Who's Who in America®

Who's Who in America®

2004

MARQUIS Who's Who 21st Century Editions Since 1899 The Chronicle of Human Achievement

58th Edition

Volume 1

A-K

MARQUIS Who's Who®

121 Chanlon Road
New Providence, NJ 07974 U.S.A.
www.marquiswhoswho.com

Who'sWho in America®

Marquis Who's Who®

Chief Executive Officer	Gene M. McGovern
President	James A. Finkelstein
Senior Managing Director	Fred Marks
Director, Editorial & Product Development	Robert Docherty
Research Director	Lisa Weissbard

Editorial

Managing Editor	Karen Chassie
Senior Editor	Danielle Netta
Associate Editor	Kate Spirito
Assistant Editors	Patricia Delli Santi
	Ryan Karwell
	Deanna Richmond
	Sandy Sauchelli

Editorial Services

Director	Debby Nowicki
Production Manager	Paul Zema
Production Editors	Daniel D. Crawford
	Jeffrey Uthaichai
Freelance Manager	Mary SanGiovanni
Editorial Services Assistant	Ann Chavis
Special Projects Supervisor	Sola Osofisan
Mail Processing Manager	Kara A. Seitz
Mail Processing Staff	Betty Gray
	Hattie Walker

Creative Services

Director, Marketing & Creative Services	Michael Noerr
Creative Services Manager	Rose Butkiewicz
Production Manager	Jeanne Danzig
Marketing Specialist	Jill Tarbell

Research

Managing Editor	Kerry Nugent Morrison
Senior Research Editors	Maria L. Izzo
	Jennifer Podolsky
Associate Research Editor	Todd Kineavy

Editorial Systems

Director	Jack Zimmerman
Technical Project Leader	Ben Loh
Composition Programmer	Tom Haggerty
Database Programmer	Latha Shankar
Senior Quality Assurance Analyst	Angela Sorrenti

Published by Marquis Who's Who LLC.

For information, contact:
Marquis Who's Who
121 Chanlon Road
New Providence, New Jersey 07974
1-908-673-1001
www.marquiswhoswho.com

WHO'S WHO IN AMERICA is a registered trademark of Marquis Who's Who LLC.

International Standard Book Number	0-8379-6974-3	(Set, Classic Edition)
	0-8379-6975-1	(Volume 1, Classic Edition)
	0-8379-6978-6	(Set, Deluxe Edition)
	0-8379-6979-4	(Volume 1, Deluxe Edition)
International Standard Serial Number	0083-9841	

Manufactured in the United States of America.

Table of Contents

Volume 1

Preface vi

Board of Advisors vii

Standards of Admission viii

Key to Information ix

Table of Abbreviations x

Alphabetical Practices xvii

Who's Who in America Biographies A–K 1

Volume 2

Preface vi

Standards of Admission vii

Key to Information viii

Table of Abbreviations ix

Alphabetical Practices xvi

Who's Who in America Biographies L–Z 2929

Volume 3

Introduction vi

Alphabetical Practices vi

Geographic Index 5791

Professional Index 6169

Retiree Index 6673

Necrology 6675

Preface

"**WHO'S WHO IN AMERICA** *shall endeavor to list those individuals who are of current national reference interest and inquiry either because of meritorious achievement or because of the position they hold."*

Albert Nelson Marquis
Founder, 1899

A Standard Reference Work

When the first edition of *Who's Who in America* appeared in 1899, it presented itself as a new and untried experiment in the field of American reference book publishing. It was the first publication ever issued which claimed to be, in any comprehensive degree, a general biographical directory of notable American contemporaries. During the generations that have passed, *Who's Who in America* has garnered a worldwide reputation for presenting the most accurate, current biographical data available. Quickly establishing itself as a standard reference work, it has grown steadily in public favor, and today is recognized globally as the premier reference pertaining to notable living Americans.

The 58th Edition upholds the guiding principle set forth by A.N. Marquis in 1899: The editors of *Who's Who in America* continue to strive to identify and chronicle the achievements of men and women who have become the leaders in our society's political, cultural, and economic affairs.

One Principle Governs Selection

In 1899, Marquis Biographees numbered 8,602, or one person per 10,000 of U.S. population. In this 58th Edition, Marquis Who's Who proudly presents the biographies of over 126,000 outstanding individuals. While our Biographees have grown in number, our selection standards remain stringent. Fewer than four in 10,000 people are included in *Who's Who in America.*

Selection is based solely on reference value. Individuals become eligible for listing by virtue of their positions and/or noteworthy achievements that have proven to be of significant value to society. An individual's desire to be listed is not sufficient reason for inclusion. Similarly, wealth or social position are not criteria. Of course, Marquis Who's Who has never charged a fee for publishing a biography, nor is purchase of the book ever a factor in the selection of Biographees.

Compiling the Most Accurate Biographical Data

Through fifty-eight editions, the basic *Who's Who in America* compilation process has remained unchanged. Potential Biographees are identified by Marquis researchers and editors. Candidates are sent data forms and are invited to submit complete biographical and career information. These data are reviewed to confirm that candidates meet the stringent selection criteria. Sketches are then prepared and sent to Biographees for prepublication checking.

In some cases, Marquis staff members compile and/or verify th biographical data through independent research. Sketches com piled in this manner are denoted by asterisks (*). For a small numbe of cases, where detailed information is not available at publicatio the editors have written brief sketches with current career informa tion; these are also indicated by asterisks.

To maintain its reputation for currency, and at the same time to adhe to space limitations, *Who's Who in America* undergoes meticulou review of selection criteria with each edition. Deletion of some name is inevitable; such deletion is not arbitrary. For example, if a Biographe has retired from active participation in a career or public life, th sketch may be excluded. In large part, it is career development tha determines inclusion and continuation.

Annual publication enables *Who's Who in America* to bring use more new names and update more existing entries each edition. In al over 22,000 new names appear in the 58th Edition.

Responding to Your Reference Needs

Who's Who in America provides a number of useful referenc features. As a complement to the biographical profiles, the Ge graphic and Professional Indexes make *Who's Who in America* a even more productive research tool. Through these indexes, use can identify and locate individuals in any of thirty-eight professiona categories, as well as by country, state, or city.

This edition also contains a cumulative Retiree Index of person whose names were deleted from the 55th through 57th Edition because they have retired from active work. This index enables th user to locate the last published biographical sketch of each liste

There is also a Necrology of Biographees whose sketches appeare in the previous Edition and whose deaths were reported prior to th closing of this edition. The sketches have been removed from th book. (For those Biographees whose deaths were reported prior t May 2003, complete biographical information, including date c death and place of interment, can be found in Volume XV of *Who Wa Who in America*.)

Finally, many of the women and men profiled in *Who's Who i America* have included in their biographies a listing of their avoca tions, thus providing additional insights into their personal lives an interests. Some of the sketches also end with an italicized featur "Thoughts on My Life." The statement is written by the Biographee and reflects their own principles, goals, ideals, and values that hav been guidelines for their success and achievement.

Our Challenge

Putting together a reference source as comprehensive as *Who's Wh in America* is a monumental challenge. Over our long histor Marquis Who's Who researchers and editors have exercised dili gent care in preparing each sketch for publication. Despite a precautions, however, errors do occasionally occur. Users of thi directory are invited to notify the publisher of any such errors so tha corrections can be made in a subsequent edition.

Board of Advisors

Iarquis Who's Who gratefully acknowledges the following distin-
uished individuals who have made themselves available for review,
valuation, and general comment with regard to the publication of
e 58th Edition of *Who's Who in America*. The advisors have
nhanced the reference value of this edition by the nomination of
utstanding individuals for inclusion. However, the Board of
dvisors, either collectively or individually, is in no way responsible
or the selection of names appearing in this volume, nor does the
oard of Advisors bear responsibility for the accuracy or
omprehensiveness of the biographical information or other material
ontained herein.

lindy Aloff
reelance Writer

Villiam C. Anderson
xecutive Director
merican Academy of
Environmental Engineers
nnapolis, Maryland

teven C. Beering
resident Emeritus
urdue University
Vest Lafayette, Indiana

Villard L. Boyd
resident Emeritus
ield Museum of
Natural History

Dr. Thomas C. Dolan
resident and CEO
merican College of Healthcare
Executives

Charles C. Eldredge
Iall Distinguished Professor
of American Art and Culture
University of Kansas
awrence, Kansas

Barbara Haskell
Curator
Whitney Museum of American Art

Thomas R. Horton
Former Chairman
American Management
Association

Jill Krementz
Author and Photographer

Charles F. Larson
President
Innovative Research Intl.

Andrew Leckey
Syndicated Investment
Columnist
The Chicago Tribune

Judith P. Lotas
Founding Partner
Lotas Minard Patton
McIver, Inc.

Martin E. Marty
Professor Emeritus
University of Chicago
Divinity School

Robert G. McKinnell
Professor Emeritus
Department of Genetics, Cell Biology
and Development
University of Minnesota
Minneapolis, Minnesota

Jeremiah P. Ostriker
Plumian Prof. Astronomy
& Exptl. Philosphy
U. Cambridge, England

Louis Rukeyser
Economic Commentator
Host, Louis Rukeyser's
Wall Street

James B. Sales
Former Senior Partner
Fulbright & Jaworski
Houston, Texas

John Fox Sullivan
President and Publisher
National Journal

Elie Wiesel
Author
Professor of Philosophy
Boston University

Standards of Admission

The foremost consideration in determining who will be admitted to the pages of *Who's Who in America* is the extent of an individual's reference interest. Reference value is based on either of two factors: (1) the position of responsibility held or (2) the level of significant achievement attained in a career of noteworthy activity. The majority of Biographees qualify for admission on the basis of the first factor, a specific position of responsibility. Incumbency in the position makes the person someone of high reference interest. The factor of position includes the following categories:

1. High-ranking members of the executive, legislative, and judicial branches of the United States government. This group includes, for example, the President of the United States, members of Congress, cabinet secretaries, chief administrators of selected federal agencies and commissions, and justices of the federal courts.

2. Military officers on active duty with the rank of Major General or higher in the Army, Air Force, and Marine Corps, and of Rear Admiral or higher in the U.S. Navy.

3. Specified state government officials. Among these are governors, lieutenant governors, secretaries of state, attorneys general, and treasurers. Also included under this standard are presidents of state senates, state university system administrators, chief state health officers, and officials of American territories.

4. Judges of state and territorial courts of the highest appellate jurisdiction.

5. High-level officials of principal cities, based on population. These officials include mayors, police chiefs, school superintendents, and other selected positions.

6. Leading government officials of Canada and Mexico. In Canada, this group includes the prime minister, premiers of the provinces, ministers of departments of the federal government, and justices of the highest courts. Examples in the Mexican government are the president of the country and cabinet secretaries of the national government.

7. Principal officers of major national and international businesses as defined by several quantitative criteria.

8. Ranking administrative officials of major universities ar colleges. Some of the officers included in this category a president, provost, dean, and selected department heads.

9. Heads of leading philanthropic, cultural, educational, professiona and scientific institutions and associations. These institutio include, for example, selected foundations, museums, sympho orchestras, libraries, and research laboratories.

10. Selected members of certain honorary and profession organizations, such as the National Academy of Sciences, t National Academy of Design, the American College of Tri Lawyers, and the Royal Society of Canada.

11. Chief ecclesiastics of the principal religious denominations.

12. Recipients of major national and international awards, such the Nobel and Pulitzer Prizes, the Academy Awards and t Antoinette Perry, or Tony Awards. Also included are winne of important professional awards, such as the American Institu of Architecture's Gold Medal for Architecture.

Admission by the second factor—significant achievement—is base on the application of objective criteria established for each field. A artist whose works are included in major museums qualifies f admission for noteworthy accomplishment. The professor who h made important research contributions in his field is of referen interest because of his outstanding achievements. Qualitati standards determine eligibility for every field.

In many instances there is considerable overlap between the tw factors used for inclusion in *Who's Who in America*. For example, t head of a major library is in the book because of position, but reachi that responsibility also signifies important achievement. Similarly, state governor not only holds a position that warrants inclusio attaining that post also represents significant achievement in t political world. In both cases, the reference value of the biographic sketch is significant. Whether the person has been selected becau of position or as a mark of achievement, the Biographee in *Who's W in America* has noteworthy accomplishments beyond those of t vast majority of contemporaries.

Key to Information

1] **GIBSON, OSCAR JULIUS,** [2] physician, medical educator; [3] b. yracuse, N.Y., Aug. 31, 1937; [4] s. Paul Oliver and Elizabeth H. (Thrun) G.; 5] m. Judith S. Gonzalez, Apr. 28, 1968; [6] children: Richard Gary, Matthew Gary, Samuel Perry. [7] BA magna cum laude, U. Pa., 1960; MD, Harvard U., 964. [8] Diplomate Am. Bd. Internal Medicine, Am. Bd. Preventive Medicine. 9] Intern Barnes Hosp., St. Louis, 1964-65, resident, 1965-66; clin. assoc. Nat. Heart Inst., NIH, Bethesda, Md., 1966-68; chief resident medicine U. Okla. Hosps., 1968-69; asst. prof. cmty. health Okla. Med. Ctr., 1969-70, ssoc. prof., 1970-74, prof., chmn. dept., 1974-80; dean Coll. Medicine U. Okla., 1978-82; v.p. med. staff affairs Bapt. Med. Ctr., Oklahoma City, 1982-6, exec. v.p., 1986-88, chmn., 1988-95, chmn, CEO, 1995—; [10] mem. overning bd. Ambulatory Health Care Consortium, Inc., 1979-80; mem. Okla. Bd. Medicolegal Examiners, 1985—; mem. Okla. Bd. of Med. Ethics, 994—. [11] Contrb. articles to profl. jours. [12] Bd. dirs., v.p. Okla. Arthritis Found., 1982—; trustee N. Ctrl. Mental Health Ctr., 1985—. [13] erved U.S. Army, 1955-56. [14] Recipient R.T. Chadwick award Overlook Hosp., 1968; Am. Heart Assn. grantee, 1985-86, 88, 1995-96. [15] Fellow Assn. Tchrs. Preventive Medicine; mem. AAAS, AMA, Am. Fedn. Clin. Rsch., Assn. Med. Colls., Masons, Shriners, Sigma Xi. [16] Republican. [17] Roman Catholic. [18] Avocations: swimming, weight lifting, travelling. [19] Home: 6060 N Ridge Ave Oklahoma City OK 73126 [20] Office: Bapt Med Ctr 1986 Cuba Hwy Oklahoma City OK 73120

KEY

[1]	Name
[2]	Occupation
[3]	Vital statistics
[4]	Parents
[5]	Marriage
[6]	Children
[7]	Education
[8]	Professional certifications
[9]	Career
[10]	Career-related
[11]	Writings and creative works
[12]	Civic and political activities
[13]	Military
[14]	Awards and fellowships
[15]	Professional and association memberships, clubs and lodges
[16]	Political affiliation
[17]	Religion
[18]	Avocations
[19]	Home address
[20]	Office address

Table of Abbreviations

The following abbreviations and symbols are frequently used in this book.

**An asterisk following a sketch indicates that it was researched by the Marquis Who's Who editorial staff and has not been verified by the Biographee.*

A

A Associate (used with academic degrees only)
AA, A.A. Associate in Arts, Associate of Arts
AAAL American Academy of Arts and Letters
AAAS American Association for the Advancement of Science
AACD American Association for Counseling and Development
AACN American Association of Critical Care Nurses
AAHA American Academy of Health Administrators
AAHP American Association of Hospital Planners
AAHPERD American Alliance for Health, Physical Education, Recreation, and Dance
AAS Associate of Applied Science
AASL American Association of School Librarians
AASPA American Association of School Personnel Administrators
AAU Amateur Athletic Union
AAUP American Association of University Professors
AAUW American Association of University Women
AB, A.B. Arts, Bachelor of
AB Alberta
ABA American Bar Association
ABC American Broadcasting Company
AC Air Corps
acad. academy, academic
acct. accountant
acctg. accounting
ACDA Arms Control and Disarmament Agency
ACHA American College of Hospital Administrators
ACLS Advanced Cardiac Life Support
ACLU American Civil Liberties Union
ACOG American College of Ob-Gyn
ACP American College of Physicians
ACS American College of Surgeons
ADA American Dental Association
a.d.c. aide-de-camp
adj. adjunct, adjutant
adj. gen. adjutant general
adm. admiral
adminstr. administrator
adminstrn. administration
adminstrv. administrative
ADN Associate's Degree in Nursing
ADP Automatic Data Processing
adv. advocate, advisory
advt. advertising
AE, A.E. Agricultural Engineer
A.E. and P. Ambassador Extraordinary and Plenipotentiary
AEC Atomic Energy Commission
aero. aeronautical, aeronautic
aerodyn. aerodynamic
AFB Air Force Base
AFL-CIO American Federation of Labor and Congress of Industrial Organizations
AFTRA American Federation of TV and Radio Artists
AFSCME American Federation of State, County and Municipal Employees
agr. agriculture
agrl. agricultural
agt. agent
AGVA American Guild of Variety Artists
agy. agency
A&I Agricultural and Industrial
AIA American Institute of Architects
AIAA American Institute of Aeronautics and Astronautics
AIChE American Institute of Chemical Engineers
AICPA American Institute of Certified Public Accountants
AID Agency for International Development
AIDS Acquired Immune Deficiency Syndrome
AIEE American Institute of Electrical Engineers
AIM American Institute of Management
AIME American Institute of Mining, Metallurgy, and Petroleum Engineers
AK Alaska
AL Alabama
ALA American Library Association
Ala. Alabama
alt. alternate
Alta. Alberta
A&M Agricultural and Mechanical
AM, A.M. Arts, Master of
Am. American, America
AMA American Medical Association
amb. ambassador
A.M.E. African Methodist Episcopal
Amtrak National Railroad Passenger Corporation
AMVETS American Veterans of World War II, Korea, Vietnam
ANA American Nurses Association
anat. anatomical
ANCC American Nurses Credentialing Center
ann. annual
ANTA American National Theatre and Academy
anthrop. anthropological
AP Associated Press
APA American Psychological Association
APGA American Personnel Guidance Association
APHA American Public Health Association
APO Army Post Office
apptd. appointed
Apr. April
apt. apartment
AR Arkansas
ARC American Red Cross
arch. architect
archeol. archeological
archtl. architectural
Ariz. Arizona
Ark. Arkansas
ArtsD, ArtsD. Arts, Doctor of
arty. artillery
AS American Samoa
AS Associate in Science
ASCAP American Society of Composers, Authors and Publishers
ASCD Association for Supervision and Curriculum Development
ASCE American Society of Civil Engineers
ASHRAE American Society of Heating, Refrigeration, and Air Conditioning Engineers
ASME American Society of Mechanical Engineers
ASNSA American Society for Nursing Service Administrators
ASPA American Society for Public Administration
ASPCA American Society for the Preventio of Cruelty to Animals
assn. association
assoc. associate
asst. assistant
ASTD American Society for Training and Development
ASTM American Society for Testing and Materials
astron. astronomical
astrophys. astrophysical
ATLA Association of Trial Lawyers of America
ATSC Air Technical Service Command
AT&T American Telephone & Telegraph Company
atty. attorney
Aug. August
AUS Army of the United States
aux. auxiliary
Ave. Avenue
AVMA American Veterinary Medical Association
AZ Arizona
AWHONN Association of Women's Healt Obstetric and Neonatal Nurses

B

B. Bachelor
b. born
BA, B.A. Bachelor of Arts
BAgr, B.Agr. Bachelor of Agriculture

alt. Baltimore
apt. Baptist
Arch, B.Arch. Bachelor of Architecture
AS, B.A.S. Bachelor of Agricultural Science
BA, B.B.A. Bachelor of Business Administration
BB Better Business Bureau
BC British Broadcasting Corporation
C, B.C. British Columbia
CE, B.C.E. Bachelor of Civil Engineering
Chir, B.Chir. Bachelor of Surgery
CL, B.C.L. Bachelor of Civil Law
CLS Basic Cardiac Life Support
CS, B.C.S. Bachelor of Commercial Science
D, B.D. Bachelor of Divinity
d. board
E, B.E. Bachelor of Education
EE, B.E.E. Bachelor of Electrical Engineering
FA, B.F.A. Bachelor of Fine Arts
ibl. biblical
ibliog. bibliographical
iog. biographical
iol. biological
J, B.J. Bachelor of Journalism
klyn. Brooklyn
L, B.L. Bachelor of Letters
ldg. building
LS, B.L.S. Bachelor of Library Science
LS Basic Life Support
lvd. Boulevard
MI Broadcast Music, Inc.
MW Bavarian Motor Works (Bayerische Motoren Werke)
n. battalion
.&O.R.R. Baltimore & Ohio Railroad
ot. botanical
PE, B.P.E. Bachelor of Physical Education
Phil, B.Phil. Bachelor of Philosophy
r. branch
RE, B.R.E. Bachelor of Religious Education
rig. gen. brigadier general
rit. British, Brittanica
ros. Brothers
S, B.S. Bachelor of Science
SA, B.S.A. Bachelor of Agricultural Science
SBA Bachelor of Science in Business Administration
SChemE Bachelor of Science in Chemical Engineering
SD, B.S.D. Bachelor of Didactic Science
SEE Bachelor of Science in Electrical Engineering
SN Bachelor of Science in Nursing
ST, B.S.T. Bachelor of Sacred Theology
Th, B.Th. Bachelor of Theology
ull. bulletin
ur. bureau
us. business
.W.I. British West Indies

C

A California
AA Civil Aeronautics Administration
CAB Civil Aeronautics Board
CAD-CAM Computer Aided Design–Computer Aided Model
Calif. California
C.Am. Central America
Can. Canada, Canadian
CAP Civil Air Patrol
capt. captain
cardiol. cardiological
cardiovasc. cardiovascular
CARE Cooperative American Relief Everywhere
Cath. Catholic
cav. cavalry
CBC Canadian Broadcasting Company
CBI China, Burma, India Theatre of Operations
CBS Columbia Broadcasting Company
C.C. Community College
CCC Commodity Credit Corporation
CCNY City College of New York
CCRN Critical Care Registered Nurse
CCU Cardiac Care Unit
CD Civil Defense
CE, C.E. Corps of Engineers, Civil Engineer
CEN Certified Emergency Nurse
CENTO Central Treaty Organization
CEO chief executive officer
CERN European Organization of Nuclear Research
cert. certificate, certification, certified
CETA Comprehensive Employment Training Act
CFA Chartered Financial Analyst
CFL Canadian Football League
CFO chief financial officer
CFP Certified Financial Planner
ch. church
ChD, Ch.D. Doctor of Chemistry
chem. chemical
ChemE, Chem.E. Chemical Engineer
ChFC Chartered Financial Consultant
Chgo. Chicago
chirurg. chirurgical
chmn. chairman
chpt. chapter
CIA Central Intelligence Agency
Cin. Cincinnati
cir. circle, circuit
CLE Continuing Legal Education
Cleve. Cleveland
climatol. climatological
clin. clinical
clk. clerk
C.L.U. Chartered Life Underwriter
CM, C.M. Master in Surgery
CM Northern Mariana Islands
CMA Certified Medical Assistant
cmty. community
CNA Certified Nurse's Aide
CNOR Certified Nurse (Operating Room)
C.&N.W.Ry. Chicago & North Western Railway
CO Colorado
Co. Company
COF Catholic Order of Foresters
C. of C. Chamber of Commerce
col. colonel
coll. college
Colo. Colorado
com. committee
comd. commanded
comdg. commanding
comdr. commander
comdt. commandant
comm. communications
commd. commissioned
comml. commercial
commn. commission
commr. commissioner
compt. comptroller
condr. conductor
Conf. Conference
Congl. Congregational, Congressional
Conglist. Congregationalist
Conn. Connecticut
cons. consultant, consulting
consol. consolidated
constl. constitutional
constn. constitution
constrn. construction
contbd. contributed
contbg. contributing
contbn. contribution
contbr. contributor
contr. controller
Conv. Convention
COO chief operating officer
coop. cooperative
coord. coordinator
CORDS Civil Operations and Revolutionary Development Support
CORE Congress of Racial Equality
corp. corporation, corporate
corr. correspondent, corresponding, correspondence
C.&O.Ry. Chesapeake & Ohio Railway
coun. council
CPA Certified Public Accountant
CPCU Chartered Property and Casualty Underwriter
CPH, C.P.H. Certificate of Public Health
cpl. corporal
CPR Cardio-Pulmonary Resuscitation
C.P.Ry. Canadian Pacific Railway
CRT Cathode Ray Terminal
C.S. Christian Science
CSB, C.S.B. Bachelor of Christian Science
C.S.C. Civil Service Commission
CT Connecticut
ct. court
ctr. center
ctrl. central
CWS Chemical Warfare Service
C.Z. Canal Zone

D

D. Doctor
d. daughter
DAgr, D.Agr. Doctor of Agriculture
DAR Daughters of the American Revolution
dau. daughter
DAV Disabled American Veterans
DC, D.C. District of Columbia
DCL, D.C.L. Doctor of Civil Law
DCS, D.C.S. Doctor of Commercial Science
DD, D.D. Doctor of Divinity

DDS, D.D.S. Doctor of Dental Surgery
DE Delaware
Dec. December
dec. deceased
def. defense
Del. Delaware
del. delegate, delegation
Dem. Democrat, Democratic
DEng, D.Eng. Doctor of Engineering
denom. denomination, denominational
dep. deputy
dept. department
dermatol. dermatological
desc. descendant
devel. development, developmental
DFA, D.F.A. Doctor of Fine Arts
D.F.C. Distinguished Flying Cross
DHL, D.H.L. Doctor of Hebrew Literature
dir. director
dist. district
distbg. distributing
distbn. distribution
distbr. distributor
disting. distinguished
div. division, divinity, divorce
divsn. division
DLitt, D.Litt. Doctor of Literature
DMD, D.M.D. Doctor of Dental Medicine
DMS, D.M.S. Doctor of Medical Science
DO, D.O. Doctor of Osteopathy
docs. documents
DON Director of Nursing
DPH, D.P.H. Diploma in Public Health
DPhil, D.Phil. Doctor of Philosophy
D.R. Daughters of the Revolution
Dr. Drive, Doctor
DRE, D.R.E. Doctor of Religious Education
DrPH, Dr.P.H. Doctor of Public Health, Doctor of Public Hygiene
D.S.C. Distinguished Service Cross
DSc, D.Sc. Doctor of Science
DSChemE Doctor of Science in Chemical Engineering
D.S.M. Distinguished Service Medal
DST, D.S.T. Doctor of Sacred Theology
DTM, D.T.M. Doctor of Tropical Medicine
DVM, D.V.M. Doctor of Veterinary Medicine
DVS, D.V.S. Doctor of Veterinary Surgery

E

E, E. East
ea. eastern
E. and P. Extraordinary and Plenipotentiary
Eccles. Ecclesiastical
ecol. ecological
econ. economic
ECOSOC Economic and Social Council (of the UN)
ED, E.D. Doctor of Engineering
ed. educated
EdB, Ed.B. Bachelor of Education
EdD, Ed.D. Doctor of Education
edit. edition
editl. editorial
EdM, Ed.M. Master of Education
edn. education
ednl. educational
EDP Electronic Data Processing
EdS, Ed.S. Specialist in Education
EE, E.E. Electrical Engineer
E.E. and M.P. Envoy Extraordinary and Minister Plenipotentiary
EEC European Economic Community
EEG Electroencephalogram
EEO Equal Employment Opportunity
EEOC Equal Employment Opportunity Commission
E.Ger. German Democratic Republic
EKG Electrocardiogram
elec. electrical
electrochem. electrochemical
electrophys. electrophysical
elem. elementary
EM, E.M. Engineer of Mines
EMT Emergency Medical Technician
ency. encyclopedia
Eng. England
engr. engineer
engring. engineering
entomol. entomological
environ. environmental
EPA Environmental Protection Agency
epidemiol. epidemiological
Episc. Episcopalian
ERA Equal Rights Amendment
ERDA Energy Research and Development Administration
ESEA Elementary and Secondary Education Act
ESL English as Second Language
ESPN Entertainment and Sports Programming Network
ESSA Environmental Science Services Administration
ethnol. ethnological
ETO European Theatre of Operations
Evang. Evangelical
exam. examination, examining
Exch. Exchange
exec. executive
exhbn. exhibition
expdn. expedition
expn. exposition
expt. experiment
exptl. experimental
Expy. Expressway
Ext. Extension

F

F.A. Field Artillery
FAA Federal Aviation Administration
FAO Food and Agriculture Organization (of the UN)
FBA Federal Bar Association
FBI Federal Bureau of Investigation
FCA Farm Credit Administration
FCC Federal Communications Commission
FCDA Federal Civil Defense Administration
FDA Food and Drug Administration
FDIA Federal Deposit Insurance Administration
FDIC Federal Deposit Insurance Corporation
FE, F.E. Forest Engineer
FEA Federal Energy Administration
Feb. February
fed. federal
fedn. federation
FERC Federal Energy Regulatory Commission
fgn. foreign
FHA Federal Housing Administration
fin. financial, finance
FL Florida
Fl. Floor
Fla. Florida
FMC Federal Maritime Commission
FNP Family Nurse Practitioner
FOA Foreign Operations Administration
found. foundation
FPC Federal Power Commission
FPO Fleet Post Office
frat. fraternity
FRS Federal Reserve System
FSA Federal Security Agency
Ft. Fort
FTC Federal Trade Commission
Fwy. Freeway

G

G-1 (or other number) Division of Genera Staff
GA, Ga. Georgia
GAO General Accounting Office
gastroent. gastroenterological
GATE Gifted and Talented Educators
GATT General Agreement on Tariffs and Trade
GE General Electric Company
gen. general
geneal. genealogical
geod. geodetic
geog. geographic, geographical
geol. geological
geophys. geophysical
geriat. geriatrics
gerontol. gerontological
G.H.Q. General Headquarters
GM General Motors Corporation
GMAC General Motors Acceptance Corporation
G.N.Ry. Great Northern Railway
gov. governor
govt. government
govtl. governmental
GPO Government Printing Office
grad. graduate, graduated
GSA General Services Administration
Gt. Great
GTE General Telephone and Electric Company
GU Guam
gynecol. gynecological

H

HBO Home Box Office
hdqs. headquarters
HEW Department of Health, Education and Welfare
HHD, H.H.D. Doctor of Humanities
HHFA Housing and Home Finance Agency
HHS Department of Health and Human Services

I Hawaii
ist. historical, historic
M, H.M. Master of Humanities
MO Health Maintenance Organization
omeo. homeopathic
n. honorary, honorable
o. of Dels. House of Delegates
o. of Reps. House of Representatives
rt. horticultural
sp. hospital
.S. High School
UD Department of Housing and Urban Development
wy. Highway
ydrog. hydrographic

I

Iowa
EA International Atomic Energy Agency
TSE International Alliance of Theatrical and Stage Employees and Moving Picture Operators of the United States and Canada
M International Business Machines Corporation
RD International Bank for Reconstruction and Development
A International Cooperation Administration
C Interstate Commerce Commission
CE International Council for Computers in Education
U Intensive Care Unit
Idaho
EE Institute of Electrical and Electronics Engineers
C International Finance Corporation
Y International Geophysical Year
Illinois
. Illinois
us. illustrated
O International Labor Organization
IF International Monetary Fund
Indiana
c. Incorporated
d. Indiana
d. independent
dpls. Indianapolis
dsl. industrial
f. infantry
fo. information
s. insurance
sp. inspector
sp. gen. inspector general
st. institute
stl. institutional
stn. institution
str. instructor
strn. instruction
strnl. instructional
ternat. international
tro. introduction
E Institute of Radio Engineers
S Internal Revenue Service
T International Telephone & Telegraph Corporation

J

G Judge Advocate General
JAGC Judge Advocate General Corps
Jan. January
Jaycees Junior Chamber of Commerce
JB, J.B. Jurum Baccalaureus
JCB, J.C.B. Juris Canoni Baccalaureus
JCD, J.C.D. Juris Canonici Doctor, Juris Civilis Doctor
JCL, J.C.L. Juris Canonici Licentiatus
JD, J.D. Juris Doctor
jg. junior grade
jour. journal
jr. junior
JSD, J.S.D. Juris Scientiae Doctor
JUD, J.U.D. Juris Utriusque Doctor
jud. judicial

K

Kans. Kansas
K.C. Knights of Columbus
K.P. Knights of Pythias
KS Kansas
K.T. Knight Templar
KY, Ky. Kentucky

L

LA, La. Louisiana
L.A. Los Angeles
lab. laboratory
L.Am. Latin America
lang. language
laryngol. laryngological
LB Labrador
LDS Latter Day Saints
LDS Church Church of Jesus Christ of Latter Day Saints
lectr. lecturer
legis. legislation, legislative
LHD, L.H.D. Doctor of Humane Letters
L.I. Long Island
libr. librarian, library
lic. licensed, license
L.I.R.R. Long Island Railroad
lit. literature
litig. litigation
LittB, Litt.B. Bachelor of Letters
LittD, Litt.D. Doctor of Letters
LLB, LL.B. Bachelor of Laws
LLD, L.L.D. Doctor of Laws
LLM, L.L.M. Master of Laws
Ln. Lane
L.&N.R.R. Louisville & Nashville Railroad
LPGA Ladies Professional Golf Association
LPN Licensed Practical Nurse
LS, L.S. Library Science (in degree)
lt. lieutenant
Ltd. Limited
Luth. Lutheran
LWV League of Women Voters

M

M. Master
m. married
MA, M.A. Master of Arts
MA Massachusetts
MADD Mothers Against Drunk Driving
mag. magazine
MAgr, M.Agr. Master of Agriculture
maj. major
Man. Manitoba
Mar. March
MArch, M.Arch. Master in Architecture
Mass. Massachusetts
math. mathematics, mathematical
MATS Military Air Transport Service
MB, M.B. Bachelor of Medicine
MB Manitoba
MBA, M.B.A. Master of Business Administration
MBS Mutual Broadcasting System
M.C. Medical Corps
MCE, M.C.E. Master of Civil Engineering
mcht. merchant
mcpl. municipal
MCS, M.C.S. Master of Commercial Science
MD, M.D. Doctor of Medicine
MD, Md. Maryland
MDiv Master of Divinity
MDip, M.Dip. Master in Diplomacy
mdse. merchandise
MDV, M.D.V. Doctor of Veterinary Medicine
ME, M.E. Mechanical Engineer
ME Maine
M.E.Ch. Methodist Episcopal Church
mech. mechanical
MEd., M.Ed. Master of Education
med. medical
MEE, M.E.E. Master of Electrical Engineering
mem. member
meml. memorial
merc. mercantile
met. metropolitan
metall. metallurgical
MetE, Met.E. Metallurgical Engineer
meteorol. meteorological
Meth. Methodist
Mex. Mexico
MF, M.F. Master of Forestry
MFA, M.F.A. Master of Fine Arts
mfg. manufacturing
mfr. manufacturer
mgmt. management
mgr. manager
MHA, M.H.A. Master of Hospital Administration
M.I. Military Intelligence
MI Michigan
Mich. Michigan
micros. microscopic, microscopical
mid. middle
mil. military
Milw. Milwaukee
Min. Minister
mineral. mineralogical
Minn. Minnesota
MIS Management Information Systems
Miss. Mississippi
MIT Massachusetts Institute of Technology
mktg. marketing
ML, M.L. Master of Laws
MLA Modern Language Association
M.L.D. Magister Legnum Diplomatic
MLitt, M.Litt. Master of Literature, Master of Letters

MLS, M.L.S. Master of Library Science
MME, M.M.E. Master of Mechanical Engineering
MN Minnesota
mng. managing
MO, Mo. Missouri
moblzn. mobilization
Mont. Montana
MP Northern Mariana Islands
M.P. Member of Parliament
MPA Master of Public Administration
MPE, M.P.E. Master of Physical Education
MPH, M.P.H. Master of Public Health
MPhil, M.Phil. Master of Philosophy
MPL, M.P.L. Master of Patent Law
Mpls. Minneapolis
MRE, M.R.E. Master of Religious Education
MRI Magnetic Resonance Imaging
MS, M.S. Master of Science
MS, Ms. Mississippi
MSc, M.Sc. Master of Science
MSChemE Master of Science in Chemical Engineering
MSEE Master of Science in Electrical Engineering
MSF, M.S.F. Master of Science of Forestry
MSN Master of Science in Nursing
MST, M.S.T. Master of Sacred Theology
MSW, M.S.W. Master of Social Work
MT Montana
Mt. Mount
MTO Mediterranean Theatre of Operation
MTV Music Television
mus. museum, musical
MusB, Mus.B. Bachelor of Music
MusD, Mus.D. Doctor of Music
MusM, Mus.M. Master of Music
mut. mutual
MVP Most Valuable Player
mycol. mycological

N

N. North
NAACOG Nurses Association of the American College of Obstetricians and Gynecologists
NAACP National Association for the Advancement of Colored People
NACA National Advisory Committee for Aeronautics
NACDL National Association of Criminal Defense Lawyers
NACU National Association of Colleges and Universities
NAD National Academy of Design
NAE National Academy of Engineering, National Association of Educators
NAESP National Association of Elementary School Principals
NAFE National Association of Female Executives
N.Am. North America
NAM National Association of Manufacturers
NAMH National Association for Mental Health
NAPA National Association of Performing Artists
NARAS National Academy of Recording Arts and Sciences
NAREB National Association of Real Estate Boards
NARS National Archives and Record Service
NAS National Academy of Sciences
NASA National Aeronautics and Space Administration
NASP National Association of School Psychologists
NASW National Association of Social Workers
nat. national
NATAS National Academy of Television Arts and Sciences
NATO North Atlantic Treaty Organization
NATOUSA North African Theatre of Operations, United States Army
nav. navigation
NB, N.B. New Brunswick
NBA National Basketball Association
NBC National Broadcasting Company
NC, N.C. North Carolina
NCAA National College Athletic Association
NCCJ National Conference of Christians and Jews
ND, N.D. North Dakota
NDEA National Defense Education Act
NE Nebraska
NE, N.E. Northeast
NEA National Education Association
Nebr. Nebraska
NEH National Endowment for Humanities
neurol. neurological
Nev. Nevada
NF Newfoundland
NFL National Football League
Nfld. Newfoundland
NG National Guard
NH, N.H. New Hampshire
NHL National Hockey League
NIH National Institutes of Health
NIMH National Institute of Mental Health
NJ, N.J. New Jersey
NLRB National Labor Relations Board
NM New Mexico
N.Mex. New Mexico
No. Northern
NOAA National Oceanographic and Atmospheric Administration
NORAD North America Air Defense
Nov. November
NOW National Organization for Women
N.P.Ry. Northern Pacific Railway
nr. near
NRA National Rifle Association
NRC National Research Council
NS, N.S. Nova Scotia
NSC National Security Council
NSF National Science Foundation
NSTA National Science Teachers Association
NSW New South Wales
N.T. New Testament
NT Northwest Territories
nuc. nuclear
numis. numismatic
NV Nevada
NW, N.W. Northwest
N.W.T. Northwest Territories
NY, N.Y. New York
N.Y.C. New York City
NYU New York University
N.Z. New Zealand

O

OAS Organization of American States
ob-gyn obstetrics-gynecology
obs. observatory
obstet. obstetrical
occupl. occupational
oceanog. oceanographic
Oct. October
OD, O.D. Doctor of Optometry
OECD Organization for Economic Cooperation and Development
OEEC Organization of European Economic Cooperation
OEO Office of Economic Opportunity
ofcl. official
OH Ohio
OK Oklahoma
Okla. Oklahoma
ON Ontario
Ont. Ontario
oper. operating
ophthal. ophthalmological
ops. operations
OR Oregon
orch. orchestra
Oreg. Oregon
orgn. organization
orgnl. organizational
ornithol. ornithological
orthop. orthopedic
OSHA Occupational Safety and Health Administration
OSRD Office of Scientific Research and Development
OSS Office of Strategic Services
osteo. osteopathic
otol. otological
otolaryn. otolaryngological

P

PA, Pa. Pennsylvania
P.A. Professional Association
paleontol. paleontological
path. pathological
PBS Public Broadcasting System
P.C. Professional Corporation
PE Prince Edward Island
pediat. pediatrics
P.E.I. Prince Edward Island
PEN Poets, Playwrights, Editors, Essayists and Novelists (international association)
penol. penological
P.E.O. women's organization (full name not disclosed)
pers. personnel
pfc. private first class
PGA Professional Golfers' Association of America
PHA Public Housing Administration
pharm. pharmaceutical

harmD, Pharm.D. Doctor of Pharmacy
harmM, Pharm.M. Master of Pharmacy
hB, Ph.B. Bachelor of Philosophy
hD, Ph.D. Doctor of Philosophy
hDChemE Doctor of Science in Chemical Engineering
hM, Ph.M. Master of Philosophy
hila. Philadelphia
hilharm. philharmonic
hilol. philological
hilos. philosophical
hotog. photographic
hys. physical
hysiol. physiological
itts. Pittsburgh
k. Park
ky. Parkway
l. Place
.&L.E.R.R. Pittsburgh & Lake Erie Railroad
lz. Plaza
NP Pediatric Nurse Practitioner
.O. Post Office
O Box Post Office Box
olit. political
oly. polytechnic, polytechnical
Q Province of Quebec
R, P.R. Puerto Rico
rep. preparatory
res. president
resbyn. Presbyterian
resdl. presidential
rin. principal
rocs. proceedings
rod. produced (play production)
rodn. production
rodr. producer
rof. professor
rofl. professional
rog. progressive
ropr. proprietor
ros. atty. prosecuting attorney
ro tem. pro tempore
SRO Professional Services Review Organization
sychiat. psychiatric
sychol. psychological
TA Parent-Teachers Association
tnr. partner
TO Pacific Theatre of Operations, Parent Teacher Organization
ub. publisher, publishing, published
ub. public
ubl. publication
vt. private

Q

uar. quarterly
m. quartermaster
.M.C. Quartermaster Corps
ue. Quebec

R

adiol. radiological
AF Royal Air Force
CA Radio Corporation of America
CAF Royal Canadian Air Force
RD Rural Delivery
Rd. Road
R&D Research & Development
REA Rural Electrification Administration
rec. recording
ref. reformed
regt. regiment
regtl. regimental
rehab. rehabilitation
rels. relations
Rep. Republican
rep. representative
Res. Reserve
ret. retired
Rev. Reverend
rev. review, revised
RFC Reconstruction Finance Corporation
RFD Rural Free Delivery
rhinol. rhinological
RI, R.I. Rhode Island
RISD Rhode Island School of Design
Rlwy. Railway
Rm. Room
RN, R.N. Registered Nurse
roentgenol. roentgenological
ROTC Reserve Officers Training Corps
RR Rural Route
R.R. Railroad
rsch. research
rschr. researcher
Rt. Route

S

S. South
s. son
SAC Strategic Air Command
SAG Screen Actors Guild
SALT Strategic Arms Limitation Talks
S.Am. South America
san. sanitary
SAR Sons of the American Revolution
Sask. Saskatchewan
savs. savings
SB, S.B. Bachelor of Science
SBA Small Business Administration
SC, S.C. South Carolina
SCAP Supreme Command Allies Pacific
ScB, Sc.B. Bachelor of Science
SCD, S.C.D. Doctor of Commercial Science
ScD, Sc.D. Doctor of Science
sch. school
sci. science, scientific
SCLC Southern Christian Leadership Conference
SCV Sons of Confederate Veterans
SD, S.D. South Dakota
SE, S.E. Southeast
SEATO Southeast Asia Treaty Organization
SEC Securities and Exchange Commission
sec. secretary
sect. section
seismol. seismological
sem. seminary
Sept. September
s.g. senior grade
sgt. sergeant
SHAEF Supreme Headquarters Allied Expeditionary Forces
SHAPE Supreme Headquarters Allied Powers in Europe
S.I. Staten Island
S.J. Society of Jesus (Jesuit)
SJD Scientiae Juridicae Doctor
SK Saskatchewan
SM, S.M. Master of Science
SNP Society of Nursing Professionals
So. Southern
soc. society
sociol. sociological
S.P.Co. Southern Pacific Company
spkr. speaker
spl. special
splty. specialty
Sq. Square
S.R. Sons of the Revolution
sr. senior
S S Steamship
S S S Selective Service System
St. Saint, Street
sta. station
stats. statistics
statis. statistical
STB, S.T.B. Bachelor of Sacred Theology
stblzn. stabilization
STD, S.T.D. Doctor of Sacred Theology
std. standard
Ste. Suite
subs. subsidiary
SUNY State University of New York
supr. supervisor
supt. superintendent
surg. surgical
svc. service
SW, S.W. Southwest
sys. system

T

TAPPI Technical Association of the Pulp and Paper Industry
tb. tuberculosis
tchg. teaching
tchr. teacher
tech. technical, technology
technol. technological
tel. telephone
Tel. & Tel. Telephone & Telegraph
telecom. telecommunications
temp. temporary
Tenn. Tennessee
Ter. Territory
Ter. Terrace
TESOL Teachers of English to Speakers of Other Languages
Tex. Texas
ThD, Th.D. Doctor of Theology
theol. theological
ThM, Th.M. Master of Theology
TN Tennessee
tng. training
topog. topographical
trans. transaction, transferred
transl. translation, translated
transp. transportation
treas. treasurer
TT Trust Territory
TV television

TVA Tennessee Valley Authority
TWA Trans World Airlines
twp. township
TX Texas
typog. typographical

U

U. University
UAW United Auto Workers
UCLA University of California at Los Angeles
UDC United Daughters of the Confederacy
U.K. United Kingdom
UN United Nations
UNESCO United Nations Educational, Scientific and Cultural Organization
UNICEF United Nations International Children's Emergency Fund
univ. university
UNRRA United Nations Relief and Rehabilitation Administration
UPI United Press International
U.P.R.R. United Pacific Railroad
urol. urological
U.S. United States
U.S.A. United States of America
USAAF United States Army Air Force
USAF United States Air Force
USAFR United States Air Force Reserve
USAR United States Army Reserve
USCG United States Coast Guard
USCGR United States Coast Guard Reserve
USES United States Employment Service
USIA United States Information Agency
USMC United States Marine Corps
USMCR United States Marine Corps Reserve
USN United States Navy
USNG United States National Guard
USNR United States Naval Reserve
USO United Service Organizations
USPHS United States Public Health Service
USS United States Ship
USSR Union of the Soviet Socialist Republics
USTA United States Tennis Association
USV United States Volunteers
UT Utah

V

VA Veterans Administration
VA, Va. Virginia
vet. veteran, veterinary
VFW Veterans of Foreign Wars
VI, V.I. Virgin Islands
vice pres. vice president
vis. visiting
VISTA Volunteers in Service to America
VITA Volunteers in Technical Assistance
vocat. vocational
vol. volunteer, volume
v.p. vice president
vs. versus
VT, Vt. Vermont

W

W, W. West
WA Washington (state)
WAC Women's Army Corps
Wash. Washington (state)
WATS Wide Area Telecommunications Service
WAVES Women's Reserve, US Naval Reserve
WCTU Women's Christian Temperance Union
we. western
W. Ger. Germany, Federal Republic of
WHO World Health Organization
WI Wisconsin
W.I. West Indies
Wis. Wisconsin
WSB Wage Stabilization Board
WV West Virginia
W.Va. West Virginia
WWI World War I
WWII World War II
WY Wyoming
Wyo. Wyoming

X, Y

YK Yukon Territory
YMCA Young Men's Christian Association
YMHA Young Men's Hebrew Association
YM & YWHA Young Men's and Young Women's Hebrew Association
yr. year
YT, Y.T. Yukon Territory
YWCA Young Women's Christian Association

Z

zool. zoological

Alphabetical Practices

Names are arranged alphabetically according to the surnames and under identical surnames according to the first given name. If both surname and the first given name are identical, names are arranged alphabetically according to the second given name.

Surnames beginning with De, Des, Du (however capitalized or spaced) are recorded with the prefix preceding the surname and arranged alphabetically under the letter D.

Surnames beginning with Mac and Mc are arranged alphabetically under M.

Surnames beginning with Saint or St. appear after names that begin Sains, and are arranged according to the second part of the name, e.g., St. Clair before Saint Dennis.

Surnames beginning with Van, Von, or von are arranged alphabetically under the letter V.

Compound surnames are arranged according to the first member of the compound.

Many hyphenated Arabic names begin Al-, El-, or al-. These names are alphabetized according to each Biographee's designation of last name. Thus Al-Bahar, Neta may be listed either under Al- or under Bahar, depending on the preference of the listee.

Also, Arabic names have a variety of possible spellings when transposed to English. Spelling of these names is always based on the practice of the Biographee. Some Biographees use a Western form of word order, while others prefer the Arabic word sequence.

Similarly, Asian names may have no comma between family and given names, but some Biographees have chosen to add the comma. In each case, punctuation follows the preference of the Biographee.

Parentheses used in connection with a name indicate which part of the full name is usually deleted in common usage. Hence Chambers, E(lizabeth) Anne indicates that the usual form of the given name is E. Anne. In such a case, the parentheses are ignored in alphabetizing and the name would be arranged as Chambers, Elizabeth Anne. However, if the name is recorded Chambers, (Elizabeth) Anne, signifying that the entire name Elizabeth is not commonly used, the alphabetizing would be arranged as though the name were Chambers, Anne. If an entire middle or last name is enclosed in parentheses, that portion of the name is used in the alphabetical arrangement. Hence Chambers, Elizabeth (Anne) would be arranged as Chambers, Elizabeth Anne.

Where more than one spelling, word order, or name of an individual is frequently encountered, the sketch has been entered under the form preferred by the Biographee, with cross-references under alternate forms.

Who'sWho in America®

Biographees A - K

AABERG, THOMAS MARSHALL, SR., b. St. Paul, Sept. 5, 1936; m. Judith S. Young, June 17, 1961; children: Thomas M. Jr., Leigh, Sarah. BA, Dartmouth Coll., 1958, MS, 1959; MD, Harvard U., 1961; MSPH in Preventive Medicine, U. Okla., 1967. Diplomate Am. Bd. Ophthalmology. Asst. prof. ophthalmology Med. Coll. Wis., Milw., 1969-71, assoc. prof. ophthalmology, 1971-76, prof. ophthalmology, 1976-88; chmn. dept. ophthalmology Sch. Medicine Emory U., Atlanta, 1988—. Surgeon USPHS, 1966-68. Office: Emory Eye Ctr Ste B 4405 1365-B Clifton Rd NE Atlanta GA 30322-1013 E-mail: ophttma@emory.edu.

AADAHL, JORG, business executive; b. Trondheim, Norway, June 16, 1937; came to U.S., 1966; s. Ottar P. and Gurli (Lockra) A.; m. Inger R. Holst, July 13, 1973; children: Erik, Nina. MS in Mech. Engring., Tech. U. Norway, 1961; MBA, U. San Francisco, 1973. Rsch. fellow Tech. U. Norway, Trondheim, 1961-62; mgr. arc welding devel. NAG, Oslo, 1964-66; mfg. engr. Varian Assocs., Palo Alto, Calif., 1966-67; sr. tech. writer Lynch Comm. sys., 1967-69; indsl. engr., project mgr. United Airlines, San Francisco, 1969-74, bus. mgr., 1974-75, sr. systems analyst, 1976-81; strategic planning specialist Magnex Corp., San Jose, Calif., 1981-82; cons. in mgmt., 1982-84; founder, pres. Safeware, Inc., San Mateo, Calif., 1984—; founder, prin. CampuSafe Sys., 1996—. Dir. Safeware Sys. Ltd., U.K., 1990—; developer Safechem Hazardous Chem. Mgmt. Sys. Author: Strength Analysis, Welded Structures, 1967; editor Nordic Highlights, 1972; contbr. articles to profl. jours. Recipient Cert. of Honor, San Francisco Bd. Suprs., 1973. Mem. Leif Erikson League (pres. 1973), Norwegian Soc. Profl. Engrs., Environment and Safety Data Exch. (founding mem., dir.). Office: Safeware Inc PO Box 6745 2575 Flores St San Mateo CA 94403-2366 E-mail: safechem@aol.com.

AADLAND, KATHLEEN A. counselor, army intelligence officer; b. Britton, S.D. d. Inguald Martin and Mabel Laverne A.; widowed; 1 child, Mabel Ann Aadland Wojcik. BS, S.D. State U., 1973; MS, No. State U., Aberdeen, S.C., 1976; postgrad., U. Ill., 1982-85. Cert. guidance and counseling, tchr. Pres. Aadland & Assocs. Inc., Maddock, N.D., 1992—. Bd. dirs. 21st Century Rehamesteading Bd., Jamestown, N.D. Roman Catholic. Office: AA Inc PO Box 100 Maddock ND 57480 E-mail: knehlich@brittansd.com.

AADLAND, THOMAS VERNON, minister; b. Mpls., Dec. 24, 1950; s. Otto Sidney and Dorothy Jean (Holmquist) A.; m. Mary Joanne Pratt, June 27, 1981; children: Evangeline Faith, Brigitta Hope, Andrew Paul, Marian Joy. AB in Philosophy, Wheaton Coll., 1973; MDiv, Luther Theol. Sem., 1980. Ordained to ministry Am. Luth. Ch., 1980. Assoc. pastor Christ Luth. Ch., Duluth, Minn., 1980-91, sr. pastor, 1991—; sec. Am. Assn. Luth. Chs., Mpls., 1987-93; min. Christ. Luth. Ch., 1981—. Presiding pastor, Amer. Assn. of Lutheran Chs., 1999—, bd. dirs. Lake Superior Life Care Ctr., Duluth, Minn., 1987-90, pres. Lake Superior Chap., Lutherans for Life, 1996—. Lutheran. Home: 13986 Dallas Ave Rosemount MN 55068-7108 *I believe Americans cannot escape the religous question. The enjoyment of our freedoms—in some vitally important sense—depends upon a humble and grateful recognition that the source of our fundamental rights to life, liberty and property is transcendent: they derive not from the generosity of the State but from the magnanimity of God, in Whose image we are created.*

AADNESEN, CHRISTOPHER, rail transportation executive, consultant; b. Salt Lake City, Nov. 2, 1948; s. Grant C. and Helen Jane (Ray) Aadnesen; m. Helen Elizabeth Twelves, Aug. 14, 1973 (div. 1988); children: Aric Paul, Brian James, Nicholas Twelves; m. Betty Jean DeLeon, Aug. 19, 1988; stepchildren: Brooke Binham, Brad Binham. BA in English, U. Utah, 1971, MBA, 1973; PMD, Harvard U., 1990. Gen. mgr., founder Thaddeus Duncan Co., Salt Lake City, 1968-72; divsn. supt. Western Pacific R.R., Sacramento, 1978-82; gen. supt. of transp. Mo. Pacific R.R., Spring, Tex., 1983-84; asst. gen. mgr. So. Region Union Pacific R.R., Spring, Tex., 1984-88, gen. dir. pers. svcs. Omaha, 1988-89, asst. v.p. ops. adminstrn., 1989-90, asst. v.p. employee devel. and involvement, 1990-91, sr. asst. v.p. field ops., 1992-93, sr. asst. v.p. transp., 1993-95, pres. capitol city group, pres. capitol city mgmt. assocs., 1996—; COO Transp. Ferroviara Mexicana, S.A. de C.V., 1996-99, exec. v.p., 1999-2000; exec. v.p., COO Tex. Mexican Rlwy. Co., 1999-2000; chmn. Port Terminal R.R. Assn., 2000-01. Bd. dirs. Georgetown Rail Equipment Co. Campaign mgr. County Commr., Quincy, Calif., 1978; commr. planning and zoning Georgetown, 2001—; bd. dirs. Palace Theatre, Georgetown, Tex., 2001—. With USN, 1967—69. Mem.: Am. Assn. R.R. Supts., Georgetown C. of C., Cimarron Hills Country Club, Berry Creek Country Club, Field Club Omaha, Happy Hollow Country Club, Rotary, Beta Theta Pi. Republican. Episcopalian. Avocations: guitar, golf, fishing. Home: 30205 Oak Tree Dr Georgetown TX 78628-1143 Office: Capitol City Group 4500 Williams Dr Ste 212 PO Box 255 Georgetown TX 78628

AALBERTS, NOLA JEAN, social worker, administrator; b. Orange City, Iowa, Feb. 19, 1941; d. Gradus C. Aallberts and Auriel Mae Aalberts. BASW, Gustavus Adolphus Coll., 1963; MS in Mgmt., U. South Fla., 1977. Peace Corps vol., Guatemala, 1963—65; tchr. Am. Sch. Guatemala, Guatemala City, 1969—73; dir. Mitchell County Homemaker-Home Health Aide Svc., Osage, Iowa, 1969—73; dir., head start North Iowa Cmty. Action Orgn., Mason City, Iowa, 1973—74; program dir., homemaker-home health aide svc. Family Services Ctr., Clearwater, Fla., 1974—78; program assoc. Nat. HomeCaring Coun., N.Y.C., NY, 1978—80, program dir., 1980—83; dir., homemaker-home health aide sect. Iowa State Dept. of Health, Des Moines, 1983—85; dir., homemaker-home health aide divsn. Nat. Assn. for Home Care, Washington, 1985—89, adminstrv. dir., 1986—87; dir. of accreditation and edn. Found. for Hospice and Homecare, Washington, 1987—89; coord. for mission stewardship and supr. for native am. ministries, Ctrl. Am. and Ecuador Ref. Ch. in Am., Corona, Calif., 1989—2001, Orange City, Iowa, 1999—2001; coord. Healthy Families NW Iowa, 2001, NW Iowa Cmty. Empowerment, and Child Welfare Decategorization, Orange City, Iowa, 2001—. Adj. prof. Spanish Northwestern Coll., Orange City, Iowa, 2001—02; past advisor, state and nat. programs Health Care Financing Adminstrn.; past advisor Depts. Elderly and Adult Svcs., Social Svcs. and Health, N.H., Mo., Nebr., Iowa, N.Y., N.J.; past tchr. seminars on supervision in home care, N.H., Mo., Nebr., Iowa, N.Y., N.J. Contbr. articles to mags.; co-author: home care curricula for supervision and home care aides. State adv. com. Healthy Families Iowa program (HOPES), 2001—; mem. Mayor's Task Force on Child Care, Orange City, Iowa, 2002. Recipient Disting. Alumni award, Gustavus Adolphus Coll., 1986, Excellence in Edn. award, Nat. Assn. Home Care, Spl. Contbns. award, Mental Health Ctr. North Iowa. Mem.: Iowa Empowerment Coordinators. Avocations: walking, hiking, travel.

AALL, CHRISTIAN BERGENGREN, software company executive; b. St. Louis, Dec. 7, 1955; s. Christian Hiorth Aall and Ruth (Bergengren) Perkins; m. Esther Drugowitsch, Aug. 5, 1983; children: Christian Daniel, Nathalie Caroline. MME, Swiss Fed. Inst. Tech., Zürich, Switzerland, 1980; MBA, Internat. Mgmt. Devel. Inst., Lausanne, Switzerland, 1987. Project mgr. Cementos Apasco S.A., Apasco, Mex., 1981-82; cons. Holderbank (Switzerland) Mgmt. & Cons. Ltd., 1982-86; mgr. systems and strategic planning GM Europe Parts and Accessories, Zürich, 1988-91; comptr. GM Europe Parts & Accessories, Ruesselsheim, Germany, 1991-92; comptr. sales Adam Opel AG, Ruesselsheim, Germany, 1992-95; mng. dir. Opel Master Lease GmbH, Ruesselsheim, Germany, 1996-98; pres. Daidalos Cons., Wellesley, Mass., 1998-2001; dir. internat. ops. Daidalos Unternehmensberatung GmbH, Wolfratshausen, Germany, 1998—2001; CEO C2 Remktg., Inc., Los Altos, Calif., 2001—. Bd. trustees Frankfurt Internat. Sch., 1995-97, chmn. bldgs. and grounds com., treas., chmn. fin. com. 1997-98; treas. IMD Alumni Deutschland e.V., 1995-99. E-mail: chris@aallonline.com.

AALTO, MADELEINE, library director; BA, Wellesley Coll., 1964; BLS, U. Toronto, 1967. Clerical asst. Toronto Pub. Libr., 1964-66, children's libr. Parkdale br., 1968-69, collection libr. Spaced Out libr., 1969-73, br. head Annette St. br., 1973-74, coord. adult svcs., 1974-75; chief libr. East York Pub. Libr., 1975-84, Greater Victoria Pub. Libr., 1984-88; dir. Vancouver (B.C.) Pub. Libr., Can., 1988—. Contbr. intro. to A Geography for Children (Philippe du Fresnoy), 1968. Recipient Commemorative medal 125th Anniversary Confederation Can., 1993. Mem. B.C. Libr. Assn. Office: Vancouver Pub Libr 350 W Georgia St Vancouver BC Canada V6B 6B1

AAMODT, ROGER LOUIS, federal agency administrator; b. San Francisco, Dec. 9, 1941; s. Rodney Lee and Barbara Helen (Quinn) A.; m. Janet Roberta Hall, Sept. 15, 1962 (div. 1995); children: Sandra Marie, Aaron Lee; m. Diane Suc Dwyer, Apr. 27, 1997. Student, Antioch Coll., 1959-60; BS cum laude, U. Utah, 1966; PhD, U. Rochester, 1972. Rsch. asst. dept. radiol. health U. Utah, Salt Lake City, 1965-66; sect. chief dept. nuclear medicine Clin. Ctr., NIH, Bethesda, Md., 1971-83; grants assoc. NIH, Bethesda, 1983-84; program dir. cancer diagnosis br. Nat. Cancer Inst., NIH, Rockville, Md., 1984-96, chief resources devel. br. cancer diagnosis program, 1997—. Pres. Internat. Soc. for Biol. and Environ. Repositories, 2002—03. Author (with others): Textbook of Nuclear Medicine, 1978; contbr. refence tables to Human Health and Disease, 1977, more than 50 articles to profl. jours. Pres. Calvin Park Civic Assn., Rockville, 1974-94.—. Spl. Health Physics fellow U.S. Atomic Energy Commn., 1966-69, NDEA fellow, 1969-71. Mem. AAAS, Am. Soc. Investigative Pathology, Internat. Soc. Analytical Cytology, NIH Microcomputer Club (sec.-treas. 1983-84). Democrat. Methodist. Achievements include research on zinc absorption and metabolism in humans; organization of the NCI Cooperative Human Tissue Network, Cooperative Breast Cancer Tissue Resource, and Cooperative Prostate Cancer Tissue Network. Office: Nat Cancer Inst EPN 6135A Executive Blvd Rockville MD 20852-4910

AAMOTH, GORDON M. medical association administrator; b. Apr. 12, 1940; MD, Northwestern U., 1966. Pres. Am. Bd. of Orthopaedic Surgery; clinical prof. of orthopaedic surgery U. Minn.; intern U. Calif., San Francisco, 1966—67, fellow, 1968—69, residency, 1969—73. Office: Am Bd Orthopaedic Surgery 400 Silver Ceder Ctr Chapel Hill NC 27514

AANERUD, MELVIN BERNARD, state agency administrator; b. Spring Lake Park, Minn., Jan. 7, 1943; s. Bernard Melvin and Margaret Agnes (Beck) A.; m. Kathleen Dipprey, Aug. 19, 1978; children: Adam Curtis, Eric Christoher. BA, U. Minn., 1965. Prodn. analyst Honeywell, Inc., New Brighton, Minn., 1966-68; plant mgr. Ault, Inc., Mpls., 1968-71; gen. mgr. Mille Lacs Reservation Bus. Enterprise, Vineland, Minn., 1971-74; from bus. devel. specialist to portfolio mgr. SBA, Mpls., 1974-94, asst dist. dir., 1994—. Pres. Columbia Hts. Charter Commn., 1971-82, chmn. Minn. Minority Bus. Opportunity Com., 1976-79; treas. edn. adv. bd. McKinley Sch. Cmty., 1985-90; chmn. park bd. Ham Lake, 1986—; coach North Metro Soccer, 1990-94; founding bd. dirs. Anoka County Bus. Assn. Network; den leader, asst. pack leader, troop scoutmaster Boy Scouts Am., 1993–, vice chair recruitment and retention Three Rivers dist., 2002. With Signal Corps, AUS, 1964-66. Named one of 10 Outstanding Young Minnesotans, 1978, Scoutmaster of Yr., Viking Coun. Boy Scouts Am., Minn., 1998, 2000, recipient Dist. award of Merit, 2002, James West award, 2002; recipient Columbia Hts. Disting. Svc. award, 1970, Columbia Hts. Outstanding Civil Servant award, 1970, 2000, Blaine/Ham Lake Cmty. Hero awrd, 2002, Paul Harris award Rotary Internat., 2002. Mem. Minn. Jaycees (found. dir. 1976-82, Gold Key Man award 1971, 76, Silver Key 1973), Columbia Hts. Jaycees (nat. U.S. dir. 1972-73), Minn. Entrepreneurs Club (bd. dirs.), U. Minn. Alumni Assn., Toastmasters (treas., v.p. edn.). Mem. Democratic Farm Labor Party. Home: 15041 Fillmore St NE Anoka MN 55304-6107 Office: 100 N 6th St Minneapolis MN 55403-1505 E-mail: Melvin.Aanerud@sba.gov.

AANESTAD, SAMUEL MARK, state legislator; b. Bismarck, N.D., July 16, 1946; s. Wilhelm C.D. and Harriet E. (Witta) A.; m. Susan Lee Thompson, Aug. 30, 1969; children: Kaesa, Erik, Kirstin. AB in Zoology, UCLA, 1969, DDS, 1973; MPA, Golden Gate U., 1991. Pvt. practice, Grass Valley, Calif., 1980—; former vice chief of surgery Sierra Nevada Memorial Hospital; mem. Calif. State Sen., 2002—. Chmn. coun. on legislation, mem. dental PAC bd., Calif. Dental Assn., Sacramento, 1993—. Trustee Grass Valley Sch. Dist., 1983-94, chmn. 1986, 91. Paul Harris fellow Rotary. Mem. Pierre Fauchard Acad., Sadi Fontaine Acad. Republican. Office: 200 Providence Mine Ste 108 Nevada City CA 95959*

AANSTOOS, CHRISTOPHER MICHAEL, psychology educator; b. Saipan Island, U.S. Trust, Apr. 4, 1952; s. Anthony Matthew and Frances Henrietta (Jambrick) A.; children: Megan, Elizabeth, Lucas Matthew. BA, Mich. State U., 1974; MA, Duquesne U., 1976, PhD, 1982. Instr. Pa. State U., McKeesport, 1979—82; asst. prof. psychology State U. West Ga., Carrollton, 1982-87, assoc. prof., 1987-92, prof., 1992—, chmn., 1995-96. Contracted rschr. Pitts. Sch. Dist., 1979, Opaion, 2001; manuscript reviewer Harcourt, Brace, Jovanovich, NYC, 1983, New Ideas in Psychology, 1984—85, Saybrook Inst., 1986, Metaphor and Symbolic Activity, 1985—88, Sage, 1989, Guilford, 1990; nat. adv. panel Existential-Humanistic Inst.; adv. coun. Ctr. Study Psychology Psychiatry; program chmn. Symposium for Qualitative Rsch., Perugia, Italy, 1987, Perugia, 99; lectr. in field. Editor: Exploring the Lived World, 1984, The World of the Infant, 1987, The Humanistic Psychologist, 1985—2002, Human Growth and Development, 1990, Studies in Humanistic Psychology, 1991; editor: (assoc.) Jour. Theoretical Philos. Psychology, 1986—89; editor: (cons.) Jour. Phenomenological Psychology, 1982—, Jour. Humanistic Psychology, 1989, Jour. Psychology of Religion, 1991—94, Psychotherapy Patient, 1996—, Ethical Human Scis. and Svcs., 1999—; contbr. articles to profl. pubs. Vol. West Ga. Coll. Spkrs. Bur., 1983—; coord. fund drive Am. Heart Assn., State U. West Ga., 1985. Faculty Rsch. grantee State U. West Ga., 1983-85, 89-90, 92-93. Fellow APA (exec. bd. divs. 24, 32, program chmn. divsn. 24 1991, pres. divsn. 32 1997-98); mem. AAUP, Human Sci. Rsch. Assn. (program chmn. 1984), Southeastern Psychol. Assn., Assn. Qualitative Rsch. Psychology (chmn. program com. 1987-97), Chess Fedn. West Ga., Phi Beta Kappa. Home: 2175 Hog Liver Rd Carrollton GA 30117-9308 Office: State U West Ga Psychology Dept Carrollton GA 30118-0001

AARESTAD, JAMES HARRISON, retired educational administrator, army officer; b. Mpls., Dec. 3, 1924; s. Selmer Emil and Myrthel Perline (Olson) A.; m. Mary-Jo Finn, Oct. 20, 1951; 1 child, Elizabeth Boe. BA, U. Minn., 1949; MA, Georgetown U., 1959; postgrad., Commd. and Gen. Staff Coll., Ft. Leavenworth, Kans., 1960-61, Nat. War Coll., Washington, 1970-71. Commd. 2d lt. U.S. Army, 1949, advanced through grades to col., 1970, comdr. 2d Squadron, 11th Cav., 1969; dir. strategy and policy War Plans Div., Washington, 1970; chief staff Hdqrs. 1st Armored Div., Fed. Republic Germany, 1971-72; comdr. 2d Brigade, 3d Armored Div., Fed. Republic Germany, 1972-74; dir. nat. security seminar Army War Coll., Carlisle Barracks, Pa., 1974-76; ret., 1976; dep. dir. indsl. devel. N.C. Dept. Commerce, Raleigh, 1976-79; sec., bus. mgr. Dover (Pa.) Area Sch. Dist., 1979-92; ret., 1992. Sr. strategy cons. Ketron Corp., Malvern, Pa., 1980-95. Bd. dirs., vice chmn. York County Econ. Devel. Corp., 1980-84, chmn. bd., 1986-88, treas., 1988-96, dir. emeritus, 1997—, chmn. emeritus, 2003; chmn. mgmt. com. CYBER Ctr., York, 1990-97; bd. dirs., mem. exec. com. Better York, 1989-97; charter mem. Mil. Heritage Found., 1999; bd. dirs. Susquehanna Conf.; vet. WWII, Korea, Vietnam wars. Decorated Silver Star, Legion of Merit with 3 oak leaf clusters, DFC, Bronze Star, Air medal with 9 oak leaf clusters, Presdl. Unit Citation, Vietnamese Gallantry Cross with Gold Star; recipient cert. of appreciation Gov. State of N.C., 1976, 79, resolution of appreciation York County Indsl. Devel. Corp., 1988. Mem. Nat. Assn. Sch. Bus. Ofcls. (registered sch. bus. adminstr.), Pa. Assn. Sch. Bus. Ofcls. (regional pres. 1982-83, citation 1986), Ends of Earth Club (N.Y.C.), Cavalry and Guards Club (London), Army-Navy Country Club (Arlington, Va.), Officers of the First Divsn. 11th Cavalry Vets. of Vietnam and Cambodia, U.S. Cavalry Assn., Rotary, Sigma Alpha Epsilon. Republican. Episcopalian. Avocations: golf, gardening, military history, travel. Home: 1200 Stratford Dr Carlisle PA 17013-3543 Office: York County Econ Devel Corp 160 Roosevelt Ave Ste 300 York PA 17404-3333 E-mail: coljha@webtv.net.

AARON, BENJAMIN, law educator, arbitrator; b. Chgo., Sept. 2, 1915; s. Henry Jacob and Rose (Weinstein) A.; m. Eleanor Opsahl, May 24, 1941; children: Judith, Louise. AB, U. Mich., 1937; LL.B., Harvard U., 1940; postgrad., U. Chgo., 1940-41. With Nat. War Labor Bd., 1942-45; mem. labor adv. com. to Supreme Comdr. Allied Powers, Tokyo, 1946; research assoc. Inst. Indsl. Relations; lectr. labor law, dept. econs. UCLA, 1946-51, assoc. dir., 1957-60, dir., 1960-75, prof. law, 1960-86, prof. emeritus, 1986—. Faculty mem. Salzburg (Austria) Seminar in Am. Studies, 1958, 67; arbitrator labor-mgmt. disputes, 1946— ; pub. mem. WSB, Washington, 1951-52; mem. Statutory Arbitration Bd. in R.R. Dispute, 1963-64; chmn. Calif. Farm Labor Panel, 1965-66; mem. Nat. Commn. on Tech., Automation and Economic Progress, 1965-66; pub. mem. Adv. Council on Employee Welfare and Pension Benefit Plans, 1966-68; vis. prof. Harvard U., 1972, U. Mich., 1979; mem. pub. rev. bd. U.A.W., 1975— ; mem. arbitration services adv. com. Fed. Mediation and Conciliation Service, 1974-82; mem. ILO Com. of Experts on Application of Convs. and Recommendations, 1986-94; charter emeritus fellow Coll. of Labor and Employment Lawyers, 1996—. Author: Legal Status of Employee Benefit Rights Under Private Pension Plans, 1961; Editor: The Employment Relation and The Law, 1957, Labor Courts and Grievance Settlement in Western Europe, 1970, Comparative Labor Law jour, 1979-85; co-editor: Industrial Conflict: A Comparative Legal Survey, 1972; Public-Sector Bargaining, 1979; editorial bd., Internat. Labor Law Reps., 1974— . Fellow Center for Advanced Study in Behavioral Sciences, 1966-67; vis. fellow Clare Hall, Cambridge (Eng.) U., 1973, Australian Nat. U., 1982; named First Southwestern Legal Found. Research Fellows' Disting. Scholar in Residence, 1971; first Howard W. Wissner Meml. Lectr. Tulane U., 1971; Phi Beta Kappa vis. scholar, 1978-79 Mem. ABA (sec. sect. labor rels. law 1975-76), AAUP, Internat. Soc. Labor Law and Social Security (chmn. U.S. nat. com., internat. exec. com. 1967-83, v.p. N.Am. region 1982-85, pres. 1985-88, hon. pres. 1988—), Nat. Acad. Arbitrators (pres. 1962, bd. govs.), Indsl. Rels. Rsch. Assn. (exec. bd. 1965-68, pres. 1972, mem. CCH labor law reports panel of experts 1987-92), Am. Arbitration Assn. (mem. adv. coun. L.A. 1975-76, Disting. Svc. award 1981). Home: 316 18th St Santa Monica CA 90402-2406 Office: UCLA 405 Hilgard Ave Los Angeles CA 90095-1476

AARON, BERTRAM DONALD, engineering executive, management consultant; b. Newport News, Va., Jan. 10, 1922; s. Harry and Lillian (Blackman) A.; children: Harry, Cynthia, Jill; m. Marcia Kurke, 1952 (dec. Nov. 1974); m. Judith Goldstein, Dec. 28, 1985 (dec. May 1993); m. Gladys Cohen, June, 1998. BSEE, Va. Poly. Inst., 1943. Registered profl. engr., N.Y., Pa., Va. Aero. rsch. scientist Nat. Adv. Com. for Aeros., Langley AFB, Va., 1946-50; pres. Aaron Investors, Inc., 1948-98, Pres., 2000—; elec. engr. Signal Corps Supply Agy., Phila., 1950-53; propr. Bertram D. Aaron and Co., L.A., 1953-58, pres. Plainview, N.Y., 1958-91, Aaron Tech. Cons., Williamsburg, Va., 1990—. Pres. Microwave Instrumentation Labs., 1959-80, AWS Visual Aids Inc., 1960-64, HAL Antenna Products, Inc., Aaron Tech. Market, Inc. Author: Hydrogen Thyratron Circuitry Considerations, 1953, Surveillance Under Low Light Level Conditions, 1971; editor Procs. Integration Com. on Hydrogen Thyratrons, 1951-53; patentee antenna. Dir. devel. Va. Breast Cancer Found., 1993, organizer, chmn. symposium Primary Care Perspectives, 1995; founder, chmn. Williamsburg Va. Symphony Soc., 1998—; bd. dirs. Va. Symphony, 1998—, exec. com., 2000; chair Williamsburg Area Arts Commn., 2002; chmn. Williamsburg Area Arts Com., 2001-02; bd. dirs. Williamsburg Area Performing Arts Ctr., 2002—. Capt. Signal Corps, U.S. Army, 1943-46. Mem. IEEE (sr.), Electronic Reps. Assn. NY Chpt. ERA, (pres., chmn. bd., nat. del. N.Y. chpt.), Assn. Old Crows (pres. Tidewater Va. chpt. 1993-95), Kiwanis (bd. dirs. 1998-2000). Jewish. Home and Office: Aaron Tech Cons Inc 212 Burtcher Ct Williamsburg VA 23185-8905

AARON, BUD, systems analyst; b. White Sulphur Springs, Mont., Apr. 27, 1927; m. Dina Aaron, Jan. 10, 1960; children: Alex, Roy, Erica, Bill. Owner Microkits, 1963-67; prodn. mgr. Ednl. Computer Products, 1967-68, mfg. rep., 1968-69; instr. Control Data Inst., 1969-70; supr. ICL, Kidsgrove, England, 1970-73; tech. writer Philips Small Computers, Fontenay aux Rose, France, 1973-74; designer, developer computer programs Hughes, JPL. Lawrence Livermore Labs. and others, 1974-76; programmer, mgr., sales BusinessMaster, Carlsbad, Calif., 1976-86; mgr., writer, programmer CheckMaster Corp., Oceanside, Calif., 1986—. E-mail: bud@checkmaster.com.

AARON, CYNTHIA G. judge; b. Mpls., May 3, 1957; d. Allen Harold and Barbara Lois (Perlman) A.; m. Craig D. Higgs, May 15, 1993. Student, Brandeis U., 1975-77; BA with honors and distinction, Stanford U., 1979; JD cum laude, Harvard U., 1984. Bar: Calif. 1984, U.S. Dist. Ct. (so. dist.) Calif. 1984, U.S. Ct. Appeals (9th cir.) 1984, U.S. Dist. Ct. (no. dist.) Calif. 1986, U.S. Dist. Ct. (ctrl. dist.) Calif. 1988, U.S. Supreme Ct. 1991. Rsch. asst. to Prof. Alan Dershowitz Law Sch. Harvard U., 1982-83; trial atty. Fed. Defenders San Diego, Inc., 1984-88; ptnr. Aaron & Cortez, 1988-94; U.S. magistrate judge U.S. Dist. Ct. (so. dist.) Calif., San Diego, 1994—. Instr. Nat. Inst. for Trial Advocacy, 1988—93; adj. prof. Calif. Western Sch. Law, San Diego, 1990—93, adj. prof. law sch. U. San Diego, 1993, 95. Bd. dirs. San Diego Vol. Lawyer Program, 2001—. Mem.: San Diego County Judges Assn. (bd. dirs., pres. 2001—02), Lawyers Club San Diego, City Club San Diego, Phi Beta Kappa. Office: US Dist Ct So Dist 940 Front St Ste 1185 San Diego CA 92101-8940

AARON, DAVID L. diplomat, author; b. Chgo., Aug. 21, 1938; m. Chloe W. Aaron; 1 child. BA, PhD (hon.), Occidental Coll.; MA, Princeton U. With Fgn. Svc., 1962—, polit. and econ. officer; internat. rels. officer Dept. of State, 1964-66; polit. officer NATO, Paris, 1966; with Arms Control and Disarmament Agy.; sr. staff mem. Nat. Security Coun., 1972-74; legis. asst. Senator Walter F. Mondale, Minn., 1974-75; task force leader select com. intelligence U.S. Senate, 1975-76; dep. asst. to pres. for nat. security, 1977-81; v.p. Oppenheimer and Co., Inc., 1981-85; writer, lectr. Lantz-Harris Agy., 1985-93. Sr. advisor Mondale Presdl. Campaign, 1984; cons. 20th Century Fund, 1990-92, sr. fellow, 1992-93; bd. dirs. quest value dual purpose fund Oppenheimer Capital Corp.; amb., U.S. rep. Orgn. Econ. Cooperation and Devel., Paris, 1996.; presdl. spl. envoy for cryptography, 1996; undersec. internat. trade dept. Commerce, 1997-00; sr. internat. adv. Dorsey & Whitney, 2000-2003; sr. fellow RAND, 2003—. Author: State Scarlet, Agent of Influence, Crossing By Night; contbr. articles to profl. jours. Staff mem. Carter-Mondale Presdl. Campaign; bd. dirs. Atlantic Coun. Decorated Nat. Def. medal. Mem. Nat. Dem. Inst. Internat. Affairs (bd. dirs.), Coun. Fgn. Rels., Overseas Devel. Coun., Internat. League Human Rights (bd. dirs.), Authors Guild. Democrat. Office: RAND 1700 Main St Santa Monica CA 90407-2138

AARON, HANK (HENRY L. AARON), professional baseball team executive; b. Mobile, Ala., Feb. 5, 1934; s. Herbert and Estella A. Aaron; m. Billye Suber Aaron, Nov. 1973; 1 child, Ceci;children: Gail, Hank, Lary, Gary(dec.). Ed. pub. schs. Former semi-pro baseball player; baseball player Milw. Braves (became Atlanta Braves 1966), 1954—76, v.p. player devel., 1976—89, sr. v.p., asst. to pres., 1989—, also bd. dirs. Bd. dirs. Turner Broadcasting; mem. Nat. League All-Star Team, 1955—74, Am. League All-Star Team, 1975, World Series Championship Team, 1957; broke Babe Ruth's career home run record with 715th home run, April 8, 1974; holder major league record for most home runs, most runs batted in. Author: (autobiography) I Had A Hammer: The Hank

Aaron Story, 1991. Pres. No Greater Love, 1974; nat. chmn. Friends of Fisk for Athletics; organizer Hank Aaron Scholarship Fund; sponsor Hank Aaron Celebrity Bowling Tournament for Sickle Cell Anemia, 1972; mem. exec. bd. PUSH; mem. nat. bd. Big Bros./Big Sisters Am., NAACP; state chmn. Wis. Easter Seal Soc., 1975; nat. sports chmn. Nat. Easter Seal Soc., 1974; mem. Atlanta bd. Am. Cancer Soc. Named Most Valuable Player, Nat. League, 1957, Player of Yr., Sporting News, 1956, 1963; named to Baseball Hall of Fame, 1982. Office: care Atlanta Braves PO Box 4064 Atlanta GA 30302-4064

AARON, HENRY J. medical association administrator; BA, UCLA, 1958; MA, Harvard U., 1960, PhD, 1963. Sr. fellow econ. studies The Brookings Inst., Washington. Mem. Ctr. on Budget and Policy Priorities, Abt Assocs.; former asst. sec. for planning and evaluation Dept. Health, Edn., and Welfare. Author: (book) Serious and Unstable Condition: Financing America's Health Care, 1991, The Problem that Won't Go Away: Reforming U.S. Health Care Financing, 1996; co-author: The Painful Prescription: Rationing Hospital Care, 1984, The Comparable Worth Controversy, 1986, Can America Afford to Grow Old? Paying for Social Security, 1989, Countdown to Reform: The Great Social Security Debate, 1998; editor: Setting National Priorities: Policy for the Nineties, 1990, Behavioral Dimensions of Retirement Policy, 1999; co-editor: Uneasy Compromise: Problems of a Hybrid Income-Consumption Tax, 1988, Setting Domestic Priorities: What Can Government Do?, 1992, Economic Effects of Fundamental Tax Reform, 1996, Setting National Priorities: The 2000 Election and Beyond, 1999; contbr. articles to profl. jours. Mem.: NAS (mem. Inst. Medicine), AAAS, Adv. Coun. on Social Security (former chmn.), Nat. Acad. Social Ins. (chmn. bd. dirs.), Am. Econ. Assn. (former v.p.). Office: 1775 Massachusetts Ave NW Washington DC 20036

AARON, HENRY JACOB, economics educator; b. Chgo., June 16, 1936; s. David and Betty (Cooper) A.; m. Ruth Kotell, May 5, 1963; children: Jeffrey, Melissa. AB, UCLA, 1958; MA, Harvard U., 1960, PhD, 1963. Assoc. prof. econs. U. Md., 1967-75, prof., 1975-77, 79-89; sr. fellow Brookings Instn., 1968-78, 96—, 1996—, dir. econ. studies, 1990-96; asst. sec. planning and evaluation HEW, Washington, 1977-78. Sr. staff economist Pres.'s Coun. Econ. Advisers, 1966-67; mem. Gov. Md. Coun. Econ. Advisers, 1968-75; vis. prof. econs. Harvard U., 1974; mem. bd. dirs. Abt Assocs., 1979—, Ctr. on Budget and Policy Priorities, 1994—, chmn. Adv. Coun. on Social Security, 1978-79; trustee Tchrs. Ins. and Annuity Assn., 1984-87; trustee Georgetown U., 1995-97, bd. dirs.; mem. vis. com. dept. econs. Harvard U., 1985-89; mem. Inst. Medicine, 1986—, mem. com. on econ. future of baseball, 1990-92; rsch. adv. coun. Joint Ctr. Polit. Studies, 1984-89; v.p. Nat. Acad. Social Ins., 1986-96, chmn. bd. dirs., 1998—; rsch. adv. bd. Com. Econ. Devel., 1988-92; mem. adv. com. Stanford Inst. for Econ. Policy Rsch. Stanford U., 1991—. Author: Who Pays the Property Tax?, 1974, Politics and the Professors, 1978, Serious and Unstable Condition: Financing America's Health Care; co-author: The Peculiar Problem of Taxing Life Insurance Companies, 1983, The Economic Effects of Social Security, 1984, The Painful Prescription: Rationing Hospital Care, 1984, Assessing Tax Reform, 1985, Can America Afford To Grow Old?, 1988, (with Robert Reischauer) Countdown to Reform: The Great Social Security Debate; editor: Setting National Priorities: Policies for the Nineties, 1990, Serious and Unstable Condition: Financing America's Health Care, 1991; co-editor: Setting Domestic Priorities: What Can Government Do?, 1992, Values and Public Policy, 1994. Economic Effects of Fundamental Tax Reform (edited with William Gale), 1996, (with Robert D. Reischaver) Countdown to Reform: The Great Social Security Debate, 1998, Jour. Econ. Perspectives, Jour. Pub. Econs., Jour. Health Econs.; contbr. articles to profl. jours. Mem. adv. com. Ctr. for Econ. Policy Rsch., Stanford U. Ctr. for Advanced Study in the Behavioral Scis. fellow, 1996-97, Guggenheim fellow, 1996-97. Mem. Am. Econ. Assn. (exec. com. 1978-81, v.p. 1991), Am. Acad. Arts and Scis., Assn. Pub. Policy and Mgmt. (pres. 1998-99). Home: Apt #41 2101 Connecticut Ave NW Washington DC 20008 Office: 1775 Massachusetts Ave NW Washington DC 20036-2103

AARON, KATHLEEN F. librarian; BS, Calif. State Poly. U., 1972; MLS, Calif. State U., 1975. Intern libr. Pomona (Calif.) Pub. Libr., 1972-75; libr. Riverside (Calif.) City and County Pub. Libr., 1976-79; reference libr. Inland Libr. Sys., Riverside, 1979-83, reference coord., 1983-92, exec. dir., 1992—. Pres. Tierra del Sol Regional Libr. Network, 2000—. Editor newsletter Inland Messenger, 1983-91. Mem. ALA, Calif. Libr. Assn. Office: Inland Libr Sys PO Box 468 Riverside CA 92502-0468

AARON, KENNETH ELLYOT, lawyer; b. Phila., Nov. 3, 1948; s. Neal L. and Dorothea G. Aaron; m. Phyllis A. Carroll, May 29, 1969; children: Seth Joel, Joshua Scott. BS in Econs., U. Pa., 1970, JD, 1973. Bar: Pa. 1973, U.S. Dist. Ct. (ea. dist.) Pa. 1973, U.S. Ct. Appeals (3d cir.) 1974, U.S. Supreme Ct. 1977, U.S. Dist. Ct. (we. and ea. dist.) Pa. 1993, Del. 2001, Fla. 2001, U.S. Dist. Ct. Del. 2001, U.S. Dist. Ct. (so. and no. dists.) Fla. 2001; cert. bus.bankruptcy law specialist Am. Bankruptcy Bd, Cert. Assoc. Astor & Weiss, Phila., 1973-76; ptnr. Casper & Davidson, P.C., Phila., 1976-80; pvt. practice Phila., 1980-83; ptnr. Garfinkel & Volpicelli, Phila., 1983-86, Mesirov, Gelman, Jaffe, Cramer & Jamieson, Phila., 1986-91, Buchanan Ingersoll P.C., Phila., 1991-2001, Weir & Ptnrs., Phila., 2001—. Mem. Ea. Dist. Pa. Bankruptcy Conf., vice chmn. edn. com. 1991, co-chmn. 1992, co-chmn. legis com., 1993; trustee Phila. Bar Found., 1997-2000. Author: Foreclosure and Repossession, 1989, (chpt.) Bus. Lawyer's Bankruptcy Guide, 1992, BNA's Environmental Due Diligence Guide, 1992, Matthew Bender's Environmental Law Practice Guide, 1992. Commr. Haverford (Pa.) Twp. Planning Bd., 1978—80; chmn. Lower Merion Zoning Bd., 1993—; planning commr. Lower Merion Twp. Planning Bd., Ardmore, Pa., 1992. Recipient Tax Writing award Nat. Assn. Accts., 1970, Am. Jr. award in Creditors' Rights, 1973. Mem.: Phila. Bar Found. (trustee 1997—2000), Phila. Bar Assn. (chmn. commn. on insolvency issues in real estate 1989—), Hias & Coun. (v.p. 1999—2002), Rotary (pres. Haverford Twp. 1982—83). Avocations: sports, camping, golfing. Office: Weir & Ptnrs 1339 Chestnut St Ste 500 Philadelphia PA 19107

AARON, LARRY GENE, secondary education educator, writer, minister; b. Danville, Va., Oct. 10, 1945; s. Conley Lee and Virginia Evelyn Aaron; m. Bonita Louise Becker (div.); m. Nancy Cody Ikenberry, June 3, 1989; children: Lori Cramton, Christie Wright, John. B in Biology, Va. Tech., 1968; B in Religious Edn., Midwestern Bapt. Coll., 1974; MDiv, Liberty Bapt. Theol. Sem., 1986; D in Ministry, Luther Rice Sem., 1999. Assoc. pastor, interim Christian Heritage Ch., Danville, 1993-94; tchr., chair dept. sci. Chatham (Va.) H.S., 1997—. Instr., adj. faculty Nat. Coll. Bus. Tech., Danville, 1996—. Author: Barefoot Boy: An Anthology of Blue Ridge Poems. Recipient Va. medal Va. Soc. SAR, 1997-98, Meritorious Svc. medal, 2000, Liberty medal Nat. Soc. SAR, First Place Feature Writing Series award Va. Press Assn., 2000, 02. Mem. Soc. Protozoologists. Avocations: backpacking, biking. Home: 185 Martindale Dr Danville VA 24541 E-mail: lgaar@juno.com.

AARON, M. ROBERT, electrical engineer; b. Phila., Aug. 21, 1922; s. Edward A. and Beatrice A.; m. Wilma Spiegelman, Nov. 18, 1944; children— Richard, James. BSE.E., U. Pa., 1949, MSE.E., 1951. Research engr. Franklin Inst. Research Labs., Phila., 1949-51; with Bell Telephone Labs. Inc., Murray Hill, N.J., 1951-89, supr., 1954-68, dept. head, 1968-89; ret., 1989; cons., 1989—. Lectr., tchr. in field. Mem. adv. com. Whippany (N.J.) Sch. Bd., 1950's Guest editor for tech. jours., 1971-99; contbr. articles to profl. jours., poems to various jours.; patentee in field. Tutor NAACP Program, Red Bank, N.J., 1966-68. Served to lt. (j.g.) USCG, 1942-45. Co-recipient computers and communications prize Found. for Computers and Communications Promotion, 1988. Fellow IEEE (mem. fin. bd. 1976-77, awards bd. 1987-89, 93, co-recipient Alexander Graham Bell medal 1978, Centennial medal 1984, Millenium medal 2000), Internat. Engring. Consortium; mem. Nat. Acad. Engring., IEEE Circuits and Systems Soc. (assoc. editor 1969-71, pres. 1973), IEEE Comm. Soc. (chmn. awards bd. 1975-79, 80-84, bd. govs. 1986-89, Meritorious Svc. award 1985, fellow evaluation 1992-96, disting. lectr. 1995, lifetime svc. award 1997, Christopher Columbus internat. telecomms. award 1999), Soc. of Cable Telecom. Engrs. Home and Office: 2427 Presidential Way Apt 901 West Palm Beach FL 33401-1359 E-mail: b.aaron@ieee.org.

AARON, MARCUS, II, lawyer; b. Pitts., Oct. 24, 1929; s. Marcus Lester and Maxine (Goldmark) A.; m. Barbara Goldman, Feb. 6, 1955; children: Susan, Judith, Barbara. AB, Princeton U., 1950; JD, Harvard U., 1953. Bar: Pa. 1953, D.C. 1953, U.S. Dist. Ct. (we. dist.) Pa. 1956, U.S. Supreme Ct. 1969, U.S. Ct. Appeals (3d cir.) 1971. Assoc. Glick, Berkman & Engel, Pitts., 1956-64; ptnr. Klett, Rooney, Lieber & Schorling, P.C., Pitts., 1965-99, sr. counsel, 2000—. Asst. solicitor City of Pitts., 1957—67; bd. dirs. Homer Laughlin China Co., Newell, W.Va., 1967—, sec., 1972—88, v.p., 1980—88, pres., treas., 1989—2001. Trustee Western Pa. Sch. for Blind Children, Pitts., 1969—2001, pres., 1982—90; bd. dirs. Blue Cross of Western Pa., Pitts., 1972—86, sec., 1984—86; bd. dirs. Ctr. Engring., Inc., State College, Pa., 1984—92; trustee Rodef Shalom Congregation, Pitts., 1991—2001, hon. trustee, 2002—, treas., 1996—98, v.p., 1998—2001. Mem.: ABA, Allegheny County Bar Assn., Pa. Bar Assn. Democrat. Jewish. Home: 2298 Pacific Ave #6 San Francisco CA 94115-1435 Office: Klett Rooney Lieber & Schorling 1 Oxford Ct Fl 40 Pittsburgh PA 15219-6498 E-mail: maaron@KlettRooney.com.

AARONS, STEPHEN D. lawyer; b. St. Louis, Nov. 23, 1954; s. Donald E. and Teddye W. Costello; m. Doris A. Valdez, Apr. 12, 1993; 1 child, Ian. BA, George Washington U., 1976; JD, St. Louis U., 1979; student, Oxford (Eng.) U., 1984. Bar: Mo. 1980, N.Mex. 1985, US Dist. Ct. (we. dist.) Mo. 1980, US Dist. Ct. N.Mex. 1985, US Dist. Ct. Mont. 1996, US Dist. Ct. (ea. dist.) Mich. 1997, US Ct. Appeals (10th cir.) 1985, US Ct. Appeals (5th cir.) 1992, US Mil. Ct. 1981, US Supreme Ct. 1983. VISTA lawyer Mont. Legal Svcs., Gt. Falls, 1979-80; judge advocate U.S. Army Intelligence Command, Augsburg, Germany, 1980-83; chief capital trial def. counsel N.Mex. Pub. Defender Dept., Santa Fe, 1984-89; assoc. Jones, Snead, Wertheim, Santa Fe, 1989-92; mng. atty. Aarons Law Firm, PC, Santa Fe, 1992—. Mem. faculty Nat. Inst. Trial Advocacy. Nat. pres. Coll. Dems. of Am., Washington, 1975-77. Lt. col. USAR, 1980—. Office: Aarons Law Firm PC 300 Catron St Santa Fe NM 87501-1807

AARONSON, DAVID ERNEST, law educator, lawyer; b. Washington, Sept. 19, 1940; s. Edward Allan and May (Rosett) A.; m. Laura Dine, 1991; stepchildren: Dara Prushansky, Jared Prushansky. BA in Econs, George Washington U., 1961, MA, 1964, PhD, 1970; LL.B., Harvard U., 1964; LL.M. (E. Barrett Prettyman fellow), Georgetown U., 1965. Bar: D.C. bar 1965, Md. bar 1975, U.S. Supreme Ct. bar 1969. Research asst. Office of Commr., Bur. Labor Stats., U.S. Dept. Labor, Washington, 1961; staff atty. legal intern program Georgetown Grad. Law Ctr., Washington, 1964-65; rsch. assoc. patent rsch. project dept. econ. George Washington U., Washington, 1966; assoc. firm Aaronson and Aaronson, Washington, 1965-67, ptnr., 1967-70; prof., B.J. Tennery Scholar Am. U. Law Sch., Washington, 1970—; prof. Sch. Justice, Coll. Pub. and Internat. Affairs, 1981-92; dep. dir. Law and Policy Inst., Jerusalem, summer, 1978. Interim dir. clin. programs Md. Criminal Justice Clinic, 1971-73, founder prosecutor criminal litigation clinic, 1972, co-dir. trial practice litigation program, 1982—; vis. prof. Law Sch. of Hebrew U., Jerusalem, summer, 1978; trustee Montgomery-Prince George's Continuing Legal Edn. Inst., 1983—. Author: Maryland Criminal Jury Instructions and Commentary, 1975, (with N.N. Kittrie and D. Saari) Alternatives to Conventional Criminal Adjudication: Guidebook for Planners and Practitioners, 1977, (with B. Hoff, P. Jaszi, N.N. Kittrie and D. Saari) The New Justice: Alternatives to Conventional Criminal Adjudication, 1977, (with C.T. Dienes and M.C. Musheno) Decriminalization of Public Drunkenness: Tracing the Implementation of a Public Policy, 1981, Public Policy and Police Discretion: Processes of Decriminalization, 1984, (with R. Simon) The Insanity Defense: A Critical Assessment of Law and Policy in the Post-Hinckley Era, 1988, Maryland Criminal Jury Instructions and Commentary, 2d rev. edit., 1988; contbr. articles to legal and public policy jours. Mem. council Friendship Heights Village Council, 1979. Recipient Outstanding Community Service award, 1980; Outstanding Tchr. award Am. U. Law Sch., 1978, 81, Scholar/Tchr. of the Year award Am. U., 1989; Pauline Ruyle Moore scholar in Pub. Law, 1983 Mem. ABA (mem. criminal justice sect. rules of cr. prof. and evid. com. 1991—), D.C. Bar Assn. (chmn. criminal code rev. com. 1971-73), Md. State Bar Assn. (criminal law sect. coun. 1984—, chairperson 1989-90, Robert C. Heeney award 1999), Assn. Am. Law Schs. (elected to sect. coun., criminal justice sect. 1999—), Montgomery County (Md.) Bar Assn., Am. Law Inst., Phi Beta Kappa. Office: Am U Law Sch 4801 Massachusetts Ave NW Washington DC 20016-8196 E-mail: daarons@wcl.american.edu.

AARONSON, ROBERT JAY, aviation executive; b. Temple, Tex., June 8, 1942; s. Leonard and Ruth (Lader) A.; m. Louise Elaine Loia, June 6, 1967; children: Steven Bradford, Suzanne Denise. AB, Brown U., 1964; M in Govtl. Adminstrn., Wharton Sch., U. Pa., 1965. Spl. asst. Southeastern Pa. Transp. Authority, Phila., 1965-67; transp. rep. Urban Mass Transp. Adminstrn., Washington, 1967-69; transp. adviser HUD, 1969-71; aviation adminstr. Md. Dept. Transp., Balt., 1972-78; asso. adminstr. for airports FAA, Washington, 1978-81; dir. aviation Port Authority of N.Y. and N.J., N.Y.C., 1981-89; pres. Air Transport Assn. Am., Washington, 1989-92; exec. v.p. Lockheed Air Terminal, Inc., Burbank, Calif., 1993-94, Airport Group Internat., Inc., Glendale, Calif., 1995-97; pres. Strategies For Airports, Inc., Encino, Calif., 1997-98; exec. v.p. Lufthansa Cons. GmbH, Encino, Calif., 1999—2002; dir. gen. Airports Coun. Internat., Geneva, 2002—. Lectr. Royal Aero. Transport Course, Oxford U. Samuel S. Fels fellow, 1964-65 Mem. Nat. Assn. State Aviation Ofcls. (pres. 1978), Airport Operators Coun. Internat. (chmn. 1987-88), Am. Assn. Airport Execs., Wings Club (pres. 1992). Address: Geneva Airport PO Box 4 1215 Geneva 15 Switzerland E-mail: raaronson@compuserve.com.

AARSLEFF, HANS, linguistics educator; b. Rungsted Kyst, Denmark, July 19, 1925; came to U.S., 1948, naturalized, 1964; s. Einar Faber and Inger (Lotz) A. BA, U. Copenhagen, 1945; PhD, U. Minn., 1960. Instr. English U. Minn., 1952-56; instr. Princeton U., 1956-60, asst. prof., 1960-65, assoc. prof., 1965-72, prof., 1972-97. Author: The Study of Language in England 1780-1860, 1967, From Locke to Saussure: Essays on the Study of Language and Intellectual History, 1982, Introduction to Wilhelm von Humboldt, On Language, 1988; editor, translator: Condillac, Essay on the Origin of Human Knowledge, 2001; ; assoc. editor: The Historiography of Linguistics, bd. editors: Jour. History Ideas, 1979—; contbr. articles to jours. and books. Jr. fellow Council of Humanities Princeton U., fall 1962; fellow Am. Council Learned Socs., 1964-65, 72-73, NEH, 1975-76 Fellow Am. Acad. Arts and Scis.; mem. Am. Philos. Soc., Royal Danish Acad. Scis. and Letters (fgn.). Office: Princeton U Dept English Princeton NJ 08544-0001

AASEN, ARNE, civil engineer, researcher, artist; b. Stockton, Calif., Nov. 22, 1936; s. Ivar and Doris Nkicklars Aasen. BFA, BA in Civil Engring., U. Calif., Berkeley, 1962; MFA, U. Ariz., Tempe, 1980; PhD in Fine Arts (hon.), UCLA, 1995. Civil engr. Fed. Hwy. Adminstrn., 1958—92, ret., 1992. Exhibitions include county fairs in Calif., Colo., N.Mex., Ariz., Utah and Wyo. Vol. patrolman San Joaquin County Sheriff's Dept., Calif., 1993—; commr. San Joaquin County Commn. on Aging, 2002—. Mem.: KC (inside guard 1996—97). Democrat. Roman Catholic. Avocation: golf.

AASEN, LAWRENCE OBERT, public relations executive; b. Gardner, N.D., Dec. 5, 1922; s. Theodore and Clara Olina (Brenden) A.; m. Martha Ann McMullan, Nov. 25, 1954; children— David Lawrence, Susan Clare. Ph.B., U. N.D., 1947; MS, Boston U., 1949. With McGraw Hill Publishing Co., N.Y.C., 1952-54, N.Y. Life Ins. Co., 1954-67, asst. v.p., 1965-67; exec. sec. Better Vision Inst., N.Y.C., 1967-87; pres. Publicity, Inc., Westport, Conn., 1988—. Author: North Dakota Postcards 1900-1930, 1999, North Dakota Images 1900-1940, 2000. Dem. commiteeman Westport; elected mem. Representative Town Meeting, 1970. With AUS, 1943-45. Mem. Public Relations Soc. Am., Am. Soc. Assn. Execs. Congregationalist. Home: 31 Ellery Ln Westport CT 06880-5203 E-mail: aasenm@aol.com.

AASLESTAD, HALVOR GUNERIUS, college dean, retired; b. Birmingham, Ala., Sept. 6, 1937; s. Knut and Geraldine (Dobson) Aaslestad; m. Barbara Wohn, July 30, 1960 (dec.); children: Katherine, Karen, Peter, Lauren; m. Peggy Smethie, Dec. 14, 2002. BS, La. State U., 1960, PhD, 1965; MS, Pa. State U., 1961. Asst. prof. U. Ga., Athens, 1968-70; rsch. scientist Wistair Inst., Phila., 1970-73; sr. scientist Frederick (Md.) Cancer Rsch. Ctr., 1973-76; exec. sec. NIH, Bethesda, Md., 1976-81, rev. chief, 1981-85; dir. rsch. grants Sch. Medicine Yale U., New Haven, 1985-95, asst. dean Sch. Medicine, 1987-89, assoc. dean, retired, 1989-96; sr. mem. Rsch. and Review Svcs., Staunton, Va., 1996-98; sr. assoc. United Info. Sys., Inc., Bethesda, Md., 1998-2001; sci. rev. mgr. Analytical Scis., Inc., Bethesda, Md., 2001—02, sr. sci., 2002—03; sr. rsch. sci. Constella Health Scis., Frederick, Md., 2003—. Cons. NIH, Bethesda, 1985—. NIH rsch. grantee and fellow, 1965—.

ABAD-ZAPATERO, CELERINO, crystallographer, researcher; b. Aranda de Duero, Province of Burgos, Spain, Mar. 11, 1947; arrived in U.S., 1972, permanent resident, 1983; s. Juan Abad and Amparo Zapatero; m. Maria Victoria Manterola, Dec. 28, 1970; children: Ines Abad-Manterola, Pablo Abad-Manterola. Licenciado in Physics, U. Valladolid, Spain, 1969; postgrad., U. Salamanca, Spain, 1969—72; PhD, U. Tex., 1978. Group leader Abbott Labs., Abbott Pk., Ill., 1994—97, assoc. rsch. fellow, 1995—. Bd. dirs. Can. Light Source, Saskatoon, Saskatchewan, Canada. Author: Crystals and Life: A Personal Journey, 2002. Mem. US Nat. Com. on Crystallography, Washington, 1995—98; dir. Can. Light Source, Saskatoon. Scholar Fullbright scholarship, U.S. Binational Com. between the US and Spain, 1972. Mem.: AAAS, N.Y. Acad. of Scis., Biophysical Soc., Am. Chem. Soc., Am. Crystallographic Assn. (chmn. biol. macromolecules spl. group 1999—2001). Achievements include patents for Ligand Screening and Design by X-ray Crystallography. Office: Abbott Laboratories 100 Abbott Park Road Abbott Park IL 60064-6098 Personal E-mail: xtalp1@aol.com.

ABAKANOWICZ, MAGDALENA, artist, sculptor; b. Falenty nr Warsaw, Poland, June 20, 1930; d. Konstanty and Helena (Domaszowska) A.; m. Jan Kosmowski, Sept. 22, 1956 Grad., Warsaw Acad. Fine Arts, 1954; D (hon.), Royal Coll. Art, London, 1974, RI Sch. Design, 1992, Acad. of Fine Arts, Lódz, Poland, 1998, Pratt Inst., NY, NY, 2000, Mass. Coll. Art, 2001; DHC (hon.), Sch. of the Art Inst. Chgo., Chgo., Ill., 2002, Acad. of Fine Arts, Lódz, Poland, 2002; Dr. (hon.), Acad. of Fine Arts, Poznan, Poland. Prof. Acad. Fine Art, Poznan, Poland, 1965, 1979. Prin. works include monumental space forms of woven fibres, circles of figurative sculptures of burlap, wood, metals, stone and clay drawings, paintings, exhibited in group shows at Internat. Biennale de Tapisserie, Lausanne, 1962—79, Biennale of Art, São Paulo, 1965, Venice Biennale, 1968, Biennale of Art, São Paulo, 1979, Venice Biennale, 1980, ROSC, Dublin, 1980, Nat. Gallery, Berlin, 1983, ARS '83, Helsinki, 1983, Mus. Moderner Kunst Vienne, 1984, Nürnberg Triennale of Drawing, 1985, Sydney Biennale of Art, 1986, Mus. Modern Art, NYC, 1987, County Mus., 1987, Hirshorn Mus., Washington, 1988, Olympic Pk., Seoul, 1988, Mus. Nacional Belas Artes, Rio de Janeiro, 1992, Fuji San Kei Biennial, Japan, 1993, Europa-Europa, Bonn, Germany, 1994, Muzeum Narodove, Warsaw, 1994, Centro Galego de Arte Conteporanea Santiago de Compostela, 1994, Royal Festival Hall, London, 1993, Mus. Ludwig, Cologne, Germany, 1993, Les Champs Elysees, Paris, 1996, The Nasher Collection, Guggenheim Mus., NYC, 1997, Guggenheim Mus., Bilbao, Spain, 1997—98, Mus. D'Art Moderne Ville de Paris, 1997, Arco, Madrid, 1998, Mus. Würth Künzelsau, Germany, 2000, Nat. Gallery Jeu de Paume, Paris, 2000, one-woman shows include Three Rivers Art Festival, 2001, exhibited in group shows at Les Jardins Du Palais Royal, Paris, 2000, Europalia, 201, Musee D'Art Moderne, France, 2001, Den Haag Sculpture, Haque, Holland, 2001, Maque, Holland, 2001, La Parade des Animaux, Monte Carlo, Monaco, 2002, Open 2002, Lido, Italy, one-woman shows include Kunsthaus Zurich, 1968, Nationalmuseum Stockholm, 1970, Pasadena Art Mus., Calif., 1971, Art Mus., 1971, Dusseldorf Kunsthalle, 1972, Whitechapel Art Gallery, London, 1975, Nat. Gallery of Victoria, Melbourne, 1976, Muzeum Sztuki, Lodz, Poland, 1978, Mus. d'Art Moderne de la Ville de Paris, 1982, Mus. Contemporary Art, Chgo., 1982, Mus. d'Art Contemporain, Montreal, 1983, Portland Art Mus., Oreg., 1984, Dallas Mus. Fine Arts, 1984, Xavier Fourcade Gallery, NYC, 1985, Turske & Turske Gallery, Zürich, Mücsarnok Palace, Budapest, Hungary, 1988, Städel Kunstinstitut, Frankfurt, 1989, Marlborough Gallery, NYC, 1989, Sezon Mus., Tokyo, 1991, Mus.Modern Art, Shiga, 1991, Art Tower, Mito, 1991, Hiroshima Art Mus., 1991, Walker Art Ctr., Mpls., 1992, Inst. Contemporary Art P.S. 1 Mus., NY, 1993, BWH Kraków, 1993, Hiroshima City Mus. Contemporary Art, 1993, Kordegarda, Warsaw, 1994, Marlborough Gallery, Madrid, 1994, Fundacio Miro a Mallorca, 1994, Ctr. Polish Sculpture, Oronsko, 1995, Yorkshire Sculpture Park, 1995, Manchester City Art Galleries, 1995, Ujazdowski Castle, Warsaw, 1995, Galerie Marwan Hoss, Paris, 1996, Charlottenborg Exhbn. Hall, Copenhagen, 1996, Oriel Mostyn, Wales, 1996, Marlborough Gallery, NYC, 1997, Doris Freedman Plz., NY, Galerie Marvan Moss, Paris, 1997, Gallery Starmach, Krakow, 1998, Muzeum Sztuki, Lodz, Poland, 1994, Met. Mus. Art, NYC, 1999, Jardins du Palais Royal, Paris, 1999, Marlborough Gallery, NY, 2000, NYC, 2000, Pillsbury and Peters Fine Art, Dallas, 2001, Grant Selwyn Fine Arts, LA, 2001, Gerald Peters Gallery, Santa Fe, N.Mex., 2001, Muzeum Narodowe (Nat. Mus.), Poznan, Poland, 2002, Mart, Museo di Arte Moderna e Contemporaranem, Trento, Roverepo, Italy, 2003, Beck & Eggeling, Inst. Fine Art, Dusseldorf, Germany, 2003, Beck & Eggeling, Mus. Beelden AAn Zee, Germany, Holland, 2003, Mus. Beelden Aan Zee, Haag, Holland, 2003, Marlborough Fine Art, London, Eng., 2003, Mus. of Art, Lucerne, Switzerland, 2003, Represented in permanent collections Muzeum Sztuki, Lodz, Mus. Modern Art, N.Y.C., Kyoto, Japan, Stedelijk Mus., Amsterdam, Australian Nat. Collection, Canberra, Ctr. Georges Pompidou, Paris, Mus. Contemprary Art, Chgo., Nat. Mus., Stockholm, Met. Mus., NYC, LA County Mus., Israel Mus., Jerusalem, Mus. Mderner Kunst, Vienna, Spazzi d'Arte, Italy, Va. Mus. Fine Art, Richmond, W. Lehmbruck Mus., Duisburg, Storm King Art Ctr., N.Y., Mus. Ludwig, Colgne, Hess Collection, Napa, Calif., Nasher Collection, Tex., Mus. Nacional Centro Arte Reina Sofia, Madrid, Mus. D'Art Moderne Ville Paris, Paris, Nelson-Atkins Mus. Art, Mo., Nat. Gallery Art, Washington, exhibitions include Open, exhi. of Sculptures and Installation, Venice and Lido, Italy, 2002. Mem. Presdl. Coun. for Culture, 1992—. Decorated officier de l'Ordre des Arts et Lettres (France), 1999, Comdr. Cross with Star, Order of Polonia Restituta, 1998; recipient prize 1st class Min. of Culture, Poland, 1965, Gold medal VIII Biennale of Art, Sao Paulo, 1965, Polish State prize Stiftung F.V.S. Hamburg, Vienna, 1979, Alfred Jurzykowski prize, 1982, award for distinction in sculpture, NY, 1993, Leonardo da Vinci World award of Arts, 1997, Cavaliere Nell Ordine Al Merito Della Republic Italiana, 2000, Orden Pour le Merite fur Wissenschaften und Kunste Berlin, 2000. Mem. Am. Acad. Arts and Letters (hon.), Polish Assn. Authors. Address: Bzowa 1 02-708 Warsaw Poland

ABARBANEL, GAIL, social service administrator, educator; b. L.A., Apr. 17, 1944; d. Sam and Sylvia (Cramer) A.; m. Stephen P. Klein, Jan. 31, 1975. BA magna cum laude, UCLA, 1966; MSW, U. So. Calif., 1968. Lic. clin. social worker. Clin. social worker Mental Health Agy., L.A., 1968-74; founder, dir. Rape Treatment Ctr. & Dept. Social Svcs. Santa Monica (Calif.) Hosp. Med. Ctr., L.A., 1974—. Cons., educator in field. Author successful legis. to change rape laws; producer films about campus rape; contbr. articles to profl. jours. Bd. dirs. Clare Found., 1975-77; atty. gen. task force Violence Against Women Act, 1995-2000; mem. Calif. Campus Sexual Assault Task Force, 2003; active Am. Cancer Soc., 1975-79; Child Trauma Coun., 1978-81; Sr. Health Ctr., 1981-87. Recipient Gov.'s Victim Svcs. award, 1985, Coro Found. Pub. Affairs award, 1985, Woman of Year Leadership award YWCA, 1980, 82, Status of Women award AAUW, 1978, Nat. Outstanding Achievement award Am. Cancer Soc., 1977, Disting. Citizen award L.A. County Bar Assn., 1988, Humanitarian award Nat. Conf. Christians and Jews, 1987, Soc. for Clin. Social Work award, 1989, DOJ award for Outstanding Svc., on Behalf of Vibtims of Crime, Pres. of U.S., 1991, Woman of Distinction award Soroptimist Internat., 1992, Excellence in Profl. Achievement Alumni award, UCLA, 1994, Outstanding Corp. Citizen award Pub. Rels. Soc. Am. La. chpt., 1997, Calif. Sexual Assault Investigators Assn. award, 1999; named Outstanding Alumni, U. So. Calif., 1979, one of Heroes of 1988 L.A. mag. Fellow Soc. Clin. Social Work; mem. NASW (Agy of Yr. award 1977, Social Worker of Yr. award 1995), Nat. Orgn. for Victim Assitance (Exemplary Program award 1995), Nat. Coalition Against Sexual Assault, Nat. Orgn. Victims Assistance, Phi Beta Kappa, Pi Gamma Mu. Office: Santa Monica-UCLA Med Ctr 1250 16th St Santa Monica CA 90404-1249

ABARBANEL, JUDITH EDNA, marketing executive; b. N.Y.C., Jan. 26, 1956; d. Albert Brandt and Dorothy Irene (Fennell) A.; m. Christopher George Lucas, June 17, 1984. BA, UCLA, 1977; MBA, MA, Ohio State U., 1980. Accredited pub. rels. profl., 1988. Sales mgr. Columbus Magic, Ohio, 1979; account mgr. Mktg. Centre, St. Petersburg, Fla., 1980-82; asst. mktg. dir. MBI, Inc., Golden, Colo., 1983; dir. mktg. Colo. Outward Bound Sch., Denver, 1983—89; satellite mktg. mgr. TVN Entertainment, 1998-2000; mktg. mgr. Nat. Lampoon.com, 2000—; dir. mktg. Nat. Lampoon, 2000—. Owner A Sporting Proposition, Boulder, Colo., 1984—; western region sales promotion mgr. Hinckley & Schmitt, Inc., L.A., 1990—, entertainment properties mktg. mgr., 1996—; sr. v.p. Caldirola Prodns., 1992-94; prodn. exec. Keystone Entertainment, 1994—, v.p. devel. Mem. Pub. Rels. Soc. Am. Avocations: mountain biking, race organizing, teaching. E-mail: judy@nationallampoon.com.

ABARBANELL, GAYOLA HAVENS, financial planner; b. Chgo., Oct. 21, 1939; d. Leonard Milton and Lillian Love (Leviten) Havens; m. Burton J. Abarbanell, June 1, 1965 (div. 1972); children: Jeffrey J. Reddick, Dena Reddick Lamb. Student, UCLA, 1975; student, San Joaquin Coll. Law, 1976-77. CFP; cert. sr. advisor, registered fin. advisor; lic. real estate rep. Calif.; lic. life ins. broker, Calif., Wash., Nev., N.Y., Ill., S.C.; lic. securities broker; cert. fin. advisor; cert. long term care, health ins. and disability ins. Postal clk., Van Nuys, Calif., 1966-69; regional mgr. Niagara Cyclo Massage, Fresno, Calif., 1969-72; owner, mgr. AD Enterprises, Fresno, 1970-72; agt., field supr. Equitable of Iowa, Fresno, 1972-73; rep. Ciba Pharms., Fresno, 1973-75; owner, operator Creativity Unltd., Fresno, 1975-76; registered fin. advisor Univ. Securities Corp., L.A., 1976-83, Fin. Network Inv. Corp., Torrance, Calif., 1983-99, Nat. Planning corp., Santa Monica, Calif., 1999—. Lectr. seminars for civic orgns.; mem. adv. bd. Financial Network, Torrance, Calif., 1985-88. Co-author: Guidelines to Feminist Consciousness Raising, 1985. Mem. bus. adv. bd. of 2d careers. Recipient award Women in Ins., 1972. Mem. Bus. and Profl. Assn., L.A. Internat. Assn. Fin. Planners (bd. dirs. 1993-94), Inst. Cert. Fin. Planners, So. Calif. Socially Responsible Investment Profls., Fin. Planning Assn. (L.A. chpt. bd. dirs. 2001-02), ACLU, NOW (nat. consciousness raising coord. 1975-76), Gay Acad. Union, Nat. Gay Task Force, Culver City C. of C., Internat. Assn. Fin. Planners, Social Investment Forum, Rotary (founding mem. L.A. Westside Sunrise Club sgt. at arms 1990-91, community svc. chair 1991-94, v.p. 1992-93, found. chair 1993-94). Democrat. Jewish. Avocations: photography, ceramics, painting, design. Home: 57124 Mono Wind Way North Fork CA 93643-9797 Office: Nat Planning Corp Ste 103 5625 Green Valley Cir Culver City CA 90230-7120 E-mail: gay.abarbanell@natplan.com.

ABASCAL CARRANZA, CARLOS MARIA, secretary of labor and social planning for Mexico; b. Mexico City, June 14, 1949; Studied law, Free Sch. Law; student, IPADE. Manual worker, sec. to mgmt. Editl. Jus; messenger, trainee legal area Afianzadora Insurgentes, dep. mgr., dir. dispatching, exec. dir. human devel., acctg. and sys., dep. gen. dir., CEO, gen. dir., 1994—2000, ret., 2000; prof. social tng. course USEM; prof. various diploma courses different univs.; participant transition team labor coord. office Pres. Elect Vicente Fox, 2000; sec. labor and social planning Govt. of Mex., 2000—. Nat. pres. Coparmex; v.p. Mexican Inst. Christian Social Doctrine; del. bus. sector in monitoring commn. INFONAVIT; cons. and lectr. in field. Pres. Found. Sustainable Devel., Mexico, Vertebra social movement, Mgmt. of Values (AVAL); chmn. bd. dirs. Proliber. Office: Periférico Sur 4271 Edificio A Nivel 9 Col Fuentes del Pedregal Tlalpan 14149 Mexico City Mexico*

ABATE, ANNE KATHERINE, librarian, consultant, educator; b. Cleve., Mar. 10, 1958; d. Frank M. and Cecelia (Homic) Abate; m. George S. Maley, May 17, 1980. HAB with honors, Xavier U., Cin., 1980; MSLS, U. Ky., 1986; PhD, Nova Southeastern U., Ft. Lauderdale, Fla., 1998. Asst. dept. head Kenton County Pub. Libr., Covington, Ky., 1985-87; asst. dir. Lloyd Libr. and Mus., Cin., 1987-88; libr. Dinsmore & Shohl, Cin., 1988-99; asst. prof. Xavier U., Cin., 1999—. Part time faculty Xavier U., Cin., 1997—, U. Ky., 1998—; mem. adj. faculty Nova Southeastern U., Ft. Lauderdale, Fla., 1999—; mem. adv. bd. West Pub. Corp., Eagan, Minn., 1992-95. Contbr. articles to profl. jours.; cons./author video package: Managing Emerging Technologies, 1994. Mem. Spl. Librs. Assn. (bd. dirs. 1997-99, chpt. pres. 1992-93, chair pub. rels. com. 1993-95), Am. Assn. of Law Librs. (mem. spl. ethics com. 1997-98, mem. nominating com. 1997-99), Ohio Regional Assn. Law Librs., Greater Cin. Area Law Librs. (convenor 1990-92), Beta Phi Mu. Roman Catholic. Avocations: reading, cooking, world travel. Office: Xavier U 3800 Victory Pkwy Unit 1 Cincinnati OH 45207-1092

ABATE, JOHN E. electrical and electronic engineer, communications consultant; b. Paterson, N.J., July 25, 1931; s. Joseph and Lucy Abate; m. Mary Ann Parrillo, July 9, 1955; children: John F., Robert J., Mark J., Holly A. BSEE, NCE, 1954; MSEE, Stevens Inst. Tech., 1960; ScD in Elec. Engring., N.J. Inst. Tech., 1967. Registered profl. engr., N.J. Astronautic engr. Kearfott Inc., Little Falls, N.J., 1956-63; tech. mgr., mem. tech. staff Bell Labs., Holmdel, N.J., 1963-92; dist. tech. mgr. AT&T Labs., Holmdel, N.J., 1992-98, comm. cons., 1998—2001. Chmn. synchronization standards group Am. Nat. Stds. Inst. T1X1.3, 1983-86; mem. U.S. Nat. Bur. Stds. Panel for Basic Standards, 1986-89; expert in field of communications network synchronization. Contbr. over 20 articles to profl. jours., conf. procs. and mags. Cubmaster Cub Scouts, Holmdel, 1968-70; chmn. ch. coms., Holmdel, 1968-70. 1st lt. USAF, 1954-56. Bell Labs. fellow, 1991, AT&T fellow, 1996; named to Alumni Honor Roll, N.J. Inst. Tech. Alumni Assn., Newark, 1992, Disting. Alumni, NCE, Newark, 1964; recipient commendation Nat. Security Agy., Washington, 1956. Mem. IEEE (sr., life). Roman Catholic. Achievements include invention of adaptive delta modulator used in NASA space shuttle communications system, Bell Labs fellow in 1991 for fundamental contributions national and international in area digital synchonization planning for public and private communication networks and AT&T fellow in 1996. Home: 20 Pearce Ct Manasquan NJ 08736 Office: PO Box 664 Manasquan NJ 08736

ABAUNZA, DONALD RICHARD, lawyer; b. New Orleans, Oct. 25, 1945; s. Alfred E. and Virginia (White) A.; m. Carolyn Thompson; 1 child, Richard. BA, Vanderbilt U., 1966; JD, Tulane U., 1969. Bar: La. 1969, U.S. Dist. Ct. (ea. dist.) La. 1969, U.S. Dist. Ct. (we. dist.) La. 1980, U.S. Supreme Ct. 1986. Ptnr. Liskow & Lewis, New Orleans, 1977—, mng. ptnr., 1996—2003. Adj. faculty Tulane Sch. Law, 1981-89. Fellow Am. Coll. Trial Lawyers; mem. La. Bar Assn. (Pres.'s award 1988). Office: Liskow & Lewis 1 Shell Sq 50th Fl 701 Poydras St New Orleans LA 70139-5099

ABBADESSA, CONSTANCE IMMACULATA, music educator, vocal artist; b. Englewood, N.J., Dec. 8, 1955; d. Paul C. and Rose (Maisano) Modafferi; m. Joseph Patrick Abbadessa, Aug. 13, 1977 (div. July 2001); children: Adele, Alison, Joseph. BA in Music Edn., Montclair State Coll., Upper Montclair, N.J., 1977, MA in Vocal Performance, 1993. Cert. tchr. music, N.J.; lic. in life ins., mortgage ins. Tchr. music West N.Y. Bd. Edn., 1977-79, St. John's Evangelist Grammar Sch., Leonia, N.J., 1979-81; pvt. voice, piano instr., 1981-82; studio tchr. Jan Le Winter Dance Studio, Fairview, N.J., 1981-82; elem. choral dir. West N.Y Pubn. Schs. #1, 1982—; with Primerica Fin. Planners, 2002—. Ch. soloist St. John the Evangelist, Bergenfield, 1987—, jr. choir dir., 1993—; vocal music tchr. West N.Y. Bd. Edn., 1982—; choir dir. West N.Y. Gifted and Talented Chorus, 2000. Vocalist (soprano) Opera Co. of Ft. Lee, Syracuse Players, Opera Workshop, Montclair Opera, Jersey City Town & Gown soloist, Bergenfield Coun. for Arts soloist, 1991, 92. Recipient Cert. of Achievement Gen. Fedn. Women's Clubs, 1997. Mem. Music Educators Nat. Conf., Nat. Assn. Tchrs. Singing, Nat. Music Tchrs. Assn. Roman Catholic. Avocations: opera, studying vocal production, family activities. Home: 125 Ames Ave Bergenfield NJ 07621 Office: West New York Bd Edn 100 51st St West New York NJ 07093-5223

ABBASCHIAN, REZA, materials science and engineering educator; b. Zanjan, Iran, Jan. 23, 1944; came to U.S., 1966; s. Ebrahim and Motahreh Abbaschian; m. Janette S. Johnson, Sept. 6, 1973; children: Lara S., Cyrus E. BS, U. Tehran, Iran, 1965; MS, Mich. Tech. U., 1968; PhD, U. Calif., Berkeley, 1971. Rsch. analyst U.S. Steel Corp., Gary, Ind., 1967; rsch. asst. U. Calif., 1968-71; asst. prof. Shiraz (Iran) U., 1972-74, assoc. prof., 1974-80; with U. Fla., Gainesville, 1980—, acting chmn., 1986-87, chmn., prof., 1987—2002. Vis. assoc. prof. dept. metallurgy and mining engring. U. Ill., Urbana, 1976-78; vis. scientist MIT, Cambridge, 1980, NASA Space Processing Lab., Marshall Space Flight Ctr., Huntsville, Ala., 1981; chmn. Shiraz U., 1974-76; mem. Nat. Materials Adv. Bd., 1996—. Co-author: Physical Metallurgy Principles, 1992; editor: Grain Refinement in Castings and Welds, 1983, Solidification Processing of Eutectic Alloys, 1988, Modeling and Control of Casting, 1988 (TMS Outstanding Educator award 1998, TMS Leadership award 1999, Structural Materials Divsns. Disting. Scientist/Engr. award 1998, TMS 2000 Fellow award). Recipient Vladimir A. Grodsky endowed professorship; grantee, NSF, NASA, 1984—. Office: U Fla Dept Materials Sci and Engring PO Box 116400 Gainesville FL 32611-6400 E-mail: rabba@mse.ufl.edu.

ABBASI, TARIQ AFZAL, psychiatrist, educator; b. Hyderabad, India, Aug. 13, 1946; came to U.S., 1976, naturalized, 1983; s. Shujaat Ali and Salma Khatoon (Siddiqui) A.; m. Kashifa Khatoon, Nov. 10, 1972; children— Sameena, Omar, Osman. B.S., Madrasa-I-Aliya, Hyderabad, 1964; M.B.B.S., Osmania Med. Coll., Hyderabad, 1970; Diploma in Psychol. Medicine, St. John's Hosp., U. Sheffield (Eng.), 1976. Diplomate Am. Bd. Psychiatry and Neurology; diplomate in psychiatry Royal Coll. Physicians of Eng. Sr. house officer St. John's Hosp., Lincoln, Eng., 1972-73, registrar, 1973-76; resident in psychiatry Rutgers Med. Sch., Piscataway, N.J., 1976-79, chief resident, 1979, dir. adult in-patient services Community Mental Health Ctr., Rutgers Med. Sch., also asst. prof. psychiatry, 1979-82; staff psychiatrist Northville Regional Psychiat. Hosp. (Mich.), 1982-83, div. dir., 1983-2002; cons. psychiatrist Rahway State Prison (N.J.), 1979-82; clin. instr. psychiatry Wayne State U. Med. Sch., Detroit. Mem. Am. Psychiat. Assn., Mich. Psychiat. Soc. E-mail: taabbasi@aol.com. Office: Northville Regl Psychiat Hosp 41001 7 Mile Rd Northville MI 48167-2655 also: 33200 Dequindre Rd Ste 200 Sterling Heights MI 48310-5916 also: 30700 Telegraph Rd Ste 2560 Bingham Farms MI 48025-4526

ABBASSIAN-KASHI, MANDANA, industrial engineer, systems engineer; b. Tehran, Iran, Sept. 4, 1973; arrived in U.S., 1995; d. Reza Abbassian and Zahra Navabi; m. Ali R. Nowroozi, Aug. 18, 1994; 1 child, Nasseem Emma Nowroozi. BS, Shahid Beheshti U., Tehran, 1995; MS, U. So. Calif., 1997. Inventory control analyst Mark Fabrics Inc., L.A., 1997—99; master production scheduler Boeing Satellite Sys., L.A., 2001—. Avocations: travel, skiing, water-skiing, windsurfing, movies. Home: 321 S Lilac Ct Anaheim Hills CA 92808 Office: Boeing Satellite Sys Inc 2006 E El Segundo El Segundo CA 90245-0902 E-mail: mabbassian@hotmail.com.

ABBATT, CANDYCE EWING, lawyer; b. Dearborn, Mich. BA, U. Mich., 1979; JD, Wayne State U., 1983. Ptnr. Fried Saperstein Abbatt P.C., Dearborn, Mich., 1982—. Trustee western region Henry Ford Hlth System, 2001—; bd. visitors Wayne State Law Sch., 2002—. Pres. alumni bd. Law Sch. Wayne State U., Detroit, 1998-2001; libr. commr. City of Dearborn, 1998—, pres., 2000—. Mem. Oakland County Bar Assn., Fairlane Club (bd. govs. 2002—), Dearborn Bar Assn. Office: Fried Saperstein Abbatt PC 29800 Telegraph Rd Southfield MI 48034-1338 Fax: 248-353-2514.

ABBAY, ALEMSEGED, education educator; s. Abbay Walde-Kidan and Yemar Abraha; m. Woyni Gebremariam, Aug. 24, 2001. PhD, U. of Calif. at Berkeley, 1996. Grad. asst. and lectr. Addis Ababa U., Ethiopia, 1978—83; asst. prof. Lakeland Coll., Sheboygan, Wis., 1999—. Mem.: African Studies Assn. D-Liberal. Orthodox Christianity. Achievements include research in identity politics, particularly in the Horn of Africa. Office: Lakeland College Po Box 359 Sheboygan WI 53082 Office Fax: 920-565-1206. E-mail: abbaya@lakeland.

ABBE, COLMAN, investment banker; b. N.Y.C., Sept. 24, 1932; s. Leo Theodore and Beatrice (Shiff) A.; m. Nancy Adele Hyams, June 23, 1963; children: Elizabeth, Leo, Richard. BS in Acctg., Bucknell U., 1953; MBA, NYU, 1962. CPA, N.Y. Ptnr. Belsky & Abbe CPAs, N.Y.C., 1960-70; stockbroker Loeb Rhoades, N.Y.C., 1971-72; pres. Sagittarius Fund, N.Y.C., 1973, OCG Tech. Inc., N.Y.C., 1973, Profl. Mediquip Inc., Scarsdale, N.Y., 1974-80, Abbe & Co., Inc., 1984—; mng. dir. corp. fin. Evans & Co. Inc., N.Y.C., 1985-87, Reich & Co., Inc., N.Y.C., 1988-90; vice chmn., sr. mgr., dir. investment banking Laidlaw Internat. Inc., N.Y.C., 1991-93; chmn. AB Capital Markets, N.Y.C., 1993-94. Trustee Heart Rsch. Found., N.Y.C., 1982-92, pres., 1986; pres. Am. Friends of HAIFA Med. Ctr., 1989-93. Mem. AICPA, N.Y. State Soc. CPAs. Democrat. Jewish. Office: Abbe & Co Inc 26 Lawrence Rd Scarsdale NY 10583-7209

ABBE, ELFRIEDE MARTHA, sculptor, graphic artist; b. Washington; d. Cleveland Jr. and Frieda (Dauer) A. Student, Art Inst. Chgo., 1937; B.F.A., Cornell U., 1940; postgrad., Syracuse U., 1947. Author and illustrator: books including The Plants of Virgil's Georgics, 1965; One-woman exhbns. include Carnegie-Mellon U., 1962, 69, Cornell U., 1963, Trinity Coll., Hartford, 1964, Arts Club of Washington, 1972, Cornell Club of N.Y., 1977, Copley Soc. Boston, 1978, Woods-Gerry Gallery, R.I. Sch. Design, 1983; represented in permanent collections Met. Mus. Art., Watson Library, Boston Mus. Fine Arts, Cin. Art Mus., Dumbarton Oaks, Washington, Houghton Library, Harvard U., Hunt Library, Carnegie-Mellon U., N.Y. Pub. Library, Rosenwald Collection Nat. Gallery, Kew Gardens Library, Royal Bot. Garden, Edinburgh, Nat. Library, Canberra, Australia; sculpture placed in Mann Library, Kroch Library and Morrison Hall, Cornell U., McGill U., N.Y. Bot. Gardens, Hunt Library, Pitts., Pres.'s Office, Keene (N.H.) State Coll., Herzog August Bibliothek, Wolfenbüttel, Fed. Republic Germany (bronze bust of founder), Abbe Mus., Bar Harbor, Maine (bronze bust of founder Dr. Robert Abbe). Recipient Gold medals Pen and Brush, N.Y.C., 1964, Margaret Sussman Meml. award 1987, Gold medals Nat. Arts Club, 1970, Gold medals Acad. Artists Assn., Springfield, Mass., 1976, Founders' Prize Pen and Brush, 1977; Bd. Dirs. award Salmagundi Club N.Y., 1978; Elliot Liskin award, 1979, Catherine Lorillard Wolfe Club award, 1993. Fellow Nat. Sculpture Soc. (Barrett-Colea prize 1984); mem. Nat. Soc. Mural Painters, Phi Kappa Phi.

ABBEY, G(EORGE) MARSHALL, lawyer, former health care company executive, general counsel; b. Dunkirk, N.Y., July 24, 1933; s. Ralph Ambrose and Grace A. (Fisher) A.; m. Sue Carroll, July 13, 1974; children: Mark, Steven, Michael, Lincoln BA with high distinction, U. Rochester, 1954; JD with distinction, Cornell U., 1957. Bar: N.H. 1957, Ill. 1965. Atty. McLane, Carleton, Graf, Greene & Brown, Manchester, N.H., 1957-65, Baxter Internat. Inc., Deerfield, Ill., 1965-69, gen. counsel, 1969-72, sec., gen. counsel, 1972-75, v.p., sec., gen. counsel, 1975-82, sr. v.p., gen. counsel, 1985-90, sr. v.p., sec., gen. counsel, 1990-93; of counsel Bell Boyd & Lloyd, Chgo., 1997—2000; pvt. practice Law Office of G. Marshall Abbey, 1993-97, 2000—. Editor Cornell Law Rev., 1956-57. Mem. vis. com. Law Sch., U. Chgo., 1978-81; dir. Coun. Puerto Rico-U.S. Affairs, 1988-92; mem. indsl. adv. coun. U. P.R.; dir. P.R.-USA Found., 1975-93, B.U.I.L.D., Chgo., 1980-84, bus. adv. com. B.U.I.L.D. Inc.; bd. dirs. Hundred Club of Lake County, Ill., 1976-86; dir. Food and Drug Law Inst., 1975-93; bd. dirs. Evanston Inventure, 1986-88; former trustee Winnetka Congl. Ch.; dir. Nat. Com. for Quality Health Care, 1988-93; mem. Northwestern U. Corp. Coun. adv. bd., 1976-93, dir. P.R. Cmty. Found., 1986-94; bd. dirs. Better Bus. Bur. Chgo. and No. Ill., 1991-93; mem. Conf. Bd's. Coun. Chief Legal Officers and Legal Quality Coun., 1991-93. Mem. ABA, Ill. Bar Assn., Lake County Bar Assn., Chgo. Bar Assn., Health Industry Mfrs. Assn. (chmn. legal/regulatory affairs 1976-78, bd. dirs. 1978-80, chmn. govt. affairs com. 1980-81), Univ. Club, Exmoor Country Club, Bankers Club (P.R.), Order of the Coif, Phi Beta Kappa. Office: 836 Skokie Blvd Northbrook IL 60062-4001*

ABBEY, GEORGE W. S. space center executive; b. Seattle, Aug. 21, 1932; children: George, Joyce, Suzanne, James, Andrew. BS in Gen. Sci., U.S. Naval Acad., 1954; MSEE, Air Force Inst. Tech., 1959. Commd. 2d lt. USAF, 1954, advanced through grades to maj., 1965; detailed to Johnson Space Ctr. (formerly Manned Spacecraft Ctr.), Houston, 1964-67, tech. asst. to mgr. Apollo Spacecraft program, 1967-69, tech. asst. to dir., 1969-76, dir. flight ops., 1976-85, dir. flight crew ops., 1985-88; dep. assoc. adminstr. for space flight NASA Hdqs., Washington, 1988-90, dep. for ops. for synthesis group, 1990-91; sr. dir. for civil space policy Nat. Space Coun., Exec. Office Pres., Washington, 1991-92; spl. asst. to adminstr. NASA, Washington, 1992-94; dep. dir. Johnson Space Ctr., 1994-95, acting dir., 1995, dir., 1996—2001. Sr. fellow James A. Baker III Inst. for Pub. Policy, Rice U., 2001—. Recipient Medal of Freedom, Pres. of U.S., 1970, Exceptional Performance award Fed. Women Program, 1973, Civil Servant of Yr. award managerial and exec. category Fed. Bus. Assn., 1974, Space Flight award Am. Astron. Soc., 1983, Al Merito Della Repulica Italiana award, 1996, Quasar award, 1997, Clear Lake Econ. Devel. Found. award for excellence, 1997, Rotary Nat. award for Space Achievement Found., 1997, NASA Disting. Svc. medal, 1973, 81, 2000; named Sr. Exec. Svc. Presdl. rank, meritorious, 1989, disting., 1994, Nassau Bay Citizen of Yr., 1999. Fellow Am. Astronautical Soc.; mem. U.S. Naval Inst. Office: Baker Inst Rice U MS 40 6100 Main St Houston TX 77005

ABBEY, RICHARD LAWRENCE, human resources specialist; BA in Bus. Adminstrn., U. South Fla., 1994. Cert. human resources profl. Dir. human resources Misener Marine Construction, Tampa, Fla., 1996—98; human resources mgr. Reptron Electronics, Inc., Tampa, Fla., 1998—2002; sr. human resources rep. Bausch & Lomb, 2002—.

ABBITT, ROBBYN JO FORRY, geographic information systems specialist; d. James M. and Susan A. Forry; m. Jason Todd Abbitt, Jan. 4, 1997. BS Environ. Sci. and Pub. Affairs, Ind. U., Bloomington, Ind., 1996; MS Environ. Sci., U. Idaho, Moscow, Idaho, 1999. Geog. info. systems analyst and rsch. assoc. U. Idaho Coop. Fish and Wildlife Rsch. Unit, Moscow, Idaho, 1997—2000; geog. info. systems specialist Mo. Resource Assessment Partnership, Columbia, Mo., 2000—. Vol. Habitat for Humanity, Columbia, Mo., 2001—02. Recipient Best Student Paper, Cooper Ornithol. Soc., 1999, Exemplary GIS Applications Award, Missouri GIS Conf., 2003. Mem.: Mid-Missouri GIS Users Group, Am. Inst. for Biol. Sci. Avocations: skiing, hiking, camping. Office: Missouri Resource Assessment Partnership 4200 New Haven St Columbia MO 65201 E-mail: robbyn_abbitt@usgs.gov.

ABBOT, WILLIAM WRIGHT, history educator; b. Louisville, Ga., May 20, 1922; s. William Wright and Lillian (Carswell) A.; m. Eleanor Pearre, Mar. 31, 1958; children— William Wright, John Pearre. Student, Davidson (N.C.) Coll., 1939-41; AB, U. Ga., 1943; MA, Duke U., 1949, PhD, 1953; LHD, Coll. William and Mary, 1998. Tchr. Louisville Acad., 1946-47, McCallie Sch., 1951-52; from asst. prof. to prof. history Coll. William and Mary, 1953—61, 1963—66; assoc. prof. Northwestern U., 1958-59, Rice U., 1961-63, James Madison prof. history U. Va., 1966-92, emeritus, 1992—, chmn. history dept., 1972—74. Author: The Royal Governors of Georgia, 1754-1775, 1957, The Colonial Origins of the United States, 1607-1763, 1975; editor in chief: The Papers of George Washington, 1977-92, Colonial Series, Vols. I-X, Revolutionary War Series, Vols. I-VI, Confederation, Vols. I-VI, 1992-97, Presidential, Vols. I-V, Retirement Series, Vols. I-IV, 1998; editor Jour. So. History, 1961-63; book rev. editor William and Mary Quar., 1955-61, editor, 1963-66; bd. editors Va. Quarterly Rev., 1971-90. Served to lt. USNR, 1943-46. Mem. Inst. Early Am. History and Culture (coun. 1976-79), So. Hist. Assn. (exec. coun. 1978-81), Mass. Hist. Soc., Am. Antiquarian Soc., Va. Hist. Soc. (hon.), Gridiron Club (U. Ga.), Raven Soc. (U. Va.), Phi Beta Kappa (pres. Alpha chpt. 1984-87). Home: 804 Rugby Rd Charlottesville VA 22903-1629

ABBOTT, A. DWIGHT, retired astronautical engineer; BS in Aero. Engring., Purdue U., 1958, MS in Indsl. Mgmt., 1964. Gen. mgr. systems engring. Aeronautics and Space Engring. Bd., Nat. Academies, Washington, 1960—2000; gen. mgr. bus. mgmt. for space tech. applications Aerospace Corp., LA, prin. dir. design engring., prin. dir. space transp. devel. for space launch ops.; ret., 2000. Mem. dean's vis. com. sch. engring. Purdue U., West Lafayette, Ind. Mem. planning commn. Palos Verdes Estates (Calif.) City Coun. Fellow: AIAA (assoc.; mem. pub. policy com.); mem.: Planetary Soc., AAAS. Avocation: flying. Home: 1825 Via Estudillo Palos Verdes Estates CA 90274

ABBOTT, ALDEN FRANCIS, lawyer, government official, educator; b. Bethesda, Md., Nov. 10, 1951; s. Roger Sloane and Suzanne Jeanne (Dupuy) Abbott; m. Ljubica Visich, May 3, 1980; 1 child, Roger Visich. Cert., U. Madrid, 1972; BA, U.Va., 1974; JD, Harvard U., 1977; MA in Econ., Georgetown U., 1984. Bar: D.C. 1977, U.S. Supreme Ct. 1992. Atty. Office of Legal Policy FTC, Washington, 1977-80; atty. Fried, Frank, Harris, Shriver & Kampelman, Washington, 1980-82; spl. counsel Office of Legal Policy U.S. Dept. Justice, Washington, 1982-84, spl. asst. to asst. atty. gen. antitrust divsn., 1984-86, sr. counsel Office of Legal Counsel, 1987-89; counsellor to gen. counsel U.S. Dept. Commerce, Washington, 1989-92, chief counsel Nat. Telecomm. and Info. Adminstrn., 1992-94, asst. gen. counsel fin. and litigation, 1994-2001, acting gen. counsel, 2001; asst. dir. for policy evaluation, Bur. of Competition FTC, Washington, 2001—. Adj. prof. Sch. Law George Mason U., Arlington, Va., 1991—. Comment and note editor Harvard Internat. Law Jour.; contbr. numerous articles to profl. jours. Mem. Fed. Comms. Bar Assn. (internat. sect.), U.S. Supreme Ct. Bar, Henry Simons Soc., Phi Eta Sigma, Phi Beta Kappa. Avocations: foreign languages and travel, swimming, reading, skiing. Home: 1611 Westmoreland St Mc Lean VA 22101-5166 Office: US Fed Trade Commn 6th & Penn Ave NW Washington DC 20580 E-mail: aabbott@ftc.gov.

ABBOTT, ALORIS JEAN, operating room nurse, administrator; b. Maynard, Minn., July 22, 1931; d. Bernt O. and Melvina (Gerde) Docken; m. Roy L. Abbott, Jan. 2, 1987; children: Dianne Weber, Susan Milewski. Diploma, Broadlawns Sch. Nursing, Des Moines, 1952. Cert. oper. rm. nurse; cert. nursing adminstr. Head nurse Iowa Meth. Med. Ctr., Des Moines; pvt. scrub nurse Des Moines; head nurse oper. rm., recovery rm., nursing coord. oper. rm. VA Med. Ctr., Des Moines, oper. rm.-recovery rm. coord., ret. 1991. Mem. adv. bd. Des Moines Area Community Coll.; bd. dirs. Coun. on Nursing Adminstrn. Mem. ANA, Assn. Oper. Rm. Nurses (v.p. Cen. Hawkeye chpt.), Nurses Orgn. VA. Home: 3519 Crestmoor Pl Des Moines IA 50310-4322

ABBOTT, ANN AUGUSTINE, social worker, educator; b. Green Bay, Wis., July 6, 1943; d. Walter A. and Ethel D. Augustine. BS in Psychology, St. Norbert Coll., W. DePere, Wis., 1965; MSS in Social Work, Bryn Mawr Coll., 1969, PhD (NIMH fellow), 1977, postgrad. in higher edn. adminstrn., 1978. Acad. tutor, counselor Devereux Schs., Devon, Pa., 1965-67; psychol. clin. coord. Pa. State U., University Park, 1969-71; social worker Tidewater Mental Health Clinic, Williamsburg, Va., 1971-72; adj. prof. Pa. State U., King of Prussia, 1973-75; vis. lectr. C.C. of Phila., 1975-76; asst. prof. dir. social work, cmty. psychology Widener U., Chester, Pa., 1976-81, project dir. Univ. Yr. for Action, 1976-81, project cons. Adult Competency Tng. Grant, 1976-81; with sch. social work Rutgers U., Camden, 1981—2001, assoc. prof., 1987—2001, assoc. dean, 1993—2001; prof., MSW program dir. grad. social work dept. West Chester U., Pa., 2001—. Faculty fellow NIAAA/NIDA/OSAP, 1990-93. Tennis coach Nat. Jr. Tennis League, Phila., 1974-76; budget rev. bd. United Way, vice-chair allocations com., 1979-86; trustee Ins. Trust, 1995-98, chair, 1996-98. Vocation Rehab. Tng. grantee, 1964. Fellow Am. Orthopsychiat. Assn., Coll. Physicians of Phila.; mem. NASW (nat. bd. mem. region IV 1988-91, del. assembly rep. 1979-89, pres. Pa. state chpt. 1987-89, nat. pres.-elect 1992-93, nat. pres. 1993-95), Coun. on Social Work Edn. (commn. on accreditation 1997-2000), Am. Group Psychotherapy Assn., Internat. Fed. Social Workers (v.p. for N.Am. 1994-96). Home: PO Box 637 Villanova PA 19085-0637 Office: Grad Social Work Dept West Chester U Reynolds Hall West Chester PA 19383 E-mail: aabbott@wcupa.edu.

ABBOTT, BARBARA LOUISE, artist, educator; b. San Francisco, Calif., Oct. 16, 1941; d. C. Paige and Mary Ellen Abbott; m. Edward Michael Seman, Nov. 21, 1964 (div. June 1980); children: Jill, Janet, Michael Paige. BFA, U. Utah, 1982; MFA, Ariz. State U., 1986. Prof. art Edinboro U. Pa., Edinboro, Pa., 1989—90, La. State U., Shreveport, La., 1990—96; prin., owner Abbott Art Studio, San Jose, Calif., 1996—. Prin. works include Quilt Kiosks, Shreveport, La., 1993, Great Blue Herons, Santa Cruz, Calif., 2000, Perro Feliz, San Jose, Calif., 2002, exhibitions include Award Winning Prints, Phila. Print Club, Phila., 1986, Marking Time: Making Space, South of Mkt. Cultural Ctr., San Francisco, 2001, book, Twice Descending, 1991. Fellow Fulbright-Hays fellowship, U.S. Govt., 1993. Home and Studio: 778 Crestview Drive San Jose CA 95117

ABBOTT, BARRY ALEXANDER, lawyer; b. New Haven, Aug. 20, 1950; s. Harold and Norma (Kaufman) A.; 1 child, Anne Stewart. AB, Dartmouth Coll., 1972; JD, U. Fla., 1975; MBA, Stanford U., 1977. Bar: Fla. 1975, Calif. 1976, U.S. Dist. Ct. (so. dist.) Fla. 1976, U.S. Dist. Ct. (no. dist.) Calif. 1976, U.S. Ct. Appeals (9th cir.) 1976, U.S. Supreme Ct. 1979, D.C. 1985, N.Y. 1986. Assoc. Morrison & Foerster, San Francisco, 1977-83, ptnr., 1983-94; dir. Howard Rice Nemerovski Canady Falk & Rabkin, San Francisco, 1994—. Adj. faculty mem. Boalt Hall Sch. Law, U. Calif., Berkeley, 1998; lectr. corp., comml. and fin. inst. law various orgns.; mem. Fed. Res. Bd. Consumer Adv. Coun., 1992-94, chmn. consumer credit com., 1993-94, mem. governing com. Conf. on Consumer Fin. Law; mem. Am. Coll. Consumer Fin. Svcs. Attys., 1995—, bd. regents, 1995-98, sec., 2002-. Co-author: Truth in Lending: A Comprehensive Guide; contbr. articles to profl. jours. Named One of Outstanding Young Men of Am., U.S. Jaycees, 1980. Fellow Royal Soc. Arts (Silver medal 1972); mem. ABA (chmn. young lawyers divsn. bus. law com. 1987-88, chmn. ins. products subcom. 1987-92, vice chmn. consumer fin. svcs. commn. 1995-96, active various coms.), Calif. Bar Assn. (vice chair fin. instns. com. 1991-92, chair 1992-93, mem. ins. law com. 1994-96, mem. bus. law sect. exec. com. 1996-99, treas. 1997-98, vice chair 1998-99), Fla. Bar Assn., D.C. Bar Assn., N.Y. State Bar Assn., San Francisco Bar Assn. (chmn. membership com. 1984-86, bd. dirs. 1982, 87-88, Award of Merit 1985), Barristers Club (bd. dirs. 1981-83, treas.,

pres. 1982), Order of Coif, Phi Beta Kappa, Phi Kappa Phi. Clubs: World Trade (San Francisco), Commonwealth (Calif.). Republican. Office: Howard Rice 3 Embarcadero Ctr Ste 700 San Francisco CA 94111-4024 E-mail: babbott@howardrice.com.

ABBOTT, BENJAMIN EDWARD, JR., corporate executive; b. Washington, Dec. 7, 1928; s. Benjamin Edward and Agnes (Campbell) A.; m. Ellianna Gray, May 22, 1955; children: Celeni, Dawn, Mark, Scott. B in Indsl. Engring., U. Fla., 1953. Registered profl. engr., Ala. Indsl. engr. E.I. Dupont de Nemours & Co., Martinsville, Va., 1951, Allis Chalmers, Milw., 1953, Pensacola (Fla.) Naval Air Sta., 1955-60; mem. exec. staff Dr. Wernher von Braun Marshall Space Flight Ctr., NASA, Huntsville, Ala., 1960-68; v.p., dir. Investors Corp. of Am., Birmingham, Ala., 1968-75, Internat. Resorts, Inc., Birmingham, Ala., 1970-75; pres. Profl. Realty Svcs., Inc., Birmingham, Ala., 1977-78, Energy Sys. Engrs., Inc., Birmingham, Ala., 1978-82, Income Diversification Cons., Birmingham, Ala., 1982-84, Abbott Supply Co., Birmingham, Ala., 1984-86, Abbott & Assocs., Birmingham, Ala., 1986-89, Associated Agys. Am., Inc., Birmingham, Ala., 1990-99; gen. mgr. Internet Marketed Alliance, LLC, 2001—; pres. Enriching Lives, Inc., 2002—. Bd. dirs. Pacific Am. Corp., San Francisco, Life Ins. Co. of Am., Birmingham. Lt. (j.g.) USNR, 1953-55. Mem. Phi Kappa Phi. Home: 882 Davis Acres Dr Alpine AL 35014-6096 E-mail: beaabbott@iglide.net.

ABBOTT, BEVERLY STUBBLEFIELD, artist; b. Greensboro, NC, Dec. 12, 1940; d. Robert L. and Helen W. Stubblefield; m. Ira H. A. Abbott, May 7, 1960; children: Ira Robert, Leslie Ann. Represented by Seaside Art Gallery, Nags Head, NC. Exhibitions include Leigh Yawkey Woodson Art Mus., 1996—97, Seaside Art Gallery, 1996—2003, Village Gallery, 1997—99, Germantown Gallery, 1999—2003, Fla. Wildlife Art Expo, 1999—2003, Southeastern Wildlife Expo, 2002, Miniature Art Soc. Fla., 2003, Pawprints on My Heart, 2000; featured artist Va. Living Mus. Wildlife Arts Festival, 2003. Grantee, Susan K. Black Found., 2002. Mem.: Hampton Arts League (Merit award 1997), Atlantic Wildfowl Heritage Mus., James River Camera Club (pres. 1994), Langley Kennel Club (life; show chmn. 1977, 1984). Avocations: traveling, photography. Home: 13 Delta Cir Newport News VA 23601-3117 E-mail: babbott@uici.net

ABBOTT, BOB, state supreme court justice; b. Kans., Nov. 1, 1932; BS, Emporia State U.; JD, Washburn U.; LLM, U. Va. Bar: Kans. 1960. Pvt. practice, Junction City, Kans., from 1960; former chief judge Kans. Ct. Appeals; justice Kans. Supreme Ct., 1990—2003.

ABBOTT, CHARLES FAVOUR, lawyer; b. Sedro-Wolley, Wash., Oct. 12, 1937; s. Charles Favour and Violette Doris Abbott; m. Oranee Harward, Sept. 19, 1958; children: Patricia, Stephen, Nelson, Cynthia, Lisa, Alyson. BA in Econs., U. Wash., 1959, JD, 1962. BAr: Calif. 1962, Utah 1981. Law clk. Judge M. Oliver Koelsch, U.S. Ct. Appeals (9th cir.), San Francisco, 1963; assoc. Jones, Hatfield & Abbott, Escondido, Calif., 1964; pvt. practice Escondido, 1964-77, Provo, Utah, 1983-93; of counsel Mueller & Abbott, Escondido, 1997—; ptnr. Abbott, Thorn & Hill, Provo, 1981-83, Abbott & Abbott, Provo, 1993—. Author: How to Do Your Own Legal Work, 1976, 2d edit., 1981, How to Win in Small Claims Court, 1981, How to Be Free of Debt in 24 Hours, 1981, How to Hire the Best Lawyer at the Lowest Fee, 1981, The Lawyers's Inside Method of Making Money, 1979, The Millionaire Mindset, 1987, How to Make Big Money in the Next 30 Days, 1989, Business Legal Manual and Forms, 1990, How to Make Millions in Marketing, 1990, Telemarketing Training Course, 1990, How to Form A Corporation in Any State, 1990, The Complete Asset Protection Plan, 1990, Personal Injury and the Law, 1997, Fen-Phen Fallout--The Medical and Legal Crisis, 1998; mem. editl. bd. Wash. Law Rev. and State Bar Assn. Jour., 1961-62; bd. editors Phen-fen Litigation Strategist, 1998-2000; contbr. articles to profl. jours. Mem. ATLA, Utah Bar Assn., Calif. Bar Assn., U.S. Supreme Ct. Bar Assn. Home: 4411 N Sheffield Ct Provo UT 84058 Office: Charles F Abbott PC 3651 N 100 E Ste 300 Provo UT 84604-4521

ABBOTT, CHARLES HENRY, lawyer; b. Rumford, Maine, Oct. 26, 1935; s. Warren Salisbury and Lucille (Hicks) A.; m. Mary Myers; children: Woods, Edward, Ann. AB, Bowdoin Coll., 1957; LLB, Yale U., 1963. Bar: Maine 1963, U.S. Dist. Ct. Maine 1963, U.S. Ct. Appeals (1st cir.) 1965, U.S. Supreme Ct. 1980. Ptnr. Skelton, Taintor & Abbott, Auburn, Maine, 1964—; bd. dirs. Cen. Maine Power Co.; mem. First Circuit Judge Selection Panel, Boston, 1979-80. Contbr. articles to profl. jours. Mem. Gov.'s Exec. Council, State of Maine, 1975-76. Served to lt. CIC, U.S. Army, 1958-60. Fellow Am. Coll. Trial Lawyers; mem. Am. Judicature Soc. Democrat. Office: Skelton Taintor & Abbott PO Box 3200 Auburn ME 04212-3200

ABBOTT, CHARLES WARREN, lawyer; b. Miami, Jan. 16, 1930; s. Voyle E. and Katherine (Paschall) A.; m. Betty Jo Eckholdt, Jan. 9, 1959; children: Brenda Jean, Katherine Louise, Abigail Jill. BS in Bus. Adminstrn., U. Fla., 1951, JD, 1953. Bar: Fla. 1955, U.S. Dist. Ct. (so. dist.) Fla. 1955, U.S. Dist. Ct. (ctrl. dist.) Fla., U.S. Supreme Ct. 1960, U.S. Ct. Appeals (11th cir.) 1981, U.S. Dist. Ct. (no. dist.) Fla. 1981; cert. mediator Supreme Ct. Fla. Assoc. Maguire, Voorhis & Wells, P.A., Orlando, Fla., 1955-59, ptnr., 1959-68, dir., 1968—95, of counsel, 1995—98; ptnr. Holland & Knight LLP, Orlando, Fla., 1998—. Mem. judicial nominating commn. Fifth Appellate Dist., 1984-88, chmn. 1987-88. Chmn. Goldenrod Fire Control Dist., 1966-79; mem. Orange County Emergency Med. Svcs. Coun., 1984, 91-94; dir. Fla. Found. for Spl. Children; trustee U. Fla. Law Ctr. Assn, 2002—. Served with JAGC, USAF, 1953-55; served to capt. USAFR, 1951-62. Fellow Am. Coll. Trial Lawyers; mem. ABA, Fla. Bar Assn., Orange County Bar Assns., Fla. Def. Lawyers Assn. (sec.-treas. 1983, v.p. 1984, pres. 1985), Def. Rsch. Inst. (state chmn. 1981-85, so. regional v.p. 1986-88, nat. dir. 1988-91), Fedn. Ins. Corp. Counsel, Am. Bd. Trial Advs. (charter, treas. 1991-92, sec. 1992-93), First Ctrl. Fla. Am. Inns of Ct. (charter mem., treas., pres. 1992-93), Phi Delta Phi. Democrat. Presbyterian. Home: 2035 Summerland Ave Winter Park FL 32789-1453 Office: Holland & Knight LLP PO Box 1526 200 S Orange Ave Ste 2600 Orlando FL 32801

ABBOTT, DAN-SAN, parachute designer; b. Canton, Kwantong, China, Aug. 10, 1923; came to U.S., 1925; s. Harry Wayne and Mary Alice (Carr) A.; m. Noami Irene Abbott, Mar. 15, 1946 (div. 1953); children: Sandra, Daniel, Danielle; m. Patricia Lee Brown, June 15, 1958. Parachute rigger Security Parachute Co., Oakland, Calif., 1946-49; parachute supr. Calif. Air N.G., Hayward, 1949-53; design engr. Security Parachute Co., San Leandro, Calif., 1953-64, mgr. engring., 1964-68, v.p., 1968-77; dir. ops. Guardian Parachute, Santa Ana, Calif., 1977-88; dir. mktg. FXC Corp., Santa Ana, 1986-88; cons. World War I Aviation Documentation Svc., Ceres, Calif., 1988—. Artist Oakland Nat. Engraving, 1946. Contbr. articles to profl. jours. Recipient Achievement award Don Beck Meml. award, 1990, Award for Editl. Excellence, Over the Front, 1988, 90. Mem. Soc. of the First World Aviation Historians, League of WWI Aviation Historians, WWI Aeroplances Inc, NRA. Republican. Presbyterian. Avocations: oil painting, watercolor painting, drawing, writing. Home and Office: 1800 Stone Cress Ct Ceres CA 95307 E-mail: dansanabbott@charter.net.

ABBOTT, DAVID HENRY, manufacturing company executive; b. Milton, Ky., July 6, 1936; s. Carl and Rachael (Miles) A.; m. Joan Shefchik, Aug. 14, 1976; children— Kristine, Gina, Beth, Linsey BS, U. Ky., 1960, MBA, 1961. With Ford Motor Co., Louisville, Mpls. and Dearborn, Mich., 1961-69; div. controller J I Case Co., Racine, Wis., 1970-73, gen. mgr. service parts supply div., 1973-75, v.p., 1975, v.p. and gen. mgr. constrn. equipment div., 1975-77, v.p., gen. mgr. Drott div. Wausau, Wis., 1977-79, exec. v.p. worldwide constrn. equipment, 1979-81; pres., chief operating officer Portec, Inc., Oak Brook, Ill., 1981-87, also dir.; pres., chief exec. officer, dir. E.D. Etnyre & Co., Oregon, Ill., 1988—2002, ret., 2002. Dir. Oak Brook Bank, 1982-88. Served with U.S. Army, 1958 Mem. Constrn. Industry Mfrs. Assn. (bd. dirs. 1979-81, 82—, chmn. 1992), Am. Rd. and Transpn. Builders Assn. (dir. 1988—2002). Republican. Home: 2461 Saddlewood Ct Lanark IL 61046

ABBOTT, DOUGLAS EUGENE, engineering educator; b. Glendale, Calif., Apr. 20, 1934; s. Richard Edward and Eva (Pogue) A.; m. Doris Bernice Newmark, Dec. 16, 1956; children: Sandra Lee, Jodi Frances, Shari Evalinis, Traci Bernice. B.M.E., Stanford U., 1956, M.M.E., 1957, PhD, 1961. Asst. head fluid mechanics sect. Vidya div. Itek Corp., Palo Alto, Calif., 1960-64; lectr. Stanford U., 1963-64; asso. prof. Purdue U., 1964-69, prof., 1969-77, dir. thermal scis. and propulsion center, 1972-77; prof., chmn. dept. mech. engring. and mechanics, dir. computer-aided design/computer-aided mfg. ednl. program Lehigh U., Bethlehem, Pa., 1977-83, vice provost for computing and info. services, 1983-85; assoc. vice chancellor for info. technologies U. Mass.-Amherst, 1985-96; cons. in comms. technologies Amherst, 1996—. Staff cons. Midwest Applied Sci. Corp., Lafayette, Ind., 1964-72; energy controls div. Bendix Corp., South Bend, Ind., 1967-75, Westinghouse Research and Devel. Center, Pitts., 1970-75, ERDA, 1975-77; chmn. air breathing propulsion adv. com. Air Force Office of Sci. Research, 1973-83, Tech. Concepts, Inc., Sudbury, Mass., 1985-88; bd. dirs. Univ. Programs in Computer Aided Engring., Design and Mfg., 1984-91. Mem. governing bd. Five Coll. Libr., 1991-96. Hon. research fellow Sci. Research Council, U.K., 1971-72 Fellow AAAS, Am. Phys. Soc.; mem. ASME, AIAA, N.Y. Acad. Scis., Nat. Computer Graphics Assn. (bd. dirs. 1985-87, treas. 1987-89), Nat. Computer Graphics Assn. Ednl. Found. (bd. dirs. 1989-92), Trout Unltd. (bd. dirs. Pioneer Valley chpt. 1995—), Pi Tau Sigma. Home: 307 Shutesbury Rd Amherst MA 01002-1268 E-mail: abbott@oiit.umass.edu.

ABBOTT, EDWARD LEROY, finance executive; b. Dayton, Ohio, Dec. 18, 1930; s. Roy Edward and Mildred Eileen (Filler) A.; m. Elizabeth Joan Grahame, June 8, 1957; children: Jay Edward, Julie Beth Abbott Holland. AB, Wittenberg U., 1952; postgrad., Ohio State U., 1952-53. With Northwestern Mut. Life Ins. Co., 1956-73, regional mgr., 1970-73; with Acacia Mut. Life Ins. Co., Washington, 1973-83, exec. v.p., treas., 1978-83; vice chmn., exec. v.p. CenTrust Savs. Bank, Miami, Fla., 1983-87; chmn., pres., CEO Capital-Union Savs., Baton Rouge, 1987-90; pres. CEO, dir. Firstate Fin., Orlando, Fla., 1992-97, Heritage Hill Farm, 1998—. Served with U.S. Army, 1954-55. Mem. Alpha Tau Omega. Republican.

ABBOTT, GAYLE ELIZABETH, human resources consultant and coach; b. Cleve., July 7, 1954; d. Olcott Rutherford and Eleanor Francis (Norley) A.; 1 child, Elizabeth Laura. BA, Am. U., 1976; MBA, Loyola Coll., Balt., 1983. Cert. sr. profl. in human resources; cert. profl. behavior analyst; cert. profl. values analyst. Personnel mgmt. specialist Food and Drug Adminstrn., Washington, 1975-77; personnel mgr. Computer Network Corp., Washington, 1977-78; dir. human resources STSC, Inc., Rockville, Md., 1978-84; compensation cons. Comm. Satellite Corp., Washington, 1984-85; pres., founder HURECO, Inc., Vienna, Va., 1985—. Lectr., adj. faculty Marymount U., Arlington, Va., 1990-95, Am. U., Washington, 1995-99; spkr. in field. Co-author: Deflecting Workplace Violence, 1994; contbr. articles to profl. jours. Vol., room mother Flint Hill Elem. Sch.; chair pers. com. Lewinsville Presbyn. Ch., 1987-91; troop leader Brownies Girl Scouts U.S.A., 1996-97; vol. art tchr. Flint Hill Elem. Sch., chair 6th-grade dinner dance, 2001; chair 8th-grade dance Thoreau Mid. Sch., 2002; pres. Glencannon Homeowners Assn., 2001-2002. Recipient Lodestar award Am. U., 1992, Alumni Recognition award, 2001; named Cons. of Yr. TTI Performance Systems, 2002. Mem. AAUW (bd. rec. sec. 1987, v.p. membership 1988-89), Soc. for Human Resource Mgmt. (dir. Va. state coun. 1991), No. Va. Soc. for Human Resource Mgmt. (legis. rep. 1987-88, v.p. programs 1988, pres. 1989-90, dir. 1991-93, Disting. Leadership award 1991), Am. U. Alumni Assn. (v.p. 1988-90, pres. 1990-92, bd. dirs. 1993-97). Mem. Unity Ch. Office: PO Box 2457 Vienna VA 22183-2457

ABBOTT, GEORGE LINDELL, librarian; b. Rutland, Vt., July 11, 1941; s. F. George and Eva Marie (Fields) A.; m. Sandra Jean Baker, Aug. 6, 1966; 1 child, Brian George. BA in Math., St. Michael's Coll., 1963; MLS, Syracuse U., 1966. Cataloguer St. Michael's Coll., Winooski, Vt., 1963-64; cataloguer libr. Syracuse (N.Y.) U., 1966-70, media librarian, 1970-80, head dept. media svcs., 1980—. Cons. in field. Contbr. articles to various publs.; editor Videodisc/VideoTex jour., 1980-82. Recipient Watson Davis award, Am. Soc. for Info. Sci. and Tech., 1987. Mem. ALA, Am. Soc. Info. Sci. (bd. dirs. 1981-85), Internat. Fedn. of Libr. Assns. and Instns. (standing com. audiovisual and multimedia sect., 2003—), Libr. and Info. Tech. Assn. (bd. dirs. 1985-88), Soc. Motion Picture and TV Engrs., Beta Phi Mu. Avocations: microcomputing, cinema. Office: Syracuse Univ Libr 222 Waverly Ave Syracuse NY 13210-2412

ABBOTT, GREG WAYNE, state attorney general, former state supreme court justice; b. Wichita Falls, Tex., Nov. 13, 1957; s. Calvin Roger and Doris Lacristia (Jacks) Rowley A.; m. Cecilia Therese Phalen, Aug. 15, 1981; 1 child, Audrey. BBA, U. Tex., 1981; JD, Vanderbilt U., 1984. Bar: Tex. 1985, U.S. Dist. Ct. (so. dist.) Tex. 1985. Atty. Butler & Binion, Houston, 1984-92; judge 12th State Dist. Ct., Houston, 1992-96; justice Texas Supreme Ct., 1996—2000; partner Bracewell & Patterson, LLP; atty. gen. State of Tex., 2003—. Prof. U. Tex.; mem. com. on Pub. Trust and Confidence in Tex. Cts., Jury Task Force Implementation Project; mem. cert. bd. Tex. Ct. Reporters; exec. com. Family Law 2000 Task Force. Dir. Houston Ctr. for Barrier Free Living, 1986-87; capt. March of Dimes Team Walk, Houston, 1986-87; mem. Gov.'s Com. to Promote Adoption; bd. dirs. Tex. Inst. Rehab. and Rsch., Maywood Children and Family Svcs.; bd. trustees Goodwill Industries; adv. bd. Career and Recovery Resources Inc. Named Disabled Person of the Yr. Harris County Com. on Employment of Disabled Persons, 1985, Outstanding Young Texan Tex. Jaycees, 1995; recipient Am. Jurisprudence award Am. Jur, 1983, Named Outstanding Trial Judge, Texas Assn. of Civil Trial and Appellate Specialists, 1995. Mem. State Bar Tex. (com. on legal advt. 1988, Supreme Ct. liason for com. on jud. ethics, jud. conduct commn., code of jud. conduct), Houston Bar Assn. (Houston's Outstanding Young Lawyer 1994), Houston Young Lawyers Assn., Tex. Assn. State Judges (exec. com.). Republican. Roman Catholic. Avocations: snow-skiing, travel, swimming. Office: Capitol Station PO Box 12548 Austin TX 78711*

ABBOTT, HENRY JAMES, electro-mechanical engineer; b. Phila., Aug. 23, 1948; s. Henry James Abbott, Sr. and Dorothy Jane Abbott; m. Carole Marsha Rappaport, Jan. 21, 1950 (div.); children: Brandon Eric, Carl Evans. Student, Montgomery County C.C., Blue Bell, Pa., Temple U., Parsons Coll. Electro-mechanical engring. tech. SPS Techs., Jenkintown, Pa., Southern Techs., King of Prussia, Pa. Contbr. articles to profl. jours. With USN, 1969—72. Recipient Recognition award, Boeing Aerospace Co. Republican. Home: 561 Philadelphia Ave King Of Prussia PA 19406-3620 Office: Southern Techs Electro Mechanical Engring 561 Philadelphia Ave King Of Prussia PA 19406 Fax: 610-239-7902.

ABBOTT, HIRSCHEL THERON, JR., lawyer; b. Clarksdale, Miss., Jan. 11, 1942; s. Hirschel Theron Sr. and Ona Belle (Williamson) A.; m. Mimi Eugenia DuPre, June 14, 1969; children: Barkley, Chip. BBA in Acct., U. Miss., Oxford, 1964; JD, U. Va., Charlottesville, 1971. Bar: La. 1971, Miss. 1971, U.S. Dist. Ct. (ea. dist.) La. 1971, U.S. Ct. Appeals (5th cir.) 1981, U.S. Tax Ct. 1988; bd. cert. tax law specialist. Lawyer Stone Pigman Walther Wittmann LLP, New Orleans, 1971—75, ptnr., 1975—. Bd. dirs. Episcopal Housing for Srs., Inc., Lambeth House, Inc.; past trustee, sec. Preservation Resource Ctr., New Orleans; past bd. mem., chmn. Trinity Episcopal Sch. Bd. Trustees; past trustee, treas. La. Civil Svc. League; past bd. mem. Uptown Neighborhood Improvement Assn.; past mem., chmn. La. Jefferson Scholarship Selection Com. U. Va.; past regional chmn. La. U. Va. Law Sch. Annual Giving Fund; past mem. of vestry Trinity Episcopal Ch.; past mem. Adv. Bd. Jr. League New Orleans. Recipient Monte M. Lemann award, La. Civil Svc. League, 1989. Fellow Am. Coll. Trust and Estate Counsel (past mem. charitable planning and exempt orgns. com.), La. Bar Found.; mem. ABA (tax sect., bus. law sect., real property trusts probate sect.), La. Bar Assn. (past chmn. tax law specialization commn., tax sect., corp. sect., successions, donations and trusts sect.), Miss. State Bar Assn., New Orleans Estate Planning Coun., Assn. Employee Benefit Planners. Epicopalian. Office: Stone Pigman Walther et al 546 Carondelet St New Orleans LA 70130-3588 E-mail: habbott@stonepigman.com.

ABBOTT, JAMES SAMUEL, III, marketing executive; b. Cleve., Nov. 19, 1918; s. James Samuel and Dorothy (Wilbor) A.; m. Mary Margaret Torrance, Oct. 13, 1957; 1 child, James Samuel. Student, Cornell U., 1941. Sales engr. Nat. Acme Co., Cleve., Chgo., 1945-63, chief sales engr. Cleve., 1963-67, sales mgr., 1967-69; mktg. mgr. Cleveland Twist Drill Co., Cleve., 1969-83; pres. James S. Abbott Consulting, Inc., Gates Mills, Ohio, 1983—. Contbr. articles to profl. jours. Mem. pk. bd. Village of Gates Mills, Ohio, 1979-86. Capt. USAF, 1941-45. Mem. Soc. Founders-Patriots (gov. 1968-69), Soc. Colonial Wars, Western Res. Hist. Soc., Clev. Mus. Natural History, U.S. Horse Cavalry Assn., Mayfield Country Club. Avocations: Am. history, antiques, fly fishing, golf, tennis, vintage cars. Home: 7059 Hillcreek Ln Gates Mills OH 44040-9629

ABBOTT, LAWRENCE E. lawyer; b. Miami, Fla., May 18, 1944; BA, St. Edward's U., 1967; JD, Tulane U. La., 1972. Bar: La. 1972, U.S. Dist. Ct. (ea. dist.) La. 1972, U.S. Dist. Ct. (we. dist.) La. 1974, U.S. Dist. Ct. (mid. dist.) La. 1975, U.S. Supreme Ct. 1979, U.S. Ct. Appeals (5th cir.) 1981, U.S. Ct. Appeals (11th cir.) 1984, Tex. 1996. D.C. 1996. Mem. Abbott, Simses & Kuchler, Houston, New Orleans and Covington, La. Mem. ABA (products, gen. liability and consumer law com., rail and motor carrier law com., toxic and hazardous substances and environ. law com. 1995—), Maritime Law Assn. U.S. (mem. internat. law sea com. 1984—, mem. subcom. offshore exploration and devel. 1984—, mem. com. river and ocean towing 1985—), Average Adjusters Assn. U.S. (assoc.), La. State Bar Assn. (asst. examiner com. on bar admissions 1994—), La. Assn. Def. Counsel, New Orleans Bar Assn., New Orleans Def. Counsel Assn., Southeastern Admiralty Law Inst., Def. Rsch. Inst., Inc., La. Bar Found., La. Assn. R.R. Trial Counsel, Am. Arbitration Assn., La. Assn. Bus. and Industry, Phi Delta Phi. Office: Abbott Simses Knister & Kuchler 400 Lafayette St Ste 200 New Orleans LA 70130-3229 E-mail: Larry-Abbott@abbott-simses.com.*

ABBOTT, LINDA JOY, stained glass artisan, educator, photographer; b. Hempstead, N.Y., Oct. 10, 1943; d. Edward Morton Brandstatter and Evalyne Manchik; divorced 1971; children: David Edward Black, Adam Michael Black. AAS in Design, SUNY at FIT, N.Y.C., 1963; Cert. paralegal, Tarrant County C.C., Fort Worth, Tex., 1983; student, Disney Inst. Wildlife Photog., 2000, N.Y. Inst. Photography, 2001. Fashion designer Alyssa/Little Craft, N.Y.C., 1963-65; bus. owner Virgin Islands Diving Sch., St. Thomas, V.I., 1972-76; stained glass artisan Creative Glass, Salt Lake City, 1978-81, Linda Abbott Glass Art, Willow Park, Tex., 1981-86; founder, stained glass artisan, instr. Crystal Rainbow Glass Studio, Dania, Fla., 1986-99; stained glass artisan Linda Abbott Glass Studio, 1999—; freelance photographer. Freelance calligrapher various colls., Covina, Calif., 1968—71; freelance artist, Lancaster, 1976—78; cons. various stained glass cos., 1989—; product cons. various stained glass equipment mfrs., 1994—; sem. instr. Internat. Art Glass Supplies Assn., 1994—, coord. seminars, chair, 1999; mem. steering com. Art Glass Am., Tampa, 1998; guest instr. MISC studios nationwide, 1999—; webmaster Cert. Career Inst., Clearfield, Utah; instr. in field. Author: E-Magine This! Book One, 2002 co-author: (books) Hot & Wired, 1993, Some Things Fishy, 1993, Rainforest, 1994, Stargazing, 1995, Image is Everything, 1996; prodr. (video) Hot & Wired; contbr. articles to mags. in field. Recipient Best in Show award Calif. City Art Assn., 1978, Glass Expo, Salt Lake City, 1982. Mem. So. Fla. Ferret Club, Internat. Art Glass Suppliers Assn. (com. chair 1996—), Internat. Stained Glass Designers Assn. (pres. 1995-99), Art Glass Guild Artisans (dir. 1996—), Art Glass Am. (founder), Ednl. Consumer Conf. Jewish. Avocations: scuba diving, white water rafting, animal welfare causes, wildlife photography. E-mail: LOTUS954@aol.com.

ABBOTT, MYLES BRUCE, pediatrician; b. New Haven, Aug. 7, 1947; m. Ida Offenbach, June 14, 1969; children: Jordan, David. MD, U. Miami, Fla., 1972. Pediatrician East Bay Pediat., Berkeley, Calif., 1978—, Orinda, 1978—. Office: East Bay Pediatrics 2999 Regent St Berkeley CA 94705 also: East Bay Pediatrics 96 Davis Road Orinda CA 94563 Office Fax: 925-254-1054.

ABBOTT, NELL SUTTLES, writer, poet; b. Atlanta, Feb. 14, 1927; d. William Edgar and Nelle Harris Suttles; m. Joe Montgomery Abbott, Jan. 29, 1948; children: Katherine Ann, Joe Montgomery Jr., Martin Edward. B of Comml. Sci., Ga. State U., 1949. Newspaper columnist South Fulton Recorder, Fairburn, Ga., 1960-74, Athens (Ga.) Advertiser, 1964-65, Marietta (Ga.) Daily Jour., 1963-74, short story writer, 1963-74; freelance short story writer for various mags., 1960-91. Tchr. Southeastern Writers, Atlanta, 1989, Dixie Coun.-Authors and Journalists, St. Simons Island, Ga., 1989, 1st Presbyn. Ch., Marietta, 1985-89; book reviewer Ida Belle Williams Book Club, Swainsboro, Ga. Contbr. short stories and poetry to anthologies including Golden Poetry, Southern Poets 50 and Older, 2003; editor (newsletter) Mettler (Ga.) Presbyn. Ch., 1998-2003. Newsletter editor: Metter (Ga.) Presbyn. Ch., 1998-2002. Mem. Nat. League Am. PEN Women (program chair Atlanta br. 1991-92, 92—, Jour. award 1999), Ga. Poetry Soc. (featured annually in anthology, Byron Herbert Reece prize 1999, Charles Dickson Chapbook award 2001), Metter Garden Club. Republican. Presbyterian. Avocations: reading, walking, cooking. Home: 409 S Lewis St Metter GA 30439

ABBOTT, REBECCA PHILLIPS, museum director, art consultant, photographer; b. Giessen, Germany, Jan. 10, 1950; d. Charles Leonard and Janet Alice (Praeger) Phillips. BA, Emory and Henry Coll., 1973; postgrad., Georgetown U., 1975, Am. U., 1982-88. Assoc. univ. registrar Am. U., Washington, 1977-81, assoc. dir. adminstrv. computing, 1981-84, dir. adminstrv. computing, 1984-88; dir. membership Nat. Mus. of Women in the Arts, Washington, 1988-89, dir., 1989-98; cons. in fine arts, 1998—. Fine arts photographer. Selected solo exhbns., Includes Anton Gallery, Public Places Private Views, 1992, The Wind, 1994, Canal Views, 1996, Burton Marinkovich Fine Art, Shadows at 18th and K, 1998; Selected group exhbns. includes The Annex Gallery, Metaphysical Landscapes,1989, Embassy of Japan: East Meets West, 1995, Nippon Gallery, Assimilations, 1997. Mem. Am. Assn. Mus., Mus. Art Table.

ABBOTT, REGINA A. neurodiagnostic technologist, consultant, business owner; b. Haverhill, Mass., Mar. 5, 1950; d. Frank A. and Ann (Drelick) A. Student, Pierce Bus. Sch., Boston, 1967-70, Seizure Unit Children's Hosp. Med. Ctr. Sch. EEG Tech., 1970-71. Registered electroneurodiagnostic technologist Advanced Fuller Sch. Massage Therapy, 2001, nat. cert. massage therapist Nat. Cert. Bd. Therapeutic Massage and Bodywork. Tech. dir. electrodiagnostic labs. Salem Hosp., 1972-76; lab. dir. clin. neurophysiology Tufts U. New Eng. Med. Ctr., Boston, 1976-78; clin. instr. EEG program Laboure Coll., Boston, 1977-81; adminstrv. dir. dept. Neurology Mt. Auburn Hosp., Cambridge, Mass., 1978-81; tech. dir. clin. neurophysiology Drs. Diagnostic Service, Virginia Beach, Va.; tech. dir. neurodiagnostic ctr. Portsmouth Psychiatric Ctr., 1981-87; founder, pres., owner Commonwealth Neurodiagnostic Services, Inc., 1986—, Hands on HealthCare, 2001—. Co-dir. continuing edn. program EEG Tech., Boston, 1977-78; mem. adv. com. sch. neurodiagnostic tech. Laboure Coll., 1977-81, Sch. EEG Tech. Children's Hosp. Med. Ctr., Boston, 1980-81; assoc. examiner Am. Bd. Registration of Electroencephalographic Technologists, 1977-83; mem. guest faculty Oxford Medilog Co., 1986; cons. Nihon Kohden Am., 1981-83; cons., educator Teca Corp., Pleasantville, N.Y., 1981-87; allied health prof. staff mem. Virginia Beach Gen. Hosp., Humana Hosp. Bayside, Virginia Beach; clin. evaluator Calif. Coll. for Health Scis., 1995—. Contbr. articles to profl. jours. EIL scholar, Poland/USSR, 1970; recipient Internat. Woman of Yr. award in bus. and sci. Internat. Biographical Ctr., London, 1993-94, Woman of Yr. award Am. Biographical Inst., 1993. Mem.: NAFE, New Eng. Soc. EEG Technologists (bd. dirs., sec., trip and edn. com., faculty tng. and edn.), Am. Massage Therapy Assn., Am. Soc. Electroneurodiagnostic Technologists, Epilepsy Soc. Mass. Avocations: running, art collecting, photography, reading, investing.

ABBOTT, REXFORD J. secondary school educator, mechanical engineer; b. Johnson City, N.Y., Jan. 25, 1945; s. Franklin P. and Ruth Marie Abbott; m. Carolyn Shope, Nov. 14, 1965; children: Lynore, Barbara. BS in Mech. Engring., U. Rochester; MS in Mech. Engring., U. Ariz. Engr. Boeing Co., Seattle, Hughes Aircraft, Tucson; supr. Spectra Physics, Mt. View, Calif.; mech. sys. engr. Novellus Sys., San Jose, Calif.; sr. mech. engr., mgr. Silicon Valley Group, San Jose, Calif.; tchr. Mt. Pleasant H.S., San Jose. Bd. dirs. First United Ch., Los Gatos, Calif., 1988—; comdr. Lake Merritt Sailing Club, Oakland, Calif. Recipient Bausch & Lomb Sci. award. Mem.: ASME, Acad. Model Aircraft. Methodist. Achievements include patents for improved etaler apparatus; robot gantry skew detector. Avocations: model aircrafts, photography, music, tuba. Address: 3465 Morgan Pl San Jose CA 95132-2414

ABBOTT, ROBERT DEAN, education scientist; b. Twin Falls, Idaho, Dec. 19, 1946; s. Charles Dean and Billie June (Moore) A.; m. Sylvia Patricia Keim, Dec. 16, 1967; children: Danielle, Matthew. BA, Calif. Western U., San Diego, 1967; MS, U. Wash., 1968, PhD, 1970. Asst. prof., assoc. prof. Calif. State U.-Fullerton, 1970-75; asst. prof., prof. ednl. psychology U. Wash., Seattle, 1975—; dir. Ctr. Inst. Devel. and Research, Seattle, 1983-92. Author: Elementary Multivariate Statistics, 1983; contbr. articles to profl. jours. Calif. State

scholar, 1964-67 Fellow Am. Psychol. Assn.; mem. Am. Ednl. Research Assn., Am. Stats. Assn., Psychometric Soc. Methodist. Office: Ednl Psych 312 Miller PO Box 353600 Seattle WA 98195-3600

ABBOTT, WILLIAM ANTHONY, lawyer; b. Austin, Minn., May 25, 1951; s. Robert Elmer and Marion Iris (Edel) A.; m. Deborah Lynn Hunt, Apr. 23, 1982; 1 child, Whitney Hunt. BBA with distinction, U. Wis., 1973, JD cum laude, 1975. Bar: Wis. 1976, U.S. Dist. Ct. (we. dist.) Wis. 1976, U.S. Tax Ct. 1981. Ptnr., Bell, Metzner, Gierhart & Moore, S.C., Madison, Wis., 1980— . V.p. Briarpatch, Inc. for runaway youth, Madison, 1979-87, pres. 1988; ambassador Picada; sec. Energy Assistance, Inc., Madison, 1983; committeeman United Way Pres.'s Council, Madison, 1984—. Mem. ABA, Wis. Bar Assn., Dane County Bar Assn., Middleton Jaycees (pres. 1978), Order of Coif, Airplane Owners and Pilots Assn., Phi Kappa Phi, Beta Gamma Sigma. Clubs: Bklyn. Flying (v.p. 1987—), Wis. Fun Flyers, Inc. (v.p. 1987—). Lodge: Optimists (bd. dirs. 1985-86). Office: Bell Metzner Gierhart & Moore SC 2472 Thatcher Ln Mc Farland WI 53558-9737

ABBOTT, WILLIAM SAUNDERS, lawyer; b. Medford, Mass., June 2, 1938; s. Charles Theodoric and Evelyn (Saunders) A.; m. Susan Shaw, June 24, 1961; children: Cathryn, Stephen, David. AB, Harvard U., 1960, LLB, 1966. Bar: Mass. 1967, U.S. Dist. Ct. Mass., U.S. Ct. Appeals (D.C. cir.). White House fellow, 1966-67; regional coord. U.S. Agrl. Programs Asia USDA, 1967-68; gen. counsel Cabot, Cabot & Forbes Co., Boston, 1968-77; prin. Simonds, Winslow, Willis & Abbott, Boston, 1977—. Mem. Harvard Law Review. Pres. Plymouth County Wildlands Trust, 1984—90, 1996—97, Nat. Found. to Improve TV, 1970—; mem. Arlington Bd. Selectmen, 1970—73; bd. dirs. Bay Tower Restaurant. Lt. USN, 1960—63. Mem.: Boston Bar Assn., Mass. Bar Assn., Phi Beta Kappa. Home: 33 Herring Way Plymouth MA 02360-3225 Office: Simonds Winslow Willis & Abbott 50 Congress St Ste 925 Boston MA 02109-4075 E-mail: wabbott1@aol.com.

ABBOTT-LYON, FRANCES DOWDLE, journalist, civic worker; b. Rome, Ga., Mar. 21, 1924; d. John Wesley and Lucille Elizabeth (Field) Dowdle; m. Jackson Miles Abbott, May 15, 1948; children: Medora Frances, David Field, Elizabeth Stockton, Robert Jackson; m. Archibald W. Lyon, Oct. 15, 1993. Student, Draughon's Bus. Coll., Columbia, S.C. Feature writer, Mt. Vernon corr. Alexandria Gazette, Va., 1967-75; libr., rsch. assoc. Gadsby's Tavern Mus., Alexandria, 1977-99. Chmn. ann. George Washington Birthnight Ball, Mt. Vernon, 1974-82; sec. George Washington 250th Birthday Celebration Commn., 1979-82; mem. steering com. Neighborhood Friends Hist. Mt. Vernon, 1988-92; chmn. publicity Waynewood Woman's Club, Waynewood Citizens Assn.; treas. Mt. Vernon Citizens Assn., 1967-82; dist. chmn. Mt. Vernon March of Dimes, 1960-62; sec. Waynewood Sch. PTA, 1962-64; tchr. 1st aid Girl Scouts U.S., 1964-65; den mother Cub Scouts, 1966; chmn. publicity Mt. Vernon Women's Rep. Club, 1955. Named Mrs. Waynewood by Cmty. Vote, 1969. Mem. DAR (registrar 1968-77, conservation chair 1992-98), The Nature Conservancy, SC Hist. Soc., Hat Ladies of Charleston. Episcopalian. Home: 1235 Colfax Ct Mount Pleasant SC 29466

ABBOTT-RYAN, PAT, painter, writer; b. Bloomington, Ind., Aug. 2, 1932; d. John Carl Abbott and Martha Louise Stone; m. James Herbert Ryan, June 7, 1955; 1 child, Pamela Louise. BA cum laude, U. Md., 1981. Coll. bd. mem. Mademoiselle Mag., N.Y.C., 1952. Exhibits chmn. Petersburg (Va.) Area Art League, 2000—. Contbr. articles, columns in newspapers; assoc. editor: Detective Mag., 1960—69; editor: Silver-Burdett Time/Life, 1965; contbr. chapters to books; one-woman shows include Touchstone Gallery, Washington, D.C., 1985, Foundry Gallery, 1985, PAAL Gallery, Old Towne, Petersburg, Va., 1999, exhibited in group shows at Rawls Mus. Arts, Courtland, Va., 2000, one-woman shows include others, exhibited in group shows at 1708 Gallery, Richmond, Va., 2000, St. Paul's Ch. and St. Stephen's Ch., 2001, Zenith Gallery, Washington, D.C., 2002—03, Olde Towne Pet Resort, Springfield, Va., 2002—03, many others. Scholar, Skowhegan (Maine) Sch. Painting & Sculpture, 1981. Mem.: Petersburg (Va.) Area Art League (bd. dirs. 2000—). Home: 1221 Woodland Road Petersburg VA 23805

ABBOUD, ALFRED ROBERT, banker, consultant, investor; b. Boston, May 29, 1929; s. Alfred and Victoria (Karam) A.; m. Joan Grover, June 11, 1955; children: Robert G., Jeanne Frances, Katherine Jane. BS cum laude, Harvard U., 1951, LL.B., 1956, MBA, 1958. Bar: Mass. 1957, Ill. 1959. Asst. cashier First Nat. Bank of Chgo., 1960-62, asst. v.p., 1962-64, v.p., 1964-69, sr. v.p., 1969-72, exec. v.p., 1972-73, vice chmn. bd., 1973-74, dep. chmn. bd., 1974-75, chmn. bd., CEO, 1975-80; pres., COO Occidental Petroleum Corp., L.A., 1980-84; pres. A. Robert Abboud & Co., Fox River Grove, Ill., 1984—; chmn., CEO First City Bancorp. of Tex. Inc., Houston, 1988-91. Bd. dirs. AAR Corp., Elk Grove Village. Author: Money in the Bank: How Safe Is It?, 1988. Capt. USMC, 1951-53. Decorated Purple Heart, Bronze Star; Baker scholar, 1958. Mem. Econ. Comml. Club, The Chgo. Club, Harvard Club Chgo., Harvard Club N.Y.C., Barrington Hills Country Club. Home: 209 Braeburn Rd Barrington IL 60010-9637 Office: PO Box 33 212 Stone Hill Ctr Fox River Grove IL 60021-0033

ABCARIAN, HERAND, surgeon, educator; b. Ahvaz, Iran, Jan. 23, 1941; arrived in U.S., 1966; s. Joseph and Stella (Banki) A.; m. Karen Jane Berger, May 10, 1969; children: Gregory, Ariane, Margot. MD, Teheran U., 1965. Intern Cook County Hosp., Chgo., 1966—67, resident in gen. surgery, 1967—71, resident in colon and rectal surgery, 1971—72, chmn. colon and rectal surgery, 1972—93; head dept. surgery, Turi Josefson prof. U. Ill. Coll. Med., Chgo., 1989—; exec. dir. Am. Bd. Colon & Rectal Surgery, Taylor, Mich. Assoc. editor: Diseases of Colon and Rectum, 1981—95. Fellow ACS (various coms. and offices), Am. Soc. Colon and Rectal Surgeons (sec. 1985-87, pres. 1988-89), Can. Soc. Colon and Rectal Surgeons (hon.); mem. Am. Surg. Assn., Soc. Am. Gastroendoscopic Surgeons (founder), Sydney Soc. Colon and Rectal Surgeons (hon.), Assn. Coloprotology of Gt. Britain (hon. fellow). Republican. Roman Catholic. Avocations: visual arts, music, philately. Office: U Ill 840 S Wood St # 518 Chicago IL 60612-7317 Also: Am Bd Colon & Rectal Surgery 20600 Eureka Rd Ste 713 Taylor MI 48180-5376

ABDALADZE, MERABI, physicist; b. Kutaisi, Georgia, Jan. 15, 1959; arrived in U.S., 2000; s. Grigoli and Lamara Abdaladze; m. Irine Kobulashvili, Aug. 3, 1987 (div. Feb. 1995); m. Tamar Bibilashvili, Apr. 21, 2000; 1 stepchild, David Taktakishvili. M, Georgian Tech. U., 1980; PhD of Engring. Sci., Physico-Tech. Inst., Novosibirsk, Russia, 1984; postgrad., Tbilisi Banking Inst., 1991—92. Engr. Rsch. Inst. Elec. Tech., Tbilisi, Georgia, 1980—81; engr., rsch. asst. Inst. Cybernetics of Acad. Sci., Tbilisi, 1981—89; engr. I Georgian Polytech. U., Tbilisi, 1989—91; dir. East and West Contacts Ltd., Tbilisi, 1991—. Sr. cons. Pres. Supr. Coun. of Georgia, Tbilisi, 1991; dir. Imacom Ltd., Tbilisi, 1998—, Imacom in U.S. Corp., N.Y.C., 2001—; cons. Tbilisi State U., 1997—. Contbr. Mem.: N.Y. Acad. Scis., Georgian Fedn. Profl. Accts. and Auditors, Am. Geophys. Union. Avocations: tennis, music, literature, mountain climbing.*

ABDELAAL, AHMED THARWAT, marketing educator, marketing professional, consultant; b. Cairo, Oct. 1, 1950; arrived in U.S., 1977; s. Muhammed Abdelaal; m. Caren Abdelaal, Jan. 8, 1997; 1 child, Sara. BS, Ein Shams U., Cairo, 1973; MBA, Minn. State U., 1981. Rsch. mgr. Egyptian Internat. U., Cairo, 1975—77; advt. mgr. Shopping Spree Publs., Mpls., 1982—84; market intelligence cons. MICG, Mpls., 1984—; project mgr. Export Bank Egypt, Cairo, 1984—85; instr. U. St. Thomas, St. Paul, 1990—, Mankato (Minn.) State U., 1996—98, Nat. Coll., St. Paul, 1996—99. Host, prodr. (talk show) Arab Am. TV, Mpls., 1994—. Promotion mgr. Egyptian Am. Soc., Mpls., 1994—; vol. Egyptian Illiteracy Agy., Cairo, 1972—75. Pvt. Air Def., 1973—75, Egypt. Named Best Cmty. TV program, Time Warner Cable Co., Mpls., 1996, Columnist of Yr., Pioneer Press, 2000. Achievements include first Arab-American TV show in the Midwest. Avocations: broadcasting, writing, reading, golf. E-mail: ata200221@msn.com.

ABDEL-AAL, HISHAM A, adult education educator; b. Alexandria, Egypt, Feb. 16, 1960; s. Ahmed M Abdel-Aal and Samira S Mohammad; m. Leah J Moran. PhD, U. of N.C., Charlotte, 1996—98. Vis. scholar Ohio State U., 2000—01; adj. prof. York Tech. Coll., Rock Hill, SC, 1999—. Author: (archival jour. papers) Thermal Analysis in Tribology. Pres. Egyptian Soc. of Greater Charlotte, 1999—2001; charitable El-Salam Found., Charlotte, 2000—01. Grantee Fellow, Egyptian Soc. of Mech. Engineers. Mem.: Japan Soc. of Mech. Engineers, AIAA, NY Acad. of Sciences, ASME. Muslim. Office: York Technical College 452 south AndersonRd Rock Hill SC 29730 Personal E-mail: haabdela@excite.com.

ABDEL-ATY, MOHAMED A. engineering educator; b. Alexandria, Egypt, Sept. 10, 1963; s. Ahmad Abdel-Aty and Fatma Balbaa; m. Hala ElAarag; children: Jasmine, Ahmad. PhD, U. Calif., Davis, 1995. Lectr. Alexandria U.; rschr. U. of Calif.; assoc. prof. U. Ctrl. Fla. Rschr. Traffic Safety, 2002. Contbr. articles; mem. editl. adv. bd.: Accident Analysis & Prevention. Mem.: Transp. Rsch. Bd., Phi Kappa Phi, Tau Beta Pi. Avocations: reading, travel. Office: Univ Ctrl Fla Dept Civil & Environ Engring Orlando FL 32816 Office Fax: 407-823-3315. Business E-Mail: mabdel@mail.ucf.edu.

ABDEL-KHALIK, SAID IBRAHIM, nuclear and mechanical engineering educator; b. Alexandria, Egypt, Aug. 9, 1948; came to U.S., 1969; s. Ibrahim Saad and Esha Farag (Ahmad) A.-K.; m. Sharon Lora Duncan; 1 child, Faith Austen Khalik. BS summa cum laude, Alexandria U., 1967; MS in Mech. Engring., U. Wis. Madison, 1971, PhD in Mech. Engring., 1973. Postdoctoral fellow in chem. engring. U. Wis., Madison, 1973-74, asst. prof. nuclear engring., 1976-78, assoc. prof., 1978-82, prof., 1982-87; Ga. Power disting. prof. nuclear engring. Ga. Inst. Tech., Atlanta, 1987-89, assoc. dir. sch. mech. engring., 1990-92, so. nuclear disting. prof., 1993—; instr. Alexandria U., 1967-69; sr. engr. Babcock & Wilcox, Lynchburg, Va., 1975. Guest rsch. scientist Nuclear Rsch. Ctr., Karlsruhe, Fed. Republic Germany, 1979; vis. prof. EPFL, Inst. de Genie Atomique, Lausanne, Switzerland, 1982; cons. Kewaunee Nuclear Plant, Green Bay, Wis., 1983—, numerous rsch. orgns. and govtl. agys. Contbr. articles to profl. jours. Fellow Am. Nuclear Soc., ASME; mem. Am. Soc. Engring. Edn. (Glenn Murphy award 1999), Profl. Reactor Operators Soc., Am. Inst. Physics, Assn. Egyptian-Am. Scholars, Sigma Xi, Phi Kappa Phi. Achievements include three patents for gaseous control system for nuclear reactors. Home: 3579 Midvale Cove Tucker GA 30084-3210 Office: Sch Mech Engring Ga Inst Tech Atlanta GA 30332-0405 E-mail: said.abdelkhalik@me.gatech.edu.

ABDELLAH, FAYE GLENN, retired public health service executive; d. H. B. and Margaret (Glenn) Abdellah. BS in Tchg., Columbia U., 1945, MA in Tchg., 1947, EdD, 1955; LLD (hon.), Case Western Res. U., 1967, Rutgers U., 1973; DSc (hon.), U. Akron, 1978, Cath. U. Am., 1981, Monmouth Coll., 1982, Ea. Mich U., 1987, U. Bridgeport, 1987, Georgetown U., 1989; D in Pub. Svc. (hon.), Am. U., 1987; LHD, D in Pub. Svc., U. S.C., 1991; D in Mil. Nursing (hon.), USUHS, 2002. RN N.Y., D.C. Commd. officer USPHS, Rockville, Md., 1949, advanced through grades to rear adm., 1970, asst. surgeon gen., chief nurse officer, 1970—87, dep. surgeon gen., 1981—89, chief nursing edn. br., divsn. nursing, 1949—59, surgeon gen., 1989; chief rsch. grants br. Bur. Health Manpower Edn., NIH, HEW, Rockville, 1959—69; dir. Office Rsch. Tng. Nat. Ctr. for Health Svcs. R & D, Health Svcs. Mental Health Adminstrn., Rockville, 1969; acting dep. dir. Nat. Ctr. for Health Svcs. R & D, Rockville, 1971, Bur. Health Svcs. Rsch. and Evaluation, Health Resources Adminstrn., Rockville, 1973; dir. Office Long-Term Care, Office Asst. Sec. for Health, HEW, Rockville, 1973—80; exec. dir. Grad. Sch. Nursing Uniformed Svcs. U. Health Scis., Bethesda, Md., 1993—, founding, prof., 1993—. Prof. nursing, Emily Smith chair U. S.C., Columbia, 1990—91; dean, prof. Grad. Sch. Nursing, Uniformed Svcs. U. Health Scis., 1993—2002, founding dean, prof. emerita, 1993—2002. Author: Effect of Nurse Staffing on Satisfactions with Nursing Care, 1959, Patient Centered Approaches to Nursing, 1960, Better Patient Care Through Nursing Research, 1965, 2d edit., 1979, 3d edit., 1986, Intensive Care, Concepts and Practices for Clinical Nurse Specialists, 1969, New Directions in Patient Centered Nursing, 1972, Preparing Nursing Research for the 21st Century, 1994; contbr. articles to profl. jours. Named to TC Nursing Hall of Fame, Columbia U., 1999, Nat. Women's Hall of Fame, 2000; recipient Mary Adelaide Nutting award, 1983, Oustanding Leadership award, U. Pa., 1987, 1999, Disting. Svc. award, 1973—89, Surgeon Gen.'s medal and medallion, 1989, Achievement award in aging, Allied-Signal, 1989, Gustav O. Lienhard award, Inst. Medicine NAS, 1992, Breaking Ground in Women's Health award, 2001, G.W. "Sonny" Montgomery award, Dept. Vets. Affairs, 2002. Fellow: Am. Acad. Nursing (charter, past v.p., pres.); mem.: AAAS, ANA (hon.), APA, Assn. Mil. Surgeons U.S., Douglas Soc., Phi Lambda Theta, Sigma Theta Tau (Disting. Rsch. Fellow award 1989). Home: 3713 Chanel Rd Annandale VA 22003-2024

ABDELNOUR, ZIAD KHALIL, international investment banker, financier, venture capitalist, lobbyist; b. Beirut, Jan. 8, 1961; arrived in US, 1981; s. Khalil I. and Rose S. (Salha) A.; m. Nada S. Sahyoun, Dec. 23, 1983; children: Karl, Mark. BA, Am. U. of Beirut, 1981; MBA, The Wharton Sch. Fin., 1984. Fin. cons. Am. Express Bank, N.Y.C., 1984-86; asst. v.p. Drexel Burnham Lambert, 1986-88, v.p., 1988-89, sr. v.p., 1989-90; sr. ptnr. Interbank Capital Group LLC, 1990—97; mng. dir., head pvt. fin. Ladenburg Thalmann, Inc., 1997—99; mng. dir. venture fin. THCG, Inc., 1999-2001; sr. ptnr., mng. mem. Terra Nova Capital Partners LLC, 2001—; CEO The Phoenician Group Ltd., 1992—; founder, pub., exec. dir. Middle East Intelligence Bull. Author: Ending Syria's Occupation of Lebanon: The U.S. Role, 2000; contbr. articles to profl. jours. Mem. Rep. Senatorial Inner Cir.; Rep. Presdl. Task Force, Washington; Am. Task Force for Lebanon Policy; founder, pres. U.S. Com. for Free Lebanon, Inc.; adv. bd. Mid. East Forum, N.Y.C.; Peace Works, Inc., NYC, Al Bawaba, London and Amman, Jordan. Mem. Arab Bankers Assn. N.Am. (bd. dirs., pres.), Coun. Fgn. Rels., Met. Club. Roman Catholic. Office: Terra Nova Capital Partners LLC 445 Park Ave 9th Fl New York NY 10022 E-mail: ziad@i-2000.com.

ABDELRAZEK, RAWAN, economist; d. Adnan and Zakia Abdelrazek. BA in Internat. Rels., Johns Hopkins U., 1995, MA in Internat. Econs., 2001. Cons. Pvt. Sector Investment Unit, Israel, 1995—97; diplomat UN, N.Y.C., 1997—99; economist U.S. Treasury Dept., Washington, 2000—02, World Bank, Washington, 2003—. Independent. Avocations: running, reading, sports. Home: 166 Louis St Hackensack NJ 07601

ABDELRAZIG, YASSIR A. engineering educator; b. Khartoum, Khartoum, Sudan, 1968; arrived in U.S., 1994; PhD, Purdue U., 1999. Rsch. assoc. Purdue U., West Lafayette, Ind., 1999; asst. prof. Fla. State U., Tallahassee, 1999—. Mem.: ASCE. Achievements include research in FSU Cornerstone Research Award - $100, 000. Office: Fla A &M U Fla State U Coll Civil Engring 2525 Pottsdamer St Tallahassee FL 32310

ABDERHALDEN, ROBERT THOMAS, internist; b. Lima, Ohio, Apr. 23, 1945; MD, U. Cin., 1971. Cert. internal medicine, 1976, med. oncology, 1983. Intern Good Samaritan Hosp., Cin., 1971-72; resident Cleve. Clinic, 1974-76, resident in medicine, 1976, fellow in hematology med. oncology, 1976-78; chmn. dept. internal medicine Arnot Ogden Meml. Hosp., Elmira, N.Y., 1994-95; pvt. practice Elmira, N.Y., 1981—. Mem. AMA, Am. Coll. Physicians, Acad. of Hospice Physicians and Palliative Care, Am. Soc. Clin. Oncology. Office: So Tier Oncology Falck Cancer Ctr 600 Roe Ave Elmira NY 14905-1629

ABDIN, MARIA, research service executive, publisher; b. Washington; AA, Pima C.C., Tucson, 1982; student, U. Ariz. Owner Prensa Samizdat Rsch. Svc./Pubs., various locations, 1974—. Native Am. sacred clown. Contbr. articles to profl. jours. Bd. sec., outreach, Com. de Vecinos Internat.; creator ednl. and social svcs. program Peoples Involvement Corp. Office: Prensa Samizdat Rsch Svc PO Box 21521 Seattle WA 98111-3521

ABDO, LYNDA LEE, art director, designer; b. Hollywood, Calif., Sept. 6, 1955; d. Carl Edward and Carol Jean (Bedford) Cons; children: Allexis, Athena. Degree with honors, West Valley Occupational Ctr., 1979; BA cum laude, Calif. State U., Northridge, 1985. Asst. art dir. Malibu Grand Prix, Warner Communications, Woodland Hills, Calif., 1979-85; prodn. artist CBS Studios; designer, illustrator Sulka Agy., Studio City, Calif.; designer Phil Mendez Animation Prodns., Burbank, Calif.; art dir. Shields & Yarnell, Encino, Calif.; merchandising designer Zak Designs, Disney, Universal Studios, Warner Bros., 1988-94; co-prodr. video Avio Prodns., 1995-97; computer designer Ultra Glas Inc., 1997—. Hon. co-chmn. Nat. Bus. Adv. Coun. Recipient Parents Choice award, Parent's Choice Found., 1999. Democrat. Avocations: swimming, hiking, travel, feng shui. Home and Office: 22731 Schoolcraft St West Hills CA 91307-2612

ABDOO, RICHARD A. utilities company executive; b. Port Huron, Mich., 1944; BSEE, U. Dayton, 1965; MA, U. Detroit, 1969. With Wis. Energy Corp., 1975—, chmn., pres., chief exec. officer, 1991—. Bd. dir. ARI Network Svcs., M & I Marshall & Ilsley Bank, Blue Cross Blue Shield United of Wis. Office: Wis Energy Corp PO Box 2046 231 W Michigan St Milwaukee WI 53203-2918

ABDOU, IKRAM ESCANDAR, engineering consultant; b. Beni Suef, Egypt, Apr. 22, 1948; came to U.S., 1975; s. Escandar Abdou and Amira Armanious; m. Mona Yanni, June 5, 1987; children: Irene, John. BS, Cairo U., 1970, MS, 1973; PhD, U. So. Calif., 1978. Asst. lectr. Cairo U., 1970-75; rsch. asst. U. So. Calif., L.A., 1975-78; postdoctoral fellow IBM Rsch. Lab., San Jose, Calif., 1978-80; sr. engr. Aydin Computer Systems, Ft. Washington, Pa., 1980-83; asst. prof. engring. U. Del., Newark, 1983-88; staff engr. Martin Marietta Electronic Systems, Orlando, Fla., 1989-93; sr. rsch. engr. SRI Internat., Menlo Park, Calif., 1993—; cons. in field. Scholar Egyptian Ministry Edn., 1962-65, Cairo U., 1965-70. Mem. IEEE (sr.), Sigma Xi, Eta Kappa Nu. Mem. Coptic Orthodox Christian Ch. Avocations: reading, music, traveling. Home: 1790 Lark Ln Sunnyvale CA 94087-4827 Office: SRI Internat 333 Ravenswood Ave Menlo Park CA 94025-3453 E-mail: ikram.abdou@sri.com.

ABDOU, NABIH I. physician, educator; b. Cairo, Oct. 11, 1934; came to U.S., 1962, naturalized, 1972; m. Nancy L. Layle, Aug. 26, 1939; children— Mark L., Marie L. MD, Cairo U., 1958; PhD, McGill U., 1969. Intern then resident Cairo Univ. Hosp., 1959-62; resident, fellow in allergy and immunology Hosp. U. Pa., 1963-65, Mayo Clinic, 1965-67, Royal Victoria Hosp., Montreal, Que., Can., 1967-69; asst., assoc. prof. U. Pa., 1969-75; assoc. prof. medicine U. Kans. Med. Ctr., Kansas City, 1975-78, prof. medicine, 1978-89; pvt. practice Ctr. for Rheumatic Disease and Ctr. for Allergy Immunology, Kansas City, 1989—, Clin. prof. medicine U. Mo., 1989—. Fulbright scholar, 1962-65 Fellow ACP, Am. Acad. Allergy, Am. Coll. Rheumatology; mem. Am. Assn. Immunologists, Cen. Soc. Clin. Rsch., Clin. Immunology Soc. Office: Ctr for Rheumatic Disease and Ctr Allergy Immunology 4330 Wornall Rd Ste 40 Kansas City MO 64111-3217

ABDOU, WAFIK ANDREW, anesthesiologist; b. Cairo, July 5, 1962; s. Farouk Rizkalla and Amal (Habashi) A.; m. Gail Marie Cragin, Apr. 16, 1994. Degree, U. So. Calif., 1983, MD, 1988. Diplomate Am. Bd. Anesthesiology. Intern the resident in internal medicine U. So. Calif. LAC Med. Ctr., 1988-1992; ptnr. Premier Anesthesiology Med. Group, Bakersfield, Calif., 1992—, mng. ptnr., 1994—; pres. Ctrl. Valley Profl. Med. Svcs. Corp., Bakersfield, 1995—; chief of anesthesiology Mercy Hosp., Bakersfield, 1994-99, CFO, 1999—, Kern Valley Hosp., Lake Isabella, Calif., 1994-97. Mem. at large exec. com. Mercy Hosp. Med. Ctr., 1996. Fund raising com. mem. Henrietta Weill Child Guidance Clinic, Bakersfield, 1993—. Mem. Am. Soc. Anesthesiology, Calif. Soc. of Anesthesiology, Seven Oaks Country Club, Am. Contract Bridge League (Nat. champion 1992, 97). Republican. Office: 1709 20th St Bakersfield CA 93301-3903

ABDULEZER, SUSAN BETH, communications educator; b. NYC, Sept. 27, 1949; d. George and Cecelia Irene Pomerantz; m. Loren Abdulezer, Aug. 30, 1987. BA in English, CUNY, 1971; MA in Deaf Edn., Columbia U., 1974; MA in Indsl. Tech., NYU, 1983. Lic. tchr. of deaf and hard of hearing, indsl. tech., NYC. Tchr. of deaf NJ Spl. Svc., NJ, 1974-78; tchr. graphic arts NYC Pub. Sch. for Deaf, NY, 1979-94; multimedia coord. NYC Pub. Sch., NY, 1994-2000; dir. multimedia Wholewide Worldtales.com, NYC, 2000—. Multimedia cons. Apple Computer, Inc., Calif., 1994—; mem. adv. bd. Digital Clubhouse Network, NYC, 1997—; freelance feature writer Converge. Author: (software) Street Signs: contributing edit., Converge Mag., 1997-2003; A City Kid's Guide to Am. Sign Lang., 1996, The Virtual Alphabet Book, 1997; contbg. editor Converge Mag., 2001—; author, prodr., editor: (CD-rom digital documentaries) Exemplary Programs, 1998-99; contbr. articles to profl. jour. Recipient The Apex Award for best feature story in a trade mag., 2001, Hero in Edn. award Reader's Digest, 1996; winner innovation in tech., edn. and academia award Computerworld-Smithsonian Instn., 1996, 97; Christa McAuliffe fellow, 1994-95, fellow Smithsonian Mus. Am. History, summer 1997. Jewish. Avocation: celtic fiddling. Office: Multimedia Ctr 400 1st Ave New York NY 10010-4004

ABDUL-JABBAR, KAREEM (LEWIS FERDINAND ALCINDOR), professional basketball coach; b. N.Y.C., Apr. 16, 1947; s. Ferdinand Lewis and Cora Alcindor; m. Habiba (Janice Brown), 1971 (div. 1973); children: Habiba, Kareem, Sutana, Amir. BA, UCLA, 1969. Basketball player with Milw. Bucks, 1969—75, L.A. Lakers, 1975—89; owner Kareem Productions; asst. coach L.A. Clippers, 2000—01; head coach, Okla. Storm U.S. Basketball League, 2002—. Commentator ESPN, Bristol, Conn. Actor: (TV series) Mannix, The Man from Atlantis, Diff'rent Strokes, Tales from the Darkside, Pryor's Place, The ABC Afterschool Spl.; (films) The Fish that Saved Pittsburgh, 1979, Airplane, 1980, Fletch, 1985; author (with Peter Knobler): Giant Steps: An Autobiography of Kareem Abdul-Jabbar, 1983; author: (with Mignon McCarthy) Kareem, 1990. Named Rookie of the Yr., NBA, 1970, Most Valuable Player, 1971, 1972, 1974, 1976, 1977, 1980, NBA Playoff Most Valuable Player, 1971, 1985, NCAA Tournament Most Outstanding Player, 1967, 1968, 1969; named to All-Star Game, NBA, 1970—87, 35th Anniversary All-Time Team, 1980, Basketball Hall of Fame, 1995; recipient Maurice Podoloff Cup. Moslem. Achievements include becoming NBA all-time leading scorer, 1984; being a mem. of NBA Championship Team, 1971, 80, 82, 85, 87, 88; being mem. of NCAA Championship Team, 1967, 68, 69. Avocation: jazz. Address: Oklahoma Storm PO Box 1873 Enid OK 65535

ABDUL-JABBAR, KARIM, retired professional football player; b. L.A., June 28, 1974; m. Sabria; 1 child, Ibarhim Abdullah. BS in Econs., UCLA, 1997. Running back Miami Dolphins, 1996-98, Cleve. Browns, 1998-99, Indianapolis Colts, 2000—. Holder club rookie rushing record; voted to all-rookie teams Football News Pro Football Writers Am. and Coll. and Pro Football Newsweekly; named AFC Offensive Player of the Week. Office: Indianapolis Colts RCA Dome PO Box 535000 Indianapolis IN 46253-5000

ABDULLA, JENNIFER ANN, marketing professional, consultant; b. Methuen, Mass., Jan. 5, 1978; d. Abraham John Abdulla Jr. and Nancy Claire (Provencal) Vitale. BS, Merrimack Coll., 2000; cert. in graphic design and digital imaging, U. Mass., 2003. Trade specialist Putnam Investments, Andover, Mass., 1999—2000; conf. coord. Pennwell, Nashua, NH, 2000—. Home: PO Box 522 Hampstead NH 03841 E-mail: jennifer-abdulla@yahoo.com.

ABDULLAEV, YALCHIN, neuroscientist, physician, educator; b. Baku, Azerbaijan, Aug. 19, 1960; s. Gulhuseyn and Almas Abdullaev; m. Naida Velieva, Nov. 24, 1987 (div. Aug. 12, 2002); 1 child, Mikail. MS, Azerbaijan State U., Baku, 1982; PhD, Inst. Exptl. Medicine, St. Petersburg, Russia, 1987; MD, St. Petersburg Med. Acad., 1994. Rsch. asst. Inst. Physiology, Azerbaijan Acad. Scis., Baku, 1982-84; grad. stud. Inst. Exptl. Medicine, St. Petersburg, 1984-87, jr. rsch. scientist, 1987-89, sr. rsch. scientist, 1989-90, Brain Ctr., St. Petersburg, 1990-94; asst. prof. U. Oreg., Eugene, 1994-96; asst. prof. U. Louisville, 1996—. Mem. grad. faculty U. Louisville, 1996—; rsch. dir. Cognitive Neurosci. Lab., 1996—. Mem. editl. bd.: Internat. Jour. Psychophysiology, 1992—96; mem. editl. bd. The Scientific World, 2002—; contbr. more than 60 rsch. articles to profl. jours. Mem.: Internat. Orgn. Psychophysiology, Internat. Orgn. Human Brain Mapping, Soc. Neurosci., Am. Psychol. Soc. Avocations: swimming, running, reading. E-mail: yabdullaev@yahoo.com.

ABDULLAH, BASHAR Y. pharmacist, researcher; s. Yousif A. and Rasmia S. Almanaseer; m. Muna M. Habib, July 9, 1986; children: Yasamin B., Yasser B., Taha B., Weseem B. BS in Pharmacy, U. Baghdad, 1986. Lic. pharmacist Iraqi Bd. Pharmacist, 1986. Pharmacist, formulation devel. Abbott labs, North Chicago, Ill., 1996—2001; reasearch assoc. III Baxter Healthcare, Round Lake, 2001—. Mem.: Am. Assn. Pharm. Scientists, The Sci. Adv. Bd. (assoc.; online cmty. 2001). Achievements include patents for United States patent no. 6, 008, 192 (Hydrophilic Binary Systems for the Adminstration of Lipophilic Compounds); Patent no. 98910361.9-2112 from the European Patent office, (Hydro-

philic Binary Systems for the Adminstration of Cyclosporine); Hydrophilic Binary Systems for the Administration of Lipophilic Compounds; Hydrophilic Binary Systems for the Adminstration of Cyclosporine; development of Norvir Capsules; Gengraf capsules; research in 1998 Chairman Award from Abbott labs pharmaceutical and Analytical Research and Development; first to Awarded year 2000 Abbott Achievment Award; development of Generic Veterinary products of 1% Iodine solution and Neomycin Suspention. Home: 2272 N Sarazen Dr Vernon Hills IL 60061 Office: Baxter Healthcare WG3-3S Route 120 and Wilson Rd Round Lake IL 60073 Office Fax: 847-270-5999.

ABDUL-RAHIM, SHAREEF, professional basketball player; b. Dec. 11, 1976; Forward, guard Vancouver Grizzlies. Named to NBA All-Rookie First Team, 1996—97, Third Team All-Am., AP. Avocations: pool, collecting basketball jerseys, movies. Office: Vancouver Grizzlies 800 Griffiths Way Vancouver BC Canada V6B 6G1

ABE, GREGG KOYEI, music educator; b. Honolulu, June 22, 1958; s. Charles Sadaichi and Diane Aiko Abe; m. Julie Yukiko Fujii, Apr. 30, 1988; children: Kayla, Gregg. BE, U. Hawaii, 1983. Cert. tchr. Hawaii. Asst. dir. bands Castle HS, Kaneohe, Hawaii, 1984—85; dir. bands Roosevelt HS, Honolulu, 1985—. Named Music Educator of the Yr., Hawaii Music Awards, 1996, Outstanding Educator, Oceanic TV, 2001. Mem.: Am. Sch. Band Dirs. Assn. (Tchr. of the Yr. S.W. Region 1998), Am. Fedn. Musicians, Phi Beta Mu. Office: Roosevelt High School 1120 Nehoa St Honolulu HI 96822-2566 Office Fax: 808-587-4637. E-mail: rhsband58@hotmail.com.

ABEDIN, MOHAMMAD ZAINUL, medical educator, researcher; b. Jhalakati, Barisal, Bangladesh, Mar. 4, 1942; came to U.S., 1976; s. Abdus Satter and Joyful Khatun; m. Rashida Begum, Jan. 16, 1967; 1 child, Zahidur. BS, U. Dhaka, Bangladesh, 1966, MS, 1968; cert., Nat. Inst. Nutrition, Hyderabad, India, 1975; PhD, UCLA, 1984, postdoctoral scholar, 1985—. Rsch. & tchg. fellow U. Dhaka, 1969-70, lectr., 1971-76; from chemist to sr. chemist Pharmavite Pharmaceutical Corp., Los Angeles, 1976-83, nutrition research scientist, 1983-85; research chemist VA Med. Ctr., Sepulveda, Calif., 1985—92; asst. prof. surgery Med. Coll. of Pa., Allegheny U. of Health Scis., Phildelphia, 1992—98; assoc. prof. surgery Allegheny U. of Heath Scis./MCP, Hahnemann U., 1998—2002, Drexel U. Coll. of Medicine, Philadelphia, 2002—; assoc. prof. pharmacology & physiology MCP Hahnemann U., Drexel U. Coll. of Medicine, 1998—. Rsch. chemist Med. Rsch. Service, Dept. of Veterans Affairs Med. Ctr. (DVAMC), Philadelphia, 1992—98; asst. dir., surg. rsch. DVAMC, 1995—2000; chmn. Laboratory Safety Com., Med. Coll. Pa., 1994—95, Univ. Biosafety Com., Allegheny U. of Health Scis., 1995—98, Biohazard and Safety Com., Phila. DVAMC, 1997—2000; mem. Radiation Safety Com., 1997—2000, Animal Studies Sub-Com., Phila. DVAMC, 1997—2000, Sr. Faculty Preceptors and Mentors, Nat. Ctr. Leadership in Academic Medicine, 1999—, Med. Sch. Admissions Com., 2001—, Animal Use Com., 2001—, Biomedical Grad. Edn. Com., 2002—; program dir., grad. studies in molecular pathobiology Drexel U. Coll. of Medicine, 2002—. Mng. editor Frontiers in Bioscience, 2000—; contbr. Recipient Bangladesh Talent Scholarship, 1959—69, U.S. Bureau Health Manpower Traineeship, 1979—82, Pharmavite Award for Vitamin E Rsch., 1981, Nat. Rsch. Service Award, 1983, UCLA postdoctoral fellow, Am. Cancer Rsch. Inst.; Rsch. Grant Support, Pharmavite Pharmaceutical Corp., 1981—83, Am. Inst. for Cancer Rsch., 1984—86, Dept. Veterans Affairs, 1987—96, Allegheny Singer Rsch. Inst., 1996—97, NIH/NIDDK, 1997—. Mem. Am. Gastroenterological Assn., Am. Psysiol. Soc., AAAS, N.Y. Acad. Sci., UCLA Sch. Pub. Health Alumni Assn., Salt and Water Club, Sigma Xi. Avocations: reading, photography, music. E-mail: mohammad.abedin@drexel.edu.

ABEDIN, SULTANAL, research phytotaxonomist; b. Ghaziabad, India, Apr. 29, 1937; arrived in Pakistan, 1964; s. Zainal and Muqaddas (Khatoon) Abedin; m. Tasawwur Khatoon, Feb. 21, 1970; children: Masood Al-Abedin, Mansoor Al-Abedin,, Shamaila Aamir. BSc, Muslim U., Aligarh, India, 1961, MSc, 1964, Karachi (Pakistan) U., 1967, PhD, 1976; DSc, Alternative Medicine Inst., Colombo, Sri Lanka, 1997. Lectr. Karachi U., 1964-68, 76-79, rschr., 1968-76, asst. prof. pharmacognosy, 1979-81, King Saud U., Riyadh, Saudi Arabia, 1981-89, rschr., 1989-2000. Chmn. dept. pharmacognosy, U. Karachi, 1979-81; warden Quaid-i-Azam Hostel, U. Karachi, 1976-80. Author: How to Know the Plants Around You, 1968; contbr. articles to profl. jours.; patentee in field of new species, subspecies, varieties and new ranks of various taxa. Pres. Aligarh Muslim U. Intermediate Students Union, 1957—58. Fellow Linnaeus Soc., Royal Soc. Health (London), Pakistan Acad. Pharm. Scis.; mem. Pakistan Pharmacol. Soc. Avocations: travel, bridge, reading, tv. E-mail: sultanabedin22@hotmail.com.

ABEGG, MARTIN GERALD, retired academic administrator; b. Alliance, Nebr., Oct. 3, 1925; s. Frank and Mary Anna (Newberry) A.; m. Barbara Louise Chamberlain, June 29, 1946; children: Martin Gerald, Robert Miles. BS in Gen. Engring, Bradley U., 1947; MS in Civil Engring, U. Colo., 1951; PhD in Civil Engring, Rensselaer Poly. Inst., 1960; LL.D. (hon.), Ill. Coll., 1982; L.H.D. (hon.), Bradley U., 1993. Registered profl. engr., Ill. registered land surveyor, Ill. Instr. engring. Bradley U., 1947-50, asst. prof., 1950-55, asso. prof., 1955-60, prof., 1960—, head dept. civil engring., 1960-63, dean Coll. Engring. and Tech., 1963-70, pres., 1971-92, pres. emeritus, 1992—. Engring. aide Ill. Div. Hwys., Dixon, 1946, civil engr., Peoria, Ill., 1948; park dist. engr., Peoria, 1953-55; cons. engr. Norman Porter & Assos., N.Y.C., 1956-57, 59. Served to lt. (j.g.) USNR, 1943-46. Recipient Putnam award Bradley U., 1961, Disting. Engring Alumnus award U. Colo., 1986, Disting. Alumnus award Bradley U., 1992. Mem. Am. Soc. C.E., Sigma Xi, Sigma Tau, Phi Kappa Phi, Omicron Delta Kappa, Tau Beta Pi, Chi Epsilon. Home: 116 Warbler Way Georgetown TX 78628-4804 E-mail: mgabegg@dcwis.com.

ABEL, ALAN IRWIN, film company executive; b. Zanesville, Ohio, Aug. 2, 1924; s. Louis and Ida (Hamburger) A.; m. Jeanne Allgeier, Sept. 14, 1959; 1 child, Jennifer. BE, Ohio State U., 1950. Exec. prodr. Spencer Prodn., N.Y.C., 1965-95. Author: Great American Hoax, 1966, Confessions of Hoaxer, 1971, Don't Get Mad, Get Even, 1983; composer Serenade To A Sand Dune, 1955. Recipient W. C. Fields award The New Sch., N.Y.C., 1975. Avocations: tennis, basketball. Home and Office: PO Box 2247 Westport CT 06880-0247 E-mail: abelalan2000@yahoo.com.

ABEL, ANNE ELIZABETH SUTHERLAND, pediatrician; b. Milw., June 16, 1945; d. David Hollingsworth and Mildred June (Nees) Sutherland; m. Francis Lee Abel; 1 child, Jonathan Earl. BA, Pasadena Coll., 1967; MS, Ind. U., Indpls., 1969, MD, 1973. Diplomate Am. Bd. Pediatrics. Resident in pediat. Meth. Hosp., Indpls., 1973-75, Richland Meml. Hosp., Columbia, S.C., 1975-76; pediatrician Moncrief Army Hosp., Ft. Jackson, S.C., 1976-80; child and adolescent psychiatry fellow William S. Hall Psychiat. Inst., Columbia, 1981, 82-83, U. B.C.-Vancouver Gen. Hosp., 1982; pvt. practice Columbia, S.C., 1983—; pediatrician Children's Rehabilitative Svcs., Orangeburg, S.C., 1984-91, 92-00; chief med. sect. Columbia Area Mental Health Ctr., 1987-92; assoc. prof. pediatrics, adj. assoc. prof. neuropsychiatry U. S.C., Columbia, 1992-2000; mental health dir. Abuse Recovery Ctr., Columbia, 1994-95; dir. Freddie Mac Child and Adolescent Protection Center, Children's National Medical Center, 2001—. Cons. behavioral pediatrics Epworth Children's Home, Columbia, 1983-86, 90-97; med. dir. Assessment and Resource Ctr., Columbia, 1996-2000; mem. med. adv. com., children's health rehabilitative svcs. S.C. Dept. Health & Environ. Control, Columbia, 1986-92, mem. maternal and child health adv. com., 1989-91; behavioral/devel. pediatrician Orangeburg Health Dept., 1994-96. Contbr. articles to profl. jours. Mem. S.C. Gov.'s Youth Unemployment Coun., Columbia, 1987. Recipient Alumni award Pasadena Coll., 1977, Vol. of Yr. award Mayor's Com. Employment Handicapped, 1988; grantee Ctr. Family Soc., U. S.C., 1993-95. Fellow Am. Acad. Pediatrics; mem. AMA, Am. Acad. Cerebral Palsy and Devel. Medicine, Am. Profl. Soc. on Abuse of Children, S.C. Med. Assn., S.C. Pediatric Soc., Columbia Med. Soc. Avocations: music, boating, hiking, fishing, reading. Office: Freddie Mac Child and Adolescent Protection Center Children's National Medical Center 111 Michigan Ave NW Washington DC 20010 E-mail: aabel@cnmc.org.

ABEL, CARLOS ALBERTO, immunologist; b. Buenos Aires, May 7, 1930; came to U.S., 1959, naturalized, 1969; s. Carlos Alberto and Rosa Blanca (Molinero) A.; m. Amalia Carmen Minieri, June 15, 1959. BS, M. Belgrano Coll., 1948; MD, U. Buenos Aires, 1957. Intern St. Joseph's Hosp., Providence, 1959-60; resident in pediatrics U. Md. Hosp., 1964-66; fellow in pediatrics U. Md., Balt., 1960-64, resident in pediatrics, 1964-66; advanced rsch. fellow Scripps Clinic, La Jolla, Calif., 1966-69; vis. scientist U. Oxford, Eng., 1969-70; mem. div. basic immunology Nat. Jewish Hosp., Denver, 1970-84; sr. scientist Med. Rsch. Inst., San Francisco, 1984-92; dir. immunochemistry ICR/Med. Rsch. Inst., 1986-89; chmn. sci. coun. Med. Rsch. Inst., 1993—. Biotech. cons.; vis. scholar U. Calif.-Berkeley, 1982. Contbr. articles to profl. jours. Mem. Am. Assn. Immunologists, Am. Assn. Pathologists, Biochem. Soc. (Eng.), British Soc. for Immunology, Sociedad Argentina de Immunologia, Assn. Latino Americana Immunologia, Soc. Clin. Immunology. Democrat. Roman Catholic. Achievements include research in structure and function of glycoproteins from the surfaces of lymphocytes; study of their role in cell-cell interactions, structure of antibodies, glycobiology. Home: 523 Cragmont Ave Berkeley CA 94708-1205 E-mail: c.abel@caramail.com.

ABEL, ELIE, reporter, broadcaster, educator; b. Montreal, Que., Can., Oct. 17, 1920; s. Jacob and Rose (Savetsky) A.; children: Mark, Suzanne; m. Charlotte Page Abel, July 2, 1995. BA, McGill U., 1941, LL.D., 1971; MS in Journalism, Columbia U., 1942; LL.D., U. Western Ont., 1976. Reporter Windsor (Ont.) Star, 1941; asst. city editor Montreal Gazette, 1945-46; fgn. corr. N.Am. Newspaper Alliance, Berlin, 1946-47; UN corr. Overseas News Agy., 1947-49; nat., fgn. corr. N.Y. Times, 1949-59; Washington bur. chief Detroit News, 1959-61; with NBC, 1961-69, chief London bur., 1965-67; diplomatic corr. NBC News, Washington, 1967-69; Godfrey Lowell Cabot prof., also dean Grad. Sch. Journalism, Columbia U., N.Y.C., 1969-79; Harry and Norman Chandler prof. Stanford U., 1979-91. Bd. govs. Am. Stock Exchange, 1974-78 Author: The Missile Crisis, 1966, (with Marvin Kalb) Roots of Involvement, The U.S. in Asia 1784-1971, 1971, (with Averell Harriman) Special Envoy to Churchill and Stalin, 1941-46, 1975, Leaking: Who Does It? Who Benefits? At What Cost?, 1987, The Shattered Bloc: Behind the Upheaval in Eastern Europe, 1990; editor: What's News: The Media in American Society, 1981. Recipient George Foster Peabody award for outstanding radio news, 1968; Overseas Press Club award for best interpretation of fgn. news, 1969 Mem. Coun. Fgn. Rels., Cosmos Club (Washington).

ABEL, ELIZABETH A. dermatologist; b. Hartford, Conn., Mar. 16, 1940; d. Frederick A. and Rose (Borovicka) Abel; m. Barton Lane; children: Barton Lane, Geoffrey Lane, Suzanne Lane. Student, Colby-Sawyer Coll., 1957-60; BS, Wash. Hosp. Ctr. Sch. Med. Tech., 1961, U. Md., 1965, MD cum laude, 1967. Diplomate Am. Bd. Dermatology. Intern San Francisco Gen. Hosp., 1967-68; resident in medicine, fellow in oncology U. Calif. Med. Ctr., San Francisco, 1968-69; resident in dermatology NYU Med. Ctr., 1969-72, chief resident, 1971-72, USPHS research trainee in immunology, 1972-73; dep. chief dept. dermatology USPHS Hosp., S.I., N.Y., 1973-74; instr. clin. dermatology Columbia U. Coll. Physicians and Surgeons, N.Y.C., 1974-75, Stanford (Calif.) U. Sch. Medicine, 1975-77, clin. asst. prof. dermatology, 1977-82, asst. prof. dermatology, 1982-90, clin. assoc. prof., 1990-96, clin. prof., 1996—. Asst. editor Jour. Am. Acad. Dermatology, 1993-98; mem. med. adv. bd. The Nat. Psoriasis Found., 1993-95. Contbr. articles to profl. sci. jours. Mellon Found. fellow, 1983, 87. Fellow Am. Acad. Dermatology; mem. N.Am. Clin. Dermatologic Soc., San Francisco Dermatologic Soc., Internat. Soc. Dermatology Surgery, Pacific Dermatologic Assn., Women's Dermatologic Soc., Noah Worcester Dermatologic Soc., Alpha Omega Alpha. Avocations: piano, golf, reading. Office: 2660 Grant Rd Ste D Mountain View CA 94040-4315

ABEL, ERNEST LAWRENCE, education educator; b. Toronto, Ont., Can., Feb. 10, 1943; s. Jack and Rose (Tarshes) A.; m. Barbara Ellen Buckley, Sept. 20, 1970; children: Jason Robert, Rebecca Rosanne. BA, U. Toronto, 1965, MA, 1967, PhD, 1971. Rsch. scientist Rsch. Inst. on Alcoholism, Buffalo, N.Y., 1971-83, acting dep. dir., 1983-84, rsch. scientist VI, 1984-85; prof. Wayne State U., Detroit, 1985—, dir. C.S. Mott Ctr. for human growth and devel., 1985—98, dir. reproductive toxicology, 1998—. Pres. Fetal Alcohol Study Group, 1985-86. Author: Marihuana, 1980, Alcohol Wordlore, 1987, Fetal Alcohol Syndrome, 1990, 2d edit., 1999, America's 25 Top Killers, 1991, Singing the New Nation, 2000, Jewish Genetic Disorders-A Layman's Guide, 2001, Arab Genetic Disorders-A Layman's Guide, 2003. Named Disting. Faculty fellow Bd. Govs., Wayne State U., 1989. Mem. Behavioral Teratology Soc. (pres. 1984-85). Office: CS Mott Ctr Human Growth 275 E Hancock St Detroit MI 48201-1415

ABEL, FLORENCE CATHERINE HARRIS, social worker; b. Phila., Dec. 28, 1941; d. Wilber Fiske and Melda Elizabeth (Beitzel) Harris; m. David Lynn Abel, Jan. 22, 1983. BS, High Point (N.C.) U., 1963; MSW, U. Md., 1972. LCSW; diplomate in clin. social work. Social work asst. Calvert County Dept. social Svcs., Prince Frederick, Md., 1964—69, Prince George's County Dept. Social Svc., Hyattsville, Md., 1969—71; social worker Md. Children's Aid and Family Svc., Towson, 1972—80, Crownsville Hosp. Ctr., Md., 1980—86; field instr. U. Md. Sch. Social Work, 1985—86; counselor Family Life Ctr., Columbia, Md., 1974—80; sec. bd. dirs. Christian Counseling Assocs., Columbia, 1978—90, family therapist, 1978—, social work supr., 1990—96. Chairperson Social Work Peer Rev. Com., 1982—83; cons. Contact Balt., 1974—79; mem. citizens adv. coun. N.W. Mental Health Balt. County, 1977—78; dir. Dayspring Counseling Svc., Bowie, Md., 1994—96. Author: The Beitzel Family: a History of the Descendants of John George Beitzel, 1986, The Shadow of His Hand: The Biography of Melda B. Harris, 1995. Mem. Faith at Work Team, Columbia, 1973—75, Calvert County Commn. on Aging, 1967—68, Evang. Women's Caucus, Washington, 1976—85, N.W. Coalition Social Agys., Balt. County, 1978; sec. local bd. adminstrn. Dayspring Wesleyan Ch., Bowie, Md., 1996; v.p., treas., bd. dirs. Wheaton Animal Hosp., Inc., Kensington, Md. Mem.: NASW, Christian Assocs. for Psychol. Studies, Md. Conf. Social Concern, Assn. Cert. Social Workers, Nat. Register Clin. Social Workers, Am. Assn. Christian Counselors (charter mem.). Democrat. Wesleyan. Home: 120 Hedgewood Dr Greenbelt MD 20770-1611 Office: 9630 Santiago Rd Ste 101 Columbia MD 21045-3907 E-mail: ABEL@us.net.

ABEL, FRANCIS LEE, physiology educator; b. Iowa City, Apr. 12, 1931; s. Earl Lester A.; m. Evelyn Joyce Reischauer, Sept. 11, 1954 (div. Mar. 1974); children: Wanda, Donna, Carolyn; m. Anne Elizabeth Sutherland, June 9, 1974; 1 child, Jonathan. AA, Creston Jr. Coll., 1950; BA in Physics, U. Kans., 1952; MD, Harvard U., 1957; PhD in Physiology, U. Wis., 1960. Postdoctoral fellow, postdoctoral trainee Wis. Heart Assn. USPHS, Madison, 1958-60; intern in pediatrics Children's Hosp., L.A., 1960-61; from asst. prof. to prof. dept. physiology Sch. Medicine Ind. U., Indpls., 1962-75; prof., chmn. dept. physiology Sch. Medicine U. S.C., Columbia, 1975-98, disting. prof. dept. pharm. and physiology, 1998-99, emeritus, 1999—, interim dean Sch. Medicine, 1976, assoc. dean basic sci. affairs Sch. Medicine, 1976-78; vol. faculty physiology and medicine U. Md., Balt., 2002—. Vis. prof. dept. biomed. engring. U. So. Calif., L.A., 1970; vis. prof. dept. kinesiology Simon Fraser U., Burnaby, B.C., Can., 1982; vis. prof. dept. physiology U. Limburg, Maastricht, The Netherlands, 1989-90; cons. Eli Lilly & Co., Indpls., 1965-68, VA Hosp., Columbia, 1976-80. Co-author: Basic Physiology for the Health Sciences, 1975, Cardiovascular Function, Principles and Applications, 1979, Functional Aspects of the Normal Hypertrophied and Failing Heart, 1984. Recipient Career Devel. award NIH, 1968-73, Nat. Rsch. Svc. award NIH, 1989-90. Fellow Cardiovascular sect. Am. Physiol. Soc.; mem. IEEE (life), Am. Physiol. Soc., Am. Heart Assn., Biomed. Engring. Soc. (sr.), Shock Soc. (councillor 1980-82). Avocations: fishing, hiking, water and snow skiing. Office: U Md Dept Physiology 655 W Baltimore St Baltimore MD 21201 E-mail: fabel@mdicine.umaryland.edu.

ABEL, GREGORY E. utility company executive; Degree, U. Alta., Can. Chartered acct., Can. With Price Waterhouse, San Francisco, Calif. Energy Co., Inc., 1992, sr. v.p.; pres., COO MidAm. Energy Holdings Co., Des Moines, 1997—. Office: Mid Am Energy Holdings Co 666 Grand Ave Des Moines IA 50309

ABEL, MICHAEL L. marketing executive; b. New London, Wis., Jan. 15, 1952; s. William A. and Delores R. (Shuey) A.; m. Monica L. Miller, Dec. 18, 1971; children: Richard M., David M. AAS, Joliet (Ill.) Jr. Coll., 1975; BA in Bus. Adminstrn., Lewis U., 1977, MBA, 1979. Lab. technician No. Petrochem. Co., Morris, Ill., 1975-76, tech. specialist, 1976-80, nat. account rep. Des Plaines, Ill., 1980-82; product mgr. Enron Chem. Co., Omaha, 1982-85, mktg. mgr., 1985-87; sr. account exec. Quantum Chem. Co., Rancho Mirage, Calif., 1987-89; sr. v.p. N.Am. ops. Intac Automotive Products, Inc., Lemont, Ill., 1989—; pres., chief exec. officer Desert Leisure Devel. Corp., Palm Springs, 1991—, bd. dirs. Bd. dirs. Palm Cts. Assn., Rancho Mirage, 1988-97, The Kids Business, Inc., Rancho Mirage, 1996—. Patentee in chem. engring. field. Pres. Palm Ct. Owners Assn., Rancho Mirage, 1988-97; mem. Rep. Presdl. Task Force, 1990—. Mem. ASTM, Soc. Automotive Engrs., Nat. Assn. Corrosion Engrs. (sec. 1981-82), Internat. Platform Assn. Republican. Lutheran. Home: 36845 Palm Ct Rancho Mirage CA 92270-2206

ABEL, ROBERT BERGER, science administrator; b. Providence, July 21, 1926; s. Abraham Lincoln and Betty Ruth (Berger) A.; m. Nancy Marilyn Klein, Oct. 4, 1953; children: Alan Stewart, Deborah Jane. BS in Chemistry, Brown U., 1947; MEA, George Washington U., 1961; PhD, Am. U., 1972. Chemist Woods Hole (Mass.) Oceanographic Inst., 1947-50; oceanographer U.S. Navy Hydrographic Office, Suitland, Md., 1950-55; asst. to dir. U.S. Navy Hydrog. Office, 1955-60; asst. research coordinator Office Naval Research, Washington, 1961-64; exec. sec. Interagy. Com. Oceanography, 1960-67; asst. exec. sec. Nat. Council Marine Resources and Engring. Devel., 1967-68; dir. Nat. Sea Grant Program, Dept. Commerce, 1966-77; asst. v.p. Tex. A&M U., 1977-78; v.p. N.J. Marine Scis. Consortium, Fort. Hancock, 1979-81, pres., 1981-93; sr. sci. Stevens Inst. Tech., Hoboken, N.J., 1993—, Tex. A&M U., 1993—. Instr. oceanography USNR Officers Sch., 1960-65, Fairleigh Dickinson U., 1966-83, U. Va., 1976-77; instr. ocean mgmt. Rutgers U., 1980-84; dir. Israel Oceanographic and Limnol. Rsch. Ltd., Inc.; mem. panel Nat. Acad. Scis.; mem. N.J. Dept. Agr. Adv. Bd.; mgr. Cooperative Marine Tech. Program for Middle East, 1993—; mem. N.J. Marine Fisheries Coun., 1993—; mem. N.J. Aquaculture Adv. Coun.; chmn. adv. com. Jersey Shore Partnership; cruise lectr. Cunard, Crystal, Celebrity, Lindblad and Seabourne Lines. Pres. Cris-Mar Manor Civic Assn., 1957-61; bd. dirs. Tantallon Civic Assn., 1973-74, Ctr. Ocean Law and Policy; v.p. Jewish Congregation; chmn. Zoning Bd., Shrewsbury, N.J., 1990-2001. With USNR, 1944-46. Recipient Spl. award Prince of Monaco, 1952, Superior Civilian Svc. award Navy Dept., 1963, Disting. Svc. award, 1967, Disting. Alumnus award George Washington U., 1983, Compass Disting. Svc. award, 1987, Disting. Svc. award Egyptian Nat. Inst. Oceanography and Fisheries; Gold medal Dept. Commerce, 1973; named Man of Yr. Nat. Sea Grant Program, 1977; decorated Order Jules Richard, Monaco, 1951. Mem. Am. Chem. Soc., Rsch. Soc. Am. (past pres. chpt.), Marine Tech. Soc. (pres. 1974-75), Am. Geophys. Union, Am. Soc. Oceanography (pres. 1971-72), Cosmos Club (Washington), Brown Club (N.J.). Jewish. Home: 33 Queen Ann Dr Shrewsbury NJ 07702-4127 Office: Stevens Inst Tech Davidson Labs 711 Hudson St Hoboken NJ 07030 E-mail: rbanka@aol.com.

ABEL, ROBERT HALSALL, writer; b. Painesville, Ohio, May 27, 1941; s. Robert Halsall and Lora Constance (Logan) A.; m. Joyce Keeler; children: Sarah Paxton, Charles. BA, Coll. of Wooster, 1964; MA in English, Kans. State Coll., 1967; MFA in English, U. Mass., 1974. Asst. prof. Mount Holyoke Coll., South Hadley, Mass., 1984-86; vis. lectr. Beijing Normal U., 1987; vis. writer Trinity Coll., Hartford, Conn., 1990-93; vis. lectr. Beijing Fgn. Studies U., 1993, 97. Author: Freedom Dues, 1980, The Progress of a Fire, 1984, Full-Tilt Boogie, 1989, Ghost Traps, 1991, Riding a Tiger, 1998. Democrat. Avocations: painting, surf-fishing, the Chinese language. Home and Office: 27 Stockwell Rd Hadley MA 01035-9644 E-mail: robert.abel@the-spa.com.

ABEL, ROBERT L. healthcare quality improvement professional; b. Postville, Iowa, Nov. 3, 1940; m. P. Elizabeth Abel, June 18, 1966. BA in Econs., Luther Coll., 1964; MA in Internat. Rels., U. So. Calif., L.A., 1970; MA in Econs., U. Iowa, 1974, PhD in Edn., 1979. Project dir. Tex. Higher Edn. Coord. Bd., Austin, 1978-81; rsch. assoc., dir. adminstrn. So. Regional Edn. Bd., Atlanta, 1981-83; program mgr. USN/Presearch, Washington and Charleston, S.C., 1983-88; dir. inst. rsch. Charleston (S.C.) U., 1988-90; biostatistician VA Med. Ctr., Columbia, S.C., 1991; health sepicers rsch. Columbia, S.C., Austin, Tex., 1991-93; projects coord. Tex. Med. Found., Austin, 1994—99, projects competence adminstr., 2000—02, program compliance adminstr., 2002—03, adminstr. Quality Resources, 2003—. Contbr. articles to profl. jours. Mem. Assn. of Health Svcs. Rsch., Am. Pub. Health Assn. Office: Tex Med Found Barton Oaks Plz II Ste 200 901 Mopac Expy S Austin TX 78746

ABEL, STEVEN L. lawyer, mediator; b. N.Y.C., Oct. 2, 1944; s. Wilfred and Lillian Abel; m. Susan J. Abramowitz, Apr. 3, 1966 (div. Apr. 1991); children: Michele, Gregory, Robert; m. Paula Kazdon Davis, July 4, 1991. BA, CCNY, 1966; JD, Bklyn. Law Sch., 1972. Bar: N.Y. 1973. Assoc. atty. Shapiro & Reeder, Spring Valley, N.Y., 1973-76; atty. Reeder & Abel, New City, N.Y., 1976-88, Abel & Brustein-Kampel, New City, 1990—; dir. Ctr. for Family and Divorce Mediation, New City, 1983—. Hearing examiner Rockland County Family Ct., 1981-82. Author: Friendly Divorce Guidebook, 1996; editor: Federal Family Law, 1998; contbr. articles to profl. jours. Bd. dirs. Rockland Family Shelter, New City; pres. N.Y. State Coun. on Divorce Mediation, Garden City, 1998-99. Recipient Disting. Svc. award County Legislature, Rockland County, 1986, Achievement award NAACP, 1998. Mem.: Assn. Family and Conciliation Cts. (bd. dirs. N.Y. chpt. 2002—). Democrat. Mem. Soc. Of Friends. Avocations: gardening, computers. Office: Abel & Brustein-Kampel 2 New Hempstead Rd New City NY 10956-3635 E-mail: sabel@igc.org.

ABEL, WILLIAM EDWARD, applied physicist, consultant; b. Great Falls, Mont., May 23, 1928; s. Ernest Edward and Anna Lucille (Rempel) A.; m. Theodora Louise Hartho, Mar. 24, 1964; children: Stephen Edward, Jeffrey William. BA, Whitman Coll., 1952; MFA, Cranbrook Acad. Art, 1954. Owner William Abel Design, Portland, Oreg., 1955-76, Lake Oswego, Oreg., 1976—. Co-founder Audiotrainer, Inc., Mountain View, Calif., 1967, dir., 1967-85; cons. in field, 1965—. Dir. Riverdale RFPD, Portland, 1983—, chmn., 1999-2001; chmn. bldg. and bonding com. Riverdale Sch. Dist., 1988. Served to sgt. USAF, 1946-48. Achievements include 16 patents in field. Home: 12203 SW Tryon Hill Rd Portland OR 97219-8314

ABELE, JOHN E. medical products executive; married; 3 children. BS, Amherst Coll. Founder, chmn., dir. Boston Sci., Natick, Mass., 1979—. Office: Boston Sci One Boston Scientific Pl Natick MA 01760-1537

ABELE, ROBERT CHRISTOPHER, lawyer; b. Boonville, Mo., Mar. 24, 1958; s. William Arved and Joyce (Gowan) A. AB, U. Mo., 1980; JD, U. Mo., Kansas City, 1983. Bar: Mo. 1983, U.S. Dist. Ct. (we. dist.) Mo. 1983, U.S. Dist. Ct. Kans. 1998, U.S. Ct. Appeals (8th cir.) 1983, U.S. Ct. Appeals (10th cir.) 1985, U.S. Supreme Ct. 1991, U.S. Ct. Appeals (11th cir.) 1993. Law clk. to judge U.S. Ct. Appeals (8th cir.), 1983-85; assoc. Morrison, Hecker, Curtis, Kuder & Parrish, Kansas City, Mo., 1985-90, ptnr., 1990-91, Morrison & Hecker, Kansas City, 1991-95, Badger & Levings, Kansas City, 1995-2000; gen. atty. law dept. Sprint, Kansas City, 2001—. Adj. prof. U. Mo. Kansas City Law Sch., 1988. Chmn. Mo. Coun. on Arts, 1989—94; trustee U. Mo.-Kansas City Law Found., 1986—99, pres., 1997—98; bd. dirs. Mid.-Am. Arts Alliance, 1989—98; treas. Nat. Assembly of State Art Agys., 1994—96; bd. dirs. SAVE, Inc., 2002—. Recipient Decade award U. Mo.-Kansas City Law Found., 1991. Mem. Kansas City Met. Bar Assn. (exec. com. 1999-2001). Republican. Avocation: classical vocal music. Home: 2204 W 49th St Westwood Hills KS 66251 Office: Sprint Law Dept KSOPHN0412-4A153 6450 Sprint Pkwy Overland Park KS 66251

ABELES, CHARLES CALVERT, retired lawyer; b. Norfolk, Va., Nov. 3, 1929; s. Charles T. and Sally (Taylor) A.; m. Mehitable Mackay-Smith, Sept. 30, 1961; children— Nathaniel C., Damaris S., Jessica A.K. AB, Harvard U., 1952; JD, U. Va., 1958. Bar: Va. 1958, D.C. 1958, U.S. Dist. Ct. (D.C. dist.) 1958, U.S. Ct. Appeals 1958. Assoc. Hogan & Hartson, Washington, 1958-62; assoc. Kieffer & Moroney, Washington, 1962-64, ptnr., 1964-69, Lichtman, Abeles, Anker & Nagle, Washington, 1969-77, Wald, Harkrader & Ross, Washington, 1977-85, Piper & Marbury, Washington, 1986-95. Trustee Corina Higginson Trust. Author articles in field Served to lt. (j.g.) USN, 1952-55 Mem D.C. Bar, Transplant Recipients Internat. Orgn. (past sec., nat. bd. dirs., past pres. local chpt.). Clubs: Metropolitan (Washington). Democrat. Home: 4339 Westover Pl NW Washington DC 20016

ABELES, JAMES DAVID, manufacturing company executive; b. N.Y.C., Mar. 24, 1916; s. James A. and Williemene H. (Kirtland) A.; m. Elizabeth Brunet, Aug. 24, 1940 (dec. 1978); children: James B. and Elizabeth K. (twins); m. Mary E. Ballantyne, Dec. 11, 1982. Student, Stevens Inst. Tech., 1935-36

M.I.T., 1936-37. Tool and die apprentice Electrolux Co., 1934-35; erecting engr. U.S. Fire Protection Co., 1937-38; sales engr. Thomas F. Mason Co., 1938-39; time study engr. Waterbury Button Co., 1939-40; with Purolator, Inc., Rahway, N.J., 1940-87, dir., 1954-87, pres., 1955-70, chmn. exec. com., 1970-73; pres., dir. Interpace Corp., 1973-74, chmn. bd. dirs., 1974-76. Mem. Jockey Hollow Fish and Game Protective Assn., Chi Phi. Clubs: Somerset Hills Country (Bernardsville, N.J.); Seal Harbor (Maine) Yacht. Home: 4113 Fellowship Rd Basking Ridge NJ 07920-3906

ABELES, KIM VICTORIA, artist; b. Richmond Heights, Mo., Aug. 28, 1952; d. Burton Noel Wright and Frances Elizabeth (Sander) Hoffman. BFA in Painting, Ohio U., 1974; MFA in Studio Art, U. Calif., Irvine, 1980. Free-lance artist, L.A., 1975—. Lectr. varius schs. and art ctrs., 1980—; vis. disting. artist Calif. State U., Fullerton, 1985-87; asst. prof. Calif. State U., Northridge, 1998—. Author, illustrator Crafts, Cookery and 'Country Living, 1976, Kim Abeles, 1988, Kim Abeles: Encyclopedia Persona, 1993, author, photographer: Impressions, 1979, work featured in Artery, 1979, Pacific Poetry and Fiction Review, 1980, Fiction Internat., 1985; one-woman shows include U. Calif., Irvine, 1979, 1980, Mcpl. Art Gallery, L.A., 1981, L.A. City Hall, 1982, Phyllis Kind Gallery, Chgo., 1983, Karl Bornstein Gallery, Santa Monica, Calif., 1983, 1985, 1987, one-woman shows include Pepperdine U., Malibu, Calif., 1985, A.I.R. Gallery, N.Y.C., 1986, Chapman Coll., Orange, Calif., 1986, Mount St. Mary's Coll., L.A., 1987, Atlanta Pavilion, 1990, Calif. Mus. of Sci. and Industry, L.A., 1991, Laguna Art Mus. Satellite Gallery, Costa Mesa, Calif., 1991, Turner-Krull Gallery, L.A., 1992, Lawrence Miller Gallery, N.Y.C., 1992, Santa Monica Mus. Art (15 yr. survey), L.A., 1993, Nat. Mus. Fine Arts, Santiago, Chile, 1996, Mus. Modern Art, Rio de Janeiro, 1996, Cmplejo Cultural Recoleta, Buenos Aires, 1986, Centro Cutural Consolidado, Caracas, 1997, Cepa Gallery, Buffalo, 1998, A.R.T., Inc., N.Y.C., 1989, Contemporary Arts Ctr., Cin., 2000, Art Resources Transfer, N.Y.C., 2001, Intersection, San Francisco, 2001, Calif. Sci. Ctr., L.A., 2000—01, commd., Marriott Hotels, 1999, City of Pasadena, 1999, San Fernando Valley Constituent Svc. Ctr., 2001, Marvin Braude San Fernando Valley Constituent Svc. Ctr., 2001—, City of Pasadena, 2002, exhibitions include Mus. of Contemporary Art, L.A., L.A. County Mus. Art, Calif. African-Am. Mus., Allen Meml. Art Mus., Ohio, exhibited in group shows at Silpakorn U., Bangkok, 2002. Honored for Outstanding Student Rsch. & Creative Achievement U. Calif., 1979; recipient U.S. Steel award Exhbn. of the Associated Artists of pitts., 1977, Clean Air award Air Quality Mgmt. Dist., Calif., 1992; hand Hollow Found. fellow, 1984, Design Team fellow Panorama City Libr., Calif., 1992-93, J. Paul Getty Trust Fund for the Visual Arts fellow, 1994; Pollock-Krasner Found. grantee, 1990, Calif. Arts Coun. grantee, 1990, L.A. Cultural Affairs grantee, 1991, 95, 96, U.S. Info. Agy. grantee, 1995-97; commissioned by Panorama City Pub. Libr., L.A., 1993, Met. Transp. Authority, L.A., 1995, Dept. Transp., L.A., 2000; recipient Richard Neutra award for Profl. Excellence, 2001. E-mail: kimabeles@earthlink.net.

ABELES, NORMAN, psychologist, educator; b. Vienna, Apr. 15, 1928; came to U.S., 1939, naturalized, 1944; s. Felix and Bertha (Gronich) A.; m. Jeanette Bueller, Apr. 14, 1957; children: Linda, Mark. BA, NYU, 1949; MA, U. Tex., 1952, PhD, 1958. Diplomate. Am. Bd. Profl. Psychology (Midwest regional bd. 1972-78, chmn. regional bd. 1975-77; nat. trustee 1975-77). Fellow in counseling U. Tex., Austin, 1956-57; instr. Mich. State U., East Lansing, 1957-59, asst. prof., 1959-64, asso. prof., 1964-67, prof. psychology, 1968—, dir. psychol. clinic, 1978—, co-dir, clin. tng., 1981-96, asst. dir. counseling center, 1965-71. U.S. State Dept. ednl. exch. prof. U. Utrecht, Netherlands, 1969, vis. prof., 1975; cons. Peace Corps, 1965-69; vocat. cons. Social Security Office of Hearings and Appeals, 1962—; med. advisor Social Security Office of Hearings and Appeals, 1986—; mem. Mich. Commn. Cert. of Psychologists, 1962-77, chmn., 1966-68; mem. coun. Nat. Register Health Svc. Providers in Psychology, 1974—, vice chmn., 1975-80; del. White House Conf. on Aging, 1995, 2002—; mem. geriatric and gerontology adv. com. to Sec. of VA. Editor: Acad. Psychology bull., 1978-82; cons. editor Jour. Personality Assessment, 1988—, Clin. Psychology: Sci. and Practice, 1994—, Clin. Psychology Rev., 1995-98, Profl. Psychology: Rsch. and Practice, 1979-81, 89—, editor, 1983-88; contbr. articles to profl. jours. Served with U.S. Army, 1954-56. Fulbright-Hays grantee, 1969; recipient Disting. Psychologist award Mich. Soc. Clin. Psychologists, 1984; Disting. Practitioner, Nat. Acad. Practice, 1982; Arthur Furst Ethics Lectureship medal Pacific Grad. Sch. Psychology, 1996; Dept. Vets. Affairs Spl. Contbns. award, Battle Creek Mich., 1997. Fellow APA (coun. reps. 1972-75, 77-79, 89-91, 93-95, 99—, policy and planning bd. 1975-79, chmn. 1976, rec. sec. 1980-86, chmn. edn. and tng. bd. 1988, bd. ednl. affairs 1999-2001, com. on internat. rels. in psychology 2002— pres.-elect divsn. clin. psychology 1989, pres. divsn. psychotherapy and divsn. clin. psychology 1990, publs. and comm. bd. 1990-96, chmn. 1995, pres.-elect 1996, pres. 1997, past pres. 1998, bd. dirs. divsn. psychotherapy 2000—), Coun. Sci. Socs. Pres.; mem. Midwestern Psychol. Assn., Mich. Psychol. Assn. (legis. chmn. 1964-72, pres. 1971-72, Disting. Psychologist 1974), Internat. Union Psychol. Scis. (U.S. com. 1999—), Sigma Xi. Home: 953 Rosewood Ave East Lansing MI 48823-3126 Office: Mich State U Dept Psychology 129 Psychology Research East Lansing MI 48824-1117 E-mail: abeles@msu.edu.

ABELES, RICHARD ALAN, lawyer; b. Chgo., June 28, 1937; s. Jerome Guthmann Sr. and Jeanne Katherine (Rosenbacher) Abeles; m. Kathleen Sue Koretz, Jan. 28, 1968; 1 child, Elizabeth Amy. BA, Amherst Coll., 1959; JD, Harvard U., 1963. Bar: Ill. 1963, N.Mex. 1976. Atty. Altheimer & Gray, Chgo., 1963-69; hon. consul of Costa Rica State of N.Mex., 1976-84; pvt. practice Chgo., 1971-75, Santa Fe, 1976—. Founding pres. Santa Fe Children's Mus., 1987-95; trustee Santa Fe Prep. Sch., 1993-99; elected ofcl. Santa Fe Met. Water Bd., 1988-90. Avocations: skiing, basketball, travel. Home and Office: 3730 Old Santa Fe Trl Santa Fe NM 87505-4573 Fax: 505-984-2040. E-mail: rick@abeles.net.

ABELES, SIGMUND M. painter, printmaker, sculptor; b. N.Y.C., Nov. 6, 1934; s. Samuel and Henrietta (Banner) A.; m. Anne Merck (div. 1998); children: David Paul, Shoshanna Lynn, Maxwell Merck Abeles. Student, Pratt Inst., 1952-53, Art Students' League, 1954, Skowhegan Sch. (scholar), 1955-56, Bklyn. Mus. Sch. (Graphics scholar), 1956-57; AB in Art, U. S.C., 1955; MFA, Columbia U., 1957; DA (hon.), Coastal Carolina U., 2000. Faculty Swain Sch. Design, New Bedford, Mass., 1961-64; resident artist Wellesley (Mass.) Coll., 1964-69; asst. prof. art Boston U., 1969-70, prof. U. N.H., 1970-87, prof. emeritus, 1987—; artist-in-residence U. So. Maine, Gorham, 1990. Instr. workshop Acad. Realist Art, Seattle, 1995, Art Students League, N.Y.C., 1997-2000; instr. advanced drawing workshop Nat. Acad. Sch. Fine Arts, N.Y.C., 1997-98; bd. dirs. Artist Fellowship, N.Y.C. One man show at Bates Coll. Mus., Lewiston, Maine, 1999, Thomas Williams Fine Arts, London, 2000, Art 2003, London, Thomas Williams Fine Arts and Drawing Studio, Tucson; exhibited in group show at S.C. State Mus., Columbia, 1999—; represented in permanent collections including Albert & Victoria Mus., London, The Brit. Mus., London, Libr. Congress, Washington, Mus. Modern Art, N.Y.C., Met. Mus. Art, N.Y.C., Museo de Arte, Ponce, P.R., Phila. Mus. Art, Mus. Find Art, Boston, Fitz William Mus., Cambridge, England, Munson-Proctor-Williams Inst., Ithaca, N.Y., Whitney Mus. Am. Art, N.Y.C.; vis. sculptor Johnson Atelier, Tech. Inst. for Sculpture, 1977; traveling retrospective exhbn. New Eng. Coll., Henniker, N.H., McKissick Mus., U. S.C., Columbia, Checkwood Mus. Art, Nashville, Fitchburg (Mass.) Mus. Art, 1992-93; (subject of) The Observant Hand, Forty Years of the Drawing of Sigmund Abeles, So. Meth. U. Gallery, Dallas, 1998; archive for his papers set up at South Carolinian Libr., U. S.C., 1998—, study archive for prints at Bates Coll. Mus. Art, 1998—, grant to paint Chateau Rochefort-en-tene-France, 2000. Nat. Inst. Arts and Letters grantee, 1965, Nat. Coun. Arts and Humanities sabbatical grantee, 1966, Louis Comfort Tiffany Found. grantee, 1967, U. N.H. Grad. Sch. Sculpture grantee, 1973, Am. Jewish Com. grantee for acad. seminar in Israel, 1981, Florsheim Found. grantee, 1992, residency grantee Chateau Rochefort en Terre, Brittany, France, 2000; recipient Am. Master/Printmaking award Am. Artist mag., 1996; subject of "Sigmund Abeles, A Monograph" essays by Charles Simic and Robert Doty, 1992. Mem. NAD (Leo Meisner prize 1983, academician 1990, mem. coun., corr. sec. 1991—), Soc. Am. Graphic Artists, Pastel Soc. Am. *I strive to observe life with a penetrating eye that I hope can go beyond surface reality to reveal psychological and visual truth, even some magic.*

ABEL HOROWITZ, MICHELLE SUSAN, advertising executive; b. Detroit, Mar. 31, 1950; d. Martin Louis and Phyllis (Berkowitz) A.; m. H. Jay Abel Horowitz, July 11, 1976; children— Jordan Michael, Stefanie Jennifer. Student Goucher Coll., 1967-70; B.A. in Econs., U. Mich., 1971; postgrad. in econs. U. Calif.-San Diego, 1973; M.A. in Econs., U. Detroit, 1974-76. Planning group supr. Hill Holliday Connors, Cosmopolus, Mass., 1976-78; econ. analyst Data Resources, Boston, 1978-79; v.p., media dir. Darkley & Evergreen, Southfield, Mich., 1979-80; v.p., dir. mktg. and media Yaffe/Berline, Southfield, Mich., 1980-82; pres., ptnr., corp. treas. Berline Group, Birmingham, Mich., 1982— ; instr. Oakland U., Rochester, Mich., 1982; trustee, chairperson mktg. com. Harbinger Dance Co., Farmington, Mich., 1983— . Named Advt. Woman of Yr., Women's Ad Club Detroit, 1982. Mem. Adcraft Club Detroit, Women in Communications. Democrat. Jewish. Office: The Berline Group 6100 N Adams Bloomfield Hills MI 48304 E-mail: mhorowitz@berlinenet.com.

ABELL, RICHARD BENDER (RICHARD LON WELCH), lawyer, federal judicial official; b. Phila., Dec. 2, 1943; s. Lon Edward Welch, Jr. and Charlotte Amelia (Bender) A., stepfather Ernest George Abell; m. Lucia del Carmen Lombana-Cadavid, Dec. 2, 1968; chldren David, Christian, Rachel. BA in Internat. Affairs, George Washington U., 1966, JD, 1974. Bar: Pa. 1974. Vol. Peace Corps, Colombia, 1967-69, assoc. Reilly & Fogwell, West Chester, Pa., 1974-80; asst. dist. atty. Chester County, Pa., 1974-79; staff mem. U.S. Senator Richard Schweiker, Washington, 1979-80; dir. Office of Program Devel. Peace Corp., Washington, 1981-83; dep. asst. atty. gen. U.S. Dept. Justice, Washington, 1983-86, asst. atty. gen., 1986-90; special master U.S. Ct. Fed. Claims, 1991—. Mem. adj. faculty Del. Law Sch., Wilmington, 1975-77, West Chester State U., 1976; bd. dirs. Fed. Prison Industries, Inc., 1985-91; chmn. Nat. Crime Prevention Coalition, 1986-90; mem. adv. bd. Nat. Inst. Corrections, 1986-90; co-chmn. adv. com. Nat. Ctr. for State and Local Law Enforcement Tng., 1987-90; vice chmn. rsch. and devel. rev. bd. Dept. Justice, 1987-89; mem. nat. drug policy bd. Enforcement Coordinating Group and Coordinating Group for Drug Abuse Prevention and Health, The White House, Washington, 1988-89. Author: Peter Smith of Westmoreland County, Va. (Died 1741) and Some Descendents, 1996, Sojourns of a Patriot: Field and Prison Papers of An Unreconstructed Confederate, 1998. Chmn. Young Rep. Nat. Fedn., Washington, 1979-81; mem. exec. com. Rep. Nat. Com., 1979-81; mem. fed. coordinating coun. on Juvenile Justice and Delinquency Prevention, 1986-90; mem. Pres.'s Task Force on Adoption, 1987-88; mem. Pres.'s Commn. on Agrl. Workers, 1988-93. With U.S. Army, 1969-71. Decorated Purple Heart, Army Commendation medal for heroism, Air medal; recipient Jefferson Davis Hist. gold medal, 2000. Episcopalian. Home: 8209 Chancery Ct Alexandria VA 22308-1514

ABELLA DOMINICIS, ESTEBAN MARTIN, hematologist, oncologist, pediatrician; b. Havana, Cuba, Feb. 11, 1961; s. Manuel and Alicia (Dominicis) Abella; m. Beth I. Wheeler, May 16, 1981; children: Isabel, Alicia, Carmen, Margarita. Student, U. Pa., 1979-80; MD, U. Ctrl. del Este, Dominican Republic, 1985. Diplomate Am. Bd. Pediats., Sub-bd. Pediatric Hematology-Oncology. Resident in pediats. Wayne State U. Children's Hosp., Detroit, 1985-91, fellow in hematology/oncology, 1988-91, assoc. hematologist, 1991—, asst. prof. pediats., medicine, 1991-96, assoc. prof. pediats., medicine, 1997—2003, prof. pediatrics, medicine and oncology, 2003—; assoc. hematologist/oncologist divsn. hematology/oncology Children's Hosp. Mich., Detroit, 1991, med. dir. Hospice Program, 1996-99; assoc. bone marrow transplant hematologist Harper Hosp., Detroit, 1992, clin. dir. pediatric bone marrow transplant program, 1995. Assoc. bone marrow transplant faculty Barbara Ann Karmanos Cancer Inst., Detroit, 1992—, med. dir. pediat. hospice svc., 1997-2000; mem. bone marrow transplantation adv. group Mich. Dept. Pub. Health, 1996-97; mem. cancer com. Crittenton Hosp., 1996-2000; presenter, rschr. in field. Contbr. numerous articles to profl. jours. Bd. dirs. Spl. Days Camp, 1997—; mem. med. adv. bd. J.P. McCarthy Found., 1996-2001. Grantee Children's Leukemia Found. Fellowship, Ford/Lincoln Mercury Divsn., 1988-91. Mem. Am. Soc. Clin. Oncology, Am. Soc. Hematology, AAAS, Am. soc. Blood and Bone Marrow Transplantation, Am. Acad. Pediats. Hematology/Oncology (sect. mem.), Am. Soc. Pediatric Hematology/Oncology, AAP. Roman Catholic. Achievements include research of the use of LAK cells and lymphokines in the prevention of graft versus leukemia and graft versus host disease in murine and cord blood models. Office: Children's Hosp Mich Divsn Hem/Onc 3901 Beaubien St Detroit MI 48201-2119

ABELLE, PATSY CAPLES, lawyer; b. Waukegan, Ill., Aug. 20, 1935; d. Roy Lee Caples Abelle and Lee Self (Rosamond) Henderson. BS fin., DePaul U., 1964; JD, 1967; LLM, NYU, 1968. Bar: Ill. 1967, NY 1968, US Dist. Ct. (no. idst.)/Ill. 1967, US Ct. Mil. Appeals 1968, US Supreme Ct. 1968. Chief securities Fed. Res. Bank, NYC, 1968—73; assoc. Willkie Farr & Gallagher, NYC, 1973—78; sr. atty. Fed. Res. Bd., Washington, 1978—81; sr. assoc. Cravath, Swaine & Moore, NYC, 1981—. Contbr. articles. Mem.: Blue Sky Lawyers Assn. (chmn. 1984—85), Fed. Women's Program Adv. Com. (chmn. 1980). Office: Cravath Swaine & Moore 825 8th Ave Fl 38 New York NY 10019-7475

ABELOV, STEPHEN LAWRENCE, uniform clothing company executive, consultant; b. N.Y.C., Apr. 1, 1923; s. Saul S. and Ethel (Esterman) Abelov; m. Phyllis S. Lichtenson, Nov. 18, 1945; children: Patricia C., Gary M. BS, NYU, 1945, MBA, 1950. Asst. divsn. mgr. Nat. Silver Co., NY, 1945; sales rep. Angelica Uniform Co., NY, 1945—50, asst. sales mgr., 1950—56, western regional mgr., 1956—66; v.p. Angelica Uniform Co. of Calif., 1958—66, nat. v.p. sales, 1966—72; v.p. Angelica Corp., 1958—88, cons., 1988—92, group v.p. mktg., 1972—80; exec. v.p., chief mktg. officer Angelica Uniform Group, 1980—88. Vis. lectr. mktg. NYU Grad. Sch. Bus. Adminstrn. Contbr. articles to profl. jours. Vice comdr. Am. Legion; mem. vocational adv. bd. VA; adv. bd. Woodcraft Rangers; bd. dirs. Univ. Temple. Served with USAF, 1942—44. Mem.: various trade assns., Inst. Environ. Scis., Health Industries Assn. Am. (dir.), Am. Mktg. Assn., Am. Soc. for Advancement Mgmt. (chpt. pres.), Am. Assn. Contamination Control (dir.), U.S. Power Squad., Coast Guard Aux. (Flotilla comdr., dist. officer), B'nai B'rith (past pres.), St. Louis Coun. on World Affairs, NYU Alumni Assn., Lake of the Ozarks Yachting Assn., Moorings Yacht Club (v.p.), Sales Execs. Club (bd. dirs.), Aqua Sierra Sportsmen Club, NYU Club, Men's Club (exec. v.p.), Town Hall Club, Phi Epsilon Pi (treas.). Home: 9821 Log Cabin Ct Saint Louis MO 63124-1133

ABELSON, ALAN, columnist; b. N.Y.C., Oct. 12, 1925; s. Harry Carl and Vivian (Finkelstein) A.; m. Virginia Eloise Peterson, Sept. 1, 1951; children— Justin Adams, Reed Vivian. BS in Chemistry and English, CCNY, 1946; MA in Creative Writing, U. Iowa, 1947. Reporter N.Y. Jour. Am., N.Y.C., 1949-56, stock market columnist, 1952-56; with Barron's, The Dow Jones Bus. and Fin. Weekly, N.Y.C., 1956—, mng. editor, 1965-81, editor, 1981-93; columnist Up & Down Wall St., 1966—. Bus. corres. NBC-TV News at Sunrise, 1982-90. Office: Barron's 200 Liberty St New York NY 10281-1003

ABELSON, ELIAS, lawyer; b. N.Y.C., Nov. 17, 1932; s. Harry and Lucille (Margulies) A.; m. Isobel Faith Schiffman, Sept. 8, 1957; children: Adam Samuel, Joshua Tobin, Matthew Noah. BA, U. Pa., 1954; JD, Columbia U., 1959. Bar: N.J. 1960, U.S. Dist. Ct. N.J. 1960, U.S. Ct. Appeals (3d cir.) 1969, U.S. Ct. Appeals (7th cir.) 1973, U.S. Claims Ct. 1969, U.S. Tax Ct. 1969, U.S. Supreme Ct. 1965. Dep. atty. gen. State of N.J., Trenton, 1960-63, 64-68, asst. atty. gen., 1968-88; assoc. Green, Robinson & Deitz, Trenton, 1963-64; gen. counsel Bucknell U., Lewisburg, Pa., 1988-98; mem. N.J. Supreme Ct. Dist. Ethics Com., 1985-88; lectr. in field. Contbr. articles to legal publs. Sec. Princeton Folk Music Soc., 1976-78; vice chmn. Princeton U. Concerts Com., 1978-82; trustee Gr. Princeton Youth Orch., 1984-88, vice-chmn., 1985-86, chmn., 1986-88. Served to 1st lt. U.S. Army, 1954-56. Mem. Nat. Assn. Coll. & Univ. Attys., N.J. Bar Assn., Pa. Bar Assn., Union County Bar Assn., Columbia Law Sch. Alumni Assn. N.J. (sec. 1982-84, trustee 1984-88). Jewish. Home: 100 Eastwood Dr Portsmouth NH 03801-6070

ABELSON, HERBERT TRAUB, pediatrician, educator; b. St. Louis, Feb. 19, 1941; s. Benjamin J. and Ann (Traub) Abelson; m. Constance Faye Caldwell, May 17, 1968; children: Matthew, Rebecca, Jonathan, Daniel. AB with high honors, U. Ill., 1962; MD, Washington U., St. Louis, 1966. Diplomate Diplomate Am. Bd. Pediat. (examiner 1988—, bd. dirs. 1992-97, sec.-treas. 1995, chmn.-elect 1995-96, chmn. 1996-97), Am. Bd. Pediatric Hematology-Oncology. Intern pediat. U Colo. Med. Ctr., Denver, 1966—67; resident Boston Children's Hosp., 1969—71; staff assoc. Nat. Cancer Inst. NIH, Bethesda, Md., 1967—69; Jane Childs Meml. Fund for Med. Rsch. fellow NIH, 1971, spl. postdoctoral fellow, 1972; teaching fellow Med. Sch. Harvard Coll., Boston, 1970—71, instr. pediat., 1973—74, asst. prof., 1974—79; tutor in med. scis., 1977—79; assoc. prof. Harvard Coll., Boston, 1979—83; vis. prof., Ctr. for Cancer Rsch. MIT, Cambridge, 1982—83; prof., chmn. dept. pediat. Med. Sch. U. Wash., Seattle, 1983—95; prof., chmn., physician-in-chief dept. pediat. U. Chgo., 1995—. Rsch. fellow in hematology Children's Hosp. Med. Ctr., Boston, 1971—73; rsch. assoc. in biology MIT, 1971—73; mem. pediatric residency rev. com. Accreditation Coun. for Grad. Med. Edn.; mem. exec. com. Am. Med. Sch. Pediatric Dept. Chairmen. Contbr. articles to profl. jours. Lt. comdr. USPHS, 1967—69. Recipient Rsch. Career Devel. award, NIH, 1975—80, Alumni achievement award, Washington U., 2001. Fellow: Am. Acad. Pediat.; mem.: Am. Soc. Pediat. Hematology (fin. com.), Am. Bd. Med. Spltys. (fin. com.), Am. Pediatric Soc., Soc. Pediatric Rsch., Am. Soc. Clin. Oncology, Am. Assn. Cancer Rsch., Am. Soc. Hematology (mem. sci. subcom. on pediatric hematology 1987—91). Office: Univ Chgo Dept Pediatrics 5841 S Maryland Ave # Mc1051 Chicago IL 60637-1463

ABELSON, JOHN NORMAN, biology educator; b. Grand Coulee Dam, Wash., Oct. 19, 1938; BS, Wash. State U., 1960; PhD, Johns Hopkins U., 1965; postgrad., Lb. Molecular Biology, Cambridge, Eng., 1965—68. Asst. prof. dept. chemistry U. Calif.-San Diego, 1968—73, assoc. prof., 1973—77, prof., 1977—82; prof. biology Calif. Inst. Tech., Pasadena, 1982—. Founding bd. dirs. Agouron Inst., La Jolla, Calif., 1979—; co-founder Agouron Pharmaceuticals, Inc. Asst. editor Analytical Biochemistry, 1980—87, mem. editl. bd. (Journal) Jour. Biol. Chemistry, 1981—85, mem. editl. com. Ann. Rev. Inc., 1982—; editor: Methods in Enzymology, —; contbr. ; Mem. editl. com Ann. Rev. Biochemistry. Mem.: Am. Acad. Arts and Scis., NAS, Am. Chem. Soc., Am. Soc. Biol. Chemists. Home: 1097 Blanche St Apt 316 Pasadena CA 91106-3062 Office: Calif Inst Tech 147-75 1200 E Calif Blvd Pasadena CA 91125-0001

ABELSON, PHILIP HAUGE, physicist; b. Tacoma, Wash., Apr. 27, 1913; s. Ole Andrew and Ellen (Hauge) A.; m. Neva Martin, Dec. 30, 1936; 1 child, Ellen Hauge Abelson Cherniavsky. BS, Wash. State Coll., 1933, MS, 1935; PhD, U. Calif., 1939; DS, Yale U., 1964, So. Meth. U., 1969, Tufts U., 1976, Duke U., 1981, Oregon State U., 1995; DHL, U. Puget Sound, 1968. Asst. physicist Carnegie Instn. of Washington, 1939-41, chmn. biophysics sect. dept. terrestrial magnetism, 1946-53, dir. Geophysics Lab., 1953-71, pres. instn., 1971-78; trustee from, 1978 ; assoc. physicist Naval Research Lab, Washington, 1941-42, physicist, 1942-44, sr. physicist, 1944-45, prin. physicist, 1945; civilian in charge Naval Research Lab. br. Navy Yard, Phila., 1944-45; resident fellow Resources for the Future Inc., Washington, 1985-88. Chmn. com. on radiation cataracts NRC, 1949-57, sub-com. on shock, 1950-53, mem. Plowshare adv. com., 1959-63; gen. adv. com. AEC, 1960-63; mem. biophysics and biophys. chemistry study sect. Nat. Inst. Arthritis and Metabolic Diseases, NIH, 1956-59, mem. phys. biology tng. grants com. 1958-60, bd. sci. counselors, 1960-63; cons. NASA, 1960-63; sci. advisor AAAS, from 1985, acting exec. dir., 1989. Author: Energy for Tomorrow, 1975, Enough of Pessimism, 1985; mem. adv. bd. Jour Nat. Cancer Inst., 1947-52; editor: Researches in Geochemistry, 1959, Vol. 2, 1967; Energy: Use, Conservation and Supply, 1974, Food: Politics, Economics, Nutrition, and Research, 1975; Materials: Renewable and Nonrenewable, 1976, Electronics: The Continuing Revolution, 1977; co-editor Jour. Geophys. Research, 1959-65; editor Sci. mag., 1962-85, dep. editor for engring. and applied scis., from 1985. Recipient Disting. Civilian Service medal, 1945, ann. award phys. sci. Washington Acad. Sci., 1950, Disting. Alumnus award Wash. State U., 1962, Hillebrand award Chem. Soc. Washington, 1962, Modern Medicine award, 1967, Mellon award Carnegie-Mellon U., 1970, Joseph Priestley award Dickinson Coll., 1973, Sci. Achievement award AMA, 1974, Hon. Scroll award D.C. Inst. Chemists, 1976, Kalinga prize UNESCO, 1972, Disting. Pub. Service award NSF, 1984, Nat. Medal Sci., 1989, Vannevar Bush award, 1996, PublicWelfare Medal, NAS, 1992. Fellow Am. Phys. Soc., Geol. Soc. Am., Mineral. Soc. Am., Geol. Soc. Washington, Am. Acad. Arts and Scis.; mem. Am. Nuclear Soc., Seismol. Soc. Am., Internat. Union Geol. Scis. (pres. 1972-76), Brit. Biochem. Soc., Brit. Mineral. Soc., Am. Chem. Soc., Am. Philos. Soc., Soc. Am. Bacteriologists, Am. Geophys. Union (pres. 1972-74), Am. Assn. Petroleum Geologists, Geochem. Soc., Washington Acad. Scis., Biophys. Soc., Philos. Soc. Washington, Phi Beta Kappa (senator-at-large 1972—), Sigma Xi, Nat. Acad. Scis., Nat. Inst. Medicine (sr.). Clubs: Cosmos (pres. 1972). Office: AAAS 1200 New York Ave NW Ste 100 Washington DC 20005-3941*

ABELT, RALPH WILLIAM, bank executive; b. Elmhurst, Ill., Feb. 16, 1929; s. P. Alfred and Clara S. (Springhorn) A.; m. Patricia Mitchell, Feb. 2, 1952; children: Susan E., Christopher M., Leslie A. BS, U. Colo., 1952; MBA, Ind. U., 1953. Acct. Marion Hutchinson, C.P.A., Denver, 1952; v.p. comml. banking Continental Ill., Chgo., 1953-77; pres., chief exec. officer, dir. Bank One of Northeastern Ohio, NA, Painesville, 1977-83; chmn., chief exec. officer Bank One Cleve., NA, 1983-86; pres., chief exec. officer Work in N.E. Ohio Council, 1988-91. Dir. KnowledgeWorks Found., Cin. Past pres., mem. exec. bd., area v.p. N.E. Ohio coun. Boy Scouts Am., Painesville, 1981; dir. Holden Arboretum, Kirtland, Ohio, 1982; hon. corp. dir. Ohio Motorists Assn. Served with USMC, 1946-48. Mem. Kirtland Country Club. Home: 4711 Figgie Dr Willoughby OH 44094-7947 E-mail: custcraft@aol.com.

ABEND, KENNETH, electrical engineer; b. N.Y.C., Jan. 14, 1936; s. Israel and Sarah Abend; m. Judith Segal, June 26, 1966; children: Cary, Illysa, Debra, Lori. BEE cum laude, CCNY, 1958; MSEE, U. Pa., 1963, PhD, 1966. Engring. rsch. specialist Philco-Ford Corp., Blue Bell, Pa., 1958-68; sr. engring. rsch. specialist Ford Aerospace and Comm., Willow Grove, Pa., 1968-76; prin. engr. RCA Missile and Surface Radar, Moorestown, N.J., 1976-84; dir. advanced signal processing Interspec Inc., Ambler, Pa., 1984-91; dir. advanced signal processing lab. GORCA Technologies, Moorestown, 1991—99; v.p. VueSonics Sensors, Wayne, Pa., 1999—. Assoc. mem. grad. faculty Pa. State U., Great Valley, 1967—, adj. assoc. prof. systems U. Pa., Phila., 1972—88; mem. com. on sci. and the arts Franklin Inst., Phila., 1999—. Bd. dirs. Welcome House Adoptive Parents Group, Doylestown, Pa., 1970—74. Named Outstanding Young Engr., CUNY, 1969. Mem.: IEEE (sr.), Franklin Inst. Com. on Sci. and the Arts. Achievements include 3-D Doppler ultrasound blood flow imaging device, digital processing pansceiver. Home: 623 Killdeer Ln Huntingdon Valley PA 19006-2121

ABER, ITA, multimedia designer, conservator, historian; b. Montreal, Can., Mar. 27, 1932; arrived in U.S., 1954; d. Tudick and Fannie (Zabitsky) Herschcovich; m. Joshua Aber, Dec. 8, 1954; children: Mindy Ann Barad, Judah David, Harry Asher. BA in Cultural Studies, Empire State Coll., Albany, N.Y., 1982; postgrad., Jewish Theol. Sem., N.Y.C. Asst. curator-history Hudson River Mus., Yonkers, NY, 1969-70; guest curator Yeshiva U. Mus., N.Y.C., 1976, 82, 97; adj. curator of collection Park Ave Synagogue, N.Y.C., 1983—2003; guest curator 150th Anniversary, Mpls., 1985; curator Hebrew Home for Aged, Riverdale, NY, 1989-93. Bd. dirs. Judaica Mus., Riverdale, 1989—, guest curator, docent trainer Jewish ethnography & textiles, 2003. Author: (book) The Art of Judaic Needlework, 1979; editor: The Paper Pomegranate, 1976—80; contbr. articles to profl. jours. Comm. cons. programming and fundraising PBS, Riverdale, 1964—66; bd. dirs. Textile Cons. Group, N.Y.C., AM. Friends Tel Aviv Mus., N.Y.C., 1970—72; mem. Landmarks Bd., Yonkers, 1991—94; campaign mgr. Reform Dems., Riverdale, 1965. Philip Morris grantee, Hudson River Mus., 1997, Pomegranate Guild, 2001, others. Mem.: Internat. Soc. Jewish Art (bd. dirs. 1990—, v.p. 1997—98), Textile Study Group of NY, Textile Soc. Am., N.Y. Landmark Conservancy, Pomegranate Guilds U.S. and Can. Avocations: research, training museum docents in Judaic textiles. Fax: 718-548-7888. E-mail: mjaberesq@msn.com.

ABER, JOHN WILLIAM, finance educator; b. Canonsburg, Pa., Sept. 9, 1937; s. John William and Rose (Lauda) A.; m. Cynthia Louise Sousa, Nov. 24, 1962; children: John, Valerie, Alexander. BS, Pa. State U., 1959; MBA, Columbia U., 1965; DBA, Harvard U., 1972. Cons. Univ. Affiliates, Inc., Boston, 1969-71; asst. prof. fin. Ga. State U., Atlanta, 1971-72, Boston U., 1972-78, assoc. prof., 1978-97, prof., 1997—. Fin. and bank mgmt. cons.; dir. mgrs. funds Appleton Growth Fund, 1999—; dir. Third Ave. Funds, 2001—.

McKinsey scholar Columbia U.; Bus. Sch. leadership fellow, Divsn. of Rsch. fellow. Home: 51 Columbia St Brookline MA 02446-2407 Office: Boston U 595 Commonwealth Ave Boston MA 02215-1704 E-mail: jackaber@bu.edu.

ABERCROMBIE, NEIL, congressman; s. G. Don and Vera June (Giersdorf) A.; m. Nancie Ellen Caraway, July 18, 1981; BA Union Coll., 1959, MA U. Hawaii, 1964, PhD in Am. Studies, 1974; Mem. Hawaii state legislature, 1974-86; elected to U.S. Congress 1st Hawaiian dist., 1986, 91—, mem. resources com., armed svcs com., nat. security com.; mem. Honolulu City Coun., 1988-90; Co-author Blood of Patriots. Democrat. Office: US Ho Reps 1502 Longworth House Office Building Washington DC 20515-0001*

ABERCROMBIE, STONEY ALTON, family physician, educator; b. Six Mile, S.C., Dec. 9, 1949; s. William Morris and Mildred Marette (Ellenburg) A.; m. Donna Gay Underwood, June 17, 1973; children: Jonathan Edward, Kristina Katherine. BS, Clemson U., 1972; MD, Med. U. S.C., 1976. Diplomate Am. Bd. Family Practice. Family practice intern Greenville (S.C.) Hosp. System, 1976, family practice resident, 1979-80; pvt. practice Seneca (S.C.) Med. Assocs., 1981-88; asst. residency dir. Self Meml. Hosp., Greenwood, 1989-90, residency dir. and dir. med. edn., 1990—99; prof. family medicine Med. U. S.C., Charleston, 1995—; assoc. dir. for Rural Med. Edn. Anderson Area Med. Ctr., Anderson, S.C., 1999—, residency dir., dir. med. edn., 2002—; exec. dir. S.C. Area Health Edn. Consortium, Charleston, 2000—02. Staff physician Oconee Meml. Hosp., Seneca, 1981-88, chief of staff, 1988, bd. trustees, 1987-88; mem. utilization rev. com. Oconee Geriatric Ctr., 1981-87; asst. med. dir. Greenwood Health Care Ctr., 1990-99, chmn. utilization rev. com., 1990-99; med. dir. Greenbrook Manor Nursing Home, 1989-93; lectr. in field. Contbr. articles to profl. jours. Founder Oconee County Prenatal Clinic for Indigent OB Patients, 1983; mem. Upstate S.C. Emergency Svcs. Coun., 1981-84, Upstate S.C. Perinatal Adv. Com., 1981-84, Teen Pregnancy Prevention Coun., Oconee, 1988; mem. Gov.'s Task Force on Primary Health Care in Oconee County, 1984, Med.-Industry Com. for Health Care in Oconee County, 1984-85; bd. visitors Lander U., Greenwood, 1991-93, Med. U. S.C., 1997-98; bd. advisors Vocat. Rehab. Ctr., Greenwood, 1991-94; bd. trustees Greenwood Literacy Coun., 1994-97, chmn., 1996, mem. century club Clemson U., 1981—, mem. IPTAY, 1981—, alumni loyalty fund vol., 1984; active Gideon's Internat., 1984-99. Recipient Dist. Svc. to Mankind award Rotary, 1995, Holford award excellence in humane medicine S.C. AHEC, 1996, S.C. Physician of Yr. award, 1999-2000, Top Ten Am. Physician of Yr. award, 2001. Fellow Am. Bd. Family Practice; mem. AMA, Am. Acad. Family Physicians (reviewer Huffington Libr. 1991—, pub. com. 1994-96, S.C. alt. del. 1998-2001, del. 2002—, commn. on continuing med. edn. 2000—), S.C. Acad. Family Physicians (bd. trustees 1987—, editor S.C. Family Physician, v.p. 1995, pres. 1996, 97, chair bd. dirs. 1998, Family Physician of Yr. 1999—), Soc. of Tchrs. Family Practice, S.C. Med. Assn. (liability case reviewer 1990—, assoc. chmn. CME com. 1995-97, chmn. 1997-2000), Anderson Med. Soc., Greenwood Med. Soc. (pres. 1992-93), Clemson Alumni Physicians Soc. (charter), Med. U.S.C. Alumni Assn. (Alumni Assn. Centennial Recognition List 1992, Disting. Alumni award 2001), Assn. of Family Practice Residency Dirs. (charter, S.C. chpt. chmn. 1994-96), Emerald City Rotary Club (bd. dirs. 1989-96, pres. 1992-93), Electric City Rotary Club. Republican. Ch. of God. Avocations: baseball card collecting, reading. Office: Anderson Area Med Ctr Family Practice Residency 600 N Fant St Anderson SC 29621-5704 E-mail: saberero@anmed.com.

ABERLE, DAVID FRIEND, anthropologist, educator; b. St. Paul, Nov. 23, 1918; s. David Winfield and Lisette (Friend) A.; m. Eleanor Kathleen Gough, Sept. 5, 1955 (dec. Sept. 1990); 1 son. AB summa cum laude, Harvard U., 1940; PhD in Anthropology, Columbia U., 1950; postgrad., U. N.Mex., summers 1938-40, No. Ariz. U., summers 1971, 73, Harvard U., 1946-47. Instr. dept. social rels. Harvard U., Cambridge, Mass., 1947-50, rsch. assoc. Sch. Pub. Health, 1948-50; vis. assoc. prof. Page Sch., Johns Hopkins U., Balt., 1950-52; assoc. prof., then prof. dept. sociology and dept. anthropology U. Mich., Ann Arbor, 1952-60; fellow Ctr. Advanced Study in Behavioral Scis., Stanford, Calif., 1955-56; Simon vis. prof. and hon. research assoc. dept. social anthropology Manchester U., Eng., 1960-61; prof., chmn. dept. anthropology Brandeis U., Waltham, Mass., 1961-63; prof. dept. anthropology U. Oreg., Eugene, 1963-67; prof. dept. anthropology and sociology U. B.C., Vancouver, Can., 1967-83, prof. emeritus, 1983—. Cons. Inst. Devel. Anthropology, Inc., Binghamton, N.Y., 1978-79; cons. to attys. Navajo Tribe, 1976-77; disting. lectr. Am. Anthrop. Assn., 1986. Author: The Peyote Religion Among the Navaho, 1966, (with Isidore Dyen) Lexical Reconstruction, the Case of the Proto-Athapaskan Kinship System, 1974; contbr. articles on anthropological theory and Navajo Indians to scholarly jours.; rev. editor: Am. Anthropologist, 1952-55. With U.S. Army, 1942-46. Recipient Social Sci. Research Council Demobilization award, 1946; Harvard U. Nat. scholar; NIMH grantee; USPHS grantee; Wenner-Gren Found. grantee, 1954-63; NSF grantee, 1965-72; Can. Council grantee, 1969-77; Social Scis. and Humanities Research Council Can., 1978-80, 84-86 Fellow Royal Soc. Can., Royal Anthropol. Inst. of Gt. Britain and Ireland; mem. Am. Anthropol. Assn. (mem. panel on Navajo-Hopi land dispute 1973-95), Am. Sociol. Assn., Soc. Applied Anthropology, Am. Ethnol. Assn., Can. Anthropology Soc., Soc. Lesbian and Gay Anthropologists, Phi Beta Kappa. Jewish. Office: U BC Dept Anthropology 6303 NW Marine Dr Vancouver BC Canada V6T 2B2

ABERLE, ELTON DAVID, dean; b. Sabetha, Kans., Aug. 30, 1940; s. Alphia Henry and Irene Judith A.; m. Carrie Rae Campbell, Sept. 11, 1965; children: Krista Kaye, Barbara Ann. BS, Kans. State U., 1962; MS, Mich. State U., 1965, DPhil, 1967. Asst. prof. Purdue U., West Lafayette, Ind., 1967-71, assoc. prof., 1971-76, prof., 1976-83; prof., dept. head U. Nebr., Lincoln, 1983-98; dean, dir., prof. U. Wis., Madison, 1998—. Author: Principles of Meat Science, 1975, 3d edit., 1994; contbr. articles to profl. jours. Fellow Am. Soc. Animal Sci. (pres. 1994-95, Meat Rsch. award 1982, Signal Svc. award 1998); mem. Am. Meat Sci. Assn. (dir. 1979-80, pres. 1985-86, Disting. Teaching award 1983, Disting. Rsch. award 1986), Inst. Food Tech., Coun. Agrl. Sci. & Tech. (dir. 1996-99), Kiwanis. Avocations: golf, fishing, hunting. Home: 5810 Windsona Cir Madison WI 53711-5853 Office: U Wis Office of Dean 1450 Linden Dr Madison WI 53706-1522

ABERLIN, BETTY KAY, actor; b. N.Y.C., Dec. 30, 1942; d. Harry Ageloff and Daisy Kinstein. BA in Creative Writing, Bennington Coll., 1963. Actor: (musical theater) Sandhog, 1953, I'm Getting My Act Together; (TV series) Mr. Rogers Neighborhood, 1969—2001, The Smothers Brothers; (films) Dogma, Jersey Girl; co-founder, on-air host Sta. WYEP-FM, Pitts.; author: Stop Me Before I Love Again, Girl Steps Out of Car - Gets Blown Up, The Blonding of America, Nightclub; contbr. to PoetsAgainstTheWar.com. Vol. chaplain's office Rikers Island, N.Y.C., 1986—90. Jewish Christian. Avocations: writing, art. E-mail: bettykayday@earthlink.net.

ABERMAN, HAROLD MARK, veterinarian; b. Chgo., Aug. 5, 1956; s. Howard Oscar and Goldie Esther Aberman. BS, Purdue U., 1979, MSE, 1987, BSE, 1986, DVM, 1983. NIH postdoctoral fellow Purdue U., West Lafayette, 1983-87; dir. sci. and biol. affairs Howmedica div. Pfizer, Rutherford, 1987-99; pres. Applied Biol. Concepts, Los Alamitos, Calif., 1996—; dir. devel. Orthop. Rsch. Inst., Long Beach, Calif., 1999-2001, med. device cons., 2001—. Adj. prof. N.C. State U., Raleigh, 1988—, Miss. State U., Starkville, Miss., 1990—, Purdue U., 1991—. Contbr. articles to profl. jours. Mem. ASME, AVMA, Am. Animal Hosp. Assn., Ortho. Rsch. Soc., Soc. Biomechanics, Acad. Surg. Rsch. Jewish. Home: 14 Dewberry Way Irvine CA 92612-2711 Office: Applied Biol Concepts 12581 Silver Fox Rd Los Alamitos CA 90720-5234 E-mail: haroldabc@aol.com.

ABERNATHY, CHARLES OWEN, toxicologist; b. Brunswick, Ga., Nov. 18, 1941; s. William Owen and Marcelle Louise (Francony) A.; m. Mary Mella Dees, Nov. 18, 1973. AB, Asbury Coll., Wilmore, Ky., 1964; MS, U. Ky., 1966; PhD, N.C. State U., 1970. Postdoctoral fellow U. Calif., Berkeley, 1970-73; pharmacologist VA Med. Ctr., Washington, 1973-84; pharmacologist office of toxic substances EPA, Washington, 1984-86; toxicologist Office Water, EPA, Washington, 1986—; rsch. toxicologist VA Med. Ctr., Washington, 1984-89. Co-chair of 6 internat. confs. on arsenic; chair conf. on arsenic WHO, Brisbane, Australia; chair conf. on risk assessment of essential trace elements, Marbella, Chile. Co-editor: 6 books; contbr. scientific papers. Vol. tutor Bapt. Boys Home, Raleigh, N.C., 1967-69; vol. blood drive ARC, Washington, 1978. Recipient Employee Recognition award EPA, 1988, Bronze medals, 1993, 96, 97, 98, 99, 2001, Gold and Silver medals, 2002; Nat. Environ. Edn. Achievement awardee, 1997. Mem. Soc. Toxicology (chmn. awards com. risk assessment sect. 1989-90), Soc. for Exptl. Biology and Medicine, N.Y. Acad. Scis., Soc. Environ. Geochemistry and Health. Achievements include rsch. on selective toxicity of pyrethroids, reversal of cholestatic effects of steroids by cholic acid derivatives; developed hypothesis on neonates and cholestasis, risk assessment of essential trace elements. Home: 4718 River Rd Bethesda MD 20816-3035 Office: EPA (4304T) Ariel Rios Bldg 1200 Pennsylvania Ave NW Washington DC 20460-0001 E-mail: abernathy.charles@epa.gov.

ABERNATHY, CORBIN BRETT, music educator, theater educator; b. Atlanta, Mar. 25, 1969; s. Ira Raulston and Oral Jean Abernathy, Jr.. MusB in Music Theater, U. Miami, 1993; MA in Drama, Okla. City U., 1998. Instr. drama David Fairchild Elem., Miami, Fla., 1990—92; instr. music St. Theresa Sch., Miami, Fla., 1994—95; voice instr. Okla. City U. Performing Arts Acad., 1996—97; interim dir. theatre The Casady Sch., Oklahoma City, 1998—98; dir. music St. Peter's Sch., Phila., 1998—2002; tchr. drama Bulmershe Sch., Reading, England, 2002—. Contracted soloist Liturgical, 1990—; singer, actor Drama,Musical Theatre, 1990—; contracted soloist Liturgical, 1990—; artistic dir. Okla. City Metro Men's Chorus, 1996—97; chorister Atlanta Symphony Orch. Chorus and Chamber Choir, 1998—99. Actor(whitney): (musical) Anything Goes, (mary sunshine) Chicago, (twimble/womper) How To Succeed In Business Without Really Trying, (mr. kraler) (play) The Diary of Anne Frank; singer (countertenor soloist): (oratorio) St. Matthew Passion; singer: (guest artist) (countertenor) NJ MENC State Convention; singer (countertenor soloist) (choral) Chichester Psalms/The Lark; dir.(music director): (musical) Philemon; musician (chorister): (concert) Voces Novae Et Antiquae. V.p. Phila. Gay Men's Chorus, 1999—2000. Grantee, Arcadia Found., 2000; scholar Treva Hancock Drama Scholar, Okla. City U., 1996—98, Maybelle Conger Drama Scholarship, 1996—98. Mem.: Am. Choral Dir.'s Assn. (assoc.), Music Educator's Nat. Conf. (assoc.), Voice and Speech Trainer's Assn. (assoc.), Alpha Psi Omega (assoc. Consistent Excellence in Supporting Roles 1997). Democrat. Avocations: travel, concerts, reading. Home: 129 Pemberton Street Philadelphia PA 19147 Personal E-mail: contra@onemain.com.

ABERNATHY, FREDERICK HENRY, mechanical engineering educator; b. Denver, Colo., June 19, 1930; s. Henry James and Irene Sarah (Lehman) A.; m. AnnaMaria Herbert, June 18, 1961; children: Sarah, Marian, Pauline. BSME, Newark Coll. Engring., 1951; postgrad., Oak Ridge Sch. Reactor Tech., 1952; SM, Harvard U., 1954, PhD, 1959. Gordon McKay prof. engring. Harvard U., Cambridge, Mass., 1963—, Abbott and James Lawrence prof. mech. engring., 1995—; dir. engring. divsn. NSF, Washington, 1972-73, dir. energy-realted rsch., 1973-74; prof. engring. Harvard U. Dir. Textile/Clothing Tech. Corp., Cambridge, 1985-87, Harvard Ctr. for Textile and Apparel Rsch., 1991—. Fellow Am. Phys. Soc., Am. Acad. Arts and Scis.; mem. ASME, Am. Soc. Engring. Edn., Sigma Xi. Office: Harvard Univ Divsn Engring/Applied Scis Pierce Hall Cambridge MA 02138 E-mail: fha@deas.harvard.edu.

ABERNATHY, JAMES LOGAN, public relations executive; b. Kansas City, Mo., Jan. 23, 1941; s. James Logan and Caryl (Nicolson) A. ; m. Kevin Kearns, Sept. 12, 1981; 1 child, Nell Logan. Student, Brown U., 1959-64. Assoc. dir. investor relations CBS Inc., N.Y.C., 1967-72; v.p. investor relations Warner Communications Inc., N.Y.C., 1972-74, ABC Inc., N.Y.C., 1974-79, v.p. corp. affairs, 1979-84; chmn. Abernathy/MacGregor Group Inc., N.Y.C., 1984—. Trustee, chmn., dir. Caron Found., Wernersville, Pa., 1983-6; trustee Hackley Sch., Tarrytown, N.Y., 1982-89; overseer Brown U. Sch. Medicine, 1996—; dir. Nat. Coun. on Alcoholism and Drug Addiction, 2000. Mem. Investor Relations Assn. (pres. 1979-80), Nat. Investor Relations Inst., Knickerbocker Club (N.Y.C.), Doubles Club (N.Y.C.), Devon Yacht Club (L.I.). Home: 130 E End Ave New York NY 10028-7553 Office: Abernathy MacGregor Group Inc 501 Madison Ave New York NY 10022-5602

ABERNATHY, RONALD FITTZ, pharmacist; b. Richmond, Va. s. Richard Fittz and Neta (Tarkington) A. BS in Pharmacy, Med. Coll. Va., 1970. Registered pharmacist, Va., Md. Pharmacist in charge Drug Fair, Falls Ch., Va., 1970-86, pharmacist, mgr. Arlington, Va., 1986-88, Rite Aid, Arlington, 1988-98, Safeway, Reston, Va., 1998—. Mem. Am. Pharmacist Assn., Va. Pharmacist Assn., Potomac Pharmacist Assn., Phillips Collection (assoc.), Phi Delta Chi (social chmn. 1969-70). Episcopalian. Avocations: doberman pinscher, computers.

ABERNATHY, THOMAS EDWARDS, IV, lawyer; b. Chattanooga, Feb. 18, 1941; s. Edwards Selman and Elizabeth Walker (Henry) Abernathy; 1 child, Elizabeth. BA, Vanderbilt U., 1963; JD, 1967; student, U. Va., 1963—65. Bar: Tenn. 1967, US Dist. Ct. (ea. dist.)/Tenn. 1967, US Supreme Ct. 1970, US Ct. Fed. Claims 1970, US Dist. Ct. (no. dist.)/Ga. 1972. Ptnr. Smith, Currie & Hancock, Atlanta, 1971—. Author: (Handbook) Constrn. Bus. Handbook, 1984; contbr. articles. Capt. JAGC, AUS, 1967—71. Mem.: Fed. Bar Assn., Atlanta Bar Assn., Tenn. Bar Assn., State Bar Ga., Am. Coll. Constrn. Lawyers, ABA, Me. Atlanta Area Social Svc. Adv. Coun., Salvation Army, Lawyers Club Atlanta. Presbyn. Office: Smith Currie & Hancock 233 Peachtree St NE Ste 2600 Atlanta GA 30303-1530

ABERNATHY, VICKI MARIE, retired nurse; b. L.A., Feb. 14, 1949; d. James David and Margaret Helen (Quider) Abernathy; m. Dirk Klaus Ernst Wiese, Aug. 15, 1968 (div. 1973); 1 child, Zoe Erde. Student, U. Calif., Riverside, 1966-67, L.A. City Coll., 1968-69; AA in Nursing, Riverside City Coll., 1971-74. RN, Calif.; cert. med.-surg. nurse; cert. ACLS. Staff nurse Riverside (Calif.) County Hosp., 1974, Oceanside (Calif.) Community Hosp., 1974-76; with Scripps Hosp., Encinitas, Calif., 1976—2001, ambulatory surgery unit and endoscopy coord., 1981-94, staff nurse short stay unit and endoscopy, 1994—2001, ret., 2001. Mem. Calif. Nurses Assn., San Diego Zool. Soc., San Elijo Lagoon Conservancy. Democrat. Avocations: camping, fishing, travel, reading.

ABERNETHY, HUGH C., JR., writer; b. West Chester, Pa., Nov. 10, 1947; s. Hugh Charles Abernethy and Edna Mae Shaffer. BA, Pa. State U., 1969. Reading tchr. Friends Cmty. Sch., West Chester, 1973—79; tradebook buyer U. Mass./Boston, Dorchester, 1984—87; editor Zephyr Press, Somerville, Mass., 1987—92; pub. Abbeywood Press, West Chester. Editor Puckerbrush Press, Orono, Maine. Contbr. more than 300 articles, poetry, short stories to lit. publs.; editor: The Complete Poems of Anna Akhmatova, 1992. Recipient John Davidson Poetry prize, Poet's Mag., Bitterroot Poetry prize, Bitterroot mag., Poetry prize, R.I. Arts Coun. Mem.: Acad. of Am. Poets (assoc.). Presbyterian. Home: 511 N High St West Chester PA 19380

ABERNETHY, IRENE MARGARET, civic worker, retired county official; b. Ord, Nebr., Mar. 28, 1924; d. Glen Dayton and Margaret Lillian (Jones) Auble; m. Don R. Abernethy, Aug. 8, 1954 (dec. Nov. 1980); children: Jill Adele Abernethy Johnson, Ted Verne (dec.). BA cum laude, Hastings Coll., 1946; postgrad., U. Nebr., 1950-53. Tchr. Ord High Sch., 1946-50, Scottsbluff (Nebr.) High Sch., 1950-55, Grand Island (Nebr.) Sr. High Sch., 1961-62; mem. Hall County Bd. Suprs., Grand Island, 1979-98, chmn., 1984, 95; ret., 1998. Vice-chair Hall County Rep. Ctrl. Com., Grand Island, 1971-73; chair campaign Congresswoman Virginia Smith for Hall County, 1974-80; sr. v.p. Nebr. Rep. Founders Day, Lincoln, 1981; chair Gov.'s Juv. Justice Adv. Group, Lincoln, 1981-91; mem. Nebr. Commn. on Law Enforcement and Criminal Justice, Lincoln, 1970-91, Nebr. Commn. on Local Govt. Innovation and Restructuring, 1997-2000; bd. dirs. Head Start, 1979-2002, Hall County Leadership Tomorrow, 1990-94, Indsl. Found., 1991, College Park, 1991-98, Cmty. Help Ctr., 1991-96, Family Violence Coalition, 1993-2002, Midland Area Agy. on Aging, 1993-95; adv. com. Region III Mental Health Bd., quality rev. team, 1996-99; active Nat. Coalition State Juvenile Justice Adv. Groups, 1981-91, Partners in Cmty. Planning, 1994-97, Grand Island Area Edn. 2000, Grand Island Bd. Edn., 1998-2000; task force on needs Heartland United Way. Named Woman of Yr., Grand Island Independent, 1980, Bus. and Profl. Woman, Grand Island, 1980, Beta Sigma Phi, 1982, Alpha Delta Kappa, 1982, 2000, Nebr. chpt. NASW, 1983, Merit Mother of Nebr., 2002; recipient Svc. to Mankind award Sertoma, 1983-84, recognition award PTA, 1988, Outstanding Cmty. Svc. award Rotary, 1985, Cmty. Leadership award Ak-Sar-Ben, 1995, Outstanding Alumni award Hastings Coll., 1996, Hall County Rep. Hall of Fame award, 1997, Disting. Citizenship award Grand Island Elks, 1997, cert. of appreciation Grand Island-Hall County Dept. Health, 1998, A.L. Carlisle Child Advocacy award Coalition for Juvenile Justice, 2001; honoree Nebr. Commn. on Status of Women, 1998, 2000; recipient Spirit of Youth award Girls and Boys Town, 2000. Mem. LWV (local pres. 1962-64, state bd. dirs. 1965-69), AAUW (local pres. 1966-68, state bd. dirs. 1970-71), YWCA (local pres. 1974-75, Woman of Distinction award 1988), Nebr. Assn. County Ofcls. (pres. 1985, Pres.'s award for Disting. Leadership 1997, County Ofcl. of Yr. award 1998), Assn. Child Abuse Prevention, Grand Island Area C. of C. (bd. dirs. 1992-94, Disting. Svc. award 1999), Philanthropic Ednl. Orgn. (local pres. 1970-71), Rotary, Woodland Golf Club Ladies Assn. (champion 1961, 63, 64, local pres. 1963), Riverside Golf Club (champion 1969), Grand Island Woman's Club (past bd. dirs.), Pi Lambda Theta. Republican. Methodist. Avocations: travel, music, photography, golf, spectator sports. Home: 707 S Blaine St Grand Island NE 68803-6146

ABERNETHY, ROBERT JOHN, real estate developer; b. Indpls., Feb. 28, 1940; s. George Lawrence and Helen Sarah (McLandress) A. BA, Johns Hopkins U., 1962; MBA, Harvard U., 1968; cert. in real estate fin. and constrn., UCLA, 1974. Asst. to chief scientist Phoenix missile program Hughes Aircraft Co., L.A., 1968-69, asst. program mgr. Iroquois night fighter and night tracker program, 1969-71, asst. to contr. space and comm. group, 1971-72, contr. tech. divsn., 1972-74; pres. Am. Std. Devel. Co., L.A., 1974—, Transit Cmty. Devel. Corp., 1997-2001. Bd. dirs., chmn. audit com. Pub. Storage, Inc., Glendale, Calif., Marathon Nat. Bank, L.A., 1984-2003, Tech Net, L.A. Bancorp, Met. Water Dist., So. Calif., Met. Transp. Authority, L.A. County; pres. Self Svc. Storage Assn., San Francisco, 1978-83. Active Albert Schweitzer Found.; asst. to dep. campaign mgr. Humphrey for Pres., Washington, 1968; commr. L.A. Planning Commn., 1984—88, L.A. Telecom. Commn., 1992—93, Calif. Transp. Commn., 1998—2001, Calif. State Bd. Edn., 2000—; vice chmn. L.A. Econ. Devel. Coun., 1988—93; chmn. Calif. Tech. Adv. Com. on Aeronautics, Ctr. for Study Dem. Inst., Santa Barbara, Calif., 1986—; bd. dirs. Met. Transp. Authority Los Angeles County, South Bay Civic Light Opera, L.A. Children's Mus., World Children's Transplant Fund, French Found. for Alzheimers Rsch., Pacific Coun. on Internat. Policy; adv. bd. mem. Peabody Conservatory, 1992—, Ctr. Talented Youth, 1992—, Nitze Sch. Advanced Internat. Studies, 1993—, Harvard Ptnrs., 1996—, Inst. Acad. Achievement of Youth, 1999—; bd. vis. Davidson Coll.; bd. dirs. L.A. Theatre Ctr., 1986—92, YMCA; mem. Coun. on Fgn. Rels., L.A. Com. on Fgn. Rels., Calif Arts Coun., 2001—; trustee Johns Hopkins U., 1991—. Lt. USNR, 1962—66. Mem. So. Calif. Planning Congress (bd. dirs.), Parker Found. (bd. dirs.), California Club, St. Francis Yacht Club, Jonathan Club, Calif. Yacht Club, Alpha Lambda. Address: PO Box 834 Redondo Beach CA 90277 E-mail: rabernethy@techcenter.net.

ABERNETHY, SHARRON GRAY, language educator; b. Tishomingo, Miss., Mar. 22, 1945; d. Dennis F. Gray (deceased) and Lyda Waddell Gray; m. Elliott Lee Abernethy, Jr.; children: Damon, Ryan (Deceased). BA, Secondary Edn., U. North Ala., Florence, 1966; MA in Latin and Am. Studies, U. Ala., Tuscaloosa, 1971, PhD, 1982, EdS, 1976; cert., U. Carlos III, Madrid, 2000. Cert. ESADE Barcelona, Spain, 1999. Spanish/Latin Am. history tchr. Deshler H.S., Tuscumbia, AL, Ala., 1966—68; Spanish/English tchr. Eastwood Jr. H.S., Tuscaloosa, 1968—68; rsch. asst. U. Ala., Tuscaloosa, 1969—70, tchg. asst., 1970—73, Spanish instr., 1977. Spanish prof. (part-time) Huntsville, 1988—90, 1994—96, Spanish prof., 1996—, departmental internat. internship coord., 2001—; Spanish/Am. history tchr. Eastwood Jr. H.S., Tuscaloosa, 1973—76; Spanish prof. Miss. State U., Meridian, 1982—84; Spanish instr. Meridian H.S., 1982—85; owner Sir Speedy Printing franchise, Pittsburg, 1986—87, Huntsville, 1988—93; reviewer John Wiley & Sons, Inc., New York, NY, 2002—. Faculty advisor Phi Sigma Iota, Huntsville, 1997—; participant numerous confs./workshops on curricular and instrnl. improvement, 1999—. Vol. St. Jude's Children's Hosp., Memphis, 1977—78, Riley Hosp., Meridian, 1981—83; bd. dirs. Harris Home for Children, Huntsville, 1990—92; supporter/vol. Chi-Ho Home for Children, Huntsville, 1988—2001; mem./officer Huntsville West Kiwanis, Huntsville, 1988—94; chair Huntsville West Kiwanis/Chi-Ho Benefit Golf Tournament, Huntsville, 1990—93; leader Cub Scouts, Meridian, 1981—84; mem. Rep. Women, Huntsville, 1988—89; tchr., deacon, com. mem. adminstrn., stewardship, fin., hospitality, pastoral search coms., co-editor 1993 ch. history/dire First Presbyn. Ch., Huntsville, 1988—2002. Mem.: Naita (UAH liaison to North Ala. Internat. Trade Assn. 1999—, bd. dirs. 2003, 1999—), Exec. Women Internat. (VIP award 2001). Republican. Presbyterian. Avocations: piano, travel, golf, culinary arts.

ABERSON, LESLIE DONALD, lawyer; b. St. Louis, May 30, 1936; s. Hillard and Adele (Wenneker) A.; m. Regene Jo Lowenstein, Oct. 16, 1960; children: Karen, Angie, Leslie. BS, U. Ky., 1957, JD, 1960. Bar: Ky. 1960, U.S. Dist. Ct. (we. dist.) Ky. 1964, U.S. Tax Ct. 1968, U.S. Supreme Ct. 1975. Dir. Bank of Louisville. Bd. dirs. Ky. Athletic Hall of Fame, 1965—2003, NCCJ; past bd. dirs. Jewish Hosp. Louisville, Louisville Med. Rsch. Found.; past pres. B'rith Sholom Temple; bd. dirs., past v.p. Jewish Cmty. Fedn. Louisville; bd. dirs. Louisville Free Pub. Libr. Found. Recipient Louis Cole Young Leadership award. Mem.: Louisville Bar Assn., Ky. Bar Assn., U. Ky. Law Sch. Alumni Assn. (bd. dirs.). Home: 5431 Harbortown Cir Prospect KY 40059-9257 Office: Rothschild Aberson & Miller Suite 102 5940 Timber Ridge Dr Prospect KY 40059

ABETTI, PIER ANTONIO, consulting electrical engineer, technology management and entrepreneurship educator; b. Florence, Italy, Feb. 7, 1921; came to U.S., 1946; s. Giorgio and Anna (Garino) A.; m. Elizabeth Burr Nelson, June 11, 1948; children: George E., Frank A. Student, Poly. Inst., Turin, Italy, 1940-44; D of Indsl. Engring., U. Pisa, Italy, 1945; MSEE, Ill. Inst. Tech., Chgo., 1948; PhD in Elec. Engring., Ill. Inst. Tech., 1953. Registered profl. engr., Mass. Advanced devel. engr. Gen. Electric Co., Pittsfield, Mass., 1948-56, mgr. project EHV, 1957-62, mgr. pvt. telephone sys. Lynchburg, Va., 1971-73, mgr. Europe strategic planning Brussels, 1974-79, cons. R & D Schenectady, N.Y., 1980-81; dep. gen. mgr. UNIVAC-Europe, Lausanne, Switzerland, 1963-64; prof. mgmt. of tech. and entrepreneurship Rensselaer Poly. Inst., Troy, N.Y., 1982—, dir. Ctr. for Entrepreneurship New Tech. Ventures, 1988-92. Adj. prof. MIT, Troy, N.Y., 1951-52, Berkshire C.C., Pittsfield, Mass., 1958-60; cons. Tech. Assessment Group, Schenectady, 1980—, UN Program Devel., Mex., Indonesia, South Korea, China, Poland, 1989, USIA, Ukraine, 1991-93, Internat. Atomic Energy Commn., Chile, 1994, OAS, Venezuela, 1994; vis. prof. U. Calgary, Can., 1986-87, U. Tech., Compiègne, France, 1988-92, Internat. U., Japan, 1991, 93, Elec. Rsch. Inst., Cuernavaca, Mex., 1992, Helsinki Sch. Econs. and Bus. Adminstrn., 1994-2003, U. Oulu, Finland, 1997, Korean Advanced Inst. Sci. and Tech., 1995-97, U. Stellenbosch, South Africa, 1994, Gordon Inst. Tufts U., 1987-2003, Duxx Sch. Bus. Leadership, Monterrey, Mex., 1997-2000, Queensland U. Technol., Brisbane, Australia, 1998, 2000-2003, Nat. Coll. of Ireland, Dublin, 1998-99, Danish U. Tech., 1999-2001, Technol. Inst. of Costa Rica, 1999-2000, U. Udine, Italy, 2001, Help Inst., Malaysia, 2002-2003, Nat. U. Singapore, 2003. Author: Linking Technology and Business Strategy, 1990, (with J. Maldifassi) The Defense Industries of Argentina, Brazil, Chile, 1994; author more than 150 tech. and mgmt. papers in 5 langs.; assoc. editor Internat. Jour. Entrepreneurship and Innovation Mgmt., 2001—. Pres. Berkshire Mycol. Soc., Pittsfield, 1954-59; pres. Berkshire Film Soc., 1955-58. Recipient Coffin award GE, 1952, Internat. prize Montefiore Inst., 1953, Recognition award Italian Hist. Soc. Am., 1953, Kaufmann Found. award Entrepreneurship Educator of Yr. Finalist, 1993. Fellow IEEE (chmn. Volta scholarship 1961-66, mem. awards bd. 1984-86, chmn. scholarship awards 1984-86); mem. Am. Mgmt. Assn. (R&D coun. 1985-92), Italian Soc. for Sci. Progress (hon.), Eta Kappa Nu (Recognition award 1953), Tau Beta Pi. *In my life I have always tried to learn from my predecessors in science and technology and innovate based on their teaching and my original thinking.*

ABHYANKAR, SHREERAM S. mathematics and industrial engineering educator; b. Ujjain, India, July 22, 1930; came to U.S., 1951, naturalized, 1989; s. Shankar Keshav and Uma (Tamhankar) A.; m. Yvonne Margit Kraft, June 5, 1958; children: Hari Shreeram, Kashi Shreeram. BSc, Bombay U., 1951; AM, Harvard U., 1952, PhD, 1955; DHD (hon.), U. Angers, 1998. Rsch. instr. Columbia U., N.Y.C., 1955-56, vis. asst. prof., 1956-57; asst. prof. Cornell U., Ithaca, N.Y., 1957-58; vis. asst. prof. Princeton (N.J.) U., 1958-59; assoc. prof. Johns Hopkins U., Balt., 1959-63; pres. math. Purdue U., West Lafayette, Ind., 1963-67, Marshall disting. prof. math., 1967—, prof. indsl. engring., 1987—, prof. computer scis., 1988—. Vis. lectr. Harvard U., 1960-61; vis. prof. Munster U., Erlangen U., summer 1963, Matsci., Madras, India, fall 1963, Tata Inst., Bombay, 1969-70, 75-76, spring 1974, Kyoto U., fall 1976, U. Ky., fall 1978,

U. Paris, spring 1980, ENS St. Cloud, France, spring 1982, U. Nice, spring 1983, U. Sydney, spring 1986, U. Strasbourg, spring 1991, Ohio State U., spring 1995; vis. assoc. prof. Yale U., spring 1963; spkr. numerous profl. meetings, univ., insts., symposia, confs., and congresses, 1960—. Author: Ramification Theoretic Methods in Algebraic Geometry, 1959, Local Analytic Geometry, 1964, Resolution of Singularities of Embedded Algebraic Surfaces, 1966, 2d enlarged edit. 1998, A Glimpse of Algebraic Geometry, 1971, Algebraic Space Curves, 1971, Lectures on Expansion Techniques in Algebraic Geometry, 1977, Weighted Expansions for Canonical Desingularization, 1982, Enumerative Combinatorics of Young Tableaux, 1988, Algebraic Geometry for Scientists and Engineers, 1990; also over 150 articles. Recipient Herbert Newby McCoy award Purdue U., 1973, Medal of Honor, U. Valliadolid, Spain, 1990; grantee NSF, 1960-87, 89-91, 89-2002, Office Naval Rsch., 1986-90, Army Rsch. Office, 1988-90, Nat. Security Agy., 1992-99; rsch. fellow Alfred P. Sloan Found., 1958-60. Fellow Indian Nat. Sci. Acad., Indian Acad. Scis.; mem. Am. Math. Soc., Math. Assn. Am. (Lester R. Ford prize 1977, Chauvenet award 1978), Phi Beta Kappa. Achievements include research in algebraic geometry, commutative and local algebra, theory of functions of several complex variables, quantum electrodynamics, circuit and invariant theory, combinatorics, computer aided design, and robotics. Home: 111 Waldron St West Lafayette IN 47906-2836 Office: Purdue U Div Math Sci West Lafayette IN 47907

ABID, ANN B. art librarian; b. St. Louis, Mar. 17, 1942; d. Clarence Frederick and Luella (Niehaus) Bartelsmeyer; m. Amor Abid (div. 1969); children: Rod, Kady; m. Cleon R. Yohe, Aug. 10, 1974 (div.); m. Roldo S. Bartimole, Feb. 1, 1991. Cert. in Librarianship, Washington U., St. Louis, 1976. Asst. to libr. St. Louis Art Mus., 1963-68, libr., 1968-85; head libr. Cleve. Mus. Art, 1985—. Vis. com. univ. librs. Case We. Res.U., 1987-90, co-chairperson, 1990. Co-author: Documents of Surrealism, 1918-1942, 1981, Planning for Automation of the Slide and Photograph Collections at the Cleveland Museum of Art: A Draft Marc Visual Materials Record, 1998; contbr. articles to profl. jours. Grantee Mo. Coun. Arts, 1978, Mo. Com. Humanities, 1980, Nat. Hist. Pubs. and Records Commn., 1981, Reinberger Found., 1987, Japan Found., 1996. Mem. ALA, Art Librs. Soc. N.Am. (chmn. mus.-type-of-libr. group nat. chpt. 1979-81, chmn. New Orleans 1980, nominating com. 1980, 84, Wittenborn awards com. 1981, 90, v.p., pres.-elect 1987-88, pres. 1988-89, past pres. 1989-90, chmn. N.Am. art libr. resources com. 1991-93, search com. new exec. dir. 1993-94. chmn. fin. com. 1996-98, presenter numerous papers, chmn. nominating com. 1999-2000, co-chair conf. program com. 1999-2000), Soc. Am. Archivists, Midwest Mus. Conf. (co-chmn. program com. ann. meeting 1982), Spl. Librs. Assn., Rsch. Libr. Group (shares exec. group 1996-98, shares participation com. 1997-99). Office: Cleve Mus of Art 11150 East Blvd Cleveland OH 44106-1711 E-mail: aabid@clevelandart.org.

ABIDI, S. MANZOOR, neurologist; b. Lucknow, India, Jan. 9, 1940; arrived in U.S., 1965; s. S. Maqbool and Afsar Begum (Zaki) Abidi; children: Nicholas, Zeena. MD, King George's Med. Coll., Lucknow, 1962. Rotating intern King George's Med. Coll., Lucknow, 1962-63, med. resident, 1963-65; internal medicine resident Huron Rd. Hosp., Cleve., 1965-66; psychiatry resident Phila. Gen. Hosp., 1966-68; neurology resident Temple U. Hosp., Phila., 1968-71; pvt. practice Regional Neurol. Group, NJ, 1973-78, Neurol. Regional Assocs., Maple Shade, NJ, 1978—, N.J. Med. Inst., Maple Shade, 1997—. Asst. neurologist Cooper Med. Ctr., Camden, NJ, 1972—73, assoc. neurologist, 1974, attending neurologist, 1974—75; asst. neurologist Pa. Hosp., Phila., 1972—74; neurologist Garden State Cmty. Hosp., 1973—77, chief neurology, 1977—88, attending neurologist, 1989—92, mem. exec. com. bd. trustees; chief attending neurologist Underwood Meml. Hosp., Woodbury, NJ, 1975—79, attending neurologist, 1979—82; assoc. neurologist Burlington County Meml. Hosp., Mt. Holly, NJ, 1975—84, chief divsn. neurology, 1984—94; cons. neurologist South Ocean County Hosp., Manahawkin, NJ, 1975—2002, Hampton Hosp., Rancocas, NJ, 1986—94; neurologist John F. Kennedy Meml. Hosp.-Univ. Med. Ctr., 1980—85, attending neurologist, 1985—, Zurbrugg Meml. Hosp., Riverside, NJ, 1984—85; chief neurology Marlton divsn. W. Jersey Hosp., 1993—95; chief neurology sect. W. Jersey Health Sys., Berlin, Camden, Marlton, Vorhees, NJ, 1995—2003, trustee, 1992—2000. Fellow: Royal Soc. Gt. Britian; mem.: AMA (alt. del. N.J. 1995—2000, del. N.J. 2000—), Phila. Neurol. Soc., Acad. Medicine N.J. (trustee 1999—2000, treas. 2000—01, 2d v.p. 2002—), Burlington County Med. Soc. (pres. 1990—91), N.J. Med. Soc. (trustee 1992—2001, 2d v.p. 2001—02, 1st v.p. 2002—03, pres.-elect 2003—), Am. Electroencephalography Soc., Am. Acad. Neurology. Home: 4 Silverwood Rd Moorestown NJ 08057-2118 Office: Neurol Regional Assocs 504 Route 38 E Maple Shade NJ 08052-2039 E-mail: abidi@yahoo.com.

ABI-GHANEM, GEORGES VICTOR, engineer, scientist; b. Dakar, Senegal, Feb. 16, 1954; Came to U.S. 1976. s. Victor and Souad (Syriani) Abi-G. Maitrise Es-Science with honors, Universite Claude-Bernard, Academie de Lyon, France, 1975; Diplome d'Ingénieur Civil, ESIB, Lebanon, 1976; MS in Water Resources Enging., Stanford U., 1977; MS in Structures and Mechanics, Princeton U., 1980, PhD in Continuum Physics, 1982. Rsch. engr. U. Delft, The Netherlands, 1975; rsch. assoc. U. Ariz., 1977-78; rsch. and teaching asst. Sch. of Enging. and Applied Sci. Princeton U., 1978-82; chief engr., gen. mgr. EWA, Inc., Mpls., 1983-87, prin. scientist, 1987-90, ARDI Corp., Mpls., 1983—. Cons. to fed. and state agys. and various corps. in U.S. and abroad, 1977—; tech. reviewer Water Resources Rsch., Soc. Petroleum Engrs. Jour. and SIAM, 1982—; observer Audits of U.S. DOE Contracts on High-Level Nuclear Waste Disposal Projects, 1987; tech. reviewer R&D grant applications Nat. Scis. and Enging. Rsch. Coun. of Canada, 1987—, Oversight of US DOE Environ. Restoration and Waste Mgmt. Activites, 1988-90; peer reviewer Hanford Environ. Dose Reconstruction Project, Hanford, Wash., 1990—. Co-author: (with V. V. Nguyen and H. O. Pfannkuch) Practical Solutions to Chemical Spillages and Groundwater Contamination; contbr. articles to Water Resources Research, Physical Review, Jour. of Physics, Jour. of Mathematical Physics, others; author numerous publs. in conf. proceedings and tech. reports. Recipient grad. studies scholarship, 1976-77. Mem. Am. Math. Soc., Am. Phys. Soc., Am. Geophys. Union. Achievements include development of models for simulation of flow and transport of chemicals and radionuclides in air, water and geological media, of stochastic based criteria for the evaluation of environmental/health monitoring network designs, of remedial action strategies for hazardous/nuclear wastes site clean-up; characterization of scale dependent rock properties for analysis and survivability of deep underground structures subject to shock wave impulses; structural stability criteria for the construction and performance of new and improved materials; modelling of surface physics processes and thin film growth; Neuromorphic Systems design & stability criteria; research in hazardous/nuclear waste technology and monitoring design for environmental systems, in atmospheric chemistry and physics of air pollution, in physics of state transition in solids, and in image formation, compression of complex information, and associative memory in neural webworks. Address: PO Box 50058 Minneapolis MN 55405-0058

ABIKOFF, WILLIAM, mathematician, educator; b. N.Y.C., Aug. 18, 1944; s. Allen and Hanna (Krotin) A.; m. Joan Thorne, Aug. 13, 1966 (div. Feb. 1975); m. Christine Krieger, Sept. 30, 1978 (div. Nov. 1991). BSEE, Polytech Inst., 1965, MSEE, 1966, PhD in Math., 1971. Tech. staff Bell Telephone Lab., Holmdel, N.J., 1965-70; asst. prof. Columbia U., N.Y.C., 1970-75, U. Ill., Urbana, 1975-76, assoc. prof., 1976-81; prof. U. Conn., Storrs, 1981—. Mem. Mittag-Leffler Inst., 1971-72, Inst. Hautes Etudes Sci., 1976-77, Inst. for Advanced Study, 1989; Lady Davis sr. fellow and vis. prof. Technion (Israel Inst. Tech.), 1996-1997. Author: Real Analytic Theory of Teichmuller Space, 1981; contbr. articles to profl. jours. Sloan Found. fellow, 1976-77. Mem. Am. Math. Soc., Math. Assn. Am. Achievements include design of control system for quadriplegics, studies of degeneracy of Kleinian groups and related computer graphics. Home: 280 Perry Hill Rd Ashford CT 06278-1024 Office: U Conn Math Dept 196 Auditorium Rd Storrs Mansfield CT 06269-9012

ABISH, CECILE, artist; b. N.Y.C. m. Walter Abish. B.F.A., Bklyn. Coll., 1953. Instr. art Queens Coll. Vis. artist U. Mass, Amherst, Cooper Union, Harvard U. Solo exhbns. include Newark Coll. Enging., 1968, Inst. Contemporary Art, Boston, 1974, U. Md., 1975, Alessandra Gallery, N.Y.C., 1977, Wright State U., Dayton, Ohio, 1978, Carpenter Ctr., Cambridge, Mass., 1979, Anderson Gallery, Va. Commonwealth U., Richmond, 1981, SUNY-Stony Brook, 1982, Ctr. for Creative Photography, Tucson, 1984, Books & Co., N.Y.C., 1996; group exhbns.: Detroit Inst. Art, 1969, Aldrich Mus. Art, 1971, 10 Bleecker St., N.Y.C., 1972, Lakeview Ctr. Arts, Peoria, Ill., 1972, Bykert Gallery, N.Y.C., 1971-74, Michael Walls Gallery, N.Y.C., 1975, Fine Arts Bldg. Gallery, N.Y.C., 1976, Mus. Modern Art, N.Y.C., 1976, Hudson River Mus., 1979, Atlanta Arts Festival, 1980, New Mus., N.Y.C., 1980, 81, Kuntsgebaude, Stuttgart, Fed. Republic Germany, 1981, Long Beach (Calif.) Mus., 1983, Edith C. Blum Art Inst., Bard Coll., Annandale-on-Hudson, N.Y., 1984, Mus. Modern Kunst, Vienna, Austria, 1985, U. R.I., Kingston, 1985, Art Defense Galleries, Paris, 1993, Architektur Zentrum, Vienna, 1993, Artists Space, N.Y.C., 1994, Islip Art Mus., N.Y., 1995, P.S. 1 Contemporary Art Ctr., N.Y., 1999; numerous commns.; represented in permanent collections; published photo works: First-hand, 1978, Chinese Crossing, 1986, 99: The New Meaning, 1990. Nat. Endowment Arts fellow, 1975, 77, 80; CAPS fellow, 1975. Mem. Coll. Art Assn. Office: Cooper Station PO Box 485 New York NY 10276-0485

ABISH, WALTER, writer; b. Vienna, Dec. 24, 1931; came to U.S., 1957; s. Adolph and Frieda Abish; m. Cecile Abish. LittD (hon.), SUNY, Oneonta, 1996. Writer-in-residence Wheaton Coll., Norton, Mass., spring 1977; vis. Butler prof. English, SUNY, Buffalo, fall 1977; lectr. English and comparative lit. Columbia U., N.Y.C., 1979-88; guest prof. dept. English, Yale U., New Haven, Conn., spring 1985; guest prof. dept. grad. writing Brown U., Providence, R.I., spring 1986; guest prof. The Cooper Union, N.Y.C., spring 1987, 93, 94. Author: (novels) Alphabetical Africa, 1974, How German Is It, 1980 (Pen/Faulkner award 1981), Eclipse Fever, 1993, (stories) Minds Meet, 1975, In the Future Perfect, 1977, (fiction) 99: The New Meaning, 1990. Recipient award, Nat. Endowment for Arts, 1979, 1985, Award of Merit medal for novel, Am. Acad. and Inst. Arts and Letters, 1991; Ingram Merrill fellow, 1977, C.A.P.S. grantee, 1981, Guggenheim fellowship, 1981, fellowship, John D. and Catherine T. MacArthur Found., 1987—92, D.A.A.D.-Deutscher Akademischer Austauschdienst, Berlin fellow, 1987, fellowship, Lila Wallace-Reader's Digest, 1992—95. Fellow Am. Acad. Arts and Scis.; mem. Pen Club (exec. bd. dirs. 1982-88). Office: PO Box 485 Cooper Station New York NY 10276

ABITZ, JAMES H. religious organization executive; BSBA, U. Wis., 1967. Dir. bond investments Aid Assn. Lutherans, Appleton, Wis., 1967-81, asst. v.p. bond investments, 1981-82, 2d v.p. bond investments, 1982, 2d v.p. securities, 1983-87, v.p. securities, 1987-97, sr. v.p. capital mgmt. corp. investment dept., 1997-99; chief investment officer Aid Assn. Lutherans (now Thrivent Fin. for Lutherans), Appleton, Wis., 1999—2001; Sr. V.P., chief investment officer Thrivent Fin. for Lutherans, 2002—. Vol. Fox Vly. Luth. H.S. Found.; bd. dirs. Luther Haven Retirement Cmty. Office: Thrivent Fin for Lutherans 4321 N Ballard Rd Appleton WI 54919-0001

ABIZAID, JOHN P. career officer; b. Redwood City, Calif., Apr. 1, 1951; m. Kathleen Denton; children: Sharon, Chritine, David. Commd. 2nd lt. U.S. Army, 1973, advanced through grades to gen., 2003; comdt. cadets U.S. Mil. Acad., West Point, N.Y., 1997-99; comdr. First Infantry Div., Wurzburg, Germany, 1999—2000; dir. of strategic plans and policy Joint Staff, Washington, 2000—01, dir., 2001—03; dep. comdr., Combined Forces Command U.S. Ctl. Command, MacDill AFB, Fla., 2003, comdr., 2003—. Office: 7115 S Boundary Blvd MacDill AFB Tampa FL 33621-5101*

ABLE, EDWARD H. association executive; BA in Chemistry, Emory U., 1967; MBA, George Washington U., 1973. Cert. assn. exec. Staff aide to U.S. Senator Richard B. Russell, 1967-68; staff aide to U.S. Senator Mike Mansfield, 1968; acct. exec. Exec. Cons., Inc., Washington, 1971-73; asst. dir. resident assoc. program Smithsonian Instn., Washington, 1973-77; exec. v.p. Am. Soc. Landscape Architects, Washington, 1977-86; pres., CEO Am. Assn. Mus., Washington, 1986—. Lectr. in field. Author: (with others) Principles of Association Management, 1988. Bd. dirs. Nat. Humanities Alliance, 1986—, officer, 1990—, Nat. Cultural Alliance, 1991—; mem. founding bd. dirs. Nat. Ctr. Non-profit Bds., 1987—, vice chair, 1993-99; coun. mem. U.S. Com. World Heritage, 1988—; bd. mem. Nat. Ctr. for Non-Profit Enterprise. Capt. U.S. Army, 1968-71. Decorated Bronze Star. Fellow Am. Soc. Assn. Execs. (bd. dirs. 1987-90, chmn. mgmt. conf. 1988, instr. 1985—, frequent speaker meetings and convs. 1981—, chmn. grad. studies commn. 1986-87, mem. nat. edn. com. 1984-86, vice-chmn. 1985, chmn. 1986, bd. dirs. membership dirs. sect. 1982-83, Key award 1990, vice-chmn. fellows 1987-88, chmn. 1988-89), bd. dirs., 1994—; Greater Washington Soc. Assn. Execs. (chief exec. officer conf. com. 1982-83), Univ. Club (Washington). Office: Am Assn Museums 1575 I St NW Ste 400 Washington DC 20005-1113*

ABLE, KENNETH PAUL, biology educator; b. Louisville, Feb. 5, 1944; s. William Morris and Viola (Bridwell) A.; m. Mary Allen, Jan. 27, 1967; 1 child, Joshua. BS, U. Louisville, 1966, MS, 1968; PhD, U. Ga., 1971. Asst. prof. SUNY, Albany, 1971-77, assoc. prof., 1977-84, prof., 1984—. NSF grantee, 1974—. Fellow Animal Behavior Soc., Am. Ornithologists' Union (treas. 1981-85, elective councilor 1999-2002, William Brewster medal 1996); mem. Internat. Soc. Behavioral Ecology, Am. Soc. Naturalists, Am. Birding Assn. (dir. 1986-95, 99—). Office: Univ at Albany-SUNY Dept Biology 1400 Washington Ave Albany NY 12222-0100

ABLE, LUKE WILLIAM, pediatric surgeon, consultant; b. Pt. Arthur, Tex. s. James Levert and Minnie Maude (Branson) A.; m. Mary Beth Able, June 7, 1937 (div. Dec. 1984); children: Luke William, Stephen Smith; m. Margaret Galloway, Dec. 29, 1984 (dec. Dec. 1993); m. Hester Finke, July 14, 1995. BA, U. Tex., 1933, MD, 1940. Diplomate Am. Bd. Surgery and Pediat. Surgery. Extern So. Pacific Hosp., 1939; intern, surg. resident Hermann Hosp., Houston, 1940-43; resident in gen. and cardiovasc. surgery Boston Children's Hosp., 1946-48; pvt. practice Tex., 1948; clin. prof. surgery Baylor Med. Coll., Houston, 1950—; surgeon-in-chief, head dept. surgery Tex. Children's Hosp., Houston, 1954-87, surgeon-in-chief, head dept. surgery emeritus, 1987—. Active staff/cons. St. Luke's Episcopal Hosp., Meml. Sys., Meth. Hosp., Hermann Hosp., Tex. Children's Hosp.; tchg. assoc. U. Tex., Houston. Author: Siamese Twins, 1968; contbr. numerous articles to surg. and med. jours., chpts. to med. and surg. books. Lt. USNR, 1943-46, PTO. Decorated Purple Heart, Silver Star; named Ky. Col., 1999. Mem. ACS (Outstanding Presentation award), AMA, Am. Med. Soc., Am. Acad. Pediats. (surg. sect. 1949 , Outstanding Presentation award), Am. Pediat. Surg. Assn. (charter), Am. Trauma Assn., Tex. Med. Soc., Tex. Pediat. Soc., Tex. Surg. Soc. (v.p. 1953—, pres. 1987, Comty. Svc. award), Tex. Assn. Pediat. Surgeons (past pres.), Houston Pediat. Soc., Houston Surg. Soc. (pres. 1969-70, Outstanding Surgeon of Yr. 1991, Comty. Svc. award). Harris County Med. Soc. (sec. 1958). Republican. Baptist. Avocations: ranching, forestry. Home: 22572 Murrell Rd Hockley TX 77447-3014 E-mail: hfable@yahoo.com. *Life is to be lived and enjoyed. Recognizing changes and planning future working fun. Even when critically wounded by komakazie bombs, I was happy to be alive.*

ABLE, WARREN WALTER, natural resource company executive, physician; b. Seymour, Ind., Mar. 3, 1932; s. Walter Cudwith and Edith (Harmon) A.; m. Joan Graham, May 6, 1956; children: Susan, Nancy, Cynthia, Wally. AB, Ind. U. 1953, MD, 1956, JD, 1968. Bar: Ind. 1968. Intern Indpls. Gen. Hosp., 1956-57; surgeon USPHS, 1957-59; pres. Able Ventures, Inc., Columbus, Ind., 1968—. Bd. dirs. Salin Bank & Trust. Editor: Lawyer's Medical Cyclopedia, 1967-68. Bd. dirs. Bartholomew Consol. Sch. Corp., Columbus, 1970-74; trustee Christian Theol. Sem., 1991—. Mem. AMA, Ind. Med. Soc., ABA, Ind. Bar Soc., Nat. Benevolent Assn. (bd. dirs. 1983-90). Democrat. Mem. Christian Ch. (Disciples Of Christ). Avocations: aviation, farming. Home and Office: 4253 E Windsor Ln Columbus IN 47201-9681

ABLER, RONALD FRANCIS, geography educator; b. Milw., May 30, 1939; s. Ambrose Francis and Lucille Bernice A.; m. Barbara Ruth Bailey, Apr. 23, 1983; children: Frederick F., Kenneth J. BA, U. Minn., Mpls., 1963, MA, 1966, PhD, 1968. Prof. Pa. State U., University Park, 1967-95; exec. dir. Assn. Am. Geographers, Washington, 1990—2002. Dir. geography program NSF, Washington, 1984-88; vis. prof. Stockholm Sch. Econs., 1982-83, U. Minn., Mpls., 1972-74, U. B.C., Vancouver, 1971. Editor: A Comparative Atlas of America's Great Cities, 1976; co-editor: Atlas of Pennsylvania, 1989, Geography's Inner Worlds, 1992. Councilman State College (Pa.) Borough, 1978-82. Recipient Publ. award Geog. Soc. Chgo., 1976, Centenary medal Royal Scottish Geog. Soc., 1990, Spl. Recognition award NSF, Washington, 1988, Victoria medal Royal Geog. Soc./Inst. British Geographers, 1996. Fellow AAAS, Assn. Am. Geographers (pres. 1985-86, exec. dir. 1990—, honors 1995), Cosmos Club, Internat. Geographical Union (sec. gen. and treas. 2000—). Avocation: beekeeping. Home: 2246 N Pollard St Arlington VA 22207-3805 Office: Assn Am Geographers 1710 16th St NW Washington DC 20009-3104 E-mail: rabler@aag.org.

ABLIN, RICHARD JOEL, immunologist, educator; b. Chgo., May 15, 1940, s. Robert Benjamin and Minnie Edith (Gordon) A.; m. Linda Lee Lutwack; 1 son, Michael David. AB, Lake Forest Coll., 1962; PhD in Microbiology, SUNY, Buffalo, 1967. Diplomate Am. Bd. Clin. Immunology and Allergy; cert. specialist in pub. health and med. lab. microbiology Nat. Registry Microbiologists of Am. Acad. Microbiology. Grad. asst. dept. biology SUNY-Buffalo, 1963-65, research asst., summer 1963, research fellow, 1965-66; USPHS postdoctoral fellow dept. microbiology Sch. Medicine, lectr., lab instr., 1966-68; instr., research asst. Rosary Hill Coll., 1965-66; research cons. program med. edn. AID, Paraguay, 1968; dir. div. immunology Millard Fillmore Hosp. Rsch. Inst., Buffalo, 1968-70; head sect. immunology, renal unit Meml. Hosp. of Springfield, 1970-73; dir. sect. immunobiology div. urology dept. surgery Cook County Hosp. and Hektoen Inst. for Med. Research, Chgo., 1973-75, sr. sci. officer div. immunology, 1976-83; sr. mem. sci. staff, clin. immunologist Cook County Hosp., 1973-75; asst. prof. medicine So. Ill. U., 1971-73; assoc. prof. microbiology Univ. Health Sci. (Chgo. Med. Sch.), 1973-74; research assoc. prof. urology, dir. immunology unit dept. urology SUNY, Stony Brook, 1983-89; pres., dir. Robert Benjamin Ablin Found. for Cancer Rsch., Evergreen Park, Ill., 1979—; dir. sci. investigation Innapharma, Inc., Park Ridge, N.J., 1991—. Mem. Univ. Senate, 1986-89, 89-92, Univ. Governing Coms., 1984-92; acad. del. United Univ. Professions, 1986-88, 88-90; organizer, presenter, instr., participant numerous nat. and internat. profl. meetings, symposia, seminars. Editor: Allergologia et Immunopathologia, 1980—84; contbg. editor: Current Perspectives in Allergology and Immunopathology, 1974—84, Cancer Watch, 2001—, Seminars in Immunopathology and Oncology, Ill. Med. Jour., 1975—88; assoc. editor: Jour. Investigational Allergology and Clin. Immunology (formerly Allergologia et Immunopathologia), 1985—95, adv.editor: Jour. Cancer, 1976—89, assoc. editor: Low Temperature Medicine, 1975—, Journal of Experimental Therapeutics and Oncology, 2003—, mem. editl. bd.: Medikon, 1974—80; mem. editl. bd. Advances in Therapy, 1999—, Am. Jour. Reproductive Immunology and Microbiology, 1980—91, Annals Clin. and Lab.Sci., 2000—, Bratislava Med. Jour., 1999—, Cancer Therapy, 2003—, Cellular and Molecular Biology, 1985—87, Clin. and Applied Immunology Revs., 2001—, Clin. and Diagnostic Lab. Immunology, 2002—, Current Oncology, 1998—, Early Pregnancy: Biology and Medicine, 1995—, Exptl. Biology and Medicine, 2000—, Immunology and Allergy Practice, 1979—95, Prostate Jour., 1999—2001, UroOncology, 2000—, mem. sci. bd. Chemistry Today, 1991—97, TumorDiagnostik und Therapie, 1980—98; mem. editl. acad.: Internat. Jour. Oncology, 1996—, mem. editl. adv. bd.: Med. Sci. Rsch., 1984—2000, mem. editl. bd.: Expert Rev. Anticancer Therapy, 2002—; contbr. articles to profl. jours. Chief Sangamo Nation Y-Indian Guides, Springfield, 1972-73; mgr. Skokie Indians' Boys' Baseball, Ill., 1973-74, 77, 80, 81, bd. dirs., 1979-83, exec. v.p., 1981-82; mgr. Little League Three Villages, Setauket, N.Y., 1986; cubmaster N.W. Suburban coun. Boy Scouts Am., 1974-78, asst. scoutmaster, 1975-77; mem. exploring divsn. Suffolk County coun. Boy Scouts Am., 1985-88; pres., dir. Spirit of Chgo. Hockey Club Found., Evergreen Park, Ill., 1982—. Recipient Nat. Pres. Leader's Dist. Boy Scouts Am., 1975; named Cubmaster of Yr. Boy Scouts Am., 1977 Fellow: Assn. Clin. Scientists, Am. Coll. Cryosurgery (adv. bd. 1977—78, v.p. 1977—79, parliamentarian 1977—79, adv. bd. 1980—81, 1984—99), Am. Coll. Allergy and Immunology, Indian Cryogenics Coun. (hon.); mem.: AAAS, Metastasis Rsch. Soc., Am. Assn. Cancer Rsch., Am. Assn. Immunologists, Am. Soc. Microbiology, Assn. Med. Lab Immunologists, Brit. Assn. Surg. Oncology, Buffalo Collegium Immunology, Internat. Soc. Andrology, Internat. Soc. Chronobiology, Internat. Soc. Cryosurgery (pres. 1977—80, bd. dirs. 1980—, hon. life pres.), Internat. Soc. Immunology Reprodn., Japan Soc. Low Temperature Medicine, N.Y. Acad. Scis., Soc. Cryobiology, Soc. Exptl. Biology and Medicine, Soc. Leukocyte Biology, Soc. Protozoologists, Soc. Study Reprodn., Transplantation Soc., Cryoimmunotherapeutic Study Group (chmn.), Witebsky Ctr. Microbial Pathogenesis and Immunology, Sigma Xi, Phi Beta Kappa (Theta of Ill. at Lake Forest Coll.). Achievements include identification of prostate specific antigen (PSA), used as tumor marker (diagnosis) in prostate cancer, and of human thymic specific antigen providing means for differentiation of thymic lymphocytes from other lymphoid cells and the development of antithymocyte globulin (selectively immunosuppressive for thymocytes) used in renal allograft (transplant) recipients; and development of concept of cryoimmunotherapy for treatment of cancer. Office: Innapharma Inc Ste 205 1 Maynard Dr Park Ridge NJ 07656 E-mail: rablin@innapharma.com. *One of the saddest things in life is to have the opportunity to do something and not to take advantage of it.*

ABLON, STEVEN LURIA, psychoanalyst; b. Phila., May 22, 1941; s. Ralph Emil and Sylvia (Luria) A.; m. Gridth Urwalek, Jun e29, 1963; children: Brooke, Stuart, Kimberly. AB, Amherst Coll., 1963; MD, Case Western Reserve U., 1967. Tng. analyst adult & chld supr. Boston Psychoanalytical Inst., 1985—; assoc. clin. prof. psychiatry Harvard U. Med. Sch.-Mass. Gen. Hosp., Boston, 1993—. Home: 62 Chestnut Hill Rd Chestnut Hill MA 02467-1310

ABLOW, JOSEPH, artist, educator; b. Salem, Mass., Aug. 16, 1928; s. Benjamin and Eva (Smith) A.; m. Roselyn Karol, June 23, 1956; 1 child, Rachel. BA, Bennington Coll., 1954; MA, Harvard U., 1955. Instr. Middlebury (Vt.) Coll., 1955-58; asst. prof. Bard Coll., Annandale, NY, 1959-61, Wellesley (Mass.) Coll., 1962-63; assoc. prof. Boston U., 1972-95, chmn. div. of art, 1964-67, prof. of art, 1972-95, prof. emeritus, 1996—2003. Vis. assoc. prof. MIT, Cambridge, 1969-70, vis. prof. Amherst (Mass.) Coll., 1975-76, vis. artist, 2003; vis. scholar Cambridge (Mass.) Humanities Seminar, MIT, 1973-82; mem. adv. com. Bunting Inst., Radcliffe Coll., Cambridge, 1984-87; lectr. Amherst Coll., 1975, 78, 82, Univ. N.H., 1980, 82, Inst. of Contemporary Art, Boston, 1980, Nieman Found., Harvard Univ., 1982, 83, MIT, 1984, St. John's Univ., Collegeville, Minn., 1986, Fitchburg Art Mus., 1987, Salve Regina Coll., Newport, R.I., 1990, and others. One-man shows include Boris Mirski Gallery, Boston, 1961, 65, 69, Pucker Gallery, Boston, 1979, 81, 83, 87, 91, 94, 2001, The Trustman Art Gallery, Simmons Coll., Boston, 1983, Fitchburg Art Mus., Miami U., Oxford, Ohio, 1987, Amherst Coll., 2003; represented in permanent collections Bard Coll., Middlebury Coll., DeCordova and Dana Mus., Univ. Mass. Harbor Campus, Mead Art Gallery, Amherst Coll., Rose Art Mus., Brandeis U., others; contbg. editor Bostonia Mag., Boston, 1986-89; contbr. articles to profl. jours. Mem. bd. dirs. Jewish Cultural Endowment, Boston Univ., 1988-95. Recipient Paige traveling fellowship Mus. Fine Arts, Boston, 1951, Fulbright grant in painting, Paris, 1958-59, Silver medal award for best article of the yr. Coun. for Advancement and Support of Edn., 1987, Boston U. Sch. for the Arts disting. faculty award, 1996. Avocation: music. Home: 16 Monmouth Ct Brookline MA 02446-5634 Office: Boston U Sch Visual Art 855 Commonwealth Ave Boston MA 02215-1303

ABLOW, KEITH RUSSELL, psychiatrist, journalist, author; b. Boston, Nov. 23, 1961; s. Allan Murray and Jeanette Norma (Mezansky) A. ScB, Brown U., 1983; MD, Johns Hopkins U., 1987. Reporter Newsweek, N.Y.C., 1984; columnist Balt. Evening Sun, Boston Herald, 1985-89, Washington Post, 1990—; intern in psychiatry Tufts U.-New Eng. Med. Ctr. Hosps., Boston, 1987-88, resident, 1988-91; chief resident 1991—, 1991-92; columnist Washington Post, 1990—; cons. psychiatrist WCVB TV, Boston, 1992—; med. dir. Tri-City Mental Health Ctr., 1992-94; assoc. med. dir. Heritage Health Systems, 1993-94; corr. Med. News Network, 1993—; med. dir. FHC New Eng., 1994-96; outpatient psychiatrist Boston Regional Med. Ctr., 1996—. Med. editor Lifetime Med. TV, L.A. and Astoria, N.Y., 1986-89; founder, CEO, memorymountain.com. Author: Medical School: Getting In, Staying In, Staying Human, 1987, How to Cope With Depression, 1989, To Wrestle With Demons, 1992, Anatomy of a Psychiatric Illness, 1993, The Strange Case of Dr. Kappler, 1994, Denial, 1997; columnist Mental Health Infosource Website, 1996—. Trustee White Pines Coll., Chester, N.H., 1989-91. Recipient Optimate award Am. Soc. Profl. Italians, 1990. Mem. AAAS, AMA (sr. editor, creative cons. Pulse 1986-87, Jerry L. Pettis award 1987), Am. Psychiat. Assn., Am. Med. Writers Assn. (Will Solimene award 1991, 92, Best Trade Book, 1993). Democrat. Avocation: writing fiction. Home: 12 49th St Newbury MA 01951-1412

ABLOW, ROZ KAROL (ROZ ABLOW), painter, curator; b. Allentown, Pa. BA, Bennington Coll., 1954; student, Boston U. Instr. Bunting Inst., 1988, Newton Arts Ctr., Mass., 1989-92, New Arts Ctr., Newton, Mass., 1993-95. Curator New Arts Ctr., Newton, Mass., 1994. Solo exhbns. at Amherst (Mass.) Coll., 1976, Impressions Gallery, Mass., 1979, Clark GAllery, Lincoln, Mass., 1984, Pine Manor Coll., Brookline, Mass., 1991, Miami U., Oxford, Ohio, 1995, Art Guild of Old Forge, N.Y., 2002; group shows include Smithsonian Traveling Exhbn., 1978-80, Fitchburg Art Mus., 1988, The Bunting Inst., Radcliffe Coll., 1988, David Brown Gallery, Provincetown, Mass., 1988, Pratt Graphic Ctr. Internat. Monotype Show, 1989, Gallery 30, Burlingame, Calif., 1993, New Art Ctr., Newton, Mass., 1994, others; represented in permanent collections Mobil Corp., Chemical Bank, N.Y., New Eng. Mutual Life Ins. Co., Boston, Conn. Gen. Life, Hartford, Sears, Roebuck & Co., Chgo., Broadway Crown Plaza Hotel, N.Y., The Pucker Gallery, Boston. Bunting Inst. fellow Radcliffe Coll., 1988; grantee Mass. Arts Lottery Coun., 1990-91. Address: Pucker Gallery Boston MA 02116

ABNEE, A. VICTOR, trade association executive; b. Lexington, Ky., June 12, 1923; s. A. Victor and Irene Sarah (Brogle) A.; m. Doris Heuck, Dec. 28, 1946 (deceased); children: Janice Lee Abnee Williams, A. Victor III. BA, U. Cin., 1948. With U.S. Gypsum Co., Chgo., 1948-63, dir. advt. and promotion, 1961-64; with Gypsum Assn., Evanston, Ill., 1964—, exec. v.p., 1964-83, pres., 1983-88; cons., 1988—. Served to capt. C.E., AUS, 1943-46, PTO. Named Alumna of Yr., U. Cin., 1967, Constrn. Industry Man of Yr. Wall and Ceiling Industries Assn., 1980. Mem. Nat. Assn. Mfrs. (councilman 1983—), Am. Soc. Assn. Execs., Ariz. Econ. Soc. Assn. Execs., Exec. Svc. Corps, Internat. Exec. Svc. Corps., Economic, Ariz., Chgo. Soc. Assn. Execs. (hon. life), Les Cheneaux Islands Assn. (pres. 1986-87), Bohemian Club, Sigma Chi (Significant Sig award 1986). Clubs: Les Cheneaux Yacht (bd. dirs. 1982-85), Foundation (Chgo.) (pres. 1985), University (Chgo.) (pres. 1981-83), Adventurers (Chgo.), University (Evanston) (pres. 1984-85), Skokie Country (Glencoe, Ill.), Skyline Country (Tucson), Gyro Internat. Lodges: Shriners, Masons. Office: Gypsum Assn 1603 Orrington Ave Evanston IL 60201-3841

ABNEY, FREDERICK SHERWOOD, lawyer; b. Brownwood, Tex., Dec. 2, 1919; s. DeWitt Fleetwood and Margaret (Lyles) A.; m. Jeanne Elizabeth Larson, Feb. 28, 1942; children: Stephen Frederick, James Lorntz. BA, U. Tex., Austin, 1942, LL.B., 1947. Bar: Tex. bar 1947, U.S. Supreme Ct. bar 1963. Pvt. practice, Brownwood, 1948-49, Dallas, 1949-94. Served with USAAF, 1942-45. Mem. Am., Dallas bar assns., State Bar Tex., Am. Judicature Soc., Southwestern Legal Found., Dallas Bar Found., Tex. Bar Found. (life fellow), Delta Tau Delta, Phi Delta Phi. Mem. Unity Ch. Home and Office: 6730 Orchid Ln Dallas TX 75230-4137

ABNEY, JOE L. lawyer; b. Wetumka, Okla., June 5, 1941; s. Virgil Lawrence and Wanda (Bachus) A.; m. Paula Katherine Fowler, Sept. 21, 1963; 1 child, Lisa Jo. B.A., E. Central U., 1963; J.D., S. Tex. Coll. Law, 1974. Bar: Tex. 1974. Prin., Lake Mt. Sch. Dist., Covelo, Calif., 1963; tchr. Davis Sch. Dist., Okla., 1964; claims supr. Liberty Mut. Ins., New Orleans, 1965-71, Home Ins. Co., Houston, 1971-74; mem. firm Smith, Abney & Woolf, Houston, 1974— . Advisor, Grangerland 4H Club, Conroe, 1981-83; pres. River Plantation Horse Owners Assn., 1980-81, Hughes County Young Dems., 1962-64; sec. E. Central U. Young Dems., Ada, Okla., 1963. Mem. So. Assn. Workmen's Compensation Adminstrs., Tex. Trial Lawyers Assn., Harris County Criminal Lawyers Assn. Baptist. Club: Montgomery County Genealogy, Soc. War of 1812. Lodge: Elks. Home: 150 Stonewall Jackson Dr Conroe TX 77302-1158 Office: 150 Stonewall Jackson Dr Conroe TX 77302-1158

ABO, RONALD KENT, freelance/self-employed architect; b. Rupert, Idaho, July 10, 1946; s. Isamu and Ameria (Hachiya) A.; m. Lisa A. Wiesley; children: Tamiko N., Reiko D., Ryan A., Emily A. BArch, U. Colo., 1969. Lic. architect, Colo. Designer SLP & Ptnrs., Denver, 1968-71; dir. Community Design Ctr., Denver, 1971-72; assoc. Barker, Rinker, Seacat, Denver, 1972-76; pvt. practice Denver, 1976-80; pres. Abo Gude Architects, Denver, 1980-84, Ron Abo Architects, Denver, 1984-91, Abo Architects PC, Denver, 1991-94, Abo Copeland Architecture, 1995—2002, ACLP Architecture, Inc., 2002—. Design instr., thesis advisor U. Colo., Denver. Prin. works include Morrison Horticultre Ctr., 1983 (W.O.O.D. Inc. citation 1983), Highland Square, 1982 (AIA citation 1983), Roxborough Elem. Sch., 1990, Tropical Discovery Ctr. Denver Zoo, 1992, New Denver Internat. Airport Concourse Bldgs., 1993, Nederland Middle/H.S., 1996, Julesburg Welcome Ctr., 1997, Rocky Mountain Mfg. Acad., 1998. Active Denver Comty. Leadership Forum, 1986, Colfax-on-the-Hill, 1988—, U. Colo. Alumni Bd., Workforce Devel. Bd., 1990—, Savid House. Recipient Design Excellence award W.O.O.D. Inc., Denver, 1982, Martin Luther King Bus. Social Responsibility award, 1998. Mem. AIA (bd. dirs., pres.-elect Denver chpt. 1990, pres. 1991, pres.-elect Colo. chpt. 1997, pres. 1998), Asian C. of C. (pres. 1998), Colo. Aikido Assn. (head instr. Denver Buddhist Temple Aikido), Lions Club (bd. dirs.). Democrat. Avocation: aikido (4th degree black belt). Office: Abo Copeland Architecture 1600 Downing St Ste 700 Denver CO 80218-1540 E-mail: rka@aclparchitecture.com.

ABOLINS, MARIS ARVIDS, physics researcher and educator; b. Liepaja, Latvia, Feb. 5, 1938; came to U.S., 1949, naturalized, 1956; s. Arvids Gustavs and Olga Elizabete (Grintals) A.; m. Frances Delano, Dec. 19, 1959 BS magna cum laude, U. Wash., 1960; MS, U. Calif.-San Diego, 1962, PhD, 1965. Research asst. U. Calif.-San Diego, 1960-65; physicist Lawrence Berkeley Lab., 1965-68; assoc. prof. physics Mich. State U., East Lansing, 1968-73, prof. physics, 1973—. Cons. U.S. Dept. Energy; sci. assoc. CERN, Geneva, 1976-77; vis. research scientist, Saclay, France, 1977, Fermi Nat. Accelerator Lab., 1990-92, Saclay, France, 1997; mem. tech. adv. com. Argonne Nat. Lab., 1971-72; mem. prep. com. Fermilab, 1978-79; chmn. Fermilab Users' Exec. Com., 1982-83; mem. SSC Users Exec. Com., 1988-91; chmn. bd. dirs. ATLAS Trigger/DAQ Instnl., 1997-99. NSF research grantee, 1971—; Disting. Faculty award 1998. Fellow Am. Phys. Soc. (exec. com. div. particles and fields 1984-86); mem. AAAS, Patria, Phi Beta Kappa, Sigma Xi. Home: 1430 Fairoaks Ct East Lansing MI 48823-1812 Office: Mich State U Dept Physics And Astro East Lansing MI 48824 E-mail: abolins@pa.msu.edu.

ABORN, FOSTER LITCHFIELD, insurance company executive; b. Providence, July 8, 1934; s. John Russell and Helene Cecile (Hesse) A.; m. Sara Holbrook; children: Justin, Hilary. BA, Dartmouth Coll., 1956, MBA, 1957; exec. prog., 1978. Asst. v.p. Mellon Bank N.A., Pitts., 1957-68; asst. investment officer John Hancock Ins. Co., 1968—72, second v.p., 1972—78, v.p., 1978—84, sr. v.p., Treas. & Fin. Services, 1984—87, sr. v.p., Corp. Mktg. Rsch., 1984, sector head, Investment & Pension Group, 1987—92; vice chmn. & chief investment officer John Hancock Fin. Svcs., Inc., 1992—2000; bd. dir. John Hancock Life Ins., 2000—. Dir & mem of com. of fin., John Hancock Life Insurance Co.; mem. adv. com. One Liberty Ventures; mem. investment com., Kairos Fund, L.P.; adv. dir., Debt Exchange, LLC; dir., Seniorlink Incorp. Trustee, dir., & chmn. fin. com. Beth Israel Deaconess Med. Ctr.; chmn. exec. adv. bd. & capital campaign steering com. Bay Cove Human Services; overseer Museum of Fine Arts; dir. SquashBusters; overseer Huntington Theatre Co. Mem. Univ. Club Boston. Office: John Hancock Finl Svcs PO Box 111 C-02-01 Boston MA 02117-0111

ABORN, MURRAY, social scientist, researcher; b. N.Y.C., July 15, 1919; s. Maurice and Rose (Kaufman) A.; m. Barbara Ann Soltow, Dec. 20, 1961; children: Shoshanah, David Asher. BSS, CCNY, 1942; MA, Columbia U., 1947, PhD, 1950. Instr. Mich. State Univ., East Lansing, 1950-53; rsch. psychologist USAF, Montgomery, Ala., 1953-57; sci. adminstr. NIH, Washington, 1957-63; sr. scientist NSF, Washington, 1963-90; pvt. cons. Kensington, Md., 1990—. Editor: (book) The Annals, 1987; contbr. articles Jour. Experimental Psychology, Annual Rev. of Psychology, Am. Jour. Psychology. Sgt. USAF, 1942-45. Fellow AAAS, APA, Am. Stats. Assn., N.Y. Acad. Scis. Home: 4918 Flanders Ave Kensington MD 20895-1231

ABORN, RICHARD MARK, organization executive, lawyer; b. N.Y.C., Sept. 2, 1952; s. Norman and Janice M. (Murphy) A. BS magna cum laude, U. Dubuque, 1974; JD, John Marshall Law Sch., Chgo., 1978. Bar: N.Y. 1978. Dist. atty. New York County Dist. Atty.'s Office, N.Y.C., 1978-84; ptnr. Aborn & Anesi, N.Y.C., 1984-92; pres. Handgun Control, Inc., Washington, 1992-96, Ctr. To Prevent Handgun Violence, Washington, 1992-96. Cons. Ford Found., N.Y.C., 1994; chmn. Ind. Jud. Screeing Panel, N.Y.C.; bd. dirs. Nat. Exec. Svc. Corp., WLIW, PBS. Mem. N.Y. State Com. on Injury Prevention, Albany. Fellow Italian Acad., Columbia U., 1994. Mem. N.Y. State Bar Assn. Democrat. Office: 801 2nd Ave New York NY 10017-4706

ABOTT, MICHAEL LARRY, physician; b. Bklyn., Mar. 22, 1952; s. Jerome and Lynn (Gross) A.; m. Beth Ellen Friedberg, Aug. 10, 1975; children: Stephen, Richard. BS, Bklyn. Coll., 1974; MD, Autonomous U. de Guadalajara, Mex., 1978. Diplomate Am. Bd. Internal Medicine, Am. Bd. Pulmonary Diseases, Am. Bd. Critical Care, Am. Bd. Geriatrics. Pvt. practice, Bklyn., 1984—; assoc. attending physician N.Y. Meth. Hosp., Bklyn., 1984—, Victory Meml. Hosp., Bklyn., 1984—, Maimonides Med. Ctr., Bklyn., 1995—; CEO, United Med. Assocs., 1998—. Med. dir. Lily Pond Nursing Home, S.I., 1984—, Garden of Eden Home, Bklyn., 1984-2001; dir. pulmonary Medspect Imaging, Bklyn., 1990—; mem. steering utility com. Bklyn. Physicians, Ind. Physicians Assn., 1995, mem. exec. com. Meth. Hosp., 1995; chmn. quality assurance N.Y. Meth. Hosp., 2001—. Fellow ACP, Am. Coll. Chest Physicians; mem. AMA, Am. Acad. Geriatrics, Soc. Critical Care Medicine, N.Y. State Soc. Internal Medicine, Thoracic Soc., Kings County Med. Soc. Office: 9001 3rd Ave Brooklyn NY 11209

ABOULAFIA, ELIE DAVID, vascular surgeon; b. Jerusalem, June 16, 1928; arrived in U.S., 1953, naturalized, 1958; s. David and Mathilda (Yeshaya) A.; m. Miriam Bernstein, May 19, 1953 (dec. June 1960); children: Diane Dalya, David Michael, Albert Jonathan; m. Eileen Helman, May 2, 1965. BSc in Medicine, U. Geneva, 1949, MD, 1953; MSc in Surgery, Tufts U., 1960. Diplomate Am. Bd. Surgery, Diplomate Gen. Vascular Surgery. Intern Michael Reese Hosp., Chgo., 1953-54; resident in surgery NYU-Bellevue Med. Ctr., N.Y.C., 1954-56; surg. rsch. fellow Tufts-New Eng. Med. Ctr., Boston, 1958-59, chief surg. resident, 1959-61; dir. surg. rsch. Sinai Hosp., Detroit, 1961-63; head sect. vascular surgery Betsford Gen. Hosp., Farmington Hills, Mich., 1963-95; dir. surg. edn. Highland Park (Mich.) Gen. Hosp., Detroit, 1969-73; dir. vascular med. svcs. DMC/Sinai-Grace Hosp., Detroit, 1995—. Clin. prof. surgery Mich. State U., East Lansing, 1977—; clin. prof. medicine Wayne State U., Detroit, 1998—. Mem. editl. bd. Internat. Jour. Surgery, 1972-95, Internat. Jour. Angiology, 1992—; contbr. articles to profl. jours. Bd. trustees Jewish Mus. of Greece, Athens, 1991—; bd. trustees Friends of Israel Def. Forces, N.Y.C., 1997. Lt. comdr. USNR, 1956-58. Fellow Internat. Coll. Surgeons (pres. 1991, emeritus fellow 1995, Disting. Svc. award 1992), Am. Assn. for Vascular Surgery, Soc. Clin. Vascular Surgery, Midwest Vascular Surg. Soc., Mich. Vascular Surg. Soc.; mem. U.S./Internat. Coll. Surgeons (pres. 1991), Internat. Coll. Angiology (vice chair sci. coun. 1994—, sec. 2002, pres. 2003—), Mich. State Med. Soc. (Spl. Recognition Leadership award 1991), Southeastern Mich. Surg. Soc. (pres. 1984-85), Maimonides Med. Soc. (pres. 1966-68), Sigma Xi. Home: 27501 W 14 Mile Rd Farmington Hills MI 48334 Office: Detroit Med Ctr/Sinai Grace Hosp 6071 W Outer Dr Detroit MI 48235-2624

ABOUL-ENEIN, YOUSSEF H. military officer; b. Oxford, Miss., Jan. 25, 1970; s. Hassan Youssef and Nagla Mohammed Mousa (El-Mojaddadi) Aboul-Enein; m. Cheryl Anne Pedigo, May 9, 1992; 1 child, Maryam;1 child, Omar. BBA, U. Miss., 1986; MBA, U. Ark., 1992, MHSA in Health Adminstrn., 1993; MS in Strategic Intelligence, Joint Mil. Intelligence Coll., 2002. Cons. Islamic affairs RAND Project Air Force, Santa Monica, Calif., 2001—; mem. editl. bd. for book Naval Inst. (U.S. Navy Through Eyes of Sailor), Annapolis, Md., 2003—; speaker on Mid-East U.S. Naval Acad., Annapolis, 2003—; lectr. on Mid-East Joint Mil. Intelligence Coll., Washington, 2003—. Editor: (Book) Navy Medicine Jour., 1998—; author: (Reviews and Commentary) U.S. Army Jour. Mil. Rev., 1999—, (Mid East Revs.) Marine Corps Gazette, 2001—; columnist Aerospace Power Chronicles, Air War Coll., 1999—, book columnist Naval Tng. Ctr. Bull., Great Lakes, 1998. Mem.: Naval War Coll. Found., Joint Mil. Intelligence Found., Am. Coll. Healthcare Execs. Avocations: Public speaking, reading, swimming, philately, writing. Office: Office Sec Defense ISA/NESA 2400 Defense Pentagon Washington DC 20301 Fax: 703-693-6795. E-mail: enein288@aol.com.

ABRAHAM, BRIAN M. research scientist; b. Salem, Dec. 19, 1965; s. Walter Rahets and Frances Carol Abraham; m. Jennifer Hunter, Oct. 10, 1992; children: Eliza Anderson, Conor Baker, Hunter Joseph. BA in Spanish, BA in Chemistry, Skidmore Coll., 1988; PhD in Chemistry, Tufts U., 1993; MBA summa cum laude, Babson Coll., 2002. Co-founder, v.p., COO SiteWorks, Inc., Northborough, Maine, 1993—95; v.p. Target Environ., Inc., Columbia, Md., 1995—98; divsn. mgr. Bruker Daltonics, Inc., Billerica, Maine, 1998—2001; dir. product develop. Battelle Meml. Inst., Columbus, Ohio, 2001—. Guest lectr. U. Md., College Park, Md.; transition mgr. Bruker Daltonics Inc., Billerica, Maine; develop. cons. Viking Instruments Corp., Chantilly, Va.; tech. cons. Plexus Sci., Silver Spring, Md.; analytical cons. EAI Corp., Abingdon, Md.; lectr., advisor Internat. Assn. Arson Investigators, Wachusett, Maine; expert witness Dennis & Haas, P.C., Alexandria, Va.; fullerene cons. Busek Co., Inc., Needham, Maine; lectr., advisor Neptune & Co., Denver; presenter in field. Contbr. articles. Recipient Access Venture Ptnrs. Challenge Winner, Moot Corp. Competition, 2002. Mem.: Beta Gamma Sigma. Avocation: hockey. Office: Battelle Meml Inst 505 Kino Ave Columbus OH 43201

ABRAHAM, HENRY JULIAN, political science educator; b. Offenbach am Main, Germany, Aug. 25, 1921; s. Fredrick and Louise (Kullmann) A.; m. Mildred Kosches, Apr. 13, 1954; children: Philip F., Peter D. AB summa cum laude, Kenyon Coll., 1948, LHD (hon.), 1972; MA, Columbia U., 1949; PhD, U. Pa., 1952; LLD (hon.), U. Hartford, 1982, Knox Coll., 1982; LittD (hon.), St. Joseph's U., 1987; LLD (hon.), Old Dominion U., 1996. Faculty U. Pa., 1949-72, prof. polit. sci., 1962-72; Doherty prof. govt. and fgn. affairs U. Va., 1971-78, James Hart prof., 1978-97, James Hart prof. emeritus, 1997—. Vis. prof. Swarthmore Coll., CCNY, Colo. U., Columbia U., Richmond Law Sch., Copenhagen U., U. Stockhholm, Aarhus U., Lund U., Goteborg U., U. Oslo, U. Helsinki, U. Uppsala, U. Amsterdam, U. London, univs. in India and Iran, 1978, univs. in Peru, Bolivia, Brazil, Paraguay, Argentina, 1979, univs. in japan, China, Taiwan, The Philippines, New Zealand, and Australia, 1982, univs. in Republic of Korea, 1982, 84. Author: Compulsory Voting, 1955, Government as Entrepreneur, 1956, Courts and Judges, 1959, Elements of Democratic Government, 1964, Essentials of National Government, 1971, Justices & Presidents, 1992, American Democracy, 1990, Justices, Presidents and Senators, 1999, The Judiciary, 1997, The Judicial Process, 1998, Freedom and the Court, 2003. Mem. com. on non-discrimintion Phila. Bd. Edn., 1962; mem. vis. com. on govt. Lehigh U., 1967-71; trustee fedn. Jewish Agys. Greater Phila., 1970-72, Kenyon Coll., 1987-93; mem. Va. Commn. on Bicentennial of Constn. of U.S., 1985-92, Va. Coun. on Human Rights, 1999-2002. Recipient award excellence undergrad. teaching U. Pa., 1959, 67, Kite and Key Teaching award, 1967, award excellence undergrad. teaching U. Va., 1978, Thomas Jefferson award U. Va., 1983, U. Va. Alumni Teaching award, 1986, Disting. Svc. award Va. Social Sci. Assn., 1982, Disting. Prof. award U. Va. Alumni Assn., 1986, First Lifetime Achievement award, org. sec. on law & courts, Am. polit., sci. Assn., 1993, others; NEH, 1975, 76, 78, 80, 81, NSF fellow, 1965, fellow Am. Philos. Soc., 1961-67, 79, Rockefeller Found. fellow, 1978, Earhart fellow, 1984, Bradley Found., 1989-97. Mem. Fellows in Am. Studies (pres. 1966), Am. Polit. Sci. Assn. (v.p. 1980-82), Raven Soc., Am. Soc. for Legal History, So. Polit. Sci. Ass. (rec. sec. 1980-81), Soc. of Fellows, English-Speaking Union, Met. Opera Guild, Nat. Trust, Golden Key, Greencroft Club (v.p. 1985-87, Charlottesville, Va.), Z Club, Imp Club, Yale Club (N.Y.C.), Capitol Hill Club, Phi Beta Kappa (vis. scholar 1970-71), Pi Sigma Alpha, Pi Gamma Mu, Omicron Delta Kappa. Home: 906 Fendall Ter Charlottesville VA 22903-1617 Office: Univ Va 232 Cabell Hall Charlottesville VA 22904 *Basically—a commitment to hard work; to discipline; to a maintenance of a sense of humour; to a rejection of pompousness and egomania; to a resolute embrace of merit. Above all, an abiding faith in drawing a viable line between the rights and obligations of individuals and those of society without which the democratic process can neither work nor survive.*

ABRAHAM, JACOB A. computer engineering educator, consultant; b. Kerala, India, Dec. 8, 1948; came to U.S., 1970; s. Jacob and Annamma (Chacko) A.; m. Ruth Anne Dick, July 19, 1975; children— Nathan Thomas, Sarah Anne BS, U. Kerala, 1970; MS, Stanford U., 1971, PhD, 1974. Acting asst. prof. Stanford U., Calif., 1974-75; asst. prof. computer engring. U. Ill., Urbana, 1975-80, assoc. prof., 1980-83, prof., 1983-88; prof. and Cockrell Family Regents Chair in Engring. #8 U. Tex., Austin, 1988—, dir. Computer Engring. Rsch. Ctr., 1989—. Cons. Aerospace Corp., Digital Equipment Corp., GE, GTE, Hewlett-Packard Co., IBM Corp., Intel, Sperry, 1979—; dir. rsch. program in reliable very large scale integration architectures U. Ill., 1984-88. Assoc. editor JETTA, 1992—; adv. editor Asken Assocs. Pub., 1987-89; contbr. over 200 articles to profl. confs., jours. and books. Recipient Best Paper award IEEE-Assn. Computing Machinery Design Automation Conf., 1993. Fellow IEEE (assoc. editor transactions on computer-aided design of integrated circuits and systems 1984-86, assoc. editor transactions on very large scale integration systems 1992-93, chair Computer Sci. Tech. Com. on Fault-Tolerant Computing, 1991-92); fellow Assn. Computing Machinery, Sigma Xi. Mem. Ch. of S. India Achievements include 1 patent. Office: U Tex Computer Engring Rsch Ctr Ace 6 134 Austin TX 78712

ABRAHAM, JOHN, mechanical engineer, engineering educator; came to U.S., 1981; s. Poovannal John and Sosamma Abraham; m. Regi Sara Varghese, Jan. 12, 1986. BTech with honors, Indian Inst. Tech., Kharagpur, West Bengal, 1981; MA, Princeton U., 1984, PhD, 1986. Sr. engr. John Deere Techs. Internat., Woodridge, NJ, 1986—91; rsch. staff engine lab. Princeton U., 1992—93; and Barbara Nelson asst. prof. dept. mech. engring. U. Minn., Mpls., 1993—95; assoc. prof. dept. mech. engring. Purdue U., West Lafayette, Ind., 1996—2002, prof. dept. mech. engring., 2002—. Vis. rsch. collaborator dept. mech. and aerospace engring. Princeton (N.J.) U., 1989—. Contbr. articles to profl. jours.; inventor rotary value for natural gas rotary engine, dual spark plug rotary engine, dual radius rotary engine. Mem. ASME, AIAA, Soc. Automotive Engrs., The Combustion Inst. Achievements include patents for 3 Patents Related To Rotary Engines. Avocations: reading, writing on general topics. Office: Purdue University Sch Med Engring Maurice J Zucrow Lab 500 Allison Rd West Lafayette IN 47907-2014

ABRAHAM, KAREN A. university administrator; b. Los Alamos, N.Mex., May 12, 1945; d. Lawrence T. and Wadette G. A. BS, U. N.Mex., 1967, MA, 1968, EdD, 1971; grad., Havard U., 1981. Asst. dean students U. N.Mex., Albuquerque, 1970-72, assoc. dean students, dir. student activities, 1972-87, dir. alumni rels., exec. dir. alumni assn., 1987—. Mem. faculty staff Alumni Rels. Summer Inst. Coun. for Advancement and Support of Edn., Williamstown, Mass., 1996-2000. Recipient fellowship Dept. Edn., 1967-70; Woman on the Move award YWCA Albuquerque, 1992, Student Svc. award U. N.Mex., 1991, Regent's Meritorious Svc. medal, 1982, Lobo award Mortar Bd., 1988, Mem. Am. Soc. Assn. Execs., Coun. Advancement and Support of Edn. (bd. trustees 1993-96), Coun. Alumni Assn. (exec. bd. trustees 1995-97). Presbyterian. Home: 815 Suzanne Ln SE Albuquerque NM 87123-4502 Office: U NMex Alumni Hodgin Hl # 111 Albuquerque NM 87131-0001

ABRAHAM, KENNETH SAMUEL, law educator; b. Kearny, NJ, June 19, 1946; s. Saul Jerome and Helen Beverly (Godin) A.; m. Susan R. Stein, Apr. 5, 1981. AB, Ind. U., 1967; JD, Yale U., 1971. Bar: Md. 1977, Va. 1988. Assoc. Mazer & Lesemann, Hackensack, N.J., 1971-73; asst. prof. law U. Md., Balt., 1974-77, assoc. prof., 1977-80, prof., 1980-84; prof. law U. Va., Charlottesville, 1984—. Assoc. reporter Am. Law Inst., Phila., 1986-91. Author: Distributing Risk: Insurance, Legal Theory, and Pub. Policy, 1986, Insurance Law and Regulation, 3d edit., 2000, Environmental Liability Insurance Law, 1991, The Forms and Functions of Tort Law, 2d edit., 2002; also articles. Mem. Am. Law Inst. (coun.), Phi Beta Kappa. Home: 770 Covey Hill Rd Charlottesville VA 22901-3268 Office: U Va Sch Law 580 Massie Rd Charlottesville VA 22903-1738

ABRAHAM, NATHAN SAMUEL, advertising agency and public relations executive, marketing professional; b. Worcester, Mass., Mar. 8, 1946; s. Israel and Ethel (Zellon) Tighe; 1 child, Josh D. BA, U. Mass., 1968. Sales rep. IBM Corp., Springfield, Mass., 1968-69; sales rep., trainer Mut. Benefit Life, Springfield, 1969-71, NCOA, Portsmouth, N.H., 1974-75; owner, prin. Nathan Abraham & Assocs., Worcester and Springfield, 1971-74, Brookline, Mass., 1975-77; ptnr. Abraham & Abraham Inc., Brookline, 1977-89; pres. Nathan Abraham & Assocs., 1989—2003. Co-author: Footprints for Peace (TM). Trustee Temple Ohabei Shalom, Brookline, 1987-88; bd. dirs., mem. publicity com. Early Childhood Ctr., Brookline, 1987-88; founder Footprints Peace TM Internat., 1984. Recipient Leadership tng. award, Bus. People, Ctrl. Mass., 1971, Jaycees for Course award, 1971. Jewish. Avocations: fishing, camping. E-mail: nathan@nathanabraham.com.

ABRAHAM, NICHOLAS ALBERT, lawyer, real estate developer; b. Boston, Sept. 17, 1941; s. Nicholas and Ida (Ghiz) A.; m. Evie Stathopoulos, June 30, 1968; children: Annise, Nicholas. BS, Boston U., 1963, JD, 1966. Bar: Mass. 1966, U.S. Dist. Ct. Mass. 1968, U.S. Ct. Appeals (1st cir.) 1971. Sr. ptnr. Abraham-Hanna, P.C., Boston, 1968-88; CEO Boston Investors Fund, Inc., 1988-93; pres., CEO Abraham Properties Inc., Boston, 1993—. CEO., chmn., founder STOR/GARD, Inc., 1996—. Author: Doing Business in Egypt, 1979, Doing Business in Saudi Arabia, 1980, Doing Business in Kuwait, 1982. Bd. of trustees Boston U. Coll. of Bus. Adminstrn., 1968; chmn. fund raising com. Boy Scouts Am., 1968; coach Weston Little League; founder of Weston Youth Hockey League, 1985. Served with U.S. Army, 1966-67; to lt. comdr. USN, 1967-74. Republican. Eastern Orthodox. Home: 21 Buckskin Dr Weston MA 02493-1129 Office: Abraham Properties Inc 581 Boylston St Fl 3 Boston MA 02116-3608

ABRAHAM, REBECCA JACOB, finance educator; b. Calcutta, India, Nov. 4, 1962; came to U.S., 1986; d. Connayil Mani and Susan (Varugis) Jacob; m. Anthony Zikiye, May 10, 1989 (dec. Jan. 1994); 1 child, Mark. BS in Chemistry, Women's Christian Coll., Madras; MBA, U.S. Internat., San Diego, 1984, D in Bus. Adminstrn., 1989. Asst. prof. Nova S.E. Univ., Ft. Lauderdale, Fla., 1989-94, assoc. prof., 1994—. Corr. South Fla. Bus., Ft. Lauderdale, 1995, Broward Times, Ft. Lauderdale, 1995; contbr. articles to profl. jours. Recipient Nat. Collegiate Bus. award, 1987. Mem. Acad. Mgmt. Avocations: reading, traveling, badminton. Office: Nova SE Univ 3301 College Ave Fort Lauderdale FL 33314-7721 E-mail: abraham@nova.edu.

ABRAHAM, RICHARD PAUL, lawyer; b. Phila., Oct. 27, 1945; s. Hans Alfred and Lillian Elizabeth (Fredericks) A.; divorced; children: Jacob, Daniel. BA, Temple U., 1967, JD, 1970. Bar: Pa. 1970, U.S. Dist. Ct. (ea. dist.) Pa. 1970, U.S. Ct. Appeals (3d cir.) 1971, U.S. Dist. Ct. (mid. dist.) Pa. 1979, U.S. Supreme Ct. 1989. Law clk. to judge Montgomery County Ct. Common Pleas, Norristown, Pa., 1970-71; sole practice, Phila., 1971-73; ptnr. Abraham, Pressman and Bauer, Phila., 1973—. Contbr. article to Temple U. Law Quar., 1970 (J. Howard Reber award). Mem. Phila. Bar Assn., Assn. Trial Lawyers Am., Phila. Trial Lawyers Assn., Pa. Trial Lawyers Assn. Democrat. Jewish. Club: Germantown Cricket (Phila.). Office: 1818 Market St 35th Fl Philadelphia PA 19103

ABRAHAM, SPENCER, secretary of energy; b. Lansing, Mich., June 12, 1952; BA in Social Sci.and Polit. Sci., Mich. State U., 1974; JD, Harvard U., 1979. Asst. prof. law Thomas M. Cooley Law Sch., 1981-83; chmn. Mich. Republican Party, 1983-90; dep. chief of staff to Vice President Dan Quayle, 1990-91; co-chair Nat. Republican Congressional Com., 1991-93; of counsel Canfield, Paddock & Stone, 1993-94; U.S. senator from Mich., 1995-2001; sec. U.S. Dept. Energy, 2001—. Mem.: Electricity Advisory Bd. (also secretary), 2001. Republican. Office: US Dept Energy 1000 Independence Ave SW Washington DC 20585*

ABRAHAM, TEENA, pharmacist, educator; b. New Delhi, Apr. 1, 1972; d. M.E. and Kunjamma Eappen; m. Titus Abraham, Mar. 27, 1972; 1 child, Alana Elyse. BS in Pharmacy, L.I. U., 1995, PharmD, 1998, MS in Pharmacy, 2002—02. Registered pharmacist NY, Pa., Tex., cert. Bd. Pharm. Specialties, 2001. Pharmacist Randall's, Pasadena, Tex., 1995—96; resident in critical care pharmacotherapy U. of Scis./Hahnemann U. Hosp., Phila., 1998—99; asst. prof. of pharmacy practice Arnold And Marie Schwartz Coll. Of Pharmacy, L.I. U., Bklyn., 1999—; dir. of clin. pharmacy svcs. NY Meth. Hosp., Bklyn., 1999—; adj. asst. prof. of nursing Hunter Coll., CUNY, N.Y.C., 2002—. Mem.: AAUP, Am. Coll. Clin. Pharmacy, Soc. Critical Care Medicine, Am. Soc. Health-system Pharmacists. Avocations: working out, travel. Office: NY Meth Hosp 506 Sixth Street Brooklyn NY 11215 Home Fax: 718-780-3347; Office Fax: 718-780-3347.

ABRAHAM, WILLIAM JOHN, JR., lawyer; b. Jan. 17, 1948; s. William John and Constance (Dudley) A.; m. Linda Omeis, Aug. 31, 1968; children: Richard S., Heidi K. BA with honors, U. Ill., 1969; JD magna cum laude, U. Mich., Ann Arbor, 1972. Bar: Wis. 1973, U.S. Supreme Ct. 1975. Jud. clk. U.S. Ct. Appeals (D.C. cir.), Washington, 1972-73; ptnr. Foley & Lardner, Milw., 1973—. Former mem. mgmt. com., former chmn. bus. law dept; bd. dirs. The Vollrath Co., Windway Capital Corp., Phillips Plastics Corp., Quad/Graphics, Inc., Park Bank, L'eft Bank Wine Co., Ltd., TransPro, Inc.;, Hi-Liter, LLC lectr. MBA program U. Wis. Mem. adv. bd. Wis. Policy Rsch. Inst.; mem. Greater Milw. Com.; bd. dirs. Greater Milw. Open, Children's Hosp. of Milw.; past bd. dirs. United Way of Greater Milw., Family Svc. of Milw., Milw. Zool. Soc.; bd. dirs., former chmn. Children's Hosp. Found. Named All-Am. Big 10 Fencing Champion, 1968—69. Mem. ABA, State Bar of Wis. (chmn. legis. com.), Milw. Bar Assn., Barristers, Tripoli Country Club (bd. dirs., pres.), Milw. Athletic Club, Milw. Club, Desert Mountain Country Club. Office: Foley & Lardner 777 E Wisconsin Ave Ste 3800 Milwaukee WI 53202-5367

ABRAHAMS, SAMUEL, writer, retired lawyer; b. N.Y.C., Dec. 3, 1923; s. Isaac and Ida (Ehrman) A.; m. Ida Savitsky, July 8, 1970. BA, Bklyn. Coll., 1945; MA, Columbia U., 1946; JD, Bklyn. Law Sch., 1956; LLM, NYU, 1961; PhD, Heed U., 1993. Bar: N.Y. 1957, U.S. Dist. Ct. (ea. and so. dists.) N.Y. 1962, U.S. Supreme Ct. 1976. Pvt. practice, Bklyn., 1958-90. Arbitrator Civil Ct. N.Y.C., 1982-87; part-time adminstrv. judge parking violations bur., 1976-88; lectr. on fgn. travel, law and politics. Author: Law in Family Conflict, 1970; contbr. articles to profl. and popular jours., newspapers. With U. S. Army, 1942-43. Mem. ABA, North Dade Profls. Jewish Fedn. Grtr. Miami, Bklyn. Coll. Alumni Assn., Internat. Assn. of Jewish Judges and Lawyers, Columbia U. Alumni Assn. Democrat. Avocation: world travel.

ABRAHAMSEN, ABEL, wholesale and retail import company executive; b. Trondheim, Norway, Sept. 7, 1923; came to U.S., 1944; s. Salamon Abrahamsen and Mirjam Fischer; m. Anne Katrine Gaaso, Nov. 22, 1954; children: Anne C.L., Synnove J. Student, Cathedral Sch., Trondheim, 1941; B Engring., Stockholm Tech. Inst., 1943; postgrad., U. So. Calif., 1946-47. Prodr. documentary movies Abrahamsen Family, Trondheim, 1938-41, Stockholm, 1941-44, RNAF Camp Little Norway, Toronto, Ont., Can., 1944-45; freelance cameraman N.Y.C., 1947-50; cameraman CBS-TV, N.Y.C., 1950-58; pres. Norwegian Silver Corp., N.Y.C., 1958-95, Norsk, Inc., N.Y.C., 1963-95, Ege Area Rugs, N.Y.C., 1975—. Co-chmn. Norwegian Immigration Sesquicentennial Commn., 1975; initiater cooperation between Rusk Inst. Rehab. Medicine NYU Med. Ctr. and Norwegian Sunnaas Rehab. Hosp., Oslo, 1998. Contbr. articles to Reader's Digest, 1949-53. Trustee Norwegian Seamen's Ch., N.Y.C., 1976—, Thanks to Scandinavia, N.Y.C., 1968-74; pres. Norwegian-Am. C. of C., 1973-76, Norwegian Club, N.Y.C., 1995-97. Nav. Sgt. Royal Norwegian AF, 1945-46. Hon. fellow Am. Scandinavian Found., 1946-47; recipient Knight's Cross 1st Class, Royal Norwegian Order of St. Olav, 1976, award for outstanding contbns. to development of trade rels. with Norway, Export Coun. Norway, 1984, award City of N.Y. and U.S. World Trade Fair, 1960, Gift and Art Buyer award, 1963. Mem. Norwegian Immigration Assn. (founder and chmn. 1996-98, chmn. emeritus 2000). Avocations: making movies, music, WWII and holocaust studies. Home and Office: 165 E 66th St New York NY 10021

ABRAHAMSON, A. CRAIG, lawyer; b. Washington, May 24, 1954; s. Joseph Labe and Helen Dorothy (Selis) A.; m. Mary Ellen Bernard, Dec. 29, 1979; children: Nicholas Eric, Amy Nicole. BA, U. Minn., 1976; JD, U. Tulsa, 1979. Bar: Minn. 1979, U.S. Dist. Ct. Minn. 1979, Okla. 1982, U.S. Dist. Ct. (no. and ea. dists.) Okla. 1983, Mo. 1991. Assoc. Law Office of Joseph L. Abrahamson, Mpls., 1979-82, Freese & March, Tulsa, 1982-83, Barlow & Cox, Tulsa, 1983-86; pvt. practice Tulsa, 1986-95, 2000—; ptnr. Levinson, Smith & Abrahamson, Tulsa, 1995-2000; gen. counsel, v.p. Sandman Property Svcs., Inc. & The Sanditen Cos., 2001—. V.p. program com. Youth Svcs., Tulsa, Inc., Leadership Tulsa Class XVII, 1989-92; sec. Great Expectations Educators, Inc., 1995-99; mem. bd. trustees Am. Theatre Co., 1999—. Recipient Am. Jurisprudence Evidence award Lawyers Co-operative Pub. Co. Bancroft-Whitney Co., 1978. Mem. Okla. Bar Assn. (family law sect., real property sect.), Nat. Assn. of Indsl. and Office Properties, Tulsa County Bar Assn. (family law sect., bankruptcy sect.), Rotary Internat. Democrat. Jewish. Avocations: fishing, camping, travel, tennis. Home: 7518 S 107th East Ave Tulsa OK 74133-2530 Office: A Craig Abrahamson 3314 E 51st St Ste 200-A Tulsa OK 74135 E-mail: craiga@abrahamsonlaw.com.

ABRAHAMSON, DAVID STEPHEN RODLER, journalism educator, writer, management consultant; b. Washington, May 7, 1947; s. Ernst Ludwig and Edith (Rodler) A.; m. Barbara Buzan, Aug. 8, 1980. BA in History, Johns Hopkins U., 1969; MJ, U. Calif., Berkeley, 1973; PhD in Am. Civilization, NYU, 1992. Assoc. editor Am. Boating mag., Lafayette, Calif., 1972-73; editor-in-chief AutoWeek mag., Reno, 1973; mng. editor Car and Driver mag., N.Y.C., 1973-77; journalist, author, mgmt. cons. Enfield Rsch., 1979—; asst. prof. NYU, 1988-90; assoc. prof. NYU Mgmt. Inst. Ctr. for Pub., N.Y.C., 1991-94; assoc. prof. Medill Sch. Journalism Northwestern U., 1994—; dir. Northwestern U. Ctr. for the Writing Arts, 2002—, Helen G. Brown Rsch. prof. journalism, 2002—. Author: The American Magazine: Research Perspectives and Prospects, 1995, Magazine-Made America: The Cultural Transformation of the Postwar Periodical, 1996; author numerous publs. and articles. Lt. U.S. Army, 1969-71. Poynter Inst. for Media Studies fellow, St. Petersburg, Fla., 1993; NEH fellow CUNY, 1993, AEJMC fellow, 1994, Humanities faculty fellow Northwestrn U., 1996, Alumnae professorship, 1997. Mem. Assn. for Edn. In Journalism and Mass Comm., Am. Journalism Historians Assn., Am. Hist. Assn., Orgn. Am. Historians, Am. Studies Assn., Am. Soc. Journalists and Authors. Home: 2025 Sherman Ave Evanston IL 60201-3280 Office: Northwestern U Medill Sch Journalism 1845 Sheridan Rd Evanston IL 60208-0815

ABRAHAMSON, KAREN K. theologian, editor; b. Iowa City, Iowa, June 28, 1965; d. Robert D. and Marilyn J. Abrahamson. BA in Theology, Southwestern Adventist Coll., Keene, TX, 1996; MA in Cmty. Counseling, Andrews U., 1998, PhD in Religion, 2003—. Mng. editor Jour. Christian Edn., Berrien Springs, Mich., 1996—97; asst. editor Andrews Univ. Sem. Studies, 1998—; contract prof. Religion Andrews Univ., 1999—. Editor: (scholarly reviews) Andrews Univ. Sem. Studies. Mem.: ACA, Nat. Bd. Cert. Counselors, Am. Acad. Religion, Adventist Soc. Relgious Studies, Phi Delta Kappa.

ABRAHAMSON, SHIRLEY SCHLANGER, state supreme court chief justice; b. N.Y.C., Dec. 17, 1933; d. Leo and Ceil (Sauerteig) Schlanger; m. Seymour Abrahamson, Aug. 26, 1953; 1 son, Daniel Nathan. AB, NYU, 1953; JD, Ind. U., 1956; SJD, U. Wis., 1962. Bar: Ind. 1956, N.Y. 1961, Wis. 1962. Asst. dir. Legis. Drafting Research Fund, Columbia U. Law Sch., 1957-60; since practiced in Madison, Wis., 1962-76; mem. firm LaFollette, Sinykin, Anderson & Abrahamson, 1962-76; justice Supreme Ct. Wis., Madison, 1976-96, chief justice, 1996—; prof. U. Wis. Sch. Law, 1966 92; v.p. conf. Chief Justices, 2002—. Bd. visitors Ind. U. Sch. Law, 1972—02, U. Miami Sch. Law, 1982-97, U. Chgo. Law Sch., 1988-92, Brigham Young U., Sch. Law, 1986-88, Northwestern U. Law Sch., 1989-94; chmn. Wis. Rhodes Scholarship Com., 1992-95; chmn. nat. adv. com. on ct.-adjudicated and ct.-ordered health care George Washington U. Ctr. Health Policy, Washington, 1993-95; mem. DNA adv. bd. FBI, U.S. Dept. Justice, 1995-2001; bd. dirs. Inst. Jud. Adminstrn., Inc., NYU Sch. Law; chair Nat. Inst. Justice's Commn. Future DNA Evidence, 1997-2001. Editor: Constitutions of the United States (National and State) 2 vols, 1962. Mem. study group program of rsch. mental health and the law John D. and Catherine T. MacArthur Found., 1988-96; mem. coun. fund for rsch. on dispute resolution Ford Found., 1987-91; bd. dirs. Wis. Civil Liberties Union, 1968-72; mem. ct. reform adv. panel Internat. Human Rights Law Group Cambodia Project, 1995-97. Mem. ABA (coun., sect. legal edn. and admissions to bar 1976-86, mem. commn. on undergrad. edn. in law and the humanities 1978-79, standing com. on pub. edn. 1991-95, mem. commn. on access to justice/2000 1993—02, mem. adv. bd. Ctrl. and East European law initiative 1994-99, mem. consortium on legal svcs. and the public 1995-2001, vice-chair ABA Coalition for Justice 1997-2000), Wis. Bar Assn., Dane County Bar Assn., 7th Cir. Bar Assn., Nat. Assn. Women Judges, Am. Law Inst. (mem. coun. 1985—), Am. Philos. Soc., Am. Acad. Arts and Scis. Office: Wis Supreme Ct PO Box 1688 Madison WI 53702-1688

ABRAHAMSON, WILLIAM GENE, retired school counselor; b. Billings, Mont., Dec. 14, 1936; s. John C. and Sarah (McNeil) A.; m. Elaine B. Abrahamson, Aug. 12, 1961; children: Donna Key, William Gene Jr. BS in Edn., Eastern Mont. Coll., Billings, 1958; MS in Sch. Counseling, Ind. State U., Terre Haute, 1969; diploma in Sch. Counseling, Auburn (Ala.) U., 1976. Nat. cert. counselor. Tchr. Lovell (Wyo.) Pub. Schs., 1958-59, 61-63, Ft. Benning (Ga.) Schs., 1963-68, sch. counselor, 1969-92, Muscogee County Sch. Dist., Columbus, Ga., 1992-2001; ret., 2001. Presenter local, dist. and state profl. meetings. Scout leader Boy Scouts Am., Chattahoochee Coun., 1984—; scouting coord. South Ga. Conf., United Meth. Ch., 1992-2000. With U.S. Army, 1959-61. Recipient experienced tchr. fellowship Ind. State U., 1968-69, Silver Beaver award Chattahoochee coun. Boy Scouts Am., 1988, Cross and Flame award for svc. to scouting St. Mark United Meth. Ch., 1988, Kappan of Yr. award Chattahoochee Valley Ga. chpt. Phi Delta Kappa, 1991, Svc. Key, 1994, Giwell award for svc. to scouting Boy Scouts Am., 1993, Torch award South Ga. Conf. United Meth. Ch., 2001. Mem. ACA, Am. Sch. Counselors Assn. (cert. of merit 1978), Ga. Sch. Counselors Assn. (sec. 1980-81, pres.-elect, membership chairperson 1981-82, pres. 1982-83, chairperson long range planning com. 1983-85, by-laws com. mem. 1990-91, past pres. action com. 1995—, Elem. Sch. Counselor of Yr. 1978, Mid. Sch. Counselor of Yr. 1998), Ga. Ret. Educators Assn., Masons. Avocations: scouting activities, reading, hiking, camping, Scottish cultural activities, travel. Home: 3104 Bellanca St Columbus GA 31909-5184 E-mail: wabemonty@aol.com.

ABRAHM, JANET LEE, hematologist, oncologist, palliative care specialist, educator; b. San Francisco, Mar. 14, 1949; d. Paul Milton and Helen Lesser Abrahm; m. David Rytman Slavitt, Apr. 16, 1978. Student, U. Calif., Berkeley, 1969; BA, U. Calif., San Francisco, 1970, MD, 1973. Diplomate in internal medicine, hematology and oncology Am. Bd. Internal Medicine; ciplomate Am. Bd. Hospice and Palliative Medicine. Intern and resident medicine Mass. Gen. Hosp., Boston, 1973-75, hematology fellow, 1975-76; chief resident medicine Moffitt Hosp. U. Calif., San Francisco, 1976-77; hematology/oncology fellow Hosp. U. Pa., Phila., 1977-80; postdoctoral fellow medicine U. Pa., Phila., 1977-78, postdoctoral trainee medicine, 1977-80, asst. prof. medicine, 1980-86, Hosp. U. Pa. and VA Med. Ctr., Phila., 1986-89, assoc. prof. medicine, 1989-2000; attending physician Hosp. U. Pa., Phila., 1980-93; from staff physician to faculty scholar Phila. VA Med. Ctr., 1982—97, faculty scholar Project Death in Am., 1997—2000; med. dir. Wissahickon Hospice UPHS, 1998-2000; assoc. prof. medicine and anesthesia Harvard Med. Sch., 2001—; attending physician Dana-Farber Cancer Inst., Brigham and Women's Hosp., Boston, 2001—. Prin. investigator Palliative Care Fellowship Grant, 1996-2001, 03—; mem. concensus panel on End-of-Life Care, ACP, 1997—; chmn. adv. com. Cancer Care VA Dist. 4, 1987-90, sec. subspecialty bd. hematology Am. Bd. Internal Medicine, 1987-92, sec. SEP subcom. hematology, 1993-95; mem. tech. adv. group Cancer Care Region 1, 1990-95; med. oncology cons. cancer pain consultation panel Ctr. for Continuing Edn. U. Pa. Sch. Nursing, 1990-2000; mem. quality of life and cancer edn. com. Pa. Cancer Adv. Bd., 1994-97; mem. human resources coun. of VHA VISN, 1996-97, councillor Region 1, AVOCOM, 1996-97, TAPC mem., 2000-02, Am. Acad. Hospice and Palliative Medicine, 1999-, ACP, 2000-, others; attending physician Brigham and Women's Hosp., Boston, 2001—; dir. pain and palliative care program Dana-Farber Cancer Inst., Boston, 2001—; adj. prof. medicine, U. Pa. Sch. Medicine, 2001-. Author: Clinical Care of the Terminal Patient, 1982, Pain Management in Hematology: Basic Principles and Practice, 1990, 94, 99, Pain Management in Kelley W. Textbook of Internal Medicine, 1996, 2000, Anemia, Pain Management in Geriatric Secrets, 1996, 2000, A Physician's Guide to Pain and Symptom Management in Cancer Patients, 2000; contbr. (booklets) Caring for the Terminally Ill Patient at Home - A Guide for Family Caregivers, 1986, Caring for the Cancer Patient at Home - A Guide for Patients and Families, 1986; reviewer New Eng. Jour. Medicine, JAMA, Cancer, Archives Internal Medicine, Annals Internal Medicine; contbr. numerous articles to profl. jours. Recipient Manual award Merck, 1973; Fife Medicine scholar, 1973. Fellow: ACP, Am. Acad. Hospice and Palliative Medicine (bd. dirs.); mem.: Am. Pain Soc., Am. Assn. Cancer Edn. (program com. 1993), Am. Soc. Clin. Oncology, Am. Soc. Clin. Hypnosis, Am. Soc. Hematology, Alpha Omega Alpha, Phi Beta Kappa. Home: 35 West St #5 Cambridge MA 02139 Office: Dana Farber Cancer Inst 44 Binney St Boston MA 02115 Fax: 617-632-4778. E-mail: jabrahm@partners.org.

ABRAIRA, CARLOS, endocrinologist, physician; b. Buenos Aires, Mar. 25, 1936; came to the U.S., 1963, naturalized, 1976; s. Jose B. and Maria (Cela) A.; m. Rosa Saffier, July 11, 1963; children: Daniel, Irene. Bacchalaureate, U. Buenos Aires, 1953, MD, 1962. Diplomate Am. Bd. Internal Medicine. Intern Mercy Hosp., Chgo., 1963-64; resident Mt. Sinai Hosp., Chgo., 1964-66; fellow in medicine Northwestern U. Hosp., Evanston, Ill., 1966-67; fellow in endocrinology Michael Reese Hosp., Chgo., 1967-69, attending physician medicine, 1969-70; asst. prof. medicine U. Ill. Abraham Lincoln Sch., Chgo., 1970-78, assoc. prof. medicine, 1978-83, Loyola U., Chgo., 1984—. prof. medicine, 1986—2001, U. Miami, Fla., 2001—. Chief endocrinology Hines VA Hosp. (Ill.), 1972-99; lectr. Am. Diabetes Assn., 1984, 89-90, 94, 95; Woodyard Meml. lectr. N.W. U., 1999; coord. diabetes program Chgo. Med. Soc. Midwest Clin. Conf., 1980-83. Editor: How to Be Your Own Diabetes Manager, 1983; contbr. articles to profl. jours. Chmn. Nat. VA Coop Study in Diabetes, 1989—. Grantee Allstate Found., 1966, VA, 1981, 88—, Sugar Assn., 1983. Fellow ACP, Am. Coll. Nutrition; mem. Am. Diabetes Assn. (pres. Ill. affiliate 1989-91), Am. Soc. Clin. Nutrition, Am. Inst. Nutrition, Am. Fedn. Clin. Rsch. (sr.), Endocrine Soc. Office: Miami VA Med Ctr 1201 NW 16th St Miami FL 33125-1624

ABRAM, BLANCHE SCHWARTZ, music educator, pianist; b. N.Y.C., June 28, 1925; d. Irving Al and Celia (Smith) Schwartz; m. Joseph Kushner (div. 1957); m. Irving Abram, May 19, 1957; children: Rachel, Michael, Anne Marie, David. BA, Bklyn. Coll., 1945; postgrad., NYU, 1945-46. Cert. Master Tchr. Music faculty 92d St Y Sch. Music, N.Y.C., 1945—97; music lectr. NYU Sch. Continuing Edn., N.Y.C.; sr. prof. music Hofstra U., Hempstead, N.Y., 1965—; pianist, co-dir. Am. Chamber Ensemble, N.Y.C., 1965—; pianist Drucker Trio, N.Y.C., 1980—. Judge in numerous competitions; hundreds of performances of solo and chamber music concerts. Contbr. articles to profl. jours. Founder, chmn. South Shore Cmty. Arts Coun., L.I., N.Y., 1951-56; founder creative arts program Roosevelt (N.Y.) Cmty. Rels. Coun., 1962. Recipient Pathfinder award in arts Twp. of Hempstead, 1998, citation for outstanding contgn. in artistry 92d St Y, 1966; N.Y. State Coun. on Arts grantee, 1989-2003. Mem. N.Y. State Music Tchrs. Assn., Music Tchrs. Nat. Assn. (Master Tchr.). Avocations: hiking, dancing, reading. Home: 2320 Surrey Ln Baldwin NY 11510-3024

ABRAM, DONALD EUGENE, retired federal judge; b. Des Moines, Feb. 8, 1935; s. Irwin and Freda Phyllis (Gibson) A.; m. Frances Jennette Cooley, Apr. 22, 1962; children: Karen Lynn, Susan Ann, Scott Alan, Diane Jennette. BS in Bus., U. Col., 1957, JD, 1963. Ptnr. Phelps, Fonda, Hays, Abram and Shaw (now Peterson & Fonda, PC), Pueblo, Colo., 1963-75; dist. judge Colo. 10th Jud. Dist., Pueblo, 1975-81; chief U.S. magistrate judge U.S. Dist. Ct. State of Colo., 1981-00; ret., 2000. Lectr. law in criminal procedure U. Denver Sch. of Law, 1983-90; adj. prof. sociology, instr. bus. law U. So. Colo., Pueblo, 1977-81. Mng. editor, bd. dir. Colo. Law Review, 1961-63. Vice chmn. Pueblo County Rep. Party, 1973-75; city councilman Pueblo, 1970-73; pres. Pueblo city coun., 1972-73, Pueblo Goodwill Industries, 1965, Pueblo United Fund, 1968; chmn. consolidation planning com. Pueblo County Sch. Dists. 60, 70, 1968-70; mem. gov.'s. milit. affairs adv. com., 1975-78; mem. gov.'s. commn. children and families, 1978-80. Lt. (j.g.) USN, 1957-60, capt. Res. ret. Recipient Disting. Svc. award Colo. Jaycee, 1970, Disting. Citizen Svc. award, Pueblo Rotary, 1975. Mem. Fed. Magistrate Judges Assn. (pres. 1990-91), Pueblo C. of C.(bd. dirs. 1972, chmn. edn. com. 1970-71), Colo. Bar Assn. (1st v.p. 1975-76), Nat. Coun. U. S. Magistrates (dir., officer 1984-89), Juvenile Judges Assn. Colo. (chmn. 1979-80), Colo. Navy League (state pres. 1976-78). Lutheran. Office: US Dist Ct US Courthouse C-566 1929 Stout St Denver CO 80294-1929

ABRAMOVITZ, MAX, architect; b. Chgo., May 23, 1908; s. Benjamin and Sophia (Maimon) A.; m. Anne Marie Causey, Sept. 4, 1937 (div.); children: Michael John, Katherine Paul; m. Anita Zeltner Brooks, Feb. 29, 1964. BS, U. Ill., 1929; MS, Columbia U., 1931; postgrad., Ecole des Beaux Arts, 1932-34; DFA (hon.), U. Pitts., 1961, U. Ill., 1970. Ptnr. firm Harrison & Abramovitz, Architects, 1945-76, Abramovitz-Harris-Kingsland, Architects, N.Y.C., 1976-85, 85—. Asso. prof. Yale U. Sch. Fine Arts, 1939-42; dep. dir. UN Hdqrs. Planning Office, 1947-52; Cons. Brandeis U., U. Pitts. Prin. works include U.S. Steel Bldg, Pitts., Nationwide Ins, Columbus, Ohio, Assembly Hall and Krannert Center Performing Arts, U. Ill.-Urbana; chapels Brandeis U; major campus devel. La Banque Rothschild, Paris, France, Groupe des Assurances Nationales, LaDefense, France, Jewish Chapel, U.S. Mil. Acad., West Point, N.Y., Rockeller U. Rsch. Lab., N.Y.C. Served with C.E. AUS, 1942-45; col. 1950-52; spl. asst. to asst. sec. air force Mar. 1952-July 1952. Recipient Legion of Merit; fellow Brandeis U., 1963; Achievement award U. Ill. Alumni Assn., 1963 Fellow AIA; mem. Am. Soc. C.E., Regional Plan Assn. (chmn. bd. 1966-68), Archtl. League N.Y. Clubs: Century Assn. (N.Y.C.). Home: 176 Honey Hollow Rd Pound Ridge NY 10576-1105

ABRAMOWICZ, JACQUES SYLVAIN, obstetrician, perinatologist, educator; b. Paris, Dec. 5, 1948; s. Theodore Dov and Sara Ethel (Cukiernik) A.; m. Annie Sternelicht, Aug. 1, 1972; children: Shelly, Ory. MD, Sackler Sch. Medicine, Tel-Aviv, 1975. Diplomate Israel Bd. Ob-Gyn., Am. Bd. Ob-Gyn. Rotating intern Tel-Aviv Mcpl. Med. Ctr., 1973-74; resident dept. ob-gyn. Sapir Med. Ctr., Kfar-Saba, Israel, 1978-85; rsch. registrar ultrasound dept. ob-gyn. King's Coll. Hosp., London, 1981; resident dept. gen. surgery Sapir Med. Ctr., 1982-83, resident dept. urology, 1983; cons. Timsit Inst. Reproductive Medicine, Tel-Aviv, 1986-87, dir. clin. rsch. Div. Maternal-Fetal Medicine, Ea. Va. Med. Sch., Norfolk, 1987-89; assoc. researcher Jones Inst. Reproductive Medicine, Norfolk, 1989; dir. perinatal ultrasound, asst. prof. dept. ob-gyn. U. Rochester Med. Ctr., 1990-93, assoc. prof., 1993-99, prof., 1999-2000, assoc. prof. radiology, 1995-99, prof. radiology, 1999-2000; prof. dept. ob-gyn. and dept. radiology U. Chgo., 2000—. Co-editor: Handbook of Ultrasound in Obstetrics and Gynecology, 1997, Imaging in Infertility and Reproductive Endocrinology, 1994; contbr. articles to profl. jours. including Am. Jour. Ob-Gyn., Obstet. Gynecology, Jour. Ultrasound Medicine, Prenatal Diagnosis, Am. Jour. Perinatology, Fetal Therapy, Jour. Perinatal Medicine, Jour. Clin. Ultrasound, Ultrasound Med. Biology, also chpts. to books; referee various jours. Maj. Israel Def. Forces, 1974-78. Fellow: ACOG, Am. Inst. Ultrasound in Medicine (sr.; internat. rels. com. 1988—91, stds. com. 1991—93, mfrs. commendation panel 1991—93, chair mfrs. commendation panel 1993—94, bioeffects com. 1994—, chair epidemiology subcom. 1999—); mem.: Internat. Soc. Ultrasound in Ob-Gyn. (chair bioeffects and safety com. 2001—), Internat. Fetal Med. and Surg. Soc., Internat. Perinatal Doppler Soc., Soc. Perinatal Obstetricians, N.Y. Acad. Scis. Jewish. Achievements include rsch. in prenatal diagnosis and therapy, ultrasound, Doppler velocimetry, ultrasound contrast media, placental perfusion, bioeffects of ultrasound. Office: U Chgo Dept Ob/Gyn MC 2050 5841 S Maryland Ave Chicago IL 60637-1463 E-mail: jsa@babies.bsd.uchicago.edu.

ABRAMOWITZ, HARRIET C. social worker; b. N.Y.C., Apr. 8, 1928; d. Max and Dora B. (Brownstein) Cohen; married Sept. 7, 1950; children: Mort, Corinne Abramowitz Sharp, David. BA, Bklyn. Coll., 1949; MSW, U. Pitts., 1951; postgrad., Mich. State U., 1977-79; MA, Wayne State U., 1983. Lic. social worker, Mich. Social worker Plymouth State Home and Tng. Sch., 1963-67; case worker, supr. recreation program Detroit League for Handicapped, 1967-70; clin. case and group social worker Kingswood Hosp., 1970-74; sch. social worker Bloomfield Hills (Mich.) Schs., 1974-88, South Lyons (Mich.) Community Schs., 1989-95; adj. instr. in social work Wayne State U., Detroit, 1990—. Mem. Mich. Assn. Sch. Social Workers, Nat. Assn. Social Workers, Social Work with Groups. Home: 31080 Columbia Dr Novi MI 48377-1509

ABRAMOWITZ, MORTON I. former ambassador; b. Lakewood, N.J., Jan. 20, 1933; s. Mendel and Dora (Smith) Abramowitz; m. Sheppie Glass, Sept. 13, 1959; children: Michael, Rachel. BA, Stanford U.; MA, Harvard U., 1955. Joined U.S. Fgn. Service, 1960; 3d sec., vice consul Taipei, Formosa, 1960-62; with Fgn. Area and Lang. Tng. Ctr., Taichung, Taiwan, 1962-63; consul, polit. officer Hong Kong, 1963-66; assigned Bur. Econ. Affairs, 1966-68; Sr. Inter dept. Group, 1968-69; spl. asst. under-sec. state, 1969-71; research assoc. Inst. for Strategic Studies, 1971; asst. to sec. of def., 1972-73; polit. adviser to Comdr.-in-Chief Pacific, 1973-78; also dep. asst. sec. def. for Inter-Am., E. Asia and Pacific, 1974-78; amb. to Thailand, Bangkok, 1978-83; U.S. rep. to Mutual and Balanced Force Reduction Negotiations, 1983-85; dir., asst. sec. Bur. of Intelligence and Rsch., 1985-89; amb. to Turkey, 1989-91. Author (with Richard Moorsteen): Remaking China Policy, 1972; author: Moving the Glacier, the Two Koreas and the Powers, 1972, East Asian Actors and Issues, China, Can We Have a Policy, 1997, Turkey's Transformation and American Policy, 2000, Turkey and the United States - Allies in Need, 2003; contbr. Pres. Carnegie Endowment for Internat. Peace, Washington, 1991—97; bd. dirs. Internat. Crisis Group, 1997—, Internat. Rescue Com., Nat. Endowment for Democracy, Open Soc. Inst., Freedom House. With AUS, 1957. Recipient Disting. Pub. Svc. award, Dept. Def., 1976, Sec. Def. Disting. Svc. award, 1978, Joseph C. Wilson award, 1980, Pres.'s award for Disting. Fed. Svc., 1981, 1985, 1988, Nat. Intelligence Disting. medal, 1989. Mem.: Am. Acad. Arts and Scis., Phi Beta Kappa.

ABRAMOWITZ, ROBERT LESLIE, lawyer; b. Phila., May 1950; s. Nathan P. and Lucille H. (Rader) A.; m. Susan Margaret Stewart, Dec. 1, 1974; children: David, Catherine. BA, Yale U., 1971; JD, Harvard U., 1974. Bar: Pa. 1974, N.J. 1975. Assoc. Ballard, Spahr, Andrews & Ingersoll, Phila., 1974-81, ptnr., 1981-90; ptnr. Morgan Lewis & Bockius, LLP, Phila., 1990—. Adj. prof. law Villanova U., 1986—2001. Trustee Moorestown (N.J.) Friends Sch., 1981-90, Rock Sch. of Pa. Ballet, 1990—; pres. Harvard Law Sch. Assn. Greater Phila., 1999-2001. Mem. ABA, Am. Coll. of Employee Benefits Counsel, Phila. Bar Assn. (exec. com. probate sect. 1982-85, pension com. 1985-94, chair 1987-89), Yale Club, Merion Cricket Club. Home: 623 Pembroke Rd Bryn Mawr PA 19010-3613 Office: Morgan Lewis & Bockius LLP 1701 Market St Philadelphia PA 19103-2903

ABRAMS, ARTHUR JAY, physician; b. Camden, N.J., Apr. 9, 1938; s. Morris and Sophia Sarah (Kates) A.; m. Marianne Ritto Abrams, June 8, 1963; children: Suzanne Beth, Cheryl Lyn, Robert Dwight. BA, Rutgers U., Camden, N.J., 1959; MD, Hahnemann U., 1963. Diplomate Am. Bd. Dermatology. Intern Madigan Army Med. Ctr., Tacoma, Wash., 1963-64; resident, chief resident Letterman Army Med. Ctr., San Francisco, 1964-67, dermatologist, Far East cons. 249th Gen. Hosp. U.S. Army, Tokyo, 1967-69; asst. chief dermatologist Tripler Army Med. Ctr., Honolulu, 1969-70; staff dermatologist El Camino Hosp., Mountain View, Calif., 1970—; clin. assoc. prof. dermatology Stanford U. Med. Ctr., 1979—; dermatology cons. San Jose (Calif.) State U., 1994—; maj. U.S. Army, 1963-70. Mem. AMA, Calif. Med. Assn., Pacific Dermatol. Assn., San Francisco Dermatol. Soc. Avocations: volleyball, walking. Office: 763 Altos Oaks Dr Ste 4 Los Altos CA 94024-5400

ABRAMS, BRUCE D, music educator; s. Max and Gussie Abrams. BME, MB, Univ. Hartford, 1973. Music tchr. Kingston City Schools, Kingston, NY, 1973—; adj. prof. percussion Ulster County C.C., Stone Ridge, NY, 1975—. Dir. Musicians Union Local 215, Kingston, NY, 1972—82. Spc 4 U.S. Army, 1968—70. Recipient Moshe Paranov Award, The Hartt Sch., 1972, Regents Honor Award, U. Hartford, 1973. Mem.: Ulster County Music Educators Assn., NY State Band Dirs. Assn., NY State Sch. Music Assn., Music Educators Nat. Conf. Office: JWatson Bailey Mid Sch 118 Merilina Ave Kingston NY

ABRAMS, BURTON A. economics educator; b. Chgo., Mar. 7, 1947; s. David and Viola Radosevich Abrams; m. Doris Lederer, Sept. 21, 1971 (div. Mar. 1982). BA, Ill. Inst. Tech., 1968; MA, Ohio State U., 1972, PhD, 1974. Prof. econs. U. Del., Newark, 1974—. Fulbright prof. Tianjin, China, 1985-86, Capetown, South Africa, 1994, Split, Croatia, 2002. Author: Return to Animal Farm, 1998; contbr. articles to profl. jours. Hoover Instn. nat. fellow, 1978-79; NSF grantee, 1983, 86. Office: U Del Dept Econs Newark DE 19716

ABRAMS, CYNTHIA F. KATLIN, nutrition scientist, educator; b. New York, NY, May 4, 1934; d. Leonard Edward and Sadie Ruth Katlin; m. David Abrams, Sept. 1, 1957; children: Charles, Sari, Leya, Lowell. BS, Hunter Coll., New York, NY, 1956; MS, U. Md., College Park, 1977, PhD, 1984. Staff dietitian Bellevue Hosp., New York, NY, 1956-57; food svc. super. Cornell Univ., Ithaca, NY, 1957-58; staff dietitian Sch. Lunch Prog., New York, NY, 1959, George Wash. Univ. Hosp., Washington, D.C., 1959-62; grad. rsch. asst. U. Md., College Park, 1976-78, grad. tchg. asst., 1979-80; rsch. asst. Georgetown Univ. Med. Sch., Washington, 1981-84, instr. pediats., 1984—87, asst. prof. biochem.

and molecular biology, 1987—96; assoc. prof. biochemistry and molecular biology Howard U. Coll. Medicine, Washington, 1996—, assoc. clin. prof. pediat., 1996—. Contbr. articles to profl. jours. Office: Howard U Coll Medicine Dept Bicohemistry & Molecular Biology 520 W St NW Washington DC 20059-0001

ABRAMS, DOUGLAS CARL, social studies educator; b. Tarboro, N.C., Jan. 7, 1950; s. Era Glenn and Edna Louise Abrams; m. Linda Marie Perry, Aug. 2, 1980; children: Jessica Louise, Benjamin Perry. BA, Bob Jones U., 1972; cert., Sorbonne U. Paris, 1974; MA, N.C. State U., 1974; PhD, U. Md., 1981. Prof. Bob Jones U., Greenville, SC, 1974—, dir. Africa team, 1991—, chair dept. social studies edn., 1992—; tchg. asst. U. Md., College Park, 1977—81; instr. U. Coll., U. Md., College Park, 1981—81. Outside reader Harcourt Press, N.Y.C., 1994—94; program participant Citadel, Conf. on the Civil Rights Movement in S.C., Charleston, 2003—; presenter and spkr. in field. Author: (historical monograph) Selling the Old-Time Religion: American Fundamentalists and Mass Culture, 1920-1940, Conservative Constraints: North Carolina and the New Deal; book rev. contbr. to various jours.: ; contbr. chapters to books, articles to profl. jours. Named alt. Fulbright lectr. for Kenya, Fulbright Scholar Program, 1995—96; grantee, NEH, 1983, 1986, Am. Coun. Learned Socs., 1988, So. Bapt. Hist. Commn., 1989, Inst. for the Study Am. Evangelicals, 1992; Hearst fellow, U. Md., 1980. Mem.: So. Hist. Assn. (assoc.), Orgn. Am. Historians (assoc.). Republican. Avocations: reading, gardening, walking, music, travel. Home: One Oriole Greenville SC 29609 Office: Bob Jones Univ Box 34627 Greenville SC 29614 Home Fax: 864-232-6701; Office Fax: 864-232-6701. Personal E-mail: clabrams@charter.net. E-mail: cabrams@bju.edu.

ABRAMS, ELLIOTT, governmental official; b. NYC, Jan. 24, 1948; s. Joseph and Mildred (Kauder) A.; m. Rachel Decter, Mar. 9, 1980; children: Jacob, Sarah, Joseph BA, Harvard U., 1969, JD, 1973; MS in Econs, London Sch. Econs., 1970. Assoc. Breed, Abbott & Morgan, N.Y.C., 1974-75; asst. counsel U.S. Senate Permanent Subcom. on Investigations, Washington, 1975; spl. counsel Sen. Henry M. Jackson, 1975-76, Sen. Daniel P. Moynihan, 1977-78, chief of staff, 1978-79; atty. Verner, Liipfert, Bernhard & McPherson, Washington, 1979-80; asst. sec. for internat. orgn. affairs U.S. Dept. State, Washington, 1981, asst. sec. for human rights and humanitarian affairs, 1981-85, asst sec. for InterAm. affairs, 1985-89; sr. fellow Hudson Inst., Washington, 1990-96; pres. Ethics and Pub. Policy Ctr., Washington, 1996-2001; spl. asst. to pres., sr. dir. Nat. Security Coun., Washington, 2001—. Chmn. U.S. Commn. Internat. Religious Freedom, 2000-01. Author: Undue Process, 1992, Security and Sacrifice, 1995, Faith or Fear, 1997. Mem. Coun. Fgn. Rels. Republican. Office: Nat Security Coun 351 Old Exec Office Bldg Washington DC 20506

ABRAMS, GERALD DAVID, physician, educator; b. Detroit, Apr. 27, 1932; s. Arthur and Esther (Kushner) A.; m. Gloria Sandra Turner, June 6, 1954; children— Kathryn, Nancy AB, Wayne U., 1951; MD, U. Mich., 1955. Diplomate Am. Bd. Pathology. House officer pathology U. Mich., Ann Arbor, 1955-59, instr. pathology, 1959-60, asst. prof. pathology, 1963-66, assoc. prof., 1966-69, prof., 1969—2002, prof. emeritus, 2002—, dir. anatomic pathology, 1985-89; asst. chief dept. exptl. pathology Walter Reed Army Inst. Rsch., 1961-62. Dep. med. examiner, Washtenaw County, Mich., 1963— ; cons. physician Ann Arbor VA Hosp., 1970— Served to capt. M.C., US Army, 1961-62 Markle scholar John and Mary Markle Found., 1963-68; recipient Elizabeth Crosby Teaching award U. Mich., 1969, 87, 96, Kaiser-Permanente Teaching award U. Mich., 1978; Lifetime achievement Award in Med. Edn., 2002. Mem. AAAS, US-Can. Acad. Pathology, Mich. Soc. Pathologists Office: U Mich Dept Pathology Ann Arbor MI 48109 E-mail: gabrams@umich.edu.

ABRAMS, HAROLD EUGENE, lawyer; b. Pensacola, Fla., Jan. 18, 1933; s. Samuel Ralph and Sadie (Gerhardt) A.; m. Nancy Gray, June 22, 1958; children: Shari Abrams Marx, Eric Gray. BA, U. Mich., 1954; JD, Harvard U., 1957. Bar: Ga. 1958, D.C. 1976, U.S. Supreme Ct. 1970. Law clk. to presiding judge U.S. Ct. Appeals (5th cir.), Atlanta, 1957-58; assoc. Kilpatrick & Cody, Atlanta, 1958-63; ptnr. Kilpatrick Stockton, Atlanta, 1963—. Pres. Atlanta Tax Forum, 1990-91, Atlanta Estate Planning Coun., 1991-92; bd. dirs. Randall Bros., Inc., Atlanta, Selig Enterprises, Inc., Atlanta. Contbr. articles on tax and estate planning to profl. publs. Pres. Buckhead Little League, Atlanta, 1972-73; bd. dirs. Atlanta chpt. Am. Jewish Com., 1987-2001, Atlanta Jewish Fedn., 1996—; sec. Ronald McDonald's Children's Charities, Atlanta, 1988—. With U.S. Army, 1957-58. Fellow Am. Coll. Tax Counsel; mem. State Bar of Ga. (chmn. tax sect. 1964-65), So. Fed. Tax Inst. (trustee 1964-2001, pres. 1970-71, treas. 1986-95), Peachtree Club, Atlanta Lawyers Club. Avocations: tennis, travel. Office: Kilpatrick Stockton LLP 1100 Peachtree St NE Ste 2800 Atlanta GA 30309-4530 E-mail: habrams@kilpatrickstockton.com.

ABRAMS, HERBERT KERMAN, physician, educator; b. Chgo., 1913; BS, Northwestern U.; MD, MS, U. Ill., 1940; MPH, Johns Hopkins U., 1947. Intern Cook County Hosp., Chgo., 1940-41; chief Bur. of Adult Health, Calif. Health Dept., 1947-52; dir. Chgo. Union Health Service, 1952-66; prof., chair dept. community medicine Chgo. Med. Sch.-Mt. Sinai Hosp., Chgo., 1966-68; prof., head dept. family community medicine U. Ariz., Tucson, 1968-78, prof. emeritus, 1990—; dir. Ariz. Ctr. for Occupl. Safety and Health, 1978-83. Surgeon USPHS, 1942-46. Mem.: APHA, AMA, Physicians for a Nat. Health Program, Internat. Physicians Prevention Nuclear War, Physicians for Social Responsibility, Am. Coll. Occupl. Environ. Medicine, Assn. Tchrs. Preventive Medicine, Ariz. Med. Assn. Office: U Ariz Dept Family and Cmty Medicine PO Box 245143 Tucson AZ 85724-5143 E-mail: hka@u.arizona.edu.

ABRAMS, HERBERT LEROY, radiologist, educator; b. N.Y.C., Aug. 16, 1920; s. Morris and Freda (Sugarman) Abrams; m. Marilyn Spitz, Mar. 23, 1943; children: Nancy, John. BA, Cornell U., 1941; MD, Downstate Med. Ctr., N.Y., 1946. Diplomate Am. Bd. Radiology. Intern L.I. Coll. Hosp., 1946—47; resident in internal medicine Montefiore Hosp., Bronx, NY, 1947—48; resident in radiology Stanford (Calif.) U. Hosp., 1948—51; practice medicine specializing in radiology Stanford U., Calif., 1951—67, mem. faculty Sch. Medicine, 1951—67, dir. divsn. diagnostic roentgenology Sch. Medicine, 1961—67, prof. radiology Sch. Medicine, 1962—67; Philip H. Cook prof. radiology Harvard U., 1967—85, now prof. emeritus, chmn. dept. radiology, 1967—80; prof. radiology Stanford U. Sch. Medicine, 1985—90, prof. emeritus, 1990—; clin. prof. U. Calif. Sch. Medicine, San Francisco, 1986—. Radiologist-in-chief Peter Bent Brigham Hosp., Boston, 1967—80; chmn. dept. radiology Brigham and Women's Hosp., Boston, 1981—85; radiologist-in-chief Sidney Farber Cancer Inst., Boston, 1974—85; R.H. Nimmo vis. prof. U. Adelaide, Australia; mem.-in-residence Ctr. for Internat. Security and Cooperation, Stanford U., 1985—; mem. radiation study sect. NIH, 1962—66; cons. to hosps., profl. socs. Author (with others): Angiocardiography in Congenital Heart Disease, 1956, Congenital Heart Disease, 1965, Coronary Arteriography: A Practical Approach, 1983, Brigham Guide to Diagnostic Imaging, 1986, Assessment of Diagnostic Technology in Health Care; editor: Abrams' Angiography, 3d edit., 1983; author: The President Has Been Shot: Confusion, Disability and the 25th Amendment, 1992, 1994, The History of Cardiac Radiology, 1996; mem. editl. bd.: Investigative Radiology, editor-in-chief, founder: Cardiovasc. and Interventional Radiology, 1978—88, Postgrad. Radiology, 1983—99. Named David M. Gould Meml. lectr., Johns Hopkins, 1964, William R. Whitman Meml. lectr., 1968, Leo G. Rigler lectr., Tel Aviv U., 1969, Holmes lectr., New Eng. Roentgen Ray Soc., Boston, 1970, Ross Golden lectr., N.Y. Roentgen Ray Soc., N.Y.C., 1971, Stauffer Meml. lectr., Phila. Roentgen Ray Soc., 1971, J.M.T. Finney Fund lectr., Md. Radiol. Soc., Ocean City, 1972, Aubrey Hampton lectr., Mass. Gen. Hosp., Boston, 1974, Kirklin-Weber lectr., Mayo Clinic, 1974, Crookshank lectr., Royal Coll. Radiology, 1980, Alpha Omega Alpha lectr., vis. prof., U. Calif. Med. Sch., San Francisco, 1961—65, W.H. Herbert lectr., U. Calif., Caldwell lectr., Am. Roentgen Ray Soc., 1982, Percy lectr., McMaster Med. Sch., 1983, Charles Dotter lectr., Soc. Cardiovasc. and Interventional Radiology, 1988, Philip Hodes lectr., Jefferson Med. Coll., 1988, David Gould Meml. lectr., Johns Hopkins U., 1991, Hymer Friedell lectr., Western Res. Sch. Medicine, 1993, Felix Fheischner Meml. lectr., Harvard Med. Sch., 1997, Charles Dotter Meml. lectr., Am. Heart Assn., 1998; fellow, Nat. Cancer Inst., 1950, Spl. Rsch. fellow, Nat. Heart Inst., 1960, 1973—74, Henry J. Kaiser sr. fellow, Ctr. for Advanced Study in Behavioral Sci., 1980—81. Fellow: Am. Coll. Cardiology, Am. Coll. Radiology, Royal Coll. Radiology (Gt. Britain) (hon.), Royal Coll. Surgery (Ireland) (hon.); mem.: NIH (chmn. consensus panel on MRI, internat. blue ribbon panel radiation effects rsch. found. Hiroshima 1996, working group on disability of U.S. pres. 1995—98), NAS (com. biol. effects of low-level ionizing radiation BEIR VII 1999—), Inst. of Medicine NAS (com. on biol. effects of low level ionizing radium 1999—), Nat. Coun. Health Tech. Assessment, Soc. Chmn. Acad. Radiology Depts. (pres. 1970—71), Soc. Cardiovasc. Radiology (Gold medal 2000), Internat. Physicians for Prevention of Nuc. War (founding v.p., participant Nobel Peace prize 1985), N.Am. Soc. Cardiac Radiology (pres. 1979—80), Radiol. Soc. N.Am. (Gold medal 1995), Am. Soc. Nephrology, Am. Heart Assn., Inst. Medicine, Assn. Univ. Radiologists (Gold medal 1984), Alpha Omega Alpha, Phi Beta Kappa. Achievements include Naming of Abrams Conf. Rm., radiology, bregham and women's hosp., 1984; Established of Herbert L. Abrams arrived lctr. of Harvard Med. Sch. bregham and women's hosp., 1985; Dedication of the endowed. Home: 714 Alvarado Stanford CA 94305 Office: Stanford U Sch Medicine 300 Pasteur Dr Stanford CA 94305-5105 E-mail: hlabrams@stanford.edu.

ABRAMS, JEFFREY STUART, sports medicine physician, surgeon; b. Oceanside, N.Y., Dec. 14, 1954; s. Murry M.I. and Iris M. (Weinberg) A.; m. Kathleen Ann Sweeny, Oct. 20, 1985; children: Matthew Joseph, Kimberly Beth. BS in Biology cum laude, Rensselaer Poly. Inst., 1976; MD, SUNY, Syracuse, 1980. Diplomate Am. Bd. Orthop. surgery. Surg. intern Santa Barbara (Calif.) Cottage Hosp., 1980-81; orthop. resident Thomas Jefferson U. Hosp., Phila., 1981-85; fellow shoulder surgery U. Western Ont., London, 1985; fellow sports medicine Orthop. Assn. Aspen and Glenwood, Aspen, Colo., 1985-86, Hughston Clinic, Columbus, Ga., 1986; assoc. med. dir. Princeton (N.J.) Orthop. and Rehab. Assn., 1986—; attending surgeon Princeton Med. Ctr., 1986—; chief shoulder surgery Sports Medicine Princeton, 1992—; pres. Princeton Orthopaedic Assocs., 2000—. Cons. sports sci. U.S. Tennis Assn., Key Biscayne, Fla., 1989—95; cons. exercise Music TV, N.Y.C., 1995—; cons. Internat. Mgmt. Group, N.Y.C., 1989—, Princeton U., 1986—, Mercer County C.C., West Windsor, NJ, 1986—, Peddie Sch., Hightstown, NJ, 1990—, West Windsor-Plainsboro Schs., 1986—, Med. Inter Ins. Exch., Lawrenceville, NJ, 1990—; physician World Cup Downhill Ski, Aspen, 1985—, N.J. Bell Invitational Tennis, Princeton, 1989—, NJCCA Nat. Soccer Finals, Mercer, 1986—96; cons. Penn-Jersey Spririts Soccer, NJ, 1990—92; internat. presenter in field; cons. Linvatec, Surg. Dynamics, Biomet/Arthrotek, Bionx, Oratec, Opus, Axya; lectr. Am. Acad. Orthop. Surgeons, 2001. Author: Orthopaedic Clinic of North America, 1987, Clinics in Sports Medicine, 1991, Shoulder Injuries in the Athlete, 1995, Shoulder Surgery for the Tennis Athlete, 1995, The Rotator Cuff, 1996, (CD-ROM) Shoulder Surgical Approaches, (videotapes) Instructional Arthroscopy Surgery, MTV: The Grind, Advanced Workout; patentee in field; contbr. articles to profl. jours., including Am. Jour. Sports Medicine, Jour. Bone and Joint Surgery, Orthopaedics, others; mem. rev. bd. Am. Jour. Sports Medicine, 1992—, Jour. Am. Assn. Orthop. Surgeons, 1994—, Jour. Am. Shoulder and Elbow Surgeons, 1995—. Bd. dirs. Med. Ctr. Princeton Found., 1992-95; celebrity waiter Am. Heart Assn., Princeton, 1993-94. Fellow: Hawkins Soc., Steadman-Hawkins Fellowship Soc., Am. Sports Medicine Fellowship Soc.; mem.: 20th Century Orthop. Surgeons, Am. Shoulder and Elbow Surgeons, Arthroscopic Assn. N. Am., Am. Acad. Orthoped. Surgery. Avocations: golf, tennis, skiing. Home: 23 Foulet Dr Princeton NJ 08540-7639 Office: Princeton Orthop/Rehab 325 Princeton Ave Princeton NJ 08540-1617 E-mail: rxbonz@aol.com.

ABRAMS, JOHN N. army officer; b. Ft. Knox, Ky., Sept. 3, 1946; BS in Bus., Bowling Green State U., 1972; MS in Pub. Adminstrn., Shippensburg (Pa.) State Coll.; postgrad., U.S. Army Command-Gen. Staff Coll., Ft. Leavenworth, Kans., 1975-76, U.S. Army War Coll., Carlisle Barracks, Pa., 1985-86. Enlisted man U.S. Army, 1966, commd. 2d lt., 1967, advanced through grades to gen., 1998; comdr. 1st squadron 11th Armored Cav. Rgt., U.S. Army Europe, Germany, 1983-85, asst. chief staff G-3, then chief staff 3d Armored Divsn., 1986-88, comdr. 11th Armored Cav. Rgt., V Corps, 1988-90; dep. dir. for ops., readiness and modlzn. Office Dep. Chief Staff for Ops. and Plans, U.S. Army, Washington, 1990-91; asst. divsn. comdr. 1st Cav. Divsn., Ft. Hood, Tex., 1991-93; comdg. gen. 2d Inf. Divsn., 8th U.S. Army, 1993-95; comdg. gen. V Corps U.S. Army Europe, 1995-97; dep. comdg. gen. Hdqs. Tng. and Doctrine Command, Dept. Army (TRADOC), Ft. Monroe, Va., 1997-98, comdg. gen., 1998—. Decorated D.S.M., Silver Star with oak leaf cluster, Legion of Merit with two oak leaf clusters, Bronze Star medal wiht V device and three oak leaf clusters, Purple Heart. Office: TRADOC 7 Fenwick Rd Fort Monroe VA 23651-1049

ABRAMS, LEE NORMAN, lawyer; b. Chgo., Feb. 28, 1935; s. Saul E. and Evelyn (Cohen) A.; m. Myrna Parker, Dec. 26, 1965; 1 dau., Elana Shira. AB, U. Mich., 1955, JD, 1957. Bar: Ill. 1957, U.S. Supreme Ct. 1961, U.S. Tax Ct. 1972. Assoc. firm Mayer, Brown, Rowe & Maw and predecessors, Chgo., 1957-66, ptnr., 1966—. Mem. visitors com. U. Mich. Law Sch., 1970—; bd. assocs. Nat. Coll. Edn., Chgo., 1973-80. Recipient Gold medal AICPA, 1958. Mem. ABA (coun. antitrust sect. 1975-77, fin. officer 1977-81, program chair antitrust sect. 1988-91, vice chair antitrust sect. 1991-92, chmn. forum on franchising 1982-85, chmn. antitrust com. sect. bus. law 1995-99), Chgo. Bar Assn. (antitrust law com. 1970-85), Ill. State Bar Assn. (antitrust section coun. 1994-2001), U.S. C. of C. (antitrust and trade regulation com. 1974-80), Briarwood Country Club, Royal and Ancient Golf Club of St. Andrews (Scotland). Office: Mayer Brown Rowe & Maw 190 S La Salle St Ste 3100 Chicago IL 60603-3441

ABRAMS, LEIGH JEFFREY, manufacturing company executive; b. N.Y.C., July 28, 1942; BBA, Baruch Coll., 1964. CPA, N.Y. Sr. auditor Ernest & Whinney, N.Y.C., 1964—68; exec. v.p. Drew Industries Inc., White Plains, NY, 1969—78, pres., CEO, dir., of specialty bldg. products mfg., 1979—. Bd. dirs. Impac Mortgage Holdings, Inc. Chmn., bd. dirs. YMCA; bd. dirs. Impac Mortgage Holdup Inc.; cons. Jr. Achievement Westchester, Inc., bd. dirs., 1992—, chmn. bd. Westchester chpt.; former soccer coach Dad's Club, White Plains; baseball mgr. Elmsford (N.Y.) Little League. Mem. Am. Inst. CPA's, N.Y. Soc. CPA's Home: 91 Ridge Rd Hartsdale NY 10530-2212 Office: Drew Industries Inc 200 Mamaroneck Ave White Plains NY 10601

ABRAMS, MARC, lawyer, state political party executive; b. N.Y.C., Mar. 23, 1957; s. Stephen Robert and Virginia Ornstein Abrams; m. Barbara Christopher, 1981; 1 child, Lawrence Christopher. BA magna cum laude, Wesleyan U., Middletown, Conn., 1978; MA, JD, U. Mich., 1981. Bar: Conn. 1982, N.Y. 1986, D.C. 1987, Pa. 1987, Oreg. 1989, U.S. Dist Ct. (so. dist.) N.Y. 1986, U.S. Dist. Co. (ea. dist.) Pa. 1988, U.S. Dist. Ct. Mont. 1989, U.S. Cir. Ct. (3d, 4th and 9th cirs.), U.S. Dist. Ct. Oreg. 1989, U.S. Supreme Ct. Asst. prof. U. Oreg., 1981-83; exec. dir. Student Press Law Ctr., 1983-85; pvt. practice, 1985—2002; sr. asst. atty. State of Oreg., 2002—. Co-author: Law of the Student Press, 1983, Confronting Wrongful Discharge Under Oregon and Washington Law, 1989. Vice chair Lane County (Oreg.) Dem. Ctrl. Com., 1981-82, Multnomah County (Oreg.) Dem. Ctrl. Com., 1991-92; mem. Oreg. Dem. State Ctrl. Com., 1981-82, 91—, Multnomah Edn. Svc. Dist. Bd., 1993-97, chmn., 1996-97; fin. chair Oreg. State Dem. Party, 1993-95, vice chair, 1994-97, chmn., 1997-99; mem. Portland Sch. Bd., 1995—, vice chair, 1998-2002; treas. Assn. State Dem. Chairs, 1998-99. Recipient Johnnie Phelps medal Vets. for Human Rights, 1995. Jewish. Office: 1753 NW Aspen Ave Portland OR 97210-1208

ABRAMS, MEYER HOWARD, English language educator; b. Long Branch, N.J., July 23, 1912; s. Joseph and Sarah (Shanes) A.; m. Ruth Gaynes, Sept. 1, 1937; children: Jane, Judith. AB, Harvard U., 1934, MA, 1937, PhD, 1940; postgrad. (Henry fellow), Cambridge (Eng.) U., 1934-35; D.H.L. (hon.), U. Rochester, 1978, Northwestern U., 1981, U. Chgo., 1982, Western Md. Coll., 1985, Le Moyne Coll., 1993, Carleton Coll., 2003. Instr. Harvard, 1938-42; research asso. psycho-acoustic lab. Harvard U., 1942-45; asst. prof. English, Cornell U., Ithaca, N.Y., 1945-47, asso. prof., 1947-53, prof., 1953-60, Frederic J. Whiton prof. English, 1960-73, Class of 1916 prof. English, 1973-83, prof. emeritus, 1983—. Adv. editor W.W. Norton & Co., Inc., 1961—; bd. editors various Cornell publs. Hon. sr. fellow Sch. Criticism and Theory, Cornell U., Fulbright lectr. Royal U. Malta, Cambridge U., 1953; Roache lectr. U. Ind., 1963; Alexander lectr. U. Toronto, 1964; Ewing lectures UCLA, 1975; Cecil Green lectr. U B.C., 1980; Lamont lectures Union Coll., 1995; Mem. founders group Nat. Humanities Ctr.; mem. coun. of scholars Libr. of Congress, 1980—, chmn. coun. of scholars, 1984-94. Author: The Milk of Paradise, 1934, 2d edit., 1970, The Mirror and the Lamp: Romantic Theory and the Critical Tradition, 1953, A Glossary of Literary Terms, 1957, 7th edit., 1998, Natural Supernaturalism: Tradition and Revolution in Romantic Literature, 1971, The Correspondent Breeze: Essays on English Romanticism, 1984, Doing Things with Texts: Essays in Criticism and Critical Theory, 1989, also publs. on mil. communications; editor: The Poetry of Pope, 1954; Editor: Literature and Belief, 1958, The Romantic Poets: Modern Essays in Criticism, 1960, rev. edit., 1975, The Norton Anthology of English Literature, 1962, 7th edit., 1999, Wordsworth: A Collection of Critical Essays, 1972, (with others) Wordsworth's Prelude: Norton Critical Edition, 1979. Recipient Christian Gauss prize Phi Beta Kappa, 1954, James Russell Lowell prize, 1971, Am. Acad. award humanistic studies, 1984, Disting. Scholar award Keats-Shelley Assn., 1987, Am. Acad. and Inst. Arts and Letters award for lit., 1990; Rockefeller fellow, 1946; Ford fellow, 1952; Guggenheim fellow, 1958, 60-61; fellow Center for Advanced Study in the Behavioral Scis., Palo Alto, Calif., 1967-68; vis. fellow All Soul's Coll., Oxford, 1977 Mem. AAUP, MLA (exec. council 1961-64), Am. Acad. Arts and Scis., Am. Acad. Arts and Letters, Am. Philos. Soc., Brit. Acad. (corr. fellow), Phi Beta Kappa, Sigma Xi. Home: 378 Savage Farm Dr Ithaca NY 14850-6505 E-mail: mha5@cornell.edu.

ABRAMS, NORMAN, law educator, university administrator; b. Chgo., July 7, 1933; s. Harry A. and Gertrude (Dick) A.; m. Toshka Alster, 1977; children: Marshall David, Julie, Hanna, Naomi. AB, U. Chgo., 1952, JD, 1955. Bar: Ill. 1956, US Supreme Ct. 1967. Assoc. in law Columbia U., 1955-57; rsch. assoc. Harvard U., 1957-59; sec. Harvard-Brandeis Coop. Rsch. for Israel's Legal Devel., 1957-58, dir., 1959; mem. faculty law sch. UCLA, 1959—, prof. law, 1964—, assoc. dean law, 1989-91, vice chancellor acad. pers., 1991-2001, interim exec. v. chancellor, spring 1998, co-dir. Ctr. for internat. and strategic studies, 1982-83, chmn. steering com., 1985-87, 88-89, interim dean law, 2003—; vis. prof. Hebrew U., 1969-70, Forchheimer vis. prof., 1986; vis. prof. Bar Ilan U., 1970-71, 78, U. So. Calif., 1972, Stanford U., Conn., 1977, U. Calif. at Berkeley, Calif., 1977, Loyola U., LA, summers 1974, 75, 76, 79; spl. asst. to US atty. gen., also prof.-in-residence criminal div. Dept. Justice, 1966-67. Reporter for So. Calif. indigent accused persons study Am. Bar Found., 1963; cons. Gov. Calif. Commn. L.A. Riots, 1965, Pres.'s Commn. Law Enforcement and Adminstrn. Justice, 1966-67, Nat. Commn. on Reform of Fed. Criminal Laws, 1967-69, Rand Corp., 1968-74, Ctr. for Adminstrv. Justice, ABA, 1973-77, Nat. Adv. Commn. on Criminal Justice Stds., Organized Crime Task Force, 1976; spl. hearing officer conscientious objector cases Dept. Justice, 1967-68; vis. scholar Inst. for Advanced Studies, Hebrew U., summer, 1994. Author: (with others) Evidence, Cases and Materials, 7th edit., 1983, 8th edit., 1988, 9th edit., 1997, Federal Criminal Law and Its Enforcement, 1986, 2d and 3d edits. (with S. Beale), 1993, 2000, Anti-terrorism and Criminal Enforcement, 2003; mem. editl. bd. Criminal Law Forum, 1990—. Chmn. Jewish Conciliation Bd., LA, 1975-81; bd. dir. Bet Tzedek, 1975-85, LA Hillel Coun., 1979-82, Shalhevet HS, 1998—; chmn. So. Calif. region Am. Prof. for Peace in Middle East, 1981-83; bd. dir. met. region Jewish Fedn., 1982-88, v.p. 1982-83; pres. Westwood Kehillah Congregation, 1985. Mem. Internat. Soc. for Reform of Criminal Law (mem. exec. com. 1994—), Phi Beta Kappa. Office: UCLA Law School 405 Hilgard Ave Los Angeles CA 90095-9000 E-mail: abrams@law.ucla.edu.

ABRAMS, ROBERT, lawyer, former state attorney general; b. Bronx, N.Y., July 4, 1938; s. Benjamin and Dorothy (Kaplan) A.; m. Diane B. Schulder, Sept. 15, 1974; children: Rachel Schulder, Becky Schulder. BA, Columbia U., 1960; JD, NYU, 1963; LL.D. (hon.), Hofstra U., 1979; Lugum Doctoris (hon.), Yeshiva U., 1984; LLD (hon.), L.I. U., 1989, Pace U., 1991. Mem. N.Y. State Assembly, 1965-69; pres. Borough of Bronx, 1970-78; atty. gen. State of N.Y., 1979-93; ptnr. Stroock & Stroock & Lavan, N.Y.C., 1994—. Panel mem. of disting. neutrals CPR Inst.; dir. Sterling Nat. Bank, Sterling Bancorp. Contbr. articles to profl. publs.; writer column Nat. Law Jour., N.Y. Law Jour., N.Y. Times, N.Y. Newsday, N.Y. Post, N.Y. Daily News, Buffalo News, Albany Times Union, Ganette Suburban Newspapers, The Harvard Environ. Law Rev., NYU Law Rev., Columbia Jour. Environ. Law, Pace Environ. Law Rev., Washburn Law Rev., Albany Law Rev., Pace Law Rev., The Jour. of State Gov. Pres. Citizens Union Found., Help Am. Vote Act - Impace and Potential for NY, Century Found.; del. Dem. Nat. Conv., 1972, 76, 80, 84, mem. platform com., 1988; elector Electoral Coll., 1988; co-chair Nat. Jewish Dem. Coun., N.Y.State. Recipient Adam Clayton Powell Pub. Svc. award, Interfaith award Coun. Chs., N.Y.C., Bronx Community Coll. medallion for Svc., Scroll of Honor plaque United Jewish Appeal, Benjamin Cardozo award for legal excellence Jewish Lawyers Guild, Brotherhood award B'nai B'rith, Man of Yr. award NAACP, Alumni Achievement award NYU Sch. Law, Environmentalist of Yr. award Environ. Planning Lobby N.Y., Disting. Pub. Svc. Citation Bus. Coun. N.Y. State, N.Y. State Sheriff's Assn. award, Nat. Crime Victims award, Torch of Liberty award Anti-Defamation League, Anatoly Scharansky Freedom award N.Y. Conf. Soviet Jewry, Environmentalist of Yr. award L.I. Pine Barrens Soc., Il Leone de San Marco Hon. Italian Am. award, Cavaliere medal Pres. Italy, Pres. award Marist Coll., Hubert Humphrey Humanitarian award United Fedn. Tchrs., Law Day award N.Y. State Trial Lawyers Assn., Contbns. to Urban Law award Fordham Law Jour., Deans medal Law Sch. NYU, Margaret Sanger award N.Y. State Family Planning Advocates, Lehman/LaGuardia Civic Achievement award Anti-Defamation League B'nai B'rith and Commn. on Social Justice of the Order of Sons of Italy, Father of the Yr. award Nat. Father's Day Com., B'nai Zion Bill of Rights award, Avodah award Jewish Tchr's. Assn., Man of the Yr. award N.Y. State Consumer Assembly, Rodef Tzedek Pursuer of Justice award Restructionist Rabbinical Coll., Humanitarian award Rochester Labor and Religious Coalition, Special Recognition award Profl. Women in Construction and Allied Industries, Humanitarian award Long Island Assn. for Children with Learning Disabilities, Man of the Yr. award Mental Ilness Found., N.Y. State Ct's. Man of the Yr. award Shamrai Tzedek Soc., Grand Marshall award Schenectady Labor Coun. Labor Day Parade, Louis Brandeis award Zionist Orgn. Am., Lubavich Tzivos Hashem award, Chassidius in Am. Exemplary Leadership award Bostoner Chassidum, Recognition for Pub. Svc. award Greater Buffalo AFL-CIO Coun., Effort on Behalf of the Elderly award Workmen's Circle Home & Infirmary For the Aged, Dedication Concerning Reproductive Rights award N.Y. Coun. of Jewish Women, Citation of Appreciation N.Y. State Assn. of Architects, Pesach-Tikvah Hope Developer award, Pub. Svc. award N.Y. Soc. Clin. Psychologists, Cmty. Achievement award Am. Orthodox Fedn., State Svc. award Nat. Columbus Day Com., Environmentalist of the Yr. award Sierra Club, Svc. award N.Y. State Jewish War Veterans, Cadet award N.Y.C. Mission Soc., Disting. Achievement award AMIT Women, Man of the Yr. award Nassau County Police Res. Assn., Ann. award Lubavitch Youth Orgn., Appreciation award Japanese C. of C. of N.Y., Friend of the Cmty. award Empire State Pride Agenda, Roland Smith award Capital Region chpt. N.Y. Civil Liberties Union, Scharansky Freedom award L.I. Com. on Soviet Jewry, Cert. of Honor award N.Y. League of Histadrut, Scouting For the Handicapped Outstanding Svc. award Greater N.Y. Coun. of Boy Scouts of Am., Citizen of the Yr. award We. N.Y. Labor Coalition, Svc. award Citizen's Coun. for the Cmty. of Mentally Retarded, Rockland Hosp. Guild, Man of the Yr. award The Shield Inst. for Retarded Children, Maccabean Svc. award N.Y. Bd. of Rabbis, Thurgood Marshall award Bridge Builders Albany, Pro Choice award Naral N.Y., Dist. Humanitarian award Insts. Applied Human Dynamics, Life-Long Dedication award Holocaust Meml. Com., Disting. Cmty. Svc. award Am. Friends of Bnei Akiva; named Man of Yr. St. Patrick's Home Aged and Infirm, Man of Yr. State Israel Bonds. Mem. N.Y. State Bar Assn. (Environ. Acheivement award), Assn. Bar City of N.Y., Nat. Assn. of Attys. Gen. (pres. 1988-89, chmn. environ. protection com. 1982-85, chmn. antitrust com. 1985-88, chmn. civil rights com. 1990-92, chmn. ea. regional conf. of attys. gen. 1983-84, Wyman award for Outstanding Atty. Gen. in the Nation 1991, commn. campaign fin. reform), Assn. Bar City NY. Democrat. Office: Stroock & Stroock & Lavan 180 Maiden Ln Ste 3989 New York NY 10038-4937 Office Fax: 212-806-6006.

ABRAMS, ROGER IAN, law educator, arbitrator; b. Newark, July 30, 1945; s. Avel S. and Myrna (Posner) A.; m. Frances Elise Kovitz, June 1, 1969; children: Jason, Seth. BA, Cornell U., 1967; JD, Harvard U., 1970. Bar: Mass. 1970, U.S. Dist. Ct. Mass. 1971, U.S. Ct. Appeals (1st cir.) 1971. Law clk. to Judge Frank M. Coffin U.S. Ct. Appeals (1st cir.), Boston, 1970-71; assoc. Foley, Hoag & Eliot, Boston, 1971-74; prof. law Law. Sch. Case Western Res. U., Cleve., 1974-86; dean Law Ctr. Nova U., Ft. Lauderdale, Fla., 1986-93; dean Law Sch. Rutgers U., Newark, 1993-1998; prof. law sch. Rutger U., Newark, 1993-99; Herbert J. Hannuch scholar Rutgers U., Newark, 1998-99; dean Northeastern U., Boston, 1999—2002, Richardson prof. law, 1999—. Labor arbitrator Fed. Mediation Svc., 1975—; mem. gender bias report implementation com. Fla. Supreme Ct. Author: Legal Bases: Baseball and the

Law, 1998, The Money Pitch: Baseball Free Agency and Salary Arbitration, 2000, The First World Scenes and the Baseball Fanatics of 1903, 2003; contbr. articles to law jours. Bd. dirs. Inst. for Continuing Legal Edn., N.J., 1993-98. Recipient Gen. Counsel's Advocacy award NAACP, Boston, 1974; inductee Union N.J. Hall of Fame, 1995. Mem. Am. Law Inst., Am. Bar Found., Am. Arbitration Assn. (labor arbitrator). Democrat. Jewish. Avocations: swimming, distance walking, reading. Office: Northeastern Univ Sch Law 400 Huntington Ave Boston MA 02115-5005 E-mail: rabrams@neu.edu.

ABRAMS, SHERI, lawyer; b. N.Y.C. BSBA, Boston U., 1989; JD, George Washington U., 1994. Bar: Va. 1995, D.C. 1996, U.S. Dist. Ct. (ea. dist.) Va., D.C. Ct. Appeals, U.S. Ct. Appeals (4th cir.), U.S. Supreme Ct. Pvt. practice, Fairfax, Va. Mem.: ABA, Nat. Orgn. Social Security Claimants Reps., Fairfax County Bar Assn., Ctrl. Fairfax C. of C. Office: 3915 Old Lee Hwy Ste 22A Fairfax VA 22030-4106 E-mail: sheri@sheriabrams.com.

ABRAMS, STANLEY DAVID, lawyer; b. Washington, Jan. 30, 1940; s. Norman J. and Sally (Taylor) A.; m. Patricia Dreisen, June 7, 1964; children: Suzanne Bari, Lori Paige. BS, U. Md., 1962, LLB, 1966, JD, 1969. Bar: Md. 1966. Trial atty. FTC, Washington, 1966-67; sr. asst. county atty. Montgomery County, Rockville, Md., 1967-71, adminstrv. hearing examiner, 1971-79; ptnr. Levitan, Ezrin, West & Kerxton, P.C., Bethesda, Md., 1979-84; city atty. City of Gaithersburg, Md., 1979—; ptnr. Abrams, West, Storm, and Diamond P.C., Bethesda, 1984—. Cons. Md. Nat. Capital Park and Planning Commn., Silver Spring, 1987, Washington Met. Transit Authority, 1985; mem. faculty ALI/ABA Land Use Inst., Phila., 1981—, Continuing Legal Edn. Inst. Md. Bar, Balt., 1980—. Author: Guide to Maryland Zoning Decisions, 1993, 4th edit., 2002, How to Win the Zoning Game, 1978; co-author: Handling the Land Use Case, 1984, Land Use Practice and Forms, 1997; contbg. author: Maryland Appellate Practice Handbook, 1977. With U.S. Army, 1958—62. Mem. Md. Bar Assn., Montgomery County Bar Assn. (sec. chmn. 1967—), Md. Bar Found., Urban Land Inst., Bethesda-Chevy Chase C. of C. (pres. 1983). Democrat. Jewish. Avocations: travel, writing, lecturing. Home: 15101 Emory Ln Rockville MD 20853-1655 Office: Abrams West and Storm PC 4550 Montgomery Ave Ste 760N Bethesda MD 20814-3379 E-mail: sabrams@awsdlaw.com.

ABRAMS, SYLVIA FLECK, religious studies educator; b. Buffalo, Apr. 5, 1942; d. Abraham and Ann (Hanf) Fleck; m. Ronald M. Abrams, June 30, 1963; children: Ruth, Sharon. BA magna cum laude, Western Res. U., 1963, MA, 1964, PhD, 1988; BHL, Cleve. Coll. Jewish Studies, 1976, MHL, 1983; postgrad., U. Haifa, 1975, Yad Va Shem Summer Inst., Hebrew U., 1983. Hebrew tchr. The Temple, 1959-77, Hebrew coord., 1973-77; tchr. Beachwood H.S., 1964-66; tchr. Hebrew and social studies Agnon Sch., Cleve., 1975-77, social studies resource tchr., 1976-77; ednl. dir. Temple Emanu El, Cleve., 1977-85; asst. dir. Cleve. Bur. Jewish Edn., 1985-92, acting exec. v.p., 1993-94; exec. dir. ednl. svcs. Jewish Edn. Ctr. Cleve., 1994-99; dean Siegal Coll. of Judaic Studies, 1999—. Chmn. ednl. dirs. coun. Cleve. Bd. Jewish Edn., 1982-85. Editor: You and Your Schools, 1972. Appointed to Ohio Coun. Holocaust Edn., 1986; co-chair Cmty. Holocaust Remembrance Com., 1999-2001, bd. dirs. 2001. Recipient Elbert J. Benton award Western Res. U., 1963; Fred and Rose Rosenwasser Bible award Coll. Jewish Studies, 1974; Emmanuel Gamoran Meml. Curriculum award Nat. Assn. Temple Educator, 1978; Samuel Lipson Meml. award Coll. Jewish Studies, 1981, Bingham fellow Case Western Res. U., 1984-86. Mem. ASCD, Nat. Assn. Temple Educators (bd. dirs. 1984-88), Coun. Jewish Edn. (bd. dirs. 1991—, v.p. 1995), Assn. Dirs. Ctrl. Agys. (sec.-treas. 1995-98), Coalition for Advancement of Jewish Edn. (bd. mem. at large 1989-93, chair 1996-2000, bd. dirs. 2000-03), Union Am. Hebrew Congregations (Israel curriculum task force), Cleve. Bur. Jewish Edn. (chmn. ednl. dirs. coun. 1982-85), Nat. Coun. Jewish Women (life), Hadassah (life), Phi Beta Kappa. Jewish. Office: Siegal Coll of Judaic Studies 26500 Shaker Blvd Cleveland OH 44122-7197

ABRAMS-HAKEEM, VENITA M. performing arts educator, theater producer, director, performing company executive; b. Chgo., Feb. 6, 1968; d. Alfonzo and Sandra Scales; 1 child, Cedric Abdul-Hakeem Jr. Tng. in drama, Black Theatre Workshop, 1987; BA in Comm., Columbia Coll., 1991; tng. in modeling, Cleo Johnson Charm Sch., 1995—96. Tchr. Bd. of Edn., Chgo., 1992; founder, dir., prodr. Neke Theatre Co., Chgo., 1992—; tchr. Bd. of Edn., Chgo., 1995—; family educator Maryville Acad., Chgo., 1995; instr. drama Guggenheim Elem. Sch., Chgo., 1994—96; tchr. drama Cleo Johnson Charm Sch., Chgo., 1996. Author: (1 act play) The Color of My Eyes, 1995, (children's books) Prince C.J. Take that Golden Road to Success, 2002, (poetry book) Shattered But Not Broken, 2002, (plays) Wanting Memories, 2002; dir.(prodr.): (Cable Access shows, plays) Cable Access, 1991—94, (comml.) Cross Colors, 1992, (runway) The Saber Room Cleo Johnson's 39th Anniversary Show, 1996, Daley Ctr. Ann. Modeling Downtown Showcase, 1996, Congress Hotel Lady Legends, 1998, (talent show) Be Optimistic, 1991, Any Which Way, 1992, Artists from the Underground, 1992; (plays) The Color of My Eyes, 1992, 1996; performer: Soul Mother of Poetry Black People Reuniting, 1997; performer: (narrator) Mzimu, 1998; actor(various characters): (plays) B.T.W., 1986—88, (1 character) Jamaican Girl, 1987, My Eyes, 1992, 1996, (lead character) Zooman, 1990. Motivational lectr. Israel Cmty. Ch., Chgo., 1997. Recipient Best Actree, Monologue, Poetry award, Cleo Johnson's Sch., MAAI Conv., Wash., 1987, Oratory, Extemporaneous Reading award, Black Theatre Workshop, NASDA Conv., Chgo., 1988, Monologue, Soaps, Photography, Runway award, Cleo Johnson's Sch., MAAI Conv., Chgo., 1996. Avocations: modeling, writing, acting, producing, reciting poetry.

ABRAMSON, ARTHUR SEYMOUR, linguistics educator, researcher; b. Jersey City, Jan. 26, 1925; s. Seymour Vallie (Olshan) A.; m. Ruby Melamed, June 27, 1952 (div. May 1985); children: Joseph B., David N. Student, Rutgers U., 1942-43; BA, Yeshiva U., 1949; MA, Columbia U., 1950, PhD, 1960. Tchr. English and French Pub. High Schs., Jersey City, 1950-53; research staff Haskins Labs., N.Y.C., 1959-63, 64-65, research assoc., 1963-64, 65—; assoc. prof. speech CUNY, 1963-64, prof. communication arts and scis., 1965-67, prof. linguistics U. Conn., Storrs, 1967-92, prof. emeritus, 1992—, head dept. linguistics, 1967-74. Fulbright tchr. Bangkok and Songkhla, Thailand, 1953-55; vis. prof. Lady Davis Fellowship Trust, Jerusalem, 1981. Author: The Vowels and Tones of Standard Thai: Acoustical Measurements and Experiments; editor Language and Speech, 1975-87; contbr. numerous articles to profl. jours. With U.S. Army, 1943-46, ETO. Am. Coun. Learned Socs. fellow, 1973-74, Ford Found. fellow, Thailand, 1973-74. Fellow Acoustical Soc. Am., Internat. Soc. Phonetic Scis. (v.p. 1985-91); mem. MLA, Permanent Coun. for Orgn. Internat. Congresses of Phonetic Scis., Linguistic Soc. Am. (sec.-treas. 1974-78, v.p. 1982, pres. 1983), Internat. Phonetic Assn. (coun. 1986-90), Am. Soc. Phonetic Scis., S.E. Asian Linguistics Soc., Siam Soc., Conn. Acad. Arts. and Scis., Phi Kappa Phi. Democrat. Jewish. Home: 43 Timber Dr Storrs Mansfield CT 06268-1210 Office: U Conn Dept of Linguistics U-145 337 Mansfield Rd Storrs Mansfield CT 06269-1145 also: Haskins Labs 270 Crown St New Haven CT 06511-6610 E-mail: abramson@uconnvm.uconn.edu.

ABRAMSON, CLARENCE ALLEN, pharmaceutical company executive, lawyer; b. Ft. Worth, Oct. 15, 1937; s. Samuel and Katherine (Berg) A.; m. Maureen L. Foley, May 15, 1962; children: Steven T., Eric M., Katherine M. BBA, U. Tex., 1952, JD, 1954. Bar: Tex. 1954, N.Y. 1963, N.J. 1972, Pa. 1974. Ptnr. Wynne & Wynne, Dallas, 1954-61; atty. SEC, Washington, 1961-62; of counsel Mobil Oil Corp., N.Y., The Hague and London, 1962-69; internat. gen. counsel Merck & Co., Inc., Rahway, N.J., 1970-86, assoc. gen. counsel, 1986-89, sec., chief counsel, 1989-90, v.p., sec., 1991-93; dir., founder Poly Pharm Inc., N.Y.C., 1993—; pres. Health Care Ventures Internat., Inc., Scotch Plains, N.J., 1994—; co-founder, mng. dir. Gulf Stream Pharms., LLC, Boca Raton, Fla., 1995. Bd. dirs. Handy & Harman, Inc., Polypharm, Inc., Acorda Therapeutics, Inc., Gliamed, Inc., N'Gene Pharma Inc.; bd. dirs., chmn. bd. Gulfstream Pharma LLC, Scotch Plains; mem. adv. bd. Inst. Circadian Physiology, Cambridge, Mass.; adj. prof. legal studies Montclair State U. Trustee Cmty. Health Law Project. Mem. ABA, Tex. Bar Assn., N.J. Bar Assn., Pa. Bar Assn., N.Y. State Bar Assn. Avocations: golf, tennis, squash, gardening, travel. Office: 27 Blackbirch Rd Scotch Plains NJ 07076-2941

ABRAMSON, EDWARD J. magazine publisher; Publisher Car and Driver, Ann Arbor, Home Mag., N.Y.C., 1999—2000; v.p. Hachette Filipacchi Mags., 2000—, group pub., 2000—. Office: Hachette Filipacchi Magazines Inc 1633 Broadway New York NY 10019-6708 also: Car & Driver 2002 Hogback Rd Ann Arbor MI 48105*

ABRAMSON, ELLIOTT MYRON, law educator, researcher; b. N.Y.C., Sept. 26, 1939; s. Max Abramson and Kate Heichman; m. Rochelle Linda Lattman, June 7, 1964; children: Monica, Jerome. BA, Columbia U., N.Y.C., 1960; JD, Harvard U., 1963. Bar: N.Y. 1964. Trial atty. U.S. SEC, N.Y.C., 1964—67; asst. prof. law Loyola U., L.A., 1967—69; assoc. Phillips Nizer Benjamin et al, N.Y.C., 1969—73; prof. law Willamette U., Salem, Oreg., 1973—79, DePaul U., Chgo., 1979—93; ret. Dir. New World Symphony, Miami Beach, Fla., 1999—. Contbr. articles to profl. jours. Alt. del. Dem. Nat. Conv., Miami, 1972. Harvard fellow in law and humanities, NEH, 1974—75. Mem.: John Ruskin Soc., William Morris Soc., Phi Beta Kappa. Avocations: classical music, tennis, philosophy, baseball history.

ABRAMSON, HANLEY NORMAN, pharmacy educator; b. Detroit, June 10, 1940; s. Frederick Jacob and Lillian (Kampner) A.; m. Young Hee Kim, Aug. 4, 1967; children: Nathaniel, Deborah, Stephen. BS in Pharmacy, Wayne State U., 1962; MS in Pharm. Chemistry, U. Mich., 1963, PhD in Pharm. Chemistry, 1966. Registered pharmacist. Rsch. assoc. The Hebrew U., Jerusalem, 1966-67; asst. prof. Wayne State U., Detroit, 1967-73, assoc. prof., 1973-78, prof., 1978—, chmn. dept. pharm. sci., 1986-95, interim dean Eugene Applebaum Coll. of Pharmacy and Health Scis., 1987—88, assoc. provost, 1991-95, assoc. dean, 1996-99, dep. dean pharmacy, 2000—02. Author numerous published articles in field of medicinal chemistry. Bd. trustees 1st Bapt. Ch. of Oak Park, Mich., 1974-78; deacon Bloomfield Hills (Mich.) Bapt. Ch., 1986-89; dir. Met. Detroit Alliance for Minority Participation, 1994-2000. Recipient rsch. grants Mich. Heart Assn., Detroit, 1967-76, Nat. Cancer Inst., Bethesda, Md., 1982-91. Mem. AAAS, Am. Chem. Soc., Am. Pharm. Assn., Am. Assn. Colls. Pharmacy. Baptist. Avocations: astronomy, numismatics, baseball history, classical music. Home: 5530 Hammersmith Dr West Bloomfield MI 48322-1452 Office: Wayne State U 3607 Applebaum Bldg Detroit MI 48201

ABRAMSON, HAROLD CALVIN, federal bankruptcy judge; b. 1928; Student, Ga. inst. Tech., 1944-45; BBA, U. Tex., 1948, LLB with honors, 1949. Bar: Tex. 1949, U.S. Dist. Ct. (no. dist.) Tex. 1951. Pvt. practice, 1952-85; judge U.S. Bankruptcy Ct., Dallas, 1985—. With USN, 1948-52. Mem. Nat. Assn. Bankruptcy Judges, Dallas Bar Assn., Tex. Bar Found. Office: US Bankruptcy Ct 1100 Commerce St Ste 12a24 Dallas TX 75242-1013 Fax: 214-753-2116.

ABRAMSON, HYMAN NORMAN, engineering and science research executive; b. San Antonio, Mar. 4, 1926; s. Nathan and Pearl (Westerman) A.; m. Idelle Rebecca Ringel, Apr. 20, 1947; children: Phillip David, Mark Donald. BSME, Stanford U., 1950, MS in Engring. Mechanics, 1951; PhD in Engring. Mechanics (So. Fellowship Fund fellow), U. Tex., Austin, 1956. Engr. U.S. Naval Air Missile Test Center, Point Mugu, Calif., 1947-48; project engr. Chance Vought Aircraft Co., Dallas, 1951-52; assoc. prof. aero. engring. Tex. A&M U., 1952-55; sect. mgr., dept. dir. S.W. Research Inst., San Antonio, 1956-72, v.p. div. engring. scis., 1972-85, exec. v.p., 1985-91, also bd. dirs. Mem. many research adv. coms. U.S. Govt.; bd. dirs. Broadway Nat. Bank. Author: An Introduction to the Dynamics of Airplanes, 1958, reprinted, 1971; contbr. numerous articles to profl. publs.; editor: (with others) Applied Mechanics Surveys, 1966, The Dynamic Behavior of Liquids in Moving Containers, 1966; assoc. editor: (with others) Applied Mechanics Revs, 1954-85; editorial adv. bd.: (with others) Jour. Computers and Structures, 1970—, Aeros. and Astronautics, 1975-80. Mem. Greater San Antonio C. of C., and City of San Antonio Market Sq. Adv. Com., 1973-77; mem. U.S. Bicentennial Com. of San Antonio, 1975-76; mem. adv. bd. dirs. U.S. Alamo, Inc., 1985-90; mem. adv. bd. Karta Techs., 1991—. Served with USN, 1943-45. Fellow AIAA (Disting. Service award 1973, dir., Structures, Structural Dynamics and Materials medal 1991), ASME (v.p., gov., hon. mem. 1979, Gold medal 1999); mem. Nat. Acad. Engring., Soc. Naval Architects and Marine Engrs., Nat. Acad. Engring. Mexico, AAAS, Sigma Xi. Republican. Jewish. Home: 1511 Spanish Oaks San Antonio TX 78213-1635 Office: SW Research Inst PO Box 28510 San Antonio TX 78228-0510

ABRAMSON, JILL, newspaper publishing executive; AB in History and Lit., Harvard U., 1976. Stringer Time mag., 1974-76, Boston bur. mgr., reporter, 1976-77; with NBC News Election Unit, 1979-81; sr. writer Am. Lawyer, 1981-88; editor Legal Times, 1986-88; with New York Times, Washington, 1988—, Chernoff Silver, 1988-97; dep. bur. chief The Wall Street Jour., 1993-97; enterprise editor Washington bur. New York Times, 1997—2003, mng. editor, 2003—. Co-author: Where They Are Now: The Story of Women of Harvard Law 1974, 1976, Strange Justice, 1994. Office: NY Times 229 W 43rd St New York NY 10036

ABRAMSON, PAUL ROBERT, political scientist, educator; b. St. Louis, Nov. 28, 1937; s. Harry Benjamin and Hattie Abramson; m. Janet Carolyn Schwartz, Sept. 11, 1966; children— Lee Jacob, Heather Lyn BA, Washington U., St. Louis, 1959; MA, U. Calif.-Berkeley, 1961, PhD, 1967. Asst. prof. polit. sci. Mich. State U., East Lansing, 1967-71, assoc. prof. polit. sci., 1971-77, prof. polit. sci., 1977—. Lady Davis vis. prof. Hebrew U. Jerusalem, 1994. Author: Generational Change in American Politics, 1975, The Political Socialization of Black Americans, 1977, Political Attitudes in America, 1983; co-author: Change and Continuity in the 1980 Elections, 1982, rev. edit., 1983, Change and Continuity in the 1984 Elections, 1986, rev. edit., 1987, Change and Continuity in the 1988 Elections, 1990, rev. edit., 1991, Change and Continuity in the 1992 Elections, 1994, rev. edit., 1995, Value Change in Global Perspective, 1995, Change and Continuity in the 1996 Elections, 1998, Change and Continuity in the 1996 and 1998 Elections, 1999, Change and Continuity in the 2000 Elections, 2002, Change and Continuity in the 2000 and 2003 Elections, 2003; contbr. articles to profl. jours. Served to lt. U.S. Army, 1960—62. Woodrow Wilson fellow, 1959-60; Ford Found. faculty research fellow, 1972-73; Fulbright grantee sr. lectr. Hebrew U. of Jerusalem, 1987-88. Mem. Am. Polit. Sci. Assn., Midwest Polit. Sci. Assn., So. Polit. Sci. Assn., Am. Sociol. Assn., Internat. Polit. Sci. Assn., Phi Beta Kappa Home: 2830 Turtlecreek Dr East Lansing MI 48823-6333 Office: Mich State U Dept Polit Sci East Lansing MI 48824-1032 E-mail: abramson@msu.edu.

ABRAMSON, SARA JANE, radiologist, educator; b. New Orleans, La., May 12, 1945; m. Walter Squire; children: Harrison, Russell, Zachary, Andrew. BA, Sarah Lawrence Coll., 1967; postgrad., Tulane U., 1967-69; MD, Mt. Sinai Sch. Medicine, 1971. Diplomate Am. Bd. Radiology, cert. added qualifications pediat. radiology. Intern in pediatrics Mt. Sinai Hosp., N.Y.C., 1971-72, resident in pediatrics, 1972-73; resident in radiology St. Luke's Children's Mercy Hosp., Kansas City, Mo., 1973-76; asst. prof. radiology U. Mo., 1976-79, Harvard U. Med. Sch., Cambridge, Mass., 1979-81; fellow in pediatric radiology Children's Hosp., Boston, 1979-81; asst. prof. radiology Columbia Coll. Physicians & Surgeons, N.Y.C., 1981-88, assoc. prof. radiology, 1988-93; assoc. attending radiologist Babies Hosp. Columbia Presbyn. Med. Ctr., N.Y.C., 1981-93, dep. dir. divsn. pediatric radiology, 1992-93; assoc. prof. radiology Cornell U. Med. Coll., N.Y.C., 1993-99, prof., 1999—; assoc. attending radiologist, assoc. mem. Sloan-Kettering Cancer Ctr., Meml. Hosp., N.Y.C., 1993-98, attending radiologist, mem., 1999—. Mem. radiology elective program Columbia U. Med. Sch., N.Y.C., 1981-93, radiology residency program reevaluation, 1984-93, program coord. affiliated hosps. teaching program, 1991-93, med. student advisor, 1991-93; mem. faculty coun. Columbia U., 1987-93; cons. in pediatric radiology Blythedale Children's Hosp., 1982—, Bet Israel Hosp., N.Y.C., 1983—, Harlem Hosp., N.Y.C., 1983—, N.Y. Foundling Hosp., 1988—, Lenox Hill Hosp., 1990—, Morristown Meml. Hosp., 1990—; lectr., presenter in field. Contbr. over 40 articles to profl. jours., chpts. to books. Named Radiology Tchr. of Yr., Columbia Coll. Physicians and Surgeons, 1992. Fellow Am. Coll. Radiology (del. N.Y. chpt. 1991—, alt. del. 1984-91, co-chair nominating com. 2000—); mem. AMA, Soc. for Pediat. Radiology (bd. dirs. 2000—), Radiology Soc. N.Am., European Soc. for Pediat. Radiology, Soc. Thoracic Radiology, Am. Assn. Ultrasound in Medicine, Am. Assn. Women in Radiology, N.Y. Roentgen Soc. (exec. com. 1999—, sec.-treas. 1991-94, v.p. 1996-97, pres.-elect 1997-98, pres. 1998-99, moderator, pediat. program chair spring conf. 1991), N.Y. State Radiological Soc. (chmn. residents sect. 1998—, treas. 2002—, guest lectr. spring conf. 1990-98), Nat. Children's Cancer Study Group, Caffey Soc., Neuhauser Soc., Kirkpatrick Soc. Office: Sloan-Kettering Cancer Ctr 1175 York Ave New York NY 10021-7169

ABRAMSON, STEPHANIE W. advertising executive, lawyer; b. Dec. 24, 1944; BA, Radcliffe Coll., 1966, JD, NYU, 1969. Bar: N.Y. 1969. Mem. Morgan, Lewis & Bockius, N.Y.C.; exec. v.p. and gen. counsel Young & Rubicam Inc, N.Y.C; legal officer, chief corp. devel. officer Heidrick & Struggles Internat. Inc., N.Y.C. Office: Heidrick & Struggles Internat 245 Park Ave New York NY 10167

ABRAVANEL, ALLAN RAY, lawyer; b. N.Y.C., Mar. 11, 1947; s. Leon and Sydelle (Berenson) A.; m. Susan Ava Paikin, Dec. 28, 1971; children: Karen, David. BA magna cum laude, Yale U., 1968; JD cum laude, Harvard U., 1971. Bar: N.Y. 1972, Oreg. 1976. Assoc. Paul, Weiss, Rifkind, Wharton & Garrison, N.Y.C., 1971-72, 74-76; fellow Internat. Legal Ctr., Lima, Peru, 1972-74; from assoc. to ptnr. Stoel, Rives, Boley, Fraser & Wyse, Portland, Oreg., 1976-83; ptnr. Perkins Coie, Portland, 1983—. Editor, pub. Abravanel Family Newsletter. Chair Oreg. Internat. Trade Com., Oreg. Dist. Export Coun. Mem. ABA, Portland Met. C. of C. Office: Perkins Coie 1211 SW 5th Ave Portland OR 97204-3713

ABREU, BOBBY, professional baseball player; b. Aragua, Venezuela, Mar. 11, 1974; 1 child, Emily Paola. With Astros, 1990-97, right fielder, 1997-98; outfielder Phila. Phillies Maj. Baseball League, 1998—. Office: Phila Phillies PO Box 7575 Philadelphia PA 19101-7575 also: Philadelphia Phillies Veterans Stadium 3501 South Broad Street Philadelphia PA 19148

ABREU, PAULA CRISTINA, statistician, researcher; b. Tomar, Portugal, Jan. 22, 1968; d. Benjamim Lopes and Maria Odete Spencer Salomao Abreu(Stepmother); m. Bernardo Piquet Carneiro, Oct. 7, 1969. MS in Applied Math. and Stats., SUNY, Stony Brook, 1992; DPH in Biostatistics, Columbia U., 1999. Lectr. Columbia U., N.Y.C., 1996—99; rsch. statistician Schering Plough Rsch. Inst., Kenilworth, NJ, 2000—. Instr. SUNY, Stony Brook, 1991—93, biostatistics and epidemiology cons., 1992—92; statis. cons. Mt. Sinai Sch. Medicine, N.Y.C., 1996—99. Contbr. articles to profl. jours. Scholar, SUNY, Stony Brook, 1993, Portuguese NRC, 1994—98; John W. Fertig Meml. fellow, Columbia U., 1999. Mem.: Internat. Biometric Soc., Am. Statis. Assn. Home: Apt 6B 99 Jane St New York NY 10014 Office: Schering-Plough Rsch Inst 2015 Galloping Hill Rd K-15-2445 Kenilworth NJ 07033 Personal E-mail: paula.abreu@usa.net.

ABREU, SUE HUDSON, physician, army officer, organizational and health-care consultant; b. Indpls., May 24, 1956; d. M.B. Hudson and Wilma (Jones) Hudson Black. BS in Engring., Purdue U., 1978; MD, Uniformed Services U., 1982; grad., U.S. Army Command & Gen. Staff, 1988, Armed Forces Staff Coll., 1990. Commd. 2d lt. U.S. Army, 1978, advanced to col., 1999, ret., 2002; intern Walter Reed Army Med. Ctr., Washington, 1982-83, resident in diagnostic radiology, 1983-85, fellow in nuc. medicine, 1985-87, staff nuc. medicine physician, 1987-88; med. rsch. fellow Walter Reed Army Inst. Rsch., Washington, 1988-89; chief nuc. medicine svc. Womack Army Med. Ctr., Ft. Bragg, NC, 1990—96, chief dept. radiology, 1991-92, 96-98, med. dir. quality assurance, 1998-2001, asst. dep. commdr. clin. svcs., 2001—02); orgnl. and healthcare cons., 2002—. Nuc. medicine cons. to Army Surgeon Gen., 2000-2002; bd. dirs. Intersocietal Commn. for Accreditation Nuclear Medicine Labs., 2001-, sec. 2003. Named Outstanding Interdisciplinary engr., Purdue U., 2001. Fellow Am. Coll. Nuclear Physicians (pres. 2001); mem. Am. Coll. Radiology, Soc. Nuclear Medicine, Soc. Women Engrs., Am. Soc. Nuclear Cardiology, U.S. Parachute Assn., Mortar Bd., Tau Beta Pi, Omicron Delta Kappa, Phi Kappa Phi., Sigma Gamma Tau. Avocations: calligraphy, parachuting. Home: 613 Saddlebred Ln Raeford NC 28376-5535 Fax: 910-875-3886. E-mail: sueabreu@mindspring.com.

ABRIL, MARCIA (ELA I. CARDINAS), writer; b. Jesus Maria, Santander, Colombia, Mar. 21, 1928; came to U.S., 1985; d. Jorge Benjamin and Ana Isabel (Valenzuela) Tellez; m. Rafael A. Cardenas, Mar. 12, 1959; children: Willyam, Harold, Alix, Ela, Rafael, Katiana. BA in Edn. and Psychology, Normal Superior A. Narino, Malaga, Santander, 1950. Prodr. Continental Network Channel 14 TV, Miami, Fla., 1989. Participant/writer Mcpl. Matanzas en el Exilio, Miami, Fla., 1986. Author: Para ti Cartagena, 1982, Aguilas e Ilusiones, 1986, Insolito, 1990, 2d edit., 1995, Girasol y Yo, 1994, Viento y Sol, 1995; author/composer: Colombia Aqui Esta tu Gente, Miami, 1986. Vol. Empresa Promotora de Turismo, Cartagena, 1982-83; benefactor Biblioteca Nacional, Bogota, Colombia, 1982, U. Nacional de Colombia, Bogota, 1982; guest/participant Primer Encuentro de la Cultura Hispanoamericana, Bogota, 1983. Recipient Honorary award Municipio de Matanzas en el Exilio, Miami, 1986, Meritory award Eva Am. Prodns., 1995, Cert. of Recognition, U.S. Libr. of Congress, 1995. Roman Catholic. Avocations: writing, dancing, swimming, reading. Office: 815 SW 8th St Miami FL 33130-3703

ABROHAMS, JANICE ELAINE, social work supervisor; b. Green Bay, Wis. d. Charles E. and Sadye Joyce (Glick) Abrohams. BA, MSSW, U. Wis., Madison. Lic. clin. social worker, Ill. Clin. social worker Hawthorne Cedar Knolls Residential Treatment Ctr., N.Y.C., 1962-64, Jewish Family Svcs., Milw., 1964-68, Chgo., 1968-70; social work adminstr. Children and Adolescent Unit Ill. Dept. Mental Health, Hines, 1971-91; pvt. practice, cons. Chgo., 1971—. Avocations: tennis, tap dance, ballet, piano. Home: 340 W Diversey Pky Chicago IL 60657-6241

ABRUTYN, ELIAS, infectious diseases physician, administrator; b. Jersey City, Apr. 15, 1940; s. Samuel Bruce and Eva A.; m. Leslye Silver, Dec. 23, 1978; children: Alex, Adam. BA, U. Pa., 1960; MD, U. Pitts., 1966. Intern Hosp. of U. Pa., Phila., 1966-67, resident in internal medicine, 1967-68; chief resident in internal medicine U. Pa., VA Hosp., Phila., 1970-71; asst. prof. medicine U. Pa., Phila., 1972-78, Med. Coll. Pa., Phila., 1978-79, assoc. prof. medicine, 1979-82, prof. medicine, 1982—; assoc. dean VA affairs Med. Coll. Pa., Hahnemann U., Phila., 1991-97; vice-chmn. medicine Allegheny U. Health Scis., MCP Hahnemann Sch. Medicine, Phila., 1996—, interim chmn. dept. medicine, 1998-2000; assoc. provost, assoc. dean faculty affairs Coll. Medicine Drexel U., Phila., 2000—, interim chief Infectious Diseases, 2002—. Prof. pub. health Allegheny U. Health Scis., 1997. Assoc. editor Annals of Internal Medicine, 1978—; mem. editl. bd. Infectious Disease Practice, 1991—, Clinical Performance and Quality Health Care, 1995—. With USPHS, 1968-70. Adj. scholar Ctr. Epidemiology and Biostats. U. Pa. Sch. Medicine, 2002; recipient Heard award in Surgery, 1965. Master ACP-ASIM; fellow Infectious Disease Soc.; mem. AMA (alt. del. 1991-94), Am. Fedn. Clin. Rsch., Am. Fedn. for Clin. Medicine, Am. Soc. Microbiology, Soc. Healthcare Epidmiology Am. (treas. 1991-95, v.p. 1996, pres.-elect 1997, pres. 1998), Nat. Found. Infectious Diseases (sec. Pa. chpt. 1985-91), Pa. Med. Soc., Pa. Soc. Infectious Disease, Phila. County Med. Soc., Hosp. Infection Soc. (England), Epidemic Intelligence Svc. Alumni Assn., Alpha Omega Alpha. Avocations: cooking, computers, tennis. Office: Drexel U Coll Medicine Mail Stop 441 245 N 15th St Philadelphia PA 19102-1192 E-mail: eabrutyn@drexel.edu.

ABRUZZO, MARGARET NICOLA, historian; b. Sharon, Conn., Mar. 19, 1977; d. Donald Joseph and Margaret Abruzzo. BA summa cum laude, U. of Dallas, 1999; MA, U. Notre Dame, 2003. PhD candidate in history U. of Notre Dame, 2002—. Recipient Louis J. Lekai award for History, U. of Dallas; fellow Presdl. fellowship, U. of Notre Dame, 1999—2003. Mem.: Orgn. of Am. Historians, Am. Hist. Assn., Union of Grad. Historians of Notre Dame (pres. 2002—03), Phi Alpha Theta, Phi Beta Kappa. Catholic. E-mail: mabruzzo@nd.edu.

ABSHER, DONNA ATKINS, textile designer; b. Ft. Ord, Calif., July 25, 1956; d. James Edward and Mary Ward (Shearin) Atkins; m. Glen Alan Downs, Jan. 2, 1982 (div. Nov. 1990); m. Robert Blair Martin, June 29, 1991 (div. 1998); 1 child, Parker James Blair Martin; m. Ray Grubb Absher, Oct. 20, 2002. AAS in Fashion Design, SUNY, 1977; BS in Textile Tech., N.C. State U., 1978. Head designer Chatham Mills, Pittsboro, N.C., 1978-81; dept. mgr. JC Penney, Wilson, N.C., 1982-85; house mem.'s asst. N.C. Legislature, Raleigh, N.C., 1985-86; dir. product devel. Doblin Fabrics, Morganton, N.C., 1989-94; pres., CEO Martin Textiles, Ltd., Hickory, N.C., 1994—. Freelance designer, stylist Carolina Mills, Hickory, 1995-97; automotive textile designer, CMI Industries,

Elkin, N.C., 1998-2000; design ops. mgr. Chatham-Borgstena Automotive Textiles, Mt. Airy, N.C., 2001—. Mem.: Overmountain Victory Trail Assn. Southern Baptist. Avocations: traveling, choral singing. E-mail: donna.absher@us.borgstena.com.

ABSHIRE, DAVID MANKER, diplomat, research executive; b. Chattanooga, Apr. 11, 1926; s. James Ernest and Phyllis (Patten) A.; m. Carolyn Lamar Sample, Sept. 7, 1957; children: Lupton Patten, Anna Lamra Abshire Bowman, Mary Lee Sample Abshire Jensvold, Phyllis Anderson Abshire d'Hoop, Carolyn Abshire Hall. Student, U. Chattanooga, 1945; BS, U.S. Mil. Acad., 1951; PhD, Georgetown U., 1959; DHL, Va. Theol. Sem., 1992; DCL (hon.), U. of the South, 1994. Mem. minority staff U.S. Ho. Reps., 1958-60; dir. spl. projects Am. Enterprise Inst., Washington, 1961-62; from exec. dir. to pres. and co-founder Center Strategic and Internat. Studies Georgetown U., 1962-99; vice chmn. Center Strategic and Internat. Studies, 1999—; ambassador, U.S. permanent rep. North Atlantic Council, 1983-87; spl. counsellor to pres. White House, 1987, vice chmn., bd. trustees; pres. Ctr. for the Study of the Presidency, 1999—, Richard Lounsbery Found., 2002—. Asst. sec. state for congl. rels., 1970-73; presdl. appointee Congl. Commn. on Orgn. of Govt. for Conduct of Fgn. Policy, 1973-75; chmn. U.S. Bd. for Internat. Broadcasting, 1974-77; dir. nat. security group Transition Office of Pres.-Elect Reagan, 1980-81; dir. Ogden Corp., 1987-96; mem. adv. bd. BP Am., President's Task Force on U.S. Government Internat. Broadcasting, 1991, bd. Procter and Gamble; adj. prof. Georgetown U., 1973-83. Author: The South Rejects a Prophet: The Life of Senator D.M. Key, 1967, International Broadcasting: A New Dimension of Western Diplomacy, 1976, Foreign Policy Makers: President vs. Congress, 1979, The Growing Power of Congress, 1981, Preventing World War III: A Realistic Grand Strategy, 1988, (with others) Detente, 1965, Vietnam Legacy, 1976, The Global Economy, 1990; editor: National Security, 1963, Portuguese Africa, 1969, Research Resources for the Seventies, 1971; co-editor Washington Quar., 1977-83; co-author: Putting America's House in Order, 1996; editor-in-chief: Report to the President-elect 2000: Triumphs and Tragedies of the Modern Presidency, 2000. Mem. adv. bd. Naval War Coll., 1975-79; vice-chmn. bd. Youth for Understanding, 1979-80; trustee Baylor Sch., 1980—; mem. Pres.'s Fgn. Intelligence Adv. Bd., 1981-83; bd. dirs. Spaak Found. (Brussels). With AUS, 1945-46; 1st lt. 1951-56; capt. Res. ret. Decorated Bronze Star with oak leaf cluster, with V for Valor, V commendation ribbon with metal pendant; Order of Crown, comdr. Order of Leopold (Belgium); grand ofcl. Order of Republic of Italy; recipient medal of Pres. of Italian Republic, Senate, Parliament and Govt. and of Pio Manzu Ctr.; recipient John Carroll award, Dept. Def. disting. pub. svc. medal, 1988, Presdl. Citizens medal, 1989, medal of diplomatic merit Republic of Korea, 1993; First Class Order of The Lion of Finland insignia of the Comdr., 1994, U.S. Military Acad. Castle award, 1994, Order of the Liberator, Argentina, 1999, Order of Sacred Treasure Gold and Silver Star, Japan, 2001. Mem. Coun. Am. Ambs., Coun. on Competitiveness, Coun. Fgn. Rels., Inst. Strategic Studies, Trinity Nat. Leadership Roundtable (co-founder), Gold Key Soc., Alfalfa Club, Met. Club, Cosmos Club, Alibi Club, Phi Alpha Theta. Republican. Episcopalian. Home: 311 S St Asaph St Alexandria VA 22314-3745 Office: Ctr for Study of the Presidency 1020 19th St NW Ste 250 Washington DC 20036

ABSTON, DUNBAR, JR., management executive; b. Memphis, Jan. 26, 1931; s. Dunbar and Esther (Cook) A.; m. Constance Condon, Apr. 29, 1978; children— Lauri Abston Arnold, Dunbar III, Linda Abston Larsen, Frank Norfleet; stepchildren— Selden Early Popwell, Martha McKellar Early, William Cole Early III, Elizabeth Early Gore. AB, Princeton U., 1953; MBA, Harvard U., 1955; M.Phil., Oxford U., 1989. Joined Parts Inc., Memphis, 1959, chmn., 1979; pres. parent co. Parts Industries Corp., Memphis, 1981-83, pres., chief exec. officer, 1983-87; pres., proprieter Abston Mgmt. Co., Memphis, 1987—. Pres. Tract-O-Land Plantation; ptnr. Abston Farms, Lake Coromorant, Miss., Abston-Norfleet Realty Co., Memphis. Past chmn. Memphis Symphony Orch., Memphis Plough Community Found.; trustee Rhodes Coll., Lawrenceville Sch. Baker scholar Harvard U., 1954. Mem. Automotive Warehouse Distbrs. Assn. (past chmn.), Memphis Econ. Club (past chmn.), Phi Beta Kappa. Republican. Presbyterian. Home: 4010 Dumaine Way Memphis TN 38117 Office: Abston Mgmt Co 4727 Spottswood Ave Memphis TN 38117-4818 E-mail: dabstonjr@aol.com.

ABT, CLARK C. social scientist, executive, engineer, publisher, educator; b. Cologne, Germany, Aug. 31, 1929; came to U.S., 1937, naturalized, 1945; m. Wendy Peter, Nov. 3, 1971; children: Thomas, Emily. BS, MIT, 1951, PhD, 1965; MA, Johns Hopkins U., 1952. Instr. Johns Hopkins U., Balt., 1951-52; mgr. advanced systems dept. Raytheon Co., Bedford, Mass., 1957-64; pres., treas. Abt Assocs., Inc., Cambridge, Mass., 1965-86, chmn., 1986—; pres., publisher Abt Books Inc., Cambridge, 1987-94; prof., dir. Ctr. for Study of Small States Boston U., 1991-93, rsch. prof. internat. rels., 1991-94, dir. Def. Tech. Conversion Ctr., 1993-96. Vis. lectr. Harvard U., 1968-69; vis. prof. SUNY, Binghamton, 1975-76; adj. prof. mgmt. U. Mass., 1991-93; dir. Russian Am. Boston Workshop on Def. Tech. Conversion, 1992, dir. Moscow Workshop, 1993; faculty dir. Moscow Entrepreneurial Workshop, 1993, 95; assoc. Ctr. for Sci. and Internat. Affairs Harvard U., 1991—; mem. smallpox preparedness adv com. Mass. Dept. Pub. Health, 2002—. Author: Serious Games, 1970, The Evaluation of Social Programs, 1977, The Social Audit for Management, 1977, Applied Research for Social Policy: The U.S. and the Federal Republic of Germany Compared, 1978, Costs and Benefits of Applied Social Research, 1979, A Strategy for Terminating a Nuclear War, 1985, AIDS and the Courts, 1990, Drugs and Crime CD-ROM Library, 1990, International Drug Library CD-ROM, 1990, National Portrait Gallery Permanent Collection of Notable Americans on CD-ROM, 1990, Solar-Powered Economic Growth, 1999, The Future of Energy, 2001, Economic Impacts of Biological and Nuclear Terrorist Attacks on Seaport-Based Transport, 2003. Vol. tutor Boston Pub. High Schs., 1998—. Recipient grand prize Thoreau award for landscape architecture, 1975 Mem.: Internat. Inst. Strategic Studies, Old Cambridge Shakespeare Soc., Cambridge Boat Club, Cambridge Tennis Club, Mt. Auburn Tennis Club. also: Abt Assocs Inc 55 Wheeler St Cambridge MA 02138-1192 E-mail: clarkabt@aol.com., clark_abt@abtassoc.com.

ABT, JEFFREY, art and art history educator, artist, writer; b. Kansas City, Mo., Feb. 27, 1949; s. Arthur and Lottie (Weinman) A.; m. Mary Kathleen Paquette, July 16, 1972; children: Uriel, Danya. BFA, Drake U., 1971, MFA, 1977. Curator collections Wichita (Kans.) Art Mus., 1977-78; gen. mgr. Billy Hork Galleries, Ltd., Chgo., 1978-80; exhbns. coordinator U. Chgo. Libr., 1980-86; asst. dir. Smart Mus. of Art, U. Chgo., 1986—87, acting dir., 1987—89; assoc. prof. dept. art and art history Wayne State U., Detroit, 1989—, dept. chair, 1989-94, mem. adv. bd. Humanities Ctr., 1993-95. Author: A Museum on the Verge: A Socioeconomic History of the Detroit Institute of Arts, 1882-2000, 2001; exhbn. catalogues The Printer's Craft, 1982, The Book Made Art, 1986; one-man shows include Cliff Dwellers, 1997, Cary Gallery, 1998, Wayne State U., 1999, Worthington Arts Coun. Gallery, 2000; editor ann. Book and Paper Group Am. Inst. for Conservation, 1985-86; editor exhbn. catalogue Up From the Streets: Detroit Art from the Duffy Warehouse Collection, 2001; mem. editl. bd. Wayne State U. Press, 1990-96, 2002—, chmn. editl. bd., 1996—2001; illustrator: Water: Sheba's Story, 1997; contbr. articles and book revs. to profl. jours., chpts. to books and encys. Bd. dirs. Hyde Pk. Jewish Cmty. Ctr., Chgo., 1988-89, Detroit Artists Market, 1994—, sec., 1996-99, pres. and chmn. bd. dirs., 1999-2001; trustee Ragdale Found., Lake Forest, Ill., 1985-96, mem. nat. adv. coun., 1996—; mem. intercultural programs com., 1990-92, libr. adv. com., 1990-96, mem. edn. adv. com., 1992-95, Detroit Inst. Arts; mem. visual arts com. Detroit Festival of the Arts, 1989-92; juror numerous art exhbns., 1986—. Recipient numerous purchase prizes, awards and commns. for artistic work, 1974—, award of merit Mich. Hist. Soc., 2002; Hebrew Union Coll.-Jewish Inst. Religion fellow, Jerusalem, 1971-72; grantee IMS, NEA, NEH, Rockefeller Archive Ctr., Rockefeller U., Logan Found., Wayne State U. Humanities Ctr., Kaufman Meml. Trust, Woodrow Wilson Nat. Fellowship Found. Mem. Am. Assn. Mus., Coll. Art Assn., Assn. Mus. History (co-founder). Office: Wayne State U Dept Art and Art History 150 Art Bldg Detroit MI 48202 E-mail: j_abt@wayne.edu.

ABT, RALPH EDWIN, lawyer; b. Chgo., Apr. 9, 1960; s. Wendel Peter and Hedi Lucie (Wieder) A. BA, Loyola U., Chgo., 1982; JD, John Marshall Law Sch., Chgo., 1987. Bar: Ill. 1987, U.S. Dist. Ct. (no. dist.) Ill. 1987, U.S. Ct. Appeals (7th cir.) Ill. 1988. Pvt. practice, Chgo., 1987—88; staff atty. Sec. of State's Office, Chgo., 1988—95, Ill. Dept. Pub. Aid, Chgo., 1995—. Poll watcher, Chgo., 1981, 83, precinct capt., 1983, 93-2000. Mem. ABA, Ill. Bar Assn., Chgo. Bar Assn., Trade Law Assn. (charter mem., chmn. charter membership drive 1986), Phi Alpha Delta. Lutheran. Avocations: reading, tennis, bicycling, weight lifting. Home: 5067 W Balmoral Ave Chicago IL 60630-1547 Office: Ill Dept Pub Aid 32 W Randolph St Ste 1200 Chicago IL 60601-3470

ABT, STEVEN R. civil engineering educator, dean; b. Cheyenne Wells, Colo; BCE, Colo. State U., 1973, MSCE, 1976, PhDCE, 1980. Hydraulics staff engr. Leonard Rice Engring., Denver, 1974-76; instr. Colo. State U., Ft. Collins, 1976-80, from asst. prof. to assoc. prof., 1980-88, prof., 1988—, exec. asst. dean, 1997—. Cons., Ft. Collins, 1976—. Editor, co-editor Proceedings; contbr. more than 78 articles to profl. jour. 2d lt. C.E., US Army, 1973, Brig.Gen. USAR, 1973—. Fellow ASCE; mem. Am. Water Resource Assn., Transp. Rsch. Bd., Internat. Erosion Control Assn. Office: Colo State U Office of Dean of Engring Fort Collins CO 80523-1301 E-mail: sabt@engr.colostate.edu.

ABTS, GWYNETH HARTMANN, dietitian; b. Union, Ill., Oct. 31, 1923; d. William John and Olga Anna (Krause) Hartmann; m. Rufus Heath Jr., Apr. 6, 1942 (div. Dec. 1945); m. Harold Henry Abts, Feb. 14, 1948; children: Leigh, Michael, Patricia. BS, U. Ill., 1945; postgrad., U. Oreg., 1945-46, U. Ill., Elgin, 1957, No. Ill. U., 1966, 74, 82, 87. Registered dietitian, Ill., Lic. Ill. Dietitian. Clin. dietitian St. Joseph Hosp., Elgin, 1947; asst. dietitian French Hosp., San Francisco, 1948-50, Elgin State Hosp., 1950-58; dietary cons. Ill. Youth Commn., Springfield, 1958-70; food adminstr. Ill. Dept. of Corrections, Springfield, 1970-85. Mem. Food and Nutrition Cou. on Govt. Commodities, Springfield, 1980-85; bd. dirs. Ill. Nutrition Assn., Urbana, 1983. Pres. PTO, Geneva, 1972. McHenry County Home Econ. scholar U. Ill., 1941-45. Mem. Am. Dietetic Assn. (citizens ambassador program to Australia and New Zealand and China), Fox Valley Home Economists, West Suburban Dietetic Assn., AAUW. Lutheran. Avocations: quilting, cooking, duplicate bridge. Home: Apt 107 975 N 5th Ave Saint Charles IL 60174-1284

ABTS, HENRY WILLIAM, banker; b. Columbus, Nebr., July 3, 1918; s. Matthew C. and Irene (Xanders) A.; m. Virginia Lung, Nov. 7, 1942; children: Bruce M., Susan A. (Mrs. J. Farnham). BS, Butler U. 1941. Asst. mgr. indsl. relations Union Carbide Co., Kokomo, Ind., 1945-54, personnel mgr. N.Y.C., 1954-56, dir. indsl. relations South Charleston, W.Va., 1956-60; v.p. personnel Cummins Engine Co., Inc., Columbus, Ind., 1960-68, v.p. adminstrn., sec., 1968-82, ret., 1982; v.p. Columbus Bank and Trust, 1982-87, pres., chief exec. officer, 1987-88; ret., 1988. Mem. regional adv. bd. Liberty Mut. Ins. Co. Served to capt. USAAF, 1941-45. Recipient Disting. Alumnus award Butler U., 1981, Cmty. Svc. award Columbus C. of C., 1985; named Outstanding Young Man Kokomo Jr. C. of C., 1951, Boss of Year Columbus Jr. C. of C., 1963, Athletic Hall of Fame, Butler U., 1996. Mem. Ind. C. of C., Ind. Golf Assn. (past pres., dir.), Phi Delta Theta. Mem. Christian Ch. Clubs: Otter Creek Golf (past pres.), Harrison Lakes Country (past pres.); Columbus Rotary (past pres.). Home: 9544 Raintree Dr S Columbus IN 47201-4817

ABUGHALI, NAZHA, pediatrician, consultant; b. Beirut, Aug. 27, 1960; d. Fawzi and Suliema Abughali; m. Mohamed A. Ali, June 13, 1989; children: Marwan M. Ali, Dana M. Ali, Nadeen Ali, Ahmad Ali. MD, Am. U. Of Beirut, Beirut, Lebanon, 1981—85. Diplomate in the Am.Bd. of Pediatrics 1989, Diplomate in Pediatric Inf. Dis. 1994. Pediatric infectious dis. Metro Health Med. Ctr., Cleveland, Ohio, 2001—; pediatric infectiuos dis. cons. Cleve. Clinic Found., Ohio, 2001—; pediatrician Children's Physicians, West Palm Beach, Fla., 1999—2001; pediatric infectiuos dis. staff Metrohealth Med. Ctr., Cleveland, Ohio, 1993—98. Head of pediatric tb services Cuyahoga Co. Tb Clin., Cleveland, Ohio, 2001—; med. dir. of pediatric in patient Metro Health Med. Ctr., Cleveland, Ohio, 2002—; asst. prof. of pediat. Case Western Res. U., Cleveland, Ohio, 1994—. Fellow: Am. Acad. Of Pediat. (corr.; us 1990); mem.: Pediatric Infectiuos Dis. of Pediat. (corr.; us 1993). Achievements include research in pediatric Tuberculosis. Office: Metrohealth Med Ctr 2500 Metrohealth Dr Cleveland OH 44109 Personal E-mail: nabughali@metrohealth.org. E-mail: nabughali@metrohealth.org.

ABU-HEJLEH, NASER M. civil engineer, researcher; b. Nablus, Palestine, July 1, 1964; s. Mahmood A. and Yusra F. Abu-Hejleh; m. Inam M. Samra, Aug. 19, 1969; 1 child, Omar N. BS in Civil Engring., Yarmouk U., Irbid, Jordan; MS in Civil Engring., M.E.T.U., Ankara, Turkey, 1986—88; PhD, U. of Colo., 1989—93. Cert. Colo. State, 1996. Rsch. asst., assoc. U. of Colo. at Boulder, 1989—95; mgr., geotechnical rsch. studies Colo. DOT, Denver, 1995—. Author: (software) CADA, for analysis of consolidation and desiccation of soft soils. Home: 3769 S Lisbon Ct Aurora CO 80013 Office: Colorado Dept of Transportation 4201 E Arkansas Ave Denver CO 80222 Office Fax: 303-757-9974. Personal E-mail: naserr1@aol.com. E-mail: naser.abu-hejleh@dot.state.co.us.

ABU KWAIK, YOUSEF A. microbiologist, educator, research scientist; b. Jerusalem, May 6, 1962; s. Abdel Rahman Yousef and Itaf M. Abu K.; m. Debra Jean Robinson, Dec. 16, 1963; 1 child, Sarah. BS, SUNY, Buffalo, 1985, MS, 1987, MA, 1988, PhD, 1991. Assoc. prof. U. Ky. Med. Sch., Lexington, 1994—. Contbr. articles to profl. jours. Recipient grant NIH, 95-2000, grant NIH, 2001-2005. Mem. Am. Soc. Microbiology. Office: U Ky Med Sch MS 408 Med Ctr 800 Rose St Lexington KY 40536

ABUL-HAJ, SULEIMAN KAHIL, pathologist; b. Palestine, Apr. 20, 1925; came to U.S., 1946, naturalized, 1955; s. Sheik Khalil and S. Buteina (Oda) Abul-H.; m. Elizabeth Abood, Feb. 11, 1948; children: Charles, Alan, Cary. *The roots of the Abul-Haj family date back to the 7th century, A.D. Arab armies invaded North Africa and intermarried with local inhabitants, the Berbers. The Berbers were Barbarian Germanic hords who invaded Rome and then moved into and settled in North Africa. Tarique Bin Ziyad, born to Berber mother and an Arab father, was the founding ancestor. Tarique commanded the Arab armies that conquered Spain in 711 A.D. Jabal Tarique, anglicized to Gibraltar, was named after him, which means the Mount of Tarique. The name Abul-Haj, father of the pilgrims, was dubbed in the 12th century following the treaty between Saladdin and the Crusaders.* BS, U. Calif., Berkeley, 1949; MS, U. Calif., San Francisco, 1951, MD, 1955. Intern Cook County Hosp., Chgo., 1955-56; resident U. Calif. Hosp., San Francisco, 1949, Brooke Gen Hosp., 1957-59; chief clin. and anatomic pathology Walter Reed Army Hosp., Washington, 1959-62; assoc. prof. U. So. Calif. Sch. Medicine, L.A., 1963-96; sr. surg. pathologist Los Angeles County Gen. Hosp., 1963; dir. dept. pathology Cmty. Meml. Hosp., Ventura, Calif., 1964-80, Gen. Hosp. Ventura County, 1966-74; dir. Pathology Svc. Med. Group, 1970—. Cons. Calif. Tumor Tissue Registry, 1962-96, Camarillo State Hosp., 1964-70, Tripler Gen. Hosp., Hawaii, 1963-67, Armed Forces Inst. Pathology, 1960-69. Contbr. articles to profl. jours. Bd. dirs. Tri-Counties Blood Bank, Am. Cancer Soc. Maj., M.C., U.S. Army, 1956-62. Recipient Calif. Honor Soc. award, 1949, Borden award, 1955, Achievement cert. Surgeon Gen. Army, 1962. Fellow Coll. Am. Pathologists; mem. AAAS, AMA, Internat. Coll. Surgeons, World Affairs Coun. Achievements include research in cardiovascular disease, endocrine, renal, skin diseases, also cancer. Home and Office: 105 Encinal Way Ventura CA 93001-3317

ABULHASAN, MOHAMMAD ABDULLA, ambassador; b. Kuwait, Jan. 12, 1943; m. Sabeeha Haji, Jan. 21, 1969; children: Mohammed, Maysoun, Amani, Arwa, Mariam. BA, U. Cairo, 1965. Joined Kuwaiti Ministry Fgn. Affairs, 1965; mem. mission to UN, GEneva, 1968-73; 1st sec. Embassy, Tehran, Iran, 1973-75; Kuwaiti amb. to People's Republic of China, 1975-78, Hungary and East Germany, to Yugoslavia, 1978-81, Cuba, Argentina and Mex., 1981—; A.E. and P. to UN, 1981—, non-resident amb. to the Bahamas, 1999—, v.p. 55th session gen. assembly, 2000—. Chmn. social, humanitarian and cultural com. Gen. Assembly, 1988, v.p. 44th session, 89, pres. Pledging Conf. Devel. Activities, 88, High Level Com. on Rev. TCDC, 89; chmn. Kuwaiti del. Summit for Internat. Conf. on Financing for Devel., Monterrey, Mexico, 2002, Ministerial Meeting of Non-Aligned Movement, Durban, South Africa, 2002. Decorated Order of Flag (Yugoslavia). Office: UN Permanent Mission of Kuwait 321 E 44th St New York NY 10017-4401 E-mail: kuwait@kuwaitmission.com.

ABU-MOSTAFA, AYMAN SAID, computer consultant; b. Giza, Egypt, June 1, 1953; came to U.S., 1978; s. Said S. Abu-Mostafa and Faiza A. Ibrahim. BME, Cairo U., 1976; MS in Mech. and Aerospace Engring., Okla. State U., 1980, PhD, 1984. Tchg. asst. Cairo U., Giza, Egypt, 1978, Okla. State U., Stillwater, 1978-79, rsch. assoc., 1979-81; software engr. SEAM Internat. Corp., Palos Verdes, Calif., 1984-87; computing and networking cons. Calif. State U., Los Alamitos, 1987-92; sr. sys. analyst Allied Signal Aerospace, Torrance, Calif., 1992-93; pres., CEO NeuroDollars, Inc., Huntington Beach, Calif., 1993-97; sr. programmer analyst Softnet Systems, Irvine, Calif., 1997-99; software solutions cons. Borland Software Corp. (formerly known as StarBase Corp.), Santa Ana, Calif., 1999—2003; software devel. engr. Capita Techs., Inc., 2003—. Author papers, articles in field. Undergrad. fellow Ministry of Higher Edn., Cairo, 1971, 72, 76; NASA/Ames grantee, 1979-81. Mem. AIAA, IEEE, Assn. for Computing Machinery. Avocations: reading, computers, languages, music. Office: Capita Techs Inc 17600 Gillette Irvine CA 92614-5702 E-mail: ayman1@aol.com.

ABU-MOUSTAFA, ADEL H. medical educator, dean; b. Cairo, Nov. 18, 1939; came to U.S., 1962; s. Abdulhamid and Zanab (Ayad) Abu-moustafa; m. Magda Ismail Kabbany, Oct. 10, 1962; children: Heidi, Sally, Sherief. BSc, Cairo U., 1960; MA, Harvard U., 1964; PhD, Boston U., 1969. Instr. Boston Coll., Chestnut Hill, Mass., 1964-67; from asst. prof. to assoc. prof. Salem (Mass.) State Coll., 1967-70, prof., 19770-72, dean undergrad studies, 1972-74, acting acad. dean, 1974-76, dean acad. svcs., 1976-79, exec. v.p., 1979-83; adminstrv. counselor King Faisal U., Saudi Arabia, 1983-86; dir. svcs. to higher edn. Acad. for Ednl. Devel., Washington, 1983-87; dir. assoc. dean internat. health affairs Tufts U. Sch. Medicine, Boston, 1987—, dean internat. health affairs, 1997—. Team leader consortium of U.S. Univs. and U.S. Dept. Treasury, U.S. Saudi Commn. on Econ. Cooperation to assist King Faisal U., Saudi Arabia, 1983-87. Contbr. articles to profl. jours. Mem. exec. com. Fletcher Sch. Law and Diplomacy, 1987—. Mem. Arab Am. Physicians. Moslem. Avocation: politics. Office: Tufts U Sch Medicine 136 Harrison Ave Boston MA 02111-1817

ABUNASSER, RIMA JAMIL, education educator; d. Jamil and Wanda F. Abunasser. PhD, U. of North Tex., 1999—2003. Rsch. asst. U. of North Tex., Denton, 1999—2003, tchg. fellow, 1999—. Fellow Tchg. Fellowship, U. of North Tex., 1999-2003, Tchg. Assistantship, 1998-1999; scholar Mary Patchell Departmental Scholarship, Dept. of English - U. of North Tex., 2001. Home: 2009 Colorado Blvd Apt C Denton TX 76205 Office: U of North Texas Dept of English Denton TX 76203 Personal E-mail: rima_jamil@yahoo.com.

ABUZAAKOUK, ALY RAMADAN, publishing executive; b. Misurata, Libya, Sept. 12, 1942; came to U.S., 1977; s. Ramadan Khalil and Umm Khatirha A. (Balam) A.; m. Fawzia Faraj Annahly, July 17, 1972; children: Asmaa, Ahmad, Anas, Aalaa. BA in Journalism, U. Cairo, 1968; MA in Comm., Stanford U., 1971; MA in Middle East Studies, U. Mich., 1980, postgrad., 1977-81. Lectr. Faculty Arts, U. Benghazi, Libya, 1972-76; dir. Internat. Muslim House, Ann Arbor, Mich., 1977-80; pres. New Era Publs., Ann Arbor, 1980-81; dir. info. NSFL, Chgo., 1981-87; dir. publs. Internat. Inst. Islamic Thought, Herndon, Va., 1987-93; publs. mgr. amana publ., Beltsville, Md., 1994-98; exec. dir. Am. Muslim Coun., Washington, 1998—. Elected mem. Faculty Arts Acad. Coun., Libya, 1973-75, U. Benghazi Acad. Coun., Libya, 1974-75; chmn. 1st Congress of the Libyan Students in N.Am., 1980; founding mem. Nat. Front for the Salvation of Libya, 1981; pres. N.Am. News Media, Fairfax, Va., 1993. Editor: Al INQAD, 1981—86. Mem., founder Nat. Front for the Salvation of Libya, 1980, Libyan League for Human Rights, Geneva, 1990; founder, bd. dirs. Libyan Studies Ctr., Oxford, Eng., Ctr. for Devel. of Mughrib, Montreal, 1994; mem. Amnesty Internat., 1983; mem. adv. bd. Am. Muslim Coun., Washington, 1997-98, exec. dir. 1998—; bd. dirs., v.p. Minaret of Freedm Inst., Bethesda, Md.; bd. dirs. United Assn. for Studies and Rsch., Annandale, Va., 1998—; bd. dir., treas. Nat. Coalition Protect Polit. Freedom, Washington, D.C., 2000-. Mem. Assn. Muslim Social Scientists, Fgn. Press Ctr., bd. dirs. The Minaret of Freedom Inst. Avocations: soccer, swimming, traveling. Office: North Am News Media PO Box 7148 Fairfax Station VA 22039-7148 Fax: 703-425-3280. E-mail: arab@erols.com.

ABY, ROBERT DAVIS, physician; b. Mpls., Jan. 24, 1945; s. Stanton Cadwell and Janet (Sandy) A.; m. Anne Jansen, Aug. 24, 1968; children: Meredith, Martha. BA, Carleton Coll., 1967; BS, U. S.D., 1969; MD, Tufts U., 1971. Diplomate Am. Bd. Internal Medicine. Physician USNR, Quantico, Va., 1974-76, Worthington (Minn.) Specialty Clinics, 1976—. Bush Found. fellow, 1989. Mem. ACP, Am. Acad. Family Practice, Minn. Med. Assn. Office: Worthington Specialty Clinics 508 10th St Worthington MN 56187-2343 E-mail: robert.aby@mckennan.org.

ACAIN, ANGELINE RAMOS, publishing executive; b. Honolulu, Mar. 11, 1959; d. Juan Tambo Acain and Victoria Calderon Ramos; life ptnr. Susan Goldie Eisenberg; 1 child, Jiana Acain Eisenberg. Student, Kapiolani C.C., Honolulu, 1977—79; BFA, Sch. Visual Arts, N.Y.C., 1986. Graphic designer, advt. sales rep. Fiduciary Comm. Fin. Advt., N.Y.C., 1986—91; freelance graphic designer Free Spirit Holistic Mag., Bklyn., 1990—91; graphic designer Hawaii Bride & Groom Mag., Honolulu, 1991—92; pub. Ohohia Holistic Mag., Honolulu, 1991—98, Gay Parent Mag., N.Y.C., 1998—. Pub. Ripe Mag. for Older LGBTs, 2000—01, N.Y. Gay Parent Guide, 2003. Author: My Kind of Family, 2001. Vol. graphic designer, liaison lesbian-gay cmty. Office of the Mayor, N.Y.C., 1988; vol. graphic designer Visibilities Lesbian Mag., N.Y.C., 1988—90; vol. mentor for LBGT youth AIDS Ctr. of Queens County, N.Y.C., 2003; grand marshal Queens Lesbian & Gay Pride Com., N.Y.C., 2000. John A. Burns scholar, Hawaii, 1977—78. Avocation: surfing. Office: Gay Parent Mag PO Box 750852 Forest Hills NY 11375-0852 E-mail: acain@gis.net.

ACAMPORA, RALPH JOSEPH, brokerage firm executive; b. N.Y.C., Oct. 2, 1941; s. Ralph J. and Teresa (Fusco) Acampora; m. Rosemary Sherlock; stepchildren: Mathew, Ross. BA, St. Joseph's Sem., Yonkers, N.Y., Iona Coll. With Harris, Upham & Co. (merged with Smith Barney), N.Y.C., 1969-80; sr. v.p., tech. analyst Kidder Peabody & Co., N.Y.C., 1980-90, Prudential Securities, N.Y.C., 1990—, mng. dir. tech. rsch. Tchr. N.Y. Inst. Fin., 1970—. Author: The Fourth Mega Market, 2000. Mem. Market Technicians Assn. (chartered, founder 1970s, pres. 1979-80, 2001-03, founder assn. libr. 1975, hon. award 1987), Internat. Fedn. Technician Analysts (founder, former and first chmn. 1986-92), N.Y. Soc. Security Analysts (bd. dirs.). Republican. Roman Catholic. Avocation: study of World War II. Home: 350 Albany St Ph 1 New York NY 10280-1415 Office: Prudential Securities 1 New York Plz New York NY 10004-1901

ACCARDI, JOSEPH RONALD, accountant; b. Bklyn., July 29, 1960; s. Joseph Anthony and Mary Catherine (Masotti) A.; m. Colette Possert, Oct. 9, 1988; children: Joseph Theodore, Nicolette Barbara. BS, St. John's U., 1982. CPA N.Y., N.J. Staff acct. Pannell Kerr Forster, N.Y.C., 1982-84; sr. acct. KPMG, N.Y.C., 1984-87, Siemens Corp., N.Y.C., 1987-90, mgr. fin. acctg., 1990-92, mgr. bus. adminstrn. Iselin, N.J., 1992-97; mgr. bus. planning & fin. analysis Siemens Transp. Systems, Inc., Iselin, N.J., 1998-99; vp., asst. contr., asst. sec. Siemens Capital Co. LLC, Bridgewater, NJ, 1999—. Mem. AICPA, N.J. State Soc. CPAs, St. John's Alumni Assn., Inst. Mgmt. Accts., Fin. Execs. Networking Group. Roman Catholic. Avocations: football, baseball, music. Home: 315 Church St Woodbridge NJ 07095-2437 Office: 200 Somerset Corporate Blvd Bridgewater NJ 08807-2862

ACCARDO, PASQUALE J. pediatrician, educator; b. Bklyn., Oct. 22, 1943; s. Annunziato and Julia A.; m. Patricia Leahy, June 8, 1968; children: Jennifer, Matthew, Claire. BS, St. John's U., Bklyn., 1965; MD, SUNY, Bklyn., 1969. Intern in pediats. Bklyn.-Cumberland Med. Ctr., 1969-70; resident in pediats. James Whitcomb Riley Hosp. Children, Ind., 1972-74; fellow in devel. pediats. John F. Kennedy Inst., Balt., 1974-76; instr. Johns Hopkins U., Balt., 1976-77, asst. prof., 1977-81; assoc. prof. St. Louis U. Sch. Medicine, 1981-90, prof., 1990-96, N.Y. Med. Coll., Valhalla, 1997—2002, Va, Commonwealth U, 2002—. Author: A Neurodevelopmental Perspective on Specific Learning Disabilities: Monographs in Developmental Pediatrics, vol. 3, 1980, Diagnosis and Detection: The Medical Iconography of Sherlock Holmes, 1987, The Medical Almanac: A Calendar of Dates of Significance to the Profession of Medicine including Fascinating Illustrations, Medical Milestones, Dates of Birth and Death of Notable Physicians, Brief Biographical Sketches, Quotations, Assorted Medical curiosities and Trivia, 1992, The Invisible Disability:

Understanding Learning Disabilities in the Context of Health and Education, 1996, The Spenserian Holmes, being the annotated manuscript of The Hell of the Baskervilles, 1998, The Infernal Holmes: Essays on Dante's Inferno as Reflected in the Sherlock Holmes Stories of Sir Arthur Conan Doyle, 1999; The Metamosphosis of Apuleius: Cupid and Psyche, Beauty and the Beast, King Kong, 2002, co-author: Primitive Reflex Profile Monographs in Developmental Pediatrics, vol. 1, 1978, The Pediatrician and the Developmentally Delayed Child: A Clinical Textbook on Mental Retardation, Monographs in Developmental Pediatrics, vol. 2, 1979, Dictionary of Developmental Disabilities: An Interdisciplinary Introduction to Multidisciplinary Terminology, 1996, 2d edit., 2002,; editor/co-editor: Failure to Thrive in Infancy and Early Childhood: A Multidisciplinary Team Approach, 1982, When A Parent is Mentally Retarded, 1990, Developmental Disabilities in Infancy and Childhood, 1991, Attention Deficit Disorders and Hyperactivity in Children, Monographs in Pediatric Habilitation, vol. 7, 1991, Attention Deficit Disorders and Learning Disabilities, 1994, Developmental Disabilities in Infancy and Childhood, 2 vols., 2d edit., 1996, Behavior Belongs in the Brain, 1997, Specific Reading Disability, 1998, Attention Deficits and Hyperactivity in Children and Adults, 2000, Monographs in Pediatric Habilitation, Vol. 10, 2000, Sherlock Holmes Meets Father Brown and His Creator: A Miscellany of Scholarship, Stories, and Literacy Diversions, 2000, Autism: Clinical and Research Issues, 2000, Disorders of Language Development, 2002, The Complete Annotated Father Brown, 2003. Capt. USAF, 1970-72. Roman Catholic. Avocations: sherlockian, chestertonian, dantean, carrollian. Home: 2302 Cardiff Pl Richmond VA 23236-1581 Office: Chldns Hosp 2924 Brook Rd Richmond VA 23220-1298 E-mail: paccardo@chva.org., pataccardo@earthlink.net.

ACCORDINO, FRANK JOSEPH, architect; b. Bklyn., July 14, 1946; s. Carmine Anthony and Elvira Helen (Saccone) A.; m. Sheila May Lloyd, Sept. 6, 1969. BS, SUNY, N.Y. Inst. Tech., 1969; MArch, U. N.Mex., 1971. Registered architect, N.Y., Ill.; cert. Nat. Council Archtl. Registration Bds. Project architect Gencorelli & Salo Architects, Mineola, N.Y., 1971-74, Grove Haack & Assocs., P.C., Architects, Engrs., Planners, Ft. Lauderdale, Fla., 1974-76; v.p., dir. Cashin Assocs., P.C., Architects, Engrs., Planners, Mineola, N.Y., 1976-79; prin. architect Frank Accordino, AIA, Merrick, N.Y., 1979-80; sr. architect, facilities devel. Eastern Airlines, Inc., Miami, Fla., 1980-83; sr. architect Dean Witter Reynolds, Inc., N.Y.C., 1983-84; regional dir. constrn. and engrng. Avis Rent A Car System, Inc., Garden City, NY, 1984-87, v.p. corp. facilities, 1987—2002; prin. architect Frank Accardino, AIA, Glen Cove, NY, 2002—. Mem. AIA. Republican. Roman Catholic.

ACERRA, MICHELE (MIKE ACERRA), engineering and construction company executive; b. Messina, Italy, Apr. 15, 1937; came to U.S., 1978; s. Luigi and Matilde Mazzullo A.; m. Elena Fino, May 31, 1975; children—Marco Eugenio, Matilde Enrica Jennifer. Dr. Chem. Engrng., Politecnico, Milan, Italy, 1962. Vessels designer Foster Wheeler Italiana, Milan, 1962, asst. mgr. drawing office, 1963, project engr., 1963-70, project mgr., 1970-74; pres. Glitsch Italiana, Rome, 1974-78; pres., chief oper. officer, dir. 8 subs. cos. Glitsch, Inc., Dallas, 1978-86; pres., chief exec. officer Foster Wheeler USA Corp., Perryville, N.J., 1986-89; corp. v.p. indsl. and environ. group Foster Wheeler Corp., Perryville, N.J., 1989-94; v.p. Foster Wheeler Energy Internat. Inc., 1994-97; dir. 4 subs.; v.p., mgr. BOC JV Foster Wheeler Power Sys., 1997-99; pres. Tray, Inc., Clinton, N.J., 2000—. Cons. in engrng. and contrn., expert mfg. and arbitrations. Roman Catholic. Avocations: reading, gardening, travel. Fax: 908-832-6169. E-mail: m.e.acerra@att.net.

ACETO, VINCENT JOHN, librarian, educator; b. Schenectady, N.Y., Feb. 5, 1932; s. Henry and Gilda (Maietta) A.; m. Jean Louise Rasey, Aug. 27, 1955 (div. 1974); children: David, Paul Andrew; m. Kveta Urbanova, June 16, 1993. AB, MA, SUNY, 1953, MLS, 1959; postgrad., Case Western Res. U., 1959, 62, 65-66. Tchr. Scotia (N.Y.)-Glenville Ctrl. Schs., 1956-57; high sch. libr. Burnt Hills (N.Y.)-Ballston Lake Ctrl. Schs., 1957-59; libr. dir. Town of Ballston Pub. Libr., Burnt Hills, 1958-60; Fulbright lectr. U. Dacca, East Pakistan, 1964-65; asst. prof. Sch. Libr. Sci., SUNY, Albany, 1959-62, assoc. prof. libr. sci., 1963-69, prof., 1969—, assoc. dean, 1987-93, interim dean, 1993-95, co-dir. film and TV documentation ctr., 1983—, Disting. Svc. prof., 2000—. Libr. cons. various pub. schs., N.Y. State Edn. Dept., U.S. Dept. Edn., USA Govt. of Bangladesh, 1965, Govt. of Cyprus, 1992, 94; dir. U.S. Office Edn. insts. and traineeships. Joint Editor: Film Lit. Index; contbr. articles to profl. jours. Prs., Filmdex Par II, Inc., 1973-90; bd. dirs. Freedom Forum, Schenectady, 1970-78, chmn., 1976-78; trustee Shenendehowa Pub. Libr., 1995—, v.p., 1996-97, 2000, pres., 1997-99, pres., 2002-; mem. Shenendehowa Ctrl. Pub. Schs. Bd. of Edn., 2002—. Served with AUS, 1954-56. Collins fellow U. Albany, 1997. Mem. ALA, NEA, Pakistan Libr. Assn., East Pakistan Libr. Assn. N.Y. Libr. Assn., Hudson-Mohawk Libr. Assn. (v.p. 1964-66), Am. Soc. Indexers, Am. Soc. Info. Scis., Soc. Cinema Studies, Idaka Forum, Kappa Phi Kappa, Phi Delta Kappa. Democrat. Unitarian Universalist. Home: 46 Southbury Rd Clifton Park NY 12065 Office: SUNY Albany Sch Info Sci and Policy 1400 Washington Ave Albany NY 12222-0100 E-mail: vaceto1@nycap.rr.com., aceto@albany.edu.

ACEVEDO-LOUBRIEL, SUZETTE, adult education educator; d. Francisco J. Acevedo and Sonia E. Loubriel. BA, U. of Puerto Rico, Rio Piedras, PR, 1990; MA, U. Wisc., 1993, PhD, 2000. Tchg. asst. U. Wis., Madison, Wis., 1991—96, rsch. asst., 1995—96; lectr. U. of Puerto Rico, Cayey, PR, 1997—2000, asst. prof., 2000—03, assoc. prof., 2003—. Systemic com. for the humanities U. of Puerto Rico, Cayey, PR, 2000, on line courses project rep., 2002—, editl. bd. Identidades, 2002—; mem. acad. senate Alternate Rep. Dept. Hispanic Studies; NEH fellow summer seminar for coll. and univ. tchrs. U. Kans., Lawrence, 2003. Author: (book) Cayey. 78, 1999, Cuadernos de Trabajo de la Biblioteca Victor M. Pons Gil 4, 1999; co-author: Escritura y communicion 7, 2000, Lenguaje y communicacion 8, 2000, Lenguaje y communicacion 9, 2000, Guia del maestro 10, 2001, Guia del maestro 11, 2001, Guia del maestro 12, 2001, Cuaderno de ortografia I, 2002, Cuaderno de ortografia II, 2002. Recipient Recognition Award for the Devel. and Advance of Arts and Humanities, U. of Puerto Rico, Cayey, 2001. Mem.: Twentieth Century Spanish Assn., Latin Am. Studies Assn., Modern Lang. Assn. Avocations: reading, music, pets, walking, travel. Office: U Puerto Rico-Cayey Dept Spanish Cayey PR 00736 E-mail: sacevedo@cayey.upr.edu.

ACEVEDO-VILA, ANIBAL, congressional representative, state legislator, lawyer; b. Río Piedras, P.R., Feb. 13, 1962; s. Salvador Acevedo-Colón and Elba Vilá; m. Luisa Gándara, June 29, 1987; children: Gabriela, Juan-Carlos. BA, U. P.R., 1982, JD, 1985; LLM, Harvard U., 1987. Law clk. to Hon. Federico Hernández-Denton Supreme Ct. of P.R., San Juan, 1985-86; law clk. to Hon. Levin H. Campbell U.S. Ct. Appeals (1st cir.), Boston, 1987-88; legis. affairs aide to Gov. Rafael Hernandez Colon San Juan, 1989-92; mem. at-large P.R. Ho. of Reps., San Juan, 1991—2001, ho. minority leader, 1997-2001; pres. Popular Dem. Party, 1997-99, v.p., 1999—; resident commr. U.S. Ho. of Reps from P. R., 2001—. Editor-in-chief Law Jour., U. P.R., 1984-85; columnist El Nuevo Día, 1993-96. Mem. governing bd. Popular Dem. Party, San Juan, 1995-. Mem. P.R. Bar Assn. Avocation: reading. Office: Ho of Reps Office Bldg 515 126 Cannon House Washington DC 20515-5401 E-mail: anibal@mail.house.gov.*

ACHAMPONG, FRANCIS KOFI, law educator, consultant; b. Kumasi, Ghana, Feb. 18, 1955; came to U.S., 1981; s. John Wilberforce and Salome (Mensa) A.; m. Nicole Victoria Blache. LLB, U. Ghana, 1976; LLM, U. London, 1977, PhD, 1981; LLM, Georgetown U., 1985. Bar: N.Y. 1986, Va. 1988, U.S. Dist. Ct. (ea. dist.) Va. 1988, U.S. Ct. Appeals (4th cir.) 1988, U.S. Supreme Ct. 1990. Adj. lectr. George Washington U., Washington, 1981-82; asst. prof. Howard U., Washington, 1981-85; assoc. prof. Norfolk State U., Va., 1985—92, prof., 1992—2002, chair dept. entrepreneurial studies, 1998—2001, interim dean Sch. Bus., 2001—02; of counsel Jones, Shelton, Kmetz & Malone, P.C, Norfolk, 1998—; dir. acad. affairs Pa. State U. at Mont Alto, 2002—. Cons. Aetna Life & Casualty, Hartford, Conn., 1981-82, Profl. Ins. Assn. of Md., Pa., 1986, Shapiro, Meiselman & Greene, P.C., Rockville, Md., 1987, Crowell & Moring, Washington, 1988, Clark & Stant, Virginia Beach, Va., 1988. Author: Workplace Sexual Harassment, 1999; contbr. articles to profl. jours. Mem. Am. Risk and Ins. Assn., Acad. Legal Studies in Bus. Avocations: gospel music, exercise, reading, movies. Home: 10076 Old Forge Rd Waynesboro PA 17268 Office: Pa State U at Mont Alto One Campus Dr Mont Alto PA 17237 Fax: 717-749-6069. E-mail: fka3@psu.edu.

ACHARYA, JAYANT NARAHARI, neurologist, educator; b. Pune, Maharashtra, India, Apr. 6, 1961; s. Holenarsipur Gururaja and Vasumathi Narahari; m. Vinita Jayant Thakur, June 12, 1994; children: Neil Jayant, Nathan Jayant. MB BS, B.J. Med. Coll., Pune U., India, 1983; MD, Pune U., India, 1986; DM in Neurology, NIMHANS, Bangalore U., India, 1991. Diplomate Am. Bd. Psychiatry and Neurology, Am. Bd. Clin. Neurophysiology. Resident in medicine Sassoon Gen. Hosps., Pune, 1984—86; lectr. medicine B. J. Med. Coll., Pune, 1987; resident in neurology NIMHANS, Bangalore, 1987—92; asst. prof. neurology M. S. Ramaiah Med. Coll., Bangalore U., Bangalore, 1993—94; clin. fellow in epilepsy and clin. neurophysiology Cleve. Clinic Found., 1994—97; resident in neurology Wake Forest U. Bapt. Med. Ctr., Winston-Salem, NC, 1997—2001; asst. prof. neurology U. Pitts. Med. Ctr., 2001—03; assoc. prof. neurology St. Louis Univ. Hosp., 2003—. Mem. residency task force com. U. Pitts. Med. Ctr., 2002—03; tchr. Wake Forest U. Sch. Medicine, Winston-Salem, 1998—2001; evaluator Wake Forest U. Sch. of Medicine, Winston-Salem, 1999—2000; tchr. U. Pitts. Sch. Medicine, 2001—, B. J. Med. Coll., Pune, 1985—87, NIMHANS, Bangalore, 1991—92, Cleve. Clinic Found., 1996—97; spkr. in field. Contbr. 14 articles to profl. jours., 4 chpts. to med. textbooks. Recipient Hindustan Ciba-Geigy Gold medal, Neurol. Soc. India, 1991, Internat. Young Investigator award, Internat. League Against Epilepsy, 1993. Mem.: AMA, Am. Soc. Neuroimaging, Am. Acad. Neurology, Am. Epilepsy Soc., Neurol. Soc. India (life), Indian Acad. Neurology (life), Indian Epilepsy Assn. (life). Avocations: music, painting, literature, philosophy, sports. Office: St Louis Univ Hosp Dept Neurology Greater Midwest Epilepsy Treatment Ctr 3635 Vista Ave at Grand Blvd Saint Louis MO 63110

ACHARYA, PRATHIMA S. research scientist; arrived in U.S., 1994; d. B.N.B. Vittal and Uma B.V. Rao; m. Sudhi S. Acharya, Dec. 23, 1993; 1 child, Aditya S. B in Pharmacy, Govt. Coll. Pharmacy, Bangalore, India, 1990, PharmM, 1992; PhD, U. Scis. Phila. (formerly PCPS), 2001. Registered pharmacist Drug Contr. Office, Karnataka, India, 1992. Scientist CIPLA Ltd., Bangalore, India, 1992—93; scientist protein formulations and analysis Diosynth RTP, Inc., Cary, NC, 2001—. Contbr. articles to profl. jours. Fellow, NIH, 1998—2001; Merit scholar, Govt. Karnataka, India, 1984, Sadtler Meml. fellow, U. Scis. in Phila., 1999—2000. Mem.: Am. Assn. Pharm. Scientists, Am. Chem. Soc., Indian Pharm. Assn. (life). Hindu. Office: Diosynth RTP Inc 3000 Weston Pkwy Cary NC 27513 Personal E-mail: prathima_acharya@hotmail.com. E-mail: prathima.acharya@diosynth-rtp.com.

ACHEBE, CHINUA, writer, humanities educator; b. Ogidi, Nigeria, Nov. 16, 1930; s. Isaiah Okafo and Janet N. (Iloegbunam) A.; m. Christie Chinwe Okoli, Sept. 10, 1961; children: Chinelo, Ikechukwu, Chidi, Nwando. Student, Univ. Coll., Ibadan, Nigeria, 1948 52; BA, U. London, 1953; DLitt (hon.), Dartmouth Coll., 1972; DUniv, Stirling U., U.K., 1975; DLitt (hon.), U. Southampton, Eng., 1975; LLD (hon.), U. Prince Edward Isl., Can., 1976; LHD (hon.), U. Mass., 1977; DLitt (hon.), U. Ife, Nigeria, 1978, U. Nigeria, Nsukka, 1981, U. Kent, Canterbury, Eng., 1982, Mt. Allison U., Sackville, Can., 1984, U. Guelph, Canada, 1984, Franklin Pierce Coll., 1985, Ibadan (Nigeria) U., 1989; DUniv, Open U., U.K., 1989; LLD (hon.), Georgetown U., 1990, Port Harcourt (Nigeria) U., 1991; DLitt (hon.), Skidmore Coll., 1991, CCNY, 1992, Fitchburg State Coll., 1994, Harvard U., 1996, BinghamtonU., 1996, Bates Coll., 1996, Fairleigh Dickinson U., 2002, Cape Town U., South Africa, 2002; LHD (hon.), Westfield Coll., 1989, New Sch. for Social Rsch., 1991, Hobart and William Smith Coll., 1991, Marymount Manhattan Coll., 1991, Colgate U., 1993; DLitt, Syracuse U., 1997; LHD, DLitt, Brown U., 1998, Trinity Coll., 1999, Ohio Wesleyan U., 1999, U. Witwatersrand, South Africa, 2000; LHD, Cape Town U., South Africa, 2002; DLitt, Haverford Coll., 2001. Prodr., contr., dir. Nigerian Broadcasting Co., Lagos, 1954-66; sr. rsch. fellow in African studies U. Nigeria, 1967-72, prof. dept. English, 1976-81, emeritus prof., 1985—. Vis. prof. English U. Mass., Amherst, 1972-75, U. Conn, Storrs, 1975-76, Afro-Am. studies U. Mass., Amherst, 1987-88; pro-chancellor Anambra State U. Tech., Enugu, Nigeria, 1986-88; Regent's lectr. UCLA, 1984; dir. Heinemann Ednl. Books (Nigeria) Ltd.; vis. fellow and Ashby lectr. Clare Hall, Cambridge (Eng.) U., 1993. Author: (novels) Things Fall Apart, 1958, No Longer at Ease, 1960, Arrow of God, 1964, A Man of the People, 1966, Anthills of the Savannah, 1988; (poetry) Christmas in Biafra, 1975; (short stories) Girls at War, 1972; (essays) Morning Yet on Creation Day, 1975; The Trouble with Nigeria, 1983, Hopes and Impediments-Selected Essays, 1965-87, 1988; (essay and poems) Another Africa, 1998; (non-fiction) Home and Exile, 2000, (children's stories) The Flute, 1978, The Drum 1978. Mem. coun. Lagos (Nigeria) U., 1966; mem. East Ctrl. State Libr. Bd., 1971-72, Anambra State Arts Coun., 1977-79; Goodwill amb. UN Population Fund, 1998—. Recipient Lit. award New Statesman, 1965, Commonwealth Poetry prize, 1973, Nat. Creativity award Nigeria, 1999, St. Louis Literary award 1999; Rockefeller fellow, 1960-61; UNESCO fellow, 1963. Friedenspreis(Peace Prize) Germany, 2002. Fellow: MLA (hon.), Nigerian Acad. Letters, Royal Soc. Lit. (London); mem.: Nonino Risit D'Aur, Royal African Soc. (hon.; hon. v.p. London 1998), Am. Acad. Arts and Letters (hon.). Office: Bard Coll Dept Lang and Lit Annandale On Hudson NY 12504

ACHELPOHL, STEVEN EDWARD, lawyer, political organization administrator; b. Wichita, Kans., July 15, 1950; s. Ray Edward and Juanita J. (Barnes) A.; m. Shelley R. Kiel (div. Sept. 1987); m. Sara K. Nabity, Nov. 24, 1989; children: Joseph E., Samuel B., Raechel A., Ryan Sullivan, Peter Sullivan. BA, U. Nebr., 1972, JD with distinction, 1975. Bar: Nebr. 1975, U.S. Dist. Ct. Nebr. 1975, U.S. Ct. Appeals (8th cir.) 1981. Law clk. hon. Donald R. Ross U.S. Ct. Appeals, Omaha, 1975-77; atty. McGrath, North, O'Mally, Kratz, Omaha, 1977-80, Dwyer, O'Leary & Martin, Omaha, 1980-83; ptnr. Schumacher & Achelpohl, Omaha, 1983-92; assoc. Smith Peterson, Omaha, 1992-93; pvt. practice Omaha, 1994—. Dir. Vis. Nurses Assn., Omaha, 1993—, fin. com., 1994—; chair, Neb. Dem. Party, 2001—; fellow, Neb. State Bar Found., Am. Coll. of Trial Lawyers; mem. Democratic Nat. Com., 2001-. Democrat. Avocations: golf, baseball. Home: 6420 Underwood Ave Omaha NE 68132-1812 Office: 1823 Harney St Ste 1010 Omaha NE 68102-1900 E-mail: achelpohl@usa.net.

ACHEM, SAMI RENE, internist, medical educator; b. Torreon, Coahuila, Mex., Aug. 16, 1949; arrived in U.S., 1976; s. Antonio Achem and Samia Karam; m. Pilar Ayala, May 22, 1976; children: Cristina, Diana, Sami Jr. BS magna cum laude, Inst. Frances De La Laguna, 1966; postgrad., Am. U. Beirut, 1966—67; MD summa cum laude, Facultad De Medicina De Torreon, Mex., 1974. Diplomate Am. Bd. Internal Medicine, Am. Bd. Gastroenterology, lic. physician Mex., Mich., Fla. Instr. anatomy and physiology Inst. Frances De La Laguna, 1972—75; instr. gastroenterology Facultad de Medicina de Torreon, U. Autonoma de Coahuila, 1972—74; instr. internal medicine Coll. Nursing Gomez Palacio, Durango, Mexico, 1973—74; intern Nat. Mex. Inst. Social Security, 1973—74, 1975—76; intern pub. health br. Nat. Mex. Govt., 1974—75; resident U. Cin. Med. Ctr., 1976—79; fellow in gastroenterology U. Mich. Med. Ctr., Ann Arbor, 1979—81, rsch. fellow gastrointestinal motility and hormone interactions, 1981—84; instr. internal medicine U. Mich. Sch. Medicine, Ann Arbor, 1981—84; asst. prof. medicine divsn. gastroenterology and nutrition U. Fla. Coll. Medicine, Jacksonville, 1985—92, assoc. prof. medicine, 1993—97, acting chief divsn. gastroenterology, 1995—97; sr. assoc. cons. Mayo Clinic, Jacksonville, 1997—, cons. dept. internal medicine, divsn. gastroenterology, assoc. program dir. gastroenterology fellowship tng. program, 2000—; assoc. prof. medicine Mayo Sch. Medicine, Rochester, Minn., 1998—. Chief gastrointestinal endoscopy unit VA Med. Ctr., U. Mich., Ann Arbor, 1981—84; mem. human experimentation com. U. Fla., Jacksonville, 1984—94, dir. gastrointestinal motility lab., 1985—97, mem. internal medicine housestaff selection com., 1985—87, mem. emergency medicine faculty positions search com., 1985—87, mem. fringe benefit com., 1986—87, dir. gastrointestinal endoscopy lab., 1986—96, mem. nephrology search com., chief and faculty positions, 1986—87, mem. cardiology dept. faculty search com., 1987—89, mem. pathology dept. faculty search com., 1987—90, mem. faculty diagnostic clinic com., 1987—90, chmn. instl. rev. bd., 1987—94, mem. rsch. com., 1993—97; acting chief divsn. gastroenterology U. Fla. Coll. Medicine, 1995—97; mem. staff policies and regulations com. U. Fla. Health Sci. Ctr., Jacksonville, 1997; mem. internat. com. Mayo Clinic, Jacksonville, 1998; spkr., lectr., presenter in field. Co-editor-in-chief Digestive Diseases, 1993—94, editor-in-chief, 1994—2001, mem. editl. bd. Revisiones en Gastroenterologia, 1997—, Am. Jour. Gastroenterology, 1997—, Endo-Nurse, 2001—, assoc. internat. editor Jour. Gastrointestinal Endoscopy of Mex., 2001—, reviewer jours. in field. Newspaper soccer writer El Siglo de Torreon, 1970—74; TV commentator, soccer critic Channel 4, Torreon, 1971—79; vol. coach Jacksonville Soccer League, 1990—93, vol. referee, 1990—91; co-chair fund raising Episcopal H.S., Jacksonville, 1998, chair, 1999, soccer announcer, 2000. Served with Mex. Army, 1967. Named Disting. Vis. Physician, City of San Pedro Sula, Honduras, 1998, City of Maracaibo, Venezuela, 1999; named one of Best Drs. in Am., 1995, 1997—98, 2002; recipient Pharm. award for disting. med. sch. career, A.H. Robbins, 1969—72, active tchr. recognition, Am. Acad. Family Physicians, 1987, recognition for tchg. and svcs., Mex. Gatroenterology Soc., 1989. Fellow: ACP (Best Rsch. Paper 1997), Am. Coll. Gastroenterology; mem.: AAAS, So. Med. Assn., Fla. Soc. Internal Medicine, Fla. Physicians Assn., Fla. Med. Assn., Fla. Gastroenterol. Assn., Duval County Med. Soc. (assoc. editor jour. 2001), Am. Soc. Internal Medicine, Am. Soc. Study of Liver Disease, Am. Soc. Gastrointestinal Endoscopy, Am. Soc. Contemporary Medicine and Surgery, Am. Motility Soc., Am. Liver Found., Am. Gastroenterol. Assn. (Disting. Poster Presentation 2000), Am. Fedn. Clin. Rsch., Am. Coll. Emergency Physicians. Home: 7842 James Island Way Jacksonville FL 32256 Office: Mayo Clinic 4500 San Pablo Rd Jacksonville FL 32224

ACHEN, MARK KENNEDY, city administrator, management consultant; b. Vancouver, Wash., Apr. 13, 1943; s. George Ben and Marjorie Beth (Pierson) A.; m. Mary Ann Uzzell, Aug. 14, 1971, children: Wyndi Marie, Kara Lynn. BA, U. Wash., 1967; MA, U. Mo., 1981. Asst. to city mgr. City of Ferguson, Mo., 1972-74; city adminstr. City of Mounds View, Minn., 1974-79; city mgr. City of Gladstone, Mo., 1979-84, City of Grand Junction, Colo., 1984-2000; ret.; interim city coord. City of Centennial, Colo., 2001—02. Cons. U.S. Nat. Fire Acad., Emmitsburg, Md., 1990-91, adj. faculty, 1991-92; mem. Colo. Supreme Ct. Disciplinary Hearing Bd., 1999—; nat. bd. dirs. Innovation Groups, 1999-2000. Gates Found. fellow Harvard U. Sr. Govt. Exec. Program, 1987. Mem. ASPA (Kansas City chpt. Adminstr. of Yr. 1983), Colo. City Mgmt. Assn. (pres. 1988-89, bd. dirs. 1985-91, range rider 2001—), Internat. City Mgmt. Assn. (life, chmn. 1988 internat. conf. planning com., co-chmn. 1995 internat. conf. host com., credentialing adv. bd. 2001-, range rider 2001—), Rotary (pres. 1983-84, bd. dirs. 1989-90, 92-93, Paul Harris fellow 1991), Club 20 (exec. com. 2000-02). Avocations: mountain climbing, backpacking, boating, golf. Home and Office: 3344 Northridge Dr Grand Junction CO 81506-1926 E-mail: machen8@tds.net.

ACHENBACH, JAN DREWES, engineering educator, scientist; b. Leeuwarden, Netherlands, Aug. 20, 1935; came to U.S., 1959, naturalized, 1978; s. Johannes and Elizabeth (Schipper) A.; m. Marcia Graham Fee, July 15, 1961. Candidate engr., Tech. U. Delft, 1959; PhD, Stanford U., 1962. Preceptor Columbia U., 1962-63; asst. prof. Northwestern U., Evanston, Ill., 1963, assoc. prof., 1966-69, prof. dept. civil engring., 1969—, Walter P. Murphy prof. civil engring., mech. engrng. and applied math., 1981—, dir. Ctr. for Quality Engrng. and Failure Prevention, 1986—; vis. assoc. prof. U. Calif., San Diego, 1969; vis. prof. Tech. U. Delft, 1970-71; prof. Huazhong Inst. Sci. and Tech., 1981. Mem. at large U.S. Nat. Com. Theoretical and Applied Mechanics, 1972-78, 86—. Author: Wave Propagation in Elastic Solids, 1973, A Theory of Elasticity with Microstructure for Directionally Reinforced Composites, 1975, (with A.K. Gautesen and H. McMaken) Ray Methods for Waves in Elastic Solids, 1982, (with Y. Rajapakse) Solid Mechanics Research for Quantitative Non-Destructive Evaluation, 1987; editor: (with J. Miklowitz) Modern Problems in Elastic Wave Propagation, 1978 (with S.K. Datta and Y.S. Rajapakse) Elastic Waves and Ultrasonic Nondestructive Testing, 1990; editor-in-chief: Wave Motion, 1979—. Recipient award C. Gelderman Found., 1970, C.W. McGraw Rsch. award Am. Soc. Engrng. Edn., 1975, Tempo All-Professor Team, Sciences, Chicago Tribune, 1993, Model of Excellence award McDonnell-Douglas, 1996, Disting. Svc. medal Am. Acad. Mechanics, 1997, Prager medal Soc. Engrng. Sci., 2001. Fellow AAAS, ASME (hon., Timoshenko medal 1992), Soc. Engrng. Sci., Am. Acad. Arts Scis., Acoustical Soc. Am., Soc. Engrng. Sci.; mem. Royal Dutch Acad. Scis. (corres.), U.S. Nat. Acad. Scis., US Nat. Acad. Engrng., Am. Soc. Nondestructive Testing. Home: 711 Roslyn Ter Evanston IL 60201-1721 Office: Northwestern U Room 324 2137 N Sheridan Catalysis Bldg Evanston IL 60208 E-mail: achenbach@northwestern.edu.

ACHENBAUM, ALVIN ALLEN, marketing and management consultant; b. N.Y.C., Dec. 11, 1925; s. Benjamin and Dora (Dworin) A.; m. Barbara Ann Greenwald, June 24, 1951 (dec. Apr. 1992); children: Jonathan Peter, Lisa Jane, Martha Beth; m. Leila Lebendig, June 6, 1993. BS, UCLA, 1950; MS, Columbia U., 1951. Mgr. market rsch. McCann-Erickson, N.Y.C., 1951-57; exec. v.p., sec., dir. Grey Advt., Inc., N.Y.C., 1957-71; exec. v.p. J. Walter Thompson Co., 1971-74; chmn. bd. dirs. Canter, Achenbaum, Assocs., Inc., N.Y.C., 1974-89; vice chmn. bd. dirs. Backer, Spielvogel, Bates Worldwide, N.Y.C., 1989-93; pres. Achenbaum Assocs. Inc., N.Y.C., 1992-95; chmn. Achenbaum Bogda Assocs. Inc., N.Y.C., 1996—. Bd. dirs. MARC, Inc. Mem. edit. bd. Jour. Advt. Rsch. Mem. Citizens Adv. Com. of Irvington, 1970— ; mem. Middle Eastern affairs com. Anti-Defamation League; adv. com. Assn. Consumer Research.; Trustee Mktg. Sci. Inst.; Am. Mktg. Assn. Found.; editl. bd. Mktg. Mgmt. Mag. Named to Market Research Hall of Fame. Mem. Market Rsch. Coun. N.Y., Copy Rsch. Coun. N.Y., Am. Mktg. Assn. (v.p. global mktg. div., bd. dirs., found. trustee), Am. Econ. Assn., Assn. Pub. Opinion Rsch., Beta Gamma Sigma. Home: 225 Central Park W New York NY 10024-6026 Office: Achenbaum Bogda Assocs Inc 225 Central Park W Apt 723 New York NY 10024-6033 E-mail: alvinache@aol.com.

ACHESON, ALLEN MORROW, retired engineering executive; b. Tanta, Egypt, June 12, 1926; s. Samuel Irvine and Hazel Lenore (Welker) A.; m. Mary Jean Baird, Aug. 5, 1950 (div. May 1978); children: Rebecca R., Jennifer E., Scott A., Jon M. BS in Mech. Engrng., Iowa State U., 1950; LLD, Tarkio Coll., 1985. Registered profl. engr., Mo. Sta. supt. Iowa Pub. Svc. Co., Carroll, 1950-54; engr. Proctor & Gamble Co., 1954-55, Iowa-Ill. Gas & Electric Co., 1955-56; mgr. City Power & Light Co., Independence, Mo., 1956-60; mgmt. adviser Yanhee Electricity Authority, Bangkok, Thailand, 1960-63; exec. v.p. Black & Veatch Internat., Kansas City, Mo., 1964-73, pres., 1973-88, chmn., 1989-91; gen. ptnr. Black & Veatch, Kansas City, Mo., 1974-75, exec. ptnr., 1975-91; ret., 1991. Trustee Tarkio (Mo.) Coll., 1964-77, chmn., 1975-77; elder Trinity and Rolling Hills United Presbyn. Ch. With USNR, 1944-46. Recipient Profl. Achievement citation Coll. Engrng., Iowa State U., 1976, Marston medal, 1992. Mem. Am. Cons. Engrs. Coun. (chmn. internat. engrng. divsn., past pres. award 1992); mem. ASME (life). Home: 723 W 100th St Kansas City MO 64114 E-mail: aacheson@hotmail.com.

ACHESON, DAVID CAMPION, lawyer, author, policy analyst; b. Washington, Nov. 4, 1921; s. Dean G. and Alice (Stanley) Acheson; m. Patricia Castles, May 1, 1943 (dec. 2000); children: Eleanor Dean, David Campion, Peter Wesley. BA, Yale U., 1942; LLB, Harvard U., 1948. Bar: DC, Pa., U.S. Supreme Ct. With Office Gen. Counsel AEC, 1948—49; with firm Covington & Burling, Washington, 1950—61, mem. firm, 1958—61; U.S. atty. for DC, 1961—65; spl. asst. to sec. treasury, 1965—67; v.p., sr. v.p., gen. counsel Communications Satellite Corp., 1967—74; ptnr. Jones, Day, Reavis & Pogue, Washington, 1974—78, Drinker Biddle & Reath, Phila. and Washington, 1978—87. Bd. dirs. Dulles Access Rapid Transit Inc. Author (with others): Effective Washington Representation, 1983, Acheson Country: A Memoir, 1993; co-author (CSIS report): A More Effective Civil Space Program, 1988; editor: This Vast External Realm, 1973; editor: (with David McLellan) Among Friends, 1980. Mem. presdl. commn. on Challenger accident, 1986; pres. Atlantic Coun. U.S., 1993—99. Mem.: Met. Club. Episcopalian. Home: 2700 Calvert St NW Washington DC 20008-2621 E-mail: dcampach@aol.com.

ACHGILL, RALPH KENNETH, retired research scientist; b. Indpls., June 17, 1938; s. Kenneth and Lois Ann (Philips) A.; m. Virginia Ann Swisher, July 21, 1956 (dec. Nov. 1992); children: Kenneth Edward, Douglas Alan, Kerry Wayne, Bridget Marie; m. Diane K. McCauley, Dec. 26, 1993. Student, Purdue U., 1956-60. Rsch. scientist Eli Lilly & Co., Indpls., 1956-93, internat. tech. coord., 1974-93; ret., 1993. Patentee in field. Mem. Masons (past master), Optimist Club (charter pres.). Republican. Avocation: philatelic dealer and auctioneer. Home: PO Box 6508 Lafayette IN 47903-6508 E-mail: rka@rkacovers.com.

ACHING, GERARD, language educator; BA in Polit. Sci., U. Calif., Berkeley, 1982; PhD in Romance Studies, Cornell U., 1991. Assoc. prof. Spanish and Portuguese langs. and lits. NYU, N.Y.C. Faculty fellow Ctr. for Critical Analysis of Contemporary Culture Rutgers U., 1992—93. Recipient Guggen-

heim fellowship, 2003, Howard Found. fellowship, Brown U., 1999—2000, Outstanding Tchr. award, Rutgers Coll. Parents Assn., 1993. Office: 19 University Pl 404 New York NY 10003*

ACHINSTEIN, PETER JACOB, philosopher, educator; b. N.Y.C., June 30, 1935; s. Asher and Betty (Comras) A.; children: Jonathan, Sharon, Betty; m. Katharine Rowland, 2002. AB, Harvard, 1956, AM, 1958, PhD, 1961; postgrad. (Knox Traveling fellow), Oxford U., Eng., 1959-60. Asst. prof. U. Iowa, Iowa City, 1961-62; asst. prof. philosophy Johns Hopkins Balt., 1962-64; asso. prof., 1964-68; prof., 1968—; chmn. dept. philosophy, 1968-77; vis. prof. M.I.T., Cambridge, 1965-66, Stanford (Calif.) U., 1967, City U. N.Y., 1973; mem. adv. panel NSF, 1968-70, 79-81; Lady Davis vis. prof. Hebrew U., Jerusalem, spring 1976. Author: Concepts of Science, 1968, Law and Explanation, 1971, The Nature of Explanation, 1983, Particles and Waves: Historical Essays in the Philosophy of Science, 1991 (Lakatos award 1993); The Book of Evidence, 2001; editor: (with Stephen Barker) The Legacy of Logical Positivism, 1969, The Concept of Evidence, 1983, (with Laura J. Snyder) Scientific Methods, 1994; Science rule, 2004; mem. editl. bd. Philosophy of Sci., 1973-2000. Guggenheim fellow, 1966-67 Fellow AAAS (chair history and philosophy of sci. sect. L 1995); mem. Philosophy of Sci. Assn. (bd. govs.), Internat. Union History and Philosophy (del. U.S. 1967-73, 79-86), Phi Beta Kappa. Office: Johns Hopkins U Dept Philosophy Baltimore MD 21218 E-mail: peter.achinstein@jhu.edu.

ACHOR, LOUIS JOSEPH MERLIN, psychology and neuroscience educator; b. Clarendon, Tex., Jan. 2, 1948; s. Merlin Farr and Aileen (Arneson) A.; m. Sharon Lyn Slack, Nov. 7, 1970; children: Shawn Joseph, Amy Christina. BA in Psychology, UCLA, 1971, MA in Zoology, 1972; PhD in Psychobiology, U. Calif., Irvine, 1977. NIMH predoctoral fellow U. Calif., Irvine, 1974-76, trainee, 1972-74, 76-77; asst. prof. in psychology Baylor U., Waco, Tex., 1978-85, assoc. prof. psychology, 1986-91, assoc. prof. neurosci. and psychology, 1991—, dir. undergrad. programs in neurosci. and psychology, 1992-94. Jour. and conf. reviewer; judge Ctrl. Tex. Regional Sci. Fair, 1979—, mem. sci. rev. com., 1991-92, mem. instnl. rev. bd., 1997-2002; instr. Baylor U. for Young People, 1991-93; mem. pre-med./pre-dental adv. com. Baylor U., 1994—. Contbr. articles to profl. jours. Chmn. nat. and internat. scholarships com. Baylor U., 1986-90; asst. scoutmaster Boy Scouts Am., 1989-93; trustee, tchr. Sunday sch., 2001—. Recipient Young Investigator award Baylor U., 1982; honoree Phi Beta Kappa, 2002; named Cir. of Achievement Outstanding Prof., Mortar Board, Baylor U., 2001. Mem. AAUP, Soc. for Neurosci., Faculty for Undergrad. Neurosci. (charter, funding sources com. 1992-93, councilor exec. com. 1993-94, sec. 1994-97, chmn. com. to establish nat. honor soc. in neurosci. 2001—, fellow 2002), Internat. Brain Rsch. Orgn., Tex. Assn. Advisors for Health Professions, Baylor Neurosci. Soc. (founder, advisor 1997—), Sigma Xi (Baylor U. chpt. sec.-treas. 1988-89, v.p. 1989-90, pres. 1990-92, nominating com. 2003), Psi Chi (founder, advisor 1985—, scholarship established in his honor Baylor U. 1986, Prof. of Yr. 1996, 98), Nu Rho Psi (advisor 2000—). Achievements include discovery that components of brainstem auditory evoked response have multiple generators. Home: 10005 Treeline Dr Waco TX 76712-8529 Office: Dept Psychology and Neurosci Baylor U Waco TX 76798

ACHORD, JAMES LEE, gastroenterologist, educator; b. Dayton, Ohio, Sept. 24, 1931; s. Lonnie M. and Ethel E. (Collins) A.; m. Patsy Jane Moore, Dec. 18, 1954; children: J. Michael, Ann Elizabeth, Andrew P. Student, Emory U., 1949-52, MD, 1956. Intern Emory Hosp., 1956-57; resident Emory U., Atlanta, 1959-62, instr., assoc. prof., 1962-71; med. dir. Med. Ctr. Cen. Ga., Macon, 1971-75; assoc. dean, prof. East Tenn. State Sch. Medicine, Johnson City, 1975-76; prof., dir. div. digestive diseases U. Miss. Med. Ctr., Jackson, 1976-98, prof. emeritus, 1998. Editor book revs. Am. Jour. Gastroenterology, 1985-91, Dig. Dis. Sci., 1994-96; mem. editl. bd. Am. Jour. Clin. Gastroenterology, 1999—; contbr. numerous articles and editls. to profl. jours. and chpts. to books. Capt. U.S. Army, 1957-59. Fellow ACP (gov. Miss. chpt. 1993-97), Am. Coll. Gastroenterology (pres. 1983-84); mem. Am. Assn. Subspecialty Profs., Am. Assn. Study Liver Disease, Am. Gastroent. Assn., Am. Soc. Gastroenterologic Endoscopy.

ACHORN, ROBERT COMEY, retired newspaper publisher; b. Westboro, Mass., Mar. 31, 1922; s. Edward Welt and Mabel (Comey) A.; m. Jean Mary Berlo, Sept. 23, 1950 (dec. 1980); children: Nancy Louise (Mrs. Eric Engberg), Susan Jean, Edward Christopher, Judith Joyce (Mrs. Albert Berry), Carole Lee (Mrs. Ralph Abislaiman); m. Ann Bouvier, Aug. 20, 1982. AB, Brown U., 1943. Reporter Worcester (Mass.) Telegram, 1946-53; editorial writer Evening Gazette, Worcester, 1953-60, mng. editor, 1964-67; editor editorial pages Worcester Telegram & Gazette, 1964-67, assoc. editor, 1967-70, editor, 1970-73, v.p., editor, 1973-81, assoc. pub., exec. v.p., 1981-82, pub., 1982-87, dir., 1982-88, pres., 1986-87, Beacon Communications Corp., 1984-85, vice chmn., 1985-87; pres. Worcester Telegram & Gazette, Inc., 1985-87. Bd. dirs. Blackstone Valley Regional Devel. Corp., 1991-95; mem. newspaper adv. bd. UPI, 1974-78. Pres. United Way of Ctrl. Mass., Worcester, 1973—75; v.p. The Meml. Hosp., 1976; vice chmn. Ctrl. Mass. chpt. ARC, 1976—84, chmn., 1984—86; media chmn. Mass. Bar-Press Com., 1976—77; chmn. trustees Worcester Found. Exptl. Biology, 1984—87; trustee Old. Sturbridge Village, 1986—2001, hon. trustee, 2001—; trustee U. Mass. Med. Ctr. Found., 1991—2002, Sutton Coun. on Aging, 1993—99, U. Mass. Meml. Found., 1998—2002. Fellow Acad. New Eng. Journalists; mem. UPI New Eng. Newspaper Editors (pres. 1969), Am. Soc. Newspaper Editors, New Eng. Newspaper Assn. (pres. 1986-87), New Eng. Soc. Newspaper Editors (pres. 1968), New Eng. AP News Execs. Assn. (pres. 1971), Am. Antiquarian Soc., Soc. Profl. Journalists, Worcester Club, Worcester Econ. Club (pres. 1975), Bohemian Club, Nat. Press Club, St. Wulstan Soc., Worcester Torch Club, Phi Beta Kappa.

ACHTENBERG, ROBERTA, former federal official; b. L.A., July 20, 1950; d. Louis and Beatrice A.; 1 child. AB, U. Calif., Berkeley, 1972; postgrad., U. Calif., San Francisco, 1972-73; JD, U. Utah, 1975. Bar: Calif., U.S. Dist. Ct. (no. dist.) Calif., U.S. Ct. Appeals (9th cir.). Exec. dir. Nat. Ctr. Lesbian Rights, 1989-90; asst. sec. fair housing and equal opportunity HUD, Washington, 1993-95, Sr. Adv. to Sec., 1995—; sr. v.p. pub. policy dept. San Francisco C. of C., 1995—. Mem. County Bd. Suprs., City and County of San Francisco; bd. dirs. Bay Area Air Quality Mgmt. Dist., 1991-93; trustee, Calif. State U. Mem. Order of Coir, Phi Beta Kappa. Office: San Francisco C of C Pub Policy Dept 235 Montgomery St 12th Fl San Francisco CA 94104

ACHTENHAGEN, FRANK, economics educator; b. Berlin, May 28, 1939; s. Wilhelm and Kaethe (Ulrich) A.; m. Roswitha Manski, Sept. 30, 1965 (dec. Feb. 1990); children: Claudia, Leona; m. Susanne Weber, Nov. 11, 1994. Diploma, Free U. Berlin, 1963, D in Econs., 1969; D in Econs. (hon.), U. St. Gallen, Switzerland, 1991; D in Philosophy (hon.), U. Helsinki, Finland, 2000. Referendar Senate of Berlin, 1963-65; asst. prof. econs. Free U. Berlin, 1966-69; assoc. prof. U. Münster, Germany, 1969-71; prof. econs., dir. U. Göttingen, Germany, 1971—. Author 20 books, 1969—. Mem. German Soc. for Edn. Rsch. (treas. 1980-88), Am. Ednl. Rsch. Assn., European Assn. for Rsch. on Learning and Instrn. Evangelical. Avocations: tennis, skiing. Home: Am Goldgraben II D-37073 Göttingen Germany Office: Georg August U Platz Goettinger Sieben 5 D-37073 Göttingen Germany

ACHTERMAN, GAIL LOUISE, lawyer; b. Portland, Oreg., Aug. 1, 1949; AB in Econs. with distinction, Stanford U., 1971; MS in Natural Resource Policy and Mgmt., U. Mich., 1975, JD cum laude, 1974. Bar: Oreg. 1974, U.S. Dist. Ct. Oreg. 1978, U.S. Supreme Ct. 1978, U.S. Ct. Appeals (fed. and 10th cirs.). Atty.-advisor U.S. Dept. Interior, 1975-78; asst. for natural resources Gov. Neil Goldschmidt, 1987-91; mem. Stoel Rives LLP, Portland, 1978-2000. Exec. dir. Deschutes Resources Conservancy, 2000—; adj. prof. forest policy, Coll. Forestry, Oreg. State U., 1991—. Mem. Oreg. Water Resources Commn., 1981-85, Gov.'s Growth Task Force, 1998; mem. pres.'s bd. advisors Oreg. State U., 2000—, Oreg. Transp. Commn., 2000—. Mem. bd. dirs. Sustainable Ecosystems Inst., Am. Leadership Forum, Oreg. Women's Forum, Portland C. of C. (bd. dirs. 1996-99). Office: PO Box 1560 Bend OR 97709-1560

ACIERNO, LOUIS JOSEPH, medical educator, researcher; b. N.Y.C., June 30, 1920; s. Michelangelo and Anna (Brienza) A.; m. Dorothy Theresa Monahan, June 6, 1948; children: M. Barry, Denise. BS, Manhattan Coll., 1941; MD, Georgetown U., 1944, Bologna (Italy) U., 1974. Diplomate Am. Bd. Internal Medicine. Intern Kings County Hosp., Bklyn., 1944-45, resident, 1945-46, 48-50; NIH post-doctoral rsch. fellow in cardiology SUNY-Downstate, 1950-51; prof. cardiopulmonary scis. U. Ctrl. Fla., 1979—. Author: Cardiac Rehabilitation and Prevention, 1984, The Human Machine: How It Breaks Down, History of Cardiology, 1994, Digest of Chest Diseases, 1997, Elements of Cardiac Pharmacology, 1998. Capt. U.S. Army, 1946-48. Fellow ACP, Am. Coll. Cardiology (Gifted Tchr. of Yr. award 1997). Republican. Roman Catholic. Avocations: reading, writing. Home: 245 Salvador Sq Winter Park FL 32789-5618 E-mail: acierno@pegasus.cc.ucf.edu.

ACKER, ANDREW FRENCH, III, mathematics educator, researcher; b. New London, Conn., May 9, 1943; s. Andrew French Jr. and Miriam Luce (Woodhull) A.; children: Denise, Marcella, Joseph, Laurel; m. Melissa Ann Stanton, Aug. 10, 1991; children: Michael, Christian. BS, Union Coll., Schenectady, 1965; PhD, Boston U., 1972; Prof Dr, Karlsruhe U., Germany, 1982. Lectr. Boston U., 1969-72; asst. prof. La. State U., New Orleans, 1972-73; asst. U. Karlsruhe, 1973-83; assoc. prof. math. Iowa State U., Ames, 1983-87, Wichita (Kans.) State U., 1987-91, prof., 1991—. Guest rschr. U. Heidelberg, Germany, summer 1987. Contbr. articles to math. jours. Mem. Am. Math. Soc., Sigma Xi, Pi Mu Epsilon. Achievements include contributions to the analytical treatment of free boundary problems in elliptic partial differential equations, especially flow-surface and flow-interface problems in fluid dynamics, with emphasis on the existence, uniqueness, convexity and geometry of solutions; development of operator methods for successive approximation of free boundaries. Home: 1213 Farmstead St Wichita KS 67208-2628 Office: Wichita State U Dept Math Wichita KS 67260-0033 E-mail: acker@math.twsu.edu.

ACKER, ANN, lawyer; b. Chgo., July 21, 1948; BA, St. Mary's Coll., 1970; JD, Loyola U., 1973. Bar: Ill. 1973. Partner Chapman and Cutler, Chgo. Mem.: Nat. Assoc. of Bond Lawyers, Chicago Bar Assoc., Amer. Bar Assoc. Office: Chapman and Cutler 111 W Monroe St Ste 1700 Chicago IL 60603-4006*

ACKER, CINDY SHERLINDA BERNICE, preschool administrator; b. San Francisco, Dec. 30, 1956; d. Washington and Darline (Bell) Maxwell; m. Elisabeth Middelberg; children: Jennifer Elisabeth, Brionna Roné, Jonathan-Paul. B in Phys. Edn., U. Calif., Berkeley, 1980; MEd, San Francisco State U., 1983. Tchr. Alameda (Calif.) Park & Recreation Dept., 1981; owner, founder GYMini of Alameda, 1981-83; founder, adminstr. The Child Unique Montessori Sch., Alameda, 1983—2000. Bd. dirs. Xanthos, Inc., Alameda Author: Contagious Disease, 1991; contbr. articles to mags. Bd. dirs. Memory, HIV Prevention Planning Coun. Recipient Golden Rule award J.S. Penney Co., 1992, 94. Mem. Nat. Child Care Assn. (health spokesman), Calif. Assn. Employers, Profl. Assn. Childhood Edn. (chpt. pres. 1990-91, v.p. 1991-92, legis. com. 1992, pres.- elect 1993, bd. dirs., pres. 1995), Montessori Adminstrs. Coun. Avocations: writing, walking, gardening, collecting antiques, singing. Office: The Child Unique 2226 Encinal Ave Alameda CA 94501-4413

ACKER, FREDERICK GEORGE, lawyer; b. Defiance, Ohio, May 7, 1934; s. Julius William and Orah Louise (Dowler) A.; m. Cynthia Ann Wayne, Dec. 1, 1962; children: Frederick Wayne, Mary Katherine, Richard Hoghton, Jennifer Ruth. Student, Ind. U., 1952-54; BA, Valparaiso U., 1956; MA, Harvard U., 1957, JD, 1961; postgrad., U. Manchester (Eng.), 1957-58. Bar: Ill. 1961, Ind. 1961. Ptnr. Winston & Strawn, Chgo., 1961-88, McDermott, Will & Emery, Chgo., 1988—2003, counsel, 2003—. Co-chmn. Joint Prin. and Income Act. com., Chgo., 1976-81. Co-author: (portfolio) Generation-Skipping Tax, 1991; contbr. articles to profl. jours. Bd. dirs. Max McGraw Wildlife Found., Dundee, Ill., 1984-2003, chmn., pres. 1997-2001; trustee L.S. Wood Ednl. Trust, Chgo., 1975—; trustee Ill. chpt. The Nature Conservancy, Chgo., 1981-90, chmn., 1986-90. Danforth Found. fellow, 1956; Fulbright scholar, 1957. Mem. Trout Unlimited, Fulbright Assn. (bd. dirs. 1994-2000, pres. 2000), Met. Chgo. Club, Anglers Club, Chgo. Farmers Club. Lutheran. Avocations: hunting, fishing. Home: 543 N Madison St Hinsdale IL 60521-3213 Office: McDermott Will & Emery 227 W Monroe St Ste 3100 Chicago IL 60606-5096

ACKER, JOSEPH EDINGTON, retired cardiology educator; b. Knoxville, Tenn., Oct. 19, 1918; s. Joseph Edwan and Kate Loubelle (Edington) A.; m. Elizabeth Chase Gutch, Nov. 14, 1942; children: Joseph Edington III, Judith Ann Acker Mitchell, Julia Chase Acker Van Mol, John Howard, Janet Acker Fox; m. Mary (Polly) Winters Phillips, Apr. 22, 1991. BS, MD, U. Tenn., 1941. Diplomate Am. Bd. Internal Medicine. Intern Kansas City Gen. Hosp., 1941-42; resident Cleve. City Hosp., 1946-48; pvt. practice internal medicine Knoxville, 1948-55; pvt. practice cardiology, 1955-84; mem. Knoxville Cardiovascular Group, 1962-85; chief cardiac work evaluation clinic Knoxville Gen. Hosp., 1948-56, U. Tenn., 1956-72, prof. clin. medicine Meml. Rsch. Ctr. and Hosp., 1957-84. Dir. cardiac outpatient rehab. programs U. Tenn. Meml. Hosp., 1977-84, St. Mary's Hosp., 1977-83, Fort Sanders Presbyn. Hosp., 1977-93. Author: (with Erb and Mann) Physicians Handbook for Evaluation of Cardiovascular and Physical Fitness, 1970; editor Newsletter Internat. Soc. Cardiology, 1972-80. Served to lt. comdr. USNR, 1942-46. Fellow ACP, Coun. Clin. Cardiology, Am. Heart Assn., Am. Coll. Cardiology; mem. East Tenn. Heart Assn. (pres. 1956), Tenn. Heart Assn. (pres. 1961-63), internat. Soc. Cardiology (rehab. coun. 1968-79). Home: 1276 Old Weisgarber Rd Knoxville TN 37909-2639

ACKER, LOREN CALVIN, medical instrument company executive; b. Lamar, Colo., Mar. 3, 1934; s. John C. and Ada M. (Ecton) A.; m. Judy N. Willms, Sept. 17, 1955 (dec. Oct. 1968); children: Cheryl Acker Hoge, Keith B., Karen Acker Kime; m. Darla C. Copeland, July 24, 1976. BS in Mech. Engring., Fresno State Coll., 1956; Bus. and Mgmt. cert., U. Calif., Berkeley, 1961; MBA, U. Santa Clara, 1966. Flight test NASA, Edwards, Calif., 1954-56; engring. mgr. Westinghouse, Sunnyvale, Calif., 1956—68; assoc. dir. Kitt Peak Nat. Obs., Tucson, 1968—73; chmn., CEO founder Engr. & Rsch. Assocs., Inc. (SEBRA), Tucson, 1973—. Gen. ptnr. Winged Foot Assocs., Tucson, 1974—; founder NYPA Inc., Tucson, 1986; mgr bd. Electrophysiology LLC, Tucson, 2000—; founder WoofSpa and Resort, N.Y.C., 2003. Patentee in field. Chmn. park and recreation City of Cupertino, Calif., 1968; mem. So. Ariz. Leadership Coun., 1997—; bd. dirs. Sonoran Sea Aquarium, 1999—; mem. agrl. and biosys. coun. U. Ariz., 1999—; chmn. bioindustry Greater Tucson Econ. Coun., 1994-99; mem. Ariz. tri-univ. master of engring. bd., 2000—. Entrepreneurial fellow U. Ariz., 1999. Mem.: Internat. Soc. Cellular Therapy, Am. Soc. Apherises, Am. Assn. Blood Banks, Audubon Soc., Nature Conservancy, Sierra Club. Republican. Avocations: skiing, tennis. Home: 4831 E Winged Foot Pl Tucson AZ 85718-1727 Office: 100 N Tucson Blvd Tucson AZ 85716-4740

ACKER, MARTIN HERBERT, psychotherapist, educator; b. N.Y.C., Dec. 15, 1921; s. Irving and Rose Martha (Katz) A.; m. Joan Elise Robinson, Apr. 29, 1948; children— Michael Christopher, David, Jonathon, Steven Anthony; m. Julia Ann Payne, Feb. 14, 1976 PhD, NYU, 1963. Lic. psychologist, Oreg. Prof. counseling and psychology U. Oreg., Eugene, 1961-86, prof. emeritus, 1986—, chmn. counseling, 1963-68. Vis. prof. Fed. City Coll., Washington, 1968-69, U. Victoria, B.C., Can., 1974, Fredrich Karls U., Tübingen, Germany, 1987; psychotherapist, Eugene, 1974—; dir. BeBusk Meml. Clinic, 1983-85. Mem. adv. com. Lane County Adult Corrections; bd. dirs. Lane Mental Health Assn., Pearl Buck Ctr.; mem. budget com. Sch. Dist. 4J, Eugene, 1994—. Mem. Am. Pers. and Guidance Assn. (bd. dirs. 1967-68), Soc. Sci. Study Sex, Oreg. Psychol. Assn., Am. Rehab. Counselors Assn. (pres. 1968-69), Men's Studies Assn. (co-chair 1986-90), Lane County Psychologists Assn. (pres. 1985-86), Friars Club. Home: 2733 Kismet Way Eugene OR 97405-1284 E-mail: macker@oregon.uoregon.edu.

ACKER, NATHANIEL HULL, retired educational administrator; b. Manistee, Mich., July 29, 1927; s. Carmon M. and Cathryn (Keiser) A.; m. Mary Anne Brawley, June 6, 1951; children: Kristan, Nathaniel Hull Jr., Amy. BS in Bus. Adminstrn., Miami U., Oxford, Ohio, 1951. Sales rep. Proctor and Gamble Co., 1951-52, Peninsular Steel Co., Dayton, Ohio, 1952-53; with Mutschler Bros. Co., Nappanee, Ind., 1953-70; v.p. Mutschler Midwest, Inc., Chgo., 1963-68; regional mgr. Ohio-Ky.-Mich., 1968-70; dir. Am. Peace Corps Office Vol. Placement Midwest Region, Chgo., 1970-71; assoc. dir. Northern region, New Delhi, India, 1971-72; exec. officer New Delhi, 1972-73; dir. estate planning St. Lawrence U., Canton, N.Y., 1973-78; v.p. instl. devel. Hampden-Sydney (Va.) Coll., 1978-84; dir. devel. Episcopal High Sch., Alexandria, Va., 1984-91, ret., 1991. Park commr., Lake Bluff, Ill., 1965-68, pres., 1967-68; mem. Citizen's Com. for Lake Forest-Lake Bluff High Sch., 1966, Sch. Caucus, 1963-64, Village Bd. Caucus, 1966-68, Citizens' Com. for Rockland Park, 1964; chmn. Lake Bluff United Fund, 1962-63. Mem. Sigma Alpha Epsilon. Home: 6230 Ridge Dr #31 Benzonia MI 49616 also: 761 W Desert Hills Dr Green Valley AZ 85614

ACKER, ROBERT FLINT, microbiologist; b. Chgo., Aug. 24, 1920; s. Robert Booth and Mary (Flint) A.; m. Phyllis Catharine Fry, Jan. 2, 1948; children: Catharine Elizabeth, Barbara Fenner, Robert Macdonald, James Christopher. BA, Ind. U., 1942, MA, 1948; PhD, Rutgers U., 1953. Asst. prof. Iowa State U., Ames, 1954-59; asst. chief cancer chemotherapy dept., chief quality control dept. Microbiol. Assocs., Inc., Bethesda, Md., 1959-61, chief dept. cell and media prodn., 1961-62; dir. microbiology program Office of Naval Research, Dept. Navy, Washington, 1962-69; dir. fed. program devel., asst. dean faculties for research, prof. biol. scis. Northwestern U., Evanston, Ill., 1969-74; exec. dir. Am. Soc. Microbiology, Washington, 1974-81, Nat. Found. Infectious Disease, Bethesda, Md., 1981-86; pres. Bionox Corp., Tucson, 1985-92. Author: (with R.R. Jennings) The Protistan Kingdom, 1970; editor: Proc. 24th Internat. Congress on Marine Corrosion and Fouling, 1972; editorial bd.: Applied Microbiology, 1962-73. V.p., bd. dirs. Iona House Sr. Svc. Ctr., Washington, 1978-79, pres., 1979-81; trustee Massanetta Conf. Ctr., 1983-86; bd. dirs. Am. Type Culture Collection, 1983-89; pres. Sunrise Mountain Ridge Homeowners Assn., 1994-95; bd. elders Potomac United Presbyn. Ch., Md., 1967-69, Winnetka (Ill.) Presbyn. Ch., 1972-74, Nat. Presbyn. Ch., Washington, 1983-86, St. Andrew's Presbyn. Ch., Tucson, 1989-91, 1998-2000. Eli Lilly & Co. postdoctoral fellow, 1953-54. Fellow Am. Acad. Microbiology, Soc. for Indsl. Microbiology (pres. 1986-87, Charles Porter award 2001); mem. Am. Soc. for Microbiology, Am. Inst. Biol. Sci. (coun. 1983-91), Cosmos Club. Home and Office: 6890 E Loma Del Bribon Tucson AZ 85750-6372 E-mail: rfacker@flash.net.

ACKER, RODNEY, lawyer; b. Jacksonville, Tex., Sept. 29, 1949; s. Mike and Dorothy (Kennedy) A.; m. Judy Bruyere, Sept. 2, 1972; children: Amy, Shelley, Rachel, Sam. BBA, U. Tex., Arlington, 1971; JD with honors, Tex. Tech, 1974. Bar: Tex. 1974, U.S. Dist. Ct. (no., so., ea., we. dists.) Tex., U.S. Ct. Appeals (5th and 11th cirs.), U.S. Supreme Ct.; cert. in civil trial law. Law clk. to Hon. Eldon Mahon, U.S. Dist. Ct., Ft. Worth, 1974-76; assoc. Kendrick, Kendrick & Bradley, Dallas, 1976, Jenkens & Gilcrist, Dallas, 1976-79, ptnr., then shareholder, 1979—. Fellow Am. Bar Found., Tex. Bar Found., Dallas Bar Found.; mem. ABA, Am. Coll. Trial Lawyers, State Bar Tex., Dallas Bar Assn., Am. Bd. of Trial Advocates, Patrick Higginbotham Am. Inns of Ct., Phi Delta Phi. Baptist. Office: Jenkens & Gilcrist 1445 Ross Ave Ste 3200 Dallas TX 75202-2785

ACKER, WILLIAM MARSH, JR., federal judge; b. Birmingham, Ala., Oct. 25, 1927; s. William Marsh and Estelle (Lampkin) A.; m. Martha Walters, 1957; children— William Marsh III, Stacey Reed. BA, Birmingham So. Coll., 1949; LLB, Yale U., 1952. Bar: Ala. 1952. Assoc. Graham, Bibb, Wingo & Foster, Birmingham, Ala., 1952-57, Smyer, White, Reid & Acker, 1957-72, Dominick, Fletcher, Yeilding, Acker, Wood & Lloyd, Birmingham, 1972-82; judge U.S. Dist. Ct. (no. dist.) Ala., 1982-96, sr. judge, 1996—. Mem. Ala. Republican Exec. Com.; del. to Repub. Nat. Convention, 1972, 76, 80. Mem. Birmingham Bar Assn. Office: US Dist Ct 481 Hugo L Black Courthouse 1729 5th Ave N Birmingham AL 35203-2000

ACKERLEY, BARRY, professional basketball team executive, communications company executive; Student, U. Iowa, 1956. Exec. v.p. Advan, Inc.; owner Golden West Outdoor Advt., 1968—75; chmn., CEO Ackerley Comm., Inc., 1975—; owner, chmn. bd. dirs. Seattle SuperSonics, 1984—. Office: Seattle SuperSonics 351 Elliott Ave W Seattle WA 98119-4101 also: Ackerley Group 1301 5th Ave Ste 4000 Seattle WA 98101-2634

ACKERLY, WENDY SAUNDERS, construction company executive; b. Chgo., July 23, 1960; d. Robert S. Jr. and Linda Ackerly. BS in Atmospheric Sci., U. Calif., Davis, 1982; postgrad., U. Nev., Reno, 1985. Programmer U. Calif, Davis, 1982-83; cons. software Tesco, Sacramento, 1983; software engr. Bently Nev. Corp., Minden, Nev., 1984-85; mgr. computer scis. Jensen Electric Co., Reno, 1985-86, software engr. Cameron Park, Calif., 1986-89; sr. engr. Aerojet, Sacramento, 1989-96, test ops. specialist, 1996-98; dir. design and devel. Kerry King Constrn., Inc., 1998—, sec.-treas., 1991—. Mem. Nat. Space Soc., Planetary Soc., U.S. Tennis Assn., Calif. Aggie Alumni Assn. Republican. Avocations: tennis, hiking, travel, piano. Office: PO Box 269 Rescue CA 95672-0269

ACKERMAN, ANTHONY WAYNE, secondary school educator, band director; b. Lexington, Ky., June 28, 1971; s. James Anthony Ackerman and Patricia Sue Kirby; m. Carol Elizabeth Ackerman; children: Clay, Amelia, Elizabeth. BMus Edn., Ea. Ky. U., 1995; MMus Edn., U. Tenn., 1997; Rank I, Ea. Ky. U., 2002. Asst. band dir. Knox Ctrl. H.C., Knoxville, Tenn.; band dir. Russell County Schs., Russell Springs, Ky. Musician: performing with various groups, including Knoxville Symphony Orch., So. Brass Quintet, Oak Ridge Symphony, Oak Ridge Cmty. Band, 1997—. Mem.: ITG, Music Educators Nat. Conf., Ky. Music Educators Assn. (rep. dist. 10) Marching Band Bd. Control, Russell Springs, pres. dist. 10). Home: 2166 S Hwy 127 Russell Springs KY 42642

ACKERMAN, ARLENE ALICE, accountant, business consultant, artist, writer; b. Omaha, Mar. 24, 1936; d. Walter Nelson and Mildred Eleanor (Krimlofski) A. BA in Social Sci. and Econs., San Francisco State U., 1962; MA in Polit. Sci., Purdue U., 1967; grad., U.S. Dept. Def. Info. Sch., 1973, U.S. Army Command-Gen. Staff Coll., 1977. CPA, Ind. Acct., adminstr. Peeples & MacDonald, CPAs, Sacramento, 1961-66; acct. chief acct.'s office Purdue U., West Lafayette, Ind., 1966-67; adj. gen. and info. officer, editor newspaper 123d Army Res. Command, Ind., 1972-75; mng. ptnr. Piano Showcase, Indpls., 1975-83; adminstr. Bennett Thrasher & Co. CPAs, Atlanta, 1983-86, Melvin Belli Law Offices, San Francisco, 1990; bus. cons. Ackerman & Assocs., Indpls., 1986-90; acctg. mgr., acting CFO Lera Dynalectric, San Francisco, 1991-94; CFO Nat. Home Bus. Assn., St. Helena, Calif., 1994-96; prin. Ackerman & Assocs., Fairfax, Calif., 1996-2000; fin. analyst Exodus Comm., Inc., Santa Clara, Calif., 2000—. Editor Mus. Indian Heritage Newsletter, Indpls., 1971-77; exhibited in group shows at Marin Agrl. Land Trust, San Rafael, Calif., 1993, Marin County Fair & Exposition, San Rafael, 1993, 96, Marin Soc. Artists, Ross, Calif., 1993, 94, Monterey Peninsula Mus. Art Christmas Miniature Show, 1993, Artisans Gallery, Mill Valley, Calif., 1993-95, Sonoma-Marin Fair, Petaluma, Calif., 1993-94, San Mateo (Calif.) County Fair, 1992-94, Sonoma County Fair, Santa Rosa, Calif., 1993-95; contbr. articles to Army profl. jours. Officer U.S. Army, 1956-61, 67-71; col. USAR, ret., 1988. Mem. Soc. Children's Book Writers and Illustrators (assoc.), Marin Soc. Artist, San Francisco Early Music Soc., Nat. Assn. Miniature Enthusiasts. Avocations: classical piano, painting, drawing, writing children's stories, miniature artist. Home: 1506 E Rock Springs Rd Atlanta GA 30306 E-mail: ladycolonel@attbi.com.

ACKERMAN, DAVID PAUL, lawyer; b. Chgo., June 11, 1949; s. Norman Alvin and Ruth (Renberg) A.; m. Deanna Mae Neumayer, Aug. 24, 1972; children: Paul David, Kristin Marie. AB, Princeton U., 1971; JD, Harvard U., 1974. Bar: Ill. 1974, U.S. Dist. Ct. (no. dist.) Ill. 1974. Assoc. McBride, Baker & Coles, Chgo., 1974-80, ptnr., 1980—2002; equity shareholder Jenkens & Gilchrist, Chgo., 2002—. Author various articles. Mem. ABA, Ill. Bar Assn., Chgo. Bar Assn., ESOP Assn., Nat. Ctr. for Employee Ownership, Tower Club. Office: Jenkens & Gilchrist 225 W Washington St ste 2600 Chicago IL 60606 E-mail: dackerman@jenkens.com.

ACKERMAN, DON EUGENE, venture capital executive; b. Gothenburg, Nebr., Dec. 30, 1933; s. Herman Eilert and Fern Helene (Witte) Ackerman; m. Joan Mason, June 17, 1956 (div. Sept. 1985); children: Cherilyn Kay, Michael Alan, Steven Jay; m. Janet Lorain Norman, Sept. 19, 1987. BS, U.S. Mil. Acad., 1956; MBA with honors, Harvard U., 1963. Instr. dept. econs. USAF Acad., 1963—66; systems analyst tactical air div. Dept. Def., Washington, 1966—67; resigned, 1967; assoc. J.H. Whitney & Co., N.Y.C., 1967—69, ptnr., 1969—; bd. dirs. Genigraphics Corp., 1982—; chmn. bd. Genicom Corp., 1984—, Decision Data Inc., 1988—; dir. Chem. Bank Adv. Bd., 1988—. Bd. dirs. Schlumberger, Ltd., Kraftware-Morgan, Walden Lakes, Inc., Numonics Corp.,

Prime Computer Corp., Sun City Ctr. Comdr. 2d lt. USAF, 1956, advanced through grades to maj. USAF, 1966, pilot trainee USAF, 1956—58, pilot 492 Tact. Fighter Squadron USAF, 1958—61, France and Eng. Mem.: Univ. (N.Y.C.). Avocations: tennis, skiing.

ACKERMAN, DONALD ROBERT, retired surveyor, retired real estate agent; b. Plainfield, N.J., Mar. 21, 1931; s. Philip and Lillian Augusta (Koch) Ackermann; m. Elisabeth Anna Wiesner, Nov. 27, 1956; children: Richard Dean, Nancy Jane. Student, Newark Coll. Engring., Middlesex County Coll. Lic. profl. land surveyor N.J., cert. planner and real estate salesman N.J. Rodman in fieldcrew C.J. Kupper Engr., Piscataway, NJ, 1951; transitman to chief fieldcrew Edward S. Lewis Engr., Plainfield, NJ, 1952—57; party chief in fieldcrew Kenneth McFadden, L.S., Bernard Twp., NJ, 1958—59; head survey dept. H. Thomas Carr, Inc., Perth Amboy, NJ, 1960—81; head survey dept. and assoc. Bernard Berson & Assocs., Fords, NJ, 1982—87; owner, v.p. Berson, Ackermann & Assocs., Inc., Piscataway, 1988—96; ret., 1997. Co-author: Madson, On New Jersey Real Property Boundary Law, 1991. Co-chairperson landscape com. Four Seasons at Mirage, Barnegat, NJ, 2002. With USN, 1951. Mem.: N.J. Soc. Profl. Land Surveyors, Nat. Writers Assn., Am. Legion. Avocations: singing, nature, gardening, writing. Home: 26 Aqua View Ln Barnegat NJ 08005

ACKERMAN, EUGENE, biophysics educator; b. Bklyn., July 8, 1920; s. Saul Benton and Dorothy (Salwen) A.; m. Dorothy Hopkirk, June 5, 1943; children— Francis H., Emmanuel T., Amy R. Ackerman de Canésie. BA, Swarthmore Coll., 1941; ScM., Brown U., 1943; PhD, U. Wis., 1949; postgrad., U. Pa., 1949-51, fellow, 1957-58. Instr. Brown U., 1943; from asst. prof. to prof. biophysics Pa. State U., 1951-60; mem. faculty U. Minn. Mayo Grad. Sch. Medicine, 1960-67, prof. biophysics, 1965-91, Hill Family Found. prof. biomed. computing, prof. biometry also computer scis., 1967-79, prof. dept. lab. medicine and pathology, 1969-91, prof. emeritus, 1991—, dir. div. health computer sci., 1969-79; staff cons. biophysics Mayo Found. and Mayo Clinic, 1960-67; dir. computer facility Mayo Found., 1964-65. Cons. bioacoustics USAF, 1957-62; mem. epidemiology and biometry tng. com. NIH, 1963-67, spl. study sect. ultrasonic applications, 1965-67, spl. study sect. lab. med. scis., 1967-69, computer and biomath. sci. study sect., 1969-73; dir. nat. resource for simulation of stochastic micropopulation models, 1983-90 Author: Biophysical Science, 1962, (with L. Ellis and L. Williams), 2d edit., 1979; (with L. Gatewood) Math Models in the Health Sciences, 1979, (with L. Elveback and J. Fox) Infectious Disease: Simulation of Epidemics and Vaccination Strategies, 1984; editor Biophys. Jour., 1983-87; also articles, tech. reports, chpts. in books. Rsch. grantee Am. Cancer Soc., 1953-56, NSF, 1958-64, NIH, 1954-90 Mem. Biophys. Soc., Am. Physiol. Soc., Assn. Computing Machinery, IEEE, Phi Beta Kappa, Sigma Xi, Gamma Alpha. Mem. Soc. Of Friends. Home: 11301 Park Ridge Dr W Minnetonka MN 55305-2551 Office: U Minn Health Ctr Box 511 MMC 420 Delaware St SE Minneapolis MN 55455-0374 E-mail: acker004@umn.edu.

ACKERMAN, F. DUANE, telecommunication industry executive; b. 1942; m. Kappy Ackerman; 4 children. BS, MS, Rollins Coll., MIT. With Bell South Corp., Orlando, Fla., 1964-91, vice-chmn., group pres., 1991-95, vice-chmn., COO, 1995-97, pres., CEO, 1997-98, chmn., CEO Atlanta, 1998—. Bd. dirs. Allstate Corp., Wachovia Corp. Bd. dirs. Ctrl. Atlanta Progress, The Commerce Club; trustee Rollins Coll. Mem. Atlanta C. of C. Office: BellSouth Corp 1155 Peachtree St NE Atlanta GA 30309-3610

ACKERMAN, F. KENNETH, JR., health facility administrator; b. Mansfield, Ohio, Apr. 2, 1939; m. Patricia Ackerman, Dec. 17, 1960; children: Franklin Kenneth III, Robert Christian, Peter Jonathan. BS in Biology, Denison U., 1961; MHA, U. Mich., 1963. Adminstrv. resident Henry Ford Hosp., Detroit, 1963—64; from asst. adminstrv. dir. to pres. Geisinger Med. Ctr., Danville, Pa., 1964—94; sr. v.p. adminstrv. affairs Geisinger Found., Danville, Pa., 1981—94; prin. assoc. McManis Assocs., Washington, 1994—97, v.p., 1991—2001; pres. Clark/Bardes Consulting-Healthcare Group, Mpls., 2001—, ptnr., sr. cons., 2001—02. Bd. dirs. Pa. Millers Mut. Ins. Co., Wilkes-Barre. Mem. Nat. Adv. Com. on Rural Health, Washington, 1988—94; bd. trustees Suburban Hosp. and Health Sys., Bethesda, Md., 1995—2000; Bd. dirs. Nat. Com. for Quality Healthcare, Washington, 1985—, Pa. Chamber of Bus. and Industry, Harrisburg, 1977—90, Healthcare R&D Inst., Pensacola, Fla., 1990—95. Recipient Adminstr. Yr. award Am. Group Practice Assn., 1988, Polit. Action Com. award Hosp. Assn. Pa., 1982, 85, 86, 88, 90, 91, Nat. Merit award Duke U. Hosp. and Health Adminstrn. Alumni Assn., 1991, Harry Harwick award for Excellence, 1994, Article of Yr. award Am. Coll. Med. Practice Execs., 1994. Mem. Am. Coll. Healthcare Execs. (regents adv. coun. 1989—, Hudgens' Meml. Award 1975). Office: Clark/Bardes Consulting-Healthcare Group Ste 370 608 2d Ave S Minneapolis MN 55402 Fax: (612) 339-2569. E-mail: ken.ackerman@clarkbardes.com.

ACKERMAN, GARY LEONARD, congressman; b. Brooklyn, N.Y., Nov. 19, 1942; s. Max and Eva (Barnett) A.; m. Rita Tewel, May 27, 1967; children: Lauren Meredith, Corey Brian, Ari David. BA, Queens Coll., 1965. Tchr. N.Y.C. Pub. Schs., 1966-70; founder Queens (N.Y.) Tribune, 1970—89; owner Multi Media, Queens, 1972—; mem. N.Y. Senate, 1979-83, 98th-108th Congresses from 5th N.Y. dist., Washington, 1983—; mem. internat. rels. com.; mem. banking and fin. svcs. com. Mem. Queens Coll. Alumni Assn. Democrat. Office: US States Capitol Office 2243 Rayburn Ho Office Bldg Washington DC 20515-3205 E-mail: gary_ackerman@mail.house.gov.*

ACKERMAN, GERALD MARTIN, art historian, consultant; b. Alameda, Calif., Aug. 21, 1928; s. Alois M. and Eva L. Ackerman. BA, U. Calif.-Berkeley, 1952; postgrad., U. Munich, Germany, 1955-58; PhD, Princeton U., 1964. Instr. Bryn Mawr Coll., Pa., 1960-64; asst. prof. Stanford U., Calif., 1964-70; assoc. prof. dept. art Pomona Coll., Claremont, Calif., 1970-75, prof., 1975-89, chmn. dept. art, 1972-82; prof. emeritus, 1989—. Fulbright prof. U. Leningrad, 1980; prof. Florence (Italy) Acad. Art, 1996—. Author (plays): The Life and Work of J.L. Gerome, 1986, American Orientalists, 1994, Gérôme, 2000, Les Orientalistes de l'Ecole britannique, 1991, The Barque-Gerome Drawing Course, 2003. Named Appleton eminent scholar, Fla. State U., 1994. Democrat. Home: 360 S Mills Ave Claremont CA 91711-5331 E-mail: gackerman@pomona.edu.

ACKERMAN, HAROLD A. federal judge; b. 1928; Student, Seton Hall U., 1945-46, 48; LL.B., Rutgers U., 1951. Bar: N.J. 1951. Adminstrv. asst. to Commr. of Labor and Industry, State of N.J., 1955-56; judge of compensation State of N.J., 1956-62, supervising judge of compensation, 1962-65; judge Union County Dist. Ct., 1965-70, presiding judge, 1966-70; judge Union County Ct., 1970-73, Superior Ct. law div., 1973-75, Superior Ct. Chancery div., 1975-79, U.S. Dist. Ct., Dist. of N.J., 1979—, now sr. judge. Mem. Supreme Ct. Com. on Revision of Rules, 1967; chmn. Supreme Ct. Com. on County Dist. Cts., 1968; mem. faculty Nat. Jud. Coll., 1978 Sgt. U.S. Army, 1946-48. Recipient Disting. Alumni award Rutgers U. Sch. Law, 1980. Fellow ABA; mem. Order of Coif. Office: US Dist Ct PO Box 999 Newark NJ 07101-0999

ACKERMAN, JACK ROSSIN, investment banker; b. N.Y.C., Feb. 8, 1931; s. Robert M. and Florence (Rossin) Ackerman; m. Dana Lowenthal, Nov. 29, 1974; children: Ellen, Jay, Robin, Bradley. BA, Harvard U., 1953, MBA, 1955. With Bache Halsey Stuart Shields, Inc., N.Y.C., 1955-80; mng. dir. Drexel Burnham Lambert, Inc., N.Y.C., 1980-88; pres. Bond Review Inc., N.Y.C., 1988-91; mng. dir. Ladenburg Thalmann & Co. Inc., N.Y.C., 1991-93, Brill Securities, 1993-94, Burnham Securities, Inc., 1994-96. Bd. dirs. Jewish Found. Edn. Women, 1980; trustee, treas. Jewish Bd. Family and Children's Svcs. Mem.: Harvard Club N.Y.C., Century Country Club (Purchase, N.Y.). E-mail: jack_ackerman@msn.com.

ACKERMAN, JACOB LEWIS, ophthalmologist; b. Berlin, July 22, 1947; s. Joseph and Pearl (Ziment) A.; m. Elaine Marsha Horowitz, Aug. 10, 1969 (dec. Mar. 2002); children: Rita, Karen, Steven, Julie; m. Judith Fay Rosenfeld, Oct. 6, 2002. MD, Albert Einstein Coll. Medicine, 1971. Assoc. dir. Brook Plaza Ophthalmology, Bklyn., 1975—, Brook Plaza Ambulatory Surgery Ctr., Bklyn., 1989—; asst. prof. of ophthalmology SUNY Health Sci. Ctr., Down State Med. Ctr., 1981—. Exec. bd. dirs. Met. Ophthalmic Ambulatory Surg. Ctr. Assn., Bronx. Contbr. articles to profl. jours. Sec. Young Israel of Lawrence-Cedarhurst, 1993. Avocations: tennis, writing, talmud, art, torah. Home: 400 Ocean Ave Lawrence NY 11559-2736 Office: Brook Plaza Ophthalmology Assocs 1901 Utica Ave Brooklyn NY 11234-3213

ACKERMAN, JAMES SLOSS, fine arts educator; b. San Francisco, Nov. 8, 1919; s. Lloyd S. and Louise (Sloss) A.; m. Mildred Rosenbaum, Apr. 11, 1947 (dec. Jan. 10, 1986); children: Anne, Anthony, Sarah; m. Jill Slosburg, Aug. 1987; 1 child, Jesse August. AB, Yale U., 1941; MA, NYU, 1947, PhD, 1952; LHD, Kenyon Coll., 1961; DFA, Md. Inst., 1972, Mass. Coll. Art, 1984; LHD, U. Md., 1976; DArch, U. Venice, 1985. Part-time instr. Yale U., 1946-48; rsch. fellow Am. Acad. in Rome, 1949-52; from asst. prof. to prof. U. Calif., 1952-60; editor in chief Art Bull., 1956-60; prof. fine arts Harvard U., 1960—, chmn. dept. fine arts, 1963-68, 82-84, Arthur Kingsley Porter prof. fine arts, 1984-90, prof. emeritus, 1990. Slade prof. fine art, fellow King's Coll., Cambridge U., 1969-70; vis. fellow Coun. Humanities, Princeton, 1960-61; fellow Am. Coun. Learned Socs., 1964-65, N.Y. Humanities Inst., spring 1992; Mellon sr. scholar Can. Ctr. for Architecture, 2001; vis. prof. fine arts NYU, 1992; sr. fellow NEH, 1974-75; Mellon lectr. Nat. Gallery Art, 1985; Schapiro prof. art history Columbia U., 1989-90, 91; vis. prof. architecture MIT, 1996, Harvard, 1996-97. Author: The Cortile del Belvedere, 1954, The Architecture of Michelangelo, 1961 (winner Alice D. Hitchcock award Soc. Archtl. Historians 1961, Charles R. Morey award 1963), (with Rhys Carpenter) Art and Archaeology, 1963, Palladio, 1967, Palladio's Villas, 1967, The Villa: Form and Ideology of Country Houses, 1990, Distance Points, 1991, Origins, Imitation, Conventions, 2002; co-editor: Annali d'Architettura, 1992-95, films Looking for Renaissance Rome (with Kathleen Weil-Garris), 1975, Palladio the Architect and His Influence in America. Trustee The Artists Found., pres., 1977-79; mem. council of scholars Library of Congress, 1980-82. Recipient medal for svc. in art edn. Nat. Gallery Art, 1966, Centennial citation U. Calif., 1968, Honors AIA 1987, Gold medal Inst. per la Storia dell'Arte Lombarda, 1987, Archtl. History award AIA, 1991, Paul Oskar Kristeller Lifetime Achievement award Renaissance Soc. Am., 1998, Internat. Balzan prize, 2001; decorated grand officer Order of Merit, Republic of Italy, 1985, Premio Daria Borghese, 1995; Guggenheim fellow, 1992-93. Fellow Am. Acad. Arts and Scis., Am. Philos. Soc., Brit. Acad., Accademia Olimpica (corr.), Royal Acad. Arts and Scis., Accademia of St. Luca (Rome, hon.), Ateneo Veneto, Royal Acad. Uppsala (corr.), Bavarian Acad. Scis. (corr.). Home: 12 Coolidge Hill Rd Cambridge MA 02138-5510 Office: Harvard U Sackler Mus Cambridge MA 02138 E-mail: jsackerm@fas.harvard.edu.

ACKERMAN, KENNETH EDWARD, lawyer, educator; b. Bronx, May 25, 1946; s. Kenneth L. and Anna (McCarthy) A.; m. Kathryn H. Hartnett, July 10, 1972; children: Andrew, Carl, Sheila, Edward, Daniel, Kenneth. Student, Talladega Coll., 1966; BA, Fordham Coll., 1968; JD, Cornell U., 1971. Bar: N.Y. 1972, Pa. 1994, U.S. Ct. Appeals (2d cir.) 1975, U.S. Supreme Ct. 1976; cert tchr., N.Y. State, 2002. Clk. legal dept. Port Authority N.Y. and N.J., 1969, IBM, 1970; ptnr. Mackenzie Hughes LLP, Syracuse, N.Y., 1971—. Adj. prof. banking law and negotiable instruments Am. Inst. Banking program Onondaga Community Coll., 1984—, Syracuse U. Coll., lectr.; adj. prof. white collar crime Ithaca Coll., 2002—. Author: Alcoholism-Prognosis for Recovery in the Reconstituted Soviet Republics, 1991; contbr. articles to profl. jours. Chmn. Ctrl. N.Y. chpt. March of Dimes, 1972-82; mem. A.A.-USSR Travel Group, 1987; bd. dirs. Ctrl. N.Y. Health Systems Agy., Inc., 1982-83, Syracuse Sr. Citizens Housing Corp., 1992—; trustee N.Y. State Lawyers Assistance Trust, 2003—; mem. Kaye Spl. Commn. Alcohol and Drug Abuse in the Profession, 1999-2001. Mem.: ABA, Onondaga County Bar Assn. (bd. dirs. 1990—93), N.Y. State Bar Assn. (chmn. com. lawyer alcoholism and drug abuse 1993—95). Office: 600 M & T Bldg PO Box 4967 Syracuse NY 13221-4967

ACKERMAN, LENNIS CAMPBELL, retired management consultant; b. L.A., July 28, 1917; s. Lennis Howard and Ethel (Campbell) A.; m. Barbara Bohlken, July 27, 1941; children: Nancy (Mrs. Michael H. Burnaugh), Janet (Mrs. Robert W. Lesser), John, Barbara (Mrs. H.D. Arnold), George. AB, UCLA, 1940. With Texaco Co., L.A., 1940-43, Schenley Distillers, San Francisco, 1945-48; merchandiser Richfield Oil Corp., San Francisco, 1949-52; sales rep. Walker Mfg. Co., 1952-56, mktg. adminstr., 1956-58; v.p., gen. mgr. Can. subs. Galt Metal Industries, 1958-63, v.p. internat. ops. parent co., 1963-65, v.p. mktg., 1965, pres., 1966-68; pres., chief exec. officer Newport News Shipbldg. and Dry Dock Co., 1969-73; exec. v.p. Tenneco, Inc., 1972-73; group v.p. Questor Corp., 1973-78; assoc. dean Sch. Bus. Adminstrn. Coll. William and Mary, Williamsburg, Va., 1978-83. Sec. Va. Port Authority, 1971-73; mem. Sch. Bus. Adminstrn. Sponsors, Inc., Coll. William and Mary, 1970-79, chmn., 1970-72. Served with USAAF, 1943-45. Mem. Soc. Automotive Engrs., Pine Valley Golf Club, Beta Gamma Sigma (hon.), Alpha Sigma Phi. Episcopalian. Home and Office: Apt 129 5700 Williamsburg Landing Dr Williamsburg VA 23185-8077 E-mail: budackman@msn.com.

ACKERMAN, MARSHALL, publishing company executive; b. N.Y.C., Jan. 22, 1925; s. Albert and Beatrice (Munstuk) A.; m. Carol Lipman, June 8, 1948; children: Stark, Scott, A. Marc. AB, Harvard U., 1949; MS in Journalism, Northwestern U., 1950. Dir. employee relations Gimbel Bros., N.Y.C., 1950-51; account exec. Leonard Wolf & Assoc. (advt. agy.), N.Y.C., 1951-54; with Rodale Press, Inc., 1954-91, exec. v.p., 1967-91, vice chmn. bd., 1978-91; pub. Prevention mag., 1977-86, Theatre Crafts mag., 1967-78, vice chmn., Western divsn., 1986-91; ind. cons. health food industry, health media, 1992—2002. Pres. bd. assocs. Cedar Crest Coll., Allentown, Pa., 1976—78, trustee, 1983—87; pres. Pa. Stage Co., Allentown, 1978—80; chmn. Santa Barbara chpt. Am. Inst. Wine and Food, 1998—. Charge de Presse, Confrerie de la Chaine des Rotisseurs, Bailliage de Santa Barbara, 1998—; Decorated Bronze Star, Purple Heart. Home and Office: 894 Toro Canyon Rd Santa Barbara CA 93108-1642 E-mail: mackermanm@aol.com.

ACKERMAN, MELVIN, investment company executive; b. Bronx, N.Y., Feb. 6, 1937; s. Norman Ackerman and Lilly (Ostreicher) Warshaw; m. Jennie Wang, Sept. 19, 1964; children: Lori, Julie, Melissa. Student, Bklyn. Coll., 1956, 59. Trader Myron A. Lomasney & Co., N.Y.C., 1960-62; sr. v.p. E.F. Hutton & Co., N.Y.C., 1963-88. Exch. arbitrator Am. Stock Exch., N.Y.C., 1984-88; mem. options adv. com. Phila. Stock Exch., 1980-88, Am. Stock Exch., 1975-88; ind. cons., 1988—; dir. BBFD Investment Co.; ptnr. Breckenridge Holding Co. With USMC, 1956-58. Mem. Securities Traders Assn. N.Y., Securities Industry Assn. (credit div., options and derivative products com., 1983-88). Jewish.

ACKERMAN, MICHAEL J. government executive; b. Bklyn., Apr. 11, 1946; s. Harry and Gertrude A.; m. Judy E. Lipton, July 3, 1967; children: Lorrie F., Jeremy D. BA, Hofstra U., 1966; MA, Clark U., 1969; PhD, U. N.C., 1971. Divsn. head Naval Med. Rsch. Inst., Bethesda, Md., 1979-87; br. chief Nat. Libr. of Medicine, Bethesda, Md., 1987-92, divsn. chief, 1992-94, asst. dir., 1994—. Cons. Tchg. and Technology Innovators, Bethesda, 1980—; adj. assoc. prof. George Washington U., Washington, 1987—; asst. prof. Uniformed Svcs. U. of Health Scis., 2000—. Originator and developer Visible Human Project, 1994. Pres. Parkwood Residents Assn., Kensington, Md., 1980-84. Lt. USN, 1972-75. Recipient Satava award Medicine Meets Virtual Reality, 1996, NIH Dir.'s award, 1996, NIH award of merit, 1998, Renice Crosby award Johns Hopkins U., 1998. Fellow Am. Coll. Med. Info. (treas. 1986-90), Am. Inst. Med. and Biol. Engring. (steering com. 1991-92, bd. dirs. 2000—). Avocations: model trains, sailing. Office: Nat Libr of Med 8600 Rockville Pike Bethesda MD 20894-0001 E-mail: ackerman@nlm.nih.gov.

ACKERMAN, MICHAEL JOHN, medical educator; b. Des Moines, Iowa, June 7, 1966; s. Larry Lee Ackerman and Leah Ruth Rohwer; m. Lisa Louise Hansemann, Dec. 17, 1988; children: Jaeger Philip, Nicholas Carl, Jens Michael. BA, Luther Coll., 1988; MD, Mayo Med. Sch., 1995; PhD, Mayo Grad. Sch., 1995. Pediats. Am. Bd. of Pediat., 1998, Pediat. Cardiology Am. Bd. of Pediat., 2002. Cons. Mayo Clinic, Cardiovasc. Diseases, Pediat. Cardiology, Rochester, Minn., 2000—; asst. prof. Mayo Clinic Coll. of Medicine, 2000—. Bd. of trustee Sudden Arrhythmia Death Syndrome Foundations (SADS), Salt Lake City, Utah, 2002; sci. adv. bd. Cardiac Arrhythmia Rsch. and Edn. Found. (CARE); bd. of trustee Ronald McDonald Ho., Rochester, Minn. Recipient Young Investigator award, Am. Acad. of Pediat., 2002, Doris Duke Clin. Scientist Devel. award, Doris Duke Charitable Found., 2000, Clin. Fellow Rsch. award, Soc. for Pediatric Rsch., 2000, Donald C. Balfour Rsch. award, Mayo Alumni Assn., 2000, Pediatric Resident Rsch. award, Am. Acad. of Pediat., 1999, Mayo Bros. Disting. Fellowship award, Mayo Grad. Sch. of Medicine, 1997, Internat. TaeKwonDo Club of the Yr., Am. TaeKwonDo Assn., 2000, Nat. TaeKwonDo Club of the Yr., 1990 and 1992; grantee Cardiac Channelopathies in Sudden Infant Death Syndrome, NIH, 2002, Neural Circulatory Control in Congenital Long QT Syndrome, 20002. Conservative. Achievements include patents pending for T Wave Lability Index: a sudden death risk stratifier; research in Long QT syndrome; hypertrophic cardiomyopathy; development of molecular autopsy. Avocations: my family, green lake vacations, scuba diving. Office: Mayo Clinic 200 First St SW Rochester MN 55905 Office Fax: 507-284-3757. E-mail: ackerman.michael@mayo.edu.

ACKERMAN, PAGE, librarian, educator; b. Evanston, Ill., June 30, 1912; d. John Bernard and Florence Page. BA, Agnes Scott Coll., Decatur, Ga., 1933; B.L.S., U. N.C., 1940. Cataloger Columbia Theol. Sem., 1942-43; post librarian U.S. Army, Aberdeen Proving Ground, Md., 1943-45; asst. librarian Union Theol. Sem., Richmond, Va., 1945-49; reference librarian UCLA, 1949-54, asst. univ. librarian, 1954-65, asso. univ. librarian, 1965-73, univ. librarian, 1973-77, prof. Sch. Info. and Library Sci., 1973-77, 82, 83; vis. prof. Sch. Librarianship, U. Calif., Berkeley, 1978, 80. Recipient award of distinction in libr. sci. UCLA Alumnae Assn., 1977, Disting. Career Citation, Assn. Coll. and Rsch. Librs., 1989. Mem. ALA, AAUW (Status of Women award 1973), Calif. Libr. Assn., Coun. on Libr. Resources (bd. dirs. 1975-90). Home: Royal Oaks Manor 1763 Royal Oaks Dr N Bradbury CA 91010 E-mail: page@ucla.edu.

ACKERMAN, PAUL ADAM, pharmacist; b. Cleve., Oct. 6, 1945; s. Kenneth Edwin and Jane (Hand) A.; m. Charity Reba Schierhorst, June 5, 1971; 1 child, Adam. BS, U. Fla., 1969. Lic. pharmacist, Fla., Ga. Pharmacist Robalo Pharmacy, Lake Park, Fla., 1969-73, Tru Valu Drugs, Lake Worth, 1973-77, Village Pharmacy, Tequesta, Fla., 1977-79, Shoppers Drug Mart, Palm Beach Garden, Fla., 1979-86; pharmacy mgr. Walgreen's, Palm Beach Garden, 1986-99, staff pharmacist North Palm Beach, Fla., 1999—. Member Airports and Aviation Adv. Com., Palm Beach County, Fla., 1985—; mem. adv. bd. Coll. of Pharmacy, U. Fla., 1986—; bd. dirs. Am. Cancer Soc., Palm Beach County, 1983-89. Recipient Pharmacy Disting. Svc. Alumnus award U. Fla., 1991. Mem.: Palm Beach County Pharmacy Assn. (pres. West Palm Beach chpt. 1983—85, Joe Price Pharmacist of Yr. 1985), Fla. Pharmacy Assn. (exec. com. Tallahassee chpt. 1984—85, chmn. Acad. Pharmacy Practice 1987—88, exec. com. Tallahassee chpt. 1988, bd. dirs. ho. of dels. 1988—90, vice-spkr. 1991, spkr. 1992, pres. 1997—98, Practitioner Merit award 1990), Am. Pharmacy Assn., Am. Pharmacists Assn. (mem.-at-large acad. pharmacy practice ambulatory care sect. 2001—03, chair-elect ambulatory care sect. 2003—, chmn. 2003—04), Fla. Aero Club, Shriners, Elks, Masons, Moose, Phi Lambda Sigma. Republican. Avocations: swimming, flying. Home: 12931 Inshore Dr West Palm Beach FL 33410-2005 Office: Walgreens 230 US # 1 North Palm Beach FL 33408 E-mail: packerman@prodigy.net.

ACKERMAN, PHILIP CHARLES, utilities executive, lawyer; b. Kenmore, N.Y., Feb. 14, 1944; s. Harold Lewis and Marion (Ehrhardt) Ackerman; m. Nancy Margaret Weig, Sept. 11, 1967; children: David Philip, Kathryn Elizabeth. BS in Acctg., SUNY, Buffalo, 1965; LLB, Harvard U., 1968. Bar: N.Y. 1968. Atty. Iroquois Gas Corp., Buffalo, 1968-72, asst. sec., 1972-74; sec. Nat. Fuel Gas Distbn. Corp., Buffalo, 1975—84, gen. counsel, 1978—84, sr. v.p., 1983—84, exec. v.p., 1989—95, pres., 1995—99, bd. dirs.; sr. v.p. Nat. Fuel Gas Supply Corp., 1984—88, exec. v.p., 1988—90, 1994—2002; v.p. Nat. Fuel Gas. Co., Buffalo, 1980—89, sr. v.p., 1989—99, dir., 1994—, pres., 1999—, CEO, 2001—, chmn. bd., 2002—. V.p. Seneca Resource Corp., 1978—89, pres., 1989—96, also bd. dirs.; mem. regional adv. bd. J. P. Morgan Chase. Mem.: Gas Tech. Inst. (bd. dirs. 2002—), Bus. Coun. N.Y. State (bd. dirs. 2002—), Buffalo Soc. Natural Sci. (bd. mgrs. 1982—, vice chmn. 1990—99, chmn. 1999—), N.Y. State Bar Assn., Am. Gas Assn. (bd. dirs. 1999—, security, integrity & reliability com. chmn. 2001—). Office: Nat Fuel Gas Co 10 Lafayette Sq Buffalo NY 14203-1826

ACKERMAN, RAYMOND BASIL, advertising agency executive; b. Pitts., Aug. 7, 1922; s. Charles Raymond and Teresa Jane (Grasinger) A.; m. Lucille Frances Flanagan, June 14, 1948; children: Patricia Ann Mehring, Ann Carol Adams, Ray K., Susan Marie Fuller, Mark, Amy Lou Shaver. BS, Oklahoma City U., 1951, PhD (hon.), 1996. Mem. display advt. staff Okla. Pub. Co., Oklahoma City, 1947-52; account exec. Knox-Ackerman Advt., Oklahoma City, 1952-53; pres. Ackerman Assos., Oklahoma City, 1954-74; chmn. bd. Ackerman McQueen, Inc., advt. agy., Oklahoma City, Tulsa, Dallas, Washington, 1975-92; chmn. emeritus Ackerman McQueen, Inc., 1992—. Bd. dirs. LSB Industries; past internat. pres. Worldwide Ptnrs. affil. Author: Tomorrow Belongs to Oklahoma, 1964; subject of biography Old Man River by Bob Burke with Joan Gilmore, 2002. Pres., gen. chmn. Oklahoma City United Appeal, 1964-66, trustee, 1967—; chmn. Oklahoma City Salvation Army, 1968; pres. Oklahoma City Better Bus. Bur., 1966; gen. chmn. Nat. Finals Rodeo Oklahoma City, 1965-84; past bd. dirs. Jr. Achievement, Oklahoma City, Okla. Water Devel. Found., Redlands Coun. of Girl Scouts, Urban League, Mercy Hosp.; past pres., bd. dirs. St. Anthony Hosp. Found.; past pres. Omniplex Sci. Mus., Oklahoma City; past trustee Oklahoma City Youth Park; campaign chmn., pres. Allied Arts Found., Oklahoma City, 1986-88, mem. exec. com., 1989—, Oklahoma City Cmty. Coun., 1989—; bd. dirs. Kirkpatrick Ctr. Mus. Complex, Oklahoma City, 1986—, pres. 1990-92; trustee, mem. exec. com., Oklahoma City U., 1988—; bd. dirs. Red Earth Indian Ctr., 1987—, Oklahoma City Pub. Sch. Found., 1990—; adv. bd. Enterprise Sq., 1994—. Rear Adm. USNR, ret. Recipient Silver medal Am. Adv. Fedn., 1982, Lifetime Svc. award Oklahoma City United Appeal, 1992, Pathfinder award Oklahoma County Hist. Soc., 1992, Outstanding Grad. award, Oklahoma City U., 1964, Disting. Alumnus award, 1991, Leadership Okla. award, 2001, Dean A. McGee award Downtown Now, Oklahoma City, 2000, Archbishop Beltran Cmty. Svc. award, 2000, Gov. Okla.'s Arts award, 2000, Lifetime Achievement award Nat. Assn. Fund Raising Execs., 2000, Sales and Mktg. Execs. Internat. Acad. Achievement award, 2000, Leadership Okla., 2001, Father of Yr. award Am. Diabetes Assn., 2003; named Humanitarian of Yr. Oklahoma County Arthritis Found., 1992; inducted into Okla. Hall of Fame, 1993, Okla. Commerce and Industry Hall of Honor, 1998. Mem. Naval Res. Assn. (nat. pres. 1969-71), Navy League (nat. bd. dirs. 1972-76, pres. Okla. chpt. 1974-76), Okla. Heritage Assn. (bd. dirs.), Oklahoma City C. of C. (bd. dirs., chmn. 1991), Oklahoma City Advt. Club (pres. 1954, Disting. Svc. award 1964), Am. Assn. of Advt. Agys. (past chmn. southwest coun.), Quail Creek Golf and Country Club, Rotary, Fortune Club, others. Home: 12905 Laurel Valley Ct Oklahoma City OK 73142-5167 Office: 1100 The Tower 1601 NW Expressway St Oklahoma City OK 73118-1467

ACKERMAN, RICHARD CHARLES, lawyer, state legislator; b. Long Beach, Calif., Dec. 5, 1942; s. Jay Fuller and Marge Mae (Lyon) A.; m. Linda Irene Vranesic, May 4, 1968; children: Lauren, Marc, Brett. AB in Math., U. Calif., Berkeley, 1964; JD, Hastings Sch. Law, 1967. Ptnr. Ackerman, Mordock & Bowen, Fullerton, Calif., 1982—. Mem. city coun. City of Fullerton, 1980-92; pres. Orange County Waste Mgmt., Santa Ana, Calif., 1982-95; v.p. So. Calif. Hazardous Waste Mgmt., L.A., 1982-95; mem. Calif. State Assembly, 1994-2000, mem. Calif. State Sen., 2000-. Named Ofcl. of Yr., O.C. Com. Persons with Disabilities, 1996. Mem. Orange County Bar Assn., Fullerton C. of C. (pres., Man of Yr. 1983, Educator of Yr. 1996), Fullerton Rotary Club (pres.), Elks, Fullerton Yacht Club (commodore 1976—). Republican. Presbyterian. Avocations: sailing, racquetball, reading. Office: Ackerman Mordock & Bowen 305 N Harbor Blvd Ste 303 Fullerton CA 92832-1901 also: 17821 East 17th St Tustin CA 92780*

ACKERMAN, ROBERT LLOYD, chemical engineer, environmental tree farmer; b. Greensburg, Pa., Sept. 3, 1925; s. Lloyd William and Anne Stella (Saul) A.; m. Margaret Dorothy Ansty, May 30, 1959; children: Julia Anne Ackerman Glenister, Janet Deborah Ackerman Fuhrmeister, Robert Peter. BSChE, U. Pitts., 1947. Tech. supr. Pittsburgh Plate Glass Co., Creighton, Pa., 1948-52; chem. engr. Koppers Co., Inc., Pitts., 1952-57; sr. chem. engr. Arabian Am. Oil Co., N.Y.C., also Saudi Arabia, 1957-75; sr. commg. engr. 8 oil desalting plants Oil Svc. Co. of Iran, Ahwas, Iran, 1975-77. Sr. design-commg. engr. Balikpapan oil refinery, Murchison and Beryl B Northsea oil/gas producing platforms, also Ok Tedi gold/copper refinery, Bechtel Internat., Inc., London, Indonesia, Papua New Guinea, 1978-84; tree farmer New Alexandria, Pa., 1984—. Author essays; patentee mfg. device used in glass industry; inventor of a graphical method used as a basis to plan and control daily operating parameters for an oil refinery-marine shipping complex. Pres. Westmoreland Woodlands Improvement Assn., Greensburg, Pa., 2001—; assoc.

dir. Westmoreland Conservation Dist., Greensburg, 1993—; treas. Penn West conf. United Ch. of Christ, Greensburg, 1994-2000; advocate for the Palestinian Cause; advocate for forest stewardship in Pa.. Recipient Maurice K. Goddard State award Pa. Assn. Conservation Dists., 1993, Outstanding Conservation Svc. award Westmoreland Conservation Dist., 1999. Mem. United Ch. of Christ. Avocation: reading. Home: PO Box 339 New Alexandria PA 15670-0339

ACKERMAN, ROBERT WALLACE, venture management company executive; b. N.Y.C., Sept. 14, 1938; s. Emory Graham and Margaret Wallace A.; m. Margaret Tracy Dealy, Dec. 30, 1964; children: Ashley, Graham, Todd. BS, Yale U., 1960; MBA, Harvard U., 1962. CPA, N.Y. Cons. Arthur Young & Co., N.Y.C., NY, 1962-66; asst. prof. Harvard Bus. Sch., Boston, 1968-72, lectr., 1972-74; v.p. fin. and adminstrn. Preco, Inc., West Springfield, Mass., 1974-78; pres., bd. dirs. Premoid Corp., West Springfield, Mass., 1979-86, Whitman Products Ltd., West Warwick, RI, 1977-86; sr. research fellow Harvard Bus. Sch., 1986-88; pres., CEO Lincoln Pulp & Paper, Inc., 1988-92, Sheffield Steel Corp., 1992-99, chmn., CEO, 1999-2000; ptnr. Watermill Ventures, Waltham, Mass., 2000—; chmn. Kervick Enterprises, Inc., 2003—. Author: The Social Challenge to Business, 1975, (with Hugo Uyterhoeven and John Rosenblum) Strategy and Organization, Text and Cases, General Management, 1973, 2d. edit., 1977, (with Raymond Bauer) Corporate Social Responsiveness, 1976. Deacon 1st Ch. in Cambridge Congl., 1970—; bd. dirs. Wildlife Conservation Trust, 1977—; adv. bd. Nature Conservancy, Mass., 1994—. Served with AUS, 1963 Mem.: AICPA, Steel Mfrs. Assn. (chmn. 1998—2000), N.Y. State Soc. CPA's, Am. Acad. Mgmt. (gov. 1972—73), Timber Owners of New Eng. (pres. 1977—, bd. dirs.), The Kittansett Club (Maron, Mass.), Yale Club (N.Y.C.). Home: 274 Beacon St Boston MA 02116- Office: Watermill Ctr 800 South St Waltham MA 02453-1435

ACKERMAN, ROGER G. ceramic engineer; m. Maureen Ackerman; 4 children. Grad., D, Rutgers U.; PMD program, Harvard U. Engr., sales, mgmt. positions Corning (N.Y.) Inc., 1962—72, pres. Corhart Refractories Co., 1972—75, gen. mgr., v.p. Ceramic Products Divsn., 1975—80, sr. v.p., 1980—81, dir. Mfg. and Engring. Divsn., 1981—83, pres. MetPath Inc., 1983—85, pres. Specialty Materials, 1985—90, pres., COO, 1990—96, chmn., CEO, 1996—2001; ret., 2001. Bd. dirs. Pittston Co., Mass. Mutual Life Ins. Co., Dow Corning Corp., trustee Corning Inc. Found., Corning Mus. Glass; mem. bd. overseers Rutgers U. Found. Office: Corning Inc PO Box 45 Phoenix NY 13135 E-mail: ackermanrg@corning.com.

ACKERMAN, RUDY SCHLEGEL, artist, educator; b. Allentown, Pa., Mar. 30, 1933; s. Harvey J. and Alma (Schlegel) A.; m. Rosemarie Ercolani, 1953; children: Sally Ann, Ann Marie. BS in Art Edn., Kutztown U., 1958; MS in Edn., Temple U., 1961; EdD in Art Edn., Pa. State U., 1967. Art specialist So. Lehigh State U., Coopersburg, Pa., 1958-63; prof., chmn. dept. art Moravian Coll., Bethlehem, Pa., 1963-2000, prof. arts and humanities, 1990—; exec. dir. Baum Sch. of Art, Allentown, Pa., 1965—. Commd. works include sculpture installations at Lehigh U., Pa. State U., Bethlehem Sculpture Garden, Moravian Coll., various pvt. collections; lectr. in field. Pres. Allentown Arts Commn., 1992—. With U.S. Army, 1953-55. Mem. Coll. Art Assn., Nat. Guild of Schs. of the Arts. Home: 2708 W Washington St Allentown PA 18104-3839 Office: Art Dept Moravian Coll Bethlehem PA 18018 E-mail: BaumSchool@aol.com.

ACKERMAN, SIGURD HOWARD, psychiatrist; b. Millville, N.J., Feb. 25, 1940; s. William H. and Ethel (Kessler) A.; m. Cecelia M. McCarton, Apr. 25, 1983; children: Elizabeth, Rebecca, McCarton. BA, Harvard U., 1962; MD, Tufts U., 1966. Intern Kings County Hosp., Bklyn., 1966-67, resident in medicine, 1967-68; resident in psychiatry Montefiore Med. Ctr., Bronx, 1970-73; dir. psychiatry St. Lukes/Roosevelt Hosp. Ctr., N.Y.C., 1989—98; med. dir., exec. v.p. St. Luke's Roosevelt Hosp. Ctr., N.Y.C., 1991-93; prof. clin. psychiatry Columbia U. Coll. Physicians and Surgeons, N.Y.C., 1989—, assoc. dean, 1991-93; pres., CEO St. Luke's-Roosevelt Med. Ctr., N.Y.C., 1998—2001; pres., med. dir. Silver Hill Hosp., Inc., New Canaan, Conn., 2003—. Rsch. Scientist Devel. award level I and II, NIMH, 1976-84. Home: 97 Sagamore Rd Stamford CT 06902-8007 Office: Silver Hill Hosp 208 Valley Rd New Canaan CT 06840

ACKERMAN, VALERIE B. sports association executive; m. Charlie Rappaport; children: Emily, Sally. Grad., U. Va., 1981; degree in law, UCLA, 1985. Assoc. Simpson, Thacher & Bartlett, N.Y.C.; staff atty. NBA, 1988, spl. asst. to commr., 1990-92, v.p. bus. affairs, 1992, 1994. Bd. dirs. Women's Basketball Hall of Fame; USA Basketball; bd. trustees Naismith Meml. Basketball Hall of Fame. Office: Olympic Tower 645 Fifth Ave New York NY 10022-5910 also: WNBA Enterprises LLC 450 Harmon Meadow Blvd Secaucus NJ 07094-3618

ACKERMANN, RUSSELL ALBERT, manufacturing company executive; b. Cin., Aug. 14; s. Russell Albert and Jennie Agatha (Brockmeier) A.; m. Mildred Arlene Streicher, July 24, 1948; children: Layne Anne Seifert, Kristie Allison Clepper, Leslie Arlene Gibbs. Student, U. Cin., 1944-47. Registered profl. engr., Ohio. Rsch. assoc. CHMR Rsch. Inst., Cin., 1947-54; adminstrv. svc. mgr. Cin. Milacron, 1954-76; mktg. mgr. Dresser Ind., Niagara Falls, N.Y., 1976-87; pres. Ackermann & Assoc., Cin., 1987-89; chmn. Internat. Abrasives Corp., Nashville, 1989-91, Ackermann & Assocs., Cin., 1991—. Cons. Colonial Abrasives, Aberdeen, N.C., 1987-89; chmn., CEO Greater Cin. Info. Svcs., Inc. (d.b.a. Net Results), 1996; chmn. Genesis Materials Internat., 1997—. Author: Laboratory Techniques, 1954; contbr. numerous articles to profl. jours.; patentee grinding wheels. Mem. Rep. Cen. Com., 1960-65; mem. city coun., Madeira, Ohio, 1965-76; mem. regional coun. Boy Scouts Am., Cin., 1955-60, Econ. Dev. and Export Coun., Pinehurst, N.C., 1988. Mem. American Water Works Assoc., Water Pollution Control Fed., Grinding Wheel Inst. (committee mem. 1986-89), Abrasive Grain Assoc. (committee mem. 1976-86), Abrasive Eng. Soc. (dir.), Germania Soc., Sons of Union Veterans of the Civil War, Rotary (Cin.), Alpha Phi Omega, Masons, Acacia Fraternity. Mem. United Ch. of Christ. Avocations: painting, coin collecting, golf, writing, geneology. Home: 1352 Rambling Hills Dr Cincinnati OH 45230-2359 Office: Ackermann & Assocs 2961 Madison Rd Cincinnati OH 45209-2027 E-mail: sandmon@aol.com.

ACKERSON, BARRY JAMES, social worker; b. Ogdensburg, N.Y., June 24, 1953; s. Gerald Wilson and Mary Agnes (Brown) A.; m. Linda Carol Graves, Aug. 15, 1976; 1 child, Sean Eric. BA in Sociology, U. Ala., 1975, MSW, 1978, PhD, 1998. Lic. clin. social worker, Ala. Psychiat. social work asst. I non-instl. care and svcs. dept Bryce Hosp., Tuscaloosa, Ala., 1975-76, dir. Alpha Program, 1982-85, dir. dept. non-instl. care and svcs., 1985-90; rsch. asst. Coll. of Cmty. Health Scis. U. Ala., Tuscaloosa, 1978; dir. Russellville Transitional Home Riverbend Mental Health Ctr., Florence, Ala., 1979-80; group home coord., aftercare therapist Indian Rivers Mental Health Ctr., Tuscaloosa, 1980-82; acting dir. cmty. placement Ala. Dept. Mental Health-Mental Retardation, Tuscaloosa, 1990-92, mental health specialist III, 1992-97; asst. prof. U. Ill., Urbana-Champaign, 1998—, assoc. dean, MSW program dir., 2002—. Adj. faculty U. Ala. Sch. Social Work, 1994-98. Recipient Outstanding Svc. award Boys Club of Tuscaloosa, 1974. Mem. NASW, Coun. on Social Work Edn., Alliance for Mentally Ill (nat. and Ala.), Mental Health Assn. of Tuscaloosa, U. Ala. Social Work Soc. (coun. social work edn.), Phi Beta Kappa, Phi Kappa Phi. Avocations: organic gardening, maritial arts. E-mail: backerso@uiuc.edu.

ACKERSON, BRADLEY KENT, physician; b. Fort Wayne, Ind., Apr. 30, 1956; s. Benjamin Ralph and Beverly Ann (Preston) A. BA in Biology, UCLA, 1978, MD, 1982. Intern in pediatrics Harbor-UCLA, 1982-83, residency in Pediatrics, 1983-85, felllowin infectious disease, 1985-86; pediatrician Kaiser Permanente, Harbor City, Calif, 1986—, asst. chief pediatrician, 1987-93. Conbtr. articles to profl. jours. Excellence in Rsch., U Calif. San Diego, 1982—, UCLA fellow, 1994-97. Mem. Infectious Disease Soc., Pediat. Infectious Disease Soc., L.A. Pediat. Soc., Habitat for Humanity, Sierra Club, Nature Conservancy Avocations: piano, bicycling, hiking. Office: Kaiser Permanente 25825 Vermont Ave Harbor City CA 90710-3599 E-mail: Bradley.K.Ackerson@kp.org.

ACKERSON, CHARLES STANLEY, minister, social worker; b. St. Louis, June 19, 1935; s. Charles Albert and Glenda Mae (Brown) A.; m. Carol Jean Stehlick, Aug. 18, 1957; children: Debra Lynn, Charles Mark, Heather Sue. AB, William Jewell Coll., 1957; MDiv, Colgate Rochester Div. Sch., 1961. Ordained to ministry Am. Bapt. Ch., 1961; lic. clin. social worker. Pastor Glens Falls (N.Y.) Friends Meeting, 1961-65; assoc. pastor Delmar Bapt. Ch., St. Louis, 1965-68; resource dir. Block Partnership, St. Louis, 1968-71; group home dir. Northside YMCA, St. Louis, 1971—72; group home supr. St. Louis Juvenile Ct., 1973-74; program dir. Youth Opportunities Unltd., casework supr. St. Louis County Juvenile Ct., 1974-83; youth svcs. specialist St. Louis County Dept. Human Svcs., 1985-94; assoc. dir. Gen. Protestant Children's Home, 1994-99; residential dir. Mo. Bapt. Children's Home, 1999-2000; instr. sociology, adminstrn. of justice and human svcs. Mo. Bapt. U., St. Louis, 1980—; pastor St. Jordan's and St. John's United Chs. of Christ, 1976—. Exhibit coord. Dog Mus., 1989—91; cons. Am. Youth Found., 1990—2001; mem. ordination coun. area V Great Rivers region Am. Bapt. Chs. U.S.A., 1982—84; chmn. youth focus group Interfaith Partnership Met. St. Louis, 1985—88; chmn. St. Louis Area Youth Svcs. Network, 1987—89. Chmn. group home com. Mo. Coun. on Criminal Justice, 1973-75; chmn. cts. and instns. subcom. Juvenile Delinquency Task Force for Gov. Mo. Action Plan for Pub. Safety, 1976. Mem.: Soc. for the Sci. Study Religion, Am. Correctional Assn., Mo. Juvenile Justice Assn., Nat. Coun. Juvenile and Family Ct. Judges, Mo. Conservation Fedn., Nat. Audubon Soc., Smithsonian Instn. Assn., Three Rivers Kennel Club of Mo. (past pres.), Cairn Terrier Club Am., Lambda Chi Alpha. Democrat. Baptist. Home: 1221 Havenhurst Rd Ballwin MO 63011-4402 E-mail: cackersn@swbell.net.

ACKERSON, NELS J(OHN), lawyer; b. Indpls., Apr. 12, 1944; s. Ralph D. and Mariel F. (Maze) A.; m. Sharon Carroll Ackerson, June 11, 1983; children by previous marriage: Betsy Virginia, Peter Nels; stepchildren: Stacia Carroll Loveall, Joshua Michael Loveall. BS with distinction, Purdue U., 1967, M in Pub. Policy, 1971; JD cum laude, Harvard U., 1971. Bar: Ind. 1971, U.S. Dist. Ct. (so. dist.) Ind. 1971, U.S. Ct. Appeals (7th cir.) 1971, D.C. 1985, U.S. Ct. Appeals (D.C. cir.) 1985, U.S. Supreme Ct. 1989, U.S. Ct. Internat. Trade, 1991, U.S. Ct. Appeals (6th cir.), 1996, U.S. Ct. Appeals (4th cir.) 1999. Advisor Harvard Adv. Mission to Republic of Columbia, 1970; assoc. Barnes, Hickam, Pantzer & Boyd, Indpls., 1971-76; chief counsel U.S. Senate Subcom. Constl. Amendments, Washington, 1976-77; chief counsel, exec. dir. U.S. Senate Subcom. on Constn., Washington, 1977-79; ptnr. Campbell, Kyle & Proffitt, Noblesville, Ind., 1979-82, Sidley, Austin & Naguib, Cairo, 1982-84, Sidley & Austin, Cairo, Washington, 1982-91; chmn. Ackerson & Bishop Chartered, The Ackerson Group, Chartered, Washington, 1991—, Class Corridor LLC, 2001—. Class counsel AT&T Fiber Optic Litigation; bd. advisors Telecom Real Estate Advisor, Bd. editors Harvard Law Rev., 1968-71. Dem. nominee for U.S. Congress, 5th dist., Ind., 1980; mem. liberal arts adv. coun. Purdue U., 1997-2001. Mem. ABA (litigation sect., bus. and banking sect., internat. law sect., adminstrv. law sect.), Am. Agrl. Law Assn., Ctr. Nat. Policy, Nat. Policy Assn. (food and agr. com.), Am. C. of C. in Egypt (pres. 1984), Assn. Trial Lawyers Am. Presbyterian. Office: Ackerson Group Chartered 1666 K St NW Ste 1010 Washington DC 20006-1217 Fax: (202) 833-8831.

ACKERT, T(ERRENCE) W(ILLIAM), lawyer; b. N.Y.C., June 8, 1946; s. T.W. and M. Ackert; m. MP. Ackert, July 4, 1970. BA in History, U. West Fla., 1969; JD, U. Fla., 1972. Bar: Fla. 1972, U.S. Dist. Ct. (mid. dist.) Fla. 1972, U.S. Supreme Ct. 1977, U.S. Ct. Appeals (fed. cir.) 1981. Pvt. practice, Orlando, Fla., 1972—; counsel Sharks Success, Inc., 1988-93, U.S. Ct. Internat. Trade, 2001—. Adj. prof. U. Cen. Fla., Orlando, 1988-93; gen. counsel (Fla.) Morgran Stiftung, Liechtenstein, 1991-95; law lectr. Profl. Skills Inst., Fla., 1981-85. Co-author: Florida Dissolution Manual, 1991; contbr. articles to profl. jours. Chmn. 9th Cir. Grievance Com., Orlando, 1989; mem. Human Svc. Planning Com., Orange County, Fla., 1984. Mem. Seminole County Bar (LAS pres. 1979, Pres. award 1980-83), Orange County Bar (LAS dir. 1980), Fla. Bar (trial lawyers sect., chmn. bar delivery of legal svc. com. 1986-88, chmn. mid-yr. conv. family law 1981, Pres.'s Svc. award 1985, 87). Avocations: pro bono service, travel. Office: PO Box 2548 Winter Park FL 32790-2548

ACKLEY, ROBERT O. lawyer; b. Chgo., July 24, 1952; s. William O. and Jeannette E. (Mitchell) A.; m. Patricia Ann Cerney, May 24, 1980; children: Matthew, Allison, Elizabeth, Anne, Kathryn, Kimberly. BA, No. Ill. U., 1974; MA., No. Mich. U., 1977; JD, John Marshall Law Sch., Chgo., 1988. Bar: Ill. 1988, U.S. Dist. Ct. (no. dist.) Ill. 1988, U.S. Ct. Appeals (7th cir.), 2003. Adminstrv. intern, asst. to city mgr. City of Marquette, Mich., 1976—77; adminstrv. asst. to town mgr. Town of Glastonbury, Conn., 1978; supr. Continental Bank, Chgo., 1979; chief methods analyst dept. fin. City of Chgo., 1980—81, chief supr. ops. dept. revenue, 1981—84; pres. Ackley & Assocs., Chgo., 1984—88; law clk., adminstrv. asst. to chief justice Thomas J. Moran Supreme Ct. of Ill., Lake Forest, 1988—90; atty. Cassiday, Schade & Gloor, Chgo., 1990—91; pvt. practice Chgo., 1991—2002; ptnr. Sarles & Ouimet, Chgo., 2003—, Woodstock & Dallas. Bd. dirs. Ill. Pro Bono Ctr., 1997-2002; adj. prof. Roosevelt U., Chgo., 1989-90; mem. panel arbitrators Cir. Ct. of 19th Jud. Cir., 1991-97, Cir. Ct. Cook County, 1993-97; detention screening atty. pretrial svcs. Cir. Ct. of Cook County, 1991—; drugs panel atty. Office of State Appellate Defender, 1992—. Bd. dirs. Bryn Mawr-Broadway Ridge Mchts. Assn., Chgo., 1984-87; panel mem. Capital Resource Ctr., 1991, Community Econ. Devel. Law Project. Fellow Ill. Bar Found.; mem. Nat. Assn. Counsel Children, Ill. Bar Assn., Chgo. Bar Assn., Lake County Bar Assn. (pro bono svc. award 2000), Ill. Appellate Lawyers Assn., Acad. Polit. Sci. (life), Nat. Coun. Juvenile and Family Ct. Judges, McHenry County Bar Assn. Home: 606 Buckingham Pl Libertyville IL 60048-3326 Office: 131 E Calhoun St Woodstock IL 60098 Office Fax: 815-334-9520. E-mail: roackley@calcon.net.

ACKOFF, RUSSELL LINCOLN, systems sciences educator; b. Phila., Feb. 12, 1919; s. Jack and Fannie (Weitz) A.; m. Alexandra Makar, July 17, 1949 (dec. Feb. 1987); children: Alan W., Karen B., Karla S.; m. Helen Wald, Dec. 20, 1987. BArch, U. Pa., 1941, PhD in Philosophy, 1947; DSc, U. Lancaster, 1967, Washington U., St. Louis, 1993, U. Lincolnshire and Humberside, U.K., 1999, Fla. Internat. U., 2001; DL (hon.), U. New Haven, 1997; Dr. (hon.), Pontificia U. Cath. del Peru, Lima, 1999. Asst. instr. philosophy U. Pa., Phila., 1941-42, 46-47; asst. prof. philosophy and math. Wayne U., Detroit, 1947-51; assoc. prof., prof. ops. rsch. Case Inst. Tech., Cleve., 1951-64; Silberberg prof. systems scis. U. Pa., 1964-86, chmn. dept. stats. and ops. rsch., 1964-66, chmn. grad. faculty ops. rsch., 1964-69, dir. Mgmt. Sci. Ctr., 1964-67, 69-70, chmn. Busch Ctr., 1970-74, 76-79, chmn. social systems sci. unit, 1974-78, 86—, Anheuser-Busch prof. emeritus of mgmt. scis., 1986—. Chmn. INTERACT: The Inst. Interactive Mgmt., 1986—; methodological cons. U.S. Bur. Census, 1950-51; cons. Eastern Airlines, Emerson Electric Co., Gen. Foods Co., Mobil Oil Co., Nat. Acad. Scis., Nat. U. Mex., Sci. and Tech. Rsch. Coun., Turkey, Western Electric Co.; bd. dirs. Mantua Indsl. Devel. Corp.; August A. Busch Jr. vis. prof. mktg. Washington U., St. Louis, 1989-95; mem. core faculty Union Inst., Cin., 1989-91, Ackoff Ctr. Advanced Sys. Approaches Univ. Penn., 2000—. Author: (with C.W. Churchman) Psychologistics, 1946, Methods of Inquiry, 1950, (with C.W. Churchman and M. Wax) Measurement of Consumer Interest, 1947, The Design of Social Research, 1953, (with C.W. Churchman and E.L. Arnoff) Introduction to Operations Research, 1957, Progress in Operations Research, I, 1961, Scientific Method, 1962, (with P. Rivett) A Manager's Guide to Operations Research, 1963, (with M. Sasieni) Fundamentals of Operations Research, 1968, A Concept of Corporate Planning, 1970, (with F.E. Emery) On Purposeful Systems, 1972, Redesigning The Future, 1974, (with T.A. Cowan et al) Designing a National Scientific and Technological Communication System, 1976, The Art of Problem Solving, 1978, Creating the Corporate Future, 1981, (with E. V. Finnel, J. Gharajedaghi) A Guide to Controlling Your Corporation's Future, 1984, (with P. Broholm and R. Snow) Revitalizing Western Economics, 1984, Management in Small Doses, 1986, Ackoff's Fables, 1991, The Democratic Corporation, 1994, Exploring Personality: An Intellectual Odyssey, 1998, Ackoff's Best, 1999, Re-Creating the Corporation, 1999, (with Sheldon Rovin) Redesigning Society, 2003; editor: Management Science, 1965-70, Systems and Mgmt. Ann, 1974; assoc. editor Ops. Rsch., 1953-65, Conflict Resolution, 1964-70; book rev. editor Philosophy of Science, 1947-53; mem. abstracting staff: Biological Abstracts, 1950-51; adv. editor mgmt. sci. John Wiley & Sons, 1964-86; mem. adv. bd. Math. Spectrum, 1968-86; mem. editorial bd. Management Decision, 1968-86, Reflections, 2001-; editorial assoc. European Jour. Operational Research; contbr. articles to profl. jours. Bd. dirs. Tallberg Found., Sweden, 1997—2000, Ctr. for Quality Mgmt., Cambridge, Mass., 1996—; mem. UN Devel. Adv. Coun., 1996—. Recipient award ASTD, 1993, award for outstanding achievement in sys. thinking and practice U.K. Sys. Soc., 1999. Fellow Am. Statis. Assn., Ops. Rsch. Soc. Am. (v.p., pres. 1956-57), Internat. Acad. Mgmt., Inst. Mgmt. Cons.; mem. Internat. Acad. Mgmt., Russian Acad. Natural Scis. (fgn. mem.), Inst. Mgmt. Scis. (v.p. 1965), Operational Rsch. Soc. (U.K.) (Silver medal 1971), Soc. Gen. Systems Rsch. (pres. 1987-88), Oprational Rsch. Soc. India, Peace Rsch. Soc., Sigma Xi, Tau Sigma Delta. Achievements include Ackoff Ctr. for Advancement of Sys. Approaches (2000) and the Russell L. Ackoff Endowment (2001) established at U. Pa. Home: Benson House 101 930 Montgomery Ave Bryn Mawr PA 19010-3044 Office: # 201 1021 W Lancaster Ave Ste 201 Bryn Mawr PA 19010-2635 E-mail: RLAckoff@aol.com.

ACKOUREY, PETER PAUL, lawyer; b. Scranton, Pa., Dec. 18, 1954; s. Paul Peter and Regina Helene (Dorris) A.; m. Christine Marie Van Wert, Aug. 6, 1977; children: Abigail Regina, Kenneth Jamal, Jemeille Irene, Mary Rose. BA in History, U. Scranton, 1974; JD, Harvard U., 1977. Bar: Pa. 1977, N.J. 1989. Assoc. Drinker Biddle & Reath, Phila., 1977-83; assoc. counsel Mellon Bank Corp., Phila., 1983-88; ptnr. Drinker Biddle & Reath LLP, Princeton & Florham Park, NJ, 1988—. Co-ptnr. in charge of Princeton office Drinker Biddle & Reath LLP, 1995—2000, bd. mem. mng. ptnrs., 1996—2000. Mem. ABA, Pa. Bar Assn., N.J. Bar Assn., Phila. Bar Assn. Avocations: reading and research Am. History, baseball. Office: Drinker Biddle & Reath LLP 105 Coll Rd E Princeton NJ 08542-0627

ACLIN, JEAN ANNE, cancer registrar; b. Point Pleasant, N.J., Oct. 14, 1960; d. Robert Warren and Evelyn Helen (Pritchard) Taylor; m. Keith Andrew Aclin, May 28, 1983. BS in Biology and Chemistry, Coll. Mt. St. Joseph, Ohio, 1984; BS in Med. Record Adminstrn., Tex. Woman's U., 1990; MPH in Epidemiology, U. Okla., 2000. Coder Irving (Tex.) Healthcare, 1990-91; coder II Marquette (Mich.) Gen. Hosp., 1991-92; quality mgr. Brazos Valley Med. Ctr., College Station, Tex., 1993-95; lead coder St. Anthony Hosp., Oklahoma City, 1995-2000; cancer registrar Healthalliance Leominster, Mass., 2001—. Adminstrv. officer Civil Air Patrol USAF Aux., Okla., 1995—. Mem. Am. Health Info. Mgmt. Assn. (cert.), Nat. Assn. Healthcare Quality (cert.), Mass. Health Info. Mgmt. Assn., Nat. Assn. Cancer Registrars, Cancer Registrars Assn. New Eng. Avocations: scuba diving, reading, travel, drawing, gardening. Home: 484 Richardson Rd Fitchburg MA 01420-1344 E-mail: jkaclin@juno.com.

ACLIN, KEITH ANDREW, technical service executive, educator; b. Meridan, Conn., May 9, 1960; s. John Joseph and Anne (Barr) A.; m. Jean Anne Taylor, May 28, 1983. BA in Psychology, Rutgers U., 1983; MS in Meteorology, Tex. A&M U., 1995. Cert. Microsoft sys. engr., Internet, trainer, Novell A+131 adminstr. Navigator tng. USAF, Mather AFB, Calif., 1983-86, navigator Carswell AFB, Tex., 1986-88, radar navigator, 1988-91, K.I. Sawyer AFB, Mich., 1991-92, radar meteorologist TWN Comms., Oklahoma City, 1995-96; sr. field support technician Oklahoma City Clinic, 1997-98; network computer engr. Coll. Edn. U. Ctrl. Okla., 1998-99; tech. svcs. mgr., tech. instr. ExecuTrain of Oklahoma City, 1999-2000; lead course devel./instr. Concord Comm., Mass., 2000—02; prin. edn. specialist Concord Comms., Mass., 2002—. Comdr. Edmond Composite Squadron, 1995-98, CAP, 1995-2000, Minute Man Squadron, CAP, 2000—. NSF grantee, 1993-95. Mem. DAV, Am. Meteorol. Soc., Masons, Scottish Rite. Avocations: scuba diving, flying, camping, reading. Home: 484 Richardson Rd Fitchburg MA 01420 Office: Concord Comms 600 Nickerson Rd Marlborough MA 01752 E-mail: kaclin@concord.com.

ACOBA, SIMEON RIVERA, JR., state supreme court justice, educator; b. Honolulu, Mar. 11, 1944; s. Simeon R. and Martina (Domingo) A.. BA, U. Hawaii, 1966; JD, Northwestern U., Chgo., 1969. Bar: Hawaii 1969, U.S. Dist. Ct. Hawaii, U.S. Ct. Appeals (9th cir.) Law clk. Hawaii Supreme Ct., Honolulu, 1969-70; housing officer U. Hawaii, Honolulu, 1970-71; dep. atty. gen. State of Hawaii, Honolulu, 1971-73; pvt. practice, Honolulu, 1973-80; judge 1st Circuit Ct. Hawaii, Honolulu, 1980-94, Intermediate Ct. Appeals Hawaii, Honolulu, 1994-2000; assoc. justice Hawaii Supreme Ct., 2000—. Instr. criminal law Hawaii Pacific U., 1992—; atty. on spl. contract divsn. OSHA, Dept. Labor, Honolulu, 1975—77, Pub. Utilities divsn., State of Hawaii, 1976—77; campaign spending com. State of Hawaii, 1976; staff atty. Hawaii State Legislature, 1975. Bd. dirs. Hawaii Mental Health Assn., 1975—77, Nuuanu YMCA, 1975—78, Hawaii Youth at Risk, 1990—91; mem. Gov.'s Conf. on Yr. 2000, Honolulu, 1970, Citizens Com. on Adminstrn. of Justice, 1972, State Drug Abuse Commn., 1975—76, Com. to Consider the Adoption of ABA Model Rules of Profl. Conduct, 1989—91; mem. Judicial Edn. Com., 1992—93, Hawaii State Bar Assn. Jud. Adminstrn. Com., 1992—94, Permanent Com. Rules Penal Procedure and Cir. Ct. Rules, 1992—96; subcom. chmn. Supreme Ct. Com. Pattern Jury Instrns., 1990—91; mem. Hawaii Supreme Ct. Ad Hoc Com. Jury Master List, 1991—92. Recipient Liberty Bell award, 1964. Mem.: Hawaii Bar Assn. (dir. young lawyers sect. 1973). Office: Hawaii Supreme Ct 417 S King St Honolulu HI 96813-2912

ACOMB, ROBERT BAILEY, JR., lawyer, educator; b. New Orleans, July 28, 1930; s. Robert Bailey and Catherine (Ryan) A.; m. Greta LeBlanc, Apr. 25, 1953; children: Robert III, Dwight J., Greta, William Ryan, John. BBA, Tulane U., 1951, JD, 1953. Bar: La. 1953, U.S. Dist. Ct. (ea. and mid. dist.) La. 1953, U.S. Ct. Appeals (5th cir.) 1955, U.S. Supreme Ct. 1967, U.S. Ct. Appeals (7th cir.) 1976, U.S. Ct. Appeals (11th cir.) 1981, U.S. Dist. Ct. (we. dist.) La. 1989. Assoc. Jones, Walker, Waechter, Poitevent, Carrere & Denegre, New Orleans, 1953-56, ptnr., 1956, sr. ptnr., 1968—. Adj. prof. law Tulane U., New Orleans, 1969—; bd. dirs. Attys. Liability Assurance Soc. Ltd., Hamilton, Bermuda, 1979—; pres. bd. dirs. Christian Bros. Found., Inc., New Orleans, 1976-78; trustee Christian Bros. Retirement Fund, New Orleans, 1989—. Author: Maritime Personal Injury & Death, 4th edit., 1993; editor: Damages Recovered, 1984; contbr. articles to profl. jours.; chmn. adv. editors: Tulane Maritime Law Jour., 1976-93. Chmn. Archbishop's Community Appeal, New Orleans, 1993; pres. Tulane U. Assocs., New Orleans, 1990-92. Decorated knight grand cross Equestrian Order of Holy Sepulchre of Jerusalem, knight of St. Gregory, Pope John Paul II. Fellow Am. Coll. Trial Lawyers (state chair 1972—), Am. Bar Found.; mem. ABA (mem. standing com. on admiralty, chmn. 1979-83), Tulane Maritime Law Ctr. (chmn. 1982—), Maritime Law Assn. U.S. (proctor, mem. exec. com. 1981-84), Tulane Maritime Law Inst. (chmn. 1991—), Tulane U. Alumni Assn. (pres. 1989-90, Vol. of Yr. 1992), Navy League U.S. (pres. New Orleans chpt. 1987-88, state pres. 1990-94), Assn. Average Adjusters U.S. (chmn. 1992-93), New Orleans Country Club, Boston Club, Pickwick Club, Stratford Club, Order of St. Louis, New Orleans Bar Assn. (Disting. Maritime Lawyer 1996). Roman Catholic. Avocations: photography, travel, sports, teaching. Office: Jones Walker Waechter Poitevent Carrere & Denegre 201 Saint Charles Ave Fl 48 New Orleans LA 70170-1000 Fax: 504-582-8010. E-mail: bacomb@jwlaw.com., bacomb@joneswalker.com.

ACORD, BOBBY, health science association administrator; BS in Animal Sci., W.Va. U. Dep. adminstr. for wildlife svcs. Animal and Plant Health Inspection Svc., USDA, Washington, 1990—99, assoc. adminstr., 1999—2001, acting adminstr., 2001—02, adminstr., 2002—. Office: FDA Animal and Plant Health Inspection Svc 1400 Independence Ave SW Washington DC 20250

ACOSTA, CRISTINA PILAR, artist; b. L.A., Sept. 23, 1959; d. Joaquin Enrique and Sandra Diane (Wisner) A.; m. Randall Scott Barna, May 25, 1991; 1 child, Isabella Pilar Acosta Barna. AA, Ctrl. Oreg. C.C., 1984; BFA, U. Oreg., 1988. Freelance comml. sign painter, window graphics, Bend and Eugene, Oreg., 1985-92; sign maker Safeway Corp., Bend and Eugene, Oreg., 1987-88; billboard, mural & lettering artist Carlson Sign, Bend, Oreg., 1989-91; instr. Ctrl. Oreg. C.C., Bend, 1990-96; comml. artist, fine artist Bend, 1990—. Participates in licensing art images to ceramic tile, home decor, gift markets. One-woman shows include Pinkney Gallery, Bend, 1987, Upper Gallery, Sunriver, Oreg., 1992, The Welcome Ctr., Bend, 1992, North Gallery, Grants Pass, Oreg., 1995; group shows include Sunriver Juried Art Show, 1987, Gallery 141, Eugene, Oreg., 1989, Sunbird Gallery, Bend, 1992, Ramskull Gallery, Hood River, Oreg., 1991-92, Columbia Art Gallery, Hood River, 1991-93, City Hall, Bend, 1992-93, Beaverton (Oreg.) Arts Commn. Juried Show, 1992-93, Wickman Gallery, Redmond, Oreg., 1992, Linn Benton C.C, 1992, Blue Sky Gallery, Bend, 1993, Ctrl. Oreg. C.C., Bend, 1995, Works of Faith, Portland, 1995, others, illustrator, "When Woman Became Sea", 1998; author: Paint Happy, 2002; contbr. art to mags. and books. Mem. Ctrl. Oreg. Arts Assn. (bd. dirs. 1992-93), Tile Heritage Found., Graphic Artists Guild. Studio: Cristina Acosta Art Studio PO Box 923 Bend OR 97709-0923 E-mail: cristina@cristinaAcosta.com.

ACOSTA, FRANK XAVIER, psychologist, educator; b. L.A., Apr. 2, 1945; s. Gilbert Lascurain and Virginia A.; m. MaryAnn Gonzales, June 30, 1979; children: Robert Xavier, Jeanette Marie. BS in Psychology magna cum laude, Loyola U., L.A., 1968; MA, UCLA, 1970, PhD in Clin. Psychology, 1974. Lic.

psychologist, Calif. Rsch. asst. Neuropsychiat. Inst., UCLA, 1968-71, vis. assoc. prof., 1984-85; clin. psychology intern VA Outpatient Clinic, L.A., 1971-72, Didi Hirsch Cmty. Mental Health Ctr., Culver City, Calif., 1972-73, Long Beach VA Hosp., Calif., 1973-74; clin. psychologist L.A. County/U. So. Calif. Med. Ctr., L.A., 1974—; dir. Spanish-Speaking Clinic, Adult Psychiat. Clinic, 1975-2000; dir. Hispanic psychol. svcs. Los Angeles County/U. So. Calif. Med. Ctr., 1981—, from assoc. dir. to dir. clin. psychol. internship tng. prog, 1986-96; asst. prof. psychiatry Keck Sch. Medicine, U. So. Calif., L.A., 1974-80, assoc. prof. clin. psychiatry, 1980-84, assoc. prof. psychiatry and behaviorl scis., 1984—, mem. allied health profl. staff, 1991—; dir. clin. psychology advanced clerkship/pre-internship Hispanic Psychol. Svcs., 1997—. Cons. Spanish Speaking Mental Health Rsch. Ctr., L.A., 1974-88; cons., reviewer NIMH, 1977-2000; guest lectr. U. Nacional Autonoma de Mexico, Mexico City, 1985, Tulane U. Sch. Medicine, 1985. Author: (with J. Yamamoto and L. Evans) Effective Psychotherapy for Low-Income and Minority Patients, 1982 (Behavioral Sci. Book Club selection 1983); mem. editorial bd. Hispanic Jour. Behavioral Scis., 1981-85; contbr. chpts. to books, articles to profl. jours. Cons. Nat. Coalition Hispanic Mental Health and Human Svcs. Orgns., Washington, 1976—88; mem. psychol. rev. panel med. svcs. and occupl. health and safety divsns. pers. dept. City of L.A., 1986—93; asst. scoutmaster troop com. mem.troop 31 Boy Scouts Am., 1994—2003; chair NRC evaln. panel psychology Ford Found. Doctoral Fellowships Minorities Program, Washington, 1986—89. Rsch. grantee Social Sci. Rsch. Coun., L.A., 1976, NIMH, 1977-84; Ford Found. postdoctoral minorities fellow NRC, 1984; recipient faculty rsch. prize, dept. psychiatry U. So. Calif. Sch. Medicine, 1977; disting. scholar profl. devel. program U. Calif., Berkeley, 1985. Fellow APA (mem. accreditation com. 1977-80), Am. Assn. for Applied and Preventive Psychology; mem. Western Psychol. Assn., Calif. Psychol. Assn., Los Angeles County Psychol. Assn., Alpha Sigma Nu. Office: Dept Psychiat U So Calif Keck Sch Medicine IRD Bldg 2020 Zonal Ave Los Angeles CA 90089-0121

ACOSTA, NELSON JOHN, civil engineer; b. Newark, N.J., July 8, 1947; s. Pedro Nelson and Bertha Maud (Williams) A.; m. Twyla Liasine Flaherty, June 19, 1970; children: Jeffrey Thomas, Stephen Patrick, Bryan Edward. BCE, Ga. Inst. Tech., 1969, MSCE, 1970. Registered profl. engr., Ill., Calif., Fla.; cert. aboveground storage tank insp., piping insp., pressure vessel insp. Am. Petroleum Inst. Design engr. Chgo. Bridge and Iron Co., Birmingham, Ala., 1970-73, sales estimator Oak Brook, Ill., 1973-74, contracting engr. Atlanta, 1975-79, CBI Constructors, Ltd., London, 1979-80, Arabian CBI Ltd., Al Khobar, Saudi Arabia, 1980-84, CBI Na-Con, Inc., Fontana, Calif., 1984-88; mgr. spl. projects and estimating HMT, Inc., Cerritos, Calif., 1989-94; region mgr., mgr. engring. and tech. svcs. HMT Inspection, Claremont, Calif., 1994—. Recipient traineeship NSF, Atlanta, 1969. Mem. ASCE, ASME (com. on structures for bulk solids), Am. Petroleum Inst. Republican. Roman Catholic. Office: HMT Inspection 640 Bluefield Dr Claremont CA 91711-2243 E-mail: nacosta@hmttank.com.

ACOSTA, RAYMOND LUIS, federal judge; b. N.Y.C., May 31, 1925; s. Ramon J. and Carmen J. (Acha-Jimenez) Acosta-Colon; m. Marie Hatcher, Nov. 2, 1957; children: Regina, Gregory, Ann Marie. Student, Princeton U., 1948; JD, Rutgers U., 1951. Bar: N.J. 1953, U.S. Supreme Ct. 1956, P.R. 1959. Sole practice, Hackensack, N.J., 1953-54; spl. agt. FBI, San Diego, Washington, Miami, Fla., 1954-58; asst. U.S. atty. San Juan, P.R., 1958-61; sole practice, 1961-67; trust officer Banco Credito y Ahorro Ponceno, San Juan, 1967-80; U.S. atty. Dist. P.R., Hato Rey, 1980-82; judge U.S. Dist. Ct. P.R., San Juan, 1982—. Alt. del. U.S.-P.R. Commn. on Status, 1962-63; mem. Gov.'s Spl. Com. to Study Structure and Orgn. Police Dept., P.R., 1969 Contbr. articles to profl. jours. Pres. United Fund, P.R., 1979. Served with USN, 1943-46, Normandy. Recipient Merit cert. Mayor of San Juan, 1973. Mem. Fed. Bar Assn. (pres., P.R. 1967), P.R. Bankers Assn. (chmn. trust div. 1971, 75, 77), P.R. Bar Assn., Soc. Former Spl. Agts. FBI. Office: US Courthouse & PO Bldg Ste 348 300 Recinto Sur St San Juan PR 00901

ACOSTA, RUBEN, surgeon; b. Chihuahua, Mex., Nov. 4, 1931; came to U.S., 1957, permanent resident, 1965; MD, U. Nat. Autonoma Mex., 1957. Diplomate Am. Bd. Surgery. Intern Meth. Hosp., Peoria, Ill., 1957-58, resident in surgery, 1958-60, Columbia Hosp., Milw., 1961-63; pvt. practice Chihuahua City, 1963-65; resident in surgery Tucson Hosp. Med. Edn. Program, 1965-67, Tucson VA Hosp., 1967-68; chief of staff St. Mary's Hosp., 1979-81. Mem. Ariz. Bd. Med. Examiners, 1976-81, chmn., 1980-81. Mem. Tucson Surg. Soc. Office: 325 W Rolling Hills St Tucson AZ 85737-6730

ACOSTA, URSULA, psychologist; b. Jan. 14, 1933; came to U.S., 1954, naturalized, 1958; d. Johannes Karl and Irma (Ulrich) Schmidt); m. Sebastian Acosta-Ronda, June 12, 1954; children: Johann, Dennis, Peter. BA, U. P.R., 1971, MD, 1973; PhD in Psychology, Gutenberg U., Mainz, Germany, 1979. Various occupations, 1954-66; instr. to asst. prof., assoc. prof., then prof. psychology U. P.R., Mayaguez, 1973-95; ret., 1995. Co-author: Familias de Cabo Rojo (History prize Ateneo Puertorriqueno de N.Y. 1983), Cabo Rojo: Notas para su historia, 1985; author: Quien era Cofresi?, 1984, New Voices of Old: Five Centuries of Puerto Rican Cultural History, 1987, Cofresi y Ducoudray: Dos hombres al margen de la historia, 1991; editor: Boletin de la Sociedad Puertorriquèna de Genealogia, 1994-99; contbr. articles to various jours. and newspapers. Chairperson appeal bd. SSS, to 2001; active P.R. Statehood Movement. Named Adopted Dau. of Cabo Rojo, P.R., 1999 Mem. LWV (unit chair 1977-78, 86-88), P.R. Geneal. Soc. Republican. Office: PO Box 8 Hormigueros PR 00660-0008 E-mail: uahorm@coqui.net.

ACQUAH, SARAH NIPAH, agricultural educator; b. Kumasi, Ghana, Mar. 10, 1945; d. Johan Nipah and Kate Bempah; m. Emmanuel Turkson Acquah, May 13, 1978; children: Isaac H., Catherine H. Diploma in home sci., U. Ghana, Accra, 1971; BSc, MSc, Ohio State U., 1975, PhD in Ext. Edn., 1977. Agrl. instr. Ministry Agr., Kumasi, 1966-69; asst. to v.p. acad. affairs U. Md. Ea. Shore, Princess Anne, Md., 1985-86, faculty rsch. assoc., 1987-96, dir. internat. student advisor, 1996—, project assoc. African Lang., 1992—, instr. agrl. and ext. edn., 1997—. Internat. student advisor U. Md. Ea. Shore, Princess Anne, 1996—, new student orientation com., 1997—, retention com., 1998-99, faculty rsch. com., 1998-99. Bd. mem., ch. mem. Asbury United Meth., Salisbury, 1986— Scholar Ghana Govt., 1969, U. Md. Ea. Shore, Princess Anne, Ohio State U., Columbus, 1973-74, Altrusa Internat.; grantee USDA, 1986-89, 93-96, 96-99, USAID, 1986-91, UMES, 1990-91, 98-99. Mem. Am. Vocat. Edn. Rsch. Assn., Md. Assn. for Higher Edn., U. Md. Internat. Faculty and Adminstrs. Assn., Soroptimist Internat. (bd. mem. 1992-93). Avocations: basektball, tennis, reading, traveling. Home: 614 Frene Ave Salisbury MD 21801 Office: Univ Md Eastern Shore Backbone Rd Princess Anne MD 21853 E-mail: sqacquah@mail.umes.edu.

ACRIVOS, ANDREAS, chemical engineering educator; b. Athens, Greece, June 13, 1928; m. Juana Vivo, Sept. 1, 1956. BSChemE, Syracuse U., 1950; MS, U. Minn., 1951, PhD, 1954. Instr. U. Calif., Berkeley, 1954-55, asst. prof., 1955-59, assoc. prof., 1959-62; prof. Stanford (Calif.) U., 1962-88; Einstein prof. CCNY, 1988-2001. Prof. emeritus, CCNY, 2001—. Contbr. articles to profl. jours. Guggenheim Found. fellow, 1959, 76; recipient Bingham Medal, 1994, Soc. Rheology, Nat. medal of Science, 2001. Fellow AIChE (awards 1963, 68, 84), Am. Phys. Soc. (Fluid Dynamics prize 1991); mem. NAS, NAE, Am. Acad. Arts and Scis., Am. Chem. Soc., Soc. Rheology. Office: CCNY Levich Inst 138th St at Convent Ave New York NY 10031

ACS, JOSEPH STEVEN, transportation engineering consultant, civil engineer; b. Budapest, Hungary, Apr. 26, 1936; came to U.S., 1957; s. Gyula Istvan and Gizella (Sztanek) A.; children: Joseph Steven, Stephen Martin. MS in Civil Engring., Kvassay Jeno Kozlekedes Ipari Technikum, Budapest, 1956. Profl. civil engr. With Balt. & Ohio R.R. Co., Cin., 1957-68; project engr. Balt. & Ohio Chgo. Terminal R.R. Co., 1968-75, terminal engr., 1975-88; pub. projects engr. CSX Transp., Chgo., 1988-92; prin. Allied Cons. Svcs., Ltd., Chgo., 1992—. Author: The Eleuthero Line, 1999; contbr. articles to profl. jours. Mem. NSPE, ASCE, Am. Rlwy. Engring. and Maintenance Assn. (chmn. com. 14/yard and terminals 1989-92, Profl. Svcs. award 1992), Am. Rlwy. Bridge and Bldg. Assn., Am. Right of Way Assn., Roadmasters and Maintenance of Way Assn., Chicago Heights Country Club, Eagles, Lions, Am. Legion, KC. Republican. Roman Catholic. Home: 6317 16th Ave Drive West Bradenton FL 34209 Office: Allied Cons Svcs Ltd Ste 606 4570 Pinebrook Cir Bradenton FL 34209 E-mail: josephjozsef@cs.com.

ACTON, DAVID, lawyer; b. Phila., Feb. 13, 1933; s. Kenneth Davis and Mary (Musselman) A.; m. Barbara Ann Sullivan, June 18, 1955; children— Lauren Doane, Paul Bodine; m. Jane Thomas Young, June 24, 1978. Grad., Episcopal Acad., 1951; AB, Yale, 1955; JD, U. Pa., 1960. Assoc. Krusen, Evans & Byrne, Phila., 1960-63; asst. sec., asst. gen. counsel Leeds & Northrup Co., Phila., 1963-65, sec., gen. counsel North Wales, Pa., 1965-71, v.p., gen. counsel K.S. Sweet Assos., King of Prussia, Pa., 1971-75, practice in Bryn Mawr, Pa., 1975-77; v.p. Crockett Mortgage Co., Valley Forge, Pa.; gen. mgr. Hershey's Mill, 1977-82; exec. v.p. Ultec, Inc., Exton, Pa., 1982-85; arbitrator and mediator, 1986—. Bd. dirs. Nat. Ctr. for the Am. Revolution. Mem. Phila. Bar Assn., Colonial Soc. Pa., Mensa, Union League Club, Merion Cricket Club, Yale Club (Phila.), Chevaliers du Tastevin. Home and Office: 233 Righters Mill Rd Gladwyne PA 19035-1532

ACTON, DAVID L(AWRENCE), automobile company executive; b. Detroit, Apr. 12, 1949; s. Lawrence E. and Johannah (Cassimatis) A.; m. Dianne Patience McNeill, Sept. 5, 1981; children: Andrew, Stephen, Amy. BME, Gen. Motors Inst., Flint, Mich., 1973; MBA, U. Mich., 1978. Assoc. engr. Hydramatic div. GM, Ypsilanti, Mich., 1973-74, project engr., 1974-77, supr. indsl. engring., 1977-78, asst. supt. indsl. engring., 1978-81, asst. supt. progress tracking, quality and reliability Detroit, 1981-83, sr. adminstr., 1983-85, mgr. program planning B-O-C- car group, 1985, program mgr. Allanté elec. test system, 1985-87; mgr. elec. design and processing Cadillac Motor Car Co., Detroit, 1987-91, mgr. electrical product systems, 1991-93; chief engr. elec./electronics Cadillac luxury car divsn. GM, Flint, Mich., 1993-96, dir. elec. engring. mid-luxury car group, 1996-97, dir. elec. engring. N.Am. ops. Warren, Mich., 1997-98, chief vehicle engr. OnStar divsn. Troy, Mich., 1998-2000; exec. dir. Global Telematics e-GM, Troy, Mich., 2000—. Bd. dirs. Its Am. Mem.: SAE, Convergence Transp. Electronics Assn. (bd. dirs.). Office: 1400 Stephenson Hwy Troy MI 48083-1189

ACUFF, JOHN EDGAR, lawyer; b. Chattanooga, Tenn., July 20, 1940; s. White Hollis and Estelle (Johnson) A; m. Carolyn Howell, Sept. 6, 1963; children: John E. Jr. (dec.), William Ira Howell, Karl David. BA, David Lipscomb U., Nashville, 1962; JD, Vanderbilt U., 1969. Bar: Tenn. 1969, U.S. Dist. Ct. (mid. dist.) Tenn. 1970, U.S. Ct. Appeals (6th cir.) 1970, U.S. Supreme Ct. 1982, U.S. Ct. Claims 1986. Assoc. Cable, McDaniel, Bowie & Bond (now McGuire Battle), Balt., 1969; law clk. to chief judge Harry Phillips U.S. Ct. Appeals, Nashville, Cin., 1969-70; assoc. Crawford & Barnes, Cookeville, Tenn., 1970-71; ptnr. Barnes & Acuff, Cookeville, 1971-96; pres. Acuff & Acuff PC, Cookeville, 1996-2000, 2000—. Mem. disciplinary hearing bd. Tenn. Supreme Ct., 1978-84. Author in field; contbr. book revs. Tenn. Hist. Soc., Lawyers Weekly USA, Tenn. Bar Jour., Chattanooga News Free Press, Herald Citizen, Putnam Star, Sparta Expositor. Dir. Law Students Nixon Agnew, 1968; mem. citizens com. Gov.'s Prayer Breakfast, 1980—, chmn., 1991; elder Christ's Fellowship, Cookeville, 1981-91; bd. dirs. Dismas House, Habitat of cumberlands, Lazrus House Hospice; mem. ethics com. Cooksville Gen. Hosp., 1997-99; mem. Leadership Putnam '97, White County Libr. Found., 1999—. Lt. USNR, 1962-66, Grad Citizens Police Acad., 1998, Citizens Fire Acad.; v.p. White County Libr. Found., 1999—, Bd. Triad Youth Home, 2000—. Mem. ATLA, Tenn. Bar Assn. (house of dels. 1980-99, speaker 1995-97, bd. govs. 1995-97) Tenn. Trial Lawyers Assn. (bd. dirs. 1998), Am. Judicature Soc., Christian Legal Soc., Putnam County Bar Assn. (pres. 1984-85), Putnam County C. of C., White County C. of C., White County Garden Club, Putnam County Master Gardeners, Phi Alpha Delta, Alpha Kappa Psi. Avocations: encouraging pilgrims, gardening (Master Gardner 2000, cert. horticulture tchr.), reading, writing. Home: Crossroads Farm 542 Almyra Rd Sparta TN 38583-5163 Office: Acuff & Acuff PC 101 S Jefferson Ave Cookeville TN 38501-3424 E-mail: acuffsbxr@blomand.net.

ACZÉL, JANOS DEZSÖ, mathematician; b. Budapest, Hungary, Dec. 26, 1924; s. Dezsö and Irén (Adler) A.; m. Susan Kende, Dec. 14, 1946; children: Catherine, Julie. MA, PhD, U. Budapest, 1947; DSc, Hungarian Acad. Sci., 1957; Dr. honoris causa, U. Karlsruhe, 1990; DHC, U. Graz, 1995, Silesian U. Katowice, 1996, U. Miskolc, 1999, U. Debrecen, 2003. Faculty U. Szeged, Hungary, 1948-50; prof. math. Tech. U., Miskolc, 1950-52, Kossuth U., Debrecen, Hungary, 1952-65, U. Waterloo, Ont., Can., 1965-93, disting. prof., 1969-93, disting. prof. emeritus, 1993—; vis. prof. U. Fla., Gainesville, 1963-64, 81, Stanford U., 1964, U. Köln, Germany, 1965, U. Giessen, 1966, 70, Ruhr U., Bochum, 1968, Fla. Atlantic U., 1968, U. Pavia, 1968, 69, Ist. Naz. Alta Matematica, Rome, 1971, Monash U., Clayton, Victoria, Australia, 1972, Ahmadu Bello U., Zaria, Nigeria, 1975-76, U. Lecce, Italy, 1976, Calif. Inst. Tech., 1978, Karl-Franzens U., Graz, Austria, 1979, 1986, 1991, 1993, 1999, 2003, Okayama U. (Japan), 1984, U. Milan, 1985, 91, U. Hamburg, 1985, U. Politécnica Catalunya, Barcelona, 1986, 92, U. Bern, Switzerland, 1986, U. Karlsruhe, Germany, 1992, 98, U. Calif., Irvine, 1994, 96—. Cons. Naval Ocean Systems Ctr., San Diego, 1979-81; chmn. Internat. Symposium Functional Equations, 1962-96, hon. chmn., 1997—; Jeffrey lectr. Acadia U., 1984, Marshak lectr. UCLA, 1998, Hungarian Acad. Sci. Author (with S. Gołąb): Funktionalgleichungen der Theorie der geometrischen Objekte, 1960; author: Vorlesungen über Funktionalgleichungen und ihre Anwendungen, 1961, Ein Blick auf Funktionalgleichungen und ihre Anwendungen, 1962, Lectures on Functional Equations and Their Applications, 1966, On Applications and Theory of Functional Equation, 1969; author: (with Z. Daróczy) On Measures of Information and Their Characterizations, 1975; author: A Short Course on Functional Equations Based Upon Recent Applications to Social and Behavioral Sciences, 1987; author: (with J. Dhombres) Functional Equations in Several Variables with Applications to Mathematics, Information Theory and to the Natural and Social Sciences, 1989; editor: Functional Equations: History, Applications and Theory, 1984, Aggregating Clones, Colors, Equations, Iterates, Numbers and Tiles, 1995, (jours.) Rendiconti di Matematica e delle sue Applicazioni, Inequalities and their Applications, Scientiae Mathematicae Japonicae, Theory and Decision Library, Series B, (book series) Results of Mathematics, Mathware and Soft Computing, Publicationes Mathematicae Comptes Rendus Mathématiques de l'Académie des Sciences Canada; hon. editor-in-chief: Aequationes Mathematicae. Recipient M. Beke award J. Bolyai Math. Soc., 1961, Hungarian Acad. Scis. award, 1958, 62, Cajal medal Spanish Nat. Council Sci. Research, 1988. Fellow Royal Soc. Can., Hungarian Acad. Scis. (fgn.); mem. Can. Math. Soc., Am. Math. Soc., N.Y. Acad. Scis., Austrian Math. Soc. Achievements include initiation of modern theory of functional equations; gave gen. theorems and applications to geometry, algebra, analysis, econs., mathematical psychology, utility, decision, probability, and info. theory; theories of mean values, measurement, and webs. Office: U Waterloo Pure Math Dept Waterloo ON Canada N2L 3G1 E-mail: jdaczel@math.uwaterloo.ca.

ACZEL, MOLLIE GOODMAN, educational consultant; b. Houston, Aug. 7, 1939; d. Aaron and Bess (Kaminsky) Goodman; m. Thomas Aczel (dec.); children: Joseph, Stephen, Elisabeth Aczel Wallock, Bettina Aczel Prober. BS in Edn., U. Houston, 1961, MEd in Spl. Edn., 1967. Cert. tchr., Tex., N.J. Prin. Irvin M. Shlenker Sch., Houston, 1985-88; instr. Found. of Edn., Kean Coll., Union, N.J., 1989-91; founding head of sch. Alfred and Adele Davis Acad., Atlanta, 1992-99; ind. cons. to pvt. schs., 1998—. Cons. Partnership for Excellence in Jewish Edn., Boston.

ADACHI, ATHAN KEN, civil engineer; b. Honolulu, July 18, 1951; s. Kenneth Korji and Dorothy Takako (Fujioka) Adachi; m. Marleen Takako Kuboyama, Feb. 13, 1993. BSCE, U. Hawaii, 1974; cert., Ind. U., 1989. Registered prof. engr., Hawaii. Project engr. Avanti Constrn. Co., Honolulu, 1974—77; engr. cons. Unemori Engring. Co., Wailuku, Hawaii, 1977—79; civil engr. IV County of Maui, Wailuku, 1979—85, asst. dist. engr., 1986—. Bd. dirs. Maui Assn. for Retarded Citizens, 1983—94; coord. Blood Bank of Hawaii, Maui United Way; bd. dirs. Grace Bible Ch., Maui, head disciplinary dept. Recipient Silver award, United Way, Cert. of Recognition, Cert. of Merit for Disting. svc. to Cmty. Mem.: NSPE, Christian Leadership Min., Christian Coalition, U. Hawaii Alumni Assn., Toastmasters (Disting. Competent award), U.S. Tennis Assn., Coll. Engring. Club. Home: 102 Kawalea Pl Kula HI 96790-9714 Office: Hawaii State Dept Transp Hwys 650 Palapala Dr Kahului HI 96732-2321

ADAIME, HAMED NAZIN, counselor; b. Ponce, P.R., July 15, 1960; s. Jose Juan and Ada Luz A.; m. Maria Ortiz, June 14, 1984 (div. June 1997); children: Shanie Marie, Shalimar Nicole, Amanda Guiselle; m. Betty E. Adaime, Dec. 18, 1999. BS, BA, New Hampshire Coll., 1996; MA in Cmty. Counseling, Santa Fe Coll., 1999. Petty officer third class USN, 1986; petty officer 2nd class U.S. Navy, 1993; ensign USN, 1984, anesthesia tech., 1985-89, champus supplemental care coord. Ceiba, P.R., 1989-94, med. evacuation coord. Brunswick, Maine, 1994-96; EAP counselor Buchanan & Assocs., El Paso, 1998-99; cmty. counselor Family & Youth Inc., Las Cruces, N.Mex., 1999—, Radford Acad., El Paso, 1999—. Bd. dirs. Southwest Counseling, Las Cruces; com. mem. Project Adventure, El Paso; screening team dir. Big Brothers Big Sisters, Las Cruces, 1999—. Vol. Tombaugh Elem. Sch., Las Cruces, 1998; vol. tchr. Radford Acad., El Paso. Mem. Am. Counseling Assn., Trans Pecos Counseling Assn. (liason), Phi Eta Mu, Club Deportivo (founder). Avocations: tennis, volleyball, cycling, golf, camping. Home: PO Box 6524 Las Cruces NM 88006-6524

ADAIR, CHARLES ROBERT, JR., lawyer; b. Narrows, Va., Sept. 29, 1914; s. Charles Robert and Margaret (Davis) A.; m. Lillian Adele Duffee, Sept. 19, 1942 (dec. 1993). BS, U. Ala., 1942, LLB, 1948, JD, 1969. Bar: Ala. bar 1948. Since practiced in, Dadeville; solicitor, 1955-73. Vice chmn. Ala. Securities Commn., 1969-71; mem., chmn. Ala. Jud. Compensation Commn., 1984—; v.p., bd. dirs. Dadeville Industries, Inc.; bd. dirs. Bank of Dadeville, Ala.. Chmn. Dadeville One Drive, 1960; chmn. Horseshoe Bend Regional Library, 1960-65; mem., sec. planning commn. City of Dadeville, 1965-80; hon. life mem. Bethel Vol. Fire Dept. and Rescue Service, Jackson's Gap Vol. Fire Dept. and Rescue Service; trustee Ala. Law Inst., Ala. Bar Found. Served as officer USAAF, World War II. Mem. Ala. Bar Assn. (past v.p.), Tallapoosa Bar (past pres.), 5th Cir. Bar Assn. (past pres., named Avery Country Lawyer of 1999), Farrah Law Soc., VFW, Am. Legion, East Ala. Peace Officers Assn. (hon. life), The Club, Capital City Club, Quarterback Club (past capt.), The Denny Soc., Masons, Kiwanis, Scabbard and Blade, Omicron Delta Kappa, Delta Tau Delta, Phi Alpha Delta. Presbyterian. Home: Duffee's Hill Dadeville AL 36853 Office: Old Bank Of Dadeville Dadeville AL 36853

ADAIR, CHARLES VALLOYD, retired physician; b. Lorain, Ohio, Apr. 20, 1923; s. Waite and Ella Jane (Robertson) A.; m. Contance Dean, Apr. 1, 1944; children: Allen V., Richard D. AB, Hobart Coll, Geneva, N.Y., 1944; MD, Western Res. U., 1947. Diplomate Am. Bd. Internal Medicine. Intern, then asst. resident in medicine Rochester Gen. Hosp., N.Y., 1947-49; fellow in medicine Univ. Hosps., Syracuse, N.Y., 1949-51; practice medicine specializing in internal medicine Mansfield, Ohio, 1953-85; ret., 1985. Past mem. staffs Mansfield Gen. Hosp., Peoples Hosp., Richland Neuropsychiat. Hosp.; mem. Mansfield City Bd. Health to 1985; trustee, past. pres. Mansfield Meml. Homes Capt. AUS, 1943-46, 51-53. Fellow Am. Coll. of Physicians; mem. AMA, Ohio Med. Assn., Richland County Med. Soc., Our Club, Westbrook Country Club. Republican. Congregationalist. Home: 1010 Woodland Rd Mansfield OH 44907-2242

ADAIR, DWIGHT RIAL, film director, educator; b. Winters, Tex., Mar. 1, 1950; s. J.P. and Beth (Clayton) A.; m. Sandra Estrin, Mar. 11; children: Marshall Clayton, Holly AshLyn. BA, Southwestern U., 1972; MA, Claremont Coll., 1975; ABD in Film, U. Tex., 1978. Dir. TV series Dallas, Dynasty, 1983-90; dialogue coach for various films and TV programs, including Urban Cowboy, 1979-80, Oldest Living Graduate, 1981, Member of the Wedding, 1982, A River Runs Through It, 1992; prodr. (movie) She Fought Alone, 1995, (series) Dream House, 2000. Mem. SAG, Dirs. Guild Am. Democrat. Methodist. Home: 11511 Queens Way Austin TX 78759-4468

ADAIR, EVAN EDWARD, lawyer; b. Erie, Pa., Aug. 31, 1950; s. Robert C. and Winifred A. (Ames) A.; m. Rebecca L. Nichols, Nov. 26, 1988; 1 child, Jacqueline. BA, Grove City Coll., 1972; JD, Coll. of William and Mary, 1975. Bar: Pa. 1976, U.S. Dist. Ct. (we. dist.) Pa. 1976, U.S. Ct. Appeals (3d cir.) 1982. Asst. gen. mgr. York St. Inn, Inc., Williamsburg, Va., 1975-76; ptnr. Williams & Adair, Erie, 1976—. Adj. faculty Mercyhurst Coll., Erie, 1982—89; solicitor Harborcreek (Pa.) Twp. Zoning Hearing Bd., 1990—, Millcreek (Pa.) Twp., 1992—. Crusade chmn. Am. Cancer Soc., Erie, 1979—85; pres. Millcreek Youth Athletic Assn., Erie, 1986—97; mem. program com. Boys and Girls Club of Erie, Inc., 1990—92; bd. dirs. Erie Playhouse; chmn. pub. rels. Erie County Bar Assn., 1979—85. Mem. ABA, Assn. Trial Lawyers Am., Pa. Bar Assn., Erie Maennerchor Club, East Erie Turners, Phi Delta Phi. Democrat. Presbyn. Avocation: reading. Office: Williams & Adair 332 E 6th St Erie PA 16507-1610 E-mail: eadair@warlaw.com.

ADAIR, JAMES ROBERT JR., religious studies educator; b. San Antonio, Tex., Aug. 12, 1960; s. James Robert and Vela Marie Adair; m. Rosa Magali Sierra, July 28, 1984; children: Danielle Marie, Elise Alexandra. B.S., Trinity U., San Antonio, Texas USA, 1979—80; Hons.-B.A., U. of Stellenbosch, Stellenbosch, South Africa, 1988—89; M.Div., Southwestern Bapt. Theol. Sem., Fort Worth, Texas USA, 1982—85; M.A., U. of Stellenbosch, Stellenbosch, South Africa, 1992—93; Ph.D., Southwestern Bapt. Theol. Sem., Fort Worth, Texas USA, 1985—92. Ordination Primera Iglesia Bautista, Ft. Worth, Tex., 1986. Systems programmer Datapoint, San Antonio, 1978—82; high sch. tchr. New Lives Sch., Fort Worth, Tex., 1992—94; adj. prof. Mercer U., Atlanta, 1996—; pvt. computer cons. Fort Worth, Tex., 1982—88; assoc. pastor Primera Iglesia Bautista, Fort Worth, 1986—94; lectr. Bapt. Theol. Coll., Cape Town, South Africa, 1988—89; mgr. of info. tech. services Scholars Press, Atlanta, 1994—98; dir. ATLA Ctr. for Electronic Resources in Theology and Religion, Stone Mountain, Ga., 1999—2001, Religion and Tech. Ctr., Stone Mountain, Ga., 2001—; tchg. fellow Southwestern Bapt. Theol. Sem., Fort Worth, Tex., 1986—91; adj. prof. Tex. Christian U., Fort Worth, Tex., 1993—93. Pres. Assn. of Peer-Reviewed Electronic Journals in Religion, 1999—2001, sec., 2001—03; vice chair, computer assisted rsch. sect. Soc. of Bibl. Lit., Atlanta, 2000—, editor, text-critical studies book series, 1997—; rsch. asst. Qumran Database Project, 1988—89. Editor: (electronic journal) TC: A Journal of Biblical Textual Criticism; author: (book) An Inductive Method for Reconstructing the Biblical Text; author: (editor) (blog (web log) Progressive Theology, numerous articles on textual criticism. Grantee SELA Digital Libr. Project, Mellon Found., 1996-1998, ATLAS Jour. Digitization Project, Lilly Found., 1999-2001, Tech. Grant, Soc. of Bibl. Lit., 2002. Mem.: Am. Schools of Oriental Rsch., Soc. of Bibl. Lit. D Liberal. Baptist. Avocations: reading, writing, sports. Home: 486 Castleaire Dr Stone Mountain GA 30087 Office: Religion and Technology Center 5385 Five Forks Trickum Rd Suite 202 Stone Mountain GA 30087 Office Fax: 770-925-3835. E-mail: jadair@reltech.org.

ADAIR, LARRY E. state representative; b. Prairie Grove, Ark., Oct. 17, 1946; s. Jess Eugene and Marjorie Louise (Bigby) Adair; m. Janice Faye Eversoll; children: Anesa Hooper, Carter. BA in Lang. Arts, Bus. Adminstrn., Northeastern State U., 1969, M in Secondary Edn., 1979. Former educator, sch. adminstr.; mem. Okla. Ho. of Reps., 1983—; spkr. of ho., 39th Legis. Okla. Ho. of Reps., Dist. 86, 2002—. Former voting mem. all ho. coms.; chair bd. dirs. Energy Coun. With U.S. Army, Vietnam. Mem.: VFW Post 3698, Stilwell Area C. of C., Adair County Cattlemen's Assn., Cherokee Tribe Okla., Am. Legion, Post 102, Kiwanis, 32d Degree Mason, Tulsa Conservatory, Flint Masonic Lodge, Bodouin Shrine, Masons. Democrat. Office: State Capitol 2300 N Lincoln Blvd Rm 401 Oklahoma City OK 73105 Address: 1207 Kerry Dr Stilwell OK 74960

ADAIR, ROBERT KEMP, physicist, educator; b. Ft. Wayne, Ind., Aug. 14, 1924; s. Robert Cleland and Margaret (Wiegman) Adair; m. Eleanor Reed, June 21, 1952; children: Douglas McVeigh, Margaret Guthrie, James Cleland. Ph.B., U. Wis., 1947, PhD, 1951, DSc (hon.), 1994. Instr. physics U. Wis., Madison, 1950-53; physicist Brookhaven Nat. Lab., Upton, NY, 1953-58, assoc. dir. high energy and nuc. physics, 1987-88; mem. faculty Yale U., New Haven, 1958—, prof. physics, 1961-72, Eugene Higgins prof. physics, 1972-88, Sterling prof. physics, 1988—94, Sterling prof. emeritus, 1994—, chmn. dept. physics, 1967-70, dir. divsn. phys. scis., 1977-80, sr. rsch. scientist, 1994—. Physicist Nat. Baseball League, 1987—89. Author (with Earle C. Fowler): (book) Strange Particles, 1963; author: Concepts in Physics, 1969, The Great Design, 1987, The Physics of Baseball, 1990; assoc. editor: Phys. Rev., 1963—66, Phys. Rev. Letters, 1974—76; editor, 1978—84. With inf. U.S. Army, 1943—46. Guggenheim fellow, 1954, Ford Found. fellow, 1962—63, Sloan Found. fellow, 1962—63. Fellow: Am. Acad. Arts and Scis., Am. Phys. Soc. (chmn. divsn. particles and fields 1972—73); mem.: NAS (chmn. physics sect. 1986—89, sec. class phys. scis. 1989—92, chmn. class phys. scis. 1992—94). Home: 50 Deepwood Dr Hamden CT 06517-3415 Office: Yale U Dept Physics Sloane Physics Lab PO Box 208121 New Haven CT 06520-8121

ADAIR, WENDELL HINTON, JR., lawyer; b. Ft. Benning, Ga., Mar. 17, 1944; s. Wendell H. Sr. and Jacqueline (Moore) A.; children: Elizabeth Carroll, John Michael, Benjamin David. BA, Emory U., 1966, postgrad., 1966-67; JD, U. Chgo., 1969. Bar: Ill. 1969, N.Y. 2000. Assoc. Ross, Hardies, O'Keefe, Babcock & Parsons, Chgo., 1969-72; ptnr. Mayer, Brown & Platt, Chgo., 1972-89, McDermott, Will & Emery, Chgo., 1989—99, Stroock & Stroock & Lowan LLP, 1999—. Editor: K & A Restructuring Register. Bd. dirs. ARC Mid-Am. chpt. 1991-99, Chgo. Opera Theatre, 1993-99; mem. Evanston Zoning Amendment Com., 1980-83. Mem.-ABA (bus. sect., bcy. sect., natural resources sect., pub. utilities sect.), Ill. Bar Assn., Fed. Energy Bar Assn. (bd. dirs. 1985-87, program chmn. 1990-91), NY Bar Assn., Am. Gas Assn. (bd. dirs. legal sect. 1986-89), Turnaround Mgmt. Assn. (program and publs. coms.). Clubs: Econ. (Chgo.), Chicago. Republican. Home: 5682 Sawyer Rd Sawyer MI 49125-9249 Office: Stroock Stroock & Lavan 180 Maden Ln New York NY 10038

ADAKU, CHIOMA, non-profit organization administrator; b. Oak Ridge, Tenn., Feb. 19, 1968; d. Orin Walter and Ethel Louise Sykes; m. Jarvis T. Griffin, Nov. 30, 2002; children: Daisha S. Ortiz, Willie Williams. BS, Knoxville Coll., 1990; BA, Bristol U., 1990, MBA, 1992. Contract adminstr. Dept. Energy, Oak Ridge, 1990—99; grantwriter Child & Family Tenn., Knoxville, 1999—2001; devel. dir. Tenn. Indsl. Renewal Network, Knoxville, 2002—. Cons. in organizational devel., marketing, and grassroots. Ind. film-maker : (documentaries) Apartheid in Appalachia, 2003; (film) From the Backyard to Brazil, 2003; From the Mountains to Mexico, 2003; author: (book) Emmaus in Appalachia, 2002. Candidate for state rep. Rep. Party, Knoxville, 1999; v.p. Women Polit. Caucus, Knoxville, 2001—02; chair bd. dirs. Tribe One, Knoxville, 2003; bd. dirs. Appalachian Cmty. Fund, Knoxville, 2002. Recipient Knoxville Leadership award, Cmty. Action Ctr., 1996, Knoxville's First and Next Leadership award, Sincere Seven, 2003, Leadership Award, Cmty. Action Com., YWCA Tribute to Women award, 2003. Mem.: NAACP (v.pres. Knoxville chpt. 2000—), Assn. Profl. Fundraiser (assoc.), Ea. Stars, Zeta Phi Beta (charter 1986—90). Republican. Bapist. Achievements include communitiy based research Apartheid in Appalachia on African-American history and health. Office: Tenn Indsl Renewal Network 1515 E Magnolia Ave Knoxville TN 37917 Home Fax: 865-522-7476, Office Fax: 865 522 7476 E-mail: development@tirn.org.

ADAM, JOHN, JR., insurance company executive emeritus; b. Braintree, Mass., Dec. 14, 1914; s. John and Harriet E. (Hubley) A.; m. Ruth E. Maddock, Dec. 27, 1945. AB, Oberlin Coll., 1937; LL.D. (hon.), Clark U., 1974. Underwriter Glens Falls Ins. Co., 1938-39, mgr. inland marine dept., 1939-40; with Central Mut. Ins. Co., 1940-60, v.p., 1957-60, Worcester Mut. Ins. Co., 1960, pres., 1960-79; also dir. pres., dir. Hanover Ins. Cos., 1969-79, dir., 1979, pres. emeritus, 1979—; pres. Heald, Inc., 1979-87. Chmn. adv. com. Mich. Investment Fund, M.B.W. Venture Ptnrs. Author: More Sales for You, 1949, also articles. Chmn. Mass. Bd. Higher Edn., 1972-77; past pres. Greater Worcester Community Found. Mem. Worcester C. of C. (past pres., dir.), Worcester County Music Assn. (past pres.), C.P.C.U. Soc. (nat. pres. 1967, dir.), Worcester Econ. Club (past pres.), Boston Sales Execs. Club (past pres.)

ADAM, JOHN ANTHONY, mathematician, educator; s. Albert John and Joan Kate Lydia Adam; m. Susan Anona Whidborne, Aug. 28, 1971; children: Rachel Louise Perry, Matthew Richard, Lindsay Rebecca. BS, U. London, 1971, PhD, 1974. Rsch. assistant applied math. U. St. Andrews, Scotland, 1976—78; lectr. math. New U. Ulster, Coleraine, Northern Ireland, 1978—83, sr. lectr. math., 1983—84; prof. math. Old Dominion U., Norfolk, Va., 1984—. Vis. asst. prof. mech. engring. U. Rochester, NY, 1983. Author: Mathematics in Nature: Modeling Patterns in the Natural World; editor: (research monograph) A survey of models for tumor/immune systems; contbr. articles to profl. jours. Fellow, U. Sussex, England, 1974—76. Episcopal (Charismatic). Avocations: photography, astronomy, reading, walking. Office: Old Dominion U Math Dept Hampton Blvd Norfolk VA 23529-0077 Home Fax: 757-683-3885; Office Fax: 757-683-3885. Personal E-mail: jadam@odu.edu. E-mail: jadam@odu.edu.

ADAM, PAUL JAMES, mechanical engineer; b. Kansas City, Mo., Oct. 26, 1934; s. Paul James and Adrienne (Zimmerman) Adam; m. Barbara Ann Mills, Dec. 18, 1956; children: Paul James, Blair Dodderidge, Matthew Mills. BSME, U. Kans., 1956. Registered profl. engr., Mo. Mech. engr. Black & Veatch, Engrs.-Architects, Kansas City, 1956, 1959—74, ptnr. asst. head power divsn., 1975—78, exec. ptnr., head power divsn., 1978—88, vice-chmn., CEO energy group, 1989—92, chmn., CEO, 1993—98, chmn., 1998—99. Chmn. engring. adv. bd. U. Kans., 1982—; chmn. World Energy Coun., 1998—; trustee U. Kans. Endowment Assn., 1994—. Fellow: ASME; mem.: U.S. Energy Assn. (chmn. 1996—98), U. Kans. Alumni Assn. (dir., past chmn.), River Club, Mission Hills Country Club, Alpha Tau Omega, Omicron Delta Kappa, Pi Tau Sigma, Sigma Tau, Tau Beta Pi. Episcopalian.

ADAM, WILLIAM JAMES, nuclear scientist; b. Milw., Dec. 1, 1952; s. George Henry and Elsie Ida (Schwertzel) A. BS, U. Wis., Milw., 1974; MS, Purdue U., 1976, PhD, 1978. Postdoctoral rsch. fellow Duke U., Raleigh, N.C., 1978-79; sr. health physicist/agreement state officer U.S. Nuclear Regulatory Commn., Glen Ellyn, Ill., 1979-90; prin. health physicist Westinghouse Hanford Co., Richland, Wash., 1991-94; project health physicist Bechtel Hanford, Inc., Richland, 1994-95; sr. safety analyst CH2MHill Hanford, Inc., Richland, 1995—. Contbr. articles to profl. jours. Chair working group 5, local task force on new radionuclide cancer treatments, Richland, 1997—. Recipient High Quality cert. U.S. NRC, 1987, Spl. Achievement cert., 1989, Westinghouse Hanford Engineered awrd for world-class engring. and sci. excellence, 1994; HEW Environ. Health fellow Purdue U., 1974, N.C. Heart Assn. postdoctoral fellow Duke U. Med. Ctr., 1979. Mem. Health Physics Soc., Health Physics Soc., Internat. Soc. Decontamination and Decommissioning Profls. (nominating com.), Am. Soc. Safety Engrs., Sigma Xi. Office: CH2MHill Hanford Inc 3190 George Washington Way Richland WA 99352-1659 E-mail: wjadam@mail.bhi-erc.com.

ADAMANY, DAVID WALTER, law and political science educator; b. Janesville, Wis., Sept. 23, 1936; s. Walter Joseph and Dora Marie (Mutter) Adamany. AB, Harvard U., 1958, JD, 1961; MS, U. Wis., 1963, PhD in Polit. Sci., 1967; LLD (hon.), Adrian Coll., 1984; AAS (hon.), Schoolcraft Coll., 1986; D. Engring. (hon.), Mich. Tech. U., 1987; D in Pub. Svc. (hon.), Eastern Mich. U., 1997. Bar: Wis. 1961. Spl. asst. to atty. gen. State of Wis., Madison, 1961—63, exec. pardon counsel, 1963; commr. Wis. Pub. Svc. Commn., 1963—65; instr. polit. sci. Wis. State U., Whitewater, 1965—67; asst. prof., then assoc. prof. Wesleyan U., Middletown, Conn., 1967—72, dean coll., 1969—71; assoc. prof., then prof. polit. sci. U. Wis., Madison, 1972—77; v.p. acad. affairs, prof. Calif. State U., Long Beach, 1977—80, U. Md., College Park, 1980—82; disting. prof. law and polit. sci. Wayne State U., Detroit, 1982—2000, pres., 1982—97, pres. emeritus, 1997; CEO Detroit Pub. Schs., 1999—2000; pres. Temple U., Phila., 2000—, Laura Carnall prof. law and polit. sci. Chmn. Wis. Coun. Criminal Justice, 1973—75, Wis. Elections Bd., 1976—77; sec. Wis. Dept. Revenue, 1973—75. Author: Financing Politics, 1969, Campaign Finance in America, 1972; co-author: Borzoi Reader in American Politics, 1972, American Government: Democracy and Liberty in Balance, 1975, Political Money, 1975; editl. bd.: Social Sci. Quarterly, 1973—, State and Local Govt. Rev., 1974—80; contbr. articles to profl. jours. Mem. exec. com. Detroit Med. Ctr., 1982—97; chmn. Mich. Bicentennial of U.S. Constrn. Commn., 1986—88; mem. Mich. Civil Svc. Commn., 1996—99; bd. dirs. Greater Phila. First, 2001—, African Am. Mus. Phila., 2001—; mem. Wis. Gov.'s Commn. on Campaign Fin. Reform, 1996—97; bd. dirs. Detroit Inst. Arts Founders Soc., 1983—92, Detroit Symphony Orch., 1983—89, Detroit Econ. Growth Corp., 1984—92, Karmanos Cancer Inst., 1982—97, New Detroit, 1982—95, Blue Cross Blue Shield Found. Mich., 1995—2000, Gilmour Fund, 1996—, HOPE Fund of Cmty. Found. of S.E. Mich., 1995—2000. Mem.: ABA (commn. on coll. and univ. legal studies 1992—95), ACLU, Pres.'s Coun. State Univs. (chmn. 1982—97), Am. Polit. Sci. Assn., Wis. Bar Assn., Greater Phila. C of C (exec. com. 2000—), Nat. Adv. Com. on Instl. Quality and Integrity (U.S. dept. edn. 1994—2000), Can.-U.S. Fulbright Commn. (bd. dirs. 1993—97). Democrat. Office: Temple U Rm 200 Sullivan Hall 1330 W Berks Street Philadelphia PA 19122-6087

ADAMCIK, JOE ALFRED, retired chemistry educator, retired attorney; b. Taylor, Tex., June 28, 1930; s. Joseph John Adamcik and Pearle Mae Offield. BS, U. Tex., Austin, 1951, MA, 1954; PhD, U. Ill., 1958; JD, Tex. Tech. U., 1991. Bar: Tex. 1991. Asst. prof. chemistry Tex. Tech. U., Lubbock, 1957-61, assoc. prof. chemistry, 1961-88; ret., 1988; practiced in, 1991-95; ret., 1995. Contbr. articles to profl. chemistry jours. Mediator Dispute Resolution Ctr., Lubbock, 1991—. Lt. (j.g.), USN, 1951-53. Fellow AAAS, Tex. Acad. Sci. (v.p.); mem. Am. Chem. Soc. (dir. 1981-88), Am. Geophys. Union, Royal Soc. Chemistry. Avocation: computers. Home: 5223 42d St Lubbock TX 79414 E-mail: jadamcik@aol.com.

ADAMCZYK, EDMOND DAVID, metallurgical engineer; b. Weirton, W.Va., June 16, 1957; s. Edmond and Elizabeth Marie (Kelchak) A. BS in Engring. and Econs., Carnegie-Mellon U., 1979, MS, 1980. Metall. engr., rsch. engr Nat. Steel Corp., Weirton, 1980-85; rsch. and devel. engr. Weirton Steel Corp., 1985-89, sr. product specialist, 1989-95, rsch. assoc., 1995-2000; product mgr. Sheet Products, 2000—. Mem. ASTM Internat., Nat. Coil Ctrs. Assn. (mktg. sect. container task force 1987-90, sec. 1987-90, chmn. mem. com. 1987-90, tech. sect. container task force 1987-90, chmn. statis. process control com. 1987-90), Minerals, Metals and Materials Soc. (chmn. Three Rivers sect. program com. 1984-85, treas. 1986, vice chmn. 1987, chmn. 1988, exec. com. 1984-89, Outstanding Young Mem. award 1986, mem. devel. com. 1989-92), Am. Soc. for Metals Internat., Am. Welding Soc., Soc. Automotive Engrs., Soc. Mfg. Engrs., Inst. Packaging Profls., Soc. Vacuum Coaters, Weirton Steel Corp. Mgmt. Club (bd. dirs. 1999-2000, treas. 2000-01), Iron and Steel Soc. Office: 400 Three Springs Dr Weirton WV 26062-4950

ADAMEK, CHARLES ANDREW, lawyer; b. Chgo., Dec. 24, 1944; s. Stanley Charles and Virginia Marie (Budzban) A.; m. Lori Merriel Klein; children: Donald Steven, Elizabeth Jean. BA with honors, U. Mich., 1966, JD, 1969. Bar: Ill. 1969, Calif. 1978. Clk. U.S. Dist. Judge U.S. Fed. Cts., Chgo., 1969-71; assoc. atty. Lord Bissell & Brook, Chgo., 1971-77, ptnr., 1977-78, L.A., 1978—. Mem. ABA, Ill. State Bar Assn., State Bar Calif., Nat. Assn. Railroad Trial Counsel. Roman Catholic. Avocations: Bluegrass banjo, sr. ice hockey. Office: Lord Bissell & Brook 300 S Grand Ave Ste 800 Los Angeles CA 90071-3119 E-mail: cadamek@lordbissell.com.

ADAMIAN, GREGORY HARRY, academic administrator; b. Somerville, Mass., Sept. 17, 1926; s. Adam K. and Sandy (Martin) Adamian; m. June Mouradian, July 6, 1958 (dec. Jan. 1967); children: Douglas, Daniel; m. Deborah Murdza, Jan. 1, 1978. AB, Harvard, 1947; MPA, JD, Boston U., 1951, LLD (hon.), 1991; DCS (hon.), Bentley Coll., 1991. Bar: Mass. 1951. Since practiced in, Cambridge; lectr. law and econs. Suffolk U., 1953-54; prof. law Bentley Coll., Waltham, Mass., 1955-67, chmn. dept. law, 1968-70, pres. coll., 1970-91, chancellor, 1991—. Lectr. real estate law Am. Savs. and Loan Inst.; bd. dirs. Joan Fabrics Corp. Pres. and trustee emeritus Bentley Coll. Lt. USN, 1944—47. Recipient Boyan Humanity award, Armenian Students Assn., 1973, Silver Shingle Disting. Svc. award, Boston U. Law Sch., 1986, Humanities award, 1990, Significant SIG medal, 1997, St. Sahag & St. Mesrob medal, Armenian Ch., 1998. Mem.: ABA, Am. Bus. Law Assn., Boston Bar Assn., Mass. Bar Assn., Nat. Assn. Armenian Studies and Rsch., Oakley Country Club, Shriners, Masons. Mem. Armenian Apostolic Ch. Home: 22 9th St Apt 804 Medford MA 02155-5166 Office: Bentley Coll Office of Chancellor Waltham MA 02452

ADAMO, KENNETH R. lawyer; b. Staten Island, N.Y., Sept. 27, 1950; BS, ChE, Rensselaer Polytech. Inst., 1972; JD, Union U., Albany, 1975; LLM, John Marshall Law Sch., 1989. Bar: Ill. 1975, N.Y. 1976, Ohio 1984, Tex. 1988, U.S. Patent and Trademark Office. Ptnr. Jones, Day, Reavis & Pogue, Cleve. Mem. Internat. Bar Assn. Office: Jones Day Reavis & Pogue N Point 901 Lakeside Ave Cleveland OH 44114

ADAMS, A. JOHN BERTRAND, public affairs consultant; b. Liverpool, Eng., Nov. 22, 1931; came to U.S., 1962, naturalized, 1971; s. Wilfrid and Francine Sophia (Bertrand) A.; m. Vibeke Dinsen, June 3, 1963 (div. 1975); m. Judith Ann Duff, Oct. 15, 1978; 1 dau., Caroline Louise. Corr. London Daily Telegraph, 1952-56; editor, bur. chief, asst. dir. news Radio Free Europe, Bonn and Munich, W.Ger., 1956-62; Africa corr. ABC News, 1963; writer, exec. CBS News, N.Y.C., 1964-70; assoc. dir. advt. and pub. rels. Investment Co. Inst., 1971-72; dir. pub. affairs U.S. Price Commn., Washington, 1972-73; pres. John Adams Assocs., Inc., Washington, 1973—; founding chmn. The WORLDCOM Group, N.Y.C., London, Tokyo, 1987. Bd. dirs. King Comm. Group, Washington. Author: (with J.M. Burke) Civil Rights: A Current Guide to the People, Organizations and Events, 1970; editor: Energy Policy: Industry Perspectives, 1975. Bd. dirs. Psychiat. Inst. Found., Washington, 1974-79, Nat. Coun. Fireworks Safety, 1986-96, Radio Free Europe Radio Liberty Fund, 1987—, Am. Com. for Aid to Poland, 1989-97, Am. Friends of Queen Mary Coll., U. London, 1990—, Friends of Benjamin Franklin House, London, 1990—; exec. dir. Eviron. Industry Coun., 1975-80; mem adv. bd. Gallaudet Coll. for Deaf, Washington, 1977-79. Lt. King's Shropshire Light Inf., Brit. Army, 1951-52, Korea. Recipient Knight's Cross, Order of Merit, Govt. of Poland, 1998, Disting. Svc. award U.S. Price Commn., 1973. Mem. Pub. Rels. Soc. Am. (Silver Anvil award 1978, 84, Hall of Fame, 1999), Nat. Press Club, Fed. City Club, Univ. Club (Washington), Severn River Yacht Club (Annapolis, Md.). Home: 12204 Meadow Creek Ct Potomac MD 20854-1408 Office: John Adams Assocs 807 National Press Building Washington DC 20045 E-mail: jadams@johnadams.com.

ADAMS, ALBERT T. lawyer; b. Cleve., Dec. 20, 1950; BA, Harvard U., 1973, MBA, JD, Harvard U., 1977. Bar: Ohio 1977. Ptnr. Baker & Hostetler, Cleve. Office: Baker & Hostetler 3200 Nat City Ctr 1900 E 9th St Ste 3200 Cleveland OH 44114-3475

ADAMS, ALBERT WILLIE, JR., lubrication company executive; b. Detroit, Nov. 22, 1948; s. Albert Willie and Goldie Inez (Davis) A.; m. Linda Maureen North, Sept. 2, 1972; children— Nichole Leahna, Albert Willie III, Melanie Rachel, Kimberly Monet. BA in Elem. Edn., Harris Tchrs. Coll., St. Louis, 1970; MBA, So. Ill. U., Edwardsville, 1974. Recreation leader City of St. Louis, 1967-69; recreation supr. Mo. Hills Home for Boys, 1969-70; tchr. spl. edn. St. Louis Bd. Edn., 1968-71; personnel asst. Equal Opportunity Adminstrn., Seven-Up Co., St. Louis, 1971-75, corporate equal opportunity adminstr., 1975-80, sr. employee relations adminstr., 1980-81, personnel mgr., 1981-82, mgr. indsl. relations, 1982-83, mgr. personnel programs and services, 1983-85, mgr. personnel ops., 1985-87; regional mgr. A. L. Williams, St. Louis, 1987-89; staff v.p. human resources Citicorp Mortgage Inc., St. Louis, 1989-91; v.p. human resources and quality Lincoln Indsl., Pentair Co., 1991—. Residence counselor Magdala Found., halfway house, 1971-77 Community-at-large mem. Affirmative Action Commn. Minorities St. Louis U., 1974-76; chmn. St. Louis corp. solicitation United Negro Coll. Fund, 1972; mem. adv. com. Statewide Job Placement Svc., 1979-84, Project Search, 1980-85; mem. Family and Children's Svc. N.W. Community Adv. Coun., 1982-85; mem. allocations com. United Way, 1985-90, bd. dirs., 1989-93; apptd. commr. St. Louis Civil Rights Enforcement Agy., 1988; bd. dirs. Vanderschmidt Sch., 1989-98, Habitat for Humanity, St. Louis, 1996-98, Pentair Found., 1998-01, Gateway Eagles of Mo., 2000--; statewide adv. bd. Internat. Student Internship, 2001--. U.S. Naval Acad. nominee, 1965; St. Louis Post-Dispatch scholar, 1971; Parsons-Blewett Meml. scholar tchrs., 1971; recipient Jr. Achievement scholarship award, 1966, St. Louis Sales and Mktg. Execs. award, 1966, St. Louis Sentinel achiever award, 1980 Mem.: AAIM (bd. dirs. 1998—2001), Black Pilots Am. (bd. dirs. 2002), Assn. MBA Execs., St. Louis Indsl. Rels. Assn., Kappa Alpha Psi. Baptist. Home: 2331 Albion Pl Saint Louis MO 63104-2524

ADAMS, ALFRED GRAY, lawyer; b. Winston-Salem, N.C., Feb. 28, 1946; s. Carlton Noble and Elizabeth (Walker) A.; m. Elizabeth Lark; children: Alfred Gray Jr., Amanda Laing. BA, Wake Forest U., 1968; JD, 1973. Bar: N.C. 1973; cert. splst. bus., comml., indsl. real estate property transactions. Ptnr. Van Winkle, Buck, Wall, Starnes & Davis, P.A., Asheville, N.C., 1973-94, Kilpatrick Stockton L.L.P., Winston-Salem, 1994-2000, Womble, Carlyle, Sandridge & Rice, PLLC, Winston-Salem, 2001—. Adj. prof. law Wake Forest U., 1996—. Assoc. editor: Wake Forest Law Rev., 1972. Chmn. Buncombe County Tax. Adv. Com., Asheville, 1983; Leadership Cir. chair United Way, 2000; pres.-elect Wake Forest U. Alumni Coun., 2002; bd. dirs. Downtown Winston-Salem Partnership, 2002—, Downtown Winston-Salem Found., 2003—. Named among N.C. Legal Elite N.C. Mag.; James Mason scholar Wake Forest U., 1972. Mem. N.C. Bar Assn. (bd. govs. 1987-90, real property sec. vice chmn. 1982-83, chmn. 1983-84, writer, lectr. real property and future interests bar rev. course 1981-83, mem. real property curriculum adv. com. 1984-91, chmn. 1988-91, seminar planner and lectr. real property 1987-98, chmn. cont. legal edn. com. 1991-93), Am. Coll. Real Estate Lawyers, Am. Coll. Mortgage Attys. (state chair 1995—2002, bd. regents 1996-98, sec. 1998, pres. 2000-01), Biltmore Forest Country Club (bd. govs. 1993-94), Forsyth Country Club (bd. dirs. 2003—), Old North State Club, Rhododendron Royal Brigade of Guards (capt. Ensign Class 1986). Republican. Methodist. Home: 115 Sullivan Way Winston Salem NC 27104-4911 Office: One W Fourth St Winston Salem NC 27101 E-mail: aadams@wcsr.com.

ADAMS, ALFRED HUGH, retired college president; b. Punta Gorda, Fla., Mar. 8, 1928; s. Alfred and Irene (Gatewood) A.; m. Joyce Morgan, Nov. 10, 1954; children: Joy, Al, Paul; m. Lynda K. Long, Apr. 20, 1999. AA, U. Fla., 1948; BS, Fla. State U., 1950, MS, 1956, Ed.D., 1962; L.H.D., Fla. Atlantic U., 1972. Asst. coach varsity football Fla. State U., 1955-58, asst. dir. housing, instr. edn., 1958-62, asst. dean men, asst. prof. edn., 1962-64; supt. pub. instrn. Charlotte County, Fla., 1965-68; pres. Broward Community Coll., Ft. Lauderdale, Fla., 1968-87; exec. dir. Performing Arts Ctr. Authority, Ft. Lauderdale, 1987-88; pres. Broward Performing Arts Found., Ft. Lauderdale, 1990-91. Bd. dirs. Am. Council on Edn.; vis. lectr. in higher edn. Inst. Higher Edn., U. Fla.; also mem. com. on internat. edn. relations, com. on mil-higher edn. relations; mem. adv. com. Inst. Internat. Edn.; dir. Sun Bank/South Fla., N.A.; Vice chmn. Gov. Fla. Commn. Quality Edn., 1968-70; mem. Gov.'s Adv. Com. Edn., 1966-70; mem. regional council Southeastern Edn. Corp., 1966-69; mem. commn. adminstrv. affairs Am. Council on Edn., 1973; pres. Pub. Instns. Higher Learning in So. States, 1975; mem. adv. com. Joint Council on Econ. Edn.; chmn. AACJC Internat./Intercultural Consortium, S.E. Fla. Ednl. Consortium; chmn. council pres. Fla. Community Colls.; Trustee South Fla. Edn. Center, Pub. Service TV Mem. editorial bd., Soc. for Coll. and Univ. Planning. Pres. United Way, 1973; bd. dirs. local chpt. ARC, 1971; bd. dirs. Opera Guild, Ft. Lauderdale, pres., 1983-85; bd. dirs. Coll. Consortium Internat. Studies; exec. dir. Performing Arts Ctr. Authority, Ft. Lauderdale; pres. Broward Performing Arts Found., Ft. Lauderdale. Served to comdr. USNR, 1945-46, 52-55. Decorated knight Internat. Constantinian Order, 1971; recipient Liberty Bell award, 1973, Patriot award Freedoms Found., Disting. Alumnus award Fla. State U., A. Hugh Adams Coll. Gold Key. cert. of recognition Fla. Ho. of Reps., Disting Omicron Delta Kappa Alumnus of Yr., 1987; named Patriot Fla. Bicentennial Commn., Fla. State U. Sports Hall of Fame. Mem. Fla. Tchr. Edn. Adv. Council, Fla. Edn. Council Ethics Com. Sch. Adminstrs., Am. Assn. Sch. Adminstrs., Ft. Lauderdale C. of C. (v.p.), Profl. Practices Commn., Fla. Assn. Colls. and Univs. (pres. 1975), Naval Res. Assn., Res. Officers Assn., U.S. Naval Inst. (life), Broward Minutemen (pres.), Fla. Inter-agy. Law Enforcement Planning Council, Omicron Delta Kappa, Phi Theta Kappa. Clubs: Gulfstream Sailing, Fort Lauderdale; Tower (gov. 1985-86). Lodges: Kiwanis. Methodist. Home: 16723 Seagull Bay Ct Bokeelia FL 33922-1554

ADAMS, ALICE, sculptor; b. N.Y.C., Nov. 16, 1930; d. Charles P. and Loretto G. (Tobin) A.; m. William D. Gordy, Feb. 7, 1969; 1 dau., Katherine Adams Gordy. Student, Adelphi Coll., 1948-50; BFA, Columbia U., 1953; postgrad. (French Govt. fellow), 1953-54; postgrad. Fulbright Travel grantee, L'Ecole Nat d'Art Decoratif, Aubusson, France, 1953-54. Lectr. Manhattanville Coll., Purchase, N.Y., 1960-79; instr. sculpture Sch. Visual Arts, 1980-87. One-woman shows include N.Y.C., 1972, 74, 75, Hal Bromm Gallery, N.Y.C., 1979, 80; exhibited in group shows at Whitney Mus. Am. Art, N.Y.C., 1971, 73, Indpls. Mus. Art, 1974, Nassau County Mus. Fine Arts, Roslyn, N.Y., 1977, Wave Hill, Riverdale, N.Y., 1979, Mus. Modern Art, N.Y.C., 1984, Lehman Coll. Art Gallery, N.Y.C., 2000-01; represented in permanent collections Weatherspoon Gallery U. N.C., Greensboro, U. Nebr., Everson Mus., Syracuse, N.Y., Haags Gemetemuseum, The Hague, Netherlands, Am. Craft Mus., N.Y.C., Edwin I. Ulrich Mus., Wichita, Kans.; pub. commissions include Bot. Garden, Toledo, Ohio, Design Team Seattle Transit Project, St. Louis Metro-Link Project, Midland Metro, Birmingham, Eng., Port Authority of N.Y. and N.J., Thomas Jefferson U., Phila., N.Y.C. Bd. Edn., State of Conn., Denver Internat. Airport, N.Y.C. Metro. Transp. Authority, U. Tex. San Antonio, Broward County, Fla., U. Del., Newark. Creative Artists Pub. Svc. grantee, 1973-74, 76-77, Nat. Endowment for Arts Artists grant, 1978-79, Richard Florsheim grant, 1999, Am. Acad. of Arts and Letters grant, 1984; Guggenheim fellow, 1981-82; Rockefeller Found. resident, Bellagio, Italy, 2002. Home: 3370 Fort Independence St Bronx NY 10463-4502

ADAMS, ANNE CLAIRE, lawyer; b. Santa Barbara, Calif., Dec. 15, 1956; d. John Franklin and Carol Louise (Snyder) A.; m. William Paul Thurber, Mar. 24, 1990. BA, UCLA, 1979; MBA, Golden Gate U., 1986; JD, Southwestern U., 1993. Bar: Calif., 1994. Investment exec. Wedbush, Noble, Cooke, Inc., L.A., 1980-84; affil. coord. SelecTV, Marina del Rey, Calif., 1985-86, affil. mgr., 1986-87; sales rep. Continental Cablevision, Culver City, Calif., 1987-88, acct. mgr. L.A., 1988-95; bus. affairs exec. MediaOne, L.A., 1995-99; sole practice Canoga Park, Calif., 1999—. Bd. dirs. L.A. Women's Appt. Collaboration, 1995—2001; bd. dirs. L.A. coun. Camp Fire Boys and Girls, 1996—2000, pres., 1997—99; asst. pub. policy dir. Jr. League L.A., 1998—99. Recipient Disting. Svc. award Harriet Buhai Ctr. Family Law, 1995, Cert. Recognition Calif. State Assembly, 1997, Cert. Commendation City L.A., 1997, Outstanding Vol. award L.A. coun. Camp Fire Boys and Girls, 1996-97, Spl. Congl. Recognition commendation State of Calif., 2002 Mem.: San Fernando Valley Bar Assn. (bd.dirs.cmty. legal found. 1995—2001, v.p. fundraising 2002—03). Avocations: community service, travel. Address: Law Offices of Anne C Adams 6928 Owensmouth Ave Ste 101 Canoga Park CA 91303-2095

ADAMS, ARLIN MARVIN, lawyer, arbitrator, mediator, retired judge; b. Phila., Apr. 16, 1921; s. Aaron M. and Mathilda (Landau) A.; m. Neysa Cristol, Nov. 10, 1942; children: Carol (Mrs. Howard Kirshner), Judith A., Jane C. BS in Econs. with highest honors, Temple U., 1941; LLB with honors, U. Pa., 1947, MA in Econs., 1950; DHL (hon.), Temple U., 1964; DSc (hon.), Phila. Coll. Optometry, 1965; LLD (hon.), Phila. Coll., 1966, Susquehanna U., 1985, Muhlenberg Coll., 1986, Villanova U., 1987, U. Pa., 1998. Bar: Pa. 1947; U.S. Ct. Appeals (3rd cir.), 1947. Law clk., Chief Justice Horace Stern Pennsylvania Supreme Ct., 1947; assoc. firm Schnader, Harrison, Segal & Lewis, Phila., 1947-50, sr. partner, 1950-63, 66-69; sec. pub. welfare Commonwealth of Pa., Phila., 1963-66; judge U.S. Ct. Appeals (3d cir.), Phila., 1969-87; counsel Schnader, Harrison, Segal & Lewis, Phila., 1987—. Apptd. ind. counsel to investigate Dept. HUD, 1990-95; apptd. spl. counsel Pa. Commn. of Police, 1994-95; instr. Am. Inst. Banking, Phila., 1949-52; lectr. fed. practice Law Sch., U. Pa., Phila., 1952-56, lectr. constl. law, 1972-97. Author: Law and Religion, 2 vols., 1991, A Nation Dedicated to Religious Liberty, 1990; Editor-in-chief Law Review U. Penn., 1947; contbr. articles to profl. jours. Pres. Annenberg Inst., 1988—91; chmn. bd. dirs. Moss Rehab. Hosp., Phila., 1962—63; trustee U. Pa., 1985—; chmn. U.S. Supreme Ct. Jud. Fellows Commn., 1987—93, Fels Inst. Govt., Phila., 1967—77, Sch. of Social Work, Bryn Mawr (Pa.) Coll., 1967—78, Diagnostic and Rehab. Ctr., Phila., 1971—72; chmn. overseers U. Pa. Law Sch., 1985—92; trustee Med. Coll. of Pa., 1974—80, hon. trustee, 1981—98; trustee German Marshall Meml. Fund, 1972—84, Lewis H. Stevens Trust, Bryn Mawr Coll., 1972—78, Columbia U. Ctr. for Law and Econ. Studies, U. Pa. Inst. for Law and Econs., William Penn Found.; hon. trustee Phila. Mus. Art, 1998—; mem. Cardinal's Commn. re Abuse of Children, 2002. With USNR, 1942—45, North Pacific. Recipient Disting. Service award U. Pa. Law Sch., 1981, Justice award Am. Jud. Soc., 1982, John Murray award DePaul U., 1987, Cresset award Rosemont Coll., 1988, Gold Medallion award Chapel of Four Chaplains, Founders award Temple U., 1997, Phila. award, 1997. Mem. ABA (del. ho. of dels. 1966-67, 75-77, chmn. trade assn. com.), Am. Law Inst., Am. Bar Found., Pa. Bar Assn. (pres. jr. bar 1950, del. ho. of dels. 1967-71), Phila. Bar Assn. (chancellor 1967, Gold Medal award 1999), Am. Judicature Soc. (pres. 1975-77), Am. Philos. Soc. (sec. 1980-83, v.p. 1987-92, pres. 1993-99), Am. Acad. Arts & Scis., Arlin Adams Law and Soc. Inst., Phila. Club, Union League, Sun. Breakfast Club, Legal Club (pres. 1986-91), Jr. Legal Club, Order of Coif, Beta Gamma Sigma. Office: Schnader Harrison Segal & Lewis LLP 1600 Market St Fl 36 Philadelphia PA 19103-7240

ADAMS, BARBARA, English language educator, poet, writer; b. N.Y.C., Mar. 23, 1932; d. David S. Block and Helen (Taxter) Block Tyler; m. Elwood Adams, June 6, 1952; (dec. 1993); children: Steven, Amy, Anne, Samuel. BS, SUNY,

New Paltz, 1962, MA, 1970; PhD, NYU, 1981. Prof. English Pace U., N.Y.C., 1984-2000, dir. bus. comm., 1984-2001. Poet in residence Cape Cod Writers' Conf., 1988. Author: Double Solitaire, 1982, The Enemy Self: The Poetry & Criticism of Laura Riding, 1990, Hapax Legomena, 1990, Negative Capability, 1999 (1st Prize for Fiction), (play) God's Lioness and the Crow: Sylvia Plath and Ted Hughes, 2000; contbr. poems, stories, articles to various mags. and jours. Recipient 1st prize for poetry NYU and Acad. Am. Poets, 1975, 1st prize for fiction Negative Capability contest, 1999; Penfield fellow NYU, 1977. Mem. PEN, Poetry Soc. Am., Poets and Writers. Home: 59 Coach Ln Newburgh NY 12550-3818

ADAMS, BEEJAY (MEREDITH ELISABETH JANE ADAMS), sales executive; b. Jefferson Barracks, Mo., June 9, 1920; d. Alden Humphrey and Louise Marion (Banta) Seabury; m. Merlin Francis Adams, July 10, 1948 (dec. 1977); children: S(tephen) Kent, Mark Francis. AB, Bradley U., 1942. Svc. editor Peoria (Ill.) Jour. Star, 1942-46; women's program dir. Sta. WEEK-AM, Peoria, 1946-47; on air personality Sta. KSD-AM, St. Louis, 1948; lectr. Sch. Assembly Svc., Chgo., 1948-49; pres. M.F. Adams, Inc., Quincy, Ill., 1977-85; commodities broker Quincy, 1985-87; pres. MarKent, Inc., Quincy, 1975-99; sec., treas. Miss. Belle Distbn. Co., Inc., Quincy, 1976—, v.p., treas., 1979—. Active Quincy Svc. League, 1949-57, local polit. campaigns, co-chmn. local presdl. campaigns, 1952-77; founder, past pres. Quincy Jr. Theatre, 1953-78; charter mem. Quincy Cmty. Theatre; co-chmn. coll. fund drive Quincy Coll., 1988, chmn. 1989; asst. majority leader State Mary Lou Kent; campaign chair, legis aide to Mary Lou Kent. Recipient Ill. Women of Achievement award, Mayor of Quincy, 2000. Mem. Quincy C. of C., Sales and Mktg. Execs. Club, Quincy Art Club, Atlantis Study Club, Quincy Country Club, Phi Beta Phi. Anglican. Avocations: golf, reading, home repair, traveling, politics. Home: 2303 Jersey St Quincy IL 62301-4343 Office: Miss Belle Distbn Co Inc PO Box 768 Quincy IL 62306-0768

ADAMS, BERNARD SCHRODER, retired college president; b. Lancaster, Pa., July 20, 1928; s. Martin Ray and Charlotte (Schroder) A.; m. Natalie Virginia Stout, June 2, 1951; children: Deborah Rowland, David Schroder. BA, Princeton, 1950; MA, Yale, 1951; PhD, U. Pitts., 1964; LL.D. (hon.), Lawrence U., 1967; cert., Inst. for Ednl. Mgmt., Harvard U., 1975. Asst. dir. admissions, instr. English Princeton, 1953-57; dir. admissions and student aid U. Pitts., 1957-60, spl. asst. to chancellor, 1960-64; dean students, lectr. English Oberlin (Ohio) Coll., 1964-66; pres. Ripon (Wis.) Coll., 1966-85, Ft. Lewis Coll., Colo., 1985-87; ednl. cons. pvt. practice, Colo. Springs, 1987-88; v.p. resources Goodwill Industries, Colorado Springs, Colo., 1988-96. Dir. Wis. Power & Light Co., Newton Funds, 1970-85; cons., examiner Commn. on Instns. Higher Edn., North Cen. Assn. Colls. and Secondary Schs., 1972-87, exec. commr., 1981-86; bd. dirs. Four Corners Opera Assn., 1985-87, pres., 1986-87. Contbr. articles to profl. jours. Bd. dirs. Keep Colorado Springs Beautiful, 1990—99; bd. dirs. Colo. chpt. Nat. Assn. Fundraising Execs., 1990—94; bd. dirs. Colorado Springs Symphony Vols., 1992—98, 2000—, Ctr. Prevention Domestic Violence, 1995—2001. 1st lt. USAF, 1951—53. Woodrow Wilson fellow, 1951 Mem. Assoc. Colls. Midwest (bd. dirs. 1966-85, pres. 1973-75), Wis. Assn. Ind. Colls. and Univs. (bd. dirs. 1966-85, pres. 1969-71, 83-85). Home: 90 Ellsworth St Colorado Springs CO 80906-7954

ADAMS, BRADY, bank executive, former state legislator; b. Portland, Oreg., Feb. 28, 1945; m. Pat Adams, 1965; children: Ted, Jennifer. BS in mktg., Portland State U. With Evergreen Fed. Savings and Loan, Grants Pass, Oreg., 1972—; mem. Oreg. Senate, Salem, 1992—2000; pres. of senate State of Oreg., 1997—2000; now pres. Evergreen Fed. Savings and Loan, Grants Pass, Oreg. Founder Our Valley Clin.; treas. Grants Pass Cmty. Sculpture Com. Mem. Rotary (hon.). Office: Evergreen Federal Savings attn: Pres 969 SE 6th Street Grants Pass OR 97526

ADAMS, BRENDA KAY, publishing executive; b. Chickasha, Okla., Dec. 5, 1954; d. William Opal and Frances Mahota (Greer) Pettigrew; m. Phillip Wayne Haney, May 29, 1976 (div. Feb. 1995); children: Kristin Lea, Phillip Kollin, Kasey Kay; m. Warren Lynn Adams, Feb. 3, 1996; stepchildren: Lindsay Nichelle, London Reed. BA, U. Sci. and Arts of Okla., 1976. Photographer, reporter Chickasha Daily Express, 1974, lifestyles editor, 1974-78, advt. dir., 1978-88, pub., 1992-95, Pauls Valley (Okla.) Democrat, 1988-92, Real Estate Exec., Chickasha, 1996-97, Builder/Architect, Chickasha, 1996-97; publs. dir. Nat. Rural Water Assn., Duncan, Okla., 1997-99; advt. dir. Richmond (Ind.) Palladium-Item, 1999; territorial sales mgr. R. K. Black Inc., Oklahoma City, 2000; gen. mgr./advt. dir. Bossier Press-Tribune, Bossier City, La., 2001—02; pub. M.D. News, Chickasha, 2002; advt. dir. Fort Madison (Iowa) Daily Dem., 2002—03; pub. Sweetwater (Tex.) Reporter, 2003—. Pub. cons. Adams Assocs., Ninnekah, Okla., 1995-99. Contbr. articles to profl. jours. Bd. dirs. Grady County Family YMCA, Chickasha, 1993-96, United Way of Grady County, Chickasha, 1993-96; v.p., treas. Cmty. Edn. Adv. Coun., Pauls Valley, 1990-92; bd. dirs. (alumni) U. Sci. and Arts of Okla., Chickasha, 1993-96, bd. dirs. (found.), 1993-96; founding bd. dirs. Festival of Light, Chickasha, 1993-96. Mem. Okla. Press Assn. (better newspaper contest com. chair 1992-95, newspaper in edn. com. chmn. 1992-95, advt. com. chmn. 1993-95, conv. com. 1993-95, 1st place in sales promotion 1991-92, 1st place in cmty. leadership 1991-92), Pauls Valley C. of C. (bd. dirs. 1988-92). Democrat. Mem. Christian Ch. (Disciples Of Christ). Avocations: antiques, photography, travel, country crafts, gardening. Home: 3459 Hwy 81 Ninnekah OK 73067-9504 Office: 112 W Third St Sweetwater TX 79556

ADAMS, C. LEE, marketing executive; b. Houston, Dec. 5, 1940; s. Carl Adams and Ruth (Carroll) Adams McGraw; m. Betty Leatherwood, June 1, 1963; children: Diana, Carroll Ann. BBA, Tex. A&M U., 1963. Export sales svc. asst. Comet Rice Mills, Inc., Houston, 1963-64, asst. export sales mgr., 1964-67, export sales mgr., 1967-68, gen. mgr. Country Cupboard Foods Divsn., 1968-71; sales mgr. Childers Mfg. Co., Houston, 1971-75; export sales mgr. Am. Rice, Inc., Houston, 1975-76, v.p. internat. mktg., 1976-80, group v.p. mktg., 1980-85, group v.p. internat. mktg., 1986-93, sr. v.p., 1993-99, sr. v.p., COO, 1999—. Bd. dirs. USA Rice Fedn., mem. rice com. New Orleans Commodity Exchange, 1981-84. Bd. dirs. Harris County Water Control and Improvement Dist. 93, 1974-76; mem. Chelford One Mcpl. Utility Dist. Appraisal Rev. Bd., 1982-85. Served with USMCR, 1960-66. Mem. Am. Arab C. of C. (bd. dirs. 1978-81), TAMU 12th Man Found. (bd. dirs. 1987—), USA Rice Coun. (bd. dirs. 1995—), Rice Millers Assn. (bd. dirs. 1983—, pres. 1986-87), Assn. Former Students Tex. A&M U., Elsik H.S. Ram Rods Club (pres. 1984-85), Sweetwater Country Club, KC, Am. Legion. Roman Catholic. Office: Am Rice Inc PO Box 2587 Houston TX 77252-2587 E-mail: ladams@amrice.com.

ADAMS, CHARLES FRANCIS, advertising and real estate executive; b. Detroit, Sept. 26, 1927; s. James R. and Bertha C. (DeChant) A.; m. Helen R. Harrell, Nov. 12, 1949; children: Charles Francis, Amy Ann, James Randolph, Patricia Duncan. BA, U. Mich., 1948; postgrad., U. Calif., Berkeley, 1949; student additional study, Oxford U., 1996. With D'Arcy-MacManus & Masius, Inc., 1947-80, exec. v.p., dir., 1970-76, pres., chief operating officer, 1976-80; pres. Adams Enterprises, 1971—; exec. v.p., dir. Washington Office, Am. Assn. Advt. Agys., 1980-84. Chmn., chief exec. officer Wajim Corp., Detroit; past mem. steering com. Nat. Advt. Rev. Bd.; mem. mktg. com. U.S. Info. Agy.; pres. Internat. Visitors Ctr. of the Bay Area, 1988-89. Author: Common Sense in Advertising, 1965, Heroes of the Golden Gate, 1987, California of the Year 2000, 1992, The Magnificent Rogues, 1999. Past chmn. exec. com. Oakland U. Mem. Am. Assn. Advt. Agys. (dir., mem. govt. rels. com.), Advt. Fedn. Am. (past dir.), Nat. Outdoor Advt. Bur. (past chmn.), Nat. Golf Links Am. Club (Southampton, LI), Olympic Club, The Family Club, Theta Chi, Alpha Delta Sigma, (hon.). Republican. Roman Catholic. Home: 2240 Hyde St # 5 San Francisco CA 94109-1509 Office: 10 W Long Lake Rd Bloomfield Hills MI 48304-2707

ADAMS, CHARLES GEOFFREY, minister, educator; b. Arkansas City, Kans., Aug. 23, 1948; s. Robert Nelson and Helen Louise A.; m. Cheryl Lynn Triplitt, Aug. 14, 1970; children: Sarah Wagner, Rebekah Herzog. B in Ministry, Luther Rice Sem., 1982; M in Sacred Lit., Trinity Theol. Sem., 1993, PhD, 2002; DD, Md. Bible Coll. and Sem., 1995. Youth pastor First Bible Bapt. Ch., Wichita, Kans., 1969-71; youth pastor and assoc. pastor Kansas City (Mo.) Bapt. Temple, 1971-74; sr. pastor Kansas City Bapt. Temple, 1984—; interim pastor Iglesia Bautista Emanuel, San Jose, Costa Rica, 1975; missionary Bapt. Internat. Missions, Inc., Managua, Nicaragua, 1976; pastor Iglesia Bautista Miramonte, San Salvador, El Salvador, 1976-84. Prof. Inst. Biblico Emanuel, San Jose, 1975, Inst. Biblico Por Ext. Que Dice la Biblia, Kansas City, 1990—; prof., pres. Inst. Biblico Miramonte, San Salvador, 1976-84; del. Internat. Congress on Itinerant Evangelism, Billy Graham Assn., Amsterdam, The Netherlands, 1983; pres. Shepherd Sch. Min., Kansas City, 1985—; pres. bd. dirs. Reality Living Pub., Kansas City. Author: Reality Living, 1990, Psalm 119: A Journey Into the Heart of God, 1993, Job: Adventures in the Land of Uz, 1994, Filemon, 2002. Mem. Mayor's Task Force on Drugs, City of Kansas City, 1984. Baptist. Avocations: black belt, shotokan karate, travel, alpine skiing. Home: 4607 Norwood Ct Kansas City MO 64133 Office: Kansas City Bapt Temple 5460 Blue Ridge Cutoff Kansas City MO 64133 E-mail: jadams@kcbt.org.

ADAMS, CHARLES HENRY, retired animal scientist, educator; b. Burdick, Kans., Nov. 7, 1918; s. Henry Lory and Bertha Frances (Westbrook) A.; m. Eula Mae Peters, Apr. 29, 1943 (dec. Apr. 1999); m. Beryle Irene Supple Somer Janousek, Dec. 23, 2000. BS, Kans. State U., 1941, MS, 1942; PhD, Mich. State U., 1964. Instr. Kans. State U., Manhattan, 1946-47; asst. prof. U. Nebr., Lincoln, 1947-64, assoc. prof., 1964-70, prof. animal sci., 1970-83, prof. emeritus, 1983—; asst. dean Coll. Agr., U. Nebr., Lincoln, 1973-83. Contbr. articles to profl. jours. 1st lt. AUS, 1943-46 Recipient Disting. Teaching awards Gamma Sigma Delta, 1969, U. Nebr., 1971, Am. Meat Sci. Assn., 1969, Am. Soc. Animal Sci., 1972; Disting. Svc. award U. Nebr. Lincoln Alumni Assn., 1989, Doc Elliott award, 2001; named to Nebr. Hall of Agrl. Achievement, 1990. Fellow AAAS, Am. Soc. Animal Sci.; mem. Am. Meat Sci. Assn. (R.C. Pollock award 1992), Inst. Food Technologists, Nebr. Acad. Sci., Am. Legion, VFW, Rotary, Sigma Xi, Gamma Sigma Delta, Alpha Zeta, Alpha Gamma Rho. Republican. Presbyterian. Home: 5700 Fremont St Apt 227 Lincoln NE 68507-1680

ADAMS, CHARLES JAIRUS, lawyer; b. Randolph, Vt., Feb. 17, 1917; s. Charles B. and Jeanette E. (Metzger) A.; m. Mary E. Tobey, July 5, 1942; children: Mary Jean, Carol Ann. BS in Elec. Engring, Norwich U., 1939; LL.B., Boston U., 1951. Bar: Vt. 1951. Student engr. Gen. Electric Co., also New Eng. Power Co., 1939-41; plant supt. Demeritt Co., Waterbury, Vt., 1946-48; practiced in Montpelier and Waterbury, 1951-98; partner firm Adams, Darby & Laundon, 1980-86; of counsel Darby, Laundon, Stearns, Thorndike & Kolter, 1987-98. Treas. Vt. Bar Assn., 1951-55; atty. gen. State of Vt., 1962-63; chmn. State of Vt. Legis. Apportionment Bd., 1972-80; mem. adv. com. on civil rules Vt. Supreme Ct., 1971-82 Trustee Village of Waterbury, 1956-57, 88-90, pres., 1958; moderator Town of Waterbury, 1961; mem. Waterbury Pub. Libr. Assn., 1961-93. Mem. Am. Legion, Norwich U. Gen. Alumni Assn. (pres. 1960-61), Partridge Soc. (bd. fellows), Masons. Congregationalist. Home: 16 Harbor View Rd Apt 302 South Burlington VT 05403

ADAMS, CHARLES LYNFORD, English language educator; b. Joliet, Ill., May 11, 1929; s. Charles Lynford and Eloise A. (Henault) A.; m. Joan Marie Johnson, June 6, 1953; children— Rebecca Lynn, Stephen Thomas. BA, Mich. State U., 1951; MA, U. Ill., 1952; PhD, U. Oreg., 1959. Instr. English U. Ore., 1959-60; asst. prof. U. Nev., Las Vegas, 1960-65, assoc. prof., 1965-67, prof. English, 1967-96, prof. emeritus English, 1996—. Las Vegas rep. U. Nev. System Grad. Sch., 1964-66, coordinator grad. studies, 1966-68, dean grad. studies, 1968-71 Editor: Studies in Frank Waters. Mem. adv. com. Univ. Mus. Soc. Served with AUS, 1954-56. Mem. MLA, Nat. Coun. Tchrs. English, Nev. Coun. Tchrs. English, So. Nev. Coun. Tchrs. English, Rocky Mountain MLA, Conf. Coll. Composition and Comm., AAUP, Nat. Soc. Profs., Frank Waters Soc., Phi Kappa Phi. Home: 1921 E Saint Louis Ave Las Vegas NV 89104-3805 Office: 4505 S Maryland Pkwy Las Vegas NV 89154-5011 E-mail: adamsc@unev.edu.

ADAMS, CHARLES PAUL, communications engineer, consultant; b. Kansas City, Mo., June 20, 1955; s. Henry Robert and Corlyn Leola (Holbrook) A.; m. Lanita Jill Christy, July 14, 1979 (div. 1998); children: Allison Denise, Robert Benjamin. BA, Southwestern Okla. State U., 1978. Cert. quality auditor, Am. Soc. Quality Control. Analytical chemist Mosites Rubber Co., Ft. Worth, 1978—79, Alcon Labs., Inc., Ft. Worth, 1979—82; analytical rsch. chemist Johnson and Johnson Med., Inc., Arlington, Tex., 1982—84; lead avionics quality engr. Northup-Grumman, Inc., Dallas, 1985—91; lead quality engr. EG&G Inc. (Super Conducting Super Collider Lab.), Waxahachie, Tex., 1991—95; sr. radio frequency design engr. Nokia Networks, Inc., Irving, Tex., 1995—. V.p. Adams Mgmt. Svcs., Inc., Ft. Worth, 1980-85; radio frequency cons. Midcom, Inc., Irving, 1982—; spl. cons. NFL, N.Y.C., 1996, Dallas Cowboys Football Club for Wireless Sys., 1998. Pub. Tex. 220, 1981-83; contbr. articles to profl. jours. Tech. advisor Tarrant County Radio Amateur Civil Emergency Svc., Ft. Worth, 1978—; mem. event mgmt. team, comm. team leader Ft. Worth Main St. Arts Festival, Ft. Worth Parade of Lights, Ft. Worth Fourth of July, 1991-2001. Recipient Pub. Svc. award Ft. Worth Fire Dept., 1980, 82, 84, 87, 88, 89, 90, 91; cert. commendation Ft. Worth-Tarrant County Office Civil Def., 1992, 93, 98, 99, 2001. Mem. IEEE, Am. Radio Relay League, Quarter Century Wireless Assn., Tex. VHF-FM Soc., Inc. (life mem., frequency coord. 1982-92, pres. 1984-85, v.p. 1985-86), Radio Club Am., Phi Mu Alpha. Republican. Achievements include pending patents in the telecommunications and cellular areas. Home: 4613 Collinwood Ave Fort Worth TX 76107-4160 Office: Nokia Networks Inc 6000 Connection Dr Irving TX 75039-2600 E-mail: xanaduu@xanaduu.com.

ADAMS, CHRISTINE BEATE LIEBER, psychiatrist, educator; b. Greensboro, N.C., June 20, 1949; d. Paul Lieber Adams and Marjorie Pinckney (Quackenbos) Ould; 1 child, Justin McKendree Adams-Tucker. Student, Agnes Scott Coll., 1967-69; BA in English Lit. with honors, U. Fla., 1971, MD, 1976. Diplomate Am. Bd. Psychiatry and Neurology (examiner 1985), Am. Bd. Child Psychiatry (examiner 1984, 91), Nat. Bd. Med. Examiners. Resident in gen. psychiatry U. Louisville Sch. Medicine, 1976-78, fellow in child psychiatry, 1978-80, asst. clin. prof. dept. psychiatry and behavioral scis., 1981—, attending psychiatrist consultation-liaison svc., 1992, 93; pvt. practice, Louisville, 1980—. Med. advisor Social Security Adminstrn., HHS, Louisville, 1986—; child psychiatry cons. Seven Counties Svcs., Ky. Dept. Human Resources, 1989, 93; physician advisor Nat. Health Svcs., Louisville, 1993-2000, physician reviewer in child and adult psychiatry Nat. Health Svcs., 2000-01, Lifespring Mental Health Svcs., 2001-02; reviewer Am. Jour. Psychiatry, 1983—; cons. So. Ind. Mental Health and Guidance Ctr., Jeffersonville, 1981-83, U. Fla., 1982; presenter in field. Contbr. articles to med. jours., chpts. to books. Mem dirs. Gainesville (Fla.) Women's Health Ctr., 1973-75, Discover Louisville Orch., 1999-2001; mem. Jefferson County (Ky.) Juvenile Justice Commn., 1982-86. Recipient award Nat. Psychiat. Endowment Fund, 1980. Fellow Am. Acad. Child and Adolescent Psychiatry (com. on rights and legal matters 1984-92); mem. Am. Psychiat. Assn. (mem. com. family violence and child sexual abuse 1987-94), Am. Acad. Psychiatry and Law, Nat. Com. for Prevention Child Abuse, Ky. Psychiat. Assn., Ky. Acad. Child Psychiatry (sec.-treas. 1980-81, pres.-elect 1981-82, pres. 1982-83).

ADAMS, CHRISTINE HANSON, advertising executive; b. Hackensack, N.J., May 24, 1950; d. Kenwood Alwin and Doris (Rogers) Hanson; m. L. Ashby Adams III, June 1, 1974 (div. Aug. 1993); 1 child, Nathaniel Kaufman. BA, Lafayette Coll., 1972; MBA, Duke U., 1979. Med. sales rep. Hoffman-LaRoche, Nutley, N.J., 1972-75; sr. market rsch. analyst Burroughs Wellcome Co., Research Triangle Park, N.C., 1976-77, product planner, 1978; dir. market research Sterling Drug Inc., N.Y.C., 1979-81; group product mgr. Pfizer Inc., N.Y.C., 1981-83; account supr. Kallir Philips Ross Inc., N.Y.C., 1983, v.p., account group supr., 1984-86; v.p., account supr. Baxter Gurian and Mazzei Inc., Beverly Hills, Calif., 1987-89, account group v.p., 1990-91, sr. v.p. account group, supr., 1991-93, sr. v.p. mgmt. supr., 1994; sr. v.p. group acct. dir. Kallir Philips Ross Inc, N.Y., 1994-96; sr. v.p. mgmt. supr. Torre Lazur Comm., Parsippany, N.J., 1996-98; v.p., mgmt. supr. Integrated Comm. Corp., Lawrenceville, N.J., 1998-2000; sr. v.p. mgmt. supr. Nelson Comms., Inc., Princeton, N.J., 2001—. Cons. active Wellness Cmty., Santa Monica, Calif., 1988-92. Active membership com. St. Michael's Episcopal Ch., Studio City, Calif., 1987-93, altar guild, 1988-93, tchr. Sunday sch., 1990-91. Named Young Career Woman Bus. Profl. Women's Assn., Chapel Hill, N.C., 1978. Mem. Healthcare Mktg. and Comms. Coun., Healthcare Businesswomen's Assn. Republican. Avocations: fashion design, sewing, music, 19th-century english literature. Home: 8 Villa Dr Princeton Junction NJ 08550-1241 Office: Integrated Comm Corp 989 Lenox Dr Ste 300 Lawrenceville NJ 08648-2315 E-mail: adamskaufman@home.com.

ADAMS, CHRISTOPHER STEVE, JR., retired defense electronics corporation executive, former air force officer; b. Shreveport, La., July 8, 1930; s. Christopher Steve and Armenda Lee (Tanner) A.; m. Mary Alene Mitchell, Aug. 22, 1953; children: Cynthia, Charlotte, Cheri, Christopher III. A.S., Tarleton State U., 1950; BS, Tex. A&M U., 1952. Commd. U.S. Air Force, 1952, advanced through grades to maj. gen., 1979, B-36, B-52 pilot; dir. plans and policy J-5, Def. Nuclear Agy., Washington, 1970-73; comdr. 90th Strategic Missile Wing, 1973-75; comdr. 12th Air Div., 1975-78; chief of staff SAC, 1982-83; ret., 1983; assoc. dir. Los Alamos Nat. Lab., 1983—86; v.p. bus. devel. Andrew Corp., Dallas, 1987-94, ret., 1994. Author: The Cold War Series, 4 books, 1999—2002. Decorated D.S.M., Def. Superior Service medal, Legion of Merit (2), Air Force Commendation medal, Air medal (2); recipient Disting. Alumnus award Tarleton State U., 1990, Disting. Alumnus award Tex. A&M U., 1991. Presbyterian. Home: 9408 Gimmee Ct Granbury TX 76049 *America the beautiful. I have dedicated my life through service to preserve our freedom. There is no better place on earth— I know, I've been there.*

ADAMS, CORLYN HOLBROOK, nursing facility administrator; b. Beloit, Kans., Sept. 28, 1926; d. Charles Benjamin and Hazel Marian (Brokaw) Holbrook; m. Henry Robert Adams, Oct. 28, 1961; 1 child, Charles Paul. Grad., U. Kans., 1948. Lic. nursing facility adminstr. Clk. bd. edn. Beloit City Sch., Kans., 1945-48; adminstr. Stanford Conv. Ctr., Ft. Worth, 1973-79; adminstr., owner Four Nursing Homes, Ft. Worth, 1979-84. Contbr.: Pioneer Women of Faith and Fortitude, Vol. IV; author: The Jose Family, 1994, Glen Elder Family History Book; contbr. Women of Faith and Fortitude, New England Ancestors, Vol. 3, No. 4; author: Family Chronicles, 1998; contbr. Family Chronicle; contbr.: Glen Elder History Book, contbr.: Journal of a Georgia Woman 1870-1872, rsch.: novels Jour. of a Ga. Woman, 1870-1872/ edited by S. Kitrell Rushing, contbr.: novel New England Ancestors, Negs vol. 3; co-author: The Brokaw-Smith Family Story; contbr. ; co-author: The Brokaw-Smith Family Story. Mem. Order of Ea. Star, DAR, Nat. Soc. New England Women (sec. 1975), Nat. Hugenot Soc., Gen. Soc. Mayflower Descendents, Daus. of Utah Pioneers. Republican. Avocations: genealogy, music-playing piano.

ADAMS, CYNTHIA ANN, librarian, media specialist, writing instructor; b. Thomaston, Ga., Nov. 27, 1942; d. Emory Ellis and Marian (Moseley) A. AB, Mercer U., 1964; MEd, U. Ga., 1972; EdS, Ga. State U., 1994. Cert. English tchr., career libr. media specialist, Ga. Libr. media specialist Walton County Bd. Edn., Monroe, Ga., 1972-74, Madison County Bd. Edn., Danielsville, Ga., 1974-80; tchr. English, libr. media specialist Westwood Bd. Trustees, Thomaston, 1981-82; libr. media specialist Harris County Bd. Edn., Hamilton, Ga., 1983—97; instr. writing, asst. computer lab. Gordon Coll., Barnesville, Ga., 1997—. Book reviewer Sch. Libr. Jour., 1973-74; contbr. poetry to anthologies; crafts accepted and displayed Nat. Mus. Women in the Arts, Washington. Mem. visual arts com. Thomaston Upson Arts Coun.; vol. Am. Heart Assn. Grad. study scholar. Mem. Kappa Delta Pi. Home: 630 S Center St Thomaston GA 30286-4143 Office: Gordon Coll 419 Coll Dr Barnesville GA 30204 E-mail: C_Adams@gdn.edu.

ADAMS, CYNTHIA ANN, nursing administrator; b. Duluth, Minn., Apr. 11, 1956; d. Arthur Raymond and Joyce Kathleen (Bonneville) Mattson; m. Timothy Lee Adams, Nov. 9, 1985; 1 child, Michael Stephen. BSN cum laude, Azusa Pacific U., 1978. RN, Calif. Team leader spinal cord injury unit Casa Colina Rehab. Hosp., Pomona, Calif., 1978-79; staff nurse, lead nurse orthop./neurology unit Portland (Oreg.) Adventist Med. Ctr., 1979-83; office nurse North Pacific Orthops., Portland, 1980-81; instr. Maricopa Skill Ctr., Phoenix, 1983-87; sales rep. Reed and Carnrick Pharm. Co., Phoenix, 1987-90; dir. nursing FHP Healthcare, Phoenix, 1990-93; sch. nurse Fredericksburg Christian Sch., 1999—2001; healthcare cons., 2001—. Coord. disaster action team Portland unit ARC, 1981-82. Author: New, Once-A-Day Levatol: Penbutolol Sulfate 20 mg., 1990, Dilatrate-SR (Isosorbide dinitrate) 40 mg; The One that Measures Up in Clinical Documentation, 1990. Mem. Am. Acad. Ambulatory Nursing Adminstrn., Nat. League for Nursing. Avocations: reading, music, needlework, travel, public speaking. Home: 210 Lakeshore Dr Fredericksburg VA 22405-3117

ADAMS, DANIEL CLIFFORD, music educator; b. Miami, Fla., June 28, 1956; s. Joseph Peter and Molly (Smith) A.; m. Elise Ruth Benjamin, Dec. 21, 1985 (div. Aug. 1994). MusB, La. State U., 1978; MusM, U. Miami, Coral Gables, Fla., 1981; D Mus. Arts, U. Ill., 1985. Adj. faculty Miami-Dade C.C., 1985-88, U. Miami, Coral Gables, 1986-88; mem. music faculty Tex. So. U., Houston, 1988—. Author: The Solo Snare Drum; music recorded on Capstone Records and Summit Records; contbr. articles to profl. jours. Recipient music composition awards ASCAP, N.Y.C., 1985-2002, Percussive Arts Soc., 1989, 2000. Mem. Soc. Composers, Inc. (nat. coun. 1995-97), Coll. Music Soc. (treas. South Ctrl. chpt. 1994-2003, v.p. chpt. 2003—), South Fla. Composers Alliance (bd. dirs. 1985-88), Houston Composers Alliance (bd. dirs. 1991—), Phi Mu Alpha Sinfonia. Avocations: travel, fishing, scuba diving. Home: 2301 Fountainview #20 Houston TX 77057 Office: Tex So U 3100 Cleburne St Houston TX 77004-4501 E-mail: dcadams@airmail.net.

ADAMS, DANIEL FENTON, law educator; b. Reading, Pa., July 29, 1922; s. Daniel Snyder and Carrie Betsy (Vought) A.; m. Eloise Williams, Sept. 6, 1968. AB, Dickinson Coll., 1947; LL.B., Dickinson Sch. Law, 1949. Bar: Pa. 1951, Ark. 1984. Prof. law Dickinson Sch. Law, Carlisle, Pa., 1949-65, asst. to dean, 1952-54, 56-60, acting dean, 1954-56, asst. dean, 1960-65; prof. Sch. Law U. Ark., Little Rock, 1965-70, 77-93, prof. emeritus, 1993—; asst. dean U. Ark. Sch. Law, Little Rock, 1966-70, acting dean, 1981-82, interim dean, 1989-91; prof. U. Miss. Sch. Law, Oxford, 1970-77. Vis. prof. Stetson U. Sch. Law, St. Petersburg, Fla., 1976-77, 99-00, U. Tenn. Coll. Law, 1993. Contbr. articles to profl. jours. Served with U.S. Army, 1943 44 Mem. ABA, Pa. Bar Assn., Ark. Bar Assn. Home: 4717 Osprey Dr Orange Beach AL 36561-5755

ADAMS, DANIEL LEE, lawyer; b. Beaver, Ohio, Oct. 3, 1936; s. Paul D. and Margaret (Rhea) A.; m. Julianne Faller, Aug. 13, 1960; children: Cristin Ann, Meghan Kathleen. BA, Ohio State U., 1957, JD, 1960. Bar: Fla. 1962. Atty. Attys.' Title Services, Inc., Ft. Lauderdale, Fla., 1960-62, also bd. dirs.; atty. Attys. Title Ins. Fund, Inc., 1962-69; ptnr. English, McCaughan and O'Bryan, Ft. Lauderdale, 1969—. Trustee, dir. 17th Jud. Cir. of Attys.' Title Ins. Fund, Orlando, Fla.; mem. MRTA Commn., Tallahassee, 1985-86; dir. Atty.'s Title Guaranty Fund, Inc., Colo. Mem. ABA, Broward County Bar Assn., Fla. Bar Assn. (exec. coun. real property, probate and trust law sect., grievance com.), Broward County Club 100 (pres. 1992-93, bd. dirs. 1988-94). Democrat. Roman Catholic. Avocations: bicycling, reading, wood working. Home: 600 Petunia Dr Fort Lauderdale FL 33317-1926 Office: English McCaughan & O'Bryan 100 NE 3rd Ave Ste 1100 Fort Lauderdale FL 33301-1144 E-mail: dadams@emolaw.com.

ADAMS, DANIEL NELSON, lawyer; AB, Yale U., 1932; LLB, Harvard U., 1935. Bar: N.Y. 1937. Sr. counsel Davis Polk & Wardwell, N.Y.C. Mem. ABA, N.Y. State Bar Assn., Assn. of Bar of City of N.Y., N.Y. County Lawyers Assn., Am. Law Inst. Office: Davis Polk & Wardwell 450 Lexington Ave Fl 31 New York NY 10017-3982*

ADAMS, DANIEL OTIS, chemist; b. Portland, Maine, Mar. 14, 1918; s. Charles Henry and Margaret Eshbaugh Adams; m. Elizabeth Jane Greig, Dec. 15, 1946; 4 children. AB in Chemistry, Oberlin Coll., 1939; MS, Inst. of Paper Chemistry, Appleton, Wis., 1941; PhD, Inst. of Paper Chemistry, 1943. Rsch. chemist W.Va. Pulp and Paper Co., Covington, Va., 1943—48; rsch. chemist to chief chemist Bird and Son, Inc., East Walpole, Mass., 1948—55; dir. Covington Rsch. Lab W.Va. Pulp and Paper Co., 1955—59, tech. svc. supt., 1959—80, tech. mgr., 1980—86, pvt. cons. Charleston, 1986—2000. Contbr. articles. Fellow: Tech. Assn. of the Pulp and Paper Industry. Achievements include first to develop pulping and bleaching procedures to produce commercial bleached hardwood pulp. Avocation: reading, writing, art, yard and garden, Bible study.

ADAMS, DAVID GRAY, lawyer; b. Tyler, Tex., Feb. 18, 1961; s. Ralph Judson and Laura (George) A. BBA, U. Tex., 1983; M in Taxation, Baylor U., 1987; JD, U. Houston, 1995. CPA, Tex. Fin. acct. Grant Thornton, Dallas, 1983-85; tax mgr. Ernst & Young, Dallas, 1987-91; jud. law clk. to Hon. Joe J. Fisher U.S. Dist. Ct. (ea. dist.) Tex., 1995-96; jud. law clk. to Hon. Robert M. Parker U.S. Ct. Appeals (5th cir.), 1996-97; atty. Baker & Botts, L.L.P., Dallas, 1997-2001, Jones, Day, Reavis & Pogue, Dallas, 2001—. Mem. Tex. Bd. Pub. Acctg. Mem. ABA, AICPA Episcopalian. Avocations: golf, tennis, snow skiing.

ADAMS, DAVID HARDY, voice educator, concert singer; b. Topeka, Mar. 13, 1950; s. John Richard and Norah Woodburn (Hardy) A.; m. Martha H. Good, Dec. 27, 1975; children: Jacob, Peter, Elizabeth. BS, Ind. U., 1972; postgrad., Accademia di Santa Cecilia, Rome, 1973-74; MusM, U. N.Mex., 1979. Asst. prof. of voice Coll.-Conservatory of Music, U. Cin., 1980-86, assoc. prof. voice, 1986—96, prof. voice, 1996—, head performance studies, 1987—. Singer Vienna (Austria) Chamber Opera, Palatinate Theater, Kaiserslautern, Fed. Republic Germany, Saarland Theater, Saarbrucken, Fed. Republic Germany, 1979-80; soloist Dayton Bach Soc., Pitts. Bach. Soc., Cinn. Chamber Orch., various others. Fulbright grantee, 1973-74. Home: 3532 Herschel View St Cincinnati OH 45208-1748 Office: U Cin Coll Conservatory of Music Cincinnati OH 45221-0003

ADAMS, DAVID HUNTINGTON, judge; b. Cleve., May 30, 1942; s. Donald Croxton and Nancy Adams; m. Mary Watson, Dec. 4, 1982; children from previous marriage: Ann Arendell, David Huntington, Susanna Camp. AB, Washington and Lee U., 1965, JD, 1968. Bar: Va. 1968, U.S. Dist. Ct. (ea. dist.) Va. 1968, U.S. Ct. Appeals (4th cir.) 1968, U.S. Supreme Ct. 1973. Law clk. U.S. Dist. Ct., Norfolk, Va., 1968-69; assoc. law firm Willcox, Savage, Norfolk, 1969-72; ptnr. law firm Agelasto, Bernard & Adams, Norfolk, 1972-74, Taylor, Walker, Bernard & Adams, Norfolk, 1974-78, Taylor, Walker & Adams, Norfolk, 1974-87, Clark & Stant, P.C., 1987-93; judge U.S. Bankruptcy Ct. (ea. dist. Va.), 1993—. Master of the bench James Kent Am. Inn of Ct., 1994-99, pres., 1995; lectr. bankruptcy practice joint com. on cont. legal edn. Va. Bar Found., 1981, 89, 93—; adminstrv. hearing officer Commonwealth of Va., 1974-89; mem. 4th Cir. Jud. Coun., 2003—, Adminstrv. Office Bankruptcy Judges Adv. Coun., 2001—, Bankruptcy Judges Adv. Group, 2001—, Adminstrv. Office Joint Adv. Com., 2003—. Author: Virginia Landlord/Tenant Law, 1980. Bd. dirs. Heritage Mus., Norfolk, 1991-94, Virginia Beach Neptune Fest., 1997—, King Neptune XXVI; chmn. Neptune Found., 2002; pres. Bay Colony Civic League, Virginia Beach, 1978, Princess Anne Hills Civic League, Virginia Beach, 1988; mem. 4th Cir. Jud. Conf., 1974—;, 4th Cir. Jud. Coun., 2002—; mem. 2d dist. ethics com. Va. State Bar, 1983-84. Mem.: ABA, Va. Bar Assn. (bd. dirs. bankruptcy sect. 1990—93, mem. coun. jud. sect. 1995—, chmn. 1997), Virginia Beach Bar Assn., Norfolk-Portsmouth Bar Assn., Nat. Conf. Bankruptcy Judges (bd. govs. 1996—2000, sec. 2000, pres.-elect), Am. Bankruptcy Inst., Hampton Roads Coun. Navy League U.S. (life; pres. 2000—, nat. dir. 2002—05), N.Y. Yacht Club, Cavalier Golf and Yacht Club (bd. dirs. 1993—98, commodore 1994). Episcopalian. Avocations: yachting, swimming, bicycling. Office: United States Bankruptcy Ct Walter E Hoffman US Courthouse 600 Granby St Norfolk VA 23510-1915 E-mail: david_adams@vaeb.uscourts.gov.

ADAMS, DEAN (LEWIS ADAMS), theater director; b. Seattle, July 22, 1957; s. Brockman and Mary Elizabeth (Scott) A.; m. Kristin Cook Gilbert, June 20, 1981. BA in Drama and English, Tufts U., 1980; MA in TV-Film, U. Md., 1986; MFA in Directing, Fla. State U., 2002. Stage prodn. mgr. Shakespeare and Co., Washington, 1975-79; asst. stage mgr. Arena Stage, Washington, 1976; tech. dir. St. Albans Sch., Washington, 1980-82; dir. theater Loomis Chaffee Sch., Windsor, Conn., 1982-88, Westminster Sch., Simsbury, Conn., 1989-99; freelance theater dir. Artistic dir. Centennial Theater Festival, Simsbury, 1989—; asst. prof. theater, Kennesaw State U., Kennesaw, Ga., 2002—. Dir. (U.K. tour) Dining Room, 1985; dir., producer (1st Chinese tour of Am. mus.) Once Upon a Mattress, 1987. Bd. dirs. Farmington Valley Music Found. Grantee Ford Found., 1984; scholar Tufts U., 1978-80. Mem. Internat. Brotherhood Magicians, Soc. Am. Magicians, Soc. of Stage Dirs. and Choreographers, Actors Equity Assn., Assn. of Performing Arts Presenters. Democrat. Episcopalian. Home and Office: 1512 Tennessee Walker Dr Roswell GA 30075 Office: Kennesaw State Univ 1000 Chastain Rd Kennesaw GA 30144 E-mail: deanadams@msn.com.

ADAMS, DEBORAH ROWLAND, lawyer; b. Princeton, NJ, July 28, 1952; d. Bernard S. and Natalie S. Adams; m. Charles L. Campbell, June 16, 1990. BA, Colo. Coll., Colorado Springs, 1974; JD, U. Colo., 1978. Bar: Ind. 1978, Colo. 1978, U.S. Dist. Ct. Colo. 1978. Atty. Legal Svcs. Orgn. Ind., Indpls., 1978-79, Pikes Peak Legal Svcs., Colorado Springs, 1979-80, Pub. Defender's Office, Colorado Springs, 1980-81; assoc. Ranson, Thomas, Cook and Livingston, Colorado Springs, 1982-84; pvt. practice Colorado Springs, 1985—. Mem. state Jud. Nominating Commn. for 4th Jud. Dist., 1994-99; Colo. State Grievance Com., 1997-98, Atty. Regulation Com., 1999. Bd. dirs. Domestic Violence Prevention Ctr., 1980-86, pres., 1982-84; bd. dirs. Pikes Peak Legal Svcs., 1983-88, pres., 1986-87, pro bono advocacy sch. faculty, 1990-92; co-chair Colo. Springs Devel. Com., Colo. Women's Found., 1987, grant selection com., 1988, 90; bd. dirs. Vis. Nurses Assn., 1989-91, Colo. Coll. Bus. and Cmty. Alliance Bd., 1999-2002, Citizens Project Bd., 1999-2002, CASA, 1999—, Emily Griffith Ctr., 2002-, Colo. Bar Found., 2000—, pres 2003; bd. dirs. Chins Up, 1991-97, pres., 1997-98; co-chair El Paso County sect. COLTAF Fundraising Com. for benefit of Colo. Legal Aid Found., 1991-99, chair, 1994-95; state bd. dirs. Legal Aid Found., 1994-2000, v.p., 1997-99. Recipient Pro Bono award Pikes Peak Legal Svcs., 1988; named Atty of Yr. El Paso County Legal Secs. Assn., 1990; selected to attend First Colo. Springs Leadership Class, Colorado Springs Leadership Inst., 1997. Mem. Colo. Bar Assn. (family law sect. 1991-2001, conciliation panel subcom. of profls. com. 1992, bd. govs. 1994-97, exec. com. 1995-97, nominating com. 1996), Zonta Club Colorado Springs (pres. 1989-90, co-chairperson dist. 12 regional conf. 1991-92, Zontian of Yr. 1990-91). Democrat. Avocations: reading, skiing, tennis, running, mountain biking. Office: 2 N Cascade Ave Ste 1010 Colorado Springs CO 80903-1629

ADAMS, DELPHINE SZYNDROWSKI, lawyer; b. East Chicago, Ind., May 24, 1953; d. Joseph C. and Rachael L. Szyndrowski; m. Dave Adams. BA, Ind. U., 1974; JD, Golden Gate U., 1985. Bar: Calif. 1986, U.S. dist. Ct. (all dists.) Calif. 1986, U.S. Ct. Appeals (9th cir.) 1986. Assoc. Goldberg, Stinnett & Macdonald, San Francisco, 1986-87, Bronson, Bronson & McKinnon, San Francisco, 1987-91, Santa Rosa, Calif., 1991-93, ptnr., 1993-95, San Francisco, 1995-96; atty. pvt. practice, Santa Rosa, 1996—. Co-author: (chpt.) Real Estate Litigation, 1994. Mem. adv. coun. Red Empire Ballet Assn., Santa Rosa, 1992-94. Mem. Engring. Contractors Assn. (adv. coun. 1996—), North Coast Builders Exch., Assoc. Gen. Contractors. Avocations: gardening, motorcycling, reading, music. Office: PO Box 1902 Santa Rosa CA 95402-1902 Fax: (707) 577-8010. E-mail: lawofcdsa@yahoo.com.

ADAMS, DENNIS PAUL, artist; b. Des Moines, Nov. 15, 1948; s. Paul Thomas Adams and Stella Vernita (Kirkland) MacGregor; children: Jack Walker, Todd Dennis. BFA, Drake U., 1969; MFA, Tyler Sch. Art, Phila., 1971. Assoc. prof. MIT, Cambridge, 1996-99, prof., dir. visual arts program, 1999—2001. Vis. prof. Parsons Sch., N.Y.C., 1990-99, Cooper Union, N.Y.C., 1988-90, Ecole Des Beaux-Arts, Paris, 1992, Rijksakademie, Amsterdam, 1992-94, Akademie Der Bildenden Künste, Munich, 1993-94, MIT, Cambridge, 1994—; asst. prof. Tyler Sch. Art, 1976, Ohio Sch. Art, Athens, 1972-75. One-man shows include de Appel Found., Amsterdam, The Netherlands, 1988, The Clocktower, N.Y.C., 1988, Galerie Meert-Rihoux, Brussels, 1989, John Weber Gallery, N.Y.C., 1989, Galerie Gabrielle Maubrie, Paris, 1990, Kent Fine Art, N.Y.C., 1990, Hirschhorn Mus., Washington, 1990, Mus. Modern Art, N.Y.C., 1991, Fundacio la Caixa, Barcelona, Spain, 1992, Portikus, Frankfurt, Germany, 1993, Muhka, Antwerpen, 1994, Contemporary Arts Mus., Houston, 1994, Queens Mus., N.Y.C., 1996, Kent Fine Art, 1997, Galerie, Gabrieele Maubrie, Paris, Mus. Contemporary Art, Zagreb, 1999, Galerie Lumen Travo, Amsterdam, 2000, 13 Quai Voltaire, Paris, 2000, Mus. Contemporary Art, Balt., 2001, Kent Gallery, N.Y.C., 2002; contbr. articles to profl. jours. Bd. govs. N.Y. Found. for Arts, N.Y.C., 1989-92. NEA fellowship grantee, 1984, 88, 95; recipient Visual Artists Project award N.Y. State Coun. on Arts, 1984. Home: 42 Walker St New York NY 10013-3514 E-mail: dadams@mit.edu.

ADAMS, DIANE LORETTA, physician; b. St. Louis, Nov. 3, 1948; m. William McKinley Adams; children: Kareem McKinley, Dawn Caron, Akeem Michael. BS, Howard U., 1969; MD, N.J. Med. Sch., 1976; MPH, Johns Hopkins U., 1980. Resident in family practice Howard U. Hosp., Washington, 1976-79; chief med. officer USCG Shipyard, Curtis Bay, Md., 1980-83, Bur. Engraving and Printing, Washington, 1983-85; med. officer St. Elizabeth Hosp., Washington, 1985-86; rsch. analyst Office Asst. Sec. Health, Rockville, Md., 1987-90; chief minority health svcs. rsch. program Agy. Health Care Policy and Rsch., Rockville, 1990-93; congl. fellow office of Congressman Louis Stokes U.S. Ho. of Reps., Washington, 1990; sr. med. adv. Agy. Health Care Policy and Rsch., Rockville, 1993-99, Agy. Healthcare Rsch. and Quality, Dept. Health/Human Svcs., 1999-2000, cons., 2000—; clin. assoc. prof. dept. phys. therapy U. Md., 1993—2000; dir. health policy, rsch. and profl. med. affairs Nat. Med. Assn., 2001—02. Cons. rep. AIDS Task Force, 1987-93; lectr. intensive bioethics Georgetown U. Kennedy Inst. Ethics, 1991; sr. health policy fellow, Ga. Ctr. Advanced Telecommns. Tech. Editor: Health Issues for Women of Color: A Cultural Diversity Perspective, 1995. Named to, Md. Women's Hall of Fame, 1997, Black Coll. Alumni Hall of Fame in Medicine, 2001, Women of Achievement in Md. History, 2002; recipient Adminstrs. Outstanding Cmty. Svc. award, Agy. Health Care Policy and Rsch., 1996. Mem.: APHA, Am. Coll. Preventive Medicine, Alpha Kappa Alpha (Outstanding Comt. Svc. award 1981—85). Avocation: equitation. Home: 17032 Barn Ridge Dr Silver Spring MD 20906-1106

ADAMS, DONALD ELWIN, cultural and organization development administrator, consultant; b. Sioux Falls, S.D., July 13, 1953; s. James Robert and Louise (Lewis) A.; m. Arlene Frances Goldbard, Dec. 1, 1978. Student, U. S.D., 1971-74; MA in Arts Adminstrn., Sangamon State U., 1976. Cmty. devel. dir. Arts and Humanities Coun., Baton Rouge, 1975-76; dep. dir. Calif. Arts Coun., Sacramento, 1976-77; ptnr. Adams & Goldbard, Richmond, Calif., 1978—; dir. Inst. for Cultural Democracy, San Francisco, 1987—. Writer-in-residence Blue Mountain Ctr., Blue Mountain Lake, N.Y., 1982, Rockefeller Found., Bellagio, Italy, 1994. Author: Crossroads: Reflections on the Politics of Culture, 1990, Creative Community: The Art of Cultural Development, 2001, Community, Culture and Globalization, 2002. Dir. Webster's World of Cultural Democracy, San Francisco, 1995—, San Francisco Jewish Film Festival, 2003—; treas. Congregation Fitz Or, 1998—2002. Fellow Nat. Endowment for the Arts, Washington, 1976. Office: 145 Ninth St Ste 200 San Francisco CA 94103 E-mail: don@sfjff.org.

ADAMS, DOUGLASS FRANKLIN, radiologist, educator, medical ethicist; b. Lewiston, Maine, Aug. 5, 1935; s. Shirah Devoy and Olive (Colburn) A.; m. Eleanor Pohleven, Aug. 15, 1954; children: Stanford, Jennifer, Jason. BA, Stetson U., 1957; BS, Wake Forest Coll., Winston-Salem, N.C., 1957; MD, Bowman Gray Sch. Medicine, Winston-Salem, 1960; SM, MIT, 1974; AM, Harvard U., 1990. Intern Phila. Gen. Hosp., 1960, resident in radiology, 1961; resident in radiology, then fellow Am. Cancer Soc., Stanford U. Hosp., 1963-66; radiologist Peter Bent Brigham Hosp., Boston, 1967-79, Brigham and Women's Hosp., Boston, 1981—. Instr. Stanford U. Med. Sch., 1966-67; mem. faculty Harvard U. Med. Sch., 1967-79, 81—, assoc. prof. radiology, 1976-82, prof. radiology, 1982— ; prof. radiology, chmn. dept. U. Mich. Med. Sch., 1979-81 Mem. editl. bd. profl. jours. Capt. M.C., USAF, 1961-63. Sloan fellow MIT, 1974; James Picker Found. scholar, 1967-70. Mem. Am. Coll. Radiology, Assn. Univ. Radiologists, Radiol. Soc. N.Am., Alpha Omega Alpha. Home: 9 Riverview Ter Dover MA 02030-2249 Office: 75 Francis St Boston MA 02115-6110

ADAMS, EARL WILLIAM, JR., economics educator; b. Lansing, Mich., Nov. 13, 1937; s. Earl William and V. Crystal (Woodruff) A.; m. Barbara Joan Charlton, Aug. 4, 1964; children: Earl William, III, Nicholas Charlton. BA, U. Mich., 1959; PhD, Mass. Inst. Tech., 1971. Asst. prof. econs. Amherst Coll., 1963-66, U. Pitts., 1966-72; Andrew Wells Robertson prof. econs. Allegheny Coll., Meadville, Pa., 1972—. Vis. asst. prof. U. Mass., 1966; rsch. dir. bus. taxation Pa. Tax Commn., 1979-81; mem. adv. coun. Pa. Blue Shield, 1980-82, mem. corp., 1982. Contbr. to profl. publs. Woodrow Wilson fellow, 1959 Mem. Am. Econs. Assn., Pa. Econs. Assn., Phi Beta Kappa, Phi Kappa Phi. Home: 187 Grandview Ave Meadville PA 16335-1415 Office: Allegheny Coll Dept Econs Meadville PA 16335 E-mail: eadams@allegheny.edu.

ADAMS, EDMUND JOHN, lawyer; b. Lansing, Mich., June 6, 1938; s. John Edmund and Helen Kathryn (Pavlick) A.; m. Mary Louise Riegler, Aug. 11, 1962. BA, Xavier U., 1960; LLB, U. Notre Dame, 1963. Bar: Ohio 1963. Assoc. Paxton & Seasongood, Cin., 1965-70, Frost & Jacobs (now Frost Brown Todd), 1970-71, ptnr., 1971-2000, mem. exec. com., 1985-88, 90-96, mng. ptnr., 1994-96, chmn., 1996-2000, of counsel, 2000—. Author: Catholic Trails West, The Founding Catholic Families of Pennsylvania, Vol. 1, 1988, Vol. 2, 1989. Mem. Ohio Bd. Regents, 1999—, sec., 2002—, vice chmn., 2003—; mem., com. co-chair Ohio Gov.'s Commn. on Higher Edn. and the Economy, 2003—; trustee Jewish Hosp., 1995-2001, Cin. Internat. Visitors Ctr., 1989-91, Japan Am. Soc. Greater Cin., 1988-96, Ursuline Acad., 1992-94; trustee S.W. Ohio Regional Transit Authority, 1980-91, pres., 1983, 88; trustee Sister Cities Assn. Greater Cin., 1984-91, chmn., 1984-90; trustee Greater Cin. Ctr. for Econ. Edn., 1996—, mem. exec. com., 1999-, vice chmn., 2002-; chmn. USTA Nat. Father and Son Clay Ct. Tennis Championships, 1990-92; mem. Hamilton County Rep. Exec. Com., 1982—; mem. Hamilton County Rep. Fin. Com., 1990—, chmn., 1992-94; mem. Hamilton County Rep. Ctrl. Com., 2000—. 1st lt. U.S. Army, 1963-65; adv. bd. Elder H.S., 2002—. Fellow Am. Coll. Bankruptcy; mem. ABA, Ohio Bar Assn., Cin. Bar Assn., Cin. Tennis Club (trustee 1990-98, treas. 1992-93, sec. 1994-95, pres. 1996-98, historian 2001—), Met. Club. (bd. dirs. 1996-2001). Roman Catholic. Home: 3210 Columbia Pky Cincinnati OH 45226-1042 Office: Frost Brown Todd 2500 PNC Ctr 201 E 5th St Cincinnati OH 45202-4182 E-mail: adamschoice@fuse.net., eadams@fbtlaw.com.

ADAMS, EDWARD THOMAS (EDDIE ADAMS), photographer; b. New Kensington, Pa., June 12, 1933; s. Edward I. and Adelaide (Suprano) A.; children: Susan Ann, Edward II, Amy Marie; m. Alyssa Ann Adkins; 1 child, August Everhett. Grad. H.S., New Kensington. Staff photographer New Kensington Daily Dispatch, 1950-58, Enquirer & News, 1958, Phila. Eve. Bull., 1958-62, A.P., 1962-72, Time mag., 1972-76; spl. corr. A.P., 1976-80; free-lance photographer, 1980—; prof. emeritus Daytona Beach (Fla.) C.C., 1984. Lectr. in field; creator ann. tuition free photojournalism workshop for America's most talented young photographers The Eddie Adams Workshop sponsored by Nikon, Inc., 1988—. Served with USMC, 1951-54. Recipient Pulitzer prize in photography, 1969; Grand prize World Press Photography, 1969, 1st pl. award, 1972; named 3d place World Photo Reporter, 1969; 2nd place World Photo Reporter, 1970; recipient Sigma Delta Chi award, 1969, 78, 80, several Overseas Press Club Am. awards, 1969, 74, George Polk Meml. award, 1969, 78, 79, Nat. Press Photographer award, 1969, 1st place AP Mng. Editors, 1968, 79, Best Pictures in Book or Mag. award Overseas Press Club, 1975; named Photographer of Year N.Y. Press Photographers, 1966, 67, 70, 72; Mid. Atlantic States, 1958, 59; Phila. Art Dirs. award, 1961; Nat. Headliners award, 1973; World Press Photo award, (7 times) 1974-85; Mag. Photographer of Yr. U. Mo.-Nat. Press Photographers Assn., 1975; Joseph Sprague Meml. award Nat. Press Photographers Assn., 1976; Silver Prix award Japan Advt. Assn., 1978; Robert Capa Meml. award, 1978; Am. Soc. Mag. Photographers Ann. award, 1980; W. Ger. Photokina award, 1978; 1st Pl. Hollywood Reporters Key Art English Lang. Movie Poster "Unforgiven" award, 1993, Leadership medal Internat. Photog. Coun., 2000; others; named Profl. Photographer of Yr., Photog. Mfrs. and Dealers Assn., 1996. Office: 538 E 11th St New York NY 10009-4607 E-mail: eaworkshop@aol.com. *I always hope that everytime I squeeze the shutter on my camera and once the photographs are published—that something good will happen to the subjects portrayed— or their cause.*

ADAMS, EDWIN MELVILLE, former foreign service officer, actor, author, lecturer; b. Gridley, Ill., Sept. 28, 1914; s. Edwin Melville and Crystal (Montgomery) A. AB, U. Ill., 1936, LL.B., 1939; postgrad., The Hague Acad. Internat. Law, summer 1951. Bar: Ill. 1939. Atty. State Farm Ins. Cos., Bloomington, Ill., 1939-42; officer charge Brazil area World Trade intelligence div., State Dept., Washington, 1942-43, negotiator German external assets agreements with neutral countries, 1946-48; successively assigned by State Dept. to London, Paris, Bern and Frankfort; as U.S. negotiator at internat. econ. confs., 1948-50; econ. attache Am. embassy, The Hague, 1950-52; charge Italian econ. affairs State Dept., 1952-55; dep. chief mut. def. affairs, 2d sec. Am. embassy, Rome, Italy, 1955-58, chief mut. def. affairs, 1st sec., 1958-61; officer in charge econ. affairs for N. Africa Dept. State, 1961-64, career mgmt. officer, 1964-65; spl. asst. to dep. under sec. state, 1965-67; asso. dean Fgn. Service Inst., 1967-68; cons. Dept. State, 1968-72. Host: radio show Passport, WAMU, 1972— ; author-narrator radio show, NBC-TV show, Venice, My Love, 1972; pub. broadcasting The Social Responsibility of Business; radio shows My Beloved Italy; star radio shows, CBS-TV show, The Empty Frame, 1973; appeared in films The Last Detail, 1974, Airport, 1975, Three Days of the Condor, 1975, Franklin and Eleanor, The Other Side of Midnight, Company, The Seduction of Joe Tynan, Justice for All, First Monday in October, BBC's Double Image U.S. del. Conf. of African States on Devel. of Edn. in Africa, 1961. Served to lt. (j.g.) USNR, 1943-46, PTO. Decorated cavaliere ufficiale Order of Merit of Italian Republic. Mem. Screen Actors Guild, AFTRA, Actors Equity, Phi Delta Phi, Phi Kappa Sigma. Espicopalian. Lodge: Masons (Washington).

ADAMS, ELIZABETH HERRINGTON, banker; b. Tulsa, May 25, 1947; d. James Dillon and Helen (Allderdice) Herrington; m. Phillip Hollis Hackney, Mar. 5, 1977 (dec. Jan. 1990); m. Keith R. Adams, Sept. 4, 1993. Student, No. Ariz. U., 1965-67, 68-69. With Coldwater (Kans.) Nat. Bank, summers 1964-67, The Ariz. Bank, Phoenix, 1969, Flagstaff, 1970-71; asst. cashier The Wilmore (Kans.) State Bank, 1972—, The Coldwater Nat. Bank, 1974-83, cashier, ops. officer, 1984—; v.p. The Coldwater (Kans.) Nat. Bank, 1998—. Dir. The Coldwater Nat. Bank, 1972—, The Wilmore State Bank, 1970—. Bd. dirs. Pioneer Lodge Nursing Home, Coldwater, 1984-89; mem. sch. site coun., 1993-94; life mem. Girl Scouts, chmn. Neighborhood Cookie Drive, 1991-95; bd. dirs., mem. strategic planning com. Wheatbelt Area Girl Scout Coun., 1994-96—; elder 1st Presbyn. Ch., Coldwater; Kans. Lung Assn. Vol. Speakers Bur., 1998—; mem. Church Session Bd., Coldwater, 1994-2000. Mem. Fin. Women Internat., Community Bankers Assn. Kans. (membership com. 1991-94, INPAC com. 1992-93), Kans. Ind. Bankers (gen. svcs. com. 1986-87), PEO, Alpha Omicron Pi, Lake Coldwater Archtl. Rev. Bd. Republican. Avocation: music (pianist). Office: Coldwater Nat Bank PO Box 726 Coldwater KS 67029-0726

ADAMS, F. GERARD, economist, educator; b. Apr. 28, 1929; s. Walter and Margot Adams; m. Heidi Vernon; children: Leslie, Colin, Loren, Mark. BA, U. Mich., 1949, MA, 1951, PhD, 1956. Instr. dept. econs. U. Mich., Ann Arbor, 1952—56; economist Calif. Tex. Oil Corp., N.Y.C., 1956—59; cons. economist, mgr. gen. econs. dept. Compagnie Française des Pétroles, N.Y.C. and Paris, 1959—61; mem. faculty U. Pa., Phila., 1961—98, prof. econs. and fin.; McDonald prof. Northeastern U., Boston, 1998—; Freeman Disting. prof. Johns Hopkins U., Balt., 2002. Dir. Econs. Research Unit, 1961-98, chmn. Faculty Senate, 1987-88; chmn. profl. bd. WEFA Group, Phila., 1969-91. Author: (with others) An Econometric Analysis of International Trade, 1969, (with J.R. Behrman) Econometric Models of World Agricultural Commodity Markets, 1976, Commodity Exports and Economic Development, 1982, (with L.R. Klein) Industrial Policies for Growth and Competitiveness, 1983, The Business Forecasting Revolution, 1986; editor: (with S.A. Klein) Stabilizing World Commodity Markets - Analysis, Practice and Policy, 1978, The Macroeconomic Dimensions of Arm Reduction, 1992, Economic Activity, Trade and Industry in the U.S.-Japan-World Economy, 1993, East Asian Development: Will the Miracle Survive?, 1998; Public Policies in East Asian Development: Facing New Challenges, 1999, Macroeconomics for Business and Society, 2002, The E-Business Revolution and the New Economy,2003. Home: 39 Stafford Rd Newton Center MA 02459-1818 E-mail: adams@ssc.upenn.edu., f.adams@neu.edu.

ADAMS, FRANCES GRANT, II, lawyer; b. Wheeling, W.Va., Nov. 30, 1955; d. Jack Richard and Frances Irene (Grant) A. BA, W.Va. U., 1976, JD, 1979; MA, Webster U., 1983. Bar: W.Va. 1979, U.S. Dist. Ct. (so. dist.) W.Va. 1979, U.S. Ct. Mil. Appeals 1979, U.S. Supreme Ct. 1988, D.C. 1989. Asst. staff judge advocate armament divsn. USAF, Eglin AFB, Fla., 1979-82, dep. staff judge advocate Keflavik, Iceland, 1982-83, staff judge advocate 71st Air Base Group Vance AFB, Okla., 1984-86, chief gen. torts sect. claims and tort litig. staff hdqrs. Washington, 1986-88, chief mgmt. and analysis br. claims and tort litig. divsn. Legal Svcs. Agy., 1988-92, sr. tort atty. tort claims and litig. divsn. Legal Svcs. Agy., 1992-97, chief internat. torts br., 1997—; atty. environ. law and litig. divsn., Legal Svcs. Agy. USAFR, USAF, Washington, 1992—99. Program chmn. Pentagon chpt. Fed. Bar Assn., 1989-90. Mem. DAR (chmn. procedures manual W.Va. chpt. 1989-92), Magna Carta Dames, Ancient and Honorable Arty. Co., Air Force Assn. (life), Ret. Officers Assn. (life). Avocations: photography, travel, farming, gardening.

ADAMS, FRANK, education specialist; b. Cleve., Sept. 11, 1948; s. Frank Albin and Helen (Coleman) Kovacevic. BS in Bus. Adminstrn., Bowling Green (Ohio) State U., 1970, MEd in Phys. Edn., 1978. Tech. writer Soldier Phys. Fitness Sch., Ft. Ben Harrison, Ind., 1983-85; edn. specialist Directorate of Tng. and Doctrine, Ft. Huachuca, Ariz., 1985-90, Dept. Tactics Intelligence Mil. Sci., Ft. Huachuca, 1990-93, 111th Mil. Intelligence Brigade, Ft. Huachuca, 1993-97; staff 112th Mil. Intelligence Brig. U.S. Army Intelligence Ctr., 1998—2003, staff, faculty devel. divsn., 2003—. Mem. steering com. tng. and doctrine command, staff and faculty devel. divsn., El Paso, Tex., 1987. Co-author: (field manual) Physical Fitness Training, 1984, (Internet site) Total Fitness; contbr. articles to profl. jours. and local newspapers. Recipient Civilian Achievement medal Dept. Army, Ft. Huachuca 1993, Comdr.'s award, 1995, 2003, Superior Civilian Svc. award, 1999. Mem. AAHPERD (life), Mil. Intelligence Corp. Avocations: internal martial arts, reading, reiki master-teacher. Home: 4838 Corte Vista Sierra Vista AZ 85635-5738 Office: Tng Devel & Support 112th Mil Intelligence Brig Fort Huachuca AZ 85613-6000

ADAMS, G. ROLLIE, museum executive; b. El Dorado, Ark., Sept. 11, 1941; s. George Donaghey and Floy (Kinard) A.; m. Diana Murphy, Dec. 19, 1982; children: Sara Ann, Amy Kristina Hee Sook, Tong Tong Amanda Joy. BA in Social Sci. Edn., La. Tech. U., 1963, MA in Social Sci. Edn., 1967; PhD in Am. History, U. Ariz., 1983. Tchr. El Dorado Sr. High Sch., 1963-67; libr. U. Ariz. Libr., Tucson, 1969-71; instr. U. Ariz. Continuing Edn. Dept., Tucson, 1973; dir. nat. hist. landmarks Am. Assn. State & Local Hist., Nashville, 1973-78, dir. edn. divsn., 1978-82, dir. planning & devel., 1982-83; exec. dir. Buffalo & Erie County Hist. Soc., 1984-85; dir. La. State Mus., New Orleans, 1986-87; pres., chief exec. officer The Strong Mus., Rochester, N.Y., 1987—. Mem. faculty Colonial Williamsburg Hist. Adminstrn. Seminar, 1987-88, 90-96; mem. parks adv. com. Rockefeller Inst. Govt., Albany, 1992-93; mem. faculty mus. mgmt. prog. U. Colo., 1999; chair exec. com. N.Y. Hist. Records Adv. Bd., Albany, 1992-95, mem. 1992—; chair N.Y. State Commr. Edn. Mus. Task Force, Albany, 1994-95. Author: General William S. Harney: Prince of Dragoons, 2001; co-author: Nashville: A Pictorial History, 1981, rev. edit. 1988; co-editor: Ordinary People and Everyday Life, 1983, The American Indian, Past and Present, 1971. Mem. Steering com. Goals for a Greater Rochester, 1990-95; vice chair, bd. dirs. Greater Rochester Vis. Assn., 1991-97; chair, bd. dirs. Family Svcs., Rochester, 1993-96; bd. dirs. Rochester Downtown Devel. Corp., 1995—, exec. com., 2001—; exec. com. East End Alliance, 1997-98; bd. dirs. Rochester Cemeteries Heritage Found., 2001-. Funded seminars grantee U.S. Hist. NEH, 1980, hist. interpretation, NEH, 1979, 80, 81, Mus. Exhibit Workshops NEH, 1980-82, Local Govt. Records Com. NEH, 1981-83. Mem. Mus. Assn. N.Y. (v.p. 1995-96, 2001—, chair strategic planning com. 1996-97, pres. 1997), Am. Assn. Mus. (vis. team, accreditation commn., Washington 1988, 90, 92-97, 2002; bd. dirs. 1997-2000), Am. Assn. State and Local History (audit com. 1995-2001), Orgn. Am. Historians, Assn. Childrens Mus., Western Hist. Assn. Avocations: photography, baseball. Office: The Strong Museum One Manhattan Square Rochester NY 14607 E-mail: radams@strongmuseum.org.

ADAMS, GARY LEE, systems engineering supervisor; b. Clearfield, Pa., May 23, 1947; s. William Ellsworth and Ethel Mae (Ling) A.; m. Rebecca Estelle Peppers, Dec. 29, 1967; children: William Matthew, Preston Lee. BSEE, Tulane U., 1969; Grad. of Theology, Bapt. Bible Coll., 1974. Assoc. engr. Westinghouse Electric Corp., Balt., 1969-71; asst. prin., dean edn. Hollywood (Fla.) Christian Sch., 1974-79; assoc. engr. Martin Marietta Corp., Orlando, Fla., 1979-80, engr., 1980-82, sr. engr., 1982-84, group engr., 1984-85; sr. lead engr. Harris Corp., Orlando, Fla., 1985, engring. sect. head, 1985-89; engring. br. mgr. PEI Electronics, Inc., Huntsville, Ala., 1989-98, lead sys. engr., 1998—2003, project engr., 2003—. Vice chmn. Nat. Indsl. Assn. MATE Users Group Test Program Set Com., Washington, 1986-88. Deaf interpreter First

Bapt. Ch., Hollywood, 1974-79, Tabernacle Bapt. Ch., Orlando, 1979-89, Triana Village Bapt. Ch., Huntsville, 1989-93; deacon Granite Bapt. Ch., Glen Burnie, Md., 1970-71, Friendship Bapt. Ch., Huntsville, 1995—. Recipient Jung scholarship Tulane U., 1965-68. Mem. IEEE, Assn. U.S. Army. Republican. Avocations: coin collecting, camping, rollerskating, home computing. Home: 13436 Wendy Dr Madison AL 35757-6530 E-mail: gadams@pei-idt.com., gadams@knology.net

ADAMS, GENE AUTRY, retired military officer; b. Canton, Miss., Sept. 18, 1951; s. Mamie Lee May; children: Kimberly, Eric E. Grad., C.C. USAF, 1991. Aircraft technician USAF, Travis AFB, Calif., 1970—91; group home sponsor VA Hosp., Cleve., 1999—. Author: (poetry) The Realist/At First Light, 1999 (Editor's Choice Award Nat. Libr. Poetry, 1995). Home and Office: We Write the Writestuff Pub Svcs 5409 Elmwood Ave Cleveland OH 44137-2724 E-mail: adamsfam02@aol.com.

ADAMS, GEORGE BELL, lawyer; b. N.Y.C., Sept. 16, 1930; s. George Bell and Mary Josephine (Smith) Adams; m. Lucy Elizabeth Ahearn, Sept. 10, 1952; children: Lucy S., Marea F., George B. Adams Jr., Alison E. BA, Yale U., 1952; LLB cum laude, Harvard U., 1957. Bar: N.Y. 1957, U.S. Dist. Ct. (so. and ea. dists.) N.Y. 1965, U.S. Ct. Appeals (2d cir.) 1973. Assoc. Debevoise, Plimpton, Lyons & Gates, NYC, 1957-65; ptnr. Debevoise & Plimpton, NYC, 1966-97, chmn. corp. dept., 1988-93, mng. ptnr. London, 1993-96, of counsel NYC, 1998—. Pres. Greater NY Fund, NYC, 1981—84, bd. dir. Trustee Sarah Lawrence Coll., Bronxville, NY, 1977—, chmn bd. trustees, 1987—91, vice chmn., chmn. exec. com., 1981—87; bd. dir., exec. com. United Way of NYC, 1982—95, chmn nominating com., 1985 93; bd. dir. New Amsterdam Singers, 1997—, Lawyers Alliance for World Security, 1989—98, mem. adv. bd., 1999—; bd. of dir. Am. Assn. Internat. Com. of Jurists, 1998; fellow Pierpont Morgan Libr., NYC, 1977—, coun. of fellows, 1983—87; mem. coun. of fellows Yale U. Coun., 1983—90, chmn. Yale alumni publs., 1979—83; trustee Am. Trust for Brit. Libr., 1998—. 1st lt. U.S. Army, 1952—54. Fellow, Davenport Coll., Yale U., 1983—90. Fellow: Am. Bar Found., Royal Soc. for Arts; mem.: ABA, Assn. of Bar of City of NY, Am. Arbitration Assn. (panel arbitrators), Century Assn., Pilgrim Soc., Racquet & Tennis Club, Cosmos Club. Office: Debevoise & Plimpton 919 3rd Ave Fl 44 New York NY 10022-3904 E-mail: marclar@sprynet.com.

ADAMS, GLEN CAMERON, publisher; b. Trent, Wash., June 19, 1912; s. Otto Ulysses and Mae (Cameron) Adams; m. Nina Lenore Finch, Apr. 30, 1936 (div. June 1939); 1 child, Robert Glen; m. Jean Pirie Evers, June 29, 1946 (dec. May 15, 2002). BA, Ea. Wash. U., 1938; PhD (hon.), Gonzaga U., 1990. Prin. Burbank (Wash.) Sch. Dist., 1938-39; livestock breeder Fairfield, Wash., 1939-51; postmaster Fairfield Post Office, 1951-72; printer, pub. Ye Galleon Press, Fairfield, 1972—. Hon. prof. history Ea. Wash. U., Cheney, 1983. Mayor, Fairfield, Wash., 1974—78. Named to Wash. State Hall of Honor, Wash. State Hist. Soc., 1983. Democrat. Presbyterian. Home: 103 Brewster St Fairfield WA 99012 Office: 103 E Main St Fairfield WA 99012

ADAMS, H. LESLIE, composer; b. Cleve., Dec. 30, 1932; s. Harrison and Jessie (Manease) A. MusB, Oberlin Conservatory, 1955; MusM, Long Beach State U., 1964; PhD in Music, Ohio State U., 1974. Composer opera Blake, (premiered by the Municipal Opera Co. of Balt., Inc., pian-percussion version, Oct. 24, 1997); a symphony; cantatas The Righteous Man and Hymn to Freedom; concert overture Ode to Life; chamber orchestral work Love Expressions; ballet A Kiss in Xanadu; sonatas for violin, cello and horn; etudes for piano and numerous orchestral works performed by Cleve. Orch., Buffalo Philharm., Indpls. Symphony, Savannah Symphony, Detroit Symphony, Prague Radio Symphony, Iceland Symphony. Office: care Creative Arts Inc 9409 Kempton Ave Cleveland OH 44108-2940 E-mail: CreativeArtsInc@webtv.net.

ADAMS, H. RICHARD, dean; BS in Vet. Sci., DVM in Vet. Medicine, Tex. A&M U.; PhD in Pharmacology, U. Pitts. Chmn. univ.-wide PhD grad. program in physiology area U. Mo., Columbia, 1986—90; prof. dept. pharmacology U. Mo.-Columbia Sch. Medicine, Columbia, 1986—98; assoc. dir. Dalton Rsch. Ctr. U. Mo.-Columbia, Columbia, 1989—92; chmn. dept. vet. biomed. scis. U. Mo.-Columbia Coll. Vet. Medicine, Columbia, 1984—92, interim dean, 1992—93, dean, 1993—98, Tex. A&M U. Coll. Vet. Medicine, 1998—. Recipient H. Richard Adams Conf. Ctr., U. Mo. named in his honor, Resolution of Appreciation, Mo. State Ho. Reps., 1998. Mem.: Am. Vet. Med. Assn., Am. Soc. Vet. Physiology and Pharmacology, Vet. Emergency and Critical Care Soc. (Robert Knowles lectr. and keynote spkr. 1994), Soc. for Exptl. Biology and Medicine (keynote spkr. ann. meeting 1985), Shock Soc. (pres. elect, pres. 1993—94), Mo. Vet. Med. Assn. (Mo. Vet. of Yr. 1997), Am. Coll. Vet. Emergency and Critical Care (hon. diplomate in emergency and critical care 1998), Sigma Xi. Office: Tex A&M U Coll Vet Medicine Ste 101 VMA College Station TX 77843-4461*

ADAMS, HAROLD LYNN, architect; b. Palmer, Tex., May 15, 1939; s. Charles Roy and Lola (Beck) A.; m. Janice Lindhurst, Aug. 29, 1963; children: Harold Lynn, Abigail, Ashley, Sam. BS in Architecture, Tex. A&M U., 1962. Registered architect 44 states and U.K.; 1st class registered architect Japan. Draftsman Pratt Box Henderson, Dallas, 1960; intern William B. Tabler & Assocs., N.Y.C., 1961-62; architect John Carl Warnecke & Assocs., Washington, 1962-66; pres. RTKL Assocs., Inc., Balt., 1967-87, chmn. bd., 1987—. Regent Am. Archtl. Found., 1989—, chmn., 2000—; cons. Nat. Caital Planning Commn., 1992; dir. Lincorn Elec. Corp., 2001—, Legg Mason, 1987—, Renaissance Weekend, 1996—. Contbg. author: Current Techniques in Architectural Practice, Representative Am. Speeches, 1987-88, Technology: Trap or Triumph. Chmn. archtl. divsn. United Fund Drive, 1972; mem. task force on econ. devl. Balt. C. of C., 1975; pres. Econ. Devel. Coun. of Balt.; exec. com. Mt. Washington Country Sch. for Boys, 1976-77; bd. mgrs. Black Rock YMCA, 1971; vice chmn. GBC Found.; mem. Greater Balt. Com. on Edn., 1977-80, Com. on Planning, 1980-82; bd. dirs. Greater Balt. Com., 1983-90; mem. devel. coun. Tex. A&M U., 1982-90; mem. vis. com. Dept. Architecture U. Md., 1985-87; trustee Md. Inst. Coll. Art, Balt., 1984—, Maryvale Prep. Sch., Brooklandville, Md., 1985-89, Peale Mus., Balt., 1985-92, Balt. City Life Mus., 1985-92; regent Morgan State U., Balt., 1985-87; regent Am. Architecture Found., 1989-98, chmn., 2000—; trustee Balt. Fgn. Rels. Coun., 1987-93, Walter Gallery Art, 1987—; Balt. Metro. YMCA, 1987-90; chmn. World Trade Ctr. Inst., Md., 1990-99; mem. svcs. policy adv. com. U.S. Trade Rep., 1990—; bd. dirs. Internat. Visitors Ctr., 1990-92; mem. U.S.-China Bus. Coun., U.S.-Korea Bus. Coun.; adv. bd. Korea Econ. Inst. of Am.; chmn. Downtown Partnership Balt.; commr. Md. Econ. Devel. Comm.; chair Nat. Bldg. Mus., 1998—. Recipient Featherlite Design award Tex. A&M U., 1962; recipient Davidson Design award Tex. A&M U., 1962, Alpha Rho Chi medal, 1962, Tau Sigma Delta Gold medal Assn. Collegiate Schs. Architecture, 1993, Gov.'s award World Trade Ctr. Md., 1996, Outstanding Alumni award Tex. A&M U., 1998. Fellow AIA (pres. Balt. chpt. 1973-74, chmn. large firm roundtable 1984—, chancellor Coll. of Fellows 1997-98, nat. dir. 1999—, Kemper medal 1997); mem. Urban Land Inst., Am. Inst. Architects (chmn. large firm roundtable 1984—), Soc. Am. Mil. Engrs. (Urban medal 1997), Bursar Coll. of Fellows (vice chancellor), Royal Inst. Brit. Architects, Japan Inst. Architects, Crescent Club (Dallas), Center Club (Balt.), Met. Club (Washington), Cosmos Club, Caves Valley Golf Club (Balt.), The Athenaeum (London). Democrat. Baptist. Home: 1601 The Terraces Baltimore MD 21209-3636

ADAMS, HAZARD SIMEON, English educator, writer; b. Cleve., Feb. 15, 1926; s. Robert Simeon and Mary (Thurness) A.; m. Diana White, Sept. 17, 1949; children: Charles Simeon, Perry White. AB, Princeton, 1948; MA, U. Wash., 1949, PhD, 1953. Instr. English Cornell U., 1952-56; asst. prof. U. Tex., 1956-59; vis. assoc. prof. Washington U., St. Louis, 1959; from assoc. prof. to prof. Mich. State U., 1959-64; Fulbright lectr. U. Dublin, 1962-63; prof. U. Calif.-Irvine, 1964-77, founding chmn. English dept., 1964-69; dean Sch. Humanities, 1970-72, vice chancellor acad. affairs, 1972-74; co-dir. Sch. Criticism and Theory, 1975-77; sr. fellow, 1975-88; hon. sr. fellow, 1988—; prof. English and comparative lit. U. Wash., Seattle, 1977-97, Byron W. and Alice L. Lockwood prof. humanities, 1988-97, prof. emeritus, 1997—. Prof. English U. Calif., Irvine, 1990-94. Author: Poems by Robert Simeon Adams, 1952, Blake and Yeats: The Contrary Vision, 1955, 2d edit., 1969, The Contexts of Poetry, 1963, William Blake: A Reading of the Shorter Poems, 1963, Poetry: An Introductory Anthology, 1968, The Horses of Instruction, 1968, Fiction as Process, 1968, The Interests of Criticism, 1969, William Blake: Jerusalem, Selected Poems and Prose, 1970, The Truth About Dragons, 1971, Critical Theory Since Plato, 1971, rev. edit., 1992, Lady Gregory, 1973, The Academic Tribes, 1976, 2d edit., 1988, Philosophy of the Literary Symbolic, 1983, Joyce Cary's Trilogies, 1983, Critical Theory Since 1965, 1986, The Book of Yeats's Poems, 1991, Antithetical Essays, 1991, Critical Essays on William Blake, 1991, The Book of Yeats's Vision, 1995,The Farm at Richwood and Other Poems, 1997, Many Pretty Toys, 1999, Home, 2001; mem. edtl. bd. Epoch, 1954-56, Tex. Studies Lit. and Lang., 1957-68, Studies in Romanticism, 1966—, Blake Studies, 1969-80, Modern Lang. Quar., 1977-84. Served to 1st lt. USMC, 1943-45, 51. Guggenheim fellow, 1974-75 Mem. Internat. Assn. Univ. Profs. English, Am. Conf. for Irish Studies, Phi Beta Kappa. Home: 3930 NE 157th Pl Lake Forest Park WA 98155-6730 E-mail: HAdams3048@aol.com.

ADAMS, HERBERT RYAN, mediation consultant, retired clergyman, educator, publishing executive; b. Phila., Apr. 19, 1932; s. Leander Hampton and Helen Marguerite (Richards) A.; m. Carol Anne Levine, Aug. 27, 1956; children: Ashley Pozefsky, Joshua; m. Elizabeth Ellis, Aug. 6, 1964; children: Lee Hampton, Rachel Ellis; m. Mary Ryan, Aug. 20, 1977. AB, Colby Coll., 1954; EdD, Harvard U., 1972; student, Harvard Div. Sch., 1955-56, Kent State U., 1957, Boston U., 1963. Ordained to ministry Congregationalist Ch., 1952, Unitarian Universalist Assn., 1968. Minister Fairfield and Pine Point, Maine, 1950-56, Chelsea, Mass., 1962-66, Lexington, Mass., 1967-75, Winnetka, Ill., 1978-87, South Paris, Maine, 1988-94, West Paris, Maine, 1991-94; iterim Ithaca, NY, 1997-98, Santa Fe, 1998-99, Port Charlotte, Fla., 2001-02; editor Allyn and Bacon, Boston, 1959-62; sr. editor Ginn & Co., Boston, 1962-68; v.p. mktg. Visual Learning Corp., Cambridge, Mass., 1968-71; dir. Sci. Rsch. Assocs. divsn. IBM, Chgo., 1975-83; v.p. Laidlaw Bros., River Forest, Ill., 1983-84, pres., CEO, 1984-87. Pres. Ryan-Adams Cons. Svcs., Center Lovell, Maine, 1994—. Author: Poetry on Film, 1970; Project Listening, 1975; Listening Your Way to Management Success, 1983; contbr. articles to profl. jours. Tchr. Greenville (Pa.) H.S., 1956-58, Euclid (Ohio) H.S., 1958-59, Lexington (Mass.) H.S., 1968-69, Harvard Grad. Sch. Edn., 1971-72, Oxford Hills (Maine) H.S., 1987-88; prin. Oxford Hills Jr. H.S., 1989-91. Recipient Coe Found. award DePauw U., 1958, Cert. of Merit VFW, 1989, Disting. Pres. award Norway-Paris Kiwanis, 1996. Mem. Mediators of Maine, Oxford Hills Ret. Tchrs. Assn., Unitarian Universalist Ret. Mins. Assn., Lake Kezar Country Club, Lovell Land Trust, Lovell Hist. Soc., Girard Coll. Alumni Assn. (life). Home and Office: PO Box 302 Center Lovell ME 04016-0302 Home: 252 Brentwood Dr Lake Placid FL 33852 E-mail: herbadams@webtv.net.

ADAMS, HILARY SHIELS, theater director; b. Washington, Nov. 3, 1972; d. Lawrence Curtis and Barbara (Johnston) A. BA, Evergreen State Coll., 1995. Dir.: (theatrical prodns.) Packing, 1997, Rain, 1997, Showboats, 1997, Office Work, 1997, It's Called the Sugar Plum, 1997, What Neighbors are For, 1997, Stills, 1997, 70 Scenes of Halloween, 1998, 100 Variations of a Family Theme, 1998, Women of Manhattan, 1999, Kaleidoscope and the Flying Machine (Ray Bradbury), 1999, Fahrenheit 451 (Ray Bradbury), 2001, A Boy Who is a Bird, 2001, Moby Dick, 2002, One Night at Your Local Superstore, 2002, Washington and the Crisis of Enlistments, 2002, Book Party, 2002, Trying to Find Chinatown, 2002, Love Detectives, 2002, Nocturne with Apples, 2002, April Showers, 2001, Fried Chicken, Hot or Cold, 2001, Habits, 2001, The Contract, 2001, A Singular Kind of Guy, 2001, The Philadelphia, 2001, DMV Tyrant, 2001; (plays) Still Asking for Trouble, 2003, the Worthy Matron of the Eastern Star, 2003, Moby Dick, 2003; asst. dir. off Broadway Bedfellows, 1997, asst. dir. on Broadway Titanic, 1997, asst. dir. regional Griller, 1998, asst. dir. on Broadway SDCF Observership, 2002, asst. dir. off Broadway The Fastest Clock in the Universe, 1998; asst. dir. : Griller, 1998; asst. dir. on Broadway Aida (Disney Theatrical Prodns.), 2000; asst. : Flower Drum Song, 2001—02; asst. dir. on Broadway A Little Night Music, The Kennedy Ctr., N.Y., 2002; dir.(author): Whiskey Talking, 1998. E-mail: hilaryadams@aol.com.

ADAMS, HUNTER (PATCH ADAMS), internist, health facility administrator; b. Washington, May 28, 1945; Student, Sewanee U.; BA, George Washington U., 1967; MD, Med. Coll. Va., 1971. Resident pediat. Georgetown U. Hosp., Washignton, 1971; founder, dir. Gesundheit Inst., Arlington, Va., 1971—92. Author: House Calls: How We Can All Heal the World One Visit at a Time, Gesundheit. Office: Gesundheit Inst 2630 Robert Walker Pl Arlington VA 22207 Address: Gesundheit Inst Hosp Found PO Box 98072 Washington DC 20090-8072

ADAMS, J. MACK, computer science educator; b. Marfa, Tex., Aug. 14, 1933; s. Glen Wayne and Albene Angie (Hughes) A.; m. Joe Ann Davis, Mar. 31, 1952; children: Mack Lane, Mark Wayne. BS, U. Tex., El Paso, 1954; MS, N.Mex. State U., 1960, PhD, 1963. Assoc. scientist Westinghouse Electric Corp., Pitts., 1954-56; supervising mathematician Flight Simulation Lab., White Sands Missile Range, N.Mex., 1956-60; dir. computer directorate Electronics R&D Activity, White Sands Missile Range, N.Mex., 1963-64; assoc. prof. U. Tex., El Paso, 1964-65; dir. computer ctr. N.Mex. State U., Las Cruces, 1965-70, prof., 1970-93, prof. emeritus, 1993—, assoc. dean Coll. Arts and Scis., 1990-93. Sr. Fulbright lectr., Cath. U., Santiago, Chile, 1972; vis. fellow Wolfson Coll., Oxford, England, 1978. Author: (with others) Introduction to Computer Science, 1970, Computers: Appreciation, Application, Implications, 1973, Social Effects of Computer Use and Misuse, 1976, An Introduction to Computer Science with Modula-2, 1988; contbr. articles to profl. jours. Univ. fellow N.Mex. State U., Las Cruces, 1960. Mem. Assn. Computing Machinery, Math. Assn. Am. Home: 905 Conway St Apt 7 Las Cruces NM 88005-3774

ADAMS, J. PHILLIP, oil industry executive; BA in Fin. and Acctg., Utah State U., 1978. With Brown and Davis, CPAs, 1978—80, Flying J. Inc., Brigham City, Utah, 1980—, CEO, 1992—. Office: Flying J Inc 1104 Country Hills Dr Ogden UT 84403*

ADAMS, JAMES BLACKBURN, former state government official, former federal government official, lawyer; b. Corsicana, Tex., Dec. 21, 1926; s. Lynn and Florence (Blackburn) A.; m. Ione Winistorfer, Sept. 3, 1955; children—James Blackburn, Elizabeth, Martha. Student, La. State U., 1944, Yale U., 1944-45; BA, Baylor U., 1950, LL.B., 1949, JD, 1969. Bar: Tex. bar 1949, U.S. Supreme Ct. bar 1965. Asst. county atty. Limestone County, Tex., 1950; mem. Tex. Ho. of Reps., 1951; spl. agt. FBI, Seattle and San Francisco offices, 1951-53; supervisory spl. agt. FBI (Hdqrs.), 1953-59; asst. spl. agt. in charge FBI (Mpls. field div.), 1959-61, asst. chief personnel sect., 1961-65, chief personnel sect., 1965-71; exec. asst. to asst. to dir. adminstrn. FBI, Washington, 1971-72, spl. agt. in charge San Antonio (Tex.) div., 1972-74; asst. dir., head Office of Planning and Evaluations, Washington, 1974; asst. to dir. FBI, 1974-78, assoc. dir., 1978-79, ret., 1979. Mem. Gov.'s Task Force on Drug Abuse; exec. dir. criminal justice div. Gov.'s Office, State of Tex., 1979-80; dir. Dept. Public Safety, 1980-87; guest lectr. various U.S. and fgn. law enforcement, intelligence and bus. groups, 1974-79 Served with U.S. Army, 1945-46, PTO. Recipient numerous govt. achievement awards, 1953-79, Atty. Gen.'s award for Disting. Service, 1978; Nat. Intelligence Disting. Service medal, 1979 Mem. U.S. Supreme Ct. Bar, Tex. Bar Assn., Tex. Police Assn., Soc. Former Spl. Agts. of FBI. Presbyterian.

ADAMS, JAMES CHARLES, lawyer; b. Cleve., June 20, 1949; s. Charles Otterbein and Loraine Ida (Bagnoli) A.; m. Donna Elaine Roe, Aug. 7, 1971 (dec. 1983); 1 dau., Heather Anne; Kathleen Ann Dunham, Oct. 22, 1983. B.A., Mich. State U., 1971; J.D., U. Mich., 1974. Bar: Mich. 1974, U.S. Dist. Ct. (ea. dist.) Mich., 1974. Assoc. Honigman Miller Schwartz, Detroit, 1974-75, Dykema, Gossett, Spencer, Goodnow & Trigg, Detroit, 1975-82, ptnr., 1982-86; ptnr. Simpson & Moran, Birmingham, Mich., 1986-87; prin. James C. Adams, Traverse City, Mich., 1987-93, Adams & Assocs., Traverse City, 1993—. Mem. ABA, Detroit Bar Assn., Order of Coif, Phi Kappa Phi. Presbyterian. Home: 155 Lake Village Dr Apt 201 Ann Arbor MI 48103-6538 Office: Dykema Gossett Spencer Goodnow & Trigg 400 Renaissance Ctr Ste 35 Detroit MI 48243-1501

ADAMS, JAMES FREDERICK, psychologist, educational administrator; b. Andong, Korea, Dec. 27, 1927; s. Benjamin Nyce and Phyllis Irene (Taylor) A.; m. Carol Ann Wagner, Jan. 17, 1980; children— James Edward, Dorothy Lee Adams Vanderhorst, Robert Benjamin BA In Psychology, U. Calif.-Berkeley, 1950; Ed.M. in Counseling and Psychology, Temple U., 1951; PhD in Exptl. Psychology, Wash. State U., 1959. Cert. psychologist, Wash., Pa.; lic. psychologist, Pa. Psychometrician Measurement and Research Ctr., Temple U., Phila., 1951-52; asst. prof. psychology Whitworth Coll., Spokane, Wash., 1952-55; teaching and research asst. State U. Wash., 1955-57; research assoc. Miami U., Oxford, Ohio, 1957-59; asst. prof. psychology Coll. Liberal Arts, Temple U., 1959-62, assoc. prof., 1962-66, prof., 1966-80, chmn. dept. counseling psychology, 1969-72; vis. prof. psychology Coll. Soc. Scis., U. P.R., Rio Piedras, 1963-64, Coll. Scis., Cath. U., Ponce, P.R., 1971-72; chmn. dept. counseling psychology Coll. Edn., Temple U., 1973-77, coordinator div. ednl. psychology, 1974-76; grad. dean, prof. psychology Grad. Coll., U. Nev., Las Vegas, 1980-85; acad. (sr.) v.p. Longwood Coll., Farmville, Va., 1985-86. Author: Problems in Counseling: A Case Study Approach, 1962, Instructors Manual for Understanding Adolescence, 1969; (exhbn. catalogue with J. D. Selig) Colonial Spanish Art of the Americas, 1976; (comml. pamphlet with C. L. Davis) The Use of the Vu-graph as an Instructional Aid, 1960; editor: Counseling and Guidance: A Summary View, 1965, Understanding Adolescence: Current Developments in Adolescent Psychology, 1968, 4th edit., 1980, Human Behavior in a Changing Society, 1973, Songs that had to be Sung (by B. N. Adams), 1979; contbr. chpts., articles, tests and book revs. to profl. publs. Served to cpl. USMC, 1945-46 Recipient Alexander Meiklejohn award AAUP, 1984; James McKean Cattell research fund grantee Miami U., Oxford, Ohio, 1958, Bolton fund research grantee Temple U., 1960, 62, faculty research grantee Temple U., 1961, 63, Commonwealth of Pa. research grantee Temple U., 1969, 70, 71, 72, summer research fellow Temple U., 1979; recipient scholarship U. Munich, 1955; James F. Adams endowment for psychology established at Wash. State U., Pullman, 2003. Fellow Am. Psychol. Assn. (divs. 26, 17); mem. Eastern Psychol. Assn., Western Psychol. Assn., Interam. Soc. Psychology, Sigma Xi, Psi Chi Avocations: art collecting; art restoring. Scholarship established in his name at U. Nev., Las Vegas. Home: 130 Palacio Rd Corrales NM 87048-9648

ADAMS, JAMES G., JR., judge, lawyer; b. Hopkinsville, Ky., Nov. 4, 1954; s. J. Granville Sr. and Levina (Simmons) A.; m. Betty Veatch; children: James G. III, William H. II, Robert Lynn. AA, Hopkinsville Community Coll., 1974; BA, U. Ky., 1976; JD, No. Ky. U., 1979. Bar: Ky. 1979, U.S. Dist. Ct. (we. dist.) Ky. 1980. Assoc. Trimble, Soyars, Breathitt & Foster, Hopkinsville, Ky., 1979-80; ptnr. Trimble & Foster & Adams, Hopkinsville, 1980-87, Trimble, Foster Adams & Powell, Hopkinsville, 1988-93. Asst. county atty. Christian County, 1980-93; dist. judge divsn. I 3rd Jud. Dist., 1994—. Bd. chmn. Pennyroyal Area Mus., Hopkinsville, 1984-88; pres. Buddies Inc., Hopkinsville, 1982-83. Named Boss of the Yr., Hopkinsville Legal Secs., 1983-84. Mem. Jaycees (pres. 1982-83, Outstanding Local Pres. Ky. 1982-83). Democrat. Methodist. Avocations: golf, hunting, fishing, boating, cooking. Office: Christian County Justice Center 100 Justice Way Hopkinsville KY 42240 E-mail: jamesadams@mail.aoc.state.ky.us.

ADAMS, JAMES LAMONT, educational foundation executive; b. Rocky Mount, N.C., Dec. 15, 1949; s. James Edgar Adams and Madelyn Louise Knowles; m. Donna Marie Adams, Apr. 20, 1974; children: Christian James, Ashley Marie, Colin Kent. BA, Va. Mil. Inst., 1971; MA, James Madison U., 1980; grad., Army Command and Staff Coll., 1988; EdD, U. Tenn., 1989. Pub. info. officer Va. Mil. Inst., Lexington, 1977-81; dir. univ. rels. U. Tenn., Chattanooga, 1981-84; dir. devel. The Citadel, Charleston, S.C., 1984-91; exec. dir., dir. membership Naval Inst. Found./U.S. Naval Inst., Annapolis, Md., 1991-98; exec. v.p., exec. dir. Va. Mil. Inst. Found./Va. Mil. Inst. Devel. Bd., Lexington, 1998—. Mem. exec. com. Boy Scouts of Am., Chattanooga, 1981-83, Charleston, 1985-89. lt. col. USAR. Named one of Outstanding Young Men of Am., Jaycees, 1983. Mem. Coun. for Advancement and Support of Edn., Res. Officers Assn., Army-Navy Club, The Commonwealth Club, Kappa Alpha. Republican. Episcopalian. Office: VMI Found Inc 304 Letcher Ave Lexington VA 24450-2110 E-mail: jadams@vmiaa.org.

ADAMS, JAMES MICHAEL, nuclear physicist; b. Brookline, Mass., Dec. 5, 1957; s. Michael James and Elizabeth (Corchary) A.; m. Linda Gail Sheehan Adams, Dec. 26, 1990; children: Kelley Marie, Megan Marie. AB, Coll. of the Holy Cross, Worcester, Mass., 1979; MS, Pa. State U., 1990, PhD, 1995. Lt. sr. grade USN, Washington, 1979-84; sr. engr. Westinghouse Electric Corp., Pitts., 1984-88; rsch. asst. Pa. State U., University Park, 1988-94; rsch. fellow U. Mich., Ann Arbor, Mich., 1995-96; guest rschr., physics lab. Nat. Inst. Stds. and Tech., Gaithersburg, Md., 1995-96; rsch. physicist Neutron Interactions & Dosimetry Group Physics Lab. Nat. Inst. Stds. and Tech., Gaithersburg, 1996—. Contbr. articles to profl. jours. including Phys. Rev., Applied Physics Letters, Surface Sci., Hyperfine Interactions, Ferroelectrics, Materials Sci. and Engring., Nuclear Tech. Vol. Alpha Cmty. Ambulance Svc., State College, Pa., 1994; asst. scoutmaster Boy Scouts Am., Framingham, Mass., 1975. Lt. USN, 1979-84. Recipient Grad. scholarships Am. Nuclear Soc., 1990-93, Inaugural Nuc. Energy Rsch. Initiative grant; named Inst. of Nuclear Power Op. scholar, 1988-89, Pa. State U. Grad. fellow The Pa. State U., 1991-92, Deans fellow, 1988-90. Mem. ASTM (sec., mem. com.), Am. Phys. Soc., Am. Nuc. Soc., Sigma Xi, Sigma Pi Sigma, Tau Beta Pi, Alpha Nu Sigma. Achievements include research in hyperfine interactions, surface physics, fundamental neutron physics, neutron spectroscopy and dosimetry, neutron source calibrations, and nuclear reactor analysis. Home: 21503 Fox Field Cir Germantown MD 20876-5944 Office: Nat Inst Stds and Tech 100 Bureau Dr Mail Stop 8461 Gaithersburg MD 20899

ADAMS, JAMES MILLS, retired chemicals executive; b. Sioux Falls, S.D., Aug. 4, 1936; m. Sherrell D.; 2 children. BSChemE, S.D. Sch. Mines and Tech., 1958; MS in Engring., U. Wash., 1961, PhD in Chem. Nuclear Engring., 1962. Sr. engring. specialist aerophysics rsch. Aerojet-Gen. Corp., Sacramento, 1962-68; sr. spectroscopist Hoffmann La Roche, Inc., Nutley, N.J., 1968-70, sr. scientist applied scis. dept., 1970-73, mgr. CVA engring., 1974-76; plant mgr. aroma chem. plant Haarmann and Reimer Corp., Springfield, N.J., 1976-79, v.p., gen. mgr. aroma chem. div., 1978-85, exec. v.p., 1979-80, pres., 1980-96, CEO, 1985-96; ret. Adv. bd. Cook Coll., Rutgers U., 1985-92; corp. v.p. Miles, Inc., 1989-91; chmn. bd. dirs. Creations Aromatiques, Inc., 1990-96; bd. dirs. Florasynth, Inc., 1995-96. Assoc. editor Pyrodynamics, 1966-69; contbr. over 40 articles to profl. jours.; patentee in fields of med. instrumentation, emission spectrometry, pyrometry, remote sensing, others. Mem. Charleston County Aviation Commn., 1978-79; internat. adv. coun. Monell Ctr., 1990-97. H.L. Doherty Ednl. Found. scholar 1954-58; W. Alton Jones fellow, 1959-60; recipient Centennial 100 Alumni award, S.D. Sch. Mines and Tech., 1985, Eric Bruell award for excellence U.S. Fragrance Industry, 1998. Mem. AAAS, Am. Phys. Soc., Am. Mgmt. Assn., Flavor and Extract Mfrs. Assn. (bd. govs. 1985-94, v.p., sec. 1989-90, pres. elect 1990, pres. 1992-93), Fragrance Materials Assn. (bd. dirs. 1985-96, pres. 1988-92, Spl. Award for outstanding contb. to global fragrance industry 1999), Rsch. Inst. for Fragrance Materials (chmn. bd. dirs. 1984-89, vice chmn. 1989-90), Cosmetic, Toiletries and Fragrance Assn. (bd. dirs. 1994-98), Internat. Fragrance Assn. (bd. dirs. 1990-98, pres. 1996-98), Svc. Corps Ret. Execs./Small Bus. Adminstrn., Pres. Assn., Optimists Club (pres. Watchung chpt. 1984-85), Sigma Xi (pres. Roche Rsch. Club 1973-74). Home: 5131 Chelterham Terr San Diego CA 92130-1416 Office: SymRise Corp 300 North St Teterboro NJ 07608-1204

ADAMS, JAMES ROBERT, medical organization sales professional; b. Kansas City, Mo., Dec. 4, 1946; s. James Watt and Helen Agnes (Cleary) A.; m. Mary Catherine Edwards, Mar. 27, 1971; children: Robert, Patrick. BA, Rockhurst Coll., 1970; AA in Respiratory Therapy, Penn Valley Community Coll., 1972; MA, Webster U., 1980. Registered respiratory therapist. Shift supr. Menorah Med. Ctr., Kansas City, 1970-73; asst. dir. respiratory therapy North Kansas City Meml. Hosp., 1973-77; dir. pulmonary lab. Truman Med. Ctr., Kansas City, 1977-80; clin. coordinator Nat. Med. Care, Merriam, Kans., 1980-85; br. mgr. Greene & Kellogg, Inc., Overland Park, Kans., 1985-87; sales rep. Nat. Med. Homecare (now Homedco of Kansas City), Lenexa, Kans., 1987—. Cons. Sysco, Inc., Kansas City, 1978-79. Cubmaster local coun. Boy Scouts Am., Kansas City, 1984—. Republican. Roman Catholic. Avocations: golf, fishing, bowling, building and flying radio-controlled airplanes. Home: 10417 Monroe Ave Kansas City MO 64137-1533

ADAMS, JAMES THOMAS, surgeon; b. Rochester, N.Y., Mar. 28, 1930; s. Thomas and Sarah A.; m. Jacqueline K. Stemmler, July 7, 1952; children—Pamela, Mark, Sari Lynn. AB, Washington U., St. Louis, 1951, MD, 1955. Intern, then resident in surgery Barnes Hosp., St. Louis, 1955-60; mem. faculty

U. Rochester Med. Sch., 1962—, prof. surgery, 1977—. Author papers in field, chpts. in books. Served as officer M.C. USAR, 1960-62. Mem. Am. Surg. Assn., Soc. Internat. de Chirurgie, Soc. U. Surgeons, Central Surg. Assn., Soc. Vascular Surgery, Am. Gastroenterol. Assn., Soc. Surgery Alimentary Tract, Am. Assn. Surgery Trauma, Phi Beta Kappa, Sigma Xi, Alpha Omega Alpha. Clubs: Oak Hill Country (Rochester). Achievements include co-designing inferior vena cava clip. Personal E-mail: jadams06@rochester.rr.com. E-mail: james-adams@urmc.rochester.edu.

ADAMS, JAMES WILLIAM, former chemist; b. Conover, Wis., Oct. 29, 1921; s. Aldred Henry and Pauline (Evertson) A.; m. Joyce Marie Braatz, Oct. 27, 1944 (div. Oct. 1986); children: Judy R. Adams Swank, Neal J.; m. Barbara A. Backlund, Apr. 4, 1987. BS in Chemistry, U. Wis., 1943. Analytical chemist U.S. Rubber Co., Institute, W.Va., 1943-47, rsch. chemist Naugatuck, Conn., 1947-52; sr. scientist Marathon Corp., Rothschild, Wis., 1952-53, rsch. group leader, 1953-57; sr. rsch. assoc. Am. Can Co., Rothschild, 1957-80; rsch. fellow Reed Lignin Inc., Rothschild, 1980-89; retired, 1989. Chemistry specialist J&B Cons., Schofield, Wis., 1989—. Contbr. articles to Chem. and Engring. Progress, Indsl. and Engring. Chemistry, Applied Polymer Symposium, Radiochem. Radioanalytical Letters. Alderman Schofield City Coun., 1958-74; vol. Wausau Nordic Ski Club. Recipient Meritorious Svc. award City of Schofield, 1976, Vol. of Yr. award Badger State Games, 1991. Mem. Am. Chem. Soc. (tour speaker 1986—, chmn. Ctr. Wis. sect. 1995), Am. Inst. Chemists, N.Y. Acad. Scis. Achievements include 20 patents for using Wood Pulping Liquor in Animal Feed, Process for Making Superabsorbent Fibers, Modified Wood Pulp Fibers for Plant Growth Medium, and others on industrial products and processes; development of test for measuring road wear qualities of tire rubber. Home: 2008 Clarberth St Schofield WI 54476-1211

ADAMS, JEAN RUTH, entomologist, researcher; b. Edgewater Park, N.J., Aug. 17, 1928; d. Herbert Raymond and Gertrude Gladys (Budd) A. BS, Rutgers U., 1950, PhD (Trubeck fellow), 1962. Registered profl. entomologist. Lab. technician Rohm & Haas Co., Bristol, Pa., 1951-57; postdoctoral fellow U. Pa., Phila., 1961-62; rsch. entomologist USDA Agr. Rsch. Ctr., Beltville, Md., 1962-96, collaborator, 1996—. Cons. insect pathology, electron microscopy. Mem. editl. bd. Jour. Invertebrate Pathology, 1986-89; editor: Atlas of Invertebrate Viruses, 1991, Insect Potpourri: Adventures in Entomology, 1992; contbr. articles to sci. jours. Mem. nominating com. D.C. Bapt. Conv., 1977—79; dir. Acteens, Mission Youth Orgn, D.C. Bapt. Conv., 1972—86, 1988—92, sec., 1993—97; Sunday sch. tchr. 1st Bapt. Ch., Hyatsville, Md., 1962—, chmn. Christian edn. bd., 1973—74, mem. nominating com., 1974—77, mem. bd. missions, 1977—80, ch. treas., 1973—74, mem. choir, 1979—, diaconate, 1980—86, 1998—2000, 2002—, vice chmn., 1981—82, chmn., 1982—91; trustee Bapt. Home, 1982—91, sec., 1985—91; trustee Sunday sch. bd. SBC, 1991—99; chmn. nominating com. D.C. Bapt. Conv., 2000—01. Mem. Am. Registered Profl. Entomologists (bd. dirs. Chesapeake chpt. 1989—, pres. 1991-93, sec.-treas. 1997—), Electron Microscopy Soc. Am. (chmn. sci. exhibits ann. meeting 1982), Entomol. Soc. Am., Am. Soc. for Cell. Biology, Soc. for Invertebrate Pathology (sec. 1982-84), Washington Soc. for Electron Microscopy (coun. 1976-83, sec.-treas. 1976-78, 80-82), Washington Entomol. Soc., Md. Entomol. Soc., Sigma Xi, Sigma Delta Epsilon. Home: 6004 41st Ave Hyattsville MD 20782-3058 Office: USDA Agr Rsch Ctr Bldg 011A W Insect Biocontrol Lab Rm 214 Beltsville MD 20705

ADAMS, JEFFREY ALAN, web producer, writer; b. Flint, Mich., June 25, 1968; s. William and Linda Suzanne (Montgomery) A.; m. William R. Knauss, Sept. 7, 1997. BA in Journalism, U. Ala., 1991. Editl. asst. Randall Pub. Co., Tuscaloosa, Ala., 1989-90; assoc. editor Equipment World Mag., Tuscaloosa, Ala., 1990-91, Overdrive Mag., Tuscaloosa, Ala., 1990-93; mng. editor Equipment World Mag., 1991-93, TVRO Dealer Mag., Fortuna, Calif., 1993-97; staff writer Satellite TV Week Mag., Fortuna, Calif., 1993-96, mng. editor, 1996-98, Satellite Choice Mag., Fortuna, Calif., 1996-98; web prodr. Dobbin/Bolgla Assocs., N.Y.C., 1998-2000, The Princeton Rev., N.Y.C., 2000—. Contbg. editor Equipment World Mag., Tuscaloosa, Ala., 1993-2002. Co-editor, co-pub. The First Line Literary Mag., Plano, Tex., 1999—. Sec. Ferndale (Calif.) Repertory Theater, 1994-95, bd. mem., 1993-94, media rels., 1994-97, photographer, 1993-98, publicist, web developer Redwood Curtian Theatre Consortium, 1997—. Recipient Robert F. Boger Feature Writing award, Constrn. Writers Assn., 1993. Avocations: acting, theater, travel, music, internet. Office: The Princeton Rev 2315 Broadway New York NY 10024

ADAMS, JO-ANN MARIE, lawyer; b. L.A., May 27, 1949; d. Joseph John and Georgia S. (Wein) A. AA, Pasadena C.C., 1968; BA, Pomona Coll., 1970; MA, Calif. State U., L.A., 1971; MBA, Pacific Luth. U., 1983; JD, Santa Clara U., 1996. cert. in telecom. and info. resource mgmt. Secondary tchr. South Pasadena (Calif.) Unified Schs., 1970-71; appraiser Riverside County (Calif.) Assessor's Office, 1972-74; systems and procedures analyst Riverside County Data Processing Dept., 1974-76, supr. systems analyst, 1976-79; systems analyst computer Boeing Computer Svcs. Co., Seattle, 1979-81; sr. systems analyst Thurston County Ctrl. Svcs., Olympia, Wash., 1981-83, data processing systems mgr., 1983-84; data processing systems engr. IBM Corp., 1984-87; realtor assoc. Dower Realty, 1987-92; corp. sales rep. UniGlobe Met. Travel, 1988-89; project mr. Servco Pacific, 1989-90, Scott Software Systems, 1990-91; systems analyst Dept. Atty. Gen., 1991-93; pvt. practice Honolulu, 1996—; with Bervar & Jones, 2002—03. Cons. in field, 1993—; corp. counsel RightWorks Corp., 2000-01, Law Offices Thomas R. Hogan, 1999; instr. Riverside City Coll., 1977-79; adj. prof. Santa Clara U., 1997-2000. Chair legis. task force Riverside/San Bernardino chpt. NOW, 1975-76, chpt. co-chair, 1978; mem. ethics com. Calif. NOW, Inc., 1978; alt. del. Calif. Dem. Caucus, 1978; del. Hawaii Dem. Caucus, 2002; mem. Gay, Lesbian, Bisexual and Transgender Caucus of Hawaii Dem. Party; bd. dirs. Honolulu Gay and Lesbian Cultural Found. Mem. ABA, NAFE, Santa Clara Calif. Bar Assn. (mem. rainbow com. 1994-2000, chair 1998, minority access com. 1 999-2000, nominating com. 2000), Pomona Coll. Alumni Assn., Santa Clara U. Alumni Assn. Home: 411 Hobron Ln # 801 Honolulu HI 96815-1210 Office: Seven Waterfront Plz 500 Ala Moana Blvd Ste 400 Honolulu HI 96813-4920 E-mail: jadamsesq@aol.com.

ADAMS, JOCELIA, oncological nurse, educator; b. Petaluma, Calif., Oct. 14, 1948; d. Richard Guy and Mary Lorraine (Cunha) A.; children: Janis E. Phillips, Jaime L. Phillips. ADN, Santa Rosa Jr. Coll., Calif., 1976; grad., Oreg. Nurses Cancer Edn. Program, 1984. Cert. oncology nurse clinician. Staff nurse, nurse mgr. McMinnville Cmty. Hosp., Oreg.; oncology staff nurse Petaluma Valley Hosp. Founder, clin. dir. Ctr. for Caregiver Tng., San Francisco.

ADAMS, JOHN BRETT, investment banker, company executive; b. England, Dec. 6, 1940; arrived in U.S., 1972; s. Harold Coates and Mildred B. (Jones) Adams; m. Laura Marie Schneider, July 15, 1970; children: Alexa, Caroline. BA, Oxford (England) U., 1962; MBA, Stanford U., 1964. Exec. dir. S.G. Warburg & Co., Ltd., London, 1964—72; dir. Singer & Friedlander, Ltd., London, 1972—74; sr. v.p. White, Weld & Co., Inc., N.Y.C., 1974—78; mng. dir. Merrill Lynch Capital Markets, N.Y.C., 1978—85; ptnr. M.J.H. Nightingale & Co., N.Y.C., 1986—89; v.p. corp. devel. Wyeth (formerly Am. Home Products Corp.), 1991—2002. Dir. Am. Swiss Assn., N.Y.C.; mem. internat. com. Securities Industry Assn., N.Y.C. Bd. dirs., treas. Am. Friends of the Warburg Inst.; bd. dirs. Brit. Schs. and Univs. Found., Inc., N.Y.C., 1982—98. Mem.: Devon Yacht Club, Maidstone Club, Racquet and Tennis Club. Avocations: golf, racquet sports, art, theater. Home: 224 E 68th St New York NY 10021-6001

ADAMS, JOHN C. transportation executive; b. Memphis; BA in Gov., U. Va., 1970. From mem. staff to pres., owner Gem Inc., Byhalia, Miss., 1973-78, pres., owner, 1978-82; pres. Miami divsn. Malone & Hyde, 1983-90; prin., owner NCC L.P., Atlanta, 1990-94; from exec. v.p. to chmn., CEO AutoZone, Memphis, 1994-97, chmn., CEO, 1997—. Dir. Keebler Foods Co.; bd. trustees LeMoyne-Owen Coll., Memphis. With USN, 1970-73. Office: AutoZone Inc 123 S Front St Memphis TN 38103-3618

ADAMS, JOHN CARTER, JR., insurance executive; b. Williston, Fla., June 13, 1936; s. John Carter and Katharine Anna (Beall) A.; m. Leila Nora Johnson, Nov. 28, 1958; children: Julia Katharine, Ruth Anne. BSBA, U. Fla., 1958. Agt. Pan Am Ins. Co., 1958-59; acct. exec. Guy B. Odum & Co., Inc., 1959-63, v.p., 1963-66, exec. v.p., 1966-71, pres., 1971-76, Jay Adams & Assocs., Inc., Daytona Beach, 1976-85, Hilb Rogal & Hamilton Co., Daytona Beach, 1986-89, CEO, 1986-92, chmn., 1986-98, mem. operating com., 1988-95, chmn. operating com., 1987-93, sr. v.p. ops., 1989-90, exec. v.p. sales and mktg., 1991-93, exec. v.p., COO, 1993-94, exec. v.p. ops., 1994-99; exec. v.p. Brown & Brown Inc., Daytona Bch., Fla., 1999—. Bd. dirs. Westside Atlantic Bank, 1972-76, First Atlantic Nat. Bank, 1976-81, Heritage Fed. Savings & Loan, 1981-85, Daytona Beach, 1985-90, Am. Pioneer Savings Bank, Fla., 1985-90, Consol. Tomoka Land Co., 1976—; chmn. adv. bd. Daytona Beach region Am. Pioneer Savings Bank, Orlando, Fla., 1986-90; chmn. compensation com. Consol. Tomoka Land Co., 1990—. Mem. bd. visitors Embry-Riddle Aero. U., Daytona Beach, 1967-69, trustee, 1969—, mem. exec. com., 1972—, vice chmn. bd. 1981—, chmn. exec. com, 1983—, devel. coun. chmn. fund drive Hunt Meml. Libr. Embry-Riddle Aero U., 1985; chmn. Commitment 2000 Fund Drive Embry-Riddle Aero U.; campaign chmn. Easter Seal Soc., 1969, trustee, 1970-73, pres., 1972-73; bd. dirs. YMCA, Daytona Beach, 1968-76, 78—, treas., 1970, v.p., 1971-82, pres., 1983; mem. Metro Bd. Daytona Beach YMCA, 1992-2001, trustee, 2002—; dir. Futures, Inc., 1985-93, pres., 1987; dir. Nat. Intercollegiate Sports Festival, 1985-87; gen. campaign chmn. United Way of Volusia County, Fla., 1977, pres., 1979, dir., 1976-82, trustee, 1985—; chmn. Civic League of Halifax Area, 1983-84, exec. com., 1977-92; chmn. Fla. Internat. Festivals, Inc., 1990-91, bd. dirs. 1987—, exec. com., 1991—, chmn. Lively Arts Ctr. Inc., 1997-2002, chmn. emeritus, 2003—; mem. Tourist Devel. Coun. Volusia County 1983-85, Halifax Advt. Authority, 1985; bd. dirs. Volusia County Bus. Devel. Coun., 1984-92, Daytona Beach Cmty. Found., 1984-87, Fla. State C. of C., 1985-86. Served with USNR, 1953-61. Recipient Disting. Svc. award Bd. visitors Embry-Riddle Aero. U., 1975, Champion Higher Ind. Edn. in Fla. award Ind. Colls. and Univs. of Fla., 1973, 1st Ann. Herbert M. Davidson Cmty. Svc. award United Way of Volusia County, 1992, J. Saxton Llyod Outstanding Cmty. Svc. award Civic League of the Halifax Area, 2003; named Citizen of Yr., Boys and Girls Club of Volusia-Flagler Counties, 2000, Ctrl. Fla. Coun. Boy Scouts Am., 2001; established John C. Adams Cmty. Svc. award Embry-Riddle Aero U., 1990. Mem. Daytona Beach C. of C. (bd. govs. 1968-70, v.p. bus. and govt. 1970, pres. 1975, gen. campaign chmn. devel. fund drive 1984, Louis Fuchs Man of Yr. award 1985), Volusia County Insurors Assn. (pres. 1971-72), Fla. Assn. Ins. Agts. (bd. dirs. 1978-81), Coun. Ins. Agts. and Brokers (bd. dirs. 1989-93, bd. dirs. coun. of ins. agents and brokers 1993— co-chmn. exec. liasion com., mem. fin. and audit com. 1993-94, sec. 1994-95, treas. 1995-96, vice chmn. 1996-97, chmn. 1997-98, co-chmn. nominating com. 1998-99), Rotary (bd. dirs. 1989-91). Republican. Episcopalian. Home: 1616 S Peninsula Dr Daytona Beach FL 32118-4948 Office: Brown & Brown Inc PO Box 2412 220 S Ridgewood Ave Daytona Beach FL 32115

ADAMS, JOHN COOLIDGE, composer, conductor; b. Worcester, Mass., Feb. 15, 1947; s. Carl John and Elinore Mary (Coolidge) A. Studied with Leon Kirchner, Earl Kim, Roger Sessions, Harvard U., AB magna cum laude, 1969, MA, 1971. Former composer-in-residence, condr. San Francisco Symphony Orch., 1979—85. Artistic advisor, San Francisco Symphony Orch., from 1978, former composer-in-residence, San Francisco Symphony Orch.; dir., New Music Ensemble, from 1972-81; faculty mem., San Francisco Conservatory, 1972-83; composer-in-residence, Marlboro Festival, 1970; musical compositions include Electric Wake, 1968, Heavy Metal, 1971, American Standard, 1973, Kataadn, 1973, Onyx, 1976, Phrygian Gates, 1977, Shaker Loops, 1978; Onyx, Grounding, Sermon, Common Tones, 1979, Harmonium, 1980, Grand Pianola Music, 1982, Harmonielehre, 1985, Nixon in China, 1987 (Grammy for Best Contemporary Composition, 1989), The Death of Klinghoffer, 1991, Chamber Symphony, 1993 (Royal Philharmonic Soc. Music Awd. 1994), Naive and Sentimental Music, 1999, On The Transmigration of Souls, 2002, Short Ride in a Fast Machine, Tromba Lontana, Violin Concerto (Grawemeyer Awd. for Music 1995). Named to rank of Chevalier dans l'Ordre des Artes et des Lettres, French Ministry of Culture; recipient Cyril Magnin Awd. for Outstanding Achievement in the Arts, Calif. Gov's. Awd. for Lifetime Achievement in the Arts. Office: Boosey & Hawkes 24 E 21st St New York NY 10010 also: California Artists Mgt 41 Sutter St # 420 San Francisco CA 94104-4903*

ADAMS, JOHN DAVID VESSOT, manufacturing company executive; b. Ottawa, Ont., Can., Jan. 7, 1934; s. Albert Oliver and Estelle Priscilla (Vessot) A.; m. Dorothy Marion Blyth, June 27, 1959; children: Nancy, Joel, Louis. Student, Carleton U., 1950-51; B in Engring., McGill U., 1955; MBA, U. Western Ont., 1958. Registered profl. engr., Ont. Project engr. Abitibi Paper Co., Toronto, 1962-63, Cockshutt Farm Equipment Co. Ltd., Brantford, Ont., 1958-62, Can. Industries Ltd., Kingston, Ont., 1955-58; mgr. fin. analysis and planning Rio Tinto Zinc Group, London, 1963-66; mgr. adminstrn. and planning Can. Gypsum Co. Ltd., toronto, 1966-72; mgr. logistics and fin. Massey Ferguson Co. Ltd., Toronto, 1972-79; pres. Can. Spool & Bobbin Co. Ltd., Walkerton, Ont., 1979-88, Quality Performance Engring., Inc., 1988—. Cons. mfg., Hanover Ont. Mem. Assn. Profl. Engrs. Province Ont. (councillor), Gideons. Home: 386 14th Ave Hanover ON Canada N4N 2Y1 Office: Quality Performance Engring Inc 386 14th Ave Hanover ON Canada N4N 1W8 E-mail: qpe@bmts.com.

ADAMS, JOHN HURST, bishop; b. Columbia, S.C., Nov. 27, 1929; s. Eugene Avery and Charity A. (Nash) A.; m. Dolly Desselle, Aug. 25, 1956; children: Gaye Desselle, Jann Hurst;1 child, Madelyn Rose. AB, Johnson C. Smith Coll., 1948; STB, Boston U., 1951, STM, 1953; DD, Wilberforce U., 1956, Paul Quinn Coll., 1972. Ordained deacon A.M.E. Ch., 1948, elder A.M.E. Ch., 1952, bishop A.M.E. Ch., 1972. Pastor Bethel A.M.E. Ch., Lynn, Mass., 1950—52; prof. Wilberforce (Ohio) U., 1952—56; pres. Paul Quinn Coll., Waco, Tex., 1956—62, chmn. bd., 1972—; pastor 1st A.M.E. Ch., Seattle, 1962—68, Grant A.M.E. ch., L.A., 1968—72; 87th A.M.E. bishop 10th Dist. Tex. councils chs., 1972—; bishop 2d Dist., 1986—89; sr. bishop, 1989—92, 7th Episcopal Dist., Columbia, SC, 1992—. Author: Ethnic Education in Black Church, 1970. Bd. dirs. Nat. Coun. Chs., Nat. Conf. Black Churchmen, Nat. Bd. Black United Funds, People United to Save Humanity (PUSH), Tex. Coun. Chs. Named Man of Yr., B'nai B'rith, 1964, Urban League, Seattle, 1965. Mem.: Boulé, Alpha Phi Alpha. Office: 110 Pisgah Church Rd Columbia SC 29203-9351*

ADAMS, JOHN JILLSON, lawyer; b. Toledo, Nov. 12, 1934; s. Theodore Floyd and Esther (Jillson) A.; m. Barbara Barr, June 6, 1959; children: Leigh Ann Adams Miller, Leslie, Julie. BA, Denison U., 1956; LLB, U. Va., 1959. Bar: Va. 1959, D.C. 1967, U.S. Ct. Appeals (4th, 6th and D.C. cirs.), U.S. Supreme Ct. Assoc. Hunton & Williams, Richmond, Va., 1960-65, ptnr. Washington, 1967—; assoc. dir. Am. United for Separation of Ch. and State, Washington, 1965-66; spl. asst. U.S. State Dept., Washington, 1966-67. Served with USAR, 1959-65. Mem. ABA, Va. Bar Assn., D.C. Bar Assn. Baptist. Home: 8546 Georgetown Pike Mc Lean VA 22102-1206 Office: Hunton & Williams 1900 K St NW Washington DC 20006-1110

ADAMS, JOHN M. library director; b. Chgo., June 10, 1950; s. Merlin J. and Esther (Bohn) A.; m. Nancy Ileen Coultas, June 12, 1970; 1 child, Arwen Lee BA in English, U. Ill., 1972, M.L.S., 1973. Grad. asst. U. Ill. Libr., Urbana, 1972-73; libr.-reference Sherman Oaks Libr., L.A., 1973-75; libr. philosophy dept. L.A. Pub. Libr., 1975-77, head gen. reading svc., 1977-78; dir. Moline Pub. Libr., Ill., 1978-83, Tampa (Fla.)-Hillsborough County Pub. Libr. System, 1983-91; dir., county librarian Orange County (Calif.) Public Library System, 1991—. Dir. Tampa Bay Libr. Consortium, Fla., 1983-91, Santiago Libr. System, 1991—, chmn., 1999; mem. adv. com. on pub. librs. OCLC, 1992-95; bd. govs. Am. Rsch. Ctr. in Egypt, 2003—. Contbr. articles to profl. jours. Pres. Orange County chpt. Am. Rsch. Ctr. in Egypt, 2002—; bd. dirs. Planned Parenthood of Tampa, 1984. Recipient Frontier award ALA Mag., 1981; named Outstanding Young Man, Moline Jaycees, 1983. Mem. ALA (J.C. Dana award 1982, 93), Calif. Libr. Assn., Calif. County Librs. Assn., Orange County C. of C. Avocations: music; tennis. Office: Orange County Pub Libr 1501 E Saint Andrew Pl Santa Ana CA 92705-4930 E-mail: jadams@ocpl.org.

ADAMS, JOHN MARSHALL, lawyer; b. Columbus, Ohio, Dec. 6, 1930; s. H.F. and Ada Margaret (Gregg) A.; m. Janet Hawk, June 28, 1952; children: John Marshall, Susan Lynn, William Alfred. BA, Ohio State U., 1952; JD summa cum laude, 1954. Bar: Ohio 1954. Mem. Cowan & Adams, Columbus, 1954—55; asst. city atty. City of Columbus, 1955—56; mem. Knepper, White, Richards & Miller, 1956-63; practiced in Columbus, 1963—74; ptnr. Porter, Wright, Morris & Arthur, Columbus, 1975—91, of counsel, 1992—. Vice chmn. Ohio Bar Liability Ins. Co., 1990-93, chmn., 1994-2002, chair emeritus, 2002—; trustee Ohio Legal Ctr. Inst., 1976-81, Ohio Lawpac, 1980-89. Fellow Am. Coll. Trial Lawyers, Am. Bar Found., Ohio Bar Found. (trustee 1975-84); mem. ABA, Ohio State Bar Assn. (exec. com. 1975-80, pres. 1978-79, Ohio Bar medal 1994), Columbus Bar Assn. (bd. govs. 1970-76, pres. 1974-75), Lawyers Club (pres. 1968-69), 6th Cir. Jud. Conf. (life), Order of Coif, Grey Oaks Country Club (Naples, Fla.), Scioto Country Club, Masons, Delta Upsilon, Phi Delta Phi. Republican. Home: 2535 Canterbury Rd Columbus OH 43221-3081 Office: 41 S High St Columbus OH 43215-6101

ADAMS, JOHN PLETCH, orthopaedic surgeon; b. Ashburn, Md., Feb. 22, 1922; s. John William and Norm Emma (Pletch) A.; m. Nancy Ellen Murphy; 1 child, John P., Jr. BS, U. Mo., 1943; MD, Washington U., St. Louis, 1945; MPH, Harvard U., 1978. Diplomate Am. Bd. Orthopaedic Surgery. Intern Wilmington (Del.) Gen. Hosp., 1945-46; resident Duke U., Durham, N.C., 1949-52; prof. and dept. chmn. George Washington U. Sch. of Medicine, Washington, 1953-87, prof. emeritus, 1987—. Councilman Lewes, Del., 1990-92, Mayor, 1992-94; chmn. Gov.'s Coun. Long Term Care Facilities, 1990-94. Capt. USPHSR, 1946-49. Named Am.-Brit. Exchange fellow, 1959. Fellow Am. Acad. Orthopaedic Surgery, Am. Coll. Surgeons, So. Surgical Assn.; mem. Am. Orthopaedic Assn., Am. Soc. for Surgery of the Hand (pres. 1971), Cosmos Club, Alpha Omega Alpha (chmn. gov.'s coun. long term care facilities 1990-94). Republican. Episcopalian. Avocations: sailing, tennis. Home and Office: 804 Bay Ave Lewes DE 19958-1005

ADAMS, JOHN STEPHEN, geography educator; b. Mpls., Sept. 7, 1938; s. Edward Francis and Ellen Cecilia (Cullen) A.; m. Judith Estelle Nielsen, Sept. 1, 1962; children: John D., Ellen Anastasia, Martin Francis, David Joseph Cullen. BA, U. St. Thomas, 1960; MA, U. Minn., 1962, PhD, 1966. Rsch. asst., rsch. fellow Upper Midwest Econ. Study, Mpls., 1960-64; teaching asst. dept. geography U. Minn., Mpls., 1964-66, assoc. prof., then prof. geography, 1970—, now prof. geography, planning and pub. affairs, dir. Sch. Pub. Affairs and H.H. Humphrey Inst. Pub. Affairs, 1976-79, chmn. dept. geography, 1981-84, 92-93, 99—, Fesler-Lampert prof. Urban and Regional Affairs; asst. prof. geography Pa. State U., State College, 1966-70. Rsch. asst. N. Star Rsch. and Devel., Inc., Mpls., 1964; Fulbright prof. geog. Econ. U. Vienna, Austria, 1975-76; vis. prof. geography U. Wash., Seattle, 1979; vis. prof. geography and environ. engring. U.S. Mil. Acad., West Point, N.Y., 1990-91; vis. prof. geography and earth scis. Marie Curie-Sklodowska U., Lublin, Poland, 1997, mem. nat. adv. com. H.H. Humphrey N.-S. Fellowship Program, Inst. Internat. Edn., N.Y.C., 1979-81, coord. at U. Minn., 1981-87, 89-90; econ. geographer in residence Bank of Am., San Francisco, 1980-81; mem. exec. com. Nat. Com. Rsch. on 1980 census Social Sci. Rsch. Coun., N.Y.C., 1981-88; bd. dirs. Consortium of Social Sci. Assns., Washington, 1983-85, FVB Energy Inc.; mem. geography panel Coun. for Internat. Exchange of Scholars, Washington, 1983-85, chair, 1986, mem. Soviet-Eastern European panel, 1990-93; mem. geography div. adv. com. U.S. Bur. Census, Washington, 1985; Bush sabbatical fellow, 1987-88, Fulbright prof. geography Moscow State U., 1988. Author: (with R. Abler and P. Gould) Spatial Organization, 1971, (with Abler and K. Lee) A Comparative Atlas of America's Great Cities, 1976 (Geog. Soc. Chgo. award 1977), Housing America in the 1980s, 1987); editor: Contemporary Metropolitan America, 4 vols., 1976, Urban Policy Making and Metropolitan Dynamics, 1976, (with B. Van Drasek) Minneapolis-St. Paul People, Place and Public Life, 1993; mem. editl. bd. Geographia Polonica, Govt. and Policy, Urban Geography, Post-Soviet Geography and Economics. Bd. dirs. Newman Ctr., Mpls., 1983—88, 1994—2002. Sr. Scientist Rsch. fellow NSF, Berkeley, Calif., 1980-81. Mem. Assn. Am. Geographers (nat. sec. 1975-78, v.p. 1981-82, pres. 1982-83, honors award 1988, editorial bd. Annals), Nat. Coun. Geog. Edn., Mpls. Com. Fgn. Rels. Democrat. Roman Catholic. Avocations: photography, numismatics, gardening. Home: 2611 W 49th St Minneapolis MN 55410-1902 Office: U Minn Dept Geography 267 19th Ave S Minneapolis MN 55455-0499 E-mail: adams004@umn.edu.

ADAMS, JOHN W. state representative; b. Hopkinsville, Ky., June 29, 1936; m. Mary Helen Adams; children: John, William. BS, U. Ky., 1958, MS, 1960. Adv. U. Ky.; farmer, 1963—; bus. officer, registrar Ky. C.C., 1964—69; bus. mgr. Hopkinsville C. C., 1965—69; exec. dir. planning and devel. co. Pennyrile ADD, 1969—93; real estate property appraiser, 1997—2002; mem. Ky. Ho. of Reps., 1996—. Mem. Ky. Bd. Agr., 1983—87. Mem. Heart of Hopkinsville; deacon First Christian Ch.; bd. dirs. Hopkinsville C.C. 1st lt. USAF, 1960—63. Office: Capitol Annex Rm 451 D Frankfort KY 40601 Home: 6255 Huffman Rd 11 R6 Hopkinsville KY 42240

ADAMS, JOSEPH KEITH, lawyer; b. Provo, Utah, Apr. 3, 1949; s. Joseph S. and Marian (Bellows) A.; m. Myrle June Overly, Sept. 2, 1971; children: Derek J., Bret K., Stephanie, Julie K., Scott J., Laura. BA summa cum laude, Brigham Young U., 1973; JD, Harvard U., 1976. Bar: Utah 1976, U.S. Dist. Ct. Utah 1976, U.S. Tax Ct. 1983. Assoc. Van Cott, Bagley, Cornwall & McCarthy, Salt Lake City, 1976-82, shareholder, 1982-98; also bd. dirs. Van Cott, Bagley, et al, Salt Lake City, 1993-97, chmn. tax and estate planning sect., 1995-98; ptnr. Stoel, Rives, LLP, Salt Lake City, 1998—. Adj. faculty Brigham Young U. Law Sch., Provo, 1993. Co-author: Practical Estate Planning Techniques, 1990. Planned giving com. Restoration Cathedral Madeleine, Salt Lake City, 1991-93; pres. Utah Planned Giving Roundtable, Salt Lake City, 1994, Salt Lake City Estate Planning Coun.; planned giving com. U. Utah Hosp. Found., 1994; bd. dirs. Salt Lake C.C. Found., 1982-98; stake pres. LDS Ch. David O. Mackay scholar Brigham Young U., 1967-73. Fellow Am. Coll. Trust and Estate Counsel; mem. ABA (real property, probate and trust sect., taxation sect.), Utah State Bar (exec. com., past chmn. estate planning probate sect.), Harvard Alumni Assn. Utah (chair bd. dirs. 1980-90), Harvard Law Sch. Assn. Utah (vice chair). Republican. Mem. Lds Ch. Avocations: skiing, reading, golfing. Office: Stoel Rives LLP 201 S Main St Ste 1100 Salt Lake City UT 84111-4904 E-mail: jkadams@stoel.com.

ADAMS, KENNETH FRANCIS, automobile manufacturing company executive; b. Danbury, Conn., Feb. 4, 1946; s. Donald and Evelyn Trocola (Mulvihill) A.; m. Annette Talarico, Sept. 28, 1968; children: Amy, Ella Louise, Elizabeth. Student Mt. St. Mary's Coll., 1964-68. C.P.A., Conn. Mgr., Price Waterhouse & Co., Bridgeport, Conn., 1968-74; v.p. fin. and adminstrn., dir. Saab Cars USA, Inc., Norcross, Ga., 1974—. Served with USAR, 1968-74. Mem. AICPA, Conn. Soc. CPAs, Fin. Exec. Inst., Inst. Mgmt. Accts.. Roman Catholic. Office: Saab Cars USA Inc 4405 International Blvd Ste A Norcross GA 30093-3205

ADAMS, KENNETH ROBERT, gaming analyst, writer, consultant, historian; b. Carson City, Nev., Sept. 8, 1942; s. Maurice Adams and Gertrude Aloha (Wilson) Burke; children: John Anthony, James Joseph. Prin. Ken Adams and Assoc., Sparks, Nev., 1990—. Coord. gaming history series of the oral history program U. Nev., continuing edns. gaming mgmt. program adv. com., 1988-97, chmn., 1988. Co-author: Playing the Cards That Are Dealt, 1992, Always Bet on the Butcher, 1994, War Stories, 1995, Dwayne Kling: Luck in the Residue of Design, 2001; publ., assoc. editor: Nev. Gaming Almanac, 1991—, Nev. Gaming Directory, 1997—, The Adams Report. Chmn. mktg. com. Downtown Improvement Assn., 1994—, pres., 2001—; steering com., chmn. gaming com. Festival Reno, 1984-86; mem. adv. bd. Leadership Reno Alumni Assn., 1995-97. Mem. Internat. Platform Assn. Office: Ken Adams & Assocs 210 Marsh Ave Ste 103 Reno NV 89509-1698 Fax: 775-322-7806.

ADAMS, KENNETH STANLEY, JR., (BUD ADAMS), energy company executive, football executive; b. Bartlesville, OK, Jan. 3, 1923; s. Kenneth Stanley and Blanch (Keeler) Adams; m. Nancy Neville, Oct. 26, 1946. Student, Menlo Coll., 1940—41, U. Kans., 1941—44. Chmn. bd. Adams Resources & Energy, Inc., Houston, Travel House of Houston; owner Bud Adams Ranches, KSA Industries, Inc.; owner, pres. Houston Oilers, 1946—97, Tenn. Titans, Inc., Nashville, 1997—; owner Southwest Lincoln-Mercury, Inc. Mem. exec. bd. Sam Houston Area Coun. Boy Scouts Am.; trustee Profl. Football Hall of Fame. With USNR, 1943—46. Named Houston Salesman of Yr., 1960, Mr. Sportsman of 1961, Westerner of Yr., 1969. Mem.: Houston Geol. Soc., Houston Assn. Petroleum Landmen, Ind. Petroleum Assn. Am., Tex. Ind. Producers and Royalty Owners Assn., 100 Club of Houston (dir.), River Oaks Country Club, Petroleum Club, Houston Club, Sigma Chi (named Significant Sig 1963). Office: care Tenn Titans Baptist Sports Park 460 Great Circle Rd Nashville TN 37228-1404

ADAMS, LAURA ANN, critical care nurse; b. Thibodaux, La., Mar. 17, 1960; d. John Anthony Sr. and M. Elma Theresa (Dufrene) A. AD, Nicholls State U., Thibodaux, 1981, BSN, 1988. RNC, La.; cert. neonatal intensive care; NALS instr., 1999. Staff nurse South La. Med. Ctr. (now Leonard J. Chabert Med. Ctr.), Houma, 1981-89, 90-94, Earl K. Long Med. Ctr. (now LSU/Earl K. Long Med. Ctr.), Baton Rouge, 1992—. Mem.: Acad. of neonatal Nurses. Home: PO Box 356 Cut Off LA 70345-0356

ADAMS, LEE TOWNE, lawyer; b. Chatham, Ont., Can., July 12, 1922; came to U.S., 1923; s. Lee Eugene and Josephine Towne A.; m. Muriel Kathryn Stang, June 29, 1946; children: Nancy Louise, Carol Josephine, Jane Bertha. *Parents, Lee Eugene A. and Josephine Towne A. were Native Born U.S. citizens from pioneer Western New York families.* BA, U. Rochester, 1943; JD, Yale U., 1949. Atty. pvt. practice, Forestville, N.Y., 1949-72; mcpl. atty. various towns and villages, 1955-72; judge State of N.Y., Chautauqua County, 1972-93; retired, 1993—. *During WWII served aboard U.S. submarine USSRazorback in Pacific War Zone; Released to inactive duty 1946 as Lieut.* Trustee Presbytery of Western N.Y., 1970-76; dir., vice chmn. Presbyn. Homes N.Y., 1984-90. Lt. USN, 1943-46. Mem. VFW, Am. legion, Submarine Vets. WWII, Masons, Jamestown Consistory, Ismaila Temple, Phi Beta Kappa. Republican. Avocations: gardening, reading. Home: 21 Pearl St PO Box 306 Forestville NY 14062-0306

ADAMS, LILIANA OSSES, music performer, harpist; b. Poznan, Poland, May 16, 1939; came to U.S., 1978, naturalized, 1990; d. Sylwester and Helena (Koswenda) O.; m. Edmund Pietryk, Sept. 4, 1965 (div. Aug. 1970); m. Bruce Meredith Adams, Feb. 3, 1978. MA, Music Acad. Poznan, Poland, 1971. Prin. harpist Philharm. Orch. of Szczecin, Poland, 1964-72, Imperial Opera and Ballet Orch., Tehran, Iran, 1972-78; pvt. music tchr. Riyadh, Saudi Arabia, 1979-81; soloist Austrian Radio, 1981-86; solo harpist, pvt. tchr. harp and piano Antioch, Calif., 1986—. Music cons. Schs. and Librs., Calif., 1991—. Contbr. articles to profl. jours. Mem. Am. Fedn. of Musicians, Am. Harp Soc., Music Tchrs. Assn. Calif., Internat. Soc. of Harpers, U.K. Harp Assn., Internat. Harp Ctr. (Switzerland). Home: PO Box 233 Antioch CA 94509-0023 Fax: 925-778-0174. E-mail: harpliliana@comcast.com.

ADAMS, LOGAN G. small business owner; b. Roscoe, Tex., Sept. 28, 1940; d. Thomas William Graham and Ruth (Duncan) Thyng; children: Molly Ann Jackson-Riley, Amy Ruth Krause. BA, U. Houston, 1962. Cert. appraiser of personal property. Pres. The Specialists of the South, Inc., Panama City, Fla., 1982—. Instr. antiques and collectibles Gulf Coast C.C., 2002—. Mem.: Internat. Soc. Appraisers (scholarship trustee 1994—95, scholarship com. sec. 1994—95, chair designation and rev. 1996—98, distance edn. instr. 1999—, bd. dirs. 1999—, sec. bd. dirs. 1999—2001, Outstanding Mem. 1996, Svc. award 1998), C. of C. (Leadership Bay 1996). Avocations: underwater photography, scuba diving, reading. Office: The Specialists of the South Inc 544 E 6th St Panama City FL 32401-3066

ADAMS, LOWELL P. assistant principal, music educator; b. Clinton, Iowa, Sept. 29, 1952; s. Lowell Pershing and Agnes Catherine Adams; m. Valerie Ann Rodgers, Oct. 5, 1992; 1 child, Chritopher Lowell; m. Blythe Glover Tretick, May 25, 1981 (div. Oct. 15, 1990). MusM cello performance, No. Ill. Univ., DeKalb, Ill., 1976, MusB cello performance, 1975; dip., Hartt Sch. of Music, W. Hartford, Ct., 1981; attended, Aspen Music Sch., Aspen, Colo., 1977. Asst. prin. of cello Grand Rapids Sym., Grand Rapids, Mich., 1977—79; prin. cellist Lake George Opera Festival, Saratoga Springs, NY, 1981—; asst. prin. cello Fla. Orch., Tampa, Fla., 1981—; co-founder Spectrum Contemporary Ensemble, Tampa, Fla., 1989—; instr. of cello Univ. of Tampa, Tampa, Fla., 1989—; vis. prof. of cello Univ. of Mo., Columbia, Mo., 1994—95; replacement cellist St. Louis Sym., St. Louis, 1996—97. Bd. mem. Fla. Orch., Tampa, Fla., 2002—; spl. cons. Hillsborough County Sch., Tampa, Fla., 1990—94; chamber music tchr. Tampa Youth Orch., Tampa, Fla., 2000—. Recipient Talented Student Award, N. Ill. Univ./ DeKalb, Ill., 1970; fellow Grad. asst., 1975, Hartt Sch. of Music/ W. Hartford, Ct., 1979—81. Mem.: Am. String Tchr. Assoc., Fla. Cello Club (Exec. Bd. mem. 2000—03). Avocations: cello, performance, teaching, producer. Home: 1509 W Pk Lane Tampa FL 33603

ADAMS, MARGARET BERNICE, retired museum official; b. Toronto, Ont., Can., Apr. 29, 1936; came to U.S., 1948, naturalized, 1952; d. Robert Russell and Kathleen Olive (Buffin) A.; m. Alberto Enrique Sánchez-Quiñonez, Nov. 30, 1956 (div. 1960). AA, Monterey Peninsula Coll., 1969; BA, San Jose State U., 1971; MA, U. Utah, 1972. Curator ethnic arts Civic Art Gallery, San Jose, 1971; staff asst. Utah Mus. Fine Arts, Salt Lake City, 1972; lectr., curator Coll. Seven, U. Calif., Santa Cruz, 1972-74; part-time educator Cabrillo Coll., Aptos, Calif., 1973, Monterey Peninsula Coll., 1973-84; dir. U.S. Army Mus., Presidio of Monterey, 1974-83; chief. mus. br. Ft. Ord Mil. Complex, 1983-88. Guest curator Am. Indian arts Monterey Peninsula Mus. Art, 1975-88. Author: Indian Tribes of North America and Chronology of World Events in Prehistoric Pueblo Times, 1975, Historic Old Monterey, 1976; contbg. editor Indian Am., (exhibit catalogue) Writing on the Wall: WWII Patriotic Posters, 1987; contbr. articles to jours. Mem. native Am. adv. panel AAAS, Washington, 1972-78; mem. rev. and adv. com. Project Media, Nat. Indian Edn. Assn., Mpls., 1973-78; working mem. Program for Tng. Am. Indian Counsellors in Alcoholism Counselling and Rehab. Programs, 1972-74; mem. hist. adv. com. Montery County Bd. Suprs., 1987-89. Grad. fellow, dean's scholar U. Utah, 1972; dean's scholar Monterey (Calif.) Peninsula Coll., 1969, San Jose (Calif.) State U., 1971. Mem. Am. Anthrop. Assn., Am. Assn. Museums, Soc. Am. Archeology, Nat., Calif., Indian edn. assns. Home: PO Box 192 Cedar Ridge CA 95924-0192

ADAMS, MARVIN LEE, nuclear engineer, researcher; b. Seattle, Jan. 23, 1959; s. Alton Lee Adams and Charlotte Eloise (Breazeale) Nowell; m. Jennifer Lee Pearson, June 14, 1980; children: David Carlton, Michael Pearson, John Bell. BS in Nuclear Engring., Miss. State U., 1981; MSE in Nuclear Engring., U. Mich., 1984; postgrad. student, Los Alamos (N.Mex.) Nat. Lab., summer 1984; PhD in Nuclear Engring., U. Mich., 1986. Nuclear engr. TVA, Chattanooga, 1982; physicist Lawrence Livermore (Calif.) Nat. Lab., 1986-91; from asst. prof. to assoc. head dept. nuclear engring. Tex. A&M U., College Station, 1992—. Author profl. articles, papers and computational methods. Inst. Nuclear Power Ops. fellow, 1981, Montague Ctr. for Tchg. Excellence scholar, 1995, Univ. Faculty fellow, 2000; recipient Tenneco Meritorious Tchg. award, 1997. Fellow Am. Nuclear Soc. (mem. exec. com. math. and computations divsn. 1990-99, chair, 1997-98, mem. tech. program com. various meetings, named Most Outstanding U.S. Undergrad. Nuclear Engring. Student 1981); mem. Phi Kappa Phi, Tau Beta Pi, Alpha Nu Sigma. Office: Tex A&M U Dept Nuclear Engring 3133 TAMU College Station TX 77843-3133 E-mail: mladams@tamu.edu.

ADAMS, MARY A. retired assistant principal; b. Trimble, Tenn., June 20, 1933; d. Ira Sr. and Diora (Pierce) Bingham; children: Cheryl R. Gray, Gregory S. Adams. BS, Tenn. State U., 1954; MS, Hofstra U., 1975. Cert. math. tchr. N.Y., ednl. adminstrn. N.Y. Cartographic engr. aide TVA, Chattanooga, 1954—55; asst. to placement dir. Tenn. State U., Nashville, 1955 56; statistical programmer IBM, Poughkeepsie, N.Y., 1956-59; tchr. math. Bellmore-Merrick Sch. Dist., Merrick, N.Y., 1961-80, asst. prin., 1980-94; ret., 1994. Trustee Roosevelt (N.Y.) Pub. Lib., 1993—, Nassau C.C., Garden City, N.Y., 1995—; bd. dirs. Literacy Vols. Am., Nassau County chpt.; mem. adv. bd. Nassau County, Hempstead, N.Y., 1992—; committeewoman Roosevelt (N.Y.) Dem. Com., 1991-2001; covenor Citizens in Support of African-Am. Mus., Hempstead, N.Y., 1991—. Recipient Edn. award Women on the Job, Inc., 1993, Cmty. Svc. award March of Dimes, 1993, Chi Eta Phi sorority, 1994, Martin Luther King award Nassau County, 1994, Sojourner Truth Cmty. Svc. award Profl. & Bus. Women Am. Ctrl. Nassau chpt., Hon. Resolution Recognition award N.Y. Com. Col. Trustees, 2001, Gov.'s award for Excellence, State of N.Y., 2001; named Outstanding Citizen Assembly of State of N.Y., 2000. Mem. NAACP, Am. Ethnic Coalition, Tenn. State U. Nat. Alumni Assn. (pres. 1994-98, archivist 1998—), Roosevelt Dem. Club. (treas. 1991-2001), Nat. Coun. Negro Women. Democrat. Presbyterian. Avocation: music. Home: 200 E Pennywood Ave Roosevelt NY 11575-1209

ADAMS, MARY LOU, piano teacher; b. Feb. 22, 1934; BA, Goucher Coll., Balt., 1956; BMEd, Wichita State U., 1984. Nat. cert. music tchr. Historian Ctrl. Okla. Music Tchrs. Assn., Oklahoma City, 1985-90, notification chair, 1986—98, hospitality chair, 1999—2000. Tutor, Oklahoma City Literacy Coun., 1989—. Mem. Nat. Music Tchrs. Assn., Ctrl. Okla. Music Tchrs. Assn., Ladies Music Club Oklahoma City. Home and Office: 6316 NW 83d St Oklahoma City OK 73132-4633

ADAMS, MASON, actor; b. N.Y.C., Feb. 26, 1919; m. Margot Adams; children: Betsy, Bill. BA, U. Wis., 1940, MA in Theater Arts, 1941. Instr. Neighborhood Playhouse, N.Y.C. Title role in radio serial Pepper Young's Family, 1946-60; appearances in radio dramas including Inner Sanctum, Grand Central Station, Theatre Guild of the Air, Eternal Light; appeared in Broadway plays Get Away Old Man, Career Angel, Public Relations, The Sign in, Window Inquest, Tall Story, The Trial of the Catonsville Nine, Shadow of My Enemy; appeared in off-Broadway plays Danger: Memory, Ancestral Voices, The Day Room, Lake Hollywood, Ryan: An Interview, The Last of the Thorntons, You Know I Can't Hear You When the Water's Running; appeared in (TV series) Lou Grant, 1977-82 (Emmy nominee 1979, 80, 81), Morningstar/Eventingstar, Knight & Daye, Talk of the Town, The Shining Season, Who is Julia, Under Sige, The Deadliest Season, Solomon Northup's Odyssey, Revenge of the Stepford Wives, Murder One, The West Wing; ; films include The Final Conflict, F/X, Toy Soldiers, Son in Law, House Guest, Not of This Planet, Touch, Hudson River Blues. Mem. Century Assn. N.Y.C.

ADAMS, MENDLE EUGENE, minister; b. Bath County, Va., July 1, 1938; s. Earl and Margaret M. (Godsey) A.; m. N. Ruth Williams, Feb. 2, 1957; children: David Mendle, Brian Richard, Josef Wayne, Vicki Ruth. AB, Ind. Wesleyan U., 1967; MA in Religion, Christian Theol. Sem., 1969, postgrad., Aquinas Coll., 1977, Harvard U., 1978. Ordained to ministry Meth. Ch. as deacon, 1968, as min., United Ch. of Christ, 1981; orders accepted The Old Cath. Order, 1993; received into Order of St. Francis of The Orthodox Cath. Ch., 2002. Pastor Windfall (Ind.) Pilgrim Ch., 1960-63, Mt. Olive Meth. Ch., Marion, Ind., 1963-67, Mt. Comfort United Meth. Ch., Indpls., 1967-69, United Meth. Cir., Donnybrook, Maxbass, Lansford, N.D., 1979, Hope Congl. United Ch. of Christ, Granville, N.D., 1980-82, 1st Congl. United Ch. of Christ, McPherson, Kans., 1982-87; chaplain ecumenical campus Okla. State U., Stillwater, 1987-91; interim pastor Peace United Ch. of Christ, Loyal, Okla., 1988, 1st Christian Ch. (Disciples of Christ), Stillwater, 1990, Bethel Congl. Ch., Edmond, Okla., 1991; organizing min. High Point United Ch. of Christ, Boone County, Ky., 1991-99; pastor St. Peter's United Ch. of Christ, Cin., 1997—. Ednl. trips to Israel-Palestine, 1980, Nicaragua, 1983, The Philippines, 1985, Ukraine, 2000. Co-author: Touching Center Adventures in Christ Conscious ness, 1990, Medical-educational Trip to Ukraine, 2000. Mem. Ind. Solid Waste Com., 1976, Ind. and Okla. group for Equal Rights Amendment to the U.S. Constn., 1977, 1981; bd. dirs. McPherson Family Life Ctr., 1983—84, Interfaith Chapel, Cin./No. Ky. Internat. Airport, 1992—; chmn. com. McPherson Cmty. Nursing Home, 1984; mem. Gov.'s Task Force on AIDS, Okla., 1987—88, Gov.'s Cabinet on Children's Issues, 1988—91, Ecumenical Coun. on Maternal and Infant Health, So. Gov.'s Leadership Coun., 1989—91; cert. mediator Okla. Dispute Resolution, Supreme Ct. Okla., 1991; mem. Ind. Ho. of Reps., 1975—76, Chs. Uniting in Global Mission, 1992—; co-chmn. United Ch. Assembly of Greater Cin.; mem. Earth Spirit Rising Com., 1999; bd. dirs. IMAGO, Inc., 1999—2001. Recipient Honored Legislator citation Ind. Coun. Chs., 1976. Mem.: Masons (32d degree York Rite). Democrat. Home: 6113 Webbland Pl Cincinnati OH 45213-1405 *Upon being ordained Deacon, Bishop Richard Raines counseled, "The Divine call is where your abilities intersect human needs." I have sought to discern that call and respond in Christ's name; trusting in Providence for a spiritual legacy.*

ADAMS, MICHAEL FRED, university president, political communications specialist; b. Montgomery, Ala., Mar. 25, 1948; s. Hubert W. and Jean (Taylor) A.; m. Mary Lynn Ethridge, June 7, 1969; children: David Winston, Stephen Taylor. BA, Lipscomb U., 1970; MA, Ohio State U., 1971, PhD, 1973. Asst. prof. Ohio State U., 1973-74; chief of staff for Sen. Howard Baker, Washington, 1975-79; advisor to gov. State of Tenn., Nashville, 1981-82; v.p. Pepperdine U., Malibu, Calif., 1982-88; pres. Centre Coll. Ky., Danville, 1988-97, U. Ga., Athens, 1997—. Chmn. Nat. Assn. Ind. Colls. and Univs., 1995-96, Assoc. Colls. of South; mem. coun. for advancement and support of edn. NCAA Pres. Commn., 1992-94; chmn. Commn. on Colls. of So. Assn. Colls. and Schs.; vice chmn. task force that founded Coun. for Higher Edn. Accreditation; chair Am. Coun. on Edn., 2000. Author: Rhetorical Strategies of Howard Baker, 1973; contbr. articles to various publs. Pres. Circle K Internat., Chgo., 1970; nominee for U.S. Congress, Nashville, 1980; mem. site host com. 1984 Olympiad, L.A.; elder Christian Ch. Recipient Bronze Quill award Internat. Assn. Bus. Communicators, 1986, Excellence award Nat. Sch. Pub. Relations Soc., 1985; Ohio State U. grad. fellow, 1970-73 Mem. Young Pres. Orgn., Speech Comm. Assn., Ctr. for Study of Presidency, Univ. Club (N.Y.C.), Coun. Fgn. Relations. Republican. Avocations: golf, reading, travel. Office: U Ga Adminstrn Bldg Athens GA 30602

ADAMS, MICHAEL JOHN, retired air force non-commissioned officer; b. Buffalo, May 20, 1958; s. Raymond Francis and Ruth Margaret A.; m. Heidi Luise Gehling, June 5, 1998. AS in Bus. Adminstrn., Onondaga C.C., Syracuse, N.Y., 1980; AS in Comm. Ops. Tech., Community Coll. of the Air Force, 1983. Enlisted USAF, 1981, advanced through grades to tech. sgt., 1996; operator giant talk radio ops. 2006th Communications Group, SAC, Incirlik Air Base, Turkey, 1982-83; frequency mgr. combat crew communications 2019th Communications Squadron, Griffiss AFB, NY, 1983-85; frequency mgr. info. network USAF in Europe, Comiso Air Sta., Italy, 1985-86; supr. mil. affiliate radio sys. 2045th Comm. Group, Andrews AFB, Md., 1986-87, supr. ops. satellite comm., 1987-89, unit tng. mgr., 1989-91; sr. operator Global Command and Control Sta., 1956th Comm. Group, Yokota Air Base, Japan, 1991-93; mgr. unit tng. 374th Comm. Squadron (PACAF), Yokota AFB, Japan, 1993-95; unit tng. mgr. 374th Maintenance Squadron, Yokota AFB, Japan, 1995-96; non-commd. officer-in-charge tng. systems mgmt., distance lng., civilian pers. tng. 3d Comm. Squadron, Elmendorf AFB, Ala., 1996-99, interactive video teletng. coord., 1998-99; chief tng. systems mgmt. and Air Force testing proctor 31st Spl. Ops. Squadron, OSAN AB, 1999—2001; ret. USAF, 2001; statewide tng. asst. Parents Inc., Anchorage, 2001—. Vol. local food bank, Statewide tng. corrd. and contact sys. coord. Mem. VFW, Am. Soc. Tng. and Devel., Am. Assn. People with Disabilities, Am. Evaluation Assn., Alaska Info. Users Group (info. and referral adv. bd.), Air Force Sgts. Assn., Family Ctr. on Tech. and Disability, Paws with a Cause, Am. Legion, AK Child Abuse Prevention Network. Republican. Lutheran. Avocations: computers, fishing, hunting.

ADAMS, MICHAEL KEITH, retired military officer; b. Trappe, Md., Aug. 7, 1948; s. Maurice Tarbutton and Erva Harrison Adams; m. Rebecca J. BA, Salisbury State U., 1975; MS, U. Md., 1982. Cert. environ. profl. Acad. Bd. Cert. Environ. Profls. Environ. project mgr. Md. Environ. Svc., Annapolis, 1983-84; environ. engr. David Taylor R&D, Annapolis, 1984-90; commd. 2d lt. U.S. Army, 1970, advanced through grades to col., 1997; environ. officer Office Chief Army Res., Washington, 1990-95; environ. divsn. chief U.S. Army Res. Command, Atlanta, 1995-97; dep. asst. commandant U.S. Army Engr. Ctr., Ft. Leonard Wood, Mo., 1997-99; asst. chief of staff Mancuver Support Ctr.-AR, Ft. Leonard Wood, 1999—2002; ret.; program mgr. Battelle Meml. Inst., 2002—. Adj. faculty mem. Park U., Drury U., Webster U., Ft. Leonard Wood, 1998; program Mgr. Battelle Meml. Inst., 2002-. Mem. Army Engr. Assn. (named to Officer Candidate Sch. Hall of Fame 1998), Beta Beta Beta. Achievements include patents for low flow fluid separator. Avocations: hiking, camping, water skiing, skeet shooting. Home: 125 Cardinal Ridge Ct Fayetteville GA 30214 E-mail: adamsm@battelle.org.

ADAMS, NANCY ANN, retired school system administrator; b. Syracuse, N.Y., Mar. 20, 1932; d. Percival William Normand and Marion Vivian (Arnold) Taylor; m. Walter Adams, June 19, 1959 (div. 1970); children: Norman, Laurie. BEd, U. Miami, Coral Gables, 1957; MEd, Fla. Atlantic U., 1969; PhD, U. Wyoming, 1981. Cert. tchr., Fla. Tchr. Broward County Schs., Ft. Lauderdale, Fla., 1957-62, rsch. asst., 1969-73, counselor high sch. srs., 1973-79, counselor adults, 1980-81, coord. adult program, 1981-94. Mem. Fla. Adminstrs. Adult Edn. (vice chmn. 1984-86, state chmn. 1994-96), Adult and Cmty. Educators of Fla. (bd. dirs. 1988-2000), Am. Assn. Adult and Continuing Edn., Fla. Sch. Counselor Assn. (v.p. 1987), Adult and Cmty. Educators of Fla. (bd. dirs.). Democrat. Home: 2880 NE 14th St #213 Pompano Beach FL 33062-3653 E-mail: nancyannbr@aol.com.

ADAMS, NANCY R. nurse, military officer; b. Rochester, N.Y., Apr. 20, 1945; BSN, Cornell U.; MSN, Cath. U. Am.; grad., U.S. Army War Coll. Advanced through grades to maj. gen. U.S. Army, 1991; comdr. William Beaumont Army Med. Ctr., S.W. Regional Med. Command; chief Army Nurse Corps; asst. surgeon gen. for pers. and comdr. U.S. Army Ctr. for Health Promotion and Preventive Medicine; lead agt. TRICARE Region VII U.S. Army; chief nurse Frankfurt Army Regional Med. Ctr., 1987—89; staff asst. profl. affairs and quality assurance Office of Asst. Sec. of Def., asst. inspector gen., dir. intensive care nursing course; nursing cons. Army Surgeon Gen., 1989—91; commd. Nurse Corps U.S. Army, 1967—; commdg. gen. Tripler Army Med. Ctr., Hawaii, 1998—. Decorated Legion of Merit, Meritorious Svc. medal, Def. Svc.medal. Fellow: Am. Acad. Nursing; mem.: ANA, Am. Orgn. of Nurse Execs., Assn. of Mil. Surgeons of the U.S., Sigma Theta Tau. Office: Tripler Army Med Ctr 1 Jarrett White Rd Honolulu HI 96859-5000

ADAMS, NORMAN, artist, educator; b. London, Feb. 9, 1927; s. Albert Henry Adams and Winifred Elizabeth Rose; m. Anna Teresa Butt, 1947; two children. Student, Royal Coll. Art, London, 1948-51. Tchr. St. Albans, Maidstone, Hammersmith Art Schs., 1952-61; head painting Manchester Coll. Art and Design, England, 1962-71; prof. fine art U. Newcastle Upon Tyne, 1981-86; keeper of schs. Royal Acad. Arts, London, 1986-95, prof. painting, 1986-99, prof. emeritus, 1999—. Public collections include Tate Gallery, London, Scottish Nat. Gallery Modern Art, Edinburgh, Ulster Mus., Belfast, No. Ireland, Nat. Gallery New Zealand, Wellington; commns. include St. Mary's Roman Cath. Ch., Manchester, 1995, St. Anselms Ch., Kensington, London, 1972, Our Lady of Lourdes Roman Cath. Ch., Milton Keynes, 1975; illustrator: (written by Glyn Hughes) Alibis and Convictions, 1978, (written by John Milner) A Decade of Painting, 1971-81, 1981, (written by A. Adams) Angels of Soho, 1988, Island Chapters, 1991, Life on Limestone, 1994. Avocations: art, music, literature. Home: Butts Horton-in-Ribblesdale Settle N Yorkshire BD24 0HD England Office: 6 Gainsborough Rd Chiswick W4 INJ England

ADAMS, PATRICK O. career officer; b. Cape Gireadeau, Mo. m. Jean Marie Means; children: Patrick Jr., Christine. BS in Pub. Adminstrn., U. Mo., 1968; MS in Internat. Rels., Auburn U., 1983. Commd. 2d lt. USAF, 1968; advanced through grades to brig. gen., 1995; personnel officer Air U., Maxwell AFB, Ala., 1969-71; aide-de-camp mil. assistance and adv. group Hdqs. Command, Tehran, Iran, 1971-72; personnel officer De Nang Air Base, Republic South Vietnam, 1972-73, Udorn Royal Thai Air Base, Thailand, 1973; chief field activities Air Force Mil. Personnel Ctr., Randolph AFB, Tex., 1991, mem. air staff tng. program, 1973-75; personnel officer office asst. for col. assignments Hdqs. USAF, Washington, 1975-78, dir. svc., 1995—; personnel officer office asst. for col. assignments Air Force Manpower and Personnel Ctr., Randolph AFB, Tex., 1978-80, asst. exec., exec. officer to comdr., 1980-82; chief mil. personnel Tinker AFB, Okla., 1983-84; exec. officer to comdr. in chief Mil. Airlift Command, Scott AFB, Ill., 1985-87, dir. personnel programs, asst. sr. officer matters, 1988-90; comdr. 3440th Tech. Tng. Group Lowry Tech. Tng. Ctr., Colo., 1987-88; dir. personnel Air Mobility Command, Scott AFB, Ill., 1993-94, spl. asst. to comdr., 1994-95; chief Mil. Liaison Team Bulgaria European Command, Sofia, 1994; dir. manpower and personnel Joint Staff/J1, Washington, 1995—. Decorated Legion of Merit with oak leaf cluster, Airman's medal, Bronze Star medal. Office: Joint Staff/J1 Rm 1E948 1000 Joint Staff Pentagon Washington DC 20318-1000

ADAMS, PAUL WINFREY, lawyer, business executive; b. Ozark, Ark., July 10, 1913; s. Robert Montague and Myrtle (Johnson) A.; m. Louise Forbes Barnes, Mar. 21, 1942; children: Sally B. (Mrs. T. V. O'Connor), Thomas Fuller, Edward Montague. BS, Trinity Coll., Hartford, Conn., 1935; JD, Yale, 1938. Bar: Conn. 1938, N.Y. 1964. Practiced in, Hartford, 1938-42, 45-50; asst. dean Yale Law Sch., New Haven, 1956-58; pvt. practice, New Haven, 1958-64; pvt. practice N.Y.C., 1964-72, various locations, Conn., 1972-95. Counsel Mfrs. Assn. Conn., 1939-42; pres. The Norden Labs. Corp., 1949-55. Pres. Pope-Brooks Found., 1949-89; trustee Trinity Coll., 1958-64, St. Margaret's Sch., 1967-71; founding trustee Southborough Sch., 1971-74; trustee Stone Found., 1967-92; pres. Atlantic Round, Inc., 1976-92. Served as lt. USNR, 1942-45. Dubbed Knight of White Rose by Pres. of Finland, 1993. Mem. Mountain Lake Colony (Fla.), Country Club (Fairfield, Conn.), N.Y. Yacht Club (N.Y.C.), Cruising Club of Am., N.Am. Sta. of Royal Scandinavian Yacht Clubs, Nylandska Jaktklubben (hon., Finland), Kongelig Dansk Yacht Club (hon., Denmark), Gothenburg Royal Yacht Club (hon.), Royal Norwegian Yacht Club (hon.), St. Barth Yacht Club (hon.). Home: PO Box 832 Lake Wales FL 33859-0832*

ADAMS, PETER FREDERICK, university president, civil engineer; b. Halifax, N.S., Can. m. Barbara Adams, Oct. 11, 1957; 3 sons. B.Eng., N.S. Tech. Coll., 1958, M.Engr., 1961; PhD, Lehigh U., 1966. With Internat. Nickel Co. Can., 1958-59, Dominion Bridge Co., 1974-75; mem. faculty U. Alta., Edmonton, 1960-89, prof. civil engring., 1971-89; dean Faculty of Engring., 1976-84; pres. Ctr. for Frontier Engring. Research, 1984-89, Tech. U. N.S., Halifax, 1989-92, Can. Inst. Petroleum Industry Devel. (now Can. Petroleum Inst.), Edmonton, Alta., Can., 1992—; dir. Churchill Corp., 1993—. Lectr. in field. Author: (Krentz & Kulak) Canadian Structural Steel Design, 1973, (Krentz & Kulak) Limit States Design in Structural Steel, 1977. Past pres. Aspen Gardens Community League;past chmn. Salvation Army Red Shield Appeal. Fellow Can. Soc. Civil Engring. (Sanderson award 1986), Can. Acad. Engring., Engring. Inst. Can.; mem. ASCE (A.B. Anderson award 1986), Internat. Assn. Bridge & Structural Engring. (hon.), Can. Stds. Assn., Toastmasters (past pres.). Office: Canadian Inst Petroleum 4220 98th St Edmonton AB Canada T6E 6AI

ADAMS, PHYLLIS CURL, nursing educator; b. Houston, Sept. 15, 1947; d. Kenneth H. and Helen (Phillips) Curl; m. Todd E. Adams, Aug. 28, 1982. BSN, Dillard U., 1969; MSN, Ohio State U., 1972; EdD, Tex. So. U., 1989; postmasters FNP, Tex. Woman's U., 1995. RN; cert family nurse practitioner. Charge nurse The Meth. Hosp., Houston, 1969-71, practitioner, asst. mgr., 1981—90, staff nurse, 1990—95; faculty coord. Columbus (Ohio) Tech. Inst., 1973-81; coord., asst. prof. Sch. Nursing U. Tex. Health Sci. Ctr., Houston, 1990-95, spl. asst. to pres. for Office of Campus Diversity, 1993—95; asst. prof. U. Tex. Sch. Nursing, Arlington, 1995—2001, asst. clin. prof., 2001—. FNP, Ft. Worth, 1997—2001, Cmty. Partnership of Tarrant County, Ft. Worth, 2001—; dir. FNP program U. Tex. Sch. Nursing, Arlington, 2000—. Contbr. articles to profl. jours. Mem. ANA (mem. adv. bd. ethics and human rights), Tex. Nurses Assn. (bd. dirs. 1994-95, mem. dist. 4), Minority Faculty Assn., Sickle Cell Assn. Ft. Worth (bd. dirs.), TEXGENE (mem. ethics and human rights com.), State Tex. Bd. Nursing (mem. adv. coun. on edn.), Nat. Black Orgn. Nurses, Sigma Theta Tau, Phi Delta Kappa. Avocations: frog collecting, aerobics, reading, skeet. Home: 1225 Chinkapin Pl Flower Mound TX 75028-3229 Office: U Tex-Arlington Sch Nursing PO Box 19407 411 S Nedderman Dr Arlington TX 76019 E-mail: pcadams@uta.edu.

ADAMS, QUENTIN MARK, neurologist; b. San Antonio, Jan. 23, 1956; s. Ronald Dean and Marjorie Loree Adams; m. Carol Louise Adams, Mar. 12, 1982, children: Melanie, Quentin, Dylan. BS in Chem. Engring., U. Tex., Austin, 1978; MD, U. Tex., San Antonio, 1985; MBA, Tex. Christian U., 2000. Diplomate Am. Bd. Neurology. Process design and computer engr. Dow Chem. Co., Freeport, Tex., 1978—81; intern in internal medicine Tex. Tech. U., Lubbock, 1985—86; resident in neurology U. Tex. Southwestern Med. Ctr., Dallas, 1986—89, clin. assoc. prof., 1989—; neurologist Arlington, Tex., 1989—. Med. dir. Rehab. Care Therapy Ctr., Arlington, 1992—96; healthcare analyst EIF at Tex. Christian U., 1999—2000; clinic attending, neurology U. Tex., Southwestern, 1989—; guest spkr. Peripheral Neuropathy Assn., Ft. Worth, 1999—2001. Contbr. articles to profl. jours. Asst. coach Colleyville (Tex.) Baseball, 1996—, Colleyville Basketball. Recipient 1st place rsch. award, Tex. Neurol. Soc., 1987. Mem.: Am. Acad. Clin. Neurophysiology, Nat. Headache Found., Am. Acad. Neurology. Avocations: reading, coaching, sculpture museums, security analysis. Office: 3150 Matlock Rd # 405 Arlington TX 76015

ADAMS, RANALD TREVOR, JR., retired air force officer; b. Ft. Sill, Okla., Mar. 7, 1925; s. Ranald Trevor and Mary (King) A.; m. Jeannette Malloy Chichester, May 3, 1947; children: Ranald T. III, Mary M., Jeannette M. Student, Va. Poly. Inst., 1941-43; BS, U.S. Mil. Acad., 1946; MS, George Washington U., 1966. Commd. 2d lt. USAF, 1946, advanced through grades to

lt. gen., 1978; served in Korean conflict, 1950-51, 1968-69; comdr. 408 Fighter Group, 1969-71; asst. dep. chief staff ops. N.Am. Air Def. Command, 1971-73; comdr. 26 N.Am. Air Def. Command Region/Air Div. Luke AFB, Ariz., 1973-74; dep. insp. gen. inspection and safety Norton AFB, Calif., 1974-77; dir. InterAm. Def. Coll., Ft. McNair, D.C., 1977-78; chmn. Interam. Def. Bd., Washington, 1978-81, ret., 1981; cons., 1981-91. Decorated Legion of Merit, Meritorious Service medal, D.S.M., D.F.C., Air medal. Mem. Air Force Assn., Order Daedalians (flight capt. 1973) Home and Office: 1002 Emerald Dr Alexandria VA 22308-2626

ADAMS, RENEE BLEDSOE, retired elementary school educator; b. Louisville, Mar. 7, 1947; d. Charles Henry and Irene (Russell) Bledsoe; m. Neil Douglas Adams, Apr. 13, 1968; children: Krista Lynn, Shawnda Renee. BA, U. Ky., 1970; MA, Murray State U., 1980. Cert. rank I tchr., Ky. Tchr. 1st grade Anderson County Sch., Lawrenceburg, Ky.; tchr. sci. kindergarten through 6th grades Paducah Ind. Sch., Ky., ret. Presenter workshops on space and environ. edn., performance assessment. Publ. com. Childhood Edn. mag. Mem. NEA, Assn. Childhood Ednl. Internat. (pres. Ky. chpt. 1987-89, 92-94, pres. coun. 1998-2000), Assn. Childhood Edn. (pub. com. 1988-91), Nat. Sci. Tchr. Assn., Ky. Edn. Assn., Ky. Instrnl. Results Info. System (sci. cons. adv. com.), Ky. Ednl. Reform Act (assessment fellow), Partnership in Reform Initiative in Sci. and Math. (primary level curriculum devel. specialist), Alpha Delta Kappa, Phi Delta Kappa.

ADAMS, REX M. telecommunications executive; b. Peoria, Ill., July 27, 1961; s. Kenneth E. and Ann (Meils) A.; m. Ritsuko Bates, May 25, 1987; 1 child, Miles. BS, U.S. Mil. Acad., 1983; MBA, Harvard U., 1990. Cons. Monitor Co., Cambridge, Mass., 1990-94; pres. Bell South Corp., Atlanta, 1994-96; v.p. Bell South Long Dist., Atlanta, 2000. Capt. U.S. Army, 1983-88. Baptist. Home: 12155 Oak Hollow Way Alpharetta GA 30005-7280

ADAMS, RICHARD EUGENE, aerospace engineer, project manager; b. Medford, Mass., Sept. 22, 1959; s. Eugene Henry and Martha Caroline (Brown) A.; m. Shari Renée Schneider, Apr. 29, 1960; children: Brian David, Robyn Lynn. BS in Aeronautical Engring., Embry-Riddle Aeronautical U., 1983; MS in Engring Mgmt, Drexel U., 1995; grad., U.S Naval Test Pilot Sch., 2000. Aerospace engr. Naval Air Devel Ctr., Warminster, Pa., 1983-96; project mgr. Naval Warfare Ctr. Aircraft Divsn., Patuxent River, Md., 1996—. Recipient Navy Meritorious Civilian Svc. award 1999. Mem. AIAA (chmn. Lighter-than-Air tech. com. 1985-87), Assn. Unmanned Vehicle Syss. Achievements include contributions to development of unmanned air vehicles including Predator and Global Hawk systems, expertise in lighter than air vehicle design. Office: NAVAIR 47123 Buse Rd Patuxent River MD 20670-1606 E-mail: adamsre@navair.navy.mil.

ADAMS, RICHARD GEORGE, writer; b. Newbury, Berkshire, Eng., May 9, 1920; s. Evelyn George Beadon and Lilian Rosa (Button); m. Elizabeth Acland, Sept. 26, 1949; children: Juliet Vera Lucy, Rosamond Beatrice Elizabeth. MA, Oxford U., 1948. With Brit. Home Higher Civil Svc. Ministry Housing and Local Govt., 1948-74; asst. sec. Dept. Environ., 1968-74. Writer-in-residence U. Fla., 1975, Hollins Coll., 1976. Author: Watership Down, 1972 (Guardian award Children's Lit. 1972, Carnegie Medal 1972), Shardik, 1974, (with Max Hooper) Nature Through the Seasons, 1975, The Tyger Voyage, 1976, The Adventures and Brave Deeds of the Ship's Cat on the Spanish Main: Together with the Most Lamentable Losse of the Alcestis and Triumphant Firing of the Port of Chagres, 1977, The Plague Dogs, 1977, (with Max Hooper) Nature Day and Night, 1978, Introduction to Faithful Ruslan, 1979, The Unbroken Web: Stories and Fables, 1980, Voyage Through the Antarctic, 1982, The Girl in a Swing, 1980, Maia, 1985, The Bureaucats, 1985, A Nature Diary, 1985, The Legend of Te Tuna, 1986, Traveller, 1988, The Day Gone By, 1990, Tales from Watership Down, 1996, The Outlandish Knight, 2000; editor, contbr. Occasional Poets, 1986. Served with Brit. Army, 1940-46. Fellow Royal Soc. Lit., Royal Soc. Arts; mem. Royal Soc. for Prevention of Cruelty to Animals (former pres.). Mem. Ch. Of Eng. Home: 26 Church St Whitchurch Hampshire England

ADAMS, RITA FUERST, management and fundraising consultant; b. Cleve., June 13, 1955; d. Raymond Lawrence and Mary Antoinette (Palumbo) Fuerst; m. Richard M. Adams, Mar. 10, 2000. BS in Journalism, Ohio U., 1976; MBA, Capital U., Columbus, Ohio, 1984. V.p. The Bill Heim Co., Granville, Ohio, 1980-95, pres., 1995-96; dir. devel. Am. Coun. Internat. Edn., Washington, 1996-97; pres. Charitable and Philanthropic Mgmt. Coun., Boston, 1997—. Trustee Ohio 4-H Found., 1992—95. Mem.: CIVICUS, Nat. Ctr. for Nonprofit Enterprise, Assn. Fundraising Profls. (bd. dirs. Mass. chpt. 1998—2001, chair govt. rels. 1998—), Orgn. Women in Internat. Trade, Nat. Soc. Fundraising Execs. (pres. 1993—95, trustee Hills of Ohio chpt. 1993—96, gov. rels. com. 1995, cert., Fuerst outstanding Cmty. Leader award named in her honor 1996). Roman Catholic. Avocations: travel, reading, golf, ice skating. Office: Charitable and Philanthropic Mgmt Counsel 257 Bolton St South Boston MA 02127-1303 Fax: 617-268-4961. E-mail: rita1st@worldnet.att.net.

ADAMS, ROBERT, music educator; b. Phila., Mar. 3, 1960; s. George Joseph and Catherine Grace Adams; m. Carol Costantino, July 8, 1989; children: Samantha, Benjamin. BA, Glassboro (N.J.) State Coll., 1984, MA, 1992. Cert. tchr. music K-12 N.J. Music tchr. Glen Landing Mid. Sch., Blackwood, NJ, 1987—94; band dir. Triton Regional H.S., Runnemede, NJ, 1995—. Musician Dept. Def./USO Tour, 1981, Statue of Liberty 100th Anniversary Ceremony, 1986. Author: Philadelphia Orchestra Education Advisory Council's Teachers Guide, 1997; dir.: (musical) West Side Story, 1998; singer: (opera) The Love for Three Oranges, 1988. Fireman Stratford (N.J.) Fire Co. Number One, 1978—82. Mem.: NEA, Phila. Orch. Ednl. Adv. Com., Olympic Conf. Band Directors Assn. (commr. 1998), South Jersey Band and Orch. Dirs. Assn., Music Educators Nat. Conf., N.J. Edn. Assn., Nat. Judges Assn./Tournament of Bands. Home: 231 Country Ln Mount Laurel NJ 08054 Office: Triton Regional HS 250 Schubert Ave Runnemede NJ 08078 Office Fax: 856-939-4724. Personal E-mail: maestroattriton@yahoo.com.

ADAMS, ROBERT BARRY, pathologist; b. Birmingham, Ala., July 24, 1928; m. Jean Glaze, Sept. 2, 1950; children: Jeanmarie, Robert Barry Jr. BS in Chemistry & Biology, Birmingham So., 1950; MD, Med. Coll. Ala., 1956. Rotating intern Lloyd Noland Hosp., Fairfield, Ala., 1956-57; pathology resident Bapt. Meml. Hosp., Memphis, 1957-59; mem. med. corps U.S. Army, San Antonio, 1959-61; instr., prof. Med. Coll. Ala., Birmingham, 1961-64; dir. pathology lab. Bapt. Med. Ctr., Montgomery, Ala., 1964-79, St. Margaret's Hosp., Montgomery, Ala., 1972—; med. dir. Ala. Reference Lab., Montgomery, 1972—, Ala. Reference Lab./LabSouth, Montgomery, 1995—. Pres. Ala. Assn. Pathologists, Birmingham, 1969-71, Med. Coll. Ala. Alumni Assn., 1993-95; edn. leader Sch. Med. Tech. Bapt. Hosp., St. Margaret's Hosp., Auburn U. Montgomery, Ala. Reference Lab., 1968—, Pres., bd. trustees Judson Coll., Marion, Ala., 1985-88; pres. Nat. Coll. Ala. Alumni, Birmingham, 1993-95; sec.-treas. Montgomery County Med. Soc., 1990-92. Recipient Algernon Sidney Sullivan award Judson Coll., 1985. Mem. AMA, Am. Soc. Clin. Pathology, Am. Assn. Blood Banks (inspector 1963-86), Am. Soc. Nuc. Medicine, Coll. Am. Pathologists, Med. Soc. Montgomery County, Cornerstone Soc., Alpha Omega Alpha. Baptist. Office: Lab Corp Am 543 S Hull St Montgomery AL 36104-4609

ADAMS, ROBERT BRERETON, lawyer; AB, Boston Coll., 1961; JD, NYU, 1965. Bar: N.Y. 1965. Dep. county atty. Nassau County, N.Y., 1965-67; assoc. Cullen & Dykman, 1968-70; v.p., asst. gen. counsel Chase Manhattan Corp., 1971-86, sr. v.p., dep. gen. counsel, 1986-97; ptnr. Kelley, Drye & Warren, N.Y.C., 1998—. Office: Kelley Drye & Warren 101 Park Ave Fl 30 New York NY 10178-0062

ADAMS, ROBERT EDWARD, journalist; b. Geneseo, Ill., Apr. 27, 1941; s. Horace Mann and Florence (Beidelman) A. BS, U. Ill., 1963. Reporter Champaign-Urbana Courier, 1962-64; reporter, city staff St. Louis Post-Dispatch, 1966-72, Washington corr., 1972-93, asst. Washington bur. chief, 1981-83, Washington bur. chief, 1983-93. Washington commentator Sta. KMOX, St. Louis, 1984— ; founding mem. St. Louis Journalism Rev., 1970 Recipient reporting award Nat. Civil Service League, 1975, polit. reporting award Lincoln U., Jefferson City, Mo., 1984, Raymond Clapper Meml. award for Washington Corr., 1987, citation for excellence Overseas Press Club, for series on Soviet Union, 1988; co-recipient Fgn. Corr. award Overseas Press Club Am., 1984, Nat. Headliner award, 1986. Mem. Nat. Press Club, Internat. Platform Assn., Com. to Protect Journalists, Washington Ind. Writers, The Gridiron Club, Sigma Delta Chi (Outstanding Young Reporter award St. Louis chpt. 1969). Roman Catholic. Home: Apt 707 2500 Wisconsin Ave NW Washington DC 20007-4504 Office: 529 14th St NW Washington DC 20045-1000 E-mail: badams@lwv.org.

ADAMS, ROBERT MCCORMICK, anthropologist, educator; b. Chgo., July 23, 1926; s. Robert McCormick and Janet (Lawrence) Adams; m. Ruth Salzman Skinner, July 24, 1953; 1 child, Megan. PhB, U. Chgo., 1947, MA, 1952, PhD, 1956; DSc (hon.), U. Pitts., 1985, Dartmouth Coll., 1989; LHD (hon.), Hunter Coll., CUNY, 1986, Coll. William and Mary, 1989, Brandeis U., 1992; LD (hon.), Harvard U., 1992; PhD (hon.), U. Copenhagen, 2002. Archaeol. field tng. in, Jarmo, Iraq, 1950—51, 1953; field studies history irrigation and urban settlement, 1956—77, 1956—77; reconnaissance and excavation ancient Mayan settlement patterns, 1958—61; mem. faculty dept. anthropology, Oriental Inst. U. Chgo., 1955—84, assoc. prof. Oriental Inst., 1961—62, prof., 1962—84, dir. Oriental Inst., 1962—68, 1981—83, dean div. social scis., 1970—74, 1979—80, provost, 1982—84; sec. Smithsonian Instn., Washington, 1984—94; Homewood prof. dept. anthropology and near ea. studies Johns Hopkins U., 1984—94. Adj. prof. U. Calif., San Diego, 1993—; fellow Inst. for Advanced Study, Berlin, 1995—96; resident dir. Baghdad Sch., Am. Schs. Oriental Rsch., 1968—69; chmn. assembly behavioral and social scis. NRC, 1972—76, chmn. commn. on behavioral and social scis. and edn., 1987—93. Author: The Evolution of Urban Society, 1966; author: (with H.J. Nissen) The Uruk Countryside, 1972; author: Heartland of Cities, 1981, Paths of Fire: An Anthropologist's Inquiry into Western Technology, 1996; editor (with C.H. Kraeling): City Invincible: A Symposium on Urbanization and Cultural Development in the Ancient Near East, 1960; editor: (with C.S. Schelling) Corners of a Foreign Field, 1979; editor: (with N.J. Smelser and D.J. Treiman) Behavioral and Social Science Research: A National Resource, 1982; editor: Trends in American and German Higher Education, 2002. Trustee Nat. Opinion Rsch. Ctr., 1970—94, Nat. Humanities Ctr., 1976—83, Russell Sage Found., 1978—91, Santa Fe Inst., 1984—, Am. U. Beirut, 1989—94, Morehouse Coll., 1989—94, German Am. Acad. Coun., 1993—99. Recipient UCLA medal, 1989, Great Cross of Vasco Nuñez de Balboa, Panama, 1993, Gold medal, Am. Inst. Archaeology, 2002, award of merit, Field Mus., 2003. Fellow: AAAS, Mid. East Studies Assn., Am. Acad. Arts and Scis., Iraqi Acad. (assoc.), Am. Anthrop. Assn.; mem.: NAS, Coun. Fgn. Rels., Am. Philos. Soc., German Archaeol. Inst., Soc. Am. Archaeology (Disting. Svc. award 1996), Sigma Xi. E-mail: rmadams@ucsd.edu.

ADAMS, ROBERT WAUGH, state agency administrator, economics educator; b. Johnstown, Pa., Oct. 26, 1936; s. Robert Waugh and Mary Louise (Pyle) A.; m. Karen Day, June 13, 1964; children: Robert W. and Tara Anne Adams Mason. BS in Acctg., Pa. State U., 1958; MBA, U. Louisville, 1967. Acct., comptroller, v.p. lending Citizens Fidelity Bank, Louisville, Ky., 1959-77; dir. fin., planning, and from dep. exec. dir. to exec. dir. Ky. Housing Corp., Frankfort, 1977-96; owner Adams Consulting Co., Louisville, 1996—. Past pres. Bank Adminstrv. Inst., 1966, Planning Exec. Inst., 1970, Fin. Exec. Inst., 1974. Bd. dirs. Habitat for Humanity, Ctr. for Non Profit Excellence. Capt. U.S. Army Infantry, 1958-62. Mem. Louisville Boat Club (past pres.). Republican. Roman Catholic. Home and Office: Adams Cons 5210 Tamerlane Rd Louisville KY 40207-1160

ADAMS, ROGER C. lawyer; BA cum laude, Bowdoin Coll., 1966; JD, Boston Coll., 1969. With criminal divsn. U.S. Dept. Justice, 1972-93, counsel to dep. atty. gen., 1993-97, acting pardon atty., 1997, pardon atty., 1998—. Mem. Maine Bar Assn. Office: US Dept Justice 4th Fl 500 1st St NW Fl 4 Washington DC 20530-0001

ADAMS, RONALD EMERSON, army officer, federal agency administrator; b. Lancaster, Pa., Dec. 28, 1943; s. Robert Harvey and Margaret May (Freeman) A.; m. Ardeelou Ann Christy, Sept. 6, 1970. MBA, Pa. State U., 1972; postgrad., Command and Gen. Staff Coll., Ft. Leavenworth, Kans., 1974-75; grad. student, Nat. War Coll., Washington, D.C., 1984—85; cert. in advanced mgmt., Carnegie-Mellon U., 1989. Commd. 2d lt. U.S. Army, 1965, advanced through grades to lt. gen., 1998; various field assignments, 1965-77; mil. asst., aide Office Sec. Army, Washington, 1977-81; bn. comdr. 2d Inf. Divsn., Republic of Korea, 1981-82; chief aviation br. U.S. Army Mil. Pers. Ctr., Alexandria, Va., 1982-84; brigade comdr. 25th Inf. Div., Schofield Barracks, Hawaii, 1985-87; exec. asst., chief of staff U.S. Pacific Command, Camp Smith, Hawaii, 1987-89; asst. div. comdr. 101st Airborne Div., Ft. Campbell, Ky., 1989-91; dir. requirements Hdqrs. Dept. Army, Washington, 1991-94; comdg. gen. U.S. Army Aviation Ctr. and Ft. Rucker, Fort Rucker, Ala., 1994-96; asst. dep. chief staff for ops. and plans hdqs. U.S. Army, 1996-98, dep. comdr./chief staff Allied Land Forces Europe, 1998-99; comdr. Stabilization Force Bosnia and Herzegovina, 1999-2000; dep. commdr. Joint Hdqs. Control Europe, 2000—01; commdg. gen. U.S. Army NATO, 2000—01; ret. U.S. Army, 2002; mem. sr. exec. svc. Dept. Def., Washington, 2003—. Decorated D.S.M. (2), Def. Disting. Svc. medal (2), Bronze Star (3), Def. Superior Svc. medal, Legion of Merit (5); recipient Tenn. Outstanding Achievement award, 1991, German Gold Cross of Honor, 2000, French Légion d'Honneur, 2002. Methodist. Avocations: sailing, golf, reading. Office: Secretary of Defense 4B673 Pentagon Pentagon DC 20301

ADAMS, RONALD G. middle school educator; b. Boston, July 7, 1948; s. Russell Lawrence and Alice Gertrude (LeCorn) A.; m. Patricia Marie Sullivan, Mar. 15, 1950; children: Ronald Patrick, Michael Joseph, Kevin Russell. BS, U. Mass., 1975; MEd, Cambridge Coll., 1992. Cert. tchr. English, reading, adult basic edn., Mass. Tchr. English Quincy (Mass.) Pub. Sch., 1975-81, tchr. grade 7, 1983—; tchr. grade 7/8 Lincoln (Mass.) Pub. Schs., 1981-83. Mem. adv. bd. Mass. Carnegie Coun.: Turning Points, Dept. Edn., Mass., 1991-93; founding mem. Internat. Space Educators Coun., Huntsville, Ala., 1992-93; on-air moderator PBS Annenberg documentary series Primary Sources in Teaching American History, 2001. Prodr. TV documentary Quincy Shipbuilding, 1989 (award Dept. Edn. 1990); co-author: (booklet) Not Me, I Can Handle It, 1985 (Gov.'s award 1986); cons. TV series A Century of Women, TBS, 1994 (A&E Cable award 1992). Founder Winnie the Welder Day, City of Quincy, 1991-93; coach Houghs Neck Women's Softball League, Quincy, 1980-85; vol. Cub Scouts, Weymouth, Mass., 1989-93; mem. edn. steering com. Amnesty Internat., Somerville, Mass., 1989-93; mem. adv. bd. U.S. Naval Shipbldg. Mus., Quincy, 1992-93. Recipient Nat. Ednl. award Cable in Classroom, 1992, George Washington medal Freedoms Found., 1992, Young Prodr.'s award Continental Cablevision, 1992, A World of Difference Tchr. award Anti-Defamation League, 1994, Giraffe award, Reebok Internat. Youth-in-Action Human Rights award, 1995, Minn. Advocates for Human Rights award, 1997, Domestic Partnership award US AID, 1998, Anti-defamation League's Global Activism award 1998, 99, Darryl Williams Human Rights Leadership award Northeastern U., 1999, Bearer of Light award Union of Am. Hebrew Congregations, 1999, Hero Among Us award Boston Celtics, 2000, Global Edn. award The Peace Corps, 2000; named Tchr. of Yr., Mass. Dept. Edn., 1992, Nat. Consumers League Trumpeter award, 1998, Citizen of the Yr. 2000, Quincy Sun Newspaper. Fellow Mass. Acad. Tchrs. (history coord. 1992-93), Boston Writing Project; mem. NEA (Human and Civil Rights award 2000Applegate/Dorros Peace and Global Edn. award 2000), Nat. State Tchrs. of Yr., Nat. Coun. Social Studies, Nat. Coun. Tchrs. English, Mass. Tchrs. Assn. (Human Rights award 1991), Quincy Edn. Assn. (exec. bd. 1980-81). Avocation: N.Y. Giants football. Home: 8 Coolidge Ave Weymouth MA 02188-3605 Office: Broad Meadows Middle Sch 50 Calvin Rd Quincy MA 02169-2516

ADAMS, ROSE ANN, nonprofit administrator; b. McHenry, Ill., Apr. 4, 1952; d. Clemens Jacob and Marguerite Elizabeth (Freund) A. BS in Edn., Ill. State U., 1974; MEd, U. Ark., 1979. Supt., exec. dir. Clinton County Children's Services, Wilmington, Ohio, 1979-81; dir. ednl. and adult svcs. Bost Human Devel. Svcs., Ft. Smith, Ark., 1981-87; adminstrv. officer Cen. Ark. Devel. Coun., Benton, 1987; adminstrv. officer, interim Head Start dir., dir. resource devel. Community Orgn. Poverty Elimination Pulaski, Lonoke Counties, Little Rock, 1987-93; exec. dir. So. Early Childhood Assn., 1993-94; sr. cons. Earl Moore and Assocs., Little Rock, 1994-2000, exec. v.p., 1999-2000; exec. dir. Ark. Cmty. Action Agys. Assn., Little Rock, 2000—. Coord. White House Conf. on Families, 1980; mem. Task Force Child Abuse; charter mem. Am. Lung Assn.; active Welfare adv. Bd., Clinton County, 1979—81; pres., v.p. Ark. Single Parent Scholarship Fund.; trustee Morris Found., Multiple Sclerosis Soc.; active Home Econs. Extension Svcs. Adv. Com., 1979—81; mem. adv. bd. U. Ark. Women's Ctr., 1979; chair Ark. Health Promotion Coalition; vice-chair Pulaski County Local Planning Group; chair Ark. Com. on Women's Concerns; mem. adv. com. Ark. Mentors; Ark. Hunger Coalition, 2001—. Named one of Outstanding Young Women of Am., 1982. Mem.: Am. Bus.Women's Assn. (Woman of Yr. Avant Garde chpt. 1992), U. Ark. (Little Rock) Alumni Assn. (bd. dirs., v.p. 1999—). Avocations: antique collection, sports, music. Home: Sonata Trl # 1 Little Rock AR 72205-1632 Office: Ark Cmty Action Agys Assn Ste 1020 300 S Spring St Little Rock AR 72201 E-mail: radams@acaaa.org.

ADAMS, ROSEMARY KATHLEEN, publishing executive; b. Decatur, Ga., July 14, 1965; d. Kenneth N and Irene Tuttle Adams. BA, Dominican U., River Forest, Ill., 1987; MA, DePaul U., Chgo., 2002. Project editor Nat. Restaurant Assn., Chgo., 1987—90; dir. of pubs. Chgo. Hist. Soc., 1990—. Author: (book) What George Wore and Sally Didn't: Surprising Stories from America's Past; editor: A Wild Kind of Boldness: A Chicago History Reader, (mag.) Chgo. History. Mem.: Am. Hist. Assn., Orgn. of Am. Historians. Democrat. Roman Catholic. Office: Chicago Historical Society 1601 N Clark St Chicago IL 60614

ADAMS, RUTH-ANNE, chef; Grad., Culinary Inst. Am. Pastry chef Michela's, 1993; mem. staff The Blue Rm.; chef Rialto, 1994, sous chef, 1995—99; chef Red Clay, Casablanca, Cambridge, Mass. Office: Casablanca 40 Brattle St Cambridge MA 02138*

ADAMS, S. CHARLES, lawyer, speaker, writer, financial consultant, radio and television commentator; b. Bklyn., July 10, 1934; s. Charles Joseph and Rose (Scala) A.; m. Ann Shepherdson, Aug. 3, 1957 (div. Feb. 1973); children: Mark, Scott, David, Christopher; m. Mary Jo Comstock, Dec. 8, 1990. BCE, Rensselaer Poly. Inst., 1955; MS, U. Conn., 1961; JD, U. Miami, 1968. Bar: Fla 1968, U.S. Dist. Ct. (so. dist.) Fla. 1969, U.S. Tax Ct. 1990, U.S. Ct. Appeals (11th cir.) 1974, U.S. Supreme Ct., 1974; registered profl. engr., N.Y., Conn. Pres. Motivation Cons., Miami, Fla., 1965-68; v.p. Exposition Corp., Miami, 1969-73; gen. counsel City of Pompano Beach, Fla., 1972-76; mcpl. judge Broward County, Fla., 1974-76; corp. counsel Five Star Industries, Hialeah, Fla., 1976-80; chmn., CEO Atlantic Svcs. Group, Ft. Lauderdale, Fla., 1977-86; prin. S. Charles Adams & Assocs., Ft. Lauderdale, 1986—. Bd. dir. Good Steward Ministries, The Legacy Found., Planned Giving Roundtable, Minute Man Found., In God We Trust; ; investment advisor U.S. SEC; gen. coun. Planned Giving Found., 1993—, Morgan, Howen & Co., 1993—; bd. regents nat. Heritage Found., 2003—. Author: Your Fiscal Fitness; creator radio commentary Your Fiscal Fitness; host talk show The Bus. Round Table; pub. Timely Tax and Money Strategies Newsletter, Fin. Strategies in Estate Planning, Preventing the Second Am. Revolution, One Nation Under God, Living in Paradise, The Repeal of the Income Tax, Preserving the Form of Govt. Established by the Constitution. Bd. dirs., pres. Planned Giving Coun., 1993-96, Fla. Bar Mgmt. Sect.; del. White House Conf. on Small Bus., Washington, 1986; apptd. to joint Presdl.-Congl. Com. by Pres. Reagan, 1984; pres. Broward Planned Giving Coun., 1994-95, Broward Estate Planning Coun., endowment com. Broward Performing Arts Ctr., planned giving com. United Way, 1992—, fin. com. Honda Classic, 1988—; bd. dirs. Minute Man Found., 1995—, In God We Trust Ministries. Recipient Pres.'s award Broward County Bar Assn., 1975. Mem. Nat. Soc. Fundraising Execs. (bd. dirs. 1991—), North Broward County Bar Assn. (treas., bd. dirs.), Broward County Mcpl. Judges Assn., Nat. Inst. Mcpl. Law Officers (chmn. ethics com.), Rensselaer Poly. Inst. Alumni Assn. (pres. South Fla. chpt.), Christian Stewardship Assn., Christian Legal Soc. Republican. Avocations: golf, tennis, racquetball, sailing, travel. Office: Adams & Assocs PO Box 30488 Fort Lauderdale FL 33303-0488 E-mail: salljoo@juno.com.

ADAMS, SARAH VIRGINIA, psychotherapist, family counselor; b. San Francisco, Oct. 23, 1955; d. Marco Tulio and Helen (Jorge) Zea; children: Mark Vincent, Elena Giselle, Johnathan Richard. BA, Calif. State U., Long Beach, 1978, MS in Psychology, 1980; MA in Christian Leadership, 1997; PsyD in Clin. Psychology, Fuller Sem., Pasadena, 1996, MA in Christian Leadership, 1997; PsyD in Clin. Psychology, Fuller Sem., 2000. Lic. marriage, family, child counseling. Tutor math. and sci., Montebello, Calif., 1979-82; behavioral specialist Cross Cultural Psychol. Corp., L.A., 1979-80; psychol. asst. Legal Psychology, L.A., 1980-82, Eisner Psychol. Assocs., L.A., 1982-83; assoc. dir. Legal Psychodiagnosis and Forensic Psychology, L.A., 1982-83; adminstrv. dir. Diagnostic Clinic, Calif., 1983-85; dir. Diagnostic Clinic of West Covina, Calif., 1985-87; owner Adams Family Counseling Inc., Calif., 1987—; with Health Group Psychol. Svcs., 1994—; domestic violence counselor Baldwin Park Counseling, 1996—2001; battered wives counselor Wings, 1996—2002; facilitator, vol., 1995—; facilitator in domestic violence Redlands, 2002—; program dir. Alternative Choices Together Batterers Counselor, 2002—. Tchr. piano, Montebello, 1973-84; ins. agent Am. Mut. Life Ins., Des Moines, 1982-84; DV counselor Baldwin Park Counseling, 1996-2001, Wings-Shelter for Battered Wives, 1996-, ALternatives Choices Together, Treatment Ctr. Batterers, 2002-. Fellow Am. Assn. Marriage and Family Therapists, Am. Psychol. Assn.; mem. NAFE, Calif. Assn. Marriage and Family Therapists, Calif. State Psychol. Assn., Calif. Soc. Indsl. Medicine and Surgery, Western Psychol. Assn., Psi Chi, Pi Delta Phi. Republican. Roman Catholic. Avocations: piano, creative writing, drawing, collecting coins. Office: 260 S Glendora Ave Ste 107 West Covina CA 91790-3041

ADAMS, SCOTT, cartoonist; b. Windham, N.Y. s. Paul and Virginia Adams. MBA in Econs., Hartwick Coll., 1979. Engr. Pacific Bell, San Ramon, Calif., 1986—95; cartoonist United Features Syndicate, 1989—. Cartoon, Dilbert, syndicated in 1,550 newspapers in 35 countries. Office: c/o United Media 200 Madison Ave New York NY 10016-3903

ADAMS, SCOTT LESLIE, accountant; b. Seattle, Nov. 23, 1955; s. Brock and Mary Elizabeth (Scott) A.; m. Crystal Hood, Aug. 7, 1978; children: Brock, Justin, Betsy, Brooke. BS in Acctg. magna cum laude, Jones Coll., 1984. CPA. Dist. dir. The Scott Co., Washington, 1972-75; pres. Slade Corp., Greenbelt, Md., 1977-80; shift supr. U.S. Ho. Reps., Washington, 1977-82; acct. Comprehensive Bus. Svcs., Jacksonville, Fla., 1984-85; prin. Contemporary Bus. Svcs., Jacksonville, 1985—, Tax Consultants, P.A., 1991—. Pres. Small Bus. Assocs., Jacksonville; v.p. Adams Mgmt. Svcs. Chmn. fin. com. deacon. Westside Bapt. Ch., Jacksonville, 2000—; treas. Jacksonville West Camp, Gideons U.S.A., 1987—. Mem. AICPA, Nat. Soc. Pub. Accts., Nat. Soc. Tax Practitioners, Fla. Inst. CPA's, Nat. Assn. Accts., Small Bus. Network, Jacksonville C. of C. Republican. Avocations: swimming, tennis. Home: 4984 Ortega Forest Dr Jacksonville FL 32210-8112 Office: Contemporary Bus Svcs 4070 Herschel St Ste 1 Jacksonville FL 32210-2249 E-mail: scott@cbsjax.com.

ADAMS, STEPHEN BERNARD, finance educator, consultant; b. Redwood City, Calif., Aug. 22, 1955; s. Victor Willard Adams and Lucille Ann Peterson; m. Madeleine Michele Bergman, June 25, 1988. AB, U. Calif., Davis, 1977; MBA, U. Mich., 1982; PhD, Johns Hopkins U., 1993. Valuation analyst Am. Appraisal Assocs., Walnut Creek, Calif., 1985—88; asst. prof. mgmt. Salisbury U., Franklin P. Perdue Sch. Bus., Md., 2002—. With Bus. History Conf., Columbia, Md., 1993—, ptnr., 2002—; vis. asst prof. Rutgers Bus. Sch., Newark, 2000—02. Author: Mr. Kaiser Goes to Washington: The Rise of a Government Entrepreneur, Manufacturing the Future: A History of Western Electric. Recipient W. Turrentine Jackson award, Am. Hist. Assn., 1994; fellow Gordon Cain fellow, Chem. Heritage Found., 1998—99; grantee, Henry J. Kaiser Family Found., 1991. Mem.: Bus. History Conf., Acad. Mgmt., Beta Gamma Sigma, Omicron Delta Epsilon. Office: Salisbury U 1101 Camden Ave Salisbury MD 21801-6860 Office Fax: 410-546-6208. E-mail: sbadams@salisbury.edu.

ADAMS, STEPHEN M. publishing company executive; BSBA, Mount St. Mary's Coll. Formerly, sr. v.p. fin. and adminstrn. Macmillan Pub.; former CFO Primedia Info. Inc.; sr. v.p., CFO, treas. Commonwealth Bus. Media, 2000—. Office: Commonwealth Bus Media 400 Windsor Corp Ctr 50 Millstone Rd Ste 200 East Windsor NJ 08520-1415*

ADAMS, STEWART LEE, special education educator; b. Moline, Ill., June 18, 1949; s. Robert Earl Jr and Henrietta Harriet (Jones) Adams; m. Ann Edwards, Oct. 12, 1985 (div. Nov. 1989). AA, Blackhawk Jr. Coll., Moline, Ill., 1969; BA, Ill. State U., 1971, MA, 1974, EdD, 2003. Cert. teacher elem K-9, spl. edn. K-12, educable mentally handicapped, learning disabled, behavior disabled. Spl. edn. tchr. Rock Island (Ill.)-Milan Sch. Dist. 41, 1972—; Master tchr., 1998—. Chair, vice chair Ill State Adv Coun Spec Educ, Springfield, 1984—92; Ill cong contact # 17 NEA, Washington, 1982—94; peer monitor spec educ Ill State Bd Educ, Springfield, 1992—; vpres Community Serv Options, Rock Island-Mercer County, 1994—97, pres, 1997—2002; app mem State Adv Coun Educ Children with Disabilities, 1996—99. Mem disabled transit comt Quad Cities Mass Transit Dist, Davenport, Iowa, 1993—; panel mem Gov Thompson's Educ Summits, Springfield, Ill., 1989—90. Mem.: NEA (caucus mem spec educ 1980—94), ASCD, Rock Island Educ Asn (vpres 1992—94, secy 1998—2000), Ill Educ Asn (chair region 18 1982—88, mem Ill Polit Act Comt Educ 1986—88, bd dirs, grassroots polit. activist for Region 18). Democrat. Presbyterian. Avocation: genealogy. Home: 3709 31st Ave Rock Island IL 61201-6548 E-mail: stewart.adams@mchsi.com.

ADAMS, SUSAN LOIS, music educator; b. New Albany, Ind., July 27, 1946; d. Frank Mitchell Sr. and Dorothy Stalker Adams. BA, Smith Coll., 1968; MS in Edn., Ind. U., 1970, postgrad., 1994. Cert. tchr. Ind. Tchr. Lafayette (Ind.) Sch. Corp., 1969—70, New Albany-Floyd County Consol. Sch. Corp., 1970—. Mem. editl. com. (hymnal) Chalice Hymnal, 1995; co-editor: (hymnal companion) Chalice Hymnal Worship Leaders' Companion, 1998. Elder Ctrl. Christina Ch., New Albany, 1996—98, Ctrl. Christian Ch., New Albany, 2000—02. Recipient Honored Laywoman, Commn. Women-Ind. Region Christian Ch., 1998. Mem.: Ind. Music Educators, Music Educators Nat. Conf., Nat. Assn. Disciple Musicians (pres. 1988, chair workshop 1989, 2001). Mem. Christian Ch. (Disciples Of Christ). Avocations: travel, reading.

ADAMS, THOMAS LYNCH, JR., lawyer; b. Fayette County, Ky., Nov. 22, 1941; s. Thomas Lynch and Amanda (Keith) A.; m. Anne Randolph, Aug. 13, 1974 (div. 1992); children: Thomas Lynch III, Randolph T., Alexander K., Andrew D. BA in History, U. Va., 1963; JD, Vanderbilt U., 1970. Bar: Ky. 1970, D.C. 1970, Tenn. 1970. Appellate atty. U.S. Dept. Justice, Washington, 1970-72; minority counsel U.S. Senate Commerce Commn., Washington, 1972-75; legal counsel SBA, Washington, 1975; asst. gen. counsel FTC, Washington, 1975-77; with govt. rels. Rep. Steel Corp., Washington, 1977-83; dep. gen. counsel U.S. EPA, Washington, 1983-86, asst. adminstr., presdl. appointee, 1986-89; ptnr. Dechert, Price & Rhoads, 1989-93; environ. dir. Internat. Paper, 1993; counsel to pres. America's Clean Water Found., 1994-95; of counsel Perkins Coie, Washington, 1995-2000; pres. Oxygenated Fuels Assn., Washington, 2000—02, sr. advisor dept. energy, asst. sec. environ. mgmt., 2002—. Lt. (j.g.) USNR, 1963-67. Mem. ABA, Ky. Bar Assn., D.C. Bar Assn., Met. Club, Beta Theta Pi.

ADAMS, THOMAS MERRITT, lawyer; b. St. Louis, Sept. 27, 1935; s. Galen Edward and Chloe (Merritt) A.; m. Sarah McCardell Davis, June 6, 1959; children: Mark Merritt, John Harrison, William Shields, Thomas Bondurant. AB, Washington U., St. Louis, 1956, JD, 1960; postgrad., London Sch. Econs., 1957; LLM, George Washington U., 1966. Bar: Mo. 1960, Calif. 1971. Atty. SEC, Washington, 1964-66; asst. dir., asst. gen. counsel Investment Bankers Assn., Washington, 1966-68; pres. Transamerica Investment Mgmt., 1969-80; ptnr. Lanning Adams & Peterson, 1980—. Author: State and Local Pension Funds, 1968; contbr. articles to profl. jours. Chmn. Salina (Kans.) Community Ambassador program, 1961. Served to capt. USAF, 1960-63. Decorated Air Force Commendation medal. Mem. Phi Beta Kappa. Episcopalian. Office: Lanning Adams & Peterson 11777 San Vicente Blve #750 Los Angeles CA 90049-5067

ADAMS, THOMAS TILLEY, lawyer; b. Orchard Park, N.Y., Oct. 9, 1929; s. Floyd Tilley and Clara Elizabeth (Potter) A.; m. Virginia Rives Smith, Sept. 1, 1956; children: Julia, Janet, Claire, Douglas. BA, U. Buffalo, 1951; JD, Cornell U., 1957. Bar: N.Y. 1957, U.S. Ct. Appeals (2d cir.) 1962, U.S. Supreme Ct. 1962, Conn. 1964. Tchr. Lake Shore Cen. Sch., Angola, NY, 1953-54; assoc. Davies, Hardy & Schenck, N.Y.C., 1957-63; prin. Gregory & Adams P.C., Wilton, Conn., 1963—2001, of counsel, 2002—. Lectr. Cornell U. Law Sch., Ithaca, N.Y., 1962-65, emeritus mem. adv. coun., 1990—; adj. assoc. prof. law Fordham U., N.Y.C., 1973-76; adviser Dana Fund Internat. and Comparative Legal Studies, Toledo, 1976-91; assoc. bd. dirs. Union Trust Co., Stamford, Conn., 1982-94; mem. adv. bd. Norwalk Savs. Soc., 1993-97. Town atty. Town of Wilton, 1966-71; pres. Five Town Found., Norwalk, Conn., 1983-85, trustee, 1989-91; chmn. bldg. com. Wilton High Sch., 1966; bd. dirs. Woodcock Nature Ctr., Wilton-Ridgefield, Conn., 1997-99, trustee Norwalk Hosp., 1974, Wilton Library Assn., Inc., 2000-2001. Capt. USAF, 1951—53, Korea. Recipient Silver Beaver award Boy Scouts Am., 1980, Disting. Alumnus award Cornell Law Sch., 1990. Mem. ABA, Am. Judicature Soc. (dir. 1991-92), Norwalk-Wilton Bar Assn. (pres. 1990), Stamford-Norwalk Regional Bar Assn. (bd. dirs. 1991-93), Conn. Bar Assn. (ethics com. 1970-75, 92-93, mem. coun. bar pres.'s 1988-90), N.Y. Bar Assn., Assn. Bar City of N.Y., Silver Spring Country Club (gov. 1998—, asst. sec. 2003—), Cornell Club (N.Y.), Phi Delta Phi. Episcopalian. Home: 55 Deer Run Rd Wilton CT 06897-1204 also: Rogers Rock Clb Ticonderoga NY 12883 Office: Gregory & Adams PC 190 Old Ridgefield Rd Wilton CT 06897-4023 Fax: 203-834-1628.

ADAMS, THOMAS WALTON, corrections official; b. Midland, Mich., Apr. 15, 1947; s. Lawrence Walton and Elizabeth (Miller) A.; m. Karen Lynn Perry. BS with honors, Mich. State U., 1973, MS, 1987. Probation agt. 75th Dist. Ct., Midland, 1973—2003; cmty. corrections coord. Midland County, 2003—. Mem. Midland County Alcohol Svcs. Bd., 1975-78, Midland-Gladwin County Community Mental Health Bd., 1978-87, chmn. 1980-82; mem. allocation panel Midland County United Way, 2002—; mem. adv. Mt. Pleasant Regional Ctr. for Devel. Disabiities, 1988-89; active Act 511 Bd., 1990—; adv. bd. Midland County Jail, 1991-93; bd. dirs. FACE, 1995—; mem. violence/gang task force Midland County, 1998—; co-chair Domestic Violence Coordinating Coun., Midland County, 2000—. Named One of Outstanding Young Men Am., 1982; recipient Liberty Bell award, Midland Bar Assn., 1983. Mem.: Am. Correctional Assn., Sigma Chi, Alpha Phi Sigma. Avocations: stereo equipment, music, photography. Home: 5900 Lamplighter Ln Midland MI 48642 3180 Office: Adult Probation Courthouse Midland MI 48640

ADAMS, THURMAN G., JR., state legislator; b. Bridgeville, Del., July 25, 1928; s. Thurman and Bessie Adams; m. Hilda McCabe, 1952; children: Brent, Lynn, Polly. BS, U. Del., 1950. Mem. Dist. 19 Del. Senate, Dover, 1972—, majority leader, 1999—, pres., 2003—, T.G. Adams & Sons, Inc. Named to Wall of Fame, U. Del. Mem. Lions. Home: PO Box 367 Bridgeville DE 19933-0367 Office: PO Box 1401 Dover DE 19903-1401*

ADAMS, TODD PORTER, financial and investment advisor; b. Nyack, N.Y., Oct. 11, 1955; s. Edmond Robert and Georgina (Porter) A.; m. Catherine Elizabeth Jarboe, Dec. 26, 1982 (div. Dec. 1985); 1 child, Danielle Elyce; m. Janine Marilyn Leduc, Jan. 29, 1994 (div. Jan. 2003). BS, St. Thomas Aquinas Coll., 1977; MBA, SUNY, Buffalo, 1981. CFP. Acct. trainee Allied Chem., Syracuse, N.Y., 1977-78, from acct. to supr. of acctg. Buffalo, 1978-80; pvt. practice fin. cons. Buffalo, 1980-81; account exec. Dean Witter Reynolds, Cape Coral, Fla., 1981-82, E.F. Hutton & Co., Cape Coral, 1982-85; v.p. investments Advest, Inc., Ft. Myers, Fla., 1985-90; rep. Linsco/Pvt. Ledger, Ft. Myers, 1990—; v.p. Mills-Price & Assoc., Inc., Ft. Myers, 1997-99, pres., 1999—. Investment and inf. commentator WINK-TV, 1989—94. Chmn. Jr. Olympic Torch Run, Lee County, Fla., 1990. Mem. Inst. CFPs, Nat. Assn. Investors Corp., Am. Assn. Ind. Investors, Assn. MBA Execs., Kiwanis (life, v.p. house South Ft. Myers chpt. 1984—, Kiwanian of Yr. award 1983, 95, 99). Republican. Presbyterian. Avocations: all sports, stamp and coin collecting. Office: Mills-Price & Assoc Inc 6710 Winkler Rd Ste 1 Fort Myers FL 33919-7235

ADAMS, TRACEY LINDEN, artist, educator; b. L.A., Nov. 2, 1954; d. Edwin Robert and Berna Berry Linden; m. John Stockton Adams, June 25, 1983. BA, Mt. St. Mary's Coll., 1978; MusM, New Eng. Conservatory, Boston, 1980. One-woman shows include U. Calif., Santa Cruz, 1995, Monterey (Calif.) Peninsula Coll., 1996, Winfield Gallery, Carmel, Calif., 1998, Andrea Schwartz Gallery, San Francisco, 1999, Kathryn Markel Fine Arts, N.Y.C., 2000, 2002, Bryant Street Gall., Palo Alto, 2001-03, Carson-Masuoka Gallery, Denver, 2001, Andy Warhol Mus., Medzilaborce, Slovakia, 2003; exhibited in group shows Winfield Gallery, Carmel, 1994, 95, 96, 97, 98, 99, 2001, Monterey Peninsula Coll., 1993, 94, Pacific Grove (Calif.) Art Ctr., 1994, Marjorie Evans Gallery, Carmel, 1994, Carl Cherry Center for Arts, Carmel, 1995, 98, Valdosta (Ga.) U., 1995, Miriam Perlman Gallery, Chgo., 1995, Brand Art Gallery, Glendale, Calif., 1995, Andrea Schwartz Gallery, San Francisco, 1995, Monterey Mus. Art, 1995, 96, 97, 98, 99, Calif. State U., Chico, 1995, Cabrillo Coll., Aptos, Calif., 1996, Pope Gallery, Santa Cruz, Calif., 1996, The Print Ctr., Phila., 1996, L.A. County Mus. Rental and Sales Gallery, 1996, Olga Dollar Gallery, San Francisco, 1996, 97, Nancy Solomon Gallery, Atlanta, 1996, Artspace II, Birmingham, Mich., 1997, Mt. St. Mary's Coll., 1998, Solomon Projects, Atlanta, 1998, 99, Finer Things Gallery, Nashville, 1999, Locus Gallery, St. Louis, 1999, 2000, Kathryn Markel Fine Arts, N.Y.C., 1999, 2000, Hunter Mus. Am. Art, Chatanooga, 2000, Trinity Gallery, Atl., 2001-02; represented in permanent collections Adobe Systems, AFL-CIO Housing Investment Trust, Alza Pharms., BEA Systems, Beverly Hills Pub. Libr., Broadvision, Canon Systems Globalization, Canon, Inc., Caribe Hilton, The Chubb Group, Clarify, Inc., Fidelity Investments, Ford Motor Co., Four Seasons Hotel, Fujitsu, Galaxi, GE Corp., Hambrecht and Quist, Hilton Hotel, Kaiser-Permanente Hosp., Macy's, Manatt, Monterey Mus. Art, Phelps and Phillips, Marcus and Millichap, Marriott Associa, Marshall Fields, MGM Grand Hotel and others. Mem. L.A. Printmaking Soc. Avocations: tennis, gardening. Home: PO Box 223093 Carmel CA 93922-3093 E-mail: adamstnj@pacbell.net.

ADAMS, TUCKER HART, economic research company executive; b. Prescott, Ark., Jan. 11, 1938; d. Hugh Ross and Mildred (Dunn) Hart; m. Daniel Williams Adams, Sept. 6, 1957; children: Virginia Schoenthaler, Carolyn, Catherine Adams-Gravley, Anne Green. BA in Math., Wellesley Coll., 1959; MA in Econs., U. Colo., 1977, PhD in Econs., 1979. V.p., chief economist United Banks of Colo., Denver, 1978-88; pres., chief exec. officer The Adams Group, Inc., Colorado Springs, Colo., 1988—; pres. Am. Russian Collaborative Enterprises, LLC, 1994—. Bd. dirs. Mortgage Analysis Corp., Touch Am., Tax Free Fund Colo., Rocky Mountain Equity Fund, Avista Labs. Bd. dirs. Colo. Health Facilities Authority, Denver, Rocky Mountain World Trade Ctr., U. Colo. Found., Boulder. Pendleton scholar Wellesley Coll., 1955; grad. fellowship U. Colo., 1977. Mem. Colo. Womens Forum (pres. 1988), Internat. Womens Forum. Republican. Presbyterian. Avocations: adventure travel, gardening, needlework, grandchildren. Office: The Adams Group Inc 4822 Alteza Dr Ste 300 Colorado Springs CO 80917-4002

ADAMS, VERONICA WADEWITZ, musician; b. Porto Alegre, Brazil, June 21, 1951; came to U.S., 1959; d. Werner Karl and Ella Victoria (Wasemiller) Wadewitz; m. Michael West Adams, Oct. 19, 1983. MusB, DePauw U., 1973; MusM, W.Va. U., 1978. Music instr. Huntington (Ind.) Coll., 1973-74; section cellist Ft. Wayne (Ind.) Philharm., 1973-74; prin. cellist Lima (Ohio) Symphony Orch., 1974-76; music instr. Bluffton (Ohio) Coll. & Pub. Schs., 1974-77; prin. cellist Alexandria (Va.) Symphony Orch., 1981-83, Millbrook Ctr. Chamber Orch., Shepherdstown, W.Va., 1982-83; free-lance cellist Washington, 1979-96; free-lance solo cellist, 2001—. Cellist Washington Friends of Baroque, 1980-88, Salerno Trio, 1982-91, Musikfest Trio, 1988-91, Designer Sounds, 1991-96; mem. applied music staff No. Va. C.C., 1988-96; designer, initiator and dir. Adult Orch. Workshop, 1988-98; founder Adult Music Student Resources, 1995-97. Recs. include Joy!, Joie!, Joye! for flute, cello, piano by Designer Sounds, 1991. Democrat. Avocations: cooking, reading, writing, traveling. Home and Office: 1442-B Cameron Ct Wilmington NC 28401-7925

ADAMS, W. RANDOLPH, JR., management consultant; b. Cleve., Aug. 5, 1944; s. William Randolph and Virginia (Fulcher) A.; m. Margaret Montgomery, Sept. 1, 1968; children: William Duff, Jessica Montgomery. BA, Dartmouth Coll., 1967, MBA, 1974; M in Pub. Adminstrn., Syracuse U., 1972. Cons. Towers Perrin Co. (formerly Cresap, McCormick and Paget), Chgo., 1974-78; prin. Cresap, McCormick and Paget, Chgo., 1978-82, v.p., 1982—, dir. cons. services to fin. insts., 1984—; exec. dir. St. Louis Symphony Orch., 2002—. Contbr. articles to Bankers mag. Active task force on fin. services Chgo. Civic Com. Served as lt. USN, 1968-71. Mem.: University (Chgo.); Indian Hill (Winnetka, Ill.); Dartmouth of N.Y. Home: 25 Twin Springs Ln Saint Louis MO 63124-1138 Office: St Louis Symphony Orch 718 N Grand Blvd Saint Louis MO 63103-3414

ADAMS, WARREN LYNN, alcohol/drug abuse services professional, consultant; b. Clarksville, Ark., Jan. 11, 1955; s. Warren Earnest Adams and Doris Anita (Reed) Crandall; m. Pamela Jo Sullivan, Sept. 9, 1978 (div. 1995); children: Lindsay Nichelle, London Reed; m. Brenda Kay Pettigrew, Feb. 3, 1996; stepchildren: Kristin Lea Haney, Phillip Kollin Haney, Kasey Kay Haney. BA, U. Ctrl. Okla., 1978, BS, 1994; MBA, Oklahoma City U., 1996. Dir. pub. rels. Oklahoma City Zoo, 1979-80; dir. sports info. Oklahoma City U., 1980-82; COO Fite-Davis & Assocs., Oklahoma City, 1982-84; pres., CEO Lynn Adams & Assocs., Oklahoma City, 1984-88; pub. rels. technician Runkle-Moroch Advt., Oklahoma City, 1988-89; COO Jim Fite Mktg. and Mgmt. Resources, Edmond, Okla., 1989-92; administrator Okla. Ctr. for Alcohol and Drug-Related Studies, Oklahoma City, 1992—. Publ. cons. 1st Bapt. Ch., Oklahoma City, 1984-95; bus. cons. Adams Assocs., Ninnekah, Okla., 1995—; pub., bus. mgr. Real Estate Exec. Mag., Chickasha, Okla., 1996-99, Builder/Architect Mag., Chickasha, 1996-99. Contbr. articles to profl. jours. Master mason Ancient, Free & Accepted Masons, Oklahoma City, 1981-2000; 32 Mason Okla. Scottish Rite, Guthrie, 1982-2000; recreation coord. First Baptist Ch., 1984-95; sec., bd. deacons 1988-90. Named Gov.'s Non-Profit Corp. of Yr., Okla. Fedn. of Parents for Drug-Free Youth, Oklahoma City, 1994. Mem. Outstanding Young Men of Am. (named Outstanding Young Men of Am. 1987-89, 92; nat. nom. com.), U. Okla. Health Scis. Ctr. Staff Senate. Democrat. Mem. Christian. Ch. (Disciples of Christ). Avocations: antiques, science fiction, travel, lighthouses, covered bridges. Home: RR 2 Box 6 Ninnekah OK 73067-9504 Office: Okla Ctr for Alcohol & Drug-Related Studies 800 NE 15th St Ste 410 Oklahoma City OK 73104-4602 E-mail: lynn-adams@ouhsc.edu.

ADAMS, WARREN SANFORD, II, retired food company executive, lawyer; b. Cleve., Sept. 4, 1910; s. Otis Howard and Hermine (Weis) A. AB, Princeton U., 1930; LL.B., Harvard U., 1934; J.S.D., NYU, 1941. Bar: N.Y. 1935. Pvt. practice, N.Y.C., 1934-40; counsel chems. div. WPB, 1941; with CPC Internat. Inc. (formerly Corn Products Co.), 1946-76, gen. counsel, 1960-72, v.p., 1962-72, sr. v.p., gen. counsel, dir., 1972-76. Bd. dirs. emeritus Washington Sq. Fund, N.Y.C.; trustee, counsel Whitehall Found., Inc. Served to lt. col. USMCR, 1942-46. Mem. ABA, The Pilgrims, English Speaking Union, Racquet and Tennis Club, Met. Opera Club, Princeton Club, Ekwanok Golf Club (Vermont), Am. Soc. of Order of St. John (knight), Royal and Ancient Golf Club (Scotland), Boodles (London), Newport Country Club (Rhode Island), The Austin Club (Texas). Episcopalian.

ADAMS, WAYNE VERDUN, pediatric psychologist, educator; b. Rhinebeck, N.Y., Feb. 24, 1945; s. John Joseph and Lorena Pearl (Munroe) A.; m. Nora Lee Swindler, June 12, 1971; children: Jennifer, Elizabeth. BA, Houghton Coll., 1966; MA, Syracuse U., 1969, PhD, 1970; postgrad., U. N.C., Chapel Hill, 1975. Hon. diplomate Am. Bd. Profl. Psychology; lic. psychologist, N.Y., Oreg. Asst. prof. Colgate U., Hamilton, N.Y., 1970-75; chief psychologist Alfred I. DuPont Inst., Wilmington, Del., 1976-86; dir. divsn. psychology, dept. pediat. DuPont Hosp. for Children (formerly Alfred I. DuPont Inst.), Wilmington, 1987-99; mem. Del. Bd. Licensure in Psychology, 1983-86, bd. pres., 1986; assoc. prof. pediat. Thomas Jefferson Coll. Medicine, Phila., 1995-99; prof. psychology George Fox U., Newberg, Oreg., 1999—, dept. chair grad. sch. clin. psychology, 2001—. Grant reviewer NIH, 1999—. Cons. editor Jour. Pediatric Psychology, 1980-83, guest reviewer, 1984—; co-author 4 nationally used psychol. tests in field; contbr. articles to profl. jours. Fellow APA, Nat. Acad. Neuropsychology; mem. Soc. Pediatric Psychology, Del. Psychol. Assn. (exec. com. 1979-82, pres. 1981-82), Oreg. Psychol. Assn. Office: George Fox U Grad Sch Clin Psychology 414 N Meridian St Newberg OR 97132-2697

ADAMS, WILBURN CLIFTON, communication educator; b. Huntsville, Ala., Feb. 14, 1943; s. Wilburn Clifton and Pauline Marie (Pennington) A.; m. Sara Ruth Shook, July 25, 1970; 1 child, Ami Rhae. BA, U. Ala., 1968; MS, Fla. State U., 1970, PhD, 1973. Asst. prof. Ctrl. Mo. State U., Warrensburg, 1972-77, assoc. prof., 1977-82, prof., 1982-99, prof., dir. of forensics, 1999-2000, prof. emeritus, 2000—. Chmn. curriculum com. Ctrl. Mo. State U., 1987—88, chmn. stds. com., 1992—93, sponsor speech comm. soc., 1979—99, co-dir. 1st nat. officiated debate tournament, 1993; vis. lectr. Fgn. Affairs Coll., Beijing, 2000—01; acad. advisor Chao Yang Culture Ctr., 2000—01; prof. U. Md. Univ. Coll.-Asia, 2001—03. Contbr. articles to profl. jours. and newspapers; creater games Sieze, Communication Activities Clock, timshel holiday cards. Sgt. U.S. Army, 1964-66. Named Outstanding Tchr. Speech and Theatre Assn. of Mo., 1975; receipient Podium of Honor, Ctrl. Mo. Forensics Squad, 1996. Mem. Elks (trustee 1997-99, exalted ruler 1989-90). E-mail: clifton_adams@yahoo.com.

ADAMS, WILLIAM B. author, inventor, educator, consultant, columnist, communications executive, systems architect; b. Richmond, Virginia, Feb. 4, 1941; s. William B. and Jeannette (Griffiths) A.; m. Gail (Taylor), June 4, 1966; children: Robert Taylor, Suzanne Valerie. BS, U. Md., 1962, AB, 1967; MS in math., Hamilton U., Wyo., 1989, PhD in computer sci., 1999. Lic. profl. engr.; cert. in program mgmt. and e - commerce. Cons., specializing in info. sys. and sys. arch., Springfield, Va., 1962—; prof. George Mason U., 2003—; CEO Plan B Pub. and Media Prodn. Co. CEO Symbiotic Sys. Ltd.; lectr. U. Md.; assoc. Networking Inst., 1991-94; bd. dirs., Amalgamated Conglomerates. Author: How to Become a Life Master, 1997; How to Balance Your Checkbook and Why You Should, 1998; 101 End Plays, 2002, Process for Sys. Engr., 2003; Sys. Arch. and Requirements Engr., 2004; The Truth About the Stock Market, 2001; How to Win with Options, 2002; How to Avoid Scams, Swindles, Frauds and Cheats, 2003. League dir. Braddock Rd. Youth Club, Springfield, 1982—, mem. exec. com., 1982—; bd. visitors Internat. Open U.; bd. dirs. Internat. Tax Inst., 1997—. U. Md. fellow, 1963-64; recipient 5th pl. worldwide Prisoners Dilemma Algorithm Contest; runner up 2001 Bulluer - Lytton contest. Mem. IEEE, Assn. Computing Machinery, Internat. Coun. Sys. Engring., Math. Assn. Am., Soc. Indsl. and Applied Math., Am. Math. Soc., European Soc. for Theoretical Computer Sci., Am. Assn. for Artificial Intelligence, Nat. Writers Union, Pi Mu Epsilon. Achievements include: invention of virus proof PC; invention of software method to replace hardware "test and set," now known as "two phase commit;" invention of method to control distributed networks, later discovered independently and patented by JPL. Office: PO Box 1473 Springfield VA 22151-0467

ADAMS, WILLIAM CARRYL, public relations educator; b. Chgo., Sept. 23, 1940; s. Herbert Nathanial and Virginia Mae (Weil) A.; m. Barbara Jane Baun, Nov. 19, 1966; children: Douglas, Erik, Kristofer. BS, U. Wis., 1962, MA, 1968. Editor Wis. State Employee Mag., Madison, 1964-66; sr. writer Amoco Corp., Chgo., 1966-67, pub. rels. supr. Atlanta, 1967-70, media rels. mgr. Chgo., 1970-73, Standard Oil Co. (Ind.), Washington, 1973-78; dir. pub. rels. Phillips Petroleum Co., Bartlesville, Okla., 1978-88; gen. mgr. pub. affairs ICI Americas, Inc., Wilmington, Del., 1988-90; assoc. prof. pub. rels. Fla. Internat. U., North Miami, 1990—. Bd. dirs. Pub. Affairs Coun., Washington, 1988-91, Del. State C. of C., Wilmington, 1988-90; trustee Media Inst., Washington, 1989-91; cons. Found. for Am. Comm., L.A., 1990—. Editor: Using Research in Public Relations, 1990; co-author: Media Guide for Academics; contbr.: Effective Public Relations, 1994; chmn. editorial bd., contbr. Public Affairs in an Era of Change, 1995. Member bd. advisors U. Fla. Sch. of Journalism, Gainesville, 1987-90; chmn. United Way Corp. campaign, Bartlesville, 1986; pub. rels. chair Pike Creek Valley Running Club, Wilmington, 1989-90. With USAR, 1962-68; co-founder Osage Hills Running Club, Bartlesville, Okla., 1980. Gannett Media Ctr. fellow, 1991. Fellow Publ. Rels. Soc. Am. (bd. dirs. Broward County, Fla chpt. pres. 1995, Silver Anvil award 1971, 84, chmn. Educators Acad. 2001, Outstanding Educator award 2001), Assn. for Edn. in Journalism and Mass Comm. (chmn. pub. rels. divsn. 1997), Arthur Page Soc. Avocations: jazz, reading. Home: 5150 SW 21st St Plantation FL 33317-5427 Office: Fla Internat U 151st Biscayne Blvd Miami FL 33181 E-mail: prprof@aol.com.

ADAMS, WILLIAM D. academic administrator; b. Pontiac, Mich., Aug. 18, 1947; s. Waldemar Harmon Adams and Charlotte Elizabeth (Drea) Rising; m. Catherine Spaulding Bruce, Oct. 10, 1993; children: Sean Douglass Vallant, Carmen Milena. BA magna cum laude, The Colo. Coll., 1972; PhD, U. Calif., Santa Cruz, 1982. Vis. asst. prof. dept. polit. sci. U. N.C., Chapel Hill, 1983—84, U. Santa Clara, Calif., 1984—85; instr. great works in western culture program Stanford U., Calif., 1985—86, program coord. great works in western culture program, 1986—88; exec. asst. to pres. Wesleyan U., Middletown, Conn., 1988—93, v.p., sec., 1993—95; pres. Bucknell U., Lewisburg, Pa., 1995—2000, Colby Coll., Waterville, Maine, 2000—. Contbr. articles to profl. jours. 1st lt. U.S. Army, 1966—69. Office: Colby Coll Office of Pres 4601 Mayflower Hl Waterville ME 04901-8846 E-mail: wadams@colby.edu.

ADAMS, WILLIAM GILLETTE, lawyer; b. Dallas, Tex., July 24, 1940; s. Dwight B. and Lorinda R. (Gillette) Adams; m. Barbara A. Picoli, Jan. 24, 1970. BA in Econs., Stanford U., 1963; JD, U. Utah, 1968. Bar: Calif. 1969; registered Conseil Juridique, France. Vol. Peace Corps, Morocco, 1963-65; assoc. O'Melveny & Myers, L.A., 1968-75, 2000ptnr. Newport Beach, Calif., 1979, resident ptnr. Paris, 1979-84; ptnr. Erickson, Zerfas & Adams, L.A., 1975-79. Bd. dirs. Valentine Enterprises, Inc. Editor-in-chief Utah Law Rev., 1967-68 With USCG, 1957-58. Mem. ABA, Orange County Bar Assn., L.A. Bar Assn., Calif. Bar Assn., Cercle Union Interalliee, Big Canyon Country Club, Order of Coif, Phi Kappa Phi, Phi Delta Phi. Office: O'Melveny & Myers 610 Newport Center Dr Ste 1700 Newport Beach CA 92660-6429 also: 400 S Hope St Los Angeles CA 90071-2899*

ADAMS, WILLIAM HENSLEY, ecologist, educator; b. Nashville, Aug. 14, 1929; s. William Hensley and Mary Pauline (Vaughn) A.; children: Deska Lee, Norma Dee, Anita Rice, Patricia Lynn; m. Marie-Louise A. Curfs, 1999. AB, U. Tenn., 1951; postgrad., U. Okla., 1951, Tulane U., 1953-54; MS, La. State U., 1956; PhD, Auburn U., 1959. Grad. research asst. Auburn U., 1956-59; sr. research biologist Tenn. Game and Fish Commn., 1959-60; chmn. dept. biology, prof. biology Tenn. Wesleyan Coll., 1960-64, dean Coll. Arts and Scis.; prof. biology Tenn. Technol. U., Cookeville, 1964-66; with div. pre-coll. edn. in sci. NSF, 1966-68, div. undergrad. edn. in sci., 1969-73, div. higher edn. in sci., 1973-75, div. sci. edn. devel. and research, 1975-77, div. sci. improvement, 1977-81; cons., 1981—; pres. BIADA Constrn. Devel. Co. and Empire Realty Investment Co., Vienna, Va., 1990-92; broker RE/MAX Real Estate, Hilton Head, SC, 1992—. Mem. NSF Research Participation for Coll. Tchrs. Highlands Biol. Sta., 1961, NSF Summer Inst. Radiation Biology Oak Ridge Inst. Nuclear Studies, 1961, NSF Summer Inst. Comparative Anatomy Harvard, 1962, NSF Summer Inst. Marine Biology Duke Marine Lab., 1963, NSF-Tenn. Acad. Sci. Vis. Scientist Program, 1962 66; dir. NSF Coop. Coll.- Sch. Sci. Program, 1963-65; mem. Commn. Undergrad. Edn. in Biol. Scis. Southeastern Regional Conf., 1965, Advanced Placement Reader in Biology, 1965; Oak Ridge Inst. Nuclear Scis. Radiation Biology Conf., 1965 Mem. Savanah River Site Citizens Adv. Bd. Served to lt. col. Med. Service Corps, USAF, 1951-53, 68-69. Recipient Sigma Xi-Research Engring. Soc. Am. grant-in-aid, 1960-61, Tenn. Wesleyan Coll. Faculty award, 1962, Tenn. Technol. U. faculty research grant, 1966 Fellow Explorers Club; mem. Am. Soc. Mammalogists (honorarium 1959), Am. Ornithologists Union, Cooper Ornithol. Soc., Wilson Ornithol. Soc., Wildlife Soc. Home: 4 Field Sparrow Ct Hilton Head Island SC 29926-1881 Office: 840 Wm Hilton Pkwy Hilton Head Island SC 29928 E-mail. adamshhi@hargray.com. *Increasingly, people in positions of responsibility are abdicating their concomitant role as respected leaders and thereby failing to set good examples for young people to follow, especially at a time when they need high standards for self-emulation. Therefore I challenge young people to set forceful leadership as their highest personal goal in life and remember, as I have, that attainment of this goal will require the stamina necessary to remount their white chargers each time and no matter how often they are unseated.*

ADAMS, WILLIAM LEIGH, history educator; b. New London, Conn., Aug. 25, 1946; s. Harold Leon and Clella Mae (Lyon) A.; m. Roselyn Grantham, May 7, 1969; children: Russell Paul, Kirstin Elizabeth. BA, Ctrl. Okla. State U., 1966; MA, SUNY, Binghamton, 1978, U. N.D., 1973, DA, 1975. Tchr., dep. Sale (Australia) Cath. Coll., 1975-77, 79-82; tchr. St. Joseph's Mission Sch., Tenaru, Solomon Islands, 1983-84, St. Joseph's Acad., Brownsville, Tex., 1987; prof. history U. Tex., Brownsville, 1988—. Prof. English and history Henan Normal U., Xinxiang, China, 1999-2000. Author: Portrait of a Border City: Brownsville, Texas, 1997, Valley Vets: WWII Veterans of the Rio Grande Valley, 1999, Remembering Xinxiang, 2001. Lt. USN, 1967-72. Avocations: woodworking, snorkeling, shell collecting. Home: 235 Hibiscus Ct Brownsville TX 78520 Office: U Tex Brownsville 80 Ft Brown Brownsville TX 78520

ADAMS, WILLIAM ROGER, historian, consultant; b. Mpls., Nov. 4, 1935; s. Jacob Anthony and Clara Louise (Jordan) A.; m. LaVonne May Turgeon, June 24, 1961; children: James Jacob, April Louise. BA, U. Minn., 1961, MA, 1967; PhD, Fla. State U., 1974. Analyst USIS, 1964-69; asst. prof. history Fla. State U., 1972-75; exec. dir. Fla. Bicentennial Commn., 1975-77; dir. Historic St. Augustine (Fla.) Preservation Bd., 1977-85. Pres., prin. cons. Historic Property Assocs.; dir. City of St. Augustine Dept. Hist. Preservation, 1999—; bd. dirs. Fla. Trust Historic Preservation, 1979-81, Fla. Hist. Soc., 1980-88. Served with AUS, 1955-57. Office: Historic Property Assocs PO Box 1002 Saint Augustine FL 32085-1002

ADAMS, WILLIAM WHITE, retired manufacturing company executive; b. Dubuque, Iowa, May 14, 1934; s. Waldo and Therese (White) A.; m. Susan Joanne Cole, Dec. 29, 1956; children: Nancy, Sara, Mark, Catherine. BS in Indsl. Adminstrn., Iowa State U., 1956; LHD (hon.), Millersville U., 1990, Lebanon Valley Coll., 1990; LittD, Franklin & Marshall, 1991. With Armstrong World Industries, Inc., Lancaster, Pa., 1956-94, gen. sales mgr. residential ceiling systems div., 1975-80, group v.p. bldg. products ops., 1981, exec. v.p., 1982-88, chmn., pres., CEO, 1988-93, chmn., 1993-94. Exec.-in-residence U. Tenn. Grad. Sch. Bus. Adminstrn.; bd. dirs. High Industries, Specialty Products & Insulation, Inc.; former chmn. Lancaster Alliance, 1993-98; dir. emeritus Bell Atlantic Corp. Chmn. adv. bd. Lancaster-Lebanon coun. Boy Scouts Am., 1970—; bd. dirs. United Way Lancaster County, Pa., 1977-82, WITF Pub. Broadcasting, 1986-88; bd. dirs. Lancaster Symphony Assn., 1978-87, pres., 1983-84; dir. Lancaster Health Alliance, 1988-96; bd. dirs. Pa. 2000, 1990-95. Recipient Silver Beaver award Boy Scouts Am., 1979, 93-98. Mem. Nat. Assn. Corp. Dirs. (dir.), Caves Valley Golf Club, Lancaster Country Club (dir. 1978-84).

ADAMS-ANDERSON, NIKI MARIA, communications company executive; b. Baytown, Tex., Oct. 18, 1954; d. Fred Elester and Carl Juanita (Brown) A. BS in Speech Pathology, Lamar U., Beaumont, Tex., 1978. Cert. tchr., Tex.; cert.engring. planning. Speech therapist South Park Ind. Sch. Dist., Beaumont, 1978-79; mgr. engring. design Southwestern Bell Telephone Co., Beaumont, 1979-85, mgr. engring. planning Dallas, 1985-90, Houston, 1990—. Tutor, mentor Harlem Elem Sch., Baytown, Tex., 1995; mentor Duncanville (Tex.) Mid. Sch., 1989-90; tutor Furr H.S., Houston, 1990-91. Mem. NAACP (membership recruitment nat. conv.), Telephone Pioneers Am., Tex. Soc. Telephone Engrs. Avocations: reading, music (singing in a chorale), yoga, co-founder community development corporation. Home: PO Box 1932 Baytown TX 77522-1932

ADAMSKI, GARY MATTHEW, language educator, real estate broker; b. Niagara Falls, N.Y., Aug. 5, 1947; s. Matthew George and Anne (Staknunas) A.; m. Blanche Elaine Viavada, July 14, 1973. AA, Niagara C.C., Niagara Falls, N.Y., 1967; BS in Edn., SUNY, Buffalo, 1969; MS in Adminstrn., St. Michael's Coll., Winooski, Vt., 1975; postgrad., U. de Grenoble, U. de MontrÉal, U. de Salamanca. Cert. tchr. French, Spanish, English; cert. prin., Vt.; lic. real estate broker, Vt. Tchr. grade 5 Pub. Sch. 54, Buffalo, 1969; tchr. French Main St. Mid. Sch., Montpelier, Vt., 1969-78; tchr. French, Spanish, English, asst. prin. Montpelier H.S., 1978-90; tchr. French, Spanish, English Whitcomb Jr./Sr. H.S., Bethel, Vt., 1990-93; real estate broker Town & Country Assocs., Barre, Vt., 1985—2002; tchr. French, Spanish Spaulding H.S., Barre, 1993-2000; prof. French Norwich U., Northfield, Vt., 1998-2000; tchr. French, English and Spanish St. Monica Sch., Barre, Vt., 2000—. French translator State of Vt., Montpelier, 1978—, Internat. Coins and Currency, Montpelier, 1973-82; sch. evaluator New Eng. Assn. Schs. and Colls., Cambridge, Mass., 1990—. Co-editor: Matérière et Manière, 1984; co-author: Franco-American History and Heritage Handbook, 1997. Mem. festival com. Union St. Jean-Baptiste, Barre, Barre Ethnic Heritage, 1988-93; mem. Montpelier Bicentennial Com., 1976; actor, mem. stage crew Montpelier Theater Guild, 1969-77. Mem. NEA, Vt. Edn. Assn. (polit. act organizer 1993-95, securities/investments com. 1996—), Barre Edn. Assn., Am. Assn. Tchrs. French (treas., Honor Soc. award 1984), Vt. Fgn. Lang. Assn. (pres. 1980-84), Assn. Quebecoise de Prof de Français, Ctrl. Vt. Tchrs. Credit Union (bd. dirs., pres.), Nat. Assn. Realtors, Vt. Assn. Realtors, Ctrl. Vt. Bd. Realtors. Avocations: travel, gardening, football, hockey. Home: 63 Woodland Dr Barre VT 05641-3315 E-mail: BgAdamski@charter.net.

ADAMSON, ARTHUR WILSON, chemistry educator; b. Shanghai, Aug. 15, 1919; s. Arthur Quintin and Ethel (Rhoda) A.; m. Virginia Louise Dillman, Mar. 24, 1942; children: Carol Ann, Janet Louise, Jean Elizabeth BS with honors, U. Calif.-Berkeley, 1940; PhD in Phys. Chemistry, U. Chgo., 1944; PhD (hon.), U. Ferrara, Italy, 1993. Research assoc. Manhattan Project, Oak Ridge, 1944-46; asst. prof. U. So. Calif., 1946-49, assoc. prof., 1949-53, prof., 1953-89, prof. emeritus, 1989—, chmn. dept. chemistry, 1972-75. Foster lectr. U. Buffalo, 1970; Venable lectr. U. N.C., 1975; Bikerman lectr. Case Western U., 1982; Reilly lectr. Notre Dame U., 1984. Author: Concepts of Inorganic Photochemistry, 1975, Understanding Physical Chemistry, 1980, Textbook of Physical Chemistry, 1986, Physical Chemistry of Surfaces, 1997; editor Langmuir Am. Chem. Soc., 1984-89; editor emeritus, 1990—; contbr. articles to profl. jours. Recipient Creative Scholarship and rsch. award U. So. Calif., 1971, Excellence in Teaching award, 1979, Raubenheimer award, 1984, Disting. Emeritus award, 1991; Alexander von Humboldt Sr. Scientist award, 1971, others; Gold medal Am. Inst. Chemists, 1994, Monie A. Ferst award Sigma Xi, 1999. Fellow Am. Inst. Chemists (Gold medal 1994); mem. Am. Chem Soc. (councillor So. Calif. sect. 1964-80, chmn. 1964, Tolman award 1967, Kendall award 1979, Langmuir lectr. 1981, Disting. Svc. in Inorganic Chemistry award 1982, Chem. Edn. award 1984, Agnes Ann Green Disting Svc. award 1989, Harry and Carol Mosher award 1990, Arthur W. Adamson Award for Disting. Svc. in Advancement of Surface Chemistry established in his honor 1992). Republican. Avocations: tennis, photography. Office: U So Calif Dept Chem U Park Los Angeles CA 90089-0001

ADAMSON, GEOFFREY DAVID, reproductive endocrinologist, surgeon; b. Ottawa, Ont., Can., Sept. 16, 1946; came to U.S., 1978, naturalized, 1986; s. Geoffrey Peter Adamson and Anne Marian Allan; m. Rosemary C. Oddie, Apr. 28, 1973; children: Stephanie, Rebecca, Eric. BSc with honors, Trinity Coll., Toronto, Can., 1969; MD, U. Toronto, 1973. Diplomate Am. Bd. Ob-Gyn., Am. Bd. Laser Surgery; cert. Bd. Reproductive Endocrinology. Resident in ob-gyn. Toronto Gen. Hosp., 1973-77, fellow in ob-gyn., 1977-78; fellow reproductive endocrinology Stanford (Calif.) U. Med. Ctr., 1978-80; practice medicine specializing in infertility Los Gatos, Calif., 1980-84; instr. Stanford U. Sch. Medicine, 1980-84, clin. asst. prof., 1984-92, clin. assoc. prof., 1992-95, clin. prof., 1995—; assoc. clin. prof. Sch. Medicine U. Calif., San Francisco, 1992—; founder, chmn., CEO Advanced Reproductive Care Inc., Palo Alto, Calif., 1997—. Editor: (textbook) Endoscopic Management of Gynecologic Disease, 1996; mem. editl. bd. Can. Doctor mag., 1977-83, Jour. Am. Assn. Gynecol. Laparoscopists, 1996—, Fertility and Sterility, 2000—, others; contbr. articles to profl. jours., mags. Fellow, Ont. Ministry of Health, 1977—78. Fellow ACS, Royal Coll. Surgeons Can., Am. Coll. Ob-Gyns.; mem. AAAS, AMA, Am. Assn. Gynecol. Laparoscopists (adv. bd., bd. trustees, sec., treas., 2002—, exec. com. 2002—), Am. Soc. Reproductive Medicine (com. mem., bd. dirs. 1997-99, 2000—, exec. com., 2002—), Soc. Reproductive Endocrinologists (charter), Soc. Reproductive Surgeons (charter, bd. dirs., sec., treas., v.p., pres., past pres.), Soc. Assisted Reproductive Tech. (treas., dir., v.p., pres., past pres. bd. dirs. 1991—), Nat. Coalition Oversight of Assisted Reproductive Technicians (vice-chair 2001—), Internat. Com. Monitoring Assisted Reproductive Techs., Pacific Coast Reproductive Soc. (dir., sec., v.p., pres., past pres.), Pacific NW Ob-Gyn Soc. (hon. life), Pacific Coast Ob-Gyn. Soc., Soc. Gynecologic Surgeons, San Francisco Gynecol. Soc. (past pres.), Soc. for Gynecologic Investigation, Bay Area Reproductive Endocrinologists Soc. (founding pres., hon. life), Gynecol. Laser Soc., N.Y. Acad. Scis., Shufelt Gynecol. Soc., Peninsula Gynecol. Soc. (past pres.), Calif. Med. Assn., San Mateo County Med. Assn., Santa Clara County Med. Assn., Am. Fedn. Clin. Rsch., Nat. Resolve (bd. dirs. 1991-2001, sec., treas., Lifetime Svc. award 1999), Can. Assn. Interns and Residents (hon. life, pres. 1977-79, bd. dirs. 1974-79, rep. AMA resident physician sect. 1978-79, rep. Can. Med. Protective Assn. 1975-78, rep. Can. Med. Assn. 1975-78, Disting. Svc. award 1980), Profl. Assn. Interns and Residents Ont. (bd. dirs. 1973-76, v.p. 1974-75, pres. 1975-76), Royal Coll. Physicians and Surgeons Can. (com. exams. 1977-80), Ont. Med. Assn. (sec. interns and residents sect. 1973-74). Avocations: hiking, ice hockey, skiing. Office: 540 University Ave Ste 200 Palo Alto CA 94301-1929 E-mail: gdadamson@arcfertility.com.

ADAMSON, HEIDI BETH, English educator; b. Binghamton, N.Y., Aug. 16, 1967; d. John Leslie and Irene Coleman Adamson. BA in English, George Mason U., 1988, MA in English Linguistics, 1989, postgrad., 1994—. Tchr. ESL Fairfax (Va.) County Pub. Schs., 1991-92; instr. ESL No. Va. C.C., Manassas, 1992-94, head dept. ESL, 1992-94, asst. prof., 1994-97, assoc. prof. ESL/English, 1997—, head dept. fgn. langs. and ESL, 1997-98, asst. divsn. chair ESL, 1998—. Cons. pvt. industry; presenter, spkr. in field. Creator/participant : (video) Becoming a U.S. Citizen: 100 possible questions the INS might ask in the interview, 2001; contbr. articles to profl. jours. Grantee, No. Va. C.C. Ednl. Found., 1997. Mem.: Nat. Assn. Fgn. Student Advisors, Washington Area Tchrs. English to Speakers of Other Langs., Nat. Assn. C.C. Educators. Avocations: child and adult language acquisition, masculine/feminine leadership in higher education, using technology to facilitate learning, travel. Office: No Va CC 6901 Sudley Rd Manassas VA 20109-2399 E-mail: HAdamson@nvcc.vccs.edu.

ADAMSON, JAMES B. business executive; b. 1948; Various positions The Gap, 1975-84, B. Dalton Bookseller, 1984—86, Target Stores, 1986—88; exec. v.p. mktg. Revco Inc., 1988—91; various positions, CEO Burger King Corp., 1991-95; chmn., pres., CEO Advantica Restaurant Group, Spartanburg, SC, 1995—2001; chmn, CEO Kmart Corp., 2002—03.

ADAMSON, JANE NAN, retired elementary school educator; b. Amarillo, Tex., Feb. 5, 1931; d. Carl W. and Lydie O. (Martin) Ray (dec.); 1 child, Dave R. Student, Eastfield Coll., Amarillo Coll., Richland Coll. Univ. Dallas, U. North Tex.; BS, West Tex. A&M U., Canyon, 1953; MEd, Tex. A&M U. Commerce, 1975; diploma, Inst. Children's Lit., 1991; cert., Bur. Edn. and Rsch., 1995; PhD, Am. Coll. Metaphys. Theology, 2000. Cert. elem. tchr., Tex.; lic. real estate salesman. Tchr. Dallas Ind. Sch. Dist., ret. Avocations: music, traveling, decorating, writing, dog training.

ADAMSON, JUDY, theater educator; b. Burlington, Iowa, Sept. 10, 1945; d. Victor Emanuel Lauer and Alma House; m. David A. Adamson, May 27, 1967. BA, U. No. Iowa, 1967. Costumer Unto These Hills, Cherokee, N.C., 1972-78, U. N.C., Chapel Hill, 1976-80; head grad. program costume prodn., 1993—; costume dir. PlayMakers Repertory Co., Chapel Hill, 1993—; draper Ala. Shakespeare Festival, Anniston, 1980; draper asst. Barbara Matera Ltd., N.Y.C., 1980-90, draper, 1990—; costume coord. Carolina Ballet, Raleigh, N.C., 1998—; draper Utah Shakespearean Festival, 2002, 2003. Editor, author (electronic pub.) Survey Costume Programs U.S., 1996—. Active mother's march March of Dimes, Chapel Hill, 1997, 99, 2003. Mem. U.S. Inst. Theatre Tech. (vice-commr. costume symposium 1995), U.S. Inst. Theatre Tech. S.E. (sec. 2003-), Costume Soc. Am., Southea. Theatre Conf., Theta Alpha Pi. Office: U NC CB # 3230 Ctr Dramatic Art Chapel Hill NC 27599-3230

ADAMSON, KATHLEEN FRANCES, not-for-profit developer, educator; d. Stanley Bertil and Rosemary (Wallace) Adamson; m. Thomas Patrick Moylan, Aug. 20, 1966 (div. July 1976); children: Kathleen Marie Moylan, Sarah Anne Moylan. BA in Math., Coll. St. Teresa, 1966; MS in Found. Edn., U. Wis., Milw., 1974, postgrad., 1976. Field staff mgr. Girl Scouts Am., Milw., 1976—81, program dir. Castroville, Calif., 1995—98; city ctr. dir. YWCA, Milw. County, 1981—82, exec. dir., CEO Seaside, Calif., 1998—2001; campaign mgr. Kessler for Congress, Milw., 1982; dir. student life U. Wis., Milw., 1982—95; pres., CEO Gateway Ctr., Pacific Grove, Calif., 2001—. Contbr. articles to profl. jours. Co-chair No. Calif. coun. YWCA, 1999—2000; sec. Domestic Violence Coord. Coun., Monterey, Calif., 1999—2001; exec. com. Child Care Planning Coun., Monterey, 1999—2001; cmty. adv. bd. Calif. state U., Monterey, 1995—97; bd. dirs. United Way, Monterey, 1999—2002. Recipient Rsch. award, Wis. Coll. Pers. Assn., 1985, Women Helping Women award, Soroptimists of Monterey Bay, 2002; grantee, State of Calif., 1998—. Mem.: Calif. Rehab. Assn., Rotary Internat. Avocations: reading, gardening, cooking, travel. Office: Gateway Ctr 850 Congress Ave Pacific Grove CA 93950 Office Fax: 831-372-2411. Business E-Mail: kadamson@gatewaycenter.org.

ADAMSON, MICHAEL ROBERT, history researcher, consultant, educator; b. Kenosha, Wis., Sept. 20, 1962; s. James Cantwell and Rita Marie Adamson; m. Carol Janice Adamson, June 6, 1992; children: Rachel Lynn, Samuel James. BBA, U. Wis., Milw., 1984; MBA, Ariz. State U., 1986; MA, U. Calif., Santa Barbara, 1996, PhD, 2000. Sr. Andersen Cons., Phoenix, 1986-89; sr. assoc. Coopers & Lybrand, San Francisco, 1989-90; bus. application cons. Synon, Inc., Larkspur, Calif., 1990-94. Vis. scholar U. Calif., Berkeley, 2000—02, asst. rschr., Santa Barbara, 2001—02; adj. prof. Sonoma State U., Rohnert Park, Calif., 2002—. Author govt. publs.; contbr. articles to profl. jours. Humane studies fellow Inst. for Humane Studies, 1998-99, 99-2000, Econ. History Rsch. fellow All-U. Calif. Econ. History Group, 1998, grad. fellow U. Calif., Santa Barbara, 1999. Mem.: Bus. History Conf., Econ. History Assn., Am. Hist. Assn., Soc. for Historians of Am. Fgn. Rels., Calif. Coun. for the Promotion of History, Calif. Preservation Found. Avocations: soccer and golf, running, reading, mountain biking, travel. E-mail: MichaelAdamson@comcast.net.

ADAMSON, STEPHEN CHARLES, retired sales professional; b. Boston, July 19, 1936; s. John Morrill and Irene Pauline (Gudowski) A.; m. Barbara Judith Wyman, Oct. 10, 1964 (div.); 1 child, Jennifer. BS in Econs., U. Pa., 1958, MA in Comm., 1963. Commd. ensign USNR, 1958, advanced through grades to lt. comdr., ret., 1996; sales rep. Auburn Cordage, Cambridge, Mass., 1963-65, A&A Distbrs., Holbrook, Mass., 1965-76, Interstate Distbrs., North Quincy, Mass., 1976-98. Contbr. articles to The Pen and Quill. Recipient First Pl. Lit. award Universal Autograph Collectors Club, 2000, Navy Expeditionary medal (Cuba). Mem. Soc. of Am. Baseball Rsch., Universal Autograph Collectors Club. Democrat. Jewish. Avocations: collecting autographs, running marathons and ultramarathons. Home: 39 Kristen Dr #72 Stoughton MA 02072-1285

ADAMSON, THOMAS CHARLES, JR., aerospace engineering educator, consultant; b. Cicero, Ill., Mar. 24, 1924; s. Thomas Charles and Helen Emily (Koubek) A.; m. Susan Elizabeth Huncilman, Sept. 16, 1949; children: Thomas Charles III, William Andros, Laura Elizabeth BS, Purdue U., 1949; MS, Calif. Inst. Tech., 1950, PhD, 1954. Rsch. engr. Jet Propulsion Lab., Pasadena, Calif., 1952-54; assoc. research engr. U. Mich., Ann Arbor, 1954-56, asst. prof., 1956-57, assoc. prof., 1957-61, prof., 1961-93; prof. emeritus, 1993—; chmn. dept. aerospace engring. U. Mich., Ann Arbor, 1983-92. Mem. François-Xavier Bagnoud Aerospace Prize Bd., 1992—, chmn., 1992-2000. Editor: (with M.F. Platzer) Transonic Flow Problems in Turbo Machinery, 1977; contbr. articles to profl. jours. Bd. trustees Mich. Aviation Hall of Fame, 1987—. With U.S. Army, 1943-46, ETO. Guggenheim fellow, 1950-52; recipient Disting. Faculty Achievement award U. Mich., 1980. Fellow AIAA; mem. Combustion Inst., Am. Phys. Soc., Francois-Xavier Bagnoud U.S. Found., Sigma Xi. Episcopalian. Home: 667 Worthington Pl Ann Arbor MI 48103-6138 Office: U Mich Dept Aerospace Engring 1320 Beal Ave Ann Arbor MI 48109-2140 E-mail: tcajr@umich.edu.

ADAMS-PASSEY, SUELLEN S. elementary education educator; b. Cin. d. Raymond J. and Thelma P. (Munk)Sweany; m. Douglas Passey ; children; Amy, Jacqueline, James, Sarah, Kristina, Zoya. BS in Edn., Kent State U. Cert. elem. tchr., Wash. Tchr. 4th and 5th grades Chgo. Jr. Sch., Elgin, Ill.; gen. dir., program developer Courtyard Theatre, Edmonds, Wash.; tchr. 4th grade Edmonds (Wash.) Dist. 15; tchr. 4th, 5th and 6th grades combination class Martha Lake Elem. Sch., Lynnwood, Wash. Bd. dirs. Pub. Edn. Fund for Dist. 15, 1985-87; pres. Seattle Storytellers Guild, 1985-88; bd. dirs. Seattle Folklore Soc. 1998-, founder and chair, concert com. 1988-2002, dir. Crackerbarrel Mornings, 1982-87, co-chair, student subsidy program, 1998-2000, Seattle Opera Guild.

ADAN, JOHN, consulting interventional cardiologist; b. Bratislava, Slovakia, Apr. 9, 1947; came to U.S., 1980; s. Peter Jaloviar and Helena (Votrubova) Zdan; m. Sylvia Winifred Blanche Porter, Sept. 7, 1973; children: Kellie, Mitchell, Caroline. Student, U. Komensky, Bratislava, 1965-68; MB BCh, Queens U., Belfast, No. Ireland, 1974. Diplomate Am. Bd. Internal Medicine, Am. Bd. Cardiovascular Diseases. Intern Framingham Union Hosp.-Boston U., 1980-81, resident in internal medicine, 1981-83; fellow in cardiology Bridgeport Hosp.-Yale U., 1983-86; pvt. practice Las Vegas, 1987—; mem. staff Univ. Med. Ctr., 1987—, Sunrise Hosp., Las Vegas, Nev., 1987—, Desert Springs Hosp., Las Vegas, 1987—; clin. asst. prof. dept. internal medicine U. Nev., Las Vegas, 1994—. Contbr. articles to profl. publs. Mem. Rep. Senatorial Inner Cir., Washington, 1995; capt. U.S. Vols., 1999; maj. U.S. Svc. Command, 1999; lt. col. Emergency Disaster Corps, comdr. for State of Nev., 2003. Coxswain USCG Aux., 1996—. Fellow ACP, Am. Coll. Cardiology, Am. Coll. Chest Physicians; mem. AMA, NRA. Roman Catholic. Avocations: military history, shooting, medical research. Office: Cons Interventional Cardiology LLC 2300 S Rancho Dr Ste 206 Las Vegas NV 89102-4508 E-mail: sylan@lvcm.com.

ADANIYA, KEVIN SEISHO, lawyer; b. San Francisco, Sept. 24, 1968; s. Roy Seijin and Lavern Gay Adaniya. BA in Polit. Sci., U. Calif., Santa Barbara, 1990; JD, U. of the Pacific, Sacramento, 1995. Bar: Hawaii 1996, U.S. Dist. Ct. Hawaii 1997. Law clk. State of Hawaii, Hilo, 1995-96; sole practitioner Honolulu, 1996—. Mem. faculty Inst. for Paralegal Edn., 1999; facilitator Ohana Conferencing, 1999—. Co-author: Paralegals in Family Law Practice, 1999. Vol., Kids First Program, Honolulu, 1998—, Vol. guardian Ad Litem Program, Honolulu, 1998—; atty. mem. AmeriCorps/Students and Advs. for Victims of Domestic Violence, 1996-97, 98-99. Recipient cert. of spl. commendation Vol. Legal Svcs. Hawaii, 1997,Outstanding Local V.P. award U.S. Jr. C. of C., 1998. Mem.: ATLA, ABA, Hawaii State Bar Assn. (dir. young lawyers divsn. 1999—2001, treas. child and parent adv. sect. 2000, pres. 2002), Hawaii Bus. Jaycees (v.p. 1997—2000, Edward R. Nakano Meml. award 1998, Daniel K. Inouye award 1999), Hawaii Jaycees (legal counsel 2002). Office: 33 S King St Ste 306 Honolulu HI 96813 E-mail: kevinadaniya@msn.com.

ADARKAR, ADITYA, humanities educator; PhD, U. Chgo., 1991—2001. Asst. prof., classics and gen. humanities Montclair State U., Upper Montclair, NJ, 2001—. Office: Montclair State Univ Classics and General Humanities Upper Montclair NJ 07043

ADASHEK, JOSEPH ABRAHAM, obstetrician-gynecologist, educator; b. Regina, Wis., Feb. 8, 1962; s. Richard David and Naomi Carole Adashek. BS UCLA, 1984; MD, Pa. State U., 1989. Diplomate Am. Bd. Ob-gyn., bd. cert. ob-gyn., maternal fetal medicine. Intern, resident Northwestern U., 1989-93; fellow U. Calif., Irvine, 1993-95, asst. prof. ob-gyn., 1995-96; asst. prof. U. Nev., 1996-97, assoc. prof., 2001—03. Contbr. articles to profl. jours. Fellow ACOG; mem. AMA. also: Desert Perinatal Assocs 7720 W Sahara Ste #103 Las Vegas NV 89117

ADASHI, ELI Y. obstetrician, gynecologist; MD, U. Tel Aviv, Israel, 1972. Diplomate Am. Bd. Obstetrics-Gynecology, Am. Bd. Reprodn. Endocrinology. Intern Met. Gen. Hospital, Tel Aviv, Israel, 1972-73; resident ob.-gyn. Tufts U. Sch. Medicine, Boston, 1974-77; fellow reprodn. endocrinology Johns Hopkins U., Balt., 1977-78; fellow reprodn.-endocrinology U. Calif. San Diego, La Jolla, 1978-81; mem. med. staff U. Md. Hosp., Balt., 1981-96; prof. ob.-gyn., physiology U. Md., Balt., 1981-96; pvt. practice in ob.-gyn. Balt., 1981-96; chair dept. ob-gyn. U. Utah, Salt Lake City, 1996—. Mem. IOM, ACOG, Am. Fedn. Surgeons, Endocrine Surgeons, Soc. Gastroenterology. Office: U Utah 50 N Med Dr Ste 2b200 Salt Lake City UT 84132-0001

ADATO, PERRY MILLER, documentary producer, director, writer; b. Yonkers, N.Y. d. Perry and Ida (Block) Miller; m. Neil M. Adato, Sept. 11, 1955; children: Laurie, Michelle. Student, Marshalov Sch. Drama, N.Y.C., New Sch. Social Rsch.; LHD (hon.), Ill. Wesleyan U., 1984. Film rsch. coord. CBS-TV Network, N.Y.C., 1959—64, prodr., 1964; assoc. prodr. NET, N.Y.C., 1964—68, prodr., dir., 1968—72, Sta. 13/WNET-TV (formerly NET), N.Y.C., 1972—92; writer Sta. 13/WNET-TV, N.Y.C., 1999—2001, 1989, 1996—97, prodr., dir., 1999—. Exec. prodr. Alvin H. Perlmutter Inc./Ind. Prodn. Fund, 1992-96; guest lectr. on film Harvard U., Columbia U., NYU, Yale U., U. Ill., others, 1970—; lectr. Fairfield (Conn.) U., 1974-75; film lectr. Smithsonian Assocs., Washington, 1997, 98, 99, 2001, 2003, Columbia (Md.) Festival of Arts, 1998, 99; mem. film award jury Am. Film Inst., Beverly Hills, Calif., 1974; judge film award Creative Artists Pub. Svc., N.Y.C., 1976; first chmn. UN Women in the Arts Film Com., 1976-77; pres. jury Montreal Internat. Festival Films on Art, 1990; mem. jury Pompidou Ctr., Paris Internat. Festival of Films on Art, 1994. Producer, dir.: (TV documentary films) Dylan Thomas: The World I Breathe, 1968 (Emmy award for outstanding achievement in cultural documentary 1968), Gertrude Stein: When This You See, Remember Me, 1970 (Montreal Festival Diplome d'Excellence 1970, Am. Film Festival Blue Ribbon award 1970, 2 Emmy nominations for outstanding direction and outstanding achievement in cultural documentary 1971), The Great Radio Comedians, 1972 (Am. Film Festival Red Ribbon award 1972), An Eames Celebration: Several Worlds of Charles and Ray Eames, 1973 (Chgo. Internat. Film Festival Silver Hugo award 1973, Am. Film Festival Red Ribbon award 1973), Mary Cassatt: Impressionist From Philadelphia, 1974 (Women in Communications Clarion award 1974), Georgia O'Keeffe, 1977 (Dirs. Guild Am. award for documentary achievement 1977-1st woman to receive any Dirs. Guild Am. award, NCCJ Christopher award 1978, Com. for Internat. Events Golden Eagle award 1978, Women in Communications Clarion award 1978, Alfred I. DuPont/Columbia U. citation 1978), Frankenthaler: Toward a New Climate, 1978 (Am. Film Festival Blue Ribbon award in fine arts 1979), Picasso: A Painter's Diary, 1980 (Dirs. Guild Am. award for directorial achievement in TV documentary 1980, Alfred I. DuPont/Columbia U. award for excellence in broadcast journalism 1980, Com. for Internat. Events Golden Eagle award 1980, Am. Film Festival Blue Ribbon award in fine arts 1980, Montreal Internat. Festival of Films on Art First prize for Best Biography of an Artist 1981), Carl Sandburg: Echoes and Silences, 1982 (Women in Communications Matrix award 1982, American Women in Radio and TV Pinnacle award for TV documentary 1982, Dirs. Guild Am. award for achievement in TV documentary 1983), Eugene O'Neill: A Glory of Ghosts, 1984-85, Broadcast, 1986 (Most Outstanding Achievement in TV Documentary award Dirs. Guild Am. 1986, Spl. Jury award San Francisco Film Festival 1985, Internat. Film and TV Festival of N.Y. Silver medal 1986); exec. producer (TV series) Women in Art, 1974-78, Art of the Western World, 1985-89; producer, dir., writer: A White Garment of Churches, 1989 (Clarion award 1990, Silver Plaque award Chgo. Internat. Film Festival 1990, Assn. Visual Comm. Silver Cindy award 1990); exec. prodr. rsch. and devel. 3 part series Asian Art, 1990-94; prodr., dir. Great Tales in Asian Art, 1994-96; writer Dream Journeys-Nature in East Asian Art, 1994-95; prodr. R & D Alfred Steiglitz, 1996-98, (working title) Writer, Alfred Steiglitz, 1996-98; prodr., dir., writer Alfred Steiglitz-The Eloquent Eye, 1999-2001. Comm. Internat. Events Golden Eagle award, 2002, Montreal Internat. Festival Films Art Selection, 2002; hon. bd. dirs. Weston-Westport (Conn.) Arts Coun., 1981-89. Poynter fellow Yale U., 1976; grantee NEA, 1977-78, 93, NEH, 1980, 83, 91, 93, 99; Calhoun Coll. assoc. fellow Yale U., 1993—; subject tribute, Montreal Internat. Art Film Festival, 1990; recipient Westport (Conn.) Arts Coun. Lifetime Achievement award in visual arts category, 1996; film retrospective Nat. Gallery Art, Washington, 1998, film festival award for biog. Houston World Fest, 2002, hon. award lifetime achievement Montreal Internat. Festival Films Art, 2002. Mem. Dirs. Guild Am., Writers Guild Am., N.Y. Women in Film and TV.

ADAWI, IBRAHIM HASAN, physics educator; b. Palestine, Apr. 18, 1930; came to U.S., 1951, naturalized, 1961; s. Hasan and Dabella (Miari) A.; children: Omar, Nadia, Yasmin, Rhonda, Tariq. BS in Engring. Physics, Washington U., St. Louis, 1953; PhD in Engring. Physics, Cornell U., 1957. Mem. tech. staff RCA Labs., Princeton, N.J., 1956-60; research cons. Battelle Meml. Inst., Columbus, Ohio, 1960-68; adj. prof. elec. engring. Ohio State U., 1965-68; prof. physics U. Mo., Rolla, 1968-97, emeritus prof. physics, 1997—. Vis. prof. U. Hamburg, W.Ger., winter 1977, Sch. Math. and Physics, U. East Anglia, Norwich, Eng., fall 1982; Fulbright lectr. Rabat, Morocco, 1982; sr. scientist Motorola, Phoenix, summer 1979; rsch. leader Internat. Ctr. Theoretical Physics, Trieste, Italy, summers 1982, 83, 85. Jr. fellow Cornell U., 1953-54; J. McMullen scholar, 1954-55; Sigma Xi fellow, 1955-56 Mem. Am. Phys. Soc. Home: 10540 County Road 3010 Rolla MO 65401-7754 Office: U Mo-Rolla Dept Physics Rolla MO 65401 E-mail: adawi@umr.edu. *Goals in science, and perhaps in life, are seldom reached; they are only approached asymptotically. The higher we soar the more dazzling is the panorama, but the wider is the horizon, and the frontiers of knowledge keep expanding.*

ADAWI, NADIA SHARON, energy cooperative executive; b. Princeton, N.J., Aug. 29, 1958; d. Ibrahim Hussein and Gerda (Obert) Adawi; m. Patrick John Loll, June 18, 1983. BSEE, U. Mo., 1980; MBA, Yale U., 1997. Electronics engr. FCC, Washington, 1980-81; cons. engr. Washington, 1981-89; asst. dir. advanced cellular tech. Ameritech Mobile Communications, Schaumburg, Ill., 1989-93; regional ops. mgr. Ericsson, Inc., Schaumburg, 1993-95; bus. ethics cons. Arthur Andersen, N.Y.C., 1997-99, dir. ops. The Energy Cooperative, Phila. Mem. Sustainable Bus. Network of Greater Phila.; fin. com. The Other Side. Named one of Phila. Bus. Jour. Women of Distinction, 2001. Mem.: NOW, Am. Solar Energy Soc. Avocations: music, literature. Home: 329 S 46th St Philadelphia PA 19143-1801 E-mail: nsadawi@aol.com.

ADAWI, OMAR, mathematician, educator, physicist, educator; b. Princeton, N.J., Apr. 18, 1957; s. Ibrahim Hassan Adawi and Gertrud Obert. BS in Physics, MIT, 1979; MS in Physics, U. Ill., 1980. Grad. tchg. asst. physics U. Ill., Urbana, 1979—80, grad. rsch. asst. physics, 1980—83, grad. tchg. asst. physics, 1984, grad. rsch. asst. biophysics, 1984—88; dir. peer tutoring program Parkland Coll., Champaign, 1995—, assoc. prof. math., 1995—. Adj. math. instr. Parkland Coll., 1993—95; lectr., cons. math., physics, Urbana, Ill., 2001—. Author: Linear Algebra with Business Applications, 2001. Mem.: Am. Assn. Physics Teachers, Ill. Coun. Teachers Math., Math. Assn. Am., Am. Math. Assn. Two-Year Colleges, Ill. Math. Assn. C.C. Avocations: philately, music, art. Home: 1711 B Willow Ct Urbana IL 61801-1150 Office: Parkland Coll 2400 West Bradley Ave Champaign IL 61821-1899 Office Fax: 217-373-3898. E-mail: oadawi@parkland.edu.

ADCOCK, ALBERT EUGENE (GENE), night vision equipment company executive; b. Christopher, Ill., Mar. 11, 1937; s. Omer Leon and Erva Doris Advock; m. Sylvia H. Adcock, Nov. 25, 1992; children: Mark, Chris. AA in Air Traffic Control Mgmt., Johnson County C.C., Olathe, Kans., 1972; BA in Econs. and Bus. Adminstrn., Park Coll., 1975; MBA, Webster U., 1977. Enlisted USAF, 1955, advanced through grades to master sgt.; assigned to Hdqrs. USAF Mil. Airlift Command, Scott AFB, Ill., 1975-76; ret., 1977; logistics engr. McDonnel Aircraft Co., St. Louis, 1977-79; high frequency radio networks comm. officer Hdqs. Air Force Comm. Command, Scott AFB, 1979-80; mktg. mgr. air traffic control navigational aids E-Sys. Montek Divsn., Salt Lake City, 1980-81; mktg. mgr. ground and aircraft radar transponders Govt. Electronics divsn. Motorola, Tempe, Ariz., 1981-87; regional mktg. mgr. Harris RF Comm., Sacramento, 1987-88; U.S. govt. mktg. mgr. night vision equipment Litton Electro-Optics Divsn., Tempe, 1988-91; v.p. bus. devel. Night Vision Equipment Co., Inc., Emmaus, Pa., 1991—. Author: Night Vision Reference Ency.—Optical Surveillance, 1999. Decorated Bronze Star medal with oak leaf cluster, Air medal with six oak leaf clusters. Mem. Air Commando Assn. (life), Combat Control Assn (life), Airlift-Tanker Assn. (life), Nat. Def. Indsl. Assn., Armed Forces Comm. and Electronics Assn. Office: Night Vision Equipment Co Inc PO Box 266 Emmaus PA 18049 E-mail: gene@nvec-night-vision.com.

ADCOCK, BETTY-LEE, real estate company executive, real estate broker; b. Waldo, Kans., Nov. 19, 1921; d. Ralph Preston and Hazel (Pangburn) Beatty; m. Charles Warren Adcock, Feb. 17, 1945; 1 dau., Roberta Lee. B.S. in Journalism, Kans. State Coll., 1946; grad. Realtors Inst. Lic. real estate broker, Hawaii; cert. residential specialist, residential broker. Mem. pub. relations staff Boeing Airplane Co., Wichita, Kans., 1942-45; biographical staff AP, N.Y.C., 1945-46; real estate salesman and broker, Honolulu, 1972— ; prin. broker, pres., owner Adcock, Ltd., real estate mktg., Honolulu, 1983— . Recipient Girl Scout Award of Merit, Kitzingen, Germany, 1960, spl. award Am. Cancer Soc., Middlebury, Vt., 1956. Mem. Nat. Assn. Realtors. Hawaii Assn. Realtors, Honolulu Bd. Realtors, Honolulu Zool. Soc., Friends of Waikiki Aquarium, Nat. Trust for Historic Preservation, Honolulu Art Acad., Friends of Iolani Palace, Bishop Mus., Hawaii Hist. Soc., Hawaii Humane Soc., Hist. Hawaii Found., Chi Omega. Republican. Episcopalian. Home and Office: Adcock Ltd 2415 Aha Aina Pl Honolulu HI 96821-1001

ADCOCK, DAVID FILMORE, radiologist, educator; b. Columbia, S.C., Sept. 19, 1938; s. David Filmore and Eloise (Daniel) A. BS, U. S.C., 1958, MPH, 1986; MD, Med. Coll. S.C., 1962. Diplomate Am. Bd. Radiology, Am. Bd. Nuclear Medicine, Am. Bd. Preventive Medicine. Asst. prof. radiology U. N.C.-Chapel Hill, 1970-72, assoc. prof., 1972-73; dir. nuclear medicine Richard Meml. Hosp., Columbia, 1974-79; prof., chmn. dept. radiology U. S.C.-Columbia, 1979—. Cons. in field Contbr. articles to profl. jours. Served as capt. U.S. Army, 1963-66. Fellow Am. Coll. Preventive Medicine; mem. Radiol. Soc. N.Am., Assn. Univ. Radiologists, Soc. Chmn. Acad. Radiology Depts., Alpha Omega Alpha. Office: U SC Sch Medicine Dept Radiology Columbia SC 29208-0001

ADCOCK, MURIEL W. special education educator; b. Chgo. BA, U. Calif. Sonoma State, Rohnert Park, 1979. Cert. spl. edn. tchr., Calif., Montessori spl. edn. tchr. Tchr. The Concordia Sch., Concord, Calif., 1980-85; tchr., cons. Tenderloin Community Children's Ctr., San Francisco, 1985-86; adminstr. Assn. Montessori Internat.-USA, San Francisco, 1988, tchr., advisor, 1989—. Course asst. Montessori Spl. Edn. Inst., San Francisco, 1985-87, tchr. spl. edn., 1990, tchr. cons., 1991—, rschr. 1992—. Contbr. articles to profl. jour. Sec. Internat. Forum World Affairs Coun., San Francisco, 1990-95, program chair, 1993-95, pres./founder Club of Budapest, U.S., 2000—. Mem. ASCD, Am. Orthopsychiat. Assn., Internat. Soc. Sys. Scientists, Internat. Sys. Inst., Assn. Montessori Internat., N.Am. Montessori Tchrs. Assn., Assn. Childhood Edn. Internat., Smithsonian Assocs., N.Y. Acad. Scis., Internat. Sys. Inst. Avocations: general evolutionary systems theory, sustainable development, educational systems design, ethical leadership. Office: 4040 Civic Center Dr Ste 200 San Rafael CA 94903

ADCOX, MARY SANDRA, dietitian, consultant; b. Portsmouth, Ohio, Dec. 4, 1939; d. Philip Henry and Bertha Mae (Hansgen) Riddinger; m. Steve Jordan Jr., Dec. 5, 1962 (dec. May 1972); 1 child, Michael Philip; m. Henry Lonzo Adcox Jr., Sept. 30, 1972. BS in Food and Nutrition, U. Cin., 1961; MEd, S.W. Tex. State U., 1984. Registered dietitian Commn. on Dietetic Registration. Rsch. dietitian U.S. Army Inst. Surg. Rsch., Ft. Sam Houston, 1964-65; chief dietitian Luth. Gen. Hosp., San Antonio, 1966-67; dir. dietetics Santa Rosa Med. Ctr., San Antonio, 1967-72, San Antonio Cmty. Hosp., 1972-75; adult edn. instr. San Antonio Coll., 1973-84; food svc. supr. San Antonio Ind. Sch. Dist., 1975-96, ret., 1996. Sch. food svc. cons., San Antonio, 1996—. Author: Dietetic Assistant Program, 1983, Diet Manual: San Antonio Community Hospital, 1st edit., 1973, Diet Manual: Santa Rosa Medical Center, 4th edit., 1969. Former den mother cub scouts, Boy Scouts Am.; organist Ch. of God. 1st lt. U.S. Army, 1962-64. Mem. Am. Dietetic Assn., San Antonio Dietetic Assn., U. Cin. Alumni Assn., S.W. Tex. State U. Alumni Assn., Tex. State Nutrition Coun., San Antonio Area Ret. Tchrs. Assn., Delta Zeta. Baptist. Avocations: piano, organ, herb gardening. Home: 5503 Oo-Loo-Te-Ka Dr San Antonio TX 78218-5041

ADCROFT, PATRICE GABRIELLA, former editor; b. Scranton, Pa., Apr. 15, 1954; d. Joseph Raymond and Patricia Ann (Ryan) Adcroft. BA In Mag. Journalism and Creative Writing, Syracuse U., 1976. Editor-in-chief Carbondale (Pa.) Miner Mid Valley Gazette, 1976—77; staff writer Good Housekeeping Mag., N.Y.C., 1978—80; mng. editor Family Media/Alive and Well, N.Y.C., 1980—81; freelance writer, editor N.Y.C., 1981—82; sr. editor CBS Mags. Family Weekly, N.Y.C., 1982—84, Omni Mag., N.Y.C., 1984—85, exec. editor, 1985—86, editor-in-chief, 1986—90; Editor-in-Chief Seventeen Magazine, 1998—2001. Vis. prof. Syracuse U., 1992—93. Editor-in-chief Omni Future Medical Almanac, 1987, NetGuide Mag., 1994—95, deputy editor InStyle Mag., 1995—98; author: (novels) Every Day Doughnuts; contbr. writer Arthur C. Clarke's 2019, 1986, Omni Book of Continuum, 1982. Bd. advisors SCI Ctr. for Advanced Studies in Mgmt. Wharton Sch., U. Pa. Roman Catholic.*

ADDABBO, DOMINIC LUCIAN, lawyer; b. N.Y.C., Dec. 13, 1951; s. Joseph P. and Grace (Salamone) A.; m. Marianna G. Riverso, Jan. 12, 1980; children: Grace, Lisa, Joseph. BA, St. John's U., 1973, JD, 1976. Bar: N.Y. 1977, Fla. 1978, U.S. Dist. Ct. (ea. and so. dists.) N.Y. 1978. Asst. dist. atty. Queens Dist. Attys. Office, KEw Gardens, N.Y., 1977-81; coun. to pres. Queens Borough Pres., KEw Gardens, N.Y., 1981-83; ptnr. Addabbo & Greenberg, Forest Hills, N.Y., 1983—. Pres. United Exec. Dem. Club, Ozone Park, N.Y., 1981-86, state commiteeman N.Y. State Dem. Party, Queens, 1982-86. Mem. Fla. Bar Assn., N.Y. State Bar Assn., Queens County Bar Assn., Asst. Dist. Attys. Assn. Roman Catholic. Avocations: music, songwriting, Karate. Office: Addabbo & Greenberg 11821 Queens Blvd Forest Hills NY 11375-7201

ADDABBO, NUNZIO PHILIP, civil engineer; b. N.Y.C., Sept. 4, 1924; s. Ciro and Filomena A.; m. Elizabeth Hamilton; children: Mark, Michael, Vance, Daniel. BS in Civil Engring., Columbia U., 1949. Field engr. Chile Exploration Co., Chuquicamata, 1950-53; office engr. Anaconda Co., Columbia Falls, Mont., 1954-58; chief field engr. Merritt Chapman & Scott Corp., Niagara Falls, N.Y., 1959-63; project mgr. Projections/Bonanza, Jonesboro, Ga., 1963-65; constrn. cons., chief resident engr. Parsons Jurden Corp., Chile, 1965-78; v.p., project mgr. Mtn. States Engrs., Inc., Tucson, Ariz., 1979-84, v.p., gen. mgr. Santiago, Chile, 1984-88; area mgr. Fluor Daniel Corp., Coloso, Chile, 1989-91. Patentee in navigation; co-author (with Elizabeth Addabbo): Expose Target *JFK*. Recipient NAS commendation, 1957; named 1st in U.S.A. to officially track Sputnik #1, Oct. 4, 1957. Mem.: Assn. Former Intelligence Officers, Ret. Officers Assn. Republican. Avocations: amateur radio, writing, bridge, flying. Home: 300 Meridian Ct New Bern NC 28562-2965

ADDERLEY, TERENCE E, corporate executive; b. 1933; married. BBA, U. Mich., 1951, BMA, 1956. Fin. analyst Standard Oil Co. of N.J., 1956-57; with Kelly Services, Inc., Troy, Mich., 1957-61, v.p., 1961-65, exec. v.p., 1965-67, pres., COO, 1967—, chmn., CEO, 1998—, also bd. dirs. Office: Kelly Svcs Inc 999 W Big Beaver Rd Troy MI 48084-4716

ADDICOTT, WARREN OLIVER, retired geologist, educator; b. Fresno, Calif., Feb. 17, 1930; s. Irwin Oliver and Astrid (Jensen) A.; m. Suzanne Aubin, Oct. 2, 1976; m. Susanne Smith, Aug. 20, 1956 (div. 1974); children: Eric Oliver, Carol. BA cum laude, Pomona Coll., Calif., 1951; MA, Stanford U., Calif., 1952; PhD, U. Calif.-Berkeley, 1956. Tchg. asst. U. Calif.-Berkeley, Calif., 1952-54; paleontologist Std. Oil Co. Calif., Calif., 1953; geologist Mobil Oil Co., 1954-62; rsch. geologist U.S. Geol. Survey, Menlo Pk., Calif., 1962-94; cons. prof. Stanford U., Calif., 1970-81. Dep. chmn. Circum-Pacific Map Project, Menlo Park, Calif., 1979-82, gen. chmn., 1982-86, project advisor, 1986—; adj. prof. So. Oreg. U., 1989-97; bd. dirs. Circum-Pacific Coun. Energy and Mineral Resources, 1983-86. Contbr. articles to profl. jours. Bd. dir. Peace Ho., 2001—. Fellow AAAS, Geol. Soc. Am., Calif. Acad. Scis., Paleontol. Soc. (pres. 1979-80), Paleontol. Res. Instn. (bd. dirs. 1980-81), Home: 2260 Old Siskiyou Hwy Ashland OR 97520

ADDINGTON, RONALD PAUL, mass media educator; b. Nashville, Ark., Sept. 15, 1946; s. Russell Kennedy and Myrtle Leonie (Clenney) Addington; m. Cecilia Ann Hearne, Mar. 26, 1976; children: Amie Ann, John Hearne. BS in Comm., Henderson State U., Arkadelphia, Ark., 1969; MS, Ind. U., 1972; D of Edn., U. of Ark., 1976. Journalism tchr. Lockesburg (Ark.) H.S., 1969; pub. info. instr. Dept. of Def. Info. Sch., Fort Benjamin Harrison, Ind., 1969—72; comm. instr. Ind. U. and Purdue U. at Indpls., 1973; pub. info. officer Ark. State Senate, Little Rock, 1975; pub. rels. dir. Henderson State U., Arkadelphia, 1975—77; journalism prof. Texarkana (Tex.) Coll., 1977—80; pres. Cossatot Tech, DeQueen, Ark., 1980—85; mass media prof. Henderson State U., Arkadelphia, 1996—. Bd. dirs. Henderson State Grad. Sch. Coun., Arkadelphia; panel guest TV program Hardball with Chris Matthews, 1998; guest live broadcast radio show BBC, London, 1998; conv. presenter Columbia U. Nat. Collegiate Media Conv., N.Y.C., 2000. Newspaper columnist: Daily Siftings Herald. City councilman Arkadelphia City Bd. of Dirs., 1989—94; campaign mgr. Bill Clinton for Congress primary campaign, Fayetteville, Ark., 1974; bd. dirs. Clark County Dem. Cen. Com., Arkadelphia, 1994—2000; del. Ark. Constl. Conv., Little Rock, 1979—80; nat. press spokesperson for Gov. Bill Clinton during Cuban conflict Ft. Chaffee, 1980; bd. dirs. State of Ark. Jobs Tng. Partnership Act, Little Rock, 1980—84; mem. coun. Boy Scouts Am., Hot Springs, Ark., 1990—94; mem. sch. bd. Arkadelphia Pub. Schs., Arkadelphia, 1998—2001. Capt. Signal Corp U.S. Army, 1969—72, lt. col. USAR, 1993, ret. USAR. Mem.: Ark. Press Assn. (assoc.), S.W. Edn. Coun. for Journalism and Mass Comm. (life), Assoc. Coll. Press (life), Coll. Media Advisors (life), Assn. for Edn. in Journalism and Mass Comm. (life; panelist 2002), United Way, Clark County Indsl. Coun. (life; fundraising chairperson 1987—89), Rotary Internat. (life; bd. dirs. 1982—85). Democrat. Methodist. Avocations: hunting, gardening. Home: PO Box 517 Arkadelphia AR 71923 Office: Henderson State U HSU Box 7681 Arkadelphia AR 71999-0001 Home Fax: 870-230-5549; Office Fax: 870-230-5549. Personal E-mail: addingr@hsu.edu. E-mail: addingr@hsu.edu.

ADDIS, DEBORAH JANE, management consultant, editor; b. Rahway, N.J., Jan. 29, 1950; d. Emmanuel and Stella (Oles) Addis; m. James Eldin Reed, Apr. 14, 1983. BA, Bowling Green State U., 1972; MA in Orgn., Mgmt. and Pub. Policy, Lesley U., Cambridge, Mass., 1992. cons. House Judiciary Com., Washington, 1999-2000. Pub. info. officer Dept. Transp., State of Ohio, 1972-73; dir. pub. info. and edn. Dept. Commerce, State of Ohio, 1973-75; press sec. Atty. Gen., State of Ohio, 1975-77; dep. press sec. Office of Gov., Commonwealth of Mass., Boston, 1978-79; sr. account exec. Miller Comms., Boston, 1979-80; v.p., prin. Addis & Reed Cons., Inc., Boston, 1981-91, pres., 1992—. Adj. faculty Lesley Coll. Grad. Sch., 1992-95; bd. dirs. Can. Inst. Internat. Affairs, Boston; cons. to affordable housing orgns., 1993—. Author monograph and numerous articles, congl. testimony; mng. editor The American Canada Watch, 1995—. Bd. govs. Women's City Club of Boston, 1982-85; mem. Ohio Task Force on Domestic Violence, Columbus, 1976; pres. Asbestos Victims Campaign, Boston, 1987-90. Mem. New Eng.-Can. Bus. Coun. (bd. dirs. 1994-98), Inst. Mgmt. Cons. (bd. dirs. New Eng. chpt. 1988-89), Mass. Audubon Soc., Harvard Club of Boston, Boston Atheneum. Democrat. Avocations: photography, herpetology (turtles), hiking, travel. Home: 25 Holly Ln Brookline MA 02467-2156 Office: Addis & Reed Cons Inc PO Box 85 Chestnut Hill MA 02467 E-mail: addis@addisreed.com.

ADDIS, KAY TUCKER, newspaper editor; AB in English, Coll. of William and Mary, 1970. Editor The Virginian-Pilot, Norfolk, 1996—. Office: The Virginian-Pilot 150 W Brambleton Ave Norfolk VA 23510-2075 also: Virginian Pilot P O Box 449 Norfolk VA 23501-0449*

ADDIS, LAIRD CLARK, JR., philosopher, educator, musician; b. Bath, N.Y., Mar. 25, 1937; s. Laird Clark and Dora Ersel (Webber) A.; m. Patricia Karen Peterson, Dec. 20, 1962; children— Kristin, Karin. BA, U. Iowa, 1959, PhD, 1964; MA (Woodrow Wilson fellow), Brown U., 1960. Instr. U. Iowa, Iowa City, 1963-64, asst. prof., 1964-68, assoc. prof., 1968-74, prof. philosophy, 1974—, also chmn. dept. philosophy, 1977-85. Sr. Fulbright lectr. State U. Groningen, Netherlands, 1970-71 Author: (with Douglas Lewis) Moore and Ryle: Two Ontologists, 1965, The Logic of Society, 1975, Natural Signs, 1989, Of Mind and Music, 1999; contbr. articles to profl. jours. Mem. Am. Philos. Assn., Philosophy of Sci. Assn., Am. Soc. for Aesthetics, Am. Fedn. Musicians, Quad City Symphony Orch. (ret.), Soc. Humanist Philosophers. Home: 20 W Park Rd Iowa City IA 52246-2304 Office: U Iowa Dept Philosophy Iowa City IA 52242 E-mail: laird-addis@uiowa.edu.

ADDIS, THOMAS HOMER, III, professional golfer; b. San Diego, Nov. 30, 1945; s. Thomas H. and Martha J. (Edwards) A.; m. Susan Tera Buckley, June 13, 1966; children: Thomas Homer IV, Bryan Michael. Student, Foothill Jr. Coll., 1963, Grossmont Jr. Coll., 1965; degree in profl. golf mgmt. (hon.), Ferris State U., 1995. Head golf profl., mgr. Sun Valley Golf Course, La Mesa, Calif., 1966-67; head golf profl., dir. golf Singing Hills Country Club and Lodge, 1969-98; sr. v.p. Golfstar Mgmt., 1998-99; v.p. Full Swing Golf, San Diego, 1999-2000; pres. Medallion Golf Inc., 2000—. Gen. chmn. Nat. Jr. Golf Championship, U.S. Golf Assn., 1973-89; cons. Nat. Golf Found. Far East, 1978-; pres. Nat. Golf Corp., 2001-; owner Rocky Mountain Chocolate Factory, Mammoth; spkr. in field; instr. Profl. Golfers Career Coll. Contbr. articles to profl. jours. Dir. Cuyamaca Coll. Found., Burn Inst.Prokids Golf; mem. internat. golf com. Spl. Olympics. Mem. PGA (pres. San Diego chpt. 1978-79, pres. sect. 1980-82, pres. PGA Am. 1994-96, named Profl. of Yr. So. Calif. sect. 1979, 89, Horton Smith award So. Calif. sect. 1980-81, 89, PGA Golf Profl. of Yr. 1989, Nat. Horton Smith award 1981, nat. bd. dirs. 1986-88, rules com. 1986-90, championship com. 1986—, hon. life mem. So. Calif. sect. and San Diego PGA), So. Calif. PGA Hall of Fame, Nat. Golf Found. (Joe Graffis award 1988), Nat. Amputee Golf Assn. (hon.), San Diego Jr. Golf Assn. (pres. 1997-98, 2000-2003), Golf Collectors Soc., Rotary. Office: 12312A Paseo Lucido San Diego CA 92128 E-mail: medalliongolf@aol.com.

ADDISON, DAVID DUNHAM, lawyer; b. Richmond, Va., Aug. 23, 1941; s. Grafton Dulany and Anne (Withers) A.; m. Marion Lee Wood, Aug. 21, 1965; children: David Dunham Jr., Marion Lee, Elizabeth Townshend. BA, Hampden-Sydney Coll., 1964; LLB, U. Va., 1967. Bar: Va. 1967. Assoc. Browder, Russell, Morris & Butcher, Richmond, 1967-72; ptnr., dir. Browder & Russell, P.C., Richmond, 1972-90; mem. firm, shareholder Williams, Mullen, Clark & Dobbins, P.C., Richmond, 1990—. Contbr. articles to profl. jours. Fellow Am. Coll. Trust and Estate Counsel (state chmn. 1986-92); mem. ABA (com. chmn. 1987-94), S.R., Va. Bar Assn., Richmond Bar Assn., Estate Planning Coun. Richmond (pres. 1987-88), Richmond Trust Adminstrs. Coun. (pres. 1986-87), Kiwanis Club of Richmond (pres. 1998-99), Country Club of Va., Commonwealth Club. Episcopalian. Avocations: travel, golf. Office: Williams Mullen Clark & Dobbins 2 James Center 1021 E Cary St Richmond VA 23219-4000

ADDISON, FERGUSON LOFTON LIGHTBOURNE, retired bank executive; b. Punta Gorda, Fla., Sept. 10, 1922; s. Locke and Maysoura Lofton (Hall) Addison. BA, Harvard U., 1950. Safety patrol sponsor Coconut Grove Elem. Sch., Miami, Fla., 1952—53. Author: House-Organ of Dun & Bradstreet, 1956. Safety patrol sponsor Coconut Grove Elem. Sch., Palm Beach, 1952—53; pres. Shaughnessy Club, First Nat. Bank, Palm Beach, 1962. With USNR, 1942—46. Named to, Fla. Women's Hall of Fame, 2002. Mem.: English Speaking Union, Martin County Hist. Soc., Shaughnessy Club, 1st Nat. Bank (pres. 1962), Harvard Club of Palm Beach (organizer 1962, pres. 1964—65). Avocations: genealogy, antiques. Home: 300 Forest Hill Blvd West Palm Beach FL 33405-4614

ADDISON, HERBERT JOHN, consulting editor; b. Berkeley, Calif., Nov. 21, 1932; s. Herbert and Clara Virginia (Mason) A.; m. Geraldyne Elaine Harvey, Aug. 17, 1957; children: Bradley Thomas, Gregory James. BA, U. Calif.-Berkeley, 1958; MA, NYU, 1959. Office-personnel mgr. Thomas Y. Crowell Co., N.Y.C., 1958-65; editor-in-chief coll. dept. Holt, Rinehart & Winston, Inc., N.Y.C., 1965-70; v.p., gen. mgr. coll. dept. Thomas Y. Crowell Co., N.Y.C., 1970-74; exec. editor coll. dept. John Wiley & Sons, Inc., N.Y.C., 1974-78; gen. mgr. coll. dept. Oxford U. Press, Inc., N.Y.C., 1978-82, v.p., exec. editor bus., 1982-2000, cons. editor, 2000—. Adj. lectr. NYU, 1977-83 Author: Books and Bucks: The Business of College Textbook Publishing, 1980. Trustee Adult Sch. Montclair, N.J., 1976-80; mem. Civic Conf. Com., Glen Ridge, N.J., 1974-77. Served with U.S. Army, 1953-55. Mem. Acad. Mgmt. Home: 46 Sherman Ave Glen Ridge NJ 07028-1441 Office: Oxford U Press Inc 198 Madison Ave New York NY 10016 E-mail: addisons@verizon.net.

ADDISON, LINDA LEUCHTER, lawyer, writer; b. Allentown, Pa., Nov. 25, 1951; d. Marcus and Sophie Theresa (Tisch) Leuchter; m. Max M. Addison, Sept. 10, 1977; 1 child, Alexandra Leuchter Addison. BA with honors, U. Tex., 1973, JD, 1976. Bar: Tex. 1976, U.S. Dist. Ct. (no. and so. dists.) Tex. 1977, U.S. Ct. Appeals (5th cir.) 1981, U.S. Ct. Appeals (fed. cir.) 2003. Assoc. Fulbright & Jaworski LLP, Houston, 1976—83, ptnr., 1984—, exec. com., tech. ptnr., 2002—. Expert on fed. and Tex. evidence. Author: Federal Civil Procedure and Evidence During Trial, 1997, Texas Evidence, 2003; contbr. chpt. to book; mng. editor Tex. Law Rev. 1975-76; contbr. articles to profl. jours. Trustee U. Tex. Law Sch. Found., 1994—; mem. fed. jud. evaluation com. of Sens. Hutchison and Cornyn, 1997-; exec. com. chancellor's coun., U. Tex. Sys., 1999-; bd. dirs. Holocaust Mus. Houston, 2001; mem. Commn. of 125, U. Tex., Austin, 2003—, vice chmn. task force of centennial commn., 1981-83. Named one of Am.'s Top 50 Women Litigators, Nat. Law Jour., 2001, Tex. Go To Litigators, Tex. Lawyer, 2002, Most Fascinating People in Houston, Friends of Tex. Med. Ctr. Libr., 2001, Hon. Barrister, U. Tex. Sch. Law bd. advocates, 2000, Outstanding Young Lawyer of Houston, 1984-85, Woman on the Move, Tex. Exec. Women, 2000, Woman to Watch, Jewish Women Internat., 2002; named one of Am. Bd. Trial Advs., 1986, One of Best Lawyers in Am., Woodard and White, 2003. Fellow: Tex. Bar Found. (trustee 2003—), Houston Bar Found. (life), Am. Bar Found. (life); mem.: ABA, Am. Bd. Trial Advs., World Internat. Patent Orgn. (arbitration and mediation ctr. domain name panel 2002—), Am. Intellectual Property Law Assn., Am. Arbitration Assn. (internat. panel 1992—, panel of neutrals, large complex case panel), Tex. Law Rev. Ex-Editors Assn. (life), Houston Young Lawyers Assn. (chmn. cont. legal edn. com. 1977—78, bd. dirs. 1978—81, Outstanding Chmn. award), Tex. Young Lawyers Assn. (bd. dirs. 1981—83), Houston Bar Assn. (chmn. cont. legal edn. com. 1981—82, mem. jud. evalns. com. 1982—83, Pres.'s award for outstanding svc. 1982), State Bar Tex. (chmn. bar jour. com. 1988—90, adminstr. rules evidence com. 1988—90, chmn. bar jour. com. 1991—99), United Way, deTocqueville Soc., Anti-Defamation League (bd. dirs. S.W. Region 1992—94), Friar Soc., Omicron Delta Kappa. Office: Fulbright & Jaworski LLP 1301 McKinney St Ste 5100 Houston TX 77010-3095

ADDO, CHARLES KWAME, municipal official; b. Techiman, B/A, Ghana, Feb. 16, 1957; arrived in U.S., 1977; s. James Kwabena Addo and Mary Abena Brefo-Inkum; m. Gifty Okwan Amoah (div. May 1991); children: Mavis, Judith, Lizzie, Liza, Stephanie. Student, SUNY Maritime Coll., Bronx, 1977—79; BS, Mercy Coll., Dobbs Ferry, N.Y., 1996; MBA, L.I. U., 1999; postgrad., Walden U., 2002—. Cert. merchant marine officer. Shipdeck officer Golotrade Shipping and Chartering, N.Y.C., 1981—90; contract guard security supr. McLane Assocs., N.Y.C., 1992—96; adj. prof. Mercy Coll., Dobbs Ferry, 1999—; prin. contract adminstrv. assoc. III Dept. of Design and Constrn., City of N.Y., L.I., 2001—. Cons. Diabetex Internat., Old Saybrook, Conn. Author: Corporate Mergers and Acquisitions: A Case Study, 2000, Burdens of the Mirage Dream, 2001. Methodist. Avocation: writing.

ADDUCCI, JAMES DOMINICK, lawyer; b. Chgo., Dec. 2, 1951; s. John James and Frances Mary (Violante) A.; m. Elizabeth Anne Clark, Apr. 29, 1978; children: John James, Marian Elizabeth. BA, Loyola U., Chgo., 1973; JD, Harvard U., 1976. Bar: Ill. 1976, U.S. Dist. Ct. (no. dist.) Ill. 1977, U.S. Ct. Appeals (7th cir.) 1977, U.S. Ct. Appeals (8th cir.) 1990, U.S. Ct. Appeals (3d cir.) 1991, U.S. Ct. Appeals (fed.cir.) 1991, U.S. Ct. Appeals (11th cir.) 1995, U.S. Ct. Appeals (9th cir.) 1998. Law clk. Judge Decker, U.S. Dist. Ct. (no. dist.) Ill., Chgo., 1976-77; assoc. Kirkland & Ellis, Chgo., 1977-82; assoc. Schuyler, Roche & Zwirner, Chgo., 1982-84, ptnr., 1984-96; ptnr. Adducci, Dorf, Lehner, Mitchell & Blankenship PC, Chgo., 1996—. Democrat. Roman Catholic. Office: Adducci Dorf Lehner Mitchell et al 150 N Michigan Ave Ste 2130 Chicago IL 60601

ADDUCCI, JOSEPH EDWARD, obstetrician, gynecologist; b. Chgo., Dec. 1, 1934; s. Dominee Edward and Harriet Evelyn (Kneppreth) A.; m. Mary Ann Tiertje, 1958; children— Christopher, Gregory, Steven, Jessica, Tobias BS, U. Ill., 1955; MD, Loyola U., Chgo., 1959. Diplomate Am. Bd. Ob-Gyn., Nat. Bd. Med. Examiners. Intern Cook County Hosp, Chgo., 1959-60; resident in ob-gyn Mt. Carmel Hosp., Detroit, 1960-64; practice medicine specializing in obstetrics and gynecology Williston, N.D., 1966—. Chief staff, chmn. obstetrics dept. Mercy Hosp., Williston, mem. governing bd., 1996, chmn. dept. surgery; clin. prof. U. N.D. Med. Sch., 1973—; mem. gov. bd. Mercy Hosp. Cath. Health Corp.; mem. coun. Accreditation Coun. for Gynecologic Endoscopy, 1999—. Mem. N.D. Bd. Med. Examiners, 1974—, past chmn.; project dir. Tri County Family Planning Svc.; past pres. Tri County Health Planning Coun.; mem. governing bd. Mercy Hosp., Williston, N.D. With Med. Corps, AUS, 1964-66. Fellow Am. Soc. Abdominal Surgeons, ACS (regent N.D. 1990—), Am. Coll. Obstetrics and Gynecologists (sect. chmn. N.D.), Internat. Coll. Surgeons (regent 1972-74, 88-89), Am. Fertility Soc., Am. Assn. Internat. Lazar Soc., Gynecol. Lataropists, N.D. Obstetricians and Gynecologists Soc. (pres. 1966, 76); mem. Am. Soc. for Colposcopy and Colpomicroscopy, Am. Soc. Cryosurgery, Am. Soc. Contemporary Medicine and Surgery, Am. Assn. Profl. Ob-Gyn., Pan Am. Med. Assn., Am. Coll. Surgeons (regent 1989— N.D.). Lodges: Elks. Home: 1717 Main St Williston ND 58801-4244 Office: Medical Ctr OB GYN Williston ND 58801

ADDUCCI, REGINA MARIE, medical/surgical nurse; b. Flushing, N.Y., Jan. 1, 1956; d. Robert Philip and Brenda Claire (Guinan) Hosey; m. Joseph Anthony Adducci, June 30, 1990 (div. June 14, 1995); 1 child, Sarah Elizabeth. BS, Mount St. Mary Coll., Newburgh, N.Y., 1978. RN, Conn. Staff nurse med./surg. unit Danbury (Conn.) Hosp., 1979-88, staff nurse ob./gyn./urology unit, 1988-89, asst. nurse mgr. gynecology/urology unit, 1989-92, asst. nurse mgr. general surgery unit, 1992-93, coord. quality improvement med. svcs., 1993-95, asst. dir. nursing, 1995-2000, clin. leader surg. unit, 2000—.

ADDY, ALVA LEROY, mechanical engineer; b. Dallas, S.D., Mar. 29, 1936; s. Alva Isaac and Nellie Amelia (Brumbaugh) A.; m. Sandra Ruth Turney, June 8, 1958 BS, S.D. Sch. Mines and Tech., 1958; MS, U. Cin., 1960; PhD, U. Ill., 1963. Engr. Gen. Electric Co., Cin., also Lancaster, Calif., 1958-60; prof. mech. engring. U. Ill., Urbana, 1963-98, prof. emeritus, 1998—, dir. mech. engring. lab., 1965-97, assoc. head mech. engring. dept., 1980-87, head, 1987-98. Aerodynamics cons. U.S. Army Missile Command, Redstone Arsenal, Ala., summers 1965-98; cons. U.S. Army Research Office, 1964— ; cons. in high-speed fluid dynamics to indsl. firms, 1963— ; vis. research prof. U.S. Army, 1976; lectr. Von Karman Inst. Fluid Dynamics, Brussels, 1968, 75, 76 Fellow ASME, AIAA (assoc.), Am. Soc. for Engring. Edn. (Ralph Coates Roe award 1990); mem. Sigma Xi, Pi Tau Sigma, Sigma Tau. Home: 726 Elk Run Rd Spearfish SD 57783 Office: U Ill 1206 W Green St Urbana IL 61801-2906

ADDY, FREDERICK SEALE, retired oil company executive; b. Boston, Jan. 1, 1932; s. William R. and Edith (Seale) A.; m. Joyce Marilyn Marshall, Mar. 26, 1954; children: Deborah, William, Brian. BA, Mich. State U., 1953, MBA, 1957. With Amoco Corp. and its subs., 1957-94; exec. v.p., chief fin. officer, dir. Amoco Corp., Chgo., 1990-94. Interim chmn., pres., CEO Enserch Exptl. Inc., 1996-97. Served with USAF, 1954-56.

ADDY, JO ALISON PHEARS, economist; b. Germany, May 2, 1951; d. William Phears and Paula Hubbard; m. Tralance Obuma Addy, May 25, 1979; children: Mantse, Miishe, Dwetri, Naakai. BA, Smith Coll., 1973; MBA, Adelphi U., 1975; postgrad., Stanford U., 1975-78. Econ. analyst Morgan Guaranty, N.Y.C., 1973—75; economist Young Profls. Program, World Bank, Washington, 1979—80; asst. v.p., internat. economist Crocker Bank, San Francisco, 1980—85; asst. v.p., economist for money markets 1st RepublicBank, Dallas, 1985—87; prin. SEGI Internat., Dallas, 1987—91; pres. Unimed Ventures, Inc., 1991—95; mng. dir. Alsweb Bus. Advantage, 1999—; mem. adv. bd. Plebys Internat. LLC, 2003—. Lectr. in field. Docent Bowers Mus.; vice chmn. St. John's Sch. Com.; pres. Saddleback Valley chpt. Nat. Charity League. Office: 8 Palomino Trabuco Canyon CA 92679-4837 Business E-Mail: principal@aslwebb.com.

ADEBIMPE, VICTOR ROTIMI, psychiatrist; b. Iji, Kwara, Nigeria, Nov. 6, 1945; arrived in U.S., 1972; s. Solomon Olawepo and Bolaji Adebimpe; m. Folasade Oluremi Ogunlana, Apr. 29, 1972; children: Oluseyi, Babatunde, Olajumoke. BS, U. Ibadan, Nigeria, 1968; MD, U. Ibadan, 1971. Intern Bapt. Hosp., Ogbomosho, Nigeria, 1971-72; resident Mo. Inst. Psychiatry, St. Louis, 1972-75; attending psychiatrist U. Pitts., 1975-79; med. dir. No. Commn. Mental Health Ctr., Pitts., 1979-82; sr. lectr. U. Ilorin, Ilorin, Nigeria, 1982-84; dir. psychiatry St. Johns Health & Hosp. Ctr., Pitts., 1984-90; med. dir. Charles R. Drew Community Mental Health Ctr., Phila., 1987-92; dir. adult psychiatry Mercy Psychiat. Inst., Pitts., 1990-95, pres. med. staff, 1992-95. Adj. asst. prof. psycniatry Allegheny U. Health Scis., 1996; attending psychiatrist Mercy Providence Hosp., Pitts., 1996. Contbr. chpts. to books, articles to profl. jours. Med. dir. Glade Run Luth. Svcs., Zelienople, Pa., 1996. Fellow Am. Psychiat. Assn., World Fedn. for Mental Health (life); mem. AAAS, Nat. Med. Assn. Baptist. Office: Allies Behavioral Ctr 275 Gateway Twrs Pittsburgh PA 15222-1616

ADEDEJI, ADEBAYO, economist, former government official; b. Ijebu-Ode, Ogun, Nigeria, Dec. 21, 1930; came to Ethiopia, 1975; s. L.S. and Adeola Adedeji; m. Aderinola Ogun, Aug. 11, 1957; children: Adedoyin, Funso, Adekunle, Adeleke, Adeniyi, Adeola, Adefunke, Adeyinka, Adepoju, Adedipe, Adeoye. Diploma in Local Govt. Adminstrn., Univ. Coll., U. Ibadan, 1953-54; B.Sc. in Econs., Leicester U. Coll., 1958; M.P.A., Harvard U., 1961; PhD in Econs., U. London, 1967; Litt.D. (hon.), Ahmadu Bello U., 1976; LL.D. (hon.), U. Dallhousie, 1984, U. Zambia, 1984, U. Calabar, 1987; DSc (hon.), Obafemi Awolowo U., 1989; DSc (hon.), U. Ibadan, 1997, Ogun State U., 1998. Sr. asst. sec. for revenue Nigerian Civil Service, 1958-63; dep. dir. Inst. Adminstrn. U. Ife, 1963-67, dir. Inst. Adminstrn., prof. pub. adminstrn., 1967-75; fed. commr. Nigeria Ministry for Econ. Devel. in Reconstruction, 1971-75; under-sec.-gen., exec. sec. UN Econ. Commn. for Africa, Addis Ababa, Ethiopia, 1975—91. Mem. ad hoc com. of experts fin. UN and specialized agys., 1965; mem. expert com. on restructuring econ. and spl. sectors UN, 1975; chmn. senate UN Inst. for Namibia, 1975—90; trustee dept. econs. Boston U., 1975—85; chmn. Western Nigerian Govt. Broadcasting Corp., 1966—67; mem. Nigerian Nat. Manpower Bd., 1968—71; chmn. Directorate of Nat. Youth Svc. Corps, 1973—75; exec. dir., founder African Ctr. for Devel. and Strategic Studies, 1991—; mem. panel of high level experts on restructuring UN, chmn. devel. program, 1994, mem. adv. bd. African Futures project, 1998—, team leader evaluation and assessment devel. assistance framework, 1998, 2000, team leader on future of staff coll., 00; spl. envoy of pres. Nigeria on Zimbabwe inter-party dialogue post pres. election, 02; spl. advisor on transition of Orgn. African Unity to African Union. Author: Africa, the Third World and the search for a New Econ. Order, 1976, Africa: The Crisis of Devel. and the Challenge of a New Econ. Order, 1977, The Political Class, the Higher Civil Svc. and the Challenge of Nation Building, 1981, The Deepening Internat. Econ. Crisis and its Implications for Africa, 1982; editor: Indigenization of African Econs., 1981, Econ. Crisis in Africa: African Perspectives on Devel. Problems and Potentials, 1985, Towards the Dawn of the Third Millenium and the Beginning of the 21st Century, 1986, Towards a Dynamic African Econ., 1989, Preparing Africa for the Twenty-First Century: Agenda for the 1990's, 1991, Africa Within the World: Beyond Disposession and Dependence, 1993, South Africa and Africa: Within or Apart?, 1996, Nigeria: Renewal From the Roots? The Struggle for Dem. Devel., 1997, Comprehending and Mastering African Conflicts - The Search for Sustainable Peace and Good Governance, 1999, People-Centered Democracy in Nigeria? The Search for Alternative Systems of Governance at the Grassroots, 2000. Decorated grand officer Order of Mono Togo; named a comdr. Order of Merit, Islamic Republic Mauritania, comdr., Republic of Gambia; named grand comdr. Order of Disting. Svc. first class, Zambia, grand comdr. Order of Lion, Senegal, 1987, grand comdr. most excellent Order of Eagle, Namibia, 1995, comdr., Fed. Republic Nigeria, 2001, grand officer Order of the Niger, 1988; recipient Gold Mercury Internat. award, 1982. Fellow Nigerian Inst. Mgmt. (dir. 1968-75), Nigerian Econ. Soc. (pres. 1971-72), African Assn. for Pub. Adminstrn. and Mgmt. (v.p. 1971-74, pres. 1975-85), African Acad. Sci. Home: Asiwaju Ct GRA Erunwon Rd PO Box 203 Ijebu Ode Nigeria Office: African Ctr Devel Strategic Studies PO Box 203 Ijebu Ode Nigeria E-mail: acdess@hyperia.com., executivedirector@acdess.org.

ADEKSON, MARY OLUFUNMILAYO, therapist, counselor educator; b. Ogbomoso, Nigeria; came to U.S., 1988; d. Gabriel and Deborah Williams; children: Adedayo, Babatunde. BA in English and Am. Lit., Brandeis U., 1975; MEd in Guidance and Counseling, Obafemi Awolowo U., Ile-Ife, Nigeria, 1987; PhD, Ohio U., 1997. English tchr. Ctrl. Sch. Bd., Ibadan, Nigeria, 1968-88; acting prin. Abe Tech. Coll., Ibadan, Nigeria, 1978; coord. guidance svcs. Min. Edn., Ile-Ife, 1984-88; part-time lectr. Obafemi Awolowo U., Ile-Ife, 1986-88; vice prin. Olubuse Meml. HS, Ile-Ife, 1987-88; grad. asst. Ohio U., Athens, 1988-91. Vol. contract worker, trainer Careline, Tri-County Mental Health Ctr., Athens, 1988-92; vol. My Sister's Place, Athens, 1989, Good Works Athens, 1989, Montgomery County Hotline, 1994; contract worker Tri County Activity Ctr., Athens, 1989-92, therapist II Woodland Ctr., Gallipolis, Ohio, 1991-92; part-time lectr. U. Md., 1993, coord. tutorial svc.; dir. Christian Book Ctr., Ile-Ife; vol., part-time counselor DWI program Prince George's County Health Dept., Hyattsville, Md.; counselor Potomac Healthcare Found. Mountain Manor Treatment Program; adj. prof. Bowie (Md.) State U. Counseling Program, 1997-98; asst. prof. St. Bonaventure U., 1998—; faculty adviser Chi Sigma Iota, Phi Rho chpt. Vol. Montgomery County Police Dept.; mem. Alcohol and Other Drug Abuse Adv. Coun., Montgomery County, Md.; mem. adv. com. Germantown (Md.) Libr.; mem. Gaithersburg (Md.) City Adv. Com.; chmn. bd. dir. Faith Enterprises; dir. Faith Consultancy Group. Recipient Gold medal West African Athletic Assn., 1965; Internat. Peace scholar P.E.O., 1990-91, Wien Internat. scholar Brandeis U., 1973-75. Mem. ACA, Am. Mental Health Counselors Assn. Network on Children and Teens (membership chair 1991-92, chair 1993-98), Am. Assn. Counseling and Devel. (award for internat. grad. students 1990), Counseling Assn. Nigeria (planning com. 1986), Oyo State Nigeria Assn. Guidance Counselors (chmn. Oranmiyan local govt. area 1986-88), Chi Sigma Iota (program coord. Ohio U. chpt. 1990, faculty advisor Phi Rho chpt.). Avocations: meeting people from around the world, jogging, walking, playing tennis, reading.

ADELBERG, ARNOLD MELVIN, mathematics educator, researcher; b. Bklyn., Mar. 17, 1936; s. David and Evelyn (Brass) A.; m. Harriet Diamond, June 30, 1962; children: Danielle Hamill, Erica. BA, Columbia U., 1956; MA, Princeton U., 1959, PhD, 1996. Instr. Columbia U., N.Y.C., 1959-62; instr., asst. prof., assoc. prof., prof. Grinnell (Iowa) Coll., 1962—, Myra Steele prof. math., 1991—. Chair math. dept., sci. div. several times, chmn. faculty Grinnell Coll., 1974-76, dir. Noyce vis. prof. program, 1997—. Contbr. articles to profl. jours. Mem. Math. Assn. Am., Am. Math. Soc. Avocations: bridge, chess. Home: 1930 Manor Cir Grinnell IA 50112-1136 Office: Grinnell Coll Math Dept PO Box 805 Grinnell IA 50112-0805 E-mail: adelbe@grinnell.edu.

ADELI, HOJJAT, engineer, educator, computer scientist; b. Langrood, Iran, June 3, 1950; came to U.S., 1974; s. Jafar and Mokarram (Soofi) A.; m. Nahid Dadmehr, Mar. 1979; children: Amir, Anahita, Mona, Cyrus Dean. MSCE summa cum laude, U. Teheran, Iran, 1973; PhD in Civil Engring. summa cum laude, Stanford U., 1976. Asst. prof. Northwestern U., Evanston, Ill., 1977, U. Teheran, 1978-81, assoc. prof., 1981-82, U. Utah, Salt Lake City, 1982-83, Ohio State U., Columbus, 1983-88, prof., 1988—, chmn. structures faculty, 1988-91, dir. Knowledge Engring. Lab., 1994—, exec. com., dept. civil/environ. engring., geodetic sci., 1994-95. Cons. Atomic Orgn. Iran, Teheran, 1978-79, Iran Ministry Housing, Teheran, 1970-82, U.S. Army Constrn. Engring. Rsch. Lab., 1988; keynote lectrs. in Italy, 1989, Mex., 1989, Japan, 1991, China, 1992, Can., 1992, 96, Portugal, 1992, Germany, 1993, U.S., 1993, 95, 96, Morocco, 1994, Singapore, 1994, 96, Australia, 1995, Bulgaria, 1995, New Zealand, 1995, Bahrain, 1996, Lithuania, 1996, France, 1997, Bahamas, 1997; contbr. to 100 confs. Author: Interactive Microcomputer-Aided Structural Steel Design, 1988; co-author: Expert Systems for Structural Design: A New Gerneration, 1988, Parallel Processing in Structural Engineering, 1993, Machine Learning-Neural Networks, Genetic Algorithms, and Fuzzy Systems, 1995; editor: Expert Systems in Construction and Structural Engineering, 1988, Microcomputer Knowledge-Based Expert Systems in Civil Engineering, 1988, Parallel and Distributed Processing in Structural Engineering, 1988, Knowledge Engineering, vols. 1 & 2, 1990, Supercomputing in Engineering Analysis, 1992, Parallel Processing in Computational Mechanics, 1992, Advances in Design Optimization, 1994; co-editor: Mechanics Computing in the 1990's and Beyond, vols. 1 & 2, 1991; Computing and Information Technology for Architechure, Engineering and Construction, 1996, Intelligent Information Systems, 1997, editor-in-chief, founder Internat. Jour. Computer-Aided Civil & Infrastructure Engring, 1986—, Integrated Computer-Aided Engring., 1993—; editor-in-chief Heuristics: The Jour. of Knowledge Engring., 1991-93; assoc. editor Control Engring. Practice, 1993-96, Jour. Artificial Neural Networks, 1995—; mem. editorial bd., editorial adv. bd. 30 sci. engring. jours. including Neural, Parallel, and Sci. Computations, 1993—, Parallel Algorithms and Applications, 1993—, Nanobiology-Jour. Rsch. Nanoscale Living Systems, 1993, Structural Engring. Review, 1989-91, Heuristic-Jour. Knowledge Engring., 1989-91, Engring. Analysis with Boundary Elements, 1987-92, Jour. of Condition Monitoring and Diagnostic Tech., 1990-92, Knowledge Based Systems, 1988—, ASCE Jour. of Aerospace Engring., 1989—, Internat. Jour. of Computers and Applications, 1990—, Internat. Jour. of Imaging Systems and Tech., 1990—, Mechatronics, 1991—, Advances in Engring Software, 1991-95, Neurocomputing, 1991—, Jour. of Systems Engring., 1991—, Internat. Jour. of Construction Information Tech., 1992—, Chaos, Solitons and Fractals, 1991—, Structural Optimization, 1991—, Computer Applications in Engring. Edn., 1993—, Asian Jour. of Structural Engring., 1995—, Theory and Practice of Object Systems, 1995—, IASTED Control & Computers Jour., 1996—, Internat. Jour. Computational Intelligence and Organization, 1996—, Int. Jour. of Computer Systems Science and Engineering, 1995, Iranian Jour. Sci. and Tech., 1997—, Internat. Jour. Parallel and Distributed Systems and Networks, 1998—; contbr. over 275 publs. Recipient 1st degree medal of Knowledge Iran Ministry Higher Edn., 1973, Rsch. award NSF, USAF Flight Dynamics Lab., Cray Rsch., Inc., Bethlehem Steel Corp., Ohio Dept. Devel. Thomas edison Program, Am. Inst. Steel Constrn., Am. Iron and Steel Inst., U.S. Army Constrn. Engring. Rsch. Lab., Ohio Dept. Transp., Fed. Hwy. Adminstrn. Fellow World Lit. Acad., ASCE (mem. numerous coms. including aerospace structures and materials com. Aerospace divsn. 1986—, real time data acquisition com., 1988—, inelastic behavior com. engring. mechanics divsn. 1987—, com. on metrication, 1991—, advanced composite materials com. 1994—); mem. IEEE Computer Soc. (mem. numerous coms. including computational medicine com. 1988-94, pattern analysis and machine intelligence com. 1988-94, microprocessors and microcomputers com. 1988-95, distributed processing com. 1988-95, data base engring. com. 1993-95, software engring. com. 1993-95, sys. engring. 1993-95, robotics and automation com. 1993-95, design automation com. 1994-95, optical processing and switching com. 1994-95, hon. chrmn. Nat. Com. for the Preservation of Scientific and Academic Information Resources, 1995-96), AAAI, Assn. for Computing Machinery, Earthquake Engring. Rsch. Inst., Internat. Soc. for Structural and Multidisciplinary Optimization, Int. Soc for Mini and Microcomputers (bd. dirs. 1996—). Office: Ohio State U Coll Engring 470 Hitchcock 2070 Neil Ave Columbus OH 43210-1226*

ADELL, HIRSCH, lawyer; b. Novogrodek, Poland, Mar. 11, 1931; arrived in U.S., 1937; s. Nathan and Nachama (Wager) A.; m. Judith Audrey Fuss, Feb. 8, 1963; children— Jeremiah, Nikolas, Balthasar, Valentine. Student, CCNY, 1949-52; BA, UCLA, 1955, LL.B., 1963. Bar: Calif. 1963. Adminstrv. asst. to State Senator Richard Richards, 1956-60; ptnr. Warren & Adell, Los Angeles, 1963-75, Reich, Adell, Crost & Cvitan, L.A., 1975—. Gen. counsel CVT Trust, 2003—. Served with AUS, 1953-55. Mem. ABA (labor and employment law sect.) Home: 545 S Norton Ave Los Angeles CA 90020-4610 Office: Reich Adell Crost & Cvitan 3550 Wilshire Blvd Ste 2000 Los Angeles CA 90010-2421

ADELMAN, CLIFFORD, research analyst; b. Boston, Sept. 29, 1942; s. Samuel Myron and Estaire Joan Adelman; m. Nancy Elizabeth Kilpatrick, Dec. 27, 1965; children: Jonathan Blake, Nicholas Benjamin. AB, Brown U., Providence, R.I., 1964; MA, U. Chgo., Ill., 1965, PhD, 1976. Instr. CCNY, NYC, 1968—71; vis. fellow/lectr. Yale U., New Haven, 1972—73; assoc. dean & assist acad v.p. William Paterson Univ., Wayne, NJ, 1974—79; assoc., sr. assoc., sr. rsch. analyst U.S. Dept. of Edn., Washington, 1979—. Vis. fellow The Coll. Bd., Washington, 1998; fellow Nat. Inst. for Sci. Edn., Madison, Wis., 1996—97; mem., nat. tech. adv. panels (10) Nat. Ctr. for Edn. Stats., Washington, 1991—. Author: (book) Generations: a Collage on YouthCult, Tourists in Our Own Land: Cultural Literacies and the College Curriculum, Leading, Concurrent or Lagging?: the Knowledge Content of Computer Science in Higher Education and the Labor Market, Women and Men of the Engineering Path, Answers in the Tool Box: Academic Intensity, Attendance Patterns, and Bachelor's Degree Attainment, (education/economic analysis monograph) A Parallel Postsecondary Universe: the Certification System in Information Technology, (articles) for Change Magazine, for The Chronicle of Higher Education, (op-ed articles (7) for The New York Times, (op-ed articles (3) and The Washington Post, (education analysis articles (3) for University Business, No Loaves, No Parables: Liberal Politics and the American Language; composer: (songs (music & lyrics) 14 Copyrighted Pieces; editor: Performance and Judgment, Signs and Traces: Model Indicators of College Student Learning; author: (reference work-book) A College Course Map, The New College Course Map & Transcript Files, Light and Shadows on College Athletes, Women at Thirtysomething: Paradoxes of Attainment, The Way We Are: the Community College as American Thermometer. Recipient Spl. Merit, Assn. for the Study of Higher Edn., 2001; fellow Woodrow Wilson Fellow (H), Woodrow Wilson Nat. Fellowship Found., 1964; grantee Humanities Fellow, The U. of Chgo., 1964-1967, Pilot Grant, Nat. Endowment for the Humanities, 1977-1979, Academic Program Devel., Fund for the Improvement of Postsecondary Edn., 1977-1980, Edn. Policy Fellow, The George Wash. U., 1979-1980. Mem.: European Assn. for Instl. Rsch., Assn. for the Study of Higher Edn., Assn. for Instl. Rsch. Avocations: aerobic dancing, jazz piano. Home: 3819 Archer Place Kensington MD 20895 Office: US Department of Education 555 New Jersey Ave NW Washington DC 20208-5531 Personal E-mail: cliffa42@aol.com. E-mail: clifford.adelman@ed.gov.

ADELMAN, GRAHAM LEWIS, lawyer; b. Frankfurt, Germany, Sept. 23, 1949; s. Louis and Helen (Howell) A.; m. Sharon Louise Stabile, May 16, 1975; children: Victor, Neal, Owen. BA, U. Va., 1971; JD cum laude, U. Miami, 1974. Bar: Fla. 1974. Law clk. High Ct. of Am. Samoa, 1975-76; asst. counsel Am. Fina Inc., Dallas, 1976-78; assoc. gen. counsel The Western Co. of N.Am., Ft. Worth, 1978-80, gen. counsel, 1980-86, v.p., gen., counsel, sec., 1986-90, dir., 1989—. Sr. v.p., gen. counsel, sec., 1990-95; sr. v.p., gen. counsel, Global Indsl. Techs., Inc., 1995-1998; pres., chief oper. officer, 1999-2000, 2001-; CEO Lexington Ct., Cambridge Healthcare Holdings LLC. Contbr. articles to law revs. Mem. ABA, Maritime Law Assn., Southwest Legal Found. (com. transnat. arbitration). Office: Global Industrial Technologies Inc 2121 San Jacinto St Ste 2500 Dallas TX 75201-6707 Home: 3000 Boonesville Rd Free Union VA 22940-1605

ADELMAN, HOWARD, philosophy educator; b. Toronto, Jan. 7, 1938; s. Harry Adelman and Frances (Duviner) Bromstein; m. Margaret Dorothy Smith, May 31, 1960; children: Jeremy Ian, Shonagh Eva, Rachel Esther, Eric Reuben; m. Nancy Jean Garrett, June 15, 1985; children: Daniel Jacob, Gabriel Benjamin. BA, U. Toronto, 1961, MA, 1963, PhD, 1971. From asst. prof. to assoc. prof. philosophy York U., Toronto, Ont., 1966-80, prof. North York, Ont., 1981-83, acting dean Atkinson Coll., 1973-74, dir. grad. programme in philosophy, 1980-83, 95-96, dir. Ctr. for Refugee Studies, 1986-93, chmn. senate, 1981-82. Lady Davis vis. prof. Hebrew U., 1977-78; vis. fellow, Princeton U., 2003-. Author: Beds of Academe, 1970, The Holiversity, 1973, Canada and the Indochinese Refugees, 1982; co-author: Early Warning and Conflict Management: The Genocide in Rwanda, 1996; editor: Refugee Policy: Canada and the United States, 1991, Legitimate and Illegitimate Discrimination: New Issues in Migration, 1993, Immigration Policy and Practice in Canada, 2002; co-editor: African Refugees, 1994, Immigration and Refugee Policy: Australia and Canada Compared, 1994, (with John Simpson) Multiculturalism, Jews and Canandian Identity, 1996, Immigration and Refugee Policy: Canada and Europe, 1998, The Path of a Genocide: The Rwanda Crisis from Uganda to Zaire, 1998; editor Refuge, 1982-93; contbr. articles to profl. jours. Harvard Harvey Harnick scholar, Queen Elizabeth II scholar, Can. Coun. Writing scholar; Grad. fellow Province of Ont.; grantee Ctrl. Mortgage and Housing Corp., Slater Found., 1980, SSHRC, 1983, 90-93, Aktinson Coll., 1982-86, CIDA, 1991, UNESCO, 1991, CEIC, 1982, 86-93, Ford Found., 1984, 86-89, IDRC, 1982, 92, ICMC, 1982, Ditchley Conf., 1983, OECD, 1995, Rsch. Travel grant, 1998, Rsch. grant CIC, 1999, Travel grant YUFA, 2001, Rsch. grant USIP, 2001, others; recipient Gerstein award, 1996, Marvin Gelber award, 1996, European Task Force award, 1996, John Holmes Found. award, 1997, SSHRC, 1997. Home: 64 Wells Hill Ave Toronto ON Canada M5R 3A8 Office: York U Philosophy Dept 4700 Keele St North York ON Canada M3J 1P3 E-mail: hadelman@yorku.ca.

ADELMAN, JONATHAN REUBEN, political science educator, consultant; b. Washington, Oct. 30, 1948; s. Benjamin and Kitty (Sandler) A.; m. Agota Kuperman, Aug. 3, 1997. BA, Columbia U., 1969, MA, 1972, M in Philosophy, 1974, PhD, 1976. Vis. asst. prof. Columbia U., N.Y.C., 1977; vis. asst. prof. U. Ala., Tuscaloosa, 1977-78; asst. prof. Grad. Sch. Internat. Studies U. Denver, 1978-85, assoc. prof., 1985-92, prof. polit. sci., 1992—; sr. rsch. analyst Sci. Applications, Inc., Denver, 1981-87, 96—; hon. prof. People's U., Beijing, 1996—; sr. fellow Found. for the Def. of Democracies, 2001—03; hon. prof. Beijing U., 1996—. Cons., 1988-89, 96—; Lady Davis vis. assoc. prof. Hebrew U., Jerusalem, 1986; vis. fellow Soviet Acad. Scis., 1989, 90, Chinese Inst. Contemporary Internat. Rels., Beijing, 1988, People's U., Beijing, 1990, 94, 96, 97, 98, 99, 2000; vis. prof. Beijing U., 1989, 98, U. Haifa, Israel, 1990, Ctrl. European U., Budapest, 2000; vis. spkr. Soviet Acad. Scis., 1990, Barcelona (Spain) U. and Complutense U., 1990, Cambridge (Eng.) U., 1991, Nat. Taiwan U., 1998, 99; vis. lectr., Japan, India, Hong Kong, Yugoslavia, Spain, 1990, 91, Germany, 1991, Bulgaria, 1991; vis. spkr. Conf. for Study of European Ideas, Aalborg U., Denmark, 1992; vis. prof. People's U., Beijing, 1990, 97, Janus Pannonius U., Pecs, Hungary, 1981. Author: The Revolutionary Armies, 1980, Revolution, Armies and War, 1986, Prelude to the Cold War: Tsarist, Soviet and U.S. Armies in Two World Wars, 1988, Torrents of Spring: Soviet and Post Soviet Politics, 1994; co-author: The Dynamics of Soviet Foreign Policy, 1988; editor: Communist Armies in Politics, 1982, Terror and Communist Politics, 1984, Superpowers and Revolution, 1986; co-editor: Contemporary Soviet Military Affairs: The Legacy World War II, 1989; contbr. numerous articles in fieod to profl. jours. Charles Phelps Taft fellow U. Cin., 1976-77; Am. Philos. Soc. grantee, 1980. Mem. Am. Polit. Sci. Assn., Am. Assn. Advancement Slavic Studies. Democrat. Jewish. Office: U Denver Grad Sch Internat Studies Denver CO 80208-0001

ADELMAN, LYNN, federal judge; b. Milw., Oct. 1, 1939; s. Albert B. and Edith Margoles Adelman; m. Elizabeth Halmbacher, 1976; children: Lisa, Mia. AB, Princeton U., 1961; LLB, Columbia U., 1965. State senator dist. 28 State of Wis., Milw., 1977-97; judge U.S. Dist. Ct. (Ea. Dist.) Wis., Milw., 1997—. Chmn. judiciary and consumer affairs com. Wis. State Senate; pvt. practice as atty. Democrat. also: US Cthse & Fed Bldg 517 E Wisconsin Ave Milwaukee WI 53202-4500

ADELMAN, MARTIN JEROME, law educator; b. Detroit, Feb. 22, 1937; parent Oscar Adelman, Rae Mary Bale; m. Susan Ellen Hershberg, Sept. 2, 1961. AB, U. Mich., 1958, MS, 1959, JD, 1962. Law clerk to Chief Judge Theodore Levin Fed. Dist. Ct., Detroit, 1962—63; assoc. atty. Honigman, Miller, Schwartz & Cohn, Detroit, 1962—63; patent atty. Burroughs Corp., Washington, Mich., 1964—65; assoc. and ptnr. Barnard, McGlynn & Reising, Birmingham, Mich., 1965—73; prof. law Wayne State U., Detroit, 1973—99; prof. law, co-dir. of intellectual property program and dir. of the Dean Dinwoodey Ctr. for Intellectual Property Law George Washington U., Washington, 1999—. Home: 29820 Woodland Dr Southfield MI 48034 Home Fax: 248-356-7554; Office Fax: 202-994-5654. E-mail: madelman@main.nlc.gwu.edu., ad3192@hotmail.com.

ADELMAN, MICHAEL, dean; DPM, Phila. Coll. Podiatric Medicine, 1977; DO, Coll. Osteo. Medicine and Surgery, 1981; postgrad., U. Toledo Coll. Law. V.p. acad. affairs and dean W. Va. Sch. Osteo. Medicine, 2002—. Office: W Va Sch Osteo Medicine 400 N Lee St Lewisburg WV 24901

ADELMAN, MICHAEL SCHWARTZ, lawyer; b. Cambridge, Mass., June 6, 1940; s. Benjamin Taft and Sally Frances (Schwartz) A.; m. Amy Kay, June 14, 1962; children: Robert, Jonathon. Student, Boston U., 1958-59; BA with honors in English, U. Mich., 1962, JD cum laude. Bar: Mich. 1968, Miss. 1974; cert. for death penalty post-conviction collateral relief cases. Assoc. Zwerdling, Miller, Klimist & Maurer, Detroit, 1968-69; ptnr. Philo, Maki, Ravitz, Glotta, Adelman, Cockrel & Robb, Detroit, 1969-70, Glotta, Adelman & Dinges, Detroit, 1970-74, Andalman, Adelman & Steiner P.A., Hattiesburg, Miss., 1974-86, Adelman & Steiner P.A., Hattiesburg, Miss., 1986—. V.p., bd. dirs. S.E. Miss. Legal Svcs., Hattiesburg. Contbr. short stories: The Deputy, The Detention Center to New Renaissance. Treas. Hattiesburg Area Equal Rights Coun.; mem. Hattiesburg Biracial Adv. Com., 1987-89, chmn., 1988-89; v.p. state bd. dirs. NAMI, 2000—. Recipient Ralph T. Abernathy award Jackson County (Miss.) So. Christian Leadership Conf., 1978. Mem.: ABA, South Ctrl. Miss. Bar Assn. (pres. 2002). Address: 33 Camellia Ct Hattiesburg MS 39402-6112 E-mail: ADELST33@aol.com.

ADELMAN, PAMELA BERNICE KOZOLL, education educator; b. Milw., Dec. 26, 1945; d. Harry and Rebecca (Sharp) Kozoll; m. Steven H. Adelman, June 30, 1968; children: David, Robert. BS, U. Wis., Madison, 1967; MA, Northwestern U., 1972, PhD, 1982. Cert. tchr., Ill. Chair edn. dept. Barat Coll., Lake Forest, Ill., 1986-97; tchr. Peckham Jr. High Sch., Milw., 1967-68, Fairview Sch., Skokie, Ill., 1968-70; learning disabilities specialist Sch. Dist 28, Northbrook, Ill., 1971-77; instr., rsch. asst. Northwestern U., Evanston, Ill., 1977-80; lectr., asst. prof., then assoc. prof. Barat Coll., Lake Forest, Ill., 1977-90, prof. edn., 1990-99, dir. learning opportunities program, 1985-99, chmn. edn. dept., 1986-97, grad. dean, 1997-99, chmn. edn. dept., 1986-97; founding exec. dir. Hyde Park Day Sch., 1999—. Cons. Deerfield (Ill.) Pub. Schs., 1986-90; proposal reviewer State of N.J., Trenton, 1986-87; mem. Pres.'s Com. on Hiring of Disabled, 1990; higher edn. adv. coun. State of Ill.; mem. Coun. Chgo. Area Deans of Edn., 1992-99, chair, 1998-99; comprehensive sys. of pers. devel. adv. com. Ill. State Bd. Edn.; presenter in field. Co-author: Learning Disabilities, Graduate School, and Careers, 1990; co-editor: Success for College Students with Learning Disabilities, 1993; consulting editor Learning Disabilities Focus, 1989-92, Jour. Developmental Edn., 1990-98, Jour. of Postsecondary Edn. and Disabilities, 1991-95; contbr. articles to ednl. publs. Chair Sch. Dist. 107 Caucus, Highland Park, Ill., 1982; bd. dirs. Jewish Children's Bur., Chgo., 1985—, pres., 1994-96; co-author brochure for Ill. Dept. Human Rights, Chgo., 1986; bd. dirs. Jewish Fedn. Met. Chgo., 1996. Paul A. Witty fellow Northwestern U., 1978-80; grantee Lloyd A. Fry Found.,

1985-86, McDonald's Corp., Chgo., 1986, Kraft Corp., Chgo., 1989, Thorn River Found., 1990—. Fellow Internat. Acad. for Rsch. in Learning Disabilities; mem. Internat. Dyslexia Assn. (bd. dirs. Ill. br. 2000—), Coun. Exceptional Children, Learning Disabilities Assn. Am., Coun. Learning Disabilities. Avocations: reading, walking, music, swimming. Office: Hyde Park Day Sch 1375 E 60th St Chicago IL 60637-2856

ADELMAN, RICHARD CHARLES, gerontologist, educator; b. Newark, Mar. 10, 1940; s. Morris and Elanor (Wachman) A.; m. Lynn Betty Richman, Aug. 18, 1963; children— Mindy Robin, Nicole Ann AB, Kenyon Coll., 1962; MA, Temple U., 1965, PhD, 1967. Postdoctoral fellow Albert Einstein Coll. Medicine, Bronx, N.Y., 1967-69; from asst. prof. to prof. Temple U., Phila., 1969-82, dir. Inst. Aging, 1978-82; prof. biol. chemistry U. Mich., Ann Arbor, 1982-2000, dir. Inst. Gerontology, 1982-97, prof. emeritus, 2001—; dir. univ. rels. University Assisted Living, Ann Arbor, 2002—. Mem. study sect. NIH, 1975-78; adv. coun. VA, 1981-85; chmn. Gordon Rsch. Conf. Biol. Aging, 1976; adv. com. VA, 1981-91; chmn. VA Geriatrics and Gerontology Adv. Com., 1987-91; dir. univ. rels. Univ. Living, Inc., 2001—. Mem. various editorial bds. biomed. research jours., 1972—. Bd. dirs. Botsford Continuing Care Ctrs., Inc., Farmington Hills, Mich., 1984-88. Recipient Medalist award Intrasci. Research Found., 1977; grantee NIH, 1970—; established investigator Am. Heart Assn., 1975-78 Fellow Gerontol. Soc. Am. (v.p. 1976-77, pres. elect 1986-87, Kent award 1990); mem. Am. Soc. Biol. Chemists, Gerontol. Soc. Am. (pres. 1986-87), Am. Chem. Soc., AAAS, Phila. Biochemists (pres.), Practitioners in Aging. Jewish.

ADELMAN, RICK, professional basketball coach; b. June 16, 1946; m. Mary Kay Adelman; children: Kathryn Mary, Laura, R.J., David. Master's, Loyola Marymount U. Profl. basketball player, San Diego, 1968-70, Portland (Oreg.) Trail Blazers, 1970-73, asst. coach, 1983-89, head coach, 1989-94; basketball player Chgo., New Orleans, Kansas City, and Omaha, 1973-75; head coach Chemeketa Community Coll., Salem, Oreg., 1975-83, Golden State Warriors, Oakland, Calif., 1995-97, Sacramento Kings, 1998—. Office: Sacramento Kings ARCO Arena One Sports Parkway Sacramento CA 95834

ADELMAN, ROBERT PAUL, retired construction company executive, lawyer; b. N.Y.C., Dec. 7, 1930; s. Saul and Eva (Ochs) A.; m. Renee Gratum, June 7, 1953 (dec. Apr. 1998); children: Michael, Susan, John; m. Judith A. Turner, Jan. 9, 1999. BA, Columbia U., 1952, JD, 1954. Bar: N.Y. 1954, U.S. Supreme Ct. 1960. Assoc. Winthrop, Stimson, Putnam & Roberts, N.Y.C., 1956-64; with Celanese Corp., N.Y.C., 1964-71; v.p., treas., gen. counsel Calina Industries, Inc., N.Y.C., 1971-73; chief fin. officer Rockefeller Group, Inc., N.Y.C., 1975-84; chmn., chief exec. officer, pres. Rogers Group, Inc., Nashville, 1984-88, chmn., 1988-92, vice chmn., 1992—2001, cons. to the pres. and CEO, 2001—. Mem. Fin. Execs. Inst., 1973-84, Conf. Bd. Exec. Coun., 1985-90; bd. dirs. N. European Oil Royalty Trust. Treas. and chief fin. officer N.Y. State Urban Devel. Corp., 1973-75; trustee The Jackson Lab., 1981—. Served with U.S. Army, 1954-56, instr. Corps of Cadets U.S. Mil. Acad., West Point, N.Y. Mem. University Club (N.Y.C.), Amelia Island Club. Avocations: sailing, golf. Home: 1540 Beachwalker Rd Amelia Island FL 32034-6610

ADELMAN, ROGER MARK, lawyer, educator; b. Norristown, Pa., June 25, 1941; s. Lewis D. and Mary (Butz) A. B.A., Dartmouth Coll., 1963; LL.B., U. Pa., 1966. Bar: D.C. 1967, Pa. 1969. Asst. U.S. atty. D.C., 1969-87; ptnr. Kirkpatrick & Lockhart, Washington, 1988—; adj. prof. Georgetown U. Law Ctr., Washington, 1975— . Served with U.S. Army, 1967-68. Mem. D.C. Bar Assn., Assn. Bar D.C. Office: 1800 M St NW Washington DC 20036-5802

ADELMAN, STANLEY JOSEPH, lawyer; b. Devils Lake, N.D., May 20, 1942; s. Isadore Russell Adelman and Eva Claire (Robins) Stoller; m. Mary Beth Petchaft, Jan. 30, 1972; children: Laura E., Sarah A. BS, U. Wis., 1964, JD, 1967. Bar: Ill. 1967, U.S. Dist. Ct. (no. dist.) Ill. 1967, Wis. 1968, U.S. Ct. Appeals (7th cir.), U.S. Dist. Ct. (ea. dist.) Wis. 1979, U.S. Supreme Ct. 1982, U.S. Ct. Appeals (10th cir.) 1984, U.S. Ct. Appeals (fed. cir.) 1987. Assoc. Sonnenchein, Carlin, Nath & Rosenthal, Chgo., 1967-75, ptnr., 1975-85; co-chmn. litigation dept. Rudnick & Wolfe, Chgo., 1985-91, 96-97, ptnr., 1985—, profl. responsibility ptnr., 1992-94, mem. mgmt. policy com., 1985-97, co-chmn. complex litigation practice group, 1997-98. Bd. dirs. Legal Assistance Found., Chgo., 1982—83. Fellow Nat. Inst. Trial Advocacy; mem. Chgo. Bar Assn., Chgo. Coun. Lawyers, Am. Inns of Ct. (pres. Markey/Wigmore chpt. 1998-99), Lawyers Club Chgo., Order of Coif. Jewish. Home: 115 Crescent Dr Glencoe IL 60022-1303 Office: Piper Rudnick Ste 1800 203 N La Salle St Chicago IL 60601-1210 E-mail: stanley.adelman@piperrudnick.com.

ADELMAN, STEVEN ALLEN, theoretical physical chemist, chemistry educator; b. Chgo., July 4, 1945; s. Hyman and Sarah Adelman; m. Barbara Stolberg, May 13, 1974 BS, Ill. Inst. Tech., 1967; PhD, Harvard U., 1972. Postdoctoral fellow MIT, Cambridge, 1972-73; postdoctoral fellow U. Chgo., 1973-74; asst. prof. chemistry Purdue U., West Lafayette, Ind., 1975-77, assoc. prof., 1977-82, prof., 1982—. Cons. Exxon Rsch. Co., Los Alamos Nat. Lab.; vis. prof. U. Paris, 1985; nominator 1994 Nobel Prize in Chemistry, Royal Swedish Acad. Scis. Contbr. articles to profl. jours. Vol. U.S. Peace Corp., Ankara, Turkey, 1969-70. Fellow Alfred P. Sloan Found., 1976-78, Guggenheim Found., 1982-83; NSF grantee, 1976—; named Outstanding Sr. in Chemistry, Am. Inst. Chemistry, 1967. Fellow Am. Phys. Soc.; mem. AAAS, Am. Chem. Soc., Am. Statis. Assn., Math. Assn. Am., Sigma Xi. Avocations: long-distance running, strength training, turkish language and literature. Home: 3037 Courthouse Dr W Apt 2C West Lafayette IN 47906-1035 Office: Purdue U Dept Chemistry West Lafayette IN 47907 E-mail: saa@purdue.edu.

ADELMAN, STEVEN HERBERT, lawyer; b. Dec. 21, 1945; s. Irving and Sylvia (Cohen) A.; m. Pamela Bernice Kozoll, June 30, 1968; children: David, Robert. BS, U. Wis., Madison, 1967; JD, DePaul U., 1970. Bar: Ill. 1970, U.S. Dist. Ct. (no. dist.) Ill. 1970, U.S. Ct. Appeals (7th cir.) 1975. Ptnr. Keck, Mahin & Cate, Chgo., 1970-93, Lord, Bissell & Brook, Chgo., 1993—. Bd. dirs. Bur. Jewish Employment Problems, Chgo., 1983—, pres. 1991, 92; employment relations com. Chgo. Assn. Commerce and Industry, 1982-90. Contbr. chpts. to books, articles to profl. jours. Fellow Coll. Labor and Employment Lawyers; mem. ABA (Silver key award 1969), Chgo. Bar Assn. (chmn. labor and employment law com. 1988-89), Ill. State Bar Assn., Chgo. Coun. Lawyers, Decalogue Soc. Office: Lord Bissell & Brook 115 S La Salle St Ste 3200 Chicago IL 60603-3902 E-mail: sadelman@lordbissell.com.

ADELMAN, WILLIAM J., JR., biophysicist; b. Mt. Vernon, N.Y., Jan. 29, 1928; s. William Joseph Adelman and Helen Emma Carlock; m. Jean Alma Mayo, Sept. 3, 1951; children: Everett M., John W., Willa J. BS, Fordham U., 1950; MS, U. Vt., 1952; PhD, U. Rochester, 1955. Aviation physiologist Sch. Aviation Medicine, Randolph AFB, 1955—56; instr. U. Buffalo (N.Y.) Sch. Medicine, 1956—57, asst. prof. physiology, 1957—59; neurophysiologist Lab. Biophysics Nat. Inst. Neurol. Diseases and Blindness, NIH, Bethesda, Md., 1959—62; prof. physiology dept. physiology U. Md. Sch. Medicine., Balt., 1962—72; chief lab. biophysics Nat. Inst. Neurol., Communicative Disorders, and Stroke, NIH, Bethesda, 1972—90, chief lab. biophysics emeritus, 1990—. Treas. Soc. Gen. Physiology; trustee Marine Biol. Lab., Woods Hole, Mass. Editor: Biophysics and Physiology Excitable Membranes, 1971; contbr. articles to profl. jours.; newspaper art critic:. Fellow, AAAS, 1965; grantee in field; spl. fellow, NIH, 1969. Avocation: fine art. Home: 160 Locust St Falmouth MA 02540-2674

ADELMAN, WILLIAM JOHN, university labor and industrial relations educator; b. Chgo., July 26, 1932; s. William Sidney and Annie Teresa (Goan) A.; m. Nora Jill Walters, June 26, 1952; children: Michelle, Marguerite, Marc, Michael, Jessica. Student, Lafayette Coll., 1952; BA, Elmhurst Coll., 1956; MA, U. Chgo., 1964. Tchr. Whitecross Sch., Hereford, Eng., 1956-57, Jefferson Sch., Berwyn, Ill., 1957-60, Morton High Sch., Berwyn, 1960-66; mem. faculty dept. labor and indsl. relations U. Ill., Chgo., 1966-91, prof., 1978-91, prof. emeritus, 1991—; coordinator Chgo. Labor Edn. Program, 1981-87. Lectr. Road Scholar Program, Ill. Humanities Coun., 1997. Author: Touring Pullman, 1972, Haymarket Revisited, 1976, Pilsen and the West Side, 1981; writer: film Packingtown U.S.A., 1968; narrator: Palace Cars and Paradise: Pullman's Model Town, 1983. Bd. dirs. Chgo. Regional Blood Program, 1977-80; mem. Ill. State Employment Security Adv. Bd., 1974-75; Democratic candidate U.S. Ho. of Reps. from 14th dist. Ill., 1970; organizer Haymarket Centennial Events, 1986; chmn. Jane Addams' Hull House Adv. Bd., 1991-99. Ill. Humanities Council grantee, 1977; German Marshall Fund U.S. grantee, 1977; recipient Tradition of Excellence award Oak Park/River Forest H.S., 1993, Eugene V. Debs award Midwest Labor Press assn., 1995. Mem. Ill. Labor History Soc. (founding mem., v.p., Union Hall of Honor 1993), Am. Fedn. Tchrs., Doris Humphrey Soc. (v.p. 1990—). Unitarian Universalist. Home and Office: 613 S Highland Ave Oak Park IL 60304-1524 E-mail: www.Dooper@aol.com.

ADELSBERG, HARVEY, hospital administrator; b. Bronx, N.Y., Aug. 5, 1931; s. Joseph and Becky (Rindner) Adelsberg; m. Miriam Levine, June 20, 1964; children: Jonathan, Risa, Seth. BA, NYU, 1953, MPA, 1960, postgrad., 1960—65. Adminstrv. resident Beth David Hosp., N.Y.C., 1953—54; adminstrv. asst. Met. Jewish Geriatric Center, Bklyn., 1954—58; asst. dir. Kingsbrook Jewish Med. Center, Bklyn., 1958—61, Hosp. for Joint Diseases, N.Y.C., 1961—64; exec. dir. Theresa Grotta Center for Restorative Svcs., Caldwell, NJ, 1964—70; asst. dir. Mt. Sinai Hosp., N.Y.C., 1970—72; cons. med. care and svcs. to aged Fedn. Jewish Philanthropies, N.Y.C., 1972—74; exec. dir. Daus. of Miriam Center for Aged, Clifton, NJ, 1974—76, exec. v.p., 1977—95, exec. v.p. emeritus, 1996; adj. prof. MBA health sys. mgmt. program Fairleigh Dickinson U., Coll. of Bus., 2002—. Adj. asst. prof. health care adminstrn. Bernard M. Baruch Coll., Mt. Sinai Sch. Medicine, CUNY, 1973—, U. Medicine and Dentistry, N.J., 1995; mem. adv. com. Rutgers U., 1969—; mem. adj. prof. N.J. Grad. Sch. Pub. Health, 1995; cons. Consulting Svcs. Inst., 1995; mem. N.J. Licensing Bd. for Nursing Home Adminstrs., 1969—, vice chmn., 1969—77; mem. Adv. Council on Aging, Livingston, NJ, 1977—; sr. exec. fellow long term care studies MBA Health Sys. Mgmt. Program Fairleigh Dickinson U., 2002; sr. exec. fellow long term care studies. V.p. Solomon Schechter Day Sch. of Essex and Union, 1980—; trustee Synagogue of Suburban Torah Center, Livingston, 1978—; v.p. Temple Beth Shalom, Livingston, 1970—71, 1973, trustee, 1968—70, 1975—; mem. governing com. Camp Ramah, Wingdale, NY, 1979—; exec. bd. Jewish Communal Svc. Assn., 1993—; trustee Hosp. and Council Met. N.J., 1967—70, Health and Hosp. Council So. N.Y., 1972—74, N.J. Assn. Non-Profit Homes for Aging, 1976—, Jewish Cmty. Housing Corp., Paterson, NJ, 1975—; trustee tng. Dist. 1199J, 1990; bd. govs. Greater N.Y. Hosp. Assn., 1972—74; agt. Daus. of Miriam Found., 1984. Fellow: Am. Geriatric Soc., Am. Coll. Nursing Home Adminstrs., Am. Coll. Hosp. Adminstrs.; mem.: APHA, Am., N.J. hosp. assns., B'nai B'rith (v.p. 1960—64), Hosp. Exec. Club. Home and Office: 27 Tuxedo Dr Livingston NJ 07039-2452 E-mail: harveyadelsberg@aol.com.

ADELSON, BENEDICT JAMES, retired lawyer; b. Cleve., July 3, 1930; s. Joseph Stanley and Sara J. (Joffe) A.; m. Sybil Schar, Apr. 12, 1981. BS in Econs., U. Pa., 1952; JD, Harvard U., 1955. Bar: Ohio 1955, Calif. 1970. Assoc. Schlesinger, Galvin, Kohn & Landefeld, Cleve., 1963-68, Gendel, Raskoff, Shapiro & Quittner, L.A., 1970-77, Fierstein & Sturman, L.A., 1977-87; ret., 1987. Home: 830 Glorietta Blvd Coronado CA 92118-2306

ADELSON, EDWARD, physicist, musician; b. Bklyn., Aug. 19, 1934; s. Barnet and Sarah (Strongin) A.; m. Juliane A.W. Riedel, Aug. 5, 1961 (div. June 1982). BA, NYU, 1956; postgrad. (Woodrow Wilson fellow), Eastman Sch. Music, 1956-57; MS, Ohio State U., 1965, PhD, 1974. Prin. physicist Battelle Mem. Inst., Columbus, Ohio, 1957-71; lectr. Ohio State U., Columbus, 1974-88, coord. program specialist, 1988— . Cons. in field. Author: Student Companion for Reese's University Physics, vol. 2, 2001; contbr. articles to profl. jours. Organist, choirmaster emeritus St. Alban's Episcopal Ch., Bexley, Ohio. Mem.: AAAS, Am. Guild Organists, Am. Assn. Physics Tchrs., Am. Phys. Soc., Chrichton Club, Sigma Pi Sigma, Phi Beta Kappa. Home: 6384 Falkirk Pl Columbus OH 43229-2045 Office: Ohio State U Smith Lab Columbus OH 43210

ADELSON, GLORIA ANN, financial executive; b. Savannah, Ga., Aug. 3, 1944; d. Lee Roy and Edith Thelma (Horovitz) Schraibman; m. Joseph Harvey Adelson, Mar. 19, 1967 (dec.). BA in Polit. Sci., U. Fla., 1965; MA in Bus., Webster U., 1991. Budget analyst U.S. Dept. Labor, Silver Spring, Md., 1967, mgmt. analyst U.S. Naval Supply Ctr., Charleston, S.C., 1967-69, budget analyst, 1969-70, head fin. mgmt. staff, 1970-73, head. ops. and maintenance br., 1973-75; mgmt. coord. officer So. Divsn. Naval Facilities Engring. Commd., Charleston, 1975-80, dir. budget br., 1980-85, dir. budget and programs divsn., 1985-88, dep. dir. programs and comptroller dept., 1988—. Fin. sec., treas. Synagogue Emanu-El, Charleston, 1982-88; pres. Sisterhood Emanu-El, Charleston, 1993-94, 95-96; active patron com. Am. Cancer Soc., Charleston, 1989, 91, 95, 97; mem. fed. sector com. United Way, Charleston, 1991; bd. dirs. so. br. Women's League for Conservative Judaism, 1996-98, v.p., 1998-2002, pres., 2002-, mem. Internat. bd. dirs., 2001—; mem. Trident Area Cmty. Excellence Comm. Team, 1995-99, examiner for quality awards, 1999; published fgn. interpreter's list S.C. World Trade Ctr, 1998, 99, 2001, 2002. Mem. Am. Soc. Mil. Comptrs. (chmn. coms. Charleston chpt. 1987—, v.p. Navy, 1990-91, pres., 1991-92), Charleston C. of C. (Leadership Charleston 1997-98), Arthritis Found., Arthritis Vol. Adv. Comm. (co-chair arthritis support group). Avocations: reading, fitness. Home: 4 Berwick Cir Charleston SC 29407-3414 Office: So Divsn Naval Facilities Engring Commd 2155 Eagle Dr Charleston SC 29406-4804 Personal E-mail: happygaa@aol.com.

ADELSON, ROGER DEAN, history educator, editor, historian; b. Abilene, Kans., July 11, 1942; s. Orlie Austin and Winnifred Graham (McClure) A.; m. Sally Isabelle Squires, Sept. 1966 (div. Apr. 1978). BA, George Washington U., 1964; MA, Washington U., 1967, PhD, 1972; BLitt, Oxford (Eng.) U., 1970. Danforth fellow Washington U., St. Louis, 1964-67; sr. rsch. fellow St. Antony's Coll., Oxford U., 1972-73; lectr. history Harvard U., Cambridge, Mass., summer 1974; asst. prof. Ariz. State U., Tempe, 1974-78, assoc. prof., 1978-95, prof., 1996—; editor Historian, 1990-95, cons. editor, 1995—2001, mem. editl. bd., 2002—. Vis. prof. Am. Grad. Sch. Internat. Mgmt., Glendale, Ariz., 1980s, Pepperdine U., Malibu, Calif., 1994, 95, 96; dir. Global History Project, 1995-97. Author: Mark Sykes: Portrait of an Amateur, 1975, London and the Invention of the Middle East, 1995, Speaking of History, 1996. Founding. pres. Soc. for Internat. Devel., Ariz., 1983; charter mem. Coun. Fgn. Rels., Phoenix, 1976. Mem. Conf. Hist. Jours. (pres. 1995-97), Phi Alpha Theta (historian 1990-95. editl. bd. 1997-). Avocations: cycling, swimming, gardening, entertaining. Office: Ariz State U Dept History PO Box 872501 Tempe AZ 85287-2501

ADELSTEIN, S(TANLEY) JAMES, physician, educator; b. NYC, Jan. 24, 1928; s. George and Belle (Schild) Adelstein; m. Mary Charlesworth Taylor, Sept. 20, 1957; children: Joseph Burrows, Elizabeth Dunster. BS, MS, MIT, 1949, PhD in Biophysics, 1957; MD, Harvard U., 1953. Med. house officer Peter Bent Brigham Hosp., Boston, 1953-54, sr. asst. resident physician, 1957-58, chief resident, 1959-60; fellow Howard Hughes Med. Inst., 1957-58, Henry A. and Camilus Christian fellow, 1959-60; Moseley travel fellow Harvard U. Med. Sch., Boston, 1958-59, instr. anatomy, then asst. prof., 1961-68, assoc prof. radiology, 1968-72, prof., 1972-89, Paul C. Cabot prof. med. biophysics, 1989-97, prof. pathology, Daniel S. Tosteson univ. prof., 1997—, dean for acad. program, 1978-97. Dir. Nat. Coun. for Radiation Protection Measurements, 1980—2002, v.p., 1982—2002, hon. v.p., 2002—; cons. Med. Found. fellow, 1960—63; Walter Dandy lectr. Johns Hopkins U., 1996; John Cameron lectr. U. Wis., 1998; Lauristen Taylor lectr. Nat. Coun. for Radiatide Photection, 2000; radiation rsch. bd. NAS, 1999—2002, chair, 2002—; biol. rsch. adv. com. Dept. Energy, 2001—; John Cameron lectr. U. Wis., 1998; L. Taylor lectr. Nat. Coun. for Radiation Protection, 2000; rsch. coll. adv. bd. U. Tasmania, 2003—. Mem. editl. bd.: Investigative Radiology, 1972—80, Postgrad. Radiology, Radiology Rsch., 1990—94; editor (assoc. editor): Jour. Nuc. Medicine, 1975—81; contbr. articles to profl. jours. Trustee Am. Bd. Nuc. Medicine, 1972—78; mem. fellowship adv. com. Whitaker Found., 1991—97. Recipient Career Devel. award, NIH, 1965—68; fellow Nat. Found., MIT, 1957, Fogarty Sr. Internat., 1976. Fellow: AAAS, Am. Coll. Nuc. Physician; mem.: Inst. Medicine, Boylston Med. Soc., Soc. Nuc. Medicine (trustee 1970—74, Blumgart award 1983, Aebersold award 1986, Dr. Hevesy award 1999), Radiation Rsch. Soc. (councillor 1975—78), Assn. Radiation Rsch., Biophys. Soc., Am. Chem. Soc., Alpha Omega Alpha, Tau Beta Pi, Sigma Xi. Office: Harvard Med Sch 25 Shattuck St Boston MA 02115-6027

ADERHOLT, ROBERT B. congressman, attorney; b. Haleyville, Ala., July 22, 1965; m. Caroline McDonald. BA, Birmingham Southern U., 1978; JD, Cumberland School of Law, 1990. Mem. U.S. Congress from 4th Ala. dist., 1997—; mem. appropriations com. Republican. Office: 1433 Longworth Bldg Washington DC 20515-0104*

ADERMAN, RALPH MERL, language educator; b. Malinta, Ohio, May 27, 1919; s. Rudolph Ernest and Stella Barbara (Litzenberg) Aderman; m. Alice Coralyn Rath, Nov. 26, 1942; 1 child, Jeffrey Alan. BE, U. Toledo, 1941, MA, 1945; PhD, U. Wis., 1951. Tchr. HS, Henry County, Ohio, 1941-45; grad. tchg. asst. U. Wis., Madison, 1945-47, assoc. prof. English Milw., 1956-59, prof., 1959-85, prof. emeritus, 1985—; instr. Milw. State Tchrs. Coll., 1947-52, Wis. State Coll., Milw., 1952-56. Fulbright lectr. U. Bucharest, 1965—66. Editor: (book) The Letters of James Kirke Paulding, 1961, Ion (translation), 1967, The Quest for Social Justice, 1983, From Trading Post to Metropolis: A History of Milwaukee County, 1987, Papa Floribunda: A Biography of Eugene S. Boerner, 1989, Critical Essays on Washington Irving, 1990; editor: (with Elizabeth M. Kerr) Aspects of American English, 1971; editor: (with Herbert L. Kleinfield, Jenifer S. Banks) The Letters of Washington Irving, Vol. I 1802-1823, 1978, Vol. II 1823-1838, 1979, Vol. III 1839-1845, 1982, Vol. IV 1846-1959, 1982; editor: (with Alice R. Aderman) A Geneology of the Irvings of New York: Washington Irving, His Brothers and Sisters, and Their Descendants, 1983; editor: (with Wayne R. Kime) Advocate for America: The Life of James Kirke Paudling, 2003; editor: Washington Irving Reconsidered: A Symposium, 1969. Dir. Milwaukee County Hist. Soc., 1953—85. Grantee, Am. Philos. Soc., 1954, 1957. Mem.: MLA, Manuscript Soc., Thoreau Soc., Poe Soc., Melville Soc., Wis. Acad. Scis., Arts & Letters, Phi Kappa Phi, Sigma Tau Delta. Avocations: stamp collecting, gardening, reading. Home: 8536 W Oklahoma Ave West Allis WI 53227-4659

ADERSON, SANFORD M. lawyer; b. Pitts., July 15, 1949; s. Sanford C. and Marjorie S. (Stern) A.; m. Leslie S. Sertner, Aug. 12, 1972; children: Benjamin, Jonathan. BSBA, Boston U., 1971, JD, 1974. Bar: Pa. 1974, U.S. Dist. Ct. (we. dist.) Pa. 1974, U.S. Tax Ct. 1978, U.S. Ct. Appeals (3d cir.) 1986. Law clk. to judge Ct. of Common Pleas, Pitts., 1974-83; with Aderson, Frank, Steiner & Blechman, Pitts., 1976-2001; of counsel Strassburger, McKenna, Gutnick & Potter, Pitts., 2000—; pres. Luttner Fin. Group, Pitts., 2001—. Bd. dirs. Jewish Cmty. Ctr. of Pitts., 1993-98, vice chair Make-A-Wish, 2000—; mem. bus. com. Pitts. Cultural Trust, 2001—. Mem.: ABA, Allegheny County Bar Assn. (bankruptcy sect. mem. of coun. 1993—98), Pa. Bar Assn., Westmoreland Country Club (bd. dirs. 1987—, pres. 2001—). Office: Strassburger McKenna Gurnik & Potter 244 Blvd of the Allies Pittsburgh PA 15222 E-mail: sanford_m_aderson@glic.com.

ADES, BRUCE ALLAN, engineering executive, researcher; b. San Francisco, Aug. 24, 1955; s. Nissim Harris and Muriel Joan Ades; m. Anastasia Vladimirovna Pyatova. BSEE, Northrop U., 1977, MSEE, 1979; PhD Northrop U., 1984; MBA, U. Phoenix, San Francisco, 1994. Cert. engring. contractor, Calif.; (paralegal). Sys. engr. Northrop U., L.A., 1980—88, ADES Engring., Aptos, Calif., 1988. Cons. engr. OAO Surneftegaz, Tyumen, Tyumen oblast, Russia, 1988—. Midshipman USN, 1973—74. Mem.: Rotary Internat. (Paul Harris fellow 1999). Mailing: PMB 163 1060 W Frankford Rd Ste 203 Carrollton TX 75007

ADES, JANET, social worker; b. Washington, July 26, 1938; d. Bernard and Mary (Hechler) A. BA, City Coll. N.Y., 1959; MSW, NYU, 1964; JD, DePaul U., 1976. Bar: Ill. 1976, U.S. Dist. Ct. (no. dist.) Ill. 1976, N.Y. 1978. Chief Social Work Bur. Legal Aid Soc., Hempstead, N.Y., 1978—. Field instr. Adelphi U., Sch. Social Work, Hempstead, 1978—; tng. cons. Fordham U. Sch. Social Svcs. Adminstrn., 1989-94. Pres. Nat. Orgn. Forensic Social Work, 1993—94, editor newsletter, 1990—93, 1994—97. Recipient Frank Vergata Meml. award Legal Aid Soc. Alumni Assn., Hempstead, 1996. Avocation: quilting. Office: Legal Aid Soc Nassau County 1 Helen Keller Way Fl 3 Hempstead NY 11550-3985

ADEWUYI, YUSUF GBADEBO, chemical engineering educator, researcher, consultant; b. Offa, Kwara, Nigeria, Nov. 26, 1952; came to U.S., 1975; s. Alhaji Kadiri and Sifawu (Oguntundun) A.; m. Janice Hughes, Jan. 16, 1987; 1 child, Kasim Adesegun. BSChemE, Ohio U., 1978; MSChemE, U. Iowa, 1980, PhD, 1985. Postdoc. resident assoc. Boston Coll., 1986-87; postdoc. resident fellow U. Ill., Urbana-Champaign, 1987-88; sr. staff engr. Mobil R & D Corp., Paulsboro, N.J., 1988-91, rsch. engr., 1991-93; assoc. prof. chem. engring. N.C. A & T State U., Greensboro, 1994—2002, prof. chem. engring., 2002—. Cons. Air Purification Inc., N.Y., 1996—; rev. panelist NSF, Washington, 1996—. Contbr. articles to I&E Chem. Rsch., Jour. Hazardous Materials, Atmospheric Environment, Environ. Sci. Tech., Jour. Geophysics Rsch., Chem. Engring. Comms., Applied Catalysis, others. Named to environ. del. to China by Citizen Ambassador's Program, Spokane, Wash., 1994. Mem. AAAS, AIChE (sec. Triad sect. 1996-97, pres. 1997, sec. environ. divsn. 1999-2001), Am. Chem. Soc., Am. Soc. Engring. Edn., Sigma Xi Rsch. Soc. Achievements include patent for Riser cracking for maximum C3 and C4 Olefin yields; for fluidized catalytic cracking. Home: 3916 Brass Cannon Ct Greensboro NC 27410-9229 Office: NC Agrl Tech State Univ Dept Chem Engring 1601 E Market St Dept Chem Greensboro NC 27401-3209 E-mail: adewuyi@ncat.edu.

ADEY, WILLIAM ROSS, physician; b. Adelaide, Australia, Jan. 31, 1922; s. William James and Constance Margaret (Weston) A.; m. Alwynne Sidney Morris (div. 1970); children: John, Susan, Geoffrey. MB and BS, U. Adelaide, Australia, 1943, MD, 1949. Sr. lectr. and reader, Dept. Anatomy U. Adelaide, Australia, 1947-53; sr. lectr., Dept. Anatomy U. Melbourne, Australia, 1955-56; prof. anatomy and physiology UCLA, 1957-77; dir. Space Biology Lab UCLA Space Biology Lab., 1965-77; dir. rsch. VA Med. Ctr., Loma Linda, Calif., 1977-97; adj. prof. biochemistry U. Calif., Riverside, 1997-2000; disting. prof. physiology Loma Linda U. Sch. Med., 1980—. Cons. NIH, 1961—, Office Sci. and Tech. Policy, Washington, 1964—, NAS, 1965—; dist. prof. physiology Loma Linda U. Sch. Med., 1980—. Author: Nonlinear Electrodynamics in Biological Systems, 1984, Magnetic Resonance Imaging of the Brain, Head and Neck, 1984. Surgeon lt. Australian Navy, 1944-46, South Pacific. Fellow IEEE, Royal Soc. Medicine, Nuffield Found. (London), AAAS, Am. Electroencephalographic Soc., Royal Soc. Medicine (London), Am. Assn. Neurolog. Surgeons. Avocations: radiophysics, radioastronomy, marathon running, backpacking. Home: Rte 1 Box 615 31866 3rd Ave Redlands CA 92374-8237 E-mail: RAdey43450@aol.com.

ADIBI, SIAMAK A. medical researcher; b. Tehran, Iran, Mar. 17, 1932; came to U.S., 1950; s. Sadegh and Nezhat (Kazemi) A.; m. Joan Foedisch, June 15, 1963; children: Elise W., Camron F., Jennifer J. BA, Johns Hopkins U., 1955; MD, Jefferson Med. Coll., 1959; PhD, MIT, 1966. Asst. prof. medicine U. Pitts. Sch. Medicine, 1966-71, assoc. prof. medicine, 1971-74, prof. medicine, 1974—2002, prof. clin. nutrition, 1980—2002; dir. clin. nutrition rsch. unit U. Pitts. Med. Ctr., 1991—2002, emeritus prof. medicine, 2002—; head GI unit Montefiore U. Hosp., Pitts., 1966-81. Mem. edit. bd. Am. Jour. Physiology, 1975-80; mem. Nat. Med. Rsch. Svc. Merit Review Bd. VA Hosps., 1976-80. Editor: Branched-Chain Amino and Keto Acids in Health and Disease, 1984, Dipeptides as New Substance in Nutrition Therapy, 1987; contbr. over 148 articles to profl. jours. Mem. Assn. Am. Physicians, Am. Soc. Clin. Investigation, Am. Physiology Soc., Am. Inst. Nutrition. Achievements include patents on use of peptides for enteral and parenteral nutrition. Office: U Pitts Sch Medicine 601 Kaufman Bldg 3471 Fifth Ave Pittsburgh PA 15213

ADICKES, SANDRA ELAINE, English language educator, writer; b. N.Y.C., July 14, 1933; d. August Ernst and Edythe Louise (Oberschlake) A.; children: Delores, Lily, Cynthia. BA, Douglass Coll., 1954; MA, CUNY, 1964; PhD, NYU, 1977. Asst. registrar NYU, 1954-55; sec. McCann Erickson, J. Walter Thompson Cos., N.Y.C., 1955-60; English tchr. N.Y.C. Bd. Edn., 1960-70, 1980-88; instr. edn. N.Y.C. Tech. Coll., 1970-72; asst. prof. English S.I. C.C., N.Y.C., 1972-77; dir. project chance Bklyn. Coll., 1977-80; from assoc. prof. to prof. English Winona (Minn.) State U., 1988-98, prof. emerita, 1998—. Cons. Antioch Coll. N.Y.C., 1970; guest tutor London U., 1979. Author: The Social Quest, 1991, Legends of Good Women, 1992, To Be Young Was Very Heaven, 1997; editor: By A Woman Writt, 1973; contbr. articles to profl. jours. Co-founder Tchrs'. Freedom Sch. Project, Miss., 1963-64, Tchrs'. Com. for Peace Vietnam, 1965-66. Named Woman of Yr. Nat. Assn. Negro Bus. Profl.

Women, N.J., 1966. Mem. MLA, Midwest Modern Lang. Assn., Nat Coun. Tchrs. of English, Popular Culture Assn. Democrat. Home: 19 Davids Ct Dayton NJ 08810-1302 E-mail: s.adickes@att.net.

ADIELE, MOSES NKWACHUKWU, state official; b. Umuahia, Abia, Nigeria, June 22, 1951; came to U.S. 1973; s. Robert O. and Virginia A. Adiele; m. Vickie I. Eseonu, July 7, 1984; children: Elizabeth, Robert, Casey. BS, Ga. Inst. Tech., 1976; MD, Howard U., 1980; MPH, Johns Hopkins U., 1981; MSS, U.S. Army War Coll., 2001. Diplomate Nat. Bd. Med. Examiners, Fed. Licensure Examiners Med. Bd. House officer Howard U. Hosp., Washington, 1981-84, intern in family practice, 1981-82, resident in family practice, 1982-84; asst. dir. pub. health Va. State Health Dept., Richmond, 1984-86, dist. health dir. Boydton, 1986-87, pub. health officer, clinician Richmond, 1987-90; cons., dir. med. support svcs. Va. State Dept. Med. Asst. Svcs., Richmond, 1990—. Cons. Internat. United Black Fund, Washington, 1984-90. Role model youth edn. Richmond Redevel. and Housing Authority, 1984; vol. physician Richmond Area High Blood Pressure Ctr., 1985—90; comdr. 4215th U.S. Army Hosp., Richmond, Va., 1997—2000, 348th Gen. Hosp., Pedrictown, NJ, 2000—; bd. dirs. Commonwealth coun. Girl Scouts U.S., 2002—. Col. USAR, 2001—. Named Outstanding Resident Physician, Howard U. Hosp., Washington, 1982. Fellow Am. Acad. Family Physicians (recognition award 1991), Am. Coll. Med. Quality (Recognition award 1992), Am. Coll. Preventive Medicine (Recognition award 1999); mem. AMA (physician recognition award 1984, 89, 91, 97, 2000, 2003), Am. Coll. Physician Execs. (Recognition award 1998), Assn. African Physicians in N.Am. (pres. 1982-84, recognition award 1991), Va. Pub. Health Assn. Avocations: running, reading, volleyball, singing. Home: 1305 Cedar Crossing Trl Midlothian VA 23114-3148 Office: Va State Dept Med Asst Svcs 600 E Broad St Ste 1300 Richmond VA 23219-1856

ADIGA, GIRIDHAR U. geriatrician, pharmacologist, researcher, internist; s. Krishna Uppoor Adiga; m. Mamatha Adiga. MB, BChir, Gulbarga U., Bellary, India, 1992; MD, All India Inst. Med. Scis., New Delhi, 1997. Diplomate Am. Bd. Internal Medicine, 2002, cert. Ednl. Commn. for Fgn. Med. Grads., 1994. Med. officer Dhanvanthri Nursing Home, Bellary, 1992—93; resident med. officer ophthalmology All India Inst. Med. Scis., New Delhi, 1993—93, postgrad. resident in pharmacology, 1994—97; resident med. officer cancer surgery Safdarjung Hosp., Govt. Delhi, New Delhi, 1993—93; sr. demonstrator Maulana Azad Med. Coll., New Delhi, 1998—99; resident internal medicine Our Lady Mercy Med. Ctr., N.Y. Med. Coll., Bronx, 1999—2002; fellow geriatric medicine N.Y. Med. Coll., Bronx, 2002—03; with Halifax Med. Specialists, P.A., Roanoke Rapids, NC, 2003—. Presenter in field. Contbr. articles to profl. jours. Mem.: AMA, Am. Geriat. Soc., Am. Coll. Clin. Pharmacology. Achievements include discovery of and characterization of Iatrogenic anemia in the elderly; research in diuretic activity of Benincasa hispida; role of life style factors on the occurance of diabetes in India; review on vitamin B12 deficiency in older adults; HIV disease and gastrointestinal manifestations in older adults; Review on Myths and Facts on Growth Hormone; Review on human helminthic infections; Review of clinical and toxicological aspects of snake bites; discovery of altered vitamin B12 metabolism in acute pneumonia; research in anti ulcer activity of B. hispida; anti inflammatory activity of pefloxacin; diuretic activity of Benincasa hispida; Characterization and role of IL2 therapy in skeletal complications of renal cell carcinoma; Reviewed and characterecterized Ritchter's conversion of CLL to Hodgkin's disease; Impact of iatrogenic anemia on mortality; Toxicological studies on Benincasa hispida. Office: Halifax Med Specialists PA 270 Smith Church Rd Roanoke Rapids NC 27870 Home: 127 1/2 Valley Dr Roanoke Rapids NC 27870 E-mail: adiga_69@yahoo.com.

ADILETTA, DEBRA JEAN OLSON, business analyst consultant; b. Gloucester, Mass., Oct. 1, 1959; d. Melvin Porter Jr. and Ruth Margaret (Dahlmer) Olson; m. Mark Anthony Adiletta, Aug. 25, 1984; children: Christopher Michael, Nichole Brianna, Mark Andrew. BA, Coll. of Holy Cross, Worcester, Mass., 1981; MBA, U. Rochester, 1986. Systems analyst Eastman Kodak Co., Rochester, N.Y., 1981-85, infosystems specialist, 1985-86, personal computer area mgr., 1986-87, bus. analyst cons., 1987—90, info. sys. co-dir., 1990—92, bus. sys. specialist, 1992—. Seminar instr., Rochester, 1987. Fin. advisor Sts. Peter and Paul Ch., Rochester, 1985-86; div. chairperson United Way, Rochester, 1987. Mem. Assn. Systems Mgmt., Holy Cross Alumni Assn. (class agt. 1981—, sec. 1983-84, treas. 1984-88, v.p. 1988-90, pres. 1990-91, bd. dirs. 1992—). Avocations: snow and water skiing, horseback riding. Office: Eastman Kodak Co 343 State St Rochester NY 14650-0001

ADIN, RICHARD H(ENRY), lawyer, editor, publisher; b. Kingston, N.Y., May 19, 1948; s. Aaron and Lenore (Glasner) A.; m. Mary Grace Francioli, Nov. 10, 1972 (div. 1995); children: Mariah Pompea, Justin Richard. Student Hebrew U., Jerusalem, 1968-69, BA, SUNY, Fredonia, 1970, JD, U. San Fernando Valley, 1977. Bar: Ind. 1977, U.S. Dist. Ct. (so. dist.) Ind. 1977, U.S. Ct. Appeals (7th cir.) 1979, U.S. Supreme Ct. 1980, U.S. Ct. Appeals (6th cir.) 1982. Assoc. Law Office of Jack Davis, Evansville, Ind., 1977-78; ptnr. Matthews, Shaw & Adin, Evansville, 1978-81, Fields & Adin, Evansville, 1981-82; assoc. Bates Law Office, Evansville, 1982-83; sole practice, Evansville, 1983-84; exec. editor, atty. Matthew Bender & Co., Inc., N.Y.C., 1984-89; mng. editor, atty. Prentice Hall Law & Bus., Englewood Cliffs, N.J., 1989-92; pres. Richard H. Adin Freelance Editorial Svcs., Gardiner, N.Y., 1992—; pres., publisher Rhache Publishers, Ltd., Gardiner, N.Y. 1994—; gen. counsel, sec. AmCor Land, Ltd. Plattekill, N.Y., 1986-88, also bd. dirs.; instr. in evidence, U. Evansville, 1979-80; instr. in pub. Rhinebeck (N.Y.) Ctrl. Sch. Dist., 1995—; Mem. U. San Fernando Valley Law Rev., 1976-77. Atty., bd. dirs. Deaf Social Services Agy., Evansville, 1978-80; bd. dirs. Evansville Legal Aid Soc., 1980-81, Plattekill Library Assn., Modena, N.Y., 1985, Plattekill Library Chess Club, Modena, 1986-87; litigation atty. Hoosiers for License Br. Reform, Evansville, 1981 83; social worker Hawthorne (N.Y.) Cedar Knolls Sch., 1970-72; welfare frauds investigator Ulster County Dept. Social Svcs., Kingston, N.Y., 1972-73; asst. cashier First Nat. Bank, Ellenville, N.Y., 1973-74. Scholar N.Y. State Regents, 1966-70, Friends of Hebrew U., 1968-69. Mem. Ind. State Bar Assn., Editorial Freelancers Assn., Mid-Hudson Pubs. Assn. (founder). Office: 52 Oakwood Blvd Poughkeepsie NY 12603-4112

ADINOLFI, MARION DARLYNE, research scientist; b. Bronx, NY, Oct. 16, 1941; d. Carlo and Frances Moscato; m. Vincent John Adinolfi Sr., June 1, 1956; children: Vincent John Jr., Richard Anthony. BA, Coll. of New Rochelle, New Rochelle, NY, 1979; Master of Metaphysical Sci., U. of Metaphysics, Studio City, CA, 2001, Dr. of Metaphysical Sci., 2002. Pres. Adino Asbestos, Bronx, NY; tech. rschr. N.Y.C.; 11c spl. edn. educator St. Raymond's H.S., Bronx; english educator St. Martin's of Tours, Bronx; tech. rsch. scientist Adino Asbestos, Bronx; ny realty owner F&S Crest Co., Bronx; pastoral counselor N.Y.C.; metaphysical practitioner; ordained min.; dr. of metaphysical. V.p. F&S Crest Co., New York, NY, 1974—2002; metaphysical cons. Pvt. Practice, New York, NY, 1984—2002. Author: of various Anti-aging, Performance Enhancement, & Entertainment Computer Programs; contbr. articles to profl. newspapers and jours. R-Consevative. Achievements include development of pheromonal cologne and perfume fragrances; completed 2 placebo studies in pheromonal research. Avocations: reading, pheromonal research, golf, swimming, gift wrapping. Home: 828 Calhoun Ave Bronx NY 10465 Home Fax: 718-892-7058.

ADIZES, ICHAK, management consultant, writer; PhD, Columbia U. Tchr. Hebrew U., Jerusalem, Tel Aviv U., Stanford (Calif.) U., Columbia U., N.Y.C.; founder, profl. dir. Adizes Inst., Santa Barbara, Calif., 1975—, acad. dean. Lectr. in field. Author: Self-Management, 1975, How to Solve the Mismanagement Crisis, 1979, Corporate Lifecycles: How and Why Corporations Grow and Die and What to Do About It, 1988, Mastering Change; The power of Mutual Trust and Respect in Personal Life, Business and Society, 1992, The Pursuit of Prime, 1996, Managing Corporate Life Cycles, 1999; contbr. articles to profl. jours., newspapers. Office: Adizes Inst 2815 E Valley Rd Santa Barbara CA 93108-1611 Fax: (805) 565-0741. E-mail: adizes@adizes.com.

ADJARIAN, MAUDE MADELEINE, literature educator, researcher; b. Santa Monica, Calif., Oct. 10, 1965; BA Comparative Lit., U. of Calif., Berkeley, 1987; PhD Comparative Lit., U.of Mich., Ann Arbor, 1994. Adj. instr., women's studies/program in personal devel. UC Berkeley Ext., San Francisco, 1995—97; instr., English Skyline H.S., Oakland, Calif., 1997—2000; assoc. rschr. U. of Ariz., Dept. Women's Studies, Tucson, 2000—; adj. instr., English Pima C.C., Tucson, 2000—. Reader, English lit. exam. Ednl. Testing Services, Princeton, NJ, 2000—; referee Coll. Lit., West Chester, Pa.; adj. lectr. women's studies U. Ariz., 2003—. Contbr. articles literary criticism and revs. to various jours.; editor: Michigan Feminist Studies, 1993—94. Vol.literacy tutor Berkeley Pub. Libr., Mich., 1995—97. Grantee U. of Mich. Departmental Fellowship, Program in Comparative Lit., 1988—89, Rackham Discretionary Grant, Rackham Grad. Coll., U. of Mich., 1990, Program in Comparative Lit., Departmental Block Grant, U. of Mich., 1990. Mem.: MLA, Am. Comparative Lit. Assn., African Lit. Assn., Phi Beta Kappa. Office: Univ of Ariz Dept Womens' Studies Comm 108 PO Box 210025 Tucson AZ 85721 E-mail: adjarian@u.arizona.edu.

ADKERSON, DONYA LYNN, clinical counselor; b. Mattoon, Ill., Oct. 5, 1959; d. Edwin Dwayne and Sonya Jeanne (Abernathie) Adkerson; m. George Anthony Ferguson, May 20, 1990; children: Tiana Jo Berry, Thomas A.R. Ferguson. MA, So. Ill. U., Edwardsville, 1983. Outpatient dir. Children's Ctr. for Behavioral Devel., Centerville, Ill., 1983-90; pvt. practice psychotherapy Evaluation & Therapy Svc., Edwardsville, 1991-92; dir. Alternatives Counseling, Inc., 1993—; grant coord. Ill. Sex Offender Mgmt. Bd., 2003—. Cons. St. Louis City Juvenile Ct., 1991-94, Covenant Children's Home, 1991-93, U. Ill., 1997-2000. Co-author: Adult Sexual Offender Assessment Packet, 1994. Pres. Ill. Network for Mgmt. Abusive Secuality, 1991; clin. mem. Assn. Treatment of Sex Abusers, exec. bd., 1995—2000, chair orgn. and devel. com., 1996—2000; mem. ethics and stds. com., founding mem. Ill. Assn. Treatment Sex Abusers, 1996—2001, Madison County Child Protection Task Force, 1999—; mem. 3d Jud. Cir. Family Violence steering com., 1996—; mem. Adolescent Perpetrator Network, 1987—95; exec. bd. Arts League Players Theatre, Edwardsville, 1996—; former chmn. Metro-East Task Force on Sexual Offenders; mem. Madison County Child Protection task force, Am. Profl. Soc. on Abuse of Children, Ill. Sex Offender Mgmt. Bd. assessment and treatment subcoms. Mem. Ill. Counseling Assn., Ill. Mental Health Counselors Assn. Avocations: gardening, theater, water gardening. Office: Alternatives Counseling 101 W Vandalia St Edwardsville IL 62025-1949

ADKINS, BEN FRANK, management and engineering consultant; b. West Liberty, Ky., Mar. 6, 1938; s. Stuart Kendall Adkins and Dorothy Elizabeth (Shaver) Indes; m. Judith Ann Williams, Mar. 14, 1959; children: Michelle Rene, Lori Lee. BS in Indsl. Engring., Ariz. State U., 1964; MBA, Western New Eng. Coll., Springfield, Mass., 1971; MS in Systems Mgmt., U. So. Calif., 1983. Registered profl. engr. Enlisted USAF, 1955, commd. 2d lt., 1964, advanced through grades to maj., 1975, ret., 1979; internal cons., mgr. State of Wash., Olympia, 1979-87; mgmt. and engring. cons. Olympia, 1987-88; sr. rsch. sci. Battelle Pacific N.W. Labs., Richland, Wash., 1988-89; mng. prin. Ben Adkins & Assocs., Olympia, 1989—. Decorated Bronze star USAF. Mem. Inst. Indsl. Engrs. (sr. mem., bd. dirs. Puget Sound chpt. 1984-86, asst. dir. and dir. govt. div. 1979-83, v.p. Washington chpt. 1969-76). Avocations: skiing, sailing, photography, reading. Home: 6606 Miner Dr SW Olympia WA 98512-7257 Office: Ben Adkins & Assocs PO Box 7613 Olympia WA 98507-7613

ADKINS, BRYAN E. management consultant, educator; b. Balt., Md., Nov. 5, 1959; s. Edward and Shirley Adkins; m. Trish Gilleland, Jan. 29, 1988. EdD, The George Wash. U., Washington, 2000—00. COO Family Svc., Lancaster, Pa., 1992—98; v.p. of ops. J M Perry Corp, Palo Alto, Calif., 1998—2001; regional vp of consulting Right Mgmt. Consultants, San Jose, Calif., 2001—. Home: 69 Patrick Way Half Moon Bay CA 94019 Office: Right Mgmt Consultants 5300 Stevens Creek Blvd San Jose CA 95129 Office Fax: 408-554-1201. E-mail: bryan.adkins@right.com.

ADKINS, DAVID JAY, lawyer; b. Manhattan, Kans., Mar. 11, 1961; s. James Lloyd and Elaine (Staples) A.; m. Lisa Renee Ashner, Apr. 7, 1990. BA, U. Kans., 1983, JD, 1986. Bar: Kans. 1986, U.S. Dist. Ct. Kans. 1986, U.S. Supreme Ct. 1990. Assoc. Bennett, Lytle, Wetzler, Winn & Martin, Prairie Village, Kans., 1986—. Mem. Kans. Ho. of Reps. (28th dist.). Pres. Truman Scholars Assn., Kansas City, Mo., 1985-90; bd. dirs. chpt. U. Kans. Alumni, Kansas City, 1988; exec. com. Boy Scouts Am., Johnson County, Kans., 1986—; mem. Leadership Kans., Kans. C. of C. and Industry, Topeka, 1988. Harry S. Truman scholar Truman Scholarship Found., 1981. Mem. ABA, Johnson County Bar Assn., Kans. Bar Assn., Nat. Assn. of Coll. and Univ. Attys., Bacchus Charitable Found., Kans. Alumni Assn. Republican. Baptist. Avocation: community theater. Home: 8021 Belinder Rd Shawnee Mission KS 66206-1151 Office: Bennett Lytle Wetzler Winn & Martin 5000 W 95th St Ste 300 Shawnee Mission KS 66207-3300*

ADKINS, EDWARD CLELAND, lawyer; b. Montgomery County, Iowa, Aug. 11, 1926; s. Esse Clarence and Elsie Mae (Cline) A.; m. Claudia Kangas, Sept. 17, 1955; children: Pamela, Philip, Paul. BS, U.S. Naval Acad., 1949; JD, U. Mich., 1957. Bar: Ohio 1957, U.S. Supreme Ct. 1961, Fla. 1963, Mich. 1965, U.S. Ct. Appeals (5th cir.) 1973, U.S. Ct. Appeals (8th cir.) 1974, U.S. Ct. Appeals (11th cir.) 1982, U.S. Ct. Appeals (3d cir.) 1991. Assoc. Arter & Hadden, Cleve., 1957-64; trial counsel Gen. Motors corp., 1964-70; ptnr. litigation Holland & Knight, PA, Tampa, Fla., from 1970. Served to capt. USNR. Mem. ABA, Fla. Bar, Mich. Bar, Palma Ceia Golf and Country Club, University Club. Deceased.

ADKINS, GREGORY D. higher education administrator; b. Charleston, W.Va., May 20, 1941; s. Wondel Lafayette and Corda Christenia (Carnes) A.; m. Dolores June Lowe, Sept. 9, 1961; children: Christenia Lea, Angela Dawn BS, U. Charleston, 1962; MEd, Fla. Atlantic U., 1966; M.C.S., U. Miss., 1968, EdD, 1970. Assoc. prof. edn. Palm Beach Atlantic Coll., West Palm Beach, Fla., 1972-74, chair dept. edn., 1972-73, chair div. profl. studies, dir. tchr. edn., 1973-74; assoc. dean career edn. W.Va. No. Community Coll., Wheeling, 1974-75, dean acad. affairs, 1975-79; coordinator instrn. and planning Colo. State Bd. C.C.s. and Occupational Edn., Denver, 1979-81; pres. So. W.Va. Community Coll., Logan, 1981-88, Bluefield (W.Va.) State Coll., 1988-93, Franklin County Schs., Frankfort, Ky., 1993-94, Jefferson Coll., Hillsboro, Mo., 1994—. Vice chmn. adv. coun. of pres. W.Va. Bd. Regents, 1986-87; chair legis. affairs com., 1986-87; bd. dirs. Missourians for Higher Edn., Mo. Coordinating Bd. for Higher Edn. Com. on Transfer and Articulation, 1997—, Jefferson Coll. Found. Inc. Mem. Gov.'s Labor/Mgmt. Coun., Charleston, 1986-93, W.Va. Enterprise Zone Authority, Charleston, 1987-93, Mercer County Econ. Devel. Authority, 1989-93; bd. dirs. Bluefield Regional Med. Ctr., 1988-89, W.Va. Joint Commn. for Vocat. and Occupational Edn., 1989-93, Missourians for Higher Edn., 1996—; mem. coms. on transfer and articulation Mo. Coordinating Bd. for Higher Edn., 1996—. Recipient Alumnus of Yr. award U. Charleston, 1984, award VFW, Chapmanville, 1987; NSF grad. fellow 1967-68, Richard Weaver fellow Intercollegiate Studies Inst., 1969-70. Mem. W.Va. Assn. Coll. and Univ. Pres. (pres. 1984-85), W.Va. C.C. Assn. (pres. 1985-86), Mo. C.C. Assn. (bd. dirs. 1995-97, adv. coun. of pres. 1994—), North Ctrl. Assn. (cons., evaluator 1984—, commr.-at-large 1984-90), Kiwanis, Rotary Internat., Chi Beta Phi (pres.). Mem. Ch. of Christ. Avocations: outdoor sports, gardening. Office: Jefferson Coll 1000 Viking Dr Hillsboro MO 63050-2440

ADKINS, THOMAS SAMUEL, library director; b. Portsmouth, Ohio, Oct. 24, 1965; s. Millard Elwood and Ruth Caroline (Shultz) A. BS, Ohio U., 1988; MLS, Kent (Ohio) State U., 1993. Tchr. Cmty. Action Agy., Portsmouth, Ohio, 1988, Scioto County Schs., Portsmouth, 1988-89; ext. svcs. coord. Portsmouth Pub. Libr., 1989-95; dir. G.A. Wilson Pub. Libr., Waverly, Ohio, 1996—. Chairperson Libr. Adv. Coun., Wellston, Ohio, 1997. Author: Lucasville Cemeteries, 1988; editor: A Backward Glance, vol. 1, 1987, vol. 2, 1990. Mem. Cmty. Svcs. Coun., Waverly, Ohio, 1996—; treas. Lucasville (Ohio) Hist. Soc., 1986—; mem. Valley Alumni Scholarship Com., Lucasville, 1990—; govt. rels. com. Ohio Libr. Coun., 1998—, treas. bd. dirs., 2000—; participant Libr. Leadership Inst., Snowbird, Utah, 1999. Recipient Diana Vescelius Meml. award, 1998. Mem. ALA (Emerging Leaders 2000), Pike County C. of C. (bd. dirs.). Avocations: book collecting, local history, movies, travel.

ADKINS, WILLIAM LLOYD, state official; b. Emporia, Kans., May 19, 1959; s. James Lloyd and Elaine (Staples) A. BA in Psychology, Washburn U., Topeka, Kans., 1981; MA in Adminstrn. of Justice, Wichita State U., 1996. Toll collector Kans. Turnpike Authority, Topeka, 1976-79; biofeedback technician VA, Topeka, 1979-81; career counselor U. Kans., Lawrence, 1981; resdl. coord. Dodge City (Kans.) Mental Health, 1982-83; vault adminstr. Kans. Lottery, Topeka, 1987-88; corrections officer Kans. Dept. Corrections, Lansing, 1988-91, corrections specialist I El Dorado, 1991, corrections counselor II, 1991—. Contbr. articles to profl. jours. Crisis counselor Headquarters, Inc., Lawrence, 1981-83; cadet advisor Towanda Law Enforcement, 1993-99; jail steering com. Butler County, El Dorado, 1995-96; mem. Butler County Sheriff Res., 1999—; CPR and first aid instr. ARC. With U.S. Army, 1983-87. Mem. VFW, Hostage Negotiators of Am., Kans. Correctional Assn. (facility rep. 1991—), Correctional Peace Officers Found., Kans. Peace Officers Assn., Am. Correctional Assn. (pub. screening com. 1991—), Charles F. Menninger Soc. Avocation: walking dog. Office: El Dorado Correctional Facility PO Box 311 El Dorado KS 67042-0311 E-mail: badkins@cox.net.

ADKINSON, BRIAN LEE, manufacturing company executive; b. Lebanon, Ind., July 10, 1959; s. Marion Leroy and Edith Marie (Shonkwiler) A.; m. Pamela Lea Dinkins, June 12, 1982; children: Katherin Elizabeth, Anna Mary Josephine. BS in Fin., Ind. U., 1982; postgrad., Keller Sch. Mgmt., 1992-93. Asst. bank examiner FDIC, Chgo., 1980-81; acctg. assoc. battery prodn. Union Carbide Co., Bennington, Vt., 1982-83; sr. ptnr. AC Sales Assocs., Murfreesboro, Tenn., 1983-89; spl. mkts. mgr. Chgo. Cutlery Housewares, div. Gen. Housewares Corp., Terre Haute, Ind., 1989-90; nat. sales mgr. Gerber Legendary Blades, a Fiskers Co., Portland, Oreg., 1990-91, Fiskers Inc, Wausau, Wis., 1992-94; mktg. mgr. Fiskars Inc., Wausau, Wis., 1994-98, dir. mktg., 1998-99; group dir. sales/mktg. Recreation Group, 1999-2000; gen. mgr. Fiskars Outdoor Leisure Products, 2000; mng. dir. Fiskar U.K. Ltd., 2000—02; v.p. Jensen Co., Racine, Wis., 2002—03; v.p. sales and mktg. Walnut Hollow INc., Dodgeville, Wis., 2003—. Spl. examiner-in-charge Union Carbide Credit Union, Bennington, 1982-83, acctg. adv. co. store, 1982-83; mem. stds. com. Hubby Industries Am. Patentee in field. Vol. Zionsville (Ind.) Christian Ch., 1975-82, Ctrl. Christian Ch., Murfreesboro, 1983-87; mem. edn. com. Trinity United Meth. Ch., Murfreesboro, 1987-89, chmn. fin. com., 1989-89, adminstrv. bd., 1988-89; bd. dirs. Wesley Found., Mid. Tenn. State U., Murfreesboro, 1989; mem. Rutherford County Humane Soc., Beasley, 1987-89. Mem. Am. Mgmt. Assn., Am. Mktg. Assn., Ind. U. Alumni Membership Assn. (Nashville chpt.), Sigma Pi (mem. alumni assn.). Republican. Methodist. Avocations: investments, reading, sports, computer science. E-mail: alegandron@yahoo.com.

ADKINSON, N. FRANKLIN, JR., clinical immunologist; b. Forest City, N.C., May 18, 1943; s. N. Frank and Estelle (Stembridge) A.; m. Judy F. Hyder, Aug. 20, 1966; children: Anna Estelle, Carter F. BA with highest honors, U. N.C., Chapel Hill, 1965; MD, Johns Hopkins U., 1969; M of Lit. Arts, John Hopkins U., 1982. Intern, resident in internal medicine Johns Hopkins U., Balt., 1969-71, asst. prof. medicine, 1973-81, assoc. prof., 1981-87, prof. medicine, 1987—; co-dir. div. allergy and clin. immunology Johns Hopkins Sch. of Medicine, Balt., 1991-96, program dir. grad. tng. program in clin. investigation, 1992—. Mem. immunolog. scis. study sect. NIH, Bethesda, Md., 1982-86, allergy immunology rev. com., 1987-91; clin. assoc. Lab. of Immunology, NIH, 1971-73. Mng. editor: Allergy: Principles and Practice, 6th edit., 2003; contbr. more than 250 articles to profl. jours. Lt. comdr. USPHS, 1971-73. Recipient Allergic Disease Acad. award Nat. Inst. Allergy and Infectious Disease, 1975. Fellow Am. Acad. Allergy and Immunology; mem. Am. Soc. Clin. Investigation, Collegium Allergologica Internat., Am. Clin. and Climatological Assn. Episcopalian. Office: Johns Hopkins Allergy & Asthma Ctr 5501 Hopkins Bayview Cir Baltimore MD 21224-6821 E-mail: Fadkinso@jhmi.edu.

ADKISON, LINDA RUSSELL, geneticist, consultant; b. Columbia, S.C., Apr. 28, 1951; d. George Palmer Russell, Jr. and Annie Frances (Ingram) White; m. Daniel Lee Adkison, Jan. 28, 1978; children: Emily Kathleen, Seth Adams Russell. BS, Ga. So. U., 1973, MS, 1977; PhD, Tex. A&M U., 1986. Lab. tech. VA Hosp., Gainesville, 1973-75, Shands Teaching Hosp., Gainesville, Fla., 1973-75; grad. teaching asst. Ga. So. U., Statesboro, 1975-77; rsch. assoc. U. South Ala. Med. Sch., Mobile, 1978-80; instr. St. Mary's Dominican Coll., New Orleans, 1980-81; grad. rsch. asst. Tulane Med. Sch., New Orleans, 1980-82, Tex. A&M U., College Station, 1982-86; postdoctoral fellow Jackson Lab., Bar Harbor, Maine, 1986-89; asst. prof. genetics Mercer U. Sch. Medicine, Macon, Ga., 1989-94, assoc. prof. genetics, 1994-99, prof. genetics, 1999—, assoc. prof. ob-gyn., 1995-99, asst. prof. ob-gyn., 1991-95, prof. ob-gyn., 1999—. Vol. Girl Scouts Mid. Ga., Macon, 1990—2000, Abnaki Girl Scout Coun., Bar Harbor, 1986—89, Ctrl. Ga. Boy Scouts, Macon, 1993—; mem. Leadership Macon, 2002. Exec. Leadership in Acad. Medicine for Women fellow, Phila., 1999-2000. Mem. AAAS, Am. Coll. Med. Genetics, Am. Soc. Human Genetics, Grad. Women in Sci., Internat. Mammalian Genome Soc., Genetics Soc. Ga. (bd. dirs. 1990-97, sec. 1997-2000), Ga. Acad. Sci. (councillor at large 2002—), Leadership Macon, Sigma Xi. Achievements include research in gene mapping mutational analyses, B2 element analysis, effect of stress on development. Avocations: running, gardening, softball, martial arts. Home: 1699 Wesleyan Bowman Rd Macon GA 31210-1037 Office: Mercer Univ Sch Medicine 1550 College St Macon GA 31207-1500

ADKISSON, PERRY LEE, university system chancellor; b. Hickman, Ark., Mar. 11, 1929; s. Robert Louis and Imogene (Perry) A.; m. Frances Rozelle, Dec. 29, 1956 (dec. 1995); m. Gloria Ray, May 16, 1998; 1 dau., Jean Amanda. BS, U. Ark., 1950, MS, 1954; PhD in Entomology, Kans. State U., 1956; DS (hon.), U. Ark., 1997; DHL, Tex. A&M U., 2001. Asst. prof. entomology U. Mo., 1956-58; assoc. prof. Tex. A&M U., 1958-63, prof., 1963-67, Disting. prof. entomology, 1967—, head dept. entomology, 1967-78, v.p. for agr. and renewable resources, 1978-80, dep. chancellor for agr., 1980-83, dep. chancellor, 1983-86, chancellor, 1986-91, regent's prof., 1991-95. Cons. Internat. AEC, Vienna, 1969-74; chmn. sci. adv. panel Gov. Tex. on Agrl. Chems., 1970-72; chmn. Tex. Pesticide Adv. Com., 1972; mem. panel experts on integrated pest control UN/FAO, Rome, 1971-78, chmn., 1992-96; mem. Structural Pest Control Bd., Tex., 1972-78, NRC World Food and Nutrition Study Team, 1977; chmn. com. biology pest species NRC, 1974; mem. environ. studies bd., study group problems pest control NAS-NRC, 1973-75; mem. U.S. directorate UNESCO Man and the Biosphere Program, 1975-77; mem. bd. on agr. NRC, 1985-87, mem. Nat. Sci. Bd., 1985-96; mem. governing bd. Internat. Crops Rsch. Inst. for Semi-Arid Tropics, 1982-88; mem. rsch. adv. com. Agr. for Internat. Devel., 1986; mem. com. on life scis. NRC, 1985-85; mem. Tex. Sci. and Tech. Coun., 1986-88; mem. Standing Com. for Internat. Plant Protection Congresses, 1984—, adv. dir. Export-Import Bank U.S., 1987. Mem. editorial com. Ann. Rev. Entomology, 1973-78; contbr. articles to profl. jours. Exec. dir. G.H.W. Bush Presdl. Libr. Ctr. and Bush Libr. Found., 1991-93. With M.C., U.S. Army, 1951-53. Recipient Faculty Disting. Achievement award for rsch. Tex. A&M U., 1965, Alexander Von Humboldt award, 1980; Disting. Svc. award Am. Registry Prof. Entomology, 1979, Disting. Scientist of Yr. award Tex. Acad. Scis., 1982, Disting. Alumnus Svc. award Kans. State U., 1980, Disting. Svc. award Am. Inst. Biol. Sci., 1987, Nat. 4-H Alumni award, 1988, Outstanding Alumnus award Coll. of Agr. and Home Econs., U. Ark., 1990, Disting. Alumni award U. Ark., 1990, Disting. Svc. award Am. Agrl. Editors Assn., 1992, Wolfe Prize in Agr., 1994-95, World Food prize, 1997, medallion alumni award Kans. State U., 1999; USPHS postdoctoral fellow Harvard U., 1963-64; Tex. Heritage Hall of Honor, 1998. Fellow AAAS, Entomol. Soc. Am. (governing bd. 1971-75, pres. 1974, Bussart Meml. award 1967, Founders Meml. lectr. 1985); mem. Am. Acad. Arts and Scis., Kans. Entomol. Soc., Internat. Orgn. Biol. Control, Am. Registry Profl. Entomologists (governing council 1976-78, pres. 1977), Nat. Acad. Scis., Phi Kappa Phi, Sigma Xi. Office: Tex A&M U Dept Entomology College Station TX 77843-0001

ADKISSON, RANDALL LYNN, minister; b. Atlanta, May 28, 1957; s. John Earl and Mearl (Cox) A.; m. Salee Robin Smith, Nov. 7, 1981; children: Katheryn Lynsey, Keith Alan. BA in Journalism, U. Ga., 1979; MDiv, Southwestern Bapt. Theol. Sem., Ft. Worth, 1985; PhD, New Orleans Bapt. Theol. Sem., 1990. Ordained to ministry So. Bapt. Conv., 1979. Min. of youth Bethel Bapt. Ch., Good Hope, Ga., 1976-79; assoc. pastor Orange Hill Bapt. Ch., Austell, Ga., 1979-82; pastor Shifalo Bapt. Ch., Kiln, Miss., 1985-88, 1st Bapt. Ch., Foxworth, Miss., 1988-91, Monroeville, Ala., 1991-98, sr. pastor Cookeville, Tenn., 1998—; mem. on bds. Tenn. Bapt. Conv., 2003—. Tchg. fellow New Orleans Bapt. Theol. Sem., 1985-86. Bd. dirs. Judson Coll., 1994-98, Romanian-Am. Missions, 1998. Mem. Marion Bapt. Assn. (pastoral ministries dir. 1990-91, pres. min.'s conf. 1990-91), Nat. Assn. Bapt. Profs. Religion, Soc. Bibl. Lit., Alumni Assn. New Orleans Bapt. Theol. Seminary (v.p. to pres.-elect Ala. chpt., 1993, pres. 1994), Am. Assn. Christian Counselors, Tenn. Bapt. Conv. (mem. bd. com.). Office: 1st Bapt Ch 18 S Walnut Ave Cookeville TN 38501-3284 *Christian faith is not a faith that can be separated from action and ethic. To be a "believer" must by necessity impact every area of conduct as well as attitude.*

ADLARD, CAROLE RECHTSTEINER, health education agency executive; b. Cin., Jan. 8, 1952; d. Carl John and Ruth Francis (Hucke) Rechtsteiner; m. Ed Joseph Adlard, Sept. 9, 1978; children: Tara, Chase, Brett, Eric. Diploma in bus. adminstrn. mgmt., U. Notre Dame, 1974. Sales rep. Burroughs/UNYSIS, Boston, 1973-76; acct. exec. Young Rubican, Cin., 1976-77; advt. mgr. Cincom Sys., Cin., 1977-79; cons. B. Cross Assocs., Indpls., 1979-88; exec. dir. Healthy Visions, Cin., 1986—. Bd. dirs. Common Ground Network, Washington. Editor Up-Downtowners, 1976-83; contbr. articles to profl. jours.; prodr.: (video and workbook) Adoption As An Option, The Price Tag of Casual Sex. Active Ohio Child Conservation League, Kindervelt, Cin., 1990—, The Archdiocese Cin., The Health Found., The Pfau Found., The George Riley Trust, The Sutlphin Found., Cath. Women Cin., Hamilton County Dept. Human Svcs. Grantee State of Ohio, 1990—, Greater Cin. Found., 2000, Helen Steiner Rice Found., 1994; named Up-Downtowner of Yr., Ohio Child Conservation League Citizen of Yr. Mem. Child and Family First, Adoption Awareness Alliance. Roman Catholic. Avocations: hiking, biking, swimming, boating, water skiing. Home: 9990 Zig Zag Rd Cincinnati OH 45242-6339 Office: Healthy Visions PO Box 429327 Cincinnati OH 45242-9327 E-mail: adoptiopti@aol.com.

ADLER, ALEXANDER, former federal government health service executive; b. N.Y.C., Dec. 20, 1919; s. Nicholas and Helen (Kramer) A.; m. Ruth Gratt, Jan. 8, 1942; children: Alison B., Linda J. Student, George Washington U., 1940-48, NYU, 1950-51, Am. U., 1949. Info. officer divsn. rsch. grants NIH, USPHS, HEW, Bethesda, Md., 1956-67; chief sci. and tech. comms. Bur. State Svcs. Manpower Resources Program, Washington, 1967-69; assoc. dir. office info. Bur. Health Manpower, Bethesda, 1969-73; spl. asst. to assoc. adminstr. for extramural affairs Health Resources Adminstrn., Rockville, Md., 1973-80; dep. chief Program Devel. br. div. student assistance Health Resources and Svcs. Adminstrn., USPHS, Rockville, 1980-82, dep. dir. div. student assistance Bur. Health Professions, 1982-84; ret. Mem. nat. adv. bd. Forum Advancement Students Sci. Tech., Washington, 1970-72; lectr. Fin. Svcs. Corp., (Budapest, Hungary), 1989 Bd. dirs. Montgomery Coll. Found., 1985-90; adv. coun. bd. trustees Suburban Hosp., Bethesda, 1986-89. Served with AUS, 1942-46. Fellow Am. Med. Writers Assn. (pres. Mid-Atlantic chpt. 1971-72); mem. APHA, Manpower Analysis and Planning Soc. (pres. 74-75), Am. Acad. Health Adminstrn., Pub. Rels. Soc. Am., Washington Soc. for the History of Medicine (pres. 1987-88), NIH Alumni Assn. (bd. dirs. 1999—), Nat. Press Club.

ADLER, CHARLES SPENCER, psychiatrist; b. N.Y.C., Nov. 27, 1941; s. Benjamin H. and Anne (Greenfield) A.; m. Sheila Noel Morrissey, Oct. 8, 1966 (dec.); m. Peggy Dolan Bean, Feb. 23, 1991 BA, Cornell U., 1962; MD, Duke U., 1966. Diplomate Nat. Bd. Med. Examiners, Am. Bd. Psychiatry and Neurology. Intern Tucson Hosps. Med. Edn. Program, 1966-67; psychiat. resident U. Colo. Med. Sch., Denver, 1967-70; pvt. practice medicine specializing in psychiatry and psychosomatic medicine Denver, 1970—. Chief divsn. psychiatry Rose Med. Ctr, 1982-87; co-founder Applied Biofeedback Inst., Denver, 1972-75; prof. pro tempore Cleve. Clinic, 1977; asst. clin. prof. psychiatry U. Colo. Med. Ctr., 1986—, chief psychiatry and psychophysiology Colo. Neurology and Headache Ctr., 1988-95; med. dir. Colo. Ctr. for Biobehavioral Health, Boulder, 1994—. Author: (with Gene Stanford and Sheila M. Adler) We Are But a Moment's Sunlight, 1976, (with Sheila M. Adler and Russell Packard) Psychiatric Aspects of Headache, 1987; contbr. (with S. Adler) sect. biofeedback med. and health ann. Ency. Britannica, 1986; chpts. to books, articles to profl. jours.; mem. editorial bd. Cephalalgia: an Internat. Jour. of Headache, Headache Quar. Emeritus mem. Citizen's Adv Bd. Duke U. Ctr. Aging and Human Devel. Recipient Award of Recognition, Nat. Migraine Found., 1981; N.Y. State regents scholar, 1958-62 Fellow Am. Psychiat. Assn.; mem. AAAS (rep. of AAPB to med. sect. com.), Am. Assn. Study Headache, Internat. Headache Soc. (chmn. subcom. on classifying psychiat. headaches), Am. Acad. Psychoanalysis (sci. assoc.), Biofeedback Soc. Colo. (pres. 1977-78), Assn. for Applied Psychophysiology and Biofeedback (rep. to AAAS, chmn. ethics com. 1983-87, bd. dirs. 1990-93, Sheila M. Adler cert. honor 1988). Jewish. Office: 955 Eudora St Apt 1605 Denver CO 80220-4341

ADLER, DALE ATKINS, artist; b. Birmingham, Ala., Aug. 16, 1943; d. Oliver Fraser and Marjorie Neola (Deakin) Atkins; m. David Parker Wheeler, Oct. 5, 1966 (div. Aug. 1983); children: Traci Pendelton, Steven Parker; m. Leonard Adler, Sept. 27, 1987. BS, Radford U., 1966. Group shows include Reston Art Gallery, 1992, Vienna Arts Soc., 1993, 94, Broadway Gallery, Fairfax, Va., 1997, 99, 2000—, also other shows in Md., Va. and D.C.; one-persons show Annapolis, Md., 1997, Deco Art, Oakton, Va., 2000—, Front Royal, Va., 2001, Blue Ridge Arts Coun. featuring 28 original oil paintings, 2001; featured artist in Taiwan show, Republic of China, 1998, Millwood (Va.) Art Show, 2003. Artist mem., bd. dirs. Greater Reston Arts Ctr.; bd. dirs., sec. Second Chance Employment Svcs., Washington. Recipient 2d place award Reston Art Gallery show, 1992. Mem. League Reston Artists. Avocations: horseback riding, sailing, skiing. Home: 12209 Thoroughbred Rd Oak Hill VA 20171-2006 E-mail: daleadler@cox.net.

ADLER, DAVID NEIL, lawyer; b. Bklyn., Apr. 11, 1955; s. Leonard Howard and Elaine (Holder) A. Student, Colgate U., 1973-75; BA, NYU, 1977; JD, St. John's U., 1980. Bar: N.Y. 1981, U.S. Dist. Ct. (ea. and so. dists.) N.Y. 1986, U.S. Tax Ct. 1989. Pvt. practice, Kew Gardens, N.Y., 1982—. Contbr. articles to profl. jours. Mem. Queens County Bar Assn. (com. chmn. 1983—, co-editor Queens Bar Bull. 1987—, bd. mgrs. 1989—, officer 1993—, pres. 1998), N.Y. State Bar Assn. (exec. com. trusts and estates). Office: 12510 Queens Blvd Kew Gardens NY 11415-1519

ADLER, EARL, insurance executive; b. N.Y.C., Apr. 5, 1932; s. Louis and Jenny (Fischman) A.; m. June Cohen, June 28, 1954; children: Greg, Gary, Mitchell. BSBA, Lehigh U., 1954. CLU. Life ins. supr. Bergen Agy., Mut. Trust Life Ins. Co., N.Y.C., 1959-62; ptnr., v.p. Weinshel Inc.; inst. broker N.Y.C., 1962-70; v.p. Brokerage Resources, Inc., 1962-70; pres. Congl. Life Ins. Co., 1969-70, EACO, Inc., 1971—. Trustee Columbia Gammar and Prep Sch., N.Y.C., 1974-82. 1st lt. inf. AUS, 1955-57. Mem. Million Dollar Round Table (life), Assn. Advanced Life Underwriting, Friars (gov. 1974-78), Alpine Country Club (gov.) Office: EACO Inc 180-A Main St Fort Lee NJ 07024-6932 E-mail: earlhow@aol.com.

ADLER, EDWARD I. media and entertainment company executive; b. N.Y.C., Jan. 12, 1954; s. Walter S. and Justine (Rosenberg) P.; m. Shari Goldman; children: Alexander Justin, Jillian Haly. BA, Vassar Coll., 1976; MA in Journalism, NYU, 1979. Reporter Time Mag. subs. Time Inc. N.Y.C., 1976-79; sports programming exec. Home Box Office Inc. subs. Time Inc., N.Y.C., 1979-81; news editor TV-Cable Week Mag. subs. Time Inc., N.Y.C., 1981-83; sr. assoc. corp. pub. affairs Time Inc., N.Y.C., 1983-88; mgr. media rels. corp. comm. Time Warner Inc., N.Y.C., 1989-93, dir. media rels. corp. comm., 1993-97, v.p. corp. comm., 1997-2000, sr. v.p. corp. comm., 2000-01, AOL Time Warner, N.Y.C., 2001—. Bd. dirs. N.Y. Cares, Big Apple Circus. Office: AOL Time Warner Inc 75 Rockefeller Plz New York NY 10019-6990 E-mail: edward.adler@aoltw.com.

ADLER, ERWIN ELLERY, lawyer; b. Flint, Mich., July 22, 1941; s. Ben and Helen M. (Schwartz) A.; m. Stephanie Ruskin, June 8, 1967; children: Lauren, Michael, Jonathan BA, U. Mich., 1963, LL.M., 1967; JD, Harvard U., 1966. Bar: Mich. 1966, Calif. 1967. Assoc. Pillsbury, Madison & Sutro, San Francisco, 1967-73; assoc. Lawler, Felix & Hall, L.A., 1973-76, ptnr., 1977-80, Rogers & Wells, L.A., 1981-83, Richards, Watson & Gershon, L.A., 1983—. Bd. dirs. Hollywood Civic Opera Assn., 1975-76, Children's Scholarships Inc., 1979-80 Mem. ABA (vice chmn. appellate advocacy com. 1982-87), Calif. Bar Assn., Phi Beta Kappa, Phi Kappa Phi. Jewish. Office: Richards Watson & Gershon 355 S Grand Ave Ste 4000 Los Angeles CA 90071

ADLER, FRED PETER, retired electronics company executive; b. Vienna, Mar. 29, 1925; came to U.S., 1942, naturalized, 1947; s. Michael and Ellida (Bronner) A.; m. Alicia Gulkis, 1950; children; Michael Steven, Andrew David; m. Adrienne Wilcox, 1991. BSEE with honors, U. Calif., Berkeley, 1945; MSEE (Charles A. Coffin fellow), Calif. Inst. Tech., 1948, PhD magna cum laude, 1950. Elec. engr. GE Rsch. and Cons. Labs., 1945-47; project engr. Jet Propulsion Lab., 1950; with Hughes Aircraft Co., 1950-70, sr. staff physicist, dept. mgr., 1954-57, mgr. advanced planning, 1957-59, dir. advanced projects labs., 1959-61, v.p., mgr. space systems div., 1961-66, v.p., asst. group exec. Aerospace Group, 1966-70; pres. Nadgeco Ltd., 1970-72, chmn. bd., 1973-77; v.p., group exec. aerospace groups Hughes Aircraft Co., 1973-81, sr. v.p., pres. electro-optical and data sys. group, 1981-87; dir. Jefferson Ctr. for Character Edn., Monrovia, Calif., 1973-99, chmn. bd., 1988-99; ret., 1999. Co-author: text Guided Missile Engineering, 1959; also articles tech. jours. Fellow AIAA; mem. N.Y. Acad. Scis., Sigma Xi, Tau Beta Pi. Home: 10795 Woodbine St Apt 208 Los Angeles CA 90034 E-mail: fredad690@cs.com.

ADLER, FREDA SCHAFFER (MRS. G. O. W. MUELLER), criminologist, educator; b. Phila., Nov. 21, 1934; d. David and Lucia G. (de Wolfson) Schaffer; children by previous marriage: Mark, Jill, Nancy. BA, U. Pa., 1956, MA, 1968, PhD (fellow), 1971. Instr. dept. psychiatry Temple U., Phila., 1971; research coordinator Addiction Scis. Center, 1971-72; research dir. sect. on drug and alcohol abuse Med. Coll. Pa., 1972-74, asst. prof. psychiatry, 1972-74; asso. prof. criminal justice Rutgers U., Newark, 1974-79, prof., 1979-82, disting. prof., 1982—, acting dean grad. sch. criminal justice, 1986-87. Bd. dirs. Internat. Sci. and Profl. Adv. Coun. UN Programs in Crime Prevention and Criminal Justice; vis. fellow Yale U., 1976; cons. to Nat. Commn. on Marijuana and Drug Abuse, 1972-73, NYU Sch. Law, 1972-74; mem. faculty Nat. Jud. Coll., U. Nev., 1973—, Nat. Coll. Criminal Def. Lawyers and Pub. Defenders U. Houston, 1975; mem. adv. com. Gen. Fedn. Women's Clubs, 1975-77; UN rep. Internat. Prisoner Aid Assn., 1973-75, Centro Nat. di Prevenzione e Difesa Sociale, 1989—, Internat. Soc. Social Def., regional sec. gen., 1991—, bd. dirs.; sec. bd. dirs. Inst. for Continuous Study of Man, 1974-77, v.p., 1977—. Author: Sisters in Crime, 1975, The Incidence of Female Criminality in the Contemporary World, 1981, Nations Not Obsessed with Crime, 1983; co-author: A Systems Approach to Drug Treatment, 1975, Medical Lollypop, Junkie Insuline or what?, 1974, Criminology of Deviant Women, 1978, Outlaws of the Ocean, 1985, Criminology, 1991, 4th edit., 2001, Criminal Justice, 1993, 3d edit., 2003, Criminal Justice: The Core, 1996; contbr. numerous articles on criminology and psychiatry to profl. jours.; editor Advances in Criminological Theory, 1987—; mem. editl. bd. Criminology, 1971-73, Jour. Criminal Law and Criminology, 1982—, The American Sociologist, 1999—; co-editor: Politics, Crime and the International Scene, 1972, Revue Internationale de Droit Penal, 1974, Advances in Crimonological Theory, 1987—; assoc. editor LAE Jour., 1977-85; cons. editor Jour. Criminal Law and Criminology. Recipient (with G.O.W. Mueller) Beccaria medal in Gold Deutsche Kriminologische Gesellschaft, 1979; fellow Max Planck Inst. Fgn. and Internat. Law and Criminology, 1984, Am. Soc. Criminology, 1994, Northeastern Criminal Inst. Assn., 2002; named Cecil H. and Ida Green Honors Prof., Tex. Christian U., 1998, Ind. U. Disting. Scholar of Crime, Law, and Justice, 1999, Excellence award minorities and women's sect. Acad. Criminal Justice Scis., 2001. Mem. Am. Soc. Criminology (pres. 1994-95, Herbert Bloch award 1972, fellow 1995), Am. Sociol. Assn., Internat. Assn. Penal Law, U. Pa. Alumnae Assn. (bd. dirs. 1974-77), Chi Omega Home: 30 Waterside Plz Apt 37J New York NY 10010-2628 Office: Rutgers U Sch Criminal Justice 123 Washington St Newark NJ 07102-3094

ADLER, FREDERICK RICHARD, lawyer, financier; b. N.Y.C., Apr. 4, 1926; s. Samuel and Rose (Axelrod) A.; m. Catherine R. George, Apr. 25, 1986; Christopher Wells, Frederick George Richard; children by previous marriage: Barbara Ilene, James Richard, Susan Ruth Chapman, Elizabeth Anne Wertheimer. BA, Bklyn. Coll., 1948; JD magna cum laude, Harvard U., 1951; Doctorate (hon.), Technion-Israel Inst. Tech., 1998. Bar: N.Y. 1952. Assoc. Reavis & McGrath, N.Y.C., 1951-58, ptnr., 1959-89, Fulbright, Jaworski, Reavis & McGrath, N.Y.C., 1989-91; ret. sr. ptnr. Fulbright & Jaworski, N.Y.C., 1991-95, of counsel, 1996—; dir., chmn. exec. com. Data Gen. Corp., Westbo, Mass., 1968-99; mng. ptnr. VENAD Assocs., Adler & Co., Penta Equity Ptnrs., LLC. Bd. dirs. Sentigen Holding Corp., Colo., SIT Investment Assn., MN. Trustee Tchrs. Ins. and Annuity Assn., 1977-95; bd. mgrs./overseers Meml. Sloan-Kettering Cancer Ctr.; mem. dean's adv. bd. Harvard Law Sch; trustee Horace Mann School; With U.S. Army, 1943-45. Mem. Harvard Club, Met. Club, Maroon Creek Club (Aspen, Colo.), Univ. Club (N.Y.), Atlantic Golf Club (Southampton, N.Y.), Old Oaks Country Club (Purchase, N.Y.), Palm Beach Country Club (Palm Beach, Fla.), N.Y. Athletic Club. Office: 220 Sunrise Ave Palm Beach FL 33480-3869

ADLER, HENRY JOSEPH, research scientist; b. Brussels, Sept. 3, 1963; s. Stephen Emil and Helen Caroline (Schultz) A.; m. Denise Ann Forsythe, Nov. 12, 1994; children: Rachel Margarete and Hannah Margarete (twins). BA, Harvard U., 1986; PhD, U. Pa., 1993. Lab. technician Mass. Eye and Ear Infirmary, Boston, 1986-88; postdoctoral fellow Kresge Hearing Rsch. Inst., Ann Arbor, Mich., 1993-98, Nat. Inst. on Deafness and Other Communicative Disorders, Bethesda, Md., 1998—. Contbr. articles to profl. jours. Mem.: Assn. Rsch. Otolaryngology. Avocations: reading, photography, travel, racquet sports, swimming. Office: NIH/NIDCD 50 South Dr Rm 4347 Bethesda MD 20892 E-mail: adlerh@nidcd.nih.gov.

ADLER, HILTON C. plastic surgeon; b. N.Y.C., Apr. 19, 1952; s. Leonard Adler and Helen Sherman; m. Jaimie Fisher, May 1984; children: Shelley and Nomi. BS in Biology cum laude, U. Pitts., 1974; MD, U. Monterrey, Mex., 1978; postgrad., Downstate Med. Sch., 1979. Diplomate Am. Bd. Plastic Surgeons. Resident in gen. surgery U. Miami-Jackson Meml. Hosp., Fla., 1979-80, Beth Israel Med. Ctr., N.Y.C., 1980-82; resident, then chief resident in plastic surgery Albany (N.Y.) Med. Ctr., 1983-85; fellow in head and neck surgery Beth Israel Med. Ctr., N.Y.C., 1981; fellow in burn surgery Albany Med. Ctr. Hosp., 1983; fellow in plastic surgery Westchester County Med. Ctr., Valhalla, N.Y., 1985-86; fellow in plastic/aesthetic surgeons Metropolitan Plastic Surgeons, N.Y.C., 1986; attending Brookhaven Meml. Hosp., Patchogue, N.Y., 1987—, Mather Meml. Hosp., Port Jefferson, N.Y., 1987—, St. Charles Hosp. and Rehab. Ctr., Port Jefferson, N.Y., 1987—, SUNY Hosp., Stony Brook, 1987—, N. Shore Surgi-Ctr., Smithtown, N.Y., 1991—; clin. instr. SUNY, Stony Brook. Mem. ACS, Am. Soc. Plastic Reconstructive Surgeons, Am. Soc. Aesthetic Plastic Surgeons, Am. Assn. Hand Surgery, Internat. Coll. Surgeons, Northeastern Soc. Plastic Surgeons, N.Y. Regl. Soc. Plastic Surgeons, Med. Soc. State N.Y., Suffolk Acad. Medicine. Office: Suffolk Plastic Surgeons 179 Bellemeade Rd East Setauket NY 11733-3495

ADLER, HOWARD, JR., lawyer; b. Chgo., Jan. 25, 1925; s. Howard and Martha (Grossman) A.; m. Mary E. Williamson, Oct. 30, 1955; children: Martine, Karla, Elizabeth. MA in Econs., JD, U. Chgo., 1951. Bar: Ill. 1952. Atty. U.S. Dept. Justice, Washington, 1952-54, law clk., 1954-55; ptnr. Bergson, Borkland, Margolis & Adler, Washington, 1956-85, Davis, Graham & Stubbs, Washington, 1986-96; of counsel Baker & McKenzie, Washington, 1996—2001, Ridberg, Press & Sherbill, LLP, Bethesda, Md., 2002—. Mediator, arbitrator, JAMS, Washington. 1st lt. USAAF, 1946, PTO. Fellow Am. Bar Found.; mem. ABA (vice chmn. coun. 1978-79, sect. on antitrust law 1973-77). Home: 3711 Morrison St NW Washington DC 20015-1733 E-mail: hadler@rpslaw.com., howard3771@aol.com.

ADLER, HOWARD BRUCE, lawyer; b. N.Y.C., Apr. 29, 1951; s. Mandel and Dora (Rosenblatt) A.; m. Tanya Jean Potter; 1 child, Alexandra. BA, Johns Hopkins U., 1972; JD, NYU, 1975. Bar: N.Y. 1976, U.S. Dist. Ct. (ea. and so. dists.) N.Y. 1976, D.C. 1979, U.S. Dist. Ct. D.C., 1979, U.S. Ct. Appeals (D.C. cir.) 1979. Assoc. Shearman & Sterling, N.Y.C., 1975-79, Arnold & Porter, Washington, 1979-82; mng. counsel Mellon Bank N.A., Pitts., 1982-84; exec. v.p., gen. counsel The Riggs Nat. Bank of Wash. D.C., Riggs Nat. Corp., 1984-87; ptnr. Gibson, Dunn & Crutcher LLP, Washington, 1987—. Contbr. articles to profl. jours. Mem. ABA (banking law com.), Fed. Bar Assn. (exec. coun. banking law com. 1990-98), D.C. Bar (treas. 1996-97, steering com. corp., fin. and securities law sect., 1991-96, chmn. 1994-95, vice chmn. 1993-94, budget com. 1996-97, chmn. task force of lawyers for econ. redevel. of D.C. 1997-99), Archdiocesan Legal Network of Washington (adv. bd. 1995-2002), Congl. Country Club, Met. Club, Knights of Malta. Avocation: civil war history. Home: 9517 Eagle Ridge Dr Bethesda MD 20817-3916 Office: Gibson Dunn & Crutcher LLP 1050 Connecticut Ave NW Ste 900 Washington DC 20036-5306

ADLER, IRA JAY, lawyer; b. N.Y.C., Jan. 1, 1942; s. Ralph and Beatrice (Rosenblum) A.; m. Laraine Sheila Garfinkel, July 4, 1965; children: Jodi, Michael. BA, NYU, 1963, JD, 1966. Bar: N.Y. 1966. Ptnr. Certilman, Balin, Adler & Hyman, LLP, East Meadow, N.Y., 1973—. Bd. dirs. Queens County Builders and Contractors, Flushing, N.Y. Contbr. to profl. publs. Mem. ABA, N.Y. State Bar Assn., Nassau County Bar Assn., L.I. Builders Inst. (bd. dirs. 1985—), Real Estate Inst. C.W. Post (bd. dirs. 1986—), N.Y. State Builders Assn. (bd. dirs. 1988—). Office: Certilman Balin Adler & Hyman LLP 90 Merrick Ave East Meadow NY 11554-1571

ADLER, IRVING, mathematician; b. N.Y.C., Apr. 27, 1913; s. Marcus and Celia (Kress) A.; m. Ruth Relis, June 2, 1935 (dec. 1968); children: Stephen L., Peggy A.; m. Joyce Lifshutz, Sept. 16, 1968 (dec. 1999). BS, CCNY, 1931, DHL (hon.), 2002; MA, Columbia U., 1938, PhD, 1961; DSc (hon.), St. Michael's Coll., 1990. Tchr. pub. high schs., N.Y.C., 1932-46; chmn. dept. math. Textile High Sch., N.Y.C., 1946-52; instr. math. Columbia U., N.Y.C., 1957-60, Bennington Coll., North Bennington, Vt., 1961, So. Vt. Coll., Bennington, 1983; researcher in math. biology North Bennington, 1972—. Lectr. in field. Author 49 books; co-author 34 books; contbr. articles to profl. jours.; contbg. editor Sci. and Society, 1981—; mem. editl. bd. Sci. and Nature, 1978-89. Recipient awards for outstanding sci. books for children Children's Book Coun. and Nat. Sci. Tchrs. Assn., 1972, 75, 80, 90, Townsend Harris medal for outstanding achievement CCNY Alumni Assn., 1993. Fellow AAAS, Vt. Acad. Arts and Sci.; mem. Am. Math. Soc., Math. Assn. Am., Nat. Council Tchrs. Math., Soc. for Indsl. and Applied Math., Authors League, Townsend Harris Hall of Fame, 1996, Phi Beta Kappa, Sigma Xi. Democrat. Jewish. Avocation: vegetable gardening. Home: 297 Cold Spring Rd North Bennington VT 05257-9767 E-mail: iadler@sover.net.

ADLER, JAMES BARRON, publishing executive; b. N.Y.C., Mar. 8, 1932; s. George G. and Mollie (Barron) A.; m. Esthy Lehmann, June 26, 1956; children: Laura Frances, Eric Stephen. AB magna cum laude, Harvard U., 1953. With NBC, N.Y.C., 1956-57, R.R. Bowker Co., N.Y.C., 1957-61, Random House, Inc., N.Y.C., 1961-64, G.P. Putnam's Sons, N.Y.C., 1964-67; founder James B. Adler, Inc., 1967; founder, pres., chmn. Congressional Info. Service, Inc., Washington, 1969-81; mng. partner Adler Assos., 1981—; pres. Adler & Adler Pubs., 1983—. Chmn. Greenwood Press, Inc., 1976-79; mem. U.S. Nat. Advisory Commn. Internat. Documentation Fedn., 1972-73 Served with U.S. Army, 1954-55. Recipient Profl. award Spl. Libraries Assn., 1972; Product of Yr. award Info. Industry Assn., 1971, 76 Mem. ALA, Am. Soc. Info. Sci. Clubs: Cosmos, Nat. Press. Home: 5630 Wisconsin Ave Apt 1205 Chevy Chase MD 20815-4457 Office: 5530 Wisconsin Ave Chevy Chase MD 20815-4404

ADLER, JEFFREY D. political consultant, public affairs consultant, crisis management expert; b. Cleve., July 10, 1952; s. Bennett and Edythe Joy (Eisner) A.; m. Colleen Ann Bentley, May 29, 1983. BS in Journalism, Northwestern U., 1975. Porter, waiter, bartender Amtrak, Chgo., 1975-76; reporter Enterprise-Courier, Oregon City, Oreg., 1977, Las Vegas Sun, 1977-80, O.C. Daily Pilot, Costa Mesa, Calif., 1982-85; v.p. pub. affairs Englander Comm., Newport Beach, Calif., 1985-86; pres. Adler Wilson Campaign Svcs., Laguna Hills, Calif., 1990-95, Adler Pub. Affairs, Long Beach, Calif., 1987—. Vice chair bd. dirs. Pacific Pub. Radio (KKJZ-FM), Long Beach, 2002—. Mem. Am. Assn. Polit. Cons. Democrat. Jewish. Home: 33 Pomona Ave Long Beach CA 90803-3426 Office: Adler Pub Affairs 200 Pine Ave Ste 300 Long Beach CA 90802-3038

ADLER, JILL S. psychiatric social worker, psychotherapist; b. Wheeling, W.Va., Oct. 27, 1948; d. Herbert and Doris (Abel) Sonneborn; m. David A. Adler, Oct. 5, 1975; children: Jonathan, Eliza. BS, Lesley Coll., 1970; MSW, Simmons Coll., 1972. Diplomate Assn. Cert. Social Workers; lic. clin. social worker, Mass. Social worker Mass. Mental Health Ctr., Boston, 1972-76, West Ros Park Mental Health Ctr., Boston, 1976-78; pvt. practice psychotherapy Newton, Mass., 1976—. Mem. Nat. Assn. Social Workers. Home and Office: 20 Sylvan Ave Newton MA 02465-3016

ADLER, JOHN HERBERT, lawyer, state legislator; b. Phila., Aug. 23, 1959; s. John Herbert and Mary Louise (Beatty) Adler; m. Shelley Arlene Levitan, Sept. 1, 1985; children: Jeffrey David, Alexander Samuel, Andrew Neal, Oliver Maxwell. AB, Harvard U., 1981, JD, 1984. Bar: N.J. 1984. Assoc. atty. Archer & Greiner, Haddonfield, N.J., 1984-87, McCarter & English, Cherry Hill, N.J., 1987-89, Gerstein Cohen & Grayson, Haddonfield, 1989-92; mem. N.J. Senate, Dist. 6, Trenton, 1992—; ptnr. Adler & Gold, P.C., Cherry Hill, 1992-98; sr. mem. Cozen & O'Connor, Cherry Hill, 1998-2000; pvt. practice Westmont, N.J., 2000—; ptnr. Earp Cohn, Westmont, NJ, 2000—. Councilman, Cherry Hill Twp., 1988-89; mem. N.J. State Senate, 1992—. Democrat. Jewish. Home: 231 S 70 E Cherry Hill NJ 08034-2421 Office: NJ Senate 231 Route 70 E Cherry Hill NJ 08034-2406

ADLER, JONATHAN L. physician; b. N.Y.C., Oct. 10, 1939; s. Samuel S. and Edna (Loewy) A.; m. Sara Ostroff, June 30, 1963; children: Robert, Andrea. BA, Colgate U., 1961; MD, Cornell U., 1965. Intern, resident Bellevue Hosp., N.Y.C., 1965-67; officer NCDC, Atlanta, 1967-69; physician pvt. practice, Winchester, Mass., 1971—. Chmn. dept. medicine Winchester Hosp., 1982-92. Fellow Boston City Hosp., 1969-71. Fellow Am. Coll. Physicians; mem. Infectious Disease Soc. Am.

ADLER, JULIUS, biochemist, biologist, educator; b. Edelfingen, Germany, Apr. 30, 1930; came to U.S., 1938, naturalized, 1943; s. Adolf and Irma (Stern) A.; m. Hildegard Wohl, Oct. 15, 1963; children: David Paul, Jean Susan. AB, Harvard U., 1952; MS, U. Wis., 1954, PhD, 1957; postdoctoral fellow, Washington U., St. Louis, 1957-59, Stanford U., 1959-60; hon. doctorate, U. Tübingen, Germany, 1987, U. Regensburg, 1995. Asst. prof. biochemistry and genetics U. Wis., Madison, 1960-63, assoc. prof., 1963-66, prof., 1966-96; prof. emeritus U.Wis., Madison, 1996—; Edwin Bret Hart prof. biochemistry and genetics U. Wis., Madison, 1972, Steenbock prof. microbiol. scis., 1982-92. Recipient hon. symposium on behavior and signaling in microorganisms, 1995. Research, publs. in field. Recipient Otto-Warburg medal German Soc. Biol. Chemistry, 1986, R.H. Wright award Simon Fraser U., 1988, Hilldale award U. Wis., 1988, Abbott-Am. Soc. Microbiology Lifetime Achievment award, 1995, William C. Rose award Am. Soc. Biochemistry and Molecular Biology, 1996. Mem. NAS (Selman A. Waksman Microbiology award 1980), Am. Acad. Arts and Scis., Am. Philos. Soc., Wis. Acad. Scis., Arts and Letters. Home: 1234 Wellesley Rd Madison WI 53705-2232 Office: U Wis Dept Biochemistry Madison WI 53706 E-mail: adler@biochem.wisc.edu.

ADLER, KARL PAUL, medical educator, academic administrator; b. Paterson, N.J., July 9, 1939; MD, Georgetown U., 1966. Diplomate Am. Bd. Internal Medicine. Intern 2d med. div. Bell Hosp., Cornell U., 1966-67, jr. asst. resident 2d med. div., 1967-68; jr. asst. resident Meml. Hosp., 1967-68; sr. asst. resident Cornell Cooperating Hosps., 1968-69, chief resident in medicine, 1969-70; sr. asst. resident North Shore Hosp., Manhasset, N.Y., 1968-69, chief resident in medicine, 1969-70, assoc. dir. dept. medicine, 1972-74, chief nephrology, 1972-74; med. dir. dept. emergency services Kings County Hosp. Ctr., Bklyn., 1974-77, med. dir. dept. medicine, 1974-77; asst. prof. medicine Cornell U., 1971-74, SUNY Med. Sch., Bklyn., 1974-76, assoc. prof. clin. medicine, 1976-77; chief dept. medicine Ellis Hosp., 1977-81; vice chmn. at Albany Med., 1977-81, assoc. prof. med., 1977-81; chief dept. medicine Met. Hosp. Ctr., 1981-87; dean N.Y. Med. Coll., 1987-94, prof. medicine, 1981—, v.p. for med. affairs, 1990-94; pres., CEO St. Vincent's Hosp. and Med. Ctr., N.Y.C., 1994-2000. Pres. Assoc. Med. Schs. N.Y., 1991-93. Mem. ACP, Am. Assn. Med. Colls., Alpha Omega Alpha. Office: St Vincents Hosp & Med Ctr 153 W 11th St New York NY 10011-8397

ADLER, LARRY, marketing executive; b. Frankfort, Ind., Dec. 18, 1938; s. Leon Sidney and Roslyn Jane (Woolf) A.; m. Ruthlee Figlure, Oct. 9, 1960; children: Laurie Kaye, Mark Allan, Joy Ellen. BS in Mktg. and Journalism, Ind. U., 1960. Asst. circulation and promotion mgr. McCall Corp., 1960-61; circulation and promotion mgr. Bartell-Media, Inc., 1961-63; sales promotion mgr. Golden Press, Inc., 1963-64; audio-visual dir., licensing mdse. dir., periodical publs. dir., advt. sales and mktg. dir. periodical div. Western Pub. Co., N.Y.C., 1964-74; v.p., pub., dir., treas. Washingtonian mag. and books Washington Mag., Inc., 1974-79; pres. Am. Program Bur., 1980; communications cons., 1980; pres., chmn. Adler Enterprises Ltd., 1981—, Adler Media, Inc., 1981—. Pres. Bergen Cablevision, Inc., Bergen County, N.J., 1970-72; asso. profl. lectr. Publs. Specialists program George Washington U., 1977-79 Creator, host: TV show Toy Fair News, 1968-73; exec. prodr. (TV programs) Jazz at the Smithsonian, 1981, Great Shark Hunt, 1981, Ireland by Rail, Tomb of Jesus, 1981, Operation Animal Shield, 1981. Pres. Englewood (N.J.) Jaycees, 1965-

66; mem. bd. edn. High Sch. Planning Com., Tenafly, N.J., 1969; program chmn. Tenafly Action Conf. on Edn., 1969; exec. bd. Tenafly, 1968-70; mem. steering com., long range planning com. Tenafly Bd. Edn., 1971-72; chmn. Tenafly Citizens Communications Com., 1971-72, Tenafly Townwide Com., 1972-73; chmn. bd. dirs. Capital Children's Mus., 1977-83; Bd. dirs. Englewood Boys Club, 1967-69. Mem. City and Regional Mag. Assn. (founder, pres., treas.), Ind. U. Alumni Assn., Alpha Delta Sigma, Zeta Beta Tau (v.p. 1960) Office: 6849 Old Dominion Dr Mc Lean VA 22101-3705 E-mail: adlermedia@aol.com.

ADLER, LEE, artist, educator, marketing executive; b. N.Y.C., May 22, 1926; s. Isidore and Anne (Blasser) A.; m. Florence Blumenkrantz, Dec. 28, 1956; 1 child, Derek Jonathan Tristan. BA, Syracuse U., 1948; MBA, N.Y. U., 1960. Research account exec. Amos Parrish & Co., N.Y.C., 1954-56; dir. mktg. Lewin, Williams & Saylor, Inc., N.Y.C., 1956-57; with Interpub. Group Cos., Inc., N.Y.C., 1958-68; client service dir. Marplan, 1958-63; market devel. McCann-Erickson, Inc., N.Y.C., 1963-64; v.p. research and planning Pritchard, Wood, Inc., N.Y.C., 1964-65; v.p. mktg. services McCann-ITSM, Inc., N.Y.C., 1966-67; dir. research Market Planning Corp., N.Y.C., 1967-68; pres. Flouton, Adler & Assos., N.Y.C., 1969-70; dir. mktg. research RCA Corp., N.Y.C., 1970-74; prof. mktg. Fairleigh Dickinson U., Madison, N.J., 1974-80; ptnr. Machlin-Adler Realty Co., Bklyn., 1978-82, Adler Realty Co., Bklyn., 1982—; owner, operator beef cattle ranch Climax, N.Y. Guest lectr. Columbia, Emory U., N.Y. U., U. Conn., St. John's U.; bd. govs., v.p., chmn. research com. Bklyn. Heights Assn.; trustee Mktg. Communications Research Ctr. Author, editor: Attitude Research at Sea, 1966, Plotting Marketing Strategy, 1967, Attitude Research on the Rocks, 1968, Managing the Marketing Research Function, 1977; also articles; contbg. author Modern Marketing Strategy, 1964, Handbook Modern Marketing, 1970, others; one man shows include, Ruth White Gallery, N.Y.C., 1968, Salpeter Gallery, N.Y.C., 1967, N.Y.C. Community Coll., 1967, NYU, 1972, New Bertha Schaefer Gallery, N.Y.C., 1973, 74, Hagley Mus., Wilmington, Del., 1974, Mickelson Gallery, Washington, 1975, Norton Gallery, St. Louis, 1974, Fairleigh Dickinson U., 1975, John Leech Gallery, Auckland, New Zealand, 1975, Poster Place, N.Y.C., 1975, Dallas, 1975, Canterbury Soc. Arts, Christ Church, New Zealand, 1975, Pub. Art Gallery, Dunedin, New Zealand, 1975, Waikato Art Gallery, Hamilton, New Zealand, 1975, Terrain Gallery, N.Y.C., 1973, Warwick (Eng.) Gallery, 1976, L.I. U., Bklyn., 1976, Kingpitcher Gallery, Pitts., 1976, Graham Gallery, N.Y.C., 1976, Instituto de Cultura Hispanica, Madrid, Spain, 1976, Mus. Modern Art, Mexico City, 1976, Universidad Autonoma de Nuevo Leon, Monterrey, Mex., 1976, Galeria de Arte, Saltillo, Mexico, 1976, Unidad de la Ciudadela, Monterrey, 1976, U. Monterrey, 1976, Instituto Tecnologico, Monterrey, 1976, USIA, Monterrey, 1976, Mus. Art, Torréon, Mexico, 1976, Albert White Gallery, Toronto, Ont., 1977, Centro de Arte Moderno, Guadalajara, Mexico, 1977, Mint Mus. Art, Charlotte, N.C., 1978, Heritage Found. Mus., 1978-79, Aldrich Mus. Contemporary Art, 1979, Gertrud Dorn Gallery, Stuttgart, W. Ger., 1979, Ulrich Mus. Art, Wichita, Kans. U., 1980, numerous others; exhibited in group shows, Museo de Arte Contemporanea, Bogota, Colombia, Whitney Mus. Am. Art, N.Y.C., State U. N.Y., Rochester, Bklyn. Mus., Am. Acad., Mus. Modern Art, São Paulo, Brazil, N.A.D., Soc. Am. Graphic Artists, Fine Arts, Springfield, Mass., New Eng. Exhbn., Butler Inst. Am. Art, Youngstown, Ohio, numerous others; represented in many permanent collections including Whitney Mus. Am. Art, Met. Mus. Art, Brit. Mus., Art Inst. Chgo., Corcoran Gallery, Washington, Fogg Art Mus., Harvard, Mus. Contemporary Art, São Paulo, Bklyn. Mus., Seattle Art Mus., Albion (Mich.) Coll., Andrew Dickson White Mus. Art, Ithaca, N.Y., Butler Inst. Am. Art, Indpls. Mus. Art, Columbia Tchrs. Coll., Cin. Art Mus., N.Y. U., N.Y.C., Community Coll., Jersey City Mus., DeCordova Mus., Lincoln, Mass., Syracuse Art Mus., Ithaca Art Mus., Detroit Inst. Art, Mus. Modern Art, Sao Paulo, Mus. Fine Arts, Montreal, Phila. Mus. Art, Municipal Art Gallery, Dublin, Ireland, Hagley Mus., Wilmington, Del. Art Mus., Wilmington, Art Gallery Ont., Toronto, Auckland Art Mus., Fairleigh Dickinson U., Madison, N.J., L.I. U., Bklyn., Printmakers Workshop Collection, N.Y.C., Wichita State U., Larry Aldrich Mus., Ridgefield, Conn., Colgate U., Munson-Williams-Proctor Inst., Utica, N.Y., N.Y. Pub. Library, Instituto de Cultura Hispanica, Madrid, Edwin A. Ulrich Mus. Art, Wichita, Kans., Nat. Acad. Health and Safety, Beckley, W.Va., Civic Mus., Udine, Italy, Neuberger Mus., Pratt Graphics Center, SUNY, Purchase, Weatherspoon Art Gallery at U. N.C., Mint Mus. Art, Charlotte, N.C., USIA. Recipient Burndy Corp. award, 1969; Grumbacher award, 1968; Purchase award Soc. Am. Graphic Artists, 1979; won Childe Hassam Fund competition, 1969 Mem. Am. Mktg. Assn. (v.p. 1970-71, dir. 1968-70, chmn. attitude research com. 1963-65), Am. Assn. Pub. Opinion Research, Am. Sociol. Assn., N.Y. U. Grad. Sch. Bus. Adminstrn. Alumni Assn. (dir. 1964-67) Home: Lime Kiln Farm Climax NY 12042

ADLER, LEWIS GERARD, lawyer; b. N.Y.C., Sept. 13, 1960; s. Sherman and Esther (Weiss) A.; m. Kim Adler, Sept. 5, 1988; children: Craig, Stephanie, Katie, Samantha. AS, Vanderbilt U., 1981; JD, Rutgers U., 1985. Bar: N.J. 1986, Pa. 1985, U.S. Dist. Ct. N.J. 1986, U.S. Dist. Ct. Pa. 1990, U.S. Supreme Ct. 1990, U.S. Tax Ct. 2000, U.S. Ct. Appeals (3d cir.) 2000. Solicitor Gloucester County Constrn. Bd. Appeals, Woodbury, N.J., 1987-88; atty. Gloucester County Sr. Citizen Will Program, Woodbury, 1987-88; pvt. practice Woodbury, N.J., 1989—; spl. counsel Gloucester County, 1990—. Pub. defender Deptford Township, 1996, zoning bd. solicitor, 1997-2000. Designer computer software. Pres. Haddonfield Plays & Players, 2002—. Mem. ABA, N.J. Bar Assn., Gloucester County Bar Assn., Phila. Trial Lawyers, Pa. Bar Assn. Democrat. Avocations: water and snow skiing, spelunking, chess, bicycling, rappelling. Home: 215 Douglass Ave Haddonfield NJ 08033-1626 Office: 26 Newton Ave Woodbury NJ 08096-4633

ADLER, LOUISE DECARL, judge; b. 1945; BA, Chatham Coll., Pitts.; JD, Loyola U., Chgo. Bar: Ill., 1970, Calif., 1972. Practicing atty., San Diego, 1972-84; standing trustee Bankruptcy Ct. So. Dist. Calif., San Diego, 1974-79, chief bankruptcy judge, 1996—2001. Mem. editorial bd. Calif. Bankruptcy Jour., 1991-92. Fellow Am. Coll. Bankruptcy; mem. San Diego County Bar Assn. (chair bus. law study sect. 1979, fed. ct. com. 1983-84), Lawyers Club of San Diego (bd. dirs. 1972-73, treas. 1972-75, sec. 1972-74, v.p. 1974-75), San Diego Bankruptcy Forum (bd. dirs. 1989-92), Nat. Conf. Bankruptcy Judges (bd. dirs. 1989-91, sec. 1992-93, v.p. 1993-94, pres. 1994-95). Office: US Bankruptcy Ct 325 W F St Rm 2 San Diego CA 92101-6017

ADLER, MARGOT SUSANNA, journalist, radio producer; b. Little Rock, Apr. 16, 1946; d. Kurt Alfred and Freyda (Nacque) A. BA, U. Calif., Berkeley, 1968; MS, Columbia U., 1970. Newscaster Sta. WBAI-FM, N.Y.C., 1968-71, host talk show, 1972-90; chief Washington bur. Pacifica News Svc. Network; corr., prodr. All Things Considered, Morning Edit., Nat. Pub. Radio, N.Y.C., 1978—, host Justice Talking, 1999—. Instr. radio comms. Goddard Coll., Plainfield, Vt., 1977; instr. religion and ecology Inst. for Social Ecology, Vt., 1986-93. Author: Drawing Down the Moon, 1979, Heretic's Heart, 1997; co-prodr., dir. (radio drama) War Day, 1985; contbr. articles to prof. jours. Nieman fellow Harvard U., 1982. Mem. Phi Beta Kappa. Avocations: swimming, bird watching, science fiction. Home: 333 Central Park W New York NY 10025-7145 Office: Nat Pub Radio 801 2nd Ave Rm 701 New York NY 10017-4781 E-mail: madler@npr.org.

ADLER, MARTIN WILLIAM, neuropharmacologist; b. Phila., Oct. 30, 1929; s. Jack and Sonia (Coopersmith) A.; m. Toby Wisotsky, June 28, 1953; children: Charles Howard, Eve Robin. BA, NYU, 1949; BS, Bklyn. Coll. Pharmacy, 1953; MS, Columbia U., 1957; PhD, Albert Einstein Coll. Medicine, 1960. From instr. to assoc. prof. Temple U. Sch. Medicine, Phila., 1960-73, prof., 1973—; Laura H. Carnell prof. pharmacology, 1999—. Chmn. rsch. rev. coms. NIH, 1980-2000; exec. officer Coll. on Problems of Drug Dependence, Phila., 1986—; dir. Ctr. for Substance Abuse Rsch., 1998—. Author: 5 book chpts., 6 major revs.; editor: (book) Factors Affecting Action of Narcotic Drugs, 1976, Testing of Drugs of Abuse, 1990; contbr. over 200 articles to profl. publs. Sgt. U.S. Army, 1953-55, Korea. Grantee Nat. Inst. on Drug Abuse, 1973—, Dir. Tng. grant, 1989-2002; recipient Nathan B. Eddy award Coll. on Problems of Drug Dependence, Jos. Wybran Award, Soc. Neuroimmune Pharmacology. Fellow AAAS, Coll. on Problems of Drug Dependence, Am. Coll. Neuropsychopharmacology; mem. Am. Soc. Pharmacology and Exptl. Therapeutics. Jewish. Achievements include patent for drug combination to produce profound hypothermia; discovery that endogenous opioid system has a role in analgesia, thermoregulation, and brain excitability, that opioids produce marked oscillations in size of pupil, that recovery from brain damage is accompanied by supersensitivity, that opioids are involved in immunoregulation and in the actions of cytokines and chemokines in the brain. Office: Temple U Sch Medicine 3420 N Broad St Philadelphia PA 19140-5104

ADLER, MICHAEL I. lawyer; b. San Francisco, May 10, 1949; BA in Polit. Sci. summa cum laude, UCLA, 1971, JD, 1976; MA, Columbia U., 1973. Bar: Calif. 1977. Extern to Hon. Matthew O. Tobriner Calif. Supreme Ct., 1975; law clerk to Hon. William B. Enright U.S. Dist. Ct. (so. dist.) Calif., 1976-77; mem. Lichter, Grossman, Nichols & Adler, Inc., L.A., 1977-97, now ptnr., 1997—. Mem. entertainment law symposium com. UCLA, 1979—; instr. UCLA Extension, 1980. Woodrow Wilson fellow, 1972; Columbia U. Presdl. fellow, 1973. Mem. ABA, State Bar Calif., L.A. County Bar Assn., Beverly Hills Bar Assn., Phi Beta Kappa, Phi Eta Sigma. Office: Lichter Grossman Nichols & Adler Inc 9200 W Sunset Blvd Ph 1200 Los Angeles CA 90069-3607 E-mail: madler@lgna.com.*

ADLER, MICHAEL L. family physician, educator; b. Chgo., Jan. 21, 1947; s. Aaron and Alice Gamberg Adler; m. Alice Sumberg, Mar. 3, 1984; children: Samantha Lillian, Gillian Carly, Noah Matthew. BA, Johns Hopkins U., 1, 1969; MD, U. Ill., 1973. Diplomate Am. Bd. Family Practice. Physician Regional Rural Health Ctr., Dixon, Calif., 1975-77; mem. faculty family practice residency program Ill. Masonic Med. Ctr., Chgo., 1978-85; dir. family practice residency program St. Joseph Med. Ctr., Stamford, Conn., 1985-89; med. dir. dept. family & cmty. medicine Bowman Gray Sch. Medicine Wake Forest U., Winston-Salem, NC, 1990—. Fellow Am. Acad. Famliy Physicians; mem. AMA, Soc. Tchrs. of Family Medicine. Office: Wake Forest U Sch Medicine Medical Center Blvd Winston Salem NC 27157-0001 E-mail: madler@wfubmc.edu.

ADLER, NANCY ELINOR, psychologist, educator; BA, Wellesley Coll., 1968; MA, Harvard U., 1971, PhD, 1973. Asst. prof. psychology U. Calif., Santa Cruz, 1972-76, assoc. prof. psychology, 1976-77, assoc. prof. med. psychology dept. psychiatry and pediat. San Francisco, 1977-84, prof. med. psychology depts. psychiatry and pediat., 1984—, dir. health psychology program, 1988—, program dir. NIMH tng. program, 1991—, vice chair dept. psychiatry, 1994—; dir. Ctr. for Health and Cmty., 1998—. Vis. asst. rsch. psychologist Inst. Personality Assessment and Rsch., U. Calif., Berkeley, 1975; mem. peer rev. panel Ad Hoc Sci. Study Sects., Nat. Inst. Child Health and Human Devel., 1977—, Nat. Heart, Lung and Blood Inst., 1993; adv. com. for five-yr. plan Demographic and Social Scis. Br., Ctr. for Population RSch., Nat. Inst. Child Health and Human Devel., 1986-87, adv. com., 1991-2000; sr. rsch. scientist in psychology Yale U., New Haven. 1994-95; review com. Intramural Rsch. NIMH, 1997, sci. adv. bd. Ctr. Advancement Health, Washington, 1995-96, bd. trustees, 1996—; grant reviewer NSF, Social Scis. and Humanities Rsch. Coun. Can., Soc. Behavioral Medicine, March of Dimes, Ctrs. for Disease Control, Econ. and Social Rsch. Coun.; presenter in field. Author: (with others) Health Psychology-A Handbook: Theories, Applications, and Challenges of a Psychological Approach to the Health Car System, 1979, Preventing Preterm Birth: A Parent's Guide, 1988, SES & Health in Industrialized Nations, 1999; adv. bd. Ency. Mental Health, 1995—; assoc. editor Health Psychology, 1984-90, Women's Health: Research in Gender, Behavior and Policy, 1994-98; mem. editl. bd. Jour. Population and Environment, 1982-88, Health Psychology, 1994—; manuscript reviewer Jour. Personality and Social Psychology, Jour. Nervous and Mental Disease, Personality and Social Psychology Bull., Jour. Health and Social Behavior, Jour. Applied Social Psychology, Basic and Applied Social Psychology, Psychology Women Quarterly, The Western Jour. Medicine, Jour. Am. Med. Assn., Am. Jour. Pub. Health, many others; contbr. articles in field. Recipient Best Rsch. Paper award Soc. for Adolescent Medicine, 1984; NSF fellow, 1968-72, U. Calif. Regents Summer fellow, 1974; grantee in field. Fellow: Am. Psychol. Soc., APA (sec.-treas. divsn. 34 1975—78, pres. divsn. 34 1979—80, chairperson fellow com. divsn. 34 1982—86, planning com. for nat. conf. on tng. in health psychology 1982—83, participant Arden House conf. on edn. and tng. in health psychology 1983, chairperson nominations com., mem. expert panel on psychol. effects of 1989—90, task force on promotion of population psychology 1992—97); mem.: Inst. of Medicine, Soc. for Rsch. on Adolescence, Assn. Med. Sch. Profs. Psychology, Soc. Advancement Social Psychology, Internat. Assn. Applied Psychology, Soc. Exptl. Social Psychology, Phi Beta Kappa, Sigma Xi. Office: U Ca Health Psychology Program 3333 California St San Francisco CA 94118-1981 E-mail: nadler@itsa.ucsF.edu.

ADLER, PATRICIA ANN, sociologist, educator; b. N.Y.C., Sept. 7, 1951; d. Benjamin Theodore and Judith Ann (Goldhill) Heller; m. Peter Adler, Aug. 20, 1972; children: Jori Ann, Brye Jacob. AB in Sociology summa cum laude, Washington U., St. Louis, 1973; MA in Sociology, U. Chgo., 1974, U. Calif., San Diego, 1975, PhD in Sociology, 1984. Instr. Tulsa Jr. Coll., 1981-83; rsch. assoc. U. Tulsa, 1983-84, asst. prof., 1984-85; asst. prof. sociology Okla. State U., Stillwater, 1985-86; asst. prof. U. Colo., Boulder, 1987-93, assoc. prof., 1993-99, prof., 1999—. Vis. asst. prof. sociology Washington U., St. Louis, 1986-87. Author: Wheeling and Dealing, 1985, 2d edit., 1993, (with others) The Social Dynamics of Financial Markets, 1984, The Sociologies of Everyday Life, 1980, Membership Roses in Field Research, 1987, Backboards and Blackboards, 1991, Constructions of Deviance, 1994, Peer Power, 1998, Sociological Odyssey, 2001; editor Jour. Contemporary Ethnography, 1986-94, (ann. series) Sociol. Studies of Child Devel., 1984-92; assoc. editor Social Problems Jour., 1984-87, Jour. Urban Life, 1982-86, Administrative Science Quarterly, 1989—; contbr. articles to profl. jours. Mem. Am. Sociol. Assn. (com. regulation rsch. 1992-95, chair alcohol and drug sect. 1993-94), Soc. for Study Social Problems, Am. Soc. Criminology, Sociologists for Women in Soc., Soc. for Study of Symbolic Interaction (publ. com. 1985 88, program chmn. 1984, 86), Midwest Sociol. Soc. (bd. dirs. 1993-95), Pacific Sociol. Assn. (pub. com. 1991-94, com. on coms. 1992-95), Phi Beta Kappa. Avocations: aerobics, travel, photography. Office: Dept Sociology 327 UCB U Colo Boulder CO 80309-0327 E-mail: adler@spot.colorado.edu.

ADLER, PEGGY ANN, writer, illustrator, investigator; b. N.Y.C., Feb. 10, 1942; d. Irving and Ruth (Relis) Adler; children: Tenney Whedon Walsh, Avery Denison Walsh (Mrs. Adam I. Lapidus). Student, Bennington Coll., 1959-60, Columbia U., 1962. Illustrator, author childrens books, 1958—; logistics and ticket sales and mgmt. the world premiere "Butch Cassidy and Sundance Kid", 1969; agt. Jan J. Agy., Inc., N.Y.C., 1981-82; freelance talent scout Cuzzins Mgmt., N.Y.C., 1982-83; personal mgmt. and pub. rels. cons. Madison, Conn., 1983-93. Rsch. assoc. Steve Fredericksen, Pvt. Investigator, Conn. and N.Y., 1990—96; investigative rschr., writer, lit. cons., 1986—; asst. investigator Ho. of Reps. October Surprise Task Force, Washington, 1992; pvt. investigator; child care provider, 1998—. Author (illustrator): The Adler Book of Puzzles and Riddles, 1962, The 2nd Adler Book of Puzzles and Riddles, 1963, Metric Puzzles, 1977, Math Puzzles, 1978, Geography Puzzles, 1979; author: Hakim's Connection, 1988; co-author: Skull and Bones: The Skeleton in Bush's Closet?, 1988; contbr. illustrator numerous books including Hot and Cold, 1959, Numbers New and Old, 1960, Reading Fundamentals for Teen-Agers, 1973, Do a Zoomdo, 1975, Pet Care, 1974, Caring for Your Cat, 1974 ; graphic designer : various book covers, posters, and logos; pub. rels. Sweetie, Baby, Cookie, Honey (Freddie Gershon), 1986, rschr. Passion and Prejudice: A Family Memoir (Sallie Bingham), 1989, The Village Voice, 1991, 1992, numerous others; contbr. The President's Private Eye: The Journey of Detective Tony U, from N.Y.P.D. to the Nixon White Ho., 1990; cons., rschr.: Bush's Boys Club: Skull and Bones, 1990; cons. Spy Saga (Philip H. Melanson), 1990; contbr. Lies of Our Times; licensee/story cons. 60 Minutes, 1991; cons., rschr. : London Sunday Times, 1991; contbr. The Independent London, 1994, 1995 ; rsch. assoc. for Ron Rosenbaum, I Stole the Head of Prescott Bush! More Scary Skull and Bones Tales (N.Y. Observer), 2000, Inside Skull and Bones' Secret Initiation Ritual (N.Y. Observer), 2001. Founder Shoreline Youth Theatre, Inc., 1979, bd. dirs., 1979—81, mem. adv. bd., 1981—86; bd. dirs. Greens Condominium Assn. Branford, Conn., 1975—78, Arts Coun. Greater New Haven, 1971—73, Planned Parenthood Greater New Haven, 1972—73, Assassination Archives and Rsch. Ctr., Washington, 1990—96; v.p., bd. dirs. Pub. Info. Rsch., Washington, 1989; hon. mem. Forgotten Families; chmn. majority subcom. study com. 10 Killingworth Turnpike bldg., mem. charter revision commn. Town of Clinton, 1997—98, author, charter revisions, legal notice and ballot questions, 1998, mem. design adv. bd., 2000—, chmn. design adv. bd., 2003—, mem. landing study com., 2003—, charter revision commn., 2003—; vol. Clinton Pub. Schs.; mem. hist. dist. commn. Town of Clinton, 2001—, elected constable, 2001—. Mem.: Charter Revision Commission (vice chmn. 2003—04), Conn. Soc. Genealogists Inc., Assn. Former Intelligence Officers (Gen. Richard G. Stilwell Chmn.'s award 2001), Assn. Former Intelligence Officers New Eng. Chpt. (program coord. 1997—, bd. dirs. 1997—, sec. 1998—2001, pres. 2001—), Duck Island Yacht Club (membership com. 1997—2000, social com. 1997—, Duck Stop 1997—, Don Dyson Corinthian award 1998). Home and Office: 5 Liberty St Clinton CT 06413

ADLER, POSY (ROSLYN), artist, educator; b. Chgo., Ill., Feb. 6, 1916; d. Leon and Julia (Sonnenschein) Woolf; m. Leon Adler, Nov. 1, 1937 (dec.); children: Larry, Janet. BE, Nat. Coll. Edn., Evanston, Ill., 1975; MFA in Sculpture, Goddard Coll., Plainfield, Vt., 1975; studied with Roger Armstrong, Eliot O'Hara, Barbara Neijna, Robert Stoetzer. Art tchr. Miami (Fla.)-Dade Coll., Miami, Fla., 1964-84; sculpture tchr. Saddleback Coll., Mission Viejo, Calif., 1984—. Art tchr. Newport Harbor Mus., Irvine Fine Arts Ctr., Met. Art Ctr., Dade County C.C., New Sch. Fine Arts. Exhibited sculpture and watercolors in shows at Art Angles, Calif., Artist's Unlimited, Fla., Bacardi Art Gallery, Fla., Blunt Gallery, Ctr. for the Arts, Boca Raton, Fla., Design Ctr. South, Calif., Grove House Gallery, Fla., Jockey Club Art Gallery, Fla., U. Fla. Lowe Art Gallery, Fla., Met. Art Ctr., Fla., Mus. Science, Miami, Neiman Marcus Art Gallery, Rauchbach Galleries, Tolley Gallery, Turnberry Gallery; commissions include: Sherman Gardens, Calif., Sports Clinic, Laguna Hills, Calif., Temple Or Olom, Miami. Ind. state v.p. Mental Health Soc., Frankfort, 1954-55, bd. dirs., Miami, Fla., 1957-62; hospice vol., Laguna Hills, Calif., 1990-99; vol. Adult Day Care Ctr., Laguna Hills, 1999. Mem. Am. Crafts Coun., Orange Co. Fine Arts, Ceramic League Miami, Creative Arts Guild, Dana Point Coastal Arts Coun., Florida Craftsman, Laguna Arts Assn., Miami Cultural Arts Alliance, Nat. League Am. Penwomen, Nat. Mus. Women in the Arts, Niguel Art Assn., Sculptors of Fla., Women's Caucus for Art. Democrat. Jewish. Avocations: travel, sculpting, painting, craft work.

ADLER, RAPHAEL, educator emeritus, speech pathologist; b. N.Y.C., Feb. 21, 1922; s. Marcus and Celia (Kress) A.; m. Minna Adler, Sept. 23, 1948; children: Ava Dee, Roxanne, Margo Celeste. BA, Wayne State U., 1953, M in Edn., 1962; PhD, Walden U., 1981. Cert. tchr. secondary schs., Mich.; cert. speech pathologist Am. Speech and Hearing Assn. Tchr. dept. English/speech Berkley (Mich.) Sch. Dist., 1954-68; prof. Oakland C.C., Union Lake, Mich., 1968-92, prof. emeritus, 1992—2002; pres. P.W. Mulligan Enterprises, LLC. Dir. speech and hearing St. Joseph Mercy Hosp., Pontiac, Mich.,1965-84; owner, dir., pres. Speech Pathology Svcs., Southfield, Mich., 1972-86; cons. hosps., nursing homes, VNA, S. Oakland County Health Dept.; bd. dirs. Motion Picture Inst. Mich. Author: The Magical Adventures of Pee Wee Mulligan, 2001. Com. mem. Am. Heart Assn. of Mich., past chmn.; chmn., bd. trustees State of Mich . Stroke Com. Recipient many speaking citations and awards, 1953-62, Toastmasters Internat. 1971, Mrs. Horace Elgin Dodge award Am. Heart Assn. Mich., 1989, 92, 95. Avocations: reading, dancing, gardening, volunteering, writing.

ADLER, RENATA, writer; b. Milan, Oct. 19, 1938; d. Frederick L. and Erna (Strauss) A. AB, Bryn Mawr Coll., 1959; MA, Harvard U., 1960; D.d.E.S., Sorbonne U., Paris, 1961; JD, Yale U., 1979; LLD (hon.), Georgetown U., 1989. Writer-reporter New Yorker, N.Y.C., 1962—; film critic N.Y. Times, 1968-69. Author: A Year in the Dark, 1970, Toward a Radical Middle, 1970, Speedboat, 1976, Pitch Dark, 1983, Reckless Disregard, 1986; mem. editorial bd. Am. Scholar, 1968-75 Recipient 1st prize O. Henry Short Story Collection, 1974; Acad.-Inst. award Am. Acad. and Inst. Arts and Letters, 1978; Guggenheim fellow, 1973-74, fellow Trumbull Coll., Yale U. Mem. PEN (exec. bd. 1964-70), Am. Acad. and Inst. Arts and Letters.

ADLER, RICHARD, composer, lyricist; b. N.Y.C., Aug. 3, 1921; s. Clarence and Elsa (Richard) A.; children by previous marriage: Andrew H., Christopher E. (dec.). AB, U. N.C., 1943. Mem. advt. dept. Celanese Corp. Am., 1946-50; White House cons. on the arts, 1965-69. Cons. on arts gov. N.C. Adv. bd. Inst. Outdoor Drama, 1968-83, N.C. School arts, 1963—; commd. by Harvard U. to write a march for 50th Anniversary of Neiman Found. Journalist Soc., 1989. Collaborator (with Jerry Ross); on music and lyrics for musicals John Murray Anderson's Almanac, 1953, Pajama Game, 1954, Damn Yankees, 1955; composer, lyricist Kwamina, 1961, TV prodns. Little Women, 1959, Gift of the Magi, 1959; produced and staged White House Press Corrs. and Photographers show for Pres. Kennedy and Prime Minister MacMillan, 1962, N.Y.'s Birthday Salute for Pres. Kennedy, 1962, Inaugural Anniversity Salute to Pres. Kennedy, 1963, Salutes to Pres. Johnson, 1964, Inaugural Gala for Pres. Lyndon Johnson, 1965; producer, composer, lyricist: ABC-TV Stage 67 Musical Olympus 7-0000, fall 1966; composer, lyricist: A Mother's Kisses, 1968; producer: revival Pajama Game, 1973; producer: Rex, 1976; co-producer-composer: Music Is, 1976, Yellowstone Overture (Pulitzer prize nomination); commd. by Dept. of Interior to write Wilderness Suite (Pulitzer prize nomination), 1983, recorded by Utah Symphony; commd. by Statue of Liberty/Ellis Island Found. to write The Lady Remembers (Pulitzer prize nomination), recorded by Detroit Symphony, Retrospectrum (Pulitzer prize nomination); commd. by Chgo. City Ballet to write Eight by Adler, 1984 (Emmy award for TV version 1985); commd. by City of Chgo. to write (ballet) Chicago for sesquicentennial, 1987; commd. by Olympic Com. to write fanfare and overture for U.S. Olympic Festival, 1987, commd. by U. N.C. to write suite to commemorate bicentennial, 1993, recorded by London Symphony Orch.; (author, autobiography) You Gotta Have Heart, 1990; collaborator lyrics, composer: Off Key, 1995, The House of Bernarda Alba, 1998, Wilderness Suite Ballet, 2001, Notes on My Life, 2002. Trustee John F. Kennedy Ctr. for Performing Arts, 1964-77, exec. com., 1975-77; bd. dirs. Southampton Cultural Com. Lt. (j.g.) USNR, 1943-46. Recipient Antoinette Perry award, Donaldson award, Variety Critics Poll for Pajama Game 1954, Damn Yankees 1955, Antoinette Perry nomination Kwamina 1962, Pulitzer Prize nomination Retrospectrum 1980, Yellowstone Overture 1981, Playmaker Life Time Achievement award dept. dramatic art U. N.C., 1999, Richard Rodgers award ASCAP Found., 2002; Pulitzer prize nominee for rec. The Statue of Liberty Suite; named to Songwriters Hall of Fame, 1984; Hon. Park Ranger award Nat. Park Service, 1984. Mem. Dramatists Guild (exec. coun. 1958-68), Songwriters Guild Am. (bd. dirs., exec. com., exec. v.p. 1985—), New Dramatists (bd. dirs. 1974-2001), Nat. Hypertension Assn. (bd. dirs. 1978—). Address: 8 E 83d St New York NY 10028-0418 E-mail: reldar2@aol.com.

ADLER, RICHARD MELVIN, architect, planner; b. N.Y.C., Mar. 25, 1928; s. Jacob William and Betty (Uffer) A.; children: Robin Sheryl, Joy Lois; m. Marie Fusco Cusano, 1986. Registered architect, N.Y., others. Airport architect Port Auth. N.Y., 1952-58; ptnr. Brodsky Hoff & Adler, N.Y.C., 1959-71; pres. BHA Architects & Engrs., N.Y.C., 1971-75, Brodsky & Adler, N.Y.C., 1975-80, R.M. Adler & Assocs., Peterborough, N.H., 1993—. Pres. Adler, Goodman A Kolab For Architects & Engrs., Great Neck, 1993—; chmn. bd. Geller Termotto & Adler, Teaneck, N.J., 1982—, Clendening Adler, Arlington, Tex., 1983—. Elected to budget com., Peterborough, 1998—; chmn. capital improvement com. Town of Peterborough, 1996—. Served to 1st lt., N.Y. Nat. Guard, 1948-63. Recipient disting. svc. award Engrs. News Record, 1974, creative design award ASCE, 1973. Mem. AIA (merit award 1977, bd. dirs. L.I. chpt. 1988, chair profl. practice L.I. chpt.), N.Y. Soc. Architects, Wings Club, Constrn. Specifications Inst., Queens C. of C. Republican. Jewish.

ADLER, ROBERT, electronics engineer; b. Vienna, Dec. 4, 1913; came to U.S., 1940, naturalized, 1945; s. Max and Jenny (Herzmark) A.; m. Mary F. Buehl, 1946 (dec. Jan. 1993); m. Ingrid C. Koch, 1998. PhD in Physics, U. Vienna, 1937. Asst. to patent atty., Vienna, 1937-38; lab. Sci. Acoustics, Ltd., London, Assoc. Rsch., Inc., Chgo., 1940-41; research group Zenith Radio Corp., Chgo., 1941-52, assoc. dir. research, 1952-63, v.p., 1959-77, dir. research, 1963-77, EXTEL Corp., Northbrook, Ill., 1978-79, v.p. research, 1979-82; tech. cons. Zenith Electronics Corp., 1982-97, Motorola, 1997—2001, Elo Touch Sys., 1997—. Contbr. numerous articles profl. publs. Fellow IEEE (Edison medal 1980); mem. Nat. Acad. Engring. Achievements include 200 patents: invention of ultrasonic remote control for TV sets, first electromechanical I.F. filter, electron beam parametric amplifier, ultrasonic touch system; research on improved touch system using Love waves. Home: 1380 Ridge Rd Northbrook IL 60062-4626 E-mail: rbtadler@aol.com.

ADLER, ROBERT MARTIN, lawyer; b. Toledo, Ohio, Oct. 2, 1943; s. Charles J. and Barbara (Sechback) A.; m. Andrea Rosenberg, June 12, 1966; children: Rebecca J., David C. BA, Oberlin Coll., 1965; JD, U. Mich., 1968. Bar: D.C. 1969. Trial atty. tax divsn. U.S. Dept. Justice, Washington, 1968-74; ptnr. Stiller, Adler & Schwartz, Washington, 1974-81; pvt. practice Law Offices Robert M. Adler, Washington, 1981-91; sr. ptnr. Drinker Biddle & Reath, Washington, 1991-96; ptnr. O'Connor & Hannon, L.L.P., Washington, 1996—. Chmn. Stiller Meml. Found., Washington, 1979-91. Avocation: sailing. Office: O'Connor & Hannan LLP 1666 K St NW Ste 500 Washington DC 20006-1217*

ADLER, RUTH GRATT, financial planner, securities arbitrator; b. N.Y.C., Aug. 27; d. Eugene and Bertha (Friedman) Gratt; m. Alexander Adler; children: Alison B., Linda J. BA, Hunter Coll.; postgrad., U. Pa. Cert. fin. planner. V.p. A.G. Edwards, Washington, 1970—. Securities arbitrator N.Y. Stock Exch., N.Y.C., 1988—, Am. Stock Exchange, 1999—; lectr. Fin. Svcs. Corp., Budapest; arbitrator N.Y. Stock Exch., 1985—. Author series of newspaper articles on Am. Stock Exch. prior to opening of Budapest Stock Exch., 1990-92; contbr. articles to profl. jours. and newspapers; radio and TV appearances. Pension fund trustee Washington Suburban Commn., Hyattsville, Md., 1983-90; mem. adv. coun. Suburban Hosp., Bethesda, Md., 1980-84; trustee Montgomery Coll. Found., Rockville, Md., 1979-82. Named to Hunter Coll. Hall of Fame, 1985. Mem. AAUW, Washington Soc. Investment Analysts (bd. dris. 1980-83). Avocation: travel.

ADLER, SAMUEL HANS, retired conductor, composer; b. Mannheim, Germany, Mar. 4, 1928; came to U.S., 1939, naturalized, 1945; s. Hugo Chaim and Selma (Rothschild) A.; m. Carol Ellen Stalker, Feb. 14, 1960 (div. 1989); children: Deborah Ruth, Naomi Leah; m. Emily Freeman Brown, June 8, 1991. MusB, Boston U., 1948; MA, Harvard U., 1950; MusD (hon.), So. Methodist U., 1969; DFA (hon.), Wake Forest U.; D.F.A. (hon.), St. Mary's Coll., Ind., 1986; DMus (hon.), St. Louis Conservatory, 1986. Music dir. Temple Emanu-El, Dallas, 1953-66; prof. composition North Tex. State U., Denton, 1957-66; Eastern regional dir. contemporary music project Ford Found., 1966-70; prof. composition Eastman Sch. Music, U. Rochester, N.Y., 1966-94; hon. prof. U. Wales, Cardiff, 1984-89; ret., 1994; tchr. Julliard Sch. Music, N.Y.C. Lectr., condr. throughout world Condr. Dallas Chorale, 1954—57, Dallas Lyric Theatre, 1955—59; composer: 6 symphonies, 4 operas, 8 string quartets, sonatas for piano, violin (4), cello, flute, viola, guitar, oboe, clarinet, organ, saxophone, concertos for piano (2), violin, horn, cello, flute, saxophone quartet, organ, woodwind quintet, guitar, viola, also for orch. and band, chamber and choral works, songs; author: Choral Conducting, 1971, 2d revised edit., 1985, Sight Singing, 1979, 2d revised edit., 1996, The Study of Orchestration, 1982, 3d edit., 2002. Served with AUS, 1950-52. Grantee Nat. Endowment Arts, Ford Found., Rockefeller Found.; recipient 6 1st prizes Tex. Composers Contest, Charles Ives award, 1965, Lillian Fairchild award, 1968, Deems Taylor award, 1983, Am. Acad. and Inst. Arts and Letters award, 1990; Guggenheim fellow, 1984-85 Mem.: ASCAP (awards 1960—), Music Tchrs. Nat. Assn., Music Educators Nat. Conf., Phi Beta Kappa, Phi Mu Alpha Sinfonia, Am. Acad. Arts and Letters. Jewish. E-mail: sadlercomp@yahoo.com.

ADLER, SARA, arbitrator, mediator; b. Chgo., Jan. 26, 1942; d. Matthew Michael and Mildred Paula (Eckhaus) Lewison; m. James N. Adler, Aug. 19, 1967; children: Michael, Philip, Matthew. AB, U. Chgo., 1961; JD, UCLA, 1969. Bar: Calif. Cons. Inst. Criminal Justice Adminstrn. U. Calif., Davis, 1969-71; assoc. Law Office of Sara Radin, L.A., 1971-72; assoc. dir. Paralegal Tng. Inst. U. So. Calif., L.A., 1972-74; assoc. Wyman, Bautzer, et al, L.A., 1974-78; arbitrator, mediator Dispute Resolution Svcs., L.A., 1978—. Fellow: Coll. Labor and Employment Lawyers; mem.: ABA (neutral co-chair ADR in Labor/employment Law 1995—98, neutral mem. coun. Labor & Employment sect.), L.A. County Bar Assn. (chmn. labor and employment sect. 1997—98), Indsl. Rels. Rsch. Assn. (pres. so. Calif. 1991—92), Nat. Acad. Arbitrators (regional chair 1994—96, bd. govs.), Am. Arbitration Assn. (bd. dirs., exec. com., labor mgmt. law task force, employment ADR steering com.). Avocation: Avocations: travel, theater, bridge. Office: Dispute Resolution Svcs 1034 Selby Ave Los Angeles CA 90024-3106

ADLER, SEYMOUR JACK, social services administrator; b. Chgo., Oct. 22, 1930; s. Michael L. and Sarah (Pasnick) A.; m. Barbara Fingold, Mar. 24, 1958; children: Susan Lynn Adler, Karen Sandra Adler-Marder, Michelle Lauren Adler-Morrison. BS, Northwestern U., Evanston, Ill., 1952; MA, U. Chgo., 1958. Caseworker Cook County Dept. Pub. Aid, Chgo., 1955; juv. officer Cook County Sheriff's Office, 1955-56; U.S. probation-parole officer U.S. Dist. Ct., Chgo., 1958-68; exec. dir. Youth Guidance, Chgo., 1968-73; dir. court svcs. Juv. Ct. Cook County, Chgo., 1973-75; exec. dir. Meth. Youth Svcs., Chgo., 1975-85; program mgr. Dept. Social Svcs., Kenosha, Wis., 1985-91, dir., 1992-95, Dept. Human Svcs., Kenosha, 1996-99, coord. Juvenile Justice Project, 1999—2002; cmty liaison Wis. Coun. on Children and Families, 2002—. Mem. Ill. Law Enforcement Commn., 1969-72; instr. corrections program Chgo. State U., 1972-75; instr. Harper Coll., 1977, St. Joseph's Coll., 1978; case developer Nat. Ctr. on Instns. and Alternatives, 1985-86; soc. sci. adv. com. Carthage Coll., 1997—; chair adminstrn. com. Joint Youth Devel. Program; bd. dirs. Kenosha Area Family and Aging Svcs., Inc. Bd. dirs. Child Care Assn. Ill., 1979-84; exec. bd. Kenosha br. NAACP, 1998—, W-2 steering com., 1998-99; ethics bd. Village Twin Lakes, 2003—. 1st lt. USMCR, 1952-55. Recipient Meritorious Svc. award Chgo. City Colls., 1968, Appreciation award NAACP, 1999. Mem. Ill. Acad. Criminology (pres. 1972, Morris J. Wexler award 1975, Pres.'s award 1997), Nat. Assn. Social Workers (del. Assembly 1977, 79, 81, 84, 87, chmn. Chgo. dist. 1978-80, com. inquiry Wis. chpt. 1990—, Disting. Svc. award Criminal Justice Coun. 1978), Ill. NASW (chmn. group for action planning childrens svcs. 1980-84, chmn. population study group Kenosha Jail 1993-95, leadership 1D com. 2002—), Alpha Kappa Delta, Tau Delta Phi. Home: 232 Grandview Ln Twin Lakes WI 53181-9572 Office: Kenosha Dept Human Svcs 8600 Sheridan Rd Kenosha WI 53143 E-mail: sadler@co.kenosha.wi.us.

ADLER, SOLOMON STANLEY, internist, oncologist, hematologist; b. Bronx, N.Y., May 26, 1945; MD, Albert Einstein Coll. Medicine, 1970. Diplomate Am. Bd. Internal Medicine, Am. Bd. Oncology, Am. Bd. Hematology. Intern Brookdale Hosp. Med. Ctr., N.Y.C., 1970-71, resident in internal medicine, 1971-72, resident in hematology-oncology, 1972-73; fellow in hematology Rush-Presbyn., St. Luke's Hosp., Chgo., 1973-75; internist, hematologist, oncologist Rush-Presbyn. St Luke's Med. Ctr., Chgo., 1975—. Adj. prof. medicine Rush Med. Coll. Mem. ACP, Am. Fedn. for Clin. Rsch., Am. Soc. Clin. Oncology, Am. Soc. Hematology, Ctrl. Soc. Clin. Rsch., Internat. Soc. Hematology, Internat. Soc. Exptl. Hematology. Office: Rush Presbyn St Luke Hosp 1753 W Congress Pkwy Chicago IL 60612-3809 E-mail: solomon_adler@rush.edu.

ADLER, STEPHEN LOUIS, physicist; b. N.Y.C., Nov. 30, 1939; s. Irving and Ruth Adler; children: Jessica Wendy, Victoria Stephanie, Anthony Curtis; m. Sarah C. Brett-Smith, 1995. AB summa cum laude, Harvard U., 1961; PhD, Princeton U., 1964. Jr. fellow Soc. Fellows Harvard U., 1964—66; rsch. assoc. Calif. Inst. Tech., 1966; mem. Inst. for Advanced Study, Princeton, NJ, 1966—69, prof. Sch. Natural Scis., 1969—, N.J. Albert Einstein prof. Sch. Natural Scis., 1979—2003. Vis. lectr. dept. physics Princeton U., 1969—. Author: (with R.F. Dashen) Current Algebras, 1968, Quaternionic Quantum Mechanics and Quantum Fields, 1995; contbr. articles to profl. jours. Recipient J.J. Sakurai prize Am. Phys. Soc., 1988, Dirac medal Internat. Ctr. Theoretical Physics, Trieste, Italy, 1998. Fellow Am. Acad. Arts and Scis., AAAS, Am. Phys. Soc.; mem. Nat. Acad. Scis., Phi Beta Kappa, Sigma Xi. Home: 287A Nassau St Princeton NJ 08540-4618 Office: Sch Natural Scis Inst Advanced Study Einstein Dr Princeton NJ 08540

ADLER, WILLIAM F. technology business development consultant; b. Chgo., Aug. 19, 1937; s. Fred William and Margaret Ann (Haak) A.; m. Dorothy Joanne Weinmann, June 8, 1958; 1 child, Elizabeth. BSCE, Ill. Inst. Tech., 1958, MS in Mechanics, 1961; PhD in Engring. Mechanics, Columbia U., 1965. Sr. engr. Martin-Marietta, Denver, 1961-62; sr. rsch. scientist Battelle Meml. Inst., Columbus, Ohio, 1965-71; prin. scientist Bell Aerospace/Textron, Buffalo, 1971-76; dir. materials sci. Effects Tech. Inc., Santa Barbara, Calif., 1976-83; mgr. materials sci. ops. GRC Internat., Santa Barbara, 1983-99; ind. cons. tech. assessments and new bus. devel., 1999—; sr. program mgr. AT&T Co., Santa Barbara, 2001—. Chmn. com. on conservation of materials through the reduction of erosion in energy systems Nat. Materials Adv. Bd., NAS, Washington, 1976-77; internat. advisor 5th, 6th and 7th Internat. Confs. on Erosion by Liquid and Solid Impact, 1978-79, 82-83, 86-87. Editor: Inelastic Behavior of Solids, 1970, Erosion: Prevention and Useful Applications, 1979; contbr. over 90 articles to tech. jours. and conf. proceedings. Office: AT&T 5383 Hollister Ave Ste 200 Santa Barbara CA 93111-2305 E-mail: wadler@att.com.

ADLERMAN, KIMBERLY MARIE, illustrator, writer, graphics designer; b. Niagara Falls, N.Y., Jan. 5, 1964; d. William Victor and Lillian (Strozewski) Hauck; m. Daniel Ezra Adlerman, Aug. 10, 1991; children: Rachelle Eve, Joshua S., Maxx Alec. BFA, SUNY, Buffalo, 1987. Freelance designer, N.Y.C., 1988-90; sr. designer Macmillan Pub., N.Y.C., 1990-94; creative dir. The Kids At Our House, Metuchen, N.J., 1994—. Co-author: It's Raining, It's Pouring, 1994, Hey Diddle, Diddle, 1997, Rub-a-Dub Dub, 1999, Humpty Dumpty, 1999, Songs for America's Children, 2002; illustrator Africa Calling, 1996. Mem.: Soc. Children's Book Writers and Illustrators. Home and Office: 47 Stoneham Pl Metuchen NJ 08840-1661 E-mail: KimArts@aol.com.

ADLERSHTEYN, LEON, naval architect, engineer, educator, researcher; b. St. Petersburg, Russia, Oct. 28, 1925; arrived in U.S., 1994, naturalized, 2000; s. Tsalim and Judith (Shusterovich) A.; m. Irina Bereznaya, Feb. 24, 1962. MS in Shipbuilding, Shipbuilding Inst., St. Petersburg, 1951; DSc in Engring., Ctr. Rsch. Inst. Shipbuilding Tech., St. Petersburg, 1970. Foreman, dep. chief of the hull shop Baltic Shipyard, St. Petersburg, 1951-63; chief technologist Ctrl. Rsch. Inst. for Shipbuilding Tech., St. Petersburg, 1963-65, leader of the team, 1965-74, chief rschr., 1993-94; head of the dept. Acad. of Shipbuilding, St. Petersburg, 1974-88, prof., 1988-94; ret., 1994. Chmn. state examination commn. State Marine Tech. U., St. Petersburg, 1989-94; coun. mem. Acad. of Shipbuilding, St. Petersburg, 1974-94, Ctrl. Rsch. Inst. for Shipbuilding Tech., St. Petersburg, 1963-94. Co-author (author) 11 books on shipbuilding tech., (including) Accuracy in Ship Hull Manufacturing, Mechanization and Automation of Ship Manufacturing, Modular Ship Building; contbr. articles and brochures over 150 to profl. jours. Chmn. coun. sect. Union of Scientists and Engrs., St. Petersburg, 1992-94, mem. bd., 1990-94. Pvt. Russian Army, 1943-45, WWII veteran. Decorated 12 mil. medals Pres. of USSR Supreme Soviet and Pres. of Russian Fedn., 1945-99, 3 mil. awards Am. Legion and Am. Assn. of Invalids and Vets. of WWII, 1995-2000; recipient Order of the Patriotric War 1st Class Pres. USSR Supreme Soviet, 1985, 5 Medals Russian Nat. Indsl. Exhbn., 1955-93. Fellow Inst. of Marine Engring., Sci. and Tech. (U.K.); mem. Soc. of Naval Architects and Marine Engrs., Union of Scientists and Engrs., Russian Soc. of Shipbuilders (various prizes 1955-93), Am. Assn. Invalids and Vets. of WWII from the former USSR, Internat. Biog. Ctr. (hon., adv. coun. 1999—), Am. Biog. Inst. (rsch. bd. advisors 2000—). Achievements include 9 Russian patents on shipbuilding technology; creation and leadership in development of the theory of accuracy in ship hull manufacturing; designed and developed mechanized means for ship manufacturing. Home: 72 Montgomery St Apt 1510 Jersey City NJ 07302-3827 E-mail: berez@aol.com.

ADLIS, SUSAN ANNETTE, biostatistician; b. Mpls., Mar. 7, 1951; d. Paul and Miriam A. BA, Coll. St. Catherine, St. Paul, 1972; BS, U. Minn., Mpls., 1982, MS, 1987. Med. technologist U. Minn., Mpls., 1983-85, tchg. asst., 1985-87; epidemiologist Minn. Dept. Health, Mpls., 1987-88; rsch. asst. U. Minn., Mpls., 1988-90; rsch. analyst Abbott Northwestern Hosp., Mpls., 1990-92; biostatistician Park Nicollet Inst., Mpls., 1992—. Mem. protocol rev. com. Health Sys. Minn., Mpls., 1993-98. Contbr. articles to profl. jours. Mem. AAAS, APHA, Am. Statis. Assn., Am. Soc. Clin. Lab. Scis., N.Y. Acad. Scis. Achievements include research on health services and internal medicine. Office: Park Nicollet Inst 3800 Park Nicollet Blvd Minneapolis MN 55416-2527 E-mail: adliss@parknicollet.com.

ADMAY, CATHERINE ADCOCK, law lecturer, researcher; b. Johannesburg, Oct. 16, 1965; came to U.S., 1981; d. Roger Sydney Edmund Wyatt and Patricia Laura (Tennant) Adcock; m. Thomas Raden Admay, Aug. 1997. MA, U. Strasbourg, France, 1987; BA, Yale U., 1988, JD, 1992. Atty. vol. Legal Resources Ctr., Pretoria, South Africa, 1988-89; law clk. to Hon. Betty Fletcher 9th Cir. Ct. Appeals, Seattle, 1992-93; assoc. Heller, Elvman, White & McCauliff, Seattle, 1993; law lectr. NYU Law Sch., N.Y.C., 1994-96, Duke U. Law Sch., Durham, N.C., 1996—. Rschr. Govt. of South Africa, 1996—. Co-author appendix Truth and Reconciliation Commission of South Africa Report, 1998. Numerous civic activities. Internat. Humanitarian fellow Hauser Found./ICRC, Geneva, 1998. Mem. numerous profl. orgns. Avocations: reading, hiking, kayaking, exploring. Office: Duke Law Sch PO Box 90360 Durham NC 27708-0360

ADNET, JACQUES JIM PIERRE, astronautical and electrical engineer, consultant; b. Sermaize-les-Bains, Marne, France, Dec. 12, 1929; arrived in U.S., 1947; s. Julien Charles and Aline Georgette (Klein) A.; m. Mildred Ann Pruet, June 8, 1952 (div. Apr. 1982); children: Denise E., Lisa A., Paul A.; m. Helen Ilene Milam, Nov. 3, 1990. BA with honors, U. Fla., 1951, BEE with honors, 1960; MS in Astronautics, AF Inst. Tech., 1965; grad., Indsl. Coll. Armed Forces, 1972. Interpreter (civilian) U.S. Army, France, 1945-46; enlisted USAF, 1951, commd. 2d lt., 1952, advanced through grades to lt. col., 1968, elec. warfare officer, 1954-57; with Radar Evaluation Flt./Air Def. Command, Griffiss AFB, N.Y., 1957-58; flight test engr. USAF Systems Command, Hanscom Field, Mass., 1960-61, subsystem devel. engr., 1961-63, site implementation engr., 1968; chief space systems divsn. USAF Fgn. Tech. Divsn., Dayton, 1968-71; R&D dir. aero. sys. divsn. USAF Systems Command, Dayton, Ohio, 1971-73, ret., 1973; instr., course dir. Air Force Acad., Colorado Springs, Colo., 1974-81; tech. cons. and tech. translator Adnetech, Colorado Springs, 1973—. Dir. Dept. Def. Protocol Office Paris Internat. Air and Space Show, 1969, 71, 73, 75, 77; translator for U.S. Army in France, 1945—46; recognized as expert translator fed. and city cts. Author: When I See a " Forty and Eight"..., 2001; contbr. articles to profl. jours. Dir. of protocol 1986 World Cycling Championships, Colorado Springs, 1985-86; active Tri-Lakes (Colo.) Comprehensive Plan Com., Tri-Lakes Land Use Com.; co-founder Am. Air Mus. Britain; mem. Air Force Acad. Environ. Coun., 1999—. Decorated Air Force Meritorious Svc. medal; recipient Ordre Nat. Du Mérite French Govt., Paris, 1982; named hon. citizen of Sermaize les Bains, France; Groupe Scolaire Jacques Adnet named in his honor, 2001. Mem. AIAA (sr.), VFW, Nat. Space Soc., Planetary Soc., Am. Legion, Air Force Assn., The Ret. Officers' Assn., USAF Acad. École de l'Air Exch. Assn. (hon., exec. sec.), USAF Acad. Environ. Coun., U. Fla. Alumni Assn., Air and Airways Comm. Svc. Alumni Assn., Nat. Air Intelligence Ctr. Alumni Assn. Roman Catholic. Achievements include numerous design modifications and conceptual design of electronic warfare equipment; direction of analysis of foreign space systems and equipment; design of unique passively heated solar homes. Home and Office: Adnetech 4360 Diamondback Dr Colorado Springs CO 80921-2364 Fax: 719-481-0082. E-mail: adnet@divide.net.

ADOLPH, DIANE JOYCE, retired underwriter; b. L.A. d. Erwin Lorraine and Geraldine (Kimport) Winter; m. Donald Oscar Adolph, Feb. 18, 1954; children: Donna Pembrooke, Darra Lee Buesser, Denise Bierman. Cert. gen. ins., Ins. Inst. Am., 1983; AA, Moorpark (Calif.) Coll., 1987. Forms control clk. State Farm Ins. Co., Thousand Oaks, Calif., 1977-78, pricing control clk., 1979-81, underwriting asst., 1981-83, underwriter, 1983-89. Pres. Arts League, La Quinta, Calif., 1992-94; mem. publicity, pub. rels. com. Cmty. Concerts, La Quinta, 1992; bd. dirs., v.p. Arts Found., La Quinta, 1994—; chmn. Roundtable West's Books for the Bookless Project, Coachella Valley, 1994—; v.p. Viva Found. Hist. Soc., 1994—; mem. Friends of La Quinta Sr. Ctr., 1998—, Friends of La Quinta Libr., 1996—; bd. dirs. Harvest Our Wellness Found., 1999—. Recipient Vol. of Yr. award Arts League, 1992, Most Dedicated Vol. award Arts Found., 1999. Mem. La Quinta C. of C. (exec. amb. 1993-96, Citizen of Yr. 1994), Toastmasters (Toastmaster of Yr. 1988), Soroptimist Internat. (bd. dirs. 1998—). Republican. Avocations: reading, travel, exercise, cooking and entertaining, golf. Home: 55105 Riviera La Quinta CA 92253-4764

ADOLPH, KATHRYN ANN, passenger service employee; b. Hartington, Nebr., Dec. 20, 1945; d. Edmund Leonard and Elizabeth Claire Arens; m. Lester Leroy Adolph, Jan. 2, 1965 (div. July 1998); children: Leslie Marie, Edmund Glenn. BS in Adult and Occupation Edn., Kans. State U., 1981. Passenger svc. employee Trans World Airlines, Kans. City, Mo., 1978—2001, Am. Airlines, Kans. City, Mo., 2001—. Industry expert (TV appearance) CNN. Avocations: writing, photography.

ADOMAVICIUS, JONAS, gastroenterologist, writer; b. Pernarava, Lithuania, Dec. 15, 1911; arrived in U.S., 1949; s. Anupras Adomavcius and Marija (Rimkute) Adomavicius. MD, Vytautes the Great U., Kaunes, Lithuania, 1938. Radio health show host (in Lithuanian); med. columnist in Lithuanian Lang. Weekly Newspaper. Author 8 med. books in Lithuanian publ. in Am.; med. columnist Dienovydis (Lithuanian Lang. Newspaper), Draugas Lithuanian lang. daily, Chgo., Lietuvill (bi-weekly), Ameikas Lietuvis (Lithuanian lang. weel;u; author: Die Medizinische Fakultat der Eberhard-Karls-Universitat zu Tübingen der Grad enes Doctors der Medizin, Kvieslys Sveikaton. Mem.: Am. Gastroenterology Soc. Home and Office: 6515 S California Ave Chicago IL 60629

ADOVASIO, J. M. anthropologist, archeologist, educator; b. Youngstown, Ohio; BA in Anthropology magna cum laude, U. Ariz., 1965, postgrad., 1965-66; PhD in Anthropology, U. Utah, 1970; DSc (hon.), Washington & Jefferson U., 1983. From instr. to asst. prof. anthropology Youngstown State U., 1966-68, 70-71; from asst. prof. to prof. anthropology, Latin Am. studies U. Pitts., Pa., 1972-90, chmn. dept. anthropology, 1980-89, dir. Cultural Resource Mgmt. Program, 1976-89, prof. geology and planetary scis., 1985-90; John E. Boyle prof. anthropology and archaeology, prof. geology Mercyhurst Coll., Erie, Pa., 1990—, dir. anthropology and archaeology dept., 1990—, dir. geology dept., 1991—, dir. sci. divsn., 2000—. Adj. assoc. prof. Youngstown State U., 1976-78; rsch. assoc. Smithsonian Instn., 1974—, Carnegie Mus., 1978—; expert witness Archaeol. Resources Protection Act cases U.S. Govt., Ariz., N.Mex., 1987—; exec. dir. Mercyhurst Archaeol. Inst., 1990—; dir. archaeology rsch. program So. Meth. U., Dallas, 1990-93; commr. Pa. Hist. and Mus. Commn., 1995-03; bd. dirs. Preservation Pa., Pa. State Hist. Preservation Bd., 1995-03; presenter in field. Reviewer Libr. Jour., 1973—; contbr. numerous book revs. and articles to profl. jours. Mem. Pa. Hist. and Mus. Commn., 1995—. Nat. Def. Edn. Act fellow, 1968-70, Smithsonian Instn. Post-Doctoral Rsch. fellow, 1971-72; recipient Cert. for Academic Achievement, Smithsonian Instrn., 1972, J. Alden Mason award for lifetime contbns. to Pa. Archaeology, 1997; numerous grants from 1969—. Fellow AAAS, Am. Anthrop. Assn.; mem. Soc. Am. Archaeology, Current Anthropology, Am. Quaternary Assn., Soc. Pa. Archaeology, N.Y. Acad. Scis., Knight of Malta, Sigma Xi, Phi Beta Kappa, Phi Eta Sigma. Office: Mercyhurst Coll Anthropology and Archaeology Dept Erie PA 16546 Home: 3439 North Rd Sherman NY 14781-9712

ADREON, BEATRICE MARIE RICE, pharmacist; b. Huntington, W.Va., July 23, 1929; d. Lloyd Emerson and Beatrice (Odell) Rice; student Mary Washington Coll., 1947-49; B.S. in Pharmacy, Med. Coll. Va., 1952; M.A. in Spl. Studies and Women's Studies, George Washington U., 1976; m. Harry Barnes Adreon, Jr., Dec. 27, 1952. Summer vol. worker pharmacies De Paul Hosp., Norfolk, Va., 1949, U.S. Marine Hosp., Norfolk, 1950; pharmacist Washington Clinic, 1954-71; counselor George Washington U., 1976-77, cons. gerontology health scis. dept., 1977— ; cons. medicine control traffic patterns nursing homes Cross & Adreon, Washington, 1962-87; founder, pres. Pharmacy Counseling Services, Inc., 1978—. Instr. advanced first aid ARC, 1952—, civil def. instr., 1952—; vol. Spanish Edn. Devel. Center, Washington, 1972; mem. Arlington (Va.) Community Services Bd., 1980-83; chmn. com. substance abuse. Recipient Arnold and Marie Schwartz award in pharmacy, 1980. Mem. Acad. Pharmacy Practice and Mgmt., Am. Pharm. Assn., Va. Pharm. Assn., Potomac Pharmacists Assn., Am. Inst. History of Pharmacy, Nat. Council Patient Info. and Edn. (task force pub. info.), Panhellenic Assn., Kappa Epsilon. Episcopalian (mem. bishop's com. neighborhood services 1967-69, chmn. services for aged div. 1967-69). Contbr. articles in field to profl. jours. Home: 4524 19th Rd N Arlington VA 22207-2352 Fax: 703-522-4343.

ADREON, HARRY BARNES, architect; b. Norfolk, Va., July 18, 1929; s. Harry Barnes and Helen Rae (Medairy) A.; m. Beatrice Marie Rice, Dec. 27, 1952. MS in Architecture, Va. Poly. Inst. and State U., 1952; postgrad., George Mason U. Law Sch., 1977-78; grad., USMC Pack and Equitation Sch., U.S. Army Engr. Sch., Ft. Belvoir, Va. Registered architect, Va., Md., D.C. Pvt. practice architect in Va., Md. and Washington; ptnr. Cross & Adreon, Architects, Washington, Va., 1961-87; prin. Harry B. Adreon, Architect, Arlington, Va., 1987—. Pres. Arlington Kiwanis Club, 1984; mem. com. on mgmt. Arlington YMCA, 1982-84; mem. Arlington Commn. on Physically Disabled Persons, 1987-93, Arlington County Fire Prevention Code Appeals Bd., 1990; chmn. Arlington County chpt. ARC, 1990-92, damage assessment technician Disaster Svcs. Human Resources Sys. Capt. USMCR, 1952. Recipient Dorothy Brunsman Outstanding Svc. award ARC, 1997; named Arlington Cmty. Hero, 1999. Mem. AIA (commr., dir. D.C. Met. chpt. 1978-79, Nat. Design Honor award 1968), Constrn. Specifications Inst. (pres. D.C. Met. chpt. 1972-74, Nat. Pres.'s plaque 1974, Carl Ebert award D.C. Met. chpt. 1990, cert. constrn. specifier), Kiwanis (Hixon award). Episcopalian (Vestryman 1961, 67, 71). Home and Office: 4524 19th Rd N Arlington VA 22207-2352 Fax: 703-522-4343.

ADRI, (ADRI STECKLING COEN), fashion designer; b. St. Joseph, Mo. Ed., Sch. Fine Arts, Washington U., St. Louis, Parson Sch. Design. With B.H. Wragge; owner, pres. Adri Studio, Ltd., N.Y.C., 1983—. Critic Parsons Sch. Design, 1982—; with Claire McCardell in 2-person showing, Innovative Contemporary Fashion, Smithsonian Instn., Washington, 1971. Two-woman show (with Claire McCardell) Smithsonian Instn., Washington, 1972. Recipient Coty award, 1982, Internat. Best Five award, Tokyo, 1986. Office: 143 W 20th St 11th Fl New York NY 10011-3630 E-mail: adri.studio@worldnet.att.net.

ADRIAN, CHARLES RAYMOND, political science educator; b. Portland, Oreg., Mar. 12, 1922; s. Harry Raymond and Helen K. (Petersen) A.; m. Audrey Jean Nelson, Apr. 2, 1946; children: Kristin, Nelson. BA, Cornell (Iowa) Coll., 1947, LL.D., 1973; MA, U. Minn., 1948, PhD, 1950; postdoctoral fellow, U. Copenhagen, Denmark, 1954-55. Instr., then asst. prof. govt. Wayne State U., 1949-55; from asst. prof. to prof. polit. sci. Mich. State U., 1955-66, chmn. dept., 1963-66; dir. Inst. Community Devel., 1958-63; prof. polit. sci. U. Calif.-Riverside, 1966-88, prof. emeritus, 1988—, chmn. dept., 1966-70, acad. asst. to v.p. acad. affairs, 1973-74. Cons. fed., state and local govt. ABC; research cons. Mich. Constl. Conv., 1961-62; Adminstrv. asst. to gov. Mich., 1956-57; mem. Meridian Twp. (Mich.) Planning Commn., 1957-60 Author: (with O. P Williams) Four Cities: A Comparative Study in Community Politics, 1963, State and Local Governments, 2d edit., 1967, 3d edit., 1971, 4th edit., 1976, (with Charles Press) American Political Process, 1965, 2d. edit., 1969, Governing Urban America, 4th edit., 1972, 5th edit., 1977, American Politics Reappraised, 1974, (with E.S. Griffith) History of American City Government 1775-1870, 1976, History of American City Government, 1920-45, 1987, (with Michael Fine) State and Local Politics, 1990; also articles. Mem. Riverside Environ. Protection Commn., 1976-78, Riverside Mayor's Charter Revision Commn., 1985. Served with USAAF, 1943-46, PTO. Faculty fellow Fund Advancement Edn., 1954-55; mem. Phi Beta Kappa. Home: Apt 149 El Palamino Rd 5881 Riverside CA 92509

ADRIAN, DONNA JEAN, retired librarian; b. Morden, Man., Can., Aug. 28, 1940; d. William Gordon and Dorothy Jean (Gregory) Frazer; m. James Ross Adrian, July 17, 1965. BA, Brandon (Man.) Coll., 1962; B.L.S., McGill U., Montreal, 1963, M.L.S., 1969; master tutor cert., Laubach Literacy Can., 1984. Librarian Laurenvale Sch. Bd., Rosemere, Que., 1963-66; librarian, then library coordinator Rosemere High Sch., 1966-74; library coordinator North Island Regional Sch. Bd., Laval, Que., 1974-79. Pedagogical cons. Laurenval Sch. Bd., Laval, 1979—97, now also literacy tutor; lectr. Concordia U., Montreal; mem. Laval Mayor's Library Com., 1975-84. Mem. adv. bd. Canadian Materials, Emergency Librarian. Mem. copyright com. Que. Dept. Edn., 1989-97. Mem. Canadian Library Assn., Que. Assn. Sch. Librarians, Que. Library Assn., Corp. Profl. Librarians Que., Assn. for Tchr.-Librarianship in Can. Home: 194 Roi du Nord Ste Rose Laval QC Canada H7L 1W5

ADRIAN, MITCHELL, management consultant, educator; b. Lake Charles, La., Jan. 30, 1959; s. Cecil Adrian, Ira Belle Adrian; m. Kathy Aguillard. D Bus. Adminstrn., Miss. State U., 1995. Assoc. prof. mgmt. Longwood U., Farmville, Va., 1996—. Pres. Adrian Cons. Co., Farmville, 1997—. Lt. USMC, 1982—85. Office: Longwood U 201 High St Farmville VA 23909 Office Fax: 434-395-2203. Business E-Mail: madrian@longwood.edu.

ADRIANOPOLI, BARBARA CATHERINE, librarian; b. Fort Dodge, Iowa, Jan. 27, 1943; d. Daniel Joseph and Mary Dolores (Coleman) Hogan; m. Carl David Adrianopoli, June 28, 1969; children: Carlin, Laurie. BS, Mundeline

Coll., 1966; MLS, Rosary Coll., 1975; student, Ozark Rsch. Inst., 1999-2000. Cert. in Pranic Healing and Dowsing Ozark Rsch. Inst. Dir. br. and extension svcs. Schaumburg Twp. (Ill.) Dist. Libr., 1979—. Mem. diversity com. N. Suburban/Suburban Libr. Sys., Wheeling, Ill., 1995—. Columnist local newspaper, 1995—, Sr. Connection, 2000—; contbr. articles to profl. jours. Mem. com. Schaumburg Twp. Disabled, 1981-95; historian Village of Hoffman Estates, 1986-99; adv. com. Hoffman Estates Sister Cities, 1996-98; asst. coach St. Viator H.S., 1999-2003; mem. adv. bd. Cmty. Nutrition Network, 1994—; organizer, mem. Northwest Corridor-St. Patrick's Day Parade com., 1986-2003; trainer A World of Difference Anti-Defamation League, 1994; mem. Com. For Choices For Success-Seminars For Young Women, 1996—; mem. Hoffman Estates Sr. and Disabled Commn., 2001; apptd. 8th Dist. State Dem. Com. Women, 2002. Recipient Hoffman Estates Citizen of Yr. award, VFW, 1995. Mem.: ALA, Dorothy Brown Clerk of Cook County Cts. Adv. on Womens Issues (co-chair 2002—), Ill. Libr. Assn. Democrat. Roman Catholic. Home: 1105 Kingsdale Rd Schaumburg IL 60194-2378 Office: Schaumburg Twp Pub Libr 130 S Rosedale Rd Schaumburg IL 60193

ADROUNIE, V. HARRY, public health administrator, scientist, educator, environmentalist; b. Battle Creek, Mich., Apr. 29, 1915; s. Haroutune Asadour and Dorthy (Kalaidjian) A.; m. Emalea Riley, June, 1943 (div. Jan. 1980); children: Harry Michael, Vee Patrick; m. Agnes M. Slone, June 26, 1981. BS, St. Ambrose U., 1940, BA, 1959; MS in Environ. Health, PhD in Environ. Health, PhD in Pub. Health, Western States U. Profl. Studies, 1984. Diplomate Am. Bd. Indsl. Hygiene, Am. Acad. Sanitarians; registered sanitarian, Calif., Mich., Pa. Enlisted U.S. Army, 1941, commd. 2nd. lt., 1943; advanced through grades to lt. col. USAF, ret., 1968; founder, tech. dir. ARA Environ. Svcs., 1968—72; dir. environ. health div. Chester County (Pa.) Health Dept., 1972—75, Berrien County (Mich.) Health Dept., 1975-78; prof. environ. health Sch. Pub. Health U. Hawaii, Manoa, 1978-80; dean, prof. Sch. Pub. Health, Western States U. Profl. Studies, Mo., 1980-83; vis. prof. environ. and pub. health Am. U., Armenia, 1995. USAF rep. U.S. Interdepartmental Com. on Nutrition for Nat. Def., 1959—61; cons. Health Mobilization Program USPHS Surgeon Gen., 1957—61; mem. USAF Surgeon Gen.'s med. goodwill tour all S.A.m. countries, 1960; chmn., vis. assoc. prof. dept. environ. health, faculty med. sch. Am. U. Beirut, 1963—66, chmn. dept. environ. health, 1964—66; charter mem. RSH-UN Welfare Relief Agy. Pub. Health Examining Bd. for Mid. East, 1963—66; cons. UN Welfare Relief Agy., 1964—66; founder, coord. 1st and 2nd Environ. Health Symposium of Mid. East, 1965—66; mem. Mich. Hazardous Waste Policy Com., 1990—91, Mich. Underground Storage Fin. Policy Bd., 1994—2001; adj. instr., adv. com. environ. health Ferris State Coll., Big Rapids, Mich., 1974—75, Big Rapids, 1977—78. Contbr. numerous articles to profl. jours.; author many manuals and tng. booklets for USAF and other orgns., several books. Chmn. Nat. Children's Environ. Health Com., 2002—03, Barry County Solid Waste Planning and Oversight com., 1981—; mem. Barry County Family Ind. Agy., 1996—, vice chmn., 1998—, Hastings City Planning Commn., 1984—; mem., co-founder sci. adv. and policy bd. Mich. Ground Water Survey, Inc., 1983—90, chmn., 1988—91; chmn. adv. coun. South Ctrl. Mich. Commn. on Aging, 1981—91; charter mem. UL Underwriters adv. coun. environ. and pub. health, 1996—; appointed mem. Vision 2020 Com. St. Ambrose U., 2000—01; past adult leader Boy Scouts Am. Decorated Legion of Merit, USAF; named Alumnus of Yr., Hastings H.S., 1961; recipient Walter S. Mangold award Nat. Environ. Health Assn., 1963, spl. recognition Mich. Environ. Health Assn., 1980, Concerned Citizen award World Safety Orgn., 1992, Safety Person of World Safety Orgn., 1992, State of Mich. White Pine award, 1998. Mem.: APHA (pres. 1995—97, emeritus conf., task force on aging 2002—), NRA (life; cert. rifle marksmanship instr.), VFW (life), Indonesian Environ. Health Assn. (co-founder 1979), World Safety Orgn. (bd. dirs. 1986—95, cert. bd. 1987—2000, editl. bd. 1988—2000), Global Health Assn., Internat. Pub. Health Soc. (charter-emeritus), Mich. Assn. Local Environ. Health Adminstrs. (pres., founder 1976, V. Harry Adrounie award named in his honor 2001), Mich. Environ. Health Assn. (life; pres. 1991—92), Assn. Mil. Surgeons (life), Nat. Environ. Health Assn. (life; pres. 1961—62), Am. Legion (comdr. post 45 1989—90), Air Force Assn., Mil. Officers Assn. Am. (life), Kiwanis (pres. Hastings, Mich. chpt. 1985—86), Moose, Elks (life), Lions (life). Home: 1905 N Broadway Hastings MI 49058-1086

ADSIT, RUSSELL ALLAN, landscape architect; b. Syracuse, N.Y., June 11, 1952; B of Landscape Arch., U. Ga., 1975; M of Agribus. Mgmt., Miss. State U., 1997. Registered landscape arch., Ala., Ark., Ga., Ky., Miss., Tenn.; lic. pest control operator. Landscape designer Landscape Svcs., Birmingham, Ala., 1975-76; pres., owner, gen. mgr. Adsit Landscape and Design Firm, Inc., Memphis, 1976-94; owner Natural Design Solutions, Memphis, 1995-98; prin. Fisher & Arnold, Inc., Memphis, 1998—. Instr. Toro U., 1990-91, Tenn. Fedn. Garden Clubs, 1990-92, Miss. State U., 1995-98; spkr. Hinds C.C., Jackson, Miss. Active BBB, Intern Program at Cobelskill Program, 1991-92, Co-op Program at Miss. State U., 1980-92, Econs. Amenities Task Force, 1982; mem. finance com. Asbury Meth. Ch., 1991-92. Named Outstanding Small Bus. of Yr., Memphis Bus. Jour., 1981, Outstanding Bus. Vol., Memphis Bot. Garden Found., 1988. Fellow Am. Soc. Landscape Archs. (chmn. membership application rev. com. 1978-80, water mgmt. ednl. seminar 1979, pres. Tenn. chpt. 1980-81, 84-85, chmn. nat. coun. chpt. pres. 1981, judges panel Miss. ann. awards 1981, spkr. nat. conv. Cin. 1985, Tenn. trustee 1987-93, judges facilitator Okla. ann. awards 1987, mem. ann. conf. organizing com. Tenn. chpt. 1989, chpt. membership com. 1989-91, publs. bd. 1991-92, fin. and adminstrn. com. 1991-92, v.p. 1999-2000, merit award 1979, 80, honor award 1981); mem. Assn. Turf and Ornamental Mgrs. (charter, pres. 1986), Assoc. Landscape Contractors Am. (distinction award 1990, 92, 93, merit award 1991), So. Nurserymen's Assn., Memphis Bot. Garden Found. (bd. dirs. 1984-92, chmn. master plan selection com. 1987, 2d v.p. 1989-90), West Tenn. Nursery and Landscape Assn., Tenn. Nursery Assn., Memphis Hort. Soc., Memphis Assn. Bldg. Owners and Mgrs., Memphis C. of C. (small bus. coun., chmn. small bus. connection 1992). Office: 3205 Players Club Pkwy Memphis TN 38125-8845

ADUBATO, RICHARD ADAM (RICHIE ADUBATO), professional basketball coach; b. East Orange, NJ, Nov. 23, 1937; m. Carol Begerow, July 25, 1989; children: Beth, Scott, Adam. grad., postgrad. degree, William Paterson Coll., Wayne, NJ. Head coach Our Lady of the Valley High Sch., Orange, NJ; asst. coach Upsala Coll., East Orange, NJ, 1969-72, head coach, 1972-78; asst. coach Detroit Pistons, Detroit, 1978-79, head coach, 1979-80; scout Atlanta Hawks, Atlanta, 1980-82; asst. coach New York Knicks, N.Y.C., NY, 1982-86, Dallas Mavericks, Dallas, 1986-89, head coach, 1989-93; asst. coach Cleveland Cavaliers, 1993-96; head coach Orlando Magic, 1996-97, New York Liberty (WNBA), 1998—. Named to William Paterson Hall Fame. Office: New York Liberty 2 Penn Plz New York NY 10121-0101

ADUDDLE, LARRY STEVEN, marketing and sales executive, consultant; b. Miami Beach, Fla., Oct. 21, 1946; s. William Allen and Bernice Elizabeth (Newlon) A.; m. Susan Carol Dominiak, Nov. 27, 1982; 1 child, Melissa Sue. BBA, Lake Forest Coll., 1982; MBA, Lake Forest Sch. Mgmt., 1984. Supr. Rexnord, Inc., Milw., 1974-77, product mgr., 1977-79, sales mgr., 1979-81; mktg. mgr. V/R Wesson, Fansteel, Inc., Waukegan, Ill., 1981-82; v.p. Metropolymer Labs, Inc., Milw., 1983-2000, bd. dirs.; COO Western Conversions Mo., 2000—02, also bd. dirs.; asst. ctr. dir. mgmt. MSC U.S. Dept. Justice, 2002—03; asst. ctr. dir. mgmt., Nat. Benefits Ctr. U.S. Dept. Homeland Security, 2003—. Bd. dirs., treas. Metromark, Inc.; v.p., sec. Metropolymer Labs, Inc.; cons. in field, Milw., 1982-83. Patentee insert for drill stabilizers. Vice chmn. United Fund Campaign, Milw., 1975; adv. Jr. Achievement, Milw., 1980. Served to capt. U.S. Army, 1965-69, Vietnam. Decorated Bronze Star. Mem. Reserve Officers Assn. (sec. 1977-78), Assn. Internat. Mktg. Execs. Republican. Lutheran. Avocations: golf, tennis, boating. Home: 3604 NW Lake Dr Lees Summit MO 64064 Office: US Dept Homeland Security NW Chipman Rd Lees Summit MO 64064 Business E-Mail: larry.aduddle@dhs.gov.

ADUJA, MELODIE WILLIAMS, state senator; b. Honolulu, Jan. 25, 1960; m. Lee Williams; children: William, Amber. BA, Hawaii Loa Coll., Kaneohe, 1981; ML, Golden Gate U. Sch. of Law, 1991, JD, 1987. Legis. aide State Rep. Alfred Lardizabal, 1982—83; dep. processing atty. Prosecutor's Office, Honolulu, 1987—91; atty. Law Office of Melodie R. Williams Aduja, 1992—; commr. Transport. Commn. City and County of Hawaii, 1999—2000; senator Hawaii State Senate, 2002—. Dir. Nat. Kidney Found. of Hawaii, 1997—98; bd. mem. Hina Mauka Recovery Ctr., 1998—2001; dir. No Hope in Dope, Inc., 1998—2001; mem. Kahaluu Neighborhood Bd., 1999—2001; dir. Hawaii Filipino Lawyers Assn., 1993—94; mem. San Francisco Area Women Tax Lawyers, 1992—93. Mem.: Calif. State Bar. Democrat. Roman Catholic. Office: State Capital Rm 231 415 S Beretania St Honolulu HI 96813 Fax: 808-586-7330. E-mail: senaduja@Capitol.hawaii.gov., melodie@aduja.com.*

ADUROJA, AMOS OLADIPO, healthcare educator, consultant; s. Samuel O. and Deborah S. Aduroja; m. Dorcas Fehintolu Fajuyigbe, Oct. 11, 1980; children: Grace Olubukola, Abiola Dolapo, Abi O., Bola E., Tunde Timothy. PhD, U. of Mich., 1984. Cert. health edn. specialist Nat., 1989. Prof. of health edn. Wayne State U., Detroit, 1985—90; dir. of health and substance abuse Detroit (Mich.) Urban League, 1990—96; dir. Bur. Substance Abuse, Detroit, 1996—. Pres. The Gideon's Internat., Ann Arbor, Mich., 2001—02; chair Prevention Coalition of S.E. Mich., Detroit, 1995—96. Recipient Leadership Award, FBI, 1996. Fellow: Soc. for Pub. Health Edn. Independent. Avocations: golf, soccer, tennis. Home: 6444 Enchanted Drive Ypsilanti MI 48197 Office: Western MIchigan University 4024 5 Student Recreation Center Kalamazoo MI 49008 Home Fax: 616-387-2704; Office Fax: 616-387-2704. Personal E-mail: droja@aol.com. E-mail: amos.aduroja@wmich.edu.

ADUSUMALLI, PRASAD (VENKATA), software engineer, engineering executive; b. Gandipalem, India, Nov. 19, 1968; s. Venkata Ratnam and Kondamma (Matcha) A.; m. Vidya Gorantla, Aug. 31, 1996; 1 child, Pallavi. B Tech. in Mech. Engring., V.R. Siddhartha Engring. Coll., Vijayawada, India, 1988; M Engring. in Prodn. and Indsl. Sys., U. Roorkee, India, 1990; PhD, Indian Inst. Tech., New Delhi, 1994. Rsch. scholar dept. mech. engring. Indian Inst. Tech., 1990-94, sr. sci. officer Computer Numerical Control Lab., 1994; sr. software engr. engring. data mgmt. divsn. Computervision R&D (India) Pvt. Ltd., Pune, 1994-96, sr. software engr. product and process data mgmt. divsn., 1996-97, prin. software engr. product and process data mgmt. divsn., 1997; sr. software engr. Concentus Tech. Corp., Columbus, Ohio, 1997-98, EDS PLM Solutions Divsn., Arden Hills, Minn., 1998—. Presenter at confs. in field. Contbr. articles to profl. jours. Grantee India Univ. Grants Commn.; Nat. Merit scholar India, 1982-88. Mem. Indian Soc. Mech. Engrs., Indian Soc. Tech. Edn. Office: EDS PLM Solutions Divsn 4233 Lexington Ave N Ste 3290 Saint Paul MN 55126-6160 E-mail: prasad.adusumalli@eds.com.

ADVANI, SURESH G. mechanical engineer, educator; PhD in Mech. Engring U. Ill., Urbana-Champaign, 1987. From asst. to assoc. prof. mech. engring. U. Del., Newark, 1987—92, prof. mech. engring., 1997—, acting chair mech. engring., 1998—99. Editor: Composites: Applied Science and Manufacturing. Fellow: ASME. Office: Dept Mechanical Engineering University of Delaware Newark DE 19716 Office Fax: 302-831-3619. E-mail: advani@udel.edu.

ADWAN, KENNETH OSCAR, surgeon; b. Oklahoma City, Oct. 10, 1924; BS, U. Okla., 1948; MD, U. Tex., 1952. Diplomate Am. Bd. Surgeons. Intern U. Okla. Hosp., 1952-53; resident in surgery Parkland Mem. Hosp., Dallas, 1956-59; fellow in surgery U. Tex. S.W. Med. Ctr., assoc. prof. surgery, 1959-70; mem. staff Drs. Hosp., Dallas; pvt. practice Dallas, 1959—93; ret., 1993. Fellow ACS; mem. AMA. Office: 334 Padre Blvd Bridgepoint #1201 South Padre Island TX 78597 E-mail: koadwanmd@webtv.net.

ADY, LAURENCE IRVIN, academic administrator; b. Washington, Mar. 15, 1932; s. Laurence E. and Georgiana C. (Covington) A.; m. Jan. 10. 1959; children: Marc S., Lori L. BA, U. Md., 1956; MA in Tchg., Rollins Coll., 1964, Ednl. Specialist, 1974. Cert. ednl. adminstrn. & supervision, elem. edn., early childhood edn., drivers edn., history, adult edn.; lic. police officer. Police officer Orlando Police Dept., 1958-59, Ocoee (Fla.) Police Dept., 1959-64; constable Dist. #3, Orange County, Fla., 1964-66; tchr. H.S. Sch. Bd. Orange Ct., Fla., 1967-68, from supervisor adult basic edn. to sch. adminstr., 1968—. Dep. sheriff Orange County, 1971-80; elem. sch. tchr. Sch. Bd. Orange Ct., 1959-67; pres. Commn. on Adult Basic Edn., 1984-85, treas. 1979—. Commr. City of Belle Isle, Fla., 1977—; treas. Dem. exec. com., Orange County, 1982—. Named to Fla. Adult Edn. Hall of Fame Fla. Adult Edn. Assn., Cocoa Beach, 1985. Mem. Am. Assn. for Adult/Continuing Edn. (treas. 1987-91), Tiger Bay Orlando, Kiwanis (treas., dir. 1972—). Methodist. Avocations: boating, swimming, exercising. Home: 2495 Trentwood Blvd Orlando FL 32812-4833 Office: COABE PO Box 592053 Orlando FL 32859-2053

AELION, C. MARJORIE, adult education educator; BS summa cum laude, U. Mass., 1980; MSCE, MIT, 1983; PhD, U. N.C., 1988. Park ranger Nat. Park Svc., Cape Cod Nat. Seashore, South Wellfleet, Mass., 1976-78; biologist, resource assessment divsn. Nat. Marine Fisheries, Woods Hole, Mass., 1978-84; rsch. asst. MIT, Cambridge, Mass., 1981-83, U. Mass.-Amherst, Amherst, Peru, 1983-84, U. N.C., Chapel Hill, 1986-88, tchg. asst., 1987; hydrologist U.S. Geol. Survey, Water Resources Divsn., Columbia, S.C., 1988-91, faculty mem., 1991-97; asst. prof. dept. environ. health scis. U. S.C., Columbia, 1991-97, assoc. prof., 1997-2001, prof., 2001—. Presenter in field. Contbr. articles to profl. jours. Fulbright-Hayes scholar, 1980-81; Bd. Govs.' fellow U. N.C., 1984-86, Dissertation fellow, 1988, NSF fellow in engring., 1993; grantee U.S. EPA, 1991-93, Hazardous Waste Mgmt. Rsch. Fund, 1991-94, 99-2002, Nat. Geographic Soc., 1992, S.C. Dept. Health and Environ. Control and Hazardous Waste Mgmt. Rsch. Fund, 1991-94, U. S.C., 1993-94, NSF, 1993-00, 99—, Fulbright Scholar, 2002; grad. student travel grantee award U. N.C., 1988; Rsch. Fellowship, Internat. Agrl. Ctr., The Netherlands, 2002. Mem. Am. Chem. Soc., Am. Soc. Microbiology, Assn. for Women in Sci. (sec. S.C. chpt. 1996-97, pres. S.C. chpt. 1997-98), Soc. Women Engrs., Soc. Environ. Toxicology and Chemistry, Phi Kappa Phi, Delta Omega. Office: U SC Environ Health Scis Dept Columbia SC 29208-0001

AERTS, CINDY SUE, nurse; b. Green Bay, Wis., Oct. 18, 1946; d. John and Winon (Kazilek) A. RN, St. Mary's Sch. Nursing, 1967; BSN, U. Wis., 1985; MSN in Critical Care Nursing, Med. Coll. Wis., 1987. CCRN; cert. ACLS instr.; CEN; cert. pediat. advanced life support; cert. emergency nurse pediat. course. Dir. coronary care unit St. Vincent Hosp., Green Bay, Wis., 1970-85; dir. critical care nursing Mary Washington Hosp., Fredericksburg, Va., 1986, L.W. Blake Hosp., Brodenton, Fla., 1988; RN III Sarasota Mem. Hosp., Sarasota, Fla. Recipient Linda Daniels Award 1985, Vol. of Year Am. Health Assn., Green Bay 1978. Mem. AACN (Northeastern Wis. chpt. pres. 1976, 77, manasota chpt. pres. 1991, 92), Emergency Nurses Assn. Home: 4525 Sanibel Way Bradenton FL 34203

AFELBIL, MARTIN, statistician, researcher; s. Alfred and Yaaya Afelbil; m. JoAnn Wallace, July 7, 1978. BA, U. of New Orleans, 1981, MA, 1985. Rsch. assoc. Pub. Housing Authorities Dirs. Assn., Washington, 1994—97; rsch. analyst Treasury Mgmt. Assn., Bethesda, Md., 1997—99; rsch. coord. Coun. on Founds., Washington, 1999—. Recipient Cert. of Appreciation, City of New Orleans, 1984. Mem.: Am. Statis. Assn., Assn. Rsch. on Nonprofit Orgns. and Voluntary Action. Democrat. Roman Catholic. Avocations: travel, soccer, reading.

AFFELDT, JOHN ELLSWORTH, retired physician; b. Lansing, Mich., May 26, 1918; s. John Ferdin and Pearl Heald (Gardner) Affeldt; m. Nancy Faye Spomer, Sept. 2, 1942; children: John C., Elizabeth Affeldt Westberg, Cindy L. BS, Andrews U., Berrien Springs, Mich., 1939; MD, Loma Linda (Calif.) U., 1944. Intern Detroit Gen. Hosp., 1943—44; resident in internal medicine White Meml. Hosp., Los Angeles, 1946—49; fellow in pulmonary physiology Harvard Sch. Pub. Health, 1949—51; med. dir. Rancho Los Amigos Hosp., Downey, Calif., 1956—64, Los Angeles County Dept. Hosps., 1964—72, Los Angeles County Dept. Health Services, 1972—77; pres. Joint Commn. Accreditation Hosps., Chgo., 1977—86; med. advisor Beverly Enterprises, Fort Smith, Ark., 1986—97. Served with U.S. Army, 1944—47. Mem.: ACP, AMA, Calif. Assn. Med. Dirs. (pres. 1993—94), Los Angeles County Med. Assn., We. Soc. Clin. Rsch., Ins. Medicine NAS, Am. Congress Rehab. Medicine. Home: 5140 Bareback Sq PO Box 8432 Rancho Santa Fe CA 92067-8432

AFFLECK, BEN, actor; b. Berkeley, Calif., Aug. 15, 1972; Actor: (films) School Ties, 1992, Dazed and Confused, 1993, Mallrats, 1995, Going All the Way, 1997, Chasing Amy, 1997, Armageddon, 1998 (Favorite Supporting Actor in Sci. Fiction Blockbuster Entertainment award, 1999), Phantoms, 1998, Reindeer Games, 1999, Forces of Nature, 1999 (Favorite Actor in Comedy/Romance Blockbuster Entertainment award, 2000), Dogma, 1999, 200 Cigarettes, 1999, Daddy and Them, 1999, Boiler Room, 1999, Bounce, 2000 (Favorite Actor in Drama/Romance Blockbuster Entertainment award, 2001), Jay and Silent Bob Strike Back, 2001, Pearl Harbor, 2001, The Sum of All Fears, 2002, Changing Lanes, 2002, The Third Wheel, 2002, Daredevil, 2003, Gigli, 2003; actor, writer Good Will Hunting, 1997 (Oscar award Best Writing Screenplay Written Directly for Screen, 3d pl. Boston Soc. Film Critics award Best Screenplay, Broadcast Film Critics Assn. award Best Screenplay-Motion Picture, Golden Satellite award Best Motion Picture Screenplay-Original, London Critics Cir. award Screenwriter of Yr., others); prodr. : (TV series) Project Greenlight, 2001; prodr.: Stolen Summer, 2002; writer, prodr. (TV series) Push, Nevada, 2002; exec. prodr.: (films) Crossing Cords, 2001, Speakeasy, 2002, The Battle of Shaker Heights, 2003. Office: c/o Ken Sunshine Ken Sunshine Consultants, Inc 75 Ninth Ave, 2nd Fl New York NY 10011 also: Endeavor Talent 9701 Wilshire Blvd, 10th Fl Beverly Hills CA 90212*

AFFLECK, MARILYN, sociology educator; b. Logan, Utah, July 1, 1932; d. Clark B. and Velda (Bryson) A.; children: Michelle Alisa, Kimberly Kay, Lacey Dawn. BA, U. Okla., 1954; MA, Brigham Young U., 1957; PhD, UCLA, 1966. Instr., Central State Coll., Edmond, Okla., 1958-60; asst. prof. Fla. State U., Tallahassee, 1966-68; asst. prof. sociology U. Okla., Norman, 1968-70, assoc. prof., 1971-90, interim dean Grad. Coll., 1978-79, asst. dean, 1976-82. Editor Free Inquiry in Creative Sociology Jour., 1984-90. Recipient AMOCO Good Teaching award U. Okla., 1974 Mem. Okla. Sociol. Assn. (pres. 1974-75), South Ctrl. Women's Studies Assn. (treas. 1979-83), Phi Beta Kappa. Democrat. Mem. Lds Ch. Home: 6395 Corky Dr NE Norman OK 73026-3135

AFFRONTI, JOHN PAUL, medical educator; b. Phila., Apr. 21, 1957; s. Lewis Francis and Ethel Aileen A. BA, George Washington U., 1979, MD, 1985; MS in Pharmacology, Uniformed Svcs. U. Health Sci., 1981. Diplomate Am. Bd. Internal Medicine. Resident in internal medicine George Washington U. Med. Ctr., Washington, 1985-88; fellow in gastroenterology Duke U. Med. Ctr., Durham, N.C., 1988-90, assoc. in medicine, 1991, asst. prof. medicine, dir. gastrointestinal endosonography, 1991-96; asst. prof. medicine U. Fla., Jacksonville, 1996-98; assoc. prof. medicine Emory U., Atlanta, 1998—; chief endoscopy Emory U. Hosp., Atlanta, 1998—. Author: (chpt.) Gastrointestinal Endoscop: An Endoscopic Approach to Gastrointestinal Disease, 1997; contbr. articles to profl. jours. Duke Auxiliary Svcs. grantee Duke U. Med. Ctr., 1990. Mem. Am. Coll. Gastroenterology, Am. Soc. Gastrointestinal Endoscopy, William Beaumont Soc., King Kane Hon. Soc. Avocation: sailing. Office: Divsn Digestive Diseases Emory U Sch Medicine 1365 Clifton Rd NE Ste 3430A Atlanta GA 30322-1013 Fax: 404-778-3184. E-mail: john_affronti@emory.org.

AFFRONTI, LEWIS FRANCIS, SR., microbiologist, educator; b. Rochester, N.Y., Aug. 12, 1928; s. John and Mary (Least) A.; m. Aileen Ledford, June 2, 1956; children: John, Lewis, Mary Louise, Eileen. BA, U. Buffalo, 1950, MA, 1951; PhD, Duke U., 1958. Rsch. assoc. Buffalo VA Hosp., 1951-52, Roswell Meml. Cancer Inst., 1954, TB Henry Phipps Inst. U. Pa., 1957-58; asst. prof. Sch. Medicine, George Washington U., Washington, 1962-65, assoc. prof., 1965-72, prof. microbiology, 1972-93, prof. emeritus, 1994—, chmn. dept. microbiology, 1973-93. Cons. AVCO Rsch. Corp., VA Hosp., Martinsburg, W.Va., VA Hosp. Ctr., Wilmington, Del.; U.S. rep. WHO Conf. on Skin Test Antigens and Vaccines, Geneva, 1966; mem. med. adv. bd. VA, Wilmington. Mem. editl. bd. Infection and Immunity, 1972-78. Bd. dirs. Lynchburg (Va.) unit Am. Cancer Soc., 1996. Commd. officer USPHS (CDC), 1958-62; with USAF, 1952-54. NIH Spl. fellow, 1969; Nat. Tb fellow for Internat. Conf. on Tb Moscow, 1971; Nat. Tb fellow for Internat. Conf. on Tb Tokyo, 1973; Washington Acad. Sci. fellow; Recipient WHO Exch. Rsch. Workers award, 1970, Scientist Emeritus award Soc. Expl. Biology and Medicine, Washington, 1994; interacad. exch. program award NAS, 1980. Fellow Am. Acad. Microbiology, Assn. Med. Sch. Microbiology Chmn. (sec.-treas. 1976-86, bd. dirs. 1976-86), Washington Acad. Sci.; mem. AAAS (life), Am. Soc. Microbiology, Am. Assn. Immunologists, Reticuloendothelial Soc., Am. Thoracic Soc., Assembly on Microbiologists and Immunologists (sec. 1971-72), The Protein Soc., Toastmasters Internat. (Atlanta), Mil. Order World Wars, KC, Sigma Xi (local pres. 1986-87). Office: George Washington U Med Ctr Dept Microbiology 2300 I St NW Washington DC 20037-2336

AFIELD, WALTER EDWARD, psychiatrist, service executive; b. N.Y.C., Dec. 28, 1935; s. Walter Edward and Mollie Evelyn (MCGovern) A.; m. Nancy Browning, Dec. 27, 1973; children: Walter Edward, Neva Browning. AB, U. Pa., 1956; MD, Johns Hopkins U., 1960. Intern Grady Meml. Hosp., Atlanta, 1960-61; fellow in psychiatry Harvard U., Cambridge, Mass., 1961-64, 66-67; asst. prof. psychiatry Johns Hopkins U., Balt., 1967-70, dir. dept. child psychiatry, 1967-70; prof. U. South Fla. Coll. Medicine, 1970-74, chmn. dept. psychiatry, 1970-74; exec. dir. Tampa Bay Neuropsychiat. Inst., Tampa, Fla., 1970—; chmn., chief exec. officer The Mental Health Programs Corp., Tampa, 1985-92. Author: The Children of Resurrection City, 1970; contbr. articles to profl. jours. Pres. Fla. Lyric Opera, 1976—. Capt. USAF, 1964-66. Fellow Am. Coll. Psychiatrists; mem. AMA, Am. Acad. Neurology, University Club, Tampa Yacht Club. Republican. Roman Catholic. Home: 4619 W Bay To Bay Blvd Tampa FL 33629-7610 Office: 5820 W Cypress St Ste B Tampa FL 33607-1785 E-mail: hogheavn@tampabay.rr.com.

AFIFI, ADEL KASSIM, physician; b. Akka, Palestine, Oct. 19, 1930; came to U.S., 1984; naturalized, 1988; s. Kassim and Zeinnab (Akki) A.; m. Larryanna Patten, June 17, 1960; children: Rema, Walid. MD, Am. U., Beirut, 1957; MS, U. Iowa, 1965. Intern Am. U. of Beirut, 1956-57, resident in internal medicine, 1959-61; resident in neurology U. Iowa, 1962-64, fellow in neuroanatomy, 1961-62; fellow in neurology N.Y. Neurol. Inst., 1964-65; fellow in electron microscopy Johns Hopkins U., Balt., 1967-68; asst. prof. Am. U., Beirut, 1965-69, assoc. prof., 1969-74, prof., 1974-84, asst. dean Coll. Medicine, 1969-78, chmn. Dept. Human Morphology, 1969-84; prof. U. Iowa, Iowa City, 1984—. Author: Atlas of Microscopic Anatomy, 1974, 89, Basic Neuroscience, 1980, 86, Compendium of Anatomical Variation, 1988, Atlas of Human Anatomy, 1991; contbr. articles to jours. in field. Trustee Diana Tamari Sabbagh Found., Beirut, 1979—, Med. Welfare Fund, Switzerland, 1991—; mem. King Faisal Internat. Prize in Medicine, Riyadh, Saudi Arabia, 1981-85. Fulbright scholar U. Iowa, 1980-81. Mem. Am. Neurol. Assn., Am. Acad. Neurology, Child Neurology Soc., Soc. for Neurosci., Alpha Omega Alpha. Home: 1147 Penkridge Dr Iowa City IA 52246-4933 Office: U Iowa Coll Medicine Dept Anatomy Iowa City IA 52242

AFIFI, ALAA YOUSSEF, cardiothoracic surgeon; b. Cairo, Jan. 19, 1965; arrived in U.S., 1972; s. Youssef s. Afifi Samia A. Salem. BS in Biology magna cum laude, Siena Coll., 1985; MD magna cum laude, Albany Med. Coll., 1989. Diplomate Nat. Bd. Med. Examiners, Am. Bd. Surgery, Am. Bd. Thoracic Surgery. Intern Wilford Hall USAF Med. Ctr., Lackland AFB, San Antonio, 1989-90, resident, 1990-91, Keesler USAF Med. Ctr., Keesler AFB, Biloxi, Miss., 1991-93, chief resident, instr. surgery, 1993-94; jr. fellow, instr. cardiothoracic surgery U. Rochester (N.Y.) Med. Ctr., 1994-95, chief fellow, instr. cardiothoracic surgery, 1995-96; chief cardiothoracic surgery, dir. surg. ICU Keesler USAF Med. Ctr., Biloxi, Miss., 1999-2000; asst. prof. surgery Uniformed Svcs. U. Health Scis., Bethesda, Md., 1999-2000; attending cardiothoracic surgeon Biloxi VA Med. Ctr., 1996-2000, Meml. Hosp. of Gulfport, Miss., 1998-2000, Ellis Hosp., Albany Med. Ctr., St. Peter's Hosp., Albany, N.Y., 2000—. Presenter in field. Contbr. articles to profl. jours. Presdl. scholar, 1981-85; recipient Ralph D. Alley award Cardiothoracic Surgery, 1989, Soc. Laparoendoscopic Surgeons award, 1994. Fellow Am. Coll. Surgeons, Am. Coll. Cardiology, Am. Coll. Chest Physicians, Soc. Thoracic Surgeons, So. Thoracic Surgeons Assn.; mem. AMA, Am. Heart Assn., Med. Soc. State N.Y., Monroe County Med. Soc., Soc. Air Force Clin. Surgeons, Sigma Xi, Alpha Kappa Alpha, Delta Epsilon Sigma, Alpha Omega Alpha. Avocations: travel, sports, landscaping, photography. Office: Schenectady Cardiothoracic 1101 Nott St Ste B-4 Schenectady NY 12308 Fax: 518-243-3613. E-mail: alaa.afifi@msn.com.

AFOUNA, MOHSEN M.I. pharmaceutical scientist, researcher; s. Mahmoud E-Sayed Afouna and Sabah Abdel-Hafeez Habash; m. Nadia El-Sayed Afouna, Aug. 16, 1992; children: Mahmoud Mohsen, Sohiel Mohsen, Joumanah Mohsen. PhD, Al-Azhar and Utah univs., Cairo and Salt Lake City, 1998; M in Pharm. Scis., Al-Azhar U., 1995, BS Pharmacy, 1987. Asst. prof. of pharm. scis. Al-Azhar U.-Ain Shams U., Nasr City, Egypt, 1998—, U. Ark. Med. Sch., Coll. Pharmacy, Little Rock, 2002—. Lectr., rsch. assoc. Al-Azhar U., Nasr City, 1998. Author: (novels) Topical-Transdermal-Ocular-Oral Drug Delivery sys-

tems (scholarship Egyptian Govt., 1999, fellowship U. of Utah, 1999, fellowship U. Ark. Med. Sch., 1999). Author AAPS, Little Rock, 1996—2003. Officer Med. Affairs, 1987—88, Cairo-Misr Al-Jadidah-Prsident Hosni Mubark Hospital. Recipient PhD fellowship, Egyptian Govt., 1995—98, postdoctorate fellowship, Dr. Bill Higushi-Utah U., 1999; grantee, Ther-Tech Inc., 1997, 1998. Independent. Achievements include research in Topical-Transdermal-Ocular-Oral Drug Delivery systems. Avocations: tennis, swimming, golf, volleyball, basketball. Home: 7820 W Capitol Ave Little Rock AR 72205 Office: U Ark Med Sch Coll Pharmacy and Pharm Scis 4301 W Markham St Little Rock AR 72205 Home Fax: 501-526-6510; Office Fax: 501-526-6510. Personal E-mail: mafouna@hotmail.com. E-mail: afounamohsen@uams.edu.

AFT, RICHARD NATHANIEL, professional society administrator, consultant; b. Chgo., May 22, 1938; s. Harry H. and Muriel Lorraine A.; m. Mary Lucille Hudson, June 9, 1961; children: David, Rob, Eric. PhD, The Union Inst., 2000. Pres. United Way and Cmty. Chest, Cin., 1987-2001, Philanthropic Leadership, Cin., 2001—. Chair United Way of Am. Nat. Prof. Coun., 1996-98. Home: 448 Warren Ave Cincinnati OH 45220

AFTEL, MANDY, perfumer; b. Detroit, Mar. 2, 1948; d. James Samuel Aftel and Ruth May Ellias, 1 child, Chloe. BA, U. Mich., 1969, MA, 1970. Psychotherapist for artists and writers, Berkeley, Calif., 1977—2000; perfumer Grandiflorum Perfumes, Berkeley, 1996—97, Aftelier Perfumes, Berkeley, 1997—. Author: Death of a Rolling Stone: The Brian Jones Story, 1982, When Talk Is Not Cheap, 1984, The Story of Your Life, 1995, Essence and Alchemy: A Book of Perfume, 2001 (Richard B. Solomon award, 01). Mem. adv. bd. creative writing program St. Mary's Coll., Moraga, Calif., 2001—. Mem.: Artisan Natural Performers Guild (founder). Office Fax: 510-841-2111. E-mail: mandy@aftelier.com.

AFTERMAN, ALLAN B. accountant, educator, researcher, consultant; b. Chgo., Jan. 25, 1944; s. Joseph and Ruth Gertrude (Jacobson) A.; m. Joan Elaine Hoffman, Apr. 30, 1974; children: Debra, Lori, Julie, Robin. BBA, Roosevelt U., 1964; PhD, U. Birmingham, Eng., 1989. CPA, Calif. Asst. dir. securities exchange com. practices Alexander Grant & Co., Chgo., 1967-70; nat. staff mgr. Touche Ross & Co., Chgo., 1970-73; nat. tech. dir. Practice Devel. Inst., Chgo., 1977-82; acctg. prof. U. Ill., Chgo., 1983-88, dir. exec. edn.; mem. faculty grad. sch. bus. U. Chgo., 1992-99. Cons. to govts. Author: Accounting and Auditing Disclosure Manual, 1982, Compilation and Review, 1983, Accounting and Auditing Update, 1984, SEC Accounting and Reporting Update, 1985, GAAP Practice Manual, 1985 (best looseleaf bus. reference award profl. and scholastic divsn. Assn. Am. Pubs. 1985), Accounting and Tax Highlights, 1986, Handbook of SEC Accounting and Disclosure, 1987, Credit Analyst's Report, 1988, Financial Reporting and Disclosure Manual in the United Kingdom, 1989, Public Accounting Practice Manual, 1990, Governmental Accounting & Auditing Disclosure Manual, 1991, Nonprofit Accounting and Auditing Disclosure Manual, 1992, Auditing Standards and Practices in Poland, 1993, SEC Regulation of Public Companies, 1994, International Financial Accounting, Reporting & Analysis, 1994, U.S. Securities Regulation of Foreign Issuers, 1995, Charities Accounting and Auditing Disclosure Manual in the United Kingdom, 1996, Nonprofit GAAP Practice Manual, 1998, Audit Committee Governance Report, 2000, Corporate Financial Management, 2001. Mem. AICPA, Am. Acctg. Assn., Practicing Law Inst., N.Y. Soc. CPAs. Jewish. Home: 3900 Mission Hills Rd Apt 302 Northbrook IL 60062-5721 Office: 3330 Dundee Rd Ste N6 Northbrook IL 60062-2329 E-mail: allan@ab-afterman.com.

AGADJANYAN, MICHAEL GRANT, education educator; b. Yerevan, Armenia, Sept. 6, 1950; s. Grant Michael Agadjanyan and Shushan Khachatrian; m. Irina Y Petrushina; 1 child, Anna Marie. PhD, Inst. Epidemiology and Microbiology, USSR Acad. Medicine, 1974—78; DSc, Inst. Epidemiology and Microbiology, USSR Acad. Medicine, Miscow, Russia, 1980—90. Vis. prof. The Wistar Inst., Phila., 1991—93, U. Pa,The Inst. Viral Preparations, Russia, 1993—2000; prof. Inst. Molecular Medicine, Huntington Beach, Calif., 2000. Contbr. articles to over 80 profl. jours. Recipient Sci. awards, NIH, CRDF, 1997—2001. Mem.: Armenian Acad. Sciences (hon.), Am. Assn. Microbiology, Immunology (assoc.). Achievements include patents in field. Office: The Inst for Molecular Medicine 15162 Triton Lane Huntington Beach CA 92649 Office Fax: 714-379-2082. E-mail: magadjanyan@immed.org.

AGAJANIAN, GILDA, pianist; b. Apr. 03; d. Oganes and Azatuhi (Tosunian) A. BA, U. So. Calif., 1973, Grad. Study, 1974-76; Diploma, Am. Coll. of Musicians, Austin, Tex., 1981, Artist Diploma, 1984. Russian educator, Calif., 1976-81; music educator Gilda Agajanian Piano Studio, La Habra Heights, Calif., 1987—; profl. classical pianist Calif., 1985—; entrepreneur, ptnr. Aggie's Restaurants, Calif., 1981-89. Mem. Westshore Musicians Club (pres. 1992-95), Music Tchrs. Nat. Assn., Calif. Assn. of Profl. Music Tchrs. (chmn. recitals 1992—), Dominant Club (sec. 1994-96), nat. Guild of Piano Tchrs., AAUW, Woman's Club of Hollywood. Avocations: Slavic langs. and lits., exotic birds, dogs, cats, horticulture. Office: Gilda Agajanian Piano Studio 2039 N Cypress St La Habra Heights CA 90631

AGALLIANOS, DENNIS DIONYSIOS, psychiatrist; b. Galati, Romania, Jan. 1, 1923; arrived in U.S., 1957; s. Dionysios Nicholas and Eleni (Craciun) Agallianos; m. Georgia-Lee Virginia Foden, June 20, 1964; 1 child, Helen Penelope. BA, Classical Gymnasium, Galati, Romania, 1941; MD, Victor Babes Med. Sch., Cluj, Romania, 1948. Diplomate Am. Bd. Psychiatry and Neurology. Pvt. practice, Romania, 1948-49; preparator urol. dept. Victor Babes Med. Sch., 1949-51; intern. urol. dept. U. Athens Med. Sch., Greece, 1951-54; asst. prof. urology Med. Sch. U. Athens, Greece, 1956-57; staff physician Polikliniki Athinon, Athens, 1954-56; intern, resident French Hosp., N.Y.C., 1957-58; resident in psychiatry Brattleboro Retreat, 1958-60; resident, staff psychiatrist Spring Grove State Hosp., Balt., 1960-64, chief of divsn., 1965-68; staff psychiatrist Brattleboro (Vt.) Retreat, 1969-76, chief of profl. svc., 1976-80, dir. older adult program, 1980-92; asst. prof. psychiatry Dartmouth Med. Sch., Hanover, 1978—95; pvt. practice, 1992—2000; locum tenens staff psychiatrist, 2000—. Adj. asst. prof. clin. psychiatry Dartmouth Med. Sch., Hanover, 1995—2000. Contbr. articles to profl. jours. Pres. Parish Coun. St. George Greek Orthodox Ch., Keene, NH, 1985—86; sustaining mem. Greek Orthodox Archdiocese N. and S.Am., 1966—; founding father United Greek Orthodox Charities, 1967. Recipient Exemplary Psychiatrist award, Nat. Alliance Mentally Ill, 1994; grantee, NIMH. Fellow: Am. Psychiat. Assn. (life Disting. life fellow); mem.: AMA, Vt. State Med. Soc., Vt. Psychiat. Assn. Home: PO Box 759 Brattleboro VT 05302-0759 E-mail: dagallia@sover.net.

AGANI, FATON HILMI, anatomist, educator; b. Gjakova, Kosovo, Oct. 4, 1956; arrived in U.S., 1992; s. Hilmi and Mukades Agani. MD, U. Prishtina, Kosovo, 1980; MS, U. Zagreb, Croatia, 1987; PhD, U. Prishtina, 1990. Cert. MD Yugoslavia. Rsch. fellow Brookhaven Nat. Lab., Upton, L.I., NY, 1985; postdoctoral rschr. Case Western Res. U., Cleve., 1992—95, Johns Hopkins U., Balt., 1995—98; instr. Case Western Res. U., 1998—99, asst. prof. anatomy, 2000—. Achievements include discovery of basic mechanisms of cell response to hypoxia, effects of insulin-like growth factor (IGF-1), nitric oxide (NO), role of mitochondria on regulation of transcription factor hypoxia-inducible factor 1 (HIF-1). Avocations: painting, running, reading. Office: Case Western Res U Euclid Ave 10900 Cleveland OH 44106 E-mail: fxa5@po.cwru.edu.

AGAPOS, MICHAEL ANGELO, economics educator; b. Cleve., Oct. 28, 1932; s. Emmanuel F. and Athena (Kapad) A.; m. Sharon Lee McMahon, May 21, 1961; children: Emmanuel M., Catherine E., John K.C. BS, Miami U., Oxford, Ohio, 1954, MBA, 1959; PhD, Case Western Res. U., 1967. Indsl. engr. Jones & Laughlin Steel Corp., Cleve., 1959-61; new product analyst N. Am. Rockwell, Columbus, Ohio, 1961-63; quality assurance specialist GM, Cleve., 1963; mgr. fin. analyst NASA/Lewis Rsch. Ctr., Cleve., 1963-66; prof. of econs. Ohio U., Athens, 1966-69; prof. of econs. and fin. U. New Orleans, 1969-84; prof., chmn. dept. econs. and fin. U. S. Ala., Mobile, 1984—. Cons. in field; bd. dirs. Great Lakes Laminates Co., South Bend, Acadian Magnolia Co., Inc., New Orleans; developer Greater New Orleans Symposium on Banking and Fin., 1982 Author: Government-Industry and Defense: Economics and Administration, 1975; contbr. articles, revs. to profl. publs. Bd. dirs. Helenic Arts Soc. Mem. Am. Econ. Assn. Fin. Mgmt. Assn., So. Econs. Assn., So. Fin. Assn., Southwestern Econs. Assn., Southwestern Fin. Assn. Home: 2113 Belmont Ct Mobile AL 36695-2906

AGAR, JOHN RUSSELL, JR., school district administrator; b. Camden, N.J., July 25, 1949; s. John R. and Evva L. (Wilhelm) A.; m. Beatrice A. B.; children: Rebekah A., Sarah L. BA with high honors, Rutgers U., 1971; MS, U. Pa., 1973, MS in Edn., 1975; EdD with distinction, Temple U., 1983; postgrad., U. Pa., 1989. Cert. secondary educator, supr., prin., dist. supt., Pa., N.J. Lectr. in chemistry U. Pa., Phila., 1974—75; sci. dept. head West Cath. Girls' High Sch., Phila., 1974—79; chemistry tchr. Moorestown Friends' Sch., NJ, 1979—82, West Deptford High Sch., Westville, NJ, 1982—84; visiting asst. prof. Temple U., Phila., 1983—88; lectr. in edn. U. Pa., Phila., 1988—90; curriculum supr. for math. and sci. Marple Newtown Sch. Dist., Newtown Sq., Pa., 1984—; mem. SEPUP staff U. Calif., Berkeley, 1991—96. Mem. tchrs. industry environment com. Pa. Chem. Industry Coun., 1992-95; mem. writing team for "Teaching Issue-Oriented Science", 1991; dir. Pa. Devel. Ctr. for "Issues, Evidence and You", 1995. Capt. emergency response team Marple Newtown Sch. Dist., 2001—. NIH fellow U. Pa., 1973-74, CEPUP/CHEM/NSF fellow U. Calif., Berkeley, 1990-91; recipient Nat. Tchr. award CEPUP, U. Calif., Berkeley, 1992. Mem.: Nat. Coun. Tchrs. of Math., Nat. Sci. Tchrs. Assn., Phi Delta Kappa, Phi Lambda Upsilon. Avocations: piano, studying the Bible, exercising, canoeing.

AGARD, EMMA ESTORNEL, psychotherapist; b. Bronx, N.Y. BA, Queens Coll.; MSW, Fordham U., 1962; cert. in Psychoanalytic Psychotherapy, Tng. Inst. for Mental Health, 1979; cert. in Child and Adolescent Psychotherapy, Postgrad. Ctr. for Mental Health, 1982. Supr. social work Foster Care Div., N.Y.C., 1968-72; asst. dir. Henry St. Settlement Urban Family Ctr., N.Y.C., 1972-74; tng. analyst, sr. supr. Tng. Inst. for Mental Health, N.Y.C., 1974—; pvt. practice psychotherapist N.Y.C., 1974—. Lectr. social work Columbia U., N.Y.C., 1977-90; adj. asst. prof. NYU, 1978-80; field instr. N.Y.C. Housing Authority, 1974-80; dist. dir., cons. Am. Consultation Ctrs., Bklyn. and N.Y.C., 1985—, dir. Park Slope br.; field instr. Sch. Social Svc. Fordham U., 1985—. Mem. Albemarle-Kenmore Neighborhood Assn., Bklyn., 1974—99. Fellow N.Y. State Soc. Clin. Social Work Psychotherapists (pres. Bklyn. chpt. 1988-91); mem. Profl. Soc. Tng. Inst. for Mental Health (sec.), Nat. Assn. Social Workers (diplomate), Acad. Cert. Social Workers, Nat. Coalition 100 Black Women, Delta Sigma Theta. Avocations: oil painting, tennis, yoga, swimming. Address: 109 E 36th St New York NY 10016-3447

AGARWAL, CHHAVI, pediatrician; b. Shahjahanpur, India, June 9, 1966; d. Dinesh P. and Pushpa Goel; m. Sanjeev Agarwal, Oct. 27, 1992; 1 child, Abhay Bansal. MBBS, Aligarh Muslim Univ., 1990, MD, 1993; MRCP, Royal Coll. of Physicians of United Kingdom, 1999. Intern J.N. Med. Coll. And Civil Hosp., Aligarh, India, 1989—90, resident in pediat. J.N. Med. Coll., Aligarh, 1990—93; pvt. practice New Delhi, 1994—96; sr. house officer Wycombe Gen. Hosp., High Wycombe, 1997—99; sr. house officer neonatology Royal Berkshire Hosp., Reading, 1999; sr. house officer, registrar Wycombe Gen Hosp., High Wycombe, 1999—2000; sr. house officer Darent Valley Hosp., Dartford, 2000—01; resident pediat. Flushing Hosp. Med. Ctr., NY, 2001—02, adminstrv. chief resident, attending pediatrician, 2003—. Fellow: Am. Acad. Pediat.; mem.: Am. Soc. Pediatric Hematology/Oncology, Royal Coll. Physicians, AMA.

AGARWAL, KISHAN C. physician; b. Agra, India, Mar. 15, 1948; came to U.S., 1976; s. Shyam Saran and Phoolwati (Bansal) A.; m. Sushma Bansal, June 29, 1974; children: Shradha, Rahul. MB, BS, Jiwaji U., India, 1969, MD in Internal Medicine, 1973; MS in Pediatrics, U. Minn., 1983; DIHom, British Inst. Homeopathy, 2001. Diplomate Am. Bd. Pediatrics, Am. Bd. Cardiology; cert. specialist in pediatrics and pediatric cardiology, Can. Resident in pediatrics Kings County Hosp./SUNY Downstate Med. Ctr., Bklyn., 1977-79; fellow in pediatric cardiology Mayo Clinic and Found., Rochester, Minn., 1979-81; fellow, vis. physician Children's Hosp. Med. Ctr./Harvard Med. Sch., Boston, 1981-82; mem. staff invasive and noninvasive pediatric cardiology Children's Hosp. of N.J., Newark, 1982-86; pvt. practice invasive, noninvasive and interventional cardiology, 1985—; asst. prof. pediatrics and pediatric cardiology U. Medicine and Dentistry N.J., Newark, 1982-86; chief dept. pediats. Muhlenberg Regional Med. Ctr., Plainfield, N.J., 1999-2001; clin. assoc. prof. pediatrics UMDNJ, Newark, 1992—, clin. prof. pediatrics Piscataway, 2002—. Pres. med./dental staff Children's Specialized Hosp., Mountainside, N.J., 1995, 96; adj. assoc. clinical prof. pediatrics Mt. Sinai Medica. Sch., N.Y., 1994— Mem. exec. bd., organizer for free health clinics Assn. Indians in Am., Piscataway, N.J., 1997. Fellow Am. Coll. Cardiology, British Inst. of Homeopathy. Avocations: reading, personal finance, gardening, music, alternative medicine. Home and Office: 450 Plainfield Rd Edison NJ 08820-2628 E-mail: pediatriccardiologist450@yahoo.com., doctorofhomeopathy@yahoo.com.

AGARWAL, RAJIV, physician; b. Allahabad, India, Mar. 12, 1963; came to U.S., 1991; s. Rajendra Kumar and Nisha Rani A.; m. Anuja Goyal, Feb. 15, 1989; 1 child, Radhika. MBBS, AIIMS, New Delhi, India, 1986, MD, 1989; DNB, Nat. Bd. Exam, New Delhi, India, 1990. Diplomate Am. Bd. Internal Medicine. Fellow in nephrology U. Tex. Southwestern Med. Ctr., Dallas, 1991-93; resident in medicine Presbyn. Hosp., Dallas, 1993-95; asst. prof. nephrology Ind. U., Indpls., 1995-97. Peer reviewer Kidney Internat., Little Rock, 1992—. Author: (books) Textbook of Cardiovascular Pharmacology and Therapeutics, 1993, Kokkos Tannen's Fluid Electrolyte Disorders, 1995, Brenner and Reclors Kidney, 1996. Grantee AHA, Ind., 1997. Mem. Am. Coll. Physician, Am. Soc. Nephrology. Hindu. Avocation: travel. Office: VAMC 1481 W 10th St # 111N Indianapolis IN 46202-2803

AGARWAL, RAMESH KUMAR, aeronautical scientist, researcher, educator; b. Mainpuri, India, Jan. 4, 1947; came to U.S., 1968; s. Radhakishan and Parkashvati (Goel) A.; m. Sugita Goel, Oct. 26, 1976; children: Vivek, Gautam. BS, U. Allahabad, 1965; BTech, Indian Inst. Tech., 1968; MS, U. Minn., 1969; PhD, Stanford U., 1975. Rsch. assoc. NASA Ames Rsch. Ctr., Moffett Field, Calif., 1976-78; McDonnell Douglas fellow, program dir. McDonnell Douglas Aerospace, St. Louis, 1978-94; Bloomfield disting. prof., chair aerospace engring. Wichita (Kans.) State U., 1994-96, Bloomfield disting prof., exec. dir. Nat. Inst. Aviatn Rsch., 1997—2001; William Palm prof. engring., dir. Aerospace Rsch. and Edn. Ctr. Washington U., St. Louis, 2001—. Affiliate prof. Washington U., St. Louis, 1986-95. Contbr. more than 200 articles to profl. jours. Fellow AIAA, AAAS, ASME, SME, Soc. Automotive Engring., Royal Aero. Soc., IEEE, Am. Phys. Soc.; mem. Am. Helicopter Soc., Tau Beta Pi, Sigma Gamma Tau, Pi Tau Sigma. Office: Washington U Dept Mech Engring Saint Louis MO 63130 E-mail: rka@me.wustl.edu.

AGARWAL, SANJAY KUMAR, physician; b. Kanpur, India, Nov. 3, 1962; s. Gopal Chandra and Vasantika Agarwal; m. Suzanne Gourley, Mar. 3, 1996; children: Ravi Kumar, Asha Shivani. MBBS, St. George's Hosp. Med. Sch., 1981—86. Medical Diploma U. of London, 1986. Acting dir. of reproductive medicine Cedars-Sinai Med. Ctr., Los Angeles, 1995—; asst. prof. of ob/gyn UCLA Sch. of Medicine, Los Angeles, 1995, assoc. prof. of ob/gyn, 2002—. Dir. of ctr. for reproductive medicine Cedars-Sinai Med. Ctr., Los Angeles, 2002—. Rsch. grant, Am. Soc. for Reproductive Medicine, 1996—98. Fellow: Am. Coll. of Obstetricians and Gynecologists. Achievements include patents pending for novel therapy for endometriosis. Office: Cedars-Sinai Medical Center 8700 Beverly Blvd Los Angeles CA 90048 Office Fax: 310-423-0140.

AGARWAL, SUMAN KUMAR, editor; b. Bolpur, India, Jan. 21, 1945; came to U.S., 1980; s. Hari Prasad and Rukmini (Modi) A.; children: Tripti, Samantha Rani. BSc with honors, Visva-Bharati, Santiniketan, India, 1966; MSc, Delhi U., India, 1971; PhD, U. Paris, 1975, DSc, 1979. Rsch. scholar Atomic Energy Commn. of France, Saclay, 1976-80; rsch. assoc. Purdue U., West Lafayette, Ind., 1980-82; sr. sci. info. analyst Chem. Abstracts Svc., Columbus, Ohio, 1982—; pres. Commodities Internat. Ltd. Inc., Columbus, Ohio, 1992—2002. Contbr. articles to profl. jours. Vol. Columbus Schs., 1984-85, Ohio State U. TV, Columbus, 1986-88. Scholar Govt. of France, 1973-76. Mem. Am. Chem. Soc. Avocations: bridge, photography, tennis. E-mail: suman_agarwal33@yahoo.com.

AGARWAL, YOGESH KUMAR, cardiologist, internist; b. New Delhi, India, Oct. 7, 1972; MBBS, Maulana Azad Med. Coll., 1990—95. Diplomate Am. Bd. of Internal Medicine, 1999. Ho. staff physician cardiology Westchester Med. Ctr., Valhalla, NY, 1996—. Recipient R. Vishwanathan award for Medicine, U. of Delhi, 1996. Office: Westchester Med Ctr 95 Grasslands Rd Valhalla NY 10595 E-mail: agarwaly@wcmc.com.

AGASAR, RONALD JOSEPH, mortgage banker; b. Phila., Nov. 27, 1946; s. Francis Robert and Penny Dolores (Alahverde) A.; m. Eleanor Joan Smith, Aug. 30, 1969 (div. Jan. 1982); m. Elizabeth Katherine Muhr, Apr. 20, 1989. BS, La Salle Coll., Phila., 1970; MBA in Mortgage Banking, Northwestern U., 1978. Regional v.p. Colonial Mortgage Svc. Co., Elkins Park, Pa., 1976-80, City Fed. Mortgage Corp., Cherry Hill, N.J., 1980 83; sr. v.p. Chase Manhattan Mortgage Corp., Cherry Hill, 1983-96; N.E. regional sr. v.p. CTX Mortgage Co., Cherry Hill, 1996—2002; with Homestar Mortgage Svcs., LLC, Brigantine, NH, 2002—. Mem. Mortgage Bankers Assn. N.J. (bd. govs. 1996—), Phila. Mortgage Bankers Assn. (bd. govs. 2002—), Phila. Young Mortgage Bankers Assn. (chmn. 1983-84, vice-chmn. wholesale lending com. 1992). Republican. Roman Catholic. Avocations: antique cars, coin collecting, racquetball, power boating. Office: CTX Mortgage Co 51 Haddonfield Rd Ste 338 Cherry Hill NJ 08002-4801

AGASSI, ANDRE KIRK, professional tennis player; b. Las Vegas, Nev., Apr. 29, 1970; s. Mike and Elizabeth Agassi; m. Brooke Shields, April 19, 1997 (div. 1999), m. Steffi Graf, Oct. 22, 2001; 1 child Jaden Gil. Mem. U.S. Davis Cup team, 1988—. Owner found. for children. Winner tournaments including Itaparica, 1987, Memphis, 1988, Charleston, 1988, Forest Hills, 1988, Stuttgart, 1988, Stratton Mountain, 1988, Livingston, 1988, Orlando, 1989, San Francisco, 1990, Key Biscayne, 1990, Washington, 1990, ATP Tour World Championship-Frankfurt, 1990, Orlando, 1991, Washington, 1991; Wimbledon champion, 1992, U.S. Open champion, 1994, Australian Open champion, 1995; gold medal U.S. Olympics, 1996; winner French Open/Grand Slam, 1999, U.S. Open, 1999, Australian Open, 2000, Australian Grand Slam, 2000, 2001, Australian Grand Slam, 2003 oldest player to be ranked no. 1 in the ATP entry system. Address: International Mgmt Group 1 Erieview Plz Ste 1300 Cleveland OH 44114-1715 Office: ATP Tour Internat 201 ATP Tour Blvd Ponte Vedra Beach FL 32082

AGATA, BURTON C. law educator, lawyer; b. N.Y.C., Feb. 7, 1928; s. Max and Augusta (Steger) A.; m. Dale S. Granirer, Dec. 24, 1955; children: Seth Hugh, Abby Fran. AB, U. Mich., 1947, JD, 1950; LLM in Trade Regulation, NYU, 1951. Bar: N.Y. 1951. Counsel div. N.Y. State Banking Dept., 1955-59; ptnr. firm Burstein & Agata, Mineola and N.Y.C., 1959-61; prof. Mont. U., 1961-62, N.Mex. U., 1962-63, Houston U., 1963-69; counsel Nat. Commn. on Reform Fed. Criminal Laws, 1968-70; prof. law Hofstra U., 1970-2001, Max Schmertz disting. prof. law, 1982-2001, disting. prof. emeritus, 2001—, interim dean, 1989; mem. faculty Nat. Inst. Trial Advocacy, 1977-81; dir. N.E. Regional Program, 1981-84. Spl. counsel N.Y. City Charter Revision Commn., 1987-89, N.Y. State Senate Minority, 1982-87; cons. Fed. Jud. Center, 1972, Inst. Jud. Adminstrn., 1973, HEW, 1971, White House Spl. Action Office Drug Abuse Prevention, 1973, N.Y. State Temp. Com. on Constnl. Revision, 1993-95; Chmn. N.Y. State Task Force, Standards and Go als for Prosecution and Def., 1977-79; cons. Adv. Com. on Qualifications of Counsel, 2d Ct., 1977; bd. dirs. Nassau Economic Opportunity Commn., 1972-73; reporter-cons. action unit on criminal justice system N.Y. State Bar Assn., 1986-90. Contbr. articles to law jours. With JAGC U.S. Army, 1951-54. Food Law fellow NYU, 1951, fellow U. Wis., 1963. Fellow Am. Bar Found. (life); mem. Am. Law Inst. (life), ABA (state antitrust law commn. 1980-01, vice chair com. on professionalism sr. lawyers divsn. 1996-2000), N.Y. State Bar Assn. (exec. com. criminal justice sect., chmn. com. rev. of criminal law 1987—, spl. com. on pre-sentence reports 1989-2001, Donnelly Act com. 1990-2001), Assn. of Bar of City of N.Y. (criminal cts. com. 1970-73, penology com. 1973-76, criminal justice coun. 1983-85, antitrust com. 1986-89), Fed. Jud. Coun., Assn. Am. Law Schs. (chmn. criminal law sect. 1973) Office: 209 Mt Merino Rd Hudson NY 12534 E-mail: vze2vnja@verizon.net.

AGBETSIAFA, DOUGLAS KOFI, financial and management consultant; b. Anloga, Volta, Ghana; came to the U.S., 1976; s. Benjamin K. Agbetsiafa and Rebecca Afafa Agbakpe; m. Patricia Ann Williams. BS, U. Ghana, 1971, MS, 1975; MA, Western Ontario, 1976; PhD, U. Notre Dame, 1980. Secondary sch. tchr. Mininstry Edn., Accra, Ghana, 1966-68; instr. U. Western Ontario, London, 1973-75, U. Notre Dame, 1976-80; prof. econs., acad. senate pres., spl. asst. to chancellor Ind. U., South Bend. Contbr. articles to profl. jours. Sec.-treas. United Way St. Joe County, bd. dirs., 1987—; trustee Urban League, South Bend, 1988; bd. dirs., trustee Urban League of South Bend and St. Joseph's County, 1996—. Mem. Math. Assn. Am., Am. Math. Soc., Am. Econ. Assn. Am. Statis Assn., Internat. Bus. Assn., Western Econ. Internat., Midwest Econ. Assn., Midsouth Acad. Econs. and Fin. (bd. dirs.), Ind. Acad. Soc. Sci., Bus. Assn. Latin Am. Studies, Assn. for Global Bus. (program dir. 1993-94, v.p. program dir. 1995—), South Bend-Mishawaka C. of C. (bd. dirs., mem. minority bus. devel. task force), U. Notre Dame Alumni Assn. Avocations: raquetball, reading poetry, gardening, travel. Home: 224 N Sunnyside Ave South Bend IN 46617-3332 Office: Ind U 1700 Mishawaka Ave South Bend IN 46615-1400

AGEE, BOB R. academic administrator, educator, minister; b. Brownsville, Tenn., Sept. 30, 1938; s. Edwin L. and Katie L. (Stewart) A.; m. Nelle Rose; children— Nancy Denise, Robyn Janelle BA, Union U., Tenn., 1960; M.Div., So. Bapt. Theol. Sem., 1964, D.Min., 1974; PhD, Vanderbilt U., 1986. Ordained to ministry Baptist Ch. Pastor Shively Heights Bapt. Ch., Louisville, 1964-70; pastor Ardmore Bapt. Ch., Memphis, 1970-75; dean, v.p. religious affairs Union U., Jackson, Tenn., 1975-82; pres. Okla. Bapt. U., Shawnee, 1982-98, pres. emeritus, 1998—. Mem. edn. commn. So. Bapt. Conv., 1985-93, chmn., 1987-90; bd. dirs. Co-op Svcs. Internat. Edn. Consortium, chmn., 1988-90; cons. evaluator North Ctrl. Assn. Colls. and Univs., 1987—; bd. dirs. Nat. Assn. Ind. Colls. and Univs., 1986-90, 93—. Author Bibl. study materials and articles Mem. human relations com. Memphis Bd. Edn., 1972-74; mem. Memphis Mayor's Crime Commn., 1973-75; mem. Okla. Ind. Coll. Found., 1982-98, chmn., 1985-87. Inducted into Okla. Higher Edn. Hall of Fame, 1999. Mem. Soc. Coll. and Univ. Planning, Shawnee C. of C. (bd. dirs. 1983-98), So. Bapt. Theol. Sem. Alumni Assn. (nat. pres. 1985-86), AAUP, Am. Assn. Univ. Adminstrs., Nat. Assn. Ind. Colls. and Univs. (bd. dirs. 1988-97), Coun. for Christian Colls. and Univs. (bd. dirs. 1997-2003), Assn. So. Bapt. Colls. and Schs. (exec. dir. 1998—, exec. dir. consortium global edn. 1998-2002). Republican. Avocations: racquetball, golf, fishing, writing. Office: PO Box 11655 Jackson TN 38308-0127

AGEE, EVE, anthropologist; b. Fayetteville, Ark., Sept. 1, 1967; d. Jacob Claude and Martha Jeanne Agee; m. Scott Andrew Lozen, Oct. 13, 2001. BA, Coll. William and Mary, 1990; MA, U. Va., 1994, PhD, 1999. Women's health rschr. U. Benin, Lome, Togo, 1990—91; English tchr. Am. Cultural Ctr./U.S. Embassy, Lome, Togo, 1991; instr. U. Va., Charlottesville, 1993, dir. health care rsch., 1993—94, mem. faculty, 1998—99; White House appointee Clinton Adminstrn., Washington, 1999—2001; pres. Agee Cons., Washington, 2001—. Cons. Cmty. Preservation and Devel. Corp., Washington, 1999—2001; dir. 1st Nat. Early Childhood Summit, U.S. Dept. Edn., Washington, 2001. Author: Menopause: Path to Woman's Empowerment, 2002; contbr. articles to profl. jours. Group organizer Habitat for Humanity, Va., 1999; vol. advisor and activist Dem. Nat. Com., 1996, 2000. Grantee NSF, 1993. Mem.: Am. Anthropology Assn. Avocations: yoga, hiking, sculpting, poetry, art. Office: Agee Cons 1234 19th St NW Ste 700 Washington DC 20036

AGEE, WARREN KENDALL, journalism educator; b. Sherman, Tex., Oct. 23, 1916; s. Frederic M. and Minnie E. (Logsdon) A.; m. Edda Robbins, June 1, 1941; children: Kim Kendall, Robyn Kendall Ansley. BA cum laude, Tex. Christian U., 1937; MA, U. Minn., 1949, PhD, 1955. Mem. editorial staff Ft. Worth Star-Telegram, 1937-48; instr. journalism Tex. Christian U., 1948-50, asst. prof., 1950-55, asso. prof., 1955-57, prof., 1957-58, chmn. dept., 1950-58, faculty adviser student publs., 1949-58; prof. journalism, dean sch. journalism W.Va U., 1958-60; mem. ednl. adv. com. WJPB-TV, Fairmont and Weston, W.Va., 1959-60; nat. exec. officer Soc. Profl. Journalists, Sigma Delta Chi, 1960-62; prof. journalism, dean Evening Coll., Tex. Christian U., Ft. Worth, 1962-65; dean William Allen White Sch. Journalism, U. Kans., Lawrence, 1965-69, Henry W. Grady Coll. Journalism and Mass Communication U. Ga., 1969-75, prof. journalism, 1975-87, dean and prof. emeritus, 1987—; vis. scholar U. Tex., fall 1975; copy editor Atlanta Constn., summer 1977. Combat corr. USCG Res., 1941-44; pub. info. specialist USCG Res. Hdqrs., 1944-45; mem. adv. screening com. journalism, com. internat. exchange of persons Conf. Bd. Assn. Rsch. Couns., Washington, 1958-62; mem. Am. Coun. Edn. for Journalism and Mass Communication, 1958-60, 65-67, mem. accrediting com.,

1969-76, vice chmn., 1973-74, chmn., 1974-76, chmn. appeals bd., 1977, 79, 81, 83; mng. dir. William Allen White Found., 1965-69, trustee, 1970—; mng. dir. George Foster Peabody Radio and TV awards, 1969-75, Sigma Delta Chi Nat. Journalism Awards, 1960-62; assoc. James M. Cox Jr. Ctr. Internat. Mass Comm. Tng. and Research, U. Ga., 1985—. Author: (with Edwin Emery and Phillip H. Ault) Introduction to Mass Communications, 1960, 12th rev. edit., 1997, Reporting and Writing the News, 1983, (with Dennis L. Wilcox, Ault) Public Relations: Strategies and Tactics, 1986, 8th edit., 2003, (with Nelson Traquina) O Quarto Poder Frustrado: Os Meios de Comunicacão Social No Portugal Pós-Revolucionário, 1988; also articles.; editor: The Press and the Public Interest, 1968, Mass Media In A Free Society, 1969, (with Emery and Ault) Perspectives on Mass Communications, 1982, Maincurrents in Mass Communications, 1986, rev. edit., 1989; assoc. editor, bus. mgr.: The Quill, 1960-62; press rev. columnist, contbg. editor, 1977-82; adv. editl. bd. Journalism Quar, 1955-60. Mem. Athens (Ga.) Internat. Rels. Cmty. Coun., pres., 1980-82; pres. Friends of Mus. Art U. Ga., 1974-75; mem. Howard Blakeslee Media Awards judging com. Am. Heart Assn., 1976-94, chmn. judging com., 1980-94. Recipient Journalism award Fort Worth Press, 1936; Outstanding News Writing award Ft. Worth Profl. chpt. Sigma Delta Chi, 1946; Carl Towley award Journalism Edn. Assn., 1969; Outstanding Achievement award U. Minn., 1973; Wells Meml. key Sigma Delta Chi, 1978, Disting. Teaching award Soc. Profl. Journalists, 1987; Fulbright grantee to Portugal, 1982, 85. Mem.: Soc. Profl. Journalists, Southwestern Journalism Congress (sec. 1957—58), Am. Studies Assn., Am. Soc. Journalism Sch. Adminstrs. (pres. 1956), Assn. Edn. in Journalism and Mass Comm. (pres. 1958, Disting. Leadership award 2001), Gridiron Club (Ft. Worth), Rotary, Phi Beta Delta, Alpha Sigma Lambda, Phi Kappa Sigma, Alpha Chi, Kappa Tau Alpha (50 yr. journalism edn. svc. award 1987), Sigma Delta Chi (pres. Fort Worth profl. chpt. 1954—55, sec. Tex. 1957—58, nat. v.p. campus chpt. affairs 1966—69, leader coun. 1982—, v.p. N.E. Ga. profl. chpt. 1978—79, pres. 1979—80). Presbyterian. Home and Office: 130 Highland Dr Athens GA 30606-3212 *One abiding goal has been to spread and deepen public understanding of the fundamentals of our democratic society as embodied in the Bill of Rights in general and the First Amendment in particular. That public understanding has been seriously eroded in recent decades. Only through a renewed, vastly broadened national effort to teach these principles in our schools and other social institutions, and through the media of mass communication, will this erosion be halted and our nation, as we have known it, survive.*

AGEMA, GERALD WALTON, publishing executive; b. Rockford, Ill., Sept. 9, 1947; s. Samuel W. and Lillian (Walton) A.; m. Marcia L. Vander Meer, June 14, 1969; children: Jerry, Matt and Mike (twins). BS in Acctg., No. Ill. U., 1970; MBA, U. Chgo., 1984. CPA, Ill. Staff/sr. auditor Price Waterhouse, Chgo., 1971—76, audit mgr., 1976—79, Tribune Co., 1979—80, asst. contr., 1980—85; dir., CFO Tribune Broadcasting Co., 1985—86, v.p., CFO, 1986—88, v.p. ops., CFO, 1988—97, v.p. adminstrn., CFO, 1997—2001, Tribune Pub. Co., 2001—. Bd. dirs. Mus. of Broadcast Comms., Chgo., 1986—, treas., 1986-97. Mem. AICPA, Ill. Soc. CPAs, Internat. Newspapers Fin. Exec. Assn. Avocations: reading, boating, fishing, travel. Office: Tribune Pub Co 435 N Michigan Ave Ste 1900 Chicago IL 60611-4066

AGER, DAVID SCOTT, landscape architect; b. Poughkeepsie, N.Y., Dec. 21, 1957; s. Donald Ralph and Martha Frances (Laidlaw) A.; m. Patricia Ann Reynolds, Sept. 12, 1981; children: Steven David, Gina Patricia. B.Landscape Arch., La. State U., 1980. Registered landscape architect; cert. planner. Landscape designer Hayward & Pakan Assocs., Poughkeepsie, N.Y., 1980-81; civil designer Burns & Roe Inc., Oradell, N.J., 1981-83; land design specialist Frederick County Planning Commn., Frederick, Md., 1983-84; sr. planner Dewberry & Davis, Gaithersburg, Md., 1984-86; sr. v.p. Rodgers Consulting, Gaithersburg, Mo., 1986—. Adj. prof. continuing edn. divsn. Frederick C.C. Mem. Frederick County Land Use Coun., 1989, Frederick County Affordable Housing Commn. Recipient Smart Growth award Gov. Glendening, 1996, 97. Mem. Am. Soc. Landscape Architects (Md. Chpt. Honor award 1991), Am. Planning Assn., Urban Land Inst., Nat. Assn. Homebuilders, Smart Growth Alliance. Republican. Episcopalian. Home: 6106 Trotter Ridge Ct Columbia MD 21044-4920 E-mail: dager@rodgers.com.

AGERBEK, SVEN, mechanical engineer; b. Soerabaya, Dutch Indies, Aug. 2, 1926; came to U.S., 1958, naturalized, 1964; s. Niels Magnus and Else Heidam (Nielsen) Agerbek-Poulsen; m. Helen Hadsbjerg Gerup, May 30, 1963; 1 child, Jesper. MSME, Tech. U., Denmark, 1952; LLB, LaSalle Ext. U., 1967; postgrad., UCLA, 1969. Registered profl. engr., Calif., Ohio, Fla. With Danish Refrigeration Rsch. Inst., Copenhagen, 1952; engr. B.P. Oil Co., Copenhagen, 1952-54; refrigeration insp. J. Lauritzen, Copenhagen, 1954-56; engr. Danish-Am. Gulf Oil Co., Copenhagen, 1956-58; instr. Ohio U., Athens, 1958-60; asst. prof. Calif. State Poly. U., San Luis Obispo, 1960-62; prin. engr. dept. environ. Ralph M. Parsons Co., L.A., 1962-73; engring. supr. Bechtel Power Co., Norwalk, Calif., 1973-85; pres., owner Woodcraft Cabinets, Inc., Rancho Cordova, Calif., 1985-90; owner Acrebrook Cons., Fair Oaks, Calif., 1990—; exec. v.p. U.S.E., Inc., Incline Village, Nev., 1994—. Past mem. Luth. Ch. coun., pres. Luth. Sch. bd. With Danish underground movement, WWII. Mem. ASHRAE (mem. tech. com., author Guide on Air Conditioning of Nuclear Power Plants), Danish Engring. Soc. Home and Office: Acrebrook Consulting 5201 Vista Del Oro Way Fair Oaks CA 95628-4148 E-mail: acrebrook@softcom.net.

AGERSBORG, HELMER PARELI K. pharmaceutical company executive, researcher; b. Decatur, Ill., Dec. 2, 1928; s. Helmer Pareli and Jennie E. (Dunbar) A.; m. Marcella Felchlia; children—Eric, Kristin, Karen BA, Harvard U., Cambridge, 1949; BS, So. Ill. U., Carbondale, 1953; PhD, U. Tenn., Memphis, 1957. Asst. physiology U. Tenn., Memphis, 1954-57, instr. physiology, 1957-58; clin. physiologist Wyeth Labs., Phila., 1958-61, mgr. toxicology, 1961-69, assoc. dir. research, 1969-76, v.p. research and devel., 1976-85, sr. v.p. research and devel., 1985-87; pres. Wyeth Ayerst Research, 1987-91; CEO, pres. Fieldcastle, Inc., Wayne, Pa., 1991—, Afferon Corp., 1991—, Maret Corp., 1994-98. Mem. Am. Soc. Pharmacology and Exptl. Therapy, Am. Physiol. Soc., Am. Soc. Zoology, Soc. Toxicology Home: 336 Saint Andrews Pl Blue Bell PA 19422-1290 Office: Fieldcastle Inc 200 Eagle Rd Wayne PA 19087-3115 E-mail: afferonha@aol.com.

AGERWALA, TILAK KRISHNA MAHESH, computer company executive; b. New Delhi, Mar. 8, 1950; came to U.S. 1971; s. Krishna Mahesh and Manorama (Vaish) A.; m. Geeta Heble, Jan. 6, 1974; children: Arjun Mahesh, Suneel Mahesh. B.Tech., Indian Inst. of Tech., Kanpur, India, 1971; PhD, The Johns Hopkins U., Balt., 1975. Asst. prof. U. Tex., Austin, 1975-79; rsch. staff mem. IBM Watson Rsch. Ctr., Yorktown Heights, N.Y., 1979-80, various mgmt. positions, 1980-85, dir. symbolic and numeric processing, 1985-87; mem. corp. tech. com. IBM Corp. Hdqrs., Armonk, N.Y., 1987-89; dir. future systems tech., advanced workstation div. IBM Corp., Austin, Tex., 1989-91, dir. tech., personal systems, 1991-92, dir. parallel architechture and systems design, power parallel systems Poughkeepsie, N.Y., 1992-97, dir. server arch. and sys. strategy, server devel., 1997-98, v.p. UNIX mktg. and product mgmt. Somers, N.Y., 1998-2000, v.p. tech. alliances, 2001—; v.p. sys. IBM Watson Rsch. Ctr., Yorktown Heights, 2002—. Mem. adv. com. Ctr. for Supercomputer Applications, U. Ill., Urbana-Champaign, 1985-88; mem. vis. com. dept. elec. engring. U. Tex., Austin, 1987-89, dept. of computer scis., 1989-93; mem. sci. coun. U. Space Rsch. Assn., Washington, 1988-90; mem. computer scis. adv. bd. Johns Hopkins U., 1999—, mem. adv. bd., Computing Rsch. Int., Purdue U., 2002-. Contbr. numerous articles to profl.jours., chpts. to books, IBM rsch. reports. Recipient best presentation award Internat. Conf. on Parallel Processing, 1978. Fellow IEEE (chmn. fellows com. 1988-89, disting. visitor, chmn. tech. com. on computer architecture, cert. appreciation 1976, 82, W. Wallace McDowell award 1998); mem. Assn. for Computing Machinery (Samuel Alexander award 1974). Office: IBM TJ Watson Rsch Ctr 1101 Kitchawan Rd Rte 134 Yorktown Heights NY 10598

AGGARWAL, KUL, internist, cardiologist, educator; b. Nairobi, Kenya, Jan. 2, 1952; s. Labhu Ram and Kaushalya Devi (Gupta) A.; m. Archana Goel, July 26, 1979; children: Ruchi, Neha. MB, BS, Panjab U., Amritsar, India, 1975, MD, 1978. Diplomate in internal medicine, cardiovasc. disease, interventional cardiology and echocardiograhy Am. Bd. Internal Medicine. Intern Med. Coll. and Hosp., Amritsar, 1974-75; resident in internal medicine Willingdon Hosp., New Delhi, 1981-84, N.Y. Med. Coll.-Lincoln Hosp., 1990-92, Natl Health Svc., London, 1986-89; fellow in cardiology U. Mo. Sch. Medicine, Columbia, 1992-95, mem. staff, 1995—, asst. prof. internal medicine, 1995—. Staff cardiologist Harry S. Truman Meml. VA Hosp., Columbia. Fellow ACP; mem. Am. Coll. Cardiology, Royal Coll. Physicians (London), Royal Coll. Physicians (Dublin, Ireland). Office: U Mo Health Scis Ctr 1E-66 Divsn Cardiology One Hospital Dr Columbia MO 65212 E-mail: aggarwalk@health.missouri.edu.

AGGARWAL, LALIT K. company executive, educator; b. New Delhi, Oct. 10, 1944; arrived in U.S., 1964; s. Pritam Lal and Krishna Devi Aggarwal; m. Alice Beatriz Pappalardo, Feb. 1, 1974; children: Vashali Maria, Lakshmi Christina. Faculty Architecture, Chandigarh Coll. Arch., 1964; BArch, U. Wash., 1966, M in Urban Planning, 1970; MArch, Rensselaer Poly. Inst., 1968; PhD, U. Pa., Phila., 1976, MA, 1972. Founder, chmn. Imagestatistics, Inc., Phila., 1998—, Imagem, Inc., Phila., 1998—; assoc. prof. Drexel U., Phila., prof.; ret., 2002. Contbr. articles to profl. jours. Grantee, Ben Franklin Tech. Ctr. Southeastern Pa., 1999. Fellow: Ops. Rsch. Soc. Am.; mem.: Peace Sci. Soc. Internat., Am. Statis. Assn. Achievements include patents for Automated Gem Grading; Phonograph Record Insulator; patents pending for Multivariate Analysis of Gemstones; first to Imagestatistics - A General Method Of Data Analysis; research in Measurement of Light.

AGGERGAARD, STEVEN PAUL, journalist, educator, musician; b. LeSueur, Minn., May 1, 1967; m. Lana Rosario, Aug. 8, 1998 BA, Augsburg Coll., Mpls., 1989; MSJ, Northwestern U., 1992; postgrad., William Mitchell Coll. of Law, 2000—. Newspaper reporter Ft. Dodge (Iowa) Messenger, 1989-90, weekend news editor, 1990-91; newspaper reporter-intern Chgo. Tribune, 1992; newspaper designer, copy editor Duluth (Minn.) News-Tribune, 1992-96, newspaper city editor, 1996-98; news editor St. Paul Pioneer Press, 1998—; summer assoc. Rider Bennett Law Firm, 2003. Freelance editor/writer, 1989—; sect. leader Arrowhead Chorale, Duluth, 1997-98, tenor vocalist, 1993—; guest journalism lectr. various high schs. and colls., 1994—; classical music reviewer Duluth News-Tribune, 1992-98; journalism instr. U. Wis., River Falls, 1999. Editor-in-chief: William Mitchell Law Rev., 2003—. Classrm. vol. Jr. Achievement, Duluth, 1995-98. Avocations: running, swimming, American literature, classical music, travel. Home: 1064 Dayton Ave Saint Paul MN 55104-6503 Office: St Paul Pioneer Press 345 Cedar St Saint Paul MN 55101-1057 E-mail: saggergaard@pioneerpress.com.

AGGOUR, MOHAMED SHERIF, civil engineer, educator; b. Cairo, July 14, 1943; came to U.S., 1968, naturalized, 1976; s. Mohamed Shafik and Hekmet Ibrahim (El-Defrawi) A.; m. Carol Christine Overn, Dec. 28, 1968; children: Lora, Kareem. BSCE with honors, Cairo U., 1964, MS, 1966; PhD, U. Wash., 1972. Registered profl. engr., Wash., Ind., Md. Engr. Shannon & Wilson, Seattle, 1972-75; project engr. ATEC Assocs., Indpls., 1975-76; asst. prof. civil engring. U. Md., College Park, 1977-79, assoc. prof., 1979-87, prof., 1987—. Cons. in field. Contbr. articles to profl. jours. Recipient cert. of Achievement in multi-media protection design U.S. Dept. Def., 1975. Fellow ASCE; mem. ASTM, NSPE, Am. Soc. for Engring. Edn., Earthquake Engring. Rsch. Inst., Internat. Soc. Soil Mechanics and Found. Engring., Sigma Xi, Phi Kappa Phi, Tau Beta Pi. Moslem. Home: 13464 Bregman Rd Silver Spring MD 20904-1240 Office: Univ Md Dept Civil Engring College Park MD 20742-0001 E-mail: msaggour@eng.umd.edu.

AGGREY, ORISON RUDOLPH, former ambassador, university administrator; b. Salisbury, N.C., July 24, 1926; s. J.E. Kwegyir and Rose Rudolph (Douglass) A.; m. Francoise Fratacci, Nov. 5, 1966; 1 dau., Roxane Rose. BS, Hampton Inst., 1946; MS, Syracuse U., 1948; fellow Ctr. for Internat. Affairs, Harvard U., 1964-65; LLD, Livingstone Coll., 1977. Publicity asst. United Negro Coll. Fund, 1947, 50; reporter Cleve. Call and Post, 1948-49; corr. Chgo. Defender, 1949; publicity dir. Bennett Coll., 1950; info. officer, vice consul Am. Consulate Gen., Lagos, Nigeria, 1951-53; asst. dir. USIS, Lille, France, 1953-54; asst. cultural affairs officer Am. embassy, Paris, 1954-57; dir. USIS Cultural Ctr., Paris, 1957-60; dep. pub. affairs adviser for Africa Dept. State, 1961-64; acting chief French br. Voice of Am., 1965; 1st sec., dep. pub. affairs officer Am. embassy, Kinshasa, Democratic Republic of Congo, 1966-68; program mgr. Motion Picture and TV Service, USIA, 1968-70; dir. West African affairs Dept. State, 1970-73; ambassador to The Gambia and Senegal, 1973-77; ambassador to Romania, 1977-81; career min. info., 1979; career min., 1981; Dept. State fgn. affairs sr. fellow, rsch. prof. diplomacy Georgetown U., Washington, 1981-83; spl. asst. Office Analysis Soviet Union and Eastern Europe Dept. State, Washington, 1983-84; internat. rels. cons., 1984-87, 94—; dir. Patricia Roberts Harris pub. affairs program Howard U., 1987-90; acting dir. Howard U. Press, 1988-90, dir., 1990-94. Mem. adv. coun. Joint Ctr. for Polit. and Econ. Studies. Decorated grand officer Senegalese Nat. Order of Lion, 1977; recipient Meritorious Svc. award USIA, 1955, Superior Svc. award, 1960; Hampton Inst. Alumni award, 1961, Meritorious Svc. award Pres. of U.S., 1984, Chancellor's medal Syracuse U., 1984, Meritorious Achievement award Fla. A&M U., 1985, Disting. Achievement award Dillard U., 1987. Mem. Soc. Prodigal Sons State of N.C., Acad. Jazz Paris (hon.), Assn. Black Am. Ambassadors, Assn. Diplomatic Study and Tng. (bd. dirs.), Am. Acad. Diplomacy (former trustee Phelps Stokes Fund, exec. com. Atlantic Coun.), Fed. City Club, Alpha Phi Alpha, Sigma Delta Chi, Alpha Kappa Mu, Sigma Pi Phi. Home: Apt 1406 320 Twenty-Third St S Arlington VA 22202

AGHA, ZIA, physician, researcher; b. Karachi, Pakistan, Mar. 31, 1968; arrived in US, 1993; m. Azmaira Hamid Maker, Aug. 13, 2001. MB BS, Aga Khan U., 1992; MS, Med. Coll. Wis., 1998. Diplomate Am. Bd. Internal Medicine. Intern dept. medicine L.I. Coll. Hosp., Bklyn., 1993—94; resident dept. medicine Med. Coll. Wis., Milw., 1994—96, fellow in gen. internal medicine, 1996—98, instr. dept. medicine, 1996—99, asst. prof., dir. internal medicine ambulatory immersion rotation, 1999—. Contbr. articles to profl. jours. Grantee Merit Rev. Rsch., VA Health Svcs. R&D, 2002—. Mem.: Am. Telemedicine Assn., Soc. Med. Decision Making, Soc. Gen. Internal Medicine. Office: Med Coll Wis HRC #H2745 POBox 26509 8701 Watertown Plank Rd Milwaukee WI 53226-0509

AGHABEGIAN, DIANA E. BORTNOWSKY, English language educator, publisher; b. Santa Monica, Calif., Apr. 25, 1963; d. Michael and Lillian Kristine (Panka) Bortnowsky; m. Armond Aghabegian, Mar. 7, 1986; children: Alex Michael, Nicole Eugenia. BA in English Lit., UCLA, 1984; MA in English Lit., Calif. State U., Carson, 1988. Cert. lifetime tchg. credential, Calif. Instr. English, West Los Angeles Coll., Culver City, Calif., 1989-93, El Camino Coll., Torrance, 1990-91, Santa Monica Coll., 1990—. Pub. Blue Rabbit Press, West Hills, Calif., 1997—. Editor Full Moon lit. mag., 1997-2000; contbr. poetry to lit. mags. Mem. Santa Monica Coll. Concert Chorale. Mem. MLA, L.A. Libr. Assn., UCLA Alumni Assn. Democrat. Roman Catholic. Avocations: choral singing, writing poetry, cycling. Office: Santa Monica Coll 1900 Pico Blvd Santa Monica CA 90405-1628 E-mail: aghabegian_diana@smc.edu.

AGHAJANIAN, GEORGE KEVORK, medical educator; b. Beirut, Apr. 14, 1932; Am. parents; s. Ghevont M. and Araxi (Movsessian) A.; m. Anne E. Hammond, Jan. 10, 1959; children: Michael, Andrew, Carol, Laura. AB, Cornell U., 1954; MD, Yale U., 1958. Asst. prof. psychiatry Sch. of Medicine Yale U., New Haven, 1965-68, assoc. prof. psychiatry Sch. of Medicine, 1968-70, assoc. prof. psychiatry and pharmacology Sch. of Medicine, 1970-74, prof. psychiatry and pharmacology Sch. of Medicine, 1974—, founds. fund prof. Sch. of Medicine, 1985. Contbr. more than 300 articles to profl. jours. Capt. U.S. Army, 1963-65. Recipient Hoffheimer prize Am. Psychiat. Assn., 1981, Scheele medal Swedish Acad. Pharmacy, 1981, Merit award NIH, 1990-2000, Hillarp award Internat. Amine Group, 1996, Lieber prize NARSAD, 1998. Fellow Am. Coll. Neuropsychopharmacology (Efron award 1975); mem. Soc. for Pharmacology and Exptl. Therapeutics, Soc. for Neurosci., Internat. Brain Rsch. Orgn., Inst. of Medicine, Inst. of Medicine/Nat. Acad. Sci. Achievements include research in electrophysiological and pharmacological properties of brain serotonergic, noradrenergic, and dopaminergic neurons. Office: 34 Park St New Haven CT 06519-1109 E-mail: george.aghajanian@yale.edu.

AGHASSI, WILLIAM J. mechanical engineer, consultant; b. N.Y.C., July 3, 1948; s. Norman H. and Violette (Solomon) A.; m. Marian Weston, June 17, 1979; children: Rachel, Eli. BSME, Polytech. U. Bklyn., 1969; MS in Environ. Engring., N.J. Inst. Tech., 1975. Registered profl. engr., N.Y.; cert. asbestos investigator, N.Y.C. Engr. Combustion Engring., Windsor, Conn., 1969-71, City of N.Y., 1971-74, Leeds and Northrup Co., N.Y.C., 1974-82; prin. W.J. Aghassi Cons. Engrs., N.Y.C., 1982—. Developer engring. curricula for h.s. Recipient Environ. Quality award EPA, 1998. Mem. ASME, ASHRAE, Am. Water Works Assn. Avocations: hiking, biking, outdoor activities. Home: 180 Cabrini Blvd New York NY 10033-1138

AGHAZARIAN, GREG G. state representative; b. Stockton, Calif., Sept. 10, 1964; m. Esther Aghazarian; 2 children. BS in Bus. Adminstrn., U. So. Calif., 1986; JD, U. of the Pacific, 1993. Stockbroker Drexxell-Burham Lambert, 1986—89; law clerk Dist. Atty.'s Office, San Joaquin County, Calif., 1990—91, Diehl Steinheimer et al, 1991—92, Law Office of David R. Lebeoulf, 1993, atty., 1994—96; pvt. practice, 1997—99; mem. Calif. Assembly, 2002—. Commr. Parks Rec. Commn., Stockton, Calif., 1999—; trustee Lincoln Unified Sch. Dist., 1998—; candidate Calif. Assembly, 2000. Mem.: San Joaquin County Farm Bur., San Joaquin County A+, San Joaquin Partnership for Tomorrow, Rotary. Republican. Roman Catholic. Office: PO Box 942849 Rm 2130 Sacramento CA 95814 Address: 4557 Quail Lakes Dr Ste C-3 Stockton CA 95219*

AGHDAMI, FARHAD, lawyer; b. Tehran, Iran, Jan. 4, 1968; came to U.S., 1971; s. Ali Asghar and Farideh H. Aghdami; m. Amanda North Jones, May 21, 1994. BA, U. Va., 1989; JD, Wake Forest U., 1992; LLM in Taxation, Georgetown U., 1995. Bar: Va. 1992, U.S. Tax Ct. 1997. Assoc. Florance, Gordon and Brown, PC, Richmond, Va., 1992-97, dir., shareholder, 1997-99; mem. Williams, Mullen, Clark & Dobbins, Richmond, 1999—. Contbr. articles to profl. jours. Fellwo Am. Coll. Trust and Estate Counsel; mem. ABA (tax sect. fiduciary income tax com., chair 2003—, co-chair ins. planning com. 2003—). Home: 1003 West Ave Richmond VA 23220-3717 Office: Williams Mullen Clark & Dobbins Two James Ctr PO Box 1320 1021 E Cary St Richmond VA 23218-1320 Fax: 804-783-6507. E-mail: aghdami@williamsmullen.com.

AGHIORGOUSSIS, MAXIMOS DEMETRIOS See MAXIMOS, METROPOLITAN

AGINS, BARNETT ROBERT, electrical engineer, educator; b. N.Y.C., May 19, 1922; s. Isidore Robert Agins and Rhea Katheryn Orkoa; m. Esther Klein, Mar. 26, 1945 (dec. May 1995); children: Ira Alan, Harriet Susan. BEE, N.Y. U., 1952, MEE, 1956; MS in Math., Leland Stanford Jr. U., 1961. Commd. USAF, 1950, advanced through grades to lt. col., group comm. & elec. officer 529th AC&W group, 1953—56, project engr. Wright Air Develop. Ctr., 1956—59, instr. tech. Stanford, Calif., 1959—61, chief applied math divsn., Office Sci. Rsch. Washington, 1961—67, ret., 1967; asst. to dir. Courani Inst. Math Sci., N.Y. U., N.Y.C., 1967—69; program dir. applied math & stats. Nat. Sci. Found., Washington, 1969—77; adj. prof. math. Fla. Atlantic U., Boca Raton, 1977—. Assoc. editor: Jour. Optimzation Theory & Application, 1967—2003. With USAF, 1942—45. Mem.: Soc. Indsl. & Applied Math., Inst. Elec. & Elec. Engr. (sr.).

AGISIM, PHILIP, advertising and marketing company executive; b. Newark, Jan. 12, 1919; s. Isidore and Jennie (Socket) A.; m. Blanche Tedlow, June 14, 1942; children: Leslie Wayne, Elliot Steven. BS, Rutgers U., 1941; MBA, N.Y. U., 1949. Asst. market research dir. Crowell-Collier Pub. Co., N.Y.C., 1945-49; asso. market research dir. Cowles Pub. Co., N.Y.C., 1949-54; research and planning dir. J.B. Williams Co., N.Y.C., 1954-59, v.p., advt. dir., 1970-71; research dir. Parkson Advt. Agy., N.Y.C., 1959-63, v.p., 1963-69, exec. v.p., 1971-72, vice chmn., 1972-77, pres., 1978—, chief exec. officer, 1980-84, also bd. dirs. Vice chmn. Ohlmeyer Advt., 1984; pres. Product Opportunities Unltd., Inc., 1985-92; ptnr. Ron Meyer and Assocs.; bd. dirs. Trevor, Cole, Reid & Monroe Inc., TCRM Commercial Corp., The Harlem Times Corp. Contbr. articles in field to profl. jours. Mem. Nat. Acad. TV Arts and Scis., Am. Mktg. Assn., Friars Club. Jewish. Home: 650 Park Ave New York NY 10021-6115 Office: Trevor Cole Reid & Monroe 515 Madison Ave New York NY 10022-5403

AGLER, BRIAN, professional basketball coach; m. Robin Agler; children: Bryce, Taylor. BA, Wittenberg U.; MEd, Pittsburg (Kans.) State U. Profl. basketball player, Blackpool, Eng., 1980-81; coach Northeastern Okla. A&M U., U. Mo., Kansas City; head women's basketball coach Kans. State U.; head coach Columbus Quest; head coach, gen. mgr. Minn. Lynx, Mpls., 1998—. Inductee Wittenberg U. Athletic Hall of Honor, 1995; named ABL Ea. Conf. All-Star head coach, 1997, 98, ABL Coach of the Yr., 1996-97. Mem. Women's Basketball Coaches Assn. Office: Minnesota Lynx Target Ctr 600 1st Ave N Minneapolis MN 55403-1400

AGLER, RICHARD DEAN, rabbi; b. N.Y.C., May 11, 1952; s. Eugene and Sylvia (Spieler) A.; m. Mindy Steinberg, June 19, 1976; children: Jesse Allen, Talia Faith, Sarah Suzan. BA in Polit. Sci., NYU, 1973; MA in Hebrew Lit., Hebrew Union Coll.-Jewish Inst. Religion, 1976; DDiv honoris causa, Hebrew U., 2003. Ordained rabbi, 1978. Rabbi Stephen Wise Free Synagogue, N.Y.C., 1978-80, Temple Beth Shalom, Vero Beach, Fla., 1980-82, Temple Beth El, Boca Raton, Fla., 1982-84; founding rabbi Congregation Bnai Israel, Boca Raton, 1984—. Bd. dirs. Anti Defamation League, Palm Beach County. V.p. Handgun Control of Palm Beach County, Fla., 1983-93; co-founder Boca Raton Black-Jewish Fellowship, 1984—; founder Ctr. for Justice, Boca Raton, 1989—; co-founder Black-Jewish Coalition Quality Pub. Edn.; v.p. S.E. Fla. region Am. Jewish Com., 2001-02. Named Outstanding Young Man Am., 1989. Mem. Ctr. Conf. Am. Rabbis, South Palm Beach County Rabbinical Assn. (pres. 1991-93), S.E. Assn. Ctrl. Conf. Am. Rabbis (spirituality chair 1984-2002), Assn. Reform Zionists of Am. (life, bd. dirs.), Palm Beach County Bd. Rabbis. Jewish. Avocations: literature, athletics, sailing. Office: Congregation Bnai Israel 2200 Yamato Rd Boca Raton FL 33431-4325

AGNELLO, DAVID JOHN, civil engineer; b. Niagara Falls, N.Y., Mar. 11, 1964; s. Joseph C. and Lauretta A. BS in Architecture, Wentworth Inst. of Tech., 1986, BSCE, 1988. Registered profl. engr., Mass. Drafter Vanasse, Hangen, Brustline, Watertown, Mass., 1985-86; asst. project mgr. Allen and Demujian, Woburn, Mass., 1986-88; project mgr. Design State Survey, Somerville, Mass., 1988-89; civil/hydraulics engr. Badger Engrs., Cambridge, Mass., 1989-93; sr. civil engr. Gannett Fleming, Inc., Braintree, Mass., 1993-98; sr. assoc. Edwards and Kelcey, Inc., Boston, 1998—2002; v.p. URS Corp., Boston, 2002—. Mem. ASCE, NSPE, Women's Transp. Seminar, Boston Soc. of Civil Engrs., Mass. Soc. of Profl. Engrs. (sec., v.p., pres.), New England RR Club, Ti Alpha Pi. Office: URS Corp 38 Chauncy St 5th fl Boston MA 02111

AGNEW, CHRISTOPHER MACK, minister, historian; b. Santa Barbara, Calif., Aug. 7, 1944; s. Jack and Agnes Emma (Mack) A.; m. Suzanne Marie Souder, June 1, 1974 (div.); m. Elizabeth Lewis Lyddane, Apr. 25, 1998. AB, Bucknell U., Lewisburg, Pa., 1967; MA, U. Del., Newark, 1975, PhD, 1980; STM, Gen. Theol. Sem., N.Y.C., 1991. Ordained to ministry as deacon Episcopal Ch., 1991, as priest Episcopal Ch., 1992. Reference libr. Dover (Del.) Pub. Libr., 1969—72; tchg. asst. dept. history U. Del., Newark, 1972—76; manuscript libr. Hist. Soc. Del., 1979—81; asst. prof. history and Can. studies SUNY, Plattsburgh, 1981—84; registrar Diocese of Del., Wilmington, 1985—89; assoc. ecumenical officer Episcopal Ch., N.Y.C., 1989—94; deacon St. Thomas' Ch., Newark, 1991—92; priest-in-charge St. Marks, Teaneck, NJ, 1992; priest assoc. All Angels Ch., N.Y.C., 1992—95; interim rector St. Martin's, Maywood, NJ, 1994—95, All Hallows, Wyncote, Pa., 1995, St. Michael's, Litchfield, Conn., 1995—97, Ch. of the Ascension, Norfolk, Va., 1997, St. Peter's in Great Valley, Paoli, Pa., 1997—99; priest in charge St. Paul's, Owens, Va., 2000—02; interim rector Vauter's Ch., Loretto, Va., 2002—, St. Paul's, Nomini Grove, Va., 2002—. Staff Anglican-Roman Cath. Consultation Standing Comm. Ecumenical Rels., 1989—94, Episcopal Russian Orthodox Joint Coord. Com., 1990—94; mem. Faith and Order Commn., 1991—95, NCC Christian-Muslim Rels. Commn., 1989—91, NCC Christian-Jewish Rels. Commn., 1989—99, chmn., 1991—99; mem. Parliament of the Worlds Religions, 1993, NCC Interfaith Working Group, 1990—95, Interfaith Rels. Commn., 1996—99, Planning Com., Nat. Workshop on Christian Unity, 1990—94. Editor: The Ecumenical Bull., 1989-94, Anglican Statements on the Church: Selected Documentary Sources for a Study of Anglican Ecclesiology, 1994; author: God With Us, 1986; contbr. articles to profl. jours. Mem. Ecumenical Interfaith Commn. Diocese of Va., 2000—; mem. faith and order workgroup Va. Coun. Chs., 2002—, co-chmn. workgroup, 2003—, co-chmn., 2003—. Mem. Nat. Episc. Historians Assn. (mem. exec. bd. 1995-99), Hist.

Soc. Episc. Ch., Order Crown Charlemagne U.S. (asst. chaplain 1997—), Orgn. Am. Historians, Am. Hist. Assn., N.Am. Acad. Ecumenists, Can. Hist. Assn., Assn. Can. Studies in U.S., Interim Ministry Network, Mil. Order of Loyal Legion of U.S. (chaplain-in-chief 1995—), Mil. Order of Stars and Bars, Soc. Colonial Wars, N.Am. Guild of Change Ringers. Home: 12433 Richards Ride King George VA 22485

AGNEW, HAROLD MELVIN, physicist; b. Denver, Mar. 28, 1921; s. Sam E. and Augusta (Jacobs) A.; m. Beverly Jackson, May 2, 1942; children: Nancy E. Agnew Owens, John S. AB, U. Denver, 1942; MS, U. Chgo., 1948, PhD, 1949; PhD (hon.), Coll. Santa Fe, 1980, U. Denver, 1992. With Los Alamos Sci. Lab., 1943-46, alt. div. leader, 1949-61, leader weapons div., 1964-70, dir., 1970-79; pres. Gen. Atomics, San Diego, 1979-85, also bd. dirs., 1985—. Sci. adviser Supreme Allied Comdr. in Europe, Paris, 1961-64; chmn. Army Sci. Adv. Panel, 1965-70, San Diego County adv. bd.; mem. aircraft panel President's Sci. Adv. Com., 1965-73; mem. USAF Sci. Adv. Bd., 1957-69, Def. Sci. Bd., 1965-70, Gov. of N.Mex.'s Radiation Adv. Coun., 1959-61; sec. N.Mex. Health and Social Svcs., 1971-73; chmn. gen. adv. com. ACDA, 1974-77, mem., 1977-81; mem. aerospace safety adv. panel NASA, 1964-70; mem. U.S. Army Sci. Bd., 1978-80, White House Sci. Coun., 1982-89; adj. prof. U. Calif., San Diego, 1988—. Mem. council engring. NRC, 1978-82; mem. Los Alamos Bd. Ednl. Trustees, 1950-55, pres., 1955; trustee San Diego Mus. Art, 1983-87; mem. Woodrow Wilson Nat. Fellowship Found., 1973-80; N.Mex. State senator, 1955-61; sec. N.Mex. Legis. Council, 1957-61; chmn. N.Mex. Senate Corp. Commn., 1957-61; mem. Fed. Emergency Agy., 1982-88; bd. dirs. Fedn. Rocky Mountain States, Inc., 1975-77, Charles Lee Powell Found., 1993—, chmn. U. Calif. San Diego Chancellors Assocs., 1998-2000. Recipient Ernest Orlando Lawrence award AEC, 1966; Enrico Fermi award Dept. Energy, 1978; Pres's. medal, U. of Calif., 2003. Fellow Am. Phys. Soc., AAAS; mem. Nat. Acad. Scis., Nat. Acad. Engring., Council on Fgn. Relations, Phi Beta Kappa, Sigma Xi, Omicron Delta Kappa. Home: 322 Punta Baja Dr Solana Beach CA 92075-1720

AGNEW, JENNIFER MARIE, literature educator; b. St. Louis, Mar. 8, 1971; d. Thomas Alan and Nancy Jane Agnew. BA in English, DePaul U., 1993; MA in English, St. Louis U., 1995, PhD in English, 2001. Tchg. adj. and fellow St. Louis U., 1993—2000; mng. editor Time Being Books, St. Louis, 1999—2000; freelance writer, 2000—01; vis. tchg. fellow Fontbonne U., St. Louis, 2000—01; vis. asst. prof. Marquette U., Milw., 2001—03; upper sch. English tchr. North Shore Country Day Sch., Winnetka, Ill., 2003—. Tchg. asst. St. Louis U., 1997, rhetoric and composition asst., 1997—98. Tutor YMCA Literacy Program, St. Louis, 1999—2000. Mem.: MLA, Assn. for Study of Food and Soc., Internat. Gothic Assn. Avocations: cooking, yoga, running, swimming, travel. E-mail: jenniferagnew@comcast.net.

AGNEW, JOHN A. education educator; b. Millom, Cumbria, Eng., Aug. 29, 1949; s. Herbert and Anne (MacPherson) A.; children: Katherine, Christine. BA, Exeter U., Eng., 1970; Cert. Edn., Liverpool U., Eng., 1971; MA, Ohio State U., 1973, PhD, 1976. From asst. prof. to prof. Syracuse (NY) U., 1975—96; prof. UCLA, 1996—, chair dept. geography, 1998—2002. Dir. social sci. program Syracuse U., 1981—88; vis. prof. U. Chgo., 1992, U. Durham, 2003; Hettner lectr. U. Heidelberg, 2000; chmn. dept. geography U. Chgo.; Guggenheim fellow UCLA, 2003—. Author: Place and Politics, 1987, The U.S. in World Economy, 1987, Rome: The Modern City, 1995, Geopolitics: Re-Visioning World Politics, 1998, 2d edit., 2003, Place and Politics in Modern Italy, 2002; co-author: The Geography of World Economy, 1989, 2d edit., 2003, Mastering Space, 1995; editor: The City in Cultural Context, 1984, The Power of Place, 1989, American Space/American Place, 2002, Companion to Political Geography, 2002; mem. editl. bd. Polit. Geography, Urban Geography, Soc. and Space, Nat. Identities, Global Networks, Scottish Geog. Jour., European Jour. Internat. Rels. Fellow: Royal Geog. Soc.; mem.: N.Y Acad. Sci., Am. Polit. Sci. Assn., Coun. European Studies, Social Sci. Hist. Assn., Assn. Am. Geographers. Office: UCLA 1255 Bunche Hl Los Angeles CA 90095-1524 E-mail: jagnew@geog.ucla.edu.

AGNEW, PETER TOMLIN, employee benefit consultant; b. Orange, N.J., Nov. 20, 1948; s. William Harold and Janet Elisabeth (Gittinger) A.; m. Linda W. Seyffarth; children: Jonathan, Stephen, Douglas, Karen; 1 step child, Kristin Seyffarth. BA in English cum laude, Amherst Coll., 1971; MBA in Fin., NYU, 1976. CLU. Asst. investment officer Mutual Benefit Life, Newark, 1971—78; exec. v.p., bd. dir., prin. Post & Kurtz, Inc., N.Y.C., 1978—85, exec. v.p., prin., 1993—, also bd. dirs., pres., treas., 1998—; sr. regional dir. Minet, N.Y.C., 1985—92. Pres. P. Tomlin Agnew Assocs., Glen Ridge, N.J., 1982—; mem. pension com. Croda, Inc. Contbr. articles to profl. jours. Capt. United Way, Newark, 1978; assoc. class agt. Amherst Coll. Alumni Fund, 1980—, class agt., 1993—; mem. exec. bd. Rep. Congl. Leadership Coun., 1988-92; mem. Rep. Nat. Com. Pres.'s Club, 1992—; vice chair Civic Conf. Com. of Glen Ridge, 1998-99, Glen Ridge Rep. Club; asst. treas. Glen Ridge Congl. Ch.; mem. parents coun. Hamilton Coll., 1997-2001, Skidmore Coll., 2002—. Fellow Life Mgmt. Inst.; mem. Soc. CLU (com. chmn. N.Y. chpt. 1984), Assn. Advanced Life Underwriters, Nat. Assn. Securities Dealers, Yale Ins. Group (chmn. 1988-90), Glen Ridge Country Club, Downtown Assn. Avocations: swimming, bridge, skiing, music. golf. Home: 75 Glen Ridge Pky Glen Ridge NJ 07028-1821

AGNEW, THEODORE LEE, JR., historian, educator; b. Ogden, Ill., Dec. 21, 1916; s. Theodore Lee and Agnes (Faris) A.; m. Jeanne Starrett LeCaine, Dec. 25, 1942 (dec.); children: Theodore (dec.), Theodore Lee III, Susan Elizabeth, Hugh LeCaine, Peter Wallace, Marion Jeanne. BA, U. Ill., 1937, MA, 1938; A.M., Harvard U., 1939; PhD, Harvard, 1954. Grad. research asst. U. Ill., 1938; asst prof. history Okla. State U., Stillwater, 1947-54, assoc. prof., 1954-60, prof., 1960-84, prof. emeritus, 1984—. Vis. prof. history Emory U., summer 1964, 66-67; adj. prof. Meth. history Phillips Grad. Sem., Tulsa, 1992, 94; mem. World Meth. Coun., 1976-91, 96-2001, exec. com., 1981-86; del. United Meth. Gen. Conf. and South Ctrl. Jurisdictional Conf., 1976, 80, 84, 88, 92, 96, mem. gen. commn. on archives and history, 1972-80, commn. to study ministry, 1972-76, 88-92, commn. on Christian unity and interreligious concerns United Meth. Ch., 1980-88, gen. coun. on ministries, 1984-88; mem. bds. South Ctrl. Jurisdiction and Okla. Ann. Conf., Okla. Conf. of Churches; lay mem. Okla. Ann. Conf., 1971-2002, mem. joint adminstrv. bd. Meth. Theol. Sch. in Ohio and United Theol. Sem.; lay consultation coun. St. Paul Sch. Theology; bd. dirs. Frances E. Willard Home, Tulsa. Author: The South Central Jurisdiction, 1939-1972, 1973; contbr. articles to profl. jours. and biog. dictionaries, chapters to books. Served from ensign to lt. USNR, 1942-46, comdr. Res. ret. Mem. AAUP (mem. coun. 1960-63), Am. Hist. Assn., Orgn. Am. Historians, So. Hist. Assn., Am. Soc. Ch. History, Midcontinent Am. Studies Assn. (pres. 1982), Okla. and Ill. Hist. Socs., Am. Legion, Phi Beta Kappa, Phi Kappa Phi, Phi Alpha Theta, Alpha Kappa Lambda. Democrat. Home: 1216 N Lincoln St Stillwater OK 74075-2749

AGNO, JOHN G. management consultant; b. Gloversville, N.Y., Dec. 8, 1940; s. John G. and Margretta (Luff) Anagnostopulos; m. Karen Clark Mikus, June 29, 1985 (div. Nov. 2002). BBA, U. Fla., 1962. Mktg. specialist Eastman Kodak Co., Rochester, N.Y., 1965-73; gen. mgr. sanitation appliance divsn. Thetford Corp., Ann Arbor, Mich., 1973-80; v.p. mktg. and adminstrn. Stirling Power Systems Corp. divsn. McDonnell Douglas Corp., Ann Arbor, 1980-87; pres. Signature, Inc., Ann Arbor, 1983—. Deacon First Presbyn. Ch., Ann Arbor; bd. dirs. Washtenaw United Way, 1991-95; bd. dirs. YMCA, 1995-2000. 1st lt. U.S. Army, 1963-65. Mem. Recreational Vehicle Industry Assn. (chmn. mktg. commn. 1978-82, bd. dirs. 1981-83), Turnaround Mgmt. Assn., Ann Arbor Country Club, Rotary. Republican. Home: 4701 Midway Dr Ann Arbor MI 48103-9427 Office: Signature Inc PO Box 2086 Ann Arbor MI 48106-2086 E-mail: johnagno@signatureseries.com.

AGOFF, S. NICHOLAS, surgical pathologist; b. Lebanon, Oreg., May 1, 1968; MD, Northwestern U. Med. Sch., 1996. Lic. anatomic pathologist Am. Bd. of Pathology, cytopathologist Am. Bd. of Pathology. Pathologist U. of Wash. Med. Ctr., Seattle, 2000—. Office: U Was Med Ctr 1959 NE Pacific Ave Seattle WA 98144

AGONAFER, MULUGETA GABRIEL, political scientist, educator; b. Shoa/Addis Abeba, Ethiopia; arrived in U.S., 1973; s. Gashi Agonafer and Kebede Wudnesh; m. Addis Alem Bekele, May 18, 1991; 1 child, Kokeb Mulugeta. BSc in Electronics Engring. Tech., Purdue U., 1978; BA in Polit. Sci., Ind. U., 1979; MA in Polit. Sci., Western Wash. U., 1981, PhD (hon.) in Internat. Rels., Comparative Politics and African-Polit. Economy, 2003. Tchr. April 27th H.S., Jimma, Ethiopia, 1971-73; instr. Pa. State U., McKeesport, 1987-91, Strayer Coll., Woodbridge, Va., 1991-92; prof. Sprinfield (Mass.) Coll., 1992—. Reader Ednl. Testing Svcs., Princeton, N.J., 1995—. Mem. editl. bd. Jour. Pub. Policy, 1999 2001. Bd. dirs. Ethiopian Rsch. Coun., Washington, 1992-97; dir. YMCA-Africa Project, Springfield, 1998-2000; cons. Ethiopian Refugee Ctr., Manchester, N.H., 2001. Mem. Am. Polit. Sci. Assn., African-Am. Devel. Edn., Rsch. and Tng. Inst. (founder, pres. 1994—). Democrat. Ethiopian Orthodox. Avocation: soccer. Home: 194 North St Belchertown MA 01007 Office: Springfield Coll 263 Alden St Springfield MA 01109 Home Fax: 413-256-1867; Office Fax: 413-748-3236. E-mail: aadert@hotmail.com., mulugeta_agonafer@spfldcol.edu.

AGOOS, JEFF, professional soccer player; b. Geneva, May 2, 1968; Student, U. Va. Defender DC United, Herndon, Va. Mem. U.S. Under-15, Under-17, Under-20, World Univ. and Indoor Nat. Teams; vol. asst. coach Bruce Arena, U. Va., 1995. Named Soccer Am.'s co-freshman of yr., 1986; named one of Soccer Am.'s 11 most valuable players, 1989. Achievements include competitor 13 international matches in 1996, scoring winning goal in 2d international appearance, Guatemala; mem. silver-medal U.S. Futsai Nat. Team, Hong Kong, 1992; helped lead DC United to inaugural MLS Cup title and 1996 U.S. Open Cup championship. Office: US Soccer Fedn 1801-1811 S Prairie Ave Chicago IL 60616 and: DC United 13832 Redstein Dr Herndon VA 20171

AGOSIN, MOISES KANKOLSKY, zoology educator; b. Marseilles, France, Dec. 1, 1922; came to U.S., 1968, naturalized, 1973; s. Abraham W. and Rachel S. (Kankolsky) A.; m. Frida Halpern, June 19, 1948; children— Cynthia Regina, Marjorie Stella, Mario Daniel. MD, U. Chile, 1948. Intern Salvador Hosp., Santiago, Chile, 1946, resident parasitology and med. entomology, 1948; Rockefeller Found. fellow NIH, Bethesda, Md., 1952-54, research assoc., 1955; head biochemistry sect., dept. parasitology U. Chile, 1957-59, chmn. dept. chemistry, prof. chemistry, 1960-67; research prof. zoology U. Ga., Athens, 1968—. Vis. prof. U. Calif., Berkeley, 1960, U. London, 1964; hon. prof. U. Cayetano Heredia, Peru, 1984 cons. in field. Contbg. author: The Physiology of Insecta, 1974, Comprehensive Insect Biochemistry, Physiology, Pharmacology, 1985; mem. editorial bd.: Exptl. Parasitology, 1967-73, Archives Insect Biochemistry and Physiology, 1982-86; contbr. articles to profl. jours. Recipient Lamar Dodd award for creativity in rsch. U. Ga., 1989; grantee USPHS, 1958—, WHO, 1963-67, Wellcome Trust, 1966, NSF, 1974, U.S.-Israel bi-nat. Sci. Found., 1976, Conicit, Chile, 1996; Fulbright scholar, Peru, 1991, Fondecit (Chile) grant, 1996. Fellow Am. Acad. Microbiology; mem. Am. Soc. Biol. Chemists, Biochem. Soc. (London), AAAS, N.Y. Acad. Scis., Am. Soc. Parasitology (Bueding-von Brand Meml. award 1990), Chilean Acad. Scis.(r-sch. prof. emeritus 1992). Home: 177 Deertree Dr Athens GA 30605-4501 Office: U Ga 623 Biol Scis Bldg Athens GA 30602 *Perhaps the most important driving force in my career has always been the need to find out not how phenomena occur but why. This has been coupled to my belief that there are only two types of research, good and bad, regardless of whether they are considered basic or applied.*

AGOSTA, VITO, mechanical and aerospace engineering educator; b. N.Y.C., July 26, 1923; s. John and Elizabeth (Alvares) A.; m. Mary Frago, Aug. 9, 1952; children: John, Diana, Charles. MS in Engring., U. Mich., 1949; PhD, Columbia, 1959. Registered profl. engr., N.Y. Thermodynamicist DeLaval Steam Turbine Co., 1946-47; mem. faculty Poly. Inst. N.Y., Bklyn., 1950—, prof. mech. and aerospace engring., 1962—, prof. emeritus, 1986—; pres. Propulsion Scis., Inc., Huntington, N.Y., 1966-75, Fuels Systems Design Corp., Huntington, N.Y., 1975-94, Propulsion Scis. Co., Huntington, 1989—. Cons. in field. Served with AUS, 1943-45. Mem. AIAA, Combustion Inst., ASME, Sigma Xi, Tau Beta Pi. Achievements include invention of non-miscible liquid emulsifier; modulating oil burner; design of and mfr. of modulating fuel emulsifier systems for engines and boilers; research in combustion instability in rocket motors; supersonic combustion of two phase systems; air and thermal pollution; heat transfer analysis in reacting fuels; ventilation in Boston and New York City automobile tunnels. Home: 42 Cherry Ln Huntington NY 11743-2945 Office: Propulsion Scis Co 300 Broadway Huntington Station NY 11746-1405 E-mail: vagosta@earthlink.net.

AGOSTA, WILLIAM CARLETON, chemist, educator; b. Dallas, Jan. 1, 1933; s. Angelo N. and Helen Carleton (Jones) A.; m. Karin Solveig Engstrom, July 2, 1958; children— Jennifer Ellen, Christopher William. BA, Rice Inst., 1954; AM, Harvard U., 1955, PhD, 1957. NRC postdoctoral fellow Oxford (Eng.) U., 1957-58; Pfizer postdoctoral fellow U. Ill., Urbana, 1958-59; asst. prof. U. Calif., Berkeley, 1959-61; liaison scientist U.S. Navy, Frankfurt, Germany, 1961-63; asst. prof. chemistry Rockefeller U., N.Y.C., 1963-67, assoc. prof., 1967-74, prof., 1974-98, prof. emeritus, 1998—. Vis. prof. U. Innsbruck, 1995, Princeton U., 1996; cons. in field; officer Chiron Press, Inc., 1977-85; mem. NRC Associateship Programs Chem. Scis. Panel, 1997—; mem. Noxious Weed Control Bd., San Juan County, Wash., 2002—. Author: Chemical Communication, 1992, Bombardier Beetles and Fever Trees, 1996, Thieves, Deceivers, and Killers, 2001; mem. editl. adv. bd. Jour. Organic Chemistry, 1984-88; contbr. articles to profl. jours. Bd. dirs. San Juan Cmty. Home Trust, 2003—. John Angus Erskine fellow U. Canterbury (N.Z.), 1981 Fellow AAAS; mem. Chem. Soc. London, Am. Chem. Soc., Interam. Photochem. Soc., European Photochemistry Assn., Am. Soc. Photobiology, Internat. Soc. for Chem. Ecology, Phi Beta Kappa, Sigma Xi. Home: PO Box 1547 Friday Harbor WA 98250-1547 Office: U Wash Friday Harbor Labs Friday Harbor WA 98250 E-mail: agosta@u.washington.edu.

AGOSTINO, MICHAEL ANTHONY, otolaryngologist; b. South Bend, Ind., June 29, 1963; s. Peter and Teresa Agostino; m. Jeanne Marie Capone; children: John, Anthony, Julia, Peter. BA Psychology, U. Notre Dame, 1985; MD, Ind. U., 1989. Physician Otorhinolaryngology, Inc., South Bend, Ind., 1994—. Bd. dirs. Select Health Network, South Bend, Ind. Pres. Italian Heritage Soc. Ind., Indpls., 1993. Fellow: ACS; mem.: Am. Acad. Otolaryngology, Head and Neck Surgery, Alpha Omega Alpha, Phi Beta Kappa. Home: 17455 Lancaster Ct South Bend IN 46635-1064 Office: Otorhinolaryngology Inc 621 Memorial Dr #402 South Bend IN 46601 Office Fax: 574-232-4800.

AGOSTO, JOSE A. psychiatrist; b. San Juan, Puerto Rico, Sept. 8, 1961; s. Jose Alberto Agosto and Olga Manuela Rodriguez; m. Mildred DeJesus, May 5, 1985; children: Camille, Alexandra, Jose A. Medicine Doctorate, UPR Sch. of Medicine, San Juan, Puerto Rico, 1984—88. Cert. bd. cert. psychiatrist 1996. Staff psychiatrist and major USA Air Force, Panama City, Fla., 1992—94; dir. of psychiatric emergency room PR Psychiatric State Hosp., San Juan, PR, 1994—95; staff psychiatrist ASSMCA, San Juan, PR, 1995—2000; pvt. practice NeuroPsychiatric Group, Carolina, PR; staff psychiatrist VA Hosp., San Juan, PR. Treas. Am. Psychiatric Assn. PR District branch, San Juan, PR, 1998—2000. Major USAF, 1992—94, Tyndall AFB, Fla. Decorated Commendation medal USAF. Mem.: Am. Psychiatric Assn. Office: Neuropsychiatric Group Sanchez Osorio Ave 5x-34 Fontana Park Carolina PR 00982 Office Fax: 787-769-7940. Personal E-mail: panadepepita@yahoo.com.

AGRAN, LARRY, mayor, lawyer; b. Chgo., Feb. 2, 1945; m. Phyllis Agran; 1 child, Ken. BA, U. Calif. Berkeley, 1966; JD with honors, Harvard U., 1969. Legal counsel Calif. State Senate Com. on Health and Welfare; lectr., legis. and pub. policy UCLA Sch. Law, Grad. Sch. Mgmt., U. Calif. Irvine; mem. Irvine City Coun., 1978—90; mayor City of Irvine, Calif., 1982—84, 1986—90; mem. Irvine City Coun., 1998—; mayor City of Irvine, 2000—. Office: One Civic Ctr Plz PO Box 19575 Irvine CA 92623-9575*

AGRAN, RAYMOND DANIEL, lawyer; b. Chgo., June 21, 1957; s. Paul and Esther (Poogach) A.; m. Melinda Carol Finberg, June 8, 1986; children: Alexander Everett, Meredith Bronwyn. BA magna cum laude, Yale U., 1979; JD with highest honors, Columbia U., 1982. Bar: N.Y. 1983, U.S. Dist. Ct. (so. dist.) N.Y. 1983, U.S. Ct. Appeals (2d cir.) 1983, Pa. 1987, N.J. 1995. Assoc. Shearman & Sterling, N.Y.C., 1982-84, Covington & Burling (formerly Howard, Smith & Levin), N.Y.C., 1984-86, Wolf, Block, Schorr & Solis-Cohen, Phila., 1986-92, ptnr., 1992-95, Ballard Spahr Andrews & Ingersoll LLP, Phila., 1995—, tech. and emerging co. practice group chair. Panel chair Ctr. Energy Policy U. Pa., 1992; panelist Fgn. Policy Rsch. Inst., Phila., 1991-92; spkr. in field. Contbr. chpt. book Layman's Guide to Venture Capital, 1999, Greater Philadelphia Venture Group Venture Capital Institute, 1999. Bd. dirs., mem. adv. bd. Univ. City Sci. Ctr. Incubator, Phila., 1991-95; bd. dirs. Greater Phila. Venture Group, 1998-99. Bates fellow Yale U., 1978, Sumitomo fellow of U.S.-Japan Found., 1979; Columbia U. Stone scholar, Kent scholar. Avocations: chess, cooking, reading, outdoors. Office: Ballard Spahr Andrews & Ingersoll LLP 1735 Market St Fl 51 Philadelphia PA 19103-7599 E-mail: agran@ballardspahr.com.

AGRANOFF, BERNARD WILLIAM, biochemist, educator; b. Detroit, June 26, 1926; s. William and Phyllis (Pelavin) A.; m. Raquel Betty Schwartz, Sept. 1, 1957; children: William, Adam. MD, Wayne State U., 1950; BS, U. Mich., 1954. Intern Robert Packer Hosp., Sayre, Pa., 1950-51; commd. surgeon USPHS, 1954-60; biochemist Nat. Inst. Neurol. Diseases and Blindness, NIH, Bethesda, Md., 1954-60; mem. faculty U. Mich., Ann Arbor, 1960—, prof. biochemistry, 1965—; R.W. Gerard prof. of neurosci. in psychiatry, 1991. Rsch. biochemist Mental Health Rsch. Inst., 1960—, assoc. dir., 1977-83, dir. 1983-95, dir. neurosci. lab., 1983-2000; vis. scientist Max Planck Inst. Zellchemie, Munich, 1957-58, Nat. Inst. Med. Rsch., Mill Hill, Eng., 1974-75; Henry Russel lectr. U. Mich., 1987; cons. pharm. industry, govt. Contbr. articles to profl. jours. Fogarty scholar-in-residence NIH, Bethesda, Md., 1989-95; named Mich. Scientist of Yr. Mus. of Sci., Lansing, 1992. Fellow AAAS (Am. Assn. Advanced Sci.), Am. Acad. Arts and Sci., N.Y. Acad. Sci., Am. Coll. Neuropsychopharmacology; mem. Am. Soc. Biochemistry and Molecular Biology, Am. Chem. Soc., Inst. Medicine of NAS, Internat. Soc. Neurochemistry (treas. 1985-89, chmn. 1989 91), Am. Soc. Neurochemistry (pres. 1973-75). Achievements include research in brain lipids, biochem. basis of learning, memory and regeneration in the nervous system, human brain imaging. Office: U Mich C 560 MSRB II 1150 W Medical Center Dr Ann Arbor MI 48109-0669 E-mail: agranoff@umich.edu.

AGRANOFF, ROBERT, political scientist, educator; b. Mpls., May 25, 1936; s. Phillip Paul and Rose Stern Agranoff; m. Zola O. Besco, Dec. 27, 1959 (dec. June 26, 1986); children: Karen Marie Agranoff Grimley, David; m. Susan M. Klein, Oct. 9, 1988. BS, U. Wis., River Falls, 1962; MA, U. Pitts., 1963, PhD, 1967. From asst. prof. to prof. polit. sci. No. Ill. U., DeKalb, 1966—68, 1970—80; dir. legis. affairs Minn. Dem. Party, Mpls., 1968—69; prof., PhD dir., assoc. dean Sch. Pub. and Environ. Affairs Ind. U., Bloomington, 1980—2001, prof. emeritus pub. and environ. affairs, 2001—. Author: Dimensions of Human Services Integration, 1979, Intergovernmental Management, 1986, Collaborative Public Management, 2003. V.p. Christole, Inc., Nashville, Ind., 1998—; mem. Ind. Social Svcs. Coun., Indpls., 1987—91, Ill. Social Svcs. Adv. Coun., Springfield, 1975—80. Named Fulbright scholar, 1990. Mem.: Internat. Polic. Sci. Assn. (chair federalism rsch. com. 2000—), Am. Polit. Sci. Assn. (chair federalism sect. 1994—96), Am. Soc. Pub. Adminstrn. (chair human svcs. sect. 1977—80, Donald Stone Rsch. award 2000). Democrat. Jewish. Avocations: travel, history, cooking. Home: 5747 W Lost Branch Rd Nashville IN 47448 Office: Ind U Sch Pub and Environ Affairs 1315 E 10th St Bloomington IN 47405 Fax: 812-855-7802. Business E-Mail: agranoff@indiana.edu.

AGRAST, MARK DAVID, lawyer; b. Cleve., Mar. 31, 1956; s. Harold and Charlotte Agrast; life ptnr. David Michael Hollis. BA, Case Western Res. U., 1978; JD, Yale U., 1985. Bar: Ohio 1986, D.C. 1988. Atty. Jones Day Reavis & Pogue, Washington, 1985—91; sr. legis. asst. Hon. Gerry E. Studds, U.S. Ho. of Reps., Washington, 1992—97; counsel and legis. dir. Hon. William D. Delahunt, U.S. Ho. of Reps., Washington, 1997—2003; sr. v.p. for domestic policy Ctr. for Am. Progress, Washington, 2003—. Bd. dirs. Ctr. for Human Rights, 2003—. Rhodes scholar, Oxford U., 1978—81. Fellow: Am. Bar Found.; mem.: ABA (chair sect. individual rights and responsibilities 2002—03). Office: Ctr for Am Progress 805 15th St NW Ste 400 Washington DC 20005

AGRAWAL, DHARMA PRAKASH, engineering educator; b. Balod, India, Apr. 12, 1945; came to U.S., 1976; s. Saryoo Prasad and Chandra K. Agrawal; m. Purnima Agrawal, June 7, 1971; children: Sonali, Braj. BE, Ravishankar U., Raipur, India, 1966; ME with honors, Roorkee (India) U., 1968; DSc in Tech., Fed. Inst. Tech., Lausanne, Switzerland, 1975. Lectr. M.N.R. Engring. Coll., Allahabad, India, 1968-72, Roorkee U., 1972-73; asst. Fed. Inst. Tech., Lausanne, 1973-75; instr., postdoctoral work So. Meth. U., Dallas, 1976-77; asst. prof., then assoc. prof. Wayne State U., Detroit, 1977-82; assoc. prof. N.C. State U., Raleigh, 1982-84, prof., 1984-98; OBR Disting. prof. U. Cin., 1998—. Gen. co-chair Advanced Computing Conf., 1997—2000; Fulbright sr. specialist, 2002; keynote spkr. Internat. Conf. on Parallel and Distributed Sys., 1997; presenter in field. Co-author: Introduction to Wireless and Mobile Systems, 2003; editor: Advanced Computer Architecture, 1986, Advances in Distributed System Reliability, 1990, Distributed Computing Network Reliability, 1990; editor: Jour. Parallel and Distg. Computing, 1984, Computer mag., 1986-91, Internat. Jour. High Speed Computing, IEEE Transactions on Computers, 1992-96, IEEE Computer Soc. Press Tutorials, 1992-94. Fellow IEEE (chair tech. com. on computer architecture, IEEE Computer Soc. 1991-94, chair McDowell Award and Harry Grode Award coms. 1991-99, chair Eckerdt Mauchley award in computer architecture, program chair internat. conf. on parallel processing 1994, workshop chair internat. conf. on parallel processing 1995, gen. chair fourth internat. workshop on modeling analysis and simulation of computer and telecom. sys. 1996, 2001), Assn. for Computing Machinery; mem. AAAS, Sigma Xi. Office: U Cin ECE&CS PO Box 210030 Cincinnati OH 45221-0030 E-mail: dpa@ececs.uc.edu.

AGRAWAL, GOVIND PRASAD, optics educator; b. Kashipur, India, July 24, 1951; came to U.S., 1977; s. Amarnath and Sushila (né Singhal) A.; m. Anne L. Frette-Damicourt, July 22, 1977; children: Sipra, Caroline, Claire. BS, U. Lucknow, 1969; MS, Indian Inst. of Tech., 1971, PhD, 1974. Rsch. assoc. Ecole Polytechnique, Palaiseau, France, 1974-76, CUNY, 1977-79; staff scientist Quantel, Orsay, France, 1980-81; tech. staff mem. AT&T Bell Labs., Murray Hill, N.J., 1982-88; assoc. prof. U. Rochester, 1989-91, prof., 1992—. Author: Semiconductor Lasers, 1986, 2d edit., 1993, Nonlinear Fiber Optics, 1989, 3d edit., 2001, Fiber Optic Communications, 1992, 3d edit., 2002, Applications of Nonlinear Fiber Optics, 2001, Optical Solitons, 2003; editor: Semiconductor Lasers, 1995; contbr. 300 articles to profl. jours. Fellow IEEE, Optical Soc. of Am. (topical editor 1993-98); mem. European Optical Soc. (editl. bd. 1995-98), Laser and Electro-optical Soc. (ednl. com. 1996-99). Office: The Inst of Optics U Rochester Rochester NY 14627 E-mail: gpa@optics.rochester.edu.

AGRAWAL, HARISH CHANDRA, neurobiologist, researcher, educator; b. Allahabad, Uttar Pradesh, India; came to U.S., 1964, naturalized, 1982; s. Shambhu and Rajmani Devi A.; m. Daya Kumari Bhushan, Feb. 6, 1960; children— Sanjay, Sanjeev B.Sc., Allahabad U., 1957, M.Sc., 1959, PhD, 1964. Med. research assoc. Thudichum Psychiat. Lab., Galesburg, Ill., 1964-68; lectr. dept. biochemistry Charing Cross Hosp., London, 1968-70; prof. neurology Washington U. Sch. Medicine, St. Louis, 1970—. Mem. neurology study sect. NIH, 1979-82 Author: Handbook of Neurochemistry, 1969, Developmental Neurobiology, 1970, Biochemistry of Developing Brain, 1971, Membranes and Receptors, 1974, Proteins of the Nervous System, 1980, Biochemistry of Brain, 1980, Handbook of Neurochemistry, 1984; contbr. numerous papers on various aspects of myelin proteins and their role in demyelinating disrders. Jr. research fellow Council Sci. and Indsl. Research, New Delhi, 1960-62, sr. research fellow, 1963-64; Research Career Devel. award Nat. Inst. Neurol. and Communicative Disorders, 1974-79 Mem. Internat. Soc. Neurochemistry, Internat. Brain Rsch. Orgn., Am. Soc. Neurochemistry, Am. Soc. Biol. Chemists and Molecular Biologists, Am. Soc. Physiology. Home: 3500 Mystic Pointe Dr #3207 Aventura FL 33180 Office: Washington U Dept Neurology 660 S Euclid Ave Dept Saint Louis MO 63110-1093

AGRAWAL, KRISHNA CHANDRA, pharmacology educator; b. Calcutta, India, Mar. 15, 1937; naturalized; s. Prasadi Lal and Asarfi Devi (Agrawal) A.; m. Mani Agrawal, Dec. 2, 1960; children— Sunil, Lina, Nira BS in Pharmacy, Andhra U., Waltair, India, 1959, MS, 1960; PhD, U. Fla., 1965. Cert. in pharm. chemistry. Research assoc. dept. pharmacology Yale U. Sch. Medicine, New Haven, 1966-69, instr., 1969-70, asst. prof., 1970-76, assoc. prof., 1976; assoc. prof. dept. pharmacology Tulane U. Sch. Medicine, New Orleans, 1976-81, prof., 1981—, interim chmn., 1996-99, regents prof., chmn., 1999—. Cons. mem. Southeastern Cancer Study Group, 1980—85; mem. adv. com. on instnl. grants Am. Cancer Soc., 1980—85; mem. AIDS and Related Rsch. Rev. Group

NIH, 1989—94, 1999—2002; mem. oncology merit rev. com. Vets. Adminstrn., 2002—; exptl. therapist NIH, 2002—. Conbr. articles to profl. jours.; patentee radiosensitizers for hypoxic tumor cells and compositions; novel AZT analogs. Grantee Nat. Cancer Inst., 1976-89, WHO, 1979-82, La. Bd. Regents, 1981-82, Nat. Inst. Allergy and Infectious Diseases, 1987—, Dept. Def., 1994-96, Nat. Heart Lung and Blood Inst., 1997—. Fellow Am. Inst. Chemists; mem. Am. Chem. Soc., Am. Assn. Cancer Rsch., Internat. Soc. Antiviral Rsch., Radiation Rsch. Soc., Am. Soc. Pharmacology and Exptl. Therapeutics, Am. Soc. Hematology, Sigma Xi. Home: 26 Olympic Ct New Orleans LA 70131-8614 Office: Tulane U Sch Medicine Dept Pharmacology New Orleans LA 70112 E-mail: agrawal@tulane.edu.

AGRAWAL, PIYUSH C. school system administrator; b. Khairagarh, Agra, India, June 26, 1936; arrived in U.S., 1976; s. Ram C. and Chameli (Kiran) Agrawal; m. Sudha Sita Bansal, May 18, 1963; children: Seema, Sukrit, Akhil. BSc, Agra (India) U., 1955, MSc, 1963; BEd, Delhi U., 1958; MS, SUNY, Albany, 1972, EdS, 1978, EdD, 1979. Tchr., dept. head Delhi Adminstrn., 1958-68; expert UNESCO, Liberia, 1968-76, 1968—76; dir. metric edn. Regional Planning Ctr., Albany, 1977-79; supr. math. Dade County Pub. Sch., Miami, Fla., 1979-94; assoc. supt. Piscataway Bd. Edn., 1992-94, dep. supt., 1994-97, acting supt., 1997-98; chmn. & CEO APS Tech., Inc., 2000. Cons. in field; Fla. state coord. nat. math. competition Am. Jr. HS Math. Exam., 1989—92; rev. panelist Am. 2000 proposals New Am. Schs. Devel. Corp., 1992; tchr. enhancement program NSF, 1992; mem. nat. adv. panel Md. Pub. TV, 1993—95; mem. nat. adv. coun. South Asian affairs, 1994—, vice chair, 1998—. Author: numerous books and booklets. Mem. U.S. Census 2000 Adv. Com. on Asian and Pacific Islander Populations, 1993—, chair, 1995, 1997, 1999, 2000, 2001; mem. Fla. House Spkr.'s Task Force on Math., Sci., and Computer Edn., 1982—83; nat. selection com. mem. Presdl. Awards for Excellence in Sci. and Math. Tchg., 1990, state selection com. mem., 1987, 1990, 1991; chmn. Secondary math. Fla. State Textbook Adoption Coun., 1984. Mem.: Asian Am. Cmty. Forum (founding Chair 2002), Asian Am. Found. (chair 2001—), Asian Am. Alliance (founding mem. 2001—, chair 2002—), Mid. States Assn. Colls. and Schs. (task force 1993—95), Fla. Leadership Alliance for Improving Math. Edn. (founder 1991), Dade County Sch. Adminstrs. Assn. (v.p. 1985—86), Fla. Assn. Instrnl. Supr. and Adminstrs. (bd. dirs. 1985—86), UNESCO Staff Assn. (pres. 1971—76), Fla. Assn. Math. Supr. (pres. 1986—87), Fla. Coun. Tchrs. Math. (pres. 1990—92), U.S. Metric Assn. (ann. conf. chmn. 1982), Assn. Indians in Am. (nat. v.p. 1984—88, 1992—94, trustee 1997—, nat. pres. 2000—). Home: 1625 Eagle Bnd Weston FL 33327-1615 Office: APS Techs Inc 630 W 84th St Hialeah FL 33014-3617 E-mail: sudhapca@aol.com.

AGRAWAL, PRADEEP KUMAR, chemical engineer, educator; b. Rampur, U.P., India, Jan. 25, 1954; arrived in U.S., 1974; s. Rameshwar Prasad, Parvati Devi; m. Kanchan P. Agrawal, Dec. 15, 1991; children: Parth, Monica. BChE, U. Roorkee, India, 1974; MChE, U. Del., 1976, PhD, 1979. Asst. prof. chem. engring. Ga. Inst. Tech., Atlanta, 1979—85, assoc. prof. chem. engring., 1985—. Cons. Milliken & Co., LaGrange, Ga., 1989—. Contbr. Mem.: AIChE (Outstanding Advisor 1994). Home: 2367 Doreen Ct NE Atlanta GA 30345 Office: Sch Chem Engring Ga Inst Tech Atlanta GA 30332

AGRAWAL, RAKESH, industrial researcher; b. Ara, Bihar, India, Nov. 3, 1953; came to U.S., 1975; s. Girdhar Lal and Bimla; m. Manju Agrawal, June 18, 1980; children: Udit, Numit. BTech, Indian Inst. Tech., Kanpur, 1975; MChE, U. Del., 1977; ScD, MIT, 1980. From process engr. to process mgr. Air Products and Chems., Allentown, Pa., 1980-90, sr. engring. assoc., 1990-92, prin. engring. assoc., 1992-96, chief engr. process synthesis, 1996—. Trustee Cache Corp., Austin, 1997—. Contbr. over 60 articles to profl. jours.; holder over 400 patents in field. Fellow Indian Inst. Chem. Engrs. (hon.); mem. AIChE (mem. chem. engring. operating tech. coun. 1999—, cons. editor Separations, AIChEJ 1999—, Inst. award for Excellence in Indsl. Gases Tech. 1998, Gerhold award in separations 2001), NAE. Avocations: exercise, photography, reading. Office: Air Products and Chems 7201 Hamilton Blvd Allentown PA 18195-1526 E-mail: agrawar@apci.com.

AGRAWAL, SUPHAL P. engineering company executive; b. Bareilly, India, 1946; arrived in U.S., 1968; s. Ram P. and Sushila D. Agrawal; m. Sushila J. Agrawal; children: Nisha, Nina, Naveen P. BSc, Agra U., Meerut, India, 1963; B in Tech., Indian Inst. Tech., Kanpur, India, 1968; MS, U. Ky., 1970, PhD, 1973. Postdoctoral scholar U. Mich., Ann Arbor, Mich., 1973—75; mem. tech. staff Rockwell Internat., El Segundo, Calif., 1976—80, Northrop, Hawthorne, Calif., 1980—89; dir. advanced tech. bus. and strategy devel. Air Combat Sys./Northrop Grumman Corp., El Segundo, Calif., 1989—. Editor: Superplastic Forming, Failure Analysis; contbr. articles to profl. jours. Capt. Neighborhood Watch, Rancho Palos Verdes, 1995—2000. Fellow: ASM Internat. (chmn. L.A. chpt.). Achievements include patents for superplastic forming of titanium and aluminum alloys; significant contribution to understanding of superplastic forming/diffusion bonding of titanium and aluminum alloys. Avocations: tennis, photography, travel, painting. Office: Air Combat Sys Northrop Grumman Corp 1 Hornet Way MS VF OO/W7 El Segundo CA 90245

AGRAZ, FRANCISCO JAVIER, SR., lawyer, public affairs representative; b. Laredo, Tex., Aug. 21, 1947; s. Jose Jesus and Irene (Garcia-Gomez) A.; m. Rosalinda Varela, Aug. 23, 1969 (div. Feb. 1980); children: Francisco Javier Jr., Raquel Jeanne; m. Ruth Urquidi, Jan. 1, 1984. BA in Journalism, U. Tex. at El Paso, 1970; JD, U. Houston, 1987. Bar: Tex. 1988, U.S. Dist. Ct. (so. dist.) Tex. 1988. Anchor reporter KENS-TV, San Antonio, 1970; corr. ABC Capital Cities Comms., Chgo., Houston, N.Y., 1970-77; pub. affairs analyst Exxon Corp., Houston and Memphis, 1977-83; assoc. Wood, Burney, Cohn & Bradley, Corpus Christi, Tex., 1987-89, Redford, Wray & Woolsey, P.C., Corpus Christi, 1989-91; pres., atty. at law Francisco J. Agraz P.C., Houston, 1991—; gen. mgr. The MRAM Co., Houston, 1996-98; pub. affairs officer FBI, Houston, 1998—. Bd. govs. United Way of Coastal Bend, Corpus Christi, Tex., 1987-91. Mem. State Bar of Tex. (grievance com., pub. rels. com.). Roman Catholic. Avocation: spanish translator. E-mail: agrazfj@franciscoagraz.com.

AGRE, JAMES COURTLAND, physical medicine and rehabilitation; b. Northfield, Minn., May 2, 1950; s. Courtland Leverne and Ellen Violet (Swedberg) A.; m. Patti Dee Soderberg, Aug. 6, 1982. MD, U. Minn., 1976, PhD, 1985. Diplomate Nat. Bd. Med. Examiners; bd. cert. Am. Acad. Phys. Medicine and Rehab. Rsch. fellow dept. phys. medicine and rehab. U. Minn., Mpls., 1979-80, instr. dept. phys. medicine and rehab., 1980-84; asst. prof. dept. phys. medicine and rehab. U. Wis., Madison, 1984-90, assoc. prof. dept. rehab. medicine, 1990-93, chmn. dept. rehab. medicine, 1991-97, prof. dept. rehab. medicine, 1993-97; practitioner in svc. Ministry Health Care, Rhinelander and Eagle River, Wis., 1997—. Mem. editorial bd. and contbr. articles to Archives of Phys. Medicine and Rehab., 1988-2000. Ski coord. Wis. Ski for Light, Madison, 1985-95. Fellow Am. Acad. Phys. Medicine and Rehab. (Elizabeth and Sidney Licht award 1989, Excellence in Sci. Writing award 1990), Am. Coll. Sports Medicine (New Investigator award 1991). Office: Ministry Health Care 1020 Kabel Ave Rhinelander WI 54501

AGREST, EMMANUIL M. mathematician, physicist, educator; b. Moscow, Jan. 30, 1945; s. Matest M and Riva S Agrest; m. Larisa S Shaldjian, Aug. 6, 1968; children: Igor, Yan. PhD Math. and Physics, N.N. Andreyev Acoustics Inst., Moscow, 1975; M.S. Math. and Mechanics, Moscow State U., 1968. Docent of department of Algebra and Geometry Supreme Certifying Bd. of the Coun. of Ministers of USSR, 1986. Rsch. fellow Acoustics Inst., Sukhumi, Georgia, 1969—80; asst. prof. Abkhazian State U., Sukhumi, Georgia, 1980—86, head of algebra and numerical methods dept., 1986—92; asst. prof. Johnson & Wales U., Charleston, SC, 1993—96, assoc. prof., 1996—2000, prof., 2000—; adj. faculty Coll. of Charleston, Charleston, SC, 1993—2002. Mem.: Am. Math. Soc., The Math. Assn. of Am. Achievements include invention of A device for automatic tractor navigation, inventors certificate # 1099865 USSR, 1984; research in Mathematical modelling of nonlinear effects in acoustical cavitation. Office: Johnson & Wales University 701 East Bay St Charleston SC 29403 Office Fax: 843-727-3094. E-mail: emmanuil.agrest@jwu.edu.

AGRESTA, ANTHONY JOHN, academic administrator, educational consultant, language educator; b. Jersey City, Apr. 8, 1933; s. Charles Vincent and Pauline Grace (Truncellito) Agresta; m. Carla Perls, Aug. 9, 1997; m. Elizabeth Ann Smelser, Nov. 13, 1955 (div. Sept. 23, 1965); m. Nancy Mae Laraway, Oct. 29, 1966 (div. Mar. 13, 1974); children: Anthony II, Lisane, Suzanne. BS, Fairleigh Dickinson U., Teaneck, NJ, 1955; MS, William Paterson U, Wayne, NJ, 1961; PhD, US U of Am., Wash. DC, 1974; dip. in Orthotics, New York Sch. of Med., New York, NY, 1982; rev. ordained, Universal Life Ch., Modesto, CA, 1997; DD, Am. Inst. of Holistic Theology, Youngstown, OH, 2001. Income tax prep., H & R Block, 1988; cert. tchr.: K-8 NJ, 1958, counselor: K-12 NJ, 1967, prin.: K-12 NJ, 1968, sch.administrator NJ, 1969, metaphysical psychology N.Y.C., hypnosis holistic practitioner, child psychol. Am. Assoc. of Christian Coun., 2003. Elem. guidance Rochelle Pk. Pub. Sch., Rochelle Pk., NJ, 1955—60, asst. prin., 1960—62; dir. of guidance Wallington (NJ) Elem. Schs., 1963—64; prin. Wallington Bd. of Ed., 1964—70; HS prin. Wallington HS, 1971—81; CEO B&H Shoe Shoppes, Inc., Hackensack, NJ, 1982—86, Red Bank, NJ, 1982—86; dir. of guidance Paramus Catholic HS, Paramus, NJ, 1986—89; dir. of fin. aid Gibbs Coll., Montclair, NJ, 1989—90; adj. prof. English William Paterson U., Wayne, NJ, 1991—, grad. office coord., 1992—93, ESL tchr., curriculum developer continuing edn. program, 1995—2002, writing ctr. tutor, 1996—2000; acad. coord. Hispanic Inst., Paramus, NJ, 1998—. Income tax preparer H & R Block, 1988—92, Budget Tax, Saddle Brook, NJ, 1991—; metaphysics lectr., 1996—98; co-chair Healthy Families Bergen County, Englewood, NJ, 1998—2002; pres. Master Learning Inst., Saddle Brook, NJ, 2000—, cons. owner, 2000—. Inventor (shoes) automatic shoe measure, 1980; editor: (ESL textbooks) Let's Get Down to Bus. (idioms), 2000. Councilman, chair, pub. works Mcpl. Town Coun., Emerson, NJ, 1979—81; chair, substance abuse coun. Paramus Cath. HS, Paramus, NJ, 1987—89. SFC USAR, 1953—61, vessel examiner US Coast Guard Auxilary, 1988—96. Nominee disting. prin., Wallington, NJ, 1979—80; recipient Cert. of Honor, Wallington PTA, 1971, Cert. of Merit, Md. States Assoc. of Secondary Sch./Coll., 1971, Achievement award, IRS/ Newark, NJ, 1989, Cert. of Merit, Hispanic Inst. /Paramus, NJ, 1990. Mem.: Am. Fed. of Tchr., Healthy Families Bergen Coun. (co-chair 2001—02), Tchr. of Eng. Second language. Achievements include writing of by-laws/constn. for Healthy Families Bergen County; dir. elementary sch. guidance prog; wrote grants and coord. remedial svc; development of curriculum staff evaluation, adult edn. and tech. studies curriculum writing of all final exams, course outlines, all levels, Hispanic Institute; federal title programs Wallington Schools, Rochelle Park Schools. Home: 531 Saddle River Rd Saddle Brook NJ 17663-4638 Office: Hispanic Inst for Rsch and Devel 17 Arcadian Ave Paramus NJ 17032

AGRESTI, MIRIAM MONELL, psychologist; b. N.Y.C., Mar. 23, 1926; d. James McCloud and Marion Henrietta (Zippel) Monell; children: Robert, Carol. BS, Queens Coll., 1947; MA in Sci. Edn., Columbia U., 1949; PhD in Clin. Psychology, Yeshiva U., 1976; postgrad., Ackerman Inst. Family Therapy, 1977-81, L.I. Jewish Hosp. Human Sexualality Ctr. Lic. psychologist, N.Y. Diplomate Am. Bd. Family Psychology (fellow, pres. 1984-85). Psychology intern Creedmoor Psychiat. Ctr., Queens, N.Y., 1963-64, family therapist, 1964-69; psychologist Northeast Nassau Psychiat. Ctr., Kings Park, N.Y., 1969-72; adminstrv. dir. Friendship House Day Hosp., Glen Cove, N.Y., 1972-74; psychologist and team leader Ctrl. Islip (N.Y.) Psychiatr. Ctr., 1974-75; tchr., coord. family therapy program Pilgrim Psychiat. Ctr., West Brentwood, N.Y., 1976-80; pvt. practice psychotherapy, 1977—. Pres. Nassau County Med. Ctr., 1990-95; co-dir. L.I. Family Inst., 1976-79; cons. family therapy Cath. Charities, 1979, St. Vincent's Hall, 1979, Nassau County Mental Health Assn., 1980; adj. faculty Sch. Edn., C.W. Post Coll., L.I. U., 1972, CUNY, 1978-80, St. John's U., 1983, Hofstra U., 1985-88. Exec. dir. movie/videotape Beware the Gaps in Medical Care for Older People (1st prize Am. Film Festival). Fellow Am. Orthopsychiat. Assn.; mem. APA, N.Y. State Psychol. Assn., Nassau County Psychol. Assn., Am. Assn. for Marriage and Family Therapy (pres. L.I. chpt. 1981-83, sec. N.Y. state divsn. 1996-98), Pi Lambda Theta. Unitarian Universalist. Address: 1110 Dee Ln Woodbury NY 11797

AGRUSS, NEIL STUART, cardiologist; b. Chgo., June 2, 1939; s. Meyer and Frances (Spector) A.; m. Janyce Zucker; children: David, Lauren, Michael, Joshua, Susan, Robyn, Bryan. BS, U. Ill., 1960; MD, 1963. Diplomate Am. Bd. Internal Medicine. Resident in internal medicine, 1964-65, 67-68; fellow in cardiology Cin. Gen. Hosp., 1968-70; dir. coronary care unit, 1971-74; dir. echocardiography lab., 1972-74; dir. cardiac diagnostic labs. Ctr. DuPage Hosp., Winfield, Ill., 1974—; asst. prof. medicine U. Cin., 1970-74, Rush Med. Coll., 1976—. Chmn. coronary care com. Heart Assn. DuPage County, 1974-76. Author: co-author publs. in field. Active Congregation Beth Shalom, Naperville, Ill. Capt. M.C. U.S. Army, 1965-67. Fellow ACP, Am. Coll. Cardiology, Am. Coll. Chest Physicians, Coun. Clin. Cardiology, Am. Heart Assn.; mem. AMA, DuPage County Med. Soc., Ill. Med. Soc., Am. Fend. Clin. Rsch., Chgo. Heart Assn. Office: 454 Pennsylvania Ave Glen Ellyn IL 60137-4418

AGUAS, RUBEN TECH, otolaryngologist; b. Manila, Philippines, Feb. 10, 1941; came to U.S., 1969; s. Francisco Calaguas and Lydia (Tech) A.; m. Aida Raymundo, June 12, 1967; 1 child, Ruben R. Jr. Student premedicine, U. Philippines, Quezon City, 1956-59; MD, U. Philippines, Manila, 1964. Diplomate Am. Bd. Otolaryngology. Resident in otolaryngology Philippine Gen. Hosp., 1964-68, Bellevue Hosp. Ctr., N.Y.C., 1969-71; resident gen. surgery Columbus Hosp., N.Y.C., 1971-72; resident in otolaryngology Met. Hosp. Ctr., N.Y.C., 1972-73; staff physician specializing in otolaryngology Marshfield (Wis.) Clinic, 1973-89, So. Calif. Permanente Med. Group, L.A., 1996—; locum tenens, 1993-96. Lt. col. USAF M.C., 1989-92. Roman Catholic. Avocations: tennis, golf, chess. Office: So Calif Permanente Med Grp 4900 W Sunset Blvd Los Angeles CA 90027-5814

AGUERO-ROSENFELD, MARIA E. pathologist, microbiologist; b. Melipilla, Chile, Feb. 21, 1953; d. Carlos E. Aguero and Maria I. Aldana; m. Louis Rosenfeld, June 24, 1983; children: Andrew C. Rosenfeld, Gregory A. Rosenfeld. MD, U. of Chile, Santiago, 1976. Lic. N.Y., cert. bd. cert. in clin. pathology Am. Bd. of Pathology, bd. cert. in med. microbiology Am. Bd. of Pathology, bd. cert. in med. and pub. health microbiology Am. Acad. of Microbiology. Asst. prof. of microbiology U. of Chile, Santiago, 1977—83; asst. prof. of pathology, microbiology and medicine and N.Y. Med. Coll., Valhalla, 1989—96, assoc. prof. of pathology, 1996—, assoc. prof. of microbiolgy and medicine, 2000—; assoc. dir. of clin. pathology Westchester Med. Ctr., Valhalla; dir. of clin. labs. Ellenville Regional Hosp., 2001—. Assoc. dir. of clin. labs. Westchester Med. Ctr., Valhalla, NY, 1989—. Contbr. articles to med. and sci. publs. (Fogarty Internat. fellowship, 1982). Grantee, Westchester County Dept. of Health, 1997. Mem.: Am. Soc. for Microbiology. Office: Westchester Med Ctr Rm 1J-11a Clinical Labs Valhalla NY

AGUIAR, ADAM MARTIN, chemist, educator; b. Newark, Aug. 11, 1929; s. Joaquim Ramahlo and Emilea Andrada (Nunes) A.; m. Laura E. Brand, Sept. 2, 1980; children: Justine Diane, David Laurence, Adam Albert, Erick Arthur, Aaron Benjamin, Evan Joaquim. BS, Fairleigh Dickinson U., 1955; MA, Columbia U., 1957, PhD, 1960. Chemist Otto B. May, Newark, 1948-55; asst. prof. Fairleigh Dickinson U., Rutherford, N.J., 1959-63; asst. prof. chemistry Tulane U., New Orleans, 1963-65, assoc. prof., 1965-67, prof., 1967-72, head dept. chemistry Newcomb Coll. div., 1970; dean grad. and research programs William Paterson Coll., Wayne, N.J., 1972-73; research prof. Rutgers U., Newark, 1973-75; prof. chemistry Fairleigh Dickinson U., Madison, N.J., 1975-93, chmn. dept. chemistry/geol. scis., 1984-89; pres. Seltox Corp., N.J., 1980—. Adj. prof. chemistry Monmouth U., West Long Branch, N.J., 1993—; cons. chem. firms in La. and N.J. Contbr. articles to profl. jours. Union Carbide fellow, 1957; NIH fellow, 1959; recipient other grants. Mem. AAUP, Am. Chem. Soc., AAAS, N.Y. Acad. Sci., Ctr. for Profl. Advancement, Sigma Xi, Phi Lambda Epsilon, Phi Omega Epsilon. Home: 37 Wyncrest Ln Neptune NJ 07753-7421 E-mail: adamatt@att.net.

AGUILAR, EUGENIO ALFREDO, III, plastic surgeon; b. St. Louis, June 23, 1951; s. Eugenio Alfredo Aguilar, Jr. and Josefina Natalia Aguilar; children from previous marriage: Eugenio Alfredo IV, Nicolas, Eric. BS, U. Tex., 1974; MD, Tex. Tech. Sch. Medicine, Lubbock, 1979. Physician dept. otolaryngology U. Tex. Hermann Hosp., Houston, 1979—97; owner Ermosa Ctr. Reconstructive Surgery, Houston, 1997—. Clin. asst. prof. dept. otolaryngology U. Tex., Houston, 1989—, clin. asst. prof. divsn. plastic surgery, 1996—; clin. asst. prof. dept. surgery Baylor Coll. Medicine, Houston, 2001—; dir. Cranio Facial Found., 1990—. Author: The Trancolumellar Incision in External Rhinoplasty, 1988; author: (chpt.) Facial Plastic and Reconstructive Surgery, 1992, Pediatric Facial Plastic and Reconstructive Surgery, 1993, Head & Neck Surgery-Otolaryngology, 1993, Operative Plastic Surgery, 2000; co-author: Plastic and Reconstructive Surgery of the Auricle, 1996, Surgery of Congenital Microtia, 1996; contbr. articles to profl. jours. Mem. bd. dirs. Houston Pub. Libr., 1997—2002, chmn. bd. dirs., 2002—; mem. bd. dirs. Prevent Blindness Tex., 2001—02. Named One of Houston's Top Doctors in Plastic Surgery, Inside Houston Mag., 2000, One of Houston's Top Doctors in Plastic Surgery and Otolaryngology, 2001; recipient, CIBA, 1977, Jefferson award, 1992, Kernahan award, Am. Soc. Plastic Reconstructive Surgeons, 1996. Mem.: AMA, Houston Soc. Otolaryngology-Head and Neck Surgery, Harris County Med. Assn., Am. Acad. Otolaryngology-Head and Neck Surgery, Am. Acad. Facial Plastic Reconstructive Surgery, Houston Soc. Plastic Surgeons, Am. Soc. Plastic Surgeons, Tex. Med. Assn. (coun. socioecons. 1977—79, resident del. to AMA 1979, 1983, 1984, alt. del. to ho. of dels. 1984—85). Avocations: piano, golf, skiing, flying. Office: 6410 Fannin # 927 Houston TX 77030

AGUILAR, FÉLIX, public health physician, educator; b. Tegucigalpa, Honduras, Mar. 31, 1963; s. Felix and Orbelina Aguilar; m. Clare Marie Weber; 1 child, René Aguilar-Weber. BS, U. Calif., Irvine, 1981—86; MPH, Tulane U., New Orleans, 1986—87; MD, U. Calif., Irvine, 1992—96. Bd. cert. in family medicine 2000, bd. cert. in preventive medicine 2001. Health educator Charles Drew U. of Medicine and Sci., L.A., Calif., 1988—90; project coord. Tobacco Control Program, L.A. County Dept. of Health Svcs., L.A., Calif., 1990—91; acting city health officer Long Beach Dept. of Health and Human Svcs., Long Beach, Calif., 2000, preventive health med. dir., 2000—01; affiliate staff physician Long Beach Meml. Med. Ctr., Long Beach, Calif., 2000—; asst. clin. prof. U. Calif. at Irvine Coll. of Medicine, Irvine, Calif., 2000—; dir. of child health and disability prevention program Long Beach Dept. of Health and Human Svcs., Long Beach, Calif., 2001—. Cancer control v.p. Am. Cancer Soc. of Long Beach, Long Beach, 2000—; congress del. and L.A chap. exec. com. mem. Am. Acad. of Family Practice, Long Beach, 1998—; com. mem. Calif. Dept. of Health Svcs. Preventive Medicine Residency Program Advisory Com. to the CDHS Dir., Sacramento, 2000—; v.p. and congress del. Joint Com. of Interns and Residents, Harbor-UCLA Med. Ctr., Torrance, Calif., 1997—99; grants application reviewer Profl. Rev. Bd., Office of AIDS Programs and Policy, LA County Dept. of Health Svcs., Los Angeles, Calif., 1990; com. mem. Calif. Conf. of Local Health Officers Communicable Disease and Environ. Health Com., Sacramento, 1999—2000; co-chair Chicano/Latino Med. Student Assn, Irvine, 1992—93; com. mem. L.A. County Commn. on AIDS - Education Committee, Los Angeles, 1989—90; coalition mem. Latino Tobacco-Free Coalition, L.A., Calif., 1990—91; com. mem. AIDS Awareness Month/AIDS Awareness Com., L.A., Calif., 1989—90. Author: Palabra Vigente, 1990. Del. med. dir. and mem. bd. dirs. Witness for Peace, L.A., 1990—; co-chair People of Color AIDS Conf., L.A., 1990, Chicanos for Creative Medicine, Irvine, 1986—86; mem. bd. dirs. Physicians for Social Responsibility Nat., Washington, 2002—; pres., mem. bd. dirs. Physicians for Social Responsibility, L.A., 1994—, Monsignor Oscar Romero Clinic, L.A., 1990—93; pres., bd. mem. Irvine Students Housing, Inc, Irvine, 1985—86. Named Cancer Control Vol. of the Yr., Am. Cancer Soc., 2001, Breast Health Edn. Vol. of the Yr., 2000, Outstanding Graduating Med. Student, Calif. Chicano/Latino Med. Students Assn., 1996; recipient Outstanding Achievement award, City of Long Beach, CA, 2001, Spl. Recognition award, Calif. State Senator Ralph C. Dills, 1998, Sr. Humanitarian award, U. of Calif. Irvine Coll. of Medicine, 1996. Fellow: Am. Acad. Family Medicine; mem.: APHA, Physicians for Social Responsibility (President of Los Angeles Chapter 2000—pres), Am. Coll. of Preventive Medicine, Am. Acad. of Family Practice (President, Long Beach, CA subchapter 2000—pres), Audubon Soc. Pasadena Chap. (Newsletter Editor 1990—91). Avocations: social justice, poetry, travel. Home: 771 Raymond Ave Long Beach CA 90804-4624 Office: Long Beach Dept of Health and Human Svcs 2525 Grand Ave Long Beach CA 90815-1765 Office Fax: 562-570-4310. Personal E-mail: felix.aguilar@earthlink.net. Business E-Mail: felix_aguilar@ci.long-beach.ca.us.

AGUILAR, GLADYS MARIA, counselor, educator; b. Mérida, Mexico, Mar. 16, 1965; came to the U.S., 1968; d. Francisco Javier and Gladys Maria (Salazar) Aguilar; children: Emmanuel, Daniel. BS cum laude, Loyola Marymount U., 1987; MS, Calif. State U., 1990. Cert. in pupil personnel svcs. Youth min. St. Francis of Assisi Parish, L.A., 1987-88; sch. counselor Concern Counseling Svcs., Fullerton, Calif., 1988-89; bilingual behavioral therapist Inst. for Applied Behavioral Analysis, L.A., 1988-89; sch. counselor, tchr. St. Lucy's Priory High Sch., Glendora, Calif., 1989-90; intern Cath. Psychol. Svcs. Cath. Charities of L.A., L.A., 1990-93; bilingual elem. sch. counselor L.A. Unified Sch. Dist., 1993-96; therapist Foothill Cmty. Mental Health Ctr., 1996-97; mental health cons. Plz. de la Raza Preschool Corp., 1996—; bilingual elem. sch. tchr. Ont.-Montclair Sch. Dist., 1997—2003, Azusa Unified Sch. Dist., 2003—. Marriage, family and child counseling intern Brown & Assocs., Whittier, Calif., 1989-93. Eucharistic min., lector St. Francis of Assisi Cath. Ch., 1986-92. Mem. Soc. Children Book Writers and Illustrators, Calif. Tchrs. Assn., Calif. Assn. Marriage and Family Therapists, Calif. Assn. Bilingual Educators, L.A. Sch. Counselors Assn., Psi Chi, Alpha Sigma Nu. Avocations: travel, folkloric dancing, reading. Home: 836 N Forest Hills Dr Covina CA 91724-3609

AGUILAR-BRYAN, LYDIA, medical educator, medical researcher; b. Mexico City, Feb. 25, 1951; m. Joseph Bryan; 1 child. MD, U. Nacional Autonoma de Mex., 1975; PhD in Population Studies, U. Tex., 1985. Rsch. assoc. Inst. Biomed. Rsch., U. Nacional Autonoma de Mex., Mexico City, 1985—86, Baylor Coll. of Medicine, Dept. of Medicine, Divsn. of Endocrinology, Houston, 1987—88, postdoctoral fellow, 1988—90, instr., 1990—91, asst. prof., 1991—; prof. M.D. Anderson Cancer Ctr. U. Tex. Contbr. articles to profl. jours. Recipient postdoctoral fellowship, Juvenile Diabetes Found., 1988—90. Mem.: AAAS, Endocrine Soc., Biophys. Soc., Am. Diabetes Assn. (Rsch. grantee 1995—). Office: U Tex MD Anderson Cancer Ctr 1515 Holcombe Blvd Houston TX 77030-4009

AGUILAR ZINSER, ADOLFO MIGUEL, diplomat; b. Mexico City, Dec. 2, 1949; married; 2 children. BA in Internat. Rels., El Colegio de Mex., 1975; MA in Pub. Adminstrn. and Econ. Devel., Harvard U., 1978. Researcher, tchr. internat. rels. and Mexican fgn. policy; served in various capacities nat. commns. including CONASUPO (nat. supply co. for basic consumption commodities); sec. CONASUPO; served on various commns. including T.V. and Cinematography and Comm. Spl. Commn.; cand. Partido Revolucion Dem.; mem. Congress, 1994—97; ind. cand. Partido Verde Ecologista Mexicano; mem. Senate, 1997—2000; nat. security adviser, commr. law and order Govt. of Mex., 2000—02; internat. affairs coord. transition team Pres. Fox; mem. permanent mission of Mex. UN, N.Y.C., 2002—. Guest faculty Lat. Am. studies program Georgetown U., Sch. Internat. Svc. Am. U., U. Chgo., U. Calif., Berkeley; foudner Ind. Citizens Congressmen Group, 1994—97; syndicated columnist. Author: books; contbr. articles to Reforma, Frontera de Tijuana, L.A. Times, The Washington Post, The Wall St. Jour., Le Monde Diplomatique, essays on internat. polit. and econ. rels., nat. security and refugees to books and specialized mags. Office: Permanent Mission of Mex Two United Nations Plz 28th Fl New York NY 10017*

AGUILERA, CHRISTINA, vocalist; b. Dec. 18, 1980; Vocalist New Mickey Mouse Club, 1994-96; vocalist theme song for Disney animated film Mulan, 1998 (Golden Globe nominee for best original song in a motion picture); debut album Christina Aguilera (RCA), 1999 (Grammy for Best New Artist 2000), My Kind of Christmas, 2000, Mi Reflejo, 2000, Complete, 2002, Stripped, 2002; singles: What A Girl Wants, 1999, The Christmas Song, 1999, Genie in a Bottle, 1999; video: The Genie Gets Her Wish, 1999. Recipient ALMA award, best new artist, 1999, Grammy award, best new artist, 2000. Office: 244 Madison Ave # 314 New York NY 10016-2817

AGUILERA, DONNA CONANT, psychologist, researcher; b. Kinmundy, Ill. d. Charles E. and Daisy L. (Frost) Conant; m. George Limon Aguilera; children: Bruce Allen, Craig Steven. BS, UCLA, 1963, MS, 1965; PhD, U. So. Calif., 1974. Teaching asst. UCLA, 1965, grad. rsch. asst., 1965-66; prof. Calif. State U., L.A., 1966-81; cons. crisis intervention Didi Hirsch Community Mental Health Ctr., L.A., 1967-82. Mem. Def. Adv. Com. Women in the Services, 1978-82; originator, project dir. Project Link Lab. U. Author: (books) Crisis Intervention: Theory and Methodology, 1974, Crisis Intervention: Theory and Methodology, 9th edit., 2002, Review of Psychiatric Nursing, 1977, Review of

Psychiatric Nursing, 7th edit., 1978, Crisis Intervention: Therapy for Psychological Emergencies, 1983, Clinical Depression: A Life Span Approach, 2003; contbr. articles to profl. jours. Docent Huntington Libr. San Marino, Calif. 1991-2000; mem., mgr. disaster mental health svcs. ARC. NIH fellow, 1972-75 Fellow Am. Acad. Nursing (sec. 1976-77, pres. 1977-78), Acad. Psychiat. Nurse Specialists, Internat. Acad. Eclectic Psychotherapists (pres. 1987-89); mem. Am. Nurses Assn., Faculty Women's Assn., Am. Psychol. Assn., Calif. Psychol. Assn., AAUP, Alpha Tau Delta, Sigma Theta Tau Office: Ste A175 31441 Santa Margarita Pkwy Rancho Santa Margarita CA 92688-1836 Fax: 949-766-9206. E-mail: DCA@cox.net.

AGUILERA, ELSA JUDITH, physiatrist; b. Guayaquil, Guayas, Ecuador, Nov. 12, 1937; came to U.S., 1967; d. Ernesto Placido and Judith Pastora (Mora) Aguilera; m. Albert Joseph Engelhart, Mar. 20, 1976; 1 child, Albert Abraham. MD, U. Guayaquil, 1966. Diplomate in phys. med. and rehab., spinal cord injury medicine Am. Bd. Phys. Med. and Rehab.; diplomate Ecuadorian Bd. Medicine and Surgery; cert. wound specialist. Intern Union Hosp., Fall River, Mass., 1967-68; resident Univ. Hosp., Boston, 1968-71; staff surgeon Luis Vernaza Hosp., Guayaquil, 1967; tchg. fellow in phys. medicine and rehab. Boston U. Sch. Medicine, 1970-71, instr. phys. medicine and rehab., 1973-74, staff physiatrist, 1974 77; staff physician spinal cord injury svc. Brockton (Mass.) VA Med. Ctr., 1978-79, interim chief spinal cord injury svc., 1979-80, chief spinal cord injury svc., 1980-82; spinal cord injury attending physician VA Hosp., West Roxbury, Mass., 1998—; staff physician spinal cord injury svc. Brockton/West Roxbury VA Med. Ctr., 1982-91, staff physician spinal cord injury and rehab. svcs., 1991-94, asst. chief longterm care spinal cord injury svc., 1994-98; asst. clin. prof. phys medicine and rehab. Tufts U. Sch. Medicine, Boston, 2002—. Recipient U. Guayaquil award, 1966; named Tchr. of Yr. Tuft U. Med. Sch., 2000. Mem. AMA, Mass. Med. Soc., Am. Congress of Rehab. Medicine, New Eng. Phys. Medicine and Rehab. Soc. (chmn. 1980-81, vice chmn. 1979-80), Am. Paraplegia Soc., Am. Acad. Wound Mgmt., Assn. for Advancement of Wound Care. Roman Catholic. Avocations: piano, accordion and harmonica playing, bicycling, hiking. Office: VA Boston Healthcare Sys Spinal Cord Injury Svc 1400 VFW Pkwy West Roxbury MA 02132-4927 E-mail: Elsa.Aguilera@med.va.gov.

AGUINALDO, JORGE TANSINGCO, chemical engineer, water treatment specialist; b. Paniqui, Tarlac, The Philippines, Feb. 22, 1952; s. Andres Pagaduan and Lydia Obcena (Tansingco) A.; m. Juliet Sibal, May 10, 1978; children: Janice, Jeremy. BSChemE, Adamson U., Manila, 1973; postgrad., De La Salle U., Manila, 1977-82, Calif. State U., Sacramento, 1990-91. Registered chem. engr., Philippines. Supr. Paniqui (Tarlac) Sugar Corp, 1973-77; product mgr. water treatment and pollution control Alpha Machinery & Engring. Corp., Manila, 1977-83; sr. project engr. Metito Saudi Arabia Ltd., Riyadh, 1983-85, Metito Engring., Ltd., Nicosia, Cyprus, 1985-86, Metito Arabia Industries Ltd., Riyadh, 1986-89, project mgr., 1989-90; v.p. mktg. & devel. Am. Engring. Svcs., Inc., Tampa, Fla., 1991—; v.p. Am. Water Chems., Inc., 2001—. Bd. dirs. Bios Trading & Mgmt. Svcs. Corp., Manila; cons. J.M. Templa & Assocs., Manila, 1980-99. Adult leader Boy Scouts Am. Troop 176 Gulfridge Coun., Tampa. Mem. AIChE, Soc. Indsl. Microbiology, Am. Chem. Soc., Instrument Soc. Am. (sr.), Am. Water Works Assn., Soc. Indsl. Microbiology, Water Environ. Fedn., Philippine Inst. Chem. Engrs., Indsl. Computing Soc., Knights of Columbus, Tampa Bay Fossil Club. Roman Catholic. Avocations: paleontology, photography, computers. Office: 9001 Brittany Way Tampa FL 33619

AGUINSKY, RICHARD DANIEL, electrical engineer, administrator; b. Buenos Aires, Dec. 26, 1958; s. Elias Lorenzo and Rosa Isabel Aguinsky; m. Adriana Faiman; 1 child, Marina Sasha. BSEE, U. Técnica Nacional, Avellaneda, Buenos Aires, 1984; MSEE, San Jose State U., 1991. Serial prodn. technician Norman S.A., Buenos Aires, 1978-80; prof. asst. U. Técnologica Nacional, Avellaneda, Buenos Aires, 1980-84; sr. design engr., mgr. Nortel Networks, 1983-2000; sr. engr., project leader Jetstream Comms., 2000-01; hardware mgr. Vpacket Comms., Milpitas, Calif., 2001—03; pres., CEO Cinensis, Inc., 2003—. Mentor adelante program San Jose City Coll. Contbr. articles to Revista Telegrafica Electronica, No. Telecom., Am. Nat. Std. Telecomms. Avocations: travel, sailing, flying. E-mail: raguinsky@cinensis.com.

AGUIRRE, ANTONIO AZANES, JR., physician; b. Manila, Nov. 15, 1932; came to U.S., 1968; s. Antonio B. and Rufina (Azanes) A.; m. Esperanza Rafael, Jan. 3, 1959; children: Antonio III, Germelina, Enrico, Aristeo, Gizela. AA, Letran Coll., 1951; MD, U. Santo Tomas, 1958. Pvt. practice, Manila, 1958-68; resident Oakwood Hosp., Dearborn, Mich., 1973-76; pvt. practice Dearborn, Mich., 1976-97; physician Park Family Med. Ctr., Wyandotte, Mich., 1998—. Fellow Am. Acad. Family Physicians; mem. Mich. Acad. Family Physicians, Mich. State Med. Soc., Wayne County Med. Soc., Philippine Am. Assn. Family Physicians (past pres. Mich. chpt. 1995-96). Roman Catholic. Avocation: sports. Office: Park Family Med Ctr 1475 Ford Ave Wyandotte MI 48192-3825 Fax: 734-284-3102.

AGUIRRE, EDUARDO, JR., federal agency administrator; b. Cuba; m. Tere Aguirre; 2 children. Grad., La. State U.; degree (hon.), U. Tacnologica Santiago, Dominican Rep. With Texas Commerce Bank, 1969, Bank of Am., 1978—2000, pres., 1999—2000; vice chmn., 1st v.p. Export-Import Bank of U.S., Washington, 2001—02; Dir. Bureau of Citizenship & Immigration Svcs Dept. Homeland Security, 2003—. Hon. prof. Beijing Polytech U., Ctrl. U. Nationalities, Beijing; former chmn. bd. trustees Tex. Bar Found.; Founding chmn. bd. dirs. Houston Livestock Show and Rodeo; former chmn. bd. dirs. Tex. Children's Hosp.; regent U. Houston System Bd. of Regents, 1995—2001, chmn., 1996—98. Office: Naval Security Station Nebraska & Massachusetts Avenues Washington DC 20393*

AGUIRRE-BACA, FRANCISCO, publisher, consultant; b. León, Nicaragua, Jan. 7, 1920; came to U.S., 1947; s. Horacio and Pilar (Baca) Aguirre-Muñoz; m. Gladys Sacasa Aguirre, Dec. 27, 1941; children: Gladys, Francisco Xavier, Mariangeles, Rafael Eugenio, Guiomar, Alejandra. JD, U. Granada, Nicaragua, 1947. Various sr. positions Nicaraguan Armed Forces, 1940-47; rep., coord. numerous L.Am. newspapers and mags. Washington, 1947-53; co-founder, co-pub. Diario Las Americas, Miami, Fla., 1953—; founder Francisco Aguirre & Assocs. Latin Am. Newspapers and mag., Washington, 1960; dir. Pan Am. Divsn. Am. Road Builders Assn., Washington, 1948-53; co-founder, co-pub. Diario Las Americas, Miami, Fla., 1953; founder Francisco Aguirre & Assoc., Washington, 1960; amb. to III Summit Iberoamerican Chiefs of State Del. Dominican Republic, Salvador, Bahia, Brazil, 1993, amb. to IV Summit Iberoamerican Chiefs of State, 1994, Del. Republic Panama, Cartajena, Colombia, 1994; amb. to IV Summit Iberoamerican Pres. and Heads of States Nicaraguan Del., Santiago, Chile, 1996, amb. to official visit to His Holiness John Paul II Vatican City, Italy, 1996, amb. to Summit of the Ams. Santa Cruz, Bolivia, 1997; amb. to inauguration new Pres. Nicaragua Arnoldo Aleman Lacayo U.S. Del., Managua, Nicaragua, 1997; amb. to official visit to Republic China Nicaraguan Del., Taiwan, 1998, amb. II Summit of the Ams. Santiago, Chile, 1998, amb. XXVIII Gen. Assembly OAS Caracas, Venezuela, 1998. Internam. cons. Ambassador Extraordinary and Plenipotentiary of Nicaragua in Spl. Missions, Panama in Spl. Missions, 2002. Bd. dirs. Panamerican Divsn., Am. Rd. Builders Assn., 1948. Knight Order of St. Gregory, Sovereign Order of Malta; decorated by govts. of Argentina, Ecuador, Panama, Dominican Republic, Spain, Nicarauga, Republic of China (Taiwan). Mem. Hist. Georgetown Club, City Club, Nat. Press Club, Univ. Club, Congl. C.C. Republican. Roman Catholic. Home: 4951 Rockwood Pkwy NW Washington DC 20016-3247

AGUIRRE-BATTY, MERCEDES, Spanish and English language and literature educator; b. Cd Juarez, Mex., Dec. 20, 1952; came to U.S., 1957. d. Alejandro M. and Mercedes (Péon) Aguirre; m. Hugh K. Batty, Mar. 17, 1979; 1 child, Henry B. BA, U. Tex., El Paso, 1974, MA, 1977. Cert. online tchr., Calif. Instr. ESL Paso del Norte- Prep Sch., Cd Juarez, 1973-74; tchg. asst. ESL and English U. Tex., El Paso, 1974-77; instr. ESL English Lang. Svcs., Bridgeport, Conn., 1977-80; instr. Spanish and English, coord. modern lang. Sheridan (Wyo.) Coll., 1980—, pres. faculty senate, 1989-90; pres. faculty senate, chair dist. coun. No. Wyo. C.C. Dist., 1995-96. Planning com. No. Wyo. C.C. Dist., 1996-97; mem. advanced placement faculty Spanish cons. Coll. Bd. Ednl. Testing Svc., 1996-99; adj. prof. Spanish, U. Autonoma Cd Juarez, 1975; adj. prof. Spanish and English, Sacred Heart U., Fairfield, Conn., 1977-80; spkr. in field. Bd. dirs. Wyo. Coun. for the Humanities, 1988-92; translator county and dist. cts., Sheridan; vol. Wmen's Ctr.; translator Sheridan County Meml. Hosp.; del. Citizen Ambassador Program, People to People-India, 1996. NEH fellow, 1991-92; Wyo. State Dept. Edn. grant, 1991. Mem. MLA (del. assembly 1998-2000), Wyo. Fgn. Lang. Tchrs. Assn. (pres. 1990-92), Am. Assn. Tchrs. Spanish and Portuguese (founder, 1st pres. Wyo. chpt. 1987-90), TESOL, Sigma Delta Mu (v.p. 1992-99, pres. 2000—), Sigma Delta Pi (Alpha Iota chpt. pres. 1974-75). Avocations: travel, reading, archeology, languages, geography. Office: Sheridan Coll NWCCD 3059 Coffeen Ave Sheridan WY 82801-9133

AGUIRRE-SACASA, FRANCISCO XAVIER, international banker, diplomat; b. Managua, Nicaragua, Sept. 4, 1944; s. Francisco and Gladys (Sacasa) A.; m. Maria de los Angeles, Oct. 6, 1968; children: Rafael Ignacio, Roberto Francisco, Georgiana Eugenia. BS in Fgn. Svc., Georgetown U., 1966; JD, Harvard U., 1969. Contributing writer Christian Sci. Monitor, Boston Herald Traveler, Boston Globe, Wall Street Jour., Fin. Times, Wash. Post, Wash. Times, La Prensa (Nicaragua), Diario Las Americas, 1968—; young profl. and loan officer The World Bank, Washington, 1969-76, div. chief, 1977-86, asst. dir., 1986-87, sr. ops. advisor, 1987-88, dir., external affairs, 1988-90, dir. Africa region, 1990-95, dir. ops. evalutation dept., 1995-97; ambassador to U.S., Canada govt. Nicaragua, Washington, 1997—. Named one of Nicaragua's Citizen of the Century, 2000; OAS scholar Harvard U., 1966-68. Mem. Nat. Press Club, Nicaraguan Acad. Geography and History, Am.-Nicaraguan Found. (treas.), U. Mobile Latin Am. Campus (adv. bd.), Zamorano Agrl. Sch. (internat. adv. bd.), Congl. Country Club (Bethesda, Md.), Harvard Club of Washington, Univ. Club (Wash.), Hist. Georgetown Club (Wash.). Roman Catholic. Avocations: carpentry, golf, farming. Home: 4739 Tilden St NW Washington DC 20016-2327 also: Valhalla Farm 11302 Obannons Mill Rd Boston VA 22713-4132 Office: Embassy of Nicaragua 1627 New Hampshire Ave NW Washington DC 20009-2573

AGUIRRE-SACASA, RAFAEL EUGENIO, international consultant; b. Washington, Dec. 31, 1951; s. Francisco and Gladys (Sacasa) A.; m. Patricia Duque Estrada, July 9, 1976; children: Javier Eugenio, Francisco Eduardo. BS in Fgn. Svc., Georgetown U., 1973; grad., Air Command and Staff Coll., 1985. With U.S. Air Force, 1973-83; dir. internat. sales P. Beretta SpA, Washington, 1983-87; dir. govt. rels. Beretta USA Corp., Washington, 1986-87, dir. mktg. Accokeek, Md., 1987-98; exec. v.p. INTEC Internat. Cons., Washington, 1998—. Bd. dirs. Greater Am. Bus. Coalition, 2000—. Mem. OAS Presidential Electoral Com., Ecuador, 1969, Pan-Am. Devel. Found. Emergency Earthquake Relief Team, Managua, Nicaragua, 1972; vice chmn. Rep. Nat. Hispanic Assembly, Washington, 1983.; bd. dirs. Am. Firearms Coun., 1994-98, Nat. Shooting Sports Found. Mktg. Coun., 1996-98; spl. advisor Fgn. Min. Internat. Polit. & Mil. Affairs, 1997-2001; bd.; spl. advisor to foreign ministry of Panama-rank of ambassador at large, 2001; Maj. USAF, 1973-83. Decorated Air Force Commendation with oak leaf cluster, Def. Meritorious Svc. medal with oak leaf cluster; ROTC scholar Georgetown U., 1971-73. Mem. Am. Mktg. Assn., Congl. Country Club, Army-Navy Club. Roman Catholic. Avocations: reading, jogging, hunting. Home: 7900 Greentree Rd Bethesda MD 20817-1302 Office: Global Marketing Devel 4835 Yuma St NW Washington DC 20016-2061

AGUS, DAVID BERNARD, physician; b. Balt., Jan. 29, 1965; s. Zalman S. and Sondra L. (Lebow) A. BA cum laude, Princeton U., 1987; MD, U. Pa., 1992. Fellow Rsch. Inst. of Scripps Clinic, La Jolla, Calif., 1988-90; physician scientist fellow NIH, Bethesda, Md., 1990-92, rsch. scholar Howard Hughes Med. Inst., 1990-92; Oster med. intern and resident, staff physician Johns Hopkins Hosp., Balt., 1992-94; fellow Meml. Sloan-Kettering Cancer Ctr., N.Y.C., 1994-97, instr. lymphoma svc., 1997-99, head Lab. of Tumor Biology, 1997-2000; dir. prostate cancer ctr. Cedars-Sinai Med. Ctr., L.A., 2000—; asst. prof. medicine UCLA Sch. Medicine, 2000—03, assoc. prof. medicine, 2003—. Instr. medicine Cornell U. Med. Ctr., 1997-99, asst. prof. medicine, 1999-2000; asst. mem. Meml. Sloan-Kettering Cancer Ctr., 1999-2000. Author: Interleukin-2: Cellular and Clinical Study, 1987; contbr. articles to Jour. Clin. Investigation, Cancer Cell, Jour. of Exptl. Medicine, Jour. Nat. Cancer Inst. Cancer Rsch. Recipient Achievement award Am. Assn. Allergy and Immunology, 1988, Physician Rsch. Devel. award Am. Cancer Inst., 1996, Young Investigator award CaPCURE, 1998; Nat. Cancer Inst. grantee, 1988. Mem. AAAS, AMA, ACP, Am. Soc. Hematology, Am. Soc. Clin. Oncology, Am. Assn. for Cancer Rsch. Office: Prostate Cancer Ctr Cedars-Sinai Med Ctr 8631 W 3d St Ste 1001E Los Angeles CA 90048-1804 E-mail: agusd@cshs.org.

AGVANIAN, YOURI, mathematician, educator, physicist; b. Yerevan, Armenia, Sept. 22, 1950; s. Martiros and Eranuhe Agvanian; m. Anahit Hovhanesyan; children: Zara, Elina. BS, Yerevan State U., Armenia, 1972; MS, Moscow U., 1980, PhD, 1990. Prof. physics, dean Yerevan Poly. U., 1973—92; prof. math. Pasadena City Coll., Calif., 1998—2000, L.A. Mission Coll., Sylmar, Calif., 1998—, Moor Park Coll., Calif., 1998—; prof. physics, astronomy Calif. State U., L.A., 1999—2001; prof. math. Calif. State Poly. U., Pomona, 2000—. Author: Transforamtion of Drops in NonHomogenious Temperature and Concentration Binary Vescous Environments, 1978; contbr. articles various profl. jours.; author: The Theory of Diffusive Magnetism of "Flying" High Heat Transferring Spherical Drops, 1978, The Theory of Thermal Magnetism of Spherical Drops in a Binary Liquid, 1979. Mem.: Math. Assn. Am., N.Y. Acad. Sci., Am. Math. Soc., Am. Phys. Soc. Office: Calif State Polytechnic U 3801 West Temple Ave Pomona CA 91768

AGWU, NKECHI MADONNA, mathematics educator; b. Enugu, Enugu, Nigeria, Oct. 8, 1962; d. Jacob Ukejeh Agwu and Europa Lauretta Durosimi Wilson; m. Nicholas C. B. Ogbonna; 1 child, Ngozichukwuka Jacob A. D. BS with honors, U. of Nigeria, Nsukka, 1984; MS, U. of Conn., 1991; PhD, Syracuse U., 1995. Lectr. Kaduna (Enugu) Poly., Kaduna, 1985—87; statistician Fed. Office of Stats., Enugu; assoc. prof. Borough of Manhattan C.C., N.Y.C., 1995—. Ednl. cons. New Visions for Pub. Schs., N.Y.C., 2000—01, Algebra Project, N.Y.C., 1998—2000. Author: (curriculum development) Using a Threaded Discussion Web-based Software to Teach Statistics (Am. Math. Assn. 2-Year Colls. INPUT award, 2000); editor: (jour.) Mathematics in College, American Journal of Undergraduate Research. Named to Project Kaleidoscope Faculty for the Twenty-First Century, 1997 2002; recipient Performance Excellence award, Profl. Staff Congress, CUNY, 2000, Nigerian Fed. Govt. Merit award, 1981—84, tchg. assistantship, Syracuse U., 1991—95, tchg. assistantship, U. of Conn., 1987—91, Internat. Conf. on Tech. in Collegiate Math. Travel award, Addison-Wesley, 2002, Nat. Grad. Student Dissertation Travel award, Am. Ednl. Rsch. Assn. Divsn K, 1994, N.Y.C. Literacy Assistance Ctr. mini-grant, N.Y.C. Literacy Assistance Ctr. and Profl. Devel. Consortium, 1998, N.Y.C. Literary Assistance Ctr. and Profl. Devel. Consortium, 1999. Mem.: Math. Assn. of Am. (Math. Assn. of Am. Inst. in the History of Math. and Its Uses in Tchg. Profl. Devel. award 1997—2001), Am. Math. Assn. 2-Year Colls. (life Travel award 1997). Office: Borough of Manhattan C C 199 Chambers St New York NY 10007 Office Fax: 212-748-7459. E-mail: nagwu@bmcc.cuny.edu.

AGWUNOBI, JOHN ODERAH, pediatrician; b. Dundee, Angus, Scotland, Oct. 4, 1964; arrived in U.S., 1989; MB, BChir, U. Jos, Plateau State, Nigeria, 1987; MBA, Georgetown U., 2000. Diplomate Am. Bd. Pediat. Resident in pediat. Howard U., Washington, 1990-93; attending pediatrician Hosp. for Sick Children, Washington, 1993-2000, med. dir., 1998-2000; dep. sec. Dept. of Health (Fla.), 2000—; sec. health Fla. Dept. Health, 2001—. Bd. dirs. Ct. Apptd. Spl. Advs., Montgomery County, Md., 1996. Fellow: Am. Acad. Pediat.; mem.: AMA, Am. Coll. Physician Execs., Nat. Med. Assn.

AGYENKWAH, KENNEDY SETH, communications executive; b. Accra, Ghana, May 20, 1953; came to U.S., 1989; s. Seth Kwabena Apeasah and Mercy Afua Addae; m. Sylvia Afari, June 23, 1984 (div. June 1994); m. Sandra Dee, Nov. 23, 1995; children: Osiris, Kwasi. BA in Mgmt., Met. State U., 2000. Instr. bus. edn. Ghana Edn. Svc., Somanya, 1974-76; prin. course tutor, writer Inst. Adult Edn., U. Ghana, Legon, 1978-79; founder, vice prin., dir. African Meth. Episcopal Zion U., Monrovia, Liberia, 1980-86; instr., bus. mgr., asst. dir. Don Bosco Poly., Monrovia, 1981-89; CEO Pan African Internat. Marketplace, Mpls., 1993-97, African Comm. Network, Mpls., 1997—. Project cons., writer Don Bosco Poly., Monrovia, 1988-89. Author: (poems and essays) African Personality, 1993, (book) African Ethoes, 1998, Organize the Village-Core Values Game and Rites of Passage Game, 2001. Gen. sec. Ananda Marga Yoga Soc., Monrovia, 1984-89; mem. steering com. North Washington Indsl. Park, Mpls., 1995; cons. Coun. Black Minnesotans African Resource Ctr., St. Paul, 2000-01; mem. adv. bd. race, poverty initiative, U. Minn. Law Sch., Mpls.; elder, chief organizer, facilitator Global African Village, 1998—. Fellow British Soc. Commerce. Home and Office: African Comm Network 2923 Dupont Ave N Minneapolis MN 55411-1343

AHADI, STEPHAN AHAD, psychologist, psychometrician; b. St. Louis, Oct. 6, 1962; s. Abdul Ahad and Gisela Ahadi; m. Maria D. Nuñez, July 25, 1998. BS, Baylor U., 1985; PhD, U. Ill., Urbana-Champaign, 1991. Postdoctoral fellow U. Oreg., Eugene, 1991-93; asst. prof. U. Tex., El Paso, 1994-99; psychometrician MetriTech, Inc., Champaign, Ill., 1999—. Cons. editor Jour. of Personality and Social Psychology: Personality Processes and Individual Differences, 1998-2003. Mem. Am. Psychol. Assn., Am. Ednl. Rsch. Assn., Soc. for Personality and Social Psychology, Am. Psychol. Soc. Office: MetriTech Inc 4106 Fieldstone Rd Champaign IL 61822 Fax: 217-398-5798. E-mail: sahadi@metritech.com.

AHANONU, CHUKWUMA SMART, education educator; s. Samuel Owowo Ahanonu Onyemaobi and Mgbakwa Adline Ahanonu Onyemaemeribe; m. Ijeoma Ahanonu, Sept. 18, 1970; children: Chidinmma Valerie children: Okechikanma, Cecilia Nkechinyere Isabel, Nwanyidirim Ahanonu-Acord, Nwachi. BS in Spl. Edn., Psychology, Utah State U., 1979, MS in Spl. Edn., 1983, Philosophy of Spl. Edn. degree, 1986. Profl. Adminstrv. and Supr. (K-12) UT State Office of Edn., 1990. Spl. educator Granite Sch. Dist., Salt Lake City, 1979—81; asst. pastor First Presbyn. Ch., Logan, Utah, 1983—91, Preston Presbyn. Cmty. Ch., Idaho, 1983—91; spl. educator, dept. chair, soccer coach Logan City Sch. Dist., Utah, 1984—91; spl. educator, soccer coach Davis County Sch. Dist., Farmington, Utah, 1991—93; assoc. prof. Weber State U., Ogden, Utah, 1993—2000; assoc. prof., acting dept. chair Miss. Valley State U., Itta Bena, 2000—. Edn. cons. Project Success Inc., Ogden, Utah, 1993—2000, adv. bd. mem., 1994—97, exec. bd. mem., edn. rep., 1997—2000. Author: (jour. article) UT Acad. of Scis. (Best Paper Presentation, 1999), (poems) The time is now; Early Morning; Onye Oma; Ochi Gi; Legacy; story teller (African folklore) Nwa aka-adighi ukporo. Pres. Phi Delta Kappa Weber State U. Chpt., Ogden, Utah, 1998—99; edn. divsn. chair UT Acad. of Scis., Arts and Letters, Salt Lake City, 1999—2000; miss. valley state univ. student chpt. advisor Coun. for Exceptional Children, Itta Bena, Utah, 2001—03. Recipient Best Poster Session award, Assn. for Behavior Analysis, 1985, Exemplary Collaboration Cert. and Cash Award, Weber State U., 1995; grantee Faculty Vitality Grant, Hemingway, 1998—99, Evaluative Rsch. and Capacity Bldg. Grant, NSF and Miss. Dept. of Edn., 2003—. Mem.: Kappa Delta Pi (student chpt. co-advisor 2002—03), Phi Delta Kappa Internat. Fratanity (weber state chpt. sec., v.p., del. i, pres. 1994—2000, Presdl. Plaque 1999), The Coun. for Exceptional Children (student chpt. advisor 1994—2003). Methodist. Avocations: photography, reading, sewing, computers, teaching. Office: Miss Valley State U 14000 Hwy 82 W Box 7243 Itta Bena MS 38941 Office Fax: 662-254-3613. E-mail: cahan@mvsu.edu.

AHEARN, JAMES, newspaper columnist; b. S. Bend, Ind., Dec. 26, 1931; s. Francis T. and Loretto (Lorden) A.; m. Mary Ann Boesch, June 7, 1954; children— Michael James, Mary Elizabeth, Sarah Katharine, Margaret Ann. BA, Amherst Coll., 1953; Nieman fellow, Harvard U., 1970-71. Reporter UPI, Boston, Newark and Trenton, N.J., 1957-61; state house corr. The Record, Hackensack, N.J., 1961-65, editorial writer, then editor editorial page, 1965-77, mng. editor, 1977-87, assoc. editor, 1987-91, contbg. editor, 1993—. Served with USNR, 1953-57. Office: 150 River St Hackensack NJ 07601-7110

AHEARN, JOHN FRANCIS, JR., retired oil and gas company executive; b. Waterbury, Conn., May 19, 1921; s. John Francis and Anna Elizabeth (Kane) A.; m. Mary Louise Gardner, Jan. 7, 1956 (dec. Aug. 1985); m. Margaret Bloch Bagby, Feb. 23, 1991 (div. Mar. 2001). AB, Brown U., 1944; MBA, Stanford U., 1955. Mgr. agrl. mktg. Kern County Land Co., Bakersfield, Calif., 1955-62, mgr. corp. planning San Francisco, 1962-65; dir. corp. planning J.I. Case, Racine, Wis., 1965-67, Kern County Land Co., 1968; v.p. corp. planning Sonat Inc., Birmingham, Ala., 1968-82, sr. v.p. corp. planning, 1982-85. Comdr. USNR, 1944-46, 50-53, ret. Mem.: Mountain Brook (Ala.); Shoal Creek (Ala.). Republican. Roman Catholic. Avocations: traveling, tennis; trout fishing; walking. Home: 7 Eagle View Shoal Creek AL 35242

AHEARN, MATTHEW J. assemblyman; b. Okinawa, Japan, Jan. 16, 1959; m. Susan Ahearn; children: Lauryn, Samantha, Kelly. BA in Polit. Sci., Rutgers U., 1981; JD, Hofstra U. Sch. of Law, 1991. Law clk. Constl. Law Clinic, Cmty. Legal Assistance Corp., 1990; atty., cons. eB Networks, 1998—2000; dep. mayor Borough of Fair Lawn, 1998—2000; legislator, atty. Hartman & Winnicki, PC, 2000—; gen. assembly, 2002—. Atty. Bergen County Domestic Violence Project, 1993—96. Mem. Borough of Fair Lawn Planning Bd., 1998—2000; vice chair Mil. & Vets. Affairs. Capt. 18th Airborne Corps U.S. Army, 1981—85, with USAR, 1985—92. Mem.: N.J. State Bar Assn. (internet and computer law com. 1991—), Bergen County Bar Assn. (land use law com. 1991—), 82d Airborne Divsn. Assn., Am. Legion Post. Green Party. Office: 305 Rte 17 S Unit 3-205 Paramus NJ 07652*

AHEARNE, JOHN FRANCIS, scientific research administrator, researcher; b. New Britain, Conn., June 14, 1934; s. Daniel Paul and Balbena Marian (Baloski) A.; m. Barbara Helen Drezek, June 19, 1956; children: Thomas, Paul, Mary Ann, Robert, Patricia. B of Engring. Physics, Cornell U., 1957, MS in Physics, 1958; MA, Princeton U., 1963, PhD, 1966. Nuclear weapons analyst USAF, 1959-61; assoc. prof. physics USAF Acad., 1964-69; from analyst to dir. tactical air Office Asst. Sec. Def. for Systems Analysis, 1969-72; dep. asst. sec. def. for gen. purpose programs, 1972-74; prin. dep. sec. def. manpower and res. affairs, 1974-76; staff White House Energy Office, 1977; dep. asst. sec. Dept. Energy, 1978; commr. U.S. Nuclear Regulatory Commn., 1978-83, chmn., 1980-81; mgmt. cons. Comptr. Gen of U.S., 1983-84; v.p., sr. fellow Resources for the Future, 1984-89; exec. dir. Sigma Xi, The Sci. Rsch. Soc., Research Triangle Park, N.C., 1989-96; dir. Sigma Xi Ctr., Research Triangle Park, N.C., 1995-99; dir. ethics program Sigma Xi, Research Triangle Park, N.C., 1999—; lectr. pub. policy Duke U., Durham, N.C., 1995— Adj. fellow Resources for Future, 1992—; adj. prof. civil and environ. engring. Duke U., 1996-2002; adj. prof. U. Colo., 1966-69; adj. fellow Resources for the Future, 1992—; vice-chmn. Nat. Rsch. Coun. Bd. on Radioactive Waste Mgmt., 1997-99, chmn., 2000—; chmn. adv. com. on nuclear facility safety U.S. Dept. Energy, 1988-91, environ. mgmt. adv. bd., 1994-2002, co-chmn. adv. com. on external regulation, 1995-96, nuclear energy rsch. adv. com., 1998—, vice chmn., 2002—; chmn. risk perception and comm. com. NAS, 1987-89, chmn. future nuclear power com., 1990-93, com. on tech. bases for Yucca Mountain Stds., 1993-96, com. on risk characterization, 1994-97, dual use techs. and export controls com., electrometallurg. tech. com., co-chmn. burning plasma experiment assessment com., 2002--, co-chmn. forum on the environment, 1995-97, vice-chmn. com. risk assessment and mgmt. marine sys., 1996-98, com. on battlefield radiation exposure, 1996-99, chmn. com. to rev. rsch. under EPACT, 1997-99, co-chmn. com. on end points of U.S. and Russian nuc. waste, 2001—, com. on indigenization of programs to prevent leakage, jt. acad. com. on counterterrorism challenges for Russia and the US, 2002—; pres.'s coun. for nat. labs. U. Calif., 1992—; vice-chmn. U.S. Commn. for IIASA, 1992-93, chmn., 1994-98; adv. com. Princeton Plasma Physics Nat. Lab., 1993-98; co-chmn. panel on opportunities in plasma sci. tech. NAS, 1992-96, reactor panel for disposition of weapons plutonium, 1992-96; bd. dirs. Wis. Energy Corp.; lectr. Colo. Coll., 1966-69; pres. com. adv. S&T Energy R&D panel, 1997-98; USGAO exec. coun. Info. Mgmt. and Tech., 1997—. Bd. dirs. Woodstock Theol. Ctr., chmn., 1980-85. Gen. Electric Coffin fellow, 1957-58; recipient Dept. Def. Disting. Civilian Service medal and bronze palm, Sec. Def. Meritorious Svc. medal; named Boss of Year D.C. chpt. Nat. Secs. Assn., 1976. Fellow AAAS, Am. Phys. Soc. (chmn. forum on physics and soc. 1996-97, chair panel on pub. affairs 2003—), Am. Acad. Arts and Scis., Soc. Risk Analysis; mem. NAE, Nat. Acads. (nat. assoc.), Nat. Coun. for Radiation Protection and Measurement, Am. Nuclear Soc., Soc. for Risk Analysis (past pres.), Sigma Xi. Democrat. Roman Catholic.

AHERN, ARLEEN FLEMING, retired librarian; b. Mt. Harris, Colo., Oct. 15, 1922; d. John R. and Josephine (Vidmar) Fleming; m. George Irving Ahern, June 14, 1944; 1 child, George Irving Jr. BA, U. Utah, 1943; MA, U. Denver, 1962; postgrad., U. Colo., 1967. Library asst. Colo. Women's Coll. Library (now U. Denver/CWC Campus), 1952-60, acquisitions librarian, 1960—. Rep.

Adult Edn. Council Denver, 1960-90, reference librarian Penrose Library, WEC librarian, assoc. prof. librarianship through 1987, U. Denver Penrose Libr.; assoc. prof. emeritus, U. Denver; retired. Vol. Opera Colo. Guild; treas., bd. dirs. Denver Lyric Opera; bd. dirs. U. Denver Women's Libr. Assn., 1996—, Samaritan House Guild, Jeanne Jugan (Little Sisters Poor) Aux., Colo. Symphony Guild, Cinema Study Club Colo., Carson Brierly Dance Libr.; committeewoman Rep. Com., Denver, 1958—59. Mem. AAUP, ALA, Mountain Plains Library Assn., Colo. (1st v.p., pres. 1969-70, dir. 1971—), Library Assn., Women's Libr. Assn. (bd. dirs. 1996—), Altrusa Club of Denver (2d v.p. 1968-69, dir. 1971-74, 76, 78), Soc. Am. Archivists, Mountain Plains Adult Edn. Assn., Denver Botanic Gardens. Home: 3212 S Oneida Way Denver CO 80224-2830

AHERN, F. DANIEL, JR., state agency administrator, management consultant; b. Malden, Mass., May 24, 1955; s. Francis Daniel and Barbara Ann Ahern; m. Jean Marie Hernon, May 4, 1980; children: Patrick Daniel, Cara Chisholm. BA in Polit. Sci. with highest honors, Northeastern U., Boston, 1977, MPA, 1978. Cert. govt. fin. mgr.; cert. fraud examiner; cert. inspector gen. Cons. Mass. Dept. Cmty. Affairs, Boston, 1977-79; assoc. legis. analyst Joint Legis. Audit and Rev. Commn., Richmond, Va., 1979-82; adj. prof. dept. polit. sci. Northeastern U., Boston, 1979—; sr. mgmt. analyst Mass. Office of the Insp. Gen., Boston, 1982-85, prin. mgmt. analyst, 1986-91, dep. insp. gen. for mgmt., 1991-93, 1st asst. insp. gen. for mgmt., 1993—2003; pres. Clarus Group, Hanover, Mass., 2003—. Mem. editl. bd. Pub. Integrity Ann., 1997-98, Pub. Adminstrn. Rev., 1997-2000, Chinese Pub. Adminstrn. Rev. Soccer coach Hanover Soccer Club, Hanover Youth Athletic Assn. Fellow: Nat. Acad. Pub. Adminstrn.; mem.: ASPA (nat. pres., past pres. Mass. chpt., chair Assn. on Budgeting and Fin. Mgmt. 1985—86, exec. com. sect. on ethics 1998—99), Assn. Cert. Fraud Examiners, Assn. Govt. Accts., Assn. Insps. Gen. (charter, bd. dirs., past sec., profl. stds. and practices com.). Office: Clarus Group 147 Curtis Mill Ln Hanover MA 02339-1349 Office Fax: 781-878-6103. E-mail: dahern@theclarusgroup.com.

AHERN, GEOFFREY LAWRENCE, behavioral neurologist; b. N.Y.C., Feb. 20, 1954; BA, SUNY, Purchase, 1976; MS, Yale U., 1978, PhD in Psychology, 1981, MD, 1984. Med. intern Waterbury (Conn.) Hosp., 1984-85; resident in neurology Boston U., 1985-88; fellow in behavioral neurology Beth Israel Hosp., Boston, 1988-90; instr. neurology Harvard Med. Sch., Boston, 1988-90; asst. prof. neurology and psychology U. Ariz., Tucson, 1990-96, assoc. prof. neurology and psychology, 1996-99, assoc. prof. neurology, psychology and psychiatry, 1999—2002, prof. neurology, psychology and psychiatry, 2002—. Contbr. articles to profl. jours., chapters to books. Mem.: Am. Neurol. Assn., Am. Acad. Neurology. Office: Univ Med Ctr Dept Neurology 1501 N Campbell Ave Tucson AZ 85724-5023

AHERN, JO ANN, diabetes clinical nurse specialist; b. Bridgeport, Conn., Mar. 22, 1951; d. Charles Cary and Mabel Rose (Donovan) Hickey; m. Brian Joseph Ahern, May 27, 1972; children: Sean, Jeremy, Abby. ASN, U. Bridgeport, 1979, BSN, 1989; MSN, So. Conn. State U., 1993. Cert. diabetes educator; advanced practice RN. Staff nurse Children's Clin. Rsch. Ctr. Yale/New Haven (Conn.) Hosp., 1979-82, trial coord. Diabetes Control and Complications Trial, 1982-93, pediatric and adult diabetes nurse specialist, 1993—. Author, reviewer The Diabetes Educator jour., 1990—; mem. editl. bd. Diabetes Forecast Mag. Recipient Wittnauer Diabetes Educator award, 1997; named Nat. Nurse of Yr., Nursing Spectrum mag., 1998. Mem. Am. Diabetes Assn. (Conn. affiliate 1975—, symposia com. 1994, DCCT translation task force 1993-94), Am. Assn. Diabetes Educators (bd. dirs. 1994-97), Conn. Assn. Diabetes Educators (v.p. 1993-94, chair profl. edn. 1989-98). Democrat. Roman Catholic. Avocations: walking, soccer, reading, tennis. Home: 530 Scenic Rd Orange CT 06477-2127 Office: Pediatric Diabetes Program 2 Church St S Ste 404 New Haven CT 06519-1717 E-mail: joann.ahern@yale.edu.

AHIMA, REXFORD SEFAH, neuroendocrinologist, internist; b. Accra, Ghana, Nov. 4, 1960; came to U.S., 1988; s. Lawrence and Grace (Kontoh) A.; m. Suzette Yaa Osei, June 9, 1990; 1 child, Afua Dedaa. BSc with honors, U. London, 1981; MD, U. Ghana, 1986; PhD, Tulane U., 1992. Diplomate Am. Bd. Internal Medicine with subspecialty in endocrinology, diabetes and metabolism. House physician, surgeon Korle Bu Teaching Hosp.-U. Ghana Med. Sch., Accra, 1986-87; rsch. assoc., instr./tutor in anatomy, physiology, neurosci. Tulane U. Sch. Medicine, New Orleans, 1988-92; house physician dept. medicine Albert Einstein Coll. Medicine, Yeshiva U., Bronx, N.Y., 1992-95; fellow in endocrinology, diabetes and metabolism Harvard U. Sch. Medicine-Longwood Med. Area Program, Boston, 1995-98; physician divsn. endocrinology Beth Israel Deaconess Med. Ctr., Boston, 1998-99; asst. prof. dept. medicine U. Pa. Sch. Medicine, Phila., 1999—. Instr. in medicine Harvard Med. Sch., 1998-99. Contbr. articles to med. jours. Recipient Leo M. Davidoff award Albert Einstein Coll. Medicine, 1994, Owl Club award Tulane U. Med. Sch., 1989, Gold medal Anat. Soc. West Africa, 1991; Pfizer fellow, 1997-98. Mem. Endocrine Soc., Mass. Med. Soc. Avocations: tennis, photography, art, collecting jazz. Office: U Pa Sch Med Div Endo Diabetes & Metabolism 611 CRB 415 Curie Blvd Philadelphia PA 19104 also: U Pa Divsn Endocrinology 611 CRB 415 Curie Blvd Philadelphia PA 19104

AHL, ALWYNELLE SELF, zoology, ecology and veterinary medical executive; b. Leesville, La., Mar. 18, 1941; d. Clyde and Fariebee Margaret (Parker) Self; m. James Gilmore Ahl, May 29, 1963; children— Robert C., Laura J. BS, Centenary Coll., La., 1961; MS, U. Wyo., 1963, PhD, 1967; DVM, Mich. State U., 1987. Research asst. U. Wyo., 1965-67; mem. faculty Mich. State U., East Lansing, 1967—77, asst. prof. natural scis., 1971-77, prof., 1977-87; vet. edml. specialist USDA/Animal and Plant Health Inspection Service/Vet. Svcs., 1987-89, dep. dir. recruitment and devel. for animal health and care tng., 1989-91; head risk analysis sect. USDA/Animal and Plant Health Inspection Service/Policy and Program Devel., Riverdale, Md., 1991-94; chief planning and risk sys. Riverdale, Md., 1994-95; dir. Office of Risk Assessment and Cost-Benefit analysis USDA, Washington, 1995-2000; USDA fellow Tuskegee U. Ctr. for Integrated Study of Food, Animal & Fiber Sys., 2000—. Contbr. articles to profl. jours. Recipient Mich. State U. tchr. scholar award, 1971; fellow NDEA, 1961-64, NSF, 1964-65, NIH summer fellow, 1963 Fellow AAAS, Coun. Excellence in Govt.; mem. AVMA, Soc. for Risk Analysis, Soc. Tropical Vet. Medicine, Sigma Xi. Episcopalian. Home: 9026 S Tatum Creek Rd Lyles TN 37098-3021 Office: Tuskegee U Coll Vet Medicine Food and Animal Prodn Bldg Rm 115 Tuskegee Institute AL 36088 E-mail: jaahl@centerville.net., asahl@tusk.edu.

AHL, ROGER JOHN, producer, writer; b. Paterson, N.J., Dec. 4, 1963; s. Brian R. and Marcia G. (Touw) A. BA in Communications, Fairleigh Dickinson U., 1986; diploma in broadcasting, Conn. Sch. Broadcasting, 1987. Sports producer Fox TV Stas. Inc., N.Y.C., 1985—; sportscaster Pepper Martin Prodns., Midland Park, NJ, 1986—88; sports writer Ridgewood Newspaper of N.J., Paramus, 1987-91; play-by-play announcer Paragon Cable Inc., Newburg, N.Y., 1990-91; freelance producer ABC Radio Sports, 1992—. Instr. Conn. Sch. Broadcasting, 1999—. Recipient Citizenship award Mayor of Franklin Lakes, N.J., 1978, Citizenship award Elks Club, Oakland, N.J., 1982. Mem. Writers Guild Am. Methodist. Avocations: ice hockey, writing, softball.

AHL, SALLY WEBB, religious studies educator; b. New Rochelle, N.Y., Apr. 6, 1938; d. Gertrude Voland Moffett. BS, Cornell U., 1960; BA summa cum laude, Barrington Coll., 1969; PhD, Brandeis U., 1972, MA, 1973; MS in Edn., U. Kans., 1989, PhD in Edn., 1992. Cert. tchr. Mich. County ext. agt. home econ. Coop. Ext. Svc., Scottville, Mich., 1960—62; tchr. home econ. Ludington Pub. Sch., Ludington, Mich., 1962—66; prof. of bibl. studies Tarkio (Mo.) Coll., 1973—82; libr. asst., instr. Bibl. Hebrew U. Kans., Lawrence, Kans., 1989; pvt. instr. in Bibl. Hebrew; leader of colloquia Reading Scripture in Hebrew, 2003. Author: Classical Hebrew: A Handbook for the Analysis of Words, 2000. Ministerial asst. various ch., Mo., 1975—82. Recipient Am. Bible Soc. award, Barrington Coll., 1969; fellow Mary E. Hirschfield fellow, Brandeis U.; scholar, 1970—73. Home: 3323 Iowa Street no 337 Lawrence KS 66046-5218

AHLEM, LLOYD HAROLD, psychologist; b. Moose Lake, Minn., Nov. 7, 1929; s. Harold Edward and Agnes (Carlson) A.; m. Anne T. Jensen, Dec. 29, 1952; children: Ted, Dan, Mary Jo, Carol, Aileen. AA, North Park Coll., 1948; AB, San Jose State Coll., 1952, MA, 1955; Ed.D., U. So. Calif., 1962. Tchr. retarded children Fresno County (Calif.) Pub. Schs., 1953-54; psychologist Baldwin Park (Calif.) Sch. Dist., 1955-62; prof. psychology Calif. State U., Stanislaus (formerly Stanislaus State Coll.), Turlock, Calif., 1962-70; pres. North Park U., Chgo., 1970-79, dir., 1966-70; exec. dir. Covenant Village Retirement Center, Turlock, 1979-89; dir. spl. projects Covenant Retirement Communities, Chgo., 1989-93; dir. Emanuel Med. Ctr., Turlock, Calif., 1984-99, Merced Mut. Ins. Co., Atwater, Calif., 1993—; chmn. Capital Corp. of West, Merced, Calif., 1995-2000. Author: Do I Have To Be Me, 1974, How to Cope: Managing Change, Crisis and Conflict, 1978, Help for the Families of the Mentally Ill, 1983, Living and Growing in Later Years, 1992; columnist Covenant Companion, 1972-90. Decorated comdr. Order of Polar Star Sweden; recipient Disting. Alumnus award North Park Coll., 1966 Mem. Assn. Colls. Ill. (vice chmn. 1975-79) Mem. Covenant Ch. Club: Rotary (Paul Harris fellow 1987). Home: 2125 N Olive C-11 Turlock CA 95382

AHLERS, GLEN-PETER, SR., law library director, educator, consultant; b. N.Y.C., Mar. 15, 1955; s. LeGrande Jacob and Joan (Stoltz) A.; m. Sondra Sue Wadley, May 17, 1987; children: Glen-Peter II, Sandia Marie, Gavin Patrick, Sierra Le Ann Rose, Stacia Camille, Sienna Catherine. BS, U. N.Mex., Albuquerque, 1979; MA, U. of South Fla., 1983; JD, Washburn U., 1987. Bar: Kans. 1987, U.S. Dist. Ct. Kans. 1987, U.S. Ct. Mil. Appeals 1988, D.C. 1990. Reference asst. U. N.Mex. Sch. Law, Albuquerque, 1979-83; asst. dir. Washburn Sch. Law Libr., Topeka, 1983-87; assoc. libr. dir. Wake Forest U., Winston-Salem, N.C., 1987-90; libr. dir., assoc. prof. D.C. Sch. Law, Washington, 1990-92, U. Ark., Fayetteville, 1992-2000, prof., 2001—02; assoc. dean info. services Barry U. Dwayne O. Andreas Sch. of Law, Orlando, Fla. Computer and libr. cons. Ctr. for R&D in Law-Related Edn., Winston-Salem, 1987-90; adj. prof. Sch. of Law Wake Forest U., Winston-Salem, N.C., 1987-90; Mid-Am. Law Sch. Libr. Consortium, 1992-2002, bd. dirs. Consortium of Southestern Law Librs., 1988-90, pres. 2000-02. Author: History of Law School Libraries in the United States, 2002, Election Laws of the United States, 1995; co-author: Notary Law and Practice, 1997; editor The Maall Newsletter, 1984-87, The Scrivener, 1992—; tech. editor Washburn Law Jour., 1985-86; contbr. articles to profl. jours. Mediator N.C. Neighborhood Justice Ctr., Winston-Salem, 1989-90. Mem. ABA, ALA, Fla. Bar Assn., Am. Assn. Law Librs., Southwestern Assn. Law Librs. (pres. 1995-97), Southeastern Assn. of Law Librs., Mid Am. Assn. Law Librs. (pres. 1999-2000), Scribes (exec. dir. 1997—), Phi Kappa Phi, Kappa Delta Pi, Beta Phi Mu. Avocation: writing. Home: 1069 Winding Waters Cir Winter Springs FL 32708-6326 Office: Barry U Dwayne O Andreas Sch of Law 6441 E Colonial Dr Orlando FL 32807-3650 E-mail: gahlers@mail.barry.edu.

AHLERS, GUENTER, physicist, educator; b. Bremen, Germany, Mar. 28, 1934; came to U.S., 1951; s. William Carl and Ida Pauline (Cornelson) A.; m. June Bly, Aug. 24, 1964 BS, U. Calif., Riverside, 1958; PhD, U. Calif., Berkeley, 1963. Mem. tech. staff Bell Labs., Murray Hill, N.J., 1963-79; prof. physics U. Calif.-Santa Barbara, 1979—. Contbr. numerous articles to profl. jours. Recipient Fritz London award in low temperature physics, 1978 Fellow AAAS, Am. Phys. Soc.; mem. NAS. Home: 523 Carriage Hill Ct Santa Barbara CA 93110-2022 Office: U Calif Dept Physics Santa Barbara CA 93106 E-mail: guenter@stc.ucsb.edu.

AHLERS, PAUL, emergency physician; b. Albany, N.Y., Sept. 12, 1949; s. Frederick Louis and Rose Marie (Fox) A.; m. Anne Margaret Smigaj, Aug. 9, 1980; children: Christopher, Michael, Eric, Krystyna, Kathleen, Andrew. AB in Biochemistry, Rutgers U., 1971; MD, Kans. Med. Ctr., 1974. Diplomate Am. Bd. Emergency Medicine. Postdoctoral fellow Duke U. Med. Ctr., Durham, N.C., 1974-75; resident in emergency medicine Hershey (Pa.) Med. Ctr., 1975-78; courtesy med. staff Chambersburg (Pa.) Hosp., 1976-78; physician emergency dept. Holy Spirit Hosp., Camp Hill, Pa., 1976-78; attending physician dept. emergency medicine Richland Meml. Hosp., Columbia, S.C., 1978-79; med. staff Lee Hosp., Johnstown, Pa., 1979—, dir. dept. emergency medicine, 1985-92, med. staff pres., 1989. Contbr. articles to profl. jours. Mem.: Am. Acad. Emergency Medicine.

AHLERS, ROLF WILLI, philosopher, theologian; b. Hamburg, Germany, June 22, 1936; came to U.S., 1966; s. Arthur W. and Ilse F. (Freund) A.; m. Luise Kuse, July 1965; children: Christoph Matthias, Marcus Andreas. BA, Drew U., 1958; M.Div., Princeton Theol. Sem., 1961; Dr. Theol., U. Hamburg, 1966. Wissenschaftlicher Ass. Seminar Für Systematische Theologie und Sozialethik, U. Hamburg, Fed. Republic Germany, 1962-66; asst. prof. religion Ill. Coll., Jacksonville, 1966-72; Reynolds prof. philosophy and religion Russell Sage Coll., Troy, N.Y., 1973—. Author: The Barmen Declaration of 1934: Archeology of a Confessional Text, 1986, The Community of Freedom: Karl Barth and Presuppositionless Theology, 1989; author, editor: System and Context/System und Kontext: Early Romantic and Early Idealistic Constellations, New Athenaeum/Neues Athenaeum, vol. VII, 2003. NEH grantee, 1972-73; Soc. for Health and Human Values grantee, 1975 Mem. Hegel Soc. Am., Am. Acad. Religion, Am. Philos. Soc., Internationale Hegel Vereinigung, Internationale Fichte Gesellschaft, Fichte Soc. N.Am. Presbyterian. Home: 3 Academy Rd Albany NY 12208-3102 Office: Russell Sage Coll Philosophy Dept Troy NY 12180 *The cunning of history, pure grace and keen sense of self made me the person who I am.*

AHLGREN, CHARLES STEPHEN, educator, business and public policy consultant; b. Appleton, Wis., Sept. 22, 1938; s. Theodore Carl Ahlgren and Valery Dorothey (Vanevenhoven) Knox; m. Marianne Collins, Oct. 19, 1972; children: Ingrid, Theodore. BA, Loras Coll., 1960; MIA, Johns Hopkins U., 1967; MPA, Harvard U., 1978. Comml. attache Am. Embassy, Singapore, 1974-77; consul Am. Consulate, Cape Town, South Africa, 1978-80; econ. officer Am. Embassy, South Africa, 1980-81, econ. counselor, 1981-84; vis. prof. U.S. Mil. Acad., West Point, N.Y., 1984-86; consul-gen. Am. Consulate-Gen., Chiangmai, Thailand, 1986-89; vis. prof. U.S. Naval War Coll., Newport, R.I., 1989-92, U.S. Army War Coll., Carlisle, Pa., 1992-93; econ. counselor Am. Embassy, Caracas, Venezuela, 1993-96; Dept. State advisor Air U., Montgomery, Ala., 1996-97. Vis. prof. Lawrence U., Appleton, Wis., 2001-2002; adj. prof. JWU, 2003. Mem. Naval War Coll. Found., Soc. Historians of Am. Fgn. Rels. Avocations: hiking, philately. Home: 179 Shaw Ave Cranston RI 02905-3828

AHLGREN, JAMES DAVID, oncologist; b. Washington, Feb. 17, 1934; s. Charles David and Dorothy Elizabeth (Webb) A.; m. Barbara Elizabeth Donelko, Sept. 7, 1957 (div. Mar. 1978); children: Gillian Webb, Nils William; m. Alice Duong, Sept. 1978; 1 child, Mats Erik. BSEE, MIT, 1955; MD, Georgetown U., 1977. Diplomate Am. Bd. Internal Medicine, Am. Bd. Med. Oncology. Chief engr. McIntosh Electronics, Binghamton, N.Y., 1955-56; chief circuit design Reed Rsch., Washington, 1956-58; rsch. engr., asst. dir. R&D Page Comm. Engrs., Washington, 1958-63; v.p., acting pres. Telcom, Inc., McLean, Va., 1963-73; intern Georgetown U. Med. Ctr., Washington, 1977-78, resident in internal medicine, 1979-80, from instr. to assoc. prof., 1980-88; assoc. prof. George Washington U. Med. Ctr., Washington, 1988-94, prof., 1994—. Chmn. Mid-Atlantic Oncology Program, Silver Spring, Md., 1983-95. Author: Gastrointestinal Oncology, 1992. Chmn. Mid-Atlantic Cancer Rsch. Found., Silver Spring, 1989—. Recipient Edward B. Bunn award Georgetown U., Washington, 1977, Dept. Medicine award, 1977, Jonathan M. Wainwright award Moses Taylor Hosp., 1993, Elaine Snyder Cancer Rsch. award George Washington U., 1994. Mem. ACP, IEEE (sr. mem.), Am. Soc. Clin. Oncology, Am. Geophys. Union, Am. Meteorol. Soc. Republican. Lutheran. Avocations: amateur radio, piano, cooking. Office: George Washington U Med Ctr 2150 Pennsylvania Ave NW Washington DC 20037-3201 E-mail: w4rx@alum.mit.edu.

AHLQUIST, PAUL GERALD, molecular biology researcher, educator; b. Des Moines, Jan. 9, 1954; s. Irving Elmer and Signrun Evelyn (Eidbo) A. BS in Physics, Iowa State U., 1976; PhD in Biophysics, U. Wis., 1981. Asst. sci. in biophysics U. Wis., Madison, 1981-84, asst. prof. biophysics and plant pathology, 1984-87, assoc. prof. molecular virology and plant pathology, 1987-91, prof., 1991—, prof. molecular virology, oncology and plant pathology, 1997—, chmn. molecular virology, 1996-97, Paul J. Kaesberg prof., 2000—; investigator Howard Hughes Med. Inst., 1997—. Mem. exec. com. Internat. Commn. Taxonomy of Viruses, 1987-93; van Arkel hon. faculty chair in biochemistry Leiden (The Netherlands) U., 1995. Editor: RNA Genetics, vols. I, II, III, 1988, Molecular Biology of Plant-Microbe Interactions, 1989; assoc. editor Virology, 1988-93, Molecular Plant-Microbe Interactions, 1988-95, Plant Molecular Biology, 1987-90; contbr. articles to profl. jours. Recipient Presdl. Young Investigator award NSF, 1985-90, Romnes Faculty Fellowship award, 1988, Shaw Faculty Scholar award Milw. Found., 1985-90, Allen Rsch. award Am. Phytopathology Soc., 1988, Pound Rsch. award, 1987, WARF Mid-Career Rsch. award, 1995, NIH Merit award, 1995—. Mem. NAS, Am. Soc. Virology (mem. exec. coun. 1993-96), Internat. Soc. Plant Molecular Biology (bd. dirs. 1989-93), Am. Soc. for Microbiology, Genetics Soc. Am.

AHLSCHWEDE, EARL DAVID, lawyer; b. Friend, Nebr., Nov. 12, 1940; s. Clarence Jefferson and Phyllis D. (Kleinholz) A.; m. Virginia S. Chudly, Apr. 15, 1972; children: Mathew, James and John (twins). BS, U. Nebr., 1962, JD, 1964. Bar: Nebr. 1964, U.S. Dist. Ct. Nebr. 1964. Adminstrv. asst. Nebr. Dept. Agr., Lincoln, 1964-66; county atty. York County, Nebr., 1967-68; city atty. Beatrice, Nebr., 1969-74; city mgr., atty. City of Grand Island, Nebr., 1974-77; ptnr. Ahlschwede, De Backer & Truell, Grand Island, 1977-87. Bd. dirs. St. Francis Med. Ctr., Grand Island, 1981-87; chmn. Hall County Housing Authority, Grand Island, 1983-93. Mem. ABA, 11th Jud. Dist. Bar Assn., Nebr. State Bar Assn. (ho. of dels. 1983-89), Am. Judicature Soc. Home: 1620 Coventry Ln Grand Island NE 68801-7026 Office: Mayer Burns & Ahlschwede Norwest Bank Bldg Third and Locust Sts Grand Island NE 68802

AHLSTROM, CALLIS BLYTHE, university official; b. Oct. 1, 1933; BS, Utah State U., 1958; postgrad., Rutgers U., 1959-62; MA, Columbia U., 1961. Exec. asst. to pres. Calif. State U., Chico, 1971-79; asst. prof. history Utah State U., Logan, 1964-71, asst. to pres., 1979-86, asst. provost, 1986—2001, emeritus asst. provost, 2001—. Chmn. bd. dirs.; bd. dirs. Logan area Habitat for Humanity, Logan City Libr., Utah State U. Libr. Friends, Logan City Hist. Preservation Com. Served to capt. U.S. Army, 1962-64, U.S. Army Res., 1964-73. Home: 1661 E 1650 N Logan UT 84341-2912 Office: Utah State U Provost's Office Logan UT 84322-1435 E-mail: blythea@champ.usu.edu.

AHLSTROM, MICHAEL JOSEPH, lawyer; b. N.Y.C., June 1, 1953; s. Albert Warren and Bernadette Patricia (Flynn) A.; m. Mary Lou Donnelly, Apr. 19, 1980; 1 child, Courtney Leigh. BS, St. Francis Coll., 1975; JD, U. San Francisco, 1978. Bar: N.Y. 1980, U.S. Dist. Ct. (so. and ea. dists.) N.Y. 1980, Ga. 1982, U.S. Dist. Ct. (no. dist.) Ga. 1983, U.S. Ct. Appeals (11th cir.) 1984, U.S. Supreme Ct. 1987; registered neutral, arbitration, domestic mediation and early case evaluator, Ga. Counsel Gear Design, Inc., N.Y.C., 1979-80; ptnr. Ahlstrom & Ahlstrom, N.Y.C., 1981-83; gen. counsel Network Rental, Inc., Atlanta, 1984-87; assoc. John Marshall and Assocs., P.C., Atlanta, 1987; ptnr. Marshall & Ahlstrom, P.C., Atlanta, 1987-88; mng. atty. UAW-GM-Ford Chrysler Legal Plan Ga., Atlanta, 1993-96; pvt. practice, Marietta, Ga., 1988-92, 96—. Arbitrator Nat Assn. Securities Dealers, Superior Ct. Fulton County, Ga., 1987—, Ga. Lemon Law, 1991—; panel atty. Cobb County Circuit Defender; spl. master Cobb County Superior Ct., mediator, 1966-1996; mediator domestic cases Fulton County Superior Ct., 1998—, mediator juvenile cases; guardian ad litem Cobb County Superior Ct. Mem. N.Y. Bar Assn., Ga. Bar Assn. (pub. rels. com. 1989-91), Cobb County Bar Assn., Am. Corp.Counsel Assn. (program chmn. 1986-87), Am. Arbitration Assn. (comml. panel 1987—), KC, Phi Delta Phi, Alpha Kappa Psi. Republican. Roman Catholic. Avocations: fishing, hunting, tennis, golf, croquet. Home: 613 Fairway Ct Marietta GA 30068-4159

AHLSTROM, RONALD GUSTIN, artist; b. Chgo., Jan. 17, 1922; s. Frederick Karl and Gertrude (Gustin) A.; m. Nancy Costa; 1 son, Arn Gustin. Ed., U. Chgo., Art Inst. Chgo.; B.F.A., 1955. Asst. dir. McCormick Pl. Gallery, 1960-63; dir. Tacoma Art Mus., 1963—. One-man shows include Barat Coll., Lake Forest, Ill., 1958, Blackhawk Restaurant, Chgo., 1961, collages at Main St. Galleries, Chgo., 1969, J. Faulkner Galleries, Chgo., 1970, 71, Spiesberger Gallery, Skokie, Ill., 1975, Zriny-Hayes Gallery, Chgo., 1978; group shows include Chgo. and vicinity ann., Art Inst. Chgo., 1955, 56, 59, 61, 62, 64, other shows at Art Inst., 1957, 58, Inst. Jewish Studies, 1956, 1020 Art Ctr., 1957, Navy Pier, 1957, 58, Old Town Art Center, 1959, B.C. Holland Gallery, 1961, McCormick Pl. Art Gallery, 1961, 62, 63, Hyde Park Art Ctr., 1963, Studio 22, 1970, all Chgo., C. McNider Mus., Mason City, Iowa, 1971, Touchstone Gallery, N.Y.C., 1973; exhibited in Chgo. Artists European Tour Exhibit, USIA, 1957-59, Festival of Fine Arts, Lake Forest, 1958, Soc. of Four Arts Exhibit, West Palm Beach, Fla., 1959, E. Mich. Coll. at Ypsilanti, 1960, Corcoran Gallery Art, Washington, 1961, Tacoma Art Mus., 1963, 5 Abstractionists, Main St. Galleries, 1968; represented in permanent collections Tacoma Art Mus., Barat Coll. Gallery, Gutenberg Mus., Mainz, Germany, Art Inst. Chgo., Blue Cross, Chgo., Atlantic-Richfield, Chgo., Ill. Bell Telephone, Container Corp. Am., Chgo., also in numerous pvt. collections; work represented in book Collage and Foundation Art (Meilach and Ten Hoor), 1964, Collage and Assemblage, Trend and Techniques (Meilach and Ten Hoor), 1973. Served with U.S. Army, 1942-46. Recipient Clyde M. Carr prize for painting, 1955, Alumni of Sch. Art Inst. prize, 1959, Jane Broadus Clark prize, 1958; Singer & Sons prize, Navy Pier; Abel Fagan prize Festival Fine Arts, Lake Forest, 1958; Ford Found. purchase prize Seattle Art Mus., 1964 Achievements include being represented in The Art of Collage (Gerald F. Brommer Davis) 1978, Collage and Found Art, MEilach & Tenhoor, Collage and Assemblage, Meilach & Tenhoor. Home: 121 W Park Dr Lombard IL 60148-3320

AHMAD, AYAZ, economist; b. London; s. Rashid and Tahira A.; m. Dawnette Joy Farley, Nov. 18, 2000. BA with hons. in Bus. Studies, Univ. Greenwich, Eng., 1996; MSc in Econ. Competition and Regulation, City U., London, 2000. Rsch. asst. Local Gov. Mgmt. Bd., London, 1994-95; pensions review adminstr. Hill Samuel Life Assurance Ltd., Croydon, Eng., 1997-98; internat. consultancy mgr. Office for Nat. Statistics, London, 1997-98; bus. support asst. House of Fraser, London, 1998; data analyst Office for Nat. Statistics, London, 1998—. Assoc. Inst. Mgmt., Corby, Eng., 1997- . Avocations: music, reading, travel. Home: 837 S Sunset Cir Andover KS 67002

AHMAD, IMAD ALDEAN, astronomer, educator, consultant; b. shipboard Atlantic Ocean, Aug. 11, 1948; s. Hassan and Qudsia (Holazada) A.; m. France Eddy, June 11, 1980. BA, Harvard U., 1970; PhD, U. Ariz., 1975. Rsch. assoc. Harvard Univ., Cambridge, Mass., 1975-76; staff scientist Am. Sci. and Engring., Cambridge, 1976-77; sr. scientist Univ. Md., College Park, 1977-79; sr. staff scientist Andrulis Rsch Corp, Bethesda, Md., 1979-81; pres. Imad-Ad-Dean, Inc., Bethesda, 1981—, Minaret of Freedom Inst., 1993—. Adj. prof. U. Md., 1997—; mem. orgn. com. Washington Area Astronomers, College Park, 1986-96. Author: Signs in the Heavens: A Muslim Astronomer's Perspective on Religion and Science; contbr. articles to Astrophysical Jour., Astronomers & Astrophysics; co-author: Islam and the Discovery of Freedom; co-editor: Islam and the West: A Dialog. Nat. com. mem. Libertarian Party, Washington, 1983-93; pres. East Bethesda (Md.) Citizens Assn., 1989-91, 93-95, 98-2000, Montgomery County Civic Fedn., 2000-02; chmn. Md. Libertarian Party, Bethesda, 1990-92. Harvard scholar, 1966; recipient Samual Chase Freedom award Md. Libertarian Party, Balt., 1990, Montgomery County Civic Fedn. Sentinel award, 1997, Champion of Democracy award Marylanders for Democracy, 1998, Star Cup award Montgomery County Civic Fedn., 2002. Mem. Am. Astron. Soc., Internat. Astronomers Union. Moslem. Achievements include invention of unified global Islamic calendar. Office: Minaret of Freedom Inst 4232 Rosedale Ave Bethesda MD 20814-4750 E-mail: dahmad@speakeasy.net.

AHMAD, IRSHAD, physicist, nuclear chemist; b. Azamgarh, India, Nov. 1, 1939; came to U.S., 1962; s. Aquil and Tahira (Khatoon) A.; m. Fauzia Mazhar, Jan. 23, 1969; children: Fahim, Mateen, Sabina. MS, U. Pacific, 1965; PhD, U. Calif., Berkeley, 1966. Postdoctoral fellow Lawrence Berkeley (Calif.) Lab., 1966, Argonne (Ill.) Nat. Lab., 1966-68, asst. chemist, 1968-71, chemist, 1971-85, physicist, 1985—. Mem. Am. Phys. Soc., Am. Chem. Soc., Sigma Xi. Office: Argonne Nat Lab D 203 9700 Cass Ave Argonne IL 60439-4803

AHMAD, JAMEEL, civil engineer, researcher, educator; b. Lahore, Punjab, Pakistan, May 22, 1941; came to U.S. 1962; s. Naseer and Iftikhar (Dean) Bakhsh; m. Rosalba Quiroz, March 31, 1983; 1 child, Monica. BSc, Punjab U., Lahore, 1962; MS, U. Hawaii, 1964; PhD, U. Pa., 1967. East-west ctr. fellow U. Hawaii, Honolulu, 1962-65; rsch. fellow U. Pa., Phila., 1965-67; asst. prof. Widener U., Chester, Pa., 1967-68, Cooper Union, N.Y.C., 1968-71, assoc. prof., 1971-80, chmn. civil engring., 1980—, prof. civil engring., 1979—; dir. rsch. Cooper Union Rsch. Found., N.Y.C., 1983—. Dir. High Techs., Inc., N.Y.C., 1986—; bd. dirs. Consortium of N.Y.C. Engring. Colls. and Univs.,

Mayor's Office of Constrn., 1994—, fellow Rsch. Inst. for the Study of Man, 2002. V.p. Vilmanor Community Assn., N.Y.C., 1992, West Side Community Assn., N.Y.C., 1976. Mem. ASEE, ASCE (Outstanding Svc. award 1985), Pakistan League of Am. (bd. dirs., Abdus Salam medal for disting. rsch. in engring. scis. 1993). Achievements include patents for fleximech reinforcement system, asphalt reinforcement system. Office: Cooper Union Coll 51 Astor Pl New York NY 10003-7132 E mail: ahmad@cooper.edu. *My philosophy of life is best exemplified by the great 19th century industrialist/philanthropist Peter Cooper - concentrate on giving something back to society. As the founder of the only tuition-free private college in America, his legacyhas benefited generations of young people since 1849.*

AHMAD, MIRZA MUZAFFAR, economic advisor; b. Qadian, India, Feb. 28, 1913; came to U.S., 1972; d. Mirza and Sarwar (Sultana) Bashir; m. Amatul Q. Ahmad, May 8, 1939; 1 child, Zahir Ahmad. BA, Gov. Coll., Lahore, India, 1933; BA wtih honors, London U., 1935; postgrad. law, Middle Temple, London, 1935; postgrad., Corpus Christie Coll., Oxford, London, 1938. Several govt. positions, India, 1939-47; additional chief sec. West Pakistan Province, 1959-62; sec. commerce Govt. of Pakistan, 1962, sec. fin., 1963-66, fed. minister, fin. minister planning commn., 1966—70, econ. adviser, fin. adviser to the pres., 1970 71, adviser for fgn. loans and consortium, 1971-72; exec. dir. bd. World Bank, 1972-74; dep. exec. sec., staff mem., con. Joint Ministerial Com. of Bd. Govs. World Bank and IMF, 1974-93. Mem. Pakistan del. to Commonwealth Prime Ministers' Conf., 1962, 64; negotiator with World Bank for Indus Basin Devel. Fund, 1964; leader Pakistan del. to 8th consortium meeting, Washington, 1966, Pakistan del. to meetings of Econ. Coun. of Indonesia-Pakistan Econ. and Cultural Cooperation, 1966 69, Pakistan del to ministerial meetings Colombo Plan Conf., Geneva, 1987, Pakistan del. to People's Republic of China, 1967; chmn. ministerial meetings 17th Colombo Plan Conf., 1966. Amir/pres. Ahmadiya Movement in Islam, Inc. Recipient Hilal Quaid Azam award, Sitari Pakistan award Pres. of Pakistan. Moslem. Home: 9920 New London Dr Potomac MD 20854-4845 Office: Ahmadiya Movement in Islam Baitur Rahman 15000 Good Hope Rd Silver Spring MD 20905-4120

AHMAD, MOGHISUDDIN, research chemist; b. Dhanbad, India, July 1, 1950; came to U.S., 1979; s. Moinuddin Ahmad and Zaibun Nesa; m. Athar Bano Hussain, Mar. 23, 1985; children: Waseem Ahmad, Raees Ahmad. BS with honors, Aligarh (India) Muslim U., 1971, MS, 1973, MPhil., 1975, PhD, 1978. Postdoctoral fellow Aligarh Muslim U., 1978-79; rsch. assoc. dept. biochemistry and biophysics Tex. A&M U., College Station, 1979-81; rsch. assoc. dept. food sci. Oregon State U., Corvallis, 1981-88; chemist Lipids dept. Sigma Chem. Co., St. Louis, 1988—95, chemist II bio-organics dept., 1995—2001; assoc. dir. chemistry NeoPharm, Inc. R&D, Waukegan, Ill., 2001—02, dir. chemistry, 2002—. Contbr. articles to profl. jours. Mem. Am. Oil Chemists Soc., Am. Chem. Soc. Avocation: reading writing.

AHMAD, SALAHUDDIN, nuclear scientist; b. Sylhet, Bangladesh, Nov. 25, 1954; arrived in Can., 1978; came to U.S., 1990; s. Jalal and Momtaz (Begum) A.; m. Munawar Sultana, June 1, 1978; 1 child, Nahid Rubaba. MSc, Dhaka U., Bangladesh, 1975; PhD, U. Victoria, B.C., Can., 1981. Lectr. Dhaka U., 1978; postdoctoral rsch. assoc. U. Victoria, 1981; rsch. scientist U. Paris South, Orsay, France, 1982-83; profl. rsch. assoc. U. Sask., Saskatoon, Can., 1983-84; rsch. assoc. Triumf Nat. Lab., Vancouver, 1984-86, U. B.C., Vancouver, 1987-89; faculty fellow Rice U., Houston, 1990-96; rsch. assoc. MD Anderson Cancer Ctr., U. Tex., Houston, 1996-98; asst. prof. radiology Baylor Coll. Medicine, Houston, 1999—; chief physicist VA Med. Ctr., Houston, 1999—. Contbr. more than 125 articles to sci. jours. and conf. procs., including Physics Letters, Phys. Rev., Phys. Rev. Letters. Bangladeshi rep. World Muslim Youth Conf., Abha, Saudi Arabia, 1977; founder, pres. Bangladesh-Can. Cultural Assn., Vancouver, 1988-89, Bangladesh-Am. Lit., Art and Cultural Assn., Houston, 1992-95, 98-99. Raja Kalinarayan scholar U. Dhaka, 1974-75; fellow Can. Commonwealth Fellowship Com., 1978-81. Mem. Am. Assn. Physicist in Medicine. Office: VA Med Ctr Radiotherapy 190 2002 Holcombe Blvd Houston TX 77030-4211 E-mail: sahmad@bcm.tmc.edu.

AHMAD, SHAH MAHMOOD, chemical engineer, consultant; b. Lahore, Punjab, Pakistan, Mar. 25, 1967; came to U.S., 1992; s. Syeo Muhammad and Mahmooda Begum Ahmad; m. Muzaffara Bushra Dahri, Dec. 29, 1996. BSChemE, U. Engring. Lahore, 1990; MSChemE, Western Mich. U., 1995. Profl. engr. Shift engr. Rupali (Toray) Polyester, Lahore, 1991; process engr. Glaxo Ltd. U.K., Lahore, 1991-92; rsch. asst. Western Mich. U., Kalamazoo, 1992-95; project mgr. EDM Consulting Inc., Vicksburg, Mich., 1995-96; cons. compliance Pharmacia & Upjohn, Kalamazoo, 1996—. Cons. BASF, Holland, Mich., 1995-96, Remote Control Inc., Allegan, Mich., 1997—. Asst. to editor Jour. Asia Pacific Bus., 1994-95. Vol. Western U. Mich. Librs., Kalamazoo, 1993; sec. publ. Ahmadiyya Movement Islam, Detroit, 1997—. Mem. Am. Inst. Chem. Engrs. Achievements include developer Software Program "Emergency Relief System Design Basis". Home: 5442 Antiqua Cir Kalamazoo MI 49009-9599 Office: Pharmacia & Upjohn OU1305-87-1 Kalamazoo MI 49001

AHMAD, SYEDA SULTANA, physician; b. Pakistan; d. Syed Wakil and Syeda (Begum) A. B in Medicine and Surgery, Punjab U., Lahore, Pakistan, 1977; MD, Ednl. Commn. Fgn. Med. Grads., Phila., 1982. Resident pediatrics Narain Das Mool Chand Children Hosp., Lahore, 1978; resident ob-gyn. U. Punjab, Sir Ganga Ram Hosp., Lahore, 1978-79; med. officer ob-gyn. Fertility Svcs. and Tng. Ctr., Dhaka, Bangladesh, 1980; clin. attachment staff S. Georgia Med. Ctr., Amarillo, Tex., 1983-84, Pvt. Clinic, Bedford, Tex., 1985-89; rschr. U. Tex. South Western Med. Ctr., Dallas, 1989; resident pathology U. Okla., Oklahoma City, 1989-90; resident pediatrics U. Tenn., Le Bonheur Childrens Med. Ctr., Memphis, 1990-92; resident in pediats. Tex. A&M U. and Scott and White Hosp., Temple, 1992-94, Scott and White Hosp., 1992-94. Avocations: traveling, reading, bicycling.

AHMANN, JOHN STANLEY, psychologist, educator; b. Struble, Iowa, Oct. 17, 1921; s. Henry Francis and Philomine (Wictor) Ahmann; children: Sandi Ann, Sheri Kay, Gregory Steven, Shelly Joan. *A descendant of Johann Adolph Ahmann of Marl, Germany, John Stanley Ahmann was born and raised in midwestern United States. His four children are: daughter Sandi (Ahmann) Ashley, BS Colorado State U., EdS U. of Kansas, a licensed professional counselor in Montana; daughter Sheri (Ahmann) Carmon, BA U. of Northern Colorado, is a real estate broker associate in Colorado; son Steve Ahmann, BS Montana State U., a teacher in Montana; and daughter Shelly Ahmann, BA and MD U of Colorado, a surgeon in Georgia. Each has an abiding love of the Rocky Mountain west and its environment.* BA, Trinity Coll., 1943; BS, Iowa State U., 1947, MS, 1949, PhD, 1951. Instr. profl. studies Iowa State U., 1949-51, prof. edn. and psychology, 1975—, disting. prof. edn., 1981—, chmn. dept. profl. studies, 1975-84; asst. prof. div. ednl. psychology and psychol. measurement Cornell U., 1951-54, assoc. prof., 1954-58, prof., 1958-60; prof. psychology Colo. State U., 1960-75; assoc. dir. Human Factors Rsch. Lab., 1969-71, asst. to pres., 1961-64, head dept. psychology, 1962-64, acad. v.p., 1964-69. Adj. prof. psychology and edn. U. Denver, 1971—76; vis. prof. Colo. State U., 1951, Wash. State U., 1960, Western Wash. U., 1970; cons. rsch. programs U.S. Dept. Edn.; cons. evaluation ednl programs, Colo., NY, La., Tex., Ark., Hawaii, Ga., Ariz., Ohio, Minn., Iowa; project dir. Nat. Assessment Ednl. Progress, 1971—75; dir. various fed. and state sponsored rsch. projects; hon. lectr. Mid-Am. State U. Assn., 1976—77. Author: (book) Statistical Methods in Educational and Psychological Research, 1954, Evaluating Student Progress, 6th edit., 1981, Evaluating Elementary School Pupils, 1960, Testing Student Achievement and Aptitudes, 1962, Measuring and Evaluating Educational Achievement, 2d edit., 1975, How Much Are Our Young People Learning?, 1976, Needs Assessment for Program Planning in Vocational Education, 1979, Academic Achievements of Young Americans, 1983; assoc. editor: Ednl. Studies, 1975—79. With USNR, 1943—46, PTO. Recipient Laureate award, Iowa State U., 1975. Fellow: APA, AAAS; mem.: Nat. Coun. Measurement Edn., Am. Ednl. Rsch. Assn., Psi Chi, Alpha Chi Sigma, Phi Lambda Upsilon, Phi Delta Kappa, Phi Kappa Phi, Sigma Xi. Home: 3738 Franklin Ave Loveland CO 80538-2204 Office: Iowa State Univ N243 Quadrangle Ames IA 50011-0001

AHMED, GAIL R. music educator; b. Martins Ferry, Ohio, Oct. 2, 1953; d. Edgar Milton and Margaret Elizabeth Horner; m. Bashir Gakhru Ahmed, Aug. 25, 1979; 1 child, Aisha. BA, West Liberty State Coll., 1975; MEd, U. Dayton, 1991. Cert. music profl. K-12. Music educator Edison Local Schs., Ironton, Ohio, 1975—77, Tipp City (Ohio) Schs., Tipp City, 1977—. Music dir. Tippecanoe Cmty. Band, Tipp City, 1979—; gen. music rep. Ohio Music Educator's Nat. Conf., Columbus, 1985—90; mem. gifted com. Tipp City Schs., 1999—2002; cons. curriculum devel. Dayton Islamic Sch., Beavercreek, 1997—98; dist. gen. music rep. Ohio Music Educator's Nat. Conf., Columbus, 1985—90; orchestral dir. Tippecanoe H.S. Mus., Tipp City; presenter Lesson Plans that Work TRIAD OMEA State Conv., 1995. Dir. United Meth. Church Bell Choir, Tipp City, 1985—87. Grantee Environ. Edn. grantee, Miami County Park Dist., 2001—02. Mem.: NGAC, Music Educator's Nat. Conf. (dist. gen. music rep. 1985—90, Ohio chpt. dist. II treas. 2002—, 25-Yr. mem. 2001), Friends of Libr. Avocations: travel, music, needlework, reading. Home: 790 Shirley Dr Tipp City OH 45371 Office: Tipp City Schs 90 S Tippecanoe D Tipp City OH 45371 Personal E-mail: grahmed@hotmail.com.

AHMED, IQBAL, psychiatrist, consultant; b. Tumkur, Karnataka, India, Aug. 23, 1951; came to U.S., 1976; s. Rahimuddin Ahmed and Arifa (Banu) Rahimuddin; m. Lisa Suzanne Rose, Oct. 9, 1983; children: Yasmin, Jihan. BS, MB, St. John's Med. Coll., Bangalore, India, 1975. Diplomate in gen. psychiatry and geriatric psychiatry Am. Bd. Psychiatry and Neurology. Intern St. Martha's Hosp., Bangalore, India, 1974-75; resident in psychiatry U. Nebr. Med. Ctr., Omaha, 1976-79; fellowship in consultation Boston U. Sch. Medicine, 1979-81; staff psychiatrist in consultation liaison psychiatry Boston City Hosp., 1981-87, staff psychiatrist, geriatric psychiatry, 1983-85, dir. geriatric neuropsychiatry unit, 1985 87, dir. geriatric psychiatry, 1988-92; assoc. dir. consultation liaison psychiatry New England Med. Ctr., Boston, 1989-92. Asst. prof. psychiatry Boston U. Sch. Medicine, 1981—87, Tufts U. Sch. Medicine, Boston, 1987—92; dir. med. student edn. in psychiatry Boston City Hosp., 1981—87; chief spl. svcs. Hawaii State Hosp., 1991—94, pres. med. staff, 1994—95, chief geriatric psychiatry, 1994—; assoc. prof. dept. psychiatry U. Hawaii John A. Burns Sch. Medicine, 1992—97, prof. dept. psychiatry, 1997—; vice chair for edn. dept. psychiatry U. Hawaii, 1999—2001; program dir. gen. and geriatric psychiatry residency programs U. Hawaii Med. Ctr., 1998—; dir. pyschopharmacy lab. Adult Dept. Mental Health State of Hawaii, Honolulu, 2003—; dir. geriatric psychiatry Queens Med. Ctr., Honolulu, 2003—, vice chmn. edn. Dept. Psychiatry, 1999—. Contbr. articles to profl. jours. Mem. Mass. State Dem. Party Minority Caucus, Boston, 1983. Fellow: Am. Acad. Geriatric Psychiatry, Acad. Psychosomatic Medicine, Royal Coll. Psychiatrists, Am. Psychiat. Assn.; mem.: Internat. Coll. Geriatric Psychoneuropharmacology (founding), Am. Neuropsychiat. Assn. Democrat. Avocations: web surfing, snorkeling. Office: 1356 Lusitana St Fl 4 Honolulu HI 96813-2421

AHMED, JIMMIE, health facility administrator; b. Memphis, Nov. 26, 1946; d. George and Cora (Sias) Stockley; children: Michael, Donald, Eric. Grad., Kingsborough Community Coll., 1973; student, Hunter Coll.; BS in Community Health, Empire State Coll., 1983; cert. in infection control, Winthrop U. Hosp., 1988; cert. Cath. hosp. adminstrv. program, St. John's U., 1990; MPA, Long Island U., 2001. RN, N.Y. Head nurse gerontology Margaret Tietz Ctr. for Nursing Care, Jamaica, N.Y., 1976-80; staff nurse Mary Immaculate Hosp., Jamaica, 1980-84; asst. dir. field ops. Social Concern Home Attendant Agy., Laurelton, N.Y., 1980-82; nursing care coord. ambulatory care Bklyn./Caledonian Hosp., 1982-85; night adminstrv. supr. M.I.H., Jamaica, 1985-87, infection control practitioner Cath. Med. Ctr., 1987-89; adminstr. infection control Cath. Med. Ctr. Bklyn. and Queens, Inc., Jamaica, 1989—2001; mgr. infection control SVCMC, 2001—; nursing supr. Glen Cove (NY) Ctr., 2001—; nurse cons. Casa Promesa, Bronx, NY, 2001—. Psychiat. nurse St. Claire Hosp., 1982-93; lectr. Am. Lung Assn. Queens, also others. Author abstracts in field. Mem.: ANA, Assn. Practitioners in Infection Control (cert.), N.Y. State Nurses Assn., N.C. A&T State U. Alumni Assn., Empire State Coll. Alumni Assn., Pi Alpha Alpha. Home: 17809 132nd Ave Jamaica NY 11434-5843 Office: St Vincent Cath Med Ctrs 88-25 153d St Ste 3R Jamaica NY 11432

AHMED, M. BASHEER, psychiatrist, educator; b. Hyderbad, India, June 7, 1935; came to U.S., 1968; s. M. Quameruddin and Aziz Fatima Ahmed; m. Shakila Khatoon, Dec. 7, 1967; children: Sameer, Araj. Osmania U., Hyderabad, 1954; MD, Dow Med. Coll., 1960. Diplomate Am. Bd. Psychiatry and Neurology, Am. Bd. Geriatric Psychiatry. Dir. psychiat. dept. St. Louis County Gen. Hosp., Clayton, Mo., 1969-71; dir. sound view Throngs Neck Community Mental Health Ctr., Bronx, N.Y., 1971-76; chief psychiatry VA Hosp., Dayton, Ohio, 1976-78; dir. psychiat. dept. John Peter Smith Hosp., Ft. Worth, 1978-82; pvt. practice, Ft. Worth, 1984—; dir. dept. psychiatry St. Joseph Hosp., Ft. Worth, 1985-89; chief staff Care Unit Hosp., Ft. Worth, 1989-94; dir. psych. geriatric unit Med. Plaza Hosp., Ft. Worth, 1992-96; med. dir. New Horizon PHP Program, Ft. Worth, 1997-2000, chmn. MCC for human svcs., 1995—. Asst. prof. Albert Einstein Coll. Medicine, N.Y.C., 1971-76; prof. Wright State U. Med. Sch., Dayton, 1976-78, U. Tex. Southwestern Med. Sch., Dallas, 1978-88, U. Tex. Health Sci. Ctr., Ft. Worth, 1982-98; chmn. dept. psychiatry Plaza Med. Ctr. East, 1995-97, Med. Direct New Horizon Mental Health Ctr., Ft. Worth, 1997-2000; chmn. MCC for Human Svcs. Inc., 1995—. Contbg. author: Group Counseling and Psychotherapy, 1976, Administration of Mental Health, 1980. Life mem. Rep. Presdl. Task Force, Washington, 1986—. Hogg Found. grantee, 1980-81, U. Tex. Health Sci. Ctr. grantee, 1981. Fellow Am. Psychiat. Assn.; mem. AMA (Physician's Recognition award 1971—), Tex. Med. Assn., Tex., Soc. Psychiat. Physicians (pres. Tarrant County chpt. 1989-90), Tarrant County Med. Soc. (task force for homeless 1989-90), Islamic Med. Assn. (pres. 1978-79), Internat. Inst. Islamic Medicine. Home: 10 Home Place Ct Arlington TX 76016-3913 Office: 10 Homeplace Ct Arlington TX 76016 E-mail: mbahmed@flash.net.

AHMED, MAHNAZ, bank executive; b. London, Eng., June 30, 1975; d. Farooq and Sumaira Shaheen Ahmed. BA in Acctg. with honors, London Guildhall U., 1997; MSc Fin. and Fin. Info. Sys., U. of Greenwich, London, 1998. Credit suisse first boston, llc Investment Bank, San Francisco, Calif., 1999—. Office: CSFB 600 California St San Francisco CA

AHMED, S. BASHEER, research company executive, educator; b. Kurnool, Andhra, India, Jan. 1, 1934; s. S. M. and K.A. (Bee) Hussain; m. Alice Cordelia Pearce; 1 child, Ivy Amina. BA, Osmania Coll., Kurnool, 1955; MA, Osmania U., Hyderabad, India, 1957; MS, Tex. A&M U., 1963, PhD, 1966. Asst. prof. Tenn. Tech. U., Cookeville, 1966-68, Ohio U., Athens, 1968-70; vis. fellow Princeton U., N.J., 1977-78; prof. Western Ky. U., Bowling Green, 1970-80; prof. Mgmt. Scis. Lubin Grad. Sch. Bus., dir. doctoral program Pace U., NYC, 1982-92, prof. emeritus, 1993—2003; pres. Princeton Econ. Rsch., Inc., 1980-99, Pearce Cons. Svcs., 2000—. Cons. Oak Ridge (Tenn.) Nat. Lab., 1969-77, Inst. for Energy Analysis, Oak Ridge, 1975, Honeywell Corp., Mpls., 1985. Author: Quantitative Methods for Business, 1974, Nuclear Fuel and Energy Policy, 1979; author, editor: Technology, International Stability, and Growth, 1984. Mem. cirs. bd. The Kennedy Ctr., 1997 2000. Recipient Achievement award Oak Ridge Nat. Lab., 1977, IEEE Centennial Medal, 1983, Millennium medal, 2000. Fellow AAAS, Systems, Man, and Cybernetics Soc. (pres. 1980-82). Home: 817 Albemarle Dr Bowling Green KY 42103 E-mail: sbahmed@aol.com.

AHMED, SALEEM, management consultant, educator; b. Agra, India, Mar. 16, 1945; came to U.S., 1969; s. Mohammed Wasi and Iqbal Begum Uddin; m. Joumana Chebbani; children: Nadeem Saleem, Asmahan Saleem, Nabeel Saleem. AEPT in Power Tech., Karachi Polytech Inst., Pakistan, 1965; BA in Math, U. Karachi, Pakistan, 1965; BSME, Detroit Inst. Tech., 1971; MBA in Systems Approach, Baldwin Walace Coll., 1980; PhD in Mktg. and Mgmt., Calif. Coast U., Santa Ana, 1985. Cert. mfg. engr. Project engr. Union Carbide Corp., Westlake, Ohio, 1977—85; mgmt. cons. Saleem & Assocs., Detroit, 1986—89; pres. Mich. Ctr. For Excellence, Inc., Dearborn, Mich., 1990—, Soc. for Profl. Advancement, Inc., Dearborn, Mich., 1991—. Author: Project Management Systems Approach for Plastics Engineers, 1990, The Excellence in Sales for Executives, 1991, Multi-Level Marketing, 1991, The Psychology of Winning, 1992, The Job Connection, 1992, How to Close Sale Every Time, 1992, Systems Approach Application for Engineers, 2000, Systems Approach Application for Every One, 2000, How to Achieve Zero Defects, 2000, How to Conduct Self Internal Audit, 2001, How to Conduct Tool Tryout, Process and Production Capabilities, 2001, How to Design Tools from Setup and Production Point of Views, 2001. Mem. ASTD. Avocations: wood working, photography. Home: 2024 N Silvery Ln Dearborn MI 48128-1021 Office: Soc Profls Advancement Inc PO Box 5116 Dearborn MI 48128-8727

AHMED, SHAFIQ, surgeon; b. Calcutta, India, Oct. 11, 1937; came to U.S., 1963. MD, King Edward Med. Coll., Lahore, Pakistan, 1960. Diplomate Am. Bd. Surgery. Intern Columbus Hosp., Chgo., 1963-64; resident in surgery Little County Mary Hosp., Evergreen Park, Ill., 1964-69; staff Palos Heights (Ill.) Cmty. Hosp. Address: 15300 West Ave Ste 302 Orland Park IL 60462-4684

AHMED, SYED Z. anthropologist; b. Meerut, India, Aug. 19, 1923; s. Syed Riazuddin and Shah Jehan Begum; m. Susan Ahmed, Feb. 20, 1944; 1 child, Suraiya. PhD, Eng. Leader Sahara Recon Expdn., North Africa; prodr. 40 scientific documentary films for TV, Europe; pres., exec. prodr. Xploration Internat. Rschr., traveler numerous expdns. worldwide. Author: Twilight of an Empire in India, Twilight of an Empire in China, Twilight on the Silk Road, Ruwenzori: A Land Journey Through Europe to Central Africa, Twilight on Caucausus, Incredible Journeys Around the World, Tales of Imperial China and Asia, 1997, Travel in Shangri-La, 1998, East of Tien Shan, 1998, An Imperial Affair, 1999, I Was a Geisha, 1999, Zenith of an Empire, 2001, A Daring Escape, 2002. Islamic.

AHMER, INAM, arrived in U.S., 1999; s. Inamul Haq Khan and Husnara Begum. BTech. in Mech. Engring., Jamia Millia Islamia, New Delhi, India, 1998; MS in Indsl. Engring., Texas A&M U., College Station, 2002; MS in Econs., Tex. A&M U., College Station, 2003. Rsch. asst. Arbin Inst. Tex. A&M U., College Station, 1999—2000; stats. analyst Texas A&M U., College Station, 2000—02. Rschr. Texas A&M System AMP/NSF-FC, TAMU, College Station, 2000—02. Contbr. Mem.: Am. Prodn. and Inventory Control Soc. Personal E-mail: ahmer_inam@hotmail.com.

AHMOSE, NEFERTARI A. journalism educator; b. Kingston, Jamaica, Oct. 3, 1951; arrived in U.S., 75; d. Cecil Alexander Rose and Florence Rhodian Daley. *Great-great-great grand parents enslaved Africans on Jamaican sugar plantation. Kidnapped from West Africa during the Atlantic Slave trade in 15t century. From Jamaican Creole descendants came my parents Cecil and Florence Rose. My father a mason, my mother a milliner and domestic.* Student, L.A. Valley Coll., 1975. Journalist Jamaica Daily News, 1974—80; pub. African Expression, Bronx, NY, 1982—91; politician Kemet-Kush, Ensley, Ala., 1985—2001; founder Afrikan U. in West, Bklyn., 1996—. Leader Wafrakan Empress Afrikan Diasporan Nation. *All through my education I could not find a place in society for my people. So I created areas using professionalism and entrepreneurship to enhance their political and economical status.* Author: Black Sovereign-The Black Alternative, 1992, Harmonization, Unification and Standardization in Afrikan Tribal Vernaculars into Kiafrakan Language-Dictionary and Grammar, 1996, Ki-Afrakan-English Excerxises, 1997, Ki-Afrakan Grammar, 1996, Ki-Afrakan Dictionary, 1996, Incorp. Afrakan Standard Language, 1994, Sex Education for Youngsters, 1994. Founder Afrikan Bank and Investment Trust, Merkutu Currency, Kemet-Kush (now Wafrakan Polit. Party), NY, 2000—. Mailing: PO Box 971 Bronx NY 10472

AHN, CHOONG YONG, economics educator; b. Taegu, Republic of Korea, Jan. 3, 1941; s. Wha Sun (Whang) A.; m. Sun Hye Kim, Dec. 20, 1972; 1 child, Jae Churl. BA, Kyungpook Nat. U., Taegu, 1963; MA, U. Hawaii, 1968; PhD, Ohio State U., 1972. Postdoctoral fellow Ohio State U., Columbus, 1972-74; prof. econs. Chung-Ang U., Seoul, 1974—2002. Chmn. bd. dirs. Chohung Bank, 1999-2002; cons. Bank of Korea, Seoul, 1990-92, World Bank, Washington, 1978-88; chief tech. advisor UN Indsl. Devel. Orgn., Vienna, 1985, 91; pres. Korea Inst. for Internat. Econ. Policy, 2002—; dean grad. sch. internat. studies Chung-Ang U., 1997-2000. Editor: Jour. Econ. Devel., 1985-96; contbr. articles to profl. jours. Pres. Korean Assn. East-West Ctr. Alumni, Seoul, 1986-87; pres. Korean Asn. Ohio State U. ALumni Assn., 1999-2000. 2d lt. Korean Army, 1963-65. Named Economist of Yr. Maeil Economic Daily Paper, Korea, 1984; recipient Okita Policy Rsch. award NIRA, Japan, 2000. Mem. Korean Econometric Soc. (pres. 1991-92), Fedn. Korean Industries (mem. adv. bd. 1980—), Presdl. Commn. Sci. and Tech. (mem. adv. bd. 1989-90), Korean Econ. Assn., Korean Internat. Econ. Assn. (pres. 1994), Korean Futurist Soc., Presdl. Econ. Adv. Coun. Avocations: golf, mountaineering, reading. Office: 300-04 Yomgok-dong Seocho-gu Seoul 137-747 Republic of Korea

AHN, CHUL, medical educator; PhD, Carnegie Mellon U., Pitts., 1986. Prof. U. of Tex. Med. Sch., Houston, 1996—. Office: University of Texas Medical School 6431 Fannin St MSB 1.122 Houston TX 77030

AHO, BRIEN, photojournalist; Grad., Syracuse Military Photojournalism, 2002. Just returned from a five month deployment in the Middle East. Photojournalist USN, Fleet Combat Camera, Atlantic. Recipient Two time first Pl. winner in Mil. Photography of the Yr. Competition. Mem.: Eddie Adams Workshop (staff mem.). Home: 603 Trout Run Odenton MD 21113-3617*

AHRARI, M. EHSAN, political science educator, researcher, consultant; b. Hyderabad, India, Nov. 24, 1945; came to U.S. 1968; s. Mohammed Hashmatullah and Sayyeda Ahrari; m. Sharon Leyland Ahrari. BA, Ea. Ill. U., 1971, MA, 1972; PhD, So. Ill. U., 1976. Grants specialist Jackson County Housing, Murpheesboro, Ill., 1977; vis. asst. prof. Ea. Ill. U., Charleston, 1977-79, Kean Coll. N.J., Union, 1980; asst. prof. polit. sci. Eastern Carolina U., Greenville, 1980-86; assoc. prof. polit. sci. Miss. State U., 1986-90; prof. Middle East and Southwestn Asian Studies Air War Coll., Maxwell AFB, Ala., 1990-94; prof. internat. security & strategy joint & combined warfighting sch. Joint Forces Staff Coll., Nat. Def. U., Norfolk, Va., 1994—, assoc. dean of joint and combined warfighting sch., 1995—96. Sr. rsch. fellow Ctr. for Internat. Security and Strategic Studies, Miss. State U. Author: The Dynamics of Oil Diplomacy, 1980, OPEC-The Failing Giant, 1986, Ethnic Groups and U.S. Foreign Policy, 1987, The Gulf and International Security: The 1980's and Beyond, 1989, the Persian Gulf After the Cold War, 1993, The Middle East in Transition, 1994, Change in the Continuity in the Middle East, 1996, The New Great Game in Central Asia, 1996; contbr. book revs. and articles to profl. jours. NEH fellow, 1979, 84-85. Mem. Am. Polit. Sci. Assn., Am. Soc. Pub. Adminstrn. (bd. dirs. Ea. N.C. chpt. 1985-86, pres. Ea. N.C. chpt. 1985-86, edit. bd. Internat. Jour. Pub. Adminstrn.), Pi Sigma Alpha, Pi Alpha Alpha. Democrat. Muslim. Avocations: photography, tennis, racquetball, travel. Home: 100 E Ocean View Ave Apt 907 Norfolk VA 23503-1634

AHRENS, FRANKLIN ALFRED, veterinary pharmacology educator; b. Leigh, Nebr., Apr. 27, 1936; s. Alfred Henry and Agnes Elizabeth (Higgins) A.; m. Katherine Aldene Henning, May 8, 1960; children— Jeffrey, Gregory, Matthew, Kristin D.V.M., Kans. State U., 1959; MS, Cornell U., 1965, PhD, 1968. Instr. U. Minn.-St. Paul, 1959-60; asst. prof. pharmacology Coll. Vet. Medicine, Iowa State U., Ames, 1968-70, assoc. prof. pharmacology, 1970-75, prof. pharmacology, 1975—2001, chmn. dept. vet. physiology and pharmacology, 1982-90; prof. emeritus Coll. Vet. Medicine Iowa State U., 2001—. Served as capt. USAF, 1960-63, lt. col. Air N.G., 1971-91. Recipient Norden Disting. Tchr. award Iowa State U., 1981; NIH spl. research fellow Cornell U., 1967-68 Mem. AVMA, N.Y. Acad. Scis., Assn. Mil. Surgeons U.S., Sigma Xi Democrat. Lutheran.

AHRENS, HENRY WILLIAM, art educator, consultant, puppeteer; b. Bklyn., Apr. 11, 1918; s. Otto Conrad and Caroline Johanna (Schoneck) A.; m. Marjorie June Brooks, Dec. 18, 1965. BFA, Pratt Inst., Bklyn., 1941; MA, Columbia U., 1943; EdD, NYU, 1964. Art tchr. Lincoln Sch., Tchrs. Coll. Columbia U., N.Y.C., 1941-42; art supr. Bd. Edn., South River, N.J., 1946-47, art tchr. Elizabeth, N.J., 1947-52; assoc. prof. SUNY, Buffalo, 1952-57; prof. art The Coll. of N.J., 1957-83, chmn. art dept., 1965-70, 72-75, ret., 1983, prof. emeritus, 1987—. Cons. Thomas A. Edison State Coll., Trenton, 1975-93; exch. prof. U. Frankfurt, Frankfurt Am Main, W. Ger., 1970-71; lectr. in field; mem. original puppet prodns. in Can., Europe and U.S., 1947—. Served alt. mil. duty Civilian Pub. Svc., 1943-46. Recipient Frank A. Rexford medal for Cooperation in Govt., 1937. Mem. Art Educators N.J. (hon. life, 1st v.p., pres.), Puppeteers of Am. (religious cons. 1969-76), Mercer County Ret. Tchrs. Assn. (life mem.), N.J. Edn. Assn. (life mem.), NEA (life mem.), Union Internat. Del La

Marionettes, The Greater Phila. Area Puppetry Guild (hon. life), Puppeteers of Am., Phi Delta Kappa (life). Mem. Religious Soc. Friends (Quakers). Home and Office: 139 N Main St Yardley PA 19067-1322

AHRENS, KENT, museum director, art historian; b. Martinsburg, W.Va. s. Fred E. and Mary C. (Routzahn) A. AB, Dartmouth Coll., 1961; MA, U. Md., 1966; PhD, U. Del., 1972. Mem. faculty Fla. State U., Tallahassee, 1971-74, Randolph-Macon Woman's Coll., Lynchburg, Va., 1974-77; mem. curatorial staff Wadsworth Atheneum, Hartford, Conn., 1977-78; mem. faculty Georgetown U., Washington, 1979-82; dir. Everhart Mus., Scranton, Pa., 1982-90, Rockwell Mus., Corning, N.Y., 1990-95, Civic Fine Arts Ctr., Sioux Falls, S.D., 1996-97, Kennedy Mus. of Art, Ohio U., Athens, 1997—2000; mus. cons., 2000—; dir. devel. Cmty. Action, Athens, 2002—. Mem. task force on art activities Lynchburg Bicentennial Commn., 1975-76; project evaluator Md. Com. Humanities, 1980-82; mem. adv. panel The Lucan Ctr., Scranton, Pa., 1983-84; mem. mus. adv. com. Pa. Hist. and Mus. Commn., 1984-86; trustee Williamstown (Mass.) Regional Art Conservation Lab., Inc., 1984-92; mem. art mus. adv. panel Pa. Coun. on Arts, 1984-87; mem. adv. panel Pa. Fedn. Mus. and Hist. Orgns., 1989-90; mem. adv. com. on exhbns. at Pa. Gov.'s residence, 1987-90; juror Regional Art '89, Marywood Coll. Art Galleries, Scranton, 1989, Regional 1991, Arnot Art Mus., Elmira, 1991, Cmty. Cultural Ctr,. Brookings, S.D., 1996; bd. dirs. Mus. West, 1990-95; juror Fiber and Textile Exhibn. Civic Fine Arts Ctr., Sioux Falls, S.D., 1996, Wilbur Stilwell Student Awards Exhibn., U. S.D., Vermillion, 1997, Zanesville (Ohio) Art Ctr., 2000; adj. prof. Sch. Art, Ohio U., Athens, 1997-2000, mem. percent for art com., 1997-99. Author: (with others) Rembrandt in the National Gallery of Art, 1969, The Drawings and Watercolors by Truman Seymour (1824-1891), Everhart Mus. 1986; co-author: Frederic C. Knight (1898-1979), Everhart Mus., 1987; author: The Oils and Watercolors by Edward D. Boit (1840-1915), Everhart Mus., 1990, Cyrus E. Dallin: His Small Bronzes and Plasters, Rockwell Mus., 1995, others; contbg. author: American Paintings and Sculpture: Illustrated Catalogue, Nat. Gallery of Art, 1970, Wadsworth Atheneum Paintings: The Netherlands and German-speaking Countries, 1978, Dictionary of Women Artists, 1997, Allgemeines Künsterlexikon, 1999—, Currier & Ives: Selection from the Nationwide Collection, Kennedy Mus. Art, 2000, Small Bronzes, 2001. Vol. Bosnia-Herzegovina Heritage Rescue, London, 1995-2001; trustee, bd. dirs. Bosnia-Herzegovina Heritage Rescue, Inc., USA, 2001—. Served as 1st lt. U.S. Army, 1962-64. Recipient grant-in-aid Am. Philos. Soc., 1975; Samuel H. Kress fellow Nat. Gallery of Art, 1968-69; Chester Dale fellow Nat. Gallery Art, 1970-71; NEH fellow, 1973-74, Mus. Mgmt. Inst., J. Paul Getty Trust, 1991, award for superior vol. svc. Am. Assn. Mus., 1999. Mem. Coll. Art Assn., Am. Assn. Mus. (on-site surveyor mus. assessment program 1984-89, 92—, accreditation com. 1986, 90—), Mus. Assn. Pa. (chmn. 1984-90), Mid-Atlantic Assn. Mus., Ohio Assn. Non-profit Orgns., Rotary, Elks. Office: Hocking-Athens-Perry Cmty Action PO Box 340 Athens OH 45701

AHRENS, LYNN, lyricist; b. NY, Oct. 1, 1948; m. Neil Costa. BA in Comms., Syracuse U., 1970. Author book, lyricist: Once On This Island, 1995 (Olivier award best musical, Tony nominations for best book and score, NAACP award for best playwright), Lucky Stiff, 1988 (Helen Hayes award for best musical), lyricist: Once on this Island, 1990, My Favorite Year, 1993, Ragtime, 1996 (Grammy nomination, Tony award, 1998, Drama Desk award, 1998, Outer Critics Cir. award, 1998), Anastasia, 1997 (2 Acad. award nominations, 2 Golden Globe nominations), Bartok the Magnificent, 1999, With Voices Raised, 1999, Seussical, 2000, A Man of No Importance, 2002, co-author, lyricist: A Christmas Carol, 1994, Schoolhouse Rock, 1973—85 (Emmy award, 4 Emmy nominations), 1992—98. Mem.: AMPAS, NARAS, ASCAP, Dramatists Guild Coun. Office: c/o William Morris Attn Peter Franklin 1325 Avenue Of The Americas New York NY 10019-6026

AHRENS, THOMAS H. production company executive; b. N.Y.C., Oct. 25, 1919; BA magna cum laude, U. Buffalo, 1938; JD, Harvard U., 1941; certificate in Culinary Arts, N.Y.C. Tech. Coll., 1953. Bar: N.Y. 1944. Dir. Edward F. Gallaher Prodns., 1946—; lectr. wines and beverages N.Y.C. Tech. Coll., 1953-55, prof. hotel and restaurant mgmt., 1971—; dir. rsch., security analyst Templeton, Dobbrow and Vance, 1962-64; pres. Chef Phillip, Inc., 1956-69. Author radio and TV scripts on wines, gastronomy and music, 1946— . Mem. chmn.'s coun. Lincoln Ctr. for Performing Arts. 2d lt. AUS, 1942-45. Decorated officer Chaine des Rotisseurs; Confrerie Saint Etienne d'Alsace; Chevaliers du Tastevin; Commanderie des Cordons Bleus de France; Medaille de la Ville de Paris, 1976 Mem. ABA, N.Y. Soc. Security Analysts, Phi Beta Kappa. Clubs: Harvard, Paris-American, Met., Met. Opera (all N.Y.C.); Travellers, Cercle de l'Union Interalliée (Paris). Home: 333 E 69th St New York NY 10021-5549

AHRENS, WILLIAM HENRY, architect; b. N.Y.C., May 12, 1925; s. John Karl and Sophie (Hashage) A.; m. Joyce Nolan, Mar. 27, 1951. Student, R.I. Sch. Design, 1946; AB in Architecture, Princeton U., 1950, M.F.A. in Arch. and Urban Planning, 1953; postgrad., Tehran U., 1960. Chief architect Litchfield, Whiting, Bowne, Iran, 1958-61, 1961-64; dir. internat. ops. Whiting Assos., Rome, 1964-67; architect William H. Ahrens, AIA, Rome, Italy, 1967-95. Chmn. John's Island Archtl. Review com., 1997—. Prin. archtl. works include ITT Sheraton Hotels, Tunisia and Iraq, Marriott Hotels, Egypt and Iran, Esso Hotels, Bologna, Italy and Bordeaux, France, Holiday Inn at Salalah Oman, Univ. of Dallas Rome Campus, various projects for NATO, Pontifical N.Am. Coll., Vatican City State. Trustee John Cabot U.; mem. adv. bd. U. Dallas, U. Rome; bd. regents Marymount Internat. Sch., Rome; councilman Indian River Shores, Fla., 2003—. With USAAF, World War II, PTO. Recipient award AIA, 1953, Pub. Svc. award Tehran Lions Club, 1961, Rector's award Pontifical N.Am. Coll., Rome, 1994. Mem. AIA, Princeton Club (N.Y.C.), John's Island Club, Circolo del Golf Club (Rome), Knight of Malta, Knight of St. Gregory, Met. Club (N.Y.C.). Home: John's Island 371 Silver Moss Dr Indian River Shores FL 32963-3430

AHRENSFELD, THOMAS FREDERICK, lawyer; b. Bklyn., June 30, 1923; s. Frederick Herman and Madeline Florence (Moffett) A.; m. Joan Ann McGowan, Mar. 17, 1944; 1 child, Thomas Frederick. AB, Bklyn. Coll., 1948; LL.B., Columbia U., 1948. Bar: N.Y. 1948. Assoc., then ptnr. Conboy, Hewitt, O'Brien & Boardman, N.Y.C., 1948-58; sec., assoc. gen. counsel Philip Morris Inc., N.Y.C., 1959-70, v.p., gen. counsel, 1970-76, sr. v.p., gen. counsel, 1976-85, Philip Morris Cos., Inc., N.Y.C., 1985-88; pvt. practice law Pleasantville, 1988—2000. Trustee Trinity-Pawling Sch. Corp., 1976-98; elder Presbyn. Ch. 1st lt. USAAF, 1942-45. Decorated D.F.C., Air medal with oak leaf clusters. Mem. ABA, N.Y.C. Bar Assn., N.Y. Athletic Club, Mt. Kisco (N.Y.) Country Club, Johns Island (Fla.) Club. Office: 85 Nannahagan Rd Pleasantville NY 10570-2314 Home: 450 Beach Rd # 324 Vero Beach FL 32963

AH-TYE, KIRK THOMAS, lawyer; b. L.A., Mar. 31, 1951; s. Thomas and Ruth Elizabeth (Liu) Ah-T.; m. Deborah Ann Wells, Jan. 31, 1981; 1 child, Torrey Ann. BA, U. Calif., Santa Barbara, 1973; JD, Boston Coll., 1976. Bar: Calif. 1977, U.S. Dist. Ct. (cen. dist.) Calif. 1978, U.S. Dist. Ct. (ea. dist.) Calif. 1994, U.S. Ct. Appeals (9th cir.) 1978, U.S. Supreme Ct. 1981. Co-exec. dir., mng. atty. Channel Counties Legal Svcs. Assn., Santa Barbara, 1977—; directing atty. Calif. Rural Legal Assistance, Inc. Expert witness Assembly Com. on Edn., Calif. Legis., Sacramento; panelist Ctr. for the Study of Dem. Instns., Santa Barbara; panelist, instr. CLE approved classes; past legal cons. Santa Barbara chpt. calif. Assn. Bilingual Educators; inaugural prodr., moderator Santa Barbara Law, Sta. KTMS-AM, 1994—. Editor (bar newsletter) Santa Barbara Lawyer, 1992-93, (monthly legal series) Santa Barbara News-Press; contbr. articles to profl. jours. Trustee Montessori Ctr. Sch., Santa Barbara, 1991-93; bd. dirs., v.p. Santa Barbara Internat. Film Festival, 1991-93; chair adv. bd. Santa Barbara Regional Health Authority, 1985; mem. blue-ribbon com. County Bd. Suprs., Santa Barbara, 1988; chair Santa Barbara County Affirmative Action Commn., 1987-88; mem. grant-making com. Fund for Santa Barbara, 1988-92. Recipient Local Hero award Santa Barbara Ind., 1988. Master Santa Barbara Am. Inns of Ct.; mem. State Bar Calif. (state resolutions com. to state bar conf. of dels. 1994-96, exec. com. to conf. dels. 1997, ann. legal svcs. achievement award for so. Calif. 1997, Achievement award for legal svc. 1997), Santa Barbara County Bar Assn. (jud. svc. award com. 1992, chmn. pro bono com. 1993, bd. dirs., sec., CFO 1992—, pres. 1997-98), Lawyer Referral Svc. Santa Barbara (bd. dirs., pres. 1992). Avocations: sports, film, literature, weights, tennis. Office: Calif Rural Legal Assistance Inc 324 E Carrillo St Ste B Santa Barbara CA 93101-7438

AHUJA, JAGDISH CHAND, mathematics educator; b. Rawalpindi, West Pakistan, Dec. 24, 1927; came to U.S., 1966, naturalized 1972; s. Nihal Chand and Ishwardai (Chhabra) A.; m. Sudarshan Sachdeva, May 18, 1955; children—Naina, Anita BA, Banaras U., 1953, MA, 1955; PhD, U. B.C., 1963. Sr. math. tchr. D.A.V. High Sch., Nairobi, Kenya, 1955-56; tchr. math. Tanzania, 1956-58; teaching asst. U. B.C., 1958-61, teaching fellow, 1961-63, stats. lab. instr., 1959-61, lectr. stats., 1961-63; asst. prof. math. U. Calgary, Can., 1963-66; assoc. prof. math. Portland State U., Oreg., 1966-69, prof. math., 1969—. Contbr. articles to profl. jours.; referee profl. jours., reviewer profl. jours. Mem. Inst. Math. Stats. Home: 4016 Orchard Dr Lake Oswego OR 97035-2406 Office: Portland State U Dept Math PO Box 751 Portland OR 97207-0751 E-mail: ahuja@mth.pdx.edu.

AHUJA, SANJAY, engineer, project manager, educator; b. Shevgaon, India; came to U.S., 1987; s. Jagatrilal and Mohina Ahuja; m. Anuradha Arora, July 6, 1988; children: Ankit, Shaan. BS, Bangalore (India) U., 1985, MS, 1987, U. Ala., Tuscaloosa, 1989, PhD, 1992. Tchg. asst. U. Ala., 1987-89, rsch. assoc., 1989-92; mem. tech. staff Argonne (Ill.) Nat. Lab., 1992-97, project mgr., 1994—. Mem. adj. faculty Coll. Dupage, Glen Ellyn, Ill., 1994-96, Benedictine U., Lisle, Ill., 1996-97; cons. U. Ala., 1994, Caterpillar, Inc., Peoria, Ill., 1994, mem. tech. staff Allied Signal Inc., Aerospace Equipment Sys., 1997-99 (project mgr., 1994—); mgr. software & sys. Corning Inc., 1999—. Reviewer Am. Foundrymen's Soc. Trans., 1994, Metall. Transactions, 1995; contbr. articles to profl. jours. Mem. Am. Ceramic Soc. (reviewer jour. 1996), Materials Rsch. Soc., Sunergy Sun Microsystems, Enterprise Network Computing. Achievements include hardware/software (embedded systems) integration for commercial and military avionics engine control applications; microsensor development for inert gas detection; microsensor for simultaneous detection of properties; research on the theoretical, experimental and numerical analysis of particle/interface interaction in composites, polymers and ceramics; on sensors, embedded systems, instrumentation development, extensive hardware/software/embedded systems development, multiple platform (Unix, Vax, PC) experience, micro- and nano-machining, biosensors and acoustic sensors. Office: Corning Inc Sp Td 02 2 Corning NY 14831-0001 Home: 18 Tamarron Way Pittsford NY 14534

AHUJA, SATINDER, chemist, consultant; b. Jahlum, Pakistan, Sept. 11, 1933; arrived in U.S.A., 1958; s. Jawnhar Lal and Sushil Ahuja; m. Fay Hontman Ahuja; children: Jay, Paul. BS in Pharmacy, Banaras (India) U., 1955, MS in Pharmacy, 1956; PhD, U. Scis., Phila., Pa., 1964. Asst. devel. chemist Lederle Labs., Pearl River, NY, 1964—66; sr. staff sci. Ciba Geigy Corp., Summit, NJ, 1966—91; sr. rsch. fellow Novartis, Suffern, NY, 1991—94; prin., owner Ahuja Consulting, Calbash, NC, 1994—2000. Editor (in chief): Jour. Isolation and Purification. Chmn. India Cultural Ctr. Rockland, NY, 1960. Mem.: Am. Assn. Pharm. Scientists, Am. Chem. Soc. (chmn. NY sect. 1968—94, Disting. Svc. award 1989, Outstanding Svc. award 1979).

AIBEL, HOWARD J. lawyer, arbitrator, mediator; b. N.Y.C., Mar. 24, 1929; m. Katherine Webster, June 6, 1952; children: David Webster, Daniel Walter, Jonathan Brown. AB magna cum laude, 1950; JD cum laude, Harvard U., 1951. Bar: N.Y. 1952. Assoc. White & Case, N.Y.C., 1952-57; trade regulation counsel GE, 1957-60, spl. litigation counsel elec. equipment antitrust cases, 1960-64; antitrust counsel ITT Corp., N.Y.C., 1964-66, v.p., assoc. gen. counsel, 1966-68, sr. v.p., gen. counsel, 1968-87, exec. v.p., gen. counsel, 1987-92, exec. v.p., chief legal officer, 1992-94; ptnr. LeBoeuf Lamb Greene & MacRae, N.Y.C., 1994-99, of counsel, 1999-2001. Bd. dirs. Farrel Corp., Transparancy, Internat.-USA; vice chmn. Fund for Modern Cts., 1985-95; mem. AAA/ABA/AMA Com. Health Care Dispute Resolution, 1997-2000. Mem. vis. com. Northwestern U. Law Sch., 1984—90; mem. adv. com. Corp. Counsel Ctr., chmn., 1986—87; trustee Lawyers Com. for Civil Rights, 1991—95, U. Bridgeport, 1989—91, chmn. adv. com. Sch. Law, 1987—92; cons. trustee Westport Nature Ctr. for Environ. Activities; bd. dirs. Alliance of Resident Theatres, NY, 1986—, chmn., 1989—2002, chmn. emeritus, 2002—; bd. dirs., 1st v.p. Westport Arts Ctr., 1993—96. Fellow Am. Bar Found. (life); mem. ABA (bus. law sect. corp. governance 1994-98), Am. Law Inst. (elected mem.), Am. Arbitration Assn. (chmn. exec. com. 1992-95, chmn. bd. dirs. 1995-98), Assn. Gen. Counsel, pres. Harvard Law Sch. Assn. NY, 1992-94, v.p. Harvard Law Sch. Assn., 1994-2002, Am. Judicature Soc. (bd. dirs. 1994-2001, exec. com. 1996-2001). Home and Office: 183 Steep Hill Rd Weston CT 06883-1924 E-mail: hjaibel@optonline.net.

AICHBHAUMIK, DIBYAJYOTI, metallurgical engineer; b. Netrokona, Bangladesh, Jan. 5, 1944; came to U.S., 1971, naturalized, 1977. s. Dibyenda and Jyotsna (Goon) A.; m. Nilu Datta, Feb. 4, 1971; 1 child, Niladri. BS, U. Calcutta, India, 1965; MS, Wayne State U., 1972, PhD, 1976. Foundry trainee Howrah Iron and Steel Corp., Calcutta, summers 1963-65; from jr. engr. to project engr. Kuljian Corp., Calcutta, 1965-71; fellow, rsch. asst., mem. faculty Wayne State U., Detroit, 1971-76; rsch. engr. Nat. Steel Corp., Weirton, W.Va., 1976-79, sr. rsch. metallurgist, 1979-80, supr. metall. engring. rsch., 1980-85, mgr. uncoated products/process, 1985-87; chief metall. engr. Weirton Steel Corp., 1987-89, mgr. rsch. and tech., 1989-90, mgr. quality assurance, 1990-92, mgr. metall. engring. and customer assurance, 1992-97, sr. fellow, 1997-98; tech. leader, sr. mgr., v.p. tech. Thomas Steel Strip, Warren, Ohio, 1998-99; cons. Debo Aichbhaumiks Assocs., Coraopolis, Pa., 1999—. Contbr. articles to profl. jours. Mem. AAAS, AIME, ASME, Am. Soc. Metals, Metall. Soc., Indian Inst. Metals, Sigma Xi. Hindu. Home and Office: 105 Freedom Ct Coraopolis PA 15108-9020 E-mail: deboaich@aol.com.

AIDINOFF, M(ERTON) BERNARD, retired lawyer; b. Newport, R.I., Feb. 2, 1929; s. Simon and Esther (Miller) A.; m. Celia Spiro, May 30, 1956 (dec. June 28, 1984); children: Seth G., Gail M.; m. Elsie V. Newburg, Nov. 29, 1996. BA, U. Mich., 1950; LLB magna cum laude, Harvard U., 1953. Bar: D.C. 1953, N.Y. 1954. Law clk. to Judge Learned Hand, U.S. Ct. of Appeals, N.Y.C., 1955-56; with Sullivan & Cromwell, N.Y.C., 1956-63, ptnr., 1963-96, ret. ptnr., 1997. Dir. Am. Internat. Group Inc., Gibbs & Cox, Inc., Goldman Sachs Philanthropy Fund; adv. com. to IRS commr., 1979-80, 85-86. Editor in chief The Tax Lawyer, 1974-77. Trustee Spence Sch., 1971-79; mem. adv. com. Gibbs Bros. Found., 1965-94; mem. vis. com. Harvard U. Law Sch., 1976-82, 99—; adv. dir. Met. Opera Assn., 1989-2002; chmn. bd. dirs. St. Luke's Chamber Ensemble, 1988-2001, chmn. emeritus, 2001—; nat. campaign chair Campaign to Save Touro Synagogue; pres. Soc. Friends of Touro Synagogue, 2002—; 1st lt. JAGC, AUS, 1953-55. Recipient Judge Learned Hand Human Rels. award Am. Jewish Com., 1997. Mem.: ABA (vice chmn. sect. taxation 1974—77, chmn.-elect 1981—82, chmn. 1982—83, chmn. commn. taxpayer compliance 1983—88, Ho. of Dels. 1988—91, Disting. Svc. award 2003), Am. Law Inst. (cons. fed. income tax project 1974—, chmn. tax program com. 1988—, John Minor Wisdom award 1995), Assn. Bar City of N.Y. (exec. com. 1974—78, chmn. exec. com. 1977—78, v.p. 1978—79, chmn. taxation com. 1979—81, chmn. govt. ethics com. 1988—90), N.Y. State Bar Assn., The Parks Coun. (bd. dirs. 1995—97), Lawyers Com. for Human Rights (bd. dirs. 1986—, treas. 1997—2002), Coun. Fgn. Rels., East Hampton Hist. Soc. (trustee 1983—89, 1990—95), Found. for a Civil Soc. (bd. dirs. 1994—, vice chmn. 1997—98, chmn. 1999—), Guild Hall (trustee 1989—94, 1995—, treas. 1993—94, 1995—2002), Met. Club, Century Assn., India Ho., Phi Beta Kappa. Home: 980 5th Ave New York NY 10021-0126 Office: Sullivan & Cromwell 125 Broad St New York NY 10004-2498 E-mail: aidinoffmb@sullcrom.com.

AIELLO, FRANK JOHN, music educator; b. Des Moines, May 23, 1940; s. Dominic O. and Rose D. Aiello; m. Judith Ann Grosvenor, Aug. 13, 1966; children: Dominic Grosvenor, Rose Helen. B Music Edn., Drake U., 1962, M Music, 1965; D Musical Arts, U. Okla., 1985. Choral dir. Urbandale (Iowa) Pub. Schs., 1964—66; music supr. Port Chester (N.Y.) Pub. Schs., 1966—68; prof. music U. S.D., Vermillion, 1968—2002, prof. emeritus, 2002—. Various choral workshops in pub. schs. and colls., 1968—; master classes at pub. schs. and colls., 1968—; dir. fine arts tour at various pub. schs. and colls., 1995—2000. Grantee Bush grants, England, France, Italy, 1986—90, 1992—95. Mem.: Music Tchrs. Nat. Assn. Roman Catholic. Avocations: hunting, fishing, carpentry, cooking. Home: 30174 448th Ave Volin SD 57072-5706

AIELLO, GENNARO C. insurance company executive; b. Ridgway, Pa., Dec. 16, 1953; s. Victor C. and Victoria I. (Bevacqua) A.; m. Cynthia K. Medvid, Sept. 20, 1975; children: Erin M., Kathryn T. BS, Gannon U., 1975; postgrad., Pa. State U, 1974-76. Lic. ins. agt., real estate agt. Sales rep. Met. Ins. Co., DuBois, Pa., 1975-80; owner, agt. Ins. Mktg. Assocs., Ridgway, 1980-86; acct. exec. The Pa. Mfrs. Assn. Group, Ridgway, 1986-94; acct. mgr. EBI Cos., Erie, Pa., 1994-98; comml. account mgr., ptnr. Anderson and Kime Ins., Inc., Ridgway, 1998—. Gen. mgr. Wolf Run Marina, Warren, Pa., 1978-79; controller U.S. Coal, Inc., Ridgway, 1981-83; realtor Anderson and Kime, St. Marys, Pa., 1983—; bd. dirs. Cmty. Nurses, Inc. Bd. dirs., v.p. Ridgway Action for Community Enhancement, 1986-88, W.R.C. Cmty. Health Svcs., 2000—; chmn. St. Leo's Home and Sch. Assn., Ridgway, 1989-91; bd. dirs. St. Leo's Parish Coun., 1986-90, 2000, pres. sports assn., 1988-91; pres. Elk County Coun. on the Arts, 1991-92, v.p., 1990-91, pres., 1991-92; pres. Ridgway Independence Festival Inc., 1990—; v.p., bd. dirs. Outdoor Companions Inc., 1991, Citizens Against Phys., Sexual and Emotional Abuse, 1992-93; treas. Ridgway Cmty. Nurses, 2000—,; bd. dirs. Ridgway Heritage Coun., 1997—; bd. dirs., treas. Ridgway Ambulance Corp., 2000—; vice chmn. Cmty. Nurses Homehealth Support Svcs., 2002—. Mem. Johnsonburg C. of C. (bd. dirs., pres. 1989—), Elk-Cameron Bd. Realtors, Jaycees (pres. local chpt. 1986-87), Ducks Unltd. (spons. chmn. 1987-88), Elk County Country Club (bd. dirs. 1991-95, v.p. 1992-93, pres. 1993—), Rotary (pres. Johnsonburg lodge 1980-81), K.C. (3d degree). Avocations: hunting, fishing, archery, boating, golf. Home: 220 Montmorenci Ave Ridgway PA 15853-1615 Office: Anderson and Kime Ins PO Box 507 Ridgway PA 15853-0507

AIELLO, JAMES ANDREW, lawyer; b. Phoenix, Ariz., Mar. 5, 1940; s. James Francis and Ethel Swea Aiello; m. Helene Sarah Aiello, June 21, 1964; children: James Anthony, Matthew Charles. BA, U. Ariz., 1962; JD, U. San Francisco, 1965. Bar: Calif. 1966, D.C. 1979, U.S. Supreme Ct. 1968. Dep. atty. gen. Office of Calif. Atty. Gen., San Francisco, 1965-70; asst. dist. atty. San Mateo County Calif. Dist. Atty., Redwood, City, 1970-79; chief of staff Hon. William Royer, U.S. Rep., Washington, 1979-81; dir. domestic govt. affairs Combustion Engring. Inc., Washington, 1981-92; v.p. govt. affairs Ogden Martin, Inc., Washington, 1992-95; acting CEO KBF Environtl., Inc., Washington, 1995-97; dir., chief of party PADCO, Inc., Midrand, South Africa, 1997—; acting CEO, MIIU, South Africa, 2000—. Prin. Oakton (Va.) Cons. Group, 1995-97; dir. KBF Environtl. Inc., 1995-97, DGL Internat., Inc., Washington, 1995-98; mem. environ. adv. com. Conn. State Legis., Hartford, 1994-97, legis. adv. com. 1994-95; mem. environ. adv. com. Hawaii Legis., 1992-95. Contbr. articles to profl. jours. Chair, legis. and regulations com. Integrated Waste Svcs. Assn., 1993-95. Mem. Masons (San Carlos Lodge #690), Aircraft and Pilots and Owners Assn., Bar Assn. D.C., Bar Assn. of State of Calif. (ho. adminstrv. asst. assoc.), Westwood Country Club. Republican. Episcopalian. Avocations: opera, classical music, private pilot, south african wild game conservation. Office: PO Box 95427 Waterkloof 0145 South Africa E-mail: ocgp@icon.co.za.

AIELLO, STEPHEN, public relations executive; BA in History, NYU; MA in History, Columbia U.; PhD in Urban Studies, Union Grad. Sch. Former adminstr. N.Y.C. Bd. Edn., pres., 1974-80; former prof. Fordham U., N.Y.C.; spl. asst. ethnic affairs White House, Washington, 1980-81; exec. dir. N.Y.C. Ednl. Constrn. Fund; v.p., dir., civic affairs Burson-Marsteller, 1983-86, exec. v.p., pub. affairs, 1987-89, dir. pub. affairs, 1991-92; exec. v.p., gen. mgr. Cohn & Wolfe, N.Y.C., 1989-90, exec. v.p., gen. mgr. N.Y., 1992-93, pres., CEO, 1993—. Chair ethnic/urban coun. Nat. Dem. Com.; former chmn. N.Y. Urban Coalition. Office: Cohn & Wolfe 225 Park Ave S Fl 17 New York NY 10003-1604

AIELLO, SUSAN, artist, illustrator, educator; b. Wilmington, Del., June 13; d. Albert Alexander and Mary Ann Aiello. Student, Moore Coll. Art, 1971-72; BS in Art Edn., U. Del., 1975; postgrad., Phila. Coll. Art, 1976. Art dir. Women's Experience Mag., Newark, 1976-78, Aloysius Butler & Clark, Wilmington, 1978-80; freelance illustrator Phila., 1980-82; illustrator Avenue Artists, Chgo., 1982-86; owner, illustrator Susan Aiello Studio, Chgo., 1987—. Art instr. Inst. Art Ill., Chgo., 1994—. Author, illustrator: Hat Like That, 1986, My Blanket Burt, 1986; group exhibitions included Del. Art Mus., 1978, Del. Artists of Italian Heritage, 1979, Kozuch Gallery, Chgo., 1997, Chgo. Artist Rep Show, 1999, Inst. Art Faculty Show, 1997. Com. mem. Mental Health Assn., Chgo., 1992-95, Brian Piccolo Found., Chgo., 1994—. Mem. The Palette and Chisel. Avocations: travel, antiques, collecting childrens books, photography, exercising. Office: Susan Aiello Studio 120 W Illinois St 5E Chicago IL 60610-4506

AIG, DENNIS IRA, writer, film producer; b. Bklyn., Jan. 15, 1950; s. Irving and Judith (Gran) A.; m. Ann Therese Bertagnolli, Nov. 26, 1983; children: Hannah Elena, Leah Isabella, Aaron Anthony (dec.). BA, CUNY, Flushing, 1971; MA, Ohio State U., 1973, PhD, 1983. Founder, co-exec. dir., pres. bd. trustees Community Film Assn., Columbus, Ohio, 1979-81; ind. writer, producer, 1981-83; staff writer, producer Chem. Abstracts Service, Columbus, 1983-89; asst. prof. Montana State U., Bozeman, 1989-95, assoc. prof., 1995—. Instr. continuing edn. Ohio State U., 1978; writer Frontier Press Columbus, 1980-81; media cons. Ridihalgh and Eggers, 1981-82; producer, dir. KUSM Pub. TV, Mont. State U., 1989—; pres. The Hunter Neil Co., Bozeman, 1996—. Screenwriter, exec. prodr.: KAZ vs. the Gypsy Moth, 1984 (Cert. of Excellence 1984), CAS-the World Resource, 1986 (Cine Golden Eagle award 1986); exec. prodr.: A Heartbeat Away: Health Care in Three Forks Montana, 1991 (Coll. TV award, The Mainstreet Show TV series; co-prodr./dir.: Shadow Casting: The Making of "A River Runs Through It", 1993 (Gold Hugo award, Chris award, Gold Apple award); co-dir., co-prodr.: Sacred Journey of Nez Perce, 1996 (winner Gold award N.Y. Festivals, Crystal award, Communicator awards, Regional Emmy award), Black Hawk Waltz: Tales of a Rocky Mountain Town, 1996 (Telly award); exec. prodr.: Confessions of a Stand-Up, 1994 (Regional Emmy award); location prodr. Quest for K2, Nat. Geographic TV, 2001; dir., co-prodr.: Test Pilots of the Body, 1997; exec. prodr.: Bridgehampton Suite, 1998; prod., dir., exec. prodr.: Visions of Grace: Robert Redford and The Horse Whisperer, 1998 (Chris award, Telly award), Electronic Press Kit, The Horse Whisperer, 1998; prodr. Guide Season, 2000; prodr., dir. America's Outdoor Heritage, 2000 (Telly award, Aegis award, Communicator award). Trustee Nat. Hall of Fame for Persons with Disabilities, Columbus, 1981-84; co-chmn. (photo exhibit) Anne Frank In The World: 1929-45, Columbus, 1987. Rockefeller Found. travel grantee, 1990. Mem. Univ. Film and Video Assn., Assn. Ind. Video and Filmmakers. Jewish. Avocations: photography, reading, weight training. Home: 8111 Rolling Hills Dr Bozeman MT 59715-9346 Office: KUSM Pub TV Dept Media Theatre Art Bozeman MT 59717-0001 also: The Hunter Neil Co PO Box 1245 Bozeman MT 59771-0001 E-mail: dennisaig@imt.net.

AIGNER, B. ROBERT, neurologist; b. Fürth-in-Ward, Germany, Mar. 24, 1928; came to U.S., 1929; s. Alois and Josefine Aigner; m. Martha Ann Wagner, June 24, 1952; children: Susan, Robert, David, Paul, Sarah. Student, St. Martins Coll., 1945-48; MD, St. Louis U., 1952. Resident in neurology Mayo Clinic, Rochester, Minn., 1956-59; pvt. practice neurology Seattle, 1960-97; semi-retired, cons., 1997—. Chief of staff Providence Hosp., 1989-90. Pres. Amigos, Seattle, 1982; trustee St. Martin's Coll., Lacey, Wash., 1967-94, pres., 1987. Lt. USAF, 1954-56. Mem. AMA, Am. Acad. Neurology, Wash. State Med. Soc. (mem. com.), King County Med. Soc. (mem. com.), North Pacific Soc. Neurology and Psychiatry (pres. 1981). Avocations: travel, birding, photography. Office: Panel of Cons Med Dental Bldg 509 Olive Way Seattle WA 98101-1720

AIGNER, DENNIS JOHN, economics educator, consultant; b. L.A., Sept. 27, 1937; s. Herbert Lewis and Della Geraldine (Balasek) A.; m. Vernita Lynne White, Dec. 21, 1957 (div. May 1977); children: Mitchell A., Annette N., Anita L., Angela D.; m. Gretchen Camille Bertolet, Dec. 22, 1992. BS, U. Calif.-Berkeley, 1959, MA, 1962, PhD, 1963. Asst. prof. econs. U. Ill., Urbana, 1962-67; from assoc. prof. to prof. U. Wis., Madison, 1967-76; prof., chmn. dept. econs. U. So. Calif., L.A., 1976-88; dean grad. sch. mgmt. U. Calif., Irvine, 1988-97, prof. grad. sch. mgmt., 1988—, assoc. dean sch. environ. sci. and mgmt. Santa Barbara, 1998-2000, acting dean, 2000-01, dean, 2001—. Pres. Dennis Aigner Inc., L.A., 1978—; dir. Analysis Group Econs. Author: Introduction to Statistical Decision Making, 1968, Basic Econometrics, 1971; editor: Latent Variables in Socio-Economic Models, 1977; co-editor: Jour. Econometrics, 1972-91. Fulbright fellow Belgium, 1970, Israel, 1983, Bren fellow U. Calif. Santa Barbara, 1998—; NSF grantee, 1968-70, 70-72, 73-76, 79-81, 84-86. Fellow Econometric Soc.; mem. Am. Statis. Assn., Am. Econ. Assn. Office: Sch Environ Sci Mgmt U Calif Santa Barbara CA 93106 E-mail: djaigner@bren.ucsb.edu.

AIGNER, EMILY BURKE, Christian lay minister; b. Henrico, Va., Oct. 28, 1920; d. William Lyne and Susie Emily (Willson) Burke; m. Louis Cottrell Aigner, Nov. 27, 1936; children: Lyne, Betty, D. Muriel (dec.), Willson, Norman, William, Randolph, Dorothy. Cert. in Bible, U. Richmond, 1969; postgrad., So. Bapt. Sem. Extension, Nashville, 1987, Va. Commonwealth U., 1981; diploma in Bible, Liberty Home Bible Inst., 1992, masterlife grad., 1994. Deacon Four Mile Creek Bapt. Ch., Richmond, Va., 1972—, trustee, 1991, dir. Woman's Missionary Union, 1986-94, treas., 1984-89, dir. Sunday sch., 1969-78, 84-85, 1989-93. Spl. edn. tchr., 1993-99; acctg. tech., 1959-80. Prodr. Dial-A-Devotion for pub. by telephone, 1978-85. Solicitor ARC, Henrico County, 1947-49, induction ctr. vol., 1994-97; solicitor, United Givers' Fund, Henrico County, 1945-48; sec.-treas. soliciting funds Bible Edn. in Varina Sch., 1946-49; singer Bellwood Choir, Chesterfield County, Va., 1965-70; telephone counselor Richmond Contact, 1980-82, Am. Cancer Soc., Richmond, 1980-82; program chmn. Varina (Va.) Home Demonstration Club, 1950-53; worker Vol. Visitor Program Westport Convalescent Home, 1983—; vol. patient rep. Richmond Meml. Hosp., 1994-98, chaplain, 1996-97; jail min. Richmond City Jail, 1973—; lay minister to sr. adults Four Mile Creek Ch., 2002—. Named Woman of Yr., Henrico Farm Bur., 1996. Mem. UDC, Am. Assn. Christian Counselors, Gideons Internat. (sec. Va. aux. 1977-80, 82-84, new mem. plan rep. 1981, 85, 91, 94, zone leader 1988-91, state cabinet rep. 1989-90, pres. Richmond N.E. Camp 1976-78, sec.-treas. 1980-82, 93, scripture sec. 1973-75, 87-89, v.p., 1997-98, chmn. Va. state widows com. 1993-97, pres. Richmond East Camp, 2000-02), Henrico Farm Bur. (women's com. 1994—), Alpha Phi Sigma. Home: 9717 Varina Rd Richmond VA 23231-8428 *Forgive or not to forgive. I choose to forgive that I may not become bitter and cynical within but have peace and love to share with others with whom I encounter.*

AIGRAIN, JACQUES A. banker; b. Paris, Aug. 15, 1954; arrived in Eng., 1991; s. Pierre R. and Françine E. (Bogard) A.; m. Nicoletta I. Gentinetta, Apr. 16, 1983; children: Florian, Laurène. BA in Law, Pantheon, Paris, 1975; M of Econs., Dauphine, Paris, 1976; PhD in Econs., Sorbonne, Paris, 1980. Registered SFA and NASD. Cons. Orgn. for Economic Cooperation & Development, France, 1979-80; analyst J.P. Morgan, N.Y.C., 1981-82, asst. treas. Paris, 1982-85, v.p. N.Y.C., 1986-91, London, 1991-93, mng. dir., 1993-96; chmn. J.P. Morgan SA, Paris, 1996-98, worldwide head energy, chem., healthcare London, 1998—, co-head worldwide M&A, head healthcare, chem. and energy, 1998—, co-head investment banking, 2000—; exec. bd., head fin. svc. Swissre, N.Y.C., Zurich, 2001—. Contbr. articles to fin. publs. Lt. French Navy, 1977-78. Avocations: skiing, windsurfing, mountain climbing. Home: 167 E 71st St New York NY 10021 Office: Swiss Re 55 E 52d St New York NY

AIKAWA, JERRY KAZUO, physician, educator; b. Stockton, Calif., Aug. 24, 1921; s. Genmatsu and Shizuko (Yamamoto) A.; m. Chitose Aihara, Sept. 20, 1944; 1 son, Ronald K. AB, U. Calif., 1942; MD, Wake Forest Coll., 1945. Intern, asst. resident N.C. Baptist Hosp., 1945-47; NRC fellow in med. scis. U. Calif. Med. Sch., 1947-48; NRC, AEC postdoctoral fellow in med. scis. Bowman Gray Sch. Medicine, 1948-50, instr. internal medicine, 1950-53, asst. prof., 1953; established investigator Am. Heart Assn., 1952-58; exec. officer lab. service Univ. Hosps., 1958-61, dir. lab. services, 1961-83, dir. allied health program, 1969—, assoc. dean allied health program, 1983—, pres. med. bd.; assoc. dean clin. affairs asst. prof. U. Colo. Sch. Medicine, 1953- 60, asso. prof. medicine, 1960-67, prof., 1967—, prof. biometrics, 1974—, assoc. dean clin. affairs, 1974—. Pres. Med. bd. Univ. Hosps. Fellow ACP, Am. Coll. Nutrition; mem. Western Soc. Clin. Research, So. Soc. Clin. Research, Soc. Exptl. Biology and Medicine, Am. Fedn. Clin. Research, AAAS, Central Soc. Clin. Research, AMA, Assn. Am. Med. Colls., Phi Beta Kappa, Sigma Xi, Alpha Omega Alpha Home: 3233 Lake Albano Cir San Jose CA 95135-1467 Office: U Colo Sch Medicine 4200 E 9th Ave Denver CO 80220-3706

AIKEN, JOAN (JOAN DELANO), author; b. Rye, Sussex, Eng., Sept. 4, 1924; d. Conrad Potter and Jessie (MacDonald) A.; m. Ronald George Brown, July 7, 1945 (dec. 1955); children: John Sebastian, Elizabeth Delano; m. Julius Goldstein, Sept. 2, 1976. Staff BBC, London, 1942-43; libr. UN Info. Ctr., London, 1943-49; sub-editor, features editor Argosy mag., London, 1955-60; copywriter J. Walter Thompson, London, 1960-61. Author: (juvenile fiction) All You've Ever Wanted and Other Stories, 1953, The Kingdom and The Cave, 1960, Black Hearts in Battersea, 1964, The Whispering Mountain, 1968, Night Fall, Winterthing: A Child's Play, 1970, The Cuckoo Tree, 1971, All and More, 1971, A Harp of Fishbones and Other Stories, 1972, The Skin Spinners, 1976, The Spiral Stair, 1979, The Shadow Guests, 1980, Up The Chimney Down, 1985, Give Yourself a Fright, 1989, A Foot in the Grave, 1990, Is, 1992, A Creepy Company, 1993, numerous others, (adult fiction) The Silence of Herondale, 1964, Beware of the Boquet, 1966, The Ribs of Death, 1967, The Embroidered Sunset, 1970, Castle Barebane, 1976, Last Movement, 1977, The Smile of the Stranger, 1978, The Weeping Ash, 1980, Foul Matter, 1983, Mansfield Revisted, 1984, If I Were You, 1987, Blackground, 1989, Jane Fairfax, 1990, The Shoemaker's Boy, 1991, The Midnight Moropus, 1993, Cold Shoulder Road, 1995, A Handful of Gold, 1995, Emma Watson, 1996, The Cockatrice Boys, 1996, The Jewel Seed, 1997, Moon Cake, 1998, others; translator: The Angel Inn; : The Youngest Miss Ward, 1998, The Way to Write for Children, 1998, Dangerous Games, 1999, Lady Catherine's Necklace, 2000, In Thunder's Pocket, 2000, The Song of Mat and Ben, 2002, The Scream, 2001, Bone and Dream, 2002; : Ghostly Beasts, 2002, Midwinter Nightingale, 2003. Address: The Hermitage East St Petworth West Sussex GU28 0AB England

AIKEN, LEWIS ROSCOE, JR., psychologist, educator; b. Bradenton, Fla., Apr. 14, 1931; s. Lewis Roscoe and Vera Irene (Hess) A.; m. Dorothy Ree Grady, Dec. 16, 1956; children: Christopher, Timothy BS, Fla. State U., Tallahassee, 1955, MA, 1956; PhD, U. N.C., 1960. Assoc. prof. psychology U. N.C., Greensboro, 1960-65; prof. Guilford Coll., Greensboro, 1966-74, Sacred Heart Coll., Belmont, N.C., 1974-76, U. Pacific, Stockton, Calif., 1977-79, Pepperdine U., Malibu, Calif., 1979. Author: General Psychology, 1969, Psychological and Educational Testing, 1971, Readings in Psychological and Educational Testing, 1973, Psychological Testing and Assessment, 1976, 11th edit., 2003, Later Life, 1978, 3rd edit., 1989, Dying, Death and Bereavement, 1985, 4th edit., 2000, Assessment of Intellectual Functioning, 1987, 2d edit., 1996, Personality Assessment Methods and Practices, 1989, 3d edit., 1999, Personality: Theories, Research and Applications, 1993, 2d edit., 2000, Aging: An Introduction to Gerontology, 1994, Rating Scales and Checklists, 1996, Assessment of Adult Personality, 1997, Questionnaires and Inventories, 1997, Human Development in Adulthood, 1998, Tests and Examinations, 1998, Human Differences, 1999, Personality: Theories, Assessment, Research and Applications, 2000, Aging and Later Life, 2001, Attitudes & Other Psychosocial Constructs, 2002, Morality and Ethics in Theory and Practice, 2003; contbr. articles to profl. jours. Sgt. USMC, 1951-54 Fla. Lewis scholar, 1949-51, Gen. scholar, 1954-56; Emory U. fellow, 1957-58, U.S. Office Edn. postdoctoral fellow, 1968-69; NAS-NRC postdoctoral resident rsch. assoc., 1963-64. Fellow APA, Am. Psychol. Soc.; mem. Am. Ednl. Rsch. Assn., Sigma Xi. Fax: 704-753-5633. E-mail: lewisaiken@aol.com.

AIKEN, LINDA HARMAN, nurse, sociologist, educator; b. Roanoke, Va., July 29, 1943; d. William Jordan and Betty Philips (Warner) Harman; children: June Elizabeth, Alan James. BSN, U. Fla., 1964, M in Nursing, 1966; PhD in Sociology, U. Tex., 1973. Nurse Med. Ctr. U. Fla., Gainesville, 1964-65, instr. coll. nursing, 1966-67; instr. sch. of nursing U. Mo., Columbia, 1967-70, clin. nurse specialist sch. of nursing, 1967-70; program officer Robert Wood Johnson Found., Princeton, N.J., 1974-76, dir. rsch., 1976-79, asst. v.p., 1979-81, v.p., 1981-87; Claire M. Fagin Leadership prof. nursing, prof. sociology U. Pa., Phila., 1988—, dir. Ctr. for Health Svcs. and Policy Rsch., 1988—, rsch. assoc. population studies ctr. Mem. Sec. Health and Human Svcs. Commn. on Nursing, 1988, Pres. Clinton's Nat. Health Care Reform Task Force, 1993; commr. Physician Payment Rev. Commn. nat. adv. coun. U.S. Agy. for Health Care Care Policy and Rsch. Author: Health Policy and Nursing Practice, 1981, Nursing in the 1980s, 1982, Applications of Social Science to Clinical Medicine and Health Policy, 1986, Evaluation Studies Rev. Ann., 1985, Charting Nursing's Future, 1991, Hospital Restructuring in North America and Europe, 1997; contbr. articles to profl. jours. Mem. Adv. Council Social Security, 1982-83. Recipient Joint Secretarial commendation U.S. Dept. Health and Human Services and HUD, 1987; NIH Nurse Scientist fellow, 1970-73. Mem. ANA (Jessie M. Scott award 1984), Am. Acad. Arts and Scis., Assn. Health Svcs. Rsch. (Disting. Investigator), Inst. Medicine, Nat. Acad. Scis., Nat. Acad. Social Ins., Am. Acad. Nursing (pres. 1979-80), Am. Sociol. Assn. (chair med. sociology sect. 1983-84), Sociol. Rsch. Assn., Coun. Nurse Rschrs. (Nurse Scientist of Yr. 1991), Sigma Theta Tau, Phi Kappa Phi. Home: 2209 Lombard St Philadelphia PA 19146-1107 Office: U Pa 420 Service Dr Philadelphia PA 19104-4210

AIKEN, MICHAEL THOMAS, former academic administrator; b. El Dorado, Ark., Aug. 20, 1932; s. William Floyd and Mary (Gibbs) Aiken; m. Catherine Comet, Mar. 28, 1969; 1 child, Caroline R. BA, U. Miss., 1954; MA, U. Mich., 1955, PhD, 1964. Asst. prof. U. Wis., Madison, 1963—67, assoc. prof., 1967—70, prof., 1970—84, assoc. dean coll. arts and scis., 1980—82; prof. U. Pa., Phila., 1984—93, dean sch. arts and scis., 1985—87, provost, 1987—93; chancellor U. Ill., Urbana, 1993—2001, Champaign/Urbana, 1993—2001. Co-author: The Dynamics of Idealism, 1971, Economic Failure, Alienation, and Extremism, 1968; co-editor: Complex Organizations: Critical Perspectives, 1981, The Structures of Community Power, 1970. Mem.: Am. Sociol. Assn. (sec. 1986—89). E-mail: aiken@uiuc.edu.*

AIKEN, PETER HAYNES, systems engineer, educator; b. Washington, Jan. 17, 1959; s. Benjamin Hayes and Susan (Benck) Aiken. BS, Va. Commonwealth U., 1981, MS, 1984; PhD, George Mason U., 1989. Sr. engr. Va. Commonwealth U., Richmond, 1980-85, asst. prof. info. systems Sch. Bus., 1992-98, assoc. prof. infosys., dir. Inst. for Data Rsch., 1998—; rsch. asst. George Mason U., Fairfax, Va., 1985-89, vis. asst. prof., 1989-93, dir. Hypermedia Tech. Lab., 1989-92; computer scientist Ctr. for Info. Mgmt. U.S. Dept. Def., Vienna, Va., 1992—. Cons. U.S. Army C.E., Ft. Belvoir, Va., 1985, Cuyahoga County C.C., Cuyahoga Falls, Ohio, 1985, U.S. Customs Bur., Washington, 1986, VA Ctr. Innovative Tech., Herndon, Va., 1987, Apple Computer Inc., 1989, Analytic Scis. Corp., 1990—91, U. Guam, 1990—, Deutsche Bank, 1998—. Author: (book) Data Reverse Engineering, 1995; author: (with W. C. Fikelstein) Building Corporate Portals Using XML. Recipient Internat. Achievement award, Data Mgmt. Assn., 2001; scholar George Mason Inst., 1985—88. Mem.: IEEE (sr.), Assn. Comuting Machinery. Avocations: playing electric bass, photography. Home: 1504 Sunset Ln Richmond VA 23221-3931 Office: School of Bus/Dept of ISY # 1 1015 Floyd Ave Richmond VA 23284-9000 Fax: (804) 828-8884. E-mail: paiken@acm.org.

AIKEN, SUSAN HARDY, English language educator; b. Bklyn., Nov. 4, 1943; d. Sutton Labon and Mae (Eppinger) Hardy; m. Christopher Franklin Carroll, Jan. 1, 1978; children: James Buchanan Aiken, Alden Hardy Carroll. BA, Furman U., 1964; MA, Duke U., 1966, PhD, 1971. Instr. English U. Ga., Athens, 1966-69; asst. prof. SUNY, Stony Brook, 1971-72, Suffolk Coll., Selden, N.Y., 1972-73, U. Ariz., Tucson, 1973-77, assoc. prof., 1977-90, prof., 1990—, acting head dept. French and Italian, 1992-93, Univ. Disting. prof., 1998—, dir. grad. studies in lit., 2000—. Cons. U. Ariz. Press, 1984—, U. Ariz. Women's Studies Program, 1981—, Ariz. Humanities Coun., 1978-83, Ford Found. Western States Curriculum Project, 1984, Hobart and William Smith Coll., 1988, Am. U., 1988, Rice U., 1995, 97, Univ. Press of Fla.; mem. adv. com. S.W. Inst. for Rsch. on Women, 1980-; referee John Simon Guggenheim Meml. Found., 1985, 86, 87, 88, 90, 91-92, 92, 96, Newberry Libr. Rsch. Ctr., 1989, ACLS, 1989, NEH, 1988, 89, 90, 91, 92, 96; judge Margaret Church award Modern Fiction Studies, 1995-96. Author: Isak Dinesen and the Engendering of Narrative, 1990; co-author: Dialogues/Dialogi: Literary and Cultural Exchanges Between (Ex)Soviet and American Women, 1994; editor: (with others) Changing Our Minds: Feminist Transformations of Knowledge, 1988, Making Worlds: Gender, Metaphor, Materiality, 1998; chair adv. bd. U. Ariz. Press; referee Signs: Jour. Women in Culture and Soc., Scandinavian Studies, PMLA (publications MLA), 1985—, Papers in Lang and Lit., 1988, Modern Fiction Studies, Ariel; contbr. chpts. to books and articles to profl. jours. Fellow Ford Found., 1964-65, Woodrow Wilson II, 1965-66, Duke U., 1969-70; grantee U. Ariz., 1984, WOSAC, 1987; recipient U. Ariz. Creative Tchg. award, 1985, Women's Studies Adv. Coun. award, 1987, Mortar Bd. citation for acad. excellence, Provost's Tchg. award, 1988, Faculty Achievement award Burlington No. Found., rsch. grant U. Ariz., 1999, grant Humanities Rsch. Initiative, 1999-2000; NEH interpretive rsch. grant, 1991-93. Mem. MLA (adv. com. publs. 1985-89), Nat. Women's Studies Assn., Soc. for the Advancement of Scandinavian Studies. Avocations: hiking, camping, historical preservation, architectural rehabilitation, gardening. Office: U Ariz Dept English Tucson AZ 85721-0001 E-mail: sha@u.arizona.edu.

AIKEN, VERNDY FRED, economist; b. Atlanta, Jan. 30, 1938; s. Verndy Grady and Anne Whitehead Aiken; m. Sue Carol Camp, Aug. 1, 1959; 1 child, Susan Leigh Aiken Grier. Student, U. Ga., 1960; LLB, Atlanta Law Sch., 1965; banking cert., La. State U., 1969. V.p. Cobb Bank and Trust, Smyrna, Ga., 1973—79; owner Alfredo's Restaurant, Dallas, Ga., 1975—89; state rep. Ga. State Ho. Reps., Atlanta, 1980—92; dist. rep. U.S. Congressman Newt Gingrich, 1992—97; dist. dir., sr. dist. rep. U.S. Congressman Bob Barr, Marietta, Ga., 1997—2003; econ. devel. specialist Ga. Dept. Labor, Atlanta, 2003—. Bd. dirs. Kingdom Comms., Inc. and SafePath, Marietta, 2000—. With Ga. Air Nat. Guard. Named Outstanding Legislator, Ga. Mcpl. Assn., 1980. Republican. Avocations: reading, golf, watching College football, Nascar auto racing. Home: 4020 Pineview Dr Smyrna GA 30080 Office: Ga Dept Labor Ste 650 148 International Blvd Atlanta GA 30303-1751

AIKENS, C(LYDE) MELVIN, anthropology educator, archaeologist, museum director; b. Ogden, Utah, July 13, 1938; s. Clyde Walter and Claudia Elena (Brown) A.; m. Alice Hiroko Endo, Mar. 23, 1963; children: Barton Hiroyuki, Quinn Yoshihisa. A.S., Weber Coll., 1958; BA, U. Utah, 1960; MA, U. Chgo., 1962, PhD, 1966. Curator U. Utah Mus. Anthropology, Salt Lake City, 1963-66; asst. prof. U. Nev., Reno, 1966-68; asst. prof. anthropology U. Oreg., Eugene, 1968-72, assoc. prof., 1972-78, prof., 1978—, dir. U. Oreg. Mus. Natural History, 1996—. Author: Fremont Relationships, 1966, Hogup Cave, 1970, Great Basin Archaeology, 1978, The Last 10,000 Years in Japan and Eastern North America, 1981, From Asia to America: The First Peopling of the New World, 1990, Archaeology of Oregon, 1993; co-author: Prehistory of Japan, 1982, Great Basin Numic Prehistory, 1986, Early Human Occupation in Far Western North America, 1988; editor: Archaeological Studies Willamette Valley, 1975; co-editor: Prehistoric Hunter-Gatherers in Japan, 1986, Pacific Northeast Asia in Prehistory, 1992, Archaeological Researches in the Northern Great Basin, 1994. NSF research grantee, 1970, 73, 78-80, 84; NSF Sci. Faculty fellow Kyoto U., Japan, 1971-72; Japan Found. research fellow Kyoto U., 1977-78, Tokyo U., 1986. Fellow Am. Anthrop. Assn., AAAS; mem. Soc. for Am. Archaeology Home: 3470 Mcmillan St Eugene OR 97405-3317 Office: U Oreg Museum Natural History Eugene OR 97403-1224 E-mail: maikens@oregon.uoregon.edu.

AIKENS, MARTHA BRUNETTE, national park service administrator; b. Jayess, Miss., Aug. 23, 1949; d. Walter and Elnora La Doris (Bridges) A.. BS in Social Sci., Alcorn State U., 1971; postgrad., George Williams Coll., 1974, Fla. Internat. U., 1977, George Washington U., 1979, Pa. State U., 1979, U. So. Calif., D.C. Ext., 1980. Social worker Pearl River County Devel. Corp., Picayune, Miss., 1971—72; environ. ednl. specialist Nat. Park Svc., Homestead, Fla., 1973—75, environ. ednl. coord., 1973—75, comm. specialist, 1976—78; park mgr. Bklyn., 1978—79, Dept. Interior's Mgmt. Program, 1979—80, St. Augustine, Fla., 1979—83, Washington, 1983—88. Instr., cons. Coll. African Wildlife Mgmt., Tanzania, 1980, Fed. Law Enforcement Tng. Ctr., Glynco, Ga., 1983—, Stephen T. Mather Employee Devel. Ctr., Harper's Ferry, W.Va., 1988—91; supt. Independence Nat. Hist. Pk., Phila., 1991—; chair Nat. Pk. Svc. Women's Conf., New Orleans, 1991. Author: tchrs. guides on Everglades Nat. Park, 1973—76, park brochure, 1977; contbr. chapters to books. Active Dept. Interior's Partnership in Edn. Commn., Washington, 1983—, Fed. Interagy Commn. on Edn., Washington, 1983—, Nat. Park Svc. Employee Rels. Task Force, Washington, 1983—, 21st Century Task Force, 1988—, Salt River Bay Nat. Hist. Pk. and Ecol. Preserve Adv. Commn., 1993—, Strategic Planning Task Force, Atlanta, 1981—83, S.E. Regional Equal Opportunity Commn., Atlanta, 1982—83; bd. trustees Walnut St. Theatre, Phila., 1993—; bd. dirs. Peopling of Phila., 1993—; mem. Leading by Example, 1992—. Recipient Star 104.5 Woman of Yr. award, 1993.

AIKIN, JUDITH POPOVICH, languages educator, academic administrator; b. L.A., Aug. 6, 1946; d. Milosh and Jeanne (Hartman) Popovich; m. Roger Cushing Aikin, Dec. 27, 1966; 1 child, Thomas. BA, U. Oreg., 1968, MA, 1969; PhD, U. Calif., Berkeley, 1974. Asst. prof. U. Iowa, Iowa City, 1975-81, assoc. prof., 1981-88, prof., 1988—, assoc. dean liberal arts, 1990-92, interim dean liberal arts, 1992-93, dean liberal arts, 1993-97, prof. German, 1988—. Author: The Mission of Rome in the Dramas of Daniel Casper von Lohenstein: Historical Tragedy as Prophecy and Polemic, 1978, German Baroque Drama, 1982, Scaramutza in Germany: The Dramatic Works of Caspar Stieler, 1989, A Language for German Opera: The Development of Forms and Formulas for Recitative and Aria in Seventeenth-Century German Libretti, 2002; contbr. articles to profl. jours. Fellow NEH, 1988, Am. Coun. Learned Socs., 1988-89. Mem. MLA (chair exec. com. divsn. German lit. to 1700, 1989), Soc. for German Renaissance and Baroque Lit. (pres. 1985), Am. Assn. Tchrs. German. Office: U Iowa Dept German 528 PH Iowa City IA 52242 E-mail: judith-aikin@uiowa.edu.

AIKMAN, ALBERT EDWARD, lawyer; b. Norman, Okla., Mar. 11, 1922; s. Albert Edwin and Thelma Annette (Brooke) A.; m. Shirley Barnes, June 24, 1944; children: Anita Gayle, Priscilla June, Rebecca Brooke. BS, Tex. A&M U., 1947; JD cum laude, So. Meth. U., 1948, LLM, 1954. Bar: Tex. (no. dist.) 1948, U.S. Supreme Ct. 1956, U.S. Ct. Appeals (5th dist.), U.S. Tax Ct. Tax ct. staff atty. Phillips Petroleum Co., Amarillo, Tex., 1948-49; sole practice pvt. practice, Amarillo, Tex., 1949-53; tax counsel Magnolia Petroleum Co. (Mobil), Dallas, 1953-56; pnr. Locke, Purnell, Boren, Laney & Neely, Dallas, 1973-81; of counsel Pickens Energy Corp., Dallas, 1981-96, Ptnrs. in Exploration, Dallas, 1997—; couns. Ptnrs. in Exploration, LLC, Dallas, 1997—. Contbr. articles to profl. jours. Served in inf. U.S. Army, 1943-45. Mem. ABA, Tex. Bar Assn., Dallas Bar Assn. Methodist. E-mail: aikmanae@aol.com.

AIKMAN, ELFLORA ANNA, senior citizens center administrator; b. Marion, Ill., July 21, 1929; d. John Frederick and Elsa Flora (Weber) Kaeser; m. Samuel Vick Aikman, Dec. 24, 1949; children: Vicki Ann Aikman Hayes, Vance J., Valerie Sue Aikman Henshaw, Samuel Vick III. Student, So. Ill. U., 1949, John A. Logan Coll., 1970, 80, 87, cert. food handler, 1984. Numerous positions, 1947-67; sec. Color-Craft Products, Detroit, 1967-69; admitting clk. Marion Meml. Hosp., 1969-70, appointed to task force, 1989—; co-owner, office mgr., decorating cons. House of Color, Marion, 1970-79; sec., bookkeeper, receptionist Mitchell-Hughes Funeral Home, Marion, 1979-80; receptionist Meredith Funeral Home, Marion, 1980—94; exec. dir. Marion Sr. Citizens Ctr., 1981—99. Columnist Marion Daily Republican, 1984; columnist, contbr. Sr. World, 1987; producer program Sta. WGGH, 1989. Editor monthly newsletter The Yodler, 1984-99; co-designer, decorator Meredith Funeral Home; decorator Marion Meml. Hosp. Chapel, 1971, 77; columnist, contbr. newspaper Old Friends, 1989. Organist, jr. choir dir. St. Clair, Mo., 1958-63; organist, jr. choir organizer, sr. choir organizer Trinity Episcopal Ch., Mt. Vernon, Ill., 1964-67; choir mem. United Ch. Christ, Plymouth, Mich., 1967-69; organist Myers Funeral Home, Mt. Vernon, 1964-67; com. mem. Girl Scouts Am., Mt. Vernon, 1964-67, PTA, St. Clair, Mo., 1960-63; pack officer Boy Scouts Am., Mt. Vernon, 1964-67; home rm. mother, St. Clair, Mo., Mt. Vernon, 1958-67; chmn. Vols. to Arts, Mt. Vernon, Ill., 1966-67; library asst. Plymouth (Mich.) Mid. Sch., 1968-69; com. mem. Williamson County (Ill.) Sesquicentennial Celebration, 1989; mem. Marion Meml. Hosp. Aux., 1980—2002, Hearts Helping Heart, Marion, 1987—2002; asst. organist and choir mem., Sunday sch. tchr. Zion United Ch. of Christ, Marion, mem. numerous other ch. coms.; mem. So. Ill. Easter Seal Soc., 1987. Recipient Svc. Plaque Marion Recreation Dept. Bd., 1983, cert. award svc. to Chautauqua Ill. Humanities Coun., 1986, cert. of recognition for outstanding svc. to sr. citizens 1995-1999, cert. recognition Modern Woodmen Am., Camp 3600, 1998, Mayors Svc. award (city of Marion), 1996, cert. recognition AARP Tax Counsel Elder, cert. recognition IRS, plaque 40 yrs. svc. to music ministry Zion UCC, 1999. Mem. Marion C. of C. (com. 1988), Marion S.A.L.T. (charter mem.), TRIAD (charter mem., treas.), Beta Sigma Phi. Avocations: crocheting, sewing, reading, playing piano and organ, grandchildren. Home: 516 S Market St Marion IL 62959 Office: Marion Sr Citizens Ctr 507 W Main St Marion IL 62959-2437

AIKMAN, JAMES WHITTON, composer, music educator; b. Indpls., Apr. 15, 1959; s. James Wilson Aikman and Jane Edith Adams; m. Deanna Margaret Gutheil, Nov. 30, 1985; children: Elise Kristine, Joshua Michael, Grace Alexandra. MusB, Butler U., 1981; MusM, Ind. U., 1988, Mus D, 1993; studied with Michael Schelle, 1979-81, with Earle Brown, 1982, 1989, with Frederick Fox, 1983, 1985-93, with William Bolcom, 1989, with Louis Andriessen, 1994, with Donald Erb, 1995, with Leslie Bassett, 1996-97. Assoc. instr. Ind. U., Bloomington, 1987-90; master artist fellow Ind. Arts Commn., Indpls., 1990-91; adj. prof. Butler U., Indpls., 1993, lectr. music, 1995-96; composer in residence Cathedral Arts, Indpls., 1996—. Prof. music U. Mich., Ann Arbor, 1996—. Composer: (Orchestral) A Bottle of Notes and Some Voyages, 1988 (American music Ctr. Award, Deans Prize, American Symphony Orchestra League Am. Repertoire Project, 1989, 1991), Intrada, 1993, Wedding Songs for High Voice and Orchestra, 1998; (Symphony Band) Step, 1996, Tempus Fugit, 2001; (Chamber Music) Three Sonatas for Violin and Piano, 1986 (Carmichael Competition Winner, 1994, nominated Kennedy Ctr. Friedheim Award, 2001), Elegy, 1988 for Solo Cello, Gig(ue) 1988 for Saxophone Quartet, Fantasy for Violin and Electronic Tape. 1989, Etudes 1989 for Piano. Spring is Purple Jewelry, 1990 (G. Schirmer Am. Art Song Collection, NYC Premiere, Dawn Upshaw's Carnegie Hall Debut, 1996), Glossolalia, 1991 (Deans Prize 2000, Internat. Soc. Contemporary Music/ League of Composers National Award), Concert Music for Strings, 1992-93 (Dean's Prize, Am. Music Center's Margaret Fairbanks Jory Grant), Four Wedding Songs 1995-96 for High Voice and Piano, Migratory Song 1996 for Medium Voice and Piano, piano Quintet 1997, Trio 1999 for Clarinet, Cello and Piano; (Electronic Works) Precipitando 1986, (with Armando Tranquilino) Tragoidia/Komoidia 1987 (1st prize, Groupe de Musique Experimentale de Bourges, 1988), (with David Dzubay) Hyper Mix 1991, Burton Tower Prelude and the 7th Trumpet Toccata 1997-98, Choral Missa Jubilaea, 2000; (Pop Music 1980-85) I'll Wait Til Then, Do Not Disturb, the Blame, Radioactive Love (Coca Cola Project III), Give Me a Chance, Introduce Yourself, Vacation, Take to the Air, Still the Same, Sooner or later, She, The Ritual of Music; Commissions: Pasadena Young Musicians Orchestra and the Pasadena Arts Council, Butler U. Symphonic Band, H. Robert Reynolds, u. Michigan, Alex Kerr, Concertmaster Concertgebouw Orkest, Amsterdam Holland, Indianapolis Museum of Art, Cathedral Arts for Suzuki and Friends, Cathedral Arts for the Ronen Ensemble, Cathedral Arts and Christ Church Cathedral, Indianapolis. Bd. dirs. Aikman Found., Indpls., 1997—. Recipient 1st prize Group Exptl. Music, 1988, Nat. award Internat. Soc. Contemporary Music League Composers, 2000; Fulbright fellow Dutch Royal Conservatory, 1994, Aspen fellow, 1989; Rec. grantee U. Mich., 1998-99. Fellow Mich. Soc. Fellows; mem. ASCAP, Coll. Music Soc. Avocations: chess, jogging, lifting weights, american saddlebred horses, basketball. Office: U Mich Sch Music 1100 Baits Dr Ann Arbor MI 48109-2085

AIKMAN, TROY, professional football player; b. West Covina, Calif., Nov. 21, 1966; Student, Okla. U., UCLA. Quarterback Dallas Cowboys, 1989—2000. Mem. Super Bowl Championship Team, 1992, 93, 95. Named Super Bowl Most Valuable Player, 1992; named to Sporting News Coll. All-Am. team, 1988, Pro Bowl team, 1991, 1992, 1993, 1994, 1996, Sporting News NFL All-Pro team, 1993. Office: Dallas Cowboys One Cowboys Pkwy Irving TX 75063

AIKMAN, WILLIAM FRANCIS, venture capitalist; b. Darby, Pa., Aug. 1, 1945; s. John Earl and Phyllis Rose (Miller) A. AB, Brown U., 1967; student, Harvard Law Sch., 1970-72; JD, U. Pa., Phila., 1972. Bar: Mass. 1972. Counsel Mass. Law Reform Inst., Boston, 1969-73; pres. Mass. Ctr. for Pub. Interest Law, Boston, 1973-76, Mass. Tech. Devel. Corp., Boston, 1979-84; mng. gen. ptnr. Gryphon Ventures Ltd. Partnerships, Boston, 1984—; under sec. of econ. affairs Commonwealth of Mass., Boston, 1976-79; pres. Gryphon Mgmt. Co., Boston, 1984—. Chmn. bd. Geltech, Inc., Orlando, Fla., SeasCape Realty, Inc., Boston. Bd. overseers, Mus. of Sci., Boston; bd. trustees Schepens Eye Rsch. Inst., Harvard Med. Sch., Boston. Mem. Harvard Club Boston, Brown Club Boston, Union Club Boston. Presbyterian. Home: 179 Beacon St Boston MA 02116-1423 also: Bayberry Rd Truro MA 02666-1186 Office: 101 Federal St Ste 1900 Boston MA 02108-4400 E-mail: wfa@gryphoninc.com.

AILES, ROGER EUGENE, television producer, consultant; b. Warren, Ohio, May 15, 1940; s. Robert Eugene and Donna Marie (Cunningham) A. B.F.A., Ohio U., 1962, D in Communications (hon.), 1989. Assoc. dir. Sta. KYW-TV, Cleve., 1962-63, prodr., dir., 1963-65; prodr. Mike Douglas Show Westinghouse Broadcasting Corp., Phila., 1965-67, exec. prodr., 1967-68; exec. prodr. TV for Richard M. Nixon, 1968; chmn. Ailes Comm., Inc., N.Y.C., 1969—; exec. v.p.

TV News Inc., N.Y.C., 1975-76; pres. CNBC, N.Y.C., 1993-96, America's Talking, N.Y.C., 1993; chmn., CEO, Fox News, N.Y.C., 1996—. Cons. WCBS-TV, 1978— ; communications cons. to polit. and bus. leaders; v.p. Conf. Personal Mgrs. Author: You Are the Message: Secrets of the Master Communicators, 1987; producer Broadway mus. Mother Earth, 1972; (play) Hot-L Baltimore, 1973-76; exec. producer, dir. TV spl. The Last Frontier, 1974, Television and the Presidency, 1984 (Emmy award); producer, dir. TV spl. Fellini: Wizards, Clowns and Honest Liars (Emmy nominee 1977); exec. producer The Rush Limbaugh Show, 1992—. Polit. cons. Reagan '84, Bush '88. Recipient award for Shakespeare prodn. Fine Arts Mag., 1964; Liberty Bell award Advt. Alliance of Phila., 1971; Commendation award for contbn. to communications Ohio U., 1972; 4 Obie awards for Hot-L Baltimore, 1973 Mem. AFTRA, Dirs. Guild Am., Radio and TV News Dirs. Assn. Office: Fox News 1211 Ave of Americas New York NY 10036*

AILLONI-CHARAS, DAN, marketing executive; b. Ploiesti, Romania, May 22, 1930; came to U.S., 1950, naturalized, 1960; s. Max and Felicia (Lupescu) Charas; m. Miriam C. Taytelbaum, Oct. 8, 1957; children: Ethan Benjamin, Orrin, Adam. AB with honors, U. Calif., Berkeley, 1952, MA, 1953; PhD, NYU, 1968. Mem. editl. staff San Francisco Call Bull., 1953-54; exec. sec. TAHAL, 1955-56; project dir. Marplan divsn. Interpub., N.Y.C., 1958-60; supr. advt. studies NBC, N.Y.C., 1960-62; dir. consumer and comm. rsch. Forbes Rsch., Inc., N.Y.C., 1962-63; mgr. market rsch. Chesebrough-Pond's, Inc., N.Y.C., 1963-64, new products mgr., 1964-68, mgr. internat. mktg. services dept., 1968-69; pres. Stratmar Sys., Inc., Port Chester, NY, 1969-91, CEO, 1991—2001, chmn., 2001—; asst., then prof. mktg. Pace U., 1963-85. Mem. adv. bd. Premium Incentive Show, 1986-92, Nat. Premium Incentive Show, 1987-92; lectr. Israel Inst. Tech., 1956-58, dir. extension divsn. no. region, 1956-58. Author: Promotion: A Guide to Effective Promotional Planning, Strategies and Execution, 1984; editor: Mktg. Rev., 1960-63, Proc. 1st Ann. Conf. on Rsch. Design, 1964, New Directions in Research Design, 2d Conf., 1965, Planning, 1968-71; bd. editors Jour. Consumer Mktg., 1982—, Jour. of Brand and Product Mgmt., 1991—, Jour. Svc. Mktg., 1992—; contbr. to Brandweek, Mktg. News, Chain Drug Rev., MMR, New Product News. Trustee Inst. Advanced Mktg. Studies, 1965-66, Philharmonic Symphony of Westchester, 1977-80; bd. dirs. Young Men's Bd. Trade, 1960-63, state dir., N.Y. StatJr. C. of C., 1960-63, bd. advisors Ad Expo, 1970; 1st v.p. Student World Affairs Coun. Northern Calif., 1953-54, chmn. Asilomar World Affairs conf., 1954; founder Israel Assn. Grads. Social Scis. & Humanities, 1955; pres. Haifa Jr. C. of C., 1956-57. Coro Found. fellow, 1953; Univ. honors scholar NYU, 1968. Mem. Am. Mktg. Assn. (pres. N.Y. chpt. 1965-66, nat. v.p. 1970-71), Promotion Mktg. Assn. Am. (bd. dirs. 1978-98, chmn. edn. com. 1979-81, 82-91, chmn. premium show com. 1982-91, exec. com. 1986-87, 89-93, 94-95, 96-97, 99-2000, chmn. nat. conf. 1988, 96, v.p. 1989-93, 94-95, chmn. retailers and mfrs. conf. 1992, 93, chmn. in-store mktg. coun. 1993-94), N.Am. Soc. Corp. Planning (bd. dirs. 1970-72), Nat. Assn. Chain Drug Stores (nat. industry adv. bd. 1992—), Am. Friends of the Coll. Mgmt. (chmn. 1999—), Soc. Profl. Journalists, Nat. Arts Club, Nat. Press Club, The Deadline Club, Coro Alumni Assn. (nat. bd. dirs. 1989-95), Sigma Delta Chi, Phi Sigma Alpha. Office: Stratmar Bldg 109 Willett Ave Port Chester NY 10573-4287 Home: 30600 N Pima Rd # 92 Scottsdale AZ 85262 E-mail: Dailloni@STRATMAR.com.

AILLONI-CHARAS, MIRIAM CLARA, interior designer, consultant; b. Veere, The Netherlands, July 31, 1935; arrived in US, 1958; d. Maurits and Elzina (De Groot) Taytelbaum; m. Dan Ailloni-Charas, Oct. 8, 1957; children: Ethan Benjamin, Orrin, Adam. Degree in Interiors, Pratt Inst., 1962; BSc, SUNY, Albany, 1978. Interior designer S.J. Miller Assocs., N.Y.C., 1960-63; interior design cons. Rye Brook, NY, 1963—88, 1990—2003; exec. v.p. Contract 2000 Inc., Port Chester, NY, 1988-90; interior design cons. Scottsdale, Ariz., 2003—. Treas. Temple Guild, Congregation Emanu-El, Rye, N.Y., 1979-88, co-chmn., 1988-96, chair, 1996-97, trustee, 1986-92. Recipient Cert. of Merit, U.S. Jaycees, 1962, March of Dimes, 1989, 91. Mem. Am. Soc. Interior Designers, Allied Bd. Trade, Nat. Trust for Hist. Preservation. Home and Office: 30600 N Pima Rd #92 Scottsdale AZ 85262 Office Fax: 480-437-9988. E-mail: mailloni@cox.net.

AIN, SANFORD KING, lawyer; b. Glen Cove, N.Y., July 24, 1947; s. Herbert and Victoria (Ben Susan) A.; m. Miriam Luskin, July 12, 1980; children: David Lloyd, Daniel Jason. BA cum laude, U. Wis., 1969; JD, Georgetown U., 1972. Bar: Va. 1972, D.C. 1973, Md. 1982. Ptnr. Sherman, Meehan, Curtin & Ain P.C., Washington, 1972—2003, Ain & Bank, P.C., Washington, 2003—. Mem. faculty continuing legal edn. program State Bar Va., D.C. Bar, Md. Bar. Fellow: Am. Acad. Matrimonial Lawyers (pres. D.C. chpt. 1991—94, 2002—, counsel 1999—2000, bd. govs. 2003—); mem.: Md. Bar Assn., Va. Trial Lawyers Assn., Am. Coll. Family Trial Lawyers. Office: Ain & Bank PC 1900 M St NW Ste 600 Washington DC 20036-3519

AINDOW, MARK, engineering educator; b. Barrow-in-Furness, Cumbria, Eng., June 23, 1964; s. Joseph Charles and Brenda Ann A.; m. Tai-Tsui Cheng, Mar. 23, 1991; children: Ann, Jay. BEng in Metallurgy and Materials Sci., U. Liverpool (Eng.), 1985, PhD in Materials Sci. and Engring., 1989. Rsch. fellow Case Western Res. U., Cleve., 1989, Ohio State U., Columbus, 1990; lectr. U. Birmingham (Eng.), 1990-96, sr. lectr., 1996-99; assoc. prof. U. Conn., Storrs, 1999—. Office: U Conn Dept Metallurgy & Materials 97 N Eagleville Rd Storrs Mansfield CT 06269-3136 E-mail: m.aindow@uconn.edu.

AINSLEY, JAMES ROBERT, academic administrator; b. Washington, Jan. 24, 1951; s. James Mann and Flora Spruill Ainsley; m. Donna Lou Porter, Aug. 18, 1973; children: Jessica Leigh Ainsley Skeens, Alyson Lauren. BA, Emory & Henry Coll., Emory, Va., 1973; MEd, Va. State U., 1977; MA, Cath. U., Washington, 1980, EdD, 1984; MS, Nat. Def. U., Washington, 1998. Prof. ednl. tech. Def. Systems Mgmt. Coll., Ft. Belvoir, Va., 1988—92, dir. exec. continuing edn. for leaders, 1992—94, chmn. acad. programs dept., 1994—95, dir. exec. program mgrs. course, 1995—98, program mgr. acquisition mgmt. curriculum enhancement program, 1998—99; assoc. provost Def. Acquisition U., Ft. Belvoir, 1999—2001, vice provost, 2001—. Contbr. articles. Recipient Joint Meritorious Unit award, Dept. Def., 1984, Spl. Recognition Citation, Under Sec. of Def., 1996. Mem.: U.S. Distance Learning Assn. (e-learning award 2001). Avocations: fly fishing, carving and painting decorative and working wildfowl, flower gardening. Mailing: Defense Acquisition Univ 9820 Belvoir Rd Fort Belvoir VA 22060

AINSLIE, GEORGE WILLIAM, psychiatrist, behavioral economist; b. Ithaca, N.Y., Sept. 19, 1944; s. George William and Elizabeth Lee Ainslie; m. Elizabeth Boyd Keeney, June 25, 1966; children: Matthew Forrest, Roger Scott, Eleanor Ruth. BA, Yale Coll., 1965; MD, Harvard Med. Sch., 1969. Diplomate Am. Bd. Psychiatry and Neurology; cert. adult psychiatry. Intern Mary Imogene Bassett Hosp., Cooperstown, N.Y., 1969-70; resident in psychiatry Mass. Mental Health Ctr., Boston, 1970-71, 73-75; fellow Harvard U. Health Svcs., Cambridge, Mass., 1975-76; asst. clin. dir. Mass. Mental Health Ctr., Boston, 1976-79; psychiatrist VA Med. Ctr., Coatesville, Pa., 1979-90, chief psychiatrist, 1990—. Asst. prof. Jefferson Med. Coll., Phila., 1979-85, assoc. prof., 1985-92; clin. prof. Temple U. Med. Coll., Phila., 1992—; rsch. assoc. Harvard Lab. Exptl. Psychology, Cambridge, Mass., 1967-78. Author: Picoeconomics: The Strategic Interaction of Successive Motivational States Within The Person, 1992, Breakdown of Will, 2001; contbr. articles on motivational conflict to profl. jours. Surgeon, USPHS, 1971-73. Mem. Players Club Swarthmore (stage dir.), Phi Beta Kappa. Avocations: dramatics, antiquarian book dealer. Office: Dept Psychiatry VA Med Ctr 116A Coatesville PA 19320 E-mail: Ainslie@Coatesville.va.gov.

AINSWORTH, HARRIET CRAWFORD, journalist, public relations consultant; b. Columbus, Ohio, Nov. 27, 1914; d. Harry Hoskins and Pansy Lucy (Graham) Crawford; m. J. Gordon Ainsworth, Oct. 6, 1945; children: J. Gordon Jr., Adeline Ainsworth Forrest. BA, Ohio Wesleyan U., 1934; postgrad., Columbia U. Sch. Journalism, 1934-35, Gonzaga U., 1940, Calif. Coll. Arts and Crafts, 1968; life adult edn.-C.C. tchg. credential, U. Calif., Berkeley, 1967. Reporter Portland Oregonian, 1936-37; ind. pub. rels. writer, 1937-42; fgn. corr. Oakland Tribune, Indpls. Star, Japan, China, The Philippines, 1946; pub. info. dir. Am. Cancer Soc., Contra Costa County, Calif., 1958-89, cons. Calif. divsn., 1965-77; pres. Ainsworth-Powell Pub. Rels., 1965-77, Corp. Identity Assocs., Orinda, Calif., 1966—; columnist (Sunbeams), feature writer Contra Costa Sun, Contra Costa Times, 1990—. Co-author: The Road Back, 1968; contbr. articles to profl. jours., newspaper columns. Mem. Citizen's Recreation Commn., dist. 6, Orinda, 1974-79; founder, pres. Orinda Found., 1975; chmn. spl. events Calif. Shakespeare Festival Amphitheater campaign, 1988-92. Lt. comdr. USNR, 1942-58. Named Orinda Citizen of Yr., 1976; recipient Plaque and Resolution Commendation Recreation Dist. 6, Orinda, 1979, Recognition award Plaque Pres. U.S. People-to-People Sports Com. Mem. San Francisco Pub. Rels. Round Table, Contra Costa Press Club, East Bay Women's Press Club (past pres.), Orinda Country Club, Orindawoods Tennis Club, Orinda Tennis Club, Kappa Alpha Theta (co-founder Diablo Valley chpt.). Avocation: tennis.

AINSWORTH, JOAN HORSBURGH, university development director; b. Cleve., Dec. 30, 1942; d. Donald Francis and Elaine Mildred Horsburgh; m. Richard B. Ainsworth Jr., Oct. 30, 1965; children: Richard B. III, Alison. BA, Wells Coll., 1965; MBA, Case Western Res. U., 1986. Cert. fund raising exec. Social worker San Diego County (Calif.) Welfare Dept., 1966-68; social worker, vol. coord. Washtenaw County (Mich.) Juvenile Ct., Ann Arbor, 1968-70; adminstrv. asst. to pres. Med. Ventures, Ltd., Cleve., 1985-86; dir. Project MOVE, Office of Mayor City of Cleve., 1986-89; dir. devel. and pres.'s programs Case Western Res. U., Cleve., 1989-97, dir. spl. gifts and prin. projects, 1997-98, dir. devel. Coll. Arts and Scis., 1998-2001, asst. dean for devel. Coll. Arts and Scis., 2001—. Trustee, v.p. Children's Aid Soc., Cleve., 1989—, pres., 1997—; trustee, chair devel. Project: LEARN, Cleve., 1990-96; past trustee, cmty. vol. Jr. League Cleve., Inc., 1971—; mem. Vol. Ohio, 1987-96. Named Hon. Mayor City of Cleve., 1989. Mem.: Coun. for Advancement and Support of Edn., Nat. Assn. Fundraising Profls. (cert, chair publicity Greater Cleve. chpt. 1994—96). Avocations: flying, tennis, boating, travel. Home: 2023 Lyndway Rd Cleveland OH 44121-4265 Office: Case Western Res U 10900 Euclid Ave Cleveland OH 44106-1712 E-mail: jha@po.cwru.edu.

AIONA, JAMES R., JR., lieutenant governor; b. Honolulu, June 8, 1955; m. Vivian Welsh; children: Makana, Ohulani, Kulia, Kaimilani. BA in Polit. Sci., U. of the Pacific; JD, U. Hawaii. Law clk. hon. Wendell K. Huddy Cir. Ct. Judge First Cir. Hawaii, 1981—82; dep. pros. atty. City and County Honolulu, 1982—85, dep. corp. counsel City Attys. Office, 1985—87, chief litigator, 1987—90; family ct. judge 1st Cir. State Hawaii, 1990—93, cir. ct. judge 14th divsn., 1993—96; adminstrv. judge Drug Ct. Program, 1996—98; ret., 1998; pvt. practice, 1997—2002; part time family dist. ct. judge 1999—2002; lt. gov. State of Hawaii, Honolulu, 2002—. Asst. basketball coach varsity boys St. Lous H.S.; vol. soccer coach AYSO; vol. youth baseball coach Makakilo-Kapolei; vol. judge H.S. mock trials competition State of Hawaii; bd. mem. The Salvation Army, Reid J.K. Richards Found., Youth At Risk Adv. Coun., Maryknoll Schs., 1995—98. Office: Exec Chambers Hawaii State Capitol Honolulu HI 96813

AIOSA, VINCENT NESTOR, music educator; b. Yonkers, N.Y., Dec. 26, 1938; s. Vincent Francis Aiosa and Margaret Caverella; m. Evelyn Rose Curtis, Apr. 16, 1960; children: Kathleen Marie, Jeffrey Vincent. BS in Music Edn., SUNY, 1960, MS in Music Edn., 1966. Dir. instrumental music Newfield (N.Y.) Ctrl. Sch., 1960—91; lectr. in music edn. Ithaca (N.Y.) Coll., 1992—. Mem.: N.Y.C. Sch. Music Assn. (chaperone 1990—), Seneca-Tompkins Music Tchrs. Assn. (pres. 1973—79, 1986—90). Home: 149 Shaffer Drive Newfield NY 14867 Office: Ithaca College Danby Road Ithaca NY 14850

AISENBERG, ALAN C. physician, educator, researcher; b. N.Y.C., Dec. 7, 1926; s. Jacob and Celia (Able) A.; m. Nadya Margulies, Oct. 2, 1952 (dec. Apr. 1999); children: James, Margaret. SB, Harvard U., 1945, MD, 1950; PhD, U. Wis., 1956. Diplomate Am. Bd. Internal Med. Internship and resident Presbyn. Hosp., N.Y.C., 1950-53; instr. medicine Harvard Med. Sch., Boston, 1956-62, asst. prof., 1962-69, assoc. prof., 1969-84, prof., 1984—; asst. physician Mass. Gen. Hosp., Boston, 1959-69, assoc. physician, 1969-84, physician, 1984—. Mem. Clin. Trials Com. Nat. Cancer Inst., Bethesda, Md., 1977-82. Author: Glycolysis and Respiration of Tumors, 1961, Malignant Lymphoma: Biology, Natural History and Treatment, 1991; contbr. over 150 articles on rsch. in oncology to profl. jours. Recipient Guggenheim Fellowship, Guggenheim Found. Nat. Inst. for Med. Research, London, 1964-65. Mem. Am. Coll. of Physicians, Am. Soc. of Clin. Oncology, Am. Assn. Immunologists. Home: 124 Chestnut St Boston MA 02108-3318 Office: Mass Gen Hosp Fruit St Boston MA 02114-2620 E-mail: aaisenberg@partners.org.

AISENBERG, BENNETT S. lawyer; b. Feb. 17, 1931; s. Joseph Samuel and Minna Ruth (Cohan) A. BA, Brown U., 1952; JD, Harvard U., 1955. Bar: Mass. 1955, Colo. 1958, U.S. Dist. Ct. Colo. 1958, U.S. Ct. Appeals (10th cir.) 1958. Ptnr. Gorsuch, Kirgis, Denver, 1958-80; pvt. practice Denver, 1980—. Mem. Nat. Acad. Arbitrators, Colo. Trial Lawyers Assn. (pres. 1984-85), Denver Bar Assn. (trustee 1982-85, 86-89, pres. 1991-92), Colo. Bar Assn. (pres. 1998-99). Office: 1600 Broadway Ste 2350 Denver CO 80202-4921*

AISENBERG, IRWIN MORTON, lawyer; b. Worcester, Mass., Aug. 8, 1925; s. William and Esther (Lewis) A.; m. Lois P., Sept. 4, 1955 (div. Apr. 1996); children: Karen Sue Portner, Sondra Lee, David Craig, Steven Bennett; m. Hana Jane Barton, June 19, 1999. BS in Chem Engring., Carnegie Mellon U., 1946; JD, Georgetown U., 1957. Bar: D.C. 1958, U.S. Ct. of Customs and Patent Appeals 1958, U.S. Ct. Appeals (D.C. cir.) 1958, U.S. Supreme Ct. 1964, N.J. 1965, Va. 1969, U.S. Ct. Appeals (fed. cir.) 1982; registered profl. engr., Mass. Patent examiner U.S. Patent and Trademark Office, Washington, 1954-57; assoc. atty. Wenderoth, Lind & Ponack, Washington, 1957-63; chief patent counsel Sandoz, Inc., Hanover, N.J., 1963-67; pvt. practice Washington, 1967-75; ptnr. Berman, Aisenberg & Platt, Washington, 1975-91, mng. ptnr., 1980-85; ptnr. Jacobson Holman PLLC, Washington, 1991—. Lectr. Franklin Pierce Law Sch., Concord, N.H., 1980-88; mem. appeal bd. Nat. Register of Health Svc. Providers in Psychology, 1987-89. Mem. editl. adv. bd. IDEA, Jour. Law and Tech., 1981-95; bd. editors: Patent Strategy and Mgmt.; author: Attorney's Dictionary of Patent Claims, 1985, with yearly supplements, Patent Law Precedent, 1991, 2d edit., 1992, Modern Patent Law Precedent, 3d edit., 1997, 5th edit., 2003; contbr. articles to profl. jours.; patentee in field. Served to cpl. U.S. Army, 1950-52. Mem. ABA, Internat. Assn. Protection Indsl. Property, Am. Intellectual Property Law Assn., Am. Arbitration Assn. (mem. panel arbitrators). Clubs: Kenwood Golf and Country, Am. Contract Bridge League (life master). Jewish. Home: 8508 Meadowlark Ln Bethesda MD 20817-2921 Office: Jacobson Holman Jenifer Bldg 400 7th St NW Washington DC 20004 E-mail: iaisenberg@jhip.com.

AISENSTARK, AVERY, lawyer, educator; b. Tel Aviv, May 11, 1945; came to U.S., 1947; s. Isaac Mayer and Hadasa Hinda (Goldberg) A.; m. Edith Gluck, June 19, 1968; 1 child, M. Daniel. J.D., U. Md., 1969. Bar: Md. 1969, U.S. Dist. Ct. Md. 1969. Assoc. Frank, Bernstein, Conaway & Goldman, Balt., 1969-73; asst. legis. officer Office of Gov., State of Md., Annapolis, 74; revisor statutes, dir. Gov.'s Commn. to Revise Annotated Code, 1974-77, spl. cons., 1978-79; asst. atty. gen., chief counsel for opinions and advice Office of Atty. Gen., Balt., 1979-85; ptnr. Frank, Bernstein, Conaway & Goldman, Balt., 1985—; lectr. law U. Md., 1981—; mem. standing com. on rules of practice and procedure Md. Ct. of Appeals, 1984—; mem. Gov.'s Commn. to Revise Annotated Code, 1977—. Sec., founding mem. bd. dirs. Md. Found. for Performing Arts, 1973-82; founding chmn. Balt. chpt. Nat. Jewish Commn. on Law and Pub. Affairs, 1977-79, mem. exec. bd., 1977—; v.p., bd. dirs. Collel Bayit Vegan Found., Inc.; pres., bd. dirs. Found. for Beth Jacob Tchrs. Coll., Inc. Mem. Md. State Bar Assn. (council, sect. on state and local govts. 1982—), Order of Coif. Democrat. Jewish. Office: Frank Bernstein Conaway Goldman 3908 N Charles St Apt 303 Baltimore MD 21218-1740 Home: Unit 704 7111 Park Heights Ave Baltimore MD 21215-1685

AISNER, JOSEPH, oncologist, physician; b. Munich, Jan. 5, 1944; came to U.S., 1948; s. Philip and Faye Aisner; m. Seena Feldman, Aug. 31, 1969; children: Dara Lianna, Leon Andrew. BS in Chemistry, Wayne State U., 1965, MD, 1970. Intern Sinai Hosp. Detroit, 1970-71; resident Georgetown U. Hosp., Washington, 1971-72; commd. med. officer USPHS, 1972, advanced through grades to rank 05; clin. assoc. Nat. Cancer Inst., Balt., 1972-75, sr. investigator, 1975-78, chief med. oncology, 1978-81; resigned USPHS, 1981; chief med. oncology U. Md. Cancer Ctr., Balt., 1981-92, dep. dir. clin. affairs, 1982-88, ctr. dir., 1988-93; prof. medicine U. Medicine and Dentistry of N.J., New Brunswick, 1995—, prof. environ. and cmty. medicine, 1996—. Prof. medicine U. Md., 1982-95, prof. oncology, 1982-95, prof. pharmacology, 1985-95, prof. clin. pharmacy, 1987-95, prof. epidemiology preventive medicine, 1993-95; mem. N.J. Legis. Commn. Pain Mgmt., 1998—, N.J. Com. to improve outcomes on cancer patients, 1999—. Editor books; contbr. numerous chpts. to books and articles and abstracts to profl. jours. Bd. dirs. Md. Chpt. Am. Cancer Soc., 1988-94, Am. Assn. Cancer Edn., 1990; exec. com. Md. Cancer Consortium, chmn. breast cancer sect., 1992-93, chmn., 1993-95,; mem. Gov.'s Coun. Cancer Prevention, 1991, exec. com., 1991-95; bd. dirs. Md. Children's Cancer Found., 1991-95. Nat. Cancer Inst. grantee, 1982-95. Fellow ACP; mem. Am. Fedn. Clin. Rsch., Am. Soc. Clin. Oncology (dir. edn. program 1985-86, bd. dirs. 1991-94), Am. Assn. Cancer Rsch., Cancer Leukemia Group B (bd. dirs. 1982-95, vice chair breast sect. 1980-86), Am. Radium Soc. (sci. program com. 1993-94), Ea. Cooperation Oncology Group (prin. investigator com. 1996—, sci. adv. com. 2000—, data audit com. 1999—). Home: 6 Cotswold Ln Warren NJ 07059-6900 Office: 195 Little Albany St New Brunswick NJ 08901-1914 Personal E-mail: aisner@worldnet.att.net. Business E-Mail: aisnerjo@umdnj.edu.

AITCHISON, ANNE CATHERINE, environmental activist, retired; b. Pontiac, Mich., Dec. 27, 1939; d. Willard Francis and Elizabeth (Smith) Speer; m. Robert Terrington Aitchison, Aug. 10, 1963; children: Hannah, Guy, Will. MusB, U. Mich., 1963, MusM, 1965. Chair Naperville (Ill.) Area Recycling Ctr., 1980-89, exec. dir., 1989-93, Sun Shares, Durham, N.C., 1994-96; ret., 1996; cons. Rsch. Triangle Inst., Research Triangle Park, N.C., 1996—. Mem. Citizen's Solid Waste Adv. Com., Will County, Ill., 1989-90, Task Force on Solid Waste, Ill., 1989-90, Task Force on Degradable Plastic, Ill., 1990-91, Mayor's Adv. Com. on Plastic Recycling, Chgo., 1990, Chmn.'s Environ. Com., DuPage County, 1993; cons. cmty. recycling Rsch. Triangle Inst., Durham. Co-author: Resource Recycling, 1991, Environmental Policy for DuPage County, 1993. Founding mem. Naperville Chamber Winds, 1981—93; dir. DuPage Environ. Awareness Ctr., 1987—93; mem. Chmn.'s Environ. Commn., DuPage County, 1992—93, Durham County Solid Waste Adv. Bd., 1994—96; bd. dirs. Durham Symphony, 1994—2000, 2001—, mem. edn. outreach com., 1994—, pres., 2002—03; bd. dirs. Meals on Wheels, Durham, 1999—, pres. bd., 2001—02; bd. dirs., membership chmn. Friends of Durham Libr., 1999—2001. Named Individual Recycler of Yr. Keep Am. Beautiful, 1987, Outstanding Woman Leader YWCA, 1988. Mem. Ill. Recycling Assn. (co-pres. 1987-90, founding dir. 1980—, Pied Piper of Recycling 1989), Women in Waste, Ill. Environ. Coun. (bd. dirs. 1989-90), LWV (bd. dirs. Naperville chpt. 1977-93), Kiwanis (Disting. Svc. award 1987). Avocation: flute.

AITCHISON, SUANN, elementary school educator; b. Paterson, N.J., Oct. 1, 1941; d. Archie Wilson and Isabell (Farrow) A. BA, William Paterson Coll., 1963, MEd, 1976; student, Fairleigh Dickinson U., 1991, St. Peter's Coll., 1996. Cert. elem. edn., reading tchr., elem. reading specialist. Tchr. 3d grade Fair Lawn (N.J.) Pub. Schs., 1963-64, 70-71, tchr. 2d grade, 1964-70, 71-87, tchr. reading, 1987-95, reading specialist, 1997—; tchr. reading and math. Fairlawn (N.J.) Bd. Edn., 1996—. Adj. prof. William Paterson Coll., 1977; developer curriculum guides for remedial reading, 1989, lang. arts and reading for ESL children, 1989, lang. arts and reading for gifted children, 1989, libr. skills and lit. for neurologically impaired children, 1991; mem. Coun. Basic Edn., 1997; com. mem. Bergen County Celebrates Excellence and Pride in our Pub. Schs., 1997. Active Observation and Evaluation Revision Com., 1995, Cerebral Palsy Ctr.; choir Ch. in Radburn, 1993—95; mem. Garretson Forge Found., 1993—95; assoc. Cerebral Palsy Ctr., 1993—95; mem. com. Bergen County Celebrates Excellence and Pride in Edn., 1997; mem. Coun. for Basic Edn., 1997, Borough Fair Lawn Family Aquatic Study Com., 1997—; dist. reading tchr. family literacy reading take home program grades 1-2 elem. schs., 1999—; mem. 1st class Fair Lawn Police Dept.'s Citizen's Police Acad. Course, 2002; reapptd. mem. adv. com. Ams. with Disability Act, 2002—; com. mem. Fair Lawn Rep. County Com., 1986—98, rec. sec., 1994; vol. Gov. Whitman primary and gen. election campaigns, 1992; mem. Fair Lawn mayor and coun. adv. com. Ams. With Disabilities Act, 1996. Mem. AAHPERD, ASCD (premium mem. 1995—), AAUW, N.J. Reading Assn. (North Jersey coun. 1987-95), Coun. Exceptional Children, N.J. ASCD, Math. Assn. Am., Nat. Coun. Tchrs. of English, Coun. Ednl. Diagnostic Svcs., Fair Lawn Rep. Club (trustee 1997), Fair Lawn Pride Com. Assn., Nat. Assn. Secondary Prins. Baptist. Avocations: singing, reading, restaurant dining, theater, concerts. Home: 38-56 Van Duren Ave Fair Lawn NJ 07410-5018 Office: Fair Lawn Bd Edn 37-01 Fair Lawn Ave Fair Lawn NJ 07410-4919

AIT-DAOUD, NASSIMA, psychiatrist, researcher; b. Algiers, Algeria, Jan. 18, 1968; d. Mouhoub Ait-Daoud and Larem Adel; m. Mohamed Tiouririne. MD, Algiers Med. Sch., Algeria, 1994. Diplomate Am. Bd. Psychiatry and Neurology, 1994. Post doctoral fellow in addiction U. of Tex. Health Sci. Ctr., San Antonio, 1989—2000, instr., 1999—2000, asst. prof., 2000—. Clinic dir. START Ctr., San Antonio, 1999—. Bd. mem. San Antonio Fighting Back, 2001—02; chem. dependency working group U. Hosp., San Antonio, 2002. Recipient MAAS award, U. of Tex. Health Sci. Ctr., 2000, travel award, ACNP, 1999, fellow Fellowship award, 7th World Congress of Biol. Psychiatry, 2001, NIAAA, 2001. Mem.: Rsch. Soc. on Alcoholism (mem. 2000—02). Achievements include invention of of combining ondansetron and naltrexone reduces craving among biologically predisposed alcoholics. Home: 8303 La Fleur San Antonio TX 78249 Office: Univ of Tex Health Sci Ctr 7703 Floyd Curl Dr San Antonio TX 78229-3900 Office Fax: 210-562-5430. Personal E-mail: tiouririne@uthscsa.edu. E-mail: tiouririne@uthscsa.edu.

AITKEN, DOUG, artist; Student, Marymount Coll., Palos Verdes, Calif., 1986—87; BFA, Art Ctr. Coll. Design, Pasadena, Calif., 1991. One-man shows include ACI Project Room, N.Y.C., 1993, 303 Gallery, 1994, 1997, 1998, Pasco Art Ctr., Holiday, Fla., 1994, Taka Ishil Gallery, Tokyo, 1996, 1998, Gallery Side Two, 1998, Jiri Svestka Gallery, Prague, 1998, Doug Lawing Gallery, Houston, 1999, Victoria Miro Gallery, London, 1999, Dallas Mus. Art, 1999, Pitti Discovery Series, Florence, Italy, 1999, exhibited in group shows at AC Project Room, N.Y.C., 1991, 1993, 1998, Stux Gallery, 1992, New Mus. Contemporary Art, 1992, Christopher Middendorf Gallery, Washington, 1992, Rushmore Estate, 1993, 303 Gallery, 1993, Santa Monica Mus. Art, 1994, Ma'nes Space, Prague, 1994, Espace Montjoie, Paris, 1994, Flash Art Mus., Trevi, Italy, 1994, Lisson Gallery, London, 1994, Mus. Lab. Art Contemporanea, Rome, 1995, Musee Art Ville Paris, 1995, Elga Wimmer Gallery, N.Y.C., 1996, Lauren Wittles Gallery, 1996, Basilico Fine Arts, 1996, Bard Ctr. Curatorial Studies, Annandale-on-Hudson, 1996, Kunsthalle N.Y., 1996, Kunstraum Vienna, 1996, Galleria Civica Art Modern Contemporanes Turin, Italy, 1996, Bonnefanten Mus., Maastricht, The Netherlands, 1996, Modern Gallery, Ljubljiana, 1997, Tivoli Gallery, 1997, San Casciano Dei Bagni, Italy, 1997, Taka Ishii Gallery, Tokyo, 1997, Galleri Index, Stockholm, 1997, Cubitt Gallery, 1997, Whitney Mus. Am. Art, N.Y.C., 1997, Photographer's Gallery, 1998, Mus. Ludwig, Cologne, Germany, 1998, Walker Art Ctr., 1998, Long Beach (Calif.) Mus. Art, 1998, Galerie Peter Kilchmann, Zurich, 1998. Office: c/o 303 Gallery 525 W 22nd St New York NY 10011-1100

AITKEN, ELLEN BRADSHAW, religious studies educator; b. Riverside, Calif., Feb. 17, 1961; d. Hugh George Jeffrey and Janice Hunter Aitken; m. William R. Porter, Dec. 9, 1990. AB (summa cum laude), Harvard U., 1982; MDiv, U. of the South, 1986; D in Theology, Harvard U., 1997. Ordained to Priesthood Episcopal Ch., 1986. Asst. prof. Harvard Div. Sch., Cambridge, Mass., 1998—. Editor: Philostratus: Heroikos; translator. Fellow, Episcopal Ch. Found., 1989—92. Mem.: Soc. of Bibl. Lit., Phi Beta Kappa. Office: Harvard Div Sch 45 Francis Ave Cambridge MA 02138 Office Fax: 617-496-0585. Personal E-mail: ellen_aitken@harvard.edu. E-mail: ellen_aitken@harvard.edu.

AITKEN, JOHN MALCOLM, engineer, educator; b. Staten Island, Ny, Jan. 12, 1945; s. William and Patricia Aitken; m. Dorothy Anne Knapp, Sept. 7, 1968; children: James, Sean, Patrick. BS, Fordham U., Bronx, NY, 1962—66; MS, Rensselaer Poly. Inst., Troy, NY, 1971, PhD, 1972. Post doctoral fellow Rensselaer Poly. Inst., Troy, NY, 1971—72; rsch. staff mem. IBM T.J. Watson Rsch. Ctr., Yorktown Heights, NY, 1973—82; sr. engr. IBM East Fishkill, East Fishkill, NY, 1982—91, IBM Burlington, Burlington, Vt., 1991—2000; sr. tech. staff mem. IBM Microelectronics, Burlington, Vt., 2000—03. Semiconductor rsch. tech. adv. bd. mem. SRC, Research Triangle Park, NC, 1991—99; adj. prof., ECE dept. UVM. Contbr. articles to profl. jours. Mem.: Inst. of Elec. & Electronic Engineers. Achievements include patents for Numerous semiconduc-

tor related, Expert in Gate Insulator Behavior. Avocations: skiing, running, swimming. Home: 17 Baycrest Dr South Burlington VT 05403 Office: Ibm 1000 River Rd Essex Junction VT 05452

AITKEN, ROBERT BAKER, religious studies educator, writer; b. Phila., June 19, 1917; s. Robert Thomas and Gladys Baker Aitken; m. Mary Louise Laune Aitken, June 1947 (div. Aug. 1954); 1 child, Thomas Laune; m. Anne Arundel Hopkins, Feb. 23, 1957 (dec. June 13, 1994). BA, U. Hawaii, 1947, MA, 1950. Shoshike (Zen master) Sanbokyodan, Kamakura, Japan, 1984. Exec. sec. Moiliili and Wahiawa (Hawaii) Cmty. Assns., 1948—52; tchr., adminstr. Happy Valley Sch., Ojai, Calif., 1955—57; owner Old Island Books, Honolulu, 1958—61; counselor, adminstr. East-West Ctr., Honolulu, 1962—66; tchr. Kapiolani C.C., Honolulu, 1966—67; leader, master Diamond Sangha, Honolulu and Peahi, Hawaii, 1959—95, retired master Puna, Hawaii, 1996—. Mem. archives preparation staff Hawaii Com. for the Humanities, U. Hawaii Hamilton Libr., 2003. Author: A Zen Wave: Basho's Haiku and Zen, 1978, Taking the Path of Zen, 1982, The Mind of Clover: Essays in Zen Buddhist Ethics, 1984, The Gateless Barrier: The Wu-men kuan (Mumonkan), 1990, Encouraging Words: Zen Buddhist Teachings for Western Students, 1993; author: (with David Steindl-Rast) The Ground We Share: Everyday Practice, Buddhist and Christian, 1994; author: The Practice of Perfection: The Paramitas from a Zen Buddhist Perspective, 1994, Original Dwelling Place: Zen Buddhist Essays, 1996, Zen Master Raven: Sayings and Doings of a Wise Bird, 2002, The Morning Star: New and Selected Writings, 2003; contbr. articles to jours. in field. Mem. Am. Friends Svc. Com., Phila., 1955—, Fellowship of Reconciliation, Nyack, NY, 1960—; mem. internat. adv. com. Buddhist Peace Fellowship, Berkeley, Calif., 1985—; pres. Parents and Friends of Lesbians and Gays, Hilo, Hawaii, 2001—. Fellow, Aloha United Way, 1950—51. Mem.: Internat. Network of Engaged Buddhists, Hawaii Assn. Internat. Buddhists. Avocations: reading, book collecting, zazen.

AITKEN, ROBERT CAMPBELL, engineer; b. Vancouver, B.C., Can., Apr. 21, 1963; came to U.S., 1990; s. Robert and Mary Elizabeth A.; m. Denise Kathleen Maloney, Aug. 2, 1986; children: Robert James, Colin Campbell. BS with hons., U. Victoria, B.C., Can., 1985, MS, 1986; PhD, McGill U., Montreal, Que., Can., 1990. Rsch. assoc. Alberta Rsch. Coun., Calgary, Alberta, Can., 1986-87; mem. tech. staff Agilent Technologies, Santa Clara, Calif., 1990—. Tech. program com. mem. Internat. Conf. on Computer-Aided Design, Santa Clara, 1993-94, local arrangements chmn., 1995, tutorials chmn., 1996-97, panels chmn., 1998; tech. program com. Custom Integrated Cirs. Conf., Santa Clara, 1995-97; panel and poster chmn. Test Synthesis Workshop, Santa Barbara, Calif., 1995, fin. chmn., 1996-97, vice-chair, 1998, gen. chair, 1999; mem. program com. Internat. Test Conf., 1996-2000, vice chair program com., 2001. Assoc. editor: IEEE Transactions on Comp.-Aided Design, 1997—. Recipient award for Best paper, Internat. Test Conf., Balt., 1992, Atlantic City, 2000, hon. mention, Balt., 1991; named Indsl. Mentor in Yr. Semiconductor Rsch. Corp., 1998. Mem. IEEE. Office: Agilent Technologies MS 51LGO 5301 Stevens Creek Blvd Santa Clara CA 95051-8059 E-mail: rob.aitken@agilent.com.

AITKEN, ROSEMARY THERESA, financial planner, consultant; b. June 26, 1946; d. John Francis and Mary Helen (Kinslow) A.; m. Frank Furch, June 24, 1983. AA, Mundelein Coll., 1976. CLU, ChFC; accredited estate planner. Mktg. cons. Anchor Orgn., Chgo., 1974-76; assoc. dir. Big Bros.-Big Sisters of Chgo., 1975-76; fin. planner Phoenix Co., Chgo., 1976-93. Chmn bd. Lincoln Equities, Inc., Chgo., 1985-88, also bd. dirs.; pres. Capital Interests, Inc., Chgo., 1984-87, Aitken Assocs., Chgo., 1980—; speaker, instr. Chgo. Women's Network, 1984—; cons., columnist Chgo. Tribune, 1980—, Chgo. Sun-Times, 1981—; lectr. Midwest Life Underwriters Assns., 1982—, lectr., instr. Mundelein Coll., Northwestern Univ., Oakton Community Coll., Loyola U. Contbr. articles to profl. jours. Bd. dirs. Loop YWCA, 1974-81. Mem. Women Life Underwriters Conf. (bd. dirs., 1st v.p. 1984-85), Chgo. Assn. Life Underwriters (bd. dirs. 1984—), Million Dollar Roundtable (life and qualifying mem.), Ill. St. Andrew Soc., Nat. Estate Planning Coun., Chgo. Estate Planning Coun., Midwest Bus. Brokers and Intermediaries. Republican. Roman Catholic. Avocations: marathon running, sailing, photography. Home: Morningside Island 26884 Maple Ave Mundelein IL 60060 Office: Aitken Assocs Ste 620 1901 N Roselle Rd Schaumburg IL 60195-3184 Fax: 847-884-6738.

AITKEN, RUTH ELAINE WILLSON, educational and career/job search consultant; BS in Secondary Edn., Indiana U. of Pa.; MS in Human Devel./Family Studies, postgrad., Pa. State U. Cert. tchr. Pa. Dir. field placements Pa. State U., University Park, 1972-83; edn./mktg./mgmt. cons. Aitken Assocs., State College, Pa., 1983—. Substitute tchr. in secondary edn., 1985—94; intstr. and substitute tchr. Dept. Continuing Edn. Pa. State U., 1985—94. Regional chair Am. Cancer Soc., Arthritis Found., Centre Region Health Coun.; membership com. Centre County Coun. on Human Svcs. Mem.: Chamber of Bus. and Industry of Centre County, Bus. and Profl. Women (state and dist. conv. del, newsletter editor, founds. chair), Coll. Human Devel. Alumni Assn. (bd. dirs. nominations com., chair), Pa. State Alumni Assn. (univ.-alumni-faculty task force com.), Soroptimist Club (youth scholarship com.), Alpha Kappa Delta (Nat. Woman of Excellence award), Omicron Nu. Avocation: community service projects. Office: Aitken Assocs 124 S Patterson St State College PA 16801-3911

AITKEN, THOMAS DEAN, lawyer; b. Coffeyville, Kans., July 9, 1939; s. Arthur E. and Kathleen Lucille (Bressie) A.; m. Molly Alexandrea Coston, Dec. 17, 1960; children: Molly Kym Aitken Wright, Michele Bressie Aitken McKinney. BBA, U. Okla., 1961, LLB, 1964; LLM in Taxation, NYU, 1965. Bar: Okla. 1964, Fla. 1966. Assoc. Carlton, Fields, Ward, Emmanuel, Smith & Cutler, P.A., Tampa, Fla., 1965-70, ptnr., 1971-96; of counsel Trenam, Kemker, Scharf, Barkin, Frye, O'Neill & Mullis, P.A., Tampa, Fla., 1996—. Contbr. articles, speaker NYU Tax Inst., 1972; editor NYU Intramural Law Rev., 1964-65; mng. editor Okla. Law Rev., 1963-64; articles editor ABA jour. The Tax Lawyer, 1987. Bd. dirs. ARC, Tampa, 1984-87; pres., bd. dirs. Met. Ministries, Tampa, 1979-80. Fellow Am. Coll. Trust and Estate Counsel; mem. Fla. Bar (tax sect. exec. coun. 1970-82), Tampa Bay Estate Planning Coun. (pres. 1975-76), Beta Gamma Sigma, Phi Eta Sigma. Democrat. Methodist. Avocations: choral music, opera, baritone soloist, clarinetist. Office: Trenam Kemker Scharf Barkin Frye ONeill & Mullis PA 2700 Barnett Plz 101 E Kennedy Blvd Tampa FL 33602-5179*

AIUTO, RUSSELL, science education consultant; b. Monroe, Mich., July 13, 1934; s. Crispino and Maria (d'Aiuto) A.; m. Nancy Jane Obenauf, Dec. 17, 1955 (dec. 1980); children: Mary T. Carroll, Susan M. Summa; m. Beverly Bradley, Jan. 3, 1981 BA, Ea. Mich. U., 1958, U. Mich., 1995; MA, U. N.C., 1963, PhD, 1971. Tchr. speech, drama Monroe High Sch., Mich., 1958-61; prof. biology Albion Coll., Mich., 1966-82, provost, 1982-85; pres. Hiram Coll., Ohio, 1985-88; div. dir. tchr. preparation and enhancement NSF, Washington, 1988-90; program mgr. Nat. Sci. Tchrs. Assn., Washington, 1990-93, Coun. Ind. Colls., 1993-95. Cons. Gygi Found., Dundee, Mich., 1984— Author: Mencken and Sara, 1980, Ring Lardner's America, 1984, Dorothy Parker, 1986; coauthor: Science Interactions, 3 vols., 1993; contbr. articles to profl. jours. Vice chmn. Albion Improvement Com., 1983-85 NSF grantee, 1968 Mem. Sigma Xi, Omicron Delta. Episcopalian. Avocation: collecting books. Home: 9631 Duffer Way Gaithersburg MD 20886-1309

AJAEV, VLADIMIR S. mathematician, educator; b. Moscow, July 24, 1973; s. Sergey Sossinsky and Valentina Ajaeva. BS in Physics, Moscow Inst. Physics and Tech., 1994; MS in Applied Math., Northwestern U., 1996, PhD of Applied Math., 1999. Postdoctoral fellow Stanford U., Calif., 1999—2001; asst. prof. So. Meth. U., Dallas, 2001—. Vis. rschr. U. Calif. Santa Barbara, 2001, 02; cons. Agilent Technologies, Palo Alto, Calif., 2001. Contbr. Mem.: Soc. Indsl. and Applied Math., Am. Phys. Soc. Achievements include development of innovative numerical methods for simulations of solidification; mathematical models for vapor/gas bubbles in microscopic devices. Avocations: tennis, skiing. Office: So Meth Univ Dept Math PO Box 751056 Dallas TX 75275

AJA-HERRERA, MARIE, fashion designer, educator; b. Bedford, England, Mar. 19, 1955; d. Henry and Ariadne Swiejkowski; m. Manny Anjel Aja-Herrera, Oct. 24, 1981. BA in Fashion, U. Ctrl. England, 1977; MA in Fashion/Textiles, Lodz U., 1980; MA in Design Studies, St. Martins, England, 1995. Head fashion dept. Southend Coll. Essex U., 1981—84; head womenswear design Ghirombelli/Pacanina Modas/Santini S.A., Barcelona, Milan, London, 1984—88, Jefferson Internat. PLC, Hong Kong, 1988—89; sales exec., design & edn. coord. Lectra Sys., 1989; chair fashion design, chair fashion merchandising Am. Coll. in London, 1989—92; disign dir. CAD, knitwear, textiles Jacques Vert PLC, 1992—95; dean faculty of art and design Am. U. Dubai, United Arab Emirates, 1995—96; head of design Twins Enterprise PLC, 1996—97; chair fashion design Savannah (Ga.) Coll. Art & Design, 1997—. Cons. Herrera UK Ltd., 1982-95. Fellow: Soc. Artists & Designers; mem.: Textile Inst., Polish Union Artists, The Fashion Group Internat., Clothing & Footwear Inst. Avocations: horse riding, skiing, collecting antiques, travel. Office: Savannah Coll Art & Design 516 Abercorn St Savannah GA 31401-5644 E-mail: mcajaher@scad.edu.

AJALAT, SOL PETER, lawyer; b. Chgo., July 12, 1932; s. Peter S. and Tesbina (Shahadie) Ajalat; m. Lily Mary Roum, Aug. 21, 1960; children: Stephen, Gregory, Denise, Lawrence. BS, UCLA, 1958, JD, 1962. Bar: Calif. 1963, U.S. Dist. Ct. (no., cen., ea. and so. dists.) Calif. 1963, U.S. Claims Ct. 1990. Pvt. practice, L.A., 1965—. Referee Calif. State Bar Ct., 1984-90; mem. sr. lawyers com. State Bar Calif., 2002—. Pres. bd. dirs. St. Nicholas Orthodox Cath. Ch., L.A., 1976-78; pres. Toluca Lake Elem. Adv. Coun., L.A., 1979, L.A. Unified Sch. Dist. Area I Adv. Coun., 1980, Providence High Sch. Adv. Coun., L.A., 1985; bd. dirs. Med. Ctr. North Hollywood, 1991-98, Angels of the Yr. Awards, 1996—, Life Svcs., Inc., 1997-2001; mem. improvement adv. com. Burbank City media dist., 1997-2000; chmn. Toluca Lake Neighborhood Coun., 2002—. Mem. Calif. Bar Assn., L.A. County Bar Assn. (mem. L.A. Superior Ct. bench and bar com. 1987-96, chmn. mcpl. ct. com. 1985-86, trustee 1987-88), Calif. Trial Lawyers Assn., Conf. Bar Dels. (del. 1985—), L.A. County Trial Lawyers Assn., Lawyers Club L.A. County (pres. 1985-86), Toluca Lake C. of C. (pres. 1997), Wm. A. Neima Rep. Club (pres. 1978-79), Masons, Shriners, Kiwanis (pres. North Hollywood chpt. 2002-03). Eastern Orthodox. Avocation: physical fitness. Office: 3800 W Alameda Ave Ste 1150 Burbank CA 91505-4304

AJANAKU, AMANA M. poet; b. Memphis, Tenn., Sept. 19, 1953; d. Ben Freeman and Viola Bayley; 1 child, Akida A.M. BA in speech, U. Memphis, 1977, MA in liberal studies, 2003. Author: (poems) I Am a Movement, 1989, Adventures in Africa, 2000. Acting sec. Kennedy Dem. Orgn., Memphis, 1998—. Avocations: reading, writing, poetry. Home: 892 N Claybrook St Memphis TN 38107

AJAX, ERNEST THEODORE, retired neurology educator; b. Salt Lake City, Oct. 11, 1926; s. William Theodore and Kathryn Fleming Ajax; m. Gwendolyn Quilico, June 9, 1950; children: Ted J., Katherine Ajax Steinberg, Wendy, E. Todd. BS in Basic Biol. Scis., U. Utah, 1949, MD, 1951; postgrad., Northwestern U., 1952-55. Diplomate Am. Bd. Psychiatry and Neurology. Chief neurology svc. VA Med. Ctr., Salt Lake City, 1962-86; asst. prof. neurology U. Utah, Salt Lake City, 1962-67, asst. prof. psychiatry, 1965-72, assoc. prof. neurology, 1967-71, prof. neurology, 1971-87, assoc. prof. psychiatry, 1972-87, prof. emeritus neurology, 1987—; assoc. prof. psychiatry emeritus. Vis. prof. Multiple Care Facilities, 1976-80; examiner Am. Bd. Psychiatry and Neurology, 1970, 76, 80, 81, 83. Contbr. articles to profl. publs. Capt. USAF, 1955-57. Mem. Am. Acad. Neurology, Am. Clin. Neurophysiology Soc., Salt Lake County Med. Soc., Utah State Med. Assn. Avocations: reading, travel, hunting, fishing, marksmanship.

AJELLO, EDITH H. state legislator; b. Apr. 26, 1944; d. Kenneth Aaron and Rozella Christine (Ewoldt) Hanover; children: Linell, Aaron. BA, Bucknell U., 1966. Store mgr. V George Rustigian Rugs, Inc., 1981-93, 94—; interim exec. dir. Vols. in Providence Schs., 1993; mem. R.I. Ho. of Reps., 1993—. With V. George Rustigian Rugs, 1994—. Democrat. Home and Office: 29 Benefit St Providence RI 02904-2743 E-mail: rep_ajello@rilin.state.ri.us.

AJHAR, MARSHA G. lawyer; b. Easton, Pa. m. R. Scott Johnston. BA, MA, Simmons Coll., 1977; JD, Vt. Law Sch., 1981. Bar: Mass. 1983, N.Y. 1984, U.S. Ct. Appeals (fed. cir.) 1987, U.S. Ct. Appeals (2d cir.) 2002. Assoc. Pennie & Edmonds, N.Y.C., 1983-89, Liddy Sullivan et al., N.Y.C., 1989-92; mem. Abelman Frayne & Schwab, N.Y.C., 1993—. Mem. N.Y. Intellectual Property Law Assn., Internat. Trademark Assn., Assn. of the Bar of the City of N.Y. Office: Abelman Frayne & Schwab 150 E 42d St New York NY 10017 Fax: 212-949-9190. E-mail: mgajhar@lawabel.com.

AJIMAL, GURJIT SINGH, anesthesiologist; BS, U. Western Ont., London, Can., 1979; MS, Wayne State U., 1981, MD, 1985. Diplomate Am. Bd. Anesthesia, Am. Bd. Pain Mgmt., Nat. Bd. Med. Examiners. Intern Henry Ford Hosp., Detroit, 1986, resident, 1987-89; resident anesthesia and critical care U. Chgo., 1986-87; attending anesthesiologist Genesys Med. Ctr., Flint, Mich., 1991-93, med. student edn. coord., 1992-93, chmn. dept. anesthesia, 1993; clin. asst. prof. Mich. State U., Lansing, 1992-94; chmn. dept. anesthesia, dir. pain clinic Caylor-Nickel Med. Ctr., Bluffton, Ind., 1993-98, chmn. dept. surgery, 1997—, Genesys Regional Med. Ctr., 1998—, chmn. dept. anesthesia, 2003—. Presenter in field; clinical asst. prof. Mich. State Coll. Human Medicine, 1998—, dir. pre-admission testing, 1999—. Contbr. articles to profl. publs. Network counselor Wayne State Med. Schs., Detroit, 1982-85. Recipient Dr. Henry R. Viets Rsch. award Myasthenia Gravis Found., 1982; Bd. Govs. scholar U. Western Ont., 1976. Fellow Am. Acad. Pain Medicine; mem. Am. Soc. Regional Anesthesia, Am. Soc. Anesthesiologists, Henry Ford Hosp. Med. Assn. Achievements include research on modulation of ACH receptors.

AJZENBERG-SELOVE, FAY, physicist, educator; b. Berlin, Feb. 13, 1926; came to U.S., 1940, naturalized, 1946; d. Mojzesz A. and Olga (Naiditch) A.; m. Walter Selove, Dec. 18, 1955. BS in Engring., U. Mich., 1946; MS, U. Wis., 1949, PhD, 1952; DSc (hon.), Smith Coll., 1995, Mich. State U., 1997, Haverford Coll., 1999—. Rsch. fellow Calif. Inst. Tech., 1952, 54; lectr. Smith Coll., 1952-53; cons., fellow MIT, Cambridge, 1952-53; from asst. prof. to rsch. assoc. prof. Boston U., 1953-57; mem. faculty Haverford Coll., 1957-70, prof. physics, 1962-70, acting chmn. dept. physics, 1967-69; rsch. prof. U. Pa., Phila., 1970-73, prof. physics, 1973—, assoc. chmn., 1989-93. Vis. asst. prof. Columbia, summer 1955, Nat. U. Mexico, summer 1955; lectr. U. Pa., 1957; cons. in field, 1962-63; vis. assoc. Calif. Inst. Tech., 1973-74; Exec. sec. com. physics faculties in colls. Am. Inst. Physics, 1962-65, mem. adv. com. manpower, 1963-68, adv. com. vis. scientists program, 1963-67; commr. Commn. on Coll. Physics, 1968-71; exec. sec. ad hoc panel on nuclear data compilations NAS-NRC, 1971-75; mem. Commn. on Nuclear Physics, Internat. Union Pure and Applied Physics, 1972-78, chairperson. 1978-81; mem. U.S. del. low energy nuclear physics to USSR, AEC, 1966; mem. Distinguished Faculty Awards Commn. Commonwealth of Pa., 1976; mem. nuclear sci. adv. com. Dept Energy-NSF, 1977-80; mem. numerical data adv. bd., assembly math. and phys. scis. NRC, 1977-79; lectr. U. Minn., 1994 Author: A Matter of Choice, Memoirs of a Female Physicist, 1994; editor: Nuclear Spectroscopy, vol. A and B, 1960; bd. editors Phys. Rev. C., 1981-83. Mem. Bower awards com. Franklin Nat. Meml., 1993. Recipient Christian R. and Mary F. Lindback award for disting. teaching, 1991, Nicholson medal for humanitarian svc. Am. Phys. Soc., 1999, 1st Disting. Alumni fellow in Physics, U. Wis., 2001; Smith-Mundt fellow, 1955; Guggenheim fellow, 1965-66. Fellow AAAS (mem. governing coun. 1974-80, mem. com. on coun. affairs 1977, 78), Am. Phys. Soc. (chairperson divsn. nuclear physics 1973-74); mem. AAUP, NRC (mem. phys. scis. panel, associateship program 1988-91), Am. Inst. Physics (mem. com. on pub. edn. and info. 1980-83), Phi Beta Kappa, Sigma Xi (nat. lectr. 1973-74). Home: 118 Cherry Ln Wynnewood PA 19096-1209 Office: U Pa Philadelphia PA 19104-6396

AKAIKE, MASAMI, communications technology educator; b. Kamakura, Japan, Oct. 15, 1940; s. Saburo and Suiko Akaike; m. Aya Murata, Nov. 16, 1971; 1 child, Makoto. B of Engring., U. Tokyo, 1964, M of Engring., 1966, D of Engring., 1969, PhD of Engring. (hon.). Rsch. engr. Nippon Telegraph and Telephone Co., Tokyo, 1969-72, sr. rsch. engr., 1972-81, sect. head, 1983-89; dept. head ATR Optical and Radio Comms. Rsch. Labs., Kyoto, Japan, 1989-92; prof. Sci. U. of Tokyo, 1992—. Vice-chmn. URSI Japanese Commn., Tokyo, 1996—; chmn. URSI Commn. C, 2002—. Author: Introduction to Microwave and Optical Wave Engineering, 1989; contbr. articles to profl. jours. Fellow IEEE MTT Soc. (Tokyo chpt. vice-chmn. 1986-90, chmn. 1993-95, assoc. editor Transactions on IEEE MTT, 1984-91), Inst. Electronics, Info. and Comms. Engrs. (Yonezawa Meml. prize 1972). Avocations: playing tennis, swimming, growing plants. Home: 1-36-15 Kaminomiya Tsurumi-ku Yokohama 230-0075 Japan Office: Sci Univ of Tokyo 1-3 Kagurazaka Shinjuku-ku Tokyo 162-8601 Japan E-mail: akaike@ee.kagu.sut.ac.jp.

AKAKA, DANIEL KAHIKINA, senator; b. Honolulu, Sept. 11, 1924; s. Kahikina and Annie (Kahoa) A.; m. Mary Mildred Chong, May 22, 1948; children: Millannie, Daniel, Gerard, Alan, Nicholas. BEdn, U. Hawaii, 1952, MEdn, 1966. Tchr., Hawaii, 1953-60; vice prin., then prin. Ewa Beach Elem. Sch., Honolulu, 1960-64; prin. Pohakea Elem. Sch., 1964-65, Kaneohe Elem. Sch., 1965-68; program specialist Hawaii Compensatory Edn., 1978-79, from 1985; dir. Hawaii OEO, 1971-74; spl. asst. human resources Office Gov. Hawaii, 1975-76; mem. 95th-101st Congresses from 2d Dist., Hawaii, 1977-90; U.S. senator from Hawaii, 1990—; mem. energy and natural resources com. U.S. Senate, mem. govt. affairs com., mem. Indian affairs com., mem. Indian affairs com., mem. vets. affairs com., mem. Senate dem. policy com. Chmn. Hawaii Principals' Conf. Bd. dirs. Hanahauoli Sch.; mem. Act 4 Ednl. Adv. Council, Library Adv. Council.; Trustee Kawaiahao Congl. Ch. Served with U.S. Army, 1945-47. Mem. NEA, Musicians Assn. Hawaii. Democrat. Office: US Senate 141 Hart Senate Office Bldg Washington DC 20510-0001*

AKAR, VIRGINIA MAYA, lawyer; b. Bklyn., Aug. 29, 1967; d. Aron and Luisa Maya; m. Joseph Akar, June 12, 1993; children: Kaili, Kane. BS in Journalism, U. Fla., 1990; JD, St. Thomas U., 1994. Bar: Fla. 1994. Writer Miami (Fla.) Today newspaper, 1990-91; prosecutor Office of Miami Dade State Atty., 1994-98; products liability atty. Seipp Flick & Kissane, Miami, 1998; pvt. practice Miami, 1998—. Legal cons. Accar Ltd. Inc., Miami, 1994. Editor St. Thomas Law Rev. jour., 1992-94. Mem. ABA, Dade County Bar Assn. Avocations: running, kickboxing. Office: 1 NE 1st St Ste 35 Miami FL 33132-2437

AKASOFU, SYUN-ICHI, geophysicist, educator; b. Nagano-Ken, Japan, Dec. 4, 1930; came to U.S., 1958, naturalized, 1986; s. Shigenori and Kumiko (Koike) A.; m. Emiko Endo, Sept. 25, 1961; children: Ken-Ichi, Keiko. BS, Tohoku U., 1953, MS, 1957; PhD, U. Alaska, 1961. Sr. research asst. Nagasaki U., 1953-55; research asst. Geophys. Inst., U. Alaska, Fairbanks, 1958-61, mem. faculty, 1961—, prof. geophysics, 1964—, dir. Geophys. Inst., 1986-99; dir. Internat. Arctic Rsch. Ctr., U. Alaska, Fairbanks, 1998—. Author: Polar and Magnetospheric Substorms (Russian edit. 1971), 1968, The Aurora: A Discharge Phenomenon Surrounding the Earth (in Japanese), 1975, Physics of Magnetospheric Substorms, 1977, Aurora Borealis: The Amazing Northern Lights, 1979, 2d edit., 2002, Exploring the Secrets of the Aurora, 2002; co-author: Sydney Chapman, Eighty, 1968, Solar-Terrestrial Physics (Russian edit. 1974); editor: Dynamics of the Magnetosphere, 1979; co-editor: Physics of Auroral Arc Formation, 1980—, The Solar Wind and the Earth, 1987; mem. editl. bd. Planet and Earth Sci; co-editor: Space Sci. Revs. Recipient Chapman medal Royal Astron. Soc., 1976, award Japan Acad., 1977, Japanese Fgn. Minister award, 1993; named Disting. Alumnus U. Alaska, 1980, Centennial Alumnus Nat. Assn. State Univs. and Land Grant Colls., 1987, Edith R. Bullock prize U. Alaska Fairbanks, 1997, Alaskan of Yr.-Denali award, 1999; named one of the most cited authors Am. Soc. Info. Sci., 2002. Fellow AAAS, Am. Geophys. Union (John Adam Fleming medal 1977); mem. Sigma Xi E-mail: sakasofu@iarc.uaf.edu. *As a researcher of earth sciences, I feel that an artist and a scientist have something very much in common. Both watch carefully a natural object such as the aurora, a glacier, migrating birds, the Arctic Ocean, etc., and abstract whatever they feel the most essential part from the object. Then, an artist paints his abstraction on a canvas, while a scientist puts his abstraction into the form of equations.*

AKBER, SYED FAROOQ, medical physicist; b. Patna, India, Aug. 12, 1950; came to U.S. 1980; s. Syed Mujtaba Karim and Maimoona Khatoon. MS, UCLA, 1982; PhD, U. Zagreb, Yugoslavia, 1990. Diplomate Am. Bd. of Radiology. Rsch. asst. UCLA, 1982-85; rsch. assoc. U. Ill., Chgo., 1986-87; med. physicist U. Mass. Med. Sch., Worcester, 1987-88, Nuclear Assc., N.Y., 1988-89; radiological physicist U. Tex. Med. Sch., Houston, 1989-92; chief radiol. physicist Marshfield Clinic, Wis., 1993-2000; radiation physicist Craven Regional Med. Ctr., New Bern, N.C., 2000; med. physicist St. John Med. Ctr., Tulsa, 2001—02, Lakeland Med. Ctr., St. Joseph, Mich., 2003—. Contbr. articles to over 47 profl. publs. Recipient Norman Poe Mem. award Soc. Nuclear Med., Los Angeles, 1982. Member Am. Assc. Physicists in Med. Achievements include contributions to lung metabolism, NMR relaxation time, mammography, radiation tolerance dose, instrumentation. Office: Lakeland Med Ctr Radiation Oncology Dept 1234 Napier Saint Joseph MI 49085 also: 2730 Lake Pines Path # 216 49085 E-mail: sakber@sjmc.org.

AKE, DAVID ANDREW, music educator; b. New Haven, May 11, 1961; s. Theodore and Beatrice Louise Ake; m. Hillary Louise Case, June 23, 2001. MusB, U. Miami, 1983; MFA, Calif. Inst. Arts, 1987; PhD, UCLA, 1998. Author: Jazz Cultures (Outstanding Dissertation award Soc. Am. Music, Mousel-Feltner Award for Outstanding Scholar, U. Nev., Reno). Mem.: Soc. Am. Music, Am. Musicol. Soc. Democrat. Office: Dept Music 226 Univ Nev Reno Reno NV 89507

AKEL, OLLIE JAMES, oil company executive; b. Harlan, Ky., Aug. 14, 1933; s. William M. and Jameleh (Raffih) A.; m. Mona, June 11, 1966; children: Omar James, Amanda Dalal, Roanna Lyn. BSME, U. Ky., 1954; M in Aero. Engring., Rensselaer Polytech. Inst., 1955; MS in Mgmt., Mass. Inst. Tech., 1967. Thermodynamic engr. North Am. Aviation, Columbus, Ohio, 1958-59; engr. Middle East Airlines, Beirut, Lebanon, 1959-65, Exxon Corp., N.Y., London, Arabia, 1967-80; pres. Exxon Chem. Mideast and Africa, Brussels, 1981-86, Exxon Chem. Belgium, Brussels, 1986-88; dir. corp. comm. Exxon Chem. Internat., Brussels, 1988-89; pres. Exxon Saudi Arabia, Riyadh, 1989-92, Exxon Mexicana, Mex., 1993-96, ret., 1996; pres. AB Assocs.LLC, 1998—. Author: Driving According to Oliver, 1999, Prisoners of Circumstances, 1998. Dir. United Way, Brussels, 1988-89. 2d lt. U.S. Army, 1956-58. Mem. Am. C.C. Mex. (bd. dirs., pres. 1995), Am. Businessmen's Group of Riyadh (steering com. 1979-81, 90-92), Tau Beta Pi, Pi Tau Sigma. Protestant.

AKELLA, UMASUNDARI SRIVENKATA, research scholar; arrived in U.S., 1997; d. Sriramchandramurty Venkata and Kamala Akella; m. Mukul Anand Krishna, Aug. 9, 2000. BA in Sociology with honors, U. of Delhi, 1994, MA in Sociology, 1996; MS in Sociology, Okla. State U., 1999; postgrad., SUNY, Stony Brook, 1999. Rsch. and tchg. asst. Okla. State U., Stillwater, 1997—99, SUNY, Stony Brook, NY, 1999—; instr. Ctr. For Survey Rsch., SUNY, Stony Brook, NY, 2002—, SUNY, Stony Brook, NY, 2002—. Contbr. book rev. Mem. Nat. Svc. Scheme, Delhi, 1991—94; vol. worker Cheshire Home for Mentally Challanged Children, Delhi, 1989—93; mem. SPIC MACAY, Delhi, 1991—94. Recipient Grad. Merit Tuition scholarship, SUNY, 1999, Summer Travelling fellowship, Ctr. for Devel. Econs., Delhi Sch. of Econs., 1995, Nat. Merit scholarship. Mem.: Ea. Sociol. Soc., Am. Sociol. Assn., Alpha Kappa Delta (life). Achievements include research in impact of corporate organizational structure and work policies on women executives in the United States; coalition formation between environmental organizations and labor unions in Oregon. Office: SUNY Dept Sociology Stony Brook NY 11794-43 Office Fax: 631-632-8203. E-mail: uakella@ic.sunysb.edu.

AKEMANN, DAVID R. lawyer; b. Elgin, Ill., Oct. 31, 1951; s. Theodore H. and Lois (Marr) A.; m. Vickie C. Skala, Aug. 5, 1978; children— Carrie, Julie, Collin. B.S., Brigham Young U., 1972; J.D., Lewis U., 1978. Bar: Ill. 1978, U.S. Dist. Ct. (no. dist.) Ill. 1978, U.S. Ct. Appeals (7th cir.) 1979, U.S. Supreme Ct. 1981. Clk. States Atty. Office, Kane County, Geneva, Ill., 1977-78; asst. states atty., 1978-79, chief civil divsn., 1979—87; sole practice, Elgin, 1978—92; elected states atty., 1992-2000; asst. atty. gen., 2000-03; Apptd. commnr. Ill. Industrial Commn., 2003. Recipient Am. Jurisprudence Constn. Law award Lawyers Coop. Pub. Co., 1978. Mem. ABA, Ill. Bar Assn., Kane County Bar Assn., Ill. Pub. Employers Labor Relations Assn. (prin.). Methodist. Home: 420 Hoxie Ct Elgin IL 60123-3220

AKENSON, DONALD HARMAN, historian, educator; b. Mpls., May 22, 1941; s. Donald Nels and Fern L. (Harman) A. BA, Yale U., 1962; PhD, Harvard U., 1967; LittD (hon.), McMaster U., 1995; HHD (hon.), U. Lethbridge, 1996; LittD (hon.), Guelph U., 2000; DLaws (hon.), Regina U., 2002. Allston Burr sr. tutor Dunster House, Harvard U., 1966-67; asst. prof. history,

asst. dean Yale Coll., 1967-70; assoc. prof. history Queens U., Kingston, Ont., Can., 1970-74, prof., 1974—; hon. prof. U. Aberdeen, 2002—; Beamish rsch. prof. migration studies U. Liverpool, England, 1997—2002; sr. editor McGill-Queens Univ. Press, 1982—. Hon. rsch. fellow Queens U., Belfast, 1976-77, sr. rsch. fellow, 1995-96; hon. prof. edn. Trinity Coll., Dublin, 1976-77; hon. lectr. Australian Nat. U., 1985; Cecil H. Green disting. vis. prof. Green Coll., U. B.C., 1995; guest artist Yaddo Colony, 1985; writer-in-residence Bellagio Ctr., Lake Como, Italy, 1993; hon. rsch. prof. Irish and Scottish studies U. Aberdeen, Scotland, 2002—; Freilich Found. lectr. Australian Nat. U., 2003. Author: The Irish Education Experiment: The National System of Education in the Nineteenth Century, 1970, The Church of Ireland: Ecclesiastical Reform and Revolution 1800-1885, 1971, Education and Enmity: The Control of Schooling in Northern Ireland 1920-50, 1973, The United States and Ireland, 1973, A Mirror to Kathleen's Face: Education in Independent Ireland 1922-60, 1975, Local Poets and Social History: James Orr, Bard of Ballycarry, 1977, Between Two Revolutions: Islandmagee, County Antrim, 1798-1920, 1979, The Lazar House Notebooks, 1981, A Protestant in Purgatory: Richard Whately, Archbishop of Dublin, 1981, The Irish in Ontario, 1984, Brotherhood Week in Belfast, 1984, Being Had: Historians, Evidence, and the Irish in North America, 1985, The Orangeman: The Life and Times of Ogle Gowan, 1986, The Edgerston Audit, 1987, Small Differences: Irish Catholics and Irish Protestants, 1815-1922, 1988, Half the World from Home; Perspectives on the Trial in New Zealand, 1990, At Face Value: The Life and Times of Eliza McCormack/John White, 1990 Occasional Papers on the Irish in South Africa, 1991, God's Peoples: Covenant and Land in South Africa, Israel and Ulster, 1992, The Irish Diaspora A Primer, 1993, Conor: A Biography of Conor Cruise O'Brien, 1994, If the Irish Ruled thr World: Montserrat 1630-1730, 1997, Surpassing Wonder. The Invention of the Bible and the Talmuds, 1998, Saint Saul: A Skeleton Key to the Historical Jesus, 2000; editor: Canadian Papers in Rural History, 1978-96; sr. editor McGill-Queen's U. Press, 1982—. Recipient rsch. award Can. Coun., 1974-83, 91-94, Am. Coun. Learned Socs., 1976-77, Chalmers prize, 1985, Landon prize, 1987, Grawemeyer award for improving world order, 1993, Biography medal U. B.C., 1994, Trillium prize, 1995, Molson Laureate, 1996; Guggenheim fellow, 1981-85, John David Stout rsch. fellow Victoria U., 1988-89, Univ. fellow Rhodes U., 1990. Fellow Royal Soc. Can., Royal Hist. Soc. (U.K.); mem. Am. Conf. Irish Studies, Phi Beta Kappa. Office: Queens U Dept History Kingston ON Canada K7L 3N6

AKER, SUSAN K. elementary education educator; b. Bklyn., Aug. 4, 1951; d. Mike and Rose Kriegsman; m. David Aker, Sept. 1, 1974; children: Michael, Jessica. BA, CUNY, 1973, MS, 1975, Long Island U., 1976, MS, 1991, Coll. New Rochelle, 1998. Cert. in early childhood edn., elem. edn., spl. edn., libr. sci., sch. adminstrn. and supervision. Tchr. 4th grade Yeshiva of Crown Heights, Bklyn., 1974-75; tchr. 6th grade Hebrew Acad. of Nassau County, Bethpage, N.Y., 1975-76; libr. Jericho (N.Y.) Jewish Ctr., 1978-81, Half-Hollow Hills Pub. Libr., Dix Hills, N.Y., 1978-81; libr. media specialist Uniondale (N.Y.) Free Sch. Dist., 1989-90, Hempstead (N.Y.) Union Free Sch. Dist., 1990-92; tchr. P.S. 105 N.Y.C. Bd. Edn., Bronx, 1993—; adj. prof. Mercy Coll., Yorktown. Internal geography cons. N.Y.C. Bd. Edn., 1996—, staff devel. workshop presenter, 1996—. Contbr. articles to TeacherLink. Grantee United Fedn. Tchrs., 1997, N.Y. Geographic Alliance, 1998, 99, McDonald's Corp., 2001. Mem. ASCD, N.Y. Geographic Alliance, Assn. for Early Childhood Internat., N.Y. Reading Assn., Phi Delta Kappa. Home: 23 Southern Rd Hartsdale NY 10530-2128

AKER, SUZANNE DEVERSE, physical movement educator; b. Kansas City, Mo., Sept. 19, 1926; d. Earnest Hillborn and Clara Maude Scruggs; m. Meredith Eugene Aker, Jan. 28, 1960 (div. Feb. 1977); children: Jan Morrow, Jan Ameen, John Bettis, Elizabeth Aker, Laura Greer. Student, Ballet Theater Sch., 1953; BA, Tulsa U., 1962. Cert. profl. dance tchr. Profl. dancer Burchmann Dancers, Hollywood, N.Y., 1944-45; tchr. Tulsa U., 1959-62; chmn. dept. dance Tex. Tech. U., Lubbock, 1962-69; founding artistic dir., choreographer, tchr. Ballett Lubbock, 1969-2000; phys. movement tchr. Covenant Health Sys., Lubbock, 2000—. Choreographer Tex. Tech. U., 1963-85, Lubbock Theater Ctr., 1965-76, Lubbock Christian U., 1981-90; choreographer, tchr. Wayland Bapt. U., Plainview, Tex., 1979-83. Assoc. Cmty. of Holy Spirit Episcopal Convent, 1985—. Nat. Endowment for Arts grantee, 1980; recipient Pathfinder's award Lubbock C. of C., 1987. Mem. Chi Omega (v.p. 1946), Alpha Psi Omega (hon.), Delta Psi Kappa (hon.). Avocations: icon painting, dance related artwork. Home: 5016 27th St Lubbock TX 79407

AKERLOF, CARL WILLIAM, physics educator; b. New Haven, Mar. 5, 1938; s. Gosta Carl and Rosalie Clara (Hirschfelder) A.; m. Carol Irene Ruska, Sept. 4, 1965; children— Karen Louise, William Gustav BA, Yale U., 1960; PhD, Cornell U., 1967. Research assoc. U. Mich., Ann Arbor, 1966-68, asst. prof., 1968-72, assoc. prof., 1972-78, prof. physics, 1978—. Contbr. articles to profl. jours. Incorporator Ann Arbor Hands-On Mus. Fellow Am. Phys. Soc.; mem. Am. Astron. Soc. Office: U Mich Randall Lab Physics Dept Physics Ann Arbor MI 48109

AKERLOF, GEORGE ARTHUR, economics educator; b. New Haven, June 17, 1940; s. Gosta Carl and Rosalie C. Akerlof; m. Janet Louise Yellen, July 7, 1978; 1 child, Robert. BA, Yale U., 1962; PhD, MIT, 1966; D Econs. (hon.), U. Zurich, Switzerland, 2000. Cassell prof. of money and banking London Sch. Econs., 1978-80; assist. prof. U. Calif., Berkeley, 1966—70, assoc. prof., 1970—77, prof., 1977—78, 1980—; sr. fellow Brookings Instn., Washington, 1994—. Bd. dirs. Nat. Bur. Econ. Rsch., 1997—; mem. bd. editors Quar. Jour. Econs., 1983—, Am. Econ. Rev., 1983-90. Author: An Economic Theorist's Book of Tales, 1984; co-author: Efficiency Wage Theories of Unemployment, 1988; co-editor Jour. Econs. and Politics, 1990—; contbr. articles to profl. jours. Recipient Woodrow Wilson fellow, 1962—63, Cooperative fellow NSF, 1963—66, Fulbright fellow, 1967—68, The Bank of Sweden Prize in Economic Sciences, 2001. Fellow Am. Acad. Arts and Scis.; mem. Am. Econ. Assn. (mem. exec. com. 1988-91, v.p. 1995), Can. Inst. Advanced Rsch. (assoc.), Russell Sage Round Table on Behavioral Econs. Office: U Calif Dept Econs 549 Evans Hall # 3880 Berkeley CA 94720-3880*

AKERS, JAMES ERIC, health facility administrator; b. Jonesboro, Ark., Oct. 14, 1945; s. Ward Eldridge and Dorothy Catherine (Erb) A.; 1 child, William Eric; m. Marie Oreigr, Aug. 31, 1991. BA in Social Sci., Vanderbilt U., 1968; MDiv in Strategic Planning, Louisville Presbyn. Theol. Sem, 1971. Gen. mgr. TGI Fridays, Nashville, 1972-73, Annie Tigues Restaurant & Bar, Jacksonville, Fla., 1973-77; sales rep. Northwestern Mut. Life Ins. Co., Jacksonville, 1977-79, Peter Gregg Mercedes-Benz, Jacksonville, 1979-80; dir. life flight Bapt. Med. Ctr., Jacksonville, 1980-83, dir. spl. projects, 1983-84; dir. mktg. Jacksonville Faculty Practice Assn., 1984-88, v.p. planning, devel. and mktg., 1988—; pres., CEO, Jim Akers and Assocs., Inc., Jacksonville. V.p. mktg. Profl. Biling Systems Inc. subs. JFPA, 1986—, Fin.-Med. Mgmt. Svcs., 1989—, Physician Bus. Svcs. Inc., 1990; pres. Healthcare Mktg. Cons., Jacksonville, 1990-2000; dir. of ops. Health Screen Am., 2000. Master of ceremonies Children's Miracle Network Telethon, Jacksonville, 1983, 84, 89, Am. Heart Assn., Jacksonville, 1988-90; chief auctioneer Sta. WJCT-TV, PBS, Jacksonville, 1983-98; campaign mgr. Senator Bill Bankhead, Jacksonville, 1984; pres. bd. dirs. Suicide Prevention Svcs., Jacksonville, 1983-89. Col. U.S. Army, 1966-96. Mem. Med. Group Mgmt. Assn., Acad. Practice Assembly, Am. Soc. Hosp. Based Emergency Air Med. Svcs. (bd. dirs.), Am. Coll. Healthcare Mktg., Alliance for Healthcare Strategy and Mktg., Acad. Health Svcs. Mktg., N.G. Officers Assn., Ye Mystic Revellers (team leader), Rotary (sec. Mandarin, Fla. 1983-84, Paul Harris fellow 1990). Republican. Presbyterian. Avocations: mountain climbing, flying, whitewater rafting. Home: 8629 Royalwood Dr Jacksonville FL 32256-8447 Office: Jim Akers and Assocs Inc 8795 Como Lake Dr Jacksonville FL 32256

AKERS, KEITH, writer, information technology consultant; b. Athens, Ga., May 15, 1949; s. Lawrence Keith and Jane (Woodroof) A.; m. Kate Lawrence, Feb. 11, 1989. BA magna cum laude, Vanderbilt U., 1971. Cons. Am. Mgmt. Sys., Arlington, Va., 1978-80, Pinkerton Computer Cons., Arlington, 1984-88, Ciber, Denver, 1989-99. Author: A Vegetarian Sourcebook: The Nutrition, Ecology, and Ethics of a Natural Foods Diet, 1983, e Last Religion of Jesus: Simple Living and Nonviolence in Early Christianity, 2000. Vegetarian activist. Mem.: Vegetarian Soc. DC (pres. 1986—88), Vegetarian Soc. Colo. (pres. 1995—96, 1999—2001). Office: Vegetarian Pres PO Box 61273 Denver CO 80206 E-mail: keith@compassionatespirit.com.

AKERS, MICHELLE ANNE, soccer player; b. Santa Clara, Calif., Feb. 1, 1966; BS in Liberal Studies and Health, U. Ctrl. Fla., 1989. Forward Tyreso Football Club, Sweden, 1990, 1992, 1994, Orlando (Fla.) Calibre Soccer Club, 1993, U.S. Women's Nat. Soccer Team, Chgo., 1985—. Author: Face to Face with Michelle Akers: Standing Fast; columnist: Soccer Jr. mag., 1995—, Sidekicks mag., 1994—, 1995—. Named All-Am., Ctrl. Fla. Athlete of Yr., 1988—89, MVP, CONCACAF Qualifying Championship, 1994, U.S. Soccer Female Athlete of Yr., 1990, 1991, ESPN Athlete of Yr., 1985; recipient Hermann Trophy, Golden Boot award, FIFA Women's World Championship, 1991, Silver Ball award, 1991, Gold medal, Atlanta Olympics, 1996. Mem.: Women's Sports Found. (adv. bd. 1992—), U.S. Soccer Fedn. (nat. bd. dirs. 1990—95), Soccer Outreach Internat. (founder 1998). Office: US Soccer Fedn US Soccer House 1801 S Prairie Ave Chicago IL 60616-1319

AKERS, SAMUEL LEE, lawyer; b. Chattanooga, Oct. 20, 1943; s. Shelby Russell and Helen Louise (Crumley) A.; m. Mercedes Lilia Vuksanovic, Mar. 13, 1967; children: Bradford Lee, Camby Leigh. BA, Berry Coll., 1966; JD, Memphis State U., 1974; cert. pub. adminstr., U. Tenn., 2001. Bar: Tenn. 1974, U.S. Dist. Ct. (ea. dist.) Tenn. 1976, U.S. Ct. Appeals (6th cir.) 1985, U.S. Supreme Ct. 1987, U.S. Dist. Ct. (mid. dist.) Tenn. 1989. Trust examiner Office of the Compt. of the Currency, Memphis, 1975-76; assoc. Luther, Anderson, Cleary & Ruth, Chattanooga, 1976-78, 81-84, ptnr., 1985-93, Hatfield Van Cleave & Akers, Chattanooga, 1994, Hatfield Van Cleave Akers & Adams, P.L.C., Chattanooga, 1995-96; spl. agt. FBI, Orlando, Fla., 1978-81; Clk. and Master Chancery Ct. Hamilton County, 11th Jud. Dist., Chattanooga, 1996—. Comml. panel Am. Arbitration Assn., NYC, 1986—96; adv. com. Tenn. Judicial Info., 1998—; treas. State Clerk's Assn. Ea divsn., 2000. Judge adv. Tenn. State Ct. Clk.'s Assn., 2000, County Ofcls. Assn. Tenn., 2001; County Officials Assn. of Tenn., Legis. Com. 2001-03; nominating com. Cmty. Found. Greater Chattanooga, 1999; active Estate Planning Coun. Chattanooga, 1996—; asst. instr. SCUBA cert. Lt. comdr. USNR, 1967-71. Named Outstanding Young Man of Am. Jaycees, 1977. Fellow Chattanooga Bar Assn. (bd. govs. 1995-96, sec.-treas. 1997, pres.-elect 1998, pres. 1999-2000), Chattanooga Bar Found.; mem. Tenn. Bar Assn., Soc. Former Spl. Agts. of the FBI (chmn. Chattanooga chpt. 1987-88, 95-96), County Officials Assn. Tenn. (legis. com. 2002-03). Republican. Roman Catholic. Avocations: jogging, bicycling, hiking, tennis, scuba diving. Home: 106 Westwood Dr Signal Mountain TN 37377-2323 Office: Chancery Ct Tenn 300 Courthouse Hamilton Co Chattanooga TN 37402 E-mail: leeakers@exch.hamiltontn.gov.

AKERS, SAUNDRA RUTH, disability rights advocate; b. Urbana, Ohio, July 21, 1943; d. Henry Albert and Clara Velma (Stultz) Crum; m. Larry Roger Akers, Mar. 1, 1964 (div. Feb. 1986); children: Crystal Annette Castle, H. Roger, Noel Justin, Pride A. Cert. paralegal, Am. Inst. Paralegal Practice. Mgr. Marathon Sta., Columbus, Ohio, 1972—73; nursing assoc., mental health tech., mental health tech. supr. Columbus Devel. Ctr., residential area program planner, vocat. habilitation specialist; disability rights advocate Ohio Legal Rights, Columbus. Liaison Gov.'s Coun. People with Disabilities, 1997—, Ohio Devel. Disability Coun., 1994—97. Author: book of poetry. Sec. Citizen's Com., Hilliard, Ohio, 1973. Mem.: Toastmasters Internat. Avocations: public speaking, creative writing, genealogy. Home: 3260 Colony Hill Ln Columbus OH 43204

AKERS, TOM, JR., cotton broker, consultant; b. Woodford, Okla., May 1, 1919; s. George Tom and Sadie Dean (Jones) A.; m. Eleanor Hoskins, Dec. 23, 1971; children: Tom, Alyce, Peggy, John. BS, Okla. A&M Coll., 1946; postgrad., Stanford U., 1966. Cotton classer Chickasha Cotton Oil Co., (Okla.), 1936-41; exec. v.p. Calcot. Ltd., Bakersfield, Calif., 1946-80; owner, ptnr. Tom Akers-Cotton, Bakersfield, 1980—. Cons. Algodonera Comercial Mexicana, 1980—, Central Cooperativa Nacional, Asuncion, Paraguay, 1982, Cooperativa Agropecuaria, Tegucigal, Paraguay, 1983, Algodonera Del Sur, Honduras, 1983, cons., Cotton Trading Corp., Goondiwindi, Queensland, 1990, cons. Zimbabwe Cotton Mktg. Bd., Harare, Zimbabwe, 1994, cons., ACDI/VOCA Cooperative Union Project Addis Ababa, Ethiopia, 1998. Campaign chmn. 18th Congl. Dist. Jimmy Carter for Pres., 1976-80; campaign chmn. Kern County for Tom Bradley for Gov., 1982; mem. Kern County Democratic Central Com, 1978—. Served to maj. inf. AUS, 1941-46, PTO. Named Rotarian of Yr. East Bakersfield Rotary, 1974 Mem. Nat. Cotton Mktg. Study Group of U.S. Congress, Nat. Cotton Adv. Com. Clubs: Bakersfield Trade (dir. 1960-70). Lodges: East Bakersfield Rotary. Democrat. Congregationalist. Home: 4 Greenfair Ct Bakersfield CA 93309-2423 Office: Tom Akers-Cotton 1716 Oak St Rm 7 Bakersfield CA 93301-3040

AKERSON, DANIEL F. investment company executive; With MCI Comms. Corp., 1983—93, exec. v.p., 1987—90, pres., COO, 1992—93; gen. ptnr. Forstmann Little & Co., 1993—96; CEO Nextel Comms., Inc., 1996—99, chmn., 1996—2000; investor, co-chmn. Eagle River, Inc.; chmn., CEO XO Comms., 1999—2003; mng. dir. The Carlyle Group, 2003—. Bd. dirs. Nextel Comms., Inc., Am. Express Co. Office: 1001 Pennsylvania Ave, NW Ste 220 South Washington DC 20004 Fax: 703-433-4747.

AKESSON, ANDERS GUSTAV, lawyer; b. Akarp, Skane, Sweden, Sept. 28, 1951; s. Evald and Sonja (Mansson) A.; m. Helene Bjorngren. LLB, Lund U., Copenhagen, 1975, MusM, 1983. Ednl. cons. Swedish Bd. Edn., Stockholm, Sweden, 1976-79; lawyer Malmö, Sweden, 1978—. Co-founder Nordic Acad. Food and Wine. Author: Corporate Law, 1981, Real Estate Law, 1983, European Community Law for Swedish Companies, 1991, Wine Law, 1994. Fellow: Inst. Dirs.; mem.: Nordic Food Law Assn. (chmn.), Sabre d'Or (commanderie de Bordeaux), Wine and Food Soc., Chaine des Rotisseurs, Internat. Wine Law Assn. (bd. dirs., Scandinavian chmn.), Royal Coll. Organists London. Avocations: organ playing, music, wine tasting. Office: EuroLaw PO Box 4178 S-20313 Malmö Sweden E-mail: adm@eurolaw.se.

AKESSON, NORMAN BERNDT, agricultural engineer, emeritus educator; b. Grandin, N.D., June 12, 1914; s. Joseph Berndt and Jennie (Nonthen) A.; m. Margaret Blasing, Dec. 14, 1946; children: Thomas Ryan (dec.), Judith Elizabeth. BS in Agrl. Engring., N.D. State U., 1940; MS in Agrl. Engring, U. Idaho, 1942. Registered profl. engr., Calif. Rsch. fellow U. Idaho, 1940-42; physicist U.S. Navy, Bremerton, Wash., 1942-47; asst. prof. agrl. engring. U. Calif., Davis, 1947-56, assoc. prof., 1956-62, prof., 1962-84, prof. emeritus, 1984—; engring. cons., 1984—. Cons. United Fruit Honduras, 1959, Israel, 1968, WHO Mosquito Control, 1969-84, FAO Aircraft in Agr., 1971-84, Japan, 1972, Egypt, 1980, China, 1985, Can. Forest Svc. Herbicide Application, 1987, U. Fla. Aircraft Application Herbicides, 1987; chmn. expert com. on vector control equipment WHO, 1976; chmn. com. on aircraft for agr. Coun. for Agrl. Sci. and Tech., 1982; pres. Calif. Weed Control Conf., 1966. Author: The Use of Aircraft in Agriculture, 1974, Pesticide Application Equipment and Techniques, 1979, Aircraft Use for Mosquito Control, 1981; contbr. over 330 articles to profl. jours. Recipient research and devel. award FAO, 1973-74, research and devel. award WHO, 1978; Fulbright fellow, Eng. and East Africa, 1957-58. Fellow Am. Soc. Agrl. Engrs. (chmn. Pacific region 1965, dir. 1972-74, assoc. editor tech. publs. 1983-93); mem. ASTM (chair E35-22 1982-84), Am. Chemical Soc., Nat. Agrl. Aviation Assn., Calif. Agrl. Aviation Assn., Nat. Mosquito Control Assn., Entomol. Soc. Am., Weed Sci. Soc. Am. (editl. bd. 1968-70), Western Weed Soc. (hon.), Calif. Weed Sci. Soc. (hon.), Farmers Club (London), Sigma Xi, Phi Kappa Phi, Alpha Zeta, Alpha Gamma Rho. Republican. Home: 1515 Shasta Dr # 1515 Davis CA 95616-6691 Office: U Calif Bio-Agr Engring Dept Davis CA 95616-5294 E-mail: NbAkesson@ucdavis.edu.

AKFIRAT, GOKHAN LUT, neurologist; b. Eregli, Zonguldak, Turkey, Feb. 9, 1971; s. Mehmet Salih and Aybike Akfirat; m. Umran Akfirat. MD, Hacettepe U., Ankara, Turkey, 1994. Diplomate Ednl. Commn. Fgn. Med. Grads., cert. N.Y. ltd. med. licence. Resident in internal medicine N.Y. Med. Coll., Our Lady of Mercy Med. Ctr.; resident in neurology N.Y. Med. Coll., Westchester Med. Ctr., Valhalla, 1997—2000; attending neurologist, clin. instr. N.Y. Med. Coll. Met. Hosp. Ctr., N.Y.C., 2001—; gen. med. practitioner Bolaman Health Ctr., Ordu, Turkey, 1994—95; resident in neurosurgery Uludag U., Bursa, Turkey, 1995—96; neurologist, fellow in neurorehab. NYU Hosp. for Joint Diseases, N.Y.C., 2000—01. Contbr. articles to profl. jours. Mem.: AMA, Am. Acad. Neurology. Home: 33 Barker Ave Apt 5F White Plains NY 10601 Office: NY Med Coll Metropolitan Hosp Neurology Dept 1901 First Ave Ste 1316 New York NY 10029 Home Fax: 775 406 9561. Personal E-mail gakfirat@ureach.com. Business E-Mail: neurology@doctor.com.

AKHAVAN, FARHAD, electrical engineer; b. Tehran, Iran, Dec. 30, 1967 came to U.S., 1989; s. Akbar Akhavan and Shahpar Karimi. MS in Physics MSEE, U. Mo., Rolla, 1992, PhD in Elec. Engring., 1998. Postdoctoral rsch assoc. Optical Scis. Ctr. U. Ariz., Tucson, 1998-2000, asst. rsch. scientist Optical Scis. Ctr., 2000; sr. optical engr. Nortel Networks Inc., Wilmington Mass., 2000—. Advisor Nat. Security Agy., Md., 1998-2000. Contbr. articles to profl. jours. Grantee NASA, 2000. Mem. IEEE, Optical Soc. Am., Soc. Optical Engrs. Avocation: classical readings of ancient civilizations. Office: Nortel Networks Inc 299 Ballardvale Wilmington MA 01887 E-mail farhad@nortelnetworks.com.

AKHAVI, SHAHROUGH, educator; b. Tehran, Iran, June 10, 1940; BA Brown U., 1962; MA, Harvard U., 1964; PhD, Columbia U., 1969. Lectr. U Calif., Davis, 1970-73; asst. prof. U. S.C., Columbia, 1973-77, assoc. prof. 1977-84, prof., 1984—. Editor Mid-East series SUNY Press, Albany, 1981—editor: Series in Middle East Politics, History and Law, 2001--; co-editor Oxford Ency. of the Modern Islamic World, 1995; sr. cons. editor Oxford Dictionary of Islam, 2003. Recipient Postdoctoral rsch. award, Ford Found. 1975—76, Am. Coun. Learned Soc. & Am. Rsch. Ctr., N.Y.C., 1980; Fulbright scholar, 1991, Social Sci. Rsch. Coun. sr. scholar. Mem.: Mid-East Inst. Mid-East Studies Assn., Soc. Iranian Studies (book rev. editor 1981—96 pres.-elect 2001—02, pres. 2002—03). Office: U SC Dept Govt & Internat Study Gambrell Hl Columbia SC 29208-0001

AKHIGBE, AIGBE, education educator, researcher; arrived in U.S., 1983; s Gabriel and Mercy Akhigbe. BS, Univ. Ibadan, Ibadan, Nigeria, 1978; MS Univ. La., Lafayette, La., 1984; MBA, Univ. Houston, Houston, 1985, PhD 1991. Engr. Gulf Oil Co., Lagos, Nigeria, 1978—79, Nigerian Nat. Petroleum Co., Lagos, Nigeria, 1979—82; tchg. asst. Univ. Houston, 1985—89 1990—91; vis. instr. Tex. So. Univ., Houston, 1989—90; prof. Fla. Atlantic Univ., Boca Raton, 1991—2000; Moyer chair and prof. Univ. Akron, Ohio 2000—. Contbr. articles to profl. jours. Achievements include wrote numerous academic articles on how the fin. policies made by co. impact their shareholders globally ranked among the top authors in finance. Office: Univ Akron 259 S Broadway Akron OH 44325

AKHTAR, MUHAMMAD I. neurologist, researcher; arrived in U.S., 1994; s Akhtar Hussain and Mushtary Begum; m. Huda Mohsin Qureshi; children Hadiya children: Sumaiyaa. MD, Sindh Med. Coll., Karachi, 1991; postgrad. Ohio State U., 2002. Chief resident Ohio State U. Med. Ctr., Columbus, 2001 cons. neurologist, 1999—2002, So. Ohio Med. Ctr., Portsmouth, 2003—. Scholar, Am. Neurol. Assn., 2002. Mem.: AMA, W.Va. Med. Assn., Columbus Med. Assn., Am. Acad. Neurology (resident scholarship 2002), Pakistan Internat. Neurosci. Soc., So. Med. Assn. (hon.), Am. Headache Soc. (hon.) Pakistan Med. Coun. (hon.). Home: 3351 Seneca Dr Portsmouth OH 45662 Office: So Ohio Med Ctr 1735 27th St C Ste 102 Portsmouth OH 45662 Office Fax: 740-355-9668. Personal E-mail: drakhtar@hotmail.com. Business E-Mail AkhtarM@somc.org.

AKHTER, SYED H. business educator; b. Feb. 11, 1949; came to U.S., 1976 s. Sultan and Masooda Akhter; m. Marita J. Forman. PhD, U. Okla., Norman 1985. Instr. We. Ill. U., Macomb, 1977-79, Marquette U., Milw., 1979-81, asst. prof., 1985-92, assoc. prof., 1992—; grad. asst. U. Okla., Norman, 1981-85. Author: Global Marketing, 1995. Mem. Am. Mktg. Assn., Acad. Internat. Bus. Assn. Global Bus. Avocations: tennis, reading, music, walking, yoga. Home 9455 St Michael's Ct Franklin WI 53132 E-mail: syed.akhter@marquette.edu.

AKIMOTO, MARTIN WAYNE, mental health services professional; b. Chgo., Ill., July 24, 1949; s. Ned E. and Emmy (Tsujimoto) A.; m. Barbara Wendley, June 11, 1983; children: Emily, Ellen. BS in Psychology, U. Utah 1972, MSW, 1974. Cert. suicide intervention trainer, Calif.; lic. social worker. Social worker Protective Svc. Davis County, Div. Family Svc., Utah, 1974; pvt. practice Simi Psychotherapy Group, Simi Valley, Calif., 1979-87; field work supr. U. So. Calif., 1983-85; sr. psychiat. social worker Simi Valley Mental Health, Ventura County Mental Health Dept, 1975-76, Conejo Valley Mental Health, 1976-87; coord. outpatient children's svc. Ventura County Mental Health, Thousand Oaks, Calif., 1987-88; regional supr. children's svcs. Ventura County Mental Health Dept., Thousand Oaks, Calif., 1988-92, program supr. options program, 1992-2000; clin. program mgr. Butte County Dept. Behavioral Health, Chico, Calif., 2000—. Vol. lectr., rap session leader Planned Parenthood of Utah, 1972-73. Office: Butte County Dept Behavioral Health Youth Svc Adminstrn 500 Cohasset Ste 28 Chico CA 95926 E-mail: makimoto@buttecounty.net.

AKIN, STEVEN PAUL, financial company executive; b. Hackensack, N.J., Apr. 6, 1945; s. Richard Ernest and Lucille F. (Mosher) A.; m. Jane Goddard, Nov. 24, 1973; children: Kyla, Susan. BA in Econs., Ohio Wesleyan U., 1969; postgrad., Columbia U., Harriman, N.Y., 1986. Lic. series 7 and 24, NASD, NYSE. Mgmt. trainee customer svc. mgmt. N.Y. Telephone, 1969-78; asst. v.p. customer svc. United Tel. Co. Ohio, Mansfield, 1978-85; v.p. ops. United Tel. Co. Ind., Warsaw, 1985-86, United Tel. Co. Midwest, Overland Park, Kans., 1986-87; sr. v.p., then pres. US Sprint, Kansas City, Mo., 1987-92; pres. Fidelity Retail Investor Svcs., Boston, 1992-95, Fidelity Brokerage Svcs., Inc., Boston, 1995-97, Fidelity Retail Customer Svcs., Boston, 1995-96; pres., chief info. officer Fidelity Investments Sys. Co., Boston, 1997-99; pres. Fidelity Capital, 1999—2002; pres., CEO Colt Telecomms., London, 2002—. Pres. Mansfield Symphony, 1985—86, Lyric Opera, Kansas City, Kans., 1991—92; trustee Kents Hill Sch., Kents Hill, Maine, 2002—, Boston Lyric Opera, 2002—. Office: Colt Telecomms Beaufort House 15 St Botolph St EC3A 7QN London England

AKIN, W. TODD, congressman, former state legislator; b. N.Y.C., July 5, 1947; m. Lulli Boe, 1971; six children. BS, Worcester Poly. Inst.; MDiv, Covenant Theol. Sem. Mo. State rep. Dist. 86, 1988-2000; corp. mgmt. Laclede Steel Co.; bus. mgr., educator; former mktg. profl. IBM Computer Systems; mem. U.S. Congress from 2d Mo. dist., 2001—, mem. armed svcs. com., small bus. com., sci. com., chmn. workforce, empowerment and govt. programs subcom. Officer Army Engrs. Republican. Office: 117 Cannon Ho Office Bldg Washington DC 20515-2502*

AKINAKA, ASA MASAYOSHI, lawyer; b. Honolulu, Jan. 19, 1938; s. Arthur Yoshinori and Misako (Miyoshi) A.; m. Betsy Yoshie Kurata, Oct. 7, 1967; children— David Asa Yoshio, Sarah Elizabeth Sachie. BA magna cum laude, Yale U., 1959; postgrad. (Rotary Found. fellow), Trinity Coll., Oxford U., 1959-60, Yale Law Sch., 1960-61; LL.B., Stanford Law Sch., 1964. Bar: Hawaii bar 1964. Research asst. U.S. Senator Oren Long, Washington, 1961-62; pvt. practice law Honolulu, 1964—. Bd. visitors Stanford Law Sch., 1971-74. Mem. Am. Bar Assn., Hawaii State Bar Assn. (pres. 1977), Nat. Conf. Bar Presidents, Pacific Club, YMCA (bd. dirs., v.p. 1970-81). Democrat. Episcopalian. Office: PO Box 1035 Honolulu HI 96808-1035

AKINS, GEORGE CHARLES, accountant; b. Feb. 22, 1917; s. Guy Brookins and Eugenie (Swan) A.; m. Jane Babcock, Mar. 27, 1945 (dec. May 3, 2003). AA, Sacramento City Coll., 1941. Acct., auditor Calif. Bd. Equalization, Dept. Fin., Sacramento, 1940—44; contr.-treas. DeVons Jewelers, Sacramento, 1944—73, v.p., contr., 1973—80, v.p., CFO, dir., 1980—84; individual acctg. and tax practice Sacramento, 1944—. Contbg. author: Portfolio of Accounting Systems for Small and Medium-Sized Business, 1968, Portfolio of Accounting Systems for Small and Medium-Sized Business, rev. edit., 1977. Acct., cons. Mercy Children's Hosp. Guild, Sacramento, 1957—77. With USAF, 1942. Mem.: Northwestern Pacific Railroad Hist. Soc., Internat. Platform Assn., Calif. Hist. Soc., Nat. Soc. Accts., Soc. Calif. Pioneers, Mendocino County Hist. Soc. (life), USN League (life), Drake Navigators Guild, Sacramento County Hist. Soc. (life), Crocker Art Mus. (life), Comstock, Commonwealth Club of Calif. Republican. Roman Catholic. Home and Office: 96 S Humboldt St Willits CA 95490-3539

AKINS, MARILYN PARKER, interior designer; b. Oak Park, Ill., Dec. 28, 1932; d. Clifford and Evelyn (Davenport) Parker; children: Tamlyn Akins, Caryn A., Lauralyn A. Kimont, Sharyn A. Student, Beloit Coll., 1951-53; Cert. of Grad., Harrington Inst. Interior Des., 1971. Owner/interior designer Marilyn Akins Interiors, Hinsdale, Ill., 1969-90, Akins & Assocs., Ltd., Hinsdale, 1990—. Projects pub. in Accessory Mag., Chgo. Tribune, Traditional Homes, Chgo. Home and Garden, Windows & Walls, New Ideas for Decorating, Perfect Home, Furnishings Daily, Met. Home, 1001 Home Ideas, N.Y. Times, numerous others. Mem. designer adv. bd. Burlington House, 1983-86; adv. bd. dirs. Ray Sch. Design, Chgo., 1987-90; design del. People's Rep. of China, 1985. Mem. Am. Soc. Interior Design (Young Mem. award Ill. 1979, Presdl. citation Ill. chpt. 1984, Medal of Honor 1986). Republican. Avocations: tennis, travel. Home: 424 S Garfield Ave Hinsdale IL 60521-4419 Office: 26 E 1st St Hinsdale IL 60521-4102

AKINS, VAUGHN EDWARD, retired engineering company executive; b. Gowanda, N.Y., Sept. 28, 1934; s. Elsworth D. and Alice (Carlton) A.; m. Muriel M. Hoglund, May 15, 1960 (dec. 1992); children: Sonja L., Coleen R., Joseph E. Student, U.S. Naval Schs., 1956-57, IBM Engring. Sch., 1961-65. Lab. specialist IBM, Poughkeepsie, N.Y., Boulder, Colo., East Fishkill, N.Y., 1959-65; test mgr. Semi, Phoenix, 1969-74; mgr. computer-aided mfg. and test engring. semicondr. R&D Motorola Corp., Mesa, Ariz., 1974-84; applications mgr. (SIM) Motorola Corp. New Enterprises Group, Mesa, 1984-86; mgr. computer integrated mfg. semicondr. products sector Motorola Corp., Phoenix, 1986-87; with start-up team SEMATECH, Inc., Austin, Tex., 1988-93, dir. internat. standards programs, 1989-93, mgr. incubator programs, 1992; mgr. strategic integration Motorola Ctr. Advanced Computer Products, Austin, 1993-96, ret. Motorola Wireless Sys. Ctr., Austin, 1996-98; cons. industry-strategic mktg. rsch. futurist, 2000—. Precinct committeeman N.Y. State Conservative Party, 1963; instr. first aid ARC, 1971-78; chair U.S. exec. com. S.E.M.I., Inc., mem. exec. com. internat. standard program. With USNR, 1956-59. Mem. IEEE (sr.), NRA, Mensa, Electrochem. Soc. (cons. to exec. bd., co-chmn. founding com. Automation in Mfg. chpt., exec. com. electronics divsn. 1985-92). Republican. Fundamentalist. Home: 4825 Davis Ln #1621 Austin TX 78749-4583 E-mail: vakins@austin.rr.com.

AKINS, ZANE VERNON, association executive; b. Bethel, Kans., Apr. 13, 1940; s. Gerald Vernon and Vesta Jean (Rutherford) A.; m. Kay Ellen Cowan, Aug. 17, 1963; children: Michael Scott, Deborah Lynn, Christine Sue. BS in Agriculture, U. Mo., 1962. Farmer, 1962-64; svc. technician No. Ohio Breeders Assn., Tiffin, 1964-66; program dir. Holstein Assn. Am., Brattleboro, Vt., 1966-73, mgr. sire devel. svc., 1973-77, adminstrv. asst., 1977-78, CEO, 1978-90; exec. v.p. Holstein-Friesian Svcs., Inc., Brattleboro, 1978-90; pres. Zane Akins and Assocs., West Brattleboro, 1991—. Pres., chmn. bd. dirs. Nat. Integrated Techs. Inc., 1996—; bd. dirs. Earthwide Assocs., Inc., pres. 1994—; pres. A&S Assocs., Ltd., 1995—; bd. dirs. Vt. Nat. Bank, 1987-2000, Earthwide Sys. Inc., v.p., 1995—; v.p. Earthwide Products Corp., 1996—; bd. dirs. Vt. Fin. Svcs., 1987-2000, chmn. exec. com., 1995-96, chmn. audit com., 1996-97, chmn. loan com., 1997-98; regional leader Primerica Fin. Svcs., 1991—; chmn. bd. dirs. Anitech Internat. Inc., Boulder, Colo., 1991-92; trustee N.E. Delta/Vt. Dental Soc., Inc., 1990-99, chmn., 1995-99; chmn. bd. NEDA, 1999-; pres. Vt. Natural Food Products Inc., 2001--. Bd. dirs. Windham County United Way, 1980-84; corporator Brattleboro Meml. Hosp., 1980—, chmn. pub. rels. com., 1982-83, bd. dirs., 1983-86; pres. Windham County Humane Soc., 1992-93; bd. dirs. Brattleboro Area Boys & Girls Club, 1998-2002, treas., 1999-2002. Sears & Roebuck scholar, Freshman Curators scholar, Borden's scholar, U. Mo., 1958-59, Sophomore Curators scholar, Campus Chest scholar, 1958-60; recognized as Man of the Yr. Tri-State Breeders Coop., 1984; recipient Citation of Merit U. Mo., 1986. Mem. Purebred Dairy Cattle Assn. (bd. dirs. 1978-90, Recognition award 1991), Nat. Soc. Livestock Records Assn. (v.p. 1982-84), Nat. Pedigree Livestock Coun. (pres. 1984-86, sec., treas. 1989—, Disting. Svc. award 1993), Nat. Coop. Dairy Herd Improvement Programs (policy bd. 1980-90), Genomics Inst., Boston Dist. Export Coun., Brattleboro C. of C. (bd. dirs. 1979-81), Alpha Zeta (Centennial Honor Roll 1997), Alpha Gamma Rho (regional v.p. 1980-84, bd. dirs. 1984-90, grand pres. 1986-89, Man of Yr. award Chgo. Alumni chpt. 1991). Congregationalist. Home and Office: 177 Palermo Pl Lady Lake FL 32159-0094

AKIYAMA, CAROL LYNN, motion picture industry executive; BA magna cum laude, U. So. Calif., 1968, JD, 1971. Bar: Calif. Atty. NLRB, Los Angeles, 1971-75, ABC-TV, Hollywood, Calif., 1975-79, So. Calif. Edison, Rosemead, 1980-81; asst. gen. atty. CBS Inc., Los Angeles, 1981-82; sr. v.p. Alliance of Motion Picture and TV Producers, Sherman Oaks, Calif., 1982-88; ind. producer and writer TV, motion pictures and multimedia/new techs., Woodland Hills, Calif., 1988—. Cons. entertainment industry; founding ptnr. Bierstedt, Akiyama and Assocs., Woodland Hills, 1988—. Mem.: Phi Beta Kappa, Phi Kappa Phi. E-mail: katramber@earthlink.net.

AKIYAMA, TOSHIO, cardiologist, educator, researcher; b. Shimizu, Japan, Mar. 10, 1941; came to U.S., 1968; m. Akiko Okamura Akyama; children: Naoko, Sachiko. MD, Kyoto Prefectural U. Med., 1966. Cert. in internal medicine, specialty in cardiovasc. disease. Rotating intern U.S. Naval Hosp., Yokosuka, Japan, 1966—67; med. resident, 3d internal medicine dept. Kyoto Prefectural U. Medicine, 1967; staff physician Atomic Bomb Casualty Commn., Hiroshima, Japan, 1967—68; intern Rochester Gen. Hosp., 1968-69, resident in medicine, 1969-70, Strong Meml. Hosp.-U. Rochester, 1970-71, resident in cardiology, 1972-73; fellow in cardiology Emory U., Atlanta, 1971-72, U. Chgo., 1973-75; dir. heart sta. Strong Meml. Hosp., Rochester; prof. medicine with unltd. tenure U. Rochester Sch. Medicine, 1993—. Reviewer NIH study sect. Biomed. Tech. Spl. Emphasis Panel; cons. Exec. com. for Japanese Med. Specialist Joint commn. Mem. editl. bd. Jour. Electrocardiology, Japanese Circulation Jour., Acta Medica Mem. Biologica; contbr. over 150 articles to profl. jours. Chmn. Rochester Hamamatsu Sister City Com., chmn., 1998-2000. Fellow Am. Coll. Cardiology; mem. Am. Heart Assn., N.Am. Soc. of Pacing and Electrophysiology, Japanese Med. Soc. (exec. com. joint commn. med. specialist sys.), Japanese Clin. Cardiology Soc. Office: U Rochester Med Ctr Dept Cardiology 601 Elmwood Ave Box 679 Rochester NY 14642-8679 Office Fax: 585-275-1667. E-mail: toshio_akiyama@urmc.rochester.edu.

AKKARA, JOSEPH AUGUSTINE, chemist, educator; b. Feb. 22, 1938; came to U.S., 1964; naturalized, 1980; s. Augustine Aippu Akkara and Theresa Anthony Kolapran; m. Mary Ann Malaickel, Aug. 18, 1969; children: Augustine Viju, Jeena Theresa. PhD in Biochemistry, U. Mo., 1969. Med. rschr. Med. Coll. Trivandrum, Kerala, India, 1959-61; tech. asst. Ctrl. Food Technol. Rsch. Inst., Mysore, India, 1961-64; grad. asst., rsch. assoc. Sch. Medicine U. Mo., Columbia, 1964-69; rsch. assoc. Rockefeller U., N.Y.C., 1969-71, Brookdale Hosp. Med. Ctr., Bklyn., 1971-73, chief radioassay, 1973-80; sr. scientist Med. Rsch. Inst., Worcester, Mass., 1980-81; biochemist stat. Toxicology Svc. Boston, 1981-84; rsch. chemist U.S. Army Natick Rsch. and Engring. Ctr., 1984-99; program dir. NSF, 1999—. Adj. faculty Framingham State Coll., 1996-99; mem. biotechnology adv. bd. Mass. Bay Coll.; advisor NRC; bd. dirs. Invention Evaluation. Recipient R&D award U.S. Army, 1992, 96, Inventor of Yr. award U.S. Army Soldier Sys. commd., 1998. Mem. Materials Rsch. Soc., Am. Chem. Soc., N.Y. Acad. Scis., Kerala Assn. New Eng. (pres. 1986-87), Indian Assn. Greater Boston (sec. 1986-88, 1st v.p. 1988-89), Lions Club, Rotary, Sigma Xi (pres. Natick chpt. 1998-99). Roman Catholic. Achievements include patents and publications in synthesis, modification, characterization, and applications of polymers and materials for electro-optic and high performance multifunctional applications; enzymology, nutrition, endocrinology, analytical chemistry, and research program management. Home: 7520 Walnut Hill Ln Falls Church VA 22042-3539 E-mail: jakkara@nsf.gov., jaakkara@aol.com.

AKMAKJIAN, ALAN PAUL, English language, literature and creative writing educator; b. Highland Park, Mich., July 18, 1948; s. Kizer and Mary Elizabeth (Goshgarian) A. BS, MA, Ea. Mich. U., 1974; student, Oxford (Eng.) U., 1979; PhD, Wayne State U., 1979; MA, Calif. State U., San Francisco, 1991; PhD, St. John's U., Jamaica, N.Y., 1995, U. Tex. Instr./area coord. Poets in the Schs., Santa Clara, Calif., 1984-91; asst. prof. English and creative writing St. John's U., 1996—. Appointed citizen amb. in linguistics, language and culture to India, 1996; hon. adv. coun. Am. Biographical Ctr., Internat. Biographical Ctr.; spkr. cir. adv. Nat. Rep. Congrl. Com. and Pres. George Bush; sec.-gen. Rsch. Coun. Internat. Biog. Ctr., Am. Biog. Inst., 2000—. Author: (books of poetry) Treading Pages of Water, 1992, Grounded Angels, 1993, Let the Sun Go, 1993, California Picnic, 1993, Breaking the Silence, 1993, California Picnic and Other Poems, 1996; contbr. articles to profl. jours.; translator. Mem. Rep. Nat. Com., Mich. State Rep. Com. Recipient award Cranbrook Art Acad., Mich., 1979, NEA/Calif. Arts Coun., 1984; univ. fellow U. Tex., Dallas, 1994, 95, 96, 97, St. John's U., 1994, Jordan fellow for the Arts, 1995, 96, 97, Republican of Yr. award, 2000, 02; grantee Alex Manoogian Cultural Fund, Mich., 1992, Tex. Pub. Ednl. grantee, 1995, 96, 97,cert. of recognition, Nat. Rep. Party. Mem. MLA, PEN, Acad. Am. Poets, Nat. Women's Book Club, PEN West, Poetry Soc. Am., Am. Comparative Lit. Assn., Mich. Authors and Illustrators, So. Comparative Lit. Assn., Beyond Baroque Lit. Arts Ctr., McKinney Ave. Contemporary Poets House, Detroit Hall Fame, Contemporary Authors, Writer's Garret, Associated Writing Programs, Internat. Honor Soc. Address: 1919 Greenleaf Dr Royal Oak MI 48067

AKMAN, VAROL, computer engineer, educator; b. Antalya, Turkey, June 8, 1957; s. Mustafa Mucahittin and Seviye Sevim (Ersoz) A.; m. Berrin Ozmen, Feb. 10, 1989; 2 children, Beril, Zeynep. BS, Middle East Tech. U., 1979, MS, 1980; PhD, Rensselaer Poly. Inst., 1985. Vis. asst. prof. Rijksuniversiteit Utrecht, Holland, 1985-86; sr. rschr. Centrum voor Wiskunde en Informatica, Amsterdam, 1986-88; asst. prof. Bilkent U., Ankara, Turkey, 1988-90, assoc. prof., 1990-95, prof., 1995—. Chair Dept. Phil. Bilkent U., 2003—. Author: Unobstructed Shortest Paths in Polyhedral Environments, 1987; editor: Intelligent CAD Systems II: Implementational Issues, 1989, Modeling and Using Context, 2001; mem. editl. bd. Computers & Graphics, 1988—2002, First Monday, 2002. With Turkish Armed Forces, 1989. Recipient Rsch. Excellence award Scientific and Tech. Rsch. Coun. Turkey, 1989, Middle East Tech. U. Parlar Found., 1990; scholarship grantee Fulbright Found., 1980-85. Mem.: Fulbright Alumni Assn., Am. Assn. for Artificial Intelligence. Avocations: poetry, swimming, basketball. Office: Bilkent U Dept Computer Engring Bilkent Ankara 06533 Turkey

AKOS, FRANCIS, violinist, conductor; b. Budapest, Hungary, Mar. 30, 1922; came to U.S., 1954; s. Karoly and Rose (Reti) Weinberg; m. Phyllis Malvin Sommers, June 7, 1981; children from previous marriage— Katherine Elizabeth, Judith Margaret. Baccalaureate, Budapest, 1941; MA, Franz Liszt Acad. Music, Budapest, 1940, PhD, 1941. Concertmaster, Budapest Symphony Orch., 1945-46, Royal Opera and Philharmonic Soc., Budapest, 1947-48, Gothenburg (Sweden) Symphony Orch., 1948-50, Municipal Opera (now Deutsche Oper), West Berlin, Ger., 1950-54, Mpls. Symphony Orch., 1954, asst. concertmaster, Chgo. Symphony Orch., 1955—, concertmaster emeritus, 1997—, also performed as soloist; performed at Salzburg Festival, 1948, Scandinavian Festival, Helsinki, Finland, 1950, Berlin Festival, 1951, Prades Festival, 1953, Bergen Festival, 1962, Vienna Festival, 1962, founder, condr., Chgo. Strings, chamber orch., 1961, condr., Fox River Valley Symphony, Aurora, Ill., 1965-73, Chicago Heights (Ill.) Symphony, 1975-79, Highland Park Strings, 1979—. Prizewinner Hubay competition, Budapest, 1939, Remenyi competition, Budapest, 1939 Home: 1310 Maple Ave Evanston IL 60201-4325 Office: 220 S Michigan Ave Chicago IL 60604-2596

AKRE, DONALD J. school system administrator; Supt. Selby (S.D.) Area Sch. Dist. State finalist Nat. Supt. Yr., 1992. Office: PO Box 222 Selby SD 57472-0222

AKRIDGE, PAUL BAI, business consultant; b. Chgo., July 15, 1952; s. Andrew Albert and Lois (LeMoyne) (McCrary) A.; m. Carrie O. Johnson, July 2, 1977; children: Anike Johnson, Akili Johnson BA, DePauw U., 1974; MA in Polit. Sci., U. Wis., 1975, MA in Pub. Policy and Adminstrn., 1978, PhD in Polit. Sci., 1979; cert. in bus. adminstrn., U. Pa., 1983. Tchr. Aga Khan Secondary Sch., Kampala, Uganda, 1973; policy analyst State of Wis., 1976-77; asst. prof. polit. sci. U. Mo., St. Louis, 1979-83; fellow Washington U., St. Louis, 1982-83; program mgr. pub. affairs IBM, Washington, 1983-88; mgr. corp. and sci. programs IBM Asia/Pacific Group, Tokyo, 1988-91; acad. rels. mgr. IBM U.S., Norwalk, Conn., 1991-94; program dir. pub. affairs IBM Corp. Hdqs., Washington, 1994-2000; pres. Worldwise Svcs., Inc., Mitchellville, Md., 2001—. Vice-chmn. Forum for World Affairs; bd. cons. U.S.-Japan Project, Joint Ctr. for Polit. and Econ. Studies, Washington; chmn. behavioral and social sci. panel NSF; info. policy com. U.S. Coun. for Internat. Bus., 1995—2000; policy and govt. rels. coun. Info. Industry Assn., 1995-2000; global info. infrastructure com. Info. Tech. Industry Coun., 1995—2000; telecom. task force Pacific Econ. Cooperation Coun., 1995-2000; adv. bd. internat. baccalaureate program Ctrl. H.S., Prince George's County, Md., 1995-98; adj. assoc. prof. bus., Grad. Sch. Mgmt. and Tech., U. Md. Univ. Coll., 2002-; vis. assoc. rsch. scholar, Internat. Ctr. Transcultural Edn., U. Md. College Park, 2003—. Mem. edit. bd. Pub. Adminstrn. Rev.; mem. adv. bd. AAAS Scis. Next Wave e-zine, 1999—2002. Alumni bd. dirs. DePauw U., bd. visitors; bd. dirs. Am. Lung Assn. Eastern Mo.; fellows conf. planning com. Ford Found.mem. governance and pub. policy bd. visitors LaFollette Sch. Pub. Affairs, U. Wis., Madison, 2001—. Pullman Found. scholar, 1970-73; Ford Found. fellow, 1978-79, Nat. Assn. Schs. Pub. Affairs and Adminstrn. fellow, 1981-82, fellow East-West Ctr., Hawaii, 1982, postdoctoral fellow NRC, 1982-83, Libr. fellow Yale U., 1993-94; Edison Electric Inst. grant, 1982-83. Mem. Am. C. of C. in Japan, Japan Afro-Am. Friendship Assn., Am. Soc. Pub. Adminstrn. (bd. dirs. Nat. Capital Area chpt.), St. Louis Com. on Fgn. Rels., Nat. Conf. Black Polit. Scientists, World Future Soc., Concerned Black Men, East-West Ctr. Alumni Assn., 100 Black Men of Stamford, Conn., Prince George's C. of C. (co-chmn. internat. bus. com. 2002-). Home and Office: 930 Lake Front Dr Mitchellville MD 20721-2951 Fax: 509-351-2366. E-mail: pbai@starpower.net.

AKSEN, GERALD, arbitrator, lawyer, educator; b. N.Y.C., Feb. 16, 1930; s. David and Bess (Stein) A.; m. Phyllis Schwadron, June 3, 1957 (dec.); 1 child, Lisa Susan. AB, CCNY, 1951; MA, Columbia U., 1952; LLB, NYU, 1958. Bar: N.Y. 1959, U.S. Dist. Ct. (so. and ea. dist.) N.Y. 1961, U.S. Supreme Ct. 1964. Assoc. Flood & Purvin, N.Y.C., 1958-61; assoc. gen. counsel Am. Arbitration Assn., N.Y.C., 1962-63, gen. counsel, 1964-80; ptnr. Reid & Priest L.L.P., N.Y.C., 1981-98, Thelen Reid & Priest L.L.P., N.Y.C., 1998—2002. Adj. prof. NYU, N.Y.C., 1968-2001; mem. First Dept. Jud. Screening Com., 1983-93; bd. dirs. U.S. Coun. Internat. Bus., 1982—; ICC Inst. World Bus. Law, 1992—; vice chmn. ICC Internat. Ct. Arbitration, 2000-02; pres. Coll. Coml. Arbitrators, 2002-03. Bd. dirs. Nat. Inst. Consumer Justice, 1971-72, World Arbitration Inst. 1984-2000; mem. adv. bd. Inst. for Internat. and Comparative Law, 1988—; pvt. adjudications com. Ctr. for Pub. Resources, 1988-2002. 1st lt. U.S. Army, 1952-55. Fellow Am. Bar Found; mem. ABA (ho. of dels. 1985-87, chmn. sect. internat. law and practice 1982-83), N.Y. State Bar Assn., Assn. Bar City of N.Y. (chmn. adv. com. on ADR 1992-93), London Ct. Internat. Arbitration, Am. Arbitration Assn. (bd. dirs. 1982-95), Citizens Union (bd. dirs. 1983-86), Am. Soc. Internat. Law. Office: 875 Third Ave 10th Fl New York NY 10022-6625 E-mail: gaksen@thelenreid.com.

AKST, GEORGE, operations analyst, mathematician; b. N.Y.C., Aug. 23, 1949; s. Ted and Estelle Akst; m. Barbara Blattner, Apr. 30, 1976; children: Jason, Jennifer. BS, CCNY, 1970; PhD, U. Ill., 1974. Sr. rsch. analyst Ctr. for Naval Analyses, Alexandria, Va., 1979-98; dep. dir. studies and analysis divsn. USMC, Quantico, Va., 1998—. Pres. Mill Creek Park Citizens Assn., Annandale, Va., 1991-95. Mem. Mil. Ops. Rsch. Soc. (sponsor's rep. 1998-2000). Avocations: golf, scuba diving, hiking, reading, travel. Office: Marine Corps Combat Devel Command 3300 Russell Rd Quantico VA 22134-5130 E-mail: akstg@mccdc.usmc.mil.

AKTOSUN, TUNCAY, mathematical physics educator; b. Turkey; arrived in U.S., 1978; BS, Middle East Tech. U., Ankara, Turkey, 1978; MS, Ind. U., 1981, PhD, 1986. Asst. prof. Duke U., Durham, N.C., 1986-88, U. Del., Newark, 1988-89, U. Tex., Dallas, 1989-90, So. Meth. U., Dallas, 1990-92; assoc. prof. N.D. State U., Fargo, 1992—2001; prof. Miss. State U., Miss. State, Miss., 2001—. Cons. and reviewer various pubs. Reviewer Zentralblatt, 1993—; contbr. articles to profl. jours. NSF grantee, 1990—. Office: Miss State U Dept Maths and Stats Mississippi State MS 39762 E-mail: aktosun@math.msstate.edu.

AKUKWE, CHINUA, public health physician, health service executive; b. Aug. 7, 1962; MD, U. Nigeria, Enugu, 1985; M in Pub. Health, Hebrew U., Jerusalem, Israel, 1991; cert. in Exec. Pub. Health Mgmt., Johns Hopkins U., 1998. Sci. coord. NIH, D.C. Initiative, Washington, 1993-97; sr. policy and planning advisor to dir. D.C Dept Health, Washington, 1997-98; assoc. prof. U. Md., College Park, 1997—, George Washington U. Sch. Pub. Health, Washington, 1998—, U. D.C., Washington, 1998—. Coord. Global Health Seminars George Washington U. Med. Ctr., Washington, 1997—98; vice chmn. Nat. Coun. Internat. Health, Washington, 1997—98; workshop expert minority health Dept. Health, Columbia, SC, 1998; mem. tech. rev. panels for maternal and child health and health stats. U.S. Dept. HHS, 1995—; mem. com. on faculty support and profl. devel. George Washington U. Hosp. Ctr., 1998—; vice chmn. PBS Internat. Devel. Group, 1999—; bd. dirs. Constituency for Africa, Washington; mem. expert com. HIV/AIDS in Africa and governance UN Econ. Commn. Africa; spkr. in field. Author, co-author 7 monographs on D.C. Health Svcs., mem. editl. bd. Am. Jour. Pub. Health, 1999—2003, contbr. over 50 articles on HIV/AIDS in Africa. Bd. dirs. Christian Connections for Internat. Health, 1994—96, Peace Corps Nigeria Alumni Found., Washington, 2002—. Fellow: Royal Soc. Medicine London, Royal Soc. Health (Eng.); mem.: N.Y. Acad. Scis., Am. Pub. Health Assn. (co-chair 125th Ann. Conf. 1997), Am. Coll. Epidemiology. Avocations: current affairs, soccer, reading biographies, health books. Office: PBS Internat Devel Group 901 N Washington St Alexandria VA 22314-1535 E-mail: cakukwe@att.net.

AKUNWAFOR, DANIEL DOMINIC, librarian, educator; b. Abatete, Anambra, Nigeria, Nov. 15, 1949; s. Akunwafor Ifezugo and Oyiboka Ogbasea; m. Helen Ngozi Okafor; children: Linda, Nkiruka;children: Maureen, Felicia, Amechi. BA in Econs., U. D.C., 1977; MURP in Urban and Regional Planning, U. D.C., W, 1980; MLS in Libr. and Info. Sci., Cath. U. Am., 1999; PhD in Polit. Sci., Howard U, 1989. Founder, CEOa Pro Bono Enterprises, Inc., Washington, 1988—2001; libr. D.C. Pub. Libr., Washington, 1998—; adj. asst. prof. Southeastern U., Washington, 2001—. Cons. Emy and Assocs., Inc., Hyattsville, 1984—88. Treas. Anambra State Assn. in Am., Washington, 1987—91. Mem.: ALA, Am. Polit. Sci. Assn. Roman Catholic. Avocations: playing soccer, reading novels, going to movies. Home: 10706 Hayes Ave Silver Spring MD 20902 Office: D C Pub Libr 4200 Kansas Ave NW Washington DC

AKUTSU, YOSHIHIRO, communications educator; b. Utsunomiya, Tochigi, Japan, Apr. 13, 1932; s. Miyoshi and Fumi (Owada) A.; m. Masako Ota, May 3, 1963. BA, Internat. Christian U., Mitaka, Tokyo, 1958, MA in Edn., 1960; PhD in Communication, Mich. State U., 1969. Instr. Internat. Christian U., 1969-71, asst. prof., 1971-74, assoc. prof., 1974-77, prof., 1977—2003, prof. emeritus, 2003—. Chmn. divsn. edn. Internat. Christian U., 1980-82, dir. pub. info. office, 1985-87, dean of students, 1988-90, dean Coll. of Liberal Arts, 1991-93. Co-author: Explorations in Mass Communication, 1970, Public Communication, 1975; editor Jour. Communication, 1976. Advisor social edn. Mitaka-City, 1983-91. Mem. Japan Soc. for Study of Audio-Visual Edn. (bd. dirs. 1972-94), Japan Soc. for Study of Radio-TV Edn. (bd. dirs. 1977-94), Japan Soc. Ednl. Sociology (bd. councillors 1987-97), Japan Assn. for Ednl. Media Study (bd. dirs. 1994—), Japan Soc. for Child Study (bd. dirs. 1994—). Avocations: noh song, Go. Home: 4-12-11 Josuiminami Kodaira Tokyo 187-0021 Japan Office: Internat Christian U 3-10-2 Osawa Mitaka Tokyo 181-8585 Japan

ALADJEM, HENRIETTA H. writer; b. Romania, Jan. 21, 1917; arrived in U.S., 1941, naturalized, 1947; d. Alfred and Mina Hirs; m. Albert T. Aladjem, Apr. 1941 (dec.); children: Albert T. Jr., Ingrid Winifred Nercesian, Martha Louise Climo. Student, Harvard U., 1941—45, Simmons Coll., 1943—44, U. Sofia. Founder, mem. acquisition dept. Harvard Weidner's Libr., Cambridge, Mass., 1941—45; writer, 1972—. Guest lectr. med. schs., Boston; cons. in field. Editor: Lupus News, 1973—96, Lupus World, 1996—; author: The Sun Is My Enemy, 1972, Understanding Lupus: What It Is, How to Treat It, How to Cope with It, 1982, In Search of the Sun, 1988, A Decade of Lupus, 1991, A Patient's Story, 1986, The Challenges of Lupus, 1998; contbr. articles to profl. publs. Recipient Pres.'s Vol. Action award, Pres. Ronald Reagan, The White Ho., 1985, Disting. Health Comm. award, New Eng. chpt. Am. Med. Writers Assn., 1992, Harold Swanberg Disting. Svc. award, Nat. Am. Med. Writers Assn., 1994, prize for nonfiction article, New Eng. Writer's Conf. Mem.: Lupus Found. Am. (co-founder 1972, adv. bd., Achievement award various chpts., Disting. Svc. award 1986).

ALAFOUZO, ANTONIA, marketing and business strategy professional; b. Cairo, Oct. 13, 1952; came to U.S., 1982; d. Pano Antony and Agni-Maria (Ranos) A.; m. Thomas D'Ambola Jr., May 29, 1988; 1 child, Tatiana Maryana. BSC in Econs., Brunel U., London, 1975; Diploma in Econs. and Politics, Oxford (Eng.) U., 1977, M of Philosophy, PhD, 1980. Staff reporter The Economist, London, 1973-75, contbg. writer, 1975-82; mktg. exec. Rubenstein, Wolfson Co., N.Y.C., 1982-87; founder, pres. Markcom Ltd., N.Y.C., 1987—. Contbg. writer Fin. Report, London, 1975-82; cons. writer Fin. Times, London, 1980-82; cons. communications and econs. World Gold Council, N.Y.C., 1982—. Contbr. reports to fin. publs. Mem. Inst. Journalism Internat., Oxford Union Soc. Avocations: travel, languages, tennis, marksmanship, horse riding. Office: Markcom Ltd 270 Lafayette St New York NY 10012-3327

ALAGAPPA, MUTHIAH, international politics researcher; b. Apr. 14, 1942; Diploma, U. Lancaster, U.K., 1977, MA, 1978; PhD, Tufts U., 1985. Sr. fellow Inst. Strategic Studies, Kuala Lumpur, Malaysia, 1986-89; vis. sr. fellow East-West Ctr., Honolulu, 1989-90; vis. prof. Columbia U., N.Y.C., 1990-91; from sr. fellow to dir. East-West Ctr., Washington, 1991—2000, dir., 2000—. Author, editor: Political Legitimacy in South East Asia, 1995, Asian Security Practice, 1998, Coercion and Governance, 2001, Taiwan Presidential Election, 2001, Military Professionalism in Asia, 2001, Asian Security Order, 2003; co-editor: UN and Management of International Security, 1999; series editor: Contemporary Issues in Asia and the Pacific, and Asian Security; mem. editl. bd. The Pacific Rev., The Australian Jour. Internat. Affairs, Internat. Rels. of the Asia-Pacific, Jour. East Asian Studies. Recipient Abe fellowship Ctr. for Global Partnership, 1996-97, 2001-2003; grantee Smith-Richardson Found., 1998—, Ford Found., 1998—, US-Japan Found., 1999—, Carnegie Corp., N.Y., 2002— . Mem. Internat. Studies Assn., Am. Polit. Sci. Assn., Assn. Asian Studies. Office: East West Ctr 1819 L St NW 2nd Flr Washington DC 20036 E-mail: ALAGAPPM@eastwestcenter.org.

ALAM, SHAWN, biologist; b. Lahore, Pakistan, Dec. 3, 1958; s. Fateh Mohammed and Zubeda Begum Chaudhry; m. Karyn Lynn Messner, Sept. 16, 1989; children: Zachary, Omar. MS, U. Punjab, Lahore, Pakistan, 1980, U. Wis., 1988; PhD, U. Ariz., 1991. Lectr. Punjab Govt., Pakistan, 1982-85; scientific officer fisheries Pakistan Agrl. Rsch. Coun., 1985-90; resource mgr. Pyramid Lake Fisheries, Sutcliffe, Nev., 1992-93; fishery biologist Fla. Fish and Wildlife Conservaton Commn., Lakeland, 1993-97, U.S. Fish and Wildlife Svc., Panama City, Fla., 1997-2000, fish and wildlife biologist, 2000—. Contbr. articles to profl. jours. Mem. Am. Inst. Fishery Rsch. Biologists, N.Am. Lake Mgmt. Soc. (life), Am. Fisheries Soc. (life), Soc. Wetland Scientists (life), Native Fish Conservancy (life), Sigma Xi (life). Office: US Fish & Wildlife Svc 4401 N Fairfax Dr Rm 810 Arlington VA 22203 Fax: 703-358-1800. E-mail: shawn_alam@fws.gov.

ALAMEDA, RUSSELL RAYMOND, JR., radiologic technologist; b. San Jose, Calif., Oct. 13, 1945; s. Russell Raymond and Rose Margaret (Manzone) A.; m. Gayle Evileen Allison, Feb. 16, 1969 (div. 1975); children: Lynda Rae, Anthony David. Student, San Jose City Coll., 1963-65. Served with U.S. Navy, 1966-75; x-ray technician VA Hosp., Palo Alto, Calif., 1975-78; office mgr. Orthopedic Surgery, Mountain View, Calif., 1978-99; supr., radiologic technologist Desert Orthopedic Ctr., Rancho Mirage, Calif., 2000—. Owner, operator Ren-Tech, San Jose, 1982-87; radiologic technologist San Jose (Calif.) Med. Clinic, 1982-93; part-time fin. analyst Primerica Fin. Svcs., Newark, Calif., 1998-2000. Mem. DeFrank Community Ctr. Recipient Mallinckrodt Outstanding Achievement award Mallinckrodt Corp., 1971. Mem. DAV (life), ACLU, NOW, Am. Registry of Radiologic Technologists, Lamda Legal Def., Calif. Soc. Radiologic Technologists, Am. Soc. Radiologic Technolgoist. Democrat. Lutheran. Home: 1840 S Caliente Rd Palm Springs CA 92264-9202

ALAN, MATTHEW W. A. lawyer; b. Cleve., Nov. 9, 1961; BA in History and Polit. Sci., Cleve. State U., 1984, JD, 1986. Bar: Ohio 1987, D.C. 1992, Pa. 1993. Sr. counsel CBS Corp., Pitts., 1993-98; sec., gen. counsel Westinghouse Safety Mgmt. Solutions, LLC, Aiken, S.C., 1998—, Safe Sites of Colo. L.L.C.,

Golden, 2002—, Thor Treatment Techs., LLC, Aiken, 2002—; counsel Washington Energy and Environment, 2000—. Maj. JAGC, U.S. Army, 1987-93. Office: Westinghouse Safety Mgmt Solutions LLC 2131 S Centennial Ave Aiken SC 29803-7609

ALAN, SONDRA KIRSCHNER, lawyer; b. Pitts. d. Andrew and Lora Hardy Kirschner; m. Riley L. Proffitt, July 9, 1988; children: Gregory Proffitt Alan, Victoria Jade Proffitt, Andrew Lawrence Proffitt. BA, SUNY, Buffalo, 1968; JD, Duquesne U., 1980. Bar: Pa. 1980, Va. 1983, U.S. Dist. Ct. (we. dist.) Va. 1982, U.S. Ct. Appeals (4th cir.) 1982. Art tchr. St. Gregory the Gt., Buffalo, 1966-68; mgr. visual arts lab Ind. U. Sch. of Optometry, Bloomington, 1969-71; law clk. to presiding justice Ct. Common Pleas, Waynesburg, Pa., 1979-80; assoc. Law Offices J.D. Bowie, Bristol, Va., 1980-83; pvt. practice Bristol, 1984—. Guardian ad litum for children, Va., 1995—; guardian ad litum for adults, Va., 2001—; hearing officer Va. Supreme Ct., Va., 2001—. Recipient 2d pl. award Pa. State Art Competition, 1976. Mem. Pa. Bar Assn., Va. Bar Assn., Bristol Bar Assn. (pres. 1984-85). Lutheran. Avocations: pencil sketching, stained glass, home remodeling, gardening. Office: 923 Cumberland St Bristol VA 24201-4103

ALANIS, JAVIER ROLANDO, theologian, religious studies educator; b. San Juan, Tex., June 14, 1953; s. Santiago Alanís and Manuela Treviño de Alanís; BA, Washington U., 1974; M in Internat. Bus. Adminstrn., Am. Grad. Sch. Internat. Mgmt., 1976; JD, U. Tex., 1984; MDiv, Wartburg Seminary, 1992; ThM in Ch. and Soc., Luth. Sch. Theology, Chgo., 1998, PhD in Systematic Theology and Ethics, 2002. Ordained 1992. Auditor Schering-Plough Corp., Kenilworth, NJ, 1977—78; acct. Exxon Corp., Niamey, Niger, 1978—81, Kinshasa, 1978—81; atty. Tex. Employment Commn., 1983, Office Atty. Gen., Austin, Tex., 1984, Carinhas and Morrow Law Offices, Brownsville, Tex., 1985—86, Armstrong and Ray Law Offices, Brownsville, 1986—87; asst. dist. atty. Hidalgo County Courthouse, Edinburg, Tex., 1987—88; pastor Trinity Luth. Ch., San Antonio, 1992—96; supervising pastor Parroquia Luterana La Ascension, Chgo., 1996—99; asst. prof. Hispanic studies and systematic theology Luth. Sem. Program in the S.W., Austin, 2000—, dir. Theol. Edn. for Emerging Ministries, 2002—03. Chair multicultural com. Southwestern Tex. Synod, 1992—96, chair anti-racism team, 1995—96; tchg. asst. Cath. Theol. Union, Chgo., 1996—97; mem. steering com. Commn. for Multicultural Ministries Evang. Luth. Ch. in Am., 2003. Mem.: Soc. Scholars in Religion, Spanish Assn. Theological Edn., Am. Acad. Religion. Lutheran. Avocations: travel, foreign languages, mission trips. Home: Apt H 307 E 33rd St Austin TX 78705 Office: Luth Sem Program SW Po Box 4790 Austin TX 78765 Office Fax: 512-477-6693.

ALANIZ, MIGUEL JOSÉ CASTAÑEDA, library director; b. L.A., Oct. 21, 1944; s. Francisco and Amalia (Castañeda) A.; m. Mercedes P., June 7, 1980. AA, Chabot C.C., 1972; BS in Child/Human Devel., Calif. State U., Hayward, 1974; MS in LS, Calif. State U., Fullerton, 1975; MS Pub. Admnstrn., Calif. State U., San Bernardino, 1988. Spanish svcs. libr. Alameda County Libr., Hayward, 1975-77; branch mgr. San Jose Pub. Libr., 1977-78, Santa Ana (Calif.) Pub. Libr., 1978-79; divsn. chief, tech. process San Bernardino (Calif.) County Libr., 1979-84; city libr. Azusa City (Calif.) Libr., 1984-92; libr. dir. Inglewood Pub. (Calif.) Libr., 1992—. Bd. dirs. St. Mary's Acad. With U.S. Army, 1965-71. Recipient Grad. Rsch. Fellow Clif. State U., 1974. Mem. ALA, Calif. Libr. Assn., Reforma, Nat. Exch Club. Avocations: automobiles, golf, reading, investments. Office: City of Inglewood Public Library 101 W Manchester Blvd Inglewood CA 90301-1753 E-mail: malaniz@cityofinglewood.org.

ALAO, ADEKOLA OLATUNJI, psychiatrist, educator; b. Iwo, Nigeria, June 5, 1960; s. Joseph and Deyo Alao; m. Lola Ojo; children: Deyo, Dami. MD, U. Ibadan, Nigeria, 1983; MSc in Mental Health Studies, U. London, 1995; MRCPsych, U. Oxford, U.K., 1996. Diplomate Am. Bd. Psychiatry 2001, Am. Acad. Pain Mgmt., cert. psychiat. adminstrn. and mgmt. Asst. prof. psychiatry SUNY Upstate Med. U., Syracuse, NY, 1998—. Contbr. Assoc. dir. Consultation Liaison Psychiatry, Syracuse. Recipient All Star award, 2000. Mem.: APA (treas. 2002), Am. Assn. Psychosomatic Medicine, Assn. Psychiatric Adminstrs. Avocations: travel, reading, dancing. Office: SUNY Upstate Med Univ 750 East Adams St Syracuse NY 13210

ALARCON, ARTHUR LAWRENCE, federal judge; b. L.A., Aug. 14, 1925; s. Lorenzo Marques and Margaret (Sais) A.; m. Sandra D. Paterson, Sept. 1, 1979; children— Jan Marie, Gregory, Lance BA in Polit. Sci., U. So. Calif., 1949, JD, 1951. Bar: Calif. 1952. Dep. dist. atty. L.A. County, 1952—61; legal adv. to gov. State of Calif., Sacramento, 1961—62, exec. asst. to Gov. Pat Brown, 1962—64; chmn. Calif. parole bd., 1964; judge L.A. Superior Ct., 1964—78; assoc. justice Calif. Ct. Appeals, L.A., 1978—79; judge U.S. Ct. Appeals for 9th Circuit, L.A., 1979—92; sr. judge, 1992—. Adj. prof. Southwestern U. sch. of law, L.A., 1985, Loyola Marymount sch. of law, 1993—94. Served with U.S. Army, 1943-46, ETO With U.S. Army, 1943—46, ETO. Office: US Ct Appeals 9th Cir 1607 US Courthouse 312 N Spring St Los Angeles CA 90012-4701 also: US Ct Appeals 95 Seventh St San Francisco CA 94103*

ALARCON, RICHARD, state legislator, former councilman; children: Armando, Antonio, Claudia, Andrea. Sr. mgmt. analyst Criminal Justice Planning Office, L.A.; sr. personnel analyst occupl. health and safety divsn. L.A. Personnel Dept.; San Fernando Valley coord. Mayor's Office; city councilman City of L.A., 1993-98; mem. Calif. State Senate, Sacramento, 1998-, majority whip, 1998-. Chmn. housing and cmty. devel. com., vice chair joint legis. audit com., mem. edn., energy, utilities and comm., environ. quality, indsl. rels. Adminstrv. dir. Cmty. Youth Gang Svc.; chmn. N.E. Cmty. Action Project; mem. United Way, MADD, AHA, Women's Care Cottage, Habitat for Humanity, Meet Each Need With Dignity. Office: Calif State Senate 6150 Van Nuys Blvd Ste 400 Van Nuys CA 91401-3345*

ALARCON, ROGELIO ALFONSO, physician, researcher; b. Yungay, Nuble, Chile, Feb. 14, 1926; arrived in U.S., 1954; s. Alfredo and Carmen Rosa (Carrasco) A. BS, U. Chile, Concepcion, 1943; MD, U. Chile, Santiago, 1950. Staff physician internal medicine U. Chile Hosp. Salvador, Santiago, 1951-52, Hosp. Gonzalez Cortez, Santiago, 1952-54; resident medicine Meml. Ctr. for Cancer and Allied Diseases, N.Y.C., 1955-56; fellow internal medicine George Washington U. Hops., George Washington Sch. Medicine, Washington, 1956-57; resident internal medicine Lemuel Shattuck Hosp., Boston, 1957-58; rsch. fellow pathology Children's Cancer Rsch. Found., Children's Hosp. Med. Ctr., Boston, 1958-60; rsch. assoc. Children's Cancer Rsch. Found., Boston, 1960-74, Harvard Med. Sch., Boston, 1962-76, Cancer Rsch. Inst., New Eng. Deaconess Hosp., Boston, 1974-76; staff physician Boston Children's Hosp. Med. Ctr., Wrentham, Mass., 1977-79, VA Med. Ctr., Phila., 1979-80, Bedford, Mass., 1980—2002. Contbr. articles to profl. jours. Mem. Am. Chem. Soc., Am. Assn. for Cancer Rsch., N.Y. Acad. Scis., Nat. Assn. VA Physicians. Roman Catholic. Achievements include discovery of the enzymatic generation of acrolein, a highly cytotoxic aldehyde, from biogenic polyamines; development of a fluorometric method to measure minimal amounts of acrolein; research in the growth inhibitory effects of oxidized spermine on mammalian cells, research involving acrolein in cell growth regulation, and identification of acrolein as a metabolite of cyclophosphamide and related chemotherapeutic agents. Home: 33 Pond Ave Apt B-915 Brookline MA 02445-7163

ALARIE-ANDERSON, PEGGY SUE, physician assistant; b. Flint, Mich., Feb. 8, 1957; d. Albert Joseph Jr. and Elizabeth Anna (Eksten) A.; m. John L. McAttee III, Oct. 3, 1980 (div. Aug. 1987); m. Donn P. Anderson, Aug. 23, 1997. AAS, Mott C.C., 1983; BS, Mich. State U., 1988; MS, U. Detroit-Mercy, 1994. Physician asst. supr. emergency rm. Hurley Med. Ctr., Flint, Mich., 1996—. Fellow Am. Acad. Physician Assts., Mich. Acad. Physician Assts.; mem. Soc. Emergency Physician Assts., Am. Acad. Surg. Physician Assts., Sigma Theta Tau. Avocations: dance (ballet, ballroom, tap, jazz). Home: 5072 Scott Rd Mount Morris MI 48458-9724 Office: Hurley Med Ctr 1 Hurley Plz Flint MI 48503-5902

ALATIS, JAMES EFSTATHIOS, university dean emeritus; b. Weirton, W.Va., July 13, 1926; s. Efstathios and Vasiliki (Galanoudis) A.; m. Penelope Mastorides, Dec. 30, 1951; children: William, Stephen, Anthony. BA, W.Va. U., 1948; MA, Ohio State U., 1953; PhD, 1966. Fulbright lectr. English U., Athens, 1955-57; English testing and teaching specialist Dept. State, 1959-61; specialist for lang. research U.S. Office Edn., 1961-65, chief lang. sect., 1965-66; asso. dean Sch. Langs. and Linguistics, Georgetown U., Washington, 1966-73, dean, 1973-94; dean emeritus Georgetown U., Washington, 1994—, sr. advisor to exec. v.p. internat. lang. programs and rsch., 1994-96, sr. advisor to Dean of Georgetown Coll. for internat. langs. programs and rsch., 1996—; assoc. prof. linguistics Sch. Langs. and Linguistics, Georgetown U., Washington, 1966-75; disting. prof. linguistics and modern Greek Georgetown U., Washington, 1994—. Exec. sec. TESOL, 1966-87, exec. dir. emeritus, 1987—; pres. Joint Nat. Com. for Langs., 1980-88, bd. dirs. 1998—, TESOL Internat. Rsch. Found., 1999—; mem. Greek Orthodox Archbishop's commn., 1999; bd. advisors U.S. Dept. Agriculture Grad. Sch. Author: (with Peter Lowenberg) The Three Circles of English: A Conference in honor of Braj B. Kachru, 2002; editor: Studies in Honor of Albert H. Marckwardt, 1972, (with Kristie Twaddell) English as a Second Language in Bilingual Education, 1976, (with Ruth Crymes) Human Factors in ESL, 1977, (with Gerli and Brod) Language in American Life, 1978, Internat. Dimensions of Bilingual Education, 1978, (with G. R. Tucker) Language in Public Life, 1979, Current Issues in Bilingual Education, 1980, (with others) The Second Language Classroom: Directions for the 1980s, 1981, Applied Linguistics and the Preparation of Second Language Teachers: Toward a Rationale, 1983, (with John J. Staczek) Perspectives on Bilingualism and Bilingual Education, 1985, (with Deborah Tannen) Language and Linguistics: The Interdependence of Theory, Data, and Application, 1986, Language Teaching, Testing, and Technology: Lessons from the Past with a View Toward the Future, 1989, Linguistics, Language Teaching and Language Acquisition: The Interdependence of Theory, Practice, and Research, 1990, Quest for Quality: The First 21 Years of TESOL, 1991, Linguistics and Language Pedagogy: The State of the Art, 1991, Language, Communication and Social Meaning, 1993, Strategic Interaction and Language Acquisition: Theory, Practice and Research, 1993, Educational Linguistics, Cross-Cultural Communication, and Global Interdependence, 1994, (with others) Linguistics and the Education of Language Teachers: Ethnolinguistic, Psycholinguistic, and Sociolinguistic Aspects, 1995, (with others) Linguistics, Language Acquisition and Language Variation: Current Trends and Future Prospects, 1996, (with others) Aspects of Sociolinguistics in Greece, 1997, (with others) Language in Our Time: Bilingual Education and Official English, Ebonics and Standard English, Immigration and the Unz Initiative, 1999, (with others) Linguistics, Language, and the Professions: Education, Journalism, Law, Medicine and Technology, Georgetown Univ. Round table on Languages and Linguistics, 2000, Linguistics, Language, and the Real World: Discourse and Beyond, Georgetown Univ. Round Table on Languages and Linguistics, 2001 (with Deborah Tannen) Georgetown University Round Table on Language and Linguistics, 2001; mem. editl. bd. World Englishes, English Today. Served with USNR, 1944-46. Recipient N.E. Conf. award, 1985, Pres.'s award Nat. Assn. for Bilingual Edn., 1987. Mem. MLA, Am. Coun. on Teaching Fgn. Langs., Linguistic Soc. Am (del. 1966-69), Nat. Assn. Fgn. Student Affairs (dir. 1965-66), Def. Lang. Inst. (bd. visitors), Phi Beta Kappa. Home: 5108 Sutton Pl Alexandria VA 22304-2704 Office: Georgetown U Int'l Langs Prog & Rsch 37th & 0 St Washington DC 20057-0001

ALATZAS, GEORGE, delivery service company executive; b. Salonika, Greece, Sept. 30, 1940; came to U.S., 1954; s. Gus Alatzas and Georgia Karayanidou; m. Ida Elizabeth Feldman, Sept. 26, 1965; children: Dennis, Ari. AA in Liberal Arts, Middlesex Community Coll., 1979; student, Rutgers U. Dept. mgr. Bamberger's N.J. div. Macy's Dept. Store, Newark, 1959-61, 63-65; buyer Koos Bros., Rahway, N.J., 1965-67; sales rep. Bassett (Va.) Furniture, 1967-69; store mgr. W&J Sloane, Union, N.J., 1969-72, Steinbach & Co., Freehold, N.J., 1972-78; owner, pres. Lawyers & Corp. Messenger Svc., Middlesex, N.J., 1978-84; pres., chief exec. officer Pegasus Delivery Systems, Inc., Somerville, N.J., 1984—. Pres. Just In Time Inc. fin. mgmt. and support svcs.; bd. dirs. Alternarives Inc. Instr. swimming Am. Legion Children's Camp, Newburgh, N.Y., 1957-58; instr. marksmanship reservation Boy Scouts Am., Yards Creek, and Blairstown, N.J., 1980-83; pres. Office Condominium Assn. Ctr. at Raritan. With U.S. Army, 1961—63, Command Sgt. Major USAR, 1973—75. Recipient Somerset County Businessman of Yr. award, 1999; Paul Harris fellow. Mem. Assn. U.S. Army, Nat. Alliance Businessmen, 78th Divsn. NCO Assn., 78th Divsn. Vets. Assn., N.J. Bus. and Industry Coun., Rotary (Somerville/Bridgewater chpt. pres. 2003—), Somerset County C. of C. (bd. dirs.) Greek Orthodox. Avocations: tennis, golf, walking. Office: Pegasus Delivery Systems Inc 1124 Us Highway 202 Ste B14 Raritan NJ 08869-1475 E-mail: gapegasus@aol.com.

ALAUPOVIC, ALEXANDRA VRBANIC, artist, educator; b. Slatina, Yugoslavia, Dec. 21, 1921; d. Joseph and Elizabeta (Papp) Vrbanic; m. Peter Alaupovic, Mar. 22, 1947; 1 child, Betsy. Student Bus. Sch., Zagreb, Yugoslavia, 1940-41, Acad. Visual Arts, Zagreb, Yugoslavia, 1944-48; postgrad. Acad. Visual Arts, Prague, Czechoslovakia, 1949, Art Sch., U. Ill., 1959-60; MFA, U. Okla., 1966; came to U.S., 1958. Sec., Arko Liquer & Yeast Factory and Distillery, Zagreb, 1941-44; instr. U. Okla., Norman, 1964-66; instr. three dimensional design sculpture Oklahoma City U., 1969-77, Okla. Sci. Found., Oklahoma City, 1969-75; one-woman shows at Okla. Art Ctr., Oklahoma City, U. Okla. Mus. Art, Norman, La Mandragore Internat. Galerie d'Art, Paris, 1984; exhibited art in group shows retrospective 50 yrs. Struggle, Growth and Whimsy, 1987-88, Okla. Art Ctr., Springfield (Mo.) Art Mus., Okla. U. Mus., Norman, 7th Ann. Temple Emanuel Brotherhood Arts Festival, Dallas, Salon des Nation, Paris, 1983; since statehood twevle Okla. artists Art. Mus., Okla. 1996; represented in permanent collections Okla. U. Art Mus., Okla. State Art Collection, Okla. Art Ctr., Mercy Health Ctr. Recipient Jacobson award U. Okla., 1964; hon. mention in sculpture Philbrook Art Ctr., Tulsa, 1967; 1st sculpture award Philbrook Art Ctr., Tulsa, 1970; biography included in Virginia Watson Jones' Contemporary American Women Sculptors, 1986, Jules and Nancy Heller's North American Women Artists of 20th Century, 1995; State of Okla. Art commemdation, 1996. Mem. Internat. Sculpture Center, Lausanne, Suisse, Prestige de la Peinture et de la Sculpture d'Aujourd'hui dans le Monde, 1992, Paris, 1995. Home and Office: 11908 N Bryant Ave Oklahoma City OK 73131-4823

ALAUPOVIC, PETAR, biochemist, educator; b. Prague, Czechoslovakia, Aug. 3, 1923; came to U.S., 1957; married, 1947; 1 child. ChemE, U. Zagreb, 1948, PhD in Chemistry, 1956; DHC (hon.), U. Lille, France, 1987, U. Buenos Aires, 1994, U. Goteborg, 1999. Rschr. pharms. rsch. lab. Chem Corp, Prague, 1948-49; rschr. organic lab. Inst. Indsl. Rsch., Yugoslavia, 1949-50; asst. agrl. faculty U. Zagreb, 1951-54, asst. chem. inst. med. faculty, 1954-56; rsch. biochemist U. Ill., 1957-60; with cardiovascular sect. Okla. Med. Rsch. Found., Oklahoma City, 1960—, head lipoprotein lab., 1972-92, also head Lipid and Lipoprotein Lab. Prof. rsch. biochemistry, sch. med. U. Okla., 1960—. Assoc. editor Lipids, 1974-78. Named Disting. Career Scientist Okla. Med. Rsch. Fund, 1990; NIH grantee, 1961-95. Mem. AAAS, Am. Soc. Biol. Chemists, Am. Chem. Soc., Am. Heart Assn. (Spl. Recognition award 1994), Am. Oil Chemistry Soc. Achievements include research on chemistry of naturally occuring macromolecular lipid compounds such as serum and tissue lipoproteins and bacterial endotoxins, on biochemistry of red cell membranes; isolation and characterization of tissue lipases. Office: Okla Med Rsch Found Lipid and Lipoprotein Lab 825 NE 13th St Oklahoma City OK 73104-5005 E-mail: alaupovicp@omrf.ouhsc.edu.

ALBA, BENNY, artist; b. Columbus, Ohio, 1949; Student, Kent State U., 1968-70; BA in Psychology, U. Mich., 1982. Artists in residence Mont. Artists Refuge, Basin, 2003. Artist-in-residence St. Charles Boy's Pres. Sch., Columbus, 1982-85, Mont. Artist Refuge, Basin, 2002; lectr. Columbus Cultural Arts Ctr., 1983-84, 93; presenter in field; panelist Calif. Inst. for Intergral Studies, San Francisco, 1995. One-woman shows include Columbus Cultural Arts Ctr., 1993, Apprentice Alliance, San Francisco, 1994, Las Vegas (Nev.) Mus., 1994, Artist TV Access, San Francisco, 1994, Western Wyo. Coll., Rock Springs, 1994, A Gallery in the Clock Tower, San Francisco, 1994, Ctr. for Psychol. Studies, Albany, Calif., 1994, Idyllwild (Calif.) Sch. Music and Art, 1995, Merced (Calif.) Coll. Art Gallery, 1997, North Country Mus. of Art, Park Rapids, Minn., 1997, Martinez (Calif.) City Hall, 1997, Martinez Arts and Culture Com., 1997, Office of Sup. Contra County Ct., Martinez, 1997, State Bd., Sacramento, Calif., 1997, Saginaw (Mich.) Art Mus., 1998, Met. Transp. Co., Oakland, Calif., 1998, Commonwealth Club, San Francisco, 1998, San Francisco State U. Club, 1998, Zen Ctr., San Francisco, 1998, Hastings Coll. Law, 1999, U. Oreg., Eugene, 1999, Oakland Higher Edn. Ctr., 1999, The Arts Ctr., Jamestown, N.D., 2000, North Valley Arts Coun., Grand Forks, N.D., 2000, Lake Region Heritage Ctr., Devils Lake, N.D., 2000, Bismarck (N.D.) Art and Galleries Assn., Valley Art Ctr., Clarkston, Wash., 2000, Pacific Grove Art Ctr., Calif., 2000, Rogue C.C., Grants Pass, Oreg., 2000, Sedona (Ariz.) Art Ctr., 2000, ARC Gallery, Chgo., 2000, Napa City County Libr., 2000, East Bay Mcpl. Utilities Dist., 2002, exhibited in group shows at throughout U.S.A., San Francisco, 1992, YWCA, Youngstown, Ohio, 1992, Mus. Without Walls, Bemis Pt., N.Y., 1993, Davis (Calif.) Art Ctr., 1993, Kunst für Begegnungen, Munich, 1993, Ednl. Testing Svc., Emeryville, Calif., 1993—94, Diablo (Calif.) Valley Coll. Gallery, 1994, N.Mex. Art League, Albuquerque, 1995, Nat. Congress Art & Design, Salt Lake City, 1995, Danville (Calif.) Fine Arts, 1995, Lillian Paley Ctr. Visual Arts, Oakland, 1995, Lamar U., Beaumont, Tex., 1996, John Jay Coll. of Criminal Justice, N.Y., 1996, Serra House, Stanford U., 1996, Fed. Bldgs. Window Project, Oakland, 1996, Civic & Cultural Ctr., Brea, Calif., 1997, Palm Springs (Calif.) Desert Mus., 1997, Downey (Calif.) Mus. Art, 1997, Am. Embassies Program, Rangoon, Burma, 1997, Lesotho, Africa, 1998, Bangladesh, 1999, Mus. Downtown L.A., 1998, Sun Gallery, Hayward, Calif., 1998, Hoyt Inst. Fine Arts, New Castle, Pa., 1998, Maude Kers Art Ctr., Eugene, 1998, Bolinas (Calif.) Mus., 1998, George Ohr Mus., Biloxi, 1998, Galesburg (Ill.) Civic Art Ctr., 1999, Coll. Notre Dame Md., Balt., 1999, Las Vegas Art Coun., 2000, Lincoln Ctr., Ft. Collins, Colo., 2000, Works Gallery, San Jose, Calif., 2000, Ohlone Coll., Freemont, Calif., 2000, Fredericksburg (Va.) Coll. Creative Arts, 2000, Gallery Rt. One, Pt. Reyes Ste, Calif., 2000, The Print Ctr., Phila., 2001, Palm Springs Desert Mus., 2001, Masur Mus. of Art, Monroe, La., 2001, Brownsville (Tex.) Art League, 2001, Period Gallery, Omaha, 2001, Art Assn. of Harrisburg, Pa., 2001, Fredericksburg CCA/Mary Washington Coll., Va., 2001, Palos Verdes Art Ctr., Rancho Palos Verdes, Calif., 2001, Viridian Artists Inc. Gallery, N.Y.C., 2001, South Cobb Arts Alliance, Mableton, Ga., 2001, Havre De Grace (Md.) Arts Commn., 2001, Steamboat Springs (Colo.) Arts Coun., 2001, ArtsBenecia, Calif., 2001, WomanMade Gallery, Chgo., 2001, Tex. Artists Mus., Port Arthur, 2001, MakeReady Press Gallery, Montclair, N.J., 2001, Impact Artists Gallery, Buffalo, 2001, others, Represented in permanent collections Nat. Mus. Women in Arts, Ark. Arts Ctr., Little Rock, U. Mich. Mus. Art, Kalamazoo Inst. Arts, Greenpeace, Ulli Wachter (Germany), Las Vegas Art Mus., Ctr. for Psychol. Studies, Albany, Calif., Birmingham (Ala.) Mus. Art, Portland (Oreg.) Art Mus., Tyler (Mich.) Mus. Art, Canajoharie Libr., N.Y., Mint Mus., Charlotte, N.C., others, one-woman shows include Parc, Zerox Corp., Palo Alto, Calif., 2003, U. Ariz., Montgomery, Ala., 2003, exhibited in group shows at Mountain Art, Bernardville, NJ, 2002, Fredericksburg (Va.) for Creative Arts, 2002, Wenatchee (Va.) Valley Coll., 2002, Alice Arts Ctr., Oakland, Calif., 2002, Central Mo. State U., 2002, San Pablo (Calif.) City Arts Gallery, 2003, one-woman shows include PARC Zensx Corp., Palo Alto, Claif., 2003, U. Ala., Montgomery, Ala., 2003, exhibited in group shows at Tex. Artists Mus., Port Arthur, Tex., 2002, Fredericksburg (Ba.) Ctr. for Creative Arts, 2002, Wenatchee (Wash.) Valley Coll., 2002, Alice Arts Ctr., Oakland, Calif., 2002, Ctrl. Mo. State U., Warrensburg, Mo., 2002, San Pablo (Calif.) City Gallery, 2003, U. Calif., Berkeley, Calif., 2003, Kellog G. Calif. State Polytec, Pomona, Calif., 2003. Bd. dirs. No. Calif. Women's Caucus for Art, 1991, sec. 1991-92, phone liaison, 1991-93. Recipient Lenore Miles award North Platte Valley Art Gallery, 1991, Body of Work award Women Artists, A Celebration, 1990, Merit award San Francisco Women Artist Gallery, 1986, Dr. S. Mackoff award Palm Springs Desert Mus., 1997, Junor Adobe Gallery award, 2000, San Francisco (Calif.) Women Artists, 2001, Art Assn. Palo Alto, 2001, 03, Adobe Galler, Castro Valley, Calif., 2003, Mem. Women's Caucus for Art (bd. dirs. No. Calif. 1991-94, sec. 1991-92), Calif. Soc. Printmakers (v.p. 1999). Studio: 4219 M L King Jr Way Oakland CA 94609-2321

ALBA, RICHARD DENIS, sociologist, educator; b. N.Y.C., Dec. 22, 1942; s. Richard and Mary Theresa (O'Sullivan) A.; m. Gwen Lova Moore, Dec. 31, 1976; children: Michael Moore, Sarah Dina Moore. AB summa cum laude, Columbia U., 1963, PhD, 1974. Asst. prof. sociology CUNY, 1974-77; asst. prof. Cornell U., Ithaca, N.Y., 1977-80; assoc. prof. SUNY, Albany, 1980-85, prof. sociology and pub. affairs and policy, 1985-2000, dist. prof. sociology and pub. policy, 2000—. Dir. Ctr. for Social and Demographic Analysis, Albany, 1981-90. Author: (with others) Right Versus Privilege, 1981, Remaking the American Mainstream: Assimilaton and Contemporary Immigration, 2003; Italian Americans: Into the Twilight of Ethnicity, 1985, Ethnic Identity: The Transformation of White America, 1990, (with others) Remaking the American Mainstream, 2003; editor: Race and Ethnicity in the U.S.A., 1985. Guggenheim fellow, 2000-01; recipient Fulbright awards, 1986-87, 93-94. Mem. Am. Sociol. Assn. (v.p. 2000-01), Ea. Sociol. Soc. (pres. 1997-98), Population Assn. Home: 45 Union Ave Delmar NY 12054-1628 Office: SUNY Sociology Dept 1400 Washington Ave Albany NY 12222-0100 E-mail: r.alba@albany.edu.

ALBACH, HORST, economist; b. Essen, Germany, July 6, 1931; s. Karl Albach; m. Renate Gutenberg; children: Rolf, Karin, Dirk. Student, U. Cologne, 1952-56, D of Econs., 1958; PhD (hon.), Helsinki U., Stockholm U., Graz U., Kiel U., Bielefeld U., Alcala de Henares U., Cottbus U., Bowdoin Coll. Lectr., Cologne, 1960; prof., 1961; sci. adv. com. Fed. Econs. Ministry, 1967—; vice-chmn. German Sci. Coun. Wissenschaftsrat, 1974-77, bd. econ. advisors, 1978-83; pres. Berlin Acad. Scis., 1987-90; prof. corp. policy Humboldt U., Berlin, 1994-99; dean exec. MBA program, Herbert Quandt prof. internat. mgmt. Koblenz (Germany) U., 1999-2001. Dir. Sci. Ctr. Berlin, 1990-99. Author: Wirtschaftlichkeitsrechn. bei unsich. Erwartungen, 1959, Investition u. Liquidität, 1962 (also in Japanese), Beitr. z. Unternehm. plan., 1969, 2d edit., 1978, Culture and Technical Innovation, 1994, 2d edit., 2000, Allgemeine Betriebswirfschaftslehre, 2000, 3d edit., 2001; co-author: numerous publs.; contbr. articles to profl. jours. Mem. Rhineland-Westphalian Acad. Sci., Royal Swedish Acad. Sci., Acad. Scis. Morals and Politics, Order Pour le Mérit for Arts and Scis. Office: 49 Wald St D-53177 Bonn Germany E-mail: profalbach@aol.com., horst.albach@t-online.de.

ALBACH, RICHARD ALLEN, microbiology educator; b. Chgo., Mar. 31, 1930; s. Maurice and Martha (Silverman) A.; m. Janice Elaine Boewe, Jan. 23, 1962; children: Michael, Karren, Kimala, David, Brian, Julie, Barry. BS, U. Ill., 1956, MS, 1958; PhD, Northwestern U., 1963. Asst. prof. U. Health Scis., Chgo. Med. Sch., North Chicago, Ill., 1968-69, assoc. prof., 1969-73, prof., 1973—, vice-chmn., 1975-82, acting chmn., 1982-83. Editl. cons. Yearbook Med. Pubs., Chgo., 1975-81; vis. prof. St. George's U. Sch. Medicine, Grenada, 1992—. Contbr. articles to profl. jours. With U.S. Army, 1953-55. Recipient Trustees Rsch. award Chgo. Med. Sch., 1968, Tchg. Prof. of Yr. award, 1976, 78, 82; fellow Abbott Found., 1961; grantee NIH, 1965-78. Fellow Am. Acad. Microbiology; mem. Am. Soc. Microbiology, Soc. Protozoologists (exec. com. 1984-89, chmn. awards com. 1995-1999), Am. Soc. Parasitologists, Ill. Soc. Microbiology (membership chmn. 1969-70). Achievements include research in biology of parasitic protozoa. Office: U Health Sci Chgo Med Sch 3333 Green Bay Rd North Chicago IL 60064-3037 E-mail: albachr@finchcms.edu.

ALBAN, ROGER CHARLES, small business consultant; b. Columbus, Ohio, Aug. 3, 1948; s. Charles Ellis and Alice Jacqueline (Hosfeld) A.; children: Allison Ann, Roger Charles II, Charles Michael (dec. June 1998); m. Linda Bayer Lusk, Aug. 30, 1997 (div. Nov. 2001). Student pub. schs. With Alban Equipment Co., Columbus, 1963—, sales mgr., 1972-75, gen. mgr., 1975-85, treas., 1978-85, v.p., 1980-85, pres., 1985-99, ret., 1999-00; exec. mgr. Infiniti of Dublin, Ohio, 2000—01. Mem. Grandview Heights Bd. Edn., Columbus, 1978-85, pres., 1979, v.p., 1982, legis. liaison, 1978-79, 83-84, re-elected mem., 1992-93; elected Grandview Heights City Coun., 1986; mem. Met. Ednl. Coun., Columbus Area Leadership PRogram, 1982-83; trustee Builders Exch. Benefit Trust, 1987-98, chmn., 1996. Mem. Assoc. Equipment Distbrs. (lt. dir. region 6 1980, 85, 86, 88, dir. 1989-91, chmn. light equipment dist. com. 1985, chmn. sales and mktg. com. 1988, elected dir. region 6 1989-92, chmn. lt. equipment steering com. 1998), Ohio Sch. Bds. Assn. (all-ctrl. region bd. 1984), Bldg. Industry Assn. Ctrl. Ohio, Am. Rental Assn., Builders Exch. Ctrl. Ohio (dir. 1990-99, elected treas. 1996, 2nd v.p. 1996, v.p. 1997, pres. 1998), Am. Mgmt. Assn., Nat. Right to Work Com., Nat. Fedn. Ind. Bus., Ohio Equipment Distbrs. Assn. (dir. 1982, 84-91, pres. 1983), Roundtable, Mensa (chpt. exec. com. 1979-80), Rotary (elected Columbus dir. 1994-97), Downtown Columbus Club. Home and Office: 4572 Carriage HIll Ln Columbus OH 43220-3802 Fax: 614-459-9483. E-mail: bigalban@mindspring.com.

ALBANESE, CATHERINE, religious studies educator; PhD in Am. Religious History, U. Chgo. Prof. religious studies U. Calif., Santa Barbara, 1987—. Recipient John Simon Guggenheim Meml. fellowship, 2003, Presdl. Rsch. fellowship in the humanities, Office of U. Calif. Pres. Richard Atkinson. Office: U Calif Santa Barbara Religious Studies Dept 3001 HSSB Santa Barbara CA 93106*

ALBANESE, JAY SAMUEL, criminologist, educator; b. Mineola, N.Y., Feb. 10, 1953; s. Samuel S. and Doris (Mather) A.; m. Leslie Elizabeth King, July 12, 1980; children: Thomas, Kelsey. BA, Niagara U., 1974; MA, Rutgers U., 1976, PhD, 1981. Chief Internat. Ctr. Nat. Inst. Justice, 2002—; prof. Niagara U., Niagara Falls, NY, 1981-96; prof. govt. and pub. policy Va. Commonwealth U., Richmond, 1996—. Vis. prof. Simon Fraser U., Vancouver, B.C., Can., 1988. Author: Dealing with Delinquency, 2d edit., 1993, Organized Crime in America, 3d edit., 1996 Criminal Justice, 1999, 2nd. edit., 2002; co-author: Crime in America, 1993, White Collar Crime in America, 1995; editor: Contemporary Issues in Organized Crime, 1995, Organized Crime: World Perspectives, 2003; contbr. articles to profl. jours. Recipient Sears Found. Teaching Excellence award, 1989-90, Founder's Award, Acad. Criminal Justice Scis., 2000, Elske Smith District Lectr. Award, Virginia Commonwealth U., Coll. Humanities & Scis. (for outstanding contributions to teaching and scholarship), 2001. Fellow Acad. Criminal Justice Scis., 2002/ mem. Am. Soc. Criminology, Internat. Assn. Study Organized Crime (exec. dir. 2002—), Northeastern Assn. Criminal Justice Scis. (pres. 1988-89), Acad. Criminal Justice Scis.(pres. 1995-96), White Collar Crime Res. Consortium (pres. 2000-02), Phi Kappa Phi. Office: PO Box 50484 Washington DC 20091-0484

ALBANESE, MARK ALAN, medical educator; b. Kansas City, Mo., Apr. 24, 1951; s. James A. and Delores E. Albanese; m. Aggie A. Albanese, May 11, 1974; children: Anne-Marie, Lisa, Amy, Mark James. BS, U. Nebr., 1973, MA, 1975; PhD, U. Iowa, 1981. Assoc. rsch. scientist U. Iowa, Iowa City, 1976-78, assoc. II rsch. scientist, 1978-82, asst. dir., adj. assoc. prof., 1982-86, dir., adj. assoc. prof., 1986-94; assoc. prof., dir. U. Wis., Madison, 1994-99, prof., dir., 1999—2003, prof., 2003—. Cons. APCOG, Washington, 1998—, ABMS, Chgo., 2001—. Mem. editl. bd. Evaluation and the Health Professions, Edn. Rsch. Quar., Med. Edn., Advances in Health Scis. Edn.; author: The Teaching Process: Theory and Practice in Nursing, 1986 (Best New Book 1987); dep. editor N.Am. Med. Edn., 2002—; contbr. articles to profl. jours. Coach Madison Area Youth Soccer Assn., Madison, 1994-99, YMCA, Madison, 1998-99, Kickers, Iowa City, 1985-94. Recipient John P. Hubbard award Nat. Bd. of Med. Examiners, 1998, Whitley award Assn. U. Radiologists, 1991, 92, 97, Best Rsch. Report Iowa Edn. Rsch. and Evaluation Assn., 1982. Mem. Am. Ednl. Rsch. Assn. (exec. com. 1999-2002), Soc. Dirs. of Rsch. in Med. Edn., (sec. 1989-90, pres. 1991-92). Avocations: biking, weight lifting, running, cross country skiing, history. Home: 314 N Yellowstone Dr Madison WI 53705-2446 Office: U Wis Med Sch 1300 University Ave Madison WI 53706-1532

ALBANESE, THOMAS, food industry executive, consultant; b. Passaic, N.J., June 27, 1930; s. Charles and Viola (Gueritey) A.; m. Theresa Mary Perez, Aug. 8, 1953; children: Thomas II, John, Theresa Lynn, Richard Charles, Michael Quintin. Grad. high sch., Garfield, N.J. Pres. Thomas Albanese Inc., Clifton, N.J., 1958-60; founder, pres. Albanese Products Inc., Las Vegas, Nev., 1960—; exec. cons. The Norlen Co., Las Vegas, 1971—; exec. dir. The Las Vegas Chili Co., Las Vegas, 1982—; owner The Chef Tomal Co., Las Vegas, 1995—. Creator Gourmet Chili Meals and Desserts-La Chilafesta, 1982, Mr. B's Hang All Kit, 1971; patentee plumbing sys. Founder Double TT Rancho, dir., 1986—. With USAF, 1951-55. Mem. United Assn. Plumbers and Pipefitters, Plumbers and Pipefitters Local 525. Avocations: designing, inventing. Home and Office: 804 Sunny Pl Las Vegas NV 89106-3632

ALBANI, THOMAS J. investor; b. Hartford, Conn., May 3, 1942; s. Charles A. and Marie F. Albani; m. Suzanne Beardsley, Sept. 3, 1966; children: Karin, Steven. BA, Amherst Coll., 1964; MBA, Wharton Sch. U. Pa., 1967. Asst. product mgr. Gen. Mills, Inc., Mpls., 1967-69; dir. mktg. Am. Can Co., Greenwich, Conn., 1969-73; mgmt. cons. McKinsey and Co., Inc., N.Y.C., 1973-78; gen. mgr. GE, Bridgeport, Conn., 1978-84; group v.p. Black & Decker, Inc., Bridgeport, 1984; pres. Sunbeam No. Am. Appliance Div. Allegheny Internat., Oak Brook, Ill., 1984-86; pres. appliance bus. Allegheny Internat. Inc., Pitts., 1986, exec. v.p., COO, 1986-89; prin. New Eng. Cons. Group, Westport, Conn., 1990-91; pres., CEO Electrolux Corp., Atlanta, 1991-98; pres. Canopache Cons., Siasconset, Mass., 1999—. Bd. dirs. Select Comfort Corp., Igloo Products Corp. Mem.: Chgo. Assn. Commerce and Industry (bd. dirs. 1986), Assn. Home Appliance Mfrs. (bd. dirs. 1985—87), Nat. Housewares Mfrs. Assn. (bd. dirs. 1985—90). Home: 1 S White Jewel Ct Vero Beach FL 32963-4275 Office: Canopache Cons PO Box 855 Siasconset MA 02564-0855 E-mail: tjalbani@aol.com.

ALBANO, ANTHONY WILLIAM, retired career officer, secondary school educator; b. Atlanta, Dec. 6, 1953; s. Rocco Louis and Ida Elizabeth (White) A. AA, Manatee Jr. Coll., 1973; BA, U. Fla., 1975; MA, Cen. Mich. U., 1979. Commd. 2d lt. USAF, 1975, advanced through grades to maj., 1979, ret., 1993; tchr. Venice (Fla.) Area Mid. Sch., 1995—. Scoutmaster Boy Scouts Am., Rochester, N.H., 1984-86, Ramstein AB, Germany, 1986-88, asst. dist. commr., Mt. Holly, N.J., 1988-92; vestry mem. St. Albans Epsicopal. Congregation, Ramstein AB, 1986-88. Mem. Air Force Assn., Order Daedalians, Mil Order of World Wars, Elks. Republican. Avocations: hiking, skiing, water skiing, camping, boating, travel. Home: 711 Albee Farm Rd N Nokomis FL 34275-2411

ALBANO, DAVID WARREN, financial executive, strategic business analyst; b. Orange, N.J., Mar. 16, 1959; s. Nicholas Henry Jr. and Anne (Warren) A. BA, U. Pa., 1982; MBA, NYU, 1990. Gen. sales mgr. Sta. WZIP, South Daytona, Fla., 1985-88; fin. analyst Motion Picture Assn. Am., N.Y.C., 1990-93; sr. fin. analyst Children's TV Workshop, N.Y.C., 1994-96, fin. dir., 1996-2000; asst. v.p. internat. fin. Sesame Workshop, N.Y.C., 2000—03; v.p. fin. and acctg. Consumer Product Licenscing and Internat. TV Distbn., N.Y.C., 2003—. Home: 435 W 119th St Apt 5C New York NY 10027

ALBANO, MAUREEN TERESA, artist; b. Pitts., Sept. 15, 1962; d. Joseph C. and Teresa (Merendino) A.; m. Theodore Galante; children: Lucian Albano Galante, Mia Albano Galante. BS in Art Edn., Ind. U. of Pa., 1985; postgrad., Inst. of Italian Studies, 1985; MFA in Sculpture, Cranbrook Acad. of Art, 1995. Cert. tchr. art K-12, Pa. Mus. educator Carnegie Mus. Art, Pitts., 1986-93, Mus. Fine Arts, Boston, 1996—. One-woman shows include U. Pitts., 1993, Mobius Gallery, Boston, 1997, 1999, exhibited in group shows at Pitts. Ctr. for Arts, 1992, Wayne State U., Detroit, 1996, Woman Made Gallery, Chgo., 1996, 1999, Fort Point Gallery, Boston, 1997, Fuller Mus. Art, Brockton, Mass., 1998, 2001, Kingston Gallery, Boston, 2000, 2002, Michael Price Gallery, 2001, Mills Gallery, 2002, Tremont Gallery, 2002. Grantee Ednl. grant, The Met. Mus. Art, 1991, Artist grant, Mass. Cultural Coun., 2001.

ALBANO, MICHAEL J. mayor; m. Michele Garreffi; children: Jonathan, Michael, Christopher. BS, Springfield Coll., 1974; MS, Am. Internat. Coll., 1976; MPA, U. Hartford, 1981. Probation officer Westfield Dist. Ct., 1974-82; mem. staff Office of the State Auditor, 1994-95; spl. parole bd. mem., 1993-94; mem. Mass. parole bd., 1982—94; mayor City of Springfield, Mass., 1996—. Adj. faculty mem. Asnutuck C.C., Enfield, Conn., 1979-81, 92-94, Springfield Tech. C.C., 1977-81, U. Mass., 1992; vis. lectr. criminal justice Westfield State Coll./Suffolk U., Boston. Springfield Youth commr., 1980-81; mem. Springfield Sch. com., 1985-90; commr. Springfield Conservation, 1990-92; mem. Springfield City Coun., 1991—, pres., 1994-95. Home: 36 Florentine Gdns Springfield MA 01108-2508 Office: City of Springfield 36 Court St Springfield MA 01103-1687*

ALBANO, PASQUALE CHARLES, management educator, management and organization development consultant; b. Bayonne, N.J., Dec. 3, 1941; s. Armando and Marie (Fasulo) A.; m. Norma Agnes Eichholz, July 16, 1960; children: Donna, Nancy, Susan, Carol. BS in Edn.-Social Sci. cum laude, Monmouth U., 1967; postgrad., Rutgers U., 1969-70; MA in Mgmt. magna cum laude, Pepperdine U., 1976; cert. in orgnl. cons., U.S. Army Tng. Ctr., 1979; EdD in Leadership and Policy summa cum laude, Temple U., 1987. Cert. tchr. social scis., N.J.; orgn. devel. cons. Personnel-employee devel. specialist Hdqs. Army Comm.-Electronics Command, Ft. Monmouth, N.J., 1967-69; chmn. mgmt. devel. dept. army edn. ctr. Hdqs. Army Comm. Command, Ft. Monmouth, N.J., 1969-75, dir. northeastern U.S. regional tng. ctr., 1975-78, orgnl. effectiveness officer R & D ctr., 1978-81, chief orgnl. effectiveness office, 1981—85, chief leadership rsch. office, 1985-87, chief orgnl. consulting office, 1987—94; pvt. practice cons., 1993—. Tchr. U.S. Army Pers. Mgmt. Program, Ga., Wash., Pa., NJ, Ala., Ariz., Va., NY, Okla., SC, Panama, 1976—78, Internat. Assn. Quality Cirs., Internat. Pers. Mgmt. Assn., Info. Resource Mgmt. Assn., USAR, 1981—91, Am. Mgmt. Assn., 1995—, Ctr. for Bus. and Inds., Monmouth and Ocean Counties, 1995; adj. prof. mgmt. and social psychology small bus. mgmt. Kean Coll., Union, NJ, 1981—96, Brookdale C.C., NJ, 1975—93, Pepperdine U., L.A., 1977—81, Temple U., Phila., 1987—88, grad. sch. bus. Fairleigh Dickinson U., 1990—; adj. prof. tchr. mgmt. and orgnl. psychology in MBA and spl. corp. onsite edn. programs Rutgers U., 1997—, adj. prof. M of Adminstrv. Sci. program, Jewish and Israeli fgn. student program, 2002; adj. prof. orgnl. behavior St. Peter's Coll., Jersey City, 2003—; tchr. interpersonal rels. Ocean County Coll., 1971—73; creative thinking Brookdale C.C., 1972—73; mem. small bus. adv. coun., 1996; cons. Mut. UFO Network, 1998; adj. prof. global mgmt. N.J. City Univ., St. Peter's Coll., Jersey City, 2003—; reviewer coll. textbooks Prentice-Hall Pubs., 2003—; global CEO Inst. Chartered Fin. Analysts, India, 2002—. Author: Transactional Analysis on the Job, 1974, Retention of Engineers and Scientists, 1983, The Effects of an Experimental Training Program on the Creative Thinking Abilities of Adults, 1987, Value-Adding Leadership, 1988, Tapping the Potential to Contribute, 1998, One Summer, A Thousand Days, 2001, The Cloud Shaman, 2001, Fires Burning Deep Inside, 2001, Turn the Sandglass Over, 2001, Skyline Drive: A Poetic Journey Through Business Life, 2001; contbr. poetry anthologies Anagram: Art and Literature of Asian Americans, 1998, Snow and Barn, The Golden Wings, Bytes of Poetry, 2001—02, Taj Mahal Rev., India, 2002, developer mgmt. tng. curriculum for Monmouth and Ocean County Adult Edn. Commn., 1996, also instnl. materials for tng. tel. crisis hotline ctr. workers Contact USA, ednl. programs for lab. software engrs. and orgnl. surveys of U.S. Army, 1995, merger, mgmt. and original design tng. programs, 1996—; contbr. world wide web articles to numerous publs., materials for use in tng. sr. officers, fgn. mil. officers. Tchr. human rels. ednl. assns. Monmouth and Ocean Counties, 1970-74, Fed. Women's Program, 1980, ESL Cmty. and Family Svcs., Monmouth, 1990-93; pvt. tutor English Citizenship; vol. Habitat for Humanity Internat., 1995-96, Contact USA, 1995-96, Presbyn. Youth Program, 1965; mem. NAACP, 1963-64; mem. Small Bus. Adv. Coun., Ocean County Coll., 1996. With U.S. Army, 1958-60. Recipient Bernard Watson award William Penn Found., 1987, Quality Circle Devel. commendation U.S. Army, 1981, Devel. Sci. Pers. commendation, 1983, Creative Edn. Techniques commendation, 1988, ESL Textbooks commendation U.S. Army Materiel Command, 1992, Mgmt. Devel. Curriculum commendation, 1992, numerous World Wide Net awards for creative writing, 1998. Mem. ASTD, ACLU, Creative Edn. Found., Internat. Transactional Analysis Assn., Adult Edn. Assn., Nat. Assn. Retired Fed. Employees, Nat. Speleol. Soc., Archaeol. Inst. of Am., Soc. Advancement of Mgmt., Acad. Mgmt., World Future Soc., Assn. of U.S. Army, Internat. Platform Assn. (elected), Union Concerned Scientists,Jersey Shore Quality Coun., Nat. Space Soc., Inst. Noetic Sciences, Acad. of Am. Poets, Planetary Soc. (cons. mutual UFO network 1998), Search for Extraterrestrial Intelligence Inst., Mensa, Phi Alpha Theta, Phi Delta Kappa. Avocations: investigating mysteries, exploring caves and ancient ruins, digging fossils, inventing, writing poetry. Home and Office: Adaptive Leadership 805 Woodwild Dr Point Pleasant NJ 08742 E-mail: charlesalbano@webtv.net. *There is a continuity in life that comes of one's core identity, the whispered voice of youth. When heeded, it unfailingly provides motivation, persistence, satisfaction and direction. Life's purpose is not given; it is self-determined. Compounded of breaks, burdens, chance, successes, failures, myths and realities, we are nevertheless, self-made. Living well means respecting life, living to one's potential, adding value, and reducing pain and suffering of others. Success must be measured against how well one has met his/her own standards and purposes in living.*

ALBARRACIN, DOLORES, psychologist, educator; d. Carlos and Marta R. Albarracín; m. Martin P. Repetto, June 1, 1962; children: Maria de los Angeles Repetto, Martin J. Repetto. PhD, U Ill., Champaign-Urbana, 1997. Asst. prof. Psychology Dept., U. Fla., Gainesville, Fla., 1997—; grad. asst. and fellow Psychology Dept., U. Ill., Champaign-Urbana, Ill., 1992—97. Author: (jour. article) Jour. of Personality and Social Psychology, Health Psychology, 2000, Jour. of Personality and Social Psychology, 2001, Psychol. Bull., 2001; : Personality and Social Psychology Bull., 2001, Advances in Exptl. Social Psychology, 2002, Health Psychology, 2003; editor: (book) Handbook of attitudes and attitude change, 2004. Recipient Scientist Devel. Award, NIMH, 1999-2003; grantee R 03 Rsch. Grant, 1997-1999, R 01 Rsch. Grant, NIH, 2001-2006. Mem.: Soc. of Intermerican Psychology (us rep. 2000—02), Am. Psychol. Soc., Soc. of Personality and Social Psychology, APA, Soc. of Exptl. Social Psychology. Home: 3629 SW 97th Way Gainesville FL 32608 Office: University Fla Psychology Dept Gainesville FL 32611 Office Fax: 352-392-7985. E-mail: dalbarra@ufl.edu.

ALBAUGH, BERNARD JOHN, II, social science researcher; b. Weston, W.Va., Dec. 24, 1935; s. Bernard John and Beulah Vada A. Albaugh; m. Jean Carlton, May 10, 1962 (div. Oct. 9, 1968); 1 child, John; m. Patricia L. Richards, Mar. 24, 1973; children: Bernard III, Kristina. BA in Psychology, U. Okla., 1965, MPA, 1976, MSW, 1968. Cert. clin. social work. Asst. dir. child welfare Okla. State Dept. Human Svcs., Oklahoma City, 1968-70; clin. social work Bur. Indian Affairs, Concho, Okla., 1970-72; dir. Dept. Behavioral Health U.S. Pub. Health Svc. Indian Hosp., Clinton, Okla., 1970-92, Ctr. for Human Behavior Studies, Weatherford, Okla., 1992—. Planning cons. Cheyenne and Arapaho Tribes, Concho, 1968-2001; adj. prof. U. Okla., Norman, 1975-2001; contract rschr. NIH, 1985—, NIAAA, 1985—. With U.S. Army, 1956-58. Mem. Nat. Assn. Social Work. Democrat. Roman Catholic. Avocations: scuba diving, travel. Home: Rte 5 Box 99A Weatherford OK 73096 Office: Ctr for Human Behavior Studies Box 976 Weatherford OK 73096 Office Fax: 580-772-6381. E-mail: lhasa@itlnet.net.

ALBAUGH, ED, retired journalist; b. Frederick, Md., June 9, 1935; s. Helen Opel and Edwin Albaugh; children: Strawinski, Kirsten. Editor, writer Balt. Sun, 1961—70, Wash. Star, Washington, 1970—81; editor U.S. News & World Report, Washington, 1982—97; ret. Chess columnist Wash. Star, Washington, 1973—81. Author: (poems) Li Po And That Lady (mad poets rev. competition, 2003). Pfc U.S. Army, 1957—59. Recipient Chess Journalist of Yr., Chess Journalists Am., 1986. Mem.: U.S. Chess Fedn. (life).

ALBAUM, JEAN STIRLING, psychologist, educator; b. Beijing, Jan. 11, 1932; came to U.S., 1936; d. Richard Henry and Emma Bowyer (Lueders) Ritter; m. B. Taylor Stirling, Aug. 15, 1953 (div. 1965); 1 child, Christopher Taylor Stirling; m. Joseph H. Albaum; stepchildren: Thomas Gary, Lauren Jean. BA, Beloit (Wis.) Coll., 1953; MS, Danbury (Conn.) State U., 1964, U. La Verne, Calif., 1983; PhD, Claremont (Calif.) Grad. Sch., 1985. Lic. ednl. psychologist, Calif. Spl. edn. tchr. Charter Oak (Calif.) Sch. Dist., 1966-80; psychologist, coord. elem. counseling Claremont Sch. Dist., 1980—2002; pvt. practice ednl. psychologist Encino, Calif., 1987—. Clin. supr. marriage, family and child counselor interns Claremont Grad. Sch., 1987—2002; sr. adj. prof. U. La Verne, 1988—; oral commr. Bd. Behavioral Sci. Examiners, Sacramento, 1989—2003. Contbr. articles to profl. jours. Hostess L.A. World Affairs Coun., 1980—; pres. Woodley Homeowner's Assn., Encino, 1986-89. Grantee Durfee Found., 1986, 92. Mem. Am. Psychol. Assn., Calif. Assn. Marriage, Family and Child Therapists, Calif. Assn. Lic. Ednl. Psychologists. Avocations: travel, international relations, history, sailing, skiing. Office: Edn Ctr 2080 N Mountain Ave Claremont CA 91711-2643

ALBEE, ARDEN LEROY, geologist, educator; b. Port Huron, Mich., May 28, 1928; s. Emery A. and Mildred (Tool) A.; m. Charleen H. Ettenheim, 1978; children: Janet, Margaret, Carol, Kathy, James, Ginger, Mary, George. BA, Harvard U., 1950, MA, 1951, PhD, 1957. Geologist U.S. Geol. Survey, 1950-59; prof. geology Calif. Inst. Tech., 1959—2002, prof. emeritus, 2002—; chief scientist Jet Propulsion Lab., 1978-84, dean grad. studies, 1984—2001, project scientist Mars Observer and Global Surveyor Missions, 1984—. Cons. in field, 1950; chmn. lunar sci. rev. panel NASA, 1972-77, mem. space sci. adv. com., 1976-84; mem. exam. bd. T.O.E.F.L. (Test of English as a Foreign Lang.), 1995-97; mem. Grad. Record Exam. Bd., 1995-98; mem. exec. com. Assn. Grad. Schs., 1995-97. Assoc. editor Jour. Geophys. Rsch., 1976-82, Ann. Rev. Earth Space Scis., 1978—; contbr. numerous articles to profl. jours. Bd. regents L.A. Chiropractic Coll., 1990-98. Recipient Exceptional Sci. Achievement medal NASA, 1976 Fellow Mineral Soc. Am. (assoc. editor Am. Mineralogist 1972-76), Geol. Soc. Am. (assoc. editor bull. 1972-89, councilor 1989-92), Am. Geophys. Union. Office: Calif Inst Tech Mail Code 150-21 Pasadena CA 91125-0001 E-mail: aalbee@gps.caltech.edu.

ALBEE, EDWARD FRANKLIN, author, playwright; b. Mar. 12, 1928; s. Reed A. and Frances (Cotter) Albee. Student, Trinity Coll., 1946-47. Disting. prof. U. Houston, 1988—. Author: (plays) The Zoo Story, 1958, The Death of Bessie Smith, The Sandbox, 1959, The American Dream, 1960, Who's Afraid of Virginia Woolf?, 1961—62, The Ballad of the Sad Cafe (adaption of Carson McCullers' novella), 1963, Tiny Alice, 1964, Malcolm, 1966, A Delicate Balance, 1966 (Pulitzer Prize for drama, 1967), Everything in the Garden, 1968, Box, Quotations from Chairman Mao, 1970, All Over, 1971, Seascape, 1975 (Pulitzer prize for drama), Counting the Ways, 1976, Listening, 1977, The Man Who Had Three Arms, 1981, The Lady from Dubuque, 1978—79, adaptation of Lolita (Nabokov), 1980, Finding the Sun, 1982, Marriage Play, 1986—87, Three Tall Women, 1990 91 (Pulitzer Prize for drama, 1994), Fragments, 1993, The Play about the Baby, 1996, The Goat, Or Who is Sylvia?, 2000, Occupant, 2001; dir.: (plays) Happy Days, 1993, Alley Theatre, 1991. Pres. Edward F. Albee Found. Named to Theater Hall of Fame, 1985; recipient gold medal in drama Am. Acad. and Inst. Arts and Letters, 1980, Nat. Medal of Arts, 1996, Kennedy Ctr. honoree, 1996. Mem.: Nat. Inst. Arts and Letters, Dramatists Guild Coun. Address: 14 Harrison St New York NY 10013-2842

ALBEE, GEORGE WILSON, psychology educator; b. St. Marys, Pa., Dec. 20, 1921; s. George W. and Maude (Allen) A.; m. Constance Impallaria, Aug. 6, 1955 (dec.); children: Alexander, Luke, Maud, Sarah; m. Margaret Moon-Mui Tong, Dec. 20, 1985. AB, Bethany Coll., 1943, ScD (hon.), 1969; MS, U. Pitts., 1947, PhD, 1949; PhD (hon.), Stirling U., Scotland, 1998. Rsch. psychologist Western Psychiat. Inst., Pitts., 1949-51; asst. exec. sec. Am. Psychol. Assn., Washington, 1951-53; Fulbright prof. Helsinki (Finland) U., 1953-54; assoc. prof. psychology Western Res. U., Cleve., 1954-56, prof., 1957-71, chmn. dept. psychology, 1957-60, 63-66, Ladd disting. prof. psychology, 1959-71; prof. psychology U. Vt., Burlington, 1971-92, prof. emeritus, 1992—; courtesy prof. Fla. Mental Health Inst. U. South Fla., Tampa, 1994—. Cons. VA, Surgeon Gen. of Army, Pres.'s Com. on Mental Retardation, Peace Corps, 1962-65; vis. fellow Brit. Psychol. Soc., 2003. Author: Mental Health Manpower, 1959, Emerging Concepts of Mental Disorder, 1969, The Uncertain Future of Clinical Psychology, 1970, The Future of Psychology, 1974, The Protestant Ethic, Sex, and Psychotherapy, 1978; editor: Primary Prevention of Psychopathology, 1977; gen. editor: (with Justin M. Joffe) series of books on primary prevention of psychopathology; humor columnist The Longboat Observer. Mem. Vt. Psychology Licensing Bd., 1972-75; dir. task force on manpower Joint Commn. Mental Illness and Health, Cambridge, Mass., 1957-59; program com. Nat. Assn. for Mental Health, 1968-70; dir. task group in prevention Pres.'s Commn. Mental Health, 1977-78; com. on prevention Nat. Mental Health Assn., 1985-86; bd. dirs. Internat. Coun. Psychologists, 1985-88, 98-00; prevention com. World Fedn. Mental Health, 1992—, Biennial Albee lectr. on prevention. Recipient Alumni Achievement award in sci. Bethany Coll., 2000. Fellow APA (bd. profl. affairs, coun. reps., bd. dirs. 1965-70, 77-80, pres. div. clin. psychology 1967, nat. pres. 1969-70, policy and planning bd. 1972-75, chairperson com. on human resources 1973-76, mem. com. on sci. and profl. ethics 1990-92, bd. for advancement of psychology in pub. interest 1999-2002, task force on governance 2003, Disting. Profl. Contbn. award 1975, Gold medal for lifetime contbns. in the pub. interest 1993, Presdl. citation 2001), Am. Psychol. Soc. (founding fellow); mem. AAAS, AAUP, Am. Bd. Profl. Psychology (bd. dirs. 1975-78, treas. 1976-80), Ea. Psychol. Assn., Midwestern Psychol. Assn., Ohio Psychol. Assn. (pres. 1963-64), Vt. Psychol. Assn., New Eng. Psychol. Assn. (pres. 1978-79, Disting. Contbn. award 1997), Am. Assn. Applied and Preventive Psychology (1st pres. 1990-92, Lifetime Achievement award in prevention psychology 1997), Psychologists for Social Responsibility (pres. 1999, steering com. 2001—), Phi Beta Kappa, Sigma Xi, Psi Chi. Home: 7157 Longboat Dr N Longboat Key FL 34228-1047

ALBEE, GLORIA, playwright; b. Brockton, Mass., Apr. 26, 1931; d. Earl Fredric and Rita Marie (Walls) Albee; m. Leonard Goodman, Jan. 13, 1961 (div.); 1 child, Anna Albee Goodman. Student, Boston U., 1948-49, U. Wash., 1972-74, Sarah Lawrence Coll., 1975-76, Hunter Coll., 1986-92. Playwright: Medea, 1975, Helen of Sparta, 1991; plays produced include Medea, Nothing Personal, The Yellow Wallpaper. Recipient John Golden Theatre award Hunter Coll., 1986, Mary M. Fay award in poetry Hunter Coll., 1990, Honorable Mention award Jane Chambers Playwriting Award, 1994; Rockefeller Bros. Found. grantee; Nat. Arts Club Lit. scholar, 1990. Mem. Dramatists Guild. Home: 110 W End Ave 14C New York NY 10023-6342 E-mail: GALBEE1707@aol.com.

ALBENSI, BENEDICT CHARLES, biomedical consultant, computer programmer, neuroscientist, educator, science writer, editor; b. Dover, N.J., Apr. 11, 1956; s. Benedict and Kathleen Helen (Owen) Albensi. BS in Gen. Sci., U. Oreg., 1982; MA in Biology, Sonoma State U., 1992; PhD in Neurosci., U. Utah, 1995; postgrad., Georgetown U., 1996-97, Sanders Brown Ctr. Aging, 1997-99; cert . mgmt., U. Utah. Analytical chemist Multi-Tech Labs., ETTC Corp., Rohnert Park, Calif., 1986-87; rsch. assoc., electrophysiologist NPS Pharms., Salt Lake City, 1987-92; clin. rsch. dept. Pfizer, Inc., Ann Arbor, 1999-01; faculty dept. neurol. surgery The Cleveland Clin. Found., Ohio, 2001—. Adj. instr. Salt Lake Cmty. Coll., 1994—95; cons. neurosci. U. Utah, Salt Lake City, 1990; grant reviewer study sect. NIH; adj. asst. prof. dept. biology Case Western Res. U., Cleve., 2003—. Contbr. articles to profl jours; manuscript ad hoc referee:. Adv. mental health Missoula Adv. Program, Mont. Recipient Achievement award, Multi-Tech Labs, 1987, 1st Pl. Best Poster award, U. Ky., 1998, Recognition award, Warner Lambert Colleague, 1999; fellow Grad. Rsch., U. Utah, 1993—94; grantee Surrey Med. Rsch. Travel, 1994. Mem.: AAAS, So.c Magnetic Resonance, Soc. Neurosci., Internat. Neural Network Soc., Nat. Stroke Assn., Inernat. Brain Rsch. Orgn., Regulatory Affairs Profl. Soc., Cognitive Neurosci. Soc., Brain Injury Assn., Am. Epilepsy Soc., Soc. Technology Cmomn., Drug Info. Assn., Am. Soc. Neurochemists, Am. Assn. Pharm. Scientists, Am. Chem. Soc. Avocations: painting, reading, camping, skiing, hiking.

ALBER, PHILLIP GEORGE, lawyer; b. Lansing, Mich., Dec. 10, 1948; s. Phillip Karl and Audrey Irene (Putnam) A.; m. Shari Thornton; children: Emily Nicole, Phillip George, Elisabeth Whitney, Christian Thornton. BA magna cum laude, U. Mich., 1971; JD cum laude, Wayne State U., 1974. Bar: Mich. 1975, U.S. Dist. Ct. (ea. dist.) Mich. 1975, U.S. Ct. Appeals (6th cir.) 1978, U.S. Dist. Ct. (we. dist.) Mich. 1982. Assoc. Harvey, Kruse, Westen & Milan, Detroit, 1975-79, ptnr., 1979-85, Mager, Mercer and Alber, Detroit, 1985-2000, Alber Crafton, PLLC, Troy, Mich., 2001—. Lectr. Ill. Inst. Continuing Edn., Chgo., 1980. Mem. ABA (torts ins. practice sect., vice chair fidelity and surety law com.), Detroit Bar Assn. (pub. adv. com. 1979—, cir. ct. com. 1978—), Mich. Bar Assn. (rep. assembly 1970-80), Internat. Assn. Def. Counsel (fidelity and surety com. 1984—), Surety Claims Inst., Nat. Bd. Claim Assn. (pres. 1992-94, program chair 1990—), Assn. Def. Trial Counsel, Detroit Athletic Club, Hundred Club, Goodfellows Old Newsboys Club (Detroit). Republican. Roman Catholic. Home: 673 Washington Rd Grosse Pointe MI 48230-1253 Office: Alber Crafton PLLC Ste 300 2301 W Big Beaver Rd Troy MI 48084-4906 E-mail: palber@albercrafton.com.

ALBERG, ANTHONY J. epidemiologist; s. John F. and Judith J. Alberg, Margot Alberg (Stepmother); m. Laura B. Alberg; children: Christian, Andrew. BS, U. Calif., Davis, 1980; MPH, Yale U., 1984; PhD, Johns Hopkins U., 1994. Asst. prof. of epidemiology Johns Hopkins Sch. of Pub. Health, Balt., 1999—. Author: (epidemiologic research) The influence of cigarette smoking on circulating concentrations of antioxidant micronutrients; contbr. articles to profl. jours. (Preventive Oncology Academic award, 1998). Recipient Ho-Ching Yang Faculty Fellow in Cancer Prevention. Mem.: Soc. for Epidemiologic Rsch., Am. Soc. of Preventive Oncology (exec. com. 2000—02). Achievements include research in influence of cigarette smoking on circulating concentrations of antioxidant micronutrients. Office: Johns Hopkins Sch Pub Health 615 N Wolfe St Baltimore MD 21205 Office Fax: 410-614-2632. E-mail: aalberg@jhsph.edu.

ALBERG, TOM AUSTIN, investment company executive, lawyer; b. San Francisco, Feb. 12, 1940; s. Thomas A. and Miriam A. (Twitchell) A.; m. Mary Ann Johnke, June 8, 1963 (div. July 1989); children: Robert, Katherine, John; m. Judith Beck, Aug. 8, 1989; children: Carson, Jessica. AB, Harvard Coll., 1962; JD, Columbia U., 1965. Bar: N.Y. 1965, Wash. 1967. Assoc. Cravath, Swaine & Moore, N.Y.C., 1965-67, Perkins, Cole, Stone, Olsen & Williams, Seattle, 1967-71, ptnr., 1971-90, chmn. exec. com., 1986-90; exec. v.p. legal and corp. affairs McCaw Cellular Comm. Inc., Kirkland, Wash., 1990-95; pres., CEO, dir. Personal Connect Comm. Corp., Kirkland, 1995—; prin. Madrona Investment Group, 1996—. Pres., COO, dir. Lin Broadcasting Inc., Kirkland, 1991-95; bd. dirs. Active Voice Corp., VISIO Corp., Emeritus Corp., Amazon Com., Inc.; pres. Seattle Legal Svcs., 1973-74; lectr. on securities and fin. law. Editor Law Rev., Columbia U. Contbr. articles to profl. jours. Pres. Intiman Theatre, Seattle, 1981-83, Pacific Sci. Ctr. Found., Seattle, 1982-84; chmn. Discovery Inst., 1991—, Seattle Commons, 1991-94; trustee Children's Hosp. Found., 1992-95, Pacific Sci. Ctr., 1994—, U. Puget Sound, 1994—, Sta. KING-FM, 1994—. Stone scholar Columbia U., 1963-65. Mem. ABA, Wash. State Bar Assn. (chmn. corp. sect. 1975-76, securities com. 1974-75), Univ. Club, Seattle Yacht Club. Office: Madrona Investment Group LLC 1000 2nd Ave Ste 3700 Seattle WA 98104-1053

ALBERGER, WILLIAM RELPH, lawyer, government official; b. Portland, Oreg., Oct. 11, 1945; s. Relph Griffin and Ferne (Ahlstrom) A.; children: Eric Griffin, Blake Eugene. BA, Willamette U., 1967; MBA, U. Iowa, 1971; JD, Georgetown U., 1973. Bar: D.C. 1974. Spl. asst. to U.S. Senator Bob Packwood, 1969-71; legis. asst. U.S. Rep. Al Ullman, Washington, 1972-75, adminstrv. asst., 1975-77, House Com. on Ways and Means, 1977; vice-chmn. U.S. Internat. Trade Commn., Washington, 1978-80, chmn., 1980-82; pvt. practice Washington, 1982—. Mem. ABA (chmn. standing com. customs law 1983-85), D.C. Bar Assn., Internat. Bar Assn. Democrat. E-mail: bill.alberger@gte.net.

ALBERICO, SALVATORE J. psychiatric social worker, educator, researcher; b. Utica, N.Y., Aug. 14, 1924; s. Tarquinio Elio and Amalia Maria (Casatelli) A.; m. Dorothy Garth Strite, July 24, 1954; children: Patricia Ann, Jeanne Marie, Victorine Garth. BA in Social Sci., Utica Coll., Syracuse U., 1955; MA in European History, Syracuse U., 1961; MSW in Mental Health, 1970. Cert. social worker, cert. tchr., N.Y.; qualified clin. social worker; diplomate in clin. social work. Instr. history Mohawk Valley C.C., Utica, 1965-73; social svc. cons. LTCF, 1974-87; case supr. family and child welfare Oneida County Dept. Social Svcs., Utica, 1963-70, staff devel. supr., 1970-79; psychiat. social worker, adminstr. Oneida County Dept. Mental Health, Utica, 1979-88; sr. psychiat. social worker Spring House Day Treatment, Utica, 1989-94. Pvt. U.S. Army WWII, 1943-45. Named Outstanding Profl. in Humn Svcs., Am. Acad. Human Svcs., 1975. Mem. NASW, Acad. Cert. Social Workers, Civil Svc. Employees Assn., AFSCME Retiree Program Chpt. 1000, Ret. Pub. Employees Assn., Am. Assn. Ret. Persons, Am. Legion. Democrat. Roman Catholic. Avocations: reading and research in world war ii history, swimming, downhill skiing.

ALBERNATHY, KATHLEEN Q. federal agency administrator; married; 1 child. BS magna cum laude; JD, Cath. U. Am. Dir. fed. affairs Comsat World Systems Divsn.; v.p. fed. regulatory AirTouch Comm., Inc.; v.p. regulatory affairs U.S. West, Inc.; ptnr. Wilkinson Barker Knauer; v.p. pub. policy BroadBand Office Comm.; commr. FCC, Washington, 2001—. Adj. prof. Georgetown U. Law Ctr., Cath. U. Am. Columbus Sch. Law. Mem.: D.C. Bar Assn., Fed. Comm. Bar Assn. (past pres.). Office: FCC 445 12th St SW Washington DC 20554

ALBERS, CHARLES EDGAR, investment manager; b. Flushing, N.Y., Nov. 30, 1940; s. Edwin M. and Olive F. (Van Dyke) A.; m. Judy Mae Hite, Dec. 18, 1961 (dec. June 1998); children: Robert, Karin, Laura. AB, Kenyon Coll., 1962; MBA, Columbia U., 1967. CFA. Securities analyst Arnold Bernhard & Co., N.Y.C., 1963-66; fin. analyst Baker Industries, Newark, 1967-68; securities analyst Wertheim & Co., N.Y.C., 1968-69; asst. portfolio mgr. Am. Standard, Inc., N.Y.C., 1969-71; sr. v.p. equity securities Guardian Life Ins. Co., N.Y.C., 1971-98. Portfolio mgr. Guardian Park Avenue Fund, Inc., N.Y.C., 1972-98; pres. Guardian Stock Fund, N.Y.C., 1983-98; sr. v.p. Oppenheimer Funds, 1998—; portfolio mgr. Oppenheimer Main St. Fund, 1998—. Named to honor roll Forbes Mut. Fund 9 times, Variable Annuity Mgr. of Yr. Morningstar, 1996; Woodrow Wilson fellow, 1962-63. Mem. Am. Fin. Assn., Assn. for Investment Mgmt. and Rsch., N.Y. Soc. Security Analysts, Fin. Mgmt. Assn., Beacon Hill Club, Columbia Club. Avocations: platform tennis, reading, mountain hiking.

ALBERS, DOLORES M. secondary education educator; AA, Casper Coll., 1969; BS, U. No. Colo., 1972; postgrad., U. N.C., U. Wyo., Chadron State. Physical edn. instr. for grades K-12, 6th and 8th grade sci. tchr. Bent County Sch. Dist. 2, McClave, Colo., 1972-75; physical edn./health instr. Sweetwater County Sch. Dist. # 2, Green River, Wyo., 1972—. Mem. phys. edn. coun. Mid. and Secondary Schs., 1999—2003, chmn. phys. edn. coun., 2002—03. Mem., chmn. Green River Parks and Recreation Bd.; coord. Hoops for Heart; co-chmn. United Way Sweetwater County, 1999-2001. Named Tchr. of Yr., Ctrl. Dist., 1994—95, Nat. Assn. Sport and Phys. Edn., 1995. Mem. AAHPERD, AALR, ASCD/NFOIA, NEA, Wyo. Edn. Assn., Wyo. Assn. Health, Phys. Edn., Recreation and Dance (Tchr. of Yr. award 1994-95), Green River Edn. Assn., Nat. Assn. for Sport and Phys. Edn., Mid. and Secondary Sch. Phys. Edn. Coun. (chmn. 2002-03). Home: PO Box 868 1745 Massachusetts Ct Green River WY 82935-6229 Office: Green River HS 1615 Hitching Post Dr Green River WY 82935-5771

ALBERS, EDWARD JAMES, SR., retired secondary school educator; b. Centralia, Wash., July 6, 1922; s. Otto Johnson and Nell Genevieve Albers; m. Caroline Constance Cochran, July 30, 1944; 1 child, Edward James Jr. Student, Wash. State Coll., 1942, U. Ariz., 1949-51; BA, U. Nebr., Omaha, 1959; MA, Rollins Coll., 1966. Cert. tchr., Fla. Commd. 2d lt. USAF, 1944, advanced through grades to maj., 1961, pilot, 1944-65, served command pilot SAC, ret., 1965; tchr. social studies Winter Park (Fla.) H.S., 1966-96, chmn. dept. social studies, 1973-88, ret., 1996. Decorated Yun-Hui medal, Chinese pilot wings, Chinese medal of Honor, 2001. Mem. Air Force Assn., Burma Star (Eng.), Mil. Order of the World Wars (past comdr.), Exptl. Aircraft Assn. and Warbirds, Ret. Officers' Assn., China-Burma-India Vets. Assn., Santa Ana Calif. AAF Cadet Class 44G Alumni, Train Collectors Assn., Lionel Collectors Assn., Officers' Club, Patrick AFB, Hump Pilots' Assn., Daedalians, Sigma Phi Epsilon. Democrat. Episcopalian. Avocations: antique toy train collecting, golfing, scuba diving, snow and water skiing, flying.

ALBERSHEIM, PETER, biology educator; b. N.Y.C., Mar. 30, 1934; s. Walter Julius and Alberta (Green) A.; children: Renee, Jim, Stephi. BS, Cornell U., 1956; PhD, Calif. Inst. Tech., 1959. NSF postdoctoral research fellow Swiss Fed. inst. Tech., Zurich, Switzerland, 1959; instr. biology Harvard, Cambridge, Mass., 1960-61, asst. prof., 1961-64; asso. prof. biochemistry, dept. chemistry U. Colo., Boulder, 1964-67, prof., 1967-85, prof. molecular, cellular, developmental biology, 1970-85; rsch. prof. biochemistry, chemistry, botany and plant pathology, dir. Complex Carbohydrate Rsch. Ctr. U. Ga., Athens, 1985—; co-dir. ctr. for plant and microbial complex carbohydrates Dept. Energy, Athens, 1987—; dir. resource ctr. for biomed. complex carbohydrates NIH, Athens, 1989—2002. Faculty Rsch. lectr. U. Colo. Coun. on Rsch. and Creative Work, 1980; Storrer Life Scis. lectr. U. Calif., Davis, 1977; Dupont lectr. Tex. A&M U., 1978; vis. prof. U. Tex., 1978. Author (with others): Twenty-six Afternoons of Biology - An Introductory Lab Manual, 1966; mem. editl. bd. Carbohydrate Rsch.; referee jours. : ; contbr. Recipient Robert L. Stearns award for contbns. to progress U. Colo., 1979; grantee NIH, 1960-65, 87—, NSF, 1966-67, 71-86, AEC-ERDA-Dept. Energy, 1964—, Herman Frasch Found., 1972-77, Rockefeller Found., 1975-83, USDA, 1975-78. Fellow AAAS; Mem. Am. Chem. Soc., Am. Soc. Biol. Chemists, Am. Soc. Plant Physiology (mem. exec. com. 1978—, Charles A. Shull award 1973), The Biochem. Soc., Am. Phytopathol. Soc., Sigma Xi, others. Office: U Ga Complex Carbohydrate Rsch Ctr 220 Riverbend Rd Athens GA 30602-1511

ALBERSON, BARBARA, health services professional; b. L.A., July 22, 1950; d. Solomon Nathan and Rae Spar Gimpel; m. Jack Alberson, Feb. 17, 1979. Pub. health educator San Diego Pub. Health Dept., 1974-78, Sacramento County Health Dept., 1979-81; health edn. cons. II Calif. Dept. of Aging, 1981-89, chief state and local injury control sect., 1989—. Mem. spl. panel for prevention of pediatric injuries Ctr. for Disease Control and Prevention, 1997-99; tng. cons. safe communities Nat. Hwy. Traffic Safety Adminstrn., 1998-2000. Bd. dirs. Calif. Coalition for Children's Safety and Health, 1994—, Calif. Coalition Against Driving Under the Influence, 1996—, alliance for Edn. Solutions, 1996—; Women's Am. Orgn. for Rehab. and Tng., 1974—. Fellowship Pub. Health Edn. Leadership Inst. Assn. of State and Territorial Dirs. of Health Promotion and Pub. Health Edn., 2000—; recipient Outstanding Achievement Calif. Office of Traffic Safety, 2000, Outstanding Partnership award Calif. Healthy Cities, 1998. Mem. APHA; mem. State and Territorial Dirs. of Injury Prevention. Avocations: gardening, cats. Office: Calif Dept Health Svcs 611 N 7th St Ste C Sacramento CA 95814

ALBERT, CAROLE ANNETTE, elementary school educator; b. Bronx, N.Y., Jan. 15, 1944; d. Henry and Antoinette (Lamborghini) Busto; m. Russell Alger Albert, July 20, 1968; 1 child, Laura Lydia. BS, SUNY, New Paltz, 1965; MA in reading, U. N.H., 1992. life cert. elem. tchr., N.Y., Calif.; cert. elem. tchr., N.H. Tchr. 2d grade Port Washington (L.I., N.Y.) Pub. Schs., 1965-67; tchr. 1st grade Simi Valley Unified Sch. Dist., Santa Susanna, Calif., 1967-68, Huntington Beach (Calif.) Sch. Dist., 1969-75; tchr. Big Bird Kindergarten, Rochester, N.H., 1976-80; Chpt. I coord. Sch. Adminstrv. Unit 44, Farmington, N.H., 1981-88; Title I project mgr. Sch. Adminstrv. Unit 61, Farmington, 1981-2001. Bd. dirs., sec. Farmington Child Care Ctr. Recipient Cert. of Recognition, Commr. Edn., 1984. Fellow: NEA; mem.: Internat. Reading Assn., Delta Kappa Gamma (pres. 2002—03). Avocations: travel, reading, photography. Home: 230 Gonic Rd Rochester NH 03839-4923

ALBERT, DANIEL MYRON, ophthalmologist, educator; b. Newark, Dec. 19, 1936; s. Maurice I. and Flora Albert; m. Eleanor Kagle, June 26, 1960; children: B. Steven, Michael. BS, Franklin and Marshall Coll., 1958; MD, U. Pa., 1962; MA (hon.), Harvard U., 1976; D honoris causa, Louis Pasteur U., Strasbourg, 1992; MS, U. Wis., Madison, 1997. Diplomate: Am. Bd. Ophthalmology. Intern Hosp. U. Pa., 1962-63, resident, 1963-66; surgeon USPHS, 1966-68; NIH spl. fellow in ophthalmic pathology Armed Forces Inst. Pathology, 1968-69; asst. prof. ophthalmology Yale U. Sch. Medicine, 1969-70, assoc. prof., 1970-75, prof., 1975-76; practice medicine specializing in ophthalmology; assoc. surgeon Mass. Eye and Ear Infirmary, 1976-86, surgeon, 1986-92, dir. David G. Cogan eye pathology lab., 1979-92; prof. ophthalmic pathology Harvard U. Med. Sch., 1976-84, David G. Cogan prof. ophthalmology, 1984-92; Frederick Allison Davis prof., dept. ophthalmology U. Wis., Madison, 1992—, chmn. dept. ophthalmology, 1992—2002, emeritus chmn., 2002—; dir. Mandelbaum Eye Rsch. Inst., U. Wis., 2002—. Author: (with Scheie) A History of Ophthalmology at the University of Pennsylvania, 1965, Textbook of Ophthalmology, 8th edit. 1969, 9th edit. 1977; co-author: Jaegar's Atlas of Ophthalmology, 1972, (with Puliafito) Foundations of Ophthalmology, 1979, Men of Vision, 1993, (with Jakobiec) Atlas of Clinical Ophthalmology, 1996; (with Edwards) History of Ophthalmology, 1996; editor: (with Edwards) The History of Ophthalmology, 1996, John Jeffres' Lectures on the Diseases of the Eye, 1998, Ophthalmic Surgery: Principles and Techniques, 1998, A Physician's Guide to Health Care Management, 2002; co-editor Principles and Practice of Ophthalmology, 1994, 2d edit., 1999, A Physician's Guide to Healthcare Management, 2002, Dates in Ophthalmology, 2002; editor Archives of Ophthalmology, 1994—; contbr. articles to profl. jours. Recipient Oliver Meml. medal, U. Pa., 1962, Friedenwald award, 1981, Von Sallmann award in vision and ophthalmology, Internat. Conf. for Eye Rsch., 1988, award, Humboldt Found., 1991, MacKenzie medal, Scottish Ophthal. Soc., 1992, Lighthouse Pisart Vision award, The Lighthouse Inc., 1997, Lorenz E. Zimmerman (WARF) professorship, 1999, Disting. Alumni award, U. Pa. Sch. Medicine, 2001; scholar William and Mary Greve scholar, 1978—79, Alcon Rsch. Inst., 1984—85. Fellow ACS; mem. Am. Assn. Ophthalmic Pathology (Zimmerman medal 1993), Am. Acad. Ophthalmology (Jackson Meml. lectr. 1996), Am. Bd. Ophthalmology (dir. 1997—), Macula Soc. (W. Richard Green award 2003). Jewish. Home: 1106 Wellesley Rd Madison WI 53705-2230 Office: U Wis Hosp and Clinics Dept Ophthalmology F4/334 600 Highland Ave Madison WI 53792-0001

ALBERT, DAVID SALEEBA, music educator; b. Noblesville, Ind., Aug. 3, 1958; s. Frank Joseph Albert and Iris Ann Albert Henderson, James Henderson (Stepfather); m. Heidi Sue Iseminger, Aug. 17, 2000; children: Joseph Taylor Whitley, Christopher David Saleeba. Student, Berklee Coll. of Music, Boston, MA, 1976—77; MusB, East Carolina U., 1982. Music Education NC, 1982. Condr. band Northeastern H.S., Elizabeth City, NC, 1982—92, Leesville Rd. H.S., Raleigh, NC, 1992—, chmn. arts dept., 1993—. Drummer Dave Albert All-Star Band, Raleigh, NC, 2000—. Pres. Albermarle Cmty. Concert Assn., Elizabeth City, NC, 1988—89. Named Band Dir. of Yr., 2002. Mem.: NC Bandmasters Assn. (pres. 1990—91, bd. dirs. 2002—), NC Assn. Educators, NC Music Educators Assn., The Am. Sch. Band Directors Assn., Phi Mu Alpha (hon.). Methodist. Achievements include Performance with The Leesville Road High School Symphonic Band at Midwest Band Clinic in Chicago, Il 2001; Performances with the Northeastern High School Symphonic Band and the Leesville Road High School Symphonic Band at several North Carolina Music Educators Conferences; selected by governor of North Carolina to develop the Music Standards for the National Board of Professional Teaching Standards. Avocations: reading, music, woodworking, antiques. Home: 4708 A Raleigh NC 27604 Office: Leesville Road High School Band 8409 Leesville Road Raleigh NC 27613 Office Fax: 919-870-4287. Personal E-mail: dalbert@wcpss.net. E-mail: dalbert@wcpss.net.

ALBERT, ELIZABETH FRANZ (MRS. HENRY B. ALBERT), investor, artist, conservationist; b. Chgo., Nov. 9, 1923; d. Herbert George and Louise Anders Franz; m. Henry Burton Albert, Oct. 24, 1964 (dec. July 1980). Student, Chevy Chase Jr. Coll., 1942. Investor stock market, real estate. Breeder several champion Miniature Poodles. Exhibitions include portraits, still life (various painting awards); contbr. biology textbook; editor: biology textbook. Former mem. Landmarks Preservation Coun. Chgo. Mem.: Am. Farmland Trust, Nat. Trust Hist. Preservation, Cousteau Soc. (founding mem.), Natural Resources Def. Coun., Environ. Def. Fund (Osprey Soc.), Nat. Mus. Women in the Arts (charter mem.), Chgo. Symphony Orch. Soc., Art Inst. Chgo. (life). Republican. Episcopalian. Achievements include design of a house in college within the architectural field; conservationist who campaigned against the herbicide Dacthal which causes lymphoma and Parkinson's Disease and is used by lawn care companies, home owners, farmers, and golf course greens keepers. Avocations: music, renovating houses, antiques, gardening, reading. Home: 316 Courtland Ave Park Ridge IL 60068

ALBERT, GARETT J. lawyer; b. Sept. 7, 1943; m. Eleanor Lanier Culbertson, Oct. 2, 1971. BA cum laude, Columbia U., 1965; postgrad., Harvard U. Bus. Sch., 1967-68; JD, Harvard U., 1968. Bar: D.C. 1969, N.Y. 1970. Atty. U.S. Atomic Energy Commn., 1968; assoc. Hughes Hubbard & Reed, N.Y.C., 1969-77; ptnr. Hughes Hubbard & Reed, LLP, N.Y.C., 1977—. Contbr. articles to various publs. including James Joyce Quar. Bd. dirs. Mannes Coll. Music, Nat. Acad. Design, Nat. Corp. Fund for Dance, Paul Taylor Dance Found. Winner U.S. Nat. Powerlifting Championship, Nat, Physique com., Tournament of Champions, 1996, Mr. USA, 1996, Kevin Levrone Bodybuilding Classic, 1995, and other masters powerlifting and bodybuilding championships. Mem. Union Club, Quogue (N.Y.) Field Club. Office: Hughes Hubbard & Reed LLP 1 Battery Park Plz Fl 12 New York NY 10004-1482

ALBERT, GERALD, clinical psychologist; b. N.Y.C., Nov. 13, 1917; s. Andrew I. and Eleanor (Walder) A.; divorced; m. Norma Holm Haskell, 1983; children: Jay Harvey, Laurie Ellen Albert Moxham. BA, CCNY, 1938; MA, New Sch. for Social Research, 1958; EdD, Columbia U., 1964; Cert. psychoanalytic tng. program, L.I. Inst. Mental Health, Queens, N.Y., 1964. Editor Vulcan and Creston Pubs., N.Y.C., 1939-45; nat. dir. advt., pub. relations Universal Pictures, div. ednl. films, N.Y.C., 1945-50; exec. dir. Advt. Enterprises and Continental Research Inst., Queens, N.Y., 1951-64; asst. to full prof. LIU, 1964-85, prof. Emeritus, 1985—; dir. L.I.U. C.W. Post Counseling Ctr., 1964-70. Psychologist, supervising psychologist, clin. dir. L.I. Consultation Ctr., 1966-86, clin. cons., 1986-95; pvt. practice marriage and individual therapy, 1958—. Author: (Psychology Today cassette) How To Choose and Keep a Marriage Partner, 1980, The Wonderful Magic of No-Fault Living, 1990, Japanese edit., 1996, (feature series for website) Making Your Marriage Work Better, 2001-02; editor-in-chief Jour. Contemporary Psychotherapy, 1985-87; contbr. articles to profl. jours., author booklets and other publs. Recipient 1st prize Most Effective Comms./Newsletters Cmty. Agys. Pub. Rels. Assn., 1983. Fellow Am. Assn. for Marriage and Family Therapy (L.I. Family Therapist of Yr. 1993, founder L.I. recorded telephone series "Helpful Hints for Happier Marriage" 1995, contbr. to webpage, 2001); mem. APA, Am. Soc. for Psychical Rsch., Soc. Clin. and Exptl. Hypnosis, Soc. Sci. Exploration, Internat. Soc. for Study of Subtle Energy and Energy Medicine, Inst. Noetic Scis. Office: 1900 Hempstead Tpke East Meadow NY 11554-1724

ALBERT, IRA BERNARD, social sciences educator; b. Balt., Aug. 8, 1944; s. Milton Albert and Augusta (Hillman) Poltilove; m. Sharon Eve, Dec. 23, 1970; 1 child, Mindi Lauren. BA, Johns Hopkins U., 1966; MA, U. Del., 1968, PhD, 1970. Asst. prof. Old Dominion Univ., Norfolk, Va., 1970-76, Jefferson Community Coll., Louisville, 1977-79, assoc. prof., 1979-81, C.C. of Baltimore County Dundalk Campus, Balt., 1981-89, prof., 1989—, chmn. social scis. and human svcs., 2002—. Adj. prof. Ea. Va. Med. Sch., Norfolk, 1974-76; cons. V.A. Hosp., Hampton, 1975-76, Louisville, 1977-81; sr. lectr. Towson State U., Balt., 1985-89; psychology assoc. Taylor Mental Health System, Balt., 1988-94. Contbr. articles to profl. jours. Home: 9213 Turnbull Rd Randallstown MD 21133-3307 Office: CC of Baltiore County Dundalk Campus 7200 Sollers Point Rd Baltimore MD 21222-4649

ALBERT, JANYCE LOUISE, human resources specialist, retired business educator, banker, consultant, human resources specialist; b. Toledo, July 27, 1932; d. Howard C. And Glenola Mae (Masters) Blessing; m. John R. Albert, Aug. 7, 1954; children: John R., James H. Student, Ohio Wesleyan U., 1949-51; BA, Mich. State U., 1953; MS, Iowa State U., 1980. Asst. pers. mgr./tng. sup. Sears, Roebuck & Co., Toledo, 1953-56; tchr. adult edn. Tenafly Pub. Schs. (N.J.), 1966-70; pers. officer, tng. officer, tng. and edn. mgr. Iowa Dept. Transp., Ames, 1974-77; coll. recruiting coord. Rockwell Internat., Cedar Rapids, Iowa, 1977-79, engring. adminstrn. mgr., 1979-80; employee rels. and job evaluation analyst, recruiter Phillips Petroleum Co., Bartlesville, Okla., 1980-81; v.p., dir. pers. Rep. Bancorp, Tulsa, 1981-83; sr. v.p. and dir. human resources First Nat. Bank, Rockford, Ill., 1983-94; dir. bus. divsn. Rock Valley Coll., Rockford, Ill., 1994-99, ret., 1999; human resources cons. Furst Group, Rockford, 2000—. Advisor to Nat. Profl. Secs. Assn.; bd. dirs. Riverside Cmty. Bank, 1995—; mem. adv. com. Zion Devel. Corp., 1999—. Bd. dirs. Rocvale Children's Home, 1986-97, 99-2001, pres. 1991-94, bd. dirs. United Way of Ames, 1976-77; mem. employee svc. comm., Rockford Pub. Schs., 1988-92; account exec. United Way Rockford, 1993-98, account sec. head, 1996, allocations com., 2000-01; bd. dirs. Rockford Human Resources Cmty. Action Program; chair legis. com. Rockford Human Svcs. Dept., 1989-92; chair Rockford State of Ill. Job Svcs. Employers Coun., 1990-97; publicity chmn. Tenafly 300th Ann. Celebration, 1969; mem. task force Rockford Bd. Edn., 1993-94; mem. gala com. Janet Wattles Mental Health Ctr., 1990; deacon Collegiate Presbyn. Ch., Ames, 1972-75; mem. adv. coun. Rockford YWCA, 1986, mem. fund drive task force, 1998-99, co-chair YWCA Leader Luncheon, 1986-87; advisor Rockford chpt. ARC, 1991—; mem. Mayor's Task Force for Rockford Project Self-Sufficiency, 1986-89, chmn. adv. coun., 1991; chair info. and referral com., bd. dirs. Contact, 1994-2003; bd. dirs. Rockford Symphony Orch., 1992-95, sec. 1994-95; bd. dirs. Rockford Leadership Found., 1994-96; chair pers. com. Rockford Ctrl. Area Commn., 1997-99, v.p., bd. dirs.; mem. fund drive taskforce Blackhawk Day Nursery, 1998-99; bd. dirs. Rock Valley Coll. Found., 2000-03, co-chmn. governance com., 2001-03; mem. session 1st Presbyn. Ch., Rockford, 2000-01, chair mktg. task force; mem. ctrl. steering com. Ctr. for Learning in Retirement, 2000-01. Pres.'s scholar Mich. State U., 1951-53; recipient YWCA Kate O'Connor award for Women in Labor Force, 1984; named Bd. Mem. of Yr. Rockford Human Resources Community Action Program, 1992. Mem.: Ill. Consortium Internat. Travel (mentor The Netherlands 1997), Employee Benefits Assn. No. Ill. (membership chmn.), Am. Soc. Pers. Adminstrn., Crusader Clin. Found. (bd. dirs. 1997—, v.p. bd. dirs. 2000, pres. bd. 2001—02, chmn. 2001—), Rockford Pers. Assn. (adv. coun. 1983—91, co-chmn. programs 1985—86), Rockford C. of C. (leadership program 1989, pres. coun. 1991—94, mem. internat. bus. coun. 1993—99, transp. com., human resources com., Nat. Athena Found. award 1991, Woman of Yr.), Rockford Network (past chairperson 1985—86, awards com. 1995—97), World Trade Coun. (bd. dirs. 1994—97), Womenspace (bd. dirs. 1993—95, mktg. com. 1993—99, awards com. 1995, 1996—98, adv. bd. 1996—), Rockford Panhellenic Coun. (sec. 1992—93, treas. 1993—94, v.p. 1994—95, pres. 1995—96, Woman of Yr. award 1994, Rockford Lifescape Sr. of Yr. award 1999), P.E.O., Rotary Internat. (chair Rockford Athena chpt. 1991—, membership com. 1999—, chair steering com. 2000—01, co-chair membership com. 2001—), Phi Kappa Phi, Alpha Gamma Delta, Sigma Epsilon (Rockford award). Home and Office: 5587 Thunderidge Dr Rockford IL 61107-1756 Fax: 815-282-8248. E-mail: janycealbert@hotmail.com.

ALBERT, MARGARET COOK, communications executive; b. Madison, Wis., Aug. 25, 1933; d. Hulet Hall and Esther Frances (Marhoefer) Cook; m. Walter E. Albert, Jan. 24, 1959; children: Jennifer Ann, Bryan Walter. AB in Journalism, Ind. U., 1955; postgrad., U. Bordeaux, France, 1957-58. Reporter Daily Herald-Telephone, Bloomington, Ind., 1953-55, 59-60; copy editor Cosmopolitan Mag., N.Y.C., 1955-57; copy chief, coll. advt. Houghton Mifflin, Boston, 1960-62, freelance writer, 1962-70; pub. rels. coord., editor Allegheny County Med. Soc., Pitts., 1970-75; dir. pub. info. Urban League Pitts., 1975-86; pres., owner Matrix Comms. Assocs., Pitts., 1986—. Cons. West Penn Hosp.: James I. McGuire Antiquity Ctr., Pitts., 1989-91; cons., sr. writer Comms. 2000, Agy. for Instnl. Tech., Bloomington, 1994—; cons. Family Comms., Pitts., 1992—; writer, editor 651-Arts, Bklyn. Acad. Music, 1992-95. Rschr., ghost writer: Day Breakers: The Story of the Urban League of Pittsburgh, 1983 (Matrix award 1984), 2d edit., 1999; author: A Practical Vision: The Story of Blue Cross of West Pennsylvania, 1987; contbr. articles to profl. publs.; prodr. computer graphics program African-Am. Computer Graphics, 1994; guest editor Mademoiselle Mag., 1955. Bd. dirs. Health Sys. Agy. of S.W. Pa., Pitts., 1976-86, Pa. Med. Care Found., Camp Hill, 1981-86, Animal Rescue League of S.W. Pa., Pitts., 1988-93; mem. Pa. Blue Shield Corp., Camp Hill, 1982-90, Kuumba Trust, 1998—. Fulbright scholar, 1957-58; recipient Disting. Svc. award Urban League of Pitts., 1977, Harold B. Gardner Citizens award Allegheny County Med. Soc., 1981, 1st place award Women in Comms., Inc., Pa. Assn. for Nonprofit Homes for Aging, Brotherhood award. Mem. Phi Beta Kappa. Democrat. E-mail: margaret.albert@verizon.net.

ALBERT, MARTIN LAWRENCE, behavioral neurologist; b. Lawrence, Mass., Jan. 7, 1939; s. Benjamin and Alice (Kaminsky) A.; m. Phyllis Gloria Cohen, Dec. 25, 1960; children: David, Michael, Rachel. MD, Tufts U., 1963; PhD, U. Paris, France, 1971. Diplomate Am. Bd. Psychiatry and Neurology. Intern Maimonides Med. Ctr., Bklyn., 1963-64; resident in neurology Boston U. Med. Sch./Boston VA Hosp., 1966-69; fellow in behavioral neurology Boston U. Med. Sch., 1969-71, Laboratoire de Neuropsychologie, Hopital Ste-Anne, Paris, 1969-71; chief, clin. neurology Boston VA Med. Ctr., 1978-83; clin. dir., co-prin. investigator Aphasia Rsch. Ctr. Boston U., 1979-96, prof. neurology Sch. Medicine, 1980—, dir. behavioral neuroscis., dept. neurology, 1983-92, dir. Aphasia Rsch. Ctr., 1996—; dir. med. rsch. svc. Dept. of Veterans Affairs, Washington, 1992-95. Cons. in behavioral neurosci. WHO, Geneva, Switzerland, 1981—; cons. to Pres.' Office of Sci. and Tech. Policy, Washington, 1993-95; Sackler scholar Inst. Advanced Studies Tel Aviv U., 1996; vis. prof. neurology Hebrew U. Med. Sch., Jerusalem, 1993; nat. adv. coun. Program in Bioethics Dept. VA, Washington, 1995—; nat. adv. coun. Nat. Inst. Gen. Med. Scis. NIH, 1992-93. Author: Human Neuropsychology, 1978, The Bilingual Brain, 1978, Clinical Aspects of Aphasia, 1981, Language in the Aging Brain, 1981, Manual of Aphasia Therapy, 1991, Clinical Neurology of Aging, 1984, 2d edit., 1994, Manual of Aphasia and Aphasia Therapy, 2003; contbr. over 200 articles to profl. jours. Mem. adv. bd. program in med. ethics Hebrew Coll., Boston, 1987; mem. adv. bd. U.S. Israel Mental Health Fedn., Worcester, Mass., 1991. Capt. U.S. Army, 1965-66. Grantee NIH, 1970—. Fellow Am. Acad. Neurology (co-founder, chmn. sect. geriatric neurology 1989-91); mem. Acad. Aphasia (bd. govs. 1986-88), Am. Neurol. Assn., Nat. Aphasia Assn. (v.p. 1988—). Jewish. Achievements include introduction of the concept subcortical dementia; development new treatment approaches for aphasia, including melodic intonation therapy and pharmacotherapy for aphasia; development of the field of language in aging and dementia, created popular diagnostic tests in behavioral neuroscience. Office: VA Boston Healthcare Sys 12A 150 S Huntington Ave Boston MA 02130-4817

ALBERT, MICHAEL SALVATORE, pathologist, medical laboratory executive; b. Buffalo, N.Y., Oct. 3, 1960; s. Salvatore Michael and Francine Joan (Anzalone) A.; m. Melissa Renee Albert, Sept. 20, 1996; children: Nathan, Jared, Hadley, Emma. BS in Biology, U. Dallas, 1982; MD, Albany (N.Y.) Med. Coll., 1986. Diplomate Nat. Bd. Med. Examiners, Am. Bd. Pathology. Intern dept. surgery St. Lukes-Roosevelt Hosp., N.Y.C., 1986-87; trauma clin. rsch. fellow Albany Med. Ctr., 1987-88; resident in pathology Strong Meml. Hosp., Rochester, N.Y., 1988-93; assoc. pathologist Mercy Hosp. of Buffalo, 1993-97, chmn. dept. pathology, 2001—; chief of pathology Unity Meml. Med. Ctr., Batavia, 1997—2001; pres., chmn. bd. dirs. X-Cell Lab., Amherst, NY, 2000—02; treas., bd. dirs. Ea. Great Lakes Pathology, P.C., 2002—. Medico-legal cons. Paul Beltz Attys., PC, Buffalo, 1996-2001; founding mem., shareholder Eastern Gt. Lakes Pathology, PC, Amherst, 1996—. Fellow Coll. Am. Pathologists, Am. Soc. Clin. Pathologists; mem. N.Y. State Soc. Pathologists (3d dist. coun.), Sigma Xi. Republican. Mem. Assembly of God Ch. Avocations: hunting, fishing, camping, photography, shooting sports. Home: 180 Independence Dr Orchard Park NY 14127 Office: Mercy Hosp of Buffalo 565 Abbott Rd Buffalo NY 14220 E-mail: malbert3258@adelphia.net.

ALBERT, ROBERT HAMILTON, lawyer; b. Columbus, Ohio, May 25, 1931; s. Raymond Joseph Albert and Kathryn Mary (Hildebrand) Lett; m. Patricia S. Smith, June 23, 1962; children: Julie Ann Certain, Karen Marie Groeber, Robert H. Jr. BSBA, Ohio State U., 1953; LLB, Franklin U., 1960; JD, Capital U., 1966. Bar: Ohio, 1960, U.S. Tax Ct. 1961, U.S. Dist. Ct. (so. dist.) Ohio, 1962, U.S. Ct. Appeals (6th cir.) 1966, U.S. Ct. Claims 1971, U.S. Supreme Ct. 1971. Indsl. engr. Fairmont Foods Co., Columbus, 1951-52; acct. E.C. Redmund CPA, Columbus, 1953-54; acct., contract adminstr. N.Am. Aviation, Columbus, 1956-60; ptnr. Kagay, Albert Diehl & Groeber, Columbus, 1961—. Mem. Rep. Nat. Com. Capt. USAF, 1954-56. Fellow Columbus Bar Found., Legal Advisory Comm. of the Columbus Found.; mem. Ohio State Bar Assn., Columbus Bar Assn., Order of Curia, Beta Gamma Sigma, Beta Alpha Psi. Roman Catholic. Office: Kagay Albert Diehl & Groeber 6877 N High St Ste 300 Worthington OH 43085-2411

ALBERT, ROSS ALAN, lawyer; b. Boston, Nov. 22, 1958; s. Richmond G. and Mary (Day) A.; m. Nancy Ada Christian, July 16, 1983. AB, Harvard U., 1982, postgrad., 1985-86; JD, U. Calif., Berkeley, 1986. Bar: Mass. 1986, D.C. 1988, U.S. Dist. Ct. Md. 1987, U.S. Ct. Appeals (4th cir.) 1987, U.S. Ct. Appeals (5th cir.) 1993, U.S. Ct. Appeals D.C. cir. 1994, U.S. Ct. Appeals (2d cir.) 1994, U.S. Ct. Appeals (6th cir.) 1994, U.S. Ct. Appeals (9th cir.) 1994, U.S. Ct. Appeals (11th cir.) 1994, U.S. Supreme Ct. 1994, U.S. Ct. Appeal (8th cir.) 1995. Jud. law clk. U.S. Dist. Ct. Md., Balt., 1986-88; assoc. Wilmer, Cutler & Pickering, Washington, 1988-93; spl. counsel Office of Gen. Counsel-appellate group U.S. SEC, Washington, 1993 97, counsel to commr. Norman S. Johnson, 1997-2000, sr. spl. counsel Office Internet Enforcement, 2000-01; of counsel Morris, Manning & Martin LLP, Atlanta, 2001—. Assoc. editor Calif. Law Rev., 1985-86. Democrat. Office: Morris Manning & Martin LLP 1600 Atlanta Fin Ctr 3343 Peachtree Rd Atlanta GA 30326 E-mail: ra81@post.harvard.edu. *Notable cases include: U.S. vs. Lincoln, U.S. Dist. Ct. N.D. Ga. & U.S. Ct. App. 11th Cir., assisted at trial and served as lead appellate counsel for largest securities fraud prosecution in Georgia history; Vail vs. SEC, U.S. Ct. App. 5th Cir., successfully argued novel disciplinary case arising from broker's theft of funds from a political group; SEC vs. Midwest Investments, Inc., U.S. Ct. App. 6th Cir., drafted brief and successfully argued case of first impression, a jurisdictional challenge to the SEC's ability to regulate interstate securities fraud; SEC vs. Grossman, U.S. Ct. App. 2d Cir., drafted brief and successfully argued case involving challenge to misappropriation theory of insider-trading.*

ALBERT, STEWART GARY, medical educator, internist, endocrinologist; b. N.Y.C., Dec. 14, 1946; BS, CCNY, 1967; MD, Albert Einstein Coll. Medicine, N.Y.C., 1971. Diplomate Am. Bd. Internal Medicine, Am. Bd. Endocrinology and Metabolism. Intern in internal medicine Montefiore Hosp., N.Y.C., 1971-72, resident in internal medicine, 1972-74; with USAF, Scott AFB, Ill., 1974-76; fellow in endocrinology Washington U., St. Louis, 1976-78; asst. prof. St. Louis U. Med. Sch., 1978-91, assoc. prof., 1991-97, prof., 1997—. Maj. USAF, 1974-76. Mem.: Am. Diabetes Assn. Office: 1402 S Grand Blvd Saint Louis MO 63104-1004 Business E-Mail: albertsg@slu.edu.

ALBERT, SUSAN WITTIG, writer, English educator; b. Maywood, Ill., Jan. 2, 1940; d. John H. and A. Lucille (Franklin) Webber; m. William Albert, 1986; children by previous marriage: Robert, Robin, Michael. BA, U. Ill., 1967; PhD, U. Calif.-Berkeley, 1972. Instr. U. San Francisco, 1969-71; asst. prof. to assoc. prof. U. Tex., Austin, 1971-79; assoc. dean Grad. Sch., U. Tex., Austin, 1977-79; dean Sophie Newcomb Coll., New Orleans, 1979-81; dean of faculty, grad. dean S.W. Tex. State U., San Marcos, 1981-82, v.p. acad. affairs, 1982-86, prof. English, 1981-87. Founder Story Circle Network, Inc., 1997. Author: Work of Her Own, 1992, Writing From Life, 1996; author: (China Bayles novels) Thyme of Death, 1992; author: Witch's Bane, 1993, Hangman's Root, 1994, Rosemary Remembered, 1995, Rueful Death, 1996, Love Lies Bleeding, 1997, Chile Death, 1998, Lavender Lies, 1999, Mistletoe Man, 2000, Bloodroot, 2001, Indigo Dying, 2003, An Unthymely Death, 2003; author: (Robin Paige novels) Death at Bishop's Keep, 1994; author: Death at Gallows Green, 1995, Death at Daisy's Folly, 1997, Death at Devil's Bridge, 1998, Death at Rottingdean, 1999, Death at Whitechapel, 2000, Epsom Downs, 2001, Death at Dartmoor, 2002, Death at Glamis Castle, 2003; contbr. articles to profl. jours.; editor: With Courage and Common Sense: Memoirs from the Older Women's Legacy Circles, 2003. Danforth grad. fellow, 1967-72 Home: PO Box 1616 Bertram TX 78605 E-mail: china@tstar.net.

ALBERTERNST, JUDITH ANN, pension administrator; b. Highland, Ill., Oct. 26, 1963; d. Joseph Bernard and Luetta Elizabeth (Seefeldt) A. AAS in Bus. mgmt. magna cum laude, Kaskaskia Coll., 2000. Bookkeeper William B. Kealey & Co., Belleville, Ill., 1981-86, office mgr., 1986-92; dir. pension adminstrn. Qualified Plan Svcs., Highland, Ill., 1992—. Contbr. poems published to publs. Roman Catholic. Avocations: stamp collecting, beadwork, cross-stich, geneology, gardening.

ALBERTI, PETER WILLIAM, otolaryngologist, educator, retired otolaryngologist; b. Coblenz, Germany, Aug. 23, 1934; arrived in Can., 1967; s. William Peter and Edith Elizabeth (Lachmann) A.; m. Elizabeth Margery Smith, Aug. 5, 1961; children: Andrew Peter, Fiona Elizabeth, Kathryn Penelope. MB, BS, U. Durham, Newcastle, Eng., 1957; PhD, Washington U., St. Louis, 1963. Intern Royal Victoria Infirmary, Newcastle upon Tyne, Eng., 1957-58, resident, 1958-60, 63-66; 1st asst. otolaryngology U. Newcastle, 1964-67; clin. tchr. U. Toronto, Ont., Can., 1967-68, asst. prof., 1968-70, assoc. prof., 1970-77, prof., 1977—, chmn. dept. otolaryngology, 1982-92. Otolaryngologist-in-chief Mt. Sinai Hosp., Toronto, 1970-88, Toronto Gen. Hosp., 1982-89; sr. staff otolaryngologist Toronto Gen. Hosp., 1982-2000; exec. bd. Hearing Internat., 1992—; vis. prof., sr. cons. Nat. U. Singapore, 2000—. Editor: Personal Hearing Protection in Industry, 1981; co-author: An Atlas of Otoscopy, 1984, 2d edit., 1990, Otological Medicine and Surgery, 1988; co-editor Proc. Centennial Conf. on Laryngeal Cancer, 1976. Fellow Royal Coll. Surgeons (London), Royal Coll. Surgeons Can.; mem. Can. Otolaryngol. Soc. (pres. 1988-89), Triological Soc. (v.p. ea. sect. 1988-89), Collegium Oto-Rhino-Laryngologicorum Amicitae Sacrum (dep. sec. 1991-96, pres. 1996-97), Acoustical Soc. Am.; hon. mem. Brazilian Otolaryngol. Soc., Assn. Otolaryngologists of India, Irish Otolaryngol. Soc., Internat. Fedn. Otolaryngol. Socs. (sec.-gen. 1991—), Kenyan Ear, Nose and Throat Soc. Anglican. Home: 10 Deer Park Crescent Toronto ON Canada M4V 2C2 E-mail: palberti@att.global.net.

ALBERTINI, ROBERT ELMER, medical executive, physician, consultant; b. Danville, Pa., Mar. 27, 1941; s. Elmer Oliver and Agnes Mary (Schneider) A.; m. Louise Frances Breslin, June 20, 1964; children: Robert E. Jr., John G., Kathryn M., Michael A. BS, U. Notre Dame, 1963; MD, Georgetown U., 1967. Diplomat Am. Bd. Internal Medicine. Intern internal medicine Geisinger Med. Ctr., Danville, 1967-68, resident internal medicine, 1970-72, assoc. dept. thoracic medicine, 1973-79, dir. dept. thoracic medicine, 1979-92, chmn. dept. medicine, 1992-95; sr. v.p. med. affairs north ctrl. region Pa. State Geisinger Health System, 1995-99, system v.p. med. performance and quality improvement, 1999—2001; fellow pulmonary medicine U. Calif., San Diego, 1972-73; part-time sr. cons., 2002—. Dir. internal medicine residency, dir. pulmonary fellowship Geisinger Health Sys., Danville; clin. prof. medicine Jefferson Med. Coll., Phila., 1989—; chmn. med. rev. com. Highmark-Blue Shield Corp., 1997—. Contbr. articles to profl. jours. Bd. dirs. Susquehanna Valley Divsn. Ctrl. Pa. Lung Assn., 1975-84, 86-92. Capt. USAF, 1968-70. Fellow ACP, Am. Coll. Chest Physicians; mem. Pa. Med. Soc. (chmn. commn. on accreditation 1983-86, chmn. coun. on edn.-sci. 1987-89), Pa. Thoracic Soc. (exec. com. 1983-92). Republican. Roman Catholic. Avocations: golfing, hiking, skiing, biking, camping. Home: 6 Cortland Dr Danville PA 17821-8489 Office: Geisinger Med Ctr 100 N Academy Ave Danville PA 17822-2201 E-mail: docbob@ptd.net., ralbertini@geisinger.edu.

ALBERTO, PAMELA LOUISE, oral and maxillofacial surgeon, educator; b. Somerville, Mass., Apr. 13, 1954; d. Louis Leon and Pamela Marie (Spera) A.; m. Gregory John Wroclawski, Aug. 4, 1979; children: Daniel Alberto, Catherine Marie. BS, Rensselaer Poly. Inst., 1976; DMD, U. Pa., 1980. Cert. oral and maxillofacial surgeon; diplomate Am. Bd. Forensic Dentistry. Clin. asst. prof. dept. oral/maxillofacial surgery N.J. Dental Sch., Newark, 1983-89, clin. assoc. prof. dept. oral/maxillofacial surgery, 1989—, dir. predoctoral edn. dept. oral/maxillofacial surgery, 1989—; pvt. practice Sparta, N.J., 1984—. Dir. CPR N.J. Dental Sch., Newark, 1985-90; dir. Dental Implant Ctr. Wallkill Valley Hosp., Sussex, N.J., 1988—; vice chief surgery Newton Meml. Hosp., 1998-2000, chief surgery, 2000-02. Recipient Outstanding Clin. Dentistry award Acad. Gen. Dentistry, 1980. Fellow Am. Assn. Oral and Maxillofacial Surgery, Am. Coll. Oral/Maxillofacial Surgery; mem. ADA, AAUP, Am. Assn. Dental Anesthesiology, Internat. Congress Oral Implantology, Psi Omega. Avocations: tennis, skiing, photography, scuba diving, jewelry making. Home: 14 Cherry Tree Ln Kinnelon NJ 07405-2229 Office: 171 Woodport Rd Sparta NJ 07871-2637

ALBERTS, BRUCE MICHAEL, research organization executive; b. Chicago, Ill., Apr. 14, 1938; s. Harry C. and Lillian (Surasky) A.; m. Betty Neary, June 14, 1960; children: Beth L., Jonathan B., Michael B. AB in Biochemical Scis. summa cum laude, Harvard Coll., 1960; PhD in Biophysics, Harvard U., 1965. Postdoctoral fellow NSF Institut de Biologie Moleculaire, Geneva, 1965-66; asst. prof. dept. chemistry Princeton (N.J.) U., 1966-73, assoc. prof. dept. biochemical scis., 1971-73, Damon Pfeiffer prof. life scis., 1973-76; prof., vice chmn. dept. biochemistry and biophysics U. Calif., San Francisco, 1976-81, Am. Cancer Soc. Rsch. prof., 1981-85, prof., chmn., 1985-90, Am. Cancer Soc. Rsch. prof. of biochemistry, 1990-93; pres. NAS, Washington, 1993—; chrm. NRC, Washington, 1993—. Trustee Cold Spring Harbor Lab., 1972-75; adv. panel human cell biology NSF, 1974-76; adv. coun. dept. biochemical scis. and molecular biology Princeton U., 1979-85; chmn. vis. com. dept. biochemistry and molecular biology Harvard Coll., 1983-86; chmn. mapping and sequencing the human genome Nat. Rsch. Coun. Com., 1986-88; bd. sci. couns. divsn. arthritis and metabolic diseases NIH, 1974-78, molecular cytology study sect. 1982-86, chmn. 1984-86; program adv. com. NIH Human Genome Project, 1988-91; sci. adv. bd. Jane Coffin Childs Meml. Fund for Med. Rsch., 1978-85, Markey Found., 1984—, Fred Hutchinson Cancer Rsch. Ctr., Seattle, 1988—; com. mem. corp. vis. dept. biology MIT, 1978—, dept. embryology Carnegie Inst., Washington, 1983—; faculty rsch. lectr. U. Calif., San Francisco, 1985; sci. adv. com. Marine Biological Lab., Woods Hole, Mass., 1988—; bd. dirs. Genentech Rsch. Found., Fed. Am. Socs. for Experimental Biology; adv. bd. Bethesda Rsch. Labs. Life Tech. Inc., Nat. Sci. Resources Ctr., Smithsonian Inst., 1990—; com. mem. adolescence and young adulthood/sci. standards, Nat. Bd. Profl. Teaching Standards, 1991—. Co-author: The Molecular Biology of the Cell, 1989; editor: Mechanistic Studies of DNA Replication and Genetic Recombination, 1980; editorial bd. Jour. Biological Chemistry, 1976-82, Jour. Cell Biology, 1984-87; assoc. editor Annual Reviews Cell Biology, 1984—; essay editor Molecular Biology of the Cell, 1991—; contbr. numerous articles to profl. jours. including Saunders Sci. Publ., Current Sci., Ltd. Fellow NSF, 1960-65; recipient Eli Lilly award in biological chemistry Am. Chemical Soc., 1972, Baxter award for Disting. Rsch. in Biomedical Scis. Assn. Am. Med. Colls., 1992; named Lifetime Rsch. Prof. Am. Cancer Soc., 1980, Outstanding Vol. Coord. Calif. Sch. Vol. Partnership, 1993. Gairdner Foundation International Award, 1995. Fellow AAAS; mem. NAS (commn. life scis. Nat. Rsch. Coun. 1988—, chmn. 1988-93, adv. bd. Nat. Sci. Resources Ctr. 1990—, Nat. Com. Sci. Edn. Standards and Assessment 1992—, com. mem. Nat. Edn. Support System for Tchrs. and Schs. 1992—, U.S. Steel Found. award 1975), Am. Chemical Soc., Am. Soc. for Cell Biology, Am. Soc. for Microbiology, Genetics Soc. Am., Am. Soc. Biochemistry and Molecular Biology (councilor 1984—), Am. Philos. Soc., European Molecular Biology Orgn. (assoc.), Phi Beta Kappa. Office: National Academy of Sciences/NRC Office of the President 500 Fifth St NW NAS215 Washington DC 20001*

ALBERTS, DAVID, theater director, performance artist; b. Akron, Ohio, Nov. 14, 1946; married (div. 1972); 1 child, Morgan Elizabeth; married (div. 1992); children: Sarah Aimee, Samantha Kaitlin Wynne. BA in Music, Kent State U., 1972; MA in Theatre, West Va. U., 1978; PhD in Theatre, Bowling Green State U., 1989. Instr. Akron (Ohio) U., 1970-71, W.Va. U., 1978, Va. Commonwealth U., Richmond, 1979-81, Calif. State U., Turlock, Calif., 1981-83, Kent (Ohio) State U., 1986-87, Bowling Green (Ohio) State U., 1987-89; artistic dir. Theatre of the One Actor, San Diego, 1995—. Mime artist in field. Author: Pantomime: Exercises and Elements, 1971, Talking About Mime, 1994 (San Diego Book award 1994), Rehearsal Management for Directors, 1995, The Expressive Body: Physical Characterization for the Actor, 1997, (play) Death by Arrangement, 1981; contbr. articles to profl. jours. Recipient Founders award Internat. Thespian Soc., 1972, Directing award Am. Coll. Theatre Festival, 1982. Mem.: Speech Comm. Assn., Assn. for Theatre in Higher Edn. E-mail: davidalberts_director@yahoo.com.

ALBERTS, DAVID SAMUEL, physician, pharmacologist, educator; b. Milw., Dec. 30, 1939; m. Heather Alberts; children: Tim, Sabrina. BS, Trinity Coll., Hartford, Conn., 1962; MD, U. Va., 1966. Dir. clin. pharmacology Ariz. Cancer Ctr., Tucson, 1975—, prof. medicine and pharmacology, 1982—99, Regent's prof. medicine, pharmacology and pub. health, 1999—, dir. cancer prevention and control, 1988—, dep. dir., 1989-96, assoc. dean rsch. Coll. Medicine, 1996—2002, acting chief hematology and oncology, 1998-99. External advisor U. Chgo. Cancer Ctr., 1993-98, Tulane U. Cancer Ctr., New Orleans, 1993-96, M.D. Anderson Cancer Ctr., Houston, 1994—, Norris Cotton Cancer Ct., Hanover, 1995 2000, Lee Moffit Cancer Ctr., Tampa, 2003—; mem. bd. sci. counselors divsn. Cancer Prevention and Control, Nat. Cancer Inst., NIH, 1990-94, chmn. chemoprevention external com. divsn. cancer prevention, 1997-2001; chmn. gynecologic cancer com. S.W. Oncology Group, 1977-2001; mem. monitoring and adv. panel Nat. Prostate Lung-Colon-Ovary Cancer Study, NCI-NIH, 1994—; mem. oversight com. NCI Nat. Lung Cancer Screening Trial, 2002—; chmn. cancer prevention com. Gynecologic Oncology Group, 1995—; chmn. oncologic adv. com. U.S. FDA, 1982-84, spl. cons., 1984-86; bd. dirs., chair sci. adv. bd.; mem. bd. sci. adv., Nat. Cancer Inst., NIH, 1999—; bd. dirs., Cancer Rsch. and Prevention Found., 1992—. Co-editor-in-chief Cancer Epidemiology, Biomarkers and Prevention, 2002—, co-editor-in-chief, 2002—; assoc. editor Cancer Rsch., 1989-2002, Cancer Chemother. and Pharmacol., 1992—, Clin. Cancer Rsch., 1994-96, Neoplasia, 1998—; contbr. articles to over 400 to profl. jours.; inventor azamitosene and anthracene anticancer agts., tumorimeter, hypodermic needle with automatic retracting point; tropical DFMO; two step carcinogen/HIV chemical deactivation system; method and composition for deactivating HIV infected blood and anticancer drugs; amifostine reversal of platinum-induced neuropathy; measurement of lesion progression via mapping of chromatin texture features along progression curve. Grantee NIH, 1975—, Nat. Cancer Inst.-NIH, 1987—. Mem. Am. Soc. for Clin. Pharmacology and Therapeutics, Am. Soc. Clin. Oncology, Am. Soc. Preventive Oncology, Am. Assn. for Cancer Rsch., Soc. Gynecologic Oncologists. Achievements include Listed by Sci. June 15, 2002 as 3rd highest NIH peer reviewed funded clin. rschr. in U.S. Office: Ariz Cancer Ctr 1501 N Campbell Ave Tucson AZ 85724-0001

ALBERTS, HAROLD, lawyer; b. San Antonio, Apr. 3, 1920; s. Bernard H. and Rose Alberts; m. Rose M. Gaskin, Mar. 25, 1945; children: Linda Rae, Barry Lawrence. LLB, U. Tex., 1942. Bar: Tex. 1943, U.S. Supreme Ct. 1950, U.S. Ct. Mil. Appeals 1959. Tchr. U. Tex., 1942, instr., 1941-42; legal officer Chase Field, 1944; sole practice Corpus Christi, Tex. Pres. Jewish Welfare Fund, Corpus Christi, 1948; chmn. S.W. Regional Anti-Defamation League, Tex. and Okla., 1970-71, chmn., 1969-72, chmn. Brotherhood Week, 1957; chmn. Nueces County (Tex.) Red Cross, 1959-61; mem. campaign exec. com., chmn. meetings United Cmty. Svcs., 1961; v.p. Little Theatre, Corpus Christi, 1964; chmn. Corpus Christi NCCJ, 1967-69, nat. dir., 1974-76; bd. dirs. Tex. State Assn. Mental Health; pres. Combined Jewish Appeal, Corpus Christi, 1974-76; moderator Friday Morning Group, 1975, 96. Served to lt. (sr. grade) USNR, 1942-46. Mem. ABA, Tex. Bar Assn., Corpus Christi Bar Assn., Kiwanis (pres. 1962), B'nai B'rith (pres. 1955), Masons (32d degree). Home and Office: PO Box 271477 Corpus Christi TX 78427-1477

ALBERTS, HENRY CELLER, real estate company executive; b. N.Y.C., Aug. 23, 1927; s. Alfred Edward and Helen (Masch) A.; m. Renée Mira Miller, Jan. 13, 1950; children: Jo Lee Lord, Nina Sue Charnley, Hope Anne Megonigal, Jody Beth Naleppa. BS in Physics/Math., Queens Coll., N.Y.C., 1949; MS in Physics/Math., U. Del., Newark, 1956; PhD in Sys. Sci., City U., London, 1995. Cert. mem. Def. Acquisition Corps (Level III), Level III Sys. Planning, rsch., Devel., Engring. and Test. Physicist USAF/U.S. Army, 1949-56; head ops. rsch. Avco Corp., Wilmington, Mass., 1956-60; dir. mktg./rsch. Nat. Co., Inc., Malden, Mass., 1960-62; sr. sci. staff Stanford Rsch. Inst., Menlo Park, Calif., 1962-69; pres., CEO Vertex Corp., McLean, Va., 1969-76; prin. scientist Gen. Rsch. Corp., McLean, 1975-80; dir. instrument dept. Arcata Assocs., Monterey, Calif., 1980-81; mem. tech. staff MRJ Inc., Fairfax, Va., 1981 83; prof. engring. mgmt. U.S. Govt./Dept. of Def./Def. Sys. Mgmt. Coll., Ft. Belvoir, Va., 1983-98; pres. Alco Realty Corp., McLean, Va., 1998—. Adj. prof. U. Md. Grad. Sch., 1998—, mem. com. on def. mfg. in yrs. 2010 and beyond NRC, 1997-98; lectr. in field; spl. lectr. on indsl. issues and analysis methodologies CIA, 1984—; mem. U.S. del. to NATO, 1996; mem. adv. bd. Inst. for Strategic tech. and Innovative Leadership, Coll. Engring., U. Tex., 1996; sr. fellow Inst. for Pub. Policy, George Mason U. Electronic Commerce rsch. Ctr., 1994—; cons. in field Contbr. articles to profl. jours. Mem. oversight bd. Fairfax County Govt., 1988-89. Recipient George Mason medal, Commonwealth of Va./George Mason U., 1995, Superior Civilian Svc. award, Dept. Def., 1998, Stanley J. Drazak award for tchg. excellence, U. Md., 2002. Mem. Internat. Coun. on Sys. Engring. (charter, bd. dirs. Wash. chpt., mem. tech. com. redefining sys. engring.), Internat. Test and Evaluation Assn. (charter, mem. nat. edn. com., chpt. pres. 1988-91, other coms.), Ops. Rsch. Soc. Am. (chmn. def. acquisition processes session 1992, chmn. advanced mgmt. and math. session 1992), Inst. Mgmt. Sci., Soc. Logistics Engrs., Internat. Sys. Sci. Soc. Avocations: music, art, jewelry making and design. Office: 5842 Hilldon St Mc Lean VA 22101-3324

ALBERTS, JAMES JOSEPH, scientist, researcher; b. Chgo., May 23, 1943; s. Joseph James and Lilyan (Matas) A. AB in Biology and Chemistry, Cornell Coll., 1965; MS in Organic Chemistry, Dartmouth Coll., 1967; PhD in Chem. Oceanography, Fla. State U., 1970. Rsch. assoc. Kans. State Geologic Survey, U. Kans., 1970; rsch. assoc. dept. biology U. Ga., 1970-72, asst. prof. dept. zoology, 1972-74; asst. chemist radiological and environ. rsch. div. Argonne Nat. Lab., 1974-77; assoc. rsch. ecologist Savannah River Ecology Lab., 1977-84; dir. and sr. rsch. scientist U. Ga. Marine Inst., 1984—2001, sr. rsch. scientist U. Ga. sch. marine programs, 2001—. Adj. prof. dept. biol. scis. Clemson U., 1985—, mem. coll. scis. adv. com., 1984-87; adj. prof. dept. zoology U. Ga., 1986-93, adj. prof. dept. marine sci., 1993—. Contbr. articles to publs. and chpts. to books. Mem. Marine divsn. Estuarine sub-com. Nat. Assn. State Univs. and Land Grant Colls., 1985-89, co-chmn., 1987-89; mem.-at-large exec. com. Southeastern Estuarine Rsch. Soc., 1986-88; pres. Southeastern Assn. Marine Labs., 1988; mem. Ga. dept. natural resources task force on rsch. priorities Sapelo Island Nat. Estuarine Rsch. Res., 1988-2001; mem. exec. com. SAML, 1989; mem. NSF adv. panel Equipment and Facilities for Biol. Field Stas. and Marine Labs., 1989-90, BBS Rsch. Tng. Groups, 1991; mem. steering com. Coun. on Ocean Affairs, 1989-91, Nat. Assn. Marine Labs. Recipient Alexander von Humboldt Found., Sr. U.S. Scientist award, 1989, Best of Conf. award for Best Plenary Session Presentation, 1994, Fulbright rsch. fellow award to Norway, 1997; Petroleum Rsch. Fund fellow, 1968-69. Mem.: Socs. Internat. Limnologiae Theoreticae et Applicatae, Estuarine Rsch. Fedn., Internat. Humic Substance Soc. (v.p. 1996—97, pres. 1998—99), Internat. Assn. Water Quality, Am. Soc. Limnology and Oceanography (mem. Ruth Patrick award com. 2002—), Phi Kappa Phi, Phi Beta Delta. Office: U Ga Sch Marine Programs Marine Sci Bldg Athens GA 30602 E-mail: jalberts@arches.uga.edu.

ALBERTS, MARION EDWARD, physician; b. Hastings, Nebr., Mar. 14, 1923; s. Eddie and Mary Margaret (Hilbers) A.; m. Jeannette McDaniel, Dec. 25, 1944; children: Kathryn (dec.), Brian, Deborah, Timothy BA, U. Nebr., 1944, MD, 1948. Lic. Am. Bd. Pediatrics. Intern Iowa Methodist Hosp., Des Moines, 1948-49; resident in pediatrics Raymond Blank Hosp. Children, Des Moines, 1949-50, 52-53; practice medicine specializing in pediatrics Des Moines, 1953-88; retired, 1988. Chief pediatrics Mercy Hosp., 1953-69, 74-78, chief med. staff, 1966; mem. med. staff Iowa Luth. Hosp., 1953-88, Iowa Meth. Hosp., 1953-88, Broadlawns Polk County Hosp., 1983-88; instr. clin. pediatrics Coll. Osteo. Medicine and Surgery, 1970-82 Author: History of the Polk County Medical Society 1951-2001, 2003; sci. editor Iowa Medicine, 1971—97; contbr. articles to profl. jours. Pres. Polk County Tb and Respiratory Diseases Assn., 1965, 66, 70. Comdr. USNR, 1943-45, 50-52 (ret.) 1983. Recipient Whitaker Interstate Teaching award Interstate Postgrad. Med. Assn., 1980; Service award Sisters of Mercy, 1978 Fellow Am. Acad. Pediatrics, AMA (recognition awards 1969—), Iowa Med. Soc.; mem. Masons, Kiwanis. Presbyterian (elder). Home: 5991 Pommel Cir West Des Moines IA 50266-6324

ALBERTS, RENÉE MILLER, substance abuse and mental health professional; b. N.Y.C., Oct. 17, 1930; d. Julius and Bertha (Brookner) Miller; m. Henry Celler Alberts, Jan 13, 1950; children: Jo Alberts Lord, Nina Alberts Charnley, Hope Alberts Megonical, Jody Alberts Naleppa. BA, Queens Coll., 1950; MA, U. Va., 1979; postgrad., Va. Poly. U.; cert. in community alcohol edn., Howard U. Med. Sch., 1973. Cert. substance abuse counselor, Va.; lic. profl. counselor, Va. Substance abuse counselor, asst. dir., then acting dir. Fairfax (Va.) Alcohol Safety Action Program, 1972-89; substance abuse coord. Mt. Vernon Ctr. Cmty. Mental Health, Alexandria, Va., 1989—2001; overseer mental health, mental retardation and alcohol and drug svcs. Fairfax, Falls Church Cmty. Svcs. Bd., 2001—. V.p. Va. Coalition on Women, Alcohol and Drugs, Fairfax, 1985-96; mem. dual diagnosis subcom. Met. Washington Coun. Govts., 1990—; bd. apptd. Woman's Collaborative on HIV/AIDS, 1995—. *Ms. Alberts is a noted watercolorist; she attended the high school of Music and Art in N.Y.C., and studied with Barse Miller and with Gregono Prespatino at the Brooklyn Museum Art School. She also attended classes at the Art Students League. She was the subject ay a feature story on her artwork in Elan magazine, July Aug '03 and has won awards in the FX County and McLean Art League Shows. In '02 She was awarded the Faucett Okie prize by The Rehoboth, Del. Art League.* Mem. No. Va. Clin. Counselors Assn.

ALBERTSON, CHRISTIERN GUNNAR (CHRIS ALBERTSON), broadcaster, music critic, writer; b. Reykjavik, Iceland, Oct. 18, 1931; came to U.S., 1957, naturalized, 1963; s. Thordur and Yvonne (Broberg) A.; m. Hanne Elisabeth Christensen, 1954 (div. 1958). Student, Kent Coll., Canterbury, England, 1947-49; grad., Acad. Merc. Art, Copenhagen, 1952. Gen. mgr. Storyville Club, Copenhagen, 1952-54; prodr., writer U.S. Armed Forces Radio and TV, Iceland, 1954-57, WCAU Radio, Phila., 1957-58; disc jockey WHAT-RM Radio, Phila., 1958-60; prodr. Riverside Records, N.Y.C., 1960-62; continuity dir. WNEW Radio, N.Y.C., 1963-64; gen. mgr. WBAI-FM Radio, N.Y.C., 1964-66; dir. BBC programs Hartwest Prodns., N.Y.C., 1966-67; co-prodr., host weekly TV series The Jazz Set, PBS Network, 1972-73; pres. Video One, Inc., 1976-79; prodr., co-host weekly cable TV series Doin' It, 1976-77; entertainment editor Beauty Trade Mag., 1978-79; prodr. Bessie Smith blues series Columbia Records, 1970; U.S. jazz reporter Danish Radio, 1972-75; U.S. music corr. Berlingske Tidende, Copenhagen, 1960-64. Talent cons. Dupont Show of Week, 1961. Author: Bessie-Biography of Bessie Smith, 1972, rev. edit., 2003, Empress of the Blues, 1974; contbg. author: Bluesland, 1992, Jazz: A Listener's Companion, 2000; contbg. editor: Oxford Biographical Encyclopedia of Jazz, 1998; writer story and script The Alberta Hunter Story, TV mini-series, 1980, (film) Really The Blues, 1997, (TV documentary, DVD) My Castle's Rockin', 1988, The Story of Jazz, 1994; contbg. editor Stereo Review, 1973-99, A Plus Mag., 1983-96, Sound & Vision, 1999-2000; edit. cons. Routes Mag., 1978-80, 91-95; contbr. articles to Down Beat, Saturday Rev., Rolling Stone, N.Y. Times, Jazz Forum, Sound & Image, MacWeek, N.Y. Amsterdam News, Timeline, others; assoc. producer, cons. (film) Bessie, 1974; music cons. (film) Buddy Can You Spare A Dime, 1974. Mem. adv. bd. N.Y. Jazz Mus., 1972-75. Recipient Grand Prix du Disque, Montreux Jazz Festival,

1971, Trendsetter of Yr. award Billboard, 1971, CEBA award for distinction, 1964, Critics Poll Best Liner Notes award Living Blues Mag., 1993. Mem. Nat. Acad. Rec. Arts & Scis. (Grammy award 1971, Trustees award 1971, Grammy nominations 1977, 97). Address: 444 Central Park W New York NY 10025-4378 E-mail: calbertson@nyc.rr.com.

ALBERTSON, CHRISTOPHER ADAM, librarian; b. Oak Park, Ill., Dec. 10, 1951; Student, U. New Orleans, 1969-70; BA magna cum laude, U. Tex.-Arlington, 1972; MLS, N. Tex. State U., 1973. Cataloger Orange (Tex.) Pub. Libr., 1974-75, asst. libr., 1975-79, city. libr., 1979-81, Tyler (Tex.) Libr., 1981—. Contbr. articles to profl. jours. Mem. ALA, ASPA, Am. Mgmt. Assn., Am. Soc. Info. Sci., Tex. Libr. Assn., Rotary. Presbyterian. Home: 3100 Pounds Ave Tyler TX 75701-8034 Office: Tyler Pub Library 201 S College Ave Tyler TX 75702-7381 E-mail: citylibn@tylertexas.com.

ALBERTSON, SUSAN L. retired federal government official; b. Washington, Dec. 3, 1929; d. J. Mark and Alice (Myers) A. BS, Purdue U., 1952; postgrad., George Washington U., 1956-58. Numerous profl. positions CIA, Washington, 1952-88; ret., 1988. Republican. Avocations: piano, cooking, swimming.

ALBERTY, ROBERT ARNOLD, chemistry educator; b. Winfield, Kans., June 21, 1921; s. Luman Harvey and Mattie (Arnold) Alberty; m. Lillian Jane Wind, May 22, 1944; children: Nancy Lou, Steven Charles, Catherine Ann. BS, U. Nebr., 1943, MS, 1944; PhD, U. Wis., 1947; DSc (hon.), U. Nebr., 1967, Lawrence U., 1967. Engaged in research blood plasma fractionation for U.S. Govt., 1944—46; mem. faculty U. Wis., 1946—67, prof. chemistry, 1955—67, assoc. dean letters and sci., 1961—63; dean U. Wis. (Grad. Sch.), 1963—67; prof. chemistry MIT, 1967—91, dean Sch. Sci., 1967—82, prof. emeritus, 1991—. Cons. NSF, 1958—83, NIH, 1962—72; chmn. commn. on human resources NRC, 1974—77; dir. Colt Industries, 1978—88, Inst. for Def. Analysis, 1980—86; pres. phys. chemistry divsn. Internat. Union Pure and Applied Chemistry, 1991—93. Co-author: Experimental Physical Chemistry, 1970, Physical Chemistry, 2001, Thermodynamics of Biochemical Reactions, 2003. Recipient Eli Lilly award biol. chemistry, 1955; fellow Guggenheim, Calif. Inst. Tech., 1950—51. Fellow: AAAS; mem.: NAS, Am. Acad. Arts and Scis. (coun. 1991—94), Am. Chem. Soc. (chmn. com. on chemistry and pub. affairs 1978—80), Inst. Medicine, Sigma Xi, Phi Beta Kappa. Home: 931 Massachusetts Ave Cambridge MA 02139-3171 Office: MIT 77 Massachusetts Ave Rm 6-215 Cambridge MA 02139-4307

ALBI, EMILIO, economist; b. Valencia, Spain, July 29, 1945; s. Emilio and Amparo (Ibañez) A.; m. Maria Rosa Piquer, Dec. 29, 1971; children: Rosa, Amparo, Concha, Emilio. PhD in Econs., U. York, Eng., 1975; D. in Econs., Complutense U., Madrid, 1974. Tax ptnr. Deloitte Haskins & Sells, Madrid, 1980-87; tax ptnr. Price Waterhouse, Madrid, 1987—; univ. prof. Complutense U., Madrid, 1975—. Juan March Found. fellow, Brit. Coun. fellow. Home: Veracruz 2 28036 Madrid Spain Office: Albi Sanchez y Asociados Veracruz 4 28036 Madrid Spain

ALBICOCCO, SANTA, lawyer, county official; b. Bklyn. d. Frank Vincent and Mary Lucy (LaCava) Caputo; m. Samuel J. Rozzi, Ma. r7, 1981 (dec. July 1992); m. Sam A. Albicocco, Mar. 11, 1997. BA, Marymount Manhattan Coll., N.Y.C., 1971; JD, St. John's U., Jamaica, N.Y., 1981. Bar: N.Y. 1982. Insp. Nassau County, N.Y., 1981-82, dep. county atty., 1982-84, dep. county treas., 1984-86, chief Bur. of Real Estate, Ins. and Workers Compensation, 1986-88, dep. county exec., 1988-93, treas., 1993—. Mem. N.Y. State Banking Bd., 1998—. Recipient Tenth Ann. Achievers award L.I. Ctr. for Bus. and Profl. Women, 1989, commendation Women Econ. Developers of L.I., 1988; Nassau County Women's History Month honoree Nassau County Office of Women's Svcs., 1996. Mem. Mcpl. Forum of N.Y., Govt. Fin. Officers Assn., Bar Assn. Nassau County, Columbia Lawyers Assn. Nassau County. Republican. Roman Catholic. Office: Nassau County Treas 240 Old Country Rd Mineola NY 11501-4245

ALBIG, IRINA S. music educator; b. Krasnodar, Kuban, Russia, Apr. 12, 1972; d. Sergei Victorovich and Larisa Alexeevna (Mironchenko) Kabatsky; m. Allan Ray Albig, Jan. 3, 1998; 1 child, Roxanna Ruth. BA music theory, history, Krasnodar Music Coll., Krasnodar, Russia, 1991; MA music theory, history, Krasnodar Acad. Arts, Krasnodar, Russia, 1994; BA piano performance, Wahington State Univ., Pullman, WA, 1998, MA piano performance, 1998—2000. Piano instr. Home, Pullman, Wash., 1998—2001, Regis Univ., Denver, 2001—; piano intr. Home, Denver, 2001—; music hist. Met. State Coll., Denver, 2002—. Recipient Golden Key Nat. Honor Soc., Outstanding Scholarship Achievement, Wash. State Univ., 1997. Mem.: Music Tchr. Assoc. (DAMTA) (first v.p. 2002—). Avocations: reading, attending classical concerts, bicycling, opera, ballet. Home: 1240 Garfield St Denver CO 80206

ALBIN, BARRY G. lawyer, rabbi, energetic healer; b. Wichita, Kans., Sept. 6, 1948; s. Frederick Eugene Albin and Eloise Nelda Riley; m. Marianne Kay Olish, Aug. 8, 1970 (div. Feb. 1997); children: Thomas C., Michael A., Benjamin J., Joshua S. BA, U. Kans., 1970, JD, 1973; cert. in data processing, Kansas City C.C., 1981. Bar; Kans. 1973, U.S. Dist. Ct. Kans. 1973. Staff counsel Wyandotte Legal Aid Soc., Kansas City, Kans., 1974-76; pvt. practice Kansas City, 1976-83, 85—; gen. mgr. Chameleon Dental Products, Kansas City, 1983-85; grand hierophant, CEO Modern Rite of Memphis, Inc., 2002. Lectr. bus. law Maple Woods C.C., Kansas City, Mo., 1978; staff counsel Kans. State Dept. Social and Rehab. Svcs., Kansas City, 1986-91; legal counsel Mid. Am. Gay Ecumenical Found., Kansas City, Mo., 1975-80, Phylaxis Soc., 1999—, N.E. Kans. Valley, AASR, 1995—, Chi Rho Fraternity, Grand Tribune, 2001—; energetic healer and exorcist. Author: Climbing Jacob's Ladder, 1981, Believers Commentary on Mark, 1985, Believers Commentary on Barnabas, 1986, Catechism of Nasorean Church, 1995. Mebakker rabbi Nasorean Orthodox Qahal, Kansas City, 1985—; state treas., Green Party, 2000-2002. Mem. Internat. Soc. Study of Subtle Energies and Energy Medicine, Common Cause (state sec. 1978, state v.p. 1978-79), Inst. Noetic Sci., Masons (various offices 1989—), Scottish Rite (33d degree), York Rite (Knight York Cross of Honor), Masonic Brotherhood of Blue Forget-Me-Not, Blue Lodge. Democrat. Avocations: computers, reading, hiking, teaching, scripture.

ALBIN, LESLIE OWENS, biology educator; b. Spur, Tex., Jan. 8, 1940; s. John Leslie and Ottie Maude (Lassetter) A.; m. Monta Kay Gragg, Sept. 3, 1961 (div. 1982); children: Leslie Susan Albin Gann, Kimberly Ann Albin. BA, McMurry Coll., Abilene, 1962; MA, N. Tex. State U., 1969. Instr. biology E. Cen. State U., Ada, Okla., 1969-71; rsch. assoc. M.D. Andrson Hosp. & Tumor Inst., Houston, 1971; asst. prof. biology Western Tex. Coll., Snyder, 1971-74, assoc. prof. biology, 1974-77; prof. Austin (Tex.) C.C., 1977—, chmn. divsn. natural scis., 1978-95, head dept. biology, 1977-97. NDEA fellow, 1968. Mem. Am. Inst. Biol. Scis., Faculty Assn. Western Tex. Coll. (pres. 1973-74), Faculty Assn. Austin C.C. (pres. 1987-88), Faculty Senate Austin C.C., Tex. C.C. Tchrs. Assn., Tex. Acad. Sci., Am. Soc. for Microbiology, Alpha Chi. Office: Austin Community Coll Cypress Creek Campus 1555 Cypress Creek Rd Cedar Park TX 78613-3607 Business E-Mail: lesalbin@austincc.edu.

ALBIN, WOODROW ROSS, civil engineer; b. Fairfield, Calif., Apr. 29, 1965; s. Ross Lyle and Mabel Ojanen Albin; m. Deborah Ann Pearce, Aug. 9, 1967; children: Victoria, Kayla. BSCE, U. Wyo., 1989; M. Civil Engring., U. S.C., 1996. Registered profl. engr., Wis., Wash., S.. Engr. Bechtel Savannah River Inc., Aiken, SC, 1991—95, Nelson Engring., Jackson, Wyo., 1995—96, Stone & Webster, Englewood, Colo., 1996—98, Carter & Burgess, Denver, 1998—99, Wyatt Engring., Lewiston, Idaho, 1999—2000, Crispell-Snyder Inc., Lake Geneva, Wis., 2000—02; substitute tchr. Badger H.S., Lake Geneva. Mem. Save Our Wild Salmon. Mem.: Audubon Soc., Sierra Club. Democrat. Lutheran.

ALBINI, JOSEPH LOUIS, retired medical educator; b. Vandergift, Pa., July 28, 1930; s. Albino and Theresina Albini; m. Patrica Fulton, May 28, 1963 (div. Nov. 1965). BA, Pa. State U., 1954; MA, La. State U., 1956; PhD, Ohio State U., 1963. Cert. hypnotherapist Nat. Bd. Hypnotic Anesthesiology. Prof. Wayne State U., Detroit, 1967-91, Inst. Shipboard Edn. and Semester at Sea, 1971, 74; prof. emeritus Wayne State U., Detroit, 1991—. Vis. prof. U. Nev., Las Vegas, 1992-98; cons. Ministry off the Interior, Irkutsk, Russia, 1995, Dikewood Assocs., Albuquerque, 1967, Disaster Rsch. Ctr., Columbus, 1967. Author: The American Mafia, 1971; contbr. over 25 articles to profl. jours., 10 chpts. to books; presenter profl. meetings. Mem. Am. Sociol. Assn., Am. Coll. Sports Medicine, Assn. Advancement Applied Sport Psychology, Am. Soc. Criminology, Internat. Soc. Study Organized Crime.

ALBINO, JOSEPH XAVIER, writer, educator, photographer; b. Syracuse, N.Y., Mar. 19, 1937; s. Samuel and Frances Carmella Albino; m. Mary Louise Albino, July 30, 1960; children: Mary Susan, Anne Louise, Christine, Julie Marie. MS English, Syracuse U., Syracuse, NY, 1983; BA English, Le Moyne Coll., Syracuse, NY, 1959. English educator and writer/photographer various colls., Cortland, Morrisville, and Herkimer, NY, 1982—; photographer/writer Fortune 500 firms, 1960—80. *As a professional writer-photographer, Joseph Albino has traveled coast-to-coast and shore-to-shore to obtain editorial and advertising photographic coverage for national corporations. In addition, he is constantly seeking article opportunities for national publications. Periodically, he also works abroad. He is able to provide both articles and pictures for his clients. As a general feature freelance writer, he writes for industrial, science, spiritual, and travel publications. As a college English instructor, he has developed unique writing assignments for students of his composition and literature classes. Based upon his premise that good writing is rewriting he has developed a unique grading program, which allows a student to rewrite an essay for a higher grade provided that the student receives tutoring assistance in areas of weakness. He also has a reputation as an instructor who helps a student to become all that the student is capable of becoming.* Consecrated mem. OPUS Santorum Angelorum, 1988—; vol. Mental Health Assn. of Onondaga County, Syracuse, NY, 1995—2001. Roman Catholic. Avocations: hiking, canoeing, swimming, amateur radio operator. Home: 221 Hillbrook Road Syracuse NY 13217 Home Fax: 315-487-1904.

ALBINO, JUDITH ELAINE NEWSOM, university president; b. Jackson, Tenn. m. Salvatore Albino; children: Austin, Adrian. BJ, U. Tex., 1967, PhD, 1973. Mem. faculty sch. dental medicine SUNY, Buffalo, 1972-90, assoc. provost, 1984-87, dean sch. arch. and planning, 1987-89, dean grad. sch., 1989-90; v.p. acad. affairs and rsch, dean system grad. sch. U. Colo., Boulder, 1990-91, pres., 1991-95, pres. emerita, prof. psychiatry, 1995-97; pres. Calif. Sch. Profl. Psychology Alliant Internat. U., San Francisco, 1997—. Contbr. articles to profl. jours. Acad. Adminstrn. fellow Am. Coun. on Edn., 1983, grantee NIH. Fellow APA (treas., bd. dirs.); mem. Behavioral Scientists in Dental Rsch. (past pres.), Am. Assn. Dental Rsch. (bd. dirs.). Office: Calif Sch Profl Psychology Alliant Internat U Office Pres 2728 Hyde St Ste 100 San Francisco CA 94109-1251 Fax: 415-771-5908. E-mail: jalbino@alliant.edu.

ALBORES-SAAVEDRA, JORGE, pathologist, educator; b. La Concordia, Chiapas, Mex., Dec. 15, 1933; came to U.S., 1984; s. Enrique and Aurora (Saavedra) Albores; m. Blanca Gallo, Dec. 16, 1957; children: Lilia, Ruth. MD, Nat. U. Mex., Mexico City, 1957. Assoc. prof. pathology Nat. U. Mex., 1964-67, prof. pathology, 1968-84, U. Miami (Fla.) Sch. Medicine, 1984-90; prof. pathology, dir. divsn. anatomical pathology U. Tex. Southwestern Med. Ctr., Dallas, 1990—. Chmn. dept. pathology Gen. Hosp. Mexico City, 1968-83, Nat. U. Mex., 1976-83, Hosp. Ctrl. sur de PEMEX, Mexico City, 1983-84. Author: Tumors of the Gallbladder and Extrahepatic Bile Ducts and Ampulla of Vater, 2000; co-author: Pathology of Incipient Neoplasia, 3d edit., 2001; contbr. more than 230 sci. papers to profl. publs., 39 chpts. to books. Office: Dept Pathology LSU Health Sci Ctr 1501 Kings Hwy Shreveport LA 71130 E-mail: albore@LSUHSC.edu.

ALBRECHT, ALBERT PEARSON, electronics/systems engineer, consultant; b. Bakersfield, Calif., Aug. 23, 1920; s. Albert Waldo and Elva (Shuck) A.; m. Muriel Elizabeth Grenell, June 15, 1942 (dec. Apr. 1943); m. Edith J. Dorner, July 18, 1944. BSEE, Calif. Inst. Tech., 1942; MSEE, U. So. Calif., L.A., 1947. Registered profl. engr., Calif. Rsch. assoc. radiation lab. MIT, Cambridge, 1942-43; chief engr. Gilfillan Bros., L.A., 1943-58; v.p. Space Gen. Corp., El Monte, Calif., 1958-68; exec. v.p. Telluran Cons., Santa Monica, Calif., 1968-72; dir. systems evaluation Office of Asst. Sec. of Def. for Intelligence, Washington, 1972-76; assoc. adminstr. FAA, Washington, 1976-86; cons., prin. AP Albrecht-Cons., Bellingham, Wash., 1986—. Bd. dirs. Air Traffic Control Assn.; mem. exec. bd. RADIO Tech. Commn. for Aeronautics, Washington, 1980-86; mem. aeronautics adv. com. NASA, Washington, 1980-90. Co-author: Electronic Designers Handbook-Design Compendium, 1957, 2d edit., 1974; editor Air Traffic Control Quar. Fellow AIAA (adv. com. Aerospace Am. 1984-2001), IEEE (Engr. Mgr. of Yr. 1989). Achievements include rsch. and management of the replacement and automation of the nation's air traffic control system. Home and Office: 3224 Eagleridge Way Bellingham WA 98226-7821 E-mail: asquared@nas.com.

ALBRECHT, CHRIS, broadcast executive; Sr. v.p. original programming HBO Pictures, N.Y.C., 1985—95, pres. original programming, 1995—. Office: HBO Pictures 1100 Ave of Americas New York NY 10036

ALBRECHT, DONNA G. author; b. Bridgeton, N.J. m. Michael C. Albrecht, Aug. 16, 1970; children: Katherine (dec.), Abigail. BA, Antioch U., San Francisco, 1983. Tchr. U. Calif. Ext.; lectr. in field; cons. in field. Author: Deals and Discounts: If You're 50 or Older, 1990, Buying a Home When You're Single, 1994, rev. edit., 2001, Raising A Child Who Has A Physical Disability, 1995, Overcoming the Four Deceptions: In Career Relationships (with Dwaine L. Canova), 1995, Promoting Your Business with Free (or Almost Free) Publicity, 1997, I Love to Tell the Story: Favorite Bible Stories of Famous People, 1999 (Silver Angel award Excellence in Media); contbr. over 400 articles to mags., including Entrepreneur Mag. (columnist), Ms., Modern Maturity, Real Estate Today, Calif. Bus., San Francisco Bus. Times, San Francisco Examiner, Contra Costa Times, Writer's Digest, Sharing Ideas, Exceptional Parent, Accent on Living, others. Pres. exec. com. No. Calif. chpt. Muscular Dystrophy Assn., 1992. Mem. Am. Soc. Journalists and Authors (founding co-chmn. for regional symposium 1992, chmn. 1994, chpt. pres. 1991-93, 98-2000, nat. bd. dirs. 1994-98, 2001-02), Author Guild. Lutheran. Office: PO Box 21423 Concord CA 94521-0423 E-mail: donna@albrechts.com.

ALBRECHT, KARL, automotive and household plastic parts executive; b. Kassell, Germany, Feb. 6, 1940; m. Ingrid Konrad; children: Oliver, Patrick. Diploma in Bus., PhD. Mgmt. cons. Knight, Gladieux & Smith, Dusseldorf and N.Y.C., 1969-72; plans adminstr. Continental Can Co., N.Y.C., 1972-76; v.p. European fins. Continental Group, Brossuels, 1976-78; pres., CEO Schmalbach-Lubeca GmbH, Brunswick, 1978-89; mem. exec. bd. Otto Wolff AG, Cologne, Germany, 1989; now chmn. supervisory bd. Ymos AG, Obertshausen, Germany, 1989—. Mem. supervisory bd. Stiebel Eltron GmbH, Holzminden; chair shareholders com. SMAG Salzgitter Maschinenbau GmbH, othres; mem. adv./adminstrv. bd. Deutsche Bank AG, Hanover, Karl Munte Bauunternehmung, Brunswick, Stinnes Stahhandel GMbH, Essen, others. Mem. European Recycling and Recovery Assn. (exec. com.). Office: care Ymos AG Feldstrasse D-63179 Obertshausen Germany

ALBRECHT, KATHE HICKS, art historian, visual resources manager; b. Ann Arbor, Mich., Aug. 21, 1952; d. Richard Brian and Mafalda (Brasile) Hicks; m. Mark Jennings Albrecht, July 20, 1973; children: Nicole, Alexander, Olivia. BA in Art History, UCLA, 1975; MA in Art History, Am. U., 1989. Slide libr. asst. Am. U., Washington, 1986-88, visual resources curator, 1991—; pres.-elect Visual Resources Assn., 2003. Co-coord. Mus. Ednl. Site Licensing Project (Nat. Initiative Getty), 1994; presenter Southeastern Coll. Art Conf., Georgetown U., 1995, Richmond, Va., 1997, Norfolk, Va., 1999; mem. Conf. on Fair Use (Dept. of Commerce) VRA rep. to Digital Future Coalition, 1996—; mem. Nat. Initiative for a Networked Cultural Heritage, 1996-2003. Vol. Fairfax County Pub. Sch. Sys., 1980-2000; re-election com. Rep. Nat. Com., Washington, 1984; Rep. precinct worker Mason dist., 1980s. Grantee Getty Art History Info. Program, 1994-97; Am. U. (image processing, database devel.), 1995, 2003. Mem. Art Librs. Soc. N. Am., Coll. Art Assn., Am. Assn. Mus., Southeastern Coll. Art Conf., Visual Resources Assn. (pres. Mid-Atlantic region 1995-96, 2000-02, chair nat. membership com., 1995-97, chair intellectual property rights com. 1996-2000, pres. elect 2003—). Presbyterian. Avocation: antique and prints collecting. Office: Am Univ 4400 Massachusetts Ave NW Washington DC 20016-8001 E-mail: Kalbrec@american.edu.

ALBRECHT, PETER LEFFINGWELL, lawyer; b. N.Y.C., Mar. 4, 1930; s. Ralph Gerhart and Aillinn (Leffingwell) A.; m. Constance Trowbridge, Sept. 10, 1955 (div. 1975); children— Kate, Cynthia Margaret, Mary Eugenie, David, Thomas Peter Salem, Matthew William Trotter; m. Margaret Page, Jan. 29, 1977. A.B., Harvard, 1952, LL.B., 1955. Bar: Mass. 1956. Assoc., Ropes & Gray, Boston, 1955-68, ptnr., 1968— . Mem. Lawyers Alliance for Nuclear Arms Control, ABA (mem. various coms. and subcoms. sect. corp., banking and bus. law). Office: Ropes & Gray 1 International Pl Fl 4 Boston MA 02110-2624

ALBRECHT, RICHARD RAYMOND, retired airplane manufacturing executive, lawyer; b. Storm Lake, Iowa, Aug. 29, 1932; s. Arnold Louis and Catherine Dorothea (Boettcher) A.; m. Constance Marie Berg, June 16, 1957; children: John Justin, Carl Arnold, Richard Louis, Henry Berg. BA, U. Iowa, 1958, JD with highest honors, 1961. Bar: Wash. 1961. Assoc. Perkins, Coie, Stone, Olsen & Williams, Seattle, 1961-67, ptnr., 1968-74; gen. counsel U.S. Dept. Treasury, Washington, 1974-76; v.p., gen. counsel, sec. Boeing Co., Seattle, 1976-81, v.p. fin., contracts and internat. bus., 1981-83, v.p., gen. mgr. Everett div., 1983-84; exec. v.p. Boeing Comml. Airplane Group, Seattle, 1984-97, sr. advisor, 1997-2000. Dir. Esterline Technologies Corp., Wash. Dental Svc., Magna Drive Corp. Mem. bd. regents Wash. State U., 1987-2000With AUS, 1955-58. Recipient Outstanding Citizen of Yr. award Seattle-King County Municipal League, 1968-69. Mem. ABA, Wash. State Bar Assn., Am. Judicature Soc., Order of St. John (officer 1992-99, comdr. 1999—), Order of Coif, Rainier Club, Broadmoor Golf Club, Seattle Tennis Club, Sigma Nu, Omicron Delta Kappa, Phi Delta Phi. Home: PO Box 10296 Bainbridge Island WA 98110 Office: Perkins Coie LLP 1201 3rd Ave Ste 4800 Seattle WA 98101-3099

ALBRECHT, ROBERTA J. writer; b. Bronx, May 27, 1945; d. Robert H. and Beverly (Burgess) Albrecht; m. David B. Richards, Aug. 13, 1983; m. Franklin D. Adams, Dec. 26, 1967 (div. Sept. 1980); 1 child, Emma Adams. MA in English, Stetson U., Deland, Fla., 1979. Tchg. asst. Purdue U., West Lafayette, Ind., 1979—83, Marquette U., Milw., 1979—83; instr. freshman composition Concordia Coll., Wis., 1982—84, instr., 1986—92, asst. prof., dir. honors program, 1991—92. Book reviewer Books and Coffee series Concordia Coll., 1990, dir. symposium study The Stronger, 88; spkr., presenter in field. Contbr. ; author: (book) Going Around with God: Patterns of Motion in Donne's Holy Sonnets, 1986, (novels) Mary as Alchemical Reference, 2005. Recipient prize in nonfiction book competition, The Devonshire Pub. Co., 1986. Mem.: DAV, MLA, Eastern Paralyzed Vets. Assn., The John Donne Soc. Democrat. Lutheran. Avocation: travel. Home: 3801 Hudson Manor Ter #7L Bronx NY 10463

ALBRECHT, RONALD LEWIS, financial services executive; b. Derby, Conn., Dec. 30, 1935; s. Lewis Davis and Gladys Imogene (Spear) A.; m. Mikyong Kim, Dec. 28, 1968; children: Rondi Kim, Kathryn Lynn, Karen Ann. BS in Agr., U. Vt., 1957; BBA in Bus. Mgmt., Baylor U., 1966; MA in Bus. Mgmt., Cen. Mich. U., 1975. Commd. 2d lt. USAF, 1957, advanced through grades to lt. col., 1973, comdr. detachment, 1957—60, air traffic control officer Cheveston, England, 1960—62, dir. air traffic control HQ12 Waco, Tex., 1962—66, comdr. detachment Kimpo AB, Republic of Korea, 1967—68, comdr. squadron Sewart AFB, 1969—70, comdr. squadron Holloman AFB, 1970—73, staff officer, air traffic control HQ air force systems command, 1973—75, dep. comdr. group Pentagon, 1975—77, staff officer electronics HQ joint staff Yongson, Republic of Korea, 1977—79, staff officer air traffic control communications area Rome, NY, 1979—80, retired, 1980; real estate broker Bangor, Maine, 1980—; retirement, investment and fin. planning exec. Bangor (Maine) Savs. Bank, 1981—87; pres. Maine Fin. Mgmt. Svcs.,Inc. and Albrecht Fin. Svcs., P.A., Bangor, 1987—. Instr. Los Angeles Community Coll., Seoul, Korea, 1977-79, Husson Coll. Bangor, 1981-84. Mem. loaned exec. bd. div. planning com. United Way of Penobscot Valley, Bangor, 1981—. Rep. Party, Bangor, 1981—. Hood Dairy scholar U. Vt., 1955. Mem. Fin. Planning Assn. (v.p. programs, co-founder 1985, pres. Maine chpt. 1988-89), Inst. Cert. Fin. Planners, Internat. Cert. Fin. Planners (bd. standards and practices), Ret. Officers Assn., Am. Assn. Ret. Persons, Air TrafficControl Assn., Armed Forces Communications Electronics Assn., Kiwanis (2d and 1st v.p. Bangor Club, pres. 1987-88), Masons, Anah Temple, Valley of Tokyo, Orientof Japan and Korea. Avocations: reading, hiking, gardening, travel. Home: 98 Judson Blvd Bangor ME 04401-2542

ALBRECHT, THEO, business executive; b. Mar. 28, 1922; m. Cilli Albrecht; children: Theo, Berthold. Grad., secondary sch. Owner grocery bus. eventually covering, all of Ruhr area, Germany, 1946—; founder, propr., mng. ptnr. Albrecht KG, Herten, Germany, 1961—; opened first Aldi market, Dortmund, Germany, 1962; acquired by Albrecht Group in USA, 1977; mng. ptnr. Aldi GmbH & Co., Mülheim, Germany; co-CEO, Aldi Group, Essen, Germany. Served with German Army, World War II; Am. prisoner of war. Avocations: golf, growing orchids. Office: Aldi Group Eckenbergstr 16 PB 13 01 10 D-45291 Essen Germany also: Otto-Suhr-Allee 26/28 10585 Berlin Germany

ALBRECHT, WILLIAM KENNETH, lawyer; b. San Diego, Nov. 10, 1957; s. William Price Albrecht and Alice Annette (Cooper) Richardson; m. Seta Marie Nazarian, Aug. 11, 1984; children: William Nazar, Nicholas Moses. BA cum laude, Williams Coll., 1979; JD, U. Iowa, 1984. Bar: Conn. 1984, N.J. 1992, U.S. Dist. Ct., Conn. 1985, U.S. District Ct., N.J. 1992. Pvt. practice, 1984-88; gen. counsel D'Addario Industries, Bridgeport, Conn., 1988-91; v.p., gen. counsel Everest Realty Co., Kearny, 1991—. Active St. Leon's Armenian Ch.; councilman Borough of Haworth, N.J., 2000—, pres. coun., 2003. Mem. N.J. State Bar Assn., Greater Bergen County Williams Coll. Assn (pres. 2001-03). Avocations: tennis, swimming, photography. Home: 582 Haworth Ave Haworth NJ 07641-1537

ALBRECHT, WILLIAM MELVIN, research chemist, consultant; b. Hungerford, Pa., Feb. 18, 1926; s. Walter John and Vivian Matilda (Sheffer) A.; m. Kathleen Mae Albrecht, July 3, 1948 (dec. Nov. 1995); children: Gary, Jeffery, Robert, Phillip, Cheryl, Keith, Karen, Marsha. BS in Chemistry, Lebanon Valley Coll., Annville, Pa., 1948; MS in Phys. Chemistry, U. Cin., 1950; Cert., MIT, 1970. Rsch. chemist Battelle Meml. Inst., Columbus, 1950-56, rsch. mgr., 1956-60; R&D chemist IBM, Endicott, N.Y., 1960-66, R&D mgr., 1966-82; cons. chemist Endwell, N.Y., 1982—. Mem. symposium panel Am. Electroplaters Soc., N.Y.C., 1978. Contbr. articles to profl. jours. With U.S. Army, 1944-45. Fellow Sigma Xi. Avocations: saxophone teaching, woodworking, cooking, photography. Home and Office: 414 Corey Ave Endwell NY 13760 E-mail: albrechtwm@yahoo.com.

ALBRECHT, WILLIAM PRICE, economist, educator, government official; b. Pitts., Jan. 7, 1935; s. William Price and Jane Lanier (Moses) A.; m. Alice Annette Cooper, June 14, 1956 (div. Nov. 1975); children— William, Alison, Jonathan, Jeffrey; m. Fran Jaecques, July 4, 1976 AB, Princeton U., 1956; MA, U. S.C., 1962, Yale U., 1963, PhD, 1965. Asst. prof. U. Iowa, Iowa City, 1965-70, assoc. prof., 1970-82, prof. econs., 1982-88, assoc. dean Coll. Bus. Adminstrn., 1984-88; self-employed antitrust cons., 1978-88; commr. Commodity Futures Trading Commn., Washington, 1988-93; prof. econs. U. Iowa, Iowa City, 1993—, dir. Inst. for Internat. Bus., 1998—, Justice prof. Internat. Bus., 2000—. TV fin. advisor. Author: Economics, 1974, 4th edit., 1986, Black Employment, 1970, Microeconomic Principles, 1979, Macroeconomic Principles, 1979 Candidate U.S. Ho. of Reps., 1970; legis. asst. U.S. Senator Dick Clark, 1974. Served to lt. USN, 1956-61 Mem. Am. Econ. Assn., Midwest Econ. Assn. (v.p. 1981-82). Avocations: tennis; farming. Home: 5770 NE Morse Rd Solon IA 52333-8806 Office: U Iowa Dept Econs Iowa City IA 52242

ALBRECHTA, JOSEPH FRANCIS, lawyer; b. Bklyn., Apr. 1, 1957; PhB, Miami U., 1978; JD, U. Toledo, 1984. Bar: Ohio 1984, U.S. Dist. Ct. (no. dist.) Ohio 1984, U.S. Ct. Appeals (5th cir.), U.S. Supreme Ct. 1986. Naturalist Ind. Dunes State Park, Ind. Dept. Natural Resources, Porter, 1978; polit. activist, campaign staff Ohio Alliance for Returns, Columbus, 1979; lobbyist Ohio Sierra Club, Columbus, 1980-81; tech. writer Toledo Met. Area Coun. Govts., 1981-82; legal asst. Gallon, Kalniz & Iorio Co. LPA, Toledo, 1982-84, assoc., 1984-86; ptnr. Gary and Albrechta, Toledo, 1986-95, Albrechta & Coble, Toledo and Fremont, Ohio, 1996—. Lawyer Otis Elem. Sch. PTO, Fremont, 1994—, St. Johns Luth. Ch., Fremont, 1995—. Vol. Otis Elem. Sch., Fremont, 1990—97; asst. den leader Cub Scouts Pack 312, Fremont, 1991—97; scoutmaster Boy Scouts Troop 400, Fremont, 1996—2002. Mem.: ATLA, Sandusky

County Bar Assn., Toledo Bar Assn. (grievance investigator 1992—96), Ohio Trial Lawyers Assn., Fremont Yacht Club (asst. comdr. 1991—98, comdr. 1999—2000). Democrat. Lutheran. Office: Albrechta & Coble 100 N Arch St Fremont OH 43420-9789

ALBRIGHT, JACK LAWRENCE, animal science and veterinary educator; b. San Francisco, Mar. 14, 1930; s. George Clarence and Elizabeth Ann (Murphy) A.; m. Lorraine Aylmer Hughes, Aug. 17, 1957; children: Maryann A. Williams, Amy Elizabeth. BS with honors, Calif. State Poly. U., 1952; MS, Wash. State U., 1954, PhD, 1957. Rsch. asst. Wash. State U., 1952-54, 55-57, acting instr., 1954-55; instr. Calif. State Poly. U., 1955, 57-59; asst. prof. U. Ill., Urbana, 1959-63; assoc. prof. Purdue U., West Lafayette, Ind., 1963-66, prof. animal sci. Sch. Agr., 1966-96, prof. animal mgmt. and behavior Sch. Vet. Medicine, 1974-96, prof. emeritus animal sci. and vet. medicine, 1996—. Mem. Ctr. Applied Ethology and Human-Animal Interactions, Human/Animal Bond Purdue U., 1982-96, Purdue Interdisciplinary Undergrad. Program in Animal Welfare and Societal Concerns, 1992-96, Purdue Animal Care and Use com., 1989-92, Ctr. for Rsch. on Livestock Behavior and Well-Being in Food Animals, 1992-96; vis. prof. U. Ariz., Tucson, 1995, N.Mex. State U., Las Cruces, 1995, U. Ill., Urbana, 1988-89; vis. prof. pure and applied zoology U. Reading, Eng., 1977-78; vis. scientist N.Z. Dept. Agr., Ruakura, Hamilton, 1971-72, Dairy Shrine, Ft. Atkinson, Wis., 1958—; cons., lectr. in field, animal mgmt., behavior, care and welfare; mem. Ind. Commn. Farm Animal Care, 1981-99; numerous invited lectures worldwide. Author more than 900 papers, revs., chpts., guidelines, and books; reviewer sci. jours. Vestryman St. John's Episcopal Ch., Lafayette, Ind., 1979-82; bellringer Salvation Army, 1964—; mem. judging teams Cal Poly Dairy Cattle, Dairy Products and Livestock; vol. Ind. Livestock Care Assistance Project Helpline, 1999—, Heifer Project Internat. Fulbright scholar, N.Z., 1971-72; NSF Animal Behavior grantee, summer 1964; USDA/FAS/ICD Sci. and Tech. Exch. Program awardee to Rep. of Ireland, 1994; recipient Guardian award Ind. Vet. Med. Assn., 1995, Sci., Edn. and Tech. award dept. animal scis. Washington State U., 1996; one of 7 named to inaugural Renaissance Acad. Hall of Fame, Paso Robles H.S., 1998. Fellow AAAS, Am. Dairy Sci. Assn., Ind. Acad. Sci.; mem. Am. Dairy Sci. Assn. (sec. 1972-73, chmn. profl. coun. 1973-74, Dairy Mgmt. Rsch. award 1986, invited lectrs. ann. meeting, 1982, 86-87, 92, 94, found. charter 1992), Animal Behavior Soc. (charter), Am. Soc. Animal Sci. (chmn. animal behavior com. 1970, 76, 85, Animal Mgmt. Rsch. award 1988, Found. charter 1993, animal care com. 1994-96), Am. Registry Profl. Animal Sci. (dairy and animal behavior 1993—), Humane Slaughter Assn., Am. Coll. Animal Behavior Sci. (cert., charter, diplomate 1995), Am. Soc. Vet. Ethology (charter), Internat. Soc. Applied Ethology, Chillingham Wild Cattle Assn. (life), Soc. Study Ethics and Animals, Scientist's Ctr. Animal Welfare (corr.), Univs. Fedn. for Animal Welfare, Hooved Animal Humane Soc., Los Lecheros Dairy Club Calif. State Poly. U. (hon.), Kiwanis (pres. Lafayette club 1969-70, sec. found. 1976-77, Tablet of Honor Internat. Kiwanis Found. 2000), Blue Key, Delta Soc., Sigma Xi, Alpha Zeta, Gamma Sigma Delta, Farm House. Republican. Home: 188 Blueberry Ln West Lafayette IN 47906-4810 Office: Purdue Univ Poul Bldg Dept Animal Scis West Lafayette IN 47907-1026 E-mail: jla9@juno.com.

ALBRIGHT, JOSEPH P. state supreme court justice; b. Parkersburg, W.Va., Nov. 8, 1938; s. M.P. and Catherine (Rathbone) A.; m. Patricia Ann Deem, 1958 (dec. 1993); children: Terri Albright Cavi, Lettie K., Joseph P. Jr., John Patrick (dec.); m. Nancie Gensert Divvens; stepchildren: Susan Divvens Bowman, Debbie Divvens Holcomb, Sandy Divvens Fox. BBA cum laude, U. Notre Dame, JD, 1962. Bar: W.Va. 1962, U.S. Dist. Ct. W.Va. 1962. Pvt. practice, Parkersburg, 1964-95; asst. prosecuting atty. Wood County, 1965-68; city atty. City of Parkersburg, W.Va., 1968; justice W.Va. Supreme Ct. of Appeals, Charleston, 1995—96, 2001—; pvt. practice Parkersburg and Charleston, 1997—2000. Former mem. W.Va. State Ethics Commn.; bd. dirs. Albrights of Belpre (Ohio), Inc. Former clk. Charter Bd. of Parkerburg; mem. W.Va. Ho. of Dels., 1970-86, mem. jud. com., chmn. com. on edn., 1977-78, chmn. com. on judiciary, 1979-84, 52d spkr. of Ho. of Dels., 1984-86; mem., former chmn. Blennerhassett Hist. Park Commn.; former co-chmn. Blennerhassett Hist. Commn.; mem. St. Francis Xavier Ch., Parkersburg, past pres. parish adv. coun. Named Freshman Legislator of Yr., Charleston Gazette, 1971. Office: WVa Supreme Ct Appeals State Capitol Complex Bldg 1 Room E308 1900 Kanawha Boulevard E Charleston WV 25305

ALBRIGHT, JOSEPH WILLIAM, army officer; b. Chillicothe, Ohio, Feb. 3, 1954; s. Herman LeRoy and Catherine Regina (Rieder) A.; m. Deanna Wells, Aug. 13, 1989; children: Andrea Lyn, Jason Michael; stepchildren: Jennifer Carlene, Tammy Darlene. BME, U. Dayton, 1976; M in Strategic Studies, U.S. Army War Coll., 2000; MS in Indsl. Engring., U. Tenn., 2001. Commd. 2nd lt. Ordnance br. U.S. Army, 1976; advanced through grades to col. Ordnance br. U.S. Army, 1999; accountable officer 9th ordnance co. 9th Ordnance Co., Germany, 1977-79, ops. officer, 1979-80; rsch. engr., chief integrated logistic support office large caliber weapon sys. lab., 1980-82; material officer 3rd ordnance bn. 59th ordnance brigade 3d Ordnance Bn., 59th Ordnance Brigade, 1982-85; Dept. of Army coord. for ammunition logistics Dept. of Army, 1985-87; asst. exec. officer to dep. commanding gen. Material Readiness Army Material Commd., 1987-88; commdr. 96th ordnance co. 96th Ordnance Co., 1988-90; inspector gen. Tech. Insp. divsn. Army Material Command Tech. Insp. divsn. Army Materiel Command, 1990-93, chief program mgmt. divsn., 1993-94; comdr. Milan Army Ammunition Plant Milan Army Ammunition Plant, Tenn., 1994-96; dep. support ops. officer 3rd corps support command V U.S. Army Corps, 1996-98; depot maintenance project chief Hdqrs., Dept. of Army, 1998-99, indsl. ops. project chief, office dep. chief staff logistics, 2000—02; sr. logistics analyst Office of Dep. Undersec. of Army, Washington, 2002—. Decorated Legion of Merit, Meritorious Svc. medal with 5 oak leaf clusters, Army Commendation medal with oak leaf cluster, Army Achievement medal; named Disting. Mil. Grad., 1976, Disting. Grad. Ordnance Officer Advanced Course, 1980. Mem. ASME, Pi Sigma Tau. Home: 219 Diamond Dr Walkersville MD 21793-9145 Office: Hdqrs Dept of Army Attn: SASA-BT Ste 3E614 101 Army Pentagon Washington DC 20310-0101 E-mail: joseph.albright@hqda.army.mil.

ALBRIGHT, JUDITH ANNE, writer, educator; b. Toldeo, Ohio; d. Matthew M. and Margaret Harris McMahon; m. Bill Eugene Albright, Aug. 15, 1964; children: Mary Sheila, Michael James. Tchr., Peoria, Ill., 1964, Concord Sch. System, Elkhart, Ind., 1965-67, Dows Ln. Sch., Irvington, N.Y., 1967-69, Capistrano Unified Schs., San Juan Capistrano, Calif., 1980-89; owner, dir. Albright Presch., Mission Viejo, Calif., 1984-86; tchr. St. Edwards Sch., Dana Point, Calif., 1986-87; with Premier Cruises, 1997—2000; kindergarten tchr. Longleaf Sch., 2000—01; tchr. Brevard Pub. Schs., Fla., 2000—02. Cons., spkr. in field of religion. Author: Our Lady of Medjugorje, 1988, Neustra Senora de Medjugorje, 1988, Mary and the Children of Medjugorje, 1989, Our Lady of Garabandal, 1992. Vol. St. Vincent de Paul. Roman Catholic. Avocations: travel, reading, writing, boating.

ALBRIGHT, JULIA SZUR, artist; b. Nixon-Edesen, N.J., Feb. 14, 1915; d. Kalman and Mary Kovacs Szur; m. Wilbur Elliott Albright, Mar. 1, 1909 (dec.); children: Barbara Lee, Marye Lou. One-woman shows include U. Ariz., 1965, exhibited in group shows, Las Cruces, N.Mex., Tubac, Ariz., Tucson, El Paso. Home and Studio: 8044 Coley Davis Rd 6B Nashville TN 37221-2310

ALBRIGHT, JULIE MARIE, sociologist, educator; d. Allan C. and Jacqueline M. Albright. PhD, U. So. Calif., 2001. Rsch. assoc. Annenberg Sch. Comm. U. So. Calif., L.A., 2001—03, lectr., 2001—. Lectr. Calif. State U., L.A., 1998—2002. Democrat. Presbyterian. Achievements include research in tobacco and the internet. Avocations: sailboat racing, weightlifting, travel. Office: U So Calif 3620 S Vermont KAP 352 Los Angeles CA 90089-2539 E-mail: albright@usc.edu.

ALBRIGHT, JUSTIN W. retired lawyer; b. Lisbon, Iowa, Oct. 14, 1908; m. Mildred Carlton, 1935; 1 child, Carlton J. BSC., U. Iowa, 1931, JD, 1933. Bar: Iowa 1933. Former counsel firm Simmons, Perrine, Albright & Ellwood, P.L.C., Cedar Rapids, Iowa; ret. Editor: Iowa Law Rev, 1932-33. Past trustee, bd. trustees YMCA of Met. Cedar Rapids; bd. dirs. Cedar Rapids Symphony Orch.; founding mem., past pres. St. Paul's United Meth. Ch. Found., Cedar Rapids. Served with AUS, World War II. Mem. ABA, Iowa Bar Assn., Linn County Bar Assn. (life), Am. Judicature Soc., Hoover Presdl. Libr. Assn., Cedar Rapids C. of C., Phi Delta Phi. Clubs: Cedar Rapids Country, Pickwick (Cedar Rapids) (past pres.). Lodges: Masons (32 deg.), Shriners, Rotary (Paul Harris fellow). Office: Simmons Perrine Albright & Ellwo 115 3rd St SE Ste 1200 Cedar Rapids IA 52401-1266

ALBRIGHT, KENDRA SUZANNE, educator; b. Bloomington, Ind., Apr. 13, 1956; d. Joseph F. and Marcia L. (Geckler) Albright; children: Brynne, Darcy. BS, U. Tenn., 1979, MS in Libr. Sci., 1985, PhD, 2002. Bus. info. ctr. mgr. Whittle Communications Ltd., Knoxville, 1985-86; cons. pvt. practice Oak Ridge, Tenn., 1986-92, 99—; tech. libr. Oak Ridge Nat. Lab., 1986-92; mgr. Info. Internat. Assocs., Inc., Oak Ridge, 1992—96, 1999—2001; asst. prof. U. Tenn., Knoxville, 2002—. Contbr. articles to profl. jours. Mem. Am. Libr. Assn., Soc. Competitive Intelligence Profls., Am. Soc. for Info Sci. Office: U Tenn Sch Info Scis 451 Comms Bldg Knoxville TN 37996

ALBRIGHT, LYLE FREDERICK, chemical engineering educator; b. Bay City, Mich., May 3, 1921; s. William Edward and Isabella (Sidebotham) A.; m. Jeanette Van Belle, Mar. 4, 1950; children: Christine, Diane. BS in Chem. Engring, U. Mich., 1943, MS in Chem. Engring, 1944, PhD in Chem. Engring, 1950. Lab. technician Dow Chem. Co., Midland, Mich., 1939-41; chem. engr. E.I. duPont de Nemours & Co., Hanford, Wash., 1944-46; research chem. engr. Colgate-Palmolive Co., Jersey City, 1950-51; asst. prof. U. Okla., Norman, 1951-54, assoc. prof., 1954-55, Purdue U., West Layette, Ind., 1955-58, prof. chem. engring., 1958—. Cons. to numerous chem. petroleum cos., 1960—. Author: Industrial and Laboratory Pyrolyses, 1976, Industrial and Laboratory Alkylations, 1977, Coke Formation on Metals, 1982, Pyrolysis: Theory and Industrial Practice, 1983, Processes for Major Addition Type Plastics and Their Monomers, 2d edit., 1985, Novel Production Methods for Ethylene, Light Hydrocarbons, and Aromatics, 1992, Nitrations: Recent Laboratory and Industrial Developments, 1996. Recipient Shreve prize Purdue U., 1960, 70, 88, Potter award for best instr. Schs. of Engring. Purdue U., 1988. Fellow AIChE (dir. 1982-84, Van Antwerpen award 2003); mem. Am. Chem. Soc., Internat. Brotherhood Magicians, Sigma Xi, Tau Beta Pi. Methodist. Home: 4750N N 250 W West Lafayette IN 47906-5525 Office: Purdue Univ Sch Chem Engring West Lafayette IN 47907

ALBRIGHT, MADELEINE KORBEL, former secretary of state; b. Prague, Czechoslovakia, May 15, 1937; d. Josef and Anna (Speeglova) Korbel; m. Joseph Medill Patterson Albright, June 11, 1959 (div. 1983); children: Anne Korbel, Alice Patterson, Katharine Medill. BA with honors in Polit. Sci., Wellesley Coll., 1959; student, John's Hopkins U.; MA, cert.Russian Inst., Columbia U., 1968, PhD, 1976. Washington coord. Maine for Muskie, 1975-76; chief legis. asst. to U.S. Senator Muskie, 1976-78; mem. staff NSC, 1978-81, White House, 1978-81; sr. fellow in Soviet and Eastern European Affairs Ctr. for Strategic and Internat. Studies, Ctr. for Strategic and Internat. Studies, 1981; fellow Woodrow Wilson Internat. Ctr. for Scholars, Washington, 1981-82; Research prof. internat. affairs, dir. women in fgn. service Sch. Fgn. Service Georgetown U., 1982-93; pres. Ctr. for Nat. Policy, 1985-93; fgn. policy coord. Mondale for Pres. campaign, 1984, to Geraldine A. Ferraro, 1984; vice chmn. Nat. Dem. Inst. for Internat. Affairs, Washington, 1984-93; perm. rep. of the U.S. UN, N.Y.C., 1993-97; Sec. U.S. Dept. of State, 1997-2001; founder The Albright Group, 2001—; chair Nat. Dem. Inst., Washington, 2001—; Michael and Virginia Mortara Endowed prof. in practice of diplomacy Georgetown Sch. Fgn. Svc.; Disting. scholar William Davidson Inst., U. Mich. Bus. Sch. Sr. fgn. policy advisor Dukakis for Pres. Campaign, 1988; mem. Pres.'s Cabinet, NSC. Author: Poland: The Role of the Press in Political Change, 1983, Madam Secretary: A Memoir, 2003; contbr. articles to profl. jours., chpts. to books. Bd. dirs. Beauvoir Sch., Washington, 1968-76, chmn., 1978-83; trustee Black Student Fund, 1969-78, 82-93, Dem. Forum, 1976-78, Williams Coll., 1978-82, Wellesley Coll., 1983-89; mem. exec. com. D.C. Citizens for Better Pub. Edn., 1975-76; bd. dirs. Washington Urban League, 1982-84, Atlantic Coun., 1984-93, Ctr. for Nat. Policy, 1985-93, Chatham House Fedn., 1986-88. Mem. Council Fgn. Relations, Am. Polit. Sci. Assn., Czechoslovak Soc. Arts and Scis. Am., Atlantic Council U.S. (dir.), Am. Assn. for Advancement Slavic Studies. Democrat.*

ALBRIGHT, RAYMOND JACOB, government official; b. Reading, Pa., Apr. 7, 1929; s. Raymond Wolf and Mary Catherine (Sherr) A.; m. Ruthmarie Reich, Sept. 13, 1952; children: Raymond Jacob, David Reich. BA, Yale, 1951; Fulbright scholar, U. Vienna, Austria, 1951-52; MA, Harvard, 1954, PhD; in Polit. Sci., 1961. Fgn. affairs officer (Nat. Security Council affairs and policy planning) Office Asst. Sec. Def. (Internat. Security Affairs), 1954-61; with Office Asst. Sec. State (European affairs), 1961-62; nat. security affairs adviser Treasury Dept., 1962-67; asst. to sec. treasury (Nat. Security Affairs) Office Sec. Treasury, 1967-69; counselor for econ. affairs Am. embassy, Belgrade, Yugoslavia, 1969-72; fgn. service res. officer Dept. State, 1969-73; v.p. Export-Import Bank U.S., 1973-92, sr. v.p., 1992-95; mng. dir. Lange, Mullen & Bohn, LLC/Global Fin. Solutions; exec. v.p. GlobalNet Venture Ptnrs., LLC. Lectr. Yale, 1959, George Washington U., 1960, George Mason U., 1997. Author: (with others) Forging a New Sword, 1958. Pres. Fgn. Policy Discussion Group, Washington. Mem.: Yale Club (Washington) (bd. dirs., chmn. Yale and govt. com. 1966-69). Home: 3609 Dunlop St Chevy Chase MD 20815-5926 E-mail: rj.albright@verizon.net.

ALBRIGHT, TERRILL D. lawyer; b. Lebanon, Ind., June 23, 1938; s. David Henry and Georgia Pauline (Doty) A.; m. Judith Ann Stoelting, June 2, 1962; children: Robert T., Elizabeth A. AB, Ind. U., 1960, JD, 1965. Bar: Ind. 1965, U.S. Dist. Ct. (so. dist.) Ind. 1965, U.S. Dist. Ct. (no. dist.) Ind. 1980, U.S. Ct. Appeals (7th cir.) 1981, U.S. Ct. Appeals (3d and D.C. cirs.) 1982, U.S. Supreme Ct. 1972; cert. arbitrator for large complex cse program constrn. and internat. commercial cases Am. Arbitration Assn., cert. mediator. Assoc. Baker and Daniels Law Firm, Indpls., 1965-72, ptnr., 1972—. Mem. panel of disting. neutrals. nat. panel for constrn. and regional comml. panel CPR Inst. for Dispute Resolution, N.Y.C. Pres. Christamore House, Indpls., 1979-86; bd. dirs. Greater Indpls. YMCA, 1980-82; chmn. Jordan YMCA, Indpls., 1982; pres. Community Ctrs. Indpls., 1987-90. 1st lt. U.S. Army, 1960—62. Fellow: Acad. Law Alumni, Ind. U. Sch. of Law (bd. dirs. 1974—80, pres. 1979—80), Am. Coll. Trial Lawyers, Indpls. Bar Found., Ind. Bar Found, Am. Bar Found.; mem.: Ind. State Bar Assn. (chmn. young lawyers sect. 1971—72, rep. 11th dist. 1983—85, bd. dirs., v.p. 1991—92, pres.-elect 1992—93, pres. 1993—94), Nat. Conf. Bar. Pres. (exec. coun. 1995—98). Democrat. Office: Baker & Daniels 300 N Meridian St Ste 2700 Indianapolis IN 46204-1782 E-mail: terry.albright@bakerd.com.

ALBRIGHT, TOWNSEND SHAUL, investment banker, government benefits consultant; b. Anderson, Ind., May 1, 1942; s. Townsend S. and Maxine Aree (Zimmerman) A.; m. Eileen Therese Argent, Aug. 30, 1968; children: Megan Eileen, Alexandra Michele. BA, Wabash Coll., 1964; MBA, U. Mich., 1966. With Mead Corp., Cin. and Chgo., 1966-69; mcpl. bond underwriter No. Trust Co., Chgo., 1969-71; v.p. Channer Newman Securities Co., Chgo., 1971-80; v.p., treas., dir. Croake Roberts, Inc., Chgo., 1980 86; v.p. instl. sales John Nuveen & Co., Chgo., 1986 90; with Fin. Forum, 1991—; sr. program adminstr. Ill. Devel. Fin. Authority, Chgo., 1995—; faculty mem. Loyola U., 1990—. Bd. dirs. Urban Gateways, Chgo., 1976—; dean Mcpl. Bond Sch. Chgo.; with Inst. Entrepreneurial Studies U. Ill., Chgo. Served with USAR, 1966-72. Mem. Chgo. Assn. Wabash Men, U. Mich. Alumni Assn., Mcpl. Bond Club Chgo., Phi Gamma Delta (Chgo. grad. chpt., former bd. dirs., Econ. Club. Presbyterian. Home: 2019 Beechwood Ave Wilmette IL 60091-1503 E-mail: talbright@idfa.com.

ALBRINK, MARGARET JORALEMON, medical educator; b. Warren, Ariz., Jan. 6, 1920; d. Ira Beaman and Dorothy (Rieber) Joralemon; m. Wilhelm Stockman Albrink, Sept. 16, 1944 (dec. July 1991); children: Frederick Henry, Jonathan Wilhelm, Peter Varick (dec.). BA in Psychology cum laude, Radcliffe Coll., 1941; MS in Physiol. Chemistry, Yale U., 1943, MD, 1946, MPH, 1951. Cert. Diplomate Am. Bd. Med. Examiners, Diplomate Am. Bd. Nutrition, Diplomate Am. Bd. Physician Nutrition Specialists. Intern New Haven (Conn.) Hosp., 1946-47; NIH postdoctoral fellow Yale U., New Haven, 1947-49, fellow pub. health, 1950-51, instr. medicine, 1952-58, asst. prof. medicine, 1958-61; assoc. prof. W.Va. U., Morgantown, 1961-66, prof. medicine, 1966-90, prof. emeritus, 1990—, mem. grad. faculty, 1977-92; mem. med. and dental staff W.Va. U. Hosp., Morgantown, 1961-2000. Vis. scientist Donner Lab., U. Calif., Berkeley, 1993—; assoc. physician Grace-New Haven Cmty. Hosp., 1952-61; cons. nutrition study sect. NIH; vis. scholar U. Calif., Berkeley, 1977-78; established investigator Am. Heart Assn., 1958-63. Guest editor: Clinics in Endocrinology and Metabolism, 1976; guest editor Am. Jour. Clin. Nutrition, 1968, mem. editorial bd., 1963-68; mem. editorial adv. bd. Jour. Am. Coll. Nutrition, 1988-89; reviewer jours.; contbr. articles, chpts. and abstracts to profl. jours. Recipient Rsch. Career award Nat. Heart, Lung and Blood Inst., 1963-90. Fellow ACP, Am. Heart Assn., Am. Coll. Nutrition; mem. Am. Fedn. Clin. Rsch., Am. Soc. Clin. Investigation, Am. Soc. Clin. Nutrition, Am. Heart Assn. (emeritus, fellow arteriosclerosis coun., fellow coun. epidemiology), Am. Diabetes Assn. (epidemiology coun.), Alpha Omega Alpha, Sigma Xi, Phi Beta Kappa. Democrat. Avocations: music, archeology, computers, nature conservation. Home: 817 Augusta Ave Morgantown WV 26501-6237 Office: WVa U Dept Medicine PO Box 9159 Morgantown WV 26506-9159 E-mail: mjalbrink@aol.com.

ALBRITTON, ARTHUR DALLAS, lawyer; b. Jacksonville, Fla., June 16, 1928; s. Arthur Dallas and Grace Elizabeth (Pratt) Albritton; m. Frances Gail Kelley, Dec. 21, 1951; m. Ann Elizabeth Hill, Dec. 27, 1968; m. Grace Lovelace, Jan. 26, 1991; children: Gary Callan, Andrew Brian, Laura Elizabeth, Rachel Ann, Ladoba Lehane. BS, Fla. State U., 1950, MS, 1951; JD, Yale U., 1956. Bar: Fla. 56, U.S. Dist. Ct. (so. dist.) Fla. 56, U.S. Dist. Ct. (mid. dist.) Fla. 59, U.S. Ct. Appeals (5th cir.) 59, U.S. Supreme Ct. 66, U.S. Ct. Appeals (11th cir.) 81. Ptnr. Hardee & Ott, Tampa, Fla., 1956—60; sr. ptnr. Albritton & Sessums, Tampa, Fla., 1961—82, pres. Albritton & Assocs., P.A., 1982—. Counsel Fla. Bd. Bar Examiners, 1958—68; asst. county solicitor Hillsborough County, 1960, asst. state atty., 1961—62; chmn., mem. Jud. Nominating Commn., 1972—79; pres. Albritton and Sebring, 1998—; arbitrator; lectr.; participant various seminars. Contbr. articles to legal publs. Sec.-treas., mem. Tampa Sports Authority, 1966—70; chmn. Mayor's Mgmt. Analysis Team, City of Tampa, 1962—66; pres. Egape Evangelistic Mission, 1980—. 1st lt. USAF, 1951—53. Recipient various awards of recognition for profl. svc. activities. Mem.: ATLA, ABA, Hillsborough County Bar Assn. (pres. 1965, Outstanding Trial Lawyer award 2000), Fla. Bar, Bay Area Trial Lawyers, Univ. Club, Bay Area Yale Club. Democrat. Methodist. Office: 100 E Madison St Ste 300 Tampa FL 33602-4703

ALBRITTON, DANIEL LEE, atmospheric scientist; b. Camden, Ala., June 8, 1936; BS in Elec. Engring., Ga. Inst. Tech., 1959, MS in Physics, 1963, PhD in Physics, 1967. Dir. Aeronomy Lab. NOAA, Boulder, Colo., 1986—. Leader atmospheric chemistry project Climate and Global Change Program NOAA; co-chmn. sci. assessments of stratospheric ozone U.N. Environ. Programme; mem. sci. working group Intergovtl. Panel on Climate Change; lectr. in atm scis. and policy/sci. interface. Former mem. editl. adv. bd. Jour. Molecular Spectroscopy; former co-editor Jour. Atmospheric Chemistry; contbr. 150 articles to profl. jours. Recipient pres. rank svc. award, 1990, 97, 2001, gold medal Dept. Commerce, 1977, 93, sci. freedom and responsibility award AAAS, 1993, sci. assessments award Am. Meteorol. Soc., 1993, stratospheric ozone protection award EPA, 1994, UN environ. programme ozone award, 1995, Pacesetter award Boulder Daily Camera, 2001. Fellow Am. Phys. Soc., Am. Geophys. Union. Achievements include research in laboratory investigation of atmospheric ion-molecular reactions and theoretical studies of diatomic molecular structure, investigation of atmospheric trace-gas photochemistry, sci. advisor in ozone depletion and climate change policy. Office: NOAA Aeronomy Lab 325 Broadway St Boulder CO 80305-3328

ALBRITTON, WILLIAM HAROLD, III, federal judge; b. Andalusia, Ala., Dec. 19, 1936; s. Robert Bynum and Carrie (Veal) A.; m. Jane Rollins Howard, June 2, 1958; children: William Harold IV, Benjamin Howard, Thomas Bynum. AB, U. Ala., 1959, LL.B., 1960. Bar: Ala. 1960. Assoc. firm Albrittons & Rankin, Andalusia, 1962-66, ptnr., 1966-76; ptnr. firm Albrittons & Givhan, Andalusia, 1976-86; ptnr. Albrittons, Givhan & Clifton, Andalusia, 1986-91; judge U.S. Dist. Ct. (mid. dist.) Ala., Montgomery, 1991-97, chief judge, 1998—. Mem. 11th Circuit Jud. Coun., 1998—. Pres. Ala. Law Sch. Found., 1988-91, Ala. Law Inst. Fellow Am. Coll. Trial Lawyers, Am. Bar Found.; mem. ABA, Fed. Judges Assn. (bd. dirs. 1999-2002, jud. conf. U.S. com. on ct. adminstrn. and case mgmt. 1999-), Ala. State Bar (commr. 1981-89, disciplinary commn. 1981-84, v.p. 1985-86, pres.-elect 1989-90, pres. 1990-91), Am. Judicature Soc., Am. Inns of Ct., Bluewater Bay Sailing Club, Bluewater Bay Country Club, Phi Beta Kappa, Phi Delta Phi, Omicron Delta Kappa, Alpha Tau Omega.

ALBRITTON, WILLIAM HAROLD, IV, lawyer; b. Tuscaloosa, Ala., Mar. 21, 1960; s. William Harold III and Jane Rollins (Howard) A.; m. Lucille Smith, July 23, 1983; 1 child, Elizabeth Rollins. BA, U. Ala., Tuscaloosa, 1982, JD, 1985. Ptnr. Albrittons, Clifton, Alverson, Bowden, Moody P.C., Andalusia, Ala., 1985-2001; counsel Bradley, Arant, Rose & White, Birmingham, Ala., 2001—. Bd. dirs The Bank, Andalusia; judge Mcpl. Ct. Andalusia, 1989-2000. Bd. dirs. Covington County Arts Coun., Andalusia, 1986-90, Andalusia City Schs. Found., 1991-2001, Andalusia Area C. of C., 1986-89; elder 1st Presbyn. Ch., Andalusia, 1990—. Mem. ABA, Ala. Bar Assn. (sec. pres.'s adv. task force 1986-88, chmn. com. on local bar activities 1990, task force on minority opportunity 1990-96, character and fitness com. 1991-96, chmn. 1993-96, chmn. com. solo practitioners & small firms 1997-99), Ala. Def. Lawyers Assn. (bd. dirs. young lawyers sect. 1991-96, amicus curiae com. 1992-2002), Internat. Assn. Def. Counsel, Am. Inns of Ct., Kiwanis. Avocations: scuba diving, music, photography, sailing, motorcycling. Office: One Federal Pl 1819 Fifth Ave N Birmingham AL 35203 E-mail: halbritton@bradleyarant.com.

ALBRITTON, WILLIAM HOYLE, training and consulting executive, lecturer, writer; b. Cleveland, Tenn., May 29, 1942; s. Hoyle Franklin and Marie Arlene (Mount) A.; m. June Ellington, June 20, 1964; children: Elizabeth Anne, William Hoyle. BA, Tenn. Wesleyan Coll., 1964; postgrad. in bus. adminstrn. U. Chgo., 1974-75. Assoc. Lendman Assocs., Los Angeles, 1969-70, dir. West Coast ops., 1970-71; ter. mgr. Baxter-Travenol, Deerfield, Ill., 1971-72, field sales trainer, 1972, sales edn. mgr., 1973; nat. sales recruiter The Kendall Co. div. Colgate-Palmolive, Boston, 1973-75, tng. and devel. mgr., 1975-76, dir. compensation, 1976-77, dir. staffing and mgmt. devel., 1978-81; pres. Tng. Concepts, Inc., Boston, 1981-86, chmn. bd. dirs., CEO1986—; ptnr. Ollinger Ptnrs. Mgmt. Cons., 1989-93, Choice Point, 1994-96, Duxbury, Mass., 1994—; v.p. Advtg. Systems Plus, 1994-96; sr. assoc. The Change Mgmt. Group, LLC, 1995—; v.p. Hamilton Cornell Assocs., 1996—. Host of Bill Board TV Show. Team capt. Jordan Hosp. Spl. Funds, Plymouth, Mass., 1978-82; mem. personnel bd. Town of Duxbury, Mass., 1980—, chmn., 1984—; mem. Bay Players Community Theater. Author: Managing Yourself and Others, Internal Consulting for Results, Results-Oriented Selling, Results-Oriented Management, Presenting Technical Information; host (TV show) The Bill Board, 1994—. Vestryman, lay reader, mem. choir Episcopal Ch., sr. warden, 1991-97. Served as officer USNR, 1966-69. Mem. Am. Soc. Tng. and Devel., Am. Mgmt. Assn. (Pres. Assn.), South Shore C. of C., Instrnl. Systems Assn., Exec. Club, Duxbury Yacht Club (chmn. tournament com., Ouimet Scholarship Fund 1989—, chmn. Golf com. 1992-94), Rotary (v.p. local dist. 1978-79, pres. 1979-80, group exch. com. 1983-93), Old Colony Club. Home: PO Box 2442 Duxbury MA 02331-2442 Office: PO Box 357 Duxbury MA 02331-2442 E-mail: walbritton@allianceresource.net.

ALBRIZIO, EILEEN MARIE, commentator, poet; b. Hartford, Conn., Sept. 18, 1963; d. Constance Claire Magnan-Albrizio and Francis John Albrizio; m. Wayne Edward Horgan, Sept. 22, 1989. Theatre, Ctrl. Conn. State U., 1983—87; grad., Conn. Sch. Broadcasting, 1995. Owner/propr. Heroes and Hitters - Comic Books, Rocky Hill, Conn., 1989—95; broadcast journalist and news host Newsradio WPOP, Hartford, Conn., 1995—97, WNPR Radio News, Hartford, Conn., 1997—; voice talent Conn. Pub. TV, Hartford, Conn., 1997—. Poetry tchr. Colleges, Universities and Cultural venues, Conn., 1998—; visual art dir. The Buttonwood Tree, Middletown, Conn., 2001—. Author: (books of poetry) Messy on the Inside, (play and poetry) Rain - Dark as Water in Winter. Recipient Best Newscast, Conn. AP, 1996, Best News Feature, 1998, Best Spot News, Soc. of Profl. Journalists, 1999, Best News Feature, 1999, Hon. Mention for Stage Play, Writer's Digest Mag., 1996, 1997, Hon. Mention for Poetry, 1999, Poetry fellowship, Greater Hartford Arts Coun., 2003. Mem.: Artemis Rising (life). Independent.

ALBUM, JERALD LEWIS, lawyer; b. Monroe, La., Oct. 18, 1947; s. Natt B. and Rose Marie (Pickens) A.; m. Joan Abbey Lurie, July 30, 1983; children: Nicole, Jeffrey. BS, Tulane U., 1969, JD, 1973. Bar: La. 1973, Colo. 1990, Tex. 1992, U.S. Dist. Ct. (ea. dist.) La. 1975, U.S. Dist. Ct. (mid. dist.) La. 1980, U.S. Dist. Ct. (we. dist.) La. 1983, U.S. Ct. Appeals (5th cir.) 1976. Assoc. Mmahat, Gagliano, Duffy & Giordano, Metairie, La., 1973-79; assoc. to ptnr. Lemle, Kelleher, Hunley, Moss & Frilot, New Orleans, 1980-85; shareholder Abbott Simses, Album & Knister, New Orleans, 1985-96; ptnr. Album, Stovall, Radecker & Giordano, New Orleans, Reich, Meeks & Treadaway, Metairie, La., 2001—. Mem. La. Assn. of Def. Counsel, New Orleans Bar Assn., La. State Bar Assn. Avocations: golf, volleyball, gardening. Home: 4637 Southshore Dr Metairie LA 70002-1430 Office: Reich Meeks & Treadaway 3850 N Causeway Blvd Ste 1000 Metairie LA 70002-7247

ALBUQUERQUE, EDSON XAVIER, pharmacology educator; BS, Salesiano Coll., Recife, Brazil, 1953; MD, U. Recife, 1959; PhD, Fed. U. Permambuco, U. Sao Paulo, U. Ill., 1962. Lectr. anatomy and physiology U. Recife, Pernambuco, Brazil, 1954—59; instr. pharmacology U. Ill., 1964—65; asst. prof. pharmacology U. Lund (Sweden), 1965—67; rsch. asst. prof. dept. pharmacology Schs. Medicine and Dentistry SUNY, Buffalo, 1968—69, assoc. prof. pharmacology, 1969—72, prof. pharmacology, 1972—73, prof., acting chmn., 1973—74; prof., chmn. dept. pharmacology and exptl. therapeutics U. Md., Balt., 1974—. Titular prof. Fed. U. Rio de Janeiro; dir. molecular pharmacology tng. program Joint U. Md./Fed.U. Rio de Janeiro. Mem. editl. bds. and contbr. articles to profl. jours. Recipient Order of Grand Cross, Pres. of Brazil, 1995, Order of Rio Branco, 1996; fellow C.A.P.E.S., 1959—62, Rockefeller Found., 1962—63, 1963—64; grantee Neuropharmacology, Nat. Inst. Neurol. Diseases and Blindness, 1964—65, Swedish Med. Rsch. Coun., IBRO/UNESCO, 1965—67. Mem.: AAAS, Brazilian Acad. Sci., Third World Acad. Scis., Soc. Neurosci., Soc. Toxicology, Brazilian Pharmacology Soc., L.Am. Soc. Physiol. Sci., Internat. Brain Rsch. Orgn. (L.Am. delegation), Internat. Soc. Myochemistry, Biophys. Soc. Am., Am. Men and Women of Sci., Am. Soc. Pharmacology and Exptl. Therapeutics (Otto Krayer award 1996), Am. Physiol. Soc. Office: U Md Sch Medicine Dept Pharmacology & Exptl Therapeutics 655 W Baltimore St Rm 4-202 Baltimore MD 21201-1509

ALBURTUS, MARY JO, social worker, consultant; b. Jersey City, Oct. 31, 1949; d. Wilson Vincent and Mary Therese (O'Neill) A. BA, Jersey City State U., 1973; MSW, Fordham U., 1982. Lic. clin. social worker, N.J.; diplomate in social work. Mgmt. analyst U.S. Dept. of Labor, N.Y.C., 1973-76; social worker/specialist Monmouth Family Ctr., Freehold, N.J., 1976-83, social work supr. Asbury Park, N.J., 1983-85; founder, group therapist Monmouth County Sexual Abuse Groups, Monmouth County, N.J., 1983-89; supr. cmty. and program devel. Monmouth County Bd. Social Svcs., Neptune, N.J., 1985-90; pvt. practice clin. social worker, cons. Shrewsbury, N.J., 1988—. Founder Monmouth County Sexual Abuse Coalition, 1981; social work specialist Family Svcs. Monmouth County Bd. Social Svcs., Neptune, 1990-91; adv. bd. Sexual Abuse Treatment Prog., Red Bank, 1983-89. Grantee Nat. Ctr. on Abuse and Neglect, 1980. Mem.: NASW, N.J. Soc. for Study of Dissociation, Internat. Soc. for Study of Dissociation, Task Force on Women and Alcohol, Monmouth County Sexual Abuse Coalition, Mental Health Assn., Acad. Cert. Social Workers. Office: 712 Sycamore Ave Red Bank NJ 07701 E-mail: mjalburtuslcsw@aol.com.

ALBYN, RICHARD KEITH, retired architect; b. Detroit, Apr. 8, 1927; s. Walter Harris and Corrine Henrietta (Miller) A.; m. Nancy Jane Cosby; children: Keith Cosby, Lisa Benton Albyn Drummond. Student, U. Ill., 1945-49. Registered architect, Mich., Ohio, Fla., Md., W.Va., N.C. Prin. dir. Linn Smith Assocs., Inc., Birmingham, Mich., 1962-64, TMP Assocs., Inc., Bloomfield Hills, Mich., 1964-82, HEPY Assocs., Inc., Southfield, Mich., 1982-86; ret., 1986. Co-author: Buildings of Michigan, 1987; also articles in profl. jours. and hist. publs.; illustrator: A Handbook for the Amateur Archaeologist, 1967, The Archaeologists Coloring Book, 1964. Mem. Preservation N.C., Transylvania County Arts Coun., Transylvania County Hist. Soc., Asheville Art Mus.; bd. dirs. pub. radio Sta. WCQS, 2003. Recipient citation Am. Assn. Sch. Adminstrs., 1964, 70, 1st pl. award Ch. Architects Guild, 1965, others. Fellow: AIA (lectr. 1961—65, treas. 1968, sec. 1969, pres. Detroit chpt. 1971, pres. Detroit archtl. found. 1971, host chpt. com. nat. conv. 1971, mem. past pres. com. 1971—86, mem. vocat.-tech. edn. svc. study com. 1976, honor award 1964, 1971, 1977, award of merit 1971, 1sr pl award Focus on Art Exhibit 1997, Viewer's Choice award 1997, Merchant's award 1998, Merit award 1999, Patrons award 2000); mem.: Brevard Music Ctr. Assn. (pres. 2001—02), Preservation N.C. (bd. advisors 1999—), Archaeol. Soc. N.C., Transylvania County Joint Hist. PreservationCommn. (chmn. 1993—96), Transylvania County Hist. Soc. (bd. dirs. 1919—94, bd. visitors 1999—), AIA N.C. Presbyterian. Avocations: painting, archaeology, geneology, photography, writing. Home: 60 Kentwood Ln Pisgah Forest NC 28768-9511

ALCALAY, ALBERT S. artist, design educator; b. Paris, Aug. 11, 1917; came to U.S., 1951, naturalized, 1956; s. Samuel and Lepa (Afar) A.; m. Vera Eskenazi, Nov. 11, 1950; children: Leor, Ammiel. Student in Paris, Rome. Lectr. design Carpenter Center, Harvard U., 1960—. One man shows, De Cordova and Dana Mus., Lincoln, Mass., 1968, Swetzoff Gallery, Pucker-Safrai Gallery, Pace Gallery, others; retrospective, Carpenter Ctr., Harvard U., 1982; group shows, Inst. Contemporary Art, Boston, 1960, Venice (Italy) Biennale, Mus. Modern Art., 1955, Whitney Mus. Am. Art, 1956, 58, 60, U. Ill., Urbana, Pa. Acad. Fine Arts, 1960; represented in permanent collections, Mus. Modern Art, N.Y.C., Boston Mus. Fine Arts, Fogg Art Mus., DeCordova and Dana Mus., Phillips Acad., Mus. Am. Art, Brandeis U. Rose Art Mus., U. Mass. Mus., Wellesley Coll. Mus., Colby Coll. Mus., Smith Coll., Rome Mus. Modern Art, U. Rome, Brockton Art Mus., Tufts U., Medford, Mass., Boston Pub. Library, Smithsonian Inst. Archives of Am. Artists. Guggenheim fellow, 1959-60; recipient prize Boston Arts Festival, 1960 Home: 66 Powell St Brookline MA 02446-3929 Office: Harvard U Carpenter Ctr Cambridge MA 01238

ALCAMO, FRANK PAUL, retired educational administrator; b. South Fork, Pa., May 25, 1920; s. Carmelo and Antonia (Trifiro) A.; m. Josephine Giusto, June 22, 1944; 1 child, Antoinette. Student, Johnstown Coll., 1938-39; BS, Indiana U. Pa., 1942; MEd, Pa. State U., 1954. Tchr. math. and sci. Wilmore (Pa.) H.S., 1942-54, Beaverdale (Pa.)-Wilmore H.S., 1954-56; tchr. math. South Fork-Croyle H.S., 1956-61, Triangle Area H.S., Sidman, Pa., 1961-62; asst. prin. Windber (Pa.) Area H.S., 1962-63, prin., 1963-81; ret., 1981. Bd. dirs. Allegheny Ridge Corp. Author: The Windber Story, 1983, The South Fork Story, 1987, The Summerhill Story, 1992. Treas. Windber Summer Playground Assn., 1963; chmn. Windber Police CSC, 1964-81; bd. dirs., pres. Mid-State Automobile Club Johnstown, Pa., 1965—; bd. dirs. Johnstown-Windber Indsl. Devel. Assn., Cambria County Hist. Soc., 1988-93, Sr. Activities Ctr. Cambria County, Inc., 1994-98; founder, dir. CBW Schs. Fed. Credit Union, 1956—; v.p. Windber Pub. Libr., 1976-81; bd. dirs. Windber Recreation Assn., treas., 1974-80; bd. dirs., v.p. Johnstown Area Heritage Assn., 1985—; instr., site coord. counselor IRS Tax Counseling for Elderly, 1984-96. Lt. (j.g.) USNR, 1944-46. Named to Windber Hall of Fame, 1984. Mem. NEA (life), ARC (historian Keystone chpt.), Pa. Edn. Assn. (local br. com. 1966-70, dept. adminstrn. pres. 1971-75, pres. Windber 1965-66), Somerset County Secondary Prins. Assn. (pres. 1965-66), Nat. Secondary Sch. Prins. Assn., Pa. Secondary Sch. Prins. Assn., Pa. Interscholastic Athletic Assn. (dist. treas. 1970-80), Greater Johnstown Assn. Sch. Retirees (pres. 1983-85, 88-91, 95-96), Sons of Italy, Pa. Assn. Sch. Retirees, Automobile Club So. Pa. (bd. dirs. 1988—), Rotary (dir. Windber 1964-69, pres. 1968-69), Phi Delta Kappa, Sigma Tau Gamma. Democrat. Roman Catholic. Avocations: playing the trombone swing city johnstown, model railroading. Home: 603 Harshberger St Johnstown PA 15905-3129

ALCANTARA, ANITA LUISA, human resources consultant; b. May 30, 1942; d. Francisco B. and Eleanor E. (Locke) A. AA, Wright City Coll., 1962; BEd, Northeastern Ill. U., 1964; cert. cmty. svc. mgmt., Roosevelt U., 1989; postgrad., Garrett Evangelical Theol. Sem. Field dir., edn. svcs. dir. Girl Scouts of Chgo., 1971-79; nat. tng. coord. Girl Scouts U.S.A., N.Y.C., 1979-84; mgmt. devel. cons. The Equitable Corp., N.Y.C., 1984; adminstr. United Ch. of Rogers Park, Chgo., 1985-86, min. of cmty. life, 1986—; dir. adminstrv. svcs. and cmty. life United C.h. of Rogers Park, Chgo., 2000—. Cons. Contact Chgo., 1985-86; Yule Connection mgr., 1985-86. Author: You Make the Difference, Leaders' Guide: Council Guide, 1980. Program com. Alternatives, Inc.; leader Let's Get Started print/video tng. program, 1981; collaborator exhibn. Out of the Loop: Neighborhood Voices, Chgo. Hist. Soc., 2001; exec. dir. Insight Arts, 1993-96; active Chgo. Hist. Soc.; guide Daisy Girl Scouts Coun., 1983; mem. parliament World's Religion Project in Rogers Park. Recipient Chgo. Youth award Mayor's Commn. Youth Welfare, 1968, Chgo. Pub. Libr. award, 1970, Girl Scouts Chgo. award, 1975; named Vol. of Yr. Chgo. Area Project, 1993. Office: 1545 W Morse Ave Chicago IL 60626-3306

ALCANTARA, FELICISIMA GARCIA, dietitian, nutrition consultant; b. Manila, Oct. 26, 1938; came to U.S., 1971; d. Pascual Cruz and Matilde Castro Garcia; m. Filemon Ocampo Alcantara, May 22, 1966; children: Philip, Manny. BS with honors in Food and Nutrition, Centro Escolar U., Manila, 1960; MS in Food and Nutrition, U. Ill., 1965. Lic. dietitian, Fla. Dietetic intern Ind. U. Med. Ctr., Indpls., 1960-61; staff dietitian St. Elizabeth Med. Ctr., Dayton, 1962-63; rsch. asst. U. Ill., Urbana, 1963-65; assoc. prof. St. Paul Coll., Manila, 1965-68; community nutritionist Cleve. Met. Gen. Hosp., 1973-76; cons. nutritionist various midwestern extended care facilities, 1977-83; dir. dietary svcs. Gainesville (Fla.) Nursing Ctr., 1983-84; clin. dietitian Tacachale Community of Excellence, Gainesville, 1985—. Renal dietitian cons. Fresenius Med. Care, Gainesville, 1997—. Roman Catholic.

ALCH, MARK LEE, organization executive, educator; b. Mpls., Oct. 21, 1945; s. Harry Brown and Dora Alch; m. Sharlene Rivi Eigen, June 22, 1969; children: Matthew Cary, Nikkie Shana. BA, U. Minn., 1967, MA, 1970; PhD, UCLA, 1977, C.Phil, 1973. cert. tchr., Calif.; lic. real estate sales, Calif. Asst. mgr. Eagle Cleaners & Launderers, Mpls., 1961-72; grad. asst. U. Minn., Mpls., 1969-70; program coord., tchg. asst. UCLA, 1972-76, asst. to vice chancellor for student and campus affairs, 1976—77; tng. mgr. So. Calif. divsn. Fluor-Daniel, Irvine, 1977-80, project adminstr. advanced tech. divsn., 1980-81; v.p. Drake Beam Morin, Inc., Irvine, 1981-84, sr. v.p., mng. dir., offices in San Diego, Phoenis, Tucson, Las Vegas, Riverside and San Bernardino, Calif., 1985-95; CEO, v.p. edn., tng. and devel. Uniben, Inc., Pasadena, Calif., 1996-99; instr. extension divsn. bus. mgmt. program U. Calif., Irvine, 1997—; nat. dir. edn. Am. Youth Soccer Orgn., Hawthorne, Calif., 2000—01, Kuykendall and Alch Real Estate Investments, 2000—02; realtor Team Gage Realtors, 2002; dir., exec. v.p. Hall Career Svcs. Adj. prof. Occidental Coll., Eagle Rock, Calif., 1977, instr. Calif. U. [illegible] Mark Alch & Assocs., Irvine, 1996-2000; adj. Temps Plus, 2003—; presenter in field. Author: A Financial Aid and College Planning System for Parents of High School Students, 1996, How to Become a Millionaire, 1999; contbr. more than 50 articles to profl. jours., internet and online broadcasts. Exec. com. Irvine, Newport Beach and Costa Mesa YMCA, 1992-93, fedn. chief, 1992-93; co-chmn. econ. devel. com. City of Irvine and Irvine C. of C., 1992-95; active Am. Youth Soccer Orgn., 1991—, referee com. region 213, Irvine, 1994—, area referee, 1995, sect. referee, 1996, referee assessor, 1996-2003, dir. referee instrn. region 213, 1997-98, sect. referee instr., trainer regional, area and sect. referee, 2000-03, others; beadkeeper Indian Guides, YMCA, 1989-90, asst. chief, 1990-91, chief, 1991-92, fedn. chief, 1992-93, mem. exec. com. YMCA, 1992-94, national elder, 1999-93. Mem. ASTD (membership com. Orange County chpt. 1995-96), Assn. Profl. Cons., Med. Mktg. Assn., Profl. Coach and Mentors Assn. (dir. evaluations nat. conf. 2003), Nat. Human Resources Assn., Life Sci. Industry Coun., Orange County Indsl. League, Orange County Venture Network, UCLA Alumni ASsn. (life). Democrat. Jewish. Avocations: jogging, travel, high performance and muscle car restoration, music, public speaking. Office: Temps Plus Inc 268 N Lincoln Ave Ste 12 Corona CA 92882 E-mail: mark@markalch.com., markalch@cox.net.

AL-CHALABI, SUHAIL ABDUL-JABBAR, transportation executive; b. Baghdad, Iraq, July 14, 1940; arrived in U.S., 1965; s. Abdul Jabbar and Wajeeha al-Chalabi; m. Margery Lee Pupach, Mar. 9, 1965. BArch, MIT, 1962; MSc, Athens (Greece) Tech. Inst., 1965. Planner, arch. Doxiadis Assocs., Athens, 1963-65, Skidmore Owings & Merrill, Chgo., 1965-67; rsch. dir. Northeastern Ill. Planning Commn., Chgo., 1967-74; exec. dep. dir. Chgo. Area Transp. Study, 1974-81; spl. advisor to mayor City of Chgo., 1981-82, commr. dept. econ. devel., 1982-83; exec. v.p., CFO The al Chalabi Group, Ltd., Chgo., 1983—. Mem. team planning 3d Chgo. airport, 1986—; adapted hwy. planning models for use in planning airports, commuter rail and interurban bus; initiated build/no-build analyses EIS; project mgr. for numerous transp. projects: rail, toll road, airport sys., bridges. Mem. rsch. and forecast adv. com. Northeastern Ill. Planning Commn., Chgo., 1992—. Mem.: Am. Assn. Airport Execs. (corp.), World Soc. Ekistics, Chgo. Southland C. of C., Lambda Alpha. Achievements include securing financing, overseeing restoration, operation of Chicago Theater, 1994-95. Home: 718 Wilson Ave Beverly Shores IN 46301-0232 Office: al-Chalabi Group Ltd 330 W Diversey Pkwy Ste 1403 Chicago IL 60657-6206 E-mail: acgtran@aol.com., suhail@al-chalabi.com.

ALCINDOR, LEWIS FERDINAND See ABDUL-JABBAR, KAREEM

ALCOCK, GEORGE LEWIS, JR., (PETER ALCOCK), investor, business strategist; b. Boston, Feb. 26, 1940; s. George Lewis and Louise Hall Alcock; m. Louise Stewart Bachelder, Sept. 29, 1984; children: Peter L., Caroline S. BS, Northeastern U., Boston, 1962. Prodn. supr. J.H. Winn, Winchester, Mass., 1963-65; sales staff Liberty Mutual Ins., Boston, 1966-68; fin. staff Nat. Med. Leasing, Cambridge, Mass., 1968-69; cons. Innovative Mgmt., Cambridge, Mass., 1970-73; treas. Devel. Mgmt. Consultants, Boston, 1973-80; chmn. M.B. Claff & Sons Inc., Brockton, Mass., 1980-2001; corp. fin. staff Alcock Investments, Watertown, Mass., 1980-87; pres., CEO U.S. Repeating Arms Co., New Haven, Conn., 1987-90; gen. ptnr. Alcock Ltd. Ptnrs., Weston, Mass., 1991—. Pres. Beckwood Svcs., Inc., Pliastow, N.H., 2001—. Dir. The Nat. Coun. Northeastern U., Boston, 1989—; trustee Fitchburg (Mass.) State Coll., 1999—, chmn. bd. trustees, 2001—. Mem.: Assn. for Corp. Growth, Nat. Assn. Corp. Dirs., Newcomen Soc. U.S. Avocation: outdoor sports. Office: Alcock Ltd Ptnrs 105 Cherry Brook Rd Weston MA 02493-1347 E-mail: palcock@attbi.com.

ALCON, SONJA L. retired medical social worker; b. Orange City, Iowa, Aug. 2, 1937; d. Albert Lee Gerard and Clarice Victoria (Brown) deBey; m. Richard J. Gebhardt, June 6, 1959; children: Russell, Cheryl, Kurt Gebhardt Ryan; m. George W. Ryan, Dec. 28, 1968; 1 child, Alanna (dec.); m. David E. Alcon, July 20, 1985. BA, Western Md. Coll./McDaniel Coll., 1959; MSW, U. Md., 1973. Caseworker Springfield State Hosp., Sykesville, Md., 1959-61; dir. social work dept. Hanover (Pa.) Gen. Hosp., 1966-96; ret., 1996. Part-time worker Matthews Hallmark Store, Hanover, 1997-99, 2002; field instr. Western Md. Coll., 1967-96, mem. social work adv. coun., 1979-81, 84-86; clin. assoc. prof. sch. social work and social planning U. Md., 1987-92; cons. Golden Age Nursing Home, Hanover, 1973-76, Carlisle (Pa.) Hosp., 1974-78, Hanover Vis. Nurse Assn., 1977-83, emergency svcs. Mental Health Clinic, 1972; chmn. profl. adv. com. Vis. Nurse Assn. Hanover and Spring Grove, Inc., 1986-89; ind. beauty cons. Mary Kay 1999-2000. Bd. dirs. Hospice of York, 1980-82, Hanover chpt. ARC, 1976-79, Adams-Hanover Mental Health, 1973-76; pres. Human Svcs. Orgn., 1980, v.p., 1985-86; mem. adv. coun. Hanover Hospice, 1982-85; treas. Hanover Cmty. Progress Com., 1976-80; mem. Adams-Hanover Sheltered Workshop Com., 1968-70; bd. dirs. Hanover Cmty. Players, 1974-77, sec., 1982; organizer local chpt. Make Today County and Preemie Parent Support Group, 1979; initiator, co-trustee Children's Cardiac Fund, 1979-92; mem. Hanover Oratorio Soc., 1964-85; adv. bd. United Cerebral Palsy South Ctrl. Pa., 1989-90; active YWCA, 1979-84, 96-98; co-organizer Adams-Hanover chpt. Compassionate Friends, 1983; mem. vestry All Saints Episcopal Ch., 1973-74, 76-79, 83-86, 97, vestry sec., 1975, diocesan del. Ctrl. Pa., 1978, 80-86, mem. altar guild, 1968-86, 92-93, treas. ch. women, 1979-83, ch. choir, soloist, 1975—; life mem. Hanover Gen. Hosp. Aux., Harmony Ct. No 146, Order Amaranth, Hanover Chpt. No. 378, Order of the Eastern Star, Samaria Shrine No. 43, Order of The White Shrine of Jerusalem, Westminster Assembly No. 245, Elizabethtown Assembly No. 265, Social Order of the Beauceant, Ozen Temple No. Daughters of the Nile; mem. adv. group Inst. Pastoral Care, 1976-77; mem. adv. coun. Parents Anonymous, 1976-79, 85-92; mem. bd. dirs. Episcopal Home at Shippensburg, 1979-85, Ea. Star Home at Warminster, Pa., 1987-89; mem. Queen Christina Found., Grand Court of Pa., 1995-98; adminstr. Hanover Gen. Hosp. Spl. Needs Fund, 1986-96; cmty. adv. com. Healthsouth Rehab. York, 1995-96; co-facilitator I Can Cope classes Am. Cancer Soc., 1989-92; active Cmty. Needs Coalition, 1990-96, South Ctrl. Pa. Coalition for Organ/Tissue Donation, 1994-98; mem. Case Mgmt. Network South Ctrl. Pa., 1994-96; vol. Hanover Gen. Hosp., Hanover Area Coun. Chs. Recipient York Daily Record Exceptional Citizen award, 1979, Spl. Recognition cert. Col. Richard Mcallister chpt. DAR, 1980; finalist YWCA Salute to Women, 1986, 87, Companion of the Temple award Grand Encampment, Knights Templar, 1999. Mem.: NASW, Acad. Cert. Social Workers, Pa. White Shrine Club (1st v.p. 2001—02, 2001—02, pres. 2002—03), Md. Alumni Assn. (bd. dirs. 1983), Daus. of the Nile, Elizabethtown Assembly Commandery Ladies Aux. (pres. 1989—90), Social Order of Beauceant (pres. Bethel Commandery Ladies Aux. 1989—90, Westminster Assembly worthy pres. 1999, worthy pres. Ladies Aux. Bethel Commandery Assembly 243 1999, organizer, worthy pres. Elizabethtown Assembly 2000—01), Order of Amaranth Harmony Ct. No. 146 (royal patron 1988—89, royal matron 1995—96, grand historian 1998—99, royal matron 1999—2000, grand standard bearer 2001—02, royal patron 2001—02, grand rep. to Eng. 2002—03), Order Eastern Star (Worthy Matron 1985—86), Order of White Shrine of Jerusalem (life; Worthy High Priestess 1994—95, Watchman of Shepherds 1999—2000, Supreme Worthy Herald 1999—2000, Material Objective). Home: 6308 Tamarind Dr Spring Grove PA 17362-8949

ALCORN, DONALD J. secondary school educator, band and choral director; b. Rushville, Nebr., June 26, 1959; s. Russell L. and Donna J. Alcorn; m. Echo A. Stone, May 26, 1979; children: Stephanie, Mitchell. BS, Chadron (Nebr.) State Coll., 1981. K-12 band and choir tchr. Stuart (Nebr.) Pub. Sch., 1981—85; 6-12 vocal tchr. Albion (Nebr.) Pub. Sch., 1985—97; k-12 band and choir tchr. Kenesaw (Nebr.) Pub. Sch., 1997—99; 5-12 band and 7-12 vocal tchr. Doniphan (Nebr.)-Trumbull Pub. Sch., 1999—. Dir.: sch. musicals, including Grease, Wizard of Oz, and Annie, 1995—. Singer Grand Island (Nebr.) City Singers, 1997—. Mem.: NEA, Am. Choral Directors Assn., Doniphan-Trumbull Edn. Assn. (treas. 2001—), Nebr. Band Dirs. Assn., Nebr. Choral Dirs. Assn. (treas. 1997—2001), Lions (pres. Albion chpt. 1994). Republican. Avocations: gardening, music, reading, woodworking, camping. Office: Doniphan-Trumbull Pub Schs 302 W Plum Box 300 Doniphan NE 68832

ALCORN, KAREN ZEFTING HOGAN, artist, art educator, journalist; b. Hartford, Conn., Sept. 29, 1949; d. Edward C. and Doris V. (Anderson) Zefting; m. Wendell R. Alcorn, Apr. 12, 1985. BS, Skidmore Coll., 1971; MFA, Boston U., 1976. Secondary art tchr. Scituate (Mass.) High Sch., 1971-73, Milton (Mass.) High Sch., 1973-79; engr. VEDA, Inc., Arlington, Va., 1979-80; analyst Info. Spectrum, Inc., Arlington, Va., 1980-82, Pacer Systems, Inc., Arlington, Va., 1982-84; dir. ops., mgr. tng. program Stanmark Corp., Arlington, Va., 1984; sr. systems analyst VSE Corp., Arlington, Va., 1984-85; analyst, tech. writer Allen Corp., Las Vegas and Fallon, Nev., 1987-88; mem. faculty Western Nev. C.C., 1989, 97-2000; instr. Newport (R.I.) Art Mus., 1990-92; dir. North Tahoe (Calif.) Art Ctr. Dir. Artward Bound, 1994; instr. Sierra Nevada Coll., 1995-98; acting edn. dir., instr. Brewery Arts Ctr., 1996-97; dir. Art Gallery Western Nevada C.C., Carson City, 1999-2000; trustee Western Nev. C.C. Found., 2000—. Exhibitions include Am. Artists Profl. Legue Grand. Nat., N.Y.C., 1995, 1998, Nev. Biennial, 1996, Catharine Lorillard Wolfe Art Club, N.Y.C., 1996, 2000, Nat. Oil and Acrylic Painters Soc., 1996, 1998, 2000, Nev. State Libr. and Archives, 1997, Salmagundi Club, N.Y.C., 1997, 1998, 2000, 2002, Allied Artists Am., N.Y.C., 1997, Butler Inst. Am. Art, Youngstown, Ohio, 2001, Audubon Artists Inc., 2001, Great Still Life Adventure II, 2002; columnist, writer: Artifacts Mag., 1998—2001. Finalist Artists' Mag., 1994; recipient Silver medal, Calif. Discovery Awards, 1994, Coun. Am. Artist Socs. award, Graphic Am. Artists Profl. League, 1995, 1998, Sarah Marshall and Ida Kaminski Meml. award, Salmagundi Club, 2000, award, Art Calendar Centerfold Contest, 1999; grantee Sierra Arts Found., 1996. Mem.: Capital Arts Coalition, Nat. Oil and Acrylic Painters Soc. (signature mem.), Am. Artists Profl. League, Catharine Wolfe Art Club (assoc.). Address: PO Box 8000 PMB 360 Mesquite NV 89024 E-mail: alcornart@att.net.

ALCORN, WALLACE ARTHUR, minister, writer; b. Milw., Aug. 29, 1930; s. William Keith and Dora Mildred (Brazee) Alcorn; m. Ann Margaret Carmichael, June 5, 1958; children: John Mark, Allison Alcorn-Oppedahl, Stephen, Paul. Student, Marquette U., 1950; AB, Wheaton Coll., 1952; MDiv, Grand Rapids Bapt. Theol. Sem., 1959; AM, Wheaton Grad. Sch. Theology, 1959; postgrad., Mich. State U., 1959-60, U. Mich., 1960-61; ThM, Princeton Theol. Sem., 1965; PhD, NYU, 1974; cert. in clin. pastoral edn., Fitzsimons Army Med. Ctr., 1975; postgrad., U. Minn., 1980-81. Ordained to ministry Gen. Assn. Regular Bapt. Chs., 1957; cert. advanced mediator Am. Arbit. Assn. Program sec. Wis. Heart Assn., 1954—55; field program rep. Chgo. Heart Assn., 1955—56; pastor Caddy Vista Bapt. Ch., Caldonia, Wis., 1955-57; tchr. Wyoming (Mich.) Schs., 1958-60; pastor Bloomfield Hills (Mich.) Bapt. Ch., 1960-61; English tchr. Waterford-Kettering H.S., Drayton Plaines, Mich., 1961-62; pastor Cmty. Bapt. Ch. Shark River Hills, Neptune, NJ, 1962-67, 1st Bapt. Ch., Austin, Minn., 1976-83; prof. bible Moody Bible Inst., Chgo., 1967-73; assoc. prof. N.T. N.W. Bapt. Sem., Tacoma, 1974-76; clin. pastoral care specialist Madigan Army Med. Ctr., Tacoma, 1974-76; police chaplain Tacoma, 1974-76, Austin, 1976-90; pres. Faith Acad., Mpls., 1986; prin. Wallace Alcorn Assocs., Austin, 1983—; pastoral counselor New Life Family Svcs., Rochester, Minn., 1987-92. Cons. U.S. Dept. Edn., 1953—54, N.J. Dept. Edn., 1964—67; radio tchr. Moody Radio Network, 1968—74; chmn. Minn. Assn. Regular Bapt. Chs., 1980—83; radio commentator Sta. KTIS and Northwestern Coll. Network, 1987—98; syndicated newspaper columnist, 1993—; adj. faculty Riverland C.C., 1994—99;. Author: (book) The Bible as Literature, 1965, Elijah, Prophet of God, 1972, The Life of Christ Visualized, 1973, Knowing and Using the Bible, 1975, Momentum, 1986; nat. editor: Christian Life, 1956—60, Mil. Life, 1983—86, Ampersand, 1995—99, N.T. editor: Living Bible Commentary, 1974—76, The Book We Love, 1994; contbr., articles to profl. jours. Mem. citizen's adv. coun. Neptune Bd. Edn., 1965—67; chair Austin Human Rights Commn., 1989—98; mem. profl. adv. coun. Pub. Edn. Relgion Studies Ctr., Wright State U., 1972—76; pub. mem. 10th Jud. Dist. Ethics Com., 1993—99; dir. Good News Hour, Austin, 1976—83, Minn. Human Rights Commn., 1990—98, Coop. Solutions Mediation Ctr., Austin, 1995—99. With USNR, 1947—52, with U.S. Army, 1952—54, with USAR, 1954—57, chaplain, col. USAR, 1957—90. Recipient Army Writing award, Army Found., 1988, First Pl. award, Baptist Heritage Preaching Contest, 2003. Mem.: Am. Pub. Health Assn., Hist. Soc. Minn., Hist. Soc. S.C., Hist. Soc. Ohio, Hist. Soc. Wis., Mil. Chaplains Assn. (pres. Chgo. chpt. 1970—74), Assn. Former Intelligence Officers, Soc. Profl. Journalists, Nat. Religious Broadcasters, Evang. Press Assn., Evang. Theol. Soc. Office: 500 J Oakland Place NE Austin MN 55912

ALCOTT, MARK HOWARD, lawyer; b. New York, Aug. 11, 1939; s. Harvey and Rose (Eigerman) A.; m. Susan M. (Bell), Sept. 3, 1961; children: Jill, Laura, Daniel, Elizabeth. AB, Harvard U., 1961, LLB, 1964. Bar: N.Y. 1965, U.S. Dist. Ct. (so. and ea. dists.) N.Y. 1966, U.S. Ct. Appeals (2d cir.) 1966, U.S. Ct. Appeals (9th and 10th cirs.) 1980, U.S. Ct. Internat. Trade 1980, U.S. Supreme Ct 1982, U.S. Ct. Appeals (D.C. cir.) 1983, D.C. 1984, U.S. Tax Ct. 1985; U.S. Ct. Appeals (1st. cir.),2000; U.S. Ct. Appeals (11th. cir.), 2003. Assoc. Paul, Weiss, Rifkind, Wharton, and Garrison, N.Y.C., 1964-73, ptnr., 1973—. Mediator Mandatory Mediation Program, U.S Dist. Ct. (so. dist.) N.Y.; spl. master, mediator commercial divsn. N.Y. Supreme Ct.; Spl. Master Appeals Divsn. first dept. Mem. Community Planning Bd., Riverdale, N.Y., 1970-72; comr. Larchmont, N.Y. Planning Commn., 1982-94; bd. dir. Mosholu-Montefiore Community Ctr., Bronx, N.Y., 1966-77. Fellow: N.Y. Bar Found., Am. Coll. Trial Lawyers (chmn. downstate N.Y. com., 1994-1996, chmn. internat. com., 1998-2002); mem.: Fed. Bar Coun., Internat. Bar Assn. (bus. law sect., internat. litigation com.), Assn. Bar : City of N.Y. (fed. legis. com. 1970—73), N.Y. State Bar Assn. (chmn. internat. litigation com. comml. and fed. litigation sect. 1989—92, sec. exec. com., exec. vice chmn. 1992—93, sect. chmn.-elect 1993—94, sect. chmn. 1994—95, mem. ho. of dels., mem. exec. com., v.p., spl commn. on campaign finance reform, 1997—99), ABA (litigation sect. internat. litigation com.). Avocation: sailing. Office: Paul Weiss Rifkind Wharton & Garrison 1285 Ave Americas New York NY 10019-6064

ALCOX, PATRICK JOSEPH, lawyer; b. Cleve., Oct. 27, 1946; s. William B. and Helen T. Alcox; m. Karen Woelfle, Oct. 20, 1979; children: Caitlin M., Molly C. BBA, Cleve. State U., 1970; MBA, Kent State U., 1974; JD, Cleve.-Marshall Coll. Law, 1976. Bar: Ohio, 1976, U.S. Supreme Ct., 1983. Group mgr. IRS, Cleve., 1972-76; fin. account exec. Internat. Mgmt. Group, Cleve., 1976-80; pvt. practice Cleve., 1980—. Ward leader Berea (Ohio) Republican Com., 1985-97; chmn. Berea CSC, 1988-92. Home: 448 Woodridge Cir Berea OH 44017-2227 Office: 75 Public Sq Ste 650 Cleveland OH 44113-2003

ALDAG, RAMON JOHN, management and organization educator; b. Beccles, Suffolk, Eng., Feb. 11, 1945; came to U.S., 1947; s. Melvin Frederick and Joyce Evelyn (Butcher) A.; m. Hollis Maura Jellinek, June 11, 1977; children— Elizabeth, Katherine BS, Mich. State U., 1966, MBA, 1968, PhD, 1974. Thermal engr. Bendix Aerospace div., Ann Arbor, Mich., 1966-70; teaching asst., instr. Mich. State U., East Lansing, Mich., 1966-73; asst. prof. mgmt. U. Wis., Madison, 1973-78, assoc. prof., 1978-82, prof. mgmt. and orgn., 1982—, chmn. dept. mgmt., 1986-88, assoc. dir. Indsl. Rels. Rsch. Inst., 1977-83, co-dir. Ctr. for Study of Orgnl. Performance, 1982—, faculty senator, 1980-84, Pyle Bascom prof. leadership, 1992—, student advisor, 1979—, Glen A. Skillrud Family chair in bus., 2001—, chmn. dept. mgmt. and human resources Sch. Bus., 1995—, co-dir. Weinert Ctr. for Entrepreneurship, 2000—, exec. dir. Weinert Ctr. Entrepreneurship, 2002—. Mgmt. cons. various businesses and industries, 1973— Author: Task Design and Employee Motivation, 1979, Managing Organizational Behavior, 1981, Introduction to Business, 1984, (now titled Business in a Changing World), 3d edit., 1993, 4th edit., 1996, Management, 1987, 2d edit., 1991, Leadership and Vision, 2000, Organizational Behavior and Management, 2002; contbr. articles to profl. jours.; cons. editor for mgmt. South-Western Pub. Co., 1987—; assoc. editor Jour. Bus. Rsch., 1988—, Decision Scis., 2002-; essays co-editor Jour. Mgmt. Inquiry. Bd. dirs. Family Enhancement Program, Madison, 1981— Grantee U. Wis., HEW, 1975-85; recipient Adminstrv. Rsch. Inst. award, 1976, Jerred Disting. Svc. award, 1993, NSF, 2000—; U. Wis. faculty rsch. fellow, 1985-88 Fellow. Acad. of Mgmt. (div. chmn. 1971—, bd. govs. 1986—, v.p. and program chair 1989—, pres. elect 1990, pres. 1991, past pres. 1992—, recipient Disting Svc. award, 1995); mem. Midwest Acad. Mgmt. (pres. 1973—), Decision Scis. Inst. (track chmn. 1975—), Indsl. Rels. Rsch. Assn. (elections commn. 1980—), Found. Administrn. Rsch. (pres. 1992—), Pi Tau Sigma, Tau Beta Pi, Sigma Iota Epsilon, Beta Gamma Sigma, Alpha Iota Delta. Avocations: gardening, fishing. Home: 2818 Van Hise Ave Madison WI 53705-3620 Office: U Wis 3112 Grainger Hall 975 University Ave Madison WI 53706-1323 E-mail: raldag@bus.wisc.edu.

ALDAVE, BARBARA BADER, law educator, lawyer; b. Tacoma, Dec. 28, 1938; d. Fred A. and Patricia W. (Burns) Bader; m. Rafael Aldave, Apr. 2, 1966; children: Anna Marie, Anthony John. BS, Stanford U., 1960; JD, U. Calif.-Berkeley, 1966. Bar: Oreg. 1966, Tex. 1982. Assoc. law firm, Eugene, Oreg., 1967-70; asst. prof. U. Oreg., 1970-73, prof., 2000—; vis. prof. U. Calif., Berkeley, 1973-74; from vis. prof. to prof. U. Tex., Austin, 1974-89, co-holder James R. Dougherty chair for faculty excellence, 1981-82, Piper prof., 1982, Joe A. Worsham centennial prof., 1984-89, Liddell, Sapp, Zivley, Hill and LaBoon prof. banking financial and comml. law, 1989; dean Sch. Law, prof. St. Mary's U., San Antonio, 1989-98, Ernest W. Clemens prof. corp. law, 1996-98; Loran L. Stewart prof. corp. law, dir., Ctr. for Law and Entrepreneurship U. Oreg. Sch. Law, 2000—. Vis. prof. Northeastern U., 1985-88, 98, Boston Coll. 1999-2000, Cornell U., 2002; ABA rep. to Coun. Inter-ABA, 1995-99; NAFTA chpt. 19 panelist, 1994-96. Pres. NETWORK, 1985-89; chair Gender Bias Task Force of Supreme Ct. Tex., 1991-94; bd. dirs. Tex. Alliance Children's Rights, Lawyer's Com. for Civil Rights Under Law of Tex., 1995-2000; nat. chair Gray Panthers, 1999—. Recipient tchg. excellence award U. Tex. Student Bar Assn., 1976, Appreciation awards Thurgood Marshall Legal Soc. of U. Tex., 1979, 81, 85, 87, Tchg. Excellence award Chicano Law Students Assn. of U. Tex., 1984, Hermine Tobolowsky award Women's Law Caucus of U. Tex., 1985, Ethics award Kugle, Stewart, Dent & Frederick, 1988, Leadership award Women's Law Assn. St. Mary's U., 1989, Ann. Inspirational award Women's Advocacy Project, 1989, Appreciation award San Antonio Black Lawyers Assn., 1990, Spl. Recognition award Nat. Conv. Nat. Lawyers Guild, 1990, Spirit of the Am. Woman award J. C. Penney Co., 1992, Sarah T. Hughes award Women and the Law sect. State Bar Tex., 1994, Ann. Tchg. award Soc. Am. Law Tchrs., 1996, Legal Svcs. award Mexican-Am. Legal Def. and Ednl. Fund, 1996, Woman of Justice award NETWORK, 1997, Ann. Peacemaker award Camino a la Paz, 1997, Outstanding Profl. in the Cmty. award Dept. Pub. Justice, St. Mary's U., 1997, Charles Hamilton Houston award Black Allied Law Students Assn. St. Mary's U., 1998, Woman of Yr. award Tex. Women's Polit. Caucus, 1998, award Clin. Legal Edn. Assn., 1998, lifetime achievement award Jour. Law and Religion, 1998, Harriet Tubman award African-Am. Reflections, 2002. Mem.: ABA (com. on corp laws, sect. banking and bus. law 1982—88), Tex.-Mex. Bar Assn., Bexar County Women's Bar Assn. (Belva Lockwood Outstanding Lawyers award 1991), Stanford U. Alumni Assn., Harlan Soc., Order of Coif, Delta Theta Phi (Outstanding Law Prof award St. Mary's U. chpt. 1990, 1991), Omicron Delta Kappa, Iota Sigma Pi, Phi Delta Phi. Roman Catholic. Home: 86399 N Modesto Dr Eugene OR 97402-9031 Office: U Oreg Sch Law Eugene OR 97403-1221 E-mail: baldave@law.uoregon.edu., balaw98@aol.com.

ALDAY, MARTA PERDOMO, library technology consultant, media consultant, art dealer; b. Havana, Cuba, Mar. 24, 1945; d. Jose E. and Celia (Gutierrez) Perdomo; m. Gonzalo Alday, Nov. 23, 1963; children: Marta Elena, Gonzalo Luis, Juan Antonio, Carolina Maria. AA, U. Fla., 1964, BA cum laude, 1973; MLS, Fla. State U., 1980. Cert. media specialist, Fla. Media specialist Heritage Christian, Miami, Fla., 1982-83, Palmer Sch., Miami, 1983-91; libr. dir., media specialist Jones Coll., Miami, 1991-92, Belen Jesuit Prep. Sch., Miami, 1992—2001; co-founder Consortium for Online Tech. Resources Arch. Miami Dept. Schs., Pompano Beach, Fla., 2001—. Mem. adv. bd. dor libr. stds. Fla. Coun. Ind. Schs., Miami, 1990—; panel mem. Archdiocese of Miami Schs., 1992—. Author: Handbook of Philosophy and Procedures, 1990. Coord. youth activities Big Five Club, Miami, 1988; chmn. St. Mary Cath. Hispanic Club, Miami, 1994. Recipient Outstanding Svc. award St. Mary Cathedral, Miami, 1989. Mem. ALA, Am. Assn. Sch. Librs., Fla. Assn. Media Edn., Dade County Libr. Assn., Phi Kappa Phi. Democrat. Avocations: reading, volunteering. Fax: 954-943-6685.

ALDAY, PAUL STACKHOUSE, JR., retired mechanical engineer; b. Camden, N.J., May 31, 1930; s. Paul Stackhouse and Amanda (Knocke) A.; m. Ethel Humes O'Connor, Nov. 29, 1952; children: Amy Jane, Paul Stackhouse III, Sarah Jean. BS in ME, Drexel U., 1953, MS in ME, 1957. Registered profl. engr., N.J. Engr. Naval Shipyard/Burroughs Corp., Phila., 1953-56; rsch. engr. Franklin Rsch. Labs., Phila., 1956-57, Univac, Phila., 1957-59; sr. engr. RCA Corp., Camden, 1959-68; sr. design engr. Univac/Burroughs/Control Data, southeastern Pa., 1968-74; project engr. Campbell Soup Co., Camden, 1974-90; cons. Budd Co., Phila., 1990-91; mail processing equipment U.S. Post Office, Phila., 1991-98; ret., 1998. Drexel U. scholar, 1948. Mem. Sigma Xi, Tau Kappa Epsilon Frat. Achievements include stress analysis, supports and preliminary bearing test on design of Enrico Fermi Nuclear Reactor; mechanical concept and design of digital data recorder for Gemini Spacecraft; concepts and designs of video recorder mechanisms used in surveillance satelites, digital computer input/output and memory devices, single position mail sorting machine for the U.S. Post Office. Home: 5759 Rogers Ave Pennsauken NJ 08109-2374

ALDCROFT, GEORGE EDWARD, guidance counselor; b. Toronto, Nov. 29, 1941; s. George and Margaret Aldcroft; m. Bernadette M. Cartoski, Nov. 27, 1971; children: Allison Marie, Bonnie Christine. BS in Edn., Wayne State U., 1966; MS in Guidance and Counseling, U. Mich., 1971; postgrad., Gestalt Ctr. L.I. Nat. cert. counselor, nat. cert. sch. counselor; cert. leader Developing Capable Young People. Elem. and jr. h.s. tchr. Center Line (Mich.) Pub. Sch. Sys., 1967-72; summer camp counselor, vol. worker Boys' Clubs Met. Detroit, 1967-69; guidance dir. Shelter Island (N.Y.) Union Free Sch. Dist., 1972-83; sch. counselor Westhampton Beach (N.Y.) Union Free Sch. Dist., 1983-89, Mattituck Cutchogue Sch. Dist., 1989—2002. Part-time employee Mattituck Cutchogue Sch. Dist., Cutchogue, NY, 2002—; facilitator parenting program. Mem. Shelter Island Drug Edn. Com., 1974, Southold Union Free Sch. Dist. Bd. Edn., 1983-86; bd. dirs. Human Understanding and Growth Seminars, 1985—, pres. bd. dirs., 1991-92. Recipient Outstanding Vol. Leader award Boys' Clubs Detroit, 1968. Mem. N.Y. State Counseling Assn., N.Y. State Sch. Counselors Assn., East End Counselors Assn. (pres. 1995-97), Am. Sch. Counselors Assn., U. Mich. Aumni Assn., N.Y. State United Tchrs. Roman Catholic. Home and Office: PO Box 431 Peconic NY 11958-0431 E-mail: galdcroft@aol.com.

ALDEA, GABRIEL S. cardiothoracic surgeon, educator; b. Bucharest, Romania, Nov. 7, 1956; came to U.S., 1970; s. Adrian and Blanche (Fainaru) A.; m. Susan Arnold, May 8, 1988; children: Alexander, Daniel. BA in Biochemistry summa cum laude, Columbia Coll., 1977; MD, Columbia U., 1981. Diplomate Am. Bd. Surgery, Am. Bd. Thoracic Surgery, Nat. Bd. Med. Examiners. Resident in gen. surgery N.Y. Hosp., Cornell Med. Ctr., N.Y.C., 1981—86, adminstrv. chief resident Dept. Surgery, 1985-86; cardiothoracic residency Dept. Cardiothoracic Surgery N.Y. Hosp., Cornell Med. Ctr. & Meml. Sloane Kettering Hosp., N.Y.C., 1988-90; cardiovasc. rsch. fellowship Cardiovasc. Rsch. Inst.-U. Calif. San Francisco, 1986-88; asst. vis. surgeon in cardiothoracic surgery Boston U. Med. Ctr., 1990-98; assoc. vis. surgeon in thoracic surgery Boston City Hosp., 1990-98; thoracic surgeon Jamaica Plain VA Hosp., Boston; assoc. prof. cardiothoracic surgery Boston U. Sch. Medicine, 1990-98; chief adult cardiac surgery, prof. surgery U. Wash., Seattle, 1998—; cardiac surgeon N.W. Hosp., Seattle, 1998—, Puget Sound VA Hosp., Seattle, 1998—. Contbr. articles to profl. jours. and chpts. to books. Recipient Nat. Rsch. Svc. award in heart & vascular diseases NIH, 1986-88. Fellow New Eng. Oncologic Soc.; mem. AAAS, AMA, ACS, Am. Coll. Chest Physicians, Am. Coll. Cardiology, Am. Heart Assn., Soc. for Thoracic Surgeons, Am. Assn. for Thoracic Surgery, Assn. Acad. Surgery, Am. Surg. Assn., Mass. Med. Soc., Rsch. Assocs. Southwestern Oncology Group, Western Thoracic Assn. Home: The Highlands Seattle WA 98177 Office: U Wash Dept Cardiothorasic Surgery PO Box 356310 Seattle WA 98195-6310

ALDEA, PATRICIA, architect; b. Bucharest, Romania, Mar. 18, 1947; came to U.S., 1976; d. Dan Jasmin Negreanu and Sonia (Friedgant) Philip-Negreanu; m. Val O. Aldea, Feb. 17, 1971; 1 child, Donna-Dana. March, Ion Mincu, Bucharest, 1970. Registered architect, N.Y. Architect, project. mgr. The Landmark Preservation Inst., Bucharest, 1971-76; architect Edward Durell Stone Assn., N.Y.C., 1977-79; sr. assoc. architect, project mgr. Alan Lapidus P.C., N.Y.C., 1980-2001; assoc. project arch., mgr. HLW, N.Y.C., 2001—02; plan examiner DOB, N.Y.C., 2003—. Columnist Contemporanul art jour., 1969-73. Hist. landmarks study fellow Internationes Fed. Republic of Germany, 1974. Office: DOB 120-55 Queens Blvd Kew Gardens NY 11415

AL-DELAIMY, WAEL, epidemiologist; 1 child, Emeen. PhD, Wellington Sch. Medicine, New Zealand, 2000. Asst. lectr. Otago U., Wellington, New Zealand, 1997—2000; rsch. fellow Harvard U., Cambridge, Mass., 2000—02, rsch. assoc., 2002—; scientist WHO, Lyon, France, 2003—. Recipient post-grad. award, U. Otago, 1997, Young Clin. Scientist award, Flight Attendants Med. Rsch. Found., 2001; post-grad. scholar, U. Otago, 1996—2000. Achievements include development of new biomarkers for the assessment of exposure to second hand smoke; finding that snoring can lead to type 2 diabetes; finding that bar and restaurant workers can be exposed to tobacco smoke levels similar to that of a moderate smoker. Avocation: acting.

ALDEN, DAURIL, historian; b. San Francisco, Jan. 12, 1926; s. Lawrence Chester and Edna Elizabeth (Klimcke) Thompson; m. Beata Maria Hambuschen Christ, Dec. 18, 1927; children: Sandor, Steven, Michael, Thomas; m. Alice Elinor Saphrone Shillington, Nov. 9, 1929 (div. Nov. 1978); children: Bryson, Grant. BA, U. Calif., Berkeley, 1950, MA, 1952, PhD, 1959. Vrom instr. to prof. U. Wash., Seattle, 1959—. Vis. prof. U. Calif., Berkeley, 1962—63, Columbia U., N.Y.C., 1967, U. Mich., Ann Arbor, 1969. Author: Royal Govt. in Colonial Brazil, 1968 (Honorable Mention for the Herbert E. Bolton Prize, 1968), The Making of an Enterprise: the Role of the Jesuits in Portugal, its Empire, and Beyond, 1540-1750, 1996 (John Gilmary Shea Prize, Am. Cath. Hist. Assoc., 1998, João de Castro Prize, Comissão Nacional, 1998), Charles R. Boxer: An Uncommon Life, 2001. Radarman, 2nd class USN, 1944—46. Mem.: Conf. on Latin Am. History. Avocations: baking, travel, writing, book purchases. Home: 6032 50th Ave NE Seattle WA 98115-7704

ALDEN, JOHN W. lawyer; BS, Stanford U., 1955, MS, 1956, JD, 1959. Bar: Calif. 1960. Assoc. Pillsbury, Madison & Sutro, 1959-67; assoc. gen. counsel Occidental Petroleum Corp., L.A., 1967—. Office: Occidental Petroleum Corp 10889 Wilshire Blvd Ste 1500 Los Angeles CA 90024-4216 E-mail: john_w_alden@oxy.com.

ALDEN, STEVEN MICHAEL, lawyer; b. L.A., May 19, 1945; s. Herbert and Sylvia Zina (Hochman) A.; m. Evelyn Mae Subotky, Dec. 31, 1977; children: Carissa Louise, Bramley Marshall, Darym Alexander. AB, UCLA, 1967; JD, U. Calif., Berkeley, 1970. Bar: Calif. 1971, N.Y. 1971. Assoc. Debevoise & Plimpton, N.Y.C., 1971-78, ptnr., 1979—. Lectr., seminar panelist Practising Law Inst., N.Y.C., 1981—; panelist, lectr. N.Y. State Bar, Albany, 1984. Contbr. articles to profl. jours. Mem. ABA (real estate fin. com.), Assn. of Bar of City of N.Y. (com. real property law), Am. Land Title Assn. (assoc. lender's counsel group), Am. Coll. Real Estate Lawyers, Am. Coll. Mortgage Attys., Order of Coif, Phi Beta Kappa, Sky Club (N.Y.C.). Republican. Office: Debevoise & Plimpton 919 3rd Ave Fl 42 New York NY 10022

ALDEN, VERNON ROGER, corporate director, trustee; b. Chgo., Apr. 7, 1923; s. Arvid W. and Hildur Pauline (Johnson) A.; m. Marion Frances Parson, Aug. 18, 1951 (dec. Aug. 1999); children: Robert Parson, Anne Elizabeth, James Malcolm, David Douglas. AB magna cum laude, Brown U., 1945; MBA, Harvard, 1950; LLD (hon.), Brown U., 1964, Emerson Coll., 1957, Ohio Wesleyan U., 1964, R.I. Coll., 1965, William Jewell Coll., 1965, Loyola U., 1966, Wilberforce U., 1970, Ottawa U., 1970, Babson Coll., 1972; LHD, North Park Coll., 1965; LittD, Ohio U., 1969; DPS, Bowling Green U., 1969; LittD, Bethany Coll., 1970. Admission officer Brown U., 1946-48; asst. dir. admissions Northwestern U., 1950-51; dir. fin. aid Harvard Grad. Sch. Bus. Adminstrn., assoc. dean, faculty, 1951-61; ednl. dir. U. Hawaii Advanced Mgmt. Program, summer 1960, Keio U. Advanced Mgmt. Program, Tokyo, summers 1960-61; pres. Ohio U., Athens, 1962-69; chmn. bd., chmn. exec. com. Boston Co. and subsidiary Boston Safe Deposit & Trust Co., 1969-78. Bd. dirs. Colgate-Palmolive Co., Digital Equipment Corp., Intermet Corp., Sonesta Internat. Hotels Corp., Tax-Free Trust Funds Hawaii, Oreg. and Rhode Island, ML-Lee Fund, Ind. Gen. Ptnrs.; hon. consul-gen. Kingdom of Thailand. Chmn. Pres.' Task Force Job Corps Program, com. Future of U. Mass, 1971, chmn. Mass. Coun. Arts/Humanities, 1972-84, Mass. Bus. Devel. Coun./Fgn. Bus. Coun., 1978-83; life trustee Boston Symphony Orch., Mus. Sci., Boston; chmn. arts facilities com. MIT; fellow emeritus Brown U.; life trustee French Libr., Boston; adv. com. Harvard Program Japan-U.S. Rels. Lt. USNR, 1943-46 Recipient Gov.'s award State Ohio, 1969; Founder's citation Ohio U., 1969; Bus. Statesman award Harvard Grad. Sch. Bus., 1975; named Hon. Consul-Gen. Kingdom of Thailand; decorated Order Rising Sun, Star (Japan), Most Noble Order of the Crown of Thailand, Disting. Civilian Svc. medal U.S. Army, Most Exalted Order of the White Elephant (Thailand). Mem. Nat. Assn. Japan-Am. Socs. (chmn.), Japan Soc. of Boston (chmn.), Somerset Club (Boston), Edgartown Yacht Club (Martha's Vineyard), Country Club (Brookline), Farm Neck Golf Club (Martha's Vineyard), Phi Beta Kappa, Phi Kappa Phi, Phi Delta Theta, Beta Gamma Sigma. Episcopalian. Avocations: golf, tennis, reading. Home: 37 Warren St Brookline MA 02445-5925 Office: 20 Park Plz Ste 414 Boston MA 02116-4308

ALDER, BERNI JULIAN, physicist, researcher; b. Duisburg, Germany, Sept. 9, 1925; came to U.S., 1941, naturalized, 1944; s. Ludwig and Ottilie (Gottschalk) A.; m. Esther Berger, Dec. 28, 1956; children: Kenneth, Daniel, Janet. BS, U. Calif., Berkeley, 1947, MS, 1948; PhD, Calif. Inst. Tech., 1951. Instr. chemistry U. Calif., Berkeley, 1951-54; theoretical physicist Lawrence Livermore Lab., Livermore, Calif., 1955-93; prof. dept. applied sci. U. Calif., Davis, 1987-93, prof. emeritus, 1993; van der Waals prof. U. Amsterdam, Netherlands, 1971; prof. associé U. Paris, 1972. G.N. Lewis lectr. U. Calif., Berkeley, 1984, Hinshelwood prof., Oxford, 1986, Lorentz prof., Leiden, 1990, Kistiakowsky lectr. Harvard U., 1990, Royal Soc. lectr., 1991. Author: Methods of Computational Physics, 1963; editor: Jour. Computational Physics, 1966-91. Served with USN, 1944-46. Recipient Boltzmann medal Internat. Union Pure and Applied Physics, 2001; Guggenheim fellow, 1954-55; NSF sr. postdoctoral fellow, 1963-64, Japanese Promotion of Sci. fellow, 1989; Berni J. Alder prize established by European Phys. Soc., 1999. Fellow: Am. Phys. Soc.; mem.: Rare Gas Dynamics Soc. (Grad lectr. 2000), Am. Chem. Soc. (Hildebrand award 1985), Nat. Acad. Scis. Republican. Jewish. Office: Lawrence Livermore Lab PO Box 808 Livermore CA 94551-0808 E-mail: alder1@llnl.gov.

ALDERDICE, CYNTHIA LOU, artist; b. Des Moines, Mar. 16, 1932; d. Charles Lloyd and Marion Maxine (Hinn) Sandahl; m. Lee Edward Alderdice, Jan. 30, 1954; children: Cheryl Lynn, Kirk Bryan. BA, U. Tex., 1957. Pres. Am. Art Assocs., Inc., Bethesda, Md., 1966-92; v.p. Am. Art Make-A-Frame, Inc., Rockville, Md., 1972-97; pres. Am. Art Assocs, Inc., Annapolis, Md., 1997—. V.p., bd. dirs. Pyramid Atlantic, Inc., Riverdale, Md., 1994—; com. mem. Jewelry from Walters Art Gallery and Zucker Family Collection, 1987, Greek Gold from Beenaki Mus., 1991; com. mem. tarnished vistas Hist. Annapolis, Md., 1988. One-woman shows include: Touchstone Gallery, Washington, 1993, 95, 97, 99, 2002, Marion Price Contemporary Fine Art Gallery, Centreville, Md., 1995, U. Md., University College, Annapolis, 1996, Md. Fedn. of Art, Annapolis, 1997, Robert C. Williams Am. Museum of Papermaking, Atlanta, 1998, Richards Gallery, Westbrook Gallery, Robert Ferst Ctr. for the Arts, Atlanta, 1998, Air Gallery, Annapolis, 1998, Zaruba Gallery, Rockville, Md., 1999, Ellen Noel Art Museum, Odessa, Tex., 1999, Mill River Gallery, Ellicott City, Md., 1999, 2000, Towson (Md.) U., 2000, The Morris Mechanic Theater, Balt., Md., 2002, others; exhibited in group shows Mus. Contemporary Art, Chamalieres, France, 1991, Walters Art Gallery, Balt., 1991, Inst. of the Arts George Mason U., Fairfax, Va., 1995, Montpelier Cultural Arts Ctr., Laurel, Md., 1995, Tarrytown Gallery, Austin, Tex., 1995, Fairbanks Arts Assn., Alaska, 1997, Melvin Art Gallery, Lakeland, Fla., 1997, Towson State U., Md., 1997, Montgomery Coll., Rockville, Md., 1997, Corcoran Mus. Art, Washington, 1997, Fernbank Mus. of Natural History, Atlanta, 1997, 98, Ann Arundel C.C., Annapolis, Md., 1997, 98, Tallahassee Museum of Natural History, 1998, Fed. Res. Bd., Washington, 1998, Washington Arts Club, 1998, Ellen Noel Art Museum, TX, 1999, American Swedish History Museum, 2000, Hanoi Coll. of Fine Art, 2000, Am. Swedish Hist. Mus., Phila., Pa., 2000, Red River Valley Museum, 2001, The Art Gallery at U. Md., Coll. Pk., Md., 2001, Kirkpatric Galleries at Omniplex, Okla. City, Okla., 2001, Hand Workshop Art Ctr., Richmond, Va., 2002, Carla Massoni Gallery, Chestertown, Md., 2002, numerous others; permanent collections include Musee d'Art Contemporain of Chamalieres, France, Artist Book Collection Balt. Mus. Art, Md. Fedn. Art, Internat. Monetary Fund Collection, Washington, Freedie Mac's Collection Honoring Washington Artists, U. Md., The Jane Voorhees Silmmerli Art Mus., N.J., Robert C. Williams Am. Mus. Papermaking, Ga. Tech. Univ., U. Md., Fisher Coll. Bus. Ohio State U., Columbus Ohio, D.C. Commn. for the Arts and Humanities, Washington, D.C., others; author: Best of Printmaking. Recipient individual artist award Md. Arts Coun., 1992. Mem. Md. Fedn. Art (pres., bd. dirs. 1985-87), Md. Printmakers, So. Graphics Art Coun., Friends Cardinal Gallery (hon.), Friends of Dard Hunter. Avocations: tennis, swimming, reading, working on computer. Studio: Annapolis Bus Pk 2104 Renard Ct Annapolis MD 21401-6748

ALDERFER, CLAYTON PAUL, organizational consultant, educator, writer, administrator; b. Sellersville, Pa., Sept. 1, 1940; s. Joseph Paul and Ruth Althea (Buck) A.; m. Charleen Judith Frankenfield, July 14, 1962; children: Kate, Benjamin. BS with high honors, Yale U., 1962, PhD, 1966. Cert. Am. Bd. Profl. Psychology. Asst. prof. Cornell U., Ithaca, N.Y., 1966-68, Yale U., New Haven, 1968-70, assoc. prof., 1970-78; prof. Sch. Orgn. Mgmt., Yale U., New Haven, 1978-92, assoc. dean, 1982-84; prof. II Grad. Sch. Applied and Profl. Psychology Rutgers U., 1992—, dir. Orgnl. Psychology program, 1992—. Author: Existence, Relatedness and Growth, 1972, Learning from Changing, 1975; contbr. articles to profl. jours.; mem. editl. bd. Jour. Applied Behavioral Sci., 1978-89, editor, 1990-93; mem. editl. bd. Family Bus. Rev., 1987—, Jour. Orgnl. Behavior, 1988-92; editor: Advances in Experiential Social Processes, vol. 1, 1979, vol. 2, 1980. Bd. dirs. NTL Inst., Arlington, Va., 1975-78, DATA, New Haven, 1989-92. Grantee Office Naval Research, 1970-74, 79-80, 82-86; recipient Cattell award, 1972, McGregor award, 1979, Levinson award, 1997, Helms award, 1999. Fellow Am. Psychol. Assn., Soc. Applied Anthropology, Am. Psychol. Soc.; mem. Sigma Xi, Tau Beta Pi. Independent. Lutheran. Office: Rutgers Grad Sch Applied Profl Psychology 152 Frelinghuysen Rd Piscataway NJ 08854-8020 E-mail: alderfer@rci.rutgers.edu.

ALDERMAN, ANNABEL (ELSIE HIGGS GRINER JR.), writer; b. Nashville, Ga., July 15, 1924; d. George Auley and Elsie Higgs Griner; m. Hugh Dorsey Alderman, July 20, 1952 (dec. Apr. 25, 1973); 1 child, Galen Alderman Mirate. Grad., high sch., Ga. Regional Police Acad., 1983. Stage performer Miss Peaches, Nashville, Ga., 1948—54; radio show host Miss Peaches Cafe, Moultrie, 1954—54, Houston, 1954—54; stage performer The Holy Notes, Nashville, 1954—62; editor, pub. The Nashville Herald, 1962—66; stage performer Chief Jesters of the South, 1966—75; legal investigator Griner & Alderman, 1981—95; novalist, poet The Write Pl., 1995—; polit. columnist The Valdosta Daily Times, Valdosta, 2000—01. Composer (performer): (songs) Callin' Moody Field, 1954; editor (pub.): The Nashville Herald (2nd Pl.; H. H. Dean Trophy for best editl., 1965, 2nd Pl.; James Cranston Williams Trophy for editl. page, 1965, 3rd Pl.; James Cranston Williams Trophy for editl. page, 1966, Otis Brumby Award for weekly column, 1964, 1966, Fearless Editl. Award, 1966, 3rd Pl., Gen. Excellence, 1965), author of short stories, Solemn in Gomorrah (Southeastern Writers' Assn.; Cappy Hall Award for So. Lit. Fiction, 1998), (novels) Family Man, 1999 (Nominated; Ga. Author of the Yr., 2000, Nominated; Townsend Prize for Fiction, 2000), limericks; composer (performer): (songs) It Is Well With My Soul; Holy Notes; composer: Brand New Star; composer: (performer) Focus On The South, Safari Down South; author: (book of poetry) Lost Loves Don't Count, 1997 (Writer's Digest Self Pub. award). Aide de camp Gov. Staff, Atlanta, 1963—67, 1971—74. Named Chief Jester of Ga., 1971; recipient citation Writing & Performing in Ann. Cracker Crumble Stage Prodn., Ga. Press Assn., 1963—75. Mem.: Internat. Soc. Poets, Ga. Poetry Soc., Southeastern Writers Assn., Mensa Soc. Libertarian. Episcopalian.

ALDERMAN, MINNIS AMELIA, psychologist, educator, small business owner; b. Douglas, Ga., Oct. 14, 1928; d. Louis Cleveland Sr. and Minnis Amelia (Wooten) A. AB in Music, Speech and Drama, Ga. State Coll., Milledgeville, 1949; MA in Supervision/Counseling Psychology, Murray State U., 1960; postgrad., Columbia Pacific U., 1987—. Tchr. music Lake County Sch. Dist., Umatilla, Fla., 1949-50; instr. vocal/instrumental music, dir. band, orch., choral Fulton County Sch. Dist., Atlanta, 1950-54; instr. English, speech, debate, vocal and instrumental music Elko County Sch. Dist., Wells, Nev., 1954-59, dir. drama, band, choral and orchestra, 1954-59; tchr. English and social studies Christian County Sch. Dist., Hopkinsville, Ky., 1960; instr. psychology, counselor critic prof. Murray (Ky.) State U., 1961-63, U. Nev., Reno, 1963-67; owner Minisizer Exercising Salon, Ely, Nev., 1969-71, Knit Knook, Ely, 1969—, Minimimeo, Ely, 1969—, Gift Gamut, Ely, 1977—; prof. dept. fine arts Wassuk Coll., Ely, 1986-91, assoc. dean, 1986-87, dean, 1987-90; counselor White Pine County Sch. Dist., Ely, 1960-68; dir. Child and Family Ctr. Ely Indian Tribe, 1988-93. Supr. testing Ednl. Testing Svc., Princeton, N.J., 1960-68, Am. Coll. Testing Program, Iowa, 1960-68, U. Nev., Reno, 1960-68; chmn. bd. White Pine Sch. Dist. Employees Fed. Credit Union, Ely, 1961-69; psychologist mental hygiene div. Nev. Pers., Ely, 1969-75, dept. employment secrity, 1975-80; sec.-treas. bd. dirs. Gt. Basin Enterprises, Ely, 1969-71; speaker at confs.; rep. Ely/East Ely Bus. Coun., 1997—; mem. Econ. Devel. Bd., 1998—; prof. Great Basin C.C., 1999—. Author various news articles, feature stories, pamphlets, handbooks and grants in field. Pvt. instr. piano, violin, voice and organ, Ely, 1981—. Dir. Family Resource Ctr. (Great Basin Rural Nev. Youth Cabinet), 1996—; bd. dirs. band Sacred Heart Sch., Ely, 1982-99; mem. Gov.'s Mental Health State Commn., 1963-65, Ely Shoshone Tribal Youth Camp, 1991-92, Elys Shoshone Tribal Unity Conf., 1991-92, Tribal Parenting Skills Coord., 1991; bd. dirs. White Pine County Sch. Employees Fed. Credit Union, 1961-68,, pres., 1963-68; 2d v.p. White Pine Community Concert Assn., 1965-67, pres., 1967, 85—, treas., 1975-79, dr. chmn., 1981-85; chmn. of bd., 1984; bd. dirs. White Pine chpt. ARC, 1978-82; mem. Nev. Hwy. Safety Leaders Bd., 1979-82; mem. Gov.'s Commn. on Status Women, 1968-74, Gov.'s Nevada State Juvenile Justice Adv. Commn., 1992-94; mem. White Pine C. of C.; dir. White Pine Legisl. Coalition, 2002—; mem. White Pine Overall Econ. Devel. Plan Coun., 1992-99; sec.-treas. White Pine Rehab. Tng. Ctr. for Retarded Persons, 1973-75; mem. Gov.'s Commn. on Hwy. Safety, 1979-81, Gov's. Juvenile Justice Program; sec.-treas. White Pine County Juvenile Problems Cabinet, 1994—; dir. Ret. Sr. Vol. Program, 1973-74; vice chmn. Gt. Basin Health Coun., 1973-75, Home Extension adv. Bd., 1977-80; sec.-treas. Great Basin chpt. Nev. Employees Assn.; bd. dirs. United Way, 1970-76; vice chmn. White Pine Coun. on Alcoholism and Drug Abuse, 1975-76, chmn., 1976-77, White Pine County Bus. Coun., 1998—; dir. White Pine Coalation; grants author 3 yrs. Indian Child Welfare Act, State Hist. Preservation, Fair and Recreation Bd. Centennial Fine Arts Ctr.; originator Community Tng. Ctr. for Retarded People, 1972, Ret. Sr. Vol. Program, 1974, Nutrition Program for Sr. Citizens, 1974, Sr. Citizens Ctr., 1974, Home Repairs for Sr. Citizens, 1974, Sr. Citizens Crafters Assns., 1976, Inst. Current World Affairs, 1989, Victims of Crime, 1990-92, grants author Family Resource Ctr., 1995; bd. dirs. Family coalition, 1990-92, Sacred Heart Parochial Sch., 1982—, dir. band, 1982—; candidate for diaconal ministry, 1982-93; dir. White Pine

Cmty. Chior, 1962— invited performer Branson Jubilee Nat. Ch. Chior Festival, Mo., Ely Meth. Ch. Choir, 1960-84; chior dir., organist Sacred Heart Ch., 1984—; Precinct reporter ABC News, 1966; speaker U.S. Atty. Gen. Conf. Bringing Nev. Together; bd. dirs. White Pine Juvenile Cabinet, 1993—, Ely/East Ely Bus. Coun., 1997—, Econ. Devel. Bd., 1998—. Named scholar, Nat. Trust for Hist. Preservation, 2000; recipient Recognition rose, Alpha Chi State Delta Kappa Gamma, 1994, Recognition Rose, 2002, Perserving America's Treasures in the 21st Century, 2001; grantee, Nat. Trust for Historic Preservation, L.A., 2000. Fellow Am. Coll. Musicians, Nat. Guild Piano Tchrs.; mem. NEA (life), UDC, DAR, Nat. Fedn. Ind. Bus. (dist. chair 1971-85, nat. guardian coun. 1985—, state guardian coun. 1987—), AAUW (pres. Wells br. 1957-58, pres. White Pine br. 1965-66, 86-87, 89-91, 93—, bd. dirs. 1965-87, rep. edn. 1965-67, implementation chair 1967-69, area advisor 1969-73, 89-91), Nat. Fedn. Bus. and Profl. Women (1st v.p. Ely chpt. 1965-66, pres. Ely chpt. 1966-68, 74-76, 85—, bd. dirs. Nev. chpt. 1966—, 1st v.p. Nev. Fedn. 1970-71, pres. Nev. chpt. 1972-73,nat. bd. dirs. 1972-73), White Pine County Mental Health Assn. (pres. 1960-63, 78—), Mensa (supr. testing 1965—), White Pine C. of C., Delta Kappa Gamma (br. pres. 1968-72, 94—99, state bd. 1967—, chpt. parliamentarian 1974-78, 99—, state 1st v.p. 1967-69, state pres. 1969-71, nat. bd. 1969-71, state parliamentarian 1971-73, 95—, chmn. state nominating com. 1995-97, chmn. bylaws com. 2003—, workshop presenter on aging 1995, presenter 1998-99), White Pine Knife and Fork Club (1st v.p. 1969-70, pres. 1970-71, bd. dirs. 1979—), Soc. Descs. of Knights of Most Noble Order of Garter, Nat. Soc. Magna Charta Dames. Office: PO Box 150457 East Ely NV 89315-0457 *My mission in this life: To use to the fullest good, the talents and abilities that have been given to me in order to productively help whenever and wherever the opportunity arises.*

ALDERMAN, RHENUS HOFFARD, III, investment company executive; b. Roanoke, Va., Dec. 16, 1926; s. Rhenus Hoffard Jr. and Virginia (Allen) A.; m. Mary Elizabeth Malin, Dec. 28, 1957 (div. Feb. 6, 2001); children: Elizabeth Allen b. Mar. 9, 1962, Rhenus H. IV b. Jan. 22, 1964, Sarah Malin b. Apr. 2, 1969. BS, Ga. Inst. Tech., 1953; MBA, U. Mich., 1963. Trainee GE Co., Lynn, Mass., 1953-54; sales exec. John Hancock Mut. Life Ins. Co., Boston, 1954-64; asst. v.p. Citibank N.A., N.Y.C., 1964-80; sr. v.p. The Merchants Bank & Trust Co., Norwalk, Conn., 1980-90; pres. Investors Capital Mgmt., Inc., Rowayton, Conn., 1990—. Past pres., treas. Alcoholism & Drug Dependency Coun., Westport, Conn., 1995-96. With U.S. Army, 1944-45. Mem. Am. Pension Conf., Am. Arbitration Assn., Norwalk Yacht Club. Home: 50 Green Ave New Canaan CT 06840-3311 Office: Investors Capital Mgmt Inc 71 Rowayton Ave Norwalk CT 06853-1644 E-mail: icm@incapman.com.

ALDERMAN, RICHARD MARK, legal educator, lawyer, television and radio commentator; b. Passaic, N.J., Feb. 18, 1947; s. Wilbur and Lois H. (Taub) A.; m. Janie Alderman; 1 child, Willie. B.A., Tulane U., 1968; J.D. cum laude, Syracuse U., 1971; LL.M., U. Va., 1973. Bar: N.Y. 1972, Tex. 1981, U.S. Supreme Ct. 1983. Staff atty. Legal Services, Syracuse, 1972-73; Dwight Olds chair in law U. Houston, 1973—, assoc. dean Law Ctr., 1993—; vis. prof. Loyola Law Sch., Los Angeles, 1976-77, Boston Coll., 1980-81; People's Lawyer, Sta. KTRK-TV, Houston, 1980—; It's the Law, 14 Tex. cities; dir. council on Legal Edn. Opportunity Summer Inst., Houston, 1975. Author: A Transactional Guide to the Uniform Commercial Code, 1982; Creditors' Rights in Texas, 1978; Uniform Commercial Code Series, 1984; Know Your Rights! Answers to your most Common Legal Questions, 1985, 4th rev. edit., 1995, Doing Business in Texas, 1987, 2d edit., 1992, Texas Deceptive Trade Practices, 1988, The Lawyer's Guide to the DTPA, 1990, Alderman's Texas Consumer and Commercial Laws Annotated, 1996. Contbr. articles to profl. jours. Recipient M.D. Anderson Scholarship award Found. Prof. U. Houston Law Ctr., 1977. Mem. ABA (Golden Gavel award 1985, 89), Tex. Bar Assn. (consumer law council 1984—, editor-in-chief Caveat Vendor 1984—), Order of the Coif, Phi Delta Phi. Jewish. Home: 4135 University Blvd Houston TX 77005-2713 Office: U Houston Law Ctr University Park 4800 Calhoun Rd Houston TX 77004-2610 *A teacher helps you acquire the skills that enable you to achieve success for the rest of your life.*

ALDERMAN, WALTER ARTHUR, JR., computer company and corporate rescue executive; b. Stoneham, Mass., July 29, 1945; s. Walter Arthur and Ida Ellen (Patchett) A.; m. Sandra May Johnston, Aug. 23, 1969; children: Walter Arthur III, Deborah Ellen. BSBA with honors, Northeastern U., 1968; MBA, Harvard U., 1971. Divisional controller Anken Industries, Williamstown, Mass., 1971-73; treas., controller James Hunter Machine Co., North Adams, Mass., 1973-78; gen. mgr. Petricca Industries, Pittsfield, Mass., 1978-80; chmn., pres. Alderman Assocs. Inc., Coral Springs, Fla., 1980-85, Bedford Computer Corp., 1985-90; owner, pres. Paragon Pub. Systems, Bedford, 1990—. Bd. dirs. Mahoney and Assocs., Inc., Springfield, Mass.; instr., mem. adv. bd. North Adams (Mass.) State Coll., 1976-78; registered rep. First New England Securities, Stockbridge, Mass., 1968-74. Bd. dirs. Mass. C. of C., 1976-78, YMCA, 1976-78; sect. leader United Fund, Mass., 1977; mem. N.H. Industry and Tech. Partnership, 1992—. Recipient Outstanding Svc. award C. of C., 1978, Community Svc. award United Fund, 1977, Blue Chip Enterprise award U.S. C. of C., 1993; named Turnaround Enterpreneur of Yr., Arthur Young and Venture mag., 1987, New Eng. and N.H. Small Bus. Exporter of Yr., SBA, 1992, Master Entrepreneur, Ernst & Young, Merrill Lynch and Inc. mag., 1991. Mem. Turnaround Mgmt. Assn., Phi Kappa Phi, Beta Gamma Sigma. Avocations: sports, coaching, bridge, chess, reading. Office: Paragon Pub Sys Bedford NH 03110

ALDERMAN, WILLIAM FIELDS, lawyer; b. Hamilton, Ohio, 1945; AB summa cum laude, Miami U., 1967; JD, Yale U., 1970. Bar: Calif. 1971. Ptnr. Orrick, Herrington & Sutcliffe, San Francisco, 1976—. Ct. apptd. arbitrator, mediator and evaluator, 1988—. Dir. Lawyers Com. for Civil Rights of the San Francisco Bay Area, 1985—, St. Thomas More Soc. San Francisco, 1987-94, pres. 1993; dir. San Francisco Neighborhood Legal Assistance Found., 1995—. Mem. Phi Beta Kappa. Office: Orrick Herrington & Sutcliffe Old Federal Reserve Bank Bldg 400 Sansome St San Francisco CA 94111-3143*

ALDERN, ROBERT JUDSON, architectural, liturgical and landscape artist; b. Sioux Falls, S.D., Jan. 16, 1929; s. John Olson and Emma (Dahl) A.; m. Joey Marlys Grunwald, Dec. 27, 1951; children: Bradley (dec.), Marlys, Noreen, Jared. Student, Augustana Coll., Sioux Falls, S.D., 1947-51; BFA, U. Hartford, 1957. Draftsman Spitznagel, Inc., Sioux Falls, 1957-61; dir. Civic Fine Arts Ctr., Sioux Falls, 1963-66; artist-in-residence S.D. State U., Brookings, 1966-68; prof. art U. S.D., Vermillion, 1968-80, chmn. art dept., 1968-73; chmn. dept. art Augustana Coll., 1980-88, prof. art, 1988-91, artist-in-residence, 1991—, dir. Liturgical Resource Ctr., 1991—; dir. Owner, operator Aldern Art Studio, Sioux Falls, 1957—; liturgical artist-cons. St. Michael's Cath. Ch., Gloria Dei Luth. Ch., Holy Spirit Cath. Ch., Sioux Falls. Prin. works include sound baffle design St. Mary's Cath. Ch., Sioux Falls, 1959 (Silver medal N.Y. Archtl. League), (murals) Our Savior's Luth. Ch., Sioux Falls, Grace Luth. Ch., Sturgis, S.D., Plains Clinic, Sioux Falls, First Luth. Ch., St. Peter, Minn., Augustana Coll. Chapel, Sioux Falls, Luther Ctr., Uermillion, Sch. of Mines and Tech., Rapid City, King of Glory Luth. Ch., Dallas, Sioux Valley Hosp., Sioux Falls, Good Samaritan Corp. Offices, Sioux Falls, McKennan Hosp., Sioux Falls, Gloria Dei Luth. Ch., Sioux Falls, Christ the King Catholic Church, Sioux Falls, Elizabeth Ann Seton Cath. Ch., Groton, S.D., large steel panels at rest area Chamberlain, S.D.; restoration of Eide fresco Augustana Coll. Chapel, Sioux Falls; 6 red oak panels Good Samaritan Great Rm., Sioux Falls, stained wood cross Chapel Gloria Dei Luth. Ch., Sioux Falls, Figurative Cross, Dallas. Bd. dirs. S.D. Art Mus., Brookings, 1995-99, Civic Fine Arts Ctr., Sioux Falls, 1998-99, Sioux Falls Beautiful, 2000-03. Active USAF, 1951-54. S.D. Arts Coun. grant, 1985; recipient Silver medal N.Y. Archtl. League, 1959,, Alumni Achievement award Augustana Coll., Sioux Falls, 1977, Creative Achievement award Gov. of S.D., 1997, Spitznagel award, 1997, 2002, Mayor's award, Sioux Falls, 2000. Lutheran. Studio: Augustana Coll 29th and Smt Sioux Falls SD 57197-0001 Home: Apt 209 2501 S Kiwanis Ave Sioux Falls SD 57105

ALDERSON, JO BARTELS, writer, poet; b. Janesville, Wis., Sept. 21, 1930; d. Frederick Carl William and Rose Augusta Theresa (Griesbach) Bartels; m. James Michael Alderson, Sr., June 21, 1952; children: James Jr. (Mick), Kaye, Jaye, Ann, Erica. BA, Milton Coll., 1952. Part-time reporter Janesville Gazette, 1949—52; tchr. Oshkosh (Wis.) Area Schs., 1958—59, play dir., 1962—67; proofreader The Paper for Ctrl. Wis., Oshkosh, 1968—70; tchr. writing workshops Johnson Found., Racine, Wis., 1969—70; guide/publs. editor Paine Art Ctr. and Arboretum, Oshkosh, 1974—92; freelance writer, 1960—. Pres., editor, bd. mem. Wis. Fellowship Poets, 1960—; bd. mem. Coun. for Wis. Writers, Milw., 1962—78, pres., 1976—78; judge various state and nat. literary contests; judge H.S. forensic contests; treas., dir., actor, bd. mem. The Co. for Wis. Arts, Oshkosh, 1977—94. Author: (biography) The Man Mazzuchelli, 1974, Rain From a Clear Sky, 1991 (Nat. Fedn. Press Women award, 1993), (history book) Wisconsin's Early French Habitants, 1998 (Nat. Fedn. Press Women award, 1999), (poetry book) Owls, 1980, Owls Too and II, 1984, Tri-Owls, 1988 (1st place Nat. Fedn. Press Women, 1989), Rudd Owls (1st place Nat. Fedn. Press Women, 1996); editor: (anthology) Poems Out of Wisconsin III, 1967, (history book and catalogue) 30th Anniversary Book of Paine Art Center, 1981, (mag.) inner-mission, 1983—92; contbr. poetry, articles, essays and play revs. to publs. Dir., actor 4 cmty. theatre groups, Wis., 1953—95; founder, pres., bd. mem. The Grand Opera House Com., Oshkosh, 1965—80; mem. Oshkosh Found. Arts Com., 1997—98. Recipient 4th Pl., Nat. Legacies Contest, N.Y., 1994. Mem.: Coun. for Wis. Writers (newsletter editor), Wis. Regional Writers, Wis. Fellowship Poets (bd. mem. 1951—, newsletter editor), Nat. Fedn. Press Women, Wis. Press Women (treas. 2000—, newsletter editor). Avocations: travel, remodeling houses, art, sewing, exploring nature. Home: 1950 Georgia St Oshkosh WI 54902

ALDERSON, MARJORIE JEAN, healthcare administrator, nurse; b. St. Louis, Jan. 27, 1947; d. Claude Jr. Hawkins and Doris Jean Philips; m. Philip Otis Alderson, Jun. 13, 1970; children: Kelly, Lisa. BS Nursing summa cum laude, St. Louis U., 1971, MS Nursing, 1972; MPH, Columbia U., 1991. RN, Mo., N.J., N.Y. Staff nurse Barnes Hosp., St. Louis, 1968-70, Firmin Des Loge Hosp., St. Louis, 1970-72; clin. specialist St. Louis VA Hosp., St. Louis, 1973-74; mgr. performance improvement Montefiore Med. Ctr., N.Y.C., 1991-96; dir. quality mgmt. Mt. Sinai Faculty Practice, N.Y.C., 1996-2000; asst. dir. med. quality N.Y.C. Adminstrn. for Children's Svcs., 2000—. Mem. N.Y. Assn. Healthcare Quality (pres. 1998-2000), N.Y. Assn. Ambulatory Care, Na t. Assn. Healthcare Quality (bd. dirs. 2000-02, govt. rels. com.), Am. Coll. Medical Quality, N.Y. Assn. Health Planning, Med. Group Mgmt. Assn. Avocations: reading, travel. Home: 211 Highland Ave Ridgewood NJ 07450-4003 Office: NYC Adminstrn for Children's Svcs Divsn Med Planning 150 William St 14 Fl New York NY 10038 E-mail: marjalderson@hotmail.com

ALDERSON, PHILIP OTIS, radiologist, educator; b. San Francisco, Aug. 11, 1944; s. Lloyd I. and Helen A. (Boekemeier); m. Marjorie Jean Hawkins, June 13, 1970; children: Kelly Suzanne, Lisa Joanne. AB in Zoology, Washington U., St. Louis, 1966, MD, 1970. Cert. Diplomate Am. Bd. Nuclear Medicine, Am. Bd. Radiology (Diagnosis). Intern Jewish Hosp., Washington U. Med. Sch., St. Louis, 1970-71, resident in radiology and nuclear medicine, 1971-74; instr. in radiology Mallinckrodt Inst., Washington U. Med. Sch., St. Louis, 1974-75; from asst. to assoc. prof. dept. radiology Johns Hopkins Med. Inst., Balt., 1977-80; prof. radiology Columbia-Presbyn. Med. Ctr., N.Y.C., 1980—, James Picker prof., chmn. dept. radiology, 1990—. Trustee Am. Bd. Radiology, 1998—, sec.-treas., 2002—; trustee Am. Bd. Nuc. Medicine, 1989—95. Author 4 books; contbr. articles to profl. jours. Maj. USAF, 1975—77. Recipient Alumni Achievement award, Washington U. Med. Sch., 1995; grantee, NIH, 1974—2001. Fellow: AAAS, Am. Inst. Med. and Biol. Engrs., N.Y. Acad. Medicine, Am. Coll. Radiology (bd. chancellors 1993—2000, v.p. 1999—2000), Am. Coll. Nuclear Physicians; mem.: Soc. Chmn. Acad. Radiology Depts. (rep. Coun. Acad. Socs. of Am. Assn. Med. Colls. 1990—95, pres. 1994—95), Acad. Radiology Rsch. (sec. 1998—99, v.p. 1999—2001, pres. 2001—), Am. Roentgen Ray Soc. (chmn. exec. coun. 1997—98), Assn. Residency Program Dirs. in Radiology (sec.-treas. 1996—97, pres. 1998—99), Assn. Univ. Radiologists (sec.-treas. 1994—95, pres. 1996—97), Soc. Nuclear Medicine (v.p. 1984—85, chmn. sci. program com. 1984—86), N.Y. State Radiol. Soc. (sec.-treas. 1991—93, pres. 1993—94), N.Y. City Roentgen Soc. (v.p. 1989—90, pres. 1991—92), Fleischner Soc. (sec. 1989—92, treas. 1996—99, pres. 2000—01), Omicron Delta Kappa. Office: Columbia-Presbyn Med Ctr Dept Radiology 630 W 168th St New York NY 10032-3702 E-mail: poa1@columbia.edu.

ALDINGER, WILLIAM F., III, diversified financial services company executive; b. 1947; BA, CUNY, 1969. With U.S. Trust Co., N.Y.C., 1969-75, Citibank Corp., N.Y.C., 1975-76; exec. v.p. Wells Fargo Bank NA, San Francisco, 1986-98; CEO Household Internat., Inc., Prospect Heights, Ill., 1994—, chmn. bd. dirs., 1996—. Office: Household Internat 2700 Sanders Rd Prospect Heights IL 60070-2701

ALDISERT, RUGGERO JOHN, judge; b. Carnegie, Pa., Nov. 10, 1919; s. John S. and Elizabeth (Magnacca) Aldisert; m. Agatha Maria DeLacio, Oct. 4, 1952; children: Lisa Maria, Robert, Gregory. BA, U. Pitts., 1941, JD, 1947. Bar: Pa. 1947. Gen. practice law, Pitts., 1947—61; judge Ct. Common Pleas, Allegheny County, 1961—68, U.S. Ct. Appeals (3d cir.), Pitts., 1968—84, chief judge, 1984—87, sr. judge Pitts., Santa Barbara, Calif., 1987—. Adj. prof. law U. Pitts. Sch. Law, 1964—87; faculty Appellate Judges Seminar, NYU, 1971—85, assoc. dir., 1979—85; chmn. Fed. Appellate Judges Seminar, 1972—78; mem. Pa. Civil Procedural Rules Com., 1965—84, Jud. Conf. Com. on Adminstrn. Criminal Law, 1971—77; chmn. adv. com. on bankruptcy rules Jud. Conf. U.S., 1979—84; vis. prof. univs. in U.S. and abroad, 1965—99; intensive lectures at univs in, Italy, Germany, France, Poland, Croatia and Serbia. Author: Il Ritorno al Paese, 1966—67, The Judicial Process, Readings, Materials and Cases, 1996, 2d edit., 1996, Logic for Lawyers: A Guide to Clear Legal Thinking, 1997, 3d edit., 1997, Opinion Writing, 1990, Winning on Appeal, 1999; contbr. over 30 articles to profl. publs. Allegheny dist. chmn. Multiple Sclerosis Soc., 1961—68; pres. ISDA, Cultural Heritage Found., 1965—68; trustee U. Pitts., 1968—; mem. bd. visitors Pitts. Sch. Law, 1968—, chmn., 1969—99. Maj. reserves USMC, 1942—46. Recipient Outstanding Merit award, Allegheny County Acad. Trial Lawyers, 1964. Mem.: Am. Law Inst., Italian Sons and Daus. Am. Fraternal Assn. (nat. pres. 1960—68), Omicron Delta Kappa, Phi Alpha Delta, Phi Beta Kappa. Democrat. Roman Catholic. Office: US Ct Appeals 120 Cremona Dr Ste D Santa Barbara CA 93117-5511

ALDONAS, GRANT D. federal agency administrator; b. Mpls. m. Pam Olson; children: Nicole, Kirsten, Noah. BA in Internat. Rels., U. Minn., 1975, JD, 1979. Spl. asst. Under Sec. of State for Econ. Affairs; dir. South Am. and Caribbean Affairs Office of the U.S. Trade Rep.; ptnr. Miller & Chevalier, Washington; chief internat. trade counsel Chmn. of the Senate Fin. Com.; under sec. for internat. trade adminstrn. Dept. Commerce, Washington, 2001—. Adj. prof. law Georgetown U. Law Ctr.; counsel Bipartisan Commn. on Entitlement and Tax Reform; adviser Commn. on U.S.-Pacific Trade and Investment. Mem.: ABA (chair task force on multilateral investment agreements, vice chair com. on trade and fgn. investment sect. internal law and pr). Office: Dept Commerce Internat Trade Adminstrn 14th & Constitution Ave NW Washington DC 20230

AL-DOURI, TAHA A. architect, educator; b. Baghdad, Iraq, Jan. 13, 1969; arrived in U.S., 1992; s. Abdul-Aziz Abdul-Karim Al-Douri and Rajiha Amin Abdul-Ghafur. BArch, Jordan U., Amman, 1992; MSc in Arch., Pa. State U., 1994; PhD in Arch., U. Pa., 2000. Tchg. asst. Pa. State U., State College, 1993—94; from rsch. asst. to prof. U. Pa., Phila., 1995—2000, prof., 2000—; architect Perkins Eastman Architects, N.Y.C., 1998—2002. Adj. asst. prof. N.Y. Inst. Tech., N.Y.C., 2002—. Published in book, Portfolio Design, 1996. Recipient Hon. Mention for Vassar-Brothers Ctr. for Cancer, Contract Mag. Healthcare, 2002. Avocations: reading, painting, writing, music, sports. Home: 216 Seventh Ave Apt 2H New York NE 10011 Office: New York Inst Tech PO Box 8000 Old Westbury NY

ALDOVER-AYON, MARTA, critical care nurse; b. Batangas City, Philippines, Jan. 19, 1951; d. Aurelio T. and Vicenta C. (Espino) Aldover; m. Lucito P. Ayon, Mar. 31, 1984; children: Oliver, April. BSN, Pamantasan ng Lungsod ng Maynila, Manila, Philippines, 1972. RN, Pa., N.J.; cert. critical care nurse, basic cardiac life support, instr. advanced cardiac life support. Staff nurse Bapt. Med. Ctr., Little Rock; charge nurse Parkview Hosp., Phila., 1975-77; clin. nurse II, advanced staff nurse, clin. staff nurse III Thomas Jefferson U. Hosp., Phila., 1977-88; adminstrn. nursing supr. Thomas Jefferson Univ. Hosp., Phila., 1988—. Recipient Full Scholarship, 1967-72, Outstanding Staff Nurse award, 1987. Mem. Am. Assn. Critical Care Nurses. Home: 12 Knoll Ct Sewell NJ 08080-3218

ALDREDGE, THEONI VACHLIOTIS, costume designer; b. Athens, Greec Aug. 22, 1932; d. Gen. Athanasios and Meropi (Gregoriades) Vachliotis; m Thomas E. Aldredge, Dec. 10, 1953. Student, Am. Sch., Athens, 1949-5 Goodman Theatre, Chgo.; LHD, De Paul U., 1985. Mem. design staff Goodma Theatre, 1951-53; head designer N.Y. Shakespeare Festival, 1962—. Designe numerous Broadway and off Broadway shows, ballet, opera, TV spls.; film include Girl of the Night, You're a Big Boy Now, No Way to Treat a Lad Uptight, Last Summer, I Never Sang for My Father, Promise at Dawn, Th Great Gatsby (Brit. Motion Picture Acad. award 1976), Network, The Chea Detective, The Fury, The Eyes of Laura Mars (Acad. Sci. Fiction Films award The Champ, Semi-Tough, The Rose, Monsignor, Annie, Ghostbusters, Moor struck, We're No Angels, Stanley and Iris, Other People's Money, Night and th City, Addams Family Values, Milk Money, Mrs. Winterbourne, The Mirror Ha Two Faces, The First Wives Club; over 100 Broadway shows include A Chorı Line (Theatre World award 1976), Annie (Tony award 1977), Barnum (Ton award 1979), Dream Girls, Woman of the Year, Onward Victoria, La Cage Au Folles (Tony award 1984), 42d Street, A Little Family Business, Merlin, Priva Lives, The Corn Is Green, The Rink, Blithe Spirit, Chess, Gypsy (1989 revival Oh, Kay, The Secret Garden, Nick and Nora, High Rollers, Putting It Togethe Annie Warbucks, The Flowering Peach, School for Scandal, Taking Sides, Th Three Sisters, St. Louis Woman, The Best Man, "EFX" MGM Grand, Follie 2001 Revival. Recipient Obie award for Disting. Svc. to Off-Broadway Theat Village Voice, Maharam award for Peer Gynt, N.Y.C. Liberty medal, 198 Career Achievement award Costume Designers Guild, 2000, DePaul U., 199 TDF Irene Sharaff Lifetime Achievement award, 2002, numerous Drama Des and Critic awards; inducted into Theatre Hall of Fame. Mem. United Scen Artists, Costume Designers Guild, Acad. Motion Picture Arts Scis. (Osca award Great Gatsby 1975)

ALDRICH, DAVID ALAN, accountant, consultant; b. West Haven, Conn Jan. 14, 1958; s. Harold and Janet (Candia) A. BS in Fin. Acctg., U. New Have 1980; BS in Profl. Acctg., Tampa Coll., 1990. CPA, Fla.; cert. bus. mgr. Ass Profls. in Bus. Mgmt., 2002. Acct. State Nat. Bank of Conn., Bridgepor 1981-82, Coordinated Benefit Plans Inc., Tampa, Fla., 1984-85, N.Am. Tele phone, Tampa, 1986; acctg. mgr. Coordinated Benefit Plans Inc., Tampa 1987-90; sr. acct. EPIX Inc. (formerly Payroll Transfers, Inc.), Tampa 1991—2001; cons. in acctg. to clients in employee leasing industry, 2002– Mem. AICPA, Fla. Inst. CPAs. Home and Office: 7311 Baja Ct Tampa FL 3363

ALDRICH, DAVID LAWRENCE, public relations executive; b. Lakehurs Naval Air Sta., N.J., Feb. 21, 1948; s. Clarence Edward and Sarah Stile (Andrews) A.; m. Benita Susan Massler, Mar. 17, 1974. BA in Communication Calif. State U.-Dominguez Hills, 1976. Pub. info. technician City of Carso (Calif.), 1973-77; pub. rels. dir./adminstrv. asst. Calif. Fed. Savs., L.A 1977-78; v.p., group supr. Hill & Knowlton, L.A., 1978-81; v.p., mgr. Ayer Pu Rels. western div. N.W. Ayer, L.A., 1981-84; pres. Aldrich and Assocs. Inc L.A., 1984—. Bd. dirs. Blue Devils Concord (Calif.). Mayor's task force fo strategic planning Long Beach; docent Long Beach Aquarium of the Pacific; bo govs. Theatre League Alliance of L.A., vice chmn. Home: 25 15th Pl # 70 Long Beach CA 90802 Office: Aldrich & Assocs 65 Pine Ave #320 Long Beac CA 90802 E-mail: larry@aldrichpr.com.

ALDRICH, FRANK NATHAN, banker; b. Jackson, Mich., June 8, 1923; s Frank Nathan and Marion (Butterfield) A.; m. Edna Dora DeJan, Nov. 21, 195 children: Marion Dolores, Clinton Pershing. Student, U. Md., summer 1943; A in Govt, Dartmouth Coll., 1948; postgrad., Harvard U., summer 1948. Sub-mg First Nat. Bank of Boston, Havana, Cuba, 1949-60, Rio de Janeiro, 1961-6 Sao Paulo, Brazil, 1963-64, mgr., 1965, exec. mgr. Rio de Janeiro, 1966, v. Brazilian brs., 1966-69, v.p. overseas ops. Boston, 1969-70; v.p. Latin Am Asia-Africa-Middle East div., Boston, 1970-73; sr. v.p. Latin Am. div., Bosto 1973-88; 96pres., CEO McLaughlin Bank N.V., Netherlands Antilles, 198 CEO Amicorp N.V., Netherlands Antilles, 1996—. Dir. Paradigm Fin. Svcs Netherlands Antilles; prin. Mitan Capital Corp., N.Y.C. Trustee Pan Am. Deve Found., Washington. With USAAF, 1943-46. Decorated Air medal with 4 oa leaf clusters, D.F.C. U.S.; Medalha Marechal Candido Mariano da Silv Rondon (Brazil); Ordem Nacional do Cruzeiro do Sul (Brazil). Fellow Bri Interplanetary Soc.; mem. Air Force Assn., Res. Officers Assn., Confederate A Force, Inst. Navigation, Royal Astron. Soc. Can., Soc. of the Cin., Sphinx Soc Vets of Battle of the Bulge, Squadron A Assn. of N.Y., Disting. Flying Cros Soc., Harvard Club (Boston), Dartmouth Coll. Club, Yale Club (N.Y.C.), Arm and Navy Club (Washington), Wellesley (Mass.), Country Club, Wellesley Col Club, Masons, Shriners., Beta Theta Pi. Home: 3 Indian Spring Rd Dover M 02030-2331

ALDRICH, FRANKLIN DALTON, research physician; b. Detroit, Jan. 2 1929; s. George Franklin and Ruth Markham (Dalton) A.; m. Margaret Joa Pearson, Mar. 22, 1952; children: Allison R., Janet D., George P.; m. Gertrud Suydam Melsom, Mar. 24, 1984. BS, Mich. State U., 1950; MA, Oreg. State U 1953, PhD, 1954; MD, Case Western Res. U., 1962. Diplomate Am. Bd. Me Toxicology. Intern U. Iowa Hosps., Iowa City, 1962-63; fellow in medicine U Colo., Denver, 1964-65; resident and chief resident Lemuel Shattuck Hosp Boston, 1969-71; physician Colo. Dept. Pub. Health, Denver, 1966-69; ass med. dir. MIT, Cambridge, 1971-76; med. dir. Climax (Colo.) Molybdenu Co., 1976-77; health effects research mgr. IBM, Boulder, Colo., 1977-92, ret 1992; cons. Boulder, 1992—. Mem. com. mil. environ. rsch. Nat. Acad. Scis 1976-80; mem. toxicology adv. com. U.S. Consumer Product Safety Com 1982-85; clin. assoc. prof. medicine U. Colo. Health Scis. Ctr., Denver. Contb articles to profl. jours. Served with AUS, 1954-56. Case Meml. scholar, Mich State U., 1948. Fellow ACP (Mead Johnson resident scholar 1970), Am. Acad Clin. Toxicology (pres. 1980-82). Avocations: fishing, amateur radio.

ALDRICH, GEORGE HOOVER, judge, arbitrator; b. St. Louis, Feb. 2 1932; s. Emmett Porter and Hettie Barbara (Hoover) A.; m. Rosemary Margare Balmforth Aldrich, June 6, 1959; children: Edward, Stephen, Robert. BA DePauw U., 1954; LLB, Harvard Law Sch., 1957, LLM, 1958. Bar: Ind., 1958 Atty. Dept. Navy, Washington, 1959-60, Dept. Def., Washington, 1960-63; lega adv. U.S. Delegation to NATO, Paris, 1963-65; asst. legal adv. Dept. State Washington, 1965-69, deputy legal adv., 1969-77, amb., deputy spl. rep. t pres., 1977-81; judge Iran-U.S. Claims Tribunal, The Hague, The Netherlands 1981—; commr. Eritrea-Ethiopia Claims Commn, The Hague, The Netherlands 2001—. U.S. amb. for Laws of War Negotiations, Geneva, Switzerland 1974-77; mem. UN Internat. Law Commn., Geneva, Switzerland, 1981; bd editors Am. Jour. Internat. Law, 1987—; prof. Leiden U., The Netherlands 1990-97; comr. Eritrea-Ethiopia Claims Commn., The Hague, The Netherlands 2001—. Author: The Jurisprudence of the Iran-United States Claims Tribunal 1996; author, negotiator: The Protocols to the 1973 Vietnam Peace Agreement. contbr. articles to profl. jours. Pres. Exec. com. of Am. Sch. of The hague 1987-88. Named Disting. Sr. Exec. President Carter, 1980. Mem. Coun. on Fgn Rels., Am. Soc. Internat. Law, Internat. Inst. Humanitarian Law. Avocations tennis, sailing. Home: 24389 Oakwood Park Rd Saint Michaels MD 21663 2543 Office: Iran-US Claims Trib Parkweg 13 2585 JH The Hague Netherland E-mail: GAldrich@compuserve.com.

ALDRICH, JOHN HERBERT, political science educator; b. Pitts., Sept. 24 1947; s. Herbert Canon and Ruth Eleanor (Taggart) A.; m. Cynthia Kay Aldrich June 13, 1970; 1 child, David Shawn BA, Allegheny Coll., 1969; MA, U Rochester, 1971, PhD, 1975. Asst. prof. polit. sci. Mich. State U., East Lansing 1974-78, assoc. prof., 1978-81; assoc. prof. polit. sci. U. Minn., Mpls., 1981-83 prof., 1983-87, Duke U., Durham, NC, 1987—, chmn. dept. polit. sci. 1992—96, 1999—2000, Pfizer-Pratt univ. prof., 1997—. Vis. prof. Harvard U. 1996-97. Co-author: Change and Continuity in the 1980 Elections, 1982, rev edit., 1983, Change and Continuity in the 1984 Elections, 1986, rev. edit., 1987 Change and Continuity in the 1988 elections, 1990, rev. edit., 1991, Change an Continuity in the 1992 Elections, 1994, rev. edit., 1995, Change and Continuin in the 1996 Elections, 1997, Change and Continuity in the 1996 and 199 Elections, 1999, Change and Continuity in the 2000 and 2002 Elections; author Before the Convention, 1980, Why Parties?, 1995; co-editor: Am. Jour. Poli Sci., 1985-87; contbr. articles to profl. jours. Served with U.S. Army, 1970-72 Vietnam Ctr. for Advanced Study in Behavioral Scis. fellow, 1989-90; NS rsch. grantee, 1977-79, 81-87; NEH teaching grantee, 1977-79; resident fello Rockefeller Found., 2002. Fellow: Am. Acad. Arts and Scis.; mem.: So. Poli Sci. Assn. (rec. sec. 1992—93, v.p. 1995—96, pres. 1998—99, Pi Sigma Alph

award 1997), Am. Polit. Sci. Assn. (sec. 1993—94, Eulau prize 1990, Kammerer prize 1996, CQ Press award 1996). Office: Duke U Dept Polit Sci Durham NC 27708 E-mail: aldrich@duke.edu.

ALDRICH, LOVELL W(ELD), lawyer; b. Port Chester, N.Y., Dec. 21, 1942; s. Laurence Weld and Leota A.; m. Sharon King, Aug. 20, 1966; children: Molly Colleen, Abigail Elizabeth. BBA in Fin., Tex. A&M U., 1965; JD, St. Mary's U., San Antonio, 1968. Bar: Tex. 1968, U.S. Dist. Ct. (so. dist.) Tex. 1971, U.S. Dist. Ct. (ea. dist.) Tex. 1980, U.S. Ct. Appeals (5th cir.) 1981. Assoc. Law Office of Fred Parks, Houston, 1970-72, Lloyd & Hoppess, Houston, 1972-75; pvt. practice Houston, 1975-78; ptnr. Aldrich & Buttrill, Houston, 1978-81, Aldrich, Buttrill & Kuhn, Houston, 1981-87, Lovell W. Aldrich & Assocs., A Profl. Legal Corp., Houston, 1987-98; pvt. practice Sugar Land, Tex., 1998—. Capt. U.S. Army, 1968-70, Vietnam. Mem. Tex. Bar Assn., Am. Bd. Trial Advs. Episcopalian. Avocations: travel, golf, photography, reading. Home and Office: Lovell W Aldrich PC 1007 Horseshoe Dr Sugar Land TX 77478-0377

ALDRICH, MICHAEL RAY, library curator, health educator; b. Vermillion, S.D., Feb. 7, 1942; s. Ray J. and Lucile W. (Hamm) A.; m. Michelle Cauble, Dec. 26, 1977. AB, Princeton U., 1964; MA, U. S.D., 1965, PhD, SUNY, 1970. Fulbright tutor Govt. Arts and Commerce Coll., Indore, India, 1965-66; founder Lemar Internat., 1966-71; mem. faculty Sch. Critical Studies Calif. Inst. Arts, Valencia, 1970-72; curator Fitz Hugh Ludlow Meml. Libr., San Francisco, 1974—. Cons. Commn. of Inquiry into Non-Med Use of Drugs, Ottawa, Ont., 1973; rsch. aide select com. on control marijuana Calif. Senate, 1974; mem. Princeton working group Future of Drug Policy, 1990—93; asst. dir. Nat. Inst. on Drug Abuse AIDS Project Menu, Youth Environment Study, San Francisco, 1987—88; project adminstr. YES Tng. Ctr., 1989; program. coord. Calif. AIDS Intervention Tng. Ctr. Inst. for Cmty. Health Outreach, 1990—2001; bd. dirs. Calif. Helping Alleviate Med. Problems (CHAMP), 1997, exec. dir., 2001—02; cons. on drug rsch., sociolegal reform specializing in drug laws and history various colls., drug confs., publishers, svc. groups; freelance writer, photographer; lectr. in field. Author: The Dope Chronicles 1850-1950, 1979, Coricancha, The Golden Enclosure, 1983; co-author: High Times Ency. of Recreational Drugs, 1978, Fiscal Costs of California Marijuana Law Enforcement, 1986, YES Tng. Manual, 1989, Methods of Estimating Needle Users at Risk for AIDS, 1990; editor: Marijuana Rev., 1968-74, Ludlow Libr. Newsletter, 1974-81; contbg. author: Cocaine Handbook, 1981, 2d edit., 1987, Cannabis in Medical Practice, 1997; mem. editl. rev. bd. Jour. Psychoactive Drugs, 1981—, marijuana theme issue editor, 1988; rsch. photographer Life mag., 1984; contbg. editor High Times, 1979-85; contbr. articles to prfl. publs. Office: PO Box 640346 San Francisco CA 94164-0346

ALDRICH, NANCY COOK, engineer, administrator; b. Ogden, Utah, Oct. 16, 1944; d. William Burford and Margaret (Spilker) Cook; m. Ralph E. Aldrich, Aug. 10, 1968. BA in Physics, Scripps Coll., 1966; MS in Physics, Tufts U., 1969. Physicist Naval Underwater Weapons Sta., Newport, R.I., 1966; engr. Microwave Assn., Burlington, Mass., 1967; assoc. engr. Honeywell Electro Optics (formerly Honeywell Radiation Ctr.) div. Honeywell Corp., Lexington, Mass., 1969-70, engr., 1970-71, sr. engr, 1971-72, prin. engr., 1972-75, sr. prin. engr., 1975-78, program mgr., 1978-81, bus. mgr., 1981-82, engring. mgr., 1982-84, sect. head, 1984-86; chief engr. Honeywell Electro Optics (formerly Honeywell Radiation Ctr.) div. Honeywell Corp. (name now Loral Infrared and Imaging Systems), Lexington, Mass., 1986—. Leader Girl Scouts U.S., Acton, Mass., 1972. Recipient Ed Lund Mgmt. award, 1987; named Disting. Alumna Scripps Coll., 1984. Mem. Profl. Council. Avocations: flying, wildlife photography, fly fishing. Office: Electro-Optics div Honeywell Corp 2 Forbes Rd Lexington MA 02421-7306

ALDRICH, PATRICIA ANNE RICHARDSON, retired magazine editor; b. St. Paul, Apr. 6, 1926; d. James Calvin and Anna Catherine (Eskra) Richardson; m. Edwin Chauncey Aldrich, July 31, 1948; 1 son, Mason Calvin. Student, Stout Inst., 1944-45; BS in Journalism; scholar, Northwestern U., 1948. Editor Child's World News, The Child's World, Inc., Chgo., 1952-57; assoc. editor Home Life mag. Advt. Div., Inc., Chgo., 1957-71, editor, 1971-90, ret., 1990; pres. Aldrich Enterprises, Inc., Chgo. Mem. steering com., publicity chmn. Evanston Urban League, 1961-64. Democrat.

ALDRICH, RICHARD JOHN, agronomist, educator; b. Fairgrove, Mich., Apr. 16, 1925; s. George and Eva Ann (Misner) A.; m. June Ellen Ellison, Apr. 5, 1943; children: Judith Allman, Sharon, Jeffrey. BS, Mich. State U., 1948; PhD, Ohio State U., 1950. Agronomist U.S. Dept. Agr., Rutgers U., New Brunswick, N.J., 1950-57; asst. dir. Agr. Exptl. Sta., Mich. State U., East Lansing, 1957-64; assoc. dir., dean agr. exptl. sta. U. Mo., Columbia, 1964-76; adminstr. CSRS, U.S. Dept. Agr., Washington, 1976-78; prof. agronomy U. Mo., Columbia, 1978-81; research agronomist, prof. SEA-ARS, Dept. Agr.-U. Mo., 1981-87; ret., 1987. Cons. OTA, U.S. Congress, 1979, The Standard Oil Co., 1983; mem. adv. com. Fed. Assistance Rev., 1970-71; pres. Agr. Research Inst., 1974-75 Author: Weed Crop Ecology, 1983; co-author: Principles in Weed Management, rev. edit., 1997; editor: Weed Sci. Jour., 1989-94; contbr. articles to profl. jours. Served to 1st lt. USAAF, 1943-46. Fellow AAAS, Weed Sci. Soc. Am.; mem. Am. Soc. Agronomy (dir. 1949-50), Agrl. Research Inst. (pres. 1974-75), Nat. Assn. State Univs. and Land Grant Colls. Home: PO Box 236 Marcell MN 56657-0236 also: 2663 S Fade Dr Green Valley AZ 85614-1151

ALDRICH, RICHARD KINGSLEY, lawyer; b. Denver, Dec. 31, 1943; s. Harold Eugene and Mary Frances (Kingsley) A.; m. Katherine Ann Kirwan, Sept. 26, 1970; children: Amy Marie Aldrich McAffee, Lori Ann Aldrich Selwyn, Sara Kathleen. Student, Tex. Tech. U., 1962-64; BA in History, U. Mont., 1966, JD, 1969. Bar: Mont. 1969, U.S. Dist. Ct. Mont. 1969. Staff atty. Office of Field Solicitor, Dept. of Interior, Billings, Mont., 1969-85, field solicitor, supervising atty., 1985—. Bd. dirs. Billings Pub. Edn. Found., 1992-97, Mont. State U. Parent Assn., Bozeman, 1993-96, Billings Sr. Bronc Booster Club; bd. dirs., pres. Billings Sr. High Parent Adv., 1991-95. Recipient cert. of appreciation, U.S. Dept. Justice, Nat. Park Svc. and U.S. Fish and Wildlife Svc., 1994, 96, Dept. of Interior Meritorious award, 1998. Mem. ABA (spkr. panel presentation 1997, 2001, natural resources sect., environment and energy law sect., Indian law sect., sr. lawyers divsn.), Mont. State Bar, Yellowstone County Bar, Phi Delta Phi, Sigma Nu. Avocations: long distance running, skiing, fly fishing, hiking, reading. Office: Dept of Interior Office of Field Solicitor 316 N 26th St Ste 3005 Billings MT 59101-1373

ALDRICH, ROBERT ADAMS, agricultural engineer, consultant; b. Veteran Twp., N.Y., Apr. 25, 1924; s. Luman Woodbridge and Mabel Hastings (Gibbs) A.; m. Roberta Ann Bowlby, Aug. 27, 1946; children— Susan Carol, Gail Jessica, Kathleen Lois, Margaret Louise. BS in Agrl. Engring, Wash. State U., 1950, MS, 1952; PhD, Mich. State U., 1958. Instr., then asso. prof. agrl. engring. Wash. State U., 1951-58; asso. prof. U. Ky., 1958-59, Mich. State U., 1959-62; asso. prof., then prof. Pa. State U., 1962-79; prof. agrl. engring., head dept. U. Conn., Storrs, 1979-88, prof. dept. nat. rsch., mgmt. and engring., 1988-89, ret., 1989; prin. Aldrich Engring., Mansfield Center, Conn., 1989—. Author papers in field. Served with C.E. AUS, 1942-46. Mem. Am. Soc. Agrl. Engrs., Nat. Soc. Profl. Engrs. Home: 72 Tressler Blvd Lewisburg PA 17837-1033

ALDRICH, SUSAN MILLER, entrepreneur; b. Chgo. m. Adrian A. Aldrich; children: Arlyn, Daryl. BA, DePaul U., 1981. Lic. real estate broker, Ill. Mgr. tech. support Spiegel, Inc., Chgo., 1962-71; mgr. computer planning and controls Internat. Minerals and Chemistry, Mundelein, Ill., 1974-78; pres. Adrian Aldrich & Sons, Lincolnshire, Ill., 1976—; pres., broker Aldrich Properties, Lincolnshire, 1985—; pres. Design Innovations, Lincolnshire, 1994—; designer, builder USN Lone Sailor Meml., Great Lakes, Ill., 1997. Mem. computer planning, contingency planning adv. bd. Guide Internat., 1974-78; pvt. practice computer cons., 1978-84. Charter pres. Bus. and Profl. Women Lake County, 1985-87 (Outstanding Working Woman Ill. 1998, Woman of Achievement award 1997); co-chmn. Com. to Re-elect Barbara Richardson Coroner of Lake County, Ill., 1988-2002; bd. dirs. Lake County Coun. Against Sexual Assault, 1988—, v.p., 1993-95, pres., 1995-2003, exec. com. 1992—; bd. dirs. YWCA of Lake County, 1988-95; bd. dirs. No. Ill. Coun. Against Alcohol and Substance Abuse, 1994-99; dream team vol. Camp-Make-A-Dream, Missoula, Mont., 1999. Recipient Woman of Achievement Entrepreneur award YWCA of Lake and McHenry Counties, 1998. Mem. AAUW, Women Interested in Govt. Avocations: theatre, art, architectural renovation, travel, photography. Office: Adrian Aldrich & Sons PO Box 538 Lincolnshire IL 60069-0538

ALDRICH, THOMAS ALBERT, former brewing executive, consultant; b. Rosebud, Tex., Nov. 30, 1923; s. John Albert and Georgia Opal (Hilliard) A.; m. Virginia Elaine Peterson, Mar. 1, 1944; children: Sharon Aldrich Lingis, Pamela Aldrich Williams, Thomas Charles. Student, Tex. A&M U., 1942-43, U. Chgo., 1943-44; BA in Math., George Washington U., 1961, MS in Bus. Adminstrn., 1968; student, Air War Coll., 1960-61. Commd. 2d lt. USAF, 1944, advanced through grades to maj. gen., 1974, pilot, meteorologist, 1943-57; dep. dir. air ops. Air Weather Svc., Washington, 1957-60; comdr. 57th Weather Reconnaissance Squadron, Melbourne, Australia, 1962-65; chief mil. employment div. Air Command and Staff Coll., 1965-68; dir. war plans Hdqrs. Mil. Airlift Command, Scott AFB, Ill., 1968-69; comdr. 9th Weather Reconnaissance Wing, McClellan AFB, Calif., 1969-70; vice comdr. USAF Air Weather Svc., Scott AFB, Ill., 1970-71, comdr., 1973-74, U.S. Forces Azores, Portugal, 1971-73; dep. chief of staff plans Hdqrs. Mil. Airlift Command, 1974-75; comdr. 22d Air Force, Travis AFB, Calif., 1975-78; ret., 1978; v.p., corp. rep. Anheuser-Busch Cos., Inc., Sacramento, 1978-94, ret., 1994. Decorated D.S.M., Legion of Merit with oak leaf cluster, Meritorious Service medal. Mem. Nat. Honor Soc., Brewers Inst., Calif. Mfrs. Assn. (chmn.), Calif. C. of C. (bd. dirs.), Air Force Acad. Falcon Found. (bd. dirs.), No. Calif. Ret. Officers Cmty. (vice chmn.), Phi Theta Kappa. Republican. Presbyterian. Home: 659 Lake Wilhaggin Dr Sacramento CA 95864-7226 E-mail: tomginnya@aol.com.

ALDRIDGE, ADRIENNE YINGLING, accountant, financial analyst; b. Hershey, Pa., June 10, 1959; d. Richard Terry Yingling and Dolores Jean (Ott) Brown. BA in Acctg. summa cum laude, N.C. State U., 1989. CPA, FLMI. Asst. mgr. Fast Fare, Raleigh, 1979—80; statis. analyst S.P.A.R., Elmsford, N.Y., 1980-81; relocation dir., sales assoc. Realty World, Cary, N.C., 1981-83; product mgr. Southeastern Electronics, Raleigh, 1983-84; results acct. No. Telecom, Rsch. Triangle Park, N.C., 1984-88; sr. auditor Deloitte & Touche, 1989-93; group contr. SPAR Mktg., Bloomington, Minn., 1994; pvt. practice, 1995; acctg. mgr. U. N.C. Physicians & Assocs., Chapel Hill, 1996-97, Progress Energy Svc Co, Raleigh, N.C., 1998—. Mem. AICPA, NCACPA, Phi Kappa Phi, Omicron Delta Epsilon. Avocations: photography, painting, physical fitness, travel, music. Office: PO Box 1551 PEB 4C4 411 Fayetteville St Raleigh NC 27602

ALDRIDGE, ALFRED OWEN, English language educator; b. Buffalo, Dec. 16, 1915; s. Albert and Jane (Ette) A.; m. Mary Hennen Dellinger, May 18, 1941 (div. 1956); 1 dau., Cecily (Mrs. John Ward); m. Adriana García Davila, June 7, 1963 (div. 1988). BS in Edn, Ind. U., 1937; MA, U. Ga., 1938; PhD, Duke U., 1942; D.U.P., U. Paris, France, 1955. Prof. comparative lit. U. Buffalo, 1942-47, U. Md., 1947-67, U. Ill., 1967-86, prof. emeritus, 1986—; Will and Ariel Durant chair St. Peter's Coll., Jersey City, 1986-87; prof. comp. lit. Pa. State U., 1987-88. Fulbright prof., France, 1953, Korea, 1988; Smith-Mundt prof., Brazil, 1957; vis. prof. Nihon U., Japan, 1976, 82, Kuwait U., 1983, Nat. Cheng Chi U., Taiwan, 1989-90, Nat. Tsing Hua U., Taiwan, 1991. Author: Franklin and His French Contemporaries, 1957, Man of Reason: Life of Thomas Paine, 1959, Jonathan Edwards, 1964, Benjamin Franklin: Philosopher and Man, 1965, Benjamin Franklin and Nature's God, 1967, Comparative Literature: Matter and Method, 1969, The Ibero-American Enlightenment, 1971, Voltaire and the Century of Light, 1975, Hikaku Bungaku: Comparative Literature East and West, 1979, Early American Literature: A Comparatist Approach, 1982, Thomas Paine's American Ideology, 1984, Fiction in Japan and the West, 1985, The Reemergence of World Literature, 1986, The Dragon and the Eagle: China in the American Enlightenment, 1993; editor Jour. Comparative Lit. Studies, 1963—; adv. editor: 18th Century: Theory and Interpretation, Modern Age. NEH fellow 1973-74 Mem. Am. Comparative Lit. Assn. (adv. bd. 1965-71, 74-77, v.p. 1977-80, pres. 1980-83), Internat. Comparative Lit. Assn. (adv. bd. 1970-78), Am. Soc. 18th Century Studies (adv. bd. 1968-75) Home: 101 E Chalmers St Champaign IL 61820-6001 Office: U Ill Modern Lang Bldg Urbana IL 61801

ALDRIDGE, DAVID WILLIAM, biologist, educator; b. Honolulu, July 26, 1952; s. William Solon and Cleo Barbara Aldridge; m. Linda Rae Myers, Dec. 21, 1982; children: Stuart, Lindsay, Shelley. BS in Biology, U. Tex., Arlington, 1974, MA in Biology, 1976; PhD in Biology, Syracuse U., 1980. Prof. biology N.C. A&T State U., Greensboro, 1999—. Contbr. articles to profl. jours. Grantee, NSF, 1989—93, U.S. Army Rsch. Office, 1995—98. Mem.: Pub. Responsibility in Medicine and Rsch., Applied Rsch. Ethics Nat. Assn., Malacological Soc. London. Home: 1224 Old Hwy 75 Lexington NC 27292 Office: NC A&T State U Dept Biology Greensboro NC 27411 Office Fax: 336-334-7105. Personal E-mail: laldridge@lexcominc.net. Business E-Mail: davida@ncat.edu.

ALDRIDGE, DONALD O'NEAL, military officer; b. Solo., Mo., July 22, 1932; BA in History, U. Nebr., Omaha, 1974; postgrad., Creighton U., 1975. Commd. 2d lt. USAF, 1958, advanced through grades to lt. gen., 1988, asst. dir. plans, 1978-79; spl. asst. to dir. Joinr Chiefs of Staff, Washington, 1979-80; dep. dir. Def. Mapping Agy., Washington, 1980-81; dep. U.S. rep. NATO Mil. Com., Brussels, 1981-83; rep. Joint Chiefs of Staff, Geneva, 1983-86; comdr. 1st Strat. Aerospace Divsn. USAF, Vanderberg AFB, Calif., 1986-88, vice-CINC Strategic Air Command Offutt AFB, Nebr., 1988—91; mgmt. cons. Sacramento, 1991—. Chmn. bd. dir. Octus, Inc., 1995—98, Ceracon, Inc., 1996—. E-mail: daldridge@cox.net.

ALDRIDGE, EDWARD C., JR., federal agency administrator; b. Houston, Tex., Aug. 18, 1938; BS, Tex. A&M U., 1960; MS, Ga. Inst. Tech., 1962. Mgr. missile and space div. Douglas Aircraft Co., Santa Monica, Calif., 1962-67, Washington, 1962-67; dir. strategic def. div. Dept. Def., 1967-72, dep. asst. sec. for strategic programs, 1974-76; dir. planning and evaluation Office of Sec. Def., 1976-77; sr. mgr. LTV Aerospace Corp., Dallas, 1972-73; sr. mgmt. assoc. Office Mgmt. and Budget, Washington, 1973-74; v.p. Strategic Systems Group System Planning Corp., Arlington, Va., 1977-81, undersec. Dept. Air Force, 1981-86; sec. of Air Force, 1986-88; pres. McDonnell Douglas Electronic Systems Co., McLean, Va., 1988-92; pres., CEO Aerospace Corp., El Segundo, Calif., 1992—; under secy acquisition, tech. and logistics U.S. Dept. Defense, Washington, 2001—. Formerly advisor Strategic Arms Limitation Talks, Helsinki and Vienna Recipient George M. Low Space Transp. award AIAA, 1990. Office: US Dept Defense Acquisition, Tech and Logisitics 3010 Defense Pentagon Washington DC 20301-3010 Office Fax: 703-693-2576.

ALDRIDGE, JOHN, lawyer; b. Durham, N.C., Jan. 31, 1943; BA, Duke U., 1965; JD with honors, U. N.C., 1968. Bar: Ga. 1968, D.C. 1969. Mem. Long, Aldridge & Norman (now McKenna Long & Aldridge), Atlanta. Assoc. editor N.C. Law Rev., 1967-68. Mem. ABA, State Bar Ga., D.C. Bar, Atlanta Bar Assn., Lawyers Club Atlanta, Order of Coif. Office: Long Aldridge & Norman LLP One Peachtree Ctr 303 Peachtree St NE Ste 5300 Atlanta GA 30308-3264*

ALDRIDGE, JOHN WATSON, English language educator, author; b. Sioux City, Iowa, Sept. 26, 1922; s. Walter Copher and Nell (Watson) A.; m. Leslie Felker, Dec. 10, 1954 (div. June 1968); 1 son, Geoffrey; children by previous marriages: Henry, Stephen, Leslie, Jeremy; m. Alexandra Bertash, July 13, 1968 (div. Dec. 1982); m. Patricia McGuire Eby, July 16, 1983. Student, U. Chattanooga, 1940-43; fellow, Breadloaf Sch. English, summer 1942; BA, U. Calif.-Berkeley, 1947. Lectr. English U. Vt., 1948-50, asst. prof., 1950-53, 54-55; lectr. Christian Gauss Seminars Criticism, Princeton, N.J., 1953-54; mem. lit. faculty Sarah Lawrence Coll., also New Sch. Social Research, 1957; prof. English Queens Coll., 1957; Berg prof. English NYU, 1958; Fulbright lectr. U. Munich, Fed. Republic of Germany, 1958-59; writer-in-residence Hollins Coll., 1960-62; Fulbright lectr. U. Copenhagen, Denmark, 1962-63; prof. English U. Mich., 1964-91, prof. emeritus, 1991; book critic N.Y. Herald Tribune Book Week, 1965-66, Saturday Review, 1970-79. Staff Bread Loaf Writers Conf., 1966-69; chief regional judge Book-of-the Month Writing Fellowship Program, 1966-67; spl. adviser for Am. studies U.S. Embassy, Germany, 1972-73; spl. adviser for Authors Am. Sta. WETA, 1990—; book commentator McNeil/Lehrer News Hour, 1983-84. Author: After the Lost Generation, 1951, Critiques and Essays on Modern Fiction, 1952, In Search of Heresy, 1956, The Party at Cranton, 1960, Time to Murder and Create, 1966, In the Country of the Young, 1970, The Devil in the Fire, 1972, The American Novel and the Way We Live Now, 1983, Talents and Technicians, 1992, Classics and Contemporaries, 1992; also articles.; editor: Selected Stories by P.G. Wodehouse, 1958. Served with AUS, 1943-45, ETO. Decorated Bronze Star; Rockefeller Humanities fellow, 1976-77 Mem. Authors Guild and League of Am., MLA, Nat. Book Critics Circle, P.E.N. Home: 381 N Main St Madison GA 30650

ALDRIDGE, KENNETH WILLIAM, physician; b. Birmingham, Ala., June 6, 1955; s. Carlton William Jr. and Marie (Hinote) A.; m. Julie Suzanne Dukes, May 1, 1982; children: Callie Suzanne, Caroline Frances, Kenneth William, Jr. BS with honors, U. Ala., 1977, MD cum laude, 1981. Diplomate Am. Bd. Urology. Intern Med. U. of S.C., Charleston, 1981-82, resident in surgery, 1982-83; resident in urology U. Ala., Birmingham, 1983-86; ptnr. Urology Assocs. of Tuscaloosa, Ala., 1986—; chief of staff West Ala. Hosp., Tuscaloosa, 1992—. Clin. asst. prof. surgery and urology U. Ala. Coll. Cmty. Health Scis. Fellow ACS; mem. AMA, Med. Assn. State of Ala. (v.p. 1998, sec..-treas. 2000—, bd. sensors), Ala. Bd. Pub. Health, Ala. Bd. Med. Examiners, Tuscaloosa County Med. Soc. (sec.-treas. 1988-89, pres. 1992, chmn. bd. censors 1999). Office: Urology Assocs Tuscaloosa 701 University Blvd E Ste 908 Tuscaloosa AL 35401-7423

ALDRIDGE, MELVIN DAYNE, engineering educator; b. Crab Orchard, W.Va., July 20, 1941; s. William Bert and Gladys Revelle A.; m. Nancy L. Dickinson, June 6, 1963; children: Kenrick Lee, Randal Jay. BSEE with high honors, W.Va. U., 1963; MEE, U. Va., 1965, D of Elec. Engring., 1968. Registered profl. engr., W.Va. Electronic engr. NASA, 1963-68; from asst. prof. to assoc. prof. elec. engring. W.Va. U., Morgantown, 1968-76, prof., 1976-84; dir. Energy Rsch. Ctr., 1978-84; asst. dean for rsch. Auburn (Ala.) U., 1984-87, dir. engring. expt. sta., 1984-89, prof. elec. engring., 1984-89, acting dean coll. engring., 1987-88, assoc. dean for rsch., 1988-90, assoc. dean for cross-disciplinary programs, 1989-99, dir. ctr. for tech. mgmt., 1989-99; dean, prof. Mercer U., Macon, Ga., 1999—. Chmn., officer Engring. Accreditation Commn.; cons. tp pvt. and govtl. orgns. Contbr. articles to profl. publs. Thomas Walter Eminent scholar Auburn U., 1994-99; recipient Rufus A. West award, 1963; named Outstanding Young Engr. W.Va., 1977-78. Fellow IEEE (sr.), ASEE, Accreditation Bd. for Engring. and Tech. (officer); mem. Indsl. Applications Soc. of IEEE (officer). Baptist. Home: 669 River North Blvd Macon GA 31211-6333 Office: Macon U 1400 Coleman Ave Macon GA 31207-0001

ALDRIDGE, SANDRA, civic volunteer; b. Iowa, Apr. 22, 1939; d. Maurice D. and Maureen M. (Bennett) Anderson; m. Guy E. Seymour, Jan. 8, 1960 (div. Oct. 1966); m. Victor E. Aldridge, Jr., Nov. 11, 1970 (dec. May 1995); 1 child, Victor E. III. Student, Millikin U., Decatur, Ill., 1957-58. Pres. Crawford Sch. PTA, 1976-78, Terre Haute Lawyers Aux., 1979; pres., dir. Wabash Valley Assn. for Gifted and Talented Children, 1981-83, Vigo County Task Force for Alcohol and Drug Abuse, 1983-84; treas., dir. Union Hosp. Svc. League; bd. dirs. YWCA of Terre Haute, Inc., 1987-89; v.p., fin. chair, mem. exec. coun. Wabash Valley coun. Boy Scouts Am., Inc.; mem. Vigo County Tax Adjustment Bd., 1986-88; mem. Class IX Leadership Terre Haute, 1985; bd. trustees Vigo County Sch. Corp., Terre Haute, 1985-97, v.p., 1992-93, 96; sec. Ernie Pyle Chapíer, The Ret. Officers Assn., 1998-2000; active Children's Theatre, United Way of Wabash Valley. Mem. Ind. Assn. Gifted Children, Swope Art Gallery, Vigo County Hist. Soc., Women's Dept. Club, Arts Illiana, Elks Women's Golf League. Democrat. Episcopalian. Home: 2929 Winthrop Rd Terre Haute IN 47802-3443

ALDROW-LIPUT, PRISCILLA REESE, retired elementary education educator; b. Kingston, Pa., Apr. 10, 1951; d. Thomas Edward and Martha Mae (Hadsall) Reese; children: Colin Michael, Justin John; m. Willard C. Aldrow. BS, Bloomsburg State Coll., 1973. Cert. instructional II. Tchr. grade 5 Dallas (Pa.) Sch. Dist., ret., 2001; homebound tchr., pre-K-12 Williamsb urg-James City County Sch. Dist., Va. Homebound tchr. Williamsburg-James County Sch. Dist., Va. Mem. NEA, Pa. State Edn. Assn., Dallas Edn. Assn. Home: 109 Rondane Pl Williamsburg VA 23188 E-mail: aldrow@bznt.com.

AL-DUJAILI, JAMEEL SADEQ, microbiology educator, researcher; b. Kufa, Najaf, Iraq, Sept. 22, 1952; s. Sadeq Mahdee and Madarek Hiade Al-Dujaili; m. Halema M. Ali Hussain, Mar. 19, 1980; children: Zeena, Lena, Safa, Sadeg. PhD, W.Va. U., 1989. Postdoctoral rsch. assoc. W.Va. U., Morgantown, 1990-93; prof. La. State U., Eunice, 1993—. Author: Guide to Keep Food in Home Freezer, 1978; contbr. articles to profl. jours. Recipient award La. Edn. Quality Support Funds, 1997-98, grantee, 1997, 98, Endowed Professorship award in sci., 1998; La. Enhancement Quality Support Fund grantee, 1999. Mem. Am. Soc. Microbiology. Home: 104 Galvez Dr Lafayette LA 70506 Office: La State U-Eunice PO Box 1129 Eunice LA 70535 Fax: 337-546-6620. E-mail: jdujaili@lsue.edu.

ALEANDRI, EMELISE FRANCESCA, producer, director, television personality, actress; b. Riva del Garda, Italy; d. John Baptist and Elodia (Lutterotti) A. AB in French, Coll. of New Rochelle, N.Y.; MA in Theater, Hunter Coll., N.Y.C., 1975; MPhil in Theater, CUNY, 1976, PhD in Theater, 1983. Drama instr. N.Y.C. Tech. Coll., Bklyn., Hunter Coll., N.Y.C., Borough of Manhattan C.C., N.Y.C., Bennington (Vt.) Coll., NYU, N.Y.C.; dir. Ctr. Italian-Am. Studies, Bklyn. Coll.; prodr. and host Italics Mag. Show CUNY-TV, N.Y.C., 1987-97; dir., prodr. video documentaries TEATRO, 1995, FESTA, CUNY-TV, 1997; prodr., host specials Manhattan Neighborhood Network. Artistic dir. Frizzi Lazzi: Olde Time Italian-Am. Music & Theatre Co., 1994—. Actress (TV) Penguins and Peacocks, The Sopranos, Loving, Our Family Honor, One Life to Live, All My Children, Guiding Light, Internal Affairs, Tattingers, Eischeid, Donohue, Nurse, MTV, Another World, Equalizer, Mathnet, Law and Order, Law and Order: Special Victims Unit, America's Most Wanted, Ed, 7th Avenue, Wonderland, Sex and the City, The Italian Passion for Life, New Italian-American Writers; (films) Snooze, Searching for Paradise, The Yards, The Frequency, Summer of Sam, Mickey Blue Eyes; Isn't She Great, Crooklyn, Paper Blood, 1967, Sleepers, Godfather III, My New Gun, Age of Innocence, Teenage Mutant Ninja Turtles, Hejdran, Cookie, Married to the Mob, Jerky Boys, Moonstruck, Jumping Jack Flash, Car 54, Turk 182, All That Jazz, Ft. Apache-the Bronx, John and Yoko, Raging Bull, Danger Adrift, Regarding Henry, Anger Management, Smack in the Kisser, The World According to Garp, King of the Gypsies, Night of the Juggler, Defiance, Willie and Phil, Rooftops, Two Week's Notice, A Few Good Years, Nothing But the Dress; author: The Italian-American Immigrant Theatre of New York City, 1999, Little Italy, 2002; appeared in numerous radio programs, plays, concerts, musicals including Sweatshop, N.Y.C., Festa Primavera, Shhh!, Star Collector, Hobo Christmas, The Legend of La Betana, Italian Funerals and other Festive Occasions, Phila.; translator various plays from Italian to English; contbr. articles on theatre to profl. jours., chpts. to books; author: The Italian-IAmerican Immigratn Theatre of New York City, 1999, Little Italy, 2002. translator plays and adaptations: Women of Fortune, Shhhhh!, Satin Angels Revue, Raggedy Ann and Raggedy Andy, Not Every Thief Will Bring You Grief, My Italian Uncle, Lost Honor, The Legend of La Befana, The Good Italian Christmas Witch, Festa Primavera: A Night at Olde Turne Hall, The Dreambook Revue, The Cranky Baby, Carnevale at City Hall, The Birds; past gen. editor, past theater editor TV News Mag.; past editor The Manifesto; editor: Storia Vera Memorie del Passato, 1994; editor, contbg. editor Directory of Italian-American Actors, 1997; stage dir. numerous plays & musicals. Recipient Leone di San Marco award, Match Interactive award, Etta award, Elena Coraro Osia award, Italian Gov. Disting. Svc. award, Dist. Svc. award Govt. Italy, Leisure Time Assn. Handicapped award, cert. achievement N.Y. State Commn. Hist. Observances; NEA grantee Bklyn. Coll., CUNY, Ctr. for Italian-Am. Studies, Bklyn. Coll., InterCities Performing Arts, N.J., Immigration History Rsch. Ctr. U. Minn. Mem. AGVA (bd. dirs., regional v.p.), AFTRA, SAG, Pursuing Our Italian Names Together, Nat. Italian-Am. Found., Am. Fedn. Tchrs. (theatre com., Italian-Am. studies com.), Actors Equity Assn., Soc. Stage Dirs. and Choreographers, Ennica Caruso Mus. (adv. bd.), Italian Actors Union (past councillor, bd. dirs.), N.Y. Women in Film & TV, Am. Italian Hist. Assn. (N.Y. metro chpt. pres.), Ind. Feature Project, Profl. Staff Congress (CUNY), Coalition Italo-Am. Assns., Am.-Italian Cultural Roundtable (adv. bd.), N.Y. Hist. Soc., Order Sons Holy in Am. Fax: 212-769-2078.

ALEINIKOV, ANDREI GRIGORYEVICH, science administrator, researcher, consultant; b. Sverdlovsk, Russia, Mar. 13, 1948; arrived in U.S., 1992, naturalized, 2002; s. Grigory Stepanovich Aleinikov and Nina Ivanovna Aleinikova; m. Elena Nikolayevna Kohn, Jan. 8, 1948; 1 child, Andrei Aleinikov-Kohn. BA and M.Ed, State Pedagogic U., Volgograd, Russia, 1967—72; PhD in Linguistics, State U., Tbilisi, Georgia, 1983; DSc, Mil. U., Moscow, 1992; postgrad., USAF Air War Coll., 1992—93. H.S. tchr. English and German, Volgograd, Russia; asst. prof., then assoc. prof. Mil. U., Moscow, 1984—92; lectr. in edn. Ctr. for Creative Rsch. Russian Acad. Scis., Moscow, 1989—92; adj. instr. Troy State U., Montgomery, Ala., 1994—; pres. Mega-Innovative Mind Internat. Inst., Montgomery, 1995—. Dir., innovative edn. divsn. Venturist, Inc, Montgomery, 1996—99; adj. instr. Auburn U., Montgomery, 1994—99; internat. fellow USAF Air War Coll., Maxwell AFB, Ala., 1992—93; interpreter Russian Army and Indian Navy, Visakhapatnam and Bombay, India, 1990—91; spkr., presenter in field. Author: (book) Father of Sozidolinguistics (or Creative Linguistics), in Russian, 1988, Father of Sozidolinguistics (or Creative Linguistics), in English, 1994, Father of Novology, the Science of Newness, in Russian, 1991, Father of Novology, the Science of Newness, in English, 2002, Grammar Creation and Creation Grammar, 1990, ALEANDR: Creativity Testing Program, 1990, Creativity in Teaching and Studying Theoretic Disciplines, 1990, Creating Creative Teachers, 1996, Make Your Child a Genius, 1996, Creative Problem Solving: Present, Past, and Future, 1997, Creating Yourself: Creative Compendium, 1999, Mega-Creator: From Creativity to Mega-, Giga-, and Infi-Creativity, 1999, MegaCreativity: Five Steps to Thinking Like a Genius, 2002; editor: Language Consciousness: Stereotypes and Creativity, 1988, (5 volume book) Creative Management, 1991, (book) When will it be?, 1996, Soul Poem, 1997, Run with the Wind, 1997, Microdictionary of Foreign Words (Nine languages), 1997, Mighty Colloquial Pomposity Power Words, 1997, Designing a Genius, 1996, Future Geniuses of the Earth, 1996, Mega-Creator in the Non-Profit Universe: Launch to Excellence, 2000, The Future of Creativity, 2002; author: (audiotape) Nurturing the Genius in Your Child, 2000, (keynote speech) Creativity: Breaking the World Record, 2001; contbr. numerous articles to profl. publs. Life time mem. Creative Edn. Found., Buffalo, 1999; mem. Internat. Coun. for Innovation in Higher Edn., Toronto, Canada, 1997. Col. Russian Army, 1973—93. Named Hon. Citizen of Ala., Gov. of Ala., 1992, Dr. E. Paul Torrance lectr., U. Ga., 2001; recipient 4 medals for Excellence in Svc., Supreme Soviet, USSR, 1980—90, numerous awards and certificates for excellence in svc., Russian Ministry of Def., 1975—92, Silver Medal for H.S. excellence, Russian Ministry of Edn., 1966, Guiness World record for fastest written, printed and pub. book Making the Impossible Possible, 2001, Outstanding Educator award for Innovative and Creative Tchg., Ednl. Leadership Acad., NC, 2003. Mem.: Am. Creativity Assn. (founding pres. Ala. chpt.), Air War Coll. Alumni Assn., Kiwanis, Phi Deta Kappa. Avocations: swimming, chess, travel, composing. Office: Mega-Innovative Mind Intl Institute 2125 E 6th St Montgomery AL 36106 Office Fax: 334-265-3851. Personal E-mail: aleini13@aol.com. E-mail: dr_andy@mega-creator.com.

ALEJANDRO, STEVEN B. physicist; b. San Jose, Calif., Apr. 16, 1957; s. Ernesto F. and Jane E. (Boulden) A.; m. Alison L. Godfrey, June 16, 1990. BS in Physics, U. Ariz., 1980, MS in Atmospheric Scis., 1983. Staff scientist Sys. & Applied Scis. Co., Arlington, Mass., 1983-84; physicist Air Force Geophysics Lab., Bedford, Mass., 1984-91, Air Force Rsch. Lab., Bedford, 1991-95, tech. dir., dir. energy directorate, 1995—. Mem. Am. Meterol. Soc., Optical Soc. Am. Avocations: astronomy, hiking, rock climbing. Office: Air Force Rsch Lab 3550 Aberdeen Ave SE Kirtland Afb NM 87117-5748 E-mail: steven.alejandro@kirtland.af.mil.

ALEMAN, JOSÉ VICENTE AGUINACO, legal administrator; Pres. Supreme Ct. Mex. Office: Pino Suarez 2 Centro Deleg Cuauhtemoc 06065 Mexico Fax: (5) 552-0152.

ALEMAN, MARTHANNE PAYNE, environmental planner, consultant; b. Houston, Dec. 3, 1938; d. Charles Franklin and Evelyn Inez (Dudley) Payne; m. Samuel Garza Alemán, July 5, 1968. BS in Landscape Arch. magna cum laude, Tex. A&M U., 1988; MS in Interdisciplinary Studies, Tex. Tech. U., 1989; PhD in Urban and Regional Sci., Tex. A&M U., 1995. Engring. aide City of Austin, 1966-69, Bryant-Curington Engrs., Austin, 1969-72; entrepreneur Rio Verde Farm, San Benito, Tex., 1972-83; rsch. asst. Tex. Tech. U., Lubbock, 1988-91, Tex. A&M U., College Station, 1993-94; cons. Rio Verde Land & Investment Corp., Calvert, Tex., 1995—. Sec./treas., bd. dirs. Tex. Avocado Growers Assn., Weslaco, 1979-83. *Planned a 4,384 acre community for the Lower Rio Grande Valley of Texas for a major research university. Analyzed soil types as determinants for allocation of land use for a multiplicity of human activities while preserving Class I and II agricultural farmland. Resolved problem of urban encroachment through a plan permitting development for human use while preserving limited farmland. Authored a 650 page reference work researching and analyzing the multiple causes of global problem of desertification. Originated system to guide decision making processes for land planners, policy makers, and educators through reevaluation of established procedures.* Author: Soil Salinity in the Texas Lower Rio Grande Valley: Cause for Concern, 1987, Export-Driven Development of Soil and Water Resources: Barrier to Sustainable Development and Inducement to Desertification, 1995. Mem. and active participant Robertson County Hist. Commn., Calvert, 1980-83. Smithsonian Instn. intern, Washington, 1987, Presdl. scholar U.S. Fed. Register, 1993; recipient Nat. Collegiate Archtl. and Design award, U.S. Achievement Acad., Lexington, Ky., 1989. Mem. Am. Planning Assn., Soil and Water Conservation Soc. of Am. (vol. Heart of Tex. chpt., Waco, Tex.). Avocations: breeding, showing, and training collies. Office: Rio Verde Land and Investment Corp 201 Browning Calvert TX 77837

ALENIEWSKI, MONICA IRENE, retired anesthesiologist; b. Harrison, N.J., 1928; BS, Rutgers U., 1949; MD, Hahnemann U., 1953. Diplomate Am. Bd. Anesthesiology. Intern St. Michael's Hosp., Newark, 1953-54; resident in anesthesiology Columbia-Presbyn. Med. Ctr., N.Y.C., 1955-57; pvt. practice; dir. anesthesiology VA Med. Ctr., East Orange, N.J., 1957-90; ret., 1990. Former assoc. prof. anesthesiology U. Medicine and Dentistry N.J. Mem. AMA, Am. Med. Women's Assn., Am. Soc. Anesthesiologists, N.J. Soc. Anesthesiologists. Home: Towers of Key Biscayne 1111 Crandon Blvd Apt B802 Key Biscayne FL 33149 E-mail: MAF-IJF@webtv.net.

ALENIKOFF, FRANCES, choreographer, performer, writer, dancer, artist; b. N.Y.C., Aug. 20, 1920; d. Clement Jack Lipman and Ruth (Alder) Taylor; m. Martin Freedman, 1956 (div. 1973); children: Francesca Rheannon. BA, Bklyn. Coll., 1940. Founding mem. Dance Theatre Workshop, N.Y., 1968—. Soloist and company at colls., univs., theaters, in festivals and community ctrs. in U.S. and abroad, 1959-93; soloist in films including Frekoba, 1969, Alenka, 1968, Episodes On The Edge, 1973, Shaping Things, 1978; soloist at Lincoln Ctr., 1985; choreographer for Zaide, 1956, L'Histoire Du Soldat, 1957, Josephine Baker Show On Broadway, 1964, Joan and the Devil, 1978; performer Dream Play, 1970, Oddfellows Players, 1991-95; participant in various art festival, 1966-86; dir. Eden's Expressway, 1975—; dance critic Dance News, 1970-82; staff writer Craft Horizons Mag., 1971-74; actress in Wheels Over Indian Trails, 1993, Witness, Blood Summer Rituals, 1994; dancer, choreographer St. Mark's Dancespace, 1996, 98, 2000, Frederick Loewe Theater, 1996, Dance Theatre Workshop, 1996, 97, Soho Arts Festival, 1996, 97, Judson Ch., N.Y.C., 1997, 2001, Downtown Arts Festival, 1998, 99, Dixon Place, Merce Cunningham Studio, 2000, Lifetime TV, 2000, Tribeca Performing Arts Ctr., 2000, 2001, 2002, Dixon Place, N.Y.C., 2001, Judson Meml. Ch., 2001; contbr. articles to profl. jours. Recipient Grant N.Y. State Coun. on the Arts, 1972-80, NEA, 1973-74, N.Y. City Cultural Coun., 1978, Meet the Composer, 1980, N.J. State Coun. on the Arts, 1972, Cine Internat. Golden Eagle award, 1978; named Pick of Yr. for Best in Dance, Village Voice, 1997. Mem. Dancers Over Forty, E. Hampton Artists Alliance. Home: 537 Broadway New York NY 10012-3930

ALENIUS, JOHN TODD, retired insurance executive; b. Denver, Sept. 27, 1938; s. Robert and Elizabeth Frances (Todd) A.; m. Sandra Lee Mally, June 30, 1962; children: Constance, Mark, Patricia, William. BBA, Regis. Coll., 1961; postgrad., Havard U., 1971; MA in Mgmt., Webster Coll., 1979. Commd. USAF, 1962, advanced through grades to col., personnel mgr., 1966-67, 1962-67, systems mgr. San Antonio, 1971-75; with exchange duty Canadian Armed Forces, Ottawa, Ont., Can., 1975-77; various system mgmt. positions USAF, San Antonio, 1977-83, dir. logistic mgmt. systems Sacramento, 1983-85; v.p. info. systems Vision Service Plan, Sacramento, 1985-88, exec. v.p. ops., 1988-98, exec. v.p., 1998—2001. Mem. Soc. Info. Mgmt., Am. Mgmt. Assn. Republican. Roman Catholic. Avocations: fishing, golf. Office: California Vision Service Inc 3333 Quality Dr Rancho Cordova CA 95670-7985

ALEONG, JOHN, statistician, educator; BA with honors, U. of The W.I., Trinidad; MSc, U. Toronto, Can.; PhD, Iowa State U. Prof. stats. U. Vt., Burlington, 1976—. Contbr. articles to profl. jours. (numerous awards and grants). Grantee, USDA, 1976—. Mem.: Biometrics Soc., Am. Statis. Assn. (assoc editor). Office: Univ Vt 16 Colchester Ave Burlington VT 05405

ALES, BEVERLY GLORIA RUSHING, artist; b. Laplace, La. d. William Pinckney and Clementine Marie (Madere) Rushing; m. Warren Vincent Ales (dec. June 1991); children: Merrick Vance Patrick, Sheryl Ann (dec.), Lori Patrice. Student, La State U., U. New Orleans. Office mgr. Nat. Auto Assn., New Orleans; cosmetician Labiche's Inc., New Orleans; art gallery owner, mgr. Gallery Toulouse, New Orleans, Village D'Artiste, Metairie, La.; pvt. practice Metairie. Past pres. Metairie Art Guild, Le Petit Art Guild, New Orleans, New Orleans Art Assn.; art tchr. East Jefferson H.S., T.H. Harris Mid. Sch., Magnolia Spl. Sch. Author poetry. Active Rep. Nat. Com., Rep. Pres. Trus, East Jefferson Hosp. Aux.; bd. dirs. Rep. Women's Club in Jefferson Parish; bd. dirs., bd. parliamentarian Rep. Women of Jefferson Parish, 2000—, parliamentarian, 2000—; past pres. La Soc. De Femme, Metarie. Recipient Great Lady award East Jefferson Hosp. Aux., Legion of Merit award. Mem. Nat. Mus. Women in Arts (charter), Nat. Authors Registry, Internat. Soc. Poets (bd. dirs.), Heart Ambassadors (v.p.). Roman Catholic. Home: 1500 Melody Dr Metairie LA 70002-1924

ALES, MICHAEL RAYMOND, engineering educator; b. Passaic, N.J., Sept. 20, 1958; s. Raymond Henry and Francis Elizabeth (Trembath) A.; m. Pamela Beth Jones, June 27, 1987; children: Thomas Michael, Joseph Gordon. BS in Naval Architecture, U.S. Naval Acad., 1980; MBA, U. So. Miss., 1998; MS in Ocean Engring., Va. Tech, 2001. Registered profl. engr., Wis. Commd. ensign USN, 1980, advanced through grades to lt.; missile control officer USS Callaghan, 1981-83, engr. adminstrv. officer, 1983-84; boilers div. officer USS New Jersey, 1984-85, boilers officer, 1985-86, from mil. stds. officer to dir. steam tng. Svc. Sch. Command, Naval Tng. Ctr., Great Lakes, Ill., 1986-91; sr. engr., engr. specialist, engring. supr. Northrop Grumman Ship Sys., Pascagoula, Miss., 1991—2002; asst. prof. engring. U.S. Merchant Marine Acad., Kings Point, NY, 2002—. Deacon First Presbyn. Ch. Ocean Springs, Miss., 1993-95. Mem. NSPE, Am. Soc. Naval Engrs., Soc. Naval Architects and Marine Engrs., Surface Navy Assn., U.S. Naval Acad. Alumni Assn. Republican. Presbyterian. Avocations: sailing, choral singing. Home: 3407 Queen Elizabeth Dr Ocean Springs MS 39564-3334

ALESCHUS, JUSTINE LAWRENCE, retired real estate broker; b. New Brunswick, N.J., Aug. 13, 1925; d. Walter and Mildred Lawrence; m. John Aleschus, Jan. 23, 1949; children: Verdene Jan, Janine Kimberley, Joanna Lauren. Student, Rutgers U. Dept. sec. Am. Bapt. Home Mission Soc., N.Y.C., 1947-49; claims examiner Republic Ins. Co., Dallas, 1950-52; broker Damon Homes, L.I., 1960-72; pres. Justine Aleschus Real Estate, Smithtown, NY, 1975—2002; ret. Exclusive broker estate of Kenneth H. Leeds, L.I., N.Y., 1980-90. Past pres. Nassau-Suffolk Coun. of Hosp. Aux, 1981-82; hon. mem. aux. St. Catherine of Siena, Smithtown, N.Y., past pres., hosp. adv. bd.; past pres. L.I. Coalition for Sensible Growth, Inc.; past v.p. Suffolk County coun. Boy Scouts Am. Mem. Sky Island Club (gov.), S.C. Citizen Police Acad. (alumni). Republican. Lutheran. Address: 2261 The Woods Dr East Jacksonville FL 32246 E-mail: landauntjay@aol.com.

ALESIA, JAMES H(ENRY), judge; b. Chgo., July 16, 1934; m. Kathryn P. Gibbons, July 8, 1961; children: Brian J., Daniel J. BS, Loyola U., Chgo., 1956; JD, Ill. Inst. Tech., Chgo., 1960; grad. Nat. Jud. Coll., U. Nev., 1976. Bar: Ill. 1960, Minn. 1970. Police officer City of Chgo., 1957-61; assoc. Law Office Anthony Scariano, Chicago Heights, Ill., 1960-61, Pretzel & Stouffer, Chgo., 1961-63; asst. gen. counsel Chgo. & North Western Transp. Co., 1963-70; assoc. Rerat Law, Mpls., 1970-71; asst. U.S. atty. No. Dist. Ill., Chgo., 1971-73; trial counsel Chessie Sys., Chgo., 1973; U.S. adminstrv. law judge Chgo., 1973-82; ptnr. Reuben & Proctor (merged with Isham, Lincoln & Beale), Chgo., 1982-87; judge U.S. Dist. Ct. for No. Dist. Ill., Chgo., 1987—. Mem. faculty Nat. Jud. Coll., U. Nev., Reno, 1979-80. Mem. FBA, Justinian Soc. Lawyers, Celtic Legal Soc. Republican. Roman Catholic. Office: US Dist Ct 219 S Dearborn St Chicago IL 60604-1800

ALESSANDRONI, VENAN JOSEPH, lawyer; b. N.Y.C., Mar. 1, 1915; s. Anthony P. and Andromeda (Rossini) A.; m. Alice Shaughnessy, Feb. 2, 1949 (dec. June 1973); m. Adelle Lincoln, Mar. 10, 1974. AB, Columbia U., 1937, JD, 1939. Bar: N.Y. 1941, also, Supreme Ct. of Korea 1946. Announcer CBS Artists Service, Inc., 1940; U.S. atty. Bd. Econ. Warfare, 1942; mem. U.S. Fgn. Econ. Adminstrn. Mission, Belgian Congo, 1943; sr. partner Wormser, Kiely, Alessandroni, Hyde & McCann (and predecessor firm), 1959—. Legal officer Mil. Govt. Korea, 1945-46; legal adviser to provincial gov. Kyunggi-Do, Korea, 1946; chief provost judge, City of Seoul, 1946; adj. prof., law sch. U. Miami, 1974— ; lectr. various tax insts., univs., profl. assns. Author: The Executor, 1963, Applied Estate Planning, 1963, also articles.; Departmental editor: Jour. Taxation, 1955-56. Recipient U.S. Army Commendation award, 1946; regional award N.Y. Times, 1932; Curtis medal Columbia, 1936 Home: Eggleston Ln Old Greenwich CT 06870 Office: Wormser Kiely Galef & Jacobs 825 3d Ave New York NY 10017-4014

ALESSE, JUDITH, special education educator; b. N.Y.C., Apr. 16, 1953; d. Joseph and Rose Alesse. BA cum laude, Hofstra U., 1977; MS, Adelphi U., 1979. Cert. spl. edn. tchr. N.Y. Spl. edn. tchr. Malverne (N.Y.) Sch. dist., 1980—. V.p. Nassau Reading Coun., Nassau County, NY, 2001—. Office: HT Herber Mid Sch 75 Ocean Ave Malverne NY 11565

ALESSI, GEORGE ANTHONY, financial advisor, consultant; b. N.Y.C., May 30, 1926; s. Anthony and Anna Cecilia (Li Greci) A.; m. Madeline Costanza, Nov. 21, 1953; 1 child, Anthony. BBA in Indsl. Mgmt., CCNY, 1949; cert. in elec. engring., Oreg. State U., 1945, MBA, 1952; cert., Ohio State U., 1960. Cert. profl. contract mgr., Washington. Employment interviewer City of N.Y. Dept. Social Svcs., 1949-52; various mgmt. and exec. positions U.S. Govt. Dept. of Def., 1952-86; cons., fin. advisor Galessi Enterprises, Yonkers, N.Y., 1986—. Mem. Archdiocesan Pastoral Coun., N.Y., 1985-91; chmn. Vicariate of N.E. Bronx, N.Y., 1983-91; cooperator Opus Dei, 1990—; mem. Cath. League for Religious and Civil Rights; bd. dirs. Lawrence Hosp. Aux., 1996-2002. Decorated Knight of the Holy Sepulchre, Pope John Paul II, 1984; recipient Disting. Svc. award Archdiocesan Union of Holy Name, 1985, Insignus Jesuit Community at Loyola Retreat House, Morristown, N.J., 1966, Jesuit Companion, 1998—, Rev. James A. Huvane Man of Yr. awrd, Serra Club of the Bronx, 2001. Fellow Profl. Contracts Mgmt. Assn. (cert. 1976), Cardinal Spellman Retreat League (pres. Riverdale, N.Y. 1980-82), Archdiocesan Union of Holy Name Soc. (pres. 1977-79), Male Glee Club Yonkers (v.p. 1986-87), Serra Internat. (dist. gov. 1989-92, pres. 1996-1999), Congregation of the Passion (assoc.and friend). Republican. Roman Catholic. Home and Office: 10 Massitoa Rd Yonkers NY 10710-5016

ALESSI, MARY JEAN, family life educator; b. St. Louis, Dec. 19, 1930; d. William Emerson and Edith G. (Dillon) Ricks; m. Dominick Alfred Alessi, Aug. 8, 1953; children: William, Barbara, Dominick Jr., Paula, Janet, John. BA, Washington U., St. Louis, 1952; MA, Webster U., 1976. Cert. family life educator. Parent facilitator St. Louis Bd. Edn., 1979-83; parent-study-group leader Midwest Soc. Individual Psychology, St. Louis, 1972—. Instr. Thomas Dunn Meml. Adult Edn., 1976—, De Paul Hosp. Good Health Program, 1986-98, St. Louis C.C., 1987—. Co-author: Once Upon a Memory, 1987; editor newsletter Family, 1986-90. Vol. tchr. St. Catherine Laboure Parish Sch. of Religion, St. Louis, 1970-98. Recipient scholarship Washington U., St. Louis, 1948. Mem. Nat. Coun. Family Rels., Midwest Soc. Individual Psychology (pres. 1979, 85, bd. dels. 1985—), N.Am. Soc. Adlerian Psychology (chmn. family edn. sect. 1986-92, bd. dels. 1986-92). Avocations: genealogy, video taping. Home and Office: 11834 Helta Dr Saint Louis MO 63128-1118 E-mail: djsunset1@juno.com.

ALESSI, ROBERT JOSEPH, lawyer, pharmacist, real estate developer; b. Rome, N.Y., Aug. 22, 1958; s. William John and Mary Jean A.; m. Ellen Mary Paczkowski, May 21, 1988; children: Laura C., Grace E. BS in Pharmacy, Union U., 1982; JD cum laude, Albany Law Sch., 1985. Bar: N.Y. 1986, U.S. Dist. Ct. (no. dist.) N.Y. 1986, U.S. Dist. Ct. (we. dist.) N.Y. 1986, U.S. Dist. Ct. (ea. dist.) N.Y. 1993, U.S. Dist. Ct. (so. dist.) N.Y. 1993, U.S. Ct. Appeals (2d cir.) 1995, U.S. Supreme Ct. 1996. Assoc. Nixon, Hargrave, Devans & Doyle, Albany, N.Y., 1985-90, LeBoeuf, Lamb, Greene & MacRae, Albany, 1990-93, ptnr., 1994—, mng. ptnr., 1999—; mng. dir. Hudson Heritage, L.L.C., 1999—. Adj. prof. law Albany Law Sch., 1989-94; town atty. Town of Bethlehem, 2001—. Co-author: Year 2000 Deskbook, 1998. Mem. master plan com. Town of Bethlehem, Delmar, N.Y., 1989-89, mem. planning bd. counsel, 1990-94. Mem. N.Y. State Bar Assn., Albany Law Sch. Environ. Alumni Group, Rockefeller Found. (advisor Pocantico roundtable consensus on brownfields). Avocations: tennis, fitness training, reading. Home: 8 Partridge Rd Delmar NY 12054-3919 Office: LeBoeuf Lamb Greene & MacRae LLP One Commerce Plz Ste 2020 99 Washington Ave Albany NY 12210 Fax: 518-626-9010. E-mail: ralessi@llgm.com.

ALEVIZOS, SUSAN BAMBERGER, lawyer, santouri player, author; b. N.Y.C., May 19, 1936; d. L. Richard and Helen (Thatcher) Bamberger; m. Theodore George Alevizos, May 6, 1960; children— Gregory, L. Richard, Theodore. BA, Smith Coll., 1958; postgrad., Columbia, 1959-60, Women's Lyceum, Athens, Greece, 1967-68; Master classes with, Maestro Yannis Jovenos, Naxos, Greece, 1967-74; JD, Suffolk U., 1978; grad. tax program, Boston U., 1986. Bar: Mass. 1978, Fed. 1979, U.S. Supreme Ct. 1982, U.S. Tax Ct. 1986. Assoc. editor Condé Nast, 1958-60; assoc. Alevizos & Alevizos, Boston, 1978-94, ptnr., 1994—; pres. Gnision Music Company, 1999—. Cons. Greek divsn. MGM Records; rec. divsn. Nat. Geog. Soc.; mem. adv. coun. Ctr. for Greek Studies, U. Fla., Gainesville, 1995—. Santouri player, 1967—, performed concerts, UN, N.Y.C., 1969, Am. embassy, Athens, 1968, Boston Mus. Fine Arts, 1972, Gardiner Mus., Boston, 1971, also in, Phila., Milw. and Detroit, field work, Nat. Folklore Archives of Greece, 1956— ; recs. include Songs of Greece, 1960, Folksongs of Greece, 1961, Greek Folksongs, 1969, Poetry and Song, 1973, Traditional Songs and Dances of Greece and the Grecian Islands, 1978; author: Folksongs of Greece, 1968; prodr. Greek Cultural Hour, Sta. WBCN-FM, Boston, 1965-67; legal columnist Hellenic Chronicle, Boston, 1979—; contbr. articles to profl. publs. prod., A Greek Byzantine Christmas, 2000, A Greek Byzantine Easter, 2002. Trustee Pro Arte Chamber Orch. Boston, 1990-94; mem. bus. com. for arts Palm Beach County Cultural Coun., 1993-97. Mem. ABA, NARAS, Mass. Bar Assn., Boston Bar Assn., Assn. Trial Lawyers Am., Am. Folklore Soc., Modern Greek Studies Assn. Office: Alevizos and Alevizos PO Box 391106 Cambridge MA 02139-1106

ALEVIZOS, THEODORE G. lawyer, singer, author; b. Milw., Feb. 7, 1926; s. Gregory and Mary (Passaris) A.; m. Susan Thatcher Bamberger, May 6, 1960; children: Gregory, L. Richard, Theodore. Ph.B., Marquette U., 1950; postgrad., Juilliard Sch. Music, 1950-51; MS, Columbia U., 1957; JD, Suffolk U., 1966. Bar: Mass. 1974, Fed. 1975, U.S. Supreme Ct. 1980. Mem. sales staff McKesson & Robbins, Milw., 1952-56; asst. cataloger N.Y. U. Med. Library, N.Y.C., 1956-57; asst. circulation librarian Widener Library, Harvard, 1957-61; asst. librarian Lamont Library, 1961-64, dir., 1964-74; mem. faculty Harvard U., 1966-74, lectr. modern Greek, 1969-73, lectr. voice, 1972-74, assoc. univ. librarian for pub. services, 1966-74; practiced in Boston, 1974—; ptnr. Alevizos & Alevizos, 1978—; faculty Suffolk U. Law Sch., 1986-93; instr. modern Greek, The Voice in Performance Cambridge Adult Center, 1972-86; nat. and internat. concertizing. Cons. MGM Records, Inc., 1965-71, Orgn. for Social and Tech. Innovation, Inc., Cambridge, 1968-70; mus. cons. Nat. Geographic, 1971-73; bd. dirs. Harvard Coop., 1973-74; mem. corp. Cambridge Ctr. Adult Edn.; faculty in entertainment and sports law Suffolk U. Law Sch., 1986—; mem. adv. coun. Ctr. for Greek Studies, U. Fla., Gainesville, 1995—. Author: Folksongs of Greece, 1968; legal columnist: Hellenic Chronicle, Boston, 1979— ; Recordings include: Folksingers Round Harvard Square, 1959, Songs of Greece, 1960, Folksongs of Greece, 1961, Greek Folksongs, 1969, Poetry and Song, 1973, Traditional Songs and Dances of Greece and the Grecian Islands, 1978, A Greek Byzantine Christmas, 2000, A Greek Byzantine Easter, 2002; host WBCN-FM Boston, Greek Cult. Hour, 1965-67. Mem. Adv. Congress Cambridge Community TV; trustee Dexter Sch., 1976—, v.p. bd. trustees, 1980— . Served with USNR, 1944-46, PTO. Decorated Bronze Star.; Hon. assoc. Center for Neo-Hellenic Studies, U. Tex. at Austin, 1967— Mem. NARAS, Am., Mass., Boston Bar Assns., Mass. Acad. Trial Attys., ALA, Am. Folklore Soc., Modern Greek Studies Assn., Inst. Byzantine and Modern Greek Studies (hon.) Office: Alevizos and Alevizos PO Box 391106 Cambridge MA 02139-1106

ALEWINE, JAMES WILLIAM, financial executive; b. Williamston, S.C., Apr. 26, 1930; s. David Andrew and Ruby Mae (Moore) A.; children: David, Susan. BA, Carolina Sch. Commerce, 1961. Cert. internal auditor, S.C. With Daniel Internat. Corp., Greenville, S.C., 1947-92, mgr. internal audit, 1970-72, mgr. M & M divsn., 1972-73, fin. adminstr. Jenkinsville, S.C., 1973-77, mgr. acctg. M-E-T Group Greenville, S.C., 1977-78, asst. treas., 1978-92. With USN, 1952-55, lt. col. S.C. State Guard, 1993—2003. Named Ky. Col. Mem. Inst. Internal Auditors (pres. Palmetto chpt. 1975-76), Masons (past grand high priest, knight York grand cross of honour, 32d degree), Scottish Rite, Elks. Baptist. Home: 2 Broad St Williamston SC 29697-1808

ALEX, JOANNE DEFILIPP, educator Montesorri school; m. Joseph Alex; children: Jessica, Joel, Julianna. BA in Art and Edn., Colby Coll., 1976; grad./cert., Montessori Methods, 1982; MEd, U. Maine, 2001. Tchr., kindergarten, Montessori schs., Various Cities, 1979-83; founder, tchr. Montessori Sch., Stillwater, Maine, 1983—. AMS Montessori intern supr., Univ. student tchr. placements (supr. tchr.); presenter numerous workshops and confs.; trained facilitator of Systematic Tng. for Effective Parenting; instr. parenting courses; ednl. cons.; facilitator Project Learning Tree, Project Wild, Project Aquatic, Project Wet workshops; coord 1st Maine Tchrs. Forum, 1998. Co-author: I Wonder What's Out There? A Vision of the Universe for Primary Classrooms, 2002. Selected to attend Nat. Geographic Soc. Summer Inst., 1993, Nat. Geographic Soc. Alliance Leadership Acad., 1999; named Outstanding Environ. Educator of Yr. (nat.), Am. Tree Found., 1994, Tchr. of Yr., Maine Audubon Soc., 1995, Maine Tchr. of Yr., 1998; recipient award for outstanding contbns. to child-care in Maine, 1996. Mem. Am. Montessori Soc. (cert. tchr.), N. Am. Montessori Tchrs. Assn., Maine Montessori Assn. (treas.). Avocations: biking, hiking, wild flowers, children's books, children's resources. Office: Stillwater Montessori Sch 1024 Stillwater Ave Unit 1 Old Town ME 04468-5112 E-mail: jalex1@adelphia.net.

ALEXAKOS, FRANCES MARIE, counselor, business owner, psychology educator, researcher, producer, editor; b. Fitchburg, Mass., Dec. 29, 1947; d. Samuel Rosario and Mary (Cucchiara) Sciabarrasi; m. Haritos Kyniacou Agadakos, June 5, 1988 (dec. Feb. 1987); m. Demetrios P. Alexakos, June 5, 1988 (dec. Dec. 1999); children: Katerina, Demetra, Artemis, Alexis. BA in Psychology, U. Mass., 1970; MA in Psychology, Assumption Coll., 1972; BA in Studio Art, U. R.I., 1994; cert. in humanities, Salve Regina U., 1996, PhD, 2003. Social worker, Mass.; psychologist, Mass.; cert. tchr., R.I.; cert. sch. counselor, R.I. Sr. med. social worker Roger William Hosp., Providence, 1972-78; prof. psychology Johnson & Wales U., Providence, 1991—96, C.C. R.I., Warwick; dir. mktg. Oak Internat. Academies, Guadelahara, Mex., 1996-97. Mem. vis. faculty summer ethics inst. Dartmouth Coll., 1998. Editor, Mediterranean bur. chief Slugfest lit. mag., 1997-2002; author: Medicine and Health, Rhode Island Physicians' Attitudes Toward Genetic Testing and Breast Cancer, 1999. Active Zoning Bd. of Rev., Wakefield, RI, 2001—; trustee U. R.I. Found.; health com. R.I. Women's Commn., 2001—. Daus. of Penelope scholar, 1994; NIH grantee, 1998; named Person of Yr., Wakefield C. of C., 1987, Leadership R.I. award 1995. Mem. LWV (chair ednl. grants com.), Rotary (chmn. charitable gifts 2003), Golden Key Honor Soc. Greek Orthodox.

ALEXANDER, ANDREW JAMES, investment banker; b. Bellaire, Ohio, Aug. 3, 1969; s. Daniel Richard Alexander. BSBA, Ohio State U., 1991; MBA, U. Pitts., 1999. Sales assoc. Prudential Securities, Wheeling, W.Va., 1992-93; controller 5B's Inc., Zanesville, Ohio, 1993-96; sr. fin. analyst PNC Bank, Pitts., 1996-97; relationship mgr. corp. banking Nat. City Bank, Pitts., 1997-2000; sr. assoc. PNC Capital Markets, Inc., Pitts., 2000—. MIS cons., Pitts.

Republican. Roman Catholic. Avocations: golf, tennis, reading novels. Home: 1031 Woodridge Dr Canonsburg PA 15317 Office: One PNC Plz 25th Fl 249 5th and Wood Sts Pittsburgh PA 15222 E-mail: andrew.alexander@pncbank.com.

ALEXANDER, ANNA MARGARET, artist, writer, educator; b. Greenville, Tex., Jan. 26, 1913; d. Samuel Jefferson and Elizabeth (Smith) Fooshee; m. Joseph C. Jake Alexander, Feb. 12, 1936 (dec. 1988); children: Joanna, Ellen Alexander Stein, Mardi. BA, Rice U., 1933. Cert. tchr. Tchr., Klein, Tex., 1933-38; fashion artist, writer, adv. mgr. Smart Shop, Houston, 1938-43; fashion artist, writer Kreeger's, New Orleans, 1943-45, Everitt Buelow Ralph Rupley, 1953-68; owner Ideas Ink, 1950—54; art tchr. Spring Branch, Houston, 1968-74. Founder Historic Outdoor Art Gallery, New Braunfels, Tex. Vol. literacy program, ch., hist. socs., sr. citizen groups, children's mus., food bank; leader, camp counselor Girl Scouts U.S.A., Houston, 1956-60; pres. Girl's Booster Club, Houston, 1966-68; bd. dirs. St. Francis Episc. Day Sch., 1965-70; Sunday sch. tchr. St. Francis Ch., Houston, 1958-62; active PTA. Mem. Advt. Club Houston, Univ. Women Houston, DAR, Colonial Dames New Braunfels, Garden Club, Ret. Tchrs. Assn., C. of C. Vis. Bur. (downtown design rev. commn., 45 Yrs. as Vol. award 1983), others. Avocations: ecology, church activities, gardening, volunteerism, travel, family activities. Home: 909 Allen Ave New Braunfels TX 78130-4903

ALEXANDER, ANNE A. sales consultant; b. Bartlesville, Okla., Aug. 22, 1927; d. Francis Willard and Cloe Gray Alexander; children: Josiah A. Turner, Kathleen Jane Turner, Christopher R. Turner, Dennis T. Wallace, Jennifer J. Wallace. Degree in Visual Art Edn., U. Kans., 1975, MA, 1980. Cert. tchr., Kans., Mo. Artist Hallmark Cards, Kansas City, 1963-64; art tchr. North Kansas City (Mo.) Schs., 1975-88; sales cons. Transworld Sys. Inc., Mission, Kans., 1991—. Pvt. artist and art tchr., Kansas City. Restored historic statues Old St. Mary's Ch., Kansas City, 1992—; one-woman shows include Parkville (Mo.) Art Gallery, 1986, Mo. Artists Invitational, Riverfront, Jefferson City, Mo., 1985 (award), Art in the Woods, Corporate Woods, Overland Park, Kans., 1982 (Purchase award), River Bend Art Show, Atchison, Kans., 1980 (1st pl. award); exhbns. in group shows include Cottonstone Gallery, Jefferson City, Mo., 1979; represented in pvt. collections throughout the U.S. Vol. Greater Kansas City Cmty., 1968—; bd. mem. Share, Kansas City, 1978-79, SafeHaven, Clay, Platte and Ray Counties, 1978-94, WomenSpeak Steering Com., Kansas City, 1994—, Forward Kansas City, 1994—; commr. Met. Commn. on Status of Women, Kansas City, 1980-82, Kansas City Mo. Human Rels. Commn., 1982-90, Mayor's Key to the City Commn., Kansas City, 1993-95; participant Women's Leadership Inst.-Avila, Kansas City, 1984, Consensus City Planning, Kansas City, 1994; chair Tri-County Domestic Violence Bd., Platte, Clay and Ray Counties, 1990-94; active Sosland Series, Kansas City Pub. Libr., 1998—; bd. govs. Citizen's Assn., Kansas City, 1999; mem. Gladstone (Mo.) Planning Commn., 2000—. Mem. Sales Profls. Internat. (bd. mem. 1996—, Rookie of the Yr. 1997). Episcopalian. Avocations: reading, gardening, advocate for women's issues, dining with friends. Office: Transworld Sys Inc 5799 Broadmoor St Ste 512 Mission KS 66202

ALEXANDER, ARLINE, entrepreneur, writer, real estate consultant; b. Los Angeles, Calif., Feb. 14, 1945; d. Bernard Berk; children: Lesa Ann, Raquel Manon. Propr. The Rocking Horse, Pacific Palisades, Calif., 1975—80; pres., psychic cons. Found. for Advancement of Metaphysical Enlightenment, Occidental, Calif., 1981—85; pres., real estate broker A&A Properties Inc, Westcliffe, Colo., 1986—; pres. The Loony Bin Factory Inc., Westcliffe, Colo., 1998—. Author: (book) Pig Latin as a Second Language, The Collective Works of Countess Alexandria de Duke I & II, I Can Make You Laugh, I Can Make You Think, X-Boyfriend Kit, Life Resume Workbook, Lepzars Report on Planet Earth, Say So Log, (poetry) Universal Soldier, Pegasus. Achievements include design of Prototypes For Phone Company And Greeting Card Company. Avocations: art and antique collecting, travel, architecture. Office: A&A Properties Inc PO Box 1763 Canon City CO 81215 Home Fax: 719-275-0555. Personal E-mail: arlinealexander@hotmail.com.

ALEXANDER, ARTHUR JACOB, economist; b. Carbondale, Pa., Oct. 6, 1936; s. Howard R. and Sylvia (Eisner) A.; m. Elaine Averich, Aug. 25, 1963; children: Sarah, Jonathan. BS, Mass. Inst. Tech., 1958; MSc, London Sch. Econs., 1966; PhD, Johns Hopkins U., 1969. Sys. analyst IBM, Poughkeepsie, N.Y., 1960-63; rsch. economist Rand Corp., Santa Monica, Calif., 1968-90; pres. Japan Econ. Inst., Washington, 1990—2001. Vis. prof. UCLA, 1988-90, Johns Hopkins U., 1994-97, George Mason U., 1998—, Georgetown U., 2000—; mem. U.S. Army Sci. Bd., Washington, 1978-82; rsch. assoc. Internat. Inst. Strategic Studies, London, 1976-77. With U.S. Army, 1959-60. Avocations: photographica collections, running. Office: Japan Econ Inst 3517 Raymond St Chevy Chase MD 20815-3227 E-mail: aalexander@jei.org.

ALEXANDER, BARBARA LEAH SHAPIRO, clinical social worker; b. St. Louis, May 6, 1943; d. Harold Albert and Dorothy Miriam (Leifer) Shapiro; m. Richard E. Alexander. B in Music Edn., Washington U., St. Louis, 1964; postgrad., U. Ill., 1964-66; MSW, Smith Coll., 1970; postgrad., Inst. Psychoanalysis, Chgo., 1971-73, grad., child therapy program, 1976-80; cert. therapist Sex Dysfunction Clinic, Loyola U., Chgo., 1975. Diplomate in Clin. Social Work. Rsch. asst., NIMH grantee Smith Coll., 1968-70; probation officer Juvenile Ct. Cook County, Chgo., 1966-68, 70; therapist Madden Mental Health Ctr., Hines, Ill., 1970-72; supr., therapist, field instr. U. Chgo., U. Ill. Grad. Schs. Social Work; therapist Pritzker Children's Hosp., Chgo., 1972-82; therapist, cons., also pvt. practice, 1973—; pres. On Good Authority, 1992—; intern Divorce Conciliation Svc., Circuit Ct. Cook County, 1976-77. Contbr. articles to profl. jours. Bd. dirs., Grant Park Concerts Soc.; sec. Art Resources in Teaching. Recipient Sterling Achievement award Mu Phi Epsilon, 1964. Mem. Nat. Fed. Soc. for Clin. Social Work (chmn. 20th ann. conf., exec. bd.), Ill. Soc. Clin. Social Work (pres. 1986-90, bd. dirs., chmn. svcs. to mems. com., dir. pvt. practitioners' referral service), Assn. Child Psychotherapists, Amateur Chamber Music Players Assn., Jewish Geneal. Soc., Smith Coll. Alumni Assn. (bd. dirs., v.p. 1992-94). Home and Office: 6 Horizon Ln Galena IL 61036-9258

ALEXANDER, BARBARA TOLL, investment banker; b. Little Rock, Dec. 18, 1948; d. Lawrence Jesser and Geraldine Best (Proctor) Toll; m. Lawrence Allen Alexander, Jan. 25, 1969 (div. 1980); m. Thomas Beveridge Stiles, II, Mar. 7, 1981; stepchildren: Thomas B. Stiles III, Jonathan E. Stiles. BS, U. Ark., 1969, MS, 1970. Asst. v.p. Wachovia Bank & Trust Co., Winston-Salem, N.C., 1972-77; security analyst Investors Diversified Services, Mpls., 1977-78; 1st v.p. Smith Barney Inc., N.Y.C., 1978-84; mng. dir. Salomon Bros., N.Y.C., 1984-91, Dillon Read & Co., 1992-97, UBS Warburg, 1997-99, sr. advisor, 1999—. Bd. dirs., chmn. audit com. Centex Corp.; bd. dirs., mem. audit com. Harrah's Entertainment, Inc.; former chmn. policy adv. bd. Joint Ctr. for Housing Studies of Harvard U.; exec. fellow Harvard U.; mem. nat. adv. bd., bd. dirs. HomeAid Am.; bd. dir. Habitat for Humanity Internat. Presbyterian. Home: 87 Monarch Bay Dr Monarch Beach CA 92629-3459 Address: UBS Warburg 299 Park Ave Fl 36 New York NY 10171-0002

ALEXANDER, BRUCE DONALD, real estate executive, educator; b. Hartford, Conn., May 11, 1943; BA, Yale U., 1965, MA (hon.), 1998; JD, Duke U., 1968. With Rouse Co., Balt., 1969-96, sr. v.p., dir. comml. devel. divsn., 1978-93, sr. v.p., dir. new bus., 1993-96; dir. Balt. Equitable Ins., 1987-89, Enterprise Social Investment Corp., 1995-2000, Balt. Devel. Corp., 1996-98; v.p., dir. New Haven and State Affairs Yale U., New Haven, 1998—, adj. prof. real estate, Yale Sch. Mgmt., 1998—. Trustee Goucher Coll., Balt., 1984-2001, chmn., 1991-96; trustee Columbia (Md.) Found., 1981-86, pres., 1983-85; trustee Balt. Ednl. Scholarship Trust, 1990-93; co-chair eastern region Yale U. Campaign, 1991-97; bd. dirs. Balt. Symphony Orch., 1986-91; dir. Conn. Pub. Broadcasting, 2002-. Recipient John Franklin Goucher medal. Office: Yale Univ 433 Temple St New Haven CT 06511-6803 E-mail: bruce.alexander@yale.edu.

ALEXANDER, CARL ALBERT, ceramic engineer, educator; b. Chillicothe, Ohio, Nov. 22, 1928; s. Carl B. and Helen E. Alexander; m. Dolores J. Hertenstein, Sept. 4, 1954; children: Carla C., David A. BS, Ohio U., 1953, MS, 1956; PhD, Ohio State U., 1961. Mem. staff Battelle Columbus Labs., 1956—, research leader, 1974—, mgr. physico-chem. systems, 1976—; mem. faculty Ohio State U., 1963—, prof. ceramic and nuclear engring., 1977—. Sr. research leader, chmn. tech. council of Biol. and Chem. Scis. Directorate, 1987—, chief scientist, 1987; prof. materials sci. and engring, 1988— Author; patentee in field. Served to lt. (j.g.) USNR, 1951-54. Recipient Merit award NASA, 1971, IR-100 award, 1987, R&D-100 award, 1988; citations Dept. Energy, citations AEC, citations ERDA. Mem. Am. Soc. Mass Spectrometry, Keramos, Sigma Xi Home: 4249 Haughn Rd Grove City OH 43123-3216 Office: 505 King Ave Columbus OH 43201-2696 E-mail: alexandc@battelle.org.

ALEXANDER, CECIL ABRAHAM, college official, architect, consultant; b. Atlanta, Mar. 14, 1918; s. Cecil Abraham and Julia (Moses) A.; m. Hermione Weil, Jan. 20, 1943 (dec. 1983); children: Therese, Judith, Douglas; m. Helen Eisemann, 1985. Student, Ga. Inst. Tech., 1936; AB, Yale, 1940; student, Mass. Inst. Tech., 1941; M. Arch., Harvard, 1947. Partner Alexander & Rothschild (architects), Atlanta, 1949-58; chmn. bd. Finch, Alexander, Barnes, Rothschild & Paschal, Architects and Engrs., Inc., Atlanta, 1958-86; archtl. cons. Atlanta, 1986-90; coord. continuing edn. Ga. Inst. Tech. Coll. Architecture, Atlanta, 1994-96; prin.-in-charge Leo A. Daley Archtl. Engrs., Atlanta, 1996-97; ptnr. Alexander-Weiner Baker Architects, Atlanta, 1997—, Alexander Weiner Architects, 00—. Coord.; chmn. bd. A.S.D. Inc., interior design svc.; dir. Atlanta office Leo A. Daly Archtl. Engring. Internat.; chmn. Atlanta Citizens Adv. Com. Urban Renewal, 1958-60; vice chmn. Atlanta Met. Planning Commn., 1962—; past chmn. Ga. Fgn. Trade Zone Corp. Prin. works include Ga. Power Bldg., Atlanta, 1st Nat. Bank, Atlanta, Cin. Riverfront Stadium, Coca-Cola Internat. Hdqs., Sci. Atlanta Hdqs., U.S. Pavilion Expo '82, So. Bell. Hdqs.; designer new Ga. flag, 2001. Past vice chmn. Community Coun., Atlanta, Ga.; mem. Mayor's Adv. Com. Race Relations, Nat. Citizens Com. Community Rels.; chmn. Atlanta chpt. Am. Jewish Com., 1963; chmn. housing resources com. City of Atlanta; past chmn. com. Yale Sch. Architecture; pres., founder Resurgens Atlanta; past v.p. Atlanta Symphony Orch.; Mem. Yale Nat. Alumni Bd., 1963; bd. dirs. Atlanta U.; bd. dirs. emeritus, Clark Atlanta U.; past bd. dirs. Marist High Sch., Atlanta; chmn. Com. to Combat Drugged and Drunken Driving; past pres. Atlanta's Clifton Corridor Biomed. Rsch. Coun. Served to lt. col. USMCR, World War II. Decorated Air medal, D.F.C.; (2) Recipient Brotherhood award NCCJ, 1973; Archdiocesan medal of St. Paul, 1980, Yale medal, 1980. Fellow AIA (pres. Ga. 1957, Ivan Allen award); mem. Atlanta C. of C. (dir., Whitney Young award, Nat Am. Inst. Architects). Home: 2677 Rivers Rd NW Atlanta GA 30305-3549 E-mail: hcalexander@mindspring.com.

ALEXANDER, CHARLES COMER, history educator, writer; b. Cass County, Tex., Oct. 24, 1935; s. Comer and Pauline Alexander; m. Joann Erwin, June 2, 1960; 1 child, Rachel. BA, Lamar U., 1958; PhD, U. Tex., 1962. Prof. history Ohio U., Athens, 1970-89, disting. prof. history, 1989—; Weiner disting. prof. humanities U. Mo./Rolla, 2002. Author: The Ku Klux Klan in the Southwest, 1965, Crusade for Conformity: The Ku Klux Klan in Texas, 1920-1930, 1966, This New Ocean: A History of Project Mercury, 1966, Nationalism in American Thought, 1930-1945, 1969, Holding the Line: The Eisenhower Era, 1952-1961, 1975, Here the Country Lies: Nationalism and the Arts in Twentieth-Century America, 1980, Ty Cobb, 1984, John McGraw, 1988, Our Game: An American Baseball History, 1991, Rogers Hornsby, 1995, Breaking the Slump: Baseball in the Depression Era, 2002. Recipient Seymour medal, Soc. for Am. Baseball Rsch., 2003. Mem. Orgn. Am. Historians, Ohio Hist. Soc. (trustee 1990-2000), Phi Beta Kappa. Home: 8 Ann Athens OH 45701 Office: Dept History Ohio Univ Athens OH 45701 E-mail: alexande@ohio.edu.

ALEXANDER, CHARLES JACKSON, II, lawyer; b. Winston-Salem, NC, Nov. 20, 1946; s. Jack C. and Mary Ann (Smitherman) Alexander; m. Marilyn Howard; 1 child, Kristen. BA, Wake Forest U., 1969; JD, Wake Forest Coll., 1972. Bar: NC 72. Sole practice, Winston-Salem, NC, 1972—76; sr. ptnr. Alexander & Hinshaw, Winston-Salem, 1976—82, Alexander, Wright, Parrish, Hinshaw, Tash, Kurtz & Porter, Winston-Salem, 1983—86; ptnr. Morrow, Alexander, Tash, Kuatz and Porter, Winston-Salem, 1987—. Pres. Cystic Fibrosis Found., Winston-Salem, 1994. Mem.: ATLA, ABA, Criminal Def. Lawyers (pres. 1982—83, Best Lawyers in Am. - Criminal Law), Greater Winston-Salem C. of C. (bd. dirs. 1978), NC Jaycees (legal counsel 1981—82, Outstanding Pres. award 1977—78, Disting. Svc. award 1983), NC Bar Assn., NC Acad. Trial Lawyers (sustaining patron). Republican. Presbyterian. Office: Morrow Alexander Task Kurtz & Porter 3890 Vest Mill Rd Winston Salem NC 27103-1302 Home: 240 Bullfinch Rd Mooresville NC 28177 E-mail: crimlawcja@aol.com.

ALEXANDER, CHARLES MICHAEL M, internist; b. Bronx, N.Y., May 5, 1952; s. Saunders P. and Anna Alexander; married; 3 children. BA, Johns Hopkins U., 1973; MD, U. So. Calif., 1977. Diplomate Am. Bd. Internal Medicine, Subsplty. Bd. Endocrinology and Metabolism. Intern in straight medicine LAC/U. So. Calif. Med. Ctr., L.A., 1977-78, resident in internal medicine, 1978-80, fellow in diabetes/endocrinology, 1980-82; pvt. practice Inglewood, Calif., 1982-92; med. dir. Daniel Freeman Diabetes Care Ctr. Daniel Freeman Hosps., Inglewood, Calif., 1985-92, med. dir. Daniel Freeman Wound Care Ctr., 1990-92; med. dir. diabetes unit Daniel Freeman Marina Hosp., Marina Del Rey, Calif., 1982-88; assoc. dir. profl. info. U.S. Human Health divsn. Merck & Co. Inc., West Point, Pa., 1992-93, dir. med. svcs. U.S. Human Health divsn., 1993-96, dir. Outcomes Rsch. and Mgmt. U.S. Human Health divsn., 1996—. Clin. instr. medicine U. So. Calif., 1980-82, asst. clin. prof. medicine, 1982-88, assoc. clin. prof. medicine, 1988-91, clin. prof. medicine, 1991-94. Contbr. chpt. (book) The Thyroid, 1987; contbr. numerous articles to profl. jours. Fellow ACP, Am. Coll. Endocrinology; mem. Am. Acad. Pharm. Physicians (pres. Phila. chpt. 1999—, v.p. ann. meeting 1999—), Am. Diabetes Assn. (rsch. grantee 1981-82; various positions L.A. and Calif. chpts.), Am. Heart Assn., Soc. Med. Decision Making, Microsoft Healthcare Info. Mgmt. Systems Soc., Am. Med. Informatics Assn., Drug Info. Assn., The Endocrine Soc., Am. Assn. Clin. Endocrinologists, Am. Fedn. Med. Rsch.

ALEXANDER, CHRISTINA ANAMARIA, translator, performing company executive; b. Bucuresti, Romania, June 30; naturalized U.S. citizen, 1975. d. Peter Vladimir and Maria Nicolae (Suciu) A. BA, Old Dominion U., 1990, MA, 1992; PhD in Religion (hon.), Pacific Universal Life Ch., 1996; acctg. degree, Sch. Acctg. and Bookkeeping, Atlanta, 2000. Cert. natural health cons. Translator, interpreter Word for Word, Inc., Norfolk, Va., 1990—; exec. dir. KultureKastle, Virginia Beach, Va., 1996—. Instr. lang. Prague (Czech Republic) Lang. Sch., 1990-91; adj. faculty Old Dominion U., Norfolk, 1993; cons. pub. rels. High Frequency Wavelengths, N.Y.C., 1995-96; cons. V.A.C.A., Richmond, Va., 1995-96; internat. star Oriental Dance Festival of Finland, 2002. Performing artist MARA Agy., Vienna, Austria, 1994, Joy Fund Theater, Norfolk, 1996-97, Boys and Girls Club, Inc., Newport News, Va., 1997, M.E. Cox Ctr., Virginia Beach, 1997, Waterfront Arts Festival, Virginia Beach, 1997, Cox Comm., 1997, Pepsi Island Music Festival, 1999, Frequencia Latina Network Peru, 1999, Multicultural Alliance Va. World Bazaar, 2000, Opsail 2000, Norfolk, Va., MTV Sink or Swim Talent Show, 2001; internat. star dancer Oriental Dance Festival of Finland, 2001; creator, dancer, choreographer Secret of the Lost Treasure, 1997 (award 1997); dancer Mantra, 1997; guest star Frequencia Latina Network; cons. Va. Ballet Theater, 2000. Bd. dirs., rec. sec. Bay West Condominiums, 2001—02. Named Ms. Petite Va. Beach, 1996. Mem. Hampton Roads Cultural Alliance, Multicultural Alliance of Va., Virgina Beach C. of C. Avocations: skiing, travel, costume design, nutrition. Office: 2525 W Bay Dr Apt A23 Belleair Bluffs FL 33770-1986 E-mail: christalx@juno.com.

ALEXANDER, C(LARK) EVERTS, accountant; b. New Rochelle, N.Y., Apr. 4, 1918; s. C. Clark and Emma B. (Everts) A.; m. Louise Vaught, Sept. 4, 1943; children: Dennis, Robert, Carol. BS in Acctg., NYU, 1941, MBA in Taxation, 1947. CPA, N.Y., Conn. Tax practitioner T.M. Byxbee Co., CPAs, N.Y./Conn., 1945-50, ptnr., 1950-83; pvt. practice Punta Gorda, Fla., 1983—. Treas., sec., v.p., pres. N.Y. N.E. Chpt.-N.Y. State Soc. CPAs, 1965-69. Treas. Mohawk Golf Club, Schenectady, N.Y., 1972-76; pres., treas. Camberwell Condominium Assn., Inc., 1993-98. Capt. USAF, 1941-45. Mem. AICPA, N.Y. State Soc. CPAs, Burnt Store Marina and Country Club (Punta Gorda, Fla.). Avocations: farming and cattle in W. Addison, Vt. Home: 17815 Courtside Landings Punta Gorda FL 33955-1985 Office: TM Byxbee Co CPAs 21 Aviation Rd Albany NY 12205-1141 E-mail: ale33955@sfrato.net.

ALEXANDER, CLIFFORD JOSEPH, lawyer; b. New Orleans, Oct. 2, 1943; s. Charles Ernest and Lois Primus (Boley) A.; m. Elizabeth McAnany, June 11, 1966; children: Brian, Heather, Rachel. AB, Rockhurst Coll., 1966; JD, Georgetown U., 1969. Bar: Mass. 1970, D.C. 1977. Mem. staff SEC, Washington, 1967-70; assoc. Gaston Snow & Ely Bartlett, Boston, 1970-75; mem. staff U.S. Senate Banking Com., Washington, 1975-77; mem. Kirkpatrick & Lockhart LLP (formerly Kirkpatrick, Lockhart, Hill, Christopher & Phillips, and predecessor), Washington, 1977—. Co-editor: Money Managers Compliance Manual. Mem. ABA (corp., banking and bus. law sect.), Boston Bar Assn., Fed. Bar Assn. (securities and banking law sects.), D.C. Bar Assn., Mass. Bar Assn., U.S. Supreme Ct. Bar. Home: 8721 Bluedale St Alexandria VA 22308-2307 Office: Kirkpatrick & Lockhart 1800 Massachusetts Ave NW Fl 2 Washington DC 20036-1806

ALEXANDER, CLIFFORD L., JR., management consultant, lawyer, former secretary of army; b. N.Y.C., Sept. 21, 1933; s. Clifford L. and Edith (McAllister) A.; m. Adele Logan, July 11, 1959; children— Elizabeth, Mark Clifford. AB cum laude, Harvard, 1955; LL.B., Yale U., 1958; LL.D. (hon.), Malcolm X Coll., 1972, Morgan State U., 1978, Wake Forest U., 1978, U. Md., 1980, Atlanta U., 1982. Bar: N.Y. 1960, U.S. Supreme Ct 1960, D.C. 1960. Asst. to dist. atty., N.Y. County, 1959-61; exec. dir. Manhattanville Hamilton Grange (neighborhood conservation project), 1961-62; exec. program dir. HARYOU, Inc., also pvt. practice law, 1962-63; mem. staff Nat. Security Council, 1963- 64; dep. spl. asst. to Pres. Johnson, 1964-65, assoc. spl. counsel, 1965-66, dep. spl. counsel, 1966-67; chmn. Equal Employment Opportunity Commn., 1967-69; partner firm Arnold & Porter, 1969-75, Verner, Liipfert, Bernhard, McPherson & Alexander, 1975-76; sec. army, 1977-80; pres. Alexander & Assocs., Inc. (cons.), Washington, 1981—. Dir. Pa. Power & Light Co., Dreyfus Third Century Fund., Dreyfus Gen. Money Market Fund, Dreyfus Common Stock Fund, Dreyfus Govt. Securities Fund, Dreyfus Tax Exempt Fund, MCI Corp.; adj. prof. Georgetown U.; prof. Howard U., Washington.; Mem. Pres.'s Commn. on Income Maintenance Programs, 1967-68; Pres.'s spl. ambassador to the Independence of Swaziland, 1968; mem. Pres.' Commn. for Observation Human Rights Yr., 1968; bd. dirs. Mex.-Am. Legal Def. and Ednl. Fund, NAACP Legal Def. and Ednl. Fund; bd. overseers Harvard U., 1969-75; trustee Atlanta U. Host, co-producer: TV program Cliff Alexander: Black on White, 1971-74. Served with AUS, 1958-59. Named hon. citizen Kansas City, Mo., 1965; recipient Ames award Harvard, 1955; Frederick Douglass award, 1970; Outstanding Civilian Service award Dept. Army, 1980; Disting. Public Service award Dept. Def., 1981; others. Mem. Am., D.C. bar assns. Clubs: Reveille (N.Y.C.) (Annual Outstanding Achievement award 1966). Home: 512 A St SE Washington DC 20003-1139 Office: Alexander & Assocs 400 C St NE Washington DC 20002-5818

ALEXANDER, CONSTANCE JOY (CONNIE ALEXANDER), stone sculptor; b. Hillsboro, Ohio, Oct. 13, 1939; d. Laurence Adair and Martha Ellen (Hill-Overman) Lucas; m. Anfred Agee Alexander, June 6, 1959; children: Troy Arthur, Andrea Ellen. Grad., Cin. Art Acad., 1961, postgrad., 1962, Atlanta Coll. of Art, 1977. Represented by Miller Gallery Cin., also various galleries in Ga. and Fla. Exhibited in group exhibitions at Southeastern Artists Ga. Jubilee Festival (1st in sculpture award 1974), Southeastern Arts & Crafts Festival, Macon (Ga.) Colisuem, 1977 (1st in sculpture), World's Fair, Knoxville, Tenn., 1982, David Schaeffer Gallery, Alpharetta, Ga., 1988-93, Ga. Marble Festival, Jasper, 1989 (1st place award), Ariel Gallery, Soho, N.Y., 1989 (award of excellence), 90, 45th Ann. Pen & Brush Sculpture Exhbn., Soho, N.Y., 1991 (Excalibur Bronze Sculpture Foundry award), Ariel Gallery, Soho, 1989-91, Tim Verstegen's The Dutch Framer Gallery, Canton, Ga., 1989-93, Artistic Frames & Gallery, Jasper, Ga., 1991-93, Trinity Gallery, 1994-2003, Atlanta, 1994, Gallery 300, Atlanta, 1994; represented in permanent collections Cin. Pub. Libr., Ga. Inst. Tech., Atlanta, Hartsfield Internat. Airport, North Dekalb Coll., Coca-Cola Internat. Hdqrs., State Art Collection Ga. Sculpture. Recipient Artfest award Habitat for Humanity, 1998. Mem. Soc. Of Friends. Avocations: cross country rock collecting, photography, poetry, home restoration. Home: PO Box 67 Canton GA 30169-0067 Office: Trinity Gallery 315 E Paces Ferry Rd NE Atlanta GA 30305-2307 E-mail: trinitygallery@mindspring.com.

ALEXANDER, DAVID ROBERT, astronomer, educator; b. Topeka, Kans., Feb. 9, 1945; s. R. Stanley and Helen L. Alexander; m. Elizabeth A. Alexander, June 3, 1967 (div. 1983); children: Patrick S., Stephen R.; m. Georgia L. Alexander, Mar. 7, 1987. BS, Kans. State U., 1967; AM, Ind. U., 1968, PhD, 1972. Chairperson dept. physics Wichita State U., Wichita, Kans., 1990-98, from asst. prof. to prof., 1971—; exec. dir. Fairmount Ctr. for Sci. and math. edn., Wichita, Kans., 1995—; dir. High Performanc Computing Ctr. Fairmount Ctr. for Sci. and math edn., Wichita, 1999—; exec. dir. Lake Afton Pub. Observatory, Wichita, 1979-85. Contbr. articles to profl. jours. including Astrophys. Jour. Recipient fellowship, Am. Soc. Engring. Edn., NASA-Ames Rsch. Ctr., 1986, 1987, NASA-Goddard Space Flight Ctr., 1973, 1974. Mem. Am. Astron. Soc., Assn. Edn. Tchrs. Sci., Nat. Sci. Tchrs. Assn. Office: Wichita State U 1845 Fairmount Wichita KS 67260 E-mail: david.alexander@wichita.edu.

ALEXANDER, DEBORAH RADFORD, elementary education administrator; b. Knoxville, Tenn., July 29, 1953; d. Frank Stanley and Elizabeth Anne (Poer) Radford; m. James R. Alexander, 1981 (dec. 1988); m. Bobby Davis, Jan. 3, 1992. BA in Religious Studies, U. Tenn., 1973, MS in Spl. Edn., 1975, EdS in Curriculum and Instrn., 1979, EdD in Curriculum and Instrn., 1982, postdoctoral. Cert. spl. edn. tchr., K-12 adminstr. and supr., career level III tchr., Tenn. Head Start Mideast Community Action Agy., Kingston, Tenn., 1975-77; resource tchr. Roane County Schs., Kingston, 1978-94, designated prin., 1992-94, asst. prin., 1994-96, prin., 1996—. Ednl. cons., 1998—; adj. faculty mem. Tusculum Coll., 2000—, Roane State CC, 2002—, Tenn. Technol. U., 2002—. Contbr. articles to profl. jours. Mem. NEA, ASCD, NAESP, Am. Ednl. Rsch. Assn., Tenn. Edn. Assn., Tenn. Prins. Study Coun. (pres. East Tenn. divsn. 2002-, steering com. 2001—, mem. exec. com. 2002—), Roane County Edn. Assn. (pres. 1986-87), Am. Contract Bridge League (pres. Tennessee Valley unit 1986-87), Oak Ridge Bridge Assn. (pres. 1983-84), Am. Belgian Malinois Club (sec. 1984-90, pres. 1991-95, bd. dirs. 1995-97), Phi Kappa Phi. Home: PO Box 5747 Oak Ridge TN 37831-5747 Office: Kingston Elem Sch 2000 Kingston Hwy Kingston TN 37763-4663 E-mail: alexanded01@k12tn.net.

ALEXANDER, DONALD CRICHTON, lawyer; b. Pine Bluff, Ark., May 22, 1921; s. William Crichton and Ella Temple (Fox) A.; m. Margaret Louise Savage, Oct. 9, 1946; children: Robert C., James M. BA with honors, Yale U., 1942; LLB magna cum laude, Harvard U., 1948; LLD (hon.), St. Thomas Inst., 1975, Capital U., 1989. Bar: D.C. 1949, Ohio 1954, N.Y. 1978. Assoc. Covington & Burling, Washington, 1948-54, Taft, Stettinius & Hollister, Cin., 1954-56, ptnr., 1956-66, Dinsmore, Shohl, Coates & Deupree, Cin., 1966-73; commr. IRS, 1973-77; mem. Commn. on Fed. Paperwork, 1975-77; ptnr. Olwine, Connelly, Chase, O'Donnell & Weyher, N.Y.C., Washington, 1977-79, Morgan, Lewis & Bockius, N.Y.C. and Washington, 1979-85, Cadwalader, Wickersham & Taft, Washington, 1985-93, Akin, Gump, Strauss, Hauer & Feld, Washington, 1993—. Mem. adv. bd. NYU Tax Inst., 1969-73, 77-87, Tax Mgmt., Inc., 1968-73, 77—; mem. adv. Treas. Dept., 1970-72; mem. adv. group to commr. IRS, 1969-70, chmn. exempt orgns. adv. group, 1987-89; mem. adv. bd. Mertens, 1986-2002, Maxwell Macmillan fed. Taxes 2d, 1989-92; commr. Martin Luther King, Jr. Fed. Holiday Commn., 1993-96; mem. Harvard Bd. Overseers' vis. com. to law sch., 1999—; mem. com. on univ. resources Harvard U., 2002—; mem. commn. on coal leasing, 1983-84. Author: The Arkansas Plantation, 1943, contbr. more than 50 articles on fed. taxation. Co-chmn. bd. advisors NYU/IRS Continuing Profl. Edn. Program, 1982-85; dir. Treasury Hist. Assn., 1996—. Served to maj. AUS, 1942-45. Decorated Silver Star, Bronze Star. Mem. ABA (vice chmn. taxation sect. 1967-68), Am. Law Inst. (tax adv. group), U.S. C. of C. (taxation com. 1981-91, bd. dirs. 1984-89, health and employee benefit com. 1989-94, regulatory affairs com. 1993-98), Chevy Chase Club (Md.), Met. Club, Nantucket Yacht Club (Mass.), Mill Reef Club (Antigua, B.W.I.), Yale Club N.Y. Home: 2801 New Mexico Ave NW Washington DC 20007-3921 Office: Akin Gump Strauss Hauer & Feld 1333 New Hampshire Ave NW Washington DC 20036-1564 Business E-Mail: dalexander@akingump.com.

ALEXANDER, DONALD G. state supreme court justice; Grad., Bowdoin Coll.; JD, U. Chgo. Bar: Maine 1972, U.S. Supreme Ct. 1973. Mem. Sen. Edmund Muskie's staff; asst. Maine atty. gen., 1974-76; dep. atty. gen.; judge Dist. Ct., 1979, Maine Superior Ct., 1980-98; justice Maine Supreme Jud. Ct., 1998—. Office: Cumberland County Courthouse PO Box 368 142 Federal St Portland ME 04112-0368

ALEXANDER, DONALD L. theologian, educator, minister; b. Modesto, Calif., Oct. 28, 1935; s. David William and Myrtle Estle (Stanage) Alexander; married, Sept. 8, 1964; children: Jonathan, Karin, Amy. BA, Seattle Pacific

Coll., 1959; MA, Chgo. Grad. Sch. Theology, 1963; grad., Bethel Theol. Sem., 1966; MDiv, Luther Theol. Sem., 1968; MA in Religious Studies, U. Calif., Santa Barbara, 1975, PhD, 1980. Acad. dean Alliance Bible Sem., Hong Kong, 1969—72, adminstv. v.p., 1974—82; prof. theology Crown Coll., St. Paul, 1982—87; prof. biblical theology Bethel Coll., St. Paul, 1987—; bd. dirs. Prairie Bible Coll., Alberta, Canada, 1983—93. Author: Christian Spirituality, 1989, The Pursuit of Godliness, 1999. Alumni grantee, Bethel Coll., 2002. Mem.: Am. Theol. Soc. (treas. 1992—98, mem. exec. bd. 2002—). Avocation: swimming. Home: 13930 Sunnyslope Dr Maple Grove MN 55311

ALEXANDER, DORIS MURIEL, humanities educator, writer; b. Newark, Dec. 14, 1922; d. Abraham Jacob and Marie (Joachim) A. BA, U. Mo., 1944; MA, U. Pa., 1946; PhD, NYU, 1952. Instr. Rutgers U., New Brunswick, N.J., 1950-56; prof., head dept. English CUNY, N.Y.C., 1956-62; Fulbright prof. Greek U., Athens, 1966-67; vis. prof., fellow in humanities Pa. State U., University Park, 1969; freelance writer Venice, 1971—. Lectr. in field. Author: The Tempering of Eugene O'Neill, 1962, Creating Characters With Charles Dickens, 1991, Eugene O'Neill's Creative Struggle, 1992, Creating Literature Out of Life, 1996; contbr. articles to profl. jours. Gregory scholar U. Mo., 1944, scholar U. Pa., 1944; Penfield fellow NYU, 1946. Mem. Phi Beta Kappa. Avocations: gourmet cookery, art history, window-box gardening. E-mail: dalex1@tin.it.

ALEXANDER, DRURY BLAKELEY, architectural educator; b. Paris, Tex., Feb. 4, 1924; s. Drury Blakeley and Katherine (Stone) A. B.Arch., U. Tex., 1950, BS in Art, 1951; MA, Columbia U., 1953. Instr. Kans. State U., Manhattan, 1953-55; asst. prof. architecture U. Tex., Austin, 1955-60, assoc. prof. architecture, 1960-67, prof. architecture, 1967-84, Meadows Found. prof. Architecture, 1984-94, emeritus prof., 1994—. Eugene McDermott lectr. U. Tex., 1983—85. Author: Texas Homes of the 19th Century, 1966; Sources of Classicism, 1978. Chmn., Historic Landmark Commn., Austin, 1975-85. Served with U.S. Army, 1943-46, ETO Decorated Bronze Star medal; recipient Disting. Svc. award, City of Austin, 1976, Svc. award for hist. preservation, Heritage Soc. Austin, 1976, Tex. Hist. Preservation award, Tex. Hist. Commn., 1986, Nat. Preservation Honor award, Nat. Trust for Hist. Preservation, 1991, Disting. Achievement award in archtl. edn., Tex. Soc. Architects, 1994, Disting. Prof. award, Assn. Collegiate Schs. of Arch., 1995, D.B. Alexander Lifetime Achievement award named in his honor, Heritage Soc. Austin, 2001. Mem. Soc. Archtl. Historians (bd. dirs. 1979-82), Assn. Preservation Technologists, Victorian Soc. Am. Democrat. Presbyterian. Avocations: book collecting, travel. Home: 811 E 38th St Austin TX 78705-1809 Office: U Tex Sch Architecture Austin TX 78712

ALEXANDER, DUANE FREDERICK, pediatrician, research administrator; b. Balt., Aug. 11, 1940; s. Fred Lucas and Christiana H. (Showacre) A.; m. Marianne Ellis, June 23, 1963; children: Keith Duane, Kristin Marianne. BS, Pa. State U., 1962; MD, Johns Hopkins U., 1966. Diplomate: Am. Bd. Pediatrics. Intern Johns Hopkins Hosp., Balt., 1966—67, resident, 1967—68, fellow, 1970—71; commd. officer USPHS, 1968—2000, ret. rear adm.; clin. assoc. Nat. Inst. Child Health and Human Devel., NIH, Bethesda, Md., 1968—70, asst. to sci. dir., 1971—74, asst. to dir., 1978—82, dep. dir., 1982—86, dir., 1986—; staff pediatrician Nat. Commn. for Protection of Human Subjects of Research, 1974—78. Contbr. articles to profl. jours. Recipient Commendation medal USPHS, 1970, Meritorious Svc. medal USPHS, 1985, Spl. Recognition medal USPHS, 1985, Surgeon Gen.'s Exemplary Svc. medal, 1990, Irving B. Harris Lectureship award Soc. Behavioral Pediatrics, 1991, Pub. Svc. award Am. Coll. Ob-Gyn., 1992, Surgeon Gen.'s Medallion, 1993, Disting. Pub. Svc. award Am. Acad. Phys. Medicine and Rehab., 1993, Presdl. Citation, APA, 1992, Sec.'s Disting. Svc. award HHS, 1997, 98, Disting Alumnus award Pa. State U., 1999; alumni fellow Pa. State U. Alumni Assn, 1993. Fellow Am. Acad. Pediatrics (Excellence Pub. Svc. award 1998), Soc. Devel. Pediatrics, Am. Pediatric Soc., Assn. for Retarded Citizens. Methodist. Office: Nat Inst Child Health-Human Devel 31 Center Dr Msc 2425 Bldg 31 Bethesda MD 20892-0001 E-mail: da432@nih.gov.

ALEXANDER, EDNA M. DEVEAUX, elementary education educator; d. Richard and Eva (Musgrove) DeVeaux. BBA, Fla. A & M U., 1943; BS in Elem. Edn., Fla. A&M U., 1948; MS in Supervision and Adminstrn., U. Pa., 1954; cert., U. Madrid, 1961; postgrad., Dade Jr. Coll., U. Miami. Sec. Dunbar Elem. Sch., 1943-46, tchr., 194-55, Orchard Villa Elem., 1959-66; prin. A. L. Lewis Elem. Sch., 1955-57; reading specialist North Cen. Dist., 1966-69; tchr. L. C. Evans Elem. Sch., 1969-71. First black woman newscaster in Miami, Sta. WBAY, 1948. V.p. Fla. Coun. on Human Rels. Dade County, Coun. for Internat. Visitors Greater Miami; vice chmn. Cmty. Action Agy. Dade County; chmn. Dade County Minimum Housing Appeals Bd.; active Vol. Unltd. Project Nat. Coun. Negro Women; sponsor Am. Jr. Red Cross, Girl Scouts U.S.; trustee Fla. Internat. U. Found., 1974—79; mem. Jacksonville Symphony Assn. Guild Bd., Salvation Army Women's Aux., Jacksonville U. Friends of Libr. Bd.; past pres. Episcopal Churchwomen of Christ Ch., Miami; bd. dirs. YWCA. Named to Miami Centennial Women's Hall of Fame, 1996. Mem. AAUW (life, Edna M. DeVeaux Alexander fellowship named in her honor Miami br., del. seminar 1977), NEA (life), LWV, Fla. Edn. Assn., Classroom Tchrs. Assn., Dade County Edn. Assn. (chmn. pub. rels. com.), Dade County Reading Assn., Assn. for Childhood Edn., Internat. Reading Tchr. Assn., U. Pa. Alumni Assn., Alpha Kappa Alpha. Avocations: composing lyrics and music, gardening, travel, golf, photography. Home: 805 Blue Gill Rd Jacksonville FL 32218-3660

ALEXANDER, EDWARD HARRISON, mathematician, educator; b. Natick, Mass., Oct. 10, 1939; s. Edward Harrison and Muriel Corliss Alexander; m. Betty Lynn Zorn, May 5, 1965 (div. Dec. 23, 1995); children: Chrisropher, Benjamin, Holly. MA, Salve Regina Coll., Newport, RI, 1990; MS Math, U. Ariz., Tucson, AZ, 1994, PhD, 1997; MA, Salve Regina Coll., Newport, RI, 1990; MS Math, U. Ariz., Tucson, 1994; PhD Math, U. Ariz., Tucson, AZ, 1997. Staff Comdr. Submarine Floatilla Two, USN, New London, Conn., 1965—66; divsn. officer USS Theodore Roosevelt (SSBN600), USN, 1966—69; navigator USS Patrick Henry (SSBN599), USN, 1969—73; exec. officer USS Robert E. Lee (SSBN601), USN, 1973—76, USS Theodore Roosevelt (SSBN600), USN, 1976—76; staff officer, missile patrol scheduling Comdr. Submarine Force, US Pacific Fleet, 1976—78; commdg. officer USS John Marshall (SSBN/SSN611), USN, 1979—82; rep. of the us comdr. in chief, atlantic The SAC, Offutt Air Base, Omaha, Nebr., 1982—85; strategic plans and programs officer Office Chief Naval Ops., Pentagon, Washington, 1985—87; charles a. lockwood chair submarine warfare US Naval War Coll., Newport, RI, 1987—91; grad. tchg. asst. Math. Dept., U. Ariz., Tucson, Ariz., 1991—97, adj. faculty, 1997—. Capt. USN, 1961—91. Decorated Meritorious Svc. Medal USN. Mem.: Math Assn. Am., Navy League, US Naval Inst. Episcopalian. Home: 4309 E Samantha Dr Tucson AZ 85712 Office: Mathematics Dept University of Arizona 617 N Santa Ria Tucson AZ 85721

ALEXANDER, EDWARD RUSSELL, retired disease research administrator, educator; b. Chgo., June 15, 1928; s. Russell Green and Ethelyn Satterlee (Abel) A. PhB, U. Chgo., 1948, BS, 1950, MD, 1953. Intern Cin. Gen. Hosp.; chief surveillance sect. Communicable Disease Center, Atlanta, 1955-57, 59-60; resident, instr. dept. pediatrics U. Chgo., 1954-55, 57-59; asst. prof. dept. preventive medicine and dept. pediatrics U. Wash., Seattle, 1961-65, assoc. prof., 1965-69, prof., 1969-79; chmn. dept. epidemiology U. Wash. Sch. Pub. Health, 1970-75; prof. dept. pediat. U. Ariz., Tucson, 1979-83; dir. rsch. br., venereal diseases control divsn. Ctrs. for Disease Control, Atlanta, 1983-89, asst. dir. sci. sexually transmitted diseases divsn., 1989; chief of epidemiology Seattle King County Dept. Pub. Health, Seattle, 1990-98; prof. dept. epidemiology U. Wash. Sch. Pub. Health, Seattle, 1990-98, prof. emeritus, 1998—. Contbr. articles to profl. jours. Markle scholar, 1962-67. Mem. Am. Acad. Pediatrics, Am. Pediatric Soc., Am. Pub. Health Assn. (Abraham Lilienfeld award 1988), Assn. Tchrs. Preventive Medicine, Am. Epidemiol. Soc. (pres. 1986-87), Soc. Epidemiol. Rsch., Internat. Epidemiol. Soc., Am. Venereal Disease Assn. (Thomas Parran award 1984, pres. 1985-87) E-mail: erussa@comcast.net.

ALEXANDER, ELIZABETH URBAN, education educator; b. Houston, Tex., Aug. 16, 1947; d. Carlyle Woodrow and Lois Ball Urban; m. James Elisha Alexander Jr., June 20, 1969; children: Lauren Kimball Lawhon, Elizabeth Evans. BA, Vanderbilt U., 1969, MA in Tech., 1971; MA, Tex. Christian U., 1995, PhD, 1998. Adj. prof. history Hill Coll., Cleburne, Tex., 1991—99, Tex. Wesleyan U., Ft. Worth, 1998—2001, asst. prof. history, 2001—. Author: (book) Notorius Woman: The Celebrated Case of Myra Clark Gaines, 2001 (Langum prize for Legal History, 2001, Willie Lee Rose prize best book in So. History by a Woman, 2002). Office: Tex Wesleyan Univ 1201 Wesleyan Fort Worth TX 76105

ALEXANDER, ELMORE ROSEBUR, III, business educator, dean; b. Florence, S.C., July 14, 1952; m. Pamela C. Carlson. BA, Wake Forest U., 1974; MA, U. Ga., 1976, PhD, 1978. Prof. mgmt. U. Memphis, 1977-89; prof. Am. U., Washington, 1989-96, chair mgmt. dept., 1989-93, assoc. dean Kogod Coll. Bus. Adminstrn., 1993-96; prof., dir. divsn. bus. mgmt. Johns Hopkins U., Balt., 1996-98; prof., dean Sch. Bus. Adminstrn. Phila. U., 1998—. Contbr. articles to profl. jours. Methodist. Avocations: golf, tennis. Home: 348 Valley Rd Merion Station PA 19066-1520 Office: Phila U School House Ln & Henry Ave Philadelphia PA 19144-5497 Fax: 215-951-2652.

ALEXANDER, FRED CALVIN, JR., lawyer; b. Abingdon, Va., Nov. 4, 1931; s. Fred C. and Mary F. (White) A.; m. Betsy Jones, May 17, 1957 (div.); children— Mitchell, Mary, Marjorie, Margaret; m. Janet Lee Hammond, Jan. 2, 1982 Student, Davidson Coll., 1950-52; BA, U. Va., 1954, LLB, 1959. Bar: Va. 1959, U.S. Dist. Ct. (ea. dist.) Va. 1959, U.S. Ct. Appeals (4th cir.) 1960. Assoc. Boothe, Prichard & Dudley, Alexandria, Va., 1959-64; ptnr. McGuire, Woods, Battle & Boothe LLP and predecessor firms, Alexandria, Va., 1964-97, ret. McLean, Va., 1997. Mem. jud. conf. U.S. Ct. Appeals (4th cir.), 1964-99; lectr. legal edn. Va. State Bar, 1970, 75-77, 89; chmn. adv. com. rules of ct. Supreme Ct. of Va., 1984-98; bd. dirs. Thomas Rutherfoord, Inc. Past bd. dirs. counsel to Alexandria Hosp., St. Stephens Sch. 1st lt. U.S. Army, 1954-56. Fellow Am. Coll. Trial Lawyers (chmn. Va. com. 1994-96), Va. Law Found.; mem. Alexandria Bar Assn. (pres. 1969-70), Va. Bar Assn. (chmn. civil litigation sect. 1989-92), Va. Assn. Def. Attys., Va. Trial Lawyers Assn., Nat. Assn. R.R. Trial Counsel, Def. Rsch. Inst. (chmn. railroad law com. 1989-92), Belle Haven Country Club (bd. dirs. 1997-2000, 2001--), Wyndemere Country Club. Episcopalian. Home: 1313 Gatewood Dr Alexandria VA 22307-2033 Office: McGuire Woods LLP 1750 Tysons Blvd Ste 1800 Mc Lean VA 22102-4231

ALEXANDER, GARY R. lawyer, state legislator, lobbyist; b. Washington Nov. 16, 1942; s. Orville I. and Ann Z. Alexander; m. Anita G. Alexander; children: Jennifer Paige, Cory Brooke. BA, U. Va., 1964; LLB, George Washington U., 1967. Pvt. practice, Washington, Md. and Va., 1967-69; ptnr. Giordano, Alexander, Haas, Mahoney & Bush, Oxen Hill, Md., 1970-78, Haas & Alexander, Md., 1978-82; prin. ptnr. Alexander & Cleaver, P.A., Ft. Washington, Md., 1982—. Bd. dirs., chmn. Prince George County bar legis. com., 1972-79. Del. Md. Ho. of Dels., 1983-94, spkr. pro tem, 1993-94; chmn. Dem. Cen. Com., Prince George County, 1978-86; people's counsel Md. Pub. Svc. Commn., 1974-78; apptd. Gov.'s Task Force to Study Gambling, Md., 1993; mem. taxation com. Md. C. of C., 1995; bd. dirs. U. Md. Found. Recipient Outstanding Svc. award Md. Senate, 1976, Outstanding Svc. citation, 1976, Pub. Svc. cert. Prince George County Exec. and County Coun., 1976, Local Employer of Yr. award Bus. and Profl. Woman's Club, 1993, Outstanding Atty. award Washington mag., 1997. Mem. ABA (chmn. automobile law com. 1975-77, chmn. automobile ins. legis. com. 1977-80), Nat. Conf. State Legislatures, Md. Bar Assn. (chmn. fed. laws com. 1973-79), D.C. Bar Assn., Va. Bar Assn., Md. Govt. Rels. Assn. Jewish. Avocations: history, gardening, golf. Office: Alexander & Cleaver PA 11414 Livingston Rd Fort Washington MD 20744-5145 also: Alexander & Cleaver PA 54 State Cir Annapolis MD 21401-1906

ALEXANDER, GEORGE JONATHON, law educator, former dean; b. Berlin, Mar. 8, 1931; s. Walter and Sylvia (Grill) A.; m. Katharine Violet Sziklai, Sept. 6, 1958; children: Susan Katina, George Jonathon II. AB with maj. honors, U. Pa., 1953, JD cum laude, 1969; LLM, Yale U., 1965, JSD, 1969. Bar: Ill. 1960, N.Y. 1961, Calif. 1974. Instr. law, Bigelow fellow U. Chgo., 1959-60; instr. internat. relations Naval Res. Officers Sch., Forrest Park, Ill., 1959-60; prof. law Syracuse U. Coll. Law, 1960-70, assoc. dean, 1968-69; prof. law U. Santa Clara (Calif.) Law Sch., 1970—, disting. univ. prof., 1994-95, Elizabeth H. and John A. Sutro prof. law, 1995—, pres. faculty senate, 1996-97, dean, 1970-85, dir. Inst. Internat. and Comparative Law, 1986—, dir. grad. programs, 1998-2001, co-dir., 2002. Dir. summer programs at Oxford, Geneva, Strasbourg, Budapest, Tokyo, Hong Kong, Beijing, Shanghai, Ho Chi Minh City, Singapore, Bangkok, Kuala Lumpur, Seoul, Munich; vis. prof. law U. So. Calif., 1963; vis. scholar Stanford (Calif.) U. Law Sch., 1985-86, 92; cons. in field. Author: Civil Rights, U.S.A., Public Schools, 1963, Honesty and Competition, 1967, Jury Instructing on Medical Issues, 1966, Cases and Materials on Space Law, 1971, The Aged and the Need for Surrogate Management, 1972, Commercial Torts, 1973, 2d edit. 1988, U.S. Antitrust Laws, 1980, Writing A Living Will: Using a Durable Power of Attorney, 1988, (with Scheflin) Law and Mental Disabilities, 1998; author, editor: International Perspectives on Aging, 1992; also articles, chpts. in books, one film. Dir. Domestic and Internat. Bus. Problems Honors Clinic, Syracuse U., 1966-69, Regulations in Space Project, 1968-70; ednl. cons. Comptroller Gen. U.S., 1977—; mem. Nat. Sr. Citizens Law Ctr., 1983-89, pres., 1986-90. With USN, 1953-56. U.S. Navy scholar U. Pa., 1949-52; Law Bds. scholar, 1956-59; Sterling fellow Yale, 1964-65; recipient Ralph E. Kharas Civil Liberties award, Syracuse U. Sch. Law, 1970, Owens award as Alumnus of Yr., 1984, Disting. prof. Santa Clara Univ. Faculty Senate, 1994-95, 2000 award for outstanding contbns. to cause of civil liberties Freedom of Thought Found.; named Disting. Vis. Prof. Krems Danube U., Vienna, 2001. Mem. Internat. Acad. Law Mental Health (mem. sci. com. 1997-99), Calif. Bar Assn. (first chmn. com. legal problems of aging), Assn. Am. Law Schs., Soc. Am. Law Tchrs. (dir., pres. 1979, Visionary Activist for Equality, Access and Diversity Throughout Law and Soc. award 2000), AAUP (chpt. pres. 1962), N.Y. Civil Liberties Union (chpt. pres. 1965, dir., v.p. 1966-70), Am. Acad. Polit. and Social Sci., Order of Coif, Justinian Honor Soc., Phi Alpha Delta (chpt. faculty adviser 1967-70) Home: 11600 Summit Wood Ct Los Altos Hills CA 94022 Office: U Santa Clara Sch Law Santa Clara CA 95053-0001 E-mail: gjalexander@aya.yale.edu. *I think a primary purpose of law is the protection of individual rights. That requires disproportionate attention to the interests of groups not in the mainstream of our society.*

ALEXANDER, GEORGE L. radiologist; b. Honolulu, 1921; AB, U. Calif., Berkeley, 1942; MD, U. Calif., San Francisco, 1946. Diplomate Am. Bd. Radiology. Intern U. Calif. San Francisco Hosp., 1946, resident in radiology, 1949-53. Capt. USAF, 1947-48. Fellow Am. Coll. Radiology; mem. Radiol. Soc. N.Am. E-mail: galexan772@aol.com.

ALEXANDER, GERRY L. state supreme court chief justice; b. Aberdeen, Wash., Apr. 28, 1936; BA, U. Wash., 1958, JD, 1964. Bar: Wash. 1964, U.S. Supreme Ct. 2000. Pvt. practice, Olympia, Wash., 1964—73; judge Wash. Superior Ct., Olympia, 1973—85, Wash. Ct. Appeals Divsn. II, Tacoma, 1985—95; state supreme ct. justice Wash. Supreme Ct., Olympia, 1995—2000, state supreme ct. chief justice, 2000—. Lt. U.S. Army, 1958—61. Mem.: ABA, Statute Law Com., Washington Cts. Hist. Soc., Bench-Bar-Press (chair), Puget Sound Inn of Ct. (pres. 1996), Thurston-Mason County Assn. (pres. 1973), Wash. State Bar Assn., Am. Judges Assn. Office: Temple of Justice PO Box 40929 Olympia WA 98504-0929 E-mail: j_g.alexander@courts.wa.gov.

ALEXANDER, HAROLD CAMPBELL, insurance consultant; b. Houston, Dec. 11, 1920; s. Henry Campbell and Essie Mae (Gilbert) A.; m. Dorothy Emma Schraub, Aug. 21, 1925; children: Linda Carol, Beverly Lynn Whitworth, Daniel James Alexander, William Campbell. BS, Miss. State U., 1938-42; postgrad., South Tex. Sch. Law, 1954-56, Harvard U., 1943, Navy Fin. and Supply Sch., 1942-43. Asst. div. credit mgr. Continental Emsco Co., Houston, 1953-56; gen. agt. and mgr. United Founders Life Ins. Co., 1956-69; mgr. Holt & Bridges Ins., Houston, 1960-69; owner, pres. Holt & Alexander Ins. Agy., Inc., Houston, 1969-85; ins. cons. Lawrence Ilfrey & Co., Houston, 1985—2003. Adv. bd. dirs. NBC Bank. Pres. Meyerland Cmty. Improvement Assn., 1969. Served as lt. commdr. USN, 1942-46, 1950-52. Mem. Profl. Ins. Agts. Tex. (state bd. dirs. 1973-74), Soc. Cert. Ins. Counselors, Club of Houston. Republican. Presbyterian. Avocation: golf. Home and Office: 8727 Manhattan Dr Houston TX 77096-1318

ALEXANDER, HERBERT E. political scientist; b. Waterbury, Conn., De 21, 1927; s. Nathan and Pearl (Shub) A.; m. Nancy Frances Greenfield, Dec. 1953 (dec.); children: Michael David, Andrew Steven, Kenneth Bruce. BA, U N.C., 1949; MA, U. Conn., 1951; PhD, Yale U., 1958. Asso. dir. adminstr officer money in politics research project U. N.C. at Chapel Hill, 1954-55; inst Princeton U., 1956-58; dir. Citizens' Rsch. Found., Princeton, 1958-78, L.A 1978-98, dir. emeritus, 1998—; prof. polit. sci. U. So. Calif., 1978—, pro emeritus, 1998—. Exec. dir. Pres.'s Com. on Campaign Costs, Washingto 1961-62; cons. Pres. U.S., 1962-64, House Adminstrn. Com., 1966-67, Comp troller Gen. U.S. and Office Fed. Elections at GAO, 1972-73, Senate Sele Com. on Presdl. Campaign Activities, 1973-74; vis. lectr. Princeton U., 1965, U Pa., Phila., 1967-68, Yale U., 1977; cons. N.J. Election Law Enforceme Commn., 1973-78, 82, 86, N.Y. State Bd. Elections, 1974-76, Ill. Bd. Election 1974-75, Gov. of R.I., 1987, others Author: Money in Politics, 1972, Financin the 1976 Election, 1979, Financing the 1980 Election, 1983, Financing Politic 1976, 2d edit., 1980, 3d edit., 1984 4th edit., 1992, Campaign Money, 197 (with Brian A. Haggerty) Financing the 1984 Election, 1987; editor: Studies Money in Politics, vol. 1, 1965, vol. 2, 1970, vol. 3, 1974, Comparative Politic Finance in the 1980s, 1989, (with Rei Shiratori) Comparative Political Financ Among the Democracies, 1994, (with Monica Bauer) Financing the 198 Election, 1991, Reform and Reality: The Financing of State and Loc Campaigns, 1991, (with Anthony Corrado) Financing the 1992 Election, 199 Served with AUS, 1946-47. Mem. Am. Polit. Sci. Assn., Nat. Mcpl. League, Sigma Alpha. Home: Unit 314 2904 N Leisure World Blvd Silver Spring M 20906

ALEXANDER, IAN ROBERT, lawyer; b. Skokie, Ill., Sept. 5, 1970; s. Josep David and Rhoda Carol A. BA, U. Ill., Urbana, 1992; JD, Tulane U., Ne Orleans, 1995. Bar: Ill.; U.S. Dist. Ct. (no. dist.) Ill. 1995, Fed. Trial Bar. Att Susan E. Loggans & Assocs., Chgo., 1995-99, Goldberg & Goldberg, Chgo 1999-2000, Meyers, Alexander & Kosner, Chgo., 2000—. Fellow The Rosco Pound Found., Assn. Trial Lawyers Am., Ill. Trial Lawyers Assn. Offic Meyers Alexander & Kosner 640 N LaSalle Ste 556 Chicago IL 60610 E-mai ira@maklaw.com.

ALEXANDER, JAMES H. industrial designer; b. Livermore, Calif., May 3 1945; s. James and Erin Estelle (Livingston) Alexander; m. Pauline Ann Rosil Oct. 10, 1970 (div. June 1985); m. Jeanne Marie Montgomery, Aug. 31, 200 children: James Blake, John Harvey. AA in liberal arts, Valley Forge Mil. Coll., 1965; BA in psychology, Case Western Res. U., 1969; BFA in inds design, Cleve. Inst. of Art, 1976; Grad. in indsl. design, U. Mich., 1977. Tch Youngstown Bd of Edn., Ohio, 1969—72; auto. stylist Chrysler Corp Highland Park, Mich., 1976—77; designer Richardson Smith Inc., Worthingto Ohio, 1977—78, Edward J. DeBartolo Corp., Youngstown, 1979—84; own Alexander & Co., Hubbard, Ohio, 1984; co-owner, mgr. Lex Pub. Co., Hubbar 1999—. Editor: Making Money, 1999. Recipient Cover Illustration awar Metal Progress Mag., 1976. Mem.: Indsl. Designers Soc. of Am., SAE Achievements include design of first postal drive-through fac. Avocation reading, golf, railroad historian, landscaping.

ALEXANDER, JAMES WESLEY, surgeon, educator; b. El Dorado, Kans May 23, 1934; s. Rossiter Wells and Merle Lydia Alexander; m. Maureen I Strohofer; children: Joseph, Judith, Elizabeth, Randolph, John Charles, Lor Molly. Student, Tex. Technol. Coll., 1951-53; MD, U. Tex., 1957; ScD, U. Cin 1958-64; postgrad., U. Minn., 1966-67. Diplomate Am. Bd. Surgery, Am. B Thoracic Surgery, lic. physician Ohio. Intern Cin. Gen. Hosp., 1957-58; reside U. Cin.-Cin. Gen. Hosp., 1958-64; mem. faculty Coll. Medicine, U. Cin 1962-64, 66—, prof. surgery, 1975—, dir. transplantation div., dept. surger 1967-99, dir. surg. immunology lab., 1967—2000; dir. research Shriners Burr Inst., 1979-90; practice medicine and surgery Cin., 1966—; dir. Ctr. for Surg Weight Loss, 2001—. Mem. staff U. Cin. Hosp., Bethesda Hosp., Ci Children's Hosp., Christ Hosp., Good Samaritan Hosp., Jewish Hosp.; mem study sect. NIH, 1983—87, 1989—93, chmn,, 1990—93, mem. ad hoc com 1990—99. Author (with R.A. Good): Fundamentals of Clinical Immunolog 1977; contbr. more than 650 articles to sci. jours. Capt. M.C. U.S. Arm 1964—66. Mem.: ACS, AAAS, Am. Soc. Bariatric Surgeons, Mont Reid Surg Soc., Shock Soc., Transplantation Soc., Surg. Infection Soc. (sec. 1981—8 pres.-elect 1985—86, pres. 1986—87), Soc. Univ. Surgeons, Ohio Med. Assn St. Paul Surg. Soc. (hon.), Internat. Soc. Surgery, Halsted Soc., Am. Surg. Assn Am. Soc. Parenteral and Enteral Nutrition, Am. Soc. Transplant Surgeons (se 1985—87, pres.-elect 1987—88, pres. 1988—89), Am. Burn Assn. (pres.-elec 1983—84, pres. 1984—85), Am. Assn. Immunologists, Am. Assn. for Surger of Trauma, Peruvian Acad. Surgery (hon.; hon.), Colombian Coll. Surgeon (hon.; hon.), Surg. Biology Club, Phi Eta Sigma, Alpha Epsilon Delta, Alph Chi, Alpha Omega Alpha. Home: 757 Riverwatch Dr Crescent Springs K 41017-4480 Office: U Cin Coll Medicine 231 Albert Sabin Way Cincinnati O 45267-0558 E-mail: jwesley.alexander@uc.edu.

ALEXANDER, JANE, actress, former federal agency administrator, produce author, theater educator; b. Boston, Oct. 28, 1939; d. Thomas Bartlett and Rut (Pearson) Quigley; m. Robert Alexander, July 23, 1962 (div. 1969); 1 chil Jason; m. Edwin Sherin, Mar. 29, 1975. Student, Sarah Lawrence Coll 1957-59, U. Edinburgh, 1959-60; LHD, Wilson Coll., 1984; DFA (hon.), Th Julliard Sch., 1994, N.C. Sch. Arts, 1994; PhD (hon.), U. Pa., 1995; DFA (hon. The New Sch. Social Rsch., 1996; PhD (hon.), Duke U., 1996; LHD (hon.), Th Coll. of Santa Fe, 1997; PhD, Sarah Lawrence Coll., 1998; DFA (hon.), Smit Coll., 1999, Pa. State U., 2000. Ind. TV, film and theatrical actress, 1962— chmn. Nat. Endowment for Arts, Washington, 1993-97. Guest artist in residenc Okla. Arts Inst., 1982, tchr. adult theatre workshop, 1984, 91, tchr. master clas 1990, Francis Eppes prof. Fla. Stat Univ., 2002—; bd. trustees Wildlif Conservation Soc., 1997—, Am. Bird Conservancy, 1995-98, The MacDowe Colony, 1997—, Arts Internat., 2000—. Author: (with Greta Jacobs) Th Bluefish Cookbook, 5 edits., 1979-95, ; translator: (with Sam Engelstad) Th Master Builder (Henrik Ibsen), 1978; Command Performance, An Actress in th Theater of Politics, 2000; appeared in prodns.: Charles Playhouse Bosto 1964-65, Arena Stage, Washington, 1965-68, 70—, Am. Shakespeare Festiva plays include Major Barbara, Mourning Becomes Electra, Merry Wives o Windsor, Stratford, Conn., summers 1971-72; Broadway prodns. include Th Great White Hope, 1968-69 (Tony award 1969, Drama Desk award, Theatr World award), 6 Rms Riv Vu, 1972-73 (Tony nomination), Find Your Wa Home, 1974 (Tony nomination), Hamlet, 1975, The Heiress, 1976, Firs Monday in October, 1978 (Tony nomination), Goodbye Fidel, 1980, Monda After the Miracle, 1982, Night of the Iguana, 1988, Shadowlands, 1990-91, Th Visit, 1992 (Tony nomination), The Sisters Rosensweig, 1993 (Drama Des award 1992-93, Tony award nomination, Obie award 1993), Honour (Ton nomination), 1998; also appeared in plays The Time of Your Life, Prese Laughter, 1975, The Master Builder, 1977, Losing Time, 1980, Antony an Cleopatra, 1981, Hedda Gabler, 1981, Old Times, 1984, Approaching Zanziba 1989, Mystery of the Rose Bouquet, 1989, The Cherry Orchard, 200 Mourning Becomes Electra, 2002, Rose and Walsh, 2003, Ghosts, 200 appeared in films The Great White Hope, 1970 (Acad. award nomination), Gunfight, 1970, The New Centurions, 1972, All the President's Men, 197 (Acad. award nomination), The Betsy, 1978, Kramer vs. Kramer, 1979 (Acad award nomination), Brubaker, 1980, Night Crossing, 1981, Testament, 198 (Acad. award nomination), City Heat, 1984, Sweet Country, 1986, Squar Dance, 1987, Glory, 1989, The Cider House Rules, 1999, Sunshine State, 2001 The Ring, 2002, Carry Me Home, 2003; appeared in TV films Welcome Hom Johnny Bristol, 1971, Miracle on 34th Street, 1973, Death Be Not Proud, 1974 This Was the West That Was, 1974, Eleanor and Franklin, 1976 (Emm nomination), Eleanor and Franklin: The White House Years, 1977 (Emm nomination, TV Critics Circle award), Lovey, 1977, A Question of Love, 197 Playing for Time, 1980 (Emmy award 1980), Calamity Jane: The Diary of Frontier Woman, 1981, Dear Liar, 1981, Kennedy's Children, 1981, In th Custody of Strangers, 1982, When She Says No, 1983, Mountainview, 198 Daughter of the Streets, 1990, A Marriage: Georgia O'Keeffe and Alfre Stieglitz, 1991; appeared in TV spls. A Circle of Children, 1977, Blood an Orchids, 1986, Calamity Jane, 1984 (Emmy nomination), Malice in Wonder land, 1985 (Emmy nomination), In Love and War, 1987, Open Admissions 1988, A Friendship in Vienna, 1988, Stay the Night, 1992, The Jenifer Estes Story, 2001; appeared in TV series: Law and Order Spl. Victims Unit, 2000 (Emmy nomination); Intimate Portrait, Lifetime TV Biography, 1998. Recipien Achievement in Dramatic Arts award St. Botolph Club, 1979, Israel Cultura award, 1982, Western Heritage Wrangler award, 1985, Helen Caldicott Lead ership award, 1984, Living Legacy award Women's Internat. Ctr., San Diego

1988, Environ. Leadership award Eco-Expo, 1991, Muse award N.Y. Women in Film, 1993, Torch of Hope award, 1992, Lectureship award NIH, 1994, Houseman award The Acting Co., 1994, medal UCLA, 1994, Outer Critics Circle award Disting. Voice in Theatre, 1994, Helen Hayes award Am. Express Tribute, 1994, Women of Achievement award Anti-Defamation League, 1994, Margo Jones award, 1995, Mass. Soc. award, 1995, N.Am. Mont Blanc de la Culture award, 1995, Common Wealth award, 1995, Creative Coalition: Christopher Reeve First Amendment award, 1998, Outstanding Leadership for Advancement in Arts, People for Am. Way, 1998, Lifetime Achievement award Americans for Arts and U.S. Conf. Mayors, 1999, Harry S. Truman award for pub. svc., Independence, Md., 1999; Woman of Achievement Award, San Antonio, Tex., 2000, Director's Guild of Am. award, 2002; named to Theatre Hall of Fame, 1993. Mem. AFTRA, SAG, Actors Equity Assn., Acad. Motion Picture Arts and Scis., Acad. Arts and Scis., Actors Fund. Office: William Morris Agy c/o Samuel Liff 1325 Avenue of Americas New York NY 10019

ALEXANDER, JASON (JAY SCOTT GREENSPAN), actor; b. Newark, N.J., Sept. 23, 1959; s. Alexander and Ruth Minnie (Simon) Greenspan; m. Daena E. Title, May 31, 1982;1 child, Gabriel. Student, Boston U., 1977-80. N.Y.C. stage debut in Merrily We Roll along, Alvin Theatre, 1981; other theater appearances include America Kicks Up Its Heels, 1982, On Hold With Music, 1982, Fragments, 1982, Forbidden Broadway, 1983, The Rink, 1984, D, 1985, Personals, 1985-86 season, Broadway Bound, 1986-87 season, Jerome Robbins' Broadway, 1989 (Tony award for best performance by a leading actor in a musical), Accomplice, 1990, Light Up The Sky, 1990, Give 'Em Hell, Harry, 1993 (Drama-Loge award), The Producers (Los Angeles), 2003; film debut in The Burning, 1979; other film appearances include The Mosquito Coast, 1986, Brighton Beach Memoirs, 1986, Pretty Woman, 1989, Jacobs Ladder, 1989, White Palace, 1989, I Don't Buy Kisses Anymore, 1991, Coneheads, 1993, Sexual Healing, 1993, North, 1994, The Paper, 1994, Blankman, 1994; The Last Supper, 1995, Love! Valour! Compassion!, 1996, the Hunchback of Notre Dame, 1996, For Better or Worse, 1996, Dunston Checks In, 1996, Denial, 1998, Adventures of Rocky & Bullwinkle, 1999, On Edge, 2001, Shallow Hal, 2001, How to Go Out on a Date in Queens, 2003; TV films include Senior Trip, 1981, Rockabye, 1986, Favorite Son, 1988, Bye Bye Birdie, 1995, Cinderella, 1998, Love & Action in Chicago, 1998,; TV series: E/R, 1984-85, Everything's Relative, 1987, Seinfeld, 1990-98 (Emmy nomination, Supporting Actor - Comedy, 1993, 94), Duckman (voice only), 1994—97, Bob Patterson, 2001; guest appearances include Dream On, 1993 (Emmy nomination, Guest Actor - Comedy Series, 1994), Star Trek, Voyager, 1999, actor, dir. For Better or Worse, 1995. Office: William Morris Agy 151 S El Camino Dr Beverly Hills CA 90212-2775

ALEXANDER, JOHN BRADFIELD, scientist, retired army officer; b. N.Y.C., Nov. 21, 1937; m. Victoria Lacas Alexander; children: Marc Bradfield, Joshua John. BGS in Sociology, U. Nebr., 1971; MA in Edn., Pepperdine U., 1975; PhD in Edn., Walden U., 1980; postgrad., UCLA, 1990, MIT, 1991, Harvard U., 1993; attended various milit. schs. Pvt. U.S. Army, 1956, advanced through grades to col., 1986, comdr. Army Spl. Forces Teams, 1966-69, chief human resources divsn., 1977-79, inspector gen. Dept. of Army Washington, 1980-82, chief human tech. Army Intelligence Command Arlington, Va., 1982-83, mgr. tech. integration Army Materiel Command Alexandria, Va., 1983-85, dir. advanced concepts U.S. Army Lab. Command Adelphi, Md., 1985-88, ret., 1988; mgr. nonlethal weapons def. tech. Los Alamos (N.Mex.) Nat. Lab., 1988-95 (ret.), mgr. anti-materiel tech. Def. Initiatives Office, 1988-91, program mgr. contingency missions tech. Conventional Def. Tech., 1991-92; dir. for sci. liaison Nat. Inst. for Discovery Sci., Las Vegas, Nev., 1995—2002; pres. LEADS Inc., 2002—. Vis. scientist Los Alamos, 1995-96; panelist Nat. Inst. Justice, Washington, 1994; adj. prof. Grad. Sch. Union Inst., Cin., 1992-97; U.S. del. to NATO adv. group aerospace R&D, 1994-97; chmn. NonLethal Def. Conf. Johns Hopkins Applied Physics Lab., 1993, NonLethal Def. Conf. II, 1996, III, 1998, IV, 1999; mem. tech. panel Advanced Weapons Conf., 1992, tech. opportunities in low intensity conflict panel LIC Tech. Conf., RAND Corp., 1992; cons. Office Sec. of Def., 1996—; spkr., presenter in field. Author: Future War: Non-Lethal Weapons 21st Century Warfare, 1999; co-author: The Warrior's Edge, 1990; contbr. numerous articles to profl. jours. Bd. dirs., past v.p. Children's Hospice Internat., Alexandria, 1982-96. Recipient Nat. Award for Volunteerism by Pres. Reagan, 1987, Aerospace Laureate award Aviation Week, 1993, 94, Weapons Program recognition of excellence, 1994; decorated numerous milit. awards; inducted into Laureate Hall of Fame U.S. Air and Space Mus., 1997, U.S. Army OCS Hall of Fame, 2001. Mem. NAS (study of non-lethal weapons and tech. com.), Soc. Sci. Exploration. Home: 9521 Grand Canal Dr Las Vegas NV 89117-0860 E-mail: nonlethal2@aol.com.

ALEXANDER, JOHN CHARLES, pharmaceutical company executive, physician; b. Perth Amboy, NJ, Dec. 28, 1943; s. Charles John and Agnes (Maloney) A.; m. Margaret Ann Kohler, July 19, 1969; children: Laurel, Jennifer, Anna. BS, St. Francis Coll., Loretto, Pa., 1965; MD, St. Louis U., 1970; MPH, Johns Hopkins U., 1972. Intern Barnes Hosp./Washington U., St. Louis, 1970-71; resident in gen. preventive medicine State of Va./Med. Coll. Va., Richmond, 1974-76; asst. clin. rsch. dir. Squibb Inst. Med. Rsch., Princeton, N.J., 1976-77, assoc. clin. rsch. dir., 1977-79, dir. clin. rsch., 1979-82, v.p. cardiovascular clin. rsch., 1982-86, sr. v.p. med. affairs, 1986-90; v.p. rsch. Bristol-Myers-Squibb Pharm. Rsch. Inst., Princeton, 1990-91; sr. v.p. med. rsch. Searle, Skokie, Ill., 1991-93, exec. v.p. med. rsch., 1993-99; pres. Sankyo Pharma Devel., Edison, NJ, 1999—; global head R&D Sankyo Co. Ltd., Tokyo, 2003—; also. bd. dirs. Patentee in field. Lt. comdr. USN, 1972-74. Mem. Drug Info. Assn. (pres., bd. dirs.), Alpha Omega Alpha. Home: 86 Beech Hollow Ln Princeton NJ 08540-1235 Office: Sankyo Pharma Inc 399 Thornall St Edison NJ 08837-2236 E-mail: jalexander@sankyopharma.com.

ALEXANDER, JOHN CHARLES, editor, writer; b. Lincoln, Nebr., Jan. 25, 1915; s. John Merriam Alexander and Helen (Abbott) Boggs; m. Ruth Edna McLane, Aug. 20, 1955. Student, U. Nebr., 1933-37, Chouinard Art Inst./Ben Bard Playhouse Sch., L.A., 1937-38, Pasadena Playhouse, 1939-42, UCLA, 1945-47. Aircraft assembler N. Am. aviation, Inglewood, Calif., 1941-42; engrng. writer Lockheed-Vega Aircraft, Burbank, Calif., 1942-45; prodn. mgr/actor Gryphon Playhouse, Laguna Beach, Calif., 1947-49; asst. producer/writer Young & Rubicam/ABC, Hollywood, Calif., 1949-51; editor-in-chief Grand Cen. Aircraft, Tucson, 1952-53; sr. writer/editor various cos., Calif., 1953-60; sr. editor/writer, sec. Sci. Guidance Rsch. Coun. Stanford Rsch. Inst., U.S. Army Combat Devel. Command, Menlo Park, Calif., 1962-66; editor-in-chief Litton Sci. Support Lab. USACDC, Fort Ord, Calif., 1966-70; editorial dir./sec. The Nelson Co., Film and Video Prodn., Tarzana, Calif., 1971—98. Editorial cons., dir. Human Resources Rsch. Office, George Washington U., The Presidio, Monterey, Calif., 1960-62; book editor The Dryden Press, Hinsdale, Ill., 1971-72; book editor/adaptor Gen. Learning Press, Silver Burdette Co., Morristown, N.J., 1972-74; contbg. editor West Coast Writers Conspiracy mag., Hollywood, Calif., 1975-77; contbg. editor/book reviewer Santa Ynez Valley Times, Solvang, Calif., 1976-77; participant Santa Barbara Writers Conf., Montecito, Calif., 1974, 75. Author: (TV plays) Michael Has Company for Coffee, 1948, House on the Hill, 1958, (radio drama) The Couple Next Door, 1951; co-author nine films for U.S. Dept. Justice: Under the Law, Parts I and II, 1973; co-author 10 films for Walt Disney Ednl. Media Co.: Lessons in Learning, Parts I and II, 1978-81; author: (with others) The American West Anthology, 1971; editorial cons. Strangers in Their Land: CBI Bombardier, 1939-45, 1990-92. Recipient award for short story, Writer's Digest, 1960, 61, Gold award, The Festival of the Americas, Houston Internat. Film Festival, 1977. Mem. Nat. Cowboy Hall of Fam, Nat. Geog. Soc., Nat. Soc. Lit. and Arts, Soc. Tech. Writers and Pubs., Western Hist. Soc., Calif. Acad. Sci., Nat. Air and Space Mus., Smithsonian Instn., Woodrow Wilson Internat. Ctr. for Scholars, Aircraft Owners and Pilots Assn., Air Force Assn., U. Nebr.-Lincoln Alumni Assn., Stanford Rsch. Internat. Alumni Assn., Sigma Nu, Alpha Phi Omega. Avocations: scale model building, environmental/wildlife conservation, aviation, science, foreign affairs, intelligence. Home and Office: 23123 Village 23 Camarillo CA 93012-7602

ALEXANDER, JOHN DAVID, JR., college administrator; b. Springfield, Tenn., Oct. 18, 1932; s. John David and Mary Agnes (McKinnon) A.; m. Catharine Coleman, Aug. 26, 1956; children: Catharine McKinnon, John David III, Julia Mary. BA, Southwestern at Memphis, 1953; student, Louisville Presbyn. Theol. Sem., 1953-54; DPhil (Rhodes Scholar), Oxford (Eng.) U., 1957; LLD, U. So. Calif., Occidental Coll., 1970, Centre Coll. of Ky., 1971, Pepperdine U., 1991, Albertson Coll. Idaho, 1992; LHD, Loyola Marymount U., 1983; LittD, Rhodes Coll., 1986, Pomona Coll., 1996. Assoc. prof. San Francisco Theol. Sem., 1957-65; pres. Southwestern at Memphis, 1965-69, Pomona Coll., Claremont, Calif., 1969-91. Am. sec. Rhodes Scholarship Trust, 1981—98; mem. commn. liberal learning Assn. Am. Colls., 1966—69, mem. commn. instl. affairs, 1971—74; mem. commn. colls. So. Assn. Colls. and Schs., 1966—69; mem. Nat. Commn. Acad. Tenure, 1971—72; dir. Am. Coun. on Edn., 1981—84, Nat. Assn. Ind. Colls. and Univs.; bd. dirs. Children'sm Hosp. L.A.; trustee Tchrs. Inst. and Annuity Assn., 1970—2002, Woodrow Wilson Nat. Fellowship Found., 1978—99, Seaver Inst., 1992—, Fellows of Soc. Phi Beta Kappa, 1993—, v.p., 1998—; bd. dirs. Wenner-Gren Found. for Anthrop. Rsch., 1995—, Webb Schs. Calif., 1995—; bd. overseers Huntington Libr., 1991—. Editor: The American Oxonian, 1997-2000. Decorated comdr. Order Brit. Empire; named Disting. Friend of Oxford U., 2000. Mem. Soc. Bib. Lit., Soc. Religion in Higher Edn., Phi Beta Kappa Alumni in So. Calif. (pres. 1974-76), Century Club, Calif. Club, Bohemian Club, Phi Beta Kappa, Omicron Delta Kappa, Sigma Nu. Office: Pomona Coll 333 N College Way Claremont CA 91711-4429 E-mail: dalexander@pomona.edu.

ALEXANDER, JOHN KURT, history educator; b. Vancouver, Wash., Oct. 25, 1941; s. Eugene Victor and Marta T. Alexander; m. June Granatir, Dec. 29, 1973. BS in Edn. with honors, Western Oreg. U., Monmouth, 1964; MA in History, U. Chgo., 1965, PhD in History, 1973. From asst. prof. to prof. history U. Cin., 1969—2002, Disting. tchg. prof., 2003—. Author: Render Them Submissive, 1980, The Selling of the Constitutional Convention, 1990, Samuel Adams, 2002; assoc. editor Am. Nat. Biography, Oxford U. Press, 1989-99; contbr. articles to profl. jours. Mem. Orgn. Am. Historians, Hist. Soc. Pa., Pa. Hist. Soc., Ohio Acad. History (Outstanding Tchr. award 2002), Soc. for Historians of Early Am. Republic. Home: 3410 Bishop St Cincinnati OH 45220-1831 Office: Univ Cin Dept History Ml 0373 Cincinnati OH 45221-0373 E-mail: John.K.Alexander@uc.edu.

ALEXANDER, JOHN MACMILLAN, JR., chemistry educator; b. Columbia, Mo., Aug. 17, 1931; s. John Macmillan and Victoria (Holladay) A.; m. Betty Jo Linton, Aug. 1, 1953; children: Mary Jo, John Macmillan III, Frank Linton, James Holladay. BS, Davidson Coll., 1953; PhD, MIT, 1956. Research assoc. MIT, 1956-57; research chemist Lawrence Radiation Lab., Berkeley, Calif., 1957-63; assoc. prof. chemistry SUNY at Stony Brook, 1963-67, prof., 1968—, chmn. exec. com. faculty senate, 1969, chmn. dept. chemistry, 1970-72; AEC-ERDA, Dept. Energy researcher, 1964—; research collaborator Brookhaven Nat. Lab., 1964—; chmn. Gordon Research Conf. on Nuclear Chemistry, 1966. Mem. exec. com. Berkeley Superhilac Accelerator, 1975-78, 85-87; vis. scientist Centre d'Etudes Nucléaires, Bordeaux, France, 1974; vis. prof. Centre d'Etudes Nucléaires de Bordeaux-Gradignan and Institut de Physique Nucléaire, Orsay, France, 1978; program adv. com. Tandem Van De Graaff Accelerator, Brookhaven Nat. Lab., 1977-83, Holifield Heavy Ion Research Facility, Oak Ridge Nat. Lab., 1986-87, SARA accelerator Institut des Sciences Nucléaires de Grenoble, France, 1988. Assoc. editor: Am. Chem. Soc. Monographs, 1968-69; contbr. articles to profl. jours. Recipient Great Amer. Home award Nat. Trust for Historic Preservation, 1993; Dupont teaching fellow, 1955-56, Sloan fellow, 1964-67, Guggenheim fellow Laboratoire de Chimie Nucléaire, Orsay, France, 1969-70. Fellow Am. Phys. Soc.; mem. Am. Chem. Soc. (chmn. divsn. nuclear chemistry and tech. 1988, vice chmn. 1987, nuclear chemistry award 1991), Phi Beta Kappa. Democrat. Achievements include research on radioactivity, high-energy nuclear reactions: fission, spallation and fragmentation; heavy ion reactions: elastic scattering, complete and incomplete fusion and reaction cross sections; splintering central collisions; energy thermalization mechanisms from low to relativistic energies; hot nuclei; energy and spin dissipation, evaporative deexcitation; fragmentation; emission lifetimes; nuclear equation of state; statistical and dynamical models. Home: 14 Highwood Rd East Setauket NY 11733-1512 Office: SUNY Dept Chemistry Stony Brook NY 11794-3400

ALEXANDER, JOHN STONE, retired radiologist; b. Paris, 1929; s. Drury B. and Katherine (Stone) A. BA, U. Tex., 1950; MD, U. Tex., Galveston, 1954. Diplomate Am. Bd. Radiology. Intern DC Gen. Hosp., Washington, 1954-55; resident in radiology Scott-White Clinic, Temple, Tex., 1957-60; ret., 1989. Mem. staff Harris Hosp., Ft. Worth. Fellow Am. Coll. Radiology; mem. AMA, Radiol. Soc. N.Am. Presbyterian. E-mail: jsalex947@charter.net.

ALEXANDER, JOHN THORNDIKE, historian, educator; b. Cooperstown, N.Y., Jan. 18, 1940; s. Edward Porter and Alice Wagner (Bolton) A.; m. Maria Kovalak Hreha, June 13, 1964; children— Michal Porter, Darya Ann BA, Wesleyan U., Middletown, Conn., 1961; cert. regional specialization Russian Inst., MA, Ind. U., 1963, PhD, 1966. Asst. prof. U. Kans., Lawrence, 1966-70, assoc. prof., 1970-74, prof. history, 1974—. Fellow Inter-Univ. Com. on Travel Grants, 1964-65, Internat. Research and Exchanges Bd., 1971, 75, 96. Author: Autocratic Politics, 1969, Emperor of the Cossacks, 1973, Bubonic Plague in Russia, 1980, 2003, Catherine the Great, 1989 (Byron Caldwell Smith award for best book by a Kans. author pub. in 1987-88), reissued luxury edit., 1999; translator, editor: Platonov, Time of Troubles, 1970, Anisimov, Reforms of Peter the Great, 1993, Anisimov, Empress Elisabeth, 1995. Recipient Balfour Jeffrey Higuchi Endowment Rsch. Achievement award, 1992. Mem. Am. Assn. for Advancement Slavic Studies, Brit. Study Group on 18th Century Russia, So. Conf. on Slavic Studies (ann. sr. scholar award 2001). Democrat. Roman Catholic. Avocation: sports. Home: 2216 Orchard Ln Lawrence KS 66049-2706 Office: U Kans Dept History Wescoe Hall Rm 3001 1445 Jayhawk Blvd Lawrence KS 66045-7590 E-mail: jatalex@ku.edu.

ALEXANDER, JONATHAN, cardiologist, consultant; b. N.Y.C., Nov. 29, 1947; s. Josef and Hannah (Margolis) A.; m. Karen Deborah Einhorn, Aug. 8, 1971; children: Jessica Beth, Daniel Lewis, Benjamin Joel. BA, Harvard U., 1968; MD, Albert Einstein Coll. Medicine, 1973. MD. Intern, resident Yale-New Haven Hosp., 1973-76; fellow dept. cardiology Sch. Medicine Yale U., New Haven, 1976-78, asst. clin. prof. medicine, 1978-83, assoc. clin. prof., 1983-95, clin. prof., 1995—; attending physician Danbury (Conn.) Hosp., 1978—, West Haven (Conn.) Vets. Hosp., 1978—, New Milford (Conn.) Hosp., 1980; dir. cardiac rehab. unit and nuclear cardiology Danbury (Conn.) Hosp., 1978—. Recipient Samuel Kushlan award Yale-New Haven Hosp., 1974, Revlon award 11th Internat. Congress Chemotherapy, 1983. Fellow ACP, Am. Coll. Cardiology (gov. Conn. 1993-96), Conn. chpt. Am. Coll. Cardiology (pres. 1993-96), Conn. Hosp. Assn., Found. for Cmty. Health Care. Jewish.

ALEXANDER, JOYCE MARY, illustrator; b. Pepin, Wis., Mar. 31, 1927; d. Colonel and Martha (Varnum) Yochem; m. Don Tocher, June 27, 1955 (div. 1962); m. Dorsey Potter Alexander, Nov. 1, 1963. Student, Coll. Arts and Crafts, 1946, Acad. of Art, 1961-62. Co-founder, owner Turtle's Quill Scriptorium Publishers, Berkeley, Calif., 1963—. Author: Thaddeus, 1972, Happy Bird Day, 1980; illustrator numerous books including: Soil and Plant Analysis, A Practical Guide for the Home Gardener, 1963, CAlifornia Farm and Ranch Law, 1967, Chinatown, A Legend of Old Cannery Row, 1968, The Sea: Excerpts from Herman Melville, 1969, Of Mice, 1966, David: Psalm Twenty-Four, 1970, Shakespeare: Selected Sonnets, 1974, The Blue-Jay Yarn, 1975, Psalm One Hundred Four, 1978, Messiah: Choruses from Handel's Messiah, 1985, A Flurry of Angels, Angels in Literature, 1986, Eleven Poems by Emily Dickinson, A Packet of Rhymes, 1989, Psalm Eight (A Nature Psalm), 1991, Poems, Emily Dickenson, 1992, Comfort Me With Apples-Excerpts From Literature Involving Food, 1993, Father William, 1994, Alice by Lewis Carroll, Excerpts from Alice in Wonderland, 1999; work represented in permanent collections Hunt Botan. Libr. at Carnegie-Mellon U. Republican. Office: Turtle's Quill Scriptorium PO Box 643 Mendocino CA 95460 0643

ALEXANDER, JUDD HARRIS, retired paper company executive; b. Owatonna, Minn., Mar. 23, 1925; s. Mark Hastings and Veta Enola (Harris) A.; m. Theo Mary Paltzer, May 19, 1956; children: Morah Lee, Duncan McIndoe, Todd Stewart. BA, Carleton Coll., 1949, PhD (hon.), 2001; postgrad., Harvard U., 1967. Co-founder Nu-Bilt Co., Owatonna, dir., 1942-71; sec. in pres.'s office, salesman Marathon Corp., Rothschild, Wis., 1949-57; with Am. Can Co., Greenwich, Conn., 1957-82, v.p., gen. mgr. spl. products packaging, 1972-73, sr. v.p. group exec. packaging, 1974-75, sr. v.p. office of chmn., 1975-81, exec. v.p. paper sector, 1981-82; exec. v.p. James River Corp., Norwalk, Conn., 1982-89, ret., 1989; chmn. Paperboard Packaging Council, 1976-78, Can Mfrs. Inst., 1978-80, Solid Waste Coun. of Paper Industry, 1977-88. Bd. dirs. encore Paper Co., Inc., 1992-95; adj. prof. environ. sci. SUNY, Syracuse, 1979-84. Author: In Defense of Garbage, 1993; contbr. articles to profl. and bus. jours., including Wall Street Jour., N.Y. Times, Industry Week. Trustee Carleton Coll., 1973-2000, Am. Shakespeare Theater, 1980-82; bd. dirs. New Eng. Legal Found., 1979-82, Norwalk (Conn.) Hosp., 1985-88, Ctr. for Advanced Studies U. Va., 1988—; chmn. bd. trustees Keep Am. Beautiful (bd. dirs. 1979-90), 1986-88. Decorated Bronze Star medal; Woodrow Wilson vis. fellow, 1975-82 Mem. Conn. Bus. Industry Assn. (bd. dirs. 1976-80, 85-89), Quechee Club, The Boulders Club. Republican. Congregationalist. Home: PO Box 3034 3041 Ironwood Rd Carefree AZ 85377 E-mail: jddalex@aol.com.

ALEXANDER, JUDITH ELAINE, psychologist; b. Worcester, Mass., Nov. 30, 1948; d. Frank E. and Winnona V. (Tracy) A.; divorced; children: Kimberly, Jenniferlyn. BS, Worcester State Coll., 1981; MA, Assumption Coll., Worcester, 1986; PsyD, Antioch New Eng., Keane, N.H., 1991. Lic. psychologist. Dir. mental health Indian Health Svc., Ft. Thompson, S.D., 1992-95; cons. self employed, 1995—; psychologist VAMC, Dublin, Ga., 2001—. Adj. faculty Mt. Wachusett C.C., Gardner, Mass., 1996—, Western New Eng. Coll., 1996—. Contbr. articles to profl. jours. Mem. APA, NEA, Nat. Assn. Forensic Counselors, Mass. Tchrs. Assn. Home: 207 Mimosa Dr Dublin GA 31021

ALEXANDER, KATHARINE VIOLET, lawyer; b. N.Y.C., Nov. 19, 1934; d. George Clifford and Violet (Jambor) Sziklai; m. George Jonathon Alexander, Sept. 6, 1958; children: Susan Katina, George J. II. Student, Smith Coll., Geneva, 1954-55; BA, Goucher Coll., 1956; JD, U. Pa., 1959; student specialized courses, U. Santa Clara, 1974-76. Bar: Calif. 1974, U.S. Dist. Ct. (no. dist.) Calif. 1974, U.S. Ct. Appeals (9th cir.) 1974; cert. criminal lawyer Calif. State Bar Bd. Legal Specialization. Research dir., adminstr. Am. Bar Found., Chgo., 1959-60; lectr. law San Jose (Calif.) State U., 1972-74; sr. atty. Santa Clara County, San Jose, 1974-97, ret., 1997. Editor: Mentally Disabled and the Law, 1961; contbg. author: The Aged and the Need for Surrogate Management, 1969-70, Jury Instructions on Medical Issues, 1965-67. Community rep. Office Econ. Opportunity Com., Syracuse, N.Y., 1969-70. Mem. AAUW, Food and Wine Inst., Calif. Bar Assn., Santa Clara County Bar Assn. (trustee 1981-82), Calif. Attys. for Criminal Justice (bd. govs. 1988-92), Jr. League, Anthropology and Stanford Museum of Arts. Presbyterian. Avocations: stock market, gourmet, traveling. Home and Office: 11600 Summit Wood Ct Los Altos Hills CA 94022-4500 Fax: 650-948-7596.

ALEXANDER, KENNETH LEWIS, editorial cartoonist; b. Gridley, Calif., June 16, 1924; s. Zareh and Rose (Affolter) A.; m. Dariel A. Hereford, July 15, 1949; children: Mark Kenneth, Stephen Scott, Peter Neil. Student, U. Calif. at Berkeley, 1942-43, Rutgers U., 1943-44, Calif. Coll. Arts and Crafts, 1946-47. Free-lance comml. artist, 1947-58; editor Pictorial Living mag., San Francisco Examiner, 1958-63; Sunday art dir., 1963-66, editorial cartoonist, 1966-84, syndicated Copley News Service, 1982-89; TV editorial cartoonist, Sta. KGO-TV, 1968-69; author: (with Andrew Curtin) A Gallery of Great Americans. Served with AUS, 1943-46. Mem. Nat. Cartoonists Soc., Soc. Am. Editorial Cartoonists, Am. Newspaper Guild, AFTRA, Kappa Alpha. Home: 1182 Glen Rd Lafayette CA 94549-3044 *As a relatively successful member of a profession whose sine qua non is the ability to come up with an endless supply of interesting, original ideas, I assign myself no credit whatever for having that ability. It is a God-given talent, and it is to Him I turn for the inspiration, the comfort, and the reassurance that He so generously and lovingly provides. And it is to Him I give my daily thanks.*

ALEXANDER, KENNETH SAUL, pharmaceuticals educator; b. Phila., Nov. 27, 1942; s. Martin R. and Ida Z. Alexander; m. Karen L. Haury, Aug. 18, 1968; children: Kimberly A., Kirsten R. (dec.), Kevin C. BSc, Phila. Coll. Pharmacy and Sci., 1965, MSc, 1970; PhD, U. R.I., 1972; EdS, U. Toledo, 1981. Instr. U. R.I., 1971-72; asst. prof. pharmacy U. Toledo, 1972-76, assoc. prof., 1977-92, prof. pharmacy, 1992—. Coord. indsl. pharmacy divsn., Coll. Pharmacy, U. Toledo; bd. dirs. MCO Fed. Credit Union, 1976-91, pres., 1981-84; cons. to pharm. and pharmacy industry. Mem. St. Mary's Sch. Bd., Monroe, Mich., 1985-89; mem. adv. com. Bedford Twp. Community Ctr., 1979-80; mem. Lucas County Hypertension Coordinating Com., 1985-89; mem. exec. coun. Boy Scouts Am., 1998—, troop com., 1990—. Mem. Am. Assn. Colls. aPharmacy (sec. tchrs. pharmacy sect. 1986, chmn.-elect 1987, chmn. 1988), Am. Chem. Soc., Ohio Pharm. Assn. (treas. 1986-89, v.p. 1989-90, pres. 1991), Ohio Pharmacists Assn. (pres. 1991-92), Toledo Acad. Pharmacy (bd. dirs. 1976-88, pres. 1990-91), pres. 1985-86), Toledo Area Soc. Hosp. Pharmacists (pres. 1986-87, 89-90). Home: 7924 Wiseman Rd Lambertville MI 48144-9682 Office: U Toledo Coll Pharmacy 280L W Bancroft St Toledo OH 43620-1832

ALEXANDER, KENT B. lawyer; b. Atlanta, Nov. 7, 1958; BA in Polit. Sci. magna cum laude, Tufts U., 1980; JD, U. Va., 1983. Bar: Ga. 1983. Assoc. Long & Alridge, Atlanta, 1983-85; asst. U.S. atty. for no. dist. Ga., U.S. Dept. Justice, Atlanta, 1985-92, U.S. atty., 1994-97; of counsel, ptnr. King & Spalding, Atlanta, 1992-94, ptnr., 1997-99; sr. v.p., gen. counsel Emory Univ., 2000—. Co-founder Hands On Atlanta. Office: Emory Univ 401 Administration Bldg Atlanta GA 30322-0001

ALEXANDER, LAMAR (ANDREW LAMAR ALEXANDER), senator, former secretary of education, former governor, lawyer; b. Maryville, Tenn., July 3, 1940; s. Andrew Lamar and Genevra Floreine (Rankin) A.; m. Leslee Kathryn Buhler, Jan. 4, 1969; children: Andrew, Leslee, Kathryn, Will. BA, Vanderbilt U., 1962; JD, NYU, 1965. Bar: Tenn. 1965. Law clk. to Hon. John Wisdom U.S. Ct. Appeals (5th cir.), New Orleans; assoc. Fowler, Rountree, Fowler & Robertson, Knoxville, 1965; legis. asst. to Senator Howard Baker, 1967-68; exec. asst. to Bryce Harlow, White House Congl. Liaison Office, 1969-70; ptnr. Dearborn and Ewing, Nashville, 1970-76; gov. State of Tenn., Nashville, 1979-87; chmn. Leadership Inst. Belmont Coll., Nashville, 1987-88; pres. U. Tenn., 1988-91; sec. Dept. Edn., Washington, 1991-93; counsel Baker, Donelson, Bearman & Caldwell, Nashville, 1993-98; pvt. practice Nashville, 1999—2001; U.S. senator from Tenn., 2003—. Mem. Pres.'s Task Force on Federalism; chmn. Nat. Govs. Assn., 1985-86, Pres.'s Commn. on Ams. Outdoors, 1985-87; co-director Empower Am., 1994-95; Goodman vis. prof. practice of pub. svc. Harvard U., 2001. Author: Steps Along the Way, 1986, Six Months Off, 1988, We Know What To Do, 1995; co-editor: The New Promise of American Life, 1995. Mgr. Winfield Dunn for Gov. Campaign, 1970, chief transition, 1970-71; Rep. nominee for Gov. of Tenn., 1974; chmn. Rep. Exch. Satellite Network, 1993-95; Rep. Presdl. candidate, 1995-96. Recipient Nat. Disting. Svc. to Edn. award Burger King, 1988, James B. Conant award Edn. Commn. of the States, 1988, Disting. State Leadership award Am. Assn. State Colls. and Univs., 1989, Teddy Roosevelt award Nat. Coll. Athletic Assn., 1993, honored as Silver Anniversary scholar-athlete, 1987; NYU Law Sch. Root-Tilden scholar. Fellow (sr.) Hudson Inst.; mem. Phi Beta Kappa. Republican. Presbyterian. Office: Off of Senator Alexander Dirksen 40 Ste 2 Washington DC 20510*

ALEXANDER, LESLIE LEE, professional sports team executive; b. N.Y.C., June 30, 1943; BS, NYU, 1964; JD, Western State Coll., 1977. Owner, pres. Houston Rockets, 1987—. Office: Houston Rockets Ste 400 2 Greenway Plz Houston TX 77046-3865

ALEXANDER, LEWIS MCELWAIN, geographer, educator; b. Summit, N.J., June 15, 1921; s. Harry Louis and Laura (Stryker) A.; m. Jacqueline Peterson, Dec. 30, 1950; children: Louise Anne, Lance Stryker. AB, Middlebury (Vt.) Coll., 1942; MA, Clark U., 1948, PhD, 1949. Instr. geography Hunter Coll., 1949-50; asst. prof. geography Harpur Coll., State U. N.Y., 1950-57, asso. prof., 1957-60; prof. geography U. R.I., Kingston, 1960-80, 83-91, prof. emeritus, 1991—, chmn. dept., 1960-80, dir. marine affairs program, 1968-80, dir. Ctr. for Ocean Mgmt. Studies, 1983-89; cons. State Dept., 1963-80; dir. Office of Geographer, 1980-83. Exec. dir. Law of Sea Inst., 1965-73, mem. exec. bd., 1973-82, 85-91; mem. ocean affairs adv. com. Dept. State, 1973-80; dep. dir. Pres.'s Commn. on Marine Sci., Engring. and Resources, 1967-68; cons. Nat. Coun. for Marine Resources and Engring. Devel., 1969-70; mem. adv. com. on law of sea Interagy. Law of Sea Task Force, 1973-80; mem. ocean policy com., ocean affairs bd. NRC, 1973-76; maritime boundary cons. Equatorial Guinea, 1977, Guinea, 1984-85, Nova Scotia Province(Can.), 1994-2000, Govt. of Bahrain, 1998-01, Govt. of Thailand, 2001—. Author: World Political Patterns, 2d edit, 1963, Offshore Geography of Northwestern Europe, 2d edit, 1966, The Northeastern United States, 2d edit., 1976, Regional Cooperation in Marine

Science, 1979, Navigational Restrictions within the New Los Context: Geographical Implications for the United States, 1986; mem. editorial bd. Ocean Devel. and Internat. Law Jour., 1973-99, Ocean Mgmt., 1973-87, Marine Policy, 1976-98; editor: (with J. Charney) International Maritime Boundaries, 3d edit., 1998. Served with USAAF, 1942—46. Recipient Ann. award Sea Grant Assn., 1979, U. R.I. Acad. Achievement award, 1986; Office Naval Rsch. grantee, 1958, 62, 66, 76. Mem. Assn. Am. Geographers (Honors award 1980), Am. Geog. Soc., Am. Soc. Internat. Law, Marine Tech. Soc., Cosmos Club. Home: 66 Beech Hill Rd Peace Dale RI 02879-2524 Office: U RI Washburn Hall Kingston RI 02881

ALEXANDER, LLOYD CHUDLEY, author; b. Phila., Jan. 30, 1924; s. Alan Audley and Edna (Chudley) A.; m. Janine Denni, Jan. 8, 1946; 1 dau., Madeleine (Mrs. Zohair Khalil). Student, West Chester (Pa.) State Coll., 1942, Lafayette Coll., 1943, U. Paris, 1946. Free-lance writer and translator, 1946—; cartoonist, pianist, advt. writer, mag. editor, 1948—; author-in-residence Temple U., 1970. Author: And Let The Credit Go, 1955, My Five Tigers, 1956, Janine is French, 1958, August Bondi, 1958 (Isaac Siegel Meml. award 1959), My Love Affair with Music, 1960, Aaron Lopez, 1960, Time Cat, 1963, Fifty Years in the Doghouse, 1964, (with Dr. Louis J. Camuti) Park Avenue Vet, 1962, The Book of Three, 1964 (A.L.A. notable book 1964), The Black Cauldron, 1965 (A.L.A. notable book 1965), Coll and His White Pig, 1965, The Castle of Llyr, 1966 (A.L.A. notable book 1966), Taran Wanderer, 1967, The Truthful Harp, 1967, The High King, 1968 (Newbery medal 1969), The Marvelous Misadventures of Sebastian, 1970 (Nat. Book award 1971), The King's Fountain, 1971, The Four Donkeys, 1972, The Foundling, 1973 (A.L.A. notable book 1973), The Cat Who Wished to be a Man, 1973 (A.L.A. notable book), The Wizard in the Tree, 1975, The Town Cats, 1977 (ALA notable book 1977), The First Two Lives of Lukas-Kasha, 1978, Westmark, 1981 (Am. Book award 1982), The Kestrel, 1982, The Beggar Queen, 1984, The Illyrian Adventure, 1986, The El Dorado Adventure, 1987, The Drackenberg Adventure, 1988, The Jedera Adventure, 1989, The Philadelphia Adventure, 1990, The Remakable Journey of Prince Jen, 1991, The Fortune-tellers, 1992, The Arkadians, 1995, The House Gobbaleen, 1995, The Iron Ring, 1997, Gypsy Rizka, 1999, How the Cat Swallowed Thunder, 2000, The Gawgon and the Boy, 2001, The Rope Trick, 2002; translator from French: (Paul Eluard) Selected Writings, 1950, (Jean-Paul Sartre) The Wall, 1951, Nausea, 1953, (Paul Vialar) The Sea Rose, 1951. Bd. dirs. Carpenter Lane Chamber Music Soc., Phila. Served with AUS, World War II. Recipient Golden Cat award, 1984, Regina medal, 1986, Carolyn W. Field medal, 1987, Otter award, 1993, Horn Book-Boston Globe award 1993. Mem. Authors League Am., P.E.N. Address: 1005 Drexel Ave Drexel Hill PA 19026-3306 also: E P Dutton Pub Co 345 Hudson St New York NY 10014-4502 also: Dell Pub Co 1540 Broadway New York NY 10036-4039

ALEXANDER, LORA KAY, writer, composer; b. Campton, KY; d. Dewey Raymond and Ada Ann (Bankenship) Tyra; m. James Kenneth Alexander; children: Kristi Eve, Eva Wynne, James Kenneth Jr. Video/films(hon.), Writers Digest Sch., Anacontes, Wa, 1985; HS diploma, Wolfe Co. High, Campton, KY, 1995. Spl. writer Wolfe Co. News, Campton, Ky., The Times, Kettering, Oakwood; adm. asst. Shawnee Kitchens, Centerville, Ohio; notary pub.; staff writer Blue Mountain Arts; owner Gift Shop, Roses in the Rain, 2001; prodr. and owner Country Unplugged, TV show. (films, ednl.) White Tigers, 1985; Wobbles World, 1985; Deer Daniel, 1985; author: (novels) By Appointment Only, 1985 (commonwealth publication, 1992), Until We're Free, 1986 (commonwealth publication, 1992), Roses In The Rain, 1987 (commonwealth publication, 1992); composer: (songs) Our People are Free (letter and award from Pres. Carter for song.), (video) She Won't Come Close/Trailblazer, 1992 (Video, 1992). Recipient poetry, Wolfe Co./KY, 1975, Video, Trailblazer/TN, 1992. Achievements include design of greeting card line-"Lovelines"; recorded and sang with Reba McIntire; two music videos; 1000 songs; 10-45rpm records; CD sales. Avocations: cooking, running, psycology. Office: Roses In The Rain, Music Publisher 106 Waterfront Place Centerville OH 45458

ALEXANDER, LYNN See MARGULIS, LYNN

ALEXANDER, LYNN MAE, English language educator; b. Bemidji, Minn., Aug. 5, 1956; d. John Woodrow and Cleo Mae (Wolfe) A. BA, Phillips U., Enid, Okla., 1978; MA, U. Tulsa, 1981, PhD, 1986. Tech. writer Murray Jones Murray Engrs., Tulsa, 1981; assoc. editor Continental Heritage Press, Tulsa, 1982; asst. prof. Upper Iowa U., Fayette, 1986-89; prof. English U. Tenn., Martin, 1989—, English dept. chair, 2000—. Vis. lectr. Keele U., Staffordshire, Eng., 1988; numerous presentations in field to profl. assns. Author: Women, Work, and Representation, 2003; contbr. articles and revs. to profl. jours. Sponsor English Soc., Martin, 1990—, Omega Theta chpt. Sigma Tau Delta, Martin, 1990—; mem. Weakley County Libr. Bd., Martin, 1991-2000. English Speaking Union Rsch.-Travel grantee, Gt. Britain, 1985; NEH Summer Inst. grantee, 1991. Mem. ADE, MLA, South Cen. MLA, South Atlantic MLA, Nat. Women's Studies Assn., Popular Culture Assn., Rsch. Soc. Victorian Periodicals, Tenn. Philol. Assn., Optimists Internat. Mem. Christian Ch. (Disciples Of Christ). Avocations: quilting, sailing, swimming. Office: U Tenn-Martin 131 Humanities Martin TN 38238

ALEXANDER, MARJORIE ANNE, artist, hand papermaker, art consultant; b. Chgo., Apr. 16, 1928; d. Alexander and Nancy Rebecca (Cordrey) Roberts; m. Harold Harman Alexander, June 13, 1948; children: Jeffrey C., Cassandra J., Peter B., Timothy C., Patrick J. Student, Wilson Jr. Coll., 1945-47; MFA in Painting, U. Ill., 1968, MA in Art Edn., 1972. cert. tchr. K-12: Ill., Minn. Graphic artist Barry Martin Studio, Rumson, N.J., 1963-65; instr. painting, drawing U. YMCA, Champaign, Ill., 1968-72; teaching asst. U. Ill., Urbana, 1968-72, rsch. assoc., 1972-76; instr. art Champaign High Sch., 1973-75, Urbana High Sch., 1976-80, Concordia Acad., St. Paul, Minn., 1982-84, U. Minn., Mpls., 1984-87, design, housing and apparel artist in residence St. Paul, 1984-88; craft cons. and educator tech. asstance program USAID, OAS, U. Minn., Kingston, Jamaica, 1986—. Design cons. J.A.M. Corp., Mpls., 1988—; tech. cons. OAS, Kingston, 1990-91, Blandin Found. grantee, Minn., 1989—; rsch. and product devel. agrl. unilization rsch. inst., 1992-95; tech. cons. Zabbaleen Paper Project, Assn. for the Protection of the Environment, Cairo, 1993—, St. Lucia Paper project Weyerhauser Found., 1994—, paper project YMCA, Jamaica, W.I., 1997—; co-curator Paper Trivia and Treasure exhibit Goldstein Mus. Design/U. Minn., St. Paul, 2000. Works have appeared in more than 35 solo shows, 1960—, more than 68 invitational shows nationally and internationally, 1985—; work chosen for inclusion 1996 Internat. Calendar Papierfabak Schfufelen Lenningen, Germany; work chosen for poster paper exhibit Leopold-Hoesch Mus., Doren, Germany, 1999; traveling exhibit, Bavaria, Germany, Geneva; work chosen for exhibit Mus. Santa Maria Della Scala, Siena, Italy, 2003, Augsborg Coll. Mpls., 2003; represented in permanent collection Imadate, Fukui, Japan, U. Ill., Weisman Art Mus., U. Minn., So. Cross U., NSW, Australia, Montclair (N.J.) Art Mus., Am. U, Cairo, other univs. and colls. and corp. collections; co-author (book): Selected Papers, 1994, Handcrafted paper and Paper Products Made from Indigenous Plant Fibers, 1997; contbr. articles to profl. jours, columns to newspaper. Vestry mem. St. John's Episcopal Ch., Champaign, 1975-78, St. Matthew's Episcopal Ch., St. Paul, 1989—. Recipient Celebrity award, Minn. State Fair, 1984, book First award, 1986, Honorable mention, 3d Onn/Off Paper Nat., Wis., 1984, 1st prize cmty. fine art exhibit, St. Paul, Minn., 2002, 2003; grantee, Blandin Found., U. Minn., 1989—90, OAS, 1990—91, Agrl. Utilization Rsch. Inst., 1992—95, Weyerhauser Found., 1997, Minn. Arts Bd., 1999. Mem.: Internat. Assn. Hand Papermakers and Paper Artists (v.p. 2003—), Nat. League Am. Penwomen (state v.p. 1994—96, Minn. art chair 2002—), Friends of Dard Hunter Paper Mus. (com. chair 1990—95). Episcopalian. Avocations: swimming, cooking, theatre, travel.

ALEXANDER, MARTHA SUE, retired librarian; b. Washington, June 8, 1945; d. Lyle Thomas and Helen (Goodwin) Alexander; m. David Henry Bowman, June 11, 1965 (div. 1982); 1 child, Elaine BA, U. Md., 1967; MS in Library Sci., Cath. U. Am., 1969. Librarian U. Md., College Park, 1969-72, head acquisitions, 1973-75; asst. univ. librarian George Washington U., Washington, 1975-78, assoc. univ. librarian, 1978-82; univ. librarian U. Louisville, 1983-90; dir. libraries U. Mo., Columbia, 1990—2002; ret., 2002. Chmn. bd. dirs. SOLINET (Southeastern Library Network), 1987-88. Coord. U. Louisville United Way, 1987; bd. dirs. Mo. Libr. Network Corp., 1990-2002; coord. United Way campaign U. Mo., 2002. Mem. ALA (chmn. poster sessions 1983-85, co-chmn. nat. conf. in Cin. 1989), Am. Assn. Higher Edn., Athletic Assn. U. Louisville (vice chmn., bd. dirs. 1989-90), D.C. Library Assn. (pres. 1981-82), Women Acad. Libr. Dirs. Exch. Network. Episcopalian. Home: 100 Mumford Dr Columbia MO 65203-0226

ALEXANDER, MARTIN, environmental toxicologist, consultant; b. Newark, Feb. 4, 1930; s. Meyer and Sarah (Rubinstein) A.; m. Renee Rafaela Wulf, Aug. 26, 1951; children: Miriam H., Stanley W. BS, Rutgers U., 1951; MS, U. Wis., 1953, PhD, 1955. Asst. prof. Cornell U., Ithaca, N.Y., from 1955, now L.H. Bailey prof. Advisor agys. fed. govt., Washington, 1965—, UN agys., Kenya, France, Italy, 1963—; mem. coms. Nat. Acad. Sci., Washington, 1971—; cons. Author: Microbial Ecology, 1971, Introduction to Soil Microbiology, 1977, Biodegradation and Bioremediation, 1994; editor: Advances in Microbial Ecology, 5 vols., 1977-81. Recipient Indsl. Research 100 award, 1968, Fisher award Am. Soc. Microbiology, 1980, Superior Svc. award USDA, 1989. Fellow Am. Acad. Microbiology, AAAS, Internat. Inst. Biotechnology, Am. Soc. Agronomy (Soil Sci. award 1964) Home: 301 Winthrop Dr Ithaca NY 14850-1736 Office: Cornell U Bradfield Hall Ithaca NY 14853

ALEXANDER, MARY ELSIE, lawyer; b. Chgo., Nov. 16, 1947; d. Theron and Marie (Bailey) A.; m. Lyman Saunders Faulkner, Jr., Dec. 1, 1984; 1 child, Michelle. BA, U. Iowa, 1969; MPH, U. Calif.-Berkeley, 1975; JD, U. Santa Clara, 1982. Bar: Calif. 1982, U.S. Dist. Ct. (no. dist.), Calif. 1982, U.S. Ct. Appeals (9th cir.) 1982. Rschr. U. Cin., 1969—74; dept. dir., sr. environ. health scientist Stanford Rsch. Inst., Menlo Park, Calif., 1975—80; cons. Alexander Assocs., Ambler, Pa., 1980—82; assoc. Caputo, Liccardo, Rossi, Sturges & McNeil, San Jose, Calif., 1982—84, Cartwright, Slobodin, Bokelman, et al, San Francisco, 1984—88, ptnr., 1988—96, The Cartwright & Alexander Law Firm, 1996—2001, Mary Alexander & Assocs., PC, San Francisco, 2001—. Com. mem. Cancer Soc., San Jose, 1983; elder Valley Presbyn. Ch., Portola Valley, 1987-90; active Am. Heart Assn., Santa Clara County. Named one of top 10 Trial Lawyers San Francisco Bay Area, San Francisco Chronicle, 1990; Nat. Inst. Occupl. Safety and Health scholar U. Calif., Berkeley, 1975. Mem.: ATLA (pres. 2002—), AAS, ABA, Santa Clara Trial Lawyers Assn. (bd. dirs. 1983—84), Am. Indsl. Hygiene Assn. (bd. dirs. 1979—81, treas. 1977—79), Calif. Women Lawyers, Trial Lawyers for Pub. Justice, San Francisco Trial Lawyers Assn., Consumer Attys. Calif. (PAC bd. 1989—, parliamentarian 1991, v.p. 1992, chair mem. com., editor Forum, pres. 1996). Democrat. Office: Mary Alexander & Assocs PC Ste 1303 44 Montgomery St San Francisco CA 94104-4615

ALEXANDER, MARY GERETTE BLAYDES, child therapist; b. Brunswick, Ga., Nov. 7, 1963; d. Thomas Hardy and Dorothy Ann (Behrens) B. BS in Computer Sci. and Acctg., Troy (Ala.) State U., 1986; diploma in Christian Counseling, Psychol. Studies Inst., Atlanta, 1995; MS in Cmty. Counseling, Ga. State U., 1995. Nat. cert. counselor; lic. profl. counselor. Computer programmer Fleming Foods, Atlanta, 1986-87; computer analyst Bell South, Atlanta, 1987-94; relief worker Open Gate, Marietta, Ga., 1996-97; wilderness counselor Roosevelt Wilderness Camp, Warm Springs, Ga., 1997-98; social svcs. coord. Ga. Sheriffs Pineland, 1998-2000; child therapist Tanner Behavioral Health, Villa Rica, Ga., 2000—02, mobile assessment counselor Carrollton, Ga., 2003—. Counselor in tng. Psi Mt. Paran & Briarcliff Counseling Ctr., Atlanta, 1994-95; case mgr. Euphrasia House, Phila., 1995-96. Mem.: ACA, Am. Assn. Christian Counselors. Republican. Roman Catholic. Avocations: running, volleyball, sewing, reading. Office: Tanner Behavioral Health 523 Dixie St Carrollton GA 30117 Home: 54 Marilyn Dr Dallas GA 30157 E-mail: mgblaydes@netzero.net.

ALEXANDER, MICHAEL JOZEF, neurosurgeon, radiologist; b. Cincinnati, Ohio, May 10, 1962; s. Waldemar Marian Brzezicki and Elizabeth Ann Uhlhorn; m. Joann E. Kim, Oct. 18, 1997; children: Julia Elizabeth, Emily Jane, Kathryn Kim. M.D., Georgetown Med. Sch., Washington, DC, 1987—91. Asst. prof. Duke U. Med. Ctr., Durham, NC, 2000—. Author over 20 pub. on Neurosurgery and Inerventional Neuroradiolog. Office: Duke Univ Med Center Box 3807 Durham NC 27710 Office Fax: 919-668-3392.

ALEXANDER, MILES JORDAN, lawyer; b. Reading, Pa., Nov. 20, 1931; s. Abe Alexander and Sarah (Gold) Fidlow; m. Elaine Eve Barron, May 29, 1955; children: Kent, David, Michael, Paige. BA in Polit. Sci. with honors., Emory U., 1952; LLB cum laude, Harvard U., 1955. Bar: Ga. 1955, D.C. 1977. Assoc. Kilpatrick & Stockton, Atlanta, summers 1954-55; teaching fellow Harvard U., Cambridge, 1957-58; assoc. Kilpatrick Stockton LLP, Atlanta, 1958-63; chmn. Kilpatrick & Stockton LLP, Atlanta, 1996—. Lectr. P.L.I., Internat. Trademark Assn., Am. Law Inst., ABA Internat. Franchise Assn., other seminars on trademarks and unfair competition, antitrust, franchising, dispute resolutions and litigation tactics; guest lectr. on trademark law NYU, U.Ga., Ga. State Law Sch., also bd. visitors; bd. visitors Emory U.; chmn. U.S. trademark pub. adv. com. Emory U., 2000—. Editor-in-chief: The Trademark Reporter, 1978-80; contbr. numerous articles to jours. in trademark field. Mem. City of Atlanta Ethics Bd., chmn., vice-chmn., 1980-92, Emory U. and Harvard Law Sch. Alumni Funds; legal counsel to Mayor Maynard Jackson, 1974-82, 89-93; chmn. City of Atlanta Lic. Rev. Bd., 1976-79; former pres. Am. Jewish Com.; mem. Friends of Morehouse Coll.; adv. bd. Family Outreach Ctr.; mem. adv. coun. J. Thomas McCarthy Inst. Intellectual Property and Tech. Law, 2001--. Capt. USAF, 1955-57. Recipient Human Rels. award Anti-Defamation League, 1997, Disting. Alumni award Emory U., 2000. Fellow Am. Bar Found., Am. Coll. Trial Lawyers; mem. ABA, Internat. Trademark Assn. (counsel 1997-2000, chmn. trademark pub. com. 2000—), Ga. Bar Assn., Ga. State Bar Assn. (former chmn. antitrust sect., advisor to legal counsel 1997—), Atlanta Bar Assn., Lawyers Club Atlanta, Internat. Trademark Assn. (lectr., bd. dirs. 1980-82, rev. commn. 1986, legal counsel 1987-2000, Pres.'s Lifetime Achievement award 2003), Am. Law Inst. (adv. com. restatement of law of unfair competition 1986-95), J. Thomas McCarthy Inst. for Intellectual Property and Tech. Law (charter mem. adv. coun.), 191 Club (bd. dirs.), Atlanta City Club (chmn. bd.), Commerce Club, Standard Club, Old War Horse Lawyers Club, Phi Beta Kappa. Avocations: reading, sports. Office: Kilpatrick Stockton LLP 1100 Peachtree St NE Ste 2800 Atlanta GA 30309-4530

ALEXANDER, NANCY A. information technology manager, consultant; b. Kansas City, Kans., Mar. 31, 1957; d. Carl Glenn and Norma Louise Hanks; m. Steven Dale Alexander, May 20, 1981; 1 child, Anne Louise. AS in Computer Info. Systems, Kansas City (Kans.) C.C., 1989; BS in Computer Info. Systems, Friends U., Wichita, Kans., 1999, MS in Mgmt. Info. Systems, 2001. Sec., a/c schedule control Trans World Airlines, Inc., Kansas City, Mo., 1976—79, coord. scheduling and planning group, 1979—80, planner, facilities and equipment engring., 1980—81, master planner, facility and equipment programs, 1981—82, mgr., facility and equipment programs, 1982—83; office mgr. Steven D. Alexander, Chtd., Overland Park, Kans., 1983—. Faculty adv. bd. Kansas City (Kans.) C.C., 1988—90; cons. Profl. Support, Inc., Shawnee, Kans., 1983—. Software developer Legal Billing and Analysis System, 1989; author: Think of Your Future, 1992. Troop leader Girl Scouts Am., Shawnee, 1988—92; county coun. rep., project leader 4-H, Olathe, Kans., 1994—97, judge, 1995—97; youth group leader Master's Cmty. Ch., Kansas City, Kans., 1999—2001. Avocations: travel, racquetball, swimming, painting.

ALEXANDER, ONNIE SUSAN, clinical nurse specialist; b. Akron, Ohio, Sept. 9, 1946; d. Toby Roland and Onnie Ouida (Boles) Moseley. BSN, Ohio State U., 1969; MA in Counseling and Health Psychology, Santa Clara (Calif.) U., 1987. Cert. pub. health nurse, registered nurse in AIDS Assn. Nurses in AIDS Care. Staff nurse Stanford U. Hosp., 1969—70; pub. health nurse Santa Clara County Health Dept., 1970—87; AIDS health svcs. patient care coord. Santa Clara Health and Hosp. Sys., 1987—95; HIV svcs. coord. Kaiser Santa Clara (Calif.) Marina Playa Med. Offices, 1995—2001; clin. care coord. Mendocino Cmty. Health Clinics, Lakeport, Calif., 2001—, case mgr., 2001—02; case mgr., infection control nurse Sutter Lakeside Hosp., Lakeport, Calif., 2002—03; HIV/AIDS nurse case mgr. Cmty. Care HIV/AIDS Project, Clearlake, Calif., 2003—. Home: 2301 Road E Redwood Valley CA 95470 Office: 14644 B Lakeshore Blvd Clearlake CA 95422 E-mail: cchaprn@hotmail.com.

ALEXANDER, PATRICK BYRON, university administrator; b. Texas City, Tex., May 11, 1950; s. Alvin Wesley and Mabel Bernice Alexander; m. Linda Graham, May 7, 1975. BA in Econs., George Mason Coll., U. Va., 1972. Publs. dir. George Mason U., Fairfax, Va., 1973-75, U. Okla. Health Scis. Ctr., Okla. City, 1975-78, Presbyn. Hosp. Inc., Okla. City, 1978-79; mng. dir. Okla. Symphony Orch., Okla. City, 1979-88; exec. dir. Allied Arts Found., 1988-92, Okla. Zool. Soc., 1992—2001; exec. dir. advancement Okla. City U., 2001—03, cons., 2003—. Bd. dirs. Ambassador's Concert Choir, Okla. Philharm. Found., English-Speaking Union Okla., Possibilities, Red Earth Indian Ctr. Recipient Gov.'s award for excellence in arts, 1987, Okla. Fundraiser of Yr. award, 1991; English-Speaking Union Okla. Kerr Found. fellow, 1981. Home: 1515 Glenwood Ave Oklahoma City OK 73116-5206 Office: Oklahoma City U 2501 N Blackwelder Oklahoma City OK 73106 E-mail: palexander@okcu.edu.

ALEXANDER, PAUL RICHARD, illustrator; b. Richmond, Ind., Sept. 3, 1937; s. Fred and Olive (Phillips) A. BFA, Wittenberg U., 1959; BFA in Illustration, Art Ctr. Coll. Design, 1967. Archtl. delineator Forest Studios, Chgo., 1961-64; advt. illustrator Pitt Studios, Cleve., 1967-70; freelance illustrator Chgo., 1970-76, Mendola Artist's Rep., N.Y.C., 1976—. Contbg. artist: (anthologies) Tomorrow and Beyond, 1970s, Infinite Worlds—The Fantastic Visions of Science Fiction Art, 1997, Spectrum Sci. Ficton Annual, Vol. 1-4, 1990. With USAR, 1960-66. Mem. Mensa. Avocations: art, architecture, classical music, railfan. Home and Office: 1380 Oaktree Dr Greenville OH 45331-2730

ALEXANDER, RALPH WILLIAM, JR., physics educator; b. Phila., May 17, 1941; s. Ralph William and Gladys (Robin) A.; m. Janet Erdien Bradley, Sept. 4, 1965; children: Ralph III, Margaret. BA, Wesleyan U., Middletown, Conn., 1963; PhD, Cornell U., Ithaca, N.Y., 1968; postdoctoral study, U. of Freiburg, Fed. Republic Germany, 1968-70. From asst. to assoc. prof. physics U. Mo., Rolla, 1970-80, prof., 1980—, chmn. dept., 1983-92. Contbr. articles to profl. jours. Mem. Am. Phys. Soc., Assn. Am. Physics Tchrs. Office: U Mo Dept Physics Rolla MO 65409-0640 E-mail: ralexand@umr.edu.

ALEXANDER, RICHARD C. association administrator; m. LaVera Alexander; children: Jeff, Ronald, Gail. Bachelors, Franklin U.; grad. Army Command and Gen. Staff Studies Cours, 1977; grad., Army War Coll., 1983. With USMC, 1954; commd. 2d lt. Ohio N.G., 1965, advanced through grades to maj. gen., 1992, adj. gen., 1987; pres. N.G. Assn. U.S., 1996—98, exec. dir., 1999—. Mem. policy bd. Def. Dept. Res. Forces, 1993—96. Decorated Def. Superior Svc. medal, Legion of Merit, Ohio award of merit, Meritorious Svc. medal. Mem.: NAACP, Ohio N.G. Assn., N.G. Assn. U.S. Office: NG Assn of US 1 Massachusetts Ave NW Washington DC 20001

ALEXANDER, ROBERT C. lawyer; b. Clarksville, Tenn., Aug. 7, 1947; s. Donald C. and Margaret S. Alexander; m. Rosalie Bailey, June 14, 1969. BA cum laude, Yale Coll., 1969; JD magna cum laude, Harvard U., 1972. Bar: Calif. 1972, D.C. 1973. Law clk. to Hon. Alfred T. Goodwin U.S. Ct. Appeals, 9th cir., San Francisco, 1972-73; shareholder Heller, Ehrman, White & McAuliffe, San Francisco, 1973-86, 88—; prin. Babcock & Brown, San Francisco, 1986-87. Writer in field. Mem. ABA, State Bar Calif., D.C. Bar, Internat. Fiscal Assn., Equipment Leasing Assn. Office: Heller Ehrman White & McAuliffe 333 Bush St San Francisco CA 94104-2806

ALEXANDER, ROBERT GARDNER, lawyer; b. Madison, Wis., May 19, 1949; s. Charles Kohl and Jean (Gardner) A.; m. Karen Lynn Kaminski, Sept. 30, 1989; children: Elizabeth Jean, Sarah Lynn, Rebecca Ann. BA, U. Wis., 1971, JD, 1976; ML in Taxation, DePaul U., 1984. Bar: Wis. 1976, U.S. Dist. Ct. (we. dist.) Wis. 1976, U.S. Dist. Ct. (ea. dist.) Wis. 1978, U.S. Tax Ct. 1982, U.S. Ct. Appeals (7th cir.) 1983. Rsch. atty. U. Wis., Madison, 1976-77; atty. McLario Law Offices, Menomonee Falls, Wis., 1978-87, Alexander & Klemmon, S.C., Wauwatosa, Wis., 1987—. Trustee, sec. Falls Bapt. Ch., Inc., Menomonee Falls, 1987—; Preach the Word, Inc., Downers Grove, 1992—; adv. bd. Joy Bapt. Camp, Whitewater, Wis., 1992—. Mem. ABA, Nat. Acad. Elder Law Attys., Wis. State Bar, Milw. Estate Planning Counsel, Nat. Assn. Estate Planning Counselors (accredited estate planner), Ea. Wis. Planning Giving Counsel, Phi Kappa Phi. Republican. Avocations: music, art, sports. Office: Alexander & Klemmer SC Ste 304 2675 N Mayfair Rd Wauwatosa WI 53226-1305 E-mail: alexlaw@exeepc.com.

ALEXANDER, ROBERT JACKSON, economist, educator; b. Canton, Ohio, Nov. 26, 1918; s. Ralph S. and Ruth (Jackson) A.; m. Joan O. Powell, Mar. 26, 1949; children: Anthony, Margaret. BA, Columbia U., 1940; MA, Columnbia U., 1941; PhD, Columbia U., 1950. Asst. economist Bd. Econ. Warfare, 1942, Office Inter-Am. Affairs, 1945-46; mem. faculty Rutgers U., 1947—, prof. econs., 1961-89, prof. emeritus, 1989—. Mem. Pres.-elect Kennedy's Latin Am. Task Force, 1960-61 Author 41 books including Juan Domingo Peron: A History, 1979, Romulo Betancourt and the Transformation of Venezuela, 1982, Bolivia: Past, Present and Future of Its Politics, 1982, Biographical Dictionary of Latin American and Caribbean Politics, 1988, Juscelino Kubitschek and the Development of Brazil, 1991, International Trotskyism 1929-85, 1991, The ABC Presidents, 1992, The Bolivarian Presidents, 1994, The Presidents of Central America, Mexico, Cuba and Hispaniola, 1995, Presidents, Prime Ministers and Governors of the English Speaking West Indies and Puerto Rico, 1997, The Anarchists in the Spanish Civil War, 1999, International Maoism in the Developing World, 1999, Hava de la Torre Man of the Millennium: His Life, Ideas and Continuing Relevance, 2001, A History of Organized Labor in Cuba, 2002. Mem. nat. bd. League Indsl. Democracy, 1955—; mem. nat. exec. com. Socialist Party-Social Dem. Fedn., 1957-66; bd. dirs. Rand Sch. Social Sci., 1951-56; mem. exec. com. Open Door Student Exch., 1970-94. Decorated officer Order Condor of the Andes Bolivia Mem. Am. Econ. Assn., Latin Am. Studies Assn., Mid. Atlantic Coun. Latin Am. Studies (v.p. 1986-87, pres. 1987-88), Coun. Fgn. Rels., Interam. Assn. Democracy and Freedom (chmn. N.Am. com. 1970-87), Phi Gamma Delta. Home: 944 River Rd Piscataway NJ 08854-5504 Office: Rutgers U Dept Econs New Brunswick NJ 08903 *I have sought to extend the bounds of knowledge through research and writing, and to pass on to my children and students not only what I have learned, but also, hopefully, some idea of how to behave in a civilized manner.*

ALEXANDER, ROBERT WAYNE, medical educator; b. Memphis, Mar. 19, 1941; AB, U. Miss., 1962; MS in Physiology, Emory U., 1967, PhD in Physiology, 1968; MD, Duke U., 1969. Diplomate Am. Bd. Internal Medicine, Am. Bd. Cardiovascular Disease. Intern in medicine Duke U., 1969-70, fellow in cardiology, 1974-76; resident in medicine U. Wash., 1970-71; asst. prof. medicine Harvard U., 1976-82, assoc. prof., 1982-88; assoc. phys. Brigham and Women's Hosp., Boston, 1982-88; asst. in medicine Beth Israel Hosp., Boston, 1982-88; chief of cardiology Emory U. Hosp., 1988—; dir. divsn. cardiology Emory U., 1988—, R. Bruce prof. medicine, 1988—, chmn. medicine, 1999—. Staff assoc., sr. surgeon experimental therapeutics br. Nat. Heart and Lung Inst., Nat. Inst. Health, Bethsda, Md., 1971-74; vis. prof. Duke U. Med. Ctr., 1986, U. Tex. Southwestern Med. Ctr., Dallas, 1988, Mt. Sinai Med. Ctr., N.Y.C., 1990, Kobe U., Japan, 1992, Ohio State U., 1995; Pfizer vis. prof. U. Mich., 1993; Pfizer vis. prof. Allegheny Med. Sch., 1997; Simon Dack vis. prof. Mt. Sinai Med. Ctr., 1995. Mem. editl. bd. Jour. Clin. Investigation, 1992—, Circulation Rsch., Advances in Pharmacology, Advances in Hypertension, all 1989-93; co-editor The Heart, 8th edit., 1993, sr. editor, 9th edit., 1998; circulation-cons. editor Jour. Am. Coll. Cardiology, 1993—. Recipient Rsch. Career Devel. award, 1977-82; Pfizer traveling fellow Clin. Rsch. Inst. Montreal, 1983. Fellow AAAS, Am. Coll. Cardiology, Am. Heart Assn. (v.p. rsch. 1995, bd. dirs. 1995—); mem. AMA, Assn. Am. Physicians, Am. Soc. Clin. Investigation, High Blood Pressure Rsch. Coun. Australia (hon. life), Am. Fedn. Clin. Rsch., Am. Clin. and Climatological Soc., Assoc. Univ. Cardiologists (pres. 1998—). Office: Emory U Sch Medicine EUH 1364 Clifton Rd Atlanta GA 30322-0001

ALEXANDER, ROBERTA SUE, history educator; b. N.Y.C., Mar. 19, 1943; d. Bernard Milton and Dorothy (Linn) Cohn; m. John Kurt Alexander, 1966 (div. Sept. 1972); m. Ronald Burett Fost, May 7, 1977. BA, UCLA, 1964; MA, U. Chgo., 1966, PhD, 1974; JD, U. Dayton, 2000. Instr. Roosevelt U., Chgo., 1967-68; prof. U. Dayton, Ohio, 1969—. Author: North Carolina Faces the Freedman: Race Relations During Presidential Reconstruction, 1985; mem. editl. bd. Cin. Hist. Soc., 1973—; contbr. chpt. to book and articles to law revs. Recipient summer stipend NEH, Washington, 1975, Tchg. Excellence and Campus Leadership award Sears-Roebuck Found, 1990, Tchg. Excellence in History award Ohio Acad. History, 1991, Michael and Elissa Cohen Writing award, 1999; fellow in residence NEH, 1976-77, fellow Inst. for Legal Studies, NEH, 1982, summer rsch. fellow U. Dayton, 1972, 74, 76, 80. Mem. Am. Hist.

Assn., Orgn. Am. Historians, Am. Soc. Legal History, Midwest Assn. Prelaw Advisors (pres.), So. Hist. Soc., Mortar Bd., Am. Contract Bridge Assn. (life master 1983), Phi Beta Kappa, Phi Alpha Theta. Avocations: bridge, golf. Home: 7715 Legendary Ln West Chester OH 45069-4605 Office: U Dayton Dept History Dayton OH 45469-0310 Fax: (937) 229-4298. E-mail: roberta.alexander@notes.udayton.edu.

ALEXANDER, RODNEY M. congressman; b. Jonesboro, La., Dec. 5, 1946; m. Nancy Sutton; 3 children. Grad., La. Tech. U., 1965. Mem. La. Ho. Reps., 1987—93, U.S. Ho. Reps. from 5th La. dist., 2003—. Mem. Jackson Parish, La. Police Jury, 1970—85, pres., 1978—85. With USAF, 1965—71. Named Legis. of Yr., La. Rural Health Assn., 1997. Democrat. Baptist. Office: 316 Cannon HOB Washington DC 20515*

ALEXANDER, ROGER EUGENE, oral and maxillofacial surgeon, educator; b. Wichita, Kans., Sept. 15, 1940; s. John Denzil and Bonnie Jean (Moore) Alexander; m. Barbara Frances Wehrle, June 25, 1966; children: Matthew Scott(dec.), Marc Alan, Daniel Adam(dec.). DDS, Marquette U., 1964. Diplomate Am. Bd. Oral and Maxillofacial Surgery; lic. dentist, Tex., Wis. Commd. lt. USN, 1964, advanced through grades to capt.; gen. dentist USN Dental Corps, 1964-67, exodontist, 1967-72, oral and maxillofacial surgeon, 1972-90; ret. USN, 1990; asst. prof. dept. oral-maxillofacial surgery/pharmacology Baylor Coll. Dentistry, Dallas, 1990-94, assoc. prof., 1994-96, Tex. A&M U. Health Sci. Ctr./Baylor Coll. Dentistry, Dallas, 1996-2000, prof., 2000—. Med. legal cons., 1994—; nat. lectr. to numerous dental orgns. Contbr. chpts. to books, articles to profl. jours. Pres. Naval Acad. Parents Club of No. Tex., Dallas/Ft. Worth, 1992-93, bd. dirs. Dallas divsn. Am. Heart Assn., 1996-98; chmn. Dallas/Ft. Worth Coalition Uniformed Svcs. Acads., 1994; mem. forensic identification disaster team Dallas County Med. Examiner's Office, 1994-2000. Decorated Meritorious Svc. medal. Fellow Am. Assn. Oral and Maxillofacial Surgeons, Acad. Dentistry Internat., Am. Coll. Dentists; mem. ADA, Tex. Dental Assn., Dallas Dental Soc., Marquette U. Alumni Assn., Delta Sigma Delta, Omicron Kappa Upsilon. Avocations: computer-based multimedia, photography. Office: Tex A&M U Hlth Sci Ctr/Baylor Coll Dentistry PO Box 660677 Dallas TX 75266-0677 E-mail: ralexander@tambcd.edu.

ALEXANDER, ROY, public relations executive, editor, author; b. Asheville, N.C., Feb. 3, 1930; s. William Roy and Ruth (Upshaw) A. PhB, Northwestern U., 1954. Mng. editor Daily Northwestern, 1951-52; assoc. editor Food Retailing, 1951-55; dir. pub. relations Mid-States Corp., 1952-53; editor Splty. Salesman, 1953-56, Mobile Homes mag., 1953-54; account exec. Philip Lesly Co., 1956-58; sr. v.p. Philip Lesly Co. (N.Y.C. Office), 1958-62; pres. Alexander Co., N.Y.C., 1962-93, Taggart & Alexander, N.Y.C., 1993—; editor Mktg. Times, 1970—. Mgr. N.Y. product publicity for Wurlitzer Co.; pub. relations counsel to Grad. Sch. Sales Mgmt. and Mktg., Lincoln Logs Ltd., The Maleck Group, Sturm Ruger & Co., Southport, Conn., Barter Advantage, Inc., Log Home Guide, Solar Additions, Inc., Hearthstone Homes, Dandridge, Tenn., Mantis Mfg. Co., Huntingdon Valley, Pa.; counselor Info. Industry Assn., Bethesda, Md., Environment Info., Ctr., N.Y.C., Flexmaster of Can., Toronto, Z-Flex, Manchester, N.H., Uni-Flex, Berlin, N.J., Unichem Indsl. Hose, Haw River, N.C., Sturm, Ruger & Co., Southport, Conn. Writer, exec. producer: (color motion picture) The Greening of Augusta; dir.: (pub. edn. program) Iron Mountain Stoneware, Classic Travel, N.Y.; creator: (pub. edn. program) W.Va. Coal Assn.; designer, creator (communications and promotion program) Singer Bus. Machines; dir. nationwide pub. edn. program Nat. Pest Control Assn.; author: Direct Salesman's Handbook, 1958, Mehdi: Story of Metlife's Top Salesman, 1977, Duke Medical Center's Ricer's Guide, 1984, Power Speech: Your Quickest Route to Success, 1986, Taking Your Company Public, 1990, Commonsense Time Management, 1992, More Mehdi: Everything Is Possible, 2000. Served with AUS, 1946-49; feature editor Armed Forces Press Service, 1948-49. Address: 333 E 34th St New York NY 10016-4977 *My guiding principles: (1) Do something even if it's wrong - percentages favor the activist. (2) Don't waste words or time; both are in finite supply. (3) All generalizations are false, including these. (4) Assume most people will fail their responsibilities and plan accordingly. (5) Anything worth doing is worth doing with quality. (6) Avoid all medication; solve health problem with diet and exercise. (7) Never forget: The market economy made it all possible.*

ALEXANDER, RUDOLPH, education educator; b. Savannah, Ga., Nov. 20, 1949; s. Rudolph and Thelma Alexander. PhD, U. Minn., 1989. Prof. Ohio State U., Columbus, 1989—. Author: (autobiography) To Ascend into the Shining World Again; contbr. articles. Achievements include research in understanding legal concepts that influence social welfare policy; counseling, treatment, and intervention methods with juvenile and adult offenders. Office: Coll Social Work 1947 College Rd Columbus OH 43210 E-mail: alexander.2@osu.edu.

ALEXANDER, RUTH BATCHELDER, interior decorator, environmental activist; b. Lynn, Mass., Apr. 15, 1904; d. George Prescott and Blanche Eliza (Tuttle) Batchelder; m. Donald Child Alexander, May 10, 1941; children: Donald Gilbert, Ruth. Comml. design diploma, Mass. Normal Art Sch., 1925. Understudy Allen Hall Co., Boston, 1925-31; propr. interior decorating co. Boston, 1931-67, Nahant, Mass., 1967-69, Rowley, Mass., 1969-74. Bd. dirs. Mass. Audubon Soc., 1938-63, Merrimack River Valley Council, 1980-81; organizer PTA, Nahant, 1948; Nahant br. Lynn YMCA, 1950; trustee, bd. dirs. Essex County Greenbelt Assn., 1961-84, v.p., 1978-79; founder, chmn. Nahant Conservation Commn., 1962-69; sec. Rowley Conservation Commn., 1971-77. Recipient award Lynn YMCA, 1955, Mass. Audubon Soc., 1981, Merrimac River Valley Watershed, 1981, citation Bradford Coll., 1986; environ. recipient Sol Feinstone award SUNY Coll. Environ. Scis. and Forestry, Syracuse, 1990, Art Longard Awd., Gulf of Maine Counc. on the Environment, 1999. Democrat. Avocation: birding.

ALEXANDER, SHAUN, football player; b. Florence, Ky., Aug. 30, 1977; Attended, U. Ala. Running back Seattle Seahawks, 2000—. Office: Seattle Seahawks 11220 NE 53rd St Kirkland WA 98033

ALEXANDER, SHELDON, psychology educator; b. N.Y.C., July 16, 1930; s. Saul and Sylvia Alexander; m. Donna Delores Rudig, Aug. 13, 1960; children: Joanne, Janice, Steven. BA, CUNY, 1952; PhD, U. Rochester, 1958. Grad. asst. U. Rochester, NY, 1952—57, instr., 1955—57; USPHS postdoctoral rsch. fellow U. Ill., Champaign-Urbana, 1957—59, asst. prof., 1959—60; assoc. prof. So. Ill. U., Carbondale, 1960—67; health scientist adminstr. NIH, Bethesda, Md., 1967—73; dept. chmn. Wayne State U., Detroit, 1973—83, prof. psychology, 1973—. Mem. exec. bd. Ctr. for Peace and Conflict Studies, Detroit, 1989—; mem. adv. bd. Fraser Ctr. for Workplace Issues, Detroit, 1999—. Co-author: (book chpts.) Altruism, Narcissim, Comity, 1999, Changing Employment Relations, 1995. Mem.: APA, Am. Psychol. Soc., AAAS, Sigma Xi, Phi Beta Kappa. Office: Wayne State U Psychology Dept 71 W Warren Detroit MI 48202 Fax: 313-577-7636. E-mail: sheldon.alexander@wayne.edu.

ALEXANDER, STEVEN, artist, educator; b. Stamford, Tex., Aug. 27, 1953; s. Thomas D. and Barbara J. Alexander; m. Laura Duerwald; children: Erin Marcelle, Ava Reed. BA, Austin Coll., 1975; MFA, Columbia U., 1977. Adj. prof. Austin (Tex.) C.C., 1989-93, U. Scranton, Pa., 1993-95; assoc. prof. art Marywood U., Scranton, 1995—. Studio resident P.S. 1 Contemporary Art Ctr., Long Island City, N.Y., 1978; vis. artist Studio Art Ctrs. Internat., Florence, Italy, 1999, Parsons Sch. Design, N.Y.C., 2003. Editor, designer exhbn. catalog: Rooms P.S. 1, 1976; curator, editor exhbn. catalog: The Poetic Object: Paintings of Rebecca Purdum, 1997; curator, essayist: Nature-Contemporary Art and the Natural World, 2000; essayist: Five Figure Painters, 2001; rep. by Gremillion and Co. Fine Art, Houston; solo shows at Amdur Gallery, Austin, Tex., 1993, Roxx Gallery, Balt., Md., 1994, AFA Gallery, Scranton, Pa., 1999, Gremillion and Co. Fine Art, Houston, 2000, 02, Gremillion Gallery, Austin, 2001, Contemporary Gallery, Marywood U., Scranton, 2001; exhibited in at Janus Gallery, Santa Fe, N. Mex., 1992, Takasaki (Japan) Art Ctr., 1994, Painting Ctr., N.Y.C., 1996, Everhart Mus., Scranton, 1997, Gremillion and Co. Fine Art, 1998, 2000, Macon Gallery, Atlanta, 2000, Gremillion Gallery, Austin, 2000. Chmn. Borough Planning Commn., Montrose, Pa., 1998-2000. Grant for painting F. Lammot Belin Found., 2000—. Mem. Coll. Art Assn., Founds. in Art: Theory and Edn., Susquehanna Agrl. Soc. (v.p. 1998—). Office: Marywood U Art Dept 2300 Adams Ave Scranton PA 18509-1514 E-mail: salexander@es.marywood.edu.

ALEXANDER, STEVEN RAY, chemical engineer; b. Morganton, N.C., Mar. 19, 1965; s. Ray Shirley and Mary Elizabeth (Andrews) A.; m. Christine Cary, Feb. 9, 1993; children: Christopher Ray, Stefan Charles. B of Chem. Engring., Ga. Inst. Tech., 1988, PhD in Chem. Engring., 1992. Sr. devel. engr. Hoechst Celanese, Corpus Christi, Tex., 1992-98; sr. process engr. Celanese Ltd., Houston, 1998-99; sr. prodn. engr. Celanese GmbH, Boehlen, Germany, 1999-2001; section leader Celanese Ltd., Pampa, Tex., 2001 . Contbr. articles to profl. jours.; patentee in field. Mem. AICE, Sigma Xi. Office: Celanese Ltd Pampa Plant PO Box 937 Pampa TX 79066 E-mail: sralexander.pampa@celanese.com.

ALEXANDER, STEVEN ROY, pediatric nephrology educator; b. Portsmouth, Va., Sept. 1, 1945; s. Woodrow Wilson and Frances Judson (Tremaine) A.; m. Jeanette Eleanore Kennedy; children: Heather, Phillip, Sarah. Student, Stanford U., Palo Alto, Calif., 1963-64; BA in Biology cum laude, Rice U., 1967; MD, Baylor Coll., 1971. Diplomate Am. Bd. Pediatrics, Am. Bd. Pediatric Nephrology; lic. physician, Tex., Calif., Oreg. Intern Baylor Coll. Medicine, Houston, 1971-72, resident in pediatrics, 1974-76, fellow, 1976-78; asst. prof. pediatric nephrology Oreg. Health Scis. U., 1978-83, assoc. prof. pediatric nephrology, 1983-87, U. Tex. Southwestern Med. Ctr. Dallas, 1987-93, prof. pediatrics, 1993-97; prof. pediat., chief pediat. nephrology Stanford (Calif.) U., 1997—. Med. dir. U.S. HHS, Oreg., 1986-89; dir. clin. pediatric nephrology Children's Med. ctr., Dallas, 1987-97; pediatric nephrology rep. NIH, 1988-90, Health Care Financing Adminstr., Balt., 1988—; dir., founder Annual Pediatric Peritoneal Dialysis Symposium, Dallas, 1990, Nashville, 1991, Seattle, 1992, San Diego, 1993; med. dir. dialysis and renal transplant Lucille Packard Children's Hosp., Stanford, 1997—; cons., lectr. and presenter in field. Author: Pateint Care Flow Chart Manual, 4th edit., 1988; (with others) End-Stage Renal Disease in Children, 1984, Peritoneal Dialysis, 2d edit., 1985, 3d edit., 1989, Current Therapy in Pediatrics, 2d edit., 1989, A Practical Guide to Pediatric Intensive Care, 1990, Pediatric Therapy, 3d edit., 1993; contbr. numerous articles and abstracts to publs. Bd. dirs. Am. Kidney Fund., 1989-96. Jesse H. Jones scholar, 1963-67, Nat. Assn. Corrosion Engrs. scholar, 1963-67. Mem. Am. Soc. Nephrology, Am. Soc. Pediatric Nephrology, Am. Soc. Transplant Physicians, Am. Heart Assn. (coun. kidney in cardiovascular disease), Am. Coun. Transplantation, Am. Acad. Pediatrics, Nat. Kidney Found., Internat. Soc. Nephrology, Internat. Soc. Peritoneal Dialysis, Internat. Pediatric Nephrology Assn., Oreg. Med. Assn., Oreg. Soc. Critical Care Medicine, Tex. Transplantation Soc., Multnomah County Med. Soc., N.W. Renal Soc., Western Soc. Clin. Nephrology, and others. Home: 736 Kendall Ave Palo Alto CA 94306-2725 Office: Stanford U Med Ctr Dept Pediat Divsn Pediat Nephrology 300 Pasteur Dr Rm G306A Palo Alto CA 94306-5208

ALEXANDER, THERON, behavioral scientist, psychologist, writer; s. Theron and Mary Helen (Jones) A.; m. Marie Bailey; children: Thomas, Mary. BA, Maryville Coll., 1935; MA, U. Tenn., 1939; postgrad. Naval tng., Princeton U., 1943, Harvard U., 1944; PhD, U. Chgo., 1949. Asst. prof. psychology Fla. State U., 1949-54; dir. Mental Health Clinic, 1954-57; assoc. prof. psychology in pediatrics U. Iowa, to 1965; prof. psychology in pediatrics U. Miami (Fla.), 1965-66; rsch. prof. Cmty. Studies Ctr. of Temple U., Phila., 1966-68; dir. Child Devel. Rsch. Ctr. for Headstart, 1966-69; prof. human devel., 1966-80; pres. Alexander Assocs., 1980-86; vis. scholar Stanford U., 1987-95. Dir. study tour human devel. programs, faciltiies and rsch. in govt., industry and univs. Temple U., Holland, France, Switzerland, Italy, Yugoslavia, Germany, England, Sweden, Denmark, 1969, univ. study leave for travel and writing, England, 1972, study tour in Soviet Union, 1974; invited lectr. Internat. Symposium, Brazil, 1977. Author: Psychotherapy in Our Society, 1963, Children and Adolscents, 1969, Human Development in an Urban Age, 1973, El Desarrollo Humano en la Epica del Urbanismo, 1978; co-author: Developmental Psychology, 1980; author: Psicologia evolutiva, 1984, A Better Childhood, Without Discipline, 2001. Staff of commdr. USN, World War II, PTO. Recipient cert. Gov. State of Sao Paulo (Brazil), 1977; Legion of Honor, 1979 Fellow APA (disting.), Am. Psychol. Soc. (charter). Address: 50 Gresham Ln Atherton CA 94027-3918 E-mail: alexandertr@worldnet.att.net.

ALEXANDER, THOMAS BENJAMIN, history educator; b. Nashville, July 23, 1918; s. Thomas Benjamin and Mary Christine (Sanders) A.; m. Elise Hadley Pritchett, June 16, 1941; children: Wynne Hadley Alexander Guy, Elaine Elliston Alexander Gates, Carol Pope Alexander Gajek. BA, Vanderbilt U., 1939, MA, 1940, PhD, 1947. From asst. prof. to assoc. prof. history Clemson U., S.C., 1946-49; prof., chmn. div. social scis. Ga. So. U., Statesboro, 1949-57; from assoc. prof. to prof. history U. Ala., Tuscaloosa, 1957-69; prof. history U. Mo., Columbia, 1969-88, Middlebush prof. history, 1979-82, prof. emeritus, 1988—, Sesquicentennial prof., 1990. Author: Political Reconstruction in Tennessee, 1950, Thomas A.R. Nelson of East Tennessee, 1956, Sectional Stress and Party Strength, 1836-1860, 1967, The Anatomy of the Confederate Congress, 1972 (Sydnor award 1973, Jefferson Davis award 1972). Served to lt. USNR, 1943-46, ETO. Fellow Guggenheim Found., 1955-56; grantee Social Sci. Research Council, 1947, 67-68; fellow Inst. So. History, 1968-69 Mem. AAUP, So. Hist. Assn. (pres. 1980), Am. Hist. Assn., Orgn. Am. Historians, Social Sci. History Assn. (pres. 1986), S.C. Hist. Assn. (pres. 1958). Home: 2606 Summit Rd Columbia MO 65203-1336 Office: U Mo Dept History Columbia MO 65211-0001

ALEXANDER, THOMAS G. chemist, researcher; b. Washington, Dc, Sept. 9, 1928; s. Lyle Thomas and Helen Goodwin Alexander; m. Amy Turner, June 1, 1991; m. Eleanor Carol Harkness, Aug. 25, 1951 (dec. Jan. 15, 1990); children: Lyle Steven, Helen Ruth, Carol Anne. BS, U. of Md., College Park, MD, 1946—50; MS, George Wash. U., Washington, DC, 1953—57. Analytical chemist US FDA, Washington, 1956—93; chemist USDA, Washington, 1952—56; analyst NY Dept. of Agr., Ithaca, NY, 1950—. Gen. referee Assn. of Ofcl. Analytical Chemists, Arlington, Va., 1969—94. Contbr. chapters to books. Commr. Boy Scouts of Am., Washington, 1969—94; bd. mem. Assn. of Analytical Chemists, Arlington, Va., 1986—88. Pfc U.S. Army, 1950—52, Maryland. Recipient Outstanding Gen. Referee, 1988. Fellow: Assn. of Ofcl. Analytical Chemists. United Methodist. Achievements include Developed Methods For The Analysis Of Milk Products, Ergot Alkaloids And Antibiotics. Avocation: photography.

ALEXANDER, VERA, dean, marine science educator; b. Budapest, Hungary, Oct. 26, 1932; came to U.S., 1950; d. Paul and Irene Alexander; div.; children: Graham Alexander Dugdale, Elizabeth Alexander. BA in Zoology, U. Wis., 1955, MS in Zoology, 1962; PhD in Marine Sci., U. Alaska, 1965; LLD, Hokkaido U., Japan, 1999. From asst. prof. to assoc. prof. marine sci. U. Alaska, Fairbanks, 1965-74, prof., 1974—, dean Coll. Environ. Scis., 1977-78, 80-81, dir. Inst. Marine Sci., 1979-93, acting dean Sch. Fisheries and Ocean Scis., 1987-89, dean, 1989—. Mem. adv. com. to ocean scis. divsn. NSF, 1980-84, chmn. adv. com., 1983-84; mem. com. to evaluate outer continental shelf environ. assessment program Minerals Mgmt. Svc., Bd. Environ. Sci. and Tech. NRC, 1987-91, mem. com. on geophys. and environ. Data, 1993-98; mem. adv. com. Office Health and Environ. Rsch., U.S. Dept. Energy, Washington, 1987-90; vice chmn. Arctic Ocean Scis. Bd., 1988-89; commr. U.S. Marine Mammal Commn., 1995—; U.S. del. North Pacific Marine Sci. Orgn., 1991-2002, vice-chmn., 1999-2002, chmn., 2002—; bd. dirs. Western Regional Aquaculture Ctr.; mem. sci. adv. bd. NOAA, 1998—; bd. govs. consortium for oceanographic rsch. and edn.; mem. ocean rsch. adv. panel Nat. Oceans Leadership Coun., 1998-2002; mem. internat. steering com. Census of Marine Life, 1999—; mem. Pres.'s Panel on Ocean Exloration, 2000; pres. Arctic Rsch. Consortium U.S., 2003—. Editor: Marine Biological Systems of the Far North (W.L. Rey), 1989. Sec. Fairbanks Light Opera Theatre Bd., 1987-88; chair Rhodes Scholar Selection Com., Alaska, 1986 95; pres. Arctic Rsch. Consortium U.S., 2003—. Research grantee U. Alaska. Fellow AAAS, Arctic Inst. N.Am., Explorers Club (sec., treas. Alaska/Yukon chpt. 1987-89, 91-99, pres. 1990-91); mem. Am. Soc. Limnology and Oceanography, Am. Geophys. Union, Oceanography Soc., Am. Fisheries Soc., Nature Conservancy of Alaska (bd. dirs.), Rotary (pres. 1999-2000). Avocations: classical piano, horsemanship. Home: 3875 Geist Rd Ste E Fairbanks AK 99709 Office: U Alaska PO Box 707220 Fairbanks AK 99775 E-mail: veraialex@aol.com., vera@sfos.uaf.edu.

ALEXANDER, W. M. philosophy educator; b. Jacksonville, Fla., Dec. 5, 1928; s. Leon Wilson Alexander and Ruth Louise Chesebrough; m. Katherine Alice Fryer, June 5, 1953; children: John Edward, Susan Dorman, David Leon (dec.). AB, Davidson Coll., 1950; BD, Louisville Presbyn. Sem., 1953; STM, Harvard U., 1957; PhD, Princeton Theol. Sem., 1961. From asst. to assoc. prof. to prof. philosophy St. Andrews Coll., Laurinburg, N.C., 1961-83, disting. prof., 1983. Vis. prof. philosophy U. N.C., Pembroke, 1983-93 Author: (book) Johann Georg Hamann, Philosophy and Faith, 1966, (book chpts.) The Death of God Debate, The Philosophy of Sex; contbr. articles to profl. jours. and encys. Chaplain, 1st lt. U.S. Army, 1953-56. Rsch. grantee Am. Coun. Learned Socs., 1967; fellow Coun. for Philos. Studies, 1974. Mem. Am. Philos. Assn., Metaphys. Soc. Am., Soc. for Philosophy in Pub. Affairs, Soc. for Philosophy of Sex and Love. Avocations: foreign travel, racquetball. Home: 1105 Shepherd Ave Laurinburg NC 28352 Office: St Andrews Coll Laurinburg NC 28352

ALEXANDER, WILLIAM BROOKS, lawyer, former state senator; b. Boyle, Miss., Dec. 23, 1921; s. William Brooks and Vivien (Beaver) A.; m. Belle McDonald, Mar. 12, 1950; children— Brooks, Becky, John, Jason, Grace. Student, Miss. Coll., 1940-42; LL.B., U. Miss., 1948. Bar: Miss. 1948. Ptnr. firm Alexander, Johnston & Alexander, Cleveland, 1948—; mem. Miss. Senate, 1960-83, past pres. pro tem. Past pres. Miss. Heart Assn.; bd. dirs. Miss. Coll. Served with AUS, 1942-46; bd. dirs. Delta Council, Miss. Econ. Council. Mem. Miss. Bar Assn. (Outstanding Legislator), Bolivar County Bar Assn., Am. Legion, VFW (past dep. comdr.) Clubs: Exchange. Lodges: Masons. Baptist. Office: PO Box 1737 Cleveland MS 38732-1737

ALEXANDER, WILLIAM D., III, civil engineer, consultant, former army air force officer; b. Charlotte, N.C., June 20, 1911; s. William D. Jr. and Elizabeth G. A.; m. Louise Elizabeth York, Nov. 14, 1936 (dec. 1983); 1 child, William D. IV; m. Jean DeZonia Mahan, Nov. 30, 1985 (dec. 1988); m. Alice West Dorrier, Aug. 9, 1990. BS, Va. Mil. Inst., Lexington, 1934; CE, N.C. State U., Raleigh, 1953. Registered profl. civil engr. Commd. 2d lt. U.S. Army-Air Force, 1940, advanced through grades to col., ret., 1962; from v.p. to pres. SSV&K, N.Y.C., 1962-75; asst. gen. mgr. MARTA, Atlanta, 1975-79. Bd. dirs. Georgetown County Water and Sewer, S.C., 1982-87 Fellow ASCE, Soc. Am. Mil. Engrs.; mem. The Moles, Nat. Acad. Engrs., Phi Kappa Phi (N.C. State chpt.), Tau Beta Pi (Citadel chpt.) Home: Apt 305 120 Lakes At Litchfield Dr Pawleys Island SC 29585-5526

ALEXANDER, WILLIAM HERBERT, business educator, former construction executive; b. Harrisburg, Pa., Apr. 17, 1941; s. Wallace Hale and Jeannette Kauffman (Hackenberger) A.; m. Marion Elizabeth Carey, Nov. 30, 1963; children: Charles, Elizabeth, Robert, Kathryn. BS, U.S. Mil. Acad., 1963; MBA, U. Pitts., 1969; D of Pub. Svc. (hon.), Harrisburg Community Coll., 1992. Registered profl. engr., Pa. Commd. 2d lt. U.S. Army, 1963, advanced through grades to capt., 1968; platoon leader, co. comdr. Kitzingen, Germany, 1963-66; capt., co. comdr. Officer Candidate Regiment, Ft. Belvoir, Va., 1966-67; staff officer, engr. constrn. battalion Cu Chi, Vietnam, 1968; resigned, 1968; project mgr. H.B. Alexander & Son, Inc., Harrisburg, 1970-77, chmn., 1977-94; dir. Pa. Blue Shield, Mchts. & Businessmen's Mut. Ins. Co., 1985—97; dir. family bus. programs Wharton Sch. U. Pa., 1988-94, mng. dir. Sol. C. Snider Entrepreneurial Ctr. Wharton Sch., 1994-98; chair Wharton Family Controlled Corp. Program, 1998—2002; dir. Gelsinger Health Sys., Phila., 1997—. Pres. Capital Region Econ. Devel. Corp., 1987—88; chmn. Hershey Trust Co., 1997—98; bd. dirs. Nursery Supply, Inc. Bd. dirs. AAA Ctrl. Penn Auto Club (chmn. 1991-93); pres. Tri County United Way, 1979-80, Ams. for Competitive Enterprise System, 1981-82; bd. dirs. Milton Hershey Sch., 1989-2002, chmn., 1997-98; chmn. Harrisburg C.C. Found., 1981-82. Decorated Bronze Star Mem. ASCE, Pa. Soc. Profl. Engrs. (Engr. of Yr. in Central Pa. 1986), Harrisburg C. of C. (bd. dirs., chmn. 1982-83), Harrisburg Rotary (pres. 1981-82), Beta Gamma Sigma, Delta Mu Delta. Presbyterian (elder). Home: 16 Wagner St Hummelstown PA 17036-9113 Office: 428 Vance Hall 3733 Spruce St Philadelphia PA 19104-6301

ALEXANDER, WILLIAM OLIN, finance company executive; b. Lexington, Ky., Aug. 2, 1939; s. Elby Olin and Louise (Watson) A.; m. Yvonne Davis, Jan. 26, 1961; children: Keith Davis, Hope. BS, U. Ky., 1961. CPA, Fla. Auditor Ring, Mahony & Arner (CPAs), Miami, Fla., 1961-62, sr. auditor, 1964-66; v.p., treas. Seabird Industries, Miami, 1966-70, exec. v.p., 1970-73; controller Belcher Oil Co., Miami, 1973-75, treas., 1976-83; sr. v.p., treas. Mitchell Co., Mobile, Ala., 1983-85; pres. Alexander & Co., PA, CPA, 1985— Served to 1st lt. AUS, 1962-64. Mem. AICPA, Fla. Inst. CPAs, Porsche Club Am., Beta Alpha Psi, Delta Sigma Pi, Delta Tau Delta. Republican. Home: 10910 Juniperus Pl Tampa FL 33618-3818 Office: 14033 N Dale Mabry Hwy Tampa FL 33618-2401

ALEXANDER, WILLIAM POWELL, business advisor; b. Buffalo, June 16, 1934; s. James Nelson and Helen (Johnston) A.; m. Eunice Gail Elwood, May 8, 1981; 1 child from previous marriage, Christine Alexander Johnson. BA, Gettysburg Coll., 1956; postgrad., Temple U., 1960-62. With Aetna Casualty & Surety Co., 1956-57, RCA Corp., N.Y.C., 1960-86, asst. sec., 1968-73, sr. asst. sec., 1973-78, sec., 1978-86; also sec. NBC, Coronet Industries, RCA/Ariola, Hertz, Random House; sec. to office of chmn., asst. to chmn. Marine Midland Banks, Inc., 1987-88; adminstrv. dir. The Gt. Atlantic & Pacific Tea Co. Inc., 1988-89. Served to 1st lt. USAF, 1957-59. Mem. Am. Soc. Corp. Secs., Phi Kappa Psi. Clubs: Cavalier Golf and Yacht (Virginia Beach, Va.). Home and Office: 216 61st St Virginia Beach VA 23451-2117

ALEXANDER-HAYNES, SANDRA, psychologist, educator; b. Cleve., Nov. 18, 1961; d. Winfield Edward Wright, Jr. and Mary Lee Alexander; m. Jeffery Orlando Haynes, June 27, 2003; 1 child, Michael A. Alexander-Leeks. BA cum laude, Cleve. State U., 1983, MA in Psychology, 1985, PhD in Urban Edn., 1997. Nationally cert. sch. psychologist 2003. Sch. psychology intern E. Cleve. Schs., 1985—86, summer sch. psychologist, 1986; sch. psychologist PSI Assocs., Inc., Akron, Ohio, 1986—87, Cleve. Mcpl. Schs., 1987—2000, lead psychologist, 1998—2000; sch. psychologist Orange City Schs., Pepper Pike, Ohio, 2000—03. Workshop co-facilitator Soc. for Prevention of Violence, 1997—2000; adj. prof. Kent State U., Kent, Ohio, 1999—2000, mem. sch. psychology program adv. com., 1999—2002; chair, multicultural com. Cleve. Mcpl. Schs., 1997—2000; thesis reader Notre Dame Coll., S. Euclid, Ohio, 2000—02, adj. prof., 2000—02. Bd. mem. Ratner Schs., Lyndhurst, Ohio, 1998—2000. Mem.: Ohio Sch. Psychology Assn. Office: Orange Schs 32000 Chagrin Blvd Pepper Pike OH 44124

ALEXANDRATOS, SPIRO DIONISIOS, chemistry educator, dean; b. N.Y.C., Dec. 11, 1951; m. Olga Pantos; 1 child, Jonathan. BS, Manhattan Coll., 1973; PhD, U. Calif., Berkeley, 1977. Sr. rsch. chemist Rohm and Haas Co., Phila., 1977-81; from asst. prof. to assoc. prof. U. Tenn., Knoxville, 1981-92, prof. chemistry, 1993-2000, Paul and Wilma Ziegler prof. chemistry, 2000-01; univ. dean for rsch. CUNY, 2001—03, prof. chemistry Hunter Coll., 2001—. Collaborating scientist U. Tenn./Oak Ridge Nat. Lab., 1998-2001. Holder 12 patents in field; mem. editorial adv. bd. Reactive and Functional Polymers, Separation Science and Technology, Solvent Extraction and Ion Exchange. Recipient Hoechst-Celanese Rsch. award, 1993, R & D 100 award R & D Mag., 1994, Tech. Achievement award Lockheed-Martin, 1999. Mem. Am. Chem. Soc. (chmn. divsn. indsl. engring. chemistry 1993-94, chmn. subdivsn. separation sci. 1991-92; assoc. editor Jour. of Indsl. and Engring. Chemistry Rsch.), Gordon Rsch. Conf. Reactive Polymer (chmn. 1995-97), Sigma Xi, Phi Beta Kappa (cert. merit 1993).

ALEXANIAN, RAYMOND, hematologist; b. N.Y.C., June 8, 1932; s. Hagop and Eleeza (Bynderian) A.; m. Lois Abbott, Jan. 16, 1960; 1 dau., Jane. BA with highest honors, Dartmouth Coll., 1952; MD, Harvard U., 1955. Diplomate: Am. Bd. Internal Medicine. Intern King County Hosp., Seattle, 1955-56; successively asst. resident in medicine, research fellow in hematology, instr. medicine U. Wash. Med. Sch., 1958-64; mem. faculty U. Tex. M.D. Anderson Hosp., Houston, 1964—, prof. medicine, 1975—. Contbr. numerous articles on myeloma and related disorders to med. jours. Served as capt. M.C. AUS, 1956-58. Mem. Am. Soc. Hematology, AMA, Tex. Med. Assn. (Waldenstrom award 1997). Home: 4082 Breakwood Dr Houston TX 77025-4033 Office: MD Anderson Hosp Dept Lymphoma-Myeloma 1515 Holcombe Blvd Houston TX 77030-4009

ALEX-ASSENSOH, YVETTE MARIE, political scientist; b. Lafayette, La., Feb. 12, 1967; d. Livingston and Thelma Coleman A.; m. A.B. Assensoh, May 7, 1994; children: Kwadwo Stephen, Livingston. BA summa cum laude, Dillard

U., 1988; postgrad., Columbia U., 1987-88; MA, Ohio State U., 1991, PhD, 1993. Asst. prof. Ind. U., Bloomington, 1994-2000, assoc. prof., 2001—, dir. grad. studies in polit. sci., 2003—. Rsch. assoc. Ohio State U., 1992-93; spkr. in field. Author: Neighborhoods, Family and Political Behavior, 1998; co-author: Afrian Military, 2001; co-editor: Black and Multiracial Politics, 2000; contbr. articles to profl. jours. Recipient Mays-Cook Sr. award Dillard U., New Orleans, 1998; NSF grantee, 1992-93, So. Regional Coun. grantee, 1994-95, Active Learning Teaching Strategies grantee, Ind. U., 1995, Multi Disciplinary Ventures grantee, 1997, Spencer Found. grantee, 2001; Benjamin E. Mays-Samuel DuBois Cook scholar, 1988; Ford Found. fellow, 1992-93, U. N.C. postdoctoral fellow, 1993-94, Nat. Acad. Edn./Spencer Found. postdoctoral fellow, 1999-2000, Fulbright fellow, 2001. Fellow Am. Polit. Sci. Assn.; mem. Assn. Third World Studies, Internat. PEN. Avocations: reading, tennis. Home: 4301 Cricket Knoll Dr Bloomington IN 47401 Office: Ind U Polit Sci Dept Bloomington IN 47405 Fax: 812-855-2027. E-mail: yalex@indiana.edu.

ALEXE, GABRIELA, research scientist; arrived in US, 1998; d. Gheorghe and Ecaterina Gheorghe; m. Sorin Alexe, Nov. 17, 1990. MSc in Math., U. Bucharest, Romania, 1986; MSc in Math. and Computer Sci. with honors, U. Galati, 1995; PhD in Ops. Rsch., Rutgers U., 2003. Asst. prof. U. Galati, 1990—98; rsch. asst. Rutgers U., NJ, 2000—. Contbr. articles to profl. jours. Recipient Nat. Math. Student Competition Spl. prizes, Ministry Edn., Romania; fellow Grad. Student Project, Discrete Math and Theoretical Computer Sci. Found., Rutgers U., 1998—2002; grantee, Office Naval Rsch.; Soros fellow, Rostock U., Rostock, Germany, 1997, Excellence fellow, Rutgers U., 1998—2001, TEMPUS fellow, Humboldt U., Berlin, 1998. Mem.: Inst. for Advanced Study, Inst. for Ops. Rsch. and Mgmt. Sci. (assoc.), Classification Soc. N.Am. Office: RUTCOR Rutgers Univ 640 Bartholomew Rd Piscataway NJ 08854 E-mail: alexe@rutcor.rutgers.edu.

ALEXEEV, DMITRI KONSTANTINOVICH, pianist; b. Moscow, Aug. 10, 1947; s. Konstantin and Gertrude (Bolotina) A.; m. Tatiana Sarkisova, 1970; 1 child. Studied with Dmitri Bashkirov, Moscow Conservatoire. Pianist performing USSR, U.K., Europe, U.S., touring Australia, Japan, Hong Kong, others; pianist London Philharm. Orch., Berlin Philharm., Berlin Radio Symphony Orchs., Chgo. Symphony Orch., Phila. Orch., London Symphony Orch., St. Petersburg Philharm. Orch., Royal Concertgebouw of Amsterdam, Munich Bavarian Radio Orch., Orchestre de Paris, City of Birmingham Symphony Orch., Royal Philharm. Orch., Hallé Orch., Balt. (Md.) Symphony Orch., Royal Flanders Philharm. Orch., Israel Philharm.; recordings include concertos by Schumann, Grieg, Rachmaninov, Prokofiev, Shostakovich, Scriabin, Medtner and solo works by Brahms, Rachmaninov, Schumann, Chopin, Liszt; performed at recitals in Munich, Florence, Rome, London, St. Petersburg, and Helsinki among others; worked with conductors such as Ashkenazy, Boulez, Dorati, Giulini, Muti, Rozhdestvensky, Tennstedt, Temirkanov, Tilson Tomas, and Jansons, among others. Recipient top honours Marguerite Long Competition, Paris, 1969, George Enescu Competition, Bucharest, 1970, Tchaikovsky Competition, Moscow, 1974, first prize 5th Leeds Internat. Piano Competition, Eng., 1975, Edison award The Netherlands, 1994. Office: IMG Artists/Lovell House 616 Chiswick High St London 5RX UK England

ALEXEFF, IGOR, physicist, electrical engineer, educator emeritus; b. Pitts., Jan. 5, 1931; s. Alexander and Tamara (Tchirkow) A.; m. Anne I. Fabina, Feb. 4, 1954; children: Alexander, Helen. BA with honors, Harvard U., 1952; MS, U. Wis., 1955, PhD, 1959. Registered profl. engr., Tenn. Research engr. Westinghouse Corp., Pitts., 1952-53; NSF postdoctoral fellow U. Zurich, Switzerland, 1959-60; group leader controlled thermonuclear fusion Oak Ridge Nat. Lab., 1960-71; prof. elec. engring. U. Tenn., 1971-96, prof. emeritus, 1996—. Vis. prof. Inst. Plasma Physics, Nagoya, Japan, 1973, Phys. Rsch. Lab., Ahmedabad, India, 1975, physics dept. U. Natal, Durban, South Africa, 1976, U. Fed. Fluminense Niteroi, Brazil, 1978, Birla Inst. Tech., Ranchi, India, 1991; organizer Plasma Physics Workshop, U.S. and India, 1976; chmn. Gordon Rsch. Conf. on Plasma Physics, 1974; pres. So. Appalachian Sci. and Engring. Far, 1985-86. Co-author: High Power Microwave Sources, 1987; contbr. articles to profl. jours.; over 10 patents in field. Chancellor's rsch. scholar U. Tenn., 1984; recipient Advanced Tech. award Internat. Hall of Fame, 1989, 91, (with others) R&D 100 award R&D Mag., 1989, 91; named Most Outstanding Tchr. of Yr., U. Tenn. Elec. Engring. Dept., 1992. Fellow IEEE (assoc. editor Trans. on Plasma Sci., organizer 1st Internat. Conf. on Plasma Sci. 1974, former pres. Oak Ridge sect., Centennial medal 1987, Outstanding Engr. in S.E. award 1987), Am. Phys. Soc. (past sec.-treas. div. plasma physics); mem. ASI (co-founder), Tech. Corp., Tenn. Inventors Assn. (founding pres., Inventor of Yr. award 1988), Nuclear and Plasma Scis. Soc. of IEEE (chmn. plasma sect. 1983-84, v.p. 1998, pres. 1999-2000, Shea award for outstanding svc., Plasma Scis. and Applications award 2002). Home: 2790 Turnpike Oak Ridge TN 37830 Office: U Tenn Ferris 315 Knoxville TN 37996-2100 also: 1907 Holston River Rd Knoxville TN 37914-6144 E-mail: ialexeff@comcast.net.

ALEXENBERG, MEL (MEL ALEXENBERG MENAHEM), artist, art educator; b. N.Y.C., Feb. 24, 1937; s. Abraham and Jeanne (Kahn) A.; m. Miriam Benjamin, Oct. 25, 1959; children: Iyrit, Ari, Ron, Moshe. BS, Queens Coll., CUNY, 1958; MS, Yeshiva U., 1959; EdD, NYU, 1969. Sci. tchr. N.Y.C. Pub. Schs., Queens, 1959-61; sci. supr. Manhasset (N.Y.) Pub. Schs., 1961-65; asst. prof. Adelphi U., L.I., N.Y., 1965-69; sr. lectr. Tel Aviv U., 1969-73; assoc. prof. Columbia U., N.Y.C., 1973-77; pres. Ramat Hanegev Coll., Yeroham, Israel, 1977-84; assoc. prof. Bar Ilan U., Ramat Gan, Israel, 1978-84; rsch. fellow MIT, Cambridge, Mass., 1984-88; chmn. dept. fine arts Pratt Inst., Bklyn., 1985-90; dean New World Sch. Arts, Miami, Fla., 1990-2000; prof. Coll. of Judea and Samaria, Ariel, Israel, 2000—. Chair. com. on design. edn. Israel Ministry Edn., 1983-84. Author: Light and Sight, 1969, A Semiotic Taxonomy of Contemporary Art Forms, 1976, Aesthetic Experience in Creative Process, 1981, Art with Computers: The Human Spirit and the Electronic Revolution, 1988, Miami in Ecological Perspective, 1994, Art Thrones and Legacy Scrolls, 1998; art editor Visual Computer: Internat. Jour. Computer Graphics; works include Lights Orot, 1987-89, Digitized Homage to Rembrandt, 1989-90, Four Corners of Am., 1995-96, Centers: Lebanon (Kansas) and Jerusalem (Israel), 1996, Art Thrones, Intergenerational Pub. Art with Miriam Benjamin, 1997, Legacy Scrolls, 1998, Trees of Good Deeds & Wisdom, Synagogue Designed with Arch. K. Treister, 1999, Danish Lights, Charlottenborg Mus., Copenhagen, 2000, Divine Retribution, Coll. of Santa Fe, N.Mex., 2000, Cybersight, 2003; represented in permanent collections Met. Mus. Art, N.Y.C., Mus. Modern Art, N.Y.C., Princeton (N.J.) Art Mus., Del. Art Mus., Wilmington, Phila. Mus. Art, Balt. Mus. Art, Tel Aviv Mus., Victoria and Albert Mus., London, Mus. Moderner Kunst, Vienna, Austria, Museo de Arte Contemporaneo, Caracas, Venezuela, Israel Mus., Jerusalem, Haags Gemeentemuseum, The Netherlands, Malmo (Sweden) Mus., High Mus. Art, Atlanta, Museo Nacional de Artes Plasticas Montevideo, Uruguay. The Future of Art: From Hellenistic to Hebraic Consciousness, 2002. Bd. trustees Torah Sch. for Environ. Studies, Mitzpeh Ramon, Israel; bd. dirs. Wolf Found., 2003—. Recipient award for art direction Am. Film Festival, 1964; Founders Day award NYU, 1969; MIT rsch. fellow, 1984-88. Mem. Internat. Soc. Edn. Through Art, Nat. Art Edn. Assn., Israel Soc. Painters and Sculptors. Jewish. Office: Coll of Judea and Samaria Ariel 44837 Israel E-mail: malexenberg@beethoven.com.

ALEXIOU, JAMES, electronics executive; b. Manchester, N.H., May 25, 1932; s. George Nicholas and Mary Alexiou; m. Elaine Alexiou, Feb. 4, 1962; children: Stephanie Alexiou Hubbard, Thomas James. BS in Bus. Mgmt., Boston U., 1954, MA in Econ., 1962. Prodn. mgr. Raytheon Co., Newton, Mass., 1962-65; plant mgr. Norton Co., Worcester, Mass., 1965-70; chmn., treas. New Eng. Rsch. Ctr., Sudbury, Mass., 1976-78; chmn., CEO Irvine Sensors Corp., Costa Mesa, Calif., 1970-97, chmn., 1970—, Novaloc, Inc., Costa Mesa, Calif., 1995—. Bd. dirs. Dycam Corp., Chatsworth, Calif. Bd. dirs. Phila. Soc. Orange County, Irvine, Calif. 1994—, chmn., 1999-2000, pres., 1997-99; pres. St. Paul's Greek Orthodox Ch. Found., Irvine, 1998-2001; founder, benefactor Orange County Performing Arts Ctr., Costa Mesa, 1984-2001. Recipient Disting. Svc. to Profession award Boston U. Sch. Mgmt., 1996. Mem. Center Club, Sigma Alpha Epsilon (past pres.). Avocations: hiking, movies, performing arts. Office: Irvine Sensors Corp 3001 Redhill Ave Costa Mesa CA 92626 E-mail: alexiou@aol.com.

ALEXIS, CARL ODMAN, lawyer, earth scientist; b. Valparaiso, Nebr., Aug. 8, 1918; s. Joseph Emmanual Alexander Alexis and Marjorie Edith Odman; m. May Britt Lennerup, 1954 (div. 1962); children: Carl Erik, Karin Frenze; m. Mildred Craig Bartos, 1966 (dec. 1996); m. Jeanette Strain, Apr. 24, 1999. BS, U. Nebr., 1937; MS, U. Ariz., 1940, PhD, 1949; postgrad., Calif. Inst. Tech., 1939-40, NYU, 1943-44; JD, U. Nebr., 1966. Bar: Nebr. 1966. Chemist Am. Potash and Chem. Corp., 1940-41; mucker Phelps Dodge Corp., Bisbee, Ariz., 1941; instrument man Stanolind Oil and Gas Co., Tulsa, 1941-42; sr. supr. Plum Brook Ordnance Works, Sandusky, Ohio, 1942-43; grad. asst. U. Ariz., Tucson, 1947-48; field engr. Anaconda Copper Corp., Salt Lake City, 1948-49; geologist U.S. Geol. Survey, Washington, 1949-50; phys. sci. adminstr. Office Naval Rsch., Washington, 1950-62; spl. asst. atty. gen. Atty. Gen.-Dept. Rds., 1967-71. Lt. comdr. USN, 1943-46, USNR, 1946-69, ret. Mem. Neb. Bar Assn., Lincoln Bar Assn., Audubon Soc., Am. Legion, Friends of Nebr. State Mus., Nebr. State Hist. Soc., Nebr. Art Assn., Gt. Plains Assn., Rotary, Sigma Xi, Phi Kappa Phi. Home: 1811 S Pershing Rd Lincoln NE 68502-4840

ALEXIS, GERALDINE M. lawyer; b. N.Y.C., Nov. 3, 1948; d. William J. and Margaret Daly; m. Marcus Alexis, June 15, 1969; children: Marcus L., Hilary I., Sean C. BA, U. Rochester, 1971; MBA, JD, Northwestern U., 1976. Bar: Ill. 1976, Calif. 2001, U.S. Dist. Ct. (no. dist.): Calif. 1976, Ill. 1976, U.S. Trial Bar: 1985, U.S. Ct. Appeals (7th cir.): 1986, U.S. Ct. Appeals (5th cir.): 1996, bar: (U.S. Ct. Appeals (9th cir.)) 2002. Law clk. to Hon. John F. Grady, justice U.S. Dist. Ct. (no. dist.) Ill., Chgo., 1976-77; assoc. Sidley & Austin, Chgo., 1977-79, 81-83, ptnr., 1983-2000; advisor U.S. Dept. Justice Office Legal Counsel, Washington, 1979-81; ptnr. McCutchen, Doyle, Brown & Enersen (now Bingham McCutchen LLP), San Francisco, 2001—. Mem.: ABA (vice-chair fin. mkts. and instns. com. antitrust sect.), Bar Assn. San Francisco (chair antitrust and trade regulation sect.). Democrat. Office: Bingham McCutchen LLP 3 Embarcadero Ctr San Francisco CA 94111

ALF, MARTHA JOANNE, artist; b. Berkeley, Calif., Aug. 13, 1930; d. Foster Wise and Julia Vivian (Kane) Powell; m. Edward Franklin Alf, Mar. 17, 1951; 1 child, Richard Franklin. BA with distinction, San Diego State U., 1953, MA in Painting, 1963, jr. coll. teaching credential, 1969; MFA in Pictorial Arts, UCLA, 1970. Rsch. asst. Health and Welfare Assn., Seattle, 1956; tchg. asst. in drawing, instr. design San Diego State U., 1963; instr. drawing L.A. Valley Coll., 1970-73, El Camino Coll., Hawthorne, Calif., 1971; instr. drawing and painting L.A. Harbor Coll., Wilmington, Calif., 1971-75; instr. art UCLA Extension, 1971-79. Instr. contemporary art Brand Library Art Ctr., Glendale, Calif., 1973; vis. artist Calif. State Coll., Bakersfield, 1980; freelance art critic Artweek, Oakland, Calif., 1974-77; guest curator Lang Art Gallery, Scripps Coll., Claremont, Calif., 1974. Retrospective exhbn. Fellows Contemporary Art, L.A. Mcpl. Art Gallery, San Francisco Art Inst., 1984; represented in permanent collections L.A. County Mus. Art, Chem. Bank N.Y., Ga. Mus. Art., Israel Mus. Art, Jerusalem, L.A. County Mus. Art, McCrory Corp., N.Y., Metromedic, Inc., L.A., N.Y., San Diego Mus. Art, San Jose Mus., Santa Barbara Mus. Art, Southland Corp., Dallas, Spencer Mus. Art U. Kans., Lawrence, Met. Mus. Art., N.Y., Phoenix Art Mus., Fresno Art Mus., Grand Rapids Art Mus., Orange County Mus. Art, Newport Beach, Calif., Palm Springs Desert Mus., Laguna Art Mus., U. Calif. Santa Barbara Art Gallery, Eli Broad Collection, Santa Monica, U. Va. Bayley Art Mus., Charlottesville; one-woman shows include John Berggruen Gallery, San Francisco, 1977, Forth Worth Art Mus., 1988, Susan Caldwell Gallery, N.Y., 1980, Dorothy Rosenthal Gallery, Chgo., 1982, Eloise Pickard Smith Gallery Cowell Coll. U. Calif., Santa Cruz, 1983, Newspace Gallery, L.A., 1976-85, 90-2000, 02, Tortue Gallery, Santa Monica, 1986, Jan Baum Gallery, L.A., 1988, Trabia Gallery, N.Y., 1990, 871 Fine Arts, San Francisco, 1991, Art Inst. of So. Calif., Laguna Beach, Calif., 1991, Fresno Art Mus., 1992, Mt. San Antonio Coll., Walnut, Calif., 1993; exhibited in group shows at San Diego Mus. of Art, 1964, 67-68, 70-71, 77-78, 83, Whitney Mus. Contemporary Art Biennial, 1975, Newport Harbor Art Mus., 1975, Marion Koogler McNay Art Inst., San Antonio, 1976, Long Beach Mus. Art, 1972, 82, 86, Am. Acad. Arts and Letters, N.Y., 1985, 96, Henry Art Gallery U. Wash., Seattle, 1985, L.A. County Mus. of Art, 1979 (Kay Neilson award 1979), 82, Womens Mus., Washington, 1994, Bakersfield Mus. Art, 1999, Santa Barbara Mus. Art, 2001, Calif. State U., L.A., 2001, Laguna Beach Art Mus., 2001. Nat. Endowment for Arts grantee, 1979, 89; recipient Richard Florsheim Art Fund award, 1996, Calif. Heritage Mus. print commn., 1998. Avocations: body building, walking, reading, keeping journal, bird study and videos. Home: 103 Brooks Ave Venice CA 90291-3254

ALFA, MICHELLE JOSEPHINE, microbiologist, educator; b. Winnipeg, Man., Canada, Dec. 9, 1953; d. Jim R. and Betty M. Foubert; m. Attahiru S. Alfa; children: Ismaila, Aisha. BSc, U. Man., 1975; MSC, U. NSW, Sydney, Australia, 1980; PhD, U. Alta., Edmonton, Can., 1986. Asst. prof. U. Man., 1989—96, assoc. prof., 1996—2000, prof., 2000—02; asst. dir. microbiology lab. St. Boniface Gen. Hosp., Winnipeg, 1989—2000, asst. dir., 2002—; assoc. prof. Wayne State U., Detroit, 2000—02. Contbr. articles to profl. jours. Bd. dirs., sec. Horace Patterson Found., Winnipeg. Studentship, Alta. Heritage Found., 1981—85, postgrad. fellow, Man. Health Rsch. Coun., 1986—88. Mem.: Assn. for Advancement of Med. Instrumentation., Am. Bd. Microbiology, Can. Coll. Microbiologists (mem. exec. com. 2003—, treas. 2003—). Achievements include invention of artificial test soil. Avocations: mentoring women in science, science education. Home: 51 Ravine Rd Winnipeg MB Canada R2M 5N4 Office: St Boniface Gen Hosp Microbiology Lab L4025 409 Tache Ave Winnipeg MB Canada R2H 2A6 E-mail: malfa@sbgh.mb.ca.

ALFANGE, DEAN, JR., political science educator; b. N.Y.C., May 6, 1930; s. Dean and Thalia (Perry) A.; m. Barbara Jean Vance, June 6, 1959. AB, Hamilton Coll., 1950; MA, U. Colo., 1960; PhD, Cornell U., 1967. Instr., then asst. prof. govt. Lafayette Coll., Easton, Pa., 1963-67; from asst. prof. to assoc. prof. polit. sci. U. Mass., Amherst, 1967-75, prof., 1975-99, prof. emeritus, 1999—, dean Faculty Social and Behavioral Scis., 1970-75, acting vice chancellor for acad. affairs, 1975-76, 83. Vis. scholar Yale Law Sch., 1977-78, Stanford Law Sch., 1986, 92. Served to 1st lt. USAF, 1952-57. Home: 5 Montague Rd Leverett MA 01054-9725 Office: U Mass Dept Political Science Amherst MA 01003 E-mail: dalfange@polsci.umass.edu.

ALFANO, CHARLES THOMAS, SR., lawyer; b. Suffield, Conn., June 21, 1920; s. Dominick and Rosina (Dimartino) A.; m. Mary Ann Sinatro, Nov. 13, 1954; children: Diane Elizabeth, Andrea Rose, Charles Thomas Jr., Susan Marie. Student, Ill. Coll., 1939-40; BA cum laude, U. Conn., 1943; LL.B., JD, U. Mich., 1948. Bar: Conn. 1948. Since practiced in, Hartford; partner firm Alfano Halloran & Flynn; judge Town Ct. of Suffield, 1949-51, 55-59; mem. Conn. Senate, 1959-77, asst. majority leader, 1966, pres. pro tem, 1967-73, minority leader, 1973-75, v.p. pro tem, 1975-77; corp. counsel Town of Suffield, 1977-83. Dir., chmn. bd. Suffield Savs. Bank; dir. Conn. Water Co. Bd. dirs. Conn. Pub. TV. Served with USNR, 1942-47, PTO. Mem. ABA, ATLA, Conn. Bar Assn., Hartford County Bar Assn., Conn. Trial Lawyers Assn. (bd. dirs.), Hartford Club, Mystic Yacht Club, Mason's Island Yacht Club, N.Y. Athletic Club, KC, Sigma Nu. Home: 50 Marbern Dr Suffield CT 06078-1533 Office: 89 Oak St Hartford CT 06106-1515 also: 53 Mountain Rd Suffield CT 06078-2041

ALFANO, EDWARD CHARLES, JR., elementary education educator; b. Bklyn, NY, Mar. 20, 1945; s. Edward Charles and Victoria Helen (Fanti) A.; m. Mary Fien, Aug. 27, 1983; children: Elizabeth Anne, Christina Irene. BA in Philosophy, Cathedral Coll., 1967; post grad., Bklyn. Coll., NY, 1967-70; MS in Edn., LI U., 1972, post grad., 1976, Oxford U., UK, 1973, Bklyn. Mus., NY, 1990, Pastoral Inst., 2001—03. Cert. elem. tchr., NY. Tchr. English St. Mark Sch., Bklyn., 1968-69; tchr. NYC Pub. Sch. Sys., Bklyn., 1969—2000; math. specialist Pub. Sch. 15, Bklyn., 1976-78; tchr. English as 2d lang. Pub. Sch. 169, Bklyn., 1985-86, tchr. art, 1986-94, tchr. sci., 1994-95, tchr. English, 1995-96, tchr. music movement/phys. edn. Early Childhood Learning Ctr, 1996-99, sr. sci. tchr., 1999—2000; tchr. 4th grade St. Simon and Jude Sch., Bklyn., 2000—01. Del. United Fedn. Tchr., Bklyn., 1977-78; faculty rep. policy consultation com. Pub. Sch. 169, 1979-92, dir. summer recreation program, 1989-97; presenter workshops and symposia; tchr. Murals in Park Project, Bklyn., 1990, summer literacy program, 1998-99; mem. Dist. 15 Sci. Focus Group, 1999-2000. Narrator video The Passion of Our Lord According to Saint John, 1993; contbr.poetry and articles to various publs. Pres. Friends of LI U. Libr., 1977-80; mem. vis. com. LI U., Bklyn., 1978-80; bd. dir. Hispanic Young People's Alternatives, Bklyn., 1990-95; lector Good Shepherd Ch., Bklyn., parish coord. Sanctity of Life com., 1993—; mem. Bklyn. Diocesan Pastoral Team for Charismatic Renewal, 1995—. Commissioned as a Lay Ecclesial Minister for the Diocese of Bklyn, May 2, 2003; recipient cmty. svc. award Cmty. Bd. 7, Bklyn., 1990, 91, Sanctity of Life Recognition award Roman Cath. Diocese of Bklyn., 1997, Pro-Life award Flatbush Coun. 497 KC, 1998. Mem. Cath. Tchr. Assn. (Educator of Yr. award 1992), So. Poetry Assn., Charismatic Prayer Group, Sanctity of Life Com., LI U. Alumni Assn. Democrat. Avocations: poetry, art, swimming, music, dramatics.

ALFANO, JORGE, music company executive, counselor; b. Buenos Aires; arrived in U.S., 1981; s. Eugenio Mario and Elisa Carolina Alfano; m. René Ceballos. Clin. hypnotherapist Am. Assn. Physiology and Hypnotherapy, N.Y., 1992, min. metaphysical Internat. Metaphysical Ministry, L.A., 1996, pastoral counselor Internat. Metaphysical Ministry, L.A., 1996. Prodr. Lyrichoir Records, NY, 1995—2000, The Relaxation Group, NY, 1995—2000, Sacred Sounds Records, Miami, 2001. Cons. Nickelodeon, NYC; advisor NY Met. Mus., NYC, U. Miami Mus. Author: (books) Andean Spirituality, Unconditional Love; prodr.: (over 40 recordings of world music). Avocations: kayaking, Japanese Painting, archery. Home and Office: 2612 Lincoln St Hollywood FL 33020 E-mail: sacredsounds@sprintmail.com.

ALFANO, MICHAEL CHARLES, dental school dean; b. Newark, Aug. 8, 1947; s. Michael Ferdinand and Anne Marie (Barrington) A.; m. JoAnn Mary Coletta, Mar. 30, 1969; children: Michael Anthony, Kristin Lynn. Student, Rutgers U., 1965-67; DMD, U. Medicine and Dentistry of N.J., 1971; postgrad. in periodontics, Harvard U., 1971-74; PhD, MIT, 1975. Asst. prof. dentistry Fairleigh Dickinson U., Hackensack, N.J., 1974-77, assoc. prof., 1977-80, prof. with tenure, 1980-82, dir. Oral Health Research Ctr., 1977-82, asst. dean grad. affairs and research, 1981-82; v.p. dental research Block Drug Co., Inc., Jersey City, 1982-84, sr. v.p. R&D, 1987-98, bd. dirs., 1988-98, pres. dental products div., 1985-88, cons. office of chief exec., 1990-98; dean Coll. Dentistry NYU, 1998—, prof. basic scis. & periodontology Coll. Dentistry, 1998—; bd. dirs. Dentsply Inc., 2001—. Cons. Nat. Inst. Dental Rsch., Bethesda, Md., 1976-82; apptd. nat. adv. dental rsch. coun. NIH, Bethesda, 1994-98; apptd. vis. prof. Nat. Dairy Coun., Chgo., 1981; vis. sr. scientist Fairleigh Dickinson U., 1982-88; adj. prof. U. Medicine and Dentistry of N.J., Newark, 1985-2003; mem. sci. adv. coun. Office of Gov., State of N.J., 1981-84. Editor: Symposium on Nutrition, 1976; contbr. articles to profl. jours. and chpts. to books; patentee in field. Trustee Found. of U. Medicine and Dentistry of N.J., 1988-98; adv. bd. Columbia U. Sch. Dental and Oral Surgery, 1990-98; mem. program com. Am. Fund for Dental Health, 1991-93; bd. overseers Forsyth Dental Ctr., Boston, 1992-99, U. Pa. Coll. Dental Medicine, 1997—; trustee Santa Fe Group, 1998—; founding dir. Friends of Nat. Inst. of Dental Rsch., 1998—; dir. Dentsply Internat., 2001—. Recipient Leadership citation Newark YMCA, 1966, Disting. Alumnus award U. Medicine and Dentistry of N.J., 1986, Harvard U. Sch. Dental Medicine, 1998; NIH research grantee, 1974-82; NIH postdoctoral fellow, 1971-74. Fellow Am. Coll. Dentists, Am. Coll. of Prosthodontists (hon. fellow), Internat. Congress Oral Implantologists (hon. life 2002-); mem. ADA (cons., Future of Dentistry Commn. 1999-2001, bd. govs. student clinicians 2000—, Nat. Achievement award 1978), Internat. Assn. for Dental Rsch., Am. Assn. for Dental Rsch. (pres. N.J. chpt. 1985), Am. Inst. Nutrition. Independent. Roman Catholic. Achievements include 8 patents; discovery of role of Vitamin C in mucous membrane barrier function. Home: 29 Washington Sq W Apt 5C New York NY 10011-9132 Office: NYU Coll Dentistry 345 E 24th St New York NY 10010-4086 E-mail: michael.alfano@nyu.edu.

ALFARO, FELIX BENJAMIN, retired physician; b. Managua, Nicaragua, Oct. 22, 1939; came to U.S., 1945, naturalized, 1962; s. Agustin Jose and Amanda Julieta (Barillas) A.; m. Carmen Heide Meyer, Aug. 14, 1965; children: Felix Benjamin, Mark. Student (state scholar), U. San Francisco, 1958-59, 61-62; MD, Creighton U., 1967. Diplomate Am. Bd. Family Practice. Clk. Pacific Gas & Electric Co., San Francisco, 1960-61; intern St. Mary's Hosp., San Francisco, 1967; resident Scenic Gen. Hosp., Modesto, Calif., 1967-70; pvt. practice, Watsonville, Calif., 1971—2000, ret., 2000. Hon. staff Watsonville Cmty. Hosp., 1971—. Capt. M.C., U.S. Army, 1968-69. Fellow Am. Acad. Family Practice; mem. AMA, Calif. Med. Assn., Santa Cruz Country Med. Soc., 38th Parallel Med. Soc. Korea, NRA, VFW. Republican. Roman Catholic.

ALFERS, GERALD JUNIOR, retired banker; b. Axtell, Kans., Dec. 12, 1931; s. Joseph Gerald and Olive (Gates) A.; m. Barbara Ruth Small, Aug. 20, 1955; children: Jerilyn, Joseph, Jean, John, James, Jennifer, Jeffrey. Grad. certificate, Am. Inst. Banking, 1964; grad., Pacific Coast Banking Sch., 1967, Nat. Comml. Lending Grad. Sch., U. Okla., 1976. Cert. comml. lender. With Pacific Nat. Bank, Seattle, 1949-80, asst. v.p., 1961-63, v.p., cashier, 1963-72, v.p., mgr. Univ. br., 1972-74, v.p., regional mgr., 1974-76, sr. v.p., 1976-81; exec. v.p. First Interstate Bank of Wash., Seattle, 1981-91; chmn., chief exec. officer First Interstate Ins. Agy. of Wash., Seattle, 1986-91; area pres. First Interstate Bank of Wash., Tacoma, 1991-93; ret., 1993. Instr. Seattle C.C., Shoreline C.C.; pres., dir. Seafair Fund, 1982—83. Bd. govs. YMCA, 1972-75, chmn., 1974-75; bd. dirs. Seafair, 1979-88, pres., 1981-82; trustee Seattle Youth Symphony Orch., 1984-87; bd. dirs. Am. Lung Assn., Wash., 1984-97, pres., 1992-94; sector chmn. United Way Pierce County; bd. dirs. Econ. Devel. Bd. Tacoma-Pierce County, 1991-94; mem. fin. coun. Cath. Archdiocese of Seattle, 1994—, chmn., 1997-2001; mem. pastoral coun. St. Michael's Parish, 1997-2000, mem. fin. coun., 2000—; dir. De Ette McCausland Stuart scholar fund U. Wash., 1984—. With USAR, 1950—58. Mem. Acad. Cert. Adminstrv. Mgrs., Am. Bankers Assn. (bank leadership coun. 1989-91, exec. com. retail banking divsn. 1991-94), Wash. Bankers Assn. (chmn. bank ops. com. 1967-72, bd. dirs. 1984-92, pres. 1989-90), Adminstrv. Mgmt. Soc. (bd. dirs. 1972-74), Clearing House Assn. Seattle (chmn. bank ops. com. 1969-72), Am. Inst. Banking (sec., bd. dirs. 1956-61, chmn. 1988-89), Wash. State Srs. Golf Assn. (bd. dirs. 2001--), Indian Summer Golf and Country Club (pres. 1996-97), Wash. Athletic Club. Roman Catholic. Home: 6439 Troon Ln SE Olympia WA 98501-5172

ALFIDI, RALPH JOSEPH, radiologist, educator; b. Rome, Apr. 20, 1932; s. Luca and Angeline (Panella) A.; m. Rose Esther Senesac, Sept. 3, 1956 (div. 1991); children: Suzanne, Lisa, Christine, Katherine, Mary, John; m. Mariella Boller, Aug. 29, 1992. AB, Ripon (Wis.) Coll., 1955; MD, Marquette U., Milw., 1959. Intern Oakwood Hosp., Dearborn, Mich., 1959-60; resident, chief resident, A.C.S. fellow U. Va., 1960-63; practice medicine, specializing in radiology Cleve., 1965-2000; staff mem. Cleve. Clinic, 1965-78, head dept. hosp. radiology, 1968-78; dir. dept. radiology Univ. Hosps., Cleve., 1978-92; prof. radiology U. N.Mex., Albuquerque, 2000—. Cons. VA Hosp., Cleve.; chmn. dept. radiology Case Western Res. U. Sch. Medicine, 1978-92; chmn. staff Cleve. Clinic Found., 1975-76. Author: Complications and Legal Implications of Special Procedures, 1972, Computed Tomography of the Human Body: An Atlas of Normal Anatomy, 1977; editor: Whole Body Computed Tomography, 1977; contbr. articles to radiology jours. Served to capt., M.C. U.S. Army Res., 1963-65. Picker Found. grantee, 1969-70; NRC grantee, 1969-70 Mem. Radiol. Soc. N. Am., Am. Roentgen Ray Soc., Am. Heart Assn., Soc. Cardiovascular Radiology, Soc. Gastrointestinal Radiology, Soc. Computed Body Tomography (pres. 1977-78), Eastern Radiol. Soc., Cleve. Radiol. Soc. (pres. 1976-77), Las Campanas Club. Roman Catholic. Home: 81 Calle Ventoso W Santa Fe NM 87506-0141 Office: Univ Hosp Radiology Dept Lomas Blvd Albuquerque NM 87106

ALFINITO, PETER DANIEL, neuroscientist; b. Yonkers, N.Y., Mar. 16, 1968; s. John and Diane Alfinito; m. Sharon Jill Fleischer, July 19, 1998; 1 child, Sophia. BA, Swarthmore Coll., 1991; PhD, U. Medicine and Dentistry N.J., 2000. Lab. instr. chemistry Columbia U., NY, 1991—92; analytical chemist Schering-Plough, Union, 1992—94; fellow U. Medicine & Dentistry N.J., Newark, 2000—, Cornell U., NY, 2001—02. Contbr. articles to profl. jours. Grantee, Am. Parkinsons Disease Assn., 2002—03; scholar, U. Medicine & Dentistry N.J., 2002—; Fite for Sight fellow, 2001—02. Mem.: Am. Soc. Pharmacology and Exptl. Therapeutics, Soc. for Neurosci. Avocations: reading, skiing, pencil drawings, weightlifting.

ALFONSO, ANTONIO ESCOLAR, surgeon; b. Manila, Nov. 25, 1943; came to U.S., 1968, naturalized, 1978; s. Ricardo Lagdameo and Marita (Escolar) Alfonso; m. Teresita Nazareno, Apr. 25, 1970; children: Margaretta, Roberto. AB cum laude, Ateneo U., 1963; MD cum laude, U. Philippines, 1968. Diplomate: Am. Bd. Surgery. Intern U. Philippines-Philippine Gen. Hosp., 1968; instr. surgery Temple U., Phila., 1968-72; sr. fellow surg. oncology Meml. Sloan-Kettering Cancer Ctr., N.Y.C., 1972-74; dir. head and neck surgery svc. SUNY Downstate Med. Ctr., Bklyn., 1974—, assoc. dir. divsn. surg. oncology, 1974—, asst. prof. surgery, 1974-77, assoc. prof., 1977-82, prof., 1982—,

vice-chmn. dept. surgery, 1988—. Chmn. dept. surgery Bklyn. Hosp., 1982-88; chmn. Dept. Surgery L.I. Coll. Hosp., 1988—; cons. head and neck surgery Bklyn. VA Hosp., 1974— Author: Principles of Surgery Oncology; contbr. articles to profl. med. jours., chpts. in med. books. Recipient rsch. essay prize N.Y. Colon and Rectal Surg. Soc., 1973; grantee Am. Cancer Soc., 1978 Mem. ACS (bd. govs. Bklyn.-L.I. chpt., gov. 1998—), Assn. Acad. Surgeons, Am. Soc. Clin. Oncology, Am. Assn. Cancer Edn., Soc. Head and Neck Surgeons, N.Y. Surg. Soc. (treas. 1994, v.p. 1998, pres. 1999), Bklyn. Surg. Soc. (pres. 1986-87), N.Y. Cancer Soc. (v.p. 1986-87, pres.-elect 1987-88, pres. 1988-89), Soc. Surg. Oncology, N.Y. Head and Neck Soc. (sec. 1993-97, pres. 1998), N.Y. Soc. Colon and Rectal Surgeons, Triboro Dirs. of Surgery Assn. (pres. 1989—), Phi Kappa Phi. Roman Catholic. Home: 50 Olive Pl Flushing NY 11375-5938 Office: LI Coll Hosp Dept Surgery 340 Henry St Brooklyn NY 11201-5514

ALFONSO, PETER J. educator; b. Bridgeport, Conn., June 24, 1941; m. Polly Yoder Alfonso. BA in Speech Pathology/Audiology, U Conn., 1972; MA in Speech Pathology, Western Mich. U. 1973; PhD in Speech Sci., Exptl. Phonetics, Purdue, 1977. Asst., asst. prof. U Conn., Storrs, 1977—91; prof., dept. head U Ill., Urbana-Champaign, 1991—99; Am. Council on Edn. Fellow Ind. U. Bloomington, 1997—98; assoc. provost for rsch.,prof. U N.C., Greensboro, 1999—2001; assoc. v.p. rsch., chief rsch. officer,prof. U Tenn., Knoxville, 2001—02; v.p. rsch. U N.D., Grand Forks, ND, 2002—. Grantee fellow, Am. Speech & Lang.-Hearing Assn., 1988, Fulbright Rsch. Scholar, The Netherlands, 1990—91. Mem.: Council of Fellows, Am. Council on Edn., Am. Assn. for the Advancement of Sci. (assoc.), Fulbright Alumni Assn. (assoc.). Avocation: private pilot. Home: 510 Reeves Dr 58201 Office: U ND Centennial Dr Twamley Hall Room 103 Box 8367 Grand Forks ND 58202

ALFONSO, ROBERT JOHN, university administrator; b. N.Y.C., Dec. 17, 1928; s. Robert Richard and Bertha Rose (Schmitt) A.; m. Martha Sue Ralston, June 9, 1956; children: Allison Denise, Robert John, Andrea Diane (dec.). BA, Roberts Wesleyan Coll., 1952; postgrad., N.Y. U., 1952-53; PhD, Mich. State U., 1962. High sch. English tchr. Syracuse, N.Y., 1956-58, Billings, Mont., 1958—59; asst. to dean Coll. Edn., Mich. State U., 1959-60; asst. prof. edn. Queens Coll., N.Y.C., 1962-64; assoc. exec. sec. Assn. for Supervision and Curriculum Devel., 1964-67; assoc. prof. curriculum and supervision Coll. Edn., U. Ala., 1967-68; asst. dean instrn. and grad. studies, prof. Coll. Edn., Kent State U. (Ohio), 1968-71; dean Coll. Edn. and Grad. Sch. Edn., also prof., 1971-80, assoc. v.p., dean faculties, 1980-82; v.p. acad. affairs East Tenn. State U., Johnson City, 1984-94, v.p. emeritus, 1994—. Vis. prof. U. Ga., 1982-83. Author: Instructional Supervision: A Behavior System, 1975, 2d edit., 1981; Asst. editor: Mich. Jour. Secondary Edn, 1959-62. Bd. dirs. Nat. Interagy. Council on Smoking and Health, 1964-67; Inter-Profl. Research Commn. on Pupil Personnel Services, 1965-68. Served to 1st lt. USMCR, 1953-56. Recipient Alumnus of Year award Roberts Wesleyan Coll., 1967 Mem. Assn. for Supervision and Curriculum Devel. (dir.), Am. Assn. Sch. Adminstrs., Nat. Council Tchrs. English (dir. 1965-68), Ohio Assn. for Supervision and Curriculum Devel. (pres.), Am. Ednl. Research Assn., Ohio Congress Sch. Adminstr. Orgns. (v.p.), Coun. Profs. Instrnl. Supervision (pres.), Phi Delta Kappa, Kappa Delta Pi, Phi Kappa Phi. Methodist. Home: 104 Ridgemont Rd Johnson City TN 37601-3940 Office: East Tenn State U Dossett Hall Johnson City TN 37614 E-mail: alfonso@xtn.net.

ALFONSO, ROBERTA JEAN, emergency room nurse; b. Lake County, Ohio; ADN, Lakeland Community Coll., Mentor, Ohio, 1982; BSN, Ursuline Coll., Pepper Pike, Ohio, 1989; MSN, Gannon U., 1994. RN, Ohio; cert. emergency room nurse, ACLS, trauma nurse care course provider, BLS instr., pediatric advanced life support provider, clin. nurse specialist in med.-surg. nursing, EMT-Basic. Nurse Lake Hosp. Systems, Painesville, Ohio, 1982—, emergency room nurse, 1987—. Recipient Isabell Sutch Nurse of Yr. award, 1995. Mem. Emergency Nurses Assn., Nat. League for Nursing, Am. Stroke Assn.

ALFONSO, VINCENT C, psychology educator; b. Brooklyn, N.Y., Aug. 26, 1964; s. Alfred C and Mary Alfonso. PhD, Hofstra U., 1986—90. School Psychologist NY, 1987. Assoc. prof. Fordham U., New York, NY, 1994—. Mem.: APA (divsn. newsletter editor 2000—03). Home: 75 West End Avenue R12D New York NY 10023 Office: Fordham University 113 West 60th Street New York NY 10023 E-mail: alfonso@fordham.edu.

ALFORD, BECKY DIANNE, food products executive; b. Chatanooga, Ga., Oct. 3, 1967; d. Leslie Bently and Gladys Irene Bean; m. Steve F. Alford, May 4, 1985; children: Rubin Cain, Sydni Leann. GED, Stephenville, Tex. Christian columnist Stephenville Empire Tribune, Tex., 1996—2000; mgr. Harmon & Creed, Lipan, 1999—, Jack in the Box, Palestine, 2001; gen. mgr. Dairy Queen, Tyler, 2002—. Contbr. poetry to anthologies. Sec. exec. com. Erath County Rep., Stephenville, 1999 E-mail: bek_i@hotmail.com.

ALFORD, BOBBY RAY, physician, educator, university official; b. Dallas, May 30, 1932; s. Bryant J. and Edith M. (Garrett) A.; m. Othelia Jerry Dorn, Aug. 28, 1953; children: Bradley Keith, Raye Lynn, Alan Scott. AS, Tyler Jr. Coll., 1951; postgrad., U. Tex., 1951-52; MD, Baylor U., 1956. Diplomate Am. Bd. Otolaryngology (dir. 1972-90, pres. 1985-86, exec. v.p. 1986-90). Intern Jefferson Davis Hosp., Houston, 1956-57; resident Baylor U. Coll. Medicine Affiliated Hosps. Program, 1957-60; mem. faculty Baylor U. Coll. Medicine, 1962—, prof. otolaryngology, 1966—, chmn. dept., 1967-95, 96—, v.p. and dean acad. and clin. affairs, 1984-88, exec. v.p., dean medicine, 1988—, disting. service prof., 1985—, interim chmn. dept. surgery, 1993-94; pres., CEO BaylorMedCare, Houston, 1994-96; chmn., CEO Nat. Space Biomed. Rsch. Inst., 1997—. Mem. rev. panel surgeon gen. on neurol. and sensory disease USPHS, 1965 67; cons. Nat. Inst. Neurol. Disease and Stroke, 1970-74; cons. to surgeon gen. U.S. Army, 1963-73; mem. nat. adv. coun. Neurol. and Communicative Disorders and Stroke, NIH, 1977-80, Deafness and Other Communicative Disorders, 1991-95; chmn. aerospace medicine adv. com. NASA, 1993-94, mem. nat. adv. coun., 1992-95, chmn. life microgravity scis. and applications adv. com., 1993-95. Author: Neurological Aspects of Auditory and Vestibular Disorders, 1964, Electrophysiologic Evaluation in Otolaryngology, 1997; Chief editor: A.M.A. Archives of Otolaryngology, 1970-79. Bd. dirs. Houston Acad. Medicine Tex. Med. Ctr. Libr., 1983-94. Recipient Herman Johnson award Baylor U. Coll. Medicine, 1956, NASA Disting. Pub. Svc. award, 1992, 95, Jeffries Aerospace Medicine and Life Scis. Rsch. award Am. Inst. Aeronautics and Astronautics, 2003; spl. NIH fellow Johns Hopkins Hosp., 1961-62. Fellow ACS (bd. govs. 1977-82); mem. AIAA (Jeffries Aerospace Medicine and Life Scis. Rsch. award 2003), NAS Inst. Medicine, Am. Laryngol. Assn., Soc. Univ. Otolaryngologists-Head and Neck Surgeons (sec. 1965-69), Am. Otol. Soc., Assn. Acad. Dept. Otolaryngology-Head and Neck Surgery, Am. Laryngol., Rhinol. and Otol. Soc., Am. Soc. Head and Neck Surgery (councillor 1978-80) Am. Acad. Otolaryngology-Head and Neck Surgery (pres. 1981), Am. Coun. Otolaryngology-Head and Neck Surgery (pres. 1980-81), Am. Bronchoesophagological Assn., Soc. Head and Neck Surgeons, Acoustical Soc. Am., Collegium Oto-Rhino-Laryngologicum Amicitiae Sacrum, Johns Hopkins U. Soc. Scholars, Univ. Space Rsch. Assn. (bd. dirs. 1991-95), Tex. Corinthian Yacht Club (bd. dirs. 1978-80, 94-95), Doctors Club (bd. govs. 1967-70, 91-93), Petroleum Club, Lakewood Yacht Club, Alpha Omega Alpha. Office: Baylor Coll Medicine One Baylor Plz Houston TX 77030

ALFORD, DUNCAN EARL, lawyer; b. Spartanburg, S.C., Oct. 17, 1963; s. Earl Curry and Martha Catherine (Van Ness) A.; m. Janet Lynne Gessner, Oct. 6, 1990. BA with high distinction, U. VA., 1985; postgrad., U. Calif., Berkeley, 1987; JD with honors, U. N.C., 1991; MLIS, U. SC, 2001. Bar: Ga. 1991, N.C. 1991, S.C. 1994. Bus. analyst McKinsey & Co., Inc., Atlanta, 1985-87; distbn. mgr. Eason Publs., Inc., Charlotte, N.C., 1988; law clk. to Hon. Burley B. Mitchell N.C. Supreme Ct., Raleigh, N.C., 1991-92; assoc. Kilpatrick & Cody, Atlanta, 1992-94; atty. Law Offices of Robert A. Hammett, Spartanburg, S.C., 1994-96; assoc. Robinson, Bradshaw & Hinson, PA, Rock Hill, S.C., 1997-2001, shareholder, 2001; reference law libr. Columbia U. Sch. Law, NYC, 2001—02; law librn. Princeton (N.J.) U., 2002—. Contbr. articles to profl. jours. Echols scholar U. Va. Mem. ABA, Phi Alpha Delta. Presbyterian. Avocations: running, golf, cycling. Home: 208 Loetscher Pl 1A Princeton NJ 08540 Office: Princeton U Firestone Libr 1 Washington Rd Princeton NJ 08544-2098

ALFORD, JOAN FRANZ, entrepreneur; b. St. Louis, Sept. 16, 1940; d. Henry Reisch and Florence Mary (Shaughnessy) Franz; m. Charles Hebert Alford, Dec. 28, 1978; stepchildren: Terry, David, Paul. BS, St. Louis U., 1962; postgrad., Consortium of State U., Calif., 1975-77; MBA, Pepperdine U., 1987; postgrad., Fielding Inst., 1988-90. Head user svcs. Lawrence Berkeley (Calif.) Lab., 1977-78, head software support and devel., Computer Ctr., 1978-82, dep. head, 1980-81; regional site analyst mgr. Cray Rsch., Inc., Pleasanton, Calif., 1982-83; owner, pres. Innovative Leadership, Oakland, Calif., 1983-91; realtor, assoc. Mason-McDuffie Real Estate, Inc., Oakland, Calif., 1991-96, Coldwell Banker, Oakland, Calif., 1996—. Treas. Oakland Multiple Listing Svc., 1994, pres., 1997; bd. dirs. East Bay Regional Data, Inc. Contbr. articles to profl. jours. Bd. dirs., sec., Vol. Ctrs. of Alameda County, 1985, chair nom. com., 1990-91, pres. bd. dirs., 1991—; campaign mem. Marge Gibson for County Supr., Oakland, 1984; mem. Oakland Piedmont Rep. Orgn., Alameda County Apt. Owners Assn., 1982. Mem. Assn. Computing Machinery, Spl. Interest Group on Computer Pers. Rsch. (past chmn.), Nat. Assn. Realtors, Calif. Assn. Realtors (bus. and tech. com. 1997, 2002, bd. dirs. 1997-2003, profl. awards com. 2002, membership com. 2003), Oakland Assn. Realtors (co-chair computer user com. 1992-93, chair 1993-94, bd. dirs. 1995—, chair bus. and tech. 1996, pres. 1998, co-chmn. profl. stds. com. 2001-03, Realtor of Yr. award 1998), Internat. Platform Assn., Small Owners for Fair Treatment, San Francisco Opera Guild, Claremont Pool and Tennis Club, Lakeview Club. Republican. Avocations: swimming, skiing, opera, horseback riding, gardening. Home: 2605 Beaconsfield Pl Piedmont CA 94611-2501 Office: Coldwell Banker 6137 La Salle Ave Oakland CA 94611-2801 E-mail: realtor@joanalford.com.

ALFORD, NEILL HERBERT, JR., retired law educator; b. Greenville, S.C., July 13, 1919; s. Neill Herbert and Elizabeth (Robertson) Alford; m. Elizabeth Talbot Smith, June 26, 1943; children: Neill Herbert III, Margaret Dudley, Eli Thomas Stackhouse. BA, The Citadel-Mil. Coll. S.C., 1940; LLB, U. Va., 1947; JSD, Yale U., 1966. Bar: Va 1954. Mem. faculty law U. Va. Law Sch., Charlottesville, 1947-61, 62-90, Doherty Found. prof., 1966-74, spl. cons. to pres. univ., legal adviser to rector and bd. dirs., 1972-74; Joseph Henry Lumpkin prof., dean Law Sch. U. Ga., Athens, 1974-76; Percy Brown Jr. prof. law U. Va., 1976-90; state reporter Supreme Ct. Va., 1977-84; counsel Woods, Rogers & Hazelgrove, Charlottesville, 1991-97. Spec counsel Va Code Comn, 1954—57; dir Va Bankers Asn Trust Sch, 1958—61; prof, chair int law Naval War Col, 1961—62, consult, 1962—68; summer teacher George Washington Univ, Univ NC; chmn bd dirs Univ Va Press, 1970—74, 1987—89; prof law emeritus Univ Va, 1990—; Lehmann disting vis prof law Washington Univ, St Louis, 1991; Hofstedler prof Ohio State Univ Law Sch, 1992; prof Washington and Lee Law Sch, 1992. Author: (book) Modern Economic Warfare: Law and the Naval Participant, 1967, Cases and Materials on Decedents Estates and Trusts, 8th edit, 1993; contbr. articles to profl jours. Comdr civil affairs group USAR, 1947—66, lt col AUS, 1941—46, ETO, col AUS. Decorated Bronze Star, Combat Inf Badge; fellow Ford, Univ Wis, 1958. Fellow: Am Bar Found, Va Law Found; mem.: ABA, Raven Soc, Va Bar Asn, Va State Bar, Am Law Inst, Am Judicature Soc, Am Soc Legal Hist, Selden Soc, Colonnade Club, Order Coif, Omicron Delta Kappa, Phi Alpha Delta. Home: 1868 Field Rd Charlottesville VA 22903-1619

ALFORD, PAUL LEGARE, college and religious foundation administrator; b. Tampa, Fla., Mar. 16, 1930; s. Louis Emerson and Mary (Alderman) A.; m. Grace Alford, Dec. 29, 1951; children: Rebecca Grace, Sharon Ann. Student, U. Fla., 1947; diploma, Nyack Coll., 1948-51; DD (hon.), Trinity Coll., 1964, Asbury Coll., 1978; LLD (hon.), Toccoa Falls Coll., 1976. Supt. Ind. Life, Columbus, Ga., 1951-53; founding pastor Christian & Missionary Alliance, Columbus, 1951-56; missionary Ecuador, 1956-60; dir. Spanish ministries Christian Missionary Alliance, Nyack, N.Y., 1960-70; dist. supt. Christian & Missionary Alliance, Orlando, Fla., 1970-79, v.p., 1976-86; pres. Toccoa Falls (Ga.) Coll., 1979—, chancellor, 2002—. Chmn. DeLand (Fla.) Retirement Bd., 1970-79; bd. mgrs. Christian and Missionary Alliance, Colorado Springs, Colo., 1993-99; trustee Asbury Coll., Wilmore, Ky.; chmn. bd. dirs. Lake Swan Conf. Grounds, Melrose, Fla., Shell Point Village, Ft. Myers, Fla., Trans World Radio, 1995-99; del. Congress on Edn., 1971, 86. Mem. editorial bd. New King James Bible; producer daily radio broadcast, 1975—. Mem. leadership coun. Stephens County, Toccoa, 1982—; bd. dirs. Salvation Army, Toccoa, 1986-93; pres. Ga. Assn. Colleges and Univs., 1997-98. Served with USNR, 1947-54. Honored by Ga. State Senate for outstanding contbn. to edn. in State of Ga., 2002; named to Hillsborough High Sch. Hall of Fame, Tampa, 1994. Mem. Am. Assn. Bible Colls. (bd. dirs. 1987-92), So. Assn. Colls. and Schs. (evaluation com.), Rotary. Republican. Avocations: golf, tennis. Home: 380 Carlyle Cir Toccoa Falls GA 30598 Office: Toccoa Falls Coll Chapel Dr Toccoa Falls GA 30598

ALFORD, ROBERT WILFRID, JR., elementary school educator; b. Langley, Va., Nov. 8, 1955; s. Robert Wilfrid and Ella Ramona (Coker) A.; m. Cynthia Marie Avery, Dec. 23, 1978 (div. 1999); children: Deborah Louise, Phillip Glenn. BS, Appalachian State U., 1978. Cert. social sci. tchr. Tchr. Greenville Mid. Sch. (S.C.) County Sch. Dist., 1984—. Cons. Student Svcs., Greenville, 1985-91. Scoutmaster Troop 749, 1989-93, troop 159 asst. scoutmaster, 1998-2000; deacon Fourth Presbyn. Ch. Named Boy Scouter of Yr., Reed Falls dist. Boy Scouts Am., 1994. Mem. Greenville County Edn. Assn. (bd. dirs. 1986-88, sec. 1988-89), S.C. Council Social Studies Tchrs., S.C. Council Middle Schs., S.C. Edn. Assn. (educator rights com. 1987-88), Kappa Delta Pi, Phi Alpha Theta, Alpha Phi Omega (pres. Tau Beta chpt. 1976-77). Democrat. Presbyterian. Avocations: camping, travel. Office: Greenville Mid Sch 339 Lownes Ave Greenville SC 29607

ALFORD, STEVE, college basketball coach; b. New Castle, Ind., Nov. 23, 1964; m. Tanya Frost: children: Kory, Bryce, Kayla. B in Bus., Ind. U. Mem. gold-medal U.S. basketball team Olympic Games, L.A., 1984; professional basketball player Dallas Mavericks, Golden St. Warriors; head coach Manchester (Ind.) Coll., 1992-95; conf. title champions, 1994, 95, S.W. Mo. State U. Bears, 1995-99, reached NCAA Sweet 16, 1999; headcoach U. Ia. Hawkeyes, 1999—. Named Ind. Collegiate Conf. Coach of Yr., 1993, 94, 95. Office: c/o U Ia Athletic Dept 240 Carver Hawkeye Arena Iowa City IA 52242-1020

ALFRED, RICHARD LINCOLN, education educator, educational association administrator, consultant, researcher; b. Quantico, Va., Mar. 11, 1944; s. Karl Sverre and Marjorie Elizabeth (Lincoln) A.; children: Daniel, Christie, Alexandra. BA, Allegheny Coll., 1966; MEd, Pa. State U., 1968, EdD, 1972. Dir. ednl. rsch. and devel. Metro. C.C., Kansas City, 1972-74; exec. asst. to pres. N.Y.C. C.C., 1974-77, dean finance, planning and mgmt., 1977-80; prof. U. Mich., Ann Arbor, 1981—; exec. dir. COMBASE, Ann Arbor, 1991—98. Founding dir. Community Coll. Consortium, Ann Arbor, 1986—; cons. over 400 colls., universities, founds. and gov. agys., 1974-93. Author more than 30 monographs and books; contbr. 80 articles to profl. jours. Recipient Sr. Scholar award Coun. Univs. and Colls., 1988, 94, Medallion award Nat. Coun. for Student Devel./Nat. Assn. Student Pers. Adminstrs./Am. Coll. Pers. Assn., 1992, Leadership award Am. Assn. Comty. Colls., 1994, Disting. Svc. award Coun. Univs. and Colls., 1994, Spl. Recognition award Nat. Coun. Rsch. and Planning, 1998. Avocation: gardening and landscaping. Home: 759 Mooreville Rd Milan MI 48160-9564 Office: U Mich 2108 Sch Of Edn Ann Arbor MI 48109

ALFRED, STEPHEN JAY, retired lawyer; b. NYC, Aug. 15, 1934; s. George J. Alfred and Janet (Brenner) Miller; m. Nora Richman, June 24, 1956 (div. 1980); children: Deborah Susan, Lynda Beth, Bruce David, Julianne Richman; m. Lynne Belofsky Durchslag, Jan. 10, 1981 (div. 1992), m. Rita G. Hungate, Aug. 23, 1997. AB, Princeton U., 1956; JD, Harvard U., 1959. Bar: Ohio 1959. From assoc. to ptnr. Squire, Sanders & Dempsey, Cleve., 1959—97; councilman City of Shaker Hts., Ohio, 1972—79, 1981, mayor, 1984—91; exec. dir. Common Cause/Ga., 1998—2001; ret., 2001. Gen. chmn. Cleve. Tax Inst., 1981. Contbr. articles to profl. jours. Trustee Citizens League of Cleve., 1976-83, Com. for Sandy Springs, Atlanta, 1998-2001, vice-chair, 1999-2000; trustee Beech Brook Children's Home, Orange, Ohio, 1968-84, pres., 1971-72, treas., 1979-81; pres. Lomond Assn., Shaker Hts., 1965-67; active Peoria County Govt. Study Commn., Peoria, 2000-01; govt. vision task force Peoria Area C. of C., 2001-02; bd. dirs. Ill. Campaign for Polit. Reform, Chgo., 2000—, v.p., 2002—; bd. dirs. Mayors Vision 2020, Peoria, 2002—, Counseling and Family Svcs., Peoria, 2002—, v.p., 2003—; exec. dir. Ctrl. Ill. Biomed. Rsch. Group, 2000-02, vice-chmn., 2001-02; assoc. bd. dirs. WCBU, Peoria, 2001—, v.p., 2003—. Mem. Harvard U. Law Sch. Assn. of Cleve. (pres. 1982). Democrat. Jewish. E-mail: sjalfred@aol.com.

ALFRED, SUELLEN, English education educator; b. May 2, 1941; d. Andrew and Freeda (Murray) A. BA, Carson-Newman Coll., 1963; MA, Ga. State U., 1969; EdD, U. Tenn., 1991. Cert. secondary English, gifted edn. Prof. curriculum and instrn. Tenn. Tech. U., Cookeville, 1990—. Co-editor "Personal Reading" col. English Jour. Co-author: Teaching Through Stories: Yours, Mine, and Theirs, 1998; editor Tenn. English Jour.; co-editor: Southern Voices in Every Direction, 1996; contbr. articles to profl. jours.; author poems. NEH fellow Vanderbilt U., 1984. Mem. ASCD, NEA, Nat. Coun. Tchrs. English, Internat. Reading Assn., Tenn. Edn. Assn. (comms. com. 1978-79), Tenn. Tech. U. Edn. Assn., Tenn. Coun. Tchrs. English (pres. 1993-94, co-editor Tenn. English jour., Excellence in Tchg. of English award 1996). Office: Tenn Tech U PO Box 5042 Cookeville TN 38505-0001 E-mail: salfred@tntech.edu.

ALFREY, LARRY ROBERT, physician assistant; b. Adrian, Mich., Mar. 26, 1951; s. William James and Dorothy Mae (Boomer) A. B Music and Edn., Cedarville Coll., 1973; BA in Studio Art, U. Md., 1978, postgrad., 1978-83; BS as Physician Asst. summa cum laude, George Washington U. Med. Sch., 1986. Lic. physician asst., N.Y., Conn.; cert. Nat. Commn. Cert. Physician Assts. Emergency room technician Holy Cross Hosp., Silver Spring, Md., 1976-86; surgical resident Montefiore Med. Ctr. and Albert Einstein Coll. Medicine, Bronx, N.Y., 1986-87, physician asst. Pacemaker Ctr., 1988-89, 98—; staff physician asst. dept. surgery Booth Meml. Med. Ctr., Queens, N.Y., 1987 88; physician asst. emergency room N.Y. Hosp-Cornell Med. Ctr., N.Y.C., 1988, Winthrop U. Hosp., Mineola, N.Y., 1989-90; physician asst. Meml. Sloan-Kettering Cancer Ctr., N.Y.C., 1990-95; physician asst. emergency room Good Samaritan Hosp., Suffern, N.Y., 1995-97, mem. CQI team emergency dept., 1996-97; physician asst. emergency room Greenwich (Conn.) Hosp., 1997—2000; with Innovative Directions, an Ednl. Alliance, City Island, NY, 1999—. Contbr. articles to music and med. jours. Co-dir. children's theatre Montgomery County Schs., Rockville, Md., 1977-97; vol. La Clevique Kids Opera Co., Met. Opera Guild, 1995—. Recipient recognition for abstracts Am. Soc. Clin. Oncology, 1991, 92. Fellow Am. Acad. Phys. Assts.; mem. City Island Arts Orgn., Phi Kappa Phi. Avocations: travel, sailing, painting and sculpturing, swimming, music. Home: 190 Schofield St Apt 3A Bronx NY 10464-1549

ALFREY, LYDIA JEAN, musician educator; b. Kingsport, Tenn., July 16, 1954; d. Milburn Flay and Betty Jo (Sensabaugh) Brooks; m. Charles Leonard Alfrey, Oct. 2, 1987; children: Benjamin Daniel, Tyler Nathaniel, Ryan Daniel. BA, Anderson (Ind.) U., 1977. Music tchr. Huntington Sch., Ferriday, La., 1978-80; elem. tchr. Warner Christian Acad., Daytona Beach, Fla., 1982-83; pvt. instr. Eustis, Fla., 1993—; prin. pianist First Bapt. Ch., Eustis, 1994—98, Mt. Dora, 2003—. Adjudicator piano competitions Lake County Music Tchrs., Eustis, 1994-97; dir., coord. Summer Music Camps, Eustis, 1994, 95, 97; pianist jazz orch.; guest artist numerous recitals. Mem.: Music Tchrs. Nat. Assn. (publicity chairperson, Fla. chpt. rec. sec. 1994—2001), Nat. Guild Piano Tchrs., Delta Omicron, Kappa Delta Pi, Pi Kappa Lambda. Baptist. Avocations: floral arranging, interior designing, oil painting. Home: 1375 Old Mount Dora Rd Eustis FL 32726-7949

ALGARY, RUTH WILKINS, community volunteer; b. Asheville, N.C., Apr. 10, 1938; d. William Fellows and Elizabeth (Russell) Wilkins; m. William Page Algary, Sept. 6, 1958; children: Kathryn Algary Tarleton, John Page, Sarah Algary Payne. Student, U. N.C., 1956-58. Treas. Sara Collins Elem. PTA, Greenville, S.C., 1971-76; community vol. Greenville Jr. League, 1973-74; children's ch. leader Westminster Presby. Ch., Greenville, 1975; council mem. Sara Collins Elem. Sch., Greenville, 1976-77; program devel. coordinator, bd. dirs. Greenville YWCA, 1976-77; substitute tchr. Sch. Dist. of Greenville County, 1984-89, devel. team, 1986; sec. Beck Middle Sch. PTA, Greenville, 1979-80. Pres. S.E. area PTA Coun., Greenville, 1979—80; v.p. Dist. 1 PTA, Greenville, 1980—83; tutor Greenville Literacy Assn., 1989—91. Sr. high youth leader Westminster Presbyn. Ch., Greenville, 1984-85, sanctuary com., 1991—, wedding com., 1998—; pres. Greenville Little Theatre League, 1987-88; chmn. ways and means com. Greenville County Med. Aux., 1979; pres. Colonial Dames XVII Century, 1980; bd. dirs. Piedmont Coun. for the Prevention of Child Abuse, 1991-92, 92-93, v.p., 1994-95. Mem. S.C. PTA (Life Mem. award 1983). Clubs: J.L. Mann Athletic (Greenville) (treas. 1981-86). Avocations: reading, writing poetry, sewing, gardening. Home and Office: 20 Stonehaven Dr Greenville SC 29607-3018

ALGEO, JOHN THOMAS, retired educator, association executive; b. St. Louis, Nov. 12, 1930; s. Thomas George and Julia Winifred (Wathen) A.; m. Adele Marie Silbereisen, Sept. 6, 1958; children: Thomas John, Catherine Marie. EdB cum laude, U. Miami, 1955; MA, U. Fla., 1957, PhD, 1960. Instr. Fla. State U., Tallahassee, 1959-61; from asst. to full prof. U. Fla., Gainesville, 1961-71, asst. dean grad. sch., 1969-71, dir. program in linguistics, 1969-71; prof. U. Ga., Athens, 1971-88, dir. program in linguistics, 1974-79, head dept. English, 1975-79, alumni found. disting. prof., 1988-94; nat. pres. Theosophical Soc. in Am., Wheaton, Ill., 1993—2002; internat. v.p. Theosophical Soc., Adyar, India, 2002—. Mem. gen. coun. Theosophical Soc., Adyar, India, 1993—; dir. Manor Found. Ltd., Sydney, Australia, 1995—; accreditation cons. So. Assn. Colls. and Schs., Atlanta, 1967-90; cons. NEH, Washington, 1974-94; dir. Commn. on the English Lang., Nat. Coun. Tchrs. of English, Urbana, Ill., 1976-82; del. Am. Coun. Learned Socs., N.Y.C., 1984-87; cons. in lang. and lexicography Cambridge Univ. Press, N.Y.C., 1987-93; cons. in Am. usage Kenkyusha Ltd., Tokyo, 1991-99; cons. Webster's New World Dictionary, 4th edit., Cleve., 1993-95. Author: Problems in the Origins and Development of the English Language, 1966, 4th edit., 1993, On Defining the Proper Name, 1973, Exercises in Contemporary English, 1974, Reincarnation Explored, 1987, Reincarnatie in Kaart gebracht, 1990, Fifty Years "Among the New Words": A Dictionary of Neologisms, 1941-91, 1991, Eigo no kigen to hatatsu, 1991, Reinkarnation: Evolution der Seele, 1991, 96, Reinkarnation i ny belysning, 1994, Investigando a reencarnacao, 1996, Unlocking the Door: Studies in The Key to Theosophy, 2001; co-author: English: An Introduction to Language, 1970, Spelling: Sound to Letter, 1971, The Origins and Development of the English Language, 1982, 4th edit., 1993, Elements of Literature, Sixth Course: Literature of Britain, 1989, The Power of Thought, 2001, Pensamento: Oque e como usar, 2003; editor: American Speech, 1972-81, Thomas Pyles: Selected Essays on English Usage, 1979, Among the New Words, American Speech, 1987-97, Cambridge History of the English Language, vol. 6, English in North America, 2001, 02, The Quest, 1997-2003; assoc. editor: The Oxford Companion to the English Language, 1992; mem. editl. bd. Jour. of English Linguistics, 1970—, Internat. Jour. Lexicography, 1990-93, World Englishes, 1996—, Names, 1997—, Language Problems Language Planning, 1997-99, Studies in English Language, 1987—. Sgt. U.S. Army, 1951-54, Korea. Fellow Guggenheim Found., London, 1986-87; Fulbright scholar U. Coll. London, Eng., 1986-87. Mem. Am. Dialect Soc. (pres. 1979), Am. Name Soc. (pres. 1984), Internat. Assn. Univ. Profs. English, Internat. Linguistic Assn., Ea. Order Internat. Co Freemasonry, Internat. Phonetic Assn., Linguistic Assn. of the U.S. and Can., Linguistic Soc. Am., Modern Lang. Assn. Am., Philological Soc., Southeastern Conf. on Linguistics (pres. 1970-71), Dictionary Soc. N.Am. (pres. 1995-97), Theosophical Soc. (nat. pres. 1993-2002, internat. v.p. 2002-), Ea. Order Internat. Co-Freemasonry (adminstr. 2002—). Democrat. Home: PO Box 80206 Athens GA 30608-0206 E-mail: johnalgeo@aol.com.

ALGER, CHADWICK FAIRFAX, political scientist, educator; b. Chambersburg, Pa., Oct. 9, 1924; s. Herbert and Thelma (Drawbaugh) A.; m. Elinor Reynolds, Aug. 28, 1948; children: Mark, Scott, Laura, Craig. BA, Ursinus Coll., 1949, LLD, 1979; MA, Johns Hopkins U., 1950; PhD, Princeton, 1958. Internat. relations specialist Dept. Navy, 1950-54; instr. Swarthmore Coll., 1957; faculty Northwestern U., Evanston, Ill., 1958-71, prof. polit. sci., 1966-71, dir. internat. relations program, 1967-71; Mershon prof. polit. sci. and pub. policy Ohio State U., 1971-95, emeritus prof., 1995—, dir. transnat. intellectual cooperation program, 1971-80, dir. world affairs program, Mershon Ctr., 1980-88, coord. working group on global rels. and peace studies, 1988-95, acting dir. univ. ctr. for internat. studies, 1990-91. Vis. prof. UN affairs N.Y.U., 1962-63 Author: Internationalization from Local Areas: Beyond Interstate Relations, 1987, Perceiving, Understanding and Coping with World Relations in Everyday Life, 1993, The United Nations System: Potential for the Twenty-First

Century, 1998; co-author: Simulation in International Relations, 1963, You and Your Community in the World, 1978, Conflicts and Crisis of International Order: New Tasks for Peace Research, 1985, A Just Peace Through Transformation: Cultural, Economic and Political Foundations for Change, 1988, The United Nations System: The Policies of Member States, 1995; contbr. articles to profl. jours. Mem. Trade Coun., State of Ohio, 1984-87. Served with USNR, 1943-46. Recipient Disting. Scholar award Internat. Soc. for Ednl., Cultural and Sci. Interchanges, 1980, Golden Apple award Am. Forum for Global Edn., 1993. Mem. Am. Polit. Sci. Assn. (coun. 1970-72), Internat. Polit. Sci. Assn., Internat. Studies Assn. (pres. 1978-79), Internat. Studies Assn. Midwest (Quincy Wright disting. scholar award 2000), Internat. Peace Rsch. Assn. (coun. 1971-77, sec.-gen. 1983-87), Internat. Peace Rsch. Assn. Found. (v.p. 1998—), Midwest Conf. Polit. Scis. (recipient prize 1966), Consortium on Peace Rsch., Edn. and Devel. (exec. com. 1971-77, chmn. 1976-77), Hunger and Devel. Coalition of Cen. Ohio (bd. dirs. 1983-90), Columbus Coun. on World Affairs (bd. dirs. 1974-88), UN Assn. (pres. Columbus chpt. 1991-93). Home: 2674 Westmont Blvd Columbus OH 43221-3354 Office: Ohio State U Mershon Ctr 1501 Neil Ave Columbus OH 43201-2602

ALGER, JAMES ARTHUR, computer consultant; b. Cin., Mar. 5, 1964; s. Arthur Edward and Judith Lee (Glasshof) A.; m. Gwen L. Rager, Sepc. 26, 1992; 1 child from previous marriage, Bradley James. AA, Ctrl. Tex. Coll., 1990. Cons. Data Tree, Inc., Rockville, Md., 1993-94, Adia Info. Techs., Balt., 1994-96, Alger and Assocs., Hanover, Md., 1996—. Cons. Bell Atlantic, Balt., 1994-96, United Srs. Health Coop., Washington, 1994-96, Cath. Relief Svcs., Balt., 1993-96, Agy. Svcs., Inc., Balt., 1996—, Phillip Pub., Inc., Potomac, Md., 1997—. Sgt. U.S. Army, 1986-90. Mem. Aircraft Owners and Pilots Assn. Avocations: travel, aviation. Office: 2657G Old Annapolis Rd # 264 Hanover MD 21076-1262 E-mail: jalger@avsoftinc.com.

ALGIERE, DENNIS LEE, state legislator; b. Westerly, Rhode Island, July 30, 1960; s. Joseph L. and Ida R. (Vacca) A.; m. Leigh A. Williams, Nov. 7, 1992. BA, Providence Coll., 1982; MS, Northea. U., 1984; JD, So. New England Sch. Law, 1991. Town councilor Town of Westerly, R.I., 1990-92; mem. RI Senate, Dist. 38, 1993—; minority leader R.I. Senate, 1997—. Sr. v.p. Washington Trust Co. Chmn. Westerly Rep. Town Com., 1991-92; bd. dirs. Chorus of Westerly 1990—, Westerly Hosp.; dir. adv. com. for the arts John F. Kennedy Ctr. for the Performing Arts, 2002—. Mem. Lions. Republican. Roman Catholic. Home: 6 Elm St Westerly RI 02891-2126 Office: RI Senate State House Rm 120 Providence RI 02908

ALGIERE, SCOTT G. health facility administrator; b. New London, Conn., Sept. 16, 1964; s. Fred and Patricia Algiere; m. Kimberlee Algiere, June 23, 2001; children: Matthew, Brianna McClelland. BS, Ctrl. Conn. State U., 1988. CFO Integrated Physician Mgmt. Svcs., Hartford, Conn., 1997—99; CFO, exec. v.p. fin. Simpson Healthcare Execs., Old Lyme, Conn., 1999—. Contr. Conn. Jr. Republic, Litchfield, Conn., 1994—97. Mem.: Am. Mgmt. Assn., Assn. Fin. Profls. (assoc.). Republican. Roman Catholic. Avocations: golf, biking, hiking. Office: Simpson Healthcare Execs 230 Shore Rd Old Lyme CT 06371 Office Fax: 860-434-3259. E-mail: scott@simpsonhealthcare.com.

ALGRA, RONALD JAMES, dermatologist; b. Artesia, Calif., Feb. 23, 1949; s. Cornelius and Helena Joyce (De Boom) A.; m. Phyllis Ann Brandsma, July 3l, l970; children: Brian David, Stephanie Ann. BS in Chemistry, Calvin Coll., 197l; MD, Baylor Coll. Medicine, 1974; MBA, Pepperdine U., 1989. Diplomate Am. Bd. Dermatology. Intern Gen. Hosp. Ventura County, Ventura, Calif., 1974-75; resident in dermatology Baylor Coll. Medicine, Houston, 1975-78; pvt. practice Hawthorne, Calif., 1978-88; asst. med. dir. FHP, Inc., Fountain Valley, 1988-89, assoc. med. dir., 1990-91, med. dir., 1991-93, sr. med. dir., 1993, assoc. v.p. med. affairs, 1993-95; COO, horses, zebras & unicorns, Irvine, Calif., 1995-96; exec., med. dir. Providence Health Plans, Eugene, Oreg., 1996-98; med. dir. HealthCare Ptnrs. Ltd., Torrance, Calif., 1999-2000; v.p., med. dir. THIPA, Torrance, 2000—. Fellow: Am. Acad. Dermatology; mem.: Am. Coll. Physician Execs., Am. Med. Informatics Assn., Alpha Omega Alpha. Republican. Mem. Christian Reformed Ch. Avocations: computers, photography, running, gardening, hiking. Bus. Office: TMCI 2355 Crenshaw Blvd Ste 150 Torrance CA 90501 E-mail: ralgra@thipa.com., rjalgr@mindspring.com.

ALHADEFF, DAVID ALBERT, economics educator; b. Seattle, Mar. 22, 1923; s. Albert David and Pearl (Taranto) A.; m. Charlotte Pechman, Aug. 1, 1948. BA, U. Wash., 1944; MA, Harvard U., 1948, PhD, 1950. Faculty U. Calif.-Berkeley, 1949-87, prof. bus. adminstrn., 1959-87, prof. emeritus, 1987—, assoc. dean Sch. Bus. Adminstrn., 1980-82, 85-86. Author: Monopoly and Competition in Banking, 1954, Competition and Controls in Banking, 1968, Microeconomics and Human Behavior, 1982; Contbr. articles to profl. jours., chpts. to books. Served with AUS, 1943-46. Recipient The Berkeley Citation U. Calif.-Berkeley, 1987. Home: 2101 Shoreline Dr Apt 456 Alameda CA 94501-6249 Office: Haas Sch Bus Berkeley CA 94720-0001

ALHADHERI, SHABIB ALI, pediatrician, cardiologist; s. Ali Ali Alhadheri and Mona Ali Alarashi; m. Fatima Ali Alhaj, Aug. 11, 1988; children: Ayman Shabib, Abdul Rahman Shabib, Mona Shabib, Omar Shabib. MB, BChir, King Saud U., Riyadh, Saudi Arabia, 1992. Diplomate Am. Acad. Pediat., 2001. Rotating intern King Saud U., Riyadh, 1992—93; pediat. resident Dallah Hosp., Riyadh, 1993—94; pediat. neurology extern and rsch. asst. Children's Hosp. Detroit, 1995—96; transitional resident Hurley Med. Ctr., Flint, Mich., 1996—97; pediat. resident SUNY Upstate Med. U., Syracuse, 1997—2000, pediat. cardiology fellow, 2000—. Author: (textbook) Alcohol And Diseases. Fellow: Am. Heart Assn.; mem.: AMA, Soc. Pediat. Echocardiography, Am. Coll. Cardiology, Am. Acad. Pediat. Achievements include research in Hypoplastic Left Heart Syndrome; Ventricular Tachycardia In Children; Pediatric Echocardiography; Pediatric Catheterization And Angigraphy. Home: Apt 39c 5100 Highbridge St Fayetteville NY 13066 Office: SUNY Upstate Med Univ Ste 804 725 Irving Ave Syracuse NY 13210

AL-HAFEEZ, HUMZA, minister, editor; b. N.Y.C., Feb. 28, 1931; s. Asa Mose and Rose Mae (Danielson) Weir; children: Jacqueline, Yuhanna, Rasul, Bismillah, Habib, Wardi, Larry, Don, Mariama. Student, Food Trades Vocat. Sch., 1947-48. Patrolman N.Y.C. Police Dept., from 1959; chmn. Temple of Islam, Inc. Founder Nat. Soc. Afro-Am. Policemen Inc.; also past pres.; cons. community relations to chief insp. N.Y.C. Police Dept., to; U.S. Dept. Justice; investigator of corruption among N.Y.C. police officers Knapp Commn.; undercover narcotic officer, investigator Manhattan office Dist. Atty.; investigator Office of 1st Dep. Policy Commr.; undercover investigator U.S. Dept. Justice.; insp. N.Y. State Athletic Commn.; Lectr. Princeton U., Mich. State U., N.Y. State U., Pace Coll., Bklyn. Coll., U. Chgo., NYU, Satellite Acad., N.Y.C., Kinlock Mission for Blind, City N.Y. Police Acad., Nassau Community Coll.; others Appeared on radio and TV.; Editor-in-chief: Your Muhammad Speaks newspaper; author The Slanderer, 1987, Some Things to Think About, 2003. Pastoral bd. Interfaith Hosp.; chaplain Frackville (Pa.) Correctional Facility, 1995—. Recipient Father of Yr. award Kinlock Freedom Found. for the Blind, 1973; Community Service award United Council of Chs., 1975; named Person of Yr. Nat. Assn. Black Policemen, 1982. Mem. Internat. Platform Assn. Mem. Nation of Islam; minister Muhammad's Temple of Islam, Bklyn. Home: 361 Clinton Ave Apt 12C Brooklyn NY 11238-1145 Office: 1211 Atlantic Ave Brooklyn NY 11216-2709 *To expect all of the people to cooperate is something that should be given some thought. Change comes through the efforts of a person, or a small group of people, not all of the people. However, all of the people may benefit, or suffer, from the action of a person, or a small group. History will bear me witness.*

AL-HAMID, ABU-BAKR MUHSIN, translator; s. Zahra Ahmed Al-Saqqaf and Muhsin Ali Al-Hamid; m. Queen Taha Sheba, Jan. 3, 1957. PhD, U. of SC., Usa, 1999—. Doctorate of Philosophy U. of SC., SC, 2004. Lectr. Aden U., Aden, Yemen, 1989—2003. Author (poet and translator): (creative writing and translation) Illusion and Reality (Poetry - winner, 1971). Recipient Poetry winner, Alhqaf Cultural Club, 1971. Mem.: Arab Translators (amman 1990—2003). Reform. Avocations: music, swimming, walking. Home: Aden University Aden Aden Aden Yemen Office: Aden University Aden Aden Aden Aden Yemen Personal E-mail: alhamidd@yahoo.com. E-mail: abubarmuhsin@maktoob.com.

ALHO, SISTER BONNIE KATHLEEN, pastoral associate; b. Superior, Wis., Feb. 6, 1942; d. Jack Wayne and Agnes (Osman) A. BS in Elem. Edn., Mt. Senario Coll., Ladysmith, Wis., 1970; MRE, St. Thomas U., Houston, 1978. Joined Order Servants of Mary, Roman Cath. Ch., 1959. Kindergarten tchr. St. Domitilla's Sch., Hillside, Ill., 1961-62; 3rd grade tchr. Annunciata, Chgo., 1962-67; 2nd grade tchr. St. Rose of Lima Sch., St. Paul, 1967-71; 1st grade tchr. St. Joseph's Sch., Carteret, N.J., 1971-72; mem. staff Diocese of Superior, Cameron, Wis., 1972-81; dir. religious edn. Our Lady of Sorrows, Ladysmith, 1981-93; sabbatical Boston Coll., 1993-94; pastoral assocs. St. Joseph's Parish, Rice Lake, Wis., 1994—; assoc. vocation dir. Diocese of Superior, 1996—2002; vocation dir. Servants of Mary, Ladysmith, 2001—. Mem. steering com. Wis. Dirs. of Religious Edn., State of Wis., 1979, bd. com. mem. 1987-90; bd. dirs. deacons com. Diocese of Superior, 1983-89, chair. Summit Bd., 1986-89, initiated Marriage Encounter; active in formation of retreat programs for teens; co-chair., treas. Area Clergy Assn., Ladysmith, 1991-92. Bd. dirs., chair ch. rels. com. Barron County Habitat for Humanity. Recipient Outstanding Leadership in Catechetical Ministry award Diocese of Superior, Mt. Telemark, Wis., 1988, Spirit of Teens Encounter Christ award Diocese of Superior, 1999. Mem. Wis. Dirs. Religious Edn. (bd. dirs. 1987-89), Nat. Conf. Vocation Dirs., Religious Fomation Ministers. Home: 334 N Wilson Ave Rice Lake WI 54868-1661 Office: St Joseph Parish 111 W Marshall St Rice Lake WI 54868-1648 E-mail: balho@chibardun.net. *It has been said "For all that has been Thanks...For all that will be Yes." It is important to me to approach life in this way.*

ALI, ASHRAF, psychiatrist; b. Dhaka, Bangladesh, June 7, 1951; s. Wazed Ali and Noorjahan Khatoon; m. Shada Newaz, Oct. 19, 1984; children: Sanah, Amir, Omar. MD, Rajshahi (Bangladesh) Med. Coll., 1974; diploma in child health, Nat. U. Ireland, Dublin, 1988. Cert. Am. Bd. Psychiatry and Neurology, Am. Bd. Adolescent Psychiatry. Resident psychiatry Brookdale U. Hosp., Bklyn., 1993—96; fellow in child and adolescent psychiatry SUNY, Bklyn., 1996—98; med. dir. Border Region Cmty. Ctr., 2001—; area dir. Camino Real Cmty. Mental Health Mental Retardation Ctr., Eagle Pass, Tex., 1998—2001. Fellow: Royal Soc. Health London; mem.: Am. Med. Soc. Vienna, Am. Soc. Addiction Medicine, Am. Soc. Clin. Psychopharmacology, Am. Psychiat. Assn. Moslem. Avocations: travel, fishing. Home: 1203 Crossfield Cir Laredo TX 78045 Office: Children's Program 2100 Corpus Christi St Ste 15 Laredo TX 78043

ALI, MIR MASOOM, statistician, educator; b. Bangladesh, Feb. 1, 1937; arrived in U.S., 1969; s. Mir Muazzam and Azifa Khatoon (Chowdhury) Ali; m. Firoza Chowdhury, June 25, 1959; children: Naheed, Fahima, Farah, Mir Ishtiaque. BSc, U. Dhaka, 1956, MSc, 1957, U. Toronto, 1967, PhD, 1969. Rsch. officer, Ministry of Food and Agriculture, Ministry of Commerce, Ctrl. Pub. Svc. Commn. Govt. of Pakistan, 1958—66; tchg. asst. U. Toronto, Canada, 1966—69; asst. prof. math. scis. Ball State U., Muncie, Ind., 1969—74, assoc. prof., 1974—78, prof., 1978—2000, George and Frances Ball disting. prof. stats., 2000—. Vis. prof. U. Windsor, Canada, 1972—73, U. Dhaka, 1983—84, Purdue U., 1978, Jahangirnagar U., 1991, Indian Stats. Inst., Calcutta, 1991, Yeungnam U., Republic of Korea, 1993, King Saud U., 1999. Assoc. editor Jour. Statis. Rsch., Aligarh Jour. Stats., Pakistan Jour. Stats., Jour. Info. and Optimization Sci., Jour. Korean Data and Info. Sci. Soc., overseas exec. editor Jour. Statis. Studies; editor: Parisankhyan Samikkha; contbr. articles to profl. jours. Named Sagamore of the Wabash, State of Ind., 2002; recipient Q.M. Husain Gold Medal, Bangladesh Stats. Assn., 1990. Fellow: Inst. Statisticians, Eng., Am. Statis. Assn. (meritorious svc. award from biopharm. sect. 1987, 1997, 2002), Royal Statis. Soc.; mem.: Inst. Math. Stats., Internat. Statis. Inst. Muslim. Home: 5200 W Deerbrook Dr Muncie IN 47304-3475 Office: Ball State U Dept Math Scis Muncie IN 47306-0490 Business E-Mail: mali@bsu.edu.

ALI, MUHAMMAD (CASSIUS MARCELLUS CLAY), retired professional boxer; b. Louisville, Jan. 17, 1942; s. Marcellus and Odessa (Grady) Clay; m. Sonji (div. 1966); m. Kalilah Tolona (Belinda Boyd), Apr. 18, 1967 (div. 1977); m. Veronica Porshe, June 19, 1977 (div.); m. Yolanda Williams, Nov. 19, 1986 Ed. pub. schs., Louisville. Profl. boxer, 1960—81. Appeared in movie The Greatest, 1976, TV movie Freedom Road; author: The Greatest: My Own Story, 1975. Named the greatest heavyweight champion of all time, Ring Mag., 1987; named to Olympic Hall of Fame, 1983, Internat. Boxing Hall of Fame, 1990; recipient Olympic gold medal in boxing, 1960, 6 Kentucky Golden Gloves titles, Nat. Golden Gloves titles, 1959—60, Jim Thorpe Pro Sports award, lifetime achievement, 1992, Essence award, 1997. Mem. World Community Islam. Achievements include being a light heavyweight champion AAU, 1959, 60; light heavyweight champion Golden Gloves, 1959, heavyweight champion, 1960; light heavy weight champion Olympic Games, 1960, world heavyweight champion, 1964-67, 74-78, 78-79; lost to heavyweight champion Larry Holmes, 1980.

ALIAGA-BUCHENAU, ANA-ISABEL, humanities educator; b. Hannover, Germany, Apr. 27, 1968; arrived in U.S., 1989; d. Alfredo Aliaga Burdio and Ingrid Charlotte (Waltraud) Aliaga-Weber; m. Jürgen Buchenau, July 31, 1993; children: Nicolas, Julia. BA, Georg August U., Göttingen, Germany, 1989, staatsexamen, 1993; MA, U. N.C., 1991, PhD, 1997. Vis. asst. prof. U. So. Miss., Hattiesburg, 1997—99, Davidson (N.C.) Coll., NC, 2000—02; asst. prof. comparative lit. U. N.C., Charlotte, 2002—. Grantee, So. Regional Edn. Bd., Atlanta, 2003. Mem.: Southeastern Coun. L.Am. Studies (program chair humanities 2003), Philol. Assn. of the Carolinas (mem.-at-large 2002—). Avocations: reading, travel, dancing, hiking. Office: U NC Charlotte University City Blvd Charlotte NC 28223 E-mail: aaliagab@email.uncc.edu.

ALIBER, ROBERT Z. economist, educator; b. Keene, N.H., Sept. 19, 1930; s. Norman H. and Sophie (Becker) A.; m. Deborah Baltzly, Sept. 9, 1955; children: Jennifer, Rachel, Michael. BA, Williams Coll., 1952, Cambridge U., 1954, MA, 1957; PhD, Yale U., 1962. Staff economist Commn. Money and Credit, N.Y.C., 1959-61; staff economist Com. on Econ. Devel., Washington, 1961-64; sr. econ. advisor AID, Dept. State, Washington, 1964-65; assoc. prof., then prof. internat. econs. and fin. U. Chgo., 1965—. Vis. prof. Brandeis U., 1987-93; vis. Bundesbank prof. Free U. Berlin, 1999; Houblon-Norman fellow, Bank of Eng., 1996, J.P. Morgan Internat. prize fellow, Am. Academy in Berlin, 2002. Author: The International Money Game, 1973, 76, 79, 83, 87, 2001, Exchange Risk and Corporate International Finance, 1978, Your Money and Your Life, 1982; co-author: Money, Banking, and the Economy, 1981, 84, 87, 90, 93, The Multinational Paradigm, 1993; editor: National Monetary Policies and the International Financial System, 1974, The Political Economy of Monetary Reform, 1976, The Reconstruction of International Monetary Arrangements, 1987, The Handbook of International Financial Management, 1989; co-editor Global Portfolios, 1991, Readings in International Business: A Decision Approach, 1993. With U.S. Army, 1954—56. Fulbright fellow, 1952-54. Mem. Am. Econs. Assn., Acad. Internat. Bus., Quadrangle Club, Williams Club of N.Y., Post Mills Soaring Club, Chgo. Gliding Club. Home: 5638 S Dorchester Ave Chicago IL 60637-1722 Office: 1101 E 58th St Chicago IL 60637-1511 E-mail: rza@gsb.uchicago.edu.

ALICEA, YVETTE, special education educator; b. Bronx, Aug. 27, 1962; d. Gregorio and Lucia Alicea; m. Leontitsis Eleftherios, Sept. 19, 1997. BA in Modern Langs., U. P.R., 1987; MS in Spl. Edn., CUNY, 1995. Cert. tchr. N.Y. Tchr. English José de Choudens, Arroyo, PR, 1983—84; tchr., asst. prin. St. Patrick's Bilingual Sch., Guayama, 1987—91; tchr. bilingual spl. edn. P.S. 26, N.Y.C. Bd. Edn., 1991—95; tchr. English Betsis Lang. Sch., Athens, Greece, 1996—99; tchr. spl. edn. P.S./M.S. 306, N.Y.C. Bd. Edn., 1999—2000, P.S. 46, N.Y. C. Bd. Edn., 2000—. Recipient Appreciation plaque, Parents Assn. of P.S. 26, Bronx, 1995. Avocations: reading, literature, movies. Home: 266 Bedford Park Blvd 2H Bronx NY 10458

ALICH, JOHN ARTHUR, JR., manufacturing executive; b. Cleve., Dec. 2, 1942; s. John Arthur and Jeanette Marie (Kusa) Alich; m. Susan Jane Moras, May 8, 1965; children: Michelle Monet, Amy Catherine. BS in Engring., U.S. Naval Acad., 1964; MBA, U. Del., 1971. Sr. cons./dir. Stanford Rsch. Inst., Menlo Park, Calif., 1973-77; mgr. devel. Baker Hughes Inc./Envirotech Corp., Menlo Park, 1977-80; v.p. devel. Baker Hughes Inc./Eimco Mining Machinery Internat., Menlo Park, 1980-82, v.p. mktg. Salt Lake City, 1982-85; group v.p., gen. mgr. Baker Hughes Inc./Eimco Secoma, Lyon, France, 1985-87; exec. v.p. ops. Baker Hughes Inc./Eimco Jarvis Clark, Toronto, Canada, 1987-88; pres. Baker Hughes Inc./Baker Hughes Mining Tools, Grand Prairie, Tex., 1988-92, Baker Hughes Inc/Envirotech Measurements and Controls, Austin, Tex., 1992-94, Thermo Instrument Controls Inc., Austin, 1994-95; bus. devel. dir. Thermo Instrument Sys. Inc., Austin, 1995-97; pres. Kevex Instruments, Valencia, Calif., 1998, Kevex Spectrace, Sunnyvale, Calif., 1999; prin. Performance Assocs., Carmel, Calif., 2000—03; pres., CEO Enogen, Inc., Carmel, 2000—. Bd. dirs. Serra HS Bd. Regents, San Mateo, Calif., 1975—77, Boys and Girls Club, Grand Prarie, 1988—92. Lt. USN, 1964—70. DuPont fellow, U. Del., 1970—71. Mem.: Beta Gamma Sigma. Avocations: golf, running, squash, personal computers. Office: Performance Assocs 2985 Alta Ave Carmel CA 93923-9315

ALIEV, ELDAR, artistic director, choreographer, educator; b. Azerbaijan; Grad.(hon.), Baku Choreographic Acad. CEO, artistic dir. Ballet Internationale, Indpls., 1994—. Former prin. ballet dancer with the Kirov Ballet appearing in more than 30 countries; guest star Bolshoi Ballet and the Australian Ballet; choreographer ballets 1001 Nights, 1995, The Nutcracker, 1996, The Firebird, Eugene, Oreg., 1999; choreographer operas Eugene Onegin, 1999, Samson and Deliah, 2000, Anoush, 2001; classics restaged Don Quixote, Giselle, La Sylphide, Paquita, Les Sylphides. Office: Ballet Internationale USA 502 N Capitol Ave Ste B Indianapolis IN 46204-1204

ALIG, FRANK DOUGLAS STALNAKER, retired construction company executive; b. Indpls., Oct. 10, 1921; s. Clarence Schirmer and Marjory (Stalnaker) A.; m. Ann Bobbs, Oct. 22, 1949; children: Douglas, Helen, Barbara. Student, U. Mich., 1939-41; BS, Purdue U., 1948. Registered profl. engr., Ind. Project engr. Ind. State Hwy. Commn., Indpls., 1948; pres. Alig-Stark Constrn. Co., Inc., 1949-57, Frank S. Alig, Inc., 1957-97—; ret. V.p., bd. dirs. Bo-Wit Products Corp., Edinburg, Ind.; pres., bd. dirs. Home Stone Realty, Inc. With AUS, 1943-46. Mem. Dramatic Club, Lambs Club. Republican. Presbyterian.

ALIGA, OLIVIA R. music teacher, choral director; b. Manila, Philippines, Sept. 8, 1951; d. Fernando Bellapaz Rocha and Thelma Reyes Rocha; m. Norman Asis Aliga, Apr. 24, 1976; children: Norman Vincent, Ferdinand Alphonse, Chester. AM in Music, Pilar Coll., Zamboanga City, Philippines; B of Music, U. Philippines, 1974, postgrad., Vandercook Coll. Music, Chgo. Cert. in Kindermusik. Mem. faculty Vallejo (Calif.) Conservatory of Music, 1982-83; music tchr. New Life Christian Sch., Middleton, Wis., 1985-86, choral dir. Lombard (Ill.) Chorale, 1986—. Music dir. Winfield Cmty. United Meth. Ch., 1988—, trustee, 1995—; bd. dirs. U. Philippines Club Am., Chgo., 1996—, music dir., 1999; music dir., vocal coach U. of the East Med. Chorale, Chgo., 1990-95. Pianist, performed to benefit Marklund Found., Chgo., 1997, and the U. Philippines Club Am., Chgo., 1991. Named to Filipino Am. Chicago Hall of Fame, 1999. Mem. Ill. Music Assn., Ill. State Music Tchrs. Assn., Ill. Philippine Med. Soc. Aux., Philippine Med. Assn. Chgo. Aux., U. PHilippines Club Am. (pres. 2003). Methodist. Avocations: raising orchids, flower arrangements, collecting stamps and coins.

ALIGIZAKI, KALLIOPI K. civil engineer, educator; b. Sparti, Lakonia, Greece, Nov. 3, 1963; arrived in U.S., 1991; d. Konstantinos K. Aligizakis and Chrissoula K. Aligizaki. Diploma in civil engring., Nat. Tech. U. Athens, Greece, 1987; MSCE, Pa. State U., 1995, PhDCE, 1999. Registered profl. engr., Greece, European Union. Rsch. assoc. Nat. Tech. U. Athens, 1987—90, Lab. of Assn. of Greek Cement Industry, Athens, 1988—89; structural engr. S. Kounadis and Assocs., Athens, 1989—90; scholar Pa. State U., University Park, 1999—2002; asst. prof. U. Okla., Norman, 2002—. Co-author: Durability of Reinforced Concrete, 1993; mem. editl. adv. bd. Anti-Corrosion Methods and Materials, 1999—. Mem.: Electrochem. Soc., NACE Internat., Materials Rsch. Soc., ACI Internat., Tech. Chamber Greece. Christian Orthodox. Avocations: opera, literature, travel, history. Home: PO Box 1647 Norman OK 73070 Personal E-mail: kalliopi@gmx.net.

ALIMANESTIANU, CALIN, retired hotel consultant; b. Bucharest, Roumania, Dec. 29, 1922; came to U.S., 1953, naturalized, 1961; s. Virgil and Nineta (Leon) A.; m. Cecilia Ciocalteu, 1948 (div. 1953); m. Joan Carpenter, 1955 (div. 1957); m. Bettie Nicholas, 1959 (div. 1967); 1 child, Simone; m. Maria Elizabeth Texeira, 1984 (div. 1996). Ed. in, Rome. Mgmt. trainee Woodner Hotel, Washington, 1955, Bismarck Hotel, Chgo., 1957; asst. to gen. mgr. Oxford House, Chgo., 1958-60; gen. mgr. Holiday Inn, Newburgh, N.Y., Plainview, L.I., N.Y., 1960-67, v.p. operation, gen. mgr. N.Y.C., 1967-71; mng. dir. Dering Harbor Inn, Shelter Island, N.Y.; hotel cons., 1973-90; pres. Creative Hotel Cons. Internat., St. Petersburg Beach, Fla., 1977-88. Mem. GOP Heritage Groups (nationalties div.), Julio Maniu Am. Roumanian Relief Found. Mem. Royal Automobile Club Roumania. Mem. Eastern Orthodox Ch. Home: 4370 Community Dr Apt 216 West Palm Beach FL 33409-2978

ALIMARAS, GUS, lawyer; BA, CUNY, 1979; JD, Hofstra U., 1982. Bar: N.Y. 1983, U.S. Dist. Ct. (ea. and so. dists.) N.Y. 1985, U.S. Ct. Internat. Trade 1985, U.S. Dist. Ct. (no. and we. dists.) N.Y. 1990, U.S. Supreme Ct. 1994. Assoc. John A. Sotirakis, Astoria, N.Y., 1983, George Kazazis, Astoria, 1983-87; ptnr. Kazazis & Alimaras, LLP, Astoria, 1987—. Dir. Independent Credit Union, 2001—; real estate continuing edn. instr. Queens Coll., CUNY, 1993—97; lectr. Nat. Bus. Inst. Mem. ABA, N.Y. State Bar Assn., Queens County Bar Assn., Long Island City Lawyers Club (pres. 1992-93). Ea. Orthodox Lawyers Assn., Phi Alpha Delta. Office: Kazazis & Alimaras LLP 36-12 34th Ave Ste 200 Long Island City NY 11106-1110

ALIN, ROBERT DAVID, lawyer; b. Mt. Vernon, NY, Oct. 10, 1952; s. Morris and Sylvia (Horowitz) A.; m. Arlene Susan Kerner, Feb. 14, 1988; children: Dustin, Lauren. BA in Math., U. Rochester, 1974; JD, NYU, 1977, LLM in Taxation, 1983. Bar: N.Y. Assoc. atty. Willkie Farr & Gallagher, NYC, 1977-79, Halperin Shivitz Eisenberg Schneider & Greenawalt, NYC, 1979-84, Berman Koerner Silberberg P.C., NYC, 1984-86; sr. v.p., sec., gen. counsel The Pentegra Group, White Plains, NY, 1986—. Mem. ABA, N.Y. State Bar Assn., Web Network. Democrat. Jewish. Avocations: tennis, bridge, music. Home: 7 Aspen Rd Scarsdale NY 10583-7301 Office: The Pentegra Group 108 Corporate Park Dr White Plains NY 10604-3805 E-mail: ralin@pentegra.com.

ALIPIO, GARY GLYNN, writer, consultant; b. Jefferson, La., June 7, 1968; s. Glynn Phillip Alipio and Eloise Gidiere Faciane; m. Nicol J. Breaux Alipio, Nov. 8, 1997. BJ, La. State U., 1986—91. Ddb needham/focus agy. Project Mgr., Dallas, 1996—97; sr. copywriter Pierce, DeDitius & Galyean, Arlington, Tex., 1997—98, Saunders-Ream, Dallas, 1998—99, Ackerman-McQueen, Okla. City, 1999—2001; freelance writer Galipio, New Orleans, La., 2001—. Copywriter (advertising) Six Flags Subway & Are You Getting Enough? Campaigns (Advt. ADDYs., 2001). Mem.: Soc. of Children's Book Writers and Illustrators (assoc.). Mem. Christian Ch. Avocations: golf, fishing, bicycling, swimming, painting.

ALISETTI, EDWIN LUIS, engineer, financial executive; b. Caracas, Venezuela, Aug. 10, 1969; s. Gualtiero Alisetti and Rina Esther Pacillo. BSCE, U. Catolica Andres Bello, Caracas, Venezuela, 1995; MSME, U. Miami, 1998, MBA, 2001. Pres. Casa Bella, Caracas, Venezuela, 1992-95; apt. adminstr. Miami, 1996-98; data analyst U. Miami Sch. Architecture, Coral Gables, Fla., 2000—; jr. analyst M&A dept. Royal Bank of Can., 2001; bus./fin. intern Merrill Lynch, Miami, 2001; eCommerce Latin Am. intern Fed. Express, Miami, 2000; cons. The Fin. Group, Fort Lauderdale, Fla., 2002—. Tutor econs. and fin. U. Miami Sch. Bus., 2000—; pres. Kateri Group Inc. Contbr. articles to sci. and tech. jours. Mem.: ASME. Avocations: martial arts, soccer, rugby. Home: # 120 20300 W Country Club Dr Aventura FL 33180 E-mail: ealisett@hotmail.com.

ALISKY, MARVIN HOWARD, political science educator; b. Kansas City, Mo., Mar. 12, 1923; s. Joseph and Bess June (Capp) A.; m. Beverly Kay, June 10, 1955; children: Sander Michael, Joseph. BA, U. Tex., 1946, MA, 1947, PhD, 1953; cert., Instituto Tecnologico, Monterey, Mex., 1951. News corr. S.W. and Latin Am. NBC, 1947-49, news corr. Midwest, 1954-56; news corr. NBC and Christian Sci. Monitor, Latin Am., 1957-72; asst. prof. Ind. U., 1953-57; assoc. prof. journalism and polit. sci. Ariz. State U., Tempe, 1957-60, prof. polit. sci., 1960—, founding chmn. dept. mass communication (now Sch. Journalism and Telecommunications), 1957-65, founding dir. Ctr. Latin Am. Studies, 1965-72. Vis. fellow Princeton U., 1963-64, Hoover Inst., Stanford, 1978;

Fulbright prof. Cath. U., Lima, Peru, 1958, U. Nicaragua, 1960; researcher U.S.-Mex. Interparliamentary Conf., Baja, Calif., 1965, Latin Am. Inst., Chinese Acad. Social Scis., Beijing, 1986, European Inst. Def. and Strategic Studies, London, 1985, Politics Inst., Copenhagen, Denmark, 1987, U. So. Calif., 1982—; U.S. del. UNESCO Conf., Quito, Ecuador, 1960; dir. Gov.'s Ariz.-Mex. Commn., 1975—; U.S. State Dept. lectr., Costa Rica, Peru, Argentina, Chile, 1983, 88; bd. dirs. Goldwater Inst. Pub. Policy Rsch., 1989—. Author: Governors of Mexico, 1965, Uruguay: Contemporary Survey, 1969, The Foreign Press, 1964, 70, Who's Who in Mexican Government, 1969, Political Forces in Latin America, 1970, Government in Nuevo Leon, 1971, Government in Sonora, 1971, Peruvian Political Perspective, 1975, (digital ed. 2000), Historical Dictionary of Peru, 1979, Historical Dictionary of Mexico, 1981, 2nd ed. 2000, Latin American Media: Guidance and Censorship, 1981, Global Journalism, 1983; co-author: Political Systems of Latin America, 1970, Political Parties of the Americas, 1982, Yucatan: A World Apart, 1980, (with J.E. Katz) Arms Production in Developing Nations, 1984, Mexico: Country in Crisis, 1986, (with Phil Rosen) International Handbook of Broadcasting Systems, 1988, Dictionary Latin American Political Leaders, 1988, (with W.C. Soderlund) Mass Media and the Caribbean, 1990, Censorship, A World Encyclopedia, edited by Derek Jones, 2001; columnist Thompson Corp. Newspapers in Ariz., 1999—; co-editor: (with Ron Pamachena) Federal Constitution of Mexico, 1993; contbr. numerous articles to profl. jours. and mags. Bd. dirs. Phoenix Com. on Fgn. Res., 1975—, Ariz. Acad. Town Hall, 1981, Tempe Pub. Libr., 1974-80; mem. U.S. Bd. Fgn. Scholarships Fulbright Commn. Bd., 1984—, Acad. Coun. Goldwater Inst. of Pub. Policy, 1989—. Ensign USNR, 1944-45. NSF grantee, 1984, Ariz. State U. rsch. grantee, 1962, 65, 70, Southwestern Studies Ctr. rsch. grantee, 1983, Latin Am. Rsch. in China grantee, 1986, World Media Rsch. in Soviet Union grantee, 1989, rsch. grantee, London, 1992, 94, Edinburgh, 1994, 97, 99, Vancouver, 1998, Mexico City, 2000-01. Fellow Hispanic Soc. Am.; mem. Am. Polit. Sci. Assn., Western Polit. Sci. Assn., Latin Am. Studies Assn., Pacific Coast Coun. Latin Am. Studies (bd. dirs.), Inter-Am. Press Assn., Inter-Am. Broadcasters Assn. (rsch. assoc.), Assocs. Liga de Municipios de Sonora, Friends of Mex. Art, Southwestern Polit. Sci. Assn. (chmn. 1976-77), Nat. Assn. Scholars, Ariz. Assn. Scholars, Arizonians for Nat. Security, Soc. Profl. Journalists (life), Tempe Rep. Men's Club, Knights of Sq. Roundtable, Sigma Delta Chi. Home: 44 W Palmdale Dr Tempe AZ 85282-2139 Office: Ariz State U Dept Political Sci Tempe AZ 85287-2001 *My life as an educator, writer, and journalist-broadcaster has enabled me to share and exchange important and vital thought with friends, associates, and fellow Americans.*

ALITO, SAMUEL ANTHONY, JR., federal judge; b. Trenton, N.J., Apr. 1, 1950; AB, Princeton U., 1972; JD, Yale U., 1975. Bar: NJ 1975, NY 1970. Law clk. to judge U.S. Ct. Appeals (3d cir.), Newark, 1976—77; asst. U.S. atty. U.S. Atty.'s Office, Newark, 1977—81, atty., 1987—90; asst. to solicitor gen. Office of Solicitor Gen. Dept. Justice, Washington, 1981—85; dep. asst. atty. gen. Office of Legal Counsel Dept. Justice, Washington, 1985—87; judge U.S. Ct. Appeals (3d cir.), Newark, 1990—. Office: US Courthouse PO Box 999 Newark NJ 07101-0999

ALJIAN, JAMES DONOVAN, investment company executive; b. Oakland, Calif., Nov. 5, 1932; s. George W. and Marguerite (Donovan) A.; m. Marjorie L. Townsend, Oct. 17, 1959; children: Mark Donovan, Mary Anne, Reed Townsend. BS, U. Calif., Berkeley, 1955; MBA, Golden Gate U., 1965. Office mgr. Uniroyal Co., San Francisco, 1957-60; audit supr. Ernst & Ernst, San Francisco, 1960-65; sec.-treas. Tracy Investment Co., Las Vegas, 1965-73, Internat. Leisure Corp., Las Vegas, 1967-70; sr. v.p. fin. MGM, Culver City, Calif., 1973-79; pres. Tracinda Corp., Las Vegas, 1979-82; sr. v.p. fin. planning MGM/UA Entertainment Co., Culver City, Calif., 1982-85; exec. v.p., chief fin. officer, dir. Southwest Leasing Corp., Los Angeles, 1985-87, also bd. dirs.; with Tracinda Corp., Las Vegas, Nev., 1987—. Mem. shareholder com. Daimler Chrysler AG, 1998-2000; bd. dirs. MGM Grand, Inc., Metro-Goldwyn-Mayer, Inc. Served with AUS, 1955-57. Mem. Am. Inst. C.P.A.s, Calif. Soc. C.P.A.s., Acad. Motion Picture Arts and Scis.

ALKALAY, ARIE L. pediatrician, neonatologist; b. July 23, 1946; MD, Hadassah Sch. Medicine, Jerusalem, 1971. Intern Belinson Med. Ctr./Kaplan Hosp., Israel, 1971-72, Cedars Sinai Med. Ctr., L.A., 1984-85; resident in pediatrics Kaplan Hosp., Israel, 1975-80, fellow in neonatal-perinatal medicine, 1980-82, Cedars Sinai Med. Ctr., L.A., 1982-84; assoc. dir. neonatology Cedars-Sinai Med. Ctr., L.A., 1992-97, dir. Well Baby Nursery, 1993-99; prof. pediats. UCLA, 1997—. Contbr. 40 articles to profl. jour. Recipient the Morris Press Humanism award Cedars-Sinai Med. Ctr., 1989. Office: 8700 Beverly Blvd Los Angeles CA 90048-1804

ALKANA, RONALD LEE, neuroscientist; s. Sam Alkana and Madelyn Jane Davis; m. Linda Anne Kelly, Sept. 12, 1970; children: Alexander Philippe Kelly, Lorna Jane Kelly. Student, UCLA, 1963-66; PharmD, U. So. Calif., 1970; PhD, U. Calif., Irvine, 1975. Resident asst. dir. divsn. neurochemistry U. Calif., Irvine, 1976; asst. prof. pharmacy/pharmacology U. So. Calif., L.A., 1976-82, assoc. prof. pharmacy/pharmacology and toxicology, 1982-89, prof. molecular pharmacology and toxicology, 1989—, asst. dean grad. affairs, 1995-98, asst. dean interdisciplinary programs Sch. Pharmacy, 1998-2001, assoc. dean curriculum devel., 2001—. Editl. bd. Alcholism: Clinical and Experimental Research, 1989-94; assoc. editor, 1994-98; contbr. chpts. to books, articles to profl. jours. Recipient various scholarships and grants; named Outstanding Alumnus U. So. Calif. Sch. of Pharmacy, 1999. Mem. AAAS, Soc. Neurosci., Am. Soc. Pharmacology and Exptl. Therapeutics, Internat. Soc. Biomed. Research on Alcoholism, Research Soc. Alcoholism, Internat. Brain Rsch. Organization World Fedn. Neuroscientists, Soc. of Toxicology, Am. Assn. Colls. of Pharmacy, Western Pharmacology Soc., QSAD (bd. dirs. 1998—), Sigma Xi, Phi Delta Chi (bd. dirs. Omicron alumni 1997—, Omicron chpt., Outstanding Alumnus of Yr. 1996, 99). Office: 1985 Zonal Ave Los Angeles CA 90089

AL-KAWAS, FIRAS H. physician; b. Damascus, Syria, Aug. 12, 1949; came to U.S., 1975; MD, Damascus U., 1974. Diplomate Am. Bd. Internal Medicine, Am. Bd. Gastroenterology. Intern D.C. Gen. Hosp., Washington, 1979—81, VA Med. Ctr., Washington, 1975—79; asst. prof. W.Va. U., Morgantown, 1982-87, assoc. prof., 1987, Georgetown U., Washington, 1987-95, prof. medicine, 1995—; chief of endoscopy VA Med. Ctr., Washington, 1987-90; chief clin. endoscopy NIH, Bethesda, Md., 1990-91; dir. biliary endoscopy Georgetown U. Med. Ctr., Washington, 1990-98, chief endoscopy, 1998—. Sect. editor book on gastrointestinal disease; contbr. articles to profl. jours. Fellow ACP, Am. Coll. Gastroenterology; mem. Am. Soc. for Gastrointestinal Endoscopy. Office: Georgetown U Med Ctr 3800 Reservoir Rd NW Washington DC 20007-2113

ALKER, HAYWARD ROSE, political scientist, educator; b. N.Y.C., Oct. 3, 1937; s. Hayward Rose and Dorothy (Fitzsimmons) Alker; m. Judith Ann Tickner, June 3, 1961; children: Joan Christina, Heather Jane, Gwendolyn Ann. BS, MIT, 1959; MS, Yale U., 1960, PhD, 1963. From instr. to assoc. prof. Yale U., New Haven, 1963-68; prof. polit. sci. MIT, 1968-95; John A. McCone prof. internat. rels. U. So. Calif., L.A., 1995—. Vis. prof. U. Mich., 1968; Olaf Plame vis. prof. U. Stockholm, U. Uppsala, 1989; vis. prof., scholar Brown U., 1996, 1997—2000, chmn. Math. Social Scis. Bd., 1970—71. Author: (non-fiction) Mathematics and Politics, 1965; co-author: World Handbook of Political and Social Indicators, 1966; co-author: (with Russett) World Politics in the General Assembly, 1966; co-author: (with Bloomfield and Choucri) Analyzing Global Interdependence, 1974; co-author: (with Hurwitz) Resolving Prisoner's Dilemmas, 1981; co-editor, co-author: non-fiction Journeys Through Conflict, 2001; author: Rediscoveries and Reformations, 1996; editor (mem. bd.): (jour.) Jour. Interdisciplinary History, 1969—71, Internat. Orgn., 1970—76, Quality and Quantity, 1974—, Internat. Studies Quar., 1980—89, European Jour. Internat. Rels., 1995—99, Internat. Rels. of Asia Pacific, 2000—. Congl. intern Office of Chester Bowles, 1960. Fellow, Ctr. Advanced Studies in Behavioral Scis., 1967—68. Mem.: Internat. Social Sci. Coun. (exec. com. 1990—92, coord. conflict early warning sys. rsch. program 1992—99), Internat. Studies Assn. (v.p. 1990—91, pres. 1992—93), Internat. Peace Rsch. Assn., Internat. Polit. Sci. Assn., Am. Polit. Sci. Assn. E-mail: alker@usc.edu.

AL-KHATIB, TAREQ, surgeon; b. Jerusalem, June 11, 1945; Student, Damascus (Syria) U., 1964-65, MD, 1971. Diplomate Am. Bd. Emergency Medicine, Am. Bd. Surgery. Intern Yale Affiliated Hosp., New Haven, 1971-72; resident in surgery Albert Einstein Hosp., N.Y.C., 1973-77; surgeon Port Charlotte (Fla.) Hosps., 1977—; pvt. practice Port Charlotte, Fla., 1977—. Fellow ACS; mem. AMA, Am. Coll. Emergency Physicians. Office: Emerald Sq 2852 Tamiami Trl Ste 5 Port Charlotte FL 33952-5100 Fax: 941-625-9797.

ALKIRE, BETTY JO, artist, commercial real estate broker, marketing consultant; b. Kansas City, Mo., June 20, 1942; d. Robert Emmitt and Gladys Faye (Craigg) Sharp; m. Daniel Wayne Hedrick, Nov. 15, 1968 (div.); children: Diane Laurie, Lisa Kay, Brett, Darin, Julie; m. William Edgar Alkire, Sept. 23, 1975 (dec. Dec. 7, 2001). Tchr. art Independence (Mo.) Art Edn., 1967—; portait artist Silver Dollar City Nat. Crafts Festival, 1971—; owner, operator artist's concession Kansas City Worlds of Fun, 1972-96; tchr. pvt. art classes, 1970—; tchr., lectr. mktg. art U. Mo. Extension Program, 1982—; the portrait artist Nat. Festival of Craftsmen, 1971—. Cons. mktg. and life-planning for artists; broker and cons. comml. investment real estate. Contbr. articles to mags. Mem. Bur. of Tourism; mem. edn. com. Tri-Lakes Bd. Realtors; mem. Rockaway Beach Bd. Planning and Zoning; chmn. Rockaway Beach Park and Mus. Bd. Mem. Mo. Arts Coun., Table Rock Art Guild, Ind. Profl. Artists Assn. (pres. 1980—), Branson (Mo.) C. of C. (mem. leadership program), Rockaway Beach Ladies Club, Rockaway Beach Booster Club. Methodist. Avocations: local art and history, antiques, real estate. Home: Historic Tancywood Rockaway Beach MO 65740 Address: PO Box 655 Rockaway Beach MO 65740 E-mail: BettyJoAlkire@realtor.com.

ALKON, ELLEN SKILLEN, physician; b. Los Angeles, Apr. 10, 1936; d. Emil Bogen and Jane (Skillen) Rost; m. Paul Kent Alkon, Aug. 30, 1957; children: Katherine Ellen, Cynthia Jane, Margaret Elaine. BA, Stanford U., 1955; MD, U. Chgo., 1961; MPH, U. Calif., Berkeley, 1968. Diplomate Nat. Bd. Med. Examiners, Am. Bd. Pediat., Am. Bd. Preventive Medicine in Pub. Health. Chief sch. health Anne Arundel County Health Dept., Annapolis, Md., 1970-71; practice medicine specializing in pediat. Mpls. Health Dept., 1971-73, dir. MCH, 1973-75, commr. health, 1975-80; chief preventive and pub. health Coastal Region of Los Angeles County Dept. Health Svcs., 1980-81; chief pub. health West Area Los Angeles County Dept. Health Svcs., 1981-85; acting med. dir. pub. health Los Angeles County Dept. Health, 1986-87, med. dir. pub. health, 1987-93; med. dir. Coastal Cluster Health Ctrs. L.A. County Dept. Pub. Health Svcs., 1993-96, CEO, 1996-98, med. dir., 1998-2000; dir. Pub. Health Edn. in Medicine, 2000—. Adj. prof. UCLA Sch. Pub. Health, 1981—; adminstr. vis. nurses svc., Mpls., 1975-80. Fellow Am. Coll. Preventive Medicine, Am. Acad. Pediatrics; mem. So. Calif. Pub. Health Assn. (pres. 1985-86), Minn. Pub. Health Assn. (pres. 1978-79), Am. Pub. Health Assn., Calif. Conf. Local Health Officers (pres. 1990-91), Calif. Ctr. for Pub. Health Advocacy (pres. 2002-03), Delta Omega. Office: Los Angeles County DHS 241 N Figueroa St Rm 143 Los Angeles CA 90012 E-mail: ealkon@dhs.co.la.ca.us.

ALKON, PAUL KENT, English language educator; Grad., Phillips Acad., 1953; AB, Harvard U., 1957; PhD in English Lit., U. Chgo., 1962. Instr., asst. prof. English lit. U. Calif.-Berkeley, 1962-70; assoc. prof. U. Md., 1970-71; assoc. prof. English U. Minn., Mpls., 1971-73, prof., 1973-80; Leo S. Bing prof. English U. So. Calif., Los Angeles, 1980—. Vis. prof. English, Ben Gurion U. of Negev, Israel, 1977-78 Author: Samuel Johnson and Moral Discipline, 1967, Defoe and Fictional Time, 1979, Origins of Futuristic Fiction, 1987, Science Fiction Before 1900, 1994. Mem. Am. Soc. 18th Century Studies (pres. 1989-90), Société française d'Etude du 18ème Siècle, Churchill Ctr. (bd. acad. advisers). Home: 17 Masongate Dr Palos Verdes Peninsula CA 90274-1560 Office: U So Calif Dept English Los Angeles CA 90089-0354 E-mail: alkon@usc.edu.

ALKSNE, JOHN F. medical educator, former dean; M.D., U. of Washington, Seattle. Chief neurolosurgery Harbor Gen. Hospital, UCLA, 1964—67; prof. neurological surgery Med. Coll. of Virginia, 1967—71, U. Calif., La Jolla, 1971, founding chief, Div. of Neurological Survey, 1971—95, dean Sch. of Medicine, 1995—2000, prof. surgery, 2000—. Office: Univ Calif San Diego 200 W Arbor Dr Dept 8893 San Diego CA 92103-8893*

ALLABY, STANLEY REYNOLDS, clergyman; b. Providence, Dec. 28, 1931; s. Edwin T. and Hope (Swift) A.; m. Marion Arlene Johnson, Dec. 18, 1954; children— Norman R., Darlene R., Kimberly A., Stephen R. AB, Gordon Coll., 1953; M.Div., Gordon Conwell Sem., 1956; D.D., Barrington (R.I.) Coll., 1977; D.Min., Westminster Theol. Sem., 1978. Ordained to ministry, 1956; pastor Black Rock Conglist. Ch., Fairfield, Conn., 1956-97; dir. Sudan Interior Mission, N.C., 1970—, chmn. bd., 1985—, vice chmn. internat. bd. govs., 1985-90; vice chmn. Billy Graham New Haven Crusade, 1982; exec. com. Billy Graham Hartford Crusade, 1985; prof. practical theology Bethel Sem. of the East; Ockenga lectr. Gordon-Conwell Sem., 1983; sr. cons. Wilson Ctr. for Missions, Gordon-Consell Sem., 2001—. Guest lectr. Tyndale Theol. Sem., Amsterdam, 1996; lectr. Bethel Seminary of the East, 1999—. Bd. dirs. United Neighbors for Self Devel., Bridgeport, Conn., 1963-64, Christian Freedom Found., 1960-70, Operation Hope, Fairfield, 1986-89; trustee Gordon Div. Sch., 1965-69. Recipient George Washington honor medal Freedoms Found., 1968, 69; Alumnus-of-Year award Gordon Coll., 1976 Mem. Gordon Coll. Alumni Assn. (past pres.), Nat. Assn. Evangelicals (dir. 1974-95, exec. com. 1980-82, nat. conv. coordinator 1981-82, (chmn. resolutions com. 1982-83), Bridgeport Pastors Assn. (past pres.), Greater Bridgeport Fellowship Evangelicals (past pres.) Home: 123 Lyon Rd Woodstock Valley CT 06282-2612 E-mail: stanreynolds6@juno.com.

ALLAHUT, LOUIS, lawyer; b. Bklyn., July 11, 1937; s. Max and Mary Allahut; m. Carrie Allahut, June 12, 1971. BSEE, Carnegie Inst. Tech., 1960; JD, Cath. U. Am., 1967. Bar: Ohio 1972, U.S. Dist Ct. (so. dist.) Ohio 1972, U.S. Dist Ct. (no. dist.) Ohio 1973, Ct. of Customs and Patent Appeals 1977, U.S. Ct. of Claims 1978. Patent examiner U.S. Patent Office, Washington, 1963-69; patent atty. North Electric Co., Gallion, Ohio, 1969-73, Fed. Pacific Electric Co., Newark, 1973-74, Bacon & Thomas, Arlington, Va., 1974-75, U.S. Army Material Devel. & Readiness Command, Alexandria, Va., 1976-81, Naval Air Sys. Command, Patuxent River, Md., 1981-99, Naval Sea Sys. Command, Arlington, Va., 1999—. 1st lt. U.S. Army, 1961-63. Mem. Govt. Patent Law Assn. (treas. 1992-96). Home: 800 Douglas St Fredericksburg VA 22407 Office: 1333 Isaac Hull Ave SE Washington Naval Yard DC 20376-1160

ALLAIN, JEAN PAUL, research scientist; b. Bogota, Cundinamarca, Colombia, June 17, 1970; s. John Frederick Allain and Luz Patricia Allain De La Torre; m. Monica Marie Cortez, June 21, 1997; 1 child, Karina Rae Chavez. BS, Calif. State Poly. U., Pomona, 1996; MS, PhD, U. Ill., 2001. Co-op rsch. intern Intel Corp., Santa Clara, Calif., 1997—97; grad. rsch. assoc. U. Ill., Urbana, 1996—2001, postdoctoral rsch. assoc., 2001—. Summer rsch. intern Gen. Atomics, La Jolla, Calif., 2000—00. Fellow SURGE, U. Ill., 1996—2001. Mem.: Am. Vacuum Soc., Am. Phys. Soc., Phi Kappa Phi, Sigma Chi (assoc.). Achievements include first to Low-Energy Sputtering of Liquid-Metals. Avocations: soccer, writing, poetry, reading. Office: Univ Ill 214 NEL 103 S Goodwin Ave Urbana IL 61801 E-mail: allain@uiuc.edu.

ALLAIN, LOUIS, literature educator, scientific advisor; b. Brest, France, June 28, 1933; s. Louis and Louise (Nicolas) A.; m. Annie Luc, May 21, 1964, children: Andree-Lise, Juliette, Laurence, Alexandre. B Degree, Ecole Normale Superieure, Paris, 1958, Agregation, 1957; Doctorate, Sorbonne, Paris, 1979. Sch. tchr. Lycee Lakanal, Paris, 1961; asst. lectr. Sorbonne, 1961-63, sr. lectr., 1963-69; mng. lectr. Univ. Lille, 1969-81, prof., head dept. Slavic langs., 1981-98, prof emeritus, 1998—. Contbr. Acad. Sci., Hungary, 1988, Russia, 1988, 90, 94, 96, 2000, Israel, 1994, Poland, 1995, 96, 97, 98, 2000, Montenegro, 1996, U. Houston, 1989, Cornell U., 1994, Columbia U., 1998, Dostoevsky Symposium, Cerisy-la-Salle, 1983, Ljubljana, 1989, Oslo, 1992, Kartause Gaming, 1995, N.Y. 1998, Gumilev Symposium I & II, Glasgow, 1986, St. Petersburg, 1996, Chekhov Symposium I & II, Badenweiler, 1985, 94, From Dissidence to Democracy, Paris, 1996., Jerusalem in Slavic cultures and religious traditions, 1996, others. Author: Dostoievski et Dieu, 1981, Dostoievski et l'Autre, 1984, Etiudy o russkoi literature, 1989, Dostoevsky i Bog, 1993, F.M. Dostoevsky: Poetika, mirooshchushchenie, bogoiskatel'stvo, 1996, Skvoz' prizmu vekov, 1998, Shtrikhi k portretu F.M. Dostoevskogo, 1998; editor: B. Poplavsky, I&II, 1993, N. Otsup, 1993-95, G. Adamovich, 1993, G. Ivanov, 1993, V. Vishnjak, 1993, V.V. Rozanov, (study), 1993, A. Remizov, 1994, N. Plevitskaya, 1994, N. Fedorova, 1994, V. Gippius, 1994, V. Zen'kovsky, 1994, I. Napelbaum, 1995, M. Voloshin (study), 1996, F. M. Dostoevsky: Poetika, mirooshchushchenie, bogoiskatel'stvo, 1996, Skvoz' Prizmu Vekov, 1998, Shtrikhi k portretu F.M. Dostoevskogo, 1998, D. Granin, Tajny znak Peterburga, 2000; co-editor: Jews and Slavs, vol. 2, 1994; contbr. articles to profl. jours. Lt. French Navy, 1958-61, France. Comdr. of Acad. Palms, French Ministry of Edn., 1990, medal City of Lille, 1994, Melanges offerts au Professeur Louis Allain, Lille, 1996, Am. Order of Excellence, 2000. Mem. Alumni Ecole Normale Superieure, Intra-Marine/France, Internat. Dostoevsky Soc., Inst. Slavic Studies, Paris. Avocations: cooking, gardening. Home: Rue Jules Guesde 408 Villeneuve d'Ascq 59650 France Office: Charles de Gaulle Univ BP 149 Villeneuve d'Ascq Cedex 59653 France E-mail: allain@univ-lille3.fr.

ALLAIRE, PAUL ARTHUR, office equipment company executive; b. Worcester, Mass., July 21, 1938; s. Arthur E Allaire and Elodie (LePrade) Murphy; children: Brian, Christiana. BSEE, Worcester Poly. Inst., 60; MSIA, Carnegie-Mellon U., 1966. Fin. analyst Xerox Corp., Rochester, N.Y., 1966-70; dir. fin. analysis Rank Xerox Ltd., London, N.Y., 1970-73; dir. internat. ops. fin. Xerox Corp., Stamford, Conn., 1973-75; chief staff officer Rank Xerox Ltd., London, 1975-79, mng. dir., 1979-83; sr. v.p., chief staff officer Xerox Corp., Stamford, Conn., 1983-86, pres., 1986 90, CEO, 1990, chmn. bd., 1991—, also. chmn. exec. com., CEO, bd. dirs., 2000—. Bd. dirs. Glaxo-SmithKline plc, Lucent Technologies, Priceline.com, Coun on Competitiveness. Bd dirs NY City Ballet; chmn bd dirs Ford Found; trustee Worcester Poly Inst, Carnegie Mellon Univ. Mem.: Nat. Acad. Engring., Eta Kappa Nu, Tau Beta Pi. Democrat. Office: Xerox Corp PO Box 10340 100 First Stamford Pl Stamford CT 06904

ALLAIS, MAURICE FELIX, economist; b. Paris, May 31, 1911; s. Maurice and Louise (Caubet) A.; m. Jacqueline Bouteloup, Sept. 6, 1960; 1 child, Christine. Grad. 1st pl.(hon.), Poly. Sch., Paris, 1933; grad., Nat. Higher Sch. Mines, Paris, 1936; D Eng, Faculty of Sci., Paris, 1949; D (hon.), U. Groningen, The Netherlands, 1964, U. Mons, Belgium, 1992, Am U., Paris, 1992, U. Lisbonne, Portugal, 1993; diplome d'Honneur Hautes Etudes Commls. (hon.), U. Paris, Paris, 1993. Engr. Dept. Mines and Quarries, 1937-43; dir. Bur. Documentation and Stats., 1943-48, Econ. and Social Rsch. Group, Paris, 1944-70; prof. econ. analysis Nat. Higher Sch. Mines, Paris, 1944-88; dir. Econ. Analysis Ctr., Paris, 1944—; prof. econ. theory Inst. Stats. U. Paris, Paris, 1947-58, dir. Ctr. Clement Juglar for Monetary Analysis, 1970-85; dir. rsch. Nat. Ctr. Sci. Rsch., Paris, 1954-79; prof. Grad. Inst. Internat. Studies, Geneva, 1967-70. Disting. vis. scholar Thomas Jefferson, U. Va., Charlottesville, 158-59; mem. energy commn. Econ. Coun., Paris, 1960-61; chmn. com. of experts for study of options in transport tariff policy EEC, Brussels, 1963-64. Author: A la Recherche d'une Discipline Economique, 1943, 2d edit. Traité d'Economic Pure, 1952, 3d edit., 1994, Abondance ou Misère, 1946, Economie et Intérêt, 1947, 2d edit., 1998, La Gestion des Houillères Nationalisées et la Théorie Economique, 1949, Les Fondements Comptables de la Macroéconomique, 1954, 2d edit., 1992, Fondements d'une Théorie positive des choix comportant un risque, 1955, Notes to French Academy of Sci. on the Anomalies in the Movements of the Paraconic Pendulum, 1957-58, Should the Law of Gravitation Be Reconsidered?, 1959, L'Europe Unie, Route de la Prospérité, 1959, L'Algérie d'Evian, 1962, 2d edit. 1999, The Role of Capital in Econ. Development, 1963, Reformulation de la Théorie Quantitative de la Monnaie, 1965, L'Impôt sur le Capital, 1966, Les Conditions de l'Efficacité dans l'Economie, 1967, Growth Without Inflation, 1968, Growth and Inflation, 1969, La Libéralisation des Relations Economiques Internationales, 1970, 2d edit., 1995, Les Théories de l'Equilibre Economique Général et de l'Efficacité Maximale, 1971, Inégalité et Civilisations, 1971, Inequality and Civilizations, 1973, L'Inflation Française et la Croissance, 1974, Inflation, Income Distribution and Indexation, 1976, L'Impôt sur le Capital et la Réforme Monétaire, 1977, 2d edit., 1988, Expected Utility Hypothesis and the Allais' Paradox, 1979, La Théorie Générale des Surplus, 1980, 2d edit., 1989, Frequency, Probability and Chance, 1982, Found. of Utility and Risk Theory, 1983, Détermination de l'Utilité Cardinale suivant un modèle intrinsèque invariant, 1984, Credit Mechanism, 1984, The Empirical Approaches of the Hereditary and Relativistic Theory of the Demand for Money, 1986, The Concepts of Surplus and Loss and the Reformulation of the Gen. Theory of Econ. Equilibrium and Maximum Efficiency, 1986, The Gen. Theory of Random Choices in Relation to the Invariant Cardinal Utility Function and the Specific Probability Function, 1986, The Equimarginal Principle: Meaning, Limits and Generalization, 1987, Les Conditions Monétaires d'une Economie de Marchés, 1987, My Life Philosophy, 1988, Autoportraits, 1989, Pour l'Indexation, 1990, Pour la Réforme de la Fiscalité, 1990, L'Europe face à son avenir-Que Faire?, 1991, De l'Europe des Douze à la Grande Europe, 1992, Erreurs et Impasses de la Construction Européenne, 1992, Cardinalism, 1994, Combats pour l'Europe 1994, L'anisotropie de l'espace, 1997, la crise mondiale d'aujourd'hui, 1999, L'Union européenne, la Mondialisation et le Chômage, 1999, Globalization, the Destruction of Employment and Growth: The Empirical Evidence, 1999, Des régularities très significatives dans les observations interférométriques de Dayton C. Miller, CRAS, 1999-2000; Foundements de La Dynamique Monétoire, 2001, La Passion de la Recherche, 2001, Un Savant Méconnu, 2002, Nouveaux Combats pour l'Europe, 2002; also sci. papers on risk and utility theory; mem. editl. bd. Polit. Econ. Rev., 1952—. Lt. arty., French Army, 1939-40. Named Laureate French Acad. Sci., 1933, French Acad. Moral and Polit. Sci., 1954, 59, 83, 84; recipient Lanchester prize Johns Hopkins U. and Operational Rsch. Soc. Am., 1958, Great Prize of Atlantic Community, 1959, Galabert prize French Astronautical Soc., 1959, Gravity Rsch. Found. prize, 1959, Grand Prix André Arnoux, 1968, Zerilli Marimo, 1984, Gold medal Soc. for Promotion of Nat. Industry, 1971, French Nat. Ctr. for Sci. Rsch., 1978, Prix Spl. Jury Dupuit-de Lesseps, 1987, Nobel prize in econ. scis., 1988, medal U. Paris-X, 1989, Gold medal City of Paris, 1989, Great Gold medal City of Nancy, 1990, Gold medal Etoile Civique, 1990, Amis de François Quesnay, 1994; decorated Officer of Palmes Académiques, 1949, Chevalier Nat. Economy Order, 1962, Comdr. Legion of Honor, 1989, Grand Officier Ordre Nat. du Mérite, 1998. Fellow Ops. Rsch. Soc. Am., Internat. Econometric Soc. (editl. bd. 1959-69), mem. NAS (assoc.), Nat. Acad. Sci., Morales et Politiques, Acad. Nat. dei Lincei (assoc.), Acad. Sci. Russia, French Assn. Econ. Sci. (chmn. 1972), Am. Econ. Assn. (hon.), Internat. Statis. Inst., Statis. Soc., Racing Club Paris. Avocations: history, theoretical and experimental physics. Home: 15 rue Des Gate-Ceps 92210 Saint Cloud France Office: Econ Analysis Ctr 60 Blvd Saint Michel 75272 Paris France E-mail: mgendrot@dub.internet.fr.

ALLAMONG, BETTY D. academic administrator; b. Morgantown, W.Va., Apr. 8, 1935; d. Lonnie R. and Jessie R. (Hoffman) Davis; m. Joseph K. Allamong, Sept. 12, 1954; 1 child, John Bradley. BS, W.Va. U., 1961, MA, 1964, PhD, 1971; student, Inst. for Ednl. Mgmt. Harvard U., 1984. Instr. biology Morgantown High Sch., W.Va., 1961-67; instr. edn. W.Va. U., Morgantown, 1965-67, instr. biology, 1967-72; asst. to full prof. biology Ball State U., Muncie, Ind., 1972-87, assoc. dean, scis. and humanities, 1981-86, acting dean, scis. and humanities, 1986-87; provost and v.p. acad. affairs Bloomsburg U., Pa., 1987-92. Mem. Ind. Corp. for Sci. & Tech., 1983-87. Co-author: Energy for Life, 1976; author numerous lab. manuals; contbr. articles to profl.jours. Mem. Ind. Corp. Sci. & Tech., 1983-87. Recipient Women of Achievement edn. award Women in Comms. Inc., Muncie, 1981. Fellow Ind. Acad. Sci. Home: 253 Pixler Hill Rd Morgantown WV 26508-9541

ALLAMPALLAM, KRISHNAN, biotechnology consultant; b. Lucknow, Uttar Pradesh, India, Jan. 20, 1966; came to US, 1989; s. Krishnaiyer A. and Saraswathy Varadarajan; m. Parvathy Shivaramakrishnan, May 17, 1995. BS, U. Bombay, 1986, MS, 1988; PhD, Med. Coll. Ohio, 1996; MBA in Mktg.-Entrepreneurship. Postdoc. fellow Cleve. Clinic Found., 1996-97; rsch. asst. Rush Cancer Inst., Chgo., 1997—2000, asst. prof., 2002; biotech. startup cons., 2002—. Contbr. articles to scientific jours. Mem. AAAS, Am. Soc. Haematology, Am. Soc. Biochemistry and Molecular Biology, N.Y. Acad. Scis. Home: 3649 W Cornelia Ave Unit D Chicago IL 60618

ALLAN, BARRY DAVID, research chemist, government official; b. Steubenville, Ohio, Jan. 20, 1935; s. John Young and Frances Lucy (Halbrunner) A.; m. Inge Elisabeth Bergeler, Aug. 5, 1961; children— Barbara Diane, Stephen Barry. BS, Ariz. State U., 1956; MS, U. Ala., 1964, PhD, 1968. Chemist White Sands Missile Range, N.M., 1956; aero. fuels research chemist Army Missile Command, Redstone Arsenal, Ala., 1958-62, research chemist-phys., 1962-96, research chemist, 1968-95; prof. J.C. Calhoun Coll., Decatur, Ala., 1969-73, Athens (Ala.) Coll., 1970-73, U. Ala., Huntsville, 1974-76; rsch. cons. Allan Cons., Huntsville, 1996—. Cons., 1965— ; reviewer Nat. Sci. Found., 1973—

Publs. in field. Active Huntsville Civic Assn., 1961— . Served to capt. AUS, 1956-58. Recipient Army Research And Devel. Achievement award, 1962, Navy commendation, 1968, Army commendation, 1971, 72 Mem. Am. Chem. Soc. (treas. 1969-73, pres. 1974-76), Combustion Inst., Pasteur Soc., Assn. U.S. Army, N.Y. Acad. Scis., Joint Army, Navy, NASA, Air Force Propellant Characterization Group on Fluids and Materials, Sigma Xi, Gamma Sigma Epsilon, Theta Chi. Office: Barry D Allan Cons 7803 Michael Cir SW Huntsville AL 35802-2900 Fax: 256-881-4101. E-mail: ballan@hiwaay.net.

ALLAN, JANET D. dean; BSN, Skidmore Coll., 1964; MS in Cmty. Health Nursing, U. Calif.-San Francisco, 1968; PhD in Med. Anthropology. Cert. adult nurse practitioner ANA. Former dean Health Sci. Ctr. U. Tex., San Antonio; dean Univ. of Maryland Sch. of Nursing, Baltimore, Md., 2001—. Recipient 2001 Distinguished Researcher Award. Office: Univ of Maryland Sch of Nursing 655 West Lombard St Baltimore MD 21201-1579

ALLAN, JONATHAN DAVID, autograph dealer, pop culture historian; b. Grasmere, N.H., July 23, 1948; s. David Nisbet and Natalie Mary (Chandler) A.; m. Barbara Lauderbach, 1966 (div.); 1 child, Jonathan David II; m. Nancy Page, 1982. BA magna cum laude, U. N.H., 1972. Registered dealer. Bookseller, book buyer, columnist, book reviewer, freelance writer, 1972-81; co-owner, pres. Elmer's Nostalgia, Inc., Sanford, Maine, 1981—. Author: The Rock Trivia Book, 1976; columnist; mem. adv. bd. Autograph Collector Mag., 1986-92. N.H. chmn. Nat. Com. to Reopen the Rosenberg Case, 1973-77; vol. York County Shelters, Alfred, Maine, 1993—. Served with USNR, 1966-67. Mem. ACLU, NAACP, Ams. United for Separation Ch. and State, Universal Autograph Collectors Club (Outstanding Autograph Dealer award 1998), Am. Polit. Items Collectors, Maine People's Alliance, Planned Parenthood, People for the Am. Way, So. Poverty Law Ctr., Amnesty Internat., McFarlane Clan Soc., Phi Beta Kappa. Mem. Green Party of Maine. Avocations: collecting autographs and historical ephemera, painting, gardening, doing historical research. Office: Elmer's Nostalgia Inc 3 Putnam St Sanford ME 04073-2024 E-mail: jon@elmers.net.

ALLAN, LARRY See BOERSMA, LAWRENCE

ALLAN, LIONEL MANNING, lawyer; b. Detroit, Aug. 3, 1943; AB cum laude, U. Mich., 1965; JD, Stanford U., 1968; student, U. Paris. Bar: Calif. 1969, U.S. Supreme Ct. 1972. Law clk. U.S. Dist. Ct. (no. dist.) Calif., 1969—70; pres. Allan Advisors, Inc., bd. governance and legal cons. firm. Spkr. and writer in field of corp. law; sec. adv. com. San Jose Fed. Ct., 1969-85; mem. bd. visitors Stanford Law Sch., 1985-88; mem. com. comml. code State Bar Calif., 1974-77, corps. com., 1983-86. Co-author: How to Structure the Classic Venture Capital Deal, 1983, Equity Incentives for Start-up Companies, 1985, Master Limited Partnerships, 1987. Bd. dirs. San Jose Mus. Art, 1983-87; trustee KTEH-TV Channel 54 Found., 1987—; dir. NCCJ, 1995-2001, Harker Sch., 1998—. Served to capt. JAGC, USAR, 1968-74. Mem. ABA (com. on small bus. 1980—, chmn. internat. bus. subcom. 1985-88, chmn. small bus. com. 1989-93), Santa Clara Bar Assn. (chmn. fed. ct. sect. 1971, 77), Internat. Bar Assn., San Jose C. of C. (dir.), Pi Sigma Alpha, Phi Sigma Iota, Phi Delta Phi. Office: Allan Advisors Inc 18222 Seebree Ln Monte Sereno CA 95030-3135 E-mail: lon@lonallan.com.

ALLAN, RICHMOND FREDERICK, lawyer; b. Billings, Mont., Apr. 22, 1930; s. Roy F. and Edith (Prater) A.; m. Dorothy Frost, Aug. 9, 1954; children: Richmond P., David F., Michael R. BA, U. Mont., 1954, JD, 1957; postgrad., London Sch. of Econs., 1957-58. Bar: Mont. 1957, U.S. Supreme Ct. 1961, D.C. 1965. Law clk. U.S. Ct. Appeals (9th cir.), San Francisco, 1958-59; ptnr. Kurth, Conner, Jones & Allan, Billings, 1959-61; chief asst. U.S. atty. U.S. Dept. of Justice, Billings, 1961-64; assoc. solicitor U.S. Dept. of Interior, Washington, 1965-67, dep. solicitor, 1968-69; ptnr. Weissbrodt & Weissbrodt, Washington, 1969-77, Casey, Lane & Mittendorf, Washington, 1977-78, Duncan, Weinberg, Miller & Pembroke, P.C., Washington, 1979—. Fulbright Commn. scholar, 1957. Mem. Fed. Bar Assn. (pres. Mont. chpt. 1963-65). Avocation: trap and skeet shooting. Office: Duncan Weinberg Genzer & Pembroke PC 1615 M St NW Ste 800 Washington DC 20036-3219 E-mail: rfa@dwgp.com.

ALLAN, RONALD GAGE, university research coordinator; b. Cin., May 9, 1941; s. Robert Gage Allan, William Herbert (Stepfather) and Gladys (Mosier) Anderson; life ptnr. Miriam Scholar Clinton. BS in Indsl. Mgmt., U. Cin., 1966, MBA, 1968; PhD, George Washington U., 1977; MS in Taxation, Georgetown U., 1993. Rsch. economist U.S. Dept. Commerce, Bur. Econ. Analysis, Washington, 1972-79; tax analyst Congl. Budget Office, Washington, 1979-81; planning dir. and analyst Vanguard Techs., Fairfax, Va., 1982-88; rsch. coord. Georgetown U., Washington, 1988—. Mem. rsch. com. Nat. Assn. Student Fin. Aid Adminstrs. Contbr. articles to profl. jours. Mem. Nat. Economists Club, Data Warehousing Inst., Am. Taxation Assn., Assn. Instnl. Rsch., Omicron Delta Epsilon. Episcopalian. Home: Apt 406 7401 Eastmoreland Rd Annandale VA 22003 Office: Georgetown U Office of Student Fin Svcs Washington DC 20057 E-mail: allanr@georgetown.edu.

ALLAN, SHER L. lawyer, mediator; b. Phoenix, Sept. 22, 1964; d. Earl Rodney Allan Jr. and Janice M. (Rollins) Norton. AA, Gulf Coast C.C., 1982; BS, Fla. State U., 1987, JD, 1989. Bar: Fla. 1990, U.S. Dist. Ct. (no. dist.) Fla. 1995; cert. family law mediator. Asst. state's atty. State's Atty. Office, Quincy, Fla., 1989-92; pvt. practice Panama City, 1992-93; assoc. Law Offices of Charles S. Isler & Assocs., P.A., Panama City, 1993-97; pvt. practice Panama City. Contbr. articles to profl. pubs. Mem. ABA, Fla. Bar Assn., Bay County Bar Assn. (pro bono svc. award 1995), Exch. Club of Panama City (pres.). Avocations: jogging, travel, crafts, needlework. Office: 731 Oak Ave Panama City FL 32401-2560

ALLAN, WALTER ROBERT, lawyer; b. Detroit, Aug. 1, 1937; s. Walter Francis and Henrietta (Fairchild) A. AB, U. Mich., 1959, JD, 1962. Bar: Calif. 1964, U.S. Ct. Appeals (9th Cir.) 1964, U.S. Supreme Ct. 1972, U.S. Ct. Appeals (D.C. cir.) 1973, U.S. Ct. Appeals (5th cir.) 1977, U.S. Ct. Appeals (3d cir.) 1988. From assoc. to ptnr. Pillsbury, Madison & Sutro, San Francisco, 1963—98; sole practitioner Tiburon, Calif., 1998—. Office: PO Box 771 Belvedere Tiburon CA 94920-0771

ALLARD, DAVID HENRY, judge; b. Snohomish, Wash., Jan. 10, 1929; s. Clayton Frederick and Ruth Elizabeth (Winston) A.; m. Hildred McClelland, June 19, 2003; children from previous marriage: John M., Clayton Frederick II. AB, Whitman Coll., 1951; LL.B., Duke U., 1956. Bar: Wash. 1957, U.S. Supreme Ct. 1965. Mem. staff ICC, Washington, 1958-67, adminstrv. law judge, 1967-72, 73-80, Office Hearings and Appeals, Social Security Adminstrn., 1986—; chief adminstrv. law judge ICC, 1980-86; adminstrv. chief law judge HHS, Tucson, 1986-92; regional chief adminstrv. law judge SSA, Boston, 1992-97; adminstrv. law judge FTC, 1972-73. Law reporter Presdl. Task Force on Career Advancement, 1967; mem. comml. panel Am. Arbitration Assn. Law reporter Presdl. Task Force on Career Advancement, 1967; mem. comml. panel Am. Arbitration Assn.; spl. master U.S. Ct. Appeals (1st cir.), 1992. Served with AUS, 1951-53. Mem. ABA (Achievement award young lawyers sect. 1965), Fed. Bar Assn. (editor-in-chief jour. 1972, pres. 1974, chmn. edn. bd. 1976-82), Fed. Adminstrv. Law Judges Conf., Delta Tau Delta. Presbyterian. Home: 4275 Owens Rd # 514 Evans GA 30809 E-mail: dhallard@aol.com.

ALLARD, DEAN CONRAD, historian, retired naval history center director; b. Kansas City, Mo., Oct. 19, 1933; s. Dean Conrad Sr. and Elizabeth Donaldson (Graves) A.; m. Constance Lynne Morgan, June 17, 1955; children: Scott, Hunt, Elizabeth. AB, Dartmouth Coll., 1955; MA, Georgetown U., 1959; PhD, George Washington U., 1967. Head Naval Operational Archives, Washington, 1958-82; sr. historian Naval Hist. Ctr., Washington, 1982-89; dir. naval history USN, Washington, 1989-95. Adj. prof. George Washington U., 1979-89, v.p. Internat. Commn. Mil. History, 2000—. Author: The United States Navy and the Vietnam Conflict, Vol. I, 1976, Spencer Fullerton Baird: A Study in the History of American Science, 1978; also articles on naval and maritime history; editor: U.S. Naval History Sources in the United States, 1979. Chmn. Hist. Commn., Arlington, Va., 1978-80; pres. Arlington Hist. Soc., 1974-75; mem. coun. Woodlawn Plantation, Fairfax, Va., 1976-84; mem. French-U.S. Sci. Com. on CSS, Ala., 1991-95. Lt. (j.g.) USN, 1955-58. Recipient Superior Civil Svc. award U.S. Govt., 1995, Samuel Eliot Morison award for Disting. Svc., USS Constn. Mus. Found., Boston, 1995. Mem.: Internat. Commn. Mil. History (v.p. 2000—), Internat. Commn. Maritime History (mem. exec. coun. 1990—), U.S. Commn. Mil. History (pres. 1995—99), World War II Studies Assn. (bd. dirs.), Soc. for Mil. History (v.p. 1983—86), N.Am. Soc. for Oceanic History (pres. 1985—89), Cosmos Club (Washington), Phi Beta Kappa. Avocations: gardening, hiking. Home: 2701 N Quincy St Arlington VA 22207-5046 E-mail: allard@prodigy.net.

ALLARD, JUDITH LOUISE, secondary education educator; b. Rutland, Vt., Feb. 21, 1945; d. William Edward and Orilla Marion (Trombley) A. BA, U. Vt., 1967, MS, 1969. Nat. bd. cert. tchr. in adolescent and young adulthood sci., 1999. Tchr. math., sci. Edmunds Jr. H.S., Burlington, Vt., 1969-73, biology tchr., 1973-78, sci. dept. chair, 1975-78; biology tchr. Burlington (Vt.) H.S., 1978—; instr. edn. St. Michaels Coll., Winooski, Vt., 2001—02; lectr. U. Vt., 2003—. Bd. dirs. Vt. Creative Imagination, Inc.; instr. environ. studies U. Vt., Burlington, 1988-89, lectr. Edn. U. of Vt., 2002—; adviser Nat. Honor Soc., 1986—. Co-author Favorite Labs of Outstanding Tchrs., 1991. Active Amnesty Internat., 1985—; mem. Lake Champlain Com., Burlington, 1987—, Vt. Goals 2000 Panel, 1995—99, Vt. State Licensing Commn., 1995—96, Vt. Stds. Bd. for Profl. Educators, 1996—2002, co-vice chair, 2000—01, chmn., 2001—02; state bd. dirs. Odyssey of the Mind, 1986—98. Named Outstanding Vt. Educator, U. Vt., 1983, Outstanding Vt. Sci. Tchr., Sigma Xi Soc., 1984, Vt. Tchr. Yr., 1998, Outstanding Vt. Sci. Tchr., Vt. Acad. Sci. and Engring., 2000, Tandy Tech. scholar, 1990, Genentech Access Excellence fellow, 1995, 1996, Access Excellence Retro fellow, 1996, Tchr. of Yr., Biol. Scis. Curriculum Study, 2001; recipient Presdl. Sci. Tchg. award, NSF, 1983, Tech. award, Tandy, 1998, Siemens award for Advanced Placement, 2000. Mem. NEA (bd. dirs. Vt. chpt., 1990-98), Vt. Sci. Tchrs. Assn. (bd. dirs. 1980-92, treas. 1985-92), Burlington Profl. Stds. Bd. (chair 1991-2001), Parents and Friends of Edn. (trustee), Nat. Assn. Biology Tchrs. (dir. Vt. Outstanding Biology Tchr. award program 1977—, Outstanding Biology Tchr. award 1975), Assn. Presdl. Awardees in Sci., Phi Delta Kappa. Roman Catholic. Avocations: needlework, fishing, music. Home: 221 Woodlawn Rd Burlington VT 05401-5722

ALLARD, MICHAEL ALAN, music educator, conductor; b. Waynesboro, Pa., Dec. 6, 1953; s. Nicholas Leo and Lillian Lee Allard; m. Barbara Diane Mazzotta, Aug. 29, 1976; children: Allison, Kristen. BA, Colgate U., 1976, M of Music Edn., Fla. State U., 1978; PhD, U. Tex., 1992. Orch. tchr. Washoe County Sch. Dist., Reno, 1977—79; orch. coord. Clark County Sch. Dist., Las Vegas, 1979—87; asst. instr. U. Tex., Austin, 1987—88; orch. dir. Punahou Sch., Honolulu, 1988—91; orch. condr., assoc. prof. U. Pacific, Stockton, Calif., 1991—2000; orch. tchr. Porterville Unified Sch. Dist., Calif., 2000—; adj. prof. Porterville Coll., 2000—; orch. condr. Ctrl. Valley Youth Symphony, Stockton, 1993—2000; nat. music edn. clinician The Selmer Co., Elkhart, Ind., 1978—. Musician (condr.): (performances) Carnegie Hall, Sydney Opera House. Recipient Robert G. Ingram Music Prize, Colgate U., 1976. Mem.: Am. Fedn. of Musicians, Music Educators Nat. Conf., Am. String Tchr. Assn. (pres. Calif. 1999—2000), Phi Kappa Lambda, Mu Phi Epsilon (U. Pacific chpt. adv. 1991—99).

ALLARD, NICHOLAS W. lawyer; b. Suffern, N.Y., Oct. 4, 1952; BA with honors, Princeton U., 1974; MA, Oxford U., 1976; JD, Yale U., 1979. Bar: N.Y. 1981, D.C. 1981. Law clk. to chief U.S. dist. judge Robert F. Peckham, San Francisco; law clk. to U.S. cir. judge Patricia M. Wald Washington; chair govt. rels. practice group Latham & Watkins, ptnr. Mem. minority staff counsel, prin. legal counsel to Sen. Edward Kennedy, Senate Com. on Judiciary, 1983-86; liaison Nat. Assn. State Attys. Gen.; adminstrv. asst., chief of staff to Sen. Patrick Moynihan, 1986-87; spkr. on health and comms. issues. Mem. editl. bd.; contbr. Spectrum, Pvt. Cable and Wireless Cable Mag., others; contbr. articles to profl. jours. Rhodes scholar Oxford U., 1976. Office: Latham & Watkins Ste 1300 1001 Pennsylvania Ave NW Washington DC 20004-2585*

ALLARD, ROBERT WAYNE, geneticist, educator; b. L.A., Sept. 3, 1919; s. Glenn A. and Alma A. (Roose) A.; m. Ann Catherine Wilson, June 16, 1944; children: Susan, Thomas (dec.), Jane, Gillian, Stacie. BS, U. Calif., Davis, 1941; PhD, U. Wis., 1946; ScD (hon.), U. Helsinki, 1996, U. Léon, 1997. From asst. to assoc. prof. U. Calif., Davis, 1946—, prof. genetics, 1955—. Author books; contbr. articles to profl. jours. Served to lt. USNR. Recipient Crop Sci. award Am. Soc. Agronomy, 1964, DeKalb Disting. Career award Crop Sci. Soc. Am., 1983; Guggenheim fellow, 1954, 60; Fulbright fellow, 1955 Mem. Nat. Acad. Scis., Am. Acad. Arts and Scis., Am. Soc. Naturalists (pres. 1974-75), Genetics Soc. Am. (pres. 1983-84), Am. Genetics Assn. (pres. 1989), Phi Beta Kappa, Sigma Xi, Alpha Gamma Rho, Alpha Zeta. Democrat. Unitarian Universalist. Home: Davis, Calif. Died Mar. 25, 2003.

ALLARD, WAYNE (A. WAYNE ALLARD), senator, veterinarian; b. Dec. 12, 1943; m. Joan Malcolm, Mar. 23, 1967; children: Christie, Cheryl. DVM, Colo. State U., 1968. Veterinarian Allard Animal Hosp.; mem. Colo. State Senate, 1983-90, U.S. Ho. Reps., Washington, 1991-96; U.S. senator from Colo., 1996—. Chmn. health, environment and instn. com., chmn. senate majority caucus; mem. 102nd-104th Congresses from 4th dist., Colo., 1991-96; mem. agrl. com., 1991-92, 93-94, 95-96, mem. small bus. com., 1991-92, mem. interior and insular affairs com., 1991-92, mem. com. on coms., 1991-92, 93-94, mem. budget com., 1993-94, 95-96, mem. natural resources com., 1993-94, 95-96, mem. joint com. on reorganization of Congress, 1993-94, 95-96, chmn. subcom. of agr. conservation, forest and water, 1995-96; senator 105th Congress, 1997—, mem. banking, urban affairs com., 1997—, environment and pub. works com., 1997—, intelligence select com., 1997—, Senate armed svcs. com., banking, housing and urban affairs com., select com. on intelligence; mem. select com. on intelligence, armed svcs. com., chmn. pers. subcom., banking, housing and urban affairs com., chmn. subcom. on housing and transp. 106th Congress; health officer, Loveland, Colo.; mem. regional adv. coun. on vet. medicine Western Interstate Commn. Higher Edn.; mem. Colo. Low-Level Radioactive Waste Adv. Com. Chmn. United Way; active 4-H Found. Mem. AVMA, Colo. Vet. Medicine Assn., Larimer County Vet. Medicine Assn. (past pres.), Bd. Vet. Practitioners (charter mem.), Am. Animal Hosp. Assn., Nat. Conf. State Legislatures (vice-chmn. human resources com. 1987—, healthcare cost containment com.), Loveland C. of C., Republican. Methodist. Home: PO Box 2405 Loveland CO 80539-2405 Office: US Senate 525 Dirksen Senate Office Bldg Washington DC 20510-0001*

ALLARD, WILLIAM ALBERT, photographer; b. Mnpls., Minn., 1937; Staff photographer Nat. Geo., Wash., DC, 1964—67; freelance, 1967—96; staff photographer Nat. Geo., Wash., DC, 1996—. Contbd. 25 mag. articles Nat. Geo., Wash., DC. Author: (book) Vanishing Breed, The Photographic Essay, A Time We Knew, Time at the Lake: A Minnesota Album. Recipient Meml. Award Winner, NPPA Joseph A. Sprague, 2002. Portraits of Am. features 165 of Allard's finest photographs, many of which have never been published before and are presented in chronological order, with incisive introductions to ea. section. Office: National Geographic Staff photographer 1145 17th St NW Washington DC 20036-4688*

ALLAWAY, WILLIAM HARRIS, retired university official; b. Oak Park, Ill., Mar. 31, 1924; s. William Horsford and Helen Margaret (Harris) A.; m. Olivia Woodhull Foster, June 28, 1952; children: William Harris Jr., Ben Foster, Eve Olivia. BS, U. Ill., 1949; postgrad., U. Grenoble, France, 1950-51; MA, U. Ill., 1951; EdD, U. Denver, 1957. Traveling sec. World Student Svc. Fund, 1947-48; spl. asst. to chmn. U.S. Nat. Commn. for UNESCO, 1949; asst. to field dir. World U. Svc. attached to Internat. Refugee Orgn., Salzburg, Austria, 1951; field rep. Inst.of Internat. Edn., Chgo. and Denver, 1952-54; gen. sec. U. Kans. YMCA, 1954-57; asst. dean of men and dir. Wilbur Hall Stanford (Calif.) U., 1957-61; dir. edn. abroad program U. Calif., Santa Barbara, 1961-89, spl. asst. to chancellor, 1990-93. Cons. and lectr. in field; mem. edni. assoc. adv. com. Inst. Internat. Edn., 1984-87; mem. Pres.'s Coun. for Internat. Youth Exch., 1982-85; mem. U.S. Del. to conf. on ednl. exch. between U.S. and U.K., 1970, 1974. Co-chair Peace and Justice Com., Goleta Presbyn. Ch., 1991-2000, mem. Nuclear Age Peace Found., Santa Barbara, Internat. Peace Rsch. Assn., Yellow Springs, Ohio; mem. Coun. on Internat. Ednl. Exch., 1961—, chmn. bd. dirs. 1978-83; past bd. dirs., hon. trustee Am. Ctr. for Students and Artists, Paris; bd. advisors Hariri Found., 1987—; exec. sec. Internat. Com. for Study of Edn. Exch., 1970-95, exec. com. Inter-Univ. Ctr. Postgrad. Studies, Dubrovnik, 1988-96, bd. dirs., 1996—; del. Hague Appeal for Peace, 1999; chair PAX 2100 Found., PAX 2100 Forum. With USAAF, 1943-46. Hon. DHC, U. Sussex, Eng., 1992; PhD h.c. U. Bergen, Norway, 1990; DHC, U. Bordeaux, France, 1988; Hon. Dr. of U. of Stirling, Scotland, 1981; recipient Scroll of Appreciation Leningrad State U., 1989, Award for Svc. to Internat. Ednl. Exch. Council on Internat. Ednl. Exch., 1989, Silver medal U. Lund, Sweden, 1990, Alumni Achievement award Coll. Liberal Arts and Sci. Alumni Assn. U. Ill., 1990, Gold Medal of Honor of the Complutense U. of Madrid, Spain, 1991. Mem. NAFSA Assn. Internat. Educators (hon. life mem.), Internat. Assn. Univs. (dep. mem., adminstrv. bd. 1995-2000, chair task force on internationalization of higher edn.), La Cumbre Country Club. Democrat. Presbyterian. Avocations: golf, skiing, choir, reading. Home: 2661 Tallant Rd C-871 Santa Barbara CA 93105 Fax: 805-687-5779. E-mail: boallaway@aol.com.

ALLBAUGH, JOE M. federal agency administrator; m. Diane Allbaugh; 3 children. BA Polit. Sci., Okla. State U. Deputy sec. Okla. Dept. Transp.; chief staff Gov. Bus.; dir. FEMA, Washington, 2001—02. Campaign mgr. Bush for Gov., Tex., Bush-Cheney, 2000. Republican.

ALLBEE, SANDRA MOLL, real estate broker; b. Reading, Pa., July 15, 1947; d. Charles Lewars and Isabel May (Ackerman) Frederici; m. Thomas J. Allbee, Oct. 18, 1975 (div. 1987). Exec. sec. Hamburg (Pa.) State Sch. and Hosp., 1965-73; regional mgr. Am. Bus. Service Corp., Newport Beach, Calif., 1973-78; v.p. T.A.S.A., Inc., Long Beach, Calif., 1978-86; realtor Very Important Properties, Inc., Rolling Hills Estates, Calif., 1986-90, Re/Max Palos Verdes Realty, Rolling Hills Estates, Calif., 1990—. Bd. dirs., v.p. Nat. Coun. on Alcoholism, Torrance, Calif., 1987-96; pres. Rollingwood Homeowners Assn., Rolling Hills Estates, Calif., 1985-92. Recipient 100% Club award. Mem. Palos Verdes Rep. Women's Club (bd. dirs. 1989-94). Office: Re/Max Palos Verdes Realty 4030 Palos Verdes Dr N Ste 104 Rolling Hills Estates CA 90274 E-mail: sallbee@remaxpv.com.

ALLBRIGHT, KARAN ELIZABETH, psychologist, consultant; b. Oklahoma City, Jan. 28, 1948; d. Jack Gahnal and Irma Lolene (Keesee) Allbright. BA, Oklahoma City U., 1970, MAT, 1972; PhD, U. So. Miss., 1981. Cert. sch. psychologist, psychometrist; lic. psychologist, Okla., Ark. Psychol. technician Donald J. Bertoch, PhD, Okla. City, 1973-76; asst. adminstr. Parents' Assistance Ctr., Okla. City, 1976-77; psychology intern Burwell Psycho-ednl. Ctr., Carrollton, Ga., 1980-81; staff psychologist Griffin Area Psychoednl. Ctr., Ga., 1981-85; clinic dir. Sequoyah County Guidance Clinic, Sallisaw, Okla., 1985-88; psychologist Baker Psychiat. Clinic, Ft. Smith, Ark., 1988-90; cons. Harbor View Mercy Hosp., 1988-90, Integris Bethany Med. Ctr., 1992-99; pvt. practice Okla. City, 1990—, Mercy Health Ctr., 1996—. Cons. Family Alliance (parents Anonymous) Sequoyah County, 1985-88; lectr. various orgns.; bd. dir. workshops. Mem. Task Force to Prevent Child Abuse, Fayette County, Ga., 1984-85, Task Force on Family Violence, Spalding County, Ga., 1983-85; assoc. bd. dir. Lyric Theatre. Named to Outstanding Young Women in Am., 1980. Mem. APA, Southeastern Psychol. Assn., Nat. Assn. Sch. Psychologists (cert. sch. psychologist), Okla. Psychol. Assn. Nat. Register Health Svc. Providers in Psychology, Okla. City Orchestra League, Psi Chi, Delta Zeta (chpt. dir. 1970-72). Democrat. Presbyterian. Home: 3941 NW 44th St Oklahoma City OK 73112-2517 Office: Northwest Mental Health Assocs 3832 N Meridian Ave Oklahoma City OK 73112-2849

ALLBRITTON, CLIFF, personal and organizational consultant; b. Aransas Pass, Tex., Aug. 19, 1931; BS, Okla. State U.; MDiv, Southwestern Sem.; MA, Baylor U.; PhD, Columbia Pacific U., 1994. Editor family ministry dept. Lifeway Christian Resources, Nashville, 1979-91; pres. Cliff Allbritton Rsch. Ctr., Nashville, 1991-96. V.p. Corp. Pers. Cons., Dallas, 1972-79; acct. exec. Beaver Assocs. Advt., Akron, Ohio, 1971-72. Author: How to Get Married and Stay That Way, 1982, Dare to Win-How to Live the American Dream, 1992, Personal Riches for Today's Singles, 1992, The Psychology of Grace, 1994; co-author: Solo Flight, 1981, Single Adult Ministry in Your Church, 1985. Min. 8 congregations, Tex., N.Mex., Ohio, Va., 1954-71. Named Internat. Man of Yr. by Internat. Biographical Ctr., Cambridge, Eng., 1992; recipient Presdl. Legion of Merit, 2003. Mem. Am. Assn. Christian Counselors, Am. Assn. Family Counselors, Internat. Platform Assn., Omicron Delta Kappa, Alpha Zeta, Kappa Tau Pi. Home: 865 Bellevue Rd U21 Nashville TN 37221-2794

ALLBRITTON, JOE LEWIS, diversified holding company executive; b. D'Lo, Miss., Dec. 29, 1924; s. Lewis A. and Ada (Carpenter) A.; m. Barbara Jean Balfanz, Feb. 23, 1967; 1 son, Robert Lewis. LLB, Baylor U., 1949, LLD (hon.), 1964, JD, 1969; LHD, Calif. Bapt. Coll., 1973. Bar: Tex. 1949. Dir. Perpetual Corp., Houston, 1958—, pres., 1965-76, 78-81, chmn. bd., 1973—. Chmn. Allbritton Comm. Co., 1974-98, chmn. exec. com., 1998—; chmn. Univ. Bancshares, Inc., Houston, 1975-97, Houston Fin. Svcs., Ltd., London, 1977—2003, Riggs Nat. Corp., Washington, 1981-2001, sr. chmn., 2001—; chmn. Riggs Bank, N.A., Washington, 1983-2001; dep. chmn. Riggs Bank Europe Ltd., London, 1986-92, chmn., 1992-2001; mem. Greater Washington Bd. Trade, 1983-88, 92—; trustee The Mitre Corp., Bedford, Mass., 1987-93. Trustee Fed. City Coun., Washington, 1975—, John F. Kennedy Ctr. for Performing Arts, Washington, 1985-90, Nat. Geog. Soc., 1986-99, trustee emeritus, 1999—; trustee The Ronald Reagan Presdl. Found., L.A., 1990—, George Bush Presdl. Found., College Station, Tex., 1993—; bd. dirs. Nat. Fund for U.S. Bot. Garden, 1992-95, The Lyndon Baines Johnson Found., 1989-2001, Georgetown U., Washington, 1990-96. With USN, 1943-46. Mem.: Bankers Roundtable, State Bar Tex.

ALLCHIN, JIM, information technology executive; Student, U. Fla., Stanford U., Ga. Inst. Tech.; D in Computer Sci. Prin. arch. Banyan Systems Inc.; with Microsoft, Redmond, Wash., 1990, v.p. Platform Group. Mem. Sr. Leadership Team, Bus. Leadership Team, Microsoft. Office: Microsoft One Microsoft Way Redmond WA 98052-6399

ALLCOCK, HARRY R. chemistry educator; b. Loughborough, Eng., Apr. 8, 1932; naturalized U.S. citizen; s. Claud Leonard and Nora (Clarke) A.; m. Noreen Raworth, Nov. 14, 1959. BSc, U. London, 1953, PhD, 1956. Cert. chemist. Postdoctoral fellow Purdue U., West Lafayette, Ind., 1956-58, Can. Nat. Rsch. Coun., Ottawa, Ont., 1958-60; rsch. scientist Cen. Rsch. Labs. Am. Cyanamid Co., Stamford, Conn., 1961-66; assoc. prof. chem. Pa. State U., University Park, 1966-70, prof. chem., 1970-85, Evan Pugh Prof. Chem., 1985—. Author: (books) Heteroatom Ring Systems and Polymers, 1967, Phosphorus-Nitrogen Compounds, 1972, (monograph) Chemistry and Applications of Polyphosphazenes, 2003; author: (with F.W. Lampe) (books) Contemporary Polymer Chemistry, 1981; author: (with F.W. Lampe and J.E. Mark), 2003; author: (with M. Zeldin & K.J. Wynne) Inorganic and Organometallic Polymers, 1988; author: (with P. Wisian-Neilson and K.J. Wynne) Inorganic and Organometallic Polymers II, 1994, editor Inorganic Syntheses Vol. XXV, (jours.) Phosphorous, 1973—77, Macromolecules, 1974—79, Chem. Revs., 1974—79, Biomaterials, 1980—82, Jour. of Polymer Sci., 1987—, Inorganic Chem., 1988—91, Chem. of Materials, 1988—, Heteroatom Chem., 1988—93, Jour. Inorganic and Organometallic Polymers, 1990—. Guggenheim fellow 1986-87. Fellow Am. Inst. Chemists (Chem. Pioneer award 1989); mem. Am. Chem. Soc. (nat. award polymer chemistry 1984, nat. award chemistry of materials 1992, Herman Mark award polymer chemistry 1994), Royal Soc. Chemistry (various coms.), Corp. Inorganic Syntheses. Office: Pa State U Dept Chemistry 152 Davey Lab University Park PA 16802-6300

ALLCORN, TERRY ALAN, principal, educator; b. Springfield, Mo., Dec. 7, 1952; s. Calbert and Bonnie Lee (Taylor) A.; m. Rhonda Gay Martens, May 24, 1974; children: Eric Alan, Nathan Scott. ThG, Bapt. Bible Coll., 1974, BS, 1977; MA, S.W. Mo. State U., 1980. Assoc. pastor Prairie Garden Bapt. Ch., Houston, 1974-76; purchasing agt. Fed. Enterprises, Inc., Nixa, Mo., 1976-80; prin. Christian Schs. of Springfield, 1980-85, 89—; pastor Mt. Calvary Bapt. Ch., Richmond, Mo., 1985-89. Tchr. Pisgah Christian Sch., Excelsior Springs, Mo., 1987-88, adminstr., 1988-89; prof. U.S. history Bapt. Bible Coll., Springfield, 1990—. Mem. Police Pers. Bd., Richmond, 1987-89; election judge Ray County, Richmond, 1985-89; dep. registrar Greene County Clk., Springfield, 1983-85, 89—; deacon Bapt. Temple, 1977-80; bd. dirs. Tri-State Christian Conf., 1998—. Mem. Mo. Assn. Christian Schs., Mo. Christian Schs. Athletic Assn. (bd. dirs. 1996—), Northside Springfield Betterment Assn. (bd. dirs. 2000). Avocations: softball, golf. Home: PO Box 8464 Springfield MO 65801-8464 Office: Christian Schs Springfield 739 W Talmage St Springfield MO 65803-1117 E-mail: allcorn@cnonline.com.

ALLDAY, MARTIN LEWIS, lawyer; b. El Dorado, Ark., May 30, 1926; s. Martin L. Sr. and Bess (Kavanaugh) A.; m. Patricia Pryor, May 1, 1954; children: Katherine, Elizabeth, Martin III. JD, U. Tex., Austin, 1951. Bar: Tex. 1951. Examiner oil and gas div. R.R. Commn. of Tex., Austin, 1951-53; legal dept. Superior Oil Co., Midland, Tex., 1953-57, Houston, 1957-59; ptnr. Lynch, Chappell, Allday and Alsup, Midland, Austin & Dallas, 1959-89; past solicitor Dept. of Interior, Washington, 1989; chmn. Fed. Energy Regulatory Commn., Washington, 1989-93; of counsel Scott, Douglass and McConnico, Austin, Dallas, Tex., 1993—. Past pres. Midland Jaycees, C. of C., Indsl. Found.; past trustee, gov. Midland Meml. Hosp.; bd. trustees Petroleum Mus. Hall of Fame; presiding officer Tex. State Cemetery Commn. With Inf. U.S. Army, 1944-46. Decorated Purple Heart, Bronze Star, Combat Infantry badge. Mem. ABA, Tex. Bar Assn. (chmn. oil, gas and mineral sect. 1970), Tex. Bar Found., Midland County Bar Assn. (pres. 1972-73), Midland Country Club (pres.), Petroleum Club (bd. dirs.). Republican. Episcopalian. Avocations: fishing, hunting, golf. Office: 600 Congress Ave Ste 1500 Austin TX 78701-2976 E-mail: mallday@scottdoug.com.

ALLDREDGE, LEROY ROMNEY, retired geophysicist; b. Mesa, Ariz., Feb. 6, 1917; s. Leo and Ida (Romney) A.; m. Larita Williams, Dec. 27, 1940; children— Carol, David Leroy, Joseph Leo, Gary Dean, Mark Evans, Janice, Luann. BS, U. Ariz., 1939, MS, 1940; M.Sc. in Engring, Harvard, 1953; PhD, U. Md., 1955. Instr. physics U. Ariz., 1940-41; fed. radio insp. FCC, Los Angeles, also Washington, 1941-44; radio engr. dept. terrestrial magnetism Carnegie Inst. of Washington, 1944-45; chief electricity and magnetism div. Naval Ordnance Lab., White Oak, Md., 1945-55; analyst operations research office Johns Hopkins, 1955-59; research geophysicist Coast and Geodetic Survey, Dept. Commerce, Washington, 1959-66; acting dir. Inst. Earth Scis., Environmental Sci. Services Adminstrn., Boulder, Colo., 1966; dir. Earth Scis. Labs., 1967-69, Earth Sci. Lab. Nat. Oceanographic and Atmospheric Adminstrn., 1969-73; research geophysicist U.S. Geol. Survey, 1973-88; gen. sec., dir. central bur. Internat. Assn. Geomagnetism and Aeronomy, 1963-75. Asso. editor: Jour. Geophys. Research, 1966-69. Mem. Am. Geophys. Union (sect. on geomagnetism and aeronomy 1950-56, v.p. sect. 1956-59, pres. sect. 1959-61, chmn. Eastern meeting com. 1962-66), Sigma Xi, Phi Kappa Phi. Mem. Ch. of Jesus Christ of Latter-day Saints. Home and Office: 4475 Chippewa Dr Boulder CO 80303-3616 *Science and engineering are very precise. For a man to properly help with the orderly development in any area of science he must treat his data and report them with strict honesty. The same principle is even more valuable in ordinary daily contacts with his friends and acquaintances. A performance that includes half truths or deceit in any form will very likely lead to unhappiness.*

ALLDREDGE, WILLIAM T. metal products executive; BA, Mich. St. U., 1961, MBA, 1962. Pres., CEO Mirro Corp.; v.p., finance Newell Rubbermaid Inc., Freeport, Ill., 1983, CFO, pres. corp. devel., 2001—. Office: Newell Ctr 29 E Stephenson St Freeport IL 61032-0943*

ALLEE, NANCY JANE, reference librarian, library administrator; b. Greencastle, Ind. d. Walter L. and Peggy J. (Matlock) A. BA, DePauw U., 1985; MLS, Ind. U., 1986; MPH, U. Okla., 1994. Reference libr. Northeastern State U., Tahlequah, Okla., 1987-95; dir. Pub. Health Library U. Mich., 1995—. Presenter, writer, cons. in field; mem. leadership fellows program NLM/AAHSH, 2003—. Reviewer (video reviews) Video Rating Guide for Libraries, 1990-95. Actress Tahlequah Community Playhouse, 1988-95 (Best Actress 1988); bd. dirs. Arts Coun. Tahlequah, 1992-93; chmn. pub. health tng. subcom. Ptnrs. in Info. Access, 1998—. Recipient Univ. Libr. ACE award, 1997. Mem. ALA, APHA, MLA (pub. health/health adminstrn. sect. chmn. 1997-98), Acad. Health Info. Profls., Phi Beta Kappa, Phi Delta Kappa (sec. Tahlequah chpt. 1988-89, pres. 1989-90). Office: Sch Pub Health Libr U Mich Ann Arbor MI 48109

ALLEGO, DONNA M. English educator; b. Sewickley, Pa., June 6, 1945; d. Anthony B. and Virginia M. Allego. MA, U. Denver, 1971; MS in Edn., Western Ill. U., 1978; PhD, So. Ill. U., 1997. Instr. English Western Ill. U., Macomb, 1971-75, Cameron U., Lawton, Okla., 1975-76; tchg. asst. in English So. Ill. U., Carbondale, 1992-96; instr. dept. English La. State U., Baton Rouge, 1997-2001; asst. prof. English Adrian (Mich.) Coll., 2001—. Mem. Modernist Studies Assn. Avocations: collecting rocks, walking. Office: English Dept Adrian Coll Adrian MI 49221 E-mail: dallego@adrian.edu.

ALLEGRUCCI, DONALD LEE, state supreme court justice; b. Pittsburg, Kans., Sept. 19, 1936; s. Nello and Josephine Marie (Funaro) A.; m. Joyce Ann Thompson, Nov. 30, 1963; children: Scott David, Bowen Jay. AB, Pittsburg State U., 1959; JD, Washburn U., 1963. Bar: Kans. 1963. Asst. county atty. Butler County, El Dorado, Kans., 1963-67; state senator Kans. Legislature, Topeka, 1976-80; mem. Kans. Pub. Relations Bd., 1981-82; dist. judge Kans. 11th Jud. Dist., Pittsburg, 1982-87, adminstrv. judge, 1983-87; justice Kans. Supreme Ct., Topeka, 1987—. Instr. Pittsburg State U., 1969-72; exec. dir. Mid-Kans. Community Action Program, Inc. Mem. Dem. State Com., 1974-80; candidate 5th Congl. Dist., 1978; past pres. Heart Assn.; bd. dirs. YMCA. Served with USAF, 1959-60. Mem. Kans. Bar Assn. Democrat. Office: Kansas Supreme Court 374 Kansas Judicial Ctr 301 SW 10th Ave Fl 3 Topeka KS 66612-1507

ALLEMAN, KURT G. optometrist; b. Provo, Utah, Aug. 25, 1953; s. Glenn L. and Afton B. Alleman; m. Marie B. Alleman, June 21, 1973; children: Kori, Wade, Amanda, Matthew. BS, Brigham Young U., 1975; OD, So. Calif. Coll. Optometry, Fullerton, 1981. Mem. group practice Colon & Alleman, O.D., Ltd., Elko, Nev., 1981—. Bd. dirs. Nev. Vision Svc. Plan, Elko, 1983—86; Nev. com. Vision Svc. Plan Elko, 1986—99; bd. dirs. Nev. State Bd. Optometry, Elko, 1998—; bishop Ch. Jesus Christ of Latter-Day Saints, Elko, 1983—87, stake pres., 1994—. Named Optometrist of Yr. Nev. Optometric Assn., 1998. Mem. Rotary (pres. 1995-96). Republican. Avocation: hiking. Office: Colon & Alleman Ltd 1555 College Pkwy Elko NV 89801-5033

ALLEN, ALFRED WILLIAM, chemical engineer, consultant; b. Clinton, Mich., Oct. 25, 1924; s. Charles William and Marjorie Irene (Dorr) A.; m. Elva Mae Dickinson, Sept. 21, 1947; children: Paul William, Teresa Sue. BSChemE, U. Mich., 1946, MSChemE, 1947. Process devel. engr. GE Co., Richland, Wash., 1947-51; asst. project mgr., prodn. supr. Titanium Metals Corp. of Am., Henderson, Nev., 1951-56; project mgr. NL Industries, Inc., N.Y.C., 1956-67, asst. chief engr., 1967-74; project mgr. Foster Wheeler Corp., Livingston, N.J., 1974-84; mgr. projects SCM Chems., Balt., 1984-90; pres. AWA, Inc., Murray Hill, N.J., 1990-99; project mgmt. cons. New Providence, N.J., 1999—. Lt. (j.g.) USN, 1943-46. Mem. N.J. Group Small Chem. Bus., Assn. Cons. Chemist and Chem. Engrs. (v.p. 1995-97), Project Mgmt. Inst. Republican. Avocations: hunting, fishing, wood-working, traveling. E-mail: awallen@excite.com.

ALLEN, ALICE, communications and marketing executive; b. N.Y.C., May 31, 1943; d. C. Edmonds and Helen (McCreery) A.; 1 child, Helen. Student, Conn. Coll., 1961. Pres. Alice Allen, Inc., N.Y.C., 1970-83; sr. v.p. Robert Marston, N.Y.C., 1983-84, Cunningham & Walsh, N.Y.C., 1984-86, Carl Byoir (acquired by Hill & Knowlton), N.Y.C., 1986; sr. v.p., dir. comms. and corp. mktg. Hill & Knowlton, N.Y.C., 1986-88; pres., owner Allen Comms. Group, Inc., N.Y.C., 1988-95, Alice Allen Comms, 1995—. Bd. dirs. Family Dynamics, N.Y.C., 1976-78, Veritas, 1980-85; v.p. Jr. League, N.Y.C., 1975-76; mem. adv. bd. Enterprise Found., 1992-2001. Mem. Pub. Rels. Soc. Am., Pub. Publicity Assn. (pres. 1969-71), Women's Media Group, Comm. Network. Office: Alice Allen Comms 320 E 72nd St New York NY 10021-4769

ALLEN, ANNA J. chiropractor; b. Henderson, Ky., Apr. 6, 1955; d. Harold D. and Aiko (Nakashima) A. AS, U. Ky., 1973, BS, 1976; Dr.Chiropractic, Palmer U., 1980; postgrad., Pan Am. U., 1981, San Antonio Coll., 1983, Tex. Southmost Coll., 1981. Orthopedic qualified bd., 1991-93. Health instr. Nautilus, Davenport, Iowa, 1978-80; dir. chiropractic Harlington, Tex., 1980-81, Handley Chiropractic, San Antonio, Tex., 1982-83, NE Chiropractic Ctr., El Paso, Tex., 1983-84, Viscount Chiropractic, El Paso, 1984—. Mem. exec. com. Nat. Right to Life Com., 1986; active Found. for Chiropractic Edn. and Rsch., 1989—90, 1990—91, 1992—93; mem. Rep. Bus. Adv. Coun., 2002—03; del. Rep. Nat. Congl. Com., 2000; bd. dirs. Fellowship of Christian Athletes. Named Tex. Businessman of Yr., Rep. Congl. Com., 2002—03; recipient El Paso Comty. Health Fair citation, 1989, Presdl. Cert. Appreciation, 1989, Congl. Cert. Appreciation, 1991, Comty. Leaders Am. award, Tex. Young Rep. Bus. award, 2000, Congl. medal of honor, 2000. Mem.: NAFE, El Pasoans for Life, Tex. Chiropractic Assn., Am. Chiropractic Assn., Palmer Alumni Assn., Tex. Palmer Alumni Assn., Found. for Chiropractic Rsch., Found. for Chiropractic Rsch., Christian Chiropractic Assn., Chiropractic Orthopedist Assn., Nat. Fedn. Ind. Bus., Am. Bus. Woman's Assn., Fellowship of Christian Athletics (bd. dirs.). Avocations: scuba diving, weight lifting, skiing, missionary work, playing piano. Office: Viscount Chiropractic Health Ctr 8838 Viscount Blvd El Paso TX 79925-5822

ALLEN, ANNA MARIE, financial executive; b. Ft. Scott, Kans., Aug. 3, 1955; d. Harold Laverne and Dorothy Arlene Kirk; m. John Leroy Allen, Sept. 18, 1982. AA, Johnson County C.C., Overland Park, Kans., 1976; BSBA in Fin., Pittsburg (Kans.) State U., 1979; MBA in Internat. Bus., Ohio State U., 1995. CPA, Kans. Asst. teller supr. Kans. Nat. Bank & Trust, Prairie Village, 1975-77; bookkeeper Foodtown, Pittsburg, 1978-79; sr. v.p. tax GRA, Inc., Merriam, Kans., 1979-89; sr. cons. Grant Thornton, Wichita, Kans., 1989-91; mgr. fin. ops. Legent Corp., Columbus, Ohio, 1991-94; asst. treas. CompuServe Inc., Columbus, 1994-96; v.p. fin. North Am. Baking, Cin., 1997-99; CFO Baerlocher USA, Cin., 2000—01, Vestar, Inc., 2001—. Com. bd. Kansas City (Mo.) Ballet Guild, 1985-89, Cin. Ballet; past mem. Jr. League Kans. City, Columbus Jr. League; bd. dirs. Jr. League, Cin.; charter mem. Women's Resource Ctr., Johnson County bd. dirs., 1986-89. Mem. AICPA, AAUW (bd. dirs. Shawnee Mission, Kans chpt. 1979-89), Fin. Exec. Inst., Assn. Fin. Profls., Am. Legion Aux., Tri-Health Athletic Club, Phi Kappa Phi, Delta Mu Delta. Baptist. Avocations: running, tatting, the flute. Office: Vestar Inc PO Box 960 139 E 4th St Rm 100C Cincinnati OH 45201

ALLEN, ANNE NORGAARD, social worker; b. N.Y.C., Feb. 28, 1939; d. Rudolf and Mildred (Norgaard) Hirsch; m. Robert Allen, Mar. 25, 1963 (div. 1980); 1 child, Sean Allen; m. Robert H. Schwoebel, June 12, 1981. BA, Middlebury (Vt.) Coll., 1961; MSW, Bryn Mawr (Pa.) Coll., 1970. Diplomate in clin. social work; lic. social worker, Pa.; cert. clin. hypnosis. Caseworker Family Counseling Svc. Northampton County, Easton, Bethlehem, Pa., 1970-75; coord. clin. unit spl. project Phila. Child Guidance Clinic, 1976-80; supr. social svcs. Family Support Ctr., Yeadon, Pa., 1980-81; supr. br. office Family and Community Svc. Delaware County, Media, Pa., 1982-84; pvt. practice Media, 1984—. Mem.: NASW, Am. Soc. Clin. Hypnosis, Acad. Cert. Social Work. Avocations: travel, swimming, cooking, reading. Office: 16 W Front St Media PA 19063-3306

ALLEN, B. MARC, managed care executive; b. Balt. s. Ralph A. and Frona B. Allen; m. Judy E. Luray, Jan. 24, 1967; children: Lara Ann, Mason Luray. BA, U. Balt., 1967, JD, 1971. Mgr. med. affairs Md. Blue Cross, Balt., 1967-73; cons. Am. Health Systems, Boston, 1973-74; dir. field ops. Bay State PSRO, Boston, 1974-75; exec. dir. Essex Physicians' Rev. Orgn., South Orange, N.J., 1975; chmn., CEO Holden Health Sys., Randolph, NJ; ret., 2002. Cons. in field; guest lectr. health policy Rutgers U.; expert witness U.S. Senate Fin. Com., U.S. Select Com. on Aging. Contbr. articles to profl. jours. Active SSS, 1972-73, New Democratic Coalition, 1969-70; past pres. Temple B'nai Or, Morristown, N.J. Mem. Nat. Health Lawyers Assn., Am. Med. Peer Rev., Inc. (chmn. task force on impact). Office: PO Box 351 Mount Freedom NJ 07970-0351

ALLEN, BARBARA, state legislator; Atty.; mem. Kans. Ho. of Reps. from 21st dist., 1987-2000, Kans. Senate from 8th dist., Topeka, 2001—. Mem. appropriations com., fiscal oversight com., social svcs. budget com., chairperson tourism com. Kans. Ho. of Reps. Republican. Office: Kansas Senate State Capitol Topeka KS 66612 Home: 7427 Walmer St Overland Park KS 66204-2056 Home Fax: 913 384 5400; Office Fax: 913 498 8488. E-mail: allen@house.state.ks.us.*

ALLEN, BARBARA ANN, musician, educator, personnel contractor; b. Abilene, Tex., Apr. 18, 1956; d. Ira James Jr. and Doris Mae (Reid) A. MusB with spl. honors, U. Tex., 1979; MusM, So. Meth. U., 1984. Cert. elem. and secondary tchr., Tex. Orch. instr., condr. Richardson (Tex.) Ind. Sch. Dist., 1979-81; violinist, violist Ft. Worth Symphony Orch., 1979-81; condr. U. Tex. Summer String Inst., Dallas, 1980, 81; violinist, violist AIMS Symphony Orch., Graz, Austria, 1980—; violinist Innsbruck (Austria) Symphony and Opera Orch., 1981-82, Münchner Instrumental Ensemble, Munich, 1981-82; faculty, dir. Am. Inst. of Mus. Studies, Graz, 1982—; violinist Dallas Ballet Orch., 1984-87; violinist, tenured core mem. Dallas Opera Orch., 1986—. 2d violinist Eger Artist-In-Residence String Quartet, Graz, Austria, 1983-87; rec. artist Profl. Rec. Studios, Dallas, 1984—; 1st violinist Lone Star String Quartet, Dallas, 1985-90; instr. violin and viola Arapaho Music Studios, Dallas, 1985-90; founder Studio of Barbara Allen-Violin and Viola, 1988—, The Classic Strings Ensembles, Musical Entertainment Booking, 1990—;instrumental pers. contr.Wichita Falls Symphony Orch., 2000—. Author: Auditioning in Europe for the Instrumentalist-A Guide to Professionalism in Music, 1987, Musicians' Tax Records - An Organizational Guide, 1997. Assoc. concertmaster Wichita Falls Symphony Orch., 2000—. Scholar Meadows Found. Scholar, So. Meth. Univ., 1982—84. Mem. Am. Fedn. Musicians. Methodist. Avocations: creative arts, tennis, travel, swimming, gardening. Home and Office: 2514 Murt St Irving TX 75062-7182 E-mail: barbara@classicstrings.us.

ALLEN, BARBARA KIRKMAN, politcal organization administrator; b. Asheville, N.C., July 23, 1931; d. Walter Alfred and Georgia Esmerald (Lewallen) Kirkman; m. Luke C. Allen, Jr., Sept. 9, 1949; 1 child, Michael Kirkman. With, Carolina Power and Light Co., Raleigh, N.C., 1950-96, mgr. adminstrv. svcs., 1979. Bd. dirs. N.C. Women's Forum; bd. deacons New Hope Bapt. Ch., Raleigh; mem. J.J. Singers; mem. adv. bd. Wake County coun. Girl Scouts U.S.; mem. adv. council Women in Econ. Devel; chairperson Acad. Women, YWCA; bd. dirs. N.C. Cmty. Colls., Wake County Coll. Aging; bd. assocs. Meredith Coll.; bd. dirs. N.C. State U. Humanities Found.; mem. exec. bd. N.C. Equity Inc.; Dem. chmn., N.C., 1998—. Mem. N.C. Symphony Soc., Greater Raleigh C. of C. (mem. Mayor's com. of '85), Women of Raleigh (trustee). Office: NC Democratic Party 220 Hillsborough St Raleigh NC 27603-1724*

ALLEN, BARRY MORGAN, corporate communications consultant; b. N.Y.C., June 3, 1939; s. Robert Mitchell and Edna B. (Feldman) A.; m. Rena Susan Garfinkle, June 16, 1974 children: Linda Krasno Gicca, David Krasno. BS in Journalism, U. Md., 1961. Mng. editor Diamondback, 1959; assoc. editor Old Line, 1959; reporter Radio News Assocs., 1960, Hearst Metrotone News/ABC-TV, 1961; account mgr. Burson-Marsteller, Washington, 1967-71; dir. communications Archon Pure Products Corp., Beverly Hills, Calif., 1971-73; v.p communications Glass Packaging Inst., Washington, 1973-77; 1st v.p., corp. communications Bank of Boston, 1977-86; sr. v.p. corp. affairs Hartford (Conn.) Nat. Corp., 1986-88; sr. v.p., dir. pub. affairs Manning, Selvage & Lee, N.Y.C., 1988-94; pres. Barry Allen & Assocs., Inc., Boca Raton, Fla., 1994—, Charter mem. Evanston Group, 1985-87. Mem. adv. com. Boca Raton Resort and Club, 2001—; pres. Boca Golf and Tennis Property Owners Assn., 2001—; mem. adv. bd. Palm Beach County, Fla., 2000—; mem. Gov.'s Alliance Against Drugs, Mass., 1985—86, Boca Raton Airport Authority, 2003—, chair pub. affairs com., 2003—; bd. dirs. Morgan Meml. Good Will, Boston, 1986, Bay State Games, Mass., 1986. Lt. USNR, 1961—67, Vietnam. Scholar Montgomery County, Md., 1960. Mem.: Union League Club N.Y.C., Pi Delta Epsilon. Avocations: golf, travel. Home and Office: 3752 Gorham Way Boca Raton FL 33487-1017 E-mail: ballen5458@aol.com.

ALLEN, BEATRICE, music educator, pianist; b. N.Y.C., June 30, 1917; d. Samuel and Rose (Krell) Hyman; m. Eugene Murray Allen, Jan. 23, 1937; children: Marlene Allen Galzin, Julian Lewis. Student, NYU, 1933—36; diploma (scholar), Inst. Musical Arts, N.Y.C., 1939, postgrad. (scholar), 1939—40; diploma (fellow, letter commendation), Juilliard Grad. Sch., N.Y.C., 1943; BA magna cum laude, Cedar Crest Coll., 1980. Mem. faculty prep. div. Juilliard Sch. Music, N.Y.C., 1957—69, Moravian Coll., 1967—68, Northampton County Area CC, 1968—70, Manhattan Sch. Music, N.Y.C., 1969—89. Mem. founding faculty Cmty. Music Sch., Allentown, Pa., 1982—; artist-in-residence, condr. Tchrs. Workshop, Antioch Coll., Yellow Springs, Ohio, 1966; Bach lectr., recitals various univs.; concert appearances Town Hall, N.Y.C., Chautauqua, NY, others. Named Winner, NJ Artists contest, 1936. Mem.: Pa. Music Tchrs. Assn., Music Tchrs. Nat. Assn. (program chmn. Lehigh Valley chpt. 1981—82). Address: 2100 Main St Bethlehem PA 18017-3752

ALLEN, BELLE, management consulting firm executive, communications company executive; b. Chgo. d. Isaac and Clara (Friedman) Allen. U. Chgo. Cert. conf. mgr. Internat. Inst. Conf. Planning and Mgmt., 1989. Report, spl. correspondent The Leader Newspapers, Chgo., Washington, 1960-64; cons., v.p., treas., dir. William Karp Cons. Co. Inc., Chgo., 1961-79, chmn. bd., pres., treas., 1979—; pres. Belle Allen Comms., Chgo., 1961—; nat. corr. CCA Press, 1990—. Apptd. pub. mem., com. on judicial evaluation Chgo. Bar Assn., 1998—; v.p., treas., bd. dirs. Cultural Arts Survey Inc., Chgo., 1965-79; cons., bd. dirs. Am. Diversified Rsch. Corp., Chgo., 1967-70; v.p., sec., bd. dirs. Mgmt. Performance Systems Inc., 1976-77; cons. City Club Chgo., 1962-65, Ill. Commn. on Tech. Progress, 1965-67; hearing mem. Ill. Gov.'s Grievance Panel for State Employees, 1979—; hearing mem. grievance panel Ill. Dept. Transp., 1985—; mem. adv. governing bd. Ill. Coalition on Employment of Women, 1980-88; spl. program advisor President's Project Partnership, 1980-88; mem. consumer adv. coun. FRS, 1979-82; reporter CCA Press, 1990—; panel mem. Free Press vs. Fair Trial Nat. Ctr. Freedom of Info. Studies Loyola U. Law Sch., 1993, mem. planning com. Freedom of Info. awards, 1993; conf. chair The Swedish Inst. Press Ethics: How to Handle, 1993. Editor: Operations Research and the Management of Mental Health Systems, 1968; contbr. articles to profl. jours. Mem. campaign staff Adlai E. Stevenson II, 1952, 56, John F. Kennedy, 1960; founding mem. women's bd. United Cerebral Palsy Assn., Chgo., 1954, bd. dirs., 1954-58; pres. Dem. Fedn. Ill., 1958-61; pres. conf. staff Eleanor Roosevelt, 1960; mem. Welfare Pub. Rels. Forum, 1960-61; bd. dirs., mem. exec. com., chmn. pub. rels. com. Regional Ballet Ensemble, Chgo., 1961-63; bd. dirs. Soc. Chgo. Strings, 1963-64; mem. Ind. Dem. Coalition, 1968-69; bd. dirs. Citizens for Polit. Change, 1969; campaign mgr. aldermanic election 42d ward Chgo. City Coun., 1969; mem. selection com. Robert Aragon Scholarship, 1991; mem. planning com. mem. Hutchins Era reunion U. Chgo., 1995, 2000. Recipient Outstanding Svc. award United Cerebral Palsy Assn., Chgo., 1954, 55, Chgo. Lighthouse for Blind, 1986, Spl. Comms. award The White House, 1961, cert. of appreciation Ill. Dept. Human Rights, 1985, Internat. Assn. Ofcl. Human Rights Agys., 1985; selected as reference source Am. Bicentennial Rsch. Inst. Libr. Human Resources, 1973; named Hon. Citizen, City of Alexandria, Va., 1985; selected to be photographed by Bachrach nat. exhibit for Faces of Chicago, 1990. Mem. AAAS, NOW, AAAU, Affirmative Action Assn. (bd. dirs. 1981-85, chmn. mem. and programs com. 1981-85, pres. 1983—), Fashion Group (bd. dirs. 1981-83, chmn. Restrospective View of an Hist. Decade 1960-70, editor The Bull. 1981), Indsl. Rels. Rsch. Assn. (bd. dirs., chmn. pers. placement com. 1960-61), Sarah Siddons Soc., Soc. Pers. Adminstrs., Women's Equity Action League, Nat. Assn. Inter-Group Rels. Ofcls. (nat. conf. program 1959), Publicity Club Chgo. (chmn. inter-city rels. com. 1960-61, Disting. Svc. award 1968), Ill. C. of C. (cmty. rels. com., alt. mem. labor rels. com. 1971-74), Chgo. C. of C. and Industry (merit employment com. 1961-63), Internat. Press Club Chgo. (charter 1992—, bd. dirs. 1992—), Chgo. Press Club (chmn. women's activities 1969-71), U. Chgo. Club of Met. Chgo. (program com. 1993—, chair summer quarter programs 1994), Soc. Profl. Journalists (Chgo. Headline Club 1992—, regional conf. planning com. 1993, co-chair Peter Lisagor awards 1993, program com. 1992—), Assn. Women Journalists, Nat. Trust for Historic Preservation. Office: 111 E Chestnut St Ste 29J Chicago IL 60611

ALLEN, BENNIE CARNEL, employee relations specialist; b. Detroit, Feb. 3, 1947; s. John Wilson and Rosella (Williams) Allen; 1 adopted child, Daron K. BA in Hist., Wayne State U., 1968; Grad. Studies, Wayne State U., Detroit Mich., 1972—78, Hampton U., 1991. Employee relations spec. U.S. Army Tacom, Warren, Mich., 1982—2002; supr. pers. staff. spec. US Internal Revenue Svc., Detroit, 1979; pers. staff. spec. US. Vet. Admin., Detroit, 1975—79. Adj. course mgr. instr. US Army Ctr. for Civil. Human Resource Mgmt., Cancaster, Pa., 1993—2002. Editor: (Regulations) Supr. Pers. Mgmt. Manual, 1987; author: (policy) Family Leave Update, 2000. Bd. mem. Detroit Fed. Exec. Bd., Detroit, 1975—79. Sgt.(E-5) USMC, 1968—71. Decorated Special Act Awards US. Army Tacom. Mem.: Detroit Instit. of Arts, Detroit Pub. Television, Marine Corps. League. Independent. Avocation: reading.

ALLEN, BESSIE MALVINA, music educator, church organist; b. LaKemp, Okla., Oct. 14, 1918; d. Percy J. and Mary Allen (Hagler) Gheen; m. Edgar Charles Allen, Aug. 29, 1940 (dec. May 1981); children: Stanley Charles, Stephen Wayne. BA in English, Tex. Woman's U., 1939; MA in Music, W. Tex. State U., 1970. Cert. secondary edn. Tchr. English Balko (Okla.) High Sch. and Jr. High Sch., 1939-40; pvt. practice Phillips, Tex., 1950-85; tchr. music Frank Phillips Coll., Borger, Tex., 1960-63, 65-73, 76-85; pvt. practice Borger, 1997. Organist First Bapt. Ch., Borger, 1947-65, Faith Covenant Ch.-Ind., Borger, 1970-81, First Christian Ch., Borger, 1981-82, Faith Covenant Ch., Borger, 1982-2000. Active Nat. Rep. Senatorial Com., Washington, 1988-91; organist First United Meth. Ch., Borger, 2001—. Recipient Presdl. Order of Merit, Nat. Rep. Senatorial Com., 1991; McCulley Organ scholar, W. Tex. State U., Canyon, 1969. Mem. Music Tchrs. Nat. Assn., Tex. Fedn. Music Clubs, Amarillo Music Tchrs. Assn., Borger Music Club. Avocations: gardening, reading. Home and Office: 221 Inverness St Borger TX 79007-8215

ALLEN, BETTY (MRS. RITTEN EDWARD LEE III), mezzo-soprano; b. Campbell, Ohio, Mar. 17, 1930; d. James Corr and Dora Catherine (Mitchell) A.; m. Ritten Edward Lee, III, Oct. 17, 1953; children: Anthony Edward, Juliana Catherine. Student, Wilberforce U., 1944-46; certificate, Hartford Sch. Music, 1953; pupil voice, Sarah Peck More, Zinka Milanov, Paul Ulanowsky, Carolina Segrera Holden; LHD (hon.), Wittenberg U., 1971; MusD (hon.), Union Coll., 1981; DFA (hon.), Adelphi U., 1990, Bklyn. Coll., 1991; LittD (hon.), Clark U., 1993; MusD (hon.), New Sch. Social Rsch., 1994. Faculty Phila. Mus. Acad., 1979, Manhattan Sch. Music, 1971, N.C. Sch. Arts, 1978-87; now faculty Harlem Sch. Arts. Tchr. master classes Inst. Teatro Colon, 1985-86, Curtis Inst. Music, 1987—; exec. dir. Harlem Sch. Arts, 1979, now pres.; vis. faculty Sibelius Akademie, Helsinki, Finland, 1976; mem. adv. bd. music panel Amherst Coll.; mem. music panel N.Y. State Council of the Arts, Dept. State Office Cultural Presentations, Nat. Endowment Arts.; bd. dirs. Arts Alliance, Karl Weigl Found., Diller-Quaile Sch. Music, U.S. Com. for UNICEF, Manhattan Sch. Music, Theatre Devel. Fund, Children's Storefront; mem. adv. bd. Bloomingdale House of Music; bd. vis. artists Boston U.; bd. dirs., mem. exec. com. Carnegie Hall, Nat. Found. for Advancement in the Arts; bd. dirs. Chamber Music Soc. of Lincoln Ctr., N.Y.C. Housing Authority Orch., Independent Sch. Orch., N.Y.C. Opera CO., Joy in Singing, Arts & Bus. Coun.; mem. Mayor's adv. commn. Cultural Affairs. Appeared as soloist: Leonard Bernstein's Jeremiah Symphony, Tanglewood, 1951, Virgil Thomson's Four Saints in Three Acts, N.Y.C. and Paris, 1952, N.Y.C. Light Opera Co., 1954; recitalist, also soloist with major symphonies on tours including ANTA-State Dept. tours, Europe, N. Africa, Caribbean, Can., U.S., S.Am., Far East, 1954-, S.Am. tour, 1968, Bellas Artes Opera, Mexico City, 1970; recital debut, Town Hall, N.Y.C., 1958, ofcl. debuts, London, Berlin, 1958, formal opera debut, Teatro Colon, Buenos Aires, Argentina, 1964; U.S. opera debut San Francisco Opera, 1966; N.Y.C. opera debut, 1973, Mini-Met. debut, 1973, Broadway debut in Treemonisha, 1975; opened new civic theaters in San Jose, Calif., and Regina, Sask., Can., concert hall, Lyndon Baines Johnson Library, Austin, Tex., 1971; artist-in-residence, Phila. Opera Co.; appeared with Caramoor Music Festival, summer 1965, 71, Cin. May Festival, 1972, Santa Fe Opera, 1972, 75, Canadian Opera Co., Winnipeg, Man., 1972, 77, Washington Opera Co., 1971, Tanglewood Festival, 1951, 52, 53, 67, 74, Oslo, The Hague, Montreal, Kansas City, Houston and Santa Fe operas, 1975, Saratoga Festival, 1975, Casals Festival, 1967, 68, 69, 76, Helsinki Festival, 1976, Marlboro Festival, 1967-74, numerous radio and TV performances, U.S., Can., Mex., Eng., Germany, Scandinavia; rec. artist, London, Vox, Capitol, Odeon-Pathe, Decca, Deutsche Grammophon, Columbia Records, RCA Victor records; represented U.S. in Cultural Olympics, Mexico City, 1968. Recipient Marian Anderson award, 1953-54, Nat. Music League Mgmt. award, 1953, 52 St Am. Festival Duke Ellington Meml. award, 1989, Bowery award Bowery Bank, 1989, Harlem Sch. of the Arts award Harlem Sch. and Isaac Stern, 1990, Womans Day Celebration award St. Thomas Episcopal Ch., 1990, St. Thomas Ch. award St. Thomas Catholic Ch., 1990, Men's Day Celebration award St. Paul's Ch., 1990, Martell House of Segram award Avery Fisher Hall, 1990; named Best Singer of Season Critics' Circle, Argentina and Chile, 1959, Best Singer of Season Critics' Circle, Uruguay, 1961; Martha Baird Rockefeller Aid to Music grantee, 1953, 58; John Hay Whitney fellow, 1953-54; Ford Found. concert soloist grantee,

1963-64 Mem. NAACP, Urban League, Hartford Mus. Club (life), Am. Guild Mus. Artists, Actors Equity, AFTRA, Silvermine Guild Artists, Jeunesses Musicales, Gioventu Musicale, Student Sangverein Trondheim, Unitarian-Universalist Women's Fedn., Nat. Negro Musicians Assn. (life), Concert Artists Guild, Met. Opera Guild, Amherst Glee Club (hon. life), Union Coll. Glee Club (hon. life), Met. Mus. Art, Mus. Modern Art, Am. Mus. Natural History, Century Assn., Sigma Alpha Iota (hon.) Unitarian-Universalist. Clubs: Cosmopolitan, Second. Office: Harlem Sch of Arts 645 Saint Nicholas Ave New York NY 10030-1098 *To be able to combine childhood fantasies of self-expression, to travel and roam the world, to meet again and make new friends, to serve the demanding, yet fulfilling art of music - these are some of the wonderful joys of being a singer. I have been free to be me.*

ALLEN, BONNIE LYNN, optometrist; b. L.A., Oct. 2, 1957; d. David and Lucille M. (Scott) A. BA summa cum laude, UCLA, 1979; BS, OD, U. Calif., Berkeley, 1998. Pvt. practice math. tutor, L.A., 1971—. Reader math. dept. UCLA, 1977-79; pension actuary Martin E. Segal Co., L.A., 1980-92. Author short stories and poetry. Active mentor program UCLA Alumni Assn., 1978-79. Mem.: U. Calif. Berkeley Optometry Alumni Assn, Acad. Sci. Fiction,Fantasy and Horror Films, L.A. Film Tchrs. Assn., Am. Math. Soc., Am. Optometric Assn., Calif. Optometric Assn., Math. Assn. Am., U. Calif. Berkeley Alumni Assn. (life), UCLA Alumni Assn. (life), L.A. Actuarial Club, Westside Bruins Club (bd. dirs.), Golden Key, Phi Beta Kappa, Beta Sigma Kappa.

ALLEN, BRUCE ROYL, JR., social worker; b. Houston, Jan. 24, 1952; s. Bruce R. Allen Sr. and Violet R. Aaron; m. Linda Claire Jernigan, May 20, 1978; children: Gretchen, Kelsey. BS in Psychology, U. Houston, 1974, MSW, 1978. Lic. social worker, Ark. Sr. clinician Ozark Counseling Svc., Harrison, Ark., 1978-84; psychiat. social worker Charter Vista Hosp., Fayetteville, Ark., 1984-86; clin. social worker N.W. Ark. Counseling Assocs., Fayetteville, Ark., 1986—. Faculty instr. Inst. for Reality Therapy, Canoga Park, Calif., 1988, U. Ark. at Little Rock Grad. Sch. Social Work. Mem. NASW (bd. dirs. 1986-88). Avocation: music. Office: NW Ark Counseling Assocs 34 E Center St Fayetteville AR 72701

ALLEN, BRUCE TEMPLETON, economics educator; b. Oak Park, Ill., Jan. 27, 1938; s. William Hendry and Harriet (Iverson) A.; m. Virginia Elizabeth Peterson, June 16, 1962; children: Elizabeth Rachel, Catherine Grace. AB, De Pauw U., 1960; MBA, U. Chgo., 1961; PhD, Cornell U., 1965. Asst. prof. econs. Mich. State U., East Lansing, 1965-75, assoc. prof., 1975-80, prof., 1980—2003. Mem. Am. Econ. Assn. Avocation: railroads. Office: Mich State U Dept Econs East Lansing MI 48824

ALLEN, CAMERON, genealogist, law educator; b. Springfield, Ohio, Feb. 7, 1928; s. George Badger and Mary Dorothy (Spencer) A. BA, Otterbein Coll., 1947; MA in History, U. Wis., 1951; MS in Libr. Sci., U. Ill., 1956; JD, Duke U., 1959. Mem. faculty sch. law Rutgers U., Newark, N.J., 1959-84; ptnr. Strawser-Allen Partnership, Columbus, Ohio, 1984—. Vis. prof. U. N.C., Chapel Hill, 1971-84; mem. ABA-Assn. Am. Law Schs. Joint Law Sch. Accreditation Com. Author: A History of the Holy Trinity American Episcopal Church Paris, 1858-1979, Growth in Grace, 1937-1962; The Sublett (Soblet) Family of Manakintown, Virginia, 1982, A Guide to New Jersey Legal Bibliography and Legal History, 1984; contbg. editor The Am. Genealogist, 1961-81; contbr. articles to profl. jours. Served with U.S. Army, 1952-53, Korea. Fellow: Am. Soc. Genealogists (sec. 1989-92, v.p. 1992-95, pres. 1995-98); mem. ABA, Am Assn. Law Librs. (sec. 1977-80). Republican. Episcopalian. Address: 90 Tarryton Court W Columbus OH 43228-1513

ALLEN, CAROL MARIE, radiologic technologist; b. Alma, Ark., Nov. 4, 1941; d. Rhuel Teal and Blake Marie (Hickey) Edwards; m. Richard William Varney, Oct. 4, 1965 (dec. Mar. 1978); 1 stepchild, Mary Beth Varney; m. Michael Thomas Allen, Dec. 24, 1979; stepchildren: Richard Lawrence, Peter Michael, Nicola Susan. 2 yr. cert., Sparks Regional Med. Ctr.-Sch. Radiology, 1961. Cert. Am. Registry Radiologic Technologists, State Conn. Registry Radiologic Technologists, clin. densitometry Mass. Staff technologist Sparks Regional Med. Ctr., Ft. Smith, Ark., 1961—62, La Puente (Calif.) Hosp., 1962—64; asst. chief technologist La Harbor (Calif.) Hosp., 1964—67; traffic contr. Lawrence and Meml. Hosp., Pequot Treatment Ctr., New London, Conn., 1967—; clin. densitometry technologist L&M Pequot Treatment Ctr., 1998—2003, traffic controller, 2003—. Contbr. Vol. ARC, Conn. Mem.: Am. Soc. for Radiologic Technologists, Internat. Soc. for Clin. Densitometry. Democrat. Avocations: gardening, antiques, reading. Home: 11 Route 165 Preston CT 06365-8414 Office: Lawrence & Meml Hosp 365 Montauk Ave New London CT 06320 also: Pequot Emergency Treatment Ctr 52 Hazelnut Hill Rd Groton CT 06340

ALLEN, CAROLE NEWMAN, pediatrician; b. Casablanca, Morocco, Sept. 13, 1945; came to U.S., 1946; m. Thomas Hagar Allen, June 17, 1967; children: David, Abigail. AB, Cornell U., 1967; MD, Tufts U., 1971. Diplomate Am. Bd. Pediatrics. Pediatric intern Boston City Hosp., 1971-72, resident in pediatrics, 1972-73, New Eng. Med. Ctr., Boston, 1973-74; pediatrician East Boston Neighborhood Health Ctr., 1974-88; pvt. practice Arlington, Mass., 1988—2002; dir. pediat. Harvard Vanguard Med. Assocs., 2002—. Fellow Am. Acad. Pediat. (bd. dirs. Mass. chpt. 1994—, sec. 1997-99, 2002-, treas. 1999-2002); mem. AMA, Mass. Med. Soc. (del.), Alpha Omega Alpha. Avocation: gardening. Office: Harvard Vanguard Med Assocs Pediat 40 Holland St Somerville MA 02144

ALLEN, CATHERINE JEAN, anthropologist, educator; b. Oakridge, Tenn., May 29, 1947; d. Augustine Oliver Allen and Agnes Robinson; m. Richard Mark Wagner, June 16, 1968 (div. Nov. 1979); m. Andras Sandor, May 21, 1984; 1 child, Andrea Anna Sandor. BA, St. John's Coll., 1969; MA, U. Ill., 1972, PhD, 1978. Vis. lectr. dept. anthropology U. Ill., Urbana, 1977—78; asst. prof. anthropology George Washington U., Washington, 1978—85, assoc. prof. anthropology, 1985—89, prof. anthropology, 1989—. Guest prof. anthropology and Am. studies Eötvös Loránd U., Budapest, Hungary, 1990—91; dept. chair dept. anthropology George Washington U., Washington, 1995—98; founding mem. George Washington U. Seminar in Andean Culture and Politics, Washington, 1987—. Author: (book) The Hold Life Has: Coca and Cultural Identity in an Andean Community, 1988, The Hold Life Has: Coca and Cultural Identity in an Andean Community (2nd expanded edit.), 2002; co-author: (plays) Condor Qatay: Anthropology in Performance, 1996. Fellow, Dumbarton Oaks, 1993—94, Guggenheim Found., 2001—02, Ctr. Advanced Study Visual Arts, 2001. Mem.: Soc. for Visual Anthropology, Am. Ethol. Soc., Am. Anthropol. Assn. Democrat. Achievements include interpretation of indigenous significance of coca leaf in Andean South America. Avocations: classical music, poetry, hiking. Office: George Washington U Dept Anthropology 2110 G St NW Washington DC 20082 Fax: 202-994-6097. E-mail: kitallen@gwu.edu.

ALLEN, CHARLES E. federal agency administrator; With CIA, Washington, 1958—, overseas intelligence liaison, 1974—77, directorate intelligence, 1977—80, mgr. major dlacified program, 1980—82; with Office Sec. Defense, 1982—85; nat. intelligence officer CIA, 1985—88, apptd. chief intelligence counterterrorist ctr., 1988—94, asst. dir. collection, 2000—. Office: CIA Office of Dir Washington DC 20505

ALLEN, CHARLES EUGENE, university administrator, agriculturist, educator; b. Burley, Idaho, Jan. 25, 1939; s. Charles W. and Elsie P. (Fowler) A.; m. Connie J. Block, June 19, 1960; children: Kerry J., Tamara S. BS, U. Idaho, 1961; MS, U. Wis., 1963, PhD, 1965. NSF postdoctoral fellow, Sydney, Australia, 1966-67; asst. prof. agr. U. Minn., St. Paul, 1967-69, assoc. prof., 1969-72, prof., 1972—, dean Coll. Agr., assoc. dir. Agrl. Expt. Sta., 1984-88, acting v.p., 1988-90, v.p. agriculture, forestry and home econs., dir. Minn. Agr. Expt. Sta., 1990-95, provost profl. studies, dir. Minn. Agr. Expt. Sta., 1995-97, dir. global outreach, 1997-98, exec. dir. internat. programs, 1998—. Vis. prof. Pa. State U., 1978; cons. to industry; C. Glen King lectr. Wash. State U., 1981; Univ. lectr. U. Wyo., Laramie, 1984; adj. prof. Hassan II U., Rabat, Morocco, 1984 Recipient Horace T. Morse-Amoco Found. award in undergrad. edn. U. Minn., 1984, Disting. Tchr. award U. Minn. Coll. Agr., 1984, Disting. Alumni award U. Idaho, 1989. Fellow AAAS, Inst. Food Tech.; mem. Am. Meat Sci. Assn. (dir. 1970-72; Research award 1980, Signal Service award, 1985), Am. Soc. Animal Sci. (Exceptional Research Achievement award 1972, Research award 1977), Sigma Xi. Avocations: photography, reading, outdoor sports, golf.

ALLEN, CHARLES NORMAN, television, film and video producer; b. Miami, July 13, 1944; s. Claude Braswell and Virginia Lucille (Gravitt) A.; m. Susan Carole Dorn, May 1, 1970; children: Jennifer, Brian. BS, U. Miami, 1967. V.p. Tel-Air Interests Inc., Miami, 1967-79; pres. Cinema East Corp., Miami, 1979—, World Studios Corp., Atlanta, 1987—, ADR Internat., Miami, 1991—2001. Bd. dirs. World Studios Corp. Representer prodns. U.S. internat. film events CINE-Washington, 1974, 75, 80, 81, 87, 88, 89, 92. Trustee Dade County Pub. Health Trust; commr. Biscayne Park, Fla., 1974-76; active Dade County Dem. Exec. Commn., 1976-80, Dade Dem. Treas., 1976-79; mem. Gov.'s Fla. Motion Picture and TV Adv. Coun., 1978-80. Mem. Am. Advt. Fed., South Fla. Film & Tape Producers Assn., Assn. Ind. Comml. Producers, Internat. Cinematographers Guild, Nat. Advt. Fraternity, Greater Miami Advt. Fed., Advt. Miami, Greater Miami C. of C., Sigma Chi Frat., Internat. Cinenatographers Guild, Iron Arrow Honor Soc., Alpha Delta Sigma. Democrat. Methodist. Office: Cinema East Corp 5859 Biscayne Blvd Miami FL 33137-2690

ALLEN, CHARLES WILLIAM, mechanical engineering educator; b. Newbury, Eng., July 24, 1932; s. Isaac William and Emily (Butler) A.; m. Rita Joyce Pembroke, Dec. 28, 1957; children: Malcolm Charles, Verity Simone. BS, U. London, 1957; MS, Case Inst. Tech., 1962; PhD, U. Calif., Davis, 1966. Design engr. Lear Siegler, Cleve., 1957-62; group leader Aerojet Gen., Sacramento, 1962-63; assoc. engring. U. Calif., Davis, 1965-66; assoc. prof. Calif. State U., Chico, 1966-71, prof. engring., 1971-88, prof. emeritus, 1988—, head mech. engring., 1976-79, 82-84. Vis. fellow U. Leicester, Eng., 1974; vis. lectr., rschr. U. Guadalajara, Mex., 1986, guest prof., 1997. Contbr. articles to profl. jours. Fellow NASA, 1967, 68, 69 Mem. ASME. Home: 1691 Filbert Ave Chico CA 95926-1777 Office: Calif State U Dept Mech Engring Chico CA 95629 E-mail: charlesa@ecst.csuchico.edu.

ALLEN, CLARENCE RODERIC, geologist, educator; b. Palo Alto, Calif., Feb. 15, 1925; s. Hollis Partridge and Delight (Wright) A. BA, Reed Coll., 1949; MS, Cal. Inst Tech., 1951, PhD, 1954. Asst. prof. geology U. Minn., 1954-55; mem. faculty Calif. Inst. Tech., 1955—, prof. geology and geophysics, 1964-91, prof. emeritus, 1991—; interim dir. Seismological Lab., 1965-67, acting chmn. division of geological scis., 1967-68. Phi Beta Kappa Disting. lectr., 1978; chmn. cons. bd. earthquake analysis Calif. Dept. Water Resources, 1965-74; chmn. geol. hazards adv. com. for program Cal. Resources Agy., 1965-66; mem. earth scis. adv. panel NSF, 1965-68, chmn., 1967-68, mem. adv. com. environmental scis., 1970-72; mem. U.S. Geol. Survey adv. panel to Nat. Center Earthquake Research, Calif. Cal. Mining and Geology Bd., 1969-75, chmn., 1975; mem. task force on earthquake hazard reduction Office Sci. and Tech., 1970-71; mem. Can. Earthquake Prediction Evaluation Council, 1983-88; vice-chmn. Nat. Acad. Sci. Com. on Advanced Study in china, 1981-85; chmn. geology sect. Nat. Acad. Sci., 1982-85, Com. on Scholarly Communication with People's Republic China, 1984-89, chmn., 1987-89; mem. Nat. Acad. Sci. Commn. on Phys. Scis., Math. and Resources; mem. Pres.'s Nuclear Waste Tech. Rev. Bd., 1989-97. Served to 1st lt. USAAF, 1943-46. Recipient G.K. Gilbert award seismic geology Carnegie Instn., 1960. Fellow Am. Geophys. Union, Geol. Soc. Am. (counselor 1968-70, pres. 1973-74), Am. Acad. Arts Scis.; mem. Nat. Acad. Scis., Earthquake Engring. Research Inst. (bd. dirs. 1985-88, Housner medal 2001), Seismological Soc. Am. (dir. 1970-76, pres. 1975-76, medal 1995), Nat. Acad. Engring., Phi Beta Kappa. Office: Calif Inst Tech Dept Geology Pasadena CA 91125-0001 E-mail: allen@gps.caltech.edu.

ALLEN, CLAUDE A. federal agency administrator; m. Jannese Mitchell; children: Claude Alexander III, Lila-Cjoan, Christian Isaiah. Degree in Polit. and Sci. and Linguistics, U. N.C.; LLM in Internat. and Comparative Law, JD, Duke U. Lawyer, Washington; counsel to atty. gen., dep. atty. gen. for civil litigation divsn. Office of the Atty. Gen., Va.; sec. health and human resources Commonwealth of Va.; dep. sec. HHS, Washington, 2001—. Office: Dept HHS Office of the Sec 200 Independence Ave SW Washington DC 20201-0004

ALLEN, CLAXTON EDMONDS, III, investment banker; b. N.Y.C., Aug. 27, 1944; s. C. Edmonds and Helen (McCreery) A. BA, Washington and Lee U., 1964, JD, 1967. Bar: N.Y. 1969. Assoc. Simpson Thacher & Bartlett, N.Y.C., 1967-70; assoc. gen. counsel GE Credit Corp., N.Y.C., 1970-71; investment banker Merrill Lynch, Pierce, Fenner & Smith, Inc., N.Y.C., 1971-72; pres. Gloucester Internat. Ltd., N.Y.C., 1972-82, Comanche Exploration Corp., N.Y.C., 1981-86, Compass Internat. Corp., N.Y.C., 1982—, Horizon Coal Corp., Mineral Res. Corp., N.Y.C., 1982-85, Compass Coal Corp., N.Y.C., 1986-91, Overseas & Fgn. Investors, Inc., N.Y.C., 1990—. Bd. dirs. Purbrook Ltd., Cranbrook Investments Ltd., Lupton Estates Ltd., Morehead State U. Found., Inc., L&H Internat. Ltd. Mem. Met. Club. Home: 405 E 54th St New York NY 10022-5123 Office: 123 E 54th St 8th Fl New York NY 10022-4506

ALLEN, CRAIG ADAMS, lawyer, director; b. Ironton, Ohio, June 30, 1941; s. Enoch Stanely and Margaret (Adams) Allen; m. Carol Linda Brewster, Aug. 15, 1964; children: Laura, Kathy. BA cum laude, Denison U., 1963; JD, Ohio State U., 1966. Bar: Ohio 1966. Ptnr. Edwards, Klien, Compton & Allen, Ironton, Ohio, 1966—76; sole practice Ironton, 1976—77; ptnr. Allen & Anderson, Ironton, 1977—78, Allen, Anderson & Anderson, Ironton, 1978—82, Allen & Stillpass, Ironton, 1983—84; sole practice, 1984—85; ptnr. Allen & Payne, Ironton, 1985—. Served Ohio Nat. Guard, 1966—72. Mem.: Hosp. Atty. Assn., Lawrence County Bar Assn., Ironton C. of C., Lawrence County Democratic Ctrl Com., So. Ohio AAA, Elks, Lions. Episc. Office: 311 S 3rd St Ironton OH 45638-1630

ALLEN, DANIELLE, political scientist, educator; BA, Princeton U., 1993; MA, Harvard U., 1998, PhD, 2001; MPhil, U. Cambridge, 1994, PhD, 1997. Assoc. prof. dept. politics and com. on social thought and dept. classical langs. and lits. U. Chgo., 1997—. Author: (book) The World of Prometheus: The Politics of Punishing in Democratic Athens, 2000. Fellow, NSF, 1997, Frank Inst. for Humanities fellow, U. Chgo., 1999. Office: U Chgo Dept Classics 1010 East 59 th St Chicago IL 60637

ALLEN, DAVID, systems engineer; b. York, Maine, May 15, 1942; s. Pliny Arunah and Tillie (MacQuinn) A.; m. JoAnn Moeckly, 1968 (div. 1975); children: Torrie, Heather; m. Robin Lee Perry, Mar. 11, 1983; children: Rebecca, Patrick. BA, Lake Forest Coll., 1965; MA, U. Ariz., 1967, PhD, 1968. Asst. prof. dept. psychology S.D. State U., Brookings, 1968-71; rsch. psychologist CIA, Washington, 1971-78, chief rsch. br., 1978-85, dep. chief psychol. svcs. divsn., 1985-87, chief rsch. and info. systems divsn., 1987-90, trustee investment plan, 1988-92, investigator Office of Insp. Gen., 1990-92, chief info. systems Latin Am. divsn., 1992-95; chief electronic messaging divsn., program dir. Enterprise Messaging Svcs., Office of Comm. CIA, Washington, 1995-97; dir. program devel./mktg. for Ctr. for Sci. and Tech. Mitretek Sys., Inc., 1998—2000; program dir. SRS Technologies, 2002—. Contbr. articles to profl. jours. Rsch. fellow USPHS, 1967-68; rsch. grantee NSF, 1970-71; recipient U.S. Govt. Career Intelligence medal, CIA, 1997. Republican. Avocations: choral singing, amateur radio, cosmology, mathematics, information technology. Home: 905 N Emerson St Arlington VA 22205-2562 Office: DARPA 3701 N Fairfax Dr Arlington VA 22203 E-mail: DavidAlle1@aol.com.

ALLEN, DAVID CHARLES, computer science educator; b. Jan. 15, 1944; s. Charles Robert and Jane Loretta (Doolittle) A.; m. Mary Ann Stanke, June 15, 1968 (div. Mar. 1994); children: Meredith Rae, Amelia Kathrine, Carl James; m. Barbara Ann Riis, Mar. 14, 1994. B Tech. Edn., Nat. U., San Diego, 1983; MA in Human Behavior, Nat. U., 1984. Dir. retail sales Nat. U. Alumni Assn., 1981-83; audiovisual technician Grossmont Union H.S. Dist., La Mesa, Calif., 1983-84; spl. project instr. San Diego C.C., 1985-91; instr. computer tech. Coleman Coll., 1991-98, sr. instr. computer applications and networking, 1998-2000, prof., dept. chair, 2000—02; prof. BOCES Continuing Edn., 2002—03; instr. ITT Tech. Inst., Liverpool, NY, 2003—. Mem. Presdl. Task Force; mem. Congl. Adv. Com. on Vets. Benefits for congressmen 44th. With USN, 1961-81. Mem. DAV, VFW, Am. Legion, Vietnam Vets. Am. (life), Fleet Reservation Assn., Nt. U. Student and Alumni Assn., Am. Tech. Edn. Assn. Republican. Roman Catholic. Home: 8614 Lakeport Road Lot 120 Chittenango NY 13037-9641 Office: ITT Technical Inst 235 Greenfield Pkwy Liverpool NY 13088 E-mail: dallen13@twcny.rr.com.

ALLEN, DAVID HARLOW, business educator, logistician, consultant; b. Lynn, Mass., May 26, 1930; s. Donald H. and Miriam Ellsworth (Harlow) A.; m. Roberta Arlene Miller, July 15, 1952; children: Donald Bruce, Richard Leroy, William David. BS in Gen. Edn., U. Nebr., Omaha, 1967; MBA, N.Mex. Highlands U., 1978. Cert. profl. logistician, cost analyst. Enlisted USAF, 1948-55, commd. 2d lt., 1955, advanced through grades to lt. col., 1970, aircraft and engine mechanic, tech. instr. and curricular planner, 1948—54, aircraft maintenance officer, squadron comdr., wing asst. dep. comdr. maintenace, 1955—74, dep. dir. logistics test and Evaluation AF Test and Evaluation Ctr., 1974—78, ret., 1978; sr. sys. analyst, space sys. project leader Arinc Rsch. Corp., 1978-84; airborne missile system dep. program mgr. for logistics, logistics project mgr. Ventura divsn. Northrop Corp., 1984-91; assoc. prof. West Coast U. Coll. Bus. and Mgmt., L.A., 1988-97; asst. dean West Coast U., L.A., 1988-90. Com. chmn. So. Calif. Logistics Conf. and Workshop, 1989-93; program chmn. 29th Internat. Logistics Conf. and Tech. Exposition, 1994; v.p., mem. bd. govs., trustee Logistics Edn. Found., 1993-96. Contbr. articles to profl. jours. Mem. Ventura County-Santa Barbara County Planning Com. for Nat. Engring. Week, 1990-98. Decorated Bronze Star. Mem. Internat. Soc. Logistics Engrs. (chmn. chpt. 1988-90, Pres.'s award for merit 1994), Logistics Edn. Found. (v.p., bd. trustees 1993-95, Pres.'s award for merit 1996), Soc. Cost Estimating and Analysis, Air Force Assn., Ret. Officers Assn., Am. Assn. Ret. Persons, Phi Kappa Phi. Avocations: racquetball, golf, swimming. Home and Office: 428 Moondance St Thousand Oaks CA 91360-1209

ALLEN, DAVID JAMES, lawyer; b. East Chicago, Ind. BS, Ind. U., 1957, MA, 1959, JD, 1965. Bar: Ind. 1965, U.S. Dist. Ct. (so. dist.) Ind. 1965, U.S. Ct. Appeals 1965, U.S. Tax Ct. 1965, U.S. Supreme Ct. 1965, U.S. Ct. Appeals (fed. and 7th cirs.) 1983. Of counsel Hagemier, Allen and Smith, Indpls., 1975—. Adminstrv. asst. Gov. of Ind. Mathew E. Welsh, 1961—65; counsel Ind. Gov. Roger D. Branigin, 1965—69; asst. to Gov. Edgar D. Whitcomb, 1969; univ. counsel Ind. State U., Terre Haute, 1969—70; legis. counsel Ind. Gov. Evan Bayh, 1989—90; spl. counsel Gov. Frank O'Bannon State of Ind., 1999—2002; mem. Spl. Commn. on Ind. Exec. Reorgn., 1967—69, commn. univ. counsel Ind. State U., 1969—70; commr. Ind. Utility Regulatory Commn., 1970—75; mem. Ind. Law Enforcement Acad. Bd. and Adv. Coun., 1968—85, Ind. State Police Bd., 1968—; commr. for revision Ind. Commn. Recommend Changes Ind. Legis. Process, 1990—2002; commr. Ind. Criminal Code Revision Study Commn., 1998—2002; nat. judge adv. Acacia Frat., 1980—86, 1992—2002, internat. pres., 2002—; chief counsel Ind. Ho. Reps., 1975—76, spl. counsel, 1979—89, Ind. Senate, 1990—97; adj. prof. pub. law Sch. Pub. and Environ. Affairs, Ind. U., Bloomington, 1976—. Author: (book) New Governor in Indiana: Transition to Executive Power, 1965. Mem.: ABA, Indpls. Bar Assn., Ind. State Bar Assn. (criminal justice law exec. com. 1966—72, mem. adminstrv. law com. 1968—77, chmn. adminstrv. law com. 1973—76, mem. law sch. liaison com. 1977—78). Office: Hagemier Allen & Smith 1170 Market Tower 10 W Market St Ste 1170 Indianapolis IN 46204-5924

ALLEN, DAVID JOSEPH, music educator; b. Ottawa, Ill., Oct. 4, 1969; s. Elza Joe and Marie Elaine Allen; m. Betty Jane Hood, Jan. 2, 1993. BS in Music Edn., U. Ill., 1992, MusM, 1994. Dir. bands Salem (Ill.) Cmty. H.S., Salem, 1994—99, Centennial H.S., Champaign, Ill., 1997—. Coord. Ill. Summer Youth Music Band Camps, Urbana-Champaign, 2001—. Mem.: Champaign Fedn. Tchrs., Ill. Music Educators Assn. (dist. rep. 2002). Avocation: computers. Home: 1508 White Pine Dr Champaign IL 61822 Office: Centennial H S 913 S Crescent Champaign IL 61821

ALLEN, DAVID WOODROFFE, computer scientist; b. Hampton, Iowa, Sept. 20, 1944; s. Edward DeWalt and Julia Woodroffe (Lamb) A.; m. Barbara Ann Schneider, Sept. 15, 1973. BA, Grinnell Coll., 1967; MS, U. Pitts., 1974. Assoc. engr. Westinghouse Electric Corp., Sharon, Pa., 1967-70, engr., 1970-79, sr. engr., 1979-84, sr. computer scientist Pitts., 1984-90, prin. engr., 1990-94, fellow engr., 1994-96; dir., officer, sr. engr. Propulsor Tech. Inc., Pitts., 1996—. Contbr. articles to profl. jours. Recipient George Westinghouse Signature award of excellence, 1989, 92, George Westinghouse Innovation award, 1993, James S. Cogswell award Outstanding Indsl. Security Achievement, 1998. Mem. IEEE (sect. sec.-treas. 1981-82, referee tech. papers for Computer jour.), Assn. for Computing Machinery, Silicon Graphics Users Group We. Pa. (treas. 1991-94). Democrat. Achievements include research in current transformer transient performance, magnetic and electric field computation and analysis, computer-aided geometric design, computer vision. Home: 2637 Rossmoor Dr Pittsburgh PA 15241-2572 Office: Propulsor Technology Inc 200 Old Pond Rd Ste 103 Bridgeville PA 15017-1269

ALLEN, DELMAS JAMES, anatomist, educator, university administrator; b. Hartsville, S.C., Aug. 13, 1937; s. James Paul and Sara (Segars) A.; m. Sarah Bahous, July 5, 1958; children— Carolyn, James, Susan BS in Biology, Am. U. of Beirut, Lebanon, 1965, MS, 1967; postgrad., Med. Coll. Ga., 1968; cert. in Radiation Sci., Colo. State U., 1969; PhD, U. N.D., 1974. Teaching fellow dept. biology Am. U. Beirut, Lebanon, 1965-67; instr. dept. biology Clarke Coll., Dubuque, Iowa, 1968-69, asst. prof., 1969-72, chmn. dept. biology, 1969-72; grad. teaching fellow and research asst. U. N.D., Grand Forks, 1972-74; asst. prof. dept. anatomy U. South Ala., Mobile, 1974-75, Med. Coll. Ohio, Toledo, 1975-77, assoc. prof. dept. anatomy, 1977-82, prof. dept. anatomy, 1982-86, asst. dean Grad. Sch., 1979-86; assoc. dean Coll. Health Scis. Ga. State U., Atlanta, 1986-88; v.p. academic affairs N. Ga. Coll., 1988—93; pres. North Ga. Coll., Dahlonega, 1993-97; provost, exec. v.p., dean faculty So. Calif. U. Heatlh Scis., 1996—2001. Vis. prof. Brazil, 1980, Ryad U. Sch. Medicine, Saudi Arabia, 1981, United Arab Emirates U. System, 1992. Co-author: Review of Neuroscience, 1980, 2d ed., 1988, Atlas of Human Anatomy, CT Scan and NMR, 1988; contbr. articles on neuroanatomy and electron microscopy to sci. jours.; editor: Three-Dimensional Microanatomy, 1981; contbr. chpts. in field to various textbooks. Recipient A. Rodger Denison award N.D. Acad. Sci., 1973; Ala. Heart Assn. grantee, 1974-75, Am. Cancer Soc. grantee, 1977, Am. Heart Assn. grantee, 1977-80; geriatrics-gerontology grantee, 1980-81; recipient Golden Apple award for Excellence in Teaching, Med. Coll. Ohio, 1977, 78, 79, 80, 82, 86; research award Brazilian Acad. Medicine, 1980, Northwestern Ohio Electron Microscopic Soc., 1980; Faculty Recognition award Med. Coll. Ohio, 1983 Fellow Ohio Acad. Sci. (membership chmn. med. sci. sect. 1977-78, v.p. med. sect. 1978-79); mem. Soc. for Neurosci., Am. Assn. Anatomists, So. Soc. Anatomists, Am. Soc. Cell Biology, Midwest Assn. Anatomists, Pan Am. Soc. Anatomy, N.Y. Acad. Scis., Am. Heart Assn., European Brain and Behavior Soc. (hon. mem.), Brit. Brain Research Assn. (hon. mem.), Sigma Xi (Thesis Excellence award 1967, Award of Merit 1974, pres. Med. Coll. Ohio club 1978-79), Rotary (pres. Dahlonga Club 1993, Paul Harris fellow 1992), Phi Kappa Phi, Omicron Delta Kappa, Phi Eta Sigma. Home: 365 Back Bay Dr Newport OR 97365-9476

ALLEN, DIANE BETZENDAHL, state legislator; b. Newark, Mar. 8, 1948; arrived in U.S., 1970; BA in Philosophy, Bucknell U., 1970. Pres. VidComm, Inc.; mem. N.J. Gen. Assembly, Trenton, 1996-98, N.J. Senate, Dist. 7, Trenton, 1998—; Rep. Conf. leader, 2003; mem. Senate transp. com., 2003; mem. health, sr. svcs. com., 2003. Majority whip N.J. State Senate, 1998—, vice chair environ. com., vice chair transp. com., women's issues, children and family svcs. com. Del. to Rep. Nat. Conv., 1996; bd. dirs. N.J. State Aquarium, Foster Care Consortium N.J., Family Svcs. of Burlington County, Youth Work Found., Moorestown Vis. Nurses Assn., United Way; mem. Com. to End Homelessness. Republican. Address: NJ State Senate PO Box 098 Trenton NJ 08624-0098 E-mail: SenAllen@njleg.org.*

ALLEN, DIANNA, language educator; b. San Antonio, Tex., Sept. 18, 1948; d. Lon Peck and Lou Evelyn Meriwether; m. Reid L. Allen; children: Meredith, Charissa. BA, Baylor U., 1970; MA, U. Tex. San Antonio, 1976. Cert. lifetime tchr. cert. Tex. Tchr. Spanish Northeast Ind. Sch. Dist., San Antonio, 1970—76; tchr. ESL Alachua County Sch., Gainesville, Fla., 1977—78; tchr. Spanish Round Rock Ind. Sch. Dist., Austin, Tex., 1982—. Adj. faculty Spanish Austin C.C., 1981—; instr. Southwest Tex. U., San Marcos, 1987—91; instr. Writing Virtual H.S., Concorde, Mass., 2001—02; instr. ESL Tarrytown Bapt. Ch.,

Austin, 2000—01; cons. Berry-Moon Products, Austin, 2000—, Media Corp., Austin, 1980. Dir. children's ministries Riverbend Ch., 1988—2000. Mem.: Tex. Fgn. Lang. Assn., Am. Consortium of Tchrs. Fgn. Lang.*

ALLEN, DIOGENES, clergyman, philosophy educator; b. Lexington, Ky., Oct. 17, 1932; m. Jane Mary Billing, Sept. 8, 1958; children: Mary, George, John, Timothy. BA with high distinction, U. Ky., 1954; postgrad., Princeton U., 1954-55; BA with honors, Oxford U., 1957, MA, 1961; B.D., Yale U., 1959, PhD, 1965. Ordained to ministry Presbyterian Ch., 1959; ordained priest Episcopal Ch., 2002. Minister Windham Presbyn. Ch., N.H., 1958-61; asst. prof. York U., Toronto, Ont., Can., 1964-66, assoc. prof. philosophy, 1966-67; assoc. prof. Princeton Theol. Sem., N.J., 1967-74, prof., 1974—, Stuart prof. philosophy, 1981—2002, Stuart prof. philosophy emeritus, 2002—. Author: The Reasonableness of Faith, 1968, Finding Our Father, 1974, reissued under title The Path to Perfect Love, 1992, Between Two Worlds, 1978, reissued under title Temptation, 1985, Traces of God, 1981, Three Outsiders: Pascal, Kierkegaard and S. Weil, 1983, Mechanical Explanations and Their Relation to the Ultimate Origin of the Universe According to Leibniz, 1983, Philosophy for Understanding Theology, 1985, Love, 1987, Christian Belief in a Postmodern World, 1989, Quest, 1990, Primary Reading in Philosophy for Understanding (with Eric Springsted), 1992, (with Eric Springsted) Nature, Spirit, Community: The Thought of Simone Weil, 1994, Spiritual Theology, 1997; editor: Theodicy (Leibniz), 1966, Steps Along the Way, 2002. Rhodes scholar, 1955-57, 63-64, Pew Evang. scholar, 1991-92; fellow Rockefeller Found., 1962-64, Ctr. Theol. Inquiry, Princeton, 1985-88, 94-95, Adv. Bd. Ctr. Theol. Inquiry, 1988-94. Mem. Soc. Christian Philosophers (bd. dirs.), Am. Weil Soc. (bd. dirs.), Leibniz Gellschaft, N.J. Com. for the Humanities, Phi Beta Kappa. Home: Lillie St 70 Princeton Jct Princeton Junction NJ 08550 Office: Princeton Theol Seminary Dept Theology Princeton NJ 08542 *In my life I have found there are many people who are glad to encourage and help another person in the pursuit of worthwhile tasks.*

ALLEN, DONALD VAIL, investment executive, writer, concert pianist; b. South Bend, Ind., Aug. 1, 1928; s. Frank Eugene and Vera Irene (Vail) A.; m. Betty Dunn, Nov. 17, 1956. BA magna cum laude, UCLA, 1972, MA, D (hon.), UCLA, 1973. Pres., chmn. bd. dirs. Cambridge Investment Corp.; music editor and critic Times-Herald, Washington; music critic L.A. Times. Lectr. George Washington U., Am. U., Washington, Pasadena City Coll. Transl. works of Ezra Pound from Italian into English; author of papers on the musical motifs in the writings of James Joyce; specialist in works of Beethoven, Chopin, Debussy, Liszt, and Scriabin; premiere performances of works of Paul Creston, Norman dello Joio, Ross Lee Finney, appearances in N.Y., L.A., Washington; represented by William Matthews Concert Agy., N.Y.C.; selected by William Steinway and Sascha Greiner of Steinway Piano Co. as an exclusive Steinway concert artist. Pres. Funds for Needy Children, 1974-76; mem. Am. Guild Organists. Mem. Ctr. for Study of Presidency, Am. Mgmt. Assn., Internat. Platform Assn., Nat. Assn. Securities Dealers, Am. Guild Organists, Chamber Music Soc., Am. Mus. Natural History. Avocations: languages, music, travel, writing, stock market. E-mail: DonaldVailAllen@cs.com.

ALLEN, DOROTHEA, secondary education educator; b. Rockaway, NJ, Apr. 30, 1919; d. Harrison Engleman and Caroline (Tierney) Allen. AB, Montclair U., 1941, MA, 1949. Cert. secondary, sci., math. tchr., counselor, supr., prin. N.J. Tchr. sci. and math. Denville (N.J.) Jr. High Sch., 1942-46; tchr. sci. Boonton (N.J.) High Sch., 1946-94, supr. sci. dept., 1978-94. Lab. technician Drew Chem. Corp., Boonton, 1942—47; tech. asst. Bell Telecom. Lab., Whippany, NJ, 1956; rsch. scientist Warner Lambert Rsch. Inst., Morris Plains, NJ, 1959—62; tchr. sci. enrichment Boonton Summer Sch., 1963—85; curriculum developer Morris County Vocat.-Tech. Sch., Denville, 1987; project evaluator Mid. States Assn., 1973, 79; facilitator Ptnrs. in Edn. Program; promoter Media Ctr. Open House; cons., reviewer Am. Biol. Tchr. Mag., 1975—; com. mem. Sch. Articulation Program Boonton Schs., 1991—94; media ctr. spkr. Meet the Author; sponsor Student Showcase of Excellence in Sci., 1990—94; faculty sponsor, mentor h.s. students, 1966—94; mentor Alt. Rt. Program Tchrs. N.J. Organizer Am. Dental Health Clinic, Boonton, 1968—72; presenter, spkr. in field. Author: Research Projects for High School Biology, 1971, Biology Teacher's Desk Book, 1979, Science Activities for Every Month of the School Year, 1981, Science Demonstrations for Elementary Classrooms, 1988, Hands-on Science, 1991; contbr. articles to profl. jours., including Am. Biology Tchr. Mem. career com. N.J. divsn. Theobald Smith Soc., 1975—76, mentoring program, 1992—; fundraiser Am. Hemophilia Found., Rockaway, NJ, 1985—, Am. Heart Assn., 1995—, Muscular Dystrophy Found., 1995—, Nat. Children's Cancer Soc., 1996—; mothers march vol. March of Dimes, 1990—; cons. Cmty. Mid. Sch. Planning Com., Boonton, 1988—90; bd. advisors ABI Rsch., 1995—. Named Outstanding Biology Tchr., Nat. Assn. Biology Tchrs., 1972, Outstanding Sci. Tchr., Rsch. Assn. N.Am., 1980, Woman of the Yr., 1993—98; named to Sci. Edn. Hall of Fame, 1994—98, Boonton H.S. Wall of Fame, 1996, 1997, 1998; recipient Disting. Citizen's award, Town of Rockaway, 1984, Gov.'s and Edn. award, N.J. Dept. Edn., 1984, Morris County Tchr. of the Yr. award, 1990, Presdl. award, NSF, 1984, Cert. of Honor, State of N.J., 1985, World Lifetime Achievement award, 1994, Internat. Order of Merit, 1994, Spotlight award, Boonton Bd. Edn., 1980—86, Tchr. of Yr., 1984, 1990, Women's Inner Cir. of Achievement award, 1995. Mem.: NSTA, ASCD, NEA, NEA Ret., Morris Area Sci. Alliance, N.J. Dept. Edn. Exec. Acad., N.J. Dept. Edn. Exec. Acad., N.J. Alliance for Math. and Sci., N.J. Prins. And Suprs. Assn., N.J. Edn. Assn., Assn. Presdl. Award Winners in Sci. Tchg., Nat. Assn. Secondary Sch. Prins., Morris County Ret. Educators Assn. Avocations: reading, propagating plants, collecting gold coins. Home: 115 Jackson Ave Rockaway NJ 07866-3039

ALLEN, EDGAR BURNS, records management professional; b. L.A., Sept. 1, 1929; s. Harry James and Hela Ruth (Graham) A.; m. Eleanor Angela Gregory, July 24, 1960; children: Linda Marie, Lisa Ann. AA, L.A. City Coll., 1958; student, Calif. State U., L.A., 1958, 81; BS, UCLA, 1985. Supr. records ctr. L.A. Dept. Water and Power, 1958-67, records mgr., 1967-76; records mgmt. officer City of L.A., 1976-85; records mgmt. cons., L.A., 1985-2000. Profl. creator records mgmt. systems, tax preparer, L.A., 1990—; established City Records Ctr. and City Archives. Chmn. Leimert Pk. Community Assn., L.A., 1972-75. Mem. Assn. Records Mgrs. and Adminstrs. (bd. dirs. 1975-76), Soc. Calif. Archivists, All Yr. Figure Skating Club (bd. dirs. 1970-79). Democrat. Roman Catholic. Avocations: bowling, walking, travel.

ALLEN, EDWARD JOHN BEDFORD, historian, retired educator; b. Ulverston, Eng., May 13, 1933; came to U.S., 1965; s. Bedford and Rosetta (Machell) A.; m. Heide Gelbert, Dec. 29, 1961; children: Peter, Ariane, Jacqueline. BA, Sir George Williams U., Montreal, Que., Can., 1965; MA, Brigham Young U., 1966, PhD, 1969. Asst., assoc., prof. history Plymouth (N.H.) State Coll., 1968-97. Author: Teaching & Technique: A History of American Ski Instruction, 1985, From Skisport to Skiing: 100 Years of an American Sport, New England Skiing 1870s-1940, New Hampshire on Skis; editor: International Ski History Congress 2002; contbr. articles to profl. jours. 2d lt. Eng. Army, 1952-54. Travel grantee German Acad. Exch.Svc., Europe, 1992. Mem. N.Am. Soc. Sports History, Internat. Soc. for History Phys. Edn. and Sport, New Eng. Ski Mus. (v.p.). Home: 106 Buffalo Rd PO Box 23 Rumney NH 03266-3255 E-mail: jallen@mail.plymouth.edu.

ALLEN, EDWARD LEFEBVRE, lawyer; b. Richmond, Va., May 17, 1962; s. Wilbur Coleman and Frances (Gayle) A.; m. Nancy Williams, Sept. 3, 1994; children: Parker Edward, Mason Elizabeth. BA, Vanderbilt U., 1984; JD, Washington and Lee U., 1987. Bar: Va. 1987, U.S. Ct. Appeals (4th cir.) 1989, U.S. Claims Ct. 1990, U.S. Ct. Appeals (D.C. cir.) 1996. Assoc. Allen, Allen, Allen & Allen, Richmond, 1987-96, ptnr., 1996—. Mem. ABA, ATLA, Va. Trial Lawyers Assn. (bd. govs. 1999—), Va. State Bar, Fredericksburg Bar Assn. Home: 401 Chamonix Dr Fredericksburg VA 22405-2029 Office: Allen Allen Allen & Allen 3405 Plank Rd Fredericksburg VA 22407-4959 E-mail: ELA@Allenandallen.com.

ALLEN, ELIZABETH MARESCA, marketing and telecommunications executive; b. Red Bank, N.J., Jan. 4, 1958; d. Paul William Michael and Roberta Gertrude (Abbes) Maresca; m. David D. Allen; 1 child, Brandon D. Student, Brookdale Community Coll., 1976-77; A Bus. Adminstrn., Tidewater C.C., 1988; BA in Bus. Mgmt., Va. Wesleyan Coll., 1997. Systems analyst Methods Research Corp., Farmingdale, N.J., 1977-79; divsn. mgr. Abacus Comm. L.P., Virginia Beach, Va., 1979—, dir. telecomm., dir. client svcs. V.p. Charlestowne Civic League, Virginia Beach, 1983—84, Plantation Lakes Homeowners Assn., Chesapeake, Va., 1992—; advisor Commonwealth Coll., Norfolk, 1984—91; commr. S. Norfolk Revitalization Commn., 1999—2001; del. Va. Rep. Conv., 1993—; mem. gov.'s coun. Rep. Nat. Com., 1997; bd. dirs. Arthritis Found., Norfolk, Va., 1986—90. Mem.: Williamsburg Area C. of C. (exhibit chmn. 1987), Hampton Roads C. of C. (com. chmn. 1985, 1989), Women's Network Hampton Roads (publicity chmn. 1988—91, chmn. publicity for Job Fair 1989). Republican. Roman Catholic. Avocations: tennis, Civil War history, collecting antiques, gardening. Office: Abacus Communications LP 4456 Corporation Ln Ste 200 Virginia Beach VA 23462-3151

ALLEN, FRANK CHARLES, writer; b. Evanston, Ill., Mar. 22, 1939; s. William Gordon Boas and Eathal Fern Wallace; m. Heidemarie Hafner. BA, U. Md., 1961; MA, NYU, 1963; PhD, U. Md., 1970. Asst. prof. Wilkes Coll., Wilkes-Barre, Pa., 1969-72; dean continuing edn. Allentown Coll., Center Valley, Pa., 1983-89; asst. prof. Cobleskill (N.Y.) State U., 1990-92; dir. continuing edn. W.Va. State Coll., 1993-94; adj. prof. Northampton C.C., Tannersville, Pa., 1995—. Adj. prof. Moravian Coll., Bethlehem, Pa., 1973-82; pres. Allen Assocs., East Stroudsburg, Pa., 1995—. Author: Robert Brownings Bishop Blougram's Apology, 1981, Magna Mater, 1981, Seeds of Recognition, 1984. Pres. RSVP Adv. Bd., East Stroudsburg, 1999—2002; sec. Monroe County Rail Authority, 2001—. With U.S. Army, 1961—67. Mem. Nat. Book Critics Cir. Avocation: hiking. Home: 220 Mary St East Stroudsburg PA 18301

ALLEN, GARLAND EDWARD, biology educator, science historian; b. Louisville, Feb. 13, 1936; s. Garland Edward and Virginia (Blandford) A.; children: Tania Leigh, Carin Tove. AB, U. Louisville, 1957; AMT, Harvard U., 1958, AM, 1963, PhD, 1966. Programmer, announcer WFPL-WFPK, Louisville, 1956-58; tchr. Mt. Hermon (Mass.) Sch., 1958-61; Allston-Burr sr. tutor, instr. history of sci. Harvard, 1965-67; asst. prof. biology Washington U., St. Louis, 1967-72, assoc. prof., 1972-80, prof., 1980—. Cons. Ednl. Rsch. Corp., Cleve., 1967-85; commr. Commn. Undergrad. Edn. in Biol. Scis., 1967-70; mem. NSF Panel for Social Scis., 1968-71; mem. ELSI rev. panel NIH, 2002; trustee Marine Biol. Lab., Woods Hole, Mass., 1985-93; Sigma Xi nat. lectr., 1973-74, bicentennial lectr., 1974-77; Watkins vis. prof. Wichita State U., 1984; vis. prof. dept. history of sci. Harvard U., 1989-91, Sarton Award Lecture, AAAS, 1998. Author: Life Sciences in the Twentieth Century, 1975, 1978, T.H. Morgan: The Man and His Science, 1978; author: (with J.J.W. Baker) Matter, Energy and Life, 1965, 1970, 1975, 1981; author: The Study of Biology, 1967, The Study of Biology, 4th edit., 1982, Hypnothesis, Prediction and Implication, 1969, The Process of Biology, 1970, Biology: Scientific Process and Social Issues, 2001; co-editor: Mendel Newsletter, 1989—92, Jour. History of Biology, 1996—; mem. editl. bd.: San Josè Studies, —, Jour. History of Biology, 1968—91, 1998—, Folia Medeliana, History and Philosophy of the Life Scis., 1993—; co-editor: Science, History, and Social Activism: A Tribute to Everett Mendelsohn, 2002. Fellow Charles Warren Ctr. for Studies in Am. History, Harvard U., 1981-82; sr. fellow Dibner Inst. for the History of Sci. and Tech., MIT, 2002. Mem. AAAS (coun., sect. L exec. com. 1975, Sarton award lectr. 1998), History Sci. Soc. (chmn. Schumann Prize com. 1972, Pfizer prize com. 1977, 80, 91-94, HSS coun. 1994-96, vis. lectr. program 1985-87), Sigma Xi. Home: 1526 Mississippi Ave Saint Louis MO 63104-2512 Office: Washington U Biology Dept Saint Louis MO 63130 E-mail: allen@biology2.wustl.edu.

ALLEN, GARY CURTISS, geology educator; b. Stockton, Calif., July 18, 1939; s. Curtiss Wright and Helen Lucille (McElroy) A.; m. Ruth Lee Mayeux, June 5, 1965; children: Adrienne Lucille, Christopher Gary. BS in Chemistry, Stanford U., 1961; MA in Geology, Rice U., 1963; PhD in Geochemistry, U. N.C., 1968. Head geochemistry and petrology dept. Mineral Resources div. State of Va., Charlottesville, 1966-68; asst. prof. earth scis. La. State U., New Orleans, 1968-78; assoc. prof. earth scis. U. New Orleans, 1972-78, prof. geology, 1978—, dir. environ. tng. program, 1993-94, coord. environ. sci. and policy degree program, 2000—. Coord. for radiation safety La. State U. System, 1989—, chair coun. faculty advisors, 1995-97; pres. Sunbelt Assocs. Inc., New Orleans 1978—; bd. dirs. Holocene Rsch. Inst.; pres. Assn. La. Faculty Senates, 1997-99; chair La. Bd. Regents Faculty Adv. Coun., 1997-2000 Contbr. articles to profl. jours. Mem. St. Frances Cabrini Sch. Bd., New Orleans, 1979-82. NASA fellow, 1963-66. Mem. Geol. Soc. Am., New Orleans Geol. Soc., U. New Orleans Fedn. Tchrs. (pres. 1985-87, treas. 1987—), Sigma Xi (pres. New Orleans chpt. 1977-78, v.p. 1991—). Home: 180 Devon Dr Mandeville LA 70448-3406 Office: U New Orleans Dept Geology And Geoph New Orleans LA 70148-0001

ALLEN, GEORGE FELIX, senator, former governor; b. Whittier, Calif., Mar. 8, 1952; s. George H. and Henrietta Lumbroso A.; m. Susan M. Brown; children: Tyler, Forrest, Brooke. BA cum laude in History, U. Va., 1974, JD, 1977. Mem. Va. Ho. of Dels., Richmond, 1982—91, 102d Congress from 7th Dist. Va., 1991-93; gov. State of Va., 1994-98; ptnr. McGuire Woods Battle & Boothe, LLP, Richmond, 1998-2001; U.S. senator from Va., 2001—. Chmn. Chesapeake Bay Exec. Coun., 1995—96, So. Gov.'s Assn., 1996—97. Republican. Presbyterian. Office: 204 Russell Senate Office Bldg Washington DC 20510*

ALLEN, GEORGE HOWARD, publishing management consultant; b. Boston, June 1, 1914; s. Albert Hacker and Myrtie A. (Lawton) A.; m. Virginia Russell, Sept. 7, 1940; children: Russell Lawton, Douglas Winslow (dec.). BS, U. Mass., 1936, LL.D., 1967; MBA, Harvard U., 1938. Asst. to pres. Nat. Theatre Supply Co., N.Y.C., 1938-40; research mgr. Sta. WOR, 1941, asst. dir. promotion and research, 1942-43; radio cons. U.S. Treasury Dept., 1943-45; gen. mgr., sec. bd. Coop. Analysis of Broadcasting, N.Y.C., 1944-46; N.E. sales mgr. N.Y. Herald Tribune, 1946, promotion mgr., 1947-50; chmn. 20th Nat. Bus. Conf., Harvard, 1950; dir. sales promotion McCall's mag., 1950-57, asst. pub., gen. mgr., 1957-60; pub. Better Living mag., 1956; v.p. Mass Markets Publs., Inc., 1953-54, pres., 1954-55, dir., 1953-55; spl. asst. to pres. Meredith Pub. Co., N.Y.C., 1960-61, v.p., 1961-66, bd. dirs., 1965-66, gen. mgr. mag. pub. div., 1962-66; pub. Better Homes and Gardens, Successful Farming mags., 1964-66; chmn. bd. Nat. Plan Service, Chgo., 1965-66; pub., v.p. bd. dirs. Fawcett Publs., Inc., N.Y.C., 1966-72, exec. v.p., dir., 1972-77; sr. v.p. mags. CBS Publs., 1977-84, sr. v.p., 1978-82, spl. interest group pub. (Audio, Road & Track, World Tennis, Am. Photographer, Cycle World), 1982—; pub. Woman's Day, 1966-80, Audio, Road & Track, World Tennis, Am. Photographers, Cycle World, 1982-84. Cons. pub. mgmt., 1984— ; mem. panel Pres.'s White House Conf. on Food and Nutrition, 1969; Bd. dirs. Internat. Youth for Understanding Exchange Program, Ann Arbor, chmn., 1978-79; bd. dirs. Advt. Council, 1969— ; chmn. Intercorp. Communications Group; mem. council judges Advt. Hall of Fame, 1982 Author: Individual Initiative in Business, 1950, Thoughts at the Holiday Season, 3 edits., The Nature Circuit; contbr. articles profl. mags. Mem. Chancellor's Council U. Mass, 1982, mem. bus. adv. Council Sch. Mgmt., 1983. Recipient leadership award Am. Legion, 1932; Young Advt. Man of Year, 1956; Achievement Award Wash. Ad Club, 1956; Silver Anvil award Am. Pub. Relations Assn., 1957; Bell Ringer award Salt Lake City Ad Club, 1957; Pub. Relations News award, 1957; Iowa Mgmt. Man of Year, 1965; named Pub. of Year; also recipient Henry Johnson Fisher award of mag. industry, 1980; named to Pub. Hall of Fame, 1985. Mem. Am. Mktg. Assn. (pres. N.Y. 1946), NAM (dir. 1965-66), Mag. Pubs. Assn. (dir., sec. 1974-75, chmn. 1977, chmn. Kelly awards com. 1980—), Advt. Fedn. Am. (dir. 1965-67), U.S. C. of C. (edn. com. 1964-66), Advt. Rsch. Found. (dir. 1965, sec.-treas. 1971, vice chmn. 1972, chmn. 1974-75), U. Mass. Alumni Assn. (v.p.), Harvard Bus. Sch. Assn. (pres. 1967), Pubs. Info. Bur. (dir. 1966, vice chmn. 1974), Harvard Alumni Assn. (dir. 1958-59), Sales Promotion Execs. Assn. (mem. nat. bd. 1958), Broadcast Pioneers), All Media Exec. Roundtable (chmn.), Harvard Club (N.Y.C.), Sky Club (N.Y.C.), Congregationalist. Office: Cons to Pub Mgmt 8400 Vamo Rd Apt 1108 Sarasota FL 34231-7816 E-mail: gha@home.com. *Togetherness is still the glue that structures our society.*

ALLEN, GEORGE SEWELL, neurosurgery educator; b. St. Louis, Jan. 10, 1942; s. Mitchell Vincent and Cleo (Scott) A.; m. Shannon Hersey, May 30, 1982; children: Kathrine Long, Jennifer Savage, Elizabeth Scott. BA in Chemistry, Wesleyan U., 1963; MD, Washington U., St. Louis, 1967; PhD, U. Minn., 1975. Diplomate Am. Bd. Neurol. Surgeons. Intern Duke U., Durham, N.C., 1967-68; rsch. assoc. Nat. Inst. Neurol. Disease and Stroke, NIH, 1968-70; resident dept. neurol. surgery U. Minn., Mpls., 1970-75; asst. prof. neurol. surgery Johns Hopkins U. and Hosp., Balt., 1975-79, assoc. prof., 1979-83, prof., 1983-84; prof. neurol. surgery, chmn. dept. Vanderbilt U. Med. Ctr., Nashville, 1984—. Mem. med. staff Vanderbilt U. Hosp., Met. Nashville Gen. Hosp., VA Hosp., Nashville, St. Thomas Hosp., Nashville, all 1984—; A.W. Rogers lectr. Milw. Acad. Medicine, 1988, J. Jay Keegan Meml. lectr. U. Nebr. Med. Ctr., Omaha, 1988, J. Cochran lectr. Med. Assn. Ala., Montgomery, 1988, A.B. Baker lectr. U. Minn., Mpls., 1988. Contbr. articles to profl. jours. Comdr. USPHS, 1968-70. Mem. ACS, Am. Assn. Neurol. Surgeons, Congress of Neurol. Surgeons, Brain Surgery Soc., Soc. Neurol. Surgeons, H. William Scott, Jr. Soc., Soc. Neurosurg. Anesthesia and Neurologic Supportive Care Office: Vanderbilt U Med Ctr N Dept Neurosurgery Rm T 4224 Nashville TN 37232-0001 E-mail: george.allen@vanderbilt.edu.

ALLEN, GERALD CAMPBELL FORREST, management consulting company owner; b. Boston, Jan. 1, 1924; s. Charles Francis and Sarah Ann (Campbell) A.; m. Anne Elisabeth Conrad, May 23, 1944; children: Katherine Sarah Anne, Ethan William John Campbell, Elisabeth Amy Martha Joan. BA, MA, Harvard U., 1945-49; PhD, U. Chgo., 1952. Ency. editor Consol. Book Pub., Chgo., 1952-54; advt. exec. Chgo. Tribune, 1954-59; pres. Gerald Allen Co., Chgo., 1960-66; v.p. Klau-Van Pietersom-Dunlap, Inc., Milw., 1967-71; v.p., dir. Unidex Pub. Co., Inc., Milw., 1971-80; chmn., CEO Allen Mgmt. Group, Inc., Milw., 1980—. Pres. Psychologists in Advt., Chgo., 1965; instr. mktg. and bus. adminstrn. U. Wis., 1967-68; v.p., dir. Benchmark Mfg. Co., Inc., Milw.; cons. Kellett Commn. on Higher Edn. Mem. ad hoc Low Income Energy Task Force, State of Wis.; mem. energy crisis planning com. City of Milw. Capt. royal arty. Brit. Army, 1944-45, ETO. Fellow Royal Hort. Soc.; mem. Am. Mktg. Assn., Am. Statis. Assn., AAAS, Am. Econ. Assn., N.Y. Acad. Scis., Harvard Club of Wis., Harvard Club of Chgo., Mensa. Republican. Home: 13 Linden Manor Kewaunee WI 54216-1735 Office: Allen Mgmt Group Inc 1204 Forth St Kewaunee WI 54216-1777

ALLEN, HAROLD DON, mathematics educator, science writer, monetary historian; b. Montreal, PQ, Canada, July 2, 1931; s. Harold Don and Eva Margaret (Reid) A.; m. Frances Mary Marven, June 30, 1955; children: Nigel David, Laura Margaret, Elizabeth Kathleen, Rosalie Elaine. BS, McGill U., Montreal, Que., 1952; MS in Tchg. of Math., U. Santa Clara, 1967; EdM, Rutgers U., 1968; EdD, 1977. Superior class I tchg. diploma, Que; cert. tchr. level 8, N.S. Tchr., tchg. credentials N.W.T.. Head math. Greater Montreal Sch. Bd., 1953-63; tchg. prin. Chibougamau Protestant Sch., Que., 1963-65; supervising prin. Saguenay Valley High Sch., Arvida, Que., 1965-67; assoc. prof. edn. N.S. Tchrs. coll., Truro, N.S., Can., 1969-77; prof., 1977-87; head dept. math. St. George's Sch., Montreal, 1987—93. Cons. adult edn. curriculum revision, N.S., 1985-86; cons. in numismatics, lottery history; com. mem. Metric Commn. Can., Ottawa, Ont., 1973-84; vis. prof., demonstration tchr. McGill U. Gifted Summer Sch., 1983-91, adj. prof. ednl. psychology, 1991—; coord. gifted and talented summer maths. camps. Ottawa, 1992—; instr. math. and sci. Eastern Arctic Tchr. Edn. Program, Iqaluit, 1993-96, Coral Harbour, 1996-97. Co-author: Mathematics with Metric Measure, vols. I-VI, 1973-75; compiler, contbg. author: Canadian Numismatic Digest, 1960, Expanding Mathematical Horizons, 1980, Face to Face with Giftedness, 1983, rev. edit., 1985, Sums of Yesteryear, 1984, Math for the Joy of It, 1994, School Mathematics Glossary, 1995, School Science Glossary, 1995, Coinman to Canadians: Authorized Biography of J.E. Charlton, 2001. Recipient Numismatic Literary award Can. Numismatic Assn., 1977, Numismatic Edn. award Royal Can. Mint, 1979. Fellow Can. Coll. Tchrs. (nat. councilor 1979-82), Royal Numismatic Soc.; mem. Math. Assn. Am. (emeritus mem.), Nat. Coun. Tchrs. Math., Sch. Sci. and Math Assn., Royal Philatelic Soc. Can., Am. Cryptogram Assn., (Damon award 1990, 96), Nat. Puzzlers League, Can. Sci. Writers Assn., Monarchist League Can. (life), Mu Alpha Theta (editor-in-chief Math. Log 1980-90, governing bd. 1980-90), Phi Delta Kappa, Kappa Delta Pi. Progressive Conservative. Presbyterian. Avocations: numismatics, mathematical problem solving, recreational mathematics, recreational cryptography, photography. Home: 6150 Bienville Ave Brossard QC Canada J4Z 1W8

ALLEN, HARRY ROGER, lawyer; b. Memphis, June 13, 1933; s. Sam J. and Louise (Frazier) A.; children: Julie Ferriss, Steven J., Leslie Loraine Allen Anchor; m. Emily Ann Mason, May 4, 1990; 1 stepchild, Jeremy Myrick. Student, Tulane U., 1951-53; BBA, U. Miss., 1955, LLB, 1959. Bar: Miss. 1959, U.S. Dist. Ct. (so. dist.) Miss. 1961, U.S. Ct. Appeals (5th cir.) 1981, U.S. Supreme Ct. 1981. From assoc. to ptnr. Brunini Everett, Grantam & Quinn, Vicksburg, Miss., 1959-68; ptnr. Bryan, Nelson, Allen, Schroeder, Cobb & Hood, Gulfport, Miss., 1968-91; pres. Allen, Vaughn, Cobb & Hood, P.A., Gulfport, Miss., 1992—. Spl. asst. atty. gen. State of Miss., Gulfport, 1989-91. Mem. Harrison County com. region XIII commn. Mental Health and Mental Retardation, Gulfport, 1976—; fin. chmn. Miss. Rep. Party, 1982-84; Miss. Elector Bush/Quayle Ticket, Jackson, Miss., 1984; del. Rep. Nat. Conv., Dallas, 1984. Capt. USAF, 1955-58. Named to Best Lawyer in Am. publ., 1988-97. Mem. Internat. Assn. Def. Counsel, Miss. Bar Found. (former trustee), Miss. Bar Assn. (pres. Harrison County young lawyers sect. 1969-70, jud. liaison com. 1990-91), Miss. Fed. Bar Assn. (so. dist. commr. 1980-81), Miss. Bar Leadership Conf. (chmn. 1991), Harrison County Bar Assn. (pres. 1990), Lamar Order, Am. Inns of Ct. (pres. Russell 1995-96, Blass-Walker chpt. Republican. Methodist. Avocations: golf, skiing. Office: Allen Vaughn Cobb & Hood P A PO Box 4108 Gulfport MS 39502-4108 E-mail: hallen@avchlaw.com.

ALLEN, HENRY LEE, sociology educator, consultant; b. Joiner, Ark., July 7, 1955; s. John Henry Jr. and Mahalie (Moore) A.; m. Juliet Eugenia-Agnes Cooper, July 7, 1979; children: Jonathan, Jessica, Janice, Justin, Julia, Janel, Joseph, Judith. BA cum laude, Wheaton Coll., 1977; MA, U. Chgo., 1979, PhD, 1988. Sociology instr., adminstrv. asst. to pres. Bethel Coll., St. Paul, 1982-87; assoc. prof. sociology Calvin Coll., Grand Rapids, Mich., 1987-91; asst. prof. edn. Grad. Sch. Edn., U. Rochester, N.Y., 1991-97; assoc. prof. sociology Rochester N.Y.) Inst. Tech., 1997-98, Wheaton (Ill.) Coll., 1998—. Cons. NEA, Washington, 1992—, Am. Bible Soc., 2001—, Inst. for the Black Family, Detroit, 1984—, among others. Contbr. articles to profl. jours. Bd. dirs. Genessee Settlement House, Rochester, 1993-96, Koinonia House, 2000—, African-Am. Leadership Roundtable of Dupage County, 2000—; mem. Kettering Found. Cmty. Leadership Program; mem. adv. com. United Way, Rochester, 1995-96; African-Am. Leadership Roundtable, Rochester, 1993-96; mem. Jubilee Bapt. Ch., 2002. Fellow Danforth Found., 1978-81. Mem. ASCD, Wilson Ctr. for Scholars, N.Y. Acad. Scis. Avocations: science fiction, archery, astronomy, football, museums. Home: 111 W Lincoln Ave Wheaton IL 60187-4114 Office: Wheaton Coll Dept Sociology Wheaton IL 60187 E-mail: henry.l.allen@wheaton.edu.

ALLEN, HENRY WESLEY, biomedical researcher, consultant; b. Louisville, Oct. 16, 1927; s. John Turk and Irene Victoria (Slater) A.; m. Evelyn Chen, Dec. 29, 1968 (div. Dec. 1988); children: Lillian Chen, Rosaniline Chen, Dianne Chen. Student, U. Louisville, 1945-46, U. Chgo., 1946-47, U. So. Calif., 1960-61. Rschr. Loma Linda (Calif.) U., 1962-77, Am. Biologics, Chula Vista, Calif., 1977—. Author: International Protocols in Cancer Management, 1983, The Study of Reactive Oxygen Toxic Species and Their Metabolism, 1985, 2d edit., 1997, The Biochemistry of Live Cell Therapy, 1986, Fibromyalgia, 2001; contbr. articles to Jour. of Theoretical Biology, Analytical Biochemistry, Nature, others. Achievements include patents in field. Office: Am Biologics 1180 Walnut Ave Chula Vista CA 91911-2622

ALLEN, HERBERT ELLIS, environmental chemistry educator; b. Sharon, Pa., July 19, 1939; s. Jacob Samuel and Florence (Safier) A.; m. Deena Wilner, 1962 (dec. 1983); children: Francine Joy, Julie Michelle; m. Ronnie Magil, 1984 BS in Chemistry, U. Mich., 1962; MS, Wayne State U., 1967; PhD, U. Mich., 1974. Chemist U.S. Bur. Comml. Fisheries, Ann Arbor, Mich., 1962-70; lectr. U. Mich., Ann Arbor, 1970-74; asst. prof. Ill. Inst. Tech., Chgo., 1974-76, assoc. prof., 1976-80, prof. environ. engring., 1980-83; dir. Environ. Studies Inst., Drexel U., Phila., also prof. chemistry, 1983-89; prof. civil engring. U. Del., Newark, 1990—, dir. Ctr. for Study of Metals in the Environment, 2002—; dir. Del. Waste Reduction Assistance Program, 1991-95. Vis. prof. Water Rsch. Ctr., Medmenham, Eng., 1980-81, Nankai U., Tianjin, People's Republic of China, 1993—; cons. WHO, U.S. EPA. Editor: Nutrients in Natural Waters, 1972, Analysis and Effects of Metal Speciation, Applications to Water, Waste, Soil, 1988, Metals in Groundwater, 1993, Metal Speciation and Contamination of Soil, 1994, Metal Contaminated Aquatic Sediments, 1995, Metals in Surface Water, 1998, Bioavailability of Metals in Terrestrial Ecosystems, 2002. Fellow, WHO, 1981. Mem. Am. Chem. Soc. (chmn. divsn. environ. chemistry 1972-

75), Water Environment Fedn., Soc. for Environ. Toxicology and Chemistry, Internat. Water Assn. Home: 21 E Levering Mill Rd Bala Cynwyd PA 19004-2251 Office: Univ Delaware Dept Civil & Environ Engring Newark DE 19716 E-mail: allen@ce.udel.edu.

ALLEN, HOWARD NORMAN, cardiologist, educator; b. Chgo., Nov. 19, 1936; s. Herman and Ida Gertrude (Weinstein) Allen; children: Michael Daniel, Jeffrey Scott. BS, U. Ill., Chgo., 1958, MD, 1960. Diplomate Am. Bd. Internal Medicine, Am. Bd. Cardiovasc. Disease, Nat. Bd. Med. Examiners. Intern Los Angeles County Gen. Hosp., L.A., 1960—61; resident in internal medicine Wadsworth VA Med. Ctr., L.A., 1961, 1964—66; fellow in cardiology Cedars-Sinai Med. Ctr., L.A., 1966—67, dir. cardiac care unit Cedars of Lebanon Hosp. div., 1968—74, dir. Pacemaker Evaluation Ctr., 1968—89, dir. Cardiac Noninvasive Lab., 1972—88; Markus Found. fellow in cardiology St. George's Hosp., London, 1967—68; attending physician cardiology svc. Sepulveda (Calif.) VA Med. Ctr., 1972—86; pvt. practice Beverly Hills, Calif., 1988—. Asst. prof. medicine UCLA, 1970—76, assoc. prof., 1976—84, adj. prof., 1984—88, clin. prof., 1988—; cons. Sutherland Learning Assocs., Inc., L.A., 1970—75; cardiology cons. Occidental Life Ins. Co., L.A., Calif., 1972—86. Contbr. articles to profl. jours., chapters to books. Commr. L.A. County Emergency Med. Svcs., 1989-—91. Capt. M.C. U.S. Army, 1962—63, Korea. Fellow, NSF, 1958, NIH, 1966—67. Fellow: ACP, Am. Coll. Cardiology (Calif. chpt. dist. councilor 1999—); mem.: Am. Heart Assn. (bd. dirs. 1979—94, fellow coun. clin. cardiology, pres. Greater L.A. affiliate 1987—88, Heart of Gold award 1994), Cedars-Sinai Alumni Assn. (life; exec. bd. 1999—, sec., treas. 2000, pres. 2001—02), U. Ill. Alumni Assn. (life Loyalty award 1996), Big Ten Club So. Calif. (bd. dirs.), Pi Kappa Epsilon, Alpha Omega Alpha. Office: 414 N Camden Dr Ste 1100 Beverly Hills CA 90210-4532 E-mail: allen@cvmg.com.

ALLEN, HUBERT A., JR., publishing executive, writer, statistician, consultant; b. Albuquerque, Apr. 22, 1958; s. Hubert A. and Mary S. Allen; m. Deborah Lynne Helitzer, Sept. 28, 1985 (div. June 1998); children: Nyika, Jos. BS in Applied Math. and Biology, Brown U., 1980; MS in Biostats., Johns Hopkins U., 1985. Pres. Hubert Allen and Assocs., Albuquerque, 1985—. Bd. dirs. ICON Consultants USA, Inc., Tucson, 1994—99. Author: Shadows On The Wall, 1988, The Petroglyph Calendar: An Archaeoastronomy Adventure, 1990, Breakfast with Kamuzu, 2001; co-author (with others): The Manual for Targeted Intervention on Sexually Transmitted Illnesses with Community Members, 1994, The Manual for Targeted Intervention on Sexually Transmitted Illnesses for the Setting of Commercial Sex, 1997; contbr. articles to profl. jours. Mem.: Am. Statis. Assn. Jewish. Avocation: rock climbing. Home and Office: 720-25 Tramway Ln NE Albuquerque NM 87122

ALLEN, JANICE FAYE CLEMENT, nursing administrator; b. Norfolk, Nebr., Aug. 19, 1946; d. Allen Edward and Hilda Bernice (Stange) Reeves; m. Roger Allen Clement, Oct. 6, 1968 (dec. July 1974); m. August H. Allen, Sept. 17, 1988. RN, Meth. Sch. Nursing, Omaha, 1967; BSN magna cum laude, Creighton U., 1978; MSN, U. Nebr., 1981. cert. in nursing adminstrn., cert. in infection control. With Meth. Hosp., 1967-68, 72-83, asst. head nurse, 1974-77, staff devel. nurse, 1977-81, dir. staff adminstrv. svcs., 1981-83; pub. health nurse Wichita-Sedgwick County Health Dept., Wichita, Kans., 1970-72; dir. nursing Meth. Med. Ctr., St. Joseph, Mo., 1983-84; v.p. nursing and profl. svcs. Broadlawns Med. Ctr., Des Moines, 1984-93; dir. staff mgmt./infection control Ea. N.Mex. Med. Ctr., Roswell, 1993-2000, Carl T. Hayden VA Med. Ctr., Phoenix, 2000—03; faculty mem. U. Phoenix, 2002. Adj. clin. faculty nursing Drake U. Nursing, Des Moines, 1986-93, adv. bd., 1984-93, Ctrl. Campus Practical Nursing, 1984-93; mem. adv. bd. Des Moines Area C.C. Dist., 1987—, Des Moines Area C.C. Nursing Bd., 1987-93, Grandview Coll., 1988-93; bd. dirs. Vis. Nurse Svcs., 1988-93; assoc. Am. Coll. Healthcare Execs., Dept. of Veteran Affairs VISN 18 Leadership Devel. Graduate, 2003. Mem.: ANA, Nat. Assoc. for Healthcare Quality, Nurses Orgn. Vet. Affairs, N.Mex. Orgn. Nurse Execs., Assn. Infection Control and Epidemiology, Iowa Orgn. Nurse Execs. (treas. 1987, sec. 1989, pres.-elect 1993), Iowa League for Nursing (treas. 1987—89, pres. 1989), Colloquium Nursing Leaders Ctrl. Iowa, Ctrl. Iowa Nursing Leadership Conf. (pres. 1985), N.Mex. Nurses Assn., Am. Orgn. Nurse Execs. (bd. dirs. 1995), Altrusa of Roswell, Sigma Theta Tau (pres. Zeta Chi chpt. 1990—92). Home: 20278 N 104 Ave Peoria AZ 85382 Office: Carl T Hayden VA Med Ctr 650 E Indian Sch Rd Phoenix AZ 85012 Business E-Mail: jan.allen@med.va.gov.

ALLEN, JEFFREY C. pediatric neurologist; MD, Harvard U., 1969. Diplomate Am. Bd. Psychiatry and Neurology. Resident in pediatrics Montreal Children's Hosp., McGill U.; resident in neurology Montreal Neurol. Inst., McGill U.; prof. neurology NYU Med. Ctr.; med. dir. Children's Brain Tumor Found. Prin. investigator NIH, 1992-95. Editl. bd. Jour. Neuro-oncology. Fellow Royal Coll. of Physicians and Surgeons (Can.); mem. Child Neurology Soc., Am. Acad. Neurology. Office: Beth Israel Med Ctr North Divsn 170 East End Ave at 87th St New York NY 10128 Fax: 212-870-9424. E-mail: jallen@bethisraelny.org.

ALLEN, JEFFREY MICHAEL, lawyer; b. Chgo., Dec. 13, 1948; s. Albert A. and Miriam (Feldman) A.; m. Anne Marie Guaraglia, Aug. 9, 1975; children: Jason M., Sara M. BA in Polit. Sci. with great distinction, U. Calif., Berkeley, 1970, JD, 1973. Bar: Calif. 1973, U.S. Dist. Ct. (no. and so. dists.) Calif. 1973, U.S. Ct. Appeals (9th cir.) 1973, U.S. Dist. Ct. (ea. dist.) Calif. 1974, U.S. Dist. Ct. (cen. dist.) Calif. 1977, U.S. Dist. Ct. (so. dist.) Calif., U.S. Supreme Ct.; lic. real estate broker. Prin. Graves & Allen, Oakland, Calif., 1973—. Teaching asst. dept. polit. sci. U. Calif., Berkeley, 1970-73; lectr. St. Mary's Coll., Moraga, Calif., 1976-90; mem. faculty Oakland Coll. of Law, 1996-98; bd. dirs. Family Svcs. of the East Bay, 1987-92, 1st v.p., 1988, pres., 1988-91; mem. panel arbitrators Ala. County Superior Ct.; arbitrator comml. arbitration panel Am. Arbitration Assn. Mem. editorial bd. U. Calif. Law Rev., 1971-73, project editor, 1972-73; mem. Ecology Law Quar., 1971-72; contbr. articles to profl. jours. Mem. U.S. Youth Soccer Constl. Commn., 1997—98, U.S. Youth Soccer Bylaws Com., 1998—; mem. region 4 regional coun. U.S. Youth Soccer, 1996—99, chmn. mediation and dispute resolution com., 1999—2000; treas. Hillcrest Elem. Sch. PTA, 1984—86, pres., 1986—88; past mem. GATE adv. com., strategic planning com. on fin. and budget, dist. budget adv. com., instructional strategy counsel Oakland Unified Sch. Dist., 1986—91; mem. Oakland Met. Forum, 1987—91, Oakland Strategic Planning Com., 1988—90; mem. adv. com. St. Mary's Coll.. Paralegal Prog.; commr. Bay Oaks Youth Soccer, 1988—94; asst. dist. commr. dist. 4 Calif. Youth Soccer Assn., 1990—92, also bd. dirs., pres. dist. 4 competitive league, 1990—93, sec. bd. dirs., 1993—96, chmn. bd. dirs., 1996—99; chmn. U.S. Soccer dateabase mktg. com. Calif. Soccer Assn., 1997—99; bd. dirs. Montera Sports Complex, 1988—89, Jack London Youth Soccer League, 1988—94, Calif. Soccer Assn., 1996—99. Mem.: Rotary (bd. dirs. Oakland 1992—94), Oakland C. of C., Assn. Conflict Resolution, Calif. North Referee Assn. (referee adminstr. dist. 4 1992—96, state bd. dirs. 1996—2000), U.S. Soccer Fedn. (nat. C lic. coach and state referee, state referee instr. and state referee assessor), Calif. Scholarship Fedn., U.S. Soccer Assn. (database mktg. com., constl. commn.), Alameda County Bar Assn. (past vice chmn. com. continuing edn., exec. com. alternative dispute resolution programs, panel mediator, arbitrator), Calif. Bar Assn. (mem. ADR com. 2001—), ABA (chmn. subcom. on use of computers in real estate trans. 1985—86, chmn. real property com. gen. practice sect. 1987—91, mem. programs com. 1991—93, adv. coord. 1993—96, sect. coun. 1994—98, mktg. bd. 1996—98, mem. 1998—99, editor, columnist Tech. and Practice Guide 1998—, editl. bd. GP Solo 1999—, editor, columnist Tech. e Report 2002—). Avocations: reading, computers, photography, skiing, baseball, coaching and refereeing youth soccer. Office: Graves & Allen 436 14th St Ste 1400 Oakland CA 94612-2716 E-mail: jallenlaw@aol.com., jallenlaw@gravesandallen.com.

ALLEN, JEFFREY RODGERS, lawyer; b. West Point, N.Y., Aug. 15, 1953; s. James R. and Kathryn (Lewis) A.; m. Cynthia Lynn Colyer, Aug. 10, 1975; children: Emily Rodgers, Elizabeth Colyer, Richard Byrd. BA in History, U. Va., 1975; JD, U. Richmond, 1978. Bar: Va. 1978, U.S. Ct. Mil. Appeals 1981, U.S. Ct. Appeals (4th cir.) 1982, U.S. Supreme Ct. 1982. Trial atty. Michie, Hamlett, Donato & Lowry, Charlottesville, Va., 1982-86; chief counsel Va. Dept. Mil. Affairs, Blackstone, Va., 1986-2000; U.S. property and fiscal officer for Va. Blackstone, 2001—. Atty., advisor U.S. Army Mobile Air Surg. Transport Team, Savannah, Ga., 1980-82; steering com. X-Car Litigation Group, 1983-85; lectr., organizer Law Everyone Should Know series Piedmont (Va.) C.C., Charlottesville, 1984-86; trial atty., of counsel Thorsen, Marchant & Scher, L.L.P., Richmond, 1986-98; mem. legal adv. com. Va. Gov.'s Mil. Adv. Commn., 1987-2000, judge advocate adv. coun. N.G. Bur., 1993-96, TJAG Air N.G. judge advocate adv. coun., 1997-, coord. strategic planning com.; mem. USPFO Coun. Futures Com., 2002--. Pres. Regency Woods Condominium Assn., Richmond, 1976-78, Ashcroft Neighborhood Assn., Charlottesville, 1983-86; treas. Va. N.G. Found., 1986-2002, mem. strategic planning coun. USPFO Coun., 2002—. Capt. U.S. Army, 1978-82, lt. col. JAGC, Va. Air N.G., 1982-2000, col. USAF, 2001—. Mem. Assn. Trial Lawyers Am., Va. Trial Lawyers Assn., Richmond Bar Assn. Avocations: jogging, mountain climbing, photography, fishing, swimming. Home: 2700 Cottage Cove Dr Richmond VA 23233-3318 Office: USPFO Bldg 316 Ft Pickett Blackstone VA 23824-6316 E-mail: jeff.allen@va.ngb.army.mil.

ALLEN, JIMMY R. religious studies educator; b. Little Rock, Apr. 16, 1930; s. James O. Goff and Gertrude E. Tucker; m. Marilyn J. McCluggage, Aug. 23, 1951; children: Jimmy H., Cythnia L. Payne, Michael S. BA, Harding Coll., 1952, MRE, 1959; HhD (hon.), Okla. Christian U., 1971; LLD (hon.), Harding U., 1995. Educator Harding U., Searcy, Ark., 1959—95, prof. emeritus, 1995—2003. Evangelist Ch. of Christ, national and internat., 1949—2003. Contbr. articles. Staff sgt. U.S. Army, 1947—50. Republican. Mem. Ch. Of Christ. Avocations: baseball, basketball, fishing, softball. Home: 3 Magnolia Cir Searcy AR 72143 Office: Harding Univ 900 Center St Searcy AR 72149

ALLEN, JOAN, actress; b. Rochelle, Ill., Aug. 20, 1956; Student, Ea. Ill. U., No. Ill. U. Founding mem. Steppenwolf Theatre Co., Chgo.; theater appearances include (debut) And A Nightingale Sang, N.Y.C. (Clarence Derwent award, Drama Desk award, Outer Critics Circle award 1984), Steppenwolf Theatre Co., also Hartford, 1983, The Marriage of Bette and Boo, N.Y. Shakespeare Festival, 1986, Burn This! (Tony awrd for Best Actress 1988) Mark Taper Forum, L.A., also N.Y.C., 1987, The Heidi Chronicles, N.Y.C., 1988, 89; film appearances include Compromising Positions, 1985, Peggy Sue Got Married, 1986, Manhunter, 1986, Tucker: The Man and His Dream, 1988, In Country, 1989, Ethan Frome, 1993, Searching for Bobbie Fischer, 1993, Josh and S.A.M., 1993, Nixon, 1995 (Acad. award nominee for best supporting actress 1996), Mad Love, 1995, The Crucible, 1996, Ice Storm, 1997, Face/Off, 1997, Pleasantville, 1998, Veronica Guerin, 1999, All the Rage, 1999, When the Sky Falls, 2000, The Contender, 2000, Off the Map, 2003; TV appearances include miniseries Evergreen, 1985, All My Sons, 1986, Am. Playhouse, PBS, 1987, Robert Frost, Voices and Visions, PBS, 1988, TV film The Room Upstairs, 1987, Without Warning: The James Brady Story, 1991, Say Goodnight, Gracie, PBS, The Mists of Avalon, 2001. Office: ICM care Brian Mann 8942 Wilshire Blvd Beverly Hills CA 90211-1934

ALLEN, JOCLETA DALTON, retired social worker, writer; b. Memphis, July 16, 1932; d. James Albert and Lillian Kennedy (Bass) Dalton; m. Ivy Martell Allen, July 28, 1954; children: Anna, Christopher, Susan. Student, Cen. Meth. Coll., Fayette, Mo., 1950-52, Memphis State U., 1952-54; BA, U. Mo., St. Louis, 1970; MSW, Washington U., St. Louis, 1978; postgrad., Psychoanalytic Inst., 2002—03. Pvt. practice therapist, St. Louis, 1973-76; piano studio, 1999—. Author screenplays; contbr. numerous short stories to pubs. Violist, timpanist Florissant Valley Symphony Orch., St. Louis C.C., 1961-91, violist Brentwood (Mo.) Orch., 1973-78, University City Symphony, 1982-84; bd. dirs. Gateway Festival Orch. of St. Louis, 1991—. Mem. NAMI, Psychoanalytic Inst., Depressive and Manic-Depressive Assn. (co-leader manic-depressive self-help groups, bd. dir.), Phi Beta, Psi Chi. Democrat. Episcopalian. Avocations: writing, reading, music.

ALLEN, JOHN LOGAN, geographer, department chairman; b. Laramie, Wyo., Dec. 27, 1941; s. John Milton and Nancy Elizabeth (Logan) A.; m. Anne Evelyn Gilroy, Aug. 9, 1964; children: Traci Kathleen, Jennifer Lynne. BA (Gen. Motors Corp. scholar 1959-63), U. Wyo., 1963, MA, 1964; PhD (univ. grad. fellow 1964-67), Clark U., Worcester, Mass., 1969; PhD NSF postdoctoral fellow, 1970-71. Mem. faculty U. Conn., Storrs, 1967-2000, prof. geography, 1979-2000, head dept., 1976-94, dir. grad. program in geography, 1992-2000, mem. nat. exec. com. Faculty Athletic Rep. Assn., 1987-96; parliamentarian Faculty Athletic Rep. Assn., 1996—; prof., chair dept. geography U. Wyo., Laramie, 2000—. Non-resident fellow Ctr. Great Plains Studies; scholar-in-residence Nat. Lewis and Clark Trail Interpretive Ctr. Author: Passage Through the Garden: Lewis and Clark and the Geog. Lore of the Am. N.W., 1975, Jedediah Smith and the Mountain Men of the Am. West, 1991, Lewis and Clark and the Images of the Am. N.W., 1991, Student Atlas of World Politics, 1991, 6th edit., 2003, Atlas of Econ. Devel., 1997, Atlas of Environ. Issues, 1997, Student Atlas of World Geography, 1998, 2d edit., 2000, 3d edit., 2002, Student Atlas of Anthropology, 2003; editor (ann. edits.): Environment, 1982—, Reshaping Traditions, 1994—; mem. editl. bd.: Jour. Hist. Geography, —, project dir., gen. editor: North Am. Exploration: A Comprehensive History, 3 vols., 1997—; contbr. articles to profl. jours., chpts. to books. Pres. Mansfield (Conn.) Middle Sch. Assn., 1979-80; mem. Mansfield Conservation Commn.; vice chmn. Mansfield Zoning Bd. Appeals; mem. Mansfield Planning and Zoning Commn.; adv. bd. Nat. Lewis and Clark Bicentennial Commn. Recipient Meritorious Achievement award Lewis and Clark Trail Heritage Found., 1976, Excellence in Teaching award U. Conn. Alumni Assn., 1987, Outstanding Contbn. award UCONN Club, 1993, Outstanding Alumnus award U. Wyo. Coll. Arts and Scis., 1999, Spl. Recognition award U. Conn., 2000. Fellow Am. Geog. Assn., Royal Geog. Soc.; mem. Assn. Am. Geographers, Western History Assn.(hon. life), Soc. Historians Early Am. Republic, Soc. History Discovery (nat. councilor), AAAS, Phi Beta Kappa, Phi Kappa Phi, Omicron Delta Kappa. Clubs: Elks, Masons. Democrat. Congregationalist. Home: 2703 Leslie Ct Laramie WY 82072-2979 Office: Univ of Wyoming Dept Geography PO Box 3371 Laramie WY 82071-3371 *As a scientist and educator, I have tried to abide by the principle that learning is necessary for the public good and that academicians should make their skills and knowledge available to society at large. Service to others is as important an educational function as the more frequently recognized components of teaching and research.*

ALLEN, JOHN POLK, environmental scientist; b. Carnegie, Okla., May 6, 1929; s. Paul Benight and Opal (Wall) Allen. Student, Northwestern U., Stanford U., Oklahoma U., 1946-49; BS, Colo. Sch. Mines, 1957; MBA, Harvard U., 1962. Supervising metallurgist Allegheny Ludlum Steel, Brackenridge, Pa., 1957-59; crushing, leaching dept. head Union Carbide Nuclear, Uravan, Colo., 1959-60; asst. v.p. Devel. & Resources Corp., N.Y.C., 1961-63; pres. Mountain & Manhattan, N.Y.C., 1963-66; head metallurgist Meadows Gold, Santa Fe, 1966-67; co-founder, dir. Inst. Ecotechnics, London, 1968—; co-founder, chmn. Biospheric Design, Santa Fe, 1978—; exec. chmn. Space Biospheres Ventures, Oracle, Ariz., 1984-94. Co-founder, chmn. Planetary Coral Reef Found., Santa Fe, 1991—; chmn. Global Ecotechnics, Santa Fe, 1998—. Author: The Human Experiment, 1989, Space Biospheres, 1986, Off the Road, 2000, Book of American Wisdom, 2003. Organizer UPWA-CIO Dist. 10, Chgo., 1950—52; pres. student body Colo. Sch. Mines, 1956—57. With U.S. Army, 1952—53. Named Hon. Citizen, City of Ft. Worth, 1989; Baker scholar, Harvard U. Bus. Sch., 1962. Fellow: World Acad. Art and Sci., Royal Geog. Soc., Linnean Soc. London; mem.: AAS, Explorers Club. Achievements include inventor in field; created 1st closed life system with 100% recycle of waste, water and 90% of air per year. Avocations: expeditions to remote areas, theater, cultures, Go. Office: 7 Silver Hills Rd Santa Fe NM 87508-4488

ALLEN, JOHN THOMAS, JR., lawyer; b. St. Petersburg, Fla., Aug. 23, 1935; s. John Thomas and Mary Lita (Shields) A.; m. Joyce Ann Lindsey, June 16, 1958 (div. 1985); children: John Thomas III, Linda Joyce, Catherine Lee (dec.).; m. Janice Dearmin Hudson, Mar. 16, 1987 (div. 2002). BSBA with honors, U. Fla., 1958; JD, Stetson U., 1961. Bar: Fla. 1961, U.S. Dist. Ct. (mid. dist.) Fla. 1962, U.S. Ct. Appeals (5th cir.) 1963, U.S. Ct. Appeals (11th cir.) 1983, U.S. Supreme Ct. 1970. Assoc. Mann, Harrison, Mann & Rowe and successor Greene, Mann, Rowe, Davenport & Stanton, St. Petersburg, 1961-67, ptnr., 1967-74; sole practice St. Petersburg, 1974-95; pvt. practice Allen & Maller, P.A., 1996-98, Gulfport, Fla., 1998—. Counsel Pinellas County Legis. Del., 1974-75; counsel for Pinellas County as spl. counsel on water matters, 1975-98. Mem. Com of 100, St. Petersburg, 1975-98. Mem. ABA, Fla. Bar Assn., St. Petersburg Bar Assn., St. Petersburg C. of C., Lions, Beta Gamma Sigma. Republican. Baptist. Home and Office: 5929 Bayview Cir S Gulfport FL 33707-3929

ALLEN, JOHN TIMOTHY, mechanical engineer; b. Columbus, Tex., Sept. 25, 1954; s. Jack Kenneth and Genola Marie (Gardner) A.; children: John Timothy II, Elizabeth Suzanne. BS Mech. Engring., Tex. A&M U., 1976. Sr. project engr. Halliburton Energy Svcs., Duncan, Okla., 1976-94; mgr. ops. CECO Equipment/Div. Nowsco, Kilgore, Tex., 1994-95; mgr. prodn. and tech. JM Clipper Corp., Nacogdoches, Tex., 1995-97; R&D supr. Weatherford Underbalanced Drilling Svcs., Houston, 1997-2000; sr. rsch. and devel. engr. Weatherford Underbalanced Drilling Svc., Houston, 2000—. Patentee in field. Precinct chmn. Stephens County Rep. Party, Okla., 1993; county campaign co-chmn. Nichols for U.S. Senate Com., 1980. Mem. ASME, Energy Rubber Group, Waterjet Technology Assn. Mem. Christian Ch. (Disciples Of Christ). Avocations: skeet, target shooting, metalworking, woodworking. Office: Weatherford Well Installation Svcs 11909 Spencer Rd # Fm529 Houston TX 77041-3000

ALLEN, JOSEPH H. retired radiologist, educator; b. St. Joseph, Mo., 1925; MD, Washington U., St. Louis, 1948. Diplomate Am. Bd. Radiologists. Intern Presbyn. Hosp., Chgo., 1948-49; resident in radiology Vanderbilt Hosp., Nashville, 1954-56; fellow in neuroradiology Columbia U., N.Y.C.; prof. radiology Vanderbilt U.; ret., 1990. Fellow Am. Coll. Radiologists; mem. Am. Soc. Neuroradiology.

ALLEN, JOSEPH P. psychologist, educator; b. DC, Oct. 30, 1958; s. Arthur Eugene and Elizabeth W. Allen; m. Claudia Mary Worrell, Aug. 29, 1987; children: Lucas Peter, Olivia Worrell, Eve Worrell. BS, U. Va., 1980; PhD, Yale U., 1986. Lic. Clin. Psychologist Va. Postdoc. fellow Harvard Med. Sch., Boston, 1986—89, asst. prof., 1989—96, assoc. prof., 1996—99; prof. psychology U. Va., Charlottesville, 1999—. Chair study sect. for grant revs. NIMH/NIH, 1996—2002. Contbr. articles to profl. jours.; assoc. editor: jour. Child Devel., 2002—, mem. editl. bd.: jour. Jour. Consulting and Clin. Psychology, 2000—01. Fellow, Spencer Found., 1990; scholar Faculty scholar, William T. Grant Found., 1991. Mem.: Soc. Rsch. Adolescence (program chair biennial meeting 1998), Soc. Rsch. Child Devel. Achievements include research in importance of autonomy processes in adolescent social development; the impact of social programs in the prevention of teen pregnancy. Office: Dept Psychology U Va Box 400 400 Charlottesville VA 22903

ALLEN, JOSEPH T. musician, educator; s. James W. Allen and D. Ann Warren. MusB, U. Nebr., 1983, D of Musical Arts, 2000; MusM, Eastman Sch. of Music, Rochester, N.Y., 1985. Choir accompanist Student Luth. Ctr., Lincoln, Nebr., 1980—82; pvt. piano tchr. Lincoln, 1989—95, Eagle, Nebr., 2000—; tchg. asst. U. Nebr., Lincoln, 1992—94; piano tchr. Liu Shih Kun Piano and Arts Ctr., Ltd., Hong Kong, China, 1995—98; substitute prin. keyboardist Lincoln Symphony Orch., 1999—; piano instr. Peru (Nebr.) State Coll., 2002—. Named Winner of Young Artist Audition, Omaha Symphony, 1981, Lincoln Symphony Orch., 1981, Winner, Omaha Morning Musicale, 1982, Finalist in Young Artists Competition, Ft. Collins Symphony, 1987; recipient Key, City of Omaha, 1982, 1st Prize, Internat. Piano Rec. Competition, 1986. Mem.: Music Tchrs. Nat. Assn. (Nebr. state winner 1977, 1978, 1981, 1982, 1983), Phi Eta Sigma, Alpha Lambda Delta, Pi Kappa Lambda. Lutheran. Avocations: reading, athletics, scuba diving, coin collecting, travel.

ALLEN, JOYCE DOYLE, social worker, preschool and elementary educator; b. Hollis, N.Y., Aug. 10, 1954; d. James Robert and Jeanne Ellen (Cook) Doyle; m. John Francis Allen, Jr., June 30, 1979; children: Kimberly Erin, Evan Doyle. BA cum laude, Conn. Coll., 1976; MSW, Rutgers U., 1979. Bd. cert. diplomate, ACSW, qualified clin. social worker NASW, lic. clin. social worker, Calif., Tex. Psychiat. and med. social work trainee VA Med. Ctr., Lyons, N.J., 1977-79; social caseworker Children's Bur. of New Orleans, 1979-82; psychiat. social worker Walnut Creek (Calif.) Hosp., 1982-85; tchr. Pine's Presbyn. Pre-sch., Houston, 1991-94; kindergarden aide Am. Sch. of the Hague, Netherlands, 1999—2003. Bd. dirs. Pine's Presbyn. Sch., Houston, 1990-91. Mem. NASW, Phi Beta Kappa. Avocations: sewing, crafts, dancing.

ALLEN, JOYCE SMITH, librarian; b. Englewood, N.J., Aug. 1, 1939; d. Harold Willard and Mary Elizabeth Smith; m. Jim Frank Allen, Mar. 1974 (div. 1982); 1 child, Shani Jamilla. BA, Howard U., 1961; MLS, Atlanta U., 1966; cert. in advanced studies, U. Ill., 1974. Reference librarian Howard U., Washington, 1966-73; mgr. libr. Meth. Hosp. Ind., Indpls., 1974-94; libr., dir. distance learning Aenon Bible Coll., Indpls., 1994—; libr. Rowland Design Inc., 1995—2001. Instr. Ind. Vocat. Tech. Coll., 1979, 85, Med. Library Assn., 1982-95, Martin Ctr. Coll., Indpls., 1983-84. Author career materials. Vol. Indpls. Police Dept. Libr., 1977, Children's Mus., Indpls., 1987—88, Children;'s Bureau, 2001—, Black Expo, 1995—, Minority Health Fair, 1995—. Recipient Minority Bus. and Profl. Achiever award Ctr. for Leadership Devel., Indpls., 1981, Central Ind. Area Libr. Svcs. Authority cert. of Excellence, 1990. Mem. ALA, Internat. Tng. In Comm., Ch. and Synagogue Libr. Assn. (pres. 1992-93, 95-96), Med. Libr. Assn., Coun. on Libr. Technicians, Spl. Librs. Assn., Indpls. Interdenominational Ch. Users' Assn. Democrat. Avocations: travel, reading, needlepoint, bicycling. Home: 3815 N Bolton Ave Indianapolis IN 46226-4826 Office: Aenon Bible Coll 3919 Meadows Dr Indianapolis IN 46205-3113 E-mail: jsaallen@hotmail.com.

ALLEN, JULIAN LEWIS, medical educator, researcher; b. Elizabeth, NJ, Oct. 7, 1952; s. Eugene Murray and Beatrice (Hyman) A.; m. Debra Lynne Stoll, June 4, 1978; children: Eli, Jeremy. BA, Columbia U., 1974, MD, 1978. Diplomate in pediat. and pediatric pulmonology Am. Bd. Pediat. Pediatric intern Columbia-Presbyn. Med. Ctr., N.Y.C., 1978-79, resident in pediatrics, 1979-81; fellow in pediatric pulmonology Boston Children's Hosp., 1981-84; instr. pediatrics Harvard Med. Sch., Boston, 1984-86; asst. prof. pediatrics Temple U. Sch. Medicine, Phila., 1986-90, assoc. prof., 1990-95, prof., 1995-97; prof. pediat. Hahnemann Med. Sch. Allegheny (Pa.) U. Health Scis., 1997-98; prof. pediat., Robert Gerard Morse chair in pulmonary medicine U. Pa. Sch. Medicine, 1998—; attending physician in pulmonary disease The Children's Hosp., Boston, 1984-86, St. Christopher's Hosp. for Children, Phila., 1986—98, dir. pulmonary function lab., 1986—94, sect. chief pediatric pulmonary medicine, 1994-98; attending physician, acting chief divsn. pulmonary medicine/cystic fibrosis ctr. Children's Hosp. Phila., 1998-99, chief, 1999—. Sub-bd. pediatric pulmonology Am. Bd. Pediat., 2001—. Author: numerous books; reviewer (profl. jours.), mem. editl. bd. Pediat. Pulmonology, 2002—; contbr. articles to profl. jours., chpts. in books. Recipient 1st award NIH, 1988-94, Investigator award, 1993—; Parker B. Francis Found. fellow, 1982-86, Sandoz award Coll. Phys.&Surg., N.Y.C., 1978; named Top Doc for Kids, Phila. Mag., 2002. Fellow: Am. Acad. Pediats.; mem.: Pediat. Pulmonary Tng. Dirs. Assn., Soc. for Pediat. Rsch., European Respiratory Soc. (joint com. on infant respiratory physiology 1990—, co-chmn. 1996), Am. Thoracic Soc. (program com. 1991—93, long range planning com. 1993—, chmn. 1996—98, pediat. assembly chmn. 1999—2001, bd. dirs. 1999—2001, rsch. advocacy com. 2000—). Achievements include research in lung and chest wall development in infants; pulmonary insults in childhood, pulmonary complications of sickle cell disease and respiratory function. Avocation: violin. Office: Childrens Hosp Phila Divsn Pulmonary Medicine 34th St and Civic Ctr Blvd Philadelphia PA 19104 E-mail: Allenj@email.chop.edu.

ALLEN, JULIAN MYRICK, JR., industrial engineer; b. Mobile, Ala., Mar. 29, 1956; s. Julian Myrick and Sarah Jane (Scanlan) A.; m. Betty Jo Culpepper; children: Kiesha Monique, Jaron Myrick, Nathan Ryan. AA, Jones County Jr. Coll., 1976; BSBA, U. So. Miss., 1980; MBA, Miss. State U., 1985. Store mgr. Burger King Inc., Slidell, La., 1976-78; indsl. engr. Howard Industries, Laurel, Miss., 1978-80; plant indsl. engr. Fairbanks Scale div. Colt Industries, Meridian, Miss., 1980-86; sr. indsl. engr. COMM/TEC div. Reliance Electric, Greenville, Miss., 1986-88, William L. Bonnell div. Tredegar Industries, Newnan, Ga., 1988-91; engring. and maintenace mgr. Borden Foodsvc., Jackson, Miss., 1991-92; engring. and maintenance mgr. Chambersburg, Pa., 1992-93; plant mgr. seafood divsn. Borden, Cape May, N.J., 1993-94; ops. mgr. Bama Foods, Birmingham, Ala., 1994, Snow's Doxsee Inc., Cape May, N.J., 1994-99; dir. ops. Baumer Foods Inc., New Orleans, 1999-2000; materials mgr. Danfoss Maneurop Ltd., Lawrenceville, Ga., 2000—. Author: Welding Robotics Handbook, 1986; contbr. articles to profl. jours. Tchr. United Pentecostal Ch., Meridian, 1983-86, New Life Pentecostal Ch., Newnan, 1990-91. Mem. Soc. Mfg. Engrs. (speaker confs. 1984-86, Pres. Club 1985, Outstanding Paper

Robotics Internat. 1985-86, sr. mem.), Inst. Indsl. Engrs. (sr. mem.). Republican. Office: Danfoss Maneurop Ltd 1775-G MacLeod Dr Lawrenceville GA 30043 E-mail: r.allen@danfoss-maneurop.com.

ALLEN, JULIE MICHELLE, secondary education educator; b. Ann Arbor, Mich., Feb. 27, 1969; d. Herbert E. and Deena (Wilner) Allen. BA, DePaul U., Chgo., 1993. Cert. tchr., Ill. English tchr. Chgo. Pub. Schs., 1994—; acad. decathlon coach Kelly H.S., Chgo., 2000—01; drama coach Steinmetz H.S., 2001—. Active Art Inst. Chgo., 1997—. Named Master Tchr./Mentor for the Golden Apple Found. Ill., 2000-. Mem. TESOL, Nat. Coun. Tchrs. English. Avocations: cooking, ballet, reading, writing. Home: 6740 W Diversey Apt 1N Chicago IL 60607 E-mail: ms_allen_english@yahoo.com.

ALLEN, LAURIE LOUISE, retired medical social worker; b. Appleton, Wis., Jan. 10, 1935; d. Earl Bruce Jr. and Gertrude Mary (Souliere) Brookbank; m. William Alfred Allen, Dec. 29, 1956 (div. Oct. 1984); children: Edward, William, Susan, James, Therese, Stephen. BS in Math., Marietta (Ohio) Coll., 1956; MS in Social Work, U. Tenn., Memphis, 1985. Lic. clin. social worker, Tenn. Computer programmer Air Materiel Command, Dayton, Ohio, 1956-57; med. social worker Les Passees Children's Rehab. Ctr., Memphis, 1985-87, Meth. Hosps. Memphis, 1987-97, Meth. Alliance Extended Acute Care Hosp., Memphis, 1997—2000. Registrar Bd. Elections, Memphis, 1974-82. NASW, Acad. Cert. Social Workers, Mid-South Organ Transplant Alliance, Soc. Democrat. Roman Catholic. Avocations: hiking, photography, guitar, Native American studies, wellness medicine. Office: 920 Blythe Memphis TN 38104-5233

ALLEN, LAWRENCE RICHARD, prosecutor; b. Portland, Oreg., May 13, 1952; s. Irving Courtney and Madonna Elizabeth (Walsh) A.; m. Suzanne Elise Chaffey, May 17, 1975 (div. June 1995); children: Rebecca Ann, Sarah Beth; m. Sherrie Lee Setters, Aug. 9, 1997. Student, Treasure Valley C.C., 1972; BS, Willamette U., 1974; JD, John F. Kennedy U., 1980. Bar: Calif. 1980, U.S. Dist. Ct. (no. and ea. dists.) Calif. 1980, U.S. Ct. Appeals (9th cir.) 1985. Clk. Safeway Stores, 1971-80; bus. agt., legal counsel United Foods Comml. Workers Union, Martinez, Calif., 1980-84; assoc. Patrick Beasley Law Office, Redding, Calif., 1984-85, Simpson & Maine, Redding, 1985-87; dep. dist. atty. Shasta County Dist. Atty., Redding, 1987-91, sr. dep. dist. atty., 1991-98; environ. prosecutor Calif. Dist. Atty. Assn., Sacramento, 1998—2002; dist. atty. Sierra County, Calif., 2002—. Instr. Calif. Dept. Fish and Game, 1996--, Calif. Dist. Atty.'s Assn., Sacramento, 1996—, Napa Valley Coll. Resource Protection Acad., 1997—. Editor Calif. Dist. Atty. Assn. Case Digest, 1993—. Mem. Family Support Legis. Com., Sacramento, 1995-98; bd. dirs. Wildlife Forensic DNA Found., Sacramento, 1994—, Californians Against Waste, Sacramento, 1981-84. Home: PO Box 491 Downieville CA 95936 Office: Sierra County Dist Atty Courthouse Sq Downieville CA 95936

ALLEN, LAYMAN EDWARD, law educator, research scientist; b. Turtle Creek, Pa., June 9, 1927; s. Layman Grant and Viola Iris (Williams) A.; m. Christine R. Patmore, Mar. 29, 1950 (dec.); children: Layman G., Patricia R.; m. Emily C. Hall, Oct. 3, 1981 (div. 1992); children: Phyllip A. Hall, Kelly C. Hairston; m. Leslie A. Olsen, June 10, 1995. Student, Washington and Jefferson Coll., 1945-46; AB, Princeton U., 1951; MPub. Admnstrn., Harvard U., 1952; LLB, Yale U., 1956. Bar: Conn. 1956. Fellow Ctr. for Advanced Study in Behavioral Scis., 1961-62; sr. fellow Yale Law Sch., 1956-57, lectr., 1957-58, instr., 1958-59, asst. prof., 1959-63, assoc. prof., 1963-66; assoc. prof. law U. Mich. Law Sch., Ann Arbor, 1966-71, prof., 1971—. Chmn. bd. trustees Accelerated Learning Found., 1998—; sr. rsch. scientist Mental Health Rsch. Inst., U. Mich., 1966-99; cons. legal drafting Nat. Life Ins. Co., Mich. Blue Cross & Blue Shield (various law firms); mem. electronic data retrieval com. Am. Bar Assn.; ops. rsch. analyst McKinsey & Co.; orgn. and methods analyst Office of Sec. Air Force.; trustee Ctr. for Study of Responsive Law. Editor: Games and Simulations, Artificial Intelligence and Law Jour., Theoria; author: WFF 'N Proof: The Game of Modern Logic, 1961, latest rev. edit., 1990, (with Robin B.S. Brooks, Patricia A. James) Automatic Retrieval of Legal Literature: Why and How, 1962, WFF: The Beginner's Game of Modern Logic, 1962, latest rev. edit., 1973, Equations: The Game of Creative Mathematics, 1963, latest rev. edit., 1994, (with Mary E. Caldwell) Reflections of the Communications Sciences and Law: The Jurimetrics Conference, 1965, (with J. Ross and P. Kugel) Queries 'N Theories: The Game of Science and Language, 1970, latest rev. edit., 1973, (with F. Goodman, D. Humphrey and J. Ross), On-Words: The Game of Word Structures, 1971, rev. edit., 1973; contbr. articles to profl. jours.; co-author/designer: (with J. Ross and C. Stratton) DIG (Diagnostic Instrnl. Gaming) Math; (with C. Saxon) Normalizer Clear Legal Drafting Program, 1986, MINT System for Generating Dynamically Multiple-Interpretation Legal Decision-Assistance Systems, 1991, The Legal Argument Game of Legal Relations, 1997, (with Sandra Bartlett) LawToe: the Game to Learn the Game Rules of The Legal Argument Game of Legal Relations, 2003, The New Legal Argument of Legal Relations, 2003. With USNR, 1945-46. Mem. ABA (coun. sect. sci. and tech.), AAAS, ACLU, Assn. Symbolic Logic, Nat. Coun. Tchrs. Math. Democrat. Unitarian Universalist. Home: 2114 Vinewood Blvd Ann Arbor MI 48104-2762 Office: U Mich Sch Law 625 S State St Ann Arbor MI 48109-1215 E-mail: laymanal@umich.edu.

ALLEN, LEATRICE DELORICE, psychologist; b. Chgo., July 15, 1948; d. Burt and Mildred Floy (Taylor) Hawkins; m. Allen Moore, Jr., July 30, 1965 (div. Oct. 1975); children: Chandra, Valarie, Allen; m. Armstead Allen, May 11, 1978 (div. May 1987). AA in Bus. Edn., Olive Harvey Coll., Chgo., 1975; BA in Psychology cum laude, Chgo. State U., 1977; M.Clin. Psychology, Roosevelt U., 1980; MS in Health Care Adminstrn., Coll. St. Francis, Joliet, Ill., 1993. Lic. clin. profl. counselor. Clk., U.S. Post Office, Chgo., 1967-72; clin. therapist Bobby Wright Mental Health Ctr., Chgo., 1979-80; clin. therapist Community Mental Health Council, Chgo., 1980-83, assoc. dir., 1983—; cons. Edgewater Mental Health, Chgo., 1984—, Project Pride, Chgo., 1985—; victim services coordinator Community Mental Health Council, Chgo., 1986-87; mgr. youth family services Mile Square Health Ctr., Chgo., 1987-88; coord. Evang. Health Systems, Oakbrook, Ill., 1988-93; adminstr. Human Enrichment Devel. Assn., Hazel Crest, Ill., 1993-96; dir. Ada S. McKinley, Chgo., 1996—. Scholar Chgo. State U., 1976, Roosevelt U., 1978; fellow Menninger Found., 1985. Mem. Am. Profl. Soc. on Abuse of Children, Nat. Orgn. for Victim Assistance, Ill. Coalition Against Sexual Assault (del. 1985—), Soc. Traumatic Stress Studies (treatment innovations task force), Chgo. Sexual Assault Svcs. Network (vice-chair, bd. dirs.), Chgo. Coun. Fgn. Rels. Avocations: aerobics, reading, theatre, dining, making and collecting dolls. Business E-Mail: lallen@adasmckinley.org.

ALLEN, (EDWIN) LEE, artist; b. Muscatine, Iowa, Sept. 16, 1910; s. Herman Clyde Allen and Loredo Robinson; m. Sally Boyce, Mar. 9, 1936 (divorced); children: Loredo Ann, Mary Lee, Elizabeth Jane. Student, U. Iowa, 1929-37. Mural painter Pub. Works of Art Project, Iowa City, 1933-36, U.S. Treasury Dept., Iowa City, 1936-37; med. artist dept. ophthalmology U. Iowa, Iowa City, 1937-75, instr., 1940-75, ocularist, 1945-75, ret., 1975; co-owner Iowa Eye Prosthetics Inc., Iowa City, 1975-82. Muralist Iowa post offices, 1937-38; inventor Buried Motility Ocular Implant, 1945; painting exhibited at Whitney Mus., 1999; exhibited in one man show at U. Iowa, Ames, 2000; co-author: The Hole in My Vision, 2000. Recipient East Des Moines High School Hall of Fame, 2003—. Democrat. Episcopalian. Home: Hawthorne Inn 1500 N 1st Ave # 74 Coralville IA 52241

ALLEN, LEE HARRISON, industrial consultant, wholesale company executive; b. Cleve., Oct. 12, 1924; s. Horace Joseph and Eleanor Quayle (Malone) A.; m. Marieke Sellenraad, Sept. 18, 1954; children: Horace, Jan, Adrian, Carel, Eleanor. BEngring. in Metallurgy, Yale U., 1948. With Hickman, Williams & Co., Detroit, 1948—, metallurgist, 1951-70, divsn. mgr., 1970—, v.p., dir., 1971-76, pres., 1976-84, chmn. bd., chief exec. officer, 1984-89, Hickman, Williams Can., Inc., 1980-89; owner L.H. Allen & Sons, Frankenmuth, Mich., 1969—. Chmn. bd. dirs. Mich. Shelf Distbrs. Inc., 1985—. Trustee Grosse Pinte Bd. Edn., 1968-76. Mem. Am. Arbitration Assn. (arbitrator), Country Club Detroit. Home and Office: 84 Hall Pl Grosse Pointe Farms MI 48236-3805 Fax: 313-886-5321. E-mail: Squeedunk@aya.yale.edu.

ALLEN, LEE NORCROSS, historian, educator; b. Shawmut, Ala., Apr. 16, 1926; s. Leland Norcross and Dorothy (Whitaker) A.; m. Catherine Ann Bryant, Aug. 24, 1963; children— Leland Norcross, Leslie Catherine. BS, Auburn U., 1948, MS, 1949; PhD, U. Pa., 1955. From instr. to prof. history Ea. Bapt. Coll., St. Davids, Pa., 1952-61; prof. history Samford U., Birmingham, Ala., 1961-2001, grad. dean, 1965-86; dean Howard Coll. Arts and Scis., 1975-90, rsch. prof., 2001—. Author: (with Mrs. E.S. Bee) History of Ruhama, 1969, The First One Hundred Fifty Years: First Baptist Church of Montgomery, 1979, Born for Missions, 1984; Southside Baptist Church: A Centennial History, 1985, Woodlawn Baptist Church: The First Century, 1886-1986, 1986; (with Catherine B. Allen) Courage to Care, 1988; Expanding the Dream, Montgomery Baptist Hospital, 1988, Notable Past, Bright Future: First Baptist Church 1893-1993, 1993, Born for Missions, 16th Decade, 1993, Ralph W. Beeson: A Biography, 2001, Outward Focus: Mountain Brook Baptist Church, The First Fifty Years, 1994, The First 150 Years Supplement: 1980-1995, 1996, (with Catherine B. Allen) Christ Is Our Salvation: Paul Piper, 1998, (with Catherine B. Allen) The Boaz Heritage: A Centennial History, Boaz, Alabama, 1897-1997, 1999. Served with AUS, 1944-46. Recipient Commendation cert. Am. Assn. State and Local History, Thomas Jefferson award, 1995, disting. svc. award Ala. Baptist Hist. Commn., 1996; Auburn U. rsch. fellow, 1948-49; Harrison fellow U. Pa., 1949-52. Mem. Am. Hist. Assn., Am. Bapt. Hist. Assn. (editor The Ala. Bapt. Historian 1989—), So. Bapt. Hist. Assn. (pres. 1987-88), So. Hist. Assn., Ala. Hist. Assn. (editor newsletter 1989-2001, pres. 1994-95), So. Bapt. Club, Rotary (pres. Shades Valley chpt. 1969 70), Omicron Delta Kappa, Phi Alpha Theta, Phi Kappa Phi, Pi Gamma Mu. Baptist. Home: 5025 Wendover Dr Birmingham AL 35223-1631

ALLEN, LEON ARTHUR, JR., lawyer; b. Springfield, Mass., July 15, 1933; s. Leon Arthur Sr. and Elsie (Shoemaker) A.; m. Patricia Mellion, June 23, 1961; 1 child, Christopher L. BEE, Cornell U., 1955; LLB, NYU, 1964. Bar: N.Y. 1964, U.S. Dist. Ct. (so. and ea. dists.) N.Y. 1965. Tech. editor McGraw Hill Pub. Co., N.Y.C., 1958-62; constrn. engr. Gilbert Assocs., N.Y.C., 1962-64; assoc. LeBoeuf, Lamb, Leiby & MacRae, N.Y.C., 1964-70; ptnr. LeBoeuf, Lamb, Leiby & MacRae (name changed to LeBoeuf, Lamb, Greene & MacRae), N.Y.C., 1971—. Served with U.S. Army, 1956-58. Mem. ABA, Assn. of Bar of City of N.Y. (chmn. adminstrv. law com. 1972-74). Clubs: Racquet & Tennis (N.Y.C.); Union (N.Y.C.), Tuxedo (Tuxedo Park, N.Y.). Home: 530 E 86th St New York NY 10028-7535 Office: LeBoeuf Lamb Greene MacRae 125 W 55th St New York NY 10019-5369 E-mail: laallen@llgm.com.

ALLEN, LEW, JR., laboratory executive, former air force officer; b. Miami, Fla., Sept. 30, 1925; s. Lew and Zella (Holman) A.; m. Barbara Frink Hatch, Aug. 19, 1949; children: Barbara Allen Miller, Lew III, Marjorie Allen Dauster, Christie Allen Jameson, James Allen. BS, U.S. Mil. Acad., 1946; MS, U. Ill., 1952, PhD in Physics, 1954. Commd. 2d lt. USAAF, 1946; advanced through grades to gen. USAF, 1977, ret., 1982; physicist test div. AEC, Los Alamos, N.Mex., 1954-57; sci. advisor Air Force Spl. Weapons Lab., Kirtland, N.Mex., 1957-61; with office of spl. tech. Sec. of Def., Washington, 1961-65; from dir. spl. projects to dep. dir. adv. plans Air Force Space Program, 1965-72; dir. Nat. Security Agy., Ft. Meade, Md., 1973-77; comdr. Air Force Systems Command, 1977-78; vice chief of staff USAF, Washington, 1978, chief of staff, 1978-82; dir. Jet Propulsion Lab., Calif. Inst. Tech., Pasadena, Calif., 1982-90; chmn. bd. Draper Lab, Boston, 1991-95. Decorated Def. D.S.M. with two clusters, Air Force D.S.M. with one cluster, Nat. Intelligence D.S.M., NASA D.S.M., Legion of Merit with two oak leaf clusters; recipient Robert H. Goddard Astronautics award Am. Inst. Aeronautics and Astronautics, 1995. Fellow AIAA (hon.), Am. Phys. Soc.; mem. Am. Geophys. Union, Nat. Acad. Engring., Coun. on Fgn. Rels., Sigma Xi, Sunset Club (L.A.), Alfalfa Club (Washington). Republican. Episcopalian. Avocations: ballooning, rafting.

ALLEN, LINDA GRAVES, real estate agent; b. Indpls., Oct. 8, 1959; d. Charles Edward and Barbara Jean (Antle) Graves; m. William Allen, Nov. 16, 1985 (div.); children: Clarke, Jordan. BSN, U. Mo., 1981, MHA, 1995. RN, Mo.; cert. emergency nurse, Mo.; cert. instr. trauma nurse, advanced burn life support, cert. provider pediatric advanced cardiac and trauma/pediatric advanced life support, cert. trauma nurse specialist, cert. emergency nurse, advanced cardiac life support, cert. med. transport exec.; cert. residential real estate specialist; accredited buyer's rep. grad. Realtor Inst.; cert. internet profl. Staff nurse level IV St. John's Mercy Med. Ctr., St. Louis, 1981-92; trauma coord. Barnes Hosp., St. Louis, 1992-96; re-engring. cons. Barnes Jewish Hosp., St. Louis, 1996-97; managed care specialist BJC Health Sys., St. Louis, 1997; v.p. med. svcs. ARCH Air Med. Svcs., St. Louis, 1998-2000; sales exec. Coldwell Banker Gundaker, 2000—. Named Rookie of the Yr., St. Louis Assn. Realtors, 2001. Mem. AACN, Emergency Nurses Assn., Am. Trauma Soc., Am. Coll. Healthcare Execs., Soc. Trauma Nurses, Nat. Assn. Realtors, Mo. Assn. Realtors, St. Louis Assn. of Realtors. E-mail: linda@lindagravesallen.com.

ALLEN, LOIS ARLENE HEIGHT (MRS. JAMES PIERPONT ALLEN), musician; b. Kenton, Ohio, Sept. 2, 1932; d. Robert Harold and Frances (Sims) Height; m. James Pierpont Allen, June 14, 1953; children: Daniel Pierpont, Carole Elizabeth. BS, Ohio State U., 1954, MA, 1958. Tchr. jr. and sr. high music Upper Arlington H.S., Columbus, Ohio, 1954-56; h.s. music supr. Westerville, Ohio, 1956-57; tchr. music Ohio State U. Sch., 1957-59; pvt. tchr. music Columbus, 1960—. Exec. dir. Battelle Scholars Program Trust Fund, 1983-86; ch. organist, choir dir. Mountview Bapt. Ch., Upper Arlington, Ohio, 1960-77, moderator, 1996-97; ednl. radio interviewer WOSU, 1970, 71, 72. Mem. Project Hope, Ctrl. Ohio, 1967-73; mem. sustaining bd. Maryhaven House for Alcoholic Women, 1969-73, 1st v.p.; mem. women's bd. Columbus Symphony, 1965-79, 91—, bd. trustees edn. com., 1992-2004, co-chair edn. com. women's assn., 1992-2000, charter mem. trustee's cir., 2000, bd. dir., chmn. youth coun., 1965-68, pres.-elect women's assn., 1973, chmn. edn. com., 1991—, pres., 1974-76; pres. vol. coun. Am. Symphony Orch. League, 1987-89; organist, choir master The Ch. of St. Edwards, 1990-92; chmn. juried art competition Cen. Ohio Arts Festival, 1969, 70, chmn. fine and applied arts, 1971, gen. chmn. of festival, 1972; area chmn. United Appeals Franklin County, 1966-68, Heart dr., 1968-85; pres. Ohio State U. Soc. Friends Sch. Music, 1977-78; trustee Columbus Symphony Orch., 1973-81, Opera/Columbus, 1981-85; v.p. women's guild Opera/Columbus, 1986-94, pres., 1987-88; mem. vol. coun. Am. Sympohny Orch. League, 1981—, v.p., 1983-84, mem. exec. com., 1986-88, mem. artistic affairs com., 1987-89, pres., 1987-88; organist, choir dir. North Congregational Ch., 1979-85; area leader Rep. Party, 1966-68; mem. Mayor's Award Coun. Com., 1981-84; active Connexions, Columbus Literacy Coun.; bd. dir., pres. Ohio Theatre Shop, 1995-96, publicity dir. 1996--; bd. dir., pres. Women's Bd. Columbus Mus. Art, 1991—; organist Glen Echo Presbyn. Ch., 2002--. Recipient Columbus Symphony Advocate award, 2002. Mem. Am. Guild Organists, Choristers Guild Am., Fedn. Am. Bapt. Musicians, Ctr. Sci. and Industry, Ohio State Hist. Soc., Ohio Orgn. Orchs. (treas. 1976-79, sec. 1979-82), Nat. Trust U.S.A., Mountview Bapt. Ch. (moderator 1996—), Rotary Club (Women of Yr. Upper Arlington Ohio 1995), Order Ea. Star, White Shrine of Jerusalem, Ohio State U. Alumnae of Franklin County Club (pres. 1962-64, 71-72), Tau Beta Sigma, Delta Omicron, Kappa Delta (Cen. Ohio Woman of Yr. 1970). Home: 3355 Somerford Rd Columbus OH 43221-1436 E-mail: jallen6@columbus.rr.com.

ALLEN, LOUIS ALEXANDER, management consultant; b. Glace Bay, N.S., Oct. 8, 1917; s. Israel Nathan and Emma (Greenberg) A.; m. Ruth Graham, Aug. 24, 1946; children: Michael, Steven, Ace, Terry Allen Beck, Deborah Allen. BS cum laude, Wash. State U., 1941. Cert. mgmt. cons. Asst. to dean of men Wash. State U., Pullman, 1940-42; tng. supr. Aluminum Co. Am., Pitts., 1946-49; mgr. pers. adminstrn. Koppers Co. Inc., Pitts., 1949-53; dir. rsch. projects The Conf. Bd., N.Y.C., 1953-56; dir. orgnl. planning Booz, Allen & Hamilton, Chgo., 1956-58; founder Louis Allen Assocs., Inc., Los Altos, Calif., 1958-92; ind. rschr., 1992-95. Lectr. on bus. mgmt. Stanford U., U. Chgo., NYU, Japan, China, Australia, Africa and Europe. Author: Improving Staff and Line Relationships, 1956, Preparing the Company Organization Manual, 1957, Organization of Staff Functions, 1958, Management and Organization, 1958, The Management Profession, 1964, Professional Management: New Concepts and Proven Practices, 1973, Time before Morning: Art and Myth of the Australian Aborigines, 1975, Making Managerial Planning More Effective, 1982, The Allen Guide for Management Leaders, 1989, Common Vocabulary for Management Leaders, 1989, The Louis Allen Leader's Handbook, 1995, The New Leadership, 1996; (mus. catalog) Australian Aboriginal Art, 1972; translated into Japanese, German, French, Finnish, Swedish, Dutch, Spanish, Portuguese, Bahasa; contbr. numerous articles and monographs to profl. jours. on mgmt., primitive art; exhibitor primitive art major mus. worldwide, 1969—. Maj. USAF, 1942-55, PTO. Decorated Legion of Merit; recipient McKinsey award Acad. Mgmt. Mem. Inst. Mgmt. Cons. (sr. assoc., regional pres. 1985). Achievements include first to fully classify human work into categories, a typology which facilities diagnosis and correction of organizational problems. Office: Louis Allen Rsch PO Box 11 Palo Alto CA 94302-0011 E-mail: laglaceby@aol.com.

ALLEN, LYLE WALLACE, lawyer; b. Chillicothe, Ill., June 17, 1924; s. Donald M. and Mary Ellen (McEvoy) A.; m. Helen Kolar, Aug. 16, 1947; children: Mary Elizabeth Watkins, Bryan James. Student, N.C. State Coll., 1943-44; BS, Northwestern U., 1947; postgrad., Columbia Law Sch., 1947-48; JD, U. Wis., 1950. Bar: Ill. 1950, Wis. 1950. Of counsel Heyl Royster Voelker & Allen, Peoria, Ill., 1951—. Served with 87th Inf. Div. U.S. Army, World War II. Decorated Purple Heart, Bronze star, Combat Infantry badge, Presdl. Unit Citation. Mem. ABA, Ill. State Bar Assn. (pres. 1972-73), Assn. of Ins. Attys. (pres. 1965-66), Illinois Valley Yacht Club, Wig and Pen Club (London). Democrat. Presbyterian. Office: 124 SW Adams St Ste 600 Peoria IL 61602-1392

ALLEN, MARGUERITE E. legal association administrator; b. Vicksburg, Miss., July 25, 1947; d. John Austin and Laura Frances (Martin) Holliday; 1 child, Laura-Ashley Allen. BA, Miss. State U., 1969; MA, La. Tech. U., 1995. Adminstr. asst. VA, Jackson, Miss.; residential realtor Towery Real Estate, Shreveport, La.; exec. dir. Shreveport Bar Assn., Shreveport. Bd. dirs. Shreveport Mental Health Assn., 1988-93; pub. relations Jr. League of Shreveport, 1992. Mem. Nat. Assn. Bar. Execs. Avocations: walking, reading, travel, gardening. Home: 11175 Heritage Oaks Shreveport LA 71106-8383 Office: Shreveport Bar Assn 509 Marshall St Shreveport LA 71101-3591

ALLEN, MARILYN MYERS POOL, theater director, video producer; b. Fresno, Calif., Nov. 2, 1934; d. Laurence B. and Asa (Griggs) Myers; m. Joseph Harold Pool, Dec. 28, 1955; children: Pamela Elizabeth, Victoria Anne, Catherine Marcia; m. Neal R. Allen, Apr. 1982. BA, Stanford U., 1955, postgrad., 1955-56, U. Tex., 1957-60, West Tex. State U., summer 1962, 63, Odessa Coll., 1987-88. Free-lance radio and TV actress; adj. prof. theatre Midland Coll., 1997—98; dir. Globe Theater, Odessa, 1998, 2002; asst. mng. dir. Amarillo Little Theatre, 1964—66, mng. dir., 1966—68, Horseshoe Players, touring profl. theater, 1969—73; actress multi-media prodn. Palo Duro Canyon, 1971; dir. touring children's theatre, 1978—79; guest actress in Medea at Amarillo Coll., 1981; guest reciter Amarillo Symphony, 1972, Midland-Odessa Symphony, 1984. Pres. Tex. Non-Profit Theatres, 1972 74, 75-77, bd. dirs., 1988-91; 1st v.p. High Plains Ctr. for Performing Arts, 1969-73; adv. mem. dept. fine arts Amarillo Coll., 1980-82; adv. mem. Tex. Constnl. Revision Commn., 1973-75; mem. adv. coun. U. Tex. Coll. Fine Arts, 1969-72; cmty. adv. com. for women Amarillo Coll., 1975-79; conv. program com. Am. Theatre Assn., 1978, program participant, 1978-80, bd. dirs., 1980-83; bd. dirs. Amarillo Found. Health and Sci. Edn., 1976-82, program v.p., 1979-81; bd. dirs. Domestic Violence Coun., 1979-82, March of Dimes, 1979-81, Tex. Panhandle Heritage Found., 1964-82, Friends of Fine Arts, West Tex. State U. (now West Tex. A&M U.), 1980-82, Amarillo Pub. Libr., 1980-82, Amarillo Symphony, 1981-82; publicity chmn. Midland Cmty. Theatre, 1984-87, bd. govs., 1986-92, sec., 1987-88, v.p., 1988-92; bd. dirs. Globe of the Great S.W., Odessa, 1998—, v.p. media, 2000-02, v.p. vols., 2002-; mem. Mus. of S.W., Midland Arts Assembly; bd. dirs. Midland County Rep. Women, Ways and Means Ch., 1991, 1st v.p., 1992, publicity chair, 1994; mem. Midland County Redistricting com., 1991; cultural exch. del. from Midland, Tex., to Dong Ying, China, 1993; Tex. UIL one act play adjudicator, 1974-99; mem. Diocesan Comm. Com., N.W. Tex., co-chmn. Companion Diocese Com., Spain, 2003—. Recipient cert. of appreciation Woman of Yr., Amarillo Bus. and Profl. Women's Club, 1966, Best Actress award for Hedda Gabler role Amarillo Little Theatre, 1965, Best Dir. award for Rashomon, 1967, 1st Pl. award for video spl. Tex. Press Conf., 1988, 1st Pl. award for news Tex. Press Conf., 1989, Disting. Svc. award Tex. Non-Profit Theatres, 1992; named Amarillo Woman of Yr., Beta Sigma Phi, 1980, Broadcaster of the Yr., Rocky Mountain Press Conf., 1988, Hamhock of Yr., Midland Cmty. Theatre, 1992, Outstanding Svc. award Midland Arts Assembly, 1992; Travel fellow AAUW, 1973, 78. Fellow Am. Assn. Cmty. Theatre (dir. 1969 72, 82 84, v.p. planning and devel. 1985-87, co-chair AACT/Fest '95), Internat. Amateur Theatre Assn. 23d World Congress (del. Monaco 1997); mem. USTA (sr. women's team sect. winner 1993, 94), S.W. Theatre Conf. (dir. 1973-76, 82-84, exec. com. 1982-84, Disting. Svc. award 1985), Tex. Theatre Coun. (dir. 1974-78, exec. com., pres. 1975-76), AAUW (br. pres. 1973-75, state chmn. cultural interests 1975-77, 86-88, state program v.p. 1977-79, state bd. dirs. 1984-88, program v.p. Midland 1988-89), Episc. Ch. Women (program v.p. Midland 1988-89, outreach chair 1996, program v.p., pres.-elect 1997-98, pres. 1999-2000), DAR (chpt. chaplain 1971-75, historian 1975-77), C. of C. (fine arts coun.), U.S. Tennis Assn. (sr. mixed doubles sect. winner 1999), U.S. Judo Assn., Symphony Guild, Amarillo Art Assn., Midland Symphony Guild (arrangements chmn. 1983-84), Act IX, Shakespeare As We Like It, Amarillo Law Wives Club (pres. 1976-77), Hamhocks (v.p. 1985-86).

ALLEN, MARY LOUISE HOOK, secondary education educator; b. Ironwood, Mich., July 18, 1930; d. Frank Eugene and Elsie Clara (Schneider) Hook; m. Dale Sanson Allen, June 30, 1955; children: Jack Eugene, Bradley Arthur. BS in Phys. Edn. cum laude, U. Mich., 1951; MA in Phys. Edn., U. Minn., 1970, postgrad., 1987—. Life teaching cert., coaching lic., Minn. Secondary edn. tchr. New Trier Twp. High Sch., Winnetka, Ill., 1951-55, Richfield (Minn.) Sch. Dist., 1955-59; teaching assoc. U. Minn., Mpls., 1969-70, part-time lectr., 1985-86; tchr. Bloomington (Minn.) Sch. Dist., 1961-85. Adj. prof. Concordia Coll., St. Paul, Minn., 1987-92; officiator U.S. Synchro Minn. Assn., Minn. State High Sch. League, Pan-Am. Trials Swimming Co-Chair, others; past officiating bd. chmn. North Shore (Winnetka) Basketball/Volleyball, Ill. State Basketball com., others. Co-author: Soccer/Speedball Rule Book - Creative Game, 1952; dir. Aqua Debs Synchronized swim shows, 1962-82. Mem. Atonement Luth. Ch., Bloomington, 1956—; worker Dem. Party, Bloomington, 1988—; dir. Synchronized Swimming Camp, 1980-87. Recipient numerous athletic awards, Minn. Pathfinder award Nat. Assn. Girls and Women in Sport, 1996, U. Mich. Kinesiology Alumni Achievement award, 1996. Mem. AAHPERD (mem. com. 1949—), Minn. Assn. Health, Phys. Edn., Recreation and Dance (sec. 1982-83, pres.-elect 1984, pres. 1985, past pres. 1986, conv. chmn. 1984, 86, student confs. 1988-92), Synchronized Swim Coaches Assn. (state chmn. 1980-82), Athletic Fedn. Coll. Women (chmn. nat. conv. 1951), Mortarboard, Phi Beta Kappa, Phi Kappa Phi, Pi Lambda Theta, also others. Avocations: athletics, camping, politics, gardening. Home: 10312 Wentworth Ave Bloomington MN 55420-5249 E-mail: mlhauofm@usfamily.net.

ALLEN, MARYON PITTMAN, former senator, journalist, lecturer, interior and clothing designer; b. Meridian, Miss., Nov. 30, 1925; d. John D. and Tellie (Chism) Pittman; m. Joshua Sanford Mullins, Jr., Oct. 17, 1946 (div. Jan. 1959); children: Joshua Sanford III, John Pittman, Maryon Foster; m. James Browning Allen, Aug. 7, 1964 (dec. June 1978). Student, U. Ala., 1944—47, Internat. Inst. Interior Design, 1970. Office mgr. for Dr. Alston Callahan, Birmingham, Ala., 1959-60; bus. mgr. psychiat. clinic U. Ala. Med. Center, Birmingham, 1960-61; life underwriter Protective Life Ins. Co., Birmingham, 1961-62; women's editor Sun Newspapers, Birmingham, 1962-64; v.p., ptnr. Pittman family cos., J.D. Pittman Partnership Co., J.D. Pittman Tractor Co., Emerald Valley Corp., Mountain Lake Farms, Inc., Birmingham; mem. U.S. Senate (succeeding late husband James B. Allen), 1978; dir. pub. rels. and advt. C.G. Sloan & Co. Auction House, Washington, 1981; feature writer Birmingham News, 1964; writer syndicated column Reflections of a News Hen, Washington, 1969-78; feature writer, columnist Maryon Allen's Washington, Washington Post, 1979-81; columnist McCall's Needlework Mag., 1993—. Owner The Maryon Allen Co. Cliff House (Restoration/Design), Birmingham. Contbg. editor: So. Accents Mag., 1976—78. Mem. Ladies of U.S. Senate unit ARC, Former Mems. of Congress, Ala. Hist. Commn., Blair House Fine Arts Commn.; charter mem. Birmingham Com. of 100 for Women; mem. steering com. Ala. Gov.'s Mansion; trustee Children's Fresh Air Farm; trustee, deacon, elder Ind. Presbyn. Ch., Birmingham; Dem. Presdl. elector, Ala., 1968. Recipient 1st place award for best original column Ala. Press Assn., 1962, 63, also various press state and nat. awards for typography, fashion writing, food pages, also several awards during Senate service; sponsor, U.S. Navy Nuclear submarine, U.S.S. Birmingham, S.S.N. 695, launched Newport News, Va., 1977, commissioned 1978. Mem. Nat. Press Club, 1925 F Street Club, 91st Congress Club, Congl. Club, Birmingham Country Club. Home and Office: Cliff House 3215 Cliff Rd S

Birmingham AL 35205-1405 E-mail: maryonallenco@aol.com. *You have to believe in yourself, your talents and the premise that you were put here to contribute of yourself...not always to take.*

ALLEN, MATTHEW ARNOLD, physicist; b. Edinburgh, Scotland, Apr. 27, 1930; came to U.S., 1955; s. William Wolff and Clara (Bloch) A.; m. Marcia Harriet Katzman, Sept. 15, 1957; children: Bruce William, Peter Jonathan, David Michael. BSc in Physics, U. Edinburgh, 1951; PhD in Physics, Stanford U., 1959. Rsch. assoc. Hansen Labs., Stanford (Calif.) U., 1959-61; rsch. mgr. tube div. Microwave Assocs., Burlington, Mass., 1961-65; radio frequency group leader Stanford Linear Accelerator Ctr., 1965-82, head accelerator physics dept., 1982-84, head klystron microwave dept., 1984-90, asst. dir. for elec. and electronic systems, 1989-90, assoc. dir. lab., 1990—2003, emeritus, 2003—. Cons. Microwave Assocs. Inc., 1965-71, Aerojet Gen., Azusa, Calif., 1959-62, Bechtel Corp., San Francisco, 1965-67; mem. tech. rev. com. Synchotron Radiation Rsch. Ctr., Taipei, Taiwan, 1985-98; chmn. U.S.A. Particle Accelerator Conf., 1991. Contbr. articles to profl. jours.; patentee in field. Commr. Environ. Planning Commn., Mountain View, Calif., 1971-74; councilman Mountain View City Coun., 1974-82; mayor City of Mountain View, 1977, 81; pres. Mountain View Community TV, 1989. Lt. British Army, 1953-55. Fellow IEEE, Am. Phys. Soc.; mem. IEEE Nuclear and Plasma Scis. Soc. (adminstrv. com. 1978-84, 98-2001), Dem. Club (bd. dirs. 1980-84), Sigma Xi. Democrat. Avocations: skiing, running, tv producing. Home: 325 Chatham Way Mountain View CA 94040-4471 Office: Stanford U Linear Accelerator Ctr Stanford CA 94309 E-mail: matthew.allen@slac.stanford.edu.

ALLEN, MAURICE BARTELLE, JR., architect; b. Lansing, Mich., Mar. 20, 1926; s. Maurice Bartelle and Marguerite Rae (Stahl) A.; m. Nancy Elizabeth Huff, June 29, 1951; children— Robert (dec.), Katherine, David. Student, Western Mich. U., 1944, Notre Dame U., 1944-46; BArch, U. Mich., 1950. Registered profl. architect, Mich. Draftsman, designer Smith, Hinchman & Grylls (architects), Detroit, 1950-51; designer, asso. Eero Saarinen & Assos., Bloomfield Hills, Mich., 1951-61; v.p. design and planning TMP Assos. (architects, engrs. and planners), Bloomfield Hills, 1961-92; emeritus, 1993; design critic, lectr. Coll. Architecture and Urban Planning, U. Mich., 1958—. Cons. arch. Camelback Bible Ch., Paradise Valley, Ariz. Prin. archtl. works include Gen. Motors Inst. campus devel. and bldgs, Flint, Mich., Mackinac and Manitou halls, Grand Valley State Coll, O'Dowd Hall, Oakland U, Prototype Regional Correctional Facilities, Mich. Dept. Corrections, Fine Arts Ctr. and Theater, Allied Scis. Bldg., Macomb Community Coll., Scheide Music Ctr., Coll. of Wooster, Towsley Ctr. Sch. of Music, U. Mich., Performing Arts Ctr. and Student Ctr., Lake Superior State U., Art Music Humanities Ctr., Wabash Coll., Univ. Community Ctr., U. Western Ont., Drama Theater and Arts Bldg., Concordia Coll., St. Paul. Active Detroit Area council Boy Scouts Am., 1969—, Detroit Inst. Arts, Detroit Symphony; mem. environmental arts com. Mich. Council for Arts, 1970; vice chmn. Mich. Gov.'s Spl. Commn. on Architecture, 1971. Served with USNR, 1944-47. Recipient honor awards Detroit chpt. AIA, 1970-71, Gold medal, 1994, citation for design high rise structures Am. Iron and Steel Inst., 1971, citation of excellence Architecture for Justice Exhbn., 1982. Mem. Coll. of Fellows AIA (co-chair urban priorities Detroit chpt. 1995—), Mich. Soc. Architects (honor awards 1970-71), Sr. Men's Club Birmingham, Masons, Alpha Tau Omega. Republican. Episcopalian. Home and Office: 4325 Derry Rd Bloomfield Hills MI 48302-1835

ALLEN, MERRILL JAMES, marine biologist; b. Brady, Tex., July 16, 1945; s. Clarence Francis and Sara Barbara (Finlay) A. BA, U. Calif., Santa Barbara, 1967; MA, UCLA, 1970; PhD, U. Calif., San Diego, 1982. Cert. jr. coll. tchr., Calif. Asst. environ. specialist So. Calif. Coastal Water Rsch. Project, El Segundo, 1971-77; postdoctoral assoc. Nat. Rsch. Coun., Seattle, 1982-84; oceanographer Nat. Marine Fisheries Svc., Seattle, 1984-86; sr. scientist MBC Applied Environ. Scis., Costa Mesa, Calif., 1986-93; prin. scientist So. Calif. Coastal Water Rsch. Project, Long Beach and Westminster, Calif., 1993—. Tech. adv. com. Santa Monica Bay Restoration Project, Los Angeles, Calif., 1989—; steering com. So. Calif. Bight Pilot Project, 1993-98, So. Calif. Bight 1998 Regional Marine Survey, 1998—; affiliate asst. prof. sch. fisheries U. Wash., Seattle, 1985-89; mem. sci. rev. panel for marine ecol. reserves rsch. program Calif. Sea Grant Coll., 1996-97; adj. prof. dept. biology Calif. State U., Long Beach, 1996—. Mem. Calif. Marine Life Mgmt. Act Evaluation Com., 2000—. Fellow Am. Inst. Fisheries Rsch. Biologists (dir. So. Calif. dist. 1991-93); mem. AAAS, Am. Fisheries Soc., Am. Soc. Ichthyologists and Herpetologists, So. Calif. Acad. Sci. (bd. dirs. 2000—). Achievements include development of most comprehensive atlas of marine fishes from Bering Sea to Mexico; description of state of contamination of Santa Monica Bay. Office: So Calif Coastal Water Rsch Project 7171 Fenwick Ln Westminster CA 92683-5218 E-mail: jima@sccwrp.org.

ALLEN, MICHAEL JOHN BRIDGMAN, English educator; b. Lewes, Eng., Apr. 1, 1941; came to U.S., 1966; m. Elena Hirshberg; children: William, Benjamin. BA, Oxford (Eng.) U., 1964, MA, 1966, DLitt, 1987; PhD, U. Mich., 1970. Asst. prof. UCLA, 1970-74, assoc. prof., 1974-79, prof. English, 1979—, assoc. dir. Ctr. for Medieval and Renaissance Studies, 1978-88, dir. Ctr. for Medieval and Renaissance Studies, 1988-93, 2003—. Editor Renaissance Quar., 1993-2001; faculty rsch. lectr. UCLA, 1998. Author: Marsilio Ficino: The Philebus Commentary, 1975, Marsilio Ficino and the Phaedran Charioteer, 1981, The Platonism of Marsilio Ficino, 1984, Icastes: Marsilio Ficino's Interpretation of Plato's "Sophist," 1989, Nuptial Arithmetic, 1994, Plato's Third Eye: Studies in Marsilio Ficino's Metaphysics and Its Sources, 1995, Synoptic Art: Marsilio Ficino on the History of Platonic Interpretation, 1998; co-author: Sources and Analogues of Old English Poetry, 1976, Marsilio Ficino: Platonic Theology, Vol. I, Books I-IV, 2001, Vol. 2, Books V-VIII, 2002, Vol. 3, Books IX-XI, 2003; co-editor: First Images of America, 1976, Shakespeare's Plays in Quarto, 1984, Sir Philip Sidney's Achievements, 1990, Marsilio Ficino: His Theology, His Philosophy, His Legacy, 2002. Recipient Eby award for disting. teaching UCLA, 1977; Guggenheim fellow, 1977; disting. vis. scholar Center for Reformation and Renaissance Studies, U. Toronto, 1997, Ludwig Maximilians U., Munich, 1999, Ariz. Ctr. for Medieval & Renaissance Studies, 2002. Office: UCLA 2225 Rolfe Hall 405 Hilgard Ave Los Angeles CA 90095-9000 E-mail: mjballen@humnet.ucla.edu.

ALLEN, MILTON D. music educator; b. Salina, Kans., Nov. 2, 1960; s. Deane and Cora May Allen; m. Margaret Sawyko, Nov. 28, 1998; children: Benjamin, Madeline. B in Music Edn., U. North Tex., 1985; MusM, U. Mo., 1992; diploma of fine arts in wind studies, U. Calgary, 1993. Dir. of bands Pky. South H.S., Ballwin, Mo., 1985—91; founder, music dir. & condr. St. Louis Youth Wind Ensemble, 1992—96; roving instr. Pky. Sch. Dist., St. Louis County, Mo., 1991—94; dir. of bands Orchard Farm Sch. Dist., St. Charles, Mo., 1994—97, Sacred Heart Jr./Sr. H.S., Salina, 1998—. Clinician, guest condr., 1981—; music dir. Salina Cmty. Theater, 1990—91. Honor band chair Cottonwood Valley Athletic League, 1998—99. Named to Kans. Exemplary Educators Network, Kans. Dept. of Edn., 2001—03. Mem.: Music Educators Nat. Conf., Kans. Music Educators Assn. (North Ctrl. mid. sch. honor band chair 2001—03, North Ctrl. H.S. Music Educator of Yr. 2001—02), Kans. Bandmasters Assn., Internat. Assn. Jazz Educators, Coll. Band Dirs. Nat. Assn. Avocations: triathlons, Tae Kwon Do, sports, Native American culture. Office: Sacred Heart Jr/Sr HS 234 E Cloud Salina KS 67401 Office Fax: 785-827-8648.

ALLEN, NEWTON PERKINS, lawyer; b. Memphis, Jan. 3, 1922; s. James Seddon and Sarah (Perkins) Allen; m. Malinda Lobdell Nobles, Oct. 4, 1947 (dec. Nov. 1986); children: John Lobdell, Malinda Nobles, Newton Perkins, Cannon Fairfax; m. Malinda Lobdell Crutchfield, June 23, 1990. AB, Princeton, 1943; JD, U. Va., 1948. Bar: Tenn 1947, NC 1990. Assoc. Armstrong, Allen, Prewitt, Gentry, Johnston & Holmes, Memphis, 1948, ptnr., 1950-95; assoc. Dann & Allen, 1996—2001; with Newton P. Allen Law Firm, Memphis, 2001—. Contbr. articles to profl jours. Mem Chickasaw coun Boy Scouts Am, 1958—60, mem exec bd, 1961—69; trustee LeBonheur Children's Hosp, Memphis, 1964—72, vice chmn bd, 1965; mem alumni coun Princeton, 1954—64, 1990—93; chmn Greater Memphis Coun Crime and Delinquency, 1976—80; bd dirs Memphis Orchestra Soc, pres, 1979—81; pres bd trustees St Mary's Episcopal Sch, 1966—67, vpres, 1972—73; co-chmn Memphis Conf Faith at Work, 1975, bd dirs, 1976—79. Mem.: ABA (ed bd sr lawyers div 1990, pub comt chair 1993—95, coun mem 1994—95, chair travel and leisure comt 1995—96, vice chair 1996—97, chair-elect 1997—98, chair 1998—99), Princeton Alumni Asn Memphis (pres 1992), NC Bar Asn, Tenn Def Lawyers Asn, Memphis Bar Asn, Tenn Bar Asn, Am Col Trust and Estate Coun, Memphis Lions (pres 1956). Office: Law Office 840 Valleybrook Dr Memphis TN 38120

ALLEN, NORMA ANN, librarian, educator; b. Balt., Jan. 22, 1951; d. James Crawley and Thelma Agusta (Keaton) Ghee; children: Lamont Ricardo Ghee, Alissa S. Allen, Avery O. Allen. BA in Adminstrn. Mgmt., Sojourner Douglass Coll., Balt., 1987; MS in Instrnl. Tech., Towson State U., 1999. Instr. data processing PSI Inst., Balt., 1987-88; acquisition technician Social Security Adminstrn., Balt., 1987-89, reference librarian, 1989-91, acquisitions librarian, 1991—. Instrnl. developer Computer Asst. Instrn., Towson U., 1995—; bus. computer tech. instr. Balt. City C.C., 2000—; freelance floral designer/arranger, freelance instr. basic writing skills and computer literacy; instr. bus. computer tech. Balt. City C.C., 2000—. Sec., bd. dirs. New Image Child Care Facility, Balt., 1992, chmn. bd. dirs., 2001-02; instr. active reading literacy program Enoch Pratt Libr., Balt., 1992; instr. United Missionary Bapt. Conv., 1997, libr., 2003. Multicultural scholar Towson U., 1995-96. Mem. ALA, Spl. Librs. Assn., Horizon User Group. Office: Social Security Adminstrn 6401 Security Blvd Rm 571 Baltimore MD 21235-0001 E-mail: norma.allen@ssa.gov.

ALLEN, OLIVER E. writer; b. Cambridge, Mass., June 29, 1922; s. Frederick Lewis and Dorothy Cobb Allen; m. Deborah Allen, May 8, 1948; children: Stephen(dec.), Frederick, Henry, Letitia, Jennie. AB, Harvard Coll., 1943. Writer, editor Life Mag., N.Y.C., 1947—60; editor Life World Libr. Time-Life Books, 1960—65, editor Time-Life Libr. Am., 1965—68, dir. editl. planning, 1968—76; freelance writer, 1976—. Author: Wildflower Gardening, 1977, Decorating With Plants, 1978, Pruning and Grafting, 1978, The Windjammers, 1978, Shade Gardens, 1979, Winter Gardens, 1979, The Pacific Navigators, 1980, The Airline Builders, 1981, Building Sound Bones and Muscles, 1981, Secrets of Good Digestion, 1982, The Atmosphere, 1983, The Vegetable Gardeners' Journal, 1985, Gardening With the New Small Plants, 1987, New York, New York, 1991, The Tiger, 1993, Tales of Old Tribeca, 1999. 1st lt. U.S. Army, 1943—46. Mem.: Century Club. Democrat. Home: 42 Hudson St New York NY 10013

ALLEN, PAUL ALFRED, lawyer, educator; b. New Canaan, Conn., Feb. 18, 1948; s. Alfred J. and Wilma T. (DeWaters) A. BA, Johns Hopkins U., 1970; JD, NYU, 1974; MBA, U. Colo., 1989. Bar: Md. 1974, D.C. 1978, Colo. 1984, Calif. 1992. Exec. dir. Md. Environ. Trust, Balt., 1974-75; assoc. Bergson, Borkland, Margolis & Adler, Washington, 1975-79, ptnr., 1980-82; gen. counsel Plus System, Inc., Denver, 1983-91; counsel Visa USA, Inc., San Francisco, 1991-92, exec. v.p., gen. counsel, 1992—. Lectr. Grad. Sch. of Banking, Boulder, Colo., 1984-86, U. Denver Law Sch., 1985-90. Editor: How to Keep Your Company Out of Court, 1984; contbr. articles to profl. jours. Recipient Svc. award Supreme Ct. Colo. Mem. ABA, Calif. Bar Assn., Colo. Bar Assn., Am. Corp. Counsel Assn. Democrat. Office: Visa USA Inc PO Box 194607 San Francisco CA 94119-4607

ALLEN, PAUL B. information technology executive; Co-founder Infobases, Inc., 1990, MyFamily.com (formerly Ancestry.com), 1996—97; CEO Ancestry.com, 1997. Office: Myfamily dot com 360 W 4800 N Provo UT 84604 Office Fax: 801-705-7001.

ALLEN, PAUL G. computer company executive, professional sports team executive; Student, Wash. State U. Co-founder Microsoft Corp., Redmond, Wash., 1975, exec. v.p., 1975—83; founder Asymetrix Corp., Bellevue, Wash., 1985—, Starwave Corp., Bellevue; founder, chmn. Intervas Rsch., Palo Alto, Calif.; CEO Vulcan Ventures, Bellevue, 1987—; owner, chmn. Seattle Seahawks; owner, chmn. bd. Portland (Oreg.) Trail Blazers, 1988—; owner TechTV. Bd. dirs. Egghead Discount Software, Microsoft Corp., Darwin Molecular, Inc.; founder Experience Music Project.*

ALLEN, PAUL HOWARD, financial institutions investor; b. Aldershot, Eng., Apr. 5, 1954; came to U.S., 1979; s. William and Frances Elva (Mason) A.; m. Sandra C. Allen, June 11, 1994; children: Emma Elizabeth, Mark William Philip, Caroline Victoria Frances, Edward Christopher James. BA in Jurisprudence, Oxford (Eng.) U., 1976; MA in Jurisprudence, Oxford U., 1988; MBA, Harvard U., 1981. Bar: solicitor Eng. and Wales 1977. Solicitor of Supreme Ct., London, Freshfields, Eng., 1977-79; lectr. law Exeter Coll. Oxford U., 1978-79; assoc. McKinsey and Co. Inc., London, 1981-84, N.Y.C., 1984-87, ptnr., 1987-89; founder Aston Assocs., Greenwich, Conn., 1989—. Author: Reengineering The Bank, 1995, Creating the New Bank, 1996; contbr. articles to profl. publs. Cons. CARE, N.Y.C., 1987—. McKinnon scholar Magdalen Coll. Oxford U., 1976; Harkness Fellow Commonwealth Fund N.Y., 1979-81; Baker scholar Harvard U., 1981. Mem. Brit. Inst. Mgmt. Avocations: tennis, golf, running, theatre. Office: Aston Assocs 35 Mason St Greenwich CT 06830-5433

ALLEN, PETER LEWIS, editor, educator; b. N.Y.C., June 1, 1957; s. Alvin Allen and Barbara Rappaport (Grossman) Taylor. BA in English and Classics, Haverford Coll., 1978; MA in Comparative Lit., U. Chgo., 1979; DEA in French and Comparative Lit., U. Poitiers, France, 1982; PhD in Comparative Lit., U. Chgo., 1984; MBA, U. Pa. Wharton Sch., Phila., 2000. V.p. Aero Rsch. Assocs., N.Y.C.; from asst. to assoc. prof. Pomona Coll., Claremont, Calif., 1986—98; scholar in residence Coll. Physicians of Phila., 1996—97; assoc. McKinsey & Co., N.Y.C., 1999—2002, sr. editor, 2000—. Lectr. Princeton U., NJ, 1984—86; Mellon fellow U.S.C., L.A., 1991—92. Author: (books) The Art of Love, 1992, The Wages of Sin, 2000. Mem. Congregation Beth Simchat Torah; bd. dirs. Chekhov Theatre Ensemble, 1997—99, Reaching Out Gay and Lesbian MBA Conf., 1999—. Recipient Scholarship, St. Andrew's Soc Phila., Aberdeen, Scotland, 1976—77, Rotary Found, Poirtiers, France, 1981—82. Mem.: Phi Beta Kappa. Democrat. Jewish. Avocations: athletics, cooking, writing. Office: McKinsey & Co 55 E 52d St New York NY 10055

ALLEN, PHILIP MARK, arts and humanities educator, dean, writer; b. Phila., Mar. 11, 1932; m. Susan Davidson, Feb. 1, 1986; children: Catherine Stewart, Jameson Louis. BA with highest honors, Swarthmore Coll., 1953; PhD, Emory U., 1956. Fgn. svc. officer U.S. Dept. of State, Washington, Hamburg, Antananarivo, 1956-66; regional rep. African Am. Inst., Lagos, Nigeria, 1966-67, Abidjan, Ivory Coast, 1966-68, dir. R & D N.Y.C., 1968-70; from assoc. prof. to prof. Johnson (Vt.) State Coll., 1970-87; dean sch. arts and humanities Frostburg (Md.) State U., 1987-99, disting. univ. prof., asst. to provost, coord. liberal studies, 1999—; Fulbright lectr. U. Antananarivo, Madagascar, 1999-2000. Cons., lectr. Raymond & Whitcomb Co., N.Y. and Africa, 1970-75; mem. Fulbright rev. panels for sub-Sahara Africa and sr. specialist grants. Author: The Western Indian Ocean, 1987, Madagascar: Conflicts of Authority, 1995; co-author: The Traveler's Africa, 1973; editor: Vermont and the Year 2000, 1976, Reciprocal Cultures, 1999. Mem. planning commn. Danby, Vt., 1972-74; mem. com. Md. Info. Tech. Bd., 1995-99; bd. dirs., mem. exec. com. Md. Citizens for the Arts, Balt., 1995-2000; founding bd. dirs. Cumberland (Md.) Theatre, 1987-99; mem. Global Expertise Res., 2002—. Fulbright lectr. U.S. Dept. State, Senegal, 1981-82, Algeria, 1985-86, Madagascar, 1999-2000; travel to collections grantee NEH, France, 1985. Mem. Internat. Coun. Fine Arts Deans (com. chair). Avocations: theater, music, hosting public radio opera program. Office: Frostburg State U PAC 127 Frostburg MD 21532 E-mail: pallen@frostburg.edu.

ALLEN, RALPH GILMORE, dramatist, producer, drama educator; b. Phila., Jan. 7, 1934; s. Ralph Bergen and Sara Beddoe (Walker) A.; m. Harriet Phyllis Nichols, Aug. 24, 1957. BA summa cum laude, Amherst Coll., 1955, DHL (hon.), 1980; DFA, Yale U., 1960. From asst. prof. theatre and drama to assoc. prof. U. Pitts, 1960-68; prof., chmn. dept. drama U. Victoria, B.C., Can., 1968-72; chmn. dept., prof. theatre U. Tenn., Knoxville, 1972-80; prof. drama Queens Coll., N.Y.C., 1983—, prof. emeritus, 1999—. Dir. Clarence Brown Theatre Co., Knoxville, 1972-77; theatre cons.; prodr. John F. Kennedy Ctr., Washington, 1980-83; dir. more than 40 prodns. Co-author: (with John Gassner) Theatre and Drama in the Making, 1965, rev. edit., 1992; playwright: (with Joshua Logan) Rip Van Winkle, 1976, The Tax Collector, 1977; (with David Campbell and Michael Valenti) Honky Tonk Nights, 1986, A Horse of a Different Color, 1989; dir: many plays including Everyman, 1972-75, The New Majestic Follies, 1977; author: (revue) Sugar Babies, 1979 (Tony award nomination 1980), Best Burlesque Sketches, 1994, Scandals, 1999; editor Theatre Survey, 1965-69; translator: Imaginary Invalid (Moliere), 1991, The Servant of Two Masters (Goldoni), 1992, The Gardener's Dog (Lope de Vega), 1993, The Palace of the Dead (Lope de Vega), 1994; contbr. numerous articles to profl. jours. John Golden fellow, 1957-59, Guggenehim fellow, 1965, Charles E. Merrill fellow, 1961; named Artist of Yr., Phi Kappa Phi, 1983; recipient Award for Service to Arts Mayor of Phila., 1983, Award of Merit Am. Theatre Assn., 1983. Fellow ASCAP, Dramatists Guild, Am. Theatre Assn. (v.p. 1972); mem. Am. Soc. Theatre Rsch. (dir., exec. com. 1977-80), Theatre Can. (gov. 1970-71), Nat. Theatre Conf.

ALLEN, RANDY LEE, lawyer; b. Kansas City, Kans., Oct. 19, 1963; s. William Richard and Martha Carol Allen; m. Lori B. Meendering; children: Elizabeth, Henry. BS in Petroleum Engring., Colo. Sch. Mines, 1986; JD, U. Colo., 1990. Bar: Colo. 1990, Ala. 1994. Clk. Astrella & Rice PC, Denver, 1988-90, atty., 1990-94; gen. counsel River Gas Corp., Tuscaloosa, Ala., 1994-2000; atty. Frontier Enterprises, L.L.C., Tuscaloosa, 2001—. Mem. Ind. Petroleum Assn. Am. (com. mem. 1994—), Ala. Coalbed Methane Assn. (com. mem. 1994—), Rocky Mountain Oil and Gas Assn. (com. mem. 1994—), Rocky Mountain Mineral Law Found. Office: Frontier Enterprises LLC Ste 804 509 Energy Center Blvd Northport AL 35473 E-mail: rallen@frontier-ent.com.

ALLEN, REX WHITAKER, retired architect; b. San Francisco, Dec. 21, 1914; s. Lewis Whitaker and Maude Rex (Allen) A.; m. Elizabeth Johnson, Oct. 11, 1941 (div. 1949); children: Alexandra A., Frances Lambert (Mrs. Andrew Dunn); m. Ruth Batchelor, Apr. 1, 1949 (div. 1971); children: Mark B., Susan Moore (Mrs. Kofy Lechner); m. Bettie J. Crossfield, Nov. 6, 1971. AB, Harvard U., 1936, M.Arch., 1939; student, Columbia U. Arch. Sch., 1936-37. With Research and Planning Assos., N.Y.C., 1939-42, Camloc Fastener Corp., N.Y.C., 1942-45, Isadore Rosenfield (architect), N.Y.C., 1945-48, Blanchard and Maher (architects), San Francisco, 1949-52; established pvt. practice San Francisco, 1953; pres. Rex Whitaker Allen & Assos., San Francisco, 1961-71, Archtl. Prodns., Inc., 1971-76; prin. Hugh Stubbins/Rex Allen Partnership, 1968, Rex Allen Partnership, 1971-76; pres. Rex Allen-Drever-Lechowski, Architects, 1976-85, Rex Allen/Mark Lechowski & Assocs., 1985-87; cons. architect, health facility planner, 1987—. Mem. Calif. Bldg. Safety Bd., 1973-93. Author: (with Ilona von Karolyi) Hospital Planning Handbook, 1976; Contbr. articles to profl. jours.; prin. works include French Hosp, San Francisco, Mercy Hosp, Sacramento, Roseville (Calif.) Dist. Hosp, Highland Hosp, Oakland, St. Francis Hosp, San Francisco, Dominican Hosp, Santa Cruz, Alta Bates Hosp, Berkeley, Calif., Boston City Hosp, Out-Patient bldg. Woodland (Calif.) Meml. Hosp, Stanislaus Meml. Hosp, Modesto, Calif., Madera (Calif.) Community Hosp, Sacred Heart Hosp, Eugene, Oreg., St. Joseph Hosp, Mt. Clemens, Mich., Commonwealth Health Center, Saipan, Guam Meml. Hosp. and Nursing Facility. Chmn. Mill Valley Adv. Edn. Council, 1956; mem. Blue Ribbon com. Sonoma Valley Unified Sch. Dist., 1997—. Fellow AIA (nat. pres. 1969-70, v.p. No. Calif. chpt. 1964, bd. dirs. Calif. coun. 1955-56, 1962-64); hon. fellow Royal Archtl. Inst. Can.; mem. Constrn. Specification Inst. (pres. San Francisco chpt. 1961), San Francisco Zool. Soc. (bd. dirs. 1974-86, 88-95, exhibits com. 1988—, chmn. design stds. com. Assn. Western Hosps., chmn. arch. sect. 1957-58), Calif. Hosp. Assn., Am. Hosp. Assn., Internat. Hosp. Fedn., Am. Assn. Hosp. Planning (pres. 1971-72), Union Internat. des Architectes Pub. Health Work Group (dir. 1979-80), La Sociedad de Arquitectos Mexicanos (hon. mem.), Federaciñn Panamericana de Asociaciones de Arquitectos (v.p. 1980-84), San Francisco Planning and Urban Renewal Assn., San Francisco Mus. Modern Art, Mus. Soc., Japanese Garden Soc. of Oreg., Portland Classical Chinese Garden, Asian Art Coun., Portland Art Mus., Sierra Club. Clubs: Harvard (N.Y.C. and San Francisco). Home and Office: 9946 SW 61st Ave Portland OR 97219 E-mail: rethmore@vom.com.

ALLEN, RICHARD BLOSE, legal editor, lawyer; b. Aledo, Ill., May 10, 1919; s. James Albert and Claire (Smith) A.; m. Marion Treloar, Aug. 27, 1949; children: Penelope, Jennifer, Leslie Jean. BS, U. Ill., 1941, JD, 1947; LLD, Seton Hall U., 1977. Bar: Ill. 1947. Staff editor ABA Jour., 1947-48, 63-66, exec. editor, 1966-70, editor, 1970-83, editor, pub., 1983-86; pvt. practice Aledo, 1949-57; gen. counsel Ill. Bar Assn., 1957-63; mng. editor Def. Counsel Jour., Chgo., 1987—. Editor Sr. Lawyer, 1986-90, 94-2000. Maj. Q.M.C., AUS, 1941-46. Mem. ABA (mem. ho. of dels. 1996-99, chair sr. lawyers divsn. 2000-01), Ill. Bar Assn. (mem. assembly 1972-74), Chgo. Bar Assn., Am. Law Inst., Selden Soc., Mich. Shores Club, Kappa Tau Alpha, Phi Delta Phi, Alpha Tau Omega. Office: Def Counsel Jour 1 N Franklin St Ste 1205 Chicago IL 60606-2401 E-mail: rallen@iadclaw.org.

ALLEN, RICHARD GARRETT, healthcare and education consultant; b. St. Paul, July 8, 1923; s. John and Margaretta (Taggart) A.; m. Ida Elizabeth Vernon, July 5, 1944; children— Richard Garrett, Barbara Elizabeth, Julie Frances (dec.). BS cum laude, Trinity U., 1954; M.H.A., Baylor U., 1957; postgrad., Indsl. Coll. of Armed Forces, 1962, USAF Command and Staff Coll., 1962. Commd. 2d lt. Med. Service Corps U.S. Air Force, 1948, advanced through grades to maj., 1961; served in U.S., Pacific, Germany; ret., 1964; asst. adminstr. U. Ala. Hosp. and Clinics; dir. Ctr. for Hosp. Continuing Edn., Sch. for Health Services, U. Ala., Birmingham, 1965-68; dir. edn. New Eng. Hosp. Assembly, Inc., New Eng. Ctr. for Continuing Edn., U. N.H., Durham, 1968-74; dir. Office Health Care Edn., 1970-74; exec. v.p. Edn. and Research Found., San Francisco, 1974-77, Assn. West Hosps., 1974-77. V.p. health affairs M G & M Communications, Foster City, Calif.; pres. Calif. Coll. Podiatric Medicine; chief exec. officer Calif. Podiatry Hosp. and Outpatient Clinic, San Francisco, 1977-81; prof. health care adminstrn. St. Mary's Coll. of Calif., Moraga, 1982-85; cons. health care and edn., 1985—; owner Sleepy Hollow Books, 1985—; mem. Nat. Adv. Coun. on Vocat. Edn., 1969-71; also cons.; cons. Booz, Allen & Hamilton, Washington, Ops. Rsch., Inc., Silver Spring, Md., Republic of Korea Air Force Med. Svcs., Seoul, Bio-Dynamics, Inc., Cambridge, Mass., HEALTHSAT— Appalachia Community Svcs. Network, Washington, 1980—. Pub.: Hosp. Forum, San Francisco, 1974-77; Contbr. articles to profl. jours. Decorated Air Force Commendation medal with oak leaf cluster. Fellow Am. Coll. Hosp. Adminstrs.; mem. Am. Soc. for Health Manpower Edn. and Tng., Am. Hosp. Assn., AAUP, Am. Soc. Hosp. Edn. and Tng. (pres. 1972), Am. Assn. Colls. Podiatric Medicine (pres. 1979-81), Sherlock Holmes Soc. London Lodges: Masons. Episcopalian. Home and Office: Sleepy Hollow Books 1455 Camino Peral Moraga CA 94556-2018 E-mail: dick78@earthlink.net. *Uncertainty is a fact of life; there is no progress free of the risk of change. Sharpen your sense of timing and know when it is time to let go and when to hang on. Trials and defeats are inevitable elements of the committed life; welcome these conflicts for it is your principles that are involved. Appreciate the past, but focus on today's tasks— while realizing that tomorrow will be nothing like you expect it to be. Cultivate a cheerful acceptance of your own mortality, and its attendant limitations and blessings.*

ALLEN, RICHARD LEE, JR., lawyer, consultant; b. Piqua, Ohio, Mar. 12, 1954; s. Richard Lee and Marcella Marie (Reaster) A.; m. Judith Ellen Simpkin, June 28, 1978; children— Richard Lee III, John Christopher. B.S. in Pharmacy, U. Cin., 1977; J.D., Capital Law Sch., 1980. Bar: Ohio 1980. Risk mgr. Med. Ctr. Hosp., Chillicothe, Ohio, 1978-79; Spl. counsel Ohio Hosp. Ins. Co., Columbus, 1980— ; pharmacist Med. Ctr. Hosp., Chillicothe, 1977; adj. prof. Ohio State U., Columbus, 1982— . Mem. Assn. Trial Lawyers Am., Am. Soc. Law and Medicine, Ohio Bar Assn., Ohio Pharm. Assn., Columbus Bar Assn. Home: 678 Blackoak Ct Reynoldsburg OH 43068-1509 Office: Ohio Hosp Ins Co 155 E Broad St Fl 13 Columbus OH 43215-3609

ALLEN, RICHARD STANLEY (DICK ALLEN), English language educator, author; b. Troy, N.Y., Aug. 8, 1939; s. Richard Sanders and Doris (Bishop) A.; m. Loretta Mary Negridge, Aug. 13, 1960; children: Richard Negridge, Tanya Angell. AB, Syracuse U., N.Y., 1961; MA, Brown U., 1963. Teaching assoc. Brown U., 1962-64; instr. English Wright State U., Dayton, Ohio, 1964-68; mem. faculty U. Bridgeport, Conn., 1968—, prof. English, 1976-79, Charles A. Dana prof. English, 1979—2001, also dir. creative writing, Dana prof. emeritus English, 2001—. Author: Anon and Various Time Machine Poems, 1971, Overnight in the Guest House of the Mystic, 1984, Regions with No Proper Names, 1975, Flight and Pursuit, 1987, Ode to the Cold War: Poems New and Selected, 1997, They Day Before: New Poems, 2003; also poems, articles, revs.; editor, poetry editor: Mad River Rev., 1964-68; co-editor: Detective Fiction: Crime and Compromise, 1974, Looking Ahead: The Vision of Science Fiction, 1975; contbg. editor: Am. Poetry Rev.; book reviewer: Poetry, Hudson Rev., Am. Book Rev.; editor: Science Fiction: The Future, 1982, Crosscurrents Expansive Poetry: The New Formalism and the New Narrative, 1989. Recipient

poetry prize Union Arts and Civic League, 1971, Disting. Tchg. award MLA-Assn. Depts. English, 1971, San Jose poetry prize, 1976, poetry prize Nassau Rev., 1995; Hart Crane Meml. poetry fellow, 1966, Robert Frost poetry fellow, 1972, Mellon rsch. fellow, 1981, poetry writing fellow Ingram Merrill Found., 1986; poetry writing grantee Nat. Endowment Arts, 1984, Nat. Millennium Survey Project, 2000. Mem. Associated Writers Programs, Poets and Writers, PEN, Poetry Soc. Am. (Carolyn Davies Meml. Poetry award 1986), Modern Poetry Soc. Republican. Unitarian Universalist. Home: 74 Fern Cir Trumbull CT 06611-4910

ALLEN, RICHARD VINCENT, international business consultant, policy advisor; b. Collingswood, N.J., Jan. 1, 1936; s. Charles Carroll and Magdalen (Buchman) A.; m. Patricia Ann Mason, Dec. 28,1957; children: Michael, Kristin, Mark, Karen, Kathryn, Kevin, Kimberly. BA, U. Notre Dame, 1957, MA, 1958; postgrad., U. Munich, W. Ger., 1958-61; hon. doctorate, Hanover Coll., Korea U. Instr. U. Md. Overseas Div., 1959-61; asst. prof. polit. sci. Ga. Inst. Tech., 1961-62; sr. staff mem. Center for Strategic and Internat. Studies, Georgetown U., 1962-66, Hoover Instn. on War, Revolution and Peace, Stanford U., 1966-69; fgn. policy coord. Richard Nixon Presdl. campaign, 1967-68; sr. staff mem. Nat. Security Council, White House, 1969; dep. asst. to Pres. U.S., White House, 1971-72; pres. Potomac Internat. Corp., Washington, 1972-80; sr. fgn. policy and nat. security adv. to Ronald Reagan, 1978-80; asst. for nat. security affairs Pres. U.S., White House, 1981-82; pres. Richard V. Allen Co., Washington, 1982-90, chmn., 1991—. Disting. fellow, chmn. Asian Studies Ctr. Heritage Found., 1982-98; sr. counselor for fgn. policy and nat. security Rep. Nat. Com., 1982-88; sr. fellow Hoover Instn., 1983—; vice chmn. Internat. Dem. Union, 1983-88; chmn. German-Am. Tricentennial Found., 1983; mem. Pres.'s Task Force on U.S. Govt. Internat. Broadcasting, 1991-92; mem. adv. bd. Cath. Campaign for Am., 1993—; mem. Rep. Congl. Policy Adv. Bd., 1998—. Author: Peace or Peaceful Coexistence, 1966, (with others) Communism and Democracy: Theory and Action, 1967; editor: (with David M. Abshire) National Security: Political, Military and Economic Strategies in the Decade Ahead, 1963, Yearbook on International Communist Affairs, 1969. Chmn. com. on intelligence Republican Nat. Com., 1977-80; trustee St. Francis Prep. Sch., Spring Grove, Pa. Named Patriot of Yr. SAR, 1981; H.B. Earhart fellow Relm Found., 1958-61; decorated Order of Diplomatic Merit Republic of Korea, 1982, Knight Comdr.'s Cross Fed. Republic of Germany, 1983, Badge and Star of Order of Merit Fed. Republic of Germany, 1983, Order of Brilliant Star, Republic of China, 1986, Sovereign Mil. Order of Knights of Malta, 1987. Mem. Am. Polit. Sci. Assn., Coun. on Fgn. Rels., Intercollegiate Studies Inst. (trustee), Com. on Present Danger (dir. 1976-90), Univ. Club, Fed. City Club, Farmington Country Club (Charlottesville, Va.), Burning Tree Club (Bethesda, Md.), Met. Club, Cordillera Club (Colo.). Office: 1615 L St NW Ste 900 Washington DC 20036-5623

ALLEN, ROBERT CHARLES, pathologist; b. Pueblo, Colo., Aug. 12, 1945; s. Noel Charles Allen and Gladys Louise (Puig) Jones; m. Joan Marie Lindsay, June 26, 1976; children: Robert Lindsay, Christina Marie, John Charles. MD, Tulane U., 1977, PhD, 1973. Diplomate Am. Bd. Pathology. Commd. 2d lt. U.S. Army, 1974; advanced through grades to lt. col. USAR, 1986; intern Brooke Army Med. Ctr., San Antonio, 1977-78; infectious disease officer U.S. Army Inst. Surgical Rsch., San Antonio, 1978-83, pathologist, 1985-87; resident, pathology Brooke Army Med. Ctr., San Antonio, 1983-85; dir. ExOxEmis, Inc., San Antonio, 1987—96, SmithKline Beecham Clin. Lab., San Antonio, 1993—98; med. dir. clin. pathology Grady Meml. Hosp., Atlanta, 1999—. Editor: Jour. Bioluminescence and Chemiluminescence, 1985—97; contbr. articles publ. over 50 to profl. jour. Fellow: Am. Soc. Clin. Pathology, Coll. Am. Pathologists; mem.: Am. Soc. Biochem. and Mol. Biol., Am. Soc. Investigative Pathology, Am. Assn. Immunologists. Achievements include patents in field of 10 us patents; discovery of phagocyte luminescence. Home: 2643 Varner Dr NE Atlanta GA 30345-1558 Office: Clin Lab Grady Meml Hosp 80 Jesse Hill Jr Dr SE Atlanta GA 30303-4204 E-mail: rallen3@emory.edu.

ALLEN, ROBERT DEE, lawyer; b. Tulsa, Oct. 13, 1928; s. Harve and Olive Jean (Brown) A.; m. Mary Latimer Conner, May 18, 1957; children: Scott, Randy, Blake. BA, U. Okla., 1951, LLB, 1955, JD, 1970. Bar: Okla. 1955, Ill. 1979, U.S. Dist. Ct. (we., no. and eas. dists.) Okla. 1955, U.S. Dist. Ct. (no. dist.) Ill. 1979, U.S. Ct. Appeals (10th cir.) 1956, U.S. Ct. Appeals (7th cir.) 1980, U.S. Supreme Ct. 1985. Assoc. Abernathy & Abernathy, Shawnee, Okla., 1955; law clk. to judge 10th U.S. Ct. Appeals, Denver, 1956; to judge Western Dist. Okla., 1956-57; asst. ins. commr., gen. counsel Okla. Ins. Dept., 1957-63; partner firm Quinlan, Allen & Batchelor, Oklahoma City, 1963-65, DeBois & Allen, 1965-66; counsel AT&T, Washington, 1966-67; gen. atty. Southwestern Bell Telephone Co., Okla., 1967-79; v.p., gen. counsel Ill. Bell Telephone Co., Chgo., 1979-83; sole practice law Chgo. and Oklahoma City, 1983—; mcpl. counselor Oklahoma City, 1984-89; of counsel Hartzog, Conger & Cason, 1983-90, Kimball, Wilson, Walker and Ferguson, 1990-93, Berry & Durland, 1993-94, Durland & Durland, 1994-96, White, Coffey, Galt & Fite, P.C., 1996-97, Phillips, McFall, McCaffrey, McVay & Murrah, P.C., 1997-2000; asst. general counsel Okla. Corp. Commn. Public Utilities Divsn., 2000—. Spl. counsel Okla. Mcpl. Power Authority, 1990-94, City of Altus, Okla., 1990-95; mem. Gov.'s Ad Valorem Tax Structure and Sch. Fin. Commn., 1972; bd. dirs. Taxpayers Fedn. Ill., 1980-83; adv. bd. dirs. Ctr. Am. and Internat. Law., 1985—; rsch. fellow Ctr. Am. and Internat. Law, 1994—; adj. prof. ins. law Oklahoma City U. Coll. Law, 1985—, agy. and partnership law, U. Okla. Coll. Law, 1989—; Okla. State chmn. Nat. Inst. Mcpl. Law Officers, 1984-89; apptd. mem. Legis Task Force on Okla. Adminstrv. Code, 1987; founding mem. U. Okla. Assocs., 1980. Bd. dirs. Oklahoma County Legal Aid Soc., 1973—; trustee Oklahoma City Riverfront Redevel. Authority, 1997-2003 With U.S. Army, 1946-48, 1st lt., 51-53; lt. col. USAR. Fellow Am. Bar Found.; mem. ABA, Fed. Bar Assn. (v.p. Okla. Chpt. 1977—), Okla. Bar Assn., Okla. County Bar Assn., Am. Judicature Soc., Okla. Assn. Mcpl. Attys. (bd. dirs. 1984-89), English Speaking Union (dir. 2001—), Order of Coif, Chgo. Club, Lions Club of Okla. City, 2000-. The Econs. Club of Okla., Oklahoma City Golf and Country Club, Phi Delta Phi, Sigma Phi Epsilon (dir.) Presbyterian. Home: 8101 Glenwood Ave Oklahoma City OK 73114-1107 E-mail: rdeeallen@aol.com.

ALLEN, ROBERT EUGENE BARTON, lawyer; b. Bloomington, Ind., Mar. 16, 1940; s. Robert Eugene Barton and Berth R. A.; m. Cecelia Ward Dooley, Sept. 23, 1960 (div. 1971); children: Victoria, Elizabeth, Robert, Charles, Suzanne, William; m. Judith Elaine Hecht, May 27, 1979 (div. 1984); m. Suzanne Nickolson, Nov. 18, 1995. BS, Columbia U., 1962; LLB, Harvard U., 1965. Bar: Ariz. 1965, U.S. Dist. Ct. Ariz. 1965, U.S. Tax Ct., 1965, U.S. Supreme Ct. 1970, U.S. Ct. Customs and Patent Appeals 1971, U.S. Dist. Ct. D.C. 1972, U.S. Ct. Appeals (9th cir.) 1974, U.S. Ct. Appeals (10th, and D.C. cirs.) 1984, U.S. Dist. Ct. N.Mex., U.S. Dist. Ct. (no. dist.) Calif., U.S. Dist. Ct. (no. dist.) Tex. 1991, U.S. Ct. Appeals (fed. cir.) 1992, U.S. Dist. Ct. (ea. dist.) Wis. 1995. Spl. asst. atty. gen., 1978; judge pro-tem Ariz. Ct. Appeals, 1984, 92, 99; Ptnr., dir. Allen, Price & Padden, Phoenix, 2000—. Nat. pres. Young Dems. Clubs Am., 1971-73; mem. exec. com. Dem. Nat. Com., 1972-73, Ariz. Gov.'s Kitchen Cabinet working on a wide range of state projects; bd. dirs. Phoenix Bapt. Hosp., 1981-83, Phoenix and Valley of the Sun Conv. and Visitors Bur., United Cerebral Palsy Ariz., 1984-89, Planned Parenthood of Ctrl. and No. Ariz., 1984-87, Ariz. Heart Inst. Found., 1998-2003, Cordell Hull Found. for Internat. Edn., 1996—; trustee Environ. Health Found., 1994-97, Friends of Walnut Canyon, 1991-94; bd. dirs. Ariz. Aviation Futures Task Force, chmn. Ariz. Airport Devel. Criteria Subcom.; Am. rep. exec. bd. Atlantic Alliance of Young Polit. Leaders, 1973-77, 77-80; trustee Am. Counsel of Young Polit. Leaders, 1971-76, 81-85; mem. Am. delegations to Germany, 1971, 72, 76, 79, USSR, 1971, 76, 88, France, 1974, 79, Belgium, 1974, 77, Can., 1974, Eng., 1975, 79, Norway, 1975, Denmark, 1976, Yugoslavia and Hungary, 1985; Am. observer European Parlimentary elections, Eng., France, Germany, Belgium, 1979, Moscow Congressional, Journalist delegation, 1989, NAFTA Trade Conf., Mexico City, 1993, Atlantic Assembly, Copenhagen, 1993. Contbr. articles on comml. litigation to profl. jours. Mem. ABA, Ariz. Bar Assn., Maricopa County Bar Assn., N.Mex. State Bar, D.C. Bar Assn., Am. Judicature Soc., Fed. Bar Assn., Am. Arbitration Assn., Phi Beta Kappa, Harvard Club. Democrat. Episcopalian (lay reader). Office: Allen Price & Padden 3131 E Camelback Rd Phoenix AZ 85016-4500

ALLEN, ROBERT FRANCIS, economist, educator; b. Long Pine, Nebr., Sept. 24, 1938; s. Cloyd Guy and Blanche (Elebrecht) A.; m. Merna L. Wessling, June 4, 1960; children: Michael, Edward, Jeffrey. BA, Creighton U., 1962; MA, U. Mo., 1963; PhD, Mich. State U., 1969. Asst. prof. Cen. Mo. State U., Warrensburg, 1963-65; instr. Mich. State U., East Lansing, 1966-68; assoc. prof. U. Nebr., Lincoln, 1969-79; sr. staff economist Coun. on Wage & Price Stability, Washington, 1975-77; prof., dep. dept. head Air Force Inst. Tech., Dayton, Ohio, 1980-86; prof., chmn. econs. and fin. dept. Creighton U., Omaha, 1987—. Cons. Miami Valley Regional Planning Commn., Dayton, 1980-84, Dept. Def., Dayton, 1981-87; trustee Nebr. Coun. Econ. Edn., Omaha, 1988. Contbr. articles to profl. jours. Cpl. USMC, 1956-58. Teaching Coun. fellow, 1973, Regents fellow, 1978, Maude Hammond Fling fellow, 1979 U. Nebr. Mem. Am. Econs. Assn., Midwest Econs. Assn. (2d v.p. 1986-87), Fin. Execs. Inst., Internat. Atlantic Econ. Soc. Home: 1206 N 131st Ave Omaha NE 68154-1268 Office: Creighton U Dept of Econs California St Omaha NE 68178-0001

ALLEN, ROBERT WATSON, retired textile company executive; b. Cambridge, Mass, Jan. 25, 1929; s. Ralph Watson and Dorothy Dansie Allen; m. Ann Stevens, May 17, 1958 (div. Sept. 1990); children: Dansie A. Little, Scott T.; m. Ruta Sepetys, July 20, 1991. AB, Bowdoin Coll., 1950; MBA, Harvard U., 1952. Various sales and mktg. positions Dewey & Almy Chem. Divsn. WR Grace & Co., Cambridge, Chgo., Montreal, Can., 1954-62; treas. Cryovac Divsn. WR Grace & Co., Duncan, SC, 1962—70; gen. mgr., CEO Grace Distbn. Svcs., Duncan, 1971-81; exec. v.p. Tietex Corp., Spartanburg, SC, 1982-87, pres., CEO, 1987-94, chmn. bd. dir., 1994-97; mem. City Coun., Spartanburg, SC, 1998—. Bd. dir. Vietri Inc., Chapel Hill, NC, Rocky Mount (NC) Cord Co. Coun. mem. Spartanburg City Coun., 1998—; chmn. Charles Lea Ctr. for Handicapped, Spartanburg, Salvation Army, Spartanburg, Health Planning Commn., Spartanburg. Served with US Army, 1952-54. Republican. Episcopalian. Home: 1090 Partridge Rd Spartanburg SC 29302-3326 E-mail: ballensptg@aol.com.

ALLEN, ROBERTA, fiction and nonfiction writer, conceptual artist, photographer; b. N.Y.C., Oct. 6, 1945; d. Sol and Jeanette (Waldner) A. Student, Inst. Bellas Artes, Mex., 1971. Lectr. Corcoran Sch. Art, Washington, 1975, Kutztown State Coll., 1979, C.W. Post Coll., 1979. Instr. creative writing Parsons Sch. Design, N.Y.C., 1986; instr. The Writer's Voice, 1992—97, The New Sch., 1993—, Dept. Continuing Edn., NYU, 1993—99; Tennessee Williams fellow, writer-in-residence U. of the South, Sewanee, Tenn., 1998; adj. asst. prof. Columbia U. Sch. of the Arts, 1998—99, Eugene Lang. Coll., 2000. Author: Partially Trapped Lines, 1975, Pointless Arrows, 1976, Pointless Acts, 1977, Everything in The World There Is To Know Is Known By Somebody, But Not By the Same Knower, 1981, Amazon Dream, 1993; author: (fiction) The Daughter, 1992, The Dreaming Girl, 2000, The Traveling Woman, 1986, Certain People, 1997; author: (writing guide) Fast Fiction, 1997, The Playful Way to Serious Writing, 2002, (Personal Growth) The Playful Way to Knowing Yourself, 2003; one-woman shows include Galerie 845, Amsterdam, Netherlands, 1967, John Weber Gallery, N.Y.C., 1974—75, 1977, 1979, Inst. for Art and Urban Resources, 1977, 1980, Galerie Maier-Hahn, Dusseldorf, Germany, 1977, MTL Galerie, Brussels, 1978, C.W. Post Coll., Glenvale, N.Y., 1978, Galerie Walter Storms, Munich, 1981, Kunstforum, Stadt. Galerie in Lenbachhaus, 1981, Galeria Primo Piano, Rome, 1981, Perth Inst. Contemporary Arts, 1989, Art Resources Transfer, Inc., 2001, SUNY, Binghamton, 2001. Fellow McDowell Colony, 1971—72; grantee LINE, 1985.

ALLEN, ROBERTA JANE, social worker; b. Billings, Mont., July 8, 1954; d. Nat and Jane Leone (Barker) A.; m. Steven J. Dawes, Dec. 20, 1986. BSW with honors, U. Mont., 1975; MSW, Portland State U., 1982. Nat. cert. sch. social worker; lic. in spl. edn. Colo. Social worker Fergus County Welfare, Lewistown, Mont., 1975-80, Denver Dept. Social Svcs., 1983-84; dir. community svcs. Nat. MS Soc., Denver, 1984-87; social worker Adams County Sch. Dist. 50, Westminster, Colo., 1987-91, Supra Home Care, Douglas County Schs., Highlands Ranch H.S., 1991—. Mem. Nat. Assn. Social Workers, Acad. Cert. Social Workers. Home: 3085 E Hinsdale Ave Centennial CO 80122-1944 Office: 9375 S Cresthill Ln Highlands Ranch CO 80122

ALLEN, RONALD JAY, law educator; b. Chgo., July 14, 1948; s. J. Matteson and Carolyn L. (Latchum) A.; m. Debra Jane Livingston, May 25, 1974 (div. 1982); children: Sarah, Adrienne; m. Julie O'Donnell, Sept. 2, 1984; children: Michael, Conor. BS, Marshall U., 1970; JD, U. Mich., 1973. Bar: Nebr. 1974, Iowa 1979, U.S. Ct. Appeals (8th cir.) 1980, U.S. Supreme Ct. 1981, Ill. 1986. Prof. law SUNY, Buffalo, 1974-79, U. Iowa, Iowa City, 1979-82, 83-84, Duke U., Durham, N.C., 1982-83, Northwestern U., Chgo., 1984—. John Henry Wigmore prof., 1992—. Pres. faculty senate U. Iowa, 1980-81. Author: Constitutional Criminal Procedure, 1985, 91, 95, An Analytical Approach to Evidence, 1989, Evidence: Text, Cases and Problems, 1997, Arthritis of the Hip and Knee: The Active Person's Guide to Taking Charge, 1998, Comprehensive Criminal Procedure, 2001, Evidence: Text, Problems, Cases, 2002; contbr. articles to profl. jours. Mem. ABA (rules com. criminal justice sect.), Am. Law Inst. Office: Northwestern U Sch Law 357 E Chicago Ave Chicago IL 60611-3059 E-mail: rjallen@northwestern.edu.

ALLEN, RONALD JOHN, astrophysics educator, researcher; b. Prince Albert, Sask., Can., Nov. 12, 1940; s. Arthur and Lillian May (Brown) A.; m. Janice Ruth Nielsen, Jan. 7, 1967; children: Melanie Ruth, Matthew John, Stefan Ronald. BA in Physics with honors, U. Sask., 1962; PhD in Physics, MIT, 1967. Postdoctoral fellow NRC Can., Paris, 1967-68; rsch. assoc. Kapteyn Astron. Inst., U. Groningen, The Netherlands, 1969-70, rsch. supr., 1971, lectr. in radio astronomy, 1972-80, prof. radio astronomy, 1980-85, chmn., 1982-85; prof. astronomy U. Ill., Urbana, 1985-90, head dept. astronomy, 1985-88; astronomer Space Telescope Sci. Inst., Balt., 1989—, head sci. computing divsn., 1989-95, head rsch. programs office, 1995-99, mgr. dirs. discretionary rsch. fund, 1995—; mission scientist NASA/JPL Space Interferometry Mission, 2000—. Vis. lectr. Cavendish Lab., Cambridge, Eng., 1971; mem. acad. council Ministry Edn. and Sci., The Netherlands, 1982-85; mem. vis. com. Nat. Radio Astronomy Obs., Charlottesville, Va., 1986-89; sr. scientist NATO, U.S., 1975-76; vis. prof. Kapteyn Astron. Inst., 1985-95; adjunct prof. Johns Hopkins U., 1991—; advisor NSF, NASA, Can. Nat. Sci. Engring. Rsch. Coun., Swedish Nat. Rsch. Bd., French Conseil Nat. Rsch. Sci., European Space Agy., U.K. Sci. Rsch. Coun., Academia Sinica Taiwan. Co-editor: Image Processing in Astronomy, 1979, The Milky Way Galaxy, 1985, The Restoration of HST Images and Spectra, 1991; contbr. numerous articles to sci. jours. Fellow Inst. des Hautes Etudes Scientifiques, Bures-sur-Yvette, France, 1974. Mem. Internat. Astron. Union, Am. Astron. Soc., Internat. Radio Sci. Union. Office: Space Telescope Sci Inst 3700 San Martin Dr Baltimore MD 21218-2464

ALLEN, RONALD WESLEY, financial executive; b. Jacksonville, Fla., Sept. 7, 1948; s. John Wesley and Frances Alida (Hadler) A.; m. Bonnie June Smith, Aug. 31, 1968; children: Donna Laurie, Marguerite Theresa. Student, Tulane U., 1966-67; AA with high honors, Fla. Jr. Coll., Jacksonville, 1972; BA with honors, U. North Fla., 1974; MS, U. Fla., 1976. CFP Coll. Fin. Planning, 1996. Salesman, electronic technician J.W. Allen & Assocs., Inc., Jacksonville, 1971-74, exec. v.p., 1976-88, chief exec. officer, 1988—; pres. Steamchem Products, Inc., Gainesville, Fla., 1975, A&B Carpet Cleaning, Inc., Gainesville, Fla., 1974-75; chief exec. officer Allen Wholesale Supply div. J.W. Allen & Assocs., Inc., Jacksonville, 1979-88; regional v.p. Primerica Fin. Svcs., Jacksonville, 1989-97. Dir., Inst. Fin. Studies, Fla. C.C., 2000—; dir., sec., treas. Madcem Inc., Jacksonville, 1985-87, Madcem of Fla., Inc., 1987-96; bd. dirs. Beaches Acad., Inc., Jacksonville, Crown Offshore Products, Inc., 1985-92, Forest Hills Meml. Park, Palm City, Fla., 1987-96, Forest Hills Funeral Home, Palm City, 1987-96, Crown Coast Mgmt. Inc., Jacksonville, 1983-94; gen. ptnr. First Coast Investments, Ltd., Jacksonville, 1984-92, J&R Products, Jacksonville, 1991-94; adj. faculty Nova Southeastern U., 1998-99, Fla. C.C., 1999—; prin. Bull and Bear Capital Advisers, Inc., 1998—, prin. Bull and Bear Brokerage Svc., 2001—. Vestry mem. Christ Ch., Ponte Verda Beach, Fla., 1988-91; v.p. exec. bd. Towers of Love, Inc., St. Augustine, Fla., 1984-95; vol. ann. fund Bolles Sch., Jacksonville, 1976—, Ronald McDonald Ho., Jacksonville, 1991; exec. bd. Living Waters Ministries, St. Augustine, Fla., 1991-93; lay min. Espiscopal Diocese of Fla., 1991—. Sgt. USAF, 1968-72. Mem. Jacksonville C. of C. (com. of 100, 1976-79, armed forces com. 1976-79), Northside Bus. Club, Beaches Bus. Assn. (bd. dirs. 1991-93), Alumni Coun. Bolles Sch., North Fla. Cruising Club (bd. dirs. 1979-86, Yachtsman of Yr. 1983), Navy Jacksonville Yacht Club, Performance Racing Handicap Circuit (bd. dirs. 1982-86, chmn. 1986, Yachtsman of Yr. 1983), Ponte Vedra Country Club, U. North Fla. Alumni Assn. Episcopalian. Avocations: sailing, yacht racing, music, lay ministry, motorcycling. Office: Corp Offices PO Box 3805 Jacksonville FL 32206-0805

ALLEN, ROSE LETITIA, special education educator; b. Dayton, Ohio, Oct. 10, 1960; d. Billie Wesley and Elisabeth Julia (Coler) Taylor; m. Randolph Eugene Allen, June 27, 1987; 1 child, Michelle Elisabeth. BSN, Wright State U., 1982; MS in Edn., U. Bridgeport, 1987. Cert. elem., K-12 handicapped edn., developmentally handicapped and specific LD tchr. Tchr. Hawaii Dept. of Edn., Honolulu, 1989-91; substitute tchr. Montgomery County Bd. Mental Retardation and Devel. Disabilities, Dayton, Ohio, 1993; tchr. Dayton Pub. Schs., 1994—. Mem. Faculty Coun., Dayton, 1994-95. 2d lt. USAF, 1983-84. Mem. AAUW, Alpha Xi Delta. Home: 2421 Orange Ave Dayton OH 45439-2839 E-mail: rose@joyrose.com.

ALLEN, ROY VERL, retired life insurance company executive; b. Hyrum, Utah, Aug. 3, 1933; s. Winfrd A. and Sarah Ann (Nielsen) A.; m. Judith Green, Aug. 11, 1961; children: Ann Marie Allen Webb, Michael R., Blair J. BS, Utah State U., 1958. CLU, Chartered Fin. Cons. Mgr. employee benefits Thiokol Chem. Corp., Brigham City, Utah, 1959-61; employment interviewer Hercules, Salt Lake City, 1962-63; agy. mgr. Standard Ins. Co., Salt Lake City, 1963—98. Maj. U.S. Army Res., 1962-79. Mem. CLUs (bd. mem. 1973-75), Estate Planning Coun. (bd. mem. 1979-81), Utah Gen. Agts. and Mgrs. (sec., v.p., pres. 1979-83), Utah Assn. Life Underwriters (pres. 1988-89), Exchange Club. Republican. Mem. Lds Ch. Avocations: fishing, hunting, basketball. Home: 2526 Olympus Dr Salt Lake City UT 84124-2916 E-mail: joyrud.1@hotmail.com.

ALLEN, RUSSELL G. lawyer; b. Ottumwa, Iowa, Nov. 7, 1946; BA, Grinnell Coll., 1968; JD, Stanford U., 1971. Bar: Calif. 1971. Ptnr. O'Melveny & Myers LLP, Newport Beach, Calif., 1975-2001; wealth advisor J.P. Morgan Chase & Co., Newport Beach, Calif., 2001—. Trustee Grinnell Coll. Capt. JAGC, USAF, 1971-75. Fellow Am. Coll. Trust and Estate Counsel; mem. ABA (real property, probate and trust law and taxation sects.), Orange County Bar Assn. (estate planning, probate and trust sects.) Office: JP Morgan Chase and Co Ste 200 888 San Clemente Dr Newport Beach CA 92660 E-mail: Russell.G.Allen@JPMorgan.com.

ALLEN, SONNY, professional basketball coach; Student, Marshall U. Coach freshman team Marshall U., 1959-65; coach Old Dominion U., 1965-75, So. Meth. U., 1975-80, U. Nev., Reno, 1980-87, Santa Barbara Islanders, Las Vegas Silver Streaks; NBA scout Charlotte Hornets, 1990-94, Dallas Mavericks, 1994-96, asst. coach, 1996-97, Detroit Shock, 1997-98; head coach Sacramento Monarchs, 1998—. Named Coach of the Yr., AP and Nat. Assn. Basketball Coaches, 1975, Southwest Conf. coach of the Yr., 1976, big Sky Coach of the Yr. awards, 1984, 85, Coach of the Yr., WNBA, 1990. Office: c/o Sacramento Monarchs One Sports Pkwy Sacramento CA 95834

ALLEN, STACY DALE, historian, parks director; b. Independence, Kans., Apr. 23, 1958; s. Charles Bradley and Etta JoAnn Allen; m. Diane Elizabeth Woodford, July 14, 1992; children: Jennifer Elizabeth Harrison, Jonathan C. Morton. B of Gen. Studies in Anthropology, U. of Kans., 1983. Fed. Law Enforcement Commn. Fed. Law Enforcement Tng. Ctr., 1987, Ranger Skills Nat. Pk. Svc. Albright Tng. Ctr., 1989. Pk. ranger Nat. Pk. Svc. Vicksburg (Miss.) Nat. Mil. Pk., 1984—89; lead pk. ranger Nat. Pk. Svc. Shiloh (Tenn.) Nat. Mil. Pk., 1989—92, historian, 1992—2002, supervisory (chief) pk. ranger, 2002—. Agy. Ea. Nat. coord. Ea. Nat. Bookstore Shiloh Nat. Mil. Pk., 1992—; historian, subject matter advisor Miss. Civil War Battlefield Commn., 2000—; historian NPS Core Study Team, Corinth Spl. Resource Study, Corinth, Miss., 2000—04, NPS Core Study Team: Vicksburg Campaign Trail Spl. Resource Study, Shiloh, 2000—04; historian, subject matter advisor Siege and Battle of Corinth (Miss.) Commn., 1992—; historian Lower Miss. Civil War Task Force, Shiloh, 1995—97; historian, site investigator Civil War Sites Adv. Commn., Shiloh, 1992—93. Author: (Blue & Gray Magazine) Corinth: Crossroads of the Western Confederacy, 2002, (audio cassette, CD tape tour) Battle of Shiloh (Nat. Silver Microphone award, 2001), (guidebook) Blue & Gray Magazine: Shiloh! A Visitor's Guide, 2001, (publn.) Blue & Gray Magazine: Shiloh! Campaign and First Day of Battle; Second Days Battle and Aftermath, 1997, (tour guide) A Guide to the Corinth Campaign of 1862, 1998, (publn.) The Tennessee Conservationist: Hell on the Hatchie, 1998; contbr. Atlas of the Civil War, James A. McPherson, ed.,1994, The Civil War Battlefield Guide, Francis Kennedy, Ed., 1998, Steven E. Woodworth, Ed., 2001. Recipient drama scholarship, Coffeyville C.C., Kans., 1976, Outstanding Achievement in Theater award, Field Kindley Meml. H.S., 1975. Mem.: The Civil War Fortification Study Group (assoc.; editor 1993—, pres. 1999—), Shiloh Battlefield Employees Assn. (assoc.; pres. 1990—2000, treas. 2000—02), NPS Employee and Alumni Assn. (assoc.), U. of Kans. Alumni Assn. (assoc.), Civil War Historians of the Western Theater (assoc.), Orgn. of Am. Historians (assoc.). Conservative. Achievements include research in Corinth/Battery Robinett Archaeological Investigations; Shiloh National Military Park Archaeological Investigations; Battlefield Investigations: Civil War Sites Advisory Commission; National Park Service, Corinth Special Resource Study; National Park Service, Vicksburg Campaign Trail Special Resource Study. Avocations: hunting, travel, drawing and painting, retriever training, reading. Home: 290 Residence Cir Shiloh TN 38376 Office: Shiloh Nat Mil Pk 1055 Pittsburg Landing Rd Shiloh TN 38376 Office Fax: 731-689-5450. E-mail: stacy_allen@nps.gov.

ALLEN, STANLEY T. architect, dean, educator; BA, Brown U.; BArch, Cooper Union Sch. Arch.; MArch, Princeton U. Dean, prof. Sch. Arch. Princeton U.; arch., prin. Field Ops. Recipient fellowship in arch., N.Y. Found. for Arts, 1986, fellowship in design arts, NEA, 1990, Graham Found. fellowship, 1993. Office: Princeton Univ School of Architecture Princeton NJ 08544

ALLEN, STEPHEN D(EAN), pathologist, microbiologist; b. Linton, Ind., Sept. 8, 1943; s. Wilburn and Betty Allen; m. Vally C. Autrey, June 17, 1964; children: Christopher D., Amy C. BA, Ind. U., 1965, MA, 1967; MD, Ind. U., Indpls., 1970. Diplomate Am. Bd. Pathology. Intern in pathology Vanderbilt U. Hosp., Nashville, 1970-71, resident in pathology, 1971-74; clin. asst. prof. pathology Emory U., Atlanta, 1974-77; asst. prof. clin. pathology Ind. U., Indpls., 1977-79, asst. prof. pathology, 1979-81, assoc. prof. pathology, 1981-86, prof. pathology, 1986-92, prof. pathology and lab. medicine, 1992—, assoc. dir. div. clin. microbiology, dept. pathology, 1977-92, dir. grad. progam pathology, 1986—, sr. assoc. chmn. dept. pathology, 1990-91, dir. divsn. clin. microbiology dept. pathology/lab. medicine, 1992-98, assoc. chair dept. pathology and lab. medicine & dir. labs., 1996-99; dir. disease control lab. divsn. Ind. State Dept. Health, Indpls., 1994—; dir. divsn. clin. microbiology dept. pathology/lab. medicine Clarian-Meth.-Ind U.-Riley Hosps., 1998—. Mem. residency rev. com. for pathology Accreditation Coun. for Grad. Med. Edn., 1996—, mem. residency rev. com. for molecular genetic pathology, 1999—, mem. molecular genetic pathology policy com., 1999—. Co-author: Color Atlas of Diagnostic Microbiology, 5th edit., 1997, Introduction to Diagnostic Microbiology, 1994, (CD-ROM) Direct Smear Atlas, 1998; contbr. With USPHS, 1974—77. Fellow: Binford-Dammin Soc. Infectious Disease Pathologists, Infectious Diseases Soc. Am., Am. Acad. Microbiology, Coll. Am. Pathologists, Sigma Xi; mem.: Am. Bd. Pathology (anatomic and clin. pathology and med. microbiology com., trustee 1995—, chmn. microbiology test com. 1995—, sec. bd. 2000—01, v.p. 2002—), Am. Soc. Clin. Pathologists (coun. microbiology 1983—89), Shriners, Masons (32d deg.). Avocation: musics: music, electric bass and trumpet, fly-fishing. Office: Ind U Hosp Rm 4430 550 University Blvd Indianapolis IN 46202-5149 E-mail: sallen@iupui.edu.

ALLEN, STEVEN GLEN, economics and business educator; b. Louisville, Mar. 17, 1952; s. Charles Freeman and Lois (Crask) A.; m. Linda L. Pattison, May 19, 1978. BA in Math., Mich. State U., 1973, MA in Econs., 1974; PhD in Econs., Harvard U., 1978. Asst. prof. econs. and bus. N.C. State U., Raleigh, 1978—83, assoc. prof., 1983—87, prof., 1987—, dir. MS mgmt. program, 1993—2002, dir. MBA program, 2002—, assoc. dean grad. programs and rsch., 2003—. Rsch. economist Nat. Bur. Econ. Rsch., Cambridge, Mass., 1983-86, rsch. assoc., 1986—; mem. bd. reviewers Indls. Rels., Berkeley, Calif., 1989—. Contbr. articles to profl. jours. Recipient Allyn Young award Harvard Coll., 1975, 76, Disting. Rsch. and Lit. Publ. award Sch. Humanities and Social Scis., N.C. State U., 1986, Outstanding Rsch. award Coll. Mgmt., 1993; NSF grantee,

1984-86, 87-92, five-time U.S. Dept. Labor grantee; Fulbright scholar, 1991, 93. Mem. Am. Econ. Assn., Soc. Labor Economists, Econometric Soc. Office: NC State U PO Box 7229 Raleigh NC 27695-7229

ALLEN, STEVEN JEFFREY, anesthesiologist, educator; b. Abilene, Tex., 1952; MD, U. Tex. Med. Br., Galveston, 1977. Diplomate Am. Bd. Anesthesiology, Am. Bd. Critical Care Medicine. Intern U. Utah Med. Ctr., Salt Lake City, 1977-78; resident in anesthesiology U. Wash., Seattle, 1980-82; fellow in critical care medicine U. Tex. Med. Sch., Houston, 1982-83, prof. anesthesiology, 1983—; med. staff Hermann Hosp., Houston, 1983—; med. dir. Meml. Hermann Hosp., 1996—. Mem. AMA, Am. Soc. Anesthesiologists, Soc. Critical Care Medicine. Office: U Tex HSC Anesthesiology 6431 Fannin MSMB 5 020 Houston TX 77030-1501

ALLEN, STUART (STUART ALLEN SUP), film and television company executive; b. N.Y.C., July 24, 1943; s. Rudolph and Rita Geraldine (Tellez) Sup; m. Carol Ann Terminelli, June 30, 1982. AA in Engring., NYU, 1961; BA in Communications, Pace U., 1963. Free-lance photographer, photojournalist, N.Y.C., 1963—; producer, dir. Stuart Allen Assocs., Iselin, N.J., 1967-76; pres., chief exec. officer Internat. Media Svcs., Inc., Plainfield, N.J., 1976—; pres., gen. mgr. The Legal Svcs. Group, Plainfield, N.J, 1976—. Spl. producer ABC-TV Evil Knievel Snake River Canyon Jump, 1974; author, producer Counterattack, 1978 (One to One Media award 1979), producer, dir. Eagle in the Wind, 1980 (Best Film award 1984); producer 2d unit The Girl Next Door, CBS TV Movie of the Week. Chmn. Plainfield (N.J.) Cultural and Heritage Commn., 1982-96; mcpl. liaison Union County (N.J.) Cultural and Heritage Adv. Bd., 1982-92; trustee Drake House Mus., Plainfield Hist. Soc., 1982-92; dir. Plainfield Econ. Devel. Corp., 1984—; trustee DeCret Sch. of Arts, 1990—; vice chmn. Plainfield City Coun. Budget Adv. Com., 1992-94. N.J. State Council Arts grantee, 1979, 86. Mem. Indsl. Photographers Assn. N.J. (pres. 1976-77, award of Excellence), Internat. TV Assn., Am. Film Inst., Cen. Jersey C. of C., Internat. Platform Assn., Am. Coll. Forensic Examiners, Am. Bd. Recorded Evidence, Soc. Motion Picture and TV Engrs., Marco Polo Club (Chgo.). Avocations: traveling, exploration, fishing. Home and Office: 718 Sherman Ave Plainfield NJ 07060-2232 E-mail: stuart.allen1@worldnet.att.net.

ALLEN, SUE FAY, music educator, conductor; b. Buffalo, N.Y., Sept. 8, 1940; d. Roy Henry and Betty Paula (Engelbert) Geyer; children: Elizabeth, Paula; m. Carl Elton Klingenschmitt; children: Julie, Gordon. BS, SUNY, Potsdam, 1961, MS, 1964. Music coord. Amherst (N.Y.) Ctrl. Schs., 1979-96, music tchr., 1966—; founder, conductor, choral dir. Amherst Bel Canto Choir, 1992—. Mem. editl. bd. Music Educators Nat. Conf., 1993-96; contbr. articles to profl. publs. Bd. dirs. Clarence (N.Y) Orch. Assn., 1990—. Named Outstanding Choral Conductor, Am. Choral Dir. Assn., 2002, Outstanding Tchr., Amherst Schs., 1993, Outstanding Alumni, Crane Music, SUNY, Potsdam, 1999; recipient Disting. Music Edn. award, NY State Music Assn., 1992, Outstanding Contbn. to Music award, Buffalo Philharm. Orch., 1996, Outstanding Svc. to Music Edn. award, Erie County Music Assn., 1998. Mem. Am. Choral Dirs. Assn. (sec. N.Y. chpt. 1991-93, pres. 1995-97, chair of honors 1995-97), N.Y. State Sch. Music Assn. (voice chmn. 1986-90). Avocations: gardening, sewing, writing. Home: 11520 Howe Rd Akron NY 14001-9743

ALLEN, SUZANNE, financial planning executive, insurance agent, writer; b. Santa Monica, Calif, May 31, 1963; d. Raymond A. and Ethel Allen; m. Steve Milstein Roth, Dec. 27, 1992, (div. 2000). BA, U. Calif., Santa Cruz, 1986; MA in Edn., Calif. State U., L.A., 1990; postgrad., Art Ctr. Sch. Design, Pasadena, Calif., 1994—. Cert. tchr., Calif.; lic. real estate agt., Calif. Interviewer LA Times Newspaper, 1986-88; educator LA Unified Sch. Dist., 1987-90, Burbank Unified Sch. Dist., Calif., 1990-94, 1994—; ptnr. fin. svc. Roth & Assoc./NY Life, LA, 1993-2000; educator Pasadena Unified Sch. Dist., 2001—02; ptnr. fin. svc. Pacific Life Ins. Co.; v.p. Jarvis & Mandell LLC Estate Planning Svc., Mass. Mut. Ins. Co., 2001—; agt. Mass. Mut. Ins., Beverly Hills, Calif. Ptnr. Retirement Educators Fin. Svc.; agt.-cons. Frasier Fin. Group, 2001—02. Model, actor :, 1998—; author: End of Days, 2001—; author: (pen name Quinn Allen) I Will Serve You All My Days, Black Dahlia, Alone, 2002, I Miss Him, 2003, (poem) Waiting for Godot, 2003. Mem. PTA, United Tchr. Pasadena, Civil War Trust; vol. SPCA/Humane Soc., 1999—; mem. Nat. Trust Hist. Preservation, Honor Roll mem.; bd. mem. Bungalow Heaven Neighborhood Assn.; hon. mem. Top Bus. Rep. Party for Sen. Tom Delany. Recipient 3 Silver Cups, Internat. Poet of Merit, 5 Bronze medal, Internat. Poets Soc., Silver Outstanding Achievement in Poetry Trophy, 2003, 2 silver trophies for outstanding achievement in poetry, 2003, Piece of the Roof award, N.Y. Life. Mem.: NEA, Libr. of Congress, Nat. Soc. for Hist. Preservation, Burbank Tchrs. Union, Internat. High IQ Soc., Abraham Lincoln Assn., Internat. Soc. Poets (hon.). Avocations: painting, illustrating, writing, weight training, old house renovation. Office: Jarvis & Mandell LLC 1875 Century Park E # 1550 Los Angeles CA 90067 also: Michael's Agy Mass Mut Beverly Hills Office 1875 Century Park E # 1550 90067

ALLEN, TAMMY D. psychologist; b. St. Louis, Mar. 28, 1962; d. Bobbie J. Kepford; m. Mark L. Poteet; 1 child, Ethan Sitver. PhD, U. Tenn., 1996. Asst. prof. U. S. Fla., Tampa, 1996—2001, assoc. prof., 2001—. Sr. cons. Orgnl. Rsch. & Solutions, Inc., Tampa, 1999—. Contbr. articles. Com. mem. Family Ctr. Tampa Family Friendly Bus. Awards, Tampa, 1998—2000; bd. dirs. New Tampa Soccer Assn., Tampa, 2001—02. Recipient Best Reviewer award, Acad. Mgmt. Careers Divsn., 1996—97; fellow Walter Melville Bonham Meml. Endowment, U. Tenn. Coll. Bus. Adminstrn., 1995; grantee, Soc. Human Resource Mgmt. Found., 1999; scholar, U. Tenn. Coll. Bus., 1993—96, U. S. Fla., 1997. Mem.: APA (Best Paper award 1998, Disseration Rsch. award 1995, Occpl. Health Tng. grant 2001), Acad. Mgmt. (exec. com. 1998—2001, chair interactive papers 2001, chair profl. develop. workshops careers divsn. 2001), Soc. Indsl. & Orgnl. Psychology (awards com.), So. Mgmt. Assn. Office: Univ South Florida 4202 E Fowler Ave PCD4118G Tampa FL 33620-7200 Business E-Mail: tallen@luna.cas.usf.edu.

ALLEN, TERRY DEVEREUX, urologist, educator; b. Dallas, Nov. 28, 1930; s. Lester E. and Gladys (McIver) A.; m. Carolyn Latham, June 26, 1955; children: Kevin, Kathleen, Cheryl, Robin. Student, Rice U., 1951; MD, Baylor Med. Sch., 1955. Diplomate Am. Bd. Urology. Intern Jefferson Davis Hosp., Houston, 1955-56; attending physician Terrell (Tex.) State Hosp., 1958-59; resident surgery Parkland Meml. Hosp., Dallas, 1959-60, resident urology, 1960-63; pvt. practice Dallas Med./ Surg. Clinic, 1963-70; faculty Southwestern Med. Sch., Dallas, 1971-98. Mem., chair Residency Rev. Com., 1977-83; exec. com. mem. Am. Bd. Med. Specialties, 1992-94; trustee Am. Bd. Urology, 1985-91. Assoc. editor Jour. Urology, Balt., 1983-93; contbr. numerous articles to profl. jours., chpts. to books. Capt. USAF, 1956-58. Fellow ACS (gov.), Am. Acad. Pediatrics (urology, pres. 1984-85, Pediat. Urology medal 2002); mem. Soc. Univ. Urologists (sec., pres. 1985-86), Soc. Pediatric Urology (sect. pres. 1977-79, 81-83), Am. Urol. Assn. (Edn. award 1985, Hugh Hampton Young award 1990), Am. Assn. Genitourol. Surgeons (Harry Spence award 2003). Avocations: sailing, fgn. langs. Home: 9829 Elmcrest Dr Dallas TX 75238-1831 Office: Children's Med Ctr Bank One Tower 14th Fl 6300 Harry Hines Blvd Dallas TX 75235-5259

ALLEN, THERESA OHOTNICKY, neurobiologist, consultant; b. Torrington, Conn., Apr. 27, 1948; d. Frank Richard and Helen Theresa (Drozdenko) Ohotnicky; m. Thomas Atherton Allen, Aug. 12, 1972; children: Melanie Atherton, Abigail Baldwin. BA, U. Conn., 1970; MS, Villanova U., 1975; PhD, Duke U., 1978; cert. in bus. adminstrn., U. Pa., 1983. Realtor. Rsch. assoc. U. Pa., Phila., 1981-83; sci. dir. Drexel U., Phila., 1983-84; cons. on neurobiology to sci.-oriented cos., 1984—. Contbr. articles to profl. jours., also chpts. to books. Bd. dirs. Gladwyne (Pa.) Libr. League, 1986—, Athena Inst. for Women's Wellness, Haverford, Pa., 1989-93; trustee Gladwyne Libr., 1988—, pres., 1991-93; com. chmn. Jr. League Phila., 1989-90. Fellow Inst. Neurol. Scis., U. Pa., 1978-80, NIH, 1980-81. Mem.: Phila. Country Club, Humane Soc., Phila. Skating Club, Phi Beta Kappa. Episcopalian. Avocations: skiing, gardening, antiques. Home: 1433 Waverly Rd Gladwyne PA 19035-1224

ALLEN, THOMAS B. writer; b. Bridgeport, Conn., Mar. 20, 1929; s. Walter L. and Catherine Elizabeth (Reilly) A.; m. Florence Elizabeth MacBride, June 5, 1950; children: Christopher, Constance, Roger. BA in Journalism, U. Bridgeport, 1956. Reporter, columnist Bridgeport (Conn.) Herald; feature writer N.Y. Daily News, 1956-63; mng. editor Trade divsn. Chilton Books, 1964-65; writer for book divsn. Nat. Geographic Soc., 1965-74. Author: War Games, 1987, The Blue and the Gray, 1992, Possessed, 1993, Offerings at the Wall, 1995, Animals of Africa, 1997, America From Space, 1998, The Shark Almanac, 1999, others; (with Norman Polmar) Rickover: Controversy and Genius, 1982, Merchants of Treason, 1988, World War II: America at War 1941-1945, 1991, Code-name: Downfall, 1995; Spy Book: The Encyclopedia of Espionage, 1996; (with William Cohen) Murder in the Senate, 1992; contbr. articles to Nat. Geographic, N.Y. Times Mag., Mil. History Quar., Washington Post, Washingtonian, Smithsonian, Popular Sci. Ann., A. History, others. Served with USN, 1951-53. Mem. Nat. Press Club. Democrat. Unitarian Universalist. E-mail: tballen@tballen.com.

ALLEN, THOMAS DRAPER, lawyer; b. Detroit, June 25, 1926; s. Draper and Florence (Jones) A.; m. Joyce M. Johnson, July 18, 1953; children— Nancy A. Bowser, Robert D., Rebecca A. Hubbard. BS, Northwestern U., 1949; JD, U. Mich., 1952. Bar: Ill. 1952, U.S. Supreme Ct. 1971. Assoc. Kirkland & Ellis, Chgo., 1952-60, ptnr., 1961-67, Wildman, Harrold, Allen & Dixon, Chgo., 1967-96, of counsel, 1997—. Chmn. Community Caucus, Hinsdale, Ill., 1960-61; mem. Hinsdale Bd. Edn., 1965-71, pres., 1970-71; pres. West Suburban coun. Boy Scouts Am., 1980-82, mem. nat. exec. bd., 1986—, chmn. internat. com., 1995-99, mem. world program com., 1983-93; moderator Union Ch., Hinsdale, 1983-84; trustee Chgo. Theol. Sem., 1982-97, chair, 1990-96, life trustee, 1997—. With USN, 1944-46. Recipient Silver Beaver award Boy Scouts Am., 1964, Silver Buffalo award, 1997, Bronze Wolf award World Scout Orgn., 1993. Fellow Am. Coll. Trial Lawyers (state chair 1984-85, chair internat. com. 1997-99); mem. ABA, Ill. Bar Assn., Chgo. Bar Assn. (bd. of mgrs 1989-91), Law Club of Chgo., Legal Club of Chgo., Jaycees Internat. (senator, 1965), Internat. Bar Assn., Hinsdale Golf Club. Mem. United Ch. of Christ. Home: 505 N Lake Shore Dr Chicago IL 60611-3427 Office: Wildman Harrold Allen & Dixon 225 W Wacker Dr Chicago IL 60606-1224

ALLEN, THOMAS E. obstetrician, gynecologist; b. Bairdford, Pa., July 2, 1919; s. Emerson Ray and Lillie Mabel (McIntyre) A.; m. Ruth Jenkins, 1943 (dec. 1991); m. Judi Cannava, 1995; children: Catherine, Christine, Cynthia, Carolyn, Thomas J., Candace. BS, U. Pitts., 1940, MD, 1943. Diplomate Am. Bd. Ob-Gyn. Rotating intern U. Pitts., 1944, assoc. clin. prof. ob-gyn. Sch. Medicine; resident in gynecology Magee Hosp., Pitts., 1944-45, resident in ob-gyn., 1948-51; gen. practice medicine Oakmont, Pa., 1947-48; practice medicine specializing in ob-gyn. Pitts., 1951—. Med. dir., co-founder Women's Health Service, Inc., Pitts., 1973-94, cons., 1994—; cons. ob-gyn Russelton Med. Group, New Kensington, Pa., 1953-73. Pres. Oakmont Sch. Bd., 1962-71; pres. bd. dirs. Am. Waterways Wind Orch., Pitts., 1970-93, chmn. bd. dirs., 1993—; bd. dirs. ACLU, Pitts., 1972-90. Served to capt. U.S. Army, 1945-47. Am. Legion and Buhl scholar, 1937. Fellow ACS, Am. Coll. Obstetricians and Gynecologists, Pan Pacific Surg. Assn., Pitts. Ob-gyn. Soc.; mem. AMA, county and state med. assns. Democrat. Avocations: cooking, music, reading, golf. Home: 301 Halket St Pittsburgh PA 15213-3104 Office: Planned Parenthood 933 Liberty Ave Pittsburgh PA 15222-3783 E-mail: ccann19601@aol.com.

ALLEN, THOMAS H. congressman, lawyer; b. Portland, Maine, Apr. 16, 1945; s. Charles and Genevieve A.; m. Diana Bell; children: Gwen, Kate. BA, Bowdoin Coll., 1967; BPhil, Oxford U., 1970; JD, Harvard U., 1971. Mem. Drummond, Woodsum, Plimpton and MacMahon, Maine, Portland (Maine) City Coun., 1989-95; mayor City of Portland, 1991-92; mem. U.S. Congress from 1st Maine dist., 1997—, armed svcs. com., energy & commerce com., De,. whip-at-large, former mem. govt. reform and oversight com. Dem. candidate for Gov., State of Maine, 1994; chair Clinton/Gore campaign, Maine, 1992; mem. Pres. Clinton's Agrl. Transition Team; bd. overseers Bowdoin Coll.; bd. dirs. Shalom House, United Way; chair Gov. Joseph Brennan Task Force on Foster Care for Children; pres. Portland Stage Co.; mem. exec. and legis. policy coms. Maine Mcpl. Assn. Rhodes scholar Oxford U. Mem. Phi Beta Kappa. Democrat. Office: US Ho of Reps 1717 Longworth Hse Ofc Bldg Washington DC 20515-0001 also: 234 Oxford St Portland ME 04101-3029*

ALLEN, TIM (TIMOTHY ALLEN DICK), actor, comedian; b. Denver, June 13, 1953; s. Gerald and Martha Dick; m. Laura Diebel, 1978; 1 child, Kady. Grad., Western Mich. U. Appeared in numerous Showtime spls.; actor: (TV series) Home Improvement, 1991-99 (Emmy award nomination, Lead actor - comedy 1993), exec. prodr., 1996-99, also writer; (films) The Santa Clause, 1994; (voice) Toy Story, 1995, Meet Wally Sparks, 1997, Jungle 2 Jungle, 1997, For Richer or Poorer, 1997, Toy Story 2, 1999, Galaxy Quest, 1999; exec. prodr., Who is Cletis Tout, 2001, Joe Somebody, 2001, Big Trouble, 2002, The Santa Clause2, 2002; (TV spls.) Men Are Pigs, 1990; (TV spls.) Showtime Comedy Club All-Stars II, 1988; author: I'm Not Really Here, 1996, Don't Stand Too Close to a Naked Man, 1994; TV quest appearances The Flying Doctors, 1985, The Drew Carey Show, 1995, The Front, 1996, Soul Man, 1997, The Larry Sanders Show, 1992, Spin City, 1996; exec. com. TV series Home Improvement, 1991. Recipient Golden Globe, 1995, Favorite Comedy Actor People's Choice award, 1995,97, 98, 99, TV Guide award 1999; nominated for Golden Globe awards 1993, 94, 96, 97, Blockbuster Entertainment award 1998. Office: William Morris Agy 151 El Camino Dr Beverly Hills CA 90212 Address: care Messina Baker 955 S Carillo Dr Ste 100 Los Angeles CA 90048

ALLEN, TODD M. immunologist, researcher; b. St. Catharines, Ontario, Can., Aug. 30, 1970; s. Wayne R. and Shirley W. Allen. PhD, U. Wis., Madison, Wis., 1999. Post doctoral fellow U. Wis., Madison, Wis., 1999—2001; instr. in medicine Mass. Gen. Hosp., Boston, 2001—. Grantee R01, NIH, 2003—. Achievements include research in HIV evolution and vaccine design; patents pending for Vaccine methodology for efficient induction of high frequency T-cell responses. P99079US. (provisional); A Method for making an HIV vaccine. P00187US. (provisional).

ALLEN, VICKY, sales and marketing professional; b. Springfield, Pa., May 27, 1957; d. James Joseph and Ann Marie (Cifone) Cattafesta; m. James Francis DeLeone, Aug. 11, 1979 (div. 1982); m. Dennis Ronald Allen, June 30, 1990; children: Amber, Austen. BBA in Computer Sci., Temple U., 1979. Quality assurance Burroughs Corp., Downingtown, Pa., 1977, software QA, 1978, systems analyst, 1979-81; program analyst Crocker Internal Systems, San Jose, Calif., 1981-83; sr. systems analyst Avantek, Inc., Santa Clara, Calif., 1983-84; product mktg. program specialist Micro Focus, Palo Alto, Calif., 1984-96; OEM sales account mgr. Netscape Comms. Corp., Mountain View, Calif., 1996-99; mgr. Nortel Networks Strategic Relationships, 1999—2002; inside sales Polycom, Milpitas, Calif., 2002—. Programmer cons. Fin. Group, Palo Alto, 1985-86. Active Sierra Club. Mem. Phi Sigma Sigma (sec. 1978-79). Democrat. Roman Catholic. Avocations: music, hiking, biking, race walking. Office: Polycom 1565 Barber Ln Milpitas CA E-mail: squirlr1@yahoo.com.

ALLEN, W. WAYNE, retired oil industry executive; b. 1936; BS, Okla. State U., 1959, MME, 1969. With Phillips Petroleum Co., 1961—84, regional mgr. U.K., 1984—85, gen. mgr. exploration and prodn. western divsn., 1986—89, sr. v.p. exploration and prodn., 1989—91, pres., COO, 1991—94, chmn. bd., CEO, 1994—99; ret., 1999. Capt. U.S. Army, 1959—61. Office: Profl Bldg 117 W 5th St Ste 401 Bartlesville OK 74004-0001

ALLEN, WILBUR COLEMAN, lawyer; b. Victoria, Va., Apr. 30, 1925; s. George Edward and Mary Lee (Bridgforth) Allen; m. Frances Brockenbrough Gayle, Sept. 16, 1950; children: Frances Gayle Allen Fitzgerald, Wilbur Coleman Jr., Robert Clayton, Edward Lefebvre, Courtney Allen Van Winkle. BA, U. Va., 1947, JD, 1950. Bar: Va. 1949, U.S. Ct. Appeals 1950, U.S. Dist. Ct. (ea. and we. dists.) Va. 1951, DC 1954, U.S. Supreme Ct. 1954. Ptnr. Allen, Allen, Allen & Allen, Richmond, Va., 1950—, pres., 1969—90. Sunday sch. supt. All Sts. Episc. Ch., Richmond, 1960—65, vestryman, 1964—68, 1970—74, 1980—83, sr. warden, 1967—68, chmn. stewardship com., 1980—81; bd. visitors Va. Commonwealth U., 1984—87, mem. property com., 1984—85, mem. audit com., 1984—85. Lt. (j.g.) USN, 1942—45, PTO. Fellow: Am. Coll. Trial Lawyers; mem.: ATLA, ABA, Richmond Bar Assn. (pres. 1979, Outstanding Contbn. award 1981), N.Y. State Trial Lawyers Assn., Va. Trial Lawyers Assn. (chmn. publicity com. 1968, chmn. spl. com. ins. 1981), Va. State Bar Coun., Va. Bar Assn. (chmn. spl. com. professionalism 1990—93), Va. State Bar, Am. Judicature Soc., Country Club Va., Rotary (pres. 1974—75, Rotarian of the Yr. 1980). Home: 1600 Westbrook Ave #2 Richmond VA 23227 Office: Allen Allen Allen and Allen 1809 Staples Mill Rd Richmond VA 23230-3515

ALLEN, WILLIAM, lawyer; s. Junior Richard and Margaret Wagner Allen. BS, Emory & Henry Coll., Emory VA, 1976—80. Bar Registration: Ohio 2000. Patent atty. Wood Herron & Evans LLP, Cincinnati, Ohio, 1999—.

ALLEN, WILLIAM BARCLAY, political scientist, consultant, writer; b. Fernandina Beach, Fla, Mar. 18, 1944; s. James Phillip and Rosa Lee Allen; m. Carol Michelle Pfeiffer, July 7, 2000. BA, Pepperdine Coll., 1967; MA, Claremont (Calif.) Grad. Sch., 1968, PhD, 1972. Prof. Mich. State U., East Lansing, 1993—, dean, prof. James Madison Coll., 1993-98. Dir. State Coun. Higher Edn., Richmond, Va., 1998-99. Author: The Federalist Papers: A Commentary, 2000, co-author: Habits of Mind: Fostering Access and Excellence in Higher Ed., 2003. Chmn. US Commn. Civil Rights, Washington, 1988-89. With US Army, 1968. Mem. Am. Polit. Sci. Assn. (divsn. chair 1996-97). Baptist. Avocations: reading, music, dance. Office: Mich State U Dept Polit Sci East Lansing MI 48824 Fax: (517) 432-1091. E-mail: allenwi@msu.edu.

ALLEN, WILLIAM CECIL, physician, educator; b. LaBelle, Mo., Sept. 8, 1919; s. William H. and Viola O. (Holt) A.; m. Madge Marie Gehardt, Dec. 25, 1943; children: William Walter, Linda Diane Allen Deardeuff, Robert Lee, Leah Denise Rogers. AB, U. Nebr., 1947, MD, 1951; M.P.H., Johns Hopkins U., 1960. Diplomate Am. Bd. Preventive Medicine. Intern Bishop Clarkson Meml. Hosp., Omaha, 1952; practice medicine specializing in family practice Glasgow, Mo., 1952-59; specializing in preventive medicine Columbia, Mo., 1960—; dir. sect. chronic diseases Mo. Div. Health, Jefferson City, 1960-65; asst. med. dir. U. Mo. Med. Ctr., 1965-75; assoc. coordinator Mo. Regional Med. Program, 1968-73, coordinator health programs, 1969—, clin. asst. prof. community health and med. practice, 1962-65, asst. prof. community health and med. practice, 1965-69, assoc. prof., 1969-75, prof., 1975-76, prof. dept. family and community medicine, 1976-87, prof. emeritus, 1987—. Cons. Mo. Regional Med. Program, 1966-67, Norfolk Area Med. Sch. Authority, Va., 1965-66; governing body Area II Health Systems Agy., 1977-79, mem. coordinating com., 1977-79; founding dir. Mid-Mo. PSRO Corp., 1974-79, dir., 1976-84. Contbr. articles to profl. jours. Mem. Gov.'s Adv Council for Comprehensive Health Planning, 1970-73; trustee U. Mo. Med. Sch. Found., 1976— . Served with USMC, 1943-46. Fellow Am. Coll. Preventive Medicine, Am. Acad. Family Physicians (sci. program com. 1972-75, commn. on edn. 1973-80), Royal Soc. Health, mem. Mo. Acad. Family Physicians (dir. 1956-59, 76-82, alt. del. 1982-87, pres. 1985-86, chmn. bd. 1986-87), Mo. Med. Assn., Howard County Med. Soc. (pres. 1958-59), Boone County Med. Soc. (pres. 1974-75), Am. Diabetes Assn. (pres. 1978, dir. 1974-77), Mo. Diabetes Assn. (pres. 1972-73), Soc. Tchrs. Family Medicine, AMA, Mo. Public Health Assn., Am. Heart Assn. (program com. 1979-82), Am. Heart Assn. of Mo. (sec. 1980-81), Mo. Heart Assn. (sec. 1979-82, pres.-elect 1982-84, pres. 1984-86). Methodist. Office: U Mo M218 Medical Ctr Columbia MO 65203

ALLEN, WILLIAM HAYES, lawyer, educator; b. Palo Alto, Calif., Oct. 19, 1926; s. Ben Shannon and Victoria Rose (French) A.; m. Joan Webster Emmett, July 16, 1950; children: Edwin Hayes, Neal French, William Kent. Student, Deep Springs Coll., 1942-44; BA with gt. distinction, Stanford U., 1948, LLB, 1956. Bar: D.C. 1958. Corr. AP, Fresno, Calif., 1948-49, newsman Sacramento, 1950-53; law clk. to Chief Justice Earl Warren U.S. Supreme Ct., Washington, 1956-57; assoc. Covington & Burling, Washington, 1957-64, ptnr., 1964-92; ret., 1993—. Acting. prof. Stanford U. Law Sch., 1979; adj. prof. Howard U. Law Sch., 1981—83; lectr. George Mason U. Law Sch., 1983—86; practitioner-in-residence Cornell U. Law Sch., 1992; vis. prof. Deep Springs Coll., 1973, 96; chmn. jud. rev. com. Adminstrv. Conf. U.S., 1972—82, sr. conf. fellow, 1982—95; mem. steering com. Nat. Prison Project, 1975—93. Pres. Stanford Law Rev., vol. 8, 1955-56; contbr. articles to legal jours. Trustee Deep Springs Coll., 1984-92, chmn. bd. trustees, 1992; mem. Fair Housing Bd., Arlington County, Va., 1974-79. With U.S. Army, 1945-47. Mem. ABA (mem. coun. adminstrv. law sect. 1969-72, 79-81, chmn. 1982-83), D.C. Bar (chmn. legal ethics com. 1976-78), Am. Law Inst., Am. Acad. of Appellate Lawyers, Order of Coif, Cosmos Club. Democrat. Mem. United Ch. of Christ. Office: Covington & Burling 1201 Pennsylvania Ave NW Washington DC 20004-2401 E-mail: billthedog2001@comcast.net., wallen@cov.com.

ALLEN, WILLIAM JERE, minister; b. Greenville, Miss., Apr. 23, 1934; s. Marion Goodman and Gradie Lee (Yates) A.; m. Lorena Faye Franklin, June 24, 1960; children: Lorena Lynn Brickson, Jennifer Dawn Moradi, William Jere Allen Jr. B of Bldg. Constrn., Auburn U., 1956; BDiv, So. Bapt. Theol. Sem., 1963; DMin, Union Theol. Sem., 1973. Ordained to ministry First Bapt. Ch., 1960. Pastor 45th Street Mission, Ashland, Ky., 1959-60, Rose Hill Bapt. Ch., Ashland, 1960-62, Colonial Ave. Bapt. Ch., Roanoke, Va., 1962-67, Bainbridge St. Bapt. Ch., Richmond, Va., 1967-71, Bainbridge Southampton Bapt. Ch., Richmond, 1972-75; cons., dir. spl. missions dept. Ala. Bapt. State Conv., Montgomery, 1975-79; assoc. then dir. met. mission dept. Home Mission Bd., So. Bapt. Conv., Atlanta, 1979-91; exec. dir., min. D.C. Bapt. Conv., Washington, 1992-2000; interim pastor Calvary Bapt. Ch., Washington, 2001—. Mega focus cities cons. Home Mission Bd., So. Bapt. Conv., Atlanta, 1982—2002. Co-author: Shaping a Future for Church in Changing Community, 1981, Church and Community Diagnostic Workbook, 1986; author: (with others) Shooting the Rapids: Effective Ministry in a Changing World, 1990, Faith and Social Ministry: Ten Christian Perspectives, 1990. Capt. USAF, 1956—62. Baptist. Avocations: jogging, reading, family travel, golf. Home: 3041 Chestnut St NW Washington DC 20015-1407 E-mail: allens@erols.com.

ALLEN, WILLIAM JULIUS, art history educator; b. Tuscaloosa, Ala., Nov. 8, 1945; s. Julius Page and Lucille (Daffron) Allen; m. Joanne Savannah Martindale, Sept. 18, 1970; 1 child, Benjamin Kinton. PhD, Johns Hopkins U., 1981; BA, U. Ala., 1968. Prof. art history Ark. State U., Jonesboro, 1979—, chair dept. art, 1983—87, dean Coll. Fine Arts, 1987—91, dir. Ctr. for Learning Techs. Editor: PhotoHistorians; mem. editl. com. Educause Quar., 2002—. Vol. Peace Corps, Mazar-i-Sharif, Afghanistan, 1968—71; bd. dirs. Ark. Humanities Coun., Little Rock, 1990—95. Home: 1224 S Madison St Jonesboro AR 72401 Office: Ark State U 108 Cooley Dr Jonesboro AR 72401 E-mail: wallen@astate.edu.

ALLEN, WILLIAM KENT, journalist; b. Washington, Apr. 21, 1960; s. William Hayes and Joan Webster (Emmett) A.; m. Karen Elizabeth Tanner, Apr. 27, 1991; children: Nicholas, Daniel. BA in History, Stanford U., 1982. Reporter Kingston Daily Freeman, Kingston, N.Y., 1982-86; mng. editor The Milford (Conn.) Citizen, 1986-88; copy editor The Bergen Record, Hackensack, N.J., 1989-90, chief copy editor, 1990-91; copy editor, philanthropy columnist The Washington Post, 1991-2000; news editor U.S. News & World Report, Washington D.C., 2000—. Pub. spkr. and freelance writer on nonprofits and philanthropy, 2000—; vis. media fellow Duke U., 1997. Mem. Nat. Press Club, Am. Jewish Com. Democrat. Avocations: long-distance running, swimming, presidential history. Home: 6638 Barnaby St NW Washington DC 20015-2357 Office: US News World Report 1050 Thomas Jefferson St NW Washington DC 20007 E-mail: kent.allen@stanfordalumni.org.

ALLEN, WILLIAM L. editor; Student, Ga. Tech.; BA in Govt., La. State U. Intern Ctr. for Strategic & Internat. Studies, Washington, 1964—66; editor Nat. Geog., Washington, 1995. Bd. dirs. Inst. on Nautical Archaeology. Bd. dirs. Nat. Geog. Ednl. Found., Nat. Space Biomed. Rsch. Inst., World Wildlife Fund. Lt. N. H.B. Earhart fellow, Georgetown U. Office: Nat Geog Soc 1145 17th St NW Washington DC 20036-4701*

ALLEN, WILLIAM MARION, III, retired graphic designer, artist; b. Ft. Worth, July 10, 1927; s. William Marion and Lucile Beasley Allen. Student, Southwestern U., 1944-45, Tex. Christian U., 1945-46; BFA, U. Tex., 1950; postgrad., UCLA, 1954; MFA, U. So. Calif., 1955. Art tchr. El Paso Pub. Schs., 1950-51; illustrator Ramo Wooldridge Corp., L.A., 1956-58, Space Tech. Labs., L.A., 1958-60; graphic design coord. The Aerospace Corp., L.A., 1960-89; ret., 1989. One-man shows include Comara Gallery, L.A., 1975, 76, Art Gallery-The Aerospace Corp., L.A., 1982, Atrium Gallery, U. North Tex. Health Sci. Ctr., 1999; exhibited in group shows including Long Beach Mus. Art, Calif. State Fair, Chico State Coll., Tex. Fine Arts Assn., Butler Inst. Am. Art, Youngstown, Ohio, Ft. Worth Art Assn., L.A. Art Assn., also others. With U.S. Army, 1951-53, PTO. Recipient Cash award 18th Annual Artists Show, Ft. Worth, 1957, Purchase award 19th Annual Tex. State Fair, Dallas Mus. Art, 1957, Cash award 22nd Annual Local Artists Show, Ft. Worth, Award of Merit, Mus.

N.Mex. Art Show, Santa Fe, 1959, Bertram M. Newhouse award 1st prize oil 27th Annual Local Artists Show, Ft. Worth, 1967, Third award contemporary So. Calif. Exhbn., Del Mar, Calif., 1967, Buza Cardoza Cash award 52nd Annual Calif. Nat. Watercolor Soc., 1972, Award of Merit, Templeton June Show, Ft. Worth, 1992, Award of Merit, 1996 Main St., 11th Annual Festival Exhbn., Ft. Worth, 1996, Cash award, Arches Paper award, Nat. Watercolor Soc. 77th Annual Exhbn., L.A., 1998, cash award 500X Gallery, Expo '98, Dallas, 1998. Mem. Nat. Watercolor Soc., Soc. Watercolor Artists (cash award 7th ann. membership exhbn. Ft. Worth 1998, 8th ann. juried exhbn. 1998, 18th juried exhcn. 1999, 1st place cash award mems. juried exhbn. 1999, 20th Anniversary Show Juried Competition Merit award 2001). Avocations: gardening, traveling. Home: 3754 Somerset Ln Fort Worth TX 76109-3555 E-mail: dockwatch@home.com.

ALLEN, WILLIAM RICHARD, retired economist; b. Eldorado, Ill., Apr. 3, 1924; s. Oliver Boyd and Justa Lee (Wingo) A.; m. Frances Lorraine Swoboda, Aug. 15, 1948 (dec.); children: Janet Elizabeth, Sandra Lee. AB, Cornell Coll., Iowa, 1948; PhD, Duke U., 1953. Faculty, Washington U., St. Louis, 1951-52; faculty UCLA, 1952—, prof., 1963-91, prof. emeritus, 1991—. Vis. prof. Northwestern U., 1952, U. Wis., 1964, U. Mich., 1965, So. Ill. U., 1969, Tex. A&M, 1971-73; cons. Dept. Commerce, 1962; v.p. Found. Rsch. in Econs. and Edn., 1971-73; pres. Internat. Inst. Econ. Rsch., 1974-86; v.p. Inst. for Contemporary Studies, 1986-90; assoc. Reason Found., 1990-92; newspaper, mag. columnist; nationally syndicated radio commentator, 1979-92. Author: (with others) Foreign Trade and Finance, 1959, Essays in Economic Thought, 1960, University Economics, 3d edit., 1972, Exchange and Production, 3d edit., 1983, International Trade Theory, 1965, Midnight Economist, 1981, vol. 2, 1989, vol. 3, 1997; mem. adv. bd.: History of Polit. Economy, 1969-84, Social Sci. Quar., 1975-2003; contbr. articles to profl. jours. Served with USAAF, 1943-46. Social Sci. Research Council grantee, 1950-51, 62; Ford Found. grantee, 1958-59, 72-74; NSF grantee, 1965-66; Earhart Found. grantee, 1972, 74-75 Mem. Western Econ. Soc. (pres. 1970-71), So. Econ. Assn. (v.p. 1978-79), History of Econs. Soc. (v.p. 1974-75), Phi Beta Kappa. Home: 11809 Allaseba Dr Los Angeles CA 90066-1112 E-mail: allen@econ.ucla.edu., midnightecon@cs.com.

ALLEN, WILLIAM SHERIDAN, retired social sciences educator; b. Evanston, Ill., Oct. 5, 1932; s. William S. and Rose (Brahm) Allen; m. Karen Miller, Jan. 9, 1982; children: Caitilyn, Jefferson, Rebecca, Claire. AB, U. Mich., 1955; MA, U. Conn., 1956; PhD, U. Minn., 1962. Instr. history Bay City (Mich.) Jr. Coll., 1957-58; instr. humanities MIT, Cambridge, Mass., 1960-61; asst. prof. history U. Mo., Columbia, 1961-65, assoc. prof., 1966-67, Wayne State U., Detroit, 1967-70; prof. SUNY, Buffalo, 1970-2001, chmn. history dept., 1987-90. Vis. prof. U. Mich., Ann Arbor, 1967; cons. Time-Life Books, Alexandria, Va., 1988—89. Author: (book) The Nazi Seizure of Power, 1984; editor, translator: book The Infancy of Nazism, 1976; contbr. articles to profl. jours. V.p. Holocaust Resources Ctr., Buffalo, 1985—90; publicity chmn. Buffalo Group Amnesty Internat., 1985—87; dir. Parkside Fed. Credit Union, Buffalo, 1986—87. Fellow, Alexander von Humboldt Found., 1965—66, NEH, 1979. Mem.: United Univ. Profs. (pres. Buffalo chpt. 1978—81), N.Y. State Assn. European Historians (pres. 1983—84), Am. Conf. Irish Studies. Avocations: sailing, gardening.

ALLEN, WOODY (ALLEN STEWART KONIGSBERG), director, actor, writer; b. N.Y.C., Dec. 1, 1935; s. Martin and Nettie (Cherry) Konigsberg; m. Harlene Rosen, 1954 (div. 1960); m. Louise Lasser, 1964 (div. 1969); ptnr. Mia Farrow; 1 child, Satchel; adopted children: Moses, Dylan; m. Soon-Yi Previn, 1997; adopted children: Bechet, Manzie Tio Student, NYU, 1953, CCNY, 1953. Writer TV comedy for Sid Caesar, 1957. Art Carney, 1958-59, Herb Shriner, 1953; appeared in numerous nightclubs, TV shows, from 1961; author screenplay, also appeared in motion picture What's New Pussycat?, 1964-65; screenplay, dir., actor Take the Money and Run, 1969, Bananas, 1971, What's Up Tiger Lily?, 1966, Everything You Always Wanted to Know About Sex But Were Afraid to Ask, 1972, Sleeper, 1973, Love and Death, 1975, The Front, 1976, Manhattan (Brit. Acad. award 1979, N.Y. Film Critics award), Stardust Memories, 1980; writer, dir., prodr., actor films Annie Hall (N.Y. Film Critics Circle award for Best Dir. and Best Screenplay 1977, Acad. awards for best film, best direction, Nat. Soc. Film Critics Screenwriting award), Zelig, 1983, Broadway Danny Rose, 1984, Hannah and Her Sisters, 1986 (Acad. award for best screenplay, D.W. Griffith award for best dir. Nat. Bd. Rev. of Motion Pictures), New York Stories (Oedipus Wrecks segment), 1989, Mighty Aphrodite, 1995 (Acad. award nominee for best screenplay 1996), Everyone Says I Love You. 1996, Deconstructing Harry, 1997, Count Mercury Goes to the Suburbs, 1997, Celebrity, 1998, Sweet and Lowdown, 1999, Small Town Crooks, 2000, The Curse of the Jade Scorpion, 2001, Hollywood Ending, 2002, Anytyhing Else, 2003; writer, dir., narrator film Radio Days, 1987; screenplay, dir. films Interiors, 1978, Purple Rose of Cairo, 1985, A Midsummer Night's Sex Comedy, 1982, September, 1987, Another Woman, 1988, Crimes and Misdemeanors, 1989, Alice, 1990, Shadows and Fog, 1992, Husbands and Wives, 1992, Manhattan Murder Mystery, 1993, Bullets Over Broadway, 1994, Mighty Aphrodite, 1995; author play: Don't Drink the Water, 1966 (actor, dir. of TV movie, 1994), The Floating Lightbulb, 1981, (one act) Death Defying Acts, 1995, Sounds from a Town I Love (TV movie), 2001; play, screenplay Play It Again, Sam, 1969, film, 1972; actor, film King Lear, 1988, Scenes From a Mall, 1990, Cannes...les 400 coups, 1997, Waiting for Woody, 1998, Impostors, 1998, AFI's 100 Years...100 Movies, 1998, Antz, 1998, Wild Man Blues, 1998, Stuck on You, 1998, Company Man, 1999 Picking Up the Pieces, 1999; author: Getting Even, 1971, Without Feathers, 1975, Side Effects, 1980; guest appearances (TV) Just Shoot Me, The Tonight Show; contbr. numerous pieces to Playboy, New Yorker, other mags. Recipient Sylvania award, 1957; Spl. award Berlin Film Festival, 1975; nominated for Emmy award as TV writer, 1957 Democrat.

ALLEN-CASTELLITTO, ANITA LAFRANCE, law educator; b. Ft. Warden, Wash., Mar. 24, 1953; d. Grover Cleveland Allen and Carrye Mae Cloud; m. Michael Kelly Williams, June 1982 (div. Mar. 1985); m. Paul Vincent Castellitto, June 7, 1985; children: Adam Peter Castellitto, Ophelia Anne Castellitto. BA, New Coll., 1974; MA, PhD, U. Mich., 1978; JD, Harvard U., 1984. Bar: NY 85, Pa. 85. Prof. philosophy Carnegie-Mellon U., Pitts., 1978—81; lawyer Cravath, Swaine & Moore, N.Y.C., 1984—85; prof. law U. Pitts., 1985—87; prof. Georgetown Law Ctr., Washington, 1987—96, assoc. dean, 1996—98; prof. U. Pa., Phila., 1998—. Mem. adv. bd. Nat. Inst. for Human Genome Rsch., Washington, 1994—98, Electronic Privacy Info. Ctr., Washington, 1998—2002, Bazelon Ctr. for Mental Health Law, Washington, 2002—. Author: Uneasy Access: Privacy, 1988, Why Privacy Isn't Everything, 2003; co-author: Privacy Law, 2002; co-editor: Debating Democracy's Discontent, 1998. Bd. dirs. Planned Parenthood, N.Y.C., 1992—97, Washington, 1992—97, New Coll. Found., Sarasota, Fla., 1990—95; mem. exec. com. Assn. Am. Law Schs., Washington, 1999—2002. Ford Found. fellow, N.Y., 1974—78, law and pub. affairs fellow, Princeton U., 2003—. Avocation: gardening. Office: Univ Pa 3400 Chestnut St Philadelphia PA 19104

ALLENDER, ERIC WARREN, computer science educator; b. Mt. Pleasant, Iowa, Nov. 19, 1956; s. Orville William and Odetta Gertrude (Stein) A.; m. Claire Ellen Todd, Aug. 3, 1985. BA, U. Iowa, 1979; PhD, Ga. Inst. Tech., 1985. Asst. prof. Rutgers U., New Brunswick, N.J., 1985-91, assoc. prof., 1991-97, prof., 1997—. Contbr. articles to profl. jours. Home: 80 Richmond Dr Skillman NJ 08558-1819 Office: Rutgers U Dept of Computer Sci New Brunswick NJ 08903 E-mail: allender@cs.rutgers.edu.

ALLENDER, JOHN ROLAND, lawyer; b. Boone, Iowa, Oct. 22, 1950; s. John S. and C. Corinne (Hayes) A.; m. Patti Allender; children: Susan A., Andrew J. BS, Iowa State U., 1972; JD, U. San Diego, 1975; LLM in Taxation, NYU, 1976. Bar: Calif. 1976, Tex. 1977, U.S. Ct. Claims 1977, U.S. Tax. Ct. 1977, U.S. Dist. Ct. (so. dist.) Tex. 1977. Assoc. Fulbright & Jaworski, Houston, 1976-83, ptnr., 1983—. Mem. adv. commn. Tex. Bd. Legal Specialization, 1986-2000. Bd. dirs. Ronald McDonald House, Houston, pres. 2003—. Mem. State Bar of Tex. (chmn. sect. taxation 1990), Houston Bar Assn. (chmn. sect. taxation 1979). Office: Fulbright & Jaworski 1301 Mckinney St Houston TX 77010-3031

ALLEN-MEARES, PAULA G. social work educator, dean; b. Buffalo, N.Y., Feb. 29, 1948; d. Joe N. and Mary T. (Hienz) Allen; married; children: Tracey, Nikki, Shannon. BS, SUNY, Buffalo, 1969; MSW in Child Welfare, U. Ill., Urbana-Champaign, 1971, PhD in Social Work and Ednl. Adminstrn., 1975; cert. in mgmt., Harvard U., 1990; cert. mgmt. of mgrs., U. Mich., 1993. Lic. cert. social worker, Ill.; lic. clin. social worker, Ill. Rsch. asst. SUNY, Buffalo, 1966-69; child welfare worker Dept. Children and Family Svcs., Champaign, Ill.; 1970-71; sch. social worker Urbana (Ill.) Sch. Dist. 116, 1971-78; supt. Sch. Social Work U. Ill., Urbana-Champaign, 1973-78, asst. prof. Sch. Social Work, 1978-83, chair Sch. Social Work Specialization, 1978-84, dir. doctoral program Sch. Social Work, 1985-88, 89, assoc. prof. Sch. Social Work, 1983-89, acting dean Sch. Social Work, 1989-90, prof. Sch. Social Work, 1989-93, dean, prof. Sch. Social Work, 1990-93, U. Mich., Ann Arbor, 1993—. Scholars forum vis. lectr. U. Tex., Austin, 1992; vis. scholar Sch. Social Work, U. S.C., 1994; manuscript and book reviewer; reviewer Social Casework, summers 1988-90; Children & Youth Svcs. Rev., 1988-90, Jour. Ethnic and Multicultural Concerns in Social Work, 1990, among others; cons. Ill. Office Edn., Pupil Pers. Svc. Unit, Springfield, 1977, Detroit Pub. Schs., 1979, Decatur (Ill.) Pub. Schs., 1979, Family Svcs. Champaign County, 1979, Dept. Pub. Instrn., State of N.C., 1979, Urbana Sch. Dist. 116, 1978-80, Ill. State Bd. Edn., 1979-81, Chgo. Pub. Schs., 1981, Champaign Pub. Schs., 1981, Vermillion County Spl. Edn. Coop., Danville, 1982, Pembroke Sch. Dist., Kankakee, Ill., 1982, Champaign Pub. Schs., 1982, Defferin-Pell Sch. Dist., Mississauga, Ont., Can., 1982, Mid-State Spl. Edn., 1983, Milw. Wis. Office Edn., 1983, D.C. Sch. Social Work, 1984, Ind. Office Edn. Pupil Pers. Divsn., Indpls., 1984, Glenbrook (Ill.) Sch. Dist., 1984-86, Kankakee Spl. Edn. Coop., 1985, N.J. State Dept. Edn. Office Cert., Trenton, 1985, Pub. Sch. Disvn., Mississauga, 1985, Budapest, Hungary, 1990, Dept. Def., 1991, Cath. Social Svcs., Indpls., 1991, Bd. Sch. Commrs., Indpls. Pub. Schs., 1991, Brown U. and Lilly Endowment, Indpls., 1992; external reviewer U. Calif. Berkeley, 1996; keynote spkr. N.Mex., Ga., Mo. 1997. Author: Intervention with Children & Adolescents, 1995, (with others) Social Work Services in Schools, 1986, Controversial Issues in Social Work Research, 1995; co-editor: Methods and Issues--Evaluating Social Services in Education Settins, 1988, Adolescent Sexuality--An Overview and Principles of Intervention, 1986; mem. editl. bd. Jour. of Women in Social Work, 1990-93, Arete, 1989—, Sch. Jour. Social Work, 1986—, Jour. NASW, 1984-88, Ednl. and Psychol. Rsch., 1983-89, Jour. Social Svc. Rsch., 1993—, Children and Youth Svcs. Rev., 1991—, Jour. Tchg. Social Work, 1990—; cons. editor Social Work in Edn., 1978-84; editor-in-chief Social Work in Edn., 1989-93, Jour. of Social Work Edn., 1997—; tech. adv. com. Social Work in Edn. spl. edit., 1996—; mem. editl. adv. bd. Families in Contemporary Soc., 1991—; contbr. articles to profl. jours. Human rels. dir. Urbana Edn., 1973-75; mem. regional adv. bd. Gifted, 1977-78; mem. planning com. for Ill. March of Dimes, 1978; bd. dirs. Vol. Action Ctr. Champaign County, 1978-80, chair nomination com., ad hoc com. on bd. policy; mem. program com. Girls Club of Champaign, 1978-81; mem. adv. bd. Ambulatory Care Ctr., Mercy Hosp., 1981-82; bd. dirs. devel. svcs. Champaign County, 1973-75; moderator black adoptions Children's Home & Aid Soc. Ill. and Dept. Children and Family Svcs., 1984; mem. policy com. Regional Ill. Children's Home and Aid Soc., 1980-84; bd. dirs. Family Svc. Champaign County, 1988-89; mem. Champaign county child placement rev. com. Champaign County Cir. Ct., 1985-93. Recipient scholarship SUNY, 1966, Alumni of Yr. U. Ill., 1993, Human Rels. award Ill. Edn. Assn., 1975; fellow U. Ill., 1969-71; grantee Urban Sch. Dist. 116, 1976, Dept. Children and Family Svcs., 1983, Workshops on Prevention of Teenage Pregnancy, 1985, Dept. Edn., 1986, 89, U. Ill., 1986—, NASW, 1988-92, Mich. Dept. Social Svcs., 1994. Mem. NASW (chair comms. com. 1993—, comms. bd. dirs. 1990—, coun. editors bd. 1990—, cert., editor-in-chief Social Work in Edn. 1990—; Social Worker of Yr. Illini dist. 1992), Nat. Assn. Black Social Workers, Nat. Assn. Deans and Dirs. (v.p. 1993-95, v.p. 1993—, bd. dirs. 1991-93), Coun. on Social Work Edn. (treas. 1992—, bd. dirs. 1989-91, del. assembly 1988-89), Rotary, Phi Delta Kappa, Delta Mu, Delta Kappa Gamma (Xi chpt.). Avocations: jogging, aerobics. Office: U Mich Sch Social Work 1065 Freize Bldg Ann Arbor MI 48109

ALLENTUCK, MARCIA EPSTEIN, English language and art history educator; b. N.Y.C., June 8, 1928; m. 1949; 1 child. BA, NYU, 1948; PhD, Columbia U., 1964; MA (hon.), Oxford U., 1975. Lectr. English Columbia U., N.Y.C., 1955-57, Hunter Coll., N.Y.C., 1957; from lectr. to prof. English CCNY, N.Y.C., 1959-88; prof. history of art Grad. Ctr. CUNY, N.Y.C., 1974-88, prof. emerita, 1988. Author: The Works of Henry Needler, 1961, Henry Fuseli: The Artist as Critic and Man of Letters, 1964, The Achievement of Isaac Bashevis Singer, 1969, John Graham's System and Dialectics of Art, 1971; contbr. articles to profl. jours. Morrison fellow AAUW, 1958-59, Howard fellow Brown U., 1966-67, Huntington Libr. fellow, 1968, 77, fellow Nat. Translation Ctr. U. Tex., 1968-69, Chapelbrook Found., 1970-72, Dumbarton Oaks Harvard U., 1972-73, sr. fellow NEH, 1973-74, vis. fellow Wolfson Coll. Oxford U., 1974—, fellow Brit. Acad. Newberry Libr., 1980, Murray rsch. fellow Radcliffe Coll., Harvard U., 1982, fellow Inst. Advanced Studies in the Humanities, Edinburgh (Scotland) U., 1984, rsch. fellow Swann Found., 1989—; vis. scholar Burrell Art Collection, Glasgow, Scotland, 1978, 88; Am. Philos. Soc. grantee, 1966-67. Fellow Royal Soc. Arts London; mem. MLA (del. assembly 1989—), Brit. Soc. Archtl. Historians, Milton Soc. Am., Augustan Reprint Soc., Soc. Archtl. Historians, Coll. Art Assn., Phi Beta Kappa. Home: 5 W 86th St Apt 12B New York NY 10024-3665

ALLER, MARGO FRIEDEL, astronomer; b. Springfield, Ill., Aug. 27, 1938; d. Jules and Claire (Cornick) Friedel; m. Hugh Duncan Aller, Aug. 17, 1964; 1 child, Monique Christine. BA, Vassar Coll., 1960; postgrad., Harvard U., 1961-62; MS, U. Mich., 1964, PhD, 1969. Mathematician programmer Smithsonian Astrophys. Obs., Cambridge, Mass., 1960-62; rsch. assoc. U. Mich., Ann Arbor, 1970-76, assoc. rsch. scientist, 1976-85, rsch. scientist, 1985—. Mem. users' com. Nat. Radio Astronomy Observatory, 1984-86. Mem. Internat. Union of Radio Sci., Am. Astron. Soc., Internat. Astron. Union, Sigma Xi. Avocation: skiing. Office: U Mich Dept Astronomy 817 Dennison Bldg Ann Arbor MI 48109-1090 E-mail: margo@astro.lsa.umich.edu.

ALLER, WAYNE KENDALL, psychology educator, researcher, computer education company executive, property manager; b. Slyvia, Kans., Feb. 20, 1933; s. Alvin Ray and Florence Dorothy (Snowbarger) A.; m. Sharon Cecelia Forray, Aug. 21, 1962 (div.); children: Jay Ramzi, Joyce Amal; m. Sonia Y. Konialian, Apr. 8, 1969 BA in Physics, N.W. Nazarene Coll., Nampa, Idaho, 1955; MS in Psychology, U. Wash., 1960, PhD in Psychology, 1964. Asst. prof. psychology Pacific Lutheran U., 1962-64; asst. prof., chmn. divsn. behavioral scis. Beirut Coll. for Women, 1964-67; assoc. prof. Mankato State Coll., Minn., 1967-68, Ind. State U., Terre Haute, from 1968, prof., to 1985; pres. Learning Unlimited, 1983—, CompuLearn, 1983-87. Adj. prof. psychology Calif. State U., Northridge, 1984—; sr. rsch. adv. Ctr. Ednl. R&D, Ministry Planning, Republic Lebanon, Beirut, 1974-75; sr. rsch. assoc. Ctr. Behavioral Rsch., Am. U. of Beirut, 1974-75; vis. scholar dept. psychology UCLA, 1982-83; cons. English as fgn. lang. Vietnamese Affairs Ctr., Terre Haute, 1976-78 Author: Readings and Experiments in General Psychology, 1970, rev. edit., 1971 Pres. Knollwood Property Owners Assn., 2002—; bd. mem. Granada Hills Neighborhood Coun. Ford Found. grantee, 1974-75 Mem. Western Psychol. Assn., N.Y. Acad. Scis., Soc. for Computers in Psychology, Computer Users Speech and Hearing, Wabash Valley Apple Byters Club (Terre Haute)(pres. 1981-82) (Terre Haute), Sigma Xi, Psi Chi, Sigma Phi Iota. Presbyterian. Home: 12045 Susan Dr Granada Hills CA 91344-2642 E-mail: wayneallerO7@hotmail.com.

ALLERTON, JEFFREY PAUL, oncologist; b. Catskill, N.Y., Mar. 22, 1960; s. Robert Stanley and Millie A.; children: Kelsey Lynn, Kristen Marie, Kimberly Ann. BA in Chemistry and Biology, Coll. St. Rose, Albany, N.Y., 1982; MD Tufts U., 1986. Intern St. Elizabeth's Hosp., Boston, 1986—87, resident, 1987—89, fellow in hematology/oncology, 1989—92; chief oncology Wilford Hall Md. Ctr., San Antonio, 1995—98; staff physician Rockford (Ill.) Clinic, 1998—99; chief oncology Swedish Am. Hosp., Rockford, 1999—2001; corp. v.p. ACT Med. Group, Rockford, 2001—02; oncologist Blue Ridge Med. Specialists, Bristol, Tenn., 2002—. Contbr. articles. Lt. col. USAF, 1992—98. Recipient Disting. Svc. award, SWOG, 1998, Physician's Recognition award, AMA, 1990. Fellow: ACP; mem.: Am. Cancer Soc., Am. Soc. Blood and Marrow Transplantation, Am. Soc. Hematology, Am. Soc. Clin. Oncology. Republican. Avocations: sports, reading. Office: Blue Ridge Med Specialists 271 Medical Park Blvd Bristol TN 37620

ALLERTON, JOHN STEPHEN, association executive; b. N.Y.C., Dec. 22, 1926; s. Moses Alexander and Rebecca A.; m. Juanita Grace Lee, Nov. 9, 1956. BA in Indsl. Engring, N.Y. U., 1950; grad. Advanced Mgmt. Program, Harvard Bus. Sch., 1971. With Am. Automobile Assn., Falls Church, Va., 1955-90, dir. mktg., 1957-62; CEO Automobile Club of Wash., Seattle, 1962-65; pres. Ohio Motorists Assn., 1965-78; exec. v.p., gen. mgr. Am. Automobile Assn., 1978 90. Bd. dirs. Salvation Army, Ohio, 1966-76, Am. Cancer Soc., 1966-70, Crawford Automotive-Aviation Mus., Cleve., 1973-78; Bd. govs. Found. Internat. Meetings Served with U.S. Navy, 1944-46. Mem. Harvard Club, Rotary. Presbyterian.

ALLERTON, SAMUEL ELLSWORTH, biochemist; b. Three Rivers, Mich., Aug. 21, 1933; s. Sanford Ellsworth and Virginia Mary (Dickenson) A.; m. Theresa Mary Pawlak, Aug. 20, 1966; children: Adam Sanford, Eve Samantha. BA summa cum laude, Kalamazoo (Mich.) Coll., 1955; PhD, Harvard U., 1962. Teaching fellow Harvard U. Med. Sch., Boston, 1957-61; rsch. assoc. Rockefeller U., N.Y.C., 1961-65; asst. prof. U. So. Calif., L.A., 1965-69, assoc. prof., 1969—; prof. of dentistry (ret.), 2000—. Cons. Woodroof Labs., Santa Ana, Calif., 1978-89. Contbr. articles to profl. jours. Bd. dirs. Huntington Beach (Calif.) Community Clinic, 1990-92. Named Outstanding Young Man of Am., Jaycee's, 1966. Mem. N.Y. Acad. Scis., Am. Coll. of Nutrition, Elks, Sigma Xi, Omicron Kappa Upsilon. Anglican. Achievements include rsch. on phys.-chem. characterization of proteins, tumor products, studies on absorption of copper. Office: U So Calif Dept Dentistry University Park Mc # 0641 Los Angeles CA 90089-0001

ALLEY, GLENDA PAULINE, music educator; b. Boulder, Colo., June 28, 1946; d. Glen LeRoy Taylor and Hazel Pauline Reynolds; m. Robert Lynn Alley, Aug. 22, 1965; children: Faith, Joy, Timothy. Sec. Gen. Electric, San Leandro, Calif., 1969—70, Internat. Beef Breeders, Denver, 1973—75, Northglenn (Colo.) Sch. Dist., 1975—76; pvt. practice music tchr. Tacoma, 1986—; sec. Nat. Bank Am., Anchorage, 1980—82, Humana Hosp., Anchorage, 1982—86, Puget Sound Hosp. and Multicare, Tacoma, 1986—96. Mem.: Kindermusik Educators Assn., Kindermusik Internat. (mentor 2001—), Wash. State Music Tchrs. Assn. (newsletter editor 1996—). Avocations: scrapbooks, sewing, reading, playing with grandchildren. Fax: 253-752-5749. E-mail: rgalley@bww.com.

ALLEY, JOHN-EDWARD, lawyer; b. El Dorado, Ark., Dec. 9, 1940; s. Granville Mason and Reyland (Stuppi) A.; m. Mary Elizabeth Conrad, Sept. 10, 1960 (div. 1970); 1 child, John-Edward Jr.; m. Ruth Rice, June 17, 1995. BSBA, U. Fla., 1962, JD, 1965; LLM in Labor Law, NYU, 1968. Bar: Fla. 1966, U.S. Dist. Ct. (so dist.) Fla. 1968, U.S. Supreme Ct. 1971, U.S. Ct. Appeals (5th cir.) 1972, U.S. Ct. Appeals (4th cir.) 1975, U.S. Ct. Appeals (D.C. cir.) 1975, U.S. Dist. Ct. (no. dist.) Fla. 1975, U.S. Ct. Appeals (11th cir.) 1981, U.S. Dist. Ct. (mid. dist.) Fla. 1984. Assoc. Clayton, Arnow, Duncan, Johnston, Clayton & Quincey, Gainesville, Fla., 1966-67, Bruckner & Greene, Miami, Fla., 1968; assoc., then ptnr. Paul & Thomson, Miami, 1969-74; ptnr. Alley & Alley, Chartered, Tampa, Fla., 1974-96, Alley and Alley/Ford & Harrison LLP, Tampa, 1996-98, Ford & Harrison LLP, Tampa, 1999—. Instr. U. Fla., Gainesville, 1964-66, asst. prof., 1966-67; adj. prof. Coll. Law, Stetson U., St. Petersburg, Fla., 1976-85; mem. faculty PTI Mgmt. Ctr., Houston, 1983-88. Contbr. articles to legal jours. Mem. Fla. Bus. Adv. Bd., Leading Am. Attys., Labor Lawyers Adv. Com., Coun. for Union-Free Environment. Named Leading Fla. Atty. Am. Rsch. Corp., 1996. Mem. ABA, Fla. Bar Assn. (vice chmn. continuing legal edn. com. 1984-86, 90-91, chmn. elect 1991-92, chmn. 1992-93, chmn. labor and employment law sect. 1973-74, Ralph A. Marsicano award 1988), Am. Arbitration Assn., Am. Employment Law Coun., Dade County Bar Assn., Miami City Club, Univ. Club. Avocations: flying, scuba diving, skiing, classic cars. boating. Office: Ford & Harrison LLP 101 E Kennedy Blvd Ste 900 Tampa FL 33602-5133 also: 100 SE 2d St Ste 4500 Miami FL 33131 E-mail: jalley@fordharrison.com.

ALLEY, STEVEN E. foundation administrator; b. Plymouth, Ind., Sept. 14, 1962; s. Edward G. and Reene S. Alley; m. Barbara J. Smith; children: Jennifer A., Eric S. BS, Ball State U., Muncie, IN, 1980—85. News reporter/anchor WASK Radio, Lafayette, Ind., 1985—85, WWKI Radio, Kokomo, Ind., 1985—87, news dir., 1987—88; cmty. rels. officer Kokomo-Ctr. Schs., Kokomo, 1988—92; pres./CEO Cmty. Found. Howard County, Kokomo, 1992—98; v.p. for external rels. Ctrl. Ind. Cmty. Found., Indianapolis, 1998—2000; dir., cmty. founds. inst. Ctr. on Philanthropy at Ind. U., Indianapolis, 2000—01; pres./CEO Cmty. Found. So. Ariz., Tucson, 2001—. Chmn., cmty. found. com. Ind. Grantmakers Alliance, Indianapolis, Ind., 1995—98; mem., cmty. founds. leadership team Coun. on Founds., Washington, 1996—2001. Office: Cmty Found for So AZ 2250 E Broadway Blvd Tucson AZ 85719 Office Fax: 520-770-1500. E-mail: salley@cfsoaz.org.

ALLEY, WAYNE EDWARD, federal judge, retired army officer; b. Portland, Oreg., May 16, 1932; s. Leonard David and Hilda Myrtle (Blum) A.; m. Marie Winkelmann Dommer, Jan. 28, 1978; children: Elizabeth, David, John; stepchildren: Mark Dommer, Eric Dommer. AB, Stanford U., 1952, JD, 1957. Bar: Calif. 1957, Oreg. 1957, Okla. 1985. Ptnr. Williams & Alley, Portland, 1957-59; commd. officer JAGC, U.S. Army, advanced through grades to brig. gen., ret., 1981; dean Coll. Law, dir. Law Ctr. U. Okla., Norman, 1981-85; judge U.S. Dist. Ct. Western Dist. Okla., Oklahoma City, 1985—. Decorated D.S.M., Legion of Merit, Bronze Star Mem. Fed. Bar Assn., Oreg. Bar Assn., Okla. Bar Assn., Order of Coif, Phi Beta Kappa. Office: US Dist Ct 4001 US Courthouse 200 NW 4th St Ste 4001 Oklahoma City OK 73102-3027 Home: 1316 Brookside Dr Norman OK 73072-6348

ALLGEIER, PETER F. federal agency administrator; Grad., Brown U.; Masters Degree, Johns Hopkins U.; PhD, U. N.C. Assoc. for western hemisphere, asst. rep. for Europe and the Mediterranean U.S. Trade Reps., 1981; sr. dir. internat. econ. affairs Nat. Econ. Coun.; dep. U.S. Trade Rep. Exec. Office of the Pres., Washington, 2001—. Office: Exec Office of the Pres US Trade Rep 600 17th St NW Washington DC 20508-4801

ALLGRIM, CAROLINE DENHAM, retired college official; b. Detroit, June 22, 1937; d. Athel Fredric Denham and Emma Virginia (Franck) Kuhns; m. Richard Lee Allgrim. B.Mus., U. S.C., 1973. Sec. Shawnee Press, Inc., Delaware Water Gap, Pa., 1958-61, editorial asst., 1961-68; clk. typist U. S.C., Columbia, 1969-72, rsch. asst., 1972-76, dir. instnl. rsch., 1976-93; ret., 1994. Libr. S.C. Philharm. Orch., 1970-84, pers. mgr., 1976-97, musician, 1968-2001. Treas. S.C. Assn. for Instl. Rsch., 1987-91, pres. 1992-93. Mem. S.C. State Employees Assn., Pi Kappa Lambda, Delta Omicron. Avocations: music, books, video movies, WW2 history.

ALLIGOOD, ELIZABETH ANN HIERS, retired special education educator; b. W Palm Beach, Fla, Dec. 7, 1931; d. Hubert Victor and Ethel Ruth (Palmer) Hiers; m. Jesse LeRoy Alligood, Aug. 24, 1952; children: Stephen Leon, Larry Lamar, Miriam Ruth, Julia Ann, Carol Beth. AA, Norman Coll., 1951; BS in Edn., Valdosta State, 1978; postgrad., Columbus Coll., 1987, 92. Cert. tchr., Ga. Resource educator Irwin County Bd. Edn., Ocilla, Ga., 1969-71; dir. Sunny Dale Tng. Ctr., Ocilla, Ga., 1971-78, Green Oaks Tng. Ctr., Moultrie, Ga., 1978-81; tchr. Calhoun County Bd. Edn., Edison, Ga., 1978; cons. Am. Heart Assn., Columbus, Ga., 1984-86; tchr. Thomas County Bd. Edn., Thomasville, Ga., 1987-89, Muscogee County Bd. Edn., Columbus, Ga., 1989-94, Colquitt County Bd. Edn., Moultrie, Ga., 1994-97; ret., 1997. Founder Sunny Dale Tng. Ctr., 1969; mem. adv. bd. Columbus Specialized Preschool, 1985. Chairperson W. Ga. area Mental Health Adv. Coun., Columbus, 1986-87. Named to Honors Day, Sunny Dale Tng. Ctr., 1992. Mem. Civitan, 1980, (treas. 1997-1999), Assn. Retarded Citizens Ga. (bd. dir. at large 1977-78, state sec. 1980-81.), Ga. Assn. Educators, Norman Coll. Alumni Assn. (editor Normanlite 1998—). Democrat. Baptist. Avocations: bowling, computers, writing.

ALLIGOOD, LOLA JANE LURVEY, retired educator; b. Washington, N.C., Nov. 15, 1947; d. William David and Dicie Elizabeth Latham Lurvey; m. Charles Michael Alligood, Aug. 25, 1968; 1 child, Elizabeth Anne. BS in Libr. Sci., East Carolina U., 1971, MLS, 1976. Libr. Rose H.S., Greenville, N.C., 1970-71; media coord. John Small Elem. Sch., Washington, N.C., 1971-00; dir. of christian edn. and youth Christian Ch., Washington, NC, 2002—. Mem. planning bd. City of Washington, 1985—; chmn. Beaufort County Rep. Party,

1989-99; vice-chmn. GOP 1st Congl. Dist., 1997-99, sec., 1995-97, 99-2003; chmn. historic Bath (N.C.) Commn., 1993-97; deacon Christian Ch. Inducted to N.C. GOP Hall of Fame, 1999. Mem. NEA, N.C. Assn. Educators (rep.), N.C. Libr. Assn., N.C. Fedn. Rep. Women (coastal pres. 2001--), Delta Kappa Gamma. Avocations: horses, horse drawn carriages, historic preservation. Home: 220 Simmons St Washington NC 27889-5148

ALLIK, MICHAEL, diversified industry executive; b. N.Y.C., Aug. 28, 1935; s. Michael and Alma (Busch) A.; m. Deborah Dixon, Jan. 2, 1983; children—William Michael, Timothy John, Ryan Andrew, Lauren Alexandra. BS, MIT, 1957; MBA, Harvard U., 1961. V.p. Kondu Corp., Erie, Pa., 1961-66; assoc. Booz, Allen & Hamilton, Cleve., 1966-69; gen. mgr. Textile Friction Group H.K. Porter, Pitts., 1969-71; gen. mgr. transformer div. Allis Chalmers, Pitts., 1971-75; exec. v.p. Mead Paper Group, Dayton, Ohio, 1975-78; sr. v.p. strategy and adminstrn. Mead Corp., Dayton, 1978-81; sr. v.p. fin. and adminstrn. Dart & Kraft, Inc., Northbrook, Ill., 1981-83, pres. Splty. Products Group, 1984-86; pres., chief oper. officer, dir. RTE Corp., Milw., 1986-89; pres. Premier Aluminum, Inc., Racine, Wis., 1989—. Ptnr. Harvest Capital Mgmt., Inc., Vero Beach, Fla.; mem. coun. Grad. Sch. Bus., U. Chgo., 1985-92. Pres. bd. trustees Victory Theatre, Dayton, 1980-81; bd. dirs. Chgo. Hort. Soc., 1982-86, Milw. Repertory Theater, 1991-93. Served to 1st lt. C.E. U.S. Army, 1957-59. Mem. Wis. Taxpayers Alliance (bd. dirs 1987). Clubs: Chgo. Economic. Home: 2260 Seaside St Vero Beach FL 32963-3131

ALLINDER, DAVID RANDALL, musician, educator; b. Birmingham, Ala., Apr. 28, 1970; s. Donna Allinder; m. Jennifer Leigh Frady, Mar. 23, 2002. BS Music Ed., Univ. Ala., Tuscaloosa, AL, 1993. Band dir. Shades Valley H.S., Birmingham, Ala., 1993—. Instr. Birmingham So. Coll., Birmingham, Ala., 1999—2002, Univ. Ala. at Birmingham, Birmingham, Ala., 1993—96. Cope com. Am. Fedn. of Teachers, Birmingham, Ala., 1996. Mem.: Internat. Assn. of Jazz Educators, Music Educators Nat. Conf. Office: Shades Valley High School 6100 Old Leeds Road Birmingham AL 35210 Office Fax: 205-956-4638.

ALLINGHAM, LYNN MARIE, lawyer; b. Seattle, Dec. 7, 1955; d. William D. and Ruth E. (Busse) A.; m. Gregory Joseph Galik, Mar. 2, 1986; children: Geoffrey Joseph Allingham Galik, Jonathan Paul Allingham Galik. BA magna cum laude, U. Wash., 1978, J.D., 1981. Bar: Wash. 1981, Alaska 1982; U.S. Dist. Ct. (we. dist.) Wash., 1981, Alaska, 1982, Ct. Appeals (9th cir.) 1983. Assoc. Guess & Rudd, Anchorage, 1982-86; pvt. practice, Anchorage, 1986-88; asst. atty. U.S. Attys. Office, Anchorage, 1988-91; pvt. practice, Anchorage, 1991—. Mem. ABA (dist. rep. young lawyers div. 1984-86, staate bar del. 1991—, exec. coun. gen. practice, solo and small firm 2000—), Wash. Bar Assn., Alaska Bar Assn., Anchorage Assn. Women Lawyers, Anchorage Bar Assn. (bd. dirs. 1984—, 2d v.p. 1986-87, pres. 1991-92, chmn. young lawyers sect. 1985), Alaska World Affairs Coun. (bd. dirs. 2001—), Phi Beta Kappa. Office: 645 G St Ste 201 A Anchorage AK 99501

ALLINGTON, GLORIA JEAN HAM, medical education administrator; b. Northwood, N.D., May 21, 1945; d. John Henry Ham and Selma Tina (Haabak) Thorson; m. Gary Francis Allington, June 6, 1966 (div. May 1986). Student, U. N.D., 1963-66; ADN, Miami Dade Community Coll., 1968; BCS, U. Miami, 1976, MS in Edn., 1987. RN, Fla.; cert. meeting profl. Staff nurse Jackson Meml. Hosp., Miami, Fla., 1969-71, asst. head nurse, 1971-73; nurse educator U. Miami Sch. Medicine, 1973-75, adminstrv. asst., 1975-81, asst. dir. div. continuing med. edn., 1981, dir. div. continuing med. edn., 1981—. Contbr. articles to profl. jours. Exec. bd. dirs. Project Newborn, Miami, 1977-86; bd. dirs. Ronald McDonald House of So. Fla., Miami, 1977-82; mem. Zool. Soc. of South Fla., Miami, 1986—. Recipient James W. Colbert, Jr., M.D. award, Health Edn. Media Assn., 1977. Mem. Soc. Med. Coll. Dirs. of Continuing Med. Edn. (cert. of achievement 1991, sec. 1992-93, v.p. 1993, pres.-elect 1994, pres. 1995-96), Alliance for Continuing Med. Edn., Meeting Planners Internat. (internat. dir. 1986-88). Democrat. Roman Catholic. Avocations: photography, gourmet food and wine. Office: U Miami Sch Medicine PO Box 16960 Miami FL 33101-6960

ALLINSON, CARL, radiologist; b. New Haven, Feb. 20, 1912; s. Jacob Samuel and Sophie Allinson; m. Roze Bernstene Rapaport, Nov. 11, 1986;children: Arthur, Robert, Nancy, Jeffrey. BS, Yale U., 1932; PhD in Biochemistry, Boston U., 1938; MD, U. Ark., Little Rock, 1945. Diplomate Am. Bd. Radiology. Radiologist Franklin Hosp., Benton, Ill., 1957-75; A.G. Holley State Hosp., Lantana, Fla., 1981—; instr. physiology U. Ark. Sch. Medicine, Little Rock, Ark., 1940-45; instr. biochemistry La. State U., New Orleans, 1939-40. Rschr. in field; contbr. articles to profl. jours. Avocations: playing violin, building violins.

ALLIO, ROBERT JOHN, management consultant, educator; b. N.Y.C., Sept. 1, 1931; s. Albert Joseph and Helen (Gerbereux) A.; m. Barbara Maria Littauer, Oct. 3, 1953; children: Mark, Paul, David, Michael. BMetE, Rensselaer Poly. Inst., 1952; MS, Ohio State U., 1954; PhD, Rensselaer Poly. Inst., 1957. Mgr. advanced materials Gen. Electric Co., Schenectady, 1957-60; sr. staff AEC, Washington, 1962; engrng. mgr. atomic power div. Westinghouse Corp., Pitts., 1962-68; dir. corp. planning Babcock & Wilcox, N.Y., 1968-75; v.p. Can. Wire Co., Toronto, Ont., 1975-78; pres. Canstar Communications, Toronto, 1976-78; sr. staff mem. Arthur D. Little Co., Cambridge, Mass., 1978-79; dean Rensselaer Poly. Inst. Sch. Mgmt., Troy, N.Y., 1981-83; pres. Robert J. Allio and Assoc., Providence, 1979—; prof. mgmt. Babson Coll, Wellesley, Mass., 1984—; mng. dir. Anasazi Group, 2000—. Bd. dirs. Fourth Shift, Springboard Software, GardenWay, NICON, TBS Funding Corp., Infantelligence; chmn. bd. TracRac Inc. Author: Corporate Planning: Techniques and Applications, 1979, Corporate Planning, 1985, The Practical Strategist, 1988, Leadership Myths and Realities, 1999, The Seven Faces of Leadership, 2003; editor Planning Rev. Jour.; contbg. editor Strategy and Leadership Jour. Mem.: Planning Forum (pres. 1976—77). Office: 150 Chestnut St Providence RI 02903

ALLISON, ADRIENNE AMELIA, voluntary organization administrator; b. Toronto, Ont., Can., Nov. 2, 1940; d. Harold Whitfield and Emmeline Amelia (Banister) Hedley; m. Stephen Vyvyan Allison, Jan. 2, 1960 (div. 1984); children: Mark Hedley, Myles Stephen, Alexander Andrew; m. Armin U. Kuder, Aug. 26, 1989 (div. 2002). BA, George Washington U., 1978; MA, Georgetown U., 1980; MPA, Harvard U., 1986. Social sci. analyst AID, Washington, 1980-85, project mgr., 1986-89, presdl. com. on HIV epidemic, 1987-88; program dir. Centre for Devel. and Population Activities, 1988-91; v.p. Centre for Devel. and Population Activities, 1991-98; dir. maternal and neonatal health program Johns Hopkins Program in Reproductive Health, Balt., 1998—2001; internat. cons., 2001—. Adj. prof. George Washington U. Sch. Pub. Health, Johns Hopkins U. Sch. Hygiene and Pub. Health. Co-author: Vegetable Gardening in Bangladesh, 1975. Chair peace commn. Episcopal Diocese of Washington, 2002—; mem. vestry St. Albans Parish, Washington, 1988. Mem.: APHA, Cosmos Club. Home: 8011 Glendale Rd Chevy Chase MD 20815-5902 E-mail: adrienneallison@aol.com.

ALLISON, ANDREW MARVIN, church administrator; b. Long Beach, Calif., May 21, 1949; s. Howard C. and Wilma A. (Franks) A.; m. Kathleen L. Anderson, May 28, 1971; children: Rebecca, Nathan, Joanna, Spencer, Jacob, Camilla. AA, Glendale (Ariz.) C.C., 1972; BA in History, Brigham Young U., 1974; PhD of Polit. Sci., Coral Ridge U., 1993. Cert. secondary tchr., Ariz., Utah. Adminstrv. staff, editor Brigham Young U., Provo, Utah, 1972-74; adminstrv. asst. LDS Ch., Salt Lake City, 1977-79; prin., tchr. LDS Seminaries, Ariz.,Utah, 1974-77, 79-80; assoc. editor, art dir. Bookcraft Publs., Salt Lake City, 1983-85; dir. rsch. and publs. Nat. Ctr. for Constl. Studies, Salt Lake City, 1980-83, 85-91, chmn., pres. West Jordan, Utah, 1991-95; product devel. editor Deseret Book Co., Salt Lake City, 1995-96; supr. confidential applications LDS Ch., Salt Lake City, 1996-99, mgr. confidential records, 1999—. Adj. prof. polit. sci. George Wythe Coll., Cedar City, Utah, 1993—. Author: The Real Thomas Jefferson, 1982, The Real Benjamin Franklin, 1983, The Real George Washington, 1991; contbr. articles to profl. jours. Mem. West Jordan City Coun., Utah, 2000—, mayor pro-tem, 2001. Mem.: Phi Kappa Phi.

ALLISON, ANNE MARIE, retired librarian; b. Oak Park, Ill., Oct. 3, 1931; d. Gerald Patrick and Anna Evelyn (Beam) Myers; m. James Dixon Alison, Aug. 28, 1954; children: Mark, Mary, Clare, Ruth, Edward. BA in French, St. Mary of the Woods Coll., 1951; postgrad., U. Fribourg, 1952-53; MLS, Rosary Coll., 1968. Asst. libr. Triton Coll., River Grove, Ill., 1967-68; asst. libr. tech. svcs. Moraine Valley Community Coll., Palos Hills, Ill., 1968-69; dir. learning resources, head libr. Coll. Lake County, Grayslake, Ill., 1969-71; asst. head catalog dept. Kent (Ohio) State U. Librs., 1971-73, head processing dept., 1973-79, asst. dir. libr. svcs., 1979-81; acting dir. Fla. Atlantic U. Libr., Boca Raton, 1980-81; asst. dir., head tech. svcs. Wayne State U. Librs., Detroit, 1981-83; dir. librs. U. Cen. Fla., Orlando, 1983-97, ret., 1997. Past chair, bd. dirs. Fla. Extension Libr., Tampa; bd. dirs. Ctr. for Libr. Automation, Gainesville, Fla., Cen. Fla. Holocaust Meml. Resource Ctr., Orlando; adj. prof. Libr. and Info. Sci., U. S. Fla., Tampa. Editor: OCLC: A National Library Network, 1979; contbr. articles to profl. jours. Arbitrator alternative dispute resolution program Better Bus. Bur. Cen. Fla., Maitland, 1985—; active Friends Winter Park Pub. Libr., Friends of Orlando Pub. Libr. Recognized for Outstanding Leadership in Edn. Cen. Fla. Edn. Consortium for Women, 1990. Mem. ALA (chair profl. ethics com.), Fla. Libr. Assn., Fla. Assn. Coll. and Rsch. Librs. (pres. bd. dirs.). Avocations: fruit farming, collecting china. Office: U Cen Fla PO Box 25000 Orlando FL 32816-0001

ALLISON, ANTHONY CLIFFORD, research scientist, consultant; arrived in US, 1981; s. Harold Clifford and Norah Nolan (Neylan) Allison; m. Elsie Mebel Eugui, Aug. 1, 1989; m. Helen Green, Aug. 25, 1952 (div. Jan. 1989); children: Miles Clifford, Joseph Mark Clifford. MSc, Witwatersrand U., South Africa, 1947; PhD, Oxford U., Eng., 1950, BM, B of Surgery, 1952. Staff scientist Nat. Inst. for Med. Rsch., London, 1958—68; head pathology divsn. MRC Clin. Rsch. Ctr., London, 1968—78; dir. Internat. Lab. for Rsch. on Animal Diseases, Nairobi, Kenya, 1978—81; v.p. rsch. Syntex Corp., Palo Alto, Calif., 1981—94; CEO Dawa Corp., Belmont, Calif., 1994—2000; scientist SurroMed Corp., Mountain View, Calif., 2001—. Cons. Biocon Corp., Bangalore, India, 2002—. Mem.: European Molecular Biology Orgn., Sierra Club. Achievements include research in sickle-cell heterozygotes that found they are resistant to malaria; development of genetically controlled polymorphisms of human lipoproteins; development of mycophenolate mofetil. Avocations: history, music, literature. Office: SurroMed Corp 1505 O'Brien Dr Menlo Park CA 94025 Fax: 650-230-1960. Business E-Mail: aallison@surromed.com.

ALLISON, BEVERLY GRAY, seminary president, evangelism educator; b. La., May 7, 1924; s. John Richard Preston and Ora (Byram) A.; m. Voncille Cruse; children: Suzanne Grigsby, Charlotte Miller, Gray Maloy. BS, La. Polytech. Inst. (now La. Tech. U.), 1948; BD, New Orleans Bapt. Theol. Sem., 1952, ThD, 1954. Spl. agt. N.Y. Life Ins. co., Ruston, La., 1948-49; pastor New Prospect Bapt. Ch., Hilly, La., 1951-52, Sharon (La.) Bapt. Ch., 1951-52; assoc. pastor Temple Bapt. Ch., Ruston, La., 1952-54; pastor Southside Bapt. Mission, Ruston, 1953-54; asst. prof. church history New Orleans Bapt. Theol. Sem., 1954-56, assoc. prof. missions, 1955-60, prof. evangelism, 1964-66; evangelist Allison Evangelistic Assn., Ruston, 1960-72; assoc. dir. div. evangelism Home Mission Bd. So. Baptist Convention, 1966-67; pres. Mid-Am. Bapt. Theol. Sem., Memphis, 1972-97, pres. emeritus, 1997—, prof. evangelism, 1972—. Contbr. articles to profl. jours. With USAAF, 1943-45. Baptist. Office: Mid-Am Bapt Theol Sem PO Box 381528 Germantown TN 38183-1528

ALLISON, BROOKE HASTINGS, artist, educator; b. N.Y.C., Feb. 12, 1940; s. Frederick Gay and Miriam Lorraine (Watkins) Hastings; m. John Borden Allison, Dec. 17, 1966 (dec. 1996); children: Brooke Allison Scannell, Jaime Joy; stepchildren: Jeffrey Clark, Jay Borden, Jerrianne Allison Anderson, Jane Sue. Student, Shimer Coll., 1957-58, Art Inst. Chgo., 1958-60, 81-82, Am. Acad. Art., 1960-61, Lake Forest Coll., 1961. Instr. Dunedin (Fla.) Fine Art Ctr., 1984-2001. Exhibited in groups shows Tampa Mus. Art, 1997, Jacksonville (Fla.) Mus. Art, 1998, works featured in 200 Great Painting Ideas, 1998, Artist Mag., 1998, St. Petersburg Arts Ctr., 1999 (J. Brown Meml. award), Ridge Art 50th Ann. Nat. Competition, 2000 (2d prize 2000), Broome St. Gallery, 1999, 2000, 01 (1st prize 2000), Butler Inst. Am. Art, Youngstown, Pa., 2003; curator Artists of the 3d Age, Octagon Gallery, Clearwater, Fla. Recipient award, Catharine L. Wolfe Exhbn., 1993—94, Richwood Art Inst. award, Catharine Larillard Wolfe Open Internat. Exhbn., Nat. Arts Club, N.Y.C., 2001, Award of Excellence in Fine Arts, Ocala Art Festival, 2001, Award of Excellence for Mainsail, Art Festival of St. Petersburg, Fla., 2002, award of distinction, Fine Arts for Ocala, 2001, award of excellence, Mainsail Art Festival, 2002; grantee Pinellas County Artists Resource, 1991, 1999. Mem. Pastel Soc. Am. (profl. mem.), Pastel Soc. of West Coast, Midwest Pastel Soc., Profl. Assn. Visual Artists (past. pres. 1992-94), Fla. Artist's Group, Catherine Lorillard Wolfe Art Club, Butler Inst. Am. Art, Pastel Soc. Am. Presbyterian. Avocations: reading, service work. Home: 1654 Mckay Ct Dunedin FL 34698-3529 E-mail: brookeallison@earthlink.net.

ALLISON, DIANNE J. HALL, retired insurance company official; b. Wadsworth, Ohio, June 9, 1936; d. Glenn Mackey and Dorothy Laverne (Broomall) Hall; widowed; children: Christine M. Gardner Fiocca, Jon R. Gardner; m. David L. Allison, May 8, 1998. BA in Speech, Heidelberg Coll., Tiffin, Ohio, 1958. Receptionist Buckeye Union Ins. Co., Akron, Ohio, 1966-67; adjuster Liberty Mut. Ins. Co., Akron, 1967-69; claims liaison Ostrov Agy., Akron, 1969-70; underwriter Clark Agy., Wadsworth, 1971-72; adjuster Celina Group, Wadsworth, 1972-73, Nationwide, Canton, Ohio, 1973-77; asst. claim mgr. Motorist Mut. Ins. Co., Akron, 1977-87; claim rep. Ohio Casualty Ins. Co., San Diego, 1987-88; claims adminstr. Riser Foods, Inc. Risk Mgmt., Bedford Heights, Ohio, 1989-97; claims specialist Motorists Ins. Co., Uniontown, Ohio, 1998-2000; ret. Mem. Ohio Hist. Soc., Friends of Gettysburg. Mem.: DAR (Cuyahoga Portage chpt.), Akron Claims Assn. (pres. 1985), Ohio State Claims Assn., Civil War Preservation Trust. Avocations: civil war history, genealogical research, reading, painting.

ALLISON, DONNA M. (DONNA MAUGHAN), critical care nurse; b. Doylestown, Pa., Apr. 20, 1965; d. James H. and Elsie A. (Haubeck) Maughan; m. Scott D. Allison, July 21, 1990; children: Heather M., Scott D. Jr. BSN cum laude, U. Pa., 1987. Staff nurse pediatric ICU A. I. duPont Inst., Wilmington, Del.; staff nurse neo-natal ICU Hosp. of U. of Pa., Phila.; staff nurse Children's Seashore House, Phila.; staff nurse adult ICU/trauma unit Brandywine Hosp., Caln, Pa.; nurse neonatal ICU Riddle Hosp., Pa., Chester County Hosp., Pa. Mem. Nat. Assn. Neo Natal Nurses.

ALLISON, DWIGHT LEONARD, JR., investor; b. Boston, Oct. 27, 1929; s. Dwight Leonard and Stella (DeGrasse) A.; m. Lyona G. Strohacker, June 19, 1954; children: Dwight Leonard III, Barbara Lynn, Laurie. AB, Dartmouth Coll., 1951, MBA, 1952; LLB, Harvard U., 1956; DCS (hon.), Suffolk U., 1989. Bar: Mass. 1956. Practiced in, Boston, 1956-66; assoc. Goodwin, Procter & Hoar, 1956-64, ptnr., 1965-66; v.p., dir. Gardner Assocs., Inc., Boston, 1966-68; chmn. fin. com. C.H. Sprague & Son Co., 1968-69; chmn. bd. Sprague Assoc., Inc., Boston, 1969-71; gen. ptnr. Sprague & Co., 1971-80; pvt. investor, 1973-77; pres., chief exec. officer Boston Co., 1977-81, chmn. bd., 1981-83, vice chmn., 1983-86; pvt. investor, 1986—. 1st lt. USAF, 1952—53. Office: 4015 Shelldrake Ln Boynton Beach FL 33436-5241 Home (Summer): PO Box 430 Melvin Village NH 03850-0430

ALLISON, ERIC WILLIAM, management consultant, historic preservationist; b. Rockville Centre, N.Y., Nov. 19, 1947; s. William A. and Lila E. A.; m. Mary Ann Burnet, July 17, 1971. BA, Shimer Coll., 1971; MS in City and Regional Planning, Pratt Inst., 1992; MPhil, Columbia U., 1994. Pres. The Historic Dists. Coun., N.Y.C., 1990-2000; prin. The Allison Group, Bklyn., 1980—. Vis. asst. prof. Pratt Inst., Bklyn. N.Y., 1996—, coord. hist. preservation program, 2002--. Author: The Raiders of Wall Street, 1986, Managing Up, Managing Down, 1984, Through the Valley of Death, 1983; asst. editor: The Encyclopedia of New York City, 1995. Vice chmn. The N.Y. Preservation Archives Project, N.Y.C., 1997—; steering com. The Neighborhood Preservation Ctr., N.Y.C., 1998—. Named Centennial Historian of N.Y.C., 1998. Fellow Inst. for Urban Design; mem. Salzburg Conf. on Planning and Urban Devel. Office: The Allison Group 152 Lafayette Ave Brooklyn NY 11238 E-mail: ewa@allisongroup.com.

ALLISON, FRED, JR., physician, educator; b. Abingdon, Va., Sept. 8, 1922; s. Fred and Elizabeth Harriet (Kelly) A.; m. Clara Knox, Oct. 14, 1949; children: Rebecca Allison Parsley, Martha Allison Brown, Fred III, Robert Gardiner. BS, Ala. Poly. Inst., 1944; MD, Vanderbilt U., 1946. Diplomate: Am. Bd. Internal Medicine. Intern Vanderbilt Hosp., Nashville, 1946-47; resident Peter Bent Brigham Hosp., Boston, 1949-50; practice medicine specializing in internal medicine, 1946—; asst. prof. medicine Washington U., St. Louis, 1955; prof. medicine, head infectious disease dept. U. Miss., Jackson, 1955-68; vis. scientist Rockefeller U., N.Y.C., 1966-67; Edgar Hull prof. medicine, head dept. medicine La. State U., New Orleans, 1968-87; head La. State U. div. Charity Hosp., 1968-87; prof. medicine emeritus La. State U., 1987—; prof. medicine Vanderbilt U., Nashville, 1987-96, prof. medicine emeritus, 1996—, med. cons. Zerfoss Student Health Svc., 1996-99; physician-in-chief Met. Nashville Gen. Hosp., 1987-93; chief, divsn. gen. internal medicine Vanderbilt U., 1993-96. Bd. dirs. La. State U. Health Network, 1995—01; bd. trustees Hosp. Authority of Metro. Nashville and Davidson County, 1999—. With U.S. Army, 1943-46, 47-49. Home: 418 Fairfax Ave Nashville TN 37212-4009

ALLISON, GLORIETTA TRAVIS, vocal educator, soprano; b. Big Spring, Tex., July 8, 1932; d. Arthur Edwin Travis and Emma Jewel York; m. Grady Ned Allison, June 2, 1950; children: Carroll Edwin, Melissa Louise Allison Sherman. BRE, Southwestern Bapt. Theol. Sem., Ft. Worth, Tex., 1954. Vocal instr., Grand Falls, Tex., 1954—55, Munday, Tex., 1957—59, Baytown, Tex., 1959—66; performing artist, soprano, 1954—66, Houston, 1966—73, N.Y.C., 1973—92; vocal instr., performing artist Grand Junction, Colo., 1994—2001, Alachua, Fla., 2001—. Soloist Aims Orch., Graz, Austria, 1980; prin. role Salzburg Music Festival, Austria, 1980; soloist Beethoven Ninth Flint Symphony, Mich., 1981. Mem.: Gainesville Music Tchrs. Assn., Fla. Music Tchrs. Assn., Nat. Assn. Tchrs. Singing. Democrat. Unitarian Universalist. Avocations: gardening, reading, walking, bicycling, swimming.

ALLISON, GRAHAM TILLETT, JR., federal government official; b. Charlotte, N.C., Mar. 23, 1940; s. Graham Tillett and Virginia (Wright) A.; m. Elisabeth Kovacs Smith, Aug. 23, 1968. AB, Harvard U., 1962, PhD, 1968; BA, MA, Hertford Coll., Oxford (Eng.) U., 1964. Asst. prof. John F. Kennedy Sch. Govt., Harvard U., Cambridge, Mass., 1968-70, assoc. prof., 1970-72, prof., 1972—, assoc. dean, 1975-77, dean, 1977-89, Douglas Dillon prof. govt., 1989—; spl. adviser to Sec. of Def., 1985-87; dir. Project on Strengthening Dem. Instns., 1990-93; asst. sec. of def. for policy and plans U.S. Dept. Def., Washington, 1993—. Fellow Ctr. for Advanced Studies, Stanford, Palo Alto, Calif., 1973-74; mem. Sec. Def.'s Policy Bd., 1985—; cons. Rand Corp., U.S. Dept. Def., others; mem. numerous NAS panels; mem. Trilateral Commn., 1974-84, Coun. on Fgn. Rels.; mem. Fgn. Affairs Task Force Dem. Adv. Com., 1974-00, mem. vis. com. on fgn. policy studies Brookings Instn., 1972-77. Author: Essence of Decision, 1971, Remaking Foreign Policy: The Organizational Connection, 1976, Sharing International Responsibility Among the Trilateral Countries, 1983; co-author: (with Carnesale and Nye) Hawks, Doves and Owls: An Agenda for Avoiding Nuclear War, 1985, Fateful Visions: Avoiding Nuclear Catastrophe, 1988, (with W. Ury) Windows of Opportunity: From Cold War to Peaceful Competition, 1989, (with Grigory Yavlinsky) Window of Opportunity: The Grand Bargain for Democracy in the Soviet Union, 1991, (with Greg Treverton) Rethinking America's Security, 1992, (with Konstantin Sarkisov and Hiroshi Kimura) Beyond the Cold War to Trilateral Cooperation in the Asia-Pacific Region, 1992; contbr. articles to profl. jours. Democrat. Home: 69 Pinehurst Rd Belmont MA 02478-1502 Office: US Dept of Defense Asst Sec for Policy & Plans The Pentagon Rm Arlington VA 22205

ALLISON, HERBERT MONROE, JR., investment firm executive; b. Pitts., Aug. 24, 1943; s. Herbert M. Sr. and Mary B. (Boardman) A.; m. Simin N. Nazemi, May 9, 1974; children: John, Andrew. BA, Yale U., 1965; MBA, Stanford U., 1971. With Merrill Lynch & Co., Inc., N.Y.C., Paris, London and Tehran, Iran, 1971-78, asst. to pres. N.Y.C., 1978-80, mgr. market planning, 1980-83, treas., 1983-86, sr. v.p., dir. human resources, from 1986, CFO, pres., COO until 1999; pres., CEO AllLearn.org; chmn., pres., CEO TIAA-CREF, 2002—. Bd. dirs. N.Y. Infirmary-Beekman Downtown Hosp., 1986. With USN, 1965-69, Vietnam. Mem. Wall Street Personnel Mgmt. Assn. Office: TIAA-CREF 730 Third Ave New York NY 10017*

ALLISON, JAMES CLAYBROOKE, II, broadcasting executive; b. Washington, Ky., May 26, 1942; s. James Claybrooke and Mary Frances (Orme) A.; m. Rosa Lee Parr, Aug. 29, 1965; children: Frances Michelle, James Claybrooke III. BA in Radio-TV, U. Ky., 1964. Announcer Sta. WVLK, Lexington, Ky., 1962-64; news dir. Sta. WCMI, Ashland, 1964; news reporter Sta. WLAP, Lexington, 1965, announcer, copywriter, 1966-68, dir. ops., 1967, asst. gen. mgr., 1968-70, gen. mgr., 1970-86; news dir. Sta. WLEX-TV, Lexington, 1987-92, mgr. sta. rels., 1992—2001; dir. mktg. and comms. Georgetown (Ky.) Coll., 2001—. V.p. Ky. chpt. Leukemia Soc., 1977-84, nat. trustee; bd. dirs. Big Bros./Big Sisters, Lexington, 1979-87, Central Ky. Youth Orch. Inc., United Way of Blue Grass, 1986-88; bd. dirs. Blue Grass coun. Boy Scouts Am., 1997—, exec. bd. 1997—. Mem. Sales and Mktg. Execs. Lexington (bd. dirs. 1978-85), Ky. Assn. Broadcasters (bd. dirs. 1978-82, Ky. Mike award 1986), Ky. Broadcasters Assn. (TV dir. 1987-89, pres. 1991), Radio-TV News Dirs. Assn., Lexington Advt. Club (pres. 1980-81) adv. bd. ret. sr. vol. program), Lafayette Club, Lexington Sports Club, Rotary (bd. dirs. 1988-89). Democrat. Avocations: tennis, photography, personal computers, fitness. Home: 3528 Colt Neck Ln Lexington KY 40502-3060 Office: 400 E College St Georgetown KY 40324 E-mail: jim_allison@georgetowncollege.edu.

ALLISON, JAMES PURNEY, lawyer; b. Paris, Tex., Jan. 16, 1947; s. Ardell and Billie Louise (Parker) A. BS, East Tex. State U., 1967, MS, 1968; JD, U. Tex., 1971. Bar: Tex., U.S. Dist. Ct., U.S. Ct. Appeals (5th and 11th cir.), U.S. Supreme Ct. County atty. Delta County, Cooper, Tex., 1972-79; asst. atty. gen. Atty. Gen., Austin, Tex., 1979-83; ptnr. Allison, Bass & Assocs., Austin, Tex., 1983—. Gen. counsel County Judges & Commrs. Assn. Tex., Austin, 1983—. Bd. dirs. Tex. Low-Level Radio-active Waste Disposal Authority, Austin, 1985-91; mem. Indigent Health Adv. Com., Tex. Dept. Human Resources, Austin, 1987-94. Mem. Tex. Assn. Counties (hon. life). Avocations: golf, water skiing. Office: Allison Bass & Assocs 402 W 12th St Austin TX 78701-1645 E-mail: j.allison@allison-bass.com.

ALLISON, JANE SHAWVER, medical school administrator, management consultant; b. San Angelo, Tex., Dec. 29, 1938; d. Floyd McKinzie and Bertha J. (Hicks) Shawver; m. Cecil Wayne Allison, June 22, 1957; children: Jana Lea Jones, David Wayne, Don McKinzie. Student, U. Denver, 1954, Northwestern U., 1955, Tex. Tech U., 1956-57, Midwestern U., Wichita Falls, Tex., 1958. Continuity writer Sta. KFDX-TV, Wichita Falls, 1957-58; sec. Wichita Falls Symphony, 1968-70; adminstrv. asst. Coll. of Bus. Tex. Tech U., Lubbock, 1971-74; coord. programs dept. family medicine Tex. Tech U. Health Sci. Ctr., 1974-77, adminstr. dept. family medicine, 1978-87, clin. adminstrv. dir. dept. family medicine, 1987—, asst. dir. clinic adminstrn. primary care, 1999—. Vol. faculty grad. program in health orgn. mgmt. Coll. Bus. Adminstrn., 1993—, chmn. clin. adminstrs., 1994-95, 2000-01; cons. Family Practice Residency, Amarillo, Tex., 1984, Temple, Tex., 1984-85; mem. external rev. team dept. family medicine Sch. Medicine, U. Md., Balt., 2000. Bd. dirs. Lubbock Symphony Orch., Inc., 1976-94, mem. nominating com., 1986, exec. com., 1987-88, v.p., 1988-89; bd. dirs. Helen A. Hodges Charitable Trust, Lubbock, 1983-94; mem. Tex. Tech U. Coll. Bus. Adminstrn. Lubbock Council, 1988—. Recipient Superior Achievement award Tex. Tech U. Health Ctr., 1987, HSC award of Excellence Tex. Tech. U. Health Scis. Ctr., 1987, HSC Pres.'s Quality Svc. award, 1997; honoree 75th Birthday Celebration, Cabrock Council Girl Scouts USA. Mem. Med. Group Mgmt. Assn., Acad. Practice Assembly, Am. Coll. Med. Practice Execs. (bd. cert.), Assn. Family Practice Adminstrs. (bd. dirs. 1983, 85, 87, 88, 94, 95, charter pres. 1984, chmn. steering com. 1983, chmn. 10th ann. celebration 1994, program co-chmn. and co-v.p., Jane S. Allison Ednl. Series Adminstrv. Issues established in her honor). Clubs: Soroptimist Internat. (pres. 1986-87, regional parliamentarian 1986-88, regional laws and resolutions chmn. 1988-90). Mem. Christian Ch. (Disciples Of Christ). Office: Tex Tech U Health Sci Ctr Dept Family Medicine 3601 4th St Stop 8143 Lubbock TX 79430-8143

ALLISON, JASON, hockey player; b. North York, Ont., Can., May 29, 1975; m. Christine Allison. Center Washington Capitals, 1993, Boston Bruins, 1996—2001, L.A. Kings, 2001—. Office: LA Kings Staples Ctr 1111 S Figueroa St Los Angeles CA 90015

ALLISON, JOAN KELLY, music educator, pianist; b. Denison, Iowa, Jan. 25, 1935; d. Ivan Martin and Esther Cecelia (Newborg) K.; m. Guy Hendrick Allison, July 25, 1954 (div. Apr. 1973); children: David, Dana, Douglas, Diane. MusB, St. Louis Inst. of Music, 1955; MusM, So. Meth. U., 1976. Korrepetitor

Corpus Christi (Tex.) Symphony, 1963-85; staff pianist Am. Inst. Mus. Studies, Graz, Austria, 1974-89; prof. Del Mar Coll., Corpus Christi, 1976—2002. Adj. prof. Del Mar Coll., 1959-75, Corpus Christi State U., 1978-93, Tex. A&M U., Corpus Christi, 1993—; program dir. Corpus Christi Chamber Music Soc., 1986—; piano chmn. Corpus Christi Young Artists' Competition, 1987—; chmn. Del Mar Coll. Student Programs Com., 1986-88, 91-92, 94-95, 2001-02; chmn. radio com., S.Tex. Pub. Broadcasting Svc., Corpus Christi, 1987-88; asst. mus. dir. Little Theater, Corpus Christi, 1970-74; judge, Houston Symphony Auditions, 1988, S.C. Young Artist Competition, Columbia, 1990; freelance accompanist, 1955—, adjudicator, 1960—; v.p. united fac., Del Mar Coll., 1986-88; pianist with Del Mar Trio, 1965-95, Young Audiences, Inc., 1975-83; recital tours in U.S., Mex., Austria, 1954-88. Piano soloist, St. Louis Symphony, 1956, 57, Bach Festival Orch., St. Louis, 1955, Corpus Christi Symphony; recipient Artist Presentation award, Artist Presentation Soc., St. Louis, 1956; contbr. articles to profl. jours., including Internat. Piano Quar. Co-chmn. Mayor's Com. on Recycling, Corpus Christi, 1989-91; bd. dirs. Corpus Christi Symphony; adv. bd. Corpus Christi Concert Ballet; mem. steering com. cultural devel. plan City of Corpus Christi, 1995-96. Recipient Women in Careers award YWCA, 1985. Mem. Music Tchrs. Nat. Assn., Tex. Music Tchrs. Assn., Corpus Christi Music Tchrs. Assn., Liszt Soc. (contbr. to jour.) Avocations: foreign travel, water-skiing, hiking, acting in community theatre. Home: 4709 Curtis Clark Dr Corpus Christi TX 78411-4801 E-mail: Jallison@the-i.net.

ALLISON, JOHN ANDREW, IV, bank executive; b. Charlotte, N.C., Aug. 14, 1948; s. John Andrew III and Anne Allison; m. Elizabeth Mc Donald, Aug. 19, 1973; children: Eric, William, Sarah. BBA, U. N.C., 1971; M in Mgmt., Duke U., 1974; grad. Stonier Sch. Banking, Rutgers U., 1981. Chmn., CEO BB&T Corp.; mgr. fin. analysis Br. Banking & Trust Co., Wilson, N.C., 1971-72, mgr. loan officer devel. program, 1972-73, regional loan adminstr., 1973-80, mgr. bus. loan adminstrn., 1980-81, mgr. banking div. (now Br. Banking Group), 1981—, pres., 1987—, also bd. dirs.; vice chmn. BB&T Fin. Corp., Wilson, 1987—; chmn., CEO So. Nat. Corp., Winston-Salem, N.C., 1996—, BB&T & Branch Banking & Trust Co., Winston-Salem, NC. Bd. dirs., chmn. capital campaign Children's Svcs. Ea. N.C., Greenville, 1985—; bd. dirs. Diversified Opportunities, Inc., Wilson, 1980-87; mem. exec. com. state fin. com. Com. to Reelect Gov. Martin, Raleigh, N.C., 1988; mem. N.C. bus. adv. bd. Fuqua Sch. Bus., Duke U.; bd. dirs. Med. Found. East Carolina U., Brody Found.; mem. communications, agy. and pub. rels. subcom. United Way Wilson County, Inc., 1989—; mem. So. Growth Policies Bd. Mem. Am. Bankers Assn., N.C. Bankers Assn., Robert Morris Assocs. (past bd. dirs. Carolinas-Va. chpt.), N.C. Citizens for Bus. and Industry, Phi Beta Kappa. Office: BB&T Corp 200 W 2nd St Winston Salem NC 27101-4019

ALLISON, JOHN LANGSDALE, naval architect, marine engineer; b. Sutton Coldfield, Eng., Aug. 10, 1930; came to U.S., 1966; s. Herbert Mandall and Eva May (Langsdale) A.; m. Eunice Quick, Apr. 7, 1956; children; Christopher John, Nigel Mark, Katherine Sarah. BSc in Engring., U. Nottingham, Eng., 1954; postgrad., U. Nottingham; aero. engring. cert., Royal Naval Engring. Coll., Plymouth, Eng., 1955; profl. mgmt. cert., U. Aston, Birmingham, Eng., 1959. Chartered engr., U.K. Sr. rsch. engr. Birmingham Small Arms Co./Daimler Group Rsch., 1956-58; lectr. in engring. Bromsgrove Coll. of Further Edn., Worcestshire, Eng., 1958-66; sr. rsch. engr. Bell Aerospace Textron, Buffalo, 1966-71; chief engr. ship tech. Textron Marine Sys. Inc. divsn. Bell Aerospace Textron, New Orleans, 1971-87; chief engr. Band, Lavis & Assocs., Inc., Severna Park, Md., 1987—2002, cons., 2002— . Student advisor George Washington U., Washington, 1991-92; cons. Outboard Motor Corp., Waukegan, Ill., 1994-97; presenter, cons. Inst. for Maritime Dynamics and Meml. U., St. Johns, Nfld., Can., 1995; cons. Kvaerner Mandal (Norway) A.S., 1995-99, UMOE, Mandal, Norway, 1999—; advisor H.S. students Hi-Frontiers Ann. Competition. Author numerous tech. articles, conf. procs., papers in field. Sub-lt. Royal Navy, 1954-56. Recipient Maritech award U.S. Govt./Advanced Rsch. Projects Agy., 1995. Fellow Inst. Mech. Engrs., Royal Instn. Naval Architects; mem. Am. Soc. Naval Engrs., Soc. Naval Architects and Marine Engrs. (Vice Adm. Cochrane award 1993), Navy League, U.S. Naval Inst. Republican. Presbyterian. Achievements include patents for waterjet steering and reversal for large ships, and design of heavy lift air cushion vehicle. Home: 4119 Hummingbird Ct Lebanon OH 45036 Office: Band Lavis & Assoc Inc 900 Ritchie Hwy Severna Park MD 21146-4142 Business E-Mail: david.lavis@cdicorp.com. E-mail: jla_eqa@juno.com.

ALLISON, JOHN MCCOMB, retired aeronautical engineer; b. Guthrie, Okla., Nov. 27, 1901; s. John McComb and Mary Ann (Miller) A.; m. Dorothy Louise Olson, Nov. 15, 1931; children: John, Mary Ann, David. BSME, U. Ka., 1928. Design staff Stinson Tri-Motor Airliner, 1928-29; aeronautical engr. Akron, Macon rigid airships & nonrigids U.S. Naval Air Sta., Lakehurst, N.J., 1929-33; rsch. engr. Nat. Adv. Com. for Aeronautics, Langley Field, Va., 1933—38; flight test engr. USN Test Sta., Anacostia, 1938-39; evaluator flight test performance of new Navy aircraft Anacostia, Washington, 1938-39; Bur. Aeronautics rep. various aircraft mfg. plants USNR, 1939-46; head new Navy aircraft and guided missiles test dept. U.S. Naval Air Missile Test Ctr., Pt. Mugu, Calif., 1946-50; engr. missile devel. Bur. Ordnance, Washington, 1950-57; head specifications Goodyear Aircraft Corp., Akron, 1957-59; 69proposal engr., guided missiles Rockwell Internat. (now Boeing Aircraft), Columbus, Ohio, 1959; ret., 1969. Cons. light airplane constrn. Allison Airplane Co., North Miami, Fla., 1977-85; founder Langley Fed. Credit Union, 1936. Contbr. articles to profl. jours. Del. Nat. Rep. Planning Com., Washington, 1992. Capt. USN, 1939-46. Fellow AIAA (assoc.), Ox-5 Club. Immanuel Lutheran. Achievements include patents for disclosure for a retractable hydrofoil at the normal step position of a flying boat to improve take-off; private pilot, 1931-50. E-mail: j.allison55@aol.com.

ALLISON, JOHN ROBERT, lawyer, educator, author; b. Waco, Tex., Apr. 6, 1948; s. Lloyd Burton and Mary LaBertha (Fulps) Allison; m. Margo Lu Armstrong, Dec. 22, 1971; children: Sarah Marie, Jill Elaine, Eric Forrest. Student, Tex. A&M U., 1966—69; JD, Baylor U., 1972. Bar: Tex. 1972. Asst. prof. U. Tex., Austin, 1972—77; assoc. prof., 1977—81; prof., 1981—83; prof. in bus. adminstrn. Mary John and Ralph Spence Centennial, 1983—; dir. Ctr. Legal and Regulatory Studies, 1987—; staff editor Am. Bus. Law Jour., Austin, 1974—78; co-editor, 1978—79; editor articles, 1979—81; mng. editor, 1981—83; editor in chief, 1983—85; adv. editor, 1985—; editor in chief Baylor Law Rev., 1971—72. Author: (novels) Bus. Law: Text and Cases, 1978, Bus. Law: Alt. Edit., 1979, 1992, Bus. Law: Text and Cases, 1994, The Legal Environment of Bus., 1984, 1993, Fundamentals of Bus. Law, 1984; contbr. articles. Named Outstanding Prof. Grad. Sch. Bus., U. Tex., 1984; recipient Best Article award Am. Bus. Law Jour., 1977, Holmes/Cardozo award, 1985, Faculty Excellence award, 1987. Mem.: Acad. Legal Studies in Bus. (mem., exec. com. 1983—84), Dispute Resolution Ctr. Austin/Travis County (bd. dir. 1989—90), Am. Diabetes Assn. (mem. 1981—), Assn. for Retarded Citizens (mem. and contbr. 1974—). Democrat. Home: 8616 Cameron Loop Austin TX 78745-7916 Office: U Tex Grad Sch Bus Mgmt Sci Info Systems Dept Austin TX 78712

ALLISON, JOHN ROBERT, lawyer; b. San Antonio, Feb. 9, 1945; s. Lyle (stepfather) and Beatrice (Kaliner) Forehand; m. Rebecca M. Picard; 1 child, Katharine. BS, Stanford U., 1966; JD, U. Wash., 1969. Bar: Wash. 1969, D.C. 1973, Minn. 1994, U.S. Supreme Ct. 1973. Assoc. Garvey, Schubert & Barer, Seattle, 1969-73; ptnr., 1973-86; prin. Betts, Patterson & Mines, P.S., 1986-94; sr. counsel Minn. Mining & Mfg. Co., 1994-2000, asst. gen. counsel, 2000—. Bd. dirs. So. Minn. Regional Legal Svcs., Jewish Family Svc., St. Paul, Minn., v.p.; lectr. bus. law Seattle U., 1970, U. Wash., 1970-73; judge pro tem, King County Superior Ct., 1983-94. Mem. ABA (vice chmn. toxic and hazardous substances and environ. law com. 1986-91, chair elect 1991-92, chair 1992-93), Minn. Bar Assn., Seattle-King County Bar Assn. (chmn. jud. evaln. polling com. 1982-83), Wash. State Bar Assn. (bd. bar examiners 1984-94), D.C. Bar Assn., Nat. Inst. Pollution Liability (co-chmn. 1988), Order of the Coif. Office: Minn Mining & Mfg Co 3 M Ctr Saint Paul MN 55144-1000 E-mail: jrallison@mmm.com.

ALLISON, JONATHAN, retired lawyer; b. Washington, Pa., Apr. 17, 1916; s. Albert Johnson and Etta (Tucker) A. BS, Washington and Jefferson Coll., 1937; JD, U. Pa., 1940; postgrad., Harvard Grad. Bus. Adminstrn., 1940-41. Bar: Pa. 1942. Pvt. practice, Washington, 1946-95; ret., 1995. Maj. AUS, 1941-46. Mem. ABA, Pa. Bar Assn., Washington County Bar Assn., Duquesne Club (Pitts.), Southpointe Golf Club, St. Clair Country Club (Upper St. Clair). Republican. Presbyterian. Home: 20 Fairmont Ave Washington PA 15301-3509 Office: 438 Washington Trust Bldg Washington PA 15301

ALLISON, LAIRD BURL, business educator; b. St. Marys, W.Va., Nov. 7, 1917; s. Joseph Alexander and Opal Marie (Robinson) A.; m. Katherine Louise Hunt, Nov. 25, 1943 (div. 1947); 1 child: William Lee; m. Genevieve Nora Elmore, Feb. 1, 1957 (dec. July 1994). BS in Personnel and Indsl. Relations magna cum laude, U. So. Calif., 1956; MBA, UCLA, 1958. Chief petty officer USN, 1936-51, PTO; asst. prof. to prof. mgmt. Calif. State U., L.A., 1956-83; asst. dean Calif. State U. Sch. Bus. and Econs., L.A., 1971-72, assoc. dean, 1973-83, emeritus prof. mgmt., 1983—. Vis. asst. prof. mgmt. Calif. State U., Fullerton, 1970. Co-authored the Bachelors degree program in mgmt. sci. at Calif. State U., 1963. Mem. U.S. Naval Inst., Navy League U.S. Ford Found. fellow, 1960. Mem. Acad. Mgmt., Inst. Mgmt. Sci., Western Econs. Assn. Internat., World Future Soc., Am. Acad. Polit. Social Sci., Calif. State U. Assn. Emeriti Profs., Calif. State U. L.A. Emeriti Assn. (program v.p. 1986-87, v.p. adminstrn. 1987-88, pres. 1988-89, exec. com. 1990-91, treas. 1991—), Am. Assn. Individual Investors, Am. Assn. Ret. Persons, Ret. Pub. Employees Assn. Calif. (chpt. sec. 1984-88, v.p. 1989, pres. 1990-92), Am. Legion, Phi Kappa Phi, Beta Gamma Sigma, Alpha Kappa Psi. Avocations: history, travel, photography, hiking. Home: 2176 E Bellbrook St Covina CA 91724-2346 Office: Calif State U Dept Mgmt 5151 State University Dr Los Angeles CA 90032-4226

ALLISON, MARY ANN, consulting company executive, author, speaker; b. Sept. 27, 1949; d. David S. and Mary (McNaughton) Burnet; m. Eric William Allison, July 17, 1971. BA, Shimer Coll., 1971; MBA, L.I. U., 1977; postgrad., NYU. Various positions Avis Rent-a-Car, Garden City, N.Y., 1971-80; v.p. Citicorp, N.Y.C., 1980-96; pres. Human Ordered Tech. LLC., 1996-97; chmn., chief cybernetics officer The Allison Group, LLC, 1996—; chmn. Allison-LoBue Group, LLC, 1999-2000. Co-author: Through the Valley of Death, 1983, Managing Up, Managing Down, 1984, The Complexity Advantage: How the Science of Complexity Can Help Your Business Achieve Peak Performance, 1999; contbr. articles to profl. publs. and nat. mags. Bd. advisors Human Issues in Mgmt., Inclusion Interactive, Inc., Metacourse, Inc. Mem. Media Ecology Assn. (bd. dirs.), OD Network, Authors Guild. Episcopalian. Office: The Allison Group 152 Lafayette Ave Brooklyn NY 11238-1006 E-mail: maa@allisongroup.com.

ALLISON, MICHAEL DAVID, space scientist, astronomy educator; b. Salem, Ill., Oct. 11, 1951; s. James M. and Claudine K. A.; m. Siri Wannamaker, Feb. 4, 1984; children: Hilary Kirstyn, Christopher Caleb. AB in Physics and English, Wittenberg U., 1973; SM in Physics, U. Chgo., 1976; PhD in Space Physics and Astronomy, Rice U., 1982. Resident rsch. assoc. Nat. Rsch. Coun. NASA/Goddard Inst for Space Studies, N.Y.C., 1981-83, space scientist, 1984—. Guest lectr. Am. Mus. Natural History, Hayden Planetarium, N.Y.C., 1984-88, 94—; mem. joint sci. working group for the NASA/ESA assessment study of the Cassini mission to Saturn and Titan, 1984-89; adj. prof. astronomy Columbia U., N.Y.C.- 1987—; co-investigator Huygens, Titan Doppler Wind Expt., U. Bonn., Germany, 1990—, team mem. Cassini Radar investigation, NASA, 2000—; rsch. assoc. Am. Mus. Dept. Astronomy, 1997-99. Co-editor: (conf. proceedings) The Jovian Atmospheres, 1986; contbr. articles to profl. jours. including Science, Icarus, Jour. of Atmospheric Scis., Geophys. Rsch. Letters, Planetary and Space Sci. Participating scientist Mars Observer and Surveyor '98 Missions, NASA, 1992-99. Mem. Am. Astron. Soc. (divsn. for planetary scis.), Am. Meteorol. Soc. Achievements include research in planetary atmospheric dynamics and meteorology, application of potential vorticity homogenization to planetary zonal circulation studies, first identification of Saturn's polar hexagon as a planetary Rossby wave, inference of a probable super-solar abundance of water on Jupiter based on the diagnostic analysis of equatorial waves. Home: 81 Teller Ave Beacon NY 12508-3067 Office: NASA/Goddard Inst Space Studies 2880 Broadway New York NY 10025-7848 E-mail: mallison@giss.nasa.gov.

ALLISON, PAUL DAVID, sociologist, educator, sociologist, consultant; b. Jefferson City, Mo., Oct. 28, 1948; s. Paul V. and Angeline L. Allison; m. Linda S. Prossack, May 11, 1999; children: Daniel A. Trisdorfer, Joshua T. AB, St. Louis U., 1970; PhD, U. Wis., 1975. Lectr. SUNY, Stony Brook, 1975—76; asst. to assoc. prof. Cornell U., Ithaca, NY, 1976—81; assoc. prof. U. Pa., Phila., 1981—87, prof. sociology, 1987—. Author: (book) Missing Data, Survival Analysis Using the SAS System, Event History Analysis. Fellow, J.S. Guggenheim Meml. Found., 1986—87. Mem.: Sociol. Rsch. Assn, Am. Statis. Assn., Am. Sociol. Assn. (Lazarsfeld Meml. award for Disting. Contributions to Sociol. Methodology Sect. on Methodology 2001). Office: Univ Pa - Sociology 3718 Locust Walk Philadelphia PA 19104-6299 E-mail: allison@ssc.upenn.edu.

ALLISON, RALPH BREWSTER, psychiatrist; b. Manila, May 13, 1931; s. W. Theodore and Metta L. (Brewster) A.; m. Mary Burden, Jan. 1, 1957 (div. 1997); children: Ann Allison-Marsh, Amy Allison Maiman, Jill Aguiar, John Allison. BA, Occidental Coll., L.A., 1952; MD, UCLA, 1956. Staff psychiatrist Santa Clara County Mental Health Svcs., Palo Alto, Calif., 1962-63; program chief Santa Cruz County Mental Health Svcs., Santa Cruz, Calif., 1964-67; pvt. practice Palo Alto & Santa Cruz, 1962-78; staff psychiatrist Yolo County Mental Health Svcs., Broderick, Calif., 1978-81; forensic psychiatrist Davis, Calif., 1978-81; sr. psychiatrist Calif. Men's Colony, San Luis Obispo, Calif., 1981-93, ret. annuitant psychiatrist, 1994-95. Sec. UAPD, Oakland, Calif., 1988-93; pres. SEPA, Oakland, 1990-93; mem. Mental Health adv. bd., Santa Cruz, 1964-67. Co-author: Minds in Many Pieces, 1980; contbr. articles to profl. jours. Founder Suicide Prevention Svcs., Santa Cruz, 1968-74. Capt. USAF, 1957-59. Recipient Cornelia B. Wilbur award ISSD, Skokie, Ill., 1995. Fellow Am. Psychiat. Assn. (life); mem. Am. Anthrop. Assn., Internat. Soc. for Study Dissociation (charter). Avocations: writing, personel computers. Home: 4106 Welsh Way Paso Robles CA 93446-4178 E-mail: ralfalison@tcsn.net.

ALLISON, REBECCA ANNE, cardiologist, writer; b. Greenwood, Miss., Dec. 21, 1946; d. Errol Ward and Mabel Irene (Blackwell) Atkinson. BS, U. Miss., 1968, MD, 1971. Diplomate Am. Bd. Internal Medicine. Intern. Parkland Meml. Hosp., Dallas, 1971-72; res. U. Miss. Med. Ctr., 1972-74, chief res., 1974-75, fellowship (cardiology), 1985-87; physician in internal medicine Physicians and Surgeons Clinic, Amory, Miss., 1975-79, Amory Internal Medicine Clinic, 1980-85; staff cardiologist Vets. Hosp., Jackson, Miss., 1987-89; physician in cardiology Cardiology Group Miss., Jackson, 1989-93, Cigna Healthcare, Phoenix, 1994—; sect. head cardiology CIGNA Med. Group, Phoenix, 1999—. Author: The Real Life Test, 1996; author (column) The Grace and Lace Letter, 1992—. Fellow Am. Coll. Cardiology, Am. Coll. Physicians; mem. N.Am. Soc. Pacing and Electrophysiology, Harry Benjamin Internat. Gender Dysphoria Assn. Mem. United Ch. Of Christ. Avocations: travel, music, internet web site. Home: 10636 N 11th St Phoenix AZ 85020-1180 Office: 755 E Mcdowell Rd Phoenix AZ 85006-2506

ALLISON, RICHARD CLARK, judge; b. N.Y.C., July 10, 1924; s. Albert Fay and Anice (Clark) A.; m. Anne Elizabeth Johnston, Oct. 28, 1950; children: Anne Sidney, William Scott, Richard Clark. BA, U. Va., 1944, LLB, 1948. Bar: N.Y. 1948. Practiced in, N.Y.C., 1948-52, 54-60; with CIA, 1952—54; ptnr. Reid & Priest, 1961-87; mem. Iran-U.S. Claims Tribunal, The Hague, 1988—. Trustee Inst. for Transnat. Arbitration. Lt. (j.g.) USNR, 1945—46. Fellow Am. Bar Found.(life) Southwestern Legal Found.; mem. ABA (chmn. com. Latin Am. Law 1964-68, chmn. Internat. Law Sect. 1977, chmn. Nat. Inst. on Doing Bus. in Far East 1972, chmn. internat. legal exchange program 1981-85), Internat. Bar Assn. (chmn. 1986 Conf., ethics com. 1986-89), Société Internat. des Avocats, Inter-Am. Bar Assn., Am. Arbitration Assn. (internat. panel), Am. Soc. Internat. Law, Coun. on Fgn. Rels., Assn. Bar City N.Y., Raven Soc., SAR, St. Andrew's Soc. N.Y., Manhasset Bay Yacht Club, Phi Beta Kappa, Omicron Delta Kappa, Pi Kappa Alpha, Phi Delta Phi. Republican. Congregationalist. Home: 224 Circle Dr Manhasset NY 11030-1123 Office: c/o Iran-US Claims Tribunal Parkweg 13 2585 JH The Hague Netherlands

ALLISON, ROBERT HARRY, school counselor; b. Hazleton, Pa., Oct. 26, 1952; s. Harry John and Loretta Ida (Henry) A. m. Barbara Joyce Ent, Oct. 28, 1978; 1 child, Diane Amy. BS in Rehab. Edn., Pa. State U., 1974; MS in Counselor Edn., U. Scranton, 1976; supervisory cert., Shippensburg (Pa.) U., 1981; principal's cert., Pa. State U., 1992, cert. in coop. edn., 1999. Work experience coord. Carbon County Area Vocat.-Tech. Sch., Jim Thorpe, Pa., 1974-75; rehab. counselor R.B. Nipon Assn., Phila., 1975-76; career svcs. coord. Sleighton Sch., Lima, Pa., 1976-77; sch. counselor West Perry Sch. Dist., Loysville, Pa., 1977-79; counselor/coord. Alternative Sch. Miffin County Sch. Dist., Lewistown, Pa., 1979-80; elem. counselor Jersey Shore (Pa.) Sch. Dist., 1980-82; mid. sch. counselor, spl. edn. liaison, career edn. coord. Brandywine Heights Sch. Dist., Topton, Pa., 1982-90, mid.-elem. counselor, 1990-93, sch.-to-work transition/elem. counselor, 1994-2000; career counselor, sch.-to-work transition coord., 2000—; regional mgr. Primorica Fin. Svcs., 1985—. Bd. dirs. Weatherly Area Jaycees, 1974-75; asst. dist. commr. Boy Scouts Am., 1977-83, asst. dist. commr. for exploring, 1990-94, dist. com. mem. 1994-96. Mem. Am. Sch. Counselors Assn., Assn. for Career and Tech. Edn., Pa. Coop. Edn. Assn., Pa. Sch. Counselors Assn., Phi Kappa Phi. Lutheran. Home: 104 W Jackson St Fleetwood PA 19522-1706 Office: Brandywine Heights HS PO Box 98 Mertztown PA 19539 E-mail: rha1952@ptdprolos.net., roball@bhasd-k12.pa.us.

ALLISON, ROBERT JAMES, JR., oil and gas company executive; b. Evanston, Ill., Jan. 29, 1939; s. Robert James and Mary Susan (Rohrer) A.; m. Carolyn J. Grother, June 17, 1961; children: Amy Allison Watkins, Ann Allison Stanislaw, Jane BS in Petroleum Engring., Kans. U., 1960. Engring. mgmt. Amoco Prodn. Co., U.S., Trinidad and Iran, 1960-73; v.p. ops. Anadarko Prodn. Co., Ft. Worth and Houston, 1973-76, pres., dir. Houston, 1976-79, pres., CEO, 1979 86; group v.p. Panhandle Eastern Corp., Houston, 1980-86, dir., 1986-93; chmn., CEO Andarko Petroleum Corp., Houston, 1986—2002; chmn., 2002—03; chmn., CEO, pres. Anadarko Petroleum Corp., The Woodlands, 2003—. Bd. dirs. Sam Houston Area Coun. Boy Scouts Am., Houston, 1985—; adv. coun. U. Tex. Engring. Found.; chmn. Spindletop Charities, Houston, Mr. Spindletop, 1991; mem. bd. visitors M.D. Anderson Cancer Ctr. Mem. IPAA, NGSA, Am. Petroleum Inst. (bd. dirs.), All Am. Wildcatters Assn., Tex. Mid-Continent Oil and Gas Assn., Nat. Gas Coun., Soc. Petroleum Engrs., River Oaks Club, Lochinvar Golf Club (pres. 1982-85), Houston Club, Petroleum Club (bd. dirs.), Pine Valley Golf Club, Champions Golf Club. Republican. Presbyterian. Avocations: golf, hunting, flying. Home: 6116 Bermuda Dunes Dr Houston TX 77069-1308 Office: Anadarko Petroleum Corp 1201 Lake Robbins Dr The Woodlands TX 77380*

ALLISON, STEPHEN GALENDER, broadcast executive; b. Springfield, Mo., Dec. 11, 1952; s. Edgbert Allcorn and Naomi Louise (Chamless) A.; m. Linda Lavelle, June 6, 1974 (div. Dec. 1980); children: Julie Ann, Jennifer Erin; m. Tara Rae Foster, Aug. 20, 1986 (div. Aug. 1994); m. Sibel Galinda Pisken, Apr. 6, 2002; 1 child, Fox Stephen. Cert. radio mktg. cons. Radio Advt. Bur. On-air personality Sta. WSBB, New Smyrna, Fla., 1971-72, Sta. WMFJ-AM-FM, Daytona Beach, Fla., 1972-75, Sta. KADI-FM, St. Louis, 1975-76, Sta. KAUM-FM, Houston, 1976-79, Sta. WKYS-FM, Washington, 1979-81; gen mgr. Sta. KSTM-FM, Phoenix, 1981-85; pres. Allison Broadcasting Co., Inc., Phoenix, 1985—, Allison Broadcast Group, Inc., Dallas, Del Mar, Calif., 1987—; owner Stas. KGRX-FM/KIKO, Phoenix, 1986-91, Sta. KDGE-FM, Dallas, 1989-94, WLVX-FM, Gainesville, Fla., 1994-95; mgr. talk/bus./ESPN programming ABC Radio Networks, Dallas, 1996-97; dir. Clear Channel Comms., Tampa, 1997-98; nat. dir. mktg. Metro Networks, Phoenix, 1998-99; sr. exec. analyst George S. May Internat. Co., San Jose, Calif., 1999—2002; with SLGG Cons. LLC, 2002—. Mktg. cons. St. Louis Post-Dispatch, 1975-76, Houston Chronicle, 1976-79, Washington Star, 1980-81; advt. cons. Celebrity Theatre, Phoenix, 1985-86; pres. JFM Branson (Mo.) Inc., 1993—; owner Doc Severinsen Theater. Bd. dirs. Desert-Mt. Foothills Assn., Scottsdale, Ariz., 1981-91, 98—, Alwun House Cultural Ctr., Phoenix, 1982—, Film in Ariz., Phoeniz, 1985-93, Ariz. Commn. on the Arts, Phoenix, 1986-89; active Nat. Rep. Congl. Com., 1988-93, No. Tex. Commn. Mem. Nat. Assn. Broadcasters, Ariz. Broadcasters Assn., Tex. Assn. Broadcasters, Phoenix Active 20-30 Club, Internat. Platform Assn., Las Colinas Sports Club, Pointe Royale Country Club, Preston Trails Country Club, The Heritage Club. Avocations: collecting classic cars, traveling, racquetball, golfing, boating. Home: 7241 Sanderling Ct Carlsbad CA 92009

ALLISON, STEPHEN PHILIP, lawyer; b. L.A., Jan. 4, 1947; s. Philip L. and Catherine (Lawder) A.; m. Margaret Ann Yochem, June 7, 1969; children—Brian Clayton, Todd Lawder. BA, Tex. Christian U., 1969; JD, U. Houston, 1972. Bar: Tex. 1972, U.S. Ct. Appeals (5th cir.) 1977, U.S. Supreme Ct. 1977, U.S. Dist. Ct. (we. dist.) Tex. 1981, U.S. Dist. Ct. (no. dist.) Tex. 1988, U.S. Dist. Ct. (so. dist.) Tex. 1990U.S. Dist. Ct. (ea. dist.) Tex. 2003. Asst. dist. atty. Bexar County, San Antonio, 1973-77; assoc. Dobbins, Harris & Gonzalez, San Antonio, 1977-78, Sawtelle, Goode, Davidson & Troilo, San Antonio, 1978-89; ptnr. Haynes and Boone, 1989—; mcpl. judge City of Terrell Hills, 1987-91; admissions com. Tex. Supreme Ct., 1978-82. Author: Products Liability, Texas Practice Guide, 1985, Accident Investigation and Product Education: Defendant's Perspective, 1985, Obtaining and Presenting Evidence on Geographic Markets, 1987, Nonprice Predation Under Section 2 of the Sherman Act, 1991, Representing Financial Institutions in a Usury Case, 1992, Drafting and Responding to Interrogatories and Requests for Production of Documents, 1995, Document Control and Management in Complex Cases, 1995, Managing Internal Investigation, 2002. Pres., Tex. Christian U.-San Antonio Alumni Club, 1978-83. Mem. Edn. Task Force, Greater San Antonio C. of C., 1991—; bd. advocates Phi Alpha Delta; bd. trustees Alamo Heights Ind. Sch. Dist., 1992—, pres., 1995-96, 2001-03; active Meth. Hosp. Found., 1987-94, Golden Circle, SW Found. Biomedical Rsch., 1993—; mem. vestry St. Mark's Episcopal Ch., 1988-91. Fellow Tex. Bar Found.; mem. ABA, Am. Health Lawyers Assn., Def. Research Inst., State Bar of Tex. (mem. com. PEER 1983-86, mem. com. ct. costs, efficiency and delay 1985-87, Citizens and Law Focused Edn. 1988-91), Tex. Assn. Def. Counsel (pres. def. counsel San Antonio 1998—99), San Antonio Bar Assn. (chmn. legal ethics com. 1992-94), San Antonio Bar Found.(mem. dean's adv. coun., 2000—), Tex. Assn. Sch. Bds. (mem. spl. com. on revenue and funding 1994-95, bd. trustees, 1997-2000), Tex. Christian U. Alumni Assn. (dir. 1979-83), Tex. Christian U. Frog Club (dir. 1992—, Alumni Svc. award 1996), Order of Alamo, Town Club; master Am. Inns of Ct. Republican. Home: 200 Morningside Dr San Antonio TX 78209-4734

ALLISON, STUART ANTHONY, chemistry educator, researcher; b. Kalispell, Mont., Mar. 26, 1951; s. Bruce Allan and Arretta Allison; m. Lenong Wang. BA Chemistry, U. Mont., 1973; MS Phys. Chemistry, U. Calif., Berkeley, 1975; PhD Phys. Chemistry, U. Wash., 1980. Postdoctoral fellow U. Oreg., Eugene, 1980—82, U. Houston, Houston, 1982—84; asst. prof. chemistry Ga. State U., Atlanta, 1984—90, assoc. prof. chemistry, 1990—2000, prof. chemistry, 2000—. Contbr. articles to profl. jours. Recipient Presdl. Young Investigator award, NSF, 1985. Mem.: Am. Biophysical Soc. Roman Catholic. Achievements include development of numerical methods for computing transport properties of complex model systems. Avocations: hiking, coin collecting, stamp collecting. Home: 978 Biltmore Dr Atlanta GA 30329 Office: Ga State U University Pl Atlanta GA 30303 Office Fax: 404-651-1416. Personal E-mail: chesaa@panther.gsu.edu. Business E-Mail: chesaa@panther.gsu.edu.

ALLISON NORMAN E. JR., anthropologist, educator; b. Asheville, N.C., July 24, 1934; s. Norman E. and Willie Stikeleather Allison; m. Judith Willyard, Aug. 17, 1958; children: S Mark Allison, Katherine A. Hober, Heather A. Broom. BA, Toccoa Falls (Ga.) Coll., 1961; MA, Am. U. of Beirut, 1969; PhD, U. of Ga., 1973. Aviation electronics technician USN, Norman, Okla., 1952—57; fgn. missionary Christian & Missionary Alliance, Colo. Springs, Colo., 1962—72; dir. of world missions Toccoa Falls (Ga.) Coll., 1972—; grad. coord. Columbia Internat. U., Toccoa, Ga., 2001—02. Contbr. articles to profl. jours. Pastor Valley Cmty. Ch., Tate City, Ga., 1986—2002. With USN, 1952—57, Alaska, Japan, Okinawa. Mem.: Am. Ethnol. Soc., Am. Soc. of Missiology, Evang. Theol. Soc., Am. Anthrop. Soc., Evang. Missiological Soc. (pres. 2001—). Republican. Avocations: pastoring, pastoring, pastoring. Office: Toccoa Falls College PO Box 800817 Toccoa Falls GA 30598 Office Fax: 706-282-6003. E-mail: nallison@tfc.edu.

ALLITON, VAUGHN, brokerage executive; b. Owosso, Mich., Apr. 16, 1966; s. Marjorie Anne (Jones) Sutliff; life ptnr.. BA in Econs., U. Mich., 1988; MBA in Internat. Fin., Nova U., 1992; postgrad. in tech. mgmt, Pace U., 2001—. Cert. profl. in human resources. Pers. asst. U. Mich., Ann Arbor, 1986-88; pers. generalist Vision-Ease, Ft. Lauderdale, Fla., 1988-89; human resources generalist World Omni Fin. Corp., Deerfield Beach, Fla., 1989-92; cons. IES, Tokyo, 1992; dir. Asia ops. NSU Japan Ltd., 1993-94; mktg. mgr. PTS, Tokyo,

1994-95; adminstrv. mgr. Merrill Lynch Japan, Tokyo, 1995-97, bus. mgr., 1997-98; v.p. Asia project office Merrill Lynch, Hong Kong, 1998-99, v.p. global regions project office, 1999-2000, dir. internat. pvt. client, global expansion project N.Y.C., 2000—01; chief adminstrv. officer Internat. Pvt. Client Tech., N.Y.C., 2002—03, Global Banking Tech., 2003—. Cons. Greater Orlando (Fla.) Auto Action, 1991-92; adv. bd. Born & Born Med. Personnel, West Palm Beach, Fla., 1992-93; dir. Nova U., Tokyo, 1992-94; adj. prof. Lubin Sch. Bus., Pace U., 2003—. Author: (manuals) AIDS Sensitivity Education, 1992, Self-Directed Work Teams, 1992. Office: Merrill Lynch 101 Hudson St 19th Fl Jersey City NJ 07302 E-mail: valliton@nyc.rr.com.

ALLMAN, AVIS ASIYE, artist, poet, Turkish and Islamic culture educator, human rights activist; b. Phila., Dec. 27, 1954; d. William Berthold and Margo (Hutz) A. BFA in Painting, Windham Coll., 1975; MBA in Arts, SUNY, Binghamton, 1978; postgrad., Hunter Coll., 1983, NYU, 1987-88, 91-95; cert., U.S. Peace Inst., 2003. Cert. U.S. Inst. Peace, 2003. Devel. officer The Bklyn. Mus., 1977; program analyst N.Y. State Coun. Arts, N.Y.C., 1977-80, dir. spl. projects, 1980-81; dir. adminstrn. Mus. Broadcasting, N.Y.C., 1981; sr. fin. analyst CBS TV Network, N.Y.C., 1981-82; rsch. cons. Am. Coun. on Arts, N.Y.C., 1983-84; fin. analyst Cmty. Svc. Soc., N.Y.C., 1983-84; pres. Allman Fin. Svcs., Bklyn., 1985—. Artist-in-residence (tiles) Canakkale Ceramics, Istanbul, Turkey, 1991-96, (carpets) Net Holding, Izmir, Turkey, 1989, (painter, poet) Zaman Newspaper, Ankara, Turkey, 1997; rsch. assoc. Georgetown U. Muslim-Christian Understanding, 1998-99. One-woman shows include Mus. Turkish/Islamic Arts, Istanbul, 1987, 90, 92, French Cultural Ctr., Izmir, 1992, Women's Libr., Istanbul, 1996, Mus. Calligraphy, Istanbul, 1996, Gumbo, N.Y.C., 2002, CRR Concert Salon, Istanbul, 2002; exhibited in group shows at Müsiad/IBF Forum, Istanbul, 1997, Altinpark, Ankara, 1997; represented in permanent collections at Vatican, Mus. Turkish/Islamic Arts, Indpls. Mus. Art; author: Road to Democracy, 1997, Religious Freedom in Turkey, 1999, Turkey Is Crying, 1999, Human Rights, Democracy and Islam in Turkey, 2000, Liberal Democracy and Democratic Muslim Movement in Turkey, 2001, Democratization Anatollian Peasants Turkey, 2002, Voices Silence, 2002, Kabba of My Heart, 2002. Sr. Rsch. Fulbright scholar U.S. Info. Agy, 1988-89; vis. scholar NYU, 1991-94; recipient Exhbn. grants U.S. Info. Svc., Ankara, 1987, Greek Consulate, Izmir, Turkey, 1992, Kale Group, Istanbul, 1997, 96, Glaxo Wellcome, Istanbul, 1996, Leeway Found., 2001, Istanbul Met. Municipality, 2002. Democrat. Moslem. Avocations: dancing, praying to god, mediterranean sea, walking. Office: Allman Fin Svcs 20 Henry St Apt 3G Brooklyn NY 11201-1348 Studio: Apt 3G 20 Henry St Brooklyn NY 11201-1348 E-mail: asiyeusa@worldnet.att.net.

ALLMAN, MARGARET ANN LOWRANCE, counseling administrator; b. Carmel, Calif., June 2, 1938; d. Edward Walton and Rhoda Elizabeth (Patton) Lowrance; m. Jackie Howard Hamilton, Dec. 21, 1959 (div. May 1976); children: John Scott Hamilton, David Lee Hamilton, Dennis Lynn Hamilton; m. Jack Fredrick Allman, Dec. 22, 1977; stepchildren: John Frederick, James Paul, Jeffrey Lee. AA, Christian Coll., 1958; BA in Spanish, U. Mo., 1960, MEd, 1971, EdD, 1994. Tchr. Spanish Neosho (Mo.) HS, 1961-62, asst. prin., 1974-77; florist Wallflower Shop and Greenhouse, Joplin, Mo., 1962-69; dean girls Joplin Sr. HS, 1967-69; florist, bookkeeper Mueller's Garden Ctr., Columbia, Mo., 1969-71; instr. edn., asst. dean of students Columbia Coll., 1971-74; dir. guidance Am. Cmty. Sch., Buenos Aires, 1978-81; tchr. Spanish, psychology Ava (Mo.) HS, 1982-84; tchr. Spanish, social studies McDonald County HS, Anderson, Mo., 1984-88; counselor, acad. advisor Mo. So. State Coll., Joplin, 1988—2003. Cons. Mo. So. State Univ., 1990—; mem. internat. task force Mo. So. State Coll., 1994—96; mem. adv. bd. Adult Basic Edn., Joplin, 1992—; presenter Ctr. Applications Psychol. Type Internat. Conf., 1996. Named to Outstanding Young Women Am., 1972; recipient William D. Phillips Music award, 1st Christian Ch., Columbia, 1956. Mem.: Southwest Mo. Sch. Counselor Assn. (sec. 1994—97, v.p. 1992—94, 1999—2001, mem. governing bd., chmn. publs. and rsch. com. 1997—99), Mo. Sch. Counselor Assn., Phi Theta Kappa, Sigma Delta Pi, Phi Sigma Iota (romance lang., pres. 1959—60), Delta Eta Chi, Sigma Phi Gamma, Kappa Delta Pi. Avocations: music, photographer, sketch artist, needlecrafts, jewelry crafts. Home: 1214 Circle Dr Neosho MO 64850-1301 Office: Mo So State Coll 3950 Newman Rd Joplin MO 64801-1512

ALLMAN, MARGO HUTZ, sculptor, painter; b. NYC, Feb. 23, 1933; d. Werner H. and Avis (Newcomb) Hutz; m. William B. Allman, Feb. 19, 1954; children: Avis Louise, David Drue. Student, Smith Coll., 1950-51, Moore Coll. Art, 1952-55, Hans Hofmann Sch. Art, 1953, U. Del., 1967-70. One-woman shows include Wallingford (Pa.) Art Center, 1964, Windham Coll., 1974, Bloomsburg State Coll., 1976-77, Moore Coll. Art and Design, 1979, Marian Locks Gallery, Phila., 1984, McKinney Gallery West Chester U., Pa., 1994, Gomez Gallery, Balt., 2002; exhibited in group shows at Phila. Art Alliance, 1954, Del. Art Mus., Wilmington, 1958 (Ann Show Drawing prize), 1965, 67, Print Club, Phila., 1959, U. Del., 1977, Del. State Arts Coun., Wilmington, 1981, C. Grimaldis Gallery, Balt., 1983, Art in Form Gallery, Karlsruhe, W.Ger., 1984, Contemporary Women Artists of Phila., 1986-87, Del. Art Mus., 1993, Del. Ctr. Contemporary Arts, 1995, Long Beach Island Found. Arts and Scis., Loveladies, N.J., 1995, Cecil County Arts Coun., Elkton, Md., 1998-99, Chester County Art Assn., West Chester, Pa., 1999-2001, 2003, Biennial, Del. Art Mus., 2000, Regional Ctr. Women in Arts, West Chester, Pa., 2001, 2003;, Del. Ctr. for the Contemporary Arts, Wilmington, 2002; artist-in residence Canakkale Seramik, Can., Turkey, 1995; represented in permanent collections at Del. Mus., Phila. Mus., Tidewater Pub. Co., Centerville, Md., Hercules Inc., Wilmington, Connolly Bove Lodge & Hutz LLP, Wilmington. Bd. dirs. Robert Small Dance Co., N.Y.C., 1979—80. Recipient Mildred Boericke prize Print Club, Phila., 1958, Landscape prize Wilmington Trust Bank, 1969, Disting. Alumnae award Moore Coll. Art Design, 1998. Mem.: Phila. Mus. Art, Maui Arts and Cultural Ctr., Nat. Mus. Women in the Arts (charter), Del. Art Mus., Del. Ctr. Contemporary Arts, Moore Coll. Art and Design Alumnae Assn. Home: 202 State Rd West Grove PA 19390-8906

ALLMAN, MARK C. engineer, physicist; b. Rochester, Pa., Aug. 4, 1958; s. Crawford Marcus and Darl Terresa (Hazenstab) A.; m. Mary Beth Decker, Apr. 30, 1983 (div. 1987); m. Janice Kay Hempleman, Dec. 8, 1989. BSBA, Robert Morris Coll., 1980; MS in Phys. Sci., U. Houston Clear Lake, 1991. Programmer/analyst Transcomm Data Systems, Inc., Pitts., 1980-81; ind. cons. Pitts., 1981-82; programmer/analyst, cons. ComTech Systems, Inc., Columbus, Ohio, 1982-83; systems programmer, mgr., project leader DataCom, Inc., Columbus, 1983-86; systems engr. R&D Discovery Systems, Dublin, Ohio, 1986-88; systems analyst On-Line Computer Libr. Ctr., Dublin, 1988-89; engr., physicist Rockwell Space Ops. Co., Houston, 1989-95; sr. engr. McDonnell Douglas/Boeing, 1995-98; pvt. practice Allman Profl. Cons. Inc., 1998—; pvt. pilot, 1997—. Mem. data collection team Allegheny Obs., U. Pitts., 1981-82; presenter at profl. confs. Author: Introduction to the C Programming Language, 1994; co-author: Modern Astrodynamics, 1996. Mem. campaign coun. Rep. Nat. Com., Washington, 1991—, Haw Rang Do Kung-Fu Martial Arts Team, 1991-2001. Mem. AAAS, Am. Astron. Soc. (assoc.), IEEE Project Mgmt. Inst., Ind. Computer Cons. Assn., Coun. Fgn. Rels., Wu Shu Kung Fu Fedn. (2d deg. black belt), Greater Houston Deming Alliance. Republican. Roman Catholic. Home: 45 Robbins Rd Walpole MA 02081 Office: 891 Main St # 354 Walpole MA 02081 E-mail: mcallman@allmanpc.com.

ALLMAN, RICHARD MARK, physician, gerontologist; b. Columbus, Ohio, Feb. 23, 1955; m. Connie Lou Allman; children: Justin Mark, Philip Randolph. BA in Biology magna cum laude, W.Va. U., 1977, MD, 1980. Diplomate Am. Bd. Internal Medicine, cert. of added qualification in geriatrics. Am. Bd. Internal Medicine, diplomate Nat. Bd. Med. Examiners. Intern W.Va. U. Sch. Medicine, 1980-81, resident in internal medicine, 1981-83; fellow in internal medicine Johns Hopkins U., Balt., 1983-85; asst. in medicine, staff physician Johns Hopkins U./Hosp., Balt., 1985-86; staff physician U. Ala. Hosp., VA Med. Ctr., Birmingham, 1986—; asst. prof. medicine U. Ala. Birmingham, 1986-90, assoc. prof. medicine, 1990-96, prof. medicine, 1996—, dir. gerontology/geriat., 1990—, dir. Ctr. Aging, 1992—, dir. Geriatric Edn. Ctr., 1993—; prin. clin. coord. Ala. Quality Assurance Found., Birmingham, 1995—. Chief geriatric sect. Birmingham VA Med. Ctr., 1990—2001; dir. Birmingham/Atlanta VA Geriatric Rsch., Edn. and Clin. Ctr., 2000—. Assoc. editor: Am. Jour. Medicine, 1988—92, mem. editl. bd.: Advances in Wound Care, 1989—97, Jour. Am. Geriat. Soc., 1994—97, Jour. Gerontology: Med. Sci., 1996—99, ad hoc reviewer for jours.: ; contbr. articles to profl. jours. Recipient Lange Book award, 1977, Mosby Book award, 1978, Kosiak award, 2003, others. Mem.: ACP, So. Soc. Clin. Investigation, Nat. Pressure Ulcer Adv. Panel (bd. dirs. 1991—95), Am. Health Quality Assn., Soc. Gen. Internal Medicine, Am. Fedn. Med. Rsch. (nat. com. 1992—95, Henry Christian Meml. award 1993), Assn. Dir. Geriat. Acad. Programs (nat. coun. 1993—2003, sec.-treas. 2000—03), Gerontol. Soc. Am., Am. Geriat. Soc. (rsch. com. 1996—2000), Phi Beta Kppa, Alpha Omega Alpha. Office: U Ala at Birmingham Ctr for Aging 1530 3rd Ave S CH-19 Rm 201 Birmingham AL 35294-2041

ALLMAN, WILLIAM BERTHOLD, musician, engineer, consultant; b. Phila., Feb. 16, 1927; s. Drue Nunez and Blanche (Oppenheimer) A.; m. Margo Hutz, Feb. 19, 1954; children: Avis Louise, David Drue. BSEE, Drexel U., 1949; MBA, U. Pa., 1951. Registered profl. engr., Pa. Contract engr. Atlantic Refining, Phila., 1951-55, E.I. DuPont de Nemours & Co., Inc., Wilmington, Del., 1955-58; constrn. engr. Niagra Falls, N.Y., 1958-59; cons. engr. Wilmington, 1959-82, Allman Assocs., West Grove, Pa., 1982—. Owner, mgr. Allman Bldgs., Phila., 1965-87. Contbr. numerous articles on plastic pipe to profl. mags.; drummer, washboard player with The Melton Bros. and Washboard Bill Allman band; performed with various musicians including Lionel Hampton, Brownie McGhee, Mississippi Fred McDowell, Sonny Terry. Mem. Bi-racial com. City of Newark, Del., 1963-71, chmn. 1965, London Grove Township Mcpl. Authority, Chester County, Pa., 1985-89, chmn. 1986; Dem. committeeman, Del., 1964-71, chmn., 1968; candidate Mayor City of Newark, 1970; adv. coun. Neighborhood Svcs. Ctr., Oxford, Pa., 1989—. With USNR, 1945-46. ETO. Mem. Am. Assn. Individual Investors, Del. Ctr. Contemporary Arts, Del. Art Mus., Phila. Mus. Art, Nature Conservancy. Avocations: painting, music, gardening, traveling, reading. Home and Office: 202 State Rd West Grove PA 19390-8906

ALLMAN, WILLIAM G. curator; b. Bethesda, Md. BA in hist., U. Md.; MA in Am. studies with mus. concentration, George Washington U. Curatorial asst. The White House, 1976—87, asst. curator, 1987—2002, curator, 2002—. Contbr.: book Official White House China, 1999, The White House: Its Historic Furnishings & First Families, 2000, articles to semi-annual jour. of the White House Hist. Assn. The White House History. Mailing: 1600 Pennsylvania Ave NW Washington DC 20502*

ALLMAND, LINDA F(AITH), retired library director; b. Port Arthur, Tex., Jan. 31, 1937; d. Clifton James and Jewel Etoile (Smith) Allmand. BA, North Tex. State U., 1960; MA, U. Denver, 1962. Clerical asst. Gates Meml. Libr., 1953-55; libr. asst. Houston Pub. Libr., 1955-58; children's libr. Denver Pub. Libr., 1960-63; children's coord. Anaheim Pub. Libr., Calif., 1963-65; br. mgr. Dallas Pub. Libr, 1965-71, chief br. svcs., 1971-81; dir. Ft. Worth Pub. Libr., 1981-98; instr. North Tex. State U., Denton, 1967—. Instr. Dallas County C.C., 1981; bldg. cons. Dallas Pub. Libr., 1974-80, Hurst Pub. Libr., 1977-78, Jacksonville (Tex.) Pub. Libr., 1976-79, Carrollton Pub. Libr., 1979-81, Haltom (Tex.) City Pub. Libr., 1984, Iowa Park (Tex.) Pub. Libr., 1985, S.W. Regional Libr., Ft. Worth, 1987. Author: 1981-2000, Ft. Worth Public Library— Facilities and Long-Range Planning Study, 1982; contbr. chpts. to books, articles to profl. jours. Bd. dirs. City of Dallas Credit Union, 1973-81, Sr. Citizen's Ctrs., Inc., 1982; com. chmn. Goals for Dallas, 1967-69; mem. Forum Ft. Worth, 1983; mem. Edn. Info. Task Force, Downtown Fort Worth, Inc., 1992-93. Pilot Club of Port Arthur scholar, 1954, Libr. Binding Inst. scholar, 1958; recipient Disting. Alumnus award North Tex. State U., 1983, U. North Tex., 1998, Leadership Ft. Worth, 1982-83; named Tarrant County Newsmaker of the Yr., 1984, Outstanding Leader, Ft. Worth Star Telegram, 1989, Outstanding Woman of the Yr., Mayor's Commn. on Status of Women, 1989, North Tex. Pub. Adminstr. of the Yr., 1990. Mem. ALA, AAUP, AAUW (Tarrant County pres.-elect 1998, pres. 1999), Tex. Libr. Assn. (pres. pub. libr. divsn. 1980-81, chmn. planning com. 1982-84, pres.-elect 1985-86, pres. 1986-87, Libr. of Yr. award 1985, North Tex. Pub. Adminstr. of Yr. award 1990), Tarrant Regional Librs. Assn., Am. Mgmt. Assn., Dallas County Librs. Assn. (pres. 1968-69), Downtown Ft. Worth Rotary Club (mem. edn. info. task force 1992-93), Freedom to Read Found., Ft. Worth C. of C. (bd. dirs. 1993-95), Sister Cities, Inc., Ft. Worth Pub. Libr. Found. Home: 701 Timberview Ct N Fort Worth TX 76112-1715

ALLMENDINGER, DAVID FREDERICK, JR., history educator; b. Wooster, Ohio, May 13, 1938; s. David Frederick and Marjorie Gertrude (Kidder) A.; m. Susan Alice Horsman, Dec. 29, 1965; children: Carolyn Marjorie, Nicholas Eric. Student, Wash. State U., 1956-58; BA, U. Mo., 1961; MS in History, U. Wis., 1962, PhD, 1968. Asst. prof. Reed Coll., Portland, Oreg., 1967-69, Smith Coll., Northampton, Mass., 1969-72; vis. assoc. prof. U. Mich., Ann Arbor, 1973-74; assoc. prof. history U. Del., Newark, 1974-90, dir. Am. Studies Program, 1974-80, 81-83, prof. history, 1990—2003. Vis. lectr. Flinders U. of South Australia, Adelaide, 1979, vis. prof., 1985. Editorial adv. bd. Va. Mag. of History, 1986-89; bd. editors History of Edn. Quar., 1972-79; author: Ruffin: Family and Reform in the Old South, 1990, Paupers and Scholars: The Transformation of Student Life in Nineteenth-Century New England, 1975; editor: The American People in the Antebellum North, 1973, The American People in the Industrial City, 1973, Incidents of My Life: Edmund Ruffin's Autobiographical Essays, Vol. 17, Virginia Historical Society Documents, 1990; contbr. articles to jours. Mem. Del. State Review Bd. for Historic Places, Dover, 1980-85, vice chmn., 1983-85. Recipient Lindback Found. award for disting. tchg. U. Del., 1977, Grad. Sch. award for excellence in tchg. U. Wis., 1965; Mellon Rsch. fellow Va. Hist. Soc., 1989, Shelby Cullom Davis Ctr. for Hist. Studies fellow, 1972-73. Mem. Orgn. of Am. Historians, Va. Hist. Soc. (Rachal award 1985), Wash. State Hist. Soc., Am. Coun. of Learned Socs. (exec. com. of dels. 1985-87, del. from Orgn. of Am. Historians 1984-87), Snohomish Tribe of Indians, Phi Beta Kappa. E-mail: dfa@udel.edu.

ALLMENDINGER, PAUL FLORIN, retired engineering association executive; b. Moline, Ill., Mar. 2, 1922; s. Andrew Louis A. and Nellie L. (Florin) Inman; m. Sara Jo Breazeale, Aug. 31, 1947; children: James, Glen, John. Student, Augustana Coll., Rock Island., Ill., 1940-41; BS, U.S. Naval Acad., 1944. Dir. engring. Prestolite Co.-Eltra Corp., Toledo, Ohio, 1961-67; dir. engring. Power Tool div. Rockwell Internat., Pitts., 1967-68, v.p. engring. Power Tool div., 1968-77; v.p. tech. affairs Motor Vehicle Mfrs. Assn., Detroit, 1977-81; dep. exec. dir. ASME, N.Y.C., 1981-82, exec. dir., 1982-87. Treas., bd. dirs. Nat. Alliance for the Mentally Ill, 1998—. Served to lt (j.g.) USN, 1941-47. Fellow Inst. Mech. Engrs., ASME (Centennial award 1980); mem. Soc. Automotive Engrs. (bd. dirs. 1963-66), Am. Soc. Engring. Edn., Soc. Mfg. Engrs., Engrs. Council for Profl. Devel. (bd. dirs. 1973-80, pres. 1976-78, Grinter Disting. Service award 1986), Am. Nat. Standards Inst. (bd. dirs. 1977-82), Lake Keowee Assn. (bd. dirs. 1988-91, pres. 1990-91), Tau Beta Pi Clubs: University (Washington and N.Y.C.). Republican. Presbyterian. Office: Am Soc Mech Engrs 3 Park Ave New York NY 10016-5902

ALLMON, MICHAEL BRYAN, financial consultant; b. Oceanside, Calif., July 14, 1951; s. William Bryan and Cecelia Audrey (Wright) A.; m. Monika Ann Arth, Sept. 15, 1979; children: Stefanie Michele, Danika Audrey. BBA, U. Tex., 1975; MBT, U. So. Calif., 1986. CPA, Calif., 1978. CPA Alexander Grant & Co., L.A., 1976-77, Laventhol & Horwath, CPAs, L.A., 1977-85; dir. tax, fin. planning svcs. Zusman, Cameron and Allmon, CPAs, 1985-88; CEO, dir. Essential Profl. Svcs., Inc., 1985-86; ptnr. Michael B. Allmon & Assocs. LLP, CPAs, Marina Del Rey, 1988—; pres. The MBA Group, Inc., Marina Del Rey, 1991—; trustee several pvt. trusts, 1995—. Chmn., MBA Advisors, Inc., Marina Del Rey, 1999—; mem. exec. bd. dirs. estate and gift com. of taxation sect. State Bar Calif.; numerous interviews local, nat. newspapers, mags. Contbr. articles to profl. jours. Mem. AICPAs (fed. tax divsn.), Calif. Soc. CPAs (fin. planning com., tax com., v.p., bd. dirs. L.A. chpt. 1992-99, statewide bd. dirs. 1995-97, 2000-2003, chair L.A. estate planning com. 1982—, founding chair statewide estate planning com. 2000-2003), Am. Assn. Profl. Fin. Planners (L.A. chpt. pres.), Walnut Track Club (pres. team) (L.A.), Manhattan Beach (Calif.) Country Club. Office: 4720 Lincoln Blvd Ste 300 Marina Del Rey CA 90292

ALLMON, MICHAEL W, SR., sales executive; b. Orange, Tex., Feb. 3, 1952; s. Paul James and Bobbie Jean Coe Allmon; m. Nancy Louise Ham Allmon, July 17, 1971; children: Jennifer Leigh, Michael Wayne Jr. BS, Southwest Tex. State U., 1986. Paramedic Houston Fire Dept., 1973—78; med. sales rep. Ross Labs, Sherman, Tex., 1978—79, Bristol Labs, Sherman and Temple, Tex., 1979—88; regional med. sales rep. Laborie Med. Technologies, Temple, Tex., 1992—96; regional sales mgr. Gen. Orthopedic, Temple, Tex., 1996—. Sales trainer Bristol Labs, Temple, Tex., 1983. Co-campaign chmn. Hugh Shine U.S. Congression Campaign, Temple and Waco, Tex., 1985. Mem.: Wildflower Country Club, Travis Masonic Lodge (3rd degree mason). Republican. Bible Ch. Avocations: golf, photography, gardening, travel, stain glass. E-mail: mallmon1@hot.rr.com.

ALLMOND, CORAL LEE, librarian; b. Lynchburg, Va., Mar. 28, 1946; d. Allison Holden and Isabel (White) Stephenson; m. John Glenwood Hurt, Jan. 26, 1962 (div. Aug. 1978); children: John Glenwood Jr., Richard Holden; m. Duane Vernard Allmond, Jan. 1, 1988. BS in Biology magna cum laude, Lynchburg Coll., 1966; M Secondary Sch. Adminstrn., U. Va., 1988. Cert. collegiate profl., Va. Tchr. sci. Bedford County Sch. System, Bedford, Va., 1966-68, O.T. Bonner Jr. High Sch., Danville, Va., 1970-76, George Washington High Sch., Danville, 1968-70, libr., 1976—. Vol. gifted and academically talented program Park Ave Elem. Sch., summer 1988. Mem. Va. Edn. Media Assn., Starwood Garden Club (pres.), Wednesday Club, Phi Delta Kappa. Republican. Congregationalist. Avocations: reading, knitting, gardening, golf. Home: 123 Meadowbrook Cir Danville VA 24541-7301

ALLNER, WALTER HEINZ, designer, painter, art director; b. Dessau, Germany, Jan. 2, 1909; came to U.S., 1949, naturalized, 1957; m. Colette Vasselon, Mar. 8, 1938 (div. June 1951); 1 son, Michel; m. Jane Booth Pope, Apr. 4, 1954; 1 son, Peter. Student, Bauhaus-Dessau, 1927-30. Designer Gesellschafts-und Wirtschafts-Museum, Vienna, Austria, 1929; asst. to typographer Piet Zwart, Wassenaar, Holland, 1930; editorial, painting, and advt. designer Paris, 1932-49; ptnr. Omnium Graphique, Paris, 1933-36; art dir. Formes, Editions d'Art Graphique et Photographique, Paris, 1933-36; Paris editor Swiss art mag. Graphis, 1945-48; founder, editor Internat. Poster Ann., 1948-52; co-dir. Editions Paralleles, Paris, 1948-51; mem. staff Fortune mag., N.Y.C., 1951-74, art dir., 1962-74; mem. faculty Parsons Sch. Design, N.Y.C., 1974-86. Vis. critic, mem. Comite de Parrainage Ecole Superieure d'Arts Graphiques, Paris, 1979—; free-lance designer design cons. companies; lectr. in Australia, 1983 Designer posters for traffic safety campaign, Outdoor Advt. Assn. Am., 1959-60; exhibits, Salon des Surindependants, Paris, Salon des Réalités Nouvelles, Paris, numerous others, Germany, Austria, U.S., Eng., France, Holland, Switzerland, Latin Am., Japan.; Compiler, editor: A.M. Cassandre, Peintre d'Affiches, 1948; editor: Posters, 1952; corr. Signes mag., Paris, 1990-92; contbg. editor Design Jour., Seoul, Korea, 1990-92; author numerous articles on poster art. Named Laureate 4th Block, Kharkov, Ukraine, 1997; recipient medal Bauhaus-Dessau, German Acad. Architecture, 1979, The Bruno Biennale Hon. Membership. Mem.: Am. Inst. Graphic Arts, Alliance Graphique Internat. (internat. pres., Spl. Prix of Jury for Investment in Devel. World Graphic Design, Henri Statuette 1998), Assn. Italiana Creativi Comunicazione Visiva (hon.). Home: 110 Riverside Dr New York NY 10024-3715 Home (Summer): PO Box 167 Truro MA 02666-0167

ALLNUTT, ROBERT FREDERICK, management consultant, corporate director; b. Richmond, Va., June 15, 1935; s. Robert Carhart and Evelyn Rosalie (Brooks) A.; m. Jan Latven, July 17, 1938; children: Robert David, Thomas Frederick. BS in Indsl. Engring, Va. Poly. Inst., 1957; JD with distinction, George Washington U., 1960, LL.M., 1962. Bar: D.C. 1960, Va. 1960. Patent examiner U.S. Patent Office, 1957-60; with NASA, 1960-70, 78-83, asst. adminstr. legis. affairs, 1967-70, assoc. dep. adminstr., 1978-81, assoc. adminstr. external relations, dep. gen. counsel, 1981-83; legal counsel, corp. sec. U.S. Com. Energy Awareness, 1983-84; v.p. Communication Satellite Corp., 1984-85; exec. v.p. Pharm. Mfrs. Assn., 1985-95; sr. counselor APCO Worldwide, Washington, 1995—. Assoc. gen. counsel Commn. on Govt. Procurement, 1970-73; staff dir. com. aero. and space scis. U.S. Senate, 1973-75; dep. asst. adminstr. ERDA, 1975-78; lectr. law Am. U. Law Sch., 1964; bd. dirs. Cortex Pharms., Inc., Irvine, Calif., Questor Pharms., Inc., Hayward, Calif., F. Dohmen Co., Inc., Germantown, Wis. Trustee Air and Space Heritage Coun.; bd. dirs. Nat. Health Coun., 1987-98, Nat. Coun. on Aging, 1990-98; mem. Com. of 100, Va. Poly. Inst., 1991—; mem. program coun. of Internat. Ctr. for Sci. Lit., Chgo. Acad. Scis.; bd. dirs. Nat. Medals Sci. & Technology Found., 1997—, Partnership for Caring, 1998-2001. Recipient Superior Performance award U.S. Patent Office, 1959, Apollo Achievement award NASA, 1969, Meritorious Service medal ERDA, 1976, Exceptional Service medal NASA, 1981, Disting. Service medal NASA, 1983; named Meritorious Fed. Exec. with Presdl. Rank Office of Pres., 1981 Mem. Legal Aid Soc. D.C. (bd. dirs.), Nat. Space Soc. (bd. govs.), NASA Alumni League (v.p.), Edgemoor Tennis Club (Bethesda, Md.;pres. 1987-89), Order of Coif. Home: 5415 Moorland Ln Bethesda MD 20814-1335 Office: APCO Worldwide 1615 L St NW Washington DC 20036-5610

ALLOCCA, JOHN ANTHONY, medical research scientist; b. Bklyn., Aug. 27, 1948; s. Frank and Dorothy (Aulicino) A.; children: Jennifer, Jerry. AAS, SUNY-Farmingdale, 1972; BA, SUNY-Old Westbury, 1975; MS, Poly. Inst. N.Y., 1979; DSc, Pacific Western U., 1981; PhD, St. Martin U., 1997. Adminstr. Hofstra U., 1967-71; psychotherapist Creedmore State Hosp., 1975-76; biomed. engr. Doll Rsch. Inc., 1971-77; rsch. scientist Albert Einstein Coll. Medicine, 1977-78; rsch. cons. L.I. Coll. Hosp., 1979-80; rsch. scientist, tech. dir. pulmonary labs. Mt. Sinai Med. Ctr., 1980-82; rsch. scientist Langer Biomech. Group, Inc., 1983-85; pres., rsch. scientist Andromeda Rsch., Inc., 1985-88, The Zibav Corp., 1988-89; pres. Allocca Tech. Inc., Smithtown, N.Y., 1989-99, Allocca Biotech., Inc., Northport, N.Y., 1999—. Author: Electrical/Electronic Safety, 1982, Electronic Instrumentation, 1983, Transducer Theory and Applications, 1983, Medical Instrumentation for the Health Care Professional, 1990, Physiology and Nutrition, 1986. Mem. IEEE, Assn. Advancement Med. Instrumentation, AAAS, Am. Assn. Physicists in Medicine, N.Y. Acad. Scis. Alumni Assn. Mt. Sinai Med. Ctr., Sigma Xi. Office: 19 Lorraine Ct Northport NY 11768-3141 E-mail: john@allocca.com.

ALLOTTA, JOANNE MARY, elementary education educator; b. Bklyn., Dec. 8, 1962; d. Joseph and Adela (Castagna) A.; m. Edward James Cirminiello, Mar. 23, 1991. BA in Child Study, St. Joseph's Coll., 1984; MS in Edn., Bklyn. Coll., 1987; postgrad., 1987-88; advanced cert., Bklyn. Coll. Cert. tchr., NY, sch. dist. adminstr., NY; provisional cert. sch. adminstr. and supr., NY. Tchr. Holy Family Sch., Bklyn., 1984—85; elem. tchr. Pub. Sch. 97, Bklyn., 1985—2001, cooperating tchr. for srs. majoring in edn., 1985—2001; curriculum writer for profl. devel. Sch. Dist. 21, N.Y.C., 1991—, program facilitator gifted program Bklyn., 2001—. Workshop presenter; reviewer N.Y.C. Bd. Edn., Bklyn, 1992; mem. task force com. N.Y. Partnership for Statewide Systems Change-Dist. 21, 1993-95; textbook reviewer grade 4 social studies Scott Forseman, 2002-03. Active Pub. Sch. 97 PTA, 1985-2001; fund raiser St. Jude's Children's Hosp., 1990-2001. Recipient Tchr. of Yr. award Phi Delta Kappa, 1994, Tchr. of Yr. award Pub. Sch. 97, 1999. Mem. ASCD, Am. Fedn. Tchrs., United Fedn. Tchrs., N.Y. State of United Tchrs., Kappa Delta Pi. Roman Catholic. Avocations: reading, writing, needlepoint. Office: Cmty Sch Dist 21 521 West Ave Brooklyn NY 11224

ALLOTTA, JOSEPH JOHN, lawyer; b. Rochester, N.Y., May 1, 1947; m. Elizabeth Dingwall, July 17, 1971; children: John Joseph, Leslie Denise, Jeffrey James. BA, Am. U., 1969; JD, Case Western Res. U., 1972. Bar: Ohio 1972. Law clk. to presiding judge U.S. Dist. Ct. (no. dist.) Ohio, 1972-74; assoc. Gallon, Kalniz & Iorio, 1974-79; founding sr. ptnr. Allotta & Farley, Toledo, 1979—. Instr. U. Toledo, 1975-76. Contbg. editor: Developing Labor Law. Pres., St. Matthew's Found.; Dem. precinct committeeman Sylvania Twp., 1983—. With U.S. Army, 1969-75. Fellow: Labor and Employment Law; mem.: ABA (employment law sect., chmn. subcom. publs. 1990), Internat. Found. Employee Benefits, Ohio State Bar Assn. (labor law sect., bd. govs. 1979—85), Internat. Boilermakers (hon.). Avocations: logging, writing. Home: 6127 Cross Trails Rd Sylvania OH 43560-1715 Office: Allotta & Farley 2222 Centennial Rd Toledo OH 43617-1870 E-mail: jallotta@allotta-farley.com.

ALLOWAY, ROBERT MALCOMBE, computer consulting executive; b. Cleve., Apr. 15, 1944; s. Robert Malcombe and May (Tingley) A.; divorced; children: Megan, Brook. BA, Brown U., 1967; MBA, Boston Coll., 1972; D in Bus. Adminstrn., Harvard U., 1975. Cert. data processor. Project mgr. Sealtest Foods, Rocky River, Ohio, 1968-70, First Nat. Stores, Summerville, Mass., 1970-72; research assoc. Boston Coll., Chestnut Hill, Mass., 1972-73; asst. prof. mgmt. sci. MIT, Cambridge, 1975-84; pres. Alloway Inc., Lexington, Mass., 1984-97; ret., 1997; profl. staff U.S. Ho. of Reps., 1997-98; dir. Nat. Leadership Task Force on Y2K, 1998-2000. Guest prof. Stockholm Sch. Econs., 1976-77; rsch. faculty Ctr. for Info. Systems Rsch., MIT, 1975-84. Contbr. articles to

profl. jours. Pres. World Future Soc., Boston, 1973-75. Fellow Nat. Acad. Pub. Adminstrn.; mem. Soc. for Mgmt. Info. (reviewer 1983—). Avocations: sailing, skiing, tennis. Office: Alloway Inc 3321 Dent Pl NW Washington DC 20007-2713

ALLRED, ALBERT LOUIS, chemistry educator; b. Mount Airy, N.C., Sept. 19, 1931; s. Caleb Haynes and Bessie (Brown) A.; m. Nancy Jean Willis, Aug. 30, 1958; children— Kevin Scott, Gregg Warren, Sarah Elaine. BS in Chemistry, U. N.C., 1953; A.M., Harvard, 1955, PhD, 1956. Chemist E.I. du Pont de Nemours Co., Wilmington, Del., 1952, 55, Mallinckrodt Chem. Works, St. Louis, 1954, Argonne (Ill.) Nat. Lab., 1958, 76; mem. faculty Northwestern U., 1956—, prof., 1969-91, prof. emeritus, 1991—, assoc. dean Coll. Arts and Scis., 1970-74, chmn. dept. chemistry, 1980-86, acting dean Coll. Arts and Scis., 1987-88, acting v.p. for rsch. and dean Grad. Sch., 1992, acting provost, 1995. Vis. scholar Cambridge (Eng.) U., 1987. Alfred P. Sloan fellow, 1963-65; postdoctoral fellow U. Rome, Italy, 1967; hon. research asso. Univ. Coll., London (Eng.), 1965 Mem. AAUP (pres. Northwestern U. 1968-69),, Am. Chem. Soc., Chem. Soc. (London), Coun. Chem. Rsch. (gov. bd. 1985-88), Rotary Internat., Phi Beta Kappa, Phi Lambda Upsilon, Sigma Xi, Alpha Chi Sigma. Home: 820 Milburn St Evanston IL 60201-2450

ALLRED, GLORIA RACHEL, lawyer; b. Phila., July 3, 1941; d. Morris and Stella Bloom; m. William Allred (div. Oct. 1987); 1 child, Lisa. BA, U. Pa., 1963; MA, NYU, 1966; JD, Loyola U., L.A., 1974; JD (hon.), U. West Los Angeles, 1981. Bar: Calif. 1975, U.S. Dist. Ct. (cen. dist.) Calif. 1975, U.S. Ct. Appeals (9th cir.) 1976, U.S. Supreme Ct. 1979. Ptnr. Allred, Maroko, Goldberg & Ribakoff (now Allred, Maroko & Goldberg), L.A., 1976—. Contbr. articles to profl. jours. Pres. Women's Equal Rights Legal Def. and Edn. Fund, L.A., 1978—, Women's Movement Inc., L.A. Recipient Commendation award L.A. Bd. Suprs., 1986, Mayor of L.A., 1986, Pub. Svc. award Nat. Assn. Fed. Investigators, 1986, Vol. Action award Pres. of U.S., 1986. Mem. ABA, Calif. Bar Assn., Nat. Assn. Women Lawyers, Calif. Women Lawyers Assn., Women Lawyers L.A. Assn., Friars (Beverly Hills, Calif.), Magic Castle Club (Hollywood, Calif.) Office: Allred Maroko & Goldberg 6300 Wilshire Blvd Ste 1500 Los Angeles CA 90048-5217

ALLSBROOK, OGDEN OLMSTEAD, JR., retired economics educator; b. Wilmington, NC, July 1, 1940; s. Ogden Olmstead Sr. and Elizabeth Barringer (Warren) A. BA, Wake Forest U., 1962; PhD, U. Va., 1966. Ops. rsch. analyst Dep. Def., Washington, 1966-68; asst. prof. econs. U. Ga., Athens, 1968-73, dir. grad. studies econs., 1971-81, assoc. prof., 1974-96, ret., 1996. Author: Utilization of Military Resources, 1969; contbr. articles to profl. jours. Capt. U.S. Army, 1966-68. Mem. AAUP, Nat. Soc. SAR (pres. Athens chpt. 1992-94), Cape Fear Club, So. Econ. Assn. Lutheran. Avocations: motor sports, philately, turned wood objects, numismatics, Japanese cloisonne. Home: 115 Tillman Ln Athens GA 30606-4115 E-mail: ooalls1@wmconnect.com.

ALLSHOUSE, MERLE FREDERICK, educational organization administrator; b. Pitts., Apr. 26, 1935; s. Merle Lawrence and Helen (Frederick) A.; m. Myrna Mansfield, Apr. 1, 1956; children: Frederick Scott, Kimberly Dawn. BA (Rector fellow), DePauw U., 1957; MA (Rockefeller Theol. fellow), Yale, 1959, PhD (Rockefeller fellow 1959-61, Kent fellow 1961), 1965. Instr. philosophy Dickinson Coll., 1963-65, asst. prof., 1965-68, assoc. dean of coll., asso. prof. philosophy, 1968-70; dean of coll., prof. philosophy Bloomfield (N.J.) Coll., 1970-71, pres., 1971-86, Myron Stratton Home Found., Colorado Springs, Colo., 1986-88; prof. publ adminstr. Grad. Sch. Pub. Affairs, U. Colo., 1988; v.p. U. Colo. Found., 1989-94; exec. dir. Acad. Sr. Profls., Eckerd Coll., St. Petersburg, Fla., 1994—2002. Mem. N.J. Student Assistance Bd. Bd. dirs. Presbyn. Career and Counseling Ctr., N.J. Coll. Fund, Inc., Colo. Children's Campaign-The Goodwill of Colorado Springs, The Colorado Springs Symphony Orch., Coun. Ind. Colls., N.E. region Boy Scouts Am., Colorado Springs Symphony Orch., The Broadmoor Improvement Soc.; pres., Beth El Coll. Nursing, Goodwill of Colorado Springs; moderator Broadmoor Community Ch.; div. chmn. United Way; mem. Da Vinci Quartet; trustee Montclair Kimberley Acad.; pres. Presbyn. Coll. Union. HEW fellow, 1979-80 Mem. Metaphys. Soc. Am., Am. Philos. Assn., Am. Acad. Religion, Assn. Ind. Colls. and Univs. in N.J. (dir., chmn. bd.), Nat. Assn. Ind. Colls. and Univs. (chmn. secretariat 1983-86, bd. dirs.), Council Ind. Colls. (bd. dirs.), St. Petersburg Rotary. Home: College Landings 15 Crescent Pl S Saint Petersburg FL 33711-5118 E-mail: allshomf@eckerd.edu.

ALLSHOUSE, ROBERT HAROLD, history educator; b. Erie, Pa., Apr. 30, 1940; s. Harold and Anne Marie (Dranzek) A.; m. Marcia Catherine Windsor, Aug. 17, 1963; children: Lisa Catherine, Heather A. Kenny, Todd Anthony. BBA, Cleve. State U., 1963; MA, Case Western Res. U., 1965, PhD, 1967. Instr. Russian history Alliance Coll., Cambridge Springs, Pa., 1966-67, Gannon U., Erie, 1967-70, asst. prof., 1970-77, assoc. prof., 1977-82, prof., 1982—, chmn. dept. history, 1981-89, grad. dir. social sci., 1977-96, faculty senate, v.p., 2001—02, pres., 2002—; sec., treas. Gt. Lakes Pen Sales, Inc., Erie, 1976-98; pres. Allegheny Internat. Devel. Inc., Erie, 1990—; sec., treas. Pennfoil Tech. Inc., Erie, 1993—2001. Vis. prof. Latvian State U., Riga, 1991; mem. fgn. trade com. Erie Excellence Coun., 1992—2002. Author: Aleksander Izvolskii and Russian Foreign Policy, 1910-1914, 1977; editor: A Select Bibliography of Military History Since 1715, 1977, Photographs for the Tsar, 1980 (Photog. Soc. N.Y. Merit award 1980); gen. editor A Centennial History of the Erie Yacht Club, 1996. Mem. adv. bd. United Way, Erie, 1989-1996, Erie County Historic Preservation Bd., 1983-1990; pres. Erie Mus. Authority, 1985-87; bd. trustees Flagship Niagara League, 1998-2003, sec., 1999-2000, v.p., 2000-2002; v.p. faculty senate Gannon U., 1001-02, pres., 2002-03, trustee, 2002-03. Recipient Cmty. Edn. award Erie Sch. Dist., 1986, All Russian State TV award Russian State TV Co., Moscow, 1991, cert. of honor Assn. Ind. Video Prodrs., Russia, 1991, cert. of leadership All Union Inst. TV/Radio Broadcasting, Moscow, 1991, cert. of appreciation SAR, 1992. Fellow Phi Alpha Theta, Pi Gamma Mu; mem. Internat. Order Blue Gavel, Erie C. of C., Rotary Internat., Erie Yacht Club (fleet capt. 1988-89, rear commodore 1989-90, vice commodore 1990-91, commodore 1991-92, svc. award 1992). Avocations: sailing, travel. Office: Gannon U Perry Sq Erie PA 16541

ALLUKIAN, MYRON, JR., government administrator, public health educator, dental educator; b. Cambridge, Mass., Jan. 6, 1939; s. Myron and Mary (Nahabedian) A.; m. Ruth Felice Losco, Oct. 11, 1975; children: Myron III, Kristin, Alison, Jason, Alexandra, Nathan. BS in Psychology, Tufts U., 1960; DDS, U. Pa., 1964; MPH, Harvard U., Boston, 1967. Chief dental health Bunker Hill Health Ctr., Mass. Gen. Hosp., Boston, 1969-77; dir. and asst. dep. commr. cmty. dental programs Boston Dept. Health and Hosps., 1970-96, dir. personal health svcs., 1991-93; dir. cmty. dental programs Boston Pub. Health Commn., 1996-2000, dir. oral health, 2000—; assoc. vis. dentist Boston City Hosp., 1970-96, Boston Med. Ctr., 1996-2000. Lectr. Georgetown U. Sch. Dentistry, 1979-89, clin. instr., 1972-78, lectr., 1994-, Tufts Sch. Dental Medicine, U. Mass. Sch. Pub. Health, 1984-93, U. Minn. Sch. Pub. Health, 1981-92, Forsyth Sch. for Dental Hygienists, Boston, 1970—, Boston U. Dental Sch., 1977—, Mich. Sch. Pub. Health, Ann Arbor, 1980—; assoc. clin. prof. Sch. Dental Medicine, Harvard U., 1977—, lectr. Sch. Pub. Health, 1991—; regional cons. Job Corps, U.S. Dept. Labor, New Eng., 1973-98; corp. mem. Mass. Dental Svc. Corp., 1971-79; vis. prof. Columbia U. Sch. Dentistry, N.Y.C., 1991, mem., 1978-88; chmn., sec. Mass. Bd. Registration in Dentistry, 1980-86; mem. Am. Bd. Dental Pub. Health, treas., 1991-92, v.p., 1992-93, pres., 1993-94, diplomate, 1973—; adj. prof. Boston U. Sch. Pub. Health, 1997—. Mem. editl. adv. com.: Nation's Health, 1991—92, mem. editl. bd.: Am. Jour. Pub. Health, 1979—82, 1985—89, assoc. editor: Jour. Pub. Health Dentistry, 2001—, editl. cons.: Jour. Pub. Health Policy, 1985—; contbr. articles and abstracts. Chmn. U.S. Surgeon Gen.'s Work Group on Fluoridation and Dental Health, 1990, Prevention Objectives for The Nation, 1978-80; mem. Healthy People 2000, oral health work group, 1988-90, 97-2000, Steering Com, 2000—, Healthy People 2010, tobacco control work group U.S. Dept. Health and Human Svcs., 1998—; reviewer U.S. Surgeon Gen.'s report on oral health, 1998-2000; mem. nat. dental tobacco-free steering com. Nat. Cancer Inst., 1989-2000; corp. mem. Boston Young Men's Christian Union, 1974—; clin. dental dir. New England AIDS Edn. and Tng. Ctr., 1991—, Northeast Regional Bd. Dental Examiners, mem., 1978—, steering com., 1980-86, Meritorious Svc. award, 1998, 2003; adv. com. Boston Health Care for The Homeless, 1992-96, Nat. Bd. Examiners in Optometry, examination com., 1992-97, chair pub. health/clin.- legal issues com., 1994-96, Harvard Sch. Pub. Health Alumni Assn. Coun., 1992-99, pres.- elect 1993-95, pres., 1995-97, Mass. "Assist", 1991-93, chmn. Statewide Tobacco Control Planning Com., 1992, Pub. Health Mus. Mass., bd. dirs., 1992—, pres., 1993-94, cons. commn. dental accreditation Am. Dental Assn., 1996-2001; accreditation reviewer Coun. Edn. for Pub. Health, 1996-99; bd. dirs. Urban Health Project, Harvard Med. Sch., 1996-2000. Lt. Dental Corps, USN, 1964-66. Recipient cert. of appreciation U.S. Dept. Labor, 1981, Community Svc. award Health Planning Coun. Greater Boston, 1986, Disting. Faculty award Harvard Sch. Dental Medicine, 1986, Disting. Alumni award, 1996, Alumni Merit award U. Pa. Dental Sch., 1987, Exemplary Svc. award USPHS, 1990, 97, Vision Svc. award Mass. Soc. Optometrists, 1992, Outstanding Achievement award Armenian-Am. Behavioral Sci. Assn., 1995, Kabakjian Sci. award Armenian Students Assn., 1999; postdoctoral rsch. fellow meritorious Harvard Sch. Dental Medicine, 1969. Fellow: Internat. Coll. Dentists, Royal Soc. Health (hon.); mem.: APHA (pres. 1989—90, John W. Knutson award 1998, Sedgwick Meml. award 2001), New Eng. Eye Inst. (bd. dirs. 2001—), New Eng. Coll. Optometry (bd. trustees 1999—), Armenian-Am. Dental Soc. (founding mem. 1978, pres. 1982—84, trustee 1985—), Mass. Health Coun. (pres. 1977—78, bd. dirs. 1980—, ann. award 1989), Mass. Pub. Health Assn. (pres. 1977—78, Disting. Svc. citation 1988), Am. Assn. Pub. Health Dentistry (pres. 1984—85, spl. merit award 1987, Disting. Svc. award 2002), Inst. Medicine of NAS (com. educating dentists for the future 1992—93), Harvard Alumni Assn. (bd. dirs. 1997—2001). E-mail: myron_allukian@bphc.org.

ALLUMS, JAMES A. former cardiovascular surgeon; b. Kountze, Tex., Sept. 28, 1937; m. Elizabeth Dee Walton, June 24, 1961; children: Ann Elizabeth, Sarah Dee, Benjamin Walton. BA, U. Tex., 1959; MD, U. Tex. Med. Br., 1962. Diplomate Am. Bd. Med. Examiners, Am. Bd. Surgery, Gen. Vascular Surgery, Am. Bd. Thoracic Surgery. Rotating intern Phila. Gen. Hosp., 1962-63; resident gen. surgery Med. Br. U. Tex., Galveston, 1963-66, 68-69; resident thoracic surgery Med. Branch U. Tex., Galveston, Tex., 1969—71; ptnr. Thoracic and Cardiovascular Surg. Assocs., Beaumont, Tex., 1971-97; clin. asst. prof. dept. thoracic and cardiovascular surgery U. Tex. Med. Br., Galveston, ret., 1997. Active physician St. Elizabeth Hosp., chief of staff 1976-77, 87-88; active Beaumont, Bapt. Hosp. of S.E. Tex., Beaumont, Beaumont Regional Med. Ctr., Beaumont Regional Med. Ctr., Park Place Hosp.; courtesy staff St. Mary Hosp., Port Arthur, Mid Jefferson Hosp., Nederland, Tex.; cons. staff U. Tex. Med. Br. Hosp., Galveston; mem. cardiovascular com. Bapt. Hosp., 1991-93, 1996, physician, nurse ad hoc com., 1992; clin. asst. prof. Dept. of Surgery U. Tex. Med. Br. Hosp., 1993-94; OR com. St. Elizabeth Hosp., Beaumont, 1990-91, 93-94, cardiovascular quality assurance subcom., 1991-92, cardiovascular/coronary care com., 1990-91, 92-93, CCU quality assurance subcom. Contbr. articles to profl. jours. Capt. U.S. Army, 1966-68. Recipient J.C. Crager award Am. Heart Assn., 1992, Mr. East Tex. award Tyler County Dogwood Festival, 1993. Fellow ACS (gov. 1989-94, pres. South Tex. chpt. 1987), Am. Coll. of Angiology, Am. Coll. of Cardiology, Am. Coll. of Chest Physicians, Beaumont Acad. of Medicine; mem. AMA, Assn. of Am. Physicians and Surgeons, Bapt. Hosp. P.H.O., Beaumont Regional P.H.O., Jefferson County Med. Soc., Singleton Surg. Soc., Soc. of Thoracic Surgeons, So. Assn. for Vascular Surgery, So. Med. Assn., So. Thoracic Surg. Assn., St. Elizabeth Hosp. P.H.O., Tex. Med. Assn. (coun. on med. edn. 1985-92), Tex. Surg. Soc., Alumni Assn. of the U. of Tex. Med. Br. (pres. 1984-85)Phi Eta Sigma, Alpha Epsilon Delta.

ALLWEIN, ROBERT WILLIAM, mechanical engineer; b. Lebanon, Pa., Oct. 12, 1942; s. Kenneth James and Sally Allwein; m. Judy Bandy, Oct. 6, 1946; children: Kenneth, Marci King, Joshua, Jennifer. BSME, U. Okla., 1970. Profl. engr., Okla. Indsl. services rep Okla. Natural Gas Co., Tulsa, 1978—. Project engr. Southwestern Bell Tel. Co., Oklahoma City, 1970—79; v.p. Graham Allwein Cons. Engrs., Oklahoma City, 1979—81; mech. project engr. Davis & Rountree Cons. Engrs., Inc., Oklahoma City, 1981—84; engring. mgr. Bergoust Engrs. & Co., Missoula, Mont., 1984—86. With U.S. Army, 1960—63. Mem.: ASHRAE (chpt. pres. 1978—79, Golden Gavel award 1979), Assn. Energy Engrs. (cert. energy engr.). Avocations: flight simulator, travel. Office: Okla Natural Gas Co 5848 E 15th St Tulsa OK 74112

ALMAGUER, FRANK, ambassador; m. Antoinette Gallegos, 1970; children: Francisco Daniel, Nina Suzanne. BA in Polit. Sci., U. Fla., 1967; MS in Govt. and Bus. Adminstrn., George Washington U., 1974. Vol. Peace Corps, Orange Walk Town, Belize, 1967-69; mgmt. analyst Office of Auditor Gen., USAID; mgmt. analyst for health affairs Office of Econ. Opportunity; assoc. country dir. U.S. Peace Corps, Belize City, 1974-76, country dir. Tegucigalpa, Honduras, 1976-79; dep. mission dir. USAID, Panama City, 1979-83, dir. Office of S.Am. and Mex. Affairs Washington, 1983-86, mission dir. Quito, Ecuador, 1986-90; mem. Sr. Seminar Fgn. Svc. Inst., 1990-91; regional mission dir. Eastern Europe USAID, Washington, 1991-93, acting asst. adminstrn. Bur. for Europe, 1993, dep. asst. adminstr. human resources Bur. of Mgmt., 1993-96, mission dir. La Paz, Bolivia, 1996-99; amb. Republic of Honduras Dept. State, Tegucigalpa, 1999—2002. Recipient Meritorious award U.S. Peace Corps, 1979, Disting. svc. award USAID, 1989, Spl. Act award, 1992, Presdl. Meritorious awards, 1988, 99, Roger W. Jones Exec. Leadership award, 1996, State Dept. Superior Honor award, 1999, Sec. of State's Career Achievement award, 2002, AID Adminstr.'s Disting. Career award, 2002. Home: 1503 Dulcimer Ct Vienna VA 22182-1607

AL MALEK, AMIR ISA, entrepreneur, business consultant, musician; b. Shreveport, La., Apr. 2, 1951; s. Samuel Leroy and Evelyn Cynthia (Jones) K. AA Arts and Humanities, Laney Coll., 1981, AA Social Sci., 1983, AA Language Arts, 1985, AA Theater Arts, 1989, AA in Music, 1995; student, Columbia Sch. Broadcasting, Radio & T.V. Announcing, 1986; male modeling student, Barbizon Sch. Modeling, 1994; cert., Founds. of Faith Theology, 1994. Assoc. The Heritage Group, Walnut Creek, Calif., 1974—; pres., CEO Magnetic Phi Artists, Oakland, Calif., 1988—; supr. Loomis Armored Inc., Oakland, Calif., 1991—; coach San Francisco Generals; coord.-backfields and lineman Am. Athletic League; coach Alameda County Knights. Musician, poet free-lance, Oakland, 1970—; model, actor, Laney Coll., Yosson Enterprises, Oakland, San Francisco, 1981—; actor, dir. The Mahdi Theater, Oakland, 1989 ; rschr., dir., The Oil Bandana, Oakland, 1989—. Author (book of poetry) Africa Sweet Africe Me Africa Me, 1991, (short story) Three Coins for the Fisherman, 1990; composer: Tally of the Leaves, 1994, Clown Cloud, 1999. Min. Imam Nation of Islam, San Francisco, 1975—; min.-in-tng. Allen Temple Bapt. Ch., 1981; fruit of Islam, Nation of Islam Mosque 26; asst. coach Peralta Coll. Dist., Oakland, 1986-87; active spl. svcs. Rainbow Coalition Calif., 1984; del. Students for Jesse Jackson Campaign, Calaif., 1989; candidate for mayor City of Oakland, 1994. With U.S. Army, 1975-76. Named Citizen of Yr., recipient Ambassador award Principality of the Hutt River Province, Queensland, Australia. Mem. Internat. Platform Assn., Pre-Paid Legal Svcs. (assoc., license), The Fed. Bear Sports Club (diploma), Nirvana Found. for Psychic Rsch. (life), Am. Legion (life), Smithsonian Inst., Knight of the Realm (ambassador, Citizen of Yr. 1995, Principality of Hutt River Province Australia), Phi Beta Lambda, Epsilon Alpha Phi (past pres., past v.p. state chpt.). Republican. Moslem. Avocations: martial arts, weight lifting, yoga, wrestling. Home and Office: 9437 Olive St Oakland CA 94603-1725 E-mail: oliverslang@msn.com., mahdi5@juno.com.

AL-MARAYATI, ABID A. political science educator; b. Baghdad, Iraq, Oct. 14, 1931; came to U.S., 1949; s. Amin Hussien and Badriah (Haj Ghazi) Al-M.; 1 child, Ghazi Daniel. BA, Bradley U., 1952, MA, 1954; PhD, NYU, 1959. Instr. U. Mass., Boston, 1960-62; assoc. prof. SUNY, Plattsburgh, 1962-64, Ariz. State U., Tempe, 1965-68; prof. emeritus U. Toledo, 1968—. Vis. prof. Beijing Fgn. Studies U., spring 1991; lectr. Beijing U., Fudan U., Shanghai Inst. for Internat. Studies, Fgn. Affairs Coll.; guest lectr. univ. in Australia and New Zealand, summer 1990; commentator radio and TV programs in US and abroad; liaison officer US Com. for UN U.; chaired panels, the Academic Coun. on the United Nations System, 2003; panelist Mid. East Inst. Conf. on the Mid. East and the UN, 1965, Rocky Mountain Social Sci. Assn., 1968, Bowling Green U., 1969, Peace Sci. Soc., 1973, U. Houston, 1973; cons. com. on internat. rels. Group for Advancement of Psychiatry; chairperson, panelist numerous ann. meetings including Internat. Studies Assn., Duquesne History Foru, Comparative and Internat. Edn. Soc., Midwest Regional Meeting, Midwest Polit. Sci. Assn., Mid. East Studies Assn., Acad. Coun. on the UN Sys., 1976—; rschr., lectr. Soviet Acad. Scis. and Internat. Rsch. and Exch. Bd. under the US-U.S.S.R. Ednl. Exch. Program, summer 1974; asylum officer Dept. Justice, 1999. Author: A Diplomatic History of Modern Iraq, 1961, Middle Eastern Constitutions and Electoral Laws, 1968, The Middle East: Its Government and Politics, 1972; editor: International Relations of the Middle East and North Africa, 1985; contbr. articles to profl. jours. Mem. Dem. Orgn.; trustee Toledo Coun. World Affairs. Named Outstanding Tchr., U. Toledo, 1981—82; recipient Key to Golden Door, City of Toledo, 1984, NEH Disting. Scholar award, Hawaii Pacific U., 2001; fellow Rockefeller Found., Ella Lyman Cabot Trust, Carl and Lilly Pforzheimer Found., U. Toledo, Am. Philos. Soc.; grantee NYU Rsch. Found., Ariz. State U., U. Toledo. Mem. NAACP, Assn. Student Edn., World Assn. Former UN Interns and Fellows (bd. dirs.), Popular Culture Assn., Midwest Internat. Studies Assn., Assn. for Advancement of Policy, Am. Cultural Assn., Inst. for Oriental Studies (Moscow and St. Petersburg), Arab Polit. Thought Forum (Jordan), Bus. Adminstrn. Assn., Gulf Ctr. for Strategic Studies (London), Inst. for Psychiatry and Fgn. Affairs, Group for Advancement of Psychiatry, Am. Polit. Sci. Assn., Internat. Studies Assn., Mid. East Studies Assn. N.Am., Mid. East Inst., Acad. Coun. on the UN Sys., Phi Kappa Phi. Muslim-Shi'ite. Avocations: swimming, walking, exercising, reading. Home: 2109 Terrace Vw W Toledo OH 43607-1066

ALMEIDA, JOSÉ AGUSTIN, romance languages educator; b. Waco, Tex., Aug. 28, 1933; s. Jesse M. and Teodora (Mancillas) A.; m. Maritza Barros, Sept. 5, 1964; 1 son, José Rodolfo BA, Baylor U., 1961; MA, U. Mo., 1964, PhD, 1967. Teaching asst. U. Mo., Columbia, 1961-66; instr. Baylor U., Waco, 1962-63; asst. prof. dept. Romance langs. U. N.C., Greensboro, 1966-77, assoc. prof., 1977-99, chmn. Latin Am. studies, 1979-81, emeritus, 1999. Vis. prof. Elmira (N.Y.) Coll., summer 1967; asst. prof. Inst. in Mid. Am., summers 1968-69, Cali, Colombia, summer 1973; assoc. prof. study abroad program U. N.C.-Greensboro-Guilford Coll., Madrid, 1980, dir. grad. studies in Spanish, 1991-95; cons. verbal-active teaching method Hampton Inst., 1976, 77, U. N.C.-Charlotte, 1984; lectr. 1st Internat. Conf. Picaresque Lit., Madrid, 1976, 6th Conf. Internat. Assn. Hispanists, 1977, 1st Internat. Conf. on Lope de Vega, 1980. Author: (with Stephen C. Mohler and Robert R. Stinson) Descubrir y crear, 1976, 3d edit., 1986; La crítica literaria de Fernando de Herrera, 1976 With USAF, 1953-57 Nat. Endowment for Humanities fellow, 1970 Mem. MLA, Am. Assn. Tchrs. Spanish and Portuguese, Internat. Assn. Hispanists, Cervantes Soc. Am., Hispanic Soc. Am. (hon.), Asociación de Cervantistas, Sigma Delta Pi (faculty sponsor 1989—). Democrat. Roman Catholic. Home: 1410 Valleymede Rd Greensboro NC 27410-3938

ALMEIDA, RICHARD JOSEPH, finance company administrator; b. N.Y.C., Apr. 29, 1942; s. Caetano Escudero and Grace (Maya) A.; m. Jill Farris, Mar. 17, 1979; 1 child, Alexis Farris. BA in Internat. Affairs, George Washington U., 1963; MA in Internat. Adminstrn., Maxwell Sch. Syracuse U., 1965. Comml. and internat. banker Citibank, N.Y. and South Am., 1966; area head comml. and internat. banking Citicorp/Citibank, Chgo., 1976, L.A., 1978-84, dep. strategic planning N.Y.C., 1984; head fin. inst. and investment banking origination Citicorp Investment Bank, N.Y.C., 1985-87; CFO Heller Fin., Inc., Chgo., 1987—, also bd. dirs., chmn., CEO, 1995—. Bd. dirs. Fuji Bank and Trust, N.Y. Trustee The Latin Sch. of Chgo.; chmn. bd. dirs. High Jump; bd. dirs. Chgo. Youth Programs, Execs. Club Chgo.; mem. Chgo. Coun. Fgn. Rels. With USCG, 1966-72. Mem. Chgo. Club, The Casino, Chgo. C. of C., The Racquet Club, Econ. Club Chgo., Mid Am. Club. Roman Catholic. Office: Heller Fin Inc 500 W Monroe St Chicago IL 60661-3630

ALMEN, LOWELL GORDON, church official; b. Grafton, N.D., Sept. 25, 1941; s. Paul Orville and Helen Eunice (Johnson) A.; m. Sally Arlyn Clark, Aug. 14, 1965; children: Paul Simon, Cassandra Gabrielle. BA, Concordia Coll., Moorhead, Minn., 1963; MDiv, Luther Theol. Sem., St. Paul, 1967; LittD (hon.), Capital U., 1981; DD (hon.), Carthage Coll., 1989, Concordia Coll., 1994. Ordained to ministry Luth. Ch., 1967. Pastor St. Peter's Luth. Ch., Dresser, Wis., 1967-69; asso. campus pastor, dir. communications Concordia Coll., Moorhead, Minn., 1969-74; mng. editor Luth. Standard ofcl. publ. Am. Luth. Ch., Mpls., 1974-78; editor Luth. Standard, 1979-87; sec., officer Evangelical Luth. Ch. Am., Chgo., 1987—. Author: Old Songs for a New Journey, 1990, One Great Cloud of Witnesses, 1997; author, co-editor: The Many Faces of Pastoral Ministry, 1989; editor: World Religions and Christian Mission, 1967, Our Neighbor's Faith, 1968. Recipient Disting. Alumnus award Concordia Coll., 1982; Bush Found. grantee, 1972 Lutheran. Office: Evang Luth Ch 8765 W Higgins Rd Chicago IL 60631-4101

ALMES, JUNE, retired education educator, librarian; b. Pitts., Feb. 14, 1934; d. Donald John Rowbottom and Marie Catherine (Linz) Douglas; widowed; children: Lawrence John, Douglas Alan. BS in Edn., Ind. U. of Pa., 1955; MLS, U. Pitts., 1969. Tchr. Shippensburg (Pa.) Area High Sch., 1964-68; assoc. prof. Lock Haven (Pa.) U., 1971-94; ret., 1990. Instr. Changsha U. Electric Power, Hunan, China, 1989-90, 95. Trustee Ross Pub. Libr., Lock Haven, 1975-88, community story programs, 1973-86; tutor Clinton City Literacy Found., Lock Haven, 1979; pres. Ea. Clinton Co. Democratic Women's Club, 2003—. Mem. Am. Assn. Sch. Librs., Pa. Assn. Sch. Librs., ACLU, Phi Kappa Phi, Phi Delta Kappa. Democrat. Avocations: playing bridge, reading, travel, literacy. Home: 228 East Hillside Dr Lock Haven PA 17745-1733

ALMEYDA, ELIZABETH ANN, plastic surgeon; b. N.Y.C., Sept. 2, 1952; d. Eduardo and Helen (Ramos) A.; m. George V. Digiacinto, May 7, 1989; children: Alexandra, Gregory. BS, U. Rochester, 1974, MD, 1978. Diplomate Am. Bd. Surgery, Am. Bd. Plastic Surgery. Clin. instr. surgery Columbia U., N.Y.C., 1986-94; pvt. practice N.Y.C., 1985—. Cons. Med. Liability Ins. Co., 1986—. Mem. AMA, N.Y. County Med. Soc. (treas., sec., pres. 1998-99), Am. Med. Women's Assn., Am. Soc. of Plastic and Reconstructive Surgery. Avocations: skiing, golf. Office: 75 Central Park W New York NY 10023-6011 E-mail: eaa203@aol.com.

ALMJELD, PAUL F. conductor, music educator; b. Wabasso, Minn., June 2, 1942; s. Floyd J. and Frances M. Almjeld; m. Susan J. Gartman; children: Karin, Kristin, Karl. BS, Mankato State Coll., 1964, MusM, 1973; D in Musical Arts, U. Ill., 1988. Music tchr. Taylor Jr. HS, Eielson AFB, Alaska, 1965—67; dir. choral music New London (Wis.) Pub. Schs., 1970—74, Sheboygan (Wis.) South HS, 1974—82; assoc. prof. music Lakeland Coll., Sheboygan, 1982—92, Dakota Wesleyan U., Mitchell, SD, 1997—. Founder, condr. Lakeshore Chorale, Sheboygan, 1982—97; condr. Dakota Chorale, Mitchell, 1997—. Author: (book) The Madrigals of Horatio Faa, 1988; composer: (choral music) Amazing Grace, 2002, Praise the Lord, 2002. Sgt. U.S. Army, 1967—70. Mem.: Music Educators Nat. Conf., S.D. Choral Dirs. Assn., Wis. Choral Dirs. Assn. (pres. 1987—89, bd. dirs. 1985—91), Am. Choral Dirs. Assn. (life; bd. dirs. north ctrl. divsn. 1985—89), Phi Delta Kappa. Avocations: restoring british sports cars, fishing. Home: 1509 S Miller Ave Mitchell SD 57301 Office: Dakota Wesleyan Univ 1200 W University Ave Mitchell SD 57301 Personal E-mail: palmjeld@mit.midco.net. Business E-Mail: paalmjel@dwu.edu.

ALMOAZEN, HASSAN, research scientist; b. Damascus, Syria; BS in pharmacy, Damascus U., 1991; PhD in pharm. sci., LI U., 2002. Rsch. fellow LI U., Brooklyn, NY, 1995—2000; rsch. profl. Novartis Pharm., East Hanover, NJ, 2000; rsch. scientist Wyeth Rsch., Pearl River, NY, 2002—. Tchg. fellowship, Arnold and Marie Schwartz Coll. of Pharmacy, 1995—2000, Travel grant, Am. Assn. of Pharm. Scientist, 2001. Mem.: Am. Assn. of Colleges of Pharmacy, Am. Assn. of Pharm. Scientists, Am. Chem. Soc. Achievements include research in studying the reactions in multiphasic systems; determining the factors for conversion of salts in the stomach to the hydrochloride; analytical methods for the separation of para amino hippuric acid in plasma; new methods for improving the solubility and dissolution rate of poorly soluble compounds; a new method for analysis of reaction in emulsion; improving the stability of poorly stable compounds in dosage forms; development of mathematical equations to determine the rate constants of reactions as a function of the system composition. Home: 905 41st St Brooklyn NY 11219 Office: Wyeth Research 401 N Middletown Rd Pearl River NY 10965 Home Fax: 718-853-7332; Office Fax: 845-602-5563. Personal E-mail: halmoazen@msn.com. E-mail: almoazh@wyeth.com.

ALMODOVAR, PEDRO, filmmaker; b. Calzada de Calatrava, Spain, Sept. 25, 1949; Theater group actor: Los Goliardos; short films include: Salome, 1978-83; films: Pepi, Luci, Bom y otras chicas del monton, 1980, Laberinto de pasiones, 1980, Dark Habits, 1983, What Have I Done to Deserve This?, 1985, Matador, 1986, Law of Desire, 1987, Women on the Verge of a Nervous

Breakdown, 1988 (Felix award 1988), Tie Me Up, Tie Me Down, 1990, High Heels, 1991, Kika, 1993, The Flower of My Secret, 1995, Live Flesh, 1997, All About My Mother, 1999 (Best Dir., Cannes Film Festival, 1999, Best Fgn. Lang. Film, Acad. Awards 2000), Talk To Her, 2002 (Best Original Screenplay Academy award, 2003, Best Screenplay-Original, British Acad. Film Award (BAFTA), 2003); pub. Fuego en las entrañas, 1982, Patty Diphusa and Other Stories, 1992. Address: El Deseo SA Ruiz Perello 15 Madrid 28028 Spain*

ALMOND, CARL HERMAN, surgeon, physician, educator; b. Latour, Mo., Apr. 1, 1926; s. Hugh Herman and Sylvia (Morrison) A.; m. Nancy Ginn, June 18, 1964 (div. 1990); children: Carrie, Callie, Carl, Christopher. BS, Washington U., St. Louis, 1949, MD, 1953. Diplomate: Am. Bd. Surgery, Am. Bd. Thoracic Surgery. Rotating intern Los Angeles County Gen. Hosp., 1953-54; resident surgery U. Mich., Ann Arbor, 1954-56, jr. clin. instr. surgery, 1956-57, sr. clin. instr., 1957-58; fellow surg. pathology Barnes Hosp.-Washington U., St. Louis, 1956; sr. surg. resident in urology Baylor U. Affiliated Hosps., 1958-59; resident thoracic surgery U. So. Calif., Los Angeles, 1959, fellow thoracic surgery, 1962-63; staff surgeon Univ. Hosp., Columbia, Mo., 1959-78, dir. thoracic and cardiovascular surgery, 1968-77, VA Hosp., Columbia; fellow Brompton Hosp., London, Eng., 1961; asst. prof. surgery U. Mo. Sch. Medicine, Columbia, 1959-64, asso. prof., 1964-69, prof., chief thoracic and cardiovascular surgery, from 1969; prof. and chmn. dept. surgery Sch. Medicine, U. S.C., Columbia, 1978-85, dir. gen. surgery residency program, 1979-85, assoc. dean clin. research and devel., 1986-90. Vis. prof. U. Geneva, Switzerland, 1972-73; Mem. med. adv. panel FAA, 1970-75; mem. U.S. Commn. on UNESCO, 1983 Contbr. articles to profl. jours. Served with USNR, 1944-52. Fellow A.C.S.; mem. AMA, Boone County Med. Soc., Columbia Med. Soc., S.C. Med. Assn., S.C. Thoracic Soc., Am. Assn. Med. Colls., Frederick H. Coller Surg. Soc., St. Louis Surg. Soc., Am. Coll. Cardiology, Am., S.C. heart assns., Am. Soc. Artificial Internal Organs, Soc. Med. Cons. to Armed Forces, Am. Coll. Chest Physicians, So. Thoracic Surg. Assn., Central Surg. Soc., Am. Assn. Thoracic Surgery, So. Surg. Assn., S.C. Surg. Soc., Chest Club, Soc. Surg. Chairmen, Marion S. DeWeese Surg. Soc., Southeastern Surg. Soc., So. Surg. Soc., Internat. Cardiovascular Soc., Soc. Thoracic Surgeons, Sigma Xi, Nu Sigma Nu, Sigma Chi. Home: 1829 Senate St 4E Columbia SC 29201 Office: U SC Sch Medicine Dept Surgery Two Medical Park Ste 402 Columbia SC 29203

ALMOND, LINCOLN, lawyer, lobbyist, former governor; b. Central Falls, R.I., 1936. BS, U. R.I., 1959; LLB, Boston U. Bar: R.I., 1962. Adminstr. Town of Lincoln, R.I., 1963-67; U.S. atty. R.I., Dept. Justice, Providence, 1967-78, 81-93; pvt. practice, 1967-69, 78-81; with Blackstone Valley Devel. Found., 1993-95; gov. State of R.I., Providence, 1995-2003; lobbyist, 2003-. *

ALMOND, PAUL, film director, producer, screenwriter, novelist; b. Montreal, Que., Can., Apr. 26, 1931; s. Eric and Irene Clarice (Gray) Almond; m. Joan Elkins, Sept. 11, 1976; 1 child, Matthew James. Student, McGill U., Montreal, 1948-49; BA, Balliol Coll., Oxford, 1952, MA, 1954. TV producer-dir. CBC, Toronto, also in Los Angeles, N.Y.C., London, 1954-67; pres. Quest Films, Montreal, 1967—2002. Writer, producer, dir : (films) Isabel, 1968 (DGA nomination Best Feature Dir); Act of the Heart, 1970 (Genie for Best Feature Dir., 1970); Journey, 1972; Ups & Downs, 1982; The Dance Goes On, 1991; dir.: Captive Hearts, 1984; author: (book) La Vengeance des Dieux, 1999; author: (with M Ballantyne) High Hopes, 1999. Decorated officer Order of Can.; recipient Spec Diploma of Merit, Prague for Seven Up, 1963, Genie for Best Can TV Drama Dir, 1980. Mem.: Writers Union of Can., Nat. Writers Union, Royal Can. Acad. Arts, Dirs. Guild Am., Dirs. Guild Can. (hon.). Anglican. Home: 54 Malibu Colony Malibu CA 90265-4637

ALMONY, ROBERT ALLEN, JR., librarian, businessman; b. Charleston, W.Va., Oct. 14, 1945; s. Robert Allen and Margaret Elizabeth A.; m. Carol A. Krzeminski, May 6, 1972; children— Rob, Michael, Chandra, Rachel. AA, Grossmont Coll., 1965; BA, San Diego State U., 1968; M.L.S., U. Calif.-Berkeley, 1977. Sr. div. clk. San Diego State U. Library, 1965-68; acct. Calif. Tchrs. Fin. Services, Orange County, 1968-70, v.p., gen. mgr., 1971-76; research asst. library sch. U. Calif.-Berkeley, 1976-77; reference librarian Oberlin Coll. Library, Ohio, 1977-79; asst. dir. libraries U. Mo., Columbia, 1980—; owner Almony & Assocs. Tax and Fin. Planning, Columbia, 1980—; distbr. USA Today, Columbia, 1984-88. Guest lectr. libr. budgeting, personal fin. planning; spkr. on fin. planning, U. Mo. HR seminars, 1999—; cons. libr. copy svcs.; faculty coun. exec. bd., 1994-2000, recorder Mo. U., 1994-98, chair fiscal affairs, 1998-2000, learning strategies tchr., 1986—, adj. faculty Libr. Sch., 1997—. Contbr. articles to profl. jours. Treas. Bahai's of Columbia, 1982-86, 95-97, sec., 1987-89, 93-95, 1998-2001, 2001-2002, chmn., 1989-93; coach Columbia Youth Soccer League, 1981-92; cubmaster Boy Scouts Am., Columbia, 1983-85; asst. scoutmaster, 1985-91; hon. warrior Mic-O-Say, 1986—, treas. Mo. U. Soccer Boosters, 1996—; mem. Daniel Boone Regional Libr. Devel. Bd., 1999-2000; treas. U Kickers, 1998—. Mem. ALA, Mo. Libr. Assn. (treas. 1996-97, 98-99), Assn. Coll. and Rsch. Librs. (exec. com. 1983-86), Libr. Adminstrn. and Mgmt. Assn. (chmn. mem. 1991-93, 2000-01, Outstanding Svc. award 1994, B & F Officers Group Libr. Adminstrn. and Mgmt. (chmn. 1987-91), Nat. Commn. on Ednl. Stats. Integrated Post-Secondary Edn. Data Sys. Acad. Librs. (coord. for Mo. 1992—), Mo. Assn. Coll. and Rsch. Librs. (vice chmn., chmn. 1982-84), Hickman Athletic Boosters (pres. 1991-94), Maplewood Barn Theater (bd. dirs. 1993-2000, sec., treas. 1998-2000), COE Coll. Parents (bd. dirs. 1993-95). Home: 301 Rothwell Dr Columbia MO 65203-0257 Office: U Mo 104 Ellis Libr Columbia MO 65201-5149 E-mail: almonyr@missouri.edu. *Be of service to others in everything you do. Become a person of value to others.*

ALMORE-RANDLE, ALLIE LOUISE, special education educator; b. Jackson, Miss, Apr. 20; d. Thomas Carl and Theressa Ruth (Garrett) Almore; m. Olton Charles Randle, Sr., Aug. 3, 1974. BA, Tougaloo (Miss.) Coll., 1951; MS in Edn., U. So. Calif., L.A., 1971; EdD, Nova Southeastern U., 1997. Recreation leader Pasadena Dept. Recreation, Calif., 1954-56; demonstration tchr. Pasadena Unified Sch., 1956-63; cons. spl. edn. Temple City Sch. Dist., Calif., 1967; supr. tchr. edn. U. Calif., Riverside, 1971; tchr. spl. edn. Pasadena Unified Sch. Dist., 1955-70, dept. chair spl. edn. Pasadena H.S., 1972-98, also adminstrv. asst. Pasadena HS, 1993-98, surrogate parent, 2001—; ind. rep. Am. Comm. Network, Inc., 1997—; surrogate parent Pasadena Unified Sch., Pasadena, Calif., 2001. Supr. Evelyn Frieden Ctr., U. So. Calif., LA, 1970; mem. Coun. Exceptional Children, 1993—; ednl. cons. Shelby Renee Ednl. Ctr., Gardena, Calif., 2000—. Organizer Northwest Project, Camp Fire Girls, Pasadena, 1963; leader Big Sister Program, YWCA, Pasadena, 1966; organizer, dir. March on The Boys' Club, the Portrait of a Boy, 1966; organized Dr. Allie's Book Mobile Project, 2002; pub. souvenir jours. Women's Missionary Soc., AME Ch., State of Wash. to Mo.; mem. NAACP, Ch. Women United, Afro-Am. Quilters LA, established Dr. Allie Louise Almore-Randle Scholarship Award, Pasadena HS, 1998; co-established Theressa Garrett Almore Music Scholarsip award Jackson State U., Jackson, Miss., 1989; founding mem. Cmty. Women of San Gabriel Valley, 1998, Women of Pasadena, 2002. Recipient Cert. of Merit, Pasadena City Coll., 1963, Outstanding Achievement award Nat. Coun. Negro Women, Pasadena, 1965, Earnest Thompson Seton award Campfire Girls, Pasadena, 1968, Spl. Recognition, Outstanding Community Svc. award The Tuesday Morning Club, 1967, Dedicated Svc. award AME Ch., 1983, Educator of Excellence award Rotary Club of Pasadena, 1993, Edn. award Altadena NAACP, 1994; named Tchr. of Yr., Pasadena Masonic Bodies, 1967, Woman of the Yr. for Community Svc. and Edn., Zeta Phi Beta, 1992, Commendation, City of Pasadena; grad. fellow U. So. Calif., LA, 1970, recognition Uniformly Excellent Work and Exceptional Commitment and Dedication to Altadena/Pasadena Communities, Pasadena African Amer. Sch. Administr., 1998, Cert. Achievment in Educational Leadership, First AME Ch., 1998, Fran Cook Salute Great Inspiring Educator Award, United Tchr. of Pasadena, 1998, Named Outstanding Educator, Nat. Sorority Phi Delta Kappa, 1998. Mem. NAACP (life; bd. mem., chmn. ch. workers com. 1955-63, Fight for Freedom award West Coast region 1957, NAACP Edn. award Altadena, Calif. chpt. 1994), ASCD, Calif. Tchrs. Assn., Calif. African Am. Geneal. Soc., Nat. Coun. Negro Women, African Pan Am. Doctoral Scholars, L.A. World Affairs Coun., Phi Delta Gamma (hospitality chair 1971—), U. So. Calif. Alumni Assn. (life), Tougaloo Coll. Nat. Alumni Assn. (life), Phi Delta Kappa, Alpha Kappa Alpha (life, membership com.), Phi Delta Phi (founder, organizer 1961), Phi Delta Kappa. Democrat. Mem. Ame Ch. Avocations: wedding director, photography, gardening, family history. Home: 1710 La Cresta Dr Pasadena CA 91103-1261 Fax: 626-797-5549. E-mail: akainger@acninc.net.

ALMOZLINO, AVRAHAM, neurologist; b. Tel Aviv, 1954; s. Elyau and Sarah A.; m. Naomi Almozlino, 1981. MD, Tel Aviv U., Israel, 1983. Asst. prof. neurology Tufts Sch. Medicine, Boston, 1995—. Mem. Am. Acad. Neurology. Office: Neuro-Diagnostic Ctr 2000 Washington St Newton MA 02462-1650

ALMQUIST, DON, illustrator, artist; b. Hartford, Conn., July 21, 1929; s. Nils Herbert and Jeannette Theresa (Perrow) A.; m. Kerstin Rigmor Jesslen, May 21, 1955; children— Kristina, Jan Christian BFA, R.I. Sch. of Design, 1951. Staff artist Esquire, Inc., N.Y.C., 1951; creative dir. Ahlen & Akerlund, Stockholm, Sweden, 1963-66; adj. prof. Paier Coll. of Art, Hamden, Conn., 1979-84; graphic advisor U.S. Dept. of Fish and Wildlife, Washington, 1981-83. Illustrator: Christmas With Ed Sullivan, 1960, Doomed Road of Empire, 1962, What Did I See?, 1961, Loudmouse, 1962, (new illustrations) 1967, (new edit./illustrations) 1982, Spring is Like the Morning, 1964, Summer is a Very Busy Day, 1967, Dolls from Cheyenne, 1968, Some Animals Are Vary Small, 1968, When Grandmother was Young, 1970, When Great Grandmother was Young, 1971, Getting to Know New York State, 1971, Den Förtrollade Lådan, 1967, It Never Is Dark, 1967, Not Very Much of a House, 1967, Cathy Uncovers a Secret, 1969, Ginnie and the Mystery Light, 1973, Libby Shadows a Lady, 1974, Season at the Point, 1991, The Little Red Hen, 1991, Dragged Aboard, 1998; one-man shows include Galleri Z, Ystad, Sweden, 2000, Carolynn Roberts Gallery, Hockessin, Del., 2002; exhibited paintings and drawings in group and one-man shows New Castle (Del.) Arts Gallery, Ltd., 1991, Springfield Art Mus., 1993, Soc. Devel. en Arts Contemporains, Montreal, Que., Can., 1994; one-man shows include Askersund, Sweden, 1993, Miriam Schiell Fine Arts, Toronto, 1994, Gallery M2, Stockholm, 1995, Gallery Vattern Askersund, Sweden, 1996, Montchanin (Del.) Arts, 1996, New Castle Arts, 1998, Galleri Cafe Lucas, Stockholm, 1999, Carolynn Roberts Gallery, Yorklyn, Del., 2002; juried exhbns. include Miss. Watercolor Soc., Miss. Mus. Art, Hoyt Inst. Fine Arts, 1993, Nat. Art Show, New Castle, Pa., La. Art & Artists Guild and River Show, 1993, Aqueous '95 Show, Louisville (Grumbacher gold medal), Charlotte County Art Guild, Punta Gorda, 1997, 98, New Castle Hist. Soc., Kent. Watercolor Soc., 1997, Pleiades Gallery, N.Y.C., 2002, Md. Fedn. Art Am. Landscapes, Annapolis, Md., 2002, Rosenfeld Gallery, Phila., 2003, Pleiades Gallery, N.Y.C., 2003. Served as sgt. U.S. Army, 1951-53, Korea. Recipient numerous awards of merit Soc. of Illustrators, N.Y.C., 1953-84, Silver Medal, Phila. Art Dirs., 1955, Gold Medal, Milw. Art Dirs., 1963, numerous awards of merit N.Y. Art Dirs., N.Y.C. Episcopalian. Avocation: horticulture. Home and Office: 103 The Strand New Castle DE 19720-4827 E-mail: almquistart@aol.com., don@almquistart.com.

ALMQUIST, DONALD JOHN, retired electronics company executive; b. Elwood, Ind., Aug. 30, 1933; s. Elliott John and Gladys Ione (Jones) A.; m. Charline Gail Mull, Dec. 17, 1955; children: Gregory John, Tracy Gail. B in Indsl. Engring., Gen. Motors Inst., 1955. Supr. Delco Remy div. Gen. Motors Co., Anderson, Ind., 1956-64, plant supt., 1964-69, planr mgr., 1969-72, asst. dir. personnel, 1972-74, mgr. mfg., 1974-78, gen. mgr. mfg., 1978-82, gen. mgr., 1982-84, Delco Electronics div. Gen. Motors Corp., Kokomo, Ind., 1984-86; v.p., gen. mgr. Delco Electronics Corp., Kokomo, 1986-89, chmn., pres., chief exec. officer, 1989-93. Exec. v.p. GM Hughes Electronics, 1989-93; bd. dirs. Aladdin Industries LLC, Nashville, Ind. Corp. for Sci. Tech., Indpls., Trinity Cons., Inc., Dallas, Ind. Bus. Modernization and Tech. Corp., Indpls., State Sci. and Tech. Inst., Columbus, Ohio. Bd. trustees Rose Hulman Inst. Tech., Terre Haute, Ind., 1984—; bd. dirs. St. Johns Med. Ctr., Anderson, 1982-84, Ind. Vocat. Tech. Coll., Kokomo, 1984-86, St. Joe Hosp., Kokomo, 1984-86. Mem. Ind. C. of C. (bd. dirs. 1984-93). Methodist. Home: 7249 Lands End Cir Noblesville IN 46060-9416 E-mail: almquist97@aol.com.

ALMY, EARLE VAUGHN, JR., (BUDDY ALMY), real estate executive; b. July 29, 1930; s. Earle Vaughn and Minnye Ruth (Rounsaville) A.; m. Gorden Yetive McGowan, July 31, 1964 (div. 1967). BS in Animal Husbandry, Tex. Tech. U., 1952; postgrad., Am. Inst. Banking, 1956-62; grad., Realtors Inst. Cert. real estate brokerage mgr.; accredited land cons.; cert. real estate appraiser, Texas State Certified General Real Estate Appraiser. Credit analyst First Nat. Bank, Fort Worth, 1956-62; dir. finance and poultry feed sales Burrus Feed Mills, Saginaw, Tex., 1963-69; pres., mgr. Almy and Co., Hurst, Tex., 1970-79, Granbury, Tex., 1979—; v.p., dir. Northeast Tarrant County Bd. of Realtors, Hurst, Tex., 1972-74; pres. Almy and Co. Realtors, Weatherford, Tex., 1973-78; instr. appraisal of farms and ranches Weatherford Coll., 1986-89. Mem. Fort Worth Farm and Ranch Club; usher Acton United Meth. Ch.; pres. Rep. Club Hood County, 1991. With USAF, 1952-56. Sears Roebuck scholar, 1951. Mem. Nat. Assn. Realtors, Tex. Assn. Realtors, Granbury Assn. Realtors, Nat. Realtors Land Inst., Tex. Realtor's Land Inst. (state dir.), Nat. Assn. Real Estate Appraisers (cert. real estate appraiser), Pecan Plantation Country Club. Republican. Avocations: golf, hunting, fishing, boating, swimming. Home: PO Box 129 Granbury TX 76048-0129 E-mail: almyco@hcnews.com.

ALOFF, MINDY, writer; b. Phila., Dec. 20, 1947; d. Jacob and Selma (Album) A.; m. Martin Steven Cohen, June 16, 1968 (div. June 2000); 1 child, Ariel Nikiya. AB in English, Vassar Coll., 1969; MA in English, SUNY, Buffalo, 1972. Asst. prof. English U. Portland, Oreg., 1973-75; editor Encore Mag. of the Arts, Portland, 1977-80, Vassar Quar., Poughkeepsie, N.Y., 1980-88; dance critic New Republic, Bklyn., 1993—2001; cons. The George Balanchine Found., 2000—. Coord. Portland Poetry Festival, 1974—75; adj. assoc. prof. Barnard Coll., 2000—, asst. prof. practice, 2002—03. Author: (poems) Night Lights, 1979; author essays and revs. theatrical dancing and lit. for N.Y. Times Weekend, Book Rev. and Arts & Leisure, New Republic mag., Nation mag., Threepenny Rev., Dance mag., New Yorker mag., ann. Ency. Britannica, others. Recipient Whiting Writers award Mrs. Giles Whiting Found., N.Y.C., 1987; Woodrow Wilson Found. fellow, 1969, Woodburn fellow SUNY-Buffalo, 1972, Am. Dance Festival Dance Critics Inst. fellow, New London, Conn., 1977, John Simon Guggenheim Meml. Found. fellow, 1990. Mem. PEN Am. Ctr., Nat. Book Critics Circle (bd. dirs. 1988-91), Phi Beta Kappa.

ALOIA, JOHN F. endocrinologist, academic administrator; b. Brooklyn, NY, Mar. 24, 1938; m. Elvira Theresa Aloia; children: John, Mark, Maria Davani, Linda Martinez. BA Chemistry, Brooklyn Coll., Brooklyn, NY, 1958; MD, Creighton Medical Sch., Omaha, NE, 1962. Cert. #29248 Am. Bd. Internal Med., 1969, endocrinology & metabolism Am. Bd. Internal Med., 1972. Dir. Med. Ed. Winthrop U Hosp., Mineola, NY, 1978—83, med. dir., DEC, 1978—, chmn., dept. of med., 1978—99, chief acad. officer, 1999—, mem. of bd. of dir., 1999—. Author: The Complete Guide to Prevention and Treatment, 1998, A Colour Atlas of Osteoporosis, 1993. Capt. Med. Corps., 1963—65, Fort Lee, VA. Mem.: Am. Coll. of Physicians, Am. Soc. for Bone & Mineral Rsch., Am. Med. Assoc. Office: Winthrop U Hosp 222 Station Plaza N #510 Mineola NY 11501

ALOIA, ROLAND CRAIG, scientist, administrator, educator; b. Newark, Dec. 21, 1943; s. Roland S. and Edna M. (Mahan) A. BS, St. Mary's Coll., 1965; PhD, U. Calif., Riverside, 1970. Postdoctoral fellow City of Hope, Duarte, Calif., 1971-75; research biologist U. Calif., Riverside, 1975-76; asst. prof. Sch. of Medicine Loma Linda (Calif.) U., 1976-79; assoc. prof. Loma Linda (Calif.) U., 1979-89, prof. anesthesiology and biochemistry, 1989—. Chemist VA, Loma Linda, 1979-94, chief rsch. ops., 1994-99; pres., chmn. Loma Linda VA for Rsch. and Edn., 1988-94, pres., CEO, 1994-99. Editor: Membrane Fluidity in Biology, Vols. 1-4, 1983, 85; sr. editor: (series) Advanced in Membrane Fluidity vols. 1-3, 1988, vol. 4, 1989, vol. 5, 1991, vol. 6, 1992. Pres. Riverside chpt. Calif. Heart Assn., 1979-80, 1984-86, exec. com. mem., 1973-86, bd. dirs. 1978-86, v.p. 1984-86. Calif. Heart Assn. fellow, 1971-73. Mem. N.Y. Acad. Scis., Sigma Xi (pres. Loma Linda chpt. 1991-92, pres.-elect 1990-91). Avocations: flying, jogging, reading. Office: Dept Biochemistry Loma Linda U Loma Linda CA 92350

AL-OMAIR, SALEH, trade association administrator; Chmn. governing bd. OPEC Fund Internat. Devel., Vienna, Austria. Office: OPEC Fund Internat Devel PO Box 995 A-1011 Vienna Austria

ALOMAR, ROBERTO VELAZQUEZ, professional baseball player; b. Ponce, P.R., Feb. 5, 1968; With San Diego Padres, 1988—90, Toronto Blue Jays, 1990—95, Balt. Orioles, 1996—98, Cleve. Indians, 1998—. Named to All-Star team, 1990—96, Am. League Silver Slugger Team, Sporting News, 1992, 1996, All-Star Team, 1992; recipient Gold Glove award, Am. League, 1991—94. Office: New York Mets Shea Stadium 123-01 Roosevelt Avenue Flushing NY 11368

ALOMAR, SANDY, JR., (SANTOS VELAZQUEZ ALOMAR), professional baseball player; b. Salinas, P.R., June 18, 1966; With San Diego Padres, 1988-89, Cleve. Indians, 1990—2000, Chicago White Sox, 2001—02, Colorado Rockies, 2002—. Named Rookie of Yr. Baseball Writers' Assn. Am., 1990, Sporting News, 1990, named to Am. League All-Star team, 1990, 91; recipient Am. League Gold Glove award, 1990. Office: Colorado Rockies Coors Field 2001 Blake Street Denver CO 80205-2000

AL-OMARI, RA'ED M. computer engineer, consultant, computer scientist, researcher; b. Irbid, Jordan, June 3, 1971; s. Mohammad Sh. Al-Omari, Mariam M. Al-Skran; m. Maisaa W. Hawana, May 5, 1974. BSEE, Jordan U. Sci. and Tech., Irbid, 1994, MS in Computer Engring., 1997; PhD in Computer Engineering, Iowa State U., 2001. Registered engr. Tchr.'s asst. Jordan U. Sci. and Tech., Irbid, 1994—96; sys. engr. Yarmouk U., Irbid, 1996—97; rsch., tchr.'s asst. Iowa State U., Ames, 1997—2001; simulation software engr. Levetate Design System Inc., Portland, Oreg., 2000; adv. engring., scientist IBM Inc., Austin, 2001—02. Recipient Distinction Acad. award, Jordan U. Sci. and Tech., 1991-1992. Independent. Moslem. Avocation: travel. Office: IBM Inc Bldg 45 11400 Burnet Rd Austin TX 78758 Office Fax: 512-838-7694. Personal E-mail: raedomari@hotmail.com. Business E-Mail: alomari@us.ibm.com.

ALON, ILAN, international business educator; b. Rehovote, Israel, Dec. 12, 1971; s. Ed and Mimi (Shlomo) Alon; m. Anna Alon. BS in Mktg., Fairleigh Dickinson U, Teaneck, NJ, 1993, MBA in Internat. Bus., 1994; MA in Econs., Kent State U, 1996, PhD in Bus. Adminstrn., 1998. Instr. mktg. and econs. Kent State U, 1994—98; asst. prof. internat. bus. State U. N.Y., Brockport, 1998—2002; assoc. prof. internat. bus. Crummer Grad. Sch. Bus., Winter Park, Fla., 2002—. Econ. advisor Ctr. for Econ. Develop., SUNY, Oneonta, 1999—2000; internat. bus. cons. Custom Elec. Inc., Oneonta, 1999—2002, Global Packaging Alliance, Rochester, NY, 2001—02. Author: International Franchising in Industrial Marketing, 2003, Chnese Economic Transition and International Marketing Strategy, 2003, Chinese Culture, Organizational Behavior and International Business Management, 2003. Recipient Chinese Mktg. award, Soc. for Mktg. Advances, 2002, Cert. of Appreciation, John Molson Sch. of Bus., 2002, Wilber Hall Tchr. Recognition award, SUNY Oneonta, 2003. Mem.: Acad. of Mgmt., European Internat. Bus. Acad., Acad. of Internat. Bus. Home: 351 N Phelps Ave Winter Park FL 32789 Office: Crummer Grad Sch of Bus 1000 Holt Ave Winter Park FL 32789 E-mail: ialon@rollins.edu.

ALONEFTIS, ANDREAS, financial and investment executive; b. Nicosia, Cyprus, Aug. 24, 1945; BA, Sch. Accountancy and Bus. Studies, Glasgow, Scotland, 1973; MBA, So. Meth. U., 1978; postgrad., N.Y. Inst. Fin., 1982, Henley Mgmt. Coll., U.K., 1996—2000, Middlesex U., 2002. Acct. Cyprus Devel. Bank, Nicosia, 1966-72, chief acct., 1972-76, mgr. fin., 1976-78, sr. mgr. investments, 1978-82; gen. mgr., chief executive officer Cyprus Investment and Securities Corp., Nicosia, 1982-88; minister of def. Republic of Cyprus, 1988-93; chief exec. Am. Life Ins. Co., Nicosia, Cyprus, 1993-95; mng. dir. CypriaLife Ins., Nicosia, Cyprus, 1995-99, group gen. mgr. ins., 1999-2000; mng. dir., CEO Lambousa Venture Capital and Olympos Investments, Nicosia, 2000—01; exec. chmn. Cyber Group, 2001—02, Allied Capital, 2001—; exec. vice chmn. Alliance Internat. Reinsurance, 2001—. Sec. Cyprus Stock Exchange Interim Com., 1980-82. Contbr. articles to profl. jours. and newspapers. 2nd lt. Cyprus N.G., 1964-66. Fulbright Found. grantee, 1977-78; So. Meth. U. fellow, 1977-78, Salzburg Seminaz fellow, 1984. Fellow Assn. Internat. Accts. (mem. coun.). Clubs: Propeller Club of the U.S. Lodges: Rotary. Greek Orthodox. Avocations: music, reading, cinema, jogging. Home: 10 Kastellorizo St Nicosia 2108 Cyprus Office: Allied Capital ltd 5 Prometheus St n Nicosia 1065 Cyprus E-mail: alonefan@cytanet.com.cy.

ALONSO, DANIEL R. medical educator; b. Mendoza, Argentina, Aug. 31, 1936; arrived in U.S., 1964; s. Francisco Alonso and Manuela E. Cordoba; m. Powers Peterson M.D., Mar. 26, 2001; m. Maria Lita Elaskar, Jan. 9, 1963 (div. Sept. 16, 1996); children: Daniel R., Jennifer D. MD, U. Cuyo Sch. of Medicine, Mendoza, Argentina, 1962. Cert. anatomic pathology 1974. Assoc. dean admissions Weill Med. Coll. Cornell U., NYC, 1982—87, prof. pathology, 1985—, sr. assoc. dean, 1987—2001; dean Weill Cornell Med. Coll. in Qatar, Doha, 2001—. Hon. prof. U. del Aconcagua, Mendoza, Argentina, 1999. Mem.: Alpha Omega Alpha (faculty mem. 1989). Avocations: opera, classical music, computers. Home: 1212 Botetourt Gardens Norfolk VA 23517 Office: Weill Cornell Med Coll Qatar Ste 321 425 East 61 Street New York NY 10021 Office Fax: 212-821-0910. E-mail: dalonso@med.cornell.edu.

ALONSO, DIANE LINDWARM, cognitive psychologist; b. Washington, May 19, 1962; d. Joseph and Naomi Rose (Kotch) Lindwarm; m. W. Thomas Alonso Jr., May 31, 1993; children: Lisa Lindwarm Alonso, Johanna Lynn Alonso. BS in Computer Sci., U. Md., 1985, MS in Psychology, 1995, PhD in Psychology, 1998. Systems engr. IBM, San Jose, Calif., 1983, Balt., 1984, computer programmer Gaithersburg, Md., 1985-88, systems engr., 1988-89, human factors engr. Shade Grove, Md., 1989-91; rsch. asst. Human-Computer Interaction Lab., U. Md., College Park, 1984-85, rsch. and tchg. asst., 1992-96, instr. psychology, 1997; exec. dir. Tom Alonso Music, Ellicott City, Md., 1993-99; computer scientist Computer Scis. Corp., Shade Grove, Md., 1999—2002, Balt., 2002—. Mem. Assn. Computing Machinery, Human Factors and Ergonomics Soc., Potomac chpt. Human Factors and Ergonomics Soc., Phi Kappa Phi. Avocations: music, dance, theater, tennis, aerobics. Home: 3014 Cluster Pines Ct Ellicott City MD 21042-7619 Office: Computer Scis Corp 3120 Lord Baltimore Rd Baltimore MD 21244 E-mail: dlalonso@aol.com.

ALONSO-CRESPO, EDUARDO, composer, conductor; b. San Miguel de Tucumán, Argentina, Mar. 18, 1956; s. Eduardo Alonso-Crespo and María Teresa Mastracchio. MFA, Carnegie Mellon U., Pitts., 1987—89. Music dir. and condr. Carnegie Mellon Contemporary Ensemble, Pitts., 1989—; artist lectr., music history Carnegie Mellon U. Sch. Music, Pitts., 2002—; music dir., condr. Tucumán Symphony Orch., San Miguel de Tucumán, Argentina, 1989—2000; composer in residence and prin. guest condr. Salta Symphony Orch., Argentina, 2003—. Composer: (opera) Putzi, Juana, la loca, Yubarta, (composition for string orchestra) Sinfonietta, Chacona en tiempo de tango, (string quartet) String Quartet no. 2 El Valle de los Menhires, String Quartet no. 1, (choral composition) Waynápaq Taki, Pachamama, (piano concerto) Commentaries on Three Waltzes by Alberdi, (ballet) Medea, Macbeth, (symphony) Symphony op. 18, Dowland Variations, (concerto) Concerto for Viola and String Orchestra, Concerto for Clarinet and String Orchestra, Concerto for Piano and String Orchestra, Concerto for Bassoon and Orchestra. Named Musician of the Yr., Fundación Canal 11, Salta, Argentina, 1991; recipient Alejandro Shaw Composition Prize, Nat. Acad. Fine Arts of Argentina, 1981, Second Prize for Chamber Music Composition, San Telmo Found., Argentina, 1981, Second Prize, Chamber Music Composers Competition, Nat. U. of La Plata, Argentina, 1982, Third Prize, Viotti-Valsesia Competition, Italy, 1983, Cristóbal Colón Prize for Symphonic Music, Assn. of Ibero-American Capital Cities, Spain, 1986, Symphonic Composition Commn. Award, NEA of Argentina, 1990, Best Original Score for Theater, Iris Marga Found., Argentina, 1994, Symphonic Music Composition Prize, Bahía Blanca Symphony Orch., Argentina, 1996.

ALONZO, MARTIN VINCENT, mining and aluminum company executive, investor, financial consultant; b. N.Y.C., Apr. 8, 1931; s. Mariano and Mary (Traina) A.; m. Sabina Gallucci, June 7, 1952; children: Martin Vincent, Marlene, Sabrina. BBA in Acctg. cum laude, Baruch Coll., CUNY, 1952, MBA in Fin. and Investments, 1971. CPA, N.Y. Acct. Eisner and Lubin CPAs, N.Y.C., 1952-57; treas., contr. Credit-Am. Corp., N.Y.C., 1957-60; asst. v.p. indsl. time sales, financing and leasing A.J. Armstrong Co., Inc., N.Y.C., 1960-65; treas., sec. So. Nitrogen Co., Savannah, Ga., 1965-67; asst. to v.p. fin. AMAX Inc., Greenwich, Conn., 1967-68, mgr. fin. planning, 1968-69, asst. contr., 1969, contr., 1970, v.p. and contr., 1973-78, sr. v.p. controls and adminstrn., 1978-80, sr. v.p. and pres. indsl. minerals div., 1981-82, exec. v.p. and pres. splty. and light metals ops., 1982-83, exec. v.p., chief fin. officer, 1983-87; pres. MVA Fin. Corp., 1987—; chmn., pres., CEO Chase Industries, Inc., 1990—2001; ptnr. Tri-Artisan Ptnrs., LLC, 2002—. Mem. Am. Copper Coun.; bd. dirs. Copper & Brass Fabricators Coun., Inc., Copper Devel. Assn.; pres.'s coun. MAPI, 1993;

mem. Internat. Wrought Copper Coun., 1999; trustee IPO plus aftermarket mut. fund. Bd. dirs. Greenwich Health Assn., 1978-90, Am. Found., 1993-95; active Greenwich Bd. Health, 1982-92, U.S. Nat. Com. Pacific Econ. Cooperation, 1993-99. Recipient Freedom of the Human Spirit award, Internat. Ctr. for the Disabled, 1999. Mem. Nat. Assn. Accts. (chmn. mgmt. acctg. practices com. 1976-79), Conf. Bd., Coun. Fin. Execs., Fin. Adv. Coun. (exec. com. 1984-87), Extractive Industries Luncheon Group (chmn. 1978-79), Am. Mining Congress (chmn. acctg. com. 1980-82, mem. pension com. 1978-82), Internat. Magnesium Assn. (bd. dirs. 1983-84), AICPA, Fin. Execs. Inst., AIME, Phosphate Rock Export Assn. (dir. 1982-83), Mining Club N.Y.C. (dir.), Econ. Club N.Y., Westchester Country Club, Sky Club, Roundtable of Greenwich, Beta Alpha Psi, Beta Gamma Sigma, Am. Assn. Sovereign Mil. Order of Malta, Legatus. Republican. Office: 2 Sound View Dr Ste 100 Greenwich CT 06830 Office Fax: 203-622-1341. E-mail: mvalonzo1@aol.com.

ALOTTA, ROBERT IGNATIUS, historian, educator, writer; b. Feb. 26, 1937; s. Peter Philip and Jean (Sacchetti) A.; m. Alice J. Danley, Oct. 1, 1960; children: Peter Anthony, Amy Louise. BA, LaSalle Coll., Phila., 1959; MA, U. Pa., 1981; PhD, Temple U., 1984. With Triangle Publs., Phila., 1956-67, merchandising mgr. Inquirer divsn., 1959-63, mgr. customer svc. Inquirer-Daily News, 1963-66, new bus. coord. Daily News, 1966-67; mgr. spl. projects Penn Cen. Transp. Co., Phila., 1967-72; dir. pub. info. Phila. Housing Authority, 1972-81; asst. prof. comms. Grand Valley State Coll., Allendale, Mich., 1981-84; from asst. prof. comm. to assoc. prof. Miss. State U., 1984-92; pres. Alotta Ink, 1992—. Prof., dean Sr. U., Ctr. Mil. Studies, 1996—; dir. edn. and info. svcs. Rockingham County Sheriff's Office, 1996—; adj. assoc. prof. Blue Ridge C.C., 1999—. Exec. prodr.: (TV series) The Kids Show, 1985-86; scriptwriter: (radio series) A Philadelphia Moment, 1982, Past/Prolog, 1976, other radio, TV series, 1969—; host: (TV series) Perceptions of War, 1988-89; co-host TV series Midweek, 1989, (radio show) Midday; narrator: (radio series) A Minute of Your Time, 1977-78; host, prodr.: (radio show) Point of View, 1996-98; Gimme a Break (radio show), 2001-. author: Street Names of Philadelphia, 1975, Stop the Evil, 1978, Old Names and New Places, 1979, A Look at the Vice President, 1981, Military Executions of the Union Army, 1861-1866, 1984, Civil War Justice, 1989, Mermaids, Monasteries Cherokees and Custer: The Story Behind Philadelphia's Street Names, 1990, Another Part of the Field: Philadelphia's Revolution, 1777-78, 1991, Signposts and Settlers: The History Behind the Place Names Beyond the Rockies, 1993, The Last Voyage of the Henry Bacon, 2001 (with Donald R. Foxvog), Margaret "Peggy" Eaton: The Innkeeper's Daughter, 2004; contbr. articles, book revs. to publs. Pres. Shackamaxon Soc., 1967—; mem. pres.'s coun. LaSalle Coll., 1976-81. With Security Agy., AUS, 1960-61. chmn., Rockingtom Regional Triad, 1999-. Recipient Freedom Found. at Valley Forge awards, 1970, 73, 74, 76, Legion of Honor award Chapel of 4 Chaplains, 1975, Colonial Dames, DAR awards, 1976, Americanism award County Detectives Assn. Pa., 1977, 17 Web site design awards; Comdr.'s award and medal for pub. svc. U.S. Dept. Army, 2000. Mem. Am. Name Soc. (trustee 1982-84), Coun. on Am.'s Mil. Past (bd. dirs. 1984-88, 89-92), Mil. History Inst., Orgn. Am. Historians, Am. Hist. Assn., Cross Keys, Order of Sons of Italy (trustee 1983-84), Nat. Press Club (Washington), KC, Sigma Delta Chi (bd. dirs. Golden Triangle chpt. 1984-86), Tau Alpha Pi, Alpha Phi Omega. Home: 283 Newman Ave Harrisonburg VA 22801-4027 Office: Rockingham Co Sheriff 25 S Liberty St Harrisonburg VA 22801 E-mail: bob@alottaink.com.

ALOU, FELIPE ROJAS, professional baseball manager; b. Santo Domingo, Dominican Republic, May 12, 1935; Player San Francisco Giants, 1958-62, Milw. Braves, 1964-65, Atlanta Braves, 1966-69, Oakland Athletics, 1970-71, N.Y. Yankees, 1971-73, Montreal Expos, 1973, Milw. Brewers, 1974; coach Montreal Expos, 1979-80, 84, mgr., 1992—2001; bench coach Detroit Tigers, 2002; mgr., S.F. Giants, 2002—. Named to Nat. League All-Star team Sporting News, 1966; named Nat. League Mgr. of Yr. Sporting News, 1994, Baseball Writers' Assn. Am., 1994. Office: San Francisco Giants Pacific Bell Pk 24 Willie Mays Plz San Francisco CA 94107*

ALOU, MOISES, professional baseball player; b. Atlanta, July 3, 1966; s. Felipe Alou. Outfielder Pitts. Pirates, 1990, Montreal Expos, 1990; outfielder Montreal Expos, 1992—96; outfielder Fla. Marlins, 1997, Houston Astros, 1998—2001, Chgo. Cubs, 2002—. Named Player of Yr., Montreal Expos, 1994; named to Nat. League All-Star Team, Sporting News, 1994, Nat. League Silver Slugger Team, 1994; recipient Buck Canel award for Top L. Am. Player, 1994. Office: Chicago Cubs Wrigley Field 1060 West Addison Chicago IL 60613

ALPEN, EDWARD LEWIS, biophysicist, educator; b. San Francisco, May 14, 1922; s. Edward Lawrence and Margaret Catherine (Shipley) A.; m. Wynella June Dosh, Jan. 6, 1945; children: Angela Marie, Jeannette Elise. BS, U. Calif., Berkeley, 1946, PhD, 1950. Br. chief, then dir. biol. and med. scis. Naval Radiol. Def. Lab., San Francisco, 1952-68; mgr. environ. and life scis. Battelle Meml. Inst., Richland, Wash., 1968-69, assoc. dir., then dir. Pacific N.W. div., 1969-75; dir. Donner Lab., U. Calif., Berkeley; also assoc. dir. Lawrence Berkeley Lab., 1975-87; prof. biophysics emeritus U. Calif., Berkeley, 1975—, prof. radiology emeritus San Francisco, 1976—, dir. study ctr. London, 1988-90; councillor, dir. Nat. Council Radiol. Protection, 1969-92; exec. v.p., tech. dir. Neutron Tech. Corp., Berkeley, 1990-93. Mem. Gov. Wash. Council Econ. Devel., 1973-75; bd. dirs. Wash. Bd. Trade, 1973-76. Author books, papers, abstracts in field. Served to capt. USN, 1942-46, 50-61. Recipient Navy Sci. medal, 1962, Disting. Service medal Dept. Def., 1963, Sustaining Members medal Assn. Mil. Surgeons, 1971; fellow Guggenheim Found., 1960-61; sr. fellow NSF, 1958-59 Fellow: Calif. Acad. Scis.; mem.: Biophys. Soc., Radiation Rsch. Soc., Am. Philat. Soc., Bioelectromagnetics Soc. (pres. 1979—80), Sigma Xi (nat. lectr. 1994—96). Episcopalian. Home: 1101 Ivy Ct El Cerrito CA 94530-2745 E-mail: e.alpen@attbi.com.

ALPER, BARBARA JOY, anesthesiologist; b. Milw., Aug. 31, 1958; BSRN, U. Wis., 1979; BSPAC, Touro Coll., 1981; MD, U. Tech. Santiago, 1985. Diplomate Am. Bd. Anesthesiology, Am. Bd. Internal Medicine, Am. Bd. Critical Care Medicine. Intern Booth Meml. Med. Ctr., Flushing, N.Y., 1985-86, resident in internal medicine, 1986-88; fellow in critical care medicine Norwalk (Conn.) Hosp., 1988; resident in anesthesiology Albert Einstein Coll. Medicine, Bronx, N.Y., 1989-91, fellow in critical care medicine, 1991; asst. prof anesthesiology Mt. Sinai Med. Ctr., 1999—. Fellow Am. Coll. Chest Physicians; mem. ACP, Am. Soc. Anesthesia, N.Y. State Soc. Anesthesia.

ALPER, CUNEYT M. pediatric otolaryngologist; b. Merzifon, Turkey, May 3, 1957; came to U.S., 1992; s. Zeki and Meral A.; m. Gulay Alper, Apr. 26, 1982; 1 child, Berk A. MD, Hacettepe U., Ankara, Turkey, 1982. Resident Vakif Gureba Hosp., Istanbul, Turkey, 1986-89, chief resident, 1989; ear, nose, throat, head and neck surgeon Kartal Tng. and Rsch. Hosp., Istanbul, 1989-92; staff otolaryngologist Children's Hosp. Pitts., 1995—; vis. scholar U. Pitts. Sch. of Medicine, 1992-94, vis. asst. prof. otolaryngology, Hamburg rsch. fellow, 1994-96, asst. prof., 1996-2000, assoc. prof., 2000—. Rsch. cons. pediat. otolaryngology Rangos Rsch. Ctr., Children's Hosp., Pitts., 1992-93, lab. supr., 1993-97. Contbr. numerous articles to profl. publs., including Acta Oto-Laryngology, Laryngoscope, Jour. Infectious Disease, others; presenter in field. Grantee numerous orgns., including NIH, 1992 , NIMH, 1993—, others. Mem. AAAS, AMA, Am. Acad. Otolaryngology, Assn. Rsch. in Otolaryngology, Soc. Ear, Nose, and Throat Advances in Children, Inc., European Soc. Pediatric Otolaryngology, Turkish Med. Assn., Turkish Otorhinolaryngology Assn. Office: Childrens Hosp Pitts Dept Pediat Otolaryngology 3705 5th Ave Pittsburgh PA 15213-2524 E-mail: alperc@pitt.edu.

ALPER, HOWARD, chemistry educator; b. Montreal, Oct. 17, 1941; s. Max and Frema (Weinstein) A.; m. Anne Elizabeth Fairhurst, June 4, 1966; children: Lara, Ruth. BS, Sir George Williams U., Montreal, 1963; PhD, McGill U., 1967. From asst. prof. to assoc. prof. SUNY, Binghamton, 1968-74; assoc. prof. U. Ottawa, 1975-77, prof., 1977—. Chmn. dept. chemistry U. Ottawa, 1982-85, 88-94, asst. v.p. rsch., 1995-96, v.p. rsch., 1997—. Editor: two books on organometallic chemistry and catalysis; contbr. more than 450 articles to profl. jours. Mem. adv. coun. Order of Can., 2000—02. Decorated officer Nat. Order of Merit (France); recipient Alfred Bader award in organic chemistry, 1990, Commemorative medal for significant contbns. to Can., 125th Anniversary of Can., 1992, E.W.R. Steacie award for disting. contbns. to chemistry, Can. Soc. for Chemistry, 1993, Urgel-Archambault prize in phys. scis., math. and engring., 1996, Bell Can. Forum award, 1998, Gerhard Herzberg Gold medal, 2000, Nat. Merit award Life Scis. Coun., 2001, Le Seuer meml. award, Soc. Chem. Industry, 2002; fellow NATO postdoctoral fellow Princeton U., 1967-68, E.W.R., Steacie fellow Nat. Sci. Engring. Rsch. Coun. Can., 1980-82, Guggenheim fellow, 1985-86, Killam rsch. fellow, Killam Found., 1986—88. Fellow: Acad. of Sci. (v.p. 1995—98, pres. 1999—2001, chair partnership group sci. and engring. 1995-99, pres. 2001-), Royal Soc. Can.; mem.: Order of Can. (officer 1999), European Acad. Arts Sci. Humanities (titular mem.), Chem. Inst. Can. (Alcan award 1980, Catalysis award 1984, CIC medal 1997, Montreal medal 2003), Royal Soc. Chemistry (London), Am. Chem. Soc., Natural Scis. and Engring. Rsch. Coun. Can. (group chmn. chemistry 1987-90). Jewish. Achievements include patents for holder 35 patents. Office: U Ottawa Dept Chemistry 10 Marie Curie Ottawa ON Canada K1N 6N5

ALPER, JOANNE FOGEL, lawyer; b. N.Y.C., Sept. 16, 1950; d. Ben R. and Florence D. (Schneider) Fogel; m. Paul Edward Alper, Aug. 4, 1973; children: Michael Ian, Brooke Lauren. BA, Syracuse U., 1972; JD, George Washington U., 1975. Bar: Va. 1975, U.S. Dist. Ct. (ea. dist.) Va. 1975, D.C. 1976, U.S. Dist. Ct. D.C. 1976, U.S. Ct. Appeals (4th and D.C. cirs.) 1978, U.S. Supreme Ct. 1980. Assoc. Leonard, Cohen & Gettings, Arlington, Va., 1975-79; ptnr. Cohen, Gettings, Alper & Dunham, Arlington, 1979—; subs judge Juvenile and Domestic Rels. Ct., 17th Jud. Dist. Mem. Arlington County Fair Housing Bd., 1984-88, mem. Commn. on Arlington's Future, 1986. Fellow Am. Acad. Matrimonial Lawyers; mem. Arlington Bar Assn. (pres. 1982-83), Va. State Bar (bar coun. 1989—, pres. conf. local bar assns. 1984-85, chmn. family law sect. 1985-86), Va. Trial Lawyers Assn. (dist. gov. 1983-87, gov. at large 1987—), No. Va. Young Lawyers Assn. (pres. 1979, v.p. Arlington County 1978). Home: 5601 Little Falls Rd Arlington VA 22207-1566 Office: Cohen Gettings Alper & Dunham 2200 Wilson Blvd Arlington VA 22201-3324

ALPER, MERLIN LIONEL, finance company executive; b. Bklyn., May 25, 1932; s. James B. and Rose (Mellis) Alper; m. Elaine R. Honig, Dec. 21, 1957; children: Jerome Eric, Alyssa Ellen. BBA, Adelphi U., 1955. CPA N.Y. With Arthur Andersen & Co., N.Y.C., 1955-68, comml. audit mgr., 1963-68; dir. fin. controls ITT, N.Y.C., 1968-73, asst. comptr., 1973-93, corp. v.p., 1979; v.p., contr. ITT Europe, Inc., 1978-84; corp. v.p., comptr., dir. ITT Telecom. Corp., 1984-85; v.p., dep. contr. ITT Corp., N.Y.C., 1993-95; exec. v.p., CFO Madison Sq. Garden, N.Y.C., 1995-98; mng. dir. Ind. Coll. Fund N.Y., 1999—, also chmn. bd. dirs. Mem. emerging issues task force Fin. Acctg. Stds. Bd., 1990—95. With Chem. Corps U.S. Army, 1956—58. Named to Acad. of Distinction, Adelphi U. Alumni, 1984. Mem.: AICPA, Fin. Execs. Internat. (mem. com. on corp. reporting), Inst. Mgmt. Accts. (dir. NY chpt. 1965—66), N.Y. State Soc. CPAs.

ALPERIN, IRWIN EPHRAIM, clothing company executive; b. Scranton, Pa., Apr. 29, 1925; s. Louis I. and Bessie (Wickner) A.; m. Francine Leah Friedman, Dec. 5, 1948; children: Barbara Joy, Jane Leslie. Cert. Mech. Engring., Pa. State U., 1945; BS in Indsl. Engring., Lehigh U., 1947; DHL (hon.), U. Scranton, Pa., 1991. Mgmt. trainee Mayflower Mfg. Co., Scranton, 1947-49, sec., 1952-79, pres., 1980-91. With Triple A Trouser Mfg. Co., Inc., Scranton, 1952, v.p., treas., 1958-79, pres., 1980-91; with Gold Star Mfg. Co., Inc., Scranton, 1956, pres., 1956-91; sec. Astro Warehousing, Inc., Scranton, 1962-91; sec.-treas. Bondeal, Inc., Scranton, 1978-89, pres., 1989—; v.p. RCO, Inc., 1989-91; vice chmn. Montage, Inc., 1979-92; sec. Alperin, Inc., 1982-91, pres., 1991—; sec. All Star Industries, Inc., 1989-92, pres., 1993—; treas. Calvin Clothing Co. Inc., 1996—. Bd. dirs. Econ. Devel. Coun. N.E. Pa., Avoca, 1974-96, v.p., 1978-83; bd. dirs. ARC, Scranton, 1968-88, pres. spl. adv. bd., 1988—; bd. dirs. Jewish Home Ea. Pa., Scranton, 1970—, treas., 1981-97; pres. Elan Gardens, 1995-2000, pres. emeritus, 2000—; bd. dirs. Jewish Cmty. Ctr., Scranton, 1971-86, now life mem.; bd. dirs. Pa. United Way, Harrisburg, 1973-78, Scranton Counseling Ctr., 1975-78, trustee, 1979-95; pres. Planning coun. Social Svcs. Lackawanna County, 1972-74, now life mem.; pres. Jewish Family Svc. of Lackawanna County, 1967-70, now life bd. mem.; v.p. United Way Lackawanna County, 1974-78, exec. com., 1978-86; pres. Alperin Found., Scranton, 1962-93; treas. Scranton-Lackawanna Jewish Fedn., 1973-75, life mem. bd. dirs.; trustee Amos Lodge Found., 1982—, v.p., 1989-91; trustee Found. Jewish Elderly, 1994—, v.p., 1985-2003, pres. 2003—; trustee Pocono N.E. Devel., 1983—, sec., 1986-95, pres., 1995-96; pres. Temple Hesed, 1969-71, life mem., bd. dirs., Scranton; mem. Lackawanna County Libr. Bd., 1983-85; treas. Lackawanna Regional Cultural Coun., 1988-91, bd. dirs. 1988-93; bd. dirs. Broadway Theatre League Lackawanna County, 1989-2000, vice chmn., 1994-99; bd. dirs. Masonic Temple Civic Ctr. Found., 1989-93; trustee U. Scranton, 1991-97. With C.E. AUS, 1944-46. Recipient Americanism award, 1982; named Man of Year, Jewish Community Ctr., 1973, Disting. Pennsylvanian, Phila. C. of C., 1982. Mem. Am. Inst. Indsl. Engrs. (sr.), Glen Oak Country Club (Clarks Summit, Pa.), Wave Oak Realty (Clarks Summit) (v.p. 1989-91), Masons, Shriners, Elks, B'nai B'rith (trustee, Man of Yr. 1982). Home: 1010 Victoria Ln Clarks Summit PA 18411-9248 *To know your god—know yourself.*

ALPERIN, JONATHAN LAZARE, mathematician, educator; b. Boston, June 2, 1937; s. Jordan Louis and Esther T. Alperin. AB, Harvard U., 1959; AM, Princeton U., 1960, PhD, 1961. Post doctoral rschr. Oxford (Eng.) U., 1961—62; Moore instr. MIT, Cambridge, Mass., 1962—63; asst. prof. math. U. Chgo., 1963—66, assoc. prof., 1966—70, prof., 1970—. Author: Local Representation Theory, 1986, Groups and Representations, 1995. Fellow, Guggenheim Found., 1974—75. Office: U Chgo Dept Math 5734 S University Ave Chicago IL 60637-1514 Home: 5728 Woodlawn Ave Chicago IL 60637 Office Fax: 773-702-9787. Business E-Mail: alperin@math.uchicago.edu.

ALPERIN, RICHARD MARTIN, clinical social worker, psychoanalyst; b. Mt. Vernon, N.Y., Oct. 16, 1946; s. Israel and Sara A.; children: Heather Nicole, Alexander Scott. BBA, We. Mich. U., 1968; MSW, Fordham U., 1974; DSW, Columbia U., 1982; postdoctoral diploma in psychotherapy and psychoanalysis, Adelphi U., 1988. Cert. social worker, N.Y.; lic. clin. social worker, N.J.; diplomate Am. Bd. Examiners in Clin. Social Work; cert. group psychotherapist Nat. Registry Cert. Group Psychotherapists. Cons. Mt. Vernon Youth Bd., 1972-76; adj. faculty Marymount Manhattan Coll., N.Y.C., 1974-76; psychotherapist Riverdale Mental Health Clinic, N.Y.C., 1974-77; psychol. counselor, psychotherapist Ctr. Counseling and Psychol. Svcs. Ramapo Coll. of N.J., 1976-81, adj. faculty, 1977-86, moderator evening forums, 1978, 80; counselor, psychotherapist Ctr. Counseling and Psychol. Svcs. SUNY, Purchase, 1981-82, 84-85, acting dir., 1982-84; clin. cons. Westside Ctr. for Family Svcs., N.Y.C., 1985-87; guest lectr. Cabrini Med. Ctr., 1979; pvt. practice psychotherapy and psychoanalysis Riverdale, N.Y., 1977—, Teaneck, N.J., 1980—, N.Y.C., 1984—. Guest lectr. grand rounds dept. psychiatry, Brookdale Hosp. Med. Ctr., 1996; field instr. Sch. Social Work-Columbia U., 1983-85; adj. assoc. prof. Sch. Social Svc.-Fordham U., 1985-98; adj. asst. prof. Grad. Sch. Social Work-NYU, 1989-91; mem. faculty, dean curriculum Rockland Inst. for Psychoanalysis and Psychotherapy, 1990-95; mem. faculty Advanced Inst. Analytic Psychotherapy, 1992-95, Object Rel. Inst. Psychoanalysis and Psychotherapy, 1992—, Psychoanalytic Psychotherapy Study Ctr., 1994—, N.J. Inst. for Tng. in Psychoanalysis, 1994—. Co-editor: The Impact of Managed Care on the Practice of Psychotherapy: Innovation, Implementation, and Controversy, 1996; contbr. articles to profl. jours.; rsch. on psychotherapy, suicide and provision of preventative svcs. Nat. Jewish Welfare Bd. fellow Fordham U., 1972-74. Trainee NIMH Columbia U., 1978. Mem.: NASW, Nat. Acads. Practice (disting. practitioner, diplomate), N.J. Coalition Mental Health Profls. and Consumers (mem. adv. bd.), Nat. Study Group on Social Work and Psychoanalysis, Alliance for Universal Access to Psychotherapy (founder, membership chair, mem. steering com. 1994-96), Nat. Membership Com. Psychoanalysis Clin. Social Work (treas. 1991—93, chair NY-NJ area 1992—94), Nat. Fedn. Soc. Clin. Social Work, Acad. Cert. Social Workers (cert.), Ea. Group Psychotherapy Soc., Am. Group Psychotherapy Assn., Adelphi Soc. Psychoanalysis and Psychotherapy, N.Y. State Soc. Clin. Social Work (chair aid com. on psychoanalysis 1991—96, diplomate). Office: 175 Cedar Ln Teaneck NJ 07666-4315

ALPERN, ANDREW, lawyer, architect, historian; b. NYC, Nov. 1, 1938; s. Dwight K. and Grace M. (Michelman) Alpern. BArch, Columbia U., 1964; DSc, London Coll. Applied Sci., 1971; JD magna cum laude, Benjamin N. Cardozo Sch. Law, 1992. Registered arch., N.Y.; bar: N.Y. 1993, U.S. Dist. Ct. (so. and ea. dists.) N.Y. 1994. With Haines Lundberg Waehler, archs., NYC, 1962—67; project dir. Saphier, Lerner, Schindler, Environetics, NYC, 1968—72; v.p., dir. arch. Environ. R&D, Inc., Space Planning & Design, NYC, 1972—75; dir. rsch. Corp. Planners & Coord., NYC, 1973—75; project mgr. Hellmuth, Obata & Kassabaum, P.C., NYC, 1977—78; mgr. real estate and facilities planning PricewaterhouseCoopers LLP, NYC, 1978—88; cons. arch., hist. arch. NYC, 1988—. Mem. adv. bd. Inst. Applied Psychotherapy, 1969—72; nat. panel arbitrators Am. Arbitration Assn., 1971—86; cons. lawyer, 1993; spl. counsel Hughes Hubbard & Reed LLP, 1994—2002; exec. v.p., counsel Peter Kimmelman Asset Mgmt. LLC, 2002—; lectr. CUNY, Inst. Architecture and Urban Studies, Grolier Club, Mcpl. Art Soc. Author: (book) Apartments for the Affluent: A Historical Survey of Buildings in New York, 1975, Garret Ellis Winants: 1813-1890, 1976; editor-in-chief: Legal Briefs for the Cons. Industry, 1978—92; author: (book) Alpern's Architectural Aphorisms, 1979; pub.: F.M.R.A. (Edward Gorey), 1980; author: (book) Handbook of Specialty Elements in Architecture, 1981, In the Manor Housed, 1982, Holdouts!, 1983; contbg. editor: NY Habitat, 1985—92; mem. bd. adv. Profl. Office Design Mag., 1986—89; author: (book) Fifth Avenue, 1986, New York's Fabulous Luxury Apartments, 1987, Statutes of Repose and the Cons. Industry: A Proposal for New York, 1991, Luxury Apt. Houses of Manhattan: An Illus. History, 1993, Hist. Manhattan Apt. Houses, 1996, New York's Arch. Holdouts, 1997, 101 Questions About Copyright Law, 1999; contbg. columnist: Ave. Mag., 2000—02; author: (book) The New York Apartment Houses of Rosario Candela and James Carpenter, 2001. Recipient Presdl. citation, N.Y. State Assn. Archs., 1991. Mem.: AIA, Friends Cast Iron Architecture, Mcpl. Art Soc., N.Y. Hist. Soc., Bklyn. Hist. Soc., Soc. Archtl. Historians.

ALPERN, HARVEY L. cardiologist; b. L.A., June 1, 1938; s. Sander A. and Rose K. Alpern; m. (div. 1972); 1 child, David. BA, Pomona Coll., 1960; MD, U. So. Calif., 1964. Diplomate Am. Bd. Internal Medicine, Am. Bd. Cardiovasc. Disease. Intern Cedars of Lebanon Hosp., L.A., 1964-65; resident in internal medicine Cedars-Sinai Med. Ctr., L.A., 1965-67, resident in cardiology, 1967-68; cardiology fellow St. Georges Hosp., London, 1968-69; pvt. practice Santa Monica, 1970—. Bd. dirs. Century City Hosp., L.A.; med. dir. Exec Fit Health, San Francisco, 1985-93. Contbr. articles to profl. jours. Bd. dirs. L.A. Bus. Coun., 1987-96, Nat. Health Found., L.A., 1985-95; active L.A.-Guangzhou Sister City Assn., 1994—. Capt. USAFR, 1965-70. Fellow Am. Heart Assn. (bd. dirs. L.A. chpt. 1974-75, coun. on clin. cardiology), Am. Coll. Cardiology, Am. Acad. Disability Evaluation Physicians (bd. dirs., pres.); mem. ACP, Calif. Soc. Indsl. Medicine (bd. dirs.). Jewish. Avocation: wine tasting. Office: 2811 Wilshire Blvd Ste 510 Santa Monica CA 90403 E-mail: alpernh@aol.com.

ALPERN, LINDA LEE WEVODAU, health agency administrator; b. Harrisburg, Pa., July 16, 1949; d. William Irvin Wevodau and Maretia Christine (Mills) Staley; m. Neil Stephen Alpern, Apr. 12, 1985; 1 child, Philip Wevodau. BS in Edn., Shippensburg (Pa.) U., 1971. Unit program coord. Pa. Div. Am. Cancer Soc., Harrisburg, 1973-75, unit exec. dir., 1975-76, div. svc. dir., 1976-81, div. med. affairs dir. Hershey, 1981-83; div. crusade dir. Md. Div. Am. Cancer Soc., Balt., 1983-87, div. v.p. for field ops., 1988, div. dep., exec. v.p. ops., 1988-95, divsn. chief oper. officer, 1995-96; sr. v.p. field ops. Mid-Atlantic divsn. Am. Cancer Soc., Balt., 1997—. Bd. dirs., sec. Cmty. Assn.; treas., v.p., pres. PTA; trustee Balt. Hebrew-Congregation Day Sch., 2000-03; bd. electors Balt. Hebrew Congregation, nominating com., 2001—. Democrat. Methodist. Avocations: photography, gardening, reading. Home: 4108 Colonial Rd Baltimore MD 21208-6042

ALPERN, ROBERT J. dean, medical educator; b. Nov. 3, 1950; m. Patricia Ann Preisig; chilren: Rachelle, Kyle. BA in Chemistry with honors and highest distinction, Northwestern U., 1972; MD with honors, U. Chgo., 1976. Diplomate Am. Bd. Internal Medicine; bd. cert in nephrology. Intern in internal medicine Columbia U., N.Y.C., 1976-77, resident in internal medicine, 1977-79; fellow in nephrology and renal physiology U. Calif. Cardiovascular Rsch. Inst., San Francisco, 1979-82, asst. prof. medicine divsn. nephrology, 1982-87; assoc. prof. medicine U. Tex. Southwestern Med. Ctr., Dallas, 1987-90, chief nephrology, 1987-98, prof. medicine, 1990—, Ruth W. and Milton P. Levy, Sr. chair in molecular nephrology, 1994—, dean, 1998—. Max Martin Salick vis. prof., UCLA Sch. Medicine, 1994; mem. Med. Sch. Admissions com. U. Calif. San Francisco, 1985-87, general clin. rsch. ctr. adv. com. U. Tex. Southwestern Med. Ctr., 1987-91, search com. for chief of cardiology, 1989, search com. for chmn. urology, 1993, search com. for chief of hematology/oncology, 1997, Med. Sch. Admissions com., 1994-96, chmn. 1996-98; chmn. general clin. rsch. ctr. adv. com. U. Tex. Southwestern Med. Ctr., 1988-90, search com. for chief of infectious diseases U. Tex. Southwestern Med. Ctr., 1994-96, presenter, lectr. in field. Editl. bd: Kidney Internat., 1989-90, Renal Physiology and Biochemistry, 1989-95, Am. Jour. Physiology, 1992-94, Internat. Yearbook of Nephrology, 1989-92, Seminars in Nephrology, 1990—, Am. Jour. Kidney Diseases, 1991-96, Kidney and Blood Pressure Research, 1996—, Am. Jour. Med. Scis., 1996—, Am. Jour. Medicine, 1997—; cons. editor: Jour. Clin. Investigation, 1993-99, Kidney Internat., 1990—; editl. com. Jour. Clin. Investigation, 1988-93; assoc. editor Am. Jour. Physiology, 1989-92, Hospital Practice: Physiology in Medicine, 1991-94; section editor: Annual Review of Physiology, 1993-97, Current Opinion in Nephrology and Hypertension, 1997-99; contbr. papers, chaps., articles to profl. pubs. Recipient NSF award for rsch. in developmental biology, 1971, NIH Merit award, 1996-2003. Mem. Am. Soc. Nephrology (mem. membership and awards com. 1991-93, exec. com. tng. program dirs. 1991-95, program com. 1993, chmn. 1995, nominating com. 1994, fin. com. 1996—, pubs. com. 1996—, com. on program structure, 1996—, mem. coun. 1996—, pres.-elect 2000), Internat. Soc. Nephrology, Am. Fed. Clin. Rsch. (mem. program com. renal and electrolyte nat. mtg. 1986, 90, chmn. 1993), Soc. General Physiology, Nat. Kidney Found. (mem. scientific adv. bd., 1988-91, exec. com. scientific adv. bd. 1989-92), Am. Physiological Soc., Am. Heart Assn., Am. Soc. Clin. Investigation, Assn. Am. Physicians, Alpha Omega Alpha, Sigma Xi, Phi Beta Kappa. Office: U Tex Southwestern Med Ctr 5323 Harry Hines Blvd Dallas TX 75390-7208 Fax: 214-648-8955. E-mail: robert.alpern@email.swmed.edu.

ALPEROVITZ, GAR, author, educator; b. Racine, Wis., May 5, 1936; s. Julius and Emily (Bensman) A.; m. Sharon Sosnick, Aug. 29, 1976; children by previous marriage: Kari Fai, David Joseph. BS in History, U. Wis., 1958; MA in Econs, U. Cal. at Berkeley, 1960; PhD in Polit. Economy, U. Cambridge, Eng., 1964. Congl. legis. asst., 1961-62; Senate legis. dir. U.S. Senate staff, 1964-65; spl. asst. Dept. State, 1965-66; fellow Kings's Coll., Cambridge (Eng.) U., 1964-68, Inst. Politics Harvard, 1965-68, Brookings Instn., 1966, Inst. Policy Studies, 1968-69, 89-99; co-dir. Cambridge (Mass.) Inst., 1968-71; dir. Exploratory Project Econ. Alternatives, 1973—; pres. Nat. Center Econ. and Security Alternatives, 1978—. Guest prof. Notre Dame U., 1982-83; sr. rsch. scientist, dept. govt. and politics U. Md., College Park, 1993-96, Harrison rsch. prof. dept. govt. and politics, 1996-99, Lionel R. Bauman prof. polit. economy, 1999—. Author: Atomic Diplomacy: Hiroshima and Potsdam, 1965, rev., 1985, 1994, Cold War Essays, 1970, Strategy and Program, 1973, Rebuilding America, 1984, American Economic Policy, 1985, The Decision to Use the Atomic Bomb, 1995, Making a Place for Community, 2002; also articles. Home: 2317 Ashmead Pl NW Washington DC 20009-1413 also: Univ Md 3140 Tydings Hall College Park MD 20742-7215 E-mail: garalper@ncesa.org.

ALPERS, DAVID HERSHEL, physician, educator; b. Phila., May 9, 1935; s. Bernard Jacob and Lillian (Sher) A.; m. Melanie Goldman, Aug. 12, 1977; children: Ann, Ruth, Barbara. BA, Harvard U., 1956, MD, 1960. Intern Mass. Gen. Hosp., Boston, 1960-61, resident in internal medicine, 1961-62; instr. medicine Harvard U., 1965-67, assoc. in medicine, 1967-68, asst. prof., 1968-69; asst. prof. medicine Washington U., St. Louis, 1969-72, assoc. prof., 1972-73, prof., 1973—, William B. Kountz prof., 1997—, dir. gastrointestinal divsn., 1969-97, asst. dir. clin. nutrition rsch. unit, 1999—; sr. cons. R&D GlaxoSmithKline, 1999—. Author: (with others) Manual of Nutritional Therapeutics, 4th edit., 2002; assoc. editor: Textbook of Gastroenterology, 4th edit., 2003, Physiology of the Gastrointestinal Tract, 4th edit., 1997; assoc. editor Jour. Clin. Investigation, 1977-82; editor Am. Jour. Physiology, Gastrointestinal and Liver Physiology, 1991-97; contbr. articles and revs. to profl. jours., chpts. to books. With USPHS, 1962-64. Mem. Am. Soc. Clin. Investigation, Assn. Am. Physicians, Am. Gastroent. Assn. (pres. 1990-91, Friedenwald medal 1997), Am. Soc. Biochem. Molecular Biology (editl. bd. 1998-2003), Am. Fedn. Clin. Rsch., Am. Soc. Clin. Nutrition. Office: Washington U Med Sch Dept Internal Medicine PO Box 8031 Saint Louis MO 63110-1010 E-mail: DAlpers@im.wustl.edu.

ALPERS, EDWARD ALTER, history educator; b. Phila., Apr. 23, 1941; s. Bernard Jacob and Lillian (Sher) A.; m. Ann Adele Dixon, June 14, 1963; children: Joel Dixon, Leila Sher. AB magna cum laude, Harvard U., 1963; PhD, U. London, 1966. Lectr. history Univ. Coll., Dar es Salaam, Tanzania, 1966-68; from asst. prof. to prof. history UCLA, 1968—, dean divsn. honors Coll. Letters and Sci., 1985-87, dean honors and undergrad. programs, 1987-96. Author: Ivory and Slaves in East Central Africa, 1975; editor: Walter Rodney: Revolutionary and Scholar, 1982, History, Memory and Identity, 2001, Africa and the West, 2001; (newsletter) Assn. Concerned Africa Scholars, 1983-85; contbg. editor: Comparative Studies of South Asia, Africa and the Middle East, 1997—; bd. editors The American Historical Rev., 2002—; contbr. articles to profl. jours. Fellow Ford Found., 1972-73, NEH, 1978-79, Fulbright Found., 1980; Conf. fellow Humanities Rsch. Ctr., Nat. Australia U., Canberra, 1998; Fundacao Calouste Gulbenkian grantee, Lisbon, Portugal, 1975. Mem. Am. Hist. Assn. (mem. com. Joan Kelly Meml. prize 1998-99, chair 2000), Africa Studies Assn. (bd. dirs. 1985-88, v.p. 1992-93, pres. 1993-94), Assn. Concerned Africa Scholars (bd. dirs. 1983-93), Alliance for Undergrad. Edn. (UCLA rep. 1987-95, co-chair 1989-92), Hist. Abstracts (adv. bd. 1994—). Office: UCLA Dept History Los Angeles CA 90095-1473

ALPERS, JOHN HARDESTY, JR., financial planning executive, retired military officer; b. Richmond, Va., Sept. 7, 1939; s. John Hardesty and Laura Elizabeth (Gaylor) A.; m. Sharon Kay Kurrle, May 1, 1971; 1 child, John Hardesty III. BS, U. Colo., 1963; MBA, InterAm. U., 1969; postgrad., USAF Squadron Officers Sch., 1968-69, USAF Command and Staff Coll., 1976-78, USAF Air War Coll., 1978-79; CFP, Nat. Endowment for Fin. Edn., 1989; CFS, Inst. Bus. & Fin., 1994. Registered investment adv. svc. exec. Commd. 2d lt. USAF, 1964; advanced through grades to lt. col., 1979; SAC B-52 navigator, select radar bombardier Ramey AFB, PR, 1967-70; squadron weapon systems officer Ubon RTAFB, Thailand, 1970-71; radar strike officer Linebacker II strike plans officer, 1972; prisoner of war, 1972-73; asst. wing weapons officer Seymour-Johnson AFB, N.C., 1971-72, wing command post contr., 1973-74; asst. prof. aerospace studies AFROTC U. Ariz., Tucson, 1974-78; asst. div. chief aviation sci. USAF Acad., Colorado Springs, 1978-79, spl. asst. to commandant, 1979-80; divsn. chief plans, policy and standardization/evaluation, 1980-83; ret., 1983; reg. rep. Waddell & Reed, Inc., 1986-90, Fin. Network Investment Corp., 1990-97; vice pres. FIn. Planning & Mgmt., Inc., Boulder, CO, 1990-97, chmn. Gateway Fin. Strategies LLC, Erie, Colo.; registered rep., registered investment adv. Royal Alliance Assocs., Inc., 1997—; pres. GFS Mgmt., Inc., 2000—; mng. mem. GFS Properties, LLC, 2001—. Lectr., spkr. in field. POW/MIA Activist. With USCG, 1961-63. Decorated Legion of Merit, DFC (2), Bronze Star for Valor, Purple Heart (2), Air Medal (9), Air Force Commendation medal (2), Vietnamese Cross of Gallantry; recipient ceremonial sabre U.S. Air Force Acad. Cadet Corps., 1983. Mem. Air Force Assn., Ret. Officers Assn., U.S. Strategic Inst., Am. Def. Inst., Red River Valley Fighter Pilots Assn., Arnold Air Soc., Nam-POWS, Inc., Inst. CFPs, CFP Bd. Stds., Registry Fin. Planning Practitioners, Internat. Platform Assn., Sports Car Club Am., Rocky Mountain Vintage Racing, HSR-West Racing Club, Vintage Auto Racing Assn., Nostalgia Racing, Pi Kappa Alpha. Republican. Avocations: vintage race car owner, driver and enthusiast (Can-Am thunder series). Home: 90 Baker Ln Erie CO 80516-9064 Office: Gateway Fin Strategies LLC 526 Briggs St Ste D Erie CO 80516 Address: PO Box 957 Erie CO 80516-0957

ALPERT, ANN SHARON, retired insurance claims examiner; b. Indpls., Feb. 24, 1938; d. Oscar and Adele Alpert. BS in Edn., Ind. U., 1959. Tchr. Indpls. Pub. Schs., 1959-60; libr. George Fry & Assocs., Chgo., 1960-62, DeLeuw, Cather & Co., Chgo., 1962-65, Arthur Young & Co., CPAs, Chgo., 1965-74; statis. asst. Sargent & Lundy, Chgo., 1974-81, computer liaison agt., 1981-83, tech. editor, 1983-87; sales assoc. Jewelmaster, Inc., Chgo., 1987-88; claims processor Benefit Trust Life Ins. Co., 1988-90; claims examiner Ft. Dearborn Life Ins. Co., 1990-91, sr. disability claims examiner, 1991—; ret. Fellow: Life Mgmt. Inst. (assoc.).

ALPERT, BARRY MARK, insurance company and banking executive; b. Chgo., Apr. 17, 1941; s. Isadore Daniel and Betty Shane A.; m. Judith Rae Schwartz, Dec. 24, 1969; children: Daniel Ian, Jason Bradley, Stephanie Ann. Student, Ind. U., 1958-60; BBA, Roosevelt U., 1961; MBA in Banking, U. Wis., 1965. V.p. Exch. Nat. Bank, Chgo., 1961-72; pres., CEO Belleair Bluffs Corp., Largo, Fla., 1973-77; chmn., CEO Orange State Life and Health Ins. Co., Largo, 1977-87, Home Life Fin. Assurance Corp., 1982-88; pres., CEO United Ins. Cos., Inc., Largo, 1988-89; pres. Pioneer Western Corp., Largo, 1989-91; vice chmn. Western Res. Life Assurance Co. of Ohio, Largo, 1989-91, Colony Savs. Bank, Clearwater, 1989-92. Chmn. bd., CEO Alpert Fin. Group Inc., 1988; sr. v.p. Robert W. Baird & Co., Inc., Tampa, Fla., 1991-97; chmn. bd., founder Life Savs. and Loan Assn., Clearwater, Vla., 1979-83; asst. prof. fin. Roosevelt U., Chgo., 1965-69; host radio program Ask a Banker, Sta. WBBM/CBS, Chgo., 1966-67; mng. dir. Raymond James, 1997—. Founding dir., chmn. Ruth Eckerd Hall-Pact Inc., Clearwater, 1980-86, Fla. Holocaust Mus., 1995—; founder North Suncoast Symphony Guild, Clearwater, 1974; bd. dirs. Fla. Orch., Clearwater, 1974-80, St. Petersburg (Fla.) chpt. United Way, 1975; trustee Fla. House Washington, 1984—, Tampa Bay Rsch. Inst., 1993—. Served with USAFR, 1961-65. Home and Office: Alpert Fin Group Inc 239 Bath Club Blvd N Redington Beach FL 33708

ALPERT, DANIEL, television executive; b. Chgo., June 20, 1952; s. Herbert and Miriam Florence (Nemiroff) A.; m. Doreen Marie Podolski, Apr. 30, 1976; children: Hilary Marie, Neil Andrew. BA, Mich. State U., 1973, postgrad., 1974-76. News reporter, disk jockey Sta. WITL-AM-FM, Lansing, Mich., 1973; audio producer Instructional Media Ctr. Mich. State U., East Lansing, 1973-74; dir. pub. info. Sta. WKAR-TV, East Lansing, 1974-76; v.p., dir. pub. info. Sta. WTVS, Detroit, 1976-82, sr. v.p., acting gen. mgr., 1983, sr. v.p., asst. gen. mgr., 1983-96, sr. v.p. sta. mgr., 1996-2000, COO, Sta. mgr., 2000—. Contbr. articles on travel and sci. local newspapers. Trustee Karmanos Cancer Inst., Detroit, 1984—. Recipient Devel. award Corp. for Pub. Broadcasting, 1976, Promotion award Broadcast Promotion Assn., 1978, Pub. Broadcasting Svc., 1981, Govt. Rels. awards Nat. Assn. Pub. TV Stas., 1989, 96, ACE award Mich. Assn. Broadcasters, 1991. Mem. NATAS (gov. Detroit chpt. 1980-97, Silver Circle award Mich. chpt. 2000), Mich. Assn. Broadcasters, Mich. Pub. Broadcasters (exec. com. 1995—). Office: Sta WTVS 7441 2nd Ave Detroit MI 48202-2796 E-mail: alpert@dptv.org.

ALPERT, DEIRDRE WHITTLETON (DEDE ALPERT), state legislator; b. N.Y.C., Oct. 6, 1945; d. Harry Mark and Dorothy (Lehn) Whittleton; m. Michael Edward Alpert, Jan. 1, 1964; children: Lehn, Kristin, Alison. Student, Pomona Coll., 1963-65; LLD (hon.), Western Am. U., 1994. Mem. from 78th dist. Calif. State Assembly, Sacramento, 1990-96; mem. from 39th dist. Calif. Senate, Sacramento, 1997—. Chair Women Legislators' Caucus, Sacramento, 1993, Assembly Edn. Com., 1995, Senate Revenue and Taxation Com., 1997-98, Senate Edn. Com., 1999-2000, chmn. Senate Appropriations Com., 2001—, Joint. Com. to Develop a Master Plan, 1999—; active Calif. Tourism Commn., Sacramento, 1990—, Calif. Libr. Allocations Bd., Sacramento, 1993—; mem. com. Natural Resources, Revenue and Taxation, Agr. and Water, Edn., select com. on Calif.'s Wine Industry, Econ. Devel.; chair Genetics and Pub. Policy, Family, Child and Youth Devel., Higher Edn. Admissions and Outreach, Juvenile Justice, Urban Econ. Devel.; vice chair Joint Com. on Fisheries and Aquaculture, Pacific Fisheries Legis. Task Force, Pacific States Marine Fisheries Commn. Author: Mammography Quality Assurance Act 1992, Assembly Bill 114 of 1993, Workplace Violence Safety Act, 1994, Battered Women's Protection Act, 1994, ABC, 1995, California Assessment Academic Achievement Act, 1995. Spl. advocate Voices for Children, San Diego, 1982-90; mem. bd. Solana Beach (Calif.) Sch. Bd., 1983-90, also pres.; pres. Beach and County Guild United Cerebral Palsy, San Diego, 1986. Recipient Beach and County Guild legis. award Calif. Regional Occupation Program, 1991-92, Am. Acad. Pediats., 1991-92, San Diego Psychol. Assn., 1993-94, Commitment to Children award Calif. Assn. for Edn. of Young Children, 1991-92, Legis. Commendation award Nat. Assn. for Yr.-Round Edn., 1991-92, State Commn. on Status of Women, 1993-94, Friend of Public Edn. award Calif. Sch. Bds. Assn., 1997-98, Legis. Champion award Calif. Union Safety Employees, Unsung Hero award Youth Law Ctr., 1995-96, Champion for Children award Voices for Children, 1995-96; named Friend of Yr., Children's PKU Network, 1991-92, Woman of Yr., Nat. Women's Polit. Caucus San Diego, 1991-92, Orgn. for Rehab. through Tng., 1993-94, High Tech Legislator of Yr., Am. Electronics Assn., 1991-2001, Calif. Sch.-Age Consortium, 1993-94, Women of Distinction, Soropimists Internat. of La Jolla, 1993-94, Assemblymember of Yr., Calif. Assn. Edn. Young Children, 1993-94, Calif. Tourism Hall of Fame, 1997—, Legis. of Yr., Calif. State U. Alumni Coun., 1999, Legis. of Yr., Calif. Women for Agriculture, 1999, Honored Patriot, U.S. Selective Svc. Sys., 1999, Legis. of Yr., Profl. Engrs. Calif. Govt., 1997, Outstanding Senator of Yr., Calif. Sch. Bd. Assn., 1998, Legis. of Yr., Am. Elec. Assn., 1995-96, Legis. of Yr., Calif. League Mid. Schs., 1995, Outstanding Legis. of Yr., Nat. Women's Polit. Caucus, S.D. chpt., 1995-96, Outstanding Assenbly Mem. of Yr., Calif. Sch. Bds. Assn., 1994; Recognition for Outstanding Legis. Efforts, Paw PAC, 1997. Mem. Calif. Elected Women's Assn. for Edn. and Rsch. (pres. 1995-96). Democrat. Avocations: golf, reading. Office: State Capitol Bldg Rm 5050 Senate District 39 Sacramento CA 95814 also: 1557 Columbia St San Diego CA 92101-2934 E-mail: dede.alpert@sen.ca.gov.

ALPERT, EUGENE J. academic administrator; AB, U. Rochester, 1970; MA, Mich. State U., 1972, PhD, 1977. Vis. asst. prof. polit. sci. U. Fla., Gainesville, 1975-76; asst. prof. polit. sci. Tex. Christian U., Ft. Worth, 1976-81, assoc. prof. polit. sci., 1981-93; v.p. acad. affairs The Washington (D.C.) Ctr. Internships, 1993-2000, sr. v.p., 2000—. Am. Polit. Sci. Assn. Congl. fellow U.S. Congress, Washington, 1982-83. Mem. Nat. Soc. Exptl. Edn. (bd. dirs. 1994—), Capital Area Polit. Sci. Assn. (mem. coun. 1997-2000). Office: The Washington Ctr 5th Fl 2301 M St NW Washington DC 20037

ALPERT, JOEL JACOBS, medical educator, pediatrician; b. New Haven, May 9, 1930; s. Herman Harold and Alice (Jacobs) A.; m. Barbara Ellen Wasserstrom, July 13, 1957; children: Norman, Mark, Deborah. AB, Yale U., 1952; MD, Harvard U., 1956. Diplomate Am. Bd. Pediatrics. Intern in medicine Children's Hosp. Med. Ctr., Boston, 1956-57, jr. asst. resident in medicine, 1957-58, chief resident for ambulatory svcs., fellow in medicine, 1961-62, from asst. to sr. assoc., 1962-72; exch. registrar St. Mary's Hosp. Med. Sch., London, 1958-59; from instr. to assoc. prof. Med. Sch., Harvard U., Boston, 1962-72, lectr., 1972; pediatrician in chief Boston City Hosp., 1972-92; prof. pediatrics and pub. health Boston U. Sch. Medicine, 2002—02, chmn. dept. pediatrics, 1972-93, also prof. sociomed. scis. and pub. health law, 1980—2002, prof. emeritus pediats. cmty. medicine and sociomed. scis., chmn. pediats., 2002—, prof. emeritus pub. health and health law, 2002—. Dozer vis. prof. Ben. Gurion Sch. Medicine, Beersheva, Israel, 1979; Raine Found. vis. prof. U. Western Australia, Perth, 1983; James and Jean Davis Prestige visitor U. Otago, Dunedin, New Zealand, 1995; cons. USPHS, 1972—, Children's Hosp., Boston, 1972; spl. cons. pres. N.Y.C. Health and Hosps. Corp., 1989; vis. prof. pediatrics Columbia Coll. Phys. and Surg., NYU Sch. Medicine; mem. med. adv. com. N.Y.C. Health and Hosps. Corp., 1989—. Author books, including: The Education of Physicians For Primary Care, 1974; also numerous papers Mem. Town Meeting, Winchester, Mass., 1970-72; mem. exec. com. Mass. Com. for Children and Youth, Boston, 1975-82; chmn. adv. com. Mass. Poison Info. System, Boston, 1980-92; bd. dirs. Med. Found., Boston, 1992—; cons. Commonwealth Fund and MEM Assocs., 1996—. Capt. U.S. Army, 1959-61. Recipient lifetime achievement award Mass. Poison Info. System, 1992, Hon. Mention Pub. Health Svc. award Pew Found., 1999, Pew Found. award for Achievement in Primary Care Edn.; numerous grants, 1965—; spl. fellow Nat. Ctr. Health Svcs. Rsch., London, 1971. Fellow: Royal Coll. Pediat. and Child Health (hon. 2000, U.K.), Am. Acad. Pediat. (v.p. 1997—98, pres. 1998—99, Job Lewis Smith award 1992); mem.: Mass. Assn. Pediat. Dept. Chmn. (chmn. 1976—78, 1981—93), Ambulatory Pediat. Assn. (pres. 1969, George Armstrong medal 1989, Lifetime Career Achievement award 2000, Pub. Policy and Advocacy award 2002), Philippine Ambulatory Pediat. Assn. (hon.), Soc. Pediat. Rsch., Am. Pediat. Soc., Inst. Medicine NAS (mem. governing coun. 1993—95, mem. bd. families and children 1993—95, mem. task force on future of primary care 1994—96), St. Botolph Club, Aescalapian Club, Harvard Club, Yale Club, Lancet Club, Alpha Omega Alpha. Jewish. Office: Boston U Sch Medicine Boston Med Ctr 91 E Concord St Boston MA 02118-2335 Home: 1802 Wisteria Way Wayland MA 01778

ALPERT, JONATHAN LOUIS, lawyer; b. Balt., Aug. 4, 1945; s. Leo M. and Louise (Altheimer) Alpert; children: Sara Louise, Rachel Leah. BA, Johns Hopkins U., 1966; JD, U. Md., 1969; LLM, Harvard U., 1970. Bar: Fla. 1969, Md. 1969, U.S. Supreme Ct. 1973, U.S. Ct. Appeals (5th cir.) 1970, U.S. Ct. Appeals (11th cir.) 1981, U.S. Dist. Ct. (so. dist.) Fla., 1970, U.S. dist. Ct. (mid. dist.) Fla., 1977. Ptnr. Alpert & Alpert, Miami, Fla., 1970-77; judge indsl. claims State of Fla., St. Petersburg, 1977-79; assoc. prof. Stetson Law Sch., St. Petersburg, 1979-82; ptnr. Fowler, White, Gillen, et al., Tampa, Fla., 1982-86; sr. ptnr. The Alpert Law Firm, Tampa, 1986—2003; ptnr. Alpert Elkin Law Firm, Tampa, 2003—. Reporter Gov.'s Advisors on the Workers' Compensation Bill, 1979; adj. prof. Stetson Law Sch., St. Petersburg, 1977—79; lectr. in field. Author: Florida Worker's Compensation Law, 5th edit., 1991, also supplements, Florida Law Damages, 1990, Automobile Reparations--The Law in Florida, 1991, Florida Real Estate, 1991, also supplements, Florida Settlement and Release, 1991, also supplements, Florida Motor Vehicle No Fault Law, 1992, also supplements; contbr. articles. Bd. dirs. Pinellas Safety Coun., Clearwater, Fla., 1977—80; chmn. coll. law admissions com. Stetson U., 1980—81; com. mem. Johns Hopkins U., Tampa, 1985—86. Recipient Torch award Nat. Safety Coun., Pinellas County, 1989. Mem.: ABA, Am. Judicature Soc., Fla. Bar Assn. (co-chmn. adminstrv. law sect. 1981—82, asst. sec. 1986—, others), Am. Soc. Legal History, Am. Trial Lawyers Assn. (DRI Scribes), Am. Arbitration Assn., Tampa Bay Inn of Ct. (master), Selden Soc., Scribes. Avocations: reading, writing, boating, swimming. Office: Alpert Law Firm 401 E Jackson St Ste 1825 Tampa FL 33601-3270

ALPERT, JOSEPH STEPHEN, physician, educator; b. New Haven, Feb. 1, 1942; s. Zelly Charles and Beatrice Ann (Kopsofsky) A.; m. Helle Mathiasen, Aug. 6, 1965; children: Eva Elisabeth, Niels David. BA magna cum laude, Yale U., 1963; MD cum laude, Harvard U., 1969. Diplomate internal medicine and cardiovasc. disease Am. Bd. Internal Medicine. Successively intern, resident in internal medicine, fellow in cardiovascular disease Peter Bent Brigham Hosp.-Harvard U. Med. Sch., Boston, 1969-74, dir. Samuel A. Levine cardiac unit, asst. prof. medicine, 1976-78; prof., dir. divsn. cardiovascular medicine U. Mass. Med. Sch., Worcester, 1978-92, vice-chm. dept. medicine, 1990—, Edward Budnitz prof. of cardiovascular medicine, 1988-92; Robert W. and Irene P. Flinn prof., chmn. dept. medicine U. Ariz., 1992—. Cons. West Roxbury VA Hosp., Boston, VA Med. Ctr., Tucson; sec., treas. med. staff U. Mass. Med. Ctr., 1979-81, pres. med. staff, 1981-82; bd. dirs. Am. Bd. Internal Medicine. Author: The Heart Attack Handbook, 1978, 2d edit., 1985, 3d edit., 1993, Cardiovascular Physiopathology, 1984; co-author: Manual of Coronary Care, 1977, 80, 84, 87, 93, 2000, Manual of Cardiovascular Diagnosis and Therapy, 1980, 84, 88, 96, 2003, Valvular Heart Disease, 1981, 87, 2000, Intensive Care Medicine, 1985, 2d edit., 1991, The Clinician's Companion, 1986, Modern Coronary Care, 1990, 2d edit., 1996, Diagnostic Atlas of the Heart, 1994, Cardiology for the Primary Care Physician, 1996, 2d edit., 1998, Primary Care of Native American Patients, 1999, American Heart Association's Clinical Cardiology Consult, 2001; editor-in-chief Current Cardiology Reports, 2001—; co-editor Cardiology in Rev., 2001--; assoc. editor: Jour. History of Medicine and Allied Scis., 1977-80; editl. cons. Little, Brown & Co., Appleton-Century Crofts; mem. editl. bd. Am. Jour. Cardiology, 1995—, Archives Internal Medicine, 1987—, Heart and Lung, 1987-90, Cardiology, 1985—, assoc. editor, 1987—, editor-in-chief, 1991—; mem. editl. bd. Geriatric Cardiovascular Medicine, 1988-89, Am. Jour. Noninvasive Cardiology, 1987-95, Am. Heart Jour., 1992-97, Internat. Jour. Cardiology, 1992—, European Heart Jour., 1995—, Heart Disease, 1999—; contbr. articles to profl. jours. Lt. comdr. USNR, 1974-76. Recipient Gold medal U. Copenhagen, 1968, Edward Rhodes Stitt award San Diego Naval Hosp., 1976, George W. Thorn award Peter Bent Bingham Hosp., 1977, Outstanding Tchr. award U. Mass. Med. Sch., 1981, 86, 87, 90, U. Ariz. Med. Sch., 1995, 97-2002; Fulbright scholar Copenhagen, 1963-64; USPHS-Mass. Heart Assn. fellow, 1971-72, NIH spl. rsch. fellow, 1972-73. Fellow ACP, Am. Coll. Cardiology (jour. editl. bd. mem. 1983-86, chmn. tng. dirs. com. 1991—, trustee 1996-2001), Am. Coll. Chest Physicians (gov. for Mass. 1983-85); mem. AAAS, Am. Heart Assn. (fellow coun. clin. cardiology, vice chmn. 1991-92, chmn. 1993-95, exec. com. 1986—, Disting. Achievement award 2001), Am. Assn. History of Medicine, Am. Fedn. Clin. Rsch., Assn. Univ. Cardiologists, New Eng. Cardiovascular Club, Assn. Profs. of Medicine, Danish Cardiology Assn. (hon.), Argentine Heart Assn. (fgn. corr.), Israeli Heart Soc. (hon.), Aesculapian Club, Phi Beta Kappa, Sigma Xi, Alpha Omega Alpha. Office: U Az Coll Medicine 1501 N Campbell Ave Tucson AZ 85724-0001 E-mail: jalpert@u.arizona.edu. *I have lived my life following 3 rules: (1) maintain enthusiasm for living and learning; (2) love family and friends; and (3) work hard.*

ALPERT, MARC H. surgeon; b. Newton, Mass., Jan. 23, 1949; s. Joseph and Tobe (Friedman) A.; m. Hillary Iris Blumenthal, May 3, 1981; children: Diane Elizabeth, Leslie Ellen. BSEE, BS in Biol., MIT, 1972; MD, U. Pa., 1976. Resident Boston U. Med. Ctr., 1976-79, N.Y. Med. Coll., 1979-82; vascular fellow Newark Beth Israel Med. Ctr., 1982-84; vascular surgeon Lansdale (Pa.) med. Group, 1984—. Fellow Am. Coll. Surgeons; mem. Del. Valley Vascular Soc., Ea. Vascular Soc. Avocations: bibliophile, antiques, computers. Home: 461 Brights Ln Blue Bell PA 19422-1137 Office: Central Montgomery Surg Assoc 1057 S Broad St Lansdale PA 19446

ALPERT, MARK IRA, marketing educator; b. Duluth, Minn., Nov. 6, 1942; s. Isadore L. and Lillian Alpert; m. Judith Itzkovits, Sept. 3, 1967; 1 child, Nicole Deborah. BS, MIT, 1964; MBA, U. So. Calif., 1965, MS, 1967, D of Bus. Adminstrn., 1968. Asst. prof. mktg. Calif. State U., Long Beach, 1967-68, U. Tex., Austin, 1968-72, assoc. prof., 1972-76, prof., 1976—, La Quinta Motor Inns Centennial prof. bus., 1982-87, Foley's Federated prof. in retailing, 1987—. Vis. prof. bus. U. Pitts., 1978; cons. Zenith Mgmt. Co., Duluth, 1980—. Author: Pricing Decisions, 1971; co-author: Managerial Analysis Marketing, 1970; also articles in profl. jours.; mem. editorial rev. bd. Jour. of Mktg., 1979—, Jour. of Retailing, 1979—, Jour. Mktg. Rsch., 1985-91, Jour. of Bus. Rsch., 1988—. Mem. exec. com. Congregation Agudas Achm, Austin, 1977, 78, bd. dirs., 1977-79, 85-88; bd. dirs. B'nai Brith Hillel, Austin, 1980-85. Mem. Am. Mktg. Assn. (track chmn. 1976, 87), Assn. for Consumer Research, Am. Psychol. Assn. Avocations: tennis, golf, water skiing, music. Office: Univ Tex Coll Bus Adminstrn Mktg Dept Cba 7 # 202 Mail Code B6700 Austin TX 78712-1176

ALPERT, MARK ZACHARY, performing arts executive; b. New Haven, Mar. 22, 1946; s. Aaron Lewis and Ann Shirley (Lichstein) A.; m. Cornelia Ruehlicke, Jul. 8, 1985. BA, NYU, 1969; MA, Columbia U., 1971. Asst. to pres. Am. Ballet Theatre, N.Y.C., 1970-71; gen. mgr. Erick Hawkins Dance Co., N.Y.C., 1971-73, exec. dir. Dennis Wayne's Dancers, N.Y.C., 1976-79; v.p. Columbia Artists Mgmt., N.Y.C., 1979—. Bd. dirs. Louis/Nikolais Dance Co., N.Y.C., Saeko Ichinoe Dance Co., N.Y.C., Music Theatre N.Y. Recipient Presdl. medal, Bingamton U. Avocations: travel, writing, golf, mountain hiking. Office: Columbia Artists 165 W 57th St New York NY 10019-2276

ALPERT, MARTIN JEFFREY, chiropractor; b. N.Y., Apr. 22, 1951; s. Sheldon Lee and Beatrice (Ostrager) Alpert; m. Gilberta Joachim, May 4, 2000; children: Chad, Mitchell, Eva. BA, Syracuse U., 1972; DC, N.Y. Chiropractic Coll., 1976; MS, U. Bridgeport, 1979. Diplomate Am. Bd. Disability Analysts, Am. Acad. Pain Mgmt., Am. Bd. Profl. Disability Cons., Am. Acad. Experts Traumatic Stress, Coll. Pain Mgmt., Am. Assn. Integrative Medicine. Pvt. practice, Yonkers, NY, 1977-84, Hollywood, Fla., 1985, Coconut Creek, Fla., 1987-92, Miami, Fla., 1992-95, Ft. Lauderdale, Fla., 1985—, Orlando, Fla., 1994—. Lt. col. USAR, 1970—. Fellow: Am. Assn. Integrative Medicine (diplomate), Am. Back Soc.; mem.: Fla. Chiropractic Soc., Am. Acad. Spine Physicians, Am. Acad. Chiropractic Physicians, Internat. Fedn. Sports Chiropractic, World Fedn. Chiropractic, Am. Pub. Health Assn., N.Y. Acad. Scis., Fla. Chiropractic Assn., Am. Coll. Sports Medicine, Internat. Fedn. Sports Chiropractic, Internat. Chiropractors Assn., Am. Chiropractic Assn. Democrat. Avocations: jogging, chess, basketball, piano. Home: 19674 Black Olive Ln Boca Raton FL 33498 Office: Third Ave Chiropractic Ctr Inc 300 W Sunrise Blvd Ste 7 Fort Lauderdale FL 33311-6200 also: Colonial Chiropractic Ctr 1310 W Colonial Dr Ste 21 Orlando FL 32804

ALPERT, NORMAN, chemical company executive; b. Phila., May 5, 1921; s. Barnet and Celia A.; m. Adeline Edna Gushman, Apr. 9, 1948; children: Rosalind Alice, Barbara Naomi. AB in Chemistry, Temple U., 1942, MA, 1947; PhD (AEC research fellow 1948-49), Purdue U., 1949. Devel. engr. Publicker Industries, Phila., 1942-45; group head Texaco, Inc., Beacon, N.Y., 1949-59; div. mgr. Exxon Research, Linden, N.J., 1959-79; v.p., dir. research Hooker Chem. Co., Grand Island, N.Y., 1979-82; v.p. spl. environ. projects Occidental Chem. Corp., Niagara Falls, N.Y., 1982-84, v.p. corp. environ. affairs, 1984-86. Environmental cons. Author; patentee in field. Mgr. Career Explorer Post local Boy Scouts Am., 1981. Mem. Am. Chem. Soc., Soc. Automotive Engrs., Niagara Frontier Assn. Research and Devel. Dirs. Home: 4060 Lower River Rd Youngstown NY 14174-9739

ALPERT, SEYMOUR, anesthesiologist, educator; b. N.Y.C., Apr. 20, 1918; s. Louis and Ida (Freedman) A.; m. Cecile Bernadine Cohen, Sept. 7, 1941. AB, Columbia U., 1939; MD, SUNY Health Scis. Ctr., Bklyn., 1943; LLD (hon.), George Washington U., 1984. Diplomate Am. Bd. Anesthesiology. Intern Beth Israel Hosp., N.Y.C., 1943-44; resident in anesthesiology Gallinger Mcpl. Hosp., Washington, 1946-47; mem. faculty dept. anesthesiology George Washington U. Sch. Medicine and Hosp., Washington, 1948—, prof., 1961-83, prof. emeritus, 1983—; v.p. for devel. George Washington U., 1969-83, v.p. emeritus for devel., 1983—. Cons. in anesthesiology Walter Reed Army Hosp., Washington, 1948-83, VA Hosp., Washington, 1948-70, D.C. Gen. Hosp., 1948-69, Mead Dental Hosp., 1949-69; dir. Jefferson Fed. Savs. and Loan Assn., 1979-82; adv. bd. Washington Fed. Savs. & Loan, 1982-89. Contbr. articles to med. jours. Bd. govs. Hebrew U., Jerusalem, 1968— ; bd. govs. State of Israel Bonds, 1964—, nat. chmn. med. div., 1969-86; bd. dirs. Israel Investors Corp., 1965-82, exec. com., 1974-82; bd. dirs. Am. Friends of Hebrew U., 1966—, chmn. med. div., 1969-86, v.p., 1969-90, hon. v.p. 1990—; bd. dirs. Council Jewish Fedn. and Welfare Funds, 1966-73; examining physician Met. Police Boys Clubs, 1952-76; pres. United Jewish Appeal Greater Washington, 1966-67, exec. com., 1955—; bd. dirs. United Givers Fund, 1972-74; exec. com. Jewish Community Council, 1958-75; bd. mgrs. Adas Israel Congregation, 1963—; bd. dirs. Kaufmann Camp for Boys and Girls, 1964-78; bd. dirs. Jewish Cmty. Found., 1966—, v.p., 1968-69; trustee United Jewish Endowment Fund D.C. 1984-98, trustee emeritus, 1998—, vice chmn., 1984-98, 1984-86, pres. 1986-88; mem. found. com. Jewish Fedn. Palm Bch., Fla., 1990—. Served to capt. AUS, 1944-46. Recipient Man of Yr. award State of Israel Bonds, 1964; Freedom award, 1970; Disting. Svc. award Phi Delta Epsilon, 1971, 73; Torch of Learning award Am. Friends of Hebrew U., 1975; Med. award United Jewish Appeal, 1980; Achievement award Profl. Fraternity Assn., 1995; State of Israel Bonds Salvador Dali Menorah award, 2001. Fellow Am. Coll. Anesthesiology; mem. Am. Soc. Anesthesiologists (dir. 1963-66, trustee Wood Library Mus. Anesthesiology 1968-74, v.p. 1970-74), Md.-D.C. Soc. Anesthesiologists (pres. 1968-69), AMA, Med. Soc. D.C. (mem. numerous coms.), Jacobi Med. Soc., Pan Am. Med. Soc. (pres. 1967), Assn. Am. Med. Colls. (co-dir. nat. med. library study 1965-66), Assn. Univ. Anesthetists, Phi Delta Epsilon (nat. pres. 1961-62, exec. com. 1961—, exec. sec. 1963-72, v.p. bd. trustees 1972-73, pres. bd. trustees 1973-74), Cosmos Club (Washington), Woodmont Country Club (Rockville, Md.). Home: Brighton Gardens 5555 Friendship Blvd Apt 424 Chevy Chase MD 20815

ALPERT, WARREN, oil company executive, philanthropist; b. Chelsea, Mass., Dec. 2, 1920; s. Goodman and Tena (Horowitz) Alpert. BS, Boston U., 1942; MBA, Harvard U., 1947; DBA (hon.), Bryant Coll. Mgmt. trainee Std. Oil Co. of Calif., 1947—48; financial specialist The Calif. Oil Co., 1948—52; pres. Warren Petroleum Co., 1952—54; now chmn. bd.; founder, pres., chmn. bd. Warren Equities, Inc., 1954. Chmn. emeritus Ritz Tower Hotel, 1995—; chmn. bd. Kenyon Oil Co., Inc., Mid-Valley Petroleum Corp., Puritan Oil Co., Inc., Drake Petroleum Co., Inc.; mem. U.S. Com. for UN, 1958; exec. com. Small Bus. Adminstrn., 1958; adminstr. for adminstrn. U.S. AID, 1962; former trustee, mem. exec. com. Boston U.; trustee Emerson Coll.; former v.p. Petroleum Mktg. Edn. Found.; bd. dirs., life mem. Assocs. of Harvard Bus. Sch., Mass.; mem. com. for resource and devel. Harvard Med. Sch. bd. fellows. Bd. dirs. World Coun. Synagogues; bd. overseers Albert Einstein Med. Sch.; founder Warren Alpert Found.; bd. fellows Harvard Med. Sch.; former trustee Boston U., Emerson Coll. Named Harvard Med. Sch. Rsch. Ctr. Bldg. named in his honor, 1993; recipient Andrew Wellington Cordier fellow Sch. Internat. Affairs, Columbia U. Mem.: Am. Petroleum Inst. (dir. mktg. divsn.), Young Pres. Orgn. (past dir.), Univ. Club, Met Club, Marco Polo Club, Harvard Club

(N.Y.C. mem. house com.), Am. Petroleum Industry 25 Yr. Club, Harvard Bus. Sch. Club (exec. com., dir., bd. govs., pres. 1960—61). Office: Warren Equities Inc 375 Park Ave Ste 2502 New York NY 10152-2595*

ALPERT, WILLIAM HAROLD (BILL ALPERT), artist, painter; b. N.Y.C., Dec. 21, 1934; s. Jacob Joseph and Fannie (Leff) Alperovicz. PharmD, UCLA, L.A., 1958; BA, UCLA, 1963, MA, 1965. Adj. prof. painting Cooper Union Sch. Art, N.Y.C., 1979-82; adj. instr. drawing Parsons Sch. Design, N.Y.C., 1981-82, Pratt Inst. Summer Program, 1981; instr. painting, drawing and watercolor Sch. Visual Arts, 1989-; Guest lectr. and studio visits, Yunnan Art Inst., Kunming, China, 1993, Acad. of Fine Arts, Bejing, China, 1993, The Green Horce Coll. of Art, Ulaanbaatar, Mongolia, 1998. Exhbns. include Constructs Orgn. Ind. Artists, Bleecker Renaissance, NY, 1978, CIA: 6 Artists View Devel., The Network Acad. of Scis. (NYAS), NY, 1978, Orgn. Ind. Artists Postcard Show, Bologna Art Fair, Italy, 1978, Indpls. Mus. Art, 1978, Albright-Knox Mus., 1978, Joe & Emily Lowe Art Gallery, Syracuse U., 1980, W. Paterson Collection of NJ, 1981, Coll. Charleston (S.C.), 1987, 89, The N.Y. Bot. Garden, Bronx, 1993, Yunnan Art Inst., Kunming, China, 1993, Gallery 331, NYC, 2003, Inaugural Show Gallery 331, NYC, 2003; pub. collections include Power Gallery Contemporary Art, Sydney, Australia;contbr. to NY Art Yearbook, 1975-76, The Sciences, NYAS, 1978, Airline Arte Informa, 1981. Avocations: pharmacy, photography, travel. Home: 64 Grand St # 5 New York NY 10013-2267

ALPHER, RALPH ASHER, physicist, educator; b. Washington, Feb. 3, 1921; s. Samuel and Rose (Maleson) Alpher; m. Louise Ellen Simons, Jan. 28, 1942; children: Harriet Alpher Lebetkin, Victor. BS, George Washington U, 1943, MS, 1945, PhD, 1948; ScD (hon.), Union Coll., 1992, Renssalaer Poly. Inst., 1993. Physicist Bur. Ordnance and Naval Ordnance Lab., USN, Washington, 1940-44, Applied Physics Lab., Johns Hopkins U., Silver Spring, Md., 1944-55, GE R & D Ctr., Schenectady, NY, 1955-86; disting. research prof. of physics Union Coll., Schenectady, 1986—. Adj. prof. aero engring. Renselaer Poly. Inst., 1958—63, adj. prof. physics, 1986—92. Contbr. chapters to books, articles to profl. jours. Bd. dirs. Mohawk-Hudson Coun. Ednl. TV, 1974—80, 1982—87, chmn., 1978—80, 1986—87; bd. dirs. Dudley Obs., Union U., Albany, NY, 1968—72, 1980—86, v.p., 1983—86, adminstr., disting. sr. scientist, 1987—. Recipient Magellanic Premium, Am. Philos. Soc., 1975, Georges Vanderlinden prize, Belgian Royal Acad. Scis., Letters and Fine Arts, 1975, John Price Wetherill medal, Franklin Inst., 1980, Phys. and Math. Scis. prize, N.Y. Acad. Scis., 1981, Disting. Alumnus award, George Washington U., 1987, Henry Draper medal, NAS, 1993. Fellow: AAAS (sect. B physics steering com. 1982—86), Am. Acad. Arts & Scis., Am. Phys. Soc. (councillor-at-large 1979—82, mem. exec. com. 1980—81); mem.: Internat. Astron. Union, Am. Astron. Soc., Fedn. Am. Scientists, Internat. Torch Club, Sigma Xi. Office: Union Coll Dept Physics Schenectady NY 12308 E-mail: raa1921@aol.com.

ALPHER, VICTOR SETH, consultant, clinical psychologist; b. Washington, Oct. 20, 1954; s. Ralph Asher and Louise Ellen (Simons) A. BA, U. Pa., 1976; PhD, Vanderbilt U., 1985. Diplomate in clin. psychology Am. Bd. Profl. Psychology. Grad. fellow Vanderbilt U., Nashville, 1981-85; asst. prof. U. Tex. Health Sci. Ctr., Houston, 1986-88, clin. asst. prof., 1989-96; ret., 1996. Cons. Rsch. Inst. on Addictions, Buffalo, 1990—. Meml. Geriatric Evaluation and Resource Ctr., Houston, 1991-95; bd. cons. Fla. Inst. Psychology, 1994—. Cons. reviewer Jour. Cons. and Clin. Psychology, 1996; contbr. articles to profl. jours., including Jour. Cons. and Clin. Psychology, Jour. Personality Assessment, Jour. Psychopathology and Behavioral Assessment, Psychotherapy, and Jour. Applied Physiology. Fellow Acad. Clin. Psychology; mem. Sigma Xi. E-mail: victor.s.alpher.85@alumni.vanderbilt.edu.

ALPIAR, HAL, management and marketing consultant, author; b. New Rochelle, N.Y., Apr. 29, 1941; s. Harold Peter and Vernetta (Roth) A.; divorced, 1972; children: Haley Alpiar Murphy, Christopher Kennedy and Melissa Monica (twins); m. Kathleen Ann Marshall, Oct. 10, 1987. BBA, Iona Coll., 1964; MBA, L.I. U., 1965; cert., Inst. Advanced Advt. Studies, 1971, New Sch. for Entrepreneurs, 1979. Account exec. Young & Rubicam, Inc., N.Y.C., 1965-68, Foote, Cone, Belding, Inc., N.Y.C., 1968; account supr. Lake Spiro Shurman, Inc., Memphis, 1968-69; mktg. and new bus. dir. Friedlich, Fearon, Strohmeier, Inc., N.Y.C., 1969-71; account supr. Wells, Rich, Greene, Inc., N.Y.C., 1971-73; mktg. and promotion mgr. Guidance Assocs. divsn. Harcourt, Brace Jovanovich, Inc., Pleasantville, N.Y., 1973-74; dir. coop. edn., asst. prof. bus. Ocean County Coll., Toms River, N.J., 1974-79; exec. dir. Mgmt. Tng. Ctr., Point Pleasant Beach, N.J., 1979-82; pres., chief exec. officer A&B Businessworks, Inc., Brick, N.J., 1982—. Cons. health professions; founding exec. dir. Pa. Heart Inst., Bethlehem, 1995—96; adj. prof. bus. Pace U., 1971—73, Georgian Ct. Coll., 1980—83; pub. rels. dir. Pharm. Soc. State N.Y., 1970—72; trustee, bus. cons. Ocean County First Aid Acad., Toms River, 1979—81; two fed. appointments to region II adv. coun. SBA, 1987—91; appointee Nat. Com. for Quality Health Care, Washington, 1998, Washington, 99, Washington, 2000, Washington, 01. Author: Doctor Business, 1994, Doctor Shopping, 1996 (Nat. Health Info. Book award 1997); author, editor: Job Hunter, 1971; author, producer, host 700 daily radio seminars for bus. and profl. practice mgmt.; designer, presenter: 2000 mgmt. skill devel. seminars and workshops; editor-in-chief Bus. Talk Mag., 1988; contbg. editor (cassette newsletter) M.D. Memo; columnist Healthcare Marketer's Exec. Briefing (nat. newsletter), 1998-99; mem. editl. adv. bd. Cosmetic Surgery PRactice Success newsletter. Avocations: swimming, landscaping, writing, reading, music. Office: Businessworks Inc Seawood Harbor PO Box 4211 Brick NJ 08723-1411 E-mail: hal@a-businessworks.com.

AL-RAMADAN, SAEED Y. veterinarian, researcher; b. Al-Ahsa, Saudi Arabia, July 30, 1965; arrived in U.S., 1999; s. Yaseen M. and Naemah A. Al-Ramadan; m. Fatemah A. Al-Shawaf, June 13, 1986; children: Sarah, Kawthar, Ahmed, Abdullah. DVM, King Faisal U., Al-Ahsa, Saudi Arabia, 1992, MA in vet. anatomy, 1998. Mem.: Soc. of Nat. Geography, Soc. Study of Reproduction. Office Fax: 979-847-8981.

ALSAPIEDI, CONSUELO VERONICA, psychoanalytic psychotherapist, consultant; b. N.Y.C., Nov. 9, 1927; d. Vernon Joseph Karram and Constance Agatha Taylor; m. John Romeo Alsapiedi, May 12, 1951; children: John Rino, Sharon Anne. BA, Seton Hill Coll., 1949; MSW, Fordham U., 1972; D Social Work, Psychoanalytic Inst. for Clin.Social Workers, N.Y.C., 1985. Lic. and cert. social worker, N.Y.; cert. alcoholism counselor, substance abuse counselor; bd. cert. diplomate. Case aide II, Cath. Charities, Bklyn., 1949-51, clin. social worker, 1963-70, clin. social worker rep. in Family Ct., 1965-70; inpatient and outpatient psychiat. social worker Office Mental Health, Queens Village, N.Y., 1972-95; pvt. practice psychoanalytic psychotherapy, N.Y.C., 1975—, Forest Hills, N.Y., 1989—. Ednl. lectr.; condr. workshops; psychotherapist staff outpatient psychotherapy svcs. A Family Ctr., Rosedale, NY, 1999—2002; psychotherapist-children ages 5 to adults, all ages. Vol. Nat. Mental Health Assn., Albany, N.Y., 1994. Mem. N.Y. State Soc. for Clin. Social Work Psychotherapy (diplomate 1979—, sec.-rec. sec. 1985 99, membership chmn. 1989-90, pres. Queens chpt. 1986-88, rec. sec. 1992-99), Brain Injury Assn., Menninger Soc. Roman Catholic. Avocations: piano, music, ballet and stage performances, art appreciation. Office: 71-36 110th St Ste 1K Forest Hills NY 11375-4838

AL-SARRAF, MUHYI, internist, oncologist; b. Baghdad, Iraq, Sept. 15, 1938; MD, U. Baghdad, 1961. Diplomate Am. Bd. Internal Medicine with subspecialty in oncology. Intern Providence Hosp., Washington, 1963-64; resident in internal medicine Grace Hosp., Detroit, 1964-66; fellow in oncology Wayne State U., Detroit, 1967-68; pvt. practice Southfield, Mich.; med. dir. Providence Cancer Ctr., Southfield; clin. prof. medicine Wayne State U., Detroit, 1981—. Fellow ACP, Royal Coll. Physicians; mem. Am. Soc. Clin. Oncology, Am. Assn. for Cancer Edn., Am. Assn. for Cancer Rsch., Am. Soc. Preventive Oncology. Office: 3577 W 13 Mile Rd #404 Royal Oak MI 48073

AL-SAUD, ALWALEED BIN TALAL BIN ABDULAZIZ, investment company executive; married; 2 children. Grad., Menlo Coll.; postgrad., Syracuse U. Avocations: exercise, reading. Office: Kingdom Holding Co PO Box 2 Riyadh 11321 Saudi Arabia

ALSBERG, DIETRICH ANSELM, electrical engineer, consultant; b. Kassel, Germany, June 5, 1917; came to U.S., 1939, naturalized, 1943; s. Adolf and Elisabeth (Hofmann) A.; m. Glenna Rose Le Baron, Nov. 6, 1942; children: Peter Allyn, Ronald Ashley, Terry Wayne, David James (dec.). BS in E.E, Tech. U., Stuttgart, 1938; postgrad., Case Sch. Applied Sci., Cleve., 1939-40. Engr. Wright Tool and Forge Co., Barberton, Ohio, 1940-41, Bridgwater Machine Co., Akron, Ohio, 1941 43; with Bell Labs., Holmdel, Murray Hill, Whippany (N.J.) and N.Y., 1945-82, head various depts., 1965-82. Author: (autobiography) A Witness to a Century, 1999; contbr. articles to profl. jours. and books; patentee in field of comms., electromagnetic waves, missile and space guidance and civil engring. Mem. Berkeley Heights (N.J.) Bd. Edn., 1955-58; chmn. Environ. Commn., Berkeley Heights, 1971-76; various office positions local Meth. Ch. With U.S. Army, ETO, 1943-45. Fellow IEEE (life). Methodist. Home: 8545 Carmel Valley Rd Carmel CA 93923-9556 E-mail: dalsberg@ieee.org.

ALSBRO, DONALD EDGAR, health educator; b. Detroit, May 20, 1940; s. Oscar Edgar and Alice Eleanor (Roberts) A.; m. Sharon Marie Gildea, May 18, 1963; children: Laura Lynn, Steven Dieter, Alan Keith. BA, Western Mich. U., 1963; MA, Roosevelt U., 1973; MS, Ea. Mich. U., 1973; EdS, Western Mich. U., 1980; EdD, Wayne State U., 1988. Cert. health edn. specialist. Commd. 2d lt. U.S. Army, 1963, advanced through grades to col., 1989; instr. health Lake Michigan Coll., Benton Harbor, Mich., 1973-92. Developer "Dump Your Plump" nat. worksite wellness program; bd. dirs. Rainbow Wellness, Benton Harbor. With USAR, 1972-94. Named to Western Mich. U. ROTC Hall of Fame, 1991, Lake Michigan Coll. Hall of Fame, 2001. Mem. AAHPERD, Mich. Coun. for Phys. Fitness and Health, Assn. for Mil. Surgeons. Republican. Methodist. Avocations: walking, racquet sports, weight lifting, horses. Home: 942 Sierra Dr Benton Harbor MI 49022-3539

ALSCHULER, AL, freelance/self-employed writer, marketing professional; b. Gary, Ind., Jan. 27, 1934; s. Harold Morris and Sarah N. Aschuler; m. Joy Van Wye, June 28, 1956 (div. 1986); children: Mari Lynn Aschuler, David Van Aschuler, Mark Jonathan Aschuler; m. Jacqulyn Yde, Oct. 7, 2000. BA in Journalism with honors, U. Okla., 1955. Exec. v.p. Vanleigh Furniture Showrooms, N.Y.C., 1958-71, Miami, Fla., 1971-79; advt. and pub. rels. cons., Miami Beach, Fla., 1979-82; mng. editor Fla. Designer Quar., Miami, 1982-84, Design S., Miami Beach, 1984-87; freelance writer, pub. rels. counsel Miami, 1987—. Cons. interior design adv. bd. Fla. Internat. U., Miami, 1988—, Art Inst. Ft. Lauderdale, 1991—. Editor: I.D.E.A.S., 1994—95; contbg. editor: South Fla., 1996—97; contbr. (to publs. including articles) N.Y. Times, San Francisco Chronicle, Orlando-Ft. Lauderdale Sun-Sentinel, Miami Today, others, guest expert on design WFOR-TV. Mem. media com. Superbowl '99; founding chmn. Players State Theatre Conservatory, Coconut Grove, Fla., 1975; mem. Metro Dade Performing Arts Dist. Commn., 1976—77, Miami Com. Beautification, 1977; trustee Miami Design Preservation League, 1988—98, Interior Design Guild Found., 1999—; bd. dirs. Miami's For Me, 1999—, Skyline Theatre Co.; committeeman East Rockaway (N.Y.) Dem. Com., 1968—69. Recipient Rachline Comm. award, 1996. Fellow: Interior Design Guild (past pres., Comm. award 1996); mem.: Miami Internat. Press Club (pres. 1994), Soc. Profl. Journalists, Am. Soc. Interior Designers, Mensa, Phi Beta Kappa. Avocations: theatre, sports, travel. Home and Office: 2430 Brickell Ave Apt 104A Miami FL 33129-2455 E-mail: alal34@aol.com.

ALSCHULER, STEVEN, public relations executive, communications consultant, writer, political consultant; b. NYC, Feb. 12, 1958; s. Robert and Caroline (Benjamin) A. BA, Queens Coll., CUNY, 1979. Press sec. State Senator Roy Goodman, NYC, 1979-86, NY State Senate Com. Investigations, Taxation and Govt. Ops., NYC, 1979-86; sr. v.p. Howard Rubenstein Assoc., Inc., NYC, 1986-93; pres. Linden Alschuler & Kaplan, Inc., NYC, 1993—. Pub. rels. cons. corporations and private sector clients, pub. affairs, fin. svcs. cos., founds., candidates and elected officials, nat., state and local offices, 1993—. Co-author: Lethal Medicine, 1993. Pub. rels. advisor N.Y. Rep. County Com., 1981-86. Mem. Pub. Rels. Soc. of Am. Office: Linden Alschuler & Kaplan Inc 25 W 43rd St Ste 820 New York NY 10036-7406

ALSDORF, ROBERT HERMANN, lawyer; b. Ashland, Ohio, Mar. 5, 1946; s. Howard Alton and Henrietta (Bulleit) A.; m. Sarah Jane Schlick, Nov. 27, 1970; children: Matthew William, Paul August. B.A. magna cum laude, Carleton Coll., 1967; M.A. in U.S. History, Yale U., 1973, J.D., 1973. Bar: D.C. 1973, Wash. 1975, U.S. Dist. Ct. (we. dist.) Wash. 1975, U.S. Ct. Appeals (9th cir.) 1975, U.S. Dist. Ct. (ea. dist.) Wash. 1981, U.S. Supreme Ct. 1984. Trial atty. Dept. Justice, Washington, 1973-75; assoc. Culp, Dwyer, Guterson & Grader, Seattle, 1975-79; ptnr. Armstrong, Alsdorf, Bradbury & Maier P.C. and predecessor Armstrong & Alsdorf, Seattle, 1979-84, pres., 1984— ; speaker continuing legal edn. seminars; pvt. arbitrator of disputes. Author continuing legal edn. materials. Bd. dirs. Stevens Neighborhood Housing Improvement Program, Seattle, 1979-82, pres., 1980-81. Mem. ABA (antitrust sect.), Wash. State Bar Assn. (franchise law revision subcom. corp. bus. and banking com. 1985—, exec. com., sec.-treas. consumer protection antitrust and unfair bus. practices sect. 1987—), Seattle-King County Bar Assn. (com. mem. young lawyers sect. 1978-80, continuing legal edn. 1984-87), Phi Beta Kappa. Home: 952 12th Ave E Seattle WA 98102-4516 Office: Armstrong Alsdorf Bradbury & Maier 1300 Hoge Bldg Seattle WA 98104

ALSENTZER, WILLIAM JAMES, JR., lawyer; b. Ravenna, Ohio, Mar. 15, 1942; s. William J. Alsentzer and Vivian (Guy) Soash; children: Lesley Joan, Michelle Guy. AB, Duke U., 1964, JD, 1966. Bar: Del. 1966, U.S. Dist. Ct. Del. 1967, Ariz. 1980, U.S. Dist. Ct. Ariz. 1980. Assoc. Wilson & Lynam, Wilmington, Del., 1967-70; ptnr. Bayard, Brill & Handelman, Wilmington, 1970-79; v.p., gen. counsel Bapt. Hosps. and Health Systems, Phoenix, 1979-2000; legal counsel BHHS Legacy Found., Phoenix, 2000—. Mem. Maricopa County Bar Assn., Am. Health Lawyers Assn., Fedn. Def. and Corp. Counsel. Office: 2999 N 44th St Ste 530 Phoenix AZ 85018

ALSIP, CHERYL ANN, small business owner; b. Jersey City, Aug. 1, 1957; m. Manuel Edward Alsip, May 23, 1992 (dec. Oct., 1992); 1 child, Jeremy Tyler. Student, Bergen C.C., Paramus, N.J., 1979-82, Broward C.C., Coconut Creek, Fla., 1983-84; AS in Electronic Engring., NEC-Bauder, Ft. Lauderdale, Fla., 1988; AS in Acctg., Internat. Corr. Sch., Scranton, Pa., 1997. Various clerical positions, N.Y.C. and N.J., 1979-81; pers. mgr. Universal Merchandising, Inc., Clifton, N.J., 1981-82; store mgr. Travelers Transp. Inc. doing business as The Gift Shop, Deerfield Beach, Fla., 1983; gen. mgr. Travelers Transp. Inc. doing business as Budget Rent-A-Car, Pompano Beach, Fla., 1982 84; various office and technical positions Fla., 1985-91; ind. contractor Mary Kay, Pompano Beach, Fla., 1991-92; customer svc. rep. Taleigh, Inc., Boca Raton, Fla., 1992; tech. writer, technician various Fla. Cos., 1992-93; owner, operator CALA Distinctive Enterprises, Salcha, Alaska, 1992—; freelance writer, English editor Alaska, 1999-2000; desktop pub., editor, freelance writer; owner, operator pet boarding kennel and animal rescue shelter, 2002—. Commr. Boy Scouts of Am., 1992—; mem. Comty. Emergency Response Team, Pompano Beach, Fla., 1997-98—; vol. Aux. Police Dept., Pompano Beach, 1997-98; mem. CAP, 1996— ; bd. dirs. Golden Valley Elec. Assn., Fairbanks, 2000—; bd. dirs., mem., sec. Sacha Cmty. Coun. With U.S. Army, 1975 78. Mem. Internat. Soc. Cert. Electronic Technicians, Navy League of the U.S. Republican. Roman Catholic. Avocations: camping, handcrafts, reading. Home and Office: PO Box 140097 Salcha AK 99714-0097 E-mail: calalsip@ptialaska.net.

ALSOBROOK, HENRY BERNIS, JR., lawyer; b. New Orleans, Nov. 9, 1930; s. Henry Bernis and Ethel (Smith) A.; m. Carey Turner Mackie; children: Eugenie Alsobrook Burglass, John Gleason, Emily Alsobrook. BA, Tulane U., 1952, JD, 1957. Bar: La. 1957. Since practiced in, New Orleans; sr. partner firm Adams & Reese. Past mem. faculty Tulane U. Law Sch.; bd. dirs. Def. Research Inst., 1978-81, 85-88, chmn. med.-legal com., 1967-72; lectr. in field. Author articles in field; : editorial bds. legal jours. Chmn. dean's coun. Tulane U., 1983-88; elder St. Charles Ave. Presbyn. Ch., New Orleans; 1st pres. Les Compagnons du Barreau de La Louisiane, 1985—; treas., bd. dirs. La. State Mus.; bd. dirs. New Orleans Symphony Soc., New Orleans Opera.; mem. La. Gov.'s Commn. on Med. Malpractice, 1989—; mem. Audubon Inst. Aquarium Capital Campaign Commn. With USNR, 1953. Fellow Am. Bar Found., Am. Coll. Trial Lawyers; mem. ABA (past chmn. standing com. commerce, ho. of dels. 1984-89), La. Bar Assn. (pres. 1982-83), New Orleans Bar Assn., Internat. Assn. Def. Counsel (exec. com. 1982-88, pres. 1986-87), Fedn. Ins. Counsel, New Orleans Assn. Def. Counsel (pres.), La. Assn. Def. Counsel (gov. 1965), La. Law Inst. (council 1984-89), Soc. Med. Assn. Counsel (charter), Soc. Hosp. Attys. (charter), AMA (hon.), Confrerie des Chevaliers du Tastevin (grand cellerier 1990-2001), New Orleans Country Club, Avoca Duck Club, Lakeshore Club, Pickwick Club, La. Club. Office: Adams & Reese 4500 One Shell Sq New Orleans LA 70139-4501

ALSOP, DONALD DOUGLAS, federal judge; b. Duluth, Minn., Aug. 28, 1927; s. Robert Alvin and Mathilda (Aaseng) A.; m. Jean Lois Tweeten, Aug. 16, 1952; children: David, Marcia, Robert. BS, U. Minn., 1950, LLB, 1952. Bar: Minn. 1952. Pvt. practice, New Ulm, Minn.; ptnr. Gislason, Alsop, Dosland & Hunter, 1954-75; judge U.S. Dist. Ct. Minn., St. Paul, 1975—, chief dist. judge, 1985-92, sr. dist. judge, 1992—. Mem. 8th cir. jud. coun., 1987-92, Jud. Conf. Com. to Implement Criminal Justice Act, 1979-87; mem. exec. com. Nat. Conf. Fed. Trial Judges, 1990-94. Chmn. Brown County (Minn.) Republican Com., 1960-64, 2d Congl. Dist. Rep. Com., 1968-72, Brown County chpt. ARC, 1968-74. Served with AUS, 1945-46. Mem. Minn. State Bar Assn., 8th Cir. Dist. Judges Assn. (pres. 1982-84), New Ulm C. of C. (pres. 1974-75), Order of Coif. Office: US Dist Ct 754 Fed Bldg 316 Robert St N Saint Paul MN 55101-1495

ALSOP, MARIN, conductor; d. LaMar and Ruth A. Student, Yale Univ., Julliard Sch. Debut with Symphony Space, N.Y.C., 1984; founder, artistic dir. Concordia Chamber Orchestra, N.Y.C., 1984—; asst. condr. Richmond Symphony, Va., 1987; music dir. Eugene Symphony Orchestra, Oreg., 1989—96, Long Island Philharmonic, 1989—96, Colorado Symphony Orchestra, Denver, 1993—; principal guest condr. City of London Sinfonia, 1999—; principal condr. Bournemouth Symphony Orchestra, England, 2003—. Guest condr. San Francisco Symphony Orchestra, Boston Pops, Los Angeles Philharmonic Orchestra, 1991, City Ballet Orchestra, 1992; dir. Cabrillo Music Festival, Calif., 1991—; concertmaster Northeastern Pennsylvania Philharmonic, Scranton; founder, mem. String Fever (swing band), 1980—. Recipient Koussevitzky Conducting prize Tanglewood Music Festival, 1988. Office: Colo Symphony Orch Boettcher Concert Hall 821 17th St Ste 700 Denver CO 80202-3000*

ALSOP, REESE FELL, medical educator; b. N.Y.C., Feb. 24, 1913; s. Reese Denny and Julia Chapin Alsop; m. Elise Coates, Nov. 7, 1947; children: Brooke, Elise, Jane, Anne, Penn. BA, Harvard U., 1936; MD, Columbia U., 1944. Diplomate Am. Bd. Internal Medicine. Resident Mary Imogene Bassett Hosp., Cooperstown, NY, 1944—45, Bellevue Hosp., N.Y.C., 1947—48, Bronx VA Hosp., 1948—50; asst. prof. medicine NYU, N.Y.C., 1950—60; chmn. dept. medicine Huntington Hosp., NY, 1968—98; clin. prof. medicine SUNY, Stonybrook, 1990—. Cons. in medicine Northport VA Hosp., NY, 1990—. Articles editor New Eng. Jour. Medicine, 1952—; author: (poetry) Back Talk, —, (book) George and His Horse Bill, 1948—; contbr. Reader Episcopal Ch., Cold Spring Harbor, NY, 1970—. Capt. Med. Corps U.S. Army, 1942—47. Mem.: Century Assn. (hon.). Achievements include patents for on audiocatheter; examining glove; return envelope. Avocations: reading, tennis, writing. Home: Lloyd Neck 33 Fort Hill Dr Huntington NY 11743

ALSPACH, PHILIP HALLIDAY, manufacturing company executive; b. Buffalo, Apr. 19, 1923; s. Walter L. and Jean E. (Halliday) A.; m. Jean Edwards, Dec. 20, 1947 (dec.); children: Philip Clough, Bruce Edwards, David Christopher; m. Loretta M. Hildebrand, Aug. 1982. BME, Tulane U., 1944. Registered profl. engr., Mass., Wis., La. With Gen. Electric Co., 1945-64, mgr. indsl. electronics div. planning, 1961-64; v.p., gen. mgr. constrn. machinery div. Allis Chalmers Mfg. Co., Milw., 1964-68; exec. v.p., dir., mem. exec. com. Jeffrey Galion, Inc., 1968-69; v.p. I.T.E. Imperial Corp., Springhouse, Pa., 1969-75; pres. E.W. Bliss div. Gulf & Western Mfg. Co., Southfield, Mich., 1975-79; group v.p. Katy Industries, Inc., Elgin, Ill., 1979-85; pres. Intercon Inc., Irvine, Calif., 1985—, also bd. dirs.; pres. Intercon Publ., Irvine, 1991—. Bd. dirs. All West Plastics, Inc., D&L Sheet Metal, Inc., Fortifiber Corp.; adv. bd. Diamond Stainless, Inc. Author: Swiss-Bernese Oberland, 1992, 2d edit., 2000; papers in field. Mem. pres.'s coun. Tulane U., 1982-90. Mem. IEEE, Soc. Automotive Engrs. (sr.), Soc. Mfg. Engrs., Internat. Forum Corp. Dirs., Inst. Dirs. (U.K.), Am. Mgmt. Assn., Chaîne des Rotisseurs (officier). Home: 23 Alejo Irvine CA 92612-2913 Office: Intercon Inc 2500 Michelson Dr Ste #125 Irvine CA 92612-1529 E-mail: intercon@att.net.

ALSTADT, DONALD MARTIN, business executive; b. Erie, Pa., July 29, 1921; s. Rheinhold L. and Jean M. Alstadt; m. Judith Carlow, Nov. 23, 1984; 1 child, Karen. BS, U. Pitts., 1947; Sc.D. (hon.), Thiel Coll., 1980. With Lord Corp., Erie, 1961—, v.p., gen. mgr., 1964-66, exec. v.p., 1966-68, pres., 1968-75, also chmn. bd., chief exec. officer, 1982-91, now chmn. bd., 1993—. Cons. Carborundum Co., Transistor Products Co. of Boston, 1952-56; dir. Keithley Instruments Inc.; cons. Lincoln Project, 1952-53, NSF, 1980—; guest lectr. Internat. Inst. Mgmt. Sci. Ctr., Berlin, 1979; vis. scientist MIT, 1986. Contbr. articles to profl. jours. Chmn. bd. overseers Franklin Pierce Law Ctr., 1981— ; mem. adv. bd. Ctr. for Advanced Engring. Study, MIT, 1981— ; mem. Pa. Sci. and Engring. Found., 1980— ; bd. advisors Case Western Res. Sch. Mgmt., Cleve., 1970— ; bd. visitors U. Pitts. Grad. Sch. Bus., 1972— ; trustee Poly. Inst. N.Y., Bklyn., 1973—, Kolff Found., Cleve., 1974—, Hamot Med. Center, Erie, Pa., 1973-78, Rose Poly. Inst., 1976-79; mem. adv. bd. Mellon Inst. Research; met. chmn. Nat. Alliance of Businessmen, 1969; mem. president's council Tulane U., 1976— ; mem. vis. com. Sch. Engring., M.I.T., 1980—, Sch. Engring., Duke U., 1980— ; mem. policy com. Pa. Bus. Council, 1979—; dir., pres. Lord Found. of N.C., Lord Fond. of Calif., Lord Found. of Mass., Lord Found. of Pa., Lord Found. of Ohio. Recipient Medal of Merit Edinboro State Coll., 1979; Univ. medal Pa. State U., 1981; Disting. Service award Sch. Engring. Duke U., 1985, Adhesives and Sealant Council, 1985; named Hon. Football Coach, U. So. Calif. Fellow Am. Inst. Chemists; mem. Am. Phys. Soc., Am. Chem. Soc., Faraday Soc. of Eng., Electrochem. Soc., Chemists Club N.Y., N.Y. Acad. Scis., Inst. Mgmt. Sci., Am. Security Council, Swedish Royal Acad. Engring. Sci. (guest lectr. 1984), Acad. Applied Sci. Republican. Presbyterian. Avocation: fishing. Office: Lord Corp PO Box 8012 11 Lord Dr Cary NC 27512-8012

ALSTADT, LYNN JEFFERY, lawyer; b. Erie, Pa., Dec. 27, 1951; s. Willis Harry and Norma Margaret (Linn) A.; m. Nancy Ann Weiz, Apr. 16, 1977. BS, BA, U. Pitts., 1973, JD, 1976. Bar: Pa. 1976, U.S. Dist. Ct. (we. dist.) Pa. 1976, U.S. Patent and Trademark Office 1979, U.S. Ct. Appeals (3d cir.) 1980, U.S. Ct. Appeals (6th and Fed. cirs.)1983, U.S. Supreme Ct. 1982, U.S. Ct. Internat. Trade 1983. Assoc. Blenko, Buell, Ziesenheim & Beck, Pitts., 1976-79; ptnr. Buell, Blenko, Ziesenheim & Beck, Pitts., 1979-84, Buell, Ziesenheim, Beck & Alstadt, Pitts., 1984-88, Buchanan Ingersoll, Pitts., 1988—. Adj. prof. U. Pitts. Sch. Law, 1988—, Duquesne U. Sch. Law, 1995—; dir. Internat. Congress on Tech., Pitts., 1983-84. Contbr. articles to legal jours. Treas. Moon Twp. Planning Agy., 1984; mem. Moon Twp. Vol. Fire Dept., 1981—. Recipient Samuel G. Wagner prize U. Pitts. Law Sch., 1976. Mem. ABA, Pa. Bar Assn., Allegheny County Bar Assn., Pitts. Intellectual Property Law Assn. (chmn. pub. rels. 1982-83, treas. 1993, chmn. ethics grievences and membership coms. 1994-95, dir. 2000-01, v.p. 2001-02, pres. 2002-03), Rivers Club, Phi Alpha Delta. Republican. Home: 102 Greenlea Dr Moon Township PA 15108-2610

ALSTON, GOLDIE VENESSA, early childhood educator; b. Long Branch, N.J., Apr. 5, 1970; d. Helen Clanton. BA, Rutgers U., 1992; postgrad. in MA program, Kean U. Pre-kindergarten tchr. Urban League Presch., Newark, 1994-96; tchr. Cleveland Sch. Pub. & Tech., Newark, 1996—. Workshop presenter Newark Pub. Schs.; critical friends coach mentoring program. Avocation: reading. Home: 1777B Walker Ave Irvington NJ 07111 E-mail: toldiereads@al.com

ALSTON, WILLIAM PAYNE, philosophy educator; b. Shreveport, La., Nov. 29, 1921; s. William Payne and Eunice (Schoolfield) A.; m. Mary Frances Collins, Aug. 15, 1943 (div.); 1 dau., Frances Ellen; m. Valerie Tibbetts Barnes, July 3, 1963. B.M., Centenary Coll., 1942; PhD, U. Chgo., 1951; LHD (honoris causa), Ch. Div. Sch. Pacific, 1988. Instr. philosophy U. Mich., 1949-52, asst. prof., then asso. prof., 1952-61, prof., 1961-71, acting chmn. dept., 1961-64; prof. philosophy Rutgers U., 1971-76, U. Ill., Champaign, 1976-80, chmn. dept., 1977-80; prof. philosophy Syracuse (N.Y.) U., 1980-99, prof. emeritus, 1999. Vis. asst. prof. UCLA, 1952-53; Austin Fagothey vis. prof. philosophy Santa Clara U., 1991; vis. lectr. Harvard U., 1955-56; fellow Ctr. for Advanced Study in the Behavioral Scis., 1965-66; dir. summer seminars for coll. tchrs. NEH, 1978-79, NEH Summer Inst. in Philosophy of Religion, 1986, NEH

Fellowship for Univ. Tchrs., 1988-89, Vatican Obs. Project on Divine Action in the Light of Contemporary Sci., Symposium of Chinese-Am. Philosophy and Religious Studies, 1994; dir. Calvin Coll. Summer Seminar in Christian Scholarship, 1999. Author: Religious Belief and Philosophical Thought, 1963, (with G. Nakhnikian) Readings in Twentieth Century Philosophy, 1963, Philosophy of Language, 1964, (with R.B. Brandt) The Problems of Philosophy: Introductory Readings, 1967, 3d edit., 1978; Divine Nature and Human Language, 1989, Epistemic Justification, 1989, Perceiving God, 1991, The Reliability of Sense Perception, 1993, A Realist Conception of Truth, 1996, Illocutionary Acts and Sentence Meaning, 2000, A Sensible Metaphysical Realism, 2001, Realism and Antirealism, 2002; editor: Philos. Rsch. Archives, 1974-77, Faith and Philosophy, 1982-90, Cornell Studies in Philosophy of Religion, 1987—; contbr. articles to profl. jours., chpts. in books. Served with AUS, 1942-46. Recipient Chancellor's Exceptional Acad. Achievement award Syracuse U., 1990. Mem. Am. Acad. Arts and Scis., Am. Philos. Assn. (pres. Western divsn. 1978-79), Soc. Christian Philosophers (pres. 1978-81), Scholarly Engagement Anglican Doctrine, Am. Theol. Soc., Soc. for Philosophy Religion (pres. 2001-02). Home: 8 Bittersweet Ln Fayetteville NY 13066-1702 Office: Syracuse U Dept Philosophy Syracuse NY 13244-1170

ALSTOTT, MICHAEL JOSEPH (MIKE ALSTOTT), professional football player; b. Joliet, Ill., Dec. 21, 1973; Student, Purdue U. Fullback Tampa Bay Buccaneers, 1996—. Office: Tampa Bay Buccaneers 1 Buccaneer Pl Tampa FL 33607-5797

ALSTRUM, JAMES JOSEPH, education educator; b. New Haven, Conn., Dec. 18, 1946; s. James Herbert Alstrum and Celestine Margaret Kephart; m. Elizabeth Acevedo; children: Rebecca Margaret, James Henry, Robert Michael. BA, Fairfield Univ., Conn., 1968; MA, Vanderbilt Univ., Tenn., 1973, PhD, 1977. Asst. prof. Univ. Wyo., Wyo., 1977—79, Univ. Miss., Miss., 1979—81, Ill. State Univ., Ill., 1981—86, assoc. prof., 1986—2000, prof., 2000—. Contbr. articles; translator: To Be a Worker, 2000. Grantee PhD Rsch. grant, U.S. Dept. of Edn., 1988—90; Fulbright-Hayes Fellowship, Columbia, 1975. Mem.: Assn. of Colombianists (sec. 1986—2001). Home: 809 N Sch St Normal IL 61761 Office: Foreign languages Dept Ill State Univ Campus Box 4300 Normal IL 61790-4300

ALSUA, CARLOS J. educator; s. Jesus Alsua and Angela Lobo. PhD, Ariz. State U. Asst. prof. U. of Alaska, Anchorage, 2001—. Office: U Alaska 3211 Providence Dr Anchorage AK 99508 Personal E-mail: alsua@uaa.alaska.edu.

ALSUBAIE, ABDULAZIZ MOHAMED, civil engineer; b. Qasseem, Saudi Arabia, 1945; s. Mohamed Abdullah Alsubaie; 6 children. BSCE, Seattle U., 1974. Ret. engring. dir. King Abdulaziz Mil. Acad.; dir. Ministry of Def., Riyadh, Saudi Arabia, 1974—; pres. Alsubaie Cons. Engrs. (Arabtech.), Riyadh, 1980—. Bd. dirs. Alsubaie Poultry Farms, Durma, Saudi Arabia, Alsubaie Poultry Feed Mills, Durma, Saleh M. Alsubaie Bros. and Co., Riyadh, Al Farooj Farms Muzamiah Nat. Arabian Bldg. Corp., Riyadh; active in real estate, agrobusiness, civil engring., constrn. and maintenance; civil works designs supervision, constrn. mgmt., pipelines, sewage and water, desalination works; ptnr. in advt. and pub. rels. co. Mem. ASTM, Am. Water Works Assn., Conf. Bd. N.Y., Brit. Std. Inst. Home and Office: King Fahd St PO Box 55001 Riyadh 11534 Saudi Arabia

ALT, CAROL A. actress, model, entrepreneur; d. Anthony Ted and Muriel B. Alt; m. Ronald John Greschner, Nov. 21, 1983 (div. Mar. 12, 2001). At, Hofstra U., LI, NY. Model Ford Models, NYC; actress Moress Nanan Hart Enterprises, LA; spokesperson QVC, Westchester, Pa. Reporter Fox News, 2002. Vol. Tribeca Performing Arts Ctr., NYC, MS, NYC, Am. Cancer Soc., NYC, Cerebral Palsy. With U.S. Army, 1978—79. Recipient Model Woman of Yr., 1981, Female Model of Yr., CFDA, 1986, Oscar moda New Actress of Yr., 1986, European Emmy, 1987, Cert. of the Arts, European Artistic Cmty., 1988, European Emmy, 1990, Mont Blanc award, 1991, Golden Box Office Ticket, 1993, European Emmy, 1994. Avocations: amateur race car driver, interior decorating, marketing. Office: Just Simplicity c/o Assante 280 Park Ave New York NY 10010

ALT, JAMES EDWARD, political science educator; b. N.Y.C., Aug. 16, 1946; s. Franz Leopold and Alice (Modern) A.; m. Elaine Fiore, June 26, 1968; children: Rachel, Adam. AB, Columbia U., 1968; MSc in Econs., London Sch. Econs., 1970; PhD, Essex U., Eng., 1978. Lectr. U. Essex, Wivenhoe Park, Eng., 1971-79; assoc. prof. Washington U., St. Louis, 1978-82, prof., 1982-86, Harvard U., Cambridge, Mass., 1986—; dir. Ctr. for Basic Rsch. in Social Sci., 1998—. Author: Politics of Economic Decline, 1979, (with K. Chrystal) Political Economics, 1983; editor: (with K. Shepsle) Perspectives on Positive Political Economy, 1990, (with M. Levi and E. Ostrom) Competition and Cooperation, 1999; contbr. articles to profl. jours. Rsch. grantee NSF, 1980, 85, 91, 93, 2001, 02; Guggenheim fellow, 1997-98. Mem. Brit. Politics Group (pres. 1983-85), Am. Polit. Sci. Assn. (coun. 1996-97), Midwest Polit. Sci. Assn. (exec. coun. 1985-88). Office: Harvard U Dept Govt Cambridge MA 02138 E-mail: james_alt@harvard.edu.

ALTABE, JOAN AUGUSTA BERG, artist, writer, art and architecture critic; b. N.Y.C., Apr. 27, 1935; d. Harold and Evelyn (Cooperman) Berg; m. David F. Altabe, Sept. 28, 1958; children: Richard Jonathan, Madeline Nissa. Studied with Robert Motherwell; BA, Hunter Coll., 1956, postgrad., 1956-57. Tchr. fine art N.Y.C. secondary schs., 1957-72. Vol. sculpture tchr. N.Y. Lighthouse For Blind, 1950-53; curator Bicentennial exhibit Long Beach (N.Y.) Mus. Art, 1975-76; architecure columnist Bradenton Herald, 2001-. Artist and muralist, 1982—; prin. work includes 6 stained glass window murals N.Y. Synagogue, 1973, heraldic deisgn Smithsonian Instn. Bicentennial Travelling Exhibit, 1976-78; represented in permanent collection at Santa Barbara (Calif.) Mus.; book reviewer: Leonardo, Pergamon Press, Eng., 1980-94; feature writer Art Press, Paris, 1992; art writer Art & Antiques mag., 1998, 99; art and architecture critic, feature writer Sarasota Herald Tribune, 1986-2001; book reviewer Western Humanities Rev., N.Y. Times; contbr. articles and illustrations to profl. jours. Recipient Fla. Press award, 1990, 91, 96, Chmn. award N.Y. Times, 1997. Mem. Soc. Profl. Journalists (award in criticism 1995, 96, 97, 99, Tampa Bay chpt., citation for excellence in journalism criticism 1990, 95-99, 2001, 02, 03), Fla. Soc. Newspaper Editors (columns and criticism 1997, 99, 2003 criticism award 1996, 98-2000, Sunshine State award 1999). Home: 604 Avenida De Mayo Sarasota FL 34242-1502 *To transcend my life through painting, teaching or publishing, with loyalty to my individual spirit and dedication to communication.*

ALTAFFER, LAWRENCE F., III, retired physician, artist; b. Richmond, Va., Jan. 7, 1947; s. Lawrence F. and Virgina Sydnor Altaffer; children: Anne, Elizabeth, Lawrence F. IV. BA, Univ. Va., Charlottesville, Va., 1969, MD, 1974. Physician urologist pvt. practice; ret., 1996. Contbr. articles to profl. jour.; exhibitions include, Nat. Exhbn. of Oil Painters of Am., 2000, 2002. Vol. Boys Scouts of Am., Fredericksburg, Va., 1985—96. Comdr. USN, 1974—84. Mem.: Wash. Soc. of Landscape Painters, Salmagundi Club. Christian. Avocations: gardening, hunting, fishing. Home: General Delivery Syria VA 22743

ALTALIB, OMAR HISHAM, sociologist; b. Arafa Kirkuk, Mosul, Iraq, May 16, 1967; s. Hisham Yahya and Ilham (Ismail) A.; m. Nina Abdullah, Dec. 31, 1991. BA, George Mason U., 1989; MA, U. Chgo., 1993. Rsch. asst. Nat. Opinion Rsch. Ctr., 1992-95; asst. prof. dept. criminal justice and sociology Ashland U., 2000—03. Vis. scholar Internat. Islamic U., Malaysia; instr. Daley Coll., 1998-99, Ind. U., 1999, St. Augustine Coll., 1998, Barat Coll., 2000; mem. Fgn. Policy Rsch. Inst. Advisor Muslim Youth Coun., Chgo., 1990; mem. Citizens Utility Bd., Chgo., 1992 ; explorer scout Fairfax County Police Dept.; mem. adv. bd. Ashland Dental Clinic; bd. advisors Buckeye Inst.; bd. dirs. Minaret of Freedom Inst. Grad. Student fellow NSF, 1989-92. Mem. Am. Sociol. Assn., Econs. Honor Soc., Electronic Frontier Found., Co-Op Am., Golden Key, Assn. Muslim Social Scientists. Libertarian. Moslem. Avocations: arabic language, qur'anic interpretation. Office: Ashland U Sociology Dept Ashland OH 44805 Fax: (419) 207-8840..

ALTAN, M(USTAFA) CENGIZ, mechanical engineering educator; b. Ankara, Turkey, Dec. 26, 1963; s. A. Rifki and Nursel Altan; m. Betul S. Marmara, July 4, 1992. BSME, Mid. East Tech. U., Ankara, 1985; PhD in Mech. Engring., U. Del., 1989. Tchg. asst. U. Del., Newark, 1985-86, rsch. asst., 1986-89; asst. prof. mech. engring. U. Okla., Norman, 1989-95, assoc. prof., 1995—. Editor: (conf. proc.) Developments in Non-Newtonian Fluid Mechanics, 1993, Intelligent Manufacturing and Material Processing, 1995, Processing and Design of Multicomponent Materials, 2000; contbr. articles to profl. jour. Recipient rsch. initiation award Soc. Mfg. Engr., 1990, Regents' award for superior tchg. U. Okla., 1998; rsch. grantee Okla. Ctr. for Advancement Sci. and Tech., 1991, NASA, 1996, Seagate Tech., 1996, Hawthorne York Internat., 1999, SIAC Corp., 2001, All Tech Inc., 2002, TMI Inc., 2003, USAF, 2003. Mem. ASME (assoc., chmn. materials processing com. materials div. 1994-97), Soc. R heology, Internat. Polymer Processing Soc., Am. Soc. Engring. Edn., Am. Phys. Soc., Am. Soc. for Composites, Pi Tau Sigma (hon., Most Outstanding Prof. award for U. Okla. 1997). Achievements include patents on computer-controlled curing of composite materials. Office: U Okla Sch Aero-Mech Eng 865 Asp Ave Rm 212 Norman OK 73019-1029 E-mail: altan@ou.edu.

ALTAN, TAYLAN, engineering educator, mechanical engineer, consultant; b. Trabzon, Turkey, Feb. 12, 1938; came to U.S., 1962; s. Seref and Sadife (Baysal) Kadioglu; m. Susan Borah, July 18, 1964; children: Peri Michele, Aylin Elisabeth Diploma in engring., Tech. U., Hannover, Fed. Republic Germany, 1962; MS in Mech. Engring., U. Calif.-Berkeley, 1964, PhD in Mech. Engring., 1966. Research engr. DuPont Co., Wilmington, Del., 1966-68; research scientist Battelle Columbus Labs, Ohio, 1968-72, research fellow, 1972-75, sr. research leader, 1975-86; prof. mech. engring., dir. engring. rsch. ctr. Ohio State U., Columbus, 1985—. Chmn. sci. com. N.Am. Mfg. Rsch. Inst. Soc. Mfg. Engrs., Detroit, 1982-86, pres., 1987; dir. Ctr. for Net Shape Mfg. Co-author: Forging Equipment, 1973, Metal Forming, 1983, Metal Forming and the Finite Element Method, 1989; assoc. editor Jour. Materials Processing Tech., Eng., 1978-99; contbr. over 400 tech. articles to profl. jours. Fellow Am. Soc. Metals (chmn. forging com. 1978-87), Soc. Mfg. Engrs. (Gold medal 1985), ASME. Avocations: languages, travel. Office: Ohio State U 210 Baker Bldg 1971 Neil Ave Columbus OH 43210-1210 E-mail: altan1@osu.edu.

ALTAYE, MEKIBIB, medical educator, consultant, medical researcher; s. Altalye Beyene; m. Martha Yoseph, May 23, 1993; 1 child, Mesgana Mekibib. BS, Addis Ababa U., Ethiopia, 1979—83; MS, Okla. State U., 1989—91; PhD, The U. of Western Ont., 1994—98. Asst. prof. Ea. Va. Med. Sch., Norfolk, 1999—2001, Children's Hosp. Med. Ctr. /U. of Cin., 2001—. Cons. Acad. for Ednl. Devel., Washington, 2000—03. Mem.: Internat. Biometric Soc., Am. Statis. Assn. Office: Children's Hosp Med Ctr 3333 Burnet Ave Cincinnati OH 45229 Office Fax: 513-636-7509.

ALTBACH, PHILIP, director, educator; b. Chgo., May 3, 1941; s. Milton and Josephine (Huebsch) A.; m. Edith Hoshino, June 16, 1962; children: Eric, Frederick Gabriel. BA, U. Chgo., 1962, MA, 1964, PhD, 1966. Lectr. Harvard U., Cambridge, Mass., 1967-68; from asst. prof. to assoc. prof. U. Wis., Madison, 1968-75; prof., chmn. dept. ednl. orgn., adminstrn. and policy SUNY, Buffalo, 1976-80, 86-92, dir. Comparative Edn. Ctr., 1978-94; prof. sch. edn. Boston Coll., 1994—, dir. Ctr. Internat. Higher Edn., 1995—, J. Donald Monan SJ prof. higher edn., 1996—. Fulbright rsch. prof. U. Bombay, 1968; cons. Regional Inst. Higher Edn., Singapore, 1979, 81, 82, Carnegie Found. Advancement Tchg., 1990-94, Rockefeller Found., 1991—; vis. prof. Moscow State U., 1981, Stanford U., 1989; Fulbright cons. U. Singapore, 1982; sr. assoc. Carnegie Found. Advancement Tchg., 1992-96; sec.-gen. Bellagio Publ. Network, 1992-98; guest prof. Peking U. Author: Student Politics in America, 1975, rev., 1997, Comparative Higher Education, 2000, Higher Education in Third World, 1982, Knowledge Context, 1987, International Higher Education: An Encyclopedia, 1991, Publishing and Development in the Third World, 1994, Higher Education in the 21st Century, 1999, Private Prometheus: Private Higher Education and Development, 2000, In Defense of American Higher Education, 2001, The Decline of the Guru, 2003, others; editor: Comparative Edn. Rev., 1979—89, Review of Higher Edn., 1996—, Ednl. Policy, 1989—, various newsletters and publs. Mem. capital budget rev. com. City of Buffalo, 1980. Grantee, NEH, 1976, Exxon Edn.. Found., 1982, 1984, NSF, 1987, Rockefeller Found., 1993, 1994, 1995, Ford Found., 1998, 2001, 2002, MacArthur Found., 2003, Toyota Found., 2003, Carnegie Corp. N.Y., 2003. Mem. Comparative Edn. Soc. (editor jour. 1980-89), Assn. Study Higher Edn. (editor jour. 1996—). Office: Boston Coll 207 Campion Hall Chestnut Hill MA 02467 E-mail: altbach@bc.edu.

ALTEKRUSE, JOAN MORRISSEY, retired preventive medicine educator; b. Cohoes, N.Y., Nov. 15, 1928; d. William T. Dee and Agnes Kay (Fitzgerald) Morrissey; m. Ernest B. Altekruse, Dec. 17, 1950; children— Philip, Clifford, Lisa, Janice, Charles, Sean, Lowell, Patrick, E. Caitlin. AB, Vassar Coll., N.Y., 1949; MD, Stanford U., Calif., 1960; MPH, Harvard U., Cambridge, 1965; DPH, U. Calif., Berkeley, 1973; MPS, Loyola U., New Orleans, 1999. Cons., program dir. Calif. State Health Dept., 1966-69; mem. faculty U. Heidelberg, Germany, 1970-72; med. dir. regional office Fla. State Health Dept., 1972-75; prof., dir. health adminstrn. Sch. Pub. Health, U. S.C., Columbia, 1975-77; prof. preventive medicine Univ. S.C. Sch. of Medicine, Columbia, 1975-94, chmn. dept., 1979-89, disting. prof. emerita, 1994—. Fellow, assoc. dir. Irish Peace Inst., U. Limerick, Ireland, 1990; vis. scholar Ctr. for Rsch. in Disease Prevention, Stanford U., 1992; women in medicine liaison officer Assn. Am. Med. Colls., 1980-94; mem. editl. bd. Aspen Publs. Mem. editorial bd. Family and Community Health Jour., Jour. Community Health; editorial adv. bd. VA Practitioner. Sr. docent chair, vol. bd. mem. Hunter Mus. Am. Art, Chattanooga; activist in social justice, peace and health advocacy orgns. Lt. USMC, 1949—51, sr. surgeon USPHS, 1960—64, capt. USPHS. Recipient Adminstrn. award Women in Higher Edn., 1989, Achievement award S.C. Commn. on Women, 1990, Ann. award, 1991, Life Achievement award Emma Willard Sch., 1996; WHO travel fellow, Eng., 1974; grantee NIH, NCI, Ctr. for Disease Control, pvt. founds; recipient Alumni award of merit Harvard Sch. Pub. Health, 1997. Fellow: APHA (mem. emerita), Assn. Tchrs. Preventive Medicine (pres. 1986, Spl. Recognition award 1995), Am. Coll. Preventive Medicine; mem.: Nat. Bd. Med. Examiners (comprehensive test com. 1986—92), Am. Heart Assn. (SC affiliate pres. 1986, agenda planning com. 1987—89, women and minorities leadership com. 1989—92, Lifetime Achievement award 1992), Am. Bd. Med. Specialties, Am. Bd. Preventive Medicine (trustee 1983—92), Emma Willard Sch. Alumni Assn. (bd. dirs. 2003—), Am. Womens Med. Assn., Harvard Sch. Pub. Health Alumni Assn. (pres. 1999—2001, leadership coun. 2003—), Harvard Alumni Assn. (bd. dirs. 2001—03). Democrat. Roman Catholic.

ALTEMOSE, MARK KENNETH, lawyer; b. Easton, Pa., July 21, 1965; s. Richard and Constance Irene (Silfies) Altemose; m. Jennifer Lou Abram, Nov. 24, 1995; children: Rachel Rebecca, Meghan Grace, Abigail Lynne. BA in Econ., Lafayette Coll., 1987; JD, Villanova, 1990. Bar: Pa. 1990, N.J. 1990, U.S. Dist. Ct. N.J. 1991, U.S. Dist. Ct. (ea. dist.) Pa. 1991, U.S. Ct. Appeals (3rd cir.) 1991. Assoc. Korn, Kline & Kutner, Phila., 1990-91, Brown, Brown, Solt & Ferretti, Allentown, Pa., 1991-94, Knafo Law Offices, Allentown, Pa., 1994—. Hearing com. mem. Disciplinary Bd. Supreme Ct. of Pa., Harrisburg, 1995-2000, chmn., 1999-2000. Mem.: ATLA, Northampton County Bar Assn., Pa. Bar Assn., Pa. Trial Lawyers Assn. (bd. govs. 1998—), Lehigh County Bar Assn. (co-chmn. Law Day 1995—, bd. dirs. 2001—). Democrat. Presbyterian. Avocations: weightlifting, running, golf. Office: Knafo Law Offices 4201 W Tilghman St Allentown PA 18104-4448 E-mail: maltemose@knafo.com.

ALTENBERGER, ANDRZEJ RYSZARD, physical chemist, chemistry educator; b. Warsaw, Sept. 19, 1942; came to U.S., 1980; s. Gustav Stanislav and Maria (Myszkorowski) A.; m. Alicja Sitek, Sept. 30, 1972. MSc in Nuclear Chemistry, U. Warsaw, 1966; PhD in Phys. Chemistry, Polish Acad. of Scis., 1972. Rsch. assoc. U. Warsaw, 1966-68, Inst. of Phys. Chemistry, Polish Acad. of Scis., Warsaw, 1968-72, rsch. group leader, sr. scientist, 1973-80; rsch. assoc. chemistry dept. MIT, Cambridge, 1972-73; vis. scientist, lectr. SUNY, Stony Brook, 1980-82; vis. asst. prof. chem. engring. and material sci. U. Minn., Mpls., 1982—; assoc. prof. chemistry St. Cloud (Minn.) State U., 2000—. Contbr. articles to profl. jours. Mem. Am. Chem. Soc. Roman Catholic. Avocations: Judo, Karate, tennis. Home: 2311 Territorial Rd Saint Paul MN 55114-1613

ALTENBERND, CHRIS W. judge; b. Muscatine, Iowa, Jan. 18, 1949; m. N. Sue Soileau, Feb. 14, 1979; 2 children. Student, Harvard Coll., 1967-69; BA in Psychology with honors, U. Mo., 1972; JD, Harvard U., 1975; MLS in Jud. Process, U. Va., 1998. Bar: Fla. 1975. Ptnr. Fowler, White, Gillen, Boggs, Villareal & Banker, P.A., 1976-88; appellate judge 2d dist. Fla. Ct. Appeals, Tampa, 1989—. Mem. faculty Fla. Coll. Advanced Jud. Studies, 1994—. Contbr. articles to law publs., including The Fla. Bar, Fla. State U. Law Rev., others. Bd. dirs. Conn Meml. Found., 1998—. Recipient Silver Beaver award Boy Scouts Am., 1996; Jurist of Yr. award Fla. Bd. Trial Advs., 1998, Jurist of Yr. award Am. Acad. Matrimonial Lawyers, 1999; Ann. rsch. grant named in his honor Florida Bay Area March of Dimes, 1989. Mem. ABA, Am. Bd. Trial Advocates, Am. Judicature Soc., Hillsborough County Bar Assn., William Glenn Terrell Inn of Ct., Am. Inns of Ct., Canakaris Inn of Ct. Presbyterian.

ALTENBURGER, KARL MARION, allergist, immunologist; b. Coral Gables, Fla., Nov. 13, 1949; s. Karl and Carol Altenburger; m. Carol Bauer, May 25, 1974; children: Laura Alyson, Ashley Carolyn, Elizabeth Ann, Allison Nicole. BA in Zoology, U. South Fla., 1971, MD, 1974. Diplomate Am. Bd. Pediatrics, Am. Bd. Allergy and Immunology, Nat. Bd. Med. Examiners. Intern in pediatrics U. Colo. Med. Ctr., Denver, 1975-76, resident, 1976-78, fellow in allergy and immunology, 1978-81, Nat. Jewish Hosp. and Rsch. Ctr.-Nat. Asthma Ctr., Denver, 1978-81; pvt. practice, Ocala, Fla., 1981—. Instr. dept. pediatrics U. Colo. Sch. Medicine, 1980-81; bd. dirs. Fla. Med. Polit. Action Com., 1991-2003, pres., 1998-2001, alt. del. to AMA, 2000-02, bd. dirs. Fla. Med. Assn., 2002—. Contbr. articles to profl. jours. Trustee Am. Lung Assn. Ctrl. Fla., 1985—93. Fellow Am. Acad. Allergy, Asthma and Immunology, Am. Coll. Allergy Asthma and Immunology; mem. AMA, Southeastern Allergy Assn., Am. Assn. for History Medicine, Fla. Med. Assn. (Marion County del. 1990—), Fla. Allergy Asthma and Immunology Soc. (exec. com. 1990-96, pres. 1993-94), Marion County Med. Soc. (bd. dirs. 1983-88, pres. 1985-86, editor Bull. 1986-89), U. South Fla. Coll. Medicine Alumni Assn. (pres. 1983-87), Alpha Omega Alpha. Roman Catholic. Avocations: faith, family, friends. Office: 1800 SE 17th St Ste 300 Ocala FL 34471-4173 E-mail: altenburge@aol.com.

ALTENHOFEN, JANE ELLEN, federal agency administrator, auditor; b. Seneca, Kans., Sept. 4, 1952; d. Justin Leo and Marva Mae (Sextro) A.; m. John Dean Arnette, Sept. 12, 1975 (div. Mar. 1978). BBA cum laude, Wichita (Kans.) State U., 1973; MPA, Am. U., 1982; cert., Inst. Internal Auditors, 1986. Cert. internal auditor, cert. fraud examiner, cert. govt. fin. mgr. Auditor U.S. Gen. Acctg. Office, Kansas City, Kans., 1974-76, Honolulu, 1976-80, Washington, 1980-84, Fed. Emergency Mgmt. Agy., Washington, 1984-89; insp. gen. U.S. Internat. Trade Commn., Washington, 1989-99, Nat. Labor Rels. Bd., Washington, 1999—. Mem. Adopt a Grandparent Program, Wichita, 1973; vol. reading course work to blind students, Wichita, 1973; vol. Vis. Nurse Assn., Washington, 1986—; host, traveler, Wash. area rep. SERVAS, 1987—; commr. Adv. Neighborhood Commn., Washington, 1986-89; troop leader Girl Scouts U.S., Washington, 1983-85; foster home Washington Humane Soc., 1994—. Mem. Inst. Internal Auditors, Nat. Intergovtl. Audit Forum, Assn. Govt. Accouts, Nat. Assn. Cert. Fraud Examiners, Phi Kappa Phi, Pi Alpha Pi. Home: 507 2nd St SE Washington DC 20003-1928 Office: Nat Labor Rels Bd 1099 14th St NW Rm 9820 Washington DC 20570-0001

ALTER, EDWARD T. state treasurer; b. Glen Ridge, N.J., July 26, 1941; s. E. Irving and Norma (Fisher) A.; m. Patricia R. Olsen, 1975; children: Christina Lyn, Ashly Ann, Darci Lee. BA, U. Utah., 1966; MBA, U. Utah, 1967. CPA, Calif., Utah. Sr. acct. Touche Ross & Co., Los Angeles, 1967-72; asst. treas. U. Utah, Salt Lake City, 1972-80; treas. State of Utah, Salt Lake City, 1981—; pres. Nat. Assn. State Treas., 1987-88. Bd. dirs. Utah Housing Corp., Utah State Retirement Bd., pres., 1984-93; mem. Utah State Rep. Ctrl. Com., 1981—, Anthony Com. on Pub. Fin., 1988-92. Sgt. USAR, 1958-66. Named to All-pro Govt. Team, City and State Mag., 1988, Outstanding CPA for 2000 Utah Assn. CPAs; recipient Jesse M. Uhruh Award for Svc. to State Treas., 1989, Adminstr. of Yr. award Romney Inst. Pub. Mgmt., Brigham Young U., 2003. Mem. AICPA, Nat. Assn. State Treas. (past sr. v.p., pres. 1987, Harlan E. Boyles Disting. Svc. award 2003), Utah Assn. CPAs, Utah Bond Club (pres. 1981-82), Delta Sigma Pi, Delta Phi Kappa. Clubs: Utah Bond (pres. 1981-82). Republican. Office: State Capitol 215 State Capitol Building Salt Lake City UT 84114-1202

ALTER, ELEANOR BREITEL, lawyer; b. N.Y.C., Nov. 10, 1938; d. Charles David and Jeanne (Hollander) Breitel; children: Richard B. Zabel, David B. Zabel. BA with honors, U. Mich., 1960; postgrad., Harvard U., 1960-61; LLB, Columbia U., 1964. Bar: N.Y. 1965. Atty., office of gen. counsel, ins. dept. State of N.Y., 1964-66; assoc. Miller & Carlson, N.Y.C., 1966-68, Marshall, Bratter, Greene, Allison & Tucker, N.Y.C., 1968-74, mem. firm, 1974-82, Rosenman & Colin, 1982-97, Kasowitz, Benson, Torres & Friedman, N.Y.C., 1997—. Fellow U. Chgo. Law Sch., 1988; adj. prof. law NYU Sch. Law, 1983-87; vis. prof. law U. Chgo., 1990-91, 93; lectr. in field. Editorial bd.: N.Y. Law Jour. Contbr. articles to profl. jours. Trustee Lawyers' Fund for Client Protection of the State of N.Y., 1983—, chmn., 1985—; bd. visitors U. Chgo. Law Sch., 1984-87. Mem. Am. Law Inst., Am. Coll. Family Trial Lawyers, N.Y. State Bar Assn., Assn. of Bar of City of N.Y. (libr. com. 1978-80, com. on matrimonial law 1977-81, 87-88, 2002—, judiciary com. 1981-84, 94, 95, 96, exec. com. 1988-92), Am. Acad. Matrimonial Lawyers. Office: Kasowitz Benson Et Al 1633 Broadway New York NY 10019

ALTER, JONATHAN HAMMERMAN, journalist; b. Chgo., Oct. 6, 1957; s. James M. and Joanne (Hammerman) A.; m. Emily Lazar, Oct. 18, 1986; children: Charlotte Helen, Thomas Beck, Molly Cecelia. AB in History cum laude, Harvard U., 1979. Mem. staff speech writing office The White House, 1978; editor The Washington Monthly, 1981-82; sr. editor, columnist, media critic Newsweek, N.Y.C., 1983—; on-air analyst, corr. NBC News, 1996—. Ferris vis. prof. Princeton U., 1997, Minow vis. prof., Northwestern U., 2003. Co-author: Selecting A President, 1980; editor: (with Charles Peters) Inside the System. 5th edit., 1984. Recipient Gerald Loeb award 1987, Lowell Mellett award for Improving Journalism, 1987, Clarion award, 1994, N.Y. Press Club award, 2001, ABA Silver Gavel award, 2001, John Bartlow Martin award Northwestern U., 2001; fellow U.S.-Japan Leadership program, 1992-93, Nat. Headliners Best Column award, 1997, 2001, Mentoring USA award, 1999; named 1 of Top 10 Media Critics in U.S., Columbia U., 1991. Office: care Newsweek Magazine 251 W 57th St New York NY 10019-1802 E-mail: jalter@newsweek.com.

ALTER, MARIA POSPISCHIL, language educator; b. Vienna; came to U.S., 1947; d. Karl and Ludmilla (Von Adamovic) Pospischil; divorced; children: Assunta, Sylvia, Nora. BA, U. Okla., 1948, MA, 1950; PhD, U. Md., 1961. Instr., asst. prof. Howard U., Washington, 1955-66; asst. prof. Case Western U., Cleve., 1966-70; acad. cons. Am. Assn. Tchrs. German, Phila., 1970-73; prof. Villanova (Pa.) U., 1974—. Author: The Role of the Physicians in Schnitzler's and Corossa's Work, 1961, A Modern Case for German, 1971. Mem. Assn. German, Modern Lang. Assn. Home: 830 Montgomery Ave Bryn Mawr PA 19010-3343 Office: Villanova U Lancaster Pike Villanova PA 19085

ALTER, MILTON, neurologist, educator; b. Buffalo, Nov. 11, 1929; s. Samuel and Rose (Schaffer) Alter; m. Reina Rolnick, Aug. 31, 1952; children: David S., Daniel M., Michael A., Naomi T., Joel A. BA, U. Buffalo, 1951, MD, 1955; PhD, U. Minn., 1966. Diplomate Am. Bd. Psychiatry and Neurology. Intern U. Minn., Mpls., 1955-56; sr. surgeon USPHS, Bethesda, Md., 1956-62; fellow Med. Coll. S.C., Charleston, 1956-57, Dalhousie U., Halifax, 1957, Columbia U. Coll. Physicians and Surgeons, N.Y.C., 1957-58, Hebrew U., Jerusalem, 1960-62; mem. faculty, chief neurology svc. U. Minn., Mpls., 1962—67, Mpls. VA Hosp., 1967-76; chmn. dept. neurology Temple U., Phila., 1976-87, prof. neurology, 1987—89; prof., dir. residency tng. Med. Coll. Pa., Phila., 1989-91; clin. prof. Allegheny U., 1995—. Mem. sci. adv. bd. Nat. Multiple Sclerosis Soc., N.Y.C., Dystonia Med. Rsch. Found., Alzheimer Disease Assn.; peer reviewer Epidemiology and Disease Control 1 and 2 NIH, Bethesda, Md.; adj. prof. Ctr. Clin. Epidemiology and Biostatistics U. Pa., 1995; adj. prof. Thomas Jefferson U., 1999. Guest editor: numerous profl. jours., editor-in-chief: Neuroepidemiology, 1989—96; editor emeritus Neuroepidemiology; contbr. articles to profl. jours., chapters to books. Capt. USPHS, 1962. Grantee, NIH, Multiple Sclerosis Soc. Mem.: AMA, World Fedn. Neurol. (chair rsch. group epidemiology 1998—2001), Am. Epidemiology Soc., Assn. Rsch. Nervous and Mental Diseases, Am. Neurol. Assn., Am. Acad. Neurology. Democrat. Jewish. Home: 236 Indian Creek Rd Wynnewood PA 19096-3404 also: Lankenau Med Rsch Ctr 100 E Lancaster Ave Wynnewood PA 19096-3404 E-mail: malter5280@aol.com.

ALTER, NELSON TOBIAS, jewelry retailer and wholesaler; b. San Antonio, July 14, 1926; s. William and Celia (Tobias) A.; m. Shirley Ann Jacobs, June 12, 1949; children: Dennis Ira, Keith Alan, Brian Reid, Wendy Ilene. BBA in Acctg., U. Tex., 1948, JD, 1950. Mgr. 9 coin-operated washeterias, 1960-67; mgr. Sta. KOGT radio, Orange, Tex., 1950-65; ptnr. Calder Properties, 1977—; mng. ptnr. Crow Road Devel. Co., Beaumont, Tex., 1976-77, Normandy Townhomes, Beaumont, 1978—, Griffing Devel. Co., Beaumont, 1978—, Griffing Realty Joint Venture, Beaumont, 1983—; comptroller Gem Jewelry Cos., Beaumont, 1950-58; pres. Gem Jewelry Co. of Beaumont, Inc., 1958—, chmn. of bd., 1991—; mng. ptnr. Gem Distbg. Co. Wholesale Jewelry, Beaumont, 1958—; gen. ptrn. Alter's Gem Jewelry, Ltd. (formerly Gem Jewelry Corp.), Beaumont. Also pres., chmn. of bd. Gem Jewelry Co. of Port Artur, Inc., 1991—, Gem Jewelry C. of Orange, Inc., 1991—, Gem. Jewelry C. of Alexandria (La.), Inc., 1991—, Gem. Jewelry C. of Rapides (La.) Inc., 1991, Gem Jewelry Distbg. Co. Inc., 1991—; U.S. rep. Tex. region Habsburg-Feldman Fine Art Auctioneers, Geneva, 1986, 87, 88, 89; real estate developer Normandy Townhomes, Griffing Devel. Co., Joint Venture, Griffing Realty Joint Venture, Partner Calder Properties. Past pres. Downtown Beaumont Unltd.; co-chmn. Beaumont Urban Renewal; drive chmn. United Jewish Appeal, Beaumont, 1954, 67; pres. Temple Emanuel, 1974-75, pres., 1981; mem. Beaumont Heritage Soc., Beaumont Music Commn., Beaumont Symphony Soc., Am. Cancer Soc.; co-founder, mem. BBB S.E. Tex.; bd. dirs. A.W. Schlesinger Geriatric Ctr., 1996-2003. Recipient Paul Harris Fellow, Rotary Internat. Found., 2002. Mem. Tex. Retail Jewelers Assn. (v.p. 1974-75), Jefferson County Bar Assn., Tex. Bar Assn., Edna Gladney Aux., Beaumont Jewish Fedn., Buckner Benevolences, Tower Club, Masons, B'nai Brith, Phi Eta Sigma, Beta Gamma Sigma, Phi Alpha Delta, Sigma Alpha Mu. Jewish. Avocations: art collecting, swimming, golf. Office: Alter's Gem Jewelry Ltd 3155 Dowlen Rd Beaumont TX 77706

ALTER, ORLY, theoretical physicist, geneticist; b. Tel Aviv, Apr. 12, 1964; d. Shlomo and Aliza (Avadish) A.; m. David Brickman Oberman, Dec. 30, 1997. BSc in Physics, Tel Aviv U., 1989; PhD in Applied Physics, Stanford U., 1998. Rsch. asst. dept. physics Tel Aviv U., 1989-91; rsch. asst. dept. applied physics Stanford U., 1991-98, postdoctoral fellow dept. genetics, 1998—. Co-author monograph. 1st lt. Israeli Air Force, 1982-85. Recipient Individual Mentored Rsch. Scientist Devel. award in genomic rsch. and analysis Nat. Human Genome Rsch. Inst., 2000—; postdoctoral fellow Alfred P. Sloan Found. and U.S. Dept. Energy, 1999—. Mem.: AAAS, Internat. Soc. Optical Engring., NY Acad. Sci., Am. Phys. Soc. Jewish. Achievements include establishing the quantum theoretical limits to the information which can be obtained in the measurement of a single physical system about the quantum wave function of the system, its time evolution and the classical potentials which shape this time evolution; building the first models of genome-wide expression data using singular value decomposition (SVD) and generalized SVD (GSVD), and showing that, these models provide a mathematical description of the underlying genetic networks. Home: 254 College Ave Apt D Palo Alto CA 94306-1511 Office: Stanford U Sch Medicine Dept Genetics 300 Pasteur Dr Stanford CA 94305-5120 E-mail: orly@genome.stanford.edu.

ALTER, ROBERT BERNARD, comparative literature educator, critic; b. N.Y.C., Apr. 2, 1935; s. Harry and Tillie (Zimmerman) A.; m. Judith Berkenbilt, June 4, 1961 (div. 1973); children: Miriam, Dan; m. Carol Cosman, June 17, 1973; children: Gabriel, Micha. BA, Columbia U., 1957; MA, Harvard U., 1958, PhD, 1962; LHD (hon.), Hebrew Union Coll., 1985. Instr., then asst. prof. English Columbia U., 1962-66; mem. faculty U. Calif.-Berkeley, 1967—, prof. Hebrew and comparative lit., 1969—, chmn. dept. comparative lit., 1970-73, 88-89, class of 1937 prof., 1989—; columnist Commentary mag., 1965-73, contbg. editor, 1973-86. Author: Rogue's Progress: Studies in the Picaresque Novel, 1964, Fielding and the Nature of the Novel, 1968, After the Tradition, 1969, Partial Magic: The Novel as a Self-Conscious Genre, 1975, Defenses of the Immagination, 1977, A Lion for Love, 1979, The Art of Biblical Narrative, 1981, Motives for Fiction, 1984, The Art of Biblical Poetry, 1985; co-editor: The Literary Guide to the Bible, 1987, The Invention of Hebrew Prose, 1988, The Pleasures of Reading in an Ideological Age, 1989, Necessary Angels, 1991, The World of Biblical Literature, 1992, Hebrew and Modernity, 1994, Genesis: Translation and Commentary, 1996, The David Story: A Translation with Commentary of 1 and 2 Samuel, 1999, Canon and Creativity, 2000; contbg. editor: Tri Quarterly mag., 1975—. Recipient essay prize English Inst., 1965, Nat. Jewish Book award for Jewish thought, 1982, Present Tense award for Jewish thought, 1986, Bay Area Book Reviewers Transl. award, 1997; Guggenheim fellow, 1966-67, 78-79, sr. fellow NEH, 1972-73, fellow Inst. for Advanced Studies, Jerusalem, 1982-83; scholar Nat. Found. for Jewish Culture, 1995. Fellow Am. Acad. Arts and Scis., Am. Philosoph. Soc.; mem. Council of Scholars of Library of Congress, Assn. Lit. Scholars and Critics (pres. 1996-97). Jewish. Home: 1475 Le Roy Ave Berkeley CA 94708-1911 Office: U Calif Dept Comp Lit 4408 Dwinelle Hall Berkeley CA 94720-2510 E-mail: altcos@uclink4.berkeley.edu.

ALTER, SHIRLEY JACOBS, jewelry store owner; b. Beaumont, Tex., June 23, 1929; d. Morris Louis and Helen (Dow) Jacobs; m. Nelson Tobias Alter, June 12, 1949; children: Dennis, Keith, Brian, Wendy. Student, U. Tex., Austin, 1950. Owner Alter's Gem Jewelry Co., Beaumont, 1950—. Pres. Nat. Coun. Jewish Women, Beaumont, 1965, 66, Sisterhood of Temple Emanuel, Beaumont, 1967, 68, Buckner Bapt. Benevolence Aux., Beaumont, 1970-72; bd. dirs. Temple Emanuel, pres. elect, 1994-96, pres. 1996-98; active Beaumont Music Commn., 1990; founder Beaumont Reach to Recovery, 1973; active BMW Drive for the Cure of breast cancer, 1997. Named Hero, Susan Komen Found., 1997. Democrat. Office: Alters Gem Jewelry 3155 Dowlen Beaumont TX 77706

ALTERMAN, IRWIN MICHAEL, lawyer; b. Vineland, N.J., Mar. 4, 1941; s. Joseph and Rose A.; m. Susan Simon, Aug. 6, 1972 (dec. Apr. 1997); 1 son, Owen. AB, Princeton U., 1962; LLB, Columbia U., 1965. Bar: N.Y. 1966, Mich. 1967. Law clk. to chief judge Theodore Levin U.S. Dist. Ct. (ea. dist.) Mich., 1965-67; assoc. Kaye, Scholer, Fierman, Hays & Handler, N.Y.C., 1967-70, Hyman, Gurwin, Nachman, Friedman & Winkelman, Southfield, Mich., 1970-74, ptnr., 1974-88, Kaufman and Payton, Farmington Hills, Mich., 1988-89, Kemp, Klein, Umphrey, Endelman & May, Troy, Mich., 1989—. Author: Plain and Accurate Style in Court Papers, 1987; founding editor: Mich. Antitrust, 1975—92; editor: Mich. Antitrust Digest, 3d edit., 2001; contbr. articles to profl. jours. Bd. gov. Jewish Fedn. Detroit, 1990—; mem. nat. young leadership cabinet United Jewish Appeal, 1978-79, mem. nat. exec. com., 1980; past pres. Adat Shalom Synagogue, Farmington Hills, Mich. Mem. ABA, Am. Law Inst., State Bar Mich. (past chmn. com. on plain English, past. chmn. antitrust sect.), Princeton Club (past pres. Mich.). Office: Kemp Klein Umphrey & Endelman 201 W Big Beaver Rd Ste 600 Troy MI 48084-4136 E-mail: irwin.alterman@kkue.com.

ALTÉUS, ÅKE, foundation administrator; Dep. exec. dir. The Nobel Found., Stockholm. Office: The Nobel Found Sturegatan 14 Box 5232 SE-10245 Stockholm Sweden

ALTFEST, KAREN CAPLAN, diversified financial services company executive, director; b. Mont., Que., Can. d. Philip and Betty (Gamer) Caplan; m. Lewis Jay Altfest; children: Ellen Wendy, Andrew Gamer. Tchr.'s diploma, McGill U.; BA cum laude, Hunter Coll., 1970, MA, 1972; PhD, CUNY, 1979. CFP, N.Y. V.p. L. J. Altfest & Co., Inc., N.Y.C., 1985—; dir. fin. planning program New Sch. Univ., N.Y.C., 1989—. Dir. CFP program Pace U., White Plains, N.Y., 1988-90. Author: Robert Owen, 1978, Keeping Clients for Life, 2001; co-author: Lew Altfest Answers Almost All Your Questions about Money, 1992; contbr. articles to fin. jours. Founding chmn. Yorkville Common Pantry, N.Y.C., 1980-84; v.p. PS 6 PTA, N.Y.C., 1991-92; bd. dirs. Temple Shaaray Tefila, 1993—. Named Planner of Month, Mut. Funds Mag., 2000; named one of 200 Best Fin. Planners in U.S., Worth Mag., 1996, 1997, 1998, Best Fin. Advisors, Med. Econs. Mag., 1998, 100 Top Advisors, Mut. Funds Mgrs., 2002, Best 100 Planners, Mut. Funds Mag., 2002, Top Wealth Mgrs. (firm), Bloomberg, 2003; recipient Cmty. Svc. award, Temple Shaaray Tefila, 1985; profile on cover, Fin. Planning Mag., 2001. Mem.: Women's Econ. Round Table, Fin. Women's Assn., Nat. Assn. Personal Fin. Advisors (chair N.E.-Mid Atlantic Conf. 1995, bd. dirs. N.E. region 1996—2003, v.p. 1997—99, pres. N.E.-Mid Atlantic region 1999—2001, chmn. 2001—03, Achievement cert. N.E. Region 1995, award for outstanding svc. to NE region 2001, 2003), Fin. Planning Assn. (bd. dirs. N.Y. chpt. 1994—99, bd. dirs. 2000—, dir. for pub. rels., Dedicated Svc. cert. 1998, 1999, 2000, 2001, 2002, 2003), Assn. for Women's Econ. Devel., Assn. for Can. Studies in U.S., Nat. Assn. Women Bus. Owners (chmn. FOCUS 1993—95, bd. dirs.), CUNY PhD Alumni Assn. (v.p. 1982—84), Phi Alpha Theta. Achievements include featured on cover of Fin. Planning Mag., 2001. Office: LJ Altfest & Co Inc 116 John St Rm 1120 New York NY 10038-3305 E-mail: karen@altfest.com.

ALTFEST, LEWIS JAY, financial and investment advisor; b. N.Y.C., Oct. 14, 1940; s. Sam and Ruth (Zwang) A.; m. Karen Caplan, Dec. 25, 1966; children: Ellen Wendy, Andrew Gamer. BBA with honors, CCNY, 1962; MBA, NYU, 1970; PhD, CUNY, 1978. CPA, N.Y.; chartered fin. analyst; cert. fin. planner, personal fin. specialist. Sr. investment analyst Wertheim and Co., N.Y.C., 1969-75, Lehman Bros., N.Y.C., 1975-76; dir. research, gen. ptnr. Lord Abbett and Co., N.Y.C., 1976-82; pres. L.J. Altfest and Co., Inc., N.Y.C., 1982—; assoc. prof. fin. Pace U. Grad. Sch. Bus., N.Y.C., 1984—; dir. fin. planning and investments program New Sch. for Social Rsch., N.Y.C., 1988—. Arbitrator Nat. Assn. Securities Dealers, Am. Arbitration Assn., 1985-88; bd. dirs. Consumer Fin. Edn. Found., 1994-95. Author: (with others) Introduction to Business, 1978, Capital Budgeting Handbook, 1986; author: Lew Altfest Answers Almost All Your Questions About Money, 1992, revised edit., 1994; contbr. articles to profl. jours. Pres. 240 E. 79th Coop. Bd., N.Y.C., 1983-86; bd. dirs. Consumer Fin. Edn. Found., 1993-97. With U.S. Army, 1962-63. Named One of Best Fin. Planners in U.S., Money Mag., 1987, One of Best Fin. Advisors, Worth Mag., 1996, 97, 98, One of Best Advisors for Physicians, Med. Econs., 1998, 2000, 2002, One of 100 Gt. Fin. Planners, Mut. Funds Mag., 2001, Best Wealth Mgrs. (Bloomberg), firm L.J. Altfest & Co., 2003; recipient Disting. Alumni award Ph.D. Alumni Assn. CUNY, 1992. Mem. Nat. Assn. Personal Fin. Advisors (bd. dirs. 1985-89, Outstanding Leadership award 1989), AICPA, Internat. Assn. for Fin. Planning (bd. dirs. N.Y. chpt. 1987-93), Inst. Chartered Fin. Analysts, Am. Fin. Assn., Fin. Analysts Fedn., Fin. Mgmt. Assn., N.Y. Soc. Security Analysts, Registry Fin. Planning Practitioners, CCNY Bus. Alumni Assn. (bd. dirs. 1983-87), Acad. of Fin. Svcs. Office: LJ Altfest & Co Inc 116 John St Rm 1120 New York NY 10038-3305

ALTHAGE, C. JILL, librarian; b. St. Louis, June 19, 1946; d. Irvin Grey and Joyce Jeanette (Gunderson) A.; m. Lawrence Traum Lefferts, July 10, 1983. BA, Andrews U., 1969; MLS, Western Mich. U., 1980; M in Reading, Northeastern Ill. U., 1985, M in History, 1992. Elem. sch. tchr. San Fernando Valley Acad., Northridge, Calif., 1969-71; secondary sch. tchr., libr. Battle Creek (Mich.) Acad., 1971-78; libr. Northeastern Ill. U., Chgo., 1980—, edn. bibliographer, 1989-95, social sci. bibliographer, 1995—, acad. adviser, 1985, mentor minority student mentoring program, 1989—2000, prof., 2000, tchr. women's studies, 2001—. Reviewer Sch. Libr. Jour., 1990, Video Rating Guide, 1992-95, Ill. Librs., 1992, Ill. Reading Coun., 1995, E-Streams, 1998—; Booklist, 1999-2000. Mem. Delta Kappa Gamma (pres. Alpha Chi chpt. 1995-98; sec.-treas. Cook County Coord. Coun. 1995-96), Phi Alpha Theta (pres. Pi Gamma chpt. 1993-96). Democrat. Unitarian Universalist. Avocations: gardening, ceramics, reading, walking, bicycling. Home: 1340 W Glenlake Ave Chicago IL 60660-2506 Office: Northeastern Ill U 5500 N Saint Louis Ave Chicago IL 60625-4679

ALTHAUS, DAVID STEVEN, consultant; b. Massilon, Ohio, Dec. 25, 1945; s. James Horace and Mary Jane (Horan) A.; m. Joan Elizabeth Wrenn, Aug. 4, 1973; children: D. Steven Jr., Matthew, Beth Anne; foster children: James, Elise. BA, Miami U., Oxford, Ohio, 1967; cert., Def. Lang. Inst., Monterey, Calif., 1969; MBA, Miami U., Oxford, Ohio, 1976. CPA, N.C., Ohio. Internal auditor Harris Corp., Cleve., 1976-77, sr. staff acct. Rochester, NY, 1977-78; acctg. supr. Imperial Group Ltd., Wilson, NC, 1978-80; dir. planning Am. Mortgage Ins. Cos., Raleigh, NC, 1980-83; asst. v.p., budget mgr. Gen. Electric Mortgage Ins. Cos., Raleigh, 1983-84; contr., asst. treas. Chem. Industry Inst. Toxicology, Research Triangle Park, 1984—2000, mgr. human resources, 1984-90, asst. sec., 1989—2000; dir. advanced solutions group Pomeroy Computer Resources, 2001—03; cons., 2003—. Cubmaster Boy Scouts Am., 1986-90, asst. scoutmaster, 1990-95. Capt. USMC, 1968-74, Vietnam. Decorated Cross of Galantry, Rep. of Vietnam, Da Nang, 1970. Mem. AICPA, Inst. Mgmt. Accts., Am. Compensation Assn., Contr.'s Coun., Soc. for Human Resources Mgmt. Baptist. Office: Chem Industry Inst Toxicology PO Box 12137 Durham NC 27709-2137

ALTHAUSEN, JACK HENRY, computer company executive; b. N.Y.C., Oct. 1, 1957; s. Alex and Edith Althausen. BS, U. Pa., 1979; MBA, Columbia U., 1984. Fin. exec. IBM, N.Y.C., 1984—. Home: 44 Strawberry Hill Ave Stamford CT 06902 Office: IBM 33 Maiden Ln New York NY 10038 E-mail: jacka@us.ibm.com.

ALTHAVER, LAMBERT EWING, manufacturing company executive; b. Kansas City, Mo., May 18, 1931; s. Edward William and Dorothy Lambert (Ewing) A.; m. Holly Elizabeth Walpole, Feb. 28, 1953; children: Brian, Lauren BA, Principia Coll, 1952. Account exec. Walbro Corp., Cass City, Mich., 1954-58, asst. to pres., 1958-65, v.p. fin., 1965-70, exec. v.p., 1970-77, pres., chief ops. officer, 1977-82, pres., CEO, 1982-87, chmn., pres., CEO, 1987-96, also bd. dirs., chmn., CEO, 1996-98, chmn. emeritus, 1998-2000. Councilman Village of Cass City, 1963—65, pres., 1965—84, 1987—2000; mem. Tuscola County Planning Commn., Caro, Mich., 1966—94; chmn. Cass City Econ. Devel. Corp., 1983—96, Tuscola Area Airport Authority, 1994—; co-founder, v.p. Village Bach Festival, 1979—; mem. Mich. Jobs Commn., 1996—99; bd. dirs. Tuscola Econ. Devel. Corp., 1985—; vice-chmn., sec., dir. Artrain, Inc., 1975—96, chmn., 1996—2003; v.p., bd. dirs. Lake Huron area Boy Scouts Am., 1988—94; dir. Am. Bus. Conf. Found., Washington, 1998—, Mich. Mcpl. League Found., Ann Arbor, 1999—2002; trustee Jordan Coll., 1990—95, Northwood U., 2000—, Hills & Dales Hosp., Cass City, 1998—. Served with U.S. Army, 1952—54. Recipient Silver Beaver award Boy Scouts Am., 1995, Disting. Eagle Scout award, 1989; named Citizen of Yr. Cass City C. of C., 1978; Paul Harris fellow Rotary Internat., Evanston, Ill., 1979, 94, 99, 2002; named Outstanding Bus. Leader, Northwood U., 1997. Mem. Mich. C. of C. (bd. dirs. 1986-92), Cass City C. of C. (bd. dirs. 1985—), Detroit Athletic Club, Rotary. Avocation: golf. Office: PO Box 27 Cass City MI 48726-0027 E-mail: althaver@tband.net

ALTHEIDE, PHYLLIS SAGE, computer scientist, software engineer; b. St. Louis, Apr. 13, 1963; d. Paul D. and Alvera Sage; m. Richard W. Altheide, Aug. 1984 (div. June 1999); children: Martha Elizabeth, Paul William. BS in Computer Sci., U. Mo., Rolla, 1985, MS in Computer Sci., 1992. GS-12 computer scientist U.S. Geol. Survey, Rolla, 1988-95, GS-13 computer scientist, 1996-98, GS-13 supervisory computer specialist software engring sect., 1998-2000, sci. mgr. geographic and cartographic rsch. and applications, 2000—02, chief sys. devel. integration and rsch., 2002—. Lead developer Spatial Data Transfer Standard Task Force, Rolla, 1990-95; presenter workshops Australia, 1995, New Zealand, 1995, Malaysia, 1997; technical expert ISO working group on geospatial stds., 1998—. Author: (with others) GIS Data Conversion: Strategies, Techniques, Management, 1998. Recipient Superior Svc. Honor award, Dept. of Interior, 1995, Meritorious Svc. award, 2000. Mem.: IEEE Computer Soc., Assn. for Computing Machinery, U. Mo.-Rolla Computer Sci. Indsl. Adv. Bd. Lutheran. Avocations: photography, travel, walking.

ALTHEIMER, BRIAN P. See TUTASHINDA, KWELI

ALTHOFF, J(AMES) L. construction company executive; b. McHenry, Ill., June 9, 1928; s. William H. and Eleanor M. (Smith) A.; m. Joan E. Andreen, June 18, 1949; children: Tim, Betsy, Kate, Tod, Patti, Jim Jr., Karyn. Grad., McHenry (Ill.) High Sch., 1947. Owner, pres. Althoff Gas Svc., McHenry, 1949-60, Fox Valley Propane, 1952-60, No. Equip. Corp., McHenry, 1958-72; CEO Althoff Industries, Crystal Lake, Ill., 1961—, Althoff & Assocs., McHenry, 1962—, Brookside Indsl., McHenry, 1991—. Trustee Plumbers Welfare Fund, Chgo., 1972—; dir. McHenry Bank. Pres. McHenry High Sch. Bd. Edn., 1967-79, Fire Protection Dist., McHenry, 1964-92; chmn. bd. govs. Ill. Univs., 1980-91; commr. Ill. State Lottery, 1991—. Recipient award for outstanding leadership Chgo. State U., 1986, Leadership award No. Med. Ctr., McHenry, 1984, Ea. Ill. U., 1987. Mem. Contrs. Assn. No. Ill. (pres. 1969-72), Bradley Dads' Assn., Kiwanis. Home: 508 N Green St Mchenry IL 60050-5684 Office: Althoff Industries 8001 S State Route 31 Crystal Lake IL 60014-8184

ALTIER, WILLIAM JOHN, management consultant; b. Drexel Hill, Pa., July 22, 1935; s. William John and Gertrude (Soule) A.; m. Mileen Rishel Bower, June 21, 1958; children: William Clark, Dwight Douglas. BA, Lafayette Coll., 1958; MBA, Pa. State U., 1962. Assoc. Kepner-Tregoe Inc., Princeton, N.J., 1964-68, Applied Synergetics Ctr., Waltham, Mass., 1968-69; dir. mktg. Comstock & Wescott Inc., Cambridge, Mass., 1969 70; gen. mgr. divsn. Princeton Rsch. Press, 1970-75, sr. assoc., 1975-76; pres. Princeton Assocs. Inc., Buckingham, Pa., 1976—. Grad. asst. Dale Carnegie Courses; lectr. Assn. for Media-Based Continuing Edn. for Engrs.; guest lectr. Grad. Sch. Mgmt., New Sch. for Social Rsch., Wharton Sch., U. Pa., Pa. State U.; bd. dirs., vice chmn. Inst. Mgmt. Cons., also exec. editor IMC Newsletter. Author: The Thinking Manager's Toolbox, 1999; editor, pub. The PA Perspective; abstractor Jour. Product Innovation Mgmt.; mem . editl. rev. bd. Jour. Managerial Issues; contbg. author: Management Consulting, 3d edit., 1996, The Art of M&A Integration: A Guide to Merging Resources, Processes, and Responsibilities, 1997; contbr. articles to profl. jours.; patentee in field. Co-chmn. indls. divns. United Cmty. Fund, Carlisle, Pa., 1963; elder Doylestown Presbyn. Ch.; exec. v.p. Bucks County br. ARC, also mem. planning com. Southeastern Pa. chpt.; vol. worker civic orgns. Fellow Inst. Mgmt. Cons. (cert.); mem. Acad. Mgmt., Am. Chem. Soc., Am. Vacuum Soc., Armed Forces Comm. and Electronics Assn., Am. Mgmt. Assn., Product Devel. and Mgmt. Assn. (v.p.), Nat. Spkrs. Assn., Liberty Bell Spkrs. Assn., Indsl. Mgmt. Club, Inst. Mgmt. Cons. (participative process cons. spl. interest group), Am. Arbitration Assn. (panel arbitrators), U. So. Calif. Ctr. for Futures Rsch., Assn. Mng. Cons. (trustee, editor newslette UPDATE II), Union League Phila., Mensa, Ctrl. Bucks C. of C., Tech. Coun. Greater Phila., Pa. Innovation Network, World Affairs Coun. Phila., Am. Creativity Assn., Exch. Club (bd. control 1960-64), Doylestown Toastmasters (v.p.), 1000 Club, Kappa Sigma Alumni Corp. (chpt. pres.). Office: PO Box 820 Buckingham PA 18912-0820

ALTIERI, PETER LOUIS, lawyer; b. Norwalk, Conn., Dec. 7, 1955; s. John L. and Eileen Mary (Rudden) A.; m. Sandra Shelton White, Sept. 3, 1983; children: Brianna Burr, John Shelton. AB, Georgetown U., 1977; JD, Fordham Sch. Law, 1980. Bar: N.Y. 1981, U.S. Dist. Ct. (so. and ea. dists.) N.Y. 1981, U.S. Dist. Ct. (no. and we. dists) N.Y. 1983, U.S. Dist. Ct. Conn. 1983, U.S. Supreme Ct. 1984, U.S. Ct. Appeals (2d cir.) 1986, Conn. 1987, U.S. Ct. Appeals (6th cir.) 2001. Law clk. to judge U.S. Dist. Ct., 1978; intern U.S. Attys. Office, N.Y.C., 1978; assoc. Law Firm Malcolm A. Hoffmann, N.Y.C., 1980-87; ptnr. Epstein, Becker & Green, N.Y.C., 1987—. Mem. ABA, Conn. Bar Assn. (exec. com. antitrust sect. 1988—), Assn. Bar City N.Y. (com. uniform state laws 1985-88, com. on inter-Am. affairs 1997-99), The Patterson Club Conn., Union League Club N.Y.C. Home: 140 Burr St Fairfield CT 06824-7105 Office: Epstein Becker & Green 250 Park Ave Ste 1201 New York NY 10177-0001 E-mail: paltieri@ebglaw.com.

ALTMAN, ARNOLD DAVID, business executive; b. South Bend, Ind., Dec. 10, 1917; s. David and Goldie (Mooren) A.; children: Daniel Blair, Jonathan Estes. BSEE, U. Notre Dame, 1941. With Newman and Altman, Inc., South Bend, 1946-64; pres. Avanti Motor Corp., South Bend, 1976-82, Nat. Inventory Res., Inc., South Bend, 1980—; pres., CEO Rosenstein & Co., South Bend, 1985—. Lt. USN, 1942-46. Democrat. Jewish. Home: 1527 E Colfax Ave South Bend IN 46617-2601 Office: PO Box 603 Mishawaka IN 46546

ALTMAN, BARBARA JEAN FRIEDMAN, lawyer; b. Jan. 3, 1947; d. Herbert V. and Marion (Rosenfeld) Friedman; m. Ronald F. Altman, June 13, 1968; children: Andrew Edward, Lynn Alexandra. AB cum laude, Cornell U., 1968; JD, Georgetown U., 1977. Bar: Ill. 1977, U.S. Dist. Ct. (no. dist.) Ill. 1978, U.S. Ct. Appeals (7th cir.) 1978, U.S. Dist. Ct. (we. dist.) Wis. 1983. Law clk. U.S. Dist. Ct. (no. dist.) Ill., Chgo., 1977—79; assoc. Hedlund, Hunter & Lynch, Chgo., 1979—83; asst. regional counsel Office Gen. Counsel HHS, Chgo., 1983—. Articles editor: Georgetown U. Law Jour., 1976—77; contbr. articles to profl. jours. Business E-Mail: barbara.altman@hhs.gov.

ALTMAN, BETH LEE, social worker; b. Washington, July 2, 1952; d. Harry E. and Ada (Hurwich) A. AB (magna cum laude), Washington U., 1974; MSW, Cath. U., 1978. Lic. social worker, Md., D.C. Sr. counselor State Md. Juvenile Svcs. Adminstrn., Rockville, Md., 1974-85; clin. social worker Family Stress Clinic, Oxon Hill, Md., 1982-84; rschr. Chestnut Lodge Hosp., Rockville, 1985-92; clin. social worker, psychotherapist pvt. practice Washington, Washington, 1982—. Del Ward III Dem. Com., Washington, 1986—1990. Mem. NASW, Greater Washington Soc. for Clin. Social Work, Inst. Contemporary Pshychotherapy and Psychoanalysis, Assn. for Psychoanalytic Thought. Democrat. Jewish. Office: # 310 1625 K St NW Washington DC 20006-1604

ALTMAN, BRIAN DAVID, pediatric ophthalmologist; b. Temple, Tex., Feb. 29, 1944; s. Harold and Alice A. BA, Adelphi U., 1965; MD, Yale Med. Sch., 1969. Diplomate Am. Bd. Pediatrics, Am. Bd. Opthalmologists. Pediatric ophthalmologist pvt. practice, Huntington Valley, Pa., 1976-98, Plymouth, Pa., 1976-98, Ocean City, N.J., 1992—, Cape May Courthouse, 1992—. Cons. in pediatric ophthalomogy several hosps. in Pa. and N.J., 1977—. Co-author: (with others) Medications in Pediatric Ophthalmology, 1975. Lt. cmmdr. USPHS, 1970-72. Fellow Am. Acad. Opthalmology, Am. Acad. Pediatrics, Am. Assn. Pediatric Ophthalmologists. Office: 315 Rt 9 S Cape May Court House NJ 08210 Home and Office: PO Box 1259 Ocean City NJ 08226-7259

ALTMAN, DAVID J, pharmacist, consultant; b. Buffalo, July 16, 1961; m. Susan Chameli, Nov. 14, 1987; children: Michael, Matthew, Madeline. AB, Harvard U., 1984; MD, PhD, SUNY, Buffalo, 1992; Essentials of Mgmt. Cert., U. Pa., 2000. Diplomate Am. Bd. Dermatology, Nat. Bd. Med. Examiners. Internal medicine intern Strong Meml. Hosp., U. Rochester, NY, 1992-93; resident in dermatology U. Pa., Phila., 1993-95; clin. asst. med. staff Nat Cancer Inst., NIH, Bethesda, Md., 1995-97; acting exec. dir. worldwide clin. rsch. in dermatology Bristol-Myers Squibb Co., Princeton, NJ, 1997—2000; v.p. for clin. affairs and devel. Beauty Medicines, Inc., Cohasset, Mass., 2000—02; cons., v.p. clin. affairs, chief med. officer Cognigen Corp., Williamsville, NY, 2001; pres. Altman Dermatology and Clin. Rsch., Williamsville, NY, 2002—; pvt. practice dermatology and dermatologic surgery, 2002—. Cons. for pharms and biotech. 1st Manhattan Investment Corp., NYC, 1998—; dir. Westwood-Squibb Ctr. for Dermatologic Rsch. Wake Forest U. Sch. Medicine, Winston-Salem, NC, 1998—2000. Author: (book) The Delivery of Dermatologic Health Care, 2000. Fellow Am. Acad. Dermatology, Am. Soc. for Dermatologic Surgery. Office: Georgetown Sq 5225 Sheridan Dr Williamsville NY 14221 Office Fax: 716-810-0630. E-mail: daltman@maximweb.com.

ALTMAN, EDITH G. sculptor; b. Altenberg, Germany, May 23, 1931; arrived in U.S., 1939; BA, Wayne State U., 1949; student, Marygrove Coll., 1956-57. Instr. visual arts and printing project U. Omaha, 1984; asst. prof. painting, grad. advisor U. Chgo., 1984-85; vis. asst. prof. painting Sch. Art Inst. Chgo., 1985-86. Lectr. painting U. Ill., Columbia Coll., Oakton C.C., Chgo. One-woman shows include NAME Gallery, 1987, Spertus Mus. Gallery Contemporary Art, 1988, Rockford Art Mus., 1989, State of Ill. Mus. Gallery, Chgo., 1992, Loyola U. Fine Arts Gallery, 1993, Peace Mus., Chgo., 1993, Mitchell Mus., Ill., 1995, Minn. Mus. Am. Art, 1995, Lindeau Mus., Altenburg, Germany, 2001, Frauen Mus., Bonn, Germany, 2001, Contextual Cultural Ctr., Chgo., 2001, Natl. Museum of Szczecin, Poland, 2002-. Hyde Park Art Ctr., 2002. others; exhibited in group shows Art Inst. Chgo., 1975, 79, 81, 85, Mus. Contemporary Art, Chgo., 1976, 81, 83, 97, Acad. Kunst, Berlin, 1987, Barbican Ctr., London, 1990, Knoxville Mus. Art, Tenn., 1998, N.J. State Mus., 1999, Okla. City Art Mus., 1999, Decordova Mus., 2000; represented in permanent collections Standard Oil Co., Mus. Contemporary Art, Chgo., 1997, State of Ill., Yale U. Mus., Holocaust Mus., Peace Mus.; contbr. articles to profl. jours., newspapers. Individual Artist fellow Ill. Arts. Coun., 1984, 94; Individual Artist Fellow grantee NEA, 1990-91, Art Matters fellow, 1994. Mem. Chgo. Artist Coalition (founding mem., mem. com. artists rights, 1988). Address: 811 W 16th St Chicago IL 60608-2222

ALTMAN, IRWIN, psychology educator; BA, NYU, 1951; MA, U. Md., 1954, PhD, 1957. Asst. prof. psychology Am. U., Washington, 1957-58, sr. rsch. scientist, assoc. prof., 1960-62, adj. prof., 1962-69; rsch. scientist in human scis. Arlington, Va., 1958-60; rsch. psychologist Naval Med. Rsch. Inst., Bethesda, Md., 1962-69; adj. prof. U. Md., 1968-69; prof. U. Utah, Salt Lake City, 1969-79, chmn. dept. psychology, 1969-76, dean Coll. Social and Behavioral Sci., 1979-83, v.p. for acad. affairs, 1983-87, disting. prof., 1987—. Author:

(with J.E. McGrath) Small Groups, 1966, (with D.A. Taylor) Social Penetration, 1973, Environment and Social Behavior, 1975; (with M. Chemers) Culture and Environment, 1980; (with J. Wohlwill) Human Behavior and Environment: Vol. I, 1976, Vol. II, 1977, Vol. III, 1978, Vol. IV, 1980, Vol. V, 1981, Vol. VI, 1983, Vol. VII, 1984, (with C. Werner) Vol. VIII, 1985, (with A. Wandersman) Vol. IX, 1987, (with E. Zube) Vol. X, 1989, (with K. Christensen) Vol. XI, 1990, (with S. Low) Vol. XII, 1992, (with A. Churchman) Women and the Environment, Vol. XIII, 1994; (with D. Stokols) Handbook of Environmental Psychology, Vols I and II, 1987; (with J. Ginat) Polygamous Families in Contemporary Society, 1996; mem. editl. bds.: Small Groups, 1970-79, Man-Environment Systems, 1969-73, Jour. Applied Social Psychology, 1973-85, Sociometry, 1973-76, Environment and Behavior, 1975, Jour. Personality and Social Psychology, 1974-83, Contemporary Psychology, 1975-86, Environ. Psychology and Nonverbal Behavior, Psychology, 1976-90, Am. Jour. Cmty. Psychology, 1978-81, Population and Environment, 1979, Jour. Environ. Psychology, 1982, Computers and Human Behavior, 1985, Internat. Jour. Applied Social Psychology, 1984, Communication Monographs, 1992-95; assoc. editor Am. Jour. Cmty. Psychology, 1988-92; co-editor Jour. Environ. Psychology, 1990-98; contbr. articles to profl. jours. 1st lt. Adj. Gen. Corps, AUS, 1954-56. Mem. APA (pres. divsn. population and environment), AAAS, Soc. Exptl. Social Psychology, Soc. Psychol. Study of Social Issues, Soc. Personality and Social Psychology (pres.), Environ. Design Rsch. Assn., Am. Psychol. Soc. E-mail: irwin.altman@m.cc.utah.edu.

ALTMAN, JANE R. lawyer; b. Cambridge, Mass., Mar. 14, 1945; d. Nathan and Renee (Owlick) Rotman; m. Robert A. Altman, June 13, 1965; children: Jennifer Anne, John Scott. BA, Barnard Coll., 1966; MS, Bank Street Coll., 1967; JD, Rutgers U., 1978. Bar: N.J. 1978. Assoc. Carchman, Sochor & Carchman, Princeton, N.J., 1978-82; pvt. practice Skillman, N.J., 1982-94; ptnr. Altman & Legband Attys.-at-Law, Skillman, N.J., 1994—. Adj. prof. domestic rels. law Mercer C.C., West Windsor, N.J., 1986-90; mem. family practice com. N.J. Supreme Ct., 1998—. Mem. adv. com. Womanspace, Trenton, N.J., 1979—; trustee Millhill Child and Family Devel. Ctr., 1979-83. Mem. ABA, N.J. Bar Assn. (exec. com., family law sect.), Mercer County Bar Assn. (trustee 1983-88). Office: Altman & Legband Attys at Law 148 Tamarack Cir Skillman NJ 08558-2021

ALTMAN, KENNETH A(LAN), gastroenterologist, educator; b. N.Y.C., July 2, 1929; s. Harry S. and Gertrude (Feuerstein) A.; m. Judith R. Carmely, Nov. 6, 1960; children: Laurie, David, Gil. AB, Cornell U., 1950; MD, Columbia U., 1954; JD, Fordham U., 1992. Diplomate Am. Bd. Internal Medicine, Am. Bd. Forensic Medicine, Am. Bd. Forensic Examiners. Intern then resident Lenox Hill Hosp., N.Y.C., 1954-60; chief resident Roosevelt Hosp., N.Y.C., 1960-61, from jr. asst. to sr. attending medicine & gastroenterology, 1961—. Cons. N.Y. Eye and Ear Infirmary, N.Y.C., 1961—; asst. clin. prof. medicine Columbia U. Coll. Physicians and Surgeons, N.Y.C., 1980—. Composer: Voice and Orch.; inventor self centering and advancing endoscope (U.S. patent); author: Index of Talmudic Aggadic Material; contbr. articles to profl. jours. Capt. USAF, 1955-57. Fellow ACP, Am. Coll. Gasteroenterology, Am. Endoscopic Soc., N.Y. Acad. Gastroenterology (exec. com. 1989), N.Y. Gastroent. Soc., N.Y. Acad. Medicine. Jewish. Avocations: tennis, sailing, photography, music. Home: 38 Homestead Rd Tenafly NJ 07670-1109 E-mail: lereche@aol.com.

ALTMAN, LAWRENCE GENE, biologist, educator; b. July 4, 1952; s. Mark Eugene and Roberta Mercedes (Baron) A. BA in Biology, Fordham U., 1972, MS, 1974, PhD, 1982. Rsch. biologist VA, West Haven, Conn., 1982-85; asst. prof. divsn. sci. and math. Fordham U., N.Y.C., 1986-87; postdoctoral assoc. in pathology Yale U. Med. Sch., New Haven, 1982-85; cons. Coll. New Rochelle, N.Y., 1980-81, Polyscis., Inc., Warrington, Pa., 1985-89, Columbia U. Coll. Physicians and Surgeons Dept. Microbiol., N.Y.C., 1986-88; asst. prof. biology Western Conn. State U., Danbury, 1992-93, 94-95, 98, CUNY, 1998-2000, Naugatuck Valley C.C., 2000—. Mem. part-time faculty Fordham U., N.Y.C., Western Conn. State U., Danbury, 1990-91, 96-98; pres. Cider Mill Pond Assn., Greenwich, Conn., 1994-96; mem. dean's adv. coun. Grad. Sch. Arts and Scis., Fordham U., 2003. Contbr. articles to profl. jours. Recipient Excellence award Nat. Inst. for Staff and Orgnl. Devel., U. Tex., Austin, 2003; Fordham U. fellow, 1975-77. Mem. AAAS, Am. Soc. for Cell Biology, Electron Microscopy Soc. Am., Conn. Electron Microscopy Soc., Sigma Xi. Avocations: theater, traveling, educational technology. Home: 304 Lansdowne Westport CT 06880-5649

ALTMAN, LAWRENCE KIMBALL, physician, journalist; b. Quincy, Mass., June 19, 1937; s. William S. and Esther (Kimball) A. AB cum laude, Harvard U., 1958; MD, Tufts U., 1962; medal (hon.), U. Calif., San Francisco. Diplomate: Am. Vet. Epidemiology Soc. Intern Mt. Zion Hosp., San Francisco, 1962-63; USPHS epidemic intelligence service officer Centers for Disease Control, Atlanta, 1963-66; med. resident, fellow U. Wash. Hosp., Seattle, 1966-69; med. corr., columnist The Doctors World N.Y. Times, 1969—; clin. assoc. prof. medicine NYU, 1970—. Vis. physician Serafimer Hosp., Karolinska Inst., Stockholm, Sweden, 1973; vis. scientist U. Wash., 1971; Chancellor's Disting. Lecture for Pub. Understanding of Sci., U. Calif., San Francisco, 1989; Ida Beam Disting. vis. prof. U. Iowa, 2000. Author: Science of The Times, 1981, Who Goes First? The Story of Self-Experimentation in Medicine, 1987, 98; contbr. chpts. to books, articles to profl. jours.; contbr. Ency. Brit., 1979, Grolier Ency., 1972-87. Recipient Howard W. Blakeslee award, Am. Heart Assn., 1982—83, 1994, Howard Lewis Career award, 2001, Claude Bernard award, Nat. Soc. Med. Rsch., 1971, 1974, Walter C. Alvarez award, Am. Med. Writers Assn., 1980, Vincent Downing award, 1988, journalism award, Am. Acad. Pediat., 1982, Pub. Svc. award, Nat. Kidney Found., George Polk award, 1986, Journalism award, Coll. Am. Pathologists, 1985, Med. Media Excellence award, Friends Nat. Libr. Medicine, 1993, Victor Cohn prize, Coun. for the Advancement of Sci. Writing, 2000, Howard Lewis career award, Am. Heart Assn., 2001. Master ACP; fellow Am. Coll. Epidemiology, N.Y. Acad. Medicine; mem. Inst. Medicine/NAS, Am. Soc. Tropical Medicine and Hygiene, Soc. for Epidemiology, Am. Bd. Med. Spltys. (pub. 1986-88), Century Club (N.Y.C.), Harvard Club (N.Y.C.). Home: 140 W End Ave New York NY 10023-6131 Office: New York Times 229 W 43rd St New York NY 10036-3959

ALTMAN, LESLIE JOAN, secondary school educator; b. Cambridge, Mass., May 11, 1943; d. Sidney Arnold and Irene Marie (Sullivan) Wolbarst; children: Christopher Matthew, Timothy Alexander. AB, Smith Coll., 1964; MA, NYU, 1967; PhD, Boston Coll., 1973; M in Counseling, Ariz. State U., 1981. Tchr. Emerson Sch., Bolton, Mass., 1964-65, 86-87, Needham (Mass.) H.S., 1965-66, 67-69; lectr. Ariz. State U., Tempe, 1974-77, Southampton (Eng.) U., 1978; sch. counselor Frank Sch., Guadalupe, Ariz., 1981-86; tchr. English lang. and lit., dir. of lower grades St. Sebastian's Country Day Sch., Needham, 1987-93; tchr. English, dir. mentoring program Hawken Sch., Gates Mills, Ohio, 1993—. Presenter numerous workshops; cons. English dept. Winsor Sch., 1991; mem. mid-career task force Ohio Assn. Ind. Schs. Contbr. articles to profl. jours. Vol. Habitat for Humanity, 1996—, Free Clin., Cleve., 1996—. Fulbright-Hays scholar, Africa, 1991, India, 1998; grantee NEH, 1989, 92; fellow Coun. for Basic Edn., summer 1990. Mem. Cleve. Counsel on World Affairs., New Eng. Assn. Tchrs. English (exec. bd. 1990-93, chmn. multicultural com.), Ohio Assn. Ind. Schs. (mem. profl. svcs. com.). Avocations: gardening, cooking, traveling. Office: Hawken Sch PO Box 8002 Gates Mills OH 44040-8002 E-mail: laltman@hawken.edu.

ALTMAN, LOUIS, lawyer, author, educator; b. N.Y.C., Aug. 6, 1933; s. Benjamin and Jean (Zimmerman) A.; m. Sally J. Schlesinger, Dec. 26, 1955 (dec.); 1 child: Andrew; m. Eleanor Silver, Oct. 30, 1966; 1 child: Robert. AB, Cornell U., 1955; LLB, Harvard U., 1958. Bar: N.Y. 1959, Conn. 1970, Ill. 1973. Assoc. Amster & Levy, N.Y.C., 1958-60; patent atty. Sperry Rand, N.Y.C., 1960-63; chief patent counsel Gen. Time Corp., N.Y.C., 1963-67; ptnr. Altman & Reens, Stamford, Conn., 1967-72; chief patent counsel Baxter Labs, Deerfield, Ill., 1972-76; assoc. prof. John Marshall Law Sch., 1976-79, adj. prof., 1979-96, Loyola Law Sch., 1996-97; of counsel Gerlach, O'Brien & Kleinke, Chgo., 1981-83; ptnr. Laff, Whitesel & Saret, Chgo., 1983-2001; of counsel Michael Best & Friedrich, Chgo., 2001—. Author: Callmann on Unfair Competition, Trademarks & Monopolies, 4th edit., 1981, Business Competition Law Adviser, 1983; contbr. Construction Law, 1986, Legal Compliance Checkups, 1985, articles to legal jours. Recipient Gerald Rose Meml. award John Marshall Law Sch., 1988. Home: 3005 Manor Dr Northbrook IL 60062-6947 Office: Michael Best & Friedrich 401 N Michigan Ave Chicago IL 60611-4255 E-mail: laltman@attglobal.net.

ALTMAN, MICAH, social scientist, researcher; b. St. Louis, Aug. 31, 1967; s. Jeremy Altman and Penny Shaff Morton; m. Kylie K. Mills, Aug. 26, 1995; children: Jacob(dec.), Aleph. BA in Computer Sci., Brown U., 1989; BA in Polit. Philosophy, Brown U., 1989; PhD in Social Sci., Calif. Inst. Tech., 1998. Mem. tech. staff Silocon Graphics, Mountain View, Calif., 1990—92; cons. A-Z Tech., Pasadena, Calif., 1993—96; assoc. dir. Harvard-MIT Data Ctr., Cambridge, Mass., 1993—96; rsch. assoc. Ctr. for Basic Rsch. in Social Sci., Harvard U., Cambridge, 2001—. Mem. com., data documentation initiative Interuniv. Consortium for Polit. Sci. Rsch., Ann Arbor, Mich., 2000—02. Contbr. articles to profl. jours. Recipient Best Dissertation award, Western Polit. Sci. Assn., 1998; grantee, NSF, Intel. Mem.: IEEE, Assn. for Computing Machinery, Am. Polit. Sci. Assn. (mem. coun., program chair, awards chair, Best Polit. Sci. Website 1999, Best Paper on Representation 1997). Office: Harvard U G-4 Littauer Ctr Cambridge MA 02138 E-mail: micah_altman@harvard.edu.

ALTMAN, MIMI ANGSTER, business owner; b. Chgo., Jan. 13, 1935; d. Herbert Charles and Marian Agnes (McGrath) Angster; m. Robert S. Altman, Jan. 31, 1970; 1 dau., Marian Catherine. Mus.B., DePauw U., 1957. Lic. real estate broker, Ill.; cert. piano tuner. Owner, mgr. secretarial service, Joliet, Ill., 1966-67; legal sec. various firms, Waukegan, Ill.; adminstrv. asst. to pres. Lake Forest Sch. Mgmt., Ill., 1982-84; owner, operator Exec. Mgmt. Co., Bannockburn, Ill., 1982—; owner Village Sec., Deerfield, Ill. Exec. dir. United Way of Highland Park/Highwood, Inc., 1986-88, Northbrook Leisure Found., 1986-88. Mem. Am. Bus. Women's Assn., Nat. Assn. Secretarial Svcs., Nat. Assn. Resume Svcs., Deerfield/Lincolnshire Ill. Rotary Club (pres. 1992-93), Mu Phi Epsilon (pres. North Shore chpt., internat. exec. sec.-treas. 1982—, exec. dir. 1983—), Kappa Kappa Gamma. Republican. Presbyterian. Lodges: Women of Rotary Found. Inc. (pres.), Zonta Internat. (local and dist. officer). Avocation: travel. Office: Mu Phi Epsilon 4202 Atlantic Ave Ste 202 Long Beach CA 90807-2826 also: Mu Phi Epsilon 4202 Atlantic Ave Ste 202 Long Beach CA 90807-2826

ALTMAN, RICHARD LEWIS, aeronautical engineer; b. Bklyn., Nov. 25, 1946; s. Lawrence and Helen (Namm) A.; m. Carole J. Gotham, Aug. 13, 1978; children: David Harrison, Benjamin Ian. BS in Aero. Engring., Bklyn. Poly. Inst., 1967; MSME, Rensselaer Poly. Inst., Troy, 1971; MBA, U. Conn., 1974. Aeronautical engr. United Tech./Pratt & Whitney, East Hartford, Conn., 1967-68, analytical engr., 1968-71, sr. analytical engr., 1971-74, asst. project engr., 1974-77, mgr. Washington ops., 1977-81, mgr. new product applications PW2000 program East Hartford, 1981-83, mgr. bus. devel., adv. engines, 1983—, program mgr. Japanese super/hypersonic propulsion program, 1990-92, bus. mgr. integrated product mgmt. team, 1992-97, mktg./svc. mgr. advanced programs, 1997—2000, mgr. green engine program, 2000—. Mem. com. aviation and environ. U.S. Transp. Rsch. Bd., 2002—. Contbr. articles to profl. jours. Mem. Bd. Fin., Cromwell, Conn., 1976, Capital Expenditures Commn., Cromwell, 1975-76, others. Mem. AIAA, Coalition for Intelligent Mfg. Systems (intellectual property rights subcom. 1991-92), Internat. Industry Working Group, Beta Gamma Sigma, Alpha Epsilon Pi.. Avocations: tennis, swimming, aerobics, golf, local access tv broadcasting. Office: Pratt & Whitney 400 Main St Ste 1 East Hartford CT 06118-1888 E-mail: altrich@aol.com.

ALTMAN, ROBERT B. film director, writer, producer; b. Kansas City, Mo., Feb. 20, 1925; m. Kathryn Altman; children: Robert, Matthew; children by previous marriage: Michael, Stephen, Christine. Student, U. Mo., 3 years. Owner Sandcastle 5 Prodns. Writer, prodr., dir.: (TV) Kraft Theatre; writer, prodr., dir.: (TV pilot) The Long Hot Summer; co-prodr.: (film) The James Dean Story, 1957; dir.: (films) The Delinquents, 1957, Countdown, 1968, That Cold Day in the Park, 1969, M*A*S*H, 1970 (Grand Prix award Cannes Film Festival 1970, Best Film, Nat. Soc. Film Critics 1970), Popeye, 1980, Come Back to the 5 & Dime, Jimmy Dean, Jimmy Dean, 1982, Streamers, 1983, Beyond Therapy, 1987, The Gingerbread Man, 1997, (TV series) Gun, 1997; producer: The Late Show, 1977, Welcome to L.A., 1977, Rich Kids, 1979, Remember My Name, 1979, Mrs. Parker and the Vicious Circle, 1994; prodr. and dir.: A Wedding, 1978, Quintet, 1979, A Perfect Couple, 1979, Secret Honor, 1985, The Player, 1992 (Best Dir. citation Cannes Film Festival, 1992), After Glow, 1997; prodr., dir., screenwriter: Three Women, 1977, Health, 1979, Gosford Park, 2001 (nominee Best dir. and Best Picture Acad. award 2002, Best dir. in Motion Picture Golden Globe award 2002, Dir. of Yr. AFI. Film Award 2002, BAFTA award, Evening Std. Brit. Film award NSFC award NYFCC award, Best Dir./Best Film Silver Ribbon award 2002); dir., screenwriter: Brewster McCloud, 1970, McCabe and Mrs. Miller, 1971, Images, 1972, The Long Goodbye, 1973, Thieves Like Us, 1974, California Split, 1974, Buffalo Bill and the Indians, 1976, Fool for Love, 1985, Short Cuts, 1993 (Best Dir. Acad. award nominee 1993), Ready to Wear (Prêt-à-Porter), 1994, Kansas City, 1996, Cookie's Fortune, 1999; dir. for stage: (Broadway) Come Back to the 5 & Dime, Jimmy Dean, Jimmy Dean, 1982, (Lyric Opera of Chgo.) McTeague, 1993; prodr., dir.: (TV) The Laundromat, 1984, The Dumb Waiter, 1987, The Room, 1987, Caine Mutiny Court Martial, 1987, Tanner '88, 1988; dir. film Vincent and Theo, 1990; prodr., dir. Nashville, 1976; actor: (TV movie) Frank Capra's American Dream, 1997; exec. prodr. Roads & Bridges, 2000; actor Dr. T & The Women (Golden Lion award 2000). Served with AUS, 1943-47. Recipient Lifetime Achievement award, 2000, Hon. Golden Berlin Bear award, 2002. Mem. Dirs. Guild Am. Office: Sandcastle 5 Prodns 502 Park Ave Ste 15G New York NY 10022-1108 also: ICM 8942 Wilshire Blvd Beverly Hills CA 90211-1934

ALTMAN, ROY PETER, pediatric surgeon; b. N.Y.C., Apr. 13, 1934; s. Charles and Sue (Solomon) A.; m. Hanna Diamond, Aug. 22, 1964; children: James David, Robert Ross. AB, Colgate U., 1955; MS, U. Rochester, 1958; MD, N.Y. Med. Coll., 1961. Diplomate Am. Bd. Surgery, Am. Bd. Thoracic Surgery, Am. Bd. Pediatric Surgery. Intern Mount Sinai Hosp., N.Y.C., 1961-62; surg. resident Tufts-New Eng. Med. Ctr, Boston, 1962-66, chief resident, 1966-67; postdoctoral fellow NIH, Dept. Surgery Tufts-New Eng. Med. Ct., 1964-65; chief resident in thoracic surgery George Washington U. Hosp., Washington, 1967—68; chief resident in pediatric surgery Children's Hosp. Nat. Med. Ctr., Washington, 1967-69; spl. fellow clin./rsch. surgery (transplantation) U. Colo. Health Scis. Ctr., Denver, 1974; prof. surgery in surgery and pediatrics Coll. Physicians and Surgeons, Columbia U., N.Y.C., 1980—; surgeon in chief Children's Hosp. N.Y. Presbyn. Hosp., N.Y.C., 1980—; sr. v.p. med. affairs, physician in chief Children's Health Network N.Y., Presbyn. Hosp.; physician-in-chief Children's Healthcare Sys., 1998. Prof. surgery and child health George Washington Sch. Medicine, 1977-80; sr. attending surgeon Children's Hosp., Nat. Med. Ctr., Washington, 1973-80, dir. surg. rsch., 1975-80, sr. dir. clin. rsch. ctr., 1975-80, dir. organ transplantation, 1975-80; cons. surgeon Walter Reed Army Hosp., 1974-80, Dewitt Army Hosp., Ft. Belvoir, Va., 1973-80, The Hosp. for Sick Children, Washington, 1974-80; asst. prof.surgery and child health George Washington U. Sch. Medicine, 1970-73, Tufts U. Sch. Medicine, Editl. cons. Pediat. Surgery Internat., 1985—; editl. adv. bd. Surgery Ann., 1986—, Surgery, 1992-98, Jour. Pediat. Surgery, 1996. Bd. dirs. Ronald McDonald House and Found. Children's Oncology Soc., N.Y. C.V. Mosby Scholar, N.Y. Med. Coll., 1961. Fellow: ACS, Am. Acad. Pediats.; mem.: Am. Pediat. Surg. Assn. (gov. 1996, bd. govs. 1996—99, 2003, pres. 2002—), Internat. Coll. Surgery, Soc. Univ. Surgeons, Am. Surg. Assn., Alpha Omega Alpha. Avocations: skiing, golf, tennis, music. Home: 15 W 81st St New York NY 10024-6022 Office: Childrens Hosp of NY Columbia-Presbyn Med Ctr 3959 Broadway 116 S New York NY 10032-1590 E-mail: RPA1@columbia.edu.

ALTMAN, S. MORTON, community center executive; b. N.Y.C., Jan. 30, 1938; s. Irving and Elaine (Feingold) A.; m. Marilyn Guss, May 23, 1964; children: Stephanie, Matthew. BA, Bklyn. Coll., 1960; MSW, Hunter Coll., 1962; D of Social Welfare, Columbia U., 1974. Br. dir. Wel-Met, N.Y.C., 1967-69; asst. exec. Vacations and Community Services for the Blind, N.Y.C., 1969-70; asst. prof. N.Y. State Coll. of Human Ecology, Cornell U., Ithaca, 1970-73; cons., dir. Nat. Jewish Welfare Bd., N.Y.C., 1973-80; exec. dir. North Shore Jewish Cmty. Ctr., Marblehead, Mass., 1980-88, Jewish Cmty. Ctr. of Mid-Westchester, Scarsdale, N.Y., 1988—. Contbr. articles to profl. jours. Mem. Anti-Poverty Bd., 1965, Coop. Extension, Ithaca, 1967—70, Nat. Jewish Welfare Bd., N.Y.C., 1969—70; exec. dir. Florence g. Heller-JWB Rsch. Ctr., N.Y.C., 1973—80. Mem. NASW, Assn. Jewish Ctr. Profls. Jewish. Avocations: music, travel, computers. Home: 25 Sammis Ln White Plains NY 10605-4727

ALTMAN, SIDNEY, biology educator; b. Montreal, Que., Can., May 7, 1939; BS, MIT, 1960; PhD in Biophys., U. Colo., 1967; DSc (hon.), McGill U., Montreal, 1991, York U., U. Colo., U. Montreal, U. B.C. Teaching asst. Columbia U., 1960—62; Damon Runyon Meml. Fund cancer rsch. fellow in molecular biology Harvard U., 1967—69; Anna Fuller Fund fellow, then Med. Rsch. Coun. fellow Med. Rsch. Coun. Lab. Molecular Biology, 1969—71; from asst. to assoc. prof. Yale U., New Haven, 1971—80, prof. molecular cellular and devel. biology, 1980—, Sterling prof. biology, 1990—, prof. biophysical chemistry, 1994—, chmn. dept., 1983—85; dean Yale Coll., 1985—90. Tutor Radcliffe Coll., 1968—69. Author: Transfer RNA, 1978. Recipient Nobel Prize in Chemistry, 1989. Fellow: AAAS; mem.: Am. Philos. Soc. (Rosenstiel award 1989), Nat. Acad. Scis., Genetics Soc. Am., Am. Soc. Biol. Chemists. Achievements include research in on effects of acridines on T4 DNA replication, mutants, precursors of tRNA processing by catalytic RNA and ribonuclease function. Office: Yale U Kline Biology Tower 402 New Haven CT 06520-8103*

ALTMAN, STEVEN, financial consulting company executive; b. Jacksonville, Fla., Oct. 24, 1945; s. Harold and Estelle (Avchin) A.; m. Judy Ellen Ovadenko, Feb. 8, 1969. BA, UCLA, 1967; MBA, U. So. Calif., 1969, D.BA, 1975. Asst. dean Sch. Bus. U. So. Calif., Los Angeles, 1969-72; asst. prof. div. mgmt. Fla. Internat. U., Miami, 1972-76, chmn. div. mgmt., 1972-77, assoc. prof. div. mgmt., 1976-84, prof. div. mgmt., 1984-85, asst. v.p. acad. affairs, 1977-78, assoc. v.p. acad. affairs, 1978-80; v.p. acad. affairs Fla. Internat U., 1981-85; univ. provost Fla. Internat. U., 1982-85; pres. Tex. A&M U., Kingsville, 1985-89, prof. mgmt., 1985-89; pres., prof. mgmt. U. Cen. Fla., Orlando, 1989-91; pres. SynerCo, Inc., Pasadena, Calif., 1992—94, Lynx Worldwide, Inc., L.A., 1995—96, Med. Telecomms. Assocs., Inc., L.A., 1994—; v.p. Lido Capital, Beverly Hills, Calif., 2002—. Spl. master Fla. Pub. Employees Relations Commn., 1976-85; mem. 4th quadennial evaluation com. Ala. Commn. for Higher Edn., 1986-87; bd. dirs. Internat. Ctr. of Fla., Miami, 1982-85; cons. in field Author: Organizational Behavior, 1979, 84, Readings in Organizational Behavior, 1979, Organizational Behavior, 1985, Profit Basics, 1977, Home Health Telecommunications, 1999; editor: Organization Development: Progress and Perspectives, 1982; co-author: Home Health Telecommunications, 1999. Mem. adv. bd. Assn. for Retarded Citizens, Miami, 1978-85; vice chmn. Internat. Health Com., 1984-85; exec. com. Metro-Miami Action Plan, 1983-85; bd. dirs. Found. Excellence in Pub. Edn., 1984-85, Kingsville Econ. Devel. Coun., 1986-89; mem. planning com. Spohn Kleberg Hosp., 1986-89; dir. Orange County Pub. Schs. Found., 1989-91; bd. dirs. Heart of Fla. United Way, 1989-91, Orlando/Orange County Compact, 1989-91, Orlando Ctr. for Humanities, 1989-91, Jr. Achievement Ctrl. Fla., 1989-91, Ctrl. Fla. coun. Boy Scouts Am., 1989-91; trustee WMFE/90.7 Pub. TV, Orlando, 1990-91. With USAR, 1968-74. Recipient Gold medal for econs. edn. Freedom Found., 1971, Excellence in Tchg. award Sch. Bus. Adminstrn., U. So. Calif., 1972, Labor Edn. award, 1982, Tree of Life award Nat. Jewish Found., Orlando, 1991; named Outstanding Faculty Mem. Coll. Bus. Adminstrn. Fla. Internat. U., 1975. Mem. Am. Arbitration Assn. (arbitrator 1977—), Hispanic Assn. Colls. and Univs. (v.p. 1986-89), South Miami-Kendall Area C. of C. (bd. dirs. 1982-85, pres. 1983-85), Kingsville C. of C. (bd. dirs. 1985-89, pres. 1986-87), Greater Orlando C. of C. (bd. dirs. 1989-91), Winter Park C. of C. (bd. dirs. 1989-91), BGeta Gamma Sigma, Phi Kappa Phi, Phi Theta Kappa, Omicron Delta Kappa. Home: 1540 Wabasso Way Glendale CA 91208-2439

ALTMAN, WILLIAM CARL, health facility administrator, merger and acquisitions specialist, investment manager, consultant; b. La Grange, Tex., Nov. 11, 1957; s. Lester Arthur and Goldie Bertha (Kretzschmar) A.; m. Danguole Julia Spakevicius, Sept. 2, 1989; children: Darius, Indre, Ilona, Isabella. BS, Tex. A&M U., 1979; BA, MA, Oxford U., Eng., 1982; MBA, Harvard U., 1984. Project dir. Trammell Crow Co., Houston, 1984-85; cons. McKinsey & Co., Inc., Houston, N.Y.C., 1985-89; v.p. Capital Guidance Corp., Houston, 1989-93, sr. v.p., 1993-94; COO Obstet. and Gynecol. Assocs., PA, Houston, 1994-97; exec. v.p. acquistions FemPartners, Inc., Houston, 1997—, also bd. dirs.; mng. dir. Interlaken Ventures, Inc., 2000—. Bd. dirs. Tredex Tile Corp., Houston, 1991-94, pres., 1993-94. Devel. bd. dirs. Tex. A&M U. Coll. Liberal Arts, College Station, 1987—; bd. dirs. U.S.-Baltic Found., Washington, 1990—, chmn., 1993-96, 2001—; mem. N.Y. coun. on Fgn. Rels., 2000—; mem. Houston com. Coun. on Fgn. Rels., 1990—; co-chair Houston com. Campaign for Oxford, 1990-91; mem. Tex. Rhodes Scholarship Selection com., 1990-91. Recipient Rhodes scholarship Rhodes Scholarship Trustees, Oxford, Eng., 1980. Mem. Harvard Bus. Sch. Club. Republican. Avocations: scouting, politics. Office: Interlaken Ventures Inc 4030 Case St Houston TX 77005-3606

ALTMAN, WILLIAM KEAN, lawyer; b. San Antonio, Feb. 18, 1944; s. Marion K. and Ruth (Nunnelee) A.; m. Doris E. Johnson, May 29, 1964; children: Brian, Brad, Blake. BBA, Tex. A&M U., 1965, MBA, 1967; JD, U. Tex., 1979. Bar: Tex. 1970, Okla. 1993, U.S. Dist. Ct. (no. and ea. dists.) Tex., U.S. Ct. Appeals (5th and 11th cirs.), U.S. Supreme Ct. Pres. Altman & Nix, Wichita Falls, Tex., 1970—. Bd. dirs. Beacon Ins. Group. Mem. Wichita Falls City Coun., 1998-2002; mayor of Wichita Falls, 2002–. Mem. ABA, Tex. Bar Assn., Assn. Trial Lawyers Am. (life) (bd. of govs. 1980-83, active coms. and sects.), Tex. Trial Lawyers Assn. (assoc. bd. dirs. 1977-78, bd. dirs. 1978—, active various coms. and sect.). Democrat. Baptist. Office: Altman & Nix PO Box 500 Wichita Falls TX 76307-0500

ALTMANN, STUART ALLEN, biologist, educator; b. St. Louis, June 8, 1930; s. Maurice Walter and Deborah (Freedman) A.; m. Jeanne Glaser, June 19, 1959; children: Michael Alexander, Rachel Ann BA in Zoology, UCLA, 1953, MA, 1954; PhD in Biology, Harvard U., 1960. Asst. prof. zoology U. Alta., Can., 1960-65, assoc. prof., 1965; sociobiologist Yerkes Regional Primate Rsch. Ctr., 1965-70; prof. anatomy U. Chgo., 1970-80, prof. biology, 1970-88, prof. ecology and evolution, 1988-95, prof. emeritus, 1995—; lectr., prof. ecology and evolutionary biology Princeton (N.J.) U., 1998—. Hon. rsch. assoc. Haile Sellaissie I U., Ethiopia, 1971; mem. exptl. psychology sci. adv. panel NIMH, 1969-73; mem. primate conservation com. NAS-NRC, 1970-72; grant reviewer NSF, NIH, NIMH, Spencer Found., Nat. Geog. Soc., Smithsonian Instn., others Mem. editl. bd. Behavioral Ecology and Sociobiology, 1976-79, Am. Naturalist, 1977-79, Animal Behavior, 1978-79, Ethology, Ecology and Evolution, 1989—; mem. bd. editl. commentators The Behavioral and Brain Scis., 1977-82 Fellow AAAS, Am. Acad. Arts and Scis., Animal Behavior Soc. (pres. 1977, exec. com. 1975-78); mem. Comparative Nutrition Soc. Avocations: making pottery, orchard farming. Office: Princeton U Dept Ecology Evol Biology Princeton NJ 08544-0001

ALTOMARA, RITA ECKE, library director, writer; b. Englewood, N.J., June 27, 1950; d. Russell and Rita (Walsh) Ecke; m. Gary John Altomara, Dec. 14, 1969; 1 child, Ginevra Marie. BA, Barnard Coll., 1972; MS, Columbia U., 1975. Jr. libr. Ft. Lee (N.J.) Pub. Libr., 1974-77, sr. libr., 1977-80, prin. libr., 1980-82, asst. dir., 1982-84, dir., 1984—. Coord. Women's Info and Referral Svc., Ft. Lee, 1975—. Author: Hollywood on the Palisades, 1983. Mem. exec. bd. Ft. Lee Hist. Soc., 1982—; liaison Bergen County Office Hist. and Cultural Affairs, Hackensack, NJ, 1978—. Mem.: ALA, N.J. Libr. Assn. Roman Catholic. Home: 121 Engle St Cresskill NJ 07626-2246 Office: Ft Lee Pub Library 320 Main St Fort Lee NJ 07024-4706

ALTON, ANN LESLIE, judge, lawyer, educator; b. Pipestone, Minn., Sept. 10, 1945; d. Howard Robert, Jr. and Camilla Ann (DeMong) A.; m. Gerald Russell Freeman Sr.; children: Brady Michael Alton Freeman, Matthew Alton Freeman (dec.). BA, Smith Coll., 1967; JD, U. Minn., 1970; postgrad., Nat. Jud. Coll., U. Nev., 1989. Bar: Minn. 1970, U.S. Dist. Ct. Minn. 1972, U.S. Supreme Ct. 1981. Apptd. gen. jurisdiction state trial ct. judge civil and criminal jurisdiction Dist. Ct., 4th Jud. Dist., Hennepin County, Minn., 1989—, elected, 1990, 96—; mem. exec. com., 1995—98; chair psychol. svcs. com., 1996; vice chair adminstrv. com. Dist. Ct., 4th Jud. Dist., Hennepin County, 1989-94, asst. county atty. Mpls., 1970-89, felony prosecutor, criminal divsn., 1970-75, acting chief citizen protection divsn., 1975-76, chief citizen protection/econ. crime divsn., 1976-79, chief econ. crime unit, 1979-85, sr. atty. civil divsn. handling labor and employment law, 1989-89, mem. civil com., 1989—, presiding judge probate/mental health div., 1995-98, mem. exec. com., 1995-98, chair psychol. svcs. to ct. com., 1997-2000, 2002. Adj. prof. law Hamline U. Law Sch., St. Paul, 1973-76, instr., 1977—; adj. prof. law William Mitchell Coll. Law, St. Paul, 1977—; adj. prof. U. Minn. Law Sch., 1978-82; lectr. in field, 1970—; sr. faculty Minn. Advocacy Inst., Minn. CLE, 1988—; mem. faculty Nat. Inst. Trial

Advocacy, U. Notre Dame Law Sch., 1989—, asst. team leader North Ctrl. Regional Jury Trial Advocacy Course, 1991—; sr. critiquing judge Jud. Trial Skills Tng. Program Minn. Supreme Ct. Continuing Edn. Program for State Cts., 1993—; mem. faculty intensive trial advocacy program Widener U. Sch. of Law, Wilmington, Del., 1993-96; bd. dirs. Pan-O-Gold Realty Co., 1986-89, Alton Realty Co., 1986-89, Alton Found., 1999—. Author articles, pamphlet, manual. Vice-chmn. bd. dirs. Minn. Program on Victims of Sexual Assault, 1974-76; bd. dirs. Physician's Health Plan (now Allina), Health Maintenance Orgn., 1976-80, exec. com., 1977-80; mem. legal drug abuse subcom. Gov. Minn. Adv. Com. Drug Abuse, 1972-74; bd. visitors U. Minn. Law Sch., 1979-85; mem. child abuse project coordinating com. Hennepin County Med. Soc., 1982-83, chmn. corp., labor, ins. subcom., 1982. Recipient Honorable Mention Roscoe award for Excellence in Tchg. Trial Advocacy, Roscoe Pound Inst., Washington, 2000. Mem. ABA (jud. adminstrn. divsn.), Minn. Bar Assn. (criminal law, labor and employment law, civil litigation sects.), Hennepin County Bar Assn. (ethics com. 1973-76, criminal law com. 1973—, vice chmn. 1979-80, 83-84, unauthorized practice law com. 1977-78, individual rights and responsibilities com. 1977-78, labor and employment law com. 1985—, civil litigation com. 1985—), Minn. Dist. Judges Assn. (benefits com. 1991—, mem. program and edn. com. 1993—, mem. worker compensation risk mgmt. com. 1995-97), U. Minn. Law Sch. Alumni Assn. (bd. dirs. 1979-85). Nat. Women Judges,2002 Office: 1251-C Hennepin County Govt Ctr 300 S 6th St Minneapolis MN 55487 also: 1251-C Hennepin County Govt Ctr Minneapolis MN 55487 E-mail: ann.alton@co.hennepin.mn.us. *The greatest joy and biggest challenge of my life has been the privilege of loving, nurturing and guiding my son. Motherhood is my most rewarding accomplishment. The most important lesson I've learned is that one person with vision, perseverance, and energy can cause significant changes in government, in an organization, in society. My great-grandmother told me, "You can do anything you want to do if you're willing to work hard for it, and don't let anyone tell you otherwise". She was right.*

ALTON, HOWARD ROBERT, JR., lawyer, real estate and food company executive; b. Pipestone, Minn., May 12, 1927; s. Howard Robert Sr. and Vera Edna (Boehmke) A.; m. Camilla Ann DeMong; children: Ann, Jeanine, Howard R. III, Patricia, Michelle. BBA, U. Minn., 1950; JD cum laude, Hamline U., 1975. Bar: Minn., 1975, U.S. Ct. Appeals (8th cir.) 1975, U.S. Dist. Ct. Minn. 1976. Founder Hamline Sch. Law, 1972-74, Alton, Severson & Sovis, Apple Valley, Minn., 1978-86, Freeman, Alton & Dodd, Mpls., 1987-88; sr. counsel, chief exec. officer Pan-O-Gold Baking Co., Wayzata and St. Cloud, Minn.; now ret. With U.S. Marines, 1945-46. Mem. Minn. Young Pres. Orgn. (past chmn.), Minn. Execs. Orgn. Forum (past chmn.), The Mpls. Club, Old Port Cove Yacht Club, North Palm Beach City Club, St. Lakes Cruising Club, Wayzata Country Club, Ocean Reef Club. Avocations: conservation, wildlife preservation, power boating. Home and Office: PO Box 619 Wayzata MN 55391-0619

ALTONGY, GILBERT JOSEPH, physician; b. Sept. 30, 1943; BA, Providence Coll., 1968; MD, Lyon (France) Sch. Med./Pharm., 1974. Pvt. practice in internal medicine and cardiology, Central Falls, R.I., 1979—; chief of medicine Notre Dame Hosp., Central Falls, 1981-89; clin. asst. prof. medicine Brown Med. Sch., 1982—; dir. subacute unit Oakland Grove Health Ctr., Woonsocket, R.I., 1997—. Office: 560 Cumberland Hill Rd Woonsocket RI 02895-5635

ALTOSE, MURRAY DAVID, physician, educator; b. Winnipeg, Man., Can., Oct. 1, 1941; came to U.S., 1969; m. Connie Jean Tesmer, Jan. 14, 1973; children: Michael Dov, Aaron Judah, Benjamin Isaac. BSc, MD, U. Man., 1965. Diplomate Am. Bd. Internal Medicine, Am. Bd. Pulmonary Disease. Rotating intern Winnipeg Gen. Hosp., 1965-66, asst. resident in medicine, 1966-67, resident in critical care medicine, 1968-69; asst. resident medicine Cleve. Met. Gen. Hosp., 1969-70, resident-in-charge pulmonary disease sect., 1970-71, chief pulmonary divsn. dept. medicine, 1977-88, assoc. dir. dept. medicine, 1981-88; fellow pulmonary disease sect. Hosp. U. Pa., Phila., 1971-73, co-dir. respiratory ICU, 1973-74, dir. diagnostic svcs., 1973-77; assoc. in medicine U. Pa. Sch. Medicine, Phila., 1973, asst. prof. medicine, 1973-77; assoc. prof. medicine Case Western Res. U. Sch. Medicine, Cleve., 1977-84, prof. medicine, 1984—; chief of staff Dept. Vets. Affairs Med. Ctr., Cleve., 1988—96; mgr. med.-surg. specialties care line Vets. Healthcare Sys. Ohio, 1996—. Assoc. dean Vets. Hosp. Affairs, 1988—; attending physician pulmonary in-patient svc. med. ICU and Pulmonary Cons. Svc. Cleve. Met. Gen. Hosp., 1977-78, med. dir. respiratory therapy dept., 1977-88, dir. respiratory ICU, 1977-81, attending physician med. ICU Univ. Hosps., Cleve., 1978—; mem. med. rsch. svc. rev. bd. for respiration VA, 1986-89; spl. reviewer NIH Clin. Sci., 1985, 88; cons. spl. emphasis panel NIH Nat. Heart, Lung and Blood Inst., 1996; temp. mem. NIH Respiratory and Applied Physiology Study Sect., 1996; attending physician respiratory ICU VA Med. Ctr., Cleve., 1988—, attending physician med. svc., 1988; lectr. in field. Mem. editl. bd. Jour. Applied Physiology, 1984-93, editl. referee, 1980—; contbr. articles to profl. publs., chpts. to books, abstracts. Trustee Northeast Ohio affiliate Am. Heart Assn., 1993-98, mem. rsch. allocation com., 1989-93. Mem. Am. Fedn. Clin. Rsch. (mem. program 1982, steering com. sect. on respiratory pathophysiology 1981-82, chmn. sect. 1982-84, mem. program and awards coms. ann. sci. assembly 1985), Am. Thoracic Soc. (program com. sci. assembly on respiratory structure and function 1989-90), Ohio Thoracic Soc., Am. Coll. Chest Physicians (gov. Ohio 2001-03, program com., awards com. ann. sci. assembly 1985), Am. Physiol. Soc., Am. Coll. Physician Execs., Am. Heart Assn., Nat. Assn. VA Chiefs of Staff (pres. elect 1996, pres. 1997-98). Office: Cleve VA Med Ctr 10701 East Blvd Cleveland OH 44106-1702

ALTSCHAEFFL, ADOLPH GEORGE, civil engineering educator, retired; b. Passaic, N.J., July 20, 1930; s. Ludwig and Crescenz (Liebl) A.; m. Martha Anne Filiatreau, Aug. 6, 1966. BSC.E., Purdue U., 1952, MSC.E., 1955, PhD, 1960. Instr. civil engring. Purdue U., West Lafayette, Ind., 1952-60, asst. prof. civil engring., 1960-64, assoc. prof., 1964-74, prof., 1974-2000, asst. head dept., 1983-91, head geotech. engring., 1994-2000; with Waterways Expt. Sta., C.E., Vicksburg, Miss., 1955, U.S. Geol. Survey, Indpls., 1956. Cons. civil engring. with various architect and contractor firms. Contbr. articles to profl. jours. Served with USAR, 1950-61. Mem. Am. Soc. Engring. Edn., ASCE, Nat. Soc. Profl. Engrs. Office: Purdue U Civil Engring Bldg West Lafayette IN 47907 E-mail: altsch@ecn.purdue.edu.

ALTSCHUL, ALFRED SAMUEL, airline executive; b. Chgo., Oct. 16, 1939; s. Herman and Lillian (Ginsburg) A.; m. Lynn Silverman, Sept. 8, 1968; children: Howard, Steven, Mark. BS, U. Wis., 1961; MBA, U. Chgo., 1963. CPA Ill. With G.A.T.X. Corp., Chgo., 1965-69, asst. treas., 1967-70, treas., 1970-81; v.p. fin., chief fin. officer Midway Airlines, Chgo., 1981-90, sr. v.p., chief fin. officer, 1990-92; CFO Sage Enterprises, Des Plaines, Ill., 1993-95; exec. v.p., CFO A. Epstein and Sons Internat., 1995-96; v.p., CFO Amtrak, 1996-99, Airlines Reporting Corp., 1999—. Lectr. in field. Served with AUS, 1963—69. Mem. AICPA, Fin. Execs. Inst., Alpha Epsilon Pi. Clubs: Standard (Chgo.). Jewish. Home: 3909 Highland Court NW Washington DC 20007-2268

ALTSCHUL, B J, public relations counselor; b. Jan. 28, 1948; d. Lemuel and Sylva (Behr) Student, Goucher Coll., 1965-67; BA, U. South Fla., 1970; MA, U. Md., 1995. Reporter St. Petersburg (Fla.) Times, 1973—74; dir. pub. rels. Valkyrie Press, Inc., St. Petersburg, 1974—77; founding editor Bay Life, Clearwater, Fla., 1977—79, Tampa Bay Monthly, Clearwater, 1977—79; mng. editor Fla. Tourist News, Tampa and Orlando, 1981; founder Capital Comms. of Tampa, 1981; owner, prin. b j Altschul & Assocs. (formerly Capital Comms. of Tampa), 1985—. Mgr. editl. and info. svcs. Va. Pt. Authority, Norfolk, 1985-88; dir. pub. rels. Va. Dept. Agr. and Consumer Svcs., Richmond, 1988-93; adj. faculty Old Dominion U., Norfolk, 1986-88, U. Richmond, 1990, 94, Washington Ctr. for Internships, 1995-96; mgr. pub. rels. U. Md. Biotech. Inst., 1997-99; lectr. dept. comm. U. Md., 1999-2001; asst. prof. Am. U., 2001—. Author: Cracker Cookin' & Other Favorites, 1984; contbg. author: Virginia: A Commonwealth Comes of Age, 1988. Bd. dirs. Pinellas County Big Bros.-Big Sisters, 1980-82, Fla. Folklore Soc., 1984-85. Mem. Fla. Motion Picture and TV Assn. (treas. 1976-78), Hampton Rds. C. of C. (co-chmn. pub. rels. Internat. Azalea Festival 1986, chmn. publs. 1987), Va. Conf. on World Trade (chmn. pub. rels. com.), Downtown Norfolk Devel. Corp. (chmn. urban living com.), Pub. Rels. Soc. Am. (chmn. Mid.-Atlantic Dist. 1988, chmn. govt. sect. 1989, bd. dirs., chmn. chpt. accreditation, chmn. Univ. Rels. Nat. Capital chpt., 2002-), Va. State Agy. Pub. Affairs Assn. (pres. 1990), Internat. Assn. Bus. Communicators (v.p. mem. svcs. Richmond chpt. 1996), Nat. Assn. Sci. Writers, Forum Agr. and Consumer Topics (founder, chmn. 1992). Avocations: piano, Irish set dancing, sailing, classical, folk, and jazz music. Office: B J Altschul & Assocs 14100 Beechvue Ln Silver Spring MD 20906 E-mail: sunrises111@hotmail.com.

ALTSCHUL, STEPHEN FRANK, mathematician; b. N.Y.C., Feb. 28, 1957; s. Arthur Goodhart and Stephanie (Wagner) A.; m. Caroline James; children: James Wagner, William Kershaw. AB summa cum laude, Harvard U., 1979; PhD, MIT, 1987. Intramural Rsch. Tng. Award fellow NIH, Bethesda, Md., 1987-89; staff fellow Nat. Libr. Medicine, Nat. Ctr. for Biotech. Info., NIH, Bethesda, 1989-91, sr. staff fellow, 1991-94, sr. investigator, 1994—; adj. prof. U. of Md., Coll. Park, Md., 2002—. Trustee St. Stephen's Sch., Rome, 1985—; bd. dirs. Overbrook Found., N.Y., 1986—, v.p., 2002--; bd. dirs. Amazon Conservation Team, Arlington, Va., 1998—. sci. adv. bd., Plexxikon, Berkeley, Calif. Fellow Am. Coll. Med. Informatics; mem. Phi Beta Kappa. Office: Nat Libr Medicine Nat Ctr For Biotech Info Bethesda MD 20894-0001 E-mail: altschul@ncbi.nlm.nih.gov.

ALTSCHULER, ALLAN BRUCE, society administrator; b. May 23, 1944; Student, Henry George Sch. Econs., 1984. Dir. internat. food Svc., Denver, 1976-87, Soc. Inernat., Santa Barbar, 1986-98. With U.S. Army, 1972-75. Office: PO Box 23321 Santa Barbara CA 93121-3321

ALTSCHULER, BRUCE ROBERT, research dentist; b. Bklyn., Feb. 17, 1947; s. Frank Philip and Sarah Gertrude (Cloder) A.; m. Ruth Phyllis Gass, Oct. 27, 1974; children: Joan Ellen, Wendy Karen, Cheryl Miriam. BA, Bklyn. Coll., 1967; DDS, Temple U., 1971. Lic. dentist, Md., Pa., Conn., Maine, N.Y. Commd. capt. USAF, 1971, advanced through grades to col., 1986; project scientist dental holography Dental Scis. Br., Brooks AFB, Tex., 1971-74, chief dental consultation, 1975-76; chief dental laser holography USAF Dental Investigation Svc., Brooks AFB, Tex., 1976-80; chief dental computer/laser tech. USAF Aerospace Medicine, Brooks AFB, Tex., 1980-82; chief avionics advanced systems rsch. group Info. Processing Br., Wright-Patterson AFB, Ohio, 1982-84; dep. optical processing Systems Avionics Div., Wright-Patterson AFB, 1985; dental resident Advanced Clin. Dentistry Residence Program, Eglin AFB, Fla., 1985-86; Air Force rsch. liaison, chief laser imaging U.S. Army Inst. Dental Rsch., Ft. Meade, Md., 1986-94; chief imaging robotics lab. Walter Reed Army Inst. Rsch. Dental Rsch. Detachment, Ft. Meade, Md., 1995-97; pres., dir. rsch. devel. Cobalt Rsch. Co., 1997—. Clin. asst. prof. dept. diagnosis/roentgenology U. Tex. Health Sci. Ctr., San Antonio, 1976-80, dept. dental diagnostic svc., 1980-82; mem. dental x-ray subcom. 26 Am. Nat. Standards Inst., Washington, 1980-85; reviewer NIH Computer Aided Dentistry, Washington, 1987. Editor 3-D Machine Perception; patentee in field. Bd. dirs. Am. Cancer Soc., Bexar County, Tex., 1980-82, mem. pub. edn. com., 1980-82; campaign coord. Avionics Lab. Combined Fed. Campaign, Dayton, Ohio 1984; spl. award judge Alamo Regional Sci. Fair, San Antonio, 1980-82. Mem. ADA, Internat. Assn. Dental Rsch., Soc. Photo Optical Instrumentation Engrs., Air Force Assn., Armed Forces Communications, Electronics Assn., Tex. Dental Assn., Am. Mensa. Republican. Jewish. Avocations: photography, electronics, computers. Home: PO Box 458 Simpsonville MD 21150-0458 Office: Cobalt Rsch LLC PO Box 458 Simpsonville MD 21150-0458 E-mail: cobalt-research@erols.com.

ALTSCHULER, SAMUEL, retired electronics company executive; b. N.Y.C., Aug. 13, 1927; s. Samuel and Sylvia (Sussman) A.; m. Nancy Treulich, Nov. 15, 1958; children: Jeffrey, Lisa, James, Jonathen, Pamela. BSEE, U. Conn., 1950; MBA, Northeastern U., 1958. Jr. engr. New London (Conn.) Instrument Co., 1950-51; engr. Western Electric, North Andover, Mass., 1951-56; sr. engr. Honeywell, Boston, 1956-58; chief quality control engr. L.F.E., Boston, 1958-59; v.p. mfg. Adage, Boston, 1959-70; founder, chmn., pres. Altron Inc., mfrs. printed cir. bds., backplanes, Wilmington, Mass., 1970—98. Mem. corp. Northeastern U., Boston, 1993—, Wentworth Inst., Boston. Recipient Disting. Engring. Alumni award U. Conn., 1993. Mem. Inst. for Interconnecting and Packaging Electronic Circuits (pres. 1992-94, Disting. Svc. award 1994), Eta Kappa Nu.

ALTSHILLER, ARTHUR LEONARD, secondary education educator; b. N.Y.C., Aug. 12, 1942; s. Samuel Martin and Betty Rose (Lepson) A.; m. Carol Heiser, Aug. 16, 1980. BS in Physics, U. Okla., 1963; MS in Physics, Calif. State U., Northridge, 1971. Elec. engr. Garrett Corp., Torrance, Calif., 1963-64, Volt Tech. Corp., Phoenix, 1965; engr., physicist Aerojet Gen. Corp., Azusa, Calif., 1966-68; elec. engr. Magnavox Rsch. Labs., Torrance, 1968-69; sr. engr. Litton Guidance & Control, Canoga Park, Calif., 1969; physics tchr. L.A. Unified Sch. Dist./Van Nuys Math/Sci. Magnet High Sch., 1971—; math. instr. Valley Coll., Van Nuys, Calif., 1986—. Part-time physics and chemistry tchr. West Coast Talmudical Sem., L.A., 1978-88; foster tchr. Seti Inst. and NASA Ames Rsch. Ctr., 1994; coach Van Nuys (Calif.) H.S. Nat. Championship Sci. Bowl Team, 1995; tchr. mem. U.S. Olympic Physics Team, 1996; Chicos participant Calif. Inst. Tech., 2000—. Mesa Club sponsor Math.-Engring. Sci. Achievement L.A. High Sch. and U. So. Calif., 1984-87, Van Nuys H.S., 1997-98, Calif. State U. Northridge, 1997-98. Recipient Cert. of Honor Westinghouse Sci. Talent Search, 1990, Lucent Tech. Talent Search, 1998; Eisenhower fellow NSF, 2002—. Mem. AAAS, Am. Assn. Physics Tchrs., Am. Inst. Physics (ednl. advisor 1999), United Tchrs. L.A. Avocations: cycling, tennis, weight lifting, track and field. Home: 6776 Vickiview Dr Canoga Park CA 91307-2751 Office: Van Nuys High Sch 6535 Cedros Ave Van Nuys CA 91411-1599 E-mail: altshiller@aol.com.

ALTSHULER, ALAN ANTHONY, political scientist, educator; b. Bklyn., Mar. 9, 1936; s. Leonard M. and Janet A. (Sonnenstrahl) A.; m. Julie C. Maller, June 15, 1958; children: Jennifer, David. BA, Cornell U., 1957; MA, U. Chgo., 1959, PhD, 1961. Instr. Swarthmore Coll., 1960-61; Smith-Mundt vis. asst. prof. Makerere (Uganda) Coll., 1961-62; asst. prof. Cornell U., 1962-66; assoc. prof. MIT, 1966-69, prof. polit. sci. and urban studies and planning, 1969-71, 1975-83, head dept. polit. sci., 1977-82; dean Grad. Sch. Pub. Adminstrn. NYU, 1983-88, dir. Urban Research Ctr., 1986-87; prof. urban policy and planning Kennedy Sch. Govt. and Grad. Sch. Design Harvard U., 1988—; dir. Taubman Ctr. State and Local Govt. Harvard U., 1988—, acad. dean Kennedy Sch. Govt., 1993-95; dir. Rappaport Inst. for Greater Boston, 1999—. Sec. transp. and constrn. Commonwealth Mass., 1971-75; dir. Boston Transp. Planning Rev. (part-time), 1970-71. Author: The City Planning Process: A Political Analysis, 1965, Community Control: The Black Demand for Participation in Large American Cities, 1970, The Urban Transportation System: Politics and Policy Innovation, 1979; co-author: The Future of the Automobile, 1984, Regulation for Revenue: The Political Economy of Land Development Exactions, 1993, Mega-Projects: The Changing Politics of Urban Public Investment, 2003; editor: Current Issues in Transportation Policy, 1979; co-editor: The Politics of the Federal Bureaucracy, 1977, Innovation in American Government, 1997, Governance and Opportunity in Metropolitan America, 1999; contbr. articles to profl. jours. Mem. Nat. Acad. Pub. Adminstrn., Am. Acad. Arts and Scis.

ALTSHULER, DAVID MATTHEW, geneticist, endocrinologist; b. Ithaca, N.Y., Aug. 27, 1964; s. Alan Anthony and Julie Maller Altshuler; m. Jill Suttenberg, Aug. 5, 1990; children: Zachary Miles, Jason Leonard. BS, MIT, 1986; PhD in Genetics, Harvard U., 1993, MD, 1994. Diplomate in internal medicine Am. Bd. of Internal Medicine, in endocrinology, diabetes and metabolism Am. Bd. of Internal Medicine, 2000. Intern Mass. Gen. Hosp., Boston, 1994—95, resident in internal medicine, 1995—96, fellow in diabetes, endocrinology and metabolism, 1996—99; asst. prof. genetics and medicine Med. Sch. Harvard U., Boston, 2000—; dir. program in med. and population genetics Whitehead Ctr. for Genome Rsch. MIT, Cambridge, Mass., 2000—. Chmn. personalized medicine sci. adv. bd. Marshfield (Wis.) Clinic, 2001; mem. clin. genomics adv. bd. Merck Rsch. Labs, West Point, Pa., 2001—; mem. sci. adv. bd. Genomics Collaborative, Inc, Cambridge, 2000—, Reify Corp., Cambridge, 2002—; co-chair Analysis, International Haplotype Map Project; mem. exec. com. Whitehead Ctr. for Genome Rsch. MIT, 2000—; founding mem. The Broad Inst. of Harvard and MIT, 2003—. Trustee The Commonwealth Sch., Boston, 2002. Recipient Steven Krane award, Mass. Gen. Hosp., 2002; scholar, Burroughs Welcome Fund, 2002—, Charles E. Culpeper scholar, Rockefeller Bros. Fund, 2002—. Office: Mass Gen Hosp Dept Molecular Biology Boston MA 02114

ALTSHULER, KENNETH Z. psychiatrist, educator; b. Paterson, NJ, Apr. 11, 1929; s. Jacob and Altie (Freedman) A.; m. Gloria Seigel, June 14, 1952 (div. 1981); children: Steven, Lori, Dara; m. Ruth Collins Sharp, Dec. 5, 1987. BA, Cornell U., 1948; MD, U. Buffalo, 1952; DSc (hon.), Gallaudet Coll., 1972. Intern Kings County Hosp., Bklyn., 1952-53; resident NY State Psychiat. Inst., NYC, 1955-58; asst. in psychiatry Columbia U., 1958-59, instr., 1959-63, research assoc., 1963-67, asst. clin. prof., 1967-71, assoc. clin. prof., 1971-75, prof., 1975-77; tng. analyst Columbia U. Psychoanalytic Clinic for Tng. and Rsch., 1969-77; project dir. Essential Aspects of Deafness, 1972-76, Trauma and Sleep Physiology, 1975-77; Stanton Sharp prof., chmn. psychiatry U. Tex.-Southwestern Med. Sch., Dallas, 1977-2000, Stanton Sharp prof. psychiatry, 2000—; tng. analyst New Orleans Psychoanalytic Inst., 1979-86, Dallas Psychoanalytic Inst., Tex., 1986—. Chief of deafness unit Rockland State Hosp., Orangeburg, NY, 1966-77; cons. to NIH; dir. Am. Bd. Psychiatry and Neurology, 1990-97, pres., 1996; mem. Nat. Bd. Med. Examiners, 1986-89, chmn. Part II psychiatry com., 1988-89; dir. bd. Tex. Dept. Mental Health and Mental Retardation, 1999—. Co-author: Mng. Sleep Complaints, 1982; co-editor: Family and Mental Health Problems in a Deaf Population, 1963, Comprehensive Mental Health Svc. for the Deaf, 1966, Psychiatry and the Deaf, 1968, Expanded Mental Health Care for the Deaf, 1970, Depression: Mechanisms, Diagnosis and Treatment, 1986; others.; Contbr. articles to profl. jour. Mem. governing bd. Tex. Sch. for the Deaf, 1986-90; bd. dir. Tex. Dept. Mental Health and Mental Retardation, 1999—. Served with USNR, 1953-55. Recipient Wilson award in genetics and preventive medicine, 1961, Disting. Cmty. Service award Dallas County Mental Health Assn., 1986, Prism award, 1992, Disting. Alumnus award, SUNY, Buffalo, 1993, 1st Trailblazer award named in his honor, Dallas County Mental Health and Retardation Ctr., 1996, Tex. Star award for Outstanding Cmty. Svc. Tex. Mental Health Assn., 1997; named Outstanding Psychiatrist, Tex. Soc. Psychiat. Physicians, 1996, alumnus of the decade Columbia U., 1996; Kenneth Z. Altshuler clinic named in his honor by the Dallas County Mental Health and Mental Retardation Ctr., 1997; Disting. Life Fellow Am. Psychiat. Assn.; Cert. of Achievement Bd. of Hosp. Psychiatry: Cert. of Significant Achievement for Deafness Program, NY State, 1976; for Mental Health Connections Program, 1995. Fellow Am. Psychiat. Assn. (cert. of achievement bd. hosp. psychiatry, cert. of significant achievement for deafness program, NY State, 1976, for Mental Health Connections program, 1995), Am. Coll. Psychiatrists, Am. Coll. Psychoanalysts; mem. AAAS, AMA, Am. Psychoanalytic Assn., Assn. for Psychoanalytic Medicine (Merit award 1965), Tex. Med. Soc., Dallas County Med. Soc., Am. Psychopathol. Assn., Assn. Dir. Med. Student Edn. in Psychiatry (founder, v.p. 1976-77), Am. Assn. Chmn. Dept. Psychiatry (pres. 1990-91), So. Assn. Rsch. Psychiatry (pres. 1993-94). E-mail: kenneth.altshuler@utsouthwestern.edu.

ALTURA, BELLA T. physiologist, educator; b. Solingen, Germany; came to U.S., 1948; d. Sol and Rosa (Brandstetter) Tabak; m. Burton M. Altura, Dec. 27, 1961; 1 child, Rachel Allison. BA, Hunter Coll., 1953, MA, 1962; PhD, CUNY, 1968. Instr. exptl. anesthesiology Albert Einstein Coll. Medicine, Bronx, 1970-74; asst. prof. physiology SUNY Health Sci Ctr., Bklyn., 1974-82, assoc. prof. physiology, 1982-97, rsch. prof. physiology, 1997—, rsch. prof. pharmacology, 1998—. Vis. prof. Beijing Coll. of Traditional Chinese Medicine, 1988, Jiangxi (China) Med. Coll., 1988, Tokyo U. Med. Sch., 1993, U. Brussels Esramé Hosp., 1995, Humboldt U.-Charité Hosp., 1995, Kagoshima U., Japan, 1995, U. Birmingham, England, 1996, Self Med. Def. Coll. Japan, 1996, Nat. Def. Med. Sch., Japan, 1996, Albert Szent Gyorgi Med. U., Szeged, Hungary, 1997; mem. Nat. Coun. on Magnesium and Cardiovascular Disease, 1991—; cons. NOVA Biomedical, 1989—; Niche pharm. cons. Protina GmbH, Munich, 1992—96, Otsuka Pharm. Co., Japan, 1995—97, Roberts Pharm. Co., 1999—2000; co-prin. investigator NIH, Nat. Heart, Lung and Blood Inst., NIMH, Nat. Inst. on Alcoholism and Alcohol Abuse. Contbr. over 700 articles to profl. jours. Fellowship NASA, 1966-67, CUNY, 1968; co-recipient Gold-Silver medal French Nat. Acad. Medicine, 1984, Silver medal Mayor of Paris, 1984, Seelig award for lifetime rsch. on magnesium, Am. Coll. Nutrition, 2002, Outstanding Inventor of Yr., SUNY, 2002. Mem. Am. Physiol. Soc., Am. Soc. Pharmacology and Exptl. Therapeutics, Am. Soc. for Magnesium Rsch. (founder, treas. 1984—), Hungarian Soc. Electrochemistry (hon. co-pres. 1995-96), Nat. Heart, Lung and Blood Inst., Nat. Inst. on Alcohol Abuse and Alcoholism, Phi Beta Kappa, Sigma Xi. Achievements include first measurement ionized magnesium with ion selective electrode in blood, serum and plasma in health and disease states; demonstration that substances of abuse can cause cerebrovasospasm and stroke. Office: SUNY Health Sci Ctr Box 31 450 Clarkson Ave Brooklyn NY 11203-2056 E-mail: baltura@downstate.edu.

ALTURA, BURTON MYRON, physiologist, educator; b. N.Y.C., Apr. 9, 1936; s. Barney and Frances (Dorfman) A.; m. Bella Tabak, Dec. 27, 1961; 1 child, Rachel Allison. BA, Hofstra U., 1957; MS, NYU, 1961, PhD (USPHS fellow), 1964. Diplomate Am. Bd. Forensic Med., Am. Coll. Forensic Medicine, Am. Bd. Forensic Examiners, Coll. Pharm. and Apothecary Scis., Am. Assn. Integrative Medicine. Tchg. fellow in biology NYU, N.Y.C., 1960-61, instr. exptl. anesthesiology Sch. Medicine, 1964-65, asst. prof. Sch. Medicine, 1965-66; rsch. fellow Bronx Mcpl. Hosp. Ctr., 1967-76; asst. prof. physiology and anesthesiology Albert Einstein Coll. Medicine, N.Y.C., 1967-70, assoc. prof., 1970-74, vis. prof., 1974-78; prof. physiology SUNY Health Sci. Ctr., Bklyn., 1974—, prof. medicine, 1992—; mem. Ctr. Cardiovasc. and Muscle Rsch., 1995—; prof. pharmacology SUNY Health Sci. Ctr., Bklyn., 1998—; CEO Bio-Def., Inc. Mem. spl. study sect. on toxicology Nat. Inst. Environ. Health Scis., 1977—78; mem. Alcohol Biomed. Rsch. Rev. Com. Nat. Inst. Alcohol Abuse and Alcoholism, 1978—83; mem. spl. study sect. on toxicology Nat. Inst. Environ. Health Scis., 2001; mem. spl. study sect. medications Nat. Inst. Alcohol Abuse and Alcoholism, 2002; mem. panel CNF bd. Inst. Med., NAS, 1996—97; mem. A Food bd. FTC; adj. prof. biology Queens Coll., CUNY, 1983—84; pres. (hon.) Internat. Symposium on Interactions of Magnesium and Potassium on Cardiac and Vascular Muscle, Montbazon, France, 1984; pres. (hon.), lectr. (hon.) Hungarian Soc. Electrochemistry, Budapest, 1995; organizer, condr. symposia; organizer workshop Nat. Inst. Alcohol Abuse and Alcoholism, 1992; condr., chmn. Gordon Rsch. Conf. on Magnesium in Biochem. Processes and Medicine, 1984; chmn., organizer 1st Internat. Workshop Unique Magnesium Sensitive Ion Selective Electrodes, Orlando, Fla., 1993, 2nd Internat. Workshop Unique Magnesium Sensitive Ion Selective Electrodes; chmn. symposium Am. Soc. Nephrology, 1993; v.p. 4th Internat. Symposium on Magnesium, Blacksburg, 1985; organizer 2nd Internat. Workshop Unique Magnesium Sensitive Ion Selective Electrodes, Crete, 1997; judge Am. Inst. Sci. and Tech., 1984, 85, 86, 1988—90, 1991, 93, Jr. Acad. N.Y. Acad. Scis., 1987, 89, 90; mem. adv. coun. Nat. Found. Addictive Drugs, 1986—; vis. prof. Yamaguchi U., Japan, 1988, 93, Beijing Coll. Traditional Chinese Medicine, China, 1988, Harvard U. Med. Sch., 1988, U. Tokyo, 1993, Kyoto U. Sch. Medicine, 1993, Kumamoto U., 1993, U. Copenhagen, 1994, U. Florence, 1994, Humboldt Univ., Berlin, 1995, U. Birmingham, England, 1996, Self Med. Def. Coll., Japan, 1996, U. Calif., Riverside, 1998, Fla. Atlantic U., 1998; vis. prof., lectr. (hon.) Inst. Water, Soil and Air Hygiene, Fed. Health Inst., Berlin, 1991, Max Planck Inst., Dortmund, Germany, 1992, 94, Yamanouchi Co. Ltd., Japan, 1995; mem. working group convened by Congressman Durbin III, 91; mem. Nat. Coun. Magnesium and Cardiovasc. Disease, 1991—; CEO Bio-Defense Sys., Inc.; spkr. in field; cons. NSF, Va. Grants Rev. Com., Nat. Heart, Lung, and Blood Inst., Nat. Inst. Drug Abuse, others. Author: Microcirculation, 3 vols., 1977—80, Vascular Endothelium and Basement Membranes, 1980, Pathophysiology of the Reticuloendothelial System, 1981, Ionic Regulation of the Microcirculation, 1982, Handbook of Shock and Trauma, Vol. 1: Basic Science, 1983, Magnesium and the Cardiovascular System, 1985, Cardiovascular Actions of Anesthetic Agents and Drugs Used in Anesthesia, vol. I, 1986, vol. II, 1987, Magnesium, Stress and the Cardiovascular System, 1986, Magnesium in Biochemical Processes and Medicine, 1987, Magnesium in Clinical Medicine and Therapeutics, 1992, Unique Magnesium-Sensitive Ion Selective Electrodes, 1994; editor-in-chief: Physiology and Patho-physiology Series, 1976—81, Microcirculation, 1980—84, Magnesium: Exptl. and Clin. Rsch., 1981—89, Microcirculation, Endothelium and Lymphatics, 1984—, Magnesium and Trace Elements, 1990—, mem. editl. bd.: Jour. Circulatory Shock, 1973—85, Advances in Microcirculation, 1976—92, Jour. Cardiovasc. Pharmacology, 1977—84, Prostaglandins, Leukotrienes and Fatty Acids, 1978—2001, Substance and Alcohol Actions/Misuse, 1979—84, Alcoholism: Clin. and Exptl. Rsch., 1982—87, assoc. editor: Jour. Artery, 1974—, Microvasc. Rsch., 1978—85, Agts. and Actions, 1981—88, Biogenic Amines, 1985—88, Jour. Am. Coll. Nutrition, 1982—94, Frontiers in Biosci., 1996—, Internat. Jour. Cardiovasc. Medicine, Surgery and Biomechanics, 1997—; contbr. over 900 articles to profl. jours. Recipient Rsch. Career Devel. award

USPHS, 1968-72, Silver medal for furthering French-U.S. sci. rels. Mayor of Paris, 1984, Medaille Vermeille, French Nat. Acad. Medicine, 1984, Travel awards NIH, 1968, Am. Soc. Pharm. and Exptl. Therapeutics, 1969, Golden Hippocrates award, Haifa, Israel, 2002, Chancellor's Outstanding Inventor of Yr. award SUNY, 2002, Medal for Lifetime of Basic Med. Rsch. and Tchg., Haifa, Israel, 2002; grantee NIH, 1968-, NIMH, 1974-78, Nat. Heart Lung Blood Inst., 1974-86, Nat. Inst. Drug Abuse, 1979-83, Nat. Inst. Alcohol Abuse and Alcoholism, 1990-; named Eminent Fellow, Wisdom Hall of Fame, 1999. Fellow: AAAS, Nat. Acad. Clinical BioChemistry, Am. Physiol. Soc. (mem. circulation group 1971—, pub. info. com. 1980—84, symposium organizer), Am. Coll. Nutrition (Seelig award 2002), Am. Heart Assn. (coun. basic sci. 1969—, coun. on thrombosis 1971—, mem. coun. on stroke 1973—, cardiovasc. A study sect. 1978—81, coun. on circulation 1978—, coun. on high blood pressure 1978—, coun. on cardiopulmonary circulation 1987—, coun. on arteriosclerosis, thrombosis, and vascular biology 1997—, coun. on cardiovascular basic scis. 2001—, fellow coun. on high blood pressure rsch. 2002), Am. Bd. Forensic Examiners (life), Assn. Clin. Scientists (life; Wisdom Hall of Fame 1999—, Molecular Medicine Soc. 2000—), Am. Soc. Integrative Medicine (life), Am. Coll. Forensic Examiners (life), Internat. Coll. Angiology, Am. Coll. Angiology, Am. Inst. Chemists; mem.: APHA, AAUP, Aur. Physiological Soc. (organizer several symposia), Internat. Soc. Free Radical Rsch., Am. Soc. Biochemistry and Molecular Biology, Am. Inst. Biological Sci., Special Study Med., Internat. Soc. Police Surgeons, Am. Med. Writers Assn., Nat. Coun. for Magnesium and Cardiovasc. Disease, Am. Assn. Pharm. Scis., Inter-Am. Soc. Hypertension, Am. Soc. Hypertension (founding mem.), Internat. Soc. for Hypertension, Internat. Anesthesia Soc., Coun. Biology Editors, N.Y. Soc. Electron Microscopy, N.Y. Heart Assn., N.Y. Acad. Scis. (symposium lectr.-spkr. com. mem.), Am. Soc. Magnesium Rsch. (exec. dir. 1984—, founder, organizer, pres., workshop, symposium), Am. Soc. Bone and Mineral Rsch., Am. Soc. Cell Biology, The Oxygen Soc., Am. Soc. Zoologists, Am. Microscopical Soc., Am. Assn. Lab. Animal Sci., Soc. for Xenobiotics, Internat. Platform Assn., Soc. Scholarly Pub., Soc. Nutrition Edn., Soc. of Parenteral and Enteral Nutrition, Liposome Soc., Internat. Soc. Exposure Analysis, Reticuloendothelial Soc. (hon. lectr.), Soc. Cardiovasc. Pathology, Soc. Environ. Geochemistry and Health, Soc. Leukocyte Biology, Internat. Soc. Biorheology, Biomed. Optics Soc., Internat. Soc. Biomed. Rsch. on Alcoholism (founding mem.), Am. Soc. Microbiology, Am. Inst. Nutrition (organizer mini-symposium), Fedn. Am. Soc. Exptl. Biology (pub. info. com. 1981—86), Internat. Anesthesia Rsch. Soc., Neurotrauma Soc., European Conf. Microcirculation (symposium organizer, hon. lectr.), Microscopy Soc. Am., Am. Fedn. Clin. Rsch., Shock Soc. (founder, hon. lectr.), Soc. for Neurosci., Am. Thoracic Soc., Soc. for Critical Care Medicine, Rsch. Soc. on Alcoholism, Am. Soc. Pharm. and Exptl. Therapeutics, Am. Oil Chemists Soc., Rsch. Soc. on Alcoholism (organizer several symposia), Am. Coll. Toxicology, Harvey Soc., Endocrine Soc., Am. Soc. Nutritional Scis., Am. Soc. Pharm. and Exptl. Therapeutics (symposium organizer), Am. Chem. Soc. (divsn. medicinal chemistry, divsn. analytical chemistry), Am. Soc. Headache, Am. Assn. for Clin. Chemistry (hon. lectr. 1989, 1992, 1994), Soc. Exptl. Biology and Medicine (editl. bd. 1976—83), Microcirculatory Soc. (mem. nominating com. 1973—74, past mem. exec. coun.), Am. Soc. Investigative Pathology, Soc. for Magnetic Resonance, Sigma Xi. Office: 450 Clarkson Ave Brooklyn NY 11203-2056

ALUMBAUGH, JOANN MCCALLA, magazine editor; b. Ann Arbor, Mich., Sept. 16, 1952; d. William Samuel and Jean Arliss (Guy) McCalla; m. Lyle Ray Alumbaugh, Apr. 27, 1974; children: Brent William, Brandon Jess, Brooke Louise. BA, Ea. Mich. U., 1974. Cert. elem. tch., Mich. Assoc. editor Chester White Swine Record Assn., Rochester, Ind., 1974-77; prodn. editor United Duroc Swine Registry, Peoria, Ill., 1977-79; dir., pres. Nat. Assn. Swine Records, Macomb, Ill., 1979-82; free-lance writer, artist Ill. and Nat. Specific Pathogen Free Assn., Ind. producers, Good Hope, Emden, Ill., 1982-85; editor The Hog Producer Farm Progress Publs., Urbandale, Iowa, 1985-99; exec. editor Nebr. Farmer, Kans. Farmer, Mo. Ruralist, We. Beef Prodr., Beef Prodr., Farm & Fireside, 1999—2003; dir. Communications Farms.Com, 2003—. Family Living Program, Farm Progress Show, 1985-, Master Farm Homemaker Program, 1989-99; mem. U.S. Agrl. Export Devel. Coun., Washington, 1979-82, apptd. mem. Blue Ribbon Com. on Agr., 1980-81. Contbr. numerous articles to profl. jours. Precinct chmn. Rep. Party, Linden, Iowa, 1988; mem. Keep Improving Dist. Schs., Panora, Iowa, 1990-91; v.p. Sunday sch. com. Sunset Circle, United Meth. Ch., Linden, 1990-91; pres. PTA, Panorama Schs., Panora, 1993-94; coach Odyssey of Mind Program World Competition, 1994—. Mem.: Iowa Master Farm Homemakers, Guthrie County Prok Prodrs., McDonough County and Ill. Porkettes (county pres. 1978—79, Bellerìnger award 1979), Nat. Pork Prodrs. Coun., Iowa Pork Prodrs. Assn. (legis. com. 1990—95, hon. master pork prodr.), U.S. Animal Health Assn., Am. Agrl. Editors Assn. (chmn. dist. svc. com. 1991, master writer 1997, pres.-elect 1998, pres. 1999, chmn. adv. coun. 1999—2002, co-chmn. comm. clinic, chmn. comms. clinic, trustee 2002—, World of Difference award 1995, Oscar in Agr. 1999), Internat. Platform Assn. Avocations: reading, painting, flower gardening. Home: 2644 Amarillo Ave Linden IA 50146-8029 Office: Farm Progress Publs/Wallaces Farmer 6200 Aurora Ave Ste 609E Urbandale IA 50322-2863

ALUQUIN, VINCENT PROTACIO ROY, pediatric cardiologist; b. Makati, Manila, Philippines, Aug. 28, 1969; s. Antonio and Corazon Aluquin; m. Shirley Angeles Albano, Oct. 16, 1970; children: Anton, Lindsay. MD, U. of the Philippines, Manila, Philippines, 1989—94. Diplomate in Pediatrics Amercian Bd. of Pediat., 1998, Diplomate in Pediatric Cardiology Am. Bd. of Pediat., 2002. Resident in pediat. Children's Hosp. of Mich./ Wayne State U., Detroit, Mich., 1995—98; post-doctoral fellow in pediatric cardiology Stanford U., Palo Alto, Calif., 1998—2001; fellow in pediatric interventional cardiology and pediatric cardiac intensive care Miami Children's Hosp., Miami, Fla., 2001—02; clin. assoc. prof. U. of the Philippines/ Philippine Gen. Hosp., Malate, Philippines, 2002—. Pediatric cardiologist Calamba Med. Ctr., Calamba, Laguna, Philippines, 2002—. Author: (medical article) Magnetic Resonance Imaging in the Diagnosis and Follow-up of Takayasu Arteritis in Children. Recipient Magna cum laude, U. of the Philippines, 1989; scholar Presdl. Scholarship, 1986-1989. Mem.: Philippine Pediatric Soc. (licentiate), Amercian Coll. of Cardiology (assoc.). Avocations: theater arts, cooking, spending time with family. Home: 415 Topaz Street Posadas Village Manila Sucat, Muntinlupa City 1770 Philippines Office: Philippine General Hospital Depatment of Pediatrics Taft Manila Malate Philippines Personal E-mail: vinzaluquin@pol.net.

ALURI, RAO, book publisher; b. Moparru, India, Sept. 1, 1941; s. Narayana Rao and Raghavamma (Vadlamudi) A.; m. Mary L. Reichel, Jan. 6, 1977; 1 child, Krishna P. BSc, A.M.A.L. Coll., Anakapalle, India, 1963; MSc, U. Western Ontario, Can., 1971, MLS, 1972; PhD in Higher Edn. & Libr. Sci., SUNY at Buffalo, 1981. Ref. libr. U. Nebr., Omaha, 1973-76; asst. prof. Emory U., Atlanta, 1980-86; mgr. libr. Burr-Brown Corp., Tucson, 1987-92; pub., pres. Parkway Pubs., Inc., Boone, N.C., 1992—. Co-compiler: (book) U.S. Gov. Sci. and Technical Periodicals, 1976; co-author: (book) U.S. Govt. Scientific & Technical Resources, 1983, Subject Analysis in Online Catalogs, 1991; co-editor: (book) Expert Systems in Libraries, 1992. Bd. dirs. Sta. WAMY, Inc., Boone, 1997-2001; bd. dirs. High Country United Way, 1999—, sec., 2001. Mem. Rotary (sec. Boone 1994-95, pres.-elect 1995-96, pres. 1996-97). Democrat. Hindu. Home: 421 Fairfield Ln Blowing Rock NC 28605-9755 Office: Parkway Publishers Inc PO Box 3678 Boone NC 28607-5578 E-mail: parkwaypub@hotmail.com.

ALVA, ALEJANDRO, psychiatrist; b. Mexico City, Mex., Mar. 2, 1960; came to U.S., 1971; s. Jose Gabriel Alva and Lucy Sanchez; m. Silvana Alva, Sept. 9, 1990; 1 child, Alex. MD, U. Guadalajara, Mex., 1990, MS, 1992; psychiatrist, U. Calif., Irvine, 1999. Forensic psychiat. cons. Orange County Superior Ct., Orange, Calif., 1997—, rsch. psychiatrist, 1998—; ptnr. Harbor Med. Assocs., Newport Beach, Calif., 1999; staff psychiatrist Hoag Med. Ctr., Newport Beach, 1999; med. dir. Chapman Med. Ctrs. Psychiat. Svcs., Orange, Calif., 2000. Med. dir. Virgil-Mid Town Med., L.A., 1997—98; staff psychiatrist adult svcs. Pacific Clinics, Orange, 1998—99, med. dir. children's svcs, 1999—; staff psychiatrist Fountain Valley (Calif.) Regional Med. Ctr., 1999, Garden Grove (Calif.) Hosp., 1999, Newport Bay Hosp., Newport Beach, 1999; med. dir. partial hospitalization program Coll. Hosp., Signal Hill, Calif. Mem. govt. affairs com., pub. affairs com. Orange County Psychiat. Soc., Orange, 1996—; western regional dir. Adventist Rehab. Agy., Loma Linda, Calif., 1996-97. Fellow: Am. Coll. Psychopharmacology, Am. Coll. Forensic Examiners; mem.: AAAS, AMA, N.Y. Acad. Scis., Hispanic-Am. Biomed. Assn., Calif. Hispanic Am. Med. Assn., Am. Bd. Forensic Medicine, Am. Psychiat. Assn. Avocations: scuba diving, soccer, Karate. Home: 25752 Golden Rod Cir Laguna Hills CA 92653-7523

ALVARADO, LINDA G. construction company executive; Doctorate (hon.), Dowling Coll. Pres. Alvarado Constrn., Inc., Denver, 1976—. Owner Colorado Rockies franchise; corp. dir. 3M, Pepsi Bottling Group. Chmn. bd. dirs. Denver Hispanic C. of C.; commrs. White House Initiative for Hispanic Excellence in Edn. Named Revlon Bus. Woman of Yr., 1996, Bus. Woman of Yr., U.S. Hispanic C. of C., 1996, 100 Most Influential Hispanics in Am., Hispanic Bus. Mag., others; recipient Nat. Minority Supplier Devel. Coun. Leadership award, 1996, Sara Lee Corp. Frontrunner award, 2001, Horatio Alger award, others; inducted into Nat. Women's Hall of Fame, Colo. Women's Hall of Fame. Office: Alvarado Construction 1266 Santa Fe Dr Denver CO 80204-3546

ALVARADO-JUAREZ, FRANCISCO, visual artist; b. Tela, Atlántida, Honduras, Dec. 18, 1950; arrived in U.S., 1965; s. Francisco Arturo Alvarado and María de Jesús Vásquez; 1 child, Lucas Alvarado-Farrar. BA, SUNY, Stony Brook, 1974; student, Internat. Ctr. of Photography, 1975; MFA, Md. Inst., 1993. Dir., founding editor Tláloc- lit. mag., Stony Brook, NY, 1971—74; gallery dir. Galería Inti, Wash., DC, 1981. One-man shows include Museo de Arte Contemporáneo de Oaxaca, Mex., 2002, Everson Mus. of Art, Syracuse,N.Y., 2001, Museo Pablo Serrano, Zaragoza, Spain, 2000, The Noyes Mus. of Art, Oceanville,N.J., 1998, Museo Universitario del Chopo, Mex., 1995, The Contemporary Arts Ctr., Cin.,Ohio, 1994, Islip Art Mus., Oakdale, N.Y., 1992, The Bronx Mus. of the Arts, The Bronx, N.Y., 1992, El Museo del Barrio, N.Y.C., 1986, numerous colls., univs. and galleries, 1976—2003, exhibitions include group Sotheby's, N.Y.C., 2001, The Discovery Mus., Bridgeport, CT, 1990, Fundaçao Bienal de São Paulo, Brazil, 1987, Brooklyn Mus. of Art, Brooklyn, N.Y., 1987, Museo Nacional de Bellas Artes, Cuba, 1986, Second Street Gallery, Charlottesville,Va., 1985, Museo de Arte Contemporáneo, Caracas, Venezuela, 1984, numerous group exhibitions at various galleries, Represented in permanent collections The Art Gallery, U Md., Banco Atlántida, Tegucigalpa, Biblioteca Nacional, Caracas, Bibliothèque Nationale, Paris, The Bronx Mus. of the Arts, Brooklyn Mus. of Art, Cartón de Venezuela, Caracas, Everson Mus. of Art, numerous more permanent colletions, reviews in pub., numerous reviews and publications. Grantee D.C. Comm. on the Arts and Humanities, 1982—83, Nat. Endowment for the Arts, 1985, D.C. Comm. on the Arts and Humanities, 1985—86, The Studio Mus. in Harlem - Artist in Residence, 1987, Nat. Endowment for the Arts, 1989, The Pollock-Krasner Found., 1991, Mid Atlantic Arts Found., 1993, 1998, The Pollock-Krasner Found., 2000, N.Y. Found. for the Arts, 2000. Office: 3647 Broadway No 2F New York NY 10031-2506 E-mail: franciscoaj@yahoo.com.

ALVARE, CHARLES DAGUERRE, television producer; s. Carlos J. and Mary J. H. Erskine Alvare; m. Carrie Rudolf, Oct. 10, 1999. BA, Columbia Coll., 1979; MPhil, Cambridge U., 2003. Mktg. dir. Praxis Film Works, North Hollywood, Calif., 1983—86; exec. prodr. EUE/Screen Gems, Burbank, Calif., 1986—88; prodr. Ind., LA., N.Y.C., London, 1989—99; pres. Sanctuary Media, Hollywood, 2000—02. Prodr.: (TV commls.), 1997—99. Mem.: Acad. TV Arts and Scis., Delta Psi. E-mail: sanctuarymedia@hotmail.com.

ALVAREZ, A. (AL ALVAREZ), writer; b. London, Aug. 5, 1929; s. Bertie and Katie (Levy) A.; m. Ursula Graham Barr, 1956 (div. 1961); 1 child, Adam Richard; m. Audrey Anne Adams, 1966; children: Luke Lyon, Kate. BA, Oxford (Eng.) U., 1952, MA, 1956; DLitt (hon.), U. East London, 1998. Sr. rsch. scholar Corpus Christi Coll. Oxford U., 1952-55, tutor English, 1954-55. Procter vis. fellow Princeton (N.J.) U., 1953-54, Gauss seminarian, vis. lectr., 1957-58; vis. fellow Rockefeller Found., N.Y.C., 1955-56, 58; poetry editor, critic Observer, London, 1956-66; D.H. Lawrence fellow U. N.Mex., 1958; drama critic New Statesman, 1958-60; vis. prof. Brandeis U., Waltham, Mass., 1960-61, SUNY, Buffalo, 1966. Author: Stewards of Excellence, 1958 (pub. in Eng. as The Shaping Spirit 1958), The End of It, 1958, The School of Donne, 1961, Under Pressure: The Writer in Society, Eastern Europe and the U.S.A., 1965, Lost, 1968, Twelve Poems, 1968, Beyond All This Fiddle: Essays, 1955-1967, 1968, 69, Apparition, 1971, The Savage God: A Study of Suicide, 1971, 72, Samuel Beckett, 1973 (pub. in Eng. as Beckett 1973), Hers, 1974, Autumn to Autumn and Selected Poems, 1953-1976, 1978, Hunt, 1978, Life After Marriage: Love in an Age of Divorce, 1982 (pub. in Eng. as Life after Marriage: Scenes from Divorce 1982), The Biggest Game in Town, 1983, Offshore: A North Sea Journey, 1986, Rain Forest, 1988, Feeding the Rat: Profile of a Climber, 1989, Day of Atonement, 1991, Night: Night Life, Night Language, Sleep and Dreams, 1995, Where Did It All Go Right?, 1999, 2000, Poker: Bets, Bluffs and Bad Beats, 2001, New and Selected Poems, 2002; (screenplay) The Anarchist, 1969; author: (with others) The Penguin Book of Contemporary Verse, 1918-1960, 1962, Penguin Modern Poets 18, 1970; editor, author introduction The New Poetry, 1962, Faber Book of Modern European Poetry, 1992; adv. editor Penguin Modern European Poets series, 1966-78; contbr. to numerous Am. and Brit. periodicals. Recipient Vachel Lindsay prize for poetry, 1961; hon. fellow Corpus Christi Coll., Oxford U., 2001. Mem.: Beefsteak Club, Alpine Club, Climbers' Club. Avocations: poker, classical music, cold-water swimming. Office: Gillon Aitken Assocs 29 Fernshaw Rd London SW10 0TG England

ALVAREZ, AIDA, former federal agency administrator; b. Aguadilla, P.R. BA cum laude, Harvard U., 1971; LLD (hon.), Iona Coll., 1985. News reporter, anchor Metromedia TV, N.Y.C.; reporter N.Y. Post, N.Y.C.; mem. N.Y.C. Charter Revision Commn.; v.p. N.Y.C. Health and Hosps. Corp.; investment banker 1st Boston Corp., N.Y.C., San Francisco, 1986-93; dir. Office Fed. Housing Enterprise Oversight, Washington, 1993-97; adminstr. Small Bus. Adminstrn., 1997-2001. Former mem. bd. dirs. Nat. Hispanic Leadership Agenda, N.Y. Cmty. Trust, Nat. civic League; former chmn. bd. Mcpl. Assistance Corp./Victim Svcs. Agy., N.Y.C.; N.Y. State chmn. Gore Presdl. Campaign, 1988; nat. co-chmn. women's com. Clinton Presdl. Campaign, 1992; mem. President's Econ. Transition Team, 1992. Recipient Front Page award, award for excellence AP, 1982, Emmy nomination for reporting guerrilla activities in El Salvador. Democrat. Home: 75 E Wayne Ave Apt W404 Silver Spring MD 20901-4263

ALVAREZ, BRYAN, newsletter editor, writer; b. Seattle, June 12, 1975; s. Carlos Moya Alvarez, Valerie Gibson. Co-host, Wrestling Observer Live Radio www.eyada.com, www.sportsbyline.com, N.Y.C., 1999—; Editor, publisher Figure Four Weekly Newsletter, Woodinville, Wash., 1995—; Wrestling Columnist Penthouse Magazine, New York, NY, 2000—01, Wrestlingobserver-.com, San Jose, Calif., 1998—. Editor: (Newsletter) Figure Four Weekly, 1995; author: (Penthouse wrestling articles) Mat Max!, 2000. Gymnastics coach Cascade Elite Gymnastics, Leading Edge Gymnastics, Lynnwood, WA, 1989—2001. Avocation; Wrestling, bodybuilding, gymnastics. Office: Figure Four Weekly PO BOX 426 Woodinville WA 98072 Personal E-mail: bryan@wrestlingobserver.com. Business E-Mail: Bryan@wrestlingobserver.com.

ALVAREZ, JUAN M. baseball player; b. Coral Gables, Fla., Aug. 9, 1973; Student, St. Thomas U. Baseball player Tex. Rangers, 2002—. Office: Tex Rangers 1000 Ball Pk Arlington TX 76011

ALVAREZ, KRISTIN JONES, geographer, educator; b. Lansing, Mich., Nov. 28, 1946; d. Robert Francis Jones and Dorothy Kent Park; m. Ronald Bernard Alvarez, Feb. 12, 1966; children: Paige Alvarez Hanks, Alexa Kelly, Mary Elizabeth. BA in Internat. Rels., U. of South Fla., 1964—67; MEd in Curriculum and Instrn., Social Studies, U. of So. Miss., 1993—94, PhD in Curriculum and Instrn., Geography, 1995—98. Adolescent/Young Adult Social Studies-History Nat. Bd. for Profl. Tchg. Standards, 1999, Secondary Social Studies Fla. State Bd. Edn., 1985. Social worker Divsn. of Family Services, Sarasota, Fla., 1971—73; retail bus. owner So. Touch, Fernandina Beach, Fla., 1979—83; spl. edn. /social studies tchr. Nassau County Schools, Fernandina Beach, 1985—99; asst. professor, geography edn. Keene State Coll., NH. Cons. Fla. Geog. Alliance, Tallahassee, 1990—98, Nat. Geog. Soc., Washington, 2000—02; rev. team mem. NH. Dept. of Edn. Higher Edn. Evaluation, Concord, NH, 2000—; com. mem. N.H. Ednl. Improvement and Assessment Program Test Devel., Concord. Author: (book rev.) The Failed Promise of the Am. H.S., (jour. article) An Overview of the Nat. Bd. for Prof. Tchg. Standards: An Opportunity for N.H. Teachers, Is Jeopardy in Jeopardy?, What is a Boswash?. Steering com. Episcopal Diocese of Fla., Jacksonville, 1980—86; pres. Nassau County Big Brothers-Big Sisters, Fernandina Beach, Fla., 1976—80; bd. mem. Amelia Cmty. Theatre, Fernandina Beach, Fla., 1979—99. Mem.: Fla. Geog. Alliance (exec. bd.), Assn. of Am. Geographers, N.E.-St. Lawrence Valley Geog. Soc., N.H. Coun. for the Social Studies (president-elect 2001—03), Fla. Coun. for the Social Studies (exec. bd. 1994—99, Endowment Scholarship Award 1998), Nat. Coun. for Geog. Edn., NEA, Fla. Geog. Soc., Nat. Coun. for the Social Studies (tchr. edn./profl. devel. com. 2001—03), Alpha Delta Kappa, Delta Delta Delta (life; alumni chpt. pres. 1972—74). Episcopalian. Office: Keene State Coll 229 Main St Keene NH 03435-2001 Office Fax: 603-358-2897. E-mail: kalvarez@keene.edu.

ALVAREZ, MARIA AUXILIADORA, language educator, poet, graphics designer; b. Caracas, Miranda, Venezuela, Feb. 3, 1956; arrived in U.S., 1996, permanent resident; d. Oswaldo Alvarez Rojas and Aura Maria Martinez de Alvarez; m. Angel Fernandez, Dec. 17, 1978 (div.); children: Laura, Diana, Andres. BA in fine arts, Cristobal Rojas Fine Arts Sch., Caracas, 1980; post grad. in lit. and poetry, Ctr. of Latin Am. Studies, Caracas, 1980—82; post grad. in fgn. lang., U. Ill., Urbana, 1997, MA in lit., PhD in lit., U. Ill., Urbana, 2003. Cert. Assn. of Lit. Scholars and Critics, Modern Lang. Assn. Pres. Exemplair & Co., Caracas, 1988—96, graphic designer, 1988—96; tchr. poetry Lit. Divsn. of Nat. Culture, Caracas, 1994; instr. bus. Spanish U. Ill., Urbana, 1999—2000, instr. Spanish, 1997—2002, dir. Portuguese program, 2000—01; vis. instr. Spanish Miami U., Oxford, Ohio, 2002, asst. prof. lit., 2002—. Invited poet U. Cin., 2003; spl. guest poetry Drury U., Mo., 2003; conf. participant Brown U., RI, 2002. Poet: books Cuerpo, 1985, Hunting House, 1990, Inmovil, 1996; contbr. poetry to anthologies. Recipient Maria Pia Gratton Internat. award, U. Ill., 1999, Nat. Poetry prize, Fundarte, Caracas, 1990. Roman Catholic. Avocations: painting, drawing, dancing.

ALVAREZ, RAUL ALBERTO, internist; b. Holguin, Cuba, Aug. 7, 1956; came to U.S., 1967; s. Raul and Esperanza (Sedano) Alvarez; m. Maria Jose Sanjuan, Oct. 4, 1983; children: Raul Eduardo, Jessica Maria. MD, Cadiz Faculty Medicine, Spain, 1983. Diplomate Am. Bd. Internal Medicine. Resident in internal medicine St. Luke's Hosp., St. Louis, 1984-87; dir. emergency rm. svcs. Comprehensive Am. Care-HMO, Miami, Fla., 1987-88; primary care physician Greater Miami Med. Ctrs., North Miami Beach, Fla., 1991-94, Gratigny Cmty. Med. Ctr., North Miami Beach, 1995—, Biscayne Pk. Med. Ctr., Miami, 1998—. Active med. staff Aventura Hosp. and Med. Ctr., 1991—, North Shore Hosp., Miami, 1994—, Parkway Regional Med. Ctr., Miami, 1991—; first, second yr. med. student mentor Nova Southeastern U., U. Miami; clin. asst. prof. U. Nova Southeastern U. Fellow ACP (assoc.); mem. AMA (Physician Recognition award 1990, 93), Am. Soc. Internal Medicine. Republican. Roman Catholic. Avocations: gardening, reading. Home: 8861 NW 151st St Miami Lakes FL 33018-1319 Office: Biscayne Park Med Ctr Miami FL 33161

ALVAREZ, RENÉ LUIS, historian, educator; b. Chgo., Nov. 29, 1969; s. Gregory and Lupe Alvarez; m. Beth Mischnick Alvarez, May 23, 1992. BA, Loyola U., 1991; MA, NYU, 1993; MSEd, Northwestern U., 1998; doctoral candidate, U. Pa. Cert. tchr. Ill., Pa. H.S. tchr. Wallingford-Swarthmore Sch. Dist., Wallingford, Pa., 1998—2001. Mem. Natural Resources Def. Coun., 1991. Mem.: Orgn. Am. Historians, Am. Hist. Assn., Phi Alpha Theta. Roman Catholic. Avocation: running.

ALVAREZ, RODOLFO, sociology educator, consultant; b. San Antonio, Oct. 23, 1936; s. Ramon and Laura (Lobo) A.; m. Edna Rosemary Simons, June 25, 1960 (div. 1984); children: Anica, Amira. BA, San Francisco State U., 1961; cert. European Studies, Inst. Am. Univs., Aix-en-Provence, France, 1960; MA, U. Wash., 1964, PhD, 1966. Teaching fellow U. Wash., Seattle, 1963-64; asst. prof. Yale U., New Haven, 1966-72; assoc. prof. sociology UCLA, 1972-80, prof., 1980—, dir. Chicano Studies Rsch. Ctr., 1972-74, chair undergrad. coun., 1995-97. Vis. lectr. Wesleyan U., Middletown, Conn., 1970; founding dir. Spanish Speaking Mental Health Research Ctr., 1973-75. Author: Discrimination in Organizations: Using Social Indicators to Manage Social Change, 1979; Racism, Elitism, Professionalism: Barriers to Community Mental Health, 1976; mem. editorial bd. Social Sci. Quar., 1971-86. Pres. ACLU So. Calif., 1980, 81, sec., treas. 1999, pres. Westwood Dem. Club, Calif., 1977-78, v.p. 2003-; trustee Inst. for Am. Univs., Aix-en-Provence, France, 1968—; bd. dirs. Mex. Am. Legal Def. and Ednl. Fund, 1975-79, 88-92; mem. adv. commn. on housing 1984 Olympic Organizing Com., 1982-84; chmn. bd. dirs. Narcotics Prevention Assn., L.A., 1974-77; mem. bilingual adv. com. Children's TV Workshop, N.Y.C., 1979-82; candidate rep. Nat. Dem. Platform Com., Washington, 1976; alt. del. Nat. Dem. Conv., N.Y.C., 1976; bd. dirs. Univ. Credit Union, 1985-92, chmn. strategic plan com., 1987-92. Sgt. USMC, 1954-57. Pres. Mgmt. fellow U. Calif., 1994-95; recipient citation meritorious service for devel. Nat. Fed. Offenders Rehab. and Rsch. Program, State of Wash., 1967. Mem. Internat. Sociol. Honor Soc. (pres. 1976-79), Am. Sociol. Assn. (mem. coun. 1982-85, chairperson sect. racial and ethnic minorities 1989-90, assoc. editor Am. Sociol. Rev. 1989-91, chairperson sect. on sociol. practice 1990-91), Soc. Study of Social Problems (bd. dirs. 1982-87, pres. 1985-86), Pacific Sociol. Assn. (mem. coun. 1979-83, 87-89, v.p. 1991-93, pres. 1996-97), Architectural Rev. Bd. City of Santa Monica, Calif., 2002-, Marines Meml. Club, Village Rotary Club (pres. elect. 2003-) Office: UCLA Dept Sociology 405 Hilgard Ave Los Angeles CA 90095-1551 E-mail: alvarez@soc.ucla.edu.

ALVAREZ, SCOTT G. lawyer; b. 1955; AB, Princeton U., 1977; JD cum laude, Georgetown U., 1981. Assoc. gen. counsel Fed. Res. Sys., Washington. Office: Fed Res Sys Bd Mems Office 20th & C Sts NW Ofc Washington DC 20551-0001*

ALVAREZ, THOMAS, foundation administrator, writer, consultant; b. Ft. Wayne, Ind., Jan. 1, 1948; s. Raul and Felicitas (Vargas) A. Student, Purdue U., 1965-69. Producer, dir. McGraw-Hill Broadcasting Co. Inc./WRTV-TV, Indpls., 1973-88; pres. The Alvarez Group Inc., Indpls., 1988-98; mng. dir. Edyvean Repertory Theatre, 1998-99; pres. Alvarez Resource Group, Indpls., 1999-2001; mng. dir. Ballet Internationale, 2000-2001; exec. dir. Freetown Village Living History Mus., 2001—02, Mundo Latino, 2002, Beacon Health Found., 2002—. Freelance journalist Indpls. Star, Indpls. Monthly, Nuvo, Arts Inc., Ind. Bus. Mag., Indpls. New Times, Mundo Latino, La Guia; arts reporter Across Ind., WFYI-TV, 1991-93, mem. adv. coun.; cmty. adv. coun. Sta. WRTV, 1993-96, Sta. WFYI-FM, 1991-93; adj. faculty dept. journalism Ind. U., Indps., 1995-97. Prodr., dir. (documentaries) A Portrait of La Gente, 1975, Dave Baker: A Medley, 1976, Concord Today, 1977, Nine Leaves on a Sprig: The Story of Madame C.J. Walker, 1977, Domestic Violence, 1977, 500 Miles: Yesterday and Today, 1979, Tuckaway, 1982, Under the Influence, 1983, Rag to Bop: A Memoir of Indianapolis Jazz, 1984, A Woman's Story, 1985, Indiana State Museum: Living the Legend, 1986, Indiana Repertory Theatre: The First Fifteen Years, 1986, Solid Gold Years, 1987; prod. James Dean & Me: Nineteenth Star, 1995 (Telly award 1997, Emmy award 1997), The Rythm Makers: A Chronicle of Indiana Jazz, 1996. Bd. dirs. Phoenix Theatre, Indpls., 1982-85, First Step, Inc., 1988-90, Ind. Film Soc., 1988-90, ARC, 1989, United Way Cen. Ind., Greater Indpls. Coun. on Alcoholism, 1993; founder, chair Festival of New Can. Cinema, 1988-89; active Ind. Cares, Inc., 1991-93, Indpls. Men's Chorus, 1992-96; bd. dirs. Damien Ctr., 1996-98; adv. com. Arts. Coun. Indpls., 1996. Recipient Casper award Cmty. Svc. Coun. Indpls., 1974, CEBA award of merit Advt. and Comm. to Black Cmty. Inc., 1981, Nat. Coun. on Family Rels. award, 1984, Arti award, 1991, Minority Bus. and Profl. Achievers award, 1999; Hispanic Am. Svc. Achievement award, 2003, Hispanic Edn. Ctr. Lifetime Acheivement award (HASA), 2003; Links Celebrity Barbecue & Grille, 2003, fellow media arts Ind. Arts Commn. Avocations: travel, cinema, running, gardening, photography. Home and Office: 850 Broadway St Indianapolis IN 46202 E-mail: consultoma@aol.com.

ALVAREZ, TIRSO REYES, JR., engineer; b. San Antonio, Dec. 26, 1948; s. Tirso and Casimira (Reyes) A.; m. Melinda Marie Jaurequi, May 12, 1975 (div. Feb. 1998); children: Sonya Marie, Tirso Adrian. With electro-motive divsn. GM, Commerce, Calif., 1970-82, 92-97; electronic motors technician A/R Delco, Signal Hill, Calif., 2000—; with G.M.C./U.A.W. Nat. Employee Placement Ctr. Svs. Parts Ops., Rancho Cucamonga, Calif., 2003—. Democrat. Roman Catholic. Avocations: fishing, automotive repairs, hiking, boating. Home: 2599 Walnut Ave Unit 229 Signal Hill CA 90755-3672 Mailing: PMB

337 2201 E Willow St Ste D Signal Hill CA 90755-2148 Office: GMC/UAW Nat Employee Placement Ctr Svc Parts Ops 9150 Hermosa Ave Rancho Cucamonga CA 91730 E-mail: mbplus@ix.net.com.com., tralvarezjr@aol.com.

ALVAREZ, WILSON EDUARDO, baseball player; b. Maracaibo, Venezuela, Mar. 24, 1970; m. Daihanna Alvarez; children: Vanessa, Viviana. Baseball player White Sox, Tampa Bay Devil Rays, 1989—. Office: Tampa Bay Devil Rays Tropicana Field 1 Tropicana Dr Saint Petersburg FL 33705

ALVAREZ DE DECLARIS, MARIA CLEMENCIA, writer, educator; b. Santafe de Bogota, D.C., Dec. 14, 1944; d. Luis Maria and Stella (Botero) A. de DeC.; m. Nicholas DeClaris. AA in Tchrs. Edn. cum laude, AA in Gen. Studies cum laude, Howard C.C., 1977, AA in Tchrs. Edn. cum laude, 1978; cert. translation, Georgetown U., 1978; BA cum laude, U. Md., 1982, MA in Spanish and Latin Am. Lit., 1986; PhD in Modern Langs. and Lit., Cath. U. of Am., 1995. Adj. prof. Spanish U. Md., College Park, 1983-86, 96, Montgomery Coll., Rockville, Md., 1987-95, The Cath. U., Washington, 1989, 1992, 1996—98, The Am. U., Washington, 1997—. ESL coord. Comfenalco, Santa Fe de Bogota, 1979; course designer to teach practical Spanish, 1987, 87, 88. Mem. organizing com. Internat. Book Fair, Gaithersubrg, 1998—; mem. large treasury Magdalena Found., Alexandria, 1993; vol. translator, collaboratory Colombian Assn. of Vol. Work, 1997—; vol. broadcaster, literary segment Colombia canta para el mundo, Radio Borinquen WILC, 1996-2000. Mem. MLA, Instituto Cultural Hispano, Mid. Atlantic Coun. of Latin Am., Asociacion Internat. Colombianistas. Avocations: travel, music, ancient history, arts. Home: 8518 Beaufort Dr Fulton MD 20759-9632 Office: Am Univ 4400 Massachusetts Ave Washington DC 20016 E-mail: Alvarez@american.edu.

ALVAREZ-GALLOSO, ROBERTO C. mental health professional; b. Akron, Ohio, Mar. 5, 1962; m. Marlene de la Caridad Melendez, July 25, 1992; 1 child, Veronica Maria. Student, U. Akron, 1980-81; MD, U. Cen. del Este, Dominican Republic, 1985. Cert. profl. in utilization rev. Observer VA Med. Ctr., Miami, Fla., 1990-92, mental health assoc., 1992—; office mgr. E. G. Hernandez, MD, PA, Miami, 1998-99. Mem. Nat. Assn. for Health Care Orgns. Avocations: stamps, coins, dxing, ping pong, swimming.

ALVAREZ-GOMARIZ, HUSAYN, simulation engineer, physicist; b. San Juan del Oro, Puno, Peru, Mar. 1, 1972; arrived in US, 1996; s. Fernando Alvarez-Garcia and Josefa Gomariz-Perez; m. Erika Paula Roth, Aug. 23, 1997; children: Carlos Alvarez-Roth, Emma Alvarez-Roth. BS in Physics, Northeastern U., 1999. Physicist, rschr. Mesoscopic Lab, Northeastern U., Boston, 1996—99; simulation engr. R&D Micron Tech., Inc., Boise, Idaho, 1999—. Sci. programming cons. Micron Tech., Inc., Boise, 2000—; pres. Northeastern U. chpt. Soc. Physics Students, Boston, 1997—98. Grantee, NSF, 1998. Mem.: AAAS, Am. Phys. Soc. Achievements include research in First mesoscopic computer simulation of Atomic Force Microscope (indicating not only forces but potentials); patents pending for Optical memory cell; Recursive hierarchical ordering computer algorithm; Controlled linear hierarchical ordering computer algorithm; Computer method for applying different optical models to OPC into a single stream file; Method for detecting side lobe printing in semiconductor waffers via computer simulation; Computer algorithms for LRC verification of different semiconductor process masks after OPC; research in OPC/LRC verification methods and techniques including parallel computing and neural networks; Scientific Computer Programming Methods; Computer Simulation of AFM at mesoscopic scale. Avocations: mathematics, computer emulation, sailing, science fiction, opera. E-mail: hgomariz@micron.com.

ALVARIÑO DE LEIRA, ANGELES (ANGELES ALVARIÑO), biologist, oceanographer; b. El Ferrol, Spain, Oct. 3, 1916; came to U.S., 1958, naturalized, 1966; d. Antonio Alvariño-Grimaldos and Carmen Gonzalez Diaz-Saavedra; m. Eugenio Leira-Manso, Mar. 16, 1940; 1 child, Angeles. BS in Letters summa cum laude, U. Santiago de Compostela (Spain), 1933; M in Natural Scis., U. Madrid, 1941, Doctorate cert., 1951; DSc summa cum laude, U. complutense, 1967. Cert. biologist-oceanographer, 1952, Spanish Inst. Oceanography. Prof. biology Coll. El Ferrol, Spain, 1941-48; fishery rsch. biologist dept. Sea Fisheries Spain, 1948-52; histologist Superior Coun. Sci. Rsch., 1948-52; biologist, oceanographer Spanish Inst. Oceanography, 1950-57; biologist Scripps Inst. Oceanography-U. Calif., LaJolla, 1958-69; fishery rsch. biologist Nat. Marine Fisheries Svc. S.W. Fisheries Sci. Ctr., NOAA, U.S. Dept. Commerce, La Jolla, 1970-87; emeritus scientist Nat. Marine Fisheries Svc. S.W. Fisheries Ctr., NOAA, U.S. Dept. Commerce, La Jolla, 1987—; assoc. prof. U. Nat. Autonomous Mexico, 1976, San Diego State U., 1979-82, U. San Diego, 1982—, rsch. assoc., 1982—. Vis. prof. Poly. Tech. Mexico, 1982—, U. Parana, Brazil, 1982. Author: Spain and the First Scientific Oceanic Expedition (1789-1794) Malaspina and Bustamante with the Corvettes "Descubierta" and "Atrevida", 2000, 2d deluxe edit., 2003; contbr. over 100 articles to profl. books and jours., chpts. in books; discovered 22 new species and the indicator species for various oceanic currents, ocean dynamics, and the study of the biotic environment of fish spawning grounds, study of plankton predators and the impact in fisheries, bunch of plankton populations carried by ships into exotic oceanic areas and throughout interoceanic canals, studies on Chaetognatha and Siphonophora in all world oceans and of hydromedusae in the Atlantic, Pacific and Indian oceans; studies on the reproductive processes in Chaetognatha, others. Brit. Coun. fellow, 1953-54, Fulbright fellow, 1956-57; NSF grantee, 1961-69, U.S. Office Navy grantee, 1958-69, Calif. Coop. Oceanic Fishery Investigations grantee, 1958-69, UNESCO grantee, 1979; recipient Great Silver Medal of Galicia, Spain, presented by King Juan Carlos and Queen Sofia of Spain, 1993. Fellow Am. Inst. Fishery Rsch. Biologists, Natural History Assn.; mem. Am. Assn. Rschrs. on Marine Scis. Achievements include discovery of biotic differences in the habitat of various fishes; sci. work on the fauna represented in color plates from specimens of 200 plankton, fishes, turtles, birds. It includes a total of over 100 species collected along the South Atlantic and Pacific (up to Alaska, western Pacific Islands, the Philippines, Australia and back to Spain), during oceanic sci. expedition of 1789-1794 with specific identification, description, behavior and distribution. Home: 7535 Cabrillo Ave La Jolla CA 92037-5206 Office: Nat Marine Fisheries Svc SW Fisheries Sci Ctr PO Box 271 La Jolla CA 92038-0271

ALVARO, ANTHONY JOSEPH, music educator; b. Syracuse, NY, Dec. 21, 1975; s. Nick A. Alvaro and Sandra L. Bianco, Mark S. Bianco (Stepfather) and Donna L. Alvaro(Stepmother); m. Maureen Teresa McCoy, Aug. 19, 2000; 1 child, Laura Rose. MusB in Music Ed. (Voice), Ithaca Coll., 1997, MusM in Music Edn., 2001. Permanent Teacher in Music K-12 NY State, 2001. Choral/band dir. Bishop Grimes Jr./Sr. H.S., East Syracuse, NY, 1997—99; choral dir. Cazenovia (NY) Jr./Sr. H.S., 1999—2000, West Genesee H.S., Camillus, NY, 2000—. Music ministry Holy Family Ch., Syracuse, NY; varsity boys basketball coach Holy Family CYO (Cath. Youth Orgn.), Syracuse, NY, 1997—; dir. Onondaga County Honor Choir. Composer: (choral composition and performance) My True Love Hath My Heart, 2002, How Like a Winter, 2003. Mem.: Am. Choral Dirs. Assn., NY State Sch. Music Assn., Music Educators Nat. Conf., Onondaga County Music Educators Assn. (dist. rep. 2002), Phi Mu Alpha Sinfonia (pres. 1996—97). Republican. Roman Catholic. Avocations: computers, basketball, golf, fishing, travel. Home: 101 West Way Camillus NY 13031 Office: West Genesee High School 5201 West Genesee Street Camillus NY 13031 Personal E-mail: aalvaro@aol.com.

ALVES, ABEL A. writer; b. New Bedford, Mass., Mar. 21, 1962; m. Carol J. Blakney, July 23, 1988. PhD, U. Mass., 1990. Author: Brutality and Benevolence: Human Ethology, Culture, and the Birth of Mexico, 1996. Office: Ball State U 232 Burkhardt Bldg Muncie IN 47306-0480 Office Fax: 765-285-5612. E-mail: aalves@bsu.edu.

ALVES, KYRIN JEAN, association executive, educator; b. Milw., Sept. 5, 1949; d. Donald Eugene Bailey and Lila Anna Monday; m. David Vierra Alves, Dec. 9, 1967 (div. 1973); children: Sean David, Kyle Vierra. AS in Bus. Adminstrn., Pima C.C., 1977, AAS in Computers, 1987; BA in Philosophy and Classics, U. Ariz., 1980; MEd, Northern Ariz. U., 1997. Cert. tchr. c.c., Ariz. Project controls adminstrn. Hughes Aircraft Co., Tucson, Ariz., 1973-79; prin., co-owner Computers for People, Tucson, Ariz., 1983-84; sr. budget rsch. analyst Pima County Govt., Tucson, Ariz., 1981-82, 85-88, info. sys. mgr., 1989-94; prof. Kazakh State Acad. Arch. and Construction, Almaty, Kazakhstan, 1994. Instr. Pima C.C., 1987-96. Pres., CEO Rebuilding Together Tucson, 1994—; mem. Metropolitan Housing Commn., Tucson, 1994-96, Almaty Sister City Com., Tucson, 1993-95; bd. dirs. Vets. Transitional Housing Project. Recipient Women on The Move award YWCA, Tucson, 1995, Exemplary Mgmt. award Booz Allen Hamilton, Washington, 1999, Dynamic Duo award Compass Health Care, Tucson, 1999. Mem. So. Ariz. Home Bldrs. Assn. (remodelors coun., sec. 1995-2001), So. Ariz. Collaboration Housing Opportunity, Housing Rehab. Collaborative (co-chair 1999). Democrat. Avocations: travel, reading, learning.

ALVEY, DAVID LYNN, advertising executive, artist, curator, poet; b. Ft. Worth, Tex., Sept. 19, 1956; s. Lafayette Durham and Frances Ann (Hillburn) A.; m. Marsha Rose Smith, June 3, 1977 (div. Mar. 1991); children: David Zachary, Rodger Drew, Chad Lucas; m. Carolyn Ruth Bennett, Oct. 16, 1993; children: Nicholas Wade, Samuel Hunter, Nathan Alexander. Copywriter Weekley & Assocs., Ft. Worth, 1983-85; broadcast prodr. Weekley-Champney, Dallas, 1985-89; v.p., creative dir. Champney & Assocs., Dallas, 1989-92; founder, owner Aardvark Studios, Dallas, 1992—; owner Aardvark Studios & Gallery, Garland, Tex., 1994-98. Performer ArtNow, Washington, 1997; featured poet McKinney Ave. Contemporary, Dallas, 1997, Deep Ellum Art Fest, Dallas, 1998, 99; lectr. in field. Author: Aard Times, 1997, Aard Labor, 1998; editor: Art's Alive, 1997, Kids Talk, 1998; contbr. poetry to mags.; curator exhibns., 1995—. Mem. Tex. Poetry Project, 1997-99, Garland Visual Arts Com., 1994-98; juror PTA Reflections contest, Garland, Tex., 1995-97; co-founder Aardvark Studios Celebrity Garage Sale benefiting Leukemia Soc., 1995-99. With USN, 1978-82. Recipient citation Tex. Visual Artists Assn., 1994-96; Telly award, 1988, Gold Addy, Dallas Advt. League, 1992. Mem. Garland Artists Group (founder, facilitator), Dallas Artists Rschg. and Exhibiting. Avocations: art, photography, poetry, gardening, travel. Office: Aardvark Studios PO Box 542913 Dallas TX 75354-2913 E-mail: aard1vark@aol.com.

ALVEY, DENNIS H. government agency administrator; Commd. USAF, 1962—82, advanced through grades, intelligence officer; assoc. dir. intelligence, directorate of intelligence, surveillance and reconnaissance and dep. chief of staff, air and space ops. USAF HQ, Washington; exec. dir. Air Intelligence Agy., Lackland AFB, Tex. Office: Lackland AFB 102 Hall Blvd Ste 201 San Antonio TX 78243-7009

ALVI, KHISAL AHMED, chemist; b. Karachi, Pakistan, Mar. 15, 1958; came to U.S., 1989; s. Wisal Ahmed Alvi and Abida Begum; m. Tanvir Sultana, July 4, 1989; children: Rida, Rohail. BS with honors, U. Karachi, 1981, MS, 1983, PhD, 1987. Rsch. asst. U. Southhampton, Eng., 1988-89; rsch. fellow U. Calif., Santa Cruz, 1989-91, sr. rsch. fellow, 1991-92; sr. scientist II MDS-PANLABS, Inc., Bothell, Wash., 1993-99; sr. scientist III AMRI Rsch. Ctr., Bothell, Wash., 1999—. Presenter in field. Contbr. articles to profl. jours. Spl. predoctoral scholar U. Grant Commn. Pakistan, 1986, postdoctoral scholar U. Calif. Cancer Rsch. Coordinating Com., 1989. Mem. AAAS, Am. Chem. Soc., Am. Soc. Pharmacognosy, Soc. Indsl. Microbiology, N.Y. Acad. Scis. Office: NCE Inc 18804 N Creek Pkwy Bothell WA 98011-8012 E-mail: khisal@hotmail.com.

ALVI, SHAHID ANWAR, sociology educator; b. Shoreham by Sea, Sussex, Eng., Jan. 24, 1958; arrived in U.S., 1999; s. Zaheer and Gaiti Alvi; m. Pamela Jane Corrigan, Aug. 9, 1986; children: Erin Norah, Megan Jane. BA, U. of Sask., Saskatoon, Can., 1982, MA, 1986; PhD, Carleton U., Ottawa, Can., 1994. Asst. prof. Carleton U., Ottawa, 1997—99, U. of St. Thomas, St. Paul, 1999—2002, assoc. prof., 2002—. Dir. criminal justice program U. of St. Thomas, St. Paul, 2002—. Author: (book) Youth and the Canadian Criminal Justice System, 2000 (Criticial Criminologist of the Yr., Am. Soc. of Criminology, Critical Criminology Divsn., 2002), (book chpt.) Realistic Crime Prevention Strategies through Alternative Measures for Youth, 1987, Union Perspectives on Drug Testing in the Workplace, 1994, Shaking the cage: Teaching About Alcohol, Drugs and Mental Illness in Deviance Courses, 1999, Poverty amidst plenty: results from a study of concentrated urban poverty in a Canadian city, 2000, A Criminal Justice History of Children and Youth in Canada, 2002; co-author: Joblessness, Poverty, Gender, and Inner-City Crime: The Current State of Canadian Sociological Knowledge, 2000; co-prodr. : (video documentary) Beyond crime and punishment: Toward the restoration of community in America, 2001; co-author: (book) Contemporary Social Problems in North American Society; contbr. articles to profl. jours. Mem. Domestic Abuse Project, Mpls., 2002—03. Mem.: Am. Sociol. Assn., Acad. of Criminal Justice Scis., Am. Soc. of Criminology. Achievements include research in Socio-cultural Factors Affecting Young Adults' Smoking Behavior. Avocations: reading, travel, coaching and playing soccer. Home: 1409 Mackubin St Saint Paul MN 55117 Office: U of St Thomas 2115 Summit Ave Saint Paul MN 55105 Personal E-mail: salvi@stthomas.edu.

ALVIANI, HENRY ANTHONY, music educator, choral conductor, voice instructor, baritone vocalist, composer; b. Burbank, Calif., June 15, 1949; s. Henry Francis and Clara Ann Alviani; m. Cynthia Dale Alviani, Nov. 23, 1985; children: Carl Anthony, Rebekah Ann. D in Musical Arts, Ariz. State U., 1993. Dir. choral and vocal studies Northland Coll., Ashland, Wis., 1997—2003, Clarion U. of Pa., 2003—. Composer: (choral music) Come Let Us Sing; O Come Let Us Worship; Let the Heavens Rejoice; Sweet William's Ghost; Chippewa Dream Song Medley; Four Chippewa Love Songs; Song of the Game of Silence. Pres., v.p., treas. Chequamegon Theatre Assn., Ashland, Wis., 1998—2002; mem. bd. elders, trustee Zion Luth. Ch., Ashland, 1998—2003. Master: Wis. Sch. Music Assn. (assoc.; master adjudicator 2001); mem.: Nat. Assn. Tchrs. Singing, Am. Choral Dirs. Assn. (assoc.). Home: 72 Campbell Ave Clarion PA 16214

ALVILLAR-SPEAKE, THERESA, federal agency administrator; Grad., Calif. State U.; MBA, Golden Gate U. Asst. dir. program devel. minority bus. devel. agy. Dept. Commerce, 1991—93; mgr. small bus. and disabled vet. bus. enterprise programs State Calif. Dept. Transp.; exec. dir. Calif. Employment Devel. Dept., 1994—97, asst. dir. bus. rels., 1997—2000; dir. minority econ. impact Dept. Energy, Washington, 2001—. Founder NEDA San Joaquin Valley. Office: Dept Energy Econ Impact and Diversity 1000 Independence Ave SW Washington DC 20585-0001

ALVINE, ROBERT, industrialist, entrepreneur; b. Newark, Aug. 25, 1938; s. James C. and Marie Alvine; m. Diane C. Marzulli, May 6, 1961 (div. 1995); children: Robert James, Laurie Anne. BA, Rutgers U., 1960; postgrad., Syracuse U., 1968-69; grad. PMD, Harvard Bus. Sch., 1972; DHL (hon.), U. New Haven, 2000. With Celanese Corp., 1960-77; bus. mgr. nylon products Celanese Plastics Co., Newark, 1967-69, bus. mgr. polyolefin products, 1969-72; sr. dir. mktg. and ops. Celanese Piping Systems and Fabricated Products Co., Hilliard, Ohio, 1972-75; v.p., gen. mgr. comml. Celanese Polymer Spltys. Co., Louisville, 1975-77; with Uniroyal Inc., 1977—87; pres. Uniroyal Development and Internat., 1977—82; CEO, COO Uniroyal Engineered Products & Svcs., Worldwide, 1982-87; founder, chmn., CEO I-Ten Mgmt. Corp., Woodbridge, Conn., 1987—; founder, chmn., CEO, I-Ten Capital Corp., Woodbridge, 1987, Aim Capital Group, Woodbridge, 1987—; chmn., CEO, prin. shareholder Charter Power Sys. (now C&D Techs. Inc.), Blue Bell, Pa., 1988—95; entrepreneur, prin., sr. oper. bus. leader Charterhouse Group Internat., Inc., N.Y.C., 1988—96; vice-chmn., CEO, major shareholder AP Parts Mfg. Co., Toledo, 1989 93; prin., dir. Internat. Automobile Products Holdings Corp., N.Y.C., 1990—96; prin. owner, chmn. Premier Subaru, Bradford, Conn., 2001—. Prin. Uniroyal Holdings, Waterbury, Conn., 1985—; trustee Uniroyal Liquidating Trust, 1985—; sr. oper. ptnr., mem. investment com. Desai Capital Pvt. Equity Investors, 1999—; chmn. compensation com., strategic com., exec. com., chmn. spl. com., chmn. pension com., bd. EDO Corp., 1995—; trustee Jackson Labs., Bar Harbor, Maine, 2000—, mem. exec. com. capital campaign, chmn. rsch. resources com., mem. devel. com., 1998—, bd. dirs. Jackson Labs, E.D.O. Corp., N.Y.; adv. bd. Polaris Fund, N.Y.C., 1996-99; bd. govs. U. New Haven, 1998, chmn. audit com., chmn. exec. com., chmn. commn. on future of U. New Haven, 1998-2000, bd. govs., 2000—, chmn. bd. trustees, 2000—, chmn. bd. govs., chmn. exec. com., 2000—; chmn. Henry Lee Inst. Forensic Scis., 1998—; sr. oper. ptnr., investment com. Desai Capital Mgmt. Pvt. Equity Investors Fund, 2000—. Mem. Rep. Presdl. Task Force, Pres.'s Roundtable, Citizens Against Govt. Waste, Presdl. Legion of Merit; state chmn. Congrl. Bus. Adv. Coun., 2002, Conn. chmn., 2002; bd. dirs., trustee Nat. Theater of the Deaf, Chester, Conn., 1994—, chmn. bd. dirs., 1995-98, hon. chmn., 1999-2002; bd. dirs. Wildlife Conservation Soc., N.Y., 1994-2002; trustee Long Wharf Theatre, New Haven, exec. fin. com., chmn. bus. devel. com., strategy com.; adv. bd. Arts Scis. Coun., Rutgers U., N.J.; mem. Navy War Coll. Found.; mem. sch. bus. adv. bd. U. New Haven; mem. Assn. Governing Bds. of Univs. and Colls. With U.S. Army, 1962-68. Recipient citations, awards and recognitions including Disting. Leadership award proclaimed by Congl. Bus. Adv. Coun., 2002, Man of Yr. for Outstanding Accomplishments, 1991, Disting. Bus. Achievement and Svcs. to the Nations award, 1984, Presdl. Legion Merit, Honor grad. Southeastern Signal Sch., 1962, Proclamation for Supreme Achievement Within the Internat. Cmty., 1986; named Ky. Col., Gov. Ky., 1976. Mem. Nat. Assn. Corp. Dirs., Pres.'s Assn., Nat. Adv. Coun., Assn. Governing Bds. of Univs. and Colls., Am. Inst. Mgmt., Internat. Bus. Coun., World Affairs Coun.-Conn., Nat. Planning Inst., Nat. Assn. Corp. Growth, Rubber Mfrs. Assn., Battery Coun. Internat., Newcomen Soc. Am. (Conn. com.), Soc. Plastics Industry (sr., past dir., Industry Legend Honor for plastic milk, juice and water bottles 1971), Soc. Plastics Engrs. (past dir.), Mfg. Chemists Assn., Societe de Chemie Industriale, Nat. Paint and Coatings Assn., Coun. of Ams., Nat. Maritime Hist. Soc., Nat. Trust for Hist. Preservation, New Haven Colony Hist. Soc., Columbus House, Rutgers Alumni Assn., U. New haven Legacy Soc., Harvard Bus. Sch. Alumni Assn., Harvard Bus. Sch. Club Greater N.Y. (honor roll mem.), So. Conn., Ellis Island Found. (charter), U.S. Navy Meml. Found. (charter), U.S. Senatorial Inner Circle, WWII Meml. Found. (charter, founder Nat. Law Enforcement Officers Meml.), Oaklane Country Club, Renaissance Club, Am. Legion, Commanders Club, Chi Phi. Mem. Ch. of Christ. Home: 55 N Racebrook Rd Woodbridge CT 06525-1407 Fax: 203-389-5153. E-mail: ialv@aol.com.

ALWANI, AHMED J. dean, consultant; b. Dec. 17, 1964; arrived in U.S., 1984; s. Taha Jabir and Saadia Al Alwani; m. Ilham Ahmad Totonji, June 19, 1990. BSME, King Saud U., Saudi Arabia, 1987; M in Engring. Adminstrn., George Washington U., 1990; PhD in Human Resources Develop., Va. Tech., 2003. Plant supt. Piedmont Poultry, Lumber Bridge, NC, 1990—95, Mountaire Corp., Lumber Bridge, 1995—97; exec. dean GSISS, Leesburg, Va., 1998—. Bd. trustees Heritage Edn. Trust, Va., 2002—, GSISS, 2002—. Tchrs. evaluation and selection com. Adam Ctr., Herndon, Va., 2002—03; edn. and workforce develop. com. Loudoun County Econ. Develop. Commn., Va., 2000—. Mem.: Acad. Human Resource Develop., Assn. Expl. Edn., Assn. Supervision and Curriculum Develop., Phi Kappa Phi. Office: GSISS 750A Miller Dr Leesburg VA 20175 E-mail: aalwani@siss.edu.

ALWARD, RUTH ROSENDALL, nursing consultant; d. Henry Rosendall and Freda Jonkman; m. Samuel Alward, Jan. 17, 1976. RN, Butterworth Hosp. Sch. Nursing, Grand Rapids, Mich.; BSN summa cum laude, Hunter Coll./CUNY, N.Y., 1980; MA Tchrs. Coll., Columbia U., 1982, EdM, 1983, EdD, 1986. Sr. clin. nurse Wadsworth VA Hosp., L.A., 1966-68; exec. dir. nursing Care Corp, Grand Rapids, Mich., 1968-71; nursing cons. Humana Inc., Louisville, 1972-76; asst. prof., dir. nursing adminstrn. grad. prog. Hunter Coll., CUNY, N.Y.C., 1986-90; pres. Nurse Exec. Assocs., Inc., Washington, 1990—; series editor Delmar Pubs. Inc., Albany, 1993-96. Co-author: The Nurse's Shift Work Handbook, 1993, The Nurse's Guide to Marketing, 1991; contbr. articles to profl. jours.; mem. editorial adv. bd. Jour. of Nursing Adminstrn. Bd. dirs., past pres. James Lenox House Assn.; bd. dirs. IONA Sr. Svcs. Mem. Va Nurses Assn. (mem. fin. com.), Nat. League Nursing (treas. D.C. chpt.), Am. Orgn. Nurse Execs., Sigma Theta Tau. Home and Office: 2011 N St NW Washington DC 20036-2301

ALWOOD, EDWARD MCQUEEN, writer, journalist, media specialist; b. Macon, Ga., Sept. 12, 1949; s. William Edward A. and Mary Fisher. BA in Journalism and Polit. Sci., U of NC, 1972; MA in Pub. Comm., Am U, 1994; PhD, U of NC, 2000. Corr. WHSV-TV, Harrisonburg, Va., 1973-75, WWBT-TV, Richmond, 1975-77, WTTG-TV, Washington, 1977-81, Fin. News Network, NYC, 1981-82, WFTV-TV, Orlando, Fla., 1982-85, Cable News Network, Washington, 1985-87; mgr. pub. rels. Am. Bankers Assn., Washington, 1987-95; sr. media rels. specialist office of the comptr. of the currency U.S. Dept. Treasury, Washington, 1995-97; asst. prof. broadcast journalism Temple U., 2000—02; assoc. prof. journalism Quinnipiac U., Hamden, Conn., 2002—. Adj. prof. comm. No. Va. C.C., Alexandria. Author: Straight News: Gays, Lesbians and the News Media, 1996. Mem. nat. rsch. adv. bd. Gay and Lesbian Alliance Against Defamation. Fellow econs. Carnegie Mellon U., 1980; recipient Janus award Mortgage Bankers Assn. Am., 1981, Outstanding Achievement award Gay and Lesbian Alliance Against Defamation, 1997. Mem. Am. Journalism History Assn., Speech Comm. Assn., Nat. Lesbian and Gay Journalists Assn. (founding mem.), Assn. for Edn. in Journalism and Mass. Comm. (Nafaiger White Dissertation award 2001). Home: 96 Livingston St # 7 New Haven CT 06511

ALWORTH, CHARLES WESLEY, lawyer, engineer; b. Buenos Aires, Aug. 23, 1943; s. Cecil Dwight and Kathleen Mary (Whitaker) A.; m. Sally Ann Wells, Dec. 21, 1967 (div. Nov. 1981); m. Madeline E. Wilson, Feb. 14, 1983; children: Cecil Dwight II, Barbara Diane. BSEE, U. Okla., 1965, M in Elec. Engring., 1967, PhD, 1969; JD, U. Tulsa, 1992. Bar: U.S. Patent Bar Office 1989, Tex. 1993, U.S. Dist. Ct. (ea. dist.) Tex. 1993, U.S. Dist. Ct. (no. dist.) Tex. 1997, U.S. Ct. Appeals (fed. cir.) 2001, U.S. Supreme Ct. 2003; registered profl. engr., La., Tex. Tchg. asst. elec. engring. U. Okla., Norman, 1965, grad. asst. elec. engring., 1965-67, spl. instr. elec. engring., 1967-68; asst. prof. elec. engring. Tex. A&M U., College Station, Tex., 1968-74; chief, prin. cons. Conoco, Inc., Ponca City, Okla., 1974-90; rsch. assoc. profl. engr. U. Tulsa, Okla., 1990—; chief engr. Alworth Cons., Tyler, Tex., 1990—; of counsel Sefrna & Assocs., Tyler, 1993-95; prin. Charles W. Alworth Engr. & Atty. at Law; assoc. prof. and head elec. engring. U. Tex., Tyler, 1997-98. Patentee in field; contbr. articles to profl. jours. Mem. Phi Delta Phi, Tau Beta Pi, Eta Kappa Nu, Sigma Xi. Episcopalian. Avocations: aviation, woodworking, gardening. Home: 505 Cumberland Rd Tyler TX 75703-9325

ALYKOVA, VALENTINA, musician, music educator; b. Moscow, June 22, 1949; arrived in U.S., 1991; d. Trifon Alykov and Zoya Alykova; m. Vladimir Binevitch, Jan. 19, 1991. M in Musical Arts, Moscow Conservatory, 1973; postgrad., Gnessin Musical Pedagogical Inst., Moscow, 1980. Violin instr. Music Sch. for Gifted Children, Moscow, 1973—77; asst. prof. Gnessin Musical Pedagogical Inst., Moscow, 1978—82; violinist Moscow String Quartet, 1973—96; artist-in-residence Lamont Sch. Music, Denver U., 1991—96; violin instr. Forte Acad. Music, Littleton, Colo., 1997—. Recipient Second prize, Internat. Quartet Competition, Budapest, Hungry, 1978, Grand Prix and First prize, Internat. Quartet Competition, Evian, France, 1979; grantee, Colo. Coun. on the Arts, Denver, 1999, 2000. Mem.: Music Tchrs. Nat. Assn. Russian Orthodox. Avocations: reading, travel, mahjong. Home: 14299 E Arizona Ave Aurora CO 80012 Office: Forte Acad Music Ste 15 10143 W Chatfield Ave Littleton CO 80127-4245

ALZAMORA, CARLOS, ambassador; b. Lima, Peru, May 20, 1926; s. Carlos and Pia (Traverso) Alzamora; m. Rosario Alvarado Alzamora; m. Juana Leguia (div. 1979). JD, Cath U., Lima, 1951; postgrad., Nat. U., Asuncion, Paragua. With Diplomatic Svc., Peru, 1943—2002; permanent rep. for Peru UN, Geneva, 1972—75; sec.-gen. L.Am. Econ. System, Caracas, Venezuela, 1979—83; permanent rep. of Peru UN, N.Y.C., 1985—89; amb. to U.S. Country of Peru, Washington, 2001; amb.-at-large Washington, 2001—02. Alt. dir. World Bank, Washington, 1971. Author: The Surrender of Latin America, 1998, The Agony of the Visionary, 2000. Recipient numerous decorations, Argentina, Boliva, Brazil, Colombia, Brazil, Ecuador, Spain, others. Home: 455 E 51st St New York NY 10022

AMABILE, JOHN LOUIS, lawyer; b. N.Y.C., Oct. 13, 1934; s. John A. and Rose (Singer) A.; m. Christina M. Leary, Nov. 23, 1963; children: Tracy Ann, John Christopher. BS cum laude, Coll. Holy Cross, 1956; LLB, St. John's Sch. Law, 1959. Bar: N.Y. 1959, U.S. Dist. Ct. (so. and ea. dists.) N.Y. 1961, U.S. Supreme Ct. 1964, U.S. Ct. Claims 1964, U.S. Ct. Appeals (2d cir.) 1970, U.S. Tax Ct. 1984, U.S. Ct. Appeals (9th cir.) 1984. Assoc. Law Office of Allen Taylor, N.Y.C., 1959-62; assoc. Schwartz & Frohlich, N.Y.C., 1963-69, ptnr., 1969, Summit, Solomon & Feldesman (and predecessor firms), N.Y.C., 1971-93, Putney, Twombly Hall & Hirson, N.Y.C., 1993-2000, of counsel, 2001—. Faculty mem. ann. seminar Practising Law Inst., 1987-91; mediator so. dist. U.S. Dist. Ct. N.Y., comml. divsn. Supreme Ct., N.Y.; arbitrator ea. dist. U.S. Dist. Ct., Bklyn.; panel chair appellate divsn. Disciplinary Com., 1980-85, 87-92; lectr. in field. Author: Responses to Complaints: Commercial Litigation in New York State Courts, 1995, Warranties: Business and Commercial Litigation in Federal Courts, 1998, The Record of the Association of the Bar of the City of New York, vol. 54, no. 5; editor St. John Law Rev. 1958-59.

Regional commr. Am. Youth Soccer Orgn., Chappaqua, N.Y., 1975-84; mem. New Castle Recreation and Parks Commn., 1984-90, chairperson, 1987-89, dir. Aiken County Coun. on Aging, 2003—. Mem. ABA, N.Y. State Bar Assn., Assn. Bar City N.Y. (mem. com. on state legis. 1971-74, chair 1975-78, com. on grievances 1979-80, com. on women in cts. 1988-94, com. on judiciary 1989-92, interim mem. 1992, 93, 94, 96, 97, 98, 99, 2000, chair com. on gender bias in fed. cts. 1991-93, coun. judicial adminstrn. 1996-2001, com. on symposium 1997-2000, chair 1998-2000), Fed. Bar Coun., Practising Law Inst. (chair winning strategies for depositions in corp. litigation 1991-92, co-chair seminars on art of taking and defending depositions in corp. litigation 1982-85). Democrat. Roman Catholic. Home: Woodside Plantation 308 Willow Lake Ct Aiken SC 29803

AMACHER, RICHARD EARL, literature educator; b. Ridgway, Pa., Dec. 13, 1917; s. Albert and Emma (Luchs) A.; m. Cordelia Anne Ward, Aug. 26, 1953; 1 child, Alice Marie. AB, Ohio U., 1939; postgrad., U. Chgo., 1939-42; PhD, U. Pitts., 1947. Instr. English Yale U., New Haven, 1944-45; instr. Rutgers U., New Brunswick, N.J., 1945-47, asst. prof., 1947-53, lectr., 1953-54; chmn. English dept. Henderson State Tchrs. Coll., Arkadelphia, Ark., 1954-57; asso. prof. English Auburn (Ala.) U., 1957-65, prof., 1965-78, Hargis prof. Am. Lit., 1978-84, prof. emeritus, 1984—. Fulbright prof., Würzburg, Fed. Republic Germany, 1961-62, Konstanz, W. Ger., 1969-70 Author: Franklin's Wit and Folly, 1953, Practical Criticism, 1956, Benjamin Franklin, 1962, Edward Albee, 1969, rev. edit., 1982, (with Margaret Rule) Edward Albee at Home and Abroad, 1973, (with Victor Lange) New Perspectives in German Literary Criticism, 1979, American Political Writers, 1588-1800, 1979; editor: (with G. Polhemus) J.G. Baldwin's The Flush Times of California, 1966. Chmn. Auburn Chamber Music Soc., 1980-82, 85-86, 88-89; elder Presbyterian Ch. Am. Coun. Learned Socs. grantee, 1972 Mem. Am. Studies Assn. (pres. southeastern sec. 1977-79), Société Historique d'Auteuil et de Passy, Nat. Soc. Lit. and Arts. Democrat. Home: 515 Auburn Dr Auburn AL 36830-5547

AMADA, GERALD, psychotherapist; b. Newark, Aug. 13, 1938; s. Samuel and Rose Amada; m. Marcia Rae Hirshberg, Aug. 9, 1962; children: Robin, Naomi Laurie Eric. BA, Rutgers U., Newark, 1960; MSW, Rutgers U., 1962; PhD, Wright Inst., Berkeley, Calif., 1977. Psychotherapist Mercer County Mental Health Clinic, Trenton, NJ, 1962—64, Dept. Mental Hygiene, Modesto, Calif., 1964—66, Homewood Terrace, San Francisco, 1966—68; staff devel. supr. Solano County Dept. Social Svcs., Vallejo, Calif., 1968—70; dir. Mental Health program City Coll. of San Francisco, 1970—2000; psychotherapist Mill Valley, Calif., 1980—. Cons. KPIX-TV, San Francisco, 1980—82, Mass. Mutual Life Ins. Co., San Francisco, 1980—83. Author (and book rev. editor): (jour.) Jour. of Coll. Student Psychotherapy, 1988—; book reviewer Am. Jour. Psychotherapy, 1983—; author: 8 books; contbr. articles. Commr. Marin County Human Rights Commn.; facilitator Alzheimer's Orgn., San Rafael, Calif., 1998—. Recipient Award of Excellence, Nat. Assn. of Vocat. Edn. Spl. Needs Pers., 1984. Mem.: NASW, Freedom for Individual Rights in Edn. Avocations: tennis, writing, reading, travel, classical music. Mailing: 185 Mount Lassen Dr San Rafael CA 94903 Office: 333 Miller Ave Ste 8 Mill Valley CA 94941

AMADEO, NATIAL SALVATORE, lawyer; b. Jersey City, Oct. 2, 1955; s. Nataile Michael and Gussie (Calato) A.; m. Jane Marie Drafke, Aug. 16, 1980; children:— Nataile, Anthony, Amalia, Andrew. A.B., U. Notre Dame, 1977; J.D., Duke U., 1980. Bar: N.J. 1980, Ill. 1981. Assoc. Arthur F. Lobbe, Jersey City, 1981-82; ptnr. Amadeo & Miller, Jersey City, 1982—. Officer bd. dirs. Hudson unit Assn. Retarded Citizens, Jersey City, 1983—, pres., 1985; bd. dirs. N.J. Youth Correctional Facility, 1983—. Mem. Hudson C. of C., Moose. Republican. Office: Amadeo & Miller 1767 John F Kennedy Blvd Jersey City NJ 07305-2023

AMADIO, BARI ANN, metal fabrication executive, former nurse; b. Phila., Mar. 26, 1949; d. Fred Deutscher and Celena (Lusky) Garber; m. Peter Colby Amadio, June 24, 1973; children: P. Grant, Jamie Blair. BA in Psychology, U. Miami, 1970; diploma in Nursing, Thomas Jefferson U., 1973, Johnston-Willis Sch. Nursing, 1974; BS in Nursing, Northeastern U., 1977; MS in Nursing, Boston U., 1978; JD, Quinnipiac Sch. Law, 1983. Faculty Johnston-Willis Sch. Nursing, Richmond, Va., 1974-75; staff, charge nurse Mass. Gen. Hosp., Boston, 1975-78; faculty New Eng. Deaconess, Boston, 1978-80, Lankenau Hosp. Sch. of Nursing, Phila., 1980-81; pres. Original Metals, Inc., Phila., 1985—, also bd. dirs. Owner Silver Carousel Antiques, Rochester, Minn. Treas. Women's Assn. Minn. Orch., Rochester, 1986-87, pres., 1987-89, life advisor, 1989—, editor newsnotes, 1985-87; mayor's coms. All Am. City Award Com., Rochester, 1984-88; bd. dirs. Rochester Civic League, 1988-94, pres.-elect, 1990-91, pres., 1991-92; pres. Rochester Friends of Mpls. Inst. Arts, 1989-90, Folwell PTA, 1990-91; state liaison Gateway, 1990-91; bd. dirs. Rochester Civic Theatre, 1993-99, v.p., 1994-95, pres., 1995-96; Minn. site coord. Pew Charitable Trust's Project 540, 2002—. Recipient Joe Saidy award Rochester Civic Theatre, 1999. Mem.: NAFE, Nat. Assn. Food Equipment Mfrs., Zumbro Valley Med. Soc. Aux. (Rochester, fin. chmn. 1986—90, treas. 1988—90), Am. Soc. Law and Medicine, Rotary Club Rochester, Friends of Mayowood, Order of the Eastern Star (trustee), Sigma Theta Tau, Phi Alpha Delta. Avocations: fencing, painting, writing poetry, piano, squash.

AMADO, HONEY KESSLER, lawyer; b. Bklyn., July 20, 1949; d. Bernard and Mildred Kessler; m. Ralph Albert Amado, Oct. 24, 1976; children: Jessica Reina, Micah Solomon, Gabrielle Beth. BA in Polit. Sci., Calif. State Coll., Long Beach, 1971; JD, Western State U., Fullerton, Calif., 1976. Bar: Calif. 1977, U.S. Dist. Ct. (ctrl. dist.) Calif. 1981, U.S. Ct. Appeals (9th cir.) 1981, U.S. Supreme Ct. 1994. Assoc. Law Offices of Jack M. Lasky, Beverly Hills, Calif., 1977-78; pvt. practice Beverly Hills, Calif., 1978—. Mem. family law exec. com. Calif. State Bar, 1987-91; lectr. in field. Contbr. articles to profl. jours.; mem. editl. bd. L.A. Lawyer mag., 1996—, articles coord., 1999-2000, chair, 2000-01. Mem. Com. Concerned Lawyers for Soviet Jewry, 1979-90; nat. v.p. Jewish Nat. Fund, 1995-97, 2002—; bd. dirs. Jewish Nat. Fund L.A., 1990-98, 2002—, Women's Alliance Israel; mem. pres.'s coun. Am. Jewish Com., 2002—; sec. L.A. region, bd. dirs., 1991-94, Am. Jewish Congress, Jewish Feminist Ctr., 1992-99, co-chair steering com., 1994-96; mem. Commn. on Soviet Jewry of Jewish Fedn. Coun. Greater L.A., 1977-83, chmn., 1979-81, commn. on edn., 1982-83, cmty. rels. com., 1979-83; mem. pres.'s coun. Am. Jewish Com., L.A., 2003—, bd. dirs., 2002—; co-chair European affairs subcom. Internat. Rels. Com. L.A. Region, 2003—. Mem. Calif. Women Lawyers (bd. govs. 1988-90, 1st v.p. 1989-90, jud. evaluations co-chair 1988-90), San Fernando Valley Bar Assn. (family law mediators and arbitrators planel 1983-94, judge pro-tem panel 1987-94), Beverly Hills Bar Assn. (family law mediators panel 1985-94), L.A. County Bar Assn. (family law sect., appellate cts. com. 1987—, chmn. subcom. to examine reorgn. Calif. Supreme Ct. 1990-94, judge pro tem panel 1985-95, appellate jud. evaluations com. 1989—, dist. 2 settlement program 1996—), Calif. State Bar, Calif. Ct. Appeal. Democrat. Jewish. Office: 261 S Wetherly Dr Beverly Hills CA 90211-2515

AMALDOSS, WILFRED, marketing educator; b. Madras, India, Nov. 15, 1961; s. Aea Doss; m. Nirmala Amaldoss, May 3, 1963; children: Bernard, Nicole. PhD, U. Pa., 1998. Instr. Wharton Sch. Bus. U. Pa., Phila., 1998; asst. prof. Purdue U., West Lafayette, Ind., 1998—2002, Duke U., NC, 2002—. Author: Collaborating to Compete, 2000, David Vs. Goliath, 2002. Office: Duke U A337 Fugua Bus Sch Durham NC 27708

AMALSAD, MEHER DADABHOY, writer, speaker, seminar leader; b. Karachi, Pakistan, Sept. 12, 1958; s. Dadabhoy and Nancy A.; m. Katayoon Amalsad; 1 child, Anahita Meher. BS in Engring., Nadirshaw Edulgee Dinshaw Engring. Univ., Karachi, Pakistan, 1982; MS in Engring., Northrop Univ., 1987. Program mgr. Hughes Aircraft Co., Rancho Santa, Calif., 1988-95; dist. mgr. ICM, Garden Grove, Calif., 1995-97; pres., CEO Starmasters, Garden Grove, Calif., 1997—. Mem. acad. svcs. com. The Pegasus Sch., Huntington Beach, Calif., 1991-98. Author: Gifts That Lift, Shift and Uplift, 1996, Bread for the Head, 1997, In Search of Your Quest, How to Be Your Best, 1995, Love Grows and Shows Only When it Flows, 1995; co-author: (with Shahriar Shahriari) SOUL (Success Out-of Understanding Love), 1998, Bread for the Parents' Head, 1997; inventor. Chairperson First World Zoroastrian Youth Congress, 1993, First North Am. Zoroastrian Youth Congress, 1987, Helping Hands Com. of Fedn. of Zoroastrian Assns. N.Am., 1987-93; pres. Hughes Toastmasters, 1995. Mem. Profl. Speakers Network, Relationship Building Network (sponsor), Leads Club. Avocations: music, writing, dancing, speaking, inventing, creative cooking. Home: 15842 Villanova Cir Westminster CA 92683-7616

AMAN, ALFRED CHARLES, JR., law educator; b. Rochester, N.Y., July 7, 1945; s. Alfred Charles Sr. and Jeannette Mary (Czebatul) Aman; m. Carol Jane Greenhouse, Sept. 23, 1976. AB, U. Rochester, 1967; JD, U. Chgo., 1970. Bar: (D.C.) 1971, Ga. 1972, N.Y. 1980. Law clk. U.S. Ct. Appeals, Atlanta, 1970—72; assoc. Sutherland, Asbill & Brennan, Atlanta, 1972—75, Washington, 1975—77; assoc. prof. Sch. Law, Cornell U., Ithaca, NY, 1977—82, prof. law, 1983—91, exec. dir. Internat. Legal Studies Program, 1988—90; dean Sch. Law, Ind. U., Bloomington, 1991—2002, prof. law, 1991—, Roscoe C. O'Byrne chair in law, 1999—, disting. Fulbright chair in comparative constitutional law, 1998; vis. prof. law U. Paris II, 1998; vis. fellow law and pub. affairs program Princeton U., 2002—03. Cons. U.S. Adminstrv. Conf., Washington, 1978—80, Washington, 1986—; trustee U. Rochester, 1980—; vis. fellow Wolfson Coll., Cambridge U., 1983—84, 1990—91. Author: Energy and Natural Resources, 1983, Administrative Law in a Global Era, 1992, Administrative Law Treatise, 1992, 2d edit., 2001. Chmn. Ithaca Bd. Zoning Appeals, 1980—82. Mem.: ABA, N.Y. State Bar Assn., Ga. Bar Assn., D.C. Bar Assn., Am. Assn. Law Schs., Phi Beta Kappa. Avocations: music, jazz drumming, piano, composition and arranging. Office: Ind U Sch Law 211 S Indiana Ave Bloomington IN 47405-7001

AMAN, GEORGE MATTHIAS, III, lawyer; b. Wayne, Pa., Mar. 2, 1930; s. George Matthias and Emily (Kalbach) A.; m. Ellen McMillan, June 20, 1959; children: James E., Catherine E., Peter T. AB, Princeton U., 1952; LL.B., Harvard U., 1957. Bar: Pa. 1958. Assoc. Townsend Elliot & Munson, Phila., 1960-65; ptnr. Morgan Lewis & Bockius, Phila., 1965-93; of counsel High, Swartz, Roberts & Seidel, Norristown, Pa., 1993—. Commr. Radnor Twp., Pa., 1976-80, 86-92, planning commr., 1981-86; pres. bd. trustees Wayne Presbyn. Ch., Pa., 1981-84. Served to 1st lt. U.S. Army, 1952-54. Mem. ABA, Pa. Mcpl. Authorities Assn., Phila. Regional Mcpl. Fin. Officers Assn. (dir. 1983-87). Clubs: Merion Cricket (Haverford, Pa.); Princeton (Phila.) (dir 1977-79, treas. 1985-86). Republican. Home: 246 Upland Way Wayne PA 19087-4859 Office: High Swartz Roberts Seidel 40 E Airy St Norristown PA 19401-4803 E-mail: george.aman@verizon.net gaman@highswartz.com.

AMAN, MOHAMMED MOHAMMED, dean, library and information science educator; b. Alexandria, Egypt, Jan. 3, 1940; came to U.S., 1963, naturalized, 1975; s. Mohammed Aman and Fathia Ali (al-Maghrabi) Mohammed; m. Mary Jo Parker, Sept. 15, 1972; 1 son, David. BA, Cairo U., 1961; MS, Columbia U., 1965; PhD, U. Pitts., 1968. Librarian Egyptian Nat. Libr., 1961-63, Duquesne U., Pitts., 1966-68; asst. prof. libr. sci. Pratt Inst., N.Y.C., 1968-69; from asst. prof. to assoc. prof. St. John's U., Jamaica, N.Y., 1969-73, prof., dir. divsn. libr. and info. sci., 1973-76; prof. libr. sci., dean Palmer Grad. Libr. Sch., C.W. Post Ctr., L.I. U., 1976-79; prof., dean, interim dean Sch. Edn. U. Wis., Milw., 2000—, dean Sch. Info. Studies, 1979—. Cons. UNESCO, U.S., AID and UNIDO; USIA acad. specialist, Germany, 1989; Fulbright lectr. Cairo U., 1990-91; USIA-sponsored lectr. Mohamed V. Univ., Rabat, Morocco, 1997. Author: Librarianship and the Third World, 1976, Cataloging and Classifications of Non-Western Library Material: Issues, Trends and Practices, 1980, Arab Serials and Periodicals: A Subject Bibliography, 1979, Online Access to Databases, 1983, On Developing Computer-Based Library Systems (Arabic), 1984, Information Services (Arabic), 1985, Trends in Urban Library Management, 1989, The Bibliotheca Alexandrina: A Link in the Chain of Cultural Continuity, 1991, Information Technology Use in Libraries (Arabic), 1998, Internet Use in Libraries, 2000, The Gulf War in World Literature, 2002; editor: Digest of Middle East Studies. Chmn. Black Faculty Coun., U. Wis., Milw.; mktg. com. Milw. Art Mus.; bd. dirs. Clara Mohammed Sch. Recipient Outstanding Achievement award Egyptian Libr. Assn., 1997. Mem. NAACP, ALA (chmn. internat. rels. com. 1984-86, standing com. on libr. edn., internat. subcom. 1990-91, chmn. 1991-93, internat. rels. Round Table 1993-94, John Ames Humphry/OCLC Outstanding Contbn. award 1989, Leadership award black caucus 1994, Excellence award black caucus 1995), Assn. Libr. and Sci. (Svc. award 1988), Am. Soc. for Info. Sci. (chmn. spl. interest group in internat. info. issues, internat. rels. com.), Egyptian Libr. Assn. (life, Outstanding Achievement award 1997), Arab/Jewish Dialogue, Egyptian-Am. Scholars Assn., Assn. for Libr. and Info. Sci. Edn. (chmn. internat. rels. com. 1983-85), Wis. Libr. Assn. (Svc. award 1992, P.N. Kaula Internat. award and medal 1996, Wis. Libr. of Yr. 1998), Libr. Svcs. and Constrn. Act. (adv. com. 1986-89), Internat. Archtl. Jury for Bibliotheca Alexandrina, Internat. Fedn. Libr. Assns. and Insts. (sec. on edn. and tng. 1983-92), Coun. on Egyptian Am. Rels., The Gamaliel Chair (bd. dirs. 1995-97), Leaders Forum (bd. dirs. 1995—), America's Black Holocaust Mus. (bd. dirs. 1999—), Islamic Social Family Svcs. (bd. dirs. 1999—), Milw. Tchr.'s Edn. Ctr. (bd. dirs.). Democrat. Moslem. Office: U Wis-Milw Sch Info Studies PO Box 413 Milwaukee WI 53201-0413 Business E-Mail: aman@uwn.edu.

AMAN, REINHOLD ALBERT, philologist, publisher; b. Fuerstenzell, Bavaria, Apr. 8, 1936; came to U.S., 1959, naturalized, 1963; s. Ludwig and Anna Margarete (Waindinger) A.; m. Shirley Ann Beischel, Apr. 9, 1960 (div. 1990); 1 child, Susan. Student, Chem. Engring. Inst., Augsburg, Germany, 1953-54; BS with high honors, U. Wis., 1965; PhD, U. Tex., 1968. Chem. engr., Munich and Frankfurt, Ger., 1954-57; petroleum chemist Shell Oil Co., Montreal, Que., Can., 1957-59; chem. analyst A. O. Smith Corp., Milw., 1959-62; prof. German U. Wis., Milw., 1968-74; editor, pub. Maledicta Jour., Maledicta Press Publs., Santa Rosa, Calif., 1976—; pres. Maledicta Press, Santa Rosa, 1976—. Dir. Internat. Maledicta Archives, Santa Rosa, 1975— Author: Der Kampf in Wolframs Parzival, 1968, Bayrisch-oesterreichisches Schimpfwoerterbuch, 1973, 86, 96, Talking Dirty, 1993, Opus Maledictorum, 1996, Hillary Clinton's Pen Pal, 1996; gen. editor Mammoth Cod (Mark Twain), 1976, Dictionary of International Slurs (A. Roback), 1979, Graffiti (A. Read), 1977; editor Maledicta: The Internat. Jour. Verbal Aggression, 1977—, Maledicta Monitor, 1990-92; contbr. articles to profl. jours. U. Wis. scholar, 1963-65; U. Wis. research grantee, 1973, 74; NDEA Title IV fellow, 1965-68 Mem. Internat. Maledicta Soc. (pres.), Am. Dialect Soc., Am. Name Soc., Dictionary Soc. N.Am. Home and Office: PO Box 14123 Santa Rosa CA 95402-6123 E-mail: aman@sonic.net.

AMANCIO, RUTH CARSON, safety engineer; b. Honolulu, Nov. 13, 1956; d. Caliupe Carson and Julia (Donios) Amancio; m. Rodney Mitsuo Kaneshiro, June 8, 1980 (div. June 1992); children: Alane Kapeka Kaneshiro, Jolie Mikala Kaneshiro. AS, U. Hawaii, 2001. Cert. health safety profl., AHERA asbestor project designer, supr. constrn.; OSHA 500 trainer 2003. Sales supr. Affirmed Med. Svc., Honolulu, 1982-96; safety adminstr. Albert C. Kobayashi Inc., Waipahu, Hawaii, 1996—; safety mgr., cons. OSHCON Inc., Honolulu, 1998—99; staff St. Francis Med. Ctr., Honolulu, 1999—2001, Integrated Svcs. Inc., Honolulu, 2001—03; with Oshcon Inc., Honolulu, 2002—03, Metcalf Constrn. Co., Inc., Honolulu, 2003—. Trainer ARC, Honolulu, 1994—96; rec. sec. Non-Traditional Employment Task Force, 1996—. Mem.: Gen. Contractors Assn., Am. Soc. Safety Engrs. (scholar 1992—95), Vets. Safety (scholar 1996), Phi Theta Kappa (2d v.p. 1992—96). Avocations: sewing, music, dancing, aerobic weight training, reading.

AMANDES, CHRISTOPHER BRUCE, lawyer; b. Seattle, Feb. 6, 1955; s. Richard Bruce and Joanne Vivien (Beran) A.; m. Katherine Joan Wildman, Nov. 17, 1990; children: Charlotte Beran Amandes, Grace Monroe Amandes. BA, Rice U., 1976, M of Environ. Engring., 1978; JD, UCLA, 1985. Bar: Tex. 1985, U.S. Dist. Ct. (so. dist.) Tex. 1988, U.S. Ct. Appeals (5th cir. 1988). Engr., project mgr. Espey Huston & Assocs., Houston, 1978-82; jud. clk. U.S. Ct. Appeals 5th Cir., Houston, 1985-86; assoc., ptnr. Vinson & Elkins L.L.P., Houston, 1986—. Author: Texas Environmental Law Handbook, 1997. Cochmn. City of Houston Land Redevel. Com., Houston, 1996-2000. Mem. Air and Waste Mgmt. Assn. Office: Vinson & Elkins LLP 1001 Fannin St Ste 2300 Houston TX 77002-6760 E-mail: camandes@velaw.com.

AMANN, CHARLES ALBERT, mechanical engineer, researcher; b. Thief River Falls, Minn., Apr. 21, 1926; s. Charles Alois and Bertha Ann (Oetting) Amann; m. Marilynn Ann Reis, Aug. 26, 1950; children: Richard, Barbara, Nancy, Julie. BS, U. Minn., 1946, MSME, 1948. Instr. U. Minn., Mpls., 1946-49; rsch. engr. GM Rsch. Labs., Detroit, 1949-54, supervisory rsch. engr. Warren, Mich., 1954-71, asst. dept. head, 1971-73, dept. head, 1973-89, rsch. fellow, 1989-91; prin. engr. KAB Engring., 1991—. Spl. instr. Wayne State U., Detroit, 1952—55; guest lectr. Mich. State U., 1980—; outside prof. U. Ariz., 1983; mem. adv. com. Gas Rsch. Inst., 1992—98, Oak Ridge Nat. Lab., 1996—98; invited lectr. Inst. Advanced Engring., Seoul, Republic of Korea, 1994. Author (with others): (book) Automotive Engine Alternatives, 1986, Advanced Diesel Engineering and Operations, 1988; co-editor: Combustion Modeling in Reciprocating Engines, 1980. Lt. (j.g.) USNR, 1944—46. Recipient James Clayton prize, Inst. Mech. Engrs., 1975, Oustanding Achievement award, U. Minn., 1991. Fellow: Soc. Automotive Engrs. (Arch T. Colwell merit award 1972, Disting. Spkr. award 1981, Arch T. Colwell merit award 1984, Disting. Spkr. award 1991, Forest R. McFarland award 2001); mem.: ASME (Richard S. Woodbury award 1989, Soichiro Honda lectr. 1992, Spkr. award Internal Combustion Engine Divsn. 1997, Internal Combustion Engine award 2000, Disting. lectr. 2002—), NAE, Tau Beta Pi, Tau Omega, Sigma Xi. Presbyterian. Achievements include patents in field. Avocation: music.

AMANN, LESLIE KIEFER, lawyer, educator; b. Pensacola, Fla., Dec. 21, 1955; d. Robert C. and Marilyn Joan (Franklin) K.; children: Augustus Kiefer, Nicholas Jacob. BMEd, S.W. Tex. State U., 1976; JD, U. Houston, 1987. Bar: Tex. 1987, U.S. Dist. Ct. (so. dist.) Tex. 1988, U.S. Ct. Appeals (5th cir.) 1991, U.S. Dist. Ct. (no. dist.) Tex. 1992. Legis. aide to Lindon Williams Tex. State Senate, Austin, 1977-81; tchr. The Lincoln Sch., Guadalajara, Mex., 1979-82; legal asst. Koons Rasor Fuller & McCurley, Dallas, 1983-84; clk., assoc., participating assoc. Reynolds, Allen, Cook, Reynolds & Cunningham, Houston, 1984-93; shareholder Cunningham & Amann, Houston, 1993-94; asst. gen. counsel Charter Bank, Houston, 1995-96; sr. v.p., fiduciary counsel, market trust exec. Bank of America, Houston, 1996—. Adj. faculty Law Sch., U. Houston, 1988-2000; mem. faculty Tex. Bankers Assn. Trust Sch., 1998-2003; mem. bd. dirs. U. Houston Law Alumni Assn. Contbr. articles to profl. jours. Mem. adv. bd. Probate and Trust Law Inst., South Tex. Coll. Law, Houston, 1998- 2000; vol. Annunciation Orthodox Sch., Houston, 1996-2003; vol. Greater Houston Partnership Texas Scholars, 2000-2002. Recipient Adj. Faculty award Univ. Houston Law Sch., 1999. Fellow Tex. Bar Found. (life); mem. Houston Bar Assn. (vol. lawyers in pub. schs. 1998), Tex. State Bar., Attys. in Tax and Probate, Houston Bus. and Estate Planning Coun., Houston Estate and Fin. Forum, U. Houston Law Alumni Assn. (bd. dirs. 2003). Republican. Methodist. Avocations: writing, reading, book collecting. Office: Bank of America PO Box 2510 700 Louisiana 6th Fl Houston TX 77252-2518

AMAON, GARY P. lawyer; b. Lubbock, Tex., Nov. 18, 1945; BS, Abilene Christian Coll., 1966; JD, U. Tex., 1969. Bar: Tex. 1969. Mem. Vinson & Elkins L.L.P., Houston. Mem. Chancellors, Order of Coif, Phi Delta Phi. Office: Vinson & Elkins LLP 2500 First City Tower 1001 Fannin St Ste 3300 Houston TX 77002-6706 Address: 7897 Broadway, Apt #601 San Antonio TX 78209

AMAR, A. D. finance educator, management consultant; b. Bhakkar, India; s. Prem Dutt and Kaushlya Devi Shakir; m. Sneh Lata Chopra, Mar. 16, 1975; children: Harpriye Amar Juneja, Januj Amar Juneja. Advanced Diploma, Punjab Engring. Coll., Chandigarh, India, 1966; BS Prodn. Engring., Panjab U., Chandigarh, India, 1969; MS Indsl. & Mgmt. Engring., Mont. State U., 1973; MBA, Baruch Coll., 1980; PhD, CUNY, N.Y.C., 1980. Asst. prof. Punjab Engring. Coll., Chandigarh, India, 1969—72; asst. engr. Teledyne Pacific Indsl. Controls, Oakland, Calif., 1972; design engr. Vornado-Store Decor, Fairfield, NJ, 1973—76; asst. prof. fin. & quantitative methods Montclair State U., Upper Montclair, NJ, 1978—83; dir.-editor The Mid-Atlantic Jour. Bus. Seton Hall U., South Orange, NJ, 1991—2002, prof. mgmt. Sch. Bus., 1983—. V.p. publs. & pub. rels. Am. Prodn. & Inventory Control Soc.--Ctrl. Jersey Chpt., Woodbridge, NJ, 1989—91; mem. editl. adv. bd. Computers & Ops. Rsch., Potomac, 1998—2002. Author: Managing Knowledge Workers: Unleashing Innovation & Productivity, 2001. Recipient Tech. Incubator at Seton Hall U.-Feasibility Study award, State of N.J., 2001. Mem.: Inst. Ops. Rsch. and Mgmt. Scis. (track chair 1975). Republican. Hindu. Avocation: travel. Office: Seton Hall U Stillman Sch Bus South Orange NJ 07079 Office Fax: 973-761-9217.

AMARA, LUCINE, opera and concert singer; b. Hartford, Conn., Mar. 1, 1925; d. George and Adrine (Kazanjian) Armaganian; married, Jan. 7, 1961 (div. June 1964). Student, Music Acad. of West, 1947, U. So. Calif., 1949-50. Artistic dir. N.J. Assn. Verismo Opera, Ft. Lee. Tchr. master classes, U.S., Mex., Can. Appeared at Hollywood Bowl, 1948, soloist, San Francisco Symphony, 1949-50; career includes over 1000 operatic performances; with Met. Opera, N.Y.C., from 1950, sang 800 performances, 9 new prodns., 5 opening nights, 57 radio broadcasts, 4 telecasts including appeared on Met. Opera: In Performance, 1982, 83, 84, 85, 86, 87, 88, 90, 91; recorded Pagliacci, 1951, 60; singer with New Orleans, Hartford, Pitts., Central City operas, 1952-54, appeared Glyndebourne Opera, 1954, 55, 57, 58, Edinburgh Festival, 1954, singer, Aida, Terme Di Caracalla, Rome, 1954, also Stockholm Opera, N.Y. Philharm., St. Louis Civic Light Opera, 1955-56; has appeared in leading or title roles in several operas including: Tosca, Aida, Amelia in Un Ballo in Maschera, Turandot, Riverside Opera Assn., 1986, others; appeared with St. Petersburg (Fla.) Opera, Venezuela Philharm. Orch., 1988, 93; opera and concert tour, USSR, 1965, 91, Manila, 1968, Paris, Mex., 1966, Hong Kong and China, 1983, Yugoslavia, 1988; rec. artist, Columbia, RCA, Victor, Angel records, Met. Opera Record Club; albums include: Beethoven's Symphony No. 9, Leoncavallo's, I Pagliacci, Puccini's La Bohème, Verdi Requiem. Recipient 1st prize Atwater-Kent Radio Auditions, 1948; inducted to Acad. Vocal Arts Hall Fame, 1989. Office: PO Box 3024 Fort Lee NJ 07024-9024 E-mail: lamara@nyc.rr.com. *My life has been filled with new experiences. I have been most fortunate to have achieved a career that has introduced me to so many wonderful people. Some have become close friends; others, because of time and distance, have become warm acquaintances. I am humbly grateful for all God's blessings.*

AMARAL, JOSEPH FERREIRA, surgeon; b. Pawtucket, R.I., Aug. 9, 1955; s. Joseph and Rosa (Ferreira) A.; m. Linda Watson, June 6, 1981; children: Courtney, Ashley, Gregory. BS in Biology summa cum laude, Providence Coll., 1977; MD, Brown U., 1981. Diplomate Am. Bd. Surgery, Am. Bd. Med. Examiners. Intern R.I. Hosp., Providence, 1981-82, resident, 1982-83; surg. rsch. fellow Brown U./R.I. Hosp., Providence, 1983-86; sr. surg. resident R.I. Hosp., Providence, 1986-88, adminstrv. chief surg. resident, 1988-89, ccord. surg. residency, asst. surgeon, asst. prof. Brown U., 1989-91, coord. surg. residencey, dir. laparoscopic surgery, 1991-92, dir. laparoscopic surgery, asst. surgeon, asst. prof., 1991-93, assoc. prof., surgeon, 1993-98, prof., 1998—, pres., CEO, 2000—. Treas. R.I. Hosp. Staff Assn., 1991-93; sec. R.I. Hosp. Surg. Found., 1992—; bd. dirs. R.I. Hosp. PHO; vis. surgeon hosps. in Australia, Argentina, Portugal, Austria, Rome, Singapore and Brazil. Contbr. articles to numerous profl. jours.; numerous internat., nat. and regional presentations; various scientific exhibits. Recipient Merck Clin. Achievement award, 1981, Haffenraffer Surg. Rsch. fellowship, 1983-85, 16th ACS scholarship, 1984-86, Young Investigators award Shock Soc., 1986, Residents Rsch. award Surg. Infection Soc., 1986. Fellow ACS, Internat. Coll. Surgeons; mem. AMA, AAAS, R.I. Med. Soc., Providence Surg. Soc., New Eng. Surg. Soc., Soc. Laproendoscopic Surgeons, Assn. Surg. Edn., Ctrl. N.Y. Surg. Soc. (hon.), Soc. Minimally Invasive Therapy, Am. Soc. Gastrointestinal Endoscopy, Am. Biatric Soc., Surg. Infection Soc., N.Y. Acad. Scis., Wound Healing Soc., Am. Soc. Eternal and Parenteral Nutrition, Shock Soc., Assn. Acad. Surgeons, Brown Med. Alumni Assn., Sigma Xi, Phi Sigma Tau, Sigma Pi Sigma. Office: Univ Surg Assn Ste 470 2 Dudley St Providence RI 02905-3236

AMARASEKARE, PRIYANGA, education educator; d. Gunadasa and Anual Amarasekare; m. Ranjan Wijeratne. BS in Zoology, U. of Colombo, Sri Lanka, 1987; MS in Zoology, U. of Hawaii, 1991; PhD in Ecology, U. of Calif., 1998. Post-doctoral rsch. fellow Nat. Ctr. for Ecol. Analysis and Synthesis, Santa Barbara, Calif., 1998—2000; asst. prof. ecology and evolution U. of Chgo., 2000—. Author: (jour. articles) Am. Naturalist; researcher Research On Diseases And Conservation (travel award and stipend from Nat. Ctr. for Ecol. Analysis and Synthesis); contbr. rsch. expertise (Travel award and stipend, 2003); invited seminar speaker Multi-species coexistence in patchy environments (travel award and honorarium from U. of Chgo., Yale, Princeton, Cambridge, U. of Chgo., U. of Wash., UC Davis). Fellow U. of Calif. Regents Fellowship, 1997—98; grantee Dissertation Improvement Grant, NSF, 1996—98, Natural Res. Sys. Rsch. Grant, U. of Calif., 1996—98, Rsch. grant, NSF, 2001—. Rsch. Experience for Undergraduates, 2002; scholar Fulbright/East-West Ctr., U.S. Info. Agy., 1988—90; Post-doctoral fellowship, Nat. Ctr. for Ecol. Analysis and Synthesis, 1998—2000. Mem.: Am. Soc. of

Naturalists (Young Investigator prize 2001), Ecol. Soc. of Am. Achievements include research in Host-parasite interactions funded by the Nat. Sci. Found. Avocations: reading, hiking, art, films. Office: U of Chgo 1101 East 57th St Chicago IL 60637

AMARASINGHE, AMARASINGHE A.W. psychiatrist, consultant; b. Rajagiriya, Sri Lanka, Aug. 22, 1935; arrived in U.S., 1973; s. Podiappuhamy Amarasinghe and Bethmage Nona Perera; m. Nandawathy Rajapakse, Sept. 1, 1965; children: Charm Saumya, Shyly Saubhagya. B Medicine, B Surgery, U. Ceylon, Colombo, Sri Lanka, 1961; diploma in child health, Royal Coll. Physicians, London, 1971. Diplomate Am. Bd. Psychiatry, Am. Bd. Neurology. Med. officer Govt. Health Svcs., Sri Lanka, 1962—70; sr. house officer Nat. Health Svcs., England, 1970—72; resident in psychiatry Mount Sinai Hosp., N.Y.C., 1973—76; psychiatrist VA Hosp., Augusta, Ga., 1976—97; cons. psychiatrist Ga. Dept. Corrections, 1998—. Assoc. clin. prof. Med. Coll. Ga., Augusta, 1992—97. Author: (novels) Tis Pe Tis Viya, 1992, Saudi Sat Sathiya, 1995, Ada Siya Wasa Diya, 2000. Pres. Assn. for Peace in Sri Lanka, Augusta, 1983. Col. USAR, 1991. Decorated Nat. Def. Svc. medal, Overseas Svc. ribbon; scholar A.E. Bennett scholarship, AMA on Alcoholism, 1980. Mem.: Assn. Mil. Surgeons of U.S. Buddhist. Avocations: meditation, travel. Home: 102 Bay Berry Hills Mcdonough GA 30253-4005

AMATANGELO, NICHOLAS S. retired financial printing and document management services exeutive; b. Monessen, Pa., Feb. 12, 1935; s. Sylvester and Lucy Amatangelo; m. Kathleen Driscoll, May 16, 1964; children: Amy Kathleen, Holly Megan. BA, Duquesne U., 1957; MBA, U. Pitts., 1958. Indsl. engr. U.S. Steel Co., Pitts., 1959-61; indsl. engr. mgr. Anaconda Co., N.Y.C., 1961-63; product mktg. mgr. Xerox Corp., N.Y.C., 1965-68; dir. mktg. Macmillan Co., N.Y.C., 1968-70; dir. product planning Philco-Ford Corp., Phila., 1970-72; pres., CEO Bowne San Francisco, Inc., 1972-79, Bowne Houston, Inc., Houston, 1979-87, Bowne Chgo., Inc., 1983-96, corp. cons., advisor, 1996-97; pres., CEO Bowne Detroit, Inc., 1987-96; ret., 1996. Instr. U. Pitts., Pitts., 1959—61; asst. prof. Westchester CC, N.Y.C., 1961—64, N.Y.C., 1970—72; ad. prof. grad. sch. bus. mgmt. and mktg. Roosevelt U. Grad Sch. Exec. MBA program, Chgo., 1996—. Contbr. articles to profl. jours. Bd. dirs. San Francisco Boys Club, 1974—79, Boys Town Italy, 1973—79, Alley Theatre, Houston, 1982—86; mem. pres.'s coun. Houston Grand Opera, 1980—86; mem. adv. bd. bus. sch. Roosevelt U., 1996—, vice chair, 1996—99. With U.S. Army, 1958—59, with U.S. Army, 1961—62. Mem.: Assn. Colls. Ill. (trustee 1993—), Pres. Assn., Am. Mgmt. Assn., Am. Soc. Corp. Secs., Printing Industries Am. (bd. dirs.), Duquesne U. Century Club (chmn. exec. com.), Union League Club Chgo., Econs. Club Chgo., Exec. Club Chgo. (bd. dirs.).

AMATO, CAROL JOY, writer, anthropologist; b. Portland, Oreg., Apr. 9, 1944; d. Sam Lawrence and Lena Dorothy (Dindia) A.; m. Neville Stanley Motts, Aug. 26, 1967 (div. 1978); children: Tracy, Damon. BA, U. Portland, 1966; MA, Calif. State U., 1986. Freelance writer, Westminster, Calif., 1969—; human factor cons. Design Sci. Corp., L.A., 1979-90; dir. software documentation Trans-Ed Communications, Westminster, 1980-84; pres. Advanced Profl. Software, Inc., Westminster, 1984-86, Systems Rsch. Analysis, Inc., Westminster, 1986-95, Stargazer Pub. Co., Corona, 1995—. Author: The Earth, 1992, Astronomy, 1992, The Human Body, 1992, Inventions, 1992, Inside Out: The Wonders of Modern Technologies Explained, 1992, 50 Nifty Science Fair Projects, 1993, The Super Science Project Book, 1994, The World's Easiest Guide to Using the APA, 1995, 3d edit., 2002, The Earth, 1995, Creepy Crawlies, 1995, The World's Easiest Guide to Using the MLA, 1999, The World's Easiest Guide to Using the APA, 3d edit., 2002; editor Cultural Futuristics, 1975-80, numerous articles and short stories; participant in numerous radio and TV interviews. Sec. bd. dirs. Am. Space Meml. Found., L.A., 1986-87; bd. dirs. Orange County Acad. Decathalon, 1986-94. Mem. Ind. Writers of So. Calif. (bd. dirs. Orange County sect. 1986-93), Profl. Writers Orange County (bd. dirs. 1993—, pres. 1994-97), Writers' Club of Whittier, Inc. (bd. dirs. 1991—), Internat. Pen, Pub. Mktg. Assn., Pub. Assn. LA, LA People in Pub. Office: Stargazer Pub Co PO Box 77002 Corona CA 92877-0100 E-mail: Bestseller@stargazerpub.com.

AMATO, PAULA, medical educator; b. Toronto, Ont., Can., Aug. 12, 1965; d. Dante and Egidia Amato. MD, U. of Toronto, 1989. Diplomate Am. Bd. of Obstetrics and Gynecology. Asst. adj. prof. U. Calif., San Diego, 1997—2000; asst. prof. Baylor Coll. of Medicine, Houston, 2000—. Contbr. articles to profl. jours., chpts. to books. Recipient Berlex Scholar award in Basic Sci. Rsch., Berlex Found., 2001. Mem.: Assn. Prof. of Gynecology and Obstetrics, N. Am. Menopause Soc., Am. Soc. Reproductive Medicine, Am. Coll. of Obstetricians & Gynecologists, Endocrine Soc., Alpha Omega Alpha. Office: Baylor Coll Medicine Ste #801A 6550 Fannin Houston TX 77030

AMATO, ROSALIE, educator; b. Racalmuto, Agrigento, Sicily, June 3, 1920; came to U.S., 1923; d. Nicolo and Francesca (Macaluso) A. BS, Buffalo State U., 1964, MEd, 1968. Office supr. Wm. Hengerer Co. (Sibley's), Buffalo, N.Y., 1941-51; installation personnel Remington Rand, Dayton, Ohio, 1951-53; office supr., acctg. City of Buffalo, 1953-61; home econs. tchr. Buffalo Bd. Edn., 1964-70, supr. home econs. federally funded projects, 1971—. Vol. Civil Def., State of N.Y., 1953-58 (Cert. Pub. Service, 1958). Mem. Am. Home Econs. Assn. (area coord. 1973-75), Kappa Delta (treas. 1962-63), Phi Epsilon Omicron (pres. 1968-70). Roman Catholic. Avocations: art, design, concerts, opera, bowling. Home: 327 Colvin Ave Buffalo NY 14216-2338

AMATO, VINCENT VITO, business executive; b. Bklyn., Oct. 14, 1929; s. Anthony and Josephine (Maniscalco) A.; m. Marie Dioguardi, Apr. 24, 1955; children— Stephanie, Janine, Anthony, Christopher. BBA, CCNY, 1951, MBA, 1958. Liaison to div. contr. Allied Chem. Corp., N.Y.C., 1951-59; acctg. systems rep. Olivetti-Underwood, N.Y.C., 1958-61; v.p. planning, contr., acquisitions exec. Ingredient Tech. SuCrest Corp., N.Y.C., 1961-72, v.p. planning, treas., 1972-73, pres. splty. products, 1973-78; pres., owner Market Makers Inc., Woodbridge, N.J., 1978-97; owner Animated Computer Engring. Inc., Woodbridge, N.J., 1991-97; founder imadeadifference.com. Adj. asst. prof. NYU; presenter seminars Am. Mgmt. Assn.; mem. food sci. adv. bd. Rutgers U., 1988—, also adv. bd. Cook Coll. Rutgers U. Pres. Lakeridges Civic Assn. Mem. Fin. Execs. Inst., Assn. for Corp. Growth, Am. Mgmt. Assn. (tech. adviser) Home and Office: Vincent V Amato Mktg Consulting 7 Alder Ct Matawan NJ 07747-3717 E-mail: vincemarie@aol.com.

AMATO CHIARAMONTE BORDONARO, BARON CARLO CAMILLO, ambassador, consultant; s. Giuseppe Michele Amato and Fernanda Giannini Paolini; m. Lorraine Manville-Dresselhouse, Feb. 22, 1959 (dec.). Diploma in Archaeology, Mex. U., Mexico, U. of Barcelona, Spain. Appraiser Assn. of Am., N.Y., 1978. Pres., founder Old World Internat., Yarmouth, Canada, 1968—; asst. prof. biology Ga. State U., Athens, 1971—81; amb. Soverign Mil. Order of Malta, Saint Vincent and the Grenadines, 1983—; pres., founder Old World Galleries, N.Y.C., 1977—84; editor-at-large Conde.Nast Publs., Milan and Paris, Italy, 1984—91; dir. fgn. rels. Gesfid, Lugano, Switzerland, 1984—98, fin. mgr., 1984—94; mng. dir. Canouan Resort Devel. Co. Ltd, Saint Vincent and the Grenadines, 1994—98; min. plenipotentiary at large Republic of San Marino, San Marino, 1983—2000. Author: (book) The Wild Boar: History Husbandry The Hunt; editor: (mag.) Artequia Internat., Harper-Bazaar. Named Man of Yr., World Inst. for Sci. Humanism, Fordham U., 1982; recipient Cert. of Appreciation, City of N.Y., 1977, Order of the Trinity, Imperial Ho. of Ethiopia, 1997, Knight of Real Cuerpo de la Nobleza de Madrid, Nobility of Castilla, 1998, Knight Comdr. of St. Maurice and Lazarus, The Savoy Order, 1999, Knight of Grace and Devotion of the Sacred Mil. Order of Malta, 2000. Fellow: Explorer Club; mem.: Knickerbocker Club. Roman Catholic. Avocations: landscaping, ecological research, cooking, gardening, enology.

AMATULI, ROBERT ALEXANDER, architect; b. N.Y.C., May 30, 1957; s. A. James and Catherine Amatuli; m. Jeanne Marie Amatuli, Apr. 19, 1985; children: Robert Alexander II, Nicholas Brandon. BS in Archtl. Tech., N.Y. Inst. Tech., 1979. Registered architect N.Y., Tex., Ariz., Conn., N.C.; registered interior design, Tex., Conn. Dir. archtl. dept. United Artists Comm., Dallas, 1979-85, dir. east coast constrn. N.Y.C., 1982; assoc., asst. office mgr. Page Southerland Page, Ft. Worth, 1985-87, assoc., prodn. coord. Dallas, 1987-95; v.p., dir. healthcare Gideon Toal Inc., Ft. Worth, 1995-99; sr. v.p., dir. ops., telecomm. Gideon Toal Fulwiler Oates, Ft. Worth, 1997-99; assoc., unit mgr. Carter & Burgess Inc., Hartford, Conn., 1999-2001; sr. project mgr., healthcare divsn. leader Tecton Archs., pc, Hartford, 2001—03, dir. design, 2003—. Cons. JPS Archtl. Cons., Ft. Worth, 1996—. Recipient craftsmenship award Knights of Pythius, N.Y.C., 1972. Mem. AIA (design award Ft. Worth 1999). Avocations: ambulist, golf, auto racing, hockey, baseball. Office: Tecton Architects pc One Hartford Sq W Hartford CT 06106

AMAYA, CARLOS C. education educator, researcher; b. Sensuntepeque, ElSalvador, May 14, 1965; arrived in U.S., 1988; s. Andrés Amaya-Romero and Esperanza Lemus. BA, Univ. Louisville, Louisville, Ky., 1990, MA, 1992; PhD, Ind. Univ., Bloomington, 1998. Cert. tchng. UCA El Salvador, 1987. Asst. instr. Univ. Louisville, Ky., 1990—92, Ind. Univ., Bloomington, Ind., 1992—98; asst. prof. Ea. Ill. Univ., Charleston, Ill., 2000—. Contbr. articles to profl. jour. Scholar Fulbright Scholarship, U.S. Govt., 1988—90. Mem.: Am. Assn. of Tchrs. of Spanish and Portuguese, Modern Languauge Assn., Ill. Coun. on the tchng. Foreign Languages.

AMBACH, DWIGHT RUSSELL, retired foreign service officer; b. Highland Park, Ill., Jan. 9, 1931; s. Russell William and Ethel (Repass) A.; m. Betsy Hunter, Aug. 27, 1955; children: Hunter MacKay, Nancy Cole, James Gordon. AB, Brown U., 1952; MA, Fletcher Sch., 1953; postgrad., MIT, 1963-64. Dep. dir. Office Regional Econ. Policy, Bur. Inter-Am. Affairs Dept. State, Washington, 1971-74; exec. asst. to chmn. Export-Import Bank, Washington, 1974-76, 84-86; counselor for econ. and comml. affairs Am. Embassy, Vienna, 1976-80; dean Fgn. Service Inst., Washington, 1980-84; office dir. Bur. Adminstrn. and Info. Services, 1986-88; cons., 1988-96; mem. Fgn. Svc. Res. Corps, 1995—2001. Pres. Montgomery County chpt. Md. Mcpl. League; bd. dirs. Mathews County Cmty. Found. Recipient Superior Honor award Dept. State, 1973; Disting. Service award Export-Import Bank, 1985 Mem. Am. Fgn. Service Assn., Am. Econ. Assn., Phi Beta Kappa Home: Aldendale PO Box 26 Susan VA 23163-0026

AMBACH, GORDON MAC KAY, educational association executive; b. Providence, Nov. 10, 1934; s. Russell W. and Ethel (Repass) A.; m. Lucy DeWitt Emory, Mar. 9, 1963; children: Kenneth Emory, Alison Repass, Douglas Mac Kay. BA, Yale U., 1956; MA, Harvard U. Grad. Sch. Edn., 1957, cert. advanced study, 1966. Tchr. social studies 7th and 8th grades East Williston Sch. Dist., L.I., N.Y., 1958-61; asst. program planning officer U.S. Office Edn., Washington, 1961-62, asst. legis. specialist, 1962-63, exec. sec. Higher Edn. Facilities Act Task Force, 1963-64; adminstrv. asst. to mem. Boston Sch. Com., 1964-65; staff seminar mgr., mem. staff Harvard U. Grad. Sch. Edn., Cambridge, Mass., 1966-67; spl. asst. to commr. for long range planning N.Y. State Edn. Dept., Albany, 1967-69, asst. commr. for long range planning, 1969-70, exec. dep. commr., 1970-77; commr. edn. and pres. U. State N.Y., Albany, 1977-87; exec. dir. Coun. Chief State Sch. Officers, Washington, 1987—2001. Del., chmn. resolutions com. The White House Conf. on Librs. and Info. Scis., 1991; mem. Nat. Coun. on Edn. Standards and Testing, 1993; mem. edn. com. Nat. Alliance for Bus., 1994-2001; mem. Nat. Bd. Internat. Comparative Studies in Edn., U.S. rep. to Internat. Assn. for Evaluation of Edn. Achievement, mem. standing com., 1990-2001; bd. dirs. Wallace-Reader's Digest Funds, Newspaper Assn. Am. Found., Ctr. for Naval Analysis Corp.; mem. edn. bd. NAS. With USAR, 1957-63. Mem. Acad. Polit. Scis., Am. Assn. Sch. Adminstrs., PEW Forum on Edn. Reform, Phi Delta Kappa. Home: PO Box 261 Bondville VT 05340

AMBARD, ALBERTO J, prosthodontist; s. Alberto J and Rhaiza C Ambard; m. Elizabeth R Buckley; 1 child, Leonardo J. DDS, Universidad Ctrl. de Venezuela, Caracas, Venezuela, 1990—96; MS Prosthodontry, U. Ala. at Birmingham, Birmingham, AL, 1998—2001; Maxillofacial prosthodontist, U. Chgo., Chgo., IL, 2001—02. Licensee Wash. State Bd. of Dentistry. Fellow U. Chgo., Chgo., 2001—02; resident U. Ala. at Birmingham, Birmingham, Ala., 1998—2001; pvt. practice Caracas, Venezuela, 1996—98. Author: (essay) Todo deriva de Bach (everything derives from Bach), (history) Historia de la musica Pop (Pop music history), (short stories and poetry) Reflexiones en noches de soledad (reflections during lonely nights). Recipient Jose Felix Rivas award, 2nd class, Sports achievements, Universidad Ctrl. de Venezuela, 1992; fellow Geriatric dentistry rsch. competition, Am. Coll. of Prosthodontists / Procter & Gambler, 2000. Mem.: Acad. of Osseointegration, Am. Coll. of Prosthodontists, ADA. Achievements include research in Properties of calcium phosphate cements filled with Bioglass; Cleansability of and patients' satisfaction with implant-retained overdentures; College level Karate national champion (Venezuela, 1990); Karate national champion (Venezuela, 1991-92); 5th place, Karate-do shito ryu world cup (Tokyo, Japan); Karate Black belt.

AMBER, DOUGLAS GEORGE, lawyer; b. East Chicago, Ind., Apr. 15, 1956; s. George and Margaret (Watson) A. BA in Polit. Sci., Ind. U., 1978; JD, U. Miami, 1985. Bar: Fla. 1985, US. Ct. Claims 1986, U.S. Ct. Internat. Trade 1986, U.S. Tax Ct. 1986, U.S. Ct. Appeals (11th cir.) 1986, U.S. Dist. Ct. (mid. and so. dists.) Fla. 1987, U.S. Ct. Mil. Appeals 1987, U.S. Ct. Appeals (fed. cir.) 1987, Ind. 1988, U.S. Dist. Ct. (no. and so. dists.) Ind. 1988, U.S. Ct. Appeals (7th cir.) 1989, U.S. Supreme Ct. 1989; registered civil mediator. Dep. prosecutor 31st Jud. Cir. Ind., Crown Point, 1988-93; pvt. practice Munster, 1993—. Adj. prof. polit. sci. Purdue U., 1997—. Mem. exec. bd. dirs. Calumet coun. Boy Scouts Am., 1994-96. Mem. ABA, Acad. Legal Studies in Bus., Nat. Dist. Attys. Assn., South Lake County Bar Assn., Ind. State Bar Assn., Lake County Bar Assn. (bd. dirs. 1990-96), Ind. Trial Lawyers Assn., Audio Engring. Soc., Soc. Audio Cons. (cert. video and audio cons.), Mensa, Delta Theta Phi. Avocations: bicycling, weight training. Office: Amber Golding & Hofstetter 9250 Columbia Ave Ste E-2 Munster IN 46321-3530 E-mail: amber@calumet.purdue.edu.

AMBER, LAURIE KAUFMAN, lawyer; b. N.Y.C., Apr. 15, 1954; d. Martin and Barbara (Schiffman) Kaufman; m. Henry Michael Amber, June 18, 1977; children: Ian, Kyle. BS, Cornell U., 1974, MBA, 1975; JD, U. Miami, 1978. Bar: Fla. 1978, U.S. Dist. Ct. (so. dist.) Fla. 1978, U.S. Tax Ct. 1978, U.S. Ct. Appeals (5th cir.) 1979, U.S. Ct. Customs and Patent Appeals 1979, U.S. Customs Ct. 1979, U.S. Ct. Appeals (11th cir.) 1981, U.S. Ct. Internat. Trade 1981, U.S. Supreme Ct. 1982, U.S. Claims Ct. 1985; cert. civil circuit mediator Supreme Ct. Fla.; cert. family mediator Supreme Ct. Fla. Staff mgr. Proctor & Gamble Mfg. Co., Staten Island, N.Y., 1975; adj. asst. prof. Nova U., Fort Lauderdale, Fla., 1976-77; atty., labor arbitrator Amber & Amber, P.A., South Miami, Fla., 1978—. Arbitrator nat. labor panel Am. Arbitration Assn., Miami, 1982—, Grievance Arbitration Panel of Fla. PERC, Tallahassee, 1979—; hearing examiner pers. appeals County of Dade, Miami, 1985-91, 2000—; dir. Kids That Care Pediat. Cancer Fund, 1996—. Pres. Office Village Condominium Assn., South Miami, 1994, Children's Cancer Fund, 1996-2000; bd. dirs. Jackson Meml. Found., 1996-2000, Kids That Care Pediatric and Cancer Fund, 2000—. Named Woman of Yr. ABWA, 1983. Mem. ABA, Zonta (bd. dirs. Coral Gables, Fla. club 1988). Office: Amber & Amber PA 7731 SW 62nd Ave Ste 202 Miami FL 33143-4908

AMBER, RICH, manufacturing engineer; b. McMinnville, Oreg., Feb. 23, 1949; s. Delmer Frank Isakson and Elizabeth Ann (Lambert) Madding; m. Valerie Ann Martin, Mar. 29, 1971 (div. Dec. 1979); 1 child, Samantha Jane; m. Terresa Lee Tuttle, May 23, 1986 (div. Mar. 2000). Student, Wash. State U., Portland (Oreg.) State U., La Salle U., Chgo., USAF Sch. Applied aerospace sci. design draftsman, jr. engr. SEMCO Control Systems, Tigard, Oreg., 1974-76; numerical controlled driller, profiler operator PCB mech. ctrl. mfg. Tektronix, Inc., Beaverton, Oreg., 1976-77, schematic draftsman III, tech. illustrator manuals dept. frequency domain instrumentation div., 1977-78; product support specialist II CAD-CAM devel. dept. Computer Sci. Ctr., Aloha, Oreg., 1978-80, tech. writer III, editor tech. communications Beaverton, 1980-83; tech. publs. mgr. communications network analyzers div. Tektronix, Redmond, Oreg., 1983-85, engring. svcs. mgr., 1985-89, mktg. contracts program mgr., 1989-90; front desk Grand Canyon (Ariz.) Nat. Park Lodges, 1991; mgr. Best Western Rama Inn, Redmond, Oreg., 1992; tech. writer, human interface designer Tektronix, Inc., Redmond, 1992-96; mgr. engring. svcs. Marus Dental Internat., 1997-99, international standards orgn. safety dir., 2000—01; ops./prodn. REMCO Control Systems, Bend, Oreg., 2002—03; owner, operator Amber Graphics, Redmond, 2003—. Freelance artist and photographer; part-time gunsmith; instr. Tektronix Edn. and Tng. Ctr., Portland Commun. Coll., Beaverton. Author: Dirt Bike, Visions; contbr. articles to trade publs., newspapers and mags., also poetry, cartoons. Loaned exec. campaign United Way, 1986-87; res. police officer City of Bend, Oreg., 1989-90, instr. firearms safety and personal protection, handgun Range Officer. With USAF, 1967-73. Mem. Friends of Pine Mountain Astronomers (bd. dirs.). Republican. Avocations: horseback riding, camping, woodworking, hiking, sculpting. Home: 5897 SW Mesa Way Redmond OR 97756-9045 Office: 63970 Sunset Dr Bend OR 97701

AMBERG, STANLEY LOUIS, lawyer; b. Phila., Oct. 2, 1934; s. Otto Philip and Florence (Bachrach) A.; m. Cynthia Fread, June 18, 1961; children: Stacy, Julie. BSChemE, Rensselaer Poly. Inst., 1956; MS, MIT, 1960; LLB, Harvard U., 1962. Bar: N.Y. 1963, U.S. Ct. Appeals (2d cir.) 1967, U.S. Supreme Ct. 1973. Ptnr. Davis Hoxie Faithfull & Hapgood, N.Y.C., 1962-95; counsel Orrick, Herrington & Sutcliffe, N.Y.C., 1995—2002. Contbr. articles to profl. jours. Pres. Temple Beth El of No. Westchester, Chappaqua, N.Y., 1982-83. Lt. U.S. Navy, 1956-58. Mem. ABA, Am. Intellectual Property Law Assn., Assn. of the Bar of City of N.Y., Sigma Xi, Tau Beta Pi. Avocation: photography.

AMBORSKI, LEONARD EDWARD, chemist; b. Buffalo, Aug. 23, 1921; s. Nicholas Leon and Angeline (Laskowska) A.; m. Irene Kazmierczak, Oct. 3, 1944; children: Donna Marie, David Paul. BS, Canisius Coll., 1943; MA, SUNY, Buffalo, 1949, PhD, 1951. Cert. indsl. hygienist Am. Bd. Indsl. Hygiene; cert. EPA instr. in lead abatement and hazardous materials worker tng. Instr. physics Canisius Coll., 1943-44; physicist Carnegie Mellon Inst., Washington, 1944-45; with E.I. DuPont de Nemours & Co., Buffalo, 1945-90, staff scientist, 1973-90, environ. health cons., 1973-90; cons. in environ. health, 1990—. Rsch. assoc. Toxicoloty Rsch. Ctr., SUNY, Buffalo. Patentee in field. Bd. dirs. Am. Lung Assn. of N.Y. State, Buffalo, 1985—; chmn. Tonawanda (N.Y.) Citizen Pre-Treatment Program, 1985-86, Tonawanda Hazardous Materials Adv. Com., Buffalo, 1985-88; chmn. local emergency planning commn. Buffalo and Erie County, N.Y., 1988—; mem. citizens adv. com. Remedial Action Plan for Niagara River Recipient Indsl. and Hazardous Waste award N.Y. State Water Pollution Control Assn., 1989. Mem. Air Pollution Control Assn. (chmn. 1983-84, Svc. award 1984), Am. Chem. Soc., Am. Indsl. Hygiene Assn., Am. Bd. Indsl. Hygiene, Am. Pub. Health Assn., Am. Soc. Safety Engrs., Water Pollution Control Fedn. Republican. Roman Catholic. Avocations: photography, swimming, cycling. Home: 62 Wedgewood Dr Buffalo NY 14221-1469 E-mail: lamborski@webtv.net.

AMBRO, THOMAS L. federal judge; b. Cambridge, Ohio, Dec. 27, 1949; BA, Georgetown U., 1971, JD, 1975. Bar: Del. 1976. Clk. Hon. Daniel L. Herrmann Del. Supreme Ct., 1975—76; assoc. Richards, Layton and Finger, 1976—82, ptnr., 1982—2000; judge U.S. Ct. Appeals (3d cir.), 2000—. Mem. State Del. Gov.'s Commn. on Mayor Comml. Litig. Reform, 1993, N.Y. TriBar Opinion Com., 1988—. Author: Third Party Legal Opinions in Asset Based Financing: A Transactional Guide, 1990; contbr. articles to profl. jours. Mem.: ABA (vice-chair com. on programs 1987—90, chair com. on meetings 1988—90, participant Silverado Conf. on Legal Opinions 1989, mem. drafting subcom. third-party legal opinion report 1989—91, chair subcom. on opinion letters 1989—95, mem. com. on comml. fin. svcs. 1989—95, chair com. on meetings 1990—94, chair or co-chair com. on publs. 1994—97, chair com. on legal opinions 1994—98, mem. coun. sect. bus. law 1994—98, editl. bd. The Bus. Lawyer 1998—99, editor The Bus. Lawyer 1999—2000, vice-chair sect. bus. law 1999—2000, sec. sect. bus. law 1998-99, 2000-01, immediate past chmn. 2002-, mem. com. on uniform comml. code, mem. com. on negotiated acquisitions, mem. bus. bankruptcy com., chair elect bus. law 2000—01, chair sec. bus. law 2001—02, immediate past chair 2002—), Am. Coll. Comml. Fin. Lawyers (bd. regents, charter), Am. Coll. Investment Counsel, Am. Coll. Bankruptcy, Del. State Bar Assn. (chmn. 1979—82, vice-chmn. 1982—83, comml. law sect., chair subcom. on uniform comml. code 1983—), Phi Beta Kappa. Office: Lockbox 32 5122 Fed Bldg 844 N King St Wilmington DE 19801

AMBROS, ROBERT ANDREW, pathologist, educator, writer; b. Passaic, N.J., May 21, 1959; s. Henry and Adele (Ruta) A.; m. Maryla Warszawa, Aug. 22, 1981; children: Robert, Janek, Julia. MD, Copernicus Acad. Medicine, 1982. Resident in surgery Morristown (N.J.) Meml. Hosp., 1983-85; resident in pathology N.J. Med. Sch., Newark, 1985-89; fellow in gynecologic pathology Johns Hopkins Hosp., Balt., 1989-91; asst. prof. pathology Albany (N.Y.) Med. Coll., 1991-96, asst. prof. ob-gyn., 1993-96, assoc. prof. pathology, ob-gyn., 1996—. Cons. in gynecologic pathology Albany Med. Coll., 1991—. Author: (novels) The Brief Sun, 2002 (Best Genre Fiction award Writer's Digest, 2002); contbr. articles to profl. jours.; editor: Internat. Jour. Gynecol. Pathology, 1994—. Clin. oncology fellow Am. Cancer Soc., 1990; recipient Basic Oncology Rsch. award Am. Cancer Soc., 1988. Fellow Coll. Am. Pathologists; mem. AAAS, Internat. Soc. Gynecol. Pathologists, Internat. Acad. Pathology, N.Y. Acad. Scis., Johns Hopkins Med. and Surg. Assn. Achievements include research in the surgical and molecular pathology of gynecologic malignancies. Office: Albany Med Coll Dept Pathology 43 New Scotland Ave Albany NY 12208-3412 E-mail: ambrosr@mail.amc.edu.

AMBROSE, ANDREW M. humanities educator; b. Knoxville, Tenn., Mar. 8, 1953; s. Dr. Harry Harwood and Miriam Lucile Ambrose; m. Terry Lynn Tilley, Aug. 2, 1980; children: William Kalin, Lucy Madison. PhD, Emory Univ., Atlanta, Ga., 1992; MA, Univ. of Tenn., Knoxville, Tenn., 1979, BA, 1975. Dep. dir./COO Atlanta Hist. Ctr., Atlanta, 2003, interim exec. dir., 2002—03, dep. dir., 1999—2002, dir.-rsch. & programs, 1998—99, admin. of programs & collect., 1997—98; adj. asst. prof. Emory Univ., Atlanta, 1992—; adj. instr. Dekalb Cmty. Coll., 1985—88. Grad. tchg. asst. Emory Univ., Atlanta, 1981; rsch. and writing Dept. of Ed. project on So. Women's Hist., 1981—82; rsch. asst. Emory Univ., Dept. of Hist., Atlanta, 1982; rsch. hist. Nat. Pk. Svc.-Martin Luther King, Jr. Nat. Hist. Site fand Pres. Dist., 1982—84; acad. coun. Emory Coll., Summer Scholars Program, Atlanta, 1985; computer lab tech. and acad. coun. Emory Coll., Atlanta, 1987—88; supr. Emory Univ., Media Prod. Ctr., Atlanta, 1988—92; hist. and rsch. coord. The Atlanta Hist. Ctr., Atlanta, 1992—97. Author: (book) Atlanta: An Illustrated History, 2003; co-author: Met. Frontiers, 1996; contbg. editor (assoc.): (jour.) Atlanta Hist.: A Jour. of Ga. and the South, 1994—2000. Recipient Bernadette Schmitt Hist. Scholar, Univ. of Tenn., 1974—75, High Honors Grad., 1975, Bernadette Schmitt Grant for Grad. Rsch., 1978, Nat. Pk. Svc. Spl. Achievement Award, 1984, Atlanta Hist. Soc. Pre-Publ. Award, 1991—92, Nominee, Ga. Author of the Yr., Ga. Writers, Inc., 1996; grantee Fellowship and Tuition Grant, Emory Univ./Atlanta, Ga., 1980—82. Mem.: Ga. Assoc. of Mus. and Gall., SE Mus. Conf., Am. Assoc. for State and Local Hist., Am. Assoc. of Mus., Urban Hist. Assoc., Nat. Coun. on Pub. Hist., So. Hist. Assoc., OAH So. Regional Conf. Program Comm., Org. of Am. Hist. Avocations: soccer, music, southern. Home: 3927 Thornridge Way Doraville GA 30340

AMBROSE, CHARLES STUART, sales executive; b. Jacksonville, NC, Nov. 28, 1951; s. Samuel Sheridan and Elizabeth (Stansbury) Ambrose. BBA, Emory U., 1974. Asst. mgr. Fifth Quarter Restaurant Shoney's, Birmingham, Ala., 1975; asst. chemist Mackay Paint Co., Birmingham, 1975-76; salesman, sales mgr. Francis & Lusky Co., Nashville, 1976-85, pres. SST Sales Co., Inc., Nashville, 1982—. Republican. Presbyterian. Office: SST Sales Co Inc 226 Waterview Dr Hendersonville TN 37075-5662 E-mail: sstsalesco@aol.com.

AMBROSE, DANIEL MICHAEL, publishing executive; b. Salem, Oreg., Nov. 1, 1955; s. Franklin Burnell and Jean Marie (Crakes) A.; m. Cynthia Barbara Friedman, Mar. 26, 1983; children: Robert Grant, Michael Bruce. BS in Polit. Sci., Lewis and Clark Coll., 1977. Mktg. mgr. Washington Monthly, 1978-79; advt. promotion mgr. Am. Film Mag., Washington, 1979-80, advt. mgr., 1980-81, advt. dir., 1981-83, Backpacker Mag., N.Y.C., 1983-84; advt. salesman House Beautiful, Hearst Mag., N.Y.C., 1984-85; corp. advt. dir. mag. div. Hearst Pub. Corp., N.Y.C., 1985-87; pub. Fathers Mag., N.Y.C., 1987-89; advt. dir. Cahners Pub. Co., N.Y.C., 1989-92; pub. Child Mag. Network Women's Mag. div. N.Y. Times Co., N.Y.C., 1992-94; mng. dir. ambro.com., N.Y.C., 1994—, DeSilva & Phillips Media Investment Bankers, N.Y.C., 1998—. Interactive media cons., investments and sales, N.Y.C., 1994—. Contbr. articles on mag. mgmt. to Folio mag. Bd. dirs. Kidsports. Avocation: collecting books on publishing, skiing, tennis.

AMBROSE, HENRY BARTLETT, real estate broker, writer; b. Gray Hawk, Ky., Feb. 6, 1917; s. Dow Henry Ambrose and Mary Ellen Lee; m. Avenelle Gray, May 22, 1939; 1 child, Nancy Lee; m. Margaret De Los Rios Ambrose,

July 26, 1961; children: Henry Joel, Margarita Mercedes, William Armando, Azucena Julita, Anthony Bartlett. AA, L.A. City Coll.; BS, U. Advanced Rsch., Hilo, Hawaii; MS, U. Advanced Rsch., 2001. Cert. real estate broker Calif. Clk. U.S. Post Office, 1945—54, supr., 1954—56; with Douglas Aircraft, 1956—64; real estate broker, 1964—82; pub. Success Systems at Work, Placentia, Calif., 1982—. Author: I Found Atlantis, 1994, My Garden of Love Catalogue, 2001, Success Systems that Work, 2003, I Found the Garden of Eden, 2003, Atlantians Return as Anglo-Saxons, 2003, Religions Mysteries Revealed, 2003, Anglo-Saxons Voyage to Promise Land, 2003, As Aztecs from Astlan. Cpl. Med. Corps U.S. Army, 1942—46. Mem.: Pubs. Mktg. Assn. Achievements include patents for on fish alarm. Home and Office: 1112 N Bradford Ave #107 Placentia CA 92870

AMBROSE, JUDITH ANN, designer; b. San Jose, Calif., Oct. 22, 1940; d. Howard Linse and Beula May (Russell) Shannon; m. James Paul Ambrose, Apr. 17, 1965; children: Sheryl Ann Beckey, James Paul Jr. BS, Salem Coll., Winston-Salem, N.C., 1962; postgrad., Purdue U., 1963-64. Lic. home econ tchr Fla, NC. Home econs. tchr. Broward County, Ft. Lauderdale, Fla., 1962-67; owner Decorative Accents, Ft. Lauderdale, 1984-99; wedding coord. Christ Ch. United Meth., Ft. Lauderdale, 1990—. Home econs. curriculum dir. Broward County Schs., Ft. Lauderdale, Fla., 1965—66. Pres Parent Tchr Fellowship Westminster Acad, 1982—83; mem resource group Children's Diagnostic and Treatment Ctr, Ft Lauderdale, Fla., 1997—; bd. dirs. Children's Diagnostic and Treatment Ctr., Ft. Lauderdale, Fla., 2001—; founder Friends of Jack & Jill Nursery, Ft Lauderdale, Fla.; organizer shoe fund for children in community Christ Methodist Ch, 1992—; mem. Pres's Coun. Ft. Lauderdale, 1989; bd. dirs. Jack & Jill Nursery Sch, Ft Lauderdale, Fla., 1974—2000; mem. Beaux Arts, 1986—90. Recipient Outstanding Community Serv Award, Jr League of Ft Lauderdale, 1989, Golden Rule Award, J C Penney, Ft Lauderdale, 1995, Heart of the Cmty. Vol. of Yr. award, Children's Diagnostic and Treatment Ctr., Broward, Fla., 2002. Mem.: AAUW, Charity Guild (publicity chmn. 1993—96, chmn. fall function 1992, rep to Kids in Distress, bd dirs 2001—, chmn. fall function 1997, pres. 1998—99), Coral Ridge Jr Women's Club (hon.; past pres, Clubwoman of the Yr 1975—76). Republican. Methodist. Avocations: growing orchids, volunteer work. Home: 4720 NE 25th Ave Fort Lauderdale FL 33308-4811

AMBROSE, SAMUEL SHERIDAN, JR., urologist, educator; b. Jacksonville, N.C., Oct. 2, 1923; s. Samuel Sheridan and Beatrice (Collins) A.; m. Betty Stuart Stansbury, Oct. 7, 1950; children: Charles Stuart, Ann Collins, Samuel Bruce. AB in Chemistry, Duke U., 1943, MD, 1947. Diplomate: Am. Bd. Urology, Nat. Bd. Med. Examiners. Intern in surgery, then asst. resident in urology Duke U. Hosp., 1947-50, resident in urology, 1953; instr. physiology Duke U. Med. Sch., 1947, instr. urology, 1953; mem. faculty Emory U. Med. Sch., 1954—, prof. urology, 1972-92, prof. urology surgery emeritus, 1992—, chmn. div. urology, 1985-89; mem. staff Emory U. Hosp., 1972-92, chief urology, 1972-91; pvt. practice medicine specializing in urology Atlanta, 1954-71; mem. staff Piedmont Hosp., 1954-72, chief urology, 1960; mem. staff Grady Meml. Hosp., 1954-92, Henrietta Egleston Hosp. for Children, 1956-92; retired, 1992. Contbr. numerous articles to med. jours. Served as officer M.C. USNR, 1950-52. Fellow Royal Soc. Medicine; mem. AMA, ACS, Am. Urol. Assn. (hon. mem. S.E. chpt., pres. Southeastern sect. 1974-75, chmn. nat. sci. exhibits com. 1974-83, mem. exec. com. 1983-90, Disting. Svc. award 1990, Gold Cane award 1995, hon. mem. 1996—), Soc. Pediatric Urology (pres. 1971-72), Am. Assn. Clin. Urologists, Am. Acad. Pediat., Am. Assn. Genito-Urinary Surgeons, Soc. Internat. D'Urologie, Pan-Pacific Surg. Assn., Med. Assn. Ga., Ga. Urol. Assn. (pres. 1967), So. Med. Soc. (chmn. urology sect. 1970-71), Fulton County Med. Soc., Atlanta Clin. Soc. (v.p. 1964), Soc. Univ. Urologists, Piedmont Driving Club, Cherokee Town and Country Club (pres. 1968-69), Univ. Yacht Club (commodore 1973), Homosassa Fishing Club (v.p. 1980-81, 92-94). Presbyterian. Home: 1014 Nawench Dr NW Atlanta GA 30327-1340 E-mail: sam@maclanta.com.

AMBROSE, TOMMY W. chemical engineer, executive; b. Jerome, Idaho, Oct. 14, 1926; s. Fines M. and Avice (Barnes) A.; m. Shirley Ann Ball, June 23, 1951; children: Leslie Ann, Julie Lynn, Pamela Lee. BS, U. Idaho, 1950, MS, 1951, PhD (hon.), 1981; PhD, Oreg. State U., 1957. Registered profl. engr., Wash., Ohio, Idaho. Engr. GE, Richland, Wash., 1951-54, 57-60, supr. reactor fuels, 1960-63, mgr. process and reactor devel., 1963-65, mgr. rsch. and engring., 1965; mgr. for rsch. and engring. Douglas United Nuclear Co., Richland, 1969-71; asst. dir. Battelle Seattle Rsch. Ctr., 1969-71, exec. dir., 1971-75; dir. Battelle Pacific N.W. Labs., Richland, 1975-79; corp. dir. multicomponent ops. Battelle Meml. Inst., Columbus, Ohio, 1979-88, dir. Battelle Edn. and Tng. Bus., 1988-90, v.p., 1975-90; liaison officer Lawrence Livermore (Calif.) Nat. Lab., 1990-91; spl. asst. lab. affairs U. Calif., Oakland, 1992-96. Adj. prof. grad. level Idaho State U. Coll. Engring., 1998—. Mem. adv. bd. Coll. Engring., U. Idaho, Moscow, 1974-83, 85-91, chmn. adv. bd., 1988-91, 96—; mem. vis. com. Coll. Engring., U. Wash., 1974-83; adj. prof. grad. level Idaho State U. Coll. Engring., 1998-, mem. adv. coun., 1999—; mem. gov.'s adv. coun. Dept. Commerce and Econ. Devel., 1975-79; mem. Wash. State Coun. Postsecondary Edn., 1977-79; chmn. bd. trustees Columbia Basin Coll., 1967-69; bd. dirs. N.W.Coll., U. Assn. for Sci., 1976-79; v.p., trustee, mem. exec. com. Pacific Sci. Ctr. Found.; trustee, mem. exec. com. Columbus Symphony Orch., 1980-84; trustee Ohio Wesleyan U., 1987-91; bd. dirs. Idaho State Civic Symphony, 1999—, pres., 2000-01; mem. Gov.'s Sci. and Tech. Coun. for Idaho, 1999—; mem. adv. bd. Natural Heritage Ctr., 1998—; bd. dirs. U. Idaho Found., 1996—. Recipient Profl. Achievement award Idaho State U. Coll. Engring., 2000; inductee Oreg. State U. Coll. Engring. Hall of Fame, 2001. Fellow AIChE (chmn. comms. com. mgmt. divsn. 1981-87, program evaluator and mem. Accreditation Bd. for Engring. and Tech. engring. accreditation commn. 1989-96); mem. Am. Nuclear Soc., Ohio Acad. Sci., Sigma Xi, Pi Lambda Upsilon. Methodist. Home: 2500 Spider Creek Inkom ID 83245-1740

AMBROSE, WILLIAM PATRICK, engineer; b. Santa Monica, Calif., Oct. 23, 1959; s. William Donnell and Mary Alice Ambrose; m. Carol Anne Ambrose, Jan. 24, 1960; children: Anne Katherine, Mary Rae, William Howard. BS, Calif. State U., Northridge, CA, 1982; MS, Cornell U., Ithaca, NY, 1986, PhD, 1989. Vis. scientist IBM, San Jose, Calif., 1989—91; scientist Los Alamos Nat. Lab., Los Alamos, N.Mex., 1991—2002; engr. Lawrence Livermore Nat. Lab., Livermore, Calif., 2002—. Home: PO Box 808 Livermore CA 94551-0808

AMBROSE, WILLIAM WRIGHT, JR., dean, academic administrator; b. Norfolk, Va., Oct. 13, 1947; s. William Wright and Charlotte Gertrude (Williamson) Ambrose; m. Marcelia A. Conerly, Aug. 7, 1971 (div. Dec. 1986); children: William Wright III, Xandrea M., Mark S., Ariana R., LaConda G. Fanning; m. Jacqueline D. Woodard, Dec. 28, 1998. BSBA, Norfolk State U., 1974; MBA, postgrad. in EdD program, Pepperdine U. Enrolled agt. IRS; lic. ins. broker, notary pub., cmty. coll. teaching credential, Calif.; cert. tax profl. Quality assurance mgr. mfg. Corning (N.Y.) Glass Co., 1974-78; contr., plant mgr. Phillip Morris, Auburn, N.Y., 1978-79; sr. exec. mgr. Kerr Glass Corp., L.A., 1979-84; instr. Nat. Edn. Corp., Anaheim, Calif., 1985-87; assoc. prof., chmn. dept. acctg. and bus., dean, regional dean so. Calif. DeVry U., Calif., 1987—, prof. bus., 1994—, dean of bus., 1998—. CEO Global Bus. Agents, Inc., 2000; cons. Protrans, Santa Ana, Calif., 1985—, Castillo Electronics, Los Alamitos, Calif., 1986. Co-patentee polarized contaminate viewer. Sgt. Army Security Agy., U.S. Army, 1967-71, Vietnam. Mem.: Calif. Soc. CPA's, Nat. Soc. Tax Profls., Am. Prodn. and Inventory Control Soc., Am. Mgmt. Assn., Am. Acctg. Assn., Nat. Bus. Edn. Assn., Inst. Mgmt. Accts., Nat. Assn. Acad. Affairs Adminstrs., Am. Assn. Higher Edn., Sigma Beta Delta, Phi Delta Kappa. Avocations: computer programming, golf, writing, international consulting, ebusiness. Home: 795 S Pampas Ave Rialto CA 92376-2102 Office: DeVry U 901 Corporate Center Dr Pomona CA 91768-2642 E-mail: bambrose@socal.devry.edu .

AMBROSI, SANDRA ELIZABETH, retired nurse, educator; b. Albany, N.Y., May 15, 1938; d. James Syme and Elizabeth Clare (Volwieder) Woodward; children: Lisa Marie Lawson, Ronald James Ambrosi. BS, Columbia U., 1962; MN, U. Wash., 1965; MPA, U. Hartford, Conn., 1983. RN, N.Y., Conn., Calif. Instr. Hartford Hosp. Sch. Nursing, 1965-66; dir. staff devel. Johnson Meml. Hosp., Stafford Springs, Conn., 1966-70, dir. utilization rev., 1970-75, dir. quality assurance, 1975-81; dir. delivery sys. AMI Health Advantage, San Diego, 1984-87; resource nurse Ask-A-Nurse, San Diego, 1988-91; sch. health specialist San Diego Unified Sch. Dist., 1991—2003; ret., 2003. Mem. Nat. Assn. Healthcare Quality (pres. 1978-80, cert. profl. healthcare quality), Nat. Assn. Sch. Nurses, S.D. Edn. Assn., Sigma Theta Tau.

AMBROSIO, DEBORAH ANN, critical care nurse; b. N.Y., Aug. 21, 1959; d. Raphael J. and Lydia C. (Roman) A.; m. Bruce R. Mawhirter, Oct. 2, 1983. BSN, Adelphi U., 1981, MS, 1996. RN, N.Y. Primary nurse med./surg. unit St. Francis Hosp., Roslyn, N.Y., 1981-83, primary nurse RICU, 1983-86; asst. coord. nursing care L.I. Vascular Ctr., Roslyn, 1986-88, coord. nursing care, 1988-94, clin. nurse specialist, 1994-97; performance improvement coord. nursing South Nassau Cmtys. Hosp., Oceanside, N.Y., 1996—. Adj. faculty mem. Sch. Nursing Adelphi U., 1994—. Contbr. to profl. jours. and newsletters. Mem. AACCN, Am. Heart Assn. (cert. instr. CPR), N.Y. State Nurses Assn., Soc. Peripheral Vascular Nursing, Soc. Non-Invasive Vascular Tech., Sigma Theta Tau (pres.-elect 1998-2000, pres. 2000-2002, Alpha Omega chpt., exec. com., chmn. 1995-2000, com. scholarship fund raising, corr. sec.).

AMBROSIO, MICHAEL ANGELO, judge; b. N.Y.C., Apr. 23, 1945; s. Vincent and Margaret (Carrillo) A.; m. Regina Maria Neal, Sept. 11, 1983. BA, Fordham U., 1966; JD, Harvard U., 1969. Bar: N.Y. 1970. Atty. N.Y. State Mental Hygiene Legal Svc., N.Y.C., 1969-72; atty. grievance com. Assn. of Bar City, N.Y.C., 1972-74; atty. Corp. Counsel N.Y.C., 1974-75; dep. dir. N.Y. State Mental Hygiene Legal Svc., N.Y.C., 1975-83; judge N.Y.C. Family Ct., 1983—; acting justice N.Y. Supreme Ct., 1986—. Mem. Assn. Bar City N.Y., Phi Beta Kappa. Avocations: classical music, reading, swimming. Office: Supreme Ct Kings County 120 Schermerhorn St Brooklyn NY 11201-5108

AMBROSIUS, LLOYD EUGENE, historian, educator; b. Macomb, Ill., Aug. 21, 1941; s. Sterling Elvin and Grace Elizabeth (Baxter) Ambrosius; m. Margery Grace Marzahn, Aug. 24, 1963; children: Walter Thomas, Paul William. BA, U. Ill., 1963, MA in History, 1964, PhD in History, 1967. Prof. history U. Nebr., Lincoln, 1967—; Fulbright prof. history U. Cologne, Germany, 1972—73; Mary Ball Washington prof. Am. history U. Coll., Dublin, 1977—78; Fulbright prof. history U. Heidelberg, Germany, 1996. Author: Woodrow Wilson and the American Diplomatic Tradition, 1987, Wilsonian Statecraft, 1991, Wilsonianism, 2002. Dir. Gen. Bd. Global Ministries United Meth. Ch., 1984—92; del. gen. assembly Nat. Coun. Chs., N.Y.C., 1995—2003. Recipient German Marshall Fund award, 1990. Mem.: Soc. Historians Am. Fgn. Rels., Orgn. Am. Historians, Am. Hist. Assn. Avocation: softball. Home: 6545 S 34th St Lincoln NE 68516 Office: U Nebr Dept History Lincoln NE 68588-0327 Office Fax: 402-472-8839. E-mail: lea@unlserve.unl.edu.

AMBROZIC, ALOYSIUS CARDINAL (HIS EMINENCE ALOYSIUS CARDINAL AMBROZIC), cardinal; b. Gabrje, Slovenia, Jan. 27, 1930; s. Aloysius and Helen (Pecar) Ambrozic. Student, St. Augustine Sem., 1955; STL, U. San Tommaso, Rome, 1958, Sacrae Scripturae Licentiatus, Biblicum, Rome, 1960; ThD, U. Wurzburg, 1970. Ordained priest Roman Cath. Ch., 1955. Ordained aux. bishop of Roman Cath. Ch., Toronto, 1976; appointed coadjutor archbishop of Toronto, 1986; archbishop of Toronto, 1990—; created cardinal, 1998. Faculty St. Augustines Sem., Scarborough, Ont., Canada, 1956—76, dean studies, 1971—76; rep. Synod on the Formation of Priests, Rome, 1990, Synod on Religious Life, Rome, 1994; prof. N.T. exegesis Toronto Sch. Theology, 1970—76; apptd. to Pontifical Coun. for Pastoral Care of Migrants and Itinerant People, 1990, Vatican Congregation for Clergy, 1991, Pontifical Coun. for Culture, 1993, Vatican Congregation for Divine Worship and Discipline of Sacraments, 1999, Congregation for Oriental Chs., 1999. Author: The Hidden Kingdom: A Redaction-Critical Study of the References to the Kingdom of God in Mark's Gospel, 1972, Remarks on the Canadian Catechism, 1974; past columnist: Cath. Register. Roman Catholic.

AMBRUS, CLARA MARIA, physician; b. Rome, Dec. 28, 1924; came to U.S., 1949, naturalized, 1955; d. Anthony and Charlotte (Schneider) Bayer; m. Julian Lawrence Ambrus, Feb. 17, 1945; children: Madeline Ambrus Lillie, Peter, Julian, Linda Ambrus-Broenniman, Steven, Katherine Ambrus-Cheney, Charles. Student, U. Budapest (Hungary), 1943-47; MD, U. Zurich, Switzerland, 1949; postgrad., U. Paris, 1949; PhD, Jefferson Med. Coll., 1955. Diplomate: Am. Bd. Clin. Chemists. Research asst. Inst. Histology, Embryology and Biology U. Budapest, 1943-45; demonstrator in pharmacology U. Budapest Med. Sch., 1946-47; asst. dept. pharmacology U. Zurich Med. Sch., 1947-49; asst. dept. therapeutic chemistry and virology Inst. Pasteur, Paris, 1949; asst. prof. pharmacology Phila. Coll. Pharmacy and Sci., 1950-52, asso. prof., 1952-55; research asso. Roswell Park Meml. Inst., Buffalo, 1955-58, sr. cancer research scientist, 1958-64, asso. scientist, 1964-69, prin. cancer research scientist, 1969-85; prof. pharmacology State U. N.Y., Buffalo Med. and Grad. Schs., 1955—, asso. prof. pediatrics, 1955-76, prof. pediatrics, 1976, research prof. ob-gyn, 1983—; chmn., founder, chief of R&D Hemex Inc., 1984—. Contbr. articles to med. and sci. jours. Trustee Nichols Sch., Buffalo, Community Music Sch. Named Outstanding Woman of Western N.Y. Cmty. Adv. Coun., SUNY, Buffalo, 1980, Med. Woman of Yr., Buffalo Gen. Hosp., 2000, Lady Comdr. of the Equestrian Order of the Holy Sepulchre of Jerusalem, 1991, comdr., 1996; recipient George F. Koepf, MD award Hauptman-Woodward Med. Rsch. Inst., Buffalo, 1997. Fellow: ACP, Internat. Soc. Hematology; mem.: Hungarian Acad. Sci. (fgn. mem.), Am. Med. Women's Assn., Buffalo Acad. Medicine, Am. Soc. Hematology, Am. Physiol. Soc., Am. Fedn. Clin. Rsch., Am. Soc. Cancer Rsch., Am. Soc. Pharmacology and Exptl. Therapeutics, Saturn Club, Clarksburg Country Club, Garrett Club, Sigma Xi. Home: 143 Windsor Ave Buffalo NY 14209-1020 also: West Hill Farm Boston NY 14025 Office: Buffalo Gen Hosp 100 High St Buffalo NY 14203-1154

AMBRUS, JULIAN L. physician, medical educator; b. Budapest, Hungary, Nov. 29, 1924; came to U.S., 1949, naturalized, 1955; s. Alexander and Elizabeth Ambrus; m. Clara M. Bayer, Feb. 18, 1945; children: Madeline (Mrs. David Lillie), Peter, Julian, Linda (Mrs. Edward Broenniman), Steven, Katherine (Mrs. Thomas Cheney), Charles. Student. U. Budapest, 1942-47; MD., U. Zurich, 1949; postgrad., Sorbonne, 1949-50; PhD in Med. Sci, Jefferson Med. Coll., 1954; ScD (hon.), Niagara U., 1984. Diplomate: Am. Bd. Clin. Chemistry, Am. Acad. Pain Mgmt. Research asst., instr. histology and med. biology U. Budapest, 1943-45, demonstrator pharmacology, 1946-47; asst. pharmacology U. Zurich, 1947-49; asst. dept. therapeutic chemistry, virology and tropical medicine Inst. Pasteur, Paris, 1949; asst. prof., asso. prof., prof. Phila. Coll. Pharmacology and Sci., 1950-55; prin. cancer research scientist Roswell Park Meml. Cancer Inst. and Hosp., 1955-65; asst. to the dir. Roswell Park Meml. Inst. and Hosp., 1961-65; dir. Springville Labs., 1965-75, dir. cancer research, head dept. pathophysiology, 1975-89, mem. dept. medicine, 1989-92; asst. prof. pharmacology U. Buffalo Med. Sch., 1955-61, asso. prof. pharmacology, 1961-65, prof., 1965-72; chmn. Roswell Park div. exec. com. Grad. Sch., 1955-65; assoc. in internal medicine SUNY, Buffalo, 1961-64, asst. prof. internal medicine, 1964-66, prof. biochem. pharmacology, 1964-80, assoc. prof. internal medicine, 1966-71, prof., 1971—; prof., chmn. dept. exptl. pathology Grad. Sch., 1972-92; prof. emeritus, 1992—. Attending physician Roswell Park Meml. Cancer Hosp., 1955-92, prof. emeritus Roswell Park Cancer Inst., 1992—; attending physician Buffalo Gen. Hosp., Erie County Med. Ctr., Children's Hosp. Buffalo, 1983—; cons. Millard Fillmore Hosp., Sisters of Charity Hosp., Buffalo, 1983—; dir. Instnl. Cancer Tng. Program, USPHS, 1956-65; mem. com. Thrombolytic agts. USPHS-NIH, 1960-66; cons. adv. com. on thrombosis AMA Coun. Drugs; Blood Coagulation Components, Protein Found., Cambridge, Mass.; Bur. Drugs FDA, WHO, Geneva; commr. Lake Erie chpt. U.S. Pony Clubs, mem. intercollegiate polo com. Editor-in-chief: Revs. of Hematology Jour. Medicine; contbr. articles to profl. jours. Trustee Calasanctius Prep. Sch. for Acad. Gifted, 1964-92. Decorated Order of Alexander the Great (France), knight comdr. Equestrian Order Holy Sepulcher of Jerusalem; recipient first prize med. student paper Hungarian Med. Sch., 1947, 1st prize surgery U. Budapest, 1947, Nelson lectureship and medal U. Calif. Davis, 1972, George F. Koepf award in biomed. rsch. Hauptman-Woodward Med. Rsch. Inst., 1997, Heart and Hand award EUA, 1997, Louis A. and Ruth Siegel award SUNY Buffalo Sch. Medicine, 1997; named Disting. Alumnus Thomas Jefferson U., 1990. Fellow ACP, AAAS, Am. Coll. Nuclear Physicians, Am. Coll. Angiology, Royal Soc. Medicine, Am. Coll. Pharmacology and Chemotherapy, Coun. on Clin. Cardiology, Am. Heart Assn., Internat. Coll. Angiology, Am. Geriat. Soc., N.Y. Acad. Sci., Internat. Soc. Hematology; mem. NAS (fgn. mem. Hungary), Am. Soc. Hematology, Am. Soc. Pathologists, Am. Soc. Nuclear Medicine, Am. Soc. Pharmacology and Exptl. Therapeutics, Am. Soc. Physiology, Am. Assn. Cancer Rsch., Am. Soc. Clin. Oncology, Fedn. Clin. Rsch., Soc. Exptl. Biology and Medicine, Assn. Am. Med. Colls., Cath. Physicians Guild (pres. 1985-86, 93-96), Sigma Xi, Rho Chi, Physiol. Soc. Phila., Radiation Rsch. Soc., Buffalo Zool. Soc. (chmn. Sci. Com. 1965-66), Buffalo Acad. Medicine (pres. 1976-77). Home: 143 Windsor Ave Buffalo NY 14209-1020 also: West Hill Farm Emmerling Rd Boston NY 14025 Office: Buffalo Gen Hosp Kaleida Health Sys SUNY/B 100 High St Buffalo NY 14203-1154 Fax: 716-859-1491.

AMBRUS, LORNA, medical/surgical nurse, geriatrics nurse; b. Phila., June 17, 1956; d. Walter C. and Joan B. (Watts) Beilfuss; 1 child, Victoria. LPN, Upper Bucks Vo-Tech., Perkasie, Pa., 1976; diploma, Gwynedd Mercy Coll., 1989. RN. Nurse Doylestown Hosp., 1976—78, Grandview Hosp., Sellersville, 1978—83, Quality Care, Allentown, 1983—89, Comprehensive Home Care, Doylestown, 1983—89, Doylestown Manor, 1990—99; RN psychiat. nurse Growth Horizons, Pipersville, Pa., 2002—03; pediat. nurse Harleysville Pediatric Healthcare, Allentown, 2003; nurse staff relief Howells Temp. Staffing Svcs., 2002—. Actor:. Home: 118 Jefferson Ct Quakertown PA 18951-1417

AMDAHL, DOUGLAS KENNETH, retired state supreme court justice; b. Mabel, Minn., Jan. 23, 1919; BBA, U. Minn., 1945; JD summa cum laude, William Mitchell Coll. Law, 1951, L.L.D. (hon.), 1987. Bar: Minn. 1951, Fed. Dist. Ct. 1952. Ptnr. Amdahl & Scott, Mpls., 1951-55; asst. county atty. Hennepin County, Minn., 1955-61; judge Mcpl. Ct., Mpls., 1961-62, Dist. Ct. 4th Dist., Minn., 1962-80, chief judge, 1973-75; assoc. justice Minn. Supreme Ct., 1980-81, chief justice, 1981-89; of counsel Rider, Bennett, Egan & Arundel, Mpls., 1989-99; ret. Asst. registrar, then registrar Mpls. Coll. Law, 1951-65; moot ct. instr. U. Minn.; faculty mem. and advisor Nat. Coll. State Judiciary; mem. Nat. Bd. Trial Advocacy; chmn. Nat. Ctr. for State Cts. Delay Reduction Adv. Com., 1986-88, Nat. Ctr. for State Cts. Coordinating Coun. on Life-Sustaining Decisionmaking by the Cts., 1989-93. Mem. ABA (chmn. com. on stds. of jud. adminstrn. 1987-96), Minn. Bar Assn., Hennepin County Bar Assn., Internat. Acad. Trial Judges, State Dist. Ct. Judges Assn. (pres. 1976-77), Conf. of Chief Judges (bd. dirs. 1987-88), Delta Theta Phi (assoc. justice supreme ct.). Home: 2322 W 53rd St Minneapolis MN 55410-2501 E-mail: dougamdahl@aol.com.

AMDUR, ARTHUR R. lawyer; b. Houston, Jan. 10, 1946; s. Paul S. and Florence Amdur; m. Dora B.; children— Josh, Jonny, Shira. B.A., 1967; J.D., 1970; LL.M., 1974. Bar: Tex. 1970, D.C. 1974; cert. immigration law Tex. Bd. Legal Specialization, 1988 . pvt. practice, Houston and Washington, 1970-76; asst. U.S. atty, Houston, 1976-82; pvt. practice, Houston, 1982—, lectr. on immigration law ; adj. prof. law South Tex. Coll. Law, Houston. Bd. dirs. YMCA Internat. Refugee Ctr., 1985—; spl. asst. to gen. counsel Republican Nat. Com., Washington, 1974. Named Adj. Law Prof. of Yr., South Tex. Coll. Law, 1983. Mem. Fed. Bar Assn. (pres. 1981), Tex. State Bar Assn., Am. Immigration Lawyers Assn., Immigration Law Examiner, State Bar Tex. (bd. legal specialization 1997—). Jewish. Club: Georgetown U. Alumni (pres. 1984) (Houston). Office: Amdur Law Office 6161 Savoy Dr Ste 450 Houston TX 77036-3379

AMDUR, MARTIN BENNETT, lawyer; b. N.Y.C., Aug. 19, 1942; s. Charles and Helen (Freedman) A.; m. Shirley Bell, May 25, 1975; children: Richard J., Stephen B. AB, Cornell U., 1964; LLB, Yale U., 1967; LLM in Taxation, NYU, 1968. Bar: N.Y. 1968, U.S. Tax Ct. 1970, U.S. Dist. Ct. (so. and ea. dists.) N.Y. 1971. Assoc. Weil, Gotshal & Manges LLP, N.Y.C., 1968-75, ptnr., 1975—. Lectr. various tax insts. Contbr. articles to legal jours. Mem. ABA, Am. Coll. Tax Counsel, N.Y. State Bar Assn., Assn. Bar City N.Y. Home: 983 Park Ave Apt 6B New York NY 10028-0808 Office: Weil Gotshal & Manges LLP 767 Fifth Ave New York NY 10153-0119 Office Fax: 212-310-6891. E-mail: Martin.Amdur@Weil.com.

AMEDURI, MICHAEL A, education educator, consultant; b. Youngstown, Ohio, Oct. 21, 1972; s. Robert A and Judith C Ameduri; m. Kendra L Sinopoli, June 15, 1997. BS in math., Younstown State U., 1994; MS in math., Youngstown State U., 1996. Coord. officer academic skills lab Tex. A&M-Kingsville, 1996; asst. prof. of math. Butler County C.C., Pa., 1996—. Adv. bd. mem. Act 101, Butler, Pa., 1999—2001; math. cons. McGraw Hill, 2001. Math. judge Armstrong Cable Co., Butler, Pa., 1997—2002. Mem.: Am. Math. Assn. for Two Yr. Colleges. Office: Butler County Cmty Coll PO Box 1203 Butler PA 16001 E-mail: mike.ameduri@bc3.edu.

AMELAN, BJORN G. choreographer; Ptnr. Fashion Designer Patrick Kelly, 1983—90; choreographer Bill T. Jones/Arnie Zane Dance Co., N.Y.C., 1993—. Office: Bill T Jones/Arnie Zane Co Found for Dance Promotion 803 Broadway Ste 1706 New York NY 10003

AMELAR, RICHARD DANIEL, urologist, andrologist; b. N.Y.C., July 9, 1927; m. Alice Zinman, 1952; children: Jessica, Sarah, Susanna. BA, NYU, 1946, MD, 1950. Intern in urology French Hosp., 1950-51, resident in urology, 1951-54, attending urologist, 1956—68, dir. urology, 1968—77; pvt. practice urology, N.Y.C., 1956-96; mem. faculty NYU, 1956—, prof. clin. urology, 1977—; dir. Male Infertility Clinic, Bellevue Hosp., 1958-72, dir. Free Vasectomy Clinic, 1970-72, attending urologist, 1972—96; expert urol. cons. NY State Dept. Health, Office Profl. Med. Conduct, 2001—. Dir. male infertility svcs. Margaret Sanger Rsch. Bur., 1959-68; cons. WHO, Nat. Inst. Child Health and Human Devel., drug evaluation sect. AMA, NSF. Cons. editor Urology; assoc. editor Internat. Jour. Fertility; editl. bds. Fertility and Sterility, Jour. Andrology Internat. Jour. Nephrology, Urology, Andrology. Capt. M.C., USAF, 1954-56. Grantee Irene Heinz Given and John La Porte Given Found. and N.Y. Found., 1970; recipient Disting. Andrologist award Am. Soc. Andrology, 1999; recipient Disting. Svc. award Am. Soc. Reproductive Medicine, 2002. Fellow ACS; mem. Am. Soc. Andrology, Soc. Sci. Study Sex (pres. 1970-71), Soc. Reproductive Surgeons, Am. Soc. for Study of Male Reprodn., Am. Urol. Assn., Am. Fertility Soc., Endocrine Soc., Pacific Coast Fertility Soc., Alpha Omega Alpha (alumni mem. 1991). Home: 526 Bull Mill Rd Chester NY 10918-4706 E-mail: ramelar@frontiernet.net.

AMEMIYA, TAKESHI, economist, statistician; b. Tokyo, Mar. 29, 1935; s. Kenji and Shizuko A.; m. Yoshiko Miyaki, May 5, 1969; children: Naoko, Kentaro. BA, Internat. Christian U., 1958; MA in Econs., Am. U., 1961; PhD, Johns Hopkins U., 1964. Mem. faculty Stanford U., (Calif.), 1964-66, 68—, prof. econs., 1974-86, Edward Ames Edmonds prof. econs., 1986—. Lectr. Inst. Econ. Research, Hitotsubashi U., Tokyo, 1966-68; cons. Author books and articles; mem. editl. bd. profl. jours. Recipient U.S. Sr. Scientist award Alexander von Humboldt Found., Fed. Republic Germany, 1988; Ford Found. fellow, 1963; Guggenheim fellow, 1975; NSF grantee; fellow Japan Soc. for Promotion of Sci., 1989. Fellow Econometric Soc., Am. Acad. Arts and Scis., Am. Statis. Assn.; mem. Internat. Statis. Inst., Am. Econ. Assn., Inst. Math. Stats., Phi Beta Kappa. Home: 923 Casanueva Pl Stanford CA 94305-1001 Office: Stanford Univ Dept Econs Stanford CA 94305 E-mail: amemiya@stanford.edu.

AMEND, JAMES MICHAEL, lawyer; b. Chgo., July 19, 1942; s. Nathan and Edith (Greenberg) A.; m. Sheila Rae Cohen, Apr. 4, 1971; children: Allison, Anthony. BSE, U. Mich., 1964, JD, 1967. Bar: Ill. 1968, U.S. Dist. Ct. (no. dist.) Ill. 1968, U.S. Ct. Appeals (7th cir.) 1969, U.S. Supreme Ct. 1970, U.S. Ct. Appeals (9th cir.) 1985. Ptnr. Kirkland & Ellis, Chgo., 1968—. Prof. Stanford U. Law Sch., 1996-97. Editor U. Mich. Law Rev., 1966, Patent Law: A Primer for Federal District Court Judges, 1998; author: Intellectual Property Law, 1982. Chmn. Chgo. Lawyers Com. for Civil Rights Under Law, 1985-86. Fulbright scholar, 1967. Mem. ABA, U.S. Trademark Assn., Mid-Am. Club (Chgo.). Jewish. Avocations: running, skiing, golf. Office: Kirkland & Ellis 200 E Randolph St Fl 54 Chicago IL 60601-6636

AMEND, JOSEPH H., III, BS in Civil Engring., Va. Poly. Inst. and State U., 1971, MS in Civil Engring., 1972, PhD in Civil Engring., 1973. Commd. 2d lt. USAF, 1971, advanced through grades to col., 1996; assoc. prof. civil engring., vice commandant and dean Civil Engr. and Svcs. Sch., Air Force Inst. Tech., 1997—98, assoc. prof. civil engring., dean Civil Engr. and Svcs. Sch., 1998—2001, vice commandant, 2001—. Decorated Meritorious Svc. medal with 4 oak leaf clusters, Commendation medal with one oak leaf cluster,

Achievement medal, Outstanding Unit award with 3 oak leaf clusters, Organizational Excellence award with 3 oak leaf clusters, Def. Svc. medal with svc. star, Armed Forces Expeditionary medal; named Air Force Mil. Engr. of Yr., Nat. Soc. Profl. Engrs., 1984. Fellow: ASCE; mem.: Chi Epsilon, Tau Beta Pi, Phi Kappa Phi. Office: Air Force Inst Tech Office of Pub Affairs Wright Patterson Afb OH 45433-7765

AMEND, WILLIAM JOHN CONRAD, JR., physician, educator; b. Wilmington, Del., Sept. 17, 1941; s. William John Conrad and Catherine (Broad) A.; m. Constance Roberts, Feb. 3, 1962; children— William, Richard, Nicole, Mark BA, Amherst Coll., 1963; MD, Cornell U., 1967. Diplomate Am. Bd. Internal Medicine. Asst. clin. prof. U. Calif. Med. Ctr., San Francisco, 1974-76, assoc. clin. prof., 1977-82, prof. clin. medicine and surgery, 1982—; chief divsn. nephrology U. Calif., San Francisco, 1999—; physician Falmouth Med. Assocs. Contbr. articles to med. jours. Chmn. med. adv. com. No. Calif. Kidney Found., 1987-88; mem. stewardship com. 1st Presbyn. Ch., Burlingame, Calif., 1983, 84, elder, 1982-85, 93-96. Maj. U.S. Army, 1969-71. Simpson fellow, 1963; recipient Gift of Life award No. Calif. Kidney Found., 1994. Fellow: ACP; mem.: Amherst Coll. Alumni Fund (class agt. 1973-83, reunion chmn. 2003, class pres. 2003—). Republican. Avocations: golf, gardening, hiking. Home: 2860 Summit Dr Burlingame CA 94010-6257 Office: U Calif Med Ctr 3rd & Parnassus San Francisco CA 94143-0001

AMENDOLA, SAL JOHN, artist, educator, writer; b. Fiumefreddo, Calabria, Italy, Mar. 8, 1948; came to U.S., 1948; s. Joseph and Mary (Amendola) A. Grad., Erasmus Hall H.S., Bklyn.; 3-yr. cert., Sch. Visual Arts, N.Y.C., 1966-69. Illustator, writer DC Comics, Archie Comics, Marvel, N.Y.C., 1969-86; asst. editor, prodn. DC Comics, N.Y.C., 1970; talent coord., editor DC Comics, Warner Communications, N.Y.C., 1983-86; illustration instr. Sch. Visual Arts, Fashion Inst., N.Y.C., 1974—; founder SRV plus 1, 1990. Lectr., cons., instr. seminars at librs., mus., schs., U.S., Can., 1983-86; freelance illustrator, 1987—. Writer, illustrator: (comic book) Batman Night of the Stalker, 1972 (Best Story Nominee 1973); editor: (comic books) Elvira's House of Mystery, Talent Showcase, 1984-86; co-artist: (movie adaptation) Superman III, 1983, (comic book) Star Trek, 1984; author, artist: (book) Perspective for Artists, 1984, (book) Other Intelligences/A Sociopolitical View, 1990; artist: (comic book) Archie, 1987 (Best Artist nominee 1988); creator young adult books The Yoomee Adventures; designer toys and games; book illustrator, designer, illustrator book jackets; portrait painter. Mem. Nat. Cartoonist Soc. (profl. com. 1987), Soc. Ilustrators. Liberal Democrat. Avocations: science, politics, foreign languages. Home: 1028 67th St Brooklyn NY 11219-5923 E-mail: srvplus1@aol.com.

AMENT, MARK STEVEN, lawyer; b. Louisville, Sept. 4, 1951; s. Milton and Bernice (Rosenberg) A.; m. Elaine Sue Winkler, Dec. 28, 1976; children: Aaron Samuel, Rachel Lynn. BA, Northwestern U., 1973; JD, Duke U., 1976; LLM in Taxation, U. Miami, 1977. Bar: Ky. 1976, Fla. 1977. Assoc. Greenebaum Doll & McDonald, Louisville, 1977-82, ptnr., 1982-95; mem. Greenebaum Doll & McDonald PLLC, Louisville, 1995—, co-chair emerging techs. group, 2000—. Bd. dirs., sec. Evans Furniture Co., Louisville; lectr. in field. Commr. City of Robinswood, Ky., 1986-99; active Louisville Mayor's Task Force on Low-Income Housing, 1987; v.p. Ctrl. Agy. for Jewish Edn., 1991-94; trustee Congregation Adath Jeshurun, 1995-98; exec. com. Jewish Family and Vocat. Svc. Mem. ABA (com. on comml. fin. svcs., com. on venture capital), Ky. Bar Assn., Louisville Bar Assn., Fla. Bar Assn., Am. Health Lawyers Assn., Nat. Assn. Coll. and Univ. Attys. (mem. publs. com.), Thoroughbred Owners and Breeders Assn., Northwestern U. Alumni Assn. (bd. dirs. 2000—). Democrat. Avocations: basketball, thoroughbreds. Office: Greenebaum Doll & McDonald PLLC 3300 National City Tower Louisville KY 40202 E-mail: msa@gdm.com.

AMENT, RICHARD RAND, psychologist; b. Merrill, Wis., Aug. 5, 1950; s. Jacob John and Edith Jean (Selner) A.; m. Mary Elizabeth Beau, Aug. 5, 1978; children: Adrianne Beth, Jacob John III, Breanne Beau. BS, U. Wis., Eau Claire, 1972; MSEd, U. Wis., Stout of Menominee, 1974. Sch. psychologist Wausau (Wis.) Sch. Dist., 1974—. Mem. profl. adv. bd. Children with Attention Deficit Disorders North Ctrl. Wis., 1991-92. V.p. Montessori Presch., Inc., Wausau, 1986, pres., 1987, 93-95; bd. dirs., 1992-94; treas. Marathon County Reps., Wausau, 1977-99, 2001; campaign mgr. Kasten for Assembly, Wausau, 1982; Marathon County chmn. Gov. Thompson for Wis. campaign, 1990, 94; county chmn. Bush for Pres. campaign, 1992; mem. St. Michael's Cath. Ch., 1991-92; county coord. Vannes for Congress, 1992; bd. dirs. Citizens for Neighborhood Schs., 1991-94; parent adv. bd. Horace Mann Mid. Sch., 1994-95; treas. Friends of Judge Howard campaign, 1996—, Jacobson for Assembly campaign, 1996-98. Mem. Wis. Sch. Psychologists Assn. (mem. exec. bd. 1983-85), Sch. Psychologists of Wis.'s North (v.p. 1976-77, 81-82, pres. 1983-85). Avocations: golf, fishing, hunting, tennis. Home: 1800 Forest Valley Rd Wausau WI 54403-2038 Office: Wausau Pub Schs 415 Seymour St Wausau WI 54403-6267

AMERSHEK, KATHLEEN, education educator; b. Johnstown, Pa., Dec. 1, 1929; d. Rudie J. and Helen (McKernan) Amershek; m. E.P. McLoone, 1973. BS, Western Pa. State Coll., 1951; MEd, Pa. State U., 1957; PhD, U. Minn., 1966. Tchr. Westmont-Upper Yoder Sch. Dist., Johnstown, 1951-56; grad. asst. Pa. State U., 1956-57; supr. SUNY, Brockport, 1957-60; assoc. prof. early childhood and elem. edn. U. Md., College Park, 1966-96, prof. emeritus, 1996—. Cons. Student Vol. Programs of Catholic Student Center, Pa. Dept. Pub. Health; mem. Md. Com. Early Childhood Edn., 1969—. Contbr. to Ency. Rsch. in Edn. Mem. Tri-State Assn. Student Tchg. (past rec. sec. Minn.), Md. Tchrs. Assn. (pres. higher edn. coun. 1973-75), Am. Ednl. Rsch Assn., Assn. Student Tchg. (pres. Md. state assn. 1990-91), Pi Lambda Theta. Home: 102 Clarion St Johnstown PA 15905-2220 Office: U Md Coll Edn College Park MD 20742-0001

AMES, ADELBERT, III, neurophysiologist, educator; b. Boston, Feb. 25, 1921; MD, Harvard U., 1945. Intern, then resident in internal medicine Presbyn. Hosp., 1945-52; rsch. assoc. Med. Sch. Harvard U., Boston, 1955-69, prof. physiology, dept. surgery, 1969-91, Charles Anthony Pappas prof. neurosci. Med. Sch., 1983-91, prof. emeritus, 1991—; neurophysiologist in neurosurgery Mass. Gen. Hosp., Boston, 1983—. Recipient Rsch. Scientist award NIMH, 1968-80. Mem. Am. Physiol. Soc., Am. Soc. Neurochemistry, Soc. Neurosci., Internat. Soc. Neurochemistry. Home: 84 Jenckes Rd Brattleboro VT 05301-9258 E-mail: delames@sover.net.

AMES, BRUCE N(ATHAN), biochemist, molecular biologist; b. N.Y.C., Dec. 16, 1928; s. Maurice U. and Dorothy (Andres) A.; m. Giovanna Ferro-Luzzi, Aug. 26, 1960; children: Sofia, Matteo. BA, Cornell U., 1950; PhD, Calif. Inst. Tech., 1953. Chief sect. NIH, Bethesda, Md., 1962-67; prof. biochemistry and molecular biology U. Calif., Berkeley, 1968—, chmn. biochemistry dept., 1983-89. Mem. Nat. Cancer Adv. Bd., 1976-82. Research, publs. on bacterial molecular biology, histidine biosynthesis and its control, aging, mutagenesis, detection of environ. mutagens and carcinogens, genetic toxicology, oxygen radicals and disease. Recipient Flemming award, 1966, Rosenstiel award, 1976, Felix Wankel award, 1978, John Scott medal, 1979, Corson medal, 1980, Mott prize GM Cancer Rsch. Found., 1983, Gairdner award, 1983, Tyler prize for environ. achievement, 1985, gold medal Am. Inst. Chemists, 1991, Glenn Found. Gerontology award, 1992, Roentgen prize Nat. Acad. Lincei, 1993, Lovelace award for excellence in environ. health rsch., 1995, Honda prize, 1997, Kehoe award, 1997, The U.S. Nat. Medal of Sci., 1998, Medal City of Paris, 1998, The Linus Pauling Inst. prize for health rsch., 2001, Lifetime Achievement award Abbott-ASM, 2001. Fellow Acad. Toxicol. Scis., Am. Acad. Microbiology, Gerontol. Soc. Am.; mem. NAS, Am. Soc. Biol. Chemists, Am. Soc. Microbiology (N.B. lectr. 1980, Abbott Lifetime Achievement award 2001), Environ. Mutagen Soc. (award 1977), Genetics Soc., Am. Assn. Cancer Rsch., Soc. Toxicology (Gustavus John Esselen award 1992), Am. Chem. Soc. (Eli Lilly award 1964), Royal Swedish Acad. Scis., Am. Acad. Arts and Scis. Home: 1324 Spruce St Berkeley CA 94709-1435 Office: CHORI 5700 ML King Jr Way Oakland CA 94609 E-mail: bnames@uclink4.berkeley.edu.

AMES, DONALD PAUL, retired aerospace company executive, researcher; b. Brandon, Manitoba, Can., Sept. 13, 1922; came to U.S., 1932; s. Paul and Della Johanna (Hebel) A.; m. Doris Elizabeth Ubbelohde, Dec. 30, 1949; children: Elizabeth Carol Ames Herbert, Barbara Louise Ames Jones. BS in Chemistry, U. Wis., 1944, PhD in Phys. Chemistry, 1949; LLD (hon.), U. Mo., St. Louis, 1978. AEC postdoctoral fellow, 1949-50; staff chemist Los Alamos Sci. Lab., 1950-52; asst. prof. physical chemistry U. Ky., Lexington, 1952-54; staff chemist DuPont Co., Aiken, S.C., 1954-56; sr. rsch. chemist, scientist/fellow Monsanto, St. Louis, 1956-61; from scientist to sr. scientist rsch. div. McDonnell Aircraft Co., St. Louis, 1961-68; from dep. dir. rsch. to dir. rsch. McDonnell Douglas Rsch. Labs., St. Louis, 1968-71, dir., 1971-76, staff v.p., 1976-86, staff v.p., gen. mgr., disting. fellow, 1986-89, cons., 1989—; pres. Fluotech Inc., 1991—. Adj. prof. physics U. Mo., St. Louis, 1989—; prof. physics Washington U., St. Louis, 1989-99; mem. vis. com. dept. mech. engring. Lehigh U., 1984-90; mem. adv. bd. Coll. Engring., U. Ill., Urbana, 1986-89; mem. spl. com. U. Chgo. 7 GeV Synchrotron Light Source, 1984-89; adv. com. U. Mo. Rsch. Reactor, Columbia, 1985-92; mem. indsl. adv. coun. dept. chemistry U. Mo., St. Louis, 1985-95; mem. subcom. on materials sci. and engring. needs and opportunities in aerospace industry NAS, 1985-86; bd. dirs. St. Louis Tech. Ctr., 1983-95; participant Manhattan Project U.S. Army, 1944-46. Contbr. articles to profl. jours.; patentee in field. With U.S. Army, 1944-46. Recipient Civic award St. Louis sect. AIAA, 1985, James B. Eads award Acad. Sci. St. Louis, 2003; Wis. Alumni Rsch. fellow, 1946-48, AEC fellow, 1948-49, Monsanto fellow, 1959-61, McDonnell Douglas Disting. fellow, 1986-89. Mem. Am. Phys. Soc., Am. Chem. Soc., Soc. Engring Sci., Combustion Inst., Mo. Acad. Sci., Phi Beta Kappa, Sigma Xi, Phi Eta Sigma, Phi Kappa Phi, Phi Lambda Upsilon, Gamma Alpha, Alpha Chi Sigma. E-mail: dpa922@cs.com.

AMES, GEORGE ROBERT, JR., judge; b. Westover, Md., Sept. 23, 1941; s. George Robert Ames Sr., Henrietta Lucille Ames; m. Beverly Ann Whittington, Oct. 22, 1962 (div. Oct. 1973); m. Delema Alberta Young, Apr. 10, 1976; children: Starlene, George Robert Ames III, Craig, Michael. AA in Social Sci., Chesapeake Coll., 1978, AA in Law Enforcement, 1982; AA in Ministry, Christian World Coll. of Theology, 2001. Lic. minister, cert. Christian Counselling One Christian World Coll. Theology, 2000; Criminal Justice Acad. Witness Internat. Inc., 2001. Sch. bus contractor Dorchester Md. Schs., Cambridge, 1979—2000; carrier newspaper Dorchester Md., Cambridge, 1973—2000, commr. dist. ct., 1980—89, judge orphans ct., 1994—. Notary public; judge Orphans Ct., 1994—. Contbr. Commr. Dist. Ct., 1980—89; bd. trustees Dorchester Libr. Bd., 1995—; pres. Dorchester NAACP. Airman 2d USAF, 1960—66, Vietnam. Recipient Dr. King award, TriCounty Orgn., 1987, 2000, Cmty. Svc. award, Iota Phi Lambda, Beta Epsilon chpt., 2001. Mem.: NAACP (pres. Dorchester chpt. 1987—), Dorchester Sch. Bus Contractors (pres. 1988—2000), Dorchester C. of C. (bd. dirs. 1998—), Am. Legion (life; judge advocate Cpl. Herman Hughes Post 87). Democrat. Baptist. Avocation: reading. Home: 703 High St Cambridge MD 21613

AMES, JOHN LEWIS, lawyer; b. Norfolk, Va., July 15, 1912; s. Harry Lee and Catherine I. (Betty) A.; m. Margaret Kilbon, Apr. 8, 1939 (dec. Sept. 1996); children: Margaret Lee, John Lewis. AB, Randolph-Macon Coll., 1933; JD, U. Richmond, 1937; postgrad., NYU, 1939-40. Bar: Va. 1936, N.Y. 1940. Mem. tax divsn. Home Life Ins. Co., N.Y.C., 1937-38; trial atty. Tanner, Sillocks & Friend, N.Y.C., 1938-41; house counsel Ruthrauff & Ryan, Inc., N.Y.C., 1941-42, house counsel and asst. to pres., 1945-48, sec., counsel, 1948-50, v.p., sec., 1950-55, v.p., sec., treas., 1955-57, also dir.; v.p., sec. Erwin, Wassey, Ruthrauff & Ryan, Inc., 1957-59; asst. dir. bus. affairs CBS TV Netowrk, Inc., N.Y.C., 1959-62; v.p., sec., treas. Kudner Agy., Inc., 1962-65, also dir.; sr. v.p. adminstrn. and fin. West, Weir & Bartel, Inc., N.Y.C., 1966, exec. v.p., dir., until 1968; v.p., sec. Lennen & Newell, Inc., 1968-73; v.p. bus. and legal affairs Dancer-Fitzgerald-Samplem Inc., 1973-83; legal cons. Saatchi & Saatchi DFS Inc., 1983-96. Dir. Carroll Products, Inc.; spl. agt. FBI, Washington and N.Y.C., 1942-45; spl. dept. atty. gen. N.Y. State, 1946-48; mem. Nassau County N.Y. Crime Commn., 1973-83. Trustee Randolph-Macon Coll., 1955-85, trustee emeritus, 1985—; mem. Massapequa Bd. Edn., 1952-79, pres. 1957-78; past pres. Nassau-Soffolk Sch. Bds. Assn.; past chmn. trustees Am. Assn. Advt. Agencies Group Ins.; trustee, chmn. bd. of trustees, vice chmn., chmn. adminstrv. bd. White Stone Unite Meth. Ch. Mem. N.Y. County Lawyers Assn., Am. Arbitration Assn. (mem. nat panel), Soc. Former Spl. Agts. FBI (past nat. sec.), Alumni Soc. Randolph-Macon Coll. (past pres.), Lancaster County Crime Solvers, Inc. (pres. 1991-94, 2001—), Indian Creek Yacht and Country Club, Windmill Point Yacht Club, Phi Kappa Sigma, Omicron Delta Kappa, Tau Kappa Alpha. Methodist. Home: PO Box 727 White Stone VA 22578-0727

AMES, MARC L. lawyer; b. Bklyn., Mar. 14, 1943; s. Arthur L. and Ray (Sardas) Ames; m. Eileen Moll, July 12, 1970 (div. Mar. 2000); children: Adam, Kimberly. JD, Bklyn. Law Sch., 1967; LLM, NYU, 1968. Bar: N.Y. 1967, U.S. Dist. Ct. (ea. and so. dist.) N.Y. 1973, U.S. Ct. Appeals (2nd cir.) 1973, U.S. Supreme Ct. 1973, U.S. Ct. Appeals (3d cir.) 1982, Pa. 1988; lic. radio amateur. Mem. faculty L.I. U., 1968-69, N.Y.C. Community Coll., 1969-70; pvt. practice, 1967—. Arbitrator U.S. Dist. Ct. (ea. dist.) N.Y. 1985, small claims divsn. N.Y.C. Civil Ct., N.Y.C. Civil Ct.; cons. disability retirement and pensions; arbitrator Am. Arbitration Assn.; bd. dirs. Internat. Comms. Concepts, Inc. Contbr. articles to profl. jours. Recipient cert. appreciation N.Y. State Trial Lawyers, commendation for disting. svc. as arbitrator. Mem. N.Y. State Trial Lawyers Assn., N.Y. County Lawyers, N.Y. State Bar Assn., Electronic Technol. Soc. N.J. Inc. Achievements include patents for bridge for billiards, storage materials for sport card collections, auto mirror, temporary replacement window with protective seat attachment primarily for use in automobiles; innovative expandable shopping cart. Office: PO Box 6162 Hillsborough NJ 08844 E-mail: bestesq1@aol.com.

AMES, RICHARD POLLARD, physician, educator, lecturer; b. Northampton, Mass., Aug. 4, 1932; s. Harold Leslie and Effie Melissa (Crowley) A.; m. Janet Ann Shaw, Oct. 7, 1961; children: Patricia Jean, Brian Shaw. BA cum laude, Williams Coll., 1954; MD, Columbia U., 1958. Diplomate Am. Bd. Internal Medicine, Am. Bd. Nephrology, Am. Bd. Med. Oncology, Am. Bd. Hematology, Am. Soc. of Hypertension Specialist in Clin. Hypertension. Intern Boston City Hosp., 1958-59, resident, 1959-61; fellow N.Y. Heart Assn. Presbyn. Hosp., N.Y.C., 1961-63; clin. assoc. Nat. Cancer Inst., Bethesda, Md., 1963-65; investigator Nat. Inst. Arthritis Metab., Paris, 1965-66, Whitehall Found., N.Y.C., 1967-70; nephrologist St. Luke's Roosevelt Hosp., N.Y.C., 1970—, chief hypertension clinic, 1973-94, dir. phys. diagnosis, 1981-94, assoc. dir. nephrology, 1990-93; chief nephrology St. Clare's Hosp., N.Y.C., 1998 2000. Dir. hypertension Am. Health Found., N.Y.C., 1972-82, clin. prof. Columbia U., N.Y.C., 1989—. Contributing author: Topics in Hypertension, 1980, Frontiers in Hypertension Res., 1981, Clinical Cardiovascular Therapeutics, 1989, Hypertension, 1995, Messerli's Cardiovascular Drug Therapy, 1996; co-editor: Medical Symposium Drugs, 1988. Asst. surgeon USPHS, 1963-65. Fellow ACP, AHA (mem. Coun. For High Blood Pressure Rsch., kidney coun.); mem. Am. Soc. Hypertension (charter), Phi Beta Kappa. Office: 1886 Broadway New York NY 10023-

AMES, ROGER, recording industry executive; b. Trinidad, West Indies; With EMI UK, 1975—79; with A&R dept., then head London Records PolyGram UK, 1979—93, chmn., CEO, 1993—96; pres. PolyGram Music Group, 1996—99, Warner Music Internat., 1999—; chmn., CEO Warner Music Group, 1999—. Office: Warner Mus Grp Inc 75 Rockefeller Plz New York NY 10019

AMES, SANDRA PATIENCE, sales executive; b. Quincy, Calif., May 23, 1947; d. Bruce Ray Richards and Margaret Elizabeth (Steiner) Richards Johnson; m. Martin P.M. Bettenhausen, Dec. 10, 1965 (div. 1972); m. Thomas William Ames, Nov. 28, 1975. Student, Yuba City Jr. Coll., 1965-66. Sales corr. Nat. Can Corp. (now Am. Nat. Can Co.), Seattle, 1974-76, Lehigh Valley, Pa., 1976-79, nat. acct. sales corr. Chgo., 1979-81, dist. sales office mgr., 1981-82, sales analyst I Oakbrook, Ill., 1982-84, regional sales office mgr., 1984-86, mgr. regional sales office, 1987-89, mgr. ctrl. sales adminstrn., 1989-93, inside sales assoc., 1993-95, Silgan Containers, Rosemont, Ill., 1995-98, office adminstr., 1998—. Office: Silgan Containers Mfg Corp 9700 W Higgins Rd Ste 820 Rosemont IL 60018-4736

AMES, STEVEN EDMUND, journalist, educator; b. Oakland, Calif., July 25, 1940; s. Eldridge Edmund and Eleanor Ruth Ames; m. Carol Murray Nelson, Aug. 20, 1966; children: Krista, Karen. BA in Journalism, San Jose State U., 1967, MS in Mass. Comms., 1971; EdD in Higher Edn., Nova Southeastern U., 1977; postgrad., Diablo Valley Coll., San Francisco State U., Stanford U., Oxnard Coll. Instr. in journalism Merced (Calif.) Coll., 1971—78; prof. journalism, dir. student publs. Pepperdine U., Malibu, Calif., 1978—91; instr. in journalism Calif. Luth. U., Thousand Oaks, 1993—98, Oxnard (Calif.) Coll., 2001—02, L.A. Valley Coll., Van Nuys, Calif., 2001. Adj. instr. journalism Citrus Coll., Glendora, Calif., 1998, Moorpark (Calif.) Coll., 1999—2000, U. LaVerne, Calif., 1999—2000, Am. InterContinental U., L.A., 1999—2000; lectr. in comms. Calif. State U., Dominguez Hills, 1991—93, 2001. Author: Elements of Newspaper Design, 1989. Named Journalism Tchr. of Yr., Calif. Newspaper Pubs. Assn., 1987, Coll. Media Advisers Nat. Disting. Newspaper Adviser, 1985. Mem.: Soc. Profl. Journalists (adv. Pepperdine U. student chpt. 1978—91), Journalism Assn. Cmty. Colls. (No. Calif. faculty pres. 1972—73, faculty pres. 1973—74, spkr. 1978—), Coll. Media Advisers (adv. bd. 1978—82), Assn. Edn. in Journalism and Mass. Comms. (newspaper, mag., visual comm., comm. tech. and policy divsns., small programs interest group), Calif. Intercollegiate Press Assn. (exec. sec. 1981—85), Soc. for News Design, C.C. Journalism Assn. (exec. sec.-treas. 1992—). Republican. Methodist. Avocation: baseball. Home: 3376 Hill Canyon Ave Thousand Oaks CA 91360-1119

AMES, STEVEN REEDE, financial planner; b. Washington, Aug. 15, 1951; s. Reede Maughan and Mary (Soderberg) A.; m. Marsha M. Ames, Sept. 1994. BS in Bus. Adminstrn., U. Md., 1973; MPA, Am. U., 1976; MS, Coll. Fin. Planning, 1994. Cert. fin. planner; registered investment advisor; enrolled agt. IRS. Specialist bus. financing Gov.'s Office State Del., Dover, 1978-83; exec. v.p. Econ. and Bus. Devel. Corp. Montgomery County, Rockville, Md., 1983-85; owner, operator Scarborough Ames and Assocs., Annapolis, Md., 1986-92; owner, prin. Ames Fee-Only Fin. Planning, Annapolis, 1993—. Instr. Anne Arundel Community Coll., Annapolis, 1987-98; bd. arbitrators Nat. Assn. Securities Dealers. Bd. dirs. Md. Hall for Creative Arts; mem. charitable gift planning adv. com. Anne Arundel Med. Ctr., Chesapeake Cmty. Found. Fin. and Asset Mgmt. com. Named among best fin. advisors Worth Mag., 1996-2002, one of 100 Gt. Fin. Planners, Mut. Funds Mag., 2001, 02. Mem. Nat. Assn. Personal Fin. Advisors (regional chmn. bd.), Nat. Assn. Securities Dealers (bd. arbitrators 1996—), Annapolis C. of C. (Mem. of Yr. 1990), Md. Soc. Accts., Kiwanis (bd. dirs. Annapolis club 1986-97, pres. 1989-90), Greater Annapolis C. of C. (bd. dirs.). Avocations: sports, travel, financial reading. Office: 196 West St Annapolis MD 21401-2824 E-mail: sames@feeonlyannapolismd.com.

AMES, WILLIAM FRANCIS, mathematician, educator; b. Brandon, Man., Can., Dec. 8, 1926; s. Paul Main and Della Johanna (Hebel) A.; m. Theresa Danielson, May 29, 1951; children: Karen Anne, Susan Lynn, Pamela Margaret. MS, U. Wis., 1950. Instr. U. Wis., Racine, 1953-55; sr. engr. DuPont Co., Wilmington, Del., 1955-59; prof. U. Del., Newark, 1959-67, U. Iowa, Iowa City, 1967-75, Ga. Inst. Tech., Atlanta, 1975—, Regents prof., 1980-91, prof. emeritus, 1991—, dir., 1981-87; research prof. U. Ga., Athens, 1977-79. Cons. in field. Author: Nonlinear Partial Differential Equations in Engineering, Vol. I, 1965, Vol. II, 1972, Nonlinear Ordinary Differential Equations in Transport Processes, 1968, Numerical Methods for Partial Differential Equations, 1970, 77, 92, Nonlinear Boundary Value Problems in Science and Engineering, 1989; book and jour. editor for Academic Press; editor 9 books.; contbr. articles to profl. jours. Served with USNR, 1944-46, 51-52. NSF faculty fellow, 1963-64, NATO sr. fellow, 1972-73; grantee, 1964-67, 76-79, 79-81, 83-85, 89-91, 92-95, NBS grantee, 1967-71, USPHS grantee, 1961-63, EPA grantee, 1978-81, U.S. Army grantee, 1968-75, 81-87; Humboldt sr. scientist, 1974-75. Home: 125 Tamarisk Dr NE Atlanta GA 30342-1421 Office: Ga Inst Tech Sch Math Atlanta GA 30332-0001 E-mail: williamames@hotmail.com.

AMESTOY, JEFFREY LEE, state supreme court chief justice; b. Rutland, Vt., July 24, 1946; s. William Joseph and Diana (Wood) Amestoy; m. Susan Claire Lonergan, May 24, 1980; children: Katherine Leigh, Christina Elizabeth, Nancy Claire. BA, Hobart Coll., 1968; JD, U. Calif., San Francisco, 1972; MPA, Harvard U., 1982; D of Pub. Adminstrn. (hon.), Norwich U., 1994; LLD (hon.), Vermont Law Sch., 2002. Bar: Vt. 1973, U.S. Dist. Ct. Vt. 1973. Assoc. Mahady & Klevana, Windsor, Vt., 1973—74; legal counsel Gov.'s Justice Commn., Montpelier, Vt., 1974—77; asst. atty. gen., chief of Medicaid fraud div. State of Vt., Montpelier, 1978—81, commr. labor and industry, 1982—84, atty. gen., 1985—97; chief justice Supreme Ct. Vt., 1997—. Pres. Nat. Assn. of Attys. Gen., 1992—93. Trustee Thomas Waterman Wood Gallery, Montpelier, 1986—92. With USAR, 1968—74. Mem.: Conf. Chief Justices, Vt. Bar Assn., Kennedy Sch. Govt. Harvard U. Alumni Exec. Coun. Republican. Congregationalist. Home: 503 Loomis Hill Rd Waterbury Center VT 05677-8280

AMEY, RAE, project management and development consultant; b. Shreveport, La., Sept. 26, 1947; d. Bruce Harold and Genevieve (Amey) Gentry; m. John E. Scarborough, Dec. 18, 1971 (div. Nov. 1979). Student, La. State U., 1968-70, U. Houston, 1972-74; BA in Liberal Arts, Antioch U., 1985; grad., U. So. Calif., 1987-89. Freelance photographer, Calif., 1973—; adminstrn. coord. Y.E.S. Inc., Sta. KCET-TV, L.A., 1980-83; freelance ednl. TV writer, cons. L.A., 1983-84; asst. to pres. prodn. So. Calif. Consortium, Cypress, 1984, project mgr., dir. devel., project dir. The Human Condition, 1985-87; v.p. devel. and outreach The Calif. Channel, L.A., 1990-92, project dir., 1991, 92; pres. Video Nexus, L.A., 1987—; owner Rae Amey Enterprises, L.A., 1999-2000; pres. Rae Amey Enterprises, Inc., 2000—. Editor TV guide book, 1985; photography exhbns. include: Contemporary Art Mus., Houston, 1973, Galveston (Tex.) Arts Ctr., 1975, Cameravision Gallery, L.A.,1980, Aloft, Pasadena, 1989. Co-founder Harbor Arts Alliance; mem., bd. dirs. African Am. Arts Coun.; founder, chair, bd. dirs. CIVICS: a video project for cmty. edn. and conversation, 1993—; advisor Congress on Racial Equality; sr. advisor Civil Soc. Ellen Torgenson Shaw scholar Annenberg Sch. Communications, U. So. Calif., 1989. Mem. Women in Communications (bd. dirs., v.p. campus svcs. 1987-88, exec. v.p. 1988-89, bd. dirs. scholarship and edn. fund L.A. chpt.). Democrat. Home and Office: 255 S Grand Ave Apt 1914 Los Angeles CA 90012-3096

AMGOTT, STEVEN MITCHELL, mathematics educator; b. Bklyn., Jan. 4, 1953; m. J. Hannah Moss, Aug. 5, 1984. BA in Math. and Physics summa cum laude, U. Pa., 1974; PhD in Math., Rutgers U., 1983. Instr. U. Conn., Stamford, 1981-83; asst. prof. Villanova (Pa.) U., 1983-89; asst. prof., dir. math. ctr. Widener U., Chester, Pa., 1989-94; asst prof. SUNY, Farmingdale, 1994-95; asst. prof., math. lab. coord. Haverford Coll., Pa., 1995-2000; math. and stats. lab. coord. Swarthmore Coll., 1999—. Conf. presenter in field. Named to Dean's list U. Pa. Mem. Math. Assn. Am., Phi Beta Kappa. E-mail: samgott1@swarthmore.edu.

AMHOWITZ, HARRIS J. lawyer, educator; b. N.Y.C., Mar. 19, 1934; s. Samuel and Ruth Amhowitz; m. Melanie Leigh Gale; children: Jennifer Ann, Joshua Seth. AB, Brown U., 1955; LLB, Harvard U., 1961. Bar: N.Y. 1961, U.S. Supreme Ct. 1967. Law clk. to judge U.S. Dist. Ct. N.Y., 1961-63; assoc. Hughes Hubbard & Reed, N.Y.C., 1963-69; gen. counsel Coopers & Lybrand, N.Y.C., 1970-96, dep. chmn., 1991-95, mem. internat. exec. com., 1991-95; of counsel Hughes Hubbard & Reed, 1996—. Adj. prof. NYU Sch. Law, 1975-83; receiver, spl. master U.S. Dist. Ct., 1963-70; pres. bd. dirs. Prosher Group, Ltd., 1970-71; trustee Citizens Budget Commn., Inc., 1983-97. Lt. comdr. USN, 1955—58. Mem. Assn. Bar City N.Y. (spl. com. on lawyers' role in securities transactions 1975-77, com. profl. and jud. ethics 1983-86, com. profl. discipline 1987-91), Harmonie Club. Home: 12600 E Fort Lowell Rd Tucson AZ 85749-9614 Office: Hughes Hubbard & Reed One Battery Park Plz New York NY 10004

AMICHETTI, DENNIS JOSEPH, advertising executive; b. Phila., Apr. 24, 1946; s. Frank and Margret H. (Ziegler) A.; m. Elizabeth Keefe, June 27, 1970; children: Christine, Karen. BS, Drexel U., 1969, MBA, 1973. Mfg. engr. Gen. Electric Co., Phila., 1969-70; mgr. mktg. devel. ESB, Inc., Phila., 1970-74; asst. v.p., dir. mktg. Phila. Sav. Fund Soc., 1974-78; v.p. SE Nat. Bank, Malvern, Pa., 1978-79; sr. v.p. Mel Richman Inc., Bala Cynwyd, Pa., 1979-83; v.p. Beneficial Corp., Wilmington, Del., 1983-86; pres. Amichetti, Lewis & Assocs., Wayne, Pa., 1987—. Bd. dirs. Cath. Philopatrian Literary Inst. Planning commn. East Goshen Twp., Pa., 1977-83, Cath. Philopatrian Lit. Inst. Recipient Gold Effie award for fin. advt. Mem. Am. Mktg. Assn., Acad. for Health Services Mktg., Direct Mktg. Assn., Beta Gamma Sigma. Republican. Roman Catholic. Avocations: music, theater, golf. Home: 814 Wetherill Ln Wayne PA 19087-2072 Office: Amichetti Lewis & Assocs Inc PO Box 1977 Southeastern PA 19899-1977 E-mail: ala300@aol.com.

AMICK, COLLIN HAL, civil engineer, consultant; b. Douglas, Wyo., Mar. 7, 1951; s. Roy N. and Betty Jane (Collins) A.; m. Ellen Sue Stinson (div.); 1 child, Elizabeth; m. Alison Marie Herzer, Oct. 28, 1995. BSCE, U. Wyo., 1974; MSCE, U. Calif., Berkeley, 1976, M of Engring., 1980. Registered profl. engr.

Calif. Engr. EDS Nuclear, San Francisco, 1974-76; rsch. engr. Lawrence Berkeley Nat. Lab., Berkeley, 1976-78; engr. Liftech Consultants Inc., Oakland, Calif., 1978-80; asst. prof. Chadron (Nebr.) State Coll., 1980-83; instr. Sheridan (Wyo.) C.C., 1983-85; sr. engr. Bolt Beranek and Newman, Cambridge Mass. and L.A., 1985-90; sr. consulting engr., dir. Acentech Inc., L.A., 1990-96; v.p. tech. Colin Gordon & Assocs., San Bruno, Calif., 1996—. Tech. expert, U.S. rep. Internat. Stds. Orgn., 1998—, IES Stds. Com., Working Group 24, Chgo., 1993—. Contbr. articles to profl. jours. Mem. U. Wyo. Alumni Assn., Laramie, 1980—. Mem. ASCE, Inst. Environ. Scis. and Tech. (sr.), Structural Engrs. Assn. Calif., Sigma Tau, Tau Beta Pi. Avocations: genealogy, history, writing. Home: 287 Angelita Ave Pacifica CA 94044 Office: Colin Gordon and Assocs Ste 150 883 Sneath Ln San Bruno CA 94066 Fax: 650-358-9430. E-mail: halamick@earthlink.net.

AMICK, STEVEN HAMMOND, state legislator, lawyer; b. Ithaca, N.Y., May 13, 1947; s. Arthur Hammond and Marolyn Dee (Hollingshead) A.; m. Helen Louise Masten, Aug. 9, 1969. BA, Washington Coll., 1969; JD, Dickinson Sch. of Law, 1972. Bar: Del. 1972, U.S. Dist. Ct. Del. 1973. Assoc. Daley & Lewis, Wilmington, Del., 1972-74; atty. E.I. Dupont De Nemours and Co., Wilmington, 1974-85, counsel, 1986-96; mem. Del. Ho. of Reps., Dover, 1986-94; spl. counsel Coach and Taylor, 1996—2002; mem. Del. Senate, Dover, 1994—, minority leader, 1998—2002. Pres. Com. of 39, Wilmington, 1978, Civic League for New Castle County, Wilmington, 1984-86. Mem. Del. Bar Assn. Republican. Presbyterian. Avocation: antique cars. Home: 449 W Chestnut Hill Rd Newark DE 19713-1132 Office: Legislature Hall PO Box 1401 Dover DE 19901

AMICK, WILLIAM WALKER, golf course architect; b. Scipio, Ind., June 16, 1932; s. George Ellsworth Sr. and Myrtle (Walker) A.; m. Sara Dell Rogers, Apr. 6, 1957; 1 child, David Walker. BA, Ohio Wesleyan U., 1954. Registered landscape architect, Fla. Golf course archtl. asst. William H. Diddel, GCA, Carmel, Ind., 1954-55, Charles Adams, GCA, Atlanta, 1957-58; golf course architect Daytona Beach, Fla., 1959—. Capt. USAF, 1955-57. Fellow Am. Soc. Golf Course Architects; mem. Am. Soc. of Golf Course Architects (treas., v.p., pres. 1975-77). Avocation: low handicap golf. Office: PO Box 1084 Daytona Beach FL 32115-1984

AMICO, CHARLES WILLIAM, management consultant; b. Boston, May 6, 1942; s. William Charles and Marie Josephine (Nicholas) A. Assoc. in Engring., Franklin Inst., 1962; BS, Suffolk U., 1968. Jr. chem. technician Avco Corp., Lowell, Mass., 1963-64; advanced vacuum tech. technician Nat. Rsch. Corp., Newton, Mass., 1964-68; semicondr. engr. IBM, Essex Junction, Vt., 1968-72, semicondr. mfg. engring. mgr., 1972-76, mgmt. devel. cons., 1976-86; founder, pres., CEO Creative Directions, Inc., San Francisco, Burlington, Vt., 1982—. Bd. dirs. Holiday Project, 1987-88. State chmn. Vt. Hugh O'Brian Youth Leadership Seminar; bd. dirs. Vt. Hugh O'Brian Youth Seminars, Inc., CEO, 1984-85; corp. pres. Hugh O'Brian Youth Found., No. Calif., 1994-95. Recipient Hugh O'Brian Outstanding State Chmn. in Nation award, 1984, 85. Office: Creative Directions Inc PO Box 10101 Zephyr Cove NV 89448-2101 also: 72 Cross Creek Pl Larkspur CA 94939

AMICO, JOSEPH C. obstetrician, gynecologist; b. NYC; s. Joseph and Maria (Randazzo) A.; m. Mildred Helen Cassidy, Feb. 19, 1955; children: Paul, Joseph, Phillip, Christopher, Matthew. BS, Fordham U., 1948; MD, Georgetown U., 1952. Sr. attending physician Bklyn. Hosp. Med. Ctr. Contbr. articles to profl. jours. With U.S. Army, 1943-46. Recipient Walter Reed medal Bklyn. Hosp. Med. Ctr., 1997, Disting. Svc. award Bklyn. Gynecol. Soc., 1997. Fellow Am. Coll. Ob-Gyn.; mem. Am. Fertility Soc., Bklyn. Gynecol. Soc., Kings County Med. Soc. (pres. elect 1995, 1996, pres. 1996-97). Home: 27 Prospect Park W Brooklyn NY 11215-1706 Office: 37 8th Ave Brooklyn NY 11217-3901

AMIDON, PAUL CHARLES, publishing executive; b. St. Paul, July 23, 1932; s. Paul Samuel and Eleanor Ruth (Simons) A.; m. Patricia Jean Winjum, May 7, 1960; children: Karen, Michael, Susan. BA, U. Minn., 1954. Bus. mgr. Paul S. Amidon & Assocs., Inc., St. Paul, 1956-66, pres., 1966—. Served with AUS, 1954-56. Home: 1582 Hillcrest Ave Saint Paul MN 55116-2147 Office: 1966 Benson Ave Saint Paul MN 55116-3214 E-mail: paul@amidongraphics.com.

AMIDON, ROGER LYMAN, retired health administration educator; b. Burlington, Vt., Apr. 8, 1938; s. Ellsworth L. and Mae (Liddle) A.; m. JoAnn Reiland, Aug. 1, 1968. BA, U. Vt., 1960; MA, U. Iowa, 1965, PhD (USPHS trainee), 1968. Asst. prof. hosp. and health adminstrn. U. Iowa, 1968-73, asso. prof., 1973-77; prof., chmn. dept. health adminstrn. U. Okla., 1977-81, U. S.C., 1981-88, on sabbatical, 1988-89, prof., grad. dir., 1989—2002, disting. prof. emeritus, 2002—. Exec. sec. Nat. Ctr. Health Svcs. Rsch., 1975-76; dir. Am. Indian Grad. Program in Health Adminstrn., U. Okla., 1977-81; cons. China Med. U. Hosp., 1999—, vis. scholar, Nat. Def. Med. Ctr., Taiwan, 2003-. Contbr. articles to profl. jours. Chair S.C. Ctr. for Gerontology, 1999-01. Served with M.S.C. U.S. Army, 1961-62. Mem. APHA, Am. Coll. Healthcare Execs., Am. Hosp. Assn. (life) Home: 234 Saluda Ave Columbia SC 29205-3031 Office: U SC Sch Pub Health Dept Health Adminstrn Columbia SC 29208-0001 E-mail: amidon@sc.edu.

AMIEL, DAVID, orthopaedic surgery educator; b. Alexandria, Egypt, Oct. 25, 1938; came to U.S., 1962; s. Eli and Inez (Bokey) A.; m. Nancy Joy Lyons, Nov. 27, 1966; 1 child, Michael Eli. B Math., Lycee Francais, Alexandria, 1955; PhD in Chem. Engring., U. Brussels, Belgium, 1962. Chem. engr. polymers lab. Boeing Aeorspace, Renton, Wash., 1962-63; assoc. in orthopaedics U. Wash., Seattle, 1964-66; chief chemist Laucks Testing Lab., Seattle, 1966-68; assoc. orthopaedic specialist U. Calif., La Jolla, 1968-75, orthopaedic specialist, 1975-83, from asst. prof. to assoc. prof. surgery, 1983-91, prof. orthopaedics, 1992—; exec. com. U. Calif. Sch. Medicine, La Jolla, 1988—. Dept. head biochemistry M&D Coutts Inst., San Diego, 1984—; bd. dirs. Am. Coll. Sports Medicine, Indpls., 1989-92; grant reviewer Arthritis Soc. Can., NIH NIAMS Osteoarthritis Study Sect., NIH Nat. Inst. Arth. Musculoskel Ortho and Musculoskeletal Study Sect., Ortho. Rsch. and Edn. Found., Swiss Nat. Sci. Found.; ad hoc reviewer U.S. Govt. VA. Reviewer Am. Jour. Physiology, Connect Tissue Rsch., Jour. Applied Physiology, Med. Sci. Sports Exercise, Osteoarthritis and Cartilage, Jour. Bone and Joint Surgery, Jour. Orthop. Rsch.; contbr. chpts. to books and articles to profl. jours. Recipient Excellence Basic Sci. Rsch. award Am. Orthopaedic Soc. Sports Medicine, 1983, 86, O'Donoghue award Orthopaedic Rsch. and Edn. Found., 1990, Herndon award, 1995, Marshall Urist award, 1996, Arthroscopy Assn. N.Am. Rsch. award, 1996, Depuy award Calif. Orthop. Assn., 1997, Merit award NIH, 1989-99, Rsch. in Orthopedics award SIROT, 1999, Best Basic Sci. award Soc. Francaise d'Arthros, 2001, co-author Vernon P. Thompson Award, Western Orthop Assoc., 2001, 02. Fellow Am. Coll. Sports Medicine (Citation award 1987); mem. Internat. Soc. Matrix Biology, Cartilage Repair Soc., Osteoarth Rsch. Soc., Western Orthop. Assn. (hon.), Orthop. Rsch. Soc., N.Y. Acad. Sci. Achievements include patents for Continuous Passive Motion Machine used as a rehabilitation device for post-ligamentous injuries and post total joint replacements (with others); among first to describe the response to stresses of periarticular connective tissues such as ligaments and tendons.

AMIEL, JON, film director, film producer; b. London, May 20, 1948; Motion picture dir., prodr. Prodr. film Simply Irresistible, 1999; dir. films Tandoori Nights, 1985, The Silent Twins, 1985, Queen of Hearts, 1989 (Grand Prix Paris Film Festival, 1st Film prize Montreal World Film Festival), Tune in Tomorrow, 1990 (winner critics and audience award Deauville Film Festival), Sommersby, 1993, Copycat, 1995, The Man Who Knew Too Little, 1997, Entrapment, 1999; T.V. mini-series The Singing Detective, 1986 (nominee BAFTA award best drama series). Office: care Internat Creative Mgmt care Martha Luttrell 8942 Wilshire Blvd Beverly Hills CA 90211-1934

AMIL-BARKER, JANA KAY, social worker; b. Cooper, Tex., Feb. 9, 1953; d. Bobby Elwayne and Janice Earl Banks; m. David Lewis Amil, June 5, 1971 (div. April 1999); 1 child, Tiffany Rene; m. Larry Allen Barker, May 19, 2000. BA in Psychology, U. Tex., 1988. Sec. to v.p. Employers of Wausau, Irving, Tex., 1971-77; exec. dir. Brighter Tomorrows, Grand Prairie, Tex., 1989—. Bd. dirs. Tex. Coun. on Family Violence, Austin, Tex., 1999—. Bd. dirs. Tex. Assn. Against Sexual Assault, 2001—. Mem. Rotary, Womens Divsn. Chamber (pres. 1999-2000), Soroptimist (v.p. 1999-2000, pres. 2000-01), C. of C. (vice chair cmty. devel. 1999-2000). Methodist. Office: Brighter Tomorrows Inc 1417 Densman St Grand Prairie TX 75051-2328 E-mail: Jkamil@aol.com.

AMILCAR, DAFNEY, academic administrator; d. Roland Jean and Marie Rose Amilcar; 1 child, Amil Rodriguez. BA, U. at Albany, 1996—2000, MS, 2001—03. Coord., collegiate sci. and tech. entry program U. at Albany, Dept. of Student Life, Albany, NY, 2001—, coord., suny louis stokes alliance for minority participation, 2001—. Coord., sci. summer bridge program U. at Albany, Dept. of Student Life, 2001—02, coord., sci. summer rsch. program, 2001—; student activites liaison U. at Albany, Office of Student Activities, 2001—; nat. coalition bldg. inst. facilitator U. at Albany, Dept. of Student Life, 2003—; project lead U. at Albany, Office of Student Activities, 2001—. Facilitator Nat. Coalition Bldg. Inst., Albany, NY, 2003—03. None NONE. Ednl. Opportunities, U. at Albany, EOP, 1996—2000. Mem.: Zeta Phi Beta Sorority Inc. (epistoleus 2003—03). Office: Universty at Albany 1400 Washington Ave Albany NY 12222 Personal E-mail: damilcar@nycap.rr.com. E-mail: damilcar@uamail.albany.edu.

AMIN, MAHUL B. physician, researcher, educator, consultant; b. Ahmedabad, India, Aug. 12, 1961; s. Bhanoo N. and Rama B. Amin; m. Ushma M. Amin, May 24, 1988; children: Anmol, Aneti. MBBS, G.S. Med. Sch., Bombay, 1984, MD in Pathology, 1987. Lectr. pathology G.S. Med. Coll., 1987-88; fellow in surg. pathology M.D. Anderson Cancer Ctr., Houston, 1992-93; chief resident in pathology Henry Ford Hosp., Detroit, 1990-92, sr. staff, 1993-98, assoc. chief immunohistochemistry, 1995-98, sect. chief anat. pathology edn., 1996-98; asst. prof. pathology Wayne State U., Detroit, 1993-98, Case Western U., Cleve., 1996-98; assoc. prof. pathology Emory U. Sch. Medicine, Atlanta, 1998—, assoc. prof. urology, 1999—; dir. surg. pathology Emory U. Hosp., Atlanta, 2000—. Author books; mem. editl. bds.; editor in chief Advances in Anat. Pathology; contbr. articles to profl. jours. Fellow Am. Soc. Clin. Pathologists, Coll. Am. Pathology; mem. AMA, U.S. and Can. Acad. Pathology (Cert. of Merit 1990), Arthur Sturdy Prout Soc., Assn. Dirs. Anat. and Surg. Pathology. Hindu. Avocations: hiking, reading, tennis. Office: Emory U Hosp 1364 Clifton Rd NE Atlanta GA 30322-1061

AMIN, MOHAMMAD, urology educator; b. Sargodha, Pakistan, Jan. 1, 1942; came to U.S., 1964; s. Mohammad and Gulzar (Begum) Nawaz; m. Elizabeth Anne Howarth, May 25, 1973; children: Daniel, Omar. MB, BS, King Edward Coll., Lahore, Pakistan, 1963. Diplomate Am. Bd. of Urology. Intern Muhlenberg Hosp., Plainfield, N.J., 1964-65; resident in surgery Norton Hosp., Louisville, 1965-66; asst. prof. urology U. Louisville, 1971-74, assoc. prof., 1974-80, prof. urology, 1980—. resident in urology, 1966-69; med. officer Social Security, Pakistan, 1969-70; house officer urology Southmede Hosp., Bristol, Eng., 1970-71. Contbr. articles and book chpts. to profl. jours. Recipient Health Advancement award Nat. Kidney Found., 1981. Mem.: ACS, Soc. Internat. d'Urologie, Am. Urol. Assn. Democrat. Islamic. Address: VA Med Ctr 800 Zorn Ave Louisville KY 40206

AMIN, OMAR MOHAMED, parasitologist; b. Egypt, Jan. 23, 1939; s. Mohamed Amin and Nadia Hasan (Shaker) Khalil; divorced; children: Sharif O., Karim O. BS in Zoology & Botany, Cairo U., 1959, MS in Med. Entomology, 1963; PhD in Parasitology, Ariz. State U., 1967. Rsch. asst. USN Med. Rsch. Unit # 3, Cairo, 1960-64; faculty assoc. Ariz. State U., Tempe, 1966-67; rsch. assoc. Old Dominion U., Norfolk, Va., 1967-69; vis. fellow Ctr. Disease Control, Atlanta, 1969-70; prof. U. Wis., Kenosha, 1971-92, Ariz. State U., 1993—2000; dir. Inst. Parasitic Diseases, Phoenix, 1993—, Parasitology Ctr., Inc., Tempe, Ariz., 1998—. Cons. in field. Contbr. articles to profl. jours. Mem. Am. Soc. Parasitology, Am. Microscopial Soc., Am. Soc. Tropical Medicine & Hygiene, Am. Soc. Microbiology, British Soc. Parasitology, Helimthological Soc. Wash., Ariz. Homeopathic and Integrative Med. Assn., Biol. Soc. Wash. Avocations: sports, theater, music, travel, mythology. Office: Inst Parasitic Diseases PO Box 28372 Tempe AZ 85285-8372 E-mail: Omaramin@aol.com.

AMINI, AMIR ARSHAM, biomedical engineering researcher, educator; b. Tehran, Mar. 28, 1965; came to U.S., 1979; s. Ahmad and Khadijeh R. (Rahat) A. BS, U. Mass., 1983; MSE, U. Mich., 1984, PhD, 1990. Rschr. Yale U., New Haven, 1990-92, asst. prof., 1992-96, Washington U., St. Louis, 1996—2001, assoc. prof., 2001—. Contbr. articles to profl. jours. Grantee Whitaker Found., 1993—, NSF, 1995—, NIH, 1998—. Mem. IEEE (sr., program com. and organizing com. 1994—), Internat. Soc. Magnetic Resonance in Medicine, Internat. Soc. Optical Engrs. Avocations: basketball, soccer, classical music, racquetball. Home: PO Box 24216 Saint Louis MO 63130-0216 E-mail: amini@cauchy.wustl.edu.

AMIR, HASSAN, surgeon, consultant; b. Zanzibar, Tanzania, Sept. 14, 1950; p. Amirali Alli and Fatemah Amirali (Jessa) Alli; m. Waheeda Mohamed Husien Kermali, Jan. 21, 1982; children: Taha, Mohamed. MB BS, U. Kashmir, India, 1976; M of Surgery, Muslim U., Aligarh, India, 1980. Intern Med. Coll. Hosp., Aligarh, 1976-77, resident in surgery, 1977-80; cons. surgeon Dubai Med. Ctr., Red Crescent Soc., Islamic Republic Iran, Dubai, United Arab Emirates, 1981-88; lectr., cons. surgeon Muhimbili U. Coll. Health Scis., Dar-Es-Salaam, Tanzania, 1988-92, sr. lectr., cons. surgeon, 1992-97, assoc. prof. surgery, 1997-99; rsch. assoc. dept. orthopedics U. Western Ont., London, Can., 2000, rsch. assoc. dept. emergency medicine, 2001. Chairperson rsch. dept. surgery Muhimbili U. Coll. Health Scis., Dar Es Salaam, 1997-99. Vice chmn. sci. adv. bd. Austral-Asian Jour. Cancer; contbr. articles to profl. jours. Grantee Internat. Union Against Cancer, Geneva, 1991. Fellow Assn. Surgeon of East Africa, Tanzania Surg. Assn.; mem. Med. Assn. Tanzania, Assn. Internat. Union Against Cancer Fellows (life). Achievements include research in cancer in African population; breast cancer in African population; Karposi's sarcoma in African population; HIV-asociated cancers. Home: 73 Elvira Crescent London ON Canada N6E 2N1 E-mail: hamir@sympatico.ca.

AMIRANA, M. T. surgeon; b. Bhanvad, India, Jan. 7, 1930; came to U.S., 1958; s. Tayob Amirana and Noorbai Abba; m. Annelene J. Vogt, July 30, 1959; children: Ebrahim, Omar, Jasmine. BS, Khalsa Coll., Bombay, 1953; MD, U. Heidelberg, Fed. Republic Germany, 1958. Instr. thoracic and cardiovascular surgery Albert Einstein Sch. Medicine, N.Y.C., 1966-67; pres. Rensselaer County Med. Soc., Troy, N.Y., 1975-76; chmn. dept. surger Leonard Hosp., Troy, 1972-74, St. Mary's Hosp., Troy, 1981-83; pvt. practice, Las Vegas, Nev., 1983—. Adj. rsch. assoc. prof. Rensselaer Poly. Inst., Troy, 1968-74. Active Rens. County Med. Soc., Troy, 1967. Fellow ACS, Am. Coll. Thoracic Surgeons; mem. N.Y. State Med. Soc., Rensselaer County Med. Soc. Home and Office: 10220 Los Padres Pl Las Vegas NV 89134-6905 E-mail: mtamirana@yahoo.com.

AMIRIKIA, HASSAN, obstetrician, gynecologist; b. Tehran, Iran, Dec. 10, 1937; came to U.S., 1966; d. Ahmad and Showkat (Asgari) Cheftsaz; m. Minoo Vassigh Amirikia, Apr. 4, 1964; children: Arezo, Omid. MD, Tehran U., 1964. Cert. Am. Bd. Ob-Gyn. Intern Cook County Hosp., Chgo., 1966—67; resident Wayne State U., Detroit, 1967—71, fellow, 1971—72; practice reproductive endocrine specializing in infertility Detroit, 1972—; asst. prof. Wayne State U., Detroit, 1972—, dir. ob-gyn. tng. dept. family medicine, 1979—; dir. infertility and reproductive endocrinology St. Joseph's Hosp., Pontiac, Mich., 1990—93; chief staff Detroit Med. Ctr., 1993—, pres. med. staff, 1997—; chief staff Hutzel Hosp., 1996—2002. Researcher effects of androgens on the ovary; pres. med. staff Detroit Med. Ctr., 1998—, bd. trustees, 2002—, chair med. exec. com., 1997—; alt. del. to AMA 2003, pres. Mich. State Med. Soc., 2003. Contbr. articles to profl. jours. Fellow ACS, ACOG (Mich. sect.), Royal Coll. Physicians and Surgeons, Wayne County Med. Soc. (pres. 1995-96); mem. Mich. State Med. Soc. (bd. dirs. 1996—, pres. 2003). Home: 1435 Lone Pine Rd Bloomfield Hills MI 48302-2632 Office: 4727 Saint Antoine St Ste 408 Detroit MI 48201-1461 also: 29877 Telegraph Rd Southfield MI 48034-1332 E-mail: hamirikia@.com.

AMIRKHANIAN, SERJI N. civil engineering educator; b. Aug. 1, 1957; BS in Civil Engring., Tenn. Tech. U., 1979, MS in Civil Engring., 1981; PhD in Civil Engring., Clemson U., 1987. Grad. asst. Tenn. Tech. U., Cookeville, 1979-81; asst. planner Teledyne Corp., L.A., 1982-83; grad. asst. Clemson (S.C.) U., 1983-86, lectr., 1986-87, asst. prof. civil engring., 1987—, prof., 1998—. Cons. S.C. Hwy. and Pub. Transp., Columbia, S.C., 1991. Contbr. articles to profl. jours. Recipient Outstanding Tchr. award Chi Epsilon, Clemson U., 1990, award of merit AAUP, 1992. Mem. ASCE (editor/treas. 1991-92, cert. of appreciation 1991), ASTM, Assn. Asphalt Paving Technologists, Constrn. Rsch. Coun. Office: Clemson U Civil Engring Dept 110 Lowry Hl Clemson SC 29634-0001

AMIS, EDWARD STEPHEN, JR., physician, retired naval officer; b. Baton Rouge, June 23, 1941; s. Edward Stephen and Annie Velma (Birdwhistell) Amis; m. Anne Schneider, Sept. 2, 1984. Student, U. Rochester, 1959-61; BS, U. Ark., 1963; MD, Northwestern U., 1967. Diplomate Am. Bd. Urology, Am. Bd. Radiology. Commd. ensign USN, 1966, advanced through grades to capt., 1980; resident in urology Naval Hosp., San Diego, 1968-72, resident in radiology, 1975-78, staff radiologist, 1978-80, 81-82, staff urologist Great Lakes, Ill., 1972-75; radiology fellow Mass. Gen. Hosp., Boston, 1980-81; chmn. radiology Naval Hosp., Bethesda, Md., 1982-84, exec. officer, 1984-85, comdg. officer, 1985-87; head sect. uroradiology dept. radiology Columbia U., N.Y.C., 1987-91, vice chmn. dept. radiology, 1990-91; chmn. dept. radiology Albert Enstein Coll. Medicine and Montefiore Med. Ctr., Bronx, N.Y., 1991—. Co-author: Essentials of Uroradiology, 1990, Textbook of Uroradiology, 2000; contbr. chapters to textbooks. Leadership council Montgomery County Heart Assn., Bethesda, 1986-87. Bausch and Lomb scholar, 1959. Mem.: Am. Coll. Radiology (bd. chancellors 1995—, vice chair 2000—02, chair 2002—), Am. Roentgen Ray Soc., Soc. Uroradiology, Assn. Univ. Radiologists, Radiol. Assn. N.Am. Republican. Avocations: philately, modern art. E-mail: amis@aecom.yu.edu.

AMIS, MARTIN LOUIS, author; b. Oxford, Aug. 25, 1949; s. Kingsley and Hilary (Bardwell) A.; m. Antonia Phillips, 1984 (div. 1996); 5 children; Isabel Fonseca, 1998; m. Osabel Fonscea, 1998; 2 children. BA in English with honors, Oxford U., 1971. Editorial asst. Times Literary Supplement, London, 1972-75; asst. literary editor New Statesman, London, 1975-79; spl. writer The Observer, 1980—. Actor: (film) A High Wind in Jamaica, 1965; author: The Rachel Papers, 1973 (Somerset Maugham award 1974), Dead Babies, 1975 (pub. as Dark Secrets, 1977), Success, 1978, Other People, 1981, Invasion of the Space Invaders 1982, Money: A Suicide Note, 1984, The Moronic Inferno and Other Visits to America, 1986, Einstein's Monsters, 1987, London Fields, 1989, Time's Arrow, 1991, Visiting Mrs. Nabokov and Other Excursions, 1994, The Information, 1995, Heavy Water and Other Stories, 1998, Experience, 2000; co-author: (with others) My Oxford, 1977, night Tain, 1997, Heavy Water & Other Stories, 1998, Experience, 2000, The War Against Cliche, 1971-2000, 2001; screenwriter: Saturn 3, 1980. Address: The Wylie Agy 4-8 Rodney St London NI 9JH England E-mail: mail@wylieagency.co.uk.

AMITIN, MARK HALL, cultural organization administrator, educator, writer, actor, director; b. N.Y.C., July 26, 1947; s. Ernest Jonas and Gladys Iris (Epstein) A. Diploma of profound studies, U. Paris, France, 1976, PhD, 1978. Gen. mgr. Radical Theatre Repertory, N.Y.C., 1968-69; exec. dir. Universal Movement Theatre, N.Y.C., 1971-76; coord. of troupes World Theatre Festival, Nancy, France, 1976-77; exec. dir. World of Culture, N.Y.C., 1982—. Lectr. univs., insts., festivals worldwide, 1971—; producer, Albee Directs Albee, 1978-79; cons. Am. Theatre Assn., Washington, 1970-79; adjudicator Am. Coll. Theatre Festivals, Washington, 1981—; negotiator, U.S.-China Theatre Exch., Beijing, China, 1984; tchr., lectr. Shanghai and Beijing Drama Insts., 1983-85, U.S. Embassy and Consultate, Israel, Tel Aviv U., Hebrew U., Tel Aviv Tchrs. Coll., 1995, Beit Hageffen, Haifa, 1997; mem. faculty New Sch. Social Rsch.; lectr. Yale U., Columbia U., NYU, Wellesley U., Brown U., Brigham Young U., Notre Dame U., Drew U., Cornell U., Carnegie Mellon U., Drake U., Hampshire U., numerous others; archives housed in librs. of NYU and U. Calif., Davis. Appeared in (films) L'Histoires D'Amerique, 1988, Alexa, 1988, In The Soup, 1991, Animal Factory, 1999; (TV) The Equalizer, 1989; dir., author (play) Cafe Vulgaris, 1981, Seduction, 1999; co-author (film documentary) Signals through the Flames, 1984; co-dir., co-author (TV) The Eyes of a Friend, 1985; cultural and arts contbg. editor Hamptons Mag., 1991-93; film critic Chelsea-Clinton News, The Westsider; contbg. writer The Village Voice; arts and culture writer N.Y. Black Book, 1997—; dir. plays The Dispossessed, Gaza, 1997. Mem. Nat. Conf. of Profl. Mgrs., Screen Actors Guild, Assn. for Theatre in Higher Edn. Avocations: horseback riding, sailing, swimming, poetry, drawing. Home: 463 West St Apt A509 New York NY 10014 E-mail: markamitin@aol.com., worldofcultures@aol.com.

AMLADI, PRASAD GANESH, management consulting executive, health care consultant, researcher; b. Mudhol, India, Sept. 12, 1941; came to U.S., 1967, naturalized, 1968; s. Ganesh L. and Sundari G. Amladi; m. Chitra G. Panje, Dec. 2, 1970; children: Amita, Amol. B in Engring. with honors, Indian Inst. Tech., Bombay, 1963; MS in Indsl. Engring., Ops. Rsch., Stanford U., 1968; MBA with high distinction, U. Mich., 1975. Sr. rsch. engr. Ford Motor Co., Dearborn, Mich., 1968-75; mgr. strategic planning Mich. Consol. Gas Co., Detroit, 1975-78; mgr. planning svcs. The Resources Group, Bloomfield Hills, Mich., 1978-80; project mgr., sr. cons. Mediflex Systems Corp., Bloomfield Hills, 1980-85; mgr. strategic planning svcs. Mersco Corp., Bloomfield Hills, 1985-86; mgr. corp. planning and rsch. Diversified Techs., Inc., New Hudson, Mich., 1986-87; mgr. planning and rsch. Blue Cross & Blue Shield of Mich., Detroit, 1987—. Contbr. papers to profl. publs. Recipient Kodama Meml. Gold medal, 1957; India Merit scholar Govt. of India, 1959-63, K.C. Mahindra scholar, 1967, R.D. Sethna Grad. scholar, 1968. Mem. Inst. Indsl. Engrs. (sr.), N.Am. Soc. Corp. Planning, Econ. Club Detroit, Beta Gamma Sigma. Office: Blue Cross Blue Shield Mich 27000 W Eleven Mile Rd B528 Southfield MI 48034-2200

AMLIN, MARTIN DOLPH, music educator; b. Dallas, June 12, 1953; s. Henry Marion Amlin and Constance Lee Dolph. MusD, Eastman Sch. of Music, 1977. Instr. Phillips Exeter (N.H.) Acad., 1978—85; affiliate artist MIT, Cambridge, Mass., 1980—83; assoc. prof. Boston U., Boston, 1985—. Pianist Tanglewood Festival Chorus, Boston, 1980—. Composer: (songs) Concerto for Piccolo and Orc., Time's Caravan for mixed chorus and double string quintet, Piano Sonatas Nos. 1-7, Shadowdance for orchestra. Fellow, Tanglewood Music Ctr., 1977—80; grantee, NEA, 1987—88, Mass. Cultural Coun., 1999. Mem.: ASCAP, Pi Kappa Lambda. Home: 505 Columbus Ave 1 Boston MA 02118 Office: Boston University 855 Commonwealth Ave Boston MA 02215 E-mail: mamlin@bu.edu.

AMLING, FREDERICK, economist, educator, investment advisor; b. Cleve., Dec. 23, 1926; s. Gustav and Elsie (Fischer) Amling; m. Gwendolyn Stewart, Feb. 17, 1951; children: Jeffrey, Scott, Terrance. BA, Baldwin Wallace Coll., 1948; MBA, Miami U., Oxford, Ohio, 1949; PhD, U. Pa., 1957. Instr. U. Maine, 1948-50, U. Pa., 1950- 52, U. Conn., 1952—; prof. finance and investment chmn. dept. Miami U., Oxford, 1955-66; prof. finance U. R.I., Kingston, 1966-69, dean Coll. Bus. Adminstrn., 1966-69; prof. fin. Grad. Sch. Bus. and Pub. Mgmt. George Washington U., 1970-2000, prof. emeritus, 2000—; pres. Frederick Amling & Assocs., computer models, Amling & Co. Investment Advisers. Cons. fin. and investment, 1959—; cons. Riggs Nat. Bank, 1970—90, Am. Psychiat. Assn., 1975—91; bd. advisers Rsch. Ctr. Credito Emiliano, Milan, 1991—93. Author: (book) Investments: An Introduction to Analysis and Management, 1963, Investments: An Introduction to Analysis and Management, 7th edit., 2000, Plaid on Investments, 1983, Dow Jones Irwin Guide to Personal Financial Planning and Personal Financial Management, 1986; author: (with Bill Droms) Investment Fundamentals, 1994; editor, contbr.: articles on fin. to profl. jours., newspapers and mags. Chmn. local Cancer Crusade, 1964; trustee Georgetown Prebyn. Ch., 1977—79; elder Presbyn. Ch., 1962—. With USNR, World War II, lt. (j.g.) USNR, 1955. Recipient Alumni Merit award, Baldwin Wallace Coll., 1973, Sch. Bus. and Pub. Mgmt. George Washington U., 1982. Mem.: Eastern Fin. Assn. (v.p. 1979), Am. Fin. Assn. (membership chmn. 1973—90), Fin. Mgmt. Assn., Washington Soc. Fin. Analysts (treas.), Colett Club, Cosmos Club, Turks Head Club (Providence), Univ. Club (Miami U., Oxford), George Washington U. Club, Congl. Country Club, Lambda Chi Alpha, Delta Sigma Pi, Beta Gamma Sigma (pres. George Washington U. chpt. 1985). Home: 3555 S Ocean Blvd Palm Beach FL 33480 also: 17 New Salt Rd Box 7148 Ocean Park ME 04063 Office: Apt 312 3555 S Ocean Blvd Palm Beach FL 33480-5765 *To work for family and society with God's help.*

AMLUND, CURTIS ARTHUR, law educator; b. Fargo, N.D., Nov. 29, 1927; s. Arthur Nils Amlund and Corinne Agnes Strand. BA, U. Minn., 1952, PhD, 1959. Instr. U. Minn., Mpls., 1959, U. Oreg., Eugene, 1959-60; vis. lectr. U. Wis., Milw., 1961; from asst. prof. to assoc. prof. N.D. State U., Fargo, 1961-71, prof., 1971—. Tchg. asst. U. Minn., Mpls., 1958-59. Contbr. articles to profl. jours. including Oxford, Cambridge Rev., Dalhousie Law Jour. Chair adminstr. screening com. Fargo City Govt., 1986-87. Recipient Outstanding Tchg. in Polit. Sci. award Am. Polilt. Sci. Assn./Nat. Polit. Sci. Honor Soc., 2000—, Disting. Educator award Nat. Blue Key; named Extraordinary Friend of the Ct. award U.S. Dist. Ct. N.D., 2000, Liberty Bell award N.D. Bar Assn., 2001. Mem. AAUP, Phi Beta Kappa. Office: ND State U Dept Polit Sci Fargo ND 58105 Home: 1200 Harwood Dr Apt 340 Fargo ND 58104-6294

AMM, SOPHIA JADWIGA, artist, educator; b. Czestochowa, Poland, June 13, 1932; arrived in Can., 1948; came to U.S., 1987. d. Romuald Witold and Jadwiga Wactawa (Kotowska) Sulatycki; m. Bruce Campbell Amm, Aug. 5, 1961; children: Alicia, Alexander, Christopher, Bruce Jr., Gregory. Diploma in nursing, Ont. Hosp., 1953; cert. in pub. health nursing, U. Toronto, Ont., Can., 1960; BFA with honors, York U., 1980; MFA, Norwich U., 2000. RN, 1953. Pvt. duty nurse Allied Registry, Toronto, Ont., Can., 1954-56; asst. head nurse Reddy Meml. Hosp., Mont., Que., Can., 1957-59; pub. health nurse Dist. of Sudbury, Ont., Can., 1960-62; pvt. duty nurse Gen. Hosp., Millinocket, Maine, 1962-66; counselor to new immigrants Ont. Welcome House, Toronto, 1982; vis. nurse St. Elizabeth Vis. Nurses Assn., Toronto, 1983-87; artist, tchr. YMCA, Appleton, Wis., 1994. Vol. art tchr. children with devel. disabilities, Appleton, 1988-89, disabled srs. Colony Oaks Nursing Home, Appleton, 1988-91; condr. art workshops Very Spl. Arts Wis. festivals, state and regional, 1989, 90, 92; art rental and sales Art Gallery of Hamilton, 1985-2003. One person show Bergstrom Mahler Mus., Neenah, Wis., 1991, Alfonse Gallery, Milw., 2000; exhibited in juried group shows Harbourfront Exhbn. Gallery, Toronto, Simpson's Art Gallery, Toronto, 1984, City Hall, Toronto, 1984, Ukrainian Art Found., Toronto, 1984, Art Gallery of Hamilton, Can., 1985-86, 2001, Pastel Soc. Can., Ottawa (nat. juried show), 1985, IDA Gallery, York U., Toronto, 1980-81, 86, Carnegie Gallery, Dundas, Can., 1986, Calumet Coll., York U., 1981, 84, Gallery 68, Burlington, Can., 1986, Charles A. Wustum Mus. Fine Arts, Racine, Wis., 1990-91, 94, Gallery Ten, Rockford, Ill., 1992, 94-95 (3d Pl. award 1992), New Vision Gallery, Marshfield, Wis., 1992, 2001 (nat. juried show), Neville Pub. Mus., Green Bay, Wis., 1987-89, 92, 94-96, 97, Lakeland Coll., Wis., 1994, U. Wis. Gallery, Madison, 1992, 94, Consilium Pl., Scarborough, Can., 1987, 89, 92-93, Del Bello Gallery, Toronto (internat. show), 1986-93, Butler Inst. Am. Art, Youngstown, Ohio, 1993 (nat. juried show), Alverno Coll., Milw., 1994, 97, Ariz. State U., 1995, Bergstrom Mahler Mus., 1995 96 (1st pl. award 1995, 3rd pl. award 1996, 97), Appleton Art Ctr., 1995, 96, 2002, 03, (nat. juried show 2000, hon. mention 2002), Ctr. for Visual Arts, Wausau, Wis., 1996, Marian Coll. Art, Fond du Lac, Wis., 1996, Anderson Art Ctr., Kenosha, Wis., 1997, The Stage Gallery, Merrick, N.Y., (nat. juried show), 1997, 98, Norwich U. Vt. Coll. Gallery, Montpelier, 1998, 99, 2000, T.W. Wood Gallery, 2000, Hendrickson Art Ctr., Waupaca, Wis. (hon. mention 2000, 02), West Bend Gallery, 2000, Art Quest Nat. Juried Exhib., Fort Smith, 2001, N.E. Exposure, Priebe Gallery Exhbn. (Jurors award 2001), Fulton St. Gallery, Troy, N.Y., 2002, The Paine Art Ctr., Oshkosh, Wis., 2002, Time Capsult: Delivery 2153 exhbn., The Paine Art Center, Oshkosh, Wis., 2003, Galex 39 Galesburg (Ill.) Civic Art Ctr., 2003. Vol. art tchr. People With Cancer, Appleton, Wis., 1997. Recipient Award of Excellence, North York (Can.) Arts Coun., 1982, 86, Best in Show Etobicoke (Can.) Arts Coun., 1982, 87; project grantee (2) Very Spl. Arts Wis., 1989. Mem. Nat. Mus. Women in Arts, Wis. Painters and Sculptors, Appleton Art Ctr. Roman Catholic. Avocations: golf, gardening. Home: 1109 N Briarcliff Dr Appleton WI 54915-2848

AMMANN, JEAN-CHRISTOPHE, art director; b. Berlin, Jan. 14, 1939; PhD, U. Fribourg, Switzerland, 1966. Asst. Kunsthalle Bern, Switzerland, 1967-68; dir. Kunstmuseum, Lucerne, Switzerland, 1968-77, Kunsthalle, Basle, Switzerland, 1978-88, Mus. für Moderne Kunst, Frankfurt, Germany, 1989—2001, prof., 1998—. Commr. German Pavillion of Biennial of Venice, Italy, 1995; lectr. U. Frankfurt/M. and Giessen, 1992—, U. Heidelberg, 2001—02. Author: Rèmy Zaugg—Discussion with Jean-Christophe Ammann, 1994, (with Harald Szeemann) Von Hodler zur Antiform, 1968, Louis Moilliet: Das Gesamtwerk, 1972, Bewegung im Kopf. Vom Umgang mit der Kunst, 1993, Kulturfinanzierung, 1995, Annäherung. Über die Notwendigkeit von Kunst, 1996, Remy Zaugg-Conversation with Jean Christophe Ammann, French edit., 1990, German edit., 1994, Das Glück Zu Sehen, 1998; co-organizer of documenta 5, Kassel, 1972. Decorated Officier Des Arts et Des Lettres, Goethe-medal City of Frankfurt, Germany. Office: Klettenbergstrasse 11 60322 Frankfurt Germany

AMMANN, LILLIAN ANN NICHOLSON, writer, editor, small business owner; b. Pearsall, Tex., June 20, 1946; d. Harvey Franklin and Annie Laura (Matthews) Nicholson; m. Jack Jordan Ammann Jr., May 31, 1967; 1 child, William Erik. BA magna cum laude, Southwestern U., 1968. Mgr. inventory Kelly AFB, San Antonio, 1967-70; employment counselor Tex. Employment Commn., San Antonio, 1970-75; owner, operator Lillie's Lovely Little Gardens, San Antonio, 1975-77, Lillie's Interior Landscapes, San Antonio, 1980-82, pres., 1983-96; sec. Jack Ammann Inc., 1983-87; pres. Lillie's & Sherry's Plants & Pottery, San Antonio, 1977-80; ind. bus. owner Rexall Showcase Internat., 1996—; editor-in-chief Our Mail Network, 2000—. Author: Lillie's Lovely Gardening Book, 1976, Look Beyond Tomorrow: The Carola Spencer Story, 1998, Stroke of Luck, 1999, How to Get Started in Network Marketing from Home, 2001; editor: A Bouquet of Recipes from the Diocese of the Southwest of the Anglican Church in America. Vol. All Saints Anglican Ch. Mem.: EPPRO, San Antonio Writers Guild (past pres.), Electronically Published Internet Connection. Home and Office: 603 Mauze Dr San Antonio TX 78216-3711 Fax: 210-344-1958. E-mail: lillie@lillieammann.com.

AMMAR, RAYMOND GEORGE, physicist, educator; b. Kingston, Jamaica, July 15, 1932; came to U.S., 1961, naturalized, 1965; s. Elias George and Nellie (Khaleel) A.; m. Carroll Ikerd, June 17, 1961; children: Elizabeth, Robert (dec.), David. AB, Harvard U., 1953; PhD, U. Chgo., 1959. Research assoc. Enrico Fermi Inst., U. Chgo., 1959-60; asst. prof. physics Northwestern U., Evanston, Ill., 1960-64, assoc. prof., 1964-69; prof. physics U. Kans., Lawrence, 1969—, chmn. dept. physics and astronomy, 1989—2003; (on sabbatical leave Fermilab and Deutsches Elektronen Synchrotron, 1984-85). Cons. Argonne (Ill.) Nat. Lab., 1965-69, vis. scientist, 1971-72; vis. scientist Fermilab, Batavia, Ill., summers 1976-81, Deutsches Elektronen Synchroton, Hamburg, Germany, summers 1982-88, lab. of nuclear studies Cornell U., summers 1989-98; project dir. NSF grant for rsch. in high energy physics, 1962-2001. Contbr. articles to sci. jours. Fellow Am. Phys. Soc.; mem. AAUP. Home: 1651 Hillcrest Rd Lawrence KS 66044-4525 Office: U Kans Dept Physics And Astronomy Lawrence KS 66045-0001 E-mail: ammar@ku.edu.

AMMER, WILLIAM, retired judge; b. Circleville, Ohio, May 21, 1919; s. Moses S. and Mary (Schallas) A. BS in Bus. Adminstrn., Ohio State U., 1941, JD, 1946. Bar: Ohio 1947. Atty., examiner Ohio Indsl. Commn., Columbus, 1947-51; assty. atty. gen. State of Ohio, Columbus, 1951-52; pvt. practice Circleville, 1953-57; pros. atty. Picaway County, Circleville, 1953-57, common pleas judge, 1957-95; ret., 1995. Judge by assignment Supreme Ct. Ohio, 1995—; asst. city solicitor Circleville, 1955-57. Past. pres. Pickaway County ARC, Am. Cancer Soc. Served with inf., AUS, 1942-46. Mem. ABA, Ohio Bar Assn. (chmn. criminal law com. 1964-67), Pickaway County Bar Assn. (pres. 1955-56), Ohio Common Pleas Judges Assn. (pres. 1968), Masons, K.T., Shriners, Kiwanis (Ohio dist. chmn., past lt. gov.). Methodist. Home: PO Box 87 Circleville OH 43113-0087 Office: 113 1/2 South Court St PO Box 87 Circleville OH 43113-0087

AMMERAAL, BRENDA FERNE, secondary school educator; b. Grand Rapids, Mich., Mar. 20, 1943; d. Donald and Jean (Longstreet) Bysterveld; m. Robert Neal Ammeraal, June 14, 1966; children: Audrey Jeanne Ammeraal Campbell, Bret Alan, Julia Marie Ammeraal Adamski. BA, Calvin Coll., Grand Rapids, 1963; MA in Latin, U. Mich., 1965; MA in English, U. Chgo., 1978; MA in Ednl. Adminstrn., Governor's State U., 1997. Tchr. Rehoboth (N.Mex.) Mission Sch., 1963-64, Timothy Christian H.S., Elmhurst, Ill., 1965-66, Trinity Luth. Sch., Tinley Park, Ill., 1966-67, Marist H.S., Chgo., 1981—. Adj. prof. Trinity Christian Coll., Palos Heights, Ill., 1984-85, Moraine Valley C.C., Palos Hills, 1983—; essay grader Advanced Placement Exams, Princeton, N.J., 1988-95, summer workshop leader, Leelanau, Mich., 1992—, Ind. State U., 1994-97; Midwest cons. Coll. Bd., 1991-98; contest judge Ill. Critical Thinking Essay Contest, Champaign, Ill., 1989. Contbr. articles to profl. jours.; editor Outlook, The Messenger. Mem. Friends of Worth Libr., 1967—; Sunday sch. tchr. Evergreen Park Christian Ref. Ch., 1968-70, Sunday sch. supt., 1970-71; vacation Bible sch. storyteller Orland Park Christian Reformed Ch. NEH grantee, 1985, 89, 91, 92, U. Chgo. Tuition grantee, 1978. Avocations: reading, gardening, computing, crossword puzzles.

AMMERAAL, ROBERT NEAL, biochemist; b. Grand Rapids, Mich., Oct. 11, 1936; s. Cornelius and Janet (Kolenbrander) A.; m. Brenda Ferne Bysterveld, June 14, 1966; children: Audrey Jeanne Campbell, Bret Alan, Julia Marie Adamski. BA, Calvin Coll., 1958; PhD, Wayne State U., 1963. Rsch. assoc. U. Chgo., 1962-65; asst. prof. biochemistry U. Ill., Chgo., 1965-67; asst. prof. Trinity Christian Coll., Palos Heights, Ill., 1967-69; rsch. project leader Am. Maize-Products Co., Hammond, Ind., 1969-96. Inventor in field; contbr. articles to profl. jours. and books. Lay preacher Orland Park (Ill.) Christian Reformed Ch.; lay pastor Calvary Reformed Ch., Orland Park, 1990-97. Fellow USPHS, 1963-65; cited for one of Top Ten Med. Discoveries by Time mag., 1966. Republican. Mem. Reformed Ch. Am. Avocations: molecular modeling, producing computer animation and graphics for video, electronic construction. Home: 11661 S Nagle Ave Worth IL 60482-2311

AMMON, HARRY, history educator; b. Waterbury, Conn., Sept. 4, 1917; s. Grover and Lena Mary (Pyne) Amman. BS, Georgetown U., 1939, MA, 1940; PhD, U. Va., 1948. Editor Md. Hist. Mag., Balt., 1948-50; asst. prof. So. Ill. U., Carbondale, 1950-57, assoc. prof., 1957-66, prof. history, 1967—, prof. emeritus, 1984—, chmn. dept., 1977-1983. Fulbright lectr. U. Vienna, Austria, 1954-55, Seoul Nat. U., Korea, 1984-85; vis. prof. U. Va., Charlottesville, 1968-69; guest lectr. Northeast Normal and Liaoning Univs., People's Republic of China, 1986, 88. Author: James Monroe: The Quest for National Identity, 1971, new edit. 1990, The Genet Mission, 1973, James Monroe A Bibliography, 1991. Mem.: Phi Beta Kappa. Home: 401 S Orchard Dr Carbondale IL 62901-2340 Office: So Ill U History Dept Carbondale IL 62901 E-mail: harryam@siu.edu.

AMMON, JOHN RICHARD, anesthesiologist; b. N.Y.C., 1948; MD, U. Pa., 1974. Cert. in anesthesiology. Intern Crozer Chester Med. Ctr., 1974—75; resident in anesthesiology Mass. Gen. Hosp., Boston, 1975—77; fellow in cardiac anesthesiology Stanford (Calif.) Med. Ctr., 1977—78; dir., v.p. Am. Bd. Anesthesiology, Phoenix, 1988—99; pvt. practice Valley Anesthesiology Ltd., Phoenix, 1999—. Mem.: Am. Soc. Anesthesiology, Alpha Omega Alpha. Office: Valley Anesthesiology Ltd 2200 N Central Ave Phoenix AZ 85004-1418 also: Am Bd Anesthesiology 4101 Lake Boone Trl Ste 510 Raleigh NC 27607-7506

AMODEI, MARK E. state legislator, lawyer; b. Carson City, Nev., June 12, 1958; m. Michelle Amodei; children: Ryanne, Erin, Brian, Melissa. BA, U. Nev., 1980; JD, U. Pacific, 1983. Atty. Allison & MacKenzie, 1987—; mem. Nev. State Assembly, 1996—98, Nev. Senate, Capitol Dist., 1998—; mem. commerce and labor com., mem. transp. com. Nev. Senate, mem. human resources and facilities com. Mem. Carson City Master Plan Adv. Com. Capt. JAGC, U.S. Army, 1983-87. Decorated Army Commendaiton medal. Mem. ABA. Republican. Presbyterian. Office: 402 N Division St Carson City NV 89703*

AMOLS, HOWARD IRA, medical physicist; b. N.Y.C., Feb. 11, 1949; s. Nathan and Esther Ruth (Rauchwarger) A.; children: Amy Lisa, Rachel. BS in Physics summa cum laude, Cooper Union, 1970; MS in Physics, Brown U., 1973, PhD in Physics, 1974. Postdoctoral fellow Los Alamos Nat. Lab., 1974-76, staff scientist, 1974-79; asst. prof. radiology U. N.Mex., Albuquerque, 1979-81; asst. prof. radiation medicine Brown U. and R.I. Hosp., Providence, 1981-84, assoc. prof., chief physicist dept. radiation therapy, 1984-86; assoc. prof., dir. med. physics dept. radiation oncology Columbia U., N.Y.C., 1986-91, prof., 1991-98; chief clin. phys. svcs. Meml. Sloan-Kettering Cancer Ctr., N.Y.C., 1998—. Vis. scientist Kernforshungzentum, Karlsruhe, Fed. Republic Germany, 1977-78. Contbr. articles to profl. jours. Fellow Am. Assn. Physicists in Medicine; mem. Am. Bd. Med. Phys., Am. Soc. Therapeutic Radiology, Am. Coll. Med. Physics. Jewish. Avocations: golf, tennis, cycling. Office: Memorial Sloan-Kettering Cancer Ctr Dept Med Physics 1275 York Ave New York NY 10021-6094 E-mail: amolsh@mskcc.org.

AMOLSCH, ARTHUR LEWIS, publishing executive; b. L.A., Nov. 28, 1939; s. Arthur Bruce Amolsch and Mildred Vivian (Guyott) Fry; m. Judith Ann Marolda, Aug. 27, 1963 (div. 1982); children: Christopher Bryan, Kira Leigh; m. Imelda Marie Moore Madden, Mar. 27, 1983. BS, Ea. Mich. U., 1963. Tchr. Edmondson Jr. High Sch., Ypsilanti, Mich., 1963-66; fgn. svc. officer Dept. State, Washington, 1971-72; head speech writer Com. for Re-election of the Pres., Washington, 1972; dep. dir., press rels. Presdl. Inaugural Com., Washington, 1973; dir. pub. info. FTC, Washington, 1973-76; pres., pub. Washington Regulatory Reporting Assocs., 1976—. Capt. USAF, 1967-71. Republican. Home: PO Box 356 Basye VA 22810-0356 Office: Washington Regulatory Reporting Assocs 601 Indiana Ave NW Ste 720 Washington DC 20004-2936 E-mail: frcwatch@usa.net.

AMON, CAROL BAGLEY, federal judge; b. 1946; BS, Coll. William and Mary, 1968; JD, U. Va., 1971. Bar: Va. 1971, D.C. 1972, N.Y. 1980. Staff atty. Communications Satellite Corp., Washington, 1971-73; trial atty. U.S. Dept. Justice, Washington, 1973-74; asst. U.S. atty. Ea. Dist. N.Y., 1974-86, U.S. magistrate, 1986-90, dist. ct. judge, 1990—. Recipient John Marshall award U.S. Dept. Justice, 1983. Mem. Assn. Bar of City of N.Y., Va. State Bar Assn., D.C. Bar Assn. (chair codes of conduct com. of jud. conf. 1998-2001). Office: US District Court 225 Cadman Plz E Brooklyn NY 11201-1818

AMONTE, ANTHONY LEWIS, hockey player; b. Weymouth, Mass., Aug. 2, 1970; Student, Boston U. Profl. hockey player N.Y. Rangers, NY, 1988—94, Chgo. Blackhawks, 1994—2002, Phoenix Coyotes, 2002—. Named Hockey East All-Rookie Team, 1989—90, NCAA All-Tournament Team, 1990—91, Hockey East All-Star 2d Team, 1990—91, NHL All-Star Rookie Team, 1991—92. Office: Phoenix Coyotes Alltel Ice Den 9375 E Bell Rd Scottsdale AZ 85260

AMORES, JOSE E. cultural director; b. Mexico City, Mar. 10, 1919; m. Alicia Salinas, July 10, 1947; 1 child, Beatriz. Degree in chem. engring., Nat. U., Mexico. Sch. dir. Monterrey (Mexico) Tech., 1947-59, v.p., 1960-70; social dir. Alfa Group, Monterrey, 1970-84; cultural dir. State Govt., Monterrey, 1984-87; mus. dir. Monterrey Art Mus., 1988-90; dir. Cultural Ctr., Monterrey, 1991-94, Nuevo León Pub. Broadcast System, 1996-98, Mex. History Mus., 1998—2002. Bd. trustees several univs., 1980—. Author of poems. Pres. Artistic Soc., Monterrey, 1948-80, Chem. Engring. Inst., Monterrey, 1974-76. Recipient Chemistry Nat. prize, 1970. Mem. Sembradores Internat. (pres. 1961-62, 70-72). Home: Rio Presas 305 66220 Garza Garcia Mexico Office: Ctr Cultrual Alta PO Box 1177 64000 Monterrey Mexico

AMORIM, CELSO LUIZ NUNES, government official; Student, Rio-Branco Inst., Diplomatic Acad. Vienna, London Sch. Econs. Amb. UN, Geneva, 1991-93; min. fgn. affairs Brazil, 1993—94; permanent rep. Brazil UN, N.Y.C., 1995-99, Geneva, 1999—; min. foreign affairs, 2003—. Spl. asst. to Ministry Sci. & Tech.; asst. prof. dept. polit. sci. and internat. rels. U. Brasilia, permanent mem. dept. internat. affairs Inst. Advanced Studies; pres. UN Security Coun., 1999; chmn. ILO Govt. Body, 2000; amb. Brazil to Ct. of St.James's, 2001-2002. Contbr. articles to profl. jours. Office: Ministry of Foreign Affairs Esplanada Dos Ministerios Bloco H 70170-900 Brasilia Brazil

AMOROSO, FRANK, retired communication system engineer, consultant; b. Providence, July 31, 1935; s. Michele and Angela Maria Barbara (D'Uva) A. BSEE, MSEE, MIT, 1958; postgrad., Purdue U., 1958-60, U. Turin, Italy, 1964-65. Registered profl. engr., Calif. Instr. elec. engring. Purdue U., West Lafayette, Ind., 1958-60; rsch. engr. Melpar Inc., Roxbury, Mass., 1959, MIT Instrumentation Lab., Cambridge, Mass., 1960, Litton Sys. Advanced Devel. Lab., Waltham, Mass., 1960-61; engr. Melpar Applied Sci. Divsn., Watertown, Mass., 1961; mem. tech. staff RCA Labs. David Sarnoff Rsch. Ctr., Princeton, N.J., 1962-64, Mitre Corp., Bedford, Mass., 1966-67; sr. applied mathematician Collins Radio Co., Newport Beach, 1967-68; comm. sys. engr. N.Am. Rockwell Corp., El Segundo, Calif., 1968-71, Northrop Electronics Divsn., Palos Verdes Peninsula, 1971-72; comm. sys. engr., sr. staff engr. Hughes Aircraft Co., Fullerton, 1972-89; ret., 1989; cons., developer, presenter ednl. seminars, 1989—. Cons. Lincom, Inc., L.A., 1994—96, Omnipoint Corp.; cons. client Sklar Comm. Engring., 1996—, Mascarell Microones, S.L., Tarragona, Spain; instr. continuing engring. edn. program George Washington U., San Diego, 1993; instr. ext. short courses UCLA, 1987—89, 1998—; cons. Mobile Elec. Tracking Sys., Boca Raton, Fla., 1992. Co-author: (book) Power Amplifier Design, 2002. 1st lt. U.S. Signal Corps, 1961-62. Recipient Outstanding Achievement award RCA Labs., 1964; grad. study scholar Italian Govt., 1964-66. Mem. IEEE (sr. mem., session organizer, chmn. conf. on mil. com., presenter). Achievements include patents in field. Home and Office: Digital Data Modulation Studies 271 W Alton Ave Apt D Santa Ana CA 92707-4171

AMOROSO, RICHARD LOUIS, cosmologist, educator; b. Medford, Mass., Apr. 24, 1946; s. Louis Raymond and Marjorie Lou (McCathie) A.; m. Juliette Noble Sherer, Oct. 1982 (div. 1986); 1 child, Juliette Rachael Sarah. BS in Psychology, U. Mass., 1972; postgrad. in psychology, Stanford U., 1972-74; postgrad. in physics and psysiology, Harvard U., 1980-82; PhD in Cosmology, Internat. Noetic U., 1992; MA in Consciousness Studies, J.F.K. Univ., 1994. Computer engr. Harvard Smithsonian Astrophys. Obs., Cambridge, Mass., 1980-82; instr. Peralta Coll., Oakland, Calif., 1987-88; dir. Mus. of Robotics, Berkeley, Calif., 1989—, Noetic Advanced Studies Inst., Orinda, Calif., 1992—; pres. Cereroscopic Systems, Inc., Provo, Utah; CFO Elec. Corp., Oakland, 1992-94; prof. philosophy of mind Internat. Noetic U., Oakland, 1995—. Founding editor Noetic Jour., Orinda, 1997—. Editor: Science and the Primary of Consciousness, 1998, Gravitation and Cosmology: From the Hubble Radius to the Planck Scale, 2001, The Scientific Origins of Sexual Preference, 2000, The Complementarity of Mind and Body, 2003, What Is Conciousness? Introducing the Cosmology of Being, 2003. Mem. AAAS, N.Y. Acad. Sci., Romanian Acad. Sci. (hon.). Republican. Mem. Lds Ch. Avocations: meditation, scuba, robotic sculpture, reading, sailing, flying. Office: Noetic Inst 120 Village Sq # 49 Orinda CA 94563-2502 E-mail: noeticj@mindspring.com.

AMOS, BETTY GILES, restaurant company executive, accountant; b. Lebanon, Mo., July 18, 1941; d. Clarence Edgar and Clara Mae (Gann) Giles; m. E.L. Amos, Sept. 18, 1959 (div. Oct. 1965); 1 child, Jeffrey Lee; m. Thomas R. Righetti, Jan. 2, 1983. BBA magna cum laude, U. Miami, Coral Gables, Fla., 1973, MBA, 1976; D of Bus. Adminstrn. honoris causa, Johnson & Wales U., 1990. CPA, Fla. Sec. City of Lebanon, 1959-63; dept. head Empire Gas Co., Lebanon, 1963-68; fin. analyst asst. Biscayne Assocs., Ltd., Miami, Fla., 1968-73; investment mgr. Universal Restaurants Inc., Miami, 1973-77; pvt. practice accountant, investment mgr. Miami, 1977-83; pres. The Abkey Cos., Miami, 1983—. Founder, Mega Bank, Miami, 1983-94; adv. com. Fuddruckers, Inc., Boston, 1986-2002; bd. dirs. Ivax Corp.; mem. Coun. Advancement and Support for Edn. (S.E. U.S. vol. of yr. 2003). Trustee Miami Project, 1986-89, United Fund of Dade County, 1992—; pres. Humane Soc. Greater Miami, 1994-2000, bd. dirs., 1993-2000; mem. pres. coun. U. Miami, 1994—, mem. founder's soc., 1994—, bd. trustees, 1997—; mem. presdl. search com. U. Miami, 2000—; mem. Coun. Advancement and Support Edn. (Vol. of Yr., 2003); dir., treas. Wings Over Miami Aviation Mus.; bd. dirs. IVAX Corp., 2003—. Recipient Philip J. Romano Founders award, 1988. Mem. AICPA, Fla. Inst. CPAs, Am. Women's Soc. CPAs, Coconut Grove C. of C. (trustee 1988-2001), Nat. Assn. Women Bus. Owners (Outstanding Woman Bus. award 1993), U. Miami Alumni Assn. (nat. pres. 1999-2001), Iron Arrow, Internat. Women's Forum, Women of Tomorrow (Orange Bowl com. 2002-). Republican. Roman Catholic. Avocations: snow skiing, water skiing, scuba diving, tennis, windsurfing. Home: 13724 SW 92nd Ct Miami FL 33176-6858 Office: The Abkey Cos 3444 48 Main Hwy 3d Floor PO Box 330927 Miami FL 33233-0927

AMOS, BRICE ALLEN, film company executive, writer; b. L.A., Calif., Aug. 29, 1951; s. Benjamin Allan Amos and Rosie Lee Thompson. BA in Screenwriting, Boston Inst., 1971; BA in Filmmaking, Am. Film Inst., 1976, MFA in Audio-visual Comm., 1987. Instr. media arts Compton Found., Compton, Calif., 1973—74; media editor Performing Arts Soc., L.A., 1975—76; v.p. pub. rels. Children Baptist Home, Inglewood, Calif., 1976—81; story editor Video Film Co., L.A., 1981—83; sr. clk. valuations L.A. County Assessor, L.A., 1983—99; chmn. bd. Cinema Verite Prodns., L.A., 1999—. Editor: Voices of Urban America, 1990; author: Law and Order Society, 1994, Our Function At The Junction, 1995, Flickering Images, 2000. Mem. Concern Citizens, L.A., 1988; v.p. Law & Order Soc., L.A., 1994; pres. So. Ctrl. Rep., L.A., 1995—. Recipient Meritorious Svc. award, Inglewood Police Dept., 1984, Filmmaking award, Am. Film Inst., 1987, Bus. of Yr. award, Merchants for Improvement, 1992. Republican. Avocations: skydiving, hunting, deep sea fishing. Office: Cinema Verite Productions 3432 W 71 Street Los Angeles CA 90043

AMOS, DANIEL PAUL, insurance company executive; b. Pensacola, Fla., Aug. 13, 1951; s. Paul Shelby and Mary Jean (Roberts) A.; m. Mary Shannon Landing, Sept. 12, 1972; children: Paul Shelby, Lauren Alyse BS in Risk and Ins. Mgmt., U. Ga., 1973. Co-state mgr. Am. Family Life Assurance Co., Columbus, Ga., 1973-78, state mgr., 1978-83, pres., 1983-96; dep. CEO Am. Family Corp., Columbus, Ga., 1996; vice-chmn., pres., CEO AFLAC Inc., Columbus, Ga., 1996—, CEO, 1990—, chmn., 2001—, pres., 1983—2001. Dir. Columbus Bank & Trust Co. Methodist. Avocation: bridge. Office: AFLAC Inc AFLAC Ctr 1932 Wynnton Rd Columbus GA 31999-0001

AMOS, DENNIS B. immunologist; b. Bromley, Eng., Apr. 16, 1923; s. Benjamin and Vera (Oliver) A.; m. Solange M. Labesse, Aug. 25, 1949 (dec. 1980); children: Susan V., Martin D., Christopher I., Nigel P., Irene C.; m. Kay B. Veale, Mar. 6, 1984 MBBS, Guy's Hosp., London, 1951, MD, 1963. House officer Guy's Hosp., London, 1951-52, rsch. pathologist, 1952-55; prin. cancer rsch. scientist Roswell Park Inst., Buffalo, 1955-62; prof. immunology, exptl. surgery Duke U., Durham, N.C., 1962-93, prof. emeritus, 1993—. Cons. NIH, Bethesda, Md., 1957— Mem. Nat. Acad. Scis., Inst. of Medicine Office: Duke Med Ctr PO Box 3010 Durham NC 27715-3010

AMOS, GEORGE, music educator, coach; b. Lakeland, Fla., Feb. 12, 1969; s. Albert Everett Amos and Sue Barnes Parham. MusB in Music Edn., Shenandoah U., 1991, MusM, 1993. Teaching certificate VA, 1998. Asst. music dir. Braddock St. United Meth. Ch., Winchester, Va., 1987 ; music dir. Front Royal (Va.) Oratorio Soc., 1995—. Recipient Artie Award, Shenandoah Arts Coun., 2000, Coach of Yr.-Volleyball, Delaney Athletic Conf., 1993, Coach of Yr.-Volleyball, 1997, 1999, 2000, 2002, Coach of Yr.-Basketball, 2000, 2002. Mem.: Music Educators Nat. Conf. (licentiate). Home: 90-8 Chinkapin Drive Stephens City VA 22655

AMOS, JAMES LYSLE, photographer; b. Kalamazoo, Jan. 25, 1929; s. George Elsworth and Lois Hazel (Noffsinger) A.; m. Martha Imogene (Holbrook), Sept. 1973. Attended, U. Idaho, Idaho, 1947-49; AAS, Rochester Inst. Tech., NY, 1951. Trainee Eastman Kodak Co., 1951-53, salesman, 1956, tech. sales rep. Balt., 1957-67. Free lance photographer, 1967-69, 93—; staff photographer, Nat. Geog. Soc., Washington, 1969-89, contract photographer, 1989-93; prin. photographer (books) on Hawaii and America's Inland Waterway. Served with AUS, 1953-55. Named Mag. Photographer of Yr., Nat. Press Photographers Assn., 1969, 70. Mem. White House News Photographers Assn., North Am. Nature Photography Assn., Internat. Assn. Panoramic Photographers. Home: PO Box 118 Centreville MD 21617-0118 E-mail: jlapix@dmv.com. *To achieve success we must love what we are doing, be willing to take risks and trust our instincts.*

AMOS, LINDA K. academic administrator; b. Findlay, Ohio, Sept. 7, 1940; d. Blond G. and Dorotha (Brinkman) A. BS, Ohio State U., 1962, MS, 1964; EdD, Boston U., 1977. Asst. dean of baccalaureate affairs Boston U. Coll. Nursing, 1971-74, dean, prof., 1975-80, U. Utah Coll. Nursing, Salt Lake City, 1980—2000; assoc. v.p. for health scis. U. Utah, Salt Lake City, 1998—. Cons. Social Sci. Rsch. Inst., Boston; chmn. Commn. on Collegiate Nursing Edn., 1998-2000; bd. dirs. Univ. Health Network. Contbr. articles to profl. jours. Chmn. Presdl. Commn. on Status of Women, U. Utah, 1995—99; bd. dirs. Utah Heart Assn. Served as cons. with USPHS. Named for Outstanding Contbns. to the Nursing Profession, Utah Citizen's League for Nursing, 1989; recipient VA Chief Nurse award for promoting unity between edn. and practice, Mary Tolle

Wright award for excellence in leadership Sigma Theta Tau, 1991. Fellow Am. Acad. Nursing (governing coun. 1986-90, selection com. 1995—98); mem. ANA, Am. Assn. Colls. of Nursing (pres. 1984-86), Nat. Adv. Coun. on Nurse Tng., Utah Women's Forum, Internat. Women's Forum, Salt Lake City Rotary, Sigma Theta Tau (internat. nominating com. 1995-97).

AMOS, WALLY, entrepreneur; b. Tallahassee, Fla., July 1, 1936; s. Wallace Sr. and Ruby Amos; m. Maria LaForey (div.); children: Michael, Gregory; m. Shirlee Ellis (div.); 1 child, Shawn; m. Christine Amos, 1979; 1 child, Sarah. Stockroom clk. Saks Fifth Ave., N.Y.C., 1957-58, stockroom supr., 1958-61; mail room clk. William Morris Agy., N.Y.C., 1961, sec., 1961-62, asst. agt., 1962; talent agt., 1962-67; ind personal mgr., 1967-75; founder Famous Amos Chocolate Chip Cookie Corp., Hollywood, Calif., 1975-89, Wally Amos Presents: Chip and Cookie, 1991-92, UNCLE Nonamé Cookie Co., 1992—; chmn. Uncle Wally Cookie Co. Author: The Famous Amos Story: The Face That Launched a Thousand Chips, 1983, The Power In You: Ten Secret Ingredients for Inner Strength, 1988, Man with No Name: Turn Lemons Into Lemonade, 1994. Nat. spokesman Literacy Vols. of Am., 1979. With USAF, 1953-57. Recipient Pres.' award for Entrepreneurial Excellence, 1986, Horatio Alger award 1987, Nat. Literacy Honors award 1990. Home and Office: Uncle Wally Cookie Co PO Box 897 Kailua HI 96734-0897

AMOS-GANTHER, LINDA, poet; b. York, Pa., Sept. 13, 1950; d. Herbert and Gloria (Stell) Gardner; m. Ralph Amos, Aug. 30, 1978 (dec.); 4 children; m. George William Ganther, Apr. 17, 1994. AS, York Coll. Pa., 1980, BA, 1984. Owner Grandmother Amos' Log Cabin Quilt Creations, York, Pa., The Wordwrite Shoppe, Murchison, Tex. Author: From A-to-Z, 1992, The Pieces of My Life, 1994, A Garden of New Beginnings, 1997, Spring Greetings, 1998, Of Heart and Hands, 2002, Carousel: A Free Verse Poetry Anthology, 2001, The Dance of Life, 2002, The View From Within, 2002. Local parent rep. Head Start Parents Group, York, 1982-88, state parent rep. Pa., 1984-88, nat. parent rep., 1988; mem. steering com. Olde York St. Fair, 1984-2002, Week of the Young Child, 1998-99; active Leadership York, 1985; com. mem. Boy Scouts Am. Troop #7, Margaret E. Moul Cerebral Palsy Home, 1998—. Named Healthy Hero, Susan P. Byrnes Health Edn. Ctr., 2001; recipient Gov.'s Hwy. Safety award, 2002. Mem. Poetry Soc. Tex., Poets Dust Tom Live Poets' Soc. of York. Presbyterian. Avocations: traditional hand quilting, organic gardening, humanitarian work. E-mail: amos_ganther@hotmail.com.

AMOSS, BENJAMIN MCRAE, JR., language educator; b. Atlanta, Apr. 22, 1960; s. Benjamin McRae and Sandra (Goggans) A. PhD, U. Va., 1990. Lectr. French, U. Va., Charlottesville, 1990-91; prof. dept. English and modern lang. Longwood U., Farmville, Va., 1991—. Author: Time and Narrative in Stendhal, 1992 (South Atlantic MLA Studies award 1990). Office: Longwood U 201 High St Farmville VA 23909

AMOSS, W. JAMES, JR., shipping company executive; b. 1924; married. BBA, Tulane U., 1947. With Lykes Bros. Steamship Co. Inc., New Orleans, 1947-93, v.p. traffic, 1963-70, exec. v.p., 1970-73, pres., 1973-86, chief exec. officer, dir., 1981—, chmn., 1986-93, Interocean Steamship Corp, Tampa, Fla., 1986-93; pres. Marine Logistics, Inc., New Orleans, 1993—, Sea Point LLC, New Orleans, 2001—. Dir. Hibernia Nat. Bank, 1973-95. With USN, 1942-46, 50-52. Office: Marine Logistics Inc 2 Canal St New Orleans LA 70130-1408

AMOSS, WALTER JAMES (JIM), III, editor; b. New Orleans, Oct. 22, 1947; s. Walter James Jr. and Berthe Lathrop (Marks) A.; m. Nancy Brooks Monroe, Apr. 5, 1975; children: Adam Brooks, Sophia Philomene. BA magna cum laude, Yale U., 1969. Reporter The States-Item, New Orleans, 1974-79, The Times-Picayune, New Orleans, 1980-82, city editor, 1982-83, met. editor, 1983-88, assoc. editor, 1988-90, editor, 1990—. Bd. vis. La. State U. Manship Sch. Mass. Comms.; trustee Trinity Episcopal Sch.; mem. Pulitzer Prize bd., 2003-, juror, 1994-95, 99-2000. Mem. La. Com. of Selection for Rhodes Scholarships, 1982—. Rhodes scholar Oxford (Eng.) U., 1970-71; Journalistes en Europe grantee, 1979-80; named Nat. Press Found.'s Editor of Yr., 1997. Mem. Am. Soc. Newspaper Editors, AP Mng. Editors, Phi Beta Kappa. Roman Catholic. Office: The Times-Picayune 3800 Howard Ave New Orleans LA 70125-1429

AMPARADO, KEITH D. communications company executive; b. Bklyn., Oct. 5, 1952; m. Arcadeo and Sadie J. (Browne) A. BS, SUNY, Empire State Coll. Supr. data processing Franklin Nat. Bank/European Am. Bank, 1974-78; mgr. Ctr. for Computing Activity Columbia U., N.Y.C., 1978-80; systems analyst Morgan Guaranty Trust Co., 1980-81; programmer, analyst Europen Am. Bank, 1981-83; sr. tech editor Mfrs. Hanover Trust, 1983-85; founder, pres. KDA Comm, Bklyn., 1985—. Cons. Siloam Presbyn. Ch., Bklyn., 1988—. Mem. Soc. for Tech. Communication (sr.), Am. Mgmt. Assn., Am. Mktg. Assn., Mktg. Rsch. Assn., Nat. Assn. Desktop Pubs., Qualitative Rsch. Cons. Assn., Internat. Assn. of Bus. Communicators.

AMPOLA, MARY G. pediatrician, geneticist; b. Syracuse, N.Y., Nov. 2, 1934; d. Mariangelo and Filomena (Albanese) Giambattista; m. Vincent G. Ampola, Aug. 7, 1966; children: Leanna, David. BA cum laude, Syracuse U., 1956; MD, SUNY, Syracuse, 1960. Diplomate Am. Bd. Pediatrics. Intern George Washington Univ. Hosp., Washington, 1960-61; pediatric resident Children's Nat. Med. Ctr., Washington, 1961-63, chief resident in pediatrics, 1963-64; genetics fellow Children's Hosp. Med. Ctr., Boston, 1964-66; metabolic diseases fellow Mass. Gen. Hosp., Boston, 1966-67; cytogeneticist New Eng. Med. Ctr., Boston, 1967-69, dir. pediatric amino acid lab., 1969—, pediatrician, 1969—, acting chief clin. genetics divsn. dept. pediatrics, 1989-96, chief divsn. metabolism, dept. pediatrics, 1996—; from asst. to assoc. prof. pediatrics New Eng. Med. Ctr./Tufts U. Sch. Medicine, Boston, 1967-92, prof., 1992—. Chmn. PL-1 selection com. dept. pediat. New Eng. Med. Ctr., 1975—, chmn. residency com., 1981—87, mem. curriculum com., 1981—, mem. hosp. quality assurance com., 1982—92, mem. residency com., 1987—98, bd. dirs. Ctr. Children Spl. Needs, 1987—; chmn. evaluation and promotions com. Tufts U. Sch. Medicine, 1998—. Editor: Early Detection and Management of Inborn Errors, 1976; author: Metabolic Diseases in Pediatric Practice, 1982; contbr. chpts. to books and articles to profl. jours. Named Alumna of Yr., SUNY Coll. Medicine, 1980. Fellow Am. Acad. Pediatrics (sect. genetics); mem. Am. Soc. Human Genetics, New Eng. Pediatric Soc. (sec.-treas. 1993—), Soc. Inherited Metabolic Disorders, Soc. Study Inborn Errors Metabolism, Phi Beta Kappa. Republican. Office: New Eng Med Ctr 750 Washington St Boston MA 02111-1526 E-mail: mampola@tufts-nemc.org.

AMPY, FRANKLIN ROOSEVELT, zoologist; b. Dinwiddie, Va., June 22, 1936; s. Preston and Beatrice Tucker A.; B.S., Va. State Coll., 1958; M.S., Oreg. State U., 1960, Ph.D., 1962. Asst. prof. Am. U. Beirut, 1962-68; NIH fellow U. Calif., Davis, 1968-71; assoc. prof. zoology Howard U., Washington, 1971—90, prof. biology, 1990-, acting chmn. dept. zoology, 1973-75, 84-86, 90-92, now acting chmn. dept.; geneticist Lebanese del. to World Poultry Conf., 1966; cons. NIH, 1981, 83. NASA-Ames faculty fellow, 1976; NIH grantee, 1978— ; NSF grantee, 1978,95. Mem. Bd. dirs., Project 30, Am. Genetic Assn., Am. Soc. Genetics, Environ. Mutagenesis Soc., Am. Soc. Cell Biologists, Smithsonian Assocs., Sigma Xi (pres. Howard U. cptr., 1993-94), Beta Kappa Xi, Alpha Phi Alpha. Democrat. Episcopalian. Home: PO Box 91886 Washington DC 20090-1886 Office: Dept Biology Howard Univ 415 College St Washington DC 20001

AMRAM, DAVID WERNER, composer, conductor, musician; b. Phila., Nov. 17, 1930; s. Philip and Emilie (Weyl) A.; m. Loralee Ecobelli, Jan. 7, 1979; children: Alana, Adira, Adam. Student, Oberlin Conservatory Music, 1948-49, Manhattan Sch. Music, 1955-56; BA in European History, George Washington U., 1952; LLD, Moravian Coll., Bethlehem, Pa., 1979; studied composition with Vittorio Giannini, N.Y.C., studied horn with Gunther Schuller, 1956; MusD (hon.), Muhlenberg Coll., 1988, U. Hartford, 1989; DMus (hon.), St. Lawrence U., 1994. Head Free Schooltime Concert Series, Bklyn. Philharmonic Orch., 1971—. Leo Block chair for the Arts & Humanities, U. Denver. Condr., soloist with 14 orchs. annually including Montreal Symphony, Toronto Symphony, Milw. Symphony, Indpls. Symphony, Grant Park Orch., Nat. Jewish Arts. Festival; 1st composer-in-residence, N.Y. Philharmonic Orch., 1966-67; composer incidental music for prodns., N.Y. Shakespeare Festival, 1956-67, Broadway plays, 1958—, films include The Manchurian Candidate, Splendor in the Grass, others, 1957—, also TV (collaboration with Jack Kerouac and Allen Ginsberg); compositions for orch. include Ode to Lord Buckley for saxophone and orch., Violin Concerto, numerous others; commd. composer A Little Rebellion: Thomas Jefferson for narrator/wood-wind guintel, strings and percussion for Libr. Congress, 1995, Kokopelli, 1997, Flute concerto for James Galway "Giants of the Night", 2002; operas include The Final Ingredient, 12th Night, 1996; recording artist, conductor, composer, multi-instrumentalist Newport Classic Records, 1989, Premiere Records; works performed by Phila. Orch., N.Y. Philharmonic, other maj. orchs.; plays French horn, piano, guitar, numerous flutes and whistles; combines symphony, jazz and folk music with audience participation; recs. include Recordings of Symphonic Works, 1993, 94, 95, The Holocaust Open The Final Ingredient, 1996, The Manchurian Candidate, 1997; author: (autobiography) Vibrations: Adventures and Musical Times of David Amram, 1968, rev. edit., 2000, music dir. Internat. Jewish Arts Festival, 1992, 94, conducting mem. Met. Opera Orch., music dir. Aaron Copland Festival, 1992, 94; composed music for films: Splendor in the Grass, The Manchurian Candidate, The Arrangement, The Young Savages; guest soloist nat. TV with Dizzy Gillespie and Willie Nelson, 1987. Served with AUS, 1952-54. Recipient Obie award for compositions for Phoenix Theater and N.Y. Shakespeare Festival, 1959; named One of 20 Most Performed Composers of Concert Music in U.S., BMI: Many Worlds of Music. Achievements include being subject of: 1-hour Nat. Ednl. TV Documentary The World of David Amram, 1969, David Amram and Friends, 1979, PBS Soundstage, a collection of papers at Mugar Library Boston Univ. Address: New World Music Artists 928 Peekskill Hollow Rd Putnam Valley NY 10579-1705 E-mail: edkeaneassociates@compuserve.com.

AMROZOWICZ, PAUL DOUGLAS, lawyer, electrical engineer; b. Ann Arbor, Mich., Sept. 14, 1961; married. BSEE magna cum laude, Ariz. State U., 1989; JD, George Mason U., 2000. Bar: (U.S. Patent Office). Commd. ensign USN, 1980, advanced through grades to officer, with USS Permit, 1980—86, with divsn. naval reactors Washington, 1990—95; patent examiner U.S. Patent and Trademark Office, Washington, 1995—98; law clk., patent agt. Fitzpatrick, Cella, Harper & Scinto, Washington, 1999; patent agt. Rader, Fishman & Grauer, Washington, 1999—2000; atty. Quarles & Brady Streich Lang LLP, Phoenix, 2000—03, Ingrassia, Fisher & Lorenz, PC, Scottsdale, Ariz., 2003—. Contbr. articles. Mem.: State Bar Ariz., Patent and Trademark Office Soc., Am. Intellectual Property Law Assn. Avocations: reading, writing, basketball, baseball. Home: 1683 S Boulder St Gilbert AZ 85296 Office: Ingrassia Fisher & Lorenz PC 7150 E Camelback Rd Ste 325 Scottsdale AZ 85251 Office Fax: 480-385-5061. Business E-Mail: pamrozowicz@ifllaw.com.

AMSCHLER, DENISE H. health science educator; b. Alton, Ill., Aug. 1, 1950; d. Victor V. and Delphine L. Amschler; m. Neal E. Lambert, Apr. 27, 1985. BS, So. Ill. U., 1972, MS, 1973, PhD, 1975. Adj. asst. prof. Southern Ill. U., Carbondale, 1975-76; asst. prof. Ball State U., Muncie, Ind., 1976-83, assoc. prof., 1984-93, full prof., 1994—. Contbr. articles to profl. jours. Fellow Am. Sch. Health Assn.; mem. APHA, Jacobs Inst. for Womens Health, Eta Sigma Gamma (life, editor-in-chief The Health Educator jour. 1977-92, Disting. Svc. award 1985, Warren E. Schaller Presdl. citation 1993). Office: Dept Physiology/Health Sci Ball State U Muncie IN 47306-0001 E-mail: dhamschler@bsu.edu.

AMSCHLER, JAMES RALPH, lawyer, relocation company executive; b. Mpls., June 29, 1943; s. Ralph Frank Amschler and June Ann (Naslund) Petrovich; m. Judith Claire Ketterbaugh, Aug. 19, 1967; 1 child, Christy Hamilton. BS, U. Wis., 1965; LLB, Stanford U., 1968. Bar: Wis. 1968, U.S. Dist. Ct. (we. dist.) Wis. 1968, Utah 1969, U.S. Dist. Ct. Utah 1969, N.Y. 1975, Conn. 1992, U.S. Supreme Ct. 1975. Instr. law U. Wis., Madison, 1968-69; assoc. VanCott, Bagley, Cornwall & McCarthy, Salt Lake City, 1969-73; asst. gen. counsel Carrier Corp., Syracuse, N.Y., 1973-83; assoc. gen. counsel Federated Dept. Stores, Cin., 1983-85; sr. v.p., gen. counsel PHH Homequity Corp., Wilton, Conn., 1985-96; prin. Diversified Adv. Svcs., Ltd., Westport, Conn., 1996—. Adj. prof. law Syracuse U., 1981-82; chmn. FTC/antitrust sub-com. Nat. Assn. Mfrs., 1982-83. Bd. dirs. Wilton (Conn.) United Way, 1985-91. Mem. N.Y. State Bar Assn., Utah Bar Assn., Wis. State Bar Assn., Conn. State Bar. Lutheran. Avocations: golf, tennis, sailing. Home: 17 Cardinal Ln Westport CT 06880-1714 Office: Diversified Advisory Services Ltd 17 Cardinal Ln Westport CT 06880-1714

AMSLER, KAREN MARIE, medical technologist, scientist; b. Duluth, Minn., May 10, 1960; d. Fred Ritts and Ilene Lucille (App) A.; m. Craig Alan Steensma, Aug. 31, 1986 (div. Mar. 1995). BA in Biology, Hollins (Va.) Coll., 1982; MS in Microbiology, Immunology, Thomas Jefferson U., 1996. Med. technologist Am. Med. Labs., Fairfax, Va., 1985-86, Bancroft Med. Lab., Wilmington, Del., 1986-89; rsch. technologist U. Pa. Sch. Vet. Medicine, Kennet Square, 1989-90; med. technologist Crozer-Chester Med. Ctr., Upland, Pa., 1991-93, Christiana Care Health System, Newark, Del., 1991-98, Smith Kline Beecham Clin. Labs., Norristown, Pa., 1993, Children's Hosp. Phila., 1994-96; sr. staff scientist DuPont Pharm. Co., Wilmington, Del., 1998—2001; scientist Enanta Pharms., Inc., Watertown, Mass., 2002—. Mem. DAR, Am. Soc. Clin. Pathologists (cert.), Am. Soc. Microbiology. Avocations: horseback riding, skiing, hiking, gardening. Office: Enanta Pharms Inc 500 Arsenal St Watertown MA 02472 Home: 31 Violetwood Cir Marlborough MA 01752 E-mail: kamsler@enanta.com.

AMSPACHER, JOHN CLAIR ELDER, retired human services manager; b. Hanover, Pa., Dec. 20, 1948; s. Clair and Emily Amspacher; m. Karen Groh, Apr. 26, 1980; children: Olivia, Lucas, Amelia. BA in English, BA in Psychology, Pa. State U., 1970; MA, West Chester U., 1975; MBA, Widener U., 1990. Trainer Temple U., Phila., 1986-88; county casework mgr. Chester County Children, Youth and Families, West Chester, Pa., 1978-99; mem. profl. adv. com. Neighborhood Home Health Agy., West Chester, Pa., 1998-2001; ret., 2001. Mem. Citizens Adv. Com., March of Dimes, West Chester, 1981-84; mem. blue ribbon panel for spl. edn., Chester County Intermediate Unit, Exton, Pa., 1994-95. Unitarian Universalist.

AMSTADT, NANCY HOLLIS, retired language educator; b. Chgo., Ill., Mar. 1, 1932; d. James George and Agnes Green Hollis; m. Ervin Carl Amstadt, Dec. 27, 1952; children: Elaine, Joan, Steven, Carolyn. BA, De Paul U., 1952; MA, San Diego State U., 1966. English & history tchr. Sweetwater H.S. Dist., Chula Vista, Calif., 1957—59; tchr., counselor Santa Clara City Schs., Santa Clara, Calif., 1959—63; secondary English tchr. San Diego City Schs., San Diego, 1966—91; English instr. San Diego C.C., San Diego, 1993—95; ret., 1995. Chmn. dept. English Kearny H.S., San Diego, 1985—91. Author: Confinement: Anne Frank's House, 1999; Confinement: Anne Frank's House, 1999, exhibitions include San Diego Art Inst., 1984—2003. Mem. U.N. Gender Equity, San Diego, 2001—03; docent art gallery U. Calif., San Diego, 1998—2003; program dir. San Diego Mus. Art, San Diego, 1968—2003. Democrat. Avocations: tennis, women refugees, art history, classical music, Chinese exercise. Home: 1097 Alexandria Drive San Diego CA 92107

AMSTADTER, LAURENCE, retired architect; b. Chgo., Apr. 9, 1922; s. Frank J. and Irene B. (Black) A.; m. Erma Jacqueline Kallen, Mar. 8, 1948; children: John Kallen, Marc Robert. BA in Architecture, Chgo. Tech. Coll., 1948; postgrad., Northwestern U., Evanston, Ill., 1948-49. Registered architect, Ill., 20 other states. Architect Ford Bacon & Davis Inc., Chgo., 1949-50, Skidmore Owings & Merrill, Chgo., 1950-51, Sidney Morris & Assocs., Chgo., 1951-52, Chgo. Housing Authority, 1952-53; sr. v.p. A. Epstein and Sons Inc., Chgo., 1953-87; cons., 1987—. Mem. Exec. Svc. Corps of Chgo. With Air Corps, U.S. Army, 1941-45, ETO. Mem. AIA (corp.), Svc. Corps Ret. Execs., Soc. Am. Registered Architects, Chgo. Com. on High Rise Bldgs. Democrat. Home: 1633 Cambridge Ave Flossmoor IL 60422-2127 Office: Amstadter Architects 200 W Superior St Chicago IL 60610-3553 E-mail: lekamstadter@aol.com.

AMSTER, LINDA EVELYN, newspaper executive, consultant; b. N.Y.C., May 21, 1938; d. Abraham and Belle Shirley (Levine) Meyerson; m. Robert L. Amster, Feb. 18, 1961 (dec. Feb. 1974). BA, U. Mich., 1960; M.L.S., Columbia U., 1968. Tchr. English Stamford High Sch., Conn., 1961-63; research librarian The Detroit News, 1965-67, The N.Y. Times, N.Y.C., 1967-69, supr. news research, 1969-74, news research mgr., 1974—. Bd. dirs. Council for Career Planning, N.Y.C., 1982— Editor: The New York Times Passover Cookbook, 1999, Kill Duck Before Serving, 2002, The New York Times Jewish Cookbook, 2003; contbr. articles to books, N.Y. Times and other publs. Mem. adv. com. N.Y.C. 100 Greater N.Y. Centennial Celebration. Mem. Spl. libraries Assn. Clubs: Coffee House. Home: 336 Central Park W New York NY 10025-7111 Office: The NY Times 229 W 43rd St New York NY 10036-3959

AMSTERDAM, ANTHONY GUY, law educator; b. Phila., Sept. 12, 1935; s. Gustave G. and Valla (Abel) A.; m. Lois P. Sheinfeld, Aug. 29, 1968. AB, Haverford Coll., 1957; LLB, U. Pa., 1960; LLD (hon.), John Jay Coll. Criminal Justice, 1987, Haverford Coll., 1993. Bar: D.C. 1960. Law clk. to U.S. Supreme Ct. Justice Felix Frankfurter, 1960-61; asst. U.S. atty., 1961-62; prof. law U. Pa., 1962-69, Stanford U., 1969-81, Montgomery prof. clin. legal edn., 1980-81; prof. law, dir. clin. programs and trial advocacy NYU, 1981—2001, univ. prof., 2001—. Cons. litigating atty. numerous civil rights groups; cons. govt. commns.; mem. Commn. to Study Disturbances at Columbia, 1968; trustee Death Penalty Info. Ctr., Lawyers Constl. Def. Com., NAACP Legal Def. Fund, Nat. Coalition to abolish the Death Penalty, So. Poverty Law Ctr., mem. Calif. Fed. Jud. Selection Com., 1976-80; mem. coord. coun. on lawyer competence Conf. of Chief Justices; gen. counsel N.Y. Civil Liberties Union; adv. counsel Civil Liberties Union No. Calif.; mem. ABA task force. Author: The Defensive Transfer of Civil Rights Litigation From State to Federal Courts, 1964, Trial Manual for Defense of Criminal Cases, 5th edit., 1989, (with Hertz and Guggenheim) Trial Manual for Defense Attorneys in Juvenile Court, 1991, (with Bruner) Minding the Law, 2000; editor-in-chief: U. Pa. Law Rev., 1959-60; contbr. articles to profl. jours. Named Outstanding Young Man of Year Phila. and Pa. Jaycees, 1967; recipient First Disting. Service award U. Pa. Law Sch., 1968; Haverford award Haverford Coll., 1970; Arthur V. Briesen award Nat. Legal Aid and Defender Assn., 1972, 76; named Lawyer of Year Calif. Trial Lawyers Assn., 1973; recipient 1st Earl Warren Civil Liberties award No. Calif. chpt. ACLU, 1973, Citizen of Merit award Sun Reporter, 1974, Walter J. Gores award Stanford U., 1977, William O. Douglas award Pub. Counsel, 1977, 2d ann. award Calif. Attys. Criminal Justice, 1978, award for enhancement human dignity Durfee Found., 1982, Francis Rawle award ALI-ABA, 1984, 3d ann. Civil Liberties award Pa. ACLU, 1985, clinical legal edn. award AALS Sect. on Clinical Legal Edn., 1986, August Vollmer award Am. Soc. Criminology, 1986, Disting. Tchr. award NYU, 1988, award N.Y. Criminal Bar Assn., 1989, Tchg. Achievement award Soc. Am. Law Tchrs., 1999, Kutak award ABA, 2002; named MacArthur fellow, 1989; hon. fellow for pub. interest svc. U. Pa. Law Sch., 2001. Fellow Am. Acad. Arts and Scis. Home: 68 Middle Line Hwy Southampton NY 11968-1645 Office: NYU Sch Law Clinical Ctr 161 Avenue of the Americas New York NY 10013

AMSTERDAM, DAVID ERIK, school psychologist; b. Bronx, N.Y., June 27, 1962; s. Bernard Sidney and Ruth Marlene (Zapolsky) A. BA in Psychology, St. John's U., 1984, MS in Sch. Psychology, 1987. Cert. sch. psychologist, N.Y. Sch. psychology intern Herricks (N.Y.) Pub. Sch., 1986-87; sch. psychologist The Shield Inst., Flushing, N.Y., 1987—. Author: The Miracle of Elcarim, 1996. Mem. Nat. Assn. of Sch. Psychologists, N.Y. Assn. of Sch. Psychologists, N.Y. Road Runners Club, Broadway Ulta Soc. Jewish. Avocations: running, writing, inventing products. Home: 19014 37th Ave Flushing NY 11358-2401 Office: The Shield Inst 14461 Roosevelt Ave Flushing NY 11354-6252

AMSTERDAM, MARK LEMLE, lawyer; b. N.Y.C., June 10, 1944; s. Leonard M. and Erica (Lemle) A.; children: Lauren, Matthew. AB, Columbia U., 1966, JD cum laude, 1969. Bar: N.Y. 1969, U.S. Dist. Ct. (so., ea. and no. dists.) N.Y. 1972, U.S. Dist. Ct. (no. dist.) Tex., U.S. Supreme Ct. 1973. Assoc. Fried, Frank, Harris, N.Y.C., 1969-70; staff atty. Ctr. Constl. Rights, N.Y.C., 1970-75; atty. pvt. practice, N.Y.C., 1975-76, 81—; ptnr. Rubin Hanley & Amsterdam, N.Y.C., 1976-79, Katz Amsterdam & Lewinter, N.Y.C., 1980, Amsterdam & Lewinter, N.Y.C., 1990—. Instr. N.Y. Law Sch., 1982-83. Contbr. articles to profl. jours. Fellow: N.Y. State Bar Assn.; mem.: Columbia Coll. Alumni Assn. (bd. dirs.), Columbia Law Sch. Alumni Assn. (bd. dirs.), Columbia Club, Gardeners Bay Country Club. Home: 1220 Park Ave New York NY 10128-1733 Office: 9 E 40th St New York NY 10016-0402

AMSTUTZ, DANIEL GORDON, international agriculture industry consultant, former grain dealer, government and intergovernment official; b. Cleve., Nov. 8, 1932; s. Gordon M. and Elizabeth (Kiss) A. BS, Ohio State U., 1954. Trainee Cargill, Inc., Mpls., 1954-55; grain mcht. Tradax Can., Ltd., Montreal, Que., Can., 1955-56, Tradax Geneva S.A., 1956-57; mgr. Deutsche Tradax Gmgh, Hamburg, Germany, 1957-58; grain mcht. Cargill, Inc., Ft. Worth, 1959, sr. grain mcht. Mpls., 1960-72; pres. Cargill Investor Svcs., Inc., Chgo., 1972—78; ptnr. Goldman, Sachs & Co., N.Y.C., 1978-82; undersec. Dept. Agr., Washington, 1983-87; pres. Cmty. Credit Corp., Washington, 1983-87; amb., chief trade negotiator for agr. USDA, Washington, 1987-89; exec. dir. Internat. Wheat Coun., London, 1992-95; pres., CEO N.Am. Export Grain Assn., Inc., Washington, 1995-2000; pres. Amstutz & Co., Washington, 2000—; sr. ministry adv. for Agrl. Iraq, 2003—. Mem. U.S. Agrl. Policy Adv. Com., 1998—2003; mem. com. agri-bus. U.S.-Russian Joint Commn. on Econ. and Tech. Coop., 1996—; dir. U.S. Feed Grains Coun., 1967—72. Mem. Nat. Grain and Feed Assn. (dir. 1973-82), Ohio State U. Alumni Assn. (v.p. 1989, co-chair fund raising campaign 1990-99), Ohio State U. Found. (dir. 1998—). E-mail: dan@amstutzandcompany.com.

AMSTUTZ, HAROLD EMERSON, veterinarian, educator; b. Barrs Mill, Ohio, June 21, 1919; s. Nelson David and Viola Emma (Schnitzer) A.; m. Mabelle Josephine Bower, June 26, 1949; children: Suzanne Marie, Cynthia Lou, Patricia Lynn, David Bruce. BS in Agr, Ohio State U., 1942, DVM, 1945. Diplomate Am. Coll. Vet. Internal Medicine (pres. 1972-73, chmn. bd. regents 1973-74); hon. diplomate Am. Coll. Theriogenology. Pvt. practice vet. medicine, Orrville, Ohio, 1946-47; instr. vet. medicine Ohio State U., 1947-52, asst. prof., 1952-54, asso. prof., 1954-56, prof., 1957-61, prof., head dept. vet. medicine, 1956-61; head dept. vet. clinics Purdue U., West Lafayette, Ind., 1961-75, prof. large animal clinics, 1975-89, prof. emeritus, 1989—. Editor: Bovine Medicine and Surgery Book, 1979; contbg. editor: Modern Veterinary Practice, 1979-84; mem. editorial bd. The Merck Vet. Manual, 6th, 7th and 8th edits.; contbr. to books on diseases of large domestic animals. Mem. exec. bd. Ind.-Ky. synod Luth. Ch. Am., 1986-88; pres. World Assn. for Buiatrics, 1972-84. Served with U.S. Army, 1945-46. Recipient Borden award for outstanding research in diseases of dairy cattle, 1978; named Disting. Alumnus Ohio State U. Coll. Vet. Medicine, 1974; recipient Alumni Faculty award Sch. Vet. Medicine, Purdue U., 1989, Sagamore of the Wabash Ind. Gov., 1990, Ark. Traveler award Ark. Gov., 1969, Gustav Rosenberger Meml. award Dutch Veterinary Assn., 1992, Alumni Recognition award Vet. Medicine Alumni Soc. Ohio State U., 1998. Mem. AVMA (12th Internat. Congress prize for contributing to internat. understanding of vet. medicine 1995), Am. Assn. Vet. Clinicians (pres. 1972), Am. Assn. Bovine Practitioners (exec. sec. 1971-89, exec. v.p. 1989-93, hon. mem. 1993), World Assn. Buiatrics (pres. 1972-84), Am. Coll. of Theriogenologists (hon. diplomate 1993), Sigma Xi, Phi Zeta, Gamma Sigma Delta (award of merit), Omega Tau Sigma (nat. Gamma award). Republican. Office: Purdue Univ Dept Veterinary Sci West Lafayette IN 47907 E-mail: amstutzh@purdue.edu.

AMSTUTZ, MARGARET, academic administrator; b. Knoxville, Tenn., May 22, 1967; d. Jerome David Amstutz, Margaret Jane Amstutz. MA Eng., Am. Lit., Wash. U., 1992. Publications dir. Mo. Humanities Coun., St. Louis, 1995—95, program dir., 1997—97; asst. to the pres. U. of Ga., Athens, 1997—. Bd. dirs. Centre Coll. Alumni, Danville, 1996—2000. Mem.: Ga. Assn. of Women in Higher Edn., Phi Beta Kappa. Office: U Ga Office of the President Athens GA 30602

AMTMANN, HANS HENRY, aeronautical engineer, naval architect; b. Sande, Prussia, Germany, Oct. 15, 1906; came to U.S., 1946; s. August Johann and Charlotte Mathilde (Bode) A.; m. Margret Suberg; children: Jürgen, Dieter, Gunter, Sylvia. BS, State Tech. Sch., Hamburg, Germany, 1928. Lic. naval arch. Design engr. Junkers Aircraft Co., Dessau, Germany, 1928-33; pre-design engr. Ernst Heinkel Aircraft Co., Warnemünde, Germany, 1933-34; chief pre-design Blohm & Voss Aircraft Divsn., Hamburg, 1934-45; with Project Paperclip, Wright Field, Ohio, 1946-51; design specialist Convair, San Diego, 1951-61; staff engr. Gen. Atomic, La Jolla, Calif., 1961-71, cons. engr., 1971-81, Inesco, La Jolla, 1981-83, Sparta Inc., Del Mar, Calif., 1984-86; pvt. cons., Del Mar, 1988; ret., 1988. Author: The Vanishing Paperclips, 1988; contbr. articles on aircraft to profl. jours. Elder Village Ch., Rancho Santa Fe, Calif., 1952-55.

Decorated War Merit Cross (Germany). Fellow Inst. Aerospace Sci. (assoc.). Republican. Presbyterian. Achievements include inventions in aircraft and nuclear reactors. Home: 16 Herrada Rd Santa Fe NM 87508-8204

AMTOFT, TORBEN, adult education educator, researcher; b. Copenhagen, June 6, 1963; s. Henning Hansen and Tove Amtoft. PhD, U. of Aarhus, Denmark, 1989—93. Rsch. assoc. U. of Aarhus, 1992—98, Boston U., 1999—2002, Heriot-Watt U., Edinburgh, Scotland, 2002—02; asst. prof. Kans. State U., 2002—. Avocations: reading, walking, bridge. Office: Kansas State U 234 Nichols Hall Manhattan KS 66506

AMUNDSON, BEVERLY CARDEN, artist; b. Kansas City, Kans., Dec. 31, 1937; d. Linton Franklin and Arlene Rose Carden; m. Jerry Warren Amundson; children: Sherry Camargo, Cynthia Harmison, Eric. Student, Kansas City (Mo.) Art Inst., 1955—58; studied with, Robert Byerley, Prairie Village, Kans., 1980, Harry Fredman, Overland Park, Kans., 1981—82, Daniel Greene, North Salem, N.Y., 1995—96, Burton Silverman, Hudson Valley, NY, 2002—03. Freelance illustrator, designer, Kansas City, Mo., 1958—64; founding ptnr., dir. Amundson & Assoc. Art Studio, DBA The Amundson Group, Kansas City, Mo., 1964—, AGI Inc., Kansas City, Kans., 1994—, AGI Packaging Svs. Ltd., Kansas City, Kans., 1999—. Lectr., cons. in field; pvt. lessons and workshops, Merriam, Kans. One-woman shows include, Shawnee Mission, Kans., Overland Park, Kans., 1998, Merriam (Kans.) Cmty. Gallery, 2001, Kansas City Artists Coalition, Mo., 2001, exhibitions include Endres Gallery, Prairie Village, Kans., 2001, Am. Artists Profl. League, NYC, 2001. Com. worker Rep. Party, Merriam. Recipient numerous awards; scholar, Kansas City Art Inst., 1955—58. Mem.: Degas Pastel Soc., Chgo. Artists Coalition, Kansas City Artist Coalition, Am. Soc. Classical Realism, Portrait Soc. Am., Mid-Am. Pastel Soc., Nat. Pastel Soc. Am. (signature), Kansas City Art Directors Club. Covenant Ch. Avocations: travel, textile weaving. Home: 9903 West 70th Terrace Merriam KS 66203 Office: AGI Inc AGI Packaging Svcs Home Offices 1100 Cambridge Circle Drive Kansas City KS 66103

AMUNDSON, EVA DONALDA, civic worker; b. Langdon, N.D., Apr. 23, 1911; d. Elmer Fritjof and Alma Julia (Nelson) Hultin; m. Leif Amundson, Mar. 1, 1929 (dec. 1974); children: Constance, Eleanor, Ardis, Priscilla. Bd. dirs. Opportunity Workshop, Missoula, Mont., 1950—, Rockmont Group Homes, Missoula, 1976—, Bethany L'Arche (group home for girls), 1976—; sec. bd. dirs. Opportunity Industries, 1990-91, pres. 1991—; mem. Missoula Sr. Citizen's Ctr., 1980-82, 88—, pres., 1982-85, bd. dirs., 1988—; tchr. Norwegian cooking and baking, 1954-56, Norweigan Rosemaling, 1975-79; treas. Sacakawea Homemakers Club, 1979-81; mem. Am. Luth. Ch. Women St. Pauls' Lutheran Ch., 1951—; active Easter Seal Program, Heart Fund, March of Dimes, United Way, Campfire Girls; mem. adv. council Area Agy. on Aging, Missoula, 1984—. Recipient Outstanding Sr. award Missoula Jr. C. of C., 1984, IDEA-PTA award, 1998, Lyle Heath award Missoula Sentinel Kiwanis Club, 1998, Golden Rule award J.C. Penney, 1998; Eva Amunson, Missoula Vol. Day proclaimed by city mayor and county commr., 1998. Mem. Sons. of Norway (sec. 1989—), Orchard Homes Country Club (mem. art judging com.), Order of Eastern Star, Elks. Avocations: rosemaling, oil painting, poetry. Home: 324 Kensington Ave Missoula MT 59801-5726

AMUNDSON, ROBERT A. state supreme court justice; m. Katherine Amundson; children: Robert, Beth, Amy. BBA, Augustana Coll., 1961; JD, U. S.D., 1964. Asst. atty. gen. Atty. Gen's. Office, 1965-69; mem. firm Belle Fourche and Lead, 1970-89; cir. judge 2d Jud. Cir., 1989-91; justice Supreme Ct. of S.D., Vermillion, 1991—2003.*

AMUZEGAR, JAHANGIR, economic consultant; b. Tehran, Iran, Jan. 13, 1920; came to U.S., 1946; s. Habibollah and Turan (Azmudeh) A.; m., Sept. 27, 1958. BA in Law, U. Tehran, 1941; MA in Econs., U. Wash., 1948; PhD in Econs., U. Calif., L.A., 1955; DSc, U. Bridgeport, 1976. Min. commerce Govt. of Iran, Tehran, 1961-62, min. fin., 1962; ambassador Iranian Econ. Mission, Washington, 1962-78; exec. dir. Internat. Monetary Fund, Washington, 1973-80, cons., 1980-84. Author: Iran: Economic Development, 1971, Iran: An Economic Profile, 1977, Comparative Economics, 1981, The Dynamics of the Iranian Revolution, 1991, Iran's Economy Under the Islamic Republic, 1993, Managing the Oil Wealth, 2001; contbr. articles to profl. jours.

AMY, JONATHAN WEEKES, scientist, educator; b. Delaware, Ohio, Mar. 3, 1923; s. Ernest Francis and Theresa Louise (Say) A.; m. Ruthanna Borden, Dec. 20, 1947 (dec. Apr. 1999); m. Betty Joy Flood, July 2, 2000; children— Joseph Wilbur, James Borden, Theresa BA, Ohio Wesleyan U., 1948; MS, Purdue U., 1950, PhD, 1955. Rsch. assoc. dept. chemistry Purdue U., West Lafayette, Ind., 1954-60, assoc. prof., 1960-70, prof., 1970—, assoc. dir. labs., 1960—, dir. instrumentation, 1970-84, emeritus, 1988. Cons. chem. instrumentation; sec.-treas. Technometrics, Inc., 1968-2001; mem. adv. panels AAAS, Assn. Am. Univs., NSF, Am. Chem. Soc.; vis. scholar Stanford U., 1992. Assoc. editor Ind. Chem. News; patentee elec. measuring equipment and chem. instrumentation Pres. Wabash Twp. Vol. Fire Dept., 1970-86. Served with U.S. Maritime Service, 1943-46. Recipient George award Lafayette Jour. and Courier, 1978, Sagamore of the Wabash award State of Ind., 1999. Mem. AAAS, Am. Chem. Soc. (Chem. Instrumentation award), Sigma Xi, Sigma Chi. Episcopalian. Home: 357 Overlook Dr West Lafayette IN 47906-1249 Office: Purdue U Dept Chemistry West Lafayette IN 47907

AMY, MICHAËL JACQUES, art historian, educator, art critic; b. Antwerp, Belgium, Sept. 26, 1964; s. Jean-Jacques Amy and Marie-Claire Nuyens. BA, Vrije U., Brussels, 1986; MA, NYU, 1989, PhD, 1997. Asst. to curator Mus. Contemporary Art, Ghent, Belgium, 1986-87; rsch. asst. Coe Kerr Gallery, N.Y.C., 1988-91; vis. specialist Montclair (N.J.) State U., 1996—97; adj. asst. prof. CUNY, 1997-99, Manhattanville Coll., Purchase, NY, 1997, NYU, 1997-99, The Cooper Union, 1999; vis. asst. prof. Oberlin (Ohio) Coll., 1999-2000; asst. prof. Rochester (N.Y.) Inst. Tech., 2000—. Sec. Mnemosyne, Antwerp, Belgium, 1995—; lectr. in field.; art critic Art et Culture, Brussels, 1997-99, Art in Am., N.Y.C., 1997—, Sculpture, Washington, 2001—, Tema Celeste, Milan, 2002-. Contbr. Santa Maria del Fiore: The Cathedral and its Sculpture, 2001. Recipient fellow Belgian Am. Ednl. Found., 1987-88, award Inst. Fine Arts fellow, 1988-89, 90-94, Bernard Berenson fellow, 1993-94, Samuel H. Kress Found. fellow, 1994-95; CIAS grantee, 2002. Mem. Internat. Assn. Art Critics, Renaissance Soc. Am., Coll. Art Assn., Italian Art Soc. Avocations: interest in literature, music, politics and philosophy. Home: Apt 8 123 Holyoke St Rochester NY 14615-1927 Office: Rochester Inst Tech Coll Imaging Arts and Scis 73 Lomb Memorial Dr Rochester NY 14623-5603 E-mail: mjafaa@rit.edu.

AMYES, EDWIN WESTBY, neurosurgeon; b. Edinburgh, Scotland, Nov. 2, 1920; came to U.S., 1921; s. Herbert Westby and Ruth Frieda Amyes; children: Nina, Christopher. BS, Pacific Union Coll., 1941; MD, Loma Linda U., 1944. Diplomate Am. Bd. of Neurosurgery. Intern White Meml. Hosp., Loma Linda, 1943, resident in psychiatry and neurology, 1944; staff physician St. Francis Hosp., Lynwood, Calif., 1946-48; pvt. gen. practice Huntington Park, Calif., 1946-48; resident, sr. resident in neurology U. So. Calif.-Loma Linda U., 1948-50; resident in neurosurgery L.A. County Hosp./White Meml. Hosp., 1950-53; with Rancho Los Amigos, 1955-65, organizer, designer neurosci. svcs., chief of neurosurgery, chief of staff; neurosurgeon Loma Linda U./White Meml. Hosp., St. Francis Hosp., Lynwood; staff neurosurgeon Hoag Meml. Hosp. Presbyn., Newport Beach, Calif., 1972—2000. Asst. prof. neurol. surgery Loma Linda U., L.A.; chief of neurosurgery Loma Linda U. at L.A. County Hosp., 1953-56; assoc. clin. prof. neurol. surgery U. Calif./Irvine Med. Ctr., 1972—; cons. in neurosurgery; pres., CEO Bioelectronics, Inc., Lynwood. Contbr. articles to profl. jours. 1st lt. U.S. Army, 1944-46. Recipient award for exceptional and disting. svc. Congress Neurol. Surgeons, 1980. Mem. Coun. of State Neurol. Socs. (founder, 1st chmn. 1975-80), Am. Assn. Neurol. Surgeons. Achievements include chair Calif. com. which developed the relative value scale for neurosurg. fees; development of the first edition of national guidelines for practice of neurosurgery, 1975. Home: 1220 Colony Plz Newport Beach CA 92660- Office: 320 Superior Ave Ste 310 Newport Beach CA 92663-2742 Fax: 949-642-6326. E-mail: ljacobs@nmadsl.com.

AMYLON, MICHAEL DAVID, physician, educator; b. Providence, Apr. 30, 1950; s. Sidney Robert and Mary Elisabeth (Alexander) A. AB, Brown U., 1972; MD, Stanford U., 1976. Diplomate sub-bd. hematology/oncology Am. Bd. Pediatrics. Resident physician Stanford (Calif.) U. Hosp., 1976-79; post-doctoral scholar Stanford U., 1979-81, acting asst. prof., 1981-82, asst. prof. pediat., 1982-89, assoc. prof. pediat., 1989-2001; prof. pediatrics Stanford U. Sch. Medicine, Palo Alto, Calif., 2001—02. Dir. marrow transplant svc. Children's Hosp. at Stanford, Palo Alto, Calif., 1986—; coord. nat. rsch. clin. trials in treatment pediatric leukemia and lymphoma Pediatric Oncology Group, St. Louis, Chgo., 1986—. Contbr. articles to profl. jours. Bd. dirs. Touchstone Support Network, Palo Alto, 1982-98, Robert J. Sturhahn Found., Novato, Calif., 1986-93, Okizu Found., Novato, 1993—, Parents Helping Parents, 1998—; med. dir. No. Calif. Oncology Camp, Nevada City, 1986—. Recipient For Those Who Care award Sta. KRON, 1990, "Ronnie" award Ronald McDonald House, 1992-93, Koshland prize Peninsula Cmty. Found., 1995, J.C. Penney Golden Rule award, 1996, Alwin C. Rambar-James B.D. Mark award for excellence in patient care Stanford U. Sch. Medicine, 2002. Mem. Am. Acad. Pediatrics, Am. Soc. Clin. Oncology, Am. Soc. Hematology, Am. Soc. Pediatric Hematology/Oncology, Am. Soc. Blood and Marrow Transplantation. E-mail: amylon@stanford.edu.

AN, HONG, engineer; s. Yimin An and Xiulan Huang; m. Xiangwei Zhang, Oct. 22, 1988; 1 child, Miranda Bonnie. B in Engring., Tsinghua U., Beijing, 1982; MS, U. Iowa, 1991, Wayne State U., 1993; PhD, Columbia U., 1999. Engr. Chongqing (China) Inst. Steel, 1982—85, Sichuan Inst. Antibiotics, Chengdu, China, 1985—87; rschr. Tsinghua U., Beijing, 1987—89; engr. Millipore, Bedford, Mass., 1999—. Grad. student adv. coun. mem. Columbia U. Grad. Sch., N.Y.C., 1996—97; mem. Scienceboard.net, 2002. Internat. com. mem. AIChE, N.Y.C., 1995—2000; press marshal Atlanta Olympics Com., 1996; active Hist. Dist. Com. Recipient Atlanta Olympics Vols. Recognition award, Internat. Olympic Com., Juan A. Samaranch, 1996, Fellowship award, Am. Soc. Artificial Internal Organs, 1997. Mem.: Am. Chem. Soc., Internat. Soc. for Pharm. Engring., Sigma Xi. Achievements include patents pending for Protein Aggregates Removal; research in mathematical analysis of a flame front inside a combustion chamber; cell deformation in an asymmetric thin liquid film. Avocations: swimming, painting, golf. Home: 5 Reeve St Acton MA 01720 Office: Millipore 80 Ashby Rd Bedford MA 01730 Home Fax: 781-533-3143; Office Fax: 781-533-3143. Personal E-mail: ha13@columbia.edu. E-mail: ha13@columbia.edu.

AN, MARK YUYING, economist; b. Xinhe, Hebei, China, Jan. 24, 1962; s. Weishu An and Lingguo Zhao; m. Ping An, July 19, 1988; children: Eric, Janet. MA in Stats., Zhong Nan U., Wuhan, China, 1986; PhD in Econs., Cornell U., 1993. Sect. chief Ministry Fin. China, Beijing, 1986-88; asst. prof. Duke U., Durham, N.C., 1993-2000; sr. economist Fannie Mae, Washington, 2000—. Vis. prof. U. Aarhus, Denmark, 1998-99. Contbr. articles to profl. jours. Grad. scholar The World Bank, 1988-90; disertation fellow Alfred P. Sloan Found., 1992-93. Mem. Am. Econ. Assn., Econometric Soc., Chinese Stats. Assn. (Bronze medal 1986), Phi Kappa Phi. Office: Fannie Mae 3900 Wisconsin Ave NW Washington DC 20016 E-mail: mark_y_an@fanniemae.com.

AN, SHUWANG, chemist, researcher; b. Beijing, July 25, 1964; s. Shaogong An and Hong Ying Ma; m. Lan Zhang, May 1, 1993; 1 child, Shi. B in Engring., Tsinghua U., Beijing, 1987; MSc, Chinese Acad. Sci., Beijing, 1990; PhD, U. Oxford, 1999. Rschr. Chinese Acad. Sci., Beijing, 1990—94; vis. scientist U. Oxford, England, 1994—95, Royal Inst. Tech., Stockholm, 1994—95; postdoc. rsch. fellow Harvard Med. Sch., Boston, 1999—2000, Cornell U., Ithaca, NY, 2000—01, MIT, Cambridge, Mass., 2001—. Contbr. articles to profl. jours. Fellow Postdoc. Rsch. fellow, NIH, 1999—2000, Nat. Sci. Found., 2000—01, DuPont-MIT Alliance, 2001—. Mem.: AAAS, Royal Soc. Chemistry, Am. Chem. Soc., Sigma Xi. Home: 291 Main St Charlestown MA 02129 Office: MIT 77 Mass Ave Cambridge MA 02139 Office Fax: 617-258-0249. E-mail: san@mit.edu.

AN, YUEHUI HUEY, orthopaedic surgeon, educator; b. Shenyang, China, Oct. 23, 1960; came to the U.S., 1991; s. Rongkai An and Yanyun Wang; m. Q. Kay Kang, July 20, 2002, m. Tianhua Ge, Jan. 20, 1986 (div. Aug. 1988). MB, Harbin (China) Med. U., 1983; M in Medicine, Beijing Inst. Orthopaedics, 1986. Orthop. resident Beijing Ji Shui Tan Hosp., 1984-88, chief resident, 1988-90; hand fellow Sydney (Australia) Hosp., 1990-91; fellow in orthop. Med. U. S.C., Charleston, 1991-93, asst. prof. orthop., 1993-98, assoc. prof. orthop., dir. orthop. rsch. lab., 1998—. Adj. asst. prof. bioengring. Clemson (S.C.) U., 1996—; cons. Cardiovasc. Tissue Techs., Charleston, 1997—, Organ Recovery Systems, Charleston, S.C., Cambridge Sci., Inc., Boston, 1997—. Editor: Animal Models in Orthopaedic Research, 1999, Mechanical Testing of Bone and the Bone-Implant Interface, 2000, Handbook of Bacterial Adhesion-Principles, Methods and Applications, 2000, Internal Fixation in Osteoporotic Bone, 2002, Handbook of Histologic Methods for Bone and Cartilage, 2003, Orthopaedic Issues in Osteoporosis, 2002; contbr. articles to profl. jours. including Jour. Bone Joint Surgery, Biomaterials, Clin. Orthop., Jour. Orthop. Rsch., Jour. Biomed. Material Rsch., Jour. Material Sci., others. Chmn. Ji Shui Tan Hosp., Bicycle Sports Assn., Beijing, 1990-91. Mem. Am. Soc. Biomechanics, Soc. for Biomaterials, Soc. Tissue Engring., Orthopaedic Rsch. Soc. Achievements include international patent for thermally reversible gelling cell culture media; U.S. patent for adjustable ligament anchor; 6 patent disclosures. Home: 100 Oyster Point Row Charleston SC 29412 Office: Med Univ SC Orthopaedic Surgery CSB 708 96 Jonathan Lucas St Charleston SC 29425 E-mail: any@musc.edu.

ANAGNOST, DINO, artistic director; Music dir., condr. Little Orch. Soc. N.Y., 1979—. Office: Little Orch Soc c/o Andel Mgmt Assocs 330 W 42nd St Fl 12 New York NY 10036-6902

ANAND, KANWALJEET SINGH, pediatrician, researcher; b. Ludhiana, Punjab, India, Nov. 29, 1957; s. Jaswant Singh and Tejinder Kaur Anand; m. Itinder Kaur Anand; children: Amrit K, Tejpartab S. MBBS, MGMMC, U. of Indore, India, 1980—84; PhD, Jesus Coll., U. of Oxford, U. K., 1984—87. Cert. Am. Bd. of Pediat., 1991, Pediatric Critical Care Am. Bd. of Pediat., 1994, Pediatric Advanced Life Support Am. Lung Assn., 1994, lic. Ark. State Med. Bd., 1997. Fellow, Critical Care Medicine Am. Coll. of Critical Care Medicine, 1998. Rsch. fellow, asst. tutor, dept. pediatrics U. of Oxford, 1983—85; clin. fellow in pediat. Harvard Med. Sch., 1988—91, clin. fellow, pediat., 1991—93; asst. prof., pediat., anesthesiology Emory U. Sch. of Medicine, 1993—97, asst. prof., psychiatry, behaviorial sciences, 1994—97, dir., critical care rsch., dept. of pediat., 1994—97; interim dir., office for rsch. and promotion, dept. of pediat. Emory Univ. Sch. of Medicine, 1995—96; assoc. prof., pediat., anesthesiology Coll. of Med., U. of Ark. for Med. Sciences, 1997—2000, assoc. prof., anatomy, neurobiology, 1998—2000; prof. of pediat., anesthesiology, pharmacology & neurobiology Coll. of Med., Univ. of Ark. for Med. Sciences, 2001—. Fellowship dir., pediat. critical care med. U.A.M.S., 1997—; sect. chief, critical care medicine, peds. U. of Ark. for Med. Sciences, 1997—; dir., pain neurobiology lab. Ark. Children's Hosp., 1997—; bd. of directors Ark. Children's Hosp. Rsch. Inst., 1997—; morris and hettie oakley chair, pediatric critical care medicine U. of Ark. for Med. Sciences, 2001—. Mem. editl. bd.: Biology of the Neonate, Elsevier Science publishers, mem. editl. bd.: Critical Care Med., Williams and Williams, publishers. Rhodes scholarship selection com. U.S. Rhodes Scholarship, 1997—2003. Grantee Rhodes Scholarship, India Rhodes Scholarship Com., 1982-1985, Ark. Ctr. for Pain Rsch., $100, 000, Intitiated Act I funds, July 2001 - 2003, The NEOPAIN Multi-Ctr. Trial, Nat. Inst. of Child Health and Human Devel., June 1999 - May 2003. Fellow: Am. Coll. of Critical Care Medicine (Rsch. Com. 2003—06), Am. Acad. of Pediat., Royal Coll. of Pediat. and Child Health; mem.: Soc. for Neuroscience, Soc. of Critical Care Medicine, Nat. Neonatology Forum (life), Internat. Assn. for the Study of Pain, Soc. for Pediatric Rsch., Am. Fedn. for Med. Rsch., Am. Assn. of Rhodes Scholars. Home: 4119 Longview Rd Little Rock AR 72212 Office: UAMS Pediatrics AR Children's Hospital 800 Marshall St Slot 512-12 Little Rock AR 72202 Office Fax: 501-364-3188.

ANAND, SURESH CHANDRA, physician; b. Mathura, India, Sept. 13, 1931; arrived in U.S., 1957, naturalized, 1971; s. Satchit and Sumaran Bai Anand; m. Wiltrud Anand, Jan. 29, 1966; children: Miriam, Michael. MB, BS, King George's Coll., U. Lucknow (India), 1954; MS in Medicine, U. Colo., 1962. Diplomate Am. Bd. Allergy and Immunology. Fellow pulmonary diseases Nat. Jewish Hosp., Denver, 1957-58, resident in chest medicine, 1958-59, chief resident allergy-asthma, 1960-62; intern Mt. Sinai Hosp., Toronto, Ont., Can., 1962-63, resident in medicine, 1963-64, chief resident, 1964-65, demonstrator clin. technique, 1963-64, U. Toronto fellow in medicine, 1964-65; rsch. assoc. asthma-allergy Nat. Jewish Hosp., Denver, 1967-69; clin. instr. medicine U. Colo., Denver, 1967-69; internist Ft. Logan Mental Health Ctr., Denver, 1968-69; pres. Allergy Assocs. & Lab., Ltd., Phoenix, 1974—. Mem. staff Phoenix Bapt. Hosp., chmn. med. records com., 1987; mem. staff St. Joseph's Hosp., St. Luke's Hosp., Human Hosp., John C. Lincoln Hosp., Good Samaritan Hosp., Phoenix Children's Hosp., Tempe St. Luke Hosp., Desert Samaritan Hosp., Mesa Luth. Hosp., Scottsdale Meml. Hosp., Chandler Regional Hosp., Ariz., Valley Luth. Hosp., Mesa, Ariz.; mem. staff. Phoenix Meml. Hosp., mem. med. com.; pres. NJH Fed. Credit Union, 1967—68. Contbr. articles to profl. jours. Mem. citizens adv. bd. Camelback Hosp. Mental Health Ctr., Scottsdale, Ariz., 1974—80; mem. Phoenix Symphony Coun., 1973—90, Ariz. Opera co., Boyce Thompson Southwestern Arboretum, Ariz. Hist. Soc., Phoenix Arts Mus., Smithsonian Inst. Fellow: ACP, Am. Coll. Allergy and Immunology (pub. edn. com. 1991—94, aerobiology com., internat. com.), Am. Assn. Cert. Allergists, Am. Coll. Chest Physicians (crit. care. com.), Am. Acad. Allergy (pub. edn. com.); mem.: AMA, AAAS, Ariz. Thoracic Soc., Assn. Care of Asthma, Internat. Assn. Asthmology, World Med. Assn., N.Y. Acad. Soc., Greater Phoenix Allergy Soc. (v.p. 1984—86, pres. 1986—88, med. adv. team sports medicine Ariz. State U.), West Coast Soc. Allergy and Immunology, Maricopa County Med. Soc. (bd. dirs. 1996—98, exec. com. 1996—98, pres.-elect 2002, pres. 2003, del. Ariz. Med. Assn.), Ariz. Allergy Soc. (v.p. 1988—90, pres. 1990—91), Ariz. Med. Assn., Internat. Assn. Allergy and Clin. Immunology, Ariz. Wild Life Assn., Nat. Geog. Soc., Phoenix Zoo, Village Tennis Club. Office: 1006 E Guadalupe Rd Tempe AZ 85283-3047 also: 6553 E Baywood Ave Ste 201 Mesa AZ 85206-1754 also: 7331 E Osborn Dr Ste 340 Scottsdale AZ 85251-6435 also: 4901 N 44th St Phoenix AZ 85018 also: 2248 N Alma School Rd Chandler AZ 85224-2488 Office: 4901 N 44th St Phoenix AZ 85018

ANANDAN, SANTHOSH, application developer; b. Madras, India, Mar. 28, 1977; arrived in U.S., 1998; s. Anandan Janakiraman and Renuka Devi Anandan. B in Engring., U. Madras, 1998; MS in Computer Sci., U. Houston, 2001. Cert. engr., U. Madras, 1998. Engr. Hyundai Motor India Ltd., Madras, India, 1998; programmer analyst Dell Computer Corp., Austin, Tex., 2000—. Contbr. articles to profl. jours.; interviewee (by Austin Am. Statesman newspaper) Effect of Indian Software Engrs. on U.S. Economy. Dir.-elect Sonakali Gardens & Zool. Preserve, Austin, Tex., 2000—01, Killeen Vol. Corp., Killeen, Tex., 2001, Sonakali Gardens Bath Preserve; jr. achievement volunteer tchr. bus. for sch. students; active TIE-Austin NE & JP Fund Childcare Excellence; active to Senator Primary Elections, Tex. Recipient Best Slogan award, 2000. Mem.: Toastmasters (pres. 2001—, area gov. 2002—). Achievements include created diveristy awareness amonst people; advanced work in VLSI processors, reliability software engineers, biomagnetic data visualization in collaboration with Texas Med. Ctr., Houston Acct. Avocations: swimming, travel. Home: 14100 Thermal Drive Apt 2308 Austin TX 78728 Office: 1 Dell Way HS 8228 Round Rock TX 78682 E-mail: santhosh_anandan@dell.com.

ANANDARAMAN, RAMANATHAN, retired physician; b. Bangalore, Mysore, India, Apr. 3, 1933; came to U.S., 1970; s. Apakodal Venkata and Thylammal Ramanathan; m. Kalyani Anandaraman, Sept. 25, 1961; 1 child, Neena. M.B.BS, U. Med. Coll., Mysore, 1957. Intern K.R. Gen. Hosp., Mysore, 1958-59; resident Sibley Meml. Hosp., Washington, 1959-61; sr. house officer St. Tydfil Hosp., Merthyr, Tydfil, Wales, 1961-63; med. registrar King's Lynn (Eng.) Gen. Hosp., 1963-66; staff physician K.C. Gen. Hosp., Bangalore, 1967-70; sr. fellow Georgetown U. Med. Ctr., Washington, 1970-72; med. officer Glendale (Md.) Hosp., 1972-80; chief of medicine VA Med. Ctr., Bonham, Tex., 1983-88, staff physician Waco and Bonham, 1980-95; ret., 1995. Clin. asst. prof. medicine Tex. Coll. Osteo. Medicine, Ft. Worth, 1991-93; clin. instr. medicine and oncology Georgetown U., 1976-80. Vol. Meals on Wheels, Am. Cancer Soc. Fellow Royal Coll. Physicians (Edinburgh); mem. ACP, Assn. of Physicians of India (life). Avocations: reading, tennis. Home: 2608 Skyline Dr Waco TX 76710-1137

ANANI, TARIG, lawyer; b. Riyadh, Saudi Arabia, Jan. 22, 1965; s. Faisal Anani and Diane Katherine Hill. BA cum laude, Univ. Houston, 1988, JD, 1991; MBA, Rice Univ., 1992; MS of Jurisprudence, Stanford U., 1994. Bar: Tex. 1991, Calif. 1993, D.C. 2002, U.S. Supreme Ct. 1995. Corp. assoc. Curtis, Mallet-Prevost, Colt & Mosle, Manhattan, N.Y., 1994-97; gen. counsel SAP Arabia, Dubai, United Arab Emirates, 1998—2002; pres. internat. ops., corp. gen. counsel Petroleum Place/P2 Energy Solutions, Houston, 2002—. Bd. dirs. Mail2World, Inc., Century City, 2000—. Recipient Best Enterprise Resource Planning Solution in the Mid. East, v.p. Al Gore, 2002. Home: 1300 Woodhollow Dr Apt 23202 Houston TX 77057 Office: P2 Energy Solutions 4 Houston Ctr 1221 Lamar Ste 1400 Houston TX 77010 E-mail: tarig.anani@stanfordalumni.org., tanani@pzes.com.

ANANIAS, JOSÉ, retired school system administrator; b. N.Y.C., Aug. 17, 1929; s. Jose A. and Inez Beatrice Johnson; m. Mamie Seymour, Dec. 30, 1953 (div. Feb. 1978) children: Jose III, Antonio, Ersell; m. Wilhemina Wright, June 17, 1978 (dec. June 1992); m. Ivanete do Nascimento Pena Lins, May 24, 1994. *America imploded into the Great Depression on October 29, 1929. Jose A. died in 1932. "Mommy Inez" never faltered. She lined up daily with Harlem mothers in the Bronx along Prospect and Westchester Avenues in the "Bronx Slave Market" niggling with garrulous, mercenary females for a day's wages (from 12 cents to $1) for food. My sister, Thelma, and I were "home alone" learning to live as adults instead of learning to live as children. The Federal Nursery Program refused to service Harlem mothers. Home relief was late and inequitable. This inflamed my passion for welfare work with the downtrodden, the impoverished, and those without hope. Sister, Thelma, BA 1952 Spelman; MSLS 1957, Atlanta U., Librarian 42 years Public Libraries; Brooklyn, NY, Library of Congress, San Diego, CA, Sunnyvale, CA, Assistant. Director, Binghamton, NY (1974-1988); Los Angeles, CA Public 1988 until retirement in 1999. Daughter, Ersell, BA Hunter 1983, M.S. Ed, City College 1984, Teacher, NYC Board of Education 1984 to present. Jose III, BA Morehouse 1977, Teacher, NYC Bd. of Education 1997-1978. U.S. Postal Service 1977 to present (25 years)* BA, Morehouse Coll., 1951; postgrad., NYU, 1957-59; MEd, CUNY, 1968. Cert. sch. adminstr. and supr., attendance tchr., English tchr., phys. edn. and recreation tchr., subst. attendance tchr. Social investigator St. Nicholas Welfare Ctr. N.Y.C. Dept. Welfare, 1955-60; attendance tchr. N.Y.C. Bd. Edn., 1965-67; adminstrv. asst. to supr. recreation Cmty. Sch. Dist. # 7, Bronx, 1969-75; supr. Office of High Sch. SPARK program Drug Abuse Prevention Citywide, Bronx, 1971-77; borough supr., asst. coord. Office of High Sch. SPARK program, Bklyn., 1971-77; tchr. English High Sch. Redirection, Bklyn., 1977-78, asst. prin., 1978-79; dist. supervising attendance officer Chancellor's Task Force on Attendance, Bklyn., 1978-79; dist. supervising attendance officer Evander Childs High Sch Bronx High Sch. Attendance Dist., 1979; dist. supervising attendance officer office of dir. pupil personnel svcs., 1979-84; ret., 1984. *"Mommy Inez" (a Spelman College graduate) infused us with the belief that education is not a gift. It has to be earned. The price is ambition, desire, initiative, perseverance, and hard work. Of these, attendance is most frequently neglected. The body has to be in the classroom. In the 1960's I was known as "the attendance officer who went after and retrieved absentees and placed them in school in his Rolls Royce automobile. "While some considered this odd, it fell within my belief that I had to use every lawful means to enforce the law while safeguarding the student's right to an education. I was also reluctant to leave my car unattended too long, and the kids enjoyed the ride.* Mem. Borough Pres. Sutton's Adopt a Child com., edn. com.; mem. bd. mgr. Harlem br. YMCA, 1974-96, mem. adv. com., editor, compiler brochure; founder Dist. 7 Scholarship Awards Fund, 1971-78; Dem. county committeeman 71st A.D.; edn. chmn. Com. to Rebuild Harlem, 1978; mem. parish coun. St. Charles Borromeo Cath. Ch., 1979; mem. PTA John F. Kennedy High Sch., DeWitt Clinton High Sch.; svc. officer VFW Post 1753, Las Vegas, 2000—; mem. Our Lady of Las Vegas Ch. Served with USN, 1951-55, Korea. Recipient Citation, Gov. Mario Cuomo, 1984, Citation, Mayor Edward I. Koch, 1984, Cert. Recognition Sec. of Def., Cert. Appreciation Harlem Bd. Mgrs., 1996; named Vol. of Yr., YMCA Greater N.Y., 1995; José Ananias Day proclaimed in his honor. Mem. VFW (Cmmdr.'s Spl. Merit award 2003), Assn. Black

Educators N.Y., Am. Legion, USN Meml., Holy Name Soc. St. Charles Borromeo Cath. Ch., CCNY Alumni Assn. (Las Vegas chpt.), Kappa Alpha Psi. Democrat. Roman Catholic. Home: 11-1074 1600 S Valley View Blvd Las Vegas NV 89102-1869

ANANIASHVILI, NINA, ballerina; b. Tbilisi, Republic of Georgia; Student, Choreographic Sch. of Georgia; grad., Bolshoi Ballet Sch., 1981. Ballerina Bolshoi Ballet, 1981—. Guest artist Am. Ballet Theatre, N.Y.C.; performed with Kirov Ballet, N.Y.C. Ballet, Royal Ballet, The Royal Danish Ballet, Royal Swedish Balltet, others. Roles include La Bayadere (Nikiya), Don Quixote (Kitri), Giselle, The Golden Age (Rita), Mlada, Raymonda, Romeo and Juliet, Swan Lake (Odette-Odile), The Dying Swan, A Dream of the Rose, Balanchine's Apollo, Raymonda Variations, Symphony in C, The Prince of the Pagodas, The Nutcraker. Recipient Gold medal Varna Competition, 1980, 5th Moscow Competition, 1985, Grand prix 4th Moscow Competition 1981, 3rd Jackson Competition, 1986, Outstanding Achievements in Fine Arts award Russia State, 1992, STate prize Georgia, 1993. Office: Am Ballet Theatre 890 Broadway New York NY 10003-1211

ANANTH, JAMBUR, psychiatrist, educator; b. Hassan, Mysore, India, Apr. 27, 1932; s. Venkata Subbaiah and Gundamma (Nanjundaiah) A.; m. Kamala Maroor, Apr. 23, 1971; 1 child, Kartik. MD, Kasturba Med. Sch., Manipal, India, 1960; Diploma in Psychol. Medicine, Nat. Inst. Mental Health, Bangalore, India, 1963. Diplomate Am. Bd. Psychiatry and Neurology. Asst. prof. McGill U., Montreal, Que., Can., 1969-74, assoc. prof., 1974-81; prof. UCLA, 1981—. Chief clin. investigations dept. psychiatry McGill U., 1969-71, dir. edn. and research dept. psychiatry, 1971-72; dir. edn. and research St. Mary's Hosp., Montreal, 1972-76; dir. biol. psychiatry Allan Meml. Inst., Montreal, 1976-81. Contbr. articles to profl. jours.; adv. editor: Psychosomatics, 1978-87. Grantee Dept. Mental Health State of Calif., 1983. Fellow Collegeum Internat. Neuropharmocologicum, Royal Coll. Psychiatrists, Am. Psychiat. Assn. (pres. Que. dist. br. 1978-79). Avocations: photography, stamps. Home: 2709 Via Pacheco Palos Verdes Peninsula CA 90274-4351 Office: Harbor-UCLA Med Ctr Dept Psychiat PO Box 2910 Torrance CA 90509-2910

ANASAZI, MARIA, artist, educator; b. Fokis, Greece, Oct. 16, 1956; d. Sotirios and Frosso (Tsavala) Giannopoulos. Student, Akto Art Sch., Athens, 1977; BFA, Calif. Coll. of Arts, Oakland, 1988; MA, San Francisco State U., 1993; Cert. in Expressive Arts, John F. Kennedy U., 1994. Graphic designer, Berkeley/San Francisco, 1980-93; art faculty Delaplaine Visual Arts Place, Frederick, Md., 1996-2000, Rockville (Md.) Arts Place, 1996-2000; profl. artist Berkeley, Calif., 1989-94, Frederick, Md., 1993—. Art cons. for cmty.-related art projects, Peace Resource Ctr., Frederick, 1997-98; artist-educator Advocates for the Homeless Women, Frederick, 1996-97; art tchr. in prisons, 1997-99; art tchr. to mentally-physically disabled, Md., 1999-2000. Artist: (book) Artist's Book, 1997; solo shows include Montpelier Cultural Arts Ctr., Laurel, Md., 1998, Glen View Mansion, 2000, Arlington Art Ctr., 2000, Del. Ctr. Contemporary Arts, 2001. Recipient individual award, Md. Arts Coun., 2001; grantee, 1998, 1999, artist-in-edn., 1997—2003, artist-in-residence at Youth Detention Ctrs. in Rockville, Md. State Arts Coun., 2002—03. Avocation: travel.

ANASTASI, MICHAEL ANTON, journalist; b. Kitzbuhel, Tirol, Austria, Sept. 15, 1965; s. Antone Frank and Waltraud (Salinger) A; m. Julie Hibbs Anastasi, Nov. 18, 1995; children: Grace Antonia, Alexandra Renee. BA in Internat. Rels., U. Calif., Davis, 1988; Journalism, Calif. State U., Long Beach, 2001. Reporter The Daily Democrat, Woodland, Calif., 1984-85, dep. sports editor, 1985-87; sports editor The Davis (Calif.) Ent., 1987-93; asst. sports editor L.A. Daily News, 1993-95, sports editor, 1995—. Recipient 1st prize best sports sect., Calif. Newspaper Pubrs. Assn., 1990, 1992, 2001, 2002, Best sports columns award, Nat. Newspaper Assn., 2d place award, 1992, hon. mention, 1993, Best Daily Sports section, APSE, 1995, hon. mention Best spl. section over 175,000, 1993, 1st place and honorable mention, Best Enterprise reporting, under 50,000, 1993, 4th place columnist under 50,000, honorable mention, 1989, Best Daily sect., 2000, 2001, 2002, Best Sunday sect., 2000, 2001, 2002, Top 10 100,000-250,000, 2d place best sports column, Nat. Newspaper Assn., 1992, hon. mention best sports column, 1993, 3d place best sports pages, 1993. Mem. Soc. Profl. Journalists (1st place best columnist, 1991, 93, 94,), AP Sports Editors. Roman Catholic. Office: LA Daily News 21221 Oxnard St Woodland Hills CA 91367-5015

ANASTASI, RICHARD JOSEPH, computer software consultant; b. N.Y.C., Aug. 30, 1951; s. Alfred J. and Mary T. (Lo Cicero) A. Student, Boston Coll., 1973, U. Pa., 1975. Staff cons. Arthur Andersen & Co., N.Y.C., 1975-76; customer svc. rep. Compu Serve, West Caldwell, N.J., 1976-77, Turnkey Systems Internat., Norwalk, Conn., 1977-79; tech. svcs. rep. Applied Data Rsch., Paramus, N.J., 1980-84, regional tech. mgr., 1985-86, mgr. tactical svcs. Princeton, N.J., 1986-88; tech. dir. Computer Assocs. Internat., Irving, Tex., 1988-91, product cons., 1991-93; mgr. tech. resources Integris, Phoenix, 1993; pres., CEO, InfoVantage, Dallas, 1993-94; sr. product specialist Open Vision Techs., Inc. (merger Veritas Software, Inc.), Dallas, 1994—, sr. systems engr., 1994-97, Open Vision Techs., Inc. (merger with VERITAS Software), Dallas, 1997-2000; sr. solutions architect VERITAS Software, Dallas, 2000—03; v.p., field opers. Camino Soft Corp., Westlake Village, Calif., 2003—. Roman Catholic. Home: 302 Old York Rd Irving TX 75063-4246 Office: Camino Soft Corp 600 Hampshire Rd Ste 105 Westlake Village CA 91361

ANASTASI, WILLIAM JOSEPH, artist; b. Aug. 11, 1933; s. Joseph Anthony and Jeanette (Corona) A.; m. Irene Ierardi, Aug. 15, 1951 (div. 1964); children: William, Lawrence, Jean. Student, U. Pa., 1953-61. Tchr. painting Sch. Visual Arts, N.Y.C., 1971-86; co-artistic advisor Merce Cunningham Dance Co., N.Y.C., 1984—. Presenter in field. One-man shows include Dwan Gallery, N.Y.C., 1966, 67, 70, Witherspoon Gallery, U. N.C., Greensboro, 1965, Washington Sq. Gallery, N.Y.C., 1964, PS 1 Mus., L.I., N.Y., 1977, Hetzler and Keller Gallery, Stuttgart, Germany, 1979, Whitney Mus. Am. Art, N.Y.C., 1979, 81, Kuntsmuseum Dusseldorf, Fed. Republic Germany, 1979, Bess Culter Gallery, N.Y.C., 1987, 88, The New Mus., N.Y.C., 1987, Stalke Gallery, Copenhagen, Denmark, 1988, 96, Scott Hanson Gallery, 1989, Ball State U., Muncie, Ind., 1990, Sandra Gering Gallery, N.Y.C., 1991, 93-95, Krister Fahl Gallery, Stockholm, 1994, The Sorbonne, Paris, 1994, Rosenbach Mus. & Libr., Phila., 1995, Brown U., Providence, R.I., 1995, Pier Gallery, Orkney, Stromness, Scotland, 1995, Moore Coll. Art and Design, Phila., 1995, Anders Tornberg Gallery, Lund, Sweden, 1996, Hubert Winter Gallery, Vienna, Austria, 1998, The Mus. of Judaica, Phila., 1998, Stalke Gallery, Copenhagen, 1999, Specta Gallery, Copenhagen, 1999, Galerij S65, Aalst, Belgium, 1999, Gary Tatintsian Gallery, N.Y.C., 1999, Art Agents Gallery, Hamburg, Germany, 2000, Niels Borch Jensen Gallery Berlin, 2000, Stalke Gallery, Copenhagen, 2000, Nikolaj Comtemporary Art Ctr., Copenhagen, 2001, Hubert Winter Gallery, Vienna, 2001, Thomas Rehbein Gallery, Cologne, 2002, Gary Tatintsian Gallery, N.Y.C., 2003, The Annex, N.Y.C., 2003, Quadrum Gallery, Lisbon, Portugal, 2003, Slought Gallery, Phila., 2003; represented in permanent collections Neuberger Mus., Purchase, N.Y., Met. Mus. Art, N.Y.C., Bklyn. Mus. Art, Phila. Mus. Art, Phoenix Mus. Art, Ga. Mus. Art, Walker Art Ctr., The Getty Ctr., Santa Monica, Calif., The Mus. Contemporary Art, L.A., Des Moines Art Ctr., Mus. Modern Art, N.Y.C., Art Inst. of Chgo., Nat. Gallery Art, Washington, Fogg Art Mus., Harvard Univ. Art Mus., Cambridge, Mass., Contemporary Mus., Honolulu, Musee Moderne, Stockholm, Sweden, Whitney Mus. Am. Art, Denver Art Mus., Chrysler Mus., Norfolk, Va., J.B. Speed Art Mus., Louisville, Ky., Jewish Mus., N.Y.C., Statensmuseum for Kunst, Copenhagen, Rooseum, Ctr. Contemporary Art, Malmo, Sweden, Phila. Mus. Jewish Art, Guggenheim Mus., N.Y.C., Ark. Art Ctr., Okla. City Art Mus., Milw. Art Mus., Museet for Samtidskunst, Roskilde, Denmark, Contemporary Arts Mus., Houston, The Baltimore Mus. Art, Md., Mus. Ludwig Koln, Cologne, Germany; artist in residence Sirius Art Ctr., Ireland, 2000, Statens Vaerksteder for Kunst, Copenhagen, 2000, Deutscher Akademischer Austauschdienst, Berlin, 2002. Home: 924 W End Ave New York NY 10025-3534

ANASTOS, ROSEMARY PARK, retired higher education educator; b. Andover, Mass., 1907; AB, Radcliffe Coll., 1928, AM, 1929; PhD, U. Cologne, Germany, 1934; 25 hon. degrees, Yale U., Columbia U., NYU, Brown U., Syracuse U., U. Notre Dame, Claremont Coll., U. Pa., Oberlin Coll., others. Prof. German, acad. dean Conn. Coll., New London, 1943-47, pres., 1947-62; pres. Barnard Coll., dean Columbia U., 1962-67; vice-chancellor UCLA, 1967-70, prof. higher edn. Grad. Sch. Edn., 1967-74, prof. emeritus, 1974—, prof. on recall, 1974-75. Pres. United Chpts. Phi Beta Kappa, 1970-73. Author: Das Bild von Richard Wagners Tristan und Isolde, 1935, two textbooks; contbr. ; contbg. editor (former): Change mag. Former chmn. bd. visitors Def. Intelligence Coll., U.S. Dept. Def.; former trustee Robert Coll., Istanbul, Turkey, New Sch. for Social Rsch., N.Y., Danforth Found., U. Hartford, Scripps Coll., Marlborough Sch., U. Notre Dame, Carnegie Found. for Advancement of Teaching, Mt. St. Mary's Coll., L.A.; former mem. adv. coun. and chmn. rsch. com. NEH; former mem. adv. coun. Fund for Improvement of Post-secondary Edn.; former dir. Am. Coun. on Edn. Recipient Woman of Yr. award L.A. Times, 1967, Radcliffe Coll. Alumnae award, 1974, medal U.S. Dept. Def. Fellow Am. Acad. Arts and Scis. Home: 10501 Wilshire Blvd Apt 2101 Los Angeles CA 90024-6330

ANAWALT, PATRICIA RIEFF, anthropologist, researcher; b. Ripon, Calif., Mar. 10, 1924; d. Edmund Lee and Anita Esto (Capps) Rieff; m. Richard Lee Anawalt, June 8, 1945; children: David, Katherine Anawalt Arnoldi, Harmon Fred. BA in Anthropology, UCLA, 1957, MA in Anthropology, 1971, PhD in Anthropology, 1975. Cons. curator costumes and textiles Mus. Cultural History UCLA, 1975-90, dir. Ctr. for Study Regional Dress, Fowler Mus. Cultural History, 1990—; trustee S.W. Mus., L.A., 1978-92; rsch. assoc. The San Diego Mus. Man, 1980—, UCLA Inst. Archaeology, 1994—. Trustee Archaeol. Inst. Am., U.S., Can., 1983-95, 98—; traveling lectr., 1975-86, 1994-2000, Pres.'s Lectureship, 1993-94, Charles E. Norton lectureship, 1996-97; cons. Nat. Geog. Soc., 1980-82, Denver Mus. Natural History, 1992-93; apptd. by U.S. Pres. to Cultural Property Adv. Com., Washington, 1984-93; fieldwork Guatemala, 1961, 70, 72, Spain, 1975, Sierra Norte de Puebla, Mex., 1983, 85, 88, 89, 91. Author: Indian Clothing Before Cortés: Mesoamerican Costumes from the Codices, 1981, paperback edit., 1990; co-author: The Codex Mendoza, 4 vols., 1992 (winner Archaeol. Inst. Am. 1994 James Wiseman Book award), The Essential Codex Mendoza, 1996; mem. editl. bd. Ancient Mesoamerica; contbr. articles to profl. jours. Adv. com Textile Mus., Washington, 1983-87. Grantee NEH, 1990, 96, J. Paul Getty Found. 1990, Nat. Geog. Soc., 1983, 85, 88, 89, 91, Ahmanson Found., 1996; Guggenheim fellow, 1988. Fellow Am. Anthrop. Assn.; mem. Centre Internat. D'Etude Des Textiles Anciens, Am. Ethnol. Soc., Soc. Am. Archaeology, Soc. Women Geographers (Outstanding Achievement award 1993), Textile Soc. Am. (bd. dirs. 1992-96, co-coord. 1994 biennial symposium). Avocations: ballet, reading, hiking. Office: Fowler Mus Cultural History Ctr Study Of Regional Dress Los Angeles CA 90095-0001 E-mail: panawalt@arts.ucla.edu.

ANAYA, RICHARD ALFRED, JR., accountant, investment banker; b. N.Y.C., Dec. 19, 1932; s. Ricardo Martinez and Clara (Chamarro) A.; m. Ninette Calandra, Sept. 8, 1957; children: Suzanne, Richard J. BBA, CCNY, 1958. CPA, N.Y. Tax acct. C.I.T. Fin. Corp., N.Y.C., 1964-67; asst. treas. Mut. Broadcasting System, Inc., N.Y.C., 1967-72; treas. Host Internat., Inc., Santa Monica, Calif., 1972-85; dir. fin. Windsor Fin. Corp, Encino, Calif., 1985; ind. cons. mergers and acquisitions A&I Investments, Inc, Century City, Calif., 1986-87, Anaya Assocs., Century City, Calif., 1987-90, CPA cons. mergers and acquisitions Woodlands Hills, Calif., 1990—. Founder retail store chain, Clear Connect Comms., LLC, 1995. Served with U.S. Navy, 1952-54. Mem. AICPA, Calif. State Soc. CPAs, N.Y. State Soc. CPAs. Roman Catholic. Office: Anaya Assocs 21550 Oxnard St Ste 960 Woodland Hills CA 91367-7145 E-mail: anayaassociates@pacbell.net.

ANAYA, RUDOLFO, educator, writer; b. Pastura, N.Mex., Oct. 30, 1937; s. Martin and Rafaelita (Mares) A.; m. Patricia Lawless, July 23, 1966. BA, U. N.Mex., Albuquerque, 1963, MA, 1968; PhD (hon.), U. Albuquerque, 1982; PhD, Mary Crest Coll., 1984; LLD (hon.), U. N.Mex., 1996. Prof. U. N.Mex., Albuquerque, 1974—. Author: (novels) Bless Me Ultima, 1972 (Premio Quinto sol) Heart of Aztlan, 1976, Tortuga, 1979 (Before Columbus Found. award), Alburquerque, 1992 (Pen West award for fiction), Zia Summer, 1995, The Farolitos of Christmas, 1995, Jalamanta, 1996, Rio Grande Fall, 1996, (children's picture book) Maya's Children, 1997, Shaman Winter, 1999, Roadrunner's Dance, 2000, Elegy for Cesar Chavez, 2000, Farolitos for Abuelo, 2000. NEA fellow, Nat. Medal of Arts (lit.), 2001. Home: 5324 Canada Vista Pl NW Albuquerque NM 87120-2412 Office: U NMex English Dept Albuquerque NM 87131-0001

ANBAR, MICHAEL, biophysics educator; b. Danzig, June 29, 1927; came to U.S., 1967, naturalized, 1973; s. Joshua and Chava A.; m. Ada Komet, Aug. 11, 1953; children: Ran D., Ariel D. MSc, Hebrew U., Jerusalem, 1950, PhD, 1953. Instr. chemistry U. Chgo., 1953-55; sr. scientist Weizmann Inst. Sci., 1955-67; prof. Frienberg Grad. Sch., Rehovoth, Israel, 1960-67; sr. rsch. assoc. NASA Ames Rsch. Ctr., 1967-68; dir. phys. sci. SRI Internat., Menlo Park, Calif., 1968-72, dir. mass spectrometry research ctr., 1972-77; prof. biophysical sci., chmn. dept. Sch. Medicine, SUNY, Buffalo, 1977-90, rsch. prof. dental materials, rsch. prof. ophthalmology, 1990—, exec. dir. Health Instrument and Device Inst., 1983-85, assoc. dean applied research, 1983-85; v.p. R & D AMARA Inc, Amherst, N.Y., 1992—; rsch. prof. surgery Sch. Medicine, SUNY, 1998—. Author: The Hydrated Electron, 1970, The Machine of the Bedside: Strategies for Using Technology in Parient Care, 1984, Clinical Biophysics, 1985, Computers in Medicine, 1986, Quantitative Dynamic Telethermometry in Medical Diagnosis and Management, 1994; editor-in-chief: Thermology, 1993; contbr. articles to profl. jours. With Israeli Air Force, 1947-49. Fellow, AIMBE, 2001; grantee in field. Fellow Am. Inst. Biomed. Engrs.; mem. IEEE, AAAS, IEEE Computer Soc., IEEE Engring. in Biology and Medicine Soc., Assn. Am. Med. Colls., Am. Inst. Physics, Am. Chem. Soc., Am. Inst. Ultrasound in Medicine, Am. Assn. Clin. Chemistry, Am. Assn. Dental Rsch., Am. Assn. Mass Spectrometry, Am. Acad. Thermology, Am. Assn. Med. Systems Informatics, N.Y. Acad. Scis., Internat. Assn. Dental Rsch., Radiation Rsch. Soc., Internat. Med. Informatics Assn., Internat. Soc. Optical Engring., Radiol. Soc. N.Am., Am. Soc. Clin. Oncology. Office: SUNY 118 Cary Hall Buffalo NY 14214-3023 *Any scientist should first try to understand nature and then to utilize knowledge for the betterment of the quality of life. Even a single modest contribution to medicine can help thousands, making it a worthwhile cause for any scientist. My research and teaching focus, therefore, is on the application of the physical sciences to medicine.*

ANBINDER, PAUL, publishing company executive; b. Bklyn., Apr. 19, 1940; s. Tulea Herzel and Gussie (Dandeshane) A.; m. Helen Rabinowitz, Feb. 16, 1964; children: Mark Harris, Jeffrey Todd. BA, Cornell U., 1960; postgrad., Columbia U., 1960-61. Editor Dover Publs., N.Y.C., 1961-64; editor-in-chief Shorewood Pubs., N.Y.C., 1964-69; with Harry N. Abrams, Inc., N.Y.C., 1969-71, sr. v.p., 1972-73, pres., 1974-75; v.p., editor trade paperbacks Ballantine Books, N.Y.C., 1975-78; dir. spl. projects Random House/Alfred A. Knopf, N.Y.C., 1975-78; pres., pub. Hudson Hills Press, N.Y.C., 1978—2002, chmn., founding pub., 2002—. Bd. dirs. Friends of the Neuberger Mus. of Art, Purchase, N.Y., 1986-96. Mem. Assn. Am. Pubs. (bd. dirs. N.Y.C. and Washington chpts. 1987-91), Century Assn. Democrat. Jewish. Avocations: opera, collecting art, travel. Office: 144 Southlawn Ave Dobbs Ferry NY 10522

ANCEL, JERALD IRWIN, lawyer; b. Indpls., Jan. 29, 1944; s. Harry and Margaret (Schneider) A.; m. Gayle Elizabeth Vogel, Aug. 21, 1965; children—Jason, Jennifer, Marc. B.S. in Acctg., Ind. U.-Bloomington, 1965, J.D., 1968. Bar: Ind. 1968, U.S. Dist. Ct. (so. dist.) Ind. 1968, U.S. Dist. Ct. (no. dist.) Ind. 1980. Adjudicator, State of Ind., Indpls., 1965-68; assoc. Law Offices of Steven H. Ancel, Indpls., 1968-73; ptnr. Ancel & Ancel, Indpls., 1974-76; mng. ptnr. Ancel, Friedlander, Miroff & Ancel, Indpls., 1976-80; mng. ptnr. Ancel, Miroff & Frank, P.C., Indpls., 1981— ; lectr. Ind. Continuing Legal Edn. Forum. Author: Save Our Farms, Farm Foreclosure Prevention and Reorganization, 1983; Survey of Bankruptcy Law from Creditor's View, 1983, 84. Mem. Gov.'s Com. to Study Mental Health Laws, Indpls., 1974-76, com. chmn., 1978-80; bd. dirs., sec. Marion County Assn. Retarded Citizens, Indpls., 1978-80. Mem. ABA, Ind. Bar Assn., Indpls. Bar Assn., Comml. Law League Am., Assn. Trial Lawyers Am., Am. Bankruptcy Inst., Phi Delta Phi. Club: Broad Ripple Sertoma (pres. 1973-74). Home: 11090 Queens Way Cir Carmel IN 46032-9636 Office: Ancel Miroff & Frank 1000 Two Market Sq Ctr PO Box 44219 Indianapolis IN 46244-0219

ANCELL, ROBERT MANNING, leadership organization executive; b. Phoenix, Oct. 16, 1942; s. Robert Manning and Alice (Lovett) A.; m. Janet Claire Neuber, Dec. 21, 1966 (div. Oct. 1984); children: Kevin Robert, Kristin Deann; m. Christine M. Miller, Mar. 30, 1995. BA, U. N.Mex., 1971. Lic. pvt. pilot. Reporter KOB Radio and TV, Albuquerque, 1966-72; sr. sales rep. Xerox Corp., Albuquerque, 1972-78; pub. Colo. Bus. mag., Denver, 1978-83; publ. mgr. Denver Bus. mag., 1983-84; pub. Endless Vacation mag., Indpls., 1985-88; mktg. mgr. World Pub. Co., Evanston, Ill., 1989-92; writer, 1962—; founder, exec. dir. Soc. for 4-Star Leadership, Alexandria, Va., 1998—. Cons. Cowles Mags., Harrisburg, Pa., 1994-95, Exec. Books, Mechanicsburg, Pa., 1996-98. Author: The Biographical Dictionary of World War II Generals and Flag Officers, 1997; co-author: Who Will Lead?, 1996, Four-Star Leadership for Leaders, 1997, Vol. I and II, 1999. Lt. comdr. USNR, 1971-93. Recipient 1st pl. TV Documentary award N.Mex. Broadcasters Assn., Albuquerque, 1968, UPI, Albuquerque, 1968, Washington Ind. Writers. Mem. Naval Order of U.S. (v.p. pub. affairs 1997—), Soc. for Mil. History, U.S. Naval Inst., Ret. Officers Assn., Assn. of U.S. Army, Air Force Assn., Am. Turkish Soc., Washington Ind. Writers, Christian Businessmen's Com., Surface Navy Assn., USN Pub. Affairs Alumni Assn. Republican. Presbyterian. Avocations: flying, photography, outdoors activities. Home: 7406 Salford Ct Alexandria VA 22315-4728 Office: 7406 Salford Ct Alexandria VA 22315-4728 E-mail: rmancelljr@aol.com.

ANCES, I. G(EORGE), obstetrician, gynecologist, educator; b. Balt., July 3, 1935; s. Harry and Fanny A.; m. Marlene Roth, Oct. 23, 1966; 1 son, Beau Mark. BS, U. Md., 1956, MD, 1959. Diplomate Am. Bd. Ob-Gyn. Intern Ohio State U. Hosp., 1959-60; resident in ob-gyn. Univ. Hosp., Balt., 1960-61, 63-65; faculty U. Md. Med. Sch., Balt., 1966—, prof. ob-gyn., 1975-83, dir. labs. obstetrics and gynecol. rsch. and clin. labs., 1967-83, dir. divsn. adolescent ob-gyn. and family planning, 1981-83;; prof. ob-gyn., chmn. dept. Rutgers U. Sch. Medicine, Camden, N.J., 1983—. Contbr. chpts. to books, articles to profl. jours. Capt. sustaining fund drive Balt. Symphony Orch., Opera Co. Phila.; med. adv. com. Fire Dept. Balt. City. With USAF, 1961-63. Recipient of Outstanding Tchg. and Edn. award Robert-Wood Johnson Sch. of Medicine-Cooper Hosp., 1989, 92, 96, 2000, 01, 02, Appreciation Coverage award, 1999, 2000, 2002, Nat. Faculty award for excellence in resident edn., 1996. Fellow Am. Coll. Obstetrics and Gynecology; mem. Endocrine Soc., Soc. Gynecol. Investigation, Soc. Study Reprodn. (charter), Internat. Soc. Rsch. in Biology Reprodn. (charter), Md. Obstetrics and Gynecol. Soc. (sec. 1978-81, dir. 1979—), Med. and Chirurgical Soc. Md., Soc. Adolescent Medicine, Douglas Obstet. and Gynecol. Soc. (pres. 1984—), N.J. State Med. Soc. (chmn. neo-natal coop. So. Jersey 1986—), Phila. Ob-Gyn. Soc., English Speaking Union, Cooper Found., N.J. Conservation Coun., Harbour League Club, Md. Club, Towson Golf and Country Club, Sigma Xi. Clubs: Maryland, Towson Golf and Country. Home: 1 Lane Of Acres Haddonfield NJ 08033-3504 Office: Rutgers U Sch Medicine Dept Ob-Gyn 3 Cooper Plz Camden NJ 08103-1438

ANCHETA, CAESAR PAUL, software developer; b. Manila, June 1, 1947; s. Carlos Fortunato and Rosalinda (Huliganga) A.; m. Ruth Segalman, June 1, 1969; children: Rebecca E., Amy L. BS in Physics, U. Tex., 1969; MS in Physics, UCLA, 1971. Mem. tech. staff Hughes Aircraft Co., Culver City, Calif., 1969-78; sr. staff engr. Fairchild Camera and Instrument, Simi Valley, Calif., 1978-82; software engr. Internat. Remote Imaging Systems, Chatsworth, Calif., 1982-84, Teradyne, Inc., Woodland Hills, Calif., 1984-86; sr. scientist Internat. Remote Imaging Systems, Chatsworth, 1986-88; rsch. scientist Teledyne Industries, Northridge, Calif., 1988-89; sr. systems engr. Hughes Aircraft Co., Long Beach, Calif., 1989-90; sr. software engr. GE, Milw., 1990-94; software devel. A&B Software, Brookfield, Wis., 1994—. Author: (publs.) Proceedings of the Society of Photo Optical Instrumentation Engineers, 1978, Proceedings of the International Test Conference, 1981. Mem. The Elfun Soc., Milw., 1992. Named New Elfun of Yr., Milw. chpt. The Elfun Soc., 1993; Hughes fellow Hughes Aircraft Co., 1969-71; Stevens scholar U. Tex., El Paso, 1965-68. Mem. AAAS. Achievements include patent pending (with Arthur F. Griffin) on Rectilinear Object Matcher; development of white blood cell recognition machine vision project, pap smear scanning machine vision project.

ANCHIE, TOBY LEVINE, health facility administrator; b. New Haven, Conn., Jan. 21, 1944; d. Solomon and Mary (Karlins) Levine; m. Alonzo C. Moreland III; children from previous marriage: Michael D., Robert P. BSN, U. of Conn., 1966; MA in Edn. magna cum laude, Nor. Ariz. U., 1984. RN Ariz., Conn., Ga. Coord. spl. projects, nurse coord., adult day hosp. Barrow Neurol. Inst. of St. Joseph's Hosp. and Med. Ctr., Phoenix, 1984-87, mgr., 1985-92, mgr. adminstrv. and support svcs., neuroscis., 1992-94, mgr. rsch. adminstrn., 1994-97, dir. rsch. adminstrn., 1997-2000, exec. dir. R&D, 2000—. Cons.; presenter in field; faculty mem. U. Phoenix; adv. bd. mem. Myasthenia Gravis Assn.; adv. coun. mem. Office Disability Prevention Ariz. Dept. Health Svcs., strategic planning com. mem. Contbr. . Mem.: NAFE, Ariz. Assn. Neurosci. Nurses, Assn. Clin. Rsch. Coords. (Ariz. chpt.), Soc. Rsch. Adminstrs., World Fedn. Splty. Nursing Orgn. (chair membership com. 1993—95), Am. Bd. Neurosci. Nursing (treas, 1995—96), Assn. Clin. Rsch. Profls. (continuing edn. com.), Am. Assn. Neurosci. Nurses (manuscript rev. bd. 1997—, bd. dirs., pres., nominating com. 2003). Home: 3112 S Los Feliz Dr Tempe AZ 85282-2854 E-mail: tanchie@chw.edu.

ANCHLIA, THAN MAL, wholesale distribution executive; b. Bikaner, Rajasthan, India, Oct. 18, 1918; s. Deokaran and Goura (Nahta) A.; m. Jethi Devi Sethia, Feb. 22, 1938; children: Kanchan, Chandra, Ratna. B in Commerce, St. Xavier Coll., Calcutta, India, 1938. Exec. dir. IMC, N.Y.C., 1975-90. Author: New Dictionary System, 1988. Mem. Rep. Task Force, Washington, 1979-80. Mem. Jain. Avocations: poetry, lyrics. Office: IMC PO Box 20028 New York NY 10017-0001

ANCIER, GARTH RICHARD RICHARD, television broadcast executive; b. Perth Amboy, N.J., Sept. 3, 1957; s. Sherman and Jean Ancier. BA, Princeton U., 1979. Exec. prodr. syndicated program Am. Focus, 1975—79; v.p. comedy programs NBC Entertainment, N.Y.C. and Burbank, Calif., 1979—86; pres. entertainment Fox TV Network, L.A., 1986—89; pres. network TV shows Walt Disney Studios, Burbank, 1989—90; corp. officer, prodr. Fox, Inc., L.A., 1991—92; pres. The Warner Bros. TV Network, 1994—99, NBC Entertainment, Burbank, Calif., 1999—. TV cons. Dem. Nat. Com., Washington, 1991—92; trustee Nat. Coun. Families and TV, 1991—; creator, exec. prodr. (TV show) Ricki Lake The Garth Ancier Co., 1992—97, exec. cons., 1997—. Mem.: Hollywood TV and Radio Soc. (trustee 1996—99). Democrat. Office: NBC Entertainment 3000 W Alameda Ave Burbank CA 91523-0002

ANCKER, CLINTON JAMES, JR., emeritus systems and industrial engineering educator; b. Cedar Falls, Iowa, June 21, 1919; s. Clinton James and Fern (Lalan) A.; m. Margaret Wright Rees, Apr. 11, 1947; children— Clinton James III, Evan Randolph, Megan Lalan, Scott Rees. BS in Mech. Engring, Purdue U., 1940; MS, U. Calif. at Berkeley, 1949, Mech. Engr., 1950; PhD, Stanford U., 1955. Jr. engr. Detroit Edison Co., 1941, 46; instr. Purdue U., 1946-47; asst. prof. U. Calif. at Berkeley, 1947-55; ops. analyst Ops. Research Office, Chevy Chase, Md., 1955-56; sr. engr. Booz-Allen Applied Research, Inc., Chgo., 1956-58; mgr. Analco Services Co., Chgo., 1958-59; head math. and operations research program System Devel. Corp., Santa Monica, Calif., 1959-67; dir. Nat. Hwy. Safety Inst., Dept. Transp., 1967-68; prof., chmn. dept. indsl. and systems engring. U. So. Calif., 1968-84, emeritus prof. Author papers in field. Served to capt. AUS, 1941-46. Mem. Ops. Rsch. Soc. Am. (nat. council 1970-73), Soc. Cincinnati, Mil. Ops. Rsch. Soc. (exec. com. 1964-65), Sigma Xi, Tau Beta Pi, Pi Tau Sigma, Alpha Pi Mu, Omega Rho (founding. pres. 1975-78). Home: 23908 Malibu Knolls Rd Malibu CA 90265-4823

ANCKER-JOHNSON, BETSY, physicist, engineer, retired automotive company executive; b. St. Louis, Apr. 29, 1927; d. Clinton James and Fern (Lalan) Ancker; m. Harold Hunt Johnson, Mar. 15, 1958; children: Ruth P. Johnson, David H. Johnson, Paul A. Johnson, Marti H. Johnson. BA in Physics with high honors (Pendleton scholar), Wellesley Coll., 1949; PhD in Exptl. Physics magna cum laude, U. Tuebingen, Germany, 1953; D.Sc. (hon.), Poly. Inst. N.Y., 1979, Trinity Coll., 1981, U. So. Calif., 1984, Alverno Coll., 1984; LL.D. (hon.), Bates Coll., 1980. Instr., jr. research physicist U. Calif., Berkeley, 1953-54; physicist Sylvania Microwave Physics Lab., 1956-58; mem. tech. staff RCA Labs., 1958-61; rsch. specialist Boeing Co., 1961-70, exec., 1970-73; asst. sec. U.S. Dept. Commerce for Sci. and Tech., 1973-77; dir. phys. rsch. Argonne Nat. Lab., Ill., 1977-79; v.p. environ. activities GM, Warren, Mich., 1979-92. Affiliate prof. elec. engring. U. Wash., 1961-73; mem. Energy Rsch. Adv. Bd., 1983-87, adv. com. on inertial confinement fusion Dept. Energy, 1992-94, US Safety Rev. Panel NSF, 1987-88; cons. Inland Steel Inc., 1991-96; adv. com. Rowan Sch. Engring., 1993-96; Regents vis. prof. U. Calif., Berkeley, 1988-89,

Author of 70 sci. papers; patentee in field. Mem. staff Inter-Varsity Christian Fellowship, 1954-56; mem. vis. com. elec. and computer divsn. MIT, U.S. Dept. Def. Sci. Bd.; mem. adv. bd. Stanford U. Sch. Engring., Fla. State U., Fla. A&M U., Congl. Caucus for Sci. and Tech.; trustee Wellesley Coll., 1971-77; chair bd. dirs. World Environ. Ctr., 1988-93, dir., 1988-99; founding trustee Johnson Scholarship Found., 1991-2001; founding dir. Work Place Influence, 1997—, dir. Enterprise Devel. Internat., 1992—; mem. faculty adv. coun. U. Tex. Sch. Engring., 1998—; bd. dirs. Tex. Environ. Forum, 2000-01. AAUW fellow, 1950-51; Horton Hollowell fellow, 1951-52; NSF grantee, 1967-72; recipient Chmn's. award Am. Assn. Engring. Socs., 1986. award of honor Licensing Execs. Soc. Fellow AAAS, IEEE, Am. Phys. Soc. (councillor-at-large 1973-76); mem. NRC (bd. engring. edn. 1991-95, com. on women in sci. and engring. 1990-96, office sci. and engring. pers. adv. com. 1993-96), Nat. Acad. Engring. (councillor 1995-2001), Air Pollution Control Assn., Soc. Automotive Engrs. (bd. dirs. 1979-81), Phi Beta Kappa, Sigma Xi. Home: 3502 Mount Bonnell Rd Austin TX 78731-5829 E-mail: betsyanjo@hotmail.com.

ANCOLI-ISRAEL, SONIA, psychologist, researcher; b. Tel Aviv, Dec. 25, 1951; came to U.S., 1955. m. Andrew G. Israel; 2 children. BA, SUNY, Stony Brook, 1972; MA, Calif. State U., Long Beach, 1974; PhD, U. Calif., San Francisco, 1979. Lic. psychologist, Calif. Staff psychologist U. Calif. San Diego, La Jolla, 1979-84, asst. adj. prof., 1984-88, assoc. prof., 1988-94; prof., 1994—; assoc. dir. Sleep Disorders Ctr., VA Med. Ctr., San Diego, 1981-92, dir., 1992—. Author: All I Want Is a Good Night's Sleep, 1996; contbr. numerous articles to profl. jours. Mem. bd. mgrs. Jewish Cmty. Ctr., La Jolla, 1985-91; mem. exec. bd. Nat. Sleep Found., 1990-95. Recipient Robert E. Harris Meml. award, U. Calif., San Francisco, 1978. Mem. AAAS, Am. Acad. Sleep Medicine, Sleep Rsch. Soc. (bd. dirs. 1993-96, pres.-elect, 2003—), Soc. for Light Treatment and Biol. Rhythms (bd. dirs. 1994-97, pres.-elect 1998—, pres. 2000—), Gerontol. Soc. Am., N.Y. Acad. Sci.

ANCONA, GEORGE EFRAIN, photographer, author; b. N.Y.C., Dec. 4, 1929; s. Ephraim Jose and Emma Graziana (Diaz) A.; m. Helga Von Sydow, July 20, 1968; children: Lisa, Gina, Tomas, Isabel, Marina, Pablo. Student, Academia de San Carlos, Mexico, 1949, Art Students League, 1950, Cooper Union Sch. Design, 1950. Art dir. Esquire Inc., N.Y.C., 1951-53, Seventeen mag., N.Y.C., 1953-54, Grey Advt. Agy., N.Y.C., 1954-58, Daniel & Charles Advt. Agy., N.Y.C., 1958-60; free lance photographer, film producer N.Y.C., 1960—. Lectr. graphic design, photography Rockland Community Coll., 1973—, Parsons Sch. Design, 1974—, Sch. Visual Arts, 1978— Author-illustrator: Handtalk, 1974, Monsters on Wheels, 1974, What Do You Do?, 1976, I Feel, 1977, Growing Older, 1978, It's A Baby!, 1979, Dancing Is, 1981, Bananas, from Manolo to Margie, Team Work, 1983, Monster Movers, Sheepdog, Helping Out, Freighters, 1985, Handtalk Birthday, 1986 (N.Y. Times 10 Best Illustrated Children's Books of Yr.), Turtle Watch, 1987, Handtalk Zoo, 1989, Riverkeeper, 1990, Handtalk School, 1991, The Aquarium Book, 1991, Man and Mustang, 1992, Pow Wow, 1992, My Camera, 1992, Pablo Remembers, 1993, The Pinatamaker, 1994, The Golden Lion Tamarin Comes Home, 1994, Fiesta U.S.A., 1995, Cutters, Carvers & the Cathedral, 1995, Earth Daughter, 1995, Mayeros, 1997, Fiesta Fireworks, 1998, Barrio, 1998, Let's Dance, 1998, Charro, The Mexican Cowboy, 1999, Carnaval, 1999, Cuban Kids, 2000, Harvest, 2001, Viva Mexico, The Food, The Fiestas, The Folk Arts, The People, The Past, 2001, Murals: Walls That Sing, 2002.. *Curiosity is the biggest element in my work. Watching people and making contact through my photographs have given me a sense of myself. My work keeps me in touch with the world around me. Whether a person bakes, builds, sings, or drives, people reach one another in their own way. Mine is taking pictures. Reaching out to others...I think that's what living is all about.*

ANCRUM, CHERYL DENISE, dentist; b. Bklyn., Sept. 28, 1958; d. Ida Jackson. BA in Psychology, Harvard U., 1980; DDS, Columbia U., 1986, MPH, 1989. Dentist. Credit analyst Hartford (Conn.) Nat. Bank, 1980-81; statis. coding instr., analyst Aetna Ins. Co., Hartford, 1981-82; dental asst. Gouverneur Hosp., N.Y.C., 1983; clk. typist Columbia Presbyn. Med. Ctr., N.Y.C., 1984-86; gen. practice resident Beth Israel Med. Ctr., N.Y.C., 1986-87; dental attending Montefiore Med. Ctr., Bronx, 1987-89; rsch. assoc., dentist North Ctrl. Bronx Hosp., 1989-90; dental dir. Manhattan Men's House of Detention, N.Y.C., 1989-97; pvt. practice, 1998—. Dental extern North Ctrl. Bronx. Hosp., 1985-86. Vol. St. John Episc. Hosp., Bklyn., 1974-75, Mt. Auburn Hosp., Cambridge, 1978, Harlem Hosp., N.Y.C., 1987-88; health adv. Harvard U., Cambridge, 1977-80; active Sutton for Mayor Campaign, Bklyn., 1977; mem. Girl Scouts U.S., Bklyn., 1969-75, Operation PUSH, Hartford, 1981-82, Hartford Black Women Network, 1980-82, Kuumba Singers, Harvard U., 1977-78, New Temple Singers, Cambridge, 1978-80; mem. tape commn. Bridge St. A.M.E. Ch., Bklyn., 1987-88; fin. sec. Flower Guild, Allen A.M.E. Church, Queens, 1994-97; bd. dirs. F.I.S.H. of Uniondale, 1991-96. A Better Chance scholar, 1973-76, Am. Fund for Dental Health scholar, 1982-84, Clark Found. scholar, 1983-86; selected profl. fellow AAUW, 1985-86; recipient Letter of Commendation, Columbia U., 1983, Applewhite award, 1986, William Bailey Dunning award, 1986, Lester R. Cain Pathology prize, 1986; named to Outstanding Young Women of Am., 1983. Mem. ADA, Nat. Dental Assn. (rec. sec. 1998-2000), N.Y. State Dental Soc., Acad. of Gen. Dentistry, Am. Assn. of Pub. Health Dentistry, Am. Profl. Practice Assn., Order of the Ea. Star (Elizabeth Moore chpt. sec. 1995-96), Delta Sigma Theta (Nassau alumnae chpt. journalist, 1992-96, 2d v.p., 1995-96). Democrat. Mem. African Methodist Episcopal Ch. Avocations: creative arts, writing, reading, music, skating. Office: 230 Hilton Ave Ste 203 Hempstead NY 11550-8116 E-mail: Cheryldanc@juno.com., cherlyancrumdds@verizon.net.

ANDARY, THOMAS JOSEPH, biochemist, researcher; b. Mar. 8, 1942; s. Joseph Boula and Marion (Schwifetti) A.. BS, No. Mich. U., 1966, MA, 1968; PhD, Wayne State U., 1974. Instr. biology No. Mich. U., Marquette, 1967—69; rsch. assoc. physiology Wayne State U., Detroit, 1973—76; sr. rsch. scientist, mgr. coagulation rsch. Hyland Labs., Costa Mesa, Calif., 1976—83; dir. quality control Hyland Therapeutics, Glendale, Calif., 1983—90; dir. quality assurance and regulatory affairs Baxter/Hyland Divsn., Glendale, Calif., 1990—91, v.p. quality assurance and regulatory affairs, 1991—96, responsible head, 1993—96. Cons. in regulatory affairs/quality assurance to biopharmaceutical industry, 1996—; lectr. in field. Contbr. articles to profl. jours. Recipient NDEA fellowship, 1969—72. Mem.: Drug Info. Assn., Internat. Assn. Biol. Standardization, N.Y. Acad. Scis., Am. Chem. Soc., Parenteral Drug Assn., Sigma Xi (Rsch. award 1973). Roman Catholic. Home and Office: 531 N Canyon Blvd Monrovia CA 91016-1707

ANDEL, MARK, communications specialist, educator; b. Chgo., Mar. 20, 1956; s. John Hale and Carole Imogene A.; m. Linda Visco, Oct. 6 1996; children: Jil, Meg. BA, Elmhurst Coll., 1978; MA, DePaul U., 1984. Sr. writer Dunlap, Schulze and Assocs., 1989—92; lifestyles editor, bus. reporter Jefferson County Jour., 1992—94; writer, columnist, theater critic Northwest Leader, North Loop News, Easy Mark, 1994—; Newark electronics catalog mgr. Jefferson County Jour., 1994—96; mem. faculty English dept. McHenry County Coll., Wright Coll., 1994—. Mng. ptnr. Impact Comm. Editor (lifestyles): Tenn. Star Jour., 1994; contbr. articles to mags. V.p. comm. Mercy Home for Boys & Girls, 1997—2001. Recipient Bright Idea award United Way, 1994-95. Mem.: Roosterfest (life; sec. 1997—2001), Sigma Tau Delta (pres.), Phi Kappa Phi. Democrat. Avocations: golf, boxing. Home and Office: 511Bunker St Woodstock IL 60098 Home Fax: 815-337-5908. E-mail: markandel@aol.com.

ANDELA, VALENTINE BISANGENA, medical researcher; b. Yaounde, Center, Cameroon, July 5, 1974; s. John Balinga and Blanche Rose Andela. MD, U. of Yaounde I, Cameroon, 1999. Wilmot cancer rsch. fellow U. of Rochester Med. Ctr., Rochester, NY, 2001—, postdoctoral fellow, 1999—2000. Founding mem. www.Cancer-Africa.org, Yaounde, Cameroon, 2002. Author: (rsch.) Modulation of Tumor Metastasis (Wilmot Fellowship award, 2000). Mem.: Assn. UICC Fellows, Am. Assn. Cancer Rsch. Achievements include research in AACR-AFLAC Young Investigator Award for Meritorious and Promising Cancer Research. Office Fax: 585-275-1121. E-mail: valentine_andela@urmc.rochester.edu.

ANDELSON, ROBERT VERNON, social philosopher, educator; b. Los Angeles, Feb. 19, 1931; s. Abraham and Ada (Markson) A.; m. Bonny Orange Johnson, June 7, 1964. AA, Los Angeles City Coll., 1950; AB equivalent, U. Chgo., 1952; A.M., U. So. Calif., 1954, PhD, 1960. Exec. dir. Henry George Sch. Social Sci., San Diego Extension, Calif., 1959-62; instr. philosophy and religion Northland Coll., Wis., 1962-63; asst. prof. govt. and philosophy Northwestern State U., La., 1963-65; mem. faculty Auburn (Ala.) U., 1965—; prof. philosophy Auburn U., 1973-92, prof. emeritus, 1992—, mem. grad. faculty, 1969-92; mem., dir. Robert Schalkenbach Found., 1986—, v.p., 1998-2001, Internat. Union Land Value Taxation and Free Trade, 1986-88, pres., 1997-2001. Inaugural lectr. philosophy lecture series U. Ala. at Birmingham, 1975; mem. adj. faculty Ludwig von Mises Inst., 1983— ; ordained to ministry Congregational Ch., 1959; reviewer instl. grant applications NEH, 1987; fac. assoc. Lincoln Inst. Land Policy, 1993-96. Author: Imputed Rights: An Essay in Christian Social Theory, 1971; editor, co-author: Critics of Henry George, 2d edit., 2003, Commons Without Tragedy, 1991, Land-Value Taxation Around the World, 2d edit., 1997, 3rd edit., 2000; joint author (with J.M. Dawsey) From Wasteland to Promised Land: Liberation Theology for a Post-Marxist World, 1992; mem. editl. bd. Am. Jour. Econs. and Sociology, 1969—, chmn. selection com. for editor-in-chief, 1996, mem. corp., 1999—; mem. editl. bd. The Personalist, 1975-80; contbr. articles to scholarly jours. Asst. sgt. at arms Republican Nat. Conv., 1952; mem. Lee County Rep. Exec. Com., 1967-79; trustee Henry George Found. Am., 1971-75, mem. adv. commn., 1975— . Recipient Rsch. awards Found. Social Rsch., 1959, Relm Found., 1967, 2 George Washington Honor medals Freedoms Found., 1970, 72; Disting. rsch. fellow Am. Inst. for Econ. Rsch., 1993—. Mem. So. Soc. Philosophy and Psychology, Ala. Philos. Soc. (pres. 1968-69, 78-79). Home: 534 Cary Dr Auburn AL 36830-2502 E-mail: rvandelson@mindspring.com.

ANDERBERG, ROY A. journalist; b. Camden, N.J., Mar. 30, 1921; s. Arthur R. and Mary V. (McHugh) A.; m. Louise M. Brooks, Feb. 5, 1953; children: Roy, Mary. AA, Diablo Valley Coll., 1975. Enlisted USN, 1942, commd. officer, 1960, ret., 1970; waterfront columnist Pacific Daily News, Agana, Guam, 1966-67; pub. rels. officer Naval Forces, Mariana Islands, 1967; travel editor Contra Costa (Calif.) Times, 1968-69; entertainment and restaurant editor Concord (Calif.) Transcript, 1971-75; entertainment editor Contra Costa Advertiser, 1975-76; dining editor Rossmoor News, Walnut Creek, Calif., 1977-78; free-lance non-fiction journalist, 1976—. Recipient Best Feature Story award Guam Press Assoc., 1966. Mem. VFW, DAV, U.S. Power Squadron, Ret. Officers Assn., Am. Legion, U.S. Submarine Vets. WWII (state comdr., regional dir., nat. 2d v.p.), Naval Submarine League (XO), Martinez Yacht Club (charter), Rossmoor Yacht Club (commodore 1995), Toastmasters. Democrat. Home: 1840 Tice Creek Dr Apt 2228 Walnut Creek CA 94595-2460

ANDEREGG, JULIUS FIDELIS, diplomat, consul general; b. Switzerland, Dec. 8, 1950; came to U.S., 1979; s. Julius A. and Katharina Anderegg; m. Ursula Anderegg, 1976; children: Rolf, Corinne. BA in Internal Rels., Marymount Coll., 1983; MA in Polit. Sci., CUNY, 1985; postgrad., Columbia U. Comml. attaché Swiss Consulate, N.Y.C., 1979-85; attaché Swiss Embassy, Baghdad, 1985-87, dep. head Copenhagen, 1987-90; dep. dir. European Free Trade Assn., Geneva, 1991-95; chmn. fin. econ. com. Org. for Security and Coop. in Europe, Vienna, 1996-97; consul gen., counsellor fin. and social policy Swiss Delegation to UN, N.Y.C., 1998—. Avocations: skiing, history. Office: Swiss Mission to UN 633 3rd Ave Fl 29 New York NY 10017-6706

ANDEREGG, KAREN KLOK, business executive; b. Council Bluffs, Iowa; d. George J. and Hazel E. Klok; m. George F. Anderegg Jr., Aug. 27, 1970 (div. Dec. 1993); m. William Drake Rutherford, Jan. 2, 1994. BA, Stanford U., 1963. Copywriter Vogue mag., N.Y.C., 1963-72; copy editor Mademoiselle mag., N.Y.C., 1972-77, mng. editor, 1977-80; assoc. editor Vogue Mag., N.Y.C., 1980-85; editor-in-chief Elle mag, N.Y.C., 1985-87; pres. Clinique USA, 1987-92; bus. cons. Portland, Oreg., 1993—. Bd. dirs. Oreg. Dental Svcs. Health Plans, ethicspoint; bus. adv. bd. mem. Portland State U.; bd. dirs. U. Club Found. Bd. Bd. dirs. Oreg. Hist. Soc. Mem.: Cosmetic Exec. Women.

ANDERER, JOSEPH HENRY, textile company executive; b. Phila., Oct. 12, 1924; s. Joseph L. and Catherine (Fleck) A.; m. E. T'Lene Brinson, Apr. 4, 1948; children: Joseph D., Mark H., Nancy T. B.M.E., Ga. Inst. Tech., 1947, B.I.E., 1948. Chem. engr. Atlantic Richfield Corp., 1947-55; asst. prof. mech. engring. Drexel Inst., Phila., 1949-56; fiber rsch. mgr., textile devel. lab. mgr. Am. Viscose Corp., 1955-62; with Celanese Corp., 1962-69, exec. v.p. textile mktg., 1967-68; pres. cosmetic and fragrance div., also dir. Revlon, N.Y.C., 1969-71; pres., chief operating officer dir. M. Lowenstein, 1972-77; dir. Aloe Creme Labs., Ft. Lauderdale, Fla., 1974-78, Fairfax Mills, N.Y.C., 1977-78; chmn. bd., chief exec. officer Warren Corp., Stafford Springs, Conn., 1978-89, Grendel Corp., Greenwood, S.C., 1979-88; v.p., dir. Trivest Corp., Sarasota, Fla., 1989-92. Trustee Lincoln Savs. Bank, N.Y.C., 1973-86, N.Y. Ocean Sci. Lab., Montauk, 1973-80, Mus. Am. Textile History, 1986-93; bd. dirs. U.S. Shoe Corp., Cin., 1980-95, Cleyn & Tinker Ltd., St. Laurent, Que., Can., 1990-94, Soundwaters, Stamford, Conn., 1990-93, Gen. Clutch Corp., Stamford, 1991-95, Storage Sol'ns, Inc., Stamford, 1993-95; chmn. nat. adv. bd. Ga. Inst. Tech., 1976-82; chmn. Emergency Med. Svcs., New Canaan, Conn., 1991-94. Patentee fiber technology. Asst. dist. mgr. SBA, Score, Conn., 1992-93, dist. mgr., 1993-94. Served to lt. USMCR, 1943-47. Named to Hall of Fame Ga. Tech. Coll. of Engring., 1997. Mem. Wool Mfg. Council (exec. com.), No. Textile Assn. (dir., v.p. 1986-88, chmn. 1988-90), Lugano Condominium Assn. (pres. 1997-98), N.Y. Yacht Club, Stamford Yacht Club (dir., comdr.), N.Am. Sta of Royal Scandinavian Yacht Clubs, Tau Beta Pi, Pi Tau Sigma. Congregationalist. E-mail: Wolfeboro@Juno.com.

ANDERHALTER, OLIVER FRANK, educational organization executive; b. Trenton, Ill., Feb. 14, 1922; s. Oliver Valentine and Catherine (Vollet) A.; m. Elizabeth Fritz, Apr. 30, 1945; children: Sharon, Stephen, Dennis. B.Ed., Eastern Ill. State Tchrs. Coll., 1943, Ped.D. (hon.), 1956; A.M., St. Louis U., 1947, PhD, 1949. Mem. faculty St. Louis U., 1947—, prof. edn., 1957—; dir. Bur. Instl. Research, 1949-65, 1949-65, Univ. Computer Center, 1961-69, chmn. research methodology dept., 1968-76; v.p. Scholastic Testing Service, Chgo., 1951-89; pres. Scholastic Testing Svc., Chgo. and St. Louis, 1989—. Chmn. finance com. Greater St. Louis Campfire Girls Orgn., 1958-59 Author, editor standardized tests. Served as pilot USNR, 1943-46. Mem. Am. Ednl. Research Assn., Nat. Council Measurement, Am. Statis. Assn., N.E.A. Home: 12756 Whispering Hills Ln Saint Louis MO 63146 4449 Office: Scholastic Testing Svc 4320 Green Ash Dr Earth City MO 63045-1208 E-mail: ststesting@email.com.

ANDERMAN, DAVID E. minister; b. Lansdale, Pa., Sept. 28, 1949; s. William Henry and Catharine Anderman; m. Alice Zimmerman, Apr. 28, 1979; children: Rachael E., Jonathan E. AB, U. Pa., 1971; MA in Min., U. Chgo., 1973, D in Min., 1982. Student pastor Ch. of the Good Shepherd UCC, Chgo., 1972-75; assoc. pastor St. Peter's United Ch. of Christ, Champaign, Ill., 1975-78; pastor Grace United Ch. of Christ, Balt., 1978-84; co-pastor St. Paul's United Ch. of Christ, Summit Station, Pa., 1984-90, Pennsburg United Ch. of Christ, Pennsburg, Pa., 1990-97; assoc. pastor St. Paul's United Ch. of Christ, Fleetwood, Pa., 1997-2000; sr. min. First Congl. Ch./UCC, Waterville, Maine, 2000—. Avocations: music, woodworking, gardening, auto restoration.

ANDERMANN, GREG, producer, director, consultant; BA in TV and Film Prodn., San Francisco State U., 1977. Dir., camera operator Video Image, Inc., San Francisco, 1977-78; creative dir. Cleland Advt., Inc., Los Angeles, 1978-79; prin., producer, dir. Telemar, Hollywood, Calif., 1980-84; comml. dir. Sta. KITV, Honolulu, 1984, Hawaii Prodn. Ctr., Honolulu, 1984-85; creative producer Time Warner TV, Honolulu, 1985-86; mgr. TV and film producer Volt Video Hawaii, Honolulu, 1986—2001; pres., exec. prodr. A2 Media, 2001—. Cons. 80/20 Mktg. Inc., Beverly Hills, Calif., 1980-82, Fawcett McDermott Cavanagh Advt., Inc., Honolulu, 1984-86; pres. East-West Connections, Inc., Honolulu, 2000—. Dir. (TV campaign) Sheraton Islands, 1984 (Pele award 1984), (videos) Hall of Fame Sports, 1984 (Pele award 1985); dir., dir. photography (music video) Reflections, 1986; assoc. producer (TV campaign) Aloha United Way, 1986 (Telly award 1986) Field producer Jerry Lewis Muscular Dystrophy Assn. Nat. Telethon, 1990. Recipient Pele Merit awards, 1985, 2, 1997, Star Award Nat. Cable Mktg. Assn., 1985, Gecko award, Hawaii Cable TV Assn., 1985, Telly award, TV campaign, 1986, Long Format TV, 1997, Cable Advt., Promotion award, 2, 1986, Ilima award Interna. Assn. Bus. Communicators, 1986, 94, 96, 97 (2), Silver Monitor award Internat. TV Assn., 1986, 87, 88, 89, Gold Monitor award Internat. TV Assn., 1987, 89, Silver Six Regional Internat Assn. Bus. Communicators, 1988 (2), Angel award L.A. Video Festival, 1988, 1st pl. Pub. Rels Soc. Am., 1994, 95 (2), Excellence award Internat. Assn. Bus. Communicators, 1997, award of honor, Pub. Rels. Soc. Am., 1997. Mem. Am. Film Inst., Dirs. Network, Soc. for Motion PIcture and TV Engrs., Internat. TV Assn., Am. Advtg. Fedn., Photographic Soc. Am., Honolulu Advt. Fedn., Film and Video Assn. Hawaii, Internat. Assn. Bus. Communicators.

ANDERS, CLAUDIA DEE, occupational therapist; b. Buffalo, May 2, 1951; d. Walter Gregory and Helen (Cedizlo) A.; (div. 1983); 1 child, Andrew T. Kiko. BS in Occupational Therapy (high honors), Va. Commonwealth U., 1973; postgrad., Ashland (Ohio) Coll., 1984, Walsh (Ohio) Coll., 1985, Kent (Ohio) State U., 1988, 89, Colo. State U., 1991, 92; MS, Clayton Coll., 2002. Lic. occupational therapist, Ohio; bd. cert. pediatric occupational therapist. With Children's Rehab. Ctr., Warren, Ohio, 1974-76; mem. transdisciplinary team Goodwill Rehab. Ctr., Canton, Ohio, 1976-78; pvt. practice, 1978-83; with Timken Mercy Med. Ctr., Canton, 1978-83; occupational therapist adult tng. team Stark County Bd. Mental Retardation, Canton, 1983-85; developer occupational therapy svcs. Stark County Local Schs., 1985-87; pediat. occupational therapist home health care sch. and cmty. agys., 1985-91; owner Eagle Seminars and Therapy, 1998—, Presenter in field. Vol. Nat. Park Svc., Cleve. Metroparks; sec. Rocky River Trailsiders, 1993-95. A. D. Williams scholar Va. Commonwealth U., 1972, 73, rsch. scholar Deerfield Beach, Fla., 2000. Mem.: Ohio Occupl. Therapy Assn., Am. Occupl. Therapy Assn., Nature Conservancy. Avocations: gardening, bird watching, hiking, sewing, needlecraft. Office: Eagle Selminars and Therapy PO Box 81520 Cleveland OH 44181-0520

ANDERS, EDWARD, chemist, educator; b. Libau, Latvia, June 21, 1926; came to U.S., 1949, naturalized, 1955; s. Adolph and Erica (Leventals) Alperovitch; m. Joan Elizabeth Fleming, Nov. 12, 1955; children: George Charles, Nanci Elizabeth. Student, U. Munich, Germany, 1946-49; AM, Columbia U., 1951, PhD, 1954; DrChem honoris causa, Latvian Acad. Scis., 2000. Instr. U. Ill., 1954-55; mem. faculty U. Chgo., 1955—, prof. chemistry, 1962-73, Horace B. Horton prof. chemistry, 1973-91, Horace B. Horton prof. emeritus, 1991—; vis. prof. Calif. Inst. Tech., 1960, U. Berne, Switzerland, 1963-64, 70, 78, 80, 83, 87, 89-90; research asso. Field Mus. Natural History, Chgo., 1968-91; resident research asso. NASA, 1961. Cons. NASA, 1961—69, mem. lunar sample analysis planning team, 1967—69. Assoc. editor: Geochimica et Cosmochimica Acta, 1966-73, Icarus, 1970-91, Earth, Moon and Planets, 1974-91; contbr. articles to profl. jours. Recipient Univ. medal for excellence Columbia U., 1966; Quantrell award for excellence in undergrad. tchg. U. Chgo., 1973; NASA medal for exceptional sci. achievement, 1973; Guggenheim fellow, 1973-74; Fairchild disting. scholar Calif. Inst. Tech., 1992-93. Fellow: AAAS (Newcomb Cleveland prize 1959), Am. Geophys. Union (Harry H. Hess medal 1995), Am. Acad. Arts and Scis., Meteoritical Soc. (v.p. 1968—72, 1989—90, pres. 1991—92, Leonard medal 1974); mem.: Acad. Creative Endeavors (fgn. mem.), Geochem. Soc. (hon., v.p. 1987—88, Goldschmidt medal 1990), Royal Astron. Soc. (assoc.), Internat. Astron. Union (pres. com. on moon 1976—79), NAS (J. Lawrence Smith medal 1971), Am. Astron. Soc. (chmn. divsn. planetary scis. 1971—72, Kuiper prize 1991). Achievements include research on the origin, age, composition of meteorites and lunar rocks, interstellar grains in meteorites, origin moon and planets. E-mail: marquis@anders2.com.

ANDERS, GEORGE CHARLES, writer, journalist; b. Chgo., Nov. 12, 1957; s. Edward and Joan Elizabeth (Fleming) Anders; m. Elizabeth Anne Corcoran, Aug. 27, 1988. BA in Econs., Stanford U., 1978. Nat. copyreader Wall St. Jour., N.Y.C., 1978—81, Heard on the St. columnist, 1981—82, London bur. chief European edit., 1982—85, news editor, 1985—89, sr. spl. writer, 1988—2000; sr. editor Fast Company Mag., 2000—03; writer Wall St. Jour., 2003—. Contbg. editor: SmartMoney mag., 1992—95; author: Merchants of Debt, 1992, Health Against Wealth, 1996, Perfect Enough, 2003. Co-recipient Pulitzer Prize for nat. reporting, 1997; recipient Janus award, Am. Mortgage Bankers Assn., 1987.

ANDERS, HARLEY DILLON, SR., retired federal agency administrator; b. Clarita, Okla., Nov. 9, 1918; s. Harley Anders and Malsey Fay Simmons; m. Eleanor J. Fitzwater, July 17, 1941 (div. Nov. 12, 1963); children: Harley, Vicki. Enlisted U.S. Army, 1939—42; advanced through grade to 2d lt. U. S. Army, 1942; claims examiner U.S. Dept. VA, Muskogee, 1944—66, chief claims svc. Juneau, Alaska, 1966—72, dir. Alaska region, 1972—74; ret., 1974. Cons. comprehensive health State of Alaska, Juneau, 1972—74. Author: (genealogy) The Ancestors and Descendants of Elias M. Anders of Missouri, 1985; editor: (book) Genealogical Gleanings in Southeast United States, 1997; author: The Life and Times of John Turnbull, Indian Trader, 1997. Avocations: genealogy, archaeology. Home: 17543 102nd Ave NE #224 Bothell WA 98011

ANDERS, JANE VIRGINIA, genealogist; b. Alexandria, Va., Aug. 5, 1957; d. William King Anders and Virginia Dare Currie. Student, Draughons Coll., 1981-82. Genealogy rschr. Mem. Doane Family Assn., Bladen County Hist. Soc., The Statue of Liberty-Ellis Island Found., Inc. (charter), Women in Mil. Svc. Am. Democrat. Avocations: travel, reading, puzzles. Home: 8114 Magnolia Dr Ethel LA 70730-3826

ANDERS, JERROLD P. lawyer; b. Wilkes-Barre, Pa., Sept. 21, 1953; m. Joan Anders, June 28, 1975; children: Jessica, Douglas. AB magna cum laude, Franklin & Marshall Coll., 1975; JD cum laude, U. Pitts., 1978. Jud. law clk. to Hon. Martin J. Coyne Lehigh County Ct. of Common Pleas, 1978-79; ptnr. White and Williams, LLP, Phila., 1979—. Mem. Phi Beta Kappa, Order of Coif. Office: White and Williams LLP 1 Liberty Pl 1650 Market St Ste 1800 Philadelphia PA 19103-7304 E-mail: andersj@whitewms.com.

ANDERS, LARRY ERMEL FAGG, mechanical engineer; b. Brazil, Ind., Aug. 13, 1949; s. Ermel Richard and Wanda Lou (Butt) F.; m. Leila Palmer Buck, Aug. 30, 1970; children: David Ericson, Leigh-Ann Kristin. BSME, Rose-Hulman Inst., 1971; postgrad., Nat. Radio Inst., Washington, 1973; MBA, Ea. Ill. U., 1983. Registered profl. engr., Ill., Ind.; cert. power engr., Ind. With tech. sales dept. Powered Equipment Inc., Terre Haute, Ind., 1971-72; corp. mgr. compliance, energy and projects Ill. Cereal Mills Inc., Paris, 1972-97; COO A&E Global Enterprises, Paris, 1997-99, CEO, 1999—2001; pres. AFC, 2001—. V.p. bd. Paris YMCA, 1988; campaign chmn. Paris United Way, 1987 (plaque 1987); pres. bd. Paris C. of C., 1987; co-author energy policy Ill. State C. of C., 1982; active Air Pollution Control Assn.; coach youth baseball, basketball and soccer, Paris, 1983—; election judge Edgar County, Ill., 1998—. Mem. Assn. Energy Engrs. (sr., cert. energy mgr., v.p.-at-large 1988, cogeneration cert., energy profession devel. award 1987), Assn. Operative Millers (dist. chmn. 1987), ASME, Wabash Valley Amateur Radio Assn., Am. Radio Relay League, Toastmasters (pres. 1985, toastmaster of yr. Paris chpt. 1984, competent toastmaster), Delta Mu Delta. Mem. Ch. of Christ. Avocations: sports, photography, travel, music, theater. Office: Ill Cereal Mills Inc 616 S Jefferson St Paris IL 61944-2000

ANDERS, TISA MAREE, social justice minister; b. Pueblo, Colo., Dec. 1, 1960; d. Dale Eugene Anders and Mary Elizabeth Cotton-Anders. BA, U. Nebr., Omaha, 1983, MS, 1989; MDiv, Iliff Sch. Theology, 1993; PhD, U. Denver/Iliff, 2002. Ordained minister Christian Ch. (Disciples of Christ), 1993. Social worker Nebr. Dept. Social Svcs., Omaha, 1983-90; chaplain Hospice of St. John, Lakewood, Colo., 1991; bookstore asst. Iliff Sch. Theology 1991. Bookstore, Denver, 1991-92, 95-96; devel. dir. New Founds. Nonviolence Ctr., Denver, 1993-95, assoc. dir., 1997—2003, exec. dir., 2003—; assoc. coord. justice and peace studies Iliff Sch. Theology, 1995; grad. tchg. asst. U. Denver, 1996-97. Guest preacher Christian Ch. (Disciples of Christ) Ctrl. Rocky Mountain Region, Colo., 1993—; grant writing seminar instr. New Founds. Nonviolence Ctr., 1999—, vol. nonviolence trainer, 1994—; retreat leader Covenant of Gethsemane, Colo., 1990-97, leadership coun., 1990-97. Co-chair Ctrl. Rocky Mountain Regional Global Partnerships Project, 1995-97; bd. dirs. Priority Peace. U. Nebr. Regents scholar, 1979-83, Ann E. Dickerson scholar Christian Ch. (Disciples of Christ), 1995-97, Cotner Coll. scholar, 1995-01; recipient Eastern Star award, 1996-2001. Fellow Soc. for Values in Higher Edn.; mem. Coord. Coun. for Women in History, Missionary Benedictine Oblate Program, Priority Peace. Democrat. Avocations: reading, writing, movies, friends, travel. Office: PO Box 18087 Denver CO 80218-0087

ANDERSEN, BURTON ROBERT, physician, educator; b. Chgo., Aug. 27, 1932; s. Burton R. and Alice C. (Mara) A.; m. Susan Berg; children: Ellen C., Julia A., Brian E., Jennifer Berg. Student, Northwestern U., 1950-51; BS, U. Ill., Urbana, 1953; MS, U. Ill., Chgo., 1957; MD, U. Ill., 1957. Intern Mpls. Gen. Hosp., 1957-58; resident and fellow U. Ill. Hosp., 1958-61; clin. assoc. NIH, Bethesda, Md., 1961-64; asst. prof. U. Rochester, N.Y., 1964-67; assoc. prof. Northwestern U., 1967-70; prof. medicine and microbiology U. Ill., Chgo., 1970—, chief infectious diseases, 1986-99, West Side VA Med. Ctr., 1970-90. Contbr. sci. research articles to profl. jours. Served as sr. surgeon USPHS, 1961-63. Grantee Rsch. grantee, NEH, 2000—03. Fellow ACP; mem. Am. Assn. Immunologists, Am. Soc. for Clin. Investigation, Central Soc. for Clin. Research. Achievements include research in on ancient Mesopotamian medicine. Office: U Ill Sect Infectious Diseases 808 S Wood St Chicago IL 60612-7300

ANDERSEN, HANS CHRISTIAN, chemistry educator; b. Bklyn., Sept. 25, 1941; m. June Jenny, June 17, 1967; children: Hans Christian, Albert William. SB, MIT, 1962, PhD, 1966. Jr. fellow Soc. Fellows Harvard U., Cambridge, 1965-68; asst. prof. chemistry Stanford (Calif.) U., 1968—74; assoc. prof. Stanford U., 1974—80, prof., 1980—, assoc. dean Sch. Humanities and Scis., 1996—99, chmn. dept. chemistry, 2002—. Vis. prof. chemistry Columbia U., N.Y.C., 1981-82; co-dir. Stanford Ctr. for Materials Rsch., 1988-89, dep. dir., 1989-95; mem. allocation com. San Diego Supercomputer Ctr., 1986-89, chmn., 1988-89; vice-chmn. Gordon Rsch. Conf. on Physics and Chemistry of Liquids, 1989, chmn. 1991. Mem. editl. com.: Ann. Rev. Phys. Chemistry, 1983—87, mem. editl. bd.: Procs. of the NAS, 2002—, Jour. Chem. Physics, 1984—86, Chem. Physics, 1986—96, mem. adv. bd.: Jour. Phys. Chemistry, 1987—92. Sloan fellow, 1972-74, Guggenheim fellow, 1976-77. Fellow AAAS, Am. Acad. Arts and Scis., Am. Phys. Soc.; mem. NAS, Am. Chem. Soc. (chmn. phys. chemistry divsn. 1986, Joel Henry Hildebrand award 1988).

ANDERSEN, JAMES A. retired state supreme court justice; b. Auburn, Wash., Sept. 21, 1924; s. James A. and Margaret Cecelia (Norgaard) A.; m. Billiette B. Andersen; children: James Blair, Tia Louise. BA, U. Wash., 1949, JD, 1951. Bar: Wash. 1952, U.S. Dist. Ct. (we. dist.) Wash. 1957, U.S. Ct. Appeals 1957. Dep. pros. atty. King County, Seattle, 1953-57; assoc. Lycette, Diamond & Sylvester, Seattle, 1957-61; ptnr. Clinton, Anderson, Fleck & Glein, Seattle, 1961-75; judge Wash. State Ct. of Appeals, Seattle, 1975-84; justice Wash. State Supreme Ct., Olympia, 1984-92, chief justice, 1992-95; ret., 1995. Chair Legis. Ethics Bd. Mem. Wash. State Ho. of Reps., 1958-67, Wash. State Senate, 1967-72. Served with U.S. Army, 1943-45, ETO. Decorated Purple Heart; recipient Disting. Alumnus award U. Wash. Sch. of Law, 1995. Mem. ABA, Wash. State Bar Assn., Am. Judicature Soc. Home: 3008 98th Ave NE Bellevue WA 98004-1817

ANDERSEN, JERRY RAE, music educator; d. Rex Lee and Margaret Reed Schwein; m. Gary Nicholas Wolz, May 27, 2001; m. Dennies Dale Andersen, Dec. 21, 1974 (div. July 16, 1986); children: Darin, Kendra. MusB in Edn., Ft. Hays State U., 1974, MS, 1979; cert. edn. specialist, U. Mo., Kansas City, 1996. Cert. elem. tchr. Mo., music tchr. K-9 Mo. Music educator USD of Garden City, Kans., 1974—78, USD of Coldwater, Kans., 1981—82; 2nd grade tchr. Kansas City Mo. Sch. Dist., 1987—91, 5th grade tchr., 1991—97, mid. sch. tchr., 1997—2000; music educator Kans. City Mo. Sch. Dist., 2000—. Organist St. Regis Cath. Ch., Kans. City, 1989—, Holy Spirit Cath. Ch., Lee's Summit, Mo., 1999—. Grantee Gt. Ideas grantee, Kauffman Found., 2001. Mem.: Music Educators Nat. Conf., Mo. State Tchrs. Assn. Avocations: swimming, reading, bicycling, computers, theater. Office: Kansas City Missouri Sch District 6201 E 17th St Kansas City MO 64126

ANDERSEN, K(ENT) TUCKER, investment executive; b. Manchester, Conn., June 5, 1942; s. Alfred Hans and Dorothy Emily (Ray) A.; m. Karen Ann Kirchofer, Oct. 11, 1963; children: Heather Michele, Kristen Eileen. Student, Phillips Exeter Acad., N.H., 1957-59; BA, Wesleyan U., 1963. Chartered fin. analyst. Actuarial student Travelers Ins. Co., Hartford, Conn., 1963-66; security analyst Smith Barney & Co., N.Y.C., 1968-69; ptnr. Rudman Assocs., N.Y.C., 1969-72, Cumberland Assocs. LLC, N.Y.C., 1972—, mng. ptnr., 1982-96, chief investment strategist, 1997—. Bd. dirs. Cato Inst., Washington, 1987—, exec. com., 1992—; trustee YWCA of Montclair, North Essex, N.J., 1980—, 1st United Meth. Ch., Montclair, 1976-94, Martin Luther King Scholarship Fund Montclair, 1989-94, Phillips Exeter Acad., 1989—, chmn. investment com., 1992—, bd. v.p. and chmn. exec. com., 1993—, admissions rep. N.J. area, 1983-93; exec. com. GOPAC, 1993—, bd. dirs., 1995—. With USPHS, 1966-68. Recipient Disting. Alumnus award Wesleyan U., 1988. Mem. Soc. Actuaries, N.Y. Soc. Security Analysts, Inst. Chartered Fin. Analysts, Polit. Club for Growth (mem. exec. com. 1984-94), Kappa Nu Kappa (pres. 1963). Republican. Avocation: N.Y.C. marathons. Office: Cumberland Assocs 38th Fl 1114 Avenue Of The Americas New York NY 10036-7703

ANDERSEN, KURT BYARS, writer; b. Omaha, Aug. 22, 1954; s. Robert and Jean (Swarr) A.; m. Anne (Kreamer), May 9, 1981; children: Katherine, and Lucy. AB magna cum laude, Harvard U., 1976. Writer NBC-TV, N.Y.C., 1976-80, Time Mag., N.Y.C., 1981-84, arch. critic, 1984-93, columnist, 1993-94; co-founder, co-editor Spy Mag., N.Y.C., 1986-93; editor-in-chief New York Mag., N.Y.C., 1994-96; columnist The New Yorker, N.Y.C., 1996-99; co-founder, co-chmn. Inside, N.Y.C., 1999—. Author: The Real Thing, 1980; Turn of the Century, 1999; co-author: Tools of Power, 1980; (off-Broadway revue and book) Loose Lips, 1994-95, 98; exec. prodr. TV pilots After Hours, 1987; Zero Hour; 1991, Pranks, 1992; exec. prodr., co-writer TV spl. How To Be Famous, 1990; The Hit List, 1992; host TV spl. Comedy Spotlight, 1996; radio show Studio 360, 2000—. Recipient journalism award ABA, 1983; Page One Award Newspaper Guild N.Y., 1984. Mem.: bd. of trustees Pratt Inst. E-mail: kastudio360@wnyc.org.*

ANDERSEN, LAIRD BRYCE, retired university administrator; b. Madison, S.D., Sept. 16, 1928; s. Andrew Christopher and Alyce (Farrington) A.; m. Joan Roberta Westwood, Nov. 23, 1961; children— Christopher Frederick, Elizabeth Virginia. BS, U. Minn., 1950, MS, 1951, MA, 1961; PhD, U. Ill., 1954. Registered profl. engr., Mass., N.J. Asst. prof. Lehigh U., 1954-59; assoc. prof. Rice U., 1959-60, U. Nebr., 1961-63; prof., assoc. dean engring. N.J. Inst. Tech., 1963-66, dean engring., 1966-75, dean acad. affairs, 1972-74, v.p. acad. affairs, 1974-75, prof. chem. engring., 1975-80; dean Coll. Engring. U. Mass. Dartmouth, North Dartmouth, 1980-93, interim provost, 1993-94. Co-author: Principles of Unit Operations, 1960, 2d edit., 1980, Introduction to Chemical Engineering, 1960. Mem. Am. Soc. Engring. Edn. (chmn. chem. engring. div. 1967), Am. Inst. Chem. Engrs., Sigma Xi, Phi Lambda Upsilon, Tau Beta Pi, Alpha Chi Sigma, Triangle. Home: 28 Holly Ln Mattapoisett MA 02739-2110

ANDERSEN, LEONARD CHRISTIAN, former state legislator, real estate investor; b. Waukegan, Ill., May 30, 1911; s. Lauritz Frederick and Meta Marie (Jacobsen) A.; m. Charlotte O. Ritland, June 30, 1937; children: Karen Schneider, Paul R., Charlene Olsson, Mark Luther. BA, Huron (S.D.) Coll., 1933; MA, U. S.D., 1937. Tchr. Onida (S.D.) H.S., 1934-35; dir. bus. tng. Waldorf Coll., Forest City, Iowa, 1935-39; ins. salesman, 1939-41; tchrs. econs., current history Morningside Coll., Sioux City, Iowa, 1941-43; engaged in ins. and real estate Sioux City, 1943-76. Mem. Iowa Ho. of Reps. from Woodbury County, 1961-64, 66-71; mem. Iowa Senate from 26th Dist., 1972-76, chmn. rules and adminstrn. com. Former mem. Iowa Commn. on Aging; former mem. investment adv. bd. IPERS; former mem. cen. com. Woodbury County Reps., del. county, dist. and state convs.; former mem. Simpco Projects Rev. Com.; former pres., chmn. bd. Siouxland Rental Assn.; past mem. Sioux City Housing Appeals Bd., Siouxland Council on Alcoholism; bd. regents Augustana Coll., Sioux Falls, S.D., 12 yrs., now mem., now co-chair call com., mem. fin. com.active Rep. Party Campaigns; del. to state, dist. and county Rep. convs., Iowa, 1998, 2000; bd. dirs. Human Rights Commn., Sioux City, 1997-2003. Del. Evang. Luth. Ch. Conv., 1999, 2000, 01, 03, promoter Wordalone movement; apptd. anti-violence com. Siouxland Area. Mem. Masons, Lions. Home: 3112 Nebraska St Apt 2 Sioux City IA 51104-3948 E-mail: LAnde11211@aol.com.

ANDERSEN, LUBA, electrologist, electropigmentologist; b. Germany, Mar. 29, 1945; came to U.S., 1955; d. Osyp and Justyna (Drozd) Nahorniak; m. Roger A. Andersen, Dec. 9, 1989 (div. Oct. 2001). A in Bus. and Acctg., DePaul U., 1977; BS in Commerce and Social Studies, LaSalle U., 1978; postgrad., U. Mich., 1984; cert., Ariz. Inst. Electrolysis, 1993. Cert. profl. electrologist, clin. electropigmentologist. From analyst to contr. Fed. Home Loan Bank, Chgo., 1965-83, v.p., contr., 1985-92; owner The Electrolysis Connection, Tucson, 1993—. Mem. NAFE, Am. Soc. Women Accts. (chair bylaws com. 1981), Am. Electrology Assn., Electrologists Assn. Ariz., Internat. Guild Profl. Electrologists, Inc., Fin. Mgrs. Soc., Soc. Cosmetic Profls., Assn. Clin. Electropigmentologists. Republican. Roman Catholic. Avocation: creating tapestries. Office: Electrolysis Connection 11038 N Canada Ridge Dr Tucson AZ 85737-8796 E-mail: landersensprint@earthlink.com.

ANDERSEN, MARIANNE SINGER, clinical psychologist; b. Baden nr. Vienna, Austria; came to U.S., 1940; naturalized, 1946; d. Richard L. and Jolanthe (Garda) Singer; 1 child, Richard Esten. BA, CUNY, 1950, MA, 1974; PhD, Fla. Inst. Tech., 1980. Rsch. assoc. Inst. for Rsch. in Hypnosis, N.Y.C., 1974-76, fellow in clin. hypnosis, 1976, dir. seminars, 1978-82, dir. edn., 1982—; psychotherapist specializing in hypnotherapy Morton Prince Ctr. for Hypnotherapy, dir. clin. svcs., 1981-82; dir. adminstrn. Internat. Grad. U., N.Y.C., 1974-77; pvt. practice psychotherapy, 1977—. Adminstrv. coordinator Internat. Grad. Sch. Behavior Sci., Fla. Inst. Tech., 1978; co-dir. The Melbourne Group, 1983—90; clin. instr. hypnotherapy Mt. Sinai Sch. Medicine, N.Y.C., 1996—; lectr. hypnosis and hypnotherapy to mental and phys. health profls., 1977—. Author: (with Louis Savary) Passages: A Guide for Pilgrims of the Mind, 1972; rsch. on treatment of obesity with hypnotherapy; book editor specializing in psychology and psychiatry including W.W. Norton Co., Sterling Pub. Co., E.P. Dutton Co., 1950-71. Fellow Soc. for Clin. and Exptl. Hypnosis; mem. APA, Internat. Soc. Clin. and Exptl. Hypnosis. Home: 60 W 57th St New York NY 10019-3909

ANDERSEN, MARIN (ROBYN), research scientist; d. Sidnee Lee Andersen-Crawford and Niels Hjorth Andersen; children: Kathryn, Christine Cornell. Grad. Cert. in Women's Studies, SUNY, Stony Brook, 1992, PhD, 1994; MPH, U. of Wash. Sch. of Pub. Health, 1996. Post doctoral fellow Fred Hutchinson Cancer Rsch. Ctr., Seattle, 1994—96, staff scientist, 1996—97, asst. mem., 1997—2003, assoc. mem., 2003—; clin. asst. prof. Dept. of Health Svcs., Sch. of Pub. Health and Cmty. Medicine, U. of Wash., Seattle, 1999—. Mem.: Soc. for Behavioral Medicine, APA. Office: Fred Hutchinson Cancer Rsch Ctr 1100 Fairview Ave N Seattle WA 98109-1024

ANDERSEN, NIELS HJORTH, chemistry educator, biophysics researcher, consultant; b. Copenhagen, Oct. 9, 1943; came to U.S. 1949; s. Orla and Inger (Larsen) A.; m. Sidnee Lee (div. 1986); children: Marin Christine, Beth Arkady; m. Susan Howell, July 21, 1987. BA, U. Minn., 1963; PhD, Northwestern U., 1967. Rsch. assoc and fellow Harvard U., Cambridge, Mass., 1966-68; asst. prof. U. Wash., Seattle, 1968-72, assoc. prof., 1972-76, prof., 1976—; prin. scientist ALZA Corp., Palo Alto, Calif., 1970-75. Cons. Genetic Systems, Seattle, 1984-86, Bristol-Myer Squibb, Princeton, N.J., 1984-95, Amylin Pharmaceutics, San Diego, 1992-2001 Receptron Corp., Mountain View, Calif., 1995—2001, Chiron, Seattle, 1997—2003. Mem. adv. bd. Biopolymers; contbr. articles to profl. jours. Recipient Teacher-Scholar award Dreyfus Found., 1974-79, Career Devel. award NIH, 1975-80. Mem. AAAS, Am. Chem. Soc., Am. Peptide Soc., Protein Soc. Democrat. Avocations: contemporary folk music and swing, dulcimer playing. Office: U Wash Dept Chem PO Box 351700 Seattle WA 98195-1700 E-mail: andersen@chem.washington.edu.

ANDERSEN, RICHARD ESTEN, lawyer; b. N.Y.C., Oct. 26, 1957; s. Arnold and Marianne (Singer) A.; m. Patricia Anne Woods, May 9, 1987; children: Benjamin Singer, David Woods. BA, Columbia U., 1978, JD, 1981; LLM, NYU, 1987. Bar: N.Y. 1982, U.S. Tax Ct. 1982. Ptnr. Arnold & Porter, N.Y.C. Mem. bd. advisors Jour. Internat. Taxation, Jour. Taxation Global Transactions, World Trade Exec., Tax Mgmt., Inc.; adj. prof. law grad. tax LLM program NYU. Author: Foreign Tax Credits, 1996, U.S. Income Tax Withholding (Fgn. Persons), 1997, Income Tax Treaties of the United States, revised edit., 2002. Mem.: ABA, Internat. Tax Assn. (pres. 2000—02), Internat. Fiscal Assn. (mem. USA br. coun., N.Y. exec. com.), Internat. Tax Inst., N.Y. State Bar Assn. Office: Arnold & Porter 399 Park Ave New York NY 10022 E-mail: richard_andersen@aporter.com.

ANDERSEN, ROBERT, health products, business executive; b. Bklyn., Oct. 9, 1937; s. Ingulf Bertel Andersen and Helen Jane Akin (McDowell) Miller; m. Elaine Marie Wood, June 13, 1958; children: Susan Marie, Robert Alan, Dori Ann. Grad. h.s., La Mesa, Calif. Area sales mgr. Golden Arrow Dairy, San Diego, 1958-66; retail sales mgr. Hollandia Dairy, San Marcos, Calif., 1966-69; pres. Health Best Inc., San Marcos, 1969-98; founding ptnr. Escondido Mills, San Marcos, 1980—; owner, operator Andersen Trading Co., Valley Center, Calif., 1984—; ptnr. Earth Products, Valley Center, 1989—; founding ptnr. Elaina's Snacks, San Marcos, 1991-94; owner, operator Andersen Gallery, Valley Center, 1992-98; pres. Gisé LLC, 1997—2001. Bd. dirs. Russian Art Guild, San Diego, 1992-96; pres. Kamut Assn. N.Am., San Marcos, 1997—. Republican. Avocation: poetry. Home: 30126 Castlecrest Dr Valley Center CA 92082-4923

ANDERSEN, ROBERT ALLEN, retired government official; b. Denver, Aug. 27, 1936; s. Emmett Christian and Margaret Irene (Maupin) A.; m. Jane Eng (dec.), May 13, 1967. AB in Polit Sci., U. S.C., 1958, MA in Polit Sci., 1961; postgrad. in law, U. Colo., 1958-59; PhD in Internat. Relations, Am. U., 1973. Area coordinator for econ. devel. Area Redevel. Adminstrn., Commerce Dept., 1962-64; acting dir. urban projects div., program officer, chief Project Adminstrn. VISTA (OEO), Washington, 1964-66; implementation programming, planning and budgeting system Office Program Planning and Evaluation, Office Edn., 1966-67; staff asst. to dep. postmaster gen. Postal Service, 1967-72, sr. planning officer, 1972-74; dir. evaluation Immigration and Naturalization Service, Washington, 1974-86, dir. Office of Program Inpection, 1986-88; dir. mgmt., planning and review Office Inspector Gen., Dept. Justice, Washington, 1988-90, dir. quality assurance rev., 1990-97; ret., 1997. Past pres. bd. dirs. D.C. Assn. Retarded Citizens; past. sec. The Arc. Episcopalian. Home: 5701 Nebraska Ave NW Washington DC 20015-1221

ANDERSEN, RONALD MAX, health services educator, researcher; b. Omaha, 1939; s. Max Adolph and Evangeline Dorothy (Wobbe) Andersen; m. Diane Borella, June 19, 1965; 1 child, Rachel. BS, U. Santa Clara, 1960; MS, Purdue U., 1962, PhD, 1968. Rsch. assoc. Purdue U., West Lafayette, Ind., 1962—63; assoc. study dir. Nat. Opinion Rsch. Ctr., Chgo., 1963—66; rsch. assoc. U. Chgo., 1963—77, from assoc. prof. to prof. Grad. Sch. Bus., 1974—90, dir. Program in Health Adminstrn. and Ctr. for Health Adminstrn. Studies, 1980—90; Wasserman prof. dept. health svcs. and sociology UCLA, 1991—, chmn. dept. health svcs., 1993—96. Com. mem. Agy. for Health Care Policy and Rsch., Rockville, Md., 1970—. Mem. editl. bd.: Health Adminstrn. Press, 1980—83, 1988—98, Med. Care Rsch. & Rev., 1994—; author: A Decade of Health Services, 1967, Two Decades of Health Service, 1976, Total Survey Error, 1979, Health Services in the U.S., 1980, Ambulatory Care and Insurance Coverage in an Era of Constraint, 1987, Training Physicians, 1994, Changing the U.S. Health Care System, 1996. Fellow, NIH, 1960—62; grantee, Agy. for Health Care Policy and Rsch, 1982, Robert Wood Johnson Found., 1983, Kaiser Family Found., 1983, WHO, 1990. Mem.: APHA, Assn. for Health Svcs. Rsch. (Disting. Career award 1996), Assoc. Univ. Program in Health Adminstrn. (Baxter Allegiance prize 1999), Assn. for Health Services Rsch. (dir. 1981—83), Inst. Medicine NAS, Am. Sociol. Assn. (chmn. med. sociology sect. 1980—81, Disting. Med. Sociologist 1994). Roman Catholic. Home: 10724 Wilshire Blvd Apt 312 Los Angeles CA 90024-4453 Office: UCLA Sch Pub Health Los Angeles CA 90024

ANDERSEN, RONALD MEREDITH, lawyer; b. Blair, Nebr., Nov. 26, 1943; s. Henry Leonard and Dorthea Marie (Sorensen) A. BS, U. Wis., Madison, 1966; JD, U. Denver, 1971. Bar: Colo. 1971, Ariz. 1981, U.S. Dist. Ct. Colo. 1971, U.S. Dist. Ct. Ariz. 1981, U.S. Ct. Appeals (10th cir.) 1976, U.S. Ct. Appeals (9th cir.) 1991, U.S. Supreme Ct. Ins. adjuster State Farm Ins. Cos., Greeley, Colo., 1967-69; law clk. Colo. Judiciary, Denver, 1969-71; appellate dep. Adams County Dist. Attys. Office, Brighton, Colo., 1971-73; ptnr. Johnston & Andersen, Denver, 1973-79; trial atty. EEOC, Phoenix, 1979-88; asst. atty. gen. State of Ariz., 1991-93; staff atty. Indsl. Commn. Ariz., Phoenix, 1993—. Mem. Ariz. Bar Assn. Office: Indsl Commn Ariz 800 W Washington #303 Phoenix AZ 85007 E-mail: rona@ica.state.az.us.

ANDERSEN, ROY STUART, physicist; b. Springfield, Mass., Oct. 16, 1921; s. O. William and Gladys (Merry) A.; m. Barbara Anne Norris, June 11, 1944; children: Karen Jana, Loring Dodd, Scott William. BA, Clark U., 1943; AM, Darmouth Coll., 1948; PhD, Duke U., 1951. Rsch. engr. Stanford Rsch. Inst., Palo Alto, Calif., 1951-52; from asst. prof. physics to assoc. prof. U. Md., College Park, 1952-60; prof. physics Clark U., Worcester, Mass., 1960-92, chmn. dept. phnysics, 1960-70, 71-72, dean grad. sch., 1970-71, prof. emeritus, 1992—. Rsch. assoc. Duke U., Durham, N.C., 1951, 53, 54, U. Calif., Berkeley, 1958-59, Woods Hole (Mass.) Oceangraphic Inst., 1961. Researcher of microwave spectroscopy of atoms and molecules, radiation damage; contbr. articles to profl. jours. Lt. USNR, 1943-46, PTO. Named Sr. Fellow in Sci., NATO, 1973. Fellow Am. Phys. Soc.; mem. Am. Assn. Physics Tchrs., N.Am. Soc. Ocean History, History Sci. Soc.

ANDERSEN, SUSAN MARIE, educator, researcher, clinician, policy advisor; b. Santa Monica, California, June 6, 1955; BA in psychology(hon.), U. Calif., Santa Cruz, 1977; PhD in sychology, Stanford U., 1981. Lic. psychologist Calif., N.Y. Asst. prof. psychology Univ. Calif., Santa Barbara, 1981-87; assoc. prof. NYU, N.Y.C., 1987-94, prof., 1994—, dir. grad. studies in psychology, 1993—97, 2000—02. Cons. Edn. Commn. of the States; Grantmaker Forum for Cmty. and Nat. Svc., Common Cents N.Y.; grants panel, social and group processes rev. panel NIMH, 1992-94, 96, Integrative Grad. Edn. and Rsch. Tng. rev. panel NSF, 2003; other panels. Assoc. editor Jour. Social and Clin. Psychology, 1987-92; Social Cognition, 1993; Jour. Personality and Social Psychology: Attitudes and Social Cognition, 1994-95; Psychol. Rev., 1998-2000; mem. editl. bd. Jour. Personality and Social Psychology, 1990-93, 2000-01, Nouvelle Revue de Psychologie Sociale, 2002—; ad hoc reviewer Jour. Comm. Rsch., Jour. Exptl. Psychology: Learning, Memory & Cognition, Jour. Exptl. Social Psychology, Jour. Personality, Jour. Rsch. in Personality, Motivation and Emotion, Personality and Social Psychology Bull., Psychol. Sci., NSF, Australian Social Sci. Rsch. Coun., Social Sci. and Human Rsch. Coun. of Can., Brit. Jour. Clin. Psychology, Brit. Jour. Social Psychology, Jour. Abnormal Psychology; contbr. numerous articles to profl. jour. Chair svc. learning task force White House Congl. Conf. on Character Bldg.; mem. rsch. and evaluation com. Character Edn. Partnership; mem. rsch. adv. bd. Kellogg Found. Nat. Initiative on Cmty. Svc. in Edn.; Learning in Deed; mem. edn. policy task force Inst. for Comm. Policy Studies, George Washington U.; mem. Russell Sage Found.'s Social Identity Consortium. Recipient Golden Dozen Award N.Y.Univ., 1993; Harold J. Flous Award UCEB, 1985; NIMH grantee 1985-86, 92-98; sr. fellow Inst. for Comm. Policy Studies, George Washington U. Fellow: APA, Soc. Personality and Social Psychology (mem. exec. com.), Am. Psychol. Soc.; mem.: Soc. Psychol. Study of Social Issues, Soc. Advancement of Socio Econ., Soc. Exptl. Social Psychology, Internat. Soc. Self and Identity. Office: Dept Psychology NY Univ 6 Washington Pl 4th Fl New York NY 10003-6603 E-mail: andersen@psych.nyu.edu.

ANDERSEN, THEODORE SELMER, engineering manager; b. N.Y.C., Dec. 4, 1944; s. Selmer and Irene Frances (McManus) A.; m. Elva Glenna Layden, June 19, 1965; children: Elva Irene, Theodore Christian, Caroline Elizabeth. BChemE, Cooper Union, 1965; MSChemE, U. Pitts., 1968, PhDChemE, 1971, MBA, 1977. Registered profl. engr., Pa. From engr. to mgr. compensation, evaluation and tng. Bettis Atomic Power Lab. Westinghouse, West Mifflin, Pa., 1965-77; mgr. emerging systems programs Advanced Energy Systems Div Westinghouse, Waltz Mill, Pa., 1978-84, mgr. energy program, 1985-86, mgr. stragetic program mktg., 1987-88; dep. dir. AP600 Program Nuclear and Advanced Tech. Div. Westinghouse Elec., Pitts., 1989-94; mgr. bus. devel. BECO Engring. Co., Oakmont, Pa., 1995-96; chief process engr. ChemTech Consultants, Inc., Bridgeville, Pa., 1996—. Mem. AIChE, Am. Chem. Soc., Am. Wind Energy Assn. (pres. 1981-84), Am. Nuclear Soc. Republican. Methodist. Home: 5170 Caste Dr Pittsburgh PA 15236-1646 Office: ChemTech Consultants Inc 1370 Washington Pike Bridgeville PA 15017-2839

ANDERSEN, TORBEN BRENDER, optical researcher, astronomer, software engineer; b. Naestved, Denmark, May 17, 1954; came to U.S., 1983; U.S. citizen, 1994; s. Bjarne and Anna Margrethe (Brender) A.; children: Iris, Erik. PhD, Copenhagen U., Denmark, 1979. Rsch. fellow Copenhagen U., 1980-82, sr. rsch. fellow, 1982-85; optical cons. Nordic Optical Telescope Assn., Roskilde, Denmark, 1985; optical systems analyst Telos Corp., Santa Clara, Calif., 1985-88; rsch. scientist Lockheed Martin Missiles and Space, Palo Alto, Calif., 1988-93, staff scientist, 1993-95, sr. staff scientist, 1995-96, staff software engr., 1996—. Vis. scholar Optical Scis. Ctr., U. Ariz., Tucson, 1983-85. Editor: Astronomical Papers Dedicated to Bengt Strömgren, 1978; contbr. articles to Jour. Quantitative Spectroscopy Radiation Transfer, Applied Optics, Astronomische Nachrichten. Mem. Optical Soc. Am., Internat. Astron. Union, Soc. Photo-Optical Instrumentation Engrs. Achievements include development of method for computing optical aberration coefficients to arbitrarily high orders; discovery of set of differential equations for the Voigt function; contributing to optical design software. Office: Lockheed Martin Advanced Tech Ctr O/L9-23 3251 Hanover St # B201 Palo Alto CA 94304-1121 E-mail: torben.andersen@lmco.com.

ANDERSLAND, MARK STEVEN, electrical and computer engineering educator; b. Lansing, Mich., June 9, 1961; s. Orlando Baldwin and Phyllis Elaine (Burgess) A.; m. Mary Susan Pruzinsky, Oct. 7, 1995. BSEE, U. Mich., 1983, MSEE, 1984, PhD, 1989. Asst. prof. dept. elec. and computer engring. U. Iowa, Iowa City, 1989-95, assoc. prof., 1995—. Contbr. articles to IEEE Transactions on Automatic Control, SIAM Jour. on Control and Optimization, Automatica, Sys. & Control Letters, Jour. Optimization Theory & Applications, Jour. of the Operational Rsch. Soc; patentee in field. Hewlett Packard Faculty Devel. fellow, 1984-88. Mem. IEEE, Soc. Indsl. and Applied Math., Tau Beta Pi, Eta Kappa Nu. Office: U Iowa Dept Elec and Computer Engring Iowa City IA 52242

ANDERSLAND, ORLANDO BALDWIN, civil engineering educator; b. Albert Lea, Minn., Aug. 15, 1929; s. Ole Larsen and Brita Kristine (Okland) A.; m. Phyllis Elaine Burgess, Aug. 15, 1958; children: Mark, John, Ruth BCE, U. Minn., 1952; MSCE, Purdue U., 1956, PhD, 1960. Registered profl. engr., Minn., Mich. Staff engr. NAS, Am. Assn. State Hwy. Ofcls. Road Test, Ottawa, Ill., 1956-57; rsch. engr. Purdue U., West Lafayette, Ind., 1957-59; mem. faculty Mich. State U., East Lansing, 1960—, prof. civil engring., 1968—, prof. emeritus, 1994—. Co-author: Geotechnical Software for the IBM, PC, 1987, Geotechnical Engineering and Soil Testing, 1992, An Introduction to Frozen Ground Engineering, 1994, 2d edit., 2003; co-editor: Geotechnical Engineering for Cold Regions, 1978; contbr. chpt. Ground Engineer's Handbook, 1987; contbr. articles to profl. jours.; patentee in field. 1st lt. C.E., U.S. Army, 1952-55. Decorated Nat. Def. Svc. medal; UN Svc. medal; Korean Svc. medal; recipient Best Paper award Assn. Asphalt Paving Technologists, 1956; postdoctoral fellow Norwegian Geotech. Inst., 1966; grantee NSF, EPA, Dept. of Energy. Fellow ASCE (best paper award Cold Regions Engring. Jour. 1991); mem. ASTM (sr.), Internat. Soc. Soil Mechanics and Found. Engring., Am. Soc. Engring. Edn. (life), Sigma Xi, Chi Epsilon, Tau Beta Pi. Lutheran. Home: 901 Woodingham Dr East Lansing MI 48823-1855 Office: Mich State U Dept Civil/Environ Engring East Lansing MI 48824

ANDERSON, AL H., JR., communications executive; b. Winston Salem, N.C., May 4, 1942; s. Al H. Sr. and Gladys (Harris) A.; m. Jeanette R., Nov. 25, 1971; children: April, Albert III. BS, Morehouse Coll., 1964; MBA, Rutgers U., 1970; MS (hon.), Ga. State U., 1972. Mgmt. trainee Allstate Ins. Co., Atlanta, 1968-70; loan officer C&S Bank, Atlanta, 1970-72; v.p. Citizens Trust Bank, Atlanta, 1972-73; pres. Triangle Assocs., Atlanta, 1972-75; chmn., founder Anderson Communications Media, Atlanta, 1975—; pres. The Shiloh Inst., Atlanta, 1979—. Cons. Small Bus. Adminstrn., Atlanta, 1978-85. Dir. Sickle Cell Found. of Ga., Atlanta, 1984, United Way of atlanta, 1987; pres. Cascade Youth Orgn., Atlanta, 1986. Mem. Black Pub. Relations Soc. (v.p. 1986—), Atlanta Bus. League, Atlanta Advt. Club, Pub. Relations Soc. of Am. Democrat. Avocations: classic cars, grand prix racing. Office: Anderson Communications Media 2245 Godby Rd Atlanta GA 30349-5012

ANDERSON, ALAN MARSHALL, lawyer; b. Postville, Iowa, Oct. 23, 1955; s. Hilbert Emil and Wilma Althea (Zumak) Anderson; m. Ann Marie Luken, Aug. 9, 1980. BA magna cum laude, Coe Coll., 1978; MBA with distinction, Cornell U., 1981, JD magna cum laude, 1982; cert. in internat. comml. and bus. law, U. Pacific, 1988. Bar: Minn. 1983, U.S. Dist. Ct. Minn. 1983, U.S. Ct.

Appeals (4th and 8th cirs.) 1983, U.S. Ct. Appeals (10th cir.) 1985, U.S. Ct. Appeals (fed. cir.) 1987, U.S. Supreme Ct. 1990, U.S. Ct. Appeals (7th cir.) 1992, U.S. Ct. Appeals (6th cir.) 2000. Law clk. to cir. judge US Ct. Appeals (4th cir.), Richmond, Va., 1982-83; assoc., then ptnr. Faegre & Benson, Mpls., 1983-90; ptnr. Robins, Kaplan, Miller & Ciresi, Mpls., 1990-92; shareholder Larkin, Hoffman, Daly & Lindgren, Mpls., 1992—2001; ptnr. Fulbright & Jaworski, LLP, Mpls., 2001—. Bd. dirs. Compumedics, Ltd. Contbr. articles to law revs. Named Super Lawyer, State of Minn., 2001, 2002, 2003; recipient Chatman Labor law prize, Cornell Law Sch. Faculty, 1982. Mem.: ABA, Order of Coif, Fed. Cir. Bar Assn., Am. Intellectual Property Law Assn., Minn. Bar Assn. (cert. civil trial specialist 1994, named Leading Am. Atty. 1999), US Judo Assn. (life; nat. bd. legal advisors 1989—94, Silver award), Coe Coll. Alumni Assn. (mem. alumni coun. 1998—2002), Phi Beta Kappa, Phi Kappa Phi. Republican. Lutheran. Avocations: Judo, fishing. Office: Fulbright and Jaworski LLP 225 S 6th St Ste 4850 Minneapolis MN 55402

ANDERSON, ALAN REINOLD, real estate executive, communications consultant; b. Danbury, Conn., Nov. 14, 1949; s. Charles Reinold and Lila Mae (Truesdale) A.; children: Sherry, Erick. AA, U.S. Naval Acad., 1972; BBA, Western Conn. State U., 1975, postgrad., 1977-82, Boeing 727 Flight Engr. Sch., Aviation Tng. Ctr., 1979, Lockheed P-3 Orion Schs., Naval Counterinsurgency Sch., Spl. Warfare Sch. Competitor modified and grand nat. divsns. NASCAR, 1971-79; researcher, clk. Law Offices of Gemza & Daly, Danbury, Conn., 1972-77; prin. Anderson-Ricards & Co., Danbury, 1981-86, A.R. Anderson & Co., Danbury, Conn., 1977—. Conn. liaison Courageous Challenge 1987 America's Cup, 1985-87; town coord. steering and fin. com. Bush/Quayle 88, 1992; mem. George Bush for Pres. Adv. Com. in Conn.; alt. Conn., Rep. Nat. Conv., New Orleans, 1988; town coord. Weicker Gov., Conn., 1991; vice chmn. Environ. Impact Commn., Danbury, 1985-88; co-chmn. Stamford (Conn.) Dinner Com. Bush for Pres., 1987; del. GOP State Conv., 1982; ward chmn. Town Com., 1978-84; asst. football coach Immaculate H.S., 1988; town coord. Prescot Bush for U.S. Senate; town and state coord. Labriola for Gov., 1982, 86; rep. Presdl. Legion Merit; active Rep. Presdl. Task Force, Am. Bicentennial Presdl. Inaugural Ball, Washington, 1989; advisor Forbes for Pres., 1996; sponsor U.S. Navy Meml., Washington; charter mem. U.S. Holocaust Meml. Mus. With USN, 1967-73, Vietnam. Decorated Air medals, DFC, Navy Commendation with Combat V, Vietnam Gallantry Cross, Vietnam Campaign with Silver Star, Navy Unit citation, Meritorious Unit citation. Mem. Assn. Naval Aviation (life), Tailhook Assn. (life), Naval Helicopter Assn., Nat. Sporting Clays Assn., Am. Scandinavian Found., U.S. Naval Acad. Athletic Assn. (commodore, life), Naval Acad. Alumni Assn. (life), Milford Yacht Club, Yale Club (Greater Danbury), N.Y. Sports Clubs. Congregationalist. Avocations: yacht racing, autoracing, weight training, football, golf. Home: 60 Miry Brook Rd Danbury CT 06810-7411

ANDERSON, ALAN STEWART, lawyer; b. Rockville Centre, N.Y., Feb. 26, 1948; s. Donald A. Sr. and Rose (Russo) A.; m. Barbara Lynn Sattler, May 18, 1974; children: Christopher Stewert, Brian Ross. BA, Colgate U., 1970; JD with Honors, George Washington U., 1973. Bar: D.C. 1973, U.S. Dist. Ct. D.C. 1974, U.S. Ct. Appeals (D.C. cir.) 1974, Va. 1975, U.S. Dist. Ct. (ea. dist.) Va. 1975, U.S. Ct. Appeals (4th cir.) 1975, U.S. Supreme Ct. 1977, Md. 1985, U.S. Dist. Ct. Md. 1985. Asst. county atty. Fairfax County, Fairfax, Va., 1975-77; stockholder Tucker Flyer, Washington, 1977—2000; sole propr. Alan S. Anderson, Esquire, 2000—; arbitrator, mediator pvt. practice, 2000—. Mem. 18th jud. cir. Va. State Bar Coun. (com. on lawyer advertising 2002—), 2001—. Elder Westminster Presbyn. Ch., Alexandria, Va., 1987-89, trustee, 1992-94; den leader Webelos Cub Scouts, Alexandria, 1989-91, asst. cubmaster, 1990-97, asst. scoutmaster Boy Scouts Am., 1997-2001; bd. dirs. Colgate U. Alumni Corp., 2000—. Mem. ABA (dispute resolution sect.), Nat. Inst. Trial Advocacy (cert. 1980), Am. Arbitration Assn. (mem. panel arbitrators), Alexandria Bar Assn. (bd. dirs. 1993-99, treas. 1995-96, pres. elect 1996-97, pres. 1997-98), Alexandria Bar Found. (bd. dirs. 1993—, v.p. 1999-2000, 2002—, pres. 2000-2002), Alexandria Crew Boosters (bd. dirs. 2000—), T.C. Williams Wrestling Boosters (bd. dirs. 2000-2002, pres. 2001-2002). E-mail: astewertanderson@aol.com.

ANDERSON, ALFRED OLIVER, mathematician, consultant; b. Marmon, N.D., May 18, 1928; s. Frederick Gustav and Minnie Petrine (Jensen) A. BS, Oreg. State U., 1953. Systems programmer U.S. Army Ballistics Research Lab., Aberdeen (Md.) Proving Ground, 1953-83; cons. Aberdeen, 1983—. Investment specialist, Palermo, Maine, 1983—. Mem. Mensa, Pi Mu Epsilon. Democrat. Lutheran. Avocations: wood working, investment analysis. Home and Office: 107 Banton Rd Palermo ME 04354-6521

ANDERSON, ALLAN, architectural firm executive; BArch cum laude, Carnegie-Mellon U., 1957; MArch, MIT, 1960. Cert. Nat. Coun. Archtl. Registration Bd.; lic. arch., N.Y., Conn., Mass., Pa., Vt., N.H., Fla., R.I., N.J., D.C. With Paul Schweikher, Architect, Pitts., 1957-58, Lawrence and Anthony Wolf, Architects, Pitts., 1958-59, Ulrich Franzen and Assocs., N.Y., 1960-72; pvt. practice, 1972—; ptnr. Anderson La Rocca Anderson Haynes Archs., 1978—. Tchr., lectr. MIT, 1959, Boston Archtl. Ctr., 1960, Pratt Inst., 1962, Cornell U., 1963, McGill U., 1969-76; architect-in-residence White Plains Schs., 1976-82, Bedford, 1979-80, New Rochelle, 1981-82, others; mem. archtl. adv. com. Bd. Edn., Rye, N.Y. Prin. works include Milton Sch. (Honor awards Westchester and N.Y. State chpts. AIA 1977), Microsociety Sch. (Citation Am. Assn. Sch. Bus. Ofcls. 1991, 1st Honor award AIA 1992, Citation Nat. Sch. Bds. Assn. 1993), Rye Mid. Sch. (1st Honor award AIA 1993, Hist. Preservation award City of Rye 1993). Mem. Landmarks Commn., Rye; mem. Arts Gen. Edn. Adv. Coun., City of White Plains, N.Y.; mem. Planning Adv. Com., Rye; bd. dirs. Rye Art Ctr., Rye Performing Arts Coun., Westchester Preservation League. Recipient Hist. Preservation award Rye Mid. Sch., N.Y. Preservation League, 1966, Award for Excellence in Design, N.Y. State Assn. Architects, 1972, Award for Archtl. Excellence, Archtl. Record, 1972, 1st Honor award AIA, House & Home and Am. Home, 1972, Design Excellence award for New Fairfield Mid. Sch., Nat. Sch. Bds. Assn., 1996, Bldg. Design award Pub. Sch. Dist. 15, N.Y.C., Queens County, 1994. Mem. AIA (regional coord. learning by design, mem. environ. edn. com., dir. Westchester-Mid Hudson chpt., 1st Honor award Westchester chpt. 1973, Honor award 1977, Ednl. Program Achievement award N.Y. State chpt. 1978, First Honor award for New Fairfield Mid. Sch. 1996), Coun. Ednl. Facilities Planner Internat. Office: Anderson La Rocca Anderson Haynes Arch 22 Purchase St Rye NY 10580-3003 E-mail: mail@alahrye.com.

ANDERSON, ALLAN CROSBY, hospital executive; b. Jamestown, N.Y., Sept. 18, 1932; s. Emmons E. and Gertrude (Sweet) A.; m. Pauline Culver, June 24, 1956; children: Todd Culver, Emily Ann. BS, Syracuse U., 1954; MHA, U. Minn., 1956. Asst. adminstr. Highland Hosp., Rochester, N.Y., 1959-62, adminstr., 1965-68; asst. dir. Presbyn. Hosp., Phila., 1962-65; exec. dir. Strong Meml. Hosp., U. Rochester, 1968-79; pres. Lenox Hill Hosp., N.Y.C., 1979-89; v.p., COO Milton S. Hershey Med. Ctr., dir. Univ. Hosps. Pa. State U., Hershey, 1990-96; asst. prof. health services U. Rochester Sch. Medicine and Dentistry. Mem. exec. com. Sub-Regional Adminstrs. Group, Adminstrs. Conf., Sub-Regional Exec. Conf.; chmn. bd. dirs. Rochester Regional Hosp. Assn., vice chmn. hosp. planning group; chmn. pub. rels. com., bd. dirs. Rochester Hosp. Svc. Corp.; dir. Univ. Hosp. Consortium, 1990-96, mem. exec. com., 1994-96; mem. Accreditation Coun. for Grad. MEd. Edn., 1990-96, treas., 1992-94, mem. exec. com., 1992-96, chmn., 1995; bd. dirs. Capital Blue Cross, 1993-95, United Way of the Capital Region, 1993-98, mem. exec. com., 1995-98. Mem. blood program com. Rochester-Monroe County chpt. A.R.C.; mem. med. adv. com. Planned Parenthood of Rochester and Monroe County.; Bd. dirs. Rochester Presbyn. Home, 1967-70, Home Care Assn. Rochester and Monroe County, Health Council Monroe County. Served to 1st lt., Med. Service Corps USAF, 1957-59. Mem. Am. Coll. Health Care Execs., Assn. Am. Med. Colls. (assembly) Hosp. Assn. N.Y. State (dir., regional orgns. com., govt. rels. com., trustee 1980-84), Greater N.Y. Hosp. Assn. (gov. 1980-89, treas. 1982, sec. 1983, vice chmn. 1984, 85, 86, chmn. 1987, chmn. fiscal policy com. 1982-83, chmn. ambulatory care comm. 1980), Am. Hosp. Assn. (regional adv. bd. 1986-89, regional policy bd. 1992-95, trustee 1985-89, exec. com. 1987-89), League Vol. Hosps. (chmn.-elect 1983-86, chmn. 1986-88). Presbyterian (ruling elder). Home: 1011 W Areba Ave Hershey PA 17033-2204

ANDERSON, AMY LEE, realtor; b. Tampa, Fla., July 24, 1950; d. Ernest William and Gloria June (Terrell) Denham; m. Arnold Albin Anderson Jr., Dec. 21, 1986; children: Melissa Lee, Nancy Marie. BA, U. Tampa, 1971. Lic. realtor Nat. Bd. Realtors. Sys. analyst Nat. CSS, Tampa, 1971-79; field analyst Digital Equipment Corp., Meriden, Conn., 1979-84; dir. nat. accounts Canaan Computer Corp., Stratford, Conn., 1984—92; realtor Prudential Carolinas Realty, Raleigh, N.C., 1992-95, Block & Assocs., Raleigh, 1995—97, Prudential Carolinas Realty, Raleigh, NC, 1997—2000, Midway Airlines, Raleigh, NC, 2001, Keller Williams Realty, Raleigh, NC, 2002—. Exec. staff Canaan Computer Corp., Stratford, 1987-92. Editor (manual) Corporate Policies, 1986; co-author: Start at the Top, 1989. Treas. PTA, Basking Ridge, N.J., 1989; advisor Tarheel Challenge Acad., Clinton, N.C., 1995; participant Paws Walk for Cancer, Raleigh, 1995. Mem. Data Processing Mgmt. Assn. (publicity com. 1978-92), Capital City Club (membership com. 1993—). Republican. Episcopalian. Avocations: needlework, reading, landscaping, upholstering.

ANDERSON, ANDREW HERBERT, retired army officer; b. Bklyn., Sept. 8, 1928; s. Hjalmar and Anna (Rantanen) Andreason; m. Ellen Lee Miller, Sept. 1, 1956; children— James Andrew, Glenn Robert, Steven Michael. BS in History, Park U., 1963; MS in Pers. Adminstrn., George Washington U., 1968. Commd. in N.G., 1951; entered active duty as 1st lt. U.S. Army, 1954, advanced through grades to maj. gen., 1981—; troop comdr. Ft. Benning, Ga., 1958-60; served in Korea, 1964; mem. army staff, 1965-67; bn. comdr., 1968, 1970-71; comdr. Support Command 1st Armored Div., Federal Republic Germany, 1973-74; chief of staff 1st Armored Div., 1975-76; dep. comdr. Tank-Automotive Materiel Readiness Command, Warren, Mich., 1977-79; comdr. U.S. Army Tank Automotive Research/Devel. Command, Warren, 1979-80; dep. insp. gen. Washington, 1980-81; dep. comdr. VII Corps, Fed. Republic Germany, 1981-84; comdr. Test and Evaluation Command, Aberdeen Proving Ground, Md., 1984-86; ret., 1986. Vice-pres. Talbot County Coun., 1990-98. Decorated D.S.M., Silver Star, Legion of Merit with 2 oak leaf clusters, D.F.C., Bronze Star with 3 oak leaf clusters and V device, Air medal with 7 oak leaf clusters and V device, Army Commendation medal with 3 oak leaf clusters and V device, Purple Heart, George Washington honor medal for individual achievement freedoms found. at Valley Forge, 1991, Md. Veteran of the Yr., 1992, N.Y. State Conspicuous Svc. cross, N.Y. State Meritorious Svc. medal; German Armed Forces honor Cross in Gold. Mem. VFW, DAV, Md. Vets. Home Commn., Assn. U.S. Army, Armor Assn., Am. Legion, Amvets, Order Purple Heart, Masons (32d degree), Shriners. Republican. Home: 29995 Bolingbroke Ln Trappe MD 21673-1522

ANDERSON, ANN, writer, actor; b. Denver, Calif., Oct. 14, 1951; d. Sol Cohen and Evelyn Theda Gross; m. Kenneth Ray Anderson, June 23, 1990. Student, Am. Acad. Dramatic Arts, 1972; BA in Theater Arts, Antioch U., 1985, MFA in Creative Writing, 2002; MA in Theater Arts, Calif. State U., Northridge, 1998. Owner Anderson Looping, 1983—2003, Anderson Comms. (Writing, Editing, Rsch.), 2003—. Presenters in field; voice-over actor. Author: (history book) Snake Oil, Hustlers and Hambones: The American Medicine Show; prodr.: (performance art) Transformations. Mem.: AFTRA, SAG, Actors Equity Assn., Phi Kappa Phi. Avocations: dancing, reading, animal welfare, reading for the blind.

ANDERSON, ARTHUR ALLAN, management consultant; b. Grand Rapids, Mich., Apr. 16, 1939; s. Alvin Alexander and Mildred Jane (Grice) A. AB in History, ScB in Chemistry, Brown U., 1962; LLB, Yale U., 1965. Bar: N.Y. 1966. Assoc. Fish & Neave, N.Y.C., 1965-69; co-founder, pres. Source Securities Corp., 1970-72; gen. counsel Teleprompter Corp., N.Y.C., 1973-74; ptnr. Anderson & Rubin, N.Y.C., 1975-82, Choate, Moore, Hahn & McGarry, N.Y.C., 1982-85; sole practice N.Y.C., 1985-87; prin. Morgan, Anderson & Co., N.Y.C., 1987-98, Morgan Anderson Consulting, N.Y.C., 1998—, also bd. dirs. Bd. dirs. Woodstock Artists' Assn.; mem. exec. bd. Samuel Dorsky Mus. of Art. Mem. Nat. Arts Club. Home: Moonhaw Rd West Shokan NY 12494 Office: 136 W 24th St New York NY 10011-1908 E-mail: consultants@morgananderson.com.

ANDERSON, ARTHUR OSMUND, pathologist, immunologist, army officer; b. N.Y.C., Mar. 12, 1945; s. Arthur Edmund and Florence Ranveig (Osmundsen) A.; m. Julane Kay Pynn, Oct. 4, 1969; 1 child, Phoebe MacDonald Anderson. BS, Wagner Coll., 1966; MD, U. Md., 1970; PhD (hon.), Wagner Coll., 2003. Diplomate Am. Bd. Pathology. Intern in pathology Johns Hopkins Hosp., Balt., 1970-71, fellow in exptl. pathology, 1970-74, resident in pathology, 1971-73; commd. 2d lt. U.S. Army, 1974, advanced through grades to col., 1988; asst. prof. biology and pathology U. Pa., Phila., 1980-83; prin. investigator pathology div. U.S. Army Med. Rsch. Inst. Infectious Diseases, Ft. Detrick, Md., 1974-80, chief respiratory immunity, 1983—, chmn. human investigational rev. bd., 1976-80, 84—. Appeared in (History Channel) Suicide Missions: Human Guinea Pigs, 2000; contbr. numerous articles to profl. jours., chpts. to immunology text books and websites. Decorated Meritorious Svc. medal; N.Y. State Regents scholar, 1962-66; recipient Order of Mil. Med. Merit award, 2002. Mem. Found. for Advanced Edn. in Scis., Am. Assn. Immunologists, Am. Assn. Pathologists, Applied Rsch. Ethics Nat. Assn. (treas. 2000), Kiwanis (pres. Frederick 1988-89), Beta Beta Beta, Omicron Delta Kappa. Republican. Achievements include first documented role of endothelium in immunity; first showed evidence in vivo that lymphocytes adhered to endothelial cells in lymph nodes, first showed that adjuvants could enhance mucosal secretion of IgA; contributed to medical ethics as chronicled in the book Undue Risk: Secret State Experiments on Humans, 1999. Office: US Army Med Rsch Inst Infectious Diseases Fort Detrick Frederick MD 21702 E-mail: artnscience@yahoo.com.

ANDERSON, AUSTIN GOTHARD, lawyer, university administrator; b. Calumet, Minn., June 30, 1931; s. Hugo Gothard and Turna Marie (Johnson) A.; m. Catherine Antoinette Spellacy, Jan. 2. 1954; children: Todd, Susan, Timothy, Linda, Mark. BA, U. Minn., 1954, JD, 1958. Bar: Minn. 1958, Ill. 1962, Mich. 1974. Assoc. Spellacy, Spellacy, Lano & Anderson, Marble, Minn, 1958-62; dir. Ill. Inst. Continuing Legal Edn., Springfield, 1962-64; dir. dept. continuing legal edn. U. Minn., Mpls., 1964-70, assoc. dean gen. extension divsn., 1968-70; ptnr. Dorsey, Marquart, Windhorst, West & Halladay, Mpls., 1970-73; assoc. dir. Nat. Ctr. State Cts., St. Paul, 1973-74; dir. Inst. Continuing Legal Edn. U. Mich., Ann Arbor, 1973-92; dir. Inst. on Law Firm Mgmt., 1992-95; prin. AndersonBoyer Group, Ann Arbor, 1995—; pres. Network of Leading Law Firms, 1995—. Adj. faculty U. Minn., 1974, Wayne State U., 1974-75; mem. adv. bd. Ctr. for Law Firm Mgmt. Nottingham Trent U., Eng.; draftsman ABA Guidelines for Approval of Legal Asst. Programs, 1973, Model Guidelines for Minimum Continuing Legal Edn., 1988; chair law practice mgmt. sect. State Bar Mich., 2000-2001; mem. Task Force on Court Filing, State Bar of Mich., 2000-2001; mem. Com. on Quality of Life, 2000-2001; cons. in field. Co-editor, contbg. author: Lawyer's Handbook, 1975, co-editor 3d edit., 1992; author: A Plan for Lawyer Development, 1986, Marketing Your Practice: A Practical Guide to Client Development, 1986; cons. editor, contbg. author: Webster's Legal Secretaries Handbook, 1981; cons. editor Merriam Webster's Legal Secretarial Handbook, 2d edit., 1996; co-author: The Effective Associate Training Program-Improving Firm Performance, Profits and Prospective Partners, 2000, Associate Retention. Keeping Our Best and Brightest, 2002; contbr. chpt. to book and articles to profl. jours. Chmn. City of Bloomington Park and Recreation Adv. Commn., Minn., 1970-72; chmn. Ann Arbor Citizens Recreation Adv. Com., 1981-89, Ann Arbor Parks Adv. Com., 1983-92, chair, 1991-92; rep. Class of '58 U. Minn. Law Sch., 1996-2002. Recipient Excellence award CLE sect. Assn. of Am. Law Schs., 1992. Fellow Am. Bar Found. (Mich. chmn. 2002-), State Bar Mich. Found.; mem. ABA (vice chmn. continuing legal edn. com. sect. legal edn. and admission to bar 1988-93, standing com. continuing edn. of bar 1984-90, 2000-, chmn. law practice mgmt. sect. 1981-82, Am. Law Inst.-ABA com. on continuing profl. edn. 1993-96, Am. Lw Inst.-ABA com. on continuing profl. edn. 1999—2002, spl. com. on rsch. on future of legal profession 1998-2000, sec. Coll. of Law Practice Mgmt. 1993-97, house of dels. 1993-99, commn. on lawyer advt. 1994-97, futures com., chmn. econs. of torts and ins. practice 2002—, mem. task force Lawyer Ctr. on pers. legal svcs. and client devel. 2002—, spl. advisor to standing com. on continuing edn. of the bar 2002—), Internat. Bar Assn., Mich. Bar Assn., Ill. Bar Assn., State Bar of Mich. (chair law practice mgmt. sect., 2000-2001), Minn. Bar Assn., Internat. Bar Assn., Assn. Continuing Legal Edn. Adminstrs.(pres. 1969-70), Ann Arbor Golf and Outing Club. Home: 4660 Bayberry Cir Ann Arbor MI 48105-9762 Office: AndersonBoyer Group 3840 Packard St # 110 Ann Arbor MI 48108-2280 E-mail: aga@andersonboyer.com.

ANDERSON, BARBARA ALLEN, b. Atlanta, Aug. 15, 1956; d. Cliff Cole and Jeanne Tiller Allen; m. Richard Jefferson Anderson, Oct. 20, 1984. BA, Shorter Coll., 1978; MCM, S.B.T.S., Louisville, 1981. Cert. addictions counselor, master's level addiction counselor, clin. supr. Asst. creative dir. Trilogy Entertainment Corp., Atlanta, 1984—89; spiritual dir. Breakthru Ho., Decatur, Ga., 1989—92; continuing care therapist SAFE Recovery Campus, Atlanta, 1990—93; continuing care assoc. Talbott Recovery Campus, Atlanta, 1993—95, continuing care coord., 1996—99, dir. continuing care, 2000—. World svc. del. AFG of Ga., Inc., Atlanta, 1995—97, area office bd. chmn., 1998—2000, archivist, 2001—. Vol. writer, editor Paths to Recovery, 1997, editor (newsletter) Talbott Times, 1997—99; contbr. articles to Talbott Times. Mem.: NAFE, Ga. Addiction Counselors Assn., Nat. Employee Assistance Profls. Assn., Nat. Assn. Alcohol and Drug Abuse Counselors. Avocations: music, tennis, writing, movies. Office: Talbott Recovery Campus 5448 Yorktowne Dr Atlanta GA 30349

ANDERSON, BARBARA JEANNE, music educator; b. Berkeley, Calif., Aug. 25, 1928; d. Hermanq Eston Mathis and Betty Jayne Baumann; widowed; children: Geoffrey P., Steven M., Cheryl I. Devlin, Donna Van Soelen. BA in Music, U. Calif., 1973; MusM, Holy Names Coll., 2000. Dic. sacred music 1st Presbyn. Ch., San Leandro, Calif., 1972—82; substitute tchr. Acalanes, Md. Daiblo High Sch. Dist., Contro Costa County, 1974—79; staff asst., dir. youth music Orinda Cmty. Ch., 1982—92; tchr. piano pvt. practice, 1979—; instr. Las Positas Coll., Livermore, 2001—. Mem.: Music Tchrs. Assn. (Contra Costa bd. bd. dirs., Contra Costa bd. program chmn. 2001—03), Nat. Guild Piano Tchrs., Music Tchrs. Nat. Assn. Avocations: photography, piano. Home and Office: 6 Van Tassel Ln Orinda CA 94563 E-mail: bandersonpiano@aol.com.

ANDERSON, BARBARA MCCOMAS, lawyer; b. Ft. Belvoir, Va., Dec. 18, 1950; d. Ben C. Jr. and Elsa A. McComas; m. Roy Ryden Anderson Jr., Dec. 11, 1982; 1 child, Ryden McComas Anderson. BA, Trinity U., San Antonio, 1972; JD, U. Tex., 1978. Bar: Tex. 1978; cert. in estate planning and probate Tex. Bd. Legal Specialization. From assoc. to ptnr. Locke Purnell Rain Harrell, Dallas, 1978-97; of counsel Locke Liddell & Sapp, LLP, Dallas, 1997—; pvt. practice Dallas, 1997—. Fellow: Coll. of State Bar of Tex., Tex. Bar. Found., Am. Coll. Trusts and Estates Counsel; mem.: Tex. Acad. Probate and Trust Lawyers (charter), Dallas Bar Assn., Tex. Bar Assn. (chair real estate, probate and trust law sect. 2003—). Avocations: reading mysteries, gardening. Office: PO Box 181147 Dallas TX 75218-8147

ANDERSON, BARRIE, gynecologic oncologist; b. Syracuse, N.Y., Apr. 17, 1942; d. Eric Albert and Edna (Barrie) A.; m. George Joel Wine, June 15, 1985. BS, U. Wis., 1963; MD, SUNY, Syracuse, 1967. Diplomate Am. Bd. Ob-Gyn; Nat. Bd. Med. Examiners; cert. of spl. competence in gynecologic oncology Am. Bd. Ob-Gyn. Intern in surgery New Eng. Med. Ctr. Hosp., Boston, 1967-68; resident in ob-gyn. Tufts Affiliated Hosp., Boston, 1968-71, fellow in gynecol. oncology, 1971-72, 74-75, asst. prof. ob-gyn, 1972-82, assoc. prof. ob-gyn, 1982, instr. radiation therapy, 1975-82; assoc. prof. ob-gyn U. Iowa Hosps. and Clinics, Iowa City, 1982-93, prof. ob-gyn., 1993—, dir. gynecol. oncology, 1982-90, dir. fellowship program gynecol. oncology, 1990—. Mem. ob-gyn com. part II Nat. Bd. Med. Examiners, 1984-87; examiner Am. Bd. Ob-Gyn., 1982—, mem. subsplty. divsn. gynecol. oncology, 1988-94, examiner subspecialty divsn., 1987-2000. Contbr. articles to profl. jours. Galloway fellow Meml. Hosp. Cancer and Allied Diseases, 1971, Am. Cancer Soc. Clin. fellow, 1974-75, Am. Cancer Soc. Jr. Clin. Faculty fellow, 1977-80. Mem.: Iowa Med. Soc., Mass. Med. Soc., Am. Gynecol. and Obstet. Soc., Soc. Pelvic Surgeons (sec.-treas. 1999—2002, pres.-elect 2003), New England Assn. Gynecol. Oncologists (sec.-treas. 1980—83), Soc. Gynecol. Oncologists, Western Assn. Gynecol. Oncologists (v.p. 1985, pres. 2001), Am. Coll. Ob-Gyn. Office: U Iowa Hosps and Clinics Div Gynecol Oncology Dept Ob-Gyn 4630 JCP Iowa City IA 52242

ANDERSON, BERGIE WAYNE, human factors psychologist; b. Shreveport, La., June 7, 1948; s. Bergie M. and Jean (Smith) A.; m. Carmen E. Valverde, May 16, 1992; children: Christiana Lynn, William Albertus, Keli Marie. BS, Tex. A&M U., 1970, MS, 1973. R & d coordinator US Army, 1973-76; rsch. psychologist Human Engring. Lab., Aberdeen Proving Ground, Md., 1976-86; sr. human factors psychologist, researcher U.S. Army Rsch. Lab., Ft. Monmouth, N.J., 1986—. Rschr. in speech comms., acoustics, noise environments, human behavior modeling, sensory interaction, and hearing conservation for armor crews; mem. experimental design panel/human use com. U.S. Army Human Engring. Lab., 1981-86, chmn. 1986, Tri-service working group on active noise reduction, 1996—; expert to NATO rsch. study group on impulse noise, 1996—; adv. group Aerospace Rsch. and Devel. Contbr. articles to profl. jours. Sec. to coun. on ministries Grace United Methodist Ch., 1978-79; chmn. bd. trustees Tome United Methodist Ch., 1981-85; mem. planning and zoning bd. Town of Port Deposit, Md., 1982-86; deacon First Reformed Ch., Rocky Hill, N.J., 1987-88; mem. various ch. choirs, 1965-93. Recipient MANPRINT Practitioner of Yr. award, 1997, MANPRINT Special Achievement award, 1997. Mem. Human Factors and Ergonomics Soc, Psy Chi. Presbyterian. Avocations: folk and ballroom dancing, writing. Home: 53 Harrison St Princeton NJ 08540-5356 Office: US Army Rsch Lab HRED CECOM Element AMSRL-HR-ML Fort Monmouth NJ 07703

ANDERSON, BERNARD E. economist; b. Phila. s. William and Dorothy (Gideon) Anderson; m. Verdia D. Wilson; children: Melinda D., Bernard E. II. BA with highest honors, Livingstone Coll., 1959; MA, Mich. State U., 1961; PhD, U. Pa., 1969; LHD (hon.), Shaw U., 1984, Livingstone Coll., 1995; LLD (hon.), Benedict Coll., 2002. Economist U.S. Bur. Labor Stats., Washington, 1963-65; successively asst. prof., assoc. prof., prof. Wharton Sch. U. Pa., Phila., 1969-79; dir. social sci. Rockefeller Found., N.Y.C., 1979-86; mng. ptnr. Urban Affairs Partnership, Phila., 1987-91; pres. Anderson Group, Phila., 1991-93; asst. sec. U.S. Dept. Labor, 1994-2001; chmn. Pa. Intergovernmental Cooperation Authority, Phila., 1991-93; Whitney M. Young prof. mgmt. Wharton Sch., U. Pa., Phila., 2001—. Vice chmn., bd. dirs. Manpower Demonstration Rsch. Co., N.Y.C., 1977—93, Pa. Econ. Devel. Partnership, Harrisburg, Provident Mut. Life Ins. Co., 1988—2002; vis. fellow Woodrow Wilson Sch., Princeton (N.J.) U., 1985; bd. dirs. United Bank Phila. Co-author: (book) Impact of Government Training and Employment Programs, 1975, Black Managers in American Business, 1978, Soul in Management, 1996; author: Youth Employment and Public Policy, 1980; mem. editl. bd. Rev. Black Polit. Economy, 1977—89. Mem. Pres.'s Commn. Employment Stats., Washington, 1979, Nat. Commn. Jobs and Small Bus., Washington, 1986; pres. People's Investment Fund Am.; trustee Livingstone Coll., Salisbury, NC, 1980—94; chmn. bd. trustees Lincoln U., Oxford, Pa., 1987—93; bd. dirs. Com. Fgn. Rels., Phila., 1983—94, Franklin Inst., Phila., Opportunities Industrialization Ctrs. Am., 2001—, Leon H. Sullivan Found., 2002—. With U.S. Army, 1961—63. Recipient Disting. Educator award, Citizens Urbanism, 1987, Cmty. Svc. award, Delaware Valley Housing Assn., 1989, Disting. Svc. award, A. Philip Randolph Inst., 1990, Bayard Rustin Humanitarianism award, 1996. Mem.: Nat. Econ. Assn. (pres. 1982), Indsl. Rels. Rsch. Assn. (mem. exec. com. 1979—82), Am. Econ. Assn., Union League, Princeton Club, U. Pa. Faculty Club. Democrat. A.M.E. Zion.

ANDERSON, BETH ELLEN, English literature and composition educator; b. South Weymouth, Mass., May 30, 1941; d. Allison Webster and Madeline Lois (Wilcox) Stone; m. Panagiotis A. Argentinis, June 20, 1963 (div. 1967); 1 child, Christopher A. BA, U. Mass., 1963; MEd, Cambridge U., 1994. Cert. English, French tchr. English tchr. Whitman (Mass.) Hanson Regional H.S., 1965-85, advanced placement English tchr., 1985—. Author: short story. Recipient Presdl. Citation Pres. George Bush, 1989, Golden Apple award Quincy Patriot Ledger, 1991; named Top 72 Educators in New Eng. 21st Century Newspaper, 1992. Mem. NEA, Mass. Tchrs. Assn., Nat. Coun. Tchrs. of English, Soc. of Mayflower Descendants. Republican. Home: 68 Beaver Ln Abington MA 02351-1226 Office: Whitman Hanson HS Franklin St Whitman MA 02382 E-mail: bander2068@aol.com.

ANDERSON, BEVERLY JACQUES, academic administrator; b. New Orleans, Sept. 10, 1943; d. Alvin Joseph and Dorothy Ann (Angelety) Jacques; m. Ronald Lee Anderson, Sept. 6, 1967; children: Montina Jacquel, Monique Janee, Montez Jacques. BS cum laude, Dillard U., 1965; MS, Howard U., 1967; PhD, Cath. U. Am., 1978. Instr. math. Howard U., Washington, 1967-69; from instr. to prof. U. D.C., Washington, 1969-94, dean coll. arts & scis., 1994-97,

provost, v.p. for acad. affairs, 1997—2000; sr. consortium rsch. fellow office of the chancellor for edn. and profl. devel. U.S. Dept. Def., 2000—. Instr. math. upward bound program, summer Dillard U., Howard U., Coll. V.I.; dir. minority affairs NRC, Washington, 1988—92; dir. instl. self-study U. D.C., 1992—94; bd. dirs. Prince Georges C.C., chmn.; presenter in field. Columnist Prince Georges News, 1991-95; contbr. articles to profl. jours. Chair adv. com. FDA, Washington, 1989—94; bd. dirs. Greater S.E. Healthcare Sys. Found., Washington, 1994—, Ft. Washington Hosp., 1988—, chair, 1994—98, 2000—; bd. dirs. YMCA Metro Washington, 1992—95. Named Outstanding Alumni, Howard U., 1997; recipient White House Initiative Faculty award, 1988, Outstanding Cmty. Svc. award, Washington View Mag., 1990, Citation, Assn. Women in Math., 1991, Cmty. Svc. award, Greater S.E. Healthcare Sys., 1993, Faculty Rsch. award, Nat. Assn. Equal Opportunity in Higher Edn., 1993, Stewardship award, United Negro Coll. Fund, 1996; grantee, Office Naval Rsch., NASA, Office Post Secondary Edn., Nat. Security Agy., Office Minority Health U.S. Dept. Health and Human Svcs. Mem. Pi Mu Epsilon, Beta Kappa Chi, Phi Delta Kappa. Democrat. Roman Catholic. Avocation: travel. Home: 705 Muirfield Cir Fort Washington MD 20744-7021 Office: Univ DC 4200 Connecticut Ave NW Washington DC 20008-1175

ANDERSON, BOB, state legislator, business executive; b. Wadena, Minn, Jan. 16, 1932; s. Alfred Emmanuel and Frances Agnes (Hassler) A.; m. Janet Lynn Hemquist, Aug. 3, 1967 BBA, U. Miami, 1959; student, US Army War Coll., 1996. Owner small bus., Minn., 1954-96; mem. Minn. Ho. of Reps., 1976-96; mem. steering com. House DFL Caucus, 1993-94. Vice chair, sec., mem. exec. com. Legis. Commn. on Waste Mgmt., 1980—96; chair NCSL com. Agrl., 1985; chair human svc. fin. divsn., 1985—86; dir. NCSL Found. for State Legislatures, 1987—93; mem. ways and means com., 1993—96; chair health and housing fin. divsn., 1993—94; chair health and human svc. com., 1995—96; legis. cons., 1997—; past pres. Viking-Land USA; bd. dirs. West Ctrl. Minn. Emergency Med. Svc., Inc., 1999—, mem. exec. com., 2000—; mem. Minn. Emergency Med. Svc. Regulatory Bd., 2001—02; assoc. chair Senate Dist. 10, 2002—; mem. 7th Congl. Dist. DFL Ctr. Com., 2002—. Past pres. Otter Tail Lake Property Owners Assn.; mem. Fergus Falls N.G. Citizens Com., 7th Congressional Dist. DFL Central Comm., 2002; mem. state ctrl. com. Minn. Dem.-Farmer-Labor Party, 2002—; bd. dir. Friends of History Mus. of East Otter Tail County, 2002—. With U.S. Army, 1958—61. Decorated D.S.M.; named Hon. Citizen, City of Winnipeg, Chief Author Glendalough State Pk., Fergus Falls Vets. Home, Prairie Wetlands Environ. Learning Ctr.; recipient Highroad Explorer award, Hon. Viking award, Svc. award Minn. Assn. Rehab. Facilities, West Cen. Emergency Med. Corp, Minn. Ambulance Assn., Nat. Fedn. Ind. Bus., Minn. Head Start Assn., Econ. Justice award MNCAP, Ctr. For Ind. Living, Minn. Cmty. Action award, Pub. Ofcl. Yr. award Minn. Nurses Assn., 1994, Food First Coalition award, 1995, Arrowhead Friends of EMS award, 2003. Mem. NRA (life), Nat. Conf. State Legislatures (exec. com. 1986-88, commerce, labor and regulation com. 1991-94), Nat. Parks Conservations Assn., Nat. Wild Turkey Fedn., Minn. Meat Processors Assn. (past pres.), Rocky Mountain Elk Fedn., Pioneer Heritage Conservation Trust, Nature Conservancy, Friends of Prairie Wetlands Learing Ctr., Otter Tail County Hist. Soc. (life), Am. Legion (life), VFW (life; Ladies Aux. Vet. of Yr. award 1994), Minn. Outdoor Heritage Caucus, Fergus Falls Fish and Game Club, Millerville Sportsmen Club, Evansville Sportsmen Club, Ottertail Rod and Gun Club, Knob Hill Sportsmen, Sons of Norway, Elks, Masons, Shriners, Theta Chi, Alpha Kappa Psi. Democrat. Home: PO Box 28 Ottertail MN 56571-0028

ANDERSON, BRADBURY H. retail executive; Pres., COO Best Buy Co., Inc., Eden Prairie, Minn., 1993—2002, CEO, 2002—. Office: 7075 Flying Cloud Dr Eden Prairie MN 55344-3532

ANDERSON, BRADY KEVIN, professional baseball player; b. Silver Spring, Md., Jan. 18, 1964; Student, U. Calif., Irvine. Ctr. field Boston Red Sox, 1985—88, Balt. Orioles, 1988—. Office: c/o Baltimore Orioles Oriole Park at Camden Yards 333 W Camden St Baltimore MD 21201-2435

ANDERSON, BRUCE JAMES, electrical engineer, consultant; b. Springfield, Mass., Oct. 16, 1962; s. Bruce James and Frances (Cirillo) A.; m. Susan Patricia Bauer, Apr. 28, 1990. BSEE, Western New Eng. Coll., 1984. Sr. engr. Lockheed, Plainfield, N.J., 1984-90; mng. dir. digital TV and entertainment Sarnoff Corp., Princeton, N.J., 1990-2000; v.p. broadcast products Diva Systems Corp., Princeton, 2000—01; chief tech. officer Invidi Techs. Corp., 2001—. Patentee in field. Mem. IEEE, Assn. of Computng Machines Achievements include co-design of Grand Alliance High Definition TV Sys. Office: Invidi 116 Davenport Dr Trenton NJ 08620

ANDERSON, CARL ALBERT, association executive, lawyer; b. Torrington, Conn., Feb. 27, 1951; s. Carl August and Louise Joanna (Giorcelli) A.; m. Dorian Jean Lounsbury Anderson, Aug. 19, 1972; children: Carl, Matthew, Teresa, Katherine, Clare. BA in Philosophy, Seattle U., 1972; JD, U. Denver, 1975. Bar: D.C. 1979. V.p. John Paul II Inst. for Studies on Marriage and Family, Cath. U. Am., Washington, 1999—; dir., bd. dirs. Basilica of the Nat. Shrine of Immaculate Conception, Washington, 2001—; corp. CEO KC, New Haven. Legis. asst. U.S. Senate, Washington, 1976-81; counsellor to the Undersec. U.S. Dept. Health and Human Svcs., Washington, 1981-83; staff mem. White House Office of Policy Devel., Washington, 1983-85; spl. asst. to the Pres., 1985-87; acting dir. White House Office of Pub. Liaison, 1987; commr. U.S. Commn. on Civil Rights, Washington, 1990-2000. Contbr. articles to profl. jours. Mem. transition team Office of the Pres.-Elect, Washington, 1980, 88; trustee Cath. U., 2002—; consultor Pontifical Coun. for the Family. Recipient Thomas Linacre award Nat. Fedn. Cath. Physicians' Guilds, 1992; Knight of the Equestrian Order of the Holy Sepulchre of Jerusalem, Knight of St. Gregory the Great, Pontifical Acad. for Life, Pontifical Coun. for the Laity. Mem. D.C. Bar Assn., KC (v.p. pub. policy 1987-97, state dep. for D.C. 1995-97, asst. supreme sec. 1997—). Roman Catholic. Address: KC Columbus Plz New Haven CT 06507-3326 E-mail: caa@kofc.org.

ANDERSON, CARL DENNIS, lawyer; b. Mt. Vernon, N.Y., July 4, 1942; s. Carl and Ellen Anderson; m. Karen A. Anderson, Aug. 21, 1965; children: Christopher P., Michael L., Kate K. BA, JD, U. Conn., 1967. Bar: Conn. 1967; cert. U.S. Dist. Ct., Conn., 1968. Atty. Brown, Jacobson, Jewett & Laudone, P.C., Norwich, Conn., 1967-88; pres. Carl D. Anderson & Assocs., Norwich, 1988-92, Anderson, Laffey, Eckert & Ferdon, P.C., Norwich, 1992-94, Anderson & Ferdon, P.C., Norwich, 1994—. Corporator Jewett City Savs. Bank, 1970—; consul Finland, State of Conn., 1977—; trial referee, fact finder State of Conn. Jud. Sys., 1996—. Chmn. Dem. Town Com., Voluntown, Conn., 1972—; sec. Voluntown Planning and Zoning Commn.; legal counsel indian trails coun. Boy Scouts Am., 1972-97. Mem. ATLA, ABA, Conn. Trial Lawyers Assn. (mem. bd. govs. 1988—, sec. 2002—), Conn. Bar Assn., New London County Bar Assn., Snake Meadow Club, Am. Quarter Horse Assn., Conn. Quarter Horse Assn., Tamarack Lodge, Inc. (pres.). Avocations: quarter horse breeder and exhibitor, gardening, fly fishing. Home: 880 Pendleton Hill Rd Voluntown CT 06384-2202 Office: Anderson and Ferdon PC 82 Chelsea Harbor Dr Norwich CT 06360-5730

ANDERSON, CARL JOSEPH, artist, educator; s. Joseph Steven and Sarah May Anderson; m. Sheri Michelle Kidder, July 8, 2000. BA in Art Edn., Concordia Coll., 1999. Lic. tchr. K-12 Minn. Photofinisher Qualex, Omaha, Nebr. and Fargo, N.D., 1996—98; gallery asst. Cy Running Meml. Gallery, Moorhead, Minn., 1995—98; dir.'s asst. Rourke Art Gallery Mus., Moorhead, 1996—99; cabinetmaker Big River Studio, St. Paul, 1999—2000; event maintenance, security Walker Art Ctr., Mpls., 1999—2000; edn. staff MacRostie Art Ctr., Grand Rapids, Minn., 2001—; art tchr. Northland Cmty. Sch., Remer, Minn., 2000—. Curriculum writer Arts Net Minn., 2001—; presenter Minn. Retreat for the Arts, Crystal, 2002. One-man shows include Rourke Art Gallery, Moorhead, 1999, GK Gallery, Cooperstown, N.D., 1998, 1999, 2001, Miles Rief Performing Arts Ctr., Grand Rapids, 2001, exhibited in group shows. Mem.: MacRostie Art Ctr., GK Gallery, Rourke Art Gallery Mus. Avocations: fishing, philosophy, ancient history, science fiction, antiques. Home: 2731 Audrey Ln Grand Rapids MN 55744 Office: Northland H S 316 Main St E Remer MN 56672 E-mail: anderci@yahoo.com.

ANDERSON, CAROLE ANN, nursing educator, academic administrator; b. Chgo., Feb. 21, 1938; d. Robert and Marian (Harrity) Irving; m. Clark Anderson, Feb. 14, 1973; 1 child, Julie. Diploma, St. Francis Hosp., 1958; BS, U. Colo., 1962, MS, 1963, PhD, 1977. Group psychotherapist Dept. Vocat. Rehab., Denver, 1963-72; psychotherapist Prof. Psychiatry and Guidance Clinic, Denver, 1970-71; asst. prof., chmn. nursing sch. U. Colo., Denver, 1971-75; therapist, coordinator The Genessee Mental Health, Rochester, N.Y., 1977-78; assoc. dean U. Rochester, N.Y., 1978-86; dean, prof. Coll. Nursing Ohio State U., Columbus, 1986-2001, prof., 2001—, vice provost acad. adminstrn., 2001—. Lectr. nursing sch. U. Colo., Denver, 1970-71; prin. investigator biomed. rsch. support grant, 1986-93, clin. rsch. facilitation grant, 1981-82; program dir. profl. nurse traineeship, 1978-86, advanced nurse tng. grant, 1982-85. Author: (with others) Women as Victims, 1986, Violence Toward Women, 1982, Substance Abuse of Women, 1982; editor Nursing Outlook, 1993—. Pres., bd. dirs. Health Assn., Rochester, 1984-86; mem. north sub area council Finger Lakes Health Systems Agy., 1983-86, longrange planning com., 1981-82; mem. Columbus Bd. Health; dir. Netcare Mental Health Ctr. Am. Acad. Nursing fellow. Mem. ANA, Ohio Nurses Assn., Am. Assn. Colls. Nursing (bd. dirs. 1992-94, pres.-elect 1994-96, pres. 1996-98), Sigma Theta Tau. Home: 406 W 6th Ave Columbus OH 43201-3137 Office: The Ohio State U Office Acad Affairs 203 Bricker Hall 190 N Oval Mall Columbus OH 43210-1358 E-mail: anderson.32@osu.edu.

ANDERSON, CAROLYN JOYCE, business development executive; b. Mishawaka, Ind., Mar. 14, 1947; d. Ebon Clayton and Maxine Ruth (Haag) Angel; m. Thomas Anderson (dec.); children: Charmien, Andrew, Paul. BS in Bus., Ind. U., 1978, MBA, 1998. CPA, Ind. Staff acct. Holdeman, Fulmer and Chiddister CPA's, Elkhart, Ind., 1974-78; comml. lender Midwest Commerce Bank, Elkhart, 1978-81; corp. contr. Bivouac Industries, Inc., Vandalia, Mich., 1981-84; exec. dir. Small Bus. Devel. Ctr., South Bend, Ind., 1984-98; small bus. banking officer, comml. lender 1st Source Bank, 1999—. Developer, implementer Michiana Investment Network, 1992-97, The Emerging Bus. Forum, 1992-96. Bd. dirs. Davenport Coll., Grand Rapids, Mich., 1986-94; bd. dirs. The Montessori Acad., South Bend, 1994-99, treas., 1995-99; Ind. state judge Blue Chip Enterprise Initiative, 1990-96; chmn. Small Bus. Week Awards, 1993-98; co-chair Women's Econ. Summit, St. Mary's Coll., Notre Dame, Ind., 1993; sec. South Bend Econ. Devel. Commn., 1994—, sec., 1995-98, v.p., 1998—; bd. dirs. St. Joe County Mental Health Assn., 1998—, treas. 2000—. Mem. Planned Parenthood (treas. 1987-90, pres. 1991-92), Kiwanis (sec. 1988-91, Disting. Svc. award 1989). Methodist. Home: 426 E Pokagon St South Bend IN 46617-1325 Personal E-mail: cja47@attbi.com. Business E-Mail: anderson@1stsource.com.

ANDERSON, CAROLYN RUTH HUNT, interior designer, realtor; b. Evansville, Ind., Aug. 20, 1941; d. Maurice Osborn and Fairy Helen (Burnau) Hunt; m. Gerald Lee Anderson, June 5, 1965; children: Clifford Blake, Gwendolyn Cheryl. BA, Boston U., 1963; MS, Columbia U., 1965; cert., N.Y. Sch. Interior Design, 1968; real estate cert., Norwalk (Conn.) C.C., 1986. Lic. social worker, N.Y. Marriage and child guidance counselor Family Agy. Community Service Soc., N.Y.C., 1966-67; pres. Carolyn Anderson Corp., Interior Designs, Greenwich, Conn., 1968—; real estate agt. Anderson Assocs., Greenwich, 1986—. Author: The Complete Book of Homemade Ice Cream, Milk Sherbet and Sherbet, 1972; co-author: Anderson Guide to Enjoying Greenwich, Conn., 2003. Den leader, coach Boy Scouts Am., Greenwich, 1978-80; Brownie leader Girl Scouts U.S.A., Greenwich, 1979-83; bd. dirs. Greenwich chpt. ARC, 1985. Mem. Am. Soc. Interior Designers, Greenwich Bd. Realtors (treas.), Nat. Trust Hist. Preservation, Am. Field Svc., Culinary Historians N.Y., Greenwich Hist. Soc. Congregationalist. Avocations: bicycling, skiing. Home: 138 Clapboard Ridge Rd Greenwich CT 06831-3351 Office: 164 Mason St Greenwich CT 06830-6611 also: One Glenville St Greenwich CT 06831 E-mail: Carolyn@GreenwichSpecialists.com.

ANDERSON, CATHERINE M. consulting company executive; b. N.Y.C., Feb. 28, 1937; d. Edward Charles and Elizabeth (O'Shea) McElligott; m. Robert Brown Anderson, June 22, 1963; children: Mark Robert, Jennifer Elizabeth. BA, Rutgers U., 1959, MA, 1960. Staff asst. to pres. Chatham Coll., Pitts., 1960-61; instr. urban studies ctr. Rutgers U., New Brunswick, N.J., 1961-63; prin. urban renewal coord. City of Cleve., Cleve., 1963-64; regional admisions counselor Am. Inst. Fgn. Study, Pitts., 1964-74; chief planner, mgr. emergency ops. ctr. Allegheny County Govt., Pitts., 1975-79; dir. accreditation svcs. Energy Cons., Inc., Pitts., 1981-83; pub. involvement cons. Pitts., 1983—. Contbr. articles to profl. jours. Committeewoman Mt. Lebanon (Pa.) Mcpl. Dem. Com., 1970-85; active United Way Allegheny County, Pitts., mem. rev. com., 1980—, chmn. rev. com., 1986-89; bd. dirs. Mt. Lebanon Nature Conservancy, v.p., 1985-88, pres., 1988-92; bd. dirs. Conservation Cons. Inc., v.p., 1983-92, pres., 1992-95; bd. dirs. Pitts. chpt. Women's Transp. Seminar, v.p., 1992-94, pres. 1994-95; bd. dirs. Exec. Women's Coun. Greater Pitts., v.p., 1986-88; bd. dirs. Carnegie-Mellon U. Art Gallery, 1986-89, USC Citizens for Land Stewardship, 1997-99. Recipient Robert L. Wells award Mt. Lebanon Nature Conservancy, 1991, Outstanding Svc. award Exec. Women's Coun., 1988; Eagleton Inst. Politics grad. fellow Rutgers U., 1960. Mem.: Women's Press Club Pitts., Women's Transp. Seminar (v.p. 1992—94, pres. 1994—95, nat. bd. dirs.), Exec. Women's Coun. (charter, v.p. 1987—88, Outstanding Svc. award 1988), Am. Soc. Hwy. Engrs. (sr.; bd. dirs. Pitts. chpt. 1998—, Pres.'s award Pitts. sect. 2001). Home and Office: 2061 Outlook Dr Upper Saint Clair PA 15241-2223 E-mail: kabob@adelphia.net.

ANDERSON, CHARLES, printing/publishing company executive; Pres., CEO, Anderson News. Office: Anderson News 6016 Brookvale Ln Ste 151 Knoxville TN 37919

ANDERSON, CHARLES ARTHUR, former research institute administrator; b. Columbus, Ohio, Nov. 14, 1917; s. Arthur E. and Huldah (Peterson) A.; m. Elizabeth Rushforth, Oct. 27, 1942; children: Peter C., Stephen E., Julia E. AB, U. Calif. at Berkeley, 1938; MBA, Grad. Sch. Bus. Adminstrn., Harvard U., 1940; LHD, Colby Coll., 1975. Asst. prof. Grad. Sch. Bus. Adminstrn., Harvard U., Boston, 1945-48; v.p. Magna Power Tool Corp., Menlo Park, Calif., 1948-58; prof., asso. dean Stanford Grad. Sch. Bus., 1959-61; v.p. Kern County Land Co., San Francisco, 1961-64; pres. Walker Mfg. Co., Racine, Wis., 1964-66, J.I. Case Co., Racine, 1966-68; pres., chief exec. officer SRI Internat., Menlo Park, 1968-79, also dir. Bd. dirs. KRI Internat., Japan, Eaton Corp., Conoco, Owens-Corning Fiberglas, NCR, Boise Cascade, Saga; mem. adv. council Bus. Sch., Stanford, 1966-72, 74-79; mem. industry adv. council Dept. Def., 1971-73 Author (with Anthony) The New Corporate Director. Mem. Menlo Park Planning Commn. and City Coun., 1955-61, Govs. Commn. on Reorgn. Wis. State Govt., 1965-67; bd. dirs. Calif. State C. of C., 1972-77, Internat. House, U. Calif., Berkeley, 1979-90; bd. dirs. Lucile Salter Packard Children's Hosp., Stanford, 1979-95, chmn., 1992-94. With USNR, 1941-45. Recipient Exceptional Service award USAF, 1965 Mem. Palo Alto Club, Pacific-Union Club, Menlo Country Club. Presbyterian. Office: 555 Byron St Apt 207 Palo Alto CA 94301-2037

ANDERSON, CHARLES AUSTIN, judge; b. Waynesville, Ohio; s. Charles Edward and Bess Christina (Smith) Anderson; m. Genevieve Elizabeth Nicherson, June 18, 1944; children: Charles A. Jr., Kristin Lynne Cetone. BA, Ohio State U., 1941; JD, 1944. Bar: Ohio 1944, US Supreme Ct. 1950. Assoc. Cowden, Pfarrer, Crew & Becker, Dayton, Ohio, 1944—62; judge US Bankruptcy Ct., Dayton, 1962—; city atty. Moraine, Ohio, 1958—62; chief asst. pros. atty Montgomery County, Ohio, 1960—62; exec. com. US 6th Cir. del. Nat. Conf. Spl. Ct. Judges, 1972—78. Author (lectr.): (Edn.) Centrville Bd. Edn., 1958—62. Mem.: Chancery, Lawyers, Nat. Conf. Bankruptcy Judges, Am. Acad. Polit. and Soc. Sci., Am. Judicature Soc., ABA, Ohio Bar Assn., Dayton Bar Assn., Dayton Bicycle. Meth. Office: US Bankruptcy Ct 809 Federal Bldg Dayton OH 45402

ANDERSON, CHARLES DAVID, lawyer; b. Balt., Aug. 4, 1943; s. Charles Quentin and Enid Ruth A.; m. Alison Grey, Apr. 15, 1972 (div. Oct. 1990); children: Charles Thomas, Patrick Grey; m. Kathleen McGuinness, June 8, 1991 (div. Dec. 2001); 1 child, Alexander James McGuinness. BA, Yale Coll., 1964; JD, U. Chgo., 1967. Capt. USAF, Pentagon, 1967-70; assoc. Caplin & Drysdale, Washington, 1970-72; from assoc. to ptnr. Tuttle & Taylor, L.A., 1972-2000; ptnr. Loeb & Loeb, L.A., 2000—. Lectr. Harvard Law Sch., Cambridge, Mass., 1983, U. So. Calif. Law Sch., L.A., 1976, 78, UCLA Law Sch., 1979, 81, 85. Pres. L.A. Soccer Found., 1994—. Avocations: pens, skiing. Home: 1375 Linda Vista Ave Pasadena CA 91103-2347 Office: Loeb & Loeb LLP 10100 Santa Monica Blvd Los Angeles CA 90067 E-mail: danderson@loeb.com.

ANDERSON, CHARLES HILL, lawyer; s. Ray N. and Lois M. Anderson; (div.); children: Eric S., Alicia L., Burton H. JD, U. Tenn., 1953. Bar: Tenn. 1953, U.S. Dist. Ct. Tenn. 1953, U.S. Ct. Appeals (6th cir.) 1956, U.S. Supreme Ct. 1956, U.S. Ct. Mil. 1964. Pvt. practice, Chattanooga, 1953-59, 2001—; assoc. gen. counsel Life & Casualty Ins. Co. Tenn., Nashville, 1960-69; dist. atty. U.S. Dept. Justice, Nashville, 1969-77; pvt. practice Nashville, 1977-79, 87—; asst. adj. gen. State of Tenn., Nashville, 1979-87. Mem. U.S. Atty. Gen. Adv. Com., Washington, 1973-77; del. Tenn. Constl. Conv., Nashville, 1965-66; dir. Nashville Pub. TV Coun., 1994-99; chmn. Met. Bd. of Equalization, 1998-2001. Brig. gen. AUS, ret., 1987. Mem. ABA, Tenn. Bar Assn., Nashville Bar Assn., Chattanooga Bar Assn., Fed. Bar Assn. (pres. Nashville chpt. 1972), Assn. Life Ins. Counsel, Cumberland Club (pres. 1981-82), The Federalist Soc. Presbyterian. Home: 1310 Aswan Dr Signal Mountain TN 37377-2618 Office: POB 561 Signal Mountain TN 37377

ANDERSON, CHARLES ROSS, civil engineer; b. N.Y.C., Oct. 4, 1937; s. Biard Eclare and Melva (Smith) A.; m. Susan Breinholt, Aug. 29, 1961; children: Loralee, Brian, Craig, Thomas, David. BSCE, U. Utah, 1961; MBA, Harvard U., 1963. Registered profl. engr.; cert. land surveyor. Owner, operator AAA Engring. and Drafting, Inc., Salt Lake City, 1960—. Mem. acad. adv. com. U. Utah, 1990-91, chmn. civil engring. adv. bd., 1995—, U. Utah nat. engring. adv. coun., 2001—, nat. adv. coun., 2001—. Mayoral appointee Housing Devel. Com., Salt Lake City, 1981-86; bd. dirs., vice chmn., cons. Met. Water Dist., Salt Lake City, 1985-99; bd. dirs., pres., v.p., sec. bd. Utah Mus. Natural History, Salt Lake City, 1980-92; asst. dist. commr. Sunrise Dist. Boy Scouts Am., Salt Lake City, 1985-86; fundraising coord. architects and engrs. United Fund; mem. Sunstone Nat. Adv. Bd., 1980-88; bd. dirs. Provo River Water Users Assn., 1986—, Salt Lake Convention & Visitor Bur., 2001-03; mgmt. bd., U. Utah Hosp., 2000—. Recipient Hamilton Watch award U. Utah Nat. Adv. Coun., 2001-, Merit of Honor award U. Utah Alumni Assn., 2001 ; fellow Am. Gen. Contractors, Salt Lake City, 1960. Mem.: ASCE, Harvard U. Bus. Sch. Club (pres. 1970—72), U. Utah Alumni Assn. (bd. dirs. 1989—92), U. Utah Crimson Club (bd. dirs. 1996—99), The Country Club (bd. dirs., v.p. 1998-2001), Rotary (pres. 1998—99, v.p. Club 24 1990-91, chmn. election com. 1980-81, vice chmn. and chmn. membership com. 1988-90, Salt Lake Rotary Club Found. bd. dirs. 2000-, 1st v.p. 1997-98), Tau Beta Pi, Chi Epsilon, Phi Eta Sigma, Pi Kappa Alpha (internat. pres. 1972-74, trustee endowment fund 1974-80, Outstanding Alumnus 1967, 72, mem. Hall of Fame 1995). Avocations: fly fishing, golfing, foreign travel. Home: 2689 Comanche Dr Salt Lake City UT 84108-2846 Office: AAA Engring & Drafting Inc PO Box 58171 Salt Lake City UT 84158-0171 E-mail: ross@uofu.net.

ANDERSON, CHESTER GRANT, English educator; b. River Falls, Wis., Dec. 8, 1923; s. C.A. Chester and Inga Amelia (Grant) A.; m. Carole Nygard, Apr. 23, 1945; children: Stephen, Mark, Jonathan. Student, St. Olaf Coll., 1941-43; MA, U. Chgo., 1948; PhD, Columbia U., 1962. Asst. prof. English Creighton U., Omaha, 1948-50, asst. prof., 1954-57, Fordham U., N.Y.C., 1951-52; dir. State Soc. Services, AICPAs, 1952-54; assoc. prof. Western Conn. State U., 1957-63; asst. prof. Columbia U., 1963-68; prof. English U. Minn., Mpls., 1963-96, prof. emeritus, 1996—; Fulbright prof. Helsinki (Finland) U., 1963-64. Semester-at-Sea prof., 1987; W.B. Yeats Internat. Summer Sch. prof., Sligo, Ireland, 1987; vis. prof. Odense U., Denmark, 1977-78, Curtin U., Australia, 1989. Author: James Joyce and His World, 1967, translation in Portugese and Italian, 1989, Spanish, 1990, Chinese, 1999, Critical Edit. of James Joyce's A Portrait of the Artist, 1968, corrected 1992, Growing Up in Minnesota, 1976. Ensign AC, USNR, 1943-45. Mem. MLA, MLA Helsinki, Acad. Am. Poets, James Joyce Found. Home: 660 S Sandlake Ct Mount Dora FL 32757-6085 E-mail: chestergan@aol.com.

ANDERSON, CHRISTOPHER JAMES, lawyer; b. Chgo., Nov. 26, 1950; s. James M. and Margaret E. (Anderson) A.; m. Lyn R. Buckley, Jan. 3, 1976; children: Vaughn Buckley, Weston Buckley. BA, Grinnell Coll., 1972; JD with highest distinction, U. Iowa, 1975. Bar: Mo. 1975. From assoc. to ptnr. Armstrong Teasdale LLP, Kansas City, Mo., 1975—. Mem. ABA, Mo. Bar Assn., Kans. City Bar Assn., Lawyers Assn. Kansas City, Estate Planning Soc. Office: Armstrong Teasdale, et al 2345 Grand Blvd Ste 2000 Kansas City MO 64108-2617 E-mail: canderso@armstrongteasdale.com.

ANDERSON, CHRISTOPHER JON, b. Albany, N.Y., Aug. 30, 1976; s. Richard Franz Anderson and Barbara Anne Dagastine; stepfather, Gary Paul Dagastine. AA, Hudson Valley C.C., 1996; BA, SUNY, Binghamton, 1997; MA, SUNY, Albany, 1999, PhD, 2002. Grad. asst. SUNY, Albany, 1998—2001; postdoc. assoc. Tilburg U., Netherlands, 2002—03; asst. prof. Temple U., Phila., 2003—. Adj. faculty mem. Russel Sage Coll., Troy, N.Y., Sage JCA, Albany, N.Y., 2000-01, Skidmore Coll., 2001-02, SUNY Albany, 1999-2001. Contbr. articles to profl. jours. Mem. APA, Am. Psychol. Soc. (grant rev. panel 1998-2001, grad. advocate 2001-02), Soc. for Judgment and Decision Making, Mensa. Avocations: songwriting, musical performance, philosophy. Office: Temple Univ Weiss Hall Philadelphia PA 19122 E-mail: chris.anderson@temple.edu.

ANDERSON, CHRISTOPHER RALSTON, financial consultant; b. July 13, 1954; BA in Classics, U. Utah, 1981; MBA in Acctg., Westminster Coll., 1994. Sys. adminstr. U. Utah, Salt Lake City, 1994-96, adminstrv. mgr., 1996-98; owner Anderson Sterling Co., Salt Lake City, 1990—; advisor, cons. AXA advisors, 1999-2000. Cons. Fidelity Investments, 2000-02, ING Fin. Svc., 2002-. Mem. Utah Libr. Assn. (exec. bd. 1991-99, 2002--, Spl. Recognition award 2000), Soc. Fin. Svcs. Profls., Heritage Found.

ANDERSON, CLARENCE GLEN, dean; b. Galahad, Alta., Can., Nov. 20, 1955; arrived in U.S., 1993; s. Andrew Anselm and Marilyn Clarissa Anderson; m. Judy Pearlene Newell, June 4, 1978; children: Cordel, Talea. PhD, U. Alta., Edmonton, 1996. Dean Walla Walla Coll., College Place, Wash., 1993—. Office: Walla Walla Coll 204 S College Ave College Place WA 99324

ANDERSON, CLIFTON EINAR, writer, communications consultant; b. Frederic, Wis., Dec. 17, 1923; s. Andrew John and Ida Louise (Johnson) A.; m. Phyllis Mary Nolan, Oct. 5, 1943; children: Kristine, Craig. BS, U. Wis., 1947; MA, U. Calif., Berkeley, 1954. News editor Chgo. Daily Drover's Jour., 1943-45; asst. editor The Progressive, Madison, Wis., 1946-47; dir. publs. Am. Press, Beirut, 1948-53; mgr. rural programs Houston C. of C., 1957-62; faculty Tex. A&M U., College Station, 1962-65; rsch. fellow U. Tex., Austin, 1965-68; faculty Southwestern Okla. U., Weatherford, 1968-72; extension editor U. Idaho, Moscow, 1972-97, prof. emeritus, 1997—. Speaker John Macmurray Centennial Conf. Marquette U., 1991; speaker Nat. Conf. on Peacemaking and Conflict Resolution, 1993, moderator the UN at 50 seminar, 1995; moderator Korea Today and Tomorrow Symposium Wash. State U., 1995. Editor: The Horse Interlude, 1976; author: History of the College of Agriculture at the University of Idaho, 1998, (with others) Ways Out: The Book of Changes for Peace, 1988, The Future: Opportunity Not Destiny, 1989, The Years Ahead: Perils, Problems and Promises, 1993, Eating Agendas: Food and Nutrition as Social Problems, 1995, Futurevision: Ideas, Insights, and Strategies, 1996, Frontiers of the 21st Century: Prelude to the New Millenium, 1999; contbr. articles to profl. jours. and mags. Treas. Moscow Sister City Assn., 1986—; writer campaign staff Senator R.M. La Follette, Jr., Madison, Wis., 1946; on senatorial campaign staff of Hubert H. Humphrey, Mpls., 1948; chmn. Borah Found. for Outlawry of War, U. Idaho, 1986-87, chmn. Borah Symposium, 1986-87. Recipient Rsch. award Fund for Adult Edn., 1954-55, U.S. Office Edn., 1965-68, 1st prize in newswriting competition Assn. Am. Agrl. Coll. Editors, 1976, merit award Agrl. Rels. Coun., 1995, Nat. Svc. award Washington Times Found., 1996. Fellow Martin Inst. Peace Studies and Conflict Resolution; mem. World Future Soc. (speaker 6th gen. assembly 1989, 7th gen. assembly 1993), Assn. for Humanistic Psychology, Assn. for Religion and Intellectual Life, Profs. World Peace Acad., Internat. Forum on Globalization, World Constn. and Parliament Assn. Democrat. Avocations: gardening, photography, writing poetry. Home: 234 N Washington St Moscow ID 83843-2757 E-mail: clifa@uidaho.edu.

ANDERSON, CONNIE, music educator; b. Spokane, Oct. 4, 1949; d. Edward Elias and Amy Alvira Clark; m. Lyle John Anderson, Aug. 28, 1971; children: Eric, Lori. BA, Cedarville Coll., 1973; MM, Wright State U., 1994. Tchr. piano, Spokane, 1962-68; sec. Ctrl. State U., Xenia, Ohio, 1971-73; tchr. piano Cedarville, Ohio, 1968—; prof. music Cedarville U., 1973—. Pianist Southgate Bapt. Ch., Springfield, Ohio, 1971—. Recipient Music award Cedarville Co., 1973. Mem. Am. Coll. Musicians, Nat. Fedn. Music Clubs, Nat. Cert. Bd. Adjudicator, Music Tchrs. Nat. Assn. Republican. Avocations: travel, reading, music, golf, skiing. Home: 136 Kyle Dr Cedarville OH 45314-9581 Office: Cedarville Ul 251 N Main St Cedarville OH 45314 E-mail: andersc@cedarville.edu.

ANDERSON, CRAIG W. lawyer; b. Idaho Falls, Idaho, Aug. 5, 1951; s. Wilford and Betty A.; m. Denise A. Dragoo, Nov. 25, 1977. BS magna cum laude, U. Utah, 1973, JD, 1977. Bar: Utah U.S. Ct. Appeals (10th cir.) 1977, U.S. Supreme Ct, 1985. Rsch. assoc. Environ. Law Inst., Washington, 1977; dep. county atty. Salt Lake County, 1978-81; ptnr. Suitter, Axland, Armstrong & Hanson, Salt Lake City, 1984-86, Van Wagoner & Stevens, Salt Lake City, 1986-91; dep. dist. atty. Salt Lake County, Utah, 1991—. U.S. Senate intern, 1974; adj. prof. U. Utah; vice chmn. Utah Solid and Hazardous Waste Control Bd. Contbr. articles to profl. jours.; editl. bd. Jouor. Contemporary Law, 1976-77. Mem. Utah Bar Assn., Hinckley Inst. Politics Intern Alumni Assn., Salt Lake County Bar Assn., ABA. Home: 1826 Hubbard Ave Salt Lake City UT 84108-1362 Office: Dep Dist Atty Salt Lake County 2001 S State St Ste S3600 Salt Lake City UT 84190-0001 E-mail: craiga@xmission.com.

ANDERSON, DALE ARDEN, aerospace engineer, educator; b. Alta, Iowa, Aug. 11, 1936; s. Everett and Inez Birdene (Burwell) A.; m. Marleen Marie Ankerson, June 15, 1958; children: Gregory Dale, Lisa Dawn BA in Aerospace Engring., St. Louis U., 1957; MS, Iowa State U., 1959, PhD, 1964. Registered profl. engr., Iowa. Flight test engr. Douglas Aircraft, Santa Monica, Calif., 1958-60; aerodynamicist Boeing Co., Wichita, Kans., 1959-60; mem. tech. staff Aerospace Corp., San Bernardino, Calif., 1964-65; prof. aerospace engring. Iowa State U., Ames, 1965-84, dir. Computational Fluid Dynamics Inst., 1980-84; prof. aerospace engring., dir. Computational Fluid Dynamics Ctr. U. Tex.-Arlington, 1984-96; pres. MDA Engring. Inc., Arlington, Tex., 1987-96; assoc. dean Coll. of Engring. U. Tex., Arlington, 1996-97, v.p., dean grad. studies, 1997-2000, v.p. rsch., v.p. Ft. Worth campus, 2000—01, prof. aerospace engr., 2001—. Cons. Gen. Dynamics, Fort Worth, 1984-96, Union Carbide, Chgo., Hartford, Conn., Centerville, Iowa, 1977-89, Lockheed Rsch. Lab., Palo Alto, Calif., 1984, Rockwell Internat., Thousand Oaks, Calif., 1982-91, Brit. Petroleum, Houston, 1988-94, Lockheed-Martin, Fort Worth, 1996—. Author: Computational Fluid Mechanics and Heat Transfer, 1984, 97; contbr. articles to profl. jours. Grantee NASA, Dept. Def., various indsl. firms, 1964— Fellow AIAA (assoc.); mem. Sigma Xi. Presbyterian. Office: U Tex Aerospace Engring Dept PO Box 19018 Arlington TX 76019-0001

ANDERSON, DALE C. state agency professional, travel consultant; b. Grinnell, Iowa, Sept. 13, 1953; s. Clifford Simon and Wilma Grace (Grunhaupt) A. AAS in Indsl. Mktg., Des Moines Area C.C., Ankeny, Iowa, 1973; BA in Comm. and Theatre, Cen. Coll., 1978. Asst. buyer Ardan Wholesaler, Des Moines, 1979; office mgr. Moingona Girl Scout Coun., Des Moines, 1979-82, dir. adminstrv. svcs., 1982-88, property/purchasing dir., 1988-96; travel cons. Al Travel, Des Moines, 1989-90, First Tours, Des Moines, 1990-95; clk. typist Iowa State Dept. Transp., Des Moines, 1996-97; acctg. clk. II Iowa Dept. Revenue and Fin., Des Moines, 1997-98; acct./auditor 1 Iowa Dept. Corrections, Des Moines, 1998—2003, acct. 2, 2003—. Camp visitor for camp accreditation State of Iowa, 1990-99. Campaign co-chmn. Kellogg (Iowa) Cmty. Chest, 1983-85, pub. rels. chmn., 1982; leader local club Jasper County 4-H, Kellogg, 1971-76, state leadership conf. del., 1971, nat. citizenship del., Washington, 1971, instr. county officers tng. sch. Jasper County, 1970-71, Jasper County v.p., 1970, state conv. del., Ames, Iowa, 1970, state counselor Des Moines Area 4-H, Madrid, Iowa, 1970; local club pres. Kellogg Club 4-H, 1970-71. Recipient State Leadership award Jasper County 4-H, 1970, named Outstanding 4-H'er of Yr., 1971; named Kellogg's Outstanding Citizen, 1983. Mem. Am. Camping Assn. (stds. chair for camp accreditation Iowa chpt. 1992-95, state of Iowa sec. 1996), Am. Camping Assn. (stds. camp accreditation com. Iowa chpt. 1996-99), Iowa State Grange (lectr. 1983-85, 91-93, state youth com. 1981-82, Iowa state youth rep. 1976), Richland Grange (state del. 1980, 83, sec. 1980-84, steward 1970-73, 77-79, overseer 1973-77, youth chmn. 1973, 75-76). United Methodist. Avocations: collecting horse figures, gardening, community service work, travel. Office: 686 Highway 224 S Kellogg IA 50135-8579

ANDERSON, DAMON ERNEST, lawyer; b. Minot, N.D., June 20, 1946; s. Melvin Ernest and Maxine I. (Spaulding) A.; m. Julie Kay Severson, Oct. 23, 1982; children: Joshua Daniel, Philip Kyle. BA, Dickinson State U., 1968; JD, U. N.D., 1974. Bar: N.D. 1974, Minn. 1981, U.S. Dist. Ct. N.D. 1974, U.S. Ct. Appeals (8th cir.) 1980, U.S. Supreme Ct. 1980. Pvt. practice Kessler and Anderson, Grand Forks, N.D., 1974-78, Grand Forks, N.D., 1978-98; asst. state's atty. Grand Forks County, N.D., 1978—. Past mem. divsnl. comdr. adv. coun. Salvation Army, Mpls., past mem. Salvation Army local adv. bd., Grand Forks. Sgt. U.S. Army, 1968-70. Mem. Am. Legion, Masons. Lutheran. Office: 151 S 4th St Ste 601 Grand Forks ND 58201-4715

ANDERSON, DARRELL EDWARD, psychologist, educator; b. Coleridge, Nebr., May 2, 1932; s. Roy Blenton and Ruby Grace (Cisney) A.; m. Violeta Salazar, Sept. 3, 1951; children: Robert, James, Timothy. AB, York Coll., 1953; PhD, U. Nebr., 1958. Counselor, asst. prof. U. Nebr., Lincoln, 1957-59; asst. prof. psychology Wittenberg U., Springfield, Ohio, 1959-61; chief psychologist Weld County Mental Health Ctr., Greeley, Colo., 1961-62; asst. prof. U. No. Colo., Greeley, 1962-66, assoc. prof., 1966-70, prof., 1970-77, chmn. dept. psychology, 1972-77; prof. counselor edn. U. N.Mex., Albuquerque, 1977-87, chmn. dept., 1977-85, prof. counseling and family studies, 1987-92, prof. emeritus, 1992—. Cons. psychologist Dulce (N.Mex.) Pub. Schs., 1984-85. Contbr. articles to profl. jours. Mem. APA, N.Mex. Psychol. Assn. Democrat. Methodist. Avocation: golf. Home: 4 Latir Ct Santa Fe NM 87508

ANDERSON, DAVID, Canadian government official; b. Victoria, B.C., Can., Aug. 16, 1937; m. Sandra McCallum; children: James, Zoe. Student, Victoria Coll.; student econs. and law, U. B.C.; student Inst. Oriental Studies, U. Hong Kong. With Dept. External Affairs; Fed. M.P. for Esquimalt Saanich Ho. of Commons, 1968-72, elected leader Liberal Party B.C., 1972; regional min. British Columbia, 1993—; founder, former chmn. spl. com. on environment pollution Ho. of Commons, Ont, M.P. for Victoria, 1993—; mem. Legis. Assembly for Victoria, 1972; of counsel B.C. Wildlife Fedn., 1975-78; tchr. law Sch. Pub. Adminstrn. U. Victoria, 1978-84; mem. Immigration Appeal Bd., 1984-89; spl. advisor to premier on tanker traffic Govt. of B.C., 1989; commr. Commn. Inquiry into Fraser Valley Petroleum Exploration, 1990; min. nat. revenue Govt. of Can., Ottawa, 1993-96, min. of transport, 1996-97, min. fisheries and oceans, 1997—, now min. environment. Cons. Environment Can., 1975-78, 89-93. Mem. silver-medal rowing crews Rome Olympic and Chgo. Pan Am. Games. Named One of 125 Victorians Who Have Made a Difference, 1992. Mem. U. B.C. Alumni Assn. (75th Alumni of Distinction award 1990). Achievements include establishment of Canada's first marine protected area; establishment of Pacific Rim Nat. Park.

ANDERSON, DAVID ARNOLD, law educator; b. 1939; AB, Harvard U., 1962; JD, U. Tex., 1971. Bar: Tex. 1972. Reporter, bur. chief United Press Internat., Austin, Tex., 1963-69; chief counsel Tex. Civil Jud. Coun., Austin, 1972; asst. prof. law U. Tex., Austin, 1972-75, prof., 1975-78, Thompson and Knight Centennial prof., 1987—. Vis. Lee prof. William and Mary U., 1983, Queen Mary Coll. U. London, 1988, 92; vis. scholar Trinity Coll. Cambridge U., 1988. Fellow Gannett Ctr. Media Studies. Mem. Assn. Am. Law Schs. (mass communications law sect.), Order of Coif, Phi Delta Phi. Office: U Tex Sch Law 727 Dean Keeton St Austin TX 78705-3224

ANDERSON, DAVID BOWEN, lawyer; b. Seattle, Sept. 19, 1948; s. Gordon Browne and Elizabeth Josephine (Bowen) A.; m. Laura Ann Jorgensen, May 23, 1975; children: Elizabeth Christine, Christina Louise. BA with great distinction, Stanford U., 1970; JD, U. Mich., 1974; MBA, Western Wash. U., 1982. Bar: Wash. 1974, Alaska 2000, Oreg. 2002, U.S. Dist. Ct. (we. dist.) Wash. 1974. Clk. Ctr. for Law and Social Policy, Washington, 1973; assoc. Bogle & Gates, Seattle, 1974-77; ptnr. Anderson, Connell & Murphy, Bellingham, Wash., 1977—; pres. San Juan Tug & Barge Co., 1979-85. Arbitrator Whatcom County, Am. Arbitration Assn.; instr. Pacific N.W. Admiralty Law Inst., Seattle, 1983, Nat. Fishery Law Symposium, Seattle, 1984; lectr. constnl. law Western Wash. U., 1996; mediator U.S. Dist. Ct. (we. dist.) Wash. Mem. adv. com. Bellingham Sch. Bd., 1981-82, Bellingham Vocat. Tech. Inst., 1986; mem. Bellingham Pub. Sch. Found. Bd., 1992, pres., 1992-93; bd. dirs. Interfaith Coalition, 1999-2002; mem. exec. com. Primorsky-Washington Russian Rule of Law Partnership. Mem. ATLA, ABA, Wash. State Bar Assn. (spl. dist. counsel, rules of profl. practice com.), Whatcom County Bar Assn. (pres. 1986), Maritime Law Assn. U.S. (proctor), Wash. Atheltic Club (Seattle), Bellingham Rotary Club (chmn. internat. svc. com.), Bellingham Golf and Country Club, Phi Beta Kappa. Presbyterian. Home: 500 16th St Bellingham WA 98225-6315 Office: Anderson Connell & Murphy 1501 Eldridge Ave Bellingham WA 98225-2801 E-mail: boatlaw@boatlaw.com.

ANDERSON, DAVID DANIEL, retired humanities educator, writer, editor; b. Lorain, Ohio, June 8, 1924; s. David and Nora Marie (Foster) A.; m. Patricia Ann Rittenhour, Feb. 1, 1953. BS, Bowling Green State U., 1951, MA, 1952; PhD, Mich. State U., 1960; D. Litt., Wittenberg U., 1986. From instr. to prof. dept. Am. thought and lang. to univ. disting. prof. Mich. State U., East Lansing, 1957-90; lectr. Am. Mus., Bath, Eng., 1980; editor U. Coll. Quar., 1971-80; Fulbright prof. U. Karachi, Pakistan, 1963-64. Am. del. to Internat. Fedn. Modern Langs. and Lit., 1969-93, Internat. Congress Orientalists, 1971-79, European Am. Studies Assn., 1994. Author: Louis Bromfield, 1964, Critical Studies in American Literature, 1964, Sherwood Anderson's Winesburg, Ohio, 1967, Sherwood Anderson, 1968 (Book Manuscript award, 1961), Brand Whitlock, 1968, Abraham Lincoln, 1970, Suggestions for the Instructor, 1970, Robert Ingersoll, 1972, Woodrow Wilison, 1978, Igantius Donnelly, 1980, William Jennings Bryan, 1981, Route Two, Titus, Ohio, 1993, The Path in the Shadow, 1998; editor: The Black Experience, 1969, Command Performances, 2003, The Literary Works of Abraham Lincoln, 1970, Sunshine and Smoke: American Writers and the American Environment, 1971; editor: (with others) The Dark and Tangled Path, 1971; editor: Mid America, 1974—, 27th edit., 2000, Sherwood Anderson: Dimensions of His Literary Art, 1976, Sherwood Anderson: The Writer at His Craft, 1979, Critical Essays on Sherwood Anderson, 1981, Michigan: A State Anthology, 1983, Myth, Memory and the American Earth: The Durability of Raintree County, 1998, Midwestern Miscellany, 1974—, numerous articles, essays, short stories, poems. Served with USN, 1942-45; with AUS, 1952-53. Decorated Silver Star, Purple Heart; recipient Disting. Alumnus award Bowling Green State U., 1976, Disting. Faculty award Mich. State U., 1974, Disting. Faculty award Mich. Assn. Governing Bds., 1988, Disting Research award Mich. State U., 1988. Mem. ASA, AAUP, MLA, Popular Culture Assn., Soc. Study Midwestern Lit. (founder, exec. sec., Disting. Service award 1982), Assn. Gen. and Liberal Edn. Am. Assn. Advancement Humanities, Internat. Assn. U. Profs. English, Univ. Club. Home: 6555 Lansdown Dr Dimondale MI 48821-9428 Office: Mich State U Dept Am Thought and Lang East Lansing MI 48824

ANDERSON, DAVID E. writer, musicologist; b. Muncie, Ind., Mar. 2, 1958; s. Edward E. and Violet M. Anderson. BS summa cum laude, William Jewell Coll., 1980; MusM, So. Ill. U., 1982; MA, U. Chgo., 1998. Editor Astrophys. Jour. U. Chgo. Press, 1990-95; writer, editor, 1995—; reviewer Forecasts Pubs. Weekly, N.Y.C., 1997—. Contbr. articles to book; reviewer articles for profl. jours. Bd. dirs. Seymour (Ind.) Main St., 2000—, Muscatatuck Wildlife Soc. Found., 2001—. Mem.: Seymour Noon Lions (bd. dirs. 2000—, sec. 2000—02, chair sight conservation program 1998—). Avocation: photography. Home and Office: Anderson Assocs 321 Jackson St Seymour IN 47274 E-mail: anderson_associates@yahoo.com.

ANDERSON, DAVID FENIMORE, mathematics educator; b. Ft. Dodge, Iowa, Dec. 20, 1948; s. Duane C. and Dorothy M. (Fenimore) A.; m. Konnie Lee Fiscel, June 22, 1974; children: Sarah, Jonathan. BS, Iowa State U., 1971; PhD, U. Chgo., 1976. Asst. prof. math. U. Tenn., Knoxville, 1976-82, assoc. prof., 1982-87, prof., 1987—. Contbr. numerous articles on commutative algebra to profl. jours. Mem. Am. Math. Soc., Math. Assn. Am. Lutheran. Office: U Tenn Dept Math Ayres Hall Knoxville TN 37996 E-mail: anderson@math.utk.edu.

ANDERSON, DAVID GASKILL, JR., Spanish language educator; b. Tarboro, N.C., Feb. 21, 1945; s. David G. Sr. and Lucile (Gammon) A.; m. Jonetta Gentemann, Jan. 29, 1968; children: Allene Q., David III, James H., John G. AB, U. N.C., 1967; MA, Vanderbilt U., 1974, PhD, 1985. Instr. of langs. Union U., Tenn., 1975-76; from instr. Spanish to asst. prof. Ouachita Bapt. U., Ark., 1976-85; asst. prof. fgn. langs. N.E. La. U., 1985-87; asst. prof. Spanish, John Carroll U., Cleve., 1987-93, assoc. prof., 1993—, acting chmn. dept. classical and modern langs., 1996, chmn., 1997—, George Grauel faculty fellow rsch. sabbatical, spring 1997. Tchg. fellow Vanderbilt U., 1983-84, NEH summer seminar on poetry, 1990; presenter in field. Author: On Elevating the Commonplace: A Structuralist Analysis of The Odas of Pablo Neruda, 1987; contbr. articles to profl. jours. Vol. ESL Peace Corps, Colombia, 1968-70. Named Outstanding Young Men of Am., 1979. Mem. Am. Assn. Tchrs. Spanish and Portuguese, Modern Lang. Assn., Cleve. Diocesan Fgn. Lang. Assn. (bd. mem. 1988-93), Cleve. Assn., Phi Beta Kappa. Democrat. Home: 2573 Dysart Rd Cleveland OH 44118-4446 Office: John Carroll Univ Classical & Modern Langs Cleveland OH 44118 E-mail: unc67@msn.com.

ANDERSON, DAVID LANGLEY, management consultant; b. Southbridge, Mass., Nov. 16, 1944; s. Arthur Godfrey and Gertrude Mary Langley; m. Melinda Marshman, June 17, 1967; children: Laura, Joy, Scott, Jennifer. BA in Econs., U. Conn., 1966; PhD in Econs., Boston Coll., 1973. Chief industry analysis U.S. Dept. Transp., Cambridge, Mass., 1972-75; v.p. Data Resources Inc., Lexington, Mass., 1975-82, Temple, Barker & Sloane Inc., Lexington, Mass., 1983-90; mng. ptnr. Andersen Cons., San Francisco, 1991-94, Boston, 1994—, London, 1996—, Boston, 1998—, Accenture, Boston, 2001— Bd. dirs. Industrl-Matematik Internat., Stockholm, Logispring Mgmt. Co., Geneva. Contbr. articles to profl. jours. Bd. dirs. Northwestern U. Ctr. for Transp. Studies, 1995—, Stanford U. Supply Chain Forum, 1995—; mem. tech. mgmt. coun. Boston Coll. Fellow Internat. Soc. Physical Distbrn. Mgmt.; mem. Am. Econs. Assn., Council Logistics Mgmt. Avocation: geneology. Home: 19 Glenridge Dr Bedford MA 01730-2009 Office: Accenture 100 William St Wellesley MA 02481-3701 E-mail: david.l.anderson@accenture.com.

ANDERSON, DAVID LAWRENCE, lawyer; b. Balt., Oct. 29, 1948; s. Robert L. and Ruth (Hahn) A. BS, Towson U., 1970; JD, U. Md., 1973. Bar: Md. 1973, U.S. Dist. Ct. Md. 1976, D.C. 1979, U.S. Dist. Ct. D.C. 1979, U.S. Ct. Appeals (D.C. cir.) 1976. Asst. revisor Gov.'s Commn. to Revise Md. Annotated Code, Annapolis, Md., 1973-74; counsel Gov.'s Task Force on Campaign Financing, Annapolis, Md., 1974-75; atty. Fed. Election Commn., Washington, 1975-77, Federal Energy Adminstrn., Washington, 1977; asst. chief counsel, trial atty. U.S. Dept. Energy, Washington, 1977-85; sr. trial atty., leader litigation team environ. enforcement sect., environment and natural resources div. U.S. Dept. Justice, Washington, 1986-90; lead counsel for Love Canal, Rocky Mountain Arsenal and New Bedford Harbor Superfund cases; sr. assoc. Shea & Gould, Washington, 1990-91, Arent Fox Kintner Plotkin & Kahn, Washington, 1992-93; ptnr. O'Connor & Hannan, Washington, 1993-95; mgr. regulatory and legis. svcs. group Waste Policy Inst., Arlington, 1995-99; sr. environ. counsel, sr. project mgr. Parsons, Fairfax, Va., 1999—. Adj. prof. polit. sci. Towson State U., 1971-73; adj. prof. legal rsch. and writing Am. U., 1985-87, 93-94. Recipient Outstanding Performance award Dept. Energy, 1981, medal and award Dept. Energy, 1983, spl. commendation Dept. Justice, 1989. Mem. ABA (environment, energy and resources law sect.), D.C. Bar Assn., Environ. Law Inst., Internat. Soc. of Environ. Forensics, Internat. Soc. of Envirn. Forensics Home: 3440 S Utah St Arlington VA 22206-1921 Office: Parsons Inc 10521 Rosehaven St Fairfax VA 22030-2839 E-mail: david.l.anderson@parsons.com.

ANDERSON, DAVID LESLIE, member of parliament; b. 1957; m. Sheila Anderson, 1982; children: Amy, Andrew. BA in Polit. Sci., U. Regina, 1978; MDiv, Can. Theol. Sem., 1990. Farmer; mem. 37th parliament House of Commons, Ottawa, Canada. Dep. agr. critic House of Commons. Chair bd. dirs. Eastend Sch. Divsn., 1994—2000. Avocations: woodworking, flying, snowboarding. Office: House of Commons Rm 618 Justice Bldg Ottawa ON K1A 0A6 Canada also: Cypress Hills-Grasslands 2-240 Central Ave N Swift Current SK S94 0L2 Canada

ANDERSON, DAVID MARTIN, environmental health scientist, environmental engineer; b. Boston, July 19, 1930; s. Martin Jens and Dorothy (Finnin) A.; m. Marjorie Gilbert, July 19, 1958; children: David, Michael, Anne, Stephen. Grad., Boston Latin Sch., 1948; BS, Northeastern U., 1953; SM, Harvard U., 1955, PhD, 1958. Registered profl. engr., Pa., diplomate, Am. Acad. Environ. Engrs., cert. Am. Bd. Indsl. Hygiene. Rsch. fellow Harvard Sch. Pub. Health, 1953-58; pub. health engr. USPHS, Cin., 1958-60; indsl. health engr. Bethlehem Steel Corp. (Pa.), 1960-67, asst. mgr. environ. quality control, 1967-71, mgr., 1971-80, corp. dir. environ. affairs, 1980-84, dir. environ. and govtl. affairs, 1984-87, gen. mgr. environ. affairs, 1987-94, cons. environ. health, 1994—. Vis. lectr. Pa. State U., 1966-71, Harvard U., 1969-81; chmn. coun. tech. advisers Pa. Dept. Health, 1964-70, N.Y. Dept. Environ. Conservation, 1974-75; co-chmn. OSHA/Am. Iron and Steel Inst. Task Force on coke oven emission stds., 1975-76; mem. Pa. Gov.'s Task Force on Occupl. Health and Safety, 1975-76; mem. com. on biol. effects of atmospheric pollutants NAS, 1971-74; mem. nat. air quality criteria adv. com. EPA, 1971-76; mem. Sec. Health, Edn. and Welfare Coal Mine Health Rsch. Adv. Coun., 1972-76; mem. U.S. Dept. Commerce Adv. Com. on Indsl. Innovation, 1978-79, mem. adv. com. Ctr. for Risk Analysis Harvard U., 1989-94; mem. negotiated rulemaking com. U.S. EPA, 1992-93. Contbr. articles to profl. jours. Mem. Am. Iron and Steel Inst. (com. on environ. 1971-94, chmn. 1978-80, 87-89), Internat. Iron and Steel Inst. (com. on environ. 1980-94), Am. Chem. Soc., Am. Indsl. Hygiene Assn. (dir. 1968-71), Air and Waste Mgmt. Assn. (dir. 1971-74), Sigma Xi, Delta Omega. Achievements include research in and critical evaluation of the epidemiology and control of dust disease. Home and Office: 1037 Westgate Cir Bethlehem PA 18017-3637 E-mail: DMAenvhealth@aol.com.

ANDERSON, DAVID POOLE, sportswriter; b. Troy, N.Y., May 6, 1929; s. Robert P. and Josephine (David) A.; m. Maureen Ann Young, Oct. 24, 1953; children: Stephen, Mark, Mary Jo, Jean Marie. BA, Holy Cross Coll., 1951. Sports writer Bklyn. Eagle, 1951-55, New York Jour.-Am., 1955-66, New York Times, 1966—. Author: Countdown to Super Bowl, 1969; (with Ray Robinson) Sugar Ray, 1970; (with Larry Csonka and Jim Kiick) Always On The Run, 1973; Pancho Gonzalez, 1974; (with Frank Robinson) Frank: The First Year, 1976; Sports Of Our Times, 1979; The Yankees, 1979; (with John Madden) Hey, Wait a Minute, I Wrote a Book, 1984; (with John Madden) The Story of Football, 1985; One Knee Equals Two Feet, 1986; One Size Doesn't Fit All, 1988; The Story of Basketball, 1988; In The Corner, 1991; Pennant Races, 1994; The Story of the Olympics, 1996; (with John Madden) All Madden, 1996; The Story of Golf, 1998; editor: The Red Smith Reader, 1981. Named to Nat. Sportscasters and Sportswriters Assn. Hall of Fame, 1990, N.Y. Sports Mus. and Hall of Fame, 1991; recipient Pulitzer prize for disting. commentary, 1981, Red Smith award, 1994, PGA of Am. Lifetime Achievement award in journalism, 1998, McCann Meml. award for disting. pro football reporting, Pro Football Hall of Fame, 1998, William D. Richardson award, Golf Writers Assn. of Am., 2003, Peter Kihss award, Soc. of Silurians, 2003. Office: NY Times 229 W 43rd St New York NY 10036-3959

ANDERSON, DAVID PREWITT, retired university dean; b. Twin Falls, Idaho, Sept. 14, 1934; m. Janice Gale Schmied, Dec. 21, 1962; children: Kathryn Lynn, Christopher Kyle. Student, U. Idaho, 1952-54; BS, Wash. State U., 1959, DVM, 1961; MS, U. Wis., 1964, PhD, 1965. NIH trainee U. Wis., 1961-62, asst. prof. vet. sci., asst. dir. biotron, 1965-69; prof. med. microbiology, dir. Poultry Disease Research Center, U. Ga., 1969-71, asso. dean research and grad. affairs Coll. Vet. Medicine, 1971-73, dean, 1975-96; retired, 1996. Animal health com. NAS, 1977-80; animal health sci. rsch. adv. bd. USDA, 1978-85, nat. adv. com. on meat and poultry inspection, 1990-92; adv. com. Ctr. for Vet. Medicine/FDA, 1984-88; tech. analysis group Food Safety Inspection Svc./USDA, 1994-95. Editor Avian Diseases, 1973-93. Mem. AVMA, Am. Coll. Vet. Microbiologists (diplomate), Am. Coll. Poultry Vets. (diplomate), Am. Assn. Avian Pathologists (pres. 1988-89), Nat. Acads. Practice. Home: 190 Harris St Winterville GA 30683-1549

ANDERSON, DAVID TREVOR, law educator; b. Winnipeg, Man., Can., Oct. 25, 1938; s. David and Mary (Irwin) A. BA, U. Man., 1959; BA in Jurisprudence, U. Oxford (Eng.), 1961, B in Civil Law, 1962. Asst. prof. law U. Alta., Edmonton, Can., 1962-66, assoc. prof., 1966-69, prof., 1969-71; prof. law U. Man., Winnipeg, 1971—, assoc. dean faculty of law, 1972-77, dean, 1984-89. Bd. dirs. Alta. Inst. Law Rsch. and Reform, Edmonton, 1968-71; mem. Man. Law Reform Commn., Winnipeg, 1981-84, Man. Pub. Utilities Bd., 1988-2000. Named Queen's Counsel, Province of Man., 1985; Rhodes scholar, 1959. Mem. Law Soc. Man. (dir. edn. 1977-80, bencher 1984-89), Can. Bar Assn. Conservative. Presbyterian. Office: U Man Faculty of Law Robson Hall Winnipeg MB Canada R3T 2N2

ANDERSON, DAVID WALTER, physics educator, consultant; b. Heron Lake, Minn., June 18, 1937; s. Walter Olaf and Martha Gladys (Bonnell) A.; m. Jane Louise Friedlund, Dec. 17, 1960; children: Bonnie Jean, Brian David. BS in Physics summa cum laude, Hamline U., 1959; PhD in Nuclear Physics, Iowa State U., 1965. Diplomate Am. Bd. Radiology, 1968. Postdoctoral fellow in physics Iowa State U., Ames, 1965-66; prof. U. Okla., Norman, 1966-82; prof. radiation physics U. Okla. Health Ctr., Oklahoma City, 1966-82; prof., dir. radiol. physics City of Faith Med. Ctr., Tulsa, 1982-88, Tulsa Regional Med. Ctr., 1988—. Presenter in field; advisor MS and/or PhD students, 1970-84. Author: Absorption of Ionizing Radiation, 1984; contbr. over 53 articles to profl. refereed jours. Chmn. coun. ministry McFarlin Meth. Ch., 1979, chmn. adminstrv. bd., 1978. Grantee Rsch. Corp., Am. Cancer Soc., Radiation Measurement Inc. Fellow Am. Coll. Radiology; mem. Am. Assn. Physicists in Medicine (physics com. on profl. activities 1986-90), Am. Bd. Radiology (physics examiner 1986-90), Am. Coll. Radiology, Soc. Nuclear Medicine, Phi Kappa Phi. Democrat. Achievements include responsiblity for shielding design, acceptance testing, primary data on 19 new or upgraded sites of clinical accelerators. Home: 3617 Guilford Ln Norman OK 73072-3037 Office: Tulsa Regional Med Ctr 744 W 9th St Tulsa OK 74127-9028 E-mail: dwajla@aol.com.

ANDERSON, DAVIN CHARLES, business representative, labor consultant; b. Mpls., July 26, 1955; s. Roland Lawrence Anderson and Merlyne (Aldrich) Bissell; m. Diane Elmshauser, Aug. 14, 1982; children: Kiersten Janel, Matilda Rae. Student, St. Cloud State U., Minn., 1973-76; BS, U. Minn., 1979. Technician Northwest Cinema, Mpls., 1976-78, Mann Cinemas, Mpls., 1978-81, Gen. Cinema Corp., Mpls., 1981-99, Tacora Theatre, 1999—; account exec. Van Clemens & Co., Mpls., 1987—. Sec. Assn. Entertainment Industries Unions, St. Paul, 1987—. Mem. AFL-CIO (del.), Internat Alliance Theatrical and Stage Employees (bus. rep. Local 219 1986—), Nat. Assn. Investors Clubs, Trades and Labor Council (del.), Cen. Labor Union Council (del.), Toastmasters. Lutheran. Avocations: fishing, boating, skiing, hiking, flying. Home: 201 3d Ave S PO Box 626 Biwabik MN 55708-0626

ANDERSON, DEAN WILLIAM, educational administrator; b. Mpls., Min., Aug. 28, 1946; s. Edward Marvin and Mabel (Gilland) A.; m. Elaine Heumann Gurian; children: Erik Wheeler, Matthew Edward. BA, Macalester Coll., 1968; MA, U. Calif.-Berkeley, 1970. Examiner Office Mgmt. and Budget, Washington, 1970-73; adminstrv. officer Smithsonian Instn., Washington, 1973-84, asst. sec. history and art, 1984-85, under sec., 1985-90; dep. dir. mgmt. and planning Woodrow Wilson Ctr., Washington, 1990—2001, acting dir., 1997-99; vis. lectr. Grad. Program Goteborg U., 2002—. Trustee Interlochen Ctr. for Arts. Recipient Robert Brooks award Smithsonian Instn., 1983; Minn. SPAN Assn. scholar, Israel, 1967; MacPherson Found. scholar, Mpls., 1967. Mem. Interlochen Alumni Orgn. (pres. 1994-98, nat. bd. dirs.), Phi Beta Kappa, Pi Sigma Alpha. Avocation: golf. Home: 4834 8th St S Arlington VA 22204-1432

ANDERSON, DENICE ANNA, editor; b. Detroit, Nov. 11, 1947; d. Carl Magnus and Geraldine Elizabeth (Willer) A. BA in Journalism, Mich. State U., 1970. Copy editor/reporter The State News, East Lansing, Mich., 1965-70; reporter/copy editor/photographer The Tecumseh (Mich.) Herald, 1966-68, 99—; copy editor/entertainment editor The State Jour., Lansing, Mich., 1970-76; freelance writer State Jour./Lansing Mag., 1977-79; freelance corr. Collier's

Year Book, N.Y.C., 1977-79; copy editor, proofreader Booz, Allen & Hamilton, N.Y.C., 1980-81, Rogers & Wells, N.Y.C., 1981-83, Advanced Therapeutics Comm., N.Y.C., 1983-84; freelance editor, N.Y.C., Santa Fe, Clinton, Mich., 1984—. Contbr. articles to profl. jours. Bd. dirs., sec. March of Dimes, Lansing, 1972-76; vol./writer Polio Info. Ctr., N.Y.C., 1984-88; vol. Vol. Involvement Svcs., Santa Fe, N.M., 1989. Mem. Editorial Freelancers Assn. Lutheran. Home: 210 E Church St Clinton MI 49236

ANDERSON, DENNIS, computer scientist information technology educator; b. Korea, Nov. 5, 1969; s. Nam-Ki No and Woon-Ja Choi. BA, Fordham U., 1991; MS, NYU, 1993; EdM, Columbia U., 1995, MPhil, PhD, Columbia U., 1999. Cert. MIT profl. Mem. faculty CUNY, 1993, NYU, 1993; chmn. St. Francis Coll., Bklyn.; assoc. dean PACE U. Fulbrigh Sr. Specialist; editor Assn. Info. Sys. Newsletter, N.Y.C., 1996-98; reviewer N.Y. State Edn. Dept. Institutional Accreditation, 2003; Fulbright Sr. Specialist, 2001—. Author: Introduction to Computers, 1996, Introduction to Programming, 1996; lectr., presenter in field. Tech. cons. Dem. Nat. Conv. Com., N.Y., 1992. Rsch. grantee St. Francis Coll., 1995, 96, faculty devel. grantee, 1995, 96, Microsoft Instrnl. Lab. grantee, NSF grantee; others. Mem. IEEE, Am. Soc. Engring. Edn., Assn. Info. Sys., Assn. Computer Machinery (chpt. chmn. 1995—, spl. interest group for computer sci. edn.), Nat. Coun. Tchrs. of Math., N.Y. Acad. Scis., Kappa Delta Pi. Achievements include becoming chmn. of computer info. sys. dept. at age 26. Home: 220 E 26th St Apt 4H New York NY 10010-2422 Office: Pace U 1 Pace Plz New York NY 10038

ANDERSON, DON LYNN, geophysicist; b. Frederick, Md., Mar. 5, 1933; s. Richard Andrew and Minola (Phares) Anderson; m. Nancy Lois Ruth, Sept. 15, 1956; children: Lynn Ellen, Lee Weston. BS, Rensselaer Poly. Inst., 1955; MS, Calif. Inst. Tech., 1959, PhD, 1962; DSc (hon.), Rensselaer Poly. Inst., 2000. With Chevron Oil Co., Mont., Wyo., Calif., 1955—56; with Air Force Cambridge Research Center, Boston, 1956—58, Arctic Inst. N.Am., Boston, 1958; mem. faculty Calif. Inst. Tech., Pasadena, 1962—, assoc. prof. geophysics, 1964—68, prof., 1968—, dir. seismol. lab., 1967—89, Eleanor and John R. McMillan prof. of geophysics, 1990—. Prin. investigator Viking Mars Seismic Expt.; mem. various coms. NASA; chmn. geophysics rsch. forum NAS; chmn. Arthur L. Day award com. NSF, chmn. Geosci. adv. com., 1994; chmn. adv. bd. for Sch. of Earth Scis. Stanford U., 1995, mem. adv. com. Purdue U., U. Chgo., U. Tex., Stanford U., U. Calif. Berkeley, Carnegie Instn., Washington, U. Paris, Yale U., Rice U.; Consortium for High Pressure Rsch. U. Calif.-Riverside; co-founder Inc. Rsch. Insts. for Seismology. Assoc. editor Jour. Geophys. Rsch., 1965—67, Tectonophysics, 1974—77; editor: Physics of the Earth and Planetary Interiors, 1984—94. Recipient Exceptional Sci. Achievement award, NASA, 1977, Emil Wiechert medal, German Geophys. Soc., 1986, Crafoord prize, Royal Swedish Acad. Scis., 1998, Nat. medal of Sci., 1998; fellow Guggenheim, 1998, Sloan Found., 1965—67. Fellow: AAAS (pres. tectonophysics sect. 1971—72, chmn. Macelwane award com. 1975, mem. Bowie medal com. 1985, pres.-elect 1986—88, pres. 1988—90, chair 1994, James B. Macelwane award 1966, Bowie medal 1990), Geol. Soc. Am. (assoc. editor bull. 1971—, mem. Penrose medal com. 1989, mem. Arthur L. Day medal com. 1989—90, mem. long range planning com. 1990—, Arthur L. Day medal 1987), Am. Geophys. Union; mem.: NAS (chmh. seismology com. 1975, chmn. Geophysics Rsch. Forum 1984—86), Seismol. Soc. Am., Royal Astron. Soc. (Gold medal 1988), Am. Philos. Soc., Sigma Xi. Home: 669 Alameda St Altadena CA 91001-3001 Office: Calif Inst Tech Seismol Lab 252 21 Pasadena CA 91125-0001

ANDERSON, DONALD BERNARD, oil company executive; b. Chgo., Apr. 6, 1919; s. Hugo August and Hilda (Nelson) A.; m. Patricia Gaylord, 1945 (dec. 1978); m. Sarah Midgette, 1980. BS in Mech. Engring, Purdue U., 1942. Vice pres. Hondo Oil & Gas Co. (formerly Malco Refineries, Inc.), Roswell, N.Mex.; vice pres. Hondo Oil & Gas Co. and subs. corps., Roswell, N.Mex., 1946-63; pres. Anderson Oil Co., Roswell, 1963—, Cotter Corp., 1966-70, chmn. bd., 1966-74; founder, pres. Anderson Drilling Co., Denver, 1974—, pres., chmn. bd., 1977—. Curator fine arts, mem. acquisitions com. Roswell Mus. and Art Center, 1949-56, trustee, 1956-85, pres. bd., 1960-85, 87—, trustee, pres. 1987-90; bd. dirs. Sch. Am. Rsch., Santa Fe, chmn. bd., 1985-88, bd. dirs. 1989—; bd. dirs. Jargon Soc., Penland, N.C.; regent Ea. N.Mex. U., 1966-72; commr. Smithsonian Instn., Nat. Mus. Am. Art, 1980-88. Lt. USNR, 1942-46. Office: PO Box 1 Roswell NM 88202-0001

ANDERSON, DONALD H. gas industry executive; b. 1948; Grad., U. Colo., Boulder, 1970. Acct. Peat, Marwick, Mitchell Y Co., Denver, 1970—78, Western Crude Oil Inc., Denver, 1978—82; with Lantern Petroleum Corp., Denver, 1983—; chmn, pres., ceo Pan Energy, Houston; vice-cmn. & CEO TransMontaigne Inc., Denver, 1999—, pres., vice-chmn. & CEO, 2000—. Office: TransMontaigne 2750 Republic Pl Denver CO 80202

ANDERSON, DONALD KENNEDY, JR., English educator; b. Evanston, Ill., Mar. 18, 1922; s. Donald Kennedy and Kathryn Marie (Shields) A.; m. Kathleen Elizabeth Hughes, Sept. 11, 1949; children: David J., Lawrence W. AB, Yale U., 1943; MA, Northwestern U., 1947; PhD, Duke U., 1957. Instr. Geneva Coll., Beaver Falls, Pa., 1947-49; from instr. to asst. prof. Rose Poly. Inst., Terre Haute, Ind., 1952-58; asst. prof., assoc. prof. Butler U., Indpls., 1958-65; assoc. prof. U. Mo., Columbia, 1965-67, prof. dept. English, 1967-92, prof. emeritus, 1992—, assoc. dean Grad. Sch., 1970-74. Author: John Ford, 1972; editor: John Ford's Perkin Warbeck, 1965, John Ford's The Broken Heart, 1968, Concord in Discord, The Plays of John Ford, 1586-1986, 1987. Served to lt. (j.g.) USNR, 1943-46. Folger fellow, 1965; U. Mo. Summer Research fellow, 1966, 68, 76, 79, 84 Mem. MLA (midwest regional del. 1972-75), AAUP (sec.-treas. 1962-63) Democrat. Methodist. Home: 3700 S Lenoir St Apt 223 Columbia MO 65201

ANDERSON, DONALD MEREDITH, bank executive; b. Milan, Minn., Feb. 19, 1928; s. Meredith A. and Lydia (Helseth) A.; m. Christine Skorupa; 1 child, Karen. Student, St. Olaf Coll., Northfield, Minn., 1946-48; BA, U. Minn., 1948-50; MBA, Harvard U., 1952; postgrad. Grad. Banking Sch., U. Wis.-Madison, 1965-67. Factory rep. Congoleum-Nairn, Inc., 1953-56; stockbroker J.M. Dain & Co., Mpls., 1956-58; v.p. comml. lending and corr. banking Northwestern Nat. Bank of Mpls., 1958-69; v.p. lending Santa Barbara Nat. Bank, Calif., 1969-71; pres. Santa Barbara Bank & Trust, 1971-89, chmn., 1989—. Dir. Gen. Telephone Calif., 1976—, mem. audit com., 1982— ; mem. regional adv. com. Comptroller of Currency, 1975-76 Bd. dirs. Blue Cross So. Calif., 1981— ; bd. dirs. Mission council Boy Scouts Am., 1977—, v.p. 1977-80, pres. 1985; bd. dirs. Goleta Valley Hosp., 1978—, pres., 1979-80; mem. Industry Edn. Council, 1975—, chmn., 1984— ; trustee U. Calif.-Santa Barbara, 1984— ; mem. comdr.'s adv. bd. Vandenberg AFB, 1978— ; mem. adv. bd. Vis. Nurses Assn., 1983— ; past pres. bd. dirs. Trinity Lutheran Ch., United Way; bd. dirs. Santa Barbara Zoo, 1985— . Served to 1st lt. USAF, 1952-53 Mem. Calif. Bankers Assn. (dir. 1982—, chair comml. lending com. 1977), Santa Barbara C. of C. (v.p. 1979, dir. 1972, 78—, Western Ind. Bankers Assn. (pres. 1985, sec. 1983, dir. 1981—), Am. Bankers Assn. (bank investments com. 1976-79) Republican. Home: 485 Via Hierba Santa Barbara CA 93110-2214 Office: Santa Barbara Bank & Trust 1021 Anacapa St Santa Barbara CA 93101-2102

ANDERSON, DONALD NORTON, JR., retired electrical engineer; b. Chgo., Aug. 15, 1928; s. Donald Norton and Helen Dorothy (Lehmann) A. BS, Purdue U., 1950, MS, 1952. With Hughes Aircraft Co., Culver City and El Segundo City, Calif., 1952-84, sect. head, sr. project engr., 1960-65, tech. mgr. Apollo program, 1965-66, mgr. visible systems dept., 1966-69, 70-73, project mgr., 1969-70, mgr. space sensors lab., 1973-79, mgr. space electro-optical systems labs., 1979-80, 80-84, ret., 1984. Recipient Apollo Achievement award, 1970; Robert J. Collier Landsat award, 1974. Mem. Rsch. Soc. Am., Nat. Speleological Soc., Am. Theatre Organ Soc., Sigma Xi (sec. Hughes Labs. br. 1974-75), Eta Kappa Nu, Sierra Club. Home: 1885 Craig's Store Rd Afton VA 22920-2013 E-mail: dnafactor@aol.com.

ANDERSON, DONNA ELAINE, elementary and secondary school educator; b. Lone Wolf, Okla., Mar. 26, 1935; d. William Herbert and Lois Alta (Montgomery) Tolleson; m. Frank D. Anderson, Sept. 3, 1955; 1 child, Valerie Elaine. BA cum laude, U. North Tex., 1957, MEd, 1960. Cert. edn. diagnostician, elem. tchr., bus. tchr.; registered profl. ednl. diagnostician. Tchr. White Deer (Tex.) Ind. Sch. Dist., 1957-62, Pampa (Tex.) Ind. Sch. Dist., 1962-70, ednl. diagnostician, 1973—2003. Missionette dir. First Assembly God Ch., Pampa, 1973—; mem. Pampa Fine Arts Assn., 1978—, Community Concert Assn., Pampa, 1965—. Mem. NEA (life), Tex. Ednl. Diagnosticians Assn., Tex. State Tchrs. Assn. (life), Ednl. Diagnosticians Golden Spread, Coun. Exceptional Children, Knife and Fork Club, Delta Kappa Gamma. Democrat. Mem. Assemby of God Ch. Avocations: photography, piano.

ANDERSON, DORIS EHLINGER, lawyer; b. Houston; d. Joseph Otto and Cornelia Louise (Pagel) Ehlinger; m. Wiley Anderson, Jr. (dec.); children: Wiley Newton III, Joe E. BA, Rice U., 1946; permanent high sch. tchr. cert., U. Houston, 1948; JD, U. Tex., 1950; MLS in Museology, U. Okla., 1985. Bar: Tex. 1950, U.S. Supreme Ct. Assoc. Ehlinger & Anderson, Houston, 1950-52, ptnr., 1965—; assoc. Price, Guinn, Wheat & Veltmann, Houston, 1952-55, Wheat, Dyche & Thornton, Houston, 1955-65; life mem. Rice Assocs., Houston, 1984—. Hist. lectr., Harvard Negotiation Seminar, 1992 Edn. for Ministry, U of South, 1999. Editor: Houston City of Destiny, 1980; contbr. articles to hist. pubs. and to Bayou Bend. Parliamentarian Harris County Flood Control Task Force, Houston, 1975-2003; dir. Houston Bapt. Mus Am. Architecture and Decorative Arts, 1980-90, curator costume, 1980; apptd. ambassador Inst. Texan Culture U. Tex, San Antonio; past pres. gen. San Jacinto Descendants; docent Bayou Bend Mus. Fine Arts, Houston. Recipient best interpretive exhibit award Tex. Hist. Commn., 1983, Outstanding Woman of Yr. award YWCA, Houston, 1983; named adm. Tex. Navy, 1980. Mem. ABA, UDC (chaplain, pres., parliamentarian gen. Jefferson Davis chpt.), Assn. Women Attys. Houston, Houston Bar Assn., Daus. Republic Tex., Am. Mus. Soc., Harris County Heritage Soc., Kappa Beta Pi (pres. Lamda alumni). Episcopalian. Home: 5556 Cranbrook Rd Houston TX 77056-1600 Office: Ehlinger & Anderson 5556 Sturbridge Dr Houston TX 77056-1623

ANDERSON, DORIS ELAINE, lawyer; b. Nov. 6, 1934; d. Frederick John and Hazel Elizabeth (Bergman). AB in Mus., U. Mich., 1956; JD, U. Calif.-Berkeley, 1964. Bar: Calif., 1968. Atty. Fibreboard Corp., San Francisco, 1965-79; gen. counsel Internat. Diamond Corp., San Rafael, Calif., 1980-82; legal counsel Kaiser-Crebs Mgmt. Corp., Oakland, Calif., 1983-85; asst. sec., atty. Fibreboard Corp., Concord, Calif., 1989-93; mgr. corp. affairs and asst. sec. Fair Isaac and Co., Inc., San Rafael, Calif., 1993-98. Mem. Am. SOc. Corp. Secs., Inc. Avocations: tennis, golf, music. Home: 5310 Taft Ave Oakland CA 94618-1519 : PO Box 11608 Oakland CA 94611 E-mail: dorisanderson@att.net.

ANDERSON, DOROTHY FISHER, social worker, psychotherapist; b. Funchal, Madeira, May 31, 1924; d. Lewis Mann Anker and Edna (Gilbert) Fisher (adoptive father David Henry Fisher); m. Theodore W. Anderson, July 8, 1950; children: Robert Lewis, Janet Anderson Yang, Jeanne Elizabeth. BA, Queens Coll., 1945; AM, U. Chgo., 1947. Diplomate Am. Bd. Examiners in Clin. Social Work; lic. clin. social worker, Calif.; registered cert. social worker, N.Y. Intern Cook County (Ill.) Bur. Pub. Welfare, Chgo., 1945-46, Ill. Neuropsychiat. Inst., Chgo., 1946; clin. caseworker, Neurol. Inst. Presbyn. Hosp., N.Y.C., 1947; therapist, Mental Hygiene Clinic VA, N.Y.C., 1947-50; therapist, Child Guidance Clinic Pub. Elem. Sch. 42, N.Y.C., 1950-53; social worker, counselor Cedarhurst (N.Y.) Family Service Agy., 1954-55; psychotherapist, counselor Family Service of the Midpeninsula, Palo Alto, Calif., 1971-73, 79-86, George Hexter, M.D., Inc., 1972-83; clin. social worker Tavistock Clinic, London, 1974-75, El Camino Hosp., Mountain View, Calif., 1979; pvt. practice clin. social work, 1978-92; ret., 1992. Cons. Human Resource Services, Sunnyvale, Calif., 1981-86. Hannah G. Solomon scholar U. Chgo., 1945-46; Commonwealth fellow U. Chgo., 1946-47. Fellow Soc. Clin. Social Work (Continuing Edn. Recognition award 1980-83); mem. Nat. Assn. Social Workers (diplomate in clin. social work). Avocations: sculpture, tennis, travel, drawing, pastels.

ANDERSON, DOROTHY KENTNER, architect; b. Wildwood, N.J., Sept. 25, 1937; d. William Herman and Mary (Cresse) Kentner; m. William M. Anderson, Sept. 20, 1958; children: Wendelyn, William, Richard. AB, U. Pa., 1959; student, New Eng. Sch. Art and Design, Boston, 1971-73; AA, Harrisburg Area C.C., 1976; BArch magna cum laude, Drexel U., 1996. Interior designer Anderson Designs, Lewisberry, Pa., 1973—; with Planned Interiors of Hershey, 1988-89; archtl. intern By Design Cons., Harrisburg, Pa., 1996-98, The Bink Partnership, 1999—. Designer, draftsman Bice Cabinet Co., Harrisburg, Pa., 1979-80; art sales, cons. William Ris Galleries, Camp Hill, Pa., 1977-79; design assoc. T.L. Kinsley Interiors, York, Pa. Co-dir. (self-guided walking tour book) Harrisburg, A Walk Through History, 1980—. Bd. dirs., founding mem. Masterpiece Film Series, Harrisburg, 1982—90, bd. dirs., 2002, Market Sq. Chamber Concert series, Harrisburg, 1983—89, 2002, Greater Harrisburg Art Coun., Habitat for Humanity-Ctrl. Pa. Ednl. Found. grantee AAUW, 1984. Mem.: AAUW (cultural chmn. 1976—80), AIA (assoc.), Am. Soc. Interior Designers (profl. mem.). also: Bink Architectural Partnership 133 South 32nd St Camp Hill PA 17011 E-mail: dotty@bink.net.

ANDERSON, DOUGLAS EDWIN, neurosurgeon; b. Ft. Monmouth, N.J., Sept. 2, 1952; m. Ann Leuking; children: Joseph, Ellie, David, Kjersten. MD, Chgo. Med. Sch., 1977. Diplomate Am. Bd. Neurosurgery. Intern Loyola U. Med. Ctr., Maywood, Ill., 1978, resident, 1978—83, neurosurgeon, 1983—; chief neurosurgery Hines (Ill.) VA Hosp., 1989—. Baritone Music of the Baroque, Chgo.; bd. elem. edn. Grace Luth. Ch. Sch., River Forest, Ill. Avocations: singing, boating, skiing. Office: Loyola U Med Ctr 2160 S 1st Ave Maywood IL 60153-3304

ANDERSON, DOUGLAS RICHARD, ophthalmologist, educator, scientist, researcher; b. Memphis, Apr. 7, 1938; s. William Arnold Douglas and Hariott Isabel (Gates) A.; m. Wirtley Anne Raine, Nov. 28, 1964; children: John Douglas, Wendy Anne, Michael Allen Scott. AB magna cum laude, U. Miami, Coral Gables, Fla., 1958; MD, Washington U., St. Louis, 1962. Diplomate Am. Bd. Ophthalmology (bd. dirs. 1988-95). Rotating intern U. Hosp. Cleve., 1962-63; staff assoc. Nat. Cancer Inst., Bethesda, Md., 1963-65; resident in ophthalmology U. Calif. Med. Ctr., San Francisco, 1965-68; rsch. fellow Howe lab. Mass. Eye and Ear Infirmary, Boston, 1968-69; asst. prof. U. Miami (Fla.) Sch. Medicine, 1969-75, assoc. prof., 1975-82, prof., 1982—. Mem. nat. eye adv. coun. NIH, Bethesda, 1982-86, visual sci. study sect. A, 1972-76, chmn., 1975-76; bd. govs. Anne Bates Leach Eye Hosp., Miami, 1987-93, 98—, outpatient med. dir., 1993-95. Author: Testing the Field of Vision, 1982, Perimetry With and Without Automation, 1987, Automated Static Perimetry, 1992, 2d edit., 1999; contbr. over 200 sci. articles and book chpts.; co-editor: Discussions on Glaucoma, 1977, Automatic Perimetry in Glaucoma, 1985, Encounters in Glaucoma Research I: Receptors, 1994, Optic Nerve in Glaucoma, 1995, How to Ascertain Progression and Outcome, 1996; assoc. editor Am. Jour. Opththalmology, Chgo., 1973-90. Mem., active med. staff Jackson Meml. Hosp., 1969-, Anne Bates Leach Eye Hosp., v.p., 1983-84, pres., 1984-86. Surgeon USPHS, 1963-65. Recipient William and Mary Greve Internat. Scholars award Rsch. to Prevent Blindness, Inc., 1978, Sr. Sci. Investigator award, 1986, 93, Recognition award Alcon Rsch. Inst., Ft. Worth, 1986; rsch. grantee Nat. Eye Inst., 1969-91, 93-97, Am. Health Assistance Found., 1978-95, Glaucoma Rsch. Found., 1993-94. Fellow Am. Acad. Ophthalmology (councillor 1984-86, Gold medal 1972, Honor awards 1978, 83, Sr. Honor award 1992); mem. Am. Glaucoma Soc. (v.p. 1988-90, pres. 1990-92), Assn. for Rsch. in Vision and Ophthalmology (trustee 1983-88, pres. 1987, Mildred Weisenfeld award 1997), Am. Ophthal. Soc., Internat. Perimetric Soc. Home: 11880 SW 63rd Ave Miami FL 33156-4802 Office: Bascom Palmer Eye Inst PO Box 016880 900 NW 17th St Miami FL 33101-6880 Fax: 305-326-6306.

ANDERSON, DYKE A. former medical association administrator; Dir. Nat. Assn. Bds. Pharmacy, Park Ridge, Ill., 2000—01.

ANDERSON, E. KARL, lawyer; b. Huntington, W. Va., Mar. 30, 1931; s. Earle Karl and Helen Emrie (Johnson) A.; m. Mary Elizabeth Williams, Nov. 13, 1953; children: Sharon Elizabeth, Charles Wesley. BBA, So. Methodist U., 1953, LLB, 1960. Bar: Tex. 1960, U.S. Dist. Ct. (no. dist.) Tex. 1963, U.S. Supreme Ct. 1971. Field supr. Travelers Ins. Co., Dallas, 1956-57; claim mgr. Allstate Ins. Co., Dallas, 1958-62; practiced in Dallas, 1963—; pntr. Lastelick, Anderson and Arneson, Dallas, 1968—. 1st lt. USAF, 1954—56. Fellow Tex. Bar Found.; mem. Am. Bar Assn., Dallas Assn. Trial Lawyers (dir. 1964-65, 74-75), Tex. Trial Lawyers Assn., Assn. Trial Lawyers Am., Dallas Country Club, Delta Theta Phi, Sigma Iota Epsilon, Sigma Alpha Epsilon. Presbyterian. Home: 3111 Drexel Dr Dallas TX 75205-2910 Office: Univ Twr Bldg S-402 6440 N Central Expy Dallas TX 75206-4123

ANDERSON, EDGAR RATCLIFFE, JR., career officer, hospital administrator, physician; b. Baton Rouge, Mar. 13, 1940; m. Sandra Caston; children: Melisa, Edward, Mark. MD, La. State U., 1964; grad., Industrial Coll. Armed Forces, 1972, Air War Coll., 1982. Diplomate Am. Bd. Family Practice, Am. Bd. Dermatology, Am. Bd. Preventive Medicine. Commd. 2d lt. USAF, 1965, advanced through grades to lt. gen., 1994, flight surgeon 464th Troop Carrier Wing, 1965-68, chief aerospace medicine 33d Tactical Fighter Wing Eglin AFB, Fla., 1968-69, undergrad. pilot tng. Williams AFB, Ariz., 1969-71, completed F-4 combat crew tng. MacDill AFB, Fla., 1971, aircraft comdr. 336th Tactical Fighter Squadron Seymour Johnson AFB, N.C., 1971, asst. ops. officer Ubon Royal Thai AFB, chief aeromed. svcs. USAF Regional Hosp. MacDill AFB, 1973-75, comdr. USAF Hosp. Seymour Johnson AFB, 1975-77, staff dermatologist USAF Med. Ctr. Keesler AFB, Miss., 1980-81, chief flight test ops. USAF-RAF exchange program Royal Air Force Station, Farnborough, Eng., 1981-83, comdr. USAF Regional Hosp. Langley AFB, Va., 1983-84, dir. profl. svcs. Office of Command Surgeon Tactical Air Command, 1984, command surgeon HQ Pacific Air Forces Hickam AFB, Hawaii, 1984-86, command surgeon SAC Offutt AFB, Nebr., 1986-90, comdr. Wilford Hall USAF Med. Ctr. Lackland AFB, Tex., 1990, surgeon general Washington, ret., 1996; CEO Truman Health Sys., Kansas City, Mo., 1996-98. Dean, prof. Sch. Med. U. Mo., Kansas City, 1996-97; exec. v.p., CEO AMA, Chgo., 1998—. Decorated D.S.M. with oak leaf cluster, Legion of Merit with oak leaf cluster, D.F.C. with oak leaf cluster, Meritorious Svc. Medal with two oak leaf clusters, Air medal with nine oak leaf clusters, Air Force Commendation Medal.

ANDERSON, EDWARD RILEY, state supreme court justice; b. Chattanooga, Aug. 10, 1932; BS, U. Tenn., 1955, JD, 1957. Bar: Tenn. 1958, U.S. Dist. Ct. (ea. dist.) Tenn. 1965, U.S. Ct. Appeals (4th cir.) 1985, U.S. Ct. Appeals (6th cir.), U.S. Supreme Ct. 1988. Assoc. Joyce & Wilson, Oak Ridge, Tenn., 1957—61; ptnr. Joyce, Anderson & Meredith, Oak Ridge, 1961—87; judge Tenn. Ct. Appeals, Knoxville, 1987—90; justice Tenn. Supreme Ct., Knoxville, 1990—, chief justice, 1994—2001. Mem. Tenn. Jud. Conf., 1987—; bd. dirs. Conf. of Chief Justices, 1999-2000, vice chair children and the family com., 1998-99, chmn. Tenn. Jud. Coun., 1990-95, Select Senate/House Com. on Ct. Automation,1990-94. Past commr. Oak Ridge City Charter. Recipient vocat. Svc. award Oak Ridge Rotary Club, 2000; named Judge of Yr. Am. Bd. Trial Advocates, 1998. Fellow Am. Bar Found., Tenn. Bar Found.; mem. ABA, Am. Bd. Trial Advocates (pres. Tenn. chpt. 1987-88), Tenn. Bar Assn. (William M. Leech Jr. Pub. Svc. award 2001), Anderson County Bar Assn. (pres. 1961), Tenn. Def. Lawyers Assn. (pres. 1980-81), Am. Inns of Ct. (pres. Tenn. chpt. 1988-90). Avocations: reading, golf. Office: Tenn Supreme Ct Supreme Court Bldg 501 Main St Ste 200 Knoxville TN 37902-2512

ANDERSON, EDWARD VIRGIL, lawyer; b. San Francisco, Oct. 17, 1953; s. Virgil P and Edna Pauline (Pedersen) A.; m. Kathleen Helen Dunbar, Sept. 3, 1983; children: Elizabeth D., Hilary J. AB in Econs., Stanford U., 1975, JD, 1978. Bar: Calif. 1978. Assoc. Pillsbury Madison & Sutro, San Francisco, 1978—, ptnr., 1987-94; chmn. mng. ptnr., mem. firm mgmt. com. Skjerven Morrill LLP, San Jose, 1994—2003; ptnr. Sidley Austin Brown & Wood, San Francisco, 2003—. Editor IP Litigator, 1995—; mem. bd. editors Antitrust Law Devel., 1983-86. Trustee Lick-Wilmerding H.S., San Francisco, 1980—, pres.; trustee Santa Clara Law Found., 1995—; trustee, v.p. Hamlin Sch. for Girls, San Francisco, 1998—, v.p. Mem. ABA, Calif. Bar Assn., San Francisco Bar Assn., Santa Clara Bar Assn. (counsel), City Club San Francisco, Stanford Golf Club, Phi Beta Kappa. Republican. Episcopal. Home: 330 Santa Clara Ave San Francisco CA 94127-2035 Office: Sidley Austin Brown & Wood Ste 5000 555 Calif St San Francisco CA 94104 E-mail: evanderson@sidley.com.

ANDERSON, ELLIS BERNARD, retired lawyer, pharmaceutical company executive; b. Michigan City, Ind., Aug. 30, 1926; s. A.B. and Esther Anderson; m. Adrienne Scotchbrook, Aug. 6, 1955 (dec. Aug. 1991); children: Rebecca J., Katherine V.; m. Jermain Johnson Andrews, May 22, 1993. AB cum laude, Ind. U., 1949, JD, 1952; grad., Advanced Mgmt. Program, Harvard U., 1970. Bar: Ind. 1952. Ptnr. Butt, Bowers & Anderson, Evansville, Ind., 1952-60; with Baxter Labs. Inc., Morton Grove, Ill., 1961-65; sr. v.p., gen. counsel, dir., mem. exec. com. Hoffmann-La Roche Inc., Nutley, N.J., 1965-88. With AUS, World War II. Mem. Nassau Club, Bay Head Yacht Club, Springdale Golf Club, Phi Beta Kappa. Home: 1 Larch Way Princeton NJ 08540-5053

ANDERSON, ERIC ANTHONY, city manager; b. New Orleans, June 2, 1946; s. Eric Albert and Edna (Barrie) A.; m. Linda Jane Briefstein, June 22, 1967; children: Eric Scott, Stacy Alissa. BA, Syracuse U., 1967; MPA, SUNY, Albany, 1968; MA, Maxwell Sch., Syracuse U., 1970, Harvard U., 1994. Adminstrv. intern City of Phoenix, 1970-71; asst. dir. Rsch. and Devel. Ctr., Internat. City Mgmt. Assn., Washington, 1971-73; asst. town mgr. Town of Windsor (Conn.), 1973-78; town mgr. Munster (Ind.), 1978-83; city mgr. Eau Claire (Wis.), 1984-91, Evanston, Ill., 1991-95, Des Moines, 1995—. Bd. mgrs. Windsor-Bloomfield YMCA, 1976-78; adv. coun. Urban League N.W. Ind., 1979. NEH fellow, Princeton Univ., 1977. Fellow Nat. Acad. Pub. Adminstrn., Ind. Mcpl. Mgmt. Assn. (pres. 1979-80), Conn. City Mgmt. Assn. (treas. 1977-78), Internat. City Mgmt. Assn. (v.p. midwest 1987-89, trustee retirement corp. 1989-92), Nat. League of Cities (community and econ. devel. policy com. 1984-91), League of Wis. Municipalities (com. on fin. and taxation 1984-90, bd. dirs. 1991), N.W. Mcpl. Conf. (exec. bd. 1991-92); mapping sci. com., Nat. Resource Coun., 2000-2002; fed. graphic data com., U.S. Dept. Interior, 1998—; mem local leaders for GIS, 1998—; trustee Geodata Alliance, 2001-2002. Home: 3309 Wolcott Ave Des Moines IA 50321-1949 Office: Office of the City Manager City Hall 400 E 1st St Des Moines IA 50309-1809

ANDERSON, ERIC EDWARD, psychologist, consultant; b. Mpls., Jan. 24, 1951; s. Charles Eric and Elizabeth Blanche (Engstrand) A.; m. Florence Kaye, June 18, 1978; children: Cara Elizabeth, Evan Travis. BA summa cum laude, U. Minn., 1973; MA, Fuller Theol. Sem., 1977, PhD in Clin. Psychology, 1978. Lic. psychologist Minn., Calif., Pa.; cert. community coll. teaching credential in psychology and philosophy Calif. Postdoctoral intern U. Minn., Mpls., 1978-79, asst. prof., coord. tng. in aging, 1979-83; group v.p. Kiel Profl. Svcs., Inc., St. Paul, 1983-84; pres. Primary Mental Health Care, Inc., Bloomington, Minn., 1984-86; sr. v.p. Treatment Ctrs. Am., Inc., Pasadena, Calif., 1986-88, LifeLink, Inc., Laguna Hills, Calif., 1988-89, chief operating officer, 1989-91; v.p., managed healthcare Columbia Gen., Laguna Hills, 1990-91; sr. v.p. managed health care Coll. Health Enterprises, Huntington Beach, Calif., 1991-94; exec. v.p. Medco. Behavioral Care/Merck Medco., 1994-96; pres. Anderson Health Strategies, LLC, 1996-97; pres., CEO Integra, Inc., 1997—2001, Anderson Health Strategies, LLC, 2001—; assoc. clin. prof. Widener U., 2000—. Cons. Ebenezer Soc., Mpls., 1979-82, Wilder Found., St. Paul, 1981-84; rsch. advisor Walden U., Mpls., 1982-86; assoc. prof. Sch. Psychology, Fuller Theol. Sem., Pasadena, 1989. Contbr. articles to profl. jours. Mem.: Am. Mgmt. Assn., Soc. Psychologists in Mgmt., Am. Psychol. Assn. (conf. participant 1981), Union League, Phi Beta Kappa. Avocations: tennis, gardening, bicycling, photography, golf. Address: 715 S Bryn Mawr Ave Bryn Mawr PA 19010-2005

ANDERSON, ERIC SCOTT, lawyer; b. Grand Forks, N.D., Aug. 26, 1949; s. Lyle William and Norma Sylvia (Lundeby) A.; children: Peter Scott, Nathan William. BSChE, U. Wis., 1971, JD, 1977. Bar: Wis. 1977, Minn. 1977, U.S. Dist. Ct. (we. dist.) Wis. 1977, U.S. Dist. Ct. Minn. 1978. Assoc. Fredrikson & Byron, P.A., Mpls., 1977-83, shareholder, 1983—. Mem. Wis. Bar Assn., Minn. Bar Assn., Hennepin County Bar Assn., Phi Eta Sigma, Tau Beta Pi, Phi Kappa Phi, Order of Coif. Avocations: golf, running, music. Office: Fredrikson & Byron PA 200 S 6th St Ste 4000 Minneapolis MN 55402-1425 E-mail: eanderson@fredlaw.com.

ANDERSON, ERIC SEVERIN, lawyer; b. N.Y.C., Dec. 16, 1943; s. Edward Severin and Dorothy Elvira (Ekbloom) A. BA in History summa cum laude, St. Mary's U., San Antonio, 1968; JD cum laude, Harvard U., 1971. Bar: Tex. 1971. From assoc. to ptnr. Fulbright & Jaworski, L.L.P., Houston, 1971—. Served with USAF, 1961-65. Mem. ABA, State Bar Tex., Houston Bar Assn. Clubs: Houston Ctr., Houston City. Democrat. Avocations: classical music, theater, sports. Home: 14 E Greenway Plz Unit 21-O Houston TX 77046-1406 Office: Fulbright & Jaworski LLP 1301 Mckinney St Houston TX 77010-3031

ANDERSON, ERIK W.L. web designer; b. Golden Valley, Minn., Apr. 23, 1968; s. Warren Ludwig and Lorraine Adele (Cahlander) A.; m. Kimberly Joy Anderson, Oct. 23, 1993. Cert. Enterpreneurship, Chippewa Valley Tech. Coll., Menomonie, Wis., 1989; BA in Bus. Mgmt., U. San Moritz, London, 1999. Leasee, mgr. Dairy Queen, 1982—95, 1998—99; pres. E. Warren Comms., Golden Valley, Minn., 1982—97, 2000—; materials coord. Cardinal Stritch U., Edina, 1995—97; pres. KingdomBooks, Burnsville, 1992—; web designer The QuikPages, Mpls., 1998—2002; product mgr. Innuity, 1998—2002. Recipient Agape Gold Award of Webpage Excellence, 1998, Nat. Leadership and Svc. award U.S. Achievement Acad., 1986, Golden Web award, 2001-. Mem. HTML Writers Guild, 1999. Mem. Internat. Ch. Christ. Avocations: photography, bonsai, collecting pepsi memorabilia. Office: KingdomBooks Mpls/St Paul Tape and Book Ministry 16335 Godson Dr Lakeville MN 55044 E-mail: ewla@bwca.cc., KingdomBooks@bwca.cc.

ANDERSON, ERNEST ROBERT, JR., pharmacist; b. Brockton, Mass., Sept. 21, 1953; s. Ernest Robert and June Gloria (Akerblom) A.; m. Merryle Louise Nutter, Sept. 16, 1973; children: Christopher Joseph, Betsy Heather. BS, Northeastern U., Boston, 1976, MS, 1979. Registered pharmacist. Pharmacist New Eng. Med. Ctr., Boston, 1976-81, assoc. dir. pharmacy, 1981-92; dir. pharmacy Lahey Clinic, Burlington, Mass., 1993—. Prof. Northeastern U., 1990—. Contbr. chpt. to book, articles to profl. jours. Elder Free Evang. Fellowship, Easton, Mass., 1992—, youth leader, 1988—; mission leader World Servants, Dominican Republic and Mex., 1991, 93, 95, 2000, St. Vincents, 2000. Mem. Am. Soc. Health Systems Pharmacists, Mass. Soc. Health System Pharmacists (chair corp. sponsorship com. 1995—, Mass. Hosp. Pharmacist of Yr 1985), Am. Pharm. Assn. (Pharmacist of Yr. 1985, 2001). Republican. Avocations: skiing, golf, basketball. Home: 489 Copeland St Brockton MA 02301-7016 E-mail: ernest.r.anderson@lahey.org.

ANDERSON, FLETCHER NEAL, chemical executive; b. Kansas City, Mo., Nov. 5, 1930; s. Chester Gustav and Astrid Cecilia (Crone) A.; m. Marilyn Lucille Henke; children: Karl C., Keith F., Susan L. BSChemE, U. Mo., 1951; MSChemE, Washington U., St. Louis, 1956; grad. exec. program, Stanford U., 1972. Registered profl. engr., Mo., Pa. With Mallinckrodt, Inc., St. Louis, 1951-81, group v.p. food, drug and cosmetic chems. group, 1974-76, group v.p. chem. group, 1976-78, sr. v.p. chem. group, 1978-81, also dir.; pres., dir. Chomerics, Inc., Woburn, Mass., 1981-85; pres., chief exec. officer, dir. Chemtech Industries, St. Louis, 1986-89; interim pres., CEO Brulin Corp., Indpls., 1990, bd. dirs., 1990-93; exec. v.p., COO, dir. F&C Internat., Cin., 1992-93, pres., CEO, 1993, also bd. dirs. Bd. dirs. Cytogen Corp., Princeton, N.J., 1987-95, Sepracor Inc., Malborough, Mass., 1993-95; chmn. bd. Med. Materials, Inc., Camarillo, Calif., 1992-93; mem. adv. coun. U. Mo. Engrng. Sch. Columbia, 1978-89. Mem. Florissant (Mo.) Charter Commn., 1961-63. Recipient Disting. Service to Engrng. award U. Mo., Columbia, 1978 Mem. Am. Inst. Chem. Engrs., Algonquin Golf Club. Lutheran. E-mail: marfle@earthlink.net.

ANDERSON, FRANCES SWEM, nuclear medical technologist; b. Grand Rapids, Mich., Nov. 27, 1913; d. Frank Oscar and Carrie (Strang) Swem; m. Clarence A.F. Anderson, Apr. 9, 1934; children: Robert Curtis, Clarelyn Christine (Mrs. Roger L. Schmelling), Stanley Herbert Student, Muskegon Sch. Bus., 1959-60; cert., Muskegon Community Coll., 1964; cert. adult edn. computer course, Fruitport Cmty. Schs., 1992. Registered nuclear med. technologist Am. Registry Radiol. Technologists. X-ray file clk., film librarian Hackley Hosp., Muskegon, Mich., 1957-59, radioisotope technologist and sec., 1959-65; nuclear med. technologist Butler Meml. Hosp., Muskegon Heights, Mich., 1966-70, Mercy Hosp., Muskegon, 1970-79, ret., 1979. Mem. Muskegon Civic A Capella Choir, 1932—39, Mother-Tchr. Singers, PTA, Muskegon, 1941—48, treas., 1944—48; with Muskegon Civic Opera Assn., 1950—51; office vol. Alive '88 Crusade; mem. com. for 60th H.S. Class Reunion; mem. Sr. Harvest Day Com., Muskegon County, 1995; co-chmn. Jackson Hill Old Timers Reunion, 1982—85; chmn. 70th H.S. Class Reunion; active Forest Park Covenant Ch., mem. choir, 1953—79, 1983—, pres. choir, 1992—93, Sunday sch. tchr., 1954—75, Sunday sch. supt., 1975—78, sec.-treas., 1981—86; sec. Forest Park Covenant Ch., 1991—93; chmn. master planning coun. Forest Park Covenant Ch., 1982, coord. centennial com., 1981, registrar vacation Bible sch., 1988—91. Named Female Sr. Servant of Yr., Forest Park Covenant Ch., 2002. Mem. Am. Registry Radiologic Technologists, Soc. Nuclear Medicine (cert. nuclear medicine technologist), Omni Fitness Club (10 Yr. Mem. award 1999). Home: 5757 Sternberg Rd Fruitport MI 49415-9740

ANDERSON, FRANCILE MARY, secondary education educator; b. Poland, Ind., Nov. 10, 1926; d. Matthew Henry and Emma Alvina (Dettinger) Worthman; m. Robert Charles Anderson, Aug. 23, 1953; children: Sally Quick, Sue Wilkinson, Robert Charles, Russell. BA, U. Mich., 1948. Tchr. Pontiac (Mich.) Sch. Dist., 1948-54. Co-organizer Mich. Law Related Edn. Conf., Lansing, 1978; mem. exec. bd. North Ctrl. Assn. Commn. on Schs., Tempe, Ariz., 1996-99. Trustee North Oakland Med. Ctrs., Pontiac, 1994—; campaign chair United Way of Oakland County, 1995. Recipient Disting. Svc. award Mich. Assn. Secondary Sch. Prins., 1987; named to Mich. Edn. Hall of Fame, 1990. Mem. Oakland County Hosp. Assn. (pres.), Oakland County Bar Law Libr. Found., North Ctrl. Assn. Mich., North Oakland Med. Ctrs. Found. (pres.), Delta Kappa Gamma. Republican. Presbyterian. Home: 2570 Silverside Dr Waterford MI 48328-1760 E-mail: franan@coast.net.

ANDERSON, FRANK GIST, JR., ophthalmologist, educator; b. College Station, Tex., Aug. 17, 1928; s. Frank Gist Anderson and Helen Arnett Salyer; m. Velma Cartwright Gilmore, June 10, 1953; children: Edith Anderson Wakefield, Frank Gist III. BS, Tex. A&M U., 1950; MD, U. Tex., Galveston, 1954. Intern Kans. U. Med. Ctr., Kansas City, 1954-55; resident Mayo Found., Rochester, Minn., 1958-61; ophthalmologist Kelsey-Seybold Clinic, Houston, 1961-64; pvt. practice Bryan, Tex., 1964-93. Core investigator FDA Intraocular Lens Investigations, 1978; clin. prof. ophthalmology Tex. A&M U. Coll. Medicine, College Station, 1981-2001; vis. ophthalmologist King Khalid Eye Specialist Hosp., Riyadh, Saudi Arabia, 1983; prof. humanities in medicine Tex. A&M U., College Station, 1996—; pres. med. staff St. Joseph Hosp., Bryan, 1974, Humana Hosp., Bryan-College Station, 1983 84; chief of surgery St. Joseph Hosp., Bryan, 1968, 88, Humana Hosp., Bryan-College Station, 1978-79, 83-84. Author: (book) History of Medicine in Brazos County, 2001; contbr. articles to profl. jours. Pres.Friends of Med. Scis. Libr. Tex. A&M U., College Station, 1987—88; mem. chancellor's coun. Tex. A&M U. Sys., College Station, 1996—; del. Tex. Rep. Party Conv., Ft. Worth, 1990. Capt. U.S. Army, 1955—57. Fellow ACS, Am. Acad. Ophthalmology, Tex. Soc. Ophthalmology and Otolaryngology; mem. AMA, Tex. Med. Assn. (hon., del. for ophthalmology, ho. of dels. 1989), Tex. A&M Univ. Assocs., Brazos-Robertson County Med. Soc. (pres. 1978), Tex. Longhorn Breeders Assn. Am. Home: 743 S Rosemary Dr Bryan TX 77802

ANDERSON, FRANK J., JR., career officer; BA in Bus. Mgmt. and Econ., Chapman Coll., 1972; student, Office Tng. Sch., Lackland AFB, Tex., 1973, Squadron Officer Sch., 1975; M in Mgmt., Ctrl. Mich. U., 1982; student, Air Command and Staff Coll., 1984, Def. Sys. Mgmt. Coll., 1987, Indsl. Coll. Armed Forces, 1992. Cert. lead assessor ISO 9000 quality sys., total quality mgmt. facilitator, program mgmt. level III, contracting level III. Commd. 2d lt. USAF, 1973, advanced through grades to brig. gen., 1997; base contracting officer, chief constrn. br. Washington Area Contracting Ctr., Andrews AFB, Md., 1973-76, chief specialized contracting br., 1973-76; with Edn. With Industry Program Boeing Co., Phila., 1976-77; chief subcontractor mgmt. div. then dep. chief contract adminstrn. divsn. GE Air Force Plant Rep. Office, Phila., 1977-79; stationed at Andrews AFB, Md., 1979-83, 89-91; comdr. Air Force Plant Rep. Office Rockwell Internat., Columbus, Ohio, 1984-87; dir. contracting Electronic Combat and Reconnaissance Sys. Program Office, Wright-Patterson AFB, Ohio, 1987-89; sys. program dir. Sys. Program Office Aero. Sys. Ctr., Eglin AFB, Fla., 1992-94, dir. Weapons, Air Base and Range Product Support Office, 1994-95, mgr. armament product group, 1995-96, dir. contracting Wright-Patterson AFB, 1996-97; dep. asst. sec. contracting Office Asst. Sec. Acquisition, adv. gen. Air Force Competition Hdqs. USAF, Pentagon, Washington, 1997-2000; comdt. Def. Sys. Mgmt. Coll., Ft. Belvoir, Va., 2000—. Decorated Legion of Merit. Recipient Air Force Professionalism in Contracting award, 1988; named Career Broadening Personnel Officer of Yr., Air Force Sys. Command, 1980, Co. Grade Officer of Yr., Air Force Sys. Command, 1982. Office: Comdr DSM Coll 9820 Belvoir Rd Ste 63 Fort Belvoir VA 22060-5565

ANDERSON, FRANK J(OHN), retired librarian; b. Chgo., Jan. 29, 1919; s. Charles Emil and Alida (Solomon) Anderson; m. Jeanette Irene Rioux, Feb. 17, 1944; 1 child, Maria Alida Anderson King. AB in Am. and English lit., Ind. U., 1950; MS in Libr. Sci., Syracuse U., 1951. Dir. libr. Kansas Wesleyan U., Salina, 1952—56; dir. branch libr. E. Chgo., 1956—57; dir. libr. Kansas Wesleyan U., Salina, 1960—66; dir. libr. and mus. Submarine Libr., Groton, Conn., 1957—60; dir. libr. Wofford Coll., Spartanburg, SC, 1966—84, libr. emeritus, 1984—; propr. Kitemaug Press, Spartanburg, 1965—. Author: Submarines, Diving and the Underwater World - A Bibliography, 1975, Private Presswork, 1977; contbr. numerous articles and revs. to profl. publs.; printer, pub.: more than 100 miniature books. With USN, 1943—45, PTO, with USN, 1951—52. Mem.: Guild of Book Workers, Amalgamated Printers' Assn., Am. Printing History Assn., Miniature Book Soc. Avocations: printing, book making, travel. Home and Office: 229 Mohawk Dr Spartanburg SC 29301 E-mail: kitemaugpresswhq@msn.com.

ANDERSON, FRED RICHARD, minister, writer; b. San Bernardino, Calif., Dec. 27, 1941; s. Elmer Duffield and Gladys Lucile (Lawlace) A.; m. Questa Lucile Donnelly, Sept. 4, 1965; children: Larra Anne, Rebecca Lucile; 1 foster child, James Gordon Cushman. BM in Voice, U. Redlands, 1963; MDiv, Princeton Theol. Sem., 1973, D in Ministry, 1981. Pastor Pompton Valley Presbyn. Ch., Pompton Plains, N.J., 1973-78; sr. pastor Pine St. Church, Harrisburg, Pa., 1978-92, Madison Ave. Presbyn. Ch., N.Y.C., 1992—. Bd. dirs. Liturgical Conf., 1990-94; bd. trustees Princeton Theol. Sem., 1992—; chair edn. bd. Reformed Liturgy and Music, 1983-89. Author: Singing Psalms of Joy & Praise, 1986, The Presbyterian Hymnal, 1990, assoc. editor: Book of Common Worship, 1993; contbr. articles to profl. jours.; opera, concert singer, 1963-64. Trustee Harrisburg Hosp., 1990-92, Chilton Meml. Hosp., Pompton Plains, 1976-78; pres. Pequennock (N.J.) Sr. City Housing, 1974-78; v.p. YMCA, Harrisburg, 1987-92, v.p., 1987-92. Capt. USAF, 1964-69. Recipient Fine Arts award Bank Am., 1959. Mem. Appeal Conscience Found. (trustee), N.Am. Acad. Liturgy, Presbyn. Assn. Musicians, Union League Club (N.Y.C.), The Pilgrims. Avocations: jogging, boating, fishing, hymntext writing, hiking the white mountains. Office: Madison Ave Presbyn Ch 921 Madison Ave New York NY 10021-3508

ANDERSON, FREDERICK JARRARD, historian; b. Albany, Ga., Dec. 26, 1944; m. Nancy Simmons, June 24, 1967; children: Christopher, Matthew. BS, Berry Coll., 1966; MEd, West Ga. Coll., 1973; MLS, Peabody Coll., 1974; LHD (hon.), Bluefield Coll., 2002. Divsn. head English and social studies Cherokee High Sch., Canton, Ga., 1966-73; adminstrv. asst. Henrico Pub. Libr., Richmond, Va., 1974-79; exec. dir. Va. Bapt. Hist. Soc. and Ctr. for Bapt. Heritage and Studies, Richmond, 1979—. Clk. Bapt. Gen. Assn. Va., Richmond, 1982—; sec. Va. Bapt. Gen. Bd., Richmond, 1982—; columnist Religious Herald, Richmond, 1983—. Author: A People Called Northminster, 1978, The Third Jubilee, 1983, Hearts and Hands, 1990, Land of Goshen, 1992, Across the Years, 2000, Playing Favorites and Getting Personal, 2000, Blessed by the Past, Embracing the Future, 2001. Archivist U. Richmond, 1982—; historian Richmond Bapt. Assn., 1979—; pres. So. Bapt. Hist. Soc., Nashville, 1992-93. Avocations: antiques, book collecting, historical character portrayals. Office: PO Box 34 Richmond VA 23218-0034

ANDERSON, FREDERICK RANDOLPH, JR., lawyer, law educator; b. Rutherfordton, NC, June 28, 1941; s. Frederick Randolph and Ophelia (Meeler) A.; m. Barbara Alison Rose, Nov., 1991; 1 child, Molly Elizabeth. BA with highest honors, U. N.C., 1963; BA in Jurisprudence, Oxford (Eng.) U., 1965; JD, Harvard U., 1968. Bar: DC 1969, US Supreme Ct. 1980, US Ct. Appeals (DC cir.) 1995, US Ct. Appeals (9th cir.) 1999, US Ct. Appeals (3rd cir.) 2002. Teaching fellow Harvard U., Cambridge, Mass.; editor in chief Environ. Law Reporter, Washington, 1970-73; exec. dir. Environ. Law Inst., Washington, 1973-78, pres., 1978-80, bd. dirs., 1980-86, 88-92, adv. coun., 1992—; prof. law U. Utah Coll. Law, Salt Lake City, 1980-85; dean Washington Coll. Law Am. U., 1985-88, Ann Loeb Bronfman Prof. Law, 1988-91; mem. firm Cadwalader, Wickersham & Taft, Washington, 1991-93, ptnr., 1993—, chmn. environ. and natural resources practice group, 1998—. Mem. congl. study of common law relief for hazardous waste injuries, 1980-82; mem. Adminstrv. Conf. U.S., 1978-80, cons., 1983-84, 89-91; chmn. adv. working group on environ. sanctions U.S. Sentencing Commn., 1992-94. Author: NEPA in the Courts, 1973, Environmental Improvement Through Economic Incentives, 1978, Environmental Protection: Law and Policy, 1984, 4th edit., 2003; contbg. author: Federal Environmental Law, 1974, Occupational and Environmental Health, 1982, The Southwest under Stress, 1981. Chmn. bd. dirs. Ctr. for Internat. Environ. Law, 1993—; v.p. Western Network, 1986-89; mem. Harvard Group on Risk Mgmt. Reform, 1994-96; bd. dirs. René Dubos Ctr., 1994—. Morehead scholar, Nat. Merit scholar U. N.C., Marshall scholar Oxford U. Mem. ABA (chmn. standing com. on environ. law 1980-82, chmn. commn. on inter-Am. affairs 1986-88), NAS (mem. Comm. on Life Scis. 1995-2001, mem. bd. environ. studies and toxicology 1988-94, mem. panel on sci., tech. and law 2000—), Am. Law Inst. (life), NatureServe (bd. dirs. 2000—). Office: Cadwalader Wickersham & Taft 1201 F St NW Washington DC 20004-1204

ANDERSON, GARRET, baseball player; b. L.A., June 30, 1972; Left field Anaheim Angles, 1994—. Involved Calif. Kids; visitor UCI Med. Ctr.; involved Boy Scouts Am., Responsible Fatherhood Campaign. Office: Anaheim Angels Edison Field 2000 Gene Autry Way Anaheim CA 92806

ANDERSON, GARRY MICHAEL, diagnostic radiologist; b. Houston, May 17, 1955; s. Dan Luther and Marcella Marie (Hanel) A. BS in Biology, Tarleton State U., Stephenville, Tex., 1977; BS in Medicine, Tex. A&M U., 1979, MD, 1981. Diplomate Nat. Bd. Med. Examiners, Am. Bd. Radiology. Intern in pathology Scott & White Hosp., Temple, Tex., 1981-82, resident in diagnostic radiology, 1982-86; fellow in imaging UCLA Ctr. of the Health Scis., 1986-87, asst. attending clin. prof., 1987-88; diagnostic radiologist Long Beach (Calif.) Cmty. Hosp., 1987-2000, Shannon Med. Ctr., San Angelo, Tex., 2000—. Mem. Second Decade Coun., Am. Film Inst., L.A., 1993—. Named Outstanding Young Alumnus, Tarleton State U., 1991. Mem. Am. Coll. Radiology, Radiol. Soc. N.Am. Roman Catholic. Avocation: tennis. Office: 120 E Beauregard Ave San Angelo TX 76903-5919 Address: 3124 Grandview Dr San Angelo TX 76904

ANDERSON, GARY DEAN, architect, planner, educator; b. Honolulu, Oct. 12, 1947; s. Glen John and Florence Lydia (Young) A. BArch magna cum laude, U. So. Calif., 1970, M in Urban Design, 1971; diplom in social sci., U. Stockholm, 1972; PhD in Geography and Environ. Engring., Johns Hopkins U., 1985. Registered architect, Md., DC, Va., Pa., NY, Maine, Mass. Planner, designer David Jay Flood and Assocs., L.A., 1973, Gruen Assocs., L.A., 1974; architect, planner RTKL Assocs., Balt., 1974-76; sr. planner Prince George's County, Upper Marlboro, Md., 1976, U. Md. Cen. Adminstrn., Adelphi, 1976-77; asst. prof. architecture and planning King Faisal U., Dammam, Saudi Arabia, 1977-79, head dept. urban and regional planning, 1980-85; rsch. fellow Johns Hopkins U., Balt., 1980; v.p., sr. arch., chief planner STV Inc., Balt., 1985—. Guest lectr. Clemson U., Dept. of Architecture, Charles Daniel Ctr., Genoa, Italy, 1995, Istanbul Tech. U., Environment and Urbanism Rsch. Ctr., 2000; faculty assoc. Johns Hopkins U., Allan L. Berman Real Estate Inst., Balt., 1994—; rsch. cons. Irvine Corp., Newport, Calif., 1973; cons. CH2M Hill Internat., Damman, 1978. Designer internat. recycling symbol, 1971; contbr. articles to profl. jours. Pres. No. Bolton Hill Assn., Balt., 1988-90; mem. Royal Improvement Assn., Balt., 1986—, mem. archtl. rev. bd., 1991-95, chmn. archtl. rev. bd., 1994-95; bd. dirs., 1992-94; mem. Long Point Assn., Long Point on the Severen, Md., 1994—; mem. Balt. Mus. Art, 1989—, Contemporary Mus., 1999—, Walters Art Mus., 1999—. Aspen (Colo.) Design Conf. fellow, 1969, Johns Hopkins U. fellow, 1978; recipient Bogardus Social Rsch. award U. So. Calif., 1980; named to Fulbright Roster Sr. Specialists, 2002. Mem. AIA (urban design com. Balt. chpt. 1990—, assoc. European chpt. 2002—, student prize 1970), Nat. Coun. Archtl. Registration Bds., Am. Planning Assn., Am. Inst. Cert. Planners (fed. installation planning divsn.), Soc. Am. Mil. Engrs. (Balt. post, chair program com. 2002—, internat. com., Max O. Urbahn award 2001), Urban Land Inst. (assoc.), Balt. Dist. Coun. (exec. com. 1995—, chair program com. 2001—), Engring. Soc. Balt., Balt. Econ. Soc., Johns Hopkins U. Alumni Assn., Merritt Athletic Club, Neighborhood Design Ctr., Citizens Planning & Housing Assn., 1,000 Friends of Md. (bd. dirs. 1998—, transp. and land use com., fin. com. 2002—), Lambda Alpha Nat. Land Econ. Honor Soc. Avocations: gardening, landscape design. Home: 1727 Park Ave Baltimore MD 21217-4336 Office: STV Inc 7125 Ambassador Rd Ste 200 Baltimore MD 21244-2722

ANDERSON, GARY GENE, music educator; b. Hampton, Va., Apr. 17, 1953; s. Arthur Hobert (Stepfather) and Phyllis Hartman Carmony, Harold G. Anderson; m. Melinda Ann McClain; children: Eric, Mary Beth Harley. B in Music Edn., James Madison U., 1977. Cert. tchr. Ariz., 1991. Dir. bands & gen. music Norton (Va.) City Schs., 1977—78; dir. bands Spratley Jr. HS, Hampton, Va., 1979—80, Tabb Intermediate Sch., Yorktown, Va., 1980—85, Ferguson HS, Newport News, Va., 1985—90, Ctrl. HS, Phoenix, 1990—96, North Canyon HS, Phoenix, 1996—. Adjudicator/Clinician Arizona Band and Orchestra Directors Association, AZ, United States, 2000—02; Trombonist Superjazz Band, Yorktown, VA, United States, 1980—90, Pat Curtis Big Band, Virginia Beach, VA, United States, 1983—90. Musician: Ariz. Symphic Wind Ensemble; trombonist: Superjazz Band, 1980—90, Pat Curtis Big Band, 1983—90. Mem.: Ariz. Band and Orch. Dir.'s Assn. (band chair west region 1999—2001, instrumental chair ctrl. region 1993—95, O.M. Hartsell Excellence in Tchg. Music award 1999), Music Educators Nat. Conf., Phi Mu Alpha Sinfonia (life). Avocations: music, woodworking, gardening. Office: North Canyon High Sch Band 1700 E Union Hills Dr Phoenix AZ 85024 Office Fax: 623-780-4304.

ANDERSON, GARY WILLIAM, physician; b. NJ, 1951; divorced; 1 child, Eric William George. BA, Seton Hall U., 1974; MA in Psychology, Fairleigh Dickinson U., 1977; MD, Autonomous U. Guadalajara, Mex., 1983. Intern Rutgers Med. Sch., New Brunswick, N.J., 1984; resident St. Joseph's Med. Ctr., Paterson, N.J., 1985; med. dir. Sandoz Rsch. Inst., East Hanover, N.J., 1985-96, Pfizer Pharms., N.Y.C., 2000—; global dept. exec. dir. clin. safety dept. Novartis Pharms., East Hanover, 1996-2000. Vol. med. dir., bd. trustees, exec. com. Sussex County (N.J.) Domestic Abuse Program, 1986-98. Mem.: N.J. Acad. Medicine, Am. Acad. Family Physicians, AMA, Nat. Honor Soc. Psychology. Republican.

ANDERSON, GENE S. lawyer. U.S. atty. Western Wash., Seattle. Office: US Atty Office 3600 Seafirst 5th Ave Pla 800 5th Ave Ste 3600 Seattle WA 98104-3176

ANDERSON, GEOFFREY ALLEN, retired lawyer; b. Chgo., Aug. 3, 1947; s. Roger Allen and Ruth (Teninga) A. BA cum laude, Yale U., 1969; JD, Columbia U., 1972. Bar: Ill. 1972. Assoc. Isham, Lincoln & Beale, Chgo., 1972-79, ptnr., 1980-81, Reuben & Proctor, Chgo., 1981-85; dep. gen. counsel Tribune Co., Chgo., 1985-92; gen. counsel Chgo. Cubs, 1986-90, corp. counsel, 1991-92; v.p. Timber Trails Country Club, Inc., 1992—. Elder Fourth Presbyn. Ch., Chgo., chmn. worship and music com., 1990-92, trustee, 1992-95, 99-2001, v.p., 1993-94; bd. dirs. The James Chorale, Chgo., 1993-96, chmn. program com., 1994-96. Recipient Citizenship award Am. Legion, 1965. Mem. Chgo. Bar Assn. (chmn. entertainment com. 1981-82, Best Performance award 1977), Yale Club (N.Y.C.), Phi Delta Phi.

ANDERSON, GEORGE See WEISSMAN, JACK

ANDERSON, GEORGE KENNETH, physician, foundation executive, retired air force officer; b. Providence, Feb. 17, 1946; s. George Raymond and Mildred (Caster) A.; m. Kimberly Kay Baker, May 18, 1968; children: George D., Ginger K. MD, U. Mich., 1971; MPH, Tulane U., 1973; postgrad., Nat. War Coll., Ft. McNair, Va., 1982-83. Diplomate Am. Bd. Preventive Medicine (chmn. 1991-95), Am. Bd. Med. Mgmt. (bd. dirs.). Intern Wilford Hall USAF Med Ctr., 1971-72; resident USAF Sch. Aerospace Medicine, 1973-75; commd. 2d lt. USAF, 1967, advanced through grades to maj. gen., 1993; comdr. USAF Hosp., Kunsan, Republic of Korea, 1975-76, 86th Tactical Hosp., Germany, 1976-79; mem. faculty USAF Sch. Aerospace Medicine, Brooks AFB, Tex., 1979-82; div. chief Office Surgeon Gen., Bolling AFB, Md., 1983-85, dep. dir., 1985-87; command surgeon Air Force Systems Command, Andrews AFB, Md., 1987-88; dir. med. inspection Air Force ISC, Norton AFB, Calif., 1988-90; comdr. Human Systems Ctr., Brooks AFB, 1990-94; dep. asst. sec. def. Health Svcs. Ops. and Readiness, Washington, D.C., 1994; ret. USAF, 1996; pres., CEO Koop Found. Inc., Rockville, Md., 1997-98; exec. v.p. Oceania Corp., Falls Church, Va., 1998-99; pres., CEO Oceania, Inc., Redwood City, Calif., 1999—. Bd. dir. New World Healthcare Solutions, Washington. Decorated Legion of Merit, Disting. Svc. medal; Koop Found. fellow, Fellow Am. Coll. Preventive Medicine (pres.), Am. Coll. Physician Execs. (disting.), Aerospace Med. Assn. (Julian Ward award 1975); mem. AMA, Air Force Assn. (life).

ANDERSON, GERALD DWIGHT, history educator; b. Dale, Minn., Nov. 18, 1944; s. Wilferd Dean and Violet Caria-Maria (Heigg) A.; m. Rhonda Waldahl, July 8, 1967 (div. June 1975); 1 child, Carmen Nell; m. Barbara Ann Thill, May 13, 1978; children: Karl August, Paul Martin. BA, Concordia Coll., Moorhead, Minn., 1965; MA, N.D. State U., 1966; PhD, U. Iowa, 1973. Asst. prof. history Waldorf Coll., Forest City, Iowa, 1966-70, Drake U., Des Moines, 1973, Iowa Wesleyan Coll., Mt. Pleasant, 1974; instr. Austin (Minn.) C.C., 1974-75; rschr. Minn. State Senate, St. Paul, 1976-79; asst. prof. Luther Coll., Decorah, Iowa, 1979-85; assoc. prof. history N.D. State U., Fargo, 1985—. Cons. history textbooks Harper Collins, N.Y.C., 1988-97, West Pub., St. Paul, 1988-97; cons. various hist. socs. Author: Fascists, Communists, The National Government, 1983, The Uffda trial, 1994, The Western Perspective Study Guide, Vols. I and II, 1999. Precinct chair Moorhead DFL Party, 1986-97; v.p. Gooseberry Park Players, Moorhead, 1994-97. Named Outstanding Tchr., N.D. State U., 1992; Fulbright scholar U.S. State Dept., 1991, Internat. Seminar scholar Coun. for Internat. Edn., Moscow, 1994, Berlin, 1996, Budapest, 1999, Madrid, 2002. Lutheran. Avocations: reading and writing detective fiction, scandinavian ethnic studies, acting in community theater. Home: 1320 5th St S Moorhead MN 56560-3420 Office: North Dakota State Univ Minard Hall 412H Fargo ND 58105 E-mail: gerald.anderson@ndsu.nodak.edu.

ANDERSON, GERALD EDWIN, utilities executive; b. Boston, Apr. 9, 1931; s. Clarence Gustav and Lela Pauline (Kelley) A.; m. Mary Elizabeth Iverson, May 21, 1955; children: Todd K., Timothy J., Kristin E. May. AA, Worthington (Minn.) Jr. Coll., 1950; BBA, U. Minn., 1952. C.P.A., Minn. Staff accountant, audit mgr. Arthur Andersen & Co., Mpls., 1953-65; asst. comptroller Commonwealth Energy System (formerly New Eng. Gas & Electric Assn.), Cambridge, Mass., 1966, system comptroller, 1967-71, v.p., comptroller, 1971-72, treas. parent co., financial v.p. system, 1972-74, pres., 1974-91, chief exec. officer, 1975-91; ret., 1992. Trustee parent co., 1974-91; also dir. operating subs. Commonwealth Energy Sys., 1972-91, dir. Liberty Mutual Ins. Co., Liberty Mutual Fire Ins. Co., 1980-2001, Liberty Life Assurance Co. of Boston, 1984-95, Liberty Fin. Cos., Inc., 1995-2001. Vice chmn. United Ways Ea. New Eng., 1986; mem. town fin. com., Carlisle, Mass., 1968-73, chmn., 1972-73; dir. Swedish Coun. Am., 1987-2003; mem. Corp. of Mass. Gen. Hosp., 1988-95. 1st lt. USAF, 1952-53. Mem. AICPA, Minn. Soc. CPAs, Fin. Execs. Inst., Oyster Harbors Club, The Lakes Country Club, Somerset Club, Comml. Club of Boston, Beta Alpha Psi, Beta Gamma Sigma. Episcopalian. Home: 75 Hornbeam Ln Centerville MA 02632-3521 also: 245 Wild Horse Dr Palm Desert CA 92211-3220 E-mail: ganderso3@aol.com.

ANDERSON, GERALD LESLIE, financial executive; b. Washington, May 24, 1940; s. Paul Hash and Edith (Hathaway) A.; m. Margaret Marie Curley, June 8, 1974; children: Paul Charles, Laura Marie. BS in Indsl. Mgmt., Carnegie Mellon U., 1961, MS in Indsl. Adminstrn., 1962. Econ. analyst Sun Oil Co., Phila., 1962-66; asst. treas. Selas Corp. Am., Dresher, Pa., 1966-74; treas. Midrex Corp., Charlotte, N.C., 1974-76; v.p., treas. Georgetown Industries, Inc., Charlotte, 1976-85, v.p. fin., chief fin. officer, 1985-95; prin. Anderson Investments, Charlotte, N.C., 1995—. Active Ch. at Charlotte Evangelical Free Ch. Republican. Home and Office: 4519 N Parview Dr Charlotte NC 28226-3450

ANDERSON, GERALD VERNE, retired aerospace company executive; b. Long Beach, Calif., Oct. 25, 1931; s. Gordon Valentine and Aletha Marian (Parkins) A.; m. Judith B. Marx, May 14, 1992; children by previous marriage: Lori Jean Anderson Fronk, Gregory Verne, David Harman, Lynn Elaine Anderson Lee (dec.), Brian Earl, Michael Gordon. AA, Long Beach City Coll., 1952; BS, U. Calif., Berkeley, 1958. Registered profl. engr., Calif. Tech.

specialist N. Am. Aviation Co., L.A., 1958-65; tech. specialist McDonnell Douglas Astronautics, Huntington Beach, Calif., 1965-84, mgr., 1984-87; sr. mgr. McDonnell Douglas Aerospace, Huntington Beach, 1987-94. Cons. Mitsubishi Heavy Industries, Nagoya, Japan, 1972-73, Aeritalia, Turin, Italy, 1975-76. Patentee portable vacuum chamber, electron beam welding device. Mem. Westminster (Calif.) Planning Com., 1974, Huntington Beach Citizens Adv. Com., 1975, Westminster Bicentennial Com., 1976, L.A. Classical Ballet Guild, 1992-96; vol. Long Beach Symphony, 1995—; crew top sail program L.A. Maritime Inst., 1998—, vol. Colonial Williamsburg Assn., Va., 2002—. Mem. Soc. Mfg. Engrs., Soc. Automotive Engrs., Aerospace Industries Assn., AIAA. Republican. Avocations: photography, skiing, backpacking, snorkeling, writing. Home: 3452 Falcon Ave Long Beach CA 90807-4814 also: 5312 Tower Hill Ct Williamsburg VA 23188 E-mail: GAnder1999@aol.com.

ANDERSON, GERALDINE LOUISE, medical researcher; b. Mpls., July 7, 1941; d. George M. and Viola Julie-Mary (Abel) Havrilla; m. Henry Clifford Anderson, May 21, 1966; children: Bruce Henry, Julie Lynne. BS, U. Minn., 1963. Med. technologist Swedish Hosp., Mpls., 1963-68; hematology supr. lab. Glenwood Hills Hosp., Golden Valley, Minn., 1968-70; assoc. scientist pediats. U. Minn. Hosps., Mpls., 1970-74; instr. health occupations, med. lab. asst. Suburban Hennepin County Area Vocat. Tech. Ctr., Brooklyn Park, Minn., 1974-81, 92-95, St. Paul Tech. Vocat. Inst., Brooklyn Park, 1978-81; rsch. med. technologist Miller Hosp., St. Paul, 1975-78; rsch. assoc. Children's and United Hosps., St. Paul, 1979-88; sr. lab. analyst Cascade Med. Inc., Eden Prairie, Minn., 1989-90; lab. mgr. VAMC, Mpls., 1990; tech. support scientist INCSTAR Corp., Stillwater, Minn., 1990-94; mem. network staff Clin. Design Group, Chgo., 1992-98; regulatory affairs product analysis coord. Medtronic Neurol., Mpls., 1995; quality assurance documentation coord. Lectec Corp., Minnetonka, Minn., 1995; clin. rsch. monitor Eli Lilly Rsch. Labs., Indpls., 1995-98; sr. clin. rsch. assoc. Covance, Inc., Princeton, N.J., 1998-99. Sr. clin. rsch. assoc. Parexel Internat., Inc., Chgo., 1999—2000, Med. Tech. Rsch. Assn./AAI Internat., Boston, 2000—01; regional clin. assoc. Wyeth, Collegeville, Pa., 2001—02; mem. health occupations adv. com. Hennepin Tech. Ctrs., 1975—90, chairperson, 1978—79; mem. hematology slide edn. rev. bd. Am. Soc. Hematology, 1977—96; mem. flow cytometry and clin. chemistry quality control subcoms. Nat. Com. for Clin. Lab. Stds., 1988—92; cons. FCM Specialists, 1989—99, 2002—, Clin. Design Group, 1992—98; mem. rev. bd. Clin. Lab. Sci., 1990—91, The Learning Laboratorian Series, 1991; contbr., presenter in Svc. Rev. in Clin. Lab. Sci., audio taped study program for ASMT, 1992. Contbr. articles to profl. jours. Charter orgns. rep. Viking Coun. troop 534 Boy Scouts Am., 1988—90; resource person lab. careers Robbinsdale (Minn.) Sch. Dist., 1970—79; active Women Scientists Spkrs. Bur., 1989—92, Helping Hands, 2002—, Med. Lab. Tech. Polit. Action Com., 1978—99; observer UN 4th World Conf. on Women, Beijing, 1995; del. Crest View Home Assn., 1981—; sci. and math. subcom. Minn. High Tech. Coun., 1983—88; bd. dirs. Big Pine Lake Property Owners, 1996—. Recipient Svc. awards and honors, Omicron Sigma. Mem.: NAFE (Twin Cities Network), AAUW, AAAS, Grad. Women in Sci., Inc., Great Lakes Internat. Flow Cytometry Assn. (charter mem. 1992), Internat. Soc. Analytical Cytology, Am. Soc. Hematology, Minn. Med. Tech. Alumni, Assn. Clin. Rsch. Profls., World Future Soc., Assn. Women in Sci., Twin Cities Hosp. Assn. (spkrs. bur. 1968—70), Am. Soc. Clin. Lab. Sci. (del. to ann. meetings 1972—, chmn. hematology sci. assembly 1977—79, nomination com. 1979—81, bd. dirs. 1986—88), Soc. Clin. Rsch. Assocs., Am. Soc. Profl. and Exec. Women, Minn. Soc. Med. Tech. (sec. 1969—71), Minn. Emerging Med. Orgns., Nat. Assn. Women Cons., Inc., Soc. Tech. Comm., Soc. Clin. Rsch. Assocs., Assn. Clin. Rsch. Profls., Women in Comm., Inc., Am. Med. Writers Assn., Alpha Mu Tau, Sigma Delta Epsilon (corr. sec. XI chpt. 1980—82, pres. 1982—84, nat. membership com. 1990—92, nat. nominations chair 1991—92, nat. v.p. 1992—93, nat. pres.-elect 1993—94, nat. pres. 1994—95, bd. dirs. 1996—2001, chmn. bd. dirs. 2000—01). E-mail: ander367@umn.edu.

ANDERSON, GERARD FENTON, economist, university program administrator; b. Mariemont, Ohio, June 24, 1951; s. Harry C. and Dorothy C. (Fenton) A.; m. Judith Rae Peres; 1 child, Anna. BA in Econs., Haverford Coll., 1973; PhD in Pub. Policy, U. Pa., 1978. Spl. asst. Cost of Living Coun. Exec. Office of the Pres., Washington, 1972; research analyst Fed. Reserve Bank, Washington, 1973-74; prin. investigator Phila. Health Mgmt. Corp., 1974-78; economist Office of the Sec. HHS, Washington, 1978-83; assoc. dir. Ctr. for Hosp. Fin. and Mgmt. Johns Hopkins U., Balt., 1983-87, dir., 1987—; co-dir. Johns Hopkins Program for Med. Tech. and Practice Assessment, Balt., 1986-94, 1994—. Cons. Blue Cross Greater Phila., 1978, World Bank, Washington, 1988; adj. prof. Grad. Sch. Pub. Adminstrn. Am. U., Washington, 1978-82; presenter to Congl. coms. over 30 times. Author: Health Care Cost Containment, 1990, Providing Hospital Services, 1989; contbr. over 120 articles to profl. jours. Fellow U. Pa., Phila., 1978. Mem. Am. Econ. Assn., Am. Pub. Health Assn., Assn. for Health Svcs. Rsch., Phi Beta Kappa, Delta Omega. Democrat. Mem. Soc. Of Friends. Home: 8022 Glendale Rd Chevy Chase MD 20815-5903 Office: Johns Hopkins U 624 N Broadway # 300 Baltimore MD 21205-1900 E-mail: ganderso@jhsph.edu.

ANDERSON, GORDON LOUIS, foundation administrator; b. St. Croix Falls, Wis., Nov. 16, 1947; s. Erwin Louis and Eunice Arlene (Johnson) A.; m. Mary Jane Evenson, July 1, 1982; children: Tamara, Jayna, Greta, Evan. BME, U. Minn., 1975; MDiv in Ethics, Union Theol. Sem., N.Y.C., 1980; MA in Religion, Claremont Grad. Sch., 1985, PhD Philosophy Religion, 1986. Engr. Gull Engring. Inc., Mpls., 1974-80, also bd. dirs.; owner, mgr. Aerograph Aerial Photography, Claremont, Calif., 1981-84; sec. gen., bd. dirs. Profs. World Peace Acad., N.Y.C., 1984-93, sec. gen. St. Paul, 1993—; sec., gen., bd. dirs. Internat. Cultural Found., Washington, 1986—. Lectr. Unification Theol. Sem., Barrytown, N.Y., 1987-96, bd. dirs., 1988-96; lectr. 40 countries including Europe, Africa, Asia and South America. Assoc. editor Internat. Jour. World Peace, 1985—94; editor: Internat. Jour. World Peace, 1994—2000; pub. Internat. Jour. World Peace, 2000—, assoc. editor Morality and Religion in Liberal Democratic Societies, 1992, Worldwide State of the Family, 1995, The Family in Global Transition, 1997; contbr. articles, chapters to books; contbr. book revs. to profl. jours. Mem. Citizens for Better N.J., 1986-92; bd. dirs. Paragon House Pubs., 1993—, exec. dir., 1996—; trustee U. Bridgeport, Conn., 1994—. With U.S. Army, 1969-72, Vietnam. Mem. World Future Soc., Am. Acad. Religion, Am. Polit. Sci. Assn., Internat. Studies Assn., Consortium on Peace Rsch. Mem. Unification Ch. Office: Profs World Peace Acad 2285 University Ave W Saint Paul MN 55114-1635 *Religion or culture has always defined manhood, womanhood, the relation to our neighbor, the government, the spiritual world and God. This has yet to take place in a normative way for the modern world.*

ANDERSON, GREGORY SHANE, insurance executive; b. Mpls., Feb. 8, 1947; s. Donald Manfred and Inez Marie (Dickson) A.; m. Joyce Millicent Goetz, June 15, 1968; children: Kaarin Marie, Kirsten Elise, Todd Gregory, Kathryn Joy. BS, U. Minn., 1969. CLU. Fin. rep. Northwestern Mut. Life Ins. Co., St. Paul, 1970—. V.p. Tri-Lakes Improvement Assn., Lake Elmo, Minn., 1990, pres., 1991, 92. Named Man of the Yr., St. Paul Spl. Agts. Assn., 1984, 95-96, St. Paul Gen. Agts. and Mgrs., 1978, 91. Mem. Nat. Assn. Ins. and Fin. Advisors, Minn. Assn. Ins. and Fin. Advisors (pres. 1985-86), St. Paul Ins. and Fin. Advisors Assn. (pres. 1979-80), St. Paul CLU Soc. (pres. 1992-93), Million Dollar Round Table (Top of the Table 1993, 94), 25 Million Dollar Internat. Forum, 1996, Dellwood Hills Golf Club (pres. 1996). Republican. Lutheran. Avocations: golf, racquetball, tennis, biking. Home: 11 Spyglass Rd Dellwood MN 55110-1227 Office: Northwestern Mutual Life Court Internat Ste 455 S 2550 University Ave Saint Paul MN 55114-1052 E-mail: greg.anderson@nmfn.com.

ANDERSON, GREGORY THOMAS, secondary school educator, researcher, historian; s. Ralph Curtis (Stepfather) and Darlene Dolores Miley, Thomas Lyle Anderson; m. Suzanne Marie Anderson, July 30, 1988; 1 child, Kathryn Michelle. BA, Calif. State U., 1999. Secondary Profl. Clear Tchg. Credential Calif. Commn. on Tchr. Credentialing, 1999. Asst. regional mgr. U.S. Dept. of Commerce, Bur. of the Census, San Pedro, Calif., 1988—90; tchr. Redondo Beach Unifed Sch. Dist., Calif., 1991—2000, Torrance Unifed Sch. Dist., Torrance, Calif., 2000—. Author: (book) Index to the Mayors of Redondo Beach, California; editor: (newsletter) 1812 Overtures, Golden State Patriot. Mem. Gen. Plan Adv. Com., Redondo Beach, Calif., 1989—92, South Bay Union HS Dist. Hist. Com., Redondo Beach, Calif.; state pres. Soc. of the War of 1812 in the State of Calif., 1989—92; state sec. SR in the State of Calif., 1989—92; state dep. gov. Soc. of Mayflower Descendants in the State of Calif., 1989—2003; mem. Redondo Beach Hist. Soc., Calif., 1993—95. Recipient Games of the XXIII Olympiad, LA Olympic Organizing Com., 1984, Ky. Col. Commn., Commonwealth of Ky., 1989. Mem.: New Eng. Geneal. Libr., Orgn. of Am. Historians, Sons and Daughters of the Colonial and Antebellum Bench and Bar 1565-1861, Order of the Crown of Charlemange in the U.S., Flagon and Trencher, SAR in the State of Calif., Soc. of the War of 1812 in the State of Calif. (state pres. 1991—92, Pres's. Commendation 1990), Sons the Revolution in the State of Calif. (state sec. 1989—92, Pres's. Commendation 1992), The Soc. of the Descendants of the Colonial Clergy, Soc. of Mayflower Descendants in the State of Calif. (colony gov. 1999—2003). Democrat. Congregationalist. Avocations: genealogy, travel, local politcs.

ANDERSON, GUNNAR DONALD, artist; b. Berkeley, Calif., Mar. 3, 1927; s. Sven Gunnar and Margaret (Hultien) A.; m. Virginia Fletcher Bullock, Jan. 31, 1953; children: Greta, Karin, Paul. BFA, Art Ctr. Coll. of Design, Pasadena, Calif., 1951. Art dir. McCann ERickson, N.Y.C., 1951-53, Cunningham & Walsh, N.Y.C., 1953-55, Batten, Barton, Durstine & Osborne, San Francisco, 1955-63; artist Sonoma, Calif., 1963—. Artist: (children's book) Oscar Lincoln Busby Stokes, 1970; one man shows include U. Nebr., Lincoln, Frye Mus., Seattle, Conacher Galleries, San Francisco, Guildhall Galleries, Chgo., Meredith Long Galleries, Houston, Dalzell Hatfield Galleries, L.A., Lord and Taylor Art Galleries, N.Y.C., Rosicrution Mus., San Jose, Calif., Phillips Galleries, Dallas; exhibited in group shows at Ft. Worth Art Ctr., Palace of Fine Arts, San Francisco, De Saisset Gallery, Santa Clara, Calif. With USCG, 1945-46. Recipient Best in Fine Art award Soc. Art Ctr. Alumni, 1972. Mem. Soc. Western Artists (trustee 1993—, Best Figure or Portrait award 1971, 1st place award 1985, 90, 91, Grumbacher gold medallion 1986), Soaring Soc. Am., Bohemian Club. Avocations: soaring, wine making, aircraft model building. Home: 4583 Belmont Ct Sonoma CA 95476-8904

ANDERSON, GWYN C. computer company executive, computer consultant; b. LaCrosse, Wis., Aug. 8, 1966; d. Robert Bernard and Alice Helaine Anderson. Owner Enhanced Ideas, LaCrosse, 1996—; e-commerce webmaster www.enhancedideas.com. Avocations: rollerskating, camping, horseback riding, swimming, science fiction. Office: Enhanced Ideas PO Box 3602 La Crosse WI 54602-3602 E-mail: gwyn06@earthlink.net

ANDERSON, HARRISON CLARKE, pathologist, educator, biomedical researcher; b. Louisville, Sept. 2, 1932; married, 1961. BA in Zoology, U. Louisville, 1954, MD, 1958. Diplomate Am. Bd. Pathology. Pathology intern Mass. Gen. Hosp., Boston, 1958-59; NIH rsch. trainee U. Louisville, Ky., 1959-60; resident in pathology Sloan Kettering Meml. Hosp, N.Y.C., 1960-62; postdoctoral fellow Sloan Kettering Inst., Rye, N.Y., 1962-63; from asst. prof., assoc. prof. to prof. pathology SUNY Downstate Med. Ctr., Bklyn., 1963-78; prof. pathology, chmn. dept. U. Kans. Med. Ctr., Kansas City, 1978-90, Harrington prof. orthopedic rsch., 1990—. Mem. study sect. NIH, Bethesda, Md., 1977-81, 99-; chmn. Gordon Research Conf. on Bone, Meriden, N.H., 1981. Edit. bd. Am. Jour. Pathology, others, 1981—; contbr. articles to profl. jours. Recipient Biol. Mineralization Research award Internat. Assn. Dental Research, 1985, Sr. Faulty Research award U. Kans. Med. Ctr., 1986, Kappa Delta Orthopedic Rsch. award Orthopedic Rsch. Soc., 1982, Higuchi Biomed. Rsch. award U. Kansas, 1991; NIH rsch. fellow Strangeways Lab., Cambridge, Eng., 1971-72, NIH sr. rsch. fellow in cell biology Yale U., New Haven,, 1984-85; grantee NIH, 1967—. Mem. Am. Soc. Investigative Pathologists, Assn. Pathology Chmn. (pres. 1988-90), Am. Soc. Cell Biology, Am. Soc. Bone and Mineral Research, Orthopaedic Research Soc. Clubs: Am. Yacht (Rye); Carriage (Kansas City). Avocations: tennis, skiing, sailing. Office: U of Kansas Dept of Pathology 39th & Rainbow Kansas City KS 66160-0001

ANDERSON, HARRY FREDERICK, JR., architect; b. Chgo., Feb. 4, 1927; s. Harry Frederick and Sarah Matilda (Anderson) A.; m. Frances Annette Zeilstra, Jan. 27, 1951 (div. Jan. 1979); children: Scott H., Mark S., Robert R., Grant Alan; m. Elizabeth Jane Elden, Jan. 17, 1979 (dec. Apr. 1982); m. Joanell Vivian Mangan, Mar. 22, 1983. B.Arch., Ill. Inst. Tech., 1953. Chief draftsman Stade & Cooley, Chgo., 1953-55; ptnr. Stade, Dolan & Anderson, Chgo., 1955-65; project architect Perkins & Will Partnership, Chgo., 1965-67, ptnr., v.p., 1967-85, sr. v.p., 1973-74, exec. v.p., 1974-75, pres., chief exec. officer, 1975-85, chmn. bd., 1982-85; chmn., chief exec. officer Anderson, Mikos Architects Ltd., Oak Brook, Ill., 1985—. Bd. dirs. Chgo. Bldg. Congress. Prin. works include Rockford (Ill.) Coll. Library, 1967, Sci. Bldg, 1968, Arts Complex, 1970, Women's Dormitory, 1969, Silver Cross Hosp, Joliet, Ill., 1971, Westlake Hosp, Melrose Park, Ill., 1970, Am. Soc. Clin. Pathologists bldg., Chgo., 1971, Ingalls Hosp, 1974, St. Mary of Nazareth Hosp, 1975, Childrens Meml. Hosp., Chgo., 1980, U. Chgo. Hosp, 1980, Northwestern Meml. Hosp., Chgo., 1987, Michael Reese Hosp., Chgo., 1987, Ctrl. Dupage Hosp., Winfield, Ill., 1998, Advocate Health Care Sys., Chgo., 1998. Chmn. adv. council Booth Meml. Hosp., Chgo., 1969-81; adv. bd. Chgo. Salvation Army, 1969-81. Served with USN, 1944-47. Fellow AIA; Mem. Internat. Hosp. Fedn., Am. Pub. Health Assn., Soc. Hosp. Planning and Mktg., Hinsdale Golf Club. Home: 721 W Walnut St Hinsdale IL 60521-3062 Office: Anderson Mikos Architects Ltd 1420 Kensington Rd Ste 306 Hinsdale IL 60523-2147

ANDERSON, HELEN SHARP, civic worker; b. Ennis, Tex., June 10, 1916; d. John H. and Eula (King) Sharp; m. Thomas Dunaway Anderson, Feb. 21, 1938; children: John Sharp, Helen Shaw, Lucille Streeter. AB, U. Tex., Austin, 1937. Mem. Mt. Vernon Ladies Assn. of the Union, vice regent, 1967-91, regent, 1982-86, vice regent for Tex. emerita, 1991—. Bd. dirs. Nat. Cathedral Assn., Washington, 1971-75, also mem. various spl. coms.; mem. Garden Club Am., 1945—, zone vice chmn., 1959-62, nat. dir., 1975-77, nat. v.p., 1977-79, nat. chmn. long range planning, 1979-80; bd. dirs. Japan Am. Soc. Houston, 1974-78; hon. mem. fine arts adv. com. U. Tex., Austin, 1963-95; Bayou Bend adv. com., 1988-97; chmn. Jr. Gallery, Mus. Fine Arts, Houston, 1953-54, docent, 1964-70; bd. dirs. Houston and Harris County coun. Girl Scouts U.S.A., 1966-67, Sheltering Arms, 1964-67; bd. trustees Winedale Hist. Ctr., 1987-97; bd. dirs. Harris County Heritage Soc., 1963-65, v.p., 1965-66; mem. River Oaks Garden Club, Houston, 1945—, pres., 1958, 59; vol. Vols. for Endowment for Patient Support, M.D. Anderson Cancer Ctr., 1995—; mem. St. John the Divine Epsicopal Ch., Houston; mem. Houston Jr. League. Recipient Zone IX Creative Leadership award Garden Club Am., 1983, Achievement medal Garden Club Am., 1988, Ima Hogg Hist. Achievement award for Hist. Preservation, Winedale Hist. Ctr., 1997, Citizens Environ. Coalition Synergy award, 1997. Mem. Assembly Bolero Clubs (Houston, Sulgrave, Washington, Colony, N.Y.), Pi Beta Phi. Republican. Episcopalian. Address: 3925 Del Monte Dr Houston TX 77019-1001

ANDERSON, HERBERT G. marine biologist, researcher; b. Roanoke, Ala., Dec. 29, 1931; s. Herbert Godwin and Ethel Blanche Anderson. BS, Auburn U., Auburn,Al, 1958; MS, Auburn U., Auburn, L, 1960; PhD, U. Of Miami, Miami, Fl, 1965. Prof. of biol. sci. Ctrl. Ct State U., New Britain, Conn., 1964—89, prof.of biogical sci. emeritus, 1989. Chair,univ,graduate studies comm. Ctrl. Ct State U., New Britain, Conn., chair, univ. termination, appeals.com., chair grad. scholarship subcom., secr.for state univ.marine studies com. Solo classical piano recital Jacksonville State U., Jacksonville, Ala., 1951; mem. of bd. of directors Westbay Pt.mooringsll, Holmes Beach, Fla., 1996; recipient of recognition for my Art Abstract Installed As A Stained Glass, Ann Maria, Fla., 2002. Petty officer 3rd u.s.navy, 1951—55, Lake Champlain (Cva) Korea. Recipient Rsch. Fellowship, F & W-l Bur. Of Sport Fisheries,Sandy Hook Nj, 1962 to 1964; grantee Rsch. Grant, Rsch. Dept. Ctrl. Ct State Univ. New Britain,ct, 1976. Mem.: Marquis Whos Who In The East (assoc.), The Am. Soc.of Parasitologists (assoc.), Sigma Xi) The Sci. Rsch. Soc. (assoc.). Episcopalian. Achievements include research in Meristic charactistics and marine fish parasites do not confirm color differen. Avocations: piantist(classical), artist(geomerical cubist abstract). Home: 6500 Flotilla Dr # 212 Holmes Beach FL 34217-1438

ANDERSON, HERBERT HATFIELD, lawyer, farmer; b. Rainier, Oreg., Aug. 2, 1920; s. Odin A. and Mae (Hatfield) A.; m. Barbara Stuart Bastine, June 3, 1949; children— Linda, Catherine, Thomas, Amy, Elizabeth, Kenneth BA in Bus. Adminstrn., U. Oreg., 1940; JD, Yale U., 1949. Exec. trainee U.S. Steel Co., San Francisco, 1940-41; assoc. Koerner, Young, McColloch & Dezendorf, Portland, Oreg., 1949—54; ptnr. Spears, Lubersky, Bledsoe, Anderson, Young & Hilliard, 1954-90, Lane, Powell, Spears & Lubersky, Portland, 1990—. Instr. law Lewis and Clark Coll., Portland, 1950-70. Mem. planning adv. com. Yamhill County, Oreg., 1974-82; bd. dirs. Emanuel Hosp., 1967—; bd. dirs. Flyfisher Found., 1972—, pres., 1972-84; bd. dirs. Multnomah Law Library, 1958—, sec. 1962-68, 77-95, pres., 1964-74. Served to maj., parachute inf. U.S. Army, 1942-46, ETO Fellow Am. Bar Found. (chmn. Oreg. chpt. 1988—); mem. ABA (chmn. governing com. forum on health law 1984-89, chmn. standing com. on jud. selection, tenure and compensation 1978-80, Lawyer's Conf., exec. com. 1980-94, chmn. 1989-90, judicial adminstrn. divsn. coun. 1988-94, sr. lawyer's divsn. coun. 1987-89), Am. Judicature Soc. (bd. dirs. 1981-85), Soc. Law and Medicine, Nat. Health Lawyers Assn., Am. Acad. Hosp. Attys., Oreg. Soc. Hosp. Attys. (pres. 1984-85), Multnomah Bar Found. (bd. dirs. 1955—, pres. 1959-64, 87—), Nat. Bankruptcy Conf. (conferee 1964—, exec. com. 1976-79, chmn. farmer insolvency com. 1985-88), Nat. Assn. R.R. Trial Counsel, Oreg. Bar Assn. (del. to ABA 1966-68), Multnomah Bar Assn. (pres. 1955), Western States Bar Conf. (pres. 1967), Oreg. Asian Pear Coun. (pres. 1989-91), Sigma Chi. Clubs: Multnomah Athletic, Michelbook Country, Flyfishers Oreg. (pres. 1972), Flyfisher Found. (pres. 1957-67), Willamette Amateur Field Trial (pres. 1968-72), Trial Clubs of Am. (trustee 2002-). Lodges: Masons. Democrat. Lutheran. Home: River Meadow Farm 19289 SE Neck Rd Dayton OR 97114-7815 Office: Lane Powell Spears & Lubersky 601 SW 2d Ave Ste 2100 Portland OR 97204-3158 E-mail: herband@open.org.

ANDERSON, HERSCHEL VINCENT, retired librarian; b. Charlotte, N.C., Mar. 14, 1932; s. Paul Kemper and Lillian (Johnson) A. BA, Duke U., 1954; MS, Columbia U., 1959. Library asst. Bklyn. Public Library, 1954-59; asst. bookmobile librarian King County Public Library, Seattle, 1959-62; asst. librarian Longview (Wash.) Public Library, 1962-63; librarian N.C. Mus. Art, Raleigh, 1963-64; audio-visual cons. N.C. State Library, Raleigh, 1964-68; dir. Sandhill Regional Library, Rockingham, N.C., 1968-70; asso. state librarian Tenn. State Library and Archives, Nashville, 1970-72; unit dir. Colo. State Library, Denver, 1972-73; state librarian S.D. State Library, Pierre, 1973-80; dir. Mesa (Ariz.) Public Library, 1980-99. Dir. Bibliographical Ctr. for Rsch., Denver, 1974-80, v.p. 1977; founding mem. Western Coun. St. Librs., 1975-80, v.p., 1978, pres., 1979; mem. Ariz. LSCA Adv. Coun., 1981-84, pres., 1982-83; founding mem., chief officers State Libr. Agys., 1973-80, bd. dirs.; mem. Ariz. Libr. Devel. Coun., 1991-93, Ariz. State Libr. Adv. Coun., 1998—, chair, 1999—, mem. libr. technician tng. adv. com. Mesa C.C., 1982-85, mem. commn. for excellence, 1993-2003; chmn. Serials On-Line in Ariz. Consortia, 1985-86; mem. libr. facilities adv. bd. Gilbert, Ariz., 1999—. Jr. warden St. Mark's Episcopal Ch., Mesa, 1985-87, vestryman, 1987-90, 95-98, sr. warden, 1996-98, archivist, 2000--; del. ann. conv. Episcopal Diocese of Ariz., 1989-92, 94-98, mem. archives com., 1990-97, mem. Diocesan Coun. Episcopal, Diocese of Ariz., 1996-98; mem., treas. Maricopa County Libr. Coun., 1981-99, pres., 1983, 93; mem. City of Mesa Hist. Preservation com., 2000—; mem. Valley Citizens League, 1991—; mem. Northeast Regional Parish steering com., 1994—, chair Native Am. com., 1999—. With U.S. Army, 1955-57. Recipient Emeritus Honors Ariz. Library Friends, 1987. Mem. ALA, S.D. Libr. Assn. (hon. life, Libr. of Yr. award 1977), Mountain Plains Libr. Assn. (pres. 1974, bd. dirs. 1974-77, 86-87, Intellectual Freedom award 1979), Ariz. Libr. Assn. (exe. com. 1986-87), Kiwanis (bd. dirs. Mesa 1981-86, v.p. 1983, pres. 1985-86), Phi Kappa Psi. E-mail: andersonvince@aol.com.

ANDERSON, HOLLY GEIS, women's health facility administrator, commentator, educator; b. Waukesha, Wis., Oct. 23, 1946; d. Henry H. and Hulda S. Geis; m. Richard Kent Anderson, June 6, 1969. BA, Azusa Pacific U., 1970. CEO Oak Tree Antiques, San Gabriel, Calif., 1975-82; pres., founder, CEO Premenstrual Syndrome Med. Clinic, Arcadia, Calif., 1982—, Breast Healthcare Ctr., 1986-89, Hormonal Treatment Ctrs., Inc., Arcadia, 1992-94; with Thyroid Ctr., 2001—. Lectr. radio and TV shows, L.A.; on-air radio personality Women's Clinic with Holly Anderson, 1990—. Author: What Every Woman Needs to Know About PMS (audio cassette), 1987, The PMS Treatment Program (video cassette), 1989, PMS Talk (audio cassette), 1989. Mem. NAFE, The Dalton Soc., Am. Hist. Soc. of Germans from Russia. Republican. Avocations: writing, genealogy, travel, hiking, boating. Office: PMS Treatment Clinic 150 N Santa Anita Ave Ste 755 Arcadia CA 91006-3148

ANDERSON, HOWARD WAYNE, JR., training company executive; b. Sharon, Pa., Oct. 29, 1957; s. Howard Wayne Anderson Sr and Judith Kathleen Anderson; m. Mary Elizabeth Santo, July 11, 1981; children: Jennifer, Ryan. BA in Criminal Justice, Mercyhurst Coll., 1980; MS in Sys. Mgmt., U. So. Calif., 1989; MEd in Tng. and Devel., Pa, State U., 2000; PhD in Mgmt., Madison U., 2003. Commd. 2d lt. USMC, 1980, advanced through grades to maj., exec. officer 2d marine divsn., 1982—84, commdg. gen. aide de camp Quantico, Va., 1986—88, commdg. officer air ground task force Twentynine Palms, Pa., 1989—91; sr. ops. mgr. Schneider Nat. Carriers, Inc, Carlisle, Pa., 1991—99; dir., N.E. tng. and loss prevention Schneider Tng. Acad., Carlisle, 1999—. Contbr. articles to profl. jours. Mem. Compassion Internat., Colorado Springs, Colo., 1989. Recipient 32 letters of appreciation, various civic groups, 1986—88. Mem.: Pa. Interscholastic Athletic Assn., Nat. Assn. of Sports Officials. Avocations: weightlifting, fitness, reading, writing. Office: Schneider National Carriers Inc 1 Schneider Drive Carlisle PA 17013 Home Fax: 717-691-4438. Personal E-mail: hwajr@aol.com. E-mail: wayne_anderson/schneider@schneider.com.

ANDERSON, HUGH GEORGE, bishop; b. L.A., Calif., Mar. 10, 1932; s. Reuben Leroy and Frances Sophia (Nielsen) A.; m. Synnøve Anna Hella, Nov. 3, 1956 (dec. Apr. 1982); 1 child, Erik; m. Jutta Ilse Fischer, July 2, 1983; children: Lars, Niels;1 child, Kristi. AB, Yale U., 1953; BD, Luth. Theol. Sem., Phila., 1956, STM, 1958; MA, U. Pa., 1957, PhD, 1962; LittD, Lenoir Rhyne Coll., 1971; DD, Roanoke Coll., 1971, Wagner Coll., 1987, Gen. Theol. Sem., N.Y.C., 1996, Luther Coll., Decorah, Iowa, 1996; LHD, Newberry Coll., 1979, Columbia (S.C.) Coll., 1981. Ordained Luth. min. Tchg. fellow Luth. Theol. Sem., Phila., 1956—58; prof. ch. history Luth. Theol. So. Sem., Columbia, SC, 1958—70, dir. grad. studies, pres., 1970—82, Luther Coll., Decorah, Iowa, 1982—95; presiding bishop Evang. Luth. Ch. Am., Chgo., 1995—2001; ret., 2001. Chair Pub. House of the Evang. Luth. Ch. Am., 1987—93; co-chmn. U.S. Luth.-Roman Cath. Dialogue, 1979—90; mem. Commn. for a New Luth. Ch., 1982—86; v.p. Luth. World Fedn., 1996—. Author: Lutheranism in the Southeastern States, 1969, A Good Time to be the Church, 1997; co-author: Lutherans in North America, 1975; translator: I Believe (H. Thielicke), 1968, Historical Commentary on the Augsburg Confession (W. Maurer), 1986. Bd. dirs. Minn. Pub. Radio, St. Paul, 1983—91. Mem.: Luth. World Fedn. (commn. on studies 1984—90). Lutheran. Avocations: astronomy, sailing. Home: PO Box 719 Prospect Heights IL 60070-0719 E-mail: hgeorgea@earthlink.net.

ANDERSON, IB, performing company executive; b. Denmark; Prin. dancer N.Y.C Ballet, 1980—90; tchr. various companies in Belgium, Norway, Japan, Can. and U.S., 1990—2000; artistic dir. Ballet Ariz., 2000—. Avocations: cooking, painting, music, poetry, literature. Office: Ballet Arizona 3645 E Indian Sch Rd Phoenix AZ 85018

ANDERSON, ILSE JANELL, clinical geneticist; b. Elmhurst, Ill., May 3, 1959; d. Lowell Leonard and Avis Janell Anderson; m. Nicholas Thomas Potter, June 24, 1989; children: Nils Andrew, Anders Matthew. BS in Biology, Lehigh U., 1981; MD, N.Y. Med. Coll., 1985. Diplomate Nat. Bd. Med. Examiners, Am. Bd. Pediatrics, Am. Bd. Med. Genetics. Resident pediatrics U. Conn., Farmington, 1985-88, fellow human genetics, 1988-91; clin. geneticist Med. Ctr. U. Tenn., Knoxville, 1991—. Mem. Phi Beta Kappa. Office: Univ Tenn Med Ctr 1930 Alcoa Hwy Ste 435 Knoxville TN 37920-1520

ANDERSON, IRIS ANITA, retired secondary education educator; b. Forks, Wash., Aug. 18, 1930; d. James Adolphus and Alma Elizabeth (Haase) Gilbreath; m. Donald Rene Anderson, 1951; children: Karen Christine, Susan Adele, Gayle Lynne, Brian Dale. BA in Teaching, U. Wash., 1969; MA in English, Seattle U., 1972. Cert. English teacher, adminr Calif. Tchr. Issaquah (Wash.) Sr. High Sch., 1969-77, L.A. Sr. High Sch., 1977-79. Nutrition vol Santa Monica Hosp Aux, Calif., Jules Stein Eye Inst, Los Angeles; mem Desert Beautirful, Palm Springs Panhellenic, Rancho Mirage Reps. Scholar W-Key Activities, Univ Wash. Mem.: LEV, AAUW (Anne Carpenter fellow 1998), NEA, DAR (1st vice regent Cahulla chpt), World Affairs Coun, Calif Ret Teachers Asn, Coachella Valley Hist Soc, Desert Music Guild, Palm Springs Press Women, Nat Thespians, Wash Speech Asn, Am League Pen Women,

Living Desert Wildlife And Botanical Preserve, Desert Celebrities, Bob Hope Cultural Ctr, Skeptics Soc, Round Table West (3d pl. writing award 2003), Rancho Mirage Womens Club, CPA Wives Club, Palm Desert Womens Club.

ANDERSON, IVAN VERNER, JR., newspaper publisher; b. Columbus, Ohio, Dec. 6, 1939; m. Josephine Blackwell; children: Thomas, Charlotte. BA, U. N.C., 1961; MBA, U. S.C., 1970. Sr. v.p. for loan adminstrn., regional mgr. Wachovia Bank and Trust Co., Winston-Salem, N.C., 1980-84; sr. v.p., regional exec. S.C. Nat. Bank, Charleston, 1984; exec. v.p. Evening Post Pub. Co., Charleston, 1984, pres., 1987—; asst. pub. The News and Courier, The Evening Post, Charleston, 1984; pub. The Post and Courier, 1987—. Bd. dirs. Trident United Way, S.C. Hist. Soc., Charleston Symphony Orch., Ashley Hall Sch., Enston Home, Ind. Colls. and Univs.; bd. visitors U. N.C., Chapel Hill; mem. city bd. Wachovia Bank S.C.; active U. S.C. Coll. Bus. Adminstrn. Bus. Partnership Found., Nature Conservancy. With USN, 1961-64. Mem. So. Newspaper Pub. Assn., Beta Gamma Sigma. Episcopalian. Avocations: golfing, hunting, fishing.

ANDERSON, J. TRENT, lawyer; b. Indpls., July 22, 1939; s. Robert C. and Charlotte M. (Pfeifer) Anderson; m. Judith J. Zimmerman, Sept. 8, 1962; children: Evan M., Molly K. BS, Purdue U., 1961; LLB, U. Va., 1964. Bar: Ill. 1965, Ind. 1965. Tchg. asst. Law Sch. U. Calif., Berkeley, 1964-65; assoc. Mayer, Brown & Platt, Chgo., 1965-72; ptnr. Mayer, Brown, Rowe & Maw LLP, Chgo., 1972—. Instr. Loyola U. Law Sch., Chgo., 1985. Mem.: Mich. Shores Club, Union League Club, Law Club. Home: 3037 Iroquois Rd Wilmette IL 60091-1106 Office: Mayer Brown Rowe and Maw LLP 190 S La Salle St Ste 3100 Chicago IL 60603-3441 E-mail: janderson@mayerbrown.com.

ANDERSON, JACK OLAND, retired college official; b. Mich., Aug. 5, 1921; s. Seymour and Laura (Fox) A. Student, Ferris State Coll., 1940-41; BS, Central Mich. U., 1948; MA, U. Mich., 1950; Ed.D., Mich. State U., 1962. Tchr. pub. schs. Mich., 1949-59; instr. Mich. State U., 1959-62; dir. edn. Lansing (Mich.) Bus. Inst., 1962-65; exec. dir. Lockyear Bus. Coll., 1965-66; acad. dean Detroit Coll., 1966-69; pres. Bristol (Tenn.) Coll., 1969-83, chmn. bd. dirs., 1983-88. Past chmn. Sullivan County Vocat. Adv. Com.; past vice chmn. region IV proprietary sch. coordinating coun. U.S. Dept. Edn. Past mem. Sullivan County Bd. Equalization, Bristol Power Bd., Sullivan County Hist. Commn., Tenn. Pub. Svc. Coun., bd. adminstrn. 1st Bapt. Ch., Bristol, Appalachian Regional Commn. Health Systems Aging; past chmn. dist. 757, Rotary Found. Capt. U.S. Army, 1942—46. Paul Harris fellow Rotary, 1983. Home: 1101 Indian Hill Dr Bristol TN 37620-3554

ANDERSON, JACK ROY, health care company executive; b. Mansfield, Ohio, Feb. 14, 1925; s. Roy L. and Katherine (Munson) A.; m. Rose-Marie J. Garcia, June 24, 1950; children— Gail Ellen, Neil Robert, Barbara Ann BS, Miami U., Oxford, Ohio, 1947; MS, Columbia Bus. Sch., 1949. Acctg. mgr. Time, Inc., N.Y.C., 1950-59; asst. to controller W.R. Grace & Co., N.Y.C., 1959-62; v.p., treas. Hartford Publs., Inc., N.Y.C., 1962-65; controller McCall Corp., N.Y.C., 1965-68; v.p. Reliance Group, Inc., N.Y.C., 1968-70; pres., dir. Hosp. Affiliates Internat., Inc., Nashville, 1970-76, chmn. bd., dir., 1977-81; chmn. INA Health Care Group, Dallas, 1978-81; pres. Manor Care, Inc., Silver Spring, Md., 1981-82, Calver Corp., Dallas, 1982—. Adj. faculty Vanderbilt Owen Grad. Sch. Mgmt., 1978—79. Author: The Road to Recovery, 1976. Trustee Nat. Com. for Quality Health Care, 1979—87, vice chmn., 1979—82; mem. bus. adv. coun. Miami U., 1975—78, chmn., 1978; mem. bd. overseers Hoover Instn. on War, Revolution and Peace, Stanford U.; mem. Pres.'s Cir., NAS, NAE, Inst. Medicine. Lt. (j.g.) USNR, 1943—46. Mem.: Reform Club (London), Met. Club (N.Y.C.), Double Eagle Club (Galena, Ohio), Greenwich (Conn.) Country Club, Desert Forest Golf Club (Carefree, Ariz.), Blind Brook Club (Purchase, N.Y.), Clove Valley Rd and Gun Club (LaGrangeville, N.Y.), Beta Alpha Psi, Sigma Chi, Beta Gamma Sigma (hon.). Office: 16475 Dallas Pkwy Addison TX 75001-6821

ANDERSON, JACK WARREN, dance critic, poet; b. Milwaukee, Wis., June 15, 1935; s. George William and Eleanore Myrtle Anderson; life ptnr. George E. Dorris. BS Theater, Northwestern Univ., Evanston, IL, 1953—57; MA Creative Writing, Ind. Univ., Bloomington, IN, 1957—58. Corr. Ballet Today, London, England, 1959—70; asst. drama critic Oakland Tribune, Oakland, 1960—63; staff writer Dance Mag., New York, 1964—78; dep. dance critic The Daily Mail, London, England, 1970—71; ny corr. The Dancing Times, London, England, 1971—; dance critic The NY Times, New York, 1978—. Author: (book) Dance, City Joys, The Invention of New Jersey, The Dust Dancers, Toward the Liberation of the Left Hand, The One and Only: The Ballet Russe de Monte Carlo, The Clouds of That Country, Selected Poems, Ballet and Modern Dance: A Concise History, The American Dance Festival; (book) Choreography Observed; author: (book) Field Trips on the Rapid Transit, Art Without Boundaries: The World of Modern Dance, Traffic: New and Selected Prose Poems; editor: The Dance, The Dancer, and The Poem: An Anthology of Twentieth Century Dance Poems. Recipient Marie Alexander Award for prose poetry, 1998, De la Torre Bueno Award for Dance Writing, 1980, Pushcart Prize for poetry, 1976-1977, Borestone Mountain Poetry Award, 1972, Lit. Award, Nat. Endowment for the Arts, 1968; fellow Creative Writing Fellowship, 1973-1974. Mem.: Nat. Endowment for the Arts (dance panelist 1975—78). Protestant. Avocations: reading, traveling. Home: 40 East 10th St Apt 1H New York NY 10003-6229 Office: The New York Times 229 West 43rd St New York NY 10036

ANDERSON, JACQUELINE ANNETTE, computer specialist; b. Balt., Md., Jan. 20, 1962; d. Edward Anderson and Ward Beatrice. AA in Bus. Adminstrn., Cert. in Office Skills, C.C. of Balt., 1984; BA in Mgmt. Sci., Coppin State Coll., 2001. Sec. Social Security Adminstrn., Balt., 1982—86, computer asst., 1986—99, computer specialist, 1999—. Election judge voting polls Bd. Election, Balt., 1996—99; interviewer Senatorial Scholarship Com., Balt., 1996—2000. Mem.: Black Affairs Adv. Coun., Toastmasters Club (v.p. #7046 1999—2000, treas. #7046 2000—, Trophy 2000). Avocations: sewing, helping others, movies, reading, tennis.

ANDERSON, JAMAL SHARIF, professional football player; b. Woodland Hills, Calif., Sept. 30, 1972; Student, U. Utah. Running back Atlanta Falcons, 1994—2002; NFC conf. champions, 1998—99; lost Superbowl 33 to Denver Broncos, 1999. Office: c/o Atlanta Falcons 1 Falcon Pl Suwanee GA 30024

ANDERSON, JAMES ALLEN, psychologist, writer; b. Ames, Iowa, May 20, 1965; s. Dale Lee and Sharon Joan Anderson; m. Ivy April Hanson, Sept. 17, 1995; children: John Tenner, Summer Grace, Kate Hannah. BS, Iowa State U., 1989; MS, Western Ill. U., 1991, splty. degree in sch. psychology, 1992. Psychologist Minn. Sch. psychologist. Consulting child psychologist. Author: Fifty Strategies for Quality Teaching, Talking Tools (award Am. Inst. Graphic Design, 2002); illustrator TanGraham Animals. Mem.: Soc. Children's Book Writers and Illustrators (assoc.). Avocations: sailing, music. Personal E-mail: lp4kids@earthlink.net.

ANDERSON, JAMES E., JR., lawyer; AB, Stanford U., 1969, JD, 1972. Bar: Calif. 1972, Tex. 1973, Tenn. 1985. Assoc. Akin, Gump, Strauss, Hauer & Feld, 1972-74, 76-78, ptnr., 1979-83, Wald, Harkrader & Ross, 1983-84, Dearborn & Ewing, 1984-91; v.p., gen. counsel Ingram Industries Inc., 1991-96; sr. v.p., sec., gen. counsel Ingram Micro, 1996—. Office: Ingram Micro 1600 E Saint Andrew Pl Santa Ana CA 92705-4926

ANDERSON, JAMES EVERETT, economics educator; b. Cleve., Apr. 10, 1943; s. Robert William and Mary Virginia (Robbins) A.; m. Jeanne Catherine Crossman, Nov. 30, 1968; children: Eleanor V., Cecily R. AB, Oberlin Coll., 1965; PhD, U. Wis., 1969. Asst. prof. econs. Boston Coll., Chestnut Hill, Mass., 1969-72, assoc. prof., 1972-77, prof., 1977—. Cons. World Bank, 1990—. Bd. editors: Am. Econ. Rev., 1988—. Jour. Internat. Econs., 1991—; author: The Relative Inefficiency of Quotas, 1988; contbr. articles to profl. jours. Recipient award Nat. Sci. Found., 1980-81. Mem. Am. Econ. Assn. Avocations: skiing, tennis, sailing. Home: 24 Ash Ln Sherborn MA 01770-1265

ANDERSON, JAMES FRANCIS, lawyer; b. Glen Ridge, NJ, June 13, 1965; BA, Seton Hall U., 1987, JD, 1990. Bar: N.J. 1991, U.S. Supreme Ct. 1995. Pvt. practice, Spring Lake, NJ, 1991—2001; staff atty. Ocean-Monmouth Legal Svcs., Freehold, NJ, 2001—. Pro bono atty. Ocean-Monmouth Legal Svcs., Freehold, N.J., 1991-2001; mentor Manasquan (NJ) HS, 1994. Office: 65 Mechanic St Ste 201 Red Bank NJ 07701 E-mail: janderson@monmouth.com.

ANDERSON, JAMES FREDERICK, clergyman; b. Elizabeth, N.J., Aug. 23, 1927; s. Fred and Hazel Minerva (Brown) A.; m. Bette Dillensnyder, Sept. 8, 1951; children: Judith (Mrs. Wayne Westbury) (dec.), James Frederick, Mark, Rebecca (Mrs. Patrick Williams). BA, Princeton U., 1948; BD, Princeton Theol. Sem., 1952; DD, Alma Coll., 1974. Ordained to ministry Presbyn. Ch., 1952; chaplain Hun Sch. for Boys, Princeton, 1953; instr. religion Lafayette Coll., Easton, Pa., 1954-55; pastor Presbyn. chs., Catasauqua, Pa., 1956-61, Narberth, Pa., 1961-66, Second Presbyn. Ch., Richmond, Va., 1966-72, Kirk in the Hills, Bloomfield Hills, Mich., 1972-94, pastor emeritus, 1994—. Trustee emeritus Alma (Mich.) Coll. With USNR, 1945-46. Home: 12 Surf Ave Ocean Grove NJ 07756-1629

ANDERSON, JAMES GEORGE, sociologist, educator; b. Balt., July 24, 1936; s. Clair Sherrill and Kathryn Ann (Plovanich) A.; m. Marilyn Anderson, 1984; children: Robin Marie, James Brian, Melissa Lee, Derek Clair. B in Engring. Scis. in Chem. Engring, Johns Hopkins U., 1957, MSE in Ops. Rsch. and Indsl. Engring., 1959, MAT in Chemistry and Math., 1960, PhD in Edn. and Sociology, 1964. Adminstrv. asst. to dean Eve. Coll., Johns Hopkins U., 1964-65, dir. divsn. engring., 1965-66; rsch. prof. ednl. adminstrn. N.Mex. State U., 1966-70; mem. faculty Purdue U., Lafayette, Ind., 1970—, prof. sociology, 1974—; asst. dean for analytical studies Sch. Humanities, Social Sci. and Edn., Lafayette, Ind., 1975 78. Assoc. dir. AIDS Rsch. Ctr., Purdue U., 1991—, co-dir. Rural Ctr. for AIDS/STD Prevention, 1993—; adj. prof. med. sociology grad. med. edn. program Meth. Hosp. Ind., 1991—; dir. Social Rsch. Inst., Purdue U., 1995-98; cons. in field. Guest editor spl. issue on simulation in health sci.: Simulation, Apr., 1996, spl. issues on modeling epidemics: guest editor spl issue on simulation in med. informatics, Jour. of the Am. Med. Informatics Assn, 2002; issue in simulation in health care mgmt., Health Care Mgmt. Sci., 2002. Mem. Am. Assn. for Med. Systems and Informatics Del. to the Peoples Republic of China, 1985; mem., citizens amb. People to People Med. Informatics Del. to Hungary and Russia, 1993. USPHS grant; recipient award for outstanding paper Am. Assn. Med. Sys. and Informatics, 1983, Gov. award State of Ind., 1987, T. Hale New Investigators award Assn. Am. Med. Coll., 1988, Wyeth-Ayerst/William Campbell Felch, MD award Alliance for Continuing Med. Edn., 1995. Mem.: APHA, AAAS (rep. soc. for computer simulation biol. scis. sect. 1992—99), AAUP, Social Sci. Computing Assn. (chair life scis. 1991—), Am. Sociol. Assn. (chair sect. sociology and computers 2000—01), Internat. Soc. Sys. Sci. in Health Care, Internat. Network for Social Network Analysis (chair life scis. 1997—), Am. Med. Informatics Assn. (internat. affairs com. 1993—96, chmn. sect. ethical, legal and social issues 1997—2000, sci. program com. ann. conf. 1999, mem. editl. bd. 2000—, chmn. sect. on quality improvement 2002—04, guest editor 2002, Best Theoretical Paper award 1997), Am. Ednl. Rsch. Assn. (treas. spl. interest group 1969—71), Am. Sociol. Assn., Assn. for Computing Machinery, Soc. Modeling and Computer Simulation (sr.; assoc. v.p. simulation in health care 1992—).

ANDERSON, JAMES KEITH, retired magazine editor; b. Grand Junction, Colo., June 27, 1924; s. Arnold Plumer and Helen Catherine (Enright) A.; m. Doris Mae Johnson, Aug. 5, 1952 (dec. Aug. 1999); children: Catherine E., Charles E., William H. II. AB, U. Mich., 1949. Reporter Jefferson City News and Tribune, Mo., 1949, Tampa Daily Times, Fla., 1949-51; editor Detroit Labor News, 1951-53; reporter Detroit News, 1953-68; editor VFW mag., Kansas City, Mo., 1968-89, West Mo. Spirit (Episcopal Diocese of West Mo.), 1989-91; ret., 1991. Mem. adv. bd. Diocesan Sch. for Ministry. Served with USMCR, 1942-43, inf. AUS, 1943-45. Decorated Bronze Star, Purple Heart, Combat Inf. badge, Gold Cross of Merit Polish Govt. in Exile, Royal Yugoslav Commemorative War Cross, Latvian Pro Merito; recipient numerous awards for ethnic coverage. Mem. VFW, SAR, DAV, Ancient and Honorable Artillery Co. of Mass., Sons and Daus. 1st Settlers Newbury, Mass., Sigma Delta Chi, Sigma Tau Gamma. Home: 621 W 63rd St Kansas City MO 64113-1525

ANDERSON, JAMES LINWOOD, pharmaceutical sales official; b. Bangor, Maine, June 8, 1949; s. Linwood Lamont and Helena May (Armitage) A.; m. Susan Grace Hughey, Aug. 23, 1974 (div. Aug. 1994). BS in Biology and Premedicine, U. Maine, 1971, MS in Physiology, 1972. Narcotics officer Maine State Police/Drug Enforcement Agy., 1973-74; sales rep. Wallace Labs., 1974-76, Hoechst-Roussell, Somerville, N.J., 1976-84; pharm. sales rep. I Miles (Bayer) Pharms., New Haven, 1984-90, ter. sales specialist, 1990-91, hosp. sales specialist, 1991-93, pharm. sales rep. II, 1994—. Coord. pastoral affairs Calvary Bapt. Ch., Manchester, N.H., 1976-80. Mem. USCG Aux. (flotilla comdr. New Bedford, Mass. 1992-94, divsn. capt. S.E. Mass. 1994-96, rear commodore Mass. and R.I. 1996-97, vice commodore for Maine, N.H., Mass., R.I. and part of Vt. 1998-99, dist. commodore 2000-2001, immediate past dist. commodore 2002-2003, chmn. dist. awards com. 2002-2003, coord. internat. search & rescue games adminstrn. logistics 2001, vice chair internat search & rescue adminstn. & logistics 2003—), Order of DeMolay (master councilor 1965-66, state master councilor 1966-67, chevalier 1967—). Avocations: boating, gun collecting, color guard drill team. Home: 205 Stevenson St New Bedford MA 02745-3516

ANDERSON, JAMES MILTON, lawyer; b. Chgo., Dec. 29, 1941; s. Milton H. and Eunice (Carlson) A.; m. Marjorie Henry Caldwell, Jan. 22, 1966; children: James Milton, Joseph H., Hilding F., Marjorie II. BA, Yale U., 1963; JD, Vanderbilt U., 1966. Bar: Ohio 1967. Assoc. rifm Taft, Stettinius & Hollister, Cin., 1968-75, ptnr., 1975-77, 82-96, mem. exec. com., 1975-77, 91-96; pres. U.S. ops., dir. Xomox Corp., Cin., 1977-81; sec. Access Corp., 1984-96; asst. sec. Carlisle Cos., 1985-90; bd. dirs. Cin. Stock Exch., 1978—, chmn., 1980-89. Bd. dir. Command Sys. Inc.; trustee, chmn. Monarch Found., 1988—; assoc. sr. v.p. med. affairs U. Cin., 1997—; dir. Children's Hosp. Corp. Am., 2000—; bd. adminstrs. Coun. Tchg. Hosps., 2000—. Mem. Indian Hill Coun., 1981-89, vice-mayor, 1985-87, mayor, 1987-89; mem. Hamilton County Airport Authority, 1980-85; trustee Children's Hosp. Med. Ctr., Cin., 1979—, chmn. bd. trustees, 1991-96, pres., CEO, 1996—; trustee The Children's Hosp. Found., 1990—, chmn. bd. trustees, 1990-93; trustee Cin. Ctr. for Devel. Disorders, 1969—, pres., 1974-80; trustee Dan Beard coun. Boy Scouts Am., 1982—, chmn., 1984-87, area pres. Ea. Ctrl. Region, 1989-91; trustee Cin. Mus. Natural History, 1984-87, Coll. Mt. St. Joseph, 1990-98; trustee Joy Outdoor Edn. Ctr., 1984-2000, pres., 1991-93, chmn., 1993-95. Capt. AUS, 1966-68. Decorated Bronze Star with two oak leaf clusters, Air medal. Mem. ABA, Ohio Bar Assn., Cin. Bar Assn., Valve Mfrs. Assn., Young Pres. Orgn., Camargo Club, Queen City Club, Commonwealth Club, Yale Club of N.Y., Cin. Yale Club, Order of Cof, Comml. Club. Avocation: sailing. Office: 3333 Burnet Ave Cincinnati OH 45229-3026

ANDERSON, JAMES WINGO, physician; b. Hinton, W.Va., Aug. 6, 1936; s. Fred Wingo and Georgia Lee (Whittaker) A.; m. Gay Veree Gilbert, June 7, 1957; children: Katherine, Steven. BS, W.Va. U., 1957; MD, Northwestern U., 1961; MS, Mayo Clinic, 1965. Intern Presbyn. Med. Ctr., Denver; resident, fellow Mayo Clinic, Rochester, Minn.; asst. prof. medicine U. Calif., San Francisco, 1968-73; prof. medicine, clin. nutrition U. Ky. Coll. Medicine, Lexington, 1973-96; pres., founder HCF Nutrition Found., Lexington, 1979—. Author: Diabetes-A Practical Guide to HEalty Living, 1981, Dr. Anderson's High Fiber Fitness Plan, 1994, Dr. Anderson;s Antioxident Antiaging, 1996. Trustee Georgetown (Ky.) Coll., 1988-96, chmn. bd. trustees, 1994-96. Capt. U.S. Army, 1965-68. Fellow Am. Coll. Physicians. Republican. Baptist. Home: 913 Taborlake Ct Lexington KY 40502-3032 Office: VA Med Ctr 2250 Leestown Rd Lexington KY 40511-1052

ANDERSON, JANICE LINN, real estate brokerage professional, paralegal; b. Paris, Tenn., Sept. 2, 1943; d. Orel Vernon and Rosie Elizabeth (Brockwell) L.; m. David James Anderson, June 11, 1965 (div. Oct. 1973). Entertainer, recording artist 4-Sons Record Co., Paris, Tenn., 1958-73; med. transcriptionist The Paris Clinic, 1965-73; computer operator, asst. to v.p. Medicare Adminstrn./Equitable, Nashville, 1973-74; property mgmt. asst. Dobson & Johnson, Inc., Nashville, 1974-76; dir. leasing and mgmt. Fortune-Nashville Co., 1976-78; real estate brokerage asst. J.G. Martin, Jr./Caudill Properties, Inc., Nashville, 1978—; pvt. practice med. ins. filing and collection, 1995—. Pvt. practice resume preparation, Nashville, 1982—. Bd. govs. Interant. Biog. Ctr., Cambridge, Eng.; active Girls Scouts U.S., Paris, 1967-69; mem. ARC, Nashville, 1978, Christian Appalachian Project, Lancaster, Ky., 1986; mem. citizen's adv. commn. Am. Inst. Cancer Rsch., Washington, 1985. Mem. NAFE, Bus. and Profl. Womens Club (pres. 1965-73), Profl. Musicians Union, Womens Missionary Union (bd. dirs. Paris chpt. 1970-71), Internat. Platform Assn., Realtors Secs. Assn., Am. Biog. Inst. Inc. (rsch. bd. advisors), Internat. Biographical Centre of Cambridge,Eng. (bd. govs.). Unitarian. Avocations: camping, guitar, do-it-yourself projects. Home: 812 Elissa Dr Nashville TN 37217-1323 Office: 208 3rd Ave N Ste 4 Nashville TN 37201-1617 E-mail: andersj@realtracs.com.

ANDERSON, JANICE M. freelance/self-employed photojournalist; b. Muncie, Ind., Oct. 19, 1938; d. John A. and Iva May McCreary; m. Jack W. Anderson, Dec. 1, 1974; m. Joe Bill Ewing (div.); children: Greg A. Ewing, Kathy L. Buesink, Gary J. Ewing. Student, Ball State U., 1990. Notary pub.: Ind.; Cert. Profl. Sec. Reporter, photographer Brownsburg Guide, Ind., 1964—68; reporter, circulation asst., photographer, writer Frankfort Times, 1969—71; reporter Lafayette Jour. Courier, Lafayette, 1971—72; reporter, broadcaster Kaspar Broadcasting (WILO Radio), Frankfort, 1972—75; baliff Clinton Circuit Ct., 1983—84; sec. to dean Ball State U., Muncie, 1985—2002. Freelance photojournalist, Muncie, 1969—. Sec. to city engr., asst. secy to mayor City of Frankfort, 1976—83, sec. plan commn., sec. to zoning bd.; sec., radio operator Clinton County CD, 1977—83; apptd. mem. Clinton County Area Plan Commn., sec., co-director, 1975—76; writer, coach puppet ministry First Bapt. Ch., 1977—84; bd. dirs., sec., treas. Am. Bapt. Campus Ministry at Ball State U., Muncie, 1987—2002; writer, prodr., camera, bd. operator First Bapt. Ch. TV Ministry, Frankfort, 1976—84; pub. rels. coord. Ctrl. Ind. Coun. of Campfire Girls, Indpls., 1963—68; bd. mem. Clinton County Boys Club, Frankfort. Nominee Woman of the Yr., 1995, 1997, A. Jane Morton award Excellence Staff Performance, Ball State U., 1996; named to Internat. Poetry Hall of Fame, 1996; recipient Top News Story in Ind., 1972, Key to the City, Mayor of Frankfort, 1983, Meritorious Svc. award, Ball State U., 1992, Best Poems and Poets of Yr., The Internat. Libr. of Poetry, 1995—2002, Internat. Profl. and Bus. Women's Hall of Fame, 1995—2001, Pres.'s award, Iliad Press, 1995. Mem.: Am. Women Radio & TV (state conf. chair 1975), Internat. Assn. Adminstrv. Profls. (chpt. pres. 1995—97, ind. divsn. historian 1995—2000, editor, historian local chpt. 1996—2000, ind. divsn. ann. meeting registration chair 2001). American Baptist. Achievements include Star Lecturer, Conway Diet Institute. Avocations: writing, travel, antiques. Home Fax: none. Personal E-mail: janderso@bsu.edu.

ANDERSON, J.C. oil and gas exploration company executive, rancher; b. Oakland, Nebr. Student, Midland Coll., Fremont, Nebr., 1949-51; BSc in Petroleum Engring., U. Tex., 1954. With Amoco Prodn. Co., various locations; chief engr. Amoco Can., Calgary, Alta., 1966-68; founder, chmn. bd., CEO Anderson Exploration Ltd., Calgary, 1968—2001; rancher Anderson Ranch. With Counter-Intelligence Corps, U.S. Army, 1954-56. Mem. Assn. Profl. Engrs., Geologists and Geophysicists of Alta., Soc. Petroleum Engrs., Can. Soc. Petroleum Geologists. Office: Ste 239 132-250 Shawville Blvd SE Calgary AB Canada T2Y 2Z7

ANDERSON, JEFFREY LEE, physician, anesthesiologist, consultant; b. Fontana, Calif., Feb. 3, 1959; s. Earle R. and Joyce E. Anderson; m. Crystal G. Anderson, Dec. 18, 1987; children: Kimberly, Kristin. BS, USAF Acad., 1981; MD, Loma Linda U., 1985. Cert. in anesthesiology. Resident in anesthesiology Loma Linda (Calif.) U. Med. Ctr., 1985-89; chief anesthesiologist USAF Hosp., Mather AFB, Calif., 1989-93; staff anesthesiologist Mercy Hosp. of Folsom, Calif., 1990—, Mercy Gen. Hosp., Sacramento, 1992—, Mercy San Juan Hosp., Carmichael, Calif., 1997—; chief anesthesiologist Folsom Surgery Ctr., 2001—. Medicolegal cons. Med. Bd. Calif., Sacramento, 1995—; clin. faculty U. Calif. Davis Sch. Medicine, 1993-96; anesthesia cons. Blue Shield of Calif., 1998—. Co-author: (textbook) Manual of Postanesthesia Care, 1993. Instr., course dir. ACLS, Am. Heart Assn., Sacramento, 1992—; physician Mercy White Rock Free Clin., 1994—. Mem. Calif. Soc. Anesthesiologists, C. of C. Office: 1650 Creekside Dr Folsom CA 95630-3400

ANDERSON, JERRY ALLEN, financial analyst; b. Ashland, Wis., Feb. 10, 1947; s. Elmer and Thelma Louise (Fallis) A.; m. Anne Marie Brown, June 7, 1975; 1 child, Kristen Marie. BBA, Temple U., 1969, MBA, 1975. Sr. investment officer Girard Bank, Phila., 1970-80; sr. investment analyst Sanford C. Bernstein, N.Y.C., 1980-83; dir. planning Sperry New Holland (Pa.), Inc., 1983-85, mgr. ops. analysis, 1985-87; fin. mgr. spl. markets Ford New Holland (Pa.), Inc., 1987-91; Mex. market mgr. Ford New Holland (Pa.) Inc., 1991-94; cons., 1994-96; v.p. investment rsch. Janney Montgomery Scott, 1996-99; cons. in fin., 1999—. Instr. sch. bus. Temple U., 1976-79, sch. bus. and govt. svcs., 1979-80. Recipient Cert. of Recognition Am. Mktg. Assn., 1968, 69, Outstanding Performance award Ford New Holland, 1987. Mem. Assn. for Investment Mgmt. and Rsch., Fin. Analysts of Phila., N.Y. Soc. Security Analysts, Model A Ford Club Am., Beta Gamma Sigma, Theta Chi. Avocations: model a restoration, numismatics, fishing, scuba diving, hunting. Home: 544 Norwyck Dr King Of Prussia PA 19406

ANDERSON, JERRY LEE, pianist, music educator; b. St. Louis, Dec. 24, 1941; m. Joanne Jones, Aug. 24, 1963. BS, diploma in Piano, S.W. Mo. State U., 1962; MusM, U. Wichita, 1964; postgrad., U. N.C., U. Iowa. Prof. music Augustana Coll., Rock Island, Ill., 1969-70; dir. music First Luth. Ch., Moline, Ill., 1970-72; prof., dir. keyboard studies Mo. Western State Coll., St. Joseph, 1972—; dir. music First Presbyn. Ch., St. Joseph, 1974—. Mem. Music Tchrs. Nat. Assn. (chmn. west-cen. div. auditions 1980-82), Music Tchrs. Assn. (editor Notes 1976-79, chmn. piano div. for Mo. 1984-92, univ. faculty 1996—).

ANDERSON, JERRY MAYNARD, speech educator, retired; b. Deronda, Wis., Sept. 16, 1933; s. Jens B. and Mamie P. (Hanson) A.; m. Betty Lou Schultz, Feb. 7, 1959; children: Gregory J., Timothy B. BS, Wis. State U. at River Falls, 1958; MS, No. Ill. U., 1959; PhD, Mich. State U., 1964; postgrad., U. Ariz., U. Minn. Instr. speech U. Maine, 1959-61; asst. prof. speech, dir. forensics Mich. State U., 1961-68; prof., chmn. dept. speech and dramatic arts Central Mich. U., Mt. Pleasant, 1968-72, vice provost, 1972—73; v.p. acad. affairs and prof. speech Western Wash. U., 1973-75; vice chancellor, prof. speech U. Wis., Oshkosh, 1975-79; pres., prof. speech Ball State U., Muncie, Ind., 1979-81; sr. cons. Am. Assn. State Colls. and Univs., Washington, 1981-82; rsch. adminstr. U. Wis., Stout, 1982—85; v.p. devel. Concordia Coll., Minn., 1985-88, prof. speech comm., 1988-99, prof. emeritus, 2000—; pres. Anderson and Assoc. Cons., 2000—. Author: Handbook for Forensic Students, 1963, Readings in Argumentation, 1968, Essays in Forensics, 1970, Case Studies in Public Relations: The 1994 U.S. West Crisis in Fargo, 2000; contbr. articles to profl. jours., chapters to books. Trustee Lake Wapogasset Assn.; bd. dirs. Radio Sta. WPCA. With USN, 1952—54. Recipient 1st Sr. Disting. Professionalism award Central Mich. U., 1971; Research fellow Harry S Truman Found., 1965; fellow Am. Council on Edn. Acad. Adminstrn. Internship Program, 1971-72; Recipient Disting. Alumnus award Delta Sigma Rho-Tau Kappa Alpha, 1980; Sagamore of Wabash Public Service award Gov. of Ind., 1980 Mem. Ctrl. States Speech Assn. (pres. 1973, Outstanding Young Tchr. award 1966), Mich. Speech Assn. (pres. 1967-68), Am. Forensic Assn. (pres. 1972-74, Disting. Svc. award 1994), Midwest Forensic Assn. (pres. 1969-72), Speech Comm. Assn. (legis. coun. 1967, legis. assembly 1975), Kiwanis, Rotary. *During my adult years the aphorism attributed to the late Senator Robert M. laFollette, Sr., has guided my work with others: "Give the people the facts and freedom to discuss and all will go well".*

ANDERSON, JERRY WILLIAM, JR., technical and business consulting executive, educator; b. Stow, Mass., Jan. 14, 1926; s. Jerry William and Heda Charlotte (Petersen) A. ; m. Joan Hukill Balyeat, Sept. 13, 1947; children: Katheleen, Diane. BS in Physics, U. Cin., 1949, PhD in Econs., 1976; MBA, Xavier U., 1959. Rsch. and test project engr. Wright-Patterson AFB, Ohio, 1949-53; project engr., electronics div. AVCO Corp., Cin., 1953-70, program mgr., 1970-73; program dir. Cin. Electronics Corp., 1973-78; pres. Anderson Industries Unltd., 1978—. Chmn. dept. mgmt. and mgmt. info. svcs. Xavier U., 1980-89, prof. mgmt., 1989-94, prof. emeritus, 1994—; lectr. No. Ky. U., 1977-78; tech. adviser Cin. Tech. Coll., 1971-80; co-founder, exec. v.p. Loving God "Complete Bible" Christian Ministries, 1988—. Contbr. articles on radars, lasers, infrared detection equipment, air pollution to govt. pubs. and prof. jours.; author: 3 books in field; reviewer, referee: Internat. Jour. Energy Sys., 1985—86. Mem. Madeira (Ohio) City Planning Commn., 1962-80; founder,

pres. Grassroots, Inc., 1964; active United Appeal, Heart Fund, Multiple Sclerosis Fund. With USNR, 1943-46 Named Man of Year, City of Madeira, 1964 Mem. MADD, VFW (life), Am. Mgmt. Assn., Assn. Energy Engrs. (charter), Internat. Acad. Mgmt. and Mktg., Nat. Right to Life, Assn. Cogeneration Engrs. (charter), Assn. Environ. Engrs. (charter), Am. Legion (past comdr.), Acad. Mgmt., Madeira Civic Assn. (past v.p.), Cin. Art Mus., Cin. Zoo, Colonial Williamsburg Found., Omicron Delta Epsilon. Republican. Home and Office: 7208 Sycamorehill Ln Cincinnati OH 45243-2101

ANDERSON, JEWELLE LUCILLE, musician, educator; b. Alexandria, La., Jan. 4, 1932; d. William Andrew and Ethel Dee (Hall) Anderson. Student, Springfield Coll., 1981-82; MusB, Boston U., 1984; postgrad., Harvard U., 1995-96. Cert. tchr. music and social studies Mass. Soloist Ch. of the Redeemer Episcopal Ch., Chestnut Hill, Mass., 1964-69, St. James Episcopal Ch., Cambridge, Mass., 1970-75; kindergarten tchr. and music dir. Trinity Episcopal Ch., Boston, 1984-86; chorus music dir. Spencer for Hire, Boston, 1986; music dir. Days in the Arts summer program Boston Symphony Orch., Tanglewood, Mass., summer 1991, 92; chorale dir. Boston Orch. Chorale, 1996-97; tchr. scholar Harvard Grad. Sch. of Edn., 1998-99. Founder Jewelle Anderson Found., Inc., Boston, 1996. Vol. ARC, Boston, 1994—; bd. dirs. Mattapan Cmty. Health Ctr., Boston, 1990—92; founder, pres. Dr. William and Ethel Hall Anderson Scholarship, 1989—. Recipient Am. Music award, Nat. Fedn. Music, 1970, Spl. Individual award, 1969, Outstanding Contbn. to Humanity award, Alexandria Civic Improvement Coun., 1967, Outstanding Achievement award, Boston Tchrs. Union, 2000, Cope Plaque for Outstanding Achievement, 2000. Mem.: AAUW, Black Educators Alliance of Mass., Amnesty Internat., Women Svc. Club (head youth group 1989—, 1st v.p. 2002), Alpha Kappa Alpha. Democrat. Baptist. Avocations: walking, boating. Office: Jewelle Anderson Found Inc PO Box 1181 Boston MA 02103-1181

ANDERSON, JOAN BALYEAT, religion educator, minister; b. Cin., Apr. 14, 1926; d. Hal Donal and Myrtle (Skinner) Hukill Balyeat; m. Jerry William Anderson, Jr., Sept. 13, 1947: children: Katheleen, Diane. AA, Stephens Coll., 1946. Ordained Christian minister, Ohio, 1988. Christian ch. bible tchr., Cin., 1944—; Christian counselor, advisor, 1964—; founder, pres., dir., ruling elder, and pastor Loving God "Complete Bible" Christian Ministries and First Ch., Cin., 1988—. Christian Bible tchr., preacher, pastor daily and Sunday radio throughout the east and midwest, 1988—. Mem. Am. Conservative Cause, 1998—2001, Capitol His. Soc., 2000—; legacy leader supporter George Washington's Mt. Vernon, 2001—; coord., collector Heart Fund, T.B., 1948—90; civic assn. officer, rep. edn. com. to all Madeira Schs., 1960—62; co-founder, officer Grassroots, Inc., Cin., 1962—65; mem. Cin. Art Mus., 1972—, Cin. Zoo, 1974—, Colonial Williamsburg Found., 1979—, Nat. Right to Life, 1980—, MADD, 1985—, Heritage Found., 1996—, Am. Conservative Union, 1998, Ronald Reagan Presdl. Found., 1998—, Parents TV Coun., 1998—2001, Am. Policy Ctr., 1998—2001, U.S. Justice Found., 1998—, Nat. Right to Work Legal Def. Found., 1998—, Nat. Security Ctr., 1998—, U.S. Intelligence Ctr., 1998—, Jud. Watch, 1999—, Young Ams. Found., 2000—; supporter The Liberty Com., 2001—; lifelong activist for preservation of U.S. Constn. and Bill of Rights; mem. U.S. Rep. Senatorial Adv. Com., Washington and Cin., 1987—88; mem. Rep. Senatorial Commn., Washington & Cin., 1996—2000; mem. Am. Prayer Network, 1998—. Mem. Blue Book of Cin. Avocation: touring america by car. Home: 7208 Sycamorehill Ln Cincinnati OH 45243-2101 Office: Loving God Complete Bible Christian Mins/1st Ch PO Box 43404 Cincinnati OH 45243-2101

ANDERSON, JOCK ROBERT, adult education educator, consultant; b. Monto, Queensland, Australia, Jan. 23, 1941; s. Robert William and Nellie Frances Anderson; m. Libby A Johnson, Feb. 15, 1964; children: Jules, Dianne Schreiber. MAgr, Univ Queensland, St Lucia, 1959—63; PhD, U. New Eng., Armidale, 1966—70; DEc, U. New England, 1982. Prof., agricultural econ. UNE, Armidale, Australia, 1970—88; adviser, rural devel. World Bank, Washington, 1989—. Recipient, FAAEA, 1996. Mem.: AARES (pres. 1982, Disting. Fellow 2003).

ANDERSON, JOEL E., JR., university administrator; b. Newport, Ark., Jan. 20, 1942; s. Joel E. Sr. and Norris Hall Anderson; m. Ann Gaskill, Aug. 7, 1964; children: Lincoln Jay, Deverick John, Mitchell Reid. BA, Harding Coll., 1964; MA, Am. U., 1966; PhD, U. Mich., 1974. Instr. polit. sci. Harding Coll., 1966-67; from asst. to assoc. prof. U. Ark., Little Rock, 1971-81, prof., 1981—, dean grad. sch., 1977-84, vice chancellor, provost, 1984—2002, interim chancellor, 1993, chancellor, 2003—. Pres. univ. assembly U. Ark., 1974-76; mem. vis. com. coll. bus. Abilene Christian U., 1994-97, chair, 1997; cons.-evaluator commn. instns. higher edn. North Ctrl. Assn. Colls. and Schs., 1994—; study dir. Plain Talk: The Future of Little Rock's Public Schools, 1997; study dir. Water for Our Future: Overcoming Regional Paralysis, 2000. Editor Ark. Polit. Sci. Rev., 1979-82. Charter mem. bd. trustees Kidney Found. Ark., 1975-79; mem. Pulaski County Bd. of Election Commrs., 1976-79; mem. bd. overseers Sta. KLRE-KUAR-FM, 1986-90; bd. dirs. Ark. 4-H Found., 1997—, Ark. Sci. and Tech. Authority, 1998-2001, Ark. Symphony Bd., 1999—. Mem. Am. Assn. State Colls. and Univs. (mem. acad. affairs resource ctr. adv. com. 1994-98), Ark. Polit. Sci. Assn. (pres. 1975), Rotary, Alpha Chi, Phi Kappa Phi. Mem. Ch. of Christ. Office: U Ark Little Rock Office of the Chancellor 2801 S University Ave Little Rock AR 72204-1099

ANDERSON, JOHN THOMAS, librarian, historian; b. Burlington, Iowa, Feb. 7, 1955; s. Alvin Jay and Margaret Ann (Thomas) A. BA, U. No. Iowa, 1976; MA, Coll. William and Mary, 1979; PhD, U. Va., 1982; M in Info. and Libr. Studies, U. Mich., 1987. Cert. archivist 1989. Instr., asst. prof. history Chadron (Nebr.) State Coll., 1984; asst. libr. pub. svcs. Mid. Ga. Coll., Cochran, 1989-91; temp. reference libr. U. No. Iowa, Cedar Falls, 1991; reference libr. Palm Beach County Libr. Sys., Boca Raton, Fla., 1992, Salve Regina U., Newport, R.I., 1992-93, catalog libr., 1993-94; media cataloger libr. Tex. A&M U., Commerce, 1997-98; libr. I info. svcs. Abilene (Tex.) Pub. Libr., 1998—2002. Catalog libr. Abilene Christian U., 1999—2002; rare book cataloger UB Found., SUNY-Buffalo, 2002—. Exhibits judge Nat. History Day Competition, Chadron, Nebr., 1984. Philip Francis du Pont fellow Coll. William and Mary, 1976; Philip Francis du Pont fellow U. Va., 1977; Virginia Mason Davidge fellow U. Va., 1978, 79. Mem. ALA, Soc. Historians Am. Fgn. Rels. Republican. Unitarian Universalist. Avocations: collecting postage stamps and first-edition books, public radio. Home: 5 Windham Way Apt A Amherst NY 14228-2409 Office: SUNY at Buffalo Poetry/Rare Books Dept 420 Capen Hall Univ Librs Buffalo NY 14260 E-mail: jta4@buffalo.edu.

ANDERSON, JOHN ALBERT, physician; b. Ashtabula, Ohio, Jan. 25, 1935; s. Albert Gunnard Anderson and Martha Anetta (Bieshline) White; m. Nicole Jeanne Anderson, July 10, 1963; children: Carole Beno, John-Marc, Christopher B. BS, U. Ill., 1958, MD, 1960. Diplomate Am. Bd. Pediat., Am. Bd. Allergy and Immunology. Intern U. Ill., 1960-61, resident in pediat., 1961-62, U.S. Naval Hosp., Bethesda, Md., 1964-65; fellow in allergy and immunology Children's Hosp., Washington, 1967-69; mem. sr. staff Henry Ford Hosp., Detroit, 1969-99, dir. pediat. allergy fellowship program, 1969-77, dir. allergy and immunology program, 1977-99, head divsn. allergy and immunology, dept. pediatrics, 1977-99, chmn. dept. pediatrics, 1982-90; physician Vivra Asthma and Allergy, Tucson, 1999-2000; with VIRA Asthma and Allergy, Inc., 2000—02; physician Allergy and Asthma Ctr. Ariz., Tucson, 2001—03, Aspen Med. Ctr., Fort Collins, 2003—. Clin. prof. U. Mich., Ann Arbor, 1985—94; prof. pediat. Case Western Res. U., 1994—99; dir. Am. Bd. Allergy and Immunology, 1990—96, sec., 1995—96. Contbr. articles. Lt. comdr. USN, 1962-66. Fellow Am. Acad. Allergy and Immunology (pres. 1990-91), Am. Acad. Pediat. (chmn. allergy sect. 1979-82), Mich. Allergy Soc. (pres. 1978-79); mem. Asthma and Allergy Found. Am. (dir. 1992-99, v.p. med. affairs 1992-95, v.p. rsch. 1995-99), Coun. Med. Speciality Soc. (bd. dirs. 1992-94), Am. Bd. Med. Specialists, Sci. Advisors Internat. Life Scis. (allergy sect. 1990—), ACGME-RRC for Allergy and Immunology. Home: 13866 N Bowcreek Springs Pl Tucson AZ 85737-5725 Office: 2001 S Shields Bldg H Fort Collins CO 80526 Fax: 970-498-9031. E-mail: jonicoaz@worldnet.att.net.

ANDERSON, JOHN BAYARD, lawyer, educator, former congressman; b. Rockford, Ill., Feb. 15, 1922; s. E. Albin and Mabel Edna (Ring) A.; m. Keke Machakos, Jan. 4, 1953; children: Eleanora, John Bayard, Diane, Karen, Susan Kimberly. AB, U. Ill., 1942, JD, 1946; LLM, Harvard U., 1949; hon. doctorates, No. Ill. U., Wheaton Coll., Shimer Coll., Biola Coll., Geneva Coll., North Park Coll. and Theol. Sem., Houghton Coll., Trinity Coll., Rockford Coll. Bar: Ill. 1946. Practice law Rockford, 1946-52; with U.S. Fgn. Service, 1952-55; assigned West Berlin, 1952-55; mem. 87th-95th Congresses from 16th Dist. Ill., mem. rules com.; chmn. Ho. Republican Conf., 1969-79; ind. candidate for Pres. U.S., 1980. Vis. prof. Stanford U., 1981; vis. prof. Nova-Southeastern U. Ctr. for Study Law, 1987-2003, Washington Coll. Law Am. U., 1997—; vis. prof. polit. sci. Brandeis U., 1985, Oreg. State U., 1986, U. Mass., 1985—; lectr. polit. sci. Bryn Mawr Coll., 1985. Author: Between Two Worlds: A Congressman's Choice, 1970, Vision and Betrayal in America, 1976, The American Economy We Need, 1984, A Proper Institution: Guaranteeing Televised Presidential Debates, 1988; editor: Congress and Conscience, 1970. Ind. candidate for Pres. U.S., 1980. Mem. World Federalist Assn. (pres. 1992—), Ctr. for Voting and Democracy (chmn. bd. 1996—, co-chmn. nat. adv. bd. pub. campaign for campaign fin. reform 1997—), Coun. on Fgn. Rels., Phi Beta Kappa. Mem. Evang. Free Ch. (past trustee). E-mail: jbafed@aol.com.

ANDERSON, JOHN DAVID, architect; b. New Haven, Dec. 24, 1926; s. William Edward and Norma Vere (Carson) A.; m. Florence A. Van Dyke, Aug. 26, 1950; children— Robert Stewart, David Carson. AB cum laude, Harvard U., 1949, M.Arch., 1952. Draftsman John K. Monroe, Architect, Denver, 1952-54; draftsman, designer, assoc. Wheeler & Lewis, Architects, Denver, 1954-60; prin. John D. Anderson, Denver, 1960-64; ptnr. Anderson, Barker Rinker, Architects, Denver, 1965-69, A-B-R Partnership, Architects, Denver, 1970-75; prin., CEO Anderson Mason Dale P.C., Denver, 1975-96, sr. v.p., 1997—. Vis. lectr. U. Colo., U. N.Mex., U. Nebr., U. Cape Town, Colo. State U., Plymouth Polytech., Eng.; chmn. Colo. Gov.'s Task Force on Removal of Archtl. Barriers, 1972-74; vice chmn. Colo. Bd. Non-Residential Energy Conservation Stds., 1978-80. Prin. works include: Front Range Community Coll., Westminster, 1977, Solar Energy Rsch. Inst., Golden, 1980 (award winning solar heated structures). Served with USNR, 1944-46. Fellow AIA (pres. Colo. chpt. 1967, Western Mountain region dir. 1995-97, Silver medal, 1984, Firm of Yr. award 1986 Western Mountain region); mem. AIA (Arch. of Yr. award 1987, pres. 1971, nat. v.p. 1999, 1st v.p. 2000, pres. 2001), Internat. Solar Energy Soc., Council Ednl. Facility Planners (internat. chmn. energy com. 1980). Democrat. Congregationalist. Home: 57 S Rainbow Trail Golden CO 80401-8341 Office: Anderson Mason Dale Architects 1615 17th St Denver CO 80202-1293

ANDERSON, JOHN DAVID, JR., aerospace engineer; b. Lancaster, Pa., Oct. 1, 1937; s. John David and Esther Pearl (Stoneback) A.; m. Sarah Allen West, Sept. 11; children: Katherine Josephine, Elizabeth Esther. B.Aero. Engring. with honors (Gen. Motors scholar, J. Hillis Meml. scholar), U. Fla., 1959; PhD in Aero. Engring., Ohio State U. Chief hypersonics group Naval Ordnance Lab., White Oak, Md., 1966-73; prof., chmn. dept. aerospace engring. U. Md., College Park, 1973-99; prof. emeritus U. Md., College Park, 1999—; Charles Lindbergh prof. Nat. Air Space Mus. Smithsonian Instn., 1986-87; curator for aerodynamics Nat. Air Space Mus., Smithsonian Instn., 1998—. Author: Gasdynamic Lasers: An Introduction, 1976, Introduction to Flight: Its Engineering and History, 1978, 4th edit., 2000, Modern Compressible Flow: with Historical Perspective, 1982, 2d edit., 1990, Fundamentals of Aerodynamics, 1984, 3d edit., 2001, Hypersonic and High Temperature Gasynamics, 1989, Computational Fluid Dynamics, 1995; History of Aerodynamics, and Its Impact on Flying Machines, 1997, Aircraft Performance and Design, 1999; contbr. articles to profl. jours. Served with USAF, 1959-62. Named disting. scholar/tchr. U. Md., 1981-82; NSF fellow, NASA fellow Ohio State U., 1966; recipient Meritorious Civilian Service award Naval Ordnance Lab., 1972 Fellow Washington Acad. Scis. (Engring. Sci. award 1975), AIAA, Royal Aeronaut. Soc.; mem. Am. Soc. Engring. Edn., Am. Phys. Soc., Sigma Xi, Tau Beta Pi, Sigma Tau, Phi Kappa Phi, Phi Eta Sigma. Roman Catholic. Office: U Md Dept Aerospace Engring College Park MD 20742-0001 also: Aeronautics Dept Nat Air and Space Mus Smithsonian Inst Washington DC 20560-0312 E-mail: john.anderson@nasm.si.edu. *A prescription for success in professional life involves a proper balance of hard work, long hours, awareness and clear thinking, with a goal-oriented philosophy and outright love of one's profession. In addition, one must have the desire, abilities and opportunities to accomplish his goals.*

ANDERSON, JOHN EDWARD, mechanical engineering educator; b. Chgo., May 15, 1927; s. Claus Oscar and Ruth Melvina (Engstrom) A.; m. Cynthia Louise Howard, May 24, 1975; children: Candice, James, Stanley. BME, Iowa State U., 1949; MSME, U. Minn., 1955; PhD, MIT, 1962. Registered profl. engr., Minn., Ill. Aero. research scientist Nat. Adv. Com. for Aeros., Langley Field, Va., 1949-51; devel. engr. Honeywell, Inc., Mpls., 1951-53, research engr., 1953-55, prin. research engr., 1955-58, research project engr., 1954-58, sr. staff engr., 1958-62, mgr. space systems, 1963; mem. faculty U. Minn., Mpls., 1963-86, prof. mech. engring., 1971-86, Boston U., 1986-94. Cons. Colo. Regional Transp. Dist., 1974-75, Raytheon Co., 1975-76, Mannesmann Demag, 1978-79, Arthr D. Little, Inc., 1981, Indpls. Transit Commn., 1979-81, Davy McKee Corp., 1984-85; founder, pres., CEO Taxi 2000 Corp. (formerly ATS Inc.), 1983—. Author: Magnetohydrodynamic Shock Waves, Magnetogasdynamics of Thermal Plasma, Transit Systems Theory; editor: Personal Rapid Transit II. With USN, 1945-46. Recipient Outstanding Inventor in Am. award Intellectual Property Owners Found., 1989; Convair fellow. NAS, 1967-68 Fellow AAAS; mem. ASME, Union Concerned Scientists, Mensa, World Federalists Assn., Sierra Club. Unitarian Universalist. Home: 5164 Ranier Pass NE Minneapolis MN 55421-1338

ANDERSON, JOHN EDWARD, diversified holding company executive, lawyer; b. Mpls., Sept. 12, 1917; s. William Charles and Myrtle (Grosvenor) A.; m. Margaret Stewart, Sept. 14, 1942 (dec.); children: Margaret Susan, Judith Grosvenor, John Edward, Deborah Lee (dec.), William Stewart; m. Marion Redding, Mar. 3, 1967. BS cum laude, UCLA, 1940; MBA with distinction (Baker scholar), Harvard U., 1942; JD cum laude, Loyola U., 1950. Bar: Calif. 1950; CPA, Calif. Acct. Arthur Andersen & Co., Los Angeles, 1945-48; since practiced in Los Angeles, Irvine; ptnr. Kindel & Anderson, 1953-85; ceo. Topa Equities, Los Angeles, Calif. Dir. Mellon 1st Bus. Bank, Summit Health Ltd., Topa Equities, Ltd., Topa Mgmt. Co., Easton AluminumCo, Indsl. Tools, Inc., Topa Ins. Co. Trustee Claremont McKenna Coll.; trustee St. John's Hosp. and Health Center Found.; bd. dirs. YMCA Met., Los Angeles. Served to lt. USNR, 1942-45. Mem. AICPA, ABA, State Bar Calif., Calif. Soc. CPAs, L.A. Country Club, Calif. Club, Eldorado Country Club (Palm Desert, Calif.), Outrigger Canoe Club (Honolulu). Presbyterian (elder). Office: Topa Equities Ste 1400 1800 Avenue Of The Stars Los Angeles CA 90067-4216

ANDERSON, JOHN ERLING, chemical engineer; b. Quincy, Mass., Mar. 12, 1929; s. Victor Emanuel and Elin Helen (Nelson) A.; m. Karin Henrietta Thornberg, Feb. 3, 1951; children: Mark David, Lynn Karin, Kristin Leslie, Claire Martha. BSCE, MIT, 1950, DSc in Chem. Engring., 1955; MSCE, Ill. Inst. Tech., 1951. Sr. corp. fellow Praxair, Inc., Tarrytown, NY, 1954-99; ret. Lectr. chem. engring. dept. MIT, 1977; mem. adv. com. Solar Energy Rsch. Inst., Golden, Colo., 1985-87; mem. combustion program work group DOE Office of Indusl. Programs, Wash., 1986-88. Contbr. articles to profl. jours.; patentee in field. Recipient Personal Merit award Chem. Engring. mag., 1974, Kirkpatrick Chem. Engring. award Chem. Engring. mag., 1989; named Inventor of Yr., N.Y. Patent Assn., 1989. Mem. NAE, Combustion Inst., Am. Inst. Chem. Engrs., Am. Chem. Soc. Democrat. Mem. Unitarian Ch. Avocations: hiking, reading. Home: 476E Heritage Hills Somers NY 10589-1920

ANDERSON, JOHN FIRTH, church administrator, librarian; b. Saginaw, Mich., Oct. 5, 1928; s. Harlan Firth and Irene Martha (Bowser) A.; m. Patricia Ann Goble, June 18, 1950 (dec. Oct. 1995); children: Douglas Firth, Elizabeth Ann; m. Barbara Peterson Smith, May 18, 1996. BA, Mich. State U., 1949; MS in L.S, U. Ill., 1950. Young people's librarian Enoch Pratt Free Library, Balt., 1950-52; with Balt. County Pub. Library, 1952-58, supr. adult work, 1955- 56, asst. county librarian, 1956-58; dir. Knoxville (Tenn.) Pub. Library System, 1958-62, Tucson Pub. Library, 1962-68, 73-82; city librarian San Francisco Pub. library, 1968-73; exec. presbyter, stated clk. Presbytery of Santa Barbara (Calif.), 1982-91; ret., 1991; interim exec. presbyter Presbytery de Cristo, 1993, stated clk., 1993-2000. Mem. Presbyn. Churchwide Adminstrv. Coordinating Cabinet, 1987-89; cons. on library bldgs., devel. and mgmt. Contbr. articles to profl. publs. Bd. dirs. Amigos Bibliographic Council, 1977-81, vice-chmn., 1977-79, sec., 1980-81; mem. Ariz. Library Adv. Council, 1975-81; charter mem. Freedom to Read Found.; bd. dirs. Ariz. Theatre Co., 1978-82. Recipient Disting. Citizen award U. Ariz., 1981 Mem. ALA (mem. at large coun. 1961-65, 66-70, bd. dirs. pub. libr. assn. 1961-65, bd. dirs. libr. administrn. div. 1964-65, chmn. libr. orgn. and mgmt. sect. 1964-65, pres. libr. administrn. div. 1968-69), Calif. Libr. Assn. (coun. 1970-71), Southwestern Libr. Assn. (pres. 1976-78), Ariz. Libr. Assn. (pres. pub. librs. div. 1964-65, pres. 1967-68, Libr. of Year 1968, Rosenzweig award 1981), Ariz. Assn. County Librs. (pres. 1979-80), Ariz. China Coun. (pres. 1979-80), World Alliance Reformed Chs. (mem. Caribbean and N.Am. Area Coun. 1991-93, recording clk. 1992-93), Beta Phi Mu. Presbyterian (Elder).

ANDERSON, JOHN FREDERICK, science administrator, entomologist, researcher; b. Fargo, N.D., Feb. 25, 1936; s. Oscar Frederick and Eleanor Birdee (Fiskum) A.; m. Marilynn Joy Robinson, June 30, 1958; children: Linda, John Jr., Kristin. BS, N.D. State U., 1957, MS, 1959; PhD, U. Ill., 1963. NSF postdoctoral fellow Dept. Entomology U. Ill., Urbana, 1963-64; asst. entomologist Conn. Agrl. Expt. Sta., New Haven, 1964-66, assoc. entomologist, 1966-69, chief entomologist, 1969-87, dir., 1987—. Mem. Conn. Tree Examining Bd., New Haven, 1969-79; dir., pres. Conn. Tree Protective Assn., New Haven, 1976-84. Author: (with others) Biology of Sex, 1967, Diseases Transmitted from Animals to Man, 6th edit., 1975, Perspectives in Forest Entomology, 1976, Preventing Lyme Disease, 1989, Ecology and Environmental Management of Lyme Disease, 1993, The Natural History of Ticks, 2002; editor: Perspectives in Forest Entomology, 1976; contbr. articles to profl. jours. 2d lt. Med. Svc. Corp. U.S. Army, 1959, capt. Res., 1969. Recipient award of Merit Conn. Tree Protective Assn., 1976, Bronze medal Fed. Garden Clubs Conn., 1981, Author Citation award Internat. Soc. Arboriculture, 1983, award of Merit Conn. Nurserymen's Assn., 1994, cert. recognition, Conn. Nurserymen's Found., 2000, Environ. Industry Coun. Outstanding Svc. award, 2000, Conn. Friend of Floristry award, 2002. Mem. AAAS, Entomol. Soc. Am., Am. Mosquito Control Assn., Am. Soc. Microbiology, Am. Soc. Parasitologists, Am. Soc. Tropical Medicine and Hygiene, Soc. Invertebrate Pathology, Conn. Acad. Sci. and Engring., Phi Kappa Phi. Office: Conn Agrl Expt Sta 123 Huntington St PO Box 1106 New Haven CT 06504-1106 E-mail: John.F.Anderson@PO.state.ct.us.

ANDERSON, JOHN GASTON, electrical engineer, consultant; b. Dante, Va., Aug. 21, 1922; s. Harvey Ellis and Lenora (Ingram) A.; m. Elizabeth Amelia Weller, Sept. 18, 1948 (dec. Mar. 1993); 1 son, David John; m. Avery Emma Weymouth, Sept. 24, 1994. BS with honors in Elec. Engring., Va. Poly. Inst., 1943. Registered profl. engr., Mass. With Gen. Electric Co., 1946-84, mgr. AC transmission studies, 1972-74, mgr. high voltage lab. Pittsfield, Mass., 1974-80, cons. engr. transmission systems Schenectady, 1980-84. Sr. cons. Power Techs., Inc., 1984-92; profl. cons. engr., 1992-95; cons., lectr. on high voltage and power transmission; mem. U.S. USSR Tech. Exch. for High Voltage Transmission. Co-author books in field; contbr. articles to profl. publs.; editor: GE Transmission Mag., 1972-74; patentee in field. Active Boy Scouts Am., 1960-79. Served to capt. USAAF, 1943-45. Recipient Nat. prizes for papers Am. Inst. Elec. Engrs., 1957 Fellow IEEE (chmn. transmission and distbn. com. 1980-82, Centennial medal 1984, Halperin award 1991, Excellence Engring. medal 1997, Excellence in Power Distbn. Engring. award 1999, Millennium medal 2000); mem. NAE, Power Engring. Soc. (chmn. nat. pub. affairs subcom. 1979, chmn. tech. coun. 1982-85), Tau Beta Pi, Eta Kappa Nu, Phi Kappa Phi.

ANDERSON, JOHN KERBY, talk show host; b. Berkeley, Calif., Dec. 7, 1951; s. John Albert and Mary Lorraine (Allen) A.; m. Susanne Elise Pardey, Aug. 3, 1974; children: Amy, Jonathan, Catherine. BS, Oreg. State U., 1974; MFS, Yale U., 1976; MA, Georgetown U., 1981. Pres. Probe Ministries, Richardson, Tex., 1976—; host syndicated radio program Probe, 1983—; host The Kerby Anderson Show Salem Radio Network, 1995-96; host NewsTalk satellite radio talk show Criswell Radio Network, 1989-93. Adj. prof. Dallas Theol. Sem., 1986—; guest host Point of View satellite radio talk show, USA Radio Network, Open Lane satellite radio talk show Moody Broadcasting Network. Author: Life, Death and Beyond, 1980, Genetic Engineering, 1982, Origin Science, 1987, Living Ethically in the 90s, 1990, Signs of Warning, Signs of Hope, 1994, Moral Dilemmas, 1998; contbg. author: Ency. Bibl. and Christian Ethics, 1987, Integrity of Heart, Skillfulness of Hands, 1994, Vital Contemporary Issues, 1994, Marriage, Family and Sexuality, 2000, Technology, Spirituality and Social Trends, 2002. Evangelical Christian. Avocations: archery, target shooting, computers, basketball, tennis, fishing. Office: Probe 1900 Firman Dr Ste 100 Richardson TX 75081-6796 E-mail: Kerby@probe.org.

ANDERSON, JOHN MURRAY, operations executive, former university president; b. Toronto, Ont., Can., Sept. 3, 1926; s. Murray Alexander and Eleanor Montgomery (Valentine) A.; m. Eileen Anne McFaul, Nov. 3, 1951 (dec. Nov. 1983); children: Nancy, Susan, Peter, Katherine; m. Sylvia Richard, May 10, 1986 B.Sc.F., U. Toronto, 1951, PhD, 1958; LL.D., St. Thomas U., 1974, Dalhousie U., 1979; D.Ped., U. Maine, Orono, 1976; DSc, U. N.B., Can., 2001. Asst. prof. U. N.B., Can., 1958-63; assoc. prof. Carleton U., 1963-67; dir. Fisheries Research Bd. Can. Biol. Sta., St. Andrews, N.B., 1967-72; dir. gen. Canadian Research and Devel., Fisheries and Marine Service, Dept. Environment, Ottawa, Ont., 1972-73; pres. U. N.B., 1973-79, J.M. Anderson Consultants Inc., 1980—; v.p. ops. Atlantic Salmon Fedn., 1984-96. Pres., chmn. bd. dirs. Huntsman Marine Lab., St. Andrews, N.B., 1973-77, bd. dirs., 1985—, chmn. bd. dirs., 1995-99; mem. Huntsman Adv. Bd.; bd. govs. Rothesay (N.B.) Collegiate Sch., 1976, Kenya Tech. Tchrs. Coll., Nairobi, 1977-79; chmn. Assn. Atlantic Univs., 1978-79; v.p. Biol. Coun. Can., 1977-79; mem. Sci. Coun. of Can., 1988-92. Contbr. numerous articles on fish physiology to profl. jours. Bd. dirs. Internat. Atlantic Salmon Found., 1979-83, J.R. Bradfield Edn. Fund, Noranda, 1979-86, Aquaculture Assn., N.B., 1981—; pres., chmn. bd. trustees Sunbury Shores Arts and Nature Ctr., Inc., 1982-84; chmn. bd. trustees Mackenzie King Scholarship Trust, 1986—; trustee Nature Trust N.B., Inc., 1987-91; v.p. Atlantic Aquaculture Fair, 1993, pres., 1994; bd. dirs. St. Croix Estuary Program, 1990-2002, vice chmn. sci., 2001-02. Recipient Happy Fraser award Atlantic Salmon Fedn., 2001. Fellow Royal Can. Geographic Soc.; mem. Inst. Can. Bankers (gov. 1974-79), Can. Soc. Zoologists (pres. 1973-74), Aquaculture Assn. Can. (pres. 1984-85), Assn. Univs. and Colls. Can. (dir. 1975-79, chmn. McCain Scholarship Group 1997—), Sigma Chi. Anglican. Office: Atlantic Salmon Fedn Saint Andrews NB Canada E0G 2X0 E-mail: atlsal@nbnet.nb.ca.

ANDERSON, JOHN RICHARD, entomologist, educator; b. Fargo, N.D., May 5, 1931; s. John Raymond and Mary Ann (Beaulieu) A.; m. Shereen V. Erickson, Mar. 26, 1955; children: Scott F., Lisa K., Steven F. BS, Utah State U., 1957; MS, U. Wis., 1958, PhD, 1960. Asst. prof. entomology U. Calif.-Berkeley, 1961-66, assoc. prof., 1967-70, prof., 1970-93, prof. emeritus, 1993—, assoc. dean research, 1979-85. Trustee, past chmn. Alameda County (Calif.) Mosquito Abatement Dist., 1961-73, 79-93. Editorial bd.: Jour. Med. Entomology, 1968-72, Jour. Econ. Entomology, 1977-81, Thomas Say Found, 1968-72. Served with USN, 1950-54. Rsch. grantee; recipient Berkeley citation for Disting. Achievement, 1993. Fellow AAAS, Entomol. Soc. Am. (governing bd. 1987-90, C.W. Woodworth award Pacific br. 1988), Royal Entomol. Soc. (London); mem. Can. Entomol. Soc., Am. Mosquito Control Assn., Nat. Audubon Soc., Am. Mus. Natural History, Oreg. Nat. Resources Coun., Oreg. Nat. Desert Assn., High Desert Mus., Sierra Club, Trout Unlimited. Home: 1283 NW Trenton Ave Bend OR 97701-1026 Office: U Calif Dept Insect Biology Berkeley CA 94720-0001

ANDERSON, JOHN ROBERT, retired mathematics educator; b. Stromsburg, Nebr., Aug. 1, 1928; s. Norris Merton and Violet Charlotte (Stromberg) A.; m. Bertha Margery Nore, Aug. 27, 1950; children: Eric Jon, Mary Lynn. Student, Midland Coll., 1945-46; AA, Luther Jr. Coll., 1949; BS (Regents scholar), U. Nebr., Lincoln, 1951, MA in Math, 1954; PhD, Purdue U., 1970. Tchr. math., coach Bloomfield (Nebr.) High Sch., 1951-52; control systems analyst, Allison div. Gen. Motors Corp., Indpls., 1954-60; prof. math. Depauw U., Greencastle, Ind., 1960, asst. dean, dir. grad. studies, 1973-76, dir. grad. studies, 1976-84, chmn. math. dept., 1984-90, prof. math., 1990-92, ret., 1992; adj. prof. math. IVTC, Greencastle, 1996—; resident dir. W. European studies program Depauw U., Germany, 1975, resident dir. Mediterranean Studies program, 1982, 90; dir. NSF Coop. Coll. Sch., Sci. Inst., 1969-70; instr. NSF summer inst., 1972; instr. Challenge sci. and math. program U.S. Students in Europe, 1976, 77, 78, 80, 82. Bd. dirs. Law Focused Edn., Indpls., 1975-77, Ind. Regional Math. Consortium, 1977-92; adj. prof. math. IVTC Coll., Greencastle, 1997—. Bd. dirs. Luth. Brotherhood br. 8746, United Way Of Greencastle, Ind., 1992-98, treas., Putnam Co. Food Pantry, 1993-98; officer Peace Evangel. Luth. Ch., 1960—. Served with U.S. Army, 1946-48. Danforth Tchr. fellow, 1963-64; NSF sci.

faculty fellow, 1964-65; Lilly Found. edn. grantee, summers 1961-63 Mem. Math. Assn. Am., Nat. Council Tchrs. Math., North Central Assn. (commr. 1974-78), Sigma Xi, Pi Mu Epsilon, Kappa Delta Pi, Beta Sigma Psi. Clubs: Rotary Internat. (sec. 1976-77, v.p. 1977-78, pres. 1978-79, 1998-99). Home: 1560 S Bloomington St Greencastle IN 46135-2212 E-mail: johnanderson@depauw.edu. *When you work with people, always keep in mind: "If I were in their place, is this the way I would like to be treated by someone in my position?"*

ANDERSON, JOHN ROY, grouting engineer; b. Culberson, N.C., June 22, 1919; s. Oscar Garfield and Lula Adeline (Russell) A.; m. Rheba Ulma Nichols, Dec. 31, 1951 (dec. Oct. 1989); children: Richard Allen, John Steven, Mark Garfield. Student, Berea Coll., 1950. From clk. to field inspector, then constrn. engr. Govt. Agys., 1941-51; project engr., mgr. Intrusion Prepakt, Cleve., 1951-58, 64-65; regional mgr./project mgr. Lee Turzillo Contracting Co., Breaksville, Ohio, 1957-60; engr. foundations, ops. mgr. Harza Engrng. Co., Chgo., 1960-61, 65-68, 1972-86; foundations engr. Tippetts Abbett McCarthy Stratton, N.Y.C., 1961-64, 68-72. Mem. ASCE. Baptist. Achievements include foundation engineering on dams, bridges, tunnels and high rise buildings throughout the world. Home and Office: 7770 Skipper Ln Tallahassee FL 32317-8530

ANDERSON, JOHN THOMAS, lawyer; b. Gary, Ind., July 13, 1930; s. Jack and Dorothy Genevieve (Gustafson) A.; m. Marvel Nancy Filkey, Aug. 15, 1953; children: Kirsten E. Teevens, Katherine L., Eric M. AB, DePauw U., 1952; LLB, Harvard U., 1955. Bar: Ind. 1955, Ill. 1956. Assoc. Lord, Bissell & Brook, Chgo., 1958-66, ptnr., 1966-95, of counsel, 1996-98. Trustee DePauw U., Greencastle, Ind., 1982—; chmn. bd. dirs. Joyce Found., Chgo., 1979—; Lt. USNR, 1955-58. Methodist. Home and Office: 2313 Cassia Ct Naples FL 34109-3370

ANDERSON, JOLENE SLOVER, small business owner, publishing executive, consultant; b. Tulare, Calif. James P. Sr., and Helen B. (Walters) Slover; m. Douglas R. Anderson, June 14, 1975; 1 child, Sabrina Jo. Student, Victor Valley Coll., Riverside C.C. Model Connor Sch. Modeling, Fresno, Calif., 1955-65; actress M. Kosloff Studios, Hollywood, Calif., 1965; nat. sales mgr. Armed Services Publs., 1966-68; pres., dir. Sullivan Publs., Inc., Riverside, Calif., 1970-82; pres., chief exec. officer Heritage House Publs., Riverside, 1983-84; pres. Jolene S. Anderson Pub. Cons., Inc., Riverside, 1987—. Bd. dirs. Riverside County Econ. Devel. Coun. Co-comdr. March AFB, Inland Empire Tourists and Conv.; mem. YWCA, City of Riverside Cultural Heritage Bd., Yr. 2000 Com., 1988, Riverside County Philharm. Bd., Temecula-Murrieta Econ. Devel. Corp.; mem. 101 Things to Do in Riverside com. Named Woman of Achievement YWCA, 1989, Humanitarian of Yr. Rotary, 1990 Mem. Riverside Downtown Assn., Sun City/Menifee Valley C. of C., Greater Riverside C. of C., Temecula Valley C. of C., Carson Valley C. of C., Murrieta C. of C., Soroptimists (Riverside chpt., Athena award 1989). Office: PO Box 800 Riverside CA 92502-0800

ANDERSON, JON DAVID, lawyer; b. Wichita, Kans., Oct. 29, 1952; s. Charles Henry Anderson and Patricia (Vaughan) Ross; m. Leanne Winters, Dec. 20, 1973; children: Nicklas, Scott, Brandt, Chase, Barrett, Britten, Kieryn. BA, U. Wash., Seattle, 1974; JD, Brigham Young U., 1977. Bar: Calif. 1977. Assoc. Latham & Watkins, L.A., Newport Beach, Calif., 1977-84, ptnr. Newport Beach, Costa Mesa, 1985—, mng. ptnr. Costa Mesa, Calif., 1987-93. Bd. dirs. Orange County Coun., Boy Scouts Am. Mem. Calif. Bar Assn., Orange County Bar Assn., Marbella Country Club. Republican. Ch. of Jesus Christ of Latter-day Saints. Avocations: skiing, baseball, golf. Office: Latham & Watkins 650 Town Center Dr Ste 2000 Costa Mesa CA 92626-7135 E-mail: jon.anderson@lw.com.

ANDERSON, JON ERIC, lawyer; b. Jacksonville, N.C., Feb. 1, 1956; m. Lori Jean Schumacher, June 30, 1979; children: Andrew Jon, Elizabeth Ruth, Margaret Mary. BA, U. Wis., 1978; JD, Marquette U., 1981. Bar: Wis. 1981, U.S. Dist. Ct. (ea. and we. dists.) Wis. 1981, U.S. Ct. Appeals (7th cir.) 1996, U.S. Supreme Ct. 1988. Assoc. Mulcahy & Wherry, S.C., Milw., 1981-84, mng. atty. Sheboygan, Wis., 1984-87, Madison, 1987-90; shareholder Godfrey & Kahn, S.C., Madison, 1991-99, Lafollette, Godfrey & Kahn, S.C., 2000—. Author: (with others) Comparable Worth-A Negotiator's Guide, 1985; contbg. author Pub. Sector Labor Rels., Wis., 1988. Thomas More Soc. scholar, 1979. Mem.: ABA, Nat. Assn. Coll. and Univ. Attys., Wis. Sch. Attys. Assn. (bd. dirs. 2000—, pres.-elect 2002—03), Wis. Bar Assn. (bd. dirs. labor law sect. 1988—91), Edn. Law Assn., Madison Club, Blackhawk Country Club, Alpha Sigma Nu, Phi Delta Phi. Lutheran. Avocations: woodworking, music.

ANDERSON, JON MAC, lawyer, educator; b. Rio Grande, Ohio, Jan. 10, 1937; s. Harry Rudolph and Carrie Viola (Magee) A.; m. Deborah Melton, June 1, 1961; children— Jon Gordon, Greta. AB, Ohio U., 1958; JD, Harvard Law Sch., 1961. Bar: Ohio 1961. Law clk. Hon. Kingsley A. Taft Ohio Supreme Ct., Columbus, 1961-62; assoc. Wright, Harlor, Morris & Arnold, Columbus, 1962-67, ptnr., 1968-76, Porter, Wright, Morris & Arthur, Columbus, 1977—. Adj. prof. law Ohio State U. Law Sch., Columbus, 1975-83; bar examiner State of Ohio, 1971-76, chmn., 1975-76; lectr. tax and estate planning insts.; bd. dirs. White Castle System, Inc., Columbus. Trustee Berea Coll, Ky., 1976-2000, Pro Musica Chamber Orch., Columbus, 1980-98, Opera Columbus, 1985-88, 1st Congl. Ch., Columbus, 1979-83, Greater Columbus Arts Coun., 1989-99; chmn., 1996-98; mem. adv. coun. The Textile Mus., 1996-2002. Mem. ABA, Ohio State Bar Assn., Columbus Bar Assn., The Columbus Club, Rocky Fork Hunt and Country Club. Democrat. Avocations: music, art, textiles, literature, antique collections. Office: Porter Wright Morris & Arthur 41 S High St Ste 2800 Columbus OH 43215-6194 E-mail: janderson@porterwright.com.

ANDERSON, JON STEPHEN, newswriter; b. Montreal, Que., Can., Mar. 13, 1936; came to U.S., 1963; s. William Howard and Dorothy Beatrice (Ryan) A.; m. Gail Rutherford, Feb. 20, 1960 (div. 1966); 1 child, Jon Gregory (dec.); m. Abra Prentice, Sept. 14, 1968 (div. 1976); children: Ashley Prentice Norton, Abra Cantrill, Anthony Ryan; m. Pamela Sherrod, Sept. 23, 2001. BA, Mt. Allison U., Sackville, Can., 1955; BCL, McGill U., Montreal, 1959; MAW, U. Iowa, 1991. Reporter Montreal Gazette, 1957-60, chief bur. Time Mag., Montreal, 1960-63, staff corr. Chgo., 1963-66; staff writer Chgo. Sun-Times, 1967-69; columnist Chgo. Daily News, 1969-72; pub. Chicagoan Mag., 1972-74; staff writer Chgo. Tribune, 1978—; writing instr. U. Iowa, 1989—2002. Author: City Watch: Discovering the Uncommon Chicago, 2000; contbr. articles to Readers Digest, 1977—, Chgo. Mag., 1977, Clothesline Rev., 1986. Gen. mgr. Second City Ctr. Pub. Arts, 1966-67; bd. dirs. Chgo. Internat. Film Festival, 1975-78 Recipient Stick o' Type award Newspaper Guild Am., 1969, Studs Turkel Journalism award, 1999. Mem. Order Ky. Cols. Roman Catholic. Office: Chgo Tribune 435 N Michigan Ave Chicago IL 60611-4066

ANDERSON, JONPATRICK SCHUYLER, financial consultant, therapist, archivist; b. Chgo., July 20, 1951; s. Ralph Anderson and Helena Hilda (Robinson) Hardy; children: André, Mary, David. Student, Cul. YMCA C.C., 1970, Lawrence Merrick Acad. Dramatic Arts, 1972—73, Comty. Coll. Air Force, 1974; AA, L.A. Trade Tech. Coll., 1978; student, Calif. State U., 1978—79; BA, UCLA, 1979; postgrad., San Diego City Coll., 1981—84, postgrad., 1992; student, U. Md., 1975; postgrad., San Diego State U., 1982—83, Grossmont Coll., El Cajon, Calif., 1984; student, Gov.'s State U., 1985; MRE, Internat. Sem. Coll., 1986, DMin, PhD, 1989; postdoct., Trinity Coll./U. Liverpool, 1998—99; fgn. acad. credentials evaluation, York U., Toronto, Ont., Can., 2000, Danish Ministry Edn., Copenhagen, 2002. Profl. life tchg. cert. Ariz. State C.C., cert. vocat. edn. tchr. Calif., adult edn. tchg. cert. Clerical supr. VA, L.A., 1976—80; fin. adminstr. Antioch Primitive Bapt. Ch., L.A., 1979—80; pres., exec. dir. All-Around Prodns., L.A., 1980—83; assoc. minister St. Stephen Ch., San Diego, 1983—87; stadium mgr. San Diego Jack Murphy Stadium, 1985—87; mgr. San Diego Sports Arena, 1985—87, Horton Plaza Shopping Ctr., San Diego, 1985—86; exec. dir. Christ-Immanuel Ministerial Assn., San Diego, 1983—; acting supr. psychiatry dept. VA Mental Health Clinic, San Diego, 1991—96; intern in counseling and psychiatry U. Calif.-San Diego Med. Ctr., 1992—95; supr. Enid Rockwell MD, 1992—95; tchr. K-12 City Schs. of Decatur, Ga., 1997—, Dekalb County Sch. Sys., Ga., 1998—. Pvt. investigator Merit Protective Svcs., L.A., 1972-74; adminstrv. asst. Dept. Def., 1981; cons. pvt. practice mgmt., cons. comptr., San Diego, 1981-82; cons. writer All-Around Music divsn. Broadcast Music, Inc., San Diego, 1980—; instr. San Diego Community Coll. Dist., 1984; libr. asst. San Diego State U., 1982-83; chaplain of the Day U. Calif., San Diego, 1984-85; archives technician Nat. Archives & Records Adminstrn., Laguna Niguel, Calif., 1988; ind. assoc. Pre-paid Legal Svcs., San Diego, 1994—. Mem. Am. Freedom Coalition, Washington, 1988, Causa, USA, Washington, 1985-87; mem. U.S. Navy Meml. Found.-Navy Log. With USMC, Vietnam, 1968-70; with U.S. Army, 1975-76; with USAF, 1974, 80 82; 2d lt. USAR, 1979-80. Grammy nominee NARAS, 1980; recipient Personal award former Pres. Ronald Reagan, L.A., 1988, Letter of Commendation from Duncan Hunter, U.S. Rep., 52nd Dist., Calif., 1994; named to Ga. Music Hall of Fame. Mem. NAACP (life). NARAS, AFTRA AGVA, Assn. MBA Execs. (Bus. award 1980), Assn. Christian Schs. Internat. (cert. tchg.-adminstrn./prin. K-12 1993—), Profl. Assn. Ga. Educators (life), UCLA Alumni Assn. (life, interviewing com. adv. and scholarship program 1988—, bd. dirs. scholarship chmn. 1991—), Res. Officers Assn. of U.S. (life), UCLA Black Alumni Assn. (life, bd. dirs., scholarship chmn.), N.G. Assn. Calif. (life), U. Calif.-San Diego Med. Ctr. Aux. (life), Nat. Conf. Ministry to Armed Forces, Mil. Officers Assn. Am. (life), VFW (life), DAV (life), AMVETS, Am. Legion, Nat. Assn. Evangelicals, Urban League of L.A., Nat. Music Publishers Assn., Am. Guild Authors and Composers, UCLA Coll. Fine Arts Dean's Gold Medal Soc., San Francisco Theol. Sem.—Montgomery Soc., Am. Assn. Religious Counselors, UCLA Sch. of Theater, Film, and TV Alumni Assn. (life), N.Y. Acad. Sci., Mil. Chaplains Assn. U.S.A. (life), Navy League U.S. (life). Democrat. Mem. Ch. of God. Avocations: reading, writing, gospel music, outdoor recreation, traveling. Office: PO Box 360424 Decatur GA 30036-0424 E-mail: jonpatrickanderson@email.com.

ANDERSON, JOSEPH ANDREW, JR., retired apparel company executive, retail consultant; b. Logan, Utah, Nov. 1, 1921; s. Joseph Andrew and Melicent H. (Willmore) A.; m. Gwen Elsie Smith, Sept. 29, 1954; children: Brian, Jodi, Paul, Bradley, Stacey, Jeffrey, Tiffani. BS, Utah State U., 1947; postgrad., Stanford U., 1949-50. With Zion's Coop. Mdse. Inst. Dept. Store, Salt Lake City, 1950-86, various positions, 1950-82, pres., chief exec. officer, 1982-84, vice chmn. bd., 1984-86, ret., 1986. Chmn. bd. Mr. Mac Clothiers, Inc.; ret., 1988; retail cons., Salt Lake City, 1988-90; mem. consumer bd. Utah Dept. Commerce, 1985-92; bd. dirs. Zions 1st Nat. Bank, Salt Lake City. Chmn., bd. dirs. Salt Lake City, 1985-88, Westminster Coll. Found., Salt Lake City, 1985-86, Utah Opera Co., 1998—; bd. dirs. Westminster Coll. Bus. Sch., 1985—; trustee Westminster Coll., 1989-96, L.D.S. Hosp.-Deseret Found., 1987-88, Salt Lake Visitor Bur., 1987-89; corp. solicitation state chmn. Am. Cancer Soc. of Utah, 1989-90; pres., bd. dirs. AMICUS-Deseret Found., Salt Lake City, 1986-89; adv. bd. Sta. KSL-TV, 1985-88; mem. dean's adv. council Bus. Sch. Utah State U., 1982-89; mem. Utah Employer Support of the Guard and Res. Com. Area # 3, 1986-91; bd. dirs. Utah Youth Village, Salt Lake City, 1990-93, chmn., 1994-96; chmn. Fitness Inst. L.D.S. Hosp., Salt Lake City, 1991-93, bd. of fitness inst., 1994-97; chmn. Utah Youth Village, 1994-96; bd. dirs. Utah Symphony, 2002—; lifetime trustee Utah Symphony and Opera, 2002—. 1st lt. U.S. Army, 1943-46, ETO. Named Outstanding Boss of Yr. Salt Lake Nat. Bus. Women's Club, 1972; recipient Block "A" award, 1947, Outstanding Alumnus award Utah State U., 1984, Outstanding Svc. award L.D.S. Hosp. Desert Found., 1990. Mem. Utah Retail Merchants Assn. (dir., sec. 1983-87, bd. dirs. nat. assn. 1983-87), Execs. Assn. Salt Lake City (bd. dirs. 1990-91), Sons of Utah Pioneers (pres. 1976-77), Rotary. Clubs: Alta (Salt Lake City). Lodges: Rotary, Lions (1st v.p. Salt Lake City club 1990-91, pres. 1991-92). Republican. Mem. Lds Ch. Avocations: jogging, fishing, golf, tennis. Home: 4394 Adonis Dr Salt Lake City UT 84124-3433

ANDERSON, JOSEPH NORMAN, executive consultant, former food company executive, former college president; b. Mpls., May 12, 1926; s. Joseph E. and Helen (Larson) A.; m. Ruth E. Anderson, Sept. 6, 1952; children: Peter, Timothy, Paul, Matthew, Robin, Kathryn, Charles. BBA with distinction, U. Minn., 1947. With Sears, Roebuck & Co., 1947-49, Gamble-Skogmo, Inc., 1950-64; v.p. fin., dir. Nat. Bellas Hess, Inc., 1964-67, pres., chief exec. officer, dir., 1967-69, chmn. bd., pres., chief exec. officer, 1969-75; pres. Jamestown (N.D.) Coll., 1975-83, Dakota Bake-n-Serv, Inc., 1979-86; exec. cons. Gladstone, Mo., 1986-90, Edwardsville, Ill., 1990—. Pres. Mchts. Rsch. Counc., 1961-62. With AUS, 1953-55. Mem. Phi Beta Kappa, Beta Gamma Sigma. Republican. Presbyterian.

ANDERSON, JOYCE LORRAINE, nurse aid; b. Newman Grove, Nebr., May 16, 1930; d. Fredrick Carl Stone and Hulda Caroline Nordgren; children: Bonita Lynne Peters, Richard Eugene. Student, Ctrl. C.C., Central City, Nebr., 1950. Rural tchrs. cert., cert. staff mem. Rural sch. tchr. Dist. 47 Platte County, St. Edward, Nebr., 1947—48, Dist. 40 Platte County, Lindsay, Nebr., 1948—51; nurse aid Hosp., Newman Grove, 1973—76; nurse aid, cert. staff mem. Newman Grove Mid Nebr. Luth. Home, 1977—2001. Active Newman Grove Civic Improvement Club, 1985—2001; vol. sing along leader Mid. Nebr. Luth. Home, Newman Grove, 1978—; life mem. Looking Glass United Meth. Ch., Newman Grove, 1930—; active United Meth. Women, 1950—; ch. pianist Looking Glass United Meth. Ch., Newman Grove, 1950—. Home: 53777 829 Rd Newman Grove NE 68758

ANDERSON, JUDITH ANN, artist, writer; b. Cin., Ohio, May 14, 1940; d. Clair Henry Stagge, Jean (Akeman) Stagge; m. Rondal Ambrose Anderson, June 13, 1959 (dec.); children: Andrew, Christopher, Lynn. Celebrity tutor Am. Diabete's Auction Gala, Cin., 2002; tchr. Cin. Women's Club; tchr. workshops in field, 1997—2003. Contbr.; prin. works include Cin. (Ohio) Music Hall, 2003. Mem.: Cin. Art Club, Ohio Watercolor Soc., Tex. Watercolor Soc., Northwest Watercolor Soc., Nat. Watercolor Soc. Avocation: interior design. Home: 3644 Langhorst Ct Cincinnati OH 45236

ANDERSON, JUDITH HELENA, English language educator; b. Worcester, Mass., Apr. 21, 1940; d. Oscar William and Beatrice Marguerite (Beaudry) A.; m. E. Talbot Donaldson, May 18, 1971 (dec. Apr. 1987). AB magna cum laude, Radcliffe Coll., 1961; MA, Yale U., 1962, PhD, 1965. Instr. English Cornell U., Ithaca, N.Y., 1964-66, asst. prof. English, 1966-72; vis. lectr. Coll. Seminar Program, Yale U., New Haven, 1973; vis. asst. prof. English U. Mich., Ann Arbor, 1973-74; assoc. prof. Ind. U., Bloomington, 1974-79, prof., 1979—, Chancellor's prof., 1999—, dir. grad. studies, 1986-90, 93, mem. governing bd. univ. Inst. for Advanced Study, 1983-85, 86-88. Morris W. Croll lectr. Gettysburg Coll., 1988, Kathleen Williams lectr., 1989, 95; dir. Folger Inst. Seminar, 1991. Author: The Growth of a Personal Voice, 1976, Biographical Truth, 1984, Words that Matter, 1996; editor: (with Elizabeth D. Kirk) Piers Plowman, 1990, (with Donald Cheney and David A. Richardson) Spenser's Life and the Subject of Biography, 1996; mem. editl. bd. Spenser Ency., 1979-90, Duquesne Studies in Lang. and Lit., 1976—, Spenser Studies, 1986—; mem. adv. bd. Textbase of Women Writers, Brown U., 1989-2000; contbr. articles on Renaissance lit. to profl. jours. Woodrow Wilson fellow, 1961-62, 63-64, NEH summer fellow and sr. rsch. fellow, 1979, 81-82, Dulin fellow Folger Libr., 1991; Huntington Libr. rsch. grantee, 1978, 97, NEH fellow, 1985-86, Mayers Found. fellow, 1990-91, Nat. Humanities Ctr. fellow, 1995-96, Newberry-NEH fellow, 2002-03; recipient Outstanding Scholar award Office of Women's Affairs Ind. U., 1996. Mem. MLA (mem. exec. com. Renaissance divsn. 1973-78, 86-90, del. to assembly 1991-93, publs. com. 1999-2002), AAUP, Spenser Soc. (pres. 1980, 88), Renaissance Soc. Am. (rep. for English to coun. 1991-93), Milton Soc., Donne Soc., Shakespeare Assn., Chaucer Soc., Phi Beta Kappa. Home: 2525 E 8th St Bloomington IN 47408-4214 Office: Ind U Dept English Bloomington IN 47405

ANDERSON, KARL RICHARD, aerospace engineer, consultant; b. Vinita, Okla., Sept. 27, 1917; s. Axel Richard and Hildred Audrey (Marshall) A.; m. Jane Shigeko Hiratsuka, June 20, 1953; 1 son, Karl Richard. BS, Calif. Western U., 1964; MA, 1966; PhD, U.S. Internat. U., 1970. Registered profl. engr., Calif. Engr. personnel subsystems Atlas Missile Program, Gen. Dynamics, San Diego, 1960-63; design engr. Solar divsn. Internat. Harvester, San Diego, 1964-66, sr. design engr., 1967-69, project engr., 1970-74, product safety specialist, 1975-78, aerospace engrng. cons., 1979-86; cons. engrng., 1979—. Lectr. Am. Indian Sci. and Engrng. Soc. Served to maj. USAF, 1936-60. Recipient Spl. Commendation award San Diego County Bd. Supervisors, 1985, Spl. Commendation award San Diego City Council, 1985, Spl. Commendation award City of San Diego, 1994, Grace "Peter" Sargent award San Diego City Natural Park, 1994. Home: 5886 Scripps St San Diego CA 92122-3212

ANDERSON, KARL STEPHEN, editor; b. Chgo., Nov. 10, 1933; s. Karl William and Eleanore (Grell) a.; m. Saralee Hegland, Nov. 5, 1977; children by previous marriage: Matthew, Douglas, Eric. BS in Editl. Journalism, U. Ill., 1955. Successively advt. mgr., asst. to pub., plant mgr. Pioneer Press, Oak Park, St. Charles, Ill., 1955-71; asst. to pub., then pub. Crescent Newspapers, Downers Grove, Ill., 1971-73; assoc. pub., editor Chronicle Pub. Co., St. Charles, 1973-80; assoc. pub. Chgo. Daily Law Bull., 1981-88; dir. comm., editor Ill. State Bar Assn., 1988—. Past pres. Chgo. Pub. Rels. Forum. Trustee emeritus Chi Psi Ednl. Trust; trustee Leo Sowerby Found.; bd. dirs. Ill. Press Found., Chgo. Legal Svcs. Found., Swedish Am. Hist. Soc., Copley First Amendment Ctr. Recipient C.V. Amenoff award No. Ill. U. Dept. Journalism, 1976, Bd. Govs. award Ill. State Bar, 1987, Print Media Humanitarian award Coalition Sub Bar Assns., 1987, Robert C. Preble, Jr. award Chi Psi, 1991, Asian-Am. Bar Media Sensitivity award, 1991, Liberty Bell award DuPage County Bar Assn., 1993, Glass Ceiling Busters award DuPage Women Lawyers, 1993, Disting. Svc. award Chgo. Vol. Legal Svcs. Found., 1993, Gratitude award Lawyers Assistance Program, 1993, Outstanding Achievement in Comm. award Justinian Soc., 1994, Communicator of Yr. award, 1999, 3rd prize Nat. Libr. Poetry, 1995, Svc. award Women's Bar Assn. Ill., 1998, Peoria County Bar Assn., 1998. Mem. Nat. Assn. Bar Execs., Baltic Bar Assn., Chgo. Legal Sec. Assn., Chgo. Press Vets. Assn. (bd. sec.), Ill. Press assn. (Will Loomis award 1977, 80), Kane County Bar Assn., DuPage Women Lawyers Assn., West Suburban Bar Assn., N. Suburban Bar Assn. (Pub. Svc. award 1997), Bohemian Lawyers Assn. (Liberty award 1999), No. Ill. Newspaper Assn. (past pres.), Pub. Rels. Soc. Ctrl. Ill. (Master Communicator award of achievement 1997), Soc. Profl. Journalists, Headline Club (past pres.), Nordic Law Club, Nellie Fox Soc., Union League Club of Chgo., Chi Psi. Home: 3180 N Lake Shore Dr Apt 14D Chicago IL 60657-4851 Office: Ill State Bar Assn 20 S Clark St Ste 900 Chicago IL 60603-1885

ANDERSON, KATHLEEN GAY, mediator, hearing officer, arbitrator, trainer; b. Cin., July 27, 1950; d. Harold B. and Trudi L. (Chambers) Briggs; m. J.R. Carr, July 4, 1988; 1 child, Jesse J. Anderson. Student, U. Cin., 1971-72, Antioch Coll., 1973-74; cert., Nat. Jud. Coll., U. Nev., Reno, 1987, Inst. Applied Law, 1987, Acad. Family Mediators, 1991. Cert. Lemmon Mediation Inst., Acad. Family Mediators, U.S. Postal Svc. Panel, U.S. Forest Svc. Panel, Nat. Assn. Securities Panel, State of Alaska, U. Alaska, pvt. sector panels. Paralegal Lauer & Lauer, Santa Fe, 1976-79, Wilkinson, Cragun & Barker, Anchorage, 1981-82; employment law paralegal specialist Hughes, Thorsness, Gantz, Powell & Brundin, Anchorage, 1983-91; investigator, mediator Alaska State Commn. Human Rights, 1991; mediator, arbitrator, trainer The Arbitration and Mediation Group, Anchorage, 1987—; hearing officer Municipality of Anchorage, 1993-99; State of Alaska, 1994—. Mem. faculty Nat. Jud. Coll., U. Nev., Reno, 1988-89; adj. prof. U. Alaska, Anchorage, 1985-99, Alaska Pacific U., 1990-96, Chapman U., 1990; mem. Alaska Supreme Ct. Mediation Task Force, 1991-96; adv. com. Am. Arbitration Assn. for Alaska, 1995-99, ADR subcom. Supreme Ct. Civil Justice Reform task force, 1998-99; trainer, mediator. pvt. profit and nonprofit groups, pub. groups, U.S. mil., state and fed. govt.; arbitrator Anchorage Bd. Realtors, 1997-98. Author, editor: Professional Responsibility Handbook for Legal Assistants and Paralegals, 1986; contbr. articles to profl. jours.; designer Ancients and Antiques, Trinkets and Treasures, 2000-. Lectr. Alaska Bar Assn., NLRB, Bus. and Profl. Women, Coun. on Edn. in Mgmt., Small Bus. Devel. Coun., various employers and bus. groups. Mem. Assn. for Conflict Resolution, Alaska Bar Assn. (assoc., alt. dispute resolution sect.), Alaska Dispute Settlement Assn. (v.p. 1992-93, chair com. on credentialing and stds. of practice, pres. 1997-98). Avocations: antiques, gourmet cooking. Home: PO Box 111517 Anchorage AK 99511-1517 Office: PO Box 240783 Anchorage AK 99524-0783 E-mail: tamg@gci.net.

ANDERSON, KATHRYN B. psychology educator; b. Westminster, Calif., Apr. 3, 1966; MA in Psychology, U. Mo., Columbia, 1993, PhD in Psychology, 1996. Prof. Our Lady of the Lake U., San Antonio, 1996—. Office: Our Lady of the Lake U 411 SW 24th St San Antonio TX 78207

ANDERSON, KATHRYN D. surgeon; b. Ashton-Under-Lyne, Lancashire, Eng., Mar. 14, 1939; came to U.S., 1961; m. French Anderson, June 24, 1961. BA, Cambridge (Eng.) U., 1961, MA, 1964; MD, Harvard U., 1964. Diplomate Am. Bd. Surgery with cert. in spl. competence in pediat. surgery. Intern in pediat. Children's Hosp., Boston, 1964-65; resident in surgery Georgetown U. Hosp., Washington, 1965-69, chief resident in surgery, 1969-70, attending surgeon, 1972-74; chief resident in pediat. surgery Children's Hosp., Washington, 1970-72, sr. attending surgeon, 1974-92, surgeon-in-chief L.A., 1992—; vice chmn. surgery George Washington U., Washington, 1984-92. Prof. surgery U. So. Calif. Fellow: ACS (sec. 1992—2001, first v.p. 2001—02), Royal Coll. Surgeons (Eng.); mem.: Soc. Univ. Surgeons, Am. Surg. Assn., Am. Pediat. Surg. Assn. (sec. 1988—91, pres. 1999—2000), Am. Acad. Pediat. (sec. surg. sect. 1982—85, chmn. 1985—86). Avocations: opera, yoga. Office: Childrens Hosp 4650 W Sunset Blvd Los Angeles CA 90027-6062

ANDERSON, KEITH, retired lawyer, retired banker; b. Phoenix, June 21, 1917; s. Carl and Helen (Fairchild) A.; m. Grace R. VanDenburg, 1941 (div. 1957); m. Catherine Huber, 1960; children: Fletcher F., Warren, Nicholas H. AB, Dartmouth Coll., 1939; LLB, Harvard U., 1942. Bar: N.Y. 1942, Ariz. 1946, Colo. 1950. Ret. lawyer. Mem. Univ. Club of Denver, Cactus Club. Democrat.

ANDERSON, KENNETH ALLEN, lawyer, hotel executive; b. Grand Junction, Colo., Sept. 16, 1962; s. Lila Marie and Norling Wayne A. AB in Polit. Sci., U. So. Calif., L.A., 1985; JD, Yale U., 1989. Bar: Calif. 1989, U.S. Dist. Ct. (ctrl. dist.) Calif. 1989, U.S. Ct. Appeals (9th cir.) 1989. Assoc. Irell & Manella, L.A., 1989-91; sr. assoc. Pettit & Martin, Newport Beach, Calif., 1991-94, O'Melveny & Myers, Newport Beach, 1994—98; v.p., sr. counsel Hilton Hotels Corp., Beverly Hills, Calif., 1998—. Author: White Bird, 1981. Mem. ABA, Beverly Hills Bar Assn., Assn. Corp. Counsel. Avocations: reading, hiking, travel. Home: 3723 Crownridge Dr Sherman Oaks CA 91403 Office: Hilton Hotels Corp 9336 Civic Ctr Dr Beverly Hills CA 90210 E-mail: allen_anderson@hilton.com

ANDERSON, KENNETH FRITZ, dramatic arts educator; b. Chgo., July 2, 1928; s. Fritz Nathaneal and Sylvia Cornelia (Lundberg) A.; m. Ruth Marie Pueschel, Aug. 23, 1952; children: Karen, James, John, Kenneth. Student, U. Ill., 1948-49; BS, Lawrence U., Appleton, Wis., 1952; MS, U. Wis., 1956, ABD in Theatre, 1969. Cert. secondary tchr., Wis., Iowa. Tchr., dir. Black River Falls (Wis.) High Sch., 1952-53, Waterloo (Iowa) E. High Sch., 1953-55, Neenah (Wis.) High Sch., 1955-65; assoc. prof., founding dir. theater U. Wis.-Fox Valley Cmty. Theatre, Menasha, 1965—. Founding dir. Riverside Players Community Theatre, Neenah, 1957—, Fox Valley Arts Alliance, Appleton, 1984—. Appeared in numerous plays, TV programs, films, and commls., 1949—; dir. over 290 plays, musicals and light opera and rock prodns., 1952—. Co-founder Friends of Riverside Community Theatre, 1969—. With U.S. Army, 1946-48. Recipient award in support of arts Gov. of Wis., 1987, Cutting Edge award Appleton Joint Rotary Clubs, 1990, Fox Valley Arts Alliance/AAL Renaissance award, 1995; named Young Man of Yr. Neenah-Menasha Jr. C. of C., 1963. Avocations: handball, theatre. Home: 961 Bridgewood Dr Neenah WI 54956-3711 Office: U Wis Fox Valley 1478 Midway Rd Menasha WI 54952-1224

ANDERSON, KENNETH JEFFERY, financial planner, accountant, lawyer; b. Daytona Beach, Fla., May 7, 1954; s. Kenneth E. and Petronella G. (Jeffer) A.; m. Susan Wagner, Aug. 19, 1978; children: Melissa, Kiersten. BSBA, Valparaiso U., 1976, JD, 1979. CPA, Ill. Prof. staff, mgr. Arthur Andersen & Co., Chgo., 1979-84, mgr. L.A., 1984-90, ptnr., 1990-2000, dir. individual tax fin. svcs., western region; dir. myCFO.com, 2000—02; founding ptnr. Quintile Wealth Mgmt. LLC, 2002—. Founding mem. adv. bd. U. So. Calif. Family and Closely-Held Bus. Inst.; sec. nat. coun. Valparaiso U. Sch. Law; bd. dirs. Iviewit.com, EVGlobal Motors, Inc., a Lee Iacocca Co., Schaffer Autosimulation, LLC. Bd. govs., treas. Idyllwild (Calif.) Arts, 1990—; active Step Up On Second, L.A. Philanthropic Found., 1995; profl. adv. bd. Children's Bur., 1995; adv. bd. L.A. Philharmonic, 1996—; assocs. bd. Chgo. Lung Assn., 1980-84; vol. Hospice of North Shore, Winnetka, Ill., 1981; bd. dirs. West coun. Boy Scouts Am., 2000-02. Mem. AICPA, Fla. Bar Assn., Ill. Bar Assn., Ill. CPA Soc., Calif. CPA Soc. (apptd. to state com. on personal fin. planning), Soc.

CPA-Fin. Planners (bd. dirs. 1987-89). Republican. Avocations: sports, sailing, music, golf. Home: 28 Cinch Rd Bell Canyon CA 91307-1003 Office: Quintile Wealth Mgmt 11150 Santa Monica Blvd Los Angeles CA 90025 E-mail: kanderson@quintile.com.

ANDERSON, KENNETH PAUL, nephrologist, administrator; b. Council Bluffs, Iowa, June 17, 1952; s. Kenneth Paul and and Kathleen Marie (Wyckoff) A.; children: Jennifer, Cassie, Zach. BS with honors, U. Iowa, 1974; DO, Coll. Osteo. Medicine, Des Moines, 1978; MS, U. Wis., 1996; cert., Harvard U., 1993. Diplomate Am. Bd. Family Practice. Resident, chief resident Luth. Hosp.-U. Iowa, Des Moines, 1978-81, Norwalk (Conn.) Hosp.-Yale U., 1981-83; fellow in nephrology, clin. instr. U. So. Calif., L.A., 1983-85; med. dir. Mercy Hosp., Iowa Luth. Hosp., Des Moines, 1985-96; clin. instr. Coll. Osteo. Medicine, Des Moines, 1986-96; chief of staff Mercy Hosp. Med. Ctr., Des Moines, 1992-94; sec., bd. officers Iowa Luth. Hosp., Des Moines, 1989-90; chief med. officer Ptnrs. Nat. Health Plans, South Bend, Ind., 1996—2000; v.p. Meml. Hosp., South Bend, 2000—. Chmn., mem. ESRD Network # 12 of HCFA, Kansas City, 1984-95; pres., CEO Nephrology and Internal Medicine Specialists, Des Moines, 1985-96; med. dir. SecureCare of Iowa, Des Moines, 1992-96. Contbr. articles to profl. jours. Bd. dirs. Iowa State Bd. of Health, Des Moines, 1993-96; cons. Nat. Health Policy Adv. Team, Washington, 1989-94, Ind. Perinatal Task Force, 1997-2000. Fellow Am. Acad. Family Practice; mem. AMA, Am. Soc. Hypertension, Am. Coll. Physician Execs., Am. Soc. Nephrology, Iowa Osteo. Med. Assn. Democrat. Roman Catholic. Avocations: camping, blues music, fishing, biking, writing short stories. Home: 11034 Birch Lake Dr E Granger IN 46530-6013 Office: Meml Hosp and Health System 615 N Michigan St South Bend IN 46601-1033

ANDERSON, KENNETH WARD, investor, consultant; b. Evanston, Ill., Dec. 14, 1931; s. Sydney Cleminson and Grey (Simpson) A.; m. Jean Jensen, Mar. 21, 1953; children: Kenneth Ward, Richard Scott, Wendy Lynn. BSBA, Northwestern U., 1953; postgrad. in fin., UCLA, 1955-56, U. So. Calif., 1956-58. Asst. v.p. United Calif. Bank, L.A., 1956-63; v.p. fin., asst. sect. T.I.M.E.-DC, Lubbock, Tex., 1963-70; sr. v.p. fin. Campbell-Taggart, Dallas, 1970-80; sr. v.p., CFO Galveston-Houston Co., Houston, 1980-82; pres., CFO, dir. Cook Data Svcs., Dallas, 1983-85; pres., dir. Blockbuster Entertainment Corp., Dallas, 1985-87; pres., dir., chmn. bd. Amtech Credit Corp., Dallas, 1987-90; chmn. exec. com., dir. Amtech Corp., 1987-92; bd. dirs. Lake Area Health Ctr. Found., 1993—, Fossil, Inc., 1993—, MarketQuiz, Inc., 2000—. Bd. dirs. Ch. at Horseshoe Bay Endowment Fund, 1996—; trustee Ch. at Horseshoe Bay, 1999—2002. With U.S. Army, 1953—55, Japan. Mem. Preston Trail Golf Club (Dallas), Horseshoe Bay Country Club. Republican. Methodist. Address: PO Box 8189 Horseshoe Bay TX 78657-8189

ANDERSON, KERRII B. construction company executive; b. 1957; BS, Elon Coll., 1978; MBA, Duke U., 1987. With Peat, Marwick, Mitchell & Co., Greensboro, N.C., 1978-84, RJ Reynolds Corp., Winston-Salem, N.C., 1984-85, Key Co., Greensboro, N.C., 1985-87; sr. v.p., CFO, chmn. bd. M/I Schottenstein Homes Inc., Columbus, 1987—. Address: MI Schottenstein Homes 3 Easton Oval Columbus OH 43219-6030

ANDERSON, KIMBALL RICHARD, lawyer; b. San Antonio, Aug. 20, 1952; s. Richard John and Martha (Bishop) A.; m. Karen Gatsis, Aug. 18, 1974; children: Alexis Katrina, Melissa Martha, Sophia Diane. BA, U. Ill., 1974, JD, 1977. Bar: Ill. 1977, U.S. Ct. Appeals (7th cir.) 1979, U.S. Supreme Ct. 1987; CPA, Ill. Assoc. Winston & Strawn, Chgo., 1977-84, ptnr., 1984—, mem. exec. com., 1994—, gen. counsel. Bd. dirs. Pub. Interest Law Initiative; Disting. Neutral, CPR Inst. for Dispute Resolution. Named Person of Yr. 1996 Chgo. Lawyer. Fellow Am. Coll. Trial Lawyers; mem. ABA, Ill. Bar Assn., Chgo. Bar Assn. (bd. mgrs. 1990-92), Ill. CPA Soc., Chgo. Bar Found. Home: 2045 N Seminary Ave Chicago IL 60614-4109 Office: Winston & Strawn 35 W Wacker Dr Ste 4200 Chicago IL 60601-1695 E-mail: kanderson@winston.com.

ANDERSON, KRISTINE JO, librarian; b. Aug. 1, 1945; d. Elvin Cornelius and Hilda Ellen A. MLS, U. Oreg., 1969; PhD in Comparative Lit., SUNY, Binghamton, 1983. Libr. Northeastern U., Boston, 1971-78; indexer MLA, N.Y.C., 1984-86; libr. N.Y.C. Pub. Libr., 1986-88; bibliographer for English and theatre Purdue U., W. Lafayette, Ind., 1988—. Contbr. articles to profl. jours. Mem. ALA, Soc. Utopian Studies, MLA Office: Humanities Soc Sci Edn Library Purdue U Stewart Ctr West Lafayette IN 47906 E-mail: kanderso@purdue.edu.

ANDERSON, LARRY, science educator; s. Gwendoline and Myron Anderson; children: Neil, Kyle. PhD, Phys. Chemistry, Ind. U., Bloomington, IN, 1968—72. Prof. U. Colo., Denver, 1982—; rsch. scientist Gen. Motors Rsch. Labs, Warren, Mich., 1973—82. Dir., ctr. for environ. sci. U. Colo., Denver, 1997—2002. Recipient Lyman A. Ripperton Award, Air & Waste Mgmt. Assn., 1999. Mem.: Air & Waste Mgmt. Assn. Office: Dept of Chemistry CB194 Univ of Colorado at Denver Denver CO 80217-3364 E-mail: larry.anderson@cudenver.edu.

ANDERSON, LAURIE ANN, critical care nurse; b. Duluth, Minn., Dec. 13, 1954; d. Robert Reginald and Claire Olivia (Hood) Johnson; m. Gary E. Anderson. RN, St. Luke's Hosp., Duluth, Minn., 1976. Gen. staff nurse med./neurosurgery Mercy San Juan Hosp., Citrus Hts., Calif., 1979-80; gen. staff nurse MSICU St. Luke's Hosp., Duluth, 1980-84; gen. staff nurse SICU St. Francis Hosp., Tulsa, 1984-85; gen. staff nurse bone marrow transplant Fairview U. Hosp., Mpls., 1985-98; staff nurse, med., surg., ICU Abbott Northwestern Hosp., Mpls., 1998-2000; staff nurse ICU Woodwinds Hosp. HealthEast, 2000—. Mem. Minn. Nurses Assn. E-mail: lauriea73@hotmail.com.

ANDERSON, LAWRENCE KEITH, electrical engineer, consultant; b. Toronto, Ont., Can., Oct. 2, 1935; came to U.S., 1957; s. Wallace Ray and Irene Margaret (Linn) A.; m. Katherine Florence Drechsler, Sept. 21, 1963; children— Susan Barbara, Robert Keith. B. in Engring. Physics, McGill U., 1957; PhDEE, Stanford U., 1962. With Bell Labs., 1961-85, dir. electronic components and Subsystems lab., 1981-85; v.p. component devel. Sandia Nat. Labs., Albuquerque, 1985-88; exec. dir. AT&T Bell Labs. Interconnection and Power Tech. Div., Parsippany, NJ, 1988-89; prof., dir. Alliance for Photonic Tech., Albuquerque, 1990-91; dir. Colo. Inst. Tech. Transfer and Implementation, U. Colo., Colorado Springs, 1991-95. Bd. dirs. N.M. Inst. for Lifelong Learning, 2002—. Fellow IEEE (pres. Electron Devices Soc. 1976-77, dir. 1979-80), Engring. Mgmt. Soc. (bd. govs. 1999-02, v.p. confs. 2001-02). Home: 150 Whitetail Rd NE Albuquerque NM 87122-1921 E-mail: andersnm@aol.com.

ANDERSON, LAWRENCE OHACO, magistrate judge, lawyer; b. Phoenix, Sept. 7, 1948; s. Jack M. and Viola (Ohaco) A. BS, U. San Francisco, 1971; JD, Ariz. State U., Tempe, 1974. Bar: Ariz. 1975. Prosecutor City of Phoenix, 1973-75; assoc. Jack M. Anderson, Phoenix, 1975-78; sole practice Phoenix, 1978-90; judge Superior Ct. of Ariz., Phoenix, 1990-92, judge, criminal calender, 1992-95, judge, juvenile ct., 1995-98, magistrate judge, 1998-. Natl. Wheelchair Weightlifting Championship, Spokane, Wash., 1974; Victory Achievement Award, State of Ariz., 1990; Outstanding Citizens award, Nat. Counil on Disability, 1992. Mem. ABA, Assn. Trial Lawyers Am., Ariz. Trial Lawyers Assn. (bd. dirs. 1985—). Republic. Roman Catholic. Avocations: fishing, hunting, sports. Office: 401 W Washington SPC11 Phoenix AZ 85003-2120

ANDERSON, LAWRENCE ROBERT, JR., lawyer; b. Minden, La., Oct. 30, 1945; s. Lawrence Robert and Elnora Dale (Fincher) A.; m. Constance Lorraine Fauver, Oct. 21, 1977; children: Lauren Constance, Frank Lawrence. BS, La. State U., 1967, JD, 1971. Bar: La. 1971, U.S. Dist. Ct. (ea. dist.) La. 1971, U.S. Ct. Appeals (5th cir.) 1971, U.S. Dist. Ct. (mid. dist.) La. 1972, U.S. Dist. Ct. (we. dist.) La. 1975, U.S. Supreme Ct. 1975. Assoc. Sanders, Miller, Downing & Kean, Baton Rouge, 1971, Talley, Anthony, Hughes & Knight, Bogalusa, La., 1971-74; ptnr. Newman, Duggins, Drolla, Gamble & Anderson, Baton Rouge, 1974-76, Anderson & Roberts, Baton Rouge, 1976-79, Anderson, Anderson, Hawsey, Rainach and Stakelum, Baton Rouge, 1979-83, Anderson & Rainach, 1983-88, Anderson & Duncan, 1988-89, Seale, Smith, Zuber & Barnette, Baton Rouge, 1990—. 1st lt. U.S. Army, 1972. Mem. La. Bar Assn., Bar Assn. Fed. 5th Cir., Baton Rouge Bar Assn., Am. Bankruptcy Inst., Comml. Law League Am. Home: 11937 Lake Sherwood Ave N Baton Rouge LA 70816-4340 Office: 8550 United Plaza Blvd Ste 200 Baton Rouge LA 70809-2256 Business E-Mail: lranderson@sszblaw.com.

ANDERSON, LINDA JEAN, critical care and psychiatric nurse practitioner; b. Louisville, Ky., Mar. 28, 1956; d. James Phillip and Ellabelle Jean (Crowder) Anderson; children: Bradley, Vanessa, Frances, Joseph; m. Donald W. Goodman. BSN, U. Louisville, 1989, MSN, 2000. ARNP, Ky., Ind. Staff nurse Audubon Regional Med. Ctr., Louisville, 1989-90; nurse clinician Vis. Nurses Assn. Louisville, 1990-95; staff nurse Southwest Hosp., Louisville, 1990-2000; rsch. coord. electrophysiology-cardiology U. Louisville, 1993-94; staff nurse Ctr. for Behavioral Health Bapt. East Hosp., 1996-2000; psychiat. clin. coord. U. Louisville Healthcare Univ. Hosp., 2000—02; pvt. practice Rose Island Counseling & Cons., Prospect, Ky., 2002—, Pk. View Psychiat. Svc., Jeffersonville, Ind., 2002—. Mem. alumni bd. govs. U. Louisville Sch. Nursing, 1988-97. Mem. Am. Psychiat. Nurses Assn., Sigma Theta Tau. Avocations: watercolor painting, charcoal & pencil sketching, poetry, flute. Home: PO Box 21694 Louisville KY 40221

ANDERSON, LLOYD LEE, animal science educator; b. Nevada, Iowa, Nov. 18, 1933; s. Clarence and Carrie G. (Sampson) A.; m. Janice G. Peterson, Sept. 7, 1958 (dec. Dec. 1966); m. JaNelle R. Hall, June 15, 1970; children: Marc C., James R. *The family cherished 20 years of love and loyal companionship with Cinnamon.* Student, Simpson Coll., 1951-52, Iowa State U., 1952-53, BS in Animal Husbandry, 1957, PhD in Animal Reproduction, 1961; DSc (hon.), Georgian Acad. Scis., Tbilisi, 2003. NIH postdoctoral fellow Iowa State U., Ames, 1961-62, asst. prof., 1961-65, assoc. prof., 1965-71, prof. animal sci., 1971—, Charles F. Curtiss Disting. prof. agr., 1992—, chmn. com. on coms., faculty senate, 2000—02, prof. biomed. sci., 2002—. Lalor Found. fellow Sta. Recherches Physiologie Animale, Inst. Nat. Recherche Agronomique, Jouy-en-Josas, France, 1963—64; rschr. physiology of reprodn. and ctrl. nervous sys.-pituitary regulation of growth for increased prodn. efficiency of farm animals; mem. reproductive biology study sect. NIH, 1984—88, NIH Reviewers Res. (NRR), 1988—92; mem. peer rev. panel animal health spl. rsch. grants on beef and dairy cattle reproductive diseases USDA, 1986—88; Honor lectr. representing Iowa State U. Mid-Am. State Univs. Assn., 1989—90; mem. sustainable growth agrl. panel USDA, Agrl. Rsch. Svc.., Nat. Program Staff to rev. rsch. projects, 1993; mem. referees panel for sponsored rsch. Kuwait U., 1998—; mem. Janice Peterson Anderson Excellence award and scholarship Coll. of Design Iowa State U., chair com. on coms., Faculty Senate, 2000—02; trustee Asian Inst. Nanobiosci. and Tech., Busan, Republic of Korea, 2002—. Mem. editl. bd. Biology Reprodn., 1968-70, 86-90, Jour. Animal Sci., 1982-87, 98-2001, Animal Reprodn. Sci., 1978—, Inst. for Sci. Info. Atlas of Sci., 1987-90, Domestic Animal Endocrinology, 1992-95, Endocrinology, 1993-97; contbr. articles to profl. jours. Mem. 4-H Club. With Constrn. Engrs., U.S. Army, 1953-55, Germany, Signal Corps USAR, 1955-61. Grantee, USDA, 1978—. Fellow AAAS, Am. Soc. Animal Sci. (hon. Animal Physiology and Endocrinology award 1988, Nat Pork Prodrs. Coun. Innovation award in basic rsch. 1993, Outstanding Achievement in Rsch. award 2001); mem. ACLU, NRA, VFW, Endocrine Soc., Am. Physiol. Soc., Iowa Physiol. Soc., Am. Assn. Anatomists, Am. Soc. Cell Biology, Soc. for Study of Reprodn., Soc. for Exptl. Biology and Medicine (mem. coun. 1980-83), Brit. Soc. for Study of Fertility, Soc. for Neurosci., Iowa Acad. Sci., Pituitary Soc., Asian Inst. of Nanobioscience and Tech., Busan, Korea (trustee 2002—), Am. Legion, Nat. Block and Bridle Club, Osborn Rsch. Club (chair 1994), Faculty Citation Iowa State Univ. Alumni Assn. 2003, Sigma Xi, Gamma Sigma Delta (Mission award in rsch. 2002), Alpha Tau Omega (Gold Cir. award 2002). Methodist. Home: 2812 Valley View Rd Ames IA 50014-4506 Office: Iowa State U Dept Animal Sci 2356 Kildee Hl Ames IA 50011-0001

ANDERSON, LOIS D. nursing administrator, mental health nurse; b. Fulton, Mo., July 7, 1929; d. John Henry and Flossie Margaret (Myers) Dye; m. Morris B. Anderson, Nov. 4, 1947 (dec.); children: Sheila Sesti, John Anderson. AS, St. Louis Community Coll., Florissant, Mo., 1981. RN, Mo.; cert. mental health and psychiat. nurse. Head nurse Fulton State Hosp., quality assurance coord., retired 1991. Named hon. Red Cross Nurse, 1988. Mem. ANA, Mo. Nurses Assn., Profl. Nurses Assn. (treas.). Avocations: travel, reading, sewing.

ANDERSON, LORRAINE PEARSON, dean; b. Orlando, Fla., Mar. 12, 1956; d. Embree Jones and Marilyn (Meckstroth) Pearson; m. Steve W. Smith; m. Dale A. Anderson; children: Brandon, Alexandra. BA, U. Fla., 1978; MBA, Marshall U., Huntington, W.Va., 1991; EdD, W.Va. U., 2000. Coll. rels. coord. Walt Disney World, Huntington, W.Va., 1973—85; owner, mgr. Premier Travel Co., Huntington, 1991—94; instr. Marshall U., Huntington, 1991—93, dir. undergrad. studies, 1993—96, assoc. dean, 1996—. Developer leadership tng. program U.S. Army C.E. Contbr. Recipient EntrePrep award, Kauffman Found., 1996—2003, Mini-Soc. award, 1999—2003. Mem.: ASTD, Nat. Assn. Female Execs., Acad. of Mgmt., Nat. Soc. Human Resource Mgmt., TriState Soc. for Human Resource Mgmt. (bd. dirs. 2002—), Beta Alpha Psi, Phi Beta Kappa. Office: Marshall Univ Lewis Coll of Bus One John Marshall Dr Huntington WV 25755-2300

ANDERSON, LOUIS WILMER, JR., physicist, educator; b. Houston, Dec. 24, 1933; s. Louis Wilmer and Margaret Quarles (Brockett) A.; m. Marguerite Gillespie, Aug. 30; children— Margaret Mary, Louis Charles, Elizabeth Brockett BA, Rice U., 1956; A.M., Harvard U., 1957, PhD, 1960. Asst. prof. U. Wis.-Madison, 1960-63, assoc. prof., 1963-68, prof. physics, 1968-94, Julian E. Mack prof. physics, 1994—. Cons. U. Calif.-Berkeley Lawrence Lab. Author 2 textbooks. Contbr. articles to profl. jours. Patentee type of N2 laser, collisional pumping ion source. Fellow U. Wis. Tchg. Acad.; co-recipient IEEE Particle Accelerator Conf. Tech. award for invention and devel. of optically pumped polarized H-Ion source, 1993. Fellow Am. Phys. Soc.; mem. Sigma Xi Home: 1818 Chadbourne Ave Madison WI 53726 Office: U Wis Dept Physics Madison WI 53726-4045 E-mail: lwanders@facstaff.wisc.edu.

ANDERSON, LYLE ARTHUR, retired manufacturing company executive; b. Jewell, Kans., Dec. 29, 1931; s. Arvid Herman and Clara Vera (Herman) A.; m. Harriet Virginia Robson, June 12, 1953; children— Brian, Karen, Eric. BS, U. Kans., 1953; MS, Butler U., 1961. C.P.A., Mo., Kans. Mgmt. trainee, internal auditor RCA, Camden, N.J. and Indpls., 1955-59; auditor Ernst & Ernst (C.P.A.'s), Kansas City, Mo., 1959-63; v.p. fin. and adminstrn., treas., dir. Affiliated Hosp. Products, Inc., St. Louis, 1963-71; sr. v.p. Sara Lee Corp., Deerfield, Ill., 1971-74; exec. v.p. fin. Consol. Foods Corp., Chgo., 1974-76. Pres. Autotrol Corp., Crystal Lake, Ill. Bd. dirs. Crystal Lake Civic Ctr. Authority, Raue Ctr. for the Arts. With U.S. Army, 1953-55. Mem. Omicron Delta Kappa. Republican. Methodist. Home: 9804 Partridge Ln Crystal Lake IL 60014-6627

ANDERSON, LYNDA A, geriatrician, behavioral scientist; b. Torrance, Calif., June 6, 1955; d. Kenneth and Carol Anderson; m. J. Kenneth Conover, 1983. PhD, U of NC, Chapel Hill, North Carolina, 1980—84; MS, U of Oreg., Eugene, Oreg., 1976—78; BS, U of Oreg. Health Sci. Ctr., Portland, Oreg., 1973—76. Acting dir. Prevention Rsch. Ctr., CDC, Atlanta, 2000—; sr. health sci. CDC, Atlanta, 1992—. Assoc. prof. (adj.) Emory U, Atlanta, 2000—; assoc. dir. Geriatric Rsch., edn., and Clin. Ctr.,Veterans Adminstrn., Ann Arbor, Mich., 1988—92; cons. U of Mich. Geriat. Ctr., Ann Arbor, Mich., 1991—92; asst. prof. U of Mich., Ann Arbor, Mich., 1986—91; NIH postdoctoral fellowship Duke U Med. Ctr., Durhan, NC, 1984—86. Mem.: Soc. Pub. Health Edn., Am. Pub. Health Soc., Delta Omega. Achievements include research in Trust in Physician Scales (Instrument); Multidimensional Desire for Control Scales; Body Image Silhouettes (measure); Over 50 peer reviewed pub. in public health and medicine; Eunice Tyler Practice Award from the Univ. of NC Dept. of Health Behavior and Health Edn; Secretary's Award for Distinguished Svc., US Dept. of Health and Human Services, 1997; research in Special Act of Service Award, US Dept. of Health and Human Services, 1996; Soc. of Public Health Educator's Grad. Student Rsch. Paper Award, 1984; Administn. on Aging Traineeship, 1976-78. Office: Ctrs for Disease Control & Prevention 4770 Buford Hyw NE (K-45) Atlanta GA 30341 Office Fax: 770-488-5486. E-mail: laa0@cdc.gov.

ANDERSON, LYNN L. trust company executive; B in B in Bus., JD, U. Kans. Various positions Frank Russell, 1987; chmn. Frank Russell Trust Co., Tacoma, Frank Russell Investment Mgmt. Co., Tacoma. Vice chmn. Frank Russell Co. Office: Frank Russell Co 909 A St Tacoma WA 98402

ANDERSON, MARILYN NELLE, elementary education educator, librarian, counselor; b. Las Animas, Colo., May 5, 1942; d. Mason Hadley Moore and Alice Carrie (Dwyer) Coates; m. George Robert Anderson, Sept. 4, 1974; children: Lisa Lynn, Edward Alan, Justin Patrick. BEd magna cum laude, Adams State Coll., 1962, postgrad., 1965; MEd, Ariz. State U., 1967; postgrad., Idaho State U., 1971, 86, Columbia Pacific U., 1991—. Cert. elem. tchr., K-12 sch. counselor. Tchr. Wendell (Idaho) Sch. Dist. 232, 1962-66, Union-Endicott (N.Y.) Sch. Dist., 1967-68; counselor, librarian West Yuma (Colo.) Sch. Dist., 1968-69; elem. sch. counselor Am. Falls (Idaho) Sch. Dist. 381, 1969-73; project dir. Gooding County (Idaho) Sr. Citizens Orgn., 1974-75; tchr. Castleford (Idaho) Sch. Dist. 417, 1982-92; placement specialist, referral counselor Idaho Child Care Program South Ctrl. Idaho Community Action Agy., Twin Falls, 1992—. Mem. Castleford Schs. Merit Pay Devel. program, 1983-84, Accreditation Evaluation com., 1984-85, Math. Curriculum Devel. com., 1985-86. Leader Brownie Scouts, Endicott, 1967-68; chmn. fundraising com. Am. Falls Kindergarten, 1971-73. Recipient Leader's award Nat. 4-H Conservation Natural Resources Program, 1984. Mem. NEA, ASCD, Nat. Assn. Edn. Young Children, Assn. Childhood Edn. Internat., Idaho Edn. Assn., So. Idaho Assn. for Childhood Edn. Internat. (pres.), Idaho Coun. Internat. Reading Assn., Magic Valley Reading Assn., Support Unltd. Providers and Parents. Republican. Baptist. Avocations: reading, painting, writing short stories, photography. Home: 1675 BBH Wendell ID 83355-9801

ANDERSON, MARILYN RUTH, retired multi-media specialist; b. Storm Lake, Iowa, Oct. 2, 1934; d. Ernest F. and Elvira (Getzmier) Otto; m. Leland A. Anderson, June 23, 1957; children: Pamela, Mitchell, Darren. BA, U. No. Iowa, 1975. Cert. tchr. Iowa. Tchr. 1st grade Holstein (Iowa) Comty. Sch., 1954-55, Humboldt (Iowa) Comty. Sch., 1955-57; substitute tchr. Aurelia (Iowa) Comty. Sch., 1958-66, Kanawha (Iowa) Comty. Sch., 1966-74; libr. media specialist, reading tchr. Marcus-Meriden-Cleghorn Sch., Meriden, Iowa, 1974-2000; h.s. libr. media specialist Willow Comty. Sch., Quimby, Iowa, 1984-89. Mem. Cleghorn (Iowa) Pub. Libr. Trustees, 1976—86, chair, 1982—86. Mem. planning com., leader Meriden-Cleghorn New Libr.Bldg. Campaign, 1983—85, chair libr. design com., chmn. fed. grant-writing com.; spkr. dedication ceremony Meriden-Cleghorn Cmty. Libr., 1986. Mem.: Iowa Reading Assn., N.W. Iowa Reading Coun., Iowa Edn. Media Assn. (mem. Children's Choice award com. 1976—), Area Edn. Agy. 4 Media Specialists (sec. 1980—82, pres. 1984—86), Internat. Reading Assn. Republican. Lutheran. Avocations: travel, camping, touring state capitols, reading, investing. Home: 306 South Lewis Ave Cleghorn IA 51014 E-mail: lmand@mailstation.com.

ANDERSON, MARILYN WHEELER, English language educator; b. Tulsa, Mar. 18, 1946; d. Robert Leslie and Lola Madelene (Offutt) Wheeler; m. Austin Gilman Anderson, Mar. 17, 1968; children: Guy, Lisa, Michael, Emily. BA, Calif. State U., L.A., 1968; MA, UCLA, 1972, Calif. State U., Dominguez Hills, 1989. Actress and dir., L.A., 1977-83; cons. Redondo Beach (Calif.) Beach City Schs., 1981-83; prof. of English El Camino Coll., Torrance, Calif., 1986—. Fine arts com. mem. El Camino Coll., 1992—, affirmative action officer, 1995-96; presenter in field. Author: (textbook) Keys to Successful Writing, 1998, 2d edit., 2001; contbr. articles to profl. jours. Vol. 1736 House/Crisis Ctr., Hermosa Beach, Calif., 1985-86; bd. dirs. Brain Injury Rsch. Ctr., UCLA, 1998—, spkr. Calif. Coun. for Humanities, 2002, keynote spkr. Joint Symposium of Nat. and Internat. Neurotrauma Socs., 2002. Mem. MLA, Nat. Coun. Tchrs. of English, UCLA Alumni Assn. Democrat. Avocations: jogging, travel, hiking, book club membership. Office: El Camino Coll 16007 Crenshaw Blvd Torrance CA 90506-0001

ANDERSON, MARK ALEXANDER, lawyer; b. Santa Monica, Calif., Nov. 15, 1953; s. William Alexander and Christina (Murray) A.; m. Rosalie Louise Movius, Nov. 28, 1986; 1 child, Morgan Anderson Movius. AB, U. So. Calif., 1974; JD, Yale U., 1978. Bar: Calif. 1979, U.S. Dist. Ct. (no. dist.) Calif. 1979, U.S. Ct. Appeals (9th cir.) 1979, Oreg. 1982, U.S. Dist. Ct. Oreg. 1982, Wash. 1985, U.S. Dist. Ct. (we. dist.) Wash. 1986, U.S. Supreme Ct. 1989. Law clk. U.S. Ct. Appeals (9th cir.), San Francisco, 1978-79, U.S. Dist. Ct. Oreg., Portland, 1980-82; atty. Miller, Nash, Wiener, Hager & Carlsen, Portland, 1983-92; gen. counsel, asst. sec. Dark Horse Comics, Inc., Milwaukie, Oreg., 1992-98; sr. asst. atty. gen. Oreg. Dept. Justice, Salem, Oreg., 2002—. Chair Raleigh Hills-Garden Home Citizen Participation Orgn., 1992-93. Mem. N.W. Lawyers and Artists (pres. 1988-90), State Bar Calif., Wash. State Bar Assn., Oreg. State Bar (chair antitrust, trade regulation and unfair bus. practices sect. 1991-92), City Club of Portland (chair arts and culture standing com. 1990-92, rsch. bd. 1999-2002). Home: PO Box 8154 Portland OR 97207-8154

ANDERSON, MARK ROBERT, data processing executive, biochemist; b. Oak Park, Ill., Aug. 11, 1951; s. Robert Hugo and Marilyn Pettee (Johnson) A.; m. Mary Jane Helsell, June 6, 1980; children: Berit Bracken, Evan Robert. BS, Stanford U., 1972; MS, Stanford U., Hopkins Marine Sta., 1973; postgrad., U. Brit. Columbia, Vancouver, 1973. Publisher Potlatch Press, Friday Harbor, Wash., 1974-77; assoc. prof. Western Wash. U., Bellingham, 1977, Harvard U., Boston, 1978; chief scientist Ocean Research & Edn. Soc., Boston, 1978; v.p. Moclips Cetological Soc., Friday Harbor, 1979-81; founder, exec. dir. The Whale Mus., Friday Harbor, 1979-81; pres. The Oikos Co., Friday Harbor, 1980—, San Juan Software, Friday Harbor, 1983-84; pres., bd. dirs. Island Tech. Inc., Friday Harbor, 1984—; founder, pres. Tech. Alliance Ptnrs., 1989—. Bd. dirs. Worldesign, PreText, Inc., Wa. Software Assn.; bd. advisors HIT Lab., U. Wash., 1991—; founder, pres. Strategic News Svc. LLC, 1995—; founder WSA Investment Forum; CEO, bd. dirs. Carrier Wave, Inc., 1996—; program chair Online Advantage 96; founder, exec. dir. Orca Relief Citizens Alliance, 1998-2001, pres., 2001-—; founder, mgr. The Resonance Fund, 1999—; bd. advisors Smartage, Inc., 1999—, E-CHRON, Stockholm, 1999-2001, Ignition Corp., 2000—; dir. Hybrid Vigor Inst., 2001—; mem. adv. bd. Merrill Lynch, 1999—. Author: Nineteen Fathers, 1971, (software) The Agent's Advantage, 1983; producer TV film Survivors, 1980; editor, founder Jour. Cetus, 1981; discoverer Resonance Theory, 1981; columnist ABC News.com, 1998-2000, Citywire, UK, 1999-2001, Microsoft Money Central, 2000-2002. Founder San Juan Musicians Guild, 1974-78, Anti-Spray Coalition, 1977, SNS Future in Rev. Conf., 2003—. Mem. Wash. Software Assn. (bd. dirs. 1988-90, chair pres.'s group 1989—). Avocations: theoretical physics, musical composition, skiing.

ANDERSON, MARTIN CARL, economist; b. Lowell, Mass., Aug. 5, 1936; s. Ralph and Evelyn (Anderson) A.; m. Annelise Graebner, Sept. 25, 1965 AB summa cum laude, Dartmouth Coll., 1957, MS in Engring., MSBA; PhD in Indsl. Mgmt., MIT, 1962. Asst. to dean, instr. engring. Thayer Sch. Engring. Dartmouth Coll., Hanover, N.H., 1959; research fellow Joint Ctr. for Urban Studies MIT and Harvard U., Cambridge, 1961-62; asst. prof. fin. Grad. Sch. Bus. Columbia U., N.Y.C., 1962-65, assoc. prof. bus., 1965-68; sr. fellow Hoover Inst. on War, Revolution and Peace Stanford (Calif.) U., 1971—; spl. asst. to Pres. of U.S. The White House, 1969-70, spl. cons. for systems analysis, 1970-71, asst. for policy devel., 1981-82. Mem. Pres.' Fgn. Intelligence Adv. Bd., 1982-85, Pres.' Econ. Policy Adv. Bd., 1982-88, Pres.' Gen. Adv. Com. on Arms Control and Disarmament, 1987-93; pub. interest dir. Fed. Home Loan Bank San Francisco, 1972-79; mem. Commn. on Crucial Choices for Ams., 1973-75, Def. Manpower Commn., 1975-76, Com. on the Present Danger, 1977—. Author: The Federal Bulldozer: A Critical Analysis of Urban Renewal, 1949-62, 1964, Conscription: A Select and Annotated Bibliography, 1976, Welfare: The Political Economy of Welfare Reform in the U.S., 1978, Registration and the Draft, 1982, The Military Draft, 1982, Revolution, 1988, Impostors in the Temple, 1992, Reagan in his Own Hand, 2001; columnist Scripps-Howard News Svc., 1993-94. Dir. research Nixon presdl. campaign, 1968; policy adviser Reagan presdl. campaign, 1976, 80; del. Rep. Nat. Conv., 1992-2000; policy adviser Dole Presdl. Campaign, 1996; sr. adviser Bush presdl. campaign, 1998-2000; trustee Ronald Reagan Presdl. Found., 1985-92; mem. Calif. Gov.'s Coun. Econ. Advisors, 1993-98, chmn. Congl. Policy Adv. Bd., 1998-2001. 2d lt. AUS, 1958-59. Mem. Mont Pelerin Soc., Phi Beta Kappa. Clubs: Bohemian. Office: Stanford U Hoover Instn Stanford CA 94305-6010

ANDERSON, MARY ELIZABETH, protection services official; b. Flint, Mich., Sept. 12, 1949; d. Buford Herbert and Florence Mary (DuPrey) A. AB, U. Mich. Flint, 1976. Lic. social worker, Mich. From residence dir. to cmty. affairs dir. YWCA Greater Flint, 1977-84; dep., sgt. Genesee County Sheriff Dept., Flint, 1984-96, lt., 1996—. Mem. Criminal Justice Women of Mich. (award 1995), Planned Parenthood USA, So. Poverty Law Ctr., Hope United Meth. Ch., U. Mich. Alumni Assn. Home: 3926 Arlene Ave Flint MI 48532-5263 Office: Genesee County Sheriff Dept 1002 S Saginaw St Flint MI 48502-1410 E-mail: Mea91249@aol.com.

ANDERSON, MARY HELEN STEED, volunteer; b. Pitts., July 24, 1914; d. Arthur Whitten and Helen Vincent (McKee) Steed; m. Townsend Canfield Anderson, Apr. 03, 1939 (dec. Feb. 1987). AB in Speech, Miami U., Oxford, Ohio, 1936. Elder Merritt Island Presbyn. Ch., mem. permanent jud. com. Fla. Synod, mem. com. on ministry St. Johns Presbytery, 1972-80, 1st woman moderator, 1979; sustainer Jr. League, Cocoa-Titusville, 1974—; mem. bd. Brevard Symphony Orch., 1988-90, 95—; vice chmn. adv. bd. Salvation Army, Cocoa, Fla., 1978—; chmn. adv. bd. Domestic Violence Shelter, Cocoa, 1988—; bd. past pres. Brevard Parliamentary Law Unit, 1981-82, 88-89, Ctrl. Brevard Guild, Brevard Symphony, 1978-90; pres. Brevard Mus. Guild, 1990-92, 94—. Named Woman of Yr. Panhellenic and Orlando Sentinel, 1971, Citizen of Yr. Kiwanis Club of Merritt Island, 1981, Historic Woman of Brevard, Brevard Cultural Alliance, 1991, named Woman of Yr. Brevard County Commn. on Status of Women, 2003. Mem. AAUW (bd. dirs. 1974—), Merritt Island Woman's Club (past pres. 1969-70, 87-88, Woman of Achievement 1989), Phi Beta Kappa. Home: 1200 S Courtenay Pky #415 Merritt Island FL 32952

ANDERSON, MARY JANE, public library consultant; b. Des Moines, Jan. 23, 1935; d. William Kenneth and Margaret Louise (Snider) McPherson; m. Charles Robert Anderson, Oct. 21, 1965 (div. Oct. 24, 1989); 1 child, Mary Margaret. BA in Edn., U. Fla., 1957; MLS, Fla. State U., 1963. Elem. sch. librarian Dade County Schs., Miami, Fla., 1957-61; children's/young adult librarian Santa Fe Regional Library, Gainesville, Fla., 1961-63; br. librarian Jacksonville (Fla.) Pub. Library, 1963-64, chief of children's services, 1964-66, head of circulation, 1966-67; pub. library cons. Fla. State Library, Tallahassee, 1967-70; dir. tech. processing St. Mary's Coll. of Md., St. Mary's City, 1970-72; coordinator children's services Balt. County Pub. Library, Towson, Md., 1972-73; exec. dir. young adult services div. ALA, Chgo., 1973-75, exec. dir. assn. for library service to children, 1973-82; pres. Answers Unltd., Inc., Deerfield, Ill., 1982-92; dir. Wilmington (Ill.) Pub. Libr., 1993-97; dir. media svcs. Newark (Ill.) County Sch. Dist., 1997-98; dir. Maud P. Palenske Pub. Libr., St. Joseph, Mich., 1998-2000; coord. Sr. Net Learning Ctr., Ariea IV Agy. Aging, St. Joseph, 2000—03; libr. cons., 2000—03. Instr. and cons. in field; part-time faculty No. Ill. U., 1985-86, Nat. Coll. Edn., Evanston, Ill., 1989; head youth svcs. Waukegan (Ill.) Pub. Libr., 1988-93; mem. exec. com. U.S. sect. Internat. Bd. on Books for Young People, 1973-82; mem. adv. bd. Reading Rainbow, TV series, 1981-84; mem. sch. bd. Avoca Sch. Dist. 37, 1985-87; mem. ALSC Newbery Medal Com., 1991. Editor: Top of the News, 1971-73, Fla. State Library Newsletter, 1967-70, Nor'Easter (North Suburban Library System Newsletter), 1984-88; contbr. articles to profl. jours. Bd. dirs. Child Devel. Assocs. Consortium, 1975—83, Coalition for Children and Youth, 1978—80; mem. City of Wilmington Downtown Redevel. Commn., 1996—98; with Episcopal Diocese Chgo. Diocesan Coun., 1988—94, standing com., 1994—97, dep. to gen. conv., 1997; mem. Bishop's search com., 1997—98; province V rep., 1998—99; mem. vestry St. Thomas' Episcopal Ch., Morris, Ill., 1996—98; with Episcopal Diocese West, Mich.; mem. Diocesan cons. team, 1999—, alt. dep. to gen. conv., 2003—; deanery rep. St. Paul's Episc. Ch., St. Joseph, Mich., 2000—01, lay eucharistic min., 1999—, mem. vestry, 2003—, 2003—. Mem. ALA (coun. 1992-2000, com. on orgn. 1999-01), Rotary (sec.-treas. 1994-96, pres. 1996-97), Wilmington C. of C. (bd. dirs. 1996-97, sec. 1997), Caxton Club (Chgo.), Beta Phi Mu, Sigma Kappa. Episcopalian.

ANDERSON, MAX ELLIOT, television and film production company executive; b. Nov. 3, 1946; s. Kenneth O. and Doris I. (Jones) A.; m. Claudia Lynd, Aug. 17, 1978; children: James Brightman, Sarah Lynd. BA in Psychology, Grace Coll., 1973. Advt. rep., cameraman Ken Anderson Films, Warsaw, Ind., 1969-78; prodr. Q Media Group, Rockford, Ill., 1978-83; pres. Philip Lasz Gallery, Warsaw, 1973—. Pres., owner The Market Place, Rockford, 1986—; prodr., dir. Eagle Video, Rockford, 1986—; regional product distbr. Laney Honey, 1994—; founder MVP Prodns., 1998—; prodr., writer, dir. Tracy's Choices, 1997; prodr. promotional video W.A. Whitney (German, French, Italian, Mandarin transl.), 1996; prodr. corp. video programs W.A. Whitney, Roper Whitney, Barber Colman, Longview Fibre, 1995, 96, patient video promotion and orientation Swedish Am. Hosp., 1995-96, puppet video programs Woodward Gov.; nat. distbr. home video cassettes, 1985—; mktg. dir. Alley Oop Bowling Alley Ramp for People with Disabilities. Prodr.: (videos) Tracy's Choices, 1997 (Telly award 1998, Dove Found.'s seal of approval, 1999, Best Christian documentary, 1999), Youth Haven, A Safe Place for Kids (Telly award 1999), Celebrating Our Past...Creating Our Future, 2000, The Shenandoah North Fork Project, 2000, Angels Among Us, 2000; prodr. (nat. TV spots) True Value Hardware, 1985-96, 40th anniversary TV spots for Rockford Clin. (Raddy award 1992), (TV and radio spot campaign) Judge Joe McGraw, 2002 (Telly award 2003); assoc. prodr.: Gospel at the Symphony, 1979; cinematographer: (film) Pilgrims Progress (Best Cinematographer award Christian Film Distbrs. Assn. 1978) With U.S. Army, 1967-69. Recipient 1st pl. award Video Internat. Tech. Video Assn., 1989, award for Sunstrand sales video, 1991, award for Woodward Gov. corp. video, 1991, Raddy Award of Excellence, No. Ill. Advt. Coun., 1989-90, 1st pl. video award Hosp. Satellite Network, 1990, award Ill. Soc. for Healthcare Mktg. and Pub. Rels., 1998. Mem. Internat. Christian Video Assn., Am. Beekeeping Assn., Christian Booksellers Assn. Republican. Mem. Evang. Free Ch. Home and Office: 4112 Marsh Ave Rockford IL 61114-6142

ANDERSON, MAXWELL L. museum director; b. N.Y.C., May 1, 1956; AB, Dartmouth Coll., 1977; AM, Harvard U., 1978, PhD, 1981. Asst. curator Met. Mus., 1982-87; dir. Michael C. Carlos Mus., Atlanta, 1987-95, Art Gallery Ont., Toronto, Can., 1995-98, Whitney Mus. Am. Art, N.Y.C., 1998—. Lectr. Roman art Princeton (N.J.) U., 1985; vis. prof. U. di Roma, 1987; adj. assoc. prof. Emory U., 1989—. Arranged exhbns. Treasures of the Holy Land, 1986, Roman Portraits in Context, 1988, Souls Grown Deep, 1996, Wired Mus., 1997, 2000 Biennial Exhbn. Mem.: Assn. Art Mus. Dirs. (pres.), Coll. Art Assn., Am. Assn. Mus. Office: Whitney Mus Am Art 945 Madison Ave New York NY 10021-2701*

ANDERSON, MAYNARD CARLYLE, national and international security executive; b. Hesper, Iowa, Aug. 6, 1932; s. Carl Adolph and Mathilda Theodora (Wold) A. BA, Luther Coll., 1954. Mem. spl. ops. group Hqrs. Dept. of Navy, Washington, 1966-68, supervising agt. Naval Investigative Svc. Office Guantanamo Bay, Cuba, 1968-69, asst. head internal security divsn. hqrs. Washington, 1969-73, dir. spl. security and spl. activities, 1973-78, dir. spl. security, 1978-79; dep. security policy Dept. of Def., Washington, 1979-82, dir. security plans and programs, 1982-88, asst. dep. under sec., 1988-93, acting dep. under sec. def., 1993-94; pres., mng. dir. Arcadia Group Worldwide, Inc., Chantilly, Va., 1994—; founder Arcadia Inst., Chantilly, 1997; prin. Strategic Trade Adv. Group, Inc., Washington, 1997—. Dir. Nat. Intellectual Property Law Inst., Washington, 1994; chmn. policy com. Security Affairs Support Assn., Washington, 1988—94; former chmn. adv. com. Dept. of Def. Security Inst., Dept. of Def. Polygraph Inst., Def. Pers. Security Rsch. and Edn. Ctr.; chmn. Nat. Adv. Group/Security Countermeasures; hon. faculty mem. Def. Security Inst.; lectr. Sch. Criminal Justice, Coll. Social Sci. Mich. State U., mem. rsch. task force; lectr. Luther Coll., Decorah, Iowa; del. UN Econ. Commn. for Europe, Com. on Sustained Devel., 1999—; dir. Griffin Svcs., Inc., Atlanta, 2002—, dir. multi-sector crisis mgmt. consortium, Arlington, Va., 2003—. Author/contbr.: Citizen Espionage: Studies in Trust and Betrayal, 1994; contbr. articles to profl. jours. Mem. pres. coun. Luther Coll., Decorah, Iowa, 1990—. Recipient Meritorious Exec. Presdl. Rank award, Washington, 1985, 92, Disting. Svc. award Luther Coll., Decorah, 1989, Donald B. Woodbridge award of excellence Nat. Classification Mgmt. Soc., Washington, 1990, Def. Disting. Svc. medal, 1992. Lutheran. Avocations: tennis, writing, lecturing, travel. Home: 205 S Yoakum Pky Apt 721 Alexandria VA 22304-3818 Office: Arcadia Group Worldwide Inc PO Box 222245 Chantilly VA 20153-2245 E-mail: arcadiagwi@aol.com. *Sometimes it seems that significant achievements have been realized by accident. Actually, they have resulted from taking advantage of opportunities.*

ANDERSON, MICHAEL CURTIS, computer industry analyst; b. Belton, Tex., Nov. 19, 1953; s. Curtis Raymond Anderson and Joan Evelyn (Sievers) Bleuer; m. Debra Beth Shlaes, June 7, 1975; children: Sara Joyce, John Michael. BA cum laude, Augustana Coll., 1975; postgrad., U. Iowa, 1982—. Mgmt. sci. analyst Deere & Co., Moline, Ill., 1975-80, mgr. office automation, 1980-88; sr. planner office systems IBM, Roanoke, Tex., 1988-89, mgr. strategy and requirements, planning-office systems, 1989-90; program dir. office info. systems Gartner Group, Stamford, Conn., 1990-93; dir. mkt. rsch. & competitive analysis Ameritech, Chgo., 1993-94; v.p., rsch. dir. adv. techs. Gartner Group, Stamford, Conn., 1994-99, v.p., rsch. area dir. Distributed Electronic Workplace, 1999-2000, v.p. rsch. ops., 2000—, v.p., dir. rsch., 2000—03, mng. v.p. rsch. quality, 2003—. Ill. State scholar, 1971, I.B. McGladrey Accountancy award McGladrey-Hendrickson, 1974. Avocations: tennis, golf, bicycling, fitness, coaching. Home: 1644 Byron Nelson Pkwy Southlake TX 76092 Office: Gartner Inc 125 E John Carpenter Fwy Ste 550 Irving TX 75062

ANDERSON, MICHAEL HUGH, diplomat; b. International Falls, Minn., Oct. 28, 1945; s. Paul Albert and Helen Ainsley (Tibbetts) A. BA in Journalism, U. Minn., 1968, MA in Journalism, 1974; PhD in Polit. Sci., U. Hawaii, 1979. Reporter St. Paul Dispatch, 1968, Mpls. Star, 1974; editor-in-chief Minn. Daily, Mpls., 1967-68; tchr. U.S. Peace Corps, Kuala Lumpur, Malaysia, 1968-71; rsch. scholar East-West Ctr., Honolulu, 1974-80; info. officer UNICEF/UN, N.Y.C., 1980-81; joined Fgn. Svc., U.S. Dept. State, 1981—. Served in Am. embassies and consulates in The Philippines, Papua New Guinea, India, Pakistan and Singapore. Author: Madison Avenue in Asia, 1984; editor: Crisis in International News, 1981; contbr. articles to profl. jours. Mem. Soc. Profl. Journalists, Asia Soc., Smithsonian Inst. (resident assoc. program 1991—). Lutheran. Avocations: travel, collecting autographs. Office: Shantipath Chanakyapuri New Delhi 110021 India

ANDERSON, MICHAEL R. elementary school educator, writer; b. Washington, Ill., Jan. 2, 1952; s. Roy Robert and Mildred Louise Anderson; m. Martha Elizabeth Ward; children: Samuel Ward, Anna Louise. BA, Ill. Coll., 1974; MA, St. Xavier U., 2002. Cert. tchr. K-9 Ill. Educator Sch. Dist. 117, Jacksonville, Ill., 1974—. Cons. Ill. State Bd. Edn., Springfield, Ill., 1999—2001. Author: (children's book) Construction of the Classical Whanger, 1981, The Phantom Teacher, 2001; musician: (audio recording) Solo: Not Alone, 1990, Ice Out, 1998; author: The Great Sled Race, 2000 (Parents' Choice Silver Honor award, 2000). Dir. Lincoln's New Salem Storytelling Festival, Petersburg, 1986—2002; artist dir. Claville Music and Storytelling Festival, Pleasant Plains, 1981—86. Named Ten Outstanding Young Persons, Ill. Jaycees, 1989; recipient Outstanding Young Educator, Jacksonville Jaycees, 1987—88, Innovative Instrnl. Initiative award, West Ctrl. Ill. Assn. for Supervision and Curriculum, 1994, Disting. Alumni award, Ill. Coll., 2003. Mem.: Jacksonville Ednl. Assn. (mem. chmn. 1986—90), Riverwinds Storytelling Guild, Prairie Grapevine Folklore Soc. (pres. 1985—88), Nat. Storytelling Network, Kappa Delta Pi. Home: PO Box 35 Jacksonville IL 62651 Office: MW Prodn PO Box 35 Jacksonville IL 62651 Home Fax: 217-245-9752; Office Fax: 217-245-9752. E-mail: mike@dulcimerguy.com.

ANDERSON, MICHAEL STEVEN, lawyer; b. Mpls., May 25, 1954; s. Wesley James and Lorraine Kathrine (Sword) A.; m. Gail Karin Miller, June 18, 1977; children: Mark, Steven. BA magna cum laude, Cornell U., 1976; JD, Washington U., St. Louis, 1980. Bar: Wis. 1980, U.S. Dist. Ct. (ea. and we. dists.) Wis. 1980, U.S. Ct. Appeals (7th cir.) 1986, U.S. Supreme Ct. 1991. Ptnr. Axley Brynelson, Madison, Wis., 1980—2003, mng. ptnr., 2003—; dir. Oakwood Village East (continuing care retirement cmty.), 2003. Bd. dirs. Oakwood Village East Continuing Care Retirement Comtys., 2003—. Editor, author Washington U. Law Quarterly, 1979-80. Apptd. mem. local Bd. Attys. Profl. Responsibility, 1993—2001; preliminary rev. com. mem. Office Lawyer Regulation, 2002—. Mem.: Licensing Exec. Soc., Licensing Execs. Soc., Order of Coif. Mem. Evangelical Free Ch. Avocation: family. Home: 5882 Timber Ridge Trail Madison WI 53711-5180 Office: Axley Brynelson 2 E Mifflin St Madison WI 53703-2889 E-mail: manderson@axley.com.

ANDERSON, MICHAEL THOMAS, mathematics researcher, educator; b. Boulder, Colo., Nov. 17, 1950; s. Julian Thompson and Elinor Elizabeth (Uhl) A.; m. Myong Hu Kim, Aug. 15, 1986; 1 child, Steven. BA, U. Calif., Santa Barbara, 1975; MA, U. Calif., Berkeley, 1977, PhD, 1981. Rsch. instr. Rice U., Houston, 1981-84; from asst. to assoc. prof. Calif. Inst. Tech., Pasadena, 1984-88; assoc. prof. SUNY, Stony Brook, 1988-91, prof., 1991—. Invited spkr. Internat. Congress Maths., Zurich, 1994. Assoc. editor: Duke Math. Jour., 1991—, mem. editl. bd.: Jour. Geometric and Functional Analysis, 1991—2000; contbr. articles to profl. jours. Recipient Annales Henri Poincare prize, 2000; NSF grantee, 1981—; NSF postdoctoral fellow, 1984-86. Mem. Am. Math. Soc. (rsch. fellow 1990-91). Democrat. Office: SUNY Dept Math Stony Brook NY 11794-3651 E-mail: anderson@math.sunysb.edu.

ANDERSON, MILADA FILKO, manufacturing company executive; b. Chgo, Nov. 17, 1922; d. John and Anna (Sianta) Filko; m. George Richard Anderson, Aug. 29, 1945 (dec. 1974); children: Mark (dec.), Renee, Teri. BS, Northwestern U., 1944, M in Mgmt., 1979. Tchr. history Evanston Township HS, Ill., 1946; tchr. social studies Mt. Prospect Jr. HS, Ill., 1947-48; dir. F&B Mfg. Co., Chgo., 1965—, CEO, chmn. bd., 1972—. Mem. Coun. of 100, Northwestern U. Mem. Northwestern U. Profl. Womens Assn., Nat. Assn. Investment Clubs, Zeta Tau Alpha. Republican. Lutheran. Avocations: opera, music, reading, investments, fishing. Office: F&B Mfg Co 5316 N 39th Ave Phoenix AZ 85063 E-mail: MiladaFAnderson@aol.com.

ANDERSON, MILTON ANDREW, chemical executive; b. Fond du Lac, Wis., Oct. 22, 1927; s. Andrew Andreas and Bertha Victoria (Almquist) A.; m. Dorothy Mae Verke, Nov. 27, 1954; children: Edward, Victoria. BS, U. Wis., Madison, 1954; MS in Mgmt., Lake Forest Grad. Sch. Mgmt., 1980. Registered profl. engr., Calif. Specification engr. Johns-Manville, Waukegan, Ill., 1955-59, supr., 1959-64, chemist, 1964-70, devel. engr., 1970-73; supr. Abbott Labs., North Chicago, 1973-74, quality engr., 1974-77, cons., auditing., 1977-81, mgr. rsch. auditing good lab. practices/good clin. practices, 1981-92; pres. Rsch. Compliance Svcs. Ltd., Lake Villa, Ill., 1992—. Author: GLP Quality Audit Manual, 1987, 3rd edit., 2000, GLP Essentials, 1995, 2d edit., 2002. Pres. Millburn Elem. Sch. Bd., 1971-73. Lt. naval aviator, 1948-52. Mem. Soc. Quality Assurance, Am. Soc.. for Quality Control (chmn. Northea. Ill. sect. 1980-82, sect. bd. dirs. 1982—). Republican. Home and Office: Rsch Compliance Svcs Ltd 19176 W Grass Lake Rd Lake Villa IL 60046-9242 E-mail: miltseen@aol.com.

ANDERSON, MONICA LUFFMAN, school librarian, educator, real estate broker; b. Ramsgate, Kent, U.K., Sept. 28, 1914; arrived in U.S., 1952; d. Percy Victor Luffman and Rosalind Dismorr; m. Howard Richmond Anderson, Dec. 22, 1951 (dec.); children: Monica Jane, James Stewart. BA in English with honors, London U., 1936; MS in Libr. Sci., Simmons Coll., 1968; EdM in Ednl. Media, Boston U., 1970. Evacuation officer London Borough of Acton, 1940—41; dir. Coun. for Edn. in World Citizenship, London, 1941—47; from asst. to head of sect. with diplomatic status UNESCO, Paris, 1947—50; H.S. libr. Holliston, Mass., 1968—70; coord. libr. svcs. Lincoln-Sudbury (Mass.) Regional H.S., 1970—81; real estate broker Coldwell Banker Residential Brokerage, Wayland, Mass., 1982—. Author brochures. Troop leader Girl Scouts Am., Weston, Mass., 1963—65; tutor in English Laotian Refugees, Weston, Mass., 1981—82, Literacy Unltd., Framingham, Mass., 1998—. Democrat. Avocations: gardening, reading, Boston Annual Walk for Hunger. Home: 40 Arrowhead Rd Weston MA 02493 Office: Coldwell Banker Resdl Brokerage 311 Boston Post Rd Wayland MA 01778

ANDERSON, MOSES B. bishop; b. Selma, Ala., Sept. 9, 1928; Student, St. Michael's Coll., St. Edmunds Sem., U. Legon, Ghana. Ordained priest Roman Cath. Ch., 1958. Ordained aux. bisop, Detroit; titular bishop of Vatarba, 1983; also aux. bishop of Detroit. Office: Diocese of Detroit 1234 Washington Blvd Detroit MI 48226-1825*

ANDERSON, N. C. writer, artist; b. Des Moines, Iowa; d. Donald Jay Canfield and Elsie Marie Johnson; m. Lowell Wayne Anderson, Sept. 14, 1957; 7 children. LPN, Ankey, Iowa. Nursing asst. Meth. Hosp., Des Moines, 0197—1974; LPN Luth. Hosp., Des Moines, 1978—79; artist commn. pvt., Iowa-Calif., 1975—; author Romance for the Old, 1999—2001, Pub. Am., 2002—. Author: Fixation (Eppie award, 2000). Mem.: Sisters in Corme, Romance Writers of Am., Electronically Publ. Internet Connection.

ANDERSON, N. CHRISTIAN, III, newspaper publisher; b. Montpelier, Idaho, Aug. 4, 1950; s. Nelson C. and Esther Barbara Anderson; m. Sara Ann Coffenberry, Dec. 11, 1971 (div.); children: Ryan, Erica; m. Aletha Ann Yurewicz, May 3, 1986; children: Paul, Amanda. BA in Liberal Studies with honors, Ore. State U., 1972. From asst. city editor to city editor Albany (Oreg.) Democrat-Herald, 1972—75; mng. editor Walla Walla (Wash.) Union Bulletin, 1975—77; assoc. mng. editor Seattle Times, 1977—80; from editor to exec. v.p., assoc. publisher The Orange County Register, Santa Ana, Calif., 1980—94; pub. Gazette Telegraph, Colorado Springs, 1994—98; pub., CEO, Orange County Register, Santa Ana, 1999—; sr. v.p. Freedom Comm., Inc., 1999—. Instr. Calif. State U., Fullerton, 1983, Fullerton, 87; Pulitzer Prize juror, 87, 88, 96; exec. editor Freedom Newspapers, Inc., Irvine, Calif., 1990—94; exec. v.p., CEO Golden West Publ., Irvine, 1991—94; mem. adv. bd. Poynter Inst. for Media Studies, St. Petersburg, Fla., 1994—99, also past chmn. adv. bd.; former chmn. bd. dirs. New Directions for News, newspaper think tank; mem. nominating com. AP; bd. dirs. Robert C. Maynard Inst. for Journalism Edn. Chmn. Orange County Bus. Com. for Arts; past mem., bd. dirs. Calif. First Amendment Coalition; bd. dirs. Santa Ana Rotary Found., 1984, Colorado Springs Fine Arts Ctr., 1994—98, Colorado Springs Non-Profit Ctr., 1994—98, Colorado Springs Sports Corp., 1994—98, Pike's Peak United Way, 1994—98, South Coast Repertory, Econ. Devel. Corp., Colorado Springs, chmn. bd., 1996. Named Nat. Newspaper Editor of Yr., 1989, Calif. Newspaper Exec. of Yr., Calif. Press Assn., 1993; recipient George D. Beveridge award, Nat. Press Found., 1989. Mem.: Calif. Soc. Newspaper Editors (founder, former bd. dirs. and pres.), Soc. Newspaper Design (co-founder), Am. Soc. Newspaper Editors (bd. dirs. 1996, treas. 1996, sec. 1997, v.p. 1998, pres. 1999). Office: Orange County Register 625 N Grand Ave Santa Ana CA 92701-4347

ANDERSON, NANCI LOUISE, computer analyst; b. Lynchburg, Va., Sept. 21, 1944; d. Ashby Littleton and Louise Elvin (Kirby) Marsh; 1 child, Toni Lynn Nelson. AAS in Computer Sci., Ctrl. Tex. Coll., 1983, AAS in Microcomputer Tech., 1985, BA Computer Programming, 2001. Real estate salesperson Blake Isley Real Estate, Lynchburg, Va., 1974; sec. U.S. Army, Germany, 1975-80; office mgr. Am. Solar Energy Soc., Killeen, Tex., 1981-82; programmer BDM, West Fort Hood, Tex., 1982-87; analyst, programmer PRC, Inc., West Fort Hood, Tex., 1987—96; sys. mgr. Maden Tech Consulting, 1996—. Mem. Clipper User's Group. Avocations: reading, swimming, horseback riding, walking. Home: 1202 Royal Crest Dr Killeen TX 76549-1071 Office: Maden Tech Cons USA OTC Network Ops Ctr Fort Hood TX 76544

ANDERSON, NANCY DIXON, librarian; b. Clarkesville, Ga., Oct. 7, 1938; d. Sherman Allen and Willie Mae (Black) Dixon; m. David Morris Anderson, Nov. 23, 1958 (div. June 1978); children: Wendy, Laurie, David Jr. BS in Mid. Grades Edn., Brenau Coll., 1981; MEd in Ednl. Media, U. Ga., 1985. Asst. prof. humanities, libr. Brenau Coll., Gainesville, Ga., 1979-87; also acad. tutor Learning Disability Ctr., 1985-87; head libr. Hightower Libr. Gordon Coll., Barnesville, Ga., 1987—. Children's ch. dir. 1st Presbyn. Ch., Gainesville, 1983-87; v.p. Friends of Libr., Barnesville/Lamar County, 1991; pres. Newcomers Club, Gainesville, 1974, Phoenix Soc., Ga. Fedn. Women's Club, Gainesville, 1978; pub. chmn. Barnesville Women's League, 1992-94; pres. Barnesville Garden Club, 1992; mem. Community Svcs. Bd., Barnesville, 1994—. Mem. Ga. Libr. Assn., Ctr. Ga. Associated Librs. Consortium (pres. 1992-93). Avocations: gardening, travel, reading. Home: 236 Harrell Cir Barnesville GA 30204-1751 Office: Gordon Coll Hightower Libr 419 College Dr Barnesville GA 30204-1746

ANDERSON, NED, SR., Apache tribal chairman; b. Bylas, Ariz., Jan. 18, 1943; s. Paul and Maggie (Rope) Anderson; m. Dalphina Hinton; children: Therese Kay, Linette Mae, Magdalene Gail, Ned, Sean. AA, Ea. Ariz. Coll., 1964, AAS in Computer Sci., 1989; BS, U Ariz., 1967, JD, 1973. Field dir. Nat. Study Indian Edn. dept. anthropology U. Ariz., Tucson, 1968-70, dir. Jojoba Project, Office of Arid Land Studies, 1973-76; tech. asst. Project Head Start Ariz. State U., Tempe, 1970; ethnographer Smithsonian Instn., Washington, 1970-73; with Jojoba devel. project San Carlos (Ariz.) Apache Tribe, 1976 78, tribal councilman, 1976-78, 93-98, tribal chmn., 1978-86, gen. mgr. spl. housing projects, 1991-99, coord. Ctrl. Ariz. project, 1999—. Contbr. articles to profl. jours. Mem. affirmative action com. City of Tucson, 1975—76; mem. study panel NAS, 1975—76; mem. supervisory bd. Ariz. Justice Planning Commn., 1978; mem. county govt. study commn. State of Ariz., 1981—84; mem. reinvention mgmt. lab. workgroup Nat. Housing Improvement Program, 1995—96; mem. Indian adv. bd. Intergovernmental Pers. Program, 1978; mem. adv. bd. Am. Indian Registry Performing Arts, 1985, San Carlos Fish and Game Commn., 1975, chmn., 1976; pres. Intertribal Coun. Ariz., 1979—85, 1992; pres. bd. dirs. Ft. Thomas HS Unified Dist., 1977, clk., 1987, clk. bd. dirs., 1989; bd. dirs. Southwestern Indian Devel., Inc., 1971, Indian Enterprise Devel. Corp., 1976—78, San Carlos Lake Devel., 1994—98, We. Apache Constrn. Co., 1994—98, Apache Gold Resort Pub. Authority, 1997—99, vice chmn., acting chmn., 2002—03; mem. adv. bd. Gila Pueblo CC ext. Ea. Ariz. Coll., 1979, Indian Edn., Ariz. State U., Tempe, 1978—86, U. Ariz., Tucson, 1978—86; trustee Bacone Coll. Recipient Outstanding CC Alumni award, Ariz. CC Bd./Ea. Ariz. Coll., 1982, Outstanding Coop. award, U.S. Secret Svc., 1984, Univ. Rels. award, AT&T, 1989; A. T. Anderson Meml. scholar, 1989. Mem.: Ariz. Acad., Globe C. of C., Nat. Tribal Chmn.'s Assn. (mem. bd. edn., mem. adv. bd. 1978—86), Phi Theta Kappa.

ANDERSON, ODIN WALDEMAR, sociologist, educator; b. Mpls., July 5, 1914; s. Edwin and Anna (Ormbreck) A.; m. Helen Hay, June 24, 1939; children: Kristin Alice, Thor Edwin. BA, U. Wis., 1937, MA, 1938; BA in L.S., U. Mich., 1940, PhD, 1948; PhD (hon.), U. Uppsala, Sweden, 1977. Instr., U. Mich. Sch. Pub. Health, 1944-49; assoc. prof. dept. clin. preventive medicine, med. faculty U. Western Ont., London, 1949-52; research dir. Health Info. Found., N.Y.C., 1952-62, Health Info. Found., U. Chgo., 1962-64, Ctr. Health Adminstrn. Studies, 1964-66, assoc. dir., 1966-72, dir., 1972-80, assoc. prof. sociology, dept. sociology and Grad. Sch. Bus., 1962-64, prof., 1964-80, prof. emeritus, 1980—; prof. sociology U. Wis.-Madison, 1980—, prof. emeritus, 1995—. Mem. rsch. com. Nat. Tb Assn., 1959-64, U.S. Nat. Com. Vital and Health Stats., 1959-63; vis. prof. Inst. Sociology and Polit. Sci. U. Trondheim, Norway, 1992. Author: (with Jacob J. Feldman) Family Medical Care and Voluntary Health Insurance, 1956, (with others) Family Medical Care and Health Insurance, 1963, (with Ronald Andersen) A Decade of Health Services: Social Survey Trends in Use and Expenditures, 1968, The Uneasy Equilibrium: Private and Public Financing of Health Services in the U.S., 1875-1965, 1968, Health Care: Can There Be Equity? The United States, Sweden, and England, 1972, The American Health Services, a Growth Enterprise Since 1875, 2nd edit., 1985, (with others) HMO Development: Patterns and Prospects, 1985, The Health Services Continuum in Democratic States: An Inquiry into Solvable Problems, 1989, Health Services as a Growth Enterprise in the United States Since 1875, 1990, The Evolution of Health Services Research: Personal Reflections on Applied Social Sciences, 1991; editor, translator: Sexual Customs in Rural Norway, 1993. Named Disting. Health Services Researcher, Assn. Health Services Research, 1985, One of Ten Most Admired Sr. Citizens Wis. for 1988 Wis. State Fair. Fellow Am. Sociol. Assn. (past chmn. sect. med. sociology, Disting. Med. Sociologist sect. med. sociology 1980), Am. Pub. Health Assn., Am. Coll. Hosp. Adminstrs. (hon.), AAAS, Assn. Health Svcs. Rsch.; mem. Inst. Medicine of Nat. Acad. Sci.

ANDERSON, O(RVIL) ROGER, biology educator, marine biology and protozoology researcher; b. East St. Louis, Ill., Aug. 4, 1937; s. Orvil Noel and Marie Elizabeth (Diekemper) A. BA, Washington U., St. Louis, 1959, MA, 1961, EdD, 1964. Asst. prof. sci. Columbia U. Tchrs. Coll., N.Y.C., 1964-67, assoc. prof., 1968-70, prof., 1971—, chmn. math., sci. and tech. dept., 2001—; faculty mem. at large Grad. Sch. Arts and Scis. Columbia U., N.Y.C., 1994—; rsch. assoc. Lamont-Doherty Obs., Palisades, N.Y., 1965-70, sr. rsch. scientist, 1971—; vis. prof. Tübingen (Germany) U., 1979, 84, 86. Vis. res. scientist Bermuda Biol. Station, 1970, 75, 76, 84, Bellairs Rsch. Inst., Barbados,

1972-85, 87-95, Caribbean Marine Biol. Inst., Curacao, 1980-82, Spanish Marine Biol. Inst., Tenerife, 1979, Freshwater Biol. Inst., Cumbria, Eng., 1994, Marine Biology Rsch. Inst., Isle of Cumbrae, Scotland, 1995-96; assoc. scientist in edn. Am. Mus. Natural History, N.Y.C., 1995-96. Author: Quantitative Analysis of Stucture in Teaching, 1971, Teaching Modern Ideas of Biology, 1972, The Experience of Science, 1976, Radiolaria, 1983, Protozoology: Ecology, Physiology, Life History, 1988, Modern Planktonic Foraminifera, 1989, Teaching and Learning of Biology in the United States; Second International Assessment of Biological Achievement, 1990; editor Jour. Rsch. in Sci. Teaching, 1970-75, Cytomechanics, 1987, The Biology of Foraminfera, 1991, Explore the World Using Protozoa, 1997; assoc. editor Jour. Protozoology, 1988—; mem. editorial bd. Marine Microbial Food Webs, 1987—, American Type Culture Collection (Scientific Adv. Bd. Mem., 2000—); contbr. articles to profl. jours. Chmn. NSF vis. com. Ariz. State U., 1995-00. Recipient Bermuda Biol. Sta. award for Marine Sci. Rsch., 1976, medal for Outstanding Rsch., Paleontol. Soc. Japan, 1999; NSF grantee, 1972—; Cocconeis andersonii species named in his honor for contbns. to symbiosis rsch., 1989. Fellow AAAS, Cushman Found. for Foraminiferal Rsch.; mem. NSTA (bd. dirs. 1976-77), Soc. Protozoologists (pres. 1994), Am. Soc. Limnology and Oceanography, Nat. Assn. for Rsch. in Sci. Tchg. (pres. 1976-77), Freshwater Biol. Assn. (U.K.), Black Rock Forest Consortium (exec. bd. dirs. 1998-99), Sigma Xi (internat. com. 1992-96, sec. Kappa chpt. 1987-91, pres.-elect 1992-93, pres. 1993-95). Home: 501 W 120th St New York NY 10027-6622 Office: Columbia U Tchrs Coll 525 W 120th St New York NY 10027-6625 E-mail: ora@ldeo.columbia.edu.

ANDERSON, OWEN RAYMOND, scientific and educational organization executive; b. Chestertown, Md., Aug. 27, 1919; s. Owen Raymond and Ida Frances (Jenkins) A.; m. Ida Lois Pritts, June 8, 1946; children: Penny Pritts, Jeri Alyce. BA, Washington Coll., 1940. Tchr. Garrett County Bd. Edn., Kitzmiller, Md., 1940-41, 1946; with Nat. Geog. Soc., Washington, 1946—, div. supr., 1950, adminstrv. asst., 1952-61, asst. sec., 1961-66, assoc. sec., 1966-76, v.p., sec., 1976-80, exec. v.p., 1980-91, trustee, 1981-95, vice chmn. bd., 1984-95, trustee emeritus, 1995—. Served to capt. U.S. Army, 1941-46, 50-52, ETO, Korea. Decorated Bronze Star, Purple Heart, Combat Infantry badge; recipient Alumni Citation award Washington Coll., 1981, Grosvenor medal Nat. Geog. Soc., 1991. Mem. Am. Legion, Lambda Chi Alpha. Clubs: Alfalfa. Methodist. Home: Carriage Hill of Bethesda #222 5215 Cedar Ln North Bethesda MD 20852

ANDERSON, PARKER LYNN, editorial columnist, playwright; b. Wickenburg, Ariz., Apr. 19, 1964; s. Harry Milton and Darla Raejean (Hangartner) A. Mem. prodn. com. Prescott (Ariz.) Fine Arts Assn., 1993-95, 98—, adv. mem., 1987—; columnist, theatre critic The Prescott News, 1995-96; with Cath. Social Svc. of Yavapai, 1983—. Mem. adv. com. The Blue Rose Theatre Co., Prescott, 1994—; guest on talk shows Sta. KUSK-TV, 1991—. Author: (plays) The Startled Cowboys, 1991, Voices From the Past, 1995, The Sleeping Toad, 1997, Virgil Earp, 1998, Until the Last Dog is Hung, 2000, Murder Dismissed, 2001; co-author: (plays) Lady with a Gun (with Jody Drake), 2002; freelance guest columnist and letters of comment in numerous Ariz. publs., 1990—. Home: PO Box 1285 Prescott AZ 86302-1285 E-mail: parkerr86302@yahoo.com.

ANDERSON, PATRICIA SUE, writer; b. San Springs, Okla., July 14, 1940; d. John Monroe and Annabelle A. BA in Psychology, Okla. State U., 1963. Co-owner, CEO River's West Prodns. CEO River's Bend Literary Agy., Cleveland, Okla., 1984-99. Author: Organizational Handbook, 1985, Campaign Organization, 1990, Getting Women to Participate, 1991; (screenplays) Nightmares Do Come True, Desert Conspiracy, Mriqtrishna; (novels) A Cold Wind in August, Surviving Toxic Parents. Democrat. Methodist. Home and Office: RR 1 Box 272 Cleveland OK 74020-9723 E-mail: pande86245@aol.com.

ANDERSON, PATRICIA COULTER, paralegal; b. Washington, Sept. 5, 1965; d. John Kendall and Clare Mary (O'Connor) C.; m. Darrell W. Anderson. AAS summa cum laude, J. Sargeant Reynolds Coll., 1993; BA, William and Mary Coll., 1987. Litigation paralegal Williams, Mullen, Christian and Dobbins, Richmond, Va., 1990-91; paralegal Russell, Cantor, Arkema & Edmonds, P.C., Richmond, 1991-95; litigation paralegal Duane and Shannon, Richmond, 1995-97; sr. legal asst. McGuireWoods LLP, Richmond, 1997—. Team photographer Richmond Renegades Ice Hockey Team. Paralegal vol. Ctrl. Va. Legal Aid Soc., 1991—. Maj. USAR, 1987—. Maj. USAR, 1987—. Mem.: Nat. Assn. Legal Assts. (Affiliates award 2000, 2002), Richmond Assn. Legal Assts. (sec. 1994, 1995, dir. 1995—97, 2d v.p. 1998, pres. 1999, Nat. Assn. Legal Assts. liaison 2000—03, Outstanding Legal Asst. of Yr. 2001), Phi Theta Kappa. Democrat. Avocations: ice hockey, music, photography. Home: 7062 River Pine Ct Mechanicsville VA 23111-5242 Office: McGuireWoods LLP 901 E Cary St Richmond VA 23219-4057 E-mail: panderson@mcguirewoods.com.

ANDERSON, PATRICIA FRANCIS, librarian; b. Ames, Iowa, Oct. 20, 1956; d. Arthur Raymond and Rose Ann (Cooper) Anderson; m. Patrick Henry Veninga, Apr. 27, 1991 (div. 2002); children: Zera Esther Ruth Anderson, Luke Robert Morris Veninga. BS, Iowa State U., 1979; M in Info. and Libr. Sci., U. Mich., 1987. Media libr. Galter Health Sci. Libr. Northwestern U., Chgo., 1987—88; libr. assoc. Engring Librs. U. Mich., Ann Arbor, 1985-87, head libr. Dentistry Libr., 1998—. Cons. NIH Consensus Devel. Conf. on Diagnosis and Mgmt. of Dental Caries Throughout Life, 2001; program planning com. NIH Working Conf. on Dental Informatics and Dental Rsch., 2003. Author: The Medical Library Encyclopedic Guide to Searching and Finding Health Information on the Web, 2004. Chairperson for design working group HealthWeb, 1994—2001; Editor HealthWeb: Dentistry, 1998—. Recipient Wallace H. Bonk award U. Mich., 1987, Beta Phi Mu Essay award, 1987. Mem. Am. Soc. for Info. Sci. (Nat. Student Paper award 1986), Health Scis. Comms. Assn. (biomed. librs. interest group sec. 1992-93), Med. Libr. Assn. (sec., treas. dental sect. 2000-03, centennial exhibit coord. ednl. media and techs. sect., Rittenhouse award 1989), Feminist Writers Guild (bd. dirs. 1990-93, newsletter editor 1990-94). Democrat. Roman Catholic. Avocations: poetry, music composition, fiber art, jewelry making. Office: Univ of Mich Dentistry Libr 1100 Dental Bldg Ann Arbor MI 48109-1078

ANDERSON, PAUL SCOTT, architect; b. L.A., Oct. 28, 1958; s. Gordon John and Ruth Ellen Anderson; m. Hai Rui Wu, May 28, 1999; 1 child, Kalli Bryce. BArch, Calif. Poly. State U., 1984. Lic. arch., Calif. Pvt. practice, La Quinta, Calif., 1991—98; prin. Shenzhen (China) Ocean Pearl Co. Ltd./Mission Hills Group; sr. arch. hotels Disneyland Resort Hotels, Anaheim, Calif., 1998—; assoc., mng. architect Marsh and Assoc., Inc., Newport Beach, Calif., 2001—. Mem. design rev. bd. City of La Quinta, 1991-94, mem. planning commn., 1994-96. Recipient award Desert Beautiful, Palm Desert, Calif., 1986, Award Mention Bien Ecoles D'art Americaines Fontainbleau, 1983. Mem. AIA (bd. dirs. Calif. Desert chpt. 1989-90, assoc. dir. South Calif. Coun. 1987, bd. dirs. Monterey Bay chpt. 1987). Avocations: golf, tennis, photography, painting, percussion. Office: Marsh and Assoc Inc 620 Newport Ctr Dr # 120 Newport Beach CA 92660

ANDERSON, PAUL HOLDEN, state supreme court justice; b. May 14, 1943; m. Janice M. Anderson; 2 children. BA cum laude, Macalester Coll., 1965; JD, U. Minn., 1968. Atty. Vols. in Svc. to Am., 1968—69; spl. asst. atty. gen. criminal divsn. dept. pub. safety Office Minn. Atty. Gen., 1970—71; assoc., ptnr. LeVander, Gillen & Miller, South St. Paul, Minn., 1971—92; chief judge Minn. Ct. Appeals, 1992—94; assoc. justice Minn. Supreme Ct., 1994—. Mem. PER coms. Ind. Sch. Dist. 199, 1982—84, chmn. cmty. svcs. adv. com., bd. dirs., chmn. bd.; deacon, ruling elder, clk. of session House of Hope Presbyn. Ch., St. Paul. Mem.: Dakota County Bar Assn. (bd. dirs., pres.), South St. Paul/Inver Grove Heights C. of C. (bd. dirs., exec. com.). Avocations: tennis, gourmet cooking, bike riding. Office: Minn Supreme Court 425 Saint Paul MN 55155-0001 Fax: 651-282-5115. E-mail: paul.anderson@courts.state.mn.us.

ANDERSON, PAUL IRVING, management executive; b. Portland, Oreg., Mar. 23, 1935; s. William F. and Ruth M. (Sundquist) A.; m. Lorraine A. Franz, Nov. 21, 1959; children: Todd, Susan, Cheryl, Cynthia. BS, Oreg. State U., 1956. Various positions in mktg., sales and engring. mgmt. 3M Co., St. Paul and Boston, 1956-74, gen. mgr. Brussels, Belgium, 1974-77, group bus. planning dir. St. Paul, 1977-79; sr. v.p., gen. mgr. Rayovac Corp., Madison, Wis., 1979-82; pres. Anderson Cons. Co., Madison, 1982-83; div. v.p. RCA Corp., Indpls., 1983-84; pres. Anderson & Assocs., La Costa, Calif., 1984-87; pres., CEO Electro-Imaging Advisors, Inc., La Jolla, Calif., 1987-93; CEO Strategic Catalysts Inc., La Jolla, Calif., 1993—. Mem. Am. Mgmt. Assn., Tau Beta Pi, Pi Tau Sigma, Sigma Tau Clubs: Columbia (Indpls.); Madison; Nakoma Golf (Madison). Republican. Presbyterian. Home: 6418 Cayenne Ln Carlsbad CA 92009-4301

ANDERSON, PAUL MAURICE, electrical engineering educator, researcher, consultant; b. Des Moines, Jan. 22, 1926; s. Neil W. and Buena Vista (Thompson) A.; m. Virginia Ann Worswick, July 8, 1950; children: William, Mark, James, Thomas. BSEE, Iowa State U., 1949, MSEE, 1958, PhD in Elec. Engring., 1961. Registered profl. elec. engr., Ariz., Calif., Iowa, Guam; registered control sys. engr., Calif. Elec. engr. Iowa Pub. Service Co., Sioux City, 1949-55; prof. elec. engring. Iowa State U., Ames, 1955-75; program mgr. Electric Power Research Inst., Palo Alto, Calif., 1975-78; pres., prin. engr. Power Math Assocs. Inc., Palo Alto, Tempe, Del Mar and San Diego, 1978-99; prof. elec. engring. Ariz. State U., Tempe, 1980-84. Schweitzer vis. prof. elec. engring.97 Wash. State U., 1996. Author: Analysis of Faulted Power Systems, 1973; (with others) Power System Control and Stability, 1977, 3d edit., 2003, Subsynchronous Resonance in Power Systems, 1990, Series Compensation of Power Systems, 1996, Power System Protection, 1999; cons. editor: Ency. Sci. and Tech., 1979-92; contbr. articles to profl. jours. NSF faculty fellow, 1960-61; recipient Faculty citation Iowa State U. Alumni Assn., 1973, Profl. Achievement citation Iowa State U., 1981 Fellow IEEE (life mem., chmn. Iowa sect. 1959-60), Conf. Internat. des Grands Reseaux Electriques, Sigma Xi, Phi Kappa Phi, Eta Kappa Nu, Pi Mu Epsilon. Republican. Home: 13335 Roxton Cir San Diego CA 92130-1841 E-mail: p.anderson@ieee.org.

ANDERSON, PAUL NATHANIEL, oncologist, educator; b. Omaha, May 30, 1937; s. Nels Paul E. and Doris Marie (Chesnut) A.; m. Dee Ann Hipps, June 27, 1965; children: Mary Kathleen, Anne Christen. BA, U. Colo., 1959, MD, 1963. Diplomate Am. Bd. Internal Medicine, Am. Bd. Med. Mgmt., Am. Bd. Med. Oncology. Intern Johns Hopkins Hosp., Balt., 1963-64, resident in internal medicine, 1964-65, fellow in oncology, 1970-72; rsch. assoc., staff assoc. NIH, Bethesda, Md., 1965-70; asst. prof. medicine, oncology Johns Hopkins U. Sch. Medicine, 1972-76; attending physician Balt. City Hosps., Johns Hopkins Hosp., 1972-76; dir. dept. med. oncology Penrose Cancer Hosp., Colorado Springs, Colo., 1976-86; clin. asst. prof. dept. medicine Colo. Sch. Medicine, 1976-90, clin. assoc. prof., 1990—. Dir. Penrose Cancer Hosp., 1979-86, chief dept. medicine, 1985-86; founding dir. Cancer Ctr. of Colorado Springs, 1986-95, Pikes Peak Forum for Health Care Ethics, 1996—, Rocky Mountain Cancer Ctr., Colorado Springs, 1995—; med. dir. So. Colo. Cancer Program, 1979-86; pres., chmn. bd. dirs. Preferred Physicians, Inc., 1986-92; mem. Colo. Found. for Med. Care Health Stds. Com., 1985, sec., exec. com., 1990, bd. dirs., pres., 1992-93; mem., chmn. treatment com. Colo. Cancer Control and Rsch. Panel, 1980-83; prin. investigator Cancer Info. Svc. of Colo., 1981-87; pres., founder Timberline Med. Assocs., 1986-87, Oncology Mgmt. Network, Inc., 1985-95. Editor Advances in Cancer Control; editl. bd. Jour. Cancer Program Mgmt., 1987-92, Health Care Mgmt. Rev., 1988—; contbr. articles to med. jours. Mem. Colo. Gov.'s Rocky Flats Employee Health Assessment Group, 1983-84; mem. Gov.'s Breast Cancer Control Commn. Colo., 1984-89; founder, dir. So. Colo. AIDS project, 1986-91; mem. adv. bd. Colo. State Bd. Health Tumor Registry, 1984-87; chmn. bd. dirs. Preferred Physicians, Inc., 1986-92; bd. dirs. Share Devel. Co. of Colo. Share Health Plan of Colo., 1986-90, vice chmn., 1989-91; bd. dirs., chmn. Preferred Health Care, Inc., 1991-92; mem. health care stds. com., trustee colo. Found. for Med. Care (PRO); mem. nat. bd. med. dirs. Fox Chase Cancer Ctr. Network, Phila., 1987-89; mem. tech. expert panel Harvard Resource-Based Relative Value Scale Study for Hematology/Oncology, 1991-92. With USPHS, 1965-70. Mem. AMA (mem. practice parameters forum 1989-97, adv. com. to HCFA on uniform clin. data set), AAAS, Am. Coll. Forensic Examiners, Am. Soc. Clin. Oncology (chmn. subcom. on oncology clin. practice stds., mem. clin. practice com., rep. to AMA 1991—, mem. healthcare svcs. rsch. com., chmn. clin. guidelines subcom. 1993—), Am. Assn. Cancer Rsch., Am. Assn. Cancer Insts. (liaison mem. bd. trustees 1980-82), Am. Coll. Physician Execs., Am. Hospice Assn., Am. Soc. Internal Medicine, Nat. Cancer Inst. (com. for cmty. hosp. oncology program evaluation 1982-83), Colo. Soc. Internal Medicine, Assn. Cmty. Cancer Ctrs. (chmn. membership com. 1980, chmn. clin. rsch. com. 1983-85, sec. 1983-84, pres.-elect 1984-85, pres. 1986-87, trustee 1981-88), N.Y. Acad. Scis., Johns Hopkins Med. Soc., Colo. Med. Soc., Am. Mgmt. Assn., Am. Assn. Profl. Cons., Am. Soc. Quality, Am. Acad. Med. Dirs., Am. Coll. Physician Execs., El Paso County Med. Soc., Rocky Mountain Oncology Soc. (chmn. clin. practice com. 1989-94, pres.-elect 1990, pres. 1993-95), Acad. Hospice Physicians, Coalition for Cancer, Colorado Springs Clin. Club, Alpha Omega Alpha. Office: Rocky Mountain Cancer Ctr 3027 North Circle Dr Colorado Springs CO 80909 also: 32 Sanford Rd Colorado Springs CO 80906-4233

ANDERSON, PAUL NATHANIEL, III, (TRIP ANDERSON), visual communications consultant; b. Dunkirk, N.Y., Sept. 24, 1952; s. Paul Nathaniel and Ann Marie (Paquin) Anderson; m. Susan Keefe, July 5, 1975 (div. Apr. 2001); children: Brian Joseph, Michael Paul. BA in Fine Arts cum laude, Harvard U., 1975; postgrad., Am. Mgmt. Assn. Extension Inst, 1985—91. Model maker Benjamin Thompson & Assoc.s Inc., Cambridge, Mass., 1974-75, dir. model shop, 1975-79; CEO, founder Trip Tech Models, Inc., Waltham, Mass., 1977-91; prin., founder Innoventive Design Assocs., 1991—; dir. rapid visualization The Trumbull Co., 1991-92; sr. project mgr. Jack Morton Worldwide, 1992—2001; bus. mgr. Howell Design & Bldg., 2002—; mgr. strategic alliances The Taylor Group, 2002. Instr. Boston Archtl. Ctr., 1977—80; mem. adv. com. N. Bennett St. Sch., Boston, 1981—82, Bemidji (Minn.) State U., 1985—91, Northeastern Wis. Tech. Coll., Green Bay, 1987—91; lectr. R.I. Sch. Design, 1986—91; lectr. in field. Contbr. articles on model making and audio-visual prodn. to profl. jours.; contbg. editor to newsletter Am. Engring. Model Soc., guest PBS-TV series, Adventures in Scale Modeling, 1988-91. Mem. adv. com. Weston Wing Child Care, Mass., 1985; mem. Weston Artist Assn., 1984-91, Mass. Audubon Soc., Lincoln, 1984-95. Mem. Am. Engring. Model Soc. (exec. sec. 1987-88, pres. 1989-92, chmn. edn. com. 1987-91, chmn. scholarship fund 1988, seminar chmn. 1991); Am. Mgmt. Assn., Soc. Mktg. Profl. Svcs. (membership com., 1987-92), Urban Land Inst. (assoc. 1988-92), Boston Soc. Architects (affiliate), Affiliated Industries of Mass., Nat. Trust for Hist. Preservation, Harvard Varsity Club (Cambridge, Mass.), Eastman Golf Club. Avocations: running, hiking, canoeing, skiing, golf. Home and Office: P O Box 330 60 Pintail Knob Grantham NH 03753

ANDERSON, PAUL STEWART, lawyer; b. Aug. 19, 1952; s. Robert Garfield and Ruth Helen (Hjorth) A.; m. Linda Joy Quinn, Sept. 29, 1984. BA, Wake Forest U., 1974; JD, Ill. Inst. Tech.-Chgo. Kent Law Sch., 1978; cert. in European Programs (hon.), U. Pacific, Sacramento and Salzburg, Austria, 1978. Bar: Ill. 1979, U.S. Ct. Appeals (7th cir.) 1979, U.S. Ct. Appeals (D.C. cir.) 1979, U.S. Ct. Internat. Trade 1979. Intern Mannheimer & Zetterlof, Gothenburg, Sweden, 1978; assoc. Barnes, Richardson & Colburn, Chgo., 1979-81; ptnr. Sonnenberg & Anderson, Chgo., 1981—. Supporting mem. Union League Boys' Club, Chgo., 1984. Mem. ABA, Ill. Bar Assn., Chgo. Bar Assn. (customs law com. 1981—, vice chmn. 1986-87, chmn. 1987-88), Mid.-Am. Swedish Trade Assn. (bd. dir. 1982-86), Norwegian-Am. C. of C. (v.p. 1984, pres. 1986—), Can. of Chgo. Club (bd. dir. 1984—, v.p. 1986—, Hon. consul gen. for Norway to Chgo. and Ill. 2000—). Methodist. Address: Sonnenberg & Anderson Atty At Law 333 W Wacker Dr Ste 2070 Chicago IL 60606-1293 E-mail: psa@sonnander.com.

ANDERSON, PETER D. pharmacist, forensic scientist; b. Stoughton, Mass. BS in Pharmacy, U. R.I., 1989, PharmD, 1998. Diplomate Am. Bd. Forensic Examiners; cert. psychiat. pharmacist Bd. Pharm. Spltys. Lab. asst. U. R.I., Kingston, 1988-89; staff pharmacist Mass. Eye & Ear Infirmary, Boston, 1991-2000; clin. pharmacist pvt. practice, Boston, 1994—, forensic pharmacist, 1995—; criteria mgr., Drug Utilization Rev. Program, U. Mass. Med. Sch., 1999-2000; clin. pharmacist Mass. Eye & Ear Infirmary, 2000-2001, McKesson Med. Mgmt., Inc., Taunton, Mass., 2001—; clin. instr. in psychiatry Harvard Med. Sch., Boston. Clin. asst. prof. Northeastern U. Sch. Pharmacy, Boston, 2000—; adj. instr. med. imaging Bunker Hill C.C.; adj. assoc. prof. pharmacy U. R.I., RI, 2001—; clin. instr. psychiatry Harvard Med. Sch., Boston, 2003—; acting chmn. pharmacy and therapeutics com. Taunton (Mass.) State Hosp., 2002. *Dr. Anderson has spearheaded the development of forensic pharmacy as an organized specialty. He started a website devoted to forensic pharmacy in 1997. In June 2000, Dr. Anderson was Guest Editor for the Journal of Pharmacy Practice, for an issue devoted to forensics. He was appointed Director, Division of Pharmacology with the American College of Forensic Examiners, the world's largest forensic association. Prof. Anderson has been consulted on legal cases regarding worker's compensation, professional malpractice, sexual assault, drunk driving, and fraud. He was a contributing author to the textbook Drug Injury: Liability, Analysis and Prevention.* Biomed. comms. and informatics rev. sect. editor: Jour. Pharmacy Practice, 2000—; contbg. editor: The ADHD Challenge, 1997—2002. Chmn. rsch. steering com. Taunton State Hosp., Mass., 2001—. Grantee Am. Pharm. Assn. Found., Washington, 1994-95. Fellow: Am. Coll. Forensic Examiners (dir. divsn. of pharmacology 2003—), Am. Soc. Cons. Pharmacists; mem.: Mass. Tchrs. Assn., U. R.I. Emergency Med. Svcs. (vet. mem.), Nat. Space Soc., Mass. Pharmacists Assn., Coll. Psychiat. and Neurologic Pharmacists (founding mem.), Assn. Cert. Fraud Examiners (assoc.), Am. Coll. Clin. Pharmacology, Am. Acad. Clin. Toxicology, Am. Med. Writers Assn., Am. Coll. Clin. Pharmacy, Am. Soc. Health System Pharmacists, Am. Acad. Experts Traumatic Stress. Avocations: volleyball, space flight, jogging, computers. Home and Office: 1035 Southern Artery Apt 301 Quincy MA 02169-8304 Office: Taunton State Hosp PO Box 4007 Taunton MA 02780-0997 E-mail: PAnder7291@aol.com.

ANDERSON, PETER JOSEPH, lawyer; b. Camden, N.J., Mar. 15, 1951; s. Lester Ryan and Rose Helen; m. Sheila K.; children: Elizabeth Rose, Hannah Louise. BA, Dickinson Coll., 1972; JD, Dickinson Sch. of Law, 1975. Bar: Pa. 1975, Ga. 1978, U.S. Dist. Ct. (ea. dist.) Pa. 1978, U.S. Dist. Ct. (no. dist.) Ga. 1978, U.S. Ct. Appeals (11th cir.) 1978, U.S. Tax Ct. 1986, U.S. Supreme Ct. 1989. Dep. dist. atty. Dist. Attys. Office, Harrisburg, Pa., 1974-77; ptnr. Peterson, Dillard, Young, Self & Asselin, Atlanta, 1977-92, Sutherland, Asbill & Brennan, Atlanta, 1992—. Bd. dirs. CADEF-Childhood Autism Found., 1986—; chmn. bd. trustees The Paideia Sch., Atlanta, 1997-2000. Mem. ABA (subcom. securities litigation 1978—), State Bar Ga., Pa. Bar Assn., Atlanta Bar Assn. Republican. Roman Catholic. Home: 1503 Emory Rd NE Atlanta GA 30306-2429 Office: Sutherland Asbill & Brennan 999 Peachtree St NE Ste 2300 Atlanta GA 30309-3996

ANDERSON, PETER MACARTHUR, lawyer; b. New Castle, Ind., July 15, 1937; s. Earl Canute and Catherine Elizabeth (Schultz) A.; m. Ann Warren Gibson, Sept.1, 1962; children: David, Karen. AB, Dartmouth Coll., 1959; LLB, Stanford U., 1962. Bar: Calif. 1963, Wash. 1970. Assoc. O'Melveny & Myers, L.A., 1966-70, Bogle & Gates, Seattle, 1970-74, mem., 1974-99; ptnr. Preston Gates & Ellis, Seattle, 1999—2002, sr. counsel, 2003—. Co-chmn. equal employment law com. ABA, 1983-86. Mem. Ecumenical Commn. for Seattle Archdiocese, St. Petersburg-Seattle Sister Chs. Com. Capt. U.S. Army, 1963-65. Fellow Coll. Labor and Employment Lawyers; mem. Phi Beta Kappa. Roman Catholic. Home: 9200 SE 57th St Mercer Island WA 98040-5005 Office: Preston Gates & Ellis LLP 925 4th Ave Ste 2900 Seattle WA 98104-1158

ANDERSON, PHILIP SIDNEY, lawyer; b. Little Rock, May 9, 1935; s. Philip Sidney and Frances (Walt) Anderson; m. Rosemary Gill Wright, Sept. 26, 1959; children: Sidney Walt Kenyon, Philip Wright, Catherine Gill Askew. BA, LLB, U. Ark., 1959. Bar: Ark. 1960, U.S. Supreme Ct. 1966. Assoc. Wright, Lindsey & Jennings, Little Rock, 1960—65, ptnr., 1965—88, Williams & Anderson, Little Rock, 1988—. Lectr. Ark. Law Sch., 1963—66; mem. com. on jury instrns. Ark. Supreme Ct., 1962—97; mem. panel for the 8th cir. U.S. Cir. Judge Nominating Commn., 1978—79; mem. fed. adv. com. U.S. Ct. Appeals 8th cir., 1983—88, co-chmn., 1987—88; bd. dirs. WEHCO Media, Inc., Ark. Dem.-Gazette, Inc. Co-author: Arkansas Model Jury Instructions, 1965, 1974, 1989. Pres. Friends of Little Rock Pub. Libr., 1968—69, Little Rock Unltd. Progress, Inc., 1973—74; trustee Ctrl. Ark. Libr. Sys., 1981—87, pres., 1984; trustee George W. Donaghey Found., 1976—, pres., 1979—80; trustee Ctr. for Am. and Internat. Law, 1996—, Lawyers' Com. for Civil Rights Under Law, 2001—. 2d lt. U.S. Army, 1959—60. Fellow: ABA (chair ho. of dels. 1992—94, bd. govs. 1990—94, 1997—2000, pres. 1998—99), Ark. Bar Found. (pres. 1973—74), Am. Bar Found.; mem.: Am. Law Inst. (mem. coun. 1982—), Ark. Bar Assn. (spl. award meritorious svc.). Episcopalian. Home: 4716 Crestwood Dr Little Rock AR 72207-5436 Office: Williams & Anderson LLP 111 Center St Ste 2200 Little Rock AR 72201-4429 E-mail: psa@wiiiamsanderson.com.

ANDERSON, PHILIP VERNON, retired pastor; b. Tanzania, Aug. 29, 1928; came to U.S., 1941; s. George N. and Annette L. (Elmquist) A.; m. Joan Audrey Carlson, Sept. 15, 1951; children: Christine Packwood, Karen, Carl, Janice, Erik. AB, Augustana Coll., Rock Island, Ill.; MDiv, Luth. Sch. Chgo., 1953; postgrad., U. Chgo., 1960-62. Ordained to ministry, Luth. Ch., 1953. Pastor Faith Luth. Ch., Syosset, N.Y., 1953-60; chaplain Augustana Hosp., Chgo., 1962-64; pastor Augustana Luth. Ch., Chgo., 1964-70; Luth. campus pastor U. Chgo., Ill., 1964—70; dir. pastoral care Augustana Hosp., Chgo., 1970-89; pastor Nazareth Luth. Ch., Hazel Crest, Ill., 1989-90; chaplain Hospice Care/Chicagoland, Homewood, Ill., 1990-91; pastor Bethesda Luth. Ch., Chgo., 1990-97; bereavement dir. VITAS—Innovative Hospice Care, Homewood, 1991-94; mgr. bereavement svcs. VITAS-Innovative Hospice Care, Chgo., 1994-98; assoc. chaplain St. Margaret Mercy Hosp., Hammond, Ind., 2000—. Instr. pastoral care Luth. Sch. Theology, Chgo., 1972-82; instr. field work McCormick Theol. Sem., Chgo., 1972-82. Avocation: pastoral counseling. Home: 5549 S Harper Ave Chicago IL 60637-1829

ANDERSON, PHILIP WARREN, physicist, educator; b. Indpls., Dec. 13, 1923; s. Harry W. and Elsie (Osborne) Anderson; m. Joyce Gothwaite, July 31, 1947; 1 child, Susan Osborne. BS, Harvard U., 1943, MA, 1947, PhD, 1949; DSc (hon.), U. Ill., 1979, Rutgers U., 1991, Ecole Normale Superieure, Paris, 1995, U. Sheffield, Eng., 1996; PhD (hon.), U. Tokyo, 2002. Mem. staff Naval Research Lab., 1943—45; mem. tech. staff Bell Tel. Labs., Murray Hill, NJ, 1949—84, chmn. theoretical physics dept., 1959—60, asst. dir. phys. rsch. lab., 1974—76, cons. dir., 1976—84; prof. theoretical physics Cambridge (Eng.) U., 1967—75, fellow Jesus Coll., 1969—75, hon. fellow, 1978—96; prof. physics Princeton (N.J.) U., 1975—96, prof. emeritus, 1996—; George Eastman prof. Oxford (Eng.) U., 1993—94. Rschr. in quantum theory, especially theoretical physics of solids, spectral line broadening, magnetism, superconductivity; Fulbright lectr. U. Tokyo, 1953—54; Loeb lectr. Harvard U., 1964; Overseas fellow Churchill Coll., Cambridge U., 1961—62; vice chmn. sci. bd. Santa Fe Inst., 1990—. Author: (book) Concepts in Solids, 1963, Basic Notions of Condensed Matter Physics, 1984, A Career in Theoretical Physics, 1994, The Theory of Superconductivity in High-Tc Cuprates, 1997. Chmn. bd. trustees Aspen Ctr. Physics, 1982—87. Recipient Nobel prize, 1977, Guthrie medal, Inst. Physics, 1978, Nat. medal Sci., 1982, Centennial medal, Harvard U., 1996, Bardeen prize, Internat. Com. M2S-HTS Conf., 1997, Dannie Heinemann prize, Gottingen Acad. Sci., 1975. Fellow: AAAS, Indian Acad. Scis., Japan Acad., Am. Phys. Soc., Am. Acad. Arts and Scis.; mem.: NAS, Russian Acad. Scis., N.Y. Acad. Scis. (life), Am. Philos. Soc., Accademia Lincei, Royal Soc.

ANDERSON, PT (PAUL THOMAS IV), film director; b. Studio City, Calif., Jan. 1, 1970; s. Ernie Anderson. Dir., writer: The Dirk Diggler Story, 1988, Cigarettes and Coffee (short film), 1993, Sydney/Hard Eight, 1996 (Boston Soc. Film Critics award 1997, nominated Grand Spl. prize Deauville Film Festival, 1996, nominated Ind. Spirit awards, best 1st feature, best 1st screenplay, 1996); dir., writer, prodr.: Boogie Nights, 1997 (New Generation award L.A. Film Critics Assn., 1997, Metro Media award Toronto Internat. Film Festival, 1997, Boston Soc. Film Critics Best New Filmmaker award, 1997; nominated Oscar, best writing, screenplay written directly for screen, 1998, nominated Brit. Acad. award, best screenplay-original, 1998, nominated Five Continents award, European Film awards, 1997, nominated Golden Satellite awards, best dir. motion picture, best motion picture-drama, 1998, nominated Writers Guild Am. Screen award, best screenplay written directly for screen, 1997), Magnolia, 1999 (awards for best dir. and best screenplay, best picture, Toronto Film Critics Assn.), Punch-Drunk Love, 2002 (Cannes Film Festival Best Dir. award), (TV) SNL Fanatic, 2000.*

ANDERSON, RACHAEL KELLER, retired library administrator; b. N.Y.C., Jan. 15, 1938; d. Harry and Sarah Keller; m. Howard D. Goldwyn; children: Rebecca Anderson, Michael Goldwyn, Bryan Goldwyn, David Goldwyn. AB, Barnard Coll., 1959; MS, Columbia U., 1960. Librarian CCNY, 1960-62; librarian Mt. Sinai Med. Ctr., N.Y.C., 1964-73, dir. library, 1973-79; dir. Health Scis Libr. Columbia U., N.Y.C., 1979-91, acting v.p., univ. libr., 1982; dir. Ariz. Health Scis. Libr., U. Ariz., Tucson, 1991-2001; assoc. dir. Ariz. Telemedicine

Program, 1996—2001; ret., 2001. Bd. dirs. Med. Libr. Ctr. of N.Y., N.Y.C., 1983-91; mem. biomed. libr. rev. com. Nat. Libr. Medicine, Bethesda, Md., 1984-88, chmn., 1987-88; mem. bd. regents Nat. Libr. Medicine, 1990-94, chmn., 1993-94; pres. Ariz. Health Info. Network, 1995. Contbr. articles to profl. jours. Mem. Med. Libr. Assn. (pres.-elect 1996-97, pres. 1997-98, bd. dirs. 1983-86, 98-99), Assn. Acad. Health Scis. Libr. Dirs. (bd. dirs. 1983-86, 90-93, pres. 1991-92). E-mail: rachaela@ahsl.arizona.edu.

ANDERSON, RALPH ROBERT, endocrinology educator; b. Fords, N.J., Nov. 1, 1932; s. Harry Walter and Johanna Katherine (Damgaard) A.; m. LaVeta Ann Phillips, Jan. 28, 1961; children— Richard, Laura BS, Rutgers U., 1953, MS, 1958; PhD, U. Mo., 1961. Cert. animal scientist, Ill. Research asst. Rutgers U., 1957-58; research asst. U. Mo., Columbia, 1958-61, instr. dairy sci. (endocrinology), 1961-62, asst. prof., 1965-68, assoc. prof., 1968-72, prof., 1976—97, prof. emeritus, 1997—. Asst. prof. Iowa State U., Ames, 1962-64; researcher Editor, co-editor 6 books; contbr. articles to profl. jours., chpts. to books. Served with U.S. Army, 1954-56 Recipient grad. teaching merit award U. Mo. chpt. Gamma Sigma Delta, 1982, Rsch. award, 1994; NIH postdoctoral fellow, 1964-65; Fulbright-Hays sr. research fellow, N.Z., 1973-74 Mem. Am. Physiol. Soc., Endocrine Soc., Am. Dairy Sci. Assn., Am. Soc. Animal Sci. Soc. Study Reproduction, Soc. Exptl. Biology and Medicine, Mo. Acad. Sci. (v.p. 1986-87), Sigma Xi (sec.-treas. U. Mo. chpt. 1981-83, pres. 1984-85) Clubs: Track (Columbia). Lodges: Kiwanis (pres. 1982-83). Presbyterian. Home: 2517 Shepard Blvd Columbia MO 65201-6131 Office: U Mo Animal Sci Rsch Ctr Columbia MO 65211-0001

ANDERSON, RANDI LAINE, occupational therapist; b. Omaha, July 17, 1947; children: Rebecca Jennifer, Heidi Julia (dec. Mar. 1991). BS, U. Ill., 1970; MS, Calif. Coll. for Health Scis., 1996. Registered occupational therapist. Occupl. therapist Westchester County Med. Ctr., Valhalla, N.Y., 1970-76, UCP Therapeutic Nursery, Washington, 1987-89, Edward Mazique Parent Child Ctr., Washington, 1989, Great Oak Ctr., Silver Spring, Md., 1989-93, Montgomery Primary Achievement Ctr., Silver Spring, 1993—, Pediat. Svcs. Am., Inc., Washington, 1996—. Active Easter Seals, 1999—. Mem. Am. Occupational Therapy Assn., Riverdale Presbyn. Ch. Avocations: writing poetry, painting portraits, jigsaw puzzles. Home: 9308 Cherry Hill Rd Apt 204 College Park MD 20740-1254

ANDERSON, RAYMOND QUINTUS, diversified company executive; b. Jamestown, N.Y., Nov. 27, 1930; s. Paul N. and Cecille (Ogren) A.; m. Sondra Rumsey, June 5, 1954; children: Heidi, Kristin, Gerrit, Mitchell, Tracy, Brooks. Grad., Phillips Acad., Andover, Mass., 1949; BS in Engring., Princeton U., 1953; postgrad., Sloane Sch., MIT, MIT. With Dahlstrom Corp., Jamestown, 1957-76, exec. v.p., 1965, pres., 1968-76; founder, pres. Aarque Steel Corp., Jamestown, 1976-78, Aarque Mgmt. Corp., Jamestown, 1978-96; founder, chmn. Aarque Cos., Jamestown, 1980-96, Aarque Capital Corp., 1996—. Bd. dirs. Oneida Ltd., Bus. Coun. N.Y. State, Inc., Cold Metal Products Co., Inc., Aarque Steel Group, Kardex Sys., Inc.; trustee Northwestern Mut. Life Ins. Co. Patentee in field. Chmn. Jamestown United Fund drive, 1964, 74; bd. dirs. N.Y. State Dept. Environ. Conservation; dir. Oneida, Ltd.; trustee Roger Tory Peterson Inst., Chautauqua Found. Inc.; civilian aide to Sec. of the U.S. Army; mem. adv. bd. World Econ. Forum. Served with USNR, 1954-57. Mem. Mfrs. Assn. Jamestown Area (pres. 1967-68), Empire State C. of C. (pres. 1974-76), Royal Round Table of Swedish Coun. Am., U.S. Can. Trade Coun., U.S. Dept. Commerce Ind. Sector Adv. Com., Tau Beta Pi. Clubs: Moon Brook Country (Jamestown); Sportsmen's (Chautaqua, N.Y.); Union League Met. (N.Y.C.). Republican. Episcopalian. Address: 20 W Fairmont Ave Lakewood NY 14750-0109

ANDERSON, REID BRYCE, performing company executive; b. New Westminister, B.C., Can., Apr. 1, 1949; s. Warren Nels and Phyllis Jessie Bryce (Purser) Anderson. Student dance, Dolores Kirkwood, Burnaby, B.C., Royal Ballet Sch., 1967, 68. Dancer Stuttgart (Fed. Republic Germany) Ballet, 1969-86, prin. dancer, 1975-86, ballet master, 1982-86; artistic dir. Ballet B.C., Vancouver, 1987-89, Nat. Ballet Can., Toronto, Ont., 1989—, Stuttgart Ballet, 1996—. Choreographer numerous works for performing cos. Decorated Order of Fed. Republic Germany; recipient John Cranko prize for svc. to Art of Classical Ballet and in particular teaching, coaching and maintaining the work of the late John Cranko, 1995. Office: The Stuttgart Ballet Obere Schlossgarten 6 70173 Stuttgart Germany

ANDERSON, RICHARD CARL, geophysical exploration company executive; b. Pontiac, Mich., June 6, 1928; s. Earling Adolph and Blenda Maria (Johnson) A.; m. Georgia L. Carnahan, Aug. 14, 1949; children— Laurie Ann, Gary Carl, Cynthia Murray, Denise Carla BS in Mining Engring., N.Mex. Inst. Mining & Tech., 1950, MS in Geophysics, 1953. Engr. Allis Chalmers, Milw., 1949-51; geophysicist, v.p. Geophys. Service, Inc., Dallas, 1953-71; v.p., then exec. v.p. Digicon, Houston, 1971-75; sr. v.p., exec. v.p. Seismograph Service Corp., Tulsa, from 1975, pres., 1981-85; ret., 1985-88; pres. Fairfield Industries, Houston, 1988-91, vice chmn., chief exec. officer, 1991-93; ret., 1993. Mem. Energy Advocates, Tulsa, 1981-93, coordinator, 1983, 86. Served with U.S. Army, 1946-47 Recipient Disting. Achievement award N.Mex. Inst. Mining and Tech., 1984 Mem. Soc. Exploration Geophysicists, Internat. Assn. Geophys. Contractors (hon. life mem., bd. dirs. 1977-85, 89-94, chmn. 1978-79). Home: 1111 Hermann Dr Unit 11F Houston TX 77004-6929

ANDERSON, RICHARD CHARLES, geology educator; b. Moline, Ill., Apr. 22, 1930; s. Edgar Oscar and Sarah Albertina (Olson) A.; m. Ethel Irene Cada, June 27, 1953; children: Eileen Ruth, Elizabeth Sarah, Penelope Cada. AB, Augustana Coll., Rock Island, Ill., 1952; SM, U. Chgo., 1953, PhD, 1955. Geologist Geophoto Svcs., Denver, 1955-57; from asst. prof. to prof. geology Augustana Coll., Rock Island, 1957-96; prof. emeritus, 1996—. Rsch. affiliate Ill. State Geol. Survey, Champaign, 1959—. Editor: Earth Interpreters, 1992; author reports. Recipient Neil Miner award Nat. Assn. Geology Tchrs., 1992. Fellow Geol. Soc. Am. (sect. co-chair 1990). Lutheran. Home: 2012 24th St Rock Island IL 61201-4533 Office: Augustana Coll Dept Geology 639 38th St Rock Island IL 61201-2210 E-mail: glanderson@augustana.edu.

ANDERSON, RICHARD EDMUND, city manager, management consultant; b. Ferndale, Mich., Dec. 23, 1938; s. Richard H. and Carolyn Jeanne (Figg) A.; m. Kay Clarke, Nov. 6, 1961 (div.); children: Pam, Mark, Linda; m. Linda (Hawk)Jenkins, Sept. 11, 1997; stepchildren: Travis, Todd. BA, Mich. State U., 1962; postgrad. in advanced mgmt., Harvard U., 1979. Aide to mgr. City of St. Petersburg, Fla., 1962-64; adminstrv. asst. City of Ft. Lauderdale, Fla., 1964-67, dep. mgr., 1967-75, city mgr., 1975-80; v.p. Fla. Innovation Group, Tampa, 1980-81; pres. Integrated Systems Assocs., Inc., Ft. Lauderdale, 1981-90; city mgr. City of Florida City, Fla., 1990-94, City of Brooksville, Fla., 1995—. Contbr. articles to profl. jours. Mem. Internat. City Mgmt. Assn. Office: 201 Howell Ave Brooksville FL 34601-2041 E-mail: city.mgr@cl.brooksville.fl.us.

ANDERSON, RICHARD ELLIOTT, internist, educator; b. N.Y.C., Dec. 28, 1946; MD, Stanford U., 1973. Cert. in internal medicine; subspecialty in oncology. Intern Beth Israel Hosp., Boston, 1973-74, resident in medicine, 1974-75; fellow in med. oncology Stanford U., 1975-77; sr. staff Scripps Meml. Hosp., La Jolla, Calif., 1977-98; clin. asst. prof. U. Calif., San Diego, 1977—, clin. prof. medicine, 1995-2000, chmn. dept. medicine, 1986-87. Chmn. The Doctor's Co., 1994—. Fellow ACP; mem. AMA, Am. Soc. Clin. Oncology, Calif. Med. Assn., Alpha Omega Alpha. Office: PO Box 2900 Napa CA 94558-0900 E-mail: randerson@thedoctors.com.

ANDERSON, RICHARD ERNEST, agribusiness development consultant, rancher; b. North Little Rock, Ark., Mar. 8, 1926; s. Victor Ernest and Lillian Josephine (Griffin) A.; m. Mary Ann Fitch, July 18, 1953; children: Vicki Lynn, Lucia Anita. BSCE, U. Ark., 1949; MSE, U. Mich., 1959. Registered profl. engr., Mich., Va., Tex., Mont. Commd. ensign USN, 1952, advanced through grades to capt., 1968, ret., 1974; v.p. Ocean Resources, Inc., Houston, 1974-77; mgr. maintenance and ops. Holmes & Narver, Inc., Orange, Calif., 1977-78; pres. No. Resources, Inc., Billings, Mont., 1978-81; v.p. Holmes & Narver, Inc., Orange, Calif., 1981-82; owner, operator Anderson Ranch, registered Arabian horses and comml. Murray Grey cows, Pony, Mont., 1982—; pres., dir. Carbon Resources Inc., Butte, Mont., 1983-88, Agri Resources, Inc., Butte, Mont., 1988-95, Anderson Holdings, Inc., Pony, Mont., 1995—. Trustee Lake Barcroft-Virginia Watershed Improvement Dist., 1973-74; pres. Lake Barcroft-Virginia Recreation Center, Inc., 1972-73. With USAAF, 1944-45. Decorated Silver Star, Legion of Merit with Combat V (2), Navy Marine Corps medal, Bronze Star with Combat V, Meritorious Service medal, Purple Heart; Anderson Peninsula in Antarctica named in his honor. Mem. ASCE, Soc. Am. Mil. Engrs. (Morrell medal 1965). Republican. Methodist. Office: Anderson Holdings Inc PO Box 266 Pony MT 59747-0266

ANDERSON, RICHARD H. air transportation executive; Various positions Harris County Dist. Atty.'s office, Houston; staff v.p., dep. gen. cousel Continental Airlines; v.p., dep. gen. counsel Northwest Airlines Corp, 1990, exec. v.p., COO, 1998—, CEO. Office: Northwest Airline Corp 5101 Northwest Dr Mailstop 110 Saint Paul MN 55111-3034

ANDERSON, RICHARD LOUIS, electrical engineer; b. Mpls., Feb. 4, 1927; s. Ben Walter and Anna Elizabeth (Zitcowicz) A.; m. Claire Louise Petersen, Sept. 15, 1951; children: Gretchen, Betty Lise, Karl. BS, U. Minn., 1950, MS, 1952; PhD, Syracuse (N.Y.) U., 1960; D.Sc. (hon.), U. Sao Paulo, Brazil, 1969. Research asst. U. Minn., 1950-52; research engr. IBM Corp., Poughkeepsie, N.Y., 1952-60; from. instr. to prof. elec. and computing engring. Syracuse U., 1954-79; prof. elec. engring. U. Vt., Burlington, 1979-95, prof. emeritus elec. engring. and materials sci., 1995—, dir. materials sci. program, 1981-91. Fulbright-Hayes prof. U. Madrid, 1960-61, U. Sao Paulo, 1967-69; cons. to govt. and industry; cons. UN Devel. Program, 1980-92, OAS, 1988, 91, 93. Author; patentee in field. Served with USNR, 1944-47. Recipient 1st Brazilian prize microelectronics, 1980; fellow Ford Found., 1967-69; grantee NSF, 1974-85, N.Y. State Sci. and Tech. Found., 1974-75, 77-78, Dept. Energy, 1979-83. Fellow IEEE; mem. AAUP, Am. Phys. Soc., Sigma Xi. Home: 601 Wake Robin Dr Shelburne VT 05482-7580 E-mail: anderson@emba.uvm.edu.

ANDERSON, RICHARD MCDONALD, hydrologist, engineer; b. Takoma Park, Md., Oct. 28, 1969; s. Milton and Vinette Anderson; m. Rosemarie DaCosta, Dec. 25, 1993. PhD, Johns Hopkins U., 1994—2002. Engr. in Tng., State of Pa., 1992. Nuc. safety analyst Westinghouse Electric Corp., Pitts., Pa., 1991—93; rsch. hydrologist NOAA/Nat. Weather Svc., Silver Spring, Md., 2002—. Mem.: Internat. Assoc of Gt. Lakes Rsch., Am. Geophys. Union, Inst. for Ops. Rsch. and the Mgmt. Sciences. Home: 631 Washington Blvd Apt E Baltimore MD 21230 Office: NOAA/Nat Weather Svc Silver Spring MD Personal E-mail: andersrmr@aol.com. E-mail: richard.anderson@noaa.gov.

ANDERSON, RICHARD MCLEMORE, internist; b. Gainesville, Fla., Mar. 3, 1930; s. Montgomery Drummond and Myrtle (McLemore) A.; m. Leewood Shaw, Mar. 21, 1959; children: Richard McLemore Jr., Bruce Dexter. BS, U. Fla., 1951; MD, Emory U., 1958. Diplomate Am. Bd. Internal Medicine. Chief of staff Alachua Gen. Hosp., Gainesville, Fla., 1973-75; internist Gainesville, Fla., 1962—. Chmn. of bd. Santa Fe Health Care, Gainesville, 1984-91, bd. dirs. Pres. Rotary Club of Gainesville, 1980-81. Capt. USAF, 1951-54. Mem. AMA, ACP, Alachua County Med. Soc. (v.p. 1972), Fla. Med. Assn. Presbyterian.

ANDERSON, RICHARD MICHAEL, lawyer; b. Hollywood, Fla., Dec. 21, 1958; s. R. M. and Rita M. (Kelly) Anderson; m. Margaret Ruth Hurt, Nov. 3, 1990. Student, Baylor U., 1976-78; BA, U. Fla., 1980; JD, Am. U., 1983. Bar: D.C. 1983, Tex. 1984. Assoc. Kleberg, Dyer, Redford & Weil, Austin, 1983-87, Kleberg & Head, Austin, 1988; assoc., shareholder Redford, Wray & Woolsey, P.C., Austin, 1988-93; shareholder Broyles & Pratt, P.C., Austin, 1993-99, Pratt & Grant, P.C., Austin, 2000-01; ptnr. Bickerstaff, Heath, Smiley, et. al., Austin, 2001—. Contbr. articles to profl. jours. Office: Bickerstaff Heath Smiley Pollan Kever and McDaniel LLP 1700 Frost Bank Tower 816 Congress Ave Austin TX 78701-2443

ANDERSON, RICHARD PAUL, agricultural company executive; b. Toledo, Apr. 10, 1929; s. Harold and Margaret Mary (Meilink) A.; m. Frances Mildred Heilman, Nov. 28, 1953; children— Christopher, Daniel, James, Martha, Jennifer, Timothy. BS magna cum laude, Mich. State U., 1953. With The Andersons, Maumee, Ohio, 1946—, gen. ptnr., 1951—, gen. mgr., 1980-82, mng. ptnr., 1983—, pres., CEO, 1986-96, chmn., CEO, 1996-98, chmn., 1999—. Bd. dirs. Chemfirst. Pres. Toledo Area council Boy Scouts Am., 1966-69; gen. chmn. Crusade of Mercy, Toledo, 1972; bd. dirs. Childrens Services, St. Luke's Hosp.; chmn. support council Ohio Agrl. Research and Devel. Ctr.; trustee U. Toledo Corp., 1985-98, chmn. bd. trustees, 1986—; bd. dirs. Pub. Broadcasting Found. NW Ohio, 1983—; chmn. bd. dirs., 1986-92. Served with AUS, 1954-56. Named Toledo Area Citizen of Yr. Toledo Bd. Realtors, 1974, Outstanding Lay Leader N.W. Ohio chpt. Nat. Assn. Social Workers, 1971; recipient Disting. Service award Ohio State U., 1986. Mem. Com. 100 (bd. dirs. exec. com. 1987-92). Clubs: Rotary (Toledo.) (pres. 1976-77). Republican. Roman Catholic. Home: 1833 S Holland Sylvania Rd Maumee OH 43537-1380 Office: The Andersons 480 W Dussel Dr Maumee OH 43537-1690

ANDERSON, RICHARD THEODORE, association executive, urban planner; b. Bklyn., Oct. 11, 1940; s. Charles Theodore and Lillian Elizabeth (Holmlin) A.; m. Anasta Frank, Oct. 3, 1970; childre; Erik Theodore, Leslie Elisabeth. AB, Rutgers U., 1962; M of Regional Planning, Cornell U., 1964; postgrad., NYU, 1964-67. Pres. Regional Plan Assn., N.Y.C., 1964-92; exec. dir. The Dallas Plan, Dallas, 1993-94; pres., CEO N.Y. Bldg. Congress, N.Y.C., 1994—; pres. N.Y. Bldg. Found., N.Y.C., 1998—. Vis. assoc. prof. dept. city and regional planning Pratt Inst., N.Y.C., 1974-92; chmn. Pres.' Coun. N.Y.C. Planning & Design Orgns., 1982-92. Bd. dirs. Water Resources Assn. Delaware River Basin, 1977-80, United Way, Pelham, N.Y., 1977-79, Friends of Hudson River Park, 2001—; v.p., trustee Big Bros./Big Sisters, N.Y.C., 1969—, Audrey Cohen Coll., 1998-2001; mem. coll. adv. coun. Cornell U. Coll. Architecture, Art and Planning, 1984-94; mem. Village Planning Bd., Pelham, 1977-80; mem. Times Sq. Adv. Coun., N.Y.C., 1985-89; bd. dirs. Regional Alliance Small Contractors, 1994—, ACE Mentorship Program, 1997—, Bklyn. Sports Found., 1998—; mem. Bus. Coun. N.Y. State, N.Y.C. Partnership, Architectural League of N.Y.; co-chmn. N.Y. chpt. Rebuild Am. Coalition; mem. N.Y.C. and Co., Citizens Union, Citizens Housing and Planning Coun., Nat. Bldg. Mus. Recipient Ellis Island medal of honor, 1995, George S. Lewis award N.Y. chpt. AIA, 2001; vis. scholar NYU, 1992. Fellow Am. Inst. Cert. Planners (chmn. Coll. Fellows 2003—), Inst. for Urban Design, Mus. of Modern Art; mem. AIA (N.Y. chpt. pub. dir. 2003—), Am. Planning Assn. (dir. and treas. 1978-80, pres. 1980-81, Disting. Svc. award 1985), Am. Soc. Planning Ofcls. (bd. dirs. 1977-78), N.Y. Soc. Assn. Execs., Urban Land Inst., N.Y. Acad. Scis., Met. Leadership Network, Gen. Soc. Mechanics and Tradesmen of City of N.Y., Ellis Island Medal of Hon. Soc., Rutgers Alumni Assn. (Loyal Son award 1989), N.Y.C. C. of C., Bklyn. C. of C., Empire State Transp. Alliance, Van Alen Inst., Archtl. League N.Y., Assn. for a Better N.Y. Lutheran. Home: 9 Highview Cir Dobbs Ferry NY 10522 Office: NY Bldg Congress 44 W 28th St New York NY 10001-4212 E-mail: rtanderson@buildingcongress.com.

ANDERSON, RICHARD VERNON, ecology educator, researcher; b. Julesburg, Colo., Sept. 9, 1946; s. Vernon Franklin and Charolett Iona (Jeppesen) A.; m. Arlune June Rosentreter, Jan. 23, 1971; children: Rustle R., Michael C., Theodore F. Student, Chadron State Coll., 1964-66, Western State Coll., 1970; BS, No. Ill. U., 1974, MS, 1975; PhD, Colo. State U., 1978. Grad. teaching asst. No. Ill. U., DeKalb, 1974-75; grad. rsch. asst. Colo. State U., 1975-78, postdoctoral fellow Nat. Resource Ecology Lab., 1978-79; asst. prof. Western Ill. U., Macomb, 1979-82, assoc. prof., 1982-87, prof., dir. Kibbe Life Scis. Field Sta., 1987-2001, chmn. dept. biol. scis., 2001—. Vis. asst. prof. inst. for. environ. studies Water Resources Ctr, U. Ill., 1980; mem. assoc. faculty Argonne Nat. Lab., 1985—; assoc. supportive scientist Ill. Natural History Survey, 1985—; proposal reviewer ecology, ecosystem studies, regulatory biology, divsn. internat. programs NSF, 1981—, mem. proposal panel for equipment and facilities grants, 1987; proposal reviewer U.S./Israel Binational Sci. Found., 1981-82, Natural Environ. Rsch. Coun., Eng., 1983-84; environ. cons. aquatic sect. Environ. Cons. and Planners, DeKalb, 1974; program chmn. Internat. Conf. on Ecological Integrity of Large Floodplain Rivers, 1994. Reviewer Natural Resource Ecology Lab., 1977-81, Jour. Nematology, 1977-81, Archives Environ. Contamination and Toxicology, 1978-81, Ecology, 1978-85, Argonne Nat. Lab., 1980—, Pedobiologia, 1982-87, Jour. Freshwater Ecology, 1982—, Freshwater Invertebrate Ecology, 1982—; contbr. over 250 sci. articles, reports, papers and abstracts; presenter papers in field. Grantee NSF, 1972, 73, 82, 83, 84, 85, (two grants), 86, (two grants), 87, 88, 99, 2002, Western Ill. U., 1980, (two grants), 81, Upper Miss. River Basin Comm./U. Ill., 1980, Abbott Labs., 1981, Ill. Dept. Transp., 1981, 85, Ctrl. Ill. Light Co., 1981, 82, 83, 84, Nat. Fish and Wildlife Svc., 1983, Ill. Dept. Conservation, 1985, 87, 88, 89, 91, U.S. Fish and Wildlife Svc./Ill. Dept. Conservation, 1988, 89, 90, 91, Environ. Cons. and Planners, Inc., 1988, 89, 91, Booker Assocs., Inc., 1989, (two grants), Ill. Natural History Survey, 1989, Wetlands Rsch., Inc., 1989, 90, 91, 92, 95, 98, 2002, USDA, U. Ill., 1991, 92, Hey and Assocs., Inc. Biotic Surveys, 1992, 83, 94, 95, 96, 97, 98, 99. Mem. Entomol. Soc. Am., N.Am. Benthological Soc. (program com. 1982-83, reviewer jour. 1990—), Ecol. Soc., Soc. Nematologists (ecology com. 1981-82, systematic resources com. 1981-82), Internat. Congress Ecologists, Ill. State Acad. Sci., Miss. River Rsch. Consortium (mem. exec. bd. 1981-82, v.p. bd. dirs. 1991-92, pres. bd. dirs. 1992-93, 99-2000), Internat. Conf. on Integrity of Large Floodplain River (program chmn. 1994), Xerces Soc., Sigma Xi (Rsch. of Yr. award 1984), Phi Kappa Phi. Achievements include research in invertebrate ecology, aquatic biology with an emphasis on large river ecosystems, aquatic invertebrates and freeliving nematodes, the effects of invertebrates on nutrient cycling. Home: 704 S Randolph St Macomb IL 61455-2966 Office: Western Ill U Dept Biol Scis Macomb IL 61455 E-mail: r-anderson1@wiu.edu.

ANDERSON, ROBERT BARBER, architect; b. Summit, N.J., Apr. 17, 1944; s. Robert B Anderson and Marion (Lent) Campbell; m. Dominique Astruc, June 2, 1973; children: Adriana, Joseph, Frederic. BArch, Clemson U., 1968; attended, Bklyn. Coll., 1971-72. Registered architect, Va. Ptnr. Anderson, Boyd & Assocs., Madison and Charlottesville, Va., 1976-78; prin. Kerns Group, Washington, 1979-82; v.p. The Benham Group East, Vienna, Va., 1982-85; pres. Anderson O'Brien Archs., Alexandria, Va., 1985-93, Heyward Boyd & Anderson, Charlottesville, Va., 1993—. Chmn Archit Adv Bd, Falls Church, Va., 1981—84. Prin. works include historic office bldg, 1915 Eye St, Washington, 1981; Author, illustrator: children's books OBO, When I Was a Little Boy... Recipient Design Award, Progressive Archit Mag, 1981, Masonry Inst Award, 1989, Best Bldg of the Yr Award, NAIOP, 1989, Best Brochure Award, Washington Metropolitan Area Art Dirs Club, 1989. Mem.: AIA (Design Award 1982, DC chpt Design Award 1987, Northern Va chpt Design Award 1992, 1994). Avocations: painting, pen and ink drawing, backcountry hiking, soccer, martial arts. Office: Heyward Boyd & Anderson 111 W High St Charlottesville VA 22902-5018 E-mail: bob@hbapc.com.

ANDERSON, ROBERT EDWARD, lawyer; b. Spokane, Wash., Sept. 25, 1928; s. Ewald Godried and Hazel L. A.; m. Audrey May, Nov. 29, 1947; children: Mark, Eric, Kent, Carl. B in Law, Gonzaga U., 1950, LLB, 1954, JD, 1967. Bar: Wash. 1954, U.S. Dist. Ct. (ea. dist.) Wash. 1954, U.S. Supreme Ct. 1966. Pvt. practice, Spokane, 1954—. Recipient Silver Beaver award Boy Scouts Am., 1976, Lamb award Nat. Luth. Ch. Am., 1980. Mem. Kiwanis Internat. (lt. gov. 1967). Lutheran. Office: 2024 W Northwest Blvd Spokane WA 99205-3715

ANDERSON, R(OBERT) GREGG, real estate company executive; b. St. Joseph, Mo., Oct. 3, 1928; s. Clarence William and Marie Louise (Newman) A.; m. Janice Kimrey, May 6, 2001; 1 child, Robert Gregg Jr. Student, U. Okla., 1948-49, U. Tulsa, 1950. Pres. Gregg Anderson Realty, San Diego, 1959-63; v.p. Trousdale Constrn. Co., L.A., 1963-67; pres. Amfac Properties div. Amfac, Inc., Honolulu, 1967-69; v.p. Amfac, Inc., Honolulu, 1967-69, sr. v.p., 1969-74; pres., chmn. bd. Accent Enterprises, Inc., Amfac Communities, Inc., Amfac Silverado Corp., Neilson Way Corp., 745 Fort St. Corp., Cen. Oahu Land Corp., L.A. Environ. Structures, Inc., 1969-74; chmn. bd. West Maui Properties, Inc., 1969-74; v.p. Silverado Country Club & Resort, Inc., 1969-74; pres. Gregg Anderson Realty & Devel., Inc., 1974—, Villa Pacific Bldg. Co., 1980—; gen. ptnr. Rancho Vista Devel. Co., Palmdale, Calif., 1980—; pres. Videocable, Inc., Palmdale, 1984-87; gen. ptnr. ProRep Assocs., 1991—. Bd. dirs. Antelope Valley Bd. Trade, 1991—. With USNR, 1950-54. Named Builder of Yr., Calif. Bldg. Industry Assn., 1998; inductee Calif. Bldg. Industry Hall of Fame, 1999. Mem. Bldg. Industry Assn. (bd. dirs. 1984-94), Rotary (hon.), Kiwanis (hon.). Republican. Avocations: tennis, golf, bowling. Office: Rancho Vista Devel Co 3011 Rancho Vista Blvd Ste F Palmdale CA 93551-4823 E-mail: ranchvista@qnet.com.

ANDERSON, ROBERT LANIER, III, judge; b. Macon, Ga., Nov. 12, 1936; s. Robert Lanier II and Helen Anderson; m. Nancy Briska, Aug. 18, 1962; children: Robert, William Hilliar, Browne McIntosh. AB magna cum laude, Yale U., 1958; LLB, Harvard U., 1961. Assoc. Anderson, Walkert, Reichert, Macon, Ga., 1963—79; judge U.S. Ct. Appeals (11th cir.), 1979—99, 2002—, chief judge, 1999—2002. With USAR, 1958—61, capt. U.S. Army, 1961—63. Mem.: ABA, Am. Judicature Soc., State Bar of Ga., Macon Bar Assn., Ga. Bar Assn. Office: US Ct Appeals PO Box 977 Macon GA 31202-0977

ANDERSON, ROBERT LEROY, lawyer; b. Oakland, Calif., Feb. 20, 1924; m. Elisabeth Olney, Dec. 18, 1948; children: Kimberley Riley Clement, Benjamin Olney. AB, U. Calif., Berkeley, 1948; JD, Hastings Coll. of Law, 1951. Bar: Calif. 1952. Dep. dist. atty. County of Alameda, Oakland, Calif., 1952-56; atty. Rankin, Anderson & Geary, Oakland, 1956-63; ptnr. Anderson & Geary, Oakland, 1963-74, Anderson, Galloway & Lucchese, Oakland, 1974—2000, sr. counsel, 1986—. Mem. Med.-Legal Com. Calif., 1970—. 1st lt. U.S. Army Air Corps, 1943-45. Listed in The Best Lawyers in America, 1987—. Mem. Am. Bd. Trial Advocates, Calif. Bar Assn., Contra Costa County Bar Assn. Office: Galloway Lucchese & Everson 1676 N California Blvd Ste 500 Walnut Creek CA 94596-4183

ANDERSON, ROBERT MORRIS, JR., electrical engineer; b. Crookston, Minn., Feb. 15, 1939; s. Robert Morris and Eleanor Elaine (Huotte) A.; m. Janice Ilene Pendell, Sept. 3, 1960; children— Erik Martin, Kristi Lynn. B.E.E., U. Mich., 1961, M.E.E., 1963, MS in Physics, 1965, PhD in Elec. Engring. 1967. Registered profl. engr., Ind. Asst. research engr. U. Mich., Ann Arbor, 1963-67; research engr. Conductron Corp., Ann Arbor, summer 1967; asst. prof. elec. engring. Purdue U., West Lafayette, Ind., 1967-71, assoc. prof., 1971-79, prof., 1979, engring. coordinator for continuing edn., 1973-79, Ball Bros. prof., 1976-79; mgr. engring. edn. and tng., corp. cons. services GE, Bridgeport, Conn., 1979-82, mgr. tech. edn. operation, corp. engring. and mfg., 1982-88; mgr. tech. edn., corp. mgmt. devel. Gen. Electric Co., Bridgeport, Conn., 1988-90; vice provost, dir. coop. extension Iowa State U., Ames, 1990-95, prof. elec. engring., 1990-2000, prof. emeritus, elec. engring., 2000—. Author: multi-media learning package Fundamentals of Vacuum Technology, 1973, (with others) Divided Loyalties, 1980; contbr. (with others) articles to profl. jours. Named Best Tchr. Elec. Engring. Purdue U., 1974; recipient Dow Outstanding Young Faculty award, 1974 Fellow Am. Soc. Engring. Edn. (cert. of merit 1977, Joseph M. Biedenbach Disting. Svc. award 1986), IEEE (Meritorious Achievement award in continuing edn. activities 1987). Lutheran. Home: 3321 Kingman Rd Ames IA 50014-3942 Office: Iowa State U 2218 Coover Hall Ames IA 50011-0001

ANDERSON, ROBERT ORVILLE, oil and gas company executive; b. Chgo., Apr. 13, 1917; s. Hugo A. and Hilda (Nelson) A.; m. Barbara Phelps, Aug. 25, 1939; children: Katherine, Julia, Maria, Robert Bruce, Barbara Burton, William Phelps, Beverley. BA, U. Chgo., 1939. With Am. Mineral Spirits Co., Chgo., 1939-41; pres. Malco Refineries, Inc., Roswell, N.Mex., 1963-86; with Atlantic Richfield Co., Los Angeles, retired chmn. bd., chief exec. officer. Mem. Com. Econ. Devel., Washington. Hon. chmn. Aspen Inst.; trustee Calif. Ins. Tech., U. Chgo.; chmn. Lovelace-Anderson Endowment Found. Mem. Nat. Petroleum Council, Am. Petroleum Inst. Clubs: Century (N.Y.C.); California (Los Angeles); Pacific-Union (San Francisco).

ANDERSON, ROBERT RAYMOND, artist, consultant; b. Orange, N.J., Nov. 9, 1945; s. Walter Edmund Anderson and Althea (Weimer) Casler; m. June Elizabeth Giardino, June 8, 1968. Student, N.J. Inst. Tech., 1964-66; BS, SUNY, Brockport, 1969; MFA, Pratt Inst., 1972. Represented by OK Harris Gallery, N.Y.C. Instr. Art Ctr. N.J., Summit, 1974-79, Newark (N.J.) Mus. Arts Workshop, 1976-79, County Coll. Morris, Dove, N.J., 1978-79; tech. cons. Binney & Smith, Easton, Pa., 1991-2000, Colart, 2000—. Co-author: Art of the Dot/Advanced Airbrush Techniques, 1985; one man shows include Park Gallery, N.Y.C., 1972, Newark Mus., 1975, N.J. State Mus., 1978, Jack Gallery, N.Y.C., 1984, Littlejohn-Smith Gallery, N.Y.C., 1986, 89, OK South Gallery, Bay Harbor Isle, Fla., 1989, Robin Hutchins Gallery, Maplewood, N.J., 1990, Wetherholt Gallery, Washington, 1992, OK Harris Gallery, N.Y.C., 2001-02;

exhibited in group shows at Montclair (N.J.) Mus., 1972, Hartwick Coll., N.Y.C., 1975, Morris Mus., N.J., 1976, Temple U., Pa., 1980, San Jose State U., 1982, N.J. State Mus., 1984, Noyes Mus., N.J., 1986, Schering Plough, Inc., 1988, Ea. Wash. U., 1988, Tex. A&M U., 1989, Gallery and hasting-on-Hudson, N.Y., 1989, Fairleigh Dickinson U., N.J., 1990, Trenton City Mus., N.J., 1991, Newark Mus., N.J., 1992, Marlboro Art Gallery, Md., 1993, First St. Gallery, N.Y.C., 1993, County Coll. Morris, Dover, N.J., 1994. Trustee Oakeside Cultural Ctr., Bloomfield, N.J., 1988-89; mem. Bloomfield (N.J.) Cultural Commn., 1988-89. Recipient fellowship grants N.J. State Coun. on the Arts, Trenton, 1976, 84, Nat. Endowment for the Arts, Washington, 1985. Mem. Trenton Artists Workshop Assn., Studio Montclair. Avocations: running, cross country skiing. Home: 46 Glen Rock Rd Cedar Grove NJ 07009-1638 E-mail: bob@arttekstudios.com.

ANDERSON, ROBERT THOMAS, anthropologist, researcher, physician; b. Oakland, Calif., Dec. 27, 1926; s. Victor T. and Stella Irene (Hansen) A.; m. Barbara Gallatin Anderson, Aug. 20, 1956 (div. Aug. 20, 1972); children: Andrea, Robin, Scott; m. Edna May Steiner Mitchell, Oct. 10, 1973; children: Debby, Tom, Kris. BA in Anthropology with hons., U. Calif., 1949, MA in Anthropology, 1953, PhD in Anthropology, 1956; MD, U. Autonoma Ciudad Juarez, Mex., 1986; D of Chiropractic, Life Chiropractic Coll. West, 1982. Cert. physician, surgeon Mex.; cert. physician, surgeon Internat. Commn. Fgn. Med. Grads., U.S.; cert. radiology x-ray supr., oper., Calif.; lic. chiropractor, Calif. Asst. prof. anthropology U. Wash., Seattle, 1959-60, U. Calif., Berkeley, 1960, assoc. prof., 1966-67, prof. anthropology, 1967; asst. prof. anthropology Mills Coll., Oakland, 1960-63, assoc. prof. anthropology, 1963-66, prof. anthropology, 1967—. Dir. rsch. Life Chriropractic Coll. W., 1978-83, Am. Coll. Traditional Chinese Medicine, 1989-92; dir. manual medicine San Francisco Spine Inst. at Seton Med. Ctr., 1988-91; researcher in field; med. anthropologist, Mex., Nepal, Brazil, Iceland. Author: Magic Science and Health: The Aims and Achievements of Medical Anthropology, 1996, Alternative and Conventional Medicine in Iceland: The Diagnosis and Treatment of Low Back Pain, 2000; co-editor: Conservative Care of Low Back Pain, 1991; assoc. editor: Newsletter of the Am. Back Soc., 1988-92; mem. editl. bd. Med. Anthropology, 1990-96, Yearbook of Transcultural Medicne Psychotherapy, 1991—; contbr. 8 chpts. to books, 44 articles to profl. jours. Served with USN, 1946-48. Decorated WWII Victory medal. Home: 2007 Manzanita Dr Oakland CA 94611-1148 Office: Mills Coll 5000 MacArthur Blvd Oakland CA 94613-1301 E-mail: boba@mills.edu.

ANDERSON, ROBERT WOODRUFF, playwright, novelist, screenwriter; b. N.Y.C., Apr. 28, 1917; s. James Hewston and Myra Esther (Grigg) A.; m. Phyllis Stohl, June 24, 1940 (dec. 1956); m. Teresa Wright, Dec. 11, 1959 (div. 1978). AB magna cum laude, Harvard U., 1939, MA, 1940. Tchr. playwriting Am. Theatre Wing, 1946-50; writer for radio and TV, 1947-53; ind. playwright, author, screenwriter, 1951—; mem. Playwrights Co., 1953-60; faculty Salzburg Seminar in Am. Studies, 1968, Iowa Writers Workshop, 1976. Past chmn. bd. overseer's com. to visit the performing arts Harvard U. Writer: Come Marching Home, produced N.Y.C., 1946, Love Revisited, produced Westport Country Playhouse, 1951, All Summer Long, Arena Stage, Washington, 1953, N.Y.C., 1954, Tea and Sympathy, N.Y.C., 1953, writer in residence, U. N.C., 1969; screenwriter (films) Tea and Sympathy, 1956, Until They Sail, 1957, The Nun's Story, 1959, The Sand Pebbles, 1966, (plays) Silent Night, Lonely Night, 1959, The Days Between, 1965, You Know I Can't Hear You When the Water's Running, 1967, I Never Sang for My Father, play, 1968, screenplay, 1970 (Writers Guild Am. award for best screenplay), Solitaire/Double Solitaire, 1971, Free and Clear, 1983, The Kissing Was Always the Best, 1985, The Last Act Is A Solo, 1989, (novels) After, 1973, Getting Up and Going Home, 1978, (TV drama) The Patricia Neal Story, 1979, (play) The Last Act Is A Solo (Ace award 1991), 1991, (TV drama) Absolute Strangers, 1991; co-editor: (six vol. set) Elements of Literature, 1988. Served to lt. USNR, 1942-46. Recipient 1st prize for Come Marching Home Army-Navy Playwriting Contest for servicemen overseas, 1945, William Inge Lifetime Achievement award 1985; named to Theater Hall of Fame, 1980; honoree Conn. Commn. on the Arts, 1992. Mem. Dramatists Guild Coun. (past pres.), New Dramatists Com. (past pres.), Harvard Club (N.Y.C.). Home and Office: 14 Sutton Pl S New York NY 10022-3071

ANDERSON, ROBERTA JOAN See **MITCHELL, JONI**

ANDERSON, ROBERTA JUNE, computer engineer; b. Widen, W.Va., Mar. 13, 1938; d. Virgil Arthur and Fanny Rebecca (Frame) Davis; m. William Douglas Anderson, Dec. 23, 1956 (div. 1981); children: Gaya Lynne Anderson Harriman, William Michael; m. Lewis Edward Boyle, Feb. 5, 1983; stepchildren: Rhonda Boyle Nelson, Brian Edward. BS in Math., Old Dominion U., 1973, MS in Math. Edn., 1979. Assoc. systems engr. Comptek Rsch. Inc., Virginia Beach, Va., 1979-80; systems analyst Sperry-Univac, Virginia Beach, 1980-84; computer programmer/analyst USAF, Langley, Va., 1984; instr. Tidewater C.C., Virginia Beach, 1984-85; sr. computer scientist Computer Scis. Corp., King George, Va., 1985-90; sr. program engr. Syscon Corp., Dahlgren, Va., 1990-94; prin. engr. Planning Cons. Inc., Dahlgren, 1994-99; sr. prin. engr. Logicon, Inc., Reston, Va., 1999—2001; prin. engr. Northrop Grumman IT, Dahlgren, 2001—. Adj. instr. Germanna C.C., Locust Grove, Va., 1991—, Tidewater C.C., 1981-84; tchr. Chesapeake (Va.) Pub. Schs., 1976-79, Virginia Beach Pub. Schs., 1973-76. Home: 5 Pawnee Dr Fredericksburg VA 22401-1110

ANDERSON, ROBIN MARIE, secondary education educator; b. Blue Island, Ill., Apr. 18, 1965; d. Donald Albert Anderson and Rosemary (Campbell) King. BA in English, No. Ill. U., DeKalb, 1988; MEd, U. North Tex., Denton, 1997. Cert. tchr. secondary edn., English, reading, Tex.; cert. libr., Tex. Tchr. English North Garland (Tex.) H.S., 1990-92, Lakeview Centennial H.S., Garland, 1992-93; tchr. reading Nimitz H.S., Irving, Tex., 1993-99; 8th grade reading tchr. Bowman Middle Sch., Plano, Tex., 1999—2002; libr. media specialist Ford Middle Sch., Allen, Tex., 2002—. Attendance policy violators com., student vol. svc. hour com. Nimitz H.S.; prin.'s coun. Bowman Mid. Sch., Allen, Tex., safety coun. Chmn. adv. bd. Irving C.A.R.E.S., 1995; sponsor Cultural Awareness Soc., Irving, 1995-96, Jr. Historians, Irving, 1994—; co-sponsor Bowman Raiders Are Great (BRAG); mem. Safety Coun., Bowman; mem. Bowman Reads Com. Recipient High Spirited Citizen award Irving Conv. and Visitors Bur., 1996. Mem. ASCD, Internat. Reading Assn., Assn. Tex. Profl. Educators, Tex. Assn. for Improvement of Reading (conf. spkr. 1995). Republican. Avocations: reading, music, environmental issues, aerobics, movies. Office: Ford Middle Sch 630 Park Pl Allen TX 75002

ANDERSON, ROLPH ELY, finance educator; b. Buchanan, Mich., Aug. 27, 1936; s. Eugene Jefferson and Susanna (James) Anderson; m. Sallie Durkee Warner; children: Rachel Elizabeth, Stuart James. BA, Mich. State U., 1958, MBA, 1964; PhD, U. Fla., 1971. Inventory mgr. Shell Oil Co., Detroit, 1958-59; contract adminstr. Westinghouse Elec. Corp., Pitts., 1962-63; mgr. new product devel. Quaker Oats Co., Chgo., 1964-67; prof., chmn. dept. bus. mgmt. Old Dominion U., Norfolk, Va., 1971-75; chmn. dept. mktg. Drexel U., Phila., 1975-97, Royal H. Gibson prof. bus. adminstrn., 1991—. Mem. sales com. Fin. Svcs. Advisor mag., 2000—; fellow LeBow Coll. Ctr. for Tchg. Excellence, 2003—. Author: (book) Professional Personal Selling, 1991, Essentials of Personal Selling: The New Professionalism, 1995; co-author: Introduction to Multivariate Data Analysis, 1974, Multivariate Data Analysis, 1979, 5th edit., 1998, Sales Management, 1983, Professional Sales Management, 3d edit., 1999; books transl. into fgn. langs., including Spanish and Czech. Mem. faculty adv. bd. U. Akron Fisher Inst. Profl. Selling, 1998—. Served to capt. Supply Corps. USN. Recipient award for best publ. article, Mu Kappa Tau, 1988, Excellence in Reviewing award, Personal Selling and Sales Mgmt., 1996, Rsch. Excellence award, LeBow Coll., 2000—01; fellow, LeBow Coll. Ctr. Tchg. Excellence, 2003—04. Mem.: N.E. Am. Inst. Deicision Inst. (bd. dirs. 1977—78), Acad. Mktg. Sci. (sec., mem. exec. coun. 1984—86), So. Mktg. Assn., Sales and Mktg. Execs. Internat., Am. Mktg. Assn. (interant. conf. co-chmn. 1978, v.p. programming Phila. chpt. 1984—85, bd. dirs. 1986—87, 1992—93, Sales Interest Group Inaugural Excellence in Sales award 1998), Am. Inst. Decision Scis. (nat. coun. 1977—79), S.E. Am. Inst. Decision Scis. (pres. 1977—78), Res. Officers Assn., Naval Res. Assn., Beta Gamma Sigma. Office: Drexel Univ Coll Bus and Adminstrn Philadelphia PA 19104 E-mail: andersre@drexel.edu.

ANDERSON, RON, advertising executive; Formerly exec. v.p., midwest creative dir., then pres. midwest Bozell & Jacobs (now Bozell Inc.), Mpls., until 1988; assoc. chief creative officer N.Y.C., 1987-88; vice-chmn., chief creative officer Bozell Inc., N.Y.C., 1988—; now vice chmn, exec creative dir Bozell, Kamstra, Minneapolis, MN. Office: Bozell Kamstra 100 N 6th St Ste 800A Minneapolis MN 55403-1523

ANDERSON, RONALD DELAINE, education educator; b. Poplar, Wis., Aug. 25, 1937; s. Leslie A. and Linnea A. (Bergsten) A.; m. Sandra Jean Wendt, June 1, 1963; children— Debra Jean, Timothy James, Nathan David. BS, U. Wis., 1959, PhD, 1964. Asst. prof. edn. Kans. State U., Manhattan, 1964-65; mem. faculty U. Colo., Boulder, 1965—, prof. edn., 1971—, asso. dean edn., 1972-78. Cons. to numerous ednl. agys. Author: Religion and Spirituality in the Public School Curriculum, 2003; co-author: Developing Children's Thinking Through Science, 1970, Issues of Curriculum Reform, 1994, Local Leadership for Science Education Reform, 1995, Portraits of Productive Schools, 1995, Study of Curriculum Reform, 1996; contbr. articles to profl. jours. Program dir. Nat. Sci. Found., 1989-90. Fulbright scholar, 1986-87. Fellow AAAS (chair edn. sect. 1998-99, mem. Assn. Coun. 2002—); mem. Nat. Assn. Rsch. Sci. Tchg. (pres. 1975-76), Assn. Edn. Tchrs. in Sci. (pres. 1972-73), Nat. Sci. Tchrs. Assn., Phi Delta Kappa. Home: 4800 North Creek Rd Beulah CO 81023-9601 Office: Univ Colo Sch Edn Boulder CO 80309-0001

ANDERSON, RONALD TRENT, artist, educator; b. Madison, Wis., Oct. 10, 1938; s. Delmar LeRoy and Violet (Doering) A.; m. Barbara Groffman, June 9, 1962; 1 child, Brett Erland. BS in Art Edn., U. Wis., 1961, MS in Art, 1962, MFA in Art, 1963. Tchr. Waupun (Wis.) High Sch., 1961; tchg. asst. rural art program U. Wis., Madison, 1961-63; tchr. Bloom Twp. High Sch., Chgo. Heights, Ill., 1963-67; asst. prof. art edn. Nova Scotia Coll. of Art and Design, Halifax, Nova Scotia, 1967-69; tchr. Springfield (Mass.) Pub. Schs., 1969—2000. Represented in permanent collections U. Wis., Dalhousie U., Halifax, Westfield (Mass.) Coll., Walter J. Kohler, Jr., family, work reproduced in, Prize-Winning Watercolors Book I, 1963, Prize-Winning Watercolors Book II, 1964, The Art of Written Forms, 1969, one-man shows include Arts Unlimited Gallery, Milw., Wis., 1965, Bradley Gallery, 1967, exhibited in group shows at Smithsonian Instn., Washington, D.C., 1962, Ill. State Mus., Springfield, Ill., 1963, 1967, Nat. Design Ctr., Chgo., Ill., 1967, Dalhousie U., 1967, Montreal (Can.) Mus. Fine Arts, 1968, Colo. Coll., Colo. Springs, Colo., 1998, numerous others. Recipient Beacon award for excellence in edn., Springfield Sch. Com., 1992, 20 awards for painting and printmaking in juried art exhbns. U.S. and Can., Mass. Art Educator of Yr. award, Mass. Art Edn. Assn., 1999, Sch. Edn. Alumni Achievement Award, U. Wis. Madison, 2001; fellow Tchr.-Artist Program, The Marie Walsh Sharpe Art Found., 1998. Mem.: NEA, Internat. Platform Assn. (First Prize for Graphics Exhbn. 1995, Best of Show award 2001), Nat. Art Edn. Assn., Salmagundi Club (Rita Duis Meml. award 2003, Gene Magazzini Meml. award traditional oil 2003), Phi Delta Kappa. Lutheran. Avocations: studying the arts and humanities, foreign travel, bicycling, photography, fishing. Home: 9 Autumn Ln Amherst MA 01002-3316

ANDERSON, ROSS BARRETT, healthcare environmental services manager; b. Toronto, Ont., Can., Aug. 25, 1951; came to U.S., 1956; s. John Ross and Constance (Nielson) A.; m. Gladys Jeanette Vincent, Aug. 26, 1972; children: Christopher Matthew, John Ross II, Josiah Dan. Student, Boston U., 1970-73. Housekeeping supr. Parker Hill Med. Ctr., Roxbury, Mass., 1973-76; acct. mgr. Servicemaster Inc., 1973—; housekeeping mgr. Union Hosp., Lynn, Mass., 1976-77, Quincy (Mass.) City Hosp., 1977-78, St. Joseph's Hosp., Lowell, Mass., 1978-79, Waltham Weston Hosp. and Med. Ctr., Waltham, Mass., 1979-86, support services mgr., 1986-90, dir. environ. svcs., 1991-93, chmn. customer svcs. bd., 1992; asst. dir. clin. engrng. Good Samaritan Med. Ctr., Stoughton/Brockton, Mass., 1993-95; dir. environ. svcs. Harrington Meml. Hosp., Southbridge, Mass., 1995—. Mem. Boston Latin Sch. Assn., Scots Charitable Soc. Boston, Westford Congl. Ch., Ashford, Conn. Home: 133 Old Town Rd Ashford CT 06278-2020 Office: Harrington Meml Hosp 100 South St Ste 1 Southbridge MA 01550-4047

ANDERSON, ROSS CARL, mayor, lawyer; b. Logan, Utah, Sept. 9, 1951; s. E. LeRoy and Grace (Rasmussen) A.; 1 child, Lucas Craig Arment. BS in Philosophy magna cum laude, U. Utah, 1973; JD with honors, George Washington U., 1978. Bar: U.S. Dist. Ct. Utah 1978. Assoc. Berman & Giauque, Salt Lake City, 1978-80; v.p., ptnr. Berman & Anderson, Rooker Larsen Kimball & Parr, Salt Lake City, 1980-82; ptnr. Berman & Anderson, Salt Lake City, 1982-85; ptnr., v.p. Hansen & Anderson, Salt Lake City, 1986-89, Anderson & Watkins, Salt Lake City, 1989-92; pres. Anderson & Karrenberg, Salt Lake City, 1992-98, of counsel, 1999; mayor Salt Lake City, 1999—. Columnist Enterprise, 1997—98, I-15 Mag., 0200—2001, Catalyst, 2002—. Dem. candidate for Congress, Utah 2d Congl. Dist., 1996, mayor Salt Lake City, 1999—; pres. bd. dirs. Citizens for Penal Reform, 1991-94, Guadalupe Ednl. Programs, Salt Lake City, 1985-96, 97-99, ACLU of Utah, 1980-85; bd. dirs. Common Cause of Utah, 1987-89, Planned Parenthood of Utah, 1979-83; mem. Salt Lake Com. on Fgn. Rels., 1983-95. Mem. Utah State Bar Assn. Democrat. Avocations: history, fgn. affairs, skiing. Home: 418 Douglas St Salt Lake City UT 84102-3231 Office: Office Mayor 451 S State St Rm 306 Salt Lake City UT 84111-0005 Business E-Mail: rocky.anderson@slcgov.com.

ANDERSON, ROSS S. architectural firm executive; Grad., Harvard Grad. Sch. of Design, 1977; BA Human Biol., Art, and Arch., Stanford Univ., 1973. Registered licensed, New York, Calif., Ohio. Pres. Anderson Arch., New York, NY, 1996—; vis. prof. in arch. Advanced Studios, Yale Univ., 1992; ptnr. Anderson/Schwartz Arch., New York, NY, 1984—96, San Francisco, 1984—96; vis. critic in arch. Yale Univ., 1987; head of second year Studio Parsons Sch. of Des., 1984—85; ptnr. Anderson-Wheelwright Assoc., New York, NY, 1981—84; project arch. John Carl Warnecke, New York, NY, 1980—81, Turner Brooks, Starksboro, Vt., 1979—81, MLTW/Turnbull Assoc., San Francisco, 1977—80. Exhibitions include Negotiating Domesticity, The Greenwich Arts Coun., Greenwich, Ct., 2003, Small Firms, Gt. Projects, AIA/SF Gallery, San Francisco, CA, 1992, Ann. Exhbn., Am. Acad. in Rome, Rome, Italy, 1990, exhibitions include Thumbnail Sketches AIA/SF Gallery, San Francisco, Calif., 1989, exhibitions include Arch. Art, Am. Crafts Mus., New York, NY, 1988. Recipient EDRA/Places Design Award, Abercrombie & Fitch Office campus, 2003, Build. Team Project of the Yr.- Grand Award, Abercrombie & Fitch Office campus, Build. and Des. & Construct. Mag., 2003, Good Des. is Good Bus. Award, Abercrombie & Fitch, Bus. wk/Arch. Record, 2002, Hollister Co., Bus. wk./arch. design, 2002, Project Award, Hudson River Pk., 2000 Design Awards, AIA NY Chapt. Interior Des., 2000, Interior Arch. Award, AIA NY Chapt., Design Awards, 1998, SMA Video, AIA NY Chapt., 1995, Western Home Award, Citation, Napa Valley House, 1991, AIA, 1991, Sunset Mag., 1991, 40 Under 40, Interiors Mag., 1986—87. Office: &derson 555 W 25th St New York NY 10001*

ANDERSON, ROY EVERETT, retired electrical engineer; b. Batavia, Ill., Oct. 30, 1918; s. Elof and Nellie Amanda Anderson; m. Gladys Marie Nelson, Aug. 22, 1943; children: Paul V., David L., Barbara J. Anderson Wald, Dorothy M. Anderson Presser. BA in Physics, Augustana Coll., Rock Island, Ill., 1943; MSEE, Union Coll., Schenectady, 1952. Instr. physics Augustana Coll., 1943-44, 46-47; cons. engr. GE, Schenectady, 1947-83; co-founder, v.p. Mobile Satellite Corp., Malvern, Pa., 1983-88; owner, mgr., cons. Anderson Assocs., Glenville, NY, 1988—99; pres. Rega Assocs., Glenville, 1993—2000; ret., 2000. Cons. Am. Mobile Satellite Corp., Washington, 1988-91; participant nat. and internat. regulatory and tech. orgns. leading to establishment generic mobile satellite svc. Contbr. over 125 articles to profl. jours.; patentee indsl. electronic measurement and quality control instruments, tone code ranging technique for position surveillance using satellites; developer Doppler radio direction finder. Trustee Dudley Obs., Schenectady, 1975-83, 90—, chmn. bd. trustees, 1980-83, 90. With USN, 1944-46. GE Coolidge fellow, 1970. Fellow IEEE, AAAS, Radio Club Am., Inst. Navigation; mem. AIAA. Home and Office: PO Box 2531 Glenville NY 12325-0531 E-mail: regainc@aol.com.

ANDERSON, RUDOLPH J., JR., lawyer; b. Bklyn., Apr. 15, 1924; s. Rudolph John and Nora (Cawley) A.; m. Helen O'Donnell, May 28, 1949; children: Mary Josephine Anderson Coughlin, Rudolph John III, Peter, Thomas, Michael, Rosemary, Christopher, Terrence. BS in Naval Sci., U. Notre Dame, 1945, BS in Chem. Engring., 1947; JD, Georgetown U., 1951. Bar: Va. 1950, D.C. 1955, N.J. 1963, Mo. 1985, Vt. 1989. Asst. to pres. Permacel div. Johnson & Johnson, 1955-60; assoc. gen. counsel, dir. patents Merck & Co., Inc., Rahway, N.J., 1960-83; gen. patent counsel Monsanto Co., St. Louis, 1984-87; of counsel Fitzpatrick, Cella, Harper & Scinto, N.Y.C., 1987-89. Former committeeman Scotch Plains Twp. Com., N.J. Served to lt. USNR, 1943-46 PTO. Mem. ABA (chmn. patent trademark and copyright law sect. 1984-85), Assn. Corp. Patent Counsel, Am. Intellectual Property Law Assn. Roman Catholic. Avocation: golf. Home and Office: PO Box 416 190 Foxfire Ln Stowe VT 05672-0416 E-mail: helenrudy1@aol.com.

ANDERSON, RUTH G. retired education educator, educational consultant; b. Blue Eye, Mo., Apr. 14, 1929; d. Claude B. and Sylvia J. (Hudson) Gibson; m. Lev Z. Anderson, Aug. 14, 1948 (dec. June 1989); 1 child, Richard L. BS in Edn., Southwest Mo. State, 1951; MEd, U. Mo., 1962, EdD, 1974; postgrad., Ball State U., No. Ariz. U. Cert. elementary tchr., elementary prin., sch. supt. Tchr. S. Bee Creek Sch., Mincy, Mo., 1947-48, Blue Eye (Mo.) Schs., 1951-54, Waynesville (Mo.)-FLW Schs., 1955-58, 60-63, prin., 1963—65, asst. supt., 1965-71; tchr. Am. Dependent Schs., Kaisers Lautern, Frankfurt, Germany, 1958-60; from asst. to full prof. edn. Coll. of the Ozarks, Point Lookout, Mo., 1972—2000, chmn. edn. dept., 1980-90, prof. emeritus, 2000—. Ednl. cons., Blue Eye, 1974—; lectr. CHNN, Emmen, The Netherlands, 1994. Mem. NEA (life), ASCD, Internat. Reading Assn. (state pres.), Mo. State Tchrs. Assn. (state adviser student group), Phi Delta Kappa, Delta Kappa Gamma, Kappa Kappa Iota (state pres. 1965-66). Avocations: reading, travel, sewing. Home: 176 Anderson Ln Blue Eye MO 65611-9615

ANDERSON, RUTH LUCILLE, interior designer, educator, artist, librarian, archivist; b. Cyprus Hills, N.Y. d. Arthur Albert and Marie Rose (Weston) Buehler; m. Gunnar Bohlin Anderson; children: Anna Kristine Kornblatt, Deborah Val. Grad., N.Y. Sch. Applied Design Women; Cert., N.Y. Sch. Interior Design; BA, Adelphi U., 1979, MA, 1981; postgrad., NYU, Nat. Acad. Sch. Fine Arts, 1987. Cert. pub. libr. N.Y., pub. libr. profl. cert. SUNY Edn. Dept., 2001, archives, qualified interior designer Nat. Coun. Interior Design Qualification. Fabric cons. F. Schumacher & Co., N.Y.C., 1954-60; sr. interior designer W&J Sloane, N.Y.C., 1960-83; adj. assoc. prof. Nassau C.C., 1979—, Adelphi U., 1980; instr. Hofstra U., 1990—; asst. to rsch. libr. Cradle of Civilization, Mitchel Air Field, 1998—2000; libr. Planting Fields Libr., Oyster Bay, NY, 2001—. Mem. faculty Parson (New Sch.), 1980-81; lectr. in field. Paintings and sculptures exhibited at W&J Sloane, Cold Springs Harbor, Oyster Bay Cove, Adelphi U. and 75 Varick St., N.Y.C., Garden City and Cold Spring Harbor Gallery, 1993. Mem. Nat. Trust Historic Preservation. Recipient Spl. participation award Open Door Program, N.Y.C.; named Partner in Edn. N.Y.C. Pub. Schs., 1991-92. Mem. Am. Soc. Interior Designers (profl. mem. 1976), Early Flyers.

ANDERSON, RUTH NATHAN, syndicated columnist, TV news host, writer, recording artist, lyricist; b. N.Y.C., Jan. 28; d. Solomon and Anna (Cornick) Gans; m. Arthur Aksel Anderson Jr., Sept. 11, 1971 (dec.); stepchildren—Jack Anderson, Barbara Anderson-Rouse, Terri Anderson-Sarli. Student, NYU, George Washington U. Feature editor Crusade for Freedom, Radio Free Europe, N.Y.C.; feature-series reporter N.Am. Newspaper Alliance, Women's News Svc., N.Y.C., 1961-79; writer, originator Doctor's Grapevine column Nat. Features Syndicate, Chgo., 1969-73; author-owner syndicated column VIP Med. Grapevine/Celebrity Health News, Round Lake, Ill., 1973-2001. Newsletter editor Washington Post;.chief med. writer, press officer Nat. Multiple Scierosis Soc., N.Y.C.; feature news corr. Waukegan (Ill.) News-Sun, 1977-82; writer, host Celebrity Health News, Cablenet TV, Chgo., 1985-89; feature writer Ind. News Alliance, Chgo.; Chgo. contbg. editor Music City Entertainer, Nashville, 1976-2002; writing projects dir. Comedy Hall of Fame, Chgo., 1989-2001; ethics writer, Chicago Journalist, 1998—, internet's Doctor Who's Who, 1999, chief lyricist Anderson-Fejer Musicals, 1995—; entertainment editor, columnist Emerald Coast Insider, 2003--; tchr. journalism, creative writing, speech arts Fla. State Bd. Adult Edn., 1968-79; writing instr. Bay Country Dist. Schs., 2002--; lectr. writing seminars for faculty U. Ill. at Chgo. Circle Campus, 1970-80. Author: Naked Brunch (poetry), 1996, How You Can Be a Part of Your United Nations, (booklet), book and lyrics (musical play) Menage a Trois, 1997; contbr. articles to various mags. including Parents, Pageant Mademoiselle, Science Digest, Reader's Digest, TV Guide, TV Radio Mirror, This Week, Am. Weekly, Am. Home., others; CD release Love Songs for Lovers, 2002; contbr. poems to (book) Nat. Libr. Poetry (Best poems of 1990, 2000, 2001, 2002; features on U.S. presidents in archives of Hoover, Truman, Eisenhower, Kennedy and Johnson presdl. libraries. Trustee, v.p. bd. Round Lake Pub. Library, 1977-86; mem. Nat. Trust for Hist. Prservation; Right=to-Read vol. tutor jr. high schs., Round Lake, 1977-86; singer ARC entertainment com. Beside Network, 1974-80; citizen amb. to South Africa with Creative Women of the Arts Del. under People-to-People Amb. Programs, 1999. Recipient Golden Poet Trophy award Internat. Soc. Poets, 1990, Editor's Choice award Nat. Lib. of Poetry, Rec. artist mus. comedy songs, pop for Am. Sound label. Mem. NARAS, NATAS, Chgo. Women in Broadcasting, Am. Med. Writers Assn. (Beth Fonda award, 1984), Am. Mus. Women in Arts (charter), Lake County Assn. Journalist, NAFE, Chgo. Unltd., Press Vets. Assn., Internat. Platform Assn., Future Physicians Am. (hon.) Soc. Profl. Journalists Headline Club, Panhandle Writers Guild, P.C. Profl. Writers Assn., Gulf Coast Jazz Soc., Authors League Am., Dramatists Guild. Chgo. Press Club, Chgo. Advt. Club. Home and Office: Writing Enterprises Box 124 14700 Front Beach Rd Panama City Beach FL 32413 Fax: 850-236-9258. E-mail: ruthswritings@aol.com.

ANDERSON, RUTH T. retired air traffic controller; b. Bartow, Fla., July 2, 1935; d. John Benjamin Thompson and Susan Ettie Scott; m. Malcolm Edward Jack Anderson; m. Perry Brannon, Jr. (div. Oct. 29, 1973); children: Glenda Brannon Parrish, Ronald Allen Brannon. AA Computer Acctg. Technology, SE Coll. of Tech., Mobile, Ala., 1992. Air traffic control specialist FAA, Dothan, Ala., Gulfport, Miss., Mobile, Ala., 1972—89. EEO investigator FAA, Atlanta, 1985—89. Methodist. Avocation: reading, writing, sewing and crafting, fishing. Home: 1983 Powell Tr Abbeville AL 36310

ANDERSON, SALLY MIDGETTE, social services administrator, linguist; b. N.Y.C., Jan. 9, 1938; d. William Raymond and Charlotte Noyes Driver; m. Willard Franklin Midgette, May 27, 1961 (dec. Apr. 1978); children: Anne Leland, Alexander Dameron; m. Donald Bernard Anderson, Mar. 15, 1980. BA, Vassar Coll., 1960; MA in Tchg., Reed Coll., 1968; PhD, U. N.Mex., 1987. Pers. interviewer Harvard U., Cambridge, 1960-61; tchr., adminstr. St. Ann's Sch., Bklyn., 1975-80; rschr. U. N.Mex., Albuquerque, 1988-98; youth worker The Unity Ctr. for Teens, Roswell, N.Mex., 1995-2000, Boys' and Girls' Club, 2000—01. Adj. prof. U. N.Mex., 1988-98. Author: The Navajo Progressive in Discourse, 1995; editor: Athabaskan Language Studies, 1996; asst. Analytical Lexicon of Navajo, 1992. Bd. dirs. REACH 2000, Roswell, 1992-99, Boys'/Girls' Club, Roswell, Assurance Home, Roswell, 1998-2001; mem. vestry St. Andrew's Episc. Ch., 1999-2002; mem. N.Mex. Arts Commn., 2003. Recipient Excellence in the Humanities award N.Mex. Endowment for the Humanities, 1997, Svc. to Mankind award Roswell Sertoma Club, 1999, Ea. N.Mex. West Tex. Dist., 1999, Greater Rocky Mountain Region, 1999. Democrat. Episcopal. Avocation: choral singing. Home: 3600 La Joya Rd Roswell NM 88201-9108 Office: Anderson Offices 409 E College Blvd Roswell NM 88201-7524

ANDERSON, SCOTT ROBBINS, hospital administrator; b. Fargo, N.D., Mar. 25, 1940; BA, U. N.D., 1962; M Health Adminstrn., U. Iowa, 1964. Adminstrn. res. St. Luke's Methodist Hosp., Veteran's Adminstrn. Med. Ctr., Cedar Rapids, Iowa City, 1963-64; adminstrv. asst. North Meml. Med. Ctr., Robbinsdale, Minn., 1964-65, asst. dir., 1965-69, adminstr., 1969-76, v.p., 1976-81, pres., 1981—; pres., ceo North Meml. Med. Ctr. (now North Meml. Health Care), Robbinsdale, Minn., 1981—. Adj. prof. in field. Office: N Meml Health Care 3300 Oakdale Ave N Robbinsdale MN 55422-2926

ANDERSON, SHERRI L. medical educator; d. Carl E. and Ida L. Anderson. BS, Howard U., 1988, MEd, 1990, postgrad. studies in organizational comm., 1992—97. Edn. services specialist Walter Reed Army Med. Ctr., Washington, 1992—98, edn. specialist nursing edn. and staff devel., 1998—2001. Mem.: Assn. Tchr. Preventive Medicine, Alpha Kappa Alpha. Office: Walter Reed Army Inst Rsch 503 Robert Grant Ave Rm 2A30 Silver Spring MD 20910-7500 E-mail: sherri.anderson@na.amedd.army.mil.

ANDERSON, STACEY ANN, school psychologist; b. Crestline, Ohio, Mar. 4, 1964; d. James Edward Anderson, Sr. and Mary Jane (Vangeloff) Anderson. Postgrad., Walden U., 2004; MA in Psychology, U. W.Va. (now Marshall University), 1990; BS in Edn., Ashland Coll. (now Ashland U.), 1985. Cert. sch. psychologist Ariz., W.Va. Tchr. jr. h.s. sci. Crestview Local Schs., Ashland, Ohio, 1986—88; tutor Human Resource Bur., Mansfield, Ohio, 1987—88; substitute tchr. Kanawha & Jackson County Schs., Charleston, W.Va., 1988—90; counselor Sexual Assault Unit Family Svcs. Kanawha Valley, Charleston, W.Va., 1990; sch. psychologist Kanawha County Schs., Charleston, W.Va., 1990—91; sch. psychologist Yuma County Accommodation Sch. Dist. #99, Yuma, Ariz., 1995—2002; sch. psychologist Yuma Sch. Dist. 1, Yuma, Ariz., 1991—2002. Supr. interns Yuma Sch. Dist. 1, Yuma, 1994—2002. Mem. edn. com. Gila Mountain United Meth. Ch., Yuma, 2000—02; Bd. dirs. Learning Pad Presch., Yuma, 2000—02. Mem.: APA, Am. Psychol. Assn. Grad. Students, Nat. Assn. Sch. Psychologists, Psi Chi. Methodist. Avocations: travel, shopping, cars, biking, collecting. Office: Yuma Sch Dist 1 450 Sixth St Yuma AZ 85364 Office Fax: 928-344-6930.

ANDERSON, STANFORD OWEN, architect, architectural historian, educator; b. Redwood Falls, Minn., Nov. 13, 1934; s. Carl Alfred and Dora Helena (Paulson) A. BA, U. Minn., 1957; MA in Arch., U. Calif., Berkeley, 1958, postgrad., 1958-59, PhD, Columbia U., 1968. Registered arch., Mass. Tchr. Archtl. Assn., London, 1962-63, 74-78; co-dir. research project Inst. for Architecture and Urban Studies, N.Y.C., 1970-72, fellow, 1971-81; asst. prof. history and architecture MIT, 1963-69, assoc. prof., 1969-72, prof., 1972—, head dept. architecture, 1991—. Co-dir. archtl. transl. project Am. Acad. Arts and Scis., 1977-80; mem. adv. council Mcpl. Art Soc., City N.Y., 1972-78. Author: Hermann Muthesius: Style Architecture and Building-Art, 1994, Peter Behrens: A New Architecture for the Twentieth Century, 2000; editor: Planning for Diversity and Choice, 1969, On Streets, 1978. Mem. Boston Landmarks Commn., 1980—87, Massport Designer Selection Panel, 1993—97; bd. dirs. Boston Preservation Alliance, 1989—91, Batuz Found. USA, 1997—, pres., 2000—; bd. dirs. Fulbright Assn., 1998—, Boston Soc. Architects, 1992—; mem. Nat. Register Peer Profls., U.S. Gen. Svcs. Adminstrn., 2002—. Fulbright scholar, 1961-62; John Simon Guggenheim fellow, 1969-70; Graham Found. fellow, 1971; ACLS fellow, 1977-78; festschrift pub. in his honor, 1997. Mem. Assn. Collegiate Schs. Architecture, Brit. Soc. for Philosophy of Sci., Coll. Art Assn., Soc. Archtl. Historians (dir. 1969-72, 76-77). Home: 63 Commercial Wharf Boston MA 02110-3814 Office: MIT Dept Architecture 77 Massachusetts Ave Cambridge MA 02139-4307

ANDERSON, STEFAN STOLEN, banker; b. Madison, Wis., Apr. 15, 1934; s. Theodore M. and Siri (Stolen) A.; m. Joan Timmermann, Sept. 19, 1959; children: Sharon Jill, Theodore Peter. AB magna cum laude, Harvard, 1956; MBA, U. Chgo., 1960; PhD (hon.), Ball State U., 1993. With Am. Nat. Bank & Trust Co. of Chgo., 1960-74, exec. v.p., 1969-74, 1st Mchts. Bank, Muncie, Ind., 1974, pres., 1979-98, chmn. bd. dirs., 1987—; pres., dir. First Mchts. Corp., Muncie, 1983-98, chmn. bd. dirs., 1987—; dir. Fed. Res. Bank of Chgo., 1991-97. Past pres., dir. Del. Advancement Corp., 1991-95; bd. dirs. Maxon Corp., Techpoint Inc., Pub. Radio Capital Fund. Past pres. Delaware County United Way, Muncie Symphony Orch.; trustee Roosevelt U., 1970-74, George Francis Ball Found., BMH Found., Ziegler Found., Ind. State Mus. Found.; trustee, chmn. Minnitrista Cultural Found.; past chair Ind. Nature Conservancy; past pres. Cmty. Found. of Muncie and Delaware County. Mem. Ind. Acad., Skyline Club (Indpls.), Rotary (past pres.), Phi Beta Kappa, Beta Gamma Sigma. Home: 2705 W Twickingham Dr Muncie IN 47304-1050 Office: 1st Mchts Bank 200 E Jackson St Muncie IN 47305-2800

ANDERSON, STEPHEN HALE, federal judge; b. Salt Lake City, Jan. 12, 1932; m. Shirlee Gehring; 2 children. Student, Eastern Oreg. Coll. Edn., LaGrande, 1951, Brigham Young U., Provo, 1956; LLB, U. Utah, 1960. Bar: Utah 1960, U.S. Claims Ct. 1963, U.S. Tax Ct. 1967, U.S. Ct. Appeals (10th cir.) 1970, U.S. Supreme Ct. 1971, U.S. Ct. Appeals (9th cir.) 1972. Tchr. South H.S., Salt Lake City, 1956—57; trial atty. tax divsn. U.S. Dept. Justice, 1960—64; ptnr. Ray, Quinney & Nebeker, 1964—85; judge U.S. Ct. Appeals (10th cir.), Salt Lake City, 1985—. Spl. counsel Salt Lake County Grand Jury, 1975; chmn. fed.-state jurisdiction com. Jud. Conf. U.S., 1995—98; mem. Nat. Jud. Coun. State and Fed. Cts., 1992—96; ad hoc. com. on bankruptcy appellate panels 10th Cir. Jud. Coun., 1995—97; com. mem. U.S. Ct. Appeals (10th cir.). Editor (in chief): Utah Law Rev. With U.S. Army, 1953—55. Mem.: Am. Bar Found., Salt Lake County Bar Assn. (pres. 1977—78), Utah State Bar (pres. 1983—84), U. Utah Coll. Law Alumni Assn. (trustee 1979—83, pres. 1982—83), Salt Lake Area C. of C. (bd.govs. 1984), Order of Coif. Office: US Ct Appeals 4201 Fed Bldg 125 S State St Salt Lake City UT 84138-1102

ANDERSON, STEPHEN MILLS, investment broker; b. Portland, Maine, Jan. 12, 1946; s. Stuart Mills and Elaine (Crommett) A.; m. Mary Elizabeth Carter, Aug. 23, 1969; children: Melissa A. Duffy, Hope Stuart. BA, Ohio U., 1969. Dir. admissions, dir. devel., dir. alumni affairs Gould Acad., Bethel, Maine, 1973-76; investment broker Burbank & Co., Portland, 1976-82, office mgr., 1978-82; investment broker, office mgr., v.p. A.G. Edwards & Sons, Portland, 1982—, sr. v.p., 1996—. Former pres. Stroudwater Corp.; mem. dirs. coun. A.G. Edwards and Sons; chmn. adv. coun. The Capital Group, L.A. Trustee Maine Med. Ctr., 1990, bd. corporators; bd. dirs. Brighton Med. Ctr. Found., 1992-96; chmn. ann. fund Maine Med. Ctr.; mem. adv. bd. Baxter State Park; chmn. bd. trustees Tilton Sch., 2002. Mem. Nat. Assn. Registered Reps., Cumberland Club, Masons, Severance Lodge Club. Home: PO Box 1437 Yarmouth ME 04096-2437 Office: 2 Portland Sq Portland ME 04101-4088

ANDERSON, SUELLEN, lawyer; b. L.A., Apr. 11, 1950; d. Robert Walter and Marian D. (Guild) Greiner; m. Dane Roger Anderson; children: Robert Joseph, Nicholas Drew. BA, Calif. State U., Los Angeles, 1974; JD, U. So. Calif., 1978. Bar: Calif. 1978, U.S. Dist. Ct. (cen. and ea. dist.) Calif. 1978. Corp. counsel, asst. sec. Tenneco West, Inc., Bakersfield, Calif., 1978-84; programs coordinator Greater Bakersfield Legal Assistance, 1985-89; assoc. Darling, Maclin and Thomson, Bakersfield, 1990-92; dean Calif. Pacific Sch. Laws, 1993-97; exec. dir. Kern County Bar Assn., 1997—2001; ptnr. Klein,DeNatale, Goldner, Cooper, Rosenlieb & Kimball, 2001—. Dir. Greater Bakersfield Legal Assistance, 1980-85; mem. coun. 100 Californian State U. Bakersfield, 1994—, steering com., 2001—. Cmty. mem. edtl. bd. The Bakersfield Californian, 1998. Assoc. dir. Alliance Against Family Violence, Bakersfield, 1985-89; bd. dirs. Tenneco Employees Fed. Credit Union, Bakersfield, 1981-83. Mem. Calif. Bar Assn. (vice chair legal svcs. sect. standing com. pvt. bar involvement 1992), Kern County Bar Assn. (bd. dirs. 1985—, sec.-treas. 1988-89, 1st v.p. 1991, pres. 1992), Kern County Women Lawyers Assn. (pres. 1982-83), Kern County Women Lawyers Scholarship Fund. (pres. 1988-90, treas. 1990-91), Bakersfield Rotary (bd. dirs. 1999-2000, sec. 2001-2002, bd. dirs. 2002—). Democrat. Business E-Mail: sanderso@kleinlaw.com.

ANDERSON, SUSAN LEIGH, philosophy educator; b. Portland, Oreg., Nov. 13, 1944; d. Paul Lynge and Viola Fern (Malm) Smith; m. J. Brooks Colburn, Aug. 1969 (div. Mar. 1974); m. Michael Edward Anderson, Mar. 11, 1974; 1 child, Alexander Scott. AB, Vassar Coll., 1966; MA, UCLA, 1971, PhD, 1974. Teaching assoc. UCLA, 1968-70; instr. Calif. State U., Northridge, 1970-71; instr., asst. prof., assoc. prof. philosophy U. Conn., Stamford, 1972-91, prof., 1991—. Vis. asst. prof. Mt. Holyoke Coll., South Hadley, Mass., 1977. Author: On Kierkegaard, 2000, On Mill, 2000, On Dostoevsky, 2001; contbg. author: Falling in Love with Wisdom, 1993; editor: Guidebook for Publishing Philosophy, 1986; co-author logic software: Proof Reader 1986, 88; also articles. Fellow NEH, Princeton U., 1975, Brown U., 1978, U. Calif., Santa Cruz, 1992, Lilly fellow, Yale U., 1976, vis. faculty fellow Yale U., 1990-91. Mem. Am. Philos. Assn. Avocations: book collecting, antiquing. Office: U Conn Philosophy Dept One University Pl Stamford CT 06901-2315 E-mail: susan.anderson@uconn.edu.

ANDERSON, TAD STEPHEN, landscape designer, consultant, photographer; b. Mpls., June 9, 1955; s. Rudolph Dennis and Verna Aurora (Young) A.; m. Kay Ann Weber, Jan. 22, 1987; children: Lena Mialisa, Rachel Aurora. Student, Utah State U., 1973-75, U. Minn., 1975-77. Landscape draftsman Minn. Valley Landscape, Bloomington, 1975-76; engring. draftsman Temple Assoc. Civil Engrs., Wayzata, Minn., 1976; landscape designer Minn. Valley Landscape, Shakopee, Minn., 1976-78; owner, landscape designer, landscape archtl. cons. Anderson Design Svcs., Minnetonka, Minn., 1978—. Creative devel., designer "The Anderson Horticultural Series" of copyrighted horticultural design plans; pin. projects include U. Minn. Landscape Arboretun, Mpls., Anderson Arboretum, Litchfield, Minn.; designer several projects in nat. publs. Mem. Nat. Landscape Assn., Am. Soc. Media Photographers, N.Am. Native Photographers Assn., Garden Writers Assn. of Am., Am. Assn. Nurserymen, Am. Soc. Landscape Architects, Assn. Profl. Landscape Designers, Minn. State Horticultural Soc., Minn. Builders Assn., Minn. Nursery and Landscape Assn. (award of excellence 1989, 97, 98, 99, 2000, award of merit 1989, 94, 95, 97, 98, 99, 2000, 03, award of design excellence 2003), Mpls. Builders Assn. (Roma award of excellence 1990), Internat. Sculpture Ctr. Independent. Avocations: photographer, sailor, sculptor, illustrator, skiing. Office: Anderson Design Svcs/Landscape & Anderson Photography PO Box 5264 Minnetonka MN 55343-2264 E-mail: andersondesigns@cs.com.

ANDERSON, TERENCE JAMES, law educator; b. Chgo., Feb. 26, 1940; s. James E. and Charlotte (Flatley) A.; m. Carolyn Bugh; children: Michael, Kathleen, Jamie, Andrew. BA, Wabash Coll., 1961; JD, U. Chgo., 1964. Bar: Ill. 1967, D.C. 1973, Fla. 1977. Local cts. commr. Zomba, Malawa, Africa, 1964-66; assoc. Goldberg, Weigle, Mallin & Gitles, Chgo., 1966-69, ptnr., 1970-73; att. prof. Antioch Sch. of Law, Washington, 1973-78, acad. dean, 1975-76; vis. prof. U. Miami Sch. of Law, Coral Gables, Fla., 1976-78, prof., 1978—. Spl. counsel to gen. counsel SEC, Washington, summers 1980-81; dir. Legal Svcs. of Greater Miami, Inc., 1977-83. Bd. dirs. ACLU of South Fla., 1981-85; mem. dist. admissions com. U.S. Dist. Ct. (so. dist.) Fla.; counsel to former U.S. Judge Alcee L. Hastings and now mem. Ho. of Reps., 1982—. Netherlands Inst. Advanced Studies fellow, 1994-95. Author: (with William Twining) Analysis of Evidence, 1991, The Battle of Hastings: Four Stories in Search of a Meaning, 1996. Mem. ABA, Am. Assn. Law Schs. Office: Univ Miami Sch Law PO Box 248087 Miami FL 33124-8087

ANDERSON, THEODORE ROBERT, physicist; b. Lodi, Ohio, Jan. 30, 1949; s. Robert Anderson and LaVaughn (Mitchell) Gillotti. BS in Physics, Fla. State U., 1971; postgrad. in math. physics, U. Geneva, Switzerland, 1973, 75; MS in Physics, NYU, 1979, MS in Applied Sci., 1983, PhD in Physics, 1986. Nuc. engr. Gibbs & Hill Inc., N.Y.C., 1980—83; rsch. physicist elec. boat divsn. Gen. Dynamics, Groton, Conn., 1983—88; rsch. physicist Naval Underwater Systems Ctr., New London, Conn., 1988—; co-founder, CEO, chief tech. officer Haleakala R&D Inc., Brookfield, Mass., 2002—. Adj. prof. mech. engring., astronomy U. Conn., Storrs, Groton, 1983—; adj. prof. math. Mitchell Coll., New London Conn., 1985, U. Hartford, 1990—; adj. prof. mech. and aeronautical engring., mgmt. and mech. engring. U. Bridgeport, 1989—; adj. prof. mech. and aeronautical engring. Hunter Coll.; adj. prof. physics and astronomy CUNY, 1979-83; adj. prof. physics L.I. Univ., 1980-83; adj. prof. elec. and mech. engring. Rensselaer Poly. Inst., Hartford, 1986—; adj. prof. Sch. Bus. U. New Haven, 1989—, mech. engring., 1983—, elec. engring., 1983—; rsch. prof. Rensselaer Poly. Inst., Troy, N.Y., U. Tenn., Knoxville; instr. Cooper Union Sch. Engring., N.Y.C., 1980; prin. investigator ASI Tech. Corp. Rsch. in fluid dynamics, acoustics, atomic physics, and electromagnetic interference; numerous patents in field. Active Met. Opera Guild, N.Y.C., 1986—, Mus. Modern Art, N.Y.C., 1985—, Met. Mus. Art, N.Y.C., 1984—, Am. Mus. Natural History, N.Y.C., 1987—, N.Y. Shakespeare Festival, 1987—, N.Y. Zool. Soc., 1988—, Ea. Nat. Park and Monument Assn., 1990—. Recipient Spl. Achievement award USN, 1989, 90. Mem. IEEE, Electromagnetic Compatibility Soc., Nat. Geographic Soc., Nat. Parks and Conservation Assn., Am. Phys. Soc., Soc. Rheology, Nat. Parks and Conservation Assn., The Adirondack Coun., The Nature Conservancy, The Smithsonian Assocs., World Powerlifting Alliance, Amnesty Internat., Wilderness Soc., World Wildlife Fund, Sierra Club, Greenpeace. Achievements include research in fluid dynamics, plasma physics, acoustics and atomic physics, electromagnetic interference, nuclear engineering solar cells; holder several patents on plasma antenna, plasma waveguides and plasma frequency selective surfaces. Home and Office: 7 Martin Rd Brookfield MA 01506 E-mail: AnderDrTed@aol.com.

ANDERSON, THEODORE WELLINGTON, portfolio strategist; b. Napa, Calif., Apr. 30, 1941; s. Theodore William and Donna Elorita (Dove) A.; children: Thomas Wellington, Hilary Dove. Student, Princeton U., 1959-60; BA, Stanford U., 1963; MBA, U. Calif., Berkeley, 1966. Portfolio mgr., v.p. John W. Bristol Inc., N.Y.C., 1968-77; assoc. rsch. dir., sr. v.p. Argus Rsch., N.Y.C., 1977-82; portfolio strategist The Ford Found., N.Y.C., 1982—. Mem. Fin. Analysts Fedn., N.Y. Soc. Security Analysts, DeBruce Fly Fishing Club, Angler's Club of N.Y., St. George's Soc. Episcopalian. Avocations: fly-fishing, foreign languages and history, tennis, bamboo rod building. Home: PO Box 432 Chappaqua NY 10514-0432 Office: The Ford Found 320 E 43rd St New York NY 10017-4890 E-mail: T.Anderson@Fordfound.org., TheodoreAnd@msn.com.

ANDERSON, THEODORE WILBUR, statistics educator; b. Mpls., June 5, 1918; s. Theodore Wilbur and Evelynn (Johnson) A.; m. Dorothy Fisher, July 8, 1950; children: Robert Lewis, Janet Lynn, Jeanne Elizabeth. BS with highest distinction, Northwestern U., 1939, DSc, 1989; MA, Princeton U., 1942, PhD, 1945; LittD, North Park U., 1988; PhD (honoris causa), U. Oslo, 1997; D (hon.), U. Athens, 1999. Asst. dept. math. Northwestern U., 1939-40; instr. math. Princeton U., 1941-43, rsch. assoc., 1943-45, Cowles Commn., U. Chgo., 1945-46; staff Columbia U., 1946-67, successively instr. math. stats., asst. prof., assoc. prof., 1946-56, prof., 1956-67, chmn. math. stats. dept., 1956-60, 64-65, acting chmn., 1950-51, 63; prof. stats. and econs. Stanford U., 1967-88, prof. stats. and econs. emeritus, 1988—. Dir. project Office Naval Rsch., 1950-82; prin. investigator NSF project, 1969-92, Army Rsch. Office project, 1982-92; vis. prof. math. U. Moscow, 1968; vis. prof. stats. U. Paris, 1968; vis. prof. econs. NYU, 1983-84; acad. visitor math. Imperial Coll. Sci. and Tech., U. London, 1967-68, London Sch. Econs. and Polit. Sci., 1974-75, U. So. Calif., 1989; C.G. Khatri Meml. lectr. Pa. State U., 1992; rsch. visitor Tokyo Inst. Tech., 1977; sabbaticant IBM Systems Rsch. Inst., 1984; rsch. assoc. Naval Postgrad. Sch., 1986-87; cons. RAND Corp., 1949-66; mem. com. on basic rsch. adv. Office Ordnance Rsch., Nat. Acad. Scis.-NRC, 1955-58; mem. panel on applied math. adv. Nat. Bur. Standards, 1964-65; chmn. com. on stats. NRC, 1961-63; mem. exec. com. Conf. Bd. Math. Scis., 1963-64; mem. com. on support rsch. in math. scis. Nat Acad. Scis., 1965-68; mem. com. Pres.'s Statis. Socs., 1962-64; sci. dir. NATO Advanced Study Inst. on Discriminant Analysis and Its Applications, 1972. Author: An Introduction to Multivariate Statistical Analysis, 1958, 3d edit., 2003, The Statistical Analysis of Time Series, 1971, (with Somesh Das Gupta and George P.H. Styan) A Bibliography of Multivariate Statistical Analysis, 1972, (with Stanley Sclove) Introductory Statistical Analysis, 1974, An Introduction to the Statistical Analysis of Data, 1986, (with Jeremy D. Finn) The New Statistical Analysis of Data, 1996; editor: (with Krishna B. Athreya and Donald L. Iglehart) Probability, Statistics and Mathematics: Papers in Honor of Samuel Karlin, 1989, (with Kai Tai Fang) Statistical Inference in Elliptically Contoured and Related Distributions, 1990, (with K.T. Fang and I. Olkin) Multivariate Analysis and Its Applications, 1994; editor Anns. of Math. Stats., 1950-52; assoc. editor jour. Time Series Analysis, 1980-88; mem. adv. bd. Econometric Theory, 1985—, Jour. Multivariate Analysis, 1988—; mem. editl. bd. Psychometrika, 1954-72. Recipient R.A. Fisher award Pres.'s Statis. Socs., 1985, Disting. Alumnus award North Park Coll. and Theol. Sem., 1987, Minnehaha Acad., 1992, Award of Merit Northwestern U. Alumni Assn., 1989; named Wesley C. Mitchell Vis. Prof. Columbia U., 1983-84; Guggenheim fellow, 1947-48, fellow Ctr. for Advanced Study in Behavioral Scis., 1957-58; vis. scholar, 1972-73, 80; Sherman Fairchild disting. scholar Calif. Inst. Tech., 1980; vis. disting. prof. Norwegian Coun. Sci. and Indsl. Rsch. U. Oslo; Abraham Wald Meml. lectr., 1982; S.S. Wilks lectr. Princeton U., 1983, P.C. Mahalanobis Meml. lectr., 1985, S.N. Roy Meml. lectr. Calcutta U., 1985, Allen T. Craig lectr. U. Iowa, 1991, C.G. Khatri Meml. lectr. Pa. State U., 1992, George Zyskind Meml. lectr. Iowa State U., 1995. Fellow AAAS (chmn. sect. 1990-91), Am. Statis. Assn. (v.p. 1971-73, Samuel S. Wilks Meml. medal 1988, R.A. Fisher lectr. 1985), Econometric Soc., Royal Statis. Soc., Inst. Math. Stats. (pres. 1963), Am. Acad. Arts and Scis.; mem. NAS, Am. Math. Soc., Internat. Statis. Insts., Bernouilli Soc. for Math. Stats. and Probability, Norwegian Acad. Sci. and Letters (fgn.), Phi Beta Kappa. Achievements include research in multivariate statistical analysis, time series analysis, and econometrics. Home: 746 Santa Ynez St Stanford CA 94305-8441 Office: Stanford U Dept Stats Stanford CA 94305-4065 E-mail: twa@stat.stanford.edu.

ANDERSON, THOMAS CARYL, financial and administrative systems professional; b. St. Paul, Sept. 3, 1944; s. Willis Cecil and Mary Lou (Kaun) A.; m. Catherine Sophia Hofstede, Apr. 20, 1968; children: Nicole, Jennifer, Karilyn. BS, U. Minn., 1966, MS, 1970. Asst. prof. Northeastern U., Boston, 1971-74; lectr. SUNY-Albany, 1974-87, dir. grad. program Sch. Bus., 1976-81, dir. fin. and adminstrv. svcs., 1981-85, exec. officer adminstrn. and fin., 1985-87; dir. adminstrv. svcs. MGH Inst. Health Professions, Boston, 1987-90, v.p. adminstrn. and fin., 1990-93; v.p. fin. and adminstrn. Chatham Coll., Pitts., 1993-96; v.p. finance and adminstrn. Black Hills State U., Spearfish, S.D., 1996-2000; assoc. dean, lectr. Wayne State U. Sch. Bus. Adminstrn., Detroit, 2000—02, assoc. dean and chief of staff, 2002—. Cons. various state govt. agys., Albany, 1978-87, Fund for Corp. Initiatives, N.Y.C., 1981—, GM, CPC Tarrytown, N.Y., 1988-89, U. Mass., Lowell, 1990-94, Wang Labs. Inc., Lowell, 1992-93, Wayne State U., 1998—; asst. sec. MGH Inst. Bd. Trustees, Boston, 1987-93. Co-author: Elements of Organizational Behavior, 1972; contbr. articles to profl. publs. Mem. planning bd. Town of Hopedale, Mass., 1990-93, exec. com. Cen. Mass. Regional Planning Commn., 1990-93; treas. Black Hills State U. Found. Home: 920 W Forest Ave Apt 7 Detroit MI 48201-3736 Office: Wayne State U Sch of Bus Adminstrn Prentis Bldg 208 Detroit MI 48202

ANDERSON, THOMAS DUNAWAY, retired lawyer; b. Oklahoma City, Mar. 9, 1912; s. Frank Ervin and Burdine (Clayton) A.; m. Helen Sharp, Feb. 21, 1938; children: Helen Shaw, Lucille Streeter, John Sharp. Student, Rice Inst., 1930-31; LLB, Washington and Lee U., 1934; LLD (hon.), Lambuth Coll., 1967. Bar: Va. 1933, Tex. 1934. Assoc. Andrews & Kurth, 1934-41, 46-47; sr. v.p., trust officer Tex. Commerce Bank, Houston, 1947-51, 60-65; co-founder Tex. Fund, 1949; pres. Tex. Fund Mgmt. Co., Houston, 1952-60; ptnr. Anderson Brown & Jones, Houston, 1965-93; ret. Trustee emeritus Washington and Lee U.; life mem., past pres. bd. visitors M.D. Anderson Cancer Ctr.; past pres., chmn. Kelsey Rsch. Fedn., Protestant Episcopal Ch. Coun., Diocese of Tex., Washington-on-Brazos State Park Assn., Mus. Fine Arts Houston, Houston Grand Opera; bd. dirs. Bayou Bend Gardens Endowment, Retina Rsch. Found., Harris County Hist. Commn. First recipient Leon Jaworski award for vol. cmty. svc., 1988. Mem. ABA, Tex. Bar Assn., Philos. Soc. Tex., Bayou, Eagle Lake Rod and Gun Club, Houston Country Club, Petroleum Club of Houston, River Oaks Garden Club (hon.), SAR, Omicron Delta Kappa, Phi Delta Phi. Episcopalian. Office: River Oaks Bank Bldg 2001 Kirby Dr Houston TX 77019-6033

ANDERSON, THOMAS JEFFERSON, JR., composer, educator; b. Coatesville, Pa., Aug. 17, 1928; BMus, W.Va. State Coll., 1950; MMusEd, Pa. State U., 1951; PhD, U. Iowa, 1958; D in Musical Arts (hon.), Coll. Holy Cross; D.Mus. (hon.), West Va. State Coll., 1989, Bridgewater State Coll., 1991, St. Augustine's Coll., 1996, Northwestern U., 2002. Instr. W.Va. State Coll., 1955-56; prof. music, chmn. dept. Langston U., 1958-63; prof. Tenn. State U., 1963-69; vis. prof. Morehouse Coll., 1971-72; prof. music, chmn. dept. music Tufts U., Medford, Mass., 1972-80, Fletcher prof., 1978-90, Fletcher prof. emeritus, 1990—. Scholar-in-residence The Rockefeller Found. Study and Conf. Ctr., Bellagio, Italy, 1984, 94; orchestrated 1st complete performance of opera Treemonisha by Scott Joplin, Atlanta, 1992. Author: (with others) Readings in Black American Music, 1971, Reflections on Afro-American Music, 1973, The Black Composer Speaks, 1978, Racial and Ethnic Directions in American Music, 1982, Black Music in our Culture, 1970; composer: Messages for orch., 1979, Spirituals for orch., jazz quartet, chorus children's choir, tenor and narrator, 1979, Vocalise for harp and violin, 1980, Soldier Boy, Soldier for opera, 1982, Jonestown for children's choir and piano, 1982, Call and Response for piano, 1982, Intermezzi for clarinet, alto sax and piano, 1983, Thomas Jefferson's Orbiting Minstrels and Contraband for multimedia, 1984, Sunstar for solo trumpet and cassette recorder, 1984, Bridging and Branching for flute and double bass, 1987, Chamber Concerto for Chamber Orch., 1988, Bahia, Bahia for orch., 1990, Huh! What Do You Say? for clarinet and string quartet, 1997, Whatever Happened to the Big Bands?, 1992, Walker for chamber opera, 1992, Spirit Songs for cello and piano, 1993, 7 Cabaret Songs for jazz singer, flute, viola, cello and piano, 1994, Grace for string quartet, 1994, Broke Baroque for violin and piano, 1996, Huh! for clarinet and string quartet, 1996, Shouts for oboe, violin, cello and piano, 1997, b Bop in 2 for alto saxophone, 1998, Aurelia, in memoriam for violin, 1999, Slavery Documents 2 for chorus,orch. and 4 soloists, 2002, Game Play for viola, cello, flute and harp, 2002. Guggenheim fellow, 1988-89, fellow Nat. Humanities Ctr., 1996-97. Home: 111 Cameron Glen Dr Chapel Hill NC 27516-2333 Office: Tufts U Dept Music Medford MA 02155 E-mail: tj8@aol.com.

ANDERSON, THOMAS PATRICK, mechanical engineer, educator; b. Chgo., Oct. 22, 1934; s. Clarence Kenneth and Anne (Moran) A.; m. Elizabeth Ann Toof, July 9, 1960; children— Patricia, James. BS in Mech. Engring., Northwestern U., 1956, MS, 1958, PhD, 1961. Registered profl. engr., Ill., Iowa. Engr. Askania Regulator Co., Chgo., 1953-55; research engr. Cook Research Labs., Skokie, Ill., summer, 1956; rsch. engr. ARO Inc., Tullahoma, Tenn., summers 1958, 59; asst. prof., then assoc. prof. Northwestern U., 1960-66; prof. mech. engring. U. Iowa, 1966-75, chmn. dept., 1966-70; program mgr. Office Systems Integration and Analysis, NSF, 1974-75, program mgr. div. intergovtl. sci. and pub. tech., 1975-78, acting dir. indsl. program, 1976-78; dean Sch. Sci. and engring., So. Ill. U., Edwardsville, 1978-83; prof. Sch. Engring. So. Ill. U., 1978—. Cons., assoc. dep. dir. interdeptl. energy study Office Sci. and Tech., 1963-65 Contbr. numerous articles to profl. jours. Named One of Ten Outstanding Young Men Chgo. Jr. Assn. Commerce and Industry, 1964 Fellow Iowa Acad. Sci.; mem. AAUP, Am. Geophys. Union, AIAA, Am. Phys. Soc., Am. Soc. Engring. Edn., ASME (Edward F. Obert award 1997), Inst. Indsl. Engrs., Ill. Acad. Sci., N.Y. Acad. Scis., Phi Kappa Phi, Sigma Xi. E-mail: tanders@siue.edu.

ANDERSON, TIM, airport terminal executive; Dir. of airports Mpls. St. Paul Internat. Airport, 1996, dep. exec. dir. of ops., 1998—. Office: Mpls-St Paul Internat Airport 6040 28th Ave S Minneapolis MN 55450-2701

ANDERSON, TIMOTHY CHRISTOPHER, educational association administrator; b. Hinsdale, Ill., Dec. 27, 1950; s. Paul Eugene and Mary Agnes (Donnell) Anderson. BA in Polit. Sci. with honors, Boston Coll., 1973; MPA, Harvard U., 2000. Rsch. asst. to Rep. Thomas P. O'Neill U.S. Ho. Reps., Washington, 1973; ednl. cons. E. F. Shelly Co., Washington, 1973-74; assoc. dir. Boston Zool. Soc., 1974-76, exec. dir., adminstr. Boston's two zoos, 1976-81; New Eng. regional v.p. Nat. Alliance Bus., Boston, 1981-83; pres. Dovetail Cons., Hull, Mass., 1983—2001, Boston Harbor Assocs., 1983-87; ecology coord. Hull Pub. Schs., 1992—93; dir. Hull Environment and Svc. Corps, 1992-94; founder, CEO South Shore Charter Sch., 1994-99, headmaster, 1994-97; founder, pres. World Computer Exch., Hull, 1999—. Bd. dirs. VSAarts Mass., chmn. bd. dirs., 1998—2001; spl. projects dir. South Shore Edn. Collaborative, 1993—94; cons. NEH, 1977—78; trustee, chmn. bd. dirs. South Shore Charter Sch., 1994—95; chmn. bd. dirs. W. Seavey Joyce SJ Award, 1988—. Internat. bd. advisors Ctr. Edn. and Devel., Bangladesh, 2000—; mem. Global Digital Divide Task Force World Econ. Forum, 2001—03. Named Hon. Prof. Tbilisi Orbeliani, State Pedagogical U., 2002, Hon. Citizen, Kutaisi, Georgia, recipient Cmty. Svc. award, Girl Scouts Greater Boston, 1978, Leadership Commendation award, Nat. Alliance Bus., 1983, Leadership award, Mass. Cultural Alliance, 1986, Pres.'s award, 1986, Leadership award, Franklin Pk. Coalition, 1987, Boston Mgmt. Consortium, 1992, John Ames award, Boston Harbor Assocs., 1987, Mayor's cert. of recognition, 1992, Supts. Leadership award, 1992, Excellence award, S. Shea Charter Sch. Students, 1999, badge of honor, Republic of Georgia, 2002. Office: World Computer Exch 936 Nantasket Ave Hull MA 02045-1453 E-mail: tanderson@worldcomputerexchange.org.

ANDERSON, TIMOTHY J. chemical engineering educator; Prof., chmn. dept. chem. engring. U. Fla., Gainsville. Recipient Charles M.A. Stine award in Materials Engring. and Sci. Am. Inst. Chem. Engrs., 1994. Office: U Fla Dept Chem Engring 229 Che Bldg/Box 116005 Gainesville FL 32611-6005

ANDERSON, BROTHER TIMOTHY MEL, academic administrator; b. Oakland, Calif., Sept. 28, 1928; BA, St. Mary's Coll., Moraga, Calif., 1952; DLitt, St. Albert's Coll., 1976; LHD, Lewis U., 1979; DHL (hon.), U. San Francisco, 1994; D in Pedagogy (hon.), Manhattan Coll., 1994. Joined Brothers of the Christian Schs. 1947. Joined Brothers of the Christian Schools, 1952; tchr. Sacred Heart High Sch., San Francisco, 1952-56; vice prin. La Salle High

Sch., Pasadena, Calif., 1956-62; prin. San Joaquin Meml. High Sch., Fresno, Calif., 1962-64; prin., superior St Mary's High Sch., Residence Sch., Grammar Sch., Berkeley, Calif., 1964-69; pres. St. Mary's Coll. of Calif., Moraga, 1969-97; dir. spl. projects Diocese of Oakland, Calif., 1999—. Trustee St. Mary's Coll., Moraga., 1968-97. Recipient Alemany award Dominican Sch. of Theology and Philosophy, 1992, Papal Pro Ecclesia medal, 1994, Disting. Lasallian Educator award, 1997; named Alumnus of Yr., St. Mary's Coll., 1987; inductee Contra Costa County Hall of Fame, 1988, Anti-Defamation League's Torch of Liberty award, 1993; named Citizen of Yr. town of Moraga, 1994. Fellow Assn. Ind. Calif. Colls. and Univs. (sr.; exec. com. 1973—, chmn. 1988, 89); mem. Regional Assn. East Bay Colls. and Univs. (chmn. 1979-81, 90-91), Fratres Scholarum Christianarum, Christian Brothers, 1947. Lodges: Rotary Internat. Democrat. Roman Catholic. Avocations: photography, woodworking, travel, drama, music. Office: Oakland Diocese 2900 Lakeshore Ave Oakland CA 94610-3614

ANDERSON, TONI P. music educator, vocalist; b. Orange, Tex., Sept. 1, 1957; d. Norman F and Lois M Passmore; m. Charles M Anderson, Aug. 13, 1978; children: Erin M, Wesley C, Brian P. PhD higher edn., Ga. State U., Atlanta, GA, 1993—97; MusM vocal performance, The New Eng. Conservatory of Music, Boston, MA, 1980—82; MusB edn., Lamar U., Beaumont, TX, 1975—79. Asst prof. of voice Morris Brown Coll., Atlanta, Ga., 1985—99; chair and assoc. prof. LaGrange Coll., LaGrange, Ga., 1999. Author: (journal article) The Southeastern Jour. of Music Edn., (essay) Affirmed Action: Essays on the Acad. and Social Lives of White Faculty Members at Hist. Black Colleges and Univ.; singer: (opera premier) Zabette, by Curtis Bryant (Ga. State U), The Opera Singer, by Sharon Willis (Americolor Opera Alliance); contbr. documentary video. Bd. mem. Brethren in Christ Gen. Conf. Bd. for Congl. Life, 1990—94, Brethren in Christ SE Conf. Bd. for Ministries, 1990—94; vp LaGrange Performing Arts Ctr., LaGrange, Ga., 2002—03. Recipient, Internat. Who's Who of Profl. & Bus. Women, 2000, Pi Kappa Delta Edn. Honor Soc., 1994, Cap & Gown Nat. Honor Soc., 1979-1980, Who's Who Among Am. Colleges & Universities, 1980; grantee Rsch. Grant, LaGrange Coll., 2002, Faculty Devel. Grant, United Negro Coll. Fund, 1997, Rsch. Grant, Morris Brown Coll., 1998. Mem.: Music Educators Nat. Conf., AAUP, Ga. State Chpt. of Nat. Assn. of Teachers of Singing (v.p. 2002), Soc. of Am. Music, Coll. Music Soc., Nat. Assn. of Teachers of Singing, Singers Resource Svc. (bd. mem. 1989—92), Delta Omicron Internat. Music Frat. (life). Protestant. Avocations: travel, reading. Office: LaGrange College 601 Broad Street Lagrange GA 30240 Office Fax: 706-880-8028. E-mail: tanderson@lagrange.edu.

ANDERSON, URSULA M. pediatrician; b. Cheshire, England, 1929; MB BS, Liverpool (Eng.) U., 1953, diploma in pub. health, 1956; diploma in psychol. medicine, London U., 1958; diploma in child health, Royal Coll. Physicians, London. Diplomate Am. Bd. Pediats. Intern and resident Liverpool United Tchg. Hosps., 1953—57; fellow dept. pediatrics Yale U., New Haven, 1960—63; assoc. prof. pediats. SUNY, Buffalo; dir. maternal and child health Buffalo/Erie County; med. dir. interagy. programs for children, regional med. cons. U.S. Dept. Health, Edn. and Welfare; chief divsn. cmty. pediats., assoc. prof. pediats U. Toronto, Canada; disting. prof., rsch. prof. Forest Inst. Profl. Psychology. Cons. divsn. rsch. WHO, Geneva; cons. Nat. Perinatal Assn., National and Regional Head Start Programs; chmn. N.Y. State Task Force on Health Manpower, Albany, NY; mem. pediat. delegation to USSR People to People. Author: Reading Instruction, Dimensions and Issues, 1968, Weeds and Seedlings, 1991, The Psalms of Children, Their Songs and Laments, 1997, Immunology of the Soul, The Paradigm for the Future, 2000, Taking Out the Violence, 2003; contbr. numerous articles to profl. jours. Recipient Merit of Excellence award, UN Open U.; grantee numerous grants for rsch. edn. and svc., U.S. and Can. Fellow: Am. Acad. Pediats.; mem.: Royal Coll. Surgeons. Mailing: 8275 Crumb Hill Rd East Otto NY 14729-9748

ANDERSON, URTON LIGGETT, accounting educator; b. Salem, Ohio, Dec. 10, 1951; s. Urton and Alice (Kenrich) A.; m. Deborah Mary Johnson, June 12, 1973; children: Bryony, Urton. BA in Greek and Philosophy magna cum laude, St. Olaf Coll., 1974; MA in Classics, U. Minn, 1977; PhD in Bus. Adminstrn., U. Minn., 1985. Cert. internal auditor Inst. Internal Auditors; cert. control self-assessment Inst. Internal Auditors. Instr. dept. acctg. U. Tex., Austin, 1984-85, asst. prof. dept. acctg., 1988-89, assoc. prof. dept. acctg., 1989-95, prof. dept. acctg., 1995—, assoc. dir. C. Aubrey Smith Ctr. for Auditing Edn. and Rsch., 1989-92, dir. C. Aubrey Smith Ctr. for Auditing Edn. and Rsch., 1992-93, acting dept. chair, 1996, assoc. dean ubdergrad. programs Coll. Bus., 1997—. Clark W. Thompson Jr. prof. in acctg. edn. U. Tex., Austin, 1997—. Author: Quality Assurance for Internal Auditing, 1983; co-editor: Internal Auditing, 1990—2001; contbr. articles to profl. jours.; : Implementing the Professional Practices Framework, 2002. Rsch. fellow KPMG Peat Marwick Found., 1988-89, faculty fellow, 1990-92, Rsch. Opportunities in Auditing grantee, 1991, 94, Ernst & Young faculty fellow, 1988-93, Atlantic Richfield Centennial fellow in acctg., 1993-97. Mem. Inst. Internal Auditors Rsch. Found. (bd. rsch. advisors 1985-94), Inst. Internal Auditors (bd. regents 1994-99, 2003—, chmn. 2003—, internal auditing standards bd. 1999-2003, chair 2002-03, cert. internal auditor, cert. control self-assessment, cert. govt. audit profl). Office: U Tex Austin Dept Acctg CBA 4M 202 Austin TX 78712-1172 E-mail: urton@mail.utexas.edu.

ANDERSON, VERA STRONG, retired dentist; b. Mound Bayou, Miss., Aug. 5, 1931; d. Will Clarence and Charlotte Montgomery Strong; m. Arthur Ray Anderson, Apr. 21, 1955; children: Arthur Ray Jr., Lisa LaMarr. BS, Tenn. State U., 1953; DDS, Meharry Med. Coll., 1957. Practiced dentistry, Memphis, 1960—65; intern Cambridge State Hosp.; pres., founder An-Strong Symbols, Inc., nonprofit corp., Richmond, Calif., 1992—. Designer African Am. flag, motivational spkr. in promotion of racial harmony. Recipient Offcl. Citation, Gary Common Coun., 1993, Commendation award, County of Alameda 4th Dist., 1993, Cert. Recognition, Calif. Legis. Assembly, 1994, Cert. Appreciation, Golden Gate U. NAACP, 1997. Democrat. Office: An-Strong Symbols Inc PO Box 2725 Richmond CA 94801 Office Fax: 510-620-0194.

ANDERSON, VICKI, retired librarian; b. Hazleton, Pa., June 17, 1928; d. Steven and Edith Potochney; m. Richard Anderson. BA, San Diego State Coll., 1961; MLS, U. Calif., Berkeley, 1962; postgrad., U. Pa., 1985—86. Libr. San Diego (Calif.) City Pub. Libr., 1962—64, San Diego City Schs., 1965—90; ret., 1991. Mem. Calif. State Coun. Edn., San Francisco, 1968—71, San Diego Citizen Adv. Com., 1978; spkr. San Diego City Coll., 1965; instr. Grossmont (Calif.) Coll., 1975—80, San Diego State Coll., 1981. Author: Fiction Sequels For readers 10 to16, 1989, 2d edit., 1998, Fiction Index for Readers 10 to 16, 1992, Cultures Outside the United States in Fiction, 1994, Sequels in Children's Literature K-6, 1998, Immigrants in the United States in Fiction, 1994, Native Americans in Fiction, 1994; Dime Novel: Its History and Context in Children's Literature in Production, 2003. Chmn. Public Employees Coord. Coun., San Diego, 1978—79; mem. N. Mt. Village Planning Com.; committeeman Willow Precinct Dem. Party, Phoenix, 1995; state com. mem. Dem. Party State Com., Phoenix, 1995; active Legislative Dist. 18, Phoenix, 1994; mem. exec. com. Maricopa County Dem. Party, 2002; chmn. Legis. Dist. 6, 2002; pres. Kensington-Talmadge Cmty. Assn., San Diego, 1976—78. Grantee, Dakota State Coll., 1970. Mem.: AAUW (v.p. fin.), Moon Hills Cmty. Group (chmn.), Ariz. Silver Haired Legislators (elected del.). Democrat. Avocations: reading, sewing, weaving. Home: 12833 N Fifteenth Ave Phoenix AZ 85029 Personal E-mail: valjest@aol.com.

ANDERSON, VINCENT PAUL, military officer; b. L.A., Calif., Dec. 21, 1924; s. Vincent Paul Anderson Sr. and Mary Esther (Orr) Anderson; m. Martha Janice Blake, May 21, 1953; children: Jandy Rebecca, Marion Kathleen, William Scott. Student, U. So. Calif., 1945—49; BS in Aero. Engring., Air Force Inst. Tech., 1959; MS in Indsl. Mgmt., U. N.D., 1967. Navigator 380th Heavy Bomb Group USAF, 1944—45, pilot, 1951—68, comdr. Minuteman Internat. Ballistic Missile 455th Strategic Missile Wing, 1963—68; ret. lt. col. Air Force, 1968. Dir. $130 million Airborne Long Range Input Program Aero. divsn. USAF, Dayton, Ohio, 1962—63. Author: The Better Part of Valor, 2001. Decorated Air medal with 5 oak leaf clusters USAF. Mem.: Mil. Officers Assn. Am., San Joaquin County Sheriffs Assn. Republican. Episcopalian. Avocations: tennis, sailing, hiking. Home: 3692 Wood Duck Cir Stockton CA 95207-5264

ANDERSON, W. FRENCH, biochemist, physician; b. Tulsa, Okla., Dec. 31, 1936; m. Kathryn D. Anderson, June 24, 1961. AB magna cum laude, Harvard U., 1958, MD magna cum laude, 1963; MA, Cambridge U., 1960; LHD (hon.), U. Okla., 1992; DSc (hon.), U. Tulsa, 1996, SUNY, 2002. Diplomate Nat. Bd. Med. Examiners, 1964, lic. DC, 1963. Intern pediatric medicine Children's Hosp. Med. Ctr., Boston, 1963—64; rsch. fellow Harvard Med. Sch., Boston, 1964—65; rsch. assoc. lab. biochem. genetics Nat. Heart, Lung & Blood Inst., 1965-67, rsch. med. officer, 1967-68, head sect. human biochem., 1968-71, head sect. molecular hematology, 1971-73, chief molecular hematology br., 1973-92; cons. in rsch., genetics program George Wash. U., 1975—78; prof. biochemistry and pediatrics, dir. gene therapy labs. U. So. Calif. Norris Cancer Ctr., 1992—, program coord. for gene therapy, 1995—; adj. prof., grad. genetics program George Wash. U., 1978—92. Rsch. fellow bacteriology and immunology med. sch. Harvard U., 1964—65; prof. lectr. sch. medicine George Washington U., 1967—75; mem. faculty dept. genetics Grad. Program, NIH, 1967—92; mem. dept. medicine & physiology NIH, 1981—92, chmn. dept. medicine & physiology, 1984—92; mem. heart fellow bd. Nat. Heart & Lung Inst., NIH, 1968—70; mem. task force hemoglobinopathies Nat. Heart, Lung and Blood Inst., NIH, 1972, mem. nat. task group on Cooley's anemia, 1977—78; pres. Assembly of Scientists, Nat. Heart, Lung and Blood Inst., NIH, 1982; chmn., inter-agy. coord. com. on Cooley's anemia NIH, 1972—77, chmn. inter-agy. coord. com. on Cooley's anemia, HEW, 1975—77; mem. exec. com. & bd. dirs. Found. Adv. Educ. in Scis., Inc., nih, 1984—92; mem. working group human gene therapy, recombinant DNA adv. com. NIH, 1984—86, mem. working group on viruses, recombinant DNA adv. com., 1985—86; hematology program dir. Lab Molecular Hematology, NIH, 1985; mem. coord. com. human genome NIH, 1988—92; mem. sr. exec. sci. svc. Dept. Health and Human Svc., 1980—92; cons. Pres. Commn. Study Ethical Problems Medicine & Biomed. Behavior Rsch., 1981—82, Human Gene Therapy Ctr. for Bioethics, Kennedy Inst. Ethics, Wash., DC, 1982—92; chmn. sci. adv. bd. Genetic Therapy Inc., Gaithersburg, Md., 1986—87; mem. sci. adv. bd. S/L Health Care Ventures, N.Y.C., 1986—88, N.Y.C., 1993—; cons. human gene therapy St. Jude Childrens Rsch. Hosp., Memphis, 1990—92, U. Pitt., 1990—92, Baylor Coll. Medicine, Houston, 1990—92, M.D. Anderson Hosp., Houston, 1990—92; chmn. scientific adv. com. Children's Nat. Med. Ctr., Wash., DC, 1990—92; lectr. Mider Lecture, NIH, 1992, Timely Topics Lecture, U.S. and Can. Acad. Pathology, 1992, Frontiers in Clin Sci. Lecture, Am. Fedn. Clin. Rsch., 1992, Myron Karon Meml. Lectureship, Children's Hosp., L.A., 1992, Disting. Sci. Lecture, Internat. and Am. Assns. Dental Rsch., 1993, Plenary Lecture, 17th Internat. Congress of Genetics, 1993, Martin Meml. Lecture, 79th Ann. Clin. Congress, Am. Coll. Surgeons, 1993, Plenary Lecture, Am. Acad. Pediatrics, 1993, others; bd. dirs. various; mem. Inst. Genetic Medicine, U. So. Calif. Sch. Medicine, 1992—; vis. assoc. in applied physics Calif. Inst. Tech., 2001—. Co-editor: Fifth Cooley's Anemia Symposium, 1985; mem. editl. bd. various publs. Mem. med. resources coun. Cooley's Anemia Blood & Rsch. Found for Children, 1974-77; mem. adv. bd. Cooley's Anemia Found., Inc., 1977—; mem. sci. adv. com. Children's Hosp. Rsch. Found., Cin., 1985-88; commd. officer USPHS, 1965-67. Recipient Thomas B. Cooley award Sci. Achievement Cooley's Anemia Blood & Rsch. Found. for Children, 1977, Mary Ann Liebert Biotherapeutic award, 1991, Pres. Award lectr. Am. Thoracic Soc., 1991, Maude L. Menten award U. Pitts., 1991, Ralph R. Braund award U. Tenn., 1991, Presdl. Meritorious Exec. Rank award HHS, 1991, Fed. Lab. Consortium award for Excellence in Tech. Transfer, 1992, Disting. Svc. award Nat. Ctr. Infectious Diseases, 1993, Dr. Murray Thelin award Nat. Hemophilia Found., 1993, Drew award lectr., 1993, King Faisal ibn Abdul Aziz Internat. Prize for Medicine, 1994, NORD Leadership award Nat. Orgn. Rare Disorders, 1996; named BioPharm Person of Yr. Biopharm Mag. editl. adv. bd., 1994. Fellow AAAS; mem. Assn. Am. Physicians, Am. Soc. Clin. Investigation, Am. Soc. Hematology, Am. Soc. Human Genetics, Am. Soc. Biol. Chemists, Am. Fedn. Clin. Rsch., Am. Soc. Gene Therapy, Internat. Soc. Stem Cell Rsch., Peripatetic Club. Achievements include research in regulation of RNA and protein synthesis, hemoglobin biosynthesis, thalassemia and hemoglobinopathies, gene expression in mammalian cells, genetic engineering of mammalian cells, human gene therapy. 10 patents issued. Office: U So Calif Keck Sch Medicine Norris Cancer Ctr Rm 6316 1441 Eastlake Ave Los Angeles CA 90033 E-mail: sdiaz@genome2.hsc.usc.edu.

ANDERSON, WALTER HERMAN, magazine publisher; b. Mt. Vernon, NY, Aug. 31, 1944; s. Walter Henry and Ethel Magdalena (Crolly) Anderson; m. Loretta Gritz, Sept. 9, 1967; children: Eric Christian, Melinda Christe. AA, Westchester C.C., 1970; BS summa cum laude, Mercy Coll., 1972; DHL (hon.), St. Ambrose U., 1988, Clemson U., 1990, Mercy Coll., 1989, U. of the Pacific, 1990. Reporter Reporter Dispatch, White Plains, NY, 1967—68, night city editor, 1968—69, editor, gen. mgr., 1975—77; police reporter Westchester Rockland Newspapers, White Plains, NY, 1969—70, help editor for action line, 1970—71, investigative reporter, 1971—72, mng. editor, 1973—74; editor, gen, mgr. Standard Star, New Rochelle, NY, 1974—75; sr. editor Parade mag., N.Y.C., 1977—78, mng. editor, 1978—80, editor-in-chief, 1980—2000, chmn., publ., CEO, 2000—02, chmn., CEO, 2002—. Author: Courage is a Three-Letter Word, 1986, The Greatest Risk of All, 1988, Read With Me, 1990, The Confidence Course, 1997, Meant to Be, 2003; actor(one-man show): Talkin' Stuff, 1992. Chmn. bd. trustees Mercy Coll, Dobbs Ferry, NY, 1980—88; bd. dirs. St. Vincent Hosp., 1975—80, N.Y. Vietnam Vets. Leadership Program Inc., 1984—89, Dropout Prevention Fund, 1987—, Nat. Ctr. for Family Literacy, 1990—, Very Spl. Arts, 1990—; bd. advisors Naval Postgrad. Sch., 1988—; mem. nat. adv. bd. Lit. Vols., 1990—2002; apptd. to U.S. Commn. on Librs. and Info. Sci., Pres. Clinton, 1995—2001. With USMC, 1961—66. Recipient Frank Tripp Meml. award, Gannett Group, 1971, Tree of Life award, Jewish Nat. Fund, 1988, Spirit of Am. award, 1988, Napoleon Hill Gold award, 1989, Horatio Alger award, 1994, Literacy Vols. of Am. Stars in Literacy cert., 1990, others. Mem.: Soc. Silurians, Overseas Press, Psi Chi, Sigma Delta Chi. Office: Parade Publs Inc 711 3rd Ave New York NY 10017-4014 *I hope a single driving desire remains with me always— that is, to encourage talented people. To share, even in the least of ways, in the growth of a creative talent is the highest goal of an editor, if his career is to matter at all.**

ANDERSON, WALTER LEE, environmental educator, artist, photographer; b. Mt. Vernon, Wash., Feb. 25, 1946; s. Arthur J. and Thelma E. Anderson; m. Rebecca M. Johnson, Feb. 3, 1968; children: Christopher Quill, Rowan Reed. BS with highest honors, Wash. State U., 1968; MS, U. Ariz., 1974; postgrad., U. Mich., 1976. Wildlife biologist, pub. use specialist U.S. Fish & Wildlife Svc., 1968, 70-72; co-dir. W. Butte Sanctuary Co., Colusa, Calif., 1976-78; founder, dir. Sutter Buttes Naturalists, Colusa, 1979-84; prof. environ. studies Prescott (Ariz.) Coll., 1991—. Freelance artist, photographer, 1976—; internat. expedition guide Voyagers Internat., others, 1979—; lectr. Am. Orient Express, Seattle, 1996-98; dir. emeritus Mid. Mountain Found., Yuba City, Calif., 1998—. Author, illustrator: The Sutter Buttes: A Naturalist's View, 1983; illustrator: (book) Coexisting with Urban Wildlife, 1996; contbg. author, photographer: California's Wild Gardens, 1997. Merit badge counselor Boy Scouts Am., Wash., 1960-64, Ariz., 1995—; sec., bd. dirs. Ctrl. Ariz. Land Trust, Yavapai County, 1995-97; choir mem. 1st Congl. Ch., Prescott, 1996-98. Staff sgt. U.S. Army, 1968-70, Vietnam. Recipient Best in show award Nat. Wildlife Art Show, 1980; NSF fellow U. Ariz., U. Mich., 1973-75. Mem. Soc. Conservation Biology, Nat. Wildlife Fedn. (life), Am. Ornithologists' Union (life), Nat. Geographic Soc. (life), Nature Conservancy (bd. dirs. no. Calif. chpt. 1979-81), Ariz. Riparian Coun., Phi Beta Kappa, Phi Kappa Phi, Omicron Delta Kappa, Phi Eta Sigma. Avocations: hiking, singing. Home: 1964 Sherwood Dr Prescott AZ 86303-5650 Office: Prescott Coll Environ Studies 220 Grove Ave Prescott AZ 86301-2912 E-mail: geolobo@cableone.net.

ANDERSON, WARREN LEE, II, marketing professional; b. Kansas City, Mo., Jan. 27, 1952; s. Warren Lee and Helen Jesse Anderson; m. Kathleen Ann Benson, Jan. 6, 1979; children: Jessica Lee, Ryan Joseph. BS in Biology, U. Mo., Kansas City, 1979; MA in Mktg. with distinction, Webster U., 1986. Lab. tech. Curts Labs., Kansas City, 1975-77; analytical chemist Marion Labs., Inc., Kansas City, 1977-81, internat. mktg. adminstr. product registrations, 1981-83, mgr. internat. sales adminstrn., 1983-85, mgr. internat. mktg., 1986-90, mgr., relationship mktg., 1990-93, managed care markets mgr., 1993-94; pres., founder Anderson Cons. Group, 1994—. Contbr. Marion Labs. Polit. Action Com., 1985—. Active United Way, Kansas City, 1983—; chmn. security com. River Oaks South Home Owners Assn., 1986—; mem. safety com. local PTA, 1986—; co-chmn. bus. adv. coun. NRCC, Republican Chmn. Honor Roll, 2003. Named one of Outstanding Young Men Am., 1985, Nova Marketer of Distinction award Am. Mktg. Assn., 1991, Mo. Businessman of Yr. award Rep. Congl. Com., 1998, 2003. Mem. Phi Kappa Phi; Clubs: Toastmasters. Lutheran. Avocations: outdoor sports, woodworking, poetry. E-mail: andersonKC@aol.com.

ANDERSON, WARREN MATTICE, lawyer; b. Bainbridge, N.Y., Oct. 16, 1915; s. Floyd E. and Edna (Mattice) Anderson; m. Eleanor C. Sanford, June 28, 1941 (dec. Sept. 1996); children: Warren David, Lawrence, Richard, Thomas; m. Ruth W. Bennett, Aug. 25, 2001. BA, Colgate U., 1937; JD, Albany Law Sch., 1940, LLD (hon.), 1979, Hartwick Coll., 1976, Coll. of New Rochelle, 1979, Fordham U., 1980, Union Coll., 1981, Colgate U., 1982, Hamilton Coll., 1985, Clarkson U., 1987, St. Lawrence U., 1988, Elmira Coll., 1989, St. Francis Coll., 1991; LHD (hon.), Hofstra U., 1987. Bar: N.Y., 1940. Since practiced in, Binghamton; asst. county atty. Broome County, N.Y., 1940-42; assoc. Hinman, Howard & Kattell LLP, 1949-52; ptnr. Hinman, Howard & Kattell, 1952—; mem. N.Y. State Senate, 1953-88, chmn. fin. com., 1966-72, pres. pro tem, majority leader, 1973-88. Del. Rep. Nat. Conv., 1972, 76, 80, 84, 88, mem. platform com., 1972; trustee Colgate U., 1964-70, Cornell U., 1973-88, Elmira Coll., 1989-95; mem. N.Y. State Commn. on Jud. Nominations; mem. Hartwick Coll. Coun.; mem. adv. com. Govt. Law Ctr., Albany Law Sch.; mem. bd. overseers Nelson A. Rockefeller Inst. Govt. With AUS, 1943-45, lt. JAGD, 1945-46. Recipient Alumni award Colgate U., 1972 Fellow Am. Bar Found.; mem. ABA, Broome County Bar Assn. Clubs: Binghamton; Oteyokwa Lake (Hallstead, Pa.). Presbyterian. Home: 34 Lathrop Ave Binghamton NY 13905-4343 Office: Hinman Howard & Kattell 700 Security Mut Bldg Binghamton NY 13902-5250

ANDERSON, WARREN RONALD, electrical engineering educator; b. July 31, 1914; s. Wallace Roy and Helen Adelia (Abrahamson) A.; m. Dantza Peinovich, May 28, 1945; children: Richard Godfrey, John Warren, Deborah Annete. AA, Bethel Coll., 1935; BS, U. Minn., 1939; BSEE, La. State U., 1944. Registered profl. engr., Calif. Design engr. Plant Engring. Agy., Phila., 1945-46; circuits engr. Automatic Electric, Chgo., 1946; prof. elec. engring. Calif. Polytech. State U., San Luis Obispo, 1946-76, head elec. engring. dept., 1976-79, prof. emeritus, 1979—. Design engr. GE, Ft. Wayne, Ind., 1951; rsch. analyst Northup Aircraft, Hawthorne, Calif., 1952; sys. engr. Western Gear Corp., Lynwood, Calif., 1955; edn. cons. GE, Schenectady, 1956. Leader Boy Scouts Am., San Luis Obispo, 1958-64. With U.S. Army, 1942-45. Recipient Cert of Appreciation AIEE, 1963. Mem. IEEE, NSPE, Am. Soc. Engring. Edn., Calif. Soc. Profl. Engrs. (dir. 1949-55), Calif. State Employees Assn. (dir. 1955-59), Eta Kappa Nu. Democrat. Baptist. Home: 573 Jeffrey Dr San Luis Obispo CA 93405-1003 Office: Calif Poly State Univ Elec Engring Dept San Luis Obispo CA 93407 E-mail: wanderso@charter.net.

ANDERSON, WAYNE ARTHUR, electrical engineering educator; b. Jamestown, N.Y., May 20, 1938; s. Arthur Charles and Flora Mary (Funicello) A.; m. Marilyn Mae Anderson, July 28, 1964; children: Wayne P., Leslie M. BA, SUNY, Buffalo, 1961, MS, 1965, PhD, 1970. Rsch. engr. Gt. Lakes Carbon, Niagara Falls, N.Y., 1961-65; instr. elec. engring. SUNY, 1965-70, prof., 1978—, Rutgers U., New Brunswick, N.J., 1970-78. Cons. Exxon, Linden, N.J., 1972-76, Amerace Corp., N.J., 1974-76; reviewer NSF, 1979—; dir., Ctr. for Electronic and Electro-Optic Materials, 1986-96, chmn. elec. and computer engring. dept., 1989-95. Contbr. over 150 articles to profl. jours. Chmn. Internat. Students Com., 1983—; deacon 1st Bapt. Ch., 1984-87, Westerly Road Ch., 1973-76. Grantee Solar Energy Rsch. Inst., 1975-83, NSF, 1972-74, 80-83, 92-96, 97—, Intelstat, 1980-84, Office Naval Rsch., 1986-89, NYSERDA, 1991-95, 99-00, Nat. Renewable Energy Lab., 1993-95, 98-99. Mem. IEEE (sr., bd. dirs. 1981-84), Materials Rsch. Soc., Am. Inst. Physics. Republican. Avocations: tennis, golf, biking. Home: 39 Sleepy Hollow Ln Orchard Park NY 14127-4617 Office: SUNY Elec and Computer Engring 217C Bonner Hall Buffalo NY 14260-1900 E-mail: waanders@eng.buffalo.edu.

ANDERSON, WAYNE CARL, public affairs officer, former corporate executive; b. Sheboygan, Wis., May 5, 1935; s. Chester Phillip and Mabel Mary (Edler) A.; m. Joan Dorothy Staranick, May 18, 1963; children: David Wayne, Steven Michael, Karen Colleen. BS in Bus. Adminstrn., Upsala Coll., 1977. Cert. arbitrator, mediator. Dir. state govt. rels. Nabisco Brands Co., Parsippany, N.J., 1974-78, dir. fed. govt. rels., 1978-79, dir. govt. rels., 1979-81, v.p. govt. rels., 1981-84, v.p. govt. and cmty. rels., 1984-87, v.p. pub. affairs, 1987; non-lawyer exec. Evans Kitchel & Jenckes, P.C., 1988-89; pres., CEO Ariz. C. of C., 1990-95; exec. v.p. Americare, 1996-98; exec. emeritus Thunderbird--The Am. Grad. Sch. Internat. Mgmt., 1999—. Guest lectr. in field. Editl. adv. bd. Pub. Affairs in Rev., 1980; contbr. articles to profl. jours. Mem. Roseland (N.J.) Planning Bd., 1978—79, Roseland Citizens Adv. Com., 1977—78; trustee State Govt. Rsch. and Edn. Found., 1981—82; mem. gov.'s adv. coun. on quality, 1991—95, gov.'s commn. econ. devel., 1991—95, Ariz. Space Commn., 1992—2000, commr. emeritus, 1996; bd. dirs. Quality Alliance, 1992—95, NCCJ, Fiesta Bowl Com., Ariz. Econ. Forum, Ariz. Utility Investors, Philos. Soc. Ariz., 2001—; statewide com. chmn. Superbowl XXX, 1995—96; chmn. adv. bd. NYU, Baruch Coll., U. N.Y.; pres. Grace Luth. Ch., Livingston, NJ, 1980—81, chmn. bd. elders, 1981—82; trustee Evang. Luth. Synod, 2003—; elder Redeemer Luth. Ch., Scottsdale, Ariz., 1997—98, v.p., 1998—. Served with U.S. Army, 1958—60. Mem. Internat. Jaycees (senator 1989—), U.S. Jaycees (nat. dir. 1964-65), Pub. Affairs Coun. (exec. com. 1986, bd. dirs. 1988—), Nat. Fgn. Trade Coun. (dir. 1986), State Govt. Affairs Coun. (past pres. 1978-79), Ford's Theatre (bd. govs.), Acad. Polit. Sci., Pub. Affairs Profls. Ariz. (founder 1987—), World Affairs Coun. (pres. 1994-95), Thunderbird Am. Grad. Sch. Internat. Mgmt., Thunderbird Global Coun. E-mail: azwca@worldnet.att.net.

ANDERSON, WAYNE KEITH, dean, educator; b. Pine Falls, Manitoba, Can., Apr. 4, 1941; s. Sigward Emmanuel and Verna Madelaine Anderson; m. Ellen Lorraine Robertson, Aug. 31, 1962; children: Brian Ross, Laura Elizabeth, Shari Lynn. BS in Pharmacy, U. Manitoba, 1962, MS, 1964; PhD, U. Wis., 1968. Asst. prof. to prof. medicinal chemistry Univ. at Buffalo (N.Y.), 1968-81, prof., medicinal chemistry, 1981—, prof., chemistry, 1993—, assoc. chmn., medicinal chemistry, 1994-95, dean Sch. Pharmacy and Pharm. Sci., 1995—. Peer reviewer Nat. Acad. Sci., Washington, 1995—, NIH, Washington, 1986-94, U.S. Army Med. Rsch., Washington, 1993-95, Nat. Cancer Inst., Washington, 1992—. Contbr. articles to profl. jours.; patentee in new anticancer drugs. Recipient Niagara Frontier Inventor of Yr., 1988; Drug Discovery grant Mitsubishi Kasei, 1988—; grantee NIH/Nat. Cancer Inst., 1971-95. Mem. Am. Assn. Coll. Pharmacy, Am. Chemical Soc. (medicinal chemistry divsn.), Am. Pharm. Assn., Pharmacists Soc. N.Y., Pharmacists Assn. Western N.Y. Avocations: genealogy, fishing, hockey, golf, travel. Office: Univ at Buffalo Sch Pharmacy 126 Cooke Hall Buffalo NY 14260-1300

ANDERSON, WES, film director; b. Houston, May 1, 1969; Writer, prodr., dir.: films Rushmore, 1998, The Royal Tenenbaums, 2001, writer, dir.: films Bottle Rocket, 1994. Office: UTA 5th Fl 9560 Wilshire Blvd Beverly Hills CA 90212*

ANDERSON, WILLIAM, JR., (WILLIAM ALBION ANDERSON JR.), investment banker; b. Paris, Ark., July 12, 1939; s. William A. and Maud (Rodgers) A.; m. Patricia P. Puterbaugh, July 5, 1968; stepchildren— Charles L. Kuehn, Cynthia P. Robinson. BSBA, U. Ark., 1961; MBA, Harvard U., 1963. With Blyth Eastman Dillon & Co., Inc., N.Y.C., 1963-75, exec. asst. to chief exec. officer, dir. planning, 1973-74, sr. v.p., 1974-75; sr. v.p., chief fin. officer ENSTAR Corp., Houston, 1975-84; pres. Farmers Oil Co., 1987-96; ltd. ptnr. Weller, Anderson, & Co., Ltd., Houston, 1988—. Mng. trustee J. G. Puterbaugh Trust. Mem. River Oaks Country Club (Houston), The Houston Club. Office: 811 Rusk St Ste 715 Houston TX 77002-2811 E-mail: billanderson@attglobal.net.

ANDERSON, WILLIAM, retail company executive, business education educator; b. LA, May 21, 1923; s. William Bert and Marie (Novotney) A.; m. Margaret Lillian Phillips, Aug. 16, 1951 (dec.); children: Margaret Gwen, Deborah Kay, William Keven, Denise Marie (dec.). BA in Econs., UCLA, 1948, MEd, 1957. Cert. secondary tchr. (life), Calif. Tchr. bus. edn. Big Bear Lake (Calif.) H.S., 1949-52, Ventura (Calif.) Unified Sch. Dist. Buena H.S., 1952-89; CEO Day's Aircraft Inc., Santa Paula, Calif., 1967-2001; founder, CEO Anderson Aero, 2001—. Cons. micro computers Calif. State Dept. Edn., 1983-85; pres. Dollars for Schollars, Ventura. Co-author: A Century of

International Cooperation in Business, 2001. Crew chief Olympic Games basketball stats., 1984, basketball stats. World Games for the Deaf, 1985, U.S. Olympic Festival, 1991; vol. Calif. Police Olympics, 1989. With USAAF, 1943-45, PTO. Mem. NEA (life), Calif. Bus. Edn. Assn. (hon. life, pres. So. sect. 1959-60, state sec. 1960-61), Internat. Soc. Bus. Edn. (voting del. to Soc. Internat. pour l'Enseignement Comml., Western rep. 1988-89, apptd. historian 1991, 1st Medal for Outstanding Svc. 1997), Am. Aviation Hist. Soc., Calif. Assn. Work Experience Educators (life), Air Force Assn. (life), So. Calif. Badminton Assn. (past bd. dirs.), Phi Delta Kappa, Delta Pi Epsilon (hon. life). Democrat. Lutheran. Avocations: photography, aviation history, badminton, ucla basketball stats. Home: 334 Manzanita Ave Ventura CA 93001-2227 E-mail: william.anderson@cavix.org., andersonaero@hotmail.com.

ANDERSON, WILLIAM BANKS, JR., ophthalmology educator; b. Durham, NC, June 14, 1931; s. William Banks and Mildred Ursula (Everett) A.; m. Nancy Eldridge Walker, Sept. 17, 1960; children: Mary Banks, Mark Eldridge, Elizabeth Perry. AB, Princeton U., 1952; MD, Harvard U., 1956. Diplomate: Am. Bd. Ophthalmology (dir. 1986-92). Intern Duke U. Med. Ctr., Durham, N.C., 1956-57, resident, 1959-62, asst. prof. ophthalmology, 1962-67, assoc. prof. ophthalmology, 1967-76, prof. ophthalmology, 1976—, acting chmn., 1991-92. Mem. profl. adv. com. N.C. Div. Services to the Blind, Raleigh, 1972-84 Chmn. bd. trustees Durham Acad., 1975-77. Served to capt. M.C. U.S. Army, 1957-59. Fellow ACS; mem. Am. Ophthalmol. Soc. (sec.-treas. 1989-98, v.p. 1998-99, pres. 1999-2000), Am. Acad. Ophthalmology (bd. dirs. 1986-89), Am. Bd. Ophthalmology (bd. dirs. 1986-93). Episcopalian. Home: 2401 Cranford Rd Durham NC 27705 1011 Office: Duke U Eye Ctr Erwin Rd Durham NC 27710-7102

ANDERSON, WILLIAM CARL, association executive, environmental engineer, consultant; b. Vinton, Iowa, Sept. 24, 1943; s. Ivan D. and Lois B. (Schlotterback) A.; m. Elizabeth A. Dingman, Nov. 12, 1966; children: William Carl III, Erica Dawn. BSCE, Iowa State U., 1967. Registered profl. engr., N.Y., N.J., Pa., Iowa; diplomate Am. Acad. Environ. Engrs. Dir. environ. health Cayuga County Health Dept., Auburn, N.Y., 1969-73; owner Pickard & Anderson, Auburn, 1973—; trustee Am. Acad. Environ. Engrs., Annapolis, Md., 1982-85, exec. dir., 1985—. Editor: Environmental Engineer, 1985—. Gen. chmn. Cayuga County United Way, 1982, exec. com., 1982-84, bd. dirs., 1981-84; health and safety com. Cayuga County council Boy Scouts Am., 1969-83; parish council Sacred Heart Parish, 1981-82; bd. dirs. YMCA-WEIU Cayuga County, 1982-85. Served with USNR, 1967-69. Recipient Recognition award United Way, 1982; named Honorable Conceptor, Mich. Cons. Engrs. Council, 1983. Fellow ASCE (Outstanding Service award 1981, 86); mem. Am. Water Works Assn., Air Waste Mgmt. Assn., Assn. Environ. Engring. Profs., NSPE, N.Y. Soc. Profl. Engrs., N.Y. Water Pollution Control Assn. (Lewis Van Carpenter award 1974), Water Environment Fedn. (Philip F. Morgan medal 1973), Buick Club Am. (bd. dirs. 1996—), Chi Epsilon. Republican. Roman Catholic. Office: Am Acad Environ Engrs 130 Holiday Ct Ste 100 Annapolis MD 21401-7003

ANDERSON, WILLIAM CARL, lawyer; b. Syracuse, N.Y., July 9, 1958; s. Harold Everett and Mildred Dorothy (Weller) A.; m. Deborah L. Harding, Nov. 3, 1990. BA in History, Washington Coll., Chestertown, Md., 1980; JD, Syracuse U., 1983; postgrad., U. Miami, 1993. Bar: Md. 1984, Fla. 1985. Fin. cons. Merrill Lynch, Miami, Fla., 1984-85; tax cons. Arthur Andersen & Co., Miami, 1985-87; sr. tax specialist Ryder System, Inc., Miami, 1987-90; assoc. tax counsel internat. GE Co., Schenectady, N.Y., 1990-91, tax counsel Plainville, Conn., 1991-93; gen. counsel, dir. environ. and quality programs GE Indsl. Sys. Europe, Gent, Belgium, 1993-96; gen. mgr., sr. counsel environ. health and safety GE Indsl. Systems, Plainville, Conn., 1996—. Chmn. GE Cmty. Svc. Fund, 1993-94; mem. adv. bd. BNA Environ. Due Diligence Guide, 2003—; advisor/observer Nat. Conf. Commrs. for Uniform State Laws-Environ. Covenants Act, 2002—. Treas. Big Bros./Big Sisters of Broward, Inc., Ft. Lauderdale, Fla., 1988-89, bd. dirs., 1989-90; bd. dirs. Urban League Greater Hartford, 2001—, Middlesex/Ctrl. Conn. chpt. ARC, 2003—. Mem. Md. Bar Assn., Fla. Bar Assn., Jaycees (local v.p., treas. 1984, Fla. legal counsel, 1988-89, 90-91). Republican. Lutheran. Avocations: sailing, rowing, cycling. Home: 81 Windward Pl Southington CT 06489-3853 Office: GE Legal Ops 41 Woodford Ave Plainville CT 06062-2372

ANDERSON, WILLIAM CARL, lawyer; b. Canton, Ohio, Nov. 14, 1941; s. Harry and Carrie (Magee) A.; m. Mary Ellen Graham, June 11, 1962; children: John, Dan, Emily, Adam. BA, Oberlin Coll., 1963; JD, U. Mich., 1966. Bar: Okla. 1966, U.S. Supreme Ct. 1985, U.S. Dist. Ct. (no., ea. and we. dists.) Okla., U.S. Dist. Ct. (no. dist.) Tex., U.S. Dist. Ct. D.C., U.S. Ct. Appeals (5th, 10th, and D.C. cirs.). Clk. to Hon. A.P. Murrah U.S. Ct. Appeals for 10th Circuit, Oklahoma City, 1966-67; ptnr. Doerner, Saunders, Daniel & Anderson, L.L.P., Tulsa, 1967—. Fellow Am. Coll. Trial Lawyers; mem. Am. Inns of Ct. (master Council Oaks chpt.), Order of Coif. Office: Doerner Saunders Daniel & Anderson LLP 320 S Boston Ave Ste 500 Tulsa OK 74103-3725 E-mail: wanderson@dsda.com.

ANDERSON, WILLIAM CORNELIUS, III, lawyer; b. Haddonfield, N.J., Dec. 1, 1947; s. William Cornelius Jr. and Madelyn Anna (Penny) A.; m. Christine Joan Keck, June 20, 1970; children: William C. IV, Teresa, Stephen, Geoffrey, Thomas, Matthew. BA, Georgetown U., 1969; JD, Villanova U., 1975. Bar: Del. 1975, Ill. 1979. Atty. Morris, Nichols, Arsht & Tunnell, Wilmington, Del., 1975-77, Biggs & Battaglia, Wilmington, 1978, Lord, Bissell & Brook, Chgo., 1979-85, ptnr., 1985-2000; founding ptnr. Anderson, Bennett & Ptnrs., Chgo., 2000—. Contbr. chpt. to book, articles to law jours. Capt. USAR, 1969-72. Fellow Am. Coll. Trial Lawyers; mem. ABA, Internat. Assn. Def. Counsel, Am. Acad. Healthcare Attys., Soc. Trial Attys., Union League Club of Chgo., North Shore Country Club, Kenilworth Club. Home: 717 Kent Rd Kenilworth IL 60043-1031 Office: Anderson Bennett & Ptnrs 55 E Monroe St Ste 3650 Chicago IL 60603-5713 E-mail: w.anderson@abandpartners.com.

ANDERSON, WILLIAM HENRY, psychobiologist, educator; b. Phila., Nov. 10, 1940; s. William Henry Schoen and Elizabeth Winifred (Laverty) A.; m. Catherine Sacchetti, Oct. 7, 1967 (dec. Sept. 1991); 1 child, Jennifer Ann Gist. BS, MIT, 1962; MA, U. Pa., 1967; MD, Thomas Jefferson U., 1967; MPH, Harvard U., 1977. Diplomate Am. Bd. Psychiatry and Neurology. Intern. Pa. Hosp., Phila., 1967-68; resident in psychiatry Mass. Gen. Hosp., Boston, 1968-71, assoc. psychiatrist dept. psychiatry, 1976-97, sr. psychiatrist, 1998—, dir. postgrad. edn., 1976-81; instr. psychiatry Harvard U., Boston, 1973-75, asst. prof., 1975-81, asst. clin. prof., 1981-82, lectr., 1982—; chmn. psychiatry St. Elizabeths Hosp., Boston, 1981-92. Dir. clinical svcs. Augusta Mental Health Inst., 1993-96; asst. attending psychiatrist Mclean Hosp., Belmont, Mass.; Cons. Scientists' Inst. Pub. Info.; mem. Carnegie Coun. Ethics and Internat. Affairs. Contbg. editor: The New Physician, 1977-79; editorial bd. Topics in Geriatrics, 1981-87, Jour. Geriatric Psychiatry and Neurology; co-author: (with M.T. McGuire) The U.S. Healthcare Dilemma, 1999. Lt. comdr., M.C. USNR, 1971-73. Fellow Am. Psychiat. Assn., Human Biology coun.; mem. AAAS, Am. Acad. Clin. Psychiatrists, Internat. Soc. Polit. Psychology, Coun. on Fgn. Rels. (lectr. to coms.), Med. Assn. P.R. (hon.), Mass. Med. Soc., Soc. Ethnobiology, U.S. Naval Inst., Boston Athenaeum (proprietor), Harvard Club of Boston, Union Club, Sigma Xi. Office: 34 Coolidge Hill Rd Cambridge MA 02138-5527

ANDERSON, WILLIAM HOPPLE, lawyer; b. Cin., Feb. 28, 1926; s. Robert Waters and Anna (Hopple) A.; m. Jean Koop, Feb. 3, 1951; children: Susan Hopple, Nancy, Barbara, William Hopple Jr., Francie. Student, Carleton Coll., 1946; LL.B., U. Cin., 1952. Bar: Ohio bar 1952, U.S. Supreme Ct 1964. Mem. firm Becker, Loeb, & Becker, Cin., 1952-54; asst. pros. atty. Hamilton County, Ohio, 1953-57; of counsel Graydon, Head & Ritchey, Cin.; judge Wyoming (Ohio) Mcpl. Ct., 1960-67. Mem. Ohio Ho. of Reps., 1967-69. With USMC, 1944-46. Mem. Cin. Bar Assn. Republican. Presbyterian. Home: 297 Mount Pleasant Ave Cincinnati OH 45215-4212 Office: 511 Walnut St Cincinnati OH 45202-3115

ANDERSON, WILLIAM ROBERT, career naval officer; b. Bakerville, Tenn., June 17, 1921; s. David Hensley and Mary (McKelvey) A.; m. Yvonne Etzel, June 10, 1943 (div. Apr. 1979); children: Michael David, William Robert; m. Patricia Walters, Dec. 26, 1980; children: Jane Hensley, Thomas McKelvey Grad., Columbia Mil. Acad., 1939; BSEE, U.S. Naval Acad., 1942; DSc, Defiance Coll., 1958. Commd. ensign USN, 1942, advanced through grades to capt., 1960; assigned submarines Tarpon, Narwhal, Trutta and 11 Pacific combat patrols, World War II; postwar service submarine Trutta, Sarda; comdr. attack submarine USS Wahoo, Pearl Harbor, 1953-55; head tactical dept. Submarine Sch., 1955-56; staff naval reactors br. AEC, Washington, 1956-57; comdr. USS Nautilus, 1957-59; ret. USN, 1962. Cons. to Pres. J.F. Kennedy, until 1963; mem. 89th-92d Congresses from 6th Tenn. Dist.; pvt. bus. exec., 1973—; co founder Pub. Office Corp., database mgmt. firm. Author: Nautilus 90 North, 1959, First Under the North Pole, 1959, The Useful Atom, 1966; Contbr. articles to nat. mags. and profl. publs. Decorated Bronze Star, Legion of Merit; recipient Stephen Decatur prize Navy League U.S., Distinguished Service award N.Y.C., Christopher Columbus Internat. Communications award Genoa, Italy; Elisha Kent Kane medalist Geog. Soc. Phila., 1959; Patron's medal Royal Geog. Soc., 1959; Leadership award Freedoms Found., 1960, Lowell Thomas award The Explorers Club, N.Y.C., 1997; featured in Greatest Adventures of All Times spl. edit. Life mag.

ANDERSON, WILLIAM SCOVIL, classics educator; b. Brookline, Mass., Sept. 16, 1927; s. Edgar Weston and Katrina (Brewster) A.; m. Lorna Candee Bassette, June 12, 1954 (dec. Dec. 1977); children: Judith, Blythe, Heather, Meredith, Keith; m. Deirdre Burt, May 28, 1983. BA, Yale U., 1950, PhD, 1954; AB, Cambridge U., (Eng.), 1952; MA, Cambridge (Eng.) U., 1955. Prix de Rome fellow Am. Acad. in Rome, 1954-55; instr. classics Yale U., 1955-59; resident in Rome, Morse fellow, 1959-60; mem. faculty U. Calif., Berkeley, 1960-94, prof. Latin and comparative lit., 1966-94, prof. charge Intercollegiate Ctr. Classical Studies, 1967-68, chmn. classics, 1970-73. Rsch. prof. U. Melbourne, 1984; Robson lectr. Victoria Coll., Toronto, 1987; Blegen rsch. prof. Vassar Coll., 1989-90, vice chair comparative lit., 1990-93; vis. disting. prof. Fla. State U., spring 1995; Gail Burnett lectr. San Diego State U., 2001; vis. prof. Ohio State U., 2003. Author: The Art of the Aeneid, 1969, Ovid, Metamorphoses, Critical Text, 1977, Essays on Roman Satire, 1982, Barbarian Play: Plautus' Roman Comedy, 1993, Ovid's Metamorphoses 1-5 Text and Commentary, 1997, Why Horace?, 1998; co-editor (with L.N. Quartarone) Approaches to Teaching Vergil's Aeneid, 2002. Served with U.S. Army, 1946—48, Korea. Recipient Berkeley citation, 1994; NEH sr. fellow, 1973-74. Mem. Am. Philol. Assn. (pres. 1977), Danforth Assocs., Soc. Religion Episcopalian. Office: Univ Calif Dept Classics Berkeley CA 94720 E-mail: wsa@socrates.berkeley.edu.

ANDERSON-HAROLD, BETH, composer, piano teacher; b. Lexington, Ky., Jan. 3, 1950; d. Sidney Hart Anderson and Marjorie Celeste Hoskins; m. Michael Scott Cooper, June 27, 1976 (div. 1978); m. Elliotte Rusty Harold, July 28, 1995. BA in Music, U. Calif., Davis, 1971; MFA in Piano Performance, Mills Coll., 1973, MA in Composition, 1974. Music tchr. The New Sch. for Social Rsch., N.Y.C., 1975, Coll. of New Rochelle, N.Y., 1978-86; theory tchr. NYU, 1978; dance accompanist Alvin Ailey's Am. Dance Studio, N.Y.C., 1975-89; piano tchr. Bklyn. Music Sch., 1978-85; theory tchr. Hebrew Arts Sch., N.Y.C., 1991-93; piano tchr. Greenwich Ho. Music Sch., N.Y.C., 1990—2003. Composer (orchestral music): Revel, 1979, Minnesota Swale, 1994, Three Swales, 2000, Mourning Dove Swale, 2002; composer: (chamber music) Trio and Net Work, 1981, 1982; composer: (mandolin and guitar music) September Swale, 1996. Bd. dirs. Am. Composers Alliance, N.Y.C., 1982-87. Grantee, Nat. Endowment for the Arts, Washington, 1974—75; Radio Prodn. grant, Nat. Pub. Radio Satellite Program Devel. Fund, 1982. Mem. Broadcast Musicians, Inc., Poets and Writers, Internat. Assn. Women in Music, N.Y. Women Composers (treas. 1997—). Avocations: sanskrit, astrology, birding. E-mail: beand@interport.net.

ANDERSON-SPIVY, ALEXANDRA, writer, editor; b. Boston, Mass, May 14, 1942; d. Henry and Marion Ruth (Thompson) Fuller; m. Samuel O.J. Spivy; children: Lafcadio, Genevieve, Oscar. BA, Sarah Lawrence Coll., 1961. Art editor Paris Rev., 1972-76, Village Voice, NYC, 1973-76; features assoc. Vogue mag., NYC, 1976-78; sr. editor Portfolio mag., NYC, 1979-83; editor-in-chief Arts and Antiques mag., NYC, 1983-85; exec. editor Am. Photographer, NYC, 1985-87; arts editor Smart mag., NYC, 1988-90; contbg. arts editor Esquire mag., NYC, 1990-94; NY editor The Argonaut, 1992-96; reviews editor The Art Jour., 1995-2000; editor-in-chief The Craftsman on CD-ROM, 1996—; projects editor Interactive Bur., 1996-99; editl. dir. Circle.com, 1999-2001. Chair bd. dir. Franklin Furnace; bd. gov. Colby Coll. Art Mus.; profl. fellow Morgan Libr. Author: Anderson and Archer's SoHo: The Essential Guide to Art and Life in Lower Manhattan, 1979, Living With Art, 1988, Portraits of Olga, 1992, Keith Haring, Last Works, 1995, Gardens of Earthly Delight: The Art of Robert Kushner, 1997, Foliage: Photographs by Harold Feinstein, 2001; mem. adv. bd. Rev. Mag., 1998-2000. V.p., Mus. Modern Art, Contemporary Arts Coun.; pres., Bd. of Dir., Exhibitions Internat., 2000-. Recipient Art Critics' award NEA, 1978; Travel grant Japan Found., 1976. Mem. Internat. Art Critics' Assn. (pres. Am. chpt. 1994-98).

ANDERSSON, BILLIE VENTURATOS, school learning specialist; b. Pitts., Jan. 16, 1947; d. George Steve and Aphrodite (Bon) Venturatos; m. Wolfgang Paul Andersson, July 12, 1969; children: Dita, Lise, Andrea. BA, Newcomb Coll., 1968; MEd in Counseling, La. State U., New Orleans, 1971; MEd in Spl. Edn., U. New Orleans, 1977, PhD in Curriculum and Instrn., 1981. Cert. Nat. Bd. Counselor, 1994; lic. profl. counselor, La., 1997. Biology and math tchr. Orleans Parish Sch. Bd., New Orleans, 1968-70; biology and gen. sci. tchr. Jefferson Parish Sch. Bd., Metairie, La., 1970-74, guidance counselor, 1974-78; reading specialist Trinity Episcopal Sch., New Orleans, 1978-96, admissions evaluator, ednl. evaluator, 1981-96, gifted and talented tchr., 1982-96, head student svcs., dir. curriculum. Gesell evaluator, 1985-96, learning specialist, 1994-96, lang. arts coord., 1994-96; learning specialist, head student svcs., dir. curriculum St. Martin's Epsicopal Sch., 1996—, curriculum dir., 2003—; instr. U. New Orleans, St. Mary's Dominican Coll., Holy Cross Coll., Loyola U., Xavier U.; lectr. and presenter in field. Author: Filo File for Filophiles, 1985, Simple and Classic: Greek Elegance for the Everyday Cook, 1991; editor: Greek Lagniappe, 1980, 2d edit., 1998, Greek Laginaippe, The Best of Best, 1998; dir. Author Fest, 1988-96; illustrator: The Greek Alphabet Coloring Book, 1993. Sunday sch. coord. Greek Orthodox Cathedral, New Orleans, 1984-87, chmn. gourmet booth, 1981—; developer, dir. La. Experience summer camp for girls, 1983-95. Mem. APA, ACA, Internat. Dyslexia Assn. (La. chpt. bd. mem., v.p.), Internat. Reading Assn., Nat. Assn. for Gifted Children, Assn. Supervision and Curriculum Devel., Phi Delta Kappa, Phi Kappa Phi, Kappa Delta Pi. Greek Orthodox. Avocations: batik, aerobics, pastry baking. Office: St Martins Episcopal Sch 5309 Airline Dr Metairie LA 70003-2401

ANDERSSON, CRAIG REMINGTON, retired chemical company executive; b. Winnipeg, Man., Can., June 16, 1937; came to U.S., 1937; s. Anders Einar and Doris (Pearson) A.; m. Dawn Marie Traver, June 13, 1959; children— Lee Erik, Karin Ingrid, Jon Kristien, Jenni Kate BS in Chem. Engring., U. Minn., 1960; postgrad., U. Del., 1960-66. Rschr. Sun Oil, 1960-67; v.p. ops. Custom Chems., Inc., 1967-68; Engr., supr. U.S. Steel Chems., Haverhill, Ohio, 1968-76, product mgr. Pitts., 1976-80, gen. mgr. Cin., 1980-82, v.p. Pitts., 1982-85, pres., 1985-86; pres., COO Aristech Chem. Corp., Pitts., 1986-93; vice chmn. Aristech Chem. Co., Pitts., 1994-95; ret., 1995. Cons., bd. dir. Albemarle Corp., ret., 2002, bd. dir. RTI Internat. Metals, Inc., Duquesne U. Contbr. articles to profl. jours.; patentee in field Mem. citizen's sponsoring com. Allegheny Conf. Cmty. Devel. Mem. AIChE, Alpha Chi Sigma. Lutheran. Avocations: golf, hunting, fishing, auto racing.

ANDERSSON, PER LENNART, computer engineer, consultant; b. Phila., Nov. 12, 1929; s. Albin Julius and Anna Maria (Johanson) A.; m. Dorothy Jeanne Leonard, June 21, 1952; children: Russell Lennart, James Albin. BSME, U. Pa., 1953. Engr., project mgr. RCA, Camden, N.J., 1953-55; mgr. engring. and product planning UNIVAC, Phila., 1955-62; rsch. mgr. electronics ANPA Rsch. Lab., Easton, Pa., 1962-64; ind. cons. Andersson Assocs., Paoli, Pa., 1964—. V.p. Mgmt. and Tech. Inc., Corona del Mar, Calif., 1965, Scriptomatic Corp., Phila., 1984; v.p. engring. Orca Industries, Berwyn, Pa., 1982-83; bd. dirs. Small Bus. Devel. Coun., Chester County, Pa., 1990-95. Contbg. author: Automation in Electronics and Publishing, 1965, Technological Change in Publishing and Printing, McGraw-Hill Yearbook of Science and Technology, 1970; contbr. nearly 100 articles to profl. jours.; inventor life-saving device for divers, logic keyboard for graphic arts applications, others. Mem. troop com. Boy Scouts Am., Berwyn, 1971-76. Avocations: travel, scuba diving, computers, investing.

ANDERT, DARLENE (DARLENE ANDERT-SCHMIDT), management consultant in corporate governance; BA in Bus. Mgmt. and Comms., Alverno Coll., Milw., 1983; MSA in Adminstrn., Ctrl. Mich. U., 1993; EdD, George Washington U., 2003. Cert. fin. mgr.; cert. mgmt. cons. Pres., owner Dance in Exercise, Inc., Milw., 1980-85; pres. Andert Governance Corp. (formerly Concepts in Mgmt., Inc.), Cape Coral, Fla., 1989—. Author: Diversity at Work, 1995. Trustee Lee County Electric Coop., Inc., 1994—; past pres. Healthy Start Coalition of S.W. Fla., inc. Mem.: ASTD, Nat. Assn. Bus. Women, Inst. Mgmt. Cons. Office: PO Box 100235 Cape Coral FL 33910

ANDERT, JEFFREY NORMAN, clinical psychologist; b. Aberdeen, S.D., May 21, 1950; s. Norman Joseph and Irene Eleanor (Olson) A.; m. Diane Kay Dunham, May 29, 1971; Jason Ryan, Jonathan Erik, Justin Matthew. BA in Psychology, Augsburg Coll., 1971; MA in Psychology, Mankato (Minn.) State U., 1973; PhD in Psychology, U. So. Miss., 1976. Diplomate in Clin. Psychology Am. Bd. Profl. Psychology; lic. psychologist, Mich. Grad. asst. Mankato State U., Minn., 1972-73, U. So. Miss., Hattisburg, Miss., 1974-75; psychology intern Des Moines Child Guidance Ctr., Des Moines, 1975-76; clin. psychologist Battle Creek (Mich.) Child Guidance Clinic, 1976-80; pvt. practice Battle Creek, 1978—; pres., dir. Psychol. Cons. of Mich., P.C., Battle Creek, 1979—; dir. Chem. Dependency Resources, Battle Creek, 1982—. Med. expert Office of Hearings and Appeals, Social Security Adminstrn., Lansing & Grand Rapids, Mich., 1986—. Contbr. articles to profl. jours. Trustee Lakeview Pub. Sch. Dist., Battle Creek, 1991—, pres. bd. trustees, 1995-97, 2003—; adult leader Boy Scouts Am., Battle Creek, 1988-96. Disting. Svc. award, So. Cen. Mich. Substance Abuse Commn., Jackson, Mich., 1987. Fellow Acad. Clin. Psychology; mem. Am. Psychol. Assn., Mich. Psychol. Assn. (ethics com. 1997—), South Cen. Mich. Substance Abuse Program Dirs. Assn. (pres. 1986-87). Lutheran. Avocations: music, water sports, golf. Home: 144 Waupakisco Bch Battle Creek MI 49015-3144 Office: Psychol Cons Mich PC 151 North Ave Battle Creek MI 49017-3418 E-mail: jandert@psycmi.com.

ANDERTON, JAMES FRANKLIN, IV, real estate development executive; b. Lansing, Mich., Aug. 2, 1943; s. James Franklin III and Florence Ethel (Bear) A.; m. Deborah Anne Garlock, Apr. 2, 1966 (div.); 1 child, James Franklin, V.; m. Denise Marie Thelen, July 6, 1985; 1 child, Sarah Elizabeth. BA, Hobart Coll., Geneva, N.Y., 1965; MBA, Cornell U, 1967; PhD, Mich. State U., 1997. Controller Summit Steel Processing Corp., Lansing, 1967-69, exec. v.p., 1970, pres., 1971-90, Processed Plastics Co., Ionia, Mich., 1986-90, Universal Steel Co. of Mich., Lansing, 1988-90; chmn., pres., CEO, Summit Holdings Corp., East Lansing, Mich., 1986—2001; pres. Lansing C.C., 1999-2000; mng. gen. ptnr. Summit Holdings Ltd. Partnership, 1996—; mng. mem. Maplegrove Property Mgmt., LLC, 2001—. Pres. Inst. of Scrap Recycling Industries, Washington, 1982-83, bd. dirs.; v.p. Bur. Internat. de la Recuperation, Brussels, 1984-85; bd. dirs. Alpena (Mich.) Power Co., 1978-2002, Fed. Forge Inc., Lansing, Auto-Owners Ins. Co., Lansing, Irwin Union Bank, Lansing; mem. Mich. Resource Recovery Com., 1975-77, Mich. Job Devel. Authority, 1977-79, nat. adv. coun. Mich. State U. Coll. of Edn., 1998—; mem. Mich. com. on financing postsecondary edn., 1999—; mem. Tchr. Edn. Accreditation Coun., 2001—. Pres. Lansing Met. Devel. Authority, 1971-72, Delta Twp. Econ. Devel. Authority, 1975-76; campaign chmn. Capital Area United Way, Lansing, 1976; chmn. Lansing Regional C. of C., 1977; chmn. Montessori Children's House, Lansing, 1982-85, St. Lawrence Hosp., Lansing, 1985-86, Capital Region Cmty. Found., Lansing, 1992-93; trustee Hobart and William Smith Colls., Geneva, N.Y., 1993-98. Sgt. USNG, 1968-74. Episcopalian. Avocations: reading, hiking, piano, tennis, golf, skiing. Home: 1618 Stanlake Dr East Lansing MI 48823-2018

ANDES, DERIEN ROMARIC, retired purchasing specialist; b. Cleve., Dec. 8, 1934; s. Ernest Lee and Dorothy Josephine (Martin) A.; m. Sheila Mary Glynn, June 13, 1970; children: Kathleen, William, Christopher. BA, Cath. U. Am., 1957, postgrad., 1963-70. Travel counselor Am. Automobile Assn., Washington, N.C., 1955-65, rschr., writer, editor, 1965-71; pers. asst. N.J. Depts. Human Svcs. and Corrections, Trenton and Princeton, 1974-78; sr. pers. asst. The Richard Stockton Coll. N.J., Pomona, 1978-82, adminstrv. asst. to v.p., 1982-87, asst. buyer, 1987-99. Mem. Atlantic City Urban Area Transp. Coun., Atlantic County, N.J., 1982-92; candidate Pleasantville (N.J.) City Coun., 1986, Pleasantville Sch. Bd., 1981-83. With U.S. Army, 1958-60. Democrat. Roman Catholic. Avocations: choral singing, community theatre, genealogy. Home: 831 Linden Ave Pleasantville NJ 08232-1305 E-mail: drandes@att.net.

ANDES, LARRY DALE, minister; b. Warrenton, Va., June 7, 1947; s. William Christian and Hilda Elizabeth (Beach) A.; m. Bobbi E. Stephens, July 16, 1966; 1 child, Joshua Dale. BS in Pastoral Studies, North Ctrl. U., 1970; student, U. Richmond, 1991, Bethel Theol. Sem., 1992. Ordained to ministry Assembly of God Ch., 1975, non-denominational, 1987. Assoc. pastor Calvary Assembly of God, Staunton, Va., 1971-72; youth min. Arlington (Va.) Assembly of God, 1972-75; assoc. pastor West End Assembly of God, Richmond, Va., 1975-76; founder, pres., festival dir. Fishnet Ministries Inc., Richmond, Front Royal, Va., 1976—; sr. pastor Fishnet Christian Ctr., Front Royal, 1992—. Named one of Outstanding Young Men of Am., 1984. Office: Fishnet Ministries Inc PO Box 1919 Front Royal VA 22630-1919 E-mail: fishnet@fishnetministries.org.

ANDES, PHOEBE CABOTAJE, retired women's health nurse, educator; b. Solano, Nueva Vizcaya, Philippines, Sept. 20, 1934; d. Adriano V. and Patricia Piggangay (Logan) Cabotaje; children: Edwin, Patricia. BSN, State U. of Philippines, 1956; student, NYU, 1959-61; MA, Columbia U., 1976. Exchange nurse Woman's Hosp.-St. Luke's, N.Y.C.; mem. faculty Far Eastern U., Manila; head nurse St. Elizabeth Hosp., Elizabeth, N.J.; assoc. prof. Middlesex County Coll., Edison, N.J., 1970-91; asst. prof. Passaic County C.C., Paterson, N.J., 1993-96; DON Valley Rest Nursing Home, 1996-98; ret., 1998. Adj. faculty Bloomfield Coll., 1999—, Fairleigh Dickinson U., 2000—; part time at long term facility; spkr. in field. Mem. coun. of ministries, 1979—89, 1999—, Wesley United Meth. Ch. Parent Tchr. Student Assn. Adv. Coun., 1976—80; vol. homeless health fairs. Named with a testimonial dinner dance for outstanding leadership, Found. Philippine Am. Med. Soc. N.JJ., 1992, grand marshall, Philippine Independence Day Celebration, 1996; recipient Cmty. Leadership award, Philippine-Am. Lion Club of N.Y., 1990, Outstanding Cmty. Leadership award, Asian Am. Cultural Heritage Coun. of N.J., 1996, Presdl. awards for Filipinos overseas, Pres. of Philippines, 2000. Mem.: ANA, U. Philippines Alumni Assn. N.J. (pres. 1984—86), Found. Fedn. Philippine Socs. N.J. (chairwoman 1993—), Philippine Nurses Assn. N.J. (founding pres. 1976, 1st Roll of Honor award 1992), Fedn. Philippine Socs. N.J. (pres. 1990—91), Asian Am. Polit. Coalition N.J. (pres. 1991—92), Philippine Nurses Assn. Am. (2d pres. 1982—84, founder, pres. Found. 2002—), NJ State Nurses Assn. (pres., Nurse of Yr. 1988, Solano U.S.A. 1996—98, named Diva in Nursing, Inst. for Nursing 1999), U. Philippines Nursing Alumni Assn. East Coast (founding pres. 1988—92), Sigma Theta Tau. Democrat. E-mail: phoebe459@comcast.net.

ANDING, ROBERT EUGENE, retired religion educator, minister; b. Coles, Miss., Aug. 25, 1921; s. Eugene George and Mamie David (Aldridge) A.; m. Billie Jean Brewer, Aug. 17, 1947; children: James Eugene, Skipper Dale, Robert Charles. BA, Millsaps Coll., 1948; BDiv, Emory U., 1950; MA, Miss. Coll., 1964; MDiv, Emory U., 1972; postgrad. in sociology, Miss. State Coll., Starkville, 1979, 82. Ordained min. United Meth. Ch., 1951, ordained elder Miss. Conf. Meth. Ch., 1951. Min. Shands United Meth. Ch., Jackson, Miss., 1947, United Meth. Ch., Pearl, Miss., 1948; assoc. prof. Millsaps Coll., Jackson, 1952-73; min. Mem. United Meth. Ch., Bolton, 1973-80, Galloway United Meth. Ch., Bolton, 1980-1981, Marvin United Meth. Ch., Jackson, 1980-1983, Capital St. United Meth. Ch., Jackson, 1984-86; ret., 1986. Contbr. book revs. (monthly jour.) Miss. History, 1960—. Mem. credit union bd., United Meth. Ch. Jackson, 1950-84, trustee Children's Home, 1984-85; assoc. trustee, Rust Coll., Holly Springs, Miss., 1955-65; chaplain, post 5048, VFW, Florence, Miss., 1986—. Named Citizen of Yr., Florence Fire Dept., 2000-01; recipient citation, So. Assn. Undergrad. Social Welfare Edn., 1972, Harry Denman award, Miss. Conf., Jackson, 1983. Am. Sociol. Soc., Ret. Ministerial Assn., So. Sociol. Soc., So. Geriatric Soc., Am. Legion, Lions Internat., Omicron Delta Kappa, Alpha Kappa Delta.. Democrat. Avocations: reading, research and writing, flintnapping, gardening, coins. Home: 1256 Steens Creek Dr Florence MS 39073

ANDJELIC, SASA, engineer, polymer scientist; b. Travnik, Yugoslavia, July 19, 1966; s. Sinisa and Rada Andjelic; m. Sofija Pavlovic, Dec. 14, 1992; children: Nikola, Lazar. BS in Chem. Engring., Faculty of Tech., Belgrade U., Serbia, 1992; PhD in Polymer Sci. and Engring., Poly. U., N.Y.C., 1998. Post-doctoral fellow ETHICON, Johnson & Johnson Co., Somerville, NJ, 1998—2000, sr. engr., 2000—. Reviewer Nat. Sci. Found. Grants, (jour.) Macromolecules, Biomacromelecules;, author 29 peer reviewed publs. and chpt. in 2 books. Recipient 22 Gold, Silver and Bronze medals in maj. internat. waterpolo tournaments, Various Internat. Waterpolo Orgns., 1977—93, Excellence award, Hoechst Celanese Co., 1995. Mem.: Soc. for Biomaterials (assoc.), Am. Chem. Soc. (assoc.). Achievements include patents for 1 U.S. patent; patents pending for 2 Patents pending. Avocations: sports, fishing, theater, opera, literature. Office: ETHICON a Jonhson & Jonhson Co Route 22 West Somerville NJ 08876 Office Fax: 908-218-3247. E-mail: sandjeli@ethus.jnj.com.

ANDO, KUNITAKE, consumer products company executive; Grad., Sch. of Economics, U. Tokyo, 1969. With Sony Corp., 1969—; mng. dir. Sony Life Ins. Co., Ltd. (formerly Sony Prudential Life Ins. Co.), 1979—85, dep. pres., 1985—90; gen. mgr., corp. planning Sony Electronics, Inc. (formerly Sony Corp. of Am.), 1976—79; pres. and COO Sony Engring. and Mfg. of Am. (now part of Sony Electronics Inc.), 1990—94; exec. v.p., sr. gen. mgr., corp. planning, consumer A & V Products Co. Sony Corp., 1994—96, pres., Divisional Info. Tech. Co., 1996—99, pres. and COO, Personal IT Network Co., 1999—2000, pres. and group COO (formerly COO), rep. dir., 2000—. Avocations: golf, swimming, tennis. Office: Sony Corp 6-7-35 Kitashinagawa Shinagawa-Ku TK 141-0001 Japan*

ANDO, SEIICHI, economics, Japanese history educator; b. Washington, Feb. 17, 1922; s. Kashitaro and Shizuko (Yabuki) A. BA, Kyushu U., Fukuoka, Japan, 1947; D in Econs., Osaka (Japan) U., 1961. Prof. Wakayama U., Japan, 1960-87, prof. emeritus, 1987—; prof. Osaka Sangyo U., 1987-95. Vis. prof. Stanford (Calif.) U., 1968-69, U. Calif., Berkeley, 1973. Author: A Study of Rural Commercial History of Pre-Modern Japan, 1958, The History of Farmers in Pre-Modern Japan, 1959, A Study of Rural History of Pre-Modern Japan, 1984, A Study of City History of Pre-Modern Japan, 1985, A History of Environmental Pollution in Pre-Modern Japan, 1992. Mem. Bd. Edn. of Wakayama Prefecture, 1995-99. Home: 20-38 Sanodai Izumisano Shi 598-0075 Japan

ANDOLSEN, ALAN ANTHONY, management consultant; b. Cleve., Feb. 19, 1943; s. Lloyd Anthony and Helen Mae (Kozinski) A.; m. Barbara Hilkert, Jan. 20, 1968; children: Daniel, Ruth. AB magna cum laude, Borromeo Coll., 1964; MA, U. Dayton, 1967; postgrad., Vanderbilt U., 1967-69. Cert. mgmt. cons.; cert. records mgr. V.p. Bergamo East, Marcy, N.Y., 1969-71; dir. Met. Health Dept., Nashville, 1971-76; prin. Naremco Svc., Inc., N.Y.C., 1976-79, v.p., 1979-86, pres., 1986—. Bd. dirs. Assn. Mgmt. Cons. Firms., N.Y.C. Editor: Management Consulting-A Model Course, 1989, 96; contbr. articles to profl. jours. Trustee Found. for Excellence in Cons. and Mgmt.; regent Inst. Cert. Records Mgrs. Mem. Inst. Mgmt. Cons., Assn. Records Mgrs. and Adminstrs., Assn. Image and Info. Mgmt., Am. Mensa Ltd. Roman Catholic. Avocations: music, cycling, reading. Office: Naremco Svcs Inc 60 E 42nd St New York NY 10165-0006

ANDORFER, DONALD JOSEPH, university president; b. Ft. Wayne, Ind., Dec. 31, 1937; s. Joseph and Cecil J. (Minich) A.; married Dec. 26, 1960; children: Susan, Joseph, Barbara. BS in Edn., Ball State U., 1960, MA in Edn., 1965; LLD (hon.), Tiffin U., 1989. Instr. Internat. Jr. Coll. Bus., Ft. Wayne, 1960-70, dean, dir., 1971-77; controller Ind. Inst. Tech., Ft. Wayne, 1978-81, v.p. fin., 1982-85, pres., 1985—. Mem. acad. com. Luth. Hosp. Bd., 1989-93; bd. dirs. Robert Morris Coll., Chgo., 1985—; bd. dirs. Ind. Pub. Broadcasting. Mem. Ind. Colls. Ind. (bd. dirs., chmn. 1994), Nat. Assn. Ind. Colls. and Univs., Nat. Assn. Ind. Athletics (nat. coun. pres. 1991-94), Ft. Wayne C. of C., Ind. Bus. Edn. Assn. (pres. 1980-81), Future Bus. Leaders Am. (bd. dirs. Outstanding Bus. Person for Ind. award 1981), Rotary (bd. dirs., v.p. 1994, pres.-elect 1995, pres. 1996, Paul Harris fellow 1998), Summit Club (bd. dirs. 2000—), Sci. Ctrl. (bd. drs., pres. elect./sec. 2002-); Delta Pi Epsilon. Roman Catholic. Avocations: golf, fishing, spectator sports. Home: 15423 Connors Rd Fort Wayne IN 46819-9720 Office: Ind Inst of Tech Office of the President 1600 E Washington Blvd Fort Wayne IN 46803-1228

ANDRADE, ANDRES, vocalist, educator; s. Francisco Andrade. BA in Vocal Performance, U. So. Fla., 1987; MusM in Vocal Performance, New Eng. Conservatory of Music, 1995. Tchg. asst., vocal music New Eng. Conservatory of Music, Boston, 1993—94; vocal instr., opera theatre dir. LaGuardia H.S. Music & Art and Performing Arts, N.Y.C.; pvt . vocal instr. N.Y.C.; freelance singer. Prodr.: (opera) Alcina (Handel), Orfeo ed Euridice (Gluck); contbr. articles. Instr. voice and diction First Ch. Congregational, Malden, Mass., 1991—97; music dir., cantor St. Patrick's Old Cathedral, N.Y.C., 1999—2001. Fellow, New Eng. Conservatory, 1993. Mem.: Music Tchrs. Nat. Assn., Nat. Assn. Tchrs. Singing, N.Y. Singing Tchrs. Assn. Home: PO Box 20498 Columbus Circle Sta New York NY 10023 Personal E-mail: andradeten@aol.com.

ANDRADE, EDNA, artist, art educator; b. Portsmouth, Va. d. Thomas Judson and Ruth (Porter) Wright; m. C. Preston Andrade, Jr., July 12, 1941 (div. 1960). BFA, Pa. Acad. Fine Arts/U. Pa., 1937. Supr. art elem. schs., Norfolk, Va., 1938-39; instr. drawing and painting Newcomb Art Sch., Tulane U., 1939-41; lectr. U. N.Mex., 1971; prof. Phila. Coll. Art, 1959-72, 73-82, prof. emeritus, 1982—; prof. art Temple U., 1972-73. Adj. prof. art Ariz. State U., 1986—; critic Pa. Acad. Fine Arts, 1988—89. Artist, designer, OSS, 1942-44, free-lance designer, Washington, 1944-46, free-lance painter, designer, muralist, Phila. and, N.Y.C., 1946—, artist-in-residence, Hartford Sch. Art and Tamarind Inst., 1971, U. Sask., Can., 1977, U. Zulia, Maracaibo, Venezuela, 1980, Ariz. State U., Tempe, 1981, 83, Fabric Workshop, Phila., 1984, Hollins Coll., Va., 1985; vis. artist, Skidmore Coll., 1973, 74, one-woman shows, E. Hampton Gallery, N.Y.C., Peale Galleries Pa. Acad., Rutgers U., U. Hartford,Marian Locks Gallery, 1989, 1971,74, 77, 83, 1989, Phila., Hollins Coll., 1985; retrospective Pa. Acad. Fine Arts, 1993, Locks Gallery, Phila., 1993-94, 97, 99, 2002-03, Inst. Contemporary Art, Phila., 2003; group shows include AAAL, In This Acad., Pa. Acad. Fine Arts, Phila., William Penn Meml. Mus., Harrisburg, Three Centuries Am. Art, Phila. Collects Art Since 1940, Phila. Mus. Art, Bklyn. Mus., Ft. Worth Art Center, Des Moines Art Center, Philbrook Art Center, Tulsa, Contemporary Phila. Artists, 1990, Phila. Mus. Art, Artists Choose Artists, Inst. of Contemporary Art, Phila., 1991, Klein Gallery, Univ. City Sci. Ctr., Phila., 1998, Phila. Mus. Art, 2000, others; represented in permanent collections, Phila. Mus. Art, Pa. Acad. Fine Arts, Print Club, Balt. Mus. Art, Addison Gallery Am. Art, McNay Art Inst., San Antonio, Montclair (N.J.) Art Mus., Nat. Collection Fine Arts, Library of Congress, USIA, Albright-Knox Art Gallery, Buffalo, Tamarind Collection, U. N.Mex. Mus., Woodmere Art Mus., Phila., Yale Art Gallery, Am. Tel. & Tel. Co., Bell of Pa., Phila., Fed. Res. Bank, Phila., Price-Waterhouse, Phila., Edwin A. Ulrich Mus. Wichita State U., Pepsi-Cola, Leeway Found., Phila., Please Touch Mus., Phila., Va. Mus. Fine Arts, Richmond. Mem. Mayor's Cultural Adv. Council, Phila., 1984-85. Recipient 1st and 2d Cresson European Traveling scholarships Pa. Acad., 1936, 37, Eyre medal Phila. Water Color Club, 1968, Mary Smith prize Pa. Acad. Fine Arts, 1968, Childe Hassam Meml. purchases AAAL, 1967, 68, Hazlett Meml. award in arts, 1980, Honor award Women's Caucus for Art, 1983, Hunt award visual arts Phila. Women's Way, 1984, Roland Gallimore Meml. award Interior Design Coun., Phila. Mayor's Arts and Culture award, 1991, Founders award Samuel S. Fleisher Art Meml., 1993, Disting. Daughter Pa. award, 2002.. Mem. Fellowship of Pa. Acad. Fine Arts, Coll. Art Assn. (Disting. Tchr. of Art award 1996).

ANDRADE, JUAN CARLOS, lawyer; b. Caracas, Venezuela, Mar. 29, 1971; s. German Andrade and Gloria Santamaria. Diploma, San Ignacio (Loyola), 1989; law sch., Universidad Catolica, 1995; post grad cum laude, London Sch. of Economics and Polit. Sci., 1998. Lawyer Baker & McKenzie, London, 1996—98, Caracas, 1998—. External adv. Venezuela Petroleum Chambers, Caracas, 2001—. Co-author: (book) Global Notification Handbook (Venezuelan Chpt.), 2001—03; contbr. articles to jours. Mem.: Spanish Cultural Inst. (bd. mem.). Avocations: sports, history. Office: Baker & McKenzie Av Francisco de Miranda Caracas Venezuela Office Fax: 58 212 264 1537. E-mail: juancarlos.andrade@bakernet.com.

ANDRAIN, CHARLES FRANKLIN, political science educator; b. Fortuna, Calif., Feb. 22, 1937; s. Milton D. and Alberta W. (Gatton) A. AB, Whittier Coll., 1959; MA, U. Calif., Berkeley, 1961, PhD, 1964. Asst. prof. dept. polit. sci. San Diego State U., 1964-67, assoc. prof., 1967-70, prof., 1970—98, chmn. dept., 1972—74, prof. emeritus, 1998—. Rsch. assoc. Inst. Internat. Studies, U. Calif.-Berkeley, 1975-76, 78-79, 80-81, 82, 86. Author: Children and Civic Awareness, 1971, Political Life and Social Change, 2d edit., 1975, Politics and Economic Policy in Western Democracies, 1980, Foundations of Comparative Politics: A Policy Perspective, 1983, Social Policies in Western Industrial Societies, 1985, Political Change in the Third World, 1988, Comparative Political Systems, 1994, (with David E. Apter) Political Protest and Social Change, 1995, Public Health Policies and Social Inequality, 1998. Woodrow Wilson Found. fellow, 1959-60; NDEA fellow, 1960-63; Ford Found. fellow, 1968-69; NIMH fellow, 1971-72. Mem. Am. Polit. Sci. Assn., Am. Sociol. Assn., Internat. Soc. Political Psychology, Internat. Studies Assn.

ANDRAKA, RAYMOND JOSEPH, digital electronics design engineer, consultant; b. Camden, N.J., Mar. 18, 1961; s. Romuald Kazmierz and Judith Adelaide (Oak) A.; m. Patricia Ann Puffer, Mar. 21, 1987; children: Christopher Thomas, Andrew Mark, Timothy Joseph, Sarah Catherine. BSEE, Lehigh U., 1983; MSEE, U. Mass., Lowell, 1992. Registered profl. engr. Sr. engr. Raytheon Missile Sys., Tewksbury, Mass., 1988-93, G-Tech Corp., West Greenwich, R.I., 1993-95; chmn., design cons. Andraka Cons. Group, North Kingstown, R.I., 1994-97; pres. Andraka cons. Group, Inc., Kingstown, R.I., 1997—. Capt. USAF, 1984-88. Mem. IEEE. Roman Catholic. Avocations: flying, woodworking. Office: Andraka Cons Group Inc 16 Arcadia Dr North Kingstown RI 02852-1666 E-mail: ray@andraka.com.

ANDRAS, OSCAR SIDNEY, oil company executive; b. Bogalusa, La., July 23, 1935; s. Oscar Severin and Rosalyn (Rogers) A.; m. Mary Louise Sisk, June 3, 1957; children: Louis James, David Sisk. BS, La. State U., 1957. With Gulf Oil Corp., Port Arthur, Tex., 1957-59, Dow Chem. Co., Baton Rouge, 1959-67, Dow Chem Co., Houston, 1967-74, Dow Chem. Co., Midland, Mich., 1974-77, Houston, 1977-80, Enterprise Cos. Inc., Houston, 1980—; now CEO Enterprise Products. Dir. Oasis Pipeline Co., Houston, 1974-80 Mem. Tex. Gov.'s Energy Council, Austin, 1975-77; pres. F.U.N. Football, Houston, 1972; bd.dirs. Meyerland Little League, 1970. Served to 2d lt. U.S. Army, 1958. Republican. Roman Catholic.*

ANDRASICK, JAMES STEPHEN, diversified company executive; b. Passaic, N.J., Mar. 27, 1944; s. Stephen Adam and Emily (Spolnik) A.; children: Christopher J., Gregory O.; m. Ginger Michael Simon, Feb. 22, 1997. BS, USCG Acad., 1965; MS, MIT, 1971. Commd. ensign USCG, 1965, advanced through grades to lt., 1968; assigned to Vietnam, 1967-68; sys. analyst Jamesbury Corp., 1970; corp. fin. and product devel. staffs Ford Motor Co., 1971-74; mgr. corp. devel. IU Internat. Corp., Phila., 1974-78; from v.p. planning, contr. to exec. v.p. C. Brewer & Co., Ltd., Honolulu, 1978-92, pres., 1992-2000; sr. v.p., CFO, treas. Alexander & Baldwin, Inc., Honolulu, 2000—02, exec. v.p., 2002; pres., CEO Matson Navigation Co., 2002—. Chmn. bd., mng. gen. ptnr. ML Macadamia Orchards LP, 1986-88; chmn. bd. HCPC, Olokele Sugar Co., Hawaiian Sugar and Transp. Coop., 1993-96; chmn. Hawaiian Sugar Planters Assn., 1992-93; bd. dirs. Wailuku Agribus. Co., C. Brewer Co., Ltd., Honolulu. Bd. dirs. Aloha United Way, Honolulu, 1983-89, Hawaii Opera Theater, Coast Guard Found.; treas., bd. dirs. ARC, Hawaii, 1983-94, 96-2002, chmn., 1989-90; bd. dirs. Hawaii Employers Coun., 1992-98, chmn., 1995-98; trustee UH Found., 1988-94, vice chmn., 1992-93, chmn., 1993-94; trustee Hawaii Maritime Ctr., 1993-98; bd. dirs. Coast Guard Found., Hawaii Opera Theater, Honolulu Symphony, Hawaii State chpt. March of Dimes. Office: Alexander & Baldwin Inc PO Box 3440 Honolulu HI 96801-3440

ANDRASSY, TIMOTHY FRANCIS, trade association executive; b. Cleve., Feb. 13, 1948; s. Robert Steven and Matilda A.; m. Grace Elizabeth Wills, Jan. 3, 1970; children— Timothy Francis, Courtney, Alyson. BS, John Carroll U., Cleve., 1970. Assoc. producer, prodn. asst. Sta. WKBF-TV, Cleve., 1968-69; asst. dir. public rels. Thistledown Racing Club, North Randall, Ohio, 1969-70, dir. promotions and community rels., 1976-77; asst. to pres. Gaffney Advt., Mentor, Ohio, 1970-71; stadium mgr., dir. broadcast ops. Cleve. Indians Profl. Baseball Club, 1971-74; mgr. communications Am. Soc. Metals, Metals Park, Ohio, 1974-76; exec. dir. Assn. Steel Distbrs., Cleve., 1977-81; v.p. Steel Svc. Ctr. Inst., Cleve., 1981-92; exec. dir. Steel Tube Inst. N.Am., Cleve., 1992—2002; exec. v.p. Precision Machined Products Assn., Brecksville, Ohio, 2002—. Mem. adv. coun. Cleve. Conv. Ctr. Dir. community rels. Geauga County Bi-Centennial Organizing Com., 1975-76. Mem. Am. Soc. Assn. Execs., Meeting Planners Internat., Greater Cleve. Growth Assn. (v.p. bd. dirs.), Greater Cleve. Soc. Assn. Execs., Downtown Euclid Assn., Walt Disney World Council of Advisors, Habitat for Humanity, Lake Metroparks.

ANDRAU, MAYA HEDDA, physical therapist; b. Digboi, Assam, India, Apr. 15, 1936; came to U.S., 1946; d. William Henry and Klara Irén Judit (Sima) Andrau; married, Sept. 1971 (div. July 1989); children: Francis Meher Traver, Darwin Meher Traver. BS in Phys. Therapy, Columbia U., 1958; MA in Social Anthropology, NYU, 1966. Lamaze cert. childbirth educator; lic. and registered phys. therapist. Phys. therapist Beekman-Downtown Hosp., N.Y.C., 1959-60; physiotherapist Stamford (Conn.) Hosp., 1963-64, Benedictine Hosp., Kingston, N.Y., 1966-69; pvt. practice in phys. therapy and lamaze Woodstock, NY, 1968-71; chief phys. therapist No. Duchess Hosp., Rhinebeck, NY, 1970-71; phys. therapist Waccamaw Pub. Health Dist., S.C. Dept. Health, Myrtle Beach, 1982-84; pain clinic specialist Pain Therapy Ctr. of Columbia (S.C.), Richland Meml. Hosp., 1986-87; phys. therapist Comprehensive Med. Rehab. Ctr., Conway, SC, 1988-92; phys. therapist, instr. conditioning program Pawleys Island (S.C.) Wellness Inst., 1993; phys. therapist Total Care, Inc., N. Myrtle Beach, S.C., 1993-97. Instr. phys. conditioning and therapeutic exercise courses, 1980—97; instr. conditioning program Health Focus Brief for TV, 1990; pvt. phys. therapist and instr. Conditioning-Wellness Program UNCA (Coll. for Srs.), Asheville, NC, 1998, Asheville-Buncombe Tech. C.C., Asheville, 1999, Blue Ridge C.C., Flat Rock, NC, 1999—2000, Elderhostel, Montreat, NC, 1999, 2001, 03, Crescent View Retirement Cmty., Arden, NC, 2001. Mem. Meher Spiritual Ctr., Inc., Alpha Kappa Delta. Follower of Avatar Meher Baba. Avocations: gardening, reading, swimming, handwork, singing.

ANDRE, CARL, sculptor; b. Quincy, Mass., Sept. 16, 1935; s. George Hans and Margaret Andre. Represented in public collections, Tate Gallery, London, Mus. Modern Art, N.Y.C., Rose Art Mus., Brandeis U., Columbus (Ohio) Gallery Fine Arts, Walker Art Center, Mpls., Milw. Art Center, La Jolla (Calif.) Mus. Contemporary Art, Dayton (Ohio) Art Inst., Albright-Knox Art Gallery, Buffalo, Monchengladbach Mus., Germany, Wallraf-Richartz Mus., Cologne, Haus Lange Mus., Krefeld, Germany, Kunstmus. Basel, Switzerland, Hessisches Landesmus., Darmstadt, Germany, Stedelijk Mus., Amsterdam, Van Abbe Mus., Eindhoven, Netherlands, Art Soc. Ghent, Belgium, Art Inst. Chgo., Los Angeles County Mus. Art, Musée Nat. d'Art Moderne, Paris, Carnegie Inst Mus. Art, Pitts., Musèo de Arte Moderno, Bogota, Colombia, Seattle Art Mus., High Mus. Art, Atlanta, Ohio State U. Gallery Fine Art, Bayerischen Staatsgemäldesammlungen, Munich, Kröller-Müller Mus., Otterlo, Netherlands, Detroit Inst. Arts, Guggenheim Mus., N.Y.C., City of Hartford, Conn., Mus. Boymans-van Beuningen, Rotterdam, Netherlands. Address: Paula Cooper 534 W 21st St New York NY 10011-2812 also: Konrad Fischer Platanenstr 7 Düsseldorf 40233 Germany

ANDRE, L. AUMUND, management consultant; b. Marquette, Kans., Dec. 21, 1916; s. Anders and Lillian Amanda (Johnson) A.; m. Elsie Viola (Nelson), June 1, 1941 (dec. Feb. 1986); children: Carolyn Aleda, Denise Ardis; m. Phyllis Jean Richter-Russo, Sept. 17, 1988. BS, CUNY, 1939; postgrad., Columbia U., 1940-41, George Williams Coll., 1947. Youth program dir. various YMCAs, N.Y.C., Syracuse, Chgo., 1939-51; exec. dir. YMCA Met. Chgo., 1951-65; sr. v.p. Cen. YMCA Coll., Chgo., 1965-80; pvt. practice cons. Chgo., 1980-96; ret., 1997. Instr. Sch. Edn. Syracuse (N.Y.) U., 1941-44; adj. prof. George William Coll., Chgo., 1948-55; lectr. Northwestern U., Evanston, Ill., 1978-80. Author: So Now You Are a Fund Raiser, 1977, Boys and Dogs Have Right of Way, 1987; author poetry; contbr. articles to profl. jours. Mem. county com. Am. Labor Party, Syracuse, 1943; chmn. Northwest Community Coun., 1954-56, Citizens Com. to Establish Triton Coll., River Grove, Ill., 1962-64; advisor Ill. Atty. Gen. Commn. to Study Fund Raising Laws and Enforcement., 1980. Named Father of Year Chgo. Area Father's Day Coun., 1962; recipient Svc. to Youth award, Lincolnland Assn. Profl Dirs. (YMCA), 1977. Mem. Nat. Soc. Fund Raising Execs. (officer, dir. 1968-79, Founder's award 1980). Democrat. Lutheran. Avocations: reading, music, traveling, writing poetry. Home and Office: 224 N Kenilworth Ave Oak Park IL 60302-2079

ANDRE, MICHAEL (KENNETH ANDRE), editor, publisher, writer; b. Halifax, N.S., Can., Aug. 31, 1946; s. Kenneth Bailey and Kathleen Mary (Warburton) A.; m. Erika Rothenberg, 1974 (div. 1983); m. Jane Adler (div. 1995); 1 child, Benjamin Eyton. BA, McGill U., 1968; MA, U. Chgo., 1969; PhD, Columbia U., 1973. Lectr. CCNY, N.Y.C., 1973, Baruch Coll., N.Y.C., 1974; editorial assoc. Art News, N.Y.C., 1973-77; treas. SoHo Baroque Opera Co., N.Y.C., 1980—; exec. dir. Unmuzzled Ox, N.Y.C., 1971—. Author: Experiments in Banal Living, 1990. Grantee Nat. Endowment Arts, Coordinating Coun. Lit. Mags., N.Y. State Coun. on Arts; grad. fellow Can. Coun. Fellow PEN; mem. MLA. Office: Unmuzzled Ox 105 Hudson St New York NY 10013-2331

ANDRE, MICHAEL PAUL, physicist, educator; b. Des Moines, Apr. 25, 1951; s. Paul Leo and Pauline (Vermie) A.; m. Janice Joan Hanecak, Mar. 12, 1988. BA, Cen. U. Iowa, 1972; postgrad., U. Ariz., 1972-73; MS, UCLA, 1975, PhD, 1980; cert., Am. Bd. Radiology, 1999. Rsch. assoc. Inst. Atmospheric Physics, Tucson, Ariz., 1972-73; mem. tech. staff Hughes Aircraft Co., L.A., 1973-74; postgrad. researcher UCLA, 1974-77; cons. L.A., 1975-84; med. radiologic physicist LACO/UCLA Olive View, L.A., 1977-81; sr. radiation physicist Cedars-Sinai Med. Ctr., L.A., 1979-84; chief med. physicist Dept. Vet. Affairs, San Diego, 1981—; prof. radiology, chief divsn.Physics and Engring, sch. medicine U. Calif., La Jolla, 1981—; chief scientific officer Radco Corp., 1996—; chief med. officer Almen Labs., Inc., 1999—. Qualified expert Calif. Radiol. Health Dept., Berkeley, 1979—; chmn. Nat. Physics Conf., San Diego, 1984-89. Editor: Physics and Biology of Radiology, 1988, Investigative Radiology, 1990—; guest editor: Internat. Jour. Imaging Sci. & Tech., 1997; contbr. articles to profl. jours. Mountain guide Sierra Club, L.A., 1977-80; dir. Ariz. PIRG, Tucson, 1973; mountain guide Am. Alpine Inst., Peru, 1987-90. Rsch. grantee U. Calif.-San Diego Found., 1989—, NIH, Nat. Cancer Inst., 1986—, VA, 1989—, U.S. Army, 1994—, Pfeiffer Rsch. Found., 2002—. Mem. Am. Assn. Physicists in Medicine, Am. Inst. Ultrasound in Medicine, San Diego Radiol. Soc., Am. Inst. Physics, Soc. Photo-Optical Inst. Engrs., Am. Coll. Radiology, Soc. of Breast Imaging. Avocations: himalayan and andean expeditions, BMS motorsports racing. Office: U Calif Dept Radiology 9114 La Jolla CA 92093 E-mail: mandre@ucsd.edu.

ANDRE, PAMELA Q. J. library director; b. Lewiston, Maine, Sept. 29, 1942; d. Charles Custer and Wilma (Hall) Quimby; m. Ronald E. Jensen, Dec. 26, 1966 (div. 1971); children: Stacy, Jaylyn; m. James Roch Andre, Mar. 3, 1973; 1 child, Brett. BA, U. N.H., 1964; MLS, U. Md., 1969. Computer programm U.S. Navy Dept., Washington, 1964-66; computer systems analyst Libr. Congress, Washington, 1968-81, asst. chief MARC editorial div., 1981-84; assoc. dir. for automation Nat. Agrl. Libr., USDA, Beltsville, Md., 1984-94, dir., 1994—. Cons. UN FAO Hdqrs., Rome, 1989, Egyptian Nat. Agrl. Libr., Cairo, 1990. Mem. editorial bd. Libr. Hi Tech, 1989—, Internet Rsch.: Electronic Networking Applications and Policy, 1991—, Microcomputers for Information Management, 1993—; contbr. articles to jours. in field. Recipient Superior Svc. award USDA, 1990. Mem. ALA, IAALD. Office: US Dept Agriculture Nat Agrl Libr 10301 Baltimore Ave Beltsville MD 20705-2326

ANDREA, JOYCE JOYCE See ROTHENBERG, JOYCE

ANDREA, MARIO IACOBUCCI, engineer, scientist, gemologist, appraiser; b. Haverhill, Mass., May 21, 1917; s. Andrea and Lucia (Antolini) Iacobucci; m. Muriel Grace Litchfield, June 29, 1940 (div. Dec. 1947); children: Gail, Patricia; m. Elizabeth Dwight (Bowes) Bray, Dec. 31, 1949 (div. Jan. 1986); children: Marjorie, Lucia, Janet; m. Elma Williams, Nov. 29, 1986. BSc, Webb Inst., Glen Cove, N.Y., 1939; grad., Oak Ridge Sch. Reactor Tech., 1958; MSE, Cath. U. Am., 1967; PhD, Pacific Western U., 1984. Grad. gemologist Gemological Inst. Am.; registered profl. engr., Md. Application engr. GE Co., Schenectady, 1948-52; marine engr. Mil. Sea Transp. Svc., Washington, 1952-54; supervisory naval architect Yokosuka, Japan, 1954-56; nuc. and gen. engr. R&D Maritime Adminstrn., Washington, 1956-74; project engr. nuc. reactor merchant ship N.S. Savannah; grad. gemologist, appraiser The Gem Tree, Bethesda, Md., 1974—. Patentee helical ship hull form. Pres., treas. Maritime Recreation Assn., Washington, 1970. Lt. comdr. USNR, 1941-61. Decorated naval medals. Mem. Gemol. Inst. Am. Alumni Assn. (life), Naval Res. Assn. (life), Order Sons of Italy in Am., Montgomery County Lodge #2288 (treas. 1994-97, trustee 1998-2000), Consumers Union (life). Avocations: chess, bridge, gardening.

ANDREADIS, TIM D. physicist, researcher; s. Dimitri and Irene Andreadis; m. Kimberly Anastasia Andreadis; children: Tanya, Anastasia. PhD, U. Md., 1981. Rsch. physicist Naval Rsch. Lab., Washington, 1984—92, sect. head high power microwave sect., 1992—. Dep. mgr. high power microwave program Naval Rsch. Lab., 2002; chmn. AMEREM, High Power Microwave Conf., Annapolis, Md., 2000—02, Small Boat Threat Workshop, Washington, 1999. V.p. Hellenic Am. Acad., Potomac, Md., 1993—95. Fellow, Nat. Rsch. Coun./Nat. Bur. Stds., 1981. Mem.: Directed Energy Profl. Soc., Assn. Old Crows. Greek Orthodox. Achievements include research in high power microwave effects on electronics; discovery of cause of atomic-like spectra from ion-bombardment induced Auger emission; development of EVOLVE, a time dependent ion bombardment simulation program. Avocations: computers, travel, politics. Office: Naval Rsch Lab 4555 Overlook Ave Washington DC 20375-5000 Personal E-mail: andreadi@bellatlantic.net. E-mail: tim.andreadis@nrl.navy.mil.

ANDREANO, RALPH LOUIS, economist, educator; b. Waterbury, Conn., Apr. 11, 1928; s. John and Loretta (Creasia) A.; m. Carol Jean Wessbecher, Sept. 5, 1955; children: Maria Carol, Nicholas George. AB, Drury Coll., 1952; MA, Washington U., St. Louis, 1955; MA Fulbright scholar, U. Oslo, Norway, 1952-53; PhD, Northwestern U., 1961. Instr. econs. Northwestern U., 1959-60; asst. prof. econs. Earlham Coll., 1961, asso. prof., chmn. dept., 1962-65; asst. prof. bus. adminstrn. Harvard Bus. Sch., 1961-62; Brookings Nat. Research prof., 1964-65; asso. prof. econs., dir. undergrad. program econs. U. Wis., 1965-67, prof., 1967—, dir. Health Econs. Research Ctr., 1969-87, chmn. dept. econs., 1980-83, dir. Ctr. for Devel.; emeritus prof. econs., 1994—. Ofcl. del. Am. Econ. Assn. to Am. Council Learned Socs., 1964-70; adminstr. Div. Health State of Wis., 1976-78; economist WHO, Geneva, 1973-74. Author: (with H.F. Williamson and others) A History of American Petroleum Industry, 2 vols., 1959, 63, No Joy in Mudville: The Dilemma of Major League Baseball, 1965, Student Economists Handbook, 1967, (with B.A. Weisbrod and others) Disease and Economic Development, 1973, (with B.A. Weisbrod) American Health Policy, 1973; editor, author: New Views on American Economic Development, 1965; editor: Economic Impact of the Civil War, 1963, rev., 1967, The New Economic History: Papers on Methodology, 1971, (with J. Siegfried) Economics of Crime, 1981, Essays on International Health, 2001, The International Health Policy Program: An Internal Assessment, 2001; editor, founder: Explorations in Entrepreneurial History, 2d series, 1963-71, Explorations in Economic History 1971-78; editor: Jour. Econ. History, 1974-75; sr. editor (econs.): Social Sci. and Medicine, 1983-87; contbr. articles to profl. jours. Ford Faculty Research fellow, 1968-69 Mem. Inst. Medicine of Nat. Acad. Scis. Home: 1815 Vilas Ave Madison WI 53711-2231 E-mail: rlandrea@wisc.edu.

ANDREAS, DAVID LOWELL, retired banker; b. St. Paul, Minn., Mar. 1, 1949; s. Lowell Willard and Nadine B. (Hamilton) A.; m. Debra Kelley, June 20, 1985; 2 children. BA, U. Denver, 1971; MA, Mankato State U., 1976. Credit mgmt. trainee United Calif. Bank, Los Angeles, 1976-77; comml. loan officer Nat. City Bank of Mpls., 1977-80; from v.p., sr. vp., to chmn., chief exec. officer to pres. & CEO Nat. City Bancorp., Mpls., 1980—2001. Chmn. ADAPA, Inc., Mpls., 1986-93; chmn. bd. Nat. City Bank, Mpls., 1991-94; pres., CEO Nat. City Bank, Mpls., 1994-2001. Bd. mem. Minn. Ctr. Victims of Torture, Marshall & Ilsley Corp., Milwaukee; mem. exec. com., dir. Children's Heart Link, 1988—, Ctr. Ethical Bus. Cultures, Minn. State U., Mankato Coll. Bus. Adv. Coun., Bus. Adv. Coun.; mem. Minn. State U. Mankato Coll. bus. adv. coun.; mem. Coll. of Social and Behavioral Scis. adv. bd.; trustee Breck Sch., Golden

Valley, Minn., 1997, Mpls. Coll. Art and Design. With U.S. Army, 1971-73. Mem.: Golden Valley Golf & Country Club. Avocations: swimming, snowboarding. E-mail: 5033@usinternet.com.

ANDREAS, DWAYNE ORVILLE, business executive; b. Worthington, Minn., Mar. 4, 1918; s. Reuben P. and Lydia (Stoltz) A.; m. Bertha Benedict, 1938 (div.); 1 dau., Sandra Ann Andreas McMurtie; m. Dorothy Inez Snyder, Dec. 21, 1947; children: TerryLynn, Michael D. Student, Wheaton (Ill.) Coll., 1935-36; hon. degree, Barry U. V.p., dir. Honeymead Products Co., Cedar Rapids, Iowa, 1936-46; chmn. bd., chief exec. officer Honeymead Products Co. (now Nat. City Bancorp.), Mankato, Minn., 1952-72; v.p. Cargill, Inc., Mpls., 1946-52; exec. v.p. Farmers Union Grain Terminal Assn., St. Paul, 1960-66; chmn. bd., chief exec. officer Archer-Daniels-Midland Co., Decatur, Ill., 1970-97, chmn. bd., 1997-98, chmn. emeritus, 1999—. Mem. Pres.'s Gen. Adv. Commn. of Fgn. Assistance Programs, 1965-68, Pres.'s Adv. Coun. on Mgmt. Improvement, 1969-73; chmn. Pres.'s Task Force on Internat. Pvt. Enterprise. Nat. bd. dirs. Boys' Club Am.; former chmn. U.S.-USSR Trade and Econ. Coun.; former chmn. Exec. Coun. on Fgn. Diplomats; former trustee Hoover Inst. on War, Revolution and Peace; former vice chmn. Woodrow Wilson Internat. Ctr. for Scholars; former mem. Trilateral Commn.; chmn. Found. for Commemoration of the U.S. Constitution, 1986. Mem. Fgn. Policy Assn. N.Y. (dir.), Indian Creek Country Club (Miami Beach, Fla.), Blind Brook Country Club (Purchase, N.Y.), Links, Knickerbocker, Friars (N.Y.C.).

ANDREAS, G(LENN) ALLEN, JR., agricultural company executive; b. Cedar Rapids, Iowa, June 22, 1943; s. Glenn Allen and Vera Irene (Yates) A.; m. Toni Kay Hibma, June 19, 1964; children: Bronwyn Denise, Glenn Allen III, Shannon Tori. BA, Valparaiso U., 1965, JD, 1968. Bar: Colo. 1969. Atty. U.S. Treas. Dept., Denver, 1969-73, Archer Daniels Midland Co., Decatur, Ill., 1973-75, asst. treas., 1975-86, treas., 1986—, v.p., chief fin. officer Europe, 1986-94, v.p., counsel to chief exec., 1994-96, mem. office of chief exec., 1996-97, pres., CEO, 1997-99, chmn., CEO, 1999—. Bd. dirs. Nat. City Bancorp., Mpls., Oelmühle Hamburg A.G, Hamburg, Federal Republic of Germany. Mem. ABA, Colo. State Bar Assn., Decatur Bar Assn. Clubs: Country of Decatur, Decatur. Democrat. Avocation: golf. Office: Archer Daniels Midland Co 4666 E Faries Pkwy Decatur IL 62526-5666

ANDREAS, WARREN DALE, lawyer; b. Clay Center, Nebr., Feb. 26, 1931; s. Leonard R. and Linda Helen (Ensz) A.; m. Arden Alanna Angst, Aug. 15, 1954 (dec. Nov. 1977); children: David Warren, Eric Alan, Alisyn Arden; m. Vera Colleen Andreas, July 14, 1984. BA, U. Kans., 1952, LLB, 1954, JD, 1968. Bar: Kans., U.S. Supreme Ct., U.S. Ct. Appeals (10th cir.), U.S. Dist. Ct. Kans. Ptnr. McSpadden & Andreas, LLP, Winfield, Kans., 1959-89, sr. ptnr., 1989-98; ret., 1998. City atty. City of Winfield, 1978-98; former dep. county atty.; atty. Bd. Edn., Unified Sch. Dist. 465, Winfield, 1971-98, pres., mem., 1967-71. Contbr. articles to profl. jours. Lay leader, chmn. fin. com., chmn. bldg. com., chmn. coun. on ministries, chmn. pastor-parish rels. com. First United Meth. Ch.; past pres. bd. dirs. Winfield Cmty. Theater, also performer; bd. dirs. Winfield Recreation Commn., United Way, Cowley County ARC, Salvation Army, Meth. Youthville, Inc., Snyder Meml. Rsch. Inst., Winfield Arts and Humanities Coun.; one of founding mems., past pres. bd. dirs. Cowley County Mental Health Assn. Fellow Kans. Bar Found.; mem. ABA, Kans. Bar Assn. (bd. govs, 1986-92, 94—, mem. title stds. com., awards com.), Cowley County Bar Assn. (past pres.), Kansas City Attys. Assn., Kans. Assn. Sch. Bds. (former mem. bd. govs.), Winfield C. of C. (bd. dirs.), Lions (past pres.), Rotary (bd. dirs.), Omicron Delta Kappa. Avocations: theater, reading, travel, golf, tennis. Office: Andreas Law Office LLP 303 State Bank Bldg Winfield KS 67156 E-mail: warrend@hit.net.

ANDREASEN, CHARLES PETER, retired electronics executive; b. Bklyn., Mar. 18, 1930; s. Peter Kristian and Marie Paulene (Pedersen) A; m. Julia Kerekes, Nov. 27, 1952; 1 child; Jane Andreasen Della Grotta. Student, Rutgers U., 1948-49, Middlesex County Coll., 1970-71. Quality control engr. Gorn Aircraft Controls Co., Stamford, Conn., 1962-63; quality control supr. Lily-Tulip Cup Corp., Holmdel, N.J., 1963-70; corp. quality control lab. supr. Purolator Products Co., Rahway, N.J., 1970-73; mgr. quality control Scovill Mfg. Co., Waterbury, Conn., 1973-78; quality assurance mgr. All-State Legal Supply Co., Mountainside, N.J., 1979-81, Durex, Inc., Union, N.J., 1981-82; quality and reliability engr., asst. quality mgr. Triangle Microwave, Inc., East Hanover, N.J., 1982-92; ret., 1992. Mem. Bd. Edn., Edison, N.J., 1982-91; vol. Edison Twp. Domestic Violence Crisis Team, 1993-95; vol. video coord. Rutgers Coop. Ext. Svc.; vol. TV dir. Piscataway Cmty. TV Ctr. Channel 22, 1997—. Mem. Am. Soc. for Quality Control (met. section exec. bd. dirs.), Elks (audit chmn. 1970-78). Democrat. Roman Catholic. Avocations: golf, swimming, photography, model railroading, fishing. Home: 24 Burchard St Edison NJ 08837

ANDREASEN, JAMES HALLIS, retired state supreme court judge; b. Mpls., May 16, 1931; s. John A. and Alice M. Andreasen; m. Janet Andreasen, June 25, 1961 (dec. July 1985); children: Jon A., Amy E., Steven J.; m. Marilyn McGuire, May 17, 1987. BS in Commerce, U. Iowa, 1953, JD, 1958. Bar: Iowa 1958. Pvt. practice law, Algona, Iowa, 1958-75; with Algona City Coun., 1961-68; judge 3d Jud. Dist. Ct., 1975-87, Supreme Ct. Iowa, Des Moines, 1987-98, ret., sr. judge, 1998—. Lt. col. USAFR, 1954-75. Mem. ABA, Iowa State Bar Assn., Kossuth County Bar Assn. Methodist. Office: Kossuth County Courthouse Algona IA 50511

ANDREASEN, NANCY COOVER, psychiatrist, educator, neuroscientist; d. John A. Sr. and Pauline G. Coover; children: Robin, Susan. BA summa cum laude, U. Nebr., 1958, PhD, 1963; MA, Radcliffe Coll., 1959; MD, U. Iowa, 1970. Instr. English Nebr. Wesleyan Coll., 1960-61, U. Nebr., Lincoln, 1962-63; asst. prof. English U. Iowa, Iowa City, 1963-66, resident, 1970-73, asst. prof. psychiatry, 1973-77, assoc. prof., 1977-81, prof. psychiatry, 1981-92, Andrew H. Woods prof. psychiatry, 1992-97, Andrew H. Woods chair psychiatry, 1997—. Dir. Mental Health Clin. Rsch. Ctr., 1987—; sr. cons. Northwick Pk. Hosp., London, 1983, acad. visitor Maudsley Hosp., London, 1986. Author: The Broken Brain, 1984, Introductory Psychiatry Testbook, 1991; editor: Can Schizophrenia be Localized to the Brain?, 1986, Brain Imaging: Applications in Psychiatry, 1988, Brave New Brain: Conquering Mental Illness in the Era of the Genome, 2001; Am. Jour. Psychiat., 1988—, dep. editor, 1989—93, editor-in-chief, 1993—; contbr. articles to profl. jours. Recipient Rhonda and Bernard Sarnat award NAS, 1999, C. Charles Burlingame award, 1999, Arthur P. Noyes award in schizophrenia, 1999, Lieber prize Nat. Alliance for Rsch. on Schizophrenia and Depression, 2000, Pres.'s Nat. Medal Sci., 2000, Interbrew Baillet-Latour Health Prize, 2003; Woodrow Wilson fellow, 1958-59, Fulbright fellow Oxford U., London, 1959-60. Fellow Royal Coll. Physicians Surgeons Can. (hon.), Am. Psychiat. Assn. (Adolf Meyer award 1999), Am. Coll. Neuropharmacologists, Royal Soc. Medicine; mem. Am. Acad. Arts and Scis., Am. Psychopathol. Assn. (pres. 1989-90), Inst. Medicine of NAS (coun. 1996—). Office: U Iowa Hosps and Clinics 200 Hawkins Dr Iowa City IA 52242-1057

ANDREASON, GEORGE EDWARD, university administrator; b. Seattle, July 4, 1932; s. Alfred M. Andreason and Alberta (Brewer) Andreason Thompson; m. Carolyn A. McKown, June 30, 1973; 1 son, Paul Edward. BS in Bus. Adminstrn., Tex. Wesleyan U., Ft. Worth, 1960; MPA (Ford Found. scholar), Ind. U., 1966; PhD, Clayton U., St. Louis, 1979. Program analyst U.S. Army, Washington, 1963-64; asst. chief mgmt. analysis divsn. FAA, Ft. Worth, 1964-67, chief mgmt. analysis divsn. Oklahoma City, 1968-70, exec. officer, 1970-71; asst. dir. IRS, Denver, 1971-72, asst. regional commr. adminstrn. Dallas, 1972-74, dist. dir. Denver, 1974, asst. dir. St. Louis, 1974-76; dir. adminstrv. svcs. McLennan C.C., Waco, Tex., 1976-77; v.p. bus. and adminstrn. U. Mary Hardin-Baylor, Belton, Tex., 1977-80, exec. v.p., 1980—. Mgmt. cons. Dept. Transp., 1966-67; partner McGregor Assocs., bus. and mgmt. cons., McGregor, Tex.; pres., CEO, A&A Consulting Co., 1989—. Served with USN, 1951-55. Recipient Career Edn. award FAA and Nat. Inst. Pub. Affairs, 1965. Fellow Nat. Inst. Pub. Affairs; mem. ASPA, Pers. and Mgmt. Assn., Nat. Coll. and Univ. Bus. Officers, So. Assn. Coll. and Univ. Bus. Officers, Belton C. of C., Rotary (Belton), Masons (master McGregor 1977, Tex. dist. dep. grand master 1980) (McGregor and Ft. Worth). Baptist. Home: PO Box 181 Mc Gregor TX 76657-0181 Office: U Mary Hardin-Baylor Sta Belton TX 76513

ANDREASON, JOHN CHRISTIAN, lawyer; b. Marysville, Calif., Nov. 18, 1924; s. John Christian and Sadie Louisa (Duus) A. BA, JD, Stanford U., 1958. Bar: Calif. 1958. With Aerojet-Gen. Corp., La Jolla, Calif., 1958-87, v.p., gen. counsel, 1980-87. Mem. ABA, Nat. Contract Mgmt. Assn., Am. Corp. Counsel Assn. Lodges: Masons. Republican. Home: PO Box 39 Plymouth CA 95669-0039

ANDREASSI, JOHN LAWRENCE, psychologist, educator; b. N.Y.C., Oct. 23, 1934; s. Croce and Agnes Marie Andreassi; m. Gina Maria Andreassi, Mar. 29, 1969; children: John II, Jeanine, Cristina. BA, CCNY, 1956; MA, Fordham U., 1959; PhD, Case Western Res. U., Cleve., 1964. Lic. psychologist, N.Y. Psychologist Dunlap & Assocs., Stamford, Conn., 1958-61; USPHS fellow Case Western Res. U., Cleve., 1961-64; assoc. prof. NYU, N.Y.C., 1967-73; prof. psychology CUNY, 1973—. Author: Psychophysiology, 1980, 4th edit., 2000; editor-in-chief Internat. Jour. Psychophysiology, 1988—. With USN, 1964-67. Disting. Faculty scholar Baruch Coll., CUNY, 1978; Office of Naval Rsch. grantee, 1969-73, Air Force Office of Sci. Rsch. grantee, 1973-85. Mem. APA, Internat. Orgn. Psychophysiology (v.p. 1984-94, bd. govs. 1996—, bd. dirs. 1982-94), Assn. for Applied Psychophysiology and Biofeedback, Sigma Xi. Avocations: tennis, golf, chess. Office: City Univ of New York Baruch Coll Dept Psychology Box B8-215 One Bernard Baruch Way New York NY 10010 E-mail: john_andreassi@baruch.cuny.edu.

ANDREASSON, KIM J. writer, consultant; b. Varberg, Sweden, Feb. 17, 1976; s. Kenth and Gullvi Andreasson. BA(hon.), NYU, 2000; MIA, Columbia U., 2002. Web editor Goteborgs-Posten, Sweden, 1997—98, asst. editor, 1998—98; forum coord. Fgn. Policy Assn., N.Y.C., 2001—01. Contbr. articles to profl. jours. Sustaining mem. Am.-Scandinavian Found., N.Y.C. Scholar, The Marcus Wallenberg Found., 2001. Mem.: The Columbia Club. Conservative. Home: 400 East 66th St Apt 15A New York NY 10021-9319 Personal E-mail: kim@kimandreasson.com.

ANDREATTA, SUSAN L. anthropologist; b. Syracuse, N.Y., Feb. 3, 1961; d. Antonio Geno and Ellen Jean Andreatta; m. Timothy David Johnston, June 27, 1998. B, U. Del., 1984; M. Iowa State U., 1986; PhD, Mich. State U., 1994. Asst. prof. U. N.C., Greensboro, 1996—2003, dir. Project Green Leaf, 2001—, assoc. prof., 2003—. Co-author: (book) Language and Community Building: The Migrant Farmworker Experience in North Carolina, 2001; contbr. articles to profl. jours. Planning com. U.S. Nat. Com. World Food Day, Washington, 2001—02; liaison Student Action with Farmworkers, Durham, NC, 1997—2002. Mem.: Carolina Farm Stewardship Assn. (sec. 1997—2000), Am. Anthropology Assn. (culture and agr. treas. 2001—03), Soc. Applied Anthropology (bd. dirs. 2001—).

ANDREEN, AVIVA LOUISE, dentist, researcher, academic administrator, educator; b. Frankfurt, Germany, Jan. 6, 1952; (parents Am. citizens); d. Robert Benjamin Andreen and Margie Corinne (LaPointe) Marshall; m. Merrill R. Penn, Nov. 8, 1987 (div.); 1 child from previous marriage, Robert Morton Salkin. BA, NYU, 1975; student, Westchester C.C., 1976; DDS, NYU Coll. Dentistry, 1996; postgrad., Laser Inst. Am., 1980. Cert. mobile laser operator, N.Y. Tchr. Kibbutz Regavim, D.N. Menasche, Israel, 1975-76; account rep. Traveler's Ins. Co., N.Y.C., 1976; spl. projects coordinator Sapan Engrng. Co., N.Y.C., 1976-78; sec., treas. founder J. Sapan Holographic Studios, N.Y.C., 1979; owner, pres. Universal Media Cons., White Plains, N.Y., 1980-84; dir. edn., owner Am. Ctr. for Laser Edn., Bronx, N.Y., 1984-96; pres. Penn Laser Systems Inc., 1994-96; chief dental resident St. Barnabas Hosp., Bronx, NY, 1997—98; fellow in spl. patient care Helen Hayes Hosp., West Haverstraw, N.Y., 1998-99; clin. instr. spl. patient care, oral medicine and pathology NYU Coll. Dentistry, N.Y.C., 1999; dentist Marvin Family Dentistry, Nanuet, NY, 1999—2001; owner, ptnr. Dental Arts of Suffern, LLP, NY, 2001—02; assoc. Dr. Gerald B. Greitzer, Tarrytown, NY, 2002—. Attending dentist Bronx Park Dental; faculty practice St. Barnabas Hosp., 2003—, attending dentist Helen Hayes Hosp.; lectr. Hudson River Mus., Yonkers, N.Y., 1986-87; producer laser light show, Andrus Planetarium; taught 1st laser safety course in Am. high sch., 1980; designed laser safety course for Westchester C.C., 1992. Curator Holography A New Dimension White Plains Mus. Gallery, Hudson River Mus., Yonkers, Troster Hall Sci.; vol. forensic dentist for World Trade Ctr. attack N.Y.C. Med. Examiner's Office, 2001—02. Lt. comdr. Dental Corps USNR, 2001—03. Mem. ADA, Acad. Gen. Dentistry, Alpha Omega. Avocations: reading, dental laser research, crocheting, embroidery. Office: 200 S Broadway Tarrytown NY 10591

ANDREESSEN, MARC, communications company executive; BS in Computer Sci., U. Ill., 1993. Co-founder, v.p. tech. Netscape Comms. Corp., Mountain View, Calif., 1994-97, co-founder, exec. v.p., 1997-99; chief tech. officer AOL, 1999; co-founder, chmn. Loudcloud, 1999—. Office: Loudcloud Inc 599 N Mathilda Ave Sunnyvale CA 94085-3545

ANDREEV, FEDOR, mathematician, educator; arrived in U.S., 1999; s. Vladimir Andreev and Ludmila Andreeva; m. Irina Balahontseva, May 23, 1987; children: Aleksei, Vasily. MSc, St. Petersburg State U., 1993; PhD, Russian Acad. Scis., St. Petersburg, 1996. Cert. mathematician Russian Acad. Scis., 1997. Fellow Steklov Math. Inst., St. Petersburg, 1996—99; vis. rschr., prof. Kans. State U., Manhattan, 1999—2001; asst. prof. Western Ill. U., Macomb, 2001—. Mem.: Am. Math. Soc. Achievements include research in painleve equations; control theory; algebraic solutions to the sixth painleve equation; development of online homework system. Office: Western Ill Univ Dept Math 1 University Circle Macomb IL 61455 E-mail: f-andreev@wiu.edu.

ANDREIEV, YURA (GEORGE ANDREIEV), electronics engineer; b. N.Y.C., June 21, 1961; s. Nikita and Maria (Tregubov) A.; 1 child, Morgan. BS in Engring. Physics, Cornell U., 1982; MS in Elec. Engring., George Washington U., 1987. Lic. pvt. pilot, FAA. Pres. Synersol Assocs., Denver, 1982-84; rsch. electronics engr. U.S. Army Night Vision and Electro-Optics Lab., Ft. Belvoir, Va., 1984-89; electronics engr. Office of Naval Intelligence, Washington, 1989-92; chief scientist radar technologies Def. Intelligence Agy., Washington, 1992-95; dir. R&D (Russia) Sci. Applications Internat. Corp., Moscow, 1995-97; dir. internat. programs Ukrainian Land and Resources Mgmt. Ctr., Kyiv, Ukraine, 1997-2000; chief scientist Environ. Rsch. Inst. of Mich., Ann Arbor, 1997-2000; sr. rsch. scientist Coherent Tech. Inc., Lafayette, Colo., 2001—. Solar energy cons. Synersol Assocs., Washington, 1982—; tech. advisor On-Site Inspection Agy., Washington, 1989. Patentee in field. Block coord. Neighborhood Watch, Alexandria, Va., 1993-94. Recipient 8 spl. act awards U.S. Army, 1984-89, Letter of Commendation, U.S. Joint Chiefs of Staff, 1992. Mem. IEEE, Optical Soc. Am., Amnesty Internat. Avocations: flying, skiing. Home: 3028 W 11th Ave Cir Broomfield CO 80020

ANDRÉ KILDARE, MICHEL WALTER, neurosurgeon; b. Tunis, Tunisia, Jan. 15, 1935; s. George Walter and Dedy Louise (Andre) Girault Kildare; m. Paula Stone Calahan, Aug. 29, 1983; 1 child, Marc Condit Andre Kildare. BS, U. Mass., 1957; MD, Meharry Med. Coll., 1961. Diplomate Am. Bd. Neurol. Surgery, Am. Bd. Surgery. Clin. instr. NYU, 1974-75; attending neurosurgeon Kaiser Permanente, Honolulu, 1974-76, Allegheny Gen. Hosp., Pitts., 1976-77, Meth. Med. Ctr., Des Moines, 1977-84, Robert Packer Hosp., Sayre, Pa., 1984-86; cons. Fremont/Rideout Hosps., Marysville, Calif., 1986—. Clin. instr. U. Calif., Davis, 1990—; attending neurosurgeon Sierra Nevada Meml. Hosp., Grass Valley, Calif., 1991—. Capt. U.S. Army, 1966-68, Vietnam. Fellow Am. Coll. Surgeons, N.Am. Spine Soc., Calif. Soc. Indsl. Medicine & Surgery, Am. Acad. Disability Evaluating Physicians; mem. Congress Neurol. Surgeons, Am. Assn. Neurol. Surgeons, Calif. Assn. Neurol. Surgeons, Alpha Omega Alpha. Avocations: chess, cycling, ballet, fishing, climbing. Office: 700 Zion St Nevada City CA 95959 also: Yuba-Sutter Neurosurgery Sierra Nevada PO Box 387 Marysville CA 95901-0387 also: PO Box 387 Marysville CA 95901-0387 Fax: 530-273-1646. E-mail: narfecin@hotmail.com.

ANDREOFF, CHRISTOPHER ANDON, lawyer; b. Detroit, July 15, 1947; s. Andon Anastas and Mildred Dimitry (Kolinoff) A.; m. Nancy Anne Krochmal, Jan. 12, 1980; children: Alison Brianne, Lauren Kathleen. BA, Wayne State U., 1969; postgrad. in law, Washington U., St. Louis, 1969-70; JD, U. Detroit, 1972. Bar: Mich. 1972, U.S. Dist. Ct. (ea. dist.) Mich. 1972, U.S. Ct. Appeals (6th cir.) 1974, Fla. 1978, U.S. Supreme Ct. 1980. Legal intern Wayne County Prosecutor's Office, Detroit, 1970-72; law clk. Wayne County Cir. Ct., Detroit, 1972-73; asst. U.S. atty. U.S. Dept. Justice, Detroit, 1973-80; asst. chief criminal divsn. U.S. Atty.'s Office, 1977-80; spl. atty. organized crime and racketeering sect. U.S. Dept. Justice, 1980-84, dep. chief Detroit Organized Crime Strike Force, 1982-85, mem. narcotics adv. com., 1979-80; ptnr. Evans & Luptak, Detroit, 1985-93, Jaffe, Raitt, Heuer & Weiss, Detroit, 1995—. Lectr. U.S. Atty. Gen. Advocacy Inst., 1984. Recipient numerous spl. commendations FBI, U.S. Drug Enforcement Adminstrn., U.S. Dept. Justice, U.S. ATty. Gen. Mem. ABA, FBA (spkr. trial adv. and criminal law sect. Detroit 1983—, bd. dirs. 1989-91, chmn. criminal law sect. 1990-91), Mich. Bar Assn., Fla. Bar Assn., Nat. Assn. Criminal Def. Lawyers, Detroit Bar Assn. Greek Orthodox. Home: 4661 Rivers Edge Dr Troy MI 48098-4161 Office: Jaffe Raitt Heuer & Weiss One Woodward Ave Ste 2400 Detroit MI 48226

ANDREOLI, KATHLEEN GAINOR, dean, nurse; b. Albany, N.Y., Sept. 22, 1935; d. John Edward and Edmunda Elizabeth (Ringlemann) Gainor; children: Paula Kathleen, Thomas Anthony, Karen Marie. BSN, Georgetown U., 1957; MSN, Vanderbilt U., 1959; DSN, U. Ala., Birmingham, 1979. Staff nurse Albany Hosp. Med. Ctr., 1957; instr. St. Thomas Hosp. Sch. Nursing, Nashville, 1958—59, Georgetown U. Sch. Nursing, 1959—60, Duke U. Sch. Nursing, 1960—61, Bon Secours Hosp. Sch. Nursing, Balt., 1962—64; ednl. coordinator, physician asst. program, instr. coronary care unit nursing inservice edn. Duke U. Med. Ctr., Durham, NC, 1965—70; ednl. dir. physician asst. program dept. medicine U. Ala. Med. Ctr., Birmingham, 1970—75, clin. assoc. prof. cardiovascular nursing Sch. Nursing, 1970—77, asst. prof. nursing dept. medicine, 1971, assoc. prof., 1972—, assoc. prof. nursing Sch. Pub. and Allied Health, 1973—; assoc. dir. Family Nurse Practitioner Program, 1976, assoc. prof. community health nursing Grad. Program, 1977—79, assoc. prof. dept. pub. health, 1978—79; prof. nursing, spl. asst. to pres. for ednl. affairs U. Tex. Health Sci. Ctr., Houston, 1979—82, acting dean Sch. Allied Health Scis., 1981, v.p. for ednl. services, interdisciplinary edn., internat. programs, 1983—87; v.p. nursing affairs Rush-Presbyn.-St. Lukes's Med. Ctr., Chgo., 1987—; dean Rush U. Coll. Nursing, 1987—. Mem. nat. adv. nursing coun. VHA, 1992; cons. in field. Author, editor, with others: Comprehensive Cardiac Care, 1983; editor: Heart and Lung, Jour. of Total Care, 1971; contbr. articles to profl. jours. Active Internat. Nursing Coalition for Mass Casualty Edn., 2002—; mem. adv. bd. Robert Wood Johnson Clin. Nurse Sch. Program; mem. vis. com. Vanderbilt U. Sch. Nursing; mem. Leadership Ill., 1991; mem. nat. nursing asdv. com. Voluntary Hosp. Am., 1991; mem. governing coun. Inst. for Hosp. Clin. Nursing Edn., Am. Hosp. Assn., 1993; bd. dirs. Ill. League for Nursing, 1994. Recipient Founder's award, N.C. Heart Assn., 1970, Disting. Alumni award, Vanderbilt U. Sch. Nursing, 1985, Leadership Tex. award, 1985, Disting. Alumni award, U. Ala. Sch. Nursing, 1991. Fellow: Am. Acad. Nursing; mem.: ACNA, ANA, Internat. Nursing Coalition for Mass Casualty Edn., Inst. of Medicine of Chgo., Nat. Nursing Adv. Coun. Hosps. Am., Am. Heart Assn. Coun. Cardiovasc. Nursing, Coun. Family Nurse Practitioners and Clinicians, Ala. Heart Assn., Nat. League Nursing, Inst. of Medicine of Nat. Acad. Scis., Am. Assn. Colls. Nursing, Rotary One Club Chgo., Phi Kappa Phi, Alpha Eta, Sigma Theta Tau. Roman Catholic. Home: 1212 N Lake Shore Dr Chicago IL 60610-2402 Office: Rush Presbyn-St Luke's Med Ctr 600 S Paulina St Ste 1080 Chicago IL 60612-3806 Business E-Mail: Kathleen_G_Andreoli@rush.edu.

ANDREOPOULOS, GEORGE JOHN, history educator, lawyer, political science educator; b. Athens, May 20, 1953; s. Ioannis K. and Paraskevi A.; m. Giuliana Campanelli, Aug. 15, 1992; 1 child, Elena. BA, U. Chgo., 1976; LLB, U. Cambridge, Eng., 1977, PhD, 1986. Lawyer, Athens, 1984-86; post doctoral fellow Yale U., New Haven, 1986-88, founding assoc. dir. Orville Schell Ctr. for Internat. Human Rights, 1988-93, lectr., 1990-96; asst. prof. govt. John Jay Coll. Criminal Justice, CUNY, 1996-99; asst. prof. govt. Grad. Sch. and Univ. Ctr. CUNY, 1998-99; assoc. prof. govt., John Jay Coll. Criminal Justice and Grad. Sch. and Univ. Ctr., CUNY, 2000—; dir. Ctr. Internat. Human Rights John Jay Coll. Criminal Justice, CUNY, 2000—. Author, editor: Genocide, 1994, The Aftermath of Defeat, 1994, The Laws of War, 1994, Human Rights Education for the Twenty-First Century, 1997, Concepts and Strategies in International Human Rights, 2002; mem. editl. bd. Peace Bull., 1985-86, Human Rights Rev., 1999—. Mem. fundraising com. Habitat for Humanity, New Haven, Conn., 1989-91; mem. adv. bd. Toda Inst., 2000—. With Greek Army, 1983-85. A.G. Leventis Found. fellow, 1986-87; grantee Conn. Humanities Coun. 1988, Ford Found., 1989-92, Marangopoulos Found., 1995, European Human Rights Found., 1996, Carnegie Corp. N.Y., 1997-98, Promoting Enduring Peace, 1999-2000. Mem.: Athens Bar Assn., Am. Polit. Sci. Assn. (v.p. human rights sect. 2002—03), Am. Hist. Assn. Avocations: films, theater, literature, jogging, swimming. Office: Dept Govt John Jay Coll Criminal Justice CUNY New York NY 10019 also: Grad Sch and Univ Ctr 365 Fifth Ave New York NY 10016 Business E-Mail: grandreopoulos@jjay.cuny.edu.

ANDREOPOULOS, SPYROS GEORGE, writer; b. Athens, Greece, Feb. 12, 1929; came to U.S., 1953, naturalized, 1962; s. George S. and Anne (Levas) A.; m. Christiane Loesch Loriaux, June 6, 1958; 1 child, Sophie. AB, Wichita State U., 1957. Pub. info. specialist USIA, Salonica, Greece, 1951-53; asst. editorial page editor Wichita (Kans.) Beacon, 1955-59; asst. dir. info. svcs., editor The Menninger Quar., The Menninger Found., Topeka, 1959-63;; info. officer Stanford U. Med. Ctr., 1963-83; dir. comm., editor Stanford Medicine, 1983-93, dir. emeritus comm., editor emeritus, 1993—. Editor Sun Valley Forum on Nat. Health, Inc. (Idaho), 1972-83, 85-95, editor emeritus, 1995—. Co-author, editor: Medical Cure and Medical Care, 1972, Primary Care: Where Medicine Fails, 1974, National Health Insurance: Can We Learn from Canada? 1975, Heart Beat, 1978, Health Care for an Aging Society, 1989; contbr. articles to newspapers and profl. jours. With Royal Hellenic Air Force, 1949-50. Mem. AAAS, Assn. Am. Med. Colls., Nat. Assn. Sci. Writers, Am. Med. Writers Assn., Am. Hosp. Assn., Am. Soc. Hosp. Mktg. and Pub. Rels., Coun. for Advancement and Support of Edn. Home: 1012 Vernier Pl Stanford CA 94305-1027

ANDREOZZI, LOUIS JOSEPH, lawyer; b. N.J., 1959; m. Lisa Marie Clark, Apr. 12, 1987. BS in Bus. Adminstrn. with hons., Rutgers U., 1981; JD, Seton Hall U., 1984. Bar: N.J. 1984. Asst. gen. counsel Gordon Pub., Inc., Randolph, NJ, 1984—93; dep. gen. counsel Elsevier U.S. Holdings, Morris Plains, NJ, 1985—93; v.p., sec., gen. counsel Reed Elsevier Med. Pub., Belle Mead, NJ, 1994—95; v.p., gen. counsel, sec., head ops. support and svcs., purchasing, sales force homeworking project, customer svc. integration project Lexis-Nexis, Miamisburg, Ohio, 1994—97; pub. Martindale-Hubbell, 1996; chief legal counsel Lexis-Nexis, 1997—98; COO Martindale-Hubbell, New Providence, NJ, 1997—99, Marquis, NRP, New Providence, NJ, 1998—99; vice-chmn. Reed Tech. and Info. Svcs., Inc., 1999—2000; pres., CEO Martindale-Hubbell, Marquis, NRP, New Providence, 1999—2000, Lexis, 2000—. Mem. legal adv. bd. Lexis-Nexis, 1994—, exec. bd., 1994—; mem. Friends of the Law Libr. of Congress; bd. dirs. Am. Assn. of Pub. Named to Dept. Distinction in Bus., Rutgers U., 1981, Nat. Honor Soc. in Econs. and Bus., 1981. Mem.: ABA, N.J. Employment Law Assn., Am. Corp. Counsel Assn., Internat. Bar Assn., N.J. Bar Assn. Roman Catholic. Office: Lexis Nexis Group 9443 Springboro Pike Miamisburg OH 45342-4425

ANDRES, EUGEN CHARLES, lawyer; b. Boston, Mass, July 15, 1939; BS econ., UCLA, 1961; LLB, Hastings Coll. Law, 1968. Bar: Calif. 1969. Dep. dist. atty. Orange County, Calif., 1969—71; sole practice Santa Ana, Calif., 1971—72; ptnr. Aitken, bradshaw & Andres, Santa Ana, Calif., 1972—81. Mem.: Orange County Bar Assn. (pres. 1978, 1982), Calif. State Bar, Trial Lawyers Assn., ABA, Bowers Mus. Found. (pres. 1979). Office: 2041 N Main St Santa Ana CA 92706-2746

ANDRES, KENNETH G., JR., lawyer; b. Trenton, N.J., Nov. 9, 1953; s. Kenneth George and Joan Margaret (Fredericks) A. BA, Swarthmore Coll., 1975; JD, Capitol U., 1978. Bar: N.J. 1978, Pa. 1978, U.S. Dist. Ct. N.J. 1978, U.S. Ct. Appeals (3rd cir.) 1981, U.S. Supreme Ct. 1994; cert. civil trial atty., N.J., cert. advocate Am. Bd. Trial Advocates. Ptnr. Andres & Berger PC, Haddonfield, N.J. Adj. prof. law Mercer County C.C., 1983-89; faculty mem. Am. Trial Lawyers Assn. - N.J., 1989—. Contbr. articles to profl. publs. Mem. N.J. Supreme Ct. Dist. III ethics com., 1994-98; mem. N.J. Supreme Ct. Civil Jury Charge Com., 1996—. Named Profl. Lawyer of Yr., N.J. Commn. Professionalism in Law, 1998. Mem. ATLA (nat. gov. 2001—), ABA, Assn. Trial Lawyers of Am.-N.J. (bd. govs. 1986-90, parliamentarian 1990-91, from asst. sec. to pres. 1990-1999, N.J. Gold Medal award 1999), Pa. State Bar Assn.,

N.J. State Bar Assn., Burlington County Bar Assn. (chmn. civil bench and bar com. 1992-94, trustee 1993), Mercer County Bar Assn. (trustee 1982-91). Office: Andres & Berger PC 264 Kings Hwy E Haddonfield NJ 08033-1907 E-mail: kandres@andresberger.com.

ANDRES, RONALD PAUL, chemical engineer, educator; b. Chgo., Jan. 9, 1938; s. Harold William and Amanda Ann (Breuhaus) A.; m. Jean Mills Elwood, July 15, 1961; children: Douglas, Jennifer, Mark. BS, Northwestern U., 1959; PhD, Princeton U., 1962. Asst. prof. Princeton U., 1962-68, assoc. prof., 1968-76, prof. chem. engring., 1976-81, Purdue U., West Lafayette, Ind., 1981—, head Sch. Chem. Engring., 1981-87, Engring. Research prof., 1987—. Mem. AAAS, Am. Chem. Soc., Am. Inst. Chem. Engrs., Am. Phys. Soc., Materials Rsch. Soc., Sigma Xi, Tau Beta Pi, Pi Mu Epsilon, Phi Lambda Upsilon, Phi Eta Sigma. Office: Purdue U Sch Chem Engring West Lafayette IN 47907-1283 E-mail: ronald@ecn.purdue.edu.

ANDRESEN, JULIE ANN DOTHAGER, librarian; b. Vandalia, Ill., June 3, 1965; d. August W. and Marilyn S. (Spires) Dothager; m. Scott Alan Andresen, July 10, 1999. BA in English and Libr. Sci., Mo. Bapt. Coll., 1987; MLS, U. Ill., 1990. Asst. libr. Evans Pub. Libr., Vandalia, 1987-88; grad. asst. U. Ill., Champaign, 1988-90; dir. libr. Hannibal (Mo.) LaGrange Coll., 1990—. Vol. Habitat Humanity, Greeley, Colo., 1990; mem. 1st Bapt. Ch., New London, Mo. Mem. ALA, So. Bapt. Libr. Assn., Single Adults Together (co-dir. 1992-93, exec. com. 1991-98). Republican. Avocations: reading, traveling. Office: Hannibal-La Grange Coll 2800 Palmyra Rd Hannibal MO 63401-1940

ANDRESEN, MALCOLM, lawyer; b. Medford, Wis., July 26, 1917; s. Thomas Whelen and Ethel (Malkson) A.; m. Ann Kimball, 1942 (div. 1968); children: Anthony M., Susan A. Bridges, Abbott K.; m. Barbara Brown, 1971 (div. 1976); m. Nigi Sato, 1979. BA, U. Wis., 1940, LLB, 1941. Bar: Wis. 1941, N.Y. 1946, U.S. Supreme Ct. 1958. Acct. J.D. Miller & Co., N.Y.C., 1946-47; jr. tax acct. Peat Marwick Mitchell & Co., N.Y.C., 1947-48; assoc. Davis Wagner Hallett & Russell, N.Y.C., 1948-52; tax counsel, then sr. tax counsel, sr. govt. rels. adviser Mobil Oil Corp., N.Y.C., 1952-70; dir. tax legal affairs Nat. Fgn. Trade Coun., N.Y.C., 1970-73; of counsel Delson & Gordon, N.Y.C., 1970-77; Whitman & Ransom, N.Y.C., 1977-86; pvt. practice N.Y.C., 1986— Trustee, fin. v.p. Nat. Urban League, 1959-65; trustee, treas. Cathedral Ch. of St. John the Divine, N.Y.C., 1977-84. Capt. USMCR, 1942-46. Decorated Bronze Star medal. Mem. Assn. of Bar City of N.Y., Internat. Fiscal Assn. (coun. U.S.A. br. pres. 1971-72), Univ. Club (coun. mem. 1985-89, co-chair com. women mem. admission 1988). Democrat. Episcopalian. Home: 2 Lincoln Sq Apt 24D New York NY 10023-6218 Office: 60 E 42nd St Ste 764 New York NY 10165-0799

ANDRESS, WILL K. music educator, conductor; b. El Dorado, Ark., Aug. 28, 1958; s. Willie Knox and Ruth Wooley Andress; m. Julia Ann Hamiter, Feb. 2, 1957; children: W. Knox, Elizabeth Andress Engman. BME, Centenary Coll. of La., Shreveport, 1961; MCM, So. Bapt. Sem., Louisville, 1963; MusM, East Carolina U., 1969; DM, Fla. State U., 1971. Ordained to ministry United Meth. Ch. Minister of music First Bapt. Ch., West Memphis, Ark., 1963—64, New Bern, NC, 1964—66, Talbot Park Bapt. Ch., Norfolk, Va., 1966—69, East Hill Bapt. Ch., Tallahassee, 1969—71, First United Meth. Ch., Shreveport, La., 1971—. Adj. prof. music Centenary Coll., Shreveport, 1974—; advisor for hymnal United Meth. Ch. Contbr. Mem.: Am. Choral Dirs. Assn., Shreveport Opera, Demoiselle Club, The Shreveport Club. Methodist. Avocation: golf. Home: 550 Ratcliff Shreveport LA 71104 Office: Centenary Coll of Louisiana 2911 Centenary Blvd Shreveport LA 71104

ANDRETTI, DANIEL, secondary school educator; b. Bayonne, N.J., May 20, 1971; s. Peter and Nancy Andretti. B of English/Writing, Kean U., 1997. Mgr. Luckys Ace Hardware, Bayonne, NJ, 1984—99; tchr. English Elizabeth High Sch., 2000—03. Newspaper supv. Elizabeth High Sch. Voice, 2002—03. Author: Joy, 1999, A Trip Through the Musuem, 2003. Avocations: bicycling, scuba diving, Star Trek, writing. E-mail: tomwasapaine@aol.com.

ANDRETTI, JOHN, professional race car driver; b. Bethlehem, Pa., Mar. 12, 1963; s. Aldo and Carolyn (Stofflet) A.; m. Nancy Ann Summers, Sept. 7, 1987; children: Jarett John, Olivia Elizabeth. BA in Bus. Mgmt., Moravian Coll. Vehicle maintenance Paul E. Smith Plumbing, 1977-78; gen. maintenance Firestone Tire & Rubber Co., 1978-81; sportsman stock cars, 1982; formula super vee, 1982; USAC midgets, 1983-85, 87-89, 93; sprint cars (USAC & CRA), 1983-87; IMSA GTP, 1986, 87, 89, 93; SCCA Can Am, 1984; IMSA showroom stock, 1986-87; CART Indy cars, 1987-94; chmn. bd. Andretti-Helmling Automotive Corp., 1991—. Shareholder Andretti-Laird Racing, 1997, Andretti-Laird Helmling Mfg., 1997. Winner U.S. Auto Club Midget Championship, 1983, 24 Hours of Daytona, 1989, 1st Indy car win in Australia, 1991, USAC Championship Dirt Cars, 1985, Group A, 1988, Group C, 1988-89, NHRA Top Fuel Dragster, 1993, British F2, 1993, Land Speed Record, Subaru Legacy, 1993, Nascar Winston Cup, 1993-98, first Nascar Winston Cup pole position, 1995, first win Nascar Winston Cup, 1997, many others; only driver to compete in Indy 500 and World 600 in same day, 1994; named USAC Midget rookie of yr., 1983, Dorney Park rookie of yr., 1982. Roman Catholic. Office: c/o Petty Enterprises 311 Branson Mill Rd Randleman NC 27317-8008

ANDRETTI, MARIO, retired race car driver; b. Montona, Italy, Feb. 28, 1940; came to U.S., 1955, naturalized, 1964; s. Alvise and Rina (Benvegnu) A.; m. Dee Ann Hoch, Nov. 25, 1961; children: Michael, Jeffrey, Barbra. Began racing career at age 19, Nazareth, Pa. Champ Car Nat. Champion, 1965, 66, 69, 84; Daytona 500 winner, 1967; 12 Hrs. of Sebring winner, 1967, 70, 72; Indpls. 500 winner, 1969; Indy 500 pole winner, 1966, 67, 87; USAC Nat. Dirt Track Champion, 1974; Formula One World Champion, 1978; Internat. Race of Champions titlist, 1979; Driver of the Yr., 1967, 78, 84, Driver of the Quarter Century, 1992, Driver of the Century, 1999-2000; all-time leader in Champ Car Pole Positions won (67); all-time Champ Car lap leader (7,587); all-time record holder for Champ Car starts (407); oldest race winner in recorded Champ car history (53 years 34 days, Phoenix, 1993); only driver to win Champ Car races in four decades; had 12 Formula One victories and captured 18 Grand Prix pole positions.

ANDREU-GARCIA, JOSE ANTONIO, territory supreme court chief justice; Chief justice Supreme Ct. of P.R. Office: Supreme Ct PR PO Box 9022392 San Juan PR 00902-2392 E-mail: andreujp@tld.net., josea2@tribunales.gobierno.pr.

ANDREULA-ORTIZ, JO-ELLEN, pharmaceutical company administrator, cosmetologist; b. Hoboken, NJ, Mar. 19, 1958; d. Peter Albert and Gilda Rosemary A.; m. Carlos Ruben Ortiz, Nov. 29, 1997; children: Krista-Rae, Kortney-Lyn, Kerrin Marie, Carlos II. Ptnr. Vinny's Confectionary Store, Hoboken, NJ, 1976-84; with Washington Savs. Bank, Hoboken, 1990-92; bus. bank svcs. Bank of N.Y., Weehwken, N.Mex., 1992; brand product dir. adminstr. Roche (Labs.) Pharm. Co., Nutley, NJ, 2000—; med. adminstr. Christ Hosp., Jersey City. Bus. and beauty cons. Jo-Ellen's Collectables, Hoboken, 1997—. Mem. Jehovah's Witness. Office: Roche Pharms 360 Kingsland Ave Nutley NJ 07110 also: Christ Hosp Bon Secours of Canterbury 176 Palisade Ave Jersey City NJ 07306 Fax: 201-795-8685. E-mail: Jo_ellen.ortiz@roche.com.

ANDREW, BRIAN J. information technology company executive; BS, Auckland U., 1984. CEO, pres. Triton Network Sys. Inc., Orlando, Fla., 1997—, Cavu Inc., Orlando. Office: Cavu Inc 4901 Vineland Rd Ste 600 Orlando FL 32811-7231

ANDREW, BRYAN HAYDN, astronomer; b. Glasgow, Scotland, Feb. 26, 1939; m. Moira Crawford, 1962; children: Susan, Heather. BS, Glasgow U., 1961; PhD in Radio Astronomy, Cambridge U., 1966. Asst. rsch. officer NRC Can., 1965-72, assoc. rsch. officer, 1972—82, sr. rsch. officer, 1979—82, chief program svc. br., 1984-86, dir. mgmt. svc. br., 1986-87, dir. Off. Natural Facil. Sci., asst. dir., 1987-90, dir. radio astronomy Herzberg Inst. Astrophysics, 1990-96; interim dir. gen. Inst. for Info. Tech., 1994-96; ret., 1996. Vis. lectr. U. Toronto, 1974-76. Mem. Can. Astron. Soc. Achievements include research in molecules; extragalactic variables; planets; comets. Home: 6 Florette Ottawa ON Canada K1J 7L4

ANDREW, JOHN HENRY, lawyer, retail corporation executive, author; b. Duluth, Minn., May 23, 1936; s. Frederick William and Florence Elizabeth (Phillips) A.; m. Floretta Claudette Townsend; children: Sean Townsend, Brett Townsend. BA cum laude with distinction, U. Minn., Duluth, 1958; JD, Northwestern U., 1961. Bar: Ill. 1961, Calif. 1975, N.Y. 1980. Assoc. Pattishall, McAuliffe & Hofstetter, Chgo., 1961-71; sr. atty. J.C. Penney Co., Inc., N.Y.C., 1971-74, sr. counsel legis. and regional ops., Western regional coun. L.A., Buena Park, Calif., 1974-93, sr. govt. rels. counsel Sacramento, 1993-97, chief counsel govt. rels., 1997; v.p. Calif. State U., Sacramento, 2003—. Author: The Hanging of Arthur Hodge: A Caribbean Anti-Slavery Milestone. Chmn. pub. affairs com. Planned Parenthood Assn. Chgo., 1970-71; mem. Calif. State Dem. Cen. Com., 1976-82. Mem.: ABA, Sacramento County Bar Assn. (co-chmn. history com. 2001—), Calif. State Bar (com. on consumer fin. svcs. 1982—84, 1990—93), Ill. State Bar Assn. (chmn. internat. law sect. 1969—70), Calif. C. of C. (regulatory, consumer and legal affairs com. 1974—86, mem. air and waste mgmt. com. 1994—97), Sullivan County (Pa.) Hist. Soc. (life), Renaissance Soc., Cornwall Family History Soc., Sacramento Pubs. Assn. (Best Gen. Non-Fiction award 2000—01), JCPenney Retirees Club (pres. 2003—). Home: 11359 Mother Lode Cir Gold River CA 95670-3025 E-mail: jandrew523@aol.com.

ANDREW, JOSEPH JERALD, lawyer; b. Poe, Ind., Mar. 1, 1960; s. Jerald Lee Andrew and Sylvia Huss Hanselmann; m. Anne Slaughter, Sept. 9, 1989. BA, Yale U., 1982, JD, 1985. Bar: Ind., D.C., N.Y., S.D., N.D., U.S. Ct. Appeals (7th cir.). Law clk to Judge Flaum U.S. Ct. Appeals (7th cir.), Chgo., 1985-86; assoc. Baker & Daniels, Indpls., 1986-89; chief dep. sec. of State of Ind., Indpls., 1989-91; with Bingham, Summers, Welsh & Spilman, Indpls., 1991-95, ptnr., 1992-95; chmn. Ind. Dem. Party, 1995-99; ptnr. Johnson Smith Pence, Indpls., 1997-99; nat. chmn. Dem. Nat. Com., Washington, 1999-2001; ptnr. Cadwalader, Wickersham & Taft, Washington, 2001—03; ptrn. McDermott, Will & Emery, Washington, 2003—. Author: (book) The Disciples, 1993. Candidate, office of gov. State of Ind., 2003—. Scholar Glen Peters Legal, 1983, 1984, 1985. Democrat. Office: McDermett Will & Emery 13th St NW Washington DC 20005 E-mail: jandrew@mwe.com.

ANDREW, KENNETH L. research physicist, physics educator; b. Wichita, Kans., June 14, 1919; s. I(saac) Ernest and Hulda (Cox) A.; m. Lois Ranman, Sept. 1, 1940; children— Ralph K., Dale Ernest, Nancy Lee AB, Friends U., 1940; MA, Johns Hopkins U., 1942; PhD, Purdue U., 1951. Head dept. physics Friends U., Wichita, 1942-56; chmn. dept. physics Dickinson Coll., Carlisle, Pa., 1956-57; assoc. prof. physics Purdue U., West Lafayette, Ind., 1957-68, prof. physics, 1968-89; prof. emeritus, 1989—. Exchange prof. Lab. Aimé-Cotton, Orsay, France, 1968-69; cons. Los Alamos Nat. Lab., 1965-72, 77-99, Argonne Nat. Lab. Ill., 1977-83; prin. investigator research grants in atomic emission spectroscopy NSF, 1958-83, research grants in atomic spectroscopy NASA, 1963-75, contracts in spectroscopy Office Naval Research, 1959-66; mem. com. on line spectra of elements NRC, 1961-73, chmn., 1966-68 Contbr. numerous articles to profl. jours. Recipient Disting. Alumnus award Friends U., 1971. Fellow Optical Soc. Am. (assoc. editor 1980-83); mem. European Group Atomic Spectroscopists, Am. Phys. Soc., Am. Assn. Physics Tchrs., Internat. Astron. Union, Sigma Xi. Home: 1637 May St # 1002 Wichita KS 67213-3503

ANDREW, LUCIUS ARCHIBALD DAVID, III, bank executive; b. Mar. 5, 1938; s. Lucius Archibald David Jr. and Victoria (Rollins) A.; m. Susan Ott, June 1, 1963 (div. 1973); children: Ashley W., L.A. David IV; m. Phoebe Haffner Kellogg, Dec. 21, 1974; children: Gaylord M., Charles H., Matthew K., Louise K. BS, U. Pa., 1962; MBA, NYU, 1965. Asst. treas. The Bank of N.Y., N.Y.C., 1962-68; instl. salesman Drexel, Harriman, Ripley, N.Y.C., 1968-70; v.p., br. mgr. Drexel, Firestone, Inc., Chgo., 1970-72; ptnr., br. mgr. Fannestock & Co., Chgo., 1972-74; pres. N.E.A., Inc., 1975-85; dir. First Am. Bank Corp., Seattle, 1985—. Vice chmn. Viner's, Ltd., Sheffield, Eng., 1981-82; chmn. exec. com. Cert. Mfg. Co., Shelton, Wash., 1975-85; bd. dirs. First Am. Bank, Chgo., 1965-91, chmn., 1982-91; bd. dirs. First Am. Data Corp.; chmn. FGI, Inc., Forest Grove, Oreg., 1985-86, Union St. Capital Corp., Seattle, Wash., 1986-87, Brudi Inc., Seattle, 1988-90. Trustee Brooks Sch.; past trustee Seattle Repertory Theatre; bd. dirs. Swedish Met. Ctr. Found. Mem. The Brook, Racquet and Tennis Club (N.Y.C.), Racquet Club (Chgo.), Rainier Club, Univ. Club, Golf Club (Seattle), Tennis Club (Seattle). Home: The Highlands Seattle WA 98177 Office: 200 1st Ave W Ste 400 Seattle WA 98119-4219

ANDREWS, ADELAIDE, real estate company executive; s. John Cannon Andrews and Adelaide Fuller; children: Dylan Aplin, Scarlett McCarthy, Mia Rose McCarthy. BA in Psychology, U. So. Calif., L.A., 1985. Ptnr. Cedros Realty Advisors, Encintas, Calif., 1998—, Tech. Ventures, LLC, Encintas, Calif., 1999—2002; pres. BoatGlo, Inc., Encintas, 2002—. Mem. Calif. Assn. Realtors, Sigma Xi, Delta Delta Delta. Avocations: scuba diving, writing, web design, sailing.

ANDREWS, ARCHIE MOULTON, government official; b. Greenwich, Conn., July 29, 1919; s. Archie M. and Eleanor (Underwood) A.; m. Margaret Jane Jones, Mar. 3, 1944 (dec. Sept. 1977); children: Archie Moulton III, Peter Underwood, Duncan Trumbull; m. Nike Smith Middleton, Oct. 3, 1978 (dec. Mar. 1987); m. Dorothy Johnson Conley, Sept. 30, 1989. AB, Princeton U., 1941. Exec. trainee W.R. Grace & Co., 1941-42; econ. analyst State Dept., 1942-43; U.S. rep. blacklist com. Ministry Econ. Warfare, Am. embassy, London, 1943-45; with Dictograph Products, Inc., Danbury, Conn., 1946-63, pres., 1962-63; also dir.; pres. Acousticon-Dictograph Co. Ltd., Can., 1963, dir., 1958-63, Gen. Acoustics Ltd., Eng., 1950-63; dep. dir. Bur. Internat. Commerce, Dept. Commerce, 1964-69; dir. U.S. trade mission to N. Africa, 1966; comml. counsellor Am. embassy, London, 1970-75; dir. bus. services Office Internat. Affairs, HUD, Washington, 1976-77; dir. exporters service Office Export Adminstrn., Dept. Commerce, Washington, 1978-86; sr. policy analyst Office of Tech. and Policy Analysis, 1986-88, ret., 1988. Mem. SAR Clubs: Princeton (Washington and N.Y.C.); Pilgrims; Diplomatic and Consular Officers Ret. Home: 326 Prospect Bay Dr W Grasonville MD 21638-1199

ANDREWS, BETTY BAUSERMAN, retired secondary school educator, property manager; b. Luray, Va, Dec. 29, 1935; d. Raymond Edgar Bauserman and Elizabeth Elaine Houser; m. George Norman Andrews, July 26, 1964 (dec. Apr. 1996). BS, Madison Coll., 1958; postgrad., U. Va., 1964-68, George Mason U., 1969—. Cert. coll. profl. cert., Va. Classroom tchr. Clarke County HS, Berryville, Va., 1958-64, Loudoun Valley HS, Purcellville, Va., 1964-68; proofreader Missles and Rockets mag., Washington, 1964, Loudoun County HS, Leesburg, Va., 1968-69; head libr. media specialist Broad Run HS, Ashburn, Va., 1969-2000. Cons., libr. reorganizer Logetronics Corp., Springfield, Va., 1974; mem. sch. improvement team Broad Run HS, Ashburn, 1996-2000. Adv. bd. Sterling (Va.) Pub. Libr., 1998—. Mem. NEA, James Madison U. Alumni Assn., Va. Edn. Assn. (life), Loudoun Edn. Assn. (life), Loudoun Educators Media Assn. (life), Nat. Soc. DAR, Sparlandria Investment Club, Am. Assn. Univ. Women (AAUW), Alpha Gamma Delta. Democrat. Methodist. Avocations: antique collecting, gardening, investing, sailing, reading. Home: 821 Golden Arrow St Great Falls VA 22066-2517 E-mail: striperrtripes@aol.com.

ANDREWS, BILLY FRANKLIN, pediatrician, educator; b. Graham, N.C., Sept. 22, 1932; s. Dean Franklin and Arlee (Byers) A.; m. Faye Rich, Dec. 25, 1953; children: Ann Elizabeth Feigenbaum, Billy Franklin Jr., David Ashley. Student, Brevard (N.C.) Coll., 1950, Elon Coll., 1951; BS cum laude, Wake Forest Coll., 1953; MD, Duke U., 1957. Diplomate Am. Bd. Pediat., 1963. Commd. 2nd lt. U.S. Army, 1956, advanced through grades to maj., 1962; intern Ft. Benning (Ga.) U.S. Army Hosp., 1957-58; resident in pediat. Walter Reed Gen. Hosp., Washington, 1958-60; with mil. med. and allied scis. course Walter Reed Army Inst. Rsch., Washington, 1960-61; chief pediat. svc. Rodriguez U.S. Army Hosp., Ft. Brooke, P.R., 1961-63; chief pediat. Tropical Med. Rsch. Lab., Ft. Brooke, P.R., 1963-64; res. U.S. Army, 1964; from asst. prof. pediat. to chmn. emeritus U. Louisville, 1964—93, chmn. emeritus, 1993—, dir. Comprehensive Health Care Ctr. for High Risk Infants and Children, 1968-98; chief of staff Kosair Children's Hosp., Louisville, 1969-93, chief-of-staff emeritus, 1993—. Cons. divsn. adult and child health Ky. Dept. Pub. Health, 1966—; lectr. Jour. Pediatrics Found., 1972; Staley Disting. Christian scholar Mary Baldwin Coll., Washington and Lee U., Sch. Medicine of U.Va., 1990; vis. scholar in med. history and ethics Green Coll., Oxford (Eng.) U., 1993, vis. fellow, 98. Author: Children's Bill of Rights, 1968; editor: Small-for-Date Infants, 1970, The Newborn, Pediatric Clinics of North America, 1977, Aphorisms, Tributes and Tenets of Billy F. Andrews: In Walls, M.E., 1986, Ideals and Inspiration (F.R. Andrews), 1993, Words to Live By (F.R. Andrews), 1993, A Statement on Transplantation and Organ Donors, 1994; contbr. numerous articles to profl. publs.; inventor, poet. Pres. Kornhauser Libr., Health Scis. Ctr., 1981-82, 90-91; mem., tchr., deacon, elder United Ch. of Christ. Recipient Helen B. Fraser award Norton-Children's Hosp., 1978, Award of Recognition, XVII Internat. Congress Pediat., Manila, 1983, Wisdom award of honor, eminent fellow The Wisdom Soc., 1991, The Billy F. Andrews, M.D. Endowed Chair in Pediat., U. Louisville, 1993, Winston Churchill medal of Wisdom Soc., Eminent Churchill Fellow of Wisdom Soc., 1993, Disting. Alumnus award Wake Forest U., 1983, The Billy F. Andrews, M.D. scholarship for pediat. U. Louisville Sch. Medicine, 1986, Festschrift to Billy F. Andrews, M.D., Jour. of Perinatology, 1995; Billy F. Andrews, MD, Lectureship in Neonatology Dept.Pediatrics, U. Louisville, 2002. Fellow ACP, Am. Acad. Pediat., Royal Soc. Medicine (London), Internat. Biog. Assn.; mem. AMA, Am. Pediat. Soc., Am. Osler Soc. (pres. 1996-97), Am. Soc. for Bioethics and Humanities, Soc. for Pediat. Rsch., So. Soc. Pediat. Rsch. (founding), Southeastern Perinatal Soc. (founding), Nat. Assn. Children's Hosps. and Related Instns. (founding), Ky. Med. Assn. (faculty Sci. Achievement award 1971, del. 1981-82, Ednl. Achievement award 1997), Jefferson County Med. Soc., Ky. Pediat. Soc., Louisville Pediat. Soc., U. Louisville Sch. Medicine Alumni Assn. (bd. govs. 1972-75), Univ. Pediatric Found. Inc. (pres. 1982-93), Internat. Assn. Bioethics, Am. Soc. Law, Medicine and Ethics, Order of Internat. Fellowship (Cambridge), Internat. Order of Merit (Cambridge), Alpha Omega Alpha. Achievements include invention of infant oxygen hood, iontophoresis sweat induction apparatus, radiant open infant warmer, infant blood warmer, diagnostic and treatment table with warmer and position changes, infant transport incubator, others. Office: Kosair Charities Pediat Ctr 571 S Floyd St Ste 449 Louisville KY 40202-3830 E-mail: sahabb01@louisville.edu. *Personal philosophy: "The level of civilization attained by any society will be determined by the attention it has paid to the welfare of its infants and children." Also, "The responsibility of the physician is to prevent, to diagnose, to prognosticate, to treat when and if necessary, and always to keep foremost in mind 'Primum Non Nocere'".*

ANDREWS, BRYANT AYLESWORTH, software company executive; b. N.Y.C., Dec. 28, 1938; s. F. Emerson and Edith Severance Andrews; m. Elisabeth Power, July 5, 1974; children: Christopher, Suzanne. BA in English, Cornell U., 1962. Engring. writer Pratt & Whitney Aircraft, East Hartford, Conn., 1962-79, supr. engring. writers, 1979-83, mgr. system devel., office automation, 1983-85; pres., co-founder Integrated Custom Software, Inc., Glastonbury, Conn., 1985—. Author: (software) System Minder, Formsprint. Chmn. Columbia Fin. Bd., 1979-87; mem., chmn. Columbia Planning and Zoning, 1971-77, Windham Regional Planning Agy., Willimantic, Conn., 1971-75. Republican. Congregationalist. Avocation: private pilot. Home: 99 Route 87 Columbia CT 06237-1023 Office: Integrated Custom Software Inc 12 National Dr Glastonbury CT 06033-1212 E-mail: icsandr@attglobal.net.

ANDREWS, CAROL, primary education educator; b. Galveston, Tex., Apr. 21, 1945; d. Herbert and Amy Elsie (Johnson) Gumaer; m. Harlan Andrews, Dec. 30, 1968; children: Monique, Brad. BA in English with distinction, San Jose State U., 1970. Cert. multiple subject cred., Calif. Tchr. spl. edn. Moreland Sch. Dist., San Jose, Calif.; mid. sch. tchr. English, South Valley Carden Sch., San Jose, Calif., 1986—2002, Carden Day Sch. of San Jose, 2002—. History and K-8 ednl. cons. Carden Acad., Silicon Valley, 2002-. Docent Ainsley House Outreach Program. Recipient Francis Lanyon Meml. award. Mem. Campbell Hist. Soc.

ANDREWS, CHARLES, wholesale distribution executive; CEO, pres. Sunbelt Beverage, Lutherville, Md., 1997—2002; former CEO Young's Market, Orange; pres., COO Nat. Distributing Co., Atlanta, 2003—. Office: 1 National Dr SW Atlanta GA 30336*

ANDREWS, CHARLES HAYNES, economics educator; b. Waycross, Ga., Nov. 30, 1937; s. Charles Haynes and Louise Rebecca (McQuaig) A.; m. Susan B. Gahan, Aug. 29, 1961 (div. 1973); m. Lorraine Lynn, Aug. 24, 1974; children— Charles Haynes, William Edward. BA, Mercer U., 1960; PhD. in Econ., Vanderbilt U., 1967. Assoc. prof. Stetson U., DeLand, Fla., 1964-73; dean Sch. Bus., Mercer U., Macon, Ga., 1978-88, Stetson prof. econ., 1988—; Author: The Econ. Performance of the Compania de Acero del Pacifico, 1970; contbr. scientific papers; Commr. Macon Housing Authority, 1984— . Fellow Woodrow Wilson Found., 1960-61, Earhart Found., 1961-62; fgn. area fellow Ford Found., 1963-64. Mem. Am. Econ. Assn., So. Econ. Assn., Phi Kappa Phi, Delta Sigma Pi, Omicron Delta Kappa. Methodist. Home: 121 Wesley Ann Ct Macon GA 31210-3136 Office: Mercer Univ 1400 Coleman Ave Macon GA 31207-0003

ANDREWS, CHARLES ROLLAND, library administrator; b. Scranton, Pa., July 5, 1930; s. Edgar W. and Margaret (Macheny) A.; m. Harriet Williams, Dec. 27, 1954 (dec. 1985); m. Dorothy Kramer, Dec. 10, 1988. BS in Edn., Bloomsburg U., 1954; MA in English Lit., U. Okla., 1959; MS in Lib. Sci., Case Western Res. U., 1964, PhD, 1967. Head reference dept. Cleve. Pub. Library, 1966-68, Case Western Res. Univ. Libraries, Cleve., 1968-69, librarian Freiberger Library, 1969-72, asst. dir. pub. services, 1972-74; univ. librarian Southeastern Mass. Univ. Library, North Dartmouth, 1974-76; dean library services Hofstra U. Library, Hempstead, N.Y., 1976-96, prof. emeritus, 1997—. Lectr. Hofstra U., U. Coll. Continuing Edn., 1997—. Editor: Reference Books for Small and Medium-Sized Libraries, 1973; contbr. articles, revs. to profl. jours. Bd. trustees Unitarian Universalist Congregation, Garden City, NY, 1998—, chair art exhibits com., 1999—2002, newsletter editor, 2000—. Mem. ALA, Assn. Coll. and Rsch. Librs., Archons of Colophon, L.I. Libr. Resources Coun. (chair regional automation com. 1986-92, bd. trustees 1990-94), Am. Express (sr. adv. bd. mem. 1998-99). Democrat. Avocations: calligraphy, word processing, graphics. Home and Office: 305 Hillside Ave Bellmore NY 11710-3519

ANDREWS, CHERI D. lawyer; b. Oakland, Calif., May 29, 1961; m. Jay A. Andrews, 1985; children: Sarah Renee, Rachel Susanne, Rebecca Anne. BA magna cum laude, Mt. Holyoke Coll., 1983; JD, Temple U., 1987. Bar: Pa. 1987. Atty. Manning, Kinkead, Brooks & Bradbury, Norristown, Pa., 1987-96, High, Swartz, Roberts & Seidel, Norristown, 1996—. Co-author, co-editor: (manual) Montgomery County Civil Practice Manual, 1992-01 (ABA G.P. Link Project award 1995); editor: Montgomery County Law Reporter, 1994-96. Mary Lyon scholar Mt. Holyoke Coll., 1983. Mem. Montgomery Bar Assn. (bd. dirs. 1996-98, Pres.'s award 2003, co-chmn. SideBar pub., 2001-02, com. of yr. award 2002), Bucks-Mont Mothers of Multiples (sec. 1997-98). Avocations: quilting, making scrapbooks. Office: High Swartz Roberts & Seidel 40 E Airy St Norristown PA 19401-4803 E-mail: candrews@highswartz.com.

ANDREWS, CLAUDE LEONARD, psychotherapist; b. Halifax County, NC, Jan. 13, 1943; s. Leland Waverly and Annie Grey (Hyde) Andrews; m. Carol Gladys Cooper, June 10, 1967 (dec. Nov. 1986). BA, St. Andrews Coll., 1965; MDiv, Princeton (N.J.) Theol. Sch., 1969; MEd, U. Ga., 1972, ABD, 1974. Lic. psychol. assoc. N.C., marriage and family therapist N.C., profl. counselor N.C., cert. EMT-ALS paramedic; ordained to ministry Presbyn. Ch. Intern, chaplain U. NC, Chapel Hill, 1967-68; intern, clin. chaplain Milledgeville State Hosp., 1970-71; minister Lavonia Presbyn. Ch., 1971-74; marital therapist U. Ga., Athens, 1971-73, teaching intern, 1972-74; psychologist Edgecombe-Nash Mental Health Ctr., Rocky Mount, NC, 1974-76; dir., psychologist Tarboro Unit Mental Health Ctr., 1976-77; pvt. practice Creative Living Assoc., Tarboro, 1977—. Cons. Albemarle Presbytery, Greenville, NC, 1975—87, Presbytery New Hope, Rocky Mount, 1987—, Tarboro Police Dept., 1987—, Edgecombe Sheriff's Dept., Tarboro, 1987—, Critical Incident Stress Debriefing Team, Ctrl. Carolina Team, 1987—, Elm City E.M.S., Stoney Creek E.M.S., Atlanta Beach Fire and Rescue; mental health coord. NC Critical Incident Stress Mgmt.; part-time instr. EMS law enforcement; cons. in mental health and psychology for N.E.E.D. Head Start. Min. Fountain (N.C.) Presbyn. Ch., 1991—; bd. dirs. N.C. Symphony. Mem.: Am. Assn. Marriage and Family Therapists (clin. mem., cert.), Scottish Rite, Shriners, Masons, Rotary (bd. dirs., sec., v.p., pres.). Avocations: martial arts, electronics, sailing, salt water fishing. Home: 309 E Saint John St Tarboro NC 27886-4413 Office: Creative Living Assocs 309 E Saint John St Tarboro NC 27886-4413 E-mail: tweetymedic@hotmail.com.

ANDREWS, CLINTON JAMES, public affairs educator; b. Sumter, S.C., Aug. 1, 1955; s. Peter Barnum and Barbara Dale (Kirk) A. ScB in Engring. with honors, Brown U., 1978; SM in Tech. and Policy, MIT, 1985, PhD in Planning, 1990. Registered profl. engr., Calif. Designer REDE Inc., Providence, 1978; mech. engr. MCT Engrs., Inc., San Francisco, 1979-83; cons. Xenergy Inc., Burlington, Mass., 1984; project mgr. Meridian Corp., Alexandria, Va., 1985-87; rsch. asst. MIT Energy Lab., Cambridge, 1987-90, postdoctoral assoc., 1990-91; asst. prof. Woodrow Wilson Sch., Princeton (N.J.) U., 1991-97; from asst. prof. to assoc. prof. Bloustein Sch., Rutgers U., 1997—, dir. urban planning program. Cons. TVA, Hydro Quebec, U.S. Dept. Energy, others; reviewer/adv. com. Intergovtl. Panel on Climate Change, U.S. Dept. Energy, various ours. on energy topics. Author: Humble Analysis: The Practice of Joint Fact-Finding, 2002; editor: Regulating Regional Power Systems, 1995; co-editor: Industrial Ecology and Global Change, 1994; contbr. articles to profl. jours. Bd. dirs. N.J. Sustainable State Inst., 2001—, Trenton Materials Exch., 2000—. AT&T Found. Indsl. Ecology Faculty fellow, 1993-95. Mem. AAAS, IEEE Power Engring. Soc. (3d millenium award 2000), IEEE Soc. on Social Implications of Technology (pres. 2002-03), Internat. Assn. for Energy Econs., Am. Assn. Geographers, Am. Planning Assn., Am. Collegiate Sch. Planning. Achievements include helping to launch a program in science, technology and public policy at Princeton, 1991; proponent/developer of communicative analysis to facilitate public participation in technological decisions. Office: Bloustein/Rutgers U 33 Livingston Ave New Brunswick NJ 08901-1900 E-mail: CJA1@rci.rutgers.edu.

ANDREWS, CONSTANCE ELAINE, pharmaceutical executive; b. Indpls., Feb. 7, 1953; d. Harold Eugene and Evelyn Louise (Poole) Garrett; children: Jason Paul, Stephen Ryan, Christopher Sean. BA, U.S. Internat. U., 1980; MA, Nat. U., 1982. Cert. therapist. Clin. rsch. coord. Feighner Rsch. Inst., San Diego, 1981—84; mgr. central nervous system rsch. Pharmaco, Austin, Tex., 1984-87; sr. clin. rsch. assoc. Beecham Smith Kline, Bristol, Tenn., 1987—88; assoc. dir., clin. opers. Boots Pharm., Shreveport, La., 1989—95; asoc. dir. clin. monitoring ClinTrials Rsch., Nashville, 1995—96; group dir. Omnicare Rsch., Blue Bell, Pa., 1996—99; sr. dir. project mgmt. MDS Pharma Svcs., King of Prussia, Pa., 1999—2002; dir. Pfizer Pharms., New London, Conn., 2002—03; dir. clin. ops. MedImmune, Gaithersburg, Md., 2003—. Contbr. articles to profl. jours. With USN, 1978-82. Mem. APA, Drug Info Assn., Am. Mgmt. Assn. Office: 50 Pequot Ave MS6025-A 3263 New London CT 06320

ANDREWS, DAVID RALPH, lawyer; b. Oakland, Calif., Jan. 4, 1942; m. Rozan McCurdy, July 1, 1962; children: David, Linda. BA, U. Calif., Berkeley, 1968; JD, U. Calif., 1971. Bar: Calif. 1971, D.C. 1986, U.S. Dist. Ct. (no. dist.) Calif. 1971, U.S. Dist. Ct. Hawaii 1991, U.S. Supreme Ct. 1980. Assoc. McCutchen, Doyle, Brown & Enersen, San Francisco, 1971-75; regional counsel Reg. IX U.S. EPA, San Francisco, 1975-77; legal counsel and spl. asst. for policy US EPA, Washington, 1977-79; dep. gen. counsel Dept. Health and Human Svcs., Washington, 1980-81; ptnr. McCutchen, Doyle, Brown & Enersen, San Francisco, 1981-97, chmn., 1991-95; legal adviser US Dept. State, Washington, 1997-2000; ptnr. McCutchen, Doyle, Brown & Enersen, San Francisco, 2000—02; sr. v.p., govt. affairs & sec. office of gen. counsel, Pepsi Co., Purchase, NY, 2002. Amb., spl. negotiator U.S./Iran Claims, 2000—; bd. dirs. Union Bank Calif., Kaiser Permanente, NetCel360 Holdings Ltd., PG&E Corp. Trustee San Francisco Mus. of Modern Art, 1988-97; bd. trustees Golden Gate Nat. Park Assn., 1992-95, Marin Cmty. Found., 1996-97; mem. U.S. Agy. for Internat. Devel. Energy Tng. Program Adv. Com. of the Inst. Internat. Edn.; mem. bd. dirs. Union Bank Calif., Kaiser Permanente and NetCel360 Holdings Ltd., 2000—. Fellow Max Planck Inst. of Pub. Internat. Law, Heidelberg, Fed. Republic of Germany, 1974. Mem. ABA (natural resources sect.), Calif. Bar Assn.), San Francisco Bar Assn. Avocations: photography, tennis, running. Office: Pepsi Co Office Gen Coun 700 Anderson Hill Rd Purchase NY 10577

ANDREWS, DIANE RANDALL, nursing administrator, critical care nurse; b. Clinton, Iowa, Dec. 30, 1953; d. Eugene E. and Carol Lee (Walker) Randall; m. Thomas Wescott Andrews, Oct. 2, 1982; children: Christine, Charles. BSN, U. Iowa, 1976; MS, U. Ill., Chgo., 1981; student, Univ. Ctrl. Fla., 2001—. RN, Fla., Ill. Unit leader/instr. Rush Presbyn. St. Lukes Med. Ctr., Chgo., 1976-84; cons. Longwood, Fla., 1990—. Trustee Fla. Hosp. Coll. of Health Scis., 1993 , mem. fin. com.; mem. women's ctr. adv. com. Fla. Hosp., 1992—; chair endowment oversight com. Fla. Hosp./Univ. of Ctrl. Fla., 1996—; chair founding bd. Fla. Hosp. Coll. Health Scis. Found., 1997-2001, treas. 2001-02, bd. dirs., 2002-. Author: After Anesthesia; former editor jour. Kaleidoscope; former contbg. editor Jour. of the Fla. Med. Assn.; contbr. articles to profl. publs. Bd. dirs. Fla. Hosp. Golden Cir. of Friends, Fla. Hosp. Found., Jewish Family Svcs., pres., 2000-02, mem. exec. com.; bd. dirs. Fla. Hosp. Cancer Inst. Recipient President's award Fla. Med. Assn. Alliance, 2000, William Trickle Vol. of Yr. award Fla. Hosp. Found., 2000, Summit award Women's Resource Ctr., 2001; State of Iowa scholar. Mem. Am. Soc. Post Anesthesia Nursing, Fla. Med. Assn. Alliance, Orange County Med. Soc. Alliance (past chair), Sigma Theta Tau. Home and Office: 1821 Alaqua Dr Longwood FL 32779-3105 E-mail: dcra4@aol.com.

ANDREWS, E. WYLLYS, archaeologist, educator; b. Phila., Oct. 10, 1943; s. Edward Wyllys and Ann (Wheeler) Andrews IV; m. Patricia Antell Andrews, June 15, 1965; children: Dwen Hardy Andrews-Cita, Edward VI, Ruth Wheeler. AB, Harvard U., 1964; PhD, Tulane U., 1971. Asst. prof. anthropology No. Ill. U., DeKalb, 1970-75; dir. Mid. Am. Rsch. Inst., Program Rsch. in Yucatan Tulane U., New Orleans, 1972-74, dir. Mid. Am. Rsch. Inst., gen. editor publs., 1975—, assoc. prof. anthropology, 1975-80, prof. anthropology, 1980—. Dir. excavations at Quelepa, El Salvador, Tulane U., 1967—69, dir. excavations at Komchen, Yucatan, Mex., 1980—84, dir. excavations Copan Royal Residence, Honduras, 1990—94. Author: The Archaeology of Quelepa, El Salvador, 1976, Excavations at Dzibilchaltun, Yucatan, Mexico, 1980; co-editor: Late Lowland Maya Civilization: Classic to Postclassic, 1986, Five Hundred Years After Columbus, 1994; mem. editl. bd. Rsch. and Exploration, 1984-95, Latin Am. Antiquity, 1989-95. Grantee NEA, 1978, NSF, 1980, Nat. Geog. Soc., 1992. Mem. Am. Anthropol. Assn., Soc. for Am. Archaeology, Sociedad Mexicana de Antropologia. Avocations: photography, backpacking, cross-country skiing, downhill skiing, canoeing. Office: Tulane U Mid Am Rsch Inst New Orleans LA 70118 E-mail: wandrews@tulane.edu.

ANDREWS, FRAN WOLFE, medical educator; b. Columbia, S.C., Mar. 22, 1961; m. Norman E. Andrews, Jr., June 26, 1993. A in Secretarial Sci., U. S.C., 1982, B in Health Sci., 1991. Staff technologist Bapt. Med. Ctr. Columbia (S.C.), 1984-92; radiologic tech. clin. instr. Orangeburg (S.C.)-Calhoun Tech. Coll., 1992-96, radiologic tech. program dir., 1996-2000, dir. health scis., 2000—. Mem. adv. bd. The Tech. Ctr., Orangeburg, 1996—; mem. S.C. Radiology Educators Coun., Columbia, 1996—. Mem.: Capitol Chpt. Midlands (v.p. 1995—96, treas. 1998—2001, v.p. 2001—03), S.C. Soc. Radiologic Tech. (treas. 2000—02), Am. Soc. Radiologic Tech. Office: Orangeburg-Calhoun Tech Coll 3250 Saint Matthews Rd Orangeburg SC 29118-8299 E-mail: andrewsf@octech.edu.

ANDREWS, FRED CHARLES, mathematics educator; b. Aylesbury, Sask., Can., July 13, 1924; s. Henry Marmaduke and Margaret (Van de Bogart) A.; m. Joyce Davenny, Apr. 5, 1944; children— Linda (Mrs. Pierre Dunn), David W. (dec.), Gail E.(Mrs. Gregory Crandell). BS in Math, U. Wash., 1946, MS in Math. Statistics, 1948; PhD, U. Calif., Berkeley, 1953; PhD (hon.), U. Tampere, Finland, 1985. Research asso. Applied Math. and Statistics Lab., Stanford, 1952-54; asst. prof. math., asso. statistician U. Nebr., 1954-57; asso. prof. math. U. Oreg., 1957-66; dir. U. Oreg. (Statistics Lab. and Computing Center), 1960-69, prof. math., 1966-89, prof. emeritus math., 1989—, head dept. math., 1973-80. Vis. statistician Math Centrum, Amsterdam, The Netherlands, 1963-64; Fulbright-Hays sr. lectr. U. Tampere, Finland, 1969-70; Fulbright-Hays sr. lectr. Univ. Coll., Cork, Ireland, 1976-77; Fulbright sr. lectr. U. Jordan, Amman, 1983-84 Contbr. articles to profl. jours. Pres. Met.-Civic Club, Eugene-Springfield, 1967-68; Trustee Oreg. Grad. Center, 1967-77. Served to lt. (j.g.) USNR, 1943-46. Fellow AAAS; mem. Sigma Xi. Office: U Oreg Dept Math Eugene OR 97403

ANDREWS, GAYLEN, measurable response public relations expert; Pres. Blitz Media-Direct, Middle Island, N.Y. Office: Blitz Media-Direct PO Box 102 Middle Island NY 11953-0102

ANDREWS, GEORGE EYRE, mathematics educator; b. Dec. 4, 1938; s. Raymond Leslie and Rovena Pearl (Eyre) A.; m. Joy Margaret Brown, Sept. 2, 1960; children: Amy Beth, Katherine Yvonne, Derek George. BS, MA, Oreg. State U., 1960; postgrad., Cambridge (Eng.) U., 1960-61; PhD, U. Pa., 1964; Doctorate in Physics (hon.), Parma (Italy) U., 1998; DSc (hon.), U. Fla., 2002. Asst. prof. math. Pa. State U., University Park, 1964-67, assoc. prof. math., 1967-70, prof. math., 1970-81, Evan Pugh prof. math., 1981—, math. dept. head, 1980-82, 95-97. Hedrick lectr. Math. Assn. Am., 1980, J.S. Frame lectr., 1993; adj. prof. U. Waterloo, Ont., Can., 1982-92, regional conf. lectr., NSF-Conf. Bd. Math. Scis., 1985. Author: Number Theory, 1971, Theory of Partitions, 1976, Partitions: Yesterday and Today, 1979, q-Series, 1986, (with R. Askey and R. Roy) Special Functions, 1998; editor: Collected Papers of P.A. MacMahon, Vol. I, 1978, Vol. II, 1986, Ramanujan Revisited, 1988, The Rademacher Legacy to Mathematics, 1994, (with S. Ahlgren and K. Ono) Topics in Number Theory in Honor of B. Gordon and S. Chowla, 1999. Recipient Disting. Univ. Tchg. award Allegheny mountain sect. Math. Assn. Am., 1993, Centennial award U. Pa., 1999; Guggenheim fellow, 1982-83. Mem.: NAS, Am. Acad. Arts and Scis. Avocation: boogie-woogie piano. Home: RR 2 Box 133 Centre Hall PA 16828-9763 Office: Pa State U Dept Math 410 Mcallister Bldg University Park PA 16802-6401 E-mail: andrews@math.psu.edu.

ANDREWS, GEORGE REID, historian, educator; b. New Haven, Apr. 10, 1951; s. George Reid and Barbara (Mahler) A.; m. Roye Alison Werner, June 30, 1974; children: Lena, Jesse, Eve. BA, Dartmouth Coll., 1972; MA, U. Wis., 1974, PhD, 1978. Staff assoc. Social Sci. Rsch. Coun., N.Y.C., 1978-81; from asst. to assoc. prof. U. Pitts., 1981-91, rsch. prof., 1991—. Author: The Afro-Argentines of Buenos Aires, 1980, Blacks and Whites in Sao Paulo, Brazil, 1888-1988, 1991. NEH fellow, 1995, John Simon Guggenheim Found. fellow, 1996, Rockefeller Humanities fellow, 2001. Mem. Am. Hist. Assn., Latin Am. Studies Assn., Conf. Latin Am. History. Office: U Pitts Dept History Pittsburgh PA 15260 E-mail: reid1@pitt.edu.

ANDREWS, GERALD BRUCE, SR., retired textile executive; b. Valley, Ala., Sept. 17, 1937; s. Bruce and Sara Andrews; m. Claire Smith; children: Gerald Bruce Jr., Benjamin G., Suzanne Andrews Smith. Diploma in textile mfg., Auburn U., 1956; BS in Mgmt. and Indsl. Engring., Auburn U., 1958; postgrad., Harvard U., 1979. Various positions WestPoint Pepperell, Inc., 1954-67, mgr. Opelika (Ala.) Mill, 1967-68, gen. mgr. no. ops., 1968-70, dir. indsl. engring. West Point, Ga., 1970-72, gen. mgr. towels ops. Valley, 1972-74, v.p. mfg., 1974-80, sr. v.p. merchandising and mktg. N.Y.C., 1980-87; pres. Stores div. N000, West Point, 1987-92; exec. v.p. merchandising WestPoint Pepperell, Inc., N.Y.C., 1992—; pres., COO Johnston Industries Inc., N.Y.C., 1992—, pres., CEO Columbus, Ga., 1995-97, ret., 1997; exec.-in-residence, vis. prof. Auburn U., 1998-99. Chmn. com. to evaluate Sch. Textile Engring., Auburn (Ala.) U., also lay speaker Guest Speakers Bur.; mem. president's adv. com. So. Union Coll.; chmn. Westpoint Pepperell Polit. Action Com., West Point; bd. dirs. Ala. Textile Edn. Found., Johnston Industries Inc., Tapistron Internat., Tech. Textiles U.S.A.; instr. textile mfg. and indsl. engring. Pres. bd. trustees Lanier Meml. Hosp., Valley; chmn. Chattahoochee Valley Health Care Found., Valley; mem. Ala. Gov.'s Adv. Coun., Montgomery; trustee Christian City, Atlanta; chmn. bd. trustees Atlanta Christian Coll., 1995-96; chmn. bd. dirs. Lanier Health Care Found., 2000-01. Named Citizen of Yr., Valley-Lanett C. of C.; recipient President's award Geo. H. Lanier Coun. Boy Scouts Am.; inducted Engring. Hall of Fame, 1995. Fellow Textile Inst. (Manchester, Eng.); mem. Am. Inst. Indsl. Engrs., Am. Textile Mfg. Assn. (dir. 1995, textile leader of yr. in Am. 1995), Ala. Textile Mfg. Assn. (pres.), Harvard Bus. Sch. Assn., Spring Wood Athletic Club (pres.), Rotary (pres. West Point), Harvard Club (N.Y.C.). Avocations: travel, golf, reading, architecture, painting. Home: 111 Highland Dr West Point GA 31833-6100

ANDREWS, GORDON CLARK, lawyer; b. Boston, Mar. 25, 1941; s. Loring Beal and Flora Spencer (Hinckley) A.; m. Deborah M. Devere, July 9, 1966; children: Christine Leigh, Cynthia Lyn, Carey Loring. BA, Dartmouth Coll., 1963; JD, NYU, 1969. Bar: N.Y. State bar 1970, Conn. bar 1971. Assoc. Morgan Lewis & Bockius (and predecessor), N.Y.C., 1969-72; asst. sec., asst. gen. counsel Howmet Corp., Greenwich, Conn., 1973-75; sec., asst. gen. counsel Beker Industries Corp., Greenwich, 1976—, v.p., 1978-81; gen. counsel M&T Chems., Inc., Woodbridge, N.J., 1982-86, v.p. law dept., 1986-90, sec., 1987-90; v.p., sec. Atochem Inc., Glen Rock, N.J., 1987—; gen. counsel, sec. ESSROC Corp., Bath, Pa., 1990—, sr. v.p., 1993—; ptnr. Epstein, Becker & Green, N.Y.C., 1995—; gen. counsel Troy Corp., Florham Park, N.J., 2000—. Bd. dir. San Juan Cement Co., Inc., Essroc Cement Corp.; v.chmn. legal counsel com. Portland Cement Assn. Mem. exec. com. Cemat kiln Recycling Coalition. Lt. USNR, 1963—69. Recipient Am. Law award, 1969. Mem. ABA, N.Y. State Bar Assn., Conn. Bar Assn., Am. Soc. Corp. Secs., Westchester-Fairfield Corp. Counsel Assn., Greenwich Country Club. Republican. Home: 46 Club Rd Riverside CT 06878-2034 Office: Epstein Becker & Green 250 Park Ave Ste 1201 New York NY 10177-0001

ANDREWS, GROVER JENE, adult education educator, administrator; b. Batesville, Ark., June 1, 1930; s. Grover Jones and Ruth Burlie (Ruble) A. BA, Vanderbilt U., 1963, MA, 1964; EdD, N.C. State U., 1972. Dir. univ. rels. Baylor U., Waco, Tex., 1955-61; asst. to pres. Peabody Coll. Vanderbilt U., Nashville, 1961-64; asst. prof. English, asst. acad. dean U. Ark., Little Rock, 1964-66; dir. of devel. Meredith Coll., Raleigh, N.C., 1966-67; asst. to dean of extension N.C. State U., Raleigh, 1967-68, assoc. vice chancellor for extension, assoc. prof. adult edn, 1979-89; assoc. exec. dir. commn. on colls. So. Assn. Colls. and Schs., Atlanta, 1968-79; assoc. dir. for instrn. U. Ga. Ctr. for Continuing Edn., 1989—, sr. pub. svc. assoc., chair sr. pub. svc. faculty, 1989—, adj. assoc. prof. adult edn., 1989—, asst. v.p. pub. svc. and outreach, 1998-99, interim dir., 1998—, assoc. v.p. pub. svc. and outreach, 1999—2001; ret., 2001. Bd. dirs. Am. Tech. Inst., Memphis, 1985-98; trustee Coun. for Adult and Exptl. Learning, Chgo., 1985-91; dir. rsch. Internat. Assn. for Continuing Edn. and Tng., Washington, 1987-92, pres., 1992-96. Member Raleigh Lions, 1967-68, 79-89; chair Christmas pageant Waco Jaycees, 1956-60; patron Atlanta Arts Ctr., 1968-79. With USN, 1948-50. Named Educator of the Yr., Fedn. of Women's Clubs, 1966; recipient Nat. Leadership award Assn. for Continuing Higher Edn., 1984, Gruman award N.C. Adult Edn. Assn., 1985, Pinnacle award for outstanding leadership Internat. Assn. for Continuing Edn. and Tng., 1996; named to Internat. Hall of Fame for Adult and Continuing Edn., 1996; Grover J. Andrews Rsch. Endowment established by Internat. Assn., for Continuing Edn. and Tng., 1996. Mem. Nat. Univ. Continuing Edn. Assn. (chair elect rsch. divsn. 1996-97, chair rsch. divsn. 1998-99, Julius M. Nolte award 1995, chair rsch. divsn. 1997-98), Ga. Adult Edn. Assn., So. Assn. Colls. and Schs. (chair accrediting coms. 1980—), Phi Delta Kappa, Sigma Tau Delta, Pi Kappa Alpha. Democrat. Baptist. Avocations: gardening, arts, antiques. Home: 243 Ashbrook Dr Athens GA 30605-3956 Fax: 706-369-9155.

ANDREWS, HOLDT, investment banker; b. N.Y.C., May 2, 1946; s. William Lloyd and Edna (Faulconer) A.; m. Nina Lawrence, Sept. 16, 1982; 1 child, Kelli. BS, U. Fla., 1968; MBA, Fla. Atlantic U., 1971. Asst. to v.p. mktg. Eltra Corp., Wilmington, Mass., 1972-74; v.p. Bank of Am., N.Y.C., 1974-81; group v.p. Amrobank, N.Y.C., 1981-84; exec. v.p. CenTrust Savs. Bank, Miami, Fla., 1984, KMC Group, Miami, 1985-86; sr. mng. dir. J.W. Charles Capital Corp.-Bush Securities, Boca Raton, Fla., 1986-89; v.p. corp. fin. dept. Internationale Nederlanden Bank N.V., N.Y.C., 1989-94; sr. v.p. S.N. Phelps and Co., Greenwich, Conn., 1994; chief oper. officer VHC, Ltd., West Palm Beach, Fla., 1994-99; sr. exec. mng. dir. The March Group, LLC, Nashville, 1999—. Mem. adv. bd. Tucker State Bank, Jacksonville, Fla., 1987-88; bd. dirs. Qilu-Maul, Shandong, Peoples Republic China, 1997-99. 1st lt. U.S. Army, 1968-70. Mem. Blue Key. Avocations: tennis, sailing, skiing. Office: The March Group 1900 Church St Nashville TN 37203-2234 E-mail: andrews@marchgroup.com.

ANDREWS, J. DAVID, lawyer; b. Decatur, Ill., July 5, 1933; s. Jesse D. and Louise Glenna (Mason) A.; m. Helen Virginia Migely, July 12, 1958; children: Virginia, Robert, Michael, Betsy. BA magna cum laude, U. Ill., 1955, JD with honors, 1960. Bar: Wash. 1961. Ptnr. Perkins Coie, Seattle, 1960-96, counsel, 1997—. Bd. dirs., v.p. Am. Bar Ins. Plans Cons., Inc., 1991—, also bd. dirs.; pres. Wash. Law Fund, 1997-98; bd. dirs. Cornish Inst., Seattle, 1977-83, pres. 1981-83; bd. dirs. Am. Bar Endowment, 1981-94, pres. 1985-87; bd. visitors U. Puget Sound Law Sch., 1976-94; trustee AEF Pension Fund, 1975-79. Contbr. articles to profl. jours. Bd. dirs. Leukemia Soc. Wash., 1984-99, pres. 1985-91; nat. bd. dirs. Leukemia Soc. Am., 1992-96. Capt. USAF, 1955-57. Fellow Am. Bar Found. (bd. dirs., former treas.), Am. Coll. Trial Lawyers; mem. ABA (ho. of dels. 1967-69, 75—, asst. treas. 1972-74, treas. 1975-79, bd. govs. 1975-79, fed. judiciary standing com. 1985-90), Wash. Bar Assn. (chmn. pub. rels. com. 1971-73), Seattle-King County Bar Assn., Am. Judicature Soc. (bd. dirs. 1985-89), Phi Beta Kappa, Phi Kappa Phi, Phi Eta Sigma. Home: 9413 SW Quartermaster Dr Vashon WA 98070-7081 Office: Perkins Coie 1201 3rd Ave Ste 4000 Seattle WA 98101-3029 E-mail: andrj@perkinscoie.com.

ANDREWS, JEAN, artist, writer; b. Kingsville, Tex., Dec. 23, 1923; d. Herbert and Katharine Andrews; divorced; children: Robert Fleming Wasson Jr., Jean Andrews Wasson (dec.). BS in Home Economics, U. Tex., 1944; MS in Edn., Tex. A & I Univ., 1966; PhD in Fine Arts, U. North Tex., 1976. Cert. home economist. Artist, writer, Austin, Tex. Vis. scholar dept. integrative biology U. Tex., Austin, adv. coun. Coll. Natural Sci., 1983-, past mem. exec. com., 1986-97, chmn. botany dept. vis. com., 1985-1993; presenter to seminars and confs. in field. Author: Sea Shells of the Texas Coast, 1971, Shells and Shores of Texas, 1977, Texas Shells: A Field Guide, 1981, Peppers: The Domesticated Capsicums, 1984, rev. edit., 1995, The Texas Bluebonnet, 1985, rev. edit., 1993, An American Wildflower: Florilegium, 1992, Texas Monthly Field Guide to Shells of the Texas Coast, 1992, Red Hot Peppers, 1993, Texas Monthly Field Guide to the Shells of the Florida Coast, 1994, The Peppers Lady's Pocket Pepper Primer, 1998, The Pepper Trail, 2000; also articles; one-woman shows include RGK Found. Gallery, Austin, 1993; numerous others. Nat. adv. bd. Leadership Am., 1988-95; trustee Laguna Gloria Art Mus., 1985-91, Nat. Wildflower Rsch. Ctr., 1987-94, adv. coun. 1995—; past trustee Art Mus. of S. Tex.; past bd. dirs. Planned Parenthood; mem. Austin Symphony Soc., Friends of Huntington Gallery/Univ. Tex., others. Recipient Disting. Alumna award U.North Tex., 1991, Hall of Honor award U. Tex. Coll. Natural Sci., 1991, Disting. Alumna award U. Tex. Austin, 1997; endowments include Jean Andrews vis. professorship in human nutrition, and vis. professorship in tropical and econ. botany, endowed scholar Tex. Found. for Women's Resources, U. Tex.; endowed scholar in art U. North Tex., others; named Tex. Inst. Letters. Mem. DAR, Am. Malacol. Union, Tex. Pepper Found. (life), Tex. State Tchrs. Assn. (life), U. Tex. Alumni Assn. (life), U. North Tex. Alumni Assn. (life), Colonial Dames of 17th Century, Nat. Soc. Ams. of Royal Descent, Nat. Soc. Colonial Dames in Am., Nat. Soc. Magna Charta Dames, Daus. of Cin., Huguenot Soc., Order of Descendants of Ancient Planters, Daus. of the Confederacy, Descendents of Ancient Planters, Jamestowne Soc., Descendants of Colonial Govs. E-mail: thepepperlady@aol.com.

ANDREWS, JOHN FRANK, civil and environmental engineering educator; b. Cave City, Ark., July 10, 1930; s. Frank Ferd and Ruth Lanell (Puckett) A.; m. Margery Ann Hall, June 21, 1952; children: John Patrick, Carol Ann, Laurie Lanell. BS in Civil Engring., U. Ark., 1951, MS, 1953; PhD, U. Calif., Berkeley, 1964. Instr. civil engring. U. Ark., 1953-55, asst. prof., 1955-59, assoc. prof., 1959-60; project engr. U. Calif. at Berkeley, 1962-63; assoc. prof., assoc. dir. water resources engring. program Clemson U., 1963-66, prof., dir. environmental systems engring., 1966-68, prof., dept head, 1968-74; prof. civil and environmental engring. U. Houston, 1975-81; prof. environ. sci. and engring. Rice U., 1981-91, prof. emeritus, 1991, ret., 1991. Vis. prof. McMaster U., Can., Kyoto U., Japan, 1988; vis. rschr. Water Pollution Rsch. Lab., Eng., 1970, Wastewater Tech. Ctr., Can., 1988; hon. prof. Harbin Inst. Archtl. and Civil Engring., People's Republic of China, 1990; cons. water pollution control Engring.-Sci., Inc., Los Angeles, Phila., Chgo., Mpls.; cons. U.S. Army, Bacardi Distilleries, Pan Am. Health Orgn., UN Devel. Program, Greeley & Hansen Engrs., Shell Devel. Co., Weyerhauser Co., Woodlands Devel. Co. Gulf Coast Waste Disposal Authority, Met. Sanitary Dist. Greater Chgo., others. Research, publs. in field. NSF grantee Mem. ASCE, AIChE, Am. Chem. Soc., Am. Water Works Assn., Water Environ. Fedn. (Harrison Prescott Eddy award 1975), Internat. Assn. Water Quality (U.S. editor Water Research 1974-84, vice chmn. Vienna conf. 1971, 75, 79, 83, program chmn. London conf. 1973, Stockholm conf. 1977 Munich conf. 1981, Houston conf. 1985, Kyoto conf. 1990, hon. mem. 1986), Am. Soc. Engring. Edn., Am. Acad. Environ. Engrs. (emeritus), Assn. Environ. Engring. Profs. (dir. 1967-70, chmn. workshops 1968-70, chmn. nat. conf. 1977, v.p. 1984-85, pres. 1985-86), Sigma Xi, Tau Beta Pi, Phi Kappa Phi. Methodist. Home: 1719 E Rayview Dr Fayetteville AR 72703-2625 E-mail: jand109090@aol.com.

ANDREWS, JOHN FRANK, editor, author, educator; b. Carlsbad, N.Mex., Nov. 2, 1942; s. Frank Randolph and Mary Lucille (Wimberley) A.; m. Vicky Roberta Anderson, Aug. 20, 1966 (div. 1983); children: Eric John, Lisa Gail; m. Janet Ann Denton, Oct. 15, 1994. AB, Princeton U., 1965; MAT, Harvard U., 1966; PhD, Vanderbilt U., 1971. Instr. English U. Tenn., Nashville, 1969-70; asst. prof. Fla. State U., Tallahassee, 1970-74, dir. grad. studies in English, 1973-74; dir. acad. programs Folger Shakespeare Library, Washington, 1974-84; chmn. Folger Inst., Washington, 1974-84; exec. editor Folger Books, Washington, 1974-84; dep. dir. div. edn. programs NEH, Washington, 1984-88; editor The Guild Shakespeare, 1988-92; pres. The Shakespeare Guild, 1992—; editor The Everyman Shakespeare, 1993—; exec. dir. Washington br. English-Speaking Union, 2001—. Cons. Time-Life TV, WNET/Thirteen, Corp. for Pub. Broadcasting, Pub. Broadcasting Svc., Nat. Pub. Radio, U.S. Dept. Edn., others; chmn. Nat. Adv. Panel for the Shakespeare Plays, 1979-85; core advisor The Shakespeare Hour, 1985-86; mem. adv. bd. Theatre for a New Audience, Humanities Coun. of Washington, Ctr. for Polit. and Strategic Studies, Ctr. for Renaissance and Baroque Studies, U. Md., others; cons. Shakespeare: The Globe and the World, touring exhbn., 1978-81; adminstr. program grants NEH, Andrew W. Mellon Found., Exxon Corp., Met. Life, Surdna Found., others; founder of the Guild's Gielgud Award for Excellence in the Dramatic Arts, 1994. Asst. editor: Shakespeare Studies, 1972-74; editor: Shakespeare Quar., 1974-85; editor-in-chief, contbr.: William Shakespeare: His World, His Work, His Influence, 1985; editor-in-chief: Shakespeare's World and Work, 2001; contbr. numerous articles to mags. and scholarly jours. Decorated officer Order Brit. Empire; recipient rsch. awards Folger Shakespeare Libr., Fla. State U., NEH. Fellow Royal Soc. Arts; mem. AAUP (sec. chpt. 1972-74), Modern Lang. Assn., Milton Soc. Am., Nat. Council of Tchrs. of English, Renaissance Soc. Am. (mem. council 1975-84), Internat. Shakespeare Conf., Shakespeare Assn. Am. (trustee 1979-82), The Lit. Soc., Cosmos Club. Home and Office: 2141 Wyoming Ave NW Apt 41 Washington DC 20008-3916

ANDREWS, JOSEPH LYON, JR., medical educator, writer, practiconer; b. N.Y.C., Mar. 19, 1938; s. Joseph Lyon and Katherine Louise (New) A.; m. Margareta Langert, Apr. 18, 1969 (dec. Mar. 1994); children: Joe, Sara, Jennifer. BA cum laude, Amherst Coll., 1959; MD, U. Rochester, 1963. Diplomate Am. Bd. Internal Medicine, Am. Bd. Pulmonary Medicine. Intern, resident Boston City Hosp., 1963-65, Tufts Med. Sch., Boston, 1963-65; resident, fellow Harvard Med. Sch., Boston, 1967-70; pulmonary fellow Mass. Gen. Hosp., 1967-68; sr. resident Boston VA Hosp., 1968-69; cardiology fellow West Roxbury VA Hosp., 1969-70; internist, pulmonologist Lahey Clinic, Boston, Burlington, Mass., 1971-90; dir. ambulatory care Bedford (Mass.) VA Med. Ctr., 1999-2000; internist Harvard Pilgrim Health Care, Boston, 2003—. Clin. tchg. staff Harvard Med. Sch., 1971-90, Tufts Med. Sch., 1971—, Boston U. Med. Sch., 1999-2000; chief pulmonary dept. New Eng. Deaconess Hosp., Boston, 1972-82. Author: Revolutionary Boston, Lexington and Concord, 1999; freelance writer Boston Globe Newspaper, 1971—; contbr. articles to profl. jours. Pres.'s assoc. World Learning, Inc., Brattleboro, Vt., 1987—; mem., social action com. Temple Shalom, Newton, Mass., 1988-93; mem. Human Rights Com., Newton, 1983-88; bd. dirs. Am. Lung Assn. Boston, 1977-90; lic. guide Town Concord, 1995—; mem. Concord Mill Brook Task Force, 1995—, Concord Hist. Commn., 1996-99; mem. social action com. Kerem Shalom, Concord, 1996—; mem. Am. Friends Neve Shalom, Israel, 1996—. Capt. USAF, 1965-67. Traveling fellow Am.Jewish Congress, Israel, 1959, Am. Cancer Soc., Mendoza, Argentina, 1962. Fellow Am. Coll. Physicians, Am. Coll. Chest Physicians; mem. AMA, Am. Thoracic Soc., Mass. Med. Assn., Mass. Thoracic Soc., Am. Jewish Hist. Soc., Sons Am. Revolution, Thoreau Soc., Concord Visitors Guide, Concord Guides and Press (founder, dir.). Avocations: writing, photography, swimming, tennis, hiking. Home: 28 Center Village Dr Concord MA 01742-2900 E-mail: joelandrew@aol.com.

ANDREWS, KENNETH RICHMOND, business administration educator; b. New London, Conn., May 24, 1916; s. William John and Myrtle (Richmond) A.; m. Edith May Platt, Apr. 29, 1945 (div. 1969); children: Kenneth Richmond, Carolyn; m. Carolyn Erskine Hall, Feb. 14, 1970. AB, Wesleyan U., 1936, MA,

1937; PhD, U. Ill., 1948; MA (hon.), Harvard U., 1957. Tchr. English U. Ill., 1937-41; instr. bus. adminstrn. Harvard Grad. Sch. Bus. Adminstrn., 1946-47, asst. prof., 1947-52, assoc. prof., 1952-57, prof., 1957-65, Donald K. David prof. bus. adminstrn., 1965-86, emeritus, 1986—, faculty chmn. Advanced Mgmt. Program, 1967-70, master Leverett House, 1971-81, chmn. gen. mgmt. faculty, 1981-83. Cons. on mgmt. devel. and policy problems; dir. Xerox Corp. and other cos., 1972-86. Author: Nook Farm, 1950, (with others) Problems of General Management, 1962, Business Policy Text and Cases, 1965, rev. edit., 1969, 73, 77, 79, 87, 90, The Effectiveness of University Executive Development Programs, 1966, The Concept of Corporate Strategy, 1971, rev. edit., 1980, 3d edit., 1987; editor: The Case Method of Teaching Human Relations and Administration, 1953; chmn. editorial bd.: Harvard Bus. Rev, 1972-79; editor in chief, 1979-85. Trustee Wesleyan U., 1955-72. Served from pvt. F.A. to maj. USAAF, 1941-46. Recipient Harvard medal, 1986. Disting. Alumnus award, Wesleyan U., 1986, Disting. Svc. award, Harvard Bus. Sch., 1990; Wesleyan U. scholar, 1967. Mem. Phi Beta Kappa. Office: Soldiers Field Boston MA 02163 E-mail: ceakra@aol.com.

ANDREWS, LINDA WASMER, writer; b. West Memphis, Ark., Nov. 9, 1957; d. Frederick Lark and Nettie Belle (Pittman) Wasmer; m. David Alan Smith, May 28, 1977 (div. 1998); children: Amanda Lark Smith, Michael David Smith; m. David Lee Andrews, Oct. 10, 1999. BA, U. N.Mex., 1979. Author: Of Mind and Body, 1997, Louis Pasteur: Disease Fighter, 1997, Depression: What it is, How to Beat it, 2000, New Drug Treatments for Diabetes, 2000, Diabetes Complications: Prevention and Management, 2001; contbr. chapters to books, articles to mags.; author: Intelligence, 2003. Ct. apptd. spl. adv. Bernalillo County, N.Mex., 1998—2002. Mem.: Am. Soc. Journalists and Authors, Nat. Assn. Sci. Writers, Am. Med. Writers Assn. E-mail: linda@lindaandrews.com.

ANDREWS, M. DEWAYNE, dean, internist, educator; b. Enid, Okla., May 24, 1944; s. Mitchell S. and Truel Eva (Melton) A.; m. Rebecca Ellen Meltzer, Aug. 26, 1984. BS, Baylor U., 1966; MD, U. Okla., 1970. Diplomate Am. Bd. Internal Medicine. Resident internal medicine Johns Hopkins Hosp., Balt., 1970-71, U. Okla. Health Sci. Ctr., Oklahoma City, 1971-72, 74-76; asst. prof., assoc. prof., dir. residency program dept. medicine U. Okla., Oklahoma City, 1976-84, vice chmn., chief gen. internal medicine, prof. dept. medicine, 1986—, assoc. dean grad. med. edn. Coll. Medicine, 1994—2000, sr. assoc. dean, 1996—2002, v.p. health affairs, exec. dean, 2002—; chief of medicine regional med. ctr., vice chmn. dept. medicine U. Tenn. Coll. Medicine, Memphis, 1984-86; chief of staff U. Hosp., Oklahoma City, 1992-94, med. dir., 1994-96. Bd. dirs. Nat. Commn. Certification Physician Assts., 1995—. Editor: Jour. Okla. State Med. Assn., 1991—; contbr. numerous articles to profl. jours. Bd. dirs. Chamber Orch. Oklahoma City, 1982-84, Lyric Theatre, Oklahoma City, 1996-2000, Oklahoma City Philharm. Found., 2003—; del. Okla. State Leadership Initiative to Soviet Union, 1988. Surgeon CDC, USPHS, 1972-74. Surgeon U.S. Pub. Health Svc., 1972—74, Atlanta, GA and Hartford, CT. Recipient Stollermen Award U. Tenn., 1986, Aesculapian award U. Okla. Coll. Medicine, 1989; ACP tchg. and rsch. scholar, 1976-79. Fellow ACP (bd. govs. Okla. 1995-99); mem. AMA, Alpha Omega Alpha. Episcopalian. Avocation: piano. Office: U Okla Coll Medicine RM 357 BMSB PO Box 26901 Oklahoma City OK 73126-0901

ANDREWS, MARK JOSEPH, lawyer; b. Chgo., July 27, 1944; s. Mark Lewis and Elizabeth (Glendening) A.; m. Martha Jo Shipman, Nov. 29, 1969(div. 2002); children: Eliza, Jonathan. AB, Harvard Coll., 1966; JD, Harvard U., 1969. Bar: U.S. Dist. Ct. D.C. 1970, U.S. Ct. Appeals (D.C. cir.) 1970, U.S. Ct. Appeals (5th and 11th cirs.) 1981, U.S. Ct. Fed. Claims 1983, U.S. Supreme Ct. 1990. From assoc. to ptnr. Verner, Liipfert, Bernhard, McPherson & Hand, Washington, 1969-91; ptnr. Barnes & Thornburg, Washington, 1991—2001, Strasburger & Price, LLP, Washington, 2001—. Co-chmn. federal govt. sponsored task force on regulatory aspects of transp. ins. crisis, 1986-87. Contbr. articles to profl. jours. Pres. Amadeus Concerts (formerly Gt. Falls (Va.) Concert Series), 1985-87, bd. dirs., 1984-2000. Mem. Transp. Lawyers Assn. (Disting. Svc. 1985, exec. com. 1986-99, pres. 1992-93), Assn. Transp. Law, Logistics and Policy, Can. Transport Lawyers Assn., Conf. Claims Counsel, Am. Law Inst. Avocations: photography, hiking, collecting native Am. artifacts, music. Office: Strasburger & Price LLP 1101 Pennsylvania Ave NW Fl 7 Washington DC 20004-2514 E-mail: mark.andrews@strasburger.com.

ANDREWS, MASON COOKE, mayor, obstetrician, gynecologist, educator; b. Norfolk, Va., Apr. 20, 1919; s. Charles James and Jean (Cooke) A.; m. Sabine Goodman, Sept. 24, 1949; c.Jean, Mason. BA, Princeton U., 1940; MD, Johns Hopkins U., 1943; Doctor of Laws (hon.), Eastern Virginia Med. School, 1987. Diplomate: Am. Bd. Ob-Gyn. Intern ob-gyn Johns Hopkins U., Balt., 1944, resident ob-gyn, 1946-50; pvt. practice ob-gyn Norfolk, Va., 1950-70; lectr. Johns Hopkins U. Sch. Medicine, Balt., 1971-72; prof. dept. ob-gyn. Eastern Va. Med. Sch., Norfolk, 1974—, chmn. dept. ob-gyn., 1974-90; mayor City of Norfolk, 1992-94. Bd. dirs. First Va. Bank of Tidewater, Chesapeake and Potomac Telephone Co.; mem., dir. Norfolk City Planning Commn., 1963-65, twice chmn., commr., exec. com. mem. Hampton Rds. Planning Dist. Commn., pres. (1971) Planning Coun. of United Communities, Norfolk City Coun., 1974-2000; chmn. Ea. Va. Med. Authority, 1964-70; pres. Am. Assn. Obstetricians Found., 1986-89. *As councilman, and subsequently Mayor, he led in organizing government, citizen leadership and consultants to make, adopt and implement plans for a downtown renaissance in Norfolk. He led the establishment of the Eastern Virginia Medical School, serving as founding chairman of the authority that organized and operates the school. As founding chairman of the Department of Obstetrics and Gynecology, he built a department which is recognized internationally for contributions to the knowledge of reproductive medicine including the first successful in vitro fertilization program in the United States.* Contbr. (numerous articles to sci. jours.). Councilman City of Norfolk, 1974-2000, vice mayor, 1978-82, mayor, 1992 94. Recipient First Citizen citation Norfolk Cosmopolitan Club, 1968, Norfolk citation for outstanding svc., 1964, award for cmty. svc. Med. Soc. Va., AMA, Nat. Brotherhood award Norfolk Conf. Christians and Jews. Fellow Am. Gynecol. and Obstet. Soc. (v.p. 1982-83, pres. 1992-93); mem. South Atlantic Assn. (pres. 1972), Va. Obstet. and Gynecol. Soc. (pres. 1975), Norfolk Acad. Medicine (pres. 1961), Johns Hopkins Soc. Scholars, Harbor Club, Norfolk Yacht and Country Club. Presbyterian. Home: 1011 N Shore Rd Norfolk VA 23505-3119 Office: Eastern Va Med Sch Dept Ob-Gyn 601 Colley Ave Norfolk VA 23507-1627

ANDREWS, MELINDA WILSON, human development researcher; b. N.Y.C., Aug. 12, 1956; d. William Maurice and Natalie Maxine (Amos) Wilson; m. James Robert Andrews, Dec. 3, 1977; children: Christopher Wilson Andrews, William James Andrews. BBA in Mgmt./Mktg., Abilene (Tex.) Christian U., 1977; MS in Human Devel., U. Tex., Dallas, 1988, postgrad., 1994—. Logics adminstr. Texas Instruments, Dallas, 1977-79, contract adminstr., 1979-81, 82-83; grocery mgr., co-asst. store dir. Tom Thumb, Dallas, 1981-82; teaching asst. U. Tex. at Dallas, Richardson, Tex., 1988-91, rsch. asst., 1991—. Dir. creative presch. coop., Richardson, 2000-02; dir. Waterview Christian Presch., 2002—; presenter in field. Contbr. articles to profl. jours. Mem. Richardson Symphony Orch., 1977-79, Canyon Creek Elem. PTA, 5th v.p., 1994-95, libr. rep., 1992-94; treas. exec. bd. Creative Presch. Coop., 1998-99, sec. ex. bd. 1999-2000, dir., 2000-02; Cub Scout leader, com. chmn., Pack 1001, 2002—; asst. dir. English as second lang. sch. Waterview Ch. of Christ. Mem. Soc. for Rsch. in Child Devel. (co-author paper-poster session 1991, 93 confs.), Southwest Soc. for Rsch. in Child Devel., Psi Chi. Mem. Ch. of Christ. Avocations: music, animals, carpentry. Home and Office: 2109 Flat Creek Dr Richardson TX 75080-2331 E-mail: melindaandrews@worldnet.att.net.

ANDREWS, MICHAEL WILLIAM, librarian, information specialist; b. Rome, N.Y., Mar. 22, 1948; s. Martin Joseph and Mary (Dublanica) A.; m. Karen Lynn Mauro, July 23, 1982. AB in History, Cornell U., 1970; MS in Libr. Sci., Syracuse U., 1972. Libr. govt. documents SUNY, Plattsburgh, 1971-76, L.I. U., Bklyn., 1977-79; rsch. asst. Health Info. Sharing Project, Syracuse (N.Y.) U., 1979-80; readers svcs. libr. Elizabethtown (Pa.) Coll., 1980-85; online data base libr. U. D.C., Washington, 1986-87; dir. rsch. Korn/Ferry Internat., Washington, 1987-2001; owner Andrews Consulting, Woodbridge, Va., 2001—; libr., selection svcs. Prince William (Va.) Pub. Libr. Sys., 2001—. Editor: Proceeding of the Second Annual Government Documents Workshop, 1976. Bd. dirs. Friends Chinn Pk. Regional Libr., 1998—. Mem.: ALA, Spl. Librs. Assn. Avocations: reading, photography, travel, coaching youth soccer. Home: 3825 Wagon Wheel Ln Woodbridge VA 22192-6441 Office: PWPLS 13083 Chinn Park Dr Woodbridge VA 22192-5073 E-mail: mandrews@pwcgov.org.

ANDREWS, MINERVA WILSON, retired lawyer; b. Rock Hill, S.C., Feb. 1, 1925; d. York Lowry and Minnie de Foix (Long) Wilson; m. Robert Taylor Andrews, Apr. 15, 1950; children: Susan Allison (Mrs. Robert N. Wiles), Stuart Davidson. AB, U. S.C., 1945; LLB, U. Va., 1948. Bar: Va. 1948. Trial atty. antitrust divsn. U.S. Dept. Justice, Washington, 1949—55; assoc. atty. Bauknight, Prichard, McCandlish & Williams, Fairfax, Va., 1963—72, Boothe, Prichard & Dudley, 1972—80; ptnr. Boothe, Prichard & Dudley, and McGuire, Woods, et al. (merged), McLean, Va., 1980—91; ret., 1992. Author: Carolina-Virginia Recollections, 1999, A Carolina-Virginia Genealogy, vol. 2, 2000. Pres. Nat. Soc. Arts & Letters, 1994—96; bd. dir. Mclean Citizen Asn., 1968—2000, Fairfax/Falls Church United Way, Vienna, Va., 1988—2001; life elder Lewinsville Presby. Church, McLean, 1980—. Named Citizen of the Yr. Fairfax County Fedn. Citizen Assn. and Washington Post, 1997. Mem.: Nat. Soc. Arts and Letters (pres. Wash. chpt. 1973—74), Fairfax Bar Assn. (past chmn. real estate com.), Va. Bar Assn. (chmn. real property com. 1980—82, William B. Spong Jr. Professionalism award 2001), Va. State Bar (past chmn. real property sect.). Republican. Office: McGuireWoods LLP 1750 Tysons Blvd Ste 1800 Mc Lean VA 22102-4215

ANDREWS, NEIL CORBLY, surgeon; b. Mar. 31, 1916; BA, U. Oreg., 1939, MD, 1943; MSc, Ohio State U., 1950. Intern Union Meml. Hosp., Balt., 1943, resident, 1944, Jefferson Hosp. (now Cmty. Hosp. Roanoke Valley), Va., 1945-46, Ohio State U., Columbus, 1947-50, instr. surgery, 1950-52, asst. prof. surgery, 1952-57, assoc. prof. surgery, 1957-67, prof. surgery, 1967-70, U. Calif., Davis, 1970-86, prof. emeritus surgery, 1986—. Home and Office: 44421 Clubhouse Dr El Macero CA 95618-0607

ANDREWS, OAKLEY V. lawyer; b. Cleve., Apr. 15, 1940; BA, Yale U., 1962; JD, Western Reserve U., 1965. Bar: Ohio 1965, U.S. Tax Ct. 1968, U.S. Dist. Ct. (no. dist.) Ohio 1968, U.S. Ct. Appeals (6th cir.) 1968. Ptnr. Baker & Hostetler, LLP, Cleve. Fellow Am. Coll. Trust and Estate Coun.; mem. Ohio State Bar Assn., Estate Planning Coun. Cleve. (pres. 1982-83), Cleve. Bar Assn. (chmn. Estate Planning, Probate and Trust law sect. 1984-85), Phi Delta Phi Office: Baker & Hostetler LLP 3200 Nat City Ctr 1900 E 9th St Ste 3200 Cleveland OH 44114-3475 E-mail: oandrews@bakerlaw.com.

ANDREWS, RALPH HERRICK, television producer; b. Chgo., Dec. 17, 1927; s. Henry Karl and Sylvia Angelica (Lorenzen Barth); m. Margaret Ann Belt, Feb. 5, 1951 (div. 1977); m. Aleksandra Vaz vel Wezykowska, June 1, 1986; children: William, Herrick, Phyllis, Patrice, Peter, James, Jakub, Matthew. Announcer, disc jockey, salesman radio stas. WSAM and WKNX, Saginaw, Mich.; page NBC, Hollywood; with Don Fedderson Prodns., Ralph Edwards Prodns.; dir. live programming Desilu; prin. Ralph Andrews Prodns. Co-founder, bd. dirs. Entertainment Industries Coun. Producer: Divorce Hearing, By the Numbers, Zoom, Show Me, You Don't Say, I'll Bet, Wedding Party, The Family Game, It Takes Two, It's Your Bet, Liars Club, The Mickie Finn Show, Celebrity Sweepstakes, 50 Grand Slam, Lingo, (movies) Silent Treatment, God Bless You Uncle Sam, Wild in the Sky; prodr., host: Lie Detector; host, writer (website) The TroubleMaker www.thetroublemaker.com. Cand. for Congress, 1972; nat. dir. edn. and tng. Rep. Nat. Com., Washington, 1972 (Presidential commendation). Republican. Roman Catholic. Avocations: skiing, flying, skating, running, sailing. Home and Office: 5021 Dantes View Dr Calabasas CA 91301-2311 E-mail: mrxinc@adelphia.net.

ANDREWS, RICHARD NIGEL LYON, public policy educator, environmental studies administrator; b. Newport, R.I., Dec. 6, 1944; s. Nigel Lyon and Constance Doane (Young) A.; m. Hannah Page Wheeler, June 7, 1969; children: Sarah Huntington, Christopher Page Monteith AB, Yale U., 1966; M in Regional Planning, U. N.C., 1970, PhD, 1972. Vol. U.S. Peace Corps, Bharatpur, Nepal, 1966-68; budget examiner U.S. Office of Mgmt. and Budget, Washington, 1970-72; prof. U. Mich., Ann Arbor, 1972-81; prof. pub. policy U. N.C., Chapel Hill, 1981—, dir. U. N.C. Inst. Environ. Studies, 1981-91, dir. environ. mgmt. and policy program, 1990-94, mem. exec. com. faculty coun., 1994-97, chair of faculty, 1997-00. Cons. NSF, Washington, 1982-85, AID, Yaounde, Cameroon, 1983, U.S.-Asia Environ. Partnership, 2000—, Kenan Inst. Asia, 2000—; mem. N.C. Natural Heritage Adv. Com., Raleigh, 1982-87; sr. staff mem. Commn. on Future of N.C., Raleigh, 1982-84; mem. Bd. Environ. Studies and Toxology, NAS, 1986-88; chmn. study com. on opportunities in applied environ. R&D, NAS, 1988-90; mem. risk reduction subcom. Sci. Adv. Bd., EPA, 1989-90, AID, Czech and Slovak Republics, 1991-94; mem. adv. com. Pew Conservation Scholars Program, 1991-94; mem. adv. com. EPA Decisionmaking, Nat. Acad. of Pub. Adminstrn., 1994-95; chmn. adv. panel new approach to environ. regulation Office Tech. Assessment U.S. Congress, Washington, 1993-95; mem. Multi-State Working Group Environ. Mgmt. Systems, 1997—; chmn. adv. panel U.S. registration practices for ISO 14001 environ. mgmt. sys. Nat. Acad. Pub. Adminstrn., 2000-01; mem. adv. com. Environ. Stewardship N.C. dept. environ. and natural resources, 2002-, mem. study com. on environ. decision making, NAS, 2003-. Author: Environmental Policy and Administrative Change, 1976, Managing the Environment, Managing Ourselves: A History of American Environmental Policy, 1999; editor: Land in America, 1979, Environmental Change and Public Health-The Next Fifty Years, 1990; contbr. articles to profl. jours. Vestry Episcopalian Ch., Chapel Hill, 1986-89. Resources for the Future Inc. fellow, 1971-72, Rockefeller Found. fellow, 1977-78, Fulbright fellow Vienna U. Econs., 1990, Salzburg Seminar faculty fellow, 1990, fellow Nat. Acad. of Pub. Adminstrn., 1996. Fellow AAAS (nominating com. sect. on societal impacts of sci. and engring. 1987-90, chmn. 1989-90, 96-97, ann. meeting program com. 1988-90, com. on sci. engring. and pub. policy 1997-2003, com. sect. social, econ. and polit. scis. 1998-2002); mem. Assn. Pub. Policy and Mgmt. (ann. meeting program com. 2003), Golden Key, Sigma Xi, Delta Omega. Democrat. Avocations: tennis, sailing, camping, photography, squash. Office: U NC Dept Public Policy CB3435 Abernethy Chapel Hill NC 27599-3435

ANDREWS, RICHARD VINCENT, physiologist, educator; b. Arapahoe, Nebr., Jan. 9, 1932; s. Wilber Vincent and Fern (Clawson) A.; m. Elizabeth Williams, June 1, 1954 (dec. Dec. 1994); children: Thomas, William, Robert, Catherine, James, John; m. Wyoma Upward, Oct. 18, 1997. BS, Creighton U., 1958, MS, 1959; PhD, U. Iowa, 1963. Instr. biology Creighton U., Omaha, 1958-60; instr. physiology U. Iowa, 1960-63; asst. prof. Creighton U., Omaha, 1963-65, assoc. prof., 1965-68, prof. physiology, 1968-97, asst. med. dean, 1972-75, dean grad. studies, 1975-85, dean emeritus, 1995—, prof. emeritus, 1997—. Vis. prof. Naval Arctic Rsch. Lab., 1963-72, U. B.C., 1985-86, U. Tasmania, 1993-94; cons. VA, NSF, NRC, ARS; plenary speaker USSR Symposium on Environment, 1970, Internat. Soc. Biomet., 1972. Contbr. articles to profl. jours. Served with M.C. U.S. Army, 1951-54. NSF fellow, 1962-63; NSF-NIH-ONR-AINA grantee, 1963— Fellow Explorers Club, Arctic Inst. N.Am.; mem. Am. Physiol. Soc., Am. Mammal Soc., Endocrine Soc., Soc. Exptl. Biology and Medicine, Internat. Soc. for Biometeorology, Sigma Xi.

ANDREWS, ROBERT E. congressman; b. Bellmar, N.J., Aug. 4, 1957; m. Camille Spinello, Nov., 1993. BA summa cum laude, Bucknell U., 1979; JD magna cum laude, Cornell U., 1982. Bar: N.J. 1982. Assoc. Archer & Greiner, Haddonfield, N.J., 1982-84, Charles J. Clarke & Assocs., Haddonfield, 1984-85, Kenney & Kearney, Cherry Hill, N.J., 1985-88; mem. Camden County (N.J.) Bd. Chosen Freeholders, 1987-90, freeholder dir., 1988-90; mem. U.S. Congress from 1st N.J. dist., Washington, 1991—; mem. edn. and workforce com., armed svcs. com., homeland sec. com. Contbr. articles to law jours. Bd. dirs. Camden County March of Dimes; mem. Task Force on Govt. Waste. Mem. Phi Beta Kappa. Democrat. Episcopalian. Avocation: jogging. Office: US House of Reps 2439 Rayburn House Office Bldg Washington DC 20515-0001*

ANDREWS, SCOTT MICHAEL, music educator; b. Hudson, N.Y., July 31, 1960; s. Frederick Paul and Patricia Kelly Andrews; m. Darlene Rose Stachewicz, Aug. 11, 1991; children: David Michael, Benjamin Patrick. BA, The Coll. Of St. Rose, 1982, MA, 1986. Cert. music tchr. N.Y. State Edn. Dept., 1983. Mem. staff Register-Star, Hudson, NY, 1976—82; mem. printing pubs. staff The Coll. Of St. Rose, Albany, NY, 1979—82; music tchr. Ravena-Coeymans-Selkirk Mid. Sch., Ravena, NY, 1983—. Music dept. chmn. and coord. Ravena-Coeymans-Selkirk Ctrl. Sch. Dist., 1988—92; instrumental music band dir. Ravena-Coeymans-Selkirk Mid. Sch., 1983—; guest condr. for bands and jazz ensembles, NY, 1985—; jazz ensemble dir. Siena Coll., Loudonville, NY, 1982—86; musician various bands. Composer: (songs) Studio Time. Recipient Outstanding Svc. award, The Coll. Of St. Rose, 1983; scholar, 1983. Mem.: Internat. Assn. For Jazz Edn., Ravena-Coeymans-Selkirk Teachers Assn., Greene County Music Educators Assn. (assoc.; treas. 1985—87, v.p. 1989—91, sec. 1999—2001, pres. 1991—93), N.Y. State Sch. Music Assn. (assoc.). Home: 47 Trumpeter Place Slingerlands NY 12159 Office: Ravena Coeymans Selkirk Central School Route 9W Ravena NY 12143

ANDREWS, SHARON MILLICENT PARRISH, historian, educator; d. Clarence Randolph and Mildred English Parrish; m. Nelson Montgomery Andrews, June 15, 1974; children: Elenora Louisa Walls, Ava Veronica Dorsett. B in Liberal Arts, Johnson C. Smith U., 1973; postgrad., Purdue U., 1974—75, Phoenix Coll. Notary pub.: Tex. Active Girl Scouts of Am., Tinton Falls, NJ, 1979—84. Mem.: NAACP, Girl, Inc., Links, Inc., Alpha Kappa Alpha. Home: PO Box 343 Cooper TX 75432 Office: Nutshell R&D Enterprises 1526 Leeward Ln Wylie TX 75098 Personal E-mail: spaiii@yahoo.com.

ANDREWS, STEVEN NICHOLAS, judge; b. Detroit, Dec. 4, 1932; s. Nick S. and Mary K. Andrews; m. Elisabeth McCurdy, June 28, 1959; children: Mary, Elisabeth, Nicholas. BA, Adrian Coll., 1955; LLB, JD, Cumberland U., 1959; D in Law (hon.), New Eng. Law Sch., 1983. Judge 6th Jud. Cir. Mich., Pontiac, chief judge. Guest lectr., instr. Detroit Coll. Law, Mich. State U.; bd. trustees Adrian Coll.; mem. adv. bd. Providence Hosp. Contbr. articles to profl. jours. Chmn. bd. trustees Oakland County Libr.; bd. dirs. Oakland Lit. Coun. for Advancing Adult Literacy. Named one of Most Respected Judges of Mich. Lawyers Weekly. Mem. Am. Judges Assn., Am. Judicature Soc., Mich. Bar Assn., Hellenic Bar Assn., Oakland County Bar Assn. (past pres., Outstanding Judge award), South Oakland County Bar Assn. (past pres., Outstanding Judge award), Supreme Ct. Hist. Soc., Federalist Soc., Am. Inn of Ct. (chancellor Oakland County Bar Assn. chpt.). Office: 6th Cir Oakland County Dept 404 1200 N Telegraph Rd Dept 404 Pontiac MI 48341-1032

ANDREWS, THEODORA ANNE, retired librarian, educator; b. Carroll County, Ind., Oct. 14, 1921; d. Harry Floyd and Margaret Grace (Walter) Ulrey; m. Robert William Andrews, July 18, 1940 (div. 1935); 1 child, Martin Harry. BS with distinction, Purdue U., 1953; MS, U.Ill., 1955. Asst. reference libr. Purdue U., West Lafayette, Ind., 1955-56, pharmacy libr., 1956-79, instr. libr. sci., 1956-60, asst. prof., 1960-65, assoc. prof., 1965-71, prof., 1971-79, 91-92, prof. libr. sci., pharmacy, nursing and health scis. libr., 1979-90, spl. bibliographer, 1991-92, prof. emeritus libr. sci., 1992—. Del. Ind. Gov.'s Conf. Librs. and Info. Svcs., 1978. Author: A Bibliography of the Socioeconomic Aspects of Medicine, 1975, A Bibliography of Drug Abuse Including Alcohol and Tobacco, 1977, A Bibliography of Drug Abuse, Supplement, 1977-80, 1981, Bibliography on Herbs, Herbal Remedies and Natural Foods, 1982, Substance Abuse Materials for School Libraries, An Annotated Bibliography, 1985, Guide to the Literature of Pharmacy and the Pharmaceutical Sciences, 1986; sect. editor Advances in Alcohol and Substance Abuse, 1981-92; contbr. articles to profl. jours. Mem. Purdue Women's Caucus, 1973—, v.p., 1975-76, pres., 1976-77; m. Internat. Women's Yr. Regional Planning Com., 1977. Grad. fellow U. Ill., 1954-55. Mem. ALA, AAUP, Spl. Libr. Assn. (John H. Moriatry award Ind. chpt. 1972), Med. Libr. Assn., Am. Assn. Colls. Pharmacy, Kappa Delta Pi, Delta Rho Kappa. Baptist. Office: Purdue U Sch Pharmacy West Lafayette IN 47907

ANDREWS, WILLIAM COOKE, physician; b. Norfolk, Va., June 7, 1924; s. Charles James and Jean Curry (Cooke) A.; m. Elizabeth Wight Kyle, Nov. 10, 1951; children— Elizabeth Randolph, William Cooke, Jr., Susan Carrington. AA, Princeton U., 1946; MD, Johns Hopkins U., 1947. Diplomate Am. Bd. Obstetrics and Gynecology. Intern N.Y. Hosp., 1947, resident in obstetrics and gynecology, 1948-50, 52-53; practice medicine specializing in obstetrics and gynecology Norfolk, Va., 1953-95; asst. in obstetrics and gynecology Cornell U. Med. Sch., 1948-50, 52-53; mem. attending staff Med. Ctr. Hosp.; prof. ob-gyn. Ea. Va. Med. Sch., Norfolk, 1975-95, prof. emeritus, 1995—, pres. faculty senate, 1976-77. Mem. fertility and maternal health drug adv. com. FDA, 1979-83, chmn., 1982-83, cons., 1983-87; mem. sci. adv. bd. Alan Guttmacher Inst., 1992-94; co-chair women's health measurement adv. panel Nat. Com. Quality Assurance, 1996—. Contbr. articles in field to profl. jours. Chmn. Norfolk Bicentennial Commn., 1969-71; mem. Community Facilities Commn., 1971-73, chmn., 1973-79; bd. dirs. Va. League for Planned Parenthood, 1966-68; pres. Norfolk chpt. Planned Parenthood, 1966-68; bd. govs. The Jacobs Inst. Women's Health, 1997—. With M.C., USN, 1950-52. Named Hon. Officer of the Most Excellent Order of the Brit. Empire, Queen Elizabeth II, 1967; presented Order of Andres Bello, Pres. Carlos Andres Perez of Venezuela, 1992. Fellow Am. Coll. Obstetricians and Gynecologists (vice chmn. dist. IV 1985-88, chmn. 1988-91, v.p. 1992-93, pres.-elect 1993, pres. 1994-95, exec. bd. 1988-96), Am. Assn. Obstetricians and Gynecologists, Am. Gynecol. and Obstet. Soc., Royal Coll. Obstetricians and Gynecologists (hon.); mem. AMA, Am. Fertility Soc. (bd. dirs. 1970-73, pres. 1977, med. dir. 1986-88, exec. dir. 1988-92), Nat. Osteoporosis Found. (interspecialty med. coun. 1995—), Med. Soc. Va., Norfolk Acad. Medicine, Va. Tidewater Obstetricians and Gynecologists Soc., Continental Gynecol. Soc., South Atlantic Assn. Obs.-Gyns., Norfolk C. of C. (chmn. armed forces com. 1966-68, v.p. 1968-69, pres. 1970), Internat. Fedn. Fertility Socs. (asst. treas. 1974-80, pres. 1983-86, chmn. sci. program com. 1986-89, exec. com. 1974-92), Navy League U.S. (pres. Hampton Roads coun. 1968-70, nat. dir. 1970-74), English Speaking Union U.S. (pres. Norfolk-Portsmouth br. 1964-66), Planned Parenthood Fedn. Am. (cons. nat. med. com. 1975-85, chmn. 1981-83), Norfolk Yacht and Country Club (commodore 1966). Presbyterian. Home and Office: 929 Graydon Ave Norfolk VA 23507-1207

ANDREWS, WILLIAM F. minister; b. Lansing, Mich., Apr. 13, 1921; s. Lyman LeRoy and Jennie Abigail (Fletcher) Andrews; m. Laura Virginia McManaway, Sept. 15, 1951; children: William Fletcher, David Eugene, Elizabeth Maxwell Andrews Williams. Student, Wayne U., 1939—42; BSChemE, Ill. Inst. Tech., 1947; MDiv, Union Theol. Sem., N.Y.C., 1953; DM, San Francisco Theol. Seminary, 1976; postgrad., Oxford (Eng.) U., 1988. Rsch. asst. Champion Spark Plug Co., Detroit, 1940—42; project engr. Vitro Corp. Am., N.Y.C., 1948—52; ordained min. United Meth. Ch., 1952—; exec. dir. United Meth. Found. N.W., Seattle, 1985—91; regional dir. Ednl. Opportunities, Inc., Lakeland, Fla., 1995—99; ret. Pres. PNWAC Bd. Pensions, Seattle, 1965—67; exec. dir. United Meth. Found. N.W., Seattle, 1985—91; conf. sec. Pacific N.W. Ann. Conf., Seattle, 1992—95; trustee Wesley Homes Found., DesMoines, Wash., 1997—; bd. dirs. Wesley Homes Retirement Ctr., Des-Moines. Editor: Jour. Pacific N.W. Conf., 1993, 1994, 1995. Pres. Sunnyside (Wash.) YMCA, 1964—66; mem. exec. bd. Tumwater Coun. Boy Scouts Am., Olympia, Wash., 1978; active City of Auburn Centennial Com., 1987—92; coord. docents White River Valley Mus., Auburn, 1997—2003. Lt. (j.g.) USNR, 1942—46. Named Citizen of the Month, C. of C., 2003. Fellow: Rotary Club Auburn, Wash. (bd. mem., historian, Paul Harris fellow 1998); mem.: Wash. Planned Giving Coun. (former pres.). Avocations: photography, travel, woodworking, reading. Home: 815 S 216th St WV #67 Des Moines WA 98198-6396 Office: Wesley Homes 815 S 216th St Des Moines WA 98198

ANDREWS, WILLIAM FREDERICK, manufacturing executive; b. Easton, Pa., Oct. 7, 1931; s. William Frederick and Lydia Nielson (Cross) Andrews; children: William Frederick III, Whitney, Carter, Clayton, Sloane. BS, U. Md., 1953; MBA, Seton Hall U., 1961. Product mgr. Scovill Mfg. Co., Waterbury, Conn., 1965-68, v.p., gen. mgr. Raleigh, N.C., 1968-73, group v.p. Nashville, 1973-79, pres. Waterbury, 1979-81, chmn., pres., chief exec., 1981-86; chmn., pres., CEO Singer Sewing Machine Co., 1986-89; pres. Massey Investment Co., 1989-90; pres., chief exec. officer UNR Industries Inc., 1990-92; CEO, chmn. bd. Amdura Corp., Conn., 1992-94; chmn. bd. Utica Corp., Utica, N.Y., 1992-94, Scovill Fasteners, Nashville, 1995—2001, Northwestern Steel and Wire Co., Nashville, 1998—2001; chmn. Corrections Corp. of Am., Nashville, 2000—, Katy Industries, Middlebury, Conn., 2001—; chmn. bd. Allied Aerospace, Newport News, Va., 0200—. Bd. dirs. Corrections Corp., Navistar Internat. Co., Johnson Controls, Katy Industries, Black Box, Inc., Trex Industries. Capt. USAF, 1953-56. Recipient Silver Beaver award Boys Scouts Am., 1979, Significant Sig award Sigma Chi, 1992. Mem.: Litchfield (Conn.)

Country Club, The Golf Club of Tenn., Univ. Club (N.Y.C.), Chgo. Club, Waterbury (Conn.) Country Club, Highfield Country Club (Conn.), Bellemeade Country Club (Nashville). Republican. Episcopalian.

ANDREWS REEVES, DONNA, professional golfer; b. Lynchburg, VA, Apr. 12, 1967; d. James Barclay and Helen Louise (Munsey) Andrews. BBA, U. N.C., 1989. Qualified golfer LPGA Tour, Fla., 1990; winner Ping-Cellular One Golf Tounament, Portland, Oreg., 1993, Ping-Welch's Golf Tournament, Tucson, Ariz., 1994, Dinah Shore Major Golf Tournament, Palm Springs, Calif., 1994, Longs Drugs Challenge, Lincoln, CA, 1998. Office: LPGA 100 International Golf Dr Daytona Beach FL 32124-1092

ANDREY, LADISLAV GEORGE, scientist; b. Vlaca, Saris, Czechoslovakia, July 15, 1948; s. George and Zuzana (Hermanovsky) A.; m. Helena Broulikova, Aug. 16, 1977; children: Margareta, Helena. Rerum Naturalium Dr, Charles U., Prague, Czech Republic, 1975, PhD, 1987; diploma, Japanese Lang. Sch., Osaka, Japan, 1978. Watchman Nat. Gallery, Prague, 1973-74; asst. prof. U. P.J. Safarik, Košice, Slovak Republic, 1974-78; rschr. Kyoto (Japan) U., 1978-80; analyst Orgn. for Selling Machines and Instruments, Prague, 1980-81; sr. scientist Acad. Scis., Prague, 1989—. Translator in field, Prague, 1981-89. Author: Biothermodynamics, 1980; contbr. articles to profl. jours. Named Am. Men of Sci., Bowker Ctr., Oldsmar, Fla., 1995. Mem. Am. Math. Soc., N.Y. Acad. Scis., Neurosci. Soc. Prague (com. mem. 1992). Avocations: chess, Greek philosophy, brain and mind research. E-mail: andre@cs.cas.cz.

ANDRIANO, KIRK PATRICK, pharmaceutical executive; b. Boise, Idaho, Nov. 10, 1956; s. Donald and Fae Andriano. BS, Utah State U., 1975—79; MS, U. of Utah, 1981—85, PhD, 1985—90. Post-doctoral fellow U. of Utah, 1990—91; nih - postgrad. internat. rsch. fellow Tampere U. of Tech., Finland, 1991—92; post-doctoral fellow APS Rsch. Inst., Advanced Polymer Systems, Inc., Redwood City, Calif., 1994—95; vis. rsch. scholar Kyoto U., 1995—97; scientist ii Atrix Laboratories, Inc., Fort Collins, Colo., 1997—99; sr. scientist MacroMed, Inc., Sandy, 1999—2001, exec. dir., preclinical devel., 2002—. Indsl. mentor, soc. for biomaterials Johns Hopkins U., Balt. Fogarty Internat. Rsch. fellow, NIH and Acad. of Finland. Master: Nat. Ski Patrol Sys.; mem.: Biomedical Engring. Soc., Soc. for Biomaterials, Controlled Release Soc., ASTM, Am. Assn. of Pharm. Scientists, Tissue Engring. Soc. Home: 1155 East 2100 South #214 Salt Lake City UT 84106 Office: MacroMed Inc 9520 South State St Sandy UT 84070 Office Fax: 801-565-8563. Personal E-mail: kandriano@aol.com. E-mail: kandriano@macromed.com.

ANDRIANO-MOORE, RICHARD COUNT, retired military officer, secondary school educator, elementary school educator; b. Petaluma, Calif., May 25, 1932; s. Norvel and Thelma Elizabeth Koch-Andriano (Cook) Moore; m. Janice Lynn Hironaka, Jan. 10, 1976 (div. Feb. 1990); children: Erika Lynn, Stephen Albert. BA, San Jose State U., 1956; MBA, Pepperdine U., 1977; B in Metaphysical Sci., U. Metaphysics, 1993. Commd. ensign USNR, 1957, advanced through grades to comdr.; 1st lt., gunnery officer USS Jefferson Count LST1068, 1957-60; 7th grade tchr. Oasis Sch., Riverside County, Calif., 1960-63; pers. and legal officer USS Maury AGS-16, 1963-65; commdg. officer Naval & Marine Corps Res. Tng. Ctr., Port Arthur, Tex., 1965-68; ops. officer USS Muliphen LKA 64, 1968-69; ASW & surface program officer 11th Naval Dist., San Diego, 1970-74; commdg. officer Naval Res. Ctr., Hunters Point, Calif., 1974-75, Army, Navy & Marine Corps Res. Ctr., San Bruno, Calif., 1975-79; dir. adminstrn. Nat. Com. Employer, Washington, 1979-82; comdr., regional coord. 10 western states Alameda, Calif., 1982—84; chief staff N. R. Readiness comdr., Treasure Island, Calif., 1984—85; tchr. Shoreline Unified Sch. Dist., Tomales, Calif., 1985—92, 1994—. Editor-in-chief: California Compatriot, 1976—80. Insp. Precinct Bd., Petaluma, 1987—90; scoutmaster Boy Scouts Am., 1989—92, dist. exec., 1992—94; alumni mem. Naval War Coll. Found., Newport, RI, 2002—. Decorated Def. Meritorious Svc. medal Sec. Def., Washington, Ancestral Title and Coat of Arms Counts of Andriano Wappenrolle, Austria, Rome, knight Order St. John of Jerusalem Knights Hopitalier; recipient Disting. Alumni award, San Jose State U., 1991, Scoutmaster award of Merit, Boy Scouts Am., 1992, numerous Best of Show and 1st place ribbons for acrylic paintings, Sonoma-Marin County Fair, 1989—2003. Mem.: Noble Co. of the Rose (lt. magister rosae 1998—), Naval Order U.S., Mil. Order Loyal Legion U.S. (Calif. comdr. 1982—88), Calif. Soc. SAR (pres. San Francisco chpt. 1976—77, state pres. 1986—87, Silver Good Citizenship medal 1978, Patriot medal 1985, Meritorious Svc. medal 1987, oak leaf cluster 1996, Citation of Merit 2001), Augustan Soc. Inc. (v.p. 1995—). Avocations: reading, hiking, bicycling, travel, abstract artist. Office: 2920 Carissa Ct Santa Rosa CA 95405 E-mail: cteandriano@netscape.net.

ANDRICA, JOHN DEAN, management consultant; b. Canton, Ohio, Sept. 17, 1946; s. John and Diane C. A.; m. Diane Cherney, Aug. 2, 1980; 1 child, Stephanie N. BS, Indsl. Engring. Coll., 1969; student, Allied Inst. Tech. Dir. engring. Wilson Sporting Goods, Chgo., 1974-77; v.p. A.T. Kearney, Chgo., 1977-87, mng. dir., 1987-91, sr. v.p., 1991—; with Prin. Cleve. Investment Ptnrs. LLC., 1997—; dir. Union Ptnrs. LLC., 2000—. Candidate Ill. 9th dist. U.S. Congress, 1980; candidate city treas. City of Chgo., 1977; mem. exec. com., bd. trustees Bus. Volunteerism Unltd., Cleve., 1994—; mem. corp. coun. Cleve. Mus. Art, 1996—; bd. dirs. Cleve. Playhouse Square Found., Shaker Heights, Ohio, 1994—, Hathaway Brown Sch. Girls, Shaker Heights, 1998—. Named Young Rep. of Yr. Cook County Rep. Party, 1978. Mem. Inst. Mgmt. Cons., Shaker Country Club, Shaker Skating Club, The Club, Union Club. Republican. Avocations: skiing, skeetshooting, golfing, boating, tennis. Office: AT Kearney 600 Superior Ave E Ste 1200 Cleveland OH 44114-2654

ANDRINGA, MICHAEL ROBERT, management consultant; b. Nov. 11, 1950; BBA in Mktg., U. Wis., Eau Claire, 1973. Mgr. contracts Northrop Grumman, Dallas, 1991-92, mgr. bus., 1993-97, dir. bus. mgmt., 1998-00; dir. program bus. mgmt. Vought Aircraft Inds., Inc., Dallas, 2000—.

ANDRINGA, PATRICIA PERKINS, fundraiser, consultant; b. Apr. 9, 1944; BA in Polit. Sci. cum laude, Mt. Holyoke Coll., 1966. Rsch. asst. Office Planning & Sys. Analysis U.S. Office Postmaster Gen., Washington, 1966-68; writer, editor U. Wis., Wausau, 1968-69; cons., facilitator Washington, 1992—. Bd. consultants Riggs Bank N.A., Washington, 1996—2001. Founder, pub. Potomac Pages Mag., 1984-85; editor Wickette mag., 1978-81. V.p. cmty. devel. Nat. Symphony Orch., 2001—; chmn. bd. dirs. Boys & Girls Clubs Greater Washington, 1986—89; mem. Boys & Girls Clubs Found., 1991—, sec., 2001—; founder, pres. The Washington Joffrey Bd., Washington, 1993—96; women's leadership round table D.C. Commn. for Women, 1987—91; active Leadership Washington, 1996—, bd. dirs., 1998—2000, chmn. resource devel. com.; trustee Holton-Arms Sch., 1988—97, emerita, 1997—; pres. Adas Israel Synagogue, Washington, 2003—; bd. dirs. Boys & Girls Clubs Greater Washington, 1984—, Nat. Symphony Orch., 1980—, The Joffrey Ballet, Chgo., 1993—, Population Reference Bur., 2000—, Children's Hosp., Washington, 1998—. Named Vol. Fundraiser of Yr., Nat. Soc. Fundraising Execs., 1992; named one of 9 Who Care, WUSA, 2002; recipient Svc. Youth award, Boys & Girls Clubs Am., 1994, 1999, Medallion award, 1991, Silver medallion award, 1998, Alumnae Achievement award, Mt. Holyoke Coll., 2001, Jefferson award, 2002. Mem. Jr. League Washington (bd. dirs. 1983-85, v.p., Spirit Volunteerism award 1988). Avocations: travel, hiking, swimming, performing and visual arts, reading.

ANDRIOLA, MARY R. neurologist, pediatrician; b. N.Y.C., Sept. 13, 1942; d. Anthony Francis Repole and Florence Elizabeth Elliott; m. Micheal John Andriola, July 21, 1962 (div. Jan. 1982); children: Margaret Mary Danao, Joseph Anthony, James Michael; m. Jordan I. Levine, Feb. 24, 1990. Student, Vassar Coll., 1958-60; AB, Johns Hopkins U., 1962; MD, Duke U., 1965. Diplomate Am. Bd. Pediatrics, Am. Bd. Psychiatry and Neurology, with spl. competence in child neurology and added qualification in clin. neurophysiology. Resident in pediatrs. Duke U. Sch. Medicine, Durham, N.C., 1965-66, U. Fla., Gainesville, 1966-67, resident in neurology, 1967-70; asst. prof. neurology and pediats. La. State U. Sch. Medicine, New Orleans, 1970-72; dir. electroencephalography and fellowship program U. Fla. Coll. Medicine, Gainesville, 1975-88, assoc. prof. neurology, 1975-88, assoc. prof. pediats., 1978-88; dir. pediat. neurology All Children's Hosp. U. S. Fla., St. Petersburg; assoc. prof. neurology SUNY, Stony Brook, 1988-98, dir. clin. neurophysiology, 1990-97, dir. divsn. clin. neurophysiology, 1997, prof. neurology and pediats., 1998—, dir. divsn. pediat. neurology, 2001—. Assoc. examiner Am. Bd. Qualification in EEG, 1976-85, Am. Bd. Psychiatry and Neurology, 1983—, Am. Bd. Clin. Neurophysiology, Inc., 1991—; mem. adv. com. Pinellas county Sch. Bd. Health, 1979-88; reviewer Neurology, 1997—; appeared in TV interviews; mem. People to People Women Specialist Med. Exch. to China, 1991; mem. profl. adv. bd. Epilepsy Found L.I., 1991—; mem. team to Russia, Physicians for Social Responsibility, 1992; lectr. in field. Author: Introduction to EEG and Evoked Potentials, 1983; contbr. numberous articles, abstract, revs. to profl. jours., chpts. to books. Grantee Abbott Labs., 1992, 96, Burroughs Wellcome, 1993, NIH, 1993, Parke-Davis, 1994, BECTS, 1995, Hoechst Marion Roussel, 1995, Warner Lambert, 1995, Cyberonics, 1998. Fellow: Am. Clin. Neurophysiology Soc. (program com. 1980—81, practice com. 1980—82, EEG lab. accreditation bd. 1980—90, liaison Child Neurology Soc. 1982—88), Am. Acad. Pediats.; mem.: So. Clin. Neurol. Soc. (bd. dirs.), Suffolk County Pediat. Soc., Tri-State Child Neurology Soc., Ea. Assn. Electroencephalographers, Child Neurology Soc., Am. Epilepsy Soc., So. EEG Soc. (sec.-treas. 1975—78, program chmn. 1979, pres. 1980, edn. chmn. 1981—89), Women's Am. Med. Assn. (sec.-treas. Suffolk County chpt. 1992). Office: SUNY Stony Brook Sch Medicine Dept Neurology Stony Brook NY 11794-0001 E-mail: mandriol@notes.cc.sunysb.edu.

ANDRIOLE, STEPHEN JOHN, information systems executive; b. Phila., Oct. 22, 1949; s. Frank Richard and Grace Marie A.; m. Denise Marie De Felice, Aug. 7, 1971. BA magna cum laude, LaSalle Coll., 1971; MA, U. Md., 1973, PhD, 1974. NDEA research fellow U. Md., 1971-74, instr., 1974, asst. prof., 1975; research analyst Decisions and Designs, Inc., McLean, Va., 1975-76, project dir., 1975-76; program mgr. Def. Advanced Research Projects Agy., Dept. Def., Arlington, Va., 1977-78; dir. Cybernetics Tech. Office, 1977-79; pres. Internat. Info. Systems, Inc., 1979—; prof. info. tech. George Mason U., Fairfax, Va., 1986-90, chmn. dept. info. systems and systems engring., 1987-89; prof. info. studies Drexel U., 1990—; chief technology officer Cigna Corp., 1995—97; sr. v.p., chief tech. officer Safeguard Scientifics, Inc., 1998—2000; prin. TL Ventures, 1998—2000; prof. Villanova U., 2001—. Participant profl. panels and seminars. Author or co-author 28 books on sys. design and analytical methods; contbr. articles to profl. publs.; reviewer Automatica, 1983—, Large Scale Systems, 1983—, mem. editl. bd., 1975—. Mem. IEEE Systems, Man Cybernetics Soc., Armed Forces Communications and Electronics Assn., Am. Assn. Artificial Intelligence. Roman Catholic. *Tenacity is the real secret of "success".*

ANDRIOLE, VINCENT THOMAS, medical educator, researcher; b. Scranton, Pa., Aug. 3, 1931; s. Vincent Anthony and Josephine M. (Cinquegrani) A.; m. Daria Louise DeRose; children: V. Charles, Katherine, David, Christina. BS, Coll. of the Holy Cross, 1953; MD, Yale U., 1957. Diplomate Am. Bd. Internal Medicine, Am. Bd. Infectious Diseases. Resident in medicine U. N.C. Meml. Hosp., Chapel Hill, 1957-59; clin. assoc. NIAID/NIH, Bethesda, Md., 1959-61; rsch. fellow Sch. Medicine Yale U., New Haven, Conn., 1961-63, instr. medicine, 1963-64, from asst. prof. to prof. medicine, 1964—, chief infectious diseases, 1973-87. Chief Fitkin Med. Svc., Yale-New Haven (Conn.) Hosp., 1987-; cons. Pfizer Pharms., 1982-, Hoffmann La Roche, 1985-, Bristol Myers Squibb, 1987-, Bayer Pharmaceuticals. Author 9 books, 90 chpts. in books; contbr. more than 300 articles to profl. jours.; editor Mediguide to Infectious Diseases, Cliniguide to Fungal Infections, Current Opinion in Infectious Diseases. Lt. USN, 1959-61. Recipient Laureate award ACP, Established Investigator award Am. Heart Assn., 1966-71, Santae Crucius award, Coll. of the Holy Cross. Fellow AAAS; mem. Infectious Diseases Soc. Am. (sec. 1987-92, v.p. 1992-93, councillor 1985-87, pres.-elect 1993-94, pres. 1995, Bristol award), Alpha Omega Alpha, British Soc. Antimicrobial Chemotherapy (Am. Garrod award). Avocation: golf. Office: Yale U Sch Medicine 333 Cedar St New Haven CT 06510-3289

ANDRISANI, JOHN ANTHONY, editor, author, golf consultant; b. Bayshore, N.Y., Sept. 24, 1949; s. Pat and Gwendoline Mary (Rose) A. Student, SUNY, Stony Brook, 1968-71. Instr. golf in country club, N.Y., 1971-78; freelance writer golf mags., 1977—; asst. editor Golf Illustrated mag., London, 1980-82; sr. editor instrn. Golf mag., N.Y.C., 1982-98. Co-author: (with Sandy Lyle) Learning Golf: The Lyle Way, 1986, (with Seve Ballesteros) Natural Golf, 1987 (Book of Month Club 1987), (with Chi Chi Rodriguez) 101 Supershots, 1990, (with Robin McMillan) The Golf Doctor, 1990 (Brentanos bestseller 1990), (with Mike Dunaway) Hit It Hard!, 1991, (with Phil Ritson) Golf Your Way, 1992, (with John Daly) Grip It, and Rip It!, 1992, (with Fred Couples) Total Shotmaking, 1994, (with Craig Stadler) I Am The Walrus, 1995, (with Claude "Butch" Harmon Jr.), The Four Cornerstones of Winning Golf, 1996, (with Jim McLean) The X-Factor Swing, 1996, The Tiger Woods Way, 1997, The Short Game Magic of Tiger Woods, 1998, (with Mark Russell) Golf Rules Plain and Simple, 1999, The Hogan Way, 2000, (with John Anselmo) "A-Game" Golf, 2001, The Bobby Jones Way, 2002, Think Like Tiger, 2002, Everything I Learned about People, I Learned From a Round of Golf, 2002, The Nicklaus Way, 2003, Play Like Sergio Garcia, 2004; contbr. articles to jours. and mags. Mem. Golf Writers Assn. (assn. champion 1985), Ballybunion Golf Club (life, Ireland). E-mail: jagolf3238@aol.com.

ANDRISANI, PAUL J. business educator, management consultant; b. Wilmington, Del., Oct. 19, 1946; s. Paul and Mary (Tavani) A.; m. Barbara Lee Frank, Nov. 23, 1968; children: Nathan, Damian, Danielle. BS, U. Del., 1968, MBA, 1970; PhD, Ohio State U., 1973, postgrad., 1973-74. Sr. rsch. assoc. Ctr. for Human Resource Rsch. Ohio State U., Columbus, 1973-74, vis. rsch. assoc., 1979; asst. prof. Sch. Bus., Temple U., Phila., 1974-76, assoc. prof., 1977-83, prof., 1983—; dir. Bur. Econ. Rsch., Phila., 1977-78, Ctr. for Labor and Human Resource Studies, 1987—; co-dir. Ctr. for Competitive Govt., Phila., 1997—2002, assoc. dean, 1989-91, chmn. dept. mgmt., 1993-95. Pres. Paul J. Andrisani Mgmt. Cons. Svcs., Wilmington, Del., 1974—, St. Anthony's Edn. Fund, 1986—; pres. West End Neighborhood House Social Svc. Agy., 1995-97; cons. Price Waterhouse, U.S. EEOC, UPS, U.S. Army Recruiting Command, Acme Markets, CBS, Coca-Cola, City of Tucson, City of Phila., Chevron, Chrysler, Olsten, La. Power and Light, La. Land and Exploration, PanAm, Smith Kline, Carpenter Tech., The Aerospace Corp. of Am., Boeing Co., Dynalectron Corp., Lukens Steel, Nordstrom, Phila. Police Dept., Shoney's Inc., Martin Marietta, CIGNA, Airline Pilots Assn., Prudential Ins., Traveler's Ins., Suffolk County Police Dept., Internat. Comms. Agy., N.Y. Times, U.S. Steel, Readers Digest, K-Mart, Wal-Mart, Russell Sage Found., United Food and Comml. Workers Union, Del. Econ. and Fin. Adv. Com., New Orleans Pub. Svc. Inc., Disability and Pension Rev. Com., Rockwell Internat., ARCO, Nationwide Ins., ICI Ams., DuPont, Witco Chem., Westinghouse, GTE, Inco, Gould Electronics, Chrysler, Dollar Bank, Rhone-Poulenc Rorer, Ohio Edison, Delmarva Power, LaSalle Univ., Carter Wallace, Nortel Networks, Enterprise Rent-a-Car, Gulfstream Aerospace Technologies, We. Digital, govt. agys., others; lectr. Internat. Comms. Agy., Japan, Portugal, Italy, Can., Brandeis U., Pa. State U., Columbia U., William and Mary Coll., U. So. Calif., U. Pa., Nat. Employment Law Inst., San Francisco and Washington; testimony before U.S. Congress, 1991; presentation on new economy to Pa. Legis., 2000. Author: Pre-Retirement Years, vol. III, 1973, vol. IV, 1974, Career Thresholds, 1975, Work Attitudes and Labor Market Experience, 1978, Making Government Work, 2000; mem. editl. bd. Jour. Econs. and Bus., 1979-83; reviewer U. Mich. Press, Ohio State U. Press, Temple U. Press and various scholarly jours.; contbr. over 40 papers to profl. jours. and socs. Temple U. Law Sch. Bd. Visitors, 1997—. With U.S. Army, 1972-73. Recipient Wilmington Man of Yr. award, 1995, West End Neighborhood House Leadership award, 1997, Prof. of Yr. award Temple U. Chpt. Soc. for Advancement of Mgmt., 1997, awards for vol. svc., Thomas J. Reese award for cmty. svc., 2000, U. Del. Alumni Hall of Fame award, 1999; Salzburg fellow, Roosevelt Youth Policy fellow; grantee U.S. Dept. Labor, 1974-77, Nat. Commn. for Employment Policy, 1979-83, Adminstrn. on Aging, 1981-82, Social Sci. Rsch. Coun., 1982, U.S. Dept. Army, 1986, 98, Human Resource Rsch. Orgn., 1989-90, PriceWaterhouse Coopers Endowment for the Bus. of Govt., 1998-2000. Mem. Am. Econs. Assn., Indsl. Rels. Rsch. Assn., Acad. of Mgmt., Soc. Labor Economists, Strategic Mgmt. Soc., U. Del. Alumni Assn. (bd. dirs. 2001—). Office: Temple U Fox Sch Bus & Mgmt Speakman Hall Rm 366 Philadelphia PA 19122

ANDRUS, CECIL DALE, academic administrator; b. Hood River, Oreg., Aug. 25, 1931; s. Hal Stephen and Dorothy (Johnson) A.; m. Carol Mae May, Aug. 27, 1949; children: Tana Lee, Tracy Sue, Kelly Kay. Student, Oreg. State U., 1948-49; LLD (hon.), Gonzaga U., U. Idaho, U. N.Mex., Coll. Idaho, Idaho State U., Whitman Coll. State gen. mgr. Paul Revere Life Ins. Co., 1969-70; gov. State of Idaho, 1971-77, 87-95; sec. of interior, 1977-81; chmn. Andrus Ctr. for Pub. Policy, Boise (Idaho) State U., 1995—. Bd. dirs. KeyCorp., Albertson's, Inc., Coeur d'Alene Mines; mem. Idaho Senate, 1961-66, 69-70; mem. exec. com. Nat. Gov.'s Conf., 1971-72, chmn., 1976; chmn. Fedn. Rocky Mountain States, 1971-72. Author: Cecil Andrus: Politics Western Style, 1998. Chmn. bd. trustees Coll. of Idaho, 1985-89; bd. dirs. Sch. Forestry, Duke U. With USN, 1951-55. Recipient Disting. Citizen award Oreg. State U., 1980, Collier County Conservancy medal, 1979, Ansel Adams award Wilderness Soc., 1985, Audubon medal, 1985, Statesman of the Yr. award Idaho State U., 1990, Torch of Liberty award B'nai B'rith, 1991, William Penn Mott award, Nat. Parks Conservation Assn., 2000; named Conservationist of Yr. Nat. Wildlife Fedn., 1980, Idaho Wildlife Fedn., 1972, Man of Yr., VFW, 1959. Mem. VFW, Idaho Taxpayers Assn. (bd. dirs. 1964-66). Democrat. Office: Boise State U Andrus Ctr Pub Policy 1910 University Dr Boise ID 83725-0399

ANDRUS, ROGER DOUGLAS, lawyer; b. Floral Park, N.Y., Dec. 3, 1945; s. Winfield and Julia Margaret (Arduino) A.; m. Stephanie Andrus, Jan. 20, 1969 (div. 1983); children: Justin, Sarah; m. Patricia Ann McDonough, Oct. 4, 1986; children: Michael, David, Molly. AB cum laude, Wagner Coll., 1966; JD, NYU, 1969. Bar: N.Y. 1970, U.S. Dist. Ct. (ea. and so. dists.) 1975, U.S. Ct. Appeals 2d cir.) 1975. Assoc. Cahill Gordon & Reindel, N.Y.C., 1970-78, ptnr., 1978—. Mem. N.Y. State Bar Assn., Canoe Brook Country Club, Down Town Assn., Omicron Delta Kappa. Office: Cahill Gordon & Reindel 80 Pine St New York NY 10005-1790

ANDRUS, SUSAN JOYCE, librarian; b. Dover, N.J., July 10, 1964; d. James Ellsworth and Jean Lucille (Dahler) A. BS in Edn., Clarion U. of Pa., 1986, MLS, 1988. Cert. libr., S.C. Automation coord. Oconee County Pub. Libr., Walhalla, S.C., 1989, system mgr., 1991—; office mgr. Wildwater Ltd., Long Creek, S.C., 1990-91. Mem. Piedmont Libr. Assn., S.C. Libr. Assn., Foothills Mopar Club. Avocations: muscle car restoration, gourmet cooking. Office: Oconee County Libr 501 W North Broad St Walhalla SC 29691-1836

ANDRYSIAK, FRANK LOUIS, videographer; b. Balt., Sept. 6, 1934; s. Francis Thomas and Clara (Weber) A.; m. Janice Rosa Hunt, Nov. 22, 1958; children: Alan, Karen, Jean. BS in bus. adminstrn., Loyola Coll., 1956; grad. U.S. Army Comman, Gen. Staff Coll., 1971; grad., Indsl. Coll. Armed Forces, 1973, U.S. Air War Coll., 1976. Control buyer Montgomery Ward, Balt., 1958-63; U.S. customs svc. Dept. Treasury, Washington, 1963-93; pres. All Occasions Video, Crofton, Md., 1993—. EEO adv. com. U.S. Customs Svc., Washington, 1990-93. Editor various family and wedding photo collages, wedding video montages (selected for showing on tv show "Here Comes the Bride-There Goes the Groom", Feb., 1996). Col. USAR, 1956-85. Mem. Wedding & Event Videographers' Assn. (ret.), K of C. Independent. Roman Catholic. Avocation: indoor and outdoor model railroading. Home and Office: 1572 Farlow Ave Crofton MD 21114-1536 E-mail: fandrysiak@aol.com.

ANDRZEJAK, MICHAEL RICHARD, insurance agent; b. Royal Oak, Mich., Mar. 20, 1962; s. Francis Jacob and Jean Ann (Lewandowski) A.; m. Yvonne L. Macks, May 23, 1992 (div. Mar. 1995). Student, Cen. Mich. U., 1980-85. Assoc. agt. State Farm Ins., Madison Heights, Mich., 1992-97; agt., owner Farmers Ins. Group of Cos., Royal Oak, 1997—. City commr. City of Royal Oak, 1995—, mayor pro tem., 1997—; bd. trustees Royal Oak Pub. Libr., 1993—; bd. dirs. Boys and Girls Club of South Oakland County, 1995—; exec. bd. dirs. Oakland County Reps., 1996—. Republican. Roman Catholic. Home: 1912 Guthrie Ave Royal Oak MI 48067-3586

ANDSNES, LEIF OVE, concert pianist; b. Karmoy, Norway, Apr. 7, 1970; Student, Bergen Music Conservatory. Concert pianist Oslo Philharm., Edinburgh Festival, 1989, Cleve. Orch. Philharm., Berlin Philharm., London Philharm., Chgo. Symphony, N.Y. Philharm., Boston Philharm., Kirov Orch., London Symphony Orch., Vienna Symphony Orch., L.A. Philharmonic, City of Birmingham Symphony, Brahms Piano Concerto No. 1 with CBSO and Simon Rattle, 1998; records for EMI classics, including Schumann Pianoworks and the Long Long Winter Night (a collection of Norwegian music), 1997, Haydn Piano Sonatas, 1999, Britten Piano Concerto and Shostakovich Concerto for Piano, Trumpet and Strings, 1999, Haydn Piano Concertos, 2000, Liszt Piano Pieces, 2001; recs. Virgin Classics include: Grieg: A minor and Liszt A major, Janacek: Piano Works (Deutschen Schallplaten award), Chopin: Sonatas, Nielsen Piano Works, Grieg Piano Works; maj. tours in Australia, Japan, Europe, U.S. Recipient First prize Hindemith Competition, Frankfurt-am-Main, prizewinner others, Dorothy Chandler award, L.A.; named The 1998 Gilmore Artist by Irving S. Gilmore Internat. Keyboard Festival of Kalamazoo. Home: IMG Artists Lovell House 616 Chiswick High Rd London London W4 2TH England W4 5RX

ANEMA-GARTEN, DURLYNN C. communications educator, counselor, writer; b. San Diego, Dec. 23, 1935; d. Durlin L. Flagg and Carolyn L. Owen; m. Charles Jay Anema, May 5, 1955 (dec. 09061986); children: Charlynn Anema Raimundi, Charles Jay, Richard F.; m. Vernon Ray Garten, July 30, 1988. BA, Calif. State U., Hayward, 1968, MS, 1977; EdD, U. Pacific, 1984; PhD, Trinity Theol. Sem., Evansville, Ind., 1994. Cert. Christian therapist; cert. life secondary tchr., life sch. adminstr., Calif. Columnist San Leandro (Calif.) Morning News, 1960-62; secondary tchr. San Leandro and Hayward Sch. Dists., 1970-75; sch. adminstr. Hayward and Lodi (Calif.) Sch. Dists., 1975-80; dir. lifelong learning U. Pacific, Stockton, Calif., 1981-84, prof. comm., 1984-89; pvt. sch. cons., 1989—; pvt. Christian counselor, 1994—. Pres., bd. dirs. Valley Cmty. Counseling Svcs., Stockton, 1982-92; cons., assoc. Raphael Coun. Ctr., Sacramento, 1994-98; adj. prof. Western Theol. Sem., Sacramento, 1999—. Author: Don't Get Fired, 1978, Get Hired, 1979, Sharing an Apartment, 1982, Harriet Chalmers Adams, 2nd edit., 2003, Louise Arner Boyd, 2000; co-author: California Yesterday and Today, 1984, Options, 1993. Pres., mem. bd. San Leandro Libr., 1970—75; pres. Homeowners Assn. San Leandro, 1973—75, Homeowners Assn. Garden Valley, Calif., 1980—97; ch. counselor Good Samaritan Covenant Ch., 1993—98; bd. dirs. Children's Commn., San Joaquin County, Calif., 1986—92, Sr. Citizens Commn., Calaveras County, Calif., 1998, Valley Mountain Regional Ctr., Stockton, Calif., 2000—. Recipient Susan B. Anthony award San Joaquin County Commn. on Women, 1989. Mem. Soc. Profl. Journalists, Soc. Christian Therapists, Nat. Writers Assn., Calif. Writers Club, James Monroe PTA (life), Phi Kappa Phi, Phi Delta Kappa. Avocations: travel, hiking, bicycling, reading. Office: 401 Oakridge Ct Valley Springs CA 95252-9362

ANFINSEN, LIBBY ESTHER SHULMAN, social worker, clinical administrator; b. Jersey City, Dec. 20, 1937; d. Herman and Shirley Ann (Stiskin) Shulman; 2d m. Christian Boehmer Anfinsen, Mar. 1, 1979; children: Mark H. Ely, Tobie R. Beckerman, Daniel J. Ely, David A. Ely. BA, Bklyn. Coll., 1954; MSW, NYU, 1956. Lic. cert. clin. social worker, Md.; diplomat in clin. social work; lic. clin. social worker. Clin. social worker NIH Clin. Ctr., Bethesda, Md., 1966-81; pvt. practice individual and group therapy Balt., Silver Spring, Md., 1980-95; dir. social svcs. Children's Hosp. and Ctr. for Reconstructive Surgery, Balt., 1983-85; social worker Balt. County Health Dept., Towson, Md., 1985-91. Devel. disabilities adminstr. Balt. County Health Dept., Balt. City Dept. Edn. Spl. Svcs. for Children with Learning Disorders, 1993-2001; interviewer child Devel. Rsch. Jerome Riker Found. for Persecution of Holocaust Children, Balt. and N.Y.C., 1983-95; mem. med. bd. NIH Clin. Ctr., Bethesda, Md.; organizer Israeli delegation Confs. of Nobel Prize Laureates, Lindau, 2002-. Contbr. articles to profl. publs. Comdr. USPHS, 1974-81. Mem. ACSW, NASW, Zionist Orgn. Am., Vols. for Israel, Israel Bond Prime Ministers Club, Israel Investment Club (Balt.). Jewish. Avocations: travel, reading, sailing, music, sports, writing. Home: 11205 Tildencrest Ct Potomac MD 20854-2770 E-mail: lesa18@msn.com.

ANFINSON, THOMAS ELMER, government financial administrator; b. Stockton, Calif., Aug. 16, 1941; s. Elmer and Elizabeth (Killebrew) A.; m. Lawrene Nixon, July 27, 1970; children: Kathleen, Rebecca, Thomas Edward. BS, U. So. Calif., 1964. CPA, Calif., Va. With Price Waterhouse, 1964-70; tax mgr. Toyota Motor Sales, USA, 1971-72; acct. Renegotiation Bd., L.A., 1972-76; pres. Anfinson Accountancy Corp., Newport Beach, Calif., 1976-81; exec. asst. to gen. mgr. New Cmty. Devel. Corp. HUD, Washington, 1981-83, spl. asst. to asst. sec. for pub. housing, 1985; dep. treas. Reagan-Bush 84 Presdl. Re-election Campaign., 1983-85; spl. asst. to asst. sec. for employment and tng. U.S. Dept. Labor, 1985-86; spl. asst. to dep. adminstr. Health Care Fin.

Adminstrn., HHS, 1986; chmn. fed. prevailing rate adv. com. U.S. Office Pers. Mgmt., 1986-89; dep. under sec. for mgmt., chief fin. officer U.S. Dept. Edn., 1989-91; exec. dir. U.S. Savs. Bonds divsn. Dept. Treasury, 1991-93; assoc. adminstr. fin., dir. fin. U.S. Ho. Reps., Washington, 1995-97, fin. adminstr., 1997—. Bd. dirs. CapitolWatch Found., 1993—, Nixon Ednl. Found., Seattle. Staff sgt. USAF, 1965—70. Mem. AICPA, D.C. Inst. CPAs, Assn. Govt. Accts. (cert. govt. fin. mgr.), Fed. exec. Inst. Alumni Assn., U. So. Calif. Alumni Assn. Republican. Avocations: gardening, camping, travel. Home: PO Box 817 Great Falls VA 22066-0817 Office: Us House Reps Washington DC 20515-0001 E-mail: teacpa@msn.com.

ANFUSO, VICTOR L'EPISCOPO, lawyer, business consultant; b. Bklyn., Sept. 17, 1932; s. Victor L'Episcopo and Frances (Stallone) A.; m. Kathy Ann Shea, Apr. 8, 1967; children— Dina, Michelle, Victor T., William P., Adrienne. A.B. magna cum laude, St. John's U., 1954, J.D., 1959. Bar: N.Y. 1959, Oreg. 1986. Ptnr., Warner Birdsall & Anfuso, N.Y.C., 1959-62, Anfuso & Kroll, N.Y.C., 1965-69, Anfuso & Posmantur, N.Y.C., 1971-73; sole practice, N.Y.C., 1974-80; ptnr. Wildes Weinberg & Anfuso, N.Y.C., 1980-84; ch. adminstr. Bible Temple, Portland, Oreg., 1984-86; sr. cons. Anfuso Cons., Yuba City, Calif., 1981-82; pres., co-founder Portland Consulting Group, 1988. Contbr. articles to law jours. Pres., N.Y. State Young Citizens for Johnson, 1964; bd. dirs. World Rehab. Fund, 1972-78. Served to lt. USNR, 1955-57. Mem. N.Y. State Bar Assn., Oreg. State Bar Assn., Assn. Immigration and Nationality Lawyers, Full Gospel Businessmen's Assn. Mem. Christian Ch. Home: 3101 NE 156th Ave Portland OR 97230-5167 Office: 1515 SW 5th Ave Portland OR 97201-5406

ANGEL, ALLEN ROBERT, mathematics educator, author, consultant; b. NYC, Oct. 13, 1942; s. Isaac and Sylvia (Budnick) A.; m. Kathryn Mary Pollinger, Feb. 14, 1966; children: Robert Allen, Steven Scott. AAS in Electrical Tech., N.Y.C. Community Coll., 1962; BS in Physics, SUNY, New Paltz, 1965; MS in Math., SUNY, 1967; postgrad., Rutgers U., 1969. Tchr. physics Rhineback (N.Y.) Cen. Sch., 1965-66; instr. physics, math. Sullivan County Community Coll., Loch Sheldrake, N.Y., 1967-70; prof. math. Monroe Community Coll., Rochester, N.Y., 1970—, chmn. math./computer sci., 1988—. Asst. dir. nat. sci. found., math. summer insts. Rutgers U., New Brunswick, N.J., 1970-72; cons. reviewer various pub. cos. including Prentice-Hall Pub. Co., Englewood Cliffs, N.J., 1983—, Addison-Wesley Pub. Co., Reading, Mass., 1978—; bd. dirs. Am. Math. Assn. Two Yr. Colls. Found. Author: (textbooks) A Survey of Mathematics with Applications, 6th edit., 2001, Elementary Algebra-A Practical Approach, 1985, Intermediate Algebra-A Practical Approach, 1986, Elementary Algebra for College Students, 6th edit., 2003, Intermediate Algebra for College Students, 6th edit., 2003, Algebra for College Students, 2000, Elementary and Intermediate Algebra for College Students, 2000, 2d edit., 2003, Elementary Algebra for College Students, Early Graphing, 2000, 2d edit., 2003. Recipient Excellence in Tchg. award Nat. Inst. for Staff and Organizational Devel., 1991. Mem. Am. Math. Assn. of Two Yr. Colls. (v.p. 1985—, chmn. conv. 1984, bd. dirs., Pres.'s award), N.Y. State Math. Assn. of Two Yr. Colls. (pres. 1978-80, chmn. summer inst. 1976-78, Outstanding Contributions award), Math. Assn. of Am., Nat. Council of Tchrs. of Math., Assn. Math. Tchrs. of N.Y. State, New England Math. Assn. of Two Yr. Colls., Nat. Inst. Staff & Organizational Devel. (Excellence award 1991, 92). Avocations: camping, travel, investing. Home: 4036 Wellington Pkwy Palm Harbor FL 34685-1174 Office: Monroe Community Coll 1000 E Henrietta Rd Rochester NY 14623-5701

ANGEL, ARMANDO CARLOS, rheumatologist, internist; b. Las Vegas, N.Mex., Mar. 25, 1940; s. Edmundo Clemente and Pauline Teresa (Flores) Sanchez A.; m. Judith Lee Weedin, Aug. 5, 1961; children: Stephanie, Renee. BA, San Jose State U., 1963; MS, U. Ariz., 1970, PhD, 1971, MD, 1977. Diplomate Am. Bd. Internal Medicine, Am. Bd. Rheumatology. Chemist Tracerlab, Inc., Richmond, Calif., 1963-67; prof. chemistry Pima Coll., Tucson, 1971-74; intern U. N.Mex., Albuquerque, 1977-78, resident, 1978-80, VA Hosp., Lovelace Med. Ctr., 1978-80; pvt. practice rheumatology and internal medicine, Las Cruces, N.Mex., 1980-88, El Paso, Tex., 1990—. Dir. pain program Rio Vista Rehab. Hosp., 1992; med. dir. Ctr. for Rehab. and Evaluation, 1992—; chief of staff Rio Vista Rehab. Hosp., 1997-99; with Estrella Cons. Group, 1999—; cons. minority biomed. sci. project NIH, Washington, 1970-74, Ednl. Assocs., Tucson, 1971-74; CARF program surveyor, Tucson, 1999—. Author: Llevve Tlaloc No. 2, 1973. Treas. Nat. Chicago Health Orgn., L.A., 1974-75; v.p. Mexican-Am. Educators, Tucson, 1973-74; pres. N.Mex. affiliate Am. Diabetes Assn., Albuquerque, 1983-85. Fellow U. Ariz., 1988-90. Fellow ACP, Am. Coll. Rheumatology; mem. AMA, Am. Diabetes Assn., Am. Assn. Internal Medicine, Tex. Med. Soc., El Paso County Med. Soc., Dona Ana County Med. Soc. (pres. 1983), Alpha Chi Sigma. E-mail: angelarman@aol.com.

ANGEL, ARTHUR RONALD, lawyer, consultant; b. Long Beach, Calif., May 10, 1948; s. Morris and Betty Estelle (Unger) A.; 1 child, Jamie Kathryn. BA, U. Calif.-Berkeley, 1969; JD, Harvard U., 1972. Bar: Mass. 1972, D.C. 1975, Okla. 1979, Calif. 2001, U.S. Dist. Ct. (we. dist.) Okla. 1980, U.S. Dist. Ct. (no. dist.) Okla. 1981, U.S. Dist. Ct. (ctrl. dist.) Calif. 2001, U.S. Supreme Ct. 1983. Atty. FTC, Washington, 1972-78; pvt. practice Oklahoma City, 1978-87; ptnr. Angel & Ikard, Oklahoma City, 1987-93; of counsel Abel, Musser Sokolosky & Assoc., L.A., 1994-2000; ptnr. Carrick Law Group, L.A., 2001—02; atty. Nagler & Assocs., L.A., 2002—. Mem. adv. panel on cardiovascular devices, Washington, 1979-82; cons. FTC, 1978-79; adminstrv. law judge Okla. Dept. Labor, 1999-2000; spl. mcpl. judge City of Oklahoma City, 1999-2001. Recipient Meritorious Service award FTC, Washington, 1978. Fellow: Inst. Law and Social Scis.; mem.: Calif. Bar Assn., Mass. Bar Assn., D.C. Bar Assn., Assn. Trial Lawyers Am., Am. Arbitration Assn. Democrat. Jewish. Home: 1236 N Fairfax Ave Los Angeles CA 90046 Office: Nagler & Assocs 2300 S Sepulveda Blvd Los Angeles CA 90064 E-mail: aangel@nagler.com.

ANGEL, AUBIE, physician, academic administrator; b. Winnipeg, Man., Can., Aug. 28, 1935; s. Benjamin and Minnie (Kaplan) A.; m. Esther-Rose Newhouse; children: Jennifer, Jonathan, Suzanne, Steven, Michael. BSc in Medicine, MD, U. Man., 1959; MSc, McGill U., 1963. Speciality resident in diabetes and endocrinology Montreal Gen. Hosp., 1961-62; postgrad. dept. exptl. medicine McGill U., 1962-63; asst. resident in medicine Royal Victoria Hosp., Montreal, 1963-64; asst. prof. pathology McGill U., Montreal, Que., Can., 1965-68; staff physician Royal Victoria Hosp., Montreal, 1965-68; sr. physician and staff endocrinologist Toronto Gen. Hosp., 1968-90; asst. prof. medicine U. Toronto, Canada, 1968-72, assoc. prof., 1972-81, prof. medicine, 1981-90, dir. Inst. Med. Sci. and clin. scis. divsn., 1983-90; prof., head dept. medicine U. Man., Canada, 1991-95, sr. fellow Ctr. for Advancement ofMedicine, 2002—; physician in chief Health Sci. Ctr., Winnipeg, Man., 1991-95. Vis. scientist U. Calif., San Diego, 1977—78, Hammersmith Hosp., London, 1978; founding pres. Diabetes Rsch. and Treatment Ctr., Winnipeg, 1991—; founding pres., chmn. bd. dirs. Friends of CIHR, 1994—; scholar-in-residence MRC, Canada, 1996; pres. 7th Internat. Congress on Obesity, 1994; co-chair Internat. Conf. Diabetes and Cardiovascular Disease, 1999. Editor (with C.H. Hollenberg and D.A.K. Roncari): (novels) The Adipocyte and Obesity: Cellular and Molecular Mechanisms, 1983; editor: (with J. Frohlich) Lipoprotein Deficiency Syndromes: Advances in Experimental Medicine and Biology, 1986; editor: (with N. Sakamoto and N. Hotta) New Directions in Research and Clinical Works for Obesity and Diabetes Mellitus, 1991; editor: (with H. Anderson, C. Bouchard, D. Lau, L. Leiter, R. Mendels) Progress in Obesity Research, 1996; editor: (with N. Dhalla, G. Grant, P. Singal) Diabetes and Cardiovascular Disease, 2001. Project dir. Can. Internat. Devel. Agy., Toronto and Costa Rica, 1987-94. Recipient Outstanding Svc. award Heart and Stroke Found. Ont., 1985; U. Toronto Med. Rsch. Coun. scholar, 1965-71; Trinity Coll., Toronto, fellow, 1989— Fellow Royal Coll. Physicians and Surgeons Costa Rica (hon.), N.Am. Assn. Study Obesity (pres. 1986-87), Can. Soc. Clin. Investigation (councillor 1977-80), Am. Soc. Clin. Investigation, Can. Inst. Acad. Medicine (founding pres. 1990-92), Internat. Assn. Study Obesity (bd. govs. 1986—), Internat. Acad. Cardiovasc. Scis., Juvenile Diabetes Found. Internat. (hon. bd. dirs. 1987-90), Obesity Canada (founding bd. dirs. 1999-2001). Office: U Man Dept Internal Med 820 Sherbrook St Rm GB-409 Winnipeg MB Canada R3A 1R9 E-mail: aangel@hsc.mb.ca.

ANGEL, CARLOS ALBERTO, pediatric surgeon, urologist; b. Bogota, Colombia, Mar. 16, 1953; came to U.S., 1986; s. Carlos Eduardo and Margarita (De Greiff) A.; m. Claudia Malkun, 1987; children: Santiago, Catalina. BS, Presbyn. Coll., Clinton, S.C., 1974; MD, Univ. del Rosario, Bogota, 1980. Resident in gen. surgery U. del Rosario, Bogota, 1983-86; fellow in pediat. surgery U. Tenn., Memphis, 1986-88, chief fellow pediat. surgery, 1988-89, fellow pediat. urology, 1990-91; fellow in pediat. oncologic surgery St. Jude's Children's Rsch. Hosp., Memphis, 1989-90; pediat. surgeon, pediat. urologist U. T ex. Med. Br., Galveston, Tex., 1993. Contbr. articles to profl. jours., chpts. to books. Active vol. colombian Red Cross Surg. Brigades, Chocó, 1985, Meta, 1986. Mem. Soc. Critical Care Medicine, Soc. for Surgery of the Alimentary Tract, Singleton Surg. Soc., Brit. Assn. Pediat. Surgeons, Internat. Pediat. Endosurgery Group. Democrat. Roman Catholic. Avocations: tennis, jogging, reading, music. Office: Univ of Texas Med Br Rt 0353 301 University Blvd Galveston TX 77555-5302

ANGEL, DENNIS, lawyer; b. Bklyn., Feb. 14, 1947; s. Morris and Rosalyn (Sobiloff) A.; m. Linda Marlene Lobel, May 15, 1977; children: Stephanie Lee, Michele Bari, Rebecca Jo. Diplome d'etudes françaises, U. Rouen, France, 1967; BA, St. Lawrence U., 1968; JD, Washington and Lee U., 1972. Cert. pratique de langue française ler Degre U. Rouen, France, 1967; bar: N.Y. 1972, U.S. Dist. Ct. (so. dist.) N.Y. 1977. Assoc. Johnson & Tannenbaum, N.Y.C., 1972-77; sole practice N.Y.C., 1978—. Contbr. articles to profl. jours. With USAR, 1969-75. Mem. ABA (subcommittee chmn. 1977-82), N.Y. State Bar Assn., Copyright Soc. U.S.A., Phi Alpha Delta. Home: 8 High Point Ln Scarsdale NY 10583-3122 Office: 1075 Central Park Ave Ste 306 Scarsdale NY 10583-3232 E-mail: dangelesq@aol.com.

ANGEL, JACK EASTON, publishing executive; b. Knoxville, Tenn., Aug. 17, 1938; s. George Harold and Rosa Lou (Crowson) A.; m. Dorothy Ann Dullaghan, May 27, 1962; children: Leeann, Laura, Stephen, Scott. B in Mech. Engring., SUNY, N.Y.C., 1960; MBA, NYU, 1963. Engr. Babcock and Wilcox, N.Y.C., 1960-65; pers. mgr. Avon, Rye, N.Y., 1965-67; staff mgr. Avon Products, N.Y.C., 1967-70; various positions Med. Econs. Co., Montvale, N.J., 1970-83, v.p. Oradell, N.J., 1980-82, sr. v.p., 1982-84; pres. Internat. Thomson Tech., Inc., N.Y.C., 1984-85, Patient Care, Darien, Conn., 1985-87; sr. v.p. Med. Econs. Co., 1987-89, exec. v.p., 1989-91; pres. Greenwich (Conn.) Comm., Ltd., 1991—. Cons. Vol. Urban Cons. Group, N.Y.C., 1974-78; mem. adv. bd. Healthcare BusinessWomens Assn.; advisor Assn. of Med. Publs.; bd. dirs. Current Psychiatry, Gold Std. Multimedia, Global Edge. Chmn. com. Nat. Coun. Patient Info. and Edn., Washington, 1982—84; coach Mid-Fairfield Hockey Assn., Darien, 1983; bd. dirs. Nat. Task Force on CME Provider/Industry Collaboration, 1997—. Lt. j.g. USN, 1961—67. Recipient Svc. to Industry award, Med. Advt. Hall of Fame. Mem. Pharm. Advt. Coun. (pres. 1988), Med. Mktg. Assn., Midwest Health Mktg. Assn., Assn. Med. Publs. (pres. 1987), Coalition Healthcare Communications (exec. dir.), Quonochontaug Tennis Club (v.p. bd.). Avocations: gardening, running, tennis, golf. Home: 8 Windsor Ln Cos Cob CT 06807-1816 Office: Greenwich Comm Ltd PO Box 967 Greenwich CT 06836-0967

ANGEL, JAMES JOSEPH, lawyer; b. Racine, Wis., Apr. 1, 1956; s. William J. and Dorothy P. (Potman) A.; m. Catherine Anne Cowan, Oct. 17, 1981; children: Carter Anne, Riley James, Spenser Catherine. BA, W.Va. Wesleyan Coll., 1977; JD, U. Richmond, 1979. Dep. commonwealth atty. City of Lynchburg (Va.) Commonwealth Atty. Office, 1979-84; ptnr. Smith, Angel & Falcone, P.C., Lynchburg, 1984-87; pvt. practice Lynchburg, 1987—. Chmn. Boonsboro-Peakland Neighborhood Assn., Lynchburg, 1990-99. Mem. ATLA, Va. Trial Lawyers Assn., Va. Bar Assn., Va. Coll. Criminal Def. Attys., Lynchburg Bar Assn. (past pres. criminal law sect. 1992). Avocations: golf, whitewater rafting. Office: 725 Church St Lynchburg VA 24504-1417 also: Allied Arts Bldg PO Box 1042 Lynchburg VA 24505-1042 Office Fax: 434-528-1665.

ANGEL, JAMES ROGER PRIOR, astronomer; b. St. Helens, Eng., Feb. 7, 1941; came to U.S., 1967; s. James Lee and Joan (Prior) A.; m. Ellinor M. Goonan, Aug. 21, 1965; children: Jennifer, James. BA, Oxford (Eng.) U., 1963, D.Phil., 1967; MS, Calif. Inst. Tech., 1966. From rsch. assoc. to assoc. prof. physics Columbia U., 1967-74; prof. astronomy U. Ariz., 1975—, prof. optical sci., 1984—, Regents prof., 1990—. Sloan fellow, 1970-74; hon. fellow St. Peter's Coll., Oxford U.; MacArthur fellow, 1996. Fellow Royal Soc., Royal Astron. Soc., Am. Acad. Arts and Scis.; mem. NAS, Am. Astron. Soc. (v.p. 1987-90, Pierce prize 1976). Achievements include research on white dwarf stars, quasars, the search for extra-solar planetary systems, astronomical mirrors, telescopes and their instruments, and adaptive optics. Office: Univ Ariz Steward Obs Tucson AZ 85721-0001

ANGEL, MICHAEL GONZALEZ, cultural organization administrator; b. Seattle, Dec. 21, 1960; s. Jose Vincente Gonzalez and Maria (del Carmen Romero de Villa) A.; m. Leni Alcantara Alonzo, May 1, 1992; 1 child, Catherine Isabella. BS in Bus. Adminstrn. magna cum laude, Creighton U., 1981; MBA, Harvard Bus. Sch., 1983. Project mgr. Harvard Group Devel., Manchester, NH, 1984-85, sales, leasing and mktg. mgr., 1986-87, gen. mgr., 1988-90; export product line mgr. Otto GmbH and Gebr. Otto KG, Cologne, Germany, 1991-92; export sales mgr. Latin Am. Otto Industries, Inc., Charlotte, NC, 1991-95; dir. N.Am. mktg. and sales Hyundai, San Diego, 1995-96; dir. wireless sales and internet applications Digital Sound Corp., Santa Barbara, CA, 1996-97; v.p. internat. bus. devel. and sales Messer/Hoechst AG, L.A., 1998-2000; v.p. technology devel. and investment Verizon Comms., N.Y.C., 2000-01; pres., CEO Nat. Assn. Advancement Hispanic People, 2001—. Mem. Harvard Club (N.Y. and Boston). Republican. Roman Catholic. Office: PO Box 893460 Temecula CA 92589-3460 E-mail: mgangel@adnc.com.

ANGEL, STEVEN, musician; b. Bklyn., Aug. 2, 1953; s. Morris and Rosalyn (Sobiloff) A. Grad. H.S., L.I. Pres. Daystar Records, Santa Monica, Calif., 1991—98. Profl. drummer, 1960—; lectr. The Whole Life Expo, Pasadena, 1992-95, Inst. for the Advanced Studies of Human Sexuality, San Francisco, 1993—; founder Drumming For Your Life Inst., 2002—; creator Rhythm of Connection for elem. schs. in L.A.. Author (music and book) Angels Rejoice, 1976-80; wrote music for tv show Another World, 1987-91; writer, recorder, prodr.: three songs for album Music for Lovers, 1993, album The Erotic God, 1993; editor Unity and Difference Jour., 1994-97; began program on CNN, Drumming For Your Life; featured on KNBC-TV Stop the Violence, KCBS Hometown Heroes, 1998, BBC Radio. Avocations: tennis, hiking, running. Home and Office: Drumming for Your Life Inst 2132 Montana Ave Ste B Santa Monica CA 90403-2017 E-mail: sangel@adelphia.net.

ANGELES, LOUIS DEAN, conductor; b. Virginia, Minn., Jan. 29, 1944; s. Helen (Canelake) P.; m. Kree Ann Lilley, June 5, 1966; children: Justin Dean, Sarah Suzanne, John Taylor. AS, Garden City (Kans.) Community Coll., 1964; MusB in Music Edn., Southwestern Coll., 1967; MS in Music Edn., Ft. Hays State U., 1969. Dir. orch. Hays (Kans.) High Sch., 1967-73, Spartanburg (S.C.) High Sch., 1973-80; condr. orch. Loyola U., New Orleans, 1980—; clinician The Selmer Co., Elkhart, Ind., 1982—. Orch. dir. at music clinics Furman U., Greenville, S.C., 1975, 77, U. Wis., Madison, 1979, U. Ill., Urbana, 1984, U. Ind., Bloomington, 1986, 87, 95 Contbr. articles to Instrumentalist mag. Pres. Collegiate Young Dems., Winfield, Kans., 1966, Hays Arts Council, 1971, S.C. Music Educators Orch., 1975-76. Recipient Good Citizen award Town of Spartanburg, 1980, Lifetime Achievement award Big Easy Awards, New Orleans, 2003; named Outstanding Young Educator Spartanburg Jaycees, 1977, one of Outstanding Young Men in Am. US Jaycees, 1978. Mem. Nat. Sch. Orch. Dirs. Assn., Music Educators Nat. Conf., Am. String Tchrs. Assn., La. Music Educators Assn. Clubs: Lakeshore Country (Metairie, La.). Democrat. Episcopalian. Avocations: traveling, movies. Office: Loyola U 6363 Saint Charles Ave New Orleans LA 70118-6195

ANGELICO, DENNIS MICHAEL, lawyer; b. New Orleans, Dec. 19, 1950; s. John Blase and Gladys (Dehring) A.; B.A., Tulane U., 1974, J.D., 1974. Bar: La. 1974, U.S. Dist. Ct. (ea., mid. and we. dists.) La. 1974, U.S. Supreme Ct. 1983, U.S. Ct. Appeals (5th cir.) 1975. Assoc., then ptnr. Hess & Washofsky, New Orleans, 1974— . Bd. dirs. Dashiki Project Theatre, New Orleans, 1982-85. Mem. ABA, La. Bar Assn. (sec.-treas. labor law sect. 1983, vice chmn. labor law sect. 1984, chmn. labor law sect. 1985), De La Salle Alumni Assn. (rec. sec. 1982), Tulane Alumni Assn. (Fellows Club), Phi Alpha Delta. Democrat. Roman Catholic. Home: PO Box 13945 New Orleans LA 70185-3945

ANGELINE, MICHAEL E. social worker, bereavement facilitator; divorced; 1 child. BA, U. Cin., 1979. Cert. forensic counselor, sports counselor. Case mgr. AIDS Vols. of Cin. Mem. exec. com. Ryan White Consortia, Cin.; chair Cmty. Adv. Bd. Holmes Hosp., Cin.; mem. Sovereign Queen City Ct. of the Buckeye Empire, Cin.; mem. Ohio Drug Adv. Coun. Office: AVOC 2183 Central Pkwy Cincinnati OH 45214

ANGELINI, MARCELLO, artistic director; b. Naples, Italy, Feb. 11, 1962; Grad., Kiev Inst. Dance, 1980-81. Dancer Maggio Musicale Fiorentino, 1979, soloist, 1981; prin. dancer Deutsche Oper Berlin, 1983-84, No. Ballet Theater, Eng., 1984-87, Ballet West, Salt Lake City, 1988-89, Les Grands Ballets Danadiens, Montreal, 1991-94, Cin. Ballet, 1983-95; artistic dir. Tulsa Ballet, 1995—. Guest prin. dancer San Carlo Opera House, Rome Opera House, the Arena of Verona, Italy, Basler Ballet, Switzerland, English Nat. Ballet, Scottish Ballet, Ballet Ariz., Santiago Teatro Mcpl., Chile. Performer (leading roles in classical repertoire including): Giselle, Sleeping Beauty, Romeo and Juliet, Cinderella; choreographer leading role in Death and the Maiden. Recipient Golden Rose award, Internat. Ballet Competition, Rome, 1982, Leonide Massine Positano prize, 1989. Office: Tulsa Ballet 4512 S Peoria Ave Tulsa OK 74105-4563*

ANGELINI, MICHAEL P. insurance company executive; BA, Wesleyan U., 1964; JD, Duke U., 1968. Bar: (Mass.) 1968. With Bowditch & Dewey and predecessor firm Bowditch, Gowetz & Lane, 1968—2002, mng. ptnr., 1990—96, chmn., 1997—, Allmerica Fin. Corp., 2002—. Fellow: Am. Coll. Trial Lawyers; mem.: ABA, Worcester County Bar Found., Worcester County Bar Assn. (pres. 1983—84, bd. dirs.). Office: 440 Lincoln St Worcester MA 01653*

ANGELIS, MICHAEL, surgeon; b. Montreal, Que., Can., Sept. 27, 1965; came to the U.S., 1988; s. Harry and Polixeni (Katravas) A.; m. Julia Laing Gallaudet, June 15, 1991; children: Harrison, Emily. BS, McGill U., Mont., Can., 1987; MD, Jefferson Med. Coll., Phila., 1992. Surg. resident U. Hawaii, Honolulu, 1992-98; transplant fellow U. Miami, Fla., 1998-00; asst. prof. surgery divsn. transplant Tufts U. Sch. Medicine, dir. pancreas transplantation. Contbr. articles to profl. jours. Mem.: ACS (2nd prize essay contest Hawaii chpt. 1990, 1st prize essay contest Hawaii chpt. 1997), Am. Soc. Transplant Surgeons, McGill Alumni Assn., Jefferson Med. Coll. Alumni, Internat. Liver Transplant Soc. Avocation: swimming. Home: 204 Hillcrest Rd Needham MA 02492 Office: New England Med Ctr 750 Washington St NEMC 40 Boston MA 02111

ANGELIS, VICTORIA SARIS, restaurant manager, consultant; b. Wilmington, N.C., Dec. 24, 1952; d. James Nicholas Saris and Ruby Lee Pressley; m. Nick Dimitrios Angelis, Dec. 1, 1974; children: Maria Victoria, Alexandra Rubina, Demetra Nicole. A in Bus. Adminstrn.(hon.), Blanton's Jr. Coll., Asheville, NC, 1987. Lic. Realtor N.C. Mgr., creative cons. Winner's Gourmet Deli, Asheville, 1983—86; owner, concept designer, sr. mgr. Max's Celebrity Deli, Asheville, 1989—94; editor, advisor The Am. Coll. of Greece, Athens, 1993—95; teacher ESL Eleytheria Paidia Sch. Fgn. Langs., Athens, 1993—97; sr. mgr. Mayflower Seafood Restaurant, Raleigh, NC, 1997—98; concept designer, gen. mgr. Bay Breeze Seafood Restaurant, Sanford, NC, 1999—2002, Ocean Stars Seafood Restaurant and Banquets, Apex, NC. Restaurant cons., NC, 1997—. Organizer, chpt. pres. Daus. of Evrytania-Evrytanian Assn. of Am., Asheville; counselor, organizer Greek Orthodox Youth of Am. -Southea. States, Asheville, 1989—92; vol. March of Dimes, Planned Parenthood, Scared Straight Program, Battered Women, Rape Crisis Hotline, soup kitchens, Project Headstart, nursing homes, Martin Luther King March on Washington tent city, 1971—80; organizer Dems. Abroad-Greece, Athens, 1994—97; del.-elect Dem. Nat. Conv., Atlanta, 1986; Buncombe county chairperson Michael Dukakis presdl. campaign, Asheville, 1984—86; tchr., counselor Holy Trinity Greek Orthodox Ch., Asheville, 1982—92. Achievements include discovery of Achievements are not always measured by awards or degrees: compassionate perserverance allows me to hear the heartbeat of others and, there is value in each. Avocations: writing, walking, ancient history, mythology, travel.

ANGELL, ELLEN, interior designer; b. Centralia, Mo., Mar. 16, 1927; d. Robert Loren and Margaret Amanda Jane (Smith) A. Cert., N.Y. Sch. Design, 1946. Interior designer Denver Dry Goods, 1946-49; cons. home furnishings Barker Bros., Los Angeles, 1950-52; interior designer Joske's, Houston, 1952-55, Showroom Finer Furniture, Corpus Christi, Tex., 1955-66, Braslau's, Corpus Christi, 1966-70, Browning Bros., Corpus Christi, 1970—. Lectr. in field. Author: The Layman's Handbook of Interior Design, 1972. Fellow Am. Soc. Interior Designers (long range planning nat. com. 1987-89, nat. bd. dirs. 1984-86, regional v.p., Medalist award 1984, Commendation for Outstanding Service 1986); mem. Am. Inst. Interior Designers (sec., chmn., bd. dirs. Tex. chpt. 1959-75, Outstanding Interior Designer 1974). Democrat. Avocations: meditation, writing. Home: 346 Southern St Corpus Christi TX 78404-1853 Office: Browning Bros 2001 S Staples St Corpus Christi TX 78404-3000

ANGELL, KENNETH ANTHONY, bishop; b. Providence, Aug. 3, 1930; s. Henry L. and Mae T. (Cooney) Angell. AB in Philosophy, St. Mary's Sem., Balt., 1952, STB, 1954; STD (hon.), Our Lady of Providence Sem., 1975; JCD (hon.), Providence Coll., 1975; DHL (hon.), St. Michael's Coll., 1999, Salve Regina, 2000. Ordained priest Roman Cath. Ch., 1956, consecrated bishop Roman Cath. Ch., 1974. Vicar St. Mark Ch., Jamestown, RI, 1956; parochial vicar Sacred Heart Ch., Pawtucket, RI, 1956—60; asst. pastor St. Mary Ch., Newport, RI, 1960—68; asst. chancellor and sec. to bishop Diocese of Providence, 1968—72, chancellor, 1972—74, titular bishop Settimunicia, aux. bishop, 1974—92; pastor St. John Ch., Providence, 1975—81; bishop Diocese of Burlington (Vt.), 1992—. Trustee Wadhams Hall Sem. Coll., 1995—2002, Champlain Coll., 1995—98; v.p. Vt. Ecumenical Coun. & Bible Soc., 1997—99, pres., 1999—2000; bd. dirs. Sr. Thea Bowman Black Cath. Ednl. Fund, 1995—99. Mem.: U.S. Cath. Conf., Nat. Conf. Cath. Bishops. Roman Catholic. Office: Diocese of Burlington PO Box 526 351 North Ave Burlington VT 05402-0526*

ANGELL, LOIS LOUISE, writer, speaker, poet, comedian; b. Riceville, Iowa; d. Kenneth Edwin and Marie E. (Dynes) A.; 1 child, Jim Barrett. Student, Am. U., 1959-60, 62-63, U. Alberta, 1978. Staff dir. Justice Rehnquist U.S. Supreme Ct., 1971-80; pub. rels. dir. Better Comm. Found., Silver Spring, Md., 1984; free lance writer and performer Arlington, Va. Talk and news show guest. Performer at comedy and supper clubs, radio and TV. Recipient Spl. Achievement award U.S Dept. Justice, 1971, Outstanding Svc. to the Arts in Comm. award Capital Hill Arts Workshop, 1984. Mem. NAFE, Washington Ind. Writers, The Capitol Hill Club, Internat. Platform Assn., Capitol Hill Poetry Group (founder), Nat. Conf. Rsch. on Women, Nat. Capitol Spkrs. Assn., Washington Conv. and Visitors Assn., World Affairs Coun., The Cato Inst. Episcopalian. Home: The Georgetown 2512 Q St NW Washington DC 20007 E-mail: owner@termis.com.

ANGELL, M(ARY) FAITH, federal magistrate judge; b. Buffalo, May 7, 1938; d. San S. and Marie B. (Caboni) A.; m. Kenneth F. Carobus, Oct. 27, 1973; children: Andrew M. Carobus, Alexander P. Carobus. AB, Mt. Holyoke Coll., 1959; MSS, Bryn Mawr Coll., 1965; JD, Temple U., 1971. Bar: Pa. 1971, U.S. Dist. Ct. (ea. dist) Pa. 1971, U.S. Ct. Appeals (3rd cir.) Pa. 1974, U.S. Supreme Ct. 1979; Acad. Cert. Social Workers. Dir. social work, vol. svcs. Wills Eye Hosp., Phila., 1961-64, 65-69; dir. soc. work dept. juvenile divsn. Defender Assoc., Phila., 1969-71; asst. dist. atty. City of Phila., 1971-72; asst. atty. gen. Commonwealth of Pa., Phila., 1972-74, deputy atty. gen., 1974-78; regional counsel ICC, Phila., 1978-80, regional dir., 1980-88; adminstrv. law judge Social Security Adminstrn., Phila., 1988-90; U.S. magistrate judge U.S. Dist. Ct. (ea. dist.) Pa., Phila., 1990—. Adj. prof. Temple U. Law Sch., Phila., 1976-94, clin. instr., 1973-76; co-chmn. Commn. on Gender, 3d Cir. Task Force on Equal Treatment in Cts., 1994—; mem. com. on racial and gender bias in the justice sys. Supreme Ct. of Pa., 2000. Federal trustee Defender Assn. Phila., 1985-90; bd. dirs. Child Welfare Adv. Bd., Phila., 1984-90, Federal Cts. 200 Adv. Bd., Phila., 1987-88, Phila. Woman's Network, 1986-88. Recipient Sr. Exec. Svc. award U.S. Govt., 1980. Mem. NASW, FBA (chair exec. com., pres. 1990-92, recognition 1992), Nat. Assn. Women Judges, Fed. Magistrate Judges Assn. (dist. dir. 1994-98), Phila. Bar Assn. (chmn. com. 1976-77), Temple Am. Inn of Cts. (master 1993-98), Third Circuit Task Force on Equal Treatment in

the Courts (co-chair Commn. on Gender 1994-97), Temple Law Alumni Exec. Bd. (Women's Law Caucus Honoree 1996). Office: US District Court 601 Market St 3030 US Courthouse Philadelphia PA 19106

ANGELL, RICHARD BRADSHAW, philosophy educator; b. Scarsdale, N.Y., Oct. 14, 1918; s. Stephen LeRoy and Alice (Angel) A.; m. Imogene Lucille Baker, June 4, 1949; children: John Baker, Paul McLean, James Bigelow, David Bradshaw, Kathryn Elizabeth. BA, Swarthmore Coll., 1940; M in Govt. Adminstrn., U. Pa., 1948; PhD in Philosophy, Harvard U., 1954. Acting asst. prof. Fla. State U., 1949-51; asst. prof. Ohio Wesleyan U., 1954-58, asso. prof., 1958-63, prof., 1963-68; chmn. philosophy dept. Wayne State U., 1968-73, 76-78, prof., 1968-89, prof. emeritus, 1989—. Author: Reasoning and Logic, 1964, A-Logic, 2002. Mem. AAUP, Am. Philos. Assn., ACLU., Mem. Soc. of Friends.

ANGELL, SUSAN L. lawyer; b. San Francisco, Feb. 8, 1955; d. Vincent H. and Margaret A. Angell; m. Larry Kastelic, June 18, 1983 (div. Jan. 1994); children: Danny, Katie, Timmy. BSN, U. San Francisco, 1977; MSN, Calif. State U. Long Beach, 1988; JD, Thomas Jefferson Sch. Law, 1996. cert. RN; Bar: Calif. RN Oakland Children's Hosp., 1977-80; RN, nurse practitioner Children's Hosp. Orange Co., 1982-85; hosp. mgr. FHP Hosp., Fountain Valley, Calif., 1986-88; RN ProCare, Santa Ana, Calif., 1989-95; atty. O'Flaherty, Cross, Martinez, Ovando & Hatton, Anaheim, Calif., 1997-98, Ginsberg, Stephan, Oringher & Richman, Costa Mesa, Calif., 1998—. Mem. Nursing Alumni Assn. (v.p.), Orange Co. Bar Assn., So. Calif. Assn. Health Care Risk Mgrs. Office: 535 Anton Blvd Ste 800 Costa Mesa CA 92626-7110 E-mail: sangwll@gsor.com.

ANGELL, WAYNE D. economist, banker; b. Liberal, Kans., June 28, 1930; s. Charlie Francis and Adele Thelma (Edwards) A.; children: Patrice, Wynne, Ryan, Wiley. BA, Ottawa U., 1952; MA, U. Kans., 1953, PhD, 1957. Instr. econ. U. Kans., Lawrence, 1954-56; prof. econ. Ottawa U., Kans., 1956-85, dean, 1969-72; pres., bd. dir. Hume Bancshares, Inc., Mo., 1972-85; bd. dir. Fed. Res. Bank, Kans. City, Mo., 1979-86, mem. bd. gov., 1986-94; chmn. com. on Fed. Res. Bank activities FRS, Washington, 1986-94; chmn. G-10 Com. on Payment and Settlement Systems, Basle, Switzerland, 1988-94; sr. mng. dir. Bear, Stearns & Co., NYC, 1994—2001; with Angell Econ., Arlington, Va., 2001—. Econ. cons. Rep. Kans. Ho. of Reps., Topeka, 1961-67; vice chmn. Rep. State Legis. Campaign Com., Topeka, 1964; chmn. Rep. Congl. Conv. 3d Dist., Overland Park, Kans., 1964. Mem. Am. Econ. Assn., Phi Beta Kappa. Republican. Baptist. Avocations: pvt. piloting, tennis, cycling. Office: Angell Econs 1600 N Oak St # 1915 Arlington VA 22209-2751 E-mail: wangell@comcast.net.

ANGELO, CHRISTOPHER EDMOND, lawyer, consultant; b. L.A., Dec. 19, 1949; s. Edmond James and Shirley Ann (Richards) A.; m. Patrice Lonnette Brown, Apr. 26, 1980; 1 child, Alexander Bradshaw. BA, U. Calif., Riverside, 1972; JD, Loyola U., 1975. Bar: Calif. 1976, U.S. Dist. Ct. Calif. 1976. Trial atty. Spray, Gould & Bowers, L.A., 1976-78, Harrington, Foxx, Dubrow & Canter, L.A., 1978-83, Gage & Mazursky, Beverly Hills, Calif., 1983-85; trial atty., ptnr. Gage, Mazursky, Schwartz, Angelo & Kussman, Beverly Hills, Calif., 1986-88; trial atty., gen. ptnr. Mazursky, Schwartz & Angelo, L.A., 1988—. Faculty lectr. Calif. Judges Assn., 1989; mem. Loyola Law Sch. Law Review, L.A., 1974-75. Author books and articles in field of tort and ins. bad faith liability. Cons. Bet Tzedak Legal Aid Found., L.A., 1992; counsel Christopher Sampson Non-Profit Found. for Catastrophically Injured, L.A., 1991, dir., founder; trustee U.C.R. Found., Inc., 1998—. Recipient Highlander scholarship U. Calif., 1968-72. Mem. ABA, Italian Am. Lawyers Assn. (bd. govs. 1979-83), Calif. Trial Lawyers Assn. (lectr. 1983—, Cert. of Appreciation), Calif. Bar Assn., Consumer Attys. Assn. L.A. (lectr. 1983—, Cert. of Appreciation), Autism Soc. Am. (mem. adv. bd.). Office: Mazursky Schwartz & Angelo 10990 Wilshire Blvd Ste 1200 Los Angeles CA 90024-3919

ANGELO, E. JOANNE, child, adolescent and adult psychiatrist; b. Boston, Feb. 11, 1936; d. Gaspar and Eda (Polcari) A. AB, Mt. Holyoke Coll., 1957; MD, Tufts U., 1961. Diplomate Am. Bd. Psychiatry and Neurology. Pvt. practice, Boston, 1969—; med. dir. Canarsie Mental Health Ctr., Bklyn., 1967—69; staff psychiatrist Cmty. Mental Health Svc. Ctr., Boston, 1969—73; psychiat. dir. Laboure Ctr., South Boston, Mass., 1974—78. Cons. Chandler Sch. for Women, Boston, 1971-72, Kennedy Meml. Hosp., Boston, 1971-74, St. Margaret's Hosp., Boston, 1976-83, North Suffolk Health Ctr., Boston, 1978-79; mem. staff St. Elizabeth's Hosp., Boston, Good Samaritan Hospice Boston. Mem. editl. bd. (Jour.) Nat. Cath. Bioethics Quar. Mem. Pontifical Acad. for Life (corr.). Office: 403 Commonwealth Ave Boston MA 02215-2326

ANGELO, GEORGE, pediatric sales representative, lawyer; b. L.A. s. Gilbert Dorie and Sara Arroyo G. BA, Whittier Coll., 1980; JD, Trinity Law Sch., Orange County, Calf., 1990; cert. participation internat. human rights, U Strasbourg, Strasbourg, France, 1994; cert. of Bibl. Studies, Talbot Sch. Theology, LaMirada, Calf., 2002. Pediatric sales rep. Ross Products divsn., Abbott Labs., Columbus, Ohio, 1983—. Pres. Friends of the Persecuted Ch., Downey, Calif., 1998—; intern, vol. Moscow Rsch. Ctr. Human Rights, 1995. Mem. Amnesty Internat., Toastmasters (area gov. 1999-2000). Avocation: writing. E-mail: g.angelo@worldnet.att.net.

ANGELO, JIM, construction company executive; b. Detroit, June 23, 1956; s. Richard James and Edith Marlene (Schaefflin) A.; m. Brenda Angelo Wood, Sept. 15, 1985; 1 child, Nathan Miller. BS, Ctrl. Mich. U., 1978; AAS in Bldg. Constrn. Tech., Ferris State U., Big Rapids, Mich., 1982. Lic. home builder, Mich. Laborer, then carpenter Vail (Colo.) Valley Constrn., 1978-80; home builder, Canadien Lakes, Mich., 1980-82; supt. Sikes Constrn., Denver, 1982-85; project mgr. Bronco Constrn., Denver, 1985-87, Ashwood Homes, Hampstead, N.H., 1987-90; constrn. mgr. Lincoln Labs., Lexington, Mass., 1990-95; project mgr. Elzinga and Volkers Constrn., Holland, Mich., 1995-96, Triangle Assocs., Inc., Grand Rapids, Mich., 1997 2002, sr. project mgr., 1998—2002, project mgr. Skanksa USA, Kalamazoo, 2002—. Author: My Thoughts, 1978 Chmn. Hwy. Bldg. Com., Hampstead, 1988; cons. Hampstead Bd. Edn., 1990-95, Hampstead Bd. Selectmen, 1990-95; officer Hampstead Civic Club, 1991; chmn. Hampstead Libr. Bldg. Com., 1992; chmn. Nat. Youth Sports Coaches Assn., Hampstead, 1993-95, Hampstead Capital Needs Com., 1994-95; clk. of works Hampstead Pub. Works Projects, 1994. Mem. Am. Inst. Constructors (cert. profl. constructor), Assoc. Builders and Contractors (polit. action com. 1999-2001), NRA, Theta Chi. Republican. Avocations: hunting, fishing, golf, snow skiing, fly tieing. Office: Skanska USA 6376 Quail Run Dr Kalamazoo MI 49009-9451 Fax: 269-342-5799. E-mail: jimangelo165@msn.com.

ANGELO, LARIAN, economist; b. N.Y.C., Oct. 9, 1953; d. Lawrence and Jeanette Angelo. BA, Bklyn. Coll., 1975; PhD, New Sch. for Social Rsch., 1990. Rsch. dir. United Elec. Radio Workers, Pitts., 1986-90; chief economist N.Y. City Coun./Fin., N.Y.C., 1990-94, spl. advisor, 1994-99, dep. dir., 1999-2001, dir. coun. fin. divsn., 2002—; cons. on urban issues City of Amsterdam, The Netherlands, 2000—. Lectr. John Jay Coll., N.Y.C., 1991-95, Queens Coll., N.Y.C., 1996-99; cons. urban issues City of Amsterdam, 2000. Contbr. articles to profl. jours. Chmn. bd. Pub. Access TV Sta., N.Y.C., 1999. Mem. Gay and Lesbian Ind. Dems. Democrat. Roman Catholic. Avocations: fencing, opera, reading club. Office: NY City Coun Fin Divsn 250 Broadway New York NY 10007-2516 E-mail: finangel@council.nyc.ny.us.

ANGELOFF, DANN VALENTINO, investment banking executive; b. Hollywood, Calif., Nov. 15, 1935; m. Jo Jeanne Ahlstrom, Sept. 26, 1964; children: Jennifer J., Dann V., Julie A. BS in Fin., U. So. Calif., 1958, MBA, 1963. Trainee Dean Witter & Co., Inc., L.A., 1957-60; v.p. Dempsey-Tegeler & Co., Inc., L.A., 1960-70; mng. dir. West Coast corp. fin. dept. Reynolds Securities, Inc., L.A., 1970-76; pres., bd. dirs. The Angeloff Co., L.A., 1976—. Bd. dirs. Softbrands Inc., Mpls., Ready Pac Produce, Irwin Dale, Calif., Pub. Storage, Glendale, Calif., Nicholas-Applegate Fund, San Diego, Retirement Capital Corp., San Diego; chmn. bd. Marshall Assocs./Univ. So. Calif. Trustee U. So. Calif., 1979-86, univ. counselor; bd. dirs., chmn. Trojan Bd. Govs., 1990-92. Mem. Bond Club L.A., Commerce Assocs. U. So. Calif., Skull and Dagger, Cardinal and Gold, Calif. Club, Pacific Club, Valley Hunt Club, San Marino City Club, Kappa Beta Phi. Office: The Angeloff Co 727 W 7th St Los Angeles CA 90017-3707

ANGELOS, PETER G. professional sports team executive, lawyer; b. Pitts., July 4, 1929; LLB, U. Balt. Bar: Md. 1961, D.C. 1974, Tenn. 1990, U.S. Dist. Ct. Md. 1964, U.S. Supreme Ct. 1974, U.S. Tax Ct. 1975, U.S. Ct. Appeals 1990. Pvt. practice atty., Balt., 1961—; mng. ptnr. Baltimore Orioles, 1993—; chmn., CEO Balt. Orioles, 1993—. Mem. Balt. City Coun., 1959—63; trustee Loyola Coll., Md. Mem.: Bar Assn. Balt. City, Tenn. Bar Assn., Md. Trial Lawyers Assn., Md. Trial Lawyers Assn., N.Y. State Trial Lawyers Assn., Criminal Def. Lawyers Assn., Assn. Trial Lawyers Am., Am. Judicature Soc. Office: 100 N Charles St # 22D Baltimore MD 21201-3805 also: Baltimore Orioles 333 W Camden St Baltimore MD 21201-2435

ANGELOU, MAYA, writer; b. St. Louis, Missouri, Apr. 4, 1928; d. Bailey and Vivian (Baxter) Johnson; 1 son, Guy Johnson. Studied dance with, Pearl Primus, N.Y.C.; hon. degrees, Smith Coll., 1975, Mills Coll., 1975, Lawrence U., 1976. Taught modern dance The Rome Opera House and Hambina Theatre, Tel Aviv; writer-in-residence U. Kans.-Lawrence, 1970; disting. vis. prof. Wake Forest U., 1974, Wichita State U., 1974, Calif. State U.-Sacramento, 1974; apptd. mem. Am. Revolution Bicentennial Council by Pres. Ford, 1975-76; 1st Reynolds prof. Am. Studies, Wake Forest U. since 1981, a lifetime appointment. Author: I Know Why the Caged Bird Sings, 1970, Just Give Me A Cool Drink of Water 'Fore I Diiie (nominated for Pulitzer Prize), 1971, Georgia, Georgia, 1972, Gather Together in My Name, 1974, Oh Pray My Wings are Gonna Fit Me Well, 1975, Singin' and Swingin' and Gettin' Merry Like Christmas, 1976, And Still I Rise, 1978, The Heart of a Woman, 1981, Shaker, Why Don't You Sing?, 1983, All God's Children Need Traveling Shoes, 1986, Now Sheba Sings the Song, 1987, I Shall Not Be Moved, 1990, On the Pulse of Morning: The Inaugural Poem, 1992, Lessons in Living, 1993, Wouldn't Take Nothing for My Journey Now, 1993, My Painted House, My Friendly Chicken, and Me, 1994, The Complete Collected Poems of Maya Angelou, 1994, Phenomenal Women: Four Poems for Women, 1995, A Brave and Startling Truth, 1995, From a Black Women to a Black Man, 1996, Kofi and His Magic, 1996, Extravagant Spirits, 1997, Making Magic in the World, 1998; prodr.: Moon on a Rainbow Shawl, 1988 (by Errol John); appeared on TV in The Richard Pryor Special, guest appearances Sister, Sisters, 1982, Touched By An Angel, 1995, Moesha, 1999, Runaway, 2000; author/prodr. Three Way Choice, Afro-American in the Arts (Golden Eagle award), in ltd. series Roots; appeared in revue Cabaret for Freedom and The Blacks (Obie award) with Godfrey Cambridge; adatped Ajax for Mark Taper Forum in L.A.; librettist, lyricist and composer: And Still I Rise, 1976; wrote and presented Trying to Make it Home, 1988; writer for Oprah Winfrey's Harpo Prodns.; poetry writer for film Poetic Justice, 1993; appeared in plays: Porgy and Bess, 1954-55 (Europe), 1957 (U.S.), Calypso, 1957, The Blacks, 1960, Mother Courage, 1964, Medea, Look Away, 1973, Ajax, 1974, And Still I Rise, 1976, Moon on a Rainbow Shawl, 1988; films: Roots (Emmy Nomination Best Supporting Actress), 1977, How to Make an American Quilt, 1995; spoken word albums include The Poetry of Maya Angelou, 1969, Women in Business, 1981, Been Found, 1996; contr. short stories and poems to mags.; also numerous appearances on network and local talk shows; articles, short stories, poems to Black Scholar, Chgo. Daily News, Cosmopolitan, Harper's Bazaar, Life Mag., Redbook, Sunday N.Y. Times, Mademoiselle Mag., Essence, Ebony Mag., Calif. Living Mag, Ghanaian Times. Mem. adv. bd. Women's Prison Assn.; apptd. by Dr. Martin Luther King Jr. No. Coord. Southern Christian Leadership Conf., 1959-60, apptd. by Pres. Ford to Bicentennal Commn., by Pres. Carter to Nat. Commn. on Observance of Internat. Women's Yr. Chubb fellowship award Yale U., 1970, named Woman of Yr. in Comm., 1976; Ladies Home Jour. Top 100 Most Influential Women, 1983, The Matric award, 1983, The North Carolina Award in Lit., 1987; named 1st Reynolds prof. Wake Forest U., 1981, a lifetime appointment, Woman of the Yr. Essence Mag., 1992, Disting. Woman of N.C., 1992, Horatio Alger award, 1992, Grammy award Best Spoken Word or Non-Traditional Album, 1994 (for recording of "On the Pulse of the Morning"), Grammy award Best Spoken or Non-Traditional Album, 1994 (for recording of "Phenomonal Woman"), NAACP Image Award for Outstanding Literary Work for "Even the Stars Look Lonesome", 1997, National Medal of Art, 2000. Mem. AFTRA, Dirs. Guild Am., Equity, Harlem Writers Guild, Am. Film Inst. (trustee), Women's Prison Assn., Horatio Alger Assn. Dist. Americans, Nat. Soc. Prevention of Cruelty to Children (Maya Angelou Ctr. opened 1992), ambassador, Unicef Internat., 1996. Office: care Dave La Camera Lordly and Dame Inc 51 Church St Boston MA 02116-5417

ANGELOV, GEORGE ANGEL, pediatrician, anatomist, teratologist; b. Bulgaria, May 12, 1925; came to U.S., 1978; s. Angel Christov and Maria Angelov; m. Olga Valerie Minkova, Dec. 21, 1952; 1 child, Angel. MD, Sch. of Medicine, Sofia, Bulgaria, 1952. Pediatrician Distric Hosp., Bulgaria, 1952-53; asst. prof. Sch. of Medicine, Sofia, Bulgaria, 1953-64; prof. anatomy and anthropology Sch. of Biology, Sofia, Bulgaria, 1964-77; mgr. reproductive toxicology Lederle Labs., Pearl River, N.Y., 1979-89; cons. reproductive toxicology pvt. practice, Laguna Niguel, Calif., 1989—. Assoc. dean Sch. of Biology, Sofia, 1970-72; vis. scientist Sch. of Medicine, Geneva, 1971, 74. Author: (textbook) Anatomy, 1970; mem. glossary com. Teratology Glossary, 1987-89; reviewer several sci. jours.; contbr. numerous sci. publs. on anatomy, teratology, and growth and devel. of adolescents to profl. jours. Mem. Teratology Soc. USA, European Teratology Soc., Human Biology Coun. USA, Free Union of Univ. Profs. of Anatomy. East Orthodox. Avocations: bridge, chess, 20th century history.

ANGERMEIER, PATRICIA, occupational therapist; b. Phila., July 29, 1952; d. Leo and Patricia McCarthy; m. John Angermeier, Nov. 30, 1974; children: Michael, Matthew. BS in Occupl. Therapy, Temple U., 1976. Cert. sensory integration, neurodevel. treatment Neurodevel. Assn. Staff occupl. therapist Temple U. Hosp., Phila., 1977—80; occupl. therapy cons. Bapt. Home, Phila., 1980—85; sch. occupl. therapist So. N.J. Coun. for Edn., Marlton, NJ, 1985—92; occupl. therapy dir. Children in Motion, Medford, NJ, 1992—97; owner, dir. Functionally Able Rehab., Inc., Shamong, NJ, 1996—. Continuing edn. presenter, Shamong, 1993—2002; presenter in field. Author: Learning in Motion. Organizer for football program Shawnee H.S., Medford, 1998, 1999. Mem.: N.J. Occupl. Therapy Assn. (presenter 1998), Am. Occupl. Therapy Assn. (OTR, bd. cert. pediat.).

ANGERMÜLLER, RUDOLPH, music foundation executive; b. Gadderbaum/Bielefeld, Westphalia, Germany, Sept. 2, 1940; Grad. in piano, contrabass, music theory, Forsterling Conservatory Music; MA in Romance langs. and History, U. Münster, Germany, 1967; PhD, Salzburg U., Austria, 1970. Asst. instr. Musicological Inst., Salzburg (Austria) U., 1967-72, lectr., 1968-75; dir. musicology dept. Internationale Stiftung Mozarteum, Salzburg, 1982-88, sec.-gen., 1988—. Author: Sigismund Neukomm, 1977, Mozart und seine Pariser Umwelt - 1778, 1978, Figaro, 1986, Don Juan Register, 1987, Mozart: Die Opern von der Uraufführung bis heute, 1988, Vom Kaiser zum Sklaven: Personen in Mozarts Opern, 1989, Ich johannes Chrisostomus Amadeus Wolfgangus sigismundus Mozart: Eine Autobiografie, 1991, Delitiae Italiae: Mozarts Reisen in Italien, 1994, W. A. Mozart, Reisetagebuch 1819-1821, 1994, Mozart auf der Reise nach Prag, Dresden, Leipzig und Berlin, 1995, Antonio Saleiri, Die Dokumente Seines Lebens, 3 vols., 2000; contbr. articles to profl. jours., numerous programme notes; designer countless exhbns. Decorated Disting. Svc. Cross for Sci. and Art (Austria); Paul Harris fellow Rotary Internat.; recipient Mozart prize Province of Lower Austria, Mozart medallion Mozart Soc. of Vienna, Silver medallion of honor Salzburg Province, Silver Mozart medallion Internationale Stiftlung Mozarteum. Office: Internat Stiftung Mozarteum Schwarzstrasse 26 5020 Salzburg Austria E-mail: rudolph@angermueller.at.

ANGERS, WINSTON THOMAS, lawyer; b. Franklin, La., June 21, 1952; s. Robert John Angers, Jr. and Geraldine Beaulieu Angers; 1 child, Austen John. BA in Polit. Sci. cum laude, U. La., 1974; JD, La. State U., 1976. Bar: La. 1977. Rsch. asst. Inst. for Civil Law Studies La. State U. Law Ctr., Baton Rouge, 1975—76; law clk. 15th Jud. Dist. Ct., New Iberia, La., 1976—77; pvt. practice Lafayette, La., 1977—; pres. Beau Bayou Pub. Co., Lafayette, 1985—. Author: Cajun Cuisine, 1986; editor: History of the Louisiana Society of the Sons of the American Revolution, 1997; contbr. articles to mags. Bd. mem. Coun. for the Devel. of French in La.; past chmn. Bd. Zoning Adjustments City of Lafayette; pres. Acadiana Arts Coun., Lafayette, 1990—91; co-founder Citizens of South Lafayette; pres. Attakapas chpt. SAR, 1994; pres. Acadian Civitan Club, Lafayette, 1997—98; alt. del. Rep. Nat. Conv., Dallas, 1984, del. Houston, 1992; past chmn. by laws com. La. Rep. State Ctrl. Com.; chmn. Lafayette Parish Rep. Exec. Com., 1995—96; past chmn. Lafayette Parish Rep. Polit. Action Coun.; del.-attendee Young Rep. Nat. Fedn. Conv., 1971; del. numerous state convs. La. Rep. Party; chair U. La. at Lafayette Coll. Reps., 1971—72. Recipient Bronze Good Citizenship medal, Attakapas Chpt. SAR, 1992, Oak Leaf Cluster, 1993, Meritorious Svc. medal, 1994, Oak Leaf Cluster, 1995, Oak Leaf Cluster for Meritorious Svc. medal, La. Soc. SAR, 1996. Mem.: ABA, Civitan Internat., Rotary Internat., Phi Eta Sigma, Phi Delta Phi. Republican. Avocation: collecting rare documents and political memorabilia. Home: 116 Teche Dr Lafayette LA 70503 Office: 1126 Coolidge St Lafayette LA 70503

ANGEVINE, ROGER LEE, mathematician, educator; b. Columbus, Ohio, July 21, 1946; s. Ruth Sannan and Thomas Walls Angevine; m. Janice Sue Prather. B Math. and Physics, Western Ky. U., 1968; M in Math., U. Ill., 1974. Instr. math. Bates Coll., Lewiston, Maine, 1974—76; asst. and assoc. prof. Houston Bapt. U., 1976—91; assoc. prof., prof. of math. Somerset C.C., Ky., 1991—. Dir. acad. computing Houston Bapt. U., 1985—91; sacs steering com. chair Somerset C.C., 1999—2003, divsn. chair math. and phys. sciences, 1996—2002, divsn. chair math. and computer sci., 2002—, Perkins grant coord. Fellow, Woodrow Wilson Nat. Fellowship Found., 1968—69. Mem.: Am. Math. Assn. Two Yr. Colleges, Assn. Computing Machinery, Ky. Math. Assn. Two Yr. Colleges, Math. Assn. Am., Alpha Phi Omega (pres. 1967—68), Sigma Pi Sigma (hon.). Avocations: travel, birdwatching, hiking, fishing. Office: Somerset CC 808 Monticello St Somerset KY 42501 E-mail: roger.angevine@kctcs.edu.

ANGHELESCU, DORALINA LUCIA, anesthesiologist; b. Bucharest, Romania, Aug. 1, 1961; d. Liviu Veneriu and Aurelia Niculina (Arseni) Gontea; m. Mircea Vladimir Anghelescu, June 6, 1987 (div. July 1991); 1 child, Andrei. MD, Bucharest Sch. Medicine, 1985. Intern Elias Found. Hosp., Bucharest, 1985—87; staff physician in anesthesiology Inst. Endocrinology, Bucharest, 1987—93; resident in anesthesiology U. N.Mex., Albuquerque, 1993—97, fellow in pain mgmt., 1998—99; fellow in pediat. anesthesia Childrens Nat. Med. Ctr., Washington, 1997—98; pediat. anesthesiologist, dir. pain mgmt. svc. St. Jude Children's Rsch. Hosp., Memphis, 1999—. Co-author: The Pain Clinic Manual, 2d edit., 2000; contbr. articles to profl. jours. Grantee, Jenssen Found., 2001. Mem.: Internat. Assn. for the Study Pain, Am. Acad. Pain, Soc. Pediat. Anesthesia, Am. Soc. Anesthesiologists. Office: St Jude Childrens Rsch Hosp 332 N Lauderdale St Memphis TN 38105

ANGIE, JILL ELIZABETH, quality assurance professional; b. Rochester, NY, Nov. 11, 1967; d. Charles John and Mildred Ansell Angie. BS in Chemistry, Clarkson U., 1989, MS in Chemistry, 1992; MS in Quality Assurance and Regulatory Affairs, Temple U., 1998. Chemist Rochester (NY) Gas and Electric, 1989; tchg. asst. Clarkson U., Potsdam, NY, 1989—91; chemist Atlantic Testing Labs., Canton, NY, 1991—92, quality assurance/quality control supr., 1992—94; quality assurance specialist Lancaster (Pa.) Labs., 1994—2000, sr. chemist, 2000, sr. date rev. specialist, coord., 2000—01; stability coord. Immune Response Corp., King of Prussia, Pa., 2001—02, quality control mgr., 2002—. Office: Immune Response Corp 680 Allendale Rd King Of Prussia PA 19406

ANGIER, CAROL C. volunteer; b. Summit, N.J., June 28, 1933; d. Elmer Douglas and Lauretta (Stagg) Chattin; m. Edward Herbert Angier, June 2, 1956; children: Wendi Paterno, Kenneth, Bruce. BA in Polit. Sci., Duke U., 1955. With CIA, Washington, 1955—56; survey mgr. Arbitron, Beltsville, Md., 1970—74; real estate sales Merrill Lynch, Crofton, Md., 1974—88. Vol., Palm Harbor Libr., 1988—; vol. dir. Clothing Depot, Presbyn. Ch. of Palm Harbor, 1994—; horticulture chair Palm Harbor Garden Club, 1996-2001; alto Presbyn. Ch. of Palm Harbor Choir, 1992—; vol. Tampa Bay Harvest, 1996-2002. Named Woman of Yr., Palm Harbor Jr. Women's Club, 1996, Vol. of Month, Palm Harbor Libr., 1999. Republican. Avocations: gardening, travel, reading. Home: 3254 Pine Forest Dr Palm Harbor FL 34684-1853

ANGIER, JOSEPH, television producer, writer; b. LA, Sept. 10, 1953; s. Keith and Adele (Rosenthal) A. BA, SUNY, Binghamton. Prodr. HBO Am. Undercover, 1986-87, PBS-KCET, 1988-93, ABC News Turning Point, 1994-97, The Great War (PBS/BBC), 1996, Vital Signs, 1997, A&E Biography, 1998, Fox Files, 1998, ABC News 20/20, 1999-2000; prodr. NBC spl. Father's Day--Now and Forever, 2001; prodr. Channel One News, 2003, Calif. Connected; writer/prodr. Becoming American, PBS, 2003. Author: Hollywood Remembers the Blacklist, 1997. Recipient Writers Guild Am. award, 1989, 91, Cine Golden Eagles. Mem. Writers Guild Am. (Best Documentary Script 1989, 91), Acad. TV Arts and Scis. (Emmy for best documentary script 1984), Am. Film Inst. Home: 2268 28th St Apt 6 Santa Monica CA 90405-1947 Office: PO Box 377 Santa Monica CA 90406-0377

ANGINO, ERNEST EDWARD, retired geology and engineering educator; b. Winsted, Conn., Feb. 16, 1932; s. Alfred and Filomena Mabel (Serluco) A.; m. Margaret Mary Lachat, June 26, 1954; children— Cheryl Ann, Kimberly Ann. BS in Mining Engring., Lehigh U., Bethlehem, Pa., 1954; MS in Geology, U. Kans., 1958, PhD in Geology, 1961. Instr. geology U. Kans., Lawrence, 1961-62, prof. civil engring., 1971-99, prof. geology, 1972-99, prof. emeritus, 1999—, chmn. dept. geology, 1972-86, dir. water resources ctr., 1990-99; asst. prof. Tex. A&M U., College Station, 1962-65; chief geochemist Kans. Geol. Survey, Lawrence, 1965-70, assoc. state geologist, 1970-72. Cons. on water chemistry and pollution to various cos. and govt. agys. including Dow Chem. Co., Ocean Mining Inc., Envicon, Oak Ridge Lab., Fisheries Research Bd. Can., Midwest Research Inst., Coast and Geodetic Survey, U.S. Geol. Survey Author: (with G.K. Billings) Atomic Absorption Spectrometry in Geology, 1967; author, editor: (with D.T. Long) Geochemistry of Bismuth, 1979; editor: (with R.K. Hardy) Proc. 3d Forum Geol. Industrial Minerals, 1967, (with G.K. Billings) Geochemistry Subsurface Brines, 1969; contbr. more than 125 articles to sci. and profl. jours. Mem. Lawrence City Police Rels. Commn., 1970-76, Lawrence City Commn., 1983-87, mayor, 1984-85; mem. Lawrence 2020 Planning Commn., 1992-94, Police Adv. Coun., 1994—, Crimestoppers Bd., 1994-2003, Lawrence Tax Abatement Commn., 2001-02, Lawrence-Douglas County Planning Commn. 2002—, Health Care Access Bd., 1997-2002. With U.S. Army, 1955-57. NSF fellow Oak Ridge Lab., 1963; recipient Antarctic Service medal Dept. Def., 1969; Angino Buttress in Antarctica named in his honor, 1967 Mem. Geochem. Soc. (sec. 1970-76), Soc. Environ. Geochemistry and Health (pres. 1978-79), Internat. Assn. Geochemistry and Cosmochemistry (treas. 1980-94), Am. Polar Soc., Am. Philatelist Soc., Am. Soc. Polar Philatelists, Meter Stamp Soc., Forum Club (Factotum 1978-79), Rotary (pres. 1993-95). Republican. Roman Catholic. Avocations: philately, Western history, Indian lore. Home: 4605 Grove Dr Lawrence KS 66049-3777 Office: U Kans Dept Geology Lindley 120 Lawrence KS 66045-0001 E-mail: rockdoc@sunflower.com. *Knowledge is what really counts. The world does not owe anyone anything!.*

ANGIOLILLO, PAUL F. retired language educator; b. N.Y.C., July 1, 1917; s. Joseph S. and Diletta (Priore) Angiolillo; m. Birgitta J. Brunskog, Feb. 29, 1948; children: Carl J., Paul F. Jr., Joel S., Dea F. AB, Columbia U., 1938, MA, 1939, PhD, 1946. Tchr. secondary schs., NY, 1939—46; prof. Am. studies Internat. Sch. of Geneva, 1947—48; prof. French and Italian U. Louisville, 1948—62; prof., chmn. modern langs. Dickinson Coll., Carlisle, Pa., 1962—81, emeritus prof., 1981—. Vis. prof. French Tchrs. Coll., Columbia U., N.Y.C., 1949, 50, 51, 52; vis. prof. French and English Am. Coll. of Switzerland, Leysin, 1976—77. Author: Armed Forces Foreign Language Teaching, 1947, Criminal as Hero, 1979; contbr. articles to profl. jours. Decorated Officier d'Académie French Govt., Officier des Palmes Acads. Avocations: cooking, gardening, reading. Home: 206 Waltham St West Newton MA 02465 E-mail: angiolillo3@msn.com.

ANGIONE, HOWARD FRANCIS, lawyer, editor; b. N.Y.C., Aug. 3, 1940; s. Charles Francis Angione and Genevieve Rita (McCarthy) A.; m. Maryann Allgaier, June 24, 1971; children: Charles Francis, Mary Christine, Kathleen Elizabeth. BA in History, Holy Cross Coll., 1962; MA in Internat. Relations, Clark U., 1966; JD cum laude, St. John's U., Jamaica, N.Y., 1989. Bar: Conn. 1989, N.Y. 1990, D.C. 1991. Reporter, sci. writer Worcester Telegram, Mass.,

1961-65; writer, day editor, sci. writer AP, Boston, 1965-69, editor, shift supr. Gen. Desk N.Y.C., 1969-77; tech. editor N.Y. Times, 1977-87; assoc. Weil, Gotshal & Manges, N.Y.C., 1989-93; pvt. practice, 1997—. Pub. N.Y. Region Lawyers Coop. Practice Guides, 1993-96; editor AP Stylebook, 1977; editor-in-chief N.Y. State Bar Jour., 1998—. Sec. Class of 1962 Holy Cross Coll., 1966-80. Mem. Harris Users Group (pres. 1980-84) Roman Catholic. Home and Office: 80-47 192d St Jamaica NY 11423-1042 E-mail: angione@nyelderlaw.com.

ANGLE, JOHN CHARLES, retired life insurance company executive; b. N.Y.C., Aug. 22, 1923; s. Everett Edward and Catharine Elizabeth (Dodge) A.; m. Catherine Anne Sellers, Oct. 4, 1945; children: Margaret Susan, James Sellers. SB, U. Chgo., 1944. With Union Nat. Life Ins. Co., Lincoln, Nebr., 1948-51; v.p., actuary Woodmen Accident and Life Co., Lincoln, 1953-73, dir., 1969-73; sr. v.p., chief actuary Guardian Life Ins. Co. Am., N.Y.C., 1973-77, exec. v.p., 1977-80, pres., 1980-84, chmn. bd., chief exec. officer, 1985-88, also bd. dirs.; pres. Probe, Inc. (ins. newsletter), 1990-97. Adv. dir. Guardian Life Ins. Co., 1999-2000. Consulting editor: Life and Health Insurance Handbook, 2d edit., 1964. Pres. Lincoln Community Chest, 1965, Lincoln Community Coun., 1966-68, 14th St. -Union Sq. Bus. Improvement Dist., 1985-88, Nebr. Art Assn., 1992-94; trustee Am. Coll., 1987-92; bd. dirs. Lincoln Gen. Hosp., 1970-73, Nebr. Traisl Found., 1995—; bd. visitors U. Nebr., Lincoln, 1994-98. 1st lt. USAF, 1943-46, capt., 1951-52. Fellow Soc. Actuaries (dir. publs. 1975-79, bd. govs. 1980-83, 84-87); mem. Am. Acad. Actuaries (bd. dirs. 1977-79), Internat. Actuarial Assn. (v.p. U.S. sect., 1984-88), Health Ins. Assn. Am. (bd. dirs. 1985-88), Life Office Mgmt. Assn. (bd. dirs. 1983-89, chmn. 1987), Am. Coun. Life Ins. (bd. dirs. 1986-88), Life Ins. Coun. N.Y. (bd. dirs. 1985-88), Lincoln Country Club. Home: 3800 S 42nd St Lincoln NE 68506-4209 E-mail: jangle@alltel.net.

ANGLEMAN, SHARON ANN, journalist; b. Houston, Apr. 14, 1961; d. Hildred Bruce Lockhart and Elizabeth Ann Davis; children: Justin Angleman, Thomas Angleman, Robert Angleman. BS in Journalism magna cum laude, Ark. State U., Jonesboro, 1998. Freelance journalist NobleInk Co., Jonesboro, 1997—. Chair diversity SPJ, Jonesboro, 1997-98. Author numerous poems; photo editor Herald, 1997-98; contbr. articles to profl. jours. Recipient Udell Smith award Nat. Assn. Retired Employees, 1995, Roy Howard award Housing and Devel., 1996, 97, award Ark. Assn. Press, 1996, 97, 98. Mem. Ark. Press Photographer's Assn., Photographic Soc. (pres. 1998, Outstanding Sr. 1997), Bus. Profl. Women (Scholarship award 1997). Home: 111 Woodside Ln Rogers AR 72756-0711 Office: 111 Woodside Ln Rogers AR 72756-0711 E-mail: sharon@jrily.com.

ANGLIN, LINDA MCCLUNEY, retired elementary school educator; b. Turrell, Ark., Apr. 20, 1929; d. Denton Sims and Helen Louise (Davis) McCluney; m. Joe Van Anglin, Aug. 30, 1952; children: Van, Cheryl, Dent, George. BA magna cum laude, Millsaps Coll., 1951; MEd, Miss. Coll., 1970; Edn. Specialist, Miss. State U., 1974. Cert. tchr., Miss. Tchr. St. Andrew's Episcopal. Sch., Jackson, Miss., 1952-53, Carthage Elem. Sch., 1956-57, Jackson Pub. Schs., 1957-94. Founder Miss. Profl. Educators, 1979, pres., 1979-82; dir. Pub. Edn. Forum Miss., Jackson, 1989-93; classroom cons. Scholastic Tchr.; bd. dirs. 1st Am. Bank, Jackson. Lobbyist for edn. and children's issues State of Miss., 1980—; charter mem. Jackson Assn. for Children with Learning Disabilities, bd. dirs., historian, mem. adv. bd. Miss. chpt.; active many civic groups. Recipient Book of Golden Deeds award Exch. Club North Jackson, 1989, Disting. Tchr. award White House Commn. Presdl. Scholars, 1996. Mem. Jackson Profl. Educators (pres. 1988-90), Jackson Area Reading Coun. (pres. 1975-76, Outstanding Svc. award 1987), Miss. Hist. Soc. (bd. dirs. 1998-2000), Jackson-Hinds Ret. Tchrs. Assn., Miss. Ret. Tchrs. Assn., Sigma Lambda, Kappa Delta Pi, Phi Kappa Phi, Delta Kappa Gamma (workshop presenter 1985, pres. Tau chpt. 1986-88, Woman of Distinction 1990, Disting. Svc. to Edn. award 1984). Methodist. Avocations: volunteer activities, church activities, reading. Home: 785 Cedarhurst Rd Jackson MS 39206-4954

ANGLIN, MICHAEL WILLIAMS, lawyer; b. Chelsea, Mass., Dec. 3, 1946; s. John M. and Lillian Rogene (Williams) A. BS, Tex. A&M Commerce, 1969; JD, U. Tex., 1976. Bar: Tex. 1976, U.S. Dist. Ct. (no. dist.) Tex. 1979, U.S. Dist. Ct. (we. and ea. dists.) Tex. 1987, U.S. Dist. Ct. Ariz. 1992, U.S. Ct. Appeals (5th and 11th cirs.) 1981, U.S. Supreme Ct. 1986. With Passman & Jones, Dallas, 1976-87; ptnr. Fulbright & Jaworski, LLP, Dallas, 1987—. Trustee Ofcl. Panel Bankruptcy Trustees for No. Dist. Tex., 1980—. Corp. mem. Dallas Mus. Fine Arts, 1984; ct. apptd. spl. advocate, 1990—; bd. dirs. Dallas Opera, 1992-95; mem. Greater Dallas Planning Coun., 1994—; mem. Greater Dallas Crime Commn., 1994—; mem. Youth Crime Coun., 1994—; chair bd. dirs. The Kessler Sch., 2001--. Mem. ABA, Tex. Bar Assn., Dallas Bar Assn., Am. Bankruptcy Inst. Office: Fulbright & Jaworski LLP 2200 Ross Ave Ste 2800 Dallas TX 75201-2784

ANGOFF, GERALD HARVEY, cardiologist; b. Cambridge, Mass., Feb. 6, 1944; s. Nathan Robert and Evelyn (Kanter) A.; m. Rosalind Norma Tarko, Nov. 23, 1975; children: Elizabeth, Rebekah. AB, Harvard Coll., 1966; MD, Harvard U., 1970. Diplomate Am. Bd. Internal Medicine, Am. Bd. Cardio Vascular Disease, Nat. Bd. Echocardiography. Resident internal medicine Cleve. Met. Gen. Hosp., 1970-72; fellow in cardiology Harvard Med. Sch., Peter Bent Brigham Hosp., Boston, 1975-77, Harvard Sch. Pub. Health, Boston, 1977-78; cardiologist The Heart Ctr., Manchester, N.H., 1978-99; dir. noninvasive cardiology New England Heart Inst., 1999—. Chief cardiology Elliot Hosp., Manchester, 1979-82, 86-93; instr. Harvard Med. Sch., Boston, 1978-96; pres. The Heart Ctr., 1995-99. Bd. dirs. Jewish Fedn. Greater Manchester, 1984-94; v.p. Temple Adath Yeshurun, Manchester, 1994-96, pres., 1996-98. Maj. U.S. Army, 1975-78. Fellow Am. Coll. Cardiology, Am. Heart Assn. (Coun. on clin. cardiology). Avocations: computers, skiing. Office: New Eng Heart Inst 100 Mcgregor St Manchester NH 03102-3730 E-mail: gangoff@cmc-nh.org.

ANGONES, GEORGINA ALFONSIN, educational association administrator; b. Havana, Cuba, Nov. 29, 1950; came to U.S., 1961; d. Ramon Alfonsin and Georgina Rivera; m. Frank R. Angones, Aug. 25, 1972; 1 child, Frank R. Jr. BA, U. Miami, 1972, postgrad., 1974. Assoc. dir. alumni rels. U. Miami, Fla., 1974-80, exec. dir. alumni rels. and devel. Sch. Law, 1980-95, asst. dean Sch. of Law, 2002—; fundraising cons. G.A. & Assocs., Coral Gables, Fla., 1995—2002. Mem. jud. nominating commn. 3d dist. Ct. Appeals, 1988. Contbr. articles to profl. publs. Mem. Dade County (Fla.) Libr. Bd., 1987—, chairwoman, 1996—; vice chair Fla. State Libr. Coun., 1996; trustee St. John's Vienney Coll. Seminary, MAST Acad.; mem. devel. coun. Archdiocese of Miami; bd. dirs., chmn. pub. affairs com. Miami Childrens Hosp., trustee; del. Belen Jesuit Preparatory Sch. Recipient Citizenship award Am. Legion, 1969. Mem. Fla. Bar Found. (mem. adminstrn. of judtice com., devel. com.), Archdiocese of Miami Ednl. Found., Jr. League of Miami (past chair endowment fund, membership outreach com.), Coun. and Support for Edn., Nat. Assn. Fundraising Execs., Epiphany Ch. Women's Club, Iron Arrow Honor Soc., Omicron Delta Kappa. Roman Catholic. Home: 1203 Santona St Coral Gables FL 33146-3106 Office: 66 W Flagler St Fl 8 Miami FL 33130-1807

ANGOTTI, CATHERINE MARIE, occupational health director; b. Arlington, Va., Nov. 9, 1946; d. Frank William and Catherine Jeannette (Kolakoski) Poos; 1 child, Heather Jeannette. BS, James Madison U., 1968; RD, Med. Coll. Va., 1969. Home economist Washington Gas Light Co., 1968; clin. dietitian Fairfax (Va.) Hosp., 1969-73; pvt. practice as nutrition cons. Va., 1972-98; nutrition cons. Manassas (Va.) Manor Nursing Home, 1973-74, Bio-Tech., Inc., Falls Church, Va., 1977-78; nutrition surveyor JWK Internat., Annandale, Va., 1980-81; nutrition cons. NASA, Washington, 1977-92, program exec. occupl. health, 1992—2000, dir. occupl. health, 2000—. Pres. Nutrion Cons., Inc., 1980-98; nutrition lectr. state and nat. meetings. Contbr. artidles to Jour. Am. Dietetic Assn., Jour. health Promotion, Jour. Occupl. and Environ. Medicine. Del. for Va. Dietetic Assn. to Va. Coun. on State Legis., 1974-76; mem. Com. for Pub. of Regional Diet Manual, 1971-73. Recipient Spl. Svcs. award NASA, 1989, 94, Exceptional Performance awards, 1996-2003, Space Flight Awareness award, 1996, Spl. Achievement award, 1997, Superior Accomplishment award, 1997-2003, Exceptional Performance medal, 1999, Sr. Exec. Fellowship award, 2000. Mem. NAFE, Am. Dietetic Assn. (named Recognized Young Dietitian of Yr. award, 1975, state rep. for nutrition svcs. payment sys. 1984-87, del. 1987-90, chmn. dels. 1988-90, Outstanding Svc. award 1990, Occupation Health award 1990, Disting. Dietitian award 1992), Va. Assn. Allied Health Profls. (del. 1974-79, bd. dirs. 1975-77), Cons. Nutritionists (Va. state coord. 1976-79), D.C. Dietetic Assn., Va. Dietetic Assn. (exec. bd. 1974-76, 82-96, legis. chmn. 1974-76, nominating com. 1982-84, licensure com. 1983-89, chmn. nutrition svcs. com. 1983-97, payment sys. 1984-87, del., pres.-elect 1993-94, pres. 1994-95, chmn. nominating com. 1995-96), No. Dist. Dietetic Assn. (exec. bd. 1977-86, 88-95, treas. 1980-82, pres. 1983-84, chmn. nominating com. 1984-85, Dietetic Appreciation award 1987, awards com. 1988), Fairfax County Nutrition Com., Cons. Nutritionists of the Chesapeake Bay Area (nominating com. 1983, sec. 1986-87), Soc. for Nutrition Edn. Home: 2727 Oak Valley Dr Vienna VA 22181-5339 Office: 300 E St SW Washington DC 20546 E-mail: cangotti@hq.nasa.gov.

ANGRESS, DINA DASBERG, retired social worker; b. Amsterdam, The Netherlands, Oct. 12, 1928; came to U.S., 1948; d. Isaac and Bertha (Nystad) Dasberg; m. Herbert Hans Angress, Dec. 15, 1947 (div. Apr. 1979); children: Eric E., Norah M. Moore, Madelyn R. Hodges, Ingrid E. Noyes, Rachel K. Nunes, Jesse J. AA, Marin Jr. Coll., 1979; BS cum laude, U. San Francisco, 1980; MSW, San Francisco State U., 1983. Ranch operator Blake's Landing Farms, Marshall, Calif., 1948-69; social worker Marin County Dept. Social Svcs., Point Reyes Station, Calif., 1983-84, Sonoma County Heath Dept., Santa Rosa, Calif., 1984-85; counselor, cmty.organizer Sonoma & Marin Counties, 1983-86; telemktg. Ann Dick Jewelry, Point Reyes Station, 1984—96; mgr. dist. sales World Book Edn. Products, Chgo., 1986-96; social worker Ptnrs. for Adoption, Santa Rosa, 1993-99; ret., 1999. Mem. adv. bd. Hospice, Petaluma, Calif., 1989-95. Cmty leader 4-H Club, U. Calif. Ext., Marin County, 1958-78;pres., treas. PTA Elem. & High Schs., Tomales, Calif., 1964-77; elected bd. dirs. Park & Recreation Dist., Camp Meeker, Calif., 1984-88; bd. dirs. Calif. Parenting Inst., 1999-; mem. film com. Sonoma County Jewish Agy., 1998—. Mem. ACLU, NOW, Common Cause, Petaluma Progressives, Amnesty Internat., Child Reach Plan Internat. Democrat. Jewish. Avocations: reading, swimming, outdoor activities, politics, travel. Home: 720 Petaluma Blvd S Apt 29 Petaluma CA 94952-5147

ANGRILLI, ALBERT, psychology educator; b. N.Y.C., Dec. 4, 1917; s. Peter and Antoinette (Levant) A.; m. Dorothy Sevush, Sept. 15, 1945 (dec. Aug. 1971); 1 child, Robert M.; m. Alma Shapiro, Aug., 1977. BS, NYU, 1949, MA, 1950, PhD, 1958. Lic. psychologist, N.Y., diplomate Am. Bd. Profl. Psychology. Rsch. investigator Bellevue Hosp. Rapid Treatment Ctr., N.Y.C., 1945-49; clin. psychologist N.Y. State Traveling Child Guidance Clinics, Albany and Binghamton, N.Y., 1949-53; lectr. Queens Coll., CUNY, Flushing, 1953-58, asst. prof. edn., assoc. prof., prof., 1958-84, dir. Ednl. Clinic, 1964-76, prof. emeritus, 1984—, resident prof., adj. prof. grad. program in sch. psychology, 1984—. Exam. asst. N.Y.C. Bd. Edn., 1962-80; cons., mem. faculty, vis. prof. Internat. Grad. Sch., Lugano, Switzerland, 1976-79, Bar Ilan U., Israel, 1972, P.R., 1979; cons. psychologist Sherut La'am, Israel, 1972, sch. systems, N.Y. State, 1951; adj. prof. Fla. Inst. Tech. Sch. Profl. Psychology, Melbourne, 1979-90. Co-author: Child Psychology, 1981, Psychologia Infantil, 1984; also articles. Past pres. and bd. dirs. Queens County Mental Health Soc.; past liaison supr. Ferrini League; past bd. dirs. N.Y. State Mental Health Assn. Staff sgt. USAAF, 1942-45. Recipient cert. of merit N.Y.C. Dept. Health, 1957, cert. of honors contbn. Queens Coll. Sch. Edn., 1987. Fellow Am. Orthopsychiat. Assn. (life), Am. Acad. Sch. Psychologists; mem. APA, N.Y. State Psychol. Assn. Avocations: tennis, classical music, books, travel. Home: 105 Stone Oaks Dr Hartsdale NY 10530-1148 Office: Queens Coll Dept Edn and Community Programs Kissena Blvd Flushing NY 11367

ANGRIST, BURTON MORRIS, retired physician, educator; b. N.Y.C., July 15, 1936; s. Alfred A. and Sylvia M. (Kasdan) A.; m. Anna Marie Katan, Apr. 2, 1976; 1 child, Laurel S. AB, Colby Coll., 1958; MD, Albert Einstein Coll. Medicine, 1962. Diplomate Am. Bd. Psychiatry and Neurology. Prof. Dept. Psychiatry NYU Sch. Medicine, 1980—; staff psychiatrist N.Y. VA Med. Ctr., 1980-98. Editor: Schizophrenia & Pharmacologic Treatment; contbr. articles to profl. jours. and book chpts. Grantee NIMH, VA. Fellow Am. Coll. Neuropsychopharmacology, Collegium Internat. Neuropsychopharmacologium; mem. Psychiatry Rsch. Soc., Soc. Biol. Psychiatry. Achievements include rsch. on effects of ctrl. nervous system stimulant drugs and schizophrenia. Office: Psychiatry 116A NY VA Med Ctr 423 W 23rd St New York NY 10011-1401

ANGST, GERALD L. lawyer; b. Chgo., Dec. 29, 1950; s. Gerald L. Sr. and Audrey M. (Hides) A.; m. Candace Simning, Jan. 29, 1983. BA magna cum laude, Loyola U., Chgo., 1972, JD cum laude, 1975. Assoc. Sidley Austin Brown & Wood, Chgo., 1975-82, ptnr., 1982—. Mem.: ABA (constrn. litigation com. litigation sect.), Chgo. Bar Assn. (civil practice com.). Office: Sidley Austin Brown & Wood Bank One Plz 47th Fl 10 So Dearborn St Chicago IL 60603-2000 E-mail: gangst@sidley.com.

ANGST, KAREN K. mental health nurse, hospice nurse; b. Houston, Tex., May 16, 1948; d. Conrad Wilbur and Wanda Lee (Sullivan) A. Student, Sacred Heart Dominican Coll., Houston, 1966-68; cert., Houston C.C., 1972; student, U. Houston, 1977-78; ADN, Alvin (Tex.) C.C., 1979. RN, LVN, Tex.; cert. mental health nurse; RNC, ANCC. Staff nurse Gready Clinic, Houston, 1969-71, St. Joseph Hosp., Houston, 1967-68, charge nurse cognitive impaired care unit and psychiat. acute care unit, 1971-98; staff nurse Vitas Hospice, Houston, 1998—. Mem. planning com. Cognitive Impaired Care Unit, St. Joseph Hosp., Houston; mem. ethics com. Vitas Inoovative Hospice. Mem. Am. Assn. Ret. Persons, Alzheimer Assn., Houston Gerontol. Soc., Chi Sigma Nu. Lutheran.

ANGSTADT, FRANCES VIRGINIA, language arts and theatre arts educator; b. Dover, Del., Oct. 11, 1953; d. T. Richard Sr. and Frances Virginia (Kohout) A. BA, Del. State U., 1976; MFA, Cath. U. Am., 1982; postgrad. in PhD program, Tex. U. Tech. Lighting designer, assoc. dir. écarté dance Theatre, Dover, 1981-93; alternative tchr. Lake Forest H.S., Felton, Del., 1982-87; English tchr. Dover H.S., 1987-89; lang. arts and theater tchr. Ctrl. Mid. Sch., Dover, 1989—2003; lighting designer Harrisburg (Pa.) Ballet, 1991-93. Lighting designer, artistic advisor Act I Players, Dover, 1983-93, lighting designer Balt. Shakespeare Festival, 1994, Kimberly Mackin Dance Co., Balt., Axis Theatre, 1996-99, Women's Project at Theatre Project, Balt., 1997-2000; adj. faculty Del. State U., Dover, 1985-89, Wilmington Coll., Dover, 1996-2001; tech. advisor 2d St. Players, Milford, Del., 1994-2001; dance leadership Visual and Performing Arts Commn., Dover, 1994-2000; English devel. com. state (testing) assessment team Dover Dept. of Edn., 1997-2000, ESL assessment team, 2000-2001, intern visual and performing arts, 2002-2003. Mem. Vietnam Vets. Meml. Com., Dover, 1985-87; sec., founding mem. Dover Arts Coun., 1988-93, tech. advisor, 1988-94; sec. Capital Educators Assn., Dover, 1993-2001; tech. advisor City of Dover First Night, 1997-2001; mem. Balt. Theatre Alliance. All Am. Youth Honor Band scholar, 1972, Del. State U. scholar, Dover, 1974-76; Chancellor's guaranteed fellow 2001—; apptd. to adjudicator Del. Theatre Assn., 1986. Mem. ACLU, AAUW, HRC, NGLIF, Nat. Coun. Tchrs. English, U.S. Inst. Tech. Theatre, Assn. Theatre Higher Edn., Theatre Communicators Group. Avocations: swimming, biking, voice, visual art, dance lighting. Address: 3011 25th St Lubbock TX 79410

ANGSTROM, WAYNE RAYMOND, communications executive; b. Chgo., Mar. 26, 1939; s. Raymond Harry and Dorothy Louise (Dixon) A.; m. Sandra Sue Weber, Oct. 5, 1963; children: Mark, Carl, David, Kristina. AA in Bus. Adminstrn., Chgo. City Coll., 1962; student, Northwestern U., 1963-68. Mfg. mgr. R.R. Donnelley & Sons Co., Chgo., 1962, div. dir., v.p., 1981-87; exec. v.p. Maxwell Communications Corp., St. Paul, 1987-90, Quebecor Printing Inc., Boston, 1990-91; pres., CEO, St. Ives Inc. U.S.A., 1992—; also bd. dirs. Home: 7082 Valencia Dr Boca Raton FL 33433-7404 Office: Saint Ives Inc 2025 Mckinley St Hollywood FL 33020-3139

ANGUIANO, LUPE, business executive; b. La Junta, Colo., June 12, 1929; d. Jose and Rosario (Gonzalez) A. Student, Ventural (Calif.) Jr. Coll., 1948, Victory Noll Jr. Coll., Huntington, Ind., 1949-52, Marymount Coll., Palos Verdes, Calif., 1958-59, Calif. State U., L.A., 1965-67; MA, Antioch-Putney, Yellow Springs, Ohio, 1978. S.W. regional dir. NAACP Legal Def. and Ednl. Fund, L.A., 1965-69; civil rights specialist HEW, Washington, 1969-73; S.W. regional dir. Nat. Coun. Cath. Bishops, Region X, San Antonio, 1973-77; pres. Nat. Women's Employment and Edn. Inc., L.A., 1979-91; cons. Cisco Sys. Inc., 1998-99; pres., cons. Lupe Anguiano & Assocs., 1981—; dir. devel. La Jolla Inst., Van Nuys, Calif., West Valley Alliance; fund devel. dir. Girl Scouts of the San Fernando Valley, Chatsworth, Calif.; rep. Primerica, Valencia, Calif. Cons. Tex. Dept. Human Resources, Dept. Labor, Women's Bur., U.S. Office Pers. Mgmt., USCG, Washington, 1990-92; tech. cons. Cisco Sys. Inc.; developer regional networking acad., Oxnard Coll.; part-time faculty mem. Ventura (Calif.) Coll.; proposal reader U.S. Office Edn., Women's Equity Act; mem. Tex. Adv. Coun. on Tec.-Vocat. Edn., Calif. del. White House Conf. on Status of Mex.-Ams. in U.S., 1967; founding mem. policy coun. Nat. Women's Polit. Caucus, 1971—; Tex. and nat. del. Intrnat. Women's Yr., 1976-77; chmn. Nat. Women's Polit. Caucus Welfare Reform Task Force, 1977—; co-developer Cisco Networking Acad. in Ventura County high schs. Author (with others): U.S. Bilingual Edn. Act, 1967, Tex. AFDC Employment and Edn. Act, 1977; manuals for Women's Employment and Edn. Model program. Co-chmn. Nat. Peace Acad. Campaign, 1977-81; founder, bd. dirs. Nat. Chicana Found. Inc., 1971-78; bd. dirs. Calif. Coun. Children and Youth, 1967, Rio Grande Fedn. Chicano Health Ctrs., S.W. rural states, 1974-76, Women's Lobby, Washington, 1974-77, Rural Am. Women, Washington, 1978—, Small Bus. Coun. Greater San Antonio; mem. Pres.'s Coun. on Pvt. Sector Initiatives, 1983. Recipient Cmty. award Coalition Mex.-Am. Orgns., 1967, Outstanding Svc. award Washington, 1968, Thanksgiving award Boys' Club, 1976, Outstanding Svc. award Tex. Women's Polit. Caucus, 1977, Liberty Bell award San Antonio Young Lawyers, 1981, Vista award for Exceptional Svc. to end poverty, 1980, Headliner award San Antonio Women in Comm., 1978, Woman of Yr. award Tex. Women's Polit. Caucus, 1978, Pres.'s Vol. Action award 1983, Leadership award Nat. Network Hispanic women, 1989; named Outstanding Woman of Yr., L.A. County, 1972, Woman of the 80's, Ms. Mag., 1980, Nat. Pres.'s award Nat. Image Inc., 1981, Wonder Woman Found. award, 1982, Pres.'s Vol. Action award, 1983, Adv. of Yr., San Antonio SBA, 1984; selected one of Am.'s 100 Most Important Women, Ladies Home Jour., 1988, 89; featured in CBS TV series An American Portrait, 1985, Leadership award Nat. Network Hispanic Women, 1989. Mem. Nat. Assn. Female Execs., Pres.'s Assn., Am. Mgmt. Assn. Republican. Roman Catholic. Office: Primerica 25060 Stanford Ave Valencia CA 91355-3411 E-mail: languian@gte.net.

ANGULO, CHARLES BONIN, foreign service officer, lawyer; b. N.Y.C., Aug. 6, 1943; s. Manuel R. and Carolyn C. (Bonin) A.; m. Penelope Snare, June 28, 1986. BA, U. Va., 1966; cert. U. Madrid, 1966; JD, Tulane U., 1969. Bar: Va. 1969. Assoc. Michael & Dent, Charlottesville, Va., 1969-73; assoc. editor The Michie Pub. Co., Charlottesville, 1973; fgn. svc. officer U.S. Dept. State, Washington, 1973-75, Am. Embassy U.S. Dept. State, Brussels, 1976-78, Santo Domingo, 1981-85, Office of the Legal Advisor, U.S. Dept. State, Washington, 1978-81; exec. dir. office of insp. gen. U.S. Dept. State, Washington, 1985-86; asst. chief protocol U.S. State Dept., Washington, 1986-88, Am. Consulate Gen. U.S. Dept. State, Jeddah, Saudi Arabia, 1988-93; fgn. svc. officer Am. Embassy U.S. Dept. State, Quito, Ecuador, 1993—. Home and Office: Ste 701 2320 Terra Ceia Bay Blvd Palmetto FL 34221 E-mail: cpangulo@aol.com.

ANGUS, JOHN COTTON, chemical engineering educator; b. Grand Haven, Mich., Feb. 22, 1934; s. Francis Clark and Margaret (Cotton) A.; m. Caroline Helen Gezon, June 25, 1960; children: Lorraine Margaret, Charles Thomas. BSChemE, U. Mich., 1956, MS, 1958, PhD in Engring, 1960; DSc (hon.), Ohio U., 1998. Registered profl. engr., Ohio. Research engr. Minn. Mining & Mfg. Co., St. Paul, 1960-63; prof. Case Inst. Tech. (now Case Western Res. U.), Cleve., 1963-67, prof. chem. engring., 1967—, chmn. dept., 1974-80, interim dean engring., 1986-87. Vis. lectr. U. Edinburgh, Scotland, 1972-73; vis. prof. Northwestern U., 1980-81; pres. Angus Engring., Inc. Trustee Ohio Scottish Games. NSF fellow, 1956-57; NATO sr. fellow, 1972-73 Fellow AIChE, Electrochem. Soc. (Pioneer award); mem. NAE, Am. Chem. Soc., Materials Rsch. Soc., Sigma Xi, Tau Beta Pi, Phi Lambda Upsilon. Achievements include research in fields of crystal growth, diamond synthesis, conducting diamond, electrochemical devices, thermodynamics. Office: Case Western Res U Dept Chem Engring Cleveland OH 44106-7217

ANGUS, ROBERT CARLYLE, JR., naturopathic physician, health administrator; b. Grand Rapids, Mich., July 23, 1946; s. Robert Carlyle Sr. and Vicki I. (Weidman) Deiters; m. Elizabeth T. Angus, May 1995; children: Tamra Ann, Robert M. BS, Donsbach U., Huntington Beach, Calif., 1985; PhD in Therapeutic Philosophy, World U., 1982. Registered cardiovascular technologist, pulmonary technologist, cardiology technologist; cert. respiratory therapist; lic. radiographer, respiratory care practitioner, Pa.; cert. occupl. hearing conservationist; bd. cert. naturopathic physician Am. Naturopathic Med. Assn.; nat. bd. cert. colon hydrotherapist advanced level; cert. thermographer. Dir. cardiopulmonary St. Mary's Hosp., Grand Rapids, Mich., 1970-74; Lectr. Muskegon (Mich.) Community Coll., 1974-76; dir. respiratory therapy Hackley Hosp., 1974-76; dir. cardiovascular, cardiopulmonary Am. Internat. Hosp., Zion, Ill., 1976-78; physician's asst. Dr. William J. Mauer; dir. med. svcs., clinic adminstr. Kingsley Med. Ctr., Arlington Heights, Ill., 1978-90; dir. med. diagnostics, naturopathic physician Celebration of Health Ctr., Inc., Bluffton, Ohio, 1990—. Edn. cons. Brookhaven Med. Care Facility; lectr., advisor Muskegon C.C., 1974-76; mem. Nat. Bd. Respiratory Care; bd. dirs. Nat. Bd. for Colon Hydrotherapy, 2000—. Active Big Bros. Am., Muskegon, 1974-76. Mem. Am. Acad. Thermology, Nat. Bd. Cardiovascular Testing, Am. Cardiology Technologists Assn., Am. Assn. Respiratory Therapy, Am. Naturopathic Med. Assn., Nat. Soc. Cardiopulmonary Technologists, Coun. for Accreditation in Occupational Hearing Conservation, Internat. Assn. for Colon Hydrothrapy, Soc. for Noninvasive Vascular Tech., Cardiovascular Credentialing Internat. Avocations: canoeing, horses, antiques, old radios, reading. E-mail: rangus@cohc.cc.

ANGUS, W. DAVID, Queen's Counsel; AB cum laude, Princeton, 1959; BCL, McGill Univ., 1962. Mem. Senate of Can., 1993—; sr. ptnr. Stikeman Elliott LLP. Pres., bd. dirs. Madeg Holdings, Inc.; bd. dirs. AON Reed Stenhouse, Inc., McGill U. Health Ctr., Montreal Gen. Hosp. Corp., AirCanada, Autoskill Internat. Inc., Delphe Tech. Inc., Security Biometrics, Inc. Mem. St. Andrews Presbyn. Homes Found. Office: The Senate of Canada 903 Victoria Bldg Ottawa ON K1A 0A4 Canada

ANGYAL, CHARLES, architect; AA Bus. Admin., Cuesta Coll., San Luis Obispo, Calif.; BS Landscape Architecture, Cal. Polytechnic State Univ., San Luis Obispo, Calif. License # C12653, State of Calif., 1982. Pres. and mng. prin. arch. Charles Angyal Arch. and Assoc., San Diego, 1980—92; intern arch. Homer Delawie and Assoc., San Diego, 1979—80, Dale Cox, Architechs, Lake Tahoe, Calif., 1977—79, William F. Morris Architects, Reno, 1975—77; chief architect, new constrn. energy-efficiency programs Sempra Energy utilities, 1992—. Co-developer Calif. Savings by Design program, 1998—99, co-adminstr., 1999—; project facilitator Ridgehaven Green Bldg. Demonstrnation, 1994—96, co-sponsor, 1996—2000. Fellow: AIA (founder San Diego Energy Efficiency Integration awards 1994, founder Coun. Savs. by Design Energy Efficiency Integration awards 2000); mem.: U.S. Green Bldg. Coun. (founding bd. dirs. 1993—94), Collaborative for high Performance Schs. (co-founder, bd. dirs. 2000—02). Office: San Diego Gas & Electric 8335 Century Park Ct San Diego CA 92123-1569 also: SDG&E 8335 Century Pk Ct, 2nd Fl CP12G San Diego CA 92123-1569 also: SDG&E 4173 Falcon St San Diego CA 92103

ANIGBOGU, ANGELA NGOZI, research scientist; arrived in U.S., 1995; d. Vincent Akpujekwu and Elizabeth Anubena Anigbogu. BSc in Biochemistry and Pharmacology, U. Nigeria, Nsukka, 1984; BPharm with 1st class honors, U. Ibadan, Nigeria, 1989; PhD in Pharmacy, U. Bradford, Eng., 1994. Bd. cert. pharmacist Pharm. Soc. Nigeria. Postdoctoral rsch. fellow U. Calif., San Francisco, 1995—2000; sr. rsch. scientist Watson Pharms. Inc., Salt Lake City, 2000—. Jour. reviewer Internat. Jour. Pharmacy, 1997—2000, Acad. Dermatology, 1997—2000; grant reviewer NIH, 2001. Author: Handbook of Occupational Dermatology, 2000, Drug Therapy in Dermatology, 2000, Toxicology of Skin, 2001; contbr. articles to profl. jours. Gen. sec. Igbo Cath. Found., San Francisco, 1998—2000. Scholar, Assn. Vice Chancellors of Brit. Univs., Cambridge, Eng., 1991; Commonwealth scholar, Commonwealth Commn., Eng., 1990. Mem.: Am. Assn. Pharm. Scientists, Acad. Pharm. Scis., Controlled Release Soc., Assn. Nigerians in Utah (fin. sec. 2000—). Roman Catholic. Achievements include patents in field of transdermal drug delivery. Avocations: reading, exercising. Office: Watson Pharms Inc 417 Wakara Way Salt Lake City UT 84108

ANIKEEFF, ANTHONY HOTCHKISS, lawyer; b. Washington, Dec. 30, 1952; s. Nicholas Michael and Nancy Brodie Wales (Hotchkiss) A. BA with distinction, U. Va., 1975; JD, Coll. William and Mary, 1980; LLM, U. London, Eng., 1981. Bar: Va. 1980, D.C. 1983, U.S. Dist. Ct. D.C. 1986, U.S. Ct. Internat. Trade 1985, U.S. Ct. Fed. Claims 1987, U.S. Ct. Appeals (fed. cir.) 2001. Law clk. U.S. Dist. Ct. (ea. dist.) Va., Richmond, Va., 1981-82; assoc. Kilpatrick and Cody, Washington, 1982-87; trial atty. civil divsn. comml. litig. br. Dept. Justice, Washington, 1987-91, sr. trial counsel civil divsn. comml. litig. br., 1991-93, asst. br. dir. civil divsn. comml. litigation, 1993-99; v.p., gen. counsel Alliance of Automobile Mfrs., 1999-2000; ptnr. Bracewell & Patterson, LLP, 2000—. Mem. ABA, S.R., Squadron A N.Y., U. Club, Fed. Am. Inn Ct. Home: 905 Seneca Rd Great Falls VA 22066-1318 E-mail: ahatlw@mindspring.com., aanikeeff@bracepatt.com.

ANISIMOV, MIKHAIL A. physicist, educator, research scientist; b. Baku, Russia, Nov. 2, 1941; arrived in U.S., 1994; d. Alexei Anisimov and Elena Timonina; m. Zoya Islamova, Mar. 21, 1963 (dec. May 13, 1981); 1 child, Tanya; m. Elena Jouravleva, Mar. 4, 1983; children: Ruslan, Alexei, Elena. PhD in Chem. Physics, Moscow State U., 1969; D in Physics and Math., USSR State Testimonial Commn., Moscow, 1976. Head dept. USSR Bur. Stds., Moscow, 1968—77; chair dept. physics State Acad. for Oil and Gas, Moscow, 1978—93; vis. prof. U. Md., College Park, 1994—95, sr. rsch. scientist, 1996—2000, prof., 2001—. Cons. Caltech/JPL, Pasadena, Calif., 1999—, Inst. for Regulatory Sci., Columbia, Miss., 2001—. Author: Critical Phenomena in Liquids and Liquid Crystals, 1991, Thermodynamics of the Critical State, 1995; mem. editl. bd.: Phase Transitions, 1988 —, Internat. Jour. Thermophysics, 1990—, Molecular Crystals and Liquid Crystals, —. Fellow: AAAS, Am. Phys. Soc. Office: Univ Md Inst for Phys Sci and Tech College Park MD 20742

ANISMAN, MARTIN JAY, academic administrator; b. Bklyn., Nov. 4, 1942; s. Harry and Florence (Dobin) A.; m. Cheryl Anisman; children: Steve, Beth, Jamie. BA, Syracuse U., 1963; MA, NYU, 1964, PhD, 1970. Asst. prof. English So. Conn. State U., New Haven, 1967-73, assoc. prof. English, 1973-77, prof. English, 1977-86, dean Sch. Arts and Scis., 1978-86; v.p. acad. affairs, dean of faculty Springfield (Mass.) Coll., 1986-89; pres. Sam Houston State U., Huntsvile, Tex., 1989-95, Daemen Coll., Amherst, N.Y., 1996—. Bd. dirs. Houston Advanced Rsch. Ctr., Tex. Internat. Ednl. Consortium; chmn. adv. com. Tex. Higher Edn. Coordinating Bd. Tchr. Edn. Editor: The Luck of Barry Lyndon: A Critical Edition, 1970. Divsn. chair United Way, 1996-99—; bd. dirs. Buffalo Conv. Ctr., 1997-2000, Erie Count YMCA, 1997—, Park Sch., 1999-2003, Studio Arena Theater, 1999—, Atlantic Corridor, 1999—. N.Y. State Regents fellow, 1963-67. Mem. MLA (bibiography com., sect. 6 1969-74), Edn. for Tomorrow Alliance (bd. dirs.). Avocations: photography, bicycling. Office: Daemen Coll 4380 Main St Amherst NY 14226-3544

ANISON, GEORGE C. retired otolaryngologist; b. Socorro, N.Mex., June 13, 1919; MD, Northwestern U., 1945. Diplomate Am. Bd. Otolaryngology. Intern Cook County Hosp., Chgo., 1944-45; resident eye ear nose and throat St. Luke's Hosp., Chgo., 1945-46; resident otolaryngologist U. Ill. Rsch. Edn. Hosp., Chgo., 1948-49. Fellow ACS; mem. AMA, Am. Acad. Otolaryngology-Head and Neck Surgery.

ANISTON, JENNIFER, actress; b. Sherman Oaks, Calif., Feb. 11, 1969; d. John Aniston; m. Brad Pitt, July 29, 2000. Actor: (TV series) Ferris Bueller, 1990, The Edge, 1992, Molloy, 1992, Friends, 1994— (Emmy award, 2002, People's Choice award, 2001, Golden Globe award, 2003); TV appearances : Herman's Head; Quantum Leap; Burke's Law; actor: (films) She's the One, 1996, Dream for an Insomniac, 1996, Til There Was You, 1996, Picture Perfect, 1997, The Object of My Affection, 1998, Office Space, 1999, Rock Star, 2001, The Good Girl, 2002, Bruce Almighty, 2003; (plays) For Dear Life, Dancing on Checkers' Grave. Office: 5750 Wilshire Blvd #580 Los Angeles CA 90036*

ANITESCU, MIHAI, computer scientist, mathematician; b. Bals, Romania, Aug. 10, 1968; arrived in U.S., 1993; s. Ilie and Marioara Anitescu; m. Magdalena Anitescu, Nov. 14, 1992; 1 child, Julia Christine. MS, Poly. U., Bucharest, Romania, 1992; PhD, U. Iowa, 1997. Asst. prof. math. U. Pitts., 1999—; computer scientist Argonne (Ill.) Nat. Lab., 2002—. Contbr. articles to profl. jours. Sgt. Inf. Romanian Mil., 1986—87. Fellow Wilkinson fellow, Argonne Nat. Laboratoty, 1997. Office: Argonne Nat Lab MCS Bdg 221 9700 S Cass Avenue Lemont IL 60439 Office Fax: 630-252-5986. E-mail: anitescu@mcs.anl.gov.

ANJARIA, SHAILENDRA J. international finance official; b. Bombay, July 17, 1946; s. Jashwantrai J. and Harvidya Anjaria; m. Nishigandha Pandit, 1972; 2 children. BS, U. Pa., 1966; MA, Yale U., 1967; MS in Econs., London Sch. Econs., 1968. Economist dept. exch. and trade rels. IMF, 1968-73, economist, 1973-75, asst. divsn. chief dept. exch. and trade rels., 1976-80, divsn. chief, 1980-86, asst. dir. and advisor dept. exch. and trade rels., 1986-88, asst. dir. North African divsn. African dept., 1988-91, dir. dept. external rels., 1991-99, sec., 1999—. Office: IMF 700 19th St NW Washington DC 20431-0001

ANKROM, BARBARA BURKE, journalist; b. Upper Darby, Pa., May 30, 1943; d. Joseph Anthony and Teresa Gertrude (Smart) Burke; children: Joseph Burke Nied, Laura Ann Nied, Michele Marie Nied; m. Robert W. Ankrom, Sr. (dec.). AB, Wheeling (W.Va.) Coll., 1965. Asst. editor Jones & Laughlin Steel Corp., Pitts., 1965-66; editor, reporter, pub. Dem. Messenger, Waynesburg, Pa., 1976, reporter/photographer, 1976-77; corr. McGraw-Hill & World News Pubs., N.Y.C., 1976—; writer Pitts. Bus. Times, 1981-82; tech. editor, writer JWK Internat. Corp., Pitts., 1982-84; writer-editor W.Va. U. Energy and Water Rsch. Ctr., 1985-88, Mining Ext. Svc. W.Va. U., 1988-89; staff writer News and Info. Svcs., 1989-98; freelance writer, 1976—'. Author: Individual Mine Rescue Team Training Module, 1989, Surface Oranization, 1989, Mine Gases, 1989, Mine Ventilation, 1989, Mine Exploration, 1989, Fires, Firefighting and Explosions, 1989, Rescue of Survivors and Recovery of Bodies, 1989, Mine Recovery, 1989, Mining Voice mag., 1997; asst. editor Men and Steel mag., 1965-66, DuPont's Safety Training Observation Program for Cyprus-Emerald Coal Company, 1989; editor Pa. chpts. Pan American's U.S.A. Guide Book, 1978, 80. Pub. rels. dir. Boy Scouts Am., Greene County, Pa., 1977—84. Mem.: AAUW.

ANKROM, CHARLES FRANKLIN, golf course architect, consultant; b. Parkersburg, W.Va., Nov. 7, 1936; s. Donsel and Elva Dale (Cale) A.; m. Alice Lynell Glass, Aug. 24, 1968; children: Steven Charles, Cheryl Lyn, Jan Ellen Lambert, Beverly Lyn Webster. Student, W.Va. U., 1955, Eli Frank Sch. Design Arts, Tampa, Fla., 1956, Indian River C.C., Stuart, Fla., 1993—94. Exec. dir. golf, corp. golf course arch. Gen. Devel. Corp., Miami, Fla., 1964-70; exec. dir. golf, golf course arch. Boise Cascade Recreation Communities Group, Palo Alto, Calif., 1970-73; pres. Charles F. Ankrom, Inc., Internat. Golf Course Archs., Cons. & Planners, Stuart, Fla., 1973—, ptnr. Palm City, Fla., 2003—. Prin. works include Sabal Trace C.C., Port Charlotte, Fla., Sun 'N Lake Country Club, Turtle Run Golf Course, Sebring, Fla., Cocoa Beach Mcpl. Golf Course, Cocoa Beach City, Fla., Ft. Lauderdale (Fla.) Country Club, Boca Raton (Fla.) Mcpl. Golf Course, Woodmont Country Club, Tamarac, Fla., The Club at Emerald Hills, Hollywood, Fla., The Habitat Golf Course, Brevard County, Fla., Aquarina Country Club, Melbourne, Fla., Crane Creek C.C., Palm City, Fla., Panther Woods Country Club, Ft. Pierce, Fla., Indian River Plantation Resort, Hutchinson Island Marriott Beach Resort and Marina, Jensen Beach, Fla., Metro Country Club Resort, Dominican Republic, Osprey Creek Golf Course, Palm City, Fla., San Miguel Country Club, Venezuela, numerous others; over 60 planned cmtys. including Indian River Plantation Marriott Resort, Hutchinson Island, Fla., Joe's Point, Hutchinson Island, Stuart West, Martin County, Fla., Pinecrest Lakes, Jensen Beach, Crystal Lakes, Okeechobee, Fla., Panther Woods, Ft. Pierce, Crane Creek, Palm City, Fla., River Ridge, Tequesta, Fla., River Landing, Palm City. Donated design & adminstrv. svcs. for Bulldog Sportsturf Complex, Martin County (Fla.) Schs. Recipient Outstanding Achievement by Ind. in Bus. or Industry award State of Fla. Coun. on Vocat. Edn., 1992, Bus. Ptnr. award Martin County Sch. Dist., 1991. Achievements include profl. svc. multi-disciplinary cons. assignments provided to clients in 28 states and 9 countries or territories, including approxmamtely 270 assignments to both the govt. and pvt. sectors, profl. orgns., coll. and univ. and the edn. industry, natl. and internat. conf. as the lectr. for seminars, including svcs. to resort ops., pvt. amenities and public ops., 2001; formed AMI (Ankrom and Miartus Internat.) for the internat. design of golf course projects, with offices in Fla. and Venezuela. Office: Charles F Ankrom Inc PO Box 898 Stuart FL 34995-0898

ANKUDINOV, VLADIMIR KONSTANTINOVICH, naval architect; b. Vladivostok, Russia, June 5, 1938; came to U.S., 1974; s. Konstantin Pavlovich and Nina Davidovna (Reva) A.; m. Galina F. Uljanovskaja, Aug. 28, 1963; 1 child, Dimitry; m. Joanne Grace Petrie, June 8, 1982; 1 child, Katherine. M in Naval Arch. Shipbuilding Inst., U. Leningrad, 1961; PhD in Ship Hydrodynamics, Maritime Tech. Inst., Leningrad, 1967. Rsch. engr. Ctrl. Rsch. Shipbuilding, Inc., Leningrad, 1961-63; asst. prof. ship hydrodynamics, dean fgn. students St. Petersburg Maritime U., Leningrad, 1963-72; rsch. prof. Tech. U., Trondheim, Norway, 1973-74; sci. cons. USN, Frankfurt, Germany, 1973-74; asst. prof. U. Mich., Ann Arbor, 1974; prin. rsch. scientist Hydronautics, Inc., Laurel, Md., 1974-90; dir. R&D, Designers & Planners, Inc., Arlington, Va., 1990—. Vis. rsch. scientist Tech. U., Delft, The Netherlands, 1968-69. Contbr. over 150 articles to profl. jours. Mem. Soc. Naval Architects (award 1994). Republican. Achievements include developments in ship design, production and operations, also corporate research and development for various U.S. Governmental agencies. Home: 1701 Colesberg St Silver Spring MD 20905-4104 Office: Designers & Planners Inc 2120 Washington Blvd Ste 200 Arlington VA 22204-5708

ANLIAN, STEVEN JAMES, urban planner, consultant; b. Jersey City, N.J., Sept. 18, 1953; s. Haig Anlian and Virginia Catherine States; m. Nune Vaganovna Anlian, Apr. 10, 1990; children: David Steven, Tigran John. BS in Environ. Sci., Syracuse U., 1975; B of Land Arch., SUNY, Syracuse, 1976; MPA, Harvard U., 1998. Internat. advisor Internat. City/County Mgmt. Assn., Washington, 1992-97; v.p. HOH Assocs. Inc., Alexandria, Va., 1976-92; sr. assoc. The Urban Inst., Washington, 1998—. Advisor to govt. of Republic of Armena, U.S. Agy. for Internat. Devel., Yerevan, 1992—. Grants bd. mem. Eurasia Found., Washington, 1995-96. Fulbright fellow Coun. for Internat. Exch. of Scholars, 1989. Mem. Am. Inst. Cert. Planners, Am. Planning Assn., Fulbright Assn. Office: The Urban Inst 2100 M St NW Washington DC 20037 E-mail: Anlian@alumni.ksg.harvard.edu.

ANLYAN, WILLIAM GEORGE, surgeon, university administrator; b. Alexandria, Egypt, Oct. 14, 1925; s. Armand and Emmeraude (Nazar) A.; children: William George, John Peter, Louise. BS magna cum laude, Yale U., 1945, MD, 1949; DSc (hon.), Rush Med. Coll., 1973. Diplomate Am. Bd. Surgery, Am. Bd. Thoracic Surgery. Intern, resident, instr., assoc. in surgery Duke Hosp., Durham, N.C., 1949-53, asst. prof. surgery, 1953-58, prof. surgery, 1961-89; assoc. dean Sch. Medicine Duke, 1963, dean, 1964-69, v.p. health affairs, 1969-83, chancellor health affairs, 1983-88, exec. v.p., 1987-88; chancellor Duke U., 1988-90, chancellor emeritus, 1990—. Chmn. Durham VA Chancellor's Com., 1963—89; chmn. Pearle Health Svcs., Inc., 1983—85; surg. cons. Durham VA Hosp.; Markle scholar med. sci., 1953—58; bd. regents Nat. Libr. Medicine, 1971—72; trustee N.C. Sch. Sci. and Math., 1978—85, chmn. phys. facilities com., 1979, fice-chmn. bd. trustees, 1981—84; mem. bd. visitors The U. Tex. Health Sci. Ctr. at Houston, 1980—88, Stanford U., 1985—87; chmn. Yale U. Coun. Com. on Med. Affairs, 1985—93. Mem. editorial bd. Pharos, 1968-93. Trustee The Duke Endowment, 1990—. Commn. on Future Structure of Vet. Health Care, 1990-92; chmn. Gov.'s Task Force on Better Health for N.C. in 2000, 1991-97; mem. White House Sci. Coun., 1988-89. Recipient award for disting. achievement Modern Medicine, 1974; Gov.'s award for disting. meritorious service, 1978; Abraham Flexner award, 1980, Disting. Surgeon Alumnus award Yale U. Sch. Medicine, 1979, Award of Merit Duke U. Hosp. and Health Adminstrn. Alumni Assn., 1987, Lifetime Achievement award Duke U. Med. Alumni, 1995, Lifetime Achievement award Rsch. Am., 1997, medal for disting. meritorius svc., Duke Univ., 2002, N.C. award in sci., presented by the gov., 2002.Lifetime Achievement award, Cty. of Medicine, 2003. Fellow ACS; mem. AMA (adv. com. med. sci. 1972—), Soc. Univ. Surgeons, Soc. Vascular Surgery, Internat. Cardiovascular Soc., Soc. Clin. Surgery, Am. Heart Assn., Soc. Med. Adminstrs. (pres. 1983-85), Inst. Medicine of Nat. Acad. Sci., Coun. Deans (chmn. 1968-69), AAMC Coun. Deans (chmn. 1968-69), So. Med. Assn., Coord. Coun. Med. Edn. (chmn. 1973-74), Surg. Biology Club II, Am. Surg. Assn., So. Surg. Assn., Halsted Soc., Allen O. Whipple Surg. Soc., Assn. Am. Med. Colls. (chmn. 1970-71), Ind. Rsch. Roundtable NAS, Assn. Acad. Health Ctrs. (pres. 1975), Rsch. Am. (bd. dirs. 1989—, chmn. 1992-96), Rotary, Phi Beta Kappa, Sigma Xi, Alpha Omega Alpha. Home: 1516 Pinecrest Rd Durham NC 27705-5817 Office: Duke Med Ctr PO Box 3626 Durham NC 27710-0001 E-mail: anlya001@mc.duke.edu.

ANMA, SO, engineer consultant; b. Hamamatsu, Shizuoka, Japan, Nov. 7, 1936; s. Yu and Chie (Matsumoto) A.; m. Fumie Kishikawa, Mar. 15, 1964; children: Ryo, Akitsu, Mizuho, Yashima. BS, Hokkaido U., Sapporo, Japan, 1959; DEng, Tokai U., Tokyo, 1987. Registered enging. geologist; profl. civil engr. Rschr. Hukada Chisitsu Inst., Tokyo, 1959-67; pres. Kisokogaku Co., Tokyo, 1967-70; exec. Kensetsu Kiso Chosa Sekkei Co., Shizuoka, Japan, 1970-91, pres., 1991—. Lectr. Tokai U., Shizuoka, 1988—, Shizuoka U., 2000—; bd. dirs. Shizuoka Environ. and Resources, 1989—. Co-author: The First Ascent of Mt. Chamlang, 1965, Geology of Nepal Himalaya, 1967 (Chichibunomiya prize 1968), Patagonian Mountain Climb, 1968, Mt. Dhaulagiri-I Midwinter, 1985. Hazard reduction adviser Shizuoka Prefecture, 1984—. Recipient Chichibunomiya prize Chichibunomiya Meml. Found., Tokyo, 1968, Hokkaido prize Hokkaido Regional Govt., 1983, Asahi Sports prize Asahi Newspaper Inc., Tokyo, 1984. Mem. Internat. Geosynthetic Soc., Internat. Soc. Soil Mechanics and Found. Engring., Internat. Assn. Engring. Geology and Environment, Geol. Soc. Japan, Japanese Soc. Snow and Ice, Japanese Alpine Club (chpt. chmn. 1986-95). Avocations: mountaineering, forest watching. Office: 241-7 Shimizu-Kusuno Kishinden Shizuoka 424-0882 Japan E-mail: anma.sf@tx.thn.ne.jp.

ANNABLE, CHARLES ROY, pathologist; b. Hastings, Mich., Mar. 3, 1932; s. Charles Roy and Verta Irene (Metster) A.; m. Toni Marie Pohl, June 8, 1985; children: Beverly, Rolf, Irene, Kelley, Monica, James, Jane, Sara. BS, U. Mich., 1957, MD, 1961; postgrad., Walter Reed Army Inst. Rsch., Washington, 1969 70, U. Conn., 1970-73, PhD, 1982. Cert. Am. Bd. Pathology, Surgery and Thoracic Surgery. Commd. 2d lt. U.S. Army, 1960, advanced through grades to col., 1974, ret., 1980; intern Womack Army Hosp., Fort Bragg, N.C., 1961-62; resident gen. surgery Walter Reed Army Med. Ctr., Washington, 1962-66, resident thoracic surgery, 1967-69, staff surgeon, dir. rsch. lab. transplantation svc., 1973-79; chief surgery 85th Evacuation Hosp., Qui Nhon, Vietnam, 1966-67; asst. chief medicine and surgery divsn. Acad. Health Scis., Fort Sam Houston, Tex., 1979-80; resident instr. dept. pathology U. Tex. Health Sci. Ctr., San Antonio, 1980-87; asst. prof. dept. pathology U. Tex. Med. Br., Galveston, 1987-90; dir. dept. pathology Driscol Children's Hosp., Corpus Christi, Tex., 1990-99; ret., 1999. Mem. Phi Beta Kappa, Alpha Omega Alpha, Phi Kappa Phi. Home: 31345 River Pines Dr Springfield LA 70462-8881

ANNAKIN, KENNETH COOPER, film director, writer; b. Beverly, Yorkshire, England; came to U.S., 1979; s. Edward C. and Hannah J. (Gains) A.; m. Pauline Mary Carter, 1960; children: Jane, Deborah. DLitt(hon.), Hull U., 1934-35. Dir. The Swiss Family Robinson, 1960, A Very Important Person, 1961, The Hellions, 1961, Crooks Anonymous, 1962, The Fast Lady, 1962, The Longest Day, 1962, Those Magnificent Men in Their Flying Machines, 1965, The Battle of the Bulge, 1965, The Biggest Bundle of Them All, 1967, Those Daring Young Men in Their Jaunty Jalopies, 1969, Call of the Wild, 1972, Paper Tiger, 1974, The Fifth Musketeer, 1977, The Pirate Movie, 1982, Pippi Longstocking, 1986, 99; screenwriter Coco Chanel, 1999, Chiffon, 2001, Fair Play, 2001, Redwing, 2002; author (autobiography): So You Wanna Be A Director?, 2001. Decorated Order Brit. Empire. Office: 9233 Swallow Dr West Hollywood CA 90069-1145 E-mail: flyingmachines@earthlink.net.

ANNAN, KOFI A. international organization official; b. Ghana, 1938; married; 3 children. Grad., U. Sci. and Tech., Kumasi, Macalester Coll., St. Paul, Inst. des Hautes Etudes Internationales, Geneva; MS, Alfred P. Sloan fellow, MIT, 1971-72. Held posts UN Econ. Commn. for Africa, Addis Ababa, Ethiopia, UN, NYC, WHO, Geneva, 1962-71; adminstrv. mng. officer UN, Geneva, 1972-74; chief civilian pers. officer UN Emergency Force, Cairo, 1974; mng. dir. Ghana Tourist Devel. Co., 1974-76; dep. chief staff svc. Office Pers. Svc., Office of UN High Commn. for Refugees, Geneva, 1976-80, dep. dir. divsn. adminstrn., head pers. svc., 1980-83; chmn. bd. trustees UN Internat. Sch., 1987-95; dir. adminstrn. mgmt. svc., dir. budget Office Fin. Svcs. UN, NYC, 1984-87, asst. sec-gen. Office Human Resources Mgmt., security coord., 1987-90, asst. sec-gen. & contr. Office Program Planning., 1990-92, asst. sec.-gen. dept. peace-keeping ops., 1993-94, under-sec.-gen. dept. peace-keeping ops., 1994-95, spl. rep. of sec.-gen. to former Yugolslavia, 1995-96, spl. envoy to NATO, 1995-96, sec. gen, 1997—. Recipient Nobel Peace Prize, 2001. Office: UN Pub Inquiries Unit Rm GA-57 UN Plz 46th St at First Ave New York NY 10017

ANNANDALE, GEORGE WILLIAM, engineer; b. Kimberly, South Africa, Aug. 2, 1951; s. George and Bernice Martha A.; m. Itha Mentz, Nov. 1970 (div. Jan. 1979); m. Linda Mouton, Dec. 12, 1980 (dec. Jan. 1985); m. Nicolene Maree, Jan. 11, 1986; children: Jacques, Graham, Lahne. BSCE, U. Pretoria, South Africa, 1974; MS in Engring., U. Witwatersrand, Johannesburg, South Africa, 1979; D of Engring., U. Pretoria, 1984. prof. engr. Engr. van Wyk & Louw, Pretoria, South Africa, 1975-76, Indsl. Devel. Corp., Johannesburg, 1976-77; sr. lectr. U. Pretoria, South Africa, 1979-81; prof., dept. head Rand Afirkaans U., South Africa, 1981—85; specialist engr. Bruinette Kruger Stoffberg, Pretoria, South Africa, 1986—87; ptnr. Steffen Roberston and Kirsten, Inc., Denver, 1988-93; mgr. water resources HDR Engring., Sacramento, 1993-95; assoc., dir. water resource engring. Golder Assocs., Lakewood, Colo., 1995-2001; pres. Engring. and Hydrosystems, Inc., Highlands Ranch, Colo., 2001—. Author: Reservoir Sedimentation, 1987; contbg. author: Guidelines for the Retirement of Dams and Hydroelectric Facilities, 1997, Reservoir Sedimentation Handbook, 1997, Stream Stability and Scour at Highway Bridges, 1999, Rock Scour due to High Velocity Falling Jets, 2002; mem. editl. bd. Internat. Assn. Hydraulic Rsch., 1985—; contbr. over 100 articles to profl. jours.; inventor in field. Bd. dirs. Arapahoe/Douglas Mental Health Network, Littleton, Colo., 1998-2000. Mem. ASCE (sedimentation com. 1993--), Internat. Assn. Hydraulic Rsch. (editl. bd. 1985—), U.S. Soc. Dams (hydraulics com. 1995—). Achievements include developer of the erodibility index method, known as Annandale's method. Home: 2374 E Lansdowne Pl Littleton CO 80126 Office: Engring & Hydrosystems Inc 8122 South Park Lane 208 Littleton CO 80120

ANNAUD, JEAN-JACQUES, film director, screenwriter, producer; b. Juvisy, France, Oct. 1, 1943; s. Pierre and Madeleine (Tripoz) A.; m. Monique Rossignol, 1970 (div. 1980); 1 child, Mathilde; m. Laurence Duval; 1 child, Louise. Student, Ecole Louis Lumière, Institut Des Hautes Etudes Cinematographiques, Paris, 1966; Lic. Lettres, The Sorbonne, Paris, 1967. Freelance film dir., screenwriter, Paris, 1967—. Screenwriter, dir.: Black and White in Color, 1976 (Oscar award Best Fgn. Film 1977), Hot head, 1978, Quest for Fire, 1981, (César award 1982), Name of the Rose, 1986 (César award 1987, Donatello award), The Bear, 1988 (César award best dir. 1988), The Lover, 1991 (Best Dir. award Japan Critics Assn., 1992); screenwriter, dir., prodr.: Wings of Courage, 1994 (in IMAX 3D), Seven Years in Tibet, 1997 (Best Fgn. Film Gilde Filmpreis, Germany, 1998); dir., prodr., screenwriter Enemy at the Gates, 2000. Decorated commandeur Ordre des Arts et Lettres; recipient Grand Prix Nat. du Cinema, prix du Cinéma de L'Académie Française. Home: 9 rue Guénégaud 75006 Paris France also: Repérage SA 10 rue Lincoln 75008 Paris France also: ICM care Jeff Berg 8899 Beverly Blvd Los Angeles CA 90048-2412

ANNENBERG, NORMAN, lawyer; b. N.Y.C., Aug. 13, 1912; s. George J. and Jeannette (Lazarus) A. J.D., Harvard U., 1935. Bar: N.Y. 1936, U.S. Ct. Appeals (2d cir.) 1948, U.S. Supreme Ct., 1966. Sole practice, N.Y.C., 1936— . Mem. N.Y. County Lawyers Assn., N.Y. State Bar Assn. E-mail: anormally@aol.com. Office: 145 W 55th St New York NY 10019-5342

ANNESE, DOMENICO, landscape architect; b. N.Y.C., June 9, 1919; s. Fedele and Antonia (Angelini) A.; m. Serafina Villanova, July 16, 1944; children: Donald F., Loretta S. Ed., SUNY Coll. Environ. Sci. and Forestry, 1942; BS in Landscape Architecture, Syracuse U., 1942. Registered landscape architect, N.Y., Pa., Conn., Mass., Ohio, Tenn. Landscape architect Clarence C. Combs, N.Y.C., 1946-50, asso., 1955-56; asst. chief landscape architect Nat. Capital Parks, Washington, 1950-55; asso. Clarke and Rapuano, Inc., N.Y.C., 1956-72, v.p., 1972-91. Vice chmn. N.Y. State Bd. Landscape Architects, 1961-67, chmn., 1967-71; mem. Pleasantville (N.Y.) Parks and Recreation Bd., 1974-83; adj. prof. urban landscape architecture CCNY, 1975-76; vis. prof., lectr. in landscape architecture Sch. Planning and Architecture, New Delhi, India, 1977; pres. Landscape Architecture Found., 1973-1975; dir. N.Y. State Coun. Landscape Architects; dir. coll. environ. sci. and forestry ESF Found., 1987-2000; dir. N.Y. Parks and Conservation Assn., 1991-1995 Served with Coast Arty., F.A. U.S. Army, 1942-46, ETO. Fellow Am. Soc. Landscape Architects, Sigma Lambda Alpha. Lutheran. Home: 315 Bedford Rd Pleasantville NY 10570-2212

ANNING, ROBERT DOAN HOPKINS, brokerage company executive; b. Cin., Apr. 16, 1940; m. Sydney Ann Fish, July 6, 1963; children: Sydney M., Robert H., John H., Elizabeth M. BA, Trinity Coll., 1963. 1st v.p. investments Merrill Lynch Pvt. Client Group, 1967—. Bd. trustees Convalescent Hosp. for Children, 1985—, chmn., 1988—94; bd. trustees The Children's Hosp. Cin., 1989—, Cin. Children's Hosp. Med. Ctr., 1990—, Cerebral Palsy Svcs. Ctr., United Cerebral Palsy Cin., 1994—2003, Cin. Parks Found., 1995—, pres., 1999—; bd. trustees Found. Family Svc., 1997—98, Family Svc. Cin. Area, 1998—99. Named one of All-Pro Stockbrokers Money mag., 1990, All-Star Brokers, 1994, Blue-Chip Brokers Town and Country mag., 1992, All-Star Brokers Money mag., 1995; named an All Star Broker, Money mag., Forecast 1996. Home: 25 Weebetook Ln Cincinnati OH 45208-3330

ANNOTICO, RICHARD ANTHONY, legal administrator, real estate investor; b. Cleve., Sept. 17, 1930; s. Anthony and Grace (Kovarik) A. AB in Bus. with hons., Ohio U., 1953; LLB, Southwestern Law Sch., 1963; JD, UCLA, 1965. Dir. internat. sales then v.p. Liberty Records, L.A., 1957-64; real estate investment counselor Calif. Land Sales, Beverly Hills, 1964-66, R.A. Annotico & Assocs., L.A., 1966-68, real estate investor, 1969—. Spkr. in field.; mem. Bd. of Governors State Calif.; expert witness State Legis. Calif. Contbr. numerous articles to profl. jours. Commr. L.A. Transp. Commn., 1984-88, v.p. 1985-87; commr. L.A. Human Rels. Comm n., 1977-84, pres. 1983-84; mem. Calif. State Senate Small Bus. Adv. Bd., 1978-82, L.A. City County Adv. Commn. on Consolidation, 1976-77; pres. Federated Italian-Americans So. Calif., 1975-76; mem. Mayors Exec. Com. Christopher Columbus Quincentenary 1992. Lt. USAF, 1954-55. Decorated Cavaliere Ufficiale Order of Merit (Italy), Comdr. St. Lazarus Internat. Chivalric, Hospitaller and Mil. Order. Mem. Calif. State Bar Assn. (bd. govs., 1983-86, 86-89, 89-92, v.p. 1986, 89, 92). Office: Admiralty Suites 4170 Admiralty Way # 1G Marina Del Rey CA 90292

ANNS, PHILIP HAROLD, international trading executive, former pharmaceutical company executive; b. London, Eng., June 24, 1925; came to U.S., 1950; s. Harold Falkner and Dorothy Louise (Torckler) A.; m. Jacqueline Estelle Wyrtzen, Dec. 27, 1952 (div. 1975); 1 child, Jean Anns; m. Arlene Claire Eiserman, Apr. 1, 1978. BA in Econs., Christ Coll., Cambridge, Eng., 1948, MA in Econs., 1950. Asst. to pres. BASF Inc., N.Y.C., 1954-58; gen. mgr. Squibb Australia E.R. Squibb and Sons, Princeton, N.J., 1958-68, dir. animal health New Brunswick, N.J.; gen. mgr. animal health Am. Hoechst, Kansas City, Mo., 1968-72; exec. v.p. Lakeside Labs., Milw., 1972-75; sr. v.p., gen. mgr. internat. div. A.H. Robins Co., Inc., Richmond, Va., 1975-85, sr. v.p. corp. govt. relations Washington, 1986-90; pres. Phase Ltd., Arlington, Va., 1990—. With Va. Dist. Export Coun.; mem. Congl. staff U.S. Ho. of Reps., 1990—. Mem. Indsl. Devel. Authority, Greene County, Va. Served to lt. Brit. Royal Navy, 1943-46, ETO. Mem. Rotary. Republican. Episcopalian. Home and Office: 6653 Celt Rd Stanardsville VA 22973-3638

ANOATUBBY, BILL, governor of Chickawaw Nation; b. Nov. 8, 1945; m. Janice Marie Loman, Dec. 23, 1967; children: Chris, Brian. AS, Murray State Coll., 1970; BS, East Ctrl. State Coll., 1972. Acct., office mgr. Am. Plating Co., 1972-74; acct., systems & budgetary contr. Little Giant Corp., 1974-75; dir. health svcs. The Chickasaw Nation, Ada, Okla., 1975-76, dir. acctg., 1976-78, spl. asst. to gov., 1978-79, lt. gov., 1979-87, gov., 1987—. Trustee Morris K. Udall Scholarship and Excellence in Nat. Environ. Policy Found., 1994-2000. Mem. adv. com. Okla. Dept. Commerce, 1990; mem. Trail of Tears Nat. Historic Adv. Com., 1990-92; trustee Oklahoma City U., 1991-98. Recipient Gov.'s ARTS award, 1997; named Okla. Minority Bus. Advocate of Yr., U.S.

SBA, 1995. Mem. Inter-Tribal Coun. of Five Civilized Tribes (past v.p., pres.), Ada Area C. of C. (bd. dirs.), Okla. Indian Affairs Commn. Democrat. Office: Chickasaw Nation PO Box 1548 Ada OK 74821-1548 E-mail: bill.anoatubby@chickasaw.net.

ANSARY, CYRUS A. investment company executive, lawyer; b. Shoraz, Oram, Nov. 20, 1933; s. A. R. and Jamali (Mostmand) Ansary; m. Janet C. Hodges, Aug. 1, 1970; children: Douglas C., Pary Ann, Jeffrey C., Bradley C. BS, Am. U., 1955; LLB, Columbia U., 1958. Bar: Md. 1959, D.C. 1960, Va. 1961. Pvt. practice, Washington, 1959-72; sr. ptnr. firm Ansary, Kirkpatrick and Rosse, 1964-72; chmn. bd. Industry Reports, Inc., Washington, 1960-72; organizer, 1st chmn. bd., pres. Woodland Nat. Bank, Alexandria, Va., 1963-67; lectr. Sch. Bus. Adminstrn., Am. U., 1967-71; chmn. bd. Fin. Dynamics Corp., Washington, 1967-72, Campbell Music Co., Washington, 1968-72, John L. Lindstrom and Assocs., Inc., Washington, 1962-86; pres. IK Investment A.G., Zurich, Switzerland, 1974-79, Investment Svcs. Internat. Co., Washington, 1973—; chmn. MACO Bancorp, Washington, 1988—95. Bd. dirs. Washington Mut. Investors Fund, J. P. Morgan Value Opportunities Fund, Am. Funds Tax-Exempt Series I; chmn. bd. dirs. CorPay Solutions, Inc. Trustee Am. U., 1968—96, chmn. bd., 1982—91; trustee Internat. Law Inst., 1976—88, Wolf Trap Found., Vienna, Va., 1977—82, Fried Krupp Found., Essen, Germany, 1977—79, Washington Opera Soc., 1982—89; pres. Ansary Found., Washington, 1983—; mem. Woodrow Wilson Coun., Washington, 2000—. With USMCR, 1959—64. Mem.: Nat. Press Club, Econ. Club Washington, Washington Soc. Investment Analysts, City Club, Chevy Chase Country Club (Bethesda), Met. Club (Washington), Rotary. Office: 1725 K St NW Ste 410 Washington DC 20006-1401 E-mail: cyrus817@aol.com.

ANSARY, HANSON JABER, transportation and telecommunications executive; b. Tehran, Iran, May 3, 1949; arrived in Can., 1973; s. Aman-al-Allah J. and Robabeh (Naimi) A.; 1 child, Farrah R. BA in Bus., Tehran Bus. Coll., 1971; MA in Econ., Meml. U. Nfld., St. Johns, Can., 1975; MBA, Pitts. (Kans.) State U., 1976; PhD in Bus., Calif. Western U., 1982. Policy advisor Gov. Ont., Toronto, Can., 1977-78; mgr. strategic planning Domtar Inc., Montreal, Que., Can., 1978-81; mgr., planning coord. Polysar Ltd., Sarnia, Ont., 1981-83, mgr. planning and devel., 1983-84; dir. corp. devel. Ports Can., Ottawa, Ont., 1984-85, v.p. corp. svcs., 1985-88, exec. v.p., 1988-92, [illegible] COO, 1992-95; pres., CEO Canol Internat., Ottawa, Ont., Can., 1995-96, AmeriTest, Inc., Rock Springs, Wyo., 1996-97; COO Acosta Med. Testing Corp., Chgo., 1998—; sr. ptnr. The Maxxus Group, 1999—. Bd. dirs., chmn. Electronic Data Interchange Coun. Can., Toronto, 1990; chmn. Total Electronic Commerce Svc. for Transp., 1993—. Founder, editor-in-chief quar. Portus, 1985-92. Bd. dirs. Carleton Condominium Corp., 1991-93, Can. Grain Coun., 1992—, Containerization and Intermodal Inst., 1993-94, The Van Horne Inst., 1993—. 2d lt. Armed Forces Iran, 1971-73. Fellow Chartered Inst. Transport; mem. Strategic Mgmt. Soc., Planning Forum, Am. Assn. Port Authorities (chmn. commerce com. 1993-94), Internat. Cargo Handling Coords. Assn. (internat. vice chmn. London 1992-94, chmn. 1994—, pres. Can. 1988—). Avocations: cinema, jogging. Home: 18216 Lange St #3A Lansing IL 60438-3347

ANSBACHER, RUDI, physician; b. Sidney, N.Y., Oct. 11, 1934; s. Stefan and Beatrice (Michel) A.; m. Elisabeth Cornelia Vellenga, Nov. 19, 1965; children—R. Todd, Jeffrey N. Grad., Harvard Coll., 1951; BA, Va. Mil. Inst., 1955; MD, U. Va., 1959; MS, U. Mich., 1970. Diplomate Am. Bd. Ob-Gyn. Staff ob-gyn, chief clin. investigation Brooke Med. Ctr., San Antonio, 1971-75, asst. chief ob-gyn, 1975-77; chief dept. ob-gyn Letterman Army Med. Ctr., San Francisco, 1977-80; from prof. ob-gyn to prof. emeritus U. Mich., Ann Arbor, 1980—2001, prof. emeritus, 2002—. Cons. Biomed. Adv. Com. Population Resource Ctr., 1978-81; bd. dirs. Health Policy Internat., Physician's Rev. Orgn. Mich., Inc., 2000—. Contbr. articles to profl. jours., chpts to books; mem. editorial bds., reviewer jours. Served to col. U.S. Army, 1960-80. Named Disting. Mil. Grad. Va. Mil. Inst., Lexington, Va., 1955; NIH grantee, 1973-78 Fellow ACOG (Chmn.'s award 1970), AAAS; mem. Am. Fertility Soc. (dir. 1979-82), Am. Soc. Andrology (sec. 1978-80, pres. 1984-85), Central Assn. Ob-Gyn, Assn. Mil. Surgeons U.S., Soc. for Study Reprodn., Mich. State Med. Soc. (bd. dirs. 1995—), Mich. State Med. Soc. Found. (bd. dirs. 2003—). Republican. Presbyterian. Avocations: tennis, softball, gardening, skiing. Home: 3755 Tremont Ln Ann Arbor MI 48105-3022 Fax: 734-647-9727. E-mail: ansbache@med.umich.edu.

ANSBACHER, SIDNEY FRANKLYN, lawyer; b. Jacksonville, Fla., May 28, 1961; m. Theresa Marie Rooney; stepchildren: Emily Matchett, Katelyn Matchett;1 child from previous marriage, Benjamin Alexander. BA, U. Fla., 1981; JD, Hamline U., 1985; LLM in Agrl. Law, U. Ark., 1989. Bar: Fla., U.S. Dist. Ct. (mid. dist.) Fla., U.S. Ct. Appeals (D.C. cir.). Atty. Fla. Dept. Natural Resources, Tallahassee, 1986-87; assoc. Turner, Ford, Buckingham, Jacksonville, Fla., 1987-90; ptnr., assoc. Brant, Moore et al, Jacksonville, Fla., 1990-95; ptnr. Mahoney Adams & Criser, Jacksonville, Fla., 1995-97, Upchurch Bailey & Upchurch, St. Augustine, Fla., 1997—. Contbr. articles to profl. jours.; mng. editor Fla. Bar Environ. and Land Use CLE Manual, 1998—. Bd. dirs. Fla. Forestry Found., 1993-96. Recipient Outstanding Achievement award Fla. Wildlife Fedn., 1990. Mem.: Jacksonville Bar Assn. (chair environ. and land use law sect. 1994—96), Fla. Bar (bd. dirs. 1994—98, chair environ. and land use law sect. 2001—02, Judy Florence Outstanding Svc. award 1992, 2000). Avocations: bicycling, tennis, reading. Office: Upchurch Bailey & Upchurch PA 780 N Ponce De Leon Blvd Saint Augustine FL 32084-3519 E-mail: sfansbacher@ubulaw.com.

ANSBRO, JOHN JOSEPH, philosopher, educator; b. N.Y.C., Nov. 16, 1932; s. Thomas and Katherine (Reilly) Ansbro. BA, St. Joseph's Sem., Yonkers, N.Y., 1954, postgrad., 1955; MA, Fordham U., 1957, PhD, 1964. Lectr. philosophy Manhattan Coll., Riverdale, NY, 1958-59, instr., 1959-63, asst. prof., 1963-68, assoc. prof., 1968-79, prof., 1979-96; ret., 1996; writer, 1996—. Curriculum guidance supr. faculty counselors Sch. Arts & Scis. Manhattan Coll., 1962—73, chmn. co-curricular interdisciplinary arts program, 1962—70, chmn. com. faculty rsch. projects and grants, 1976—78, 1989—92, chmn. dept. philosophy, 1977—81, chmn. sabbatical leave com., 1989—91, dir. rsch. peace studies program, 1990—91, com. faculty rsch. projects, mem. instnl. rev. bd. human subjects, task force acad. programs, liaison officer Danforth Found., others; adj. asst. prof. philos. resources contemporary problems program Grad. Sch. Arts & Scis., Fordham U., 1975; chmn. Met. Round Table Philosophy, 1972—75; project field coord. N.Y. State Dept. Edn., 1965—67; founder, pres. Manhattan Coll. Coun. World Hunger, 1977—85. Author: (book) Martin Luther King, Jr.: The Making of a Mind, 1982, Martin Luther King, Jr.: The Making of a Mind, Mex. trans., 1985, Martin Luther King, Jr.: Nonviolent Strategies and Tactics for Social Change, 2d edit., 2000; contbr. some 40 articles to publs. including N.Y. Times. Grantee Travel and Study, Ford Found., 1973, Summer, Am. Can. Co. Found., 1985, Samuel Rubin Found., 1985; scholar, Fordham U. Grad. Sch., 1956—57. Mem.: AAUP, Gandhi-King Soc., Soren Kierkegaard Soc., Soc. Ancient Greek Philosophy, Hegel Soc. Am., Am. Philos. Assn., Soc. Advancement Am. Philosophy.

ANSCHER, BERNARD, manufacturing executive, investor, management consultant; b. Bklyn., June 9, 1922; s. Abraham and Esther (Draznin) A.; children: William, Marlene, Joseph. Student, Sch. Tech., CCNY, 1939-42; BS in Mech. Engring., NYU, 1948, MBA, 1953, postgrad., 1953-65, Fla. Internat. U., 1997—. Cert. mfg. engr. robotics, mfg. engr. Chief metall. and fabrication devel. reactor materials br. U.S.A.E.C., N.Y.C., 1946-50; devel. mgr., gen. sales mgr. domestic sales, asst. v.p. Loewy-Hydropress, Inc., N.Y.C., 1950-55; cons., mfrs.' rep. Mercury Engring. Co., N.Y.C., 1955-65; founder, chmn. bd. dirs., pres. Nat. Molding Corp., Farmingdale, N.Y., 1965-87; pres. Anscher Mgmt. Corp. (formerly Custom Molds), Opa Locka, Fla., 1975—; founder, pres. Nat. Indsl. Robotic Controls, 1983-90; mfg. cons., 1991—. Founder, instr. mktg. program in cmty. coll., N.Y.C., 1962-65; mem. industry adv. group Underwriters Labs.; mem. robotics standards com. Robot Inst.; corp. mem. Automotive Industry Action Group, 1984-87. Reviewing editor Die Design Handbook, 1954-55; polit. columnist Miami Beach Sunpost, 1991-92; contbr. articles to profl. jours.; patentee in field. Queens County committeeman Rep. Party, 1960-68; mem. Dem. Exec. Com., Dade County, Fla., 1990-92; Dem. party nominee for Congress, 18th Dist., Fla., 1990; ind. candidate Congress, 22d Dist., Fla., 1992; mem. platform com. Dem. Party Presdl. Election, 1992; treas. Temple Emanu-el, 1994-95, Lehrman Day Sch., 1994-95. With AUS, 1943-46, PTO. Recipient Spl. award Manhattan Project, 1946; cert. mfg. engr. Mem. N.Y. State Mktg. Educators (chmn. curriculum rsch. com. 1964), Soc. Mfg. Engrs., Soc. Plastics Engrs., Robotics Internat., Am. Jewish Congress (commn. law and social action, chmn. edn. com. S.E. region 1999), Pres.' Club U. Miami, NYU Alumni Assn., Stuyvesant H.S. Alumni. Office: Anscher Mgmt Corp PO Box 610157 Miami FL 33261-0157

ANSCHUETZ, HAROLD FREDRIC, JR., family physician; b. Milw., Oct. 9, 1945; s. Harold F. and Martha M. (Miller) A.; m. Ruth Ann Schneider, May 15, 1976; children: Jodi, Wesley. BS, Carroll Coll., Waukesha, Wis., 1967; MA, U. Ga., 1971; MD, Med. Coll. Wis., 1977. Diplomate Am. Bd. Family Practice. Intern and residency Deacons Hosp., Milw., 1977—80; pvt. practice Ft. Atkinson Med. Ctr., Wis., 1980—. Capt. USAF, 1969-73. Mem. Am. Acad. Family Physicians. Avocations: sports, woodworking, gardening. Home: 700 Mcmillen St Fort Atkinson WI 53538-1261 Office: Fort Atkinson Med Ctr 211 Memorial Dr Fort Atkinson WI 53538-1949

ANSCHUTZ, PHILIP F. transportation executive, communications executive; b. Russell, Kansas, 1939; BS, Univ. Kansas, 1961. Dir. chair. QCC, 1993—, Anschutz Co., Denver, 1991—; ceo, dir. Anschutz Corp., Denver, 1992—; dir. So. Pacific Rail Corp., San Francisco, 1988-96; chair. So Pacific Rail Corp., 1988-96; vice chmn. (merger with So Pacific Rail Corp) Union Pacific, San Francisco, 1996—; dir. Forest Oil Corp., 1995—; dir., chair. Qwest Communications, 1997—; co-owner L.A. Kings, 1995—; owner L.A. Galaxy, 1996—; investor-operator Major League Soccer, 1995—. Board Mem: Am. Petroleum Inst., Nat. Petroleum Council, Nat. Hockey League, Kansas Univ. Endowment Assoc. Office: Southern Pacific Rail Corp 49 Stevenson St Fl 15 San Francisco CA 94105-2909 also: 555 17th St Ste 2400 Denver CO 80202-3941 also: Quest Communication 1801 Calif St Inglewood CA 80202

ANSCOMBE, RODERICK JOHN, psychiatrist, educator; b. Manchester, England, Dec. 28, 1947; arrived in U.S., 1976; MA, Oxford U., England, 1970, BM, BChir, 1974. Assoc. psychiatrist Beth Israel Hosp., Boston; staff psychiatrist Bridgewater (Mass.) State Hosp.; asst. clin. prof. Harvard Med. Sch., Boston. Author: The Secret life of Laszlo, Count Dracula, 1994, Shank, 1996. Office: 31 Eastern Point Rd Gloucester MA 01930-4134

ANSELL, EDWARD ORIN, lawyer; b. Superior, Wis., Mar. 20, 1926; s. H. S. and Mollie (Rudnitzky) A.; m. Hanne B. Baer, Dec. 23, 1956; children: Deborah, William. BSEE, U. Wis., 1948; JD, George Washington U., 1955. Bar: D.C. 1955, Calif. 1960. Electronic engr. FCC, Buffalo and Washington, 1948-55; patent atty. RCA, Princeton, NJ, 1955-57; gen. mgr. AeroChem. Rsch. Labs., Princeton, 1957-58; patent atty. Aerojet-Gen. Corp., La Jolla, Calif., 1958-63, corp. patent counsel, 1963-82, asst. sec., 1970-79, sec., 1979-82, assoc. gen. counsel, 1981-82; dir. patents and licensing Calif. Inst. Tech., Pasadena, Calif., 1982-92; pvt. practice Claremont, Calif., 1992—; co-founder Gryphon Pharms., South San Francisco, 1993, Ciphergen BioSystems, Fremont, Calif., 1993. Adj. prof. U. La Verne (Calif.) Coll. Law, 1972-78; spl. advisor, task force chmn. U.S. Commn. Govt. Procurement, 1971 Editor: Intellectual Property in Academe: A Legal Compendium, 1991; contbr. articles to profl. publs. Recipient Alumni Svc. award George Washington U., 1975. Mem. Am. Intellectual Property Law Assn., Assn. Corp. Patent Counsel, Ea. Bar Assn. Los Angeles County, L.A. Intellectual Property Law Assn., Assn. Univ. Tech. Mgrs., State Bar Calif. (exec. com. intellectual property sect. 1983-86), Athenaeum Club Pasadena, Univ. Club Claremont. Office: 427 N Yale Ave # 204 Claremont CA 91711 E-mail: anselaw@att.net.

ANSELL, JULIAN S. physician, retired urology educator; b. Portland, Maine, June 30, 1922; s. Jacob M. and Anna Gertrude (Fieldman) A.; m. Eva Ruth Ballin, June 17, 1951; children: Steven, Jody, Carol, Ellen, Peter. BA, Bowdoin Coll., 1946; MD, Tufts U., 1951; PhD, U. Minn., 1959. Intern in surgery U. Minn. Hosps., Mpls., 1951-52, resident in urology, 1952-54; NIH fellow U. Minn., Mpls., 1954, instr., 1956-59; asst. prof., head urology U. Wash., Seattle, 1959-62, assoc. prof., head urology, 1962-64, prof., chair urology, 1965-87, prof. urology, 1987-92, prof. emeritus, 1992—. With U.S. Army, 1943-46. Mem. Am. Alpine Club. Office: 3827 49th Ave NE Seattle WA 98105-5233

ANSELME, JEAN-PIERRE LOUIS MARIE, chemist; b. Port-au-Prince, Haiti, Sept. 22, 1936; came to U.S., 1955, naturalized, 1960; s. Pierre F. and Jeanne (Kieffer) A.; m. Marie-Celine Carrie, Dec. 31, 1960; children: Fabienne, Veronika, Vanessa. BA, St. Martial Coll., Haiti, 1955; BS, Fordham U., 1959; PhD, Poly. Inst., Bklyn., 1963. Research asso. Poly. Inst. Bklyn., 1963, 65, sr. instr., 1965. NSF fellow Institut fur Organische Chemie, Munich, 1964; asst. prof. chemistry U. Mass. at Boston, 1965-68, asso. prof., 1968-70, prof., 1970— ; pres. Organic Preparations and Procedures, Inc., Newton, Mass.; vis. prof. Research Inst. Indsl. Sci., Kyushu U., Fukuoka, Japan, 1972, U. Miami, Coral Gables, Fla., 1979 Author: (with others) Organic Compounds with Nitrogen-Nitrogen Bonds, 1966, N-Nitrosamines, 1979; founder, editor: Organic Preparations and Procedures, 1969-70, Organic Preparations and Procedures Internat, 1971— ; contbr. (with others) articles to profl. jours. Recipient Seymour Shapiro award as outstanding grad. student organic chemistry Poly. Inst. Bklyn., 1963; Sloan fellow, 1969-71 Fellow Japan Soc. for Promotion Sci.; mem. Am. Chem. Soc., Chem. Soc. London, Sigma Xi, Phi Lambda Upsilon. Office: U Mass Dept Chemistry Harbor Campus Boston MA 02125-3393 E-mail: jp.anselme@umb.edu.

ANSINGKAR, KAMLESH G. health facility administrator, otolaryngologist; b. Nainpur, India, June 12, 1964; s. Govind B. and Indumati G. Ansingkar; m. Kalyani K. Marathe, Dec. 4, 1994; 1 child, Koyal K. BSc, B Surgery, Govt. Med. Coll., Nagpur, India, 1987; Diploma in Otolaryngology, Govt. Med. Coll., Nagpur, India, 1989; MSc in Health Informatics, U. of Ala., 2002. Resident in otolaryngology Govt. Med. Coll., Nagpur, 1988—89; sr. resident in otolaryngology Mcpl. Gen. Hospitals, Bombay, 1990—91; jr. med. officer, asst lectr. NKP Salve Inst. of Med. Sciences, Nagpur, 1991—93; pvt. practice Nagpur, 1992—95; observer in internal medicine St. Catherine Hosp., Garden City, Kans., 1997; observer in emergency rm. Elmore Cmty. Hosp., Wetumpka, Ala., 1998—99; rsch. fellow in echocardiography U. Ala. Hosp., Birmingham, 1999—2001; internship in health informatics U. Ala., Birmingham, 2002; data mgmt. specialist Alegent Health Immanuel Med. Ctr., Omaha, 2002—; family practice resident Creighton U., Omaha, 2003—. Contbr. articles to profl. jours. Scholar Nat. Merit scholarship, Govt. of India, 1981—87. Office: Alegent Health Immanuel Med Ctr 6901 N 72nd Street Omaha NE 68022 Personal E-mail: kansingkar@yahoo.com.

ANSLEY, DARLENE H. marketing and communications executive; b. Anderson, Ind., Aug. 21, 1942; d. Byron J. and Edith O. (Earlywine) Howell; children: David, Bradley, Lisa. Student, Anderson U., 1960-61; BS in Communications, Fla. State U., 1978. Asst. project Boydston Advt. & Creative Svcs., Tallahassee, 1978; asst. dir. Pub. Broadcasting Svc., Alexandria, Va., 1982-85, assoc. dir., 1985-87, advt. mgr., nat. programming & promotion svcs., 1987-93; prin. Ansley Comms., Inc., 1993-97; dir. mktg. and comms. Divsn. of continuing edn. George Washington U., Washington, 1997; dir. mktg. and publs. Nat. Office Orthotics and Prosthetics, Alexandria, Va., 1997-98; creative dir., mktg. promotions Bur. Nat. Affairs, Washington, 1999—2000; dir. mktg. comms. i2, Inc., Springfield, Va., 2000—01; brand mgr. U.S. Internat. Broadcasting Bur., Washington, 2002—03. Home: 5707 Walnut Wood Ln Burke VA 22015-2710 Office: US Internat Broadcasting Bur 330 Independence Ave SW Washington DC 20237

ANSLEY, SHEPARD BRYAN, lawyer; b. July 31, 1939; s. William Bonneau and Florence Jackson (Bryan) A.; m. Boyce Lineberger, May 9, 1970; children: Anna Ansley Davis, Florence Bryan. BA, U. Ga., 1961; LLB, U. Va., 1964. Bar: Ga. 1967. Assoc. Carter & Ansley and predecessor firm Carter, Ansley, Smith & McLendon, Atlanta, 1967-73, ptnr., 1973-84, of counsel, 1984-91; with Attkisson Carter & Akers Inc., Atlanta, 1997—2000, Attkisson Carter & Co., Atlanta, 2001—. Bd. dirs. Prime Bancshares, Inc., Prime Bank, FSB; chmn. bd. dirs., pres. Sodamaster Co. Am.; exec. v.p. Woodridge Realty, Inc.; sr. v.p., ACA Consulting, Inc.; fin. cons. Attkisson, Carter & Co. Inc.; bd. dirs., sec. CRM Co., LLC, L.A. County, Calif. Vestry mem. St. Luke's Episcopal Ch., Atlanta, 1971-74; treas., exec. com., bd. dirs. Alliance Theatre Co., Atlanta, 1974-85; trustee Atlanta Music Festival Assn., Inc., 1975—; v.p., bd. dirs. Atlanta Preservation Ctr. Inc., pres., 1988-90; bd. vis. Lineberger Cancer Rsch. Ctr. U. N.C., Chapel Hill, 1987-92; pres., Study Hall at Emmaus House, Inc., 1988-1992, bd. 1992— ; bd. dirs. Margaret Mitchell House, Inc.; bd. govs. Ga. Pub. Policy Found., Inc., 1999-2001. Capt. U.S. Army, 1965-67. Mem. ABA, Ga. Bar Assn., Atlanta Bar Assn., Piedmont Driving Club. E-mail: sbansley@mindspring.com.

ANSON, WAYNE MELVIN, social welfare administrator; b. O'Neill, Nebr., Sept. 9, 1950; s. Walter Melvin and Dorothy Mae Cole Anson; m. Patricia Ann Reynolds, June 12, 1970; children: Kristi Dawn, Kristin Dale, Kory Drew, Kari Danielle. AA, Miltonvale Wesleyan Coll., 1970; BA, Ind. Wesleyan U., 1972; MDiv, Columbia Internat. U., 1994. Ordained missionary Bapt. Ch., 1997. Chapel mgr. USAF, 1972-78; assoc. pastor Booker (Tex.) Friends Ch., 1979-80; pastor Pleasant Plain Friends Ch., Byers, Kans., 1980-81, Riverton (Kans.) Friends Ch., 1981-82, Bear Creek Friends Ch., Earlham, Iowa, 1982-86; dir. adult residential svcs. and program devel. Alston Wilkes Soc., Columbia, SC, 1986-97; founder Alston Wilkes Vets. Home and Social Svcs. Ctr., Columbia, SC, 1996; dir. World Relief Chgo., 1998-2001; freelance writer, orgn. and adminstrv. cons. Presenter spiritual devel. workshops. Scoutmaster Boy Scouts Am., Columbia, 1987-94; project coord. Listening Project, Columbia, 1995-96; founding ptnr. S.C. Homeless Coalition, 1996-97; organizing cons. for regional homeless coalitions, S.C., 1997. Recipient Best Practices award U.S. HUD, 1997. Mem. Christian Cmty. Devel. Assn. Avocations: public speaking, fine hand crafts, art collecting.

ANSPACH, ERNST, economist, lawyer; b. Glogau, Germany, Feb. 4, 1913; came to U.S., 1936, naturalized, 1943; s. Hermann and Margarete (Gurassa) A.; m. Ruth Pietsch, Dec. 20, 1950; children: Paul David, Margaret Louise. Js.D., D Polit. Sci., U. Freiburg, Berlin, Munich, Breslau, 1935; M.Sc., New Sch. Social Research, N.Y.C., 1943. With German jud. service, 1934-36; fin. analyst Loeb, Rhoades & Co., N.Y.C., 1936-43; reorgn. of adminstrn. Justice in Bavaria and Hesse, 1946-49; gen. counsel and polit. adviser Dept. State, U.S. Land Commr. for Hesse, 1949-52; chief economist, gen. ptnr. Loeb, Rhoades & Co., Investment Bankers, N.Y.C., 1952-79; cons., 1980—. Tchr. adult edn. program Henry St. Settlement, N.Y.C., 1939-43; lectr. Univs. Munich, Marburg, Frankfurt, 1948-52; lectr. fields econs., polit. sci., theology and primitive art, 1955—. Contbr. articles to sci. jours.; collection African Tribal Art; exhibited, Mus. Primitive Art, N.Y.C., 1967-68. Trustee Bleuler Psychotherapy Ctr., 1953-85, chmn. bd. 1956-65; trustee Nightingale-Bamford Sch., 1971-77; trustee Madison Ave. Presbyn. Ch., 1966—, chmn. bd. trustees, 1975-80, fellow in perpetuity and mem. vis. com. dept. primitive art Met. Mus. Art, N.Y.C.; bd. dirs. Mus. African Art, 1982-91, treas., 1982-87. Capt. AUS, 1943-46. Recipient Army commendation medal. Mem. Conf. Bus. Economists. Home: 118 W 79th St New York NY 10024-6445

ANSPACH, ROBERT MICHAEL, lawyer; b. Tiffin, Ohio, Feb. 29, 1948; s. William Charles and Evelyn Helen (Smith) A.; m. Jane Evelyn Friedman, Oct. 29, 1983; children: Michael Robert, Robert Joseph, John William. BA, Cornell U., 1970, JD, 1973. Bar: Ohio 1973, U.S. Dist. Ct. (no. dist.) Ohio 1974, U.S. Ct. Appeals (6th cir.) 1976, U.S. Supreme Ct. 1976, U.S. Tax Ct. 1985. Assoc. Shumaker, Loop & Kendrick, Toledo, 1973-79, ptnr., 1979-83, mng. ptnr., 1984, adminstr. trial dept., 1985; founder, mng. ptnr. Anspach, Serraino, Meeks & Nunn, L.L.P. and predecessor firm, Toledo, 1986—. Co-author: Winning in Court—The Accountant's Role in Litigation, Arbitration and Dispute Resolution, 1986. Trustee Toledo Repertoire Theatre, 1993—96, Boys and Girls Clubs Toledo, 1993—, Historic Perrysburg, Inc., 1998—99, pres., 1998—2000; trustee Toledo Cultural Arts Commn. at the Valentine Theatre, bd. chmn., 2001—. Recipient award of merit Ohio Legal Ctr., 1986. Fellow: Am. Bar Found., Ohio State Bar Found.; mem.: ABA, Def. Rsch. Inst., Nat. Assn. R.R. Trial Counsel, Toledo Bar Assn., Ohio Bar Assn. (vice chmn. jud. adminstrn. and legal reform com. 1982, lawyer's assistance com. 1986—). Avocations: singing, piano, art collecting, musical composition, tennis. Home: 535 E Front St Perrysburg OH 43551-2135 Office: Anspach Serraino Meeks & Nunn LLP 1600 Edison Plz 300 Madison Ave Toledo OH 43604-2633

ANSPAUGH, LYNN RICHARD, research biophysicist; b. Rawlins, Wyo., May 25, 1937; s. Solon Earl and Alice Henrietta (Day) A.; m. Barbara Anne Corrigan, Nov. 2, 1965 (div.); children: Gregory, Heidi; m. Larisa Fedorovna Kornushina, Sept. 27, 1993. BA, Nebr. Wesleyan U., 1959; M in Bioradiology, U. Calif., Berkeley, 1961, PhD, 1963. Biophysicist Lawrence Livermore (Calif.) Nat. Lab., 1963-74, group leader, 1974-75, sect. leader, 1976-82, div. leader, 1982-92, dir. Risk Scis. Ctr., 1992-95, dir. Dose Reconstruction program, 1995-96; rsch. prof. radiobiology divsn. Univ. Utah, Salt Lake City, 1997—. Tchr. extension U. Calif., Berkeley, 1966-69; lectr. San Jose (Calif.) State U., 1975; guest lectr. UCLA, Stanford U., U. Calif., Davis, 1992-96; faculty affiliate Colo. State U., Ft. Collins, 1979-83; cons. EPA, Washington, 1984-85, U. Utah, Salt Lake City, 1983-88, NAS/NRC, 1998; mem. U.S. del. UN Sci. Com. on Effects of Radiation, Vienna, 1987—; mem. Nat. Coun. on Radiation Protection and Measurements, 1989-2001, hon. mem., 2002—; mem. radiation adv. com. EPA, 1999—. Contbr. articles to profl. jours. AEC fellow, 1959-61; fellow NSF, 1961-63. Fellow Health Physics Soc. (pres. environ. radiation sect. 1984-85, pres. No. Calif. chpt. 1986-87); mem. AAAS, Soc. for Risk Analysis, Internat. Union Radioecology, Radiation Rsch. Soc., Sigma Xi. Home: PO Box 171319 Salt Lake City UT 84117-1319 Office: U Utah 729 Arapeen Dr Ste 2334 Salt Lake City UT 84108-1218 E-mail: LAnspaugh@aol.com.

ANSTATT, PETER JAN, marketing services executive; b. Haworth, N.J., Feb. 9, 1942; s. Herman E. and Margaret (Dunham) A.; m. Jean Ann Sorchiotti, Aug. 13, 1966; children: Christopher Ryan, Holley Elizabeth. BS in Printing Mgmt., Carnegie Mellon U., 1963; grad. program for mgmt. devel., Harvard U. Bus. Sch., 1977. Estimator Einson Freeman Inc., N.Y.C., 1963, project mgr., 1965-66, account exec. Fairlawn, N.J., 1966-71, gen. mgr., 1971-76, pres., chief exec. officer, 1977-78, chmn., chief exec. officer Paramus, N.J., 1978-93; pres. Enterprise Comms., Inc., Wyckoff, N.J., 1994-95; exec. dir. Buehler Challenger & Sci. Ctr., Paramus, 1995-2000; mem. Ednovations, LLC, Morristown, NJ, 2000—01, Wilmington, NC, 2002—. V.p. ops. EAC Industires, Paramus, 1978 Mem. alumni bd. govs. Blair Acad., 1974-77; bd. dirs. Ridgewood YMCA, 1981-90, bd. trustees, 1991—. Served with C.E., U.S. Army, 1963-65, Korea. Recipient Jacob Van Dyke award for Outstanding Service, Ridgewood YMCA, 1985. Mem. Point of Purchase Advt. Inst. (chmn. trade ethics com. 1973-78, chmn. ann. exhibit com. 1979, dir. 1973-81, vice chmn. bd. 1979, chmn. 1980, speaker ann. industry seminar 1977-88, Producer/Supplier of Yr. 1984, inducted into Hall of Fame, 1994), Beta Theta Pi (pres. 1962-63). Republican. Methodist. Home: 603 Gunston Ln Wilmington NC 28405-5317 E-mail: janstatt@ednovations.com. *Undying belief in God, country and the free enterprise system. Adherence to the principles of respect, fairness, achievement through teamwork, and happiness.*

ANSTEAD, HARRY LEE, state supreme court justice; b. Jacksonville, Fla., Nov. 4, 1937; Judge, then chief judge Fla. Ct. Appeals. (4th dist.), Fla., 1976—94; justice Fla. Supreme Ct., Tallahassee, 1994—, chief justice. Office: Supreme Ct Bldg 500 S Duval St Tallahassee FL 32399-6556

ANSTICE, DAVID W. pharmaceutical executive; B of Econs., U. Sydney, Australia, 1970. Economist Australian Pharm. Mfrs. Assn., 1969—74; various positions Merck Sharp & Dohme Australia, 1974—81; with corp., domestic divsn. Merck Rsch. Labs., 1981—82; dir. mktg. and sales Merck Sharp & Dohme South Africa, 1982—84; dir. sales Merck Sharp & Dohme Australia, 1984—85, dir. mktg. and sales, 1985—86, mng. dir., 1986—88; v.p. internat. human health mktg. Merck Sharp & Dohme Internat., 1988—89; v.p. mktg. Merck Sharp & Dohme USA, 1989—91; sr. v.p. human health divsn., pres. human health Merck & Co., Inc., 1991—92, sr. v.p. Europe human health divsn., 1993, pres. human health U.S./Can., 1994—97, pres. human health, 1997—. Bd. dirs. Am. Found. Pharm. Edn.; bd. dirs., exec. com. Biotech. Industry Orgn., Washington; bd. dirs. Nat. Pharm. Coun., Reston, Va., chmn., 1997; bd. trustees U. Scis., Phila., Found. for Managed Care Pharmacy, Alexandria, Va., U.S. Found. of U. of Valley of Guatemala ; mem. pres.'s coun. Gwynedd-Mercy Coll., Ambler, Pa.; mem. corp. adv. coun. COSSMHO, Nat. Coalition Hispanic Health and Human Svcs. Orgn., Washington; mem. corp. exec. bd. Phila. Mus. Art; mem. corp. coun. Children's Health Fund., Pitts. Chmn. steering com. Merck United Way, 1995—97. Office: Merck and Co Inc One Merck Dr Whitehouse Station NJ 08889-0100

ANSTROM, DECKER, broadcast executive; Grad., Macalester Coll., 1972; post grad., Princeton U. Sr. staff mem. Office Mgmt. and Budget, 1977—79; asst. dir. White House Office Presdl. Pers., 1979—81; pres. Pub. Strategies, Washington; exec. v.p. Nat. Cable TV Assn., 1987—93, pres., CEO, 1993—94, The Weather Channel, Atlanta, 1999—, Landmark Comm.; pres. The Weather Channel Companies. Recipient Am. Horizon Award, The Media Inst., 1999. Office: The Weather Channel 300 Interstate N. Pkwy. S.E. Atlanta GA 30339-2403*

ANTALEK, EILEEN ELIZABETH, educational consultant; b. Burtonwood, Eng., Jan. 16, 1957; d. Henry and Sarah Louise O'Connor; m. Michael Antalek, Feb. 16, 1980; children: Peter, Sarah. BA, Framingham State Coll., 1991; M in English, Clark U., 1994, EdD, 2003. House maintenance, Grafton, Mass., 1989-90; tutor Framingham (Mass.) State Coll., 1990-91, Clark U., Worcester, 1991-93, asst. dir. spl. needs, 1993-94, tchg. asst., 1994-95; asst. dir. Educational Directions, Westborough, Mass., 1995—. Cable access prodr. Grafton Cable Network, 1986—88. Publicity dir. North Grafton United Meth. Ch., 1986—88, Sunday sch. tchr., 1989—95, Sunday sch. supt., 1992—95, chair bd. edn., 1988—92, chair pastor parish rels., 1999—, chair space needs com., 2000—. Scholar Resident, Clark U., 1991—96, Nat. Merit, 1975, 1976, David O. Wilson, Anderson Coll., 1976. Mem.: Consortium for Learning Disabilities, Phi Eta Sigma. Avocations: textile art, motorcycling, painting, music, hiking. Office: Educational Directions 57 E Main St Ste 224 Westborough MA 01581 Fax: 508-870-1505.

ANTAR, GHASSAN YOUSSEF, research scientist; b. Zgharta, Lebanon, Nov. 29, 1965; arrived in U.S., 2000, s. Youssef Antar and Latife Merheb; m. Anne-Marie Pier-Antar, Aug. 6, 1994; children: Gabrielle, Firaas. MS, Lebanese U., 1990; diploma in advanced studies, U. Paris VI, 1994; PhD, Ecole Poly., Palaiseau, France, 1996. Postgrad. scientist Ecole Poly., Palaiseau, 1997; engr. CEA, Cadarache, France, 1998—99; postgrad. scientist U. Calif., San Diego, 2000, rsch. scientist, 2001—. Mem.: Am. Phys. Soc. Avocation: art.

ANTELL, DARRICK EUGENE, plastic surgeon, educator; b. Cleve., Feb. 22, 1951; s. E. James and Wanda H. (Kociecki) A.; m. Elizabeth Ann Sobottka, July 14, 1984; children: Gillian Elizabeth, Darrick Eugene Jr., Leslie Jane, Helen Greer, Meredith James. BS in Biology, Hobart Coll., 1973; DDS, Case Western Res. U. Dental, 1978; MD, Med. Coll. of Ohio, 1982. Cert. Am. Bd. Plastic Surgery. Surgery intern Stanford (Calif.) U. Med. Ctr., 1982-83, surgery resident, 1983-85; plastic surgery resident N.Y. Hosp. Cornell, N.Y.C., 1985-87; plastic and reconstructive surgeon St. Luke's/Roosevelt, N.Y.C., 1987—; asst. clin. prof. plastic surgery Columbia U., N.Y.C., 1989—; med. dir., founder 850 Park Surg. Ctr., N.Y.C. Author: Plastic Surgery, 1991; contbr. articles to profl. jours. Trustee East Side House Settlement, N.Y.C., 1991, Hist. Soc. of the Town of Greenwich, 1999, Univ. Sch. Cleve., 2000; trustee adv. Girl Scouts U.S.A., N.Y.C., 1991. Facial Proportions grantee Am. Soc. for Aesthetic Plastic Surgery, 1987; Maliniac fellow Plastic Surgery Edn. Found.; recipient Pres. Citizenship award N.Y. State Med. Soc., 1992. Fellow: ACS, Plastic Surgery Ednl. Found.; mem.: AMA, Lipoplasty Soc., Interplast, Am. Acad. Cosmetic Dentistry, Internat. Acad. Dental Facial Aesthetics (founding), Internat. Soc. for Aestheic Plastic Surgery, N.Y. Regional Soc. Plastic and Reconstructive Surgeons, Am. Soc. Maxillofacial Surgeons Parliamentarian, Am. Soc. Aesthetic Plastic Surgery, Am. Soc . Plastic and Reconstructive Surgeons, Univ. Sch. Alumni Adv. Coun., Herbert Conway Soc., Greenwich Skating Club, Mill Reef Club (Antigua, W.I.), Cleve. Skating Club, Fishers Island Yacht Club, Stanwich Country Club, Union Club. Avocations: squash, fly fishing, golf, skiing. Office: 850 Park Ave New York NY 10021-1845 E-mail: dea@antell-md.com.

ANTHOINE, ROBERT, lawyer, educator; b. Portland, Maine, June 5, 1921; s. Edward S and Sara B (Pinkham) Anthoine; m. Rebecca S Rudnick, Dec. 2, 1990; children from previous marriage: Alison, Robert Neal, Nelson, Nina. AB, Duke U., 1942; JD, Columbia U., 1949. Bar: NY 1949, US Ct Appeals (2d cir) 1956, US Supreme Ct 1970. Research assoc. Am. Law Inst. fed income tax project Columbia U., N.Y.C., 1949-50; assoc. Cleary, Gottlieb, Friendly and Cox, N.Y.C., 1950-52; assoc. prof. law Columbia U., N.Y.C., 1952-56, prof. law, 1956-64, adj. prof., 1964-93; ptnr. Winthrop, Stimson, Putnam and Roberts, N.Y.C., 1963-86, sr. counsel, 1987-2000, in charge London office, 1972-76; sr. counsel Pillsbury Winthrop LLP, 2001—. Vis prof Univ Tex Law Sch, Austin, 1988, Univ NC Law Sch, Chapel Hill, 1991, Univ Pa Law Sch, Philadelphia, 1996, Seattle Univ Law Sch, 1997. Auth, ed: survey Tax Incentives for Investment in Developing Countries, 1979; contbr. articles to profl jours. Active Coun Foreign Relations; chmn. emeritus, bd. dirs. Aperture Found.; pres Lucid Art Found, S K Yee Found; dir Hazen Polsky Found; hon gov Royal Shakespeare Theatre, Stratford-upon-Avon, England; vice-chmn, bd dirs Am Friends Theater; trustee, dir Grosvenor Gallery (Fine Arts) Ltd, London; vice chair, trustee Int Photog Coun, Royal Shakespeare Theatre Trust, Sevenarts, Ltd, London; bd dirs emeritus Eric and Salome Estorick Found, Vol Lawyers Arts; bd. dirs., v.p. Morris Graves Found. Lt. USN, 1942—46. Mem.: ABA, Asn Litéraire et Artistique Int (US), Int Fiscal Asn, Asn Bar City NY, Am Law Inst (life), Queen's, Hurlingham Club (London), River Club (New York, NY), Century Asn Club. Democrat. Office: Pillsbury Winthrop LLP One Battery Park Plz New York NY 10004-1490 E-mail: robert.anthoine@pillsburywinthrop.com.

ANTHONISEN, GEORGE RIOCH, sculptor, artist; b. Boston, July 31, 1936; s. Niels Landmark and Margaret (Rioch) A.; m. Ellen Friedman, Feb. 16, 1966; children: Rachel, Daniel. BA, U. Vt., 1961; postgrad., Nat. Acad. Design, N.Y.C., 1961—62, Art Students League, 1962—64, Dartmouth Coll. Med. Sch., 1967. One-man shows include Hopkins Ctr. Dartmouth Coll., 1966, Ctr. Art Gallery, N.Y.C., 1969, Moody Gallery, Pasadena, Calif., 1979, Bjorn Lindgren Gallery, N.Y.C., 1981, 82, U. Scranton (Pa.) Art Gallery, 1986, Rotunda Cannon House Office Bldg., U.S. Capitol, Washington, 1989, The Woodmere Art Mus., Phila., 1992, Bianco Gallery, Buckingham, Pa., 1994, 98, Phila. Flower Show-Gale Nurseries, 1995, Berman Mus. Art, Collegeville, Pa., 1996, Festival of Faiths, The Gardens of Louisville, 1999; exhibited in group shows NAD, N.Y., 1971, Port of History Mus., Phila., 1987, James A. Michener Art Mus., Doylestown, 1988, 00, Millersville (Pa.) U., 1991, Nat. Sculpture Soc., 1993, Morani Gallery, Med. Coll. Pa., 1994, Monuments Conservancy, Samuel Dorsky Symposium on Pub. Monuments/Time and Life Bldg., N.Y.C., 1997, Bianco Gallery, Buckingham, Pa., 1995-2002, Salmagundi Club, N.Y.C., 2000, Travis Gallery, 2002, 03; represented in permanent collections at WHO, Geneva, U.S. Capitol Bldg. Hall of Columns, Washington, Carnegie Hall, N.Y.C., Rittenhouse Hotel, Phila., Cathedral Heritage Found., Louisville, Please Touch Mus., Phila., Dartmouth-Hitchcock Med. Ctr., Lebanon, N.H., Washington Sch. Psychiatry, Germantown Hosp., Med. Ctr., Phila., Doylestown (Pa.) Hosp., Atlanta U. Trevor Arnett Libr., Trevor Arnett Libr., U. Alaska, Fairbanks, James Michener Art Mus., Doylestown, Phila. Coll. Osteo. Medicine, Berman Mus. Art, Collegeville, N.Y., Martin Art Gallery, Muhlenberg Coll., Allentown, Pa. With U.S. Army, 1955-57. Sculptor-in-residence Augustus St. Gaudens Nat. Hist. Site, U.S. Dept. Interior, 1971; recipient James Augustus Suydam bronze medal, 1968, Sen. Ernest Gruening award Alaska State Coun. on Arts, 1976, Exemplary Achievement in Arts award Bucks County (Pa.) C. of C., 1985. Fellow Nat. Sculpture Soc. (bd. dirs. 1993-94), hon. mem. Phila. Sketch Club. 2002. Avocations: fishing, baseball. Home and Office: PO Box 147 Solebury PA 18963-0147 Fax: 215-297-5162. E-mail: ellena@voicenet.com.

ANTHONY, ANDREW JOHN, lawyer; b. Newark, Jan. 26, 1950; s. Andrew and Mary (Norton) A.; m. Raquel Perez Montoya, Sept. 29, 1990; children: Nicholas, Natalie. BA, Kean Coll., 1973; JD cum laude, U. Miami, 1976. Bar: Fla. 1977, U.S. Dist. Ct. (so. dist.) Fla. 1977. Assoc. Knight, Peters, Hoeveler, Pickle, Niemoeller & Flynn, Miami, Fla., 1977-79, Vernis & Bowling, Miami, 1979, Ligman, Martin, Shiley & McGee, Coral Gables, Fla., 1979-86; sole practice Coral Gables, 1986—. Mem. ABA, Fla. Bar Assn. Democrat. Roman Catholic. Avocations: numismatics, fishing, reading. Home: 3703 Anderson Rd Coral Gables FL 33134-7052 Office: 866 S Dixie Hwy Coral Gables FL 33146 E-mail: ajanthony@ajalaw.com.

ANTHONY, DONALD BARRETT, engineering executive; b. Kansas City, Kans., Jan. 28, 1948; s. Donald W. and Marjorie (Lifsey) A.; m. Darla S. Donovan, Dec. 16, 1972; children: Jennifer L., Danielle S. BSChemE, U. Toledo, 1970; MS, MIT, 1971, DSc, 1974. Asst. prof., practice sch. dir. dept. chem. engring. MIT, Cambridge, Mass., 1974-75; group supr. coal R&D Std. Oil Co. Ohio, Cleve., 1976-77, mgr. marine planning, 1978-79, mgr. synthetic fuels devel., 1980-83, v.p., gen. mgr. Pfaudler Divsn. Rochester, N.Y., 1983-85; v.p. R&D Std. Oil Co., Cleve., 1985-87, BP Am., Inc., Cleve., 1987-88, BP Exploration, Inc., Cleve., 1989-90; v.p. tech. Bechtel, Inc., Houston, 1990-94, v.p. ops., 1994-95, v.p. ref., 1995-96; pres. Bailey Controls Co., 1996-98, Process Ind. Group, ABB Automation, 1999—2000; pres., CEO NineSigma, Inc., Cleve., 2001—. Contbr. articles to profl. jours.; patentee in field. Capt. AUS, 1970-78. MIT Esso fellow, 1970-71, Little rsch.-devel. fellow, 1971-72, Procter & Gamble fellow, 1972-73, Bechtel fellow, 1992. Mem. AIChE, Am. Chem. Soc., Sigma Xi, Phi Kappa Phi, Tau Beta Pi, Pi Mu Epsilon, Phi Eta Sigma. Lutheran. Home: 6336 Canterbury Dr Hudson OH 44236-3488 Office: NineSigma Inc 29145 Chagrin Blvd Cleveland OH 44122

ANTHONY, DONALD BRUCE, humanities educator; b. East Cleveland, Ohio, Aug. 8, 1936; s. Donald Elliot and Arvella Mae (Coffin) Anthony; BA in Music, Oberlin (Ohio) Coll., 1958; MA in Music, Stanford (Calif.) U., 1959, PhD in Music, 1968. Pvt. tchr. piano and music theory, Palo Alto, Calif., 1960-92; cons. music software Soundware Corp., Menlo Park, Calif., 1988-96; adminstr. Ctr. for Computer Assisted Rsch. in Humanities, Stanford, 1996—. Mem. Soc. for Performance of Contemporary Music (pres. bd. 1960-70), Music Now (bd. dirs.). Democrat. Home: 2721 Midtown Ct 313 Palo Alto CA 94303 Office: CCARH Braun Music Ctr # 129 Stanford CA 94305 E-mail: wushujia@earthlink.net.

ANTHONY, DONALD CHARLES, librarian, educator; b. N.Y.C., Mar. 29, 1926; s. Charles and Margaret Evelyn (Gleason) A.; m. Mary Miserez, Apr. 18, 1957; children— Stephen, Sheila, Irene. BA, U. Wis., 1951, MA, 1954; postgrad., U. Geneva, Switzerland, 1952-53. Library asst. Enoch Pratt Free Library, Balt., 1954-55; librarian Eleutherian Mills-Hagley Found., Wilmington, Del., 1955-59; dir. Fargo (N.D.) Pub. Library, 1959-61; asso. librarian N.Y. State Library, Albany, 1961-66; asst. dir. Columbia Libraries, 1966-69, acting dir., 1969, asso. dir., 1970-74; dir. Syracuse U. Libraries, 1974-85; cons. on preservation of library materials, 1986—; pres. Donmar Assocs., Clinton, N.Y., 1987—. Adj. faculty Mohawk Valley Community Coll., Utica, N.Y., 1989-97; docent Munson-Williams-Proctor Arts Inst., Utica, 1999—; cons. N.Y. State Edn. Dept., 1967-97. Producer; host: TV Museum, KXGO-TV, Fargo, 1960; Contbr. articles to profl. jours. Trustee N.Y. Met. Reference and Research Library Agy., 1969-74, Cen. N.Y. Library Resources Council, 1983-86; chmn. bd. dirs. Five Asso. U. Libraries, Syracuse, 1975-76, 77-79; trustee Bd. Edn., Dobbs Ferry, N.Y., 1971-74, v.p., 1973-74. Served with USNR, 1944-46. Fellow Coun. on Libr. Resources. Home: 3654 State Route 12 Clinton NY 13323-4245

ANTHONY, EDWARD MASON, linguistics educator; b. Cleve., Sept. 1, 1922; s. Edward Mason and Elsie (Haas) A.; m. Ann Louise Terbrueggen, Sept. 18, 1946; children: Lynn Diane Anthony Higgins, Janice Louise, Edward Mason, 4th. AB, U. Mich., 1944, MA, 1946, PhD, 1954. From instr. English to prof. linguistics U. Mich., 1945-64; prof. U. Pitts., 1964-90, prof. emeritus, 1990—, chmn. dept. gen. linguistics, 1964-74; dir. Lang. Acquisition Inst., 1970, dir. lang. orientation programs, 1974-82, dir. Asian Studies program, 1977-82, dir. Lang. and Culture Inst, 1982-90. Vis. lectr., Afghanistan, 1951, Thailand, 1955-57, Mexico, 1964, 65, Poland, 1977, Greece and Yugoslavia, 1981, Singapore and Thailand, 1984, Hong Kong, 1985, 86; dir. S.E. Asian English Project, Thailand, Laos, Vietnam, 1958-61, Rockefeller Found. Thai Project, 1967-72; vis. prof. Regional English Lang. Centre, Singapore, 1974-75, Peking Inst. Fgn. Lang., 1979-80; cons. in field; mem. Nat. Adv. Council Teaching English as a Fgn. Lang.; resource person Detroit Bd. Edn., 1964, Pitts. Bd. Edn., 1965; mem. adv. screening com. in linguistics Council for Internat. Exchange of Scholars, 1976; mem. adv. panel in English teaching to dir. USIA, 1987-93. Author: Reading Thai Syllables, 1962, (with others) Foundations of Thai, 2 vols, 1968, Towards a Theory of Lexical Meaning, 1975, About Thai, 2001; book rev. editor: Lan. Learning, 1948; editor, 1949. Smith-Mundt grantee, 1951; recipient Fulbright award, 1955-57; NDEA lang. Rsch. grantee, 1965-67; State Dept. grantee, 1964, 65, 77, 81, 84, 90; plaque of Honor Ramkhamhaeng U., Bangkok, Thailand, 1986, USIA cert. appreciation, 1992. Mellon fellow Nat. Fgn. Language Ctr. Washington, 1990; mem. Linguistic Soc., Am. Assn. Applied Linguistics, Assn. Asian Studies, Siam Soc. (life), Assn. Tchrs. English to Speakers of Other Langs. (pres. 1967, Alatis award 1991), Nat. Council Tchrs. English. Democrat. Presbyterian. Home: 4118 Northampton Dr Allison Park PA 15101-1532 Office: Dept Linguistics U Pitts Pittsburgh PA 15260 E-mail: ema1@pitt.edu.

ANTHONY, ETHAN, architect; b. Iowa City, Oct. 14, 1950; s. Frank and Carol (Kessler) A.; m. Luz Eugenia Rey, Feb. 18, 1984; children: Winston Eugene, Alexandra Luce, Edward Rey. Student, Boston Architecture Ctr., 1971-77; BArch, U. Oreg., 1980. Project architect Payette Assocs., Boston, 1980-83; prin. Anthony Assocs., Boston, 1983-90; pres. HDB/Cram & Ferguson Inc., Boston, 1998—; cons. architect Phillips Exeter Acad., 1998—2003, St. George's Sch., 1999—2001, The Canterbury Sch., Greensboro, NC, 1999—2003, Syon Abbey, Roanoke, Va., 2001—, Casady Sch., Oklahoma City, 2001—; pres. Kalmia Woods Corp., 2001—. Cons. N.E. Worldcom, 1994-2000; instr. design Roger Williams U., Bristol, R.I., 1984-89; thesis advisor Boston Archtl. Ctr., 1985-87; speaker in field. Cons. architect Russell Sage First Presbyn. Ch., N.Y.C., 1994-98, All Saints Ch., Peterborough, N.H., 1998-2001. Recipient honor award Interfaith Forum on Religion, Art and Arch., 1993. Mem. AIA, Boston Soc. Archs. Avocations: painting, history, professional speaking. Office: Hoyle Doran and Berry Inc 83 Newbury St Boston MA 02116-3007

ANTHONY, FRANCIS POLIPNICK (FRANCIS ANTHONY POLIPNICK), poet, writer; b. Breckenridge, Minn., June 6, 1922; s. Alois Leo Polipnick and Loretta Pauline Miksche; m. Carol Louise Kessler, 1950 (div.); children: Ethan, Karen, Bryan, Leslie; m. Susan Carter Hall, June 30, 1985; 1 child, Frederick. BA, U. Minn., 1950; MALS, Dartmouth Coll., 1984; PhD, Fla. State U., 1990. TV prodr. Sta. KKTV, Colorado Springs, Colo., 1953-54; specifications engr. Douglas Aircraft, El Segundo, Calif., 1954-55; pers. mgr. Raytheon Co., Waltham, Mass., 1955-60; columnist, editor Beacon Publs., Acton, Mass., 1960—70; owner Small Cars of Stow, Mass., 1960-76; prodr. Vt. Pub. Radio, Windsor, 1977-80; pres. New Eng. Writers, Windsor, 1986—. Interviews of celebrities archived in spl. collections Dartmouth Coll., 1980—. Author: Terminus, 1976, books of poetry, essays and interviews, 1980—. Mem. nat. adv. bd. Boy Scouts Am., Boston, 1960—62; fund raiser State Red Feather, Boston, 1962—64; Windsor Planning Commn., 1995—; mem. Windsor Zoning Bd., 1995—, S.W. Regional Transp. Adv. Bd., 1995—; Rep. nominee to U.S. Ho. of Reps. Mass., 1964. Staff sgt. USAF, 1942—46. Arts coun. grantee State of Minn., 1982; recipient Lambda Iota Tau, 1988, Hon. award Paradox Internat., 1999. Mem. Acad. Am. Poets, New Eng. Poetry Club, Bay Area Poetry Coalition (Poets prize 1996). Avocations: flying, oil painting, guns, interviewing. Home and Office: 151 Main St Box 5 Windsor VT 05089 E-mail: newvtpoet@aol.com.

ANTHONY, HARRY ANTONIADES, city planner, architect, educator; b. Skyros, Greece, July 28, 1922; arrived in U.S., 1951, naturalized, 1954; s. Anthony G. and Maria G. (Ftoulis) Antoniades; m. Anne C. Skoufis, Sept. 23, 1950; children: Mary Anne Anthony Smith, Kathryn Harriet. B.Arch., Nat. Tech. U., Athens, Greece, 1945; student, Ecole Nat. Supérieure des Beaux Arts, Paris, 1945-46; M.City Planning, U. Paris, 1947; Docteur de l'Université, Sorbonne, Paris, 1949; PhD in Arch. and Urban Planning, Columbia, 1955. Architect-planner with Constantinos A. Doxiadis, Athens, 1943-45, LeCorbusier, Paris, 1946-47, ECA, Paris, 1949-51; city planner with Maurice E.H. Rotival, N.Y.C., 1951-52; chief planner Brown & Blauvelt, N.Y.C., 1952-54; city planner, urban designer Skidmore, Owings & Merrill, N.Y.C., 1954-56; prin. planning cons. Brown Engrs. Internat., N.Y.C., 1956-60; prin. Brown & Anthony City Planners, Inc., N.Y.C., 1960—69; v.p. Doxiadis Assocs., Inc., Washington, 1971—72; mem. faculty Columbia U., 1953-72, from asst. to assoc. prof., 1956-63, prof. urban planning, 1963-72, dir. grad. div. urban planning Grad. Sch. Architecture and Planning, 1962-65; prof. urban planning Calif. State Poly. U., Pomona, 1972-83, prof. emeritus urban and regional planning, 1983—, chmn. dept., 1972-76. Vis. prof. urban design Tulane U., 1967-68; vis. lectr. U. Calif. at Berkeley, Stanford U., Dartmouth, San Diego State U., CUNY, U. Okla., Ohio U., Auburn U., Salk Inst. Biol. Studies, U.S. Internat. U.; lectr. urban studies and planning U. Calif., San Diego, 1980-82, Chancellor's Assoc., 2001—; scholar-in-residence U. B.C., Vancouver, 1978; planning, zoning, urban renewal and urban design cons. to several cities, U.S. and abroad; also cons. to UN, Am. Med. Bldg. Guild, corps. and pvt. firms, to govts. and univs.; planning commr., Leonia, N.J., 1958-64; master planner, cons. arch. for Ss. Constantine and Helen Greek Orthodox Ch. and Village for the Elderly, Cardiff-by-the-Sea, Calif., 1983-97 (AIA design awareness program orchid award 1997). Author, co-author, contbr.: Four Great Makers of Modern Architecture: Gropius, Le Corbusier, Mies Van Der Rohe, Wright, Dictionary of American History, The Challenge of Squatter Settlements-With Special Reference to the Cities of Latin America, La Défense à Paris et le Quartier d'Affaires de Vancouver: Une Comparaison Urbaine, New Orleans Air Rights Study, Woodstock Growth Plan and Land Use Controls, Mt. Vernon Planning Study, Corning Area, N.Y.: Conditions and Prospects, Corning Region: Development Plans, Metairie Shore, La.: Lakefront Recreation and Comty. Devel., U.S. Navy Multiple Activity Master Plan: Norfolk Complex, Aqaba, Jordan: Future Devel., Lands of Kapua, Hawaii: Feasibility Study for Urban, Agricultural and Recreational Devel.; several master plans, city and regional planning reports, urban design plans and programs, environ. impact reports, zoning ordinances, educational videocassettes on urban planning subjects; contbr. articles to profl. jours., mags., newspapers; acad. profl. writings, awards, plans, designs and reports included in Spl. Collections Libr., U. Calif. (San Diego), 1998. Recipient Premier Grand Prix Internat. Exhbn. Housing and City Planning, Paris, 1947, St. Paul's Gold Medal award Greek Orthodox Archdiocese Am., 2003; William Kinne Fellows travelling fellow in planning N.Am., 1956, French Govt. fellow, 1945-47; research award Urban Center of Columbia U., 1969; named Outstanding Prof. Calif. State Poly. U., 1975; founder Met. Opera House, Lincoln Ctr. for the Performing Arts, N.Y.C. Mem. AIA (Arnold W. Brunner scholar 1958), Am. Inst. Cert. Planners (bd. examiners), Am. Planning Assn. (Disting. Svc. award 1984, San Diego Cmty. Design Awareness Program Orchid award 1997), Order of Am. Hellenic Ednl. Progressive Assn., Hellenic Cultural Soc. (Dedication to Perpetuating the Greek Lang. award 2003), Internat. Land Econs. Soc. of Lambda Alpha (Richard T. Ely Disting. Educator award 1988), Univ. Calif. San Diego Faculty Club. Home: 7665 Caminito Avola La Jolla CA 92037-3956 E-mail: hanthony@ucsd.edu.

ANTHONY, JACK RAMON, mechanical engineer, retired; b. Hobbs, N.Mex., Dec. 9, 1932; s. Wadie Fowler and Zelma Ray Anthony; m. Peggy Lou Berryhill, July 17, 1953; children; Vera Lynn Anthony Robertson, Michael Ray. BSME, U. N.Mex., 1959; ME, Tex. Tech. U., 1974. Registered profl. engr., Tex. Engr. Chrysler, New Orleans, 1963-65, Eberline Instruments, Santa Fe, 1959-63, Dresser Golf, Houston, 1965-67; project engr. Mason & Hagner co., Amarillo, Tex., 1967-90, Nuclear Fuel Svcs., Erwin, Tenn., 1990-95; retired, 1995—. With U.S. Army, 1953-55. Mem. NSPE (chpt. pres. 1973-74), Pi Tau Sigma. Republican. Methodist. Achievements include patent for Ditigal Plotter and Drive System. Home: PO Box 308 Buffalo OK 73834-0308

ANTHONY, JOAN CATON, administrative judge; b. South Bend, Ind., July 28, 1939; d. Joseph Robert and Margaret Catherine (McMeel) Caton; m. Robert Armstrong Anthony, Jan. 3, 1980; 1 child, Peter. BA, Marquette U., 1961; MA, Northwestern U., 1963; JD, Catholic U. Am., 1979. Bar: D.C. 1980, Va. 1982. Instr. English Marquette U., Milw., 1963-65, George Washington U., Washington, 1965-69, asst. prof., 1969-70; spl. asst. student affairs HEW, Washington, 1970-72; dir. Office Student and Youth Affairs U.S. Office Edn., Washington, 1972-74, legis. specialist, 1974-78; chief mgmt. ops. br. Fed. Wildlife Permit Office U.S. Fish and Wildlife Svc., Washington, 1978-81; assoc. Cate and Goodbread, Washington, 1981—85; atty., advisor office legis. counsel U.S. Dept. Interior, 1991-95; staff atty. Interior Bd. Land Appeals, 1995—2003; adminstrv. judge Def. Office of Hearings and Appeals, U.S. Dept. Def., 2003—. Mem. U.S. del. to 2d meeting Conf. Parties to Conv. on Internat. Trade in Endangered Species of Wild Fauna and Flora, San Jose, Costa Rica, 1979. Contbr. lit. revs., essays and articles on univ.-cmty. rels., western settlement and internat. negotiations to various publs. Pres. Franklin Forest Frolickers, 1985—86; den leader Cub Scouts, mem. com. Boy Scouts Am., 1990—2000; parent vol. Fairfax County Pub. Schs., 1987—2001; treas. Greater McLean Rep. Women's Club, 1987—88; bd. dirs. McLean Citizens Assn., 1982—83, Fairfax County Humane Soc., 1983. Recipient Spl. Achievement award U.S. Fish and Wildlife Svc., 1981. Mem. D.C. Bar, Va. Bar, DAR (Freedom Hill chpt.). Roman Catholic. Home: 2011 Lorraine Ave Mc Lean VA 22101-5331

ANTHONY, J(ULIAN) DANFORD, JR., lawyer; b. Boston, Oct. 23, 1935; s. Julian Danford and Eleanor Caroline (Hopkins) A.; m. Ellen Nora Brown, Apr. 8, 1961; children: Julian Danford III, Sarah Dodge, David Campbell. AB, Wesleyan U., 1957; LLB, Harvard U., 1960. Bar: Minn. 1961, Conn. 1965. Atty.-advisor U.S. Tax Ct., Washington, 1962-64; assoc. Day, Berry & Howard LLP, Hartford, Conn., 1965-70, ptnr., 1971—. Chmn. Conn. Red Cross Blood Svcs., Farmington, 1981—82; trustee J. Walton Bissell Found., Hartford, 1987—, pres., 1987—; mem. adv. bd. dirs. Salvation Army, Hartford, 1990—96; elector Wadsworth Atheneum, Hartford, 1986—95; corporator Hartford Hosp., 1988—; trustee Amistad Found., Hartford, 1997—; bd. dirs. Hartford Symphony Orch., 1993—99, Conn. Children's Med. Ctr., 1994—, chmn., 1999—2002; bd. dirs. Conn. Children's Med. Ctr. Found., 1998—, Coordinating Coun. for Founds., Hartford, 1994—99. Mem. ABA, Nat. Assn. Bond Lawyers, Nat. Assn. Coll. and Univ. Attys., Fed. Tax Inst. New Eng. (exec. com. 1987—), Conn. Bar Assn. (chmn. tax sect. 1988-91), IRS Exempt Orgns. Liaison Group, Tax Club Hartford (pres. 1970-71). Office: Day Berry & Howard LLP Cityplace Hartford CT 06103

ANTHONY, KATHRYN HARRIET, architecture educator; b. NYC, Sept. 11, 1955; d. Harry Antoniades and Anne (Skoufis) Anthony; m. Barry Daniel Riccio, May 24, 1980 (dec. Jan. 2001). AB in Psychology, U. Calif., Berkeley, 1976, PhD in Architecture, 1981. Rsch. promotion Kaplan/McLaughlin/Diaz Architects and Planners, San Francisco, 1980-81; vis. lectr. U. Calif., Berkeley, Calif., 1980-81, 82-83, San Francisco State U., Calif., 1981; assoc. prof. Calif. State Poly. U., Pomona, Calif., 1981-84; asst. prof. U. Ill., Urbana-Champaign, Ill., 1984-89, assoc. prof., 1989-96, chair bldg. rsch. coun., 1994-97, prof. architecture, 1996—, chair design faculty, 2002—. Guest lectr. numerous orgns., coll. and univ.; mem. numerous comm. Coll. of Fine and Applied Arts, Sch. Architecture, Housing Rsch. and Devel. Program, Dept. Landscape Architecture. Author: Design Juries on Trial: The Renaissance of the Design Studio, 1991, Designing for Diversity: Gender, Race, and Ethnicity in the Architectural Profession, 2001; co-editor Jour. Archtl. Edn. 47:1, 1993; mem. editl. bd. Jour. Archtl. and Planning Rsch., 1989-92, Jour. Archtl. Edn., 1990-95, Environ. and Behavior Jour., 1991—; reviewer Landscape Jour., 1990; contbr. articles to profl. jours; co-designer, co-prodr. (exhibit) Shattering the Glass Ceiling: The Role of Gender and Race in the Archtl. Profession, Nat. Conv. AIA, 1996. Recipient Collaborative Achievement award AIA, 2003; Creative Achievement award Assn. Collegiate Sch. Architecture, 1992; grant US Army C.E.R.L., 1993, grant U. Ill., 1984, 87, 92, 93, 95, 96, grant Graham Found., 1989-91, 93-96, grant Decatur Housing Authority, 1988, grant Upgrade Cos., Peoria, Ill., 1987, grant Nat. Endowment for Arts, 1986-87, grant LA County Cmty. Devel. Commn., 1984, grant Calif. State U. and Coll., 1982, 83, summer grant U. Calif., Berkeley, 1980; fellow Acad. Leadership Program Com. Instnl. Coop., 1996-97. Mem. Environ. Design Rsch. Assn. (bd. dir. 1989-92, treas. 1990-92, co-editor Coming of Age: Proceedings of 21st Ann. Conf. 1990), Chgo. Women in Architecture. Home: 309 W Pennsylvania Ave Urbana IL 61801-4918 Office: U Ill Sch Architecture 611 Taft Dr Champaign IL 61820-6922 E-mail: kanthony@uiuc.edu.

ANTHONY, KENNETH C., JR., lawyer; b. Spartanburg, S.C., Jan. 23, 1954; s. Kenneth C. Sr. and Carol Ferguson (Burnside) A.; m. Monta Lorraine Moody, Mar. 15, 1980; children: Jay, Mary Sullivan, Dunk, Grady. Student, Rice U., 1972-74; BA, Wofford Coll., 1975; JD, U. S.C., 1977. Bar: S.C. 1978, U.S. Dist. Ct. S.C. 1978, U.S. Ct. Appeals (4th cir.) 1988, U.S. Supreme Ct. 1996; cert. civil and family mediator; cert. civil arbitrator. Ptnr. The Anthony Law Firm, P.A., Spartanburg, 1978—. Adj. prof. Wofford Coll., Spartanburg, 1978-98; bd. advisors U. S.C. Law Sch., Columbia, 1988-92. Recipient Compleat Lawyer award, USC Law School, 2001. Fellow S.C. Bar Found. (life); mem. ABA (mem. editl. bd.ABA/BNA Lawyers; Manual on Professional Conduct, 1995-98), S.C. Bar Assn. (ho. dels. 1985-96, chmn. Law Related Edn. Commn. 1999-2000, bd. govs. 1996-99, sec. 2000-01, treas. 2001-02, past chmn. ethic adv. com., pres. 2003—), S.C. Trial Lawyers Assn. (bd. govs. 1996-98), Am. Trial Lawyers Assn. Office: The Anthony Law Firm PA 250 Magnolia St PO Box 3565 Spartanburg SC 29304-3565 Fax: 864-583-9772. E-mail: kanthony@anthonylaw.com.

ANTHONY, LEWIS GEORGE, retired internist, cardiologist; b. Jim Thorpe, Pa., Jan. 3, 1936; MD, Jefferson Med. Coll., 1961. Diplomate Am. Bd. Internal Medicine, Am. Bd. Cardiology. Intern Allentown Hosp., 1961-62; resident Tripler Army Hosp., Honolulu, 1964-67; fellow in cardiology Med. Ctr. Hosp. Vt., Burlington, 1970-72; mem. staff Bellin Meml. Hosp., Green Bay, Wis., 1973-2000; ptnr. Cardiol. Assoc., Green Bay, 1972-2000; mem. staff St. Vincent Hosp., 1973-2000; ret., 2000. Cons. staff mem. Dickinson County Hosp., 1985-2000, Door County Meml. Hosp., 1987-2000, Holy Family Hosp., 1993-2000. Fellow Am. Coll. Cardiology; mem. AMA, Am. Soc. Internal Medicine. Office: Cardiol Assocs Green Bay 704 S Webster Ave Green Bay WI 54301-3528 E-mail: lightkeeper36@aol.com.

ANTHONY, MICHAEL FRANCIS, lawyer; b. Chgo., Dec. 19, 1950; s. Rudolph A. and Margaret M. (Shea) A.; m. Megan P. O'Connell; children: Erin Christine, Ian O'Connell, Connor Cullerton, Madeline Shea, McKenzie Galligan. BS cum laude, Xavier U., Cin., 1972, MHA, 1974; JD, U. Balt., 1978. Bar: Md. 1978, Fla. 1979, Ill. 1980, D.C. 1989. Adminstrv. positions Johns Hopkins Hosp., Balt., 1973-78; assoc. Ober Kaler Grimes & Shriver, Balt., 1978-80; from assoc. to ptnr. McDermott, Will & Emery, Chgo., 1980-87, 1989—91, nat. head health law dept., 1991—2001; sr. v.p. for legal affairs Am. Hosp. Assn., Chgo., 1987-89. Contbr. articles to profl. jours. Mem. adv. bd. De Paul Inst. for Health Law. Fellow Am. Coll. Healthcare Execs. (various coms.), Am. Health Lawyers Assn. (past pres.). Office: McDermott Will & Emery 227 W Monroe St Ste 3100 Chicago IL 60606-5096 E-mail: manthony@mwe.com.

ANTHONY, RICHARD E. bank executive; b. May 6, 1946; BS in Fin., U. Ala., 1968; MBA, U. Va., 1971. Various position including exec. v.p. AmSouth Bank, N.A., Birmingham, 1971—85; pres. First Comml. Bancshares, Inc., 1985; chmn. bd., CEO First Comml. Bank, 1985; chmn. First Comml. Bank. (acquired by Synovus), Birmingham, 1985—93; pres. Synovus Finl. Corp., Ala., 1993—95; vice chmn. Synovus, Columbus, Ga., 1995—. Dir. Econ. Develop. Partnership Ala.; mem. Fin. Svc. Roundtable, U. Ala. Nat. Adv. Coun., U. Ala. Pres.'s Cabinet; mem. bd. vistors U. Ala. Sch. Commerce and Bus. Adminstrn. ; bd. dirs. Bux. Coun. Ala. Mem.: Kiwanis (pres. Birmingham club), Morning Quarterback Club (capt. 1993). Office: Synovus Finl Corp PO Box 120 Columbus GA 31902 Office Fax: 703-641-6555.

ANTHONY, ROBERT ARMSTRONG, lawyer, educator; b. Washington, Dec. 28, 1931; s. Emile Peter and Martha Graham (Armstrong) Anthony; m. Ruth Grace Barrons, Feb. 7, 1959 (div.); 1 child, Graham Barrons; m. Joan Patricia Caton, Jan. 3, 1980; 1 child, Peter Christopher Caton. BA, Yale U., 1953; BA in Jurisprudence, Oxford U., 1955; JD, Stanford U., 1957. Bar: Calif. 1957, N.Y. 1971, DC 1972. Assoc. Pillsbury, Madison & Sutro, San Francisco, 1957-62, Kelso, Cotton & Ernst, San Francisco, 1962-64; assoc. prof. law Cornell U. Law Sch., 1964-68, prof., 1968-75, dir. internat. legal studies, 1964-74; chief counsel, later dir. Office Fgn. Direct Investments, Dept. Commerce, 1972-73; cons. Adminstrv. Conf. U.S., Washington, 1968-71, chmn., 1974-79; ptnr. McKenna, Conner & Cuneo, Washington, 1979-82; pvt. practice Washington, 1982-83; prof. law George Mason U., Arlington, Va., 1983—2002, prof. emeritus, 2002—. Fulbright lectr., Slovenia, 1994; lectr. Acad. Am. and Internat. Law, Southwestern Legal Found., Dallas, 1967—72; instr. Golden Gate U., 1961; cons., chmn. pubs. adv. bd. Internat. Law Inst., 1984—; cons. Inst. Pub. Adminstrn., Slovenia, 1994—. Mem. editl. adv. bd. Jour. Law and Tech., 1986—91; contbr. articles to profl. jours. Active Pres.'s Inflation Program Regulatory Coun., 1978—79; chmn. panel U.S. Dept. Edn. Appeal Bd., 1981—83; commr. Sausalito (Calif.) City Planning Commn., 1962—64; active Fairfax County (Va.) Rep. Com., 1984—86; bd. dirs. Nat. Ctr. Adminstrv. Justice, 1974—79, Marin Shakespeare Festival, San Rafael, Calif., 1961—64, Va. Assn. Scholars, 1990—98. Mem.: ABA (coun., sec. sect. adminstrv. law and regulatory practice 1988—94), Stanford U. Law Soc. Washington (pres. 1982), Am. Law Inst., Assn. Am. Rhodes Scholars, Cosmos Club. Home: 2011 Lorraine Ave Mc Lean VA 22101-5331 Office: George Mason U Law Sch 3301 N Fairfax Dr Arlington VA 22201-4426 E-mail: ranthony@gmu.edu.

ANTHONY, ROBERT NEWTON, management educator emeritus; b. Orange, Mass., Sept. 6, 1916; s. Charles H. and Grace (Newton) A.; m. Gretchen Lynch, Aug. 28, 1943; children: Robert N., Victoria Stewart; m. Katherine Worley, Aug. 4, 1973. AB, Colby Coll., 1938, MA (hon.), 1959, LHD (hon.), 1963; MBA, Harvard U., 1940, DCS, 1952. Mem. faculty Bus. Sch., Harvard U., 1940-42, 46-67, 68-83, Ross Graham Walker prof. mgmt. control, prof. emeritus, 1983—. Pres. Mgmt. Analysis Ctr., Inc., 1955-63; asst. sec., contr. Dept. Def., 1965-68; prof. Mgmt. Devel. Inst., Switzerland, 1957-58; with Stanford Exec. Devel. Program, 1962; mem. adv. com. IMEDE, Switzerland, 1961-65, 68-77; spl. asst. to chmn. Price Commn., 1971-73; mem. educators cons. com. GAO, 1973-87; dir., chmn. audit com. Carborundum Co., 1971-77; dir. Warnaco, Inc., 1971-86; mem. adv. com. Kyoto Rsch. Inst., 1987-90, IPMI (Jakarta), 1983-90. Author: Management Controls in Industrial Research Organization, 1952, (with Dearborn and Kneznek) Shoe Machinery: Buy or Lease?, 1955, (with Reece) Accounting, Text and Cases, 1956, 11th edit. (with Hawkins and Merchant), 2004, Office Equipment, Buy or Rent?, 1957, Essentials of Accounting, 1964, 8th edit., 2003, Accounting Principles, 1965, 7th edit., 1995, Planning and Control Systems: A Framework for Analysis, 1965, (with Govindarajan) Management Control Systems, (with Vijay Govindarajan) 11th edit., 2004, (with Hekimian) Operations Cost Control, 1967, Plaid in Management Accounting, (with Welsch) Fundamentals of Financial Accounting, 1974, Fundamentals of Management Accounting, 1974, (with Young) Management Control in Nonprofit Organizations, 1975, 7th edit., 2003, Accounting for the Cost of Interest, 1976, Financial Accounting in Nonbusiness Organizations, 1978, Tell It Like It Was, 1983, Future Directions for Financial Accounting, 1984, Teach Yourself the Essentials of Accounting (computer software), 1999; (with Anderson) The New Corporate Director, 1986, The Management Control Function, 1988, Should Business and Nonbusiness Accounting Be Different?, 1989, Rethinking the Rules of Financial Accounting, 2003; editor Richard D. Irwin, Inc.; mem. bd. Harvard Bus. Rev., 1947-60; contbr. articles to profl. jours. Trustee Colby Coll., 1959-74, 75—, chmn., 1978-83; trustee Dartmouth Hitchcock Med. Ctr., 1983-93, treas., 1993; town auditor Town of Waterville Valley, N.H., 1976-92; mem. audit com. City of N.Y., 1977-85. Lt. comdr. USNR, 1941-46. Recipient Disting. Leadership award Fed. Govt. Accts. Assn., Disting. Pub. Svc. medal Dept. Def., Disting. Svc. award Harvard Bus. Sch., Marriner Disting. Svc. award Colby Coll., Meritorious Svc. award Exec. Office of Pres., CINPAC Letter of Commendation, Baker Scholar; named to Acctg. Hall of Fame. Fellow Acad. Mgmt.; mem. Am. Acctg. Assn. (v.p. 1959, pres. 1973-74, Outstanding Acctg. Educator of Yr. 1989, acctg. sect. Lifetime Achievement award 2003), Fin. Exec. Inst., Inst. Mgmt. Accts. (chmn. cost concepts subcom., mgmt. acctg. practices com.), Assn. Govt. Accts., Am. Soc. Mil. Compts., Cosmos Club, Phi Beta Kappa, Pi Gamma Mu, Beta Alpha Psi. Home: 80 Lyme Rd Apt 332 Hanover NH 03755-1233 E-mail: rnanthony@valley.net.

ANTHONY, SHEILA FOSTER, government official; b. Hope, Ark., Nov. 8, 1940; m. Beryl F. Anthony; children: Alison, Lauren. BA, U. Ark., 1962; JD, Am. U., 1984. Bar: Ark. 1985, D.C. 1985, U.S. Ct. Appeals (D.C. cir.) 1987, U.S. Supreme Ct. 1992. Tchr. Ark. Pub. Schs., 1962-63, 74-76; with Dow, Lohnes & Albertson, Washington, 1985-93; asst. atty. gen. Dept. of Justice, Washington, 1993-95; commr. FTC, Washington, 1997—. Del. Dem. Nat. Conv., 1980; justice of the peace Union County, Ark., 1969; trustee South Ark. U., 1971-75. Democrat. Office: FTC 600 Pennsylvania Ave NW Washington DC 20580-0001

ANTHONY, STAVROS, protective services official; b. Kansas City, Missouri, Jan. 13, 1957; s. Eracles P. and Helen Anthony; m. Bernadette D. Anthony, May 31, 1956; children: Irene, Elizabeth. BS, Wayne St. U., Detroit, MI., 1980; MA polit. sci., U. Nev.Las Vegas, Las Vegas, NV., 1987; PhD sociology, U. Nev. Las Vegas, Las Vegas, NV., 1999. Adj. faculty U. Nev. Las Vegas, Las Vegas, Nev., 1987—2002, Comm. Coll. So. Nev., Las Vegas, Nev., 1998—2002; police capt. Las Vegas Metro Police, Las Vegas, Nev., 1980—. Bd. of dir. Goodwill of So. NV., Las Vegas, Nev., 1998—. Author: Nights of Fire, 1992. U. regent U. Nev., Las Vegas, Nev., 2002. Grantee Phi Kappa Phi, U. Nev. Las Vegas, Nev., 1987. Republican. Greek Orthodox. Achievements include grad. FBI Nat. Acad. 205th So.Police Inst. 1992 AOC. Avocations: golf, reading, working out. Office: Las Vegas Metro Police Dept Regent 3141 Sunrise Ave Las Vegas NV 89101-4833 Office Fax: 702-229-4039. Business E-Mail: 52197A@LVMPD.com.

ANTHONY, STEPHEN PIERCE, lawyer; b. Concord, Mass., Aug. 30, 1961; s. Reed Pierce and Barbara (Beatley) Anthony; m. Lisa Ann Battalia, June 2, 1990; children: Matthew William, Caroline Grace. AB, Dartmouth Coll., 1983; JD, Columbia U., 1988. Bar: Md. 1989, D.C. 1991, U.S. Dist. Ct. D.C. 1991, U.S. Dist. Ct. Md. 2000, U.S. Ct. Appeals (D.C. Cir.) 1991. Law clk. to Hon. Patricia M. Wald, U.S. Ct. Appeals for D.C. Cir., Washington, 1988—89; assoc. Wilmer, Cutler & Pickering, Washington, 1989—91; asst. U.S. Atty. U.S. Atty.'s Office for D.C., Washington, 1991—96; trial atty. pub. integrity sect. criminal divsn. U.S. Dept. Justice, Washington, 1996—2000; with Covington & Burling, Washington, 2000—. Barrister Edward Bennett Williams Am. Inn of Ct., Washington, 1997—. Notes and comments editor Columbia Law Rev., 1987-88. Harlan Fiske Stone scholar Columbia U., 1985-86, 87-88, James Kent scholar, 1986-87. Office: Covington & Burling 1201 Pennsylvania Ave NW Washington DC 20004 E-mail: santhony@cov.com.

ANTHONY, SYLVIA, social welfare organization executive; b. Boston, Oct. 5, 1929; d. Charles and Josephine (Guastaferro) Caccamesi; children: Lyn Newbury, Edward Charles Souza Jr., Dean Souza. Student, Northeastern U., Boston, 1968-69, Lee Inst., 1966, 86-87. Lic. real estate broker, Mass. Founder, pres. Life for the Little Ones, Inc., Everett, Mass., 1987-94, Sylvia's Haven, Everett, 1994—2003, Devens, Mass., 1997—. Recipient Arthur L. Whitaker award Am. Bapt. Ch. of Mass., 1992, Recognition award Commonwealth of Mass. State Senate, Ho. of Reps., Gov. of Mass., 1997, 99, Mass. Gov.'s Hwy Safety Bur., 1998, Mayor Dean J. Mazzarella City of Leominster, 1999, named Hometwon Hero WBZ TV, Boston, 2001; Daily Point of Light award Points of Light Found., 2002, Amb. for Peace award The Interreligious and Internat. Fedn. for World Peace, 2002; Commendation from Pres. George Bush, 2002. Address: PO Box 1166 Groton MA 01450 Office: Sylvia's Haven PO Box 2163 Ayer MA 01432-2163

ANTHONY, THOMAS DALE, lawyer; b. Cleve., July 23, 1952; m. Susan Shelly; children: Lara, Elizabeth. BS, Miami U., Oxford, Ohio, 1974; JD, Case Western Res. U., 1977. Bar: Ohio 1977. Tax specialist Ernst & Young, Cleve., 1977—79; ptnr. Benesch, Friedlander, Coplan and Aronoff, Cin., 1979—89, Frost and Jacobs, Cin., 1989—98; exec. v.p., chief legal officer, sec. Choice Care, 1996—98; pres., CEO PacifiCare of Ohio, 1998—2002; counsel, vice chair corp. dept. Frost Brown Todd LLC, 2001— . Speaker various orgns. Mem. Cin. Coun. on World Affairs, 1980-82; vol. fundraising drive Sta. WVIZ, 1978-79, Sta. WCET, 1980-82; legal counsel Children's Internat. Summer Villages, 1979—; account capt. United Way of Hamilton County, 1986-88, cabinet mem., 1993; pres. State Libr. Bd., Ohio, 1987-89; mem. bus. adv. coun., subcom. ednl. legis. Mariemont City Schs. and Bd. of Edn.; bd. dirs. Greater Cin. Ctr. for Econ. Edn., Am. Heart Assn. (Cin. chpt.), Juvenile Diabetes Found. Mem. ABA (taxation sect., tax acctg. problems com., tax shelter subcom., small bus. com., mem. health law forum), Ohio State Bar Assn. (health law com., ins. sect.), Cin. Bar Assn. (chmn. tax. inst. com. 1990, adminstrn. and fin. com. 1991-93, chmn. tax sect. 1993, health law com.), Cin. C. of C., Miami U. Alumni Assn. (bd. dirs., treas. 1989-91, v.p. 1991-92), Nat. Health Lawyers Assn., Rotary (co-chair youth in city govt. program), Omicron Delta Kappa, Sigma Phi Epsilon. Home: 4337 Ashley Oaks Dr Cincinnati OH 45227-3947 Office: PacifiCare 11260 Chester Rd Ste 800 Cincinnati OH 45246-4096

ANTHONY, VIRGINIA QUINN BAUSCH, medical association executive; b. Odessa, Tex., June 9, 1945; d. William Francis and Florence Elizabeth (Decker) Quinn; m. E. James Anthony; 1 child, Justin. BA, Mt. Holyoke Coll., 1967. Exec. dir. Am. Acad. Child and Adolescent Psychiatry, Washington, 1973—. Recipient Spl. Presdl. citation Am. Psychiat. Assn., 1995, Exec. Achievement award AMA, 1999. Mem. Am. Soc. Assn. Execs. Office: Am Acad Child & Adolescent Psychiatry 3615 Wisconsin Ave NW Washington DC 20016-3007

ANTHONY, WILLIAM GRAHAM, artist; b. Ft. Monmouth, N.J., Sept. 25, 1934; s. Emile Peter and Martha Graham (Armstrong) A.; m. Norma Neuman, Jan. 16, 1983. BA in European History, Yale U., 1958; student, San Francisco Art Inst., 1959. Author: A New Approach to Figure Drawing, 1965, Bible Stories, 1978, Bill Anthony's Greatest Hits, 1988, War is Swell, 2000; exhibited in one-man shows: Legion of Honor, San Francisco, 1962, Berland /Hall Gallery, N.Y.C., 1991, Stuart Katz Gallery, Laguna Beach, Calif., 1992, Cokkie Snoie Gallery, Rotterdam, 1995, 99, Dorfman Gallery, N.Y.C., 2002, others; exhibited in group shows: San Francisco Mus. Modern Art, Art Inst. Chgo., Whitney Mus. Am. Art, N.Y.C., Allan Stone Gallery, N.Y.C., St. Paul Art Center; works represented in collections: Art Inst. Chgo., Bklyn. Mus., Cleve. Mus. Art, Corcoran Gallery Art, Washington, Detroit Inst. Arts, Mus. Fine Arts, Houston, Met. Mus. Art, N.Y.C., Seattle Art Mus., Whitney Mus. Am. Art, N.Y.C., Guggenheim Mus., N.Y.C., others. Served with U.S. Army, 1953-55. Republican. Home: 463 West St Apt 903 New York NY 10014-2010

ANTHONY, YANCEY LAMAR, minister; b. Cordova, Ala., Feb. 13, 1922; s. Clifford Elmo and Tula (Barton) A.; m. Betty Pratt. BA, Samford U., 1944; BTh, So. Bapt. Theol. Sem., 1947; Dr es Scis, U. Paris; DTh, Pioneer Theol. Sem., Rockford, Ill., Vanderbilt U., 1956; DPh, Accademia Universitaria Intl., Rome, 1957; DD, Ministerial Tng. Coll., Sheffield, Eng., 1973; PhD in History, Gt. China World U., Hong Kong. Ordained to ministry Bapt. Ch., 1942. Pastor Valley Grove Bapt. Ch., Tuscumbia, Ala., 1942-44, Walnut Grove Bapt. Ch., Lodiburg, Ky., 1945-47, First Bapt. Ch., Fort Walton Beach, Fla., 1947-53, Harsh Chapel Bapt. Ch., Nashville, 1953-56, Ctrl. Bapt. Ch., Fort Walton Beach, 1957-67; amb. to all the Americas, Republic Danzig in Exile, N.Y.C., 1973-80; amb.-at-large Principality of Sealand, 1980-98; moderator Oskaloosa County Bapt. Assn., 1949-50; pres. Fort Walton Beach Ministerial Assn., 1952-55; mem. exec. bd. Fla. Bapt. Conv., 1948-56; pres. The Albert Schweitzer Internat. Open U., El Salvador, 1989—. Mem. bd. editors Study Centre for Am. Indians, Antwerp, Belgium, 1989—; mem. editl. bd. UN News, 1998—. Pres. Okaloosa County Bettr Govt. League, 1950-52; mem. Fla. Bd. Social Welfare, 1959-68, chmn., 1960-64; dir. Ch. Missions Fund Bapt. Found., 1947—; dir. Ch. Devel. Found. Fla., 1962—; lt. col. and a.d.c. Gov. Ala.; a.d.c. Gov. Miss., 1976. Decorated Knights of Malta, knight Ordre de la Courtoisie Francais; Ordine INternazionale della Legion d'Onore du l'Immacolata (Italy); Gold medal of Labour (Netherlands); grand officier Ordre du Merite Afraicain; d'Honneur de l'Institut des Relations Diplomatiques (Belgium); recipient Lit. award Belgian High Fidelity Inst., 1976; Legion of Honor, Chapel of Four Chaplains, Phila., 1981, numerous others; hon. academician W.A. Mozart (Germany), French Acad. Golden Letters. Fellow Brit. Inst. Adv. Cons.; mem. Accademia Delle Scienze di Roma (life), Inst. Diplomatic Rels. Brussels (hon.), Royal Acad. Golden Letters (hon.), Accademia Gentium Populorum Progressie, Accademia Gentium Pro Pace, Nobility Acad. of Kaspis, Nat. Soc. Univ. Profs. (pres. 1981), Albert Schweitzer Soc. Internat. (pres. 1982-85, 90—), Internat. Assn. Educators for World Peace (v.p. fin. affairs 1989—), Sons of the Confederate Vets., Mt. Kenya Safari Club (exec. com.), Rep. Presdl. Roundtable, 2002—. Home: 2328 River Rd Cordova AL 35550-3904 E-mail: bobmurton@aol.com.

ANTIA, KERSEY H. industrial and clinical psychologist, consultant; b. Surat, Gujarat, India, Jan. 7, 1936; came to U.S., 1965; s. Hormasji and Dinsi R. (Mistry) A.; m. Dilshad K. Khambalta, Dec. 18, 1966; children: Anahita, Mazda, Jimmy. AB with honors, U. Bombay, 1958; MS, Tata Inst. Social Scis., Bombay, 1960, N.C. State U., 1969; PhD, Ind. No. U., 1976. Lic. psychologist, Ill.; cert. social worker, Ill. Personnel mgr., welfare officer Tata Steel and Tata Chem., 1960-65; research asst. psychology dept. N.C. State U., 1966-67, U. N.C., 1967-69; project dir. Behavior Systems, Inc., Raleigh, N.C., 1969-70; dir. Midwest Inst. Human Resources, Tinley Park, Ill., 1972—. Lang. scholar U. Bombay, 1954-56. Mem. Am. Psychol. Soc., Assn. for the Advancement of Psychology, Am. Acad. of Pain Mgmt., Am. Bd. of Profl. Disability Cons. Zoroastrian. Avocations: photography, yoga, jogging, hiking, traveling. Home: 8318 138th Pl Orland Park IL 60462-1746

ANTIKAJIAN, SARKIS SEROP, artist, retired pharmacist; b. Amman, Jordan, June 15, 1933; came to U.S., 1958; s. Serop and Nazouhi Antikajian; m. Karen Joy Albach, May 27, 1961; children: Kyle Sarkis, Garrick Serop. BS in Chemistry, Am. U. Beirut, 1956; BS in Pharmacy, U. N.Mex., 1961. Registered pharmacist N.Mex., Oreg. Pharmacist William's Drugs, Farmington, N.Mex., 1961-62, Cato's Pharmacy, Gallup, N.Mex., 1962-66, Tiffany's Drugs and Pay Less Pharmacy, Eugene, Oreg., 1966-95; artist Cheshire, Oreg., 1970—. Exhibited at various galleries, including Portland Art Mus. Rental/Sales Gallery, Alder Gallery, Coburg, Oreg. Recipient 3d pl. award Pastel Soc. of West Coast, 1987. Mem. Watercolor Soc. Oreg. (Sweepstakes awards 1984). Avocations: pottery, gardening. Home: PO Box 247 Cheshire OR 97419-0247 E-mail: santikajian@att.net.

ANTIN, DAVID, poet, critic; b. Bklyn., Feb. 1, 1932; s. Max and Mollie (Kitzes) A.; m. Eleanor Fineman, Dec. 16, 1961; 1 son, Blaise BA, CCNY, 1955; MA (Herbert Lehman fellow), NYU, 1966. Prof. visual art U. Calif.-San Diego, 1968—; contbg. editor Alcheringa, 1972-80, New Wilderness 1979—; editorial com. U. Calif. Press, 1972-76; prof. emeritus visual arts U. Calif.-San Diego. Author: Definitions, 1967, Autobiography, 1967, Code of Flag Behavior, 1968, Meditations, 1971, Talking, 1972, Talking at the Boundaries, 1976, Tuning, 1984, Selected Poems 1963-73, 1991, What It Means to be Avant Garde, 1993, (with Charles Bernstein) A Conversation with David Antin, 2002. Recipient Creative Arts award U. Calif., 1972; Guggenheim fellow, 1976-77; Nat. Endowment Humanities fellow, 1983-84, Getty Rsch. fellow, 2002. Home: PO Box 1147 Del Mar CA 92014-1147 Office: U Calif San Diego Visual Arts Dept La Jolla CA 92037

ANTIN, MICHAEL, lawyer; b. Milw., Nov. 30, 1938; s. David Boris and Pauline (Mayer) A.; m. Evelyne Judith Hirsch, June 19, 1960; children: Stephanie, Bryan, Randall BS, Univ. Calif., 1960; JD, U. Calif., 1963. Bar: Calif. 1963; cert. tax specialist. Tax atty. Cruikshank, Antin & Grebow, Beverly Hills, Calif., 1963-81, Antin, Litz & Grebow, Beverly Hills, 1981-91, Antin & Taylor, L.A., 1993—99; sole practice L.A., 1999—. Bd. dirs. Small Bus. Counsel Am., Washington, The Group, Inc.; speaker in field; instr. Solomon S. Heubner Sch. CLU Studies, 1977-86. Author: How to Operate Your Trust or Probate, 1983; contbr. articles to profl. jours. With U.S. Air Force, 1959-67. Fellow Am. Coll. Tax Counsel, Am. Coll. of Trust and Estate Counsel, L.A. County Bowlers Assn. (bd. dirs. 1996-99). Avocations: jogging, tennis, cross country skiing, bowling. Office: Ste 2000 1925 Century Park East Blvd Fl 20 Los Angeles CA 90067-2721

ANTIOCO, JOHN F. entertainment company executive; b. Brooklyn, Nov. 1, 1949; Grad. in Bus. adminstrn., N.Y. Inst. of Tech., 1970. Mgr. tng., v.p. of mktg., sr. v.p. oper. Southland Corp., 1970—90; CEO Pearle Vision, Dallas, 1990; pres., CEO Cir. K Corp, Phoenix, 1991-96, Taco Bell Corp., 1996-97; chmn., CEO Blockbuster Entertainment, Dallas, 1997—. Recipient Phoenix Award, Pub. Rel. Soc. of Am., Valley of the Sun Chap.*

ANTIPAS, CONSTANTINE GEORGE, lawyer, civil engineer; b. N.Y.C., Mar. 8, 1962; s. George Spyro and Katina (Petropoulos) A.; m. Amy Lisa Scott, June 15, 1991. BSE, U. Conn., 1984; JD, Pace U., 1990. Bar: Conn. 1991, Mo. 1991, U.S. Dist. Ct. (we. dist.) Mo. 1991, N.Y. 1991, Kans. 1992, U.S. Dist. Ct. Kans. 1992, U.S. Dist. Ct. Conn. 1993; registered profl. engr. N.Y. Project engr./project mgr. Chas. H. Sells, Inc., Bedford Hills, N.Y., 1985-91, chmn. computer com., 1986-91; pvt. practice Overland Park, Kans., 1991-92; atty. Garcia & Assocs., P.C., New Haven, 1993-96, The Antipas Law Firm, Groton, Conn., 1996—. Dir. Family Counseling Greater New Haven, Inc. Author: (legislation) Stamford Historic Preservation Ordinance, 1989. Active Vol.-Atty. Project, Kansas City, Mo., 1992. Named Stamford Found. Scholar, 1982. Mem.: ASCE, ABA, Conn. Design/Build Coalition, Conn. Bldg. Congress (bd. dirs. 1998—, treas.), Conn. Bar Assn. (legis. liaison, mem. exec. com. constrn. law sect.), Mo. Bar, Order of Ahepa (sec. Rose of New Eng. chpt. 1997—2000, v.p. chpt. 2000—01, pres. chpt. 2001—02, lt. gov. Yankee dist. 7 2002—03). Republican. Greek Orthodox. Avocations: sailing, history, linguistics, mountain hiking, scuba diving. Home: 164 Payer Ln Mystic CT 06355-1643

ANTLE, CHARLES EDWARD, statistics educator; b. East View, Ky., Nov. 11, 1930; s. Bayard Pierpoint and Mary Elizabeth (Blaydes) A.; m. Elna Thomas Hall, Nov. 25, 1953; children— James, Rebecca, Susan Hall, Mark Edward. AA, Lindsey Wilson Coll., 1950; BS, Eastern Ky. State U., 1954, MA, 1955; postgrad., U. Ky., 1954-55; PhD (NDEA fellow), Okla. State U., 1962. Sr. aerophysics engr. Gen. Dynamics Corp., Fort Worth, 1955-57; mem. faculty U. Mo., Rolla, 1957-60, 62-68, prof. math., 1966-68; asso. prof. statistics Pa. State U., University Park, 1968-70, prof., 1970-92, prof. emeritus of stats., 1992—. Contbr. articles to profl. jours. Served with AUS, 1951-52. Decorated Bronze Star medal. Mem. Am. Statis. Assn. Home: 2303 W Branch Rd State College PA 16801-8043 Office: Pa State U Dept Stats University Park PA 16802 E-mail: cea@psu.edu.

ANTLIFF, ROBERT MARK, humanities educator; b. Victoria, B.C., Can., Sept. 29, 1957; BA, McGill U., Montreal, Que., Can., 1981; M, Queen's U., Kingston, Ont., Can., 1984; PhD, Yale U., 1990. Asst. prof. Johns Hopkins U., Balt., 1993—95, Queen's U., Kingston, 1995—96, assoc. prof., 1996—98, Duke U., Durham, NC, 1998—. Author: Inventing Bergson, 1993; co-author: Cubism and Culture, 2001; co-editor: Fascist Visions, 1997. Fellow, CASVA, 1988—90, Guggenheim Found., 1995—96, Inst. Advanced Studies, Princeton, N.J., 2000.

ANTMAN, STUART SHELDON, mathematician, educator; b. Bklyn., June 2, 1939; s. Mitchell and Gertrude (Siegel) A.; m. Wilma Gail Richlin, Mar. 24, 1968; children: Rachel Alexandra, Melissa Dora. BS, Rensselaer Poly. Inst., 1961; MS, U. Minn., 1963, PhD, 1965. Lectr. U. Minn., 1965; vis. mem. Courant Inst. of NYU, 1965-67; asst. prof. math. and aeros. NYU, 1967-69, assoc. prof. math., 1969-72; sr. vis. fellow U. Oxford, 1969-70, Heriot-Watt U., Edinburgh, 1972, 77; prof. math. U. Md., College Park, 1972—2001, disting. prof., 2001—. Prin. investigator NSF grants, 1972—; mem. Applied Math. Summer Inst., Dartmouth Coll., 1973; prof. Ecole d'Eté d'Analyse Numérique, Bréau, France, 1974; vis. prof. U. Paris-Sud, Orsay, 1975, Brown U., Providence, 1978-79, Ecole Polytechnique, Palaiseau, France, 1979, U. Nacional Autónoma de México, 1981, Math. Scis. Rsch. Inst., Berkeley, Calif., 1983, Univ. P. and M. Curie, Paris, 1983, 92, Math. Rsch. Ctr., U. Wis., 1984, Inst. Math. and Applications, U. Minn., 1985, U. Bonn, Germany, 1987, U. Leipzig, Germany, 1995, Tech. U. Darmstadt, Germany, 1999, Max Planck Inst., Leipzig, 1999, City Univ. of Hong Kong, 2000, U. Dortmund, Germany, 2001; mem. U.S. Nat. Com. on Theoretical and Applied Mechanics, 1980-88. Author: The Theory of Rods, 1972, Nonlinear Problems of Elasticity, 1995; co-editor: Bifurcation Theory and Nonlinear Eigenvalue Problems, 1969, Metastability and Improperly Posed Problems, 1987, Analysis and Continuum Mechanics, 1989; mem. editl. bd. Archive for Rational Mechanics and Analysis, 1972-89, 99—, editor in chief, 1989-99; mem. editl. bd. Springer Tracts in Natural Philosophy, 1972-80, Acta Applicandae Mathematicae, 1982—, Jour. Elasticity, 1996—, Electronic Rsch. Announcements of Am. Math. Soc., 1997—, Quar. of Applied Math., 1999—, assoc. editor Notices of Am. Math. Soc., 1985-87; mem. editl. com. Proc. of Symposia on Applied Math, 1986-88; mem. editl. adv. bd. (Springer series) Applied Math. Scis., 1998-2001, co-editor-in-chief, 2001—; mem. editl. bd. Interdisciplinary Applied Math., 1998-2001, co-editor-in-chief, 2001—; co-editor-in-chief Texts in Applied Math, 2001. Recipient D. Alcaraz medal Nat. Autónoma U. Mex., 1997; John S. Guggenheim Meml. Found. fellow, 1978-79. Mem. Am. Math. Soc., Soc. Indsl. and Applied Math. (T. von Kármán prize 1999), Soc. for Natural Philosophy (sec. 1974-76), Soc. for Interaction of Mechanics and Math. (mem. exec. com. 1986-90), Math. Assn. Am. (L.R. Ford award 1987), Pi Mu Epsilon. Office: U Md Dept Math College Park MD 20742-0001 E-mail: ssa@math.umd.edu.

ANTOKOLETZ, ELLIOTT MAXIM, music educator; b. Jersey City, Aug. 3, 1942; s. Jack and Esther (Leiter) A.; m. Juana Canabal, May 28, 1972; 1 child, Eric. Student, Juilliard Sch. Music, 1960-65; BA in Musicology, Hunter Coll., 1968, MA in Musicology, 1970; PhD in Musicology, CUNY, 1975. Instr. violin Brearley Sch., N.Y.C., 1970-76; theory lectr., instr. chamber music Queens Coll., N.Y.C., 1973-76; prof. musicology U. Tex., Austin, 1976—. Author: The Music of Béla Bartók, 1984, Béla Bartók: A Guide to Research, 1988, Twentieth-Century Music, 1992, Musical Symbolism in the Operas of Debussy and Bartok, 2003; editor: Bartók Perspectives, 2000, Internat. Jour. of Musicology; contbr. articles to prof. jours. and mags. Recipient Béla Bartók Memorial award Hungarian Govt., 1981, Tacquard Endowed Centennial Chair, U. Tex., 1983-84, Tching. Excellence award U. Tex., 1981, Achievement PhD Alumni award CUNY, 1987. Mem. Am. Musicol. Soc. (Subvention award 1982), Coll. Music Soc., Internat. Alban Berg Soc., Sonneck Soc., Internat. Musicol. Soc. Avocation: oil and water-color painting. Office: U Tex Music Dept Austin TX 78712

ANTOKOL-MECKLER, SHIRLEY, humanities educator; b. Altoona, Pa., Oct. 8, 1940; d. Julius and Faye (Falk) Antokol; m. Jack Meckler, Dec. 1, 1963; children: Janine Lynn, Philip Richard (dec.), David Zvi. Degree in Nursing, U. Md., 1960; AA, Catonsville C.C., Balt., 1978; BS, Towson State U., 1989; MA, Morgan State U., 1995. Staff nurse Md. Ge. Hosp., Balt., 1961-64; mkt. rsch. interviewer Venick Assocs., Balt., 1980-83; pub. rels. staff Shaare Zedek Med. Ctr. in Jerusalem, Balt., 1989-92; lectr. English Coppin State Coll., Balt., 1995—. Tutor Towson State U., 1988-89. Contbr. articles to newspapers. Mem. steering com. Jewish Am. Festival, Balt., 1979-84, auction com. co-chair, 1979-80, chair raffle com., 1981-84; donor, chair, bd. dirs. Amit Women, Balt., 1978-86. All-Am. Scholar Collegiate award, 1994. Mem. Phi Alpha Theta (past pres.), Lambda Iota Tau. Democrat. Jewish. Avocations: reading, crocheting, music, opera, symphony. Office: Coppin State College 2500 W North Ave Baltimore MD 21216-3698 Personal E-mail: santokol@earthlink.net.

ANTOLIN, STANISLAV, patent lawyer; b. Toronto, Ont., Can., Mar. 27, 1960; came to U.S., 1962; BS, Drexel U., 1983; MS, Carnegie Mellon U., 1985; JD, Widner U., 1994. Bar: Pa. 1994, N.C. 2000, U.S. Patent Office 1991, U.S. Dist. Ct. (we. dist.) Pa 1994. Rsch. engr. Lanxide Corp., Newark, Del., 1985-89, patent agt., 1989-94; patent counsel Kennametal Inc., Latrobe, Pa., 1994-99; assoc. Rhodes & Mason, P.L.L.C., Greensboro, N.C., 1999-2001, MacCord Mason, P.L.L.C., Greensboro, 2001—. Contbr. articles to profl. jours. Mem.: Assn. Univ. Tech. Mgrs., Nat. Assn. Patent Practitioners, N.C. Bar Assn. E-mail: santolin@maccordmason.com.

ANTOLINI, ANTHONY FREDERICK, music educator, editor; b. N.Y.C., Jan. 25, 1942; s. Alberto Gastone and Margaret (Fishback) Antolini; m. Holly Lyman, Nov. 26, 1976 (div.); children: Christina Elizabeth, Anastasia Teresa. AB, Bowdoin Coll., 1963; AM, Stanford U., 1965, AM, 1972, PhD, 1975. Instr. music and Russian Cabrillo Coll., Aptos, Calif., 1968—91; dir. music St. Bede's Episc. Ch., Menlo Park, Calif., 1982—91, St. John Bapt. Episc. Ch., Thomaston, Maine, 1991—; dir. Bowdoin Chorus Bowdoin Coll., Brunswick, Maine, 1992—; dir. Down East Singers Thomaston, Maine, 1991—. Program annotator Bay Chamber Concerts, Rockport, Maine, 1997—; coord., cons. Odeon Youth String Orch., Rockport, Maine, 2000—. Editor: Icons in Sound, 1994—, Russian Choral Music, 1988; author, editor Rediscovering Rachmaninoff, 1992; contbr. articles to profl. jours. Bd. dirs. Lincoln St. Ctr. Arts and Edn., Rockland, Maine, 1997—; co-chair, liturgy com. Episc. Diocese of Maine, 1998—2002. Recipient Disting. Alumni medal, Moscow State U., 1988. Mem.: Am. Guild Organists, Am. Choral Dirs. Assn. (presenter Chgo. 1999, Condr. of Yr., ME chpt. 2000—). Achievements include editor-translator first bilingual editions of the choral works of Sergei Rachmaninoff. Avocations: farming, hiking, kayaking, cross country skiing, bicycling. Office: Bowdoin Coll Music Dept 9200 College Station Brunswick ME 04011-8492 E-mail: aantolin@bowdoin.edu.

ANTON, BARBARA, writer; b. Pocono Pines, Pa., Apr. 3, 1926; d. Walter B. and Emma Agnes (Hess) Miller; m. Albert Anton, June 23, 1949. Grad. Gemologist, Gemol. Inst. of Am., 1964. Fashion and design editor Nat. Jeweler Mag., N.Y.C., 1956-58; freelance writer novels/plays, 1956—; staff writer Writer's Guidelines and News Mag.; instr. sr. divsn. U. South Fla., 2000—. Writing instr. Sr. Acad./Elderhostel U. South Fla., 1999—. Contbr. articles;, author plays, (novels) Egrets to the Flames (Top Ten/Fla. Writers Festival, 1995), short stories, 13 plays produced off-Broadway, 1995—2003. Recipient First Prize Humor, Manatee Writers Contest, 2000—01, 1st prize, Father's Hall of Fame Contest, 2000—01, over 100 awards for various writings, 14 awards, Fla. Studio Theatre Shorts Contest. Mem. Dramatists Guild.

ANTON, BRYAN LARRY, music educator, musician; b. Fort Riley, Kans., Mar. 22, 1963; s. Larry Irving and Dorothy Judith Anton; m. Lori Elizabeth Henderson, Dec. 30, 1988. B in Music Edn., U. No. Iowa, 1985; MusM, Pa. State U., 1988. Music instr. Wise County Schs., Big Stone Gap, Va., 1985—86; grad. asst. Pa. State U., University Park, 1986—88; band dir. Concord (Mich.) Schs., 1988—90; mgr. Pizza Hut, Lansing, Mich., 1990—92; Cook Dante's Inc., State College, Pa., 1992—93; music instr. Windber (Pa.) Area Elem., 1993—. Free-lance bass trombonist, 1992—2002; bass trombonist Williamsport (Pa.) and Altoona (Pa.) Symphony, 1992—2002, Laurel Brass, 1997—2002. Band dir. Windber Town Band, 1995—98; soloist Johnstown Civic Band-Blue Topaz; ch. musician Mid-Pa. Ch., 1992—2002. Named Tchr. of Autistic Children, Cambria Chpt. Autism Soc. Am., 1997. Mem.: NEA (rep. Windber, mem. exec. com.), Pa. Music Educators, Internat. Trombone Assn. Republican. Methodist. Avocations: running, gardening, tropical fish, reading.

ANTON, CAROL J. small business owner, writer; b. Rice Lake, Wis., June 12, 1949; d. Edward Burton and Clementine Emma (Kuhrt) McManus; m. Jimmy Eugene Anton, Oct. 31, 1965; children: David E., Brandi J. Grad. high sch., Dora, N. Mex. Cert. marine mechanic; ceramics instr. Beauty councilor Vanda Beauty Councilors, Fla., 1967-69; owner Sunshine Ceramics, Elephant Butte, N. Mex., 1980-84; freelance writer, 1994—, Sierra County Sentinel, T-or-C, N. Mex., 1995—; co-owner, office mgr. Anton's Marine, Elephant Butte, 1969—. Cub scout leader, 1976; scout leader Rio Grande Girl Scout Coun., N. Mex., 1981-83; project chmn. children's grant T-or-C community theater, N. Mex., 1997, theater dir., 1991—, sec., treas.; pres. Truth or Consequence Cmty. Theatre, Inc., chmn. writers group; spl. chmn. Sierra Santas Inc. Recipient Hearts and Hands Acting Out award N.Mex. Arts Coun., 1997. Mem. Sierra Shooters Club (sec., treas.), Women of the Moose. Republican. Baptist. Avocations: reading, writing, crocheting, quilting, theater projects. Office: Anton's Marine PO Box 1063 Elephant Butte NM 87935-1063 Personal E-mail: sunnianton@zianet.com. Business E-Mail: jeanton@zianet.com.

ANTON, DAVID, lawyer; b. Tampa, Fla., Nov. 25, 1958; s. Leonard Morton Anton and Joyce (Schonbrun) Hartmann. BS in Econs., U. Fla., 1981, JD, 1984. Cert. mediator; securities arbitrator Nat. Assn. Securities Dealers. Pvt. practice, Tampa. Mem. Fla. Bar Assn., Hillsborough County Bar Assn. Office: S David Anton PA 1802 N Morgan St Tampa FL 33602-2328 E-mail: david@schonbrun.com.

ANTON, HARVEY, textile company executive; b. N.Y.C., Nov. 10, 1923; s. Abraham J. and Byrdie (Casin) A.; student Western State Coll. Colo., 1941, Savage Sch. Edn., 1941 42; B.S., N.Y. U., 1949; m. Betty L. Weintraub, Dec. 18, 1949; children: Bruce Norman, Lynne Beth. Pres., Anton Yarn Corp. (merged with Robison Textile Co. to form Robison-Anton Textile Co. 1959), N.J., 1949-50, chmn. bd., 1989—; v.p. Arrow Spinning, Susquehanna, Pa.; adv. bd. 1st Jersey Nat. Bank; v.p. Mid-Valley Textile; sec. Bloomsburg Dye; chmn. bd. Robison-Anton Textile Co. Trustee Erza Charitable Found.; pres. Anton Found.; bd. dirs. Pascock Valley Hosp., Westwood, N.J. Served to 1st lt. AUS, 1943-46. Clubs: Masons, KP; Leonia Tennis; N.Y. Univ. Letter (N.Y.C.). Home: 41 Longview Dr Emerson NJ 07630-1507 Office: Robison Anton Textile Co 175 Bergen Blvd Fairview NJ 07022-1684

ANTON, JOHN PETER, philosopher, educator; b. Canton, Ohio, Nov. 2, 1920; s. Peter C. and Christine (Giannopoulos) A.; m. Helen Vezos, Nov. 26, 1955; children: James, Christopher, Peter. BS, Columbia U., 1949, MA, 1950, PhD, 1954; PhD, LHD (hon.), U. Athens, 1992. Instr. Pace Coll., 1953-54; vis lectr. U. N.Mex., 1954-55; asst. prof. U. Nebr., 1955-58; assoc. prof. Ohio Wesleyan U., 1958-62; prof. SUNY, Buffalo, 1962-67, assoc. dean grad. sch., prof., 1967-69; Fuller E. Callaway prof. Emory U., 1969-81, chmn. dept. philosophy, 1969-76; prof., provost New Coll., U. South Fla., Tampa, 1982-83, disting. prof. Greek philosophy and culture, 1983—, dir. Ctr. Greek Studies. Woods vis. prof. Mills Coll., 1981; vis. prof. Columbia U., 1966. Author: Aristotle's Theory of Contrariety, 1957, Science, Philosophy and Educational Tasks, 1966, Naturalism and Historical Understanding, 1967, Philosophical Essays, 1969, Essays in Ancient Greek Philosophy (5 vols.), 1971-92, Science and the Sciences in Plato, 1980, Critical Humanism as a Philosophy of Culture, 1981, Upward Panic: The Autobiography of Eva Palmer-Sikelianos, 1993, The Poetry and Poetics of C.P. Cavafy, 1995, Categories and Experience, 1996, Archetypal Principles and Hierarchies, 2000; co-editor (jour.) Diotima: editl. cons. Jour. History of Philosophy, 1968—, The Humanist, 1967—; mem. editl. bd. So. Jour. Philos., 1974—, Eidos, 1974—, Ancient Philosophy, 1979, Idealistic Studies, 1981, Philos. Inquiry, 1981; founding editor (jours.) Jour. of Neoplatonic Studies, 1991, Revue de Philosophie Ancienne, 1984—, Skepsis, 1997. Bd. govs. St. Lawrence Coll., 1989. With U.S. Army, 1946—47. Named Disting.scholar U. South Fla., 1985; recipient Gold medal Hon. Citizen of Samos, Greece, 1988. Mem. Am. Philos. Assn., Soc. Advancement of Am. Philosophy (founding mem.), Am. Philol. Assn., Am. Soc. Aesthetics (trustee 1973-76, 81-84), Ga. Philos. Soc. (v.p. 1972, pres. 1973), Internat. Soc. Neoplatonic Studies (chmn. exec. com., pres. 1997—), Soc. Ancient Greek Philosophy (sec., treas. 1973-81, pres. 1981-83), Internat. Assn. Sports Law (hon.), Modern Greek Studies Assn. (v.p. 1969—), Soc. Macedonian Studies (hon.), Acad. Athens (corr.), Internat. Assn. Greek Philos. (hon. pres. 1993), Soc. Internat. pour l'Etude de la Philosophie Medievale, Parnassos Lit. Soc. (hon.), Phi Beta Kappa, Eta Sigma Phi, Phi Sigma Tau. Home: 10012 Oxford Chapel Dr Tampa FL 33647-2870 Office: U South Fla Dept Philosophy Tampa FL 33620 E-mail: hanton1@tampabay.rr.com.

ANTON, THOMAS JULIUS, political science and public policy educator, consultant; b. Worcester, Mass., Sept. 28, 1934; s. Julius and Irene (Dupsha) A.; m. Barbara Jane Lindblom, June 22, 1957; children: Lynn Allison, Leslie Carol, Thomas Rolf. AB, Clark U., 1956; MA, Princeton U., 1959; PhD, Prnceton U., 1961. Lectr. U. Pa., Phila, 1960-61; asst. prof. U. Ill., Urbana, 1961-63, assoc. prof. Urbana, Chgo., 1964-67; from assoc. prof. to prof. U. Mich., Ann Arbor, 1967-83, dir. PhD program in urban planning, 1977-80; prof. polit. sci., dir. A. Alfred Taubman Ctr. for Pub. Policy and Am. Instns. Brown U., Providence, 1983—, dean of faculty, 1990-91. Vis. prof. U. Stockholm, 1968, 71; cons. State of Ill., Springfield, Chgo., 1963 70, State of Mich., Lansing, 1972-83, HEW, Washington, 1976-80, Brookings Instn., Washington, 1970—; cons. NAS, Washington, 1976-80, panel mem., 1981-82; mem. Swedish Fulbright Commn., Stockholm, 1971; vice chmn., bd. trustees Clark Univ., 1995-2001. Author: The Politics of State Expenditure in Illinois, 1966, Governing Greater Stockholm, 1975, Moving Money, 1980, Administered Politics, 1980, American Federalism and Public Policy: How the System Works, 1989; editor: Policy Scis., Amsterdam, 1977-80. Commr. Providence Housing Authority, 1986—, chmn., 1990—. J.F. Kennedy fellow Gov. of Sweden, 1977; NSF grantee, 1980; recipient Individual Recognition award HUD, 1992. Mem. Am. Polit. Sci. Assn. (Gladys M. Kammerer award 1989, Disting. Federalism scholar award 2000), Assn. Pub. Policy and Mgmt., Midwest Polit. Sci. Assn., Nat. Acad. Pub. Adminstrn. (panel on info. mgmt. 1993—), Princeton Club (N.Y.C.), Phi Beta Kappa. Democrat. Home: 50 Park Row W Providence RI 02903-1177 Office: Brown Univ Pub Policy Ctr PO Box 1977 Providence RI 02912-1977

ANTONACCI, ANTHONY EUGENE, engineer; b. Sept. 21, 1949; s. Salvatore Natali and Odile Estella (Stanton) A.; m. Sherry Lee Kessler, Mar. 6, 1971; children: Don Warren, Lance Anthony. Cadet, USAF Acad., 1968-69; AS, Forest Park Coll., 1971. Lic. power engr. Asst. supr. data processing ops. 1st Nat. Bank, St. Louis, 1969-71; engr. Installation & Svc. Engring. (Mech. & Nuclear) divsn. Gen. Electric Corp., St. Louis, 1971-76; engr. Anheuser-Busch Corp., St. Louis, 1976—. Author software. Trustee, treas. Antonette Hills Trusteeship, Affton, Mo., 1976-80. Mem. Brewers and Maltsters Local 6 (del. 1982-83), Nat. Aerospace Edn. Coun., Apple Programmers and Developers Assn., Am. Legion. Republican. Roman Catholic. Avocations: classic auto restoration, trumpet music. Home: 8971 Antonette Hills Dr Saint Louis MO 63123-6503 E-mail: TonyA2@aol.com.

ANTONAKOS, STEPHEN, sculptor; b. So., Greece, Nov. 1, 1926; came to U.S., 1930; Ed., Bklyn. C.C. Lectr. Yale, New Haven, 1968; sculptor, working primarily in neon; vis. artist; artist-in-residence (U. Wis.), Madison, 1971, U. Calif.-Fresno, 1972. One-man shows U. Maine, 1958, Avant-Garde Gallery, N.Y., 1958, Miami Mus. Modern Art, 1964, Schramm Gallery, Ft. Lauderdale, 1964, Byron Gallery, N.Y.C., 1964, Fischbach Gallery, N.Y.C., 1967, 68, 69, 70, 72, John Weber Gallery, N.Y.C., 1974, 75, 76, 77, Ft. Worth Art Mus., 1970, 74-75, Contemporary Art Mus., Houston, 1971, SUNY, Albany, 1973, Bernier Gallery, 1977, Young Hoffman Gallery, Chgo., 1978, U. Mass., 1978, Bernier Gallery, 1977, Gillespie/de Laage Gallery, Paris, 1979, Albright-Knox Art Gallery, Buffalo, 1975, Wright State U., Dayton, Ohio, 1975, Galleria Marilena Bonomo, Bari, Italy, 1975, Galerie 26, Paris, 1975, Galleriaforma, Genoa, Italy, 1975, Galerie December, Dusseldorf, Germany, 1976, Art & Project, Amsterdam, 1976, Galerie Bonnier, Geneva, 1976, Nancy Lurie Gallery, Chgo., 1976, Galerie Aronowitsch, Stockholm, 1977, Galerie Tanit, Munich, 1978, 80, Lowe Art Mus., Miami, Fla., 1980, Nassau County Mus. Fine Art, Roslyn, N.Y., 1982, Maison de Culture de Nevers (France), 1983, Le Coin du Miroir, Dijon, France, 1983, Bonnier Gallery, N.Y.C., 1983, Jean Bernier Gallery, Athens, 1983, La Jolla (Calif.) Mus. Contemporary Art, 1984, Davenport (Iowa) Art Gallery, 1985, Ileana Tounta Contemporary Art Ctr., Athens, Greece, 1988, Rose Art Mus., Brandeis U., 1986, Elvehjem Mus. Art U. Wis., Madison, 1986, Burnett Miller Gallery, L.A., G.H. Dalsheimer Gallery, Balt., 1987, Kouros Gallery, N.Y.C., 1989, Galerie d'Art Contemporain, Geneva, 1990, Ileana Tounta Gallery, Athens, Greece, 1992, Carpenter Ctr., Harvard U., 1992-93, Rhodes (Greece) Contemp. Art Space, 1993, Mus. Contemporary Art, Salonika, 1993, Malibu (Calif.) Internat. Sculpt. Exhibition, 1993, Macedonian Mus. Modern Art, Salonika, Greece, 1993, The New Fort, Corfu, Greece, 1995, The Art Inst. Boston, 1996, Smith Coll. Mus. Art, Northampton, Mass., 1997, The Harn Mus., Gainesville, Fla., 1997, Stux Gallery, Athens Greece, 1997, Lucas Gallery Princeton U., 1998, Mitchell Algus Gallery, 1998, Gallery Camino Real, Boca Raton, Fla., 1999, St. Peter's Ch., 1999, Pub. Sch. 1, Long Island City, N.Y., 1999, others; exhibited in group shows Miami Mus. Modern Art, 1958, Martha Jackson Gallery, N.Y., 1960, Allan Stone Gallery, 1961, 62, 64, Byron Gallery, 1963, 64, PVI Gallery, N.Y., 1964, 65, Whitney Mus. Am. Art, 1966, 68, 69, 73, Newark Coll. Engring., 1968, U. N.C., 1968, R.I. Sch. Design, 1969, Worcester Art Mus., 1965, Nelson Gallery of Art, Kansas City, Mo., 1966, 68, Stedelijk von Abbemuseum, Eindhoven, 1966, Walker Art Ctr., Mpls., 1967, L.A. County Mus., 1967, N.J. State Mus. Cultural Ctr., 1967, Carnegie Internat. Mus., Pitts., 1967, Wadsworth Atheneum, Hartford, Conn., 1968, Fort Worth Art Mus., 1969, Smithsonian Instn., 1970, Portland Mus., Maine, 1971, Anne-Marie Verna Gallery, Zurich, 1972, San Francisco Mus. Art, 1973, Indpls. Mus. Art, 1974, Stadtischen Mus., Leverkusen, Federal Republic of Germany, 1975, MIT, Arts on the Line, 1980, Aldrich Mus., Ridgefield, Conn., 1979, 84, Corcoran Gallery of Art, Washington, 1987, Am. Craft Mus., N.Y.C., 1988, UCLA Art Gallery, 1969, U. Nebr., Lincoln, 1969, 70, Documenta 6, Kassel, W.Ger., 1977, Galerie Nancy Gillespie/Elisabeth de Laage, Paris, 1979, Wellesley (Mass.) Coll. Mus., 11th Internat. Sculpture Conf., Washington, 1980, Creative Time Inc., N.Y.C., Mus. Mod. Art, N.Y.C., 1981, Europalia, Brussels, 1982, Mus. Mod. Art of the City of Paris, 1983, 24th Annual Print Exbn. Bklyn. Mus., 1986, Sao Paulo Internat. Biennale, Brazil, 1987, Rose Art Mus. Brandeis U., 1987, archtl. show Montreal, 1988, Boston Atheneum, 1988, Ileana Tounta Contemporary Arts Ctr., Athens, Greece, 1988, Artec, Nagoya, Japan, 1989, Fawbush Gallery, N.Y.C., 1990, Nat. Gallery, Athens, 1992, Harn Mus. Art, Gainesville, Fla., 1998, Chrysler Mus. Art., Norfolk, 1999; represented in permanent collections Fed. Bldg., Dayton, Ohio, Hampshire Coll., Amherst, Mass., U. Mass., Amherst, Atlanta Internat. Airport, Whitney Mus. Am. Art, Mus. Modern Art,N.Y.C., Wadsworth Atheneum, Hartford, Conn., Phoenix Art Mus., Weatherspoon Art Gallery, U. N.C., Greensboro, Newark Mus., Milw. Art Center, Guggenheim Mus., La Jolla Mus. Contemporary Art; pub. commns. include Fed. Bldg., Dayton, Ohio, U. Mass., Amherst, Harstfield Internat. Airport, Atlanta, The Atheneum, U. Dijon, France, 14th Dist. Police Sta., Chgo., Hampshire Coll., U. Mass., 42d St, N.Y.C., Bagley Wright Theatre, Seattle, Tacoma (Wash.) Dome, La Jolla Mus. Contemporary Art, Rose Art Mus., Columbus (Ohio) Mus. Arts, Greektown Sta., Detroit, 59th St. Marine Transfer Sta., N.Y., 7475 Wis. Ave., Bethesda, Md., Back Bay/South Sta., Boston, Exch. Pl. Sta., Jersey City, 5th/Hill Sta. L.A., Lawrence St., Denver, Southwestern Bell, Dallas, Davenport (Iowa) Transit Ctr., Charles St. Sta., Balt., South Campus Sta., Buffalo, York Coll., Jamaica, N.Y., Embassy Stes., San Diego, Neon for the 59th St. Marine Transfer Station, N.Y., 1990, Neons for Buttonwood, Phila., 1990, Neons and Drawings Galerie d'Art Contemporain, Geneva, 1990, Neons for Momoci, Fukuoka, Japan, 1992, Neons for Messe Turm Frankfurt, Ger., 1993, Neons for the Stadtsparkasse, Cologne, 1993, Neons for Tachikawa, Tokyo, 1994, San Antonio Pub. Libr., 1995, Neons for Providence Convention Ctr., 1995, Neon for Granpark, Tokyo, 1996, Neon for William Paterson Coll., Wayne, N.J., 1995, Neuberger Gallery SUNY, Purchase, 1997, Neons Reading Power Plant, Tel Aviv, 1998—, Hot Glass, Flat Glass & Neon, Chrysler Mus., Norfolk, Va., 1999, Blue Cross: Meditation Chapel, Courthouse Gallery, Portsmouth, Va., 1999. Recipient award NEA, 1973, N.Y. Creative Artists Pub. Svc. Program, Lifetime Achievement award Neuberger Mus. Art, 2000. Home: 435 W Broadway New York NY 10012-5902

ANTONE, NAHIL PETER, lawyer, civil engineer; b. Baghdad, Iraq, Jan. 17, 1952; came to U.S., 1978; s. Peter and Salima (Kammoo) A. BS in Civil Engring. with highest distinction, U. Baghdad, 1971; MS in Structural Engring., U. Surrey, 1974; JD summa cum laude, Detroit Coll. Law, 1985. Bar: Mich. 1985, U.S. Dist. Ct. (ea. dist.) Mich. 1985; registered profl. engr., Mich. Constrn. engr. Ministry Constrn., Baghdad, 1971-73; project mgr. Ministry Oil, Baghdad, 1974-78; design engr. Harley Ellington Pierce Yee, Southfield, Mich., 1978-79; v.p. Hennessey Engring. Co., Trenton, Mich., 1979-85; assoc. Bodman, Longley & Dahling, Detroit, 1985-88; owner N. Peter Antone Profl. Corp., Southfield, 1988—; ptnr. Antone & Kuhn Law Offices, Farmington Hills, Mich., 1989-93; pvt. practice Southfield, 1993—. Lectr. Detroit Coll. Law, 1986-87. Govt. of Iraq scholar, 1974; scholar Det. Coll. Law, 1982. Mem. ABA, Detroit Bar Assn., ASCE (chmn. legis. com. Southeast Mich. chpt. 1981). Avocations: tennis, swimming, exercise, travel, music. Office: 16445 W 12 Mile Rd Southfield MI 48076-2949 Home: 7084 Yarmouth Dr West Bloomfield MI 48322-1077

ANTONELLI, ANGELA MARIA, federal agency administrator; b. Aug. 4, 1963; BA, Cornell U., 1985; MPA, Princeton U., 1988. Asst. br. chief White House Office of Mgmt. and Budget, 1989-93; cons. Lewin-VHI, Inc., Vienna, Va., 1993-95; dir. Roe Inst. for Econ. Policy Studies Heritage Found., 1995—; chief financial off. U.S. Dept. H.U.D., Washington, 2001—. Office: US Dept HUD Financial Off 451 7th St SW Washington DC 20410-9000 E-mail: angela.antonelli@heritage.org.

ANTONELLI, CRISTIANO, economist, educator; b. Firenze, Italy, Dec. 24, 1951; s. Enzo and Ludovica (Boccardo) Antonelli; m. Anna Rissone, Apr. 3, 1951; children: Paolo, Emanuele, Francesco. Laurea, U. Torino, 1974. Prof. econs. U. Torino, 1990-95, chair prof. econs., 1995—. Rockefeller Found. fellow, 1983-85. Mem. Internat. Schumpeter Soc. (v.p. 2000—). Home: Via Bava 9 10124 Torino Italy Office: U Torino Dept Economics Via Po 53 10124 Torino Italy

ANTONELLI, G. ALDO, logic and philosophy of science educator; b. Turin, Italy, Feb. 10, 1962; came to U.S., 1987; s. Edilio Antonelli and Fanny Ascarelli; m. Giovanna Fogli Antonelli, May 16, 1987; children: Federico, Riccardo. Bachelor, U. Turin, 1986; PhD, U. Pitts., 1992. Lectr. Yale U., New Haven, 1993—96; vis. asst prof. Stanford (Calif.) U., 1996—97; asst. prof. Mich. State U., East Lansing, 1997—98; asst. prof. dept. logic and philosophy sci. U. Calif., Irvine, 1998—2000, assoc. prof., 2000—. Contbr. articles to profl. jours., including Jour. Philos. Logic, Artificial Intelligence, Jour. Symboli Logic, others. Rotary Internat. scholar, 1987-88. Mem. Am. Philos. Assn., Assn. Symbolic Logic. Office: U Calif 3151 Social Science Plz Irvine CA 92697-5100

ANTONELLI, JOSEPH K. musician, educator; b. Chicago, Ill., Jan. 15, 1944; s. Joseph Antonelli and Concetta Chodur; m. Patricia Nelson, Aug. 0, 1969 (div. Oct. 0, 1980); children: Colleen, Jeffrey. BM, DePaul U., Chicago, IL, 1969; Masters Music Edn., Vander Cook Music Coll., Chicago, IL, 1973. Band dir. Lisle Sch. Dist., Lisle, Ill., 1969—70; music dir. jazz band Broadview Pk. Dist., Broadview, Ill., 1973—77; music dir. Lindop Sch. Dist. #92, Broadview, Ill., 1970—99; pres. Sound Cir. Inc., Villa Park, Ill., 1980—. Treas. Midwest Suburban Music Fest Assn., Broadview, Ill., 1970—99; music cons. SCI Inc., Villa Park, Ill., 1980—90; editor / pub. Music Lovers' Network, Oak Brook, Ill., 1993—95. Contbr. articles to profl. jours. Mem. Rotary Internat., Glen Lo Park, Ill., 1984, Iea, Nea, Broadview, Ill., 1970—99, M.E.N.C., 1980—89. Recipient Best in Class Jazz Band, Chgo. Area Jazz Festival, 1974, Wright Coll. Merit Award, Wright Coll. Music Dept., 1965. Mem.: Phi Mu Alpha Symphonia. Avocations: creating stained glass projects, continuing education, psychology, philosophy. Home: 1136 S Euclid Villa Park IL 60181 Personal E-mail: josepha334@aol.com.

ANTONELLI, PATRICK JOSEPH, otolaryngologist, educator; b. Mpls., Oct. 16, 1962; s. Jordan Joseph and Sandra Ann Antonelli; m. Ann Woodring McGuire, July 14, 1984. BS, U. Minn., 1984, MD, 1988, MS, 1993. Diplomate Nat. Bd. Med. Examiners, Am. Bd. Otolaryngology. Sr. lab. technician U. Minn., Mpls., 1984-86, med. fellow, 1988-93; clin. fellow Mich. Ear Inst., Farmington Hills, 1993-94; asst. prof. U. Fla., Gainesville, 1994-98, assoc. prof., 1998—2003, prof., 2003—; v.p. health info. sys. Shands Healthcare, Gainesville, 2001—. Contbr. articles to profl. jours. Vol. lectr. for numerous charitable orgns. Grantee in field. Fellow ACS, Am. Acad. Otolaryngology/Head and Neck Surgery (Honor award 1997). Office: U Fla Dept Otolaryngology PO Box 100264 Gainesville FL 32610-0264 E-mail: antonpj@ent.ufl.edu.

ANTONELLI, ROSEMARY, writer; b. Hazleton, Pa. d. Dominic A. and Carmella Antonelli. BA in Journalism, Pa. State U. Newspaper reporter Hazleton (Pa.) Standard-Speaker, Inc.; writer, pub. rels. cons. Orlando, Fla. Contbr. articles to consumer mags., newspapers, and profl. jours. including Design Times, Health Facilities Mgmt., Bldr./Arch., Orbus, Hosp. News of Fla., Fla. Design, Orlando Mag., Orlando Bus. Jour., The Lion, Hazleton (Pa.) Standard-Speaker. Recipient newswriting award Pa. affiliate Nat. Fedn. Press Women; named Woman of the Yr., Soroptimist Internat. of Greater Hazleton, 1979; featured in Editor and Pub. mag., 1979.

ANTONIC, JAMES PAUL, international marketing consultant; b. Milw., Mar. 29, 1943; s. George Paul and Betti Ware (Littler) A.; m. Irene Robson, Dec. 26, 1970; 1 child, Glenn. BS in Psychology, U. Wis., 1964; MBA, Boston U., 1976. Owner JPA Supply and Warehouse Co., Milw., 1966-68; product mgr., market mgr. Delta Oil Products, Milw., 1968-74, v.p. internat. ops. Brussels, 1974—2003; pres. Internat. Market Devel. Group, Barrington, Ill., 1976—2003; CEO Internat. Market Devel. Group, LLC, Ft. Myers, Fla., 1998—; pres., COO, Advanced Composite Tech., Inc., Ft. Myers, 2003—. Bd. dirs. ASG LLC, Schaumburg, Ill.; lectr. Cast Metals Inst., Am. Mgmt. Assn., U.S. Dept. Commerce, Ga. World Congress Inst., various colls. Contbr. articles to profl. jours. With U.S. Army Combat Engrs., 1964-66. Fellow Anglo-Am. Acad.; mem. Licensing Execs. Soc., Internat. Trade Club Chgo., MIT Enterprise Forum, World Trade Assn., Japan Mgmt. Cons. Assn., Am. Foundrymen's Assn. (chair legis. task force), Oak Brook Hounds (pres.). Home: 9111 Southmont Cv Apt 406 Fort Myers FL 33908-6298 Office: One University Park Ste 550 12800 University Dr Fort Myers FL 33907 Fax: 603-388-0385. E-mail: jamesantonic@msn.com.

ANTONIJEVIC, ALEKSANDAR, dancer; Trained at, Nat. Ballet Sch., Novi Sad, Yugoslavia. Ballet dancer Zurich Ballet; second soloist Nat. Ballet, 1991—95, prin. dancer, 1995—. Dancer English Nat. Ballet, Japan's Inoue Ballet, Singapore Dance Theatre, Mich. State Opera. Dancer (ballets) Romeo and Juliet, The Sleeping Beauty, Swan Lake, 1999, Onegin, Giselle, Manon, La Bayadère, Apollo, The Four Seasons. Office: The Walter Carsen Ctr for Nat Ballet Can 470 Queens Quay West Toronto ON M5V 3K4 Canada

ANTONIO, DOUGLAS JOHN, lawyer; b. N.Y.C., Sept. 14, 1955; s. John and Joan (Deitz) A.; m. Sarah Kathrine Nadelhoffer, Aug. 31, 1986; children: Zachary Douglas, Sophia Marie. BS, BA, U. Md., 1977, JD, 1980, MBA, 1981; LLM in Taxation, Georgetown U., 1983. Bar: Md. 1980, D.C. 1981, Mo. 1983, U.S. Ct. Claims 1983, Ill. 1984. Atty.-advisor U.S. Labor Dept., 1980-83; atty. Thompson & Mitchell, St. Louis, 1983-84; assoc. Blumenfeld, Sandweiss, Marx, Tureen, Ponfil & Kaskowitz, St. Louis, 1984-86, Sugar, Friedberg and Felsenthal, Chgo., 1986-87, ptnr., 1988-95; owner Antonio and Assocs., Chgo., 1995-98; ptnr. Holleb & Coff, Chgo., 1998-2000, Duane Morris LLP, Chgo., 2000—. Adj. prof. law John Marshall Sch. Law, Chgo. Contbr. articles to profl. jours. Mem. Chgo. Bar Assn. (mem. exec. com. 1996—, chair fed. taxation com. 1999-2000). Home: 1316 N Sutton Pl Chicago IL 60610-2008 Office: Duane Morris LLP 227 W Monroe St Ste 3400 Chicago IL 60606-5098

ANTONIO, ROBERT JOHN, sociology educator; b. New Haven, Conn., June 20, 1945; s. Joseph and Mary A. BA, Miami U., 1967; MA, U. Notre Dame, 1970, PhD, 1972. Asst. prof. U. Kans., Lawrence, 1971-74, assoc. prof., 1975-86, prof., 1989—. Chancellors tchg. prof. Co-author, editor: (with G. Ritzer) Social Problems, 1975, (with R. Glassman) A Weber-Marx Dialogue, 1985, Marx and Modernity, 2003. Younger Humanist fellow NEH, 1974-75. Mem. Am. Sociol. Assn., Midwest Sociol. Assn. Avocations: birdwatching, hiking. Home: 1629 Alabama St Lawrence KS 66044-4033 Office: U Kans Sociol Dept Lawrence KS 66045-0001 E-mail: anto@ku.edu.

ANTONIOU, ANDREAS, electrical engineering educator; b. Yerolakkos, Nicosia, Cyprus, 1938; immigrated to Can., 1969; s. Antonios and Eleni Hadjisavva; m. Rosemary C. Kennedy, 1964 (dec.); children: Anthony, David, Constantine, Helen BSc with honors, U. London, 1963, PhD, 1966, Nat. Tech. U. Greece, 2002. Mem. sci staff GEC Ltd., London, 1966; sr. sci. officer P.O. Rsch. Dept., London, 1966-69; sci. staff in R & D No. Electric Co., Ottawa, Canada, 1969-70; from asst. prof. elec. engring. to prof., dept. chmn. Concordia U., Montreal, Canada, 1970-83; prof. U. Victoria, Canada, 1983—2003, founding chmn. elec. and computer engring. dept., 1983-90, prof. emeritus, 2003—. Author: Digital Filters: Analysis, Design, and Applications, 1979, 2d edit., 1993; co-author: Two-Dimensional Digital Filters, 1992; contbr. articles to profl. jours. Recipient Chmn.'s award for Career Achievement, B.C. Sci. Coun., 2000. Fellow: IEEE (assoc. editor Trans. on Cirs. and Sys. 1983—85, editor 1985—87, bd. govs. Cirs. Sys. Soc. 1995—97, Golden Jubilee award Cirs. Sys. Soc. 2000, Disting. Lectr. Sig. Proc. Soc. 2003); mem.: Assn. Profl. Engrs. and Geoscientists B.C. (councilor 1988—90), Instn. Elec. Engrs. (Ambrose Fleming premium 1969). Greek Orthodox. Home: 4058 Jason Pl Victoria BC Canada V8N 4T6 Office: U Victoria Dept Elec & Computer Engring PO Box 3055 STN CSC Victoria BC Canada V8W 3P6 E-mail: aantoniou@ece.uvic.ca.

ANTONOVA, NATALYA, music educator, musician; b. Moscow, Aug. 24, 1945; arrived in U.S., 1991; d. Alex Antonov and Sofia Antonova; m. Edward L. Pavia, Mar. 13, 2002; 1 child, Katerina Sidorovich. BM, MM, Leningrad (Russia) Conservatory, 1968, DMA, 1971. Prof. St. Petersburg (Russia) Conservatory, 1971—81, Russian Acad. Music (formerly State Guessin Inst. Music), Moscow, 1981—91; vis. prof. Eastman Sch. Music, Rochester, NY, 1991, prof., 1993—, Converse Coll., Greenvile, SC, 1992—93. Lectr. in field. Contbr. articles to profl. jours. Mem.: Music Tchrs. Union Russia, Music Tchrs. Nat. Assn. Office: Eastman Sch Music 26 Gibbs St Rochester NY 14604

ANTONOVICH, MICHAEL DENNIS, county official; b. L.A. m. Christine Hu; children: Michael Dennis, Jr., Mary Christine. BA, Calif. State U., L.A., 1963; secondary tchg. cert., Cail. State U., 1966; MA, Calif. State U., L.A., 1967; grad., Pasadena Police Acad., 1967; postgrad., Harvard U., 1984, 87; postgrad. Hoover Inst., Stanford U., 1968-70. Cert. secondary tchr. 1966. Govt. and history instr. L.A. Unified Sch. Dist., 1966-72; Republican whip Calif. State Assembly, 1976-78, assemblyman, 1972-78, mem. bd. suprs. 5th Dist. L.A. County, 1980—; mem. Gov. George Bush- Cheney State Steering Com., 2000. Instr. Calif. State U., 1979, 85, Pepperdine U., 1979; trustee L.A. C.C.s Dist., 1969-72. Trustee L.A. C.C., 1969-73; mem. Tournament of Roses Com., Glendale Symphony, L.A. Zoo. Assn., South Pasadena Police Dept. Res., Good Shepherd Luth. Home for Retarded Children; mem. Met. Transp. Authority, 1993—, chmn., 1994-95; mem. L.A. County Transp. Commn., 1980-93, chmn., 1984, 92; chmn. Calif. State Rep. Party, 1985-86; mem. L.A. Coliseum Commn., South Coast Air Quality Mgmt. Dist.; presdl. appointee U.S. Del. to UN Internat. Conf. on Indo-Chinese Refugees, Geneva, 1989, Com. on Privatization, 1987-88, U.S.-Japan Adv. Com., 1984, J. Fulbright Fgn. Scholarship Bd., 1991-93; mem. adv. bd. Atty. Gen.'s Missing Children, 1987-88; mem. delegation Rep. Nat. Com., 1972, 76, 84, 88, 92, 96, 2000, mem. platform com., 1976, co-chmn. human resources com. Recipient Pub. Ofcl. Yr., Nat. Fedn. Indian-Ams., 1989, Outstanding and Invaluable Svc. award Home Visitation Ctr., 1990, Brother's Keeper award Chaplain's Eagles, 1990, Responsible Citizen award Thomas Jefferson Rsch. Ctr., 1990, Outstanding Citizen award Internat. Footprint Assn., 1991, Recognition award Salvation Army, Leadership awards United Way, 1987, 91, 93, Hon. Svc. award PTA, 1991, San Fernando Valley Outstanding Leadership award Min.'s Fellowship and Focus 90s, 1991, Mental Health Assn. award of appreciation Antelope Valley Social Ctr., 1991, Recognition award MADD, 1992, Appreciation award Soc. Hispanic Profl. Engrs., L.A. chpt., 1992, awards Boy Scouts Am., 1992, 93, 2001, Recognition award Mex. Am. Correctional Assn., 1996, Outstanding Leader award SER/Jobs Progress, 2002, Person of Yr. award Met. News-Enterprise, 2002, Counties Care Kids award Nat. Assn. Counties, 2003, others; named Man of Yr. Pasadena NAACP, 1999. Mem. County Suprs. Assn. Calif. (bd. dirs.), Phila. Soc., Glendale C. of C., Blue Key, Elks, Sigma Nu. Lutheran. Office: LA County 5th Dist 869 Hall of Adminstrn 500 W Temple St Los Angeles CA 90012-2713

ANTONS, PAULINE MARIE, mathematics educator; b. Monticello, Iowa, Jan. 15, 1926; d. Henry and Eliza (Zimmerman) Tobiason; m. Richard William Antons, Aug. 13, 1950 (dec. 1999); children: Sharon Kay, Karen Lyn. BS, U. Dubuque, 1948. Cert. secondary tchr., Iowa. Tchr. math. Elkader (Iowa) Community Sch., 1948-50, Onslow (Iowa) Ind. Schs., 1950-60, Midland Community, Wyoming, 1960-90, Kirkwood Coll., Cedar Rapids, Iowa, 1982-90. Mem. scholarship adv. bd. Jones County Health Assn., Anamosa, Iowa, 1983—. Mem. adv. bd. Evang. Luth. Ch. Women; mem. Limestone Bluffs Resource Conservation and Devel.; co-treas. Jones County Soil and Water Commn., 1992-97 (Region 4 Commn. award 1997); sec. Iowa League, sec. Recipient Pres. award for excellencein math. edn., 1988, Friends of Math. award Iowa Tchrs. of Math., 1992, Jones County Conservation Outstanding Tchr. award, 1988, 93; Pres.'s scholar U. Dubuque, 1945-48, NSF scholar Drake U., 1967, Clarke Coll., 1968, U. Iowa, 1969. Mem. Delta Kappa Gamma (treas. Beta Nu chpt.). Lutheran. Avocations: gardening, reading, travel. Home and Office: 13481 105th Ave Center Junction IA 52212-7502 E-mail: pantons@netins.net.

ANTONSEN, ELMER HAROLD, Germanic languages and linguistics educator; b. Glens Falls, N.Y., Nov. 17, 1929; s. Haakon and Astrid Caroline Emilie (Sommer) A.; m. Hannelore Gertrude Adam, Mar. 24, 1956; children: Ingrid Carol, Christopher Walter. BA, Union Coll., Schenectady, N.Y., 1951; postgrad., U. Vienna, 1951-52, U. Goettingen, 1956; MA, U. Ill., 1957, PhD, 1961. Instr. German, Northwestern U., Evanston, Ill., 1959-61; asst. prof. U. Iowa, Iowa City, 1961-64, assoc. prof., 1964-67, U. Ill., Urbana, 1967-70, prof. Germanic langs. and linguistics, 1970—, head dept. Germanic langs., 1973-82, head dept. linguistics, 1990-96, assoc. Ctr. for Advanced Studies, 1984. Vis. prof. U. N.C., Chapel Hill, 1972-73, U. Goettingen, 1988. Author: A Concise Grammar of the Older Runic Inscriptions, 1975, Runes and Germanic Linguistics, 2002; editor: The Grimm Brothers and the Germanic Past, 1989, Studies in the Linguistic Sciences, 1995—2002; co-editor: Staefcraeft: Studies in Germanic Linguistics, 1991; contbr. articles to profl. jours. Served with AUS, 1953-56. Fulbright scholar, 1951-52 Mem. Linguistic Soc. Am., Royal Norwegian Soc. Scis. and Letters, Soc. Advancement of Scandinavian Study, Institut für Deutsche Sprache (corr. mem.), Selskab for nordisk filologi, Soc. for Germanic Linguistics, Phi Beta Kappa. Home: 2210 Plymouth Dr Champaign IL 61821-6542 Office: Univ Ill 4088 Flb Urbana IL 61801 E-mail: antonsen@uiuc.edu.

ANTONUCCI, RON, librarian, editor; b. Akron, Ohio, Apr. 16, 1951; s. Dominic and Louisa (Conti) A.; m. Katherine Jean Lambert, Oct. 18, 1973 (div. Dec. 1991); four children. BS in Journalism, Ohio U., 1973; MLS, Kent State U., 1998. Owner, operator The Old Book Store, Akron, 1978-85; editor, reporter Maple Heights (Ohio) Press, 1985-89; mng. editor City Express Publs., Bklyn., 1989-90; cataloguer, bibliographer Strand Bookstore, N.Y.C., 1990-91; asst. dir. Hudson (Ohio) Libr. and Hist. Soc., 1991—; fiction editor Artful Dodge, 2001—. Editor Ohio Writer Mag., 1996-2001. Mem. lit. jury Cleve. Arts Prize. Mem. ALA, Ohio Libr. Coun. (mem. intellectual freedom com.), Nat. Book Critics Cir., Poets League Greater Cleve. Home: PO Box 2115 Hudson OH 44236-0115 E-mail: ron@hudson.lib.oh.us.

ANTONUCCIO, JOSEPH ALBERT, management consultant; b. San Pier Niceto, Sicily, Italy, Apr. 25, 1932; came to U.S., 1935, naturalized, 1941; s. Joseph and Nancy (Calogero) A.; m. Patricia B. Damon, June 1, 1957 (div. 1987); children—Joseph Russell, Louise Shaffer, Timothy Damon AB, Rutgers U., 1954. Vice pres. Deluxe Reading Corp., Elizabeth, N.J., 1962-67; ptnr. Peat, Marwick, Mitchell & Co., N.Y.C., 1967-88; exec. v.p. Lex Electronics Inc., Westbury, N.Y., 1988-90; v.p. Princess Hotels Internat., N.Y.C., 1990-98; mng. ptnr. Veritas Cons., N.Y.C., 1998—. Contbr. aticles on computers to profl. jours. Vice pres., bd. dirs. Sutton-Area Community, Inc., N.Y.C., 1983— ; mem. N.Y.C. Bd. Elections task force N.Y.C. Partnership, Inc., 1985. Served to sgt. U.S. Army, 1954-56 Mem. Data Processing Mgmt. Assn. (bd. dirs. 1962-67), Computer Security Inst. (lectr. 1979—), Assn. Systems Mgmt. (project chmn. 1972-79) Clubs: University (N.Y.C.). Avocations: hiking, skiing. Home and Office: 405 E 56th St New York NY 10022-2412 E-mail: jantonuccio@msn.com.

ANTONY, AJIT IVAN, urologist; b. May 1, 1945; B Medicine B Surgery, Seth Gordhandas Sunderdas Med., Bombay, 1967; M Surgery, King Edward IV Meml. Hosp., Bombay, 1972. Intern KEM Hosp., Bombay, 1967-68, Beth Israel Med. Ctr., N.Y.C., 1972-73, resident in urology, 1973-77; physician Hudson Valley Urology Assoc., New Windsor, N.Y., 1977—. Fellow ACS; mem. Am. Urol. Assn., Orange County Med. Soc., Med. Soc. State of N.Y. Office: Hudson Valley Urology Assoc PC 3074 Route 9W Ste 100 New Windsor NY 12553-6751

ANTONY, LOUISE MARIE, education educator; b. Melrose, Mass., Apr. 1, 1953; d. Paul Urban and Elizabeth Louise Antony; m. Joseph Levine, June 2, 1979; children: Paul Samuel Antony-Levine, Rachel Katherine Antony-Levine. PhD, Harvard U., 1975—80. Instr. U. of Ill., 1980—81; asst. prof. Boston U., 1981—83, Bates Coll., 1983—86; asst./assoc. prof. NC State U., 1986—93; assoc./full prof. U. of NC, 1993—2000; prof. Ohio State U., 2000—. Editor: (book) Chomsky and His Critics. Fellowship, Am. Coun. of Learned Societies, 1985, Andrew W. Mellon fellowship, Nat. Humanities Ctr., 1989—90, Rsch. fellowship, Humanities Rsch. Ctr., Australian Nat. U., 1999. Mem.: Soc. for Analytical Feminism (exec. com. 1994—97), Soc. for Philosophy and Psychology (exec. com. 1994—97), Soc. for Philosophy and Psychology (exec. com. 1989—92), Am. Philos. Assn. Independent. None. Avocations: knitting, music, flute. Home: 870 Franklin Ave Columbus OH 43205 Office: Dept of Philosophy Ohio State U 230 North Oval Mall U Hall Columbus OH 43210-1335 Home Fax: 614-292-7502; Office Fax: 614-292-7502. E-mail: antony.3@osu.edu.

ANTOUN, ANNETTE AGNES, newspaper editor, publisher; b. Franklin, Pa., Mar. 7, 1927; d. Adrien Uriel and Charlotte Mary (McMullen) Adelman; m. Frederic George Antoun, July 19, 1947 (dec.); children: Frederic G., Gregory S., Lawrence J., Mark J. (dec.), Laureace A., Scott J., Jonathan M., Lisa A. Student, Allegheny Coll., Meadville, Pa. Founder, editor-pub. Paxton Herald, Harrisburg, Pa., 1960—; founder, owner Graphic Svcs., advt. and graphics, Harrisburg, 1972—; owner Comms. Sys. Design, 1978—; pres. Susquehanna Valley Assocs., Inc., 1978—. Co-editor French Creek Patriot, cmty. newspaper, Cochranton, Pa., 1972. Mem. comms. com. Tri-County United Fund, 1973, mem. com. children's svcs., 1975-79; bd. dirs. Pa. Am. Lung Assn., 1973-98, treas., 1976, sec., 1979-80, v.p., 1980-81, treas., 1996-98; counselor to bd. Am. Lung Assn., 1989-90; bd. dirs. Harris Commn., 1975-79, Cath. Social Svc. Harrisburg, 1972-76; mem. extension planning com. YMCA, 1975-79; mem. bd. govs. Camp Curtin YMCA, 1980-85; mem. exec. bd. Lower Paxton Coalition Cmty. Groups, 1973-93; mem. comms. bd. Cath. Diocese Harrisburg, 1971-80; co-chmn. Dauphin County Ethics Com., 1979-81; chmn. bldg. com. Juvenile Detention Home, 1976-80; chmn. fund raising com. Greater Harrisburg Arts Coun., 1977-79; mem. Dauphin County bd. com. children and youth, 1982-85; vice chmn. Dauphin County Election Voting Machine Com., 1982—; mem. Tri-County Solid Waste Mgmt. Com., 1983-87; bd. dirs. Salvation Army Rehab. Svcs., 1992—, Capitol Pavilion Rehab., 1992—; mem. exec. com. spl. events United Negro Coll. Fund, 1993-98; spl. events chmn. Ctrl. Pa. UNCF, 1993-94, bd. dirs. H. John Heinz Ctr., 1994—; vice chmn. Millenium commn. City of Harrisburg, 1999—. Recipient Advocate award Paxton Area Jaycees, 1969, 73, citation Am. Legion Pa., 1971, 74, CAP, 1972, medallion Am. Legion Pa., 1972; award Am. Cancer Soc., 1969-89, March of Dimes award, 1969-89, AARP award, 1988, MADD award Hist. Preservation award, All Am. City Participation award, Nat. award Am. Lung Assn., 1992, Am. Legion REgional award, 1994, Pioneer award John Heinz Ctr., 1996, Cmty. Svc. award VFW, 1996, award for historic rehab. City Harrisburg, 1992, Cit of Harrisburg award, 1998, Gettysburg Monument Preservation award, 1998; numerous others. Mem. Am. Lung Assn. Pa. (treas. 1995-98), Internat. Platform Assn. Home: 4910 Earl Dr Harrisburg PA 17112-2123 Office: 101 Lincoln St Harrisburg PA 17112-2543

ANTOUN, MIKHAIL, medicinal chemistry and pharmacognosy educator; b. Khartoum, Sudan, Aug. 20, 1946; came to U.S., 1979; s. Daoud and Badia (Boulos) A.; m. Slavomira Kucerova, Sept. 14, 1973; children: Helena, David Emmanuel, Anna Maria. B in Pharm. with distinction, U. Khartoum, 1968; PhD, U. London, 1974. Asst. prof. pharm. U. Khartoum (Sudan), 1974—78, assoc. prof., 1978—81; sr. rsch. scientist Purdue U., West Lafayette, Ind., 1981—86; assoc. prof. medicinal chemistry and pharmacognosy U. P.R. Sch. Pharm., San Juan, 1986—92, prof. medicinal chemistry and pharmacognosy, faculty chairprof., dept. head, 1993—. Vis. prof., rsch. assoc. Sch. Pharmacy & Pharm. Sci. Purdue U., West Lafayette, 1979-81. Contbr. articles to profl. jours. Sr. scholar U. Khartoum, 1968-69; teaching fellow U. London, 1969-73. Fellow Linnean Soc.; mem. Am. Assn. Colls. Pharmacy, Am. Soc. Pharmacognosy, Sigma Xi. Avocations: piano, classical music, reading, chess, swimming.

ANTREASIAN, GARO ZAREH, artist, lithographer, art educator; b. Indpls., Feb. 16, 1922; s. Zareh Minas and Takouhie (Daniell) A.; m. Jeanne Glascock, May 2, 1947; children: David Garo, Thomas Berj. BFA, Herron Sch. Art, 1948; DFA (hon.), Ind. U.-Purdue U. at Indpls., 1972. Instr. Herron Sch. Art, 1948-64; tech. dir. Tamarind Lithography Workshop, Los Angeles, 1960-61; prof. art U. N.Mex., 1964-87, chmn. dept. art, 1981-84; tech. dir. Tamarind Inst., U. N.Mex., 1970-72; vis. lectr., artist numerous univs. Bd. dirs. Albuquerque Mus., 1980-90; printmaker emeritus Southern Graphics Coun., 1994; Fulbright vis. lectr. U. São Paulo and Found. Armando Alvares Penteado, Brazil, 1985. Prin. author: The Tamarind Book of Lithography: Art and Techniques, 1970; one-man shows include Malvina Miller Gallery, San Francisco, 1971, Marjorie Kauffman Gallery, Houston, 1975-79, 84, 86, U. Colo., Boulder, 1972, Calif. Coll. Arts & Crafts, Oakland, 1973, Miami U., Oxford, Ohio, 1973, Kans. State U., 1973, Atlanta Coll. Art, 1974, U. Ga., Athens, 1974, Alice Simsar Gallery, Ann Arbor, 1977-79, Elaine Horwich Gallery, Santa Fe, 1977-79, Mus. of N.Mex., Santa Fe, 1979, Robischon Gallery, Denver, 1984, 86, 90, Moss-Chumley Gallery, Dallas, 1987, Rettig-Martinez Gallery, Santa Fe, 1988, 91, 92, U. N.Mex. Art Mus., 1988, Albuquerque Mus., 1988, Louis Newman Gallery, L.A., 1989, Expositum Gallery, Mexico City, 1989, State U. Coll., Cortland, N.Y., 1991, Mus. Art, U. Ariz., Tucson, 1991, Indpls. Mus. Art, 1994, Ruschmon Gallery, Indpls., 1994, Mitchell Mus. Art, Vernon, Ill., 1995, Cline-Lewallen Gallery, Santa Fe, 1997, 2002, Anderson Gallery, Albuquerque, 1997, Fenix Gallery, Taos, NM State U., Las Crucis, 1998, Lewallen Gallery, Santa Fe, 2002, Cline Gallery, Scottsdale, 2002, 03, Cline Fine Art, Scottsdale, Ariz., 2002, Santa Fe, 2003; exhibited group shows Phila. Print Club, 1960-63, Ind. Artists, 1947-63, White House, 1966, Nat. Lithographic Exhbn. Fla. State U., 1965, Library Congress, 1961-66, Bklyn. Mus., 1958-68, 76, U.S. Pavilion Venice Biennale, 1970, Internat. Biennial, Bradford, Eng., 1972-74, Internat. Biennial, Tokyo, 1972, City Mus. Hong Kong, 1972, Tamarind UCLA, 1985, Roswell Mus., 1989, Pace Gallery, 1990, Worcester (Mass.) Art Mus., 1990, Amon Carter Mus., Ft. Worth, 1990, Albuquerque Mus., 1991, 92, Art Mus. U. N.Mex., 1991, 92, 99, 2001, Norton Simon Mus., Pasadena, Calif., 1999, U. N.H., 1999, Cline Fine Art, Scottsdale, Ariz., 2002, 03, Fenix Gallery, Taos, 2003; represented in permanent collections: Albuquerque Mus., Bklyn. Mus., Guggenheim Mus., N.Y.C., Cin. Mus., Chgo. Art Inst., Ind. State Mus., Mus. Modern Art, N.Y.C., Library of Congress, Met. Mus., N.Y.C., N.Y. Pub. Libr., Mus. Fine Arts, Santa Fe, also, Boston, Indpls., Seattle, Phila., San Diego, Dallas, N.Mex., Worcester Art Museums, Los Angeles County Mus., Roswell Mus. and Art Ctr., Tucson Mus., murals, Ind. U., Butler U., Ind. State Office Bldg., Nat. Acad. Design, N.Y.C., N.Y., 2003. Combat artist with USCGR, World War II, PTO. Recipient Distinguished Alumni award Herron Sch. Art, 1972, N.Mex. Annual Gov.'s award, 1987; Grantee Nat. Endowment for Arts, 1983. Fellow NAD; mem. World Print Coun. (bd. dirs. 1980-87), Nat. Print Coun. Am. (co-pres. 1980-82), Coll. Art Assn. Am. (bd. dirs. 1977-80). Home: 5900 Canyon Vista Dr NE Albuquerque NM 87111-6621

ANTWEILER, DENNIS FRANCIS, mechanical engineer; b. Cleve., June 16, 1949; s. Ralph Joseph and Marie Leola (Freeman) A.; m. Karen Lisa Porter, Feb. 27, 1971 (div. Feb. 2000); children: Christopher J., Brandon D., Jamie A. BSME, U. Calif. Berkeley, 1972. Mech. engr. Altare Sys., Inc., Oakland, Calif., 1973; controls and instrumentation engr. Exxon, USA Corp., Benicia, Calif., 1973-78, Hess Oil Virgin Islands Corp., St. Croix, V.I., 1978-79, Union Camp Corp., Savannah, Ga., 1979-81; mgr. ops. Stanford (Calif.) U., 1981-86; v.p. Cascade Controls, Inc., Sunnyvale, Calif., 1986—. Mem. ASME, Instrument Soc. Am. Avocation: windsurfing. Office: Cascade Controls Inc 1132 N 7th St San Jose CA 95112-4427

ANTZELEVITCH, CHARLES, research center executive; b. Israel, Mar. 25, 1951; came to U.S., 1959; s. Chaim and Frida (Hassman) A.; m. Brenda Reisner, June 24, 1973; children: Daniel Avi, Lisa Rachel. BA, Queens Coll., 1973; PhD, SUNY, Syracuse, 1977. Postdoctoral fellow Masonic Med. Rsch. Lab., Utica, N.Y., 1977-80, rsch. scientist, 1980-83, sr. rsch. scientist, 1984, exec. dir., dir. rsch., 1984—; asst. prof. SUNY Health Scis. Ctr. Pharmacology, Syracuse, N.Y., 1980-83, assoc. prof., 1983-86; prof. of Pharmacology SUNY Health Scis. Ctr., Syracuse, N.Y., 1987—. Mem. editl. bd. Jour. Cardiovasc. Electrophysiology, 1990, NASPETAPES, Jour. of Cardiovascular Pharmacology and Therapeutics; contbr. articles to profl. jours. Com. mem. N.Y. State Heart Assn., Syracuse, 1982-87; bd. dirs. Clin. Med. Network, Utica, 1987-94, Jewish Cmty. Ctr., Utica, 1987-92, Royal Arch Masons Med. Rsch. Found., 1989, Ctrl. N.Y. Heart Assn., 1989; v.p. Temple Beth El, Utica, v.p., 1993-95, pres., 1995-97, mem. com., 1991—; mem. instnl. rev. bd. Faxton Hosp., Utica, 1990—. Recipient Van Horne award Ctrl. N.Y. Heart Assn., 1981-84, numerous grants; Gordon K. Moe scholar chair in exptl. cardiology, Masonic Med. Rsch. Lab., 1987—, Disting. Svc. award RAM Med. Rsch. Found., 1994, Charles Henry Johnson medal Grand Lodge Free and Accepted Masons N.Y., 1996, Disting. Achievement medal, 2001. Fellow: Am. Coll. Cardiology (editl. bd. jour. 1989—92, program com. 2001—); mem.: N.Am. Soc. Pacing and Electrophysiology (chmn. sci. com. 1995—98, long range planning com. 1995—98, nominations com. 1997—99, bd. dirs. 1997—2003, program com. 1998—2002, sec. 2000—03, exec. com. 2000—03, fin. com. 2000—03, Disting. Scientist award 2002), Internat. Cardiac Electrophysiology Soc. (sec.-treas. 1994—96, pres. 1996—98, sec.-treas. 1998—), Cardiac Electrophysio. Soc., Internat. Soc. for Heart Rsch., N.Y. Acad. Scis., Am. Heart Assn. (chmn. peer rev. com. 1997—, Excellence in Cardiovascular Sci. award). Avocation: swimming. Office: Masonic Med Rsch Lab 2150 Bleecker St Utica NY 13501-1738 E-mail: ca@mmrl.edu.

ANUSZKIEWICZ, RICHARD JOSEPH, artist; b. Erie, Pa., May 23, 1930; s. Adam Jacob and Victoria (Jankowski) A.; m. Sarah Feeney, Nov. 26, 1960; children: Adam John, Stephanie, Christine. B.F.A., Cleve. Inst. Art, 1953; M.F.A., Yale U., 1955; BS in Edn., Kent State U., 1956. One-man shows at, Butler Art Inst., Youngstown, Ohio, 1955, The Contempories, N.Y.C., 1960, 61, 63, Sidney Janis Gallery, N.Y.C., 1965-67, Dartmouth Coll., 1967, Cleve. Mus. Art, 1967, Kent State U., 1968, Andrew Crispo Gallery, N.Y.C., 1975, 77, La Jolla (Calif.) Mus. Contemporary Art, 1976, Univ. Art Mus., Berkeley, Calif., 1977, Columbus (Ohio) Gallery of Fine Arts, 1977, Charles Foley Gallery, Columbus, 1982, Graham Modern, N.Y.C., 1984, Heckscher Mus., Huntington, N.Y., 1984, Schweyer-Galdo Galleries, Pontiac, Mich., 1985, Tampa (Fla.) Mus., 1986, Richard Green Gallery, N.Y.C., 1987, Galleria Sagittaria, Pordenone, Italy, 1988, Charles Foley Gallery, Columbus, 1988, Galleie Civiche D'Arte Moderna, Ferrara, Italy, 1989, Newark Mus., 1990, Maruzen Co., Ltd., Tokyo, 1990, 91, Abante Fine Art, Portland, Oreg., 1992, Ctr. fro Arts, Vero Beach, Fla., 1993, others; exhibited in group shows at, Mus. Modern Art, 1960-61, 63, 65, U. Ill., 1961, NYU, 1961, Pa. Acad. Design, 1962, Whitney Mus. Am. Art, 1962, 63-64, 70, 71, Inst. Contemporary Arts, Boston, 1962, Columbus (Ohio) Gallery Fine Arts, 1962, City Art Mus., St. Louis, 1962, Munson-Williams-Proctor Inst., Utica, N.Y., 1962, Tweed Gallery U. Minn., 1962, Silvermine (Conn.) Guild Artists, 1962, 63, Atheneum Sch., Helsinki, Finland, 1962, Mus. Modern Art, Sarasota, Fla., 1962, J.B. Speed Art Mus., Louisville, 1962, Meml. Art Gallery, Rochester, N.Y., 1962, Allentown (Pa.) Art Mus., 1963, Krannert (Ill.) Art Mus., 1963, De Cordova Mus., Lincoln, Mass., 1963, Washington Gallery Modern Art, 1963, U. Mich. Mus. Art, 1964, Sidney Janis Gallery, N.Y.C., 1964, 65, Art Inst., Chgo., 1964, 71, Tate Gallery, London, 1964, Far Gallery, 1964, Carnegie Inst., Pitts., 1964,, Corcoran Gallery Art, Washington, 1965, Art Fair Cologne, Germany, 1967, Larry Aldrich Mus., Ridgefield, Conn., 1968, 71, Hopkins Center Art Galleries Dartmouth Coll., Hanover, N.H., 1969, Denver Art Mus., 1969, Va. Mus. Fine Arts, Richmond, 1970, Ind. State U., Terre Haute, 1970, Masur Modern Art, Monroe, La., 1970, Birmingham (Ala.) Mus., 1971, Whitney Mus. Am. Art, N.Y.C., 1972, Hirshhorn Mus. and Sculpture Garden, N.Y.C., 1974, Bklyn. Mus., 1977, Albright-Knox Gallery, Buffalo, 1979, Met. Mus. Art, N.Y.C., 1982, Museo de Arts Moderno, Ciudad Bolivar, Venezuela, 1984, Tel Aviv Mus., 1986, Paris-New York-Kent Gallery, Kent, Conn., 1987, Guggenheim Mus., N.Y.C., 1987-88, Marilyn Pearl Gallery, N.Y.C., 1988, James A. Michener Arts Ctr. Bucks County, Doylestown, Pa., 1988, Centre d'Art Contempora, Geneva, 1989, Provincaal Mus., Hasselt, Belgium, Ctr. d'Art en Sante Monica, Barcelona, Spain, 1989, Galleri Civiche D'Arte Moderna, 1989, Samuel P. Harn Mus. Art, Gainesville, Fla., 1990, 92, DeCordova Mus., Lincoln, Mass., 1991, Nat. Gallery Art, Washington, 1991, Cummer Gallery Art, Jacksonville, Fla., 1992, Harmon Meek Gallery, Naples, Fla., 1993, Nat. Acad. Design, Washington, 1993, Camino Real Gallery, Boca Raton, Fla., 1993, 96, 98, Center for the Arts, Vero Beach, Fla., 1993, Intermission Gallery, John Harms Ctr. Arts, Englewood, N.J., 1993, Williams Center Arts, Lafayette Coll., Easton, P.A., 1994, N.J. State Mus., Trenton, 1994, Harmon Meek Gallery, Naples, Fla., 1995, 2000, others; represented in permanent collections, Mus. Modern Art, Whitney Mus. Am. Art, Cleve. Mus. Art, Corcoran Gallery Art, Allentown Art Mus., Albright-Knox Art Gallery, Butler Art Inst., Akron (Ohio) Art Inst., Yale Art Gallery, Chgo. Art Inst., Larry Aldrich Mus., Ridgefield, Conn., Fogg Art Mus. of Harvard U., Hirshhorn Mus. and Sculpture Garden, artist-in-residence, Dartmouth Coll., 1967, U. Wis., 1968, Cornell U., 1968, Kent State U., 1968; Contbr. articles to profl. jours. Home and Office: 76 Chestnut St Englewood NJ 07631-3045

ANUTA, KARL FREDERICK, lawyer; b. Menominee, Mich., May 16, 1935; s. Michael J. and Marianne Anuta; m. Barbara L. Olds Anuta, June 23, 1956; children: Karl Gregory Anuta, Natasha Louise Anuta. BA, Macalester Coll., 1957; LLB, U. Colo. Sch. Law, 1960. Bar: U.S. Supreme Ct., U.S. Dist. Ct., U.S. Ct. Appeals (D.C. and 10th cirs.). Staff atty. Office of Regional Solicitor U.S. Dept. Interior, Denver, 1960-63, Frontier Refining Co., Denver, 1963-67, gen. counsel, 1967-68; sr. atty. Husky Oil Co., Denver, 1968-79, chief regional atty., 1979-83, gen. counsel, 1983-84; of counsel Duncan, Weinberg & Miller, Denver, 1985-87; atty. pvt. practice, Boulder, Colo., 1987—. Pres. Interfaith Coun. Boulder, 1964; pres. Hist. Boulder, Inc., 1980; mem. and chmn. City Boulder Landmarks Bd., 1981-91; bd. dirs. Colo. Chautauqua Assn., 1980-83, 1999-2002; bd. trustees Boulder Hist. Soc., 1992-96, 2001—; chmn. Boulder Coun. Internat. Visitors, 1986-88; bd. dirs. Spl. Transit Sys. Boulder County, 1988-95, pres. 1995; mem., chmn. County Hist. Preservation Adv. Bd., 1992-2000; mem. coun. Presbytery of Plains and Peaks, 1996-99; bd. dirs. Copper Mountain Consol. Met. Dist, bd. dirs. land use coalation. Named Boulder County Pacesetter, Boulder Daily Camera, 1996. Mem. ABA, Colo. Bar Assn. Presbyterian. Avocations: bicycling, skiing, fishing. Office: 1720 14th St PO Box 1001 Boulder CO 80306-1001

ANUTTA, LUCILE JAMISON, lawyer; b. Nashville, July 10, 1943; d. Frederick Thomas and Roberta Bogle (Jamison) A.; m. Gerald Patrick McCarthy, May 21, 1977. BA, Duke U., 1965; MA, Middlebury Coll., 1966; JD, U. Mich., 1975. Bar: Va. 1976. Assoc. Hunton & Williams, Richmond, Va., 1975-79; tax atty. Reynolds Metal Co., Richmond, 1979-2000; of counsel McGuire Woods LLP, Richmond, 2000—. Home: 305 Marston Ln Richmond VA 23221-3705 Office: McGuire Woods LLP One James Ctr 901 E Cary St Richmond VA 23219-4030 E-mail: lanutta@mcguirewoods.com.

ANVARIPOUR, M. A. lawyer; b. Tehran, Iran, Jan. 23, 1935; arrived in U.S., 1957; s. Ahmed and Monir (Georgi) A.; m. Patricia Matson Lynch (div. 1971); 1 dau., Sandra M.; m. Guilda Eshtehardi, Mar. 31, 1978 (div. 1984); 1 son, Cyrus Ramsey; m. Tess Temel, May 15, 1995. LLB, U. Tehran, 1956; BS, U. San Francisco, 1959; student, U. Calif. Hastings Coll. Law, San Francisco, JD, 1973. Bar: Ill. 1973, Fed. cts. Asst. field dir. Am. Friends of Middle East, Inc., Iran, 1962-64, field dir., 1964-66; asst. dean students, dean internat. students and faculty affairs Ill. Inst. Tech., Chgo., 1966-81; practiced in Chgo., 1973—, in San Francisco, 1985—; ednl. and legal adviser Consulate Gen. Iran, Chgo., 1973-79; aux. lawyer NAACP, Chgo., 1973-74. Lectr. immigration and law seminar Ill. Inst. Tech.-Chgo.-Kent Coll. Law Sch., 1974 Mem. Am., Iran-Am. (sec.-gen. 1964-66), Chgo. Bar Assn. (chmn. immigration com. 1982-83), Iran Am. Alumni Assn. (sec. 1964-66), Nat. Assn. Fgn. Student Affairs (Ill. chmn. 1968-69), U. Tehran, U. San Francisco, Idaho State U. (hon.), Ill. Inst. Tech., Chgo.-Kent Coll. Law alumni assns., Am. Immigration Lawyers Assn. (sec.-treas. Chgo. chpt. 1976-78, v.p. 1978-80, pres. 1980-81), Armour Faculty Club (pres. 1977-78), Phi Delta Phi. Home: 512 N McClurg Ct Chicago IL 60611-3051 Office: 180 N La Salle St Chicago IL 60601-2501 *My biases have*

made my life extremely rewarding. I have several. I have a strong bias against intolerance. I have a deep-seated bias against hate and bigotry, a bias against war, a bias for peace, and a bias which guides me to have faith in the basic goodness of my fellow human beings.

ANWYL-DAVIES, MARCUS JOHN, judge, arbitrator; b. London, July 11, 1923; came to U.S., 1993; s. Thomas Anwyl-Davies and Kathleen Beryl Oakshott; m. Eva Hilda Paulson, June 5, 1954 (div. Jan. 1974); children: Alexander Cornelia Eva, Nicholas Thomas Gustav; m. Myrna Ruth Berenbeim, Aug. 7, 1983 (dec. June 2002). MA, Oxford U., 1956. Barrister Inner Temple, London, 1949, Queen's Counsel, 1967; cir. judge, 1972-93; arbitrator, 1993. Pub. arbitrator Am. Arbitration Assn., 1993, Nat. Assn. Securities Dealers, 1994, Pacific Stock Exch., 1995; arbitrator Korean Comml. Arbitration Bd., 1996; mem. Indian Coun. Arbitration, 1999. Pres. Coun. of Her Majesty's Cir. Judges, Eng. and Wales, 1989; legal assessor Gen. Med. Coun., U.K., 1968-71, Gen. Dental Coun., U.K., 1968-71. Fellow Chartered Inst. Arbitrators; mem. Hertfordshire Magistrates Assn. (v.p.), Ctr. for Internat. Comml. Arbitration (bd. dirs.), London Ct. Internat. Arbitration. Avocations: photography, golf. Home and Office: 16624 Calle Arbolada Pacific Palisades CA 90272-1923 E-mail: marcus.anwyldavies@verizon.net.

ANYALEWECHI, PATRICK OKECHUKWU, psychology educator; b. Umunevo, Nvosi, Abia State, Nigeria, Mar. 4, 1955; came to U.S., 1983; s. John Ija and Hannah (Nma) A.; m. Ifeyinwa Anyalewechi, Aug. 26, 1989. BA, God's Bible Sch. & Coll., Cin., 1986, ThB, 1987; MEd, U. Cin., 1987, EdD, 1994. Lectr. Calvery Coll. of theology, Port Harcourt, Nigeria, 1982-83; tchg. asst. Coll. of Edn. U. Cin., 1987-89, adj. prof. dept. humanities and social sci., Summer 1992, asst. to assoc. dean Coll. Edn., 1990-92, asst. to asst. dean, 1992-93; asst. prof. psychology Wilberforce (Ohio) U., 1993-98, assoc. prof., 1998—. Author: A Comparative Study of Teachers and Principals, 1994. Mem.: AAUP, Am. Psychol. Soc., Am. Edn. Studies Assn., Am. Edn. Rsch. Assn., Phi Delta Kappa. Avocations: reading, travel, music, games, soccer. Office: PO Box 1001 Wilberforce OH 45384-1001 E-mail: panyalew@wilberforce.edu.

ANYANWU, CHUKWUKRE, alcohol and drug abuse facility administrator; b. Ogbor-Ugiri, Nigeria, Apr. 14, 1943; came to U.S., 1963; s. Peter Ebo and Eunice Ikwuaha (Madu) A.; m. Ngozi G. Nwaike, Jan. 10, 1980; children: Okechukwu-Pat, Adaku Cathy, Ikechukwu-Uzo, Uremegbulem, Kingsley-Ugo, Ucheckukwu. BS in Biology and Chemistry, St. Joseph's Coll., 1971; MS in Biochemistry, Fairleigh Dickenson U., 1972; postgrad., Temple U., 1979; MD, Cetec U., Dominican Republic, 1981. Internationally cert. alcohol and other drug counselor. Postdoctorate Temple Hosp.; diplomatic envoy Nigeria, 1973-75; extern various hosps., Phila. area, 1977-79; obstetrician-gynecologist, cons. Lagos U. Teaching Hosp., Nigeria, 1983-84; cons. psychiatry St. Mary's Hosp., Phila., 1981-82; rsch. nuclear medicine Temple U. Hosp., Phila., 1980-81; chmn. A-B Assocs. Inc., Phila., 1970—; chief exec. officer, owner, founder A-B Assocs., Inc., Phila., 1989—; virolog rsch. A-B Assocs. Inc., Phila., 1979-82, owner, chief exec. officer, dir.; mem. staff dept. of psychiatry JFK Mental Health/Retardation, Phila., 1985-88; mem. staff dept. of drug and alcohol addiction Giuffré Med. Ctr., 1988-89; counselor in psychiatry Misericordia Hosp., Phila., 1987-88; mem. staff addiction svcs. Guiffre Med. Ctr., Phila., 1988—; founder, chief exec. officer AB Assocs. Am. Beats Addiction, Inc., Phila., 1989—. Paper rev. cons. NIH, Alcohol, Drug Abuse and Mental Health Adminstrn.; mem. com. peer rev. Dept. HHS, USPHS, NIH; mem. healthy start-reduction of infant mortality Pub. Policy Phila. Dept. Pub. Health; panelist Phila. Empowerment Zone for HealthCare Providers. Author numerous poems; contbr. articles profl. jours. Senate candidate Imo State Govt., Nigeria, 1983; mem. free standing steering com, pub. policy com. and providers com. Health Start Initiative-Phila. Dept. Pub. Health, vice chmn. programs, federally funded programs for maternal infant child care; Olympian athlete competing in pole vault, 1500 meters and 400 meter hurdles, Mex., 1968; bd. dirs. March of Dimes Birth Defects Found.; mem. adv. bd. Mayor's Office of Cmty. Svcs., City of Phila., 1994—; founder African Congress, 1995, chmn.; founder State Our Family Unity, 1999; ; rep. Area D., Phila.; treas. Phila. Health Consortium; candidate for City Coun., City of Phila., 1999; candidate city coun. City of Phila., 1999. First African immigrant of 20th century to run for City Council-at-Large, Phila., 1999. Mem. AAAS, Am. Coll. Healthcare Execs., Pa. Cert. Addiction Counselors, Orgn. Nigerian Profs. USA (chmn. jud. com.), Fedn. Police Law Enforcement, Phila. Fraternal Order of Police, Interagy. Coun. Homeless. Democrat. Roman Catholic. Office: 1523-25 W Erie Ave Philadelphia PA 19140 E-mail: nnaenyonna@yahoo.com., nnanyereugo@netzero.net.

ANZAI, EARL I. former state attorney general; b. Honolulu; Student, Emroy U., Oreg. State U.; BA, U. Hawaii, 1964, MA, 1966. Planning prog. coord. Oahu Metropolitan Planning Org., 1967—77; mgmt. analyst/investigator U.S. Gen. Accounting Office, 1968—70; sr. legislative analyst Hawaii state Office of the Legislative Auditor, 1970—75; special asst. exec. dir. Comprehensive Planning Org. San Diego, 1975—76; chief clerk/staff dir. state senate Ways and Means Com., 1979—81; com. clerk Hawaii com. on environment, agriculture, conservation and land, constitution convention of 1978, 1978; atty./chief investigator special senate com. investigating the pesticide heptachlor in milk, 1982—83; law clk. First Cir. Ct., Honolulu, 1982—83; sr. assoc. Schutter & Glickstein, 1983—88; ptnr. Anzai & Evangelista fka Anzai Ahn Holt & Evangelista fka Anzai Holt & Evangelitsta; dir. Dept. Budget and Fin., Honolulu, 1995—99; atty. gen. State Senate Hawaii, Honolulu, 1999—2002; com. clerk state senate Com. on Health, 1981—82; chief coun. com. on judiciary state senate, 1987.*

ANZALDI, JAMES ANTHONY, mayor; b. Clifton, N.J., Feb. 15, 1950; s. Vincent R. and Josephine (Bianco) A. BA in Polit. Sci., Fairleigh Dickinson U., 1974. Mem. City Coun., Clifton, 1978—; mayor Clifton, 1990—. Bd. dirs. Boys and Girls Club of Clifton, 1972; mem. exec. bd. N.J. League Municipalities, 2002. Named Citizen of Yr., Jaycees, Clifton, 1976, Clifton War Vets. Alliance, 1996; named to, N.J. League of Municipalities Mayor's Hall of Fame, N.J. Elected Ofcls. Hall of Fame. Mem. Elks, Moose, KC (Man of Yr. 1996), Italian Family Assn., Clifton Rotary. Republican. Roman Catholic. Avocations: golf, fishing, jersey shore recreation. Home: 156 Day St Clifton NJ 07011-2524 Office: City of Clifton 900 Clifton Ave Clifton NJ 07013-2708

ANZALDO-GONZALEZ, DEMETRIO, literature educator; b. Mexico City, Dec. 22, 1958; arrived in U.S., 1989; s. Pablo Alberto Anzaldo-Rivera and Beatriz Jesus González-Arzate; m. Guadalupe Perez-Martinez de Anzaldo, Aug. 29, 1986; children: David Ricardo Anzaldo-Perez, Elaine Diana Anzaldo-Perez. Grad., Coll. Scis. and Humanities, Mexico City, 1983. Instr. UNAM/DDF, Mexico City, 1983—85, Bartow (Calif.) C.C., Bartow, 1989—90, U. Calif., Riverside, 1991—94, U. Wash., Seattle, 1994—95, U. Calif., Irvine, 1995—2001, Pomana Coll., Claremont, Calif., 2001—02, U. Memphis, 2002—, asst. prof. L.Am. lit. and Spanish, 2002—. Author: Genero y Giudad en la Noveln Mexicana, 2003. Avocations: reading, movies, travel, soccer, music. Home: 6314 Adobe Cir ND-DS Irvine CA 92612 Office: Univ Memphis 375 Dunn Hall Memphis TN 38152

AOURIRI, CHEDLEY, software engineer, computer science educator; b. Tunis, Tunisia, Nov. 30, 1950; came to U.S., 1980; s. Abdelkader B. Bachir and Jenina (Brahimi) A.; m. Samira Dalel, July 4, 1980; children: Heykel, Sonia. B. Math., U. Louis Pasteur, Strasbourg, France, 1971; MS, U. Tunis, 1976; MBA, NYU, 1986. Prof. of math. Dept. Edn./Coll., Tunis, 1972-78; systems analyst NCR Corp., Tunis, 1978-80; software engineer Reliable Communications, Franklin Park, Ill., 1980-82; design engr. Rockwell Internat./Wescom, Oak Brook, Ill., 1982-83; sr. tech. staff mem. ITT/ATC, Shelton, Conn., 1984-86; sr. engr. Intel Corp., Hillsboro, Oreg., 1986 . Adj. prof. computer Sci. Portland (Oreg.) State U., 1987—; gen. sec. Assn. Tunisienne des Sciences Mathematiques, 1974-78. Mem. IEEE, U.S. Chess Fedn., Tunisian Sci. Soc., City Club of Portland. Moslem. Achievements include research in catastrophy theory, design of ISDN network operating system, digital satellite communication systems, multimedia network systems.

APARICIO, JULIO L. systems analyst; b. N.Y.C., Apr. 25, 1952; s. Fernando Oscar Aparicio and Mercedes Gloria Ortega; m. Marianne J. Aparicio, Nov. 11, 2000. BA in Music, NYU, 1974, diploma in computer tech., 1984; MS in Edn., L.I. U., 1979. Bilingual elem. tchr. Pub. Sch. 123, Bklyn., 1976-81; claims rep. Social Security Adminstrn., N.Y.C., 1981-85; computer programmer IRS, Newark, 1985-88; tech. cons. Cin. Bell Info. Sys., Piscataway, N.J., and Maitland, Fla., 1988-90, programmer, analyst Maitland, 1990-93; sys. analyst Convergys (formerly Cin. Bell Info. Sys.), Lake Mary, Fla., 1995—. Mem. IEEE, Am. Assn. Individual Investors. Democrat. Avocations: piano, bowling, weightlifting, investing. Home: 1222 Stonehaven Ct Heathrow FL 32746 Office: Convergys 285 International Parkway Lake Mary FL 32746

APASSA, CYRIL OMO-OSAGIE, clergyman, educator; b. Aba, Abbia, Nigeria, Feb. 4, 1944; s. Emmanuel Agbonfiro and Agnes (Amobo) A. BD, Urban U., 1971; diploma in edn., U. Nigeria, 1977, MEd, 1986; EdD, U. San Francisco, 1996. Ordained to ministry, Roman Cath. Ch., 1971. Tchr. govt. h.s., Nigeria, 1964, 73-77; pastor Roman Cath. chs., Nigeria, 1971-81; prin. Govt. H.S., Nigeria, 1981-90; assoc. pastor Our Lady of Lourdes Parish, Aba, Nigeria, 1990-91, Holy Angel's Parish, Arcadia, Calif., 1991, St. John Eudes Parish, Chatsworth, Calif., 1991-92, St. Theresa Little Flower Ch., Reno, 1996—. Sch. counselor, chmn. disciplinary com. St. Ephrem's Secondary Sch., Owerrinta, Nigeria, 1975-79; mem. bd. govs. Mbutu Ngwa (Nigeria) Secondary Sch., 1984-89; mem. grad. coun. U. San Francisco, 1995-96. Bd. dirs. Scholz Found. and Project Restart, 1998—. Mem. ASCD, K.C. (chaplain 1991—, Svc. award 1991, 96, 99), Phi Delta Kappa. Avocations: photography, table tennis, traveling, soccer. Office: St Therese Ch of the Little Flower 875 E Plumb Ln Reno NV 89502-3507 Fax: 775-322-0196.

APATOFF, MICHAEL JOHN, b. Harvey, Ill., June 12, 1955; s. William and Frances (Brown) A. BA, Reed Coll., 1980. Chief legis. asst. to U.S. Congressman Al Ullman, Chmn. Ways and Means Com., Washington, 1978-80; spl. asst. to U.S. Congressman Tom Foley, Majority Whip, Washington, 1981-85, exec. v.p., COO Chgo. Merc. Exch., 1986-90; pres., COO Dresdner RCM Global Investors, San Francisco, 1991-98, fin. entrepreneur, 1998—. Democrat. Office: 11 Edwards Ave Sausalito CA 94965 E-mail: mapatoff@msn.com.

APEL, HARRY JAMES, composer; b. Mitchel Field, N.Y., Apr. 17, 1946; s. Harold Robert Apel and Santa Sarah Falcone; 1 child, Angelica Valentino. Student, Miricosta Coll., 1969—70, Western Bible Coll., 1971—73; AA, Pima Coll., 1978; student, U. Ariz., 1979, student, 1984—85. Cert. substitute tchr. grades K-12 Ariz., martial arts instr. Japan. Substitute tchr. Ariz. Schs., 1973—2001; publicity dir. Kids Ind. of Drugs, Oceanside, Calif., 1987—88; actor, comedian Fosi's Talent Agy., Tucson, 1987—2003; instr. martial arts YMCA and Marana (Ariz.) Schs., Tucson, 1993—97. Founder Am. Shu-do-Kan, Tucson, 1993—. Composer: songs (APEL Music), 1993—. Sgt. USAF, 1964—68. Avocations: reading, horseback riding, guitar, music. Home: #602 2650 N Oracle Rd Tucson AZ 85705

APEL-BRUEGGEMAN, MYRNA L. entrepreneur; b. Cleve., July 19, 1942; d. Melvin Arthur and Merle Ruth (Hoffman) Rehlender; children: Timothy, Kristen, Michelle, Kim; m. Earl L. Brueggeman, May 7, 1994. BS in Edn., Kent State U., 1965, M. in Edn. Counseling, 1987. Cert. tchr., Ohio; lic. minister, Ohio. Owner, mgr. real estate investments, Kent, Ohio; wner, founder IHS Counseling Ctr., Ravenna, Ohio; owner, mgr., founder IHS Home Sweet Home, Ravenna, Ohio; owner IHS Bookstore; co-owner Chapel on the Lakes. Owner Stow Estates, LLC, Southington Estates, LLC, Orchard Estates, Orchard Plaza, LLC. Mem. NAFE, Ohio Manufactured Housing Assn. (bd. dirs., pres. We. Res. chpt.), Internat. Soc. Profl. Hypnotists, Sigma Epsilon, Chi Sigma Iota.

APFEL, GARY, lawyer; b. N.Y.C., June 2, 1952; s. Willy and Jenny (Last) A.; m. Serena Jakobovits, June 16, 1980; children: Alyssa J., I. Michael, Alanna J., Stephen J., Alexander. BA, NYU magna cum laude, 1973; JD, Columbia U., 1976. Bar: N.Y. 1977, Calif. 1988, U.S. Dist. Ct. (so. and ea. dists.) N.Y. 1977, U.S. Dist. Ct. (cen. dist.) Calif. 1988, U.S. Ct. Appeals (9th cir.) 1988. Assoc. Sullivan & Cromwell, N.Y.C., 1976-80, LeBoeuf, Lamb, Leiby & MacRae, N.Y.C., 1980-84, ptnr., 1985-88, Kaye, Scholer, Fierman, Hays & Handler LLP, L.A., 1988-97, Akin, Gump, Strauss, Hauer & Feld, L.L.P., L.A., 1997—2000; chmn. bd. ELSA, Inc., 2000—01; ptnr. LeBoeuf, Lamb, Greene & MacRae, 2001—. Kent scholar Columbia U., 1976. Mem. ABA, Calif. State Bar Assn. (bus. law sect. corps. com.), Phi Beta Kappa. Office: LeBoeuf Lamb Greene & MacRae 725 S Figueroa St Los Angeles CA 90017 E-mail: gapfel@llgm.com.

APFEL, MERI F, not-for-profit developer; b. Newark, N.J., June 6, 1948; d. Simon Coleman Frank and Shirley Metz; m. Kenneth Scott Apfel, Dec. 25, 1969; children: Seth, Carrie, Jessica. BS, Syracuse U., 1970. Dir. of spl. events Hole in the Wall Gang Camp, New Haven, 1987—97; personal asst. Joanne Woodward and Paul Newman, N.Y.C., 1996—98; dir. of devel. Interreligious Fellowship for the Homeless of Bergen County, Teaneck, NJ, 1998—2000, People for the Am. Way, N.Y.C., 2000—. Bd. mem. Interreligious Fellowship for the Homeless of Bergen County, 2002—. Vol. Bill Bradley for Pres., Montclair, NJ, 1999—2000; bd. mem. Pascack Valley Regional H.S., Montvale, NJ, 1994—98, Rivervale Bd. of Edn., Rivervale, NJ, 1985—96, Blue Light Theater Co., N.Y.C., 1997—2001.

APGAR, JEAN E. artist, consultant; b. Rockford, Ill., May 19, 1949; m. Richard R. Apgar, May 30, 1969; 1 child, Daniel. BFA, No. Ill. U., 1971, MA in Painting, 1978. Instr. continuing edn. Rock Valley Coll., Rockford, 1971-78; ptnr. Gallery Ten, Rockford, 1990-94. Artist's cons. Jester Pubs., Rockford, 1995—; lectr. in field; condr. workshops in field. Co-author: Now What? This Art Business, 1994; one-woman shows include Third Floor Gallery, Union League Club Chgo., 1981, Rockford Area Arts Coun., 1990, Gallery Ten, Rockford, 1991, Cannova's, Loves Park, Ill., 1992, La Petite Gallery, Rockford, 1992, North End Gallery, Leonardtown, Md., 1992, Prairie Ctr. Arts, Schaumburg, 1992, Gallery 451, Rockford, 1994, 1995, exhibited in group shows at Freeport Art Mus., 1980, The Parsonage, Rockford, 1981, Byron (Ill.) Gallery, 1981—82, Rockford Pub. Libr. Gallery Three, 1981—82, Images/4, 1980—82, North End Gallery, 1992, Charlotte Hackin Fine Arts Gallery, 1992, Gallery 451, 1991, Yvette's, Barrington, 1994, 317 Market St. Gallery, 1994, 1995, Artisan Gallery, Paoli, Wis., 1996, past Ptnrs. Plus, Gallery Ten, Rockford, 1996, 1998, Kebby Gallery, 1996, Colonade Gallery, Chautauqua, N.Y., 1996, East Bank Gallery, Rockford, 1997, Gambino Gallery, 1998, Womanspace, Rockford, 1999, Silk Painters Internat., 1999, 2000, UIC Coll. Medicine, Rockford, 2000, Freeport (Ill.) Arts Ctr., 2000, Represented in permanent collections Beverly Bank, Chgo., Baarstad & Harris, Cherry Valley, Ill., Solar Flame, Genoa, Ill., Kishwaukee Coll., Malta, Ill., Winnebao County Title Ins., Swedish Am. Hosp., Rockford, Crusader Clinic, U.S. Amb. Residence, Niamey, Niger, Rangoon, Burma, pvt. collections in U.S., Sweden, Eng. Advisor/cons. Arts against Violence, Rockford Area Arts Coun., 1994. Rockford Area Arts coun. City ArtsAction grantee, 1995, 96. Mem.: Silk Painters Internat., Am. Watercolor Soc. (assoc.), Nat. Watercolor Soc. (assoc.). Avocation: horseback riding. Home: 2513 Knight Ave Rockford IL 61101-4244

APICELLA, MICHAEL ALLEN, physician, educator; b. Bklyn., Apr. 4, 1938; s. Anthony D. and Fay (Kahn) A.; m. Agnes Dengler, Aug. 19, 1961; children: Michael P., Christopher A., Peter N. AB, Holy Cross Coll., 1959; MD, SUNY, Bklyn., 1963. Diplomate Am. Bd. Internal Medicine, Am. Bd. Infectious Disease. Postdoctoral fellow Johns Hopkins Hosp., Balt., 1966-68; asst. prof. microbiology SUNY, Buffalo, 1970-74, assoc. prof., 1974-78, prof., 1981-92; prof., chmn. dept. microbiology Coll. Medicine U. Iowa, Iowa City, 1993—. Contbr. over 150 articles to profl. jours. Maj. USAF, 1968-70. Office: U Iowa Coll Medicine Dept Microbiology Coll Medicine 3-403 Science Bldg Iowa City IA 52242

APLAN, FRANK FULTON, metallurgical engineering educator; b. Boulder, Colo., Aug. 11, 1923; s. Frank Fulton Sr. and Helen Elizabeth (Fischer) A.; m. Clare Marie Donaghue, July 30, 1955; children: Susan M., Peter D., Lucy A., Margaret Ann (dec.). BS, S.D. Sch. Mines and Tech., 1948; MS, Mont. Sch. Mines, 1950; ScD, MIT, 1957; hon. degree in mineral engring., Mont. Tech. of U. of Mont., 1968. Mill engr. Climax Molybdenum Co., Climax, Colo., 1950-51, 53; asst. prof. U. Wash., Seattle, 1951-53; sr. scientist Kennecott Copper Corp., Salt Lake City, 1957; group mgr. mineral engring. R & D Mining and Metals div., Union Carbide Corp., Niagara Falls, Tuxedo, N.Y., 1957-67; prof. metallurgy and mineral processing Pa. State U., University Park, 1968—, Disting. prof., 1990, head dept. mineral preparation, 1968-71, chmn. mineral processing sect. University Pk., 1971-77, chmn. metallurgy sect. University Park, 1973-75. Bd. dirs. Engring. Found., N.Y.C., 1977-90, chmn. 1985-87. Contbr. articles to profl. jours.; patentee in field. T/Sgt. U.S. Army, 1942-46, ETO. Decorated Bronze Star; recipient Engring. Found. award, 1989, Percy H. Nicholls award AIME/ASME Joint Soc., 1998; inductee S.D. Hall of Fame, 1998. Mem. Nat. Acad. Engring., AIME (hon. mem. 1991, Robert H. Richards award 1978, Mineral Industry Edn. award 1992), AIChE, ASM Internat., Archaeol. Inst. Am., Am. Filtration Soc., Am. Chem. Soc., Soc. Mining, Metallurgy & Exploration Engrs. (bd. dirs. 1973-76, chmn. mineral processing divsn. 1972-73, Arthur F. Taggart award 1985, Disting. Mem. award 1978, Antoine M. Gaudin award 1991), Minerals, Metals & Materials Soc., Mining History Assn. Home: 432 W Fairmount Ave State College PA 16801-4612 Office: Pa State U Dept Energy & Geo-Environ Engring 155 Hosler Bldg University Park PA 16802-5000 E-mail: ffa1@psu.edu.

APODACA, PATRICK VINCENT, lawyer; b. El Paso, Tex., Mar. 11, 1951; s. Richard Felix and Isabel (Ortega) A. B.S. in Fgn. Service, Georgetown U., 1972; J.D., Harvard U., 1975. Bar: D.C. 1975, N.Mex. 1984. Assoc. Silverstein & Mullens, Washington, 1975-76; spl. asst. Carter-Mondale Transition Group, Washington, 1976-77; assoc. counsel to pres., The White House, Washington, 1977-81; assoc. Finley, Kumble, Wagner, Washington, 1981-84, Keleher & McLeod, Albuquerque, 1984-86, ptnr., 1986—. Asst. coordinator get-out-the vote com. Dem. Nat. Com., Washington, 1976; voter registration coordinator N.Mex. Dem. Com., Albuquerque, 1984; mem. N.Mex. State Dem. Party Cen. Com., 1987—; del. Dem. Nat. Conv., 1988; mem. Pres.'s Adv. Com. on Arts, Washington, 1981; bd. dirs. Tex. Tech U. and Health Scis. Ctr. Research Found., 1987—, Presbyn. Heart Inst., 1986—. Mem. D.C. Bar Assn. (chmn. internat. law com. young lawyers div. 1982-84), ABA, N.Mex. Bar Assn. (com. on minority involvement in bar 1987—, com. on Lawyer Referral Project for Elderly 1986—), Albuquerque Bar Assn. Roman Catholic.

APONE, CARL ANTHONY, journalist; b. Brownsville, Pa., July 9, 1923; s. Peter P. and Carmela (Puglia) A.; m. Kathleen King, Jan. 23, 1965; 1 dau., Elizabeth. BA cum laude, U. Notre Dame, 1949; MA, Boston U., 1950. Dir. pub. rels., lectr. journalism and Am. lit. St. Mary's Coll., Notre Dame, Ind., 1950-53; staff writer UP, Detroit, 1953; city editor Brownsville Telegraph, 1953-57; staff writer Pitts. Sun- Telegraph, 1958-60; music editor Pitts. Press, 1960-89; mem. faculty journalism Duquesne U., 1967-72; free-lance writer, 1950—; artistic dir. Music for Mt. Lebanon, Pitts., 1990—. Mem. penal com. St. Vincent DePaul Soc., 1963— Served with inf. AUS, 1943-46. Recipient Golden Quill Journalism awards; Pa. Newspaper Pubs. Assn. awards. Home: 2016 Worcester Dr Pittsburgh PA 15243-1542 Office: Music for Mt Lebanon 2016 Worcester Dr Pittsburgh PA 15243-1542

APONTE, ABRAHAM, secondary school educator; b. NYC, Aug. 6, 1953; s. Abraham and Gladys (Ayala) Aponte; m. Ana María Acevedo, June 15, 1985; children: Amitza, Abie. BA, Fordham U., 1975; MA, NYU, 1976. Tchr. NYC Pub. Sch., 1977—79, Colegio San José pvt. sch., Rio Piedras, PR, 1980—83, Ramey Sch., Aguadilla, PR, 1983—. EEO counselor Dept. Def. Ednl. Activity, Aguadilla, 1989—92. Mem.: Orgn. Am. Historians, Am. Hist. Assn., Phi Delta Kappa. Democrat. Mem. Christian Ch. (Disciples Of Christ). Avocations: photography, basketball, reading. Office: Ramey Sch 201 Arch Rd Ramey PR 00603

APONTE MARTINEZ, LUIS CARDINAL, archbishop emeritus; b. Lajas, P.R., Aug. 4, 1922; s. Santiago E. Aponte and Rosa Martinez. Student, San Ildefonso Sem., San Juan, P.R., 1944, St. John's Sem., Boston, 1950; LLD (hon.), Fordham U., 1965. Ordained priest Roman Cath. Ch., 1950. Asst. in Patillas, PR; pastor in Maricao, PR, Sta. Isabel, PR, 1953—55; sec. to bishop of Ponce, PR, 1955—57; pastor in Aibonito, PR, 1957—60; from aux. bishop to bishop of Ponce, 1960—64; archbishop of San Juan, 1964—; elevated to cardinal, 1973. Chancellor Cath. U., Ponce, 1963—; pres. Puerto Rican Episcopal Conf. Chaplain P.R. N.G., 1957—60. Mem.: Lions. Roman Catholic. Address: SER Urpanizacion 1763 Calle Fan Alejahbeo San Juan PR 00926*

APOSTOLAKIS, JAMES JOHN, shipping company executive, pharmaceutical executive; b. N.Y.C., May 31, 1942; s. John George and Ann (Lampros) A. AB, U. Pa., 1962; LLB, Harvard U., 1965. Bar: N.Y. 1965. Atty. Dewey, Ballantine, Bushby, Palmer & Wood, N.Y.C., 1965-67; pres. Transoceanic Tank Ship Mgmt. Group, N.Y.C., 1968-72, Koplik Group Ltd., N.Y.C., 1983-84, A.G. Palmer & Co., Inc., N.Y.C., 1976—, Bradford Shipping, Inc., N.Y.C., 1973—, Bradmar Trading Corp., N.Y.C., 1975—; mng. dir. Poseidon Capital Corp., N.Y.C., 1998—; vice chmn., pres. Columbia Labs, Inc., Miami, Fla., 1999—; pres. Columbia Labs., Inc., Fla., 2000—, vice chmn. Pres. Lexington Shipping and Trading Corp., N.Y.C., 1980—, Bedford Capital Corp., N.Y.C., 1989—93; vice chmn. Koplik Group Ltd., N.Y.C., 1988—93, Columbia Labs. Inc., Livingston, NJ, 1999—; bd. dirs. Macmillan, Inc., Grow Group, Inc., Columbia Labs., Inc. Mem. Phi Beta Kappa. Clubs: Union, Metropolitan. Home: 150 E 69th St New York NY 10021-5704 E-mail: apostolakis@att.net.

APOSTOLOS-CAPPADONA, DIANE PAN, religion and art educator; b. Trenton, NJ, May 10, 1948; d. Vasilios Daniel and Stacia Elaine (Pappayliou) Apostolos. BA with spl. honors in religion, George Washington U., 1970, MA in Religion, 1973, PhD in Am. Civilization, 1988; MA in Religion and Culture, Cath. U. Am., 1979. Editl. asst. The George Washington U., 1970-73; asst. to dir. devel. Bellarmine Coll., 1974-75; professorial lectr. religion and art Georgetown U., 1978—, adj. prof. religion, art and gender studies, 1985—, adj. prof. Ctr. for Muslim-Christian U., 1996—. Lectr. religion and art Ctr. for Cmty. Edn., Bellarmine Coll., 1974, Humanities Inst., 1979-80; vis. lectr. in religion and art Inst. Religious Studies U. St. Thomas, 1979, Cath. U. Am., 1985-86, 89; lectr. in religion Mount Vernon Coll., 1980-85, George Washington U., 1981-86; tchg. fellow Grad. Theol. Found., 1989-93; residential fellow Alden B. Dow Creativity Ctr., 1982, Edward F. Albee Found., 1983; core cons. PBS/BBC series Dancing, 1993; co-curator Noguchi at the Dance, N.Y. Pub. Libr. for the Performing Arts, 1994; sr. fellow Ctr. Study World Religions Harvard U., 1996-97; cons. Religion and Art Ency. of Religion, 2002--; adv. Art/World Iconography Dictionary of the History of Ideas, 2002--; presenter, lectr., cons. in field. Author: Dictionary of Christian Art, 1994, The Spirit and the Vision: The Influence of Christian Romanticism on the Development of 19th-century American Art, 1995, Encyclopedia of Women in Religious Art, 1996, Dictionary of Women in Religious Art, 1998; author, curator In Search of Mary Magdalene: Images and Traditions, 2002; editor: The Sacred Play of Children, 1983, Art, Creativity, and the Sacred, 1984, 95, Symbolism, the Sacred, and the Arts, 1985, Image and Spirit in Sacred and Secular Art, 1990; co-editor: Isamu Noguchi: Essays and Conversations with Bruce Altshuler, 1994; editor: World Spirituality: An Encyclopedic History of the Religious Quest, 25 vols., 1985-94; co-translator A History of Religious Ideas, Vol. III, 1985; contbr. articles to profl. jours. Presenter adult edn. programs Blessed Sacrament Cath. Cmty., First Presbyn. Ch. Arlington, First Unitarian Ch. Washington, Smithsonian Resident Assoc. Program, Christ Episcopal Ch., others. Recipient Excellence award, Newington-Cropsey Found., 2000; Travel grant, NEH, 1990, Coll. Art Assn., 1997, Rsch. grant, ACLS, 1989, Am. Acad. Religion, 1990, Cultural Studies Ctr. Newington-Cropsey Found., 2003—. Mem. AAUW, Am. Acad. Religion, Am. Assn. Mus., Am. Studies Assn., Assocs. for Religion and Intellectual Life, Coll. Art Assn., Coll. Theology Soc., Congress on Rsch. in Dance, Soc. for Art, Religion and Contemporary Culture. Office: Ctr Muslim-Christian Understanding Georgetown Univ Icc # 260 Washington DC 20057-1052 E-mail: apostold@georgetown.edu.

APPACHANA, ANJANA, writer, educator; b. Mercara, India; d. Somayandra T. and Parvathy Appachana; m. Rajiv K. Sinha; 1 child, Malavika. BA in English with honors, Delhi U., 1976; MA in Sociology, Jawaharlal Nehru U., 1978; MFA in fiction, Pa. State U., 1988. Asst. orgnr. World Wildlife Fund India, New Delhi, 1980-81; personnel officer DCM Data Products, New Delhi, 1981-84; tchg. asst. Pa. State U., State College, 1985-88; vis. prof. Ariz. State U., Tempe, 1998-99; tchr. Tempe (Ariz.) Preparatory Acad., 2000—. Author: Incantations and Other Stories, 1991, Listening Now, 1998; contbr. numerous short stories to anthologies. Fellow NEA, 1995-96, Hawthornden Found., 1993, 98; recipient O'Henry Festival prize, 1989.

APPATOV, SEMYEN IOSIFOVICH, historian; b. Pervomaisk, Ukraine, Jan. 24, 1930; s. Josif and Hanna (Goichman) A.; m. Ninel Michailovna Mazur, Apr. 4, 1956; two children. PhD, Inst. Internat. Rels., 1966; DSc, Russia Acad. Scis., 1980. Tchr., lectr. high sch., Odessa, Ukraine, 1952-58; dir., lectr. State Courses Fgn. Lang., Odessa, 1958-66; from asst. prof. to prof., chmn. dept. internat. rels. Odessa U., Ukraine, 1966-99, ret., 1999. Author: USA and Europe, 1979,

Analysis of American Historiography, 1984, The USA Middle East Policy in American Historiography, 1986; editor, author: American Foreign Policy Mentality in the 1980s, 1992, Ukraine and European Security, 1999. E-mail: appatov_semen@yahoo.com.

APPEADU, CHARLES EDWARD, finance educator, researcher; b. Kwasi-buokrom, Brong Ahafo Region, Ghana, Mar. 27, 1959; s. Kwame Ampomah and Grace Akosuah Kyeremaah; m. Christina Agyeiwaa; children: Edward, Michael, Sarah. BSc in Civil Engring., U. Sci. and Tech., Kumasi, Ghana, 1984; MASc, U. B.C., Vancouver, Can., 1989; PhD in Fin., U. Wash., 1996. CFA. Full time tchg. asst. U. of Sci. and Tech., Kumasi, 1984—86; asst. rsch. officer BRRI, Coun. for Sci. and Indsl. Rsch., Kumasi, 1986—87; tchg./rsch. assoc. Sch. Bus. Adminstrn. U. Wash., Seattle, 1991—94; asst. prof. fin. U. of Wis., Milw., 1994—98; U.S. equity rsch. mgr./portfolio mgr. Parametric Portfolio Assocs., Seattle, 1998—2000; asst. prof. of fin. Ga. State U., Atlanta, 2000—. CFA exam. grader/sr. grader Aimr, Charlottesville, 2000—02. Contbr. articles to scholarly jours. Asst. sr. prefect St. Augustine's Coll., Cape Coast, Ghana, 1978—79. Fellow Michael G. Foster fellow, U. of Wash., 1993—94; scholar Commonwealth scholar, Can. Govt., 1987—89. Mem.: Ghana Engring. Students Assn. (pres. 1982—84), Assn. for Investment Mgmt. and Rsch. Home: 525 Meadows Creek Dr Alpharetta GA 30005 Office: Ga State U 35 Broad St Atlanta GA 30303 Personal E-mail: cappeadu@gsu.edu. Business E-Mail: cappeadu@gsu.edu.

APPEL, ALBERT M. lawyer; b. N.Y.C., May 26, 1945; s. Morris and Belle (Kaplan) A.; m. Irena Uhl, June 10, 1979; 1 child, Elliott. BS in Econs., U. Pa., 1966; JD, NYU, 1969. Bar: N.Y. 1969, U.S. Dist. Ct. (so. and ea. dists.) N.Y. 1971, U.S. Ct. Appeals (2d cir.) 1974, U.S. Ct. Appeals (4th cir.) 1979, U.S. Ct. Appeals (11th Cir.) 2002. Assoc. Spear and Hill, N.Y.C., 1969-75, Webster & Sheffield, N.Y.C., 1976-80, ptnr., 1981-91; spl. counsel Stroock & Stroock & Lavan LLP, N.Y.C., 1991-97, ptnr., 1998—. Mem. ABA, Am. Health Lawyers Assn., N.Y. State Bar Assn., Assn. of Bar of City of N.Y., Beta Alpha Psi. Home: 670 W End Ave New York NY 10025-7313 Office: Stroock & Stroock & Lavan LLP 180 Maiden Ln New York NY 10038-4925 E-mail: aappel@stroock.com.

APPEL, BERNARD SIDNEY, marketing consultant, former electronic company executive; b. Boston, Jan. 10, 1932; s. Max and Sophia (Altshuler) A.; m. Ellen Carey, July 1988; children: Ann, Sharon; children by previous marriage: Arlene R., Gerald I. AA Commercial Sci., Boston U., 1959; D Comml. Sci. (hon.), McKenzie Coll., 1991. Store mgr., buyer S & W Distbg. Co., Boston, 1949-59; buyer Radio Shack Co., Boston, 1959-66, mdse. mgr., 1966-70, v.p. merchandising Ft. Worth, 1970-78, sr. v.p. merchandising and advt., 1978-80, exec. v.p. mktg., 1980-84, pres., 1984-92, chmn., 1992-93; sr. v.p. Tandy Corp., 1992-93; bd. dirs. Uniview Corp., 1995—; pres. Appel Assocs., Mktg. Cons., 1993—; vice chmn., bd. dirs. Integrated Tech. Inc., 1994-99. V.p. Holbrook (Mass.) Jewish Cmty. Ctr., 1958-59; bd. dirs. Dan Danciger Jewish Cmty. Ctr., Ft. Worth, 1989-98; v.p., founder Temple Aliyah, Needham, Mass., 1969-70; pres. Congregation Ahavath Sholom, Ft. Worth, 1979-81, bd. dirs., 1972—; bd. dirs. Jewish Fedn. Ft. Worth, 1975-97, v.p., 1981-85, pres., 1985-87; bd. dirs. Casa Manana Mus., 1978-79; mem. adv. bd. Arts Coun. Ft. Worth, 1985—; project renewal cluster chmn. Acco-East, Israel, 1981-94; mem. exec. com. so. regional campaign cabinet United Jewish Appeal, 1980-89; so. regional chmn. United Jewish Appeal's Passage to Freedom Campaign for Soviet Jewry, 1989; co-chmn. fin. rels. United Jewish Appeal Western Region, Jewish Agy. Com., 1992-93, United Jewish Appeal Ctrl. Region, Jewish Agy Com., 1993; mem. exec. com. Network of Ind. UJA Coms., 1994—; bd. dirs. Family Svcs., Inc., 1990—; mem. internat. bd. visitors M.J. Neeley Sch. Bus., Tex. Christian U., 1990—; hon. life mem. nat. commn. Anti-Defamation League, 1992. With USCG, 1951-54. Recipient Torch of Liberty award Anti-Defamation League of B'nai B'rith, 1988, Defender of Jerusalem award, 1990, Alumni award Boston U. Sch. Mgmt., 1994; named Man of Yr., B'nai B'rith Ft. Worth Jewish, 1984, Anti-Defamation League Ft. Worth, 1990; named to Consumer Electronics Hall of Fame, 2002. Mem. Electronic VIP Club, Ft. Worth C. of C. (bd. dirs. 1981-84), Masons, Shriners, Frog Club (Tex. Christian U.), Colonial Country Club, City Country Club, Ft. Worth. Home: 4917 Ranch View Rd Fort Worth TX 76109-3117 Office: Appel Assocs 301 Commerce St Ste 1415 Fort Worth TX 76102-4114 E-mail: bappel@flash.net.

APPEL, CAROLE STEIN, writer, political organizer; b. Phila., Jan. 23, 1937; d. Joseph George and Charlotte Stein; m. Kenneth I. Appel, June 21, 1959; children: Andrew, Laurel, Peter. BS, Temple U., 1958; MA, U. Mich., 1959. From asst. editor to sr. editor, jours. mgr. U. Ill. Press, Urbana, 1969-93; cons. Writing Ctr., U. N.H., Durham, 1995—. Mem. com. on bias free lang. Assn. Am. Univ. Presses, N.Y.C., 1991-93. Author: (chpt.) University Press Editing and Publishing, 1994; contbr. articles to profl. jours. Bd. dirs. Champaign County chpt. ACLU, 1980-89; chair Strafford County Dem. Com., Dover, N.H., 1996—; sec. N.H. Dem. Party, 2003--; mem. allocations com. United Way Greater Seacoast, Portsmouth, N.H., 1999-2002. Woodrow Wilson Nat. Fellowship Found. fellow, 1958; recipient Horace W. Norton Meml. award ACLU, 1990, Jefferson-Jackson award N.H. Dem. Party, 2000. Mem. NOW (pres. Champaign County chpt. 1976). Democrat. Avocation: photography. Home: 16 Isaac Lucas Cir Dover NH 03820-4910

APPEL, GERALD, investment advisor; b. N.Y.C., June 2, 1933; s. Samuel and Vivian (Adlerstein) A.; m. Judith Kane, May 26, 1956; children: Marvin Laurence, Marion Fran. BA, Bklyn. Coll., 1954; MSW, NYU, 1956. Adminstr. social agy. Jewish Family Svc., Bklyn., 1958-73; pvt. practice as psychoanalyst Great Neck, N.Y., 1963-95; pres. Signalert Corp., Great Neck, 1973—, Appel Asset Mgmt. Corp., 1995—. Author: Winning Market Systems, 1972, Double Your Money Every Three Years, 1973, 99 Ways to Make Money in a Depression, 1974, Stock Option and No-Load Switch Fund Scalpers Manual, 1979, Winning Stock Selection Systems, 1979, The Big Move, 1981, Time-Trend III, 1988, Portraits of Nature, 1992, American Photographers at the Turn of the Century, Travel and Trekking, 1994, (with others) The Art of the Human Form, 1995, New Directions in Technical Analysis, 1976, Stock Market Trading Systems, 1980, Far Away Faces—A Guide to Better Travel Portraits, 1998; (video) The MACD Trading System, 1990, Power Tools, 1992, Day Trading, 1990; contbr. articles to profl. jours. Bd. dirs. Keystone Ctr. of Music and Arts, 1998-2000, Mountain Laurel Ctr. Performing Arts, 2000—, The Great Neck Ctr. Performing Arts, 2000—. Mem. Nat. Psychol. Assn. for Psychoanalysis (bd. dirs., v.p.), Am. Assn. Media Photographers. Avocations: photography, tennis, sailing, music. Home: 97 Myrtle Dr Great Neck NY 11021-1805 Office: Signalert Corp 150 Great Neck Rd Ste 301 Great Neck NY 11021-3339 E-mail: gappel6@optonline.net., gappel@signalert.com.

APPEL, KENNETH I. mathematician, educator; b. Bklyn., Oct. 8, 1932; s. Irwin and Lillian (Sender) A.; m. Carole Stein, June 21, 1959; children— Andrew, Laurel, Peter BS, Queens Coll., 1953; MA, U. Mich., 1956, PhD, 1959. Mem. tech. staff Inst. for Def. Analyses, Princeton, N.J., 1959-61; asst. prof. math U. Ill., Urbana, 1961-67, assoc. prof., 1967-77, prof., 1977-93, prof. emeritus, 1993; prof. U. N.H., 1993—2003, chair dept. math., 1993—2002, prof. emeritus, 2003. Alderman, City of Urbana, 1971-75, mem. zoning bd. of appeals, 1975— . Served as pfc. U.S. Army, 1953-55 Recipient Delbert Ray Fulkerson prize Am. Math. Soc. and Math. Programming Soc., 1979, Disting. Alumnus award Queens Coll., 1979 Mem. Am. Math. Soc., Math. Assn. Am., Assn. Symbolic Logic Democrat. Jewish. Office: Univ New Hampshire Dept Math Kingsbury Hall Durham NH 03824 E-mail: kia@oregano.unh.edu.

APPEL, MARSHA CEIL, association executive; b. N.Y.C., Dec. 3, 1953; d. Albert and Stella Joy (Glaser) A.; m. Mark D. Marcellus, Sept. 10, 1978; children: Sam, Jill. BA, SUNY, Albany, 1974; MSLS, Syracuse U., 1975. Info. specialist Am. Assn. Advt. Agys., N.Y.C., 1976-79, mgr. member info svc., 1979-89, v.p., 1989-97, sr. v.p., 1997—. Author: Illustration Index IV, 1980, Illustration Index V, 1984, Illustration Index VI, 1988, Illustration Index VII, 1993, Illustration Index VIII, 1998; editor What's New in Advertising and Marketing, 1978-80; mem. adv. bd., contbr. Ency. Advt., 2002; contbr. Super Searchers on Madison Avenue, 2003. Mem. Spl. Librs. Assn. (chmn. advt. and mktg. div. 1982-83). Office: Am Assn Advt Agys 405 Lexington Ave New York NY 10174-0002

APPEL, NINA SCHICK, law educator, dean; b. Feb. 17, 1936; d. Leo and Nora Schick; m. Alfred Appel Jr.; children: Karen Oshman, Richard. Student, Cornell U.; JD, Columbia U., 1959. Instr. Columbia Law Sch., 1959-60; adminstr. Stanford U., mem. faculty, prof. law, 1973—, assoc. dean, 1976-83; dean Sch. Law Loyola U., 1983—. Mem. Am. Bar Found., Ill. Bar Found., Chgo. Bar Found., Chgo. Legal Club, Chgo. Network. Jewish. Office: Loyola U Sch Law 1 E Pearson St Chicago IL 60611-2055

APPEL, ROBERT EUGENE, lawyer, educator; b. Cleve., Oct. 18, 1958; s. Robert Donald and Jean Ann (Crites) Appel; m. Margaret Rose Curley, Aug. 24, 1985. BS, Cen. Conn. State U., 1980; JD, U. Bridgeport, Conn., 1982; MBA, U. Conn., 1984; LLM, Boston U., 1984. Bar: Conn. 1983. Asst. mgr. fin. services Lexington Ins. Co., Boston, 1984-85; tax. cons. Touche Ross and Co., Stamford, Conn., 1985-86; asst. dir. nat. design CIGNA Corp., Bloomfield, Conn., 1986—88, dir. nat. design, 1988—97; asst. v.p. Lincoln Nat. Life Ins. Co., Hartford, 1998—2002, 2d v.p., 2002—. Lectr. Real Estate Tng. and Ednl. Svcs., Bridgeport, 1985—88; lectr. real estate Danr Inst., Southbury, 1991—. Divsn. coord. United Way, 1988. Mem.: ABA, Conn. Bar Assn. Republican. Roman Catholic. Avocations: investing, running, weightlifting, motorcycling. Home: 80 Kingston Dr East Hartford CT 06118-2450 Office: Lincoln Fin Group 350 Church St Hartford CT 06103-1106

APPEL, ROBERT JOSEPH, lawyer; b. Phila., June 15, 1951; s. Frederick and Celeste Evelyn (Hirsch) A.; m. Constance Marie Keresey, June 1, 1980; children: Benjamin Joseph, Lucas John. BA, Goddard Coll., 1980. Bar: Vt. Fgn. car mechanic, Barre, Vt., 1970-77; def. investigator Office of Defender Gen., Montpelier, Vt., 1977-80, asst. to defender gen., 1984-85, correctional defender, 1985-86, pub. defender St. Johnsbury, Vt., 1986-88, defender gen. Montpelier, 1993—2001; civil rights investigator Officer of Atty. Gen., Montpelier, 1980-84, asst. atty. gen. for civil rights, 1988-92; exec. dir. Vt. Human Rights Commn., 2001—. Adj. faculty Woodbury Coll., Montpelier, 1989-91. Chair Planning Commn., Woodbury, 1989-93; mem. Sch. Bd. Woodbury, 1998—, chair, 1999—. Mem. Vt. Assn. of Criminal and Def. Lawyers, ACLU (Vt. chpt. 1993—), Vt. Bar. Assn. (Svc. award 2001), Vt. Trial Lawyers Assn. (Outstanding Pub. Svc. award 1996). Office: Office of Defender Gen 120 State St Montpelier VT 05658

APPEL, TRUMAN FRANK, surgeon; b. St. Louis, Apr. 4, 1936; s. Myron Henry and Ida Doris (Pearline) A.; children: Leslie Carol, Sarah Elizabeth. BS, Tulane U., 1956; MD, St. Louis U., 1960. Diplomate Am. Bd. Surgery, Am. Bd. Colon and Rectal Surgery. Pvt. practice, Corpus Christi, Tex., 1969—. Treas., bd. dirs. Coastal Bend Health Plan, Corpus Christi, 1984-92. Served to capt. USAF, 1961-64. Fellow AMA, ACS, Am. Soc. Colon and Rectal Surgeons Tex., Tex. Med. Assn., Masons, Shriners, Tex. Surg. Soc. Jewish. Avocations: hunting, fishing. Office: 101 Med Arts Bldg 1001 Louisiana St Corpus Christi TX 78404 E-mail: tfappel@earthlink.net.

APPEL, WILLIAM FRANK, pharmacist; b. Mpls., Oct. 8, 1924; s. William Ignatius and Elna Antonia (Mulzahn) A.; m. Louise D. Altman, Sept. 24, 1949; children— Nancy, Peggy, James, Elizabeth. BS in Pharmacy, U. Minn., 1949; D.Sc. (hon.), Phila. Coll. Pharmacy and Sci., 1978. Intern in pharmacy Northwestern Hosp., Mpls.; pres., pharmacist, mgr. Appel Com-Pharm, Inc., Mpls., 1949—; pres. Pharm. Cons. Services, P.A., St. Paul, 1960—. Mem. Minn. Bd. Pharmacy, 1960-65, pres., 1965; preceptor internship requirement program; chmn. Minn. Gov.'s. Commn. on Drug Abuse, 1971-73; mem. Mpls. Health Dept. Task Force on Pub. Health Approaches to Chem. Dependency; clin. instr. U. Minn. Coll. Pharmacy, 1970— ; cons. HEW; long term care facilities; rep. Nat. Pharmacy/Industry Com. on Nat. Health Ins.; mem. revision com. U.S. Pharmacopeial Conv., 1980— Served with USN, 1942-46. Recipient Good Neighbor award, Sta. WCCO, Mpls., 1973. Mem. Twin City Met. Drug Assn., Minn. Pharm. Assn. (v.p., Harold R. Popp award 1974, mem. continuing edn. faculty 1970—), Am. Pharm. Assn. (pres. N.W. br., nat. pres. 1976-77, Daniel B. Smith award 1970, treas. 1979—) pharm. assns), Minn. Gerontol. Soc., U. Minn. Coll. Pharmacy Alumni Assn. (v.p., Distinguished Pharmacist award 1971) Home: 7204 Trillium Ln Minneapolis MN 55435-4020 Office: Preferred Choice Pharmacy 900 Long Lake Rd #150 New Brighton MN 55112

APPELBAUM, ANN HARRIET, lawyer; b. Decatur, Ill., 1948; d. Irving and Cecelia (Hecht) A.; m. Neal Borovitz, July 4, 1982; children: Abby, Jeremy. BA, Barnard Coll., 1970; JD, Boston U., 1973. Bar: N.Y. 1974, U.S. Dist. Ct. (so. dist.) N.Y. 1975, U.S. Ct. Appeals (2nd cir.) 1975, U.S. Supreme Ct. 1978. Assoc. Hart & Hume, N.Y.C., 1974-76, Warshaw, Burstein, N.Y.C., 1976-80; counsel Jewish Theol. Sem. & Jewish Mus., N.Y.C., 1980—. Mem. Nat. Assn. Coll. and Univ. Attys. Office: The Jewish Theological Seminary 3080 Broadway New York NY 10027-4650

APPELBAUM, BRUCE DAVID, physician; b. Lincroft, N.J., Apr. 24, 1957; s. John S. and Shirley B. (Wolfson) A.; m. Renee P., 1997; children: Alexa, Aniessa. BS in pharmacy, Rutgers Coll., 1980; MS in pharmacology, Emory U., 1983, PhD in pharmacology, 1985; MD, Medical Coll. Ga., 1989. Diplomate Nat. Bd. Med. Examiners, Am. Bd. Psychiatry and Neurology. Rsch. assoc. Emory U. Dept. Pharmacology, Atlanta, 1985; resident physician U. Calif. Dept. Psychiatry, Irvine, Calif., 1989-93; pvt. practice Huntington Beach, Calif., 1993—. Med. dir. Coll. Cmty. Svcs., Anaheim, Calif., 1995—. Contbr. articles to profl. jours. Recipient Nat. Rsch. Svc. award Nat. Inst. Health, 1982-83, Ea. Student Rsch. Forum U. Miami Medical Sch., 1984, Nat. Student Rsch. Forum, 1987. Mem. AMA, Am. Psychiat. Assn., Orange County Psychiat. Soc., N.Y. Acad. Scis., Sigma Xi. Avocations: travel, photography, bicycling, reading. Office: 18811 Huntington St Ste 200 Huntington Beach CA 92648-6003

APPELBAUM, JUDITH PILPEL, editor, consultant, educator; b. N.Y.C., Sept. 26, 1939; d. Robert Cecil and Harriet Florence (Fleischl) Pilpel; m. Alan Appelbaum, Apr. 16, 1961; children: Lynn Stephanie, Alexander Eric. BA with honors, Vassar Coll., 1960. Editor Harper's Mag., N.Y.C., 1960-74; mng. editor Harper's Weekly, 1974-76; sr. cons. Atlas World Press Rev., 1977; mng. editor Pubs. Weekly, 1978-81, contbg. editor, 1981-82; columnist N.Y. Times Book Rev., 1982-84; founder Sensible Solutions, Inc., 1979, mng. dir., 1984—. Assoc. dir. Ctr. for Book Rsch., U. Scranton, 1985—88; book rev. editor Pub. Rsch. Quar., 1984—86; editor in chief, 1986—88; cons. editor, 1988—; chair book industry sys. adv. com. royalty subcom., 1996—98; chair Book Industry Standards and Comm. Rights Com., 1998—; mem. exec. com. BISAC, 1998—; vice chair, 1999—2002; contbg. editor Small Press mag., 1991—96; adv. bd. Foreward Mag., 1999—2001; mem. faculty Pub. Inst., U. Denver, 1981—; mem. CUNY Edn. in Publs. Program, 1982; chair Book Industry Study Group Publs., 1980—; adv. coun. mem. Small Press Ctr., 1998—; mem. rsch. com. Book Industry Study Group, 1984—, bd. dirs., 1997—, exec. com., 1998—; adv. bd. Coordinating Coun. Lit. Mags., 1980—84, PEN Ctr. USA West, 1988—90. Author: How to Get Happily Published, 1978, 5th edit., 1998, (with Fl. Janovic) The Writer's Workbook: A Full and Friendly Guide to Boosting Your Book's Sales, 1991; editor: (with T. Jones and G. Cravens) The Big Picture: A Wraparound Book, 1976, The Question of Size in the Book Industry Today, 1978, Getting a Line on Backlist, 1979, Paperback Primacy, 1981, Small Publisher Power, 1982; editor-at-large Publishers Mktg. Assn. Newsletter, 2001—. Mem.: PEN, Pubs. Mktg. Assn. (bd. dirs. 1990—92, Benjmain Franklin Lifetime Achievement award 1995), Women's Media Group (bull. editor 1990—92), Authors Guild. Office: Sensible Solutions Inc 500 Croton Lake Rd Mount Kisco NY 10549-4233 E-mail: verysensibly@aol.com.

APPELBAUM, KENNETH LLOYD, psychiatrist; b. N.Y.C., Mar. 18, 1951; BA, Goddard Coll., 1972; MD, U. Wash., 1981. Diplomate in psychiatryn and forensic psychiatry Am. Bd. Psychiatry and Neurology. Resident in family medicine Maine Dartmouth Family Practice Residency, Augusta, 1981-82; resident in psychiatry U. Vt., Burlington, 1983-86; fellow in forensic psychiatry Yale U., New Haven, 1986-87; asst. prof. psychiatry U. Mass. Sch. Medicine, Worcester, 1987-96; dir. forensic svc. Worcester State Hosp., 1987-98; dir. forensic psychiatry fellowship U. Mass. Sch. Medicine, Worcester, 1993-98; supr. forensic mental health Commonwealth of Mass., Dept. Mental Health, Boston, 1988—. Mem. experts panel ABA, Benchbook for State Courts on Psychiatric and Psychological Evidence and Testimony, 1998; co-dir. Law and Psychiatry program U. Mass. Sch. Medicine, 1992-99, dir. Correctional Mental Health program, 1998—, assoc. prof. clin. psychiatry, 1996-2002 prof., 2002—; mental health program dir. Commonwealth of Mass. Dept. of Correction, Boston, 1998—; pres. profl. staff orgn. Worcester State Hosp., 1992-95; mem. com. subsplty. cert. in forensic psychiatry Am. Bd. Psychiatry and Neurology, Inc. Contbr. articles to profl. jours. Chairperson Sunday sch., Kahal B'raira, Boston, 1996-98, human rights adv. commn. Cmty. Health Link, Worcester, 1997-99. Fellow: Am. Psychiat. Assn. (disting.); mem.: Mass. Psychiat. Soc., Am. Acad. of Psychiatry and the Law (councillor 1997—2000, dep. editor jour. 1997—, treas. 2001—). Office: U Mass Correctional Health One Research Dr Ste 120C Westborough MA 01581 E-mail: Kenneth.Appelbaum@umassmed.edu.

APPELBAUM, MARGERY FREEMAN, artist; b. Washington, July 15, 1953; d. Jacob J. and Rose Freeman BFA, U. Md., 1975, MFA in Printmaking, 1978. Coord. Art for Pub. Places Md.-Nat. Capital Park and Planning Commn., Riverdale, Md., 1978-80, coord. visual arts program, 1980-86; adj. prof. Montgomery Coll., Takoma Park, Md., 1986-98. Chair visual arts grant panel State of Md., Balt., 1978-80, joint mgmt. coun., 1981-88; artist-in-resident Md. State Arts Coun., Balt., 1997; adj. prof. Marymount Coll., Tarrytown, N.Y., 20000-02, Grad. Sch., Coll. New Rochelle, N.Y., 2000—. SUNY Westchester Art Workshop, 2001—. One/two/three-person shows include Plum Gallery, Kensington, Md., 1985, Montpelier Cultural Arts Ctr., Laurel, Md., 1986, Md. Art Place, Balt., 1987, Montgomery Coll., Takoma Park, 1987, Sande Webster Gallery, Phila., 1988, Catonsville C.C., Balt., 1989, Franlin Square, Washington, 1993, Glen View Mansion, Rockville, Md., 1997; group exhbns. include Md. State Arts Coun., Balt., 1979, Balt. Mus. Art, 1979, 83, Corcoran Gallery Art, Washington, 1980, Woodmere Art Gallery, 1983, Athenaeum Gallery, Alexandria, Va., 1984, Fendrick Gallery, Washington, 1985, SUNY, Buffalo, 1985, Musee cantonal des Beaux-Arts, Lausanne, Switzerland, 1985, Md. Crafts Coun., Balt., 1986, Parson's Gallery, N.Y.C., 1986, Three Rivers Art Fesitval, Pitts., 1986, David Adamson Gallery, Washington, 1987, Md. Inst. Art, Balt., 1987, Hand Workshop, Richmond, Va., 1987, Washington Project for Arts, Washington, 1987, 89, Sotheby's, N.Y.C., 1987, Md. Art Place, Balt., 1988, Renwick Mus. Shop, Washington, 1988, Phila. Art Alliance, 1988, Anderson Gallery and Franklin Gallery, Richmond, Va., 1989, Bergstrom-Mahler Mus., Neenah, Wis., 1990, Del. Ctr. for Contemporary Arts, Wilmington, 1991, Rockville (Md.) Arts Place, 1995, 96, Marymount Coll., 2001, Islip (N.Y.) Mus. Contemporary Art, 2002; represented in permanent collections Washington Post, Inc., Woodholm Ctr., IBM Corp. Collection, Hyatt Regency, Inc., Gannett Co./USA Today, Environs, Health Tech. Assn. Recipient fellowship in visual arts Md. State Arts Coun., 1996. Office: SUNYn Westchester Art Workshop White Plains NY 10606 also: Grad Sch New Rochelle NY 10805

APPELBAUM, MICHELLE GELLMAN, family nurse practitioner; b. Monticello, N.Y. d. Emanuel and Sally Gellman; m. Joel Appelbaum, June 8, 1980; 1 child, Edward. BA in English, SUNY, Binghamton, 1977; MS, Pace U., N.Y. Med. Coll., 1980; postgrad., Columbia U., 1998—. Cert. family and pediat. nurse practitioner ANCC; lic. in prescription writing privileges including controlled substances, N.Y. Nursing supr. Wellness Home Care, Liberty, N.Y., 1986-89; FNP Sullivan Diagnostic Treatment Ctr., Harris, N.Y., 1989—; pediat. nurse practitioner pediat. and adolescent medicine office Dr. Louis Rodrigues Monticello, NY. Instr., cons. phys. assessment in employment and ednl. settings; adj. instr. nursing divsn. Sullivan County C.C., Loch Sheldrake, N.Y., 1988; 1st nurse practitioner med. staff Cmty. Gen. Hosp., Harris. Contbr. articles to profl. jours. Developer parent aide program for high risk families, Sullivan County. Named N.Y. State Nurse Practitioner of Yr., Am. Acad. Nurse Practitioners, 2002. Mem. N.Y. State Coalition Nurse Practitioners, Sigma Theta Tau. Avocations: weight training, reading, traveling.

APPELBAUM, PAUL STUART, psychiatrist, educator; b. Bklyn., Nov. 30, 1951; s. Isidore W. and Celia (Bressler) A.; m. Diana Muir Karter, Nov. 9, 1953; children: Binyamin, Yonaton, Avigail. AB, Columbia U., 1972; MD, Harvard U., 1976. Diplomate Am. Bd. Psychiatry and Neurology. Intern Soroka Med. Ctr., Beersheva, Israel, 1976-77; resident Mass. Mental Health Ctr., Boston, 1977-80; Clin. fellow psychiatry Harvard Med. Sch., Boston, 1977-80; from asst. prof. to assoc. prof. psychiatry and law U. Pitts., 1980-84; assoc. prof. psychiatry Harvard Med. Sch., Boston, 1984-85; Zeleznik prof. psychiatry, dir. law and psychiatry program U. Mass. Med. Sch., Worcester, 1985—, chmn. dept., 1992—; vis. interdisciplinary prof. Law Ctr. Georgetown U., Washington, 1988-89. Mem. commn. on mentally disabled ABA, Washington, 1982-87; task force on involuntary civil commitment Nat. Ctr. for State Cts., Williamsburg, Va., 1984-89, Rsch. Network on Mental Health and Law, John D. and Catherine T. Macarthur Found., Chgo., 1988-96; fellow Ctr. for Advanced Study in the Behavioral Scis., Stanford, Calif., 1996-97;rsch. network on mandatory outpatient treatment John D. and Catherine T. MacArthur Found., Chgo., 2000--. Author: Clinical Handbook of Psychiatry and the Law, 1982 (M.F. Guttmacher award 1982), 3d edit., 2000, Informed Consent: Legal Theory and Clinical Practice, 1987, 2d edit., 2001, Paul Appelbaum on Law and Psychiatry, 1989, Almost A Revolution: Mental Health Law and Limits of Change, 1994 (M.F. Guttmacher award 1996), Trauma and Memory: Clinical and Legal Controversies, 1997, Assessing Patients' Capacities to Consent to Treatment, 1998 (M.F. Guttmacher award 2000), Rethinking Risk Assessment, 2001 (M.F. Guttmacher award 2002); contbr. articles to profl. jours. Nat. coord. Med. Mobilization for Soviet Jewry, Waltham, Mass., 1974-80; bd. dirs. Action for Soviet Jewry, Waltham, 1984-85, Torah Ctr., Sharon, Mass., 1987-88, Cmty. Health Link, Worcester, Mass., 1992—, Am. Psychiat. Press, 2001-03, Am. Psychiat. Inst. on Rsch. and Edn., 2001-03. Recipient rsch. scientist devel. award NIMH, 1983; rsch. grantee President's Commn. on Ethical Problems in Medicine, Washington, 1982, John D. and Catherine T. MacArthur Found., 1988, 2003; fellow Ctr. for Advanced Study in Behavioral Scis., Palo Alto, Calif., 1996-97. Mem. NAS (elected to Inst. Medicine 2000), Internat. Acad. Law and Mental Health (Philippe Pinel award 2000), Am. Psychiat. Assn. (bd. dirs. 1997--, chair commn. on jud. action 1984-90, joint reference com. 1984-94, chair coun. on psychiatry and law 1990-94, sec. 1997-99, v.p. 1999-2001, pres. 2002-03, Isaac Ray award 1990), Am. Acad. Psychiatry and the Law (councillor 1987-90, pres. 1995-96, Seymour Pollock award 2001), Am. Soc. Law and Medicine, Mass. Psychiat. Soc. (pres. 1992-93). Jewish. Avocation: writing for popular mags. Office: U Mass Med Sch Dept Psychiatry Worcester MA 01655 E-mail: appelbap@ummhc.org.

APPELDORN, CLAUDIA J. nursing administrator, editor; b. Pipestone, Minn., Apr. 14, 1947; d. Louis H. and Barbara B. Appeldorn. Diploma, Sioux Valley Hosp. Sch Nursing, Sioux Falls, S.D., 1968; BSN, S.D. State U., Brookings, 1972; MSN, U. Tex., San Antonio, 1977. Nursing asst. Sioux Valley Hosp., 1967-68, staff and charge nurse, 1968-70, 70-72; charge nurse Kingsbury Manor, Lake Preston, S.D., 1970; instr. Bapt. Meml. Hosp. Sch. Nursing, San Antonio, 1972-74, asst. dir., 1974-81; asst. dir., acting dir. and dir. nursing St. Anne's Hosp., Chgo., 1981-82, asst. adminstr., 1983-85; dir. edn. Am. Assn. Neurosci. Nurses, Chgo., 1985-90, assoc. exec. dir., 1990-94; pres. Los Gatos, Inc., Chgo., 1993—. Mem. adv. bd. Summit Home Health Care, Chgo., 1981-95. Co-editor: Core Curriculum for Neuroscience Nursing, 1990; mng. editor Jour. Neurosci. Nursing, 1988-94. Named Nurse of Yr., Bapt. Meml. Hosp. Sys., San Antonio, 1979. Mem. Nat. League for Nursing, Ill. League for Nursing (v.p. 1992-96), Ill. Orgn. Nurse Execs. (program com. 1988-90, bylaws com. 1990-92). Home: 891 121st St Pipestone MN 56164-

APPELL, LOUISE SOPHIA, consulting company executive; b. Northampton, Mass., Sept. 22, 1930; d. Romeo Edward and Phyllis Teresa (Szynal) Fortier; m. Melville Joseph Appell, July 26, 1953 (div. 1975); children: Melissande Foglio, David Maxcim; m. Clifford Harding Querolo, June 1, 1991 (dec. 1992). BA, Smith Coll., 1951; MA, U. Ky., 1966, PhD, 1972. Instr. U. Ky., 1966-68; dir. spl. edn. grad. program Catholic U. Am., Washington, 1969-76; assoc. dir. nat. com. Arts for the Handicapped, Washington, 1976-80; owner, pres. Louise Appell Cons. Svcs., Washington, 1980-82; assoc. Macro Systems, Inc., Silver Spring, Md., 1982-84, dir. edn. product devel., 1984-85, dir. ednl. product devel., 1985—, v.p., 1985—, ret., 1996. E-mail: lsapell@patriot.net.

APPELMAN, EVAN HUGH, retired chemist; b. Chgo., June 6, 1935; s. Harry Louis and Mollie Sarah (Hirsch) A.; m. Mary Frances Goold, Sept. 2, 1960; children: Harold Stewart, Hilary Louise. AB, U. Chgo., 1953, MS, 1955; PhD, U. Calif. at Berkeley, 1960. With Argonne (Ill.) Nat. Lab., 1960-95, chemist, 1963-76, sr. chemist, 1976-95, ret., 1995. Contbr. articles to profl. jours. Guggenheim fellow, 1973-74; Recipient award for service at Argonne Nat. Lab., U. Chgo., 1975, E.O. Lawrence award ERDA, 1976, Alexander von Humboldt Research award Fed. Republic Germany, 1988-89; vis. sr. rsch. fellow Brit. Sci. Rsch. Coun.-U. Oxford, 1983-84. Fellow AAAS; mem. Am. Chem. Soc., Phi Beta Kappa, Sigma Xi. Jewish. Home: 224 Lake Dr Kensington CA 94708-1132 E-mail: evhap@anl.gov.

APPELT, GLENN DAVID, pharmacologist, consultant, medical educator; b. Yoakum, Tex., Aug. 24, 1935; s. Leonard William and Josephine Mildred Appelt; m. Jennifer Sue McNew, Feb. 2, 1983; 1 stepchild, Christy Ann Allen. BS in Pharmacy, U. Tex., 1957, MS in Pharmacology, 1959; PhD, U. Colo., 1963. Registered pharmacist Ala. Asst. prof. pharmacy U. Tex., Austin, 1963—67; assoc. prof. pharmacy U. Colo., Boulder, 1967—77, prof. pharmacy, 1978—92; prof. emeritus U. Colo. Health Scis. Ctr., Denver, 1992—; lectr. allied health U. South Ala., Mobile, 1994—; prof., program dir. Columbia So. U., Orange Beach, Ala., 1997—. Cons. Dixie Dunes Consulting Group, Gulf Shores, Ala., 1993—; mem. adv. bd. Herb Rsch. Found., Boulder, 1985—; mem. rev. panels herbs and natural products NIH, Bethesda, Md., 1997, 99. Co-author: Therapeutic Pharmacology, 1988, Nature's Medicine Chest-A Sampler, 2000. Vol. Ft. Morgan (Ala.) Vol. Fire Dept., 1993—96; vol. campaigner Dem. Party, Boulder, 1975—82. Named Disting. Coloradan in Pharmacy, Sch. Pharmacy U. Colo.; fellow, Armour Inc., 1959, Danforth Found., 1968—74. Democrat. Unitarian Universalist. Avocations: hiking, fly fishing, reading. Home: 3120 Ponce de Leon Ct Gulf Shores AL 36542

APPENZELLER, OTTO, neurologist, researcher; b. Czernowitz, Romania, Dec. 11, 1927; came to U.S., 1963; s. Emmanuel Adam and Josephine (Metsch) A.; m. Judith Bryce, Dec. 11, 1956; children: Timothy, Martin, Peter. MBBS, Sydney U., Australia, 1957, MD, 1966; PhD, U. London, 1963. Diplomate Am. Bd. Psychiatry and Neurology. Prof. U. N. Mex., Albuquerque, 1970-90; vis. prof. McGill U., Montreal, 1977; hon. rsch. fellow U. London, 1983; vis. scientist Oxygen Transport Program Lovelace Med. Found., Albuquerque, 1990-92; pres. N.Mex. Health Enhancement and Marathon Clinics Rsch. Found., Albuquerque, 1992—; prof. exptl. neurobiology Bogomoletz Inst., Ukrainian Acad. Sci., Kiev, 1995-2000. U.S.-India exch. scientist NSF, 1992; Fogarty internat. exch. scientist, Kiev, Ukraine, 1993; rsch. com. UNESCO Internat. Coun. Sports and Phys. Edn., 1978-99; ref. Med. Rsch. Coun. New Zealand, 1986-99, reviewer, 1988-99; participant individual health scientist exch. program Fogarty Internat. Ctr., NIH to A.A. Bogomoletz Inst. Physiology, Kiev, 1993. Author: The Autonomic Nervous System, 5th edit., 1997; co-author: Headache, 1984; editor: Pathogenesis and Management of Headache, 1976, Health Aspects of Endurance Training, 1978, Sports Medicine, 3d edit., 1988, Jour. Headache, 1975-77, Annals of Sports Medicine, 1984-88; translator: Neurologic Differential Diagnosis (M. Mumentaler), 2nd edit., 1992; vol. editor: Handbook of Clinical Neurology: The Autonomic Nervous System, Parts I and II, 1998-2000; mem. editl. bd. numerous med. jours. Grantee Diabetes Rsch. and Edn. Found., 1988, Inst. C. Mondino, U. Pavia, Italy, 1992, 95-96, 2000, NMHEMC Rsch. Found., 1992, 93-2001, 2002, 2003. Fellow ACP (sr.), Am. Acad. Neurology (sr.), Royal Australasian Coll. Physicians (sr.). Achievements include discovery of disease affecting peripheral nerves of Navajo children, of release of opioids and endothelin in human circulatory system after exercise, of chronic neurodegenerative disease in human T-lymphotropic viral II (HTLV II) infection, of peptidergic innervation of blood vessels supplying blood to peripheral nerves in present day and ancient mummified tissues of neurologic dis. in mummy portraits, of neuropathy in chronic pulmonary disease and chronic mountain sickness of human fossilized biological rhythm in ancient human teeth, of the neurobiology of migraines in the Andes; leader of Mt. Everest research expedition in 1987, Khachenjunga research expedition, 1989, Stock Kangri research expedition, 1992, Tso Moriri Lake (Ladakh) research expedition, 1994, Cerro de Pasco research expedition, 1997, 99, 2000, 2003. E-mail: ottoarun12@aol.com.

APPERSON, BERNARD JAMES, lawyer; b. Washington, June 28, 1956; s. Bernard James Jr. and Ann Wentworth (Anderson) A. BA in Polit. Sci., Am. U., 1978; JD, Cumberland Sch. Law, 1981; LLM in Internat. Law, Georgetown U., 1985. Bar: Fla. 1981, Ga. 1981, D.C. 1983, U.S. Supreme Ct. 1985. Atty., U.S. trustee for so. dist. N.Y. U.S. Dept. Justice, N.Y.C., 1981; atty. EPA, Washington, 1981-83; atty. civil rights div. U.S. Dept. Justice, Washington, 1983-84, atty. office legis. affairs, 1986-87; asst. U.S. atty. Ea. Dist. Va., Alexandria, 1987-97; counsel to dir. Legal Services Corp., Washington, 1985-86; commr. U.S. Dist. Ct., Ea. Dist. Va., Alexandria, 1996-97; sr. counsel com. on govt. reform and oversight, spl. counsel subcom. Nat. Econ. Growth, Natural Resources etc. U.S. Ho. of Reps., Washington, 1997-98; assoc. ind. counsel Office of the Ind. Counsel, Washington, 1998-99, dep. ind. counsel, 1999-2000; chief counsel oversight and investigations Com. on Jud., U.S. Ho. of Reps., Washington, 2001, chief counsel subcom. on crime, terrorism & homeland security, 2001—. Instr. FBI Tng. Acad., Quantico, Va., 1990; lectr. law U. London and U. Ga., 1990. Assoc. editor Am. Jour. Trial Advocacy Cumberland Sch. Law, 1979-81. County chmn. Paula Hawkins for U.S Senate, Volusia County, Fla., 1974; nat. staff Citizens for Reagan, Fla., Kansas City, Mo., 1976; cons. Reagan for Pres., Detroit, 1980; dep. northeastern regional dir. Reagan-Bush 1984, Washington, 1984, Lawyers for Bush-Cheney, Washington, 2000. Lewis F. Powell Medal for Excellence in Advocacy Am. Coll Trial Lawyers, 1980. Mem. Federalist Soc. for Law and Pub. Policy Studies, Order of Barristers, St. Andrew's Soc. Republican. Anglican. Home: 545 E Braddock Rd Apt 704 Alexandria VA 22314-2171 Office: US Ho of Reps Jud Com Subcom Crime Terrorism and Homeland Secu 207 Cannon House Office Bld Washington DC 20515

APPERSON, JACK ALFONSO, retired army officer, business executive; b. Fredericksburg, Va., Dec. 21, 1934; s. Claude Heywood and Mary Louise (Farmer) A.; m. Alexandra Maynard, Aug. 31, 1957 (dec. Aug. 1992); children: Melissa Heywood, Amy Alexandra, Robert Randall (dec.), Eric Edward; m. Marguerite M. Legin, Nov. 25, 1995. BS, U.S. Mil. Acad., 1957; MS in Nuclear Physics, U. Ala., 1962; AA (hon.), Texarkana C.C., 1979. Commd. 2d lt. U.S. Army, 1957, advanced through grades to brig. gen., platoon leader, 1957-58, Ft. Knox, Ky., 1958-59; comdg. officer 546th Ordnance Co. U.S. Army-Europe, 1963-64, materiel officer 66th Maintenance Bn., 1964-65, exec. officer bn., 1965-66; asst. prof., instr. dept. ordnance U.S. Mil. Acad., 1967-69; bn. comdr. and materiel officer 801st Maintenance Bn., Vietnam, 1969-70; assignment officer ordnance br. Office of Personnel Ops., Dept. Army, Washington, 1970-71, chief co. grade assignments, 1971-72; bn. comdr. 1st Inf. Div., Ft. Riley, Kans., 1973-74; office dep. chief of staff for logistics Dept. Army, Washington, 1974-75; chief war res. office Office Dep. Chief of Staff for Logistics, Dept. Army, Washington, 1975-76; exec. to asst. sec. Army Installations and Logistics, Washington, 1976-77; comdr. Red River Army Depot, Texarkana, Tex., 1977-79; dep. comdg. gen. U.S. Army Missile Materiel Readiness Command, Redstone Arsenal, Ala., 1979-81; comdg. gen. U.S. Army Depot System Command, Chambersburg, Pa., 1981-82; sr. v.p. ops. mgmt. div. Day & Zimmermann, Phila., 1982-83, also bd. dirs.; pres. Govt. Systems Group Day and Zimmerman, Phila., 1991-95, Systems Engrng. Assocs. Corp., Mt. Laurel, NJ, 1983-91. Bd. dirs. Redstone Fed. Credit Union; vestryman Sharon Chapel Episcopal Ch., Alexandria, Va., 1975-77, St. Paul's Episcopal Ch., Phila., 1984-1988. Decorated DSM, Legion of Merit, Bronze Star (2), Meritorious Svc. medal, others; inducted into U.S. Army Ordnance Hall of Fame, 1994. Mem. Assn. Grads. U.S. Mil. Acad., West Point Soc. Phila. (bd. dirs.), Assn. U.S. Army (pres. chpt. 1983-85), Am. Def. Preparedness Assn., Alumni Assn. U.S. Army War Coll., Phila C. of C., Cherry Hill C. of C., Narragansett C. of C. (pres. 1996—2000), South County Hosp. Found.; trustee R.I. State Investment Commn., Rotary (pres. West Bay Rotary Coun. 2000), Rehoboth-Lewes Rotary, Sigma Pi Sigma. Republican. Home: 817 Riverton Rd Moorestown NJ 08057

APPERSON, JEAN, psychologist; b. Durham, N.C., June 8, 1934; d. James Harry and Dorothy Elizabeth (Johnson) Apperson; m. Calvin Adams Pope, Mar. 23, 1956 (div. 1967); 1 child, Richard Allan. BA, U. S. Fla., 1966; MA, Mich. State U., 1970, PhD, 1973. Cert. in psychoanalysis Mich. Psychoanalytic Coun., 1990. Teaching asst. Mich. State U., E. Lansing, 1968-69; psychiatric technician St. Lawrence Community Mental Health Ctr., Lansing, Mich., 1968-69, psychology intern, 1969-71, Mich. State U. Counseling Ctr., 1971-73; clin. psychologist U. Mich. Counseling Ctr., Ann Arbor, 1973-81; pvt. practice psychology and psychoanalysis Ann Arbor, 1974—. Mem., chmn. Mich. Bd. Psychology, Lansing, 1984-91. Contbr. articles to profl. jours.; cons. editor Am. Psychol. Assn. Catalog of Selected Documents, 1975-80. USPHS grantee, 1969-70; NIMH grantee, 1970-71. Fellow Mich. Psychol. Assn. (chmn. women's issues com. 1981-83); mem. APA (com. on sci. and profl. ethics and conduct 1977-80), Mich. Soc. Psychoanalytic Psychology (treas. 1982-86), Mich. Psychoanalytic Coun. (tchg. and supervising analyst, mem. at large 1991-93, tng. com. 1992-2001, pres. 1995-97, v.p. for edn. and tng. 1998-2001), Assn. for Advancement of Psychology, Am. Women in Psychology, Mich. Women Psychologists. Democrat. Unitarian Universalist. Avocations: french language and culture, gardening, nature study, music. Home: 7224 Chelsea Manchester Rd Manchester MI 48158-9443 Office: Ste 23E 555 E William St Ann Arbor MI 48104-2428 E-mail: jeanatapp@aol.com.

APPEZZATO, MARC ROBERT, graphic artist; b. Rahway, N.J., Jan. 22, 1973; s. Robert and Edith (Nardone) A. AA, Union County Coll., Cranford, N.J., 1995; BS, Kean Coll., Union, N.J., 1997. Graphic artist Vantage Custom Classics, Avenel, NJ, 1997—2001, Ideal Jacobs Corp., Maplewood, NJ, 2001—. Patentee in field. Avocations: photography, writing, moviemaking/film, web design, illustration, design. Home: 1027 Leesville Ave Rahway NJ 07065-1810 E-mail: mrock_1@yahoo.com.

APPLE, DAINA DRAVNIEKS, government agency official; b. Kuldiga, Latvia, July 6, 1944; came to U.S., 1951; d. Albins Dravnieks and Alina A. (Bergs) Zelmenis; divorced; 1 child, Almira Moronne; m. Martin A. Apple, Sept. 2, 1986. BSc, U. Calif., Berkeley, 1977, MA, 1980. Economist Pacific S.W. Rsch. U.S. Forest Svc., Berkeley, 1976-85, mgr. regional land use appeals San Francisco, 1986-88, program analysis officer, engring., 1988-90, asst. regulatory officer, 1990-95, strategic planner nat. forest sys. resources program, 1995-98, policy analyst, 1998—2002; adminstr. workplace rels. Pacific Southwest Region, Vallejo, Calif., 2002—. Author: Public Involvement in the Forest Service-Methodologies, 1977, Public Involvement, Selected Abstracts for Natural Resource Managers, 1979, The Management of Policy and Direction in the Forest Service, 1982, An Analysis of the Forest Service Human Resource Management Program, 1984, Organization Design-Abstracts for Natural Resources Users, 1986, Social and Legal Forces Changing the Management of National Forests, 1996, Water and the Forest Service, 2000, The Forest Service as a Learning Organization, 2000, Evolution of U.S. Water Policy, 2001; contbg. editor Jour. Women in Natural Resources, 1987—. Fellow Soc. Am. Foresters (chair Nat. Capital Soc. 2000), Phi Beta Kappa Soc.; mem. AAAS, ESA, AWIS, N.Y. Acad. Sci., Am. Water Resources Assn., Am. Forestry Assn., m. Latvian Assn. (bd. dirs. 1995-97), Phi Beta Kappa Assocs. (nat. sec. 1985-88, pres. No. Calif. 1982-84), Commonwealth Club of Calif., Exch. Club of Capitol Hill, Sigma Xi. Avocations: organization and political theory, ballroom dancing, tennis, film. Office: US Forest Svc 1323 Club Dr Vallejo CA 94592 E-mail: dapple@fs.fed.us.

APPLE, JACKI (JACQUELINE B. APPLE), artist, writer, educator; b. N.Y.C. Student, Syracuse U.; BFA, Parsons Sch. Design. Curator exhbns. and performance Franklin Furnace, N.Y.C., 1977-80; prodr., host Sta. KPFK-FM, North Hollywood, Calif., 1982-95; mem. core faculty Art Ctr. Coll. Design, Pasadena, Calif., 1983—. Mem. faculty adv. com. Art Ctr. Coll. Design, Pasadena, 1993, Faculty Coun. rep., 2000—; vis. faculty UCSD, LaJolla, 1995-99. Contbg. writer: L.A. Weekly, 1983-89; contbg. editor: Artweek, 1983-90, High Performance Mag., 1984-95; performance works include The Garden Planet Revisited, 1982, The Amazon, the Mekong, the Missouri and the Nile, 1985, Palisade, 1987, Fluctuations of the Field, 1989, (with J. Adler) A Stone's Throw..., 2000; writer, performer, dir., prodr.: (record) The Mexican Tapes, 1979-80, (performance/installation/audio work) Voices in the Dark, 1989-97, (radio art work) Swan Lake, 1989; artist, prodr.: (installations and audio work) The Culture of Disappearance, # 1-5, 1991-95; author, designer: (book, installation) Trunk Pieces, 1975-78, (cd) Thank You for Flying American, 1995, Ghost Dances/On the Event Horizon 1996; six part radio art series Redefining Democracy in America Parts, 1991-92; (site specific installation) Zeitghosts: Angels in the Architecture, 1996, Sanctuary, 1996, Hidden Desires, 1998, A Stone's Throw...The Last Witnesses, 2001; (photowork) ghost.dance series 1995—, (photo/audio performance) You Don't Need a Weatherman, 1999; pub. art projects Aliso-Pico Cmty. Ctr., 1997-2000, Venice Oakwood Cmty. Ctr., 2000-03, Martin Luther King Rehab Ctr., 2000-03, Queen Anne Cmty. Ctr., L.A., 2001-, Little Tokyo Br., L.A. Public Libr., 2002-; author: Doing it Right in L.A., 1990; prodr. EarJam Music Festival, 2000, 01, 02. Recipient Vesta award Media Arts Women's Bldg., 1990, Faculty Enrichment grant Art Ctr. Coll. Design, 2001; NEA visual artists fellow, 1979, 81; InterArts program grantee NEA, 1984-85, 91-92; Calif. Arts Coun. Visual Arts/New Genres fellowship, 1996; grantee Durfee Foundation, 2003. Mem. Internat. Art Critics Assn., Nat. Writers Union, Coll. Art Assn., Am. Composers Forum. Home: 3532 Jasmine Ave Los Angeles CA 90034-4947

APPLE, JAMES GLENN, lawyer, educator; b. Huntington, W.Va., Sept. 20, 1937; s. David French and Bernice (Stewart) A.; m. Emory O'Shee, June 9, 1959 (div. May 15, 1990); children: Meredith Ellen, Miles Stewart; m. Elizabeth Fitzpatrick Jones, Nov. 10, 1990. BA (with honors), U. Va., 1959, JD, 1962; LLM, U. Edinburgh, Scotland, 1990. Bar: Va. 1962, Ky. 1962, U.S. Dist. Ct. (ea. and we. dists.) Ky., U.S. Ct. Appeals (6th cir.), U.S. Supreme Ct. Pvt. practice law Wheeler & Marshall, Paducah, Ky., 1964-67; adminstrv. asst. Gov. of Ky., Frankfort, 1967-69; exec. asst. Ky. Commr. of Hwys., Frankfort, 1969-70; assoc. Stites & Harbison Law Firm, Louisville, 1970-72, ptnr., 1972-90; spl. asst., counsel to dir. Fed. Jud. Ctr., Washington, 1990-92; chief Interjudicial Affairs Office, Fed. Jud. Ctr., 1992-99; chmn., pres. Internat. Jud. Acad., Washington, 1999—. Adj. prof. Bellarmine Coll., Louisville, 1988-90; adj. prof. internat. law dept. polit. sci. George Washington U., 1995, Am. U., 1996. Editor State-Fed. Jud. Observer, 1993-99, Internat. Jud. Observer, 1994-98; co-author: A Primer on the Civil Law System (Fed. Jud. Ctr.), Manual for Cooperation Between State and Federal Courts (Fed. Jud. Ctr.; contbr. articles to profl. jours. Bd. dirs. Ky. Authority for Ednl. TV, Lexington, 1971-75; chmn. bd. Transit Authority of River City, Louisville, 1981-85; pres. Louisville Bar Found., 1986-87; mem. Leadership Louisville, 1983-84; treas. Jud. Leadership Devel. Coun., Washington, 2001—. Lt. USAR, 1963-68. Recipient Award of Merit, Louisville Bar Assn., 1980, Citation for work in pub. transp., U.S. Senate, Senator Mitch McConnell, 1988, Pres.'s award Washington Combined Fed. Campaign, 1990, 91, Spl. Svc. award, 1990; first prize Brit. Red Cross Essay Contest, 1990. Fellow Am. Coll. Trial Lawyers; mem. Am. Law Inst., Am. Soc. Internat. Law (chair, tillar house com.), Am. Bd. Trial Advocates, Nat. Press Club. Avocations: reading, writing, gardening, travel, walking. Office: Interna Jud Acad 1616 H St NW Ste 204 Washington DC 20006 Fax: 202-628-7803. E-mail: jasgapple@aol.com.

APPLE, MARTIN ALLEN, science executive, scientist, educator; b. Duluth, Minn., Sept. 17, 1938; m. M. Daina; children: Deborah Dawn, Pamela Ruth, Nathan, Rebeccah Lynn AB, ALA, U. Minn., 1959, MSc, 1962; PhD, U. Calif., 1968. Chmn. Multidisciplinary Drug Rsch. Group U. Calif., San Francisco, 1974-78; pres. IPRI, San Carlos, Calif., 1978-81; with EAN-Tech., Inc., Daly City, Calif., 1982-84, chmn. bd., 1983-84; with Adytum Internat., Mountain View, Calif., 1982-90, CEO, 1983-90, LEADERS, Washington, 1989—; pres., Coun. Sci. Soc. Presidents, Washington, 1993—; CEO Sci. Watch, Inc., 1996-98. With Hon. Doug Walgren co-chair Leadership Network, 1995-97; adj. prof. U. Calif., San Francisco, 1982-84; cons. SRI Internat. Dept. Edn., EPA, NIH, NSF, The Network, Hughes-GM, Nat. Cancer Inst., AAAS, Nat. Sci. Tchrs. Assn., others; adj. rsch. prof. George Mason U., Fairfax, Va., 1991-92; vis. scholar Nat. Humanities Ctr., 1990-91; nat. project mgr. NSTA Scope Sequence and Coordination Project, 1991-92; bd. dirs. Am. Med. Progress Ednl. Found.; bd. dirs. ACCTION, Inc., chmn. trustees, 1995-96; expert advisor Dept of Edn., 1996-2001; mem. blue ribbon panel USDA, 2000-01; chmn. bd. trustees Ctr. Advanced Rsch. Behavioral Neurobiology U. Ill., Chgo., 2002-03; chmn. bd. visitors U. Md./U. Md. Biotech. Inst., 1999-2003. Author: (with F. Myers) Review Medical Pharmacology, 1976; (with M. Fink) Immune RNA in Neoplasia, 1976; (with F. Becker et al) Cancer: A Comprehensive Treatise, 1977; (with M. Keenberg et al) Investing in Biotechnology, 1981; (with F. Ahmad et al) From Genes to Proteins: Horizons in Biotechnology, 1983; (with J. Kureczka) Status of Biotechnology, 1987; (with M. Baum) Business Advantage, 1987 (winner Excellence award Software Pubs. Assn. 1987), (with R. Yager) Translating and Using Research for Improving Teacher Education in Science and Mathematics, 1998; mem. editl. bd. Computers in Medicine Mem. Calif. Coun. Indsl. Innovation, 1982. Recipient citation, East West Ctr. Bd. of Govs., 1988, Leadership citation, Coun. Sci. Soc. Pres., 1995, Support of Sci. award, 2002. Fellow Am. Coll. Clin. Pharmacology, Am. Inst. Chemists, Phi Beta Kappa Assocs. (Disting. Svc. award 1984, 85); mem. Assn. Venture Founders (bd. govs. 1982-83), East-West Ctr. Assn. (trustee 1982-88, vice chmn. 1983-85), Profl. Software Programmers Assn., Leaders of Tomorrow (chmn. 1987-88), Commonwealth Club Calif., Phi Beta Kappa, Sigma Xi (bd. dirs., chmn. long-range strategic planning com. 1988-92). Office: Coun Sci Soc Presidents PO Box 33999 Washington DC 20033-0999 also: PO Box 905 Benicia CA 94510-0905 E-mail: cssp@acs.org.

APPLE, RAYMOND WALTER, JR., journalist; b. Akron, Ohio, Nov. 20, 1934; s. Raymond Walter and Julia (Albrecht) A.; m. Betsey Pinckney Brown, July 14, 1982; stepchildren: Catherine Brown Collins, John Preston Brown. Student, Princeton U., 1952-56; AB, Columbia U., 1961; LHD (hon.), Denison U., 1989; LLD, Knox Coll., 1993, Gettysburg Coll., 1995, Marquette U., 2000. Reporter Wall St. Jour., 1956 57, 59 61; writer, corr. NBC News, 1961-63; mem. staff N.Y. Times, 1963—, Albany bur. chief, 1964-65, Vietnam corr., 1965-66, Vietnam bur. chief, 1966-68, Africa bur. chief, 1969, nat. polit. corr., 1970-76, London bur. chief, 1977-80, 81-85, Moscow bur. chief, 1980-81, Washington bur. chief, 1992-97, chief Washington corr., 1985-97, chief corr., 1998—. Assoc. edit. Theodore H. White Meml. lectr. Harvard U., 1989, Joe Alex Morris Jr. Meml. lectr., 1993; Herzberg lectr. Columbia U.; Kent Meml. lectr. Johns Hopkins U., 1990. Author: Apple's Europe, 1986; contbr. to nat. mags., books. Bd. visitors Western Res. Acad.; chmn. Rhodes Scholarship Com., Mid-Atlantic States. With AUS, 1957-59; judge James Beard Restaurant Awards. Recipient Krout prize history Columbia U., 1961, award NATAS, 1963, George Polk Meml. award, 1967, Overseas Press Club award, 1967, Outstanding Alumnus award Columbia U., 1988, Western Res. Acad., 1976, Weintal award for diplomatic reporting, 1993, Lowell Thomas award for travel writing, Am. Soc. Travel Writers, 1999; Chubb fellow Yale U., 1998. Mem. AFTRA, Am. Inst. Wine and Food, Gridiron Club, Princeton Club, Century Assn. N.Y., Met. Club. Office: NY Times Washington Bur 1627 I St NW Washington DC 20006-4007 E-mail: rwappl@nytimes.com.

APPLEBAUM, CHARLES, lawyer; b. Newark, May 19, 1947; s. Harry I. and Francis (Gastwirth) A.; m. Patricia (Gyurko) Applebaum; children: Matthew, David, Michael, Amanda. BA, U. Pa., 1969; JD, Rutgers U., 1973; LLM, NYU, 1978. Bar: U.S. Dist. Ct. N.J. 1973. Law clk. to Hon. Samuel A. Larner, Jersey City, 1973-74; assoc., then ptnr. Greenbaum, Rowe, Smith, Ravin, Davis & Himmel LLP, Woodbridge, N.J., 1974-89; gen. counsel Alfieri Orgn., Edison, NJ, 1989—2002, Kara Homes Inc., East Brunswick, NJ, 2002—. Adj. prof. Rutgers Law Sch., Newark, 1985-88. Co-author: New Jersey Real Estate Forms, 1988; contbr. articles to profl. jours. Mem. ABA (real property probate and trust, chmn. significant lit. and publs. 1985-97, co-editor The Acrel Papers 1992-94), Am. Coll. Real Estate Lawyers (editor publs. 1991—). Office: Kara Homes Inc 197 Rte 18 Ste 101N East Brunswick NJ 08816 E-mail: capplebaum@karahomes.com.

APPLEBAUM, STUART S. public relations executive; b. N.Y.C., Sept. 19, 1949; s. Jack and Anne (Miller) A. BA, Queens Coll., 1971. Publicist Alfred A. Knopf Inc., N.Y.C., 1971-73, MGM Pictures, N.Y.C., 1973, Bantam Books Inc., N.Y.C., 1974-77, mgr. publicity, 1977-79, dir. publicity, 1979-87, v.p., dir. pub. rels. and publicity, 1983-90, v.p., dir. pub. rels., 1990-91, v.p., dir. publicity and pub. rels., 1991—; sr. v.p., dir. pub. rels. Bantam Doubleday Dell Pub. Group, N.Y.C., 1987-98, Random House, Inc., N.Y.C., 1998—, exec. v.p. comms., 2002—. Named as one of the People Who Shaped the Book Bus., Pubs. Weekly, 1997. Mem. Publishers Publicity Assn. (bd. dirs. N.Y.C. chpt. 1979-84) Office: Random House Inc 1745 Broadway New York NY 10019

APPLEBERRY, JAMES BRUCE, higher education consultant; b. Waverly, Mo., Feb. 22, 1938; s. James Earnest and Bertha Viola (Lane) A.; m. Patricia Ann Trent, June 5, 1960; children: John Mark, Timothy David. BS, Central Mo. State Coll., 1960; MS, Cen. Mo. State Coll., 1963, EdS, 1967; postgrad., U. Kans., 1967; Ed.D., Okla. State U., 1969. Tchr. Knob Noster (Mo.) Pub. Sch., 1960-62; prin. Knob Noster Elem. Sch., 1962-63, Knob Noster Jr. High Sch., 1963-64; minister edn. Wornall Rd. Bapt. Ch., Kansas City, Mo., 1964-65; grad. fellow Cen. Mo. State Coll., Warrensburg, 1965-66, asst. dir. field service, 1966-67; grad. asst. Okla. State U., 1968-69, asst. prof. ednl. adminstrn., 1969-71, assoc. prof., 1971-73, prof., head dept. adminstrn. and higher edn., 1972-75; Am. Council on Edn. fellow acad. adminstrn. internship program U. Kans., Lawrence, 1973-74, dir. planning, prof. adminstrn., founds. and higher edn., 1975-76, asst. to chancellor, prof., 1976-77; pres. Pittsburg (Kans.) State U., 1977-83, No. Mich. U., Marquette, 1983-91, Am. Assn. of State Coll. and Univs., Washington, 1991-99, Appleberry Enterprises, 1999—; sr. cons. Acad. Search Consultation Svc., 2001—. Plenary rep. Univ. Council for Ednl. Adminstrn., 1968-72, mem. exec. com., 1973-76; ednl. adminstrn. rep. Council on Tchr. Edn., 1968-75; chmn. Am. Council Edn. Commn. Leadership Devel. and Acad. Adminstrn.; abstracter Univ. Council for Ednl. Adminstrn., Columbus, Ohio, 1969-75; asst. state liaison rep. to Am. Assn. Colls. for Tchr. Edn., 1971; coordinator Interested Profs. Ednl. Adminstrn.; cons. North Cen. Okla. Assn. Sch. Adminstrs.; vice chmn. adv. council Nat. Council Edn. Stats., 1980-83; Kans. rep. to Am. Assn. State Colls. and Univs., 1980-81; pres. Nat. Coll. Athletics Assn. Pres.'s Commn., 1988-89; chmn. bd. dirs. Thoroughbred Techs., 2000-02. Contbr. articles to ednl. jours. Trustee Marquette Gen. Hosp.; bd. dirs. Actor's Theatre, 2003—. Named Outstanding Alumnus Cen. Mo. State U., 1987, Disting. Alumnus Okla. State U., 1987. Mem. NEA, Am. Assn. for Higher Edn., Am. Assn. State Colls. and Univs. (chmn. policy and purposes com.), Am. Ednl. Rsch. Assn., Nat. Conf. Profs. Ednl. Adminstrn., Exec. Club Louisville, Mace and Torch, Rotary, Masons (33 deg.), Phi Delta Kappa, Phi Kappa Phi, Kappa Delta, Phi Sigma Phi, Kappa Mu Epsilon, Alpha Kappa Psy. Home: 504 Jarvis Ln Louisville KY 40207-1313

APPLEBY, DAVID CURTIS, dentist, educator; b. Providence, R.I., Dec. 23, 1947; s. Stanley and Florence Eve Appleby; m. Alice Lillian Lafferty, Jan. 3, 1981. BA, Colgate U., Hamilton, NY, 1970; DMD, U. Pa., Phila., 1974; MSc in Prosthetic Dentistry, Boston U., 1979. Diplomate Am. Bd. of Prosthodontics, 1993. Asst. prof. Temple U. Sch. of Dentistry, Phila., 1978—84, assoc. prof., 1984—94, prof., 1994—. Contbr. articles to profl. jours. Lt. USNR Dental Corps, 1974—76. Fellow: Am. Coll. Prosthodontists. Episcopalean. Achievements include patents in field. Avocations: genealogy, travel, old house restoration. Office: Temple Univ Sch Dentistry 3223 North Broad St Philadelphia PA 19140 Office Fax: 215-707-5484. E-mail: dappleby@dental.temple.edu.

APPLEBY, JOYCE OLDHAM, historian, educator; b. Omaha, Apr. 9, 1929; d. Junius G. and Edith (Cash) Oldham; children: Ann Lansburgh Caylor, Mark Lansburgh, Frank Bell Appleby. BA, Stanford U., 1950; MA, U. Calif., Santa Barbara, 1959; PhD, Claremont Grad. Sch., 1966. With Mademoiselle mag., 1950-52; asst. prof. history San Diego State U., 1967-70, asso. prof., 1970-73; prof. history, asso. dean Coll. Arts and Letters, 1973-75, prof., 1976-81. Vis. asso. prof. U. Calif., Irvine, 1975-76; vis. prof. UCLA, 1978-79, prof. history, 1981— ; vis. fellow St. Catherine's Coll., U. Oxford, 1983; Harmsworth prof. Am. History, U. Oxford, 1990-91; Bd. fellows Claremont Grad. Sch. and U. Center, 1970-73 Author: Economic Thought and Ideology in Seventeenth-Century England, 1978, Capitalism and a New Social Order, 1983, Liberalism and Republicanism in the Historical Imagination, 1992; co-author: Telling the Truth about History, 1994; co-editor: Knowledge and Postmodernism in Historical Perspective, Inheriting the Revolution, 2000; mem. bd. editors Democracy, 1980-83, William and Mary Quar., 1980-83, 18th Century Studies, 1982-87, Ency. Am. Polit. History, Am. Hist. Rev., 1988—, Jour. Interdisciplinary History, 1989—, The Papers of Thomas Jefferson, 1988—, The Adams Papers, 1990—; contbr. articles to profl. jours.; mem. adv. bd. Am. Nat. Biography. Mem. Am. Acad. Arts and Scis., Am. Philos. Soc., Smithsonian Inst. (coun.), Am. Hist. Assn. (pres.), Orgn. Am. Historians (pres.), Inst. Early Am. History and Culture (coun. 1980-86, chmn. 1983-89). Home: 615 Westholme Ave Los Angeles CA 90024-3209 Office: UCLA Dept History Los Angeles CA 90024

APPLEGATE, CHARLES G. financial professional; b. Englewood, N.J., June 8, 1951; s. Charles M. and Betty Eleanor (Pederson) Applegate; children: Heather Diane, Christina. BS in Bus. Mgmt., Phillips U., 1975. Owner Mountain Wilderness Outfitters, Portland, Oreg., 1984—; dist. rep. Westinghouse Corp., Portland, Oreg., 1976—82; br. mgr. Met. Life, Portland, Oreg., 1982—86; owner Applegate Fin. Group, Portland, Oreg., 1986—98; br. mgr. Key Corp., Portland, Oreg., 1998—2002; regional dir. The Foresters, 2002—. Bd. dirs. programs Oreg. Assn. Underwriters, Portland. Bd. dirs. programs Kiwanis, Portland; bd. dirs. Portland Mountain Rescue; vol. Portland Art Mus. Capt. USAF, 1971—75. Avocations: mountaineering, scuba diving, skiing, jogging, piano. Home: PO Box 621 Marylhurst OR 97036

APPLEGATE, CHRISTINA, actress; b. L.A., Calif., Nov. 25, 1971; d. Nancy Priddy; m. Johnathon Schaech, Oct. 20, 2001. Film appearances include: Jaws of Satan, 1980, Streets, 1990, Don't Tell Mom the Babysitter's Dead, 1991,

Across the Moon, 1994, Vibrations, 1995, Wild Bill, 1995, Mars Attacks!, 1996, Nowhere, 1997, Claudine's Return, 1998, The Big Hit, 1998, Mafia!, 1998; TV appearances include: (series) Days of Our Lives, 1974, Washingtoon, 1985, Heart of the City, 1986, Married...With Children, 1987-97, All My Life, 1998, Jesse, 1998-2000, Friends, 2002, (TV movies) Grace Kelly, 1983, Dance 'til Dawn, 1988, (spls.) Rate the '80's Awards, 1989, MTV's 1989 Ann. Emmy Awards, 1989, Time Warner Presents the Earth Day Special, 1990, The 4th Ann. Am. Comedy Awards, 1990, The 43d Ann. Primetime Emmy Awards Presentation, 1991, (episodes) Father Murphy, 1981, Quincy, 1983, Charles in Charge, 1984, 84, All Is Forgiven, 1986, Leave It to Beaver, 1986, Amazing Stories, 1986, Silver Spoons, 1986, Family Ties, 1987, 21 Jump St., 1988, Animal Crack-Ups, 1988, Hour Magazine, 1988, Win, Lose, or Draw, 1988, The Pat Sajak Show, 1989, Live with Regis and Kathy Lee, 1989, The Arsenio Hall Show, 1989, A View From the Top, 2003; film appearances include Just Visiting, 2001, The Sweetest Thing, 2002.*

APPLEGATE, EDWARD C. education educator, researcher, writer; s. Clarice Bentley Crump and Marvin Edward Applegate; m. Eva Marie Doyle. AA, U. of Ky. C.C. Sys., 1972—73; BA, Morehead State U., 1973—75, MA, MHEd, Morehead State U., 1975—76; Ed. S., Morehead State U., Morehead, KY, 1981—81; EdD, Okla. State U., 1982—84. Instr. Westark C.C., Ft. Smith, Ark., 1976—77, Broward C.C., Ft. Lauderdale, 1978—80; asst. prof. N.W. Mo. State U., Maryville, 1981—82, Mid. Tenn. State U., Murfreesboro, 1984—90, assoc. prof., 1990—96, prof., 1997—. Reporter, editl. writer, reviewer The Trail Blazer, Morehead, Ky., 1973—75; news writer R. O. P. E. S. Region IX, Morehead, 1974—75; cons. Swap or Buy, Margate, Fla., 1978—80, Mid. Tenn. State U./ Small Bus. Devel. Ctr., Murfreesboro, 1987—92. Author: (nonfiction book) Am. Naturalistic and Realistic Novelists: A Biographical Dictionary, Personalities and Products: A Hist. Perspective on Advt. in Am., Journalistic Advocates and Muckrakers: Three Centuries of Crusading Writers, Lit. Journalism: A Biog. Dictionary of Writers and Editors, Print and Broadcast Journalism: A Critical Exam.; editor: The Ad Men and Women: A Biog. Dictionary of Advert., Advert.: Concepts, Strategies, and Issues. Fellow Fellowship, Donald and Geraldine Hedberg Found. and the Direct Mktg. Ednl. Found., 1994; grantee, Mo. Commn. on Humanities, Nat. Endowment for the Humanities, 1981-1982, Ben Snow Fellowship, Am. Press Inst., 1980, Scholarship, Freedoms Found. at Valley Forge, 1987, Am. Assn. of Advt. Agencies, 1988, Fellowship, The Annenberg Wash. Program, 1989, Gannett Found., 1989-1990, The Freedom Forum Media Studies Ctr., 1992-1993. Mem.: Assn. for Hist. Rsch. in Mktg., Am. Journalism Historians Assn., Assn. for Edn. in Journalism and Mass Comm. (cooperation with eric com. 1986—91), Am. Acad. of Advt. (membership com. 1989—91, naa rels. com. 1996—97, fin. com. 1997—98, industry rels. com. 1999—2000). Avocations: reading, writing, hiking.

APPLEGET, TERRI LYNN, elementary education educator; b. Racine, Wis., Dec. 3, 1952; d. Richard Louis and Joan Elizabeth (Seatter) Tobias; m. Patrick R. Appleget, Dec. 26, 1971 (div. May 1997); children: Brooke Elizabeth, Patrick Justin-Shaun, Katherine Bethany Anne Aisling, Keir Michael James. BA, U. Wis., 1973; MA in Tchg., Coll. of Charleston, S.C., 1991; postgrad., Trinity Coll., Dublin, Ireland, 1994. Dir. extended day Ashley Hall, Charleston, 1993; founder, dir. The Children's Ctr., Summerville, S.C., 1993-97; tchr. mid. sch. lit., grammar, history Pinewood Preparatory, Summerville, 1993-97; tchr. kindergarten, early childhood diagnostic, 1st and 3d grade inclusion Charleston County Sch. Dist., 1997—2001; tchr. Charlestowne Acad. Magnet Sch., 2001—02, Ronald McNair Elem., 2002—03, N. Charleston Elem. at McNair, 2003—. Homesch. tchr. Charleston Preparatory Sch., 1998—; freelance tutor, 1997—. Tchr. ptnr. Jr. Achievement, Charleston, 2000; sponsor Jr. Beta Club, Summerville, 1993—97; docent Historic Charleston Soc., 1988—98; v.p. Oakleaf Officers Wives Club, Orlando, Fla., 1986—87; pres. Fellowship Wartburg Spouses, Dubuque, Iowa, 1982—83; active Ladies Sewing Soc.; tchr. adult Sunday ch. sch. St. John's Luth. Ch., Charleston, 1988—, chair social ministry, 1989—, mem. vestry, 1989—. Mem. Nat. Assn. for Edn. of Young Children, Nat. Trust, Internat. Reading Assn. (S.C. coun.), Palmetto State Tchrs. Assn. Republican. Avocations: writing, studying irish history, reading. Home: 141 Palmetto Bluff Ct Charleston SC 29418-3017

APPLEHANS, DENVER LEE, military officer; b. Robbinsdale, Minn., Sept. 3, 1976; s. Kenneth Lee and Deanna Joy Applehans; m. Nicole Jean Lauer, Aug. 19, 2000. BA, Georgetown U., Washington, 1999. Ensign USNR, 1999, naval flight officer, 2000—. Mem.: Antique Telescope Soc., Georgetown Astronomy Club (pres. 1997—99). Lutheran. Avocations: hiking, kayaking, woodworking. Home: 1091 SW Kaleeton Loop # 202 Oak Harbor WA 98277

APPLEMAN, JOLENE W. patent lawyer; b. New Castle, PA, June 5, 1945; d. Lawrence B. and Bertha L. Weinstein; m. Bernard R. Appleman, Aug. 31, 1969; children: Laura I., Beth H. BA, Case Western Res. U., 1967; MS Chem., Ohio State U., 1970; JD, Duquesne U., 1990. Bar: Pa. 1990, U.S. Patent Office, 1991, N.J. 1992. Lectr. in chem. Montgomery Coll., 1977-84, Union C.C., Cranford, NJ, 1984-87, Carnegie Mellon U., 1987-90; assoc. Cohen & Grigsby, Pitts., 1990-91, Eckert Seamans, Pitts., 1992-95, Reed, Smith, Shaw & McClay, Pitts., 1995-97; sr. patent counsel Pfizer Inc., N.Y.C., 1997—. Lectr. Food and Drug in Law School, Duquesne U., 1997—; assoc. adj. prof. Fordham Law Sch., 2000—. Mem. ABA, Chem. and the Law. Office: Pfizer Inc 235 E 42nd St New York NY 10017-5755 E-mail: jolene.w.appleman@pfizer.com.

APPLEMAN, PHILIP, poet, writer, educator; b. Feb. 8, 1926; m. Marjorie Haberkorn. BS in English, Northwestern U., 1950, PhD in English, 1955; AM in English, U. Mich., 1951; postgrad., U. Lyon, France, 1951-52. Teaching asst. Northwestern U., Evanston, Ill., 1953-55; instr. English Ind. U., Bloomington, 1955-58, asst. prof., 1958-62, assoc. prof., 1962-67, prof., 1967-82, disting. prof., 1982-86, disting. prof. emeritus, 1986—. Dir., instr. in world lit. and philosophy Internat. Sch. Am., 1960-63; vis. prof. lit. SUNY, Purchase, 1973; vis. prof. English Columbia U., 1974; panelist NEH, Washington, 1968, applications judge, 1978, 80; adv. panel Ind. Arts Commn., 1971; cons. NEH-sponsored Project on Ethics and Values in Health Care Columbia U. Coll. Physicians and Surgeons, 1979-81; lectr. in field, poetry reader. Author: The Silent Explosion, 1965, 2d edit., 1966, Portuguese transl., 1973, (poetry) Kites on a Windy Day, 1967, Summer Love and Surf, 1968, Open Doorways, 1976, Darwin's Ark, 1984, Darwin's Bestiary, 1986, Let There Be Light, 1991, New and Selected Poems, 1956-96, 1996, (novels) In the Twelfth Year of the War, 1970, Shame the Devil, 1981, Apes and Angels, 1989; founding co-editor Victorian Studies, 1957—63; co-editor: 1859: Entering an Age of Crisis, 1959; editor: The Origin of Species, 1975, 2d edit., 2002, An Essay on the Principle of Population, 1976, 2d edit., 2003, Darwin, 1970, 3d edit., 2001; contbr. articles to profl. jours., chpts. to books. Co-founder Bloomington Civil Liberties Union; faculty adviser Ind. U. Civil Liberties Union, Bloomington. Served with AC U.S. Army, 1944-45; served with U.S. Mcht. Marine, 1946, 48-49. Recipient Citation for In the Twelfth Year of the War Ind. Authors's Day, 1971, Humanist Arts award, 1994, Friends of Darwin award Nat. Ctr. for Sci. Edn., 2003; Fulbright scholar France, 1951-52; Huntington Hartford Found. fellow, 1964, Nat. Endowment for Arts fellow, 1975. Mem.: PEN, MLA (sec. English sect. II 1965, chmn. 1966, chmn. exec. com. 1972), AAUP (pres. Ind. U. chpt. 1968—69, nat. coun. 1969—72), Nat. Ctr. Sci. Edn. (Friends of Darwin award 2003), Authors Guild, Acad. Am. Poets, Poets Ho. (poets adv. com. 1987—), Poetry Soc. Am. (awards judge 1970, 1971, 1974, 1976, 1979, governing bd. 1981—83, Christopher Morley Meml. award 1970, Alice Fay di Castagnola award 1975), Nat. Coun. Tchrs. English, Phi Beta Kappa. Home: PO Box 39 Sagaponack NY 11962-0039

APPLER, THOMAS L. lawyer; b. Washington, Oct. 12, 1943; m. Nancy J. Babb, Dec. 20, 1967; children: Alexandra, Whitney. AB in Politics, Princeton U., 1965; JD, George Washington U., 1968. Bar: Va. 1968. Atty. Office of Judge Adv., Surgeon Gen. of Army, 1969-70; ptnr. McGuire, Woods, Battle & Boothe (and predecessor firms), McLean, Va., 1970-99, Crews & Hancock, PLC, Fairfax, Va., 1999—2002, Hancock, Daniel, Johnson & Nagle, P.C., 2002—. Co-author: Damages for Plaintiff and Defense Attorneys, 1987. USAR, 1970-76. Fellow Am. Coll. Trial Lawyers; mem. No. Va. Def. Attys. Assn. (pres. 1975), Va. Assn. Def. Attys. (v.p., bd. dirs. 1977-83), Va. Bar Assn. (bd. dirs. young lawyers sect. 1974-76, appellate judges com. 1989-91, Boyd-Graves Conf. com. 1988—), Va. State Bar (coun. 1985-92, malpractice ins. com. 1989-99), Fairfax Bar Assn. (pres. 1984-85, bd. dirs. 1983-86), No. Va. Young Lawyers Assn. (pres. 1974). Home: 9717 Meadowlark Rd Vienna VA 22182-1951 Office: Hancock Daniel Johnson & Nagle PC 3050 Chain Bridge Rd Ste 300 Fairfax VA 22030-2834 Fax: 703-591-7646. E-mail: tappler@hdjn.com.

APPLETON, ALAN B. lawyer; b. Frankfort, Ind., Nov. 18, 1945; s. Allen A. and Wilda L. Appleton. BA, Franklin Coll., 1967; JD, U. Louisville, 1970. Bar: D.C. 1975, U.S. Supreme Ct. 1978. Law clk., intern Appleton Law Office, Frankfort, 1970-74, assoc., 1975—89; gen. counsel Appleton Group, Inc. A Pvt. Equity Firm, Frankfort, 1990—. Judge Frankfort City Ct., 1972-73. Named Clinton County Boys Club Bd. Mem. of Yr., Frankfort, 1978. Mem.: D.C. Bar Assn., Phi Alpha Delta, Sigma Alpha Epsilon. Office: Appleton Group Inc PO Box 541 Frankfort IN 46041-0541

APPLETON, R. O., JR., lawyer; b. San Francisco, Aug. 17, 1945; s. Robert Oser and Leslie Jeanne (Roth) A.; m. Susan Frelich, June 3, 1971; children: Jesse David, Seth Daniel. AB, Stanford U., 1967; JD, U. Calif., San Francisco, 1970; postgrad., NYU, 1971. Bar: Calif. 1971, U.S. Dist. Calif. (no. dist.) Calif. 1971, Mo. 1973, U.S. Dist. Ct. (ea. dist.) Mo. 1974, U.S. Ct. Appeals (8th cir.) 1975, U.S. Ct. Internat. Trade, 1980. Assoc. Dinkelspiel & Dinkelspiel, San Francisco, 1971-73, Schramm & Morganstern, St. Louis, 1973-75; pvt. practice, 1975-77; ptnr. Braun, Newman, Stewart & Appleton, St. Louis, 1977-82, Appleton, Newman & Kretmar, St. Louis, 1982-84, Appleton, Newman & Gerson, St. Louis, 1984-89, Appleton & Kretmar, St. Louis, 1989—, Appleton, Kretmar & Beatty. Adj. prof. pre-trial litigation Washington U. Sch. Law, St. Louis, 1985-88. Arbitrator, vol. Better Bus. Bur. of St. Louis, 1980—; St. Louis Gymnastic Centre, 1984—; bd. dirs. St. Louis Friends of Tibet, 1991-94. Mem. ABA, Calif. Bar Assn., Met. Bar Assn. of St. Louis, St. Louis County Bar Assn., Am. Arbitration Assn. (arbitrator comml. panel, arbitrator mass claims appeals com. 1999), Stanford Club (pres. 1991—). Democrat. Jewish. Avocations: jogging, swimming, cooking, model trains, reading. Home: 8317 Cornell Ave Saint Louis MO 63132-5025 Office: Appleton Kretmar Beatty & Stolze 8000 Maryland Ave Ste 900 Saint Louis MO 63105-3911 E-mail: roajratty1@aol.com.

APPLETON, STEVEN R. electronics executive; b. Mar. 1960; BBA, Boise State U., 1982. Fab supr., prodn. mgr., dir. mfg., v.p. mfg. Micron Tech., Inc., Boise, Idaho, 1983—91, pres., COO, 1991, chmn., CEO, pres., 1994—; chmn., CEO Micron Semiconductor, 1992. Bd. dirs. St. Luke's Hosp.; trustee Boise State U.; mem. Coll. Bus. Adv. Coun., Semiconductor Tech. Coun. Mem.: Semiconductor Industry Assn. (bd. dirs.). Office: Micron Tech PO Box 6 8000 South Federal Way Boise ID 83707*

APPLEWHITE, KIM, music company executive, educator; b. Atlantic City, N.J., Feb. 2, 1961; s. Paul C. and Ida B. Applewhite. AA specializing in tech. in video prodns., Art Inst. Phila., 2000; BA in Theology, Jameson Christian Coll., 2001; BS in Mgmt., U. Phoenix, 2002; MBA in Music Bus. Mgmt., Northwestern Internat. U., Denmark and Sweden, 2003; postgrad., Audrey Cohen Coll., 2003—. Lic. internat. evangelistic lic. Jameson Christian Coll., 1999. Pres., CEO Applewhite Entertainment Group, LLC, Atlantic City, 1995—; radio engr. WUSS 1490 Rejoice Radio, Linwood, NJ, 2002—. Author: (music bus. adminstrn. solutions) Recobizworks, 2002; contbr. poetry to anthologies. Pastor TriUnity Worship and Praise Ctr., Absecon, NJ, 2001—02. Home: PO Box 73 Pleasantville NJ 08232 Office: Prophete Music Group Inc 849 Cedar Ln Pleasantville NJ Personal E-mail: K_applewhite@yahoo.com.

APPLEY, MORTIMER HERBERT, psychologist, university president emeritus; b. N.Y.C., Nov. 21, 1921; s. Benjamin and Minnie (Albert) A.; m. Dee Gordon, June 5, 1942 (div. Oct. 1969); children: Richard Gordon, John Benton; m. Mariann B. Hundahl, Jan. 10, 1971; stepchildren: Scott, Eric, Heidi Hundahl. BS, CCNY, 1942; MA, U. Denver, 1946; PhD, U. Mich., 1950; DSc (hon.), York U., 1975; DHL (hon.), Northeastern U., 1983; LittD (hon.), Am. Internat. Coll., 1984; LLD (hon.), Clark U., 1984. Instr. U. Denver, 1945-47; instr. U. Mich., 1947-49; asst. prof. Wesleyan U., Middletown, Conn., 1949-52; prof., chmn. psychology Conn. Coll., New London, 1952-60, So. Ill. U., Carbondale, 1960-62, York U., Toronto, Ont., Can., 1962-67, dean faculty grad. studies, 1965-68; prof., chmn. psychology U. Mass., Amherst, 1967-69; dean Grad. Sch., 1969-74, asso. provost, 1973-74; pres. Clark U., Worcester, Mass., 1974-84; vis. scholar psychology Harvard U., 1984-88, lectr., extension, 1985-95, vis. prof., 1985-86; exec. dir., Commn. on the Future of the Univ. U. Mass., Boston, 1988-89. Cons. NSF, NIMH, NRC of Can., Can. Council, VA., AAAS, MacArthur Found. Author: (with C.N. Cofer) Motivation: Theory and Research, 1964, (with R. Trumbull) Psychological Stress, 1967, (with J. Rickwood) Psychology in Canada, 1967, (with R. Trumbull) Dynamics of Stress, 1986, (with L. Lasagna) Who are the Elderly, 1986, (with W.B. Maher) Social and Behavioral Sciences, 1989, Learning to Lead, 1989; editor: Adaption Level Theory: A Symposium, 1971, Motivation and Emotion, 1976-88; assoc. editor Psychol. Abstracts, 1961-62; editor, contbr. Internat. Ency. Neurology, Psychology, Psychoanalysis and Psychiatry; contbr. articles to profl. jours. Chmn. bd. mgrs. Unitarian Fellowship, Toronto; vestryman King's Chapel, Boston; trustee Nantucket Atheneum. With USAAF, 1942-45. NSF Sci. Faculty fellow, 1959-60, Fulbright fellow, Germany, 1973-74. Fellow AAAS, APA (past chmn. edn. and tng. bd.), Can. Psychol. Assn. (bd. dirs.); mem. Conn. Psychol. Assn. (past pres.), New Eng. Psychol. Assn. (past pres.), St. Botolph Club (Boston, pres. 1997-2000), Worcester Econ. Club (pres. 1980-81), Wharf Rats (Nantucket), Sigma Xi, Psi Chi, Phi Sigma. Democrat. Unitarian Universalist. Home: 221 Mt Auburn St Apt 606 Cambridge MA 02138-4851 E-mail: mappley@attbi.com.

APPLEYARD, DAVID FRANK, mathematics and computer science educator; b. South Haven, Mich., July 13, 1939; s. Edwin Ray and Hortense Ruth (Guilford) A.; m. Joey Hierlmeier, Aug. 5, 1967; children: David Wayne, Gregory Jay, Robert James. BA, Carleton Coll., 1961; MS, U. Wis., 1963, PhD, 1970. Teaching asst. in math. U. Wis., Madison, 1961-66; prof. math. and computer science Carleton Coll., Northfield, Minn., 1966—, Lloyd P. Johnson Norwest Found. prof. liberal arts, 1993—, dean students, 1977-83, faculty pres., 1988-91. Carleton Coll. faculty athletic rep. to Midwest Collegiate Athletic Conf., 1975-83, pres., 1982-83 Trustee United Ch. Christ, Northfield, 1969-72 Recipient Cowling Cup for career achievement, 2002; NSF fellow, 1964, grantee prin. investigator, 1993—; NASA traineeship, 1965-66; Sloan Found. grantee, 1969, 73, 84. Mem. Math. Assn. Am., Nat. Coun. Tchrs. Math., Sigma Xi. Avocations: long-distance running; canoeing. Home: 6450 134th St E Northfield MN 55057-4611 Office: Carleton Coll 1 N College St Northfield MN 55057-4021

APPLING, CHRISTOPHER MICHAEL, columnist, writer; b. Cleve., Aug. 7, 1966; s. John Bradford Appling and Gloriajeanne Mattibelle Wall-Appling. Student, Ohio State U., Columbus, 1984—85, Cleve. State U., 1985—86. Entertainment columnist East Side News, Cleve., 2000. Author: (short stories) Artificial Aryan, 1992, (books) Black Comic, 1994, Shades of Our Soul, 1998; filmmaker: Kate's Promise, 2000. Mem.: Cleve. Film Soc. Avocations: reading, film collecting, pop/R&B music, sketching, weightlifting. Home: 12701 Shaker Blvd Cleveland OH 44120

APPS, JEROLD WILLARD, adult education educator, writer; b. Wild Rose, Wis., July 25, 1934; s. Herman E. and Eleanor S. (Witt) A.; m. Ruth Ellen Olson, May 20, 1961; children: Susan, Steven, Jeffrey. BS, U. Wis., 1955, MS, 1957, PhD, 1967. Extension agt. U. Wis., Green Lake, 1957-60, Green Bay, 1960-62, asst. prof. Madison, 1962-67, assoc. prof., 1967-69, prof. adult and continuing edn., 1969-94; prof. emeritus, 1994—. Vis. prof. N.C. State U., Raleigh, 1979, U. Guelph, Ont., Can., 1980, U. Alta., Can., 1982, 89, U. Man., Can., 1986, U. Victoria, Can., 1991, U. Alaska, 1995, 97, No. Ill. U., 1996. Author: The Land Still Lives, 1970, How to Improve Adult Education in Your Church, 1972, Cabin in the Country, 1972, Toward a Working Philosophy of Adult Education, 1973, Ideas for Better Church Meetings, 1975, Barns of Wisconsin, 1977, rev. edit., 1995, Problems in Continuing Education, 1979, Spanish edit., 1983, Mills of Wisconsin and the Midwest, 1980, The Adult Learner on Campus: A Guide for Instructors and Administrators, 1981, Study Skills: For Adults Returning to School, 1981, Improving Your Writing Skills, 1982, Improving Practice in Continuing Education, 1985, Skiing into Wisconsin: A Celebration of Winter, 1985, Higher Education in a Learning Society, 1988, Study Skills for Today's College Student, 1990, Mastering the Teaching of Adults, 1991, Breweries of Wisconsin, 1992, Leadership for the Emerging Age, 1994, One-Room Country Schools, 1996, Rural Wisdom, 1997, Traveler's Companion, 1997, Cheese: The Making of a Wisconsin Tradition, 1998, When Chores Were Done, 1999, Symbols: Viewing a Rural Past, 2000, Humor from the Country, 2001, The People Came First: A History of Wisconsin Cooperative Extension, 2002, Eat Rutabagas, 2002, Stormy, 2002. Capt. U.S. Army, 1956. Recipient Non-Fiction Book award of merit Wis. Hist. Soc., 1978, 81, 93, 99, 2003, Wis. Idea award, 1994, Robert E. Gard Excellence in Lit. award, 1996, Wis. 4-H Alumni award, 1998, Midwest Favorite Book award Upper Midwest Booksellers, 1999, 2000, 02, Pride of Wis. award Barnes and Noble Booksellers, 2001, 02; recognized for Outstanding Lit. Achievement, Wis. Libr. Assn. Mem. Am. Assn. Adult and Continuing Edn. (mem. exec. com. 1975-76, Rsch. to Practice award 1982), Commn. Profls. of Adult Edn. (pres. 1972-74), Wis. Acad. Scis., Arts and Letters (pres. 1987), Wis. Assn. Adult and Continuing Edn. (pres. 1969, Outstanding Adult Educator of Yr. award 1986), Wis. Coun. Writers (pres. 1978-80, Best Non-Fiction Book award 1977, Scholarly Book award 1988, 2003).

APRIKYAN, ANDRANIK GOORGEN, molecular biologist, biomedical researcher; b. Yerevan, Armenia, Mar. 27, 1962; s. Goorgen Vardevan and Vera Aprikyan; m. Anoush Oganesian-Aprikyan, Feb. 27, 1988; children: Tatevik, Helen. BS(hon.), Yerevan U., 1983; MS (hon.), Moscow U., 1984; PhD in Molecular Biology, Inst. of Molecular Biology, Moscow, 1988. Scientist, sr. senior scientist dept. neurochemistry of aging Inst. of Biochemistry, Yerevan, 1989—93; sr. fellow dept. medicine and oncology U. Wash., Seattle, 1994—98, rsch. asst. prof. medicine dept. medicine and hematology, 1999—. Contbr. articles to profl. jours. Mem. supreme adv. bd. Ministry of Economy, Yerevan, 1991—93. Recipient Rsch. Grant award, Amgen, Inc, 1999—2000, Nat. Merit award, Nat. Acad. Sci. Armenia, 1991, Gold Medal of Excellency, Ministry of Sci. and Edn., 1979, Reserach Grant award, Am. Cancer Soc., Inc., 2000—01, Nat. Merit award, Nat. Acad. Sci. Armenia, 1992; grantee U.S. HHS, NIH-NCI, 2001—06. Mem.: AAAS, Internat. Soc. of Exptl. Hematology (Merit award 2001), Am. Soc. of Hematology (Merit/Travel award 1996, Merit/Travel Award 1997, 1998). Achievements include patents for substance prolonging the lifespan of experimental animals. Home: Orbeli St 63-32 Yerevan 375028 Armenia Office: U Washington Box 356422 1959 NE Pacific St Seattle WA 98195 Office Fax: 206-616-4096. Personal E-mail: apri@u.washington.edu. E-mail: apri@u.washington.edu.

APRIL, RAND SCOTT, lawyer; b. Bklyn., Feb. 10, 1951; s. Arthur and Muriel (Marmorstein) A. BA, Northwestern U., 1972; JD, Columbia U., 1975. Bar: N.Y. 1976, U.S. Dist. Ct. (so. and ea. dists.) N.Y. 1976, Calif. 1989. Assoc. Marshall, Bratter, Greene, Allison & Tucker, N.Y.C., 1975-78, Gordon, Hurwitz, Butowsky, Baker, Weitzen & Shalov, N.Y.C., 1978-81, Skadden, Arps, Slate, Meagher & Flom, N.Y.C., 1981-83, ptnr., 1983—. Stone scholar Columbia U., 1974-75. Mem. Phi Beta Kappa. Avocation: skiing. Office: Skadden Arps Slate Meagher & Flom 300 S Grand Ave Los Angeles CA 90071-3109

APRISON, MORRIS HERMAN, biochemist, experimental and theoretical neurobiologist, emeritus educator; b. Milw., Oct. 6, 1923; s. Henry and Ethel Aprison; m. Shirley Reder, Aug. 21, 1949; children— Barry, Robert. BS in Chemistry, U. Wis., 1945, tchrs. cert., 1947, MS in Physics, 1949, PhD in Biochemistry, 1952. Grad. teaching asst. in physics U. Wis., Madison, 1947-49; grad. research asst. in pathology Sch. Medicine, 1950-51, grad. research asst. in biochemistry, 1951-52; tech. asst. in physics Inst. Paper Chemistry, Appleton, Wis., 1949-50; biochemist, prin. investigator, head biophysics sect. Galesburg (Ill.) State Research Hosp., 1952-56; prin. research investigator in biochemistry Inst. Psychiat. Research; asst. prof. depts. biochemistry and psychiatry Ind. U. Med. Sch., Indpls., 1956-60, asso. prof., 1960-64, prof. biochemistry, 1964-78, distinguished prof. neurobiology and biochemistry, 1978-93, disting. prof. emeritus, 1993—, chief neurobiology sect., 1969-74. Mem. exec. com. dept. psychiatry, exec. adminstr. Inst. Psychiat. Rsch., 1973-74, dir. inst., 1974-78, chief sect. applied and theoretical neurobiology, 1978-93; co-chmn. session on neurotransmitters 23d Internat. Physiol. Congress, 1965; chmn. session neurochemistry and neuropharmacology 25th Congress, 1971; ad hoc mem. study sect. psychopharmacology NIMH, 1967-71, mem. neuropsychology study sect., 1970-74; mem. molecular and cellular neurobiology program adv. panel NSF, 1984-86; mem. com. recommendations U.S. Army sci. rsch. Nat. Rsch. Coun. Bd. Physics and Astronomy, 1987-89; mem. gov. bd. Inst. for Advanced Study Ind. U., Bloomington, 1989-92; vis. prof. 4th ASPET Workshop, Vanderbilt U., 1972; guest scholar Grad. Sch., Kans. State U., 1973. Adv. editor Neurosci. Rsch., 1968-73, Jour. Biol. Psychiatry, 1968-83, Neuropharmacology, 1969-93, Jour. Neurochemistry, 1972-75, Pharmacology, Biochemistry and Behavior, 1973-89, Jour. Comparative and General Pharmacology, 1974-75, Jour. Gen. Pharmacology, 1975-93, Jour. Developmental Psychobiology, 1974-77; regional editor Life Scis., 1970-73; co-editor Advances in Neurochemistry, 1973-92; mem. editorial bd. Jour. Neurochemistry, 1975-79, dep. chief editor, 1980-83; mem. editorial bd. Neurochem. Rsch., 1975-82, Jour. Neurosci. Rsch., 1984-92; co-editor 10 books; contbr. more than 355 rsch. articles and abstracts to profl. jours., chpts. to books, including one in History of Neuroscience in Autobiography, vol. 3, 2001. Mem. Ind. regional adv. bd. Anti-Defamation League, 1973-76; bd. overseers St. Meinrad Sem., 1974-77. Served with USNR, 1944-46. Prof. M.H. Aprison awards for best rsch. toward PhD in med. neurobiology at dept. psychiatry Ind. U. Sch. Medicine created in his honor, 1999. Mem. Am. Physiol. Soc., Biophys. Soc., Soc. Biol. Psychiatry (program com. 1974-75, co-chmn. 1975-76, gold medal 1975), Internat. Brain Rsch. Orgn., Internat. Soc. Neurochemistry (co-chmn. session 1st internat. meeting Strasbourg, France 1967, 4th meeting Tokyo 1973, 7th meeting Jerusalem 1979, coun. 1973-75, sec. 1975-79, chmn. 1979-81, publicity com. 1975-83, nominating com. 1983-87, policy adv. com. 1985-98, ad hoc and founding rules com. 1998-2000, standing rules com., 2000—), Am. Soc. Neurochemistry (co-chmn. sci. program com. 1972, mem. 1973), Soc. for Neurosci. (pres. Indpls. chpt. 1970-71), Sigma Xi. Home: 9268 Spring Forest Dr Indianapolis IN 46260-1266 E-mail: maprison@iupui.edu.

APRUZZESE, VINCENT JOHN, lawyer; b. Newark, Nov. 1, 1928; s. John and Mildred (Cerefice) A.; m. Marie A. Yeager, July 10, 1955; children: Barbara, John, Donald, Lynn, Kathy. BA, Rutgers U., 1950; LLB, U. Pa., 1953. Bar: N.J. 1954, U.S. Dist. Ct. N.J. 1954, U.S. Ct. Appeals (3d cir.) 1962, U.S. Supreme Ct. 1970, U.S. Ct. Appeals (D.C. cir. 1973), U.S. Ct. Appeals (4th cir.) 1973, D.C. 1976, N.Y. 1983. Assoc. Lum, Fairlie & Foster, Newark, 1953-54; sole practice Newark, 1954-55, 58-65; sr. ptnr. Apruzzese & McDermott, Newark, 1965-70, pres. Springfield, N.J., 1970-90, Liberty Corner and Newark. Mem. legal adv. bd. Martindale-Hubbell, 1991-98. Bd. dirs. St. Barnabas Hosp., Papermill Playhouse. With JAGC, USAF, 1956-57. Mem. ABA (mem. coun. labor and employment law sect. 1984-94, chair labor & employment law sect. 1992-93, bd. govs. 1988-91), Coll. of Labor and Employment Lawyers, Fed. Bar Assn., Internat. Labor Law Soc. (treas.), Am. Coll. Trial Lawyers, Am. Bar Found., Fed. Bar State N.J., N.J. State Bar Assn. (pres. 1982-84), Essex County Bar Assn., Somerset County Bar Assn., Baltusrol Country Club (Springfield), Chatham (Mass.) Beach and Tennis Club, Eastward Ho Country Club (Chatham). Office: Apruzzese McDermott Mastro & Murphy PO Box 112 25 Independence Blvd Liberty Corner NJ 07938 E-mail: vapruzzese@excite.com.

APT, CHARLES, artist; b. NYC, Dec. 10, 1933; s. Gustav Lee and Tami (Vera Salzman) A.; m. Ursula Edith Betz, July 24, 1959; children— Gregory, Sam. B.F.A., Pratt Inst., 1956. Exhibited in group shows at Mus. Fine Art, Springfield, Mass., 1966, Expn. Intercontinentale, Monaco, France, 1966, 68, NAD, 1965, 68, 77-81, 83, 85, 87, 99, 2001, 03, Am. Watercolor Soc., 1965-66, 68-69, Allied Artists Am., 1964-65, 67, 69-70, 72, Nat. Mus. Racing, Saratoga, N.Y., 1967, Atlantic City Race Track, 1967, Nat. Arts Club, 1967; one-man shows Ground Floor Art Gallery, N.Y.C., 1967-69, Aqueduct Race Track Art Gallery, N.Y.C., 1967, Grand Central Art Galleries, 1969, Far Gallery, N.Y.C., 1972, 78, Palm Beach (Fla.) Galleries, 1973, Talisman Gallery, Bartlesville, Okla., 1976, Gallery 52, South Orange, N.J., 1976-77, Lorings Gallery, Cedarhurst, N.Y., 1985, 87, Huntsman Gallery, Aspen Colo., Dassin Gallery, LA, Loring Gallery, Sheffield, Mass., Off the Wall Gallery, Savannah, Ga. Served with AUS, 1956-58. Recipient Gold medal Am. Vets. Soc. Artists, 1965; Best in Show award Saratoga Mus. Racing Ann., 1967; 2d Benjamin Altman award for figure painting NAD, 1968; Le Prix Prince Souverain Monaco, 1968; Bronze medal Nat. Arts Club, 1971; Sutherland prize Annual Open Oil Exhbn., 1972; Ject-key prize Salmagundi Club, 1972, prize, 1966, 68-69, 71, Williams award Salmagundi Club, 1966, 68, 1st prize Product Design award for

Aquarelle fabric collection Resource Coun., 1984, 1st prize Am. Artists Profl. League, 1965, Talens award, 1966 Mem. NAD (academician, Briggs Meml. award 1989), Artists Equity Assn. N.Y. Studio: 152 South Almont Dr Los Angeles CA 90048

APT, LEONARD, physician; b. Phila., June 28, 1922; s. Morris and Rebecca Apt. AB with honors, U. Pa., 1942; MD with honors, Jefferson Med. Coll., 1945. Diplomate Am. Bd. Pediat., Am. Bd. Ophthalmology. Intern Jefferson Med. Coll. Hosp., Phila., 1945-46; rsch. fellow in pathology-hematology, resident in pediat. Children's Hosp., Detroit, 1946-49, resident in pediat. Cin., 1949—50, Children's Med. Ctr., Boston, 1950-52, chief med. resident, 1952-53, asst. physician, 1953-55; resident in ophthalmology Wills Eye Hosp., Phila., 1955-57; first spl. fellow in Pediat. Ophthalmology NIH, and Bethesda and Children's Hosp., Washington, 1957—59; first fellow in Pediat. Ophthalmology Wills Eye Hosp., Phila., 1959—61; from asst. prof. to prof. ophthalmology Sch. Medicine, UCLA, 1961—72, prof., 1972—; disting. prof. UCLA, 1993—; attending surgeon Jules Stein Eye Inst., UCLA, dir. pediat. ophthalmology, 1961-81, dir. emeritus, 1981—. Tchg. fellow in pediat. Harvard U. Med. Sch., Boston, 1950—52, instr. pediat., 1953—55; sr. physician radioisotope unit Boston VA Hosp., 1953—55; cons. pediat. ophthalmology Cedars-Sinai Med. Ctr., L.A., St. John's Hosp., Santa Monica, Calif., Bur. Maternal and Child Health, Dept. Pub. Health Calif., Dept. Health, L.A. *Dr. Apt is recognized as one of the founders of pediatric opthalmology. He is the first physician to be board-certified in both pediatrics and ophthalmology. At UCLA, Dr. Apt established the first full-time division of pediatric ophathalmology at a medical school in the United States. Dr. Apt authored one of the first books devoted to the new subspecialty. He is the originator of the Apt test widely known especially to pediatricians and obstetricians. Dr. Apt helped develop a new antiseptic eyedrop that has appreciably reduced the incidence of pediatric blindness in developing countries.* Author: Diagnostic Procedures in Pediatric Ophthalmology, 1963; mem. editl. bd. numerous med. jours.: ; contbr. numerous articles on pediat. ophthalmology to med. books. Founder L.A. Philharmonic Assn.; presdl. circle mem. L.A. County Mus. of Art; v.p. fin. UCLA Grundwald Ctr. for Graphic Arts; steering com. UCLA Performing Arts Dept.; founder John Wooden UCLA Athletic Ctr.; exec. coun. mem. UCLA Divsn. of Humanities; judge Wines of Am. Ann. Competition. 1st lt. M.C. U.S. Army, 1943—46. Recipient Disting. Alumnus Achievement award, Jefferson Med. Coll., 1992, 1st Escalon Sci. award, 1992, Hall of Fame Distinction award, Cin. Pediat. Hist. Soc., 1994, 1st Disting. Alumni award, Sch. Arts and Scis. U. Pa., 1995, Alumni Univ. Svc. award, UCLA, 1996, William Feinbloom 1st Disting. Achievement award, 1999, Profl. Achievement award, UCLA Med. Alumni Assn., 1999, 1st Disting. Achievement award, Ethicon Inc.-Johnson & Johnson Co., 1999. Mem.: AMA, Am. Med. Writers Assn., Pacific Coast Oto-Ophthal. Soc., Internat. Strabismol. Assn., Am. Assn. Pediat. Ophthalmology and Strabismus (1st Disting. Achievement award 1996, Honor award 1995), Soc. Pediat. Rsch., Assn. for Rsch. Ophthalmology, Am. Ophthal. Soc., Am. Acad. Pediats. (Lifetime Achievement award 2000, Ann. Leonard Apt Lectureship named in his honor 2000), Am. Acad. Ophthalmology (Honor award 1968), L'Ordre Mondial des Gourmets Deguistaeurs, Confrerie de la Chaine des Rotisseurs, Internat. Wine and Food Soc., Shriner, Masons (32d deg.), Alpha Omega Alpha. Avocations: sports, art, theater, gourmet food, oenology. Office: UCLA Sch Medicine Jules Stein Eye Inst 100 Stein Plz Los Angeles CA 90095-7000 Fax: 310-206-3652.

APTED, MICHAEL DAVID, film director; b. London, Feb. 10, 1941; BA, Downing Coll., Cambridge, Eng., 1963. Dir.: (films) Triple Echo, 1972, Stardust, 1974, The Squeeze, 1976, Agatha, 1977, Coalminer's Daughter, 1980 (DGA nominee), Continental Divide, 1981, Gorky Park, 1983, Kipperbang, 1983 (Brit. Acad. TV and Film award nominee), Firstborn, 1984, Critical Condition, 1986, Gorillas in the Mist, 1988, Class Action, 1990, Thunderheart, 1991, Blink, 1993, Nell, 1994, Extreme Measures, 1996, Always Outnumbered, 1998, The World Is Not Enough, 1999, Enigma, 2000, Enough, 2002; (play) Strawberry Fields, 1978 (BAFTA, Emmy award); (documentaries) 14 UP, 21 UP (Internat. Emmy), 28 UP (Brit. Acad. award, Internat. Emmy), 1985, Bring On the Night, 1984 (Emmy, Grammy awards), The Long Way Home, 1989, Incident at Oglala, 1991, 35 UP, 1992 (BAFTA award), Moving the Mountain, 1993 (IDA award), Inspirations, 1997, 42 Up, 1998, Me & Isaac Newton, 1999, Married in America, 2002; (Brit. TV) Slattery's Mounted Foot, 1970 (Brit. Critics Best Play), The Mosedale Horshoe, 1971 (Brit. Critics Best Play), Another Sunday and Sweet F.A., 1972 (Brit. Critics Best Play), Follyfoot, 1972 (Best Children's Svcs.), Kisses at Fifty (Brit. Critics Best Play, SFTA Best Dir.), The Collection (Internat. Emmy), others.

APTEKAR, KEN, painter; b. Detroit, May 13, 1950; BFA, U. Mich., 1973; MFA, Pratt Inst., 1975. Studio artist, N.Y.C. Solo shows include Jack Shainman Gallery, N.Y.C., 1994, 96, Palmer Mus. Art Pa. State U., 1995, Corcoran Gallery of Art, 1997, Cummer Mus. of Art, Jacksonville, Fla., 1998, Steinbaum-Krauss Gallery, N.Y.C., 1999, Victoria and Albert Mus., London, 2001, Meml. Art Gallery, Rochester, N.Y., 2002, Kemper Mus., Kansas City, 2001, Coll. of Wooster, Ohio, 2002, Pamela Auchincloss Projects, N.Y.C., 2001, Contemporary ARt Ctr. of Va., 2001-02, Bernice Steinbaum Gallery, 2003; exhibited in group shows at Carnegie-Mellon U. Mus., Pitts., 1991, Corcoran Gallery, Washington, 1993-94, 97-98, Flint (Mich.) Inst. Art, 1993, Wight Gallery UCLA, 1994, Yerba Buena Ctr. Contemporary Art, San Francisco, 1994, Walters Art Gallery, Balt., 1995, Calif. Ctr. Contemporary Art, Escondido, 1996, Kohler Arts Ctr., Wis., 1996, Jewish Mus., N.Y.C., San Francisco, 1996, Armand Hammer Mus., L.A., 1996, Islip Art Mus., N.Y., 1998, Ashville Mus. Art, 2003; represented in permanent collections Kemper Mus., Kansas City, Mo., Meml. Art Gallery, Rochester, Niagara U., Denver Mus. Art, Progressive Corp., Jewish Mus., Bell Atlantic Corp., Nat. Mus. Am. Art, Washington, Harvard U. Recipient Pollock-Krasner Found. award, 1989; NEA fellow, 1987, 95, Bellagio residency Rockefeller Found., 1992, artist residency Ucross Found., Wyo., 1992, painting residency Resident Artists Program Djerassi, 1991, 94, Mid Atlantic Arts Found. award, 1998. Home: 201 W 85th St Apt 7E New York NY 10024-3909

APTEKAR, SHELDON I. speech, theatre, and performing art educator; b. Bklyn., Sept. 14, 1939; s. Al and Fanny (Horowitz) A. BA in Speech and Theatre, Bklyn. Coll., 1962; MA in Drama, Trinity U., 1964; postgrad. in Theatre, Northwestern U., 1966-68; PhD Equivalency in Theatre, CUNY, 1972. Mem. Repertory Co. Dallas Theater Ctr., 1962-64; asst. prof. speech and theatre L.I. U., Bklyn., 1964-66; lectr. in speech and theatre CUNY, Kingsborough C.C., Bklyn., 1969-70, asst. prof. speech and theatre, 1970-75, assoc. prof. speech and theatre, 1975 84, prof. speech and theatre, 1984-95, prof. speech, theatre, and performing arts, 1995—, dir. performing arts program, 2000—. Cons. theatre in edn. The Ednl. Alliance, N.Y.C., 1970-72; cons. staging spectacle Citibank's Bicentennial Spectacle, Bronx, N.Y., 1974-76; artistic advisor stand up comics No-Artificial Sweetner Co., N.Y.C., 1977-82; program developer performing arts Kingsborough C.C., 1994-98; lectr. in field. Co-prodr. Georgetown Prodns., Inc., N.Y.C., 1990-94; artistic dir. various play prodns.; awards dir. Kennedy Ctr. Am. Coll. Theatre Festival, region II, 1974, 84, 94; staged readings dir. Shakespeare's plays Genesis Repertory Ensemble, N.Y.C., 2003—. Mem., adjudicator Kennedy Ctr., Am. Coll. Theatre Festival, Region II; acting coach, 1994—, freelance dir. Recipient Cert. of Recognition, Centro Ecol. Akumal, 1998, citations in The Director as Artist, 1995, Theatre as the Essential Liberal Art in the American University, 2002; Study grant, Culture and the European Common Market in Belgium, 1985, Modern Drama and the Avant Garde, Mellon Found., 1986, Rsch. grantee, Kingsborough C., 2001—02, P.S./CUNY, 2002—. Mem. Am. Theatre Assn. (chair directing program 1981-83), Assn. for Theatre in Higher Edn., East Ctrl. Theatre Conf. (constl. com. 1985-89), Internat. Brecht Soc. Avocations: pen and ink drawing, photography, traveling, wood sculpturing. E-mail: saptekar@kbcc.cuny.edu.

APTER, EMILY, language educator; BA in History and Lit., Harvard U., 1977; PhD in Comparative Lit., Princeton U., 1983. Prof. French NYU, N.Y.C. Recipient Guggenheim fellowship, 2003, Mellon fellowship, Rockefeller fellowship, ACLS fellowship, NEH fellowship, Coll. Art Assn. fellowship. Office: 19 University Pl 634 New York NY 10003*

APTER, RONNIE SUSAN, English educator, translator; b. Hartford, Conn., June 4, 1943; d. Marvin and Rosalind Helen (Kenig) A.; m. Mark Norman Herman, June 18, 1967; children: Daniel A., Jeffry M. BA, Sarah Lawrence Coll., 1965; MA in English, NYU, 1967; PhD in English, Fordham U., 1980. Mem. English faculty Ctrl. Mich. U., Mt. Pleasant, 1986—, prof. English, 1996—. Author: Digging for the Treasure: Translation After Pound, 1984, A Bilingual Edition of the Love Songs of Bernart de Ventadorn in Occitan and English: Sugar and Salt, 1999; co-author 19 opera translations; pub. 1st performing edit. of Alessandro Scarlatti's Eraclea; contbr. articles, poems and poetry translations to profl. jours. Recipient Thomas Wolfe Poetry award NYU, 1967, award for outstanding rsch. and creative activity Ctrl. Mich. U., 2003; NEH grantee, 1986. Mem. MLA (manuscript evaluator 1987—), Am. Lit. Translator's Assn. (exec. bd. 1986-89), Am. Translator's Assn., Internat. Courtly Lit. Soc., Société Guilhem IX. Office: Ctrl Mich Univ Dept English Mount Pleasant MI 48859-0001 E-mail: ronnie.apter@cmich.edu.

APUD, JOSE ANTONIO, psychiatrist, psychopharmacologist, educator; b. San Miguel de Tucuman, Argentina, May 25, 1948; came to U.S., 1987; s. Jose and Emelin (Chagra) A.; m. Graciela Varela, Jan. 25, 1979; children: Maria Macarena, Jose Sebastian. MD, U. Tucuman, 1975; degree in pharmacology, U. Milan, 1980, degree in exptl. endocrinology, 1983; PhD, U. Buenos Aires, 1985. Diplomate Am. Bd. Psychiatry and Neurology. Investigator CONICET, Buenos Aires, 1985—98; prof. pharmacology U. Buenos Aires, 1985-93; psychiatrist in residence St. Elizabeth's Hosp., Nat. Inst. of Mental Health, Washington, 1991 95; clin. assoc. neuropsychiatry br. Nat. Inst. of Mental Health, Washington, 1995-98; faculty psychiatry residency tng. program Commn. on Mental Health Svcs., Washington, 1998—2000; dir. psychopharmacology divsn. St. Elizabeths Hosp.-Commn. on Mental Health Svcs., Washington, 1998-2000; med. dir. Schizophrenia Inpatient Rsch. Program NIMH, 2000—. Cons. Farmitalia Carlo Erba Labs, Milan, 1979-83; vis. prof. pharmacology Georgetown U., Washington, 1987-91; mem. editorial bd. Endocrinologia Clinica y Metabolism, 1982—, Neuroendocrinologia Latinoamericana, 1982—; instr. dept. psychiatry George Washington U., 1995-98, prof. psychiatry, 1998—. Contbr. numerous articles to profl. jours. Fellow Nat. Atomic Energy Commn., 1976, Dept. Endocrinology French Hosp., 1978, Inst. Pharmacology U. Milan, 1978-84, sr. staff fellow St. Elizabeth's Hosp. NIMH, 1994-98; recipient Cediquifa award in pharmacology, 1992, Upjohn award NIMH, 1993. Mem. AMA, Am. Psychiat. Assn. (sci. com. 1993-95, Burroughs Wellcome award 1993), Am. Soc. Clin. Psychopharmacology, Washington Psychiat. Soc., Italian Soc. Neurosci., Italian Soc. Pharmacology, Soc. for Neurosci., Sociedad Argentina de Farmacologia Exptl., Internat. Soc. Psychoneuroendocrinology, Internat. Soc. Neuroendocrinology, Argentina Soc. Biology and Nuclear Medicine, Serotonin Club. Roman Catholic. Achievements include identification of Gabaergic system in rats; study of the mechanism of action of psychotropic drugs; studies on schizophrenia and tardive dyskinesia; identification of an endogenous ligand for the serotonin-2 receptor in the rat brain. Office: NIMH Clin Brain Disorders Br Bldg 10 Rm 4S229 10 Center Dr Bethesda MD 20892 E-mail: apudj@intra.nimh.nih.gov.

APURON, ANTHONY SABLAN, archbishop; b. Agana, Guam, Nov. 1, 1945; s. Manuel Taijito and Ana Santos (Sablan) P.. BA, St. Anthony Coll., 1969; MDiv, Maryknoll Sem., 1972, M in Theology, 1973; MA in Liturgy, Notre Dame U., 1974; LHD, U. Guam, 1998. Ordained priest Roman Catholic Ch., 1972, bishop, 1984, installed archbishop, 1986. Chmn. Diocesan Liturgical Commn., Agana, 1974—86; vice-chmn. Chamorro Lang. Commn., Agana, 1984—86; aux. bishop Archdiocese of Agana, 1984—85, archbishop, 1986—. Chmn. Interfaith Vols. Caregivers, Agana, 1984—; active Civilian Adv. Com., Agana, 1986—, Post-Synod of Bishops of Oceania, 1998—; pres. Cath. Bishops' Conf. of Pacific, 1990—96; v.p. Cath. Bishops' Conf. of Oceania, 1990—98. Author: A Structural Analysis of the Content of Myth in the Thought of Mircea Eliade, 1973. Chmn. Cath. Ednl. Radio. Named Most Outstanding Young Man, Jaycees, Guam, 1984. Roman Catholic. Avocations: jogging, walking, swimming. Office: Archbishop's Office 196B Cuesta San Ramon Agana GU 96910-4334*

APUZZIO, JOSEPH J. obstetrician-gynecologist; b. Elizabeth, N.J., 1947; MD, N.J. Med. Coll., 1973. Resident Martland Hosp., Newark, 1973-76; with U. Hosp., Newark, Clara Mass. Hosp., Belleville, N.J., Columbus Hosp., Newark, St. Elizabeth (N.J.) Hosp., Overlook Hosp., Summit, N.J. U. Hosp. fellow, Newark, 1980-82. Fellow ACS, ACOG, Maternal-Fetal Medicine; mem. Am. Coll. Ob-gyn. Office: Dept Ob-Gyn Med Sci Bldg E506 185 S Orange Ave Newark NJ 07103-2757

AQUADRO, JEANA LAUREN, graphic designer, educator; b. Key West, Fla., June 10, 1957; d. Charles Frasure and Geraldine Ferguson (Norton) A.; m. John A. Crawford. B Environ. Design magna cum laude, N.C. State U., 1979; MFA, Yale U., 1984. Graphic designer various projects for Cooper-Hewitt Nat. Mus. Design, Whitney Mus. Am. Art, Shearson Lehman Bros., Citicorp Investment Bank, Abbeville Press, UNICEF, others, N.Y.C., 1984-91; asst. dir. graphic design dept. Mus. Modern Art, 1988-89; design cons. Solomon R. Guggenheim Mus., 1989-91; prof. Savannah Coll., Savannah, Ga., 1991—2001; graphic design cons., 2001—. Bd. dirs. Wilderness S.E. Recipient The Am. Fedn. of Arts award of Excellence, 1988, Fed. design achievement award Nat. Endowment for Arts, 1992, Presidential award for design excellence Fed. Govt., 1994. Avocations: aquatic sports, travel, gardening. Studio: 3 Pinewood Ave Savannah GA 31406

AQUILA, SAMUEL JOSEPH, bishop; b. Burbank, Calif., Sept. 24, 1950; s. Salvatore Joseph and Josephine Aquila. BA, U. Colo., Boulder, 1972; MA in Theology-Dogma, St. Thomas Sem., Denver, 1976; licentiate in Sacred Theology, San Anselmo U., Rome, 1990. Ordained priesthood Denver, 1976, apptd. coadjutor bishop Diocese of Fargo, N.D., 2001, episcopal ordination Fargo, 2001, apptd. bishop Diocese of Fargo, 2002. Asst. pastor St. Mary Parish, Colorado Springs, Colo., 1976—79, Christ the King Parish, Denver, 1979—82; pastor Guardian Angels Parish, Denver, 1982—87; dir. Office of Liturgy; Master of Ceremonies, Denver, 1990—95; co-dir. Continuing Edn. for Priests, Denver, 1990—2000, asst. sec. for Cath. edn., 1991—93, sec. for Cath. edn., 1995—99, sec. for social concerns, 1997—98; CEO Our Lady of the New Advent Theol. Inst., Denver, 1999—2001; rector St. John Vianney Sem., Denver, 1999—2001; chaplain Lagatus Chpt., Denver, 2000—01; apptd. Prelate of Honor by Pope John Paul II, 2000; coadjutor Bishop Diocese of Fargo, 2001—02, bishop, 2002—. Advisor Bishops' Com. on Liturgy, Washington, 1991—93, Washington, 2000—01, mem., 2001—; detender of the bond Met. Tribunal, Denver, 1982—83; mem., vice chmn. Presbyteral Coun., Denver, 1986—87; ad hoc com. Bishops' Life and Ministry, 2001—; mem. Bishops' Com. on Diaconate, 2001—. Mem.: U.S. Conf. Cath. Bishops (com. lay ministry 2002—, nominations com. 2002—). Office: Diocese of Fargo 1310 N Broadway Fargo ND 58102

AQUILINO, DANIEL, banker; b. Needham, Mass., Feb. 4, 1924; s. Michael Aquilino and Anna (Bruno) A.; m. Theresa H. Barberio, Nov. 9, 1946; children: Donna Lee, Daniel C., Michael D. BS magna cum laude, Northeastern U., 1949; grad., Stonier Grad. Sch. Banking, Rutgers U., 1962. With Fed. Res. Bank Boston, 1949-85, exec. v.p., 1970-85, Bank of New Eng., Boston, 1985-89; cons. Boston, 1990—. Dir. Secure Fin. Networks, Inc., Wakefield, R.I. Served with AUS, 1943-45. Recipient Sears B. Condit award Northeastern U., 1947, 49; recognition award Italian-Am. Soc., Inc., 1972. Home: 3 N Bennet Ct Apt 1 Boston MA 02113-1904

AQUILINO, THOMAS JOSEPH, JR., federal judge, law educator; b. Mt. Kisco, N.Y., Dec. 7, 1939; s. Thomas Joseph and Virginia Burr (Doughty) A.; m. Edith Luise Berndt, Oct. 27, 1965; children: Christopher T., Philip A., Alexander B. Student, Cornell U., 1957-59, U. Munich, 1960-61; BA, Drew U., 1962; postgrad., Free U., Berlin, 1965-66; JD, Rutgers U., 1969. Bar: N.Y. 1972, U.S. Dist. Ct. (so., ea. and no. dists.) N.Y. 1973, U.S. Ct. Appeals (2nd cir.) 1973, U.S. Supreme Ct. 1976, U.S. Ct. Appeals (3rd cir.) 1977, Interstate Commerce Commn. 1978, U.S. Ct. Claims 1979, U.S. Ct. Internat. Trade 1984. Law clk. to judge U.S. Dist. Ct. (so. dist.) N.Y., N.Y.C., 1969-71; atty. Davis Polk & Wardwell, N.Y.C., 1971-85; judge U.S. Ct. Internat. Trade, N.Y.C., 1985—. Adj. prof. law Benjamin N. Cardozo Sch. of Law, 1984-95; mem. bd. visitors Drew U., 1997—. With U.S. Army, 1962-65. Mem. N.Y. State Bar Assn., Fed. Bar Coun. Roman Catholic. Avocations: sports, travel, linguistics, cinema. Office: US Ct Internat Trade 1 Federal Plz New York NY 10278-0001

AQUINO, JOSEPH MARIO, clinical psychologist; b. N.Y.C., Nov. 21, 1947; s. Joseph and Rose (Nasi) A.; m. Kathleen Ann Ryan, Oct. 6, 1990; children: Joseph Patrick, Ryan Thomas, Erin Rose. BA in English, So. Ill. U., 1969, MS in Secondary Edn., 1976; PhD in Clin. Psychology, St. John's U., Jamaica, N.Y., 1987. Lic. psychologist, N.Y. Tchr. English Wappingers Cen. Schs., Wappingers Falls, N.Y., 1969-79; intern psychology Maimonides Med. Ctr., Bklyn., 1983-84; specialist in applied behavior sci. Builders for Family and Youth, Bklyn., 1984-85; trainee psychology and psychologist St. Vincent's Svcs., Bklyn., 1984-89; psychologist St. Christopher-Ottilie Svcs., Sea Cliff, N.Y., 1989-96; pvt. practice psychology N.Y.C. area, 1989—. Guest lectr. St. John's U., 1990. Co-author: Situational Leadership for Principals, 1983; mem. editl. bd. Jour. Urban Psychiatry, 1982-84; guest The Women's Line, WVOX 1460 AM, 1994; cited in newspaper articles; contbr. articles to profl. jours. Recipient citation VFW, Wappingers Falls, N.Y., 1977; Bethany House Achievement award Bethany House II, 1991; psychology teaching fellow St. John's U., 1981; cited in article Emergency mag., 1991. Mem. APA, N.Y. State Psychol. Assn., Westchester County Psychol. Assn., Nat. Register of Health Svc. Providers in Psychology, Am. Coll. of Advanced Practice Psychologists (founding fellow). Office: 10 Rye Ridge Plz Ste 213 Rye Brook NY 10573-2857

ARABIAN, ARMAND, arbitrator, mediator, lawyer; b. N.Y.C., Dec. 12, 1934; s. John and Aghavnie (Yalian) A.; m. Nancy Arabian, Aug. 26, 1962; children: Allison Ann, Robert Armand. BSBA, Boston U., 1956, JD, 1961; LLM, U. So. Calif., L.A., 1970; LLD (hon.) (hon.), Southwestern Sch. Law, 1990, Pepperdine U., 1990, U. West L.A., 1994, We. State U., 1997, Thomas Jefferson Sch. of Law, 1997, Am. Coll. Law, 2001. Bar: Calif. 1962, U.S. Supreme Ct. 1966. Dep. dist. atty. L.A. County, 1962-63, pvt. practice law Van Nuys, Calif., 1963-72; judge Mcpl. Ct., L.A., 1972-73, Superior Ct., L.A., 1973-83; assoc. justice Calif. Ct. Appeal, L.A., 1983-90, Supreme Ct. Calif., San Francisco, 1990-96; ret., 1996. Adj. prof. sch. law Pepperdine U., 1996—. Contbr. 1st lt. U.S. Army, 1956-58. Recipient Stanley Lintz Meml. award San Fernando Valley Bar Assn., 1986, Lifetime Achievement award San Fernando Valley Bar Assn., 1993; Outstanding Jurist of the Yr., Malibu Bar Assn., 1996; Pappas Disting. scholar Boston U. Sch. Law, 1987; Justice Armand Arabian Resource and Comm. Ctrs. named in honor of Van Nuys and San Fernando Calif. Courthouses, 1999; Mekhitar Gosh medal Pres. of Armenia Robert Kocharian, 2001, St. James the Apostle medal Beatitude Torkom Manoogian, Jerusalem, 2001, Mesrob Mashdots medal Aram I Catholicos, Beirut, Lebanon, 1999, Mekhitar medal Brotherhood in Venice, Italy, 1999, Gold medal of honor of Peter the Great, Russian Acad. Sci., 1999, Albert Einstein Gold medal of honor, Russian Acad. Natural Scis., 2003. Republican. Office: 6259 Van Nuys Blvd Van Nuys CA 91401-2711 Fax: 818-781-6002. E-mail: honarabian@AOL.com.

ARABIE, PHIPPS, marketing educator, researcher; b. Mar. 13, 1948; s. Wade Joseph and Betty Jo (Thomason) A.; m. Terry Feldstein, Feb. 24, 2000. Diploma, Phillips Acad., Andover, 1966; AB, Harvard U., 1970; PhD, Stanford U., 1974. Asst. prof. psychology U. Minn., Mpls., 1974-77, assoc. prof., 1977-80; prof. psychology and sociology U. Ill., Champaign-Urbana, 1980-90; prof. Rutgers U. Sch. Mgmt., Newark, 1990—; chair mktg. Rutgers U. Bus. Sch., Newark, 1990-96, 2000—02. Cons. AT&T Bell Labs, Murray Hill, N.J., 1975-82; Fulbright vis. prof. computer sci. U. Coll., Dublin, Ireland, 1986-87; vis. prof. psychology U. Santiago de Compostela, Spain, 1993; mem. adv. panel on methods, measures and stats. NSF, 1996-97. Co-author: Three-way Scaling and Clustering, 1987, Combinatorial Data Analysis: Optimization by Dynamic Programming, 2001; co-editor: Clustering and Classification, 1996; editor Jour. Classification, 1983-2002; contbr. articles to profl. jours.; author computer programs for multidimensional analysis of data. Grantee NSF, Office Naval Research, Nat. Inst. Justice, AT&T; Beckman assoc. U. Ill., 1983-84 Fellow: AAAS, APA, Am. Statis. Assn., Am. Psychol. Soc.; mem.: INFORMS, Am. Mktg. Assn., Soc. Math. Psychology, Psychonometric Soc. (trustee 1987—89, pres. 1990—91), Classification Soc. N.Am. (bd. dirs. 1983—). Office: Rutgers U Business Sch 180 University Ave Newark NJ 07102-1893

ARAC, JONATHAN, English language educator; b. N.Y.C., Apr. 4, 1945; s. Benjamin and Evelyn (Charm) A. AB, Harvard U., 1967, MA, 1968, PhD, 1974. Jr. fellow Soc. Fellows Harvard U., Cambridge, Mass., 1970-73; asst. prof. English Princeton U., 1973-79; assoc. prof. U. Ill., Chgo., 1979-85, prof., 1985-86; prof. grad. program lit. Duke U., 1986-87; prof. English and comparative lit. Columbia U., 1987-90; prof. English U. Pitts., 1989-2000, Mellon prof. English, 2000-01; Harriman prof. English and comparative lit. Columbia U., 2001—. Assoc. dir. Inst. for Humanities, U. Ill., Chgo., 1983-84, dept. chair, 2001—; Drue Heinz vis. acad. Oxford U., 2000; Avalon disting. vis. prof. humanities Northwestern U., 2000. Author: Commissioned Spirits, 1979, Critical Genealogies, 1987, Huckleberry Finn as Idol and Target, 1997; editor: The Yale Critics: Deconstruction in America, 1983, Postmodernism and Politics, 1986, After Foucault, 1988, Consequences of Theory, 1990, Macropolitics of 19th Century Literature, 1991; contbr. to Cambridge History of American Literature, Vol. 2, 1995; mem. editl. bd. Comparative Lit., 1989—, Am. Lit., 2000—; asst. editor: Boundary 2: Jour. Postmodern Lit. and Culture, 1979—. Am. Coun. Learned Socs. fellow, 1978-79, NEH fellow, 1986-87, 94-95. Mem. MLA (mem. publs. com. 1997-2000), Soc. Critical Exch. (bd. dirs. 1983-90), English Inst. (mem. supervisory com. 1985-88, chmn. 1987-88), PMLA (mem. adv. com. 1990-94). Office: Columbia U Dept English & Comp Lit 602 Philosophy Hall New York NY 10027 E-mail: ja2007@columbia.edu.

ARAGHIZADEH, FARSHID YEGANEH, surgeon; s. Mehdi and Shokoufeh Araghizadeh. MD, U. of South Ala., 1994. Diplomate Am. Bd. of Surgery, 2000, lic. surgeon Ill., 2000. Asst. prof. Dept. of Surgery U. of Miss. Med. Ctr., Jackson, Miss., 2001—. Personal E-mail: docsoc@usa.net.

ARAI, TOSHIHIKO, retired microbiology and immunology educator; b. Niigata, Japan, Sept. 12, 1937; s. Hachiro Sisido and Kazue Arai; m. Hatsue Aoki, Dec. 1, 1963; children: Masako, Tomoko, Kazuhiko. MD, Keio U., Tokyo, 1962; PhD, Keio U., 1968. Instr. dept. microbiology Keio U. Sch. Medicine, 1967-73, asst. prof., 1973-85, assoc. prof., 1985; prof. microbiology and immunology Meiji Coll. Pharmacy, Tokyo, 1985-97; ret., 1997. Rsch. assoc. U. Tex., Dallas, 1970—72; lectr. Ochanomizu U. Sch. Sci., Tokyo, 1978—79, Chiba (Japan) U. Sch. Medicine, 1978—82, Josai Dental U., Sakado, Japan, 1978—87, Aoyama Gakuin U., Tokyo, 1988—2003; cons. Kitasato Inst., Tokyo, 1981—84. Author (15 books) ; contbr. Mem.: N.Y. Acad. Scis., Am. Soc. Microbiology, Japan Antibiotic Rsch. Assn. (bd. dirs.), Japan Soc. Chemotherapy (bd. dirs.), Japan Soc. Bacteriology. Zen Buddhist. Home: 5-1-23 Yatsu Narashimo-shi Chiba 275-0026 Japan Office: Kaiyu Clinic #205 Spur 3-3-6 Saginomiya Nakano-ku Tokyo 165-0032 Japan E-mail: ya5-1-23@mxm.mesh.ne.jp.

ARAI-ABRAMSON, LUCY, artist, writer; b. Tokyo, Mar. 3, 1956; came to U.S., 1956; d. Lucian Ford Robinson and Masuko Arai; m. William John Abramson, Dec. 31, 1975. Student, Ea. Mich. U., 1974-75; BFA cum laude, U. S.C., 1979; MFA, U. Mich., 1983, grad. cert. of mus. practices, 1986. Copy editor U. Mich. Microfilms, Ann Arbor, 1979-80; mus. shop asst. mgr. U. Mich. Mus. of Art, 1983, membership coord., 1984; asst. curator Cranbrook Art Acad./Mus., Bloomfield Hills, Mich., 1985-86; cons. archives, exhbns. and mus. edn. programs, 1987—; freelance instr., 1987—; artist/designer, 1987—; with U.S. State Dept. Arts in Embassies Program, Bandar Seri Begawan, 2000—02; with arts in embassies program U.S. Embassy, Djibouti, Africa, 2001—; with Arts in Embassies Program, Brunei, 2000—02, U.S. State Dept. Arts in Embassies Program, Hong Kong, 2002—; edn. devel. cons. U. Mich. Mus. Art, 2001—02. Archive cons. Wente Bros. Winery, Livermore, Calif., 1989—92; Japanese stitching instr. nat. quilting orgns., 1989—; lectr./panelist Am. Acad. Religion, San Francisco, 1997; lectr. Holy Name Coll., Oakland, Calif., 1998; instr., lectr. Textile Mus., Washington, 2001; mus. edn. program cons. U. Mich., Ann Arbor, 2001—02. Designer/contbr.: (artist biography/slidebooks) Of Our Own Voice: Asian American Women Artists, 1996, 98; designer: (one of a kind garments) Kasuri Dyeworks, 1994—; author: (monograph) Mirrors of the Soul, 1992, Sashiko: Innovations & Refinement of a Japanese Stitchery Technique, 1994; contbr. articles to art mags. Vol. instr. Hawes and Jack London Schs., Redwood City and Antioch, Calif., 1992, 93, 94, 95; vol. arranger Calif. wildflower exhbn., Oakland, Calif., 1995, 96, 97, 98; garden designer/vol. coord. Dearborn (Mich.) Hist. Mus., 1997; vol. instr. Sansei Legacy Project, Alameda, Calif., 1991. Work judged Best in Show U. S.C., 1979; recipient grad. fellowship U. Mich., 1980, 81, 82, 83, art scholarship U. Mich. Sch. Art, 1980, 81, 82, 83, curatorial internship grant Cranbrook Acad.

Art/Mus., 1984-85. Mem. Coll. Art Assn., Asian Am. Women Artists Assn. Avocations: hiking, Calif. wildflowers, camping, travel, reading. Office: PO Box 683 Oakley CA 94561-0683 Fax: 925-737-7666. E-mail: LucyArai@aol.com.

ARAIZ, JOSEPH MICHAEL, securities company executive; b. Mexico City, Mex., Feb. 2, 1961; came to U.S., 1965; s. Francisco and Myra Hilda (Kagan) A.; m. Sandra Ramirez, May 25, 1990. BA, Brandeis U., 1983. Corp. bond trader Cowen & Co., Inc., 1983-85; exec. v.p. Gruntal & Co. Inc., 1985-88; exec. v.p., prin. M.J. Whitman & Co. Inc., N.Y.C., 1988-97, bd. dirs., 1989—; sr. exec. v.p. Whitman Security Corp., 1987-97; exec. v.p. M.J. Whitman Sr. Debt Corp., 1988—; dir. Whitman Investments; sr. exec. v.p. Whitman Structured Fin. Group; sr. mng. dir., bd. dirs. Ladenburg and Thalmann, 1997-98; sr. exec. v.p., mng. dir. Imperial Capital, N.Y.C., 1998—2001; pres.mgr. Further Lane Asset Mgmt., 2000—; pres., CEO Osprey Group Asset Mgmt., East Hampton, N.Y., 2000—; mng. ptnr. Osprey Opportunity Fund, 2000—; CEO, Further Lane Securities, 2002—. V.p. Whitman Securities Corp., exec. v.p., sr. debt corp. Mem. Nat. Trust for Historic Preservation. Mem. Am. Fine Arts Soc., Guggenheim Mus., Whitney Mus., Internat. Platform Assn., B'nai Brith. Office: Further Llane Securities 250 E 54th St 37B New York NY 10022 also: 62 Newtown Lane Suite 104 East Hampton NY 11937 Address: 295 Central Park W Apt 15G New York NY 10024-3056

ARAIZA, FRANCISCO (JOSÉ FRANCISCO ARAIZA ANDRADE), opera singer; b. Mexico City, Oct. 4, 1950; s. José and Guadalupe (Andrade) A.; m. Vivian Jaffray, Sept. 30, 1977 (div. 1995); children: José Riccardo, Maria del Carmen Cecilia; m. Ethery Inasaridse, children: Abessalom Rodrigo, Laura Imeda. Grad. in Bus. Adminstrn., U. Mexico City, 1972; grad., Nat. Sch. Music, Mexico City, 1974, Nat. Conservatory, 1974, Musikhochschule, Munich, 1975. Tenor roles (lyric repertory as well as dramatic parts till Wagner's Lohengrin in 1990) include performances in opera hos. Zurich, Munich, Vienna, Rome, Hamburg, Berlin, Milan, London, Parma, Florence, Venice, Barcelona, Madrid, Tokyo, Mexico City, Chgo., San Francisco, N.Y.C.; performed at Salzburg Festival, Bayreuth Festival; numerous recordings include works by Mozart, Rossini, Beethoven, Donizetti, Offenbach, Schubert, Verdi, Puccini, Gounod, Massenet, Weber and others; also six solo albums including opera arias, lieder, popular songs. Recipient Orphée d'Or, 1981, Deutscher Schallplattenpreis 1984, Otello d'Oro performer prize, 1995, Golden Merkur best performance award, 1996, Mozart medal of Mex., 1991; named Kammersänger of Vienna State Opera, 1988, prof. of the Music and Art Hochschule Stuttgart, Germany. Address: c/o Elene Tschaidse Opern-und Konzertagentur Tal 15 80331 Munich Germany

ARAKAKI, DENNIS A. state representative; b. Honolulu, Oct. 18, 1947; m. Michiko Toba-Arakaki; children: Jamie Leigh, Cammie Michelle. BA, U. of Hawaii, 1970. Co-propr. Venus Dry Cleaners, 1966—73; comp. supr. Pks. and Recreation City & County of Honolulu, 1971—85; planning mgr. Kapiolani Health, 1989—98; cons. Kokua Kaliha Valley Family Svcs., 1999; cmty. health planner Kokua Valley Comp. Family Svcs., 1999—. Commr. State Comm. on Children and Youth, 1970—76; bd. mem. Kalihi Valley Neighborhood Bd. #16, 1980—85; del. Dem. State and Nat. Conv., 1988; majority fl. leader, 1989—90; commr. Hawaii Commn. for Nat. and Cmty. Svcs., 1998—. Chair Hershey Youth Program, 1983—; co-chair Childern and Youth Day and Month, 1994—, Child Protection Reform, 1996—, Long Term Care Financing, 1996—2000; co-convenor Keiki Caucus, 1988—. Mem.: Kalihi Bus. Assn. (bd. mem.), Filipino C. of C., Hawaii Coun. of Chs. (bd. mem.), Hawaii Children's Cancer Found., Kalakaua Lions Club. Democrat. Office: State Capital Rm 436 415 S Beretania St Honolulu HI 96813 Fax: 808-586-6051. E-mail: reparakaki@capitol.hawaii.gov.*

ARAKAWA, KASUMI, physician, educator; b. Toyohashi, Japan, Feb. 19, 1926; came to U.S., 1954, naturalized, 1963; s. Masumi and Fayuko (Hattori) A.; m. Juen Hope Takahara, Aug. 27, 1956; children: Jane Riet, Kenneth Luke, Amy Kathryn. MD, Tokyo Med. Coll., 1953; PhD, Showa U., Tokyo, 1984. Diplomate Am. Bd. Anesthesiology. Intern Iowa Meth. Hosp., Des Moines, 1954-56; resident in internal medicine U. Kans. Med. Ctr., Kansas City, 1956-58, instr. anesthesiology, 1961-64, from asst. prof. to prof., 1964-94; prof. emeritus, 1994—; Arakawa Disting. prof. anesthesiology U. Kans. Med. Ctr., Kansas City, 1990, Kasumi Arakawa professorship, 1994, prof. emeritus, 1994—. Clin. assoc. prof. U. Mo.-Kans. City Sch. Dentistry, 1973— ; dir. Kansas City Health Care, Inc. Fulbright scholar, 1954; nat. cons. to surgeon gen., USAF, 1990—. Recipient Outstanding Faculty award Student AMA, 1970 Fellow Am. Coll. Anesthesiology; mem. Assn. Univ. Anesthetists, Acad. Anesthesiology (pres. 1986-87), Japan-Am. Soc. Midwest (v.p. 1965, 71). Home: 2913 W 112th St Leawood KS 66211-3088 Office: Univ Med Ctr 3901 Rainbow Blvd Kansas City KS 66160-0001

ARAKAWA, PETER STANHOPE, artist, educator; b. New Brunswick, N.J., Feb. 4, 1956; s. David Masaru Arakawa and Dorothy Hisako Umezawa. Student, Hampshire Coll., 1975-76; BFA, Rutgers U., 1982, MFA, 1984. Asst. in printmaking Oxbow Arts Inst., Saugatuck, Mich., 1981; asst. in ceramics Rutgrs U., New Brunswick, 1982-84, 88, Nantucket Island (Mass.) Sch. Design and Art, 1985-86; instr. drawing and sculpture Raritan Valley C.C., Somerville, N.J., 1987-88; instr. ceramics, drawing and painting Middlesex C.C., Edison, N.J., 1996, instr. painting, 2000, instr. painting and drawing, 2001, instr. drawing, 2003. One-man shows include Johnson & Johnson Internat. Hdqrs., New Brunswick, N.J., 1990, Middlesex County Coll., Edison, N.J., 1997, Highland Park (N.J.) Pub. Libr., 1998, B. Beamesderfer Gallery, Highland Park, 2000, The Francis E. Parker Meml. Home, New Brunswick, N.J., 2001, Simon Gallery, Morristown, N.J., 2001, Berrie Ctr., Ramapo Coll., Mahwah, NJ, 2002, B. Beamesderfer Gallery, Highland Park, NJ, 2002, Hunterdon Mus. Art, Clinton, NJ, 2002; exhibited in group shows at The Morris Mus., Morristown, N.J., 1988, 2003, Newark Pub. Libr., 1991, Montclair (N.J.) State U., 1995, Hunterdon Mus. Art, Clinton, N.J., 1998, 2002, 03, Artsforum, N.Y.C., 1999, Monmouth Mus., Lincroft, N.J., 2001 (prize), 2002, 03, Gary Snyder Fine Art, N.Y.C., 2002, N.J. State Mus., Trenton, 2002, Walter Wickiser Gallery, N.Y.C., 2003; represented in pub. and pvt. collections. Recipient purchase award Jane Voorhees Zimmerli Art Mus., 1984, Johnson & Johnson Corp., 1990, others; painting fellow Rutgers U., 1981, Pollock-Krasner Found., 1994; Printmaking fellow Rutgers Ctr. for Innovative Paper and Printmaking, New Brunswick, 2002. Avocations: trout fishing, plastic model building, stamp collecting. Home: 210 Horizon Dr Edison NJ 08817-5759 Studio: 1185 Stockton Pl North Brunswick NJ 08902-3238 E-mail: ptwopainters@aol.com.

ARAKI, TAKAHARU, editor, mineralogist, crystallographer, consultant; b. Kyoto, Dec. 22, 1929; arrived in U.S., 1965; s. Shiro and Kiyo (Ohmori) Araki; m. Motoko Yoshizawa, Nov. 23, 1958 (dec. Apr. 1993); m. Marlene A. Baughman, Jan. 31, 2000. MS, Kyoto U., Japan, 1957, DSc, 1961. Rsch. assoc. Kyoto U., Japan, 1960-62; sr. chemist Tekkosha Corp., Mitaka, Tokyo, Japan, 1962-65, 68-70; rsch. fellow U. Minn., Mpls., 1965-67, 70-71; sr. rsch. scientist U. Chgo., 1971-82; sr. rsch. assoc., cons. McGill U., Montreal, Can., 1983-85; sr. assoc. editor Chem. Abstracts Svc., Columbus, Ohio, 1985-94, pvt. contractor, 1995-99. Contbr. articles to profl. jours. Named for mineral arakiite. Fellow: Mineral. Soc. Am.; mem.: Friends of Mineralogy, Am. Crystallographic Assn., Am. Chem. Soc., Am. Ceramic Soc. Home: 4612 182d Pl SW Lynnwood WA 98037-4625

ARAL, MUSTAFA MEHMET, civil engineer educator; b. Ankara, Turkey, Feb. 26, 1945; came to U.S., 1978; s. Faruk and Bedia Aral; m. Sevg H. Aral (div. 1991); 1 child, Sinan K. MSCE, PhD, Ga. Inst. Tech. Asst. prof. Mid. East Tech. U., Ankara, Turkey, 1971-76, prof., 1976-78; assoc. prof. civil engring. Ga. Inst. Tech., Atlanta, 1978-95, prof., 1995—. Mem. bd. sci. advisors ASTDR/DHHS, Atlanta, 1990-92; dir. NATO Advanced Study Inst., 1995. Author: Ground Water Modeling in Multilayer, 1990, Advances in Groundwater Pollution Control and Remediation, 1996; mem. editl. bd. Jour. Engring. Sci. and Health, 1990—, Jour. Hydrologic Engring.; contbr. articles to profl. jours. Advisor, coach YMCA, Atlanta, 1980-90. NATO fellow, 1974, 78. Mem. ASCE, Am. Geophys. Union, Am. Water Resources Assn., Am. Inst. Hydrology. Office: Ga Tech Inst Sch Civil Environ Engring Atlanta GA 30332

ARAMBEL, PHYLLIS ANN, elementary education educator; b. Hays, Kans., Aug. 12, 1952; d. Melvin Joseph and Barbara Ann (Bennett) Eichman; m. Joseph John Arambel, Apr. 7, 1984; children: Jeremy Sage, Spenser Miles, Alexander Joseph. BEd, U. No. Colo., 1974; postgrad. Cert. elem. tchr., Colo., Wyo. Primary tchr. Queensland (Australia) Dept. Edn., 1974-76; 1st grade tchr. Gertrude Burns Elem. Sch., Newcastle, Wyo., 1976-77; western U.S. ednl. cons. Rand McNally, San Francisco, 1977-78; K-2 Mountain Sch. tchr. Poudre R-1 Dist., Ft. Collins, Colo., 1978-79; constrn. supr. CAR-MEL, Inc., Pierre, S.D., 1979-80; 3rd grade tchr. Sweetwater County Sch. Dist. #1, Rock Springs, Wyo., 1980-87; ret., 1987. Pres./founder The Children's Discovery Found., Rock Springs, 1991—, sec., 1991-93, fundraising chairperson, 1991—, pres., 1996—, exec. dir. Discovery Station, 1997—; pres./founder Westridge Sch. PTO, Rock Springs, 1996-97; founder Westridge Hist. Soc., 1998-2002; coord. Sch. Boxtops for Edn., 1996-2002. Tiger Cub Group coach Boys Scouts Am., Rock Springs, 1996-97; soccer team parent, 1992-97, asst. registration commr., 1996-99, newsletter editor and pub., 1996—, coach, 1997—; wolf den leader Cub Scouts, Rock Springs, 1997-98, bear leader, 1998-99, webelos leader, 1999-2001; founder, chair Cmty. Carnival, 2003; sec. bd. dirs. Competitive Soccer League, 2003; level D soccer coach, Wyo., 1996—, competitive soccer coach, 2003—. Mem. Overland Sch. Hist. Soc. (founder 2000—), Girl Scouts U.S. (life), Phi Sigma Iota (life). Avocations: travel, gardening, photography, camping, scrapbooking. Home: 904 Bonners Way Rock Springs WY 82901-4362 E-mail: jarambel@wyoming.com.

ARAMBURU, JOHN RICHARD, lawyer; b. Spokane, Wash., Mar. 8, 1945; s. Victor B. Aramburu and Virginia (Westacott) Scarpelli; m. Lesa Rae French, Aug. 23, 1991. BA, U. Wash., 1967, JD, 1970. Bar: Wash. 1970, U.S. Dist. Ct. (we. dist.) Wash. 1970, U.S. Ct. Appeals (9th cir.) 1970, U.S. Dist. Ct. (ea. dist.) Wash. 1973. Assoc. Irving M. Clark, Jr., Seattle, 1970-78; prin. Law Offices of J. Richard Aramburu, Seattle, 1978—. Author: Real Property Deskbook, 1985, rev. edit., 1996. Bd. dirs. Allied Arts of Seattle, 1987-89; legal chair Wash. Environ. Coun., Seattle, 1982-88. Mem. Wash. State Bar (chairperson CLE com. 1977, chairperson environ. and land use law sect. 1978), Avocations: squash, skiing, river rafting. Office: Law Offices of J Richard Aramburu 505 Madison St Ste 209 Seattle WA 98104-1138

ARAMINI, MICHAEL JOSEPH, software engineer; b. Hoboken, N.J., Sept. 18, 1958; s. John Martin and Arlene Joan Aramini. BS, Stevens Inst. Tech., 1980; MS, U. Ill., 1981; postgrad., U. Mass., 1982-84, Rutgers U., 1984-85. Mem. tech. staff AT&T Bell Labs., Piscataway, N.J., 1980-82; software engr. Matrix Instruments, Inc., Orangeburg, N.Y., 1983-87, Apollo Computer, Inc., Chelmsford, Mass., 1987-89; software design engr. Hewlett-Packard Co., Chelmsford, Mass., 1989-95, Andover, Mass., 1995—99, Agilent Technologies, Inc., 1999—2000; sr. software engr. NuGenesis Technologies, Inc., Westboro, Mass., 2000—01; scientific programmer veridian MIT Lincoln Lab., Lexington, 2002, software design engr. veridian, 2003—. Mem.: Amateur Telescope Makers of Boston, Internat. Dark-Sky Assn., N.H. Astron. Soc., Sigma Xi. Avocations: astronomy, photography. Home: 843 Wellman Ave North Chelmsford MA 01863-1367

ARAMS, FRANK ROBERT, electronics company executive; b. Danzig; came to U.S., 1939, naturalized, 1945; s. Richard and Alice (Frank) A.; m. Edith Knoll, July 24, 1952; children: Mark, Ronald. BEE, U. Mich., 1947; MS in Applied Physics, Harvard U., 1948; MS in Bus. Mgmt, Stevens Inst. Tech., 1953; PhD in Electrophysics, Poly. U. N.Y., 1961. Group leader RCA Microwave div., Harrison, N.J., 1948-56; cons. AIL div. Eaton Corp., Melville, N.Y., 1956-65, head electrooptics and infrared dept., 1965-71; v.p. LNR Communications, Inc., Hauppauge, N.Y., 1971-99, also bd. dirs.; mgmt. cons., patent tech. expert, 2000—. Author: Infrared-to-Millimeter Wave Detectors, 1972; contbr. articles to profl. jours. Served with AUS, 1942-44. Fellow IEEE. Home: 37 School House Ln Great Neck NY 11020-1322

ARANA, MARIE, editor, writer; b. Lima, Peru, Sept. 15, 1949; came to U.S., 1959; d. Jorge Enrique and Marie Elverine (Clapp) Arana; children: Hilary Walsh, Adam Williamson Ward; m. Wendell B. Ward Jr., Dec. 18, 1971 (d. Dec. 1998); m. Jonathan Yardley, Mar. 21, 1999. BA in Russian Lang. & Lit., Northwestern U., Evanston, Ill., 1971; cert. scholarship Mandarin lang., Yale U. in China, Hong Kong, 1976; MA in Linguistics, Brit. U. Hong Kong, 1977. Lectr. linguistics Brit. U. Hong Kong, 1978-79; sr. editor Harcourt Brace Jovanovich, Pubs., NYC, 1980-89, Harcourt Brace Jovanovich, Washington, 1980—89; v.p., sr. editor Simon & Schuster Pub., Washington, 1989—92, Simon & Schuster Pubs., NYC, 1989-92; writer, editor Washington Post, 1992-99, Book World editor-in-chief, 1999—. Bd. dir. Ctr. Policy Rsch., Washington, 1994-99; Hoover Media fellow Stanford U., 1997, 2000. Author: American Chica: Dos Mundos, Una Infacia, 2003, The Writing Life: Writers on How They Think and Work, 2003, American Chica: Two Worlds, One Childhood, 2001, Spanish edit., 2003; editor: The Writing Life: Writers on How they Think and Work, 2003; Studies in Bilingualism, 1978. Finalist National Book award, 2001, PEN OIR award, 2001; recipient award for excellence in editing, ABA, 1985, Christopher award for excellence in editing, 1986, Books for a Better Life award, 2001. Mem. Nat. Assn. Hispanic Journalists (bd. dir. 1996-99), Nat. Book Critics Cir. (bd. dir. 1996-2000). Office: Washington Post 1150 15th St NW Washington DC 20071-0002

ARANDA, JUAN M., JR., cardiologist, medical educator; b. San Juan, P.R., May 26, 1965; s. Juan M. and Carmen Aranda; m. Alysia L. Hines; children: Jennifer, Eva, Sarah. BS in Chemistry, U. P.R., 1987, MD, 1991; subsplty. degree in cardiology, U. South Fla., 1997; subsplty. degree in internal medicine, VA Med. Ctr., San Juan, 1994. Diplomate Am. Bd. Internal Medicine, Am. Bd. Cardiovascular Medicine. Resident VA Med. Ctr., San Juan, 1991—94; fellow in cardiology U. South Fla., Tampa, 1994—97; asst. prof. medicine divsn. cardiology U. Fla., Gainesville, 1997—. Chief cardiology fellow U. South Fla., 1996—97; cons. VA Med. Ctr., Gainesville, 1997— ; assoc. dir. heart transplant program U. Fla., Gainesville, 2001—. Contbr. articles to profl. jours. Named one of Best Drs., 2001—02. Fellow: Am. Coll. Cardiology (Fla. chpt. govt. rels. com., 3d party reimbursement com.); mem.: Alachua County Med. Soc., Internat. Soc. Heart Lung Transplantation. Avocation: golf. Office: U Fla 1600 SW Archer Rd Box 100277 Gainesville FL 32610

ARANGO, JORGE SANIN, architect; b. Bogota, Colombia, Nov. 29, 1916; s. Fernando Arango and Maria Sanin A.; m. Elizabeth Leighton, 1944; 1 child, Peter; m. Judith Brooks Wolpert, Dec. 14, 1951; children: Richard, Virginia; m. Penelope Corey, Aug. 18, 1976. Student, Universidad Catolica de Chile Sch. Architecture, 1935-42, Harvard Grad. Sch. Design, 1942-43. Head archtl. firm Arango & Murtra, Bogota, 1946-59; prof. architecture and urban design Nat. U., Bogota, 1945-47; vis. prof. Sch. Architecture U. Calif., Berkeley, 1956, 58; Pub. bldgs. dir. Colombia, 1948-49; pres. Colombian Soc. Architects, 1946-51, Colegio Engrs. and Architects of Colombia, 1955. Co-creator (with Le Corbusier) basic plan for devel. Bogota, 1948. Author: (with C. Martinez) Architecture in Colombia, 1951, The Urbanization of the Earth, 1970, Segunda Edad Media, 1994, Ecophila: The Future is Waiting, 2000, Villa Sofia, 2003; mem. bd. contbrs. Miami Herald, 1984-91. Recipient Excellence in Design awards Miami and Fla. chpts. AIA, 1967 Mem. AIA (mem. emeritus). Achievements include being invited to U.S. by State Dept. and Mus. Modern Art, N.Y.C. Home: 5153 SW 71st Pl Miami FL 33155-5640 E-mail: jorge.arango@gte.net.

ARANGO, RICHARD STEVEN, architect, graphic and industrial designer; b. Bogota, Colombia, June 30, 1953; s. Jorge Arango Sanin and Judith (Wolpert) Arango; m. Maria Francesca Violich, Aug. 1977; children: Ruy Rafael, Antonia. AB in Architecture with honors, U. Calif., Berkeley, 1976, MArch, 1980. Registered architect. Prin. Arango Architects, Coconut Grove, Fla., 1993—. John K. Branner traveling fellow U. Calif.-Berkeley grad. div., 1980. Contbr. articles to profl. jours.

ARANI, ARDY A. professional sports marketing executive, lawyer; b. Bklyn., July 14, 1954; BBA, U. Miami, 1975; JD, Loyola U., New Orleans, 1978. Mktg. dir. Internat. Sports Mktg. Ltd., London, 1978-80; mng. dir., CEO Championship Group Inc., Atlanta, 1980—. Mem. editl. bd. Sport Mktg. Quar.; contbr. articles to profl. jours. Bd. dirs. Atlanta Sports Coun., 1986-97, Atlanta Olympic Organizing Com., 1988-96; chmn. TEAM Ga. Recipient Reggie Promotions award, Promotion Mktg. Assn. Am., 1999. Mem. Am. Mktg. Assn., Sports Car Club of Am. (Recognition award 1988), Nat. Assn. Stock Car Auto Racing, Am. Motorcycle Assn., Internat. Motor Sports Assn. Home: PO Box 80489 Atlanta GA 30366-0489 Office: Championship Group Inc 3690 N Peachtree Rd Atlanta GA 30341-2340

ARANOVICH, GREGORY, chemical engineering educator, researcher; b. Ordzonikidze, USSR, July 11, 1952; came to U.S., 1994; s. Lev Aranovich and Sofia Tiomkina; m. Tatyana Brodskaya, June 16, 1990; 1 child, Valeriya. BS, Inst. Elec. Engring., Moscow, 1975; PhD, Moscow Inst. Steel and Alloys, 1981; DS, Moscow State U., 1992. Engr. Inst. Earth Physics, Moscow, 1975-78; rschr. Inst. Steel and Alloys, 1978-81; sr. rschr. Inst. Chromatography, Moscow, 1981-89; leading rschr. Moscow State U., 1989-94; prin. rsch. scientist (rsch. prof.) in chem. engring. Johns Hopkins U., Balt., 1994—2002, rsch. prof., 2002—. Contbr. 140 articles to profl. jours. Home: 56 Taverngreen Ct Baltimore MD 21209-5304 Office: Johns Hopkins U Dept Chem Engring 3400 N Charles St Baltimore MD 21218-2680 E-mail: aranovich@jhu.edu.

ARANT, EUGENE WESLEY, lawyer; b. North Powder, Oreg., Dec. 21, 1920; s. Ernest Elbert and Wanda (Haller) A.; m. Juanita Clark Flowers, Mar. 15, 1953; children: Thomas W., Kenneth E., Richard W. BS in Elec. Engring, Oreg. State U., 1943; JD, U. So. Calif., 1949. Bar: Calif. 1950. Mem. engring. faculty U. So. Calif., 1947-51; pvt. practice L.A., 1950—51; patent atty. Hughes Aircraft Co., Culver City, Calif., 1953-56; pvt. practice L.A., 1957—2001, Lincoln City, Oreg., 2001—. Author articles. Mem. La Mirada (Calif.) City Council, 1958-60; trustee Beverly Hills Presbyn. Ch., 1976-78. Served with AUS, 1943-46, 51-53. Mem. ABA, Am. Intellectual Property Law Assn., State Bar Calif., Lincoln City Rotary. Democrat. Home: 100 NE Indian Shores Lincoln City OR 97367 Office: Lincoln Tech Bldg Lincoln City OR 97367 E-mail: gwapat@wcn.net.

ARANTES, JOSÉ CARLOS, industrial engineer, educator; b. Itamogi, Brazil, May 10, 1955; came to U.S., 1986; s. Antonio A. and Parizina (Marinzeck) A.; m. Nadia Maria Monti, July 26, 1986; children: Ellen Kay, Alex José, Isa Carolina. MSc in Indsl. Mgmt., Katholieke U. Leuven, Belgium, 1982; PhD in Indsl. Engring., U. Mich., 1991. Product engr. Kodak Co., Brazil, 1979-81; instr., cons. U. Campinas, Brazil, 1983-86; rsch. asst., tchg. asst. U. Mich., Ann Arbor, 1987-90; asst. prof. U. Cin., 1991-98; assoc. prof. EAESP-FGV, Brazil, 1997-98. Cons. Criminal Justice Task Force, Cin., 1992; co-founder, v.p. ImpEx Co.; cons. mgmt. sci., supply chain Anheuser-Busch, 1998—. Author: Degeneracy in Gereralized Networks, 1990; contbr. articles to profl. jours. 2d lt. Brazilian armed forces, 1973-75. Grantee Westinghouse Environ., Cin., 1992, County of Hamilton, Cin., 1992, Fernald Environ. Mng. Co., Cin., 1993-94, Revco, Inc., 1996-97, CVS, Inc., 1997. Mem. Sci. Rsch. Soc., Inst. Indsl. Engrs., Inst. Mgmt. Sci., Ops. Rsch. Soc. Am. Home: 361 Meadowbrook Dr Ballwin MO 63011-2414 E-mail: jarantes@aol.com., jose.arantes@anheuser-busch.com.

ARAPOFF, JOHN RICHARD, artist; b. Beverly, Mass., June 1, 1935; s. Alexis Paul and Catherene (Green) A.; m. Rita Marie Crossman, Nov. 20, 1960; children: Anton A., Christopher J., Jason T., Alexis A.; 1 child from previous marriage, Steven P. Student, Vesper George, 1956-58. Artist Mass. Beverage Jour., Boston, 1958-60; fashion illustrator May D&F, Denver, 1961; artist A.B. Hirschfield, Denver, 1962; v.p., creative dir. South Shore Pub. Co., Scituate, Mass., 1965-88; pres. J. Arapoff Images, Marshfield, Mass., 1989—. Artist, fine arts restorer, resident restorer South Shore Arts Ctr., Cohasset, Mass., 1964—; artist North River Arts Soc., Marshfield, 1975—; pub. dir. Mass. Cultural Coun., Marshfield, 1993-97. Exhibited in group shows at Denver Mus. Art, Central City (Colo.) Art Gallery, Colo. State Coll., South Shore Arts Festivals (prize 1986, 87), Scituate Arts Festival (1st prize 1966), North River Arts Soc. (Popular prize 1988), Boston Arts Festivals, Scituate Pub. Libr. (with cartoonist Paul Szep); one man shows include Thayer Gallery, Braintree, Mass., Habitat Belmont, Mass., Belmont Hill Sch., Artica Gallery, Duxbury, Mass., South Shore Conservatory of Music Staircase Gallery; represented in permanent collections Strohs Beer, Morris Alper & Sons, Am. Automobile Assn., Realtron Multi-List, Thayer Acad., Fitchburg State Coll., Tabloid Shippers, KTB Assocs., Taunton Regency Hotel, T.J. Clark Advt., Downtown Harvard Club, Boston, Mill Pond Tennis Club, 4 wall murals on Cuttyhunk Island, Mass., Tri City Fitness Ctr.; numerous restorations including U.S. Postal Dept. and major librs. and comml. and indsl. settings. Mem. Am. Assn. Mus., Nat. Hist. Trust, Assn. Preservation Tech., Am. Inst. Conservation. Avocations: tennis, golf, biking. Office: PO Box 1080 Marshfield MA 02050-1080

ARAT, METIN, retired psychiatrist; b. Istanbul, Turkey; came to U.S., 1968; s. Esat and Saime A.; m. Sevinc Ulku, Feb. 29, 1952; children: Mustafa, Deger, Isil, Nese. MD, Med. Sch. Ankara, Turkey, 1951. Diplomate Turkish Bd. Psychiatry and Neurology. Commd. lt. Turkish Army, 1951, advanced through grades to col., 1968; intern Gulhane Mil. Med. Acad. and Sch. Medicine, Ankara, Turkey, 1952, resident, 1956-59; mil. physician Turkish Army, 1951-68, resigned, 1968; physician III, clin. dir. Farmington (Mo.) State Hosp., 1968-74; chief psychiatry VA Med. Ctr., Battle Creek, Mich., 1974-79, chief of staff Marion, Ind., 1979-97; ret., 197. Mem. Am. Psychiat. Assn. (life mem.), Turkish-Am. Cultural Assn. Fla. (pres.). Moslem. Avocations: gardening, photography. E-mail: marat1@tampabay.rr.com.

ARAZI, LORRI ROSENBERG, real estate broker; b. Bowling Green, Ohio, Apr. 5, 1958; d. Benjamin George and Peggy Lee (Hull) Rosenberg; m. Yaacov (Kobi) Arazi, June 22, 1986 (div. Dec. 1993). BA, U. Calif. Berkeley, 1979; postgrad., Antioch U., San Francisco, 1981-82; MA, San Francisco State U., 1994. Dist. mgr. ClothesFreak, Berkeley, 1977-79; asst. buyer Emporium Dept. Stores, San Francisco, 1980-82, asst. store mgr., 1983-84; dist. mgr. Maquette Leather Fashions, Tel Aviv, 1985-86; pers. mgr. Ross Stores, Walnut Creek, Calif., 1986-88; resdl. real estate broker Pacific Union, Oakland, Calif., 1993—. Democrat. Jewish. Avocations: internat. travel, gardening, art and music appreciation, film, photography. Office: Pacific Union 1900 Mountain Blvd Oakland CA 94611

ARBABI, SAMAN, surgeon, researcher; b. Aug. 28, 1966; s. Esmail and Shahnaz Arbabi; m. Sielen S. Namdar, Aug. 16, 1998; 1 child, Kavon. BA, U. Calif., 1988, MD, 1992; MPH, U. Wash., 2001. Diplomate Am. Bd. of Surgery, 1998, in surgical critical care Am. Bd. of Surgery, 2001. Resident in surgery U. of Wash., Seattle, 1992—97, rsch. fellow, 1997—2001; fellow critical care and trauma Harborview and U. Wash., Seattle, 1999—2001; asst. prof. surgery U. Mich. Health Sys., Ann Arbor, Mich., 2002—. Mem.: Am. Bd. Surgery (Best Regional Paper award 2001), Surg. Infection Soc. (assoc.; membership com. 2001). Office: University of Michigan Health System 1C421 UH Box 0033 1500 E Medical Driv Ann Arbor MI 48109 Office Fax: 734-936-9657. Personal E-mail: sarbabi@med.umich.edu. E-mail: sarbabi@med.umich.edu.

ARBEIT, ROBERT DAVID, physician; b. Jersey City, Aug. 16, 1947; s. Sidney Robert and Marie (Gluck) A.; m. Susan Abelson, Dec. 20, 1970; children: Jeffrey, Miriam. BA, Williams Coll., 1968; MD, Yale U., 1972. Diplomate Am. Bd. Internat. Medicine, Am. Bd. Infectious Disease. Intern then resident Yale-New Haven Hosp., New Haven, 1972-74; clin. assoc. Nat. Cancer Inst., Bethesda, Md., 1974-76; fellow Sidney Farber Cancer Inst., Boston, 1976-79; staff physician VA Med. Ctr., Boston, 1979-2000, asst. chief med. svcs., 1989-91, dir. infectious diseases rsch., 1991-2000, assoc. chief of staff, rsch., 1991-2000; asst. prof. Sch. Med. Boston U., 1979-87, assoc. prof. Sch. Med., 1987-95, prof. Sch. Med., 1995-2000, adj. prof. Sch. Med., 2001—; dir. med. ops. Cubist Pharms., Lexington, Mass., 2001—02, exec. med. dir., 2002—03; exec. dir. clin. rsch. Paratek Pharms., Boston, 2003—. Contbr. articles to profl. jours. and books. Fellow ACP, Infectious Diseases Soc. Am.; mem. Am. Soc. for Microbiology, Phi Beta Kappa, Alpha Omega Alpha. Avocation: personal computers. Office: Paratek Pharms Inc 75 Kneeland St Boston MA 02111

ARBEIT, WENDY SUE, researcher, writer; b. Jersey City, May 14, 1941; d. Carl and Ethel Arbeit. BA, Temple U., 1963; MA, Columbia U., 1968. Author: What Are Fronds For?, 1985, Baskets in Polynesia, 1990, Tapa in Tonga, 1994; editor: (CD) Arts of the Pacific Islands, 2000; assoc. editor Pacific Arts, 1992-98, co-editor, 1999-2002; prodr./dir. (video): From Mortal to Ancestor: The Funeral in Tonga, 1994, Pacific Passages, 1997. Mem. Pacific Arts Assn., Tongan History Assn., Cmty. TV Prodrs. Assn. (pres. 1997-2000).

ARBEITER, JOAN, artist, educator; b. N.Y.C., May 8, 1937; d. David and Winifred Arden (Lembke) Berman; m. Jay David Arbeiter, June 15, 1958 (div. May 1990); children: Lisa B. Arbeiter, Gail Arbeiter Goldstein. BA, CUNY, 1959; MFA, Pratt Inst., 1981. Lic. art tchr., N.Y., N.J. Tchr. N.Y.C. Sch. Sys. Bd.

Edn., 1959-63; dir. Joan Arbeiter Studio Sch., Metuchen, N.J., 1976-90; instr. art, coord. founds. Ducret Sch. Art, Plainfield, N.J., 1978—, instr. color and design, 1978—, instr. art history, 1981—, instr. art appreciation, 1983—; workshop instr. N.J. Teen Arts Festival, 1998—. Juror various art orgns., N.J., 1981—; cons. Ednl. Testing Svc., Princeton, N.J., 1988; curator traveling art exhibit Age As a Work of Art., Plainfield, Boston, N.Y.C., 1985-86, Lives and Works, N.Y.C., 2000; artist-in-residence Sch. Arts, N.J., 1995-2001; presenter paper, slides Coll. Art Assn. Conf., San Antonio, 1995, N.Y.C., N.Y., 2003; presenter, moderator Nat. Mus. Women in the Arts, Wash., 1997, Artists Talk on Art, N.Y.C., 2000; bd. dirs. Women's Studio Ctr. One-woman shows Ceres Gallery, N.Y.C., 1985, 87, 89, 93, 97, 2000, Columbia U., N.Y.C., 1986, Wagner Coll., S.I., N.Y., 1992, Douglass Coll. Ctr., New Brunswick, N.J., 1992, 96, Stony Brook-Millstone Watershead Assn. Gallery, Pennington, N.J., 1991 Union County Coll., Crawford, N.J., 1999; exhibited in group shows:Ramapo Coll., Mahwah, 1980, Brookdale Coll., Lincroft. N.J., 1980, Westbeth Gallery, N.Y.C., 1980. Ceres Gallery, 1983, N.Y. Feminist Art Inst., N.Y.C., 1985-88, Monmouth Mus., Lincroft, N.J., 1996, Kingsbourgh Comm. Coll., Brooklyn, N.Y., 1999, Soho 20 Gallery, N.Y.C., 1990, 98, Kunstler Forum, Bonn, Germany, 1999 Environ Protection Agency, Wash., D.C.,2001-02, Noyes Mus. Oceanville, N.J., 1995, 1998, Krasdale Corp. Gallery, Bronx, N.Y., 1995; represented in permanent collections at Noyes Mus., Oceanville, N.J., Fairmount Chem., Newark, CSR Group Architects and Builders-Leon Cohen, Nutley, N.J., JFK Med. Ctr., Edison, N.J., Muhlenberg Regional Med. Ctr., Plainfield, N.J., First Presbyterian church, Metuchen, N.J., MS Found., N.Y.C., 1995, also pvt. collections; co-author Lives and Works: Talks with Women Artists, Vol. 2, 1999. Recipient 1st place all media award Metuchen Cultural Arts Commn. Art Exhbn., 1988, best in show award Artists League Ctrl. N.J., 1989, AIA award Hunterdon Arts Ctr. N.J., 1996, excellence award Manhattan Arts Mag., 2000; grantee Vt. Studio Colony, 1987. Mem. Coll. Art Assn., Women's Caucus for Art, Art Table, Ceres Gallery, Varo Registry, Women's Studio Ctr. N.Y.C., (hon. mem. bd. dirs.) Alpha Beta Kappa. Studio: 41 Victory Ct Metuchen NJ 08840-1430

ARBER, WERNER, microbiologist; b. Gränichen, Switzerland, June 3, 1929; married; 2 children. Ed., Aargau (Switzerland) Gymnasium, Eidgenössische Technische Hochschule, Zurich, 1949—53. Asst. Lab. Biophysics, U. Geneva, 1953—58, docent, then extraordinary prof. molecular genetics, 1962—70; research assoc. dept. microbiology U. So. Calif., 1958—59; vis. investigator dept. molecular biology U. Calif., Berkeley, 1970—71; prof. microbiology U. Basel, Switzerland, 1971—96, rector, 1986—88. Co-recipient Nobel Prize for physiology or medicine, 1978. Mem.: Internat. Coun. Sci. (pres. 1996—99), Nat. Acad. Scis. (assoc.). Office: Biozentrum der Universität 70 Klingelbergstrasse CH-4056 Basel Switzerland

ARBIB, MICHAEL ANTHONY, neuroscientist, educator, computer scientist; b. Eastbourne, U.K., May 28, 1940; came to U.S., 1961; s. John R. and Helen (Arbib) A.; m. Prue Hassell, Dec. 29, 1965; children: Phillipa Jane, Benjamin Giles. BSc with honors, U. Sydney, 1960; PhD in Math., MIT, 1963. Mem. faculty Stanford (Calif.) U., 1965-70, assoc. prof. elec. engring., 1969-70; adj. prof. psychology, prof. computer and info. sci. U. Mass., Amherst, 1970-86, chmn. dept. computer and info. sci., 1970-75; dir. Ctr. for Systems Neurosci., 1974-86, dir. Cognitive Sci. Program, 1980-82, dir. Lab. Perceptual Robotics, 1982-86; prof. biomed. engring., neurobiology, psychology U. So. Calif., L.A., 1986-94, prof. computer sci., elec. engring., 1986—, dir. Ctr. for Neural Engring., 1987-94, dir. USC Brain Project, 1994—, chair computer sci., 1999-2000, Fletcher Jones prof. computer sci., prof., 1999—. Vis. prof. U. Western Australia, Perth, 1974, 96, 99, 2000, Technion, Israel, 1975, Washington U., St. Louis, 1976, U. Edinburgh, 1976-77, U. Calif., Irvine, 1980; vis. scientist Inst. Cybernetics, Barcelona, spring 1985, Cognitive Scis. Inst., U. Calif., San Diego, 1985-86; vis. lectr. U. New South Wales, Australia, 1962, 65, 68, Mont. State U., summers, 1963, 65, Imperial Coll. London, 1964; Gifford lectr. in natural theology U. Edinburgh, Scotland, 1983; John Douglas French lectr. Brain Rsch. Inst., UCLA, 1993; lectr. tours to U.S., USSR, Japan, Australia and China. Author: Brains, Machines and Mathematics, 1964, 2d. edit., 1987, Theories of Abstract Automata, 1969, The Metaphorical Brain, 1972, Computers and the Cybernetic Society, 1977, 2d edit., 1984, In Search of the Person, 1985, The Metaphorical Brain 2, 1989; (with others) Topics in Mathematical System Theory, 1969, System Theory, 1974, Discrete Mathematics, 1974, Conceptual Models of Neural Organization, 1974, Arrows, Structures and Functors, 1975, Design of Well-Structured and Correct Programs, 1978, A Basis for Theoretical Computer Science, 1981, A Programming Approach to Computability, 1982, Algebraic Approaches to Program Semantics, 1986, The Construction of Reality, 1986, From Schema Theory to Language, 1987, An Introduction to Formal Language Theory, 1988, Neural Organization: Structure, Function, Dynamics, 1997; editor: The Handbook of Brain Theory and Neural Networks, 1995, (with others) Algebraic Theory of Machines, Languages and Semigroups, 1968, Neural Models of Language Processes, 1982, Competition and Cooperation in Neural Nets, 1982, Adaptive Control of Ill-Defined Systems, 1983, Vision, Brain and Cooperative Computation, 1987, Dynamic Interactions in Neural Networks: Models and Data, 1988, Visuomotor Coordination: Amphibia, Comparisons, Models, and Robots, 1989, Natural and Artificial Parallel Computation, 1990, Visual Structures and Integrated Functions, 1991, Neuroscience: From Neural Networks to Artificial Intelligence, 1993, Neuroscience and the Person, 1999, Computing the Brain, A Guide to Neuroinformatics, 2001; contbr. articles to profl. jours. Mem. IEEE, AAAS, Soc. Neurosci., Neurosci. and the Person. Office: U So Calif Brain Project Los Angeles CA 90089-0001

ARBIT, BERYL ELLEN, legal assistant; b. L.A., Aug. 16, 1949; d. Harry A. and Norma K. (Michelson) A. BA, UCLA, 1970. From legal asst. to sr. legal asst. O'Melveny & Myers, LLP, L.A., 1977—. Guest lectr. atty. asst. tng. program UCLA, 1991. Mem. UCLA Atty. Asst. Alumni Assn. (bd. dirs. 1980-82), Alpha Omicron Pi (treas. Greater L.A. alumnae chpt. 1993—), Nu Lambda (corp. bd. pres. 1978-80, chpt. adv. 1976-78). Avocations: travel, theater, needlework, bridge. Office: O'Melveny & Myers, LLP 400 S Hope St Los Angeles CA 90071-2899 E-mail: barbit@omm.com.

ARBIT, BRUCE, direct marketing executive, consultant; b. Milw., Nov. 16, 1954; s. Saul B. and Naomi (Chase) A.; m. Tanya Arbit, children: Oren, Carmiel, Eugene. Student, U. Haifa, Israel, U. Wis. Founder, co-mgr., dir. A B Data, Ltd., Milw., 1977—. Chmn., bd. dirs. Integrated Mail Industries Ltd.; bd. dirs. State Fin. Bank, Asset Devel. Group, Inc., Integrated Mail Industries Israel, Ltd. Gen. campaign chmn., bd. dirs. Milw. Jewish Fedn. Keshet, Milw. Jewish Day Sch., Habonim Dror Found.; mem. United Jewish Appeal Young Leadership Cabinet; mem. Wexner Heritage Found., United Israel Appeal., Non-profit Mailers Fedn., Campaign Cabinet Devel. Corp. for Israel; trustee United Israel Appeal; bd. dirs., Jewish Telegraphic Agy.; bd. govs. Jewish Agy. for Israel. Recipient Benjamin E. Nickoll Young Leadership award Milw. Jewish Fedn., 1989. Mem. Direct Mktg. Assn., Israel Direct Mktg., Wis. Direct Mktg. Assn. (Direct Marketer of Yr. award 1997), Am. Assn. Polit. Cons. Office: AB Data Ltd 8050 N Port Washington Rd Milwaukee WI 53217-2600

ARBITELLE, RONALD ALAN, elementary school educator; b. Danbury, Conn., Aug. 1, 1949; s. Roxy Joseph and Janet Helen (Otto) A.; m. Ruth Ann Young, Aug. 6, 1977. BS, Western Conn. State U., 1971, MS, 1973; postgrad. in adminstrn., supervision, So. Conn. State U., 1983. Tchr. Shelter Rock Sch. Danbury (Conn.) Bd. Edn., 1977—. Mem. text selection coms., Shelter Rock Sch., Danbury. Active Shelter Rock PTO. Mem. NEA, Conn. Edn. Assn., Danbury Edn. Assn. Avocations: bowling, swimming, coin, baseball card and Jim Beam car collecting. Home: 7 Belmont Cir Danbury CT 06810-6426 Office: Shelter Rock Sch Shelter Rock Rd Danbury CT 06810

ARBITER, ANDREW RICHARD, accountant; b. Merrick, N.Y., May 12, 1958; s. Harold Irving and Marlene (Balfan) A.; m. Joan Sanalitro, Nov. 21, 1981; children: Heather, Aaron. BS in Acctg., U. Bridgeport, 1980; MBA in Taxation, Hofstra U., 1981. CPA, N.Y., N.C.; cert. secondary bus. tchr. N.Y. Supr. Deloitte & Touche (formerly Deloitte Haskins & Sells), Woodbury, N.Y., 1981-85; prof. Dowling Coll., Oakdale, N.Y., 1985-86; dir. Andrew Richard Arbiter CPA, Massapequa, N.Y., 1985—; pres. Compucount Systems, Inc., Merrick, N.Y., 1988—; co-founder The Tax Shop, Massapequa, N.Y., 1995—; founder, pres. Omni Fin. Planning Inc., 1999—. Registered rep. Royal Alliance Assn., Inc., N.Y.C., 2000—; N.Y. State lic. life and health agt. Author (computer software) lease analysis software for FASB-13 analysis, copyright, 1980; contbr. articles to mags. Councilman Day Care Coun. of Nassau County, Nassau, N.Y., 1979; v.p. CHADD (Children and Adults with Attention Deficit Disorders) of Nassau County, N.Y., fin. and oversight com., Landover, Md.; trustee Beth Sholom Ctr. of Amityville and the Massapequas, N.Y., 1996—; mem. budget and fin. com. Massapequa Pub. Sch. Bd., Massapequa, N.Y. Recipient Cert. of Qualification, Computer Assocs. Internat., San Jose, Calif., 1989. Mem. AICPA, N.Y. State Soc. CPAs, Inst. Mgmt. Accts., Nat. Soc. Pub. Accts., N.C. Assn. CPAs, N.Y. Sport Fishing Fedn., NRA (affiliate), Nat. Conf. of CPA Practitioners. Republican. Jewish. Avocations: sport fishing, target shooting, photography. Office: 601 Broadway Massapequa NY 11758-5025 E-mail: andrew@arbitercpa.com.

ARBOGAST, BRIAN, information technology executive; married; 2 children. BSc in Computer Sci., U. Waterloo, Can. Intern IBM Corp., Phillips Info. Sys., Systemhouse Graphics; from software developer to corp. v.p. Microsoft, Redmond, Wash., 1986, corp. v.p. Office: One Microsoft Way Redmond WA 98052-6399

ARBOGAST, GORDON WADE, systems engineer, educator, consultant, retired military officer; b. Charleston, SC, May 24, 1942; s. Valentine and Teresa Louise Arbogast; m. Dorothy Sheryl Blackwell, Mar. 5, 1966; children: Annette Marie, Christina Theresa, Valentine Scott. BS, U.S. Mil. Acad., 1963; MSEE, MSIM, Ga. Inst. Tech., 1971; PhD, Clemson U., 1986. Commd. 2d lt. U.S. Army, 1963, advanced through grades to col., 1983, ret., 1990; head, assoc. prof. dept. engring. U.S. Mil. Acad., 1986-89; assoc. dir. engring. and tech. Def. Comm. Agy., 1989-90; v.p. sys. tech. Pacific Bell, San Ramon, Calif., 1991—94; prof. Jacksonville (Fla.) U., 1994—. Prin. scientist Contel, Chantilly, Va., 1990; instr., cons. Learning Tree Internat., Reston, Va., 1994—. Contbr. articles to profl. jours. Lector, eucharistic min. Cursillo Cath. Ch., 1988—. Decorated Legion of Merit, Bronze Star, Air medal, Def. Superior Svc. medal. Mem.: Armed Forces Comm.-Electronics Assn. (pres. West Point chpt. 1987—89), Inst. Indsl. Engrs. (sr.), West Point Soc. of North Fla. (pres. 1998—2001). Achievements include initiating systems engineering at U.S. Military Academy and major work in transforming Defense Communications Agency to Defense Information Systems Agency. Home: 9937 Orchard Hills Rd Jacksonville FL 32256 Office: Jacksonville U Davis Coll Bus 2800 University Blvd N Jacksonville FL 32211-3394 E-mail: garboga@ju.edu.

ARBOLEYA, CARLOS JOAQUIN, lawyer, broker; b. Havana, Cuba, Aug. 16, 1958; came to U.S., 1960; s. Carlos Jose and Marta Aurora (Quintana) A. ABA, Miami Dade C.C., 1977; BBA in Fin., U. Miami, 1980, MBA in Fin., 1981, JD, 1987. Bar: Fla. 1989, U.S. Ct. Appeals (D.C. cir.) 1990. From teller to br. mgr. Barnett Bank South Fla. N.A., North Miami Beach, 1975-84; realtor, assoc. Cervera Real Estate, 1980—; pres. Owner's Box Promotions, 1993-95; owner Carlos J. Arboleya, Jr., P.A., Coconut Grove, 1988—. Adv. bd. Exec. Nat. Bank, 1994—, Linda Ray Infant Ctr., 1990—; mem 20th Anniversary Grand Prix of Miami com., 2002; bd. dirs. Pvt. Industry Coun. Jobs for Miami; Hispanic adv. com. U. Miami Sports Mktg., 1992—95. Bd. dirs. Greater Miami Tennis Found., 1995, U. Miami Ear Inst., 1993; vice chma. planning adv. bd. City of Miami, 1993-95, 98-99, chmn. 1995-98, chmn. code enforcement bd., 1990-91, vice chmn. 1989-90; asst. scoutmaster Boy Scouts Am.; participant joint civilian orientation conf. U.S. Dept. Def., 1995; pres. Cocogrove Villas Condominium Assn., 1998—; trustee United Way, Miami-Dade, 2000-01. Named One of 12 Good Men of Miami, Ronald McDonald House, 2000-01. Mem. ABA, Nat. Soc. Hispanic MBAs, Nat. Eagle Scout Assn., Cuban Am. Bar Assn., Builders Assn. South Fla., Am. Title Ins. Co., Attys. Title Ins. Fund, Inc., Fla. Bar Assn., Latin Bus. Assn., Latin Builders Assn., Hispanic Law Students Assn., Coral Gables C. of C., Greater Miami C. of C. (sports coun., chmn., homestead motorsports complex com., 1994-97, co-chmn. existing events com., 1992-94), Leadership Miami (exec. com. 1990-93, task force 1984-88, Coconut Grove Jaycees, Phi Delta Phi, Delta Sigma Pi (Outstanding Alumni award 1982). Republican. Roman Catholic. Office: Carlos J Arboleya Jr PA 2550 S Dixie Hwy Coconut Grove FL 33133-3137

ARBOUR, ALGER, professional hockey coach; b. Sudury, Ont., Can., Nov. 1, 1932; m. Claire Arbour; children: Julie, Janice, Jo-Anne, Jay. Defenseman Detroit Red Wings, Chgo. Black Hawks, Toronto Maple Leafs, St. Louis Blues of Nat. Hockey League, 1953-71; coach St. Louis Blues, 1970, 71-72, asst. gen. mgr., 1971; coach N.Y. Islanders, Uniondale, 1973-86, 1988-94, v.p. hockey opers., 1995—. Mem. 4 Stanley Cup championships teams, including Detroit Red Wings, 1954, Chgo. Black Hawks, 1961, Toronto Maple Leafs, 1964, 62; coach 4 Stanley Cup championship teams, 1980-83. Office: NY Islanders 1255 Hempstead Turnpike Nassau Vets Meml Colis Uniondale NY 11553

ARBUCKLE, AVERIL DOROTHY (COOKIE ARBUCKLE), healthcare facility administrator; b. Bklyn., May 9, 1934; d. Arnold Drummond and Mildred (Engel) Lloyd; m. Robert V. Arbuckle (dec. Mar. 1990); children: Gregory, Jody, Leann, Kathleen, Mary. Student, Lamson Coll., Phoenix, 1968-71, Colo. State U., 1964-68, U. Ctrl. Okla., 1974, Okla. State U., Oklahoma City, 1976. Flight attendant Pacific Southwest Airlines, San Diego, 1952, Am. Airlines, Chgo., 1953; social worker Dept. Human Svcs., Oklahoma City, 1972-89; mem. task force Gov.'s Task Force on AIDS, Oklahoma City, 1987-88; exec. dir. Other Options, Inc., Oklahoma City, 1989—. Mem. adv. bd. Carter Hospice, Carter Home Health, Red Rock Mental Health Homeless Com., Okla. AIDS Coalition; cons. HIV-AIDS State of Okla., 1985—96; dir. Friends Food Pantry Okla. City. Author: Aids for HIV-AIDS, 4 edit. 1989 (award 1992), Accessing the System Directory, 1995, Physician Compassionate Use Directory, 1995. Bd. dirs. AIDS Support Program, 1986-88, Okla. Epilepsy Found., 1989-93; com. chmn. Cmty. Action Agy., Oklahoma City., 1994-95; bd. mem. Ven Cor Hosp. Ethics Com., 1998; HIV Care Consortium, Okla., 1998, 99, Okla. City Housing Com. HIV/AIDS, 1998, 99; Nat. Fin. Planning Bd. for Disabilities, 1998, 99; dir. fellowship award Okla. Lions Svc. Found., 2002. Recipient Jefferson award Presbyn. Health Found., Oklahoma City, 1990, Jacqueline Kennedy award Am. Inst. Pub. Svc., Washington, 1990, Five Who Care award Gannett Found., Arlington, Va., 1992, merit award GLB Polit. Caucus, Oklahoma City, 1993, Book of Yr. award Woman's Front Page News, 1993, Friends of Libr. Book award City of Oklahoma City-Moore Libr., 1989, Cmty. Contbn. award, 1994, Individual award U. Okla. Coll. Pub. Health and Alumni Assn., 4th Annual Pub. Health award for excellence U. Okla. Health Scis. Ctr., 1999. Mem. Case Mgmt. Soc. Am., Case Mgmt. Soc. Ctrl. Okla.. Lions (v.p. Bethany Helping Hands 2002. Lion of the Yr. 2002). Democrat. Avocations: writing, lecturing, consulting, horticulture, geology. Home: PO Box 36 Bethany OK 73008-0036 Office: Other Options Inc 5915 NW 23rd St Ste 219 Oklahoma City OK 73127-1254

ARBUTHNOT, ROBERT MURRAY, lawyer; b. Montreal, Quebec, Can., Oct. 23, 1936; s. Leland Claude and Winnifred Laura (Hodges) A.; m. Janet Marie O'Keefe, Oct. 6, 1968; children: Douglas, Michael, Mary Kathleen, Allison Anne. BA, Calif. State U., San Francisco, 1959; JD, U. Calif., San Francisco, 1966. Bar: Calif. 1967, U.S. Dist. Ct. (no. and cen. dists.) Calif. 1967, U.S. Ct. Appeals (9th cir.) 1967, U.S. Supreme Ct. 1975. Assoc. trial lawyer Rankin & Craddick, Oakland, Calif., 1967-69; assoc. atty. Ericksen, Arbuthnot, Brown, Kilduff & Day, Inc., San Francisco, 1970-73, ptnr., 1973-80, chmn. bd., mng. dir., 1980—. Gen. counsel CFS Ins. Svcs., San Francisco, 1990—; pro tem judge, arbitrator San Francisco Superior Ct., 1990—; lectr. in field. Bd. regents St. Mary's Coll. High Sch., Berkeley, Calif., 1988-91. With U.S. Army, 1959-62. Recipient Honors plaque St. Mary's Coll. High Sch., 1989. Mem. Internat. Assn. of Ins. Counsel, No. Calif. Assn. of Def. Counsel, Def. Rsch. Inst., Assn. Trial Lawyers Am., San Francisco Lawyers Club. Avocations: boating, family activities. Office: Ericksen Arbuthnot Kilduff Day & Lindstrom Inc 260 California St Ste 1100 San Francisco CA 94111-4300 E-mail: eakdlsf@aol.com.

ARBUZ, JOSEPH ROBERT, lawyer; b. N.Y.C., Nov. 23, 1949; s. Jose Hernan Cortes and Rachel Dweck Arbuz; m. Millicent Luck Fornah July, 1978 (div.); 1 child, Christina. BA, Fla. State U., 1972, MS in Pub. Adminstrn., 1975; JD, Howard U., 1977; MDiv, Southwestern Bapt. Sem., 1981; postgrad. in theology, Westminster Theol. Sem., 1995; D Divinity, Cohen U. & Theol. Sem., 2000. Bar: Fla. 1978, U.S. Ct. Mil. Appeals 1983, U.S. Dist. Ct. (so. dist.) Fla. 1986, U.S. Ct. Appeals (11th cir.) 2000, U.S. Supreme Ct., 2000; lic. min. So. Bapt. Ch., 1982—. EEO investigator Smithsonian Instn., Washington, 1985; asst. atty. gen. Atty. Gen., Miami, Fla., 1986; pvt. practice Miami, Fla., 1987-90, Miami Beach, Fla., 1994—. Evangelism Gambrell St. Bapt. Ch., Ft. Worth, 1980; pastor Biscayne Bapt. Ch., Miami, 1989; choir mem. U. Bapt. Ch., Coral Gables, Fla., 1994-97; performer Miami Christmas Pageant, Miami, 1994, 96; asst. staff judge advocate. 1st lt. Signal Corps., U.S. Army, 1972-74; capt. USAF, 1982-84. J.F.K. Tchg. scholar Miami-Dade C.C., Miami, 1969. Mem. Am. Immigration Lawyer's Assn., Atty. Title Ins. Fund, South Fla. Hispanic C. of C., Dade County Bar Assn., Lions Club, Delta Theta Phi. Democrat. Presbyterian. Avocations: exercise, theatre, reading, church activities. Office: 1400 Lincoln Rd # 304 Miami Beach FL 33139 Fax: 305-675-0190. E-mail: joearbuz@aol.com.

ARCAK, MURAT, engineering educator, consultant; b. Istanbul, Turkey, Sept. 29, 1973; arrived in U.S., 1996; s. Teoman and Bihter Arcak. BS, Bogazici U., Istanbul, Turkey, 1996; MS, U. Calif., Santa Barbara, Calif., 1997, PhD, 2000. Tchg. asst. U. Calif., Santa Barbara, 1996—97, rsch. asst., 1997—2000, rsch. engr., 2000—01; asst. prof. Rensselaer Polytechnic Inst., Troy, NY, 2001—. Cons. United Technologies, Hartford, Conn., 2001—. Co-author: System Theory: Modeling, Analysis and Control, 1999; editor: IEEE Control Sys. Soc., 2000—; contbr. articles to profl. jours. Recipient Career award, NSF, 2003. Mem.: IEEE, Soc. Indsl. and Applied Math. Avocations: photography, cinematography. Office: Rensselaer Polytechnic Inst 110 8th St Troy NY 12180 E-mail: arcakm@rpi.edu.

ARCE, A. ANTHONY, psychiatrist, educator; b. San Juan, P.R., June 13, 1923; s. Angel and Juana (Baez) A.; m. Malvene Balkind, Oct. 7, 1971; children Alan I. Scheer, Judith Ann Scheer, Michael Anthony Arce. BS, Washington and Jefferson Coll., 1942; MD, Temple U., 1946. Diplomate: Am. Bd. Psychiatry and Neurology; certified in adminstrv. psychiatry. Intern Mercy Hosp., Bay City, Mich. and; Frankford Hosp., Phila., 1946-47; dir. Aguadilla (P.R.) Dist. Hosp., 1947-48; chief health officer Utuado, P.R., 1950-51; physician U.S. Mil. Acad., West Point, N.Y., 1951-52; med. officer Pa. R.R., 1952-53; practice medicine Yonkers, N.Y., 1953-59; resident psychiatrist Payne Whitney Clinic, N.Y.C., 1959-62; assoc. dir. psychiatry Grasslands Hosp., Valhalla, N.Y., 1962-67; dir. psychiatry Lincoln Hall Sch., Lincolndale, N.Y., 1967-68; dir. Bur. Aftercare Services N.Y. State Dept. Mental Hygiene, 1968-71; dir. Manhattan Psychiat. Center, Ward's Island, N.Y., 1971-76, Hahnemann Community Mental Health and Mental Retardation Center, Phila., 1976-84; pvt. practice medicine specializing in psychiatry, 1962—; prof. psychiatry, dep. chmn. dept. mental health svcs. Hahnemann U., 1976-85, prof., chmn., 1985-87, prof., dir. amb. svcs., 1987-91; prof., dep. chmn. dept. psychiatry Med. Coll., U. Pa., Phila., 1991-96; chmn. dept. behavioral medicine Girard Med. Ctr., Phila., 1996—. Mem. president's council N.Y. U. Sch. Social Work, 1963-66; bd. dirs. P.R. Family Inst., N.Y.C., 1970-72. Served with AUS, 1943-46, 48-50. Mem. Am. Coll. Mental Health Adminstrs., Am. Coll. Psychiatrists, Am. Psychiat. Assn. (chmn. task force continuing care), Phila. Psychiat. Soc., Am. Assn. Psychiat. Adminstrs. (treas., pres.). Home: 1416 Academy Ln Elkins Park PA 19027-2515 Office: Girard Med Ctr 2ADC 8th St & Girard Ave Philadelphia PA 19122-9999 E-mail: aarce@nphs.com.

ARCE, PEDRO L. economic development executive, banker; b. Guayaquil, Ecuador, Oct. 7, 1966; came to U.S., 1970; s. Pedro Luis Arce and Jeannette Rosa Arce Barahona; children: Jacquelin, Yesenia. BA, U. Mass., 1989; MA, Cambridge Coll., 1993; MS, Boston U., 1995. V.p. Fleet Bank, Boston, 1990-2000; dir. econ. devel. Nuestra Comunidad Devel. Corp., Boston, 2000—02; v.p. cmty. devel. Bankworth Group, Andover, Mass., 2002—. Pres. Adelante Inc., Lawrence, Mass., 1998—; co-chmn. MACDC/Econ. Boston; bd. dirs. devel. com. Cmty. Works Inc., Lawrence. Office: Bankworth Group 61 Main Street Andover MA 01810

ARCE, PHILLIP WILLIAM, hotel and casino executive; b. N.Y.C., June 25, 1937; s. Joseph F. and Margaret (Degnan) A.; m. Dorothy Fiss, June 25, 1966; children: Joseph, William, Serena. Student, U. Notre Dame, 1955-56; AA, San Diego Jr. Coll., 1958; student, San Diego State U., 1958-60, San Diego State U., 1960-62, LaSalle Law Sch., 1963-65. Various positions Del Webb Corp., Las Vegas and Reno, Nev., Oahu, Hawaii, 1963-75; exec. Caesars Palace, Las Vegas, 1975-78; pres. Frontier Hotel, Las Vegas, 1978-84; corp. v.p., v.p. mktg., sr. v.p. Dunes Hotel & Country Club, Las Vegas, 1985-88; hotel and gaming specialist Arce Cons., Las Vegas, 1988—. Tchr. hotel div. U. Nev., Las Vegas, 1966-67, 1976-77 Mem. exec. com. Boulder Dam Area coun. Boy Scouts Am., 1976-88; vice chmn. United Way So. Nev., 1968-70; founder, chmn. Las Vegas Events, Inc., 1980-89; pres. Easter Seals Nev., 1974-76, pres. first nat. telethon, 1975; bd. dirs. Air Force Acad. Found., 1982-89. Served with USMC, 1962. Recipient numerous awards including Appreciation awards Easter Seals, 1972, 73, United Way, 1975, Silver Beaver Boy Scouts Am., 1984 Mem. Am. Hotel and Motel Assn. (bd. dirs. 1979-82), Nev. Hotel and Motel Assn. (founder, pres. 1980, Hotelier of Yr. award 1981), Las Vegas C. of C. (dir. 1979-85, pres. 1984). Republican. Roman Catholic. Home: 4243 Ridgecrest Dr Las Vegas NV 89121-4949 also: Colo Belle Hotel & Casino PO Box 77000 Laughlin NV 89028-7000

ARCENEAUX, M(ARTIN) THOMAS, lawyer; b. Lake Charles, La., Oct. 8, 1951; s. Felix Felicien and Betty Gordon (Gunn) A.; m. Elizabeth Montgomery, June 1, 1993; children: Anna Marie, Martin Thomas Jr., Jordan M. Lewis. BS, La. State U., 1972, JD, 1976. Bar: La. 1976, U.S. Dist. . (we. dist.) La. 1976, Tex. 1978, U.S. Ct. Appeals (5th cir.) 1980, U.S. Supreme Ct. 1997, U.S. Dist. Ct. (so. Dist.) Tex. 2003. Law clk. to presiding judge U.S. Dist. Ct., Shreveport, La., 1976—78; assoc. Vinson & Elkins, Houston, 1978—79; ptnr. Beard, Arceneaux & Sutherland, Shreveport, 1979—81; land mgr., gen. counsel Despot Exploration Inc., Shreveport, 1981—83; sole practice Shreveport, 1983—87; ptnr. Davidson, Nix, Arceneaux, Jones & Askew, Shreveport, 1987—96; city atty. City of Shreveport, 1995—2003; pvt. practice Shreveport, 1995—2003; assoc. Blanchard, Walker, O'Quin & Roberts, Shreveport, 2003—; instr. La. State U.-Shreveport Paralegal Inst., 1996—; town atty. Town of Blanchard, 1996—. Exec. coun. Ark.-La.-Tex. Regional Export and Tech. Ctr., 1995—. Articles editor Law Rev., 1975-76. Mem. Shreveport City Coun., 1982—90, chmn., 1986—87, chmn. audit fin. com., 1985—86; mem. Caddo Parish Rep. Exec. Com., 1987—91; bd. dirs. Shreveport Symphony Orch., 1992—95, Holy Angels Residential Facility, 1991—95. Named Outstanding Young Man of Yr., Shreveport Jaycees, 1985; emeritus award, Aquinas Coll., 2002. Mem. La. Lawyers for Life, Rotary Club Shreveport (dir. 2000-01). Republican. Avocations: weight-lifting, writing, reading, singing. Home: 828 E Kings Hwy Shreveport LA 71105-3017

ARCENEAUX, WILLIAM, historian, educator, association official; b. Scott, La., Aug. 19, 1941; s. Teddy and Regina (Begnaud) A.; m. Patricia Boozman; children: Ted, Angelle, Leah, Scott. BA, U. La., Lafayette, 1962; MA, La. State U., 1965, PhD, 1969; LHD, Loyola U., 1982. Instr. La. State U., 1966-67; asst. prof. Northwestern State U., Natchitoches, La., 1967-69; assoc. prof., chmn. dept. history So. U., New Orleans, 1969-72; exec. dir. La. Coordinating Council for Higher Edn., Baton Rouge, 1972-75; commr. higher edn. La. Baton Rouge, 1975-87; pres. La. Assn. Ind. Colls. and Univs., 1987—. Chmn. CSLA, Inc., Lajeunesse & Assocs., Inc. Author: Acadian General-Alfred Mouton and the Civil War, 1972, 2d edit., 1981, No Spark of Malice: The Murder of Martin Begnaud, 1999; editor: Postsecondary Education in Transition: Planning for Change in Louisiana, 1975. Bd. dirs., chmn. Student Loan Mktg. Assn., 1979-97; chmn. Devel. French in La. Found., 1993—; exec. com. La. Pub. Broadcasting, chair La. Bicentennial Com. of Baton Rouge. Decorated chevalier L'Ordre de la Pleiade, Association Internationale des Parlementaires de Langue Francaise, L'Ordre des Palmes Academique (France); named one of 100 Young Leaders of Academy Change mag., 1978; recipient Jefferson Davis medal UDC, E.T. Dunlap medal Southern Okla. State U. Mem.: La. Hist. Assn., Fgn. Relations Assn. New Orleans, Am. Hist. Assn., Nat. Assn. Ind. Coll. and Univ. State Execs., Plimsol Club, City Club of Baton Rouge (bd. govs.), Country Club of La., Phi Alpha Theta, Omicron Delta Kappa. Roman Catholic. Office: La Assn Ind Colls and Univs Ste 104 320 Third St Baton Rouge LA 70801 E-mail: bill@laicu.org.

ARCHAMBAULT, JOALLYN, museum administrator, anthropologist; b. Claremore, Okla., Feb. 13, 1942; BA, U. Calif., Berkeley, 1970, MA, 1974, PhD, 1984. Dir. Am. Indian Program Nat. Mus. Natural History, Washington, 1986—; lectr. in Native Am. studies U. Calif., Berkeley, 1976—79, chair ethnic studies dept. Coll. of Arts and Crafts; rsch. assoc. Ctr. for the Study of Race, Crime and Social Policy, Cornell U., Ithaca, NY, 1980—82; asst. prof. anthropology U. Wis., Milw., 1983—86. Vis. faculty Oglala Lakota Coll., Pine

Ridge, SD, Calif. State U., Hayward, U. N.Mex., Navajo C.C., Tsaile, N.Mex., Mills Coll., Oakland, Calif., Johns Hopkins U., Balt.; lectr. in field. Contbr. ; curator (exhbn.) Plains Indian Arts: Change and Continuity, 1987, 100 Years of Plains Indian Painting, 1989, Indian Basketry and Their Makers, 1990, Seminole!, 1990. Fellow Doctoral fellow, Ford Found., 1970—75. Mem.: Plains Anthropol. Soc., Studies in Am. Indian Lit., Soc. for Applied Anthropology, Native Am. Art Studies Assn., Coun. for Mus. Anthropology, Anthropol. Soc. of Washington, Am. Ethnol. Soc., Am. Anthropol. Assn. (mem. commn. on Native Am. reburial). Office: National Museum of Natural History 10th St and Constitution Ave NW Washington DC 20560

ARCHAMBAULT, LEE JOSEPH, astronaut; b. Oak Park, Ill., Aug. 25, 1960; s. Lee and Mary Ann Archambault; m. Kelly Renee Raup; 3 children. BSc with hon. in Aero. & Astronautical Engring., U. Ill., Urbana, 1982, MSc with hon. in Aero. & Astronautical Engring., 1984. Commd. 2d lt. USAF, 1985, advanced through grades to lt. col., various assignments, 1985—90; assigned to Operation Desert Sheild/Desert Storm, Saudi Arabia, 1990—91, Saudi Arabia, 1991—92, 1992—94; various assignments USAF, 1995—98; astronaut NASA, Houston, 1998—. Mem. acad. adv. com. U. Ill. Aero. & Astronautical Engring. Dept. Decorated Flying Cross USAF, Meritorious Svc. medal with 1 oak leaf cluster, Air medal with 2 oak leaf clusters, Aerial Achievement medal with 4th oak leaf cluster, Commendation medal with 1st oak leaf cluster, Kuwaiti Liberation medal. Mem.: Soc. Exptl. Test Pilots, U. Ill. Alumni Assn., Order of Daedalians. Avocations: weightlifting, golf, running, ice hockey. Office: Astronaut Office CB NASA Johnson Space Center Houston TX 77058

ARCHAMBAULT, LOUIS, sculptor; b. Montreal, Que., Can., Apr. 4, 1915; s. Anthime Sergius and Annie (Michaud) A.; m. Mariette Provost, June 7, 1941; children: Aubert, Eloi, Eve, Patrice. Student, Coll. Jean-de-Brebeuf, Montreal; BA, U. Montreal, 1936; Diploma, Ecole des Beaux Arts, Montreal, 1939. Former mem. faculty Musée des Beaux-Arts, Montreal, Ecole des Beaux-Arts, Montreal, U. B.C., Vancouver, Can., U. Que., Montreal, Concordia U., Montreal. Works exhibited Internat. Sculpture Exhbn., Festival of Gt. Britain, London, 1951, 10th Triennale, Milan, Italy, 1954, 28th Biennial, Venice, 1956, 11th Triennale, Milan, 1957, Brussels Universal and Internat. Exhbn., 1958, Pitts. Internat., 1958, Internat. Exhbn. Contemporary Sculpture, Expo 67, Montreal, 11th Biennial, Middelheim, 1971, Musee des Beaux Arts, Montreal, 1993; several one-man shows in Can., France, Eng.; represented in permanent collections Nat. Gallery, Ottawa, Musée du Que., Quebec City, Musée d'art contemporain, Montreal, Musee des Beaux Arts, Montreal, Museo Internazionale della Ceramica, Faenza, Italy, Can. Imperial Bank of Commerce, Montreal, Art Gallery Ont., Toronto, Sun Life Bldg., Toronto, Upland Air Terminal, Ottawa, Place des Arts, Montreal, Malton Airport, Toronto, Scarborough Coll., Toronto, Macdonald Block, Queen's Park, Toronto, Centre D'Accueil, Longueuil, Que., Centre Hospitalier, Chateauguay, Que., Fed. Food and Drug Bldg., Longueuil, Can. Council Art Bank, Ottawa, Winnipeg Art Gallery, Justice Ct. Bldg., Quebec City, Faculté de Medicine Veterinaire U. de Montreal, also others; subject of TV documentary: Searching for Louis Archambault, 1999. Decorated officer Order Can., 1968; recipient Allied Arts medal Royal Archtl. Inst. of Can., 1958; Recipient Diplome d'honneur Can. Conf. Arts, 1982; Canadian Govt. fellow for travel in France, 1953-54; Can. Council grantee, 1959, 62, 69 Achievements include Academician Royal Canadian Acad. Arts. Died Jan. 27, 2003.

ARCHANGELSKY, DMITRY A, application developer, researcher; b. Kharkov, Ukraine, Nov. 29, 1960; s. Cecilia V and Avenir L Archangelsky; m. Svetlana V Loganova; 1 child, Alexander D. PhD, St.Petersburg State U., 1993. Assoc. prof. Tver State U., Tver, Russia, 1995—99; cons. Global Consulting Group, Haverhill, Mass., 1999—. Contbr. articles to profl. jours. Grant, Internat. Sci. Fund, Russian Fund of Fundamental Researches. Mem.: Am. Math. Soc. (assoc.), NY Acad. Of Sciences (assoc.). Achievements include invention of algorithm of person identification using blood vessel picture; algorithm of understanding of a natural language in a given context; development of a system for computer text book development; research in polinomial algorithm for BR-nets.

ARCHER, CHALMERS, JR., retired education educator; b. Tchula, Miss., Apr. 21, 1938; s. Chalmers Sr. and Eva Alcola (Rutherford) A. AS, Saints Jr. Coll., 1969; BS, Tuskegee Inst., 1972, MEd, 1974; PhD, U. Ala., 1980; cert., MIT, 1980; PhD, Auburn U., 1979. Asst. to the pres. Saints Coll., Lexington, Miss., 1968-72; asst. v.p. Tuskegee (Ala.) Inst., 1972-83; prof. No. Va. C.C., Manassas, 1983-2001, prof. emeritus, 2001. Author: Growing Up Black in Rural Mississippi (recipient Miss. Inst. of Arts and Letters award for Nonfiction), Green Berets in the Vanguard: Inside Special Forces, 1953-1963; contbg. editor: The Jackson Advocate; contbr. articles to profl. jours. and newspapers. Mem. Dem. Spkr.'s Bur. for Clinton/Gore Re-election Campaign. Recipient Nat. Edn. Articulation Model, Conf. on Blacks in Higher Edn., Washington, 1986. Mem. Rotary (county transportation commnr.). Democrat. Baptist. Avocations: academic and community program development, motivational speaking, writing. Home: 7885 Flager Cir Manassas VA 20109-7435 E-mail: drarcher@aol.com.

ARCHER, DAVE, artist; b. San Luis Obispo, Calif., Jan. 15, 1941; s. Palmer Stewart and Ellen Margaret Nelson; m. Michaelle Hillary Nelson, Nov. 15, 1969 (div. Apr. 1977); children: River, Forest. Student, Phil Paradise, Santa Rosa Jr. Coll., 1960. Artist, Roseburg, Oreg. One-person shows include Hayden Planetarium, N.Y., 1990, Omniversum, The Hague, The Netherlands, 1989, AT&T World Hdqs., N.Y., 1990, Nihon Garo Galleries, Japan, 1997 ; inventor high-voltage elec. painting. E-mail: dave@davearcher.com.

ARCHER, DENNIS WAYNE, lawyer, former mayor; b. Detroit, Jan. 1, 1942; s. Ernest James and Frances (Carroll) A.; m. Trudy Ann DunCombe, June 17, 1967; children: Dennis Wayne, Vincent DunCombe BS, Western Mich. U., 1965; JD, Detroit Coll. Law, 1970; LLD (hon.), Western Mich. U., 1987, Detroit Coll. Law, 1988, U. Detroit, 1988, John Marshall Law Sch., 1991, Gonzaga U., 1991, U. Mich., 1994; D in Pub. Svc. (hon.), Ea. Mich. U., 1994. Bar: Mich. 1970. Tchr. spl. edn. Detroit Bd. Edn., 1965-70; assoc. Gragg & Gardner, 1970-71; ptnr. Hall, Stone, Allen, Archer & Glenn, P.C., 1971-73, Charfoos, Christensen & Archer, P.C., 1973-85; assoc. justice Mich. Supreme Ct., 1986-90; ptnr. Dickinson, Wright, Moon, Van Dusen & Freeman, Detroit, 1991-93; chmn. Dickinson Wright PLLC, 2001—; mayor City of Detroit, 1994—2001; pres. Am. Bar Assn., 2003—04. Assoc. prof. Detroit Coll. Law, 1972-78; adj. prof. Wayne State U. Law Sch., Detroit, 1984-85; mem. Mich. Bd. Ethics, 1979-83; mem. adv. bd. U.S. Conf. Mayors, 1994—; bd. dirs. Nat. Conf. Black Mayors, 1994—; mem. intergovtl. policy adv. com. U.S. Trade Rep.; bd. dirs. Covisint, Compuware, Johnson Controls, Inc. Contbr. articles to legal jours. Bd. dirs. Legal Aid and Defenders Assn., Detroit, 1980-82, Nat. Conf. Black Mayors, 1994, CATCH, Henry Ford Health Sys.; co-chmn. Met. Detroit Cmty. Coalition for Dems., 1979-80; bd. trustees Olivet Coll., 1991-93; active numerous local Dem. campaigns, 1970-85; host local pub. svc. radio programs; co-chair platform com. Dem. Conv., 1996; pres. Nat. Conf. Dem. Mayors, 1996; mem. Nat. Com. on Crime Control and Prevention, 1995. Named Most Respected Judge in Mich. Mich. Lawyers Weekly Jour., 1990. Mem. ABA (ho. dels. 1979-93, chmn. drafting com. 1986-88, com. on scope and correlation of work sect. officers liaison 1987-90, chmn. gen. practice sect. 1987-88, chair commn. on opportunities for minorities in the profession 1987-91, sect. legal edn. and admissions to the bar, coun. mem. 1989-95, task force on profl. skills instrn. 1989-91, task force on law schs. and the profession, Narrowing The Gap, 1989-91, chmn. spl. com. prepaid legal svcs. 1981-83, chmn. sect. officers conf. 1988-90, resource devel. coun. 1988-91, bd. editors ABA Jour. 1988-94, bd. editors The Practical Litigator 1989-94, chmn. rules and calendar com. 1990-92, state del. 1990-96, pres. 2003), ATLA, Nat. Bar Assn. (pres. 1983-84), Am. Judicature Soc. (bd. dirs 1977-81), State Bar Mich. (pres. 1984-85), Wolverine Bar Assn. (pres. 1979-80), Detroit Bar Assn. (bd. dirs. 1973-75), Mich. Trial Lawyers Assn. (exec. bd. 1973-74), Econ. Club, Alpha Phi Alpha. Roman Catholic.

ARCHER, GLENN LEROY, JR., federal judge; b. Densmore, Kans., Mar. 21, 1929; s. Glenn LeRoy and Ruth Agnes (Ford) A.; m. Carole J. Thomas, 1990; children: Susan, Sharon, Glenn, Thomas. BA, Yale U., 1951; JD with honors, George Washington U., 1954. Bar: D.C. 1954. Asst. atty. gen. U.S. Dept. Justice, Washington, 1981-85; circuit judge U.S. Ct. Appeals (fed. cir.), Washington, 1985-94, chief judge, 1994-97, sr. cir. judge, 1997—. First lt. JAG Corps USAF, 1954—56. Republican. Methodist. Office: US Ct of Appeals Fed Circuit 717 Madison Pl NW Washington DC 20439-0002*

ARCHER, HUGH MORRIS, consulting engineer, retired manufacturing executive; b. Dover, N.J., June 22, 1916; s. Harvey George and Helen Thomson (Morris) A.; m. Mary Jane Reed, May 11, 1940; children: June, Ruth, Lucy. BEE, Rensselaer Poly. Inst., 1937; D Engring., Milw. Sch. Engring., 1990. Registered profl. engr., Mich. Rsch. engr. Detroit Edison Co., 1937-51; founder, ptnr. Archer-Reed Co., Dearborn, 1951-63; ind. cons. engr. Dearborn, Mich., 1951—; founder, chmn. bd. dirs. Spiratex Co., Romulus, Mich., 1954—2001. Chmn. Dearborn Bank and Trust Co., 1970-86, Alliance Fin. Corp., Dearborn, 1980-89; bd. dirs. Syncro Corp., Arab, Ala. Patentee in sci. instrumentation and mfg. processes. Active YMCA, Boy Scouts Am., others; bd. dirs. Greenfield Village Schs., 1948-52, Henry Ford Hosp., 1983-85; chmn. Fairlane Med. Ctr., 1980-85. Ensign USN, 1944-47, PTO, ETO. Recipient Gold award for engring. Affiliate Coun. Mich. Engrs., 1992. Mem. Dearborn Rotary Club (pres. 1957-58), Rotary Internat. (pres. 1989-90), Found. of Rotary Internat. (trustee 1990—). Republican. Presbyterian. Avocations: amateur radio, computer science, ancient technical books.

ARCHER, JAMES ELSON, engineering educator; b. Hedley, Tex., Dec. 1, 1922; s. James M. and Mary Minerva (Bolles) A.; m. Reta Faye Turner, Nov. 8, 1942; 1 son, James Elson. BS, Tex. Tech. U., 1947; PhD, Mass. Inst. Tech., 1950. Instr. Mass. Inst. Tech., 1950-52, Sloan fellow in indsl. mgmt., 1963-64; researcher Pitts. Plate Glass Co., Pitts., 1952-53, asst. dir., 1953-54, asso. dir., 1954-56, dir. research, 1956-62; mng. partner Archer Assos., Dallas, 1962-64; corporate dir. mgmt. systems Tex. Instruments, Dallas, 1964-68; prof. Tex. Tech U., Lubbock, 1968-95, prof. emeritus, 1995—. Served with USAAF, 1943-46. Home: 6208 Lynnhaven Dr Lubbock TX 79413-5332

ARCHER, JAMES G. lawyer; b. San Antonio, Tex., Jan. 16, 1936; BA, U. Ill., 1957, LLB, 1959. Bar: Ill. 1960, N.Y. 1994. Ptnr. Sidley & Austin Brown & Wood, N.Y.; ret. Mem. State bd. acctg. examiners, 1976-78. Mem. Order of Coif. Office: Sidley Austin Brown & Wood 10 S Dearborn St Chicago IL 60603

ARCHER, JOAN M. trade association administrator; b. Sioux Falls, S.D., Aug. 7, 1953; d. Wilbur Lewis and Beverly Jane Archer. BA in Econ., U. S.D., 1974; MA in Urban Studies, Mankato State U., 1978. Cert. assn. exec. Inst. Orgn. Mgmt. City planner City of Redfield, S.D., 1974-76; planning cons. S.M.S.Q., Northfield, Minn., 1977-78; city planner City of New Brighton, Minn., 1978-82; exec. v.p. Minn. Mfr. Housing Assn., St. Paul, 1983-88, Builders Assn. Minn., St. Paul, 1988-96; v.p. govt. rels. Minn. Bankers Assn., St. Paul, 1996-98; pres. Minn. Soft Drink Assn., St. Paul, 1998—. Bd. dirs. Minn. Govt. Rels. Coun., pres., 1998, 99; bd. dirs. coun. Girl Scouts Am., St. Croix Valley, 2d v.p., 1993-95; bd. dirs. Youth in Govt., 1998-2000. Mem. Minn. Soc. Execs. Assn. (bd. dirs., pres. 1995-96), Green Haven Women's Golf League (pres. 2001). Office: Ste 830 161 Saint Anthony Ave Saint Paul MN 55103-2300 E-mail: joan@mn.state.net.

ARCHER, KELLIE JO, education educator; b. Circleville, Ohio, Feb. 16, 1969; d. Paul Raymond and Leona Marie Lovenshimer; m. Brian Lee Archer. BA, Franklin Coll. of Ind., 1991; MAS, Ohio State U., 1993, PhD, 2001. Biostatistician Grant Med. Ctr., Columbus, Ohio, 1993—95, Pharmacia, Dublin, Ohio, 1995—96, Grant Med. Ctr., 1996—98; biostatistician & rsch. scientist Ohio State U., 1998—2002; asst. prof. Va. Commonwealth U., 2002—. Mem. Nat. Com. for Clin. Lab. Standards, Wayne, Pa., 2002—. Contbr. articles to profl. jours. Mem.: Am. Statis. Assn., Phi Kappa Phi. Office: Virginia Commonwealth University PO Box 980032 Richmond VA 23298 Office Fax: 804-828-8900. E-mail: kjarcher@vcu.edu.

ARCHER, LLOYD DANIEL, communications educator; b. Cromwell, Ind., May 15, 1942; s. Dallas Lloyd and Wilma Christine (Halsey) A.; m. Carol Sue Bonney, May 15, 1966; 1 child, Elisa Carol. BS, Ind. U., 1971, MS, 1973; EdS, U. Ga., 1992. Dir. media Ind. U. Sch. Edn., Bloomington, 1971-73; media cons. U.S. Agy. for Internat. Devel., Mali, Africa, 1982; dir. media and prof. edn. Ft. Valley (Ga.) State Coll., 1973-87, dept. chmn. mass communication, 1987-89, prof. mass communications, 1989—, dept. chmn. mass comm., 2000—. TV rsch. cons. Rsch. Comm.'s Ltd., Boston, 1989, 95; mem. evaluation team NCATE, U. N.Fla., 1986, U. N. Ala., 1986; mem. faculty devel. seminar, Zimbabwe and S. Africa, 1998; mem. Journalistic Tour Kenya, 1999. Photographer postcard views, Ft. Valley State Coll., 1981. Active Spl. Olympics, Warner Robins, Ga., 1981-87; panelist Reg. Minorities Conf., Atlanta Jour. and Const., 1988; dir. music/choir dir. Christ United Meth. Ch., Warner Robins, Ga., 1988-95. Named State Photographer of Yr., Ga. Spl. Olympics, 1986. Mem. Ga. Assn. Inst. Tech. (bd. dirs. 1986-88), Assn. for Ednl. Communications Tech., AAUP (v.p. 1975-88), Broadcast Edn. Assn. Avocations: photography, graphics, computers. Office: Mass Comm Dept Ft Valley State U Fort Valley GA 31030

ARCHER, LUCY ANN, small business owner, librarian; m. Clay Archer; children from previous marriage: Michael, Amanda, Erin, Aimee. Student, Brigham Young U., 1965—72; BA, U. Utah, 1990; MS in Instrnl. Tech., Utah State U., 2001. Cert. real estate specialist. Pres. Med. Mgmt. Assoc., San Jose, Calif., 1979—83; assoc. broker Wardley Corp. Better Homes & Gardens, Park City, Utah, 1989—94; prin. broker Silver Mountain Realty, Park City, 1994—; co-owner Archer Computer Svcs., Park City; specialist sch. libr. media ctr. Park City Sch. Dist.; head libr. Summit County Libr.; childrens libr. Salt Lake City Libr., 1998—. Editor: (newsletter) Snyderville Spirit, 1985-90. Capt. Park City Camp; vol. rep. Park City Media Ctr. XIX Winter Olympics; capt. Daus. Utah Pioneers; scoutmaster, den leader, dist. chair Boy Scouts Am.; v.p. Calif. Family Women, San Jose; vol. Salt Lake City chpt. Jr. League; Friends of the Library; SLOC (Salt Lake Olympics Com.), 2001—02; active Rep. Women, Salt Lake City, 1990—; dist. chmn., state del., election judge, registration agt. Rep. Party, 1984—. Named to Top 20 Realtors in State, Pres. Club, 1992, 93, 94, 95. Mem.: Women's Coun. Realtors, Park City Bd. Realtors (v.p., edn. com. 1991). Lds. Avocations: gardening, literature, volunteer work, family history research. Office: Archer Computer Svcs LLC PO Box 980111 Park City UT 84098-0111

ARCHER, RICHARD JOSEPH, lawyer; b. Virginia, Minn., Mar. 24, 1922; s. William John and Margaret Leanore (Duff) A.; m. Kristina Hanson, Jan. 29, 1977 (dec.); children: Alison P., Cynthia J. AB, U. Mich., 1947, JD, 1948. Bar: Calif. 1949, U.S. Supreme Ct. 1962, Hawaii 1982. Partner firm Morrison and Foerster, San Francisco, 1954-71, Sullivan, Jones and Archer, San Francisco, 1971-81, Archer Rosenak & Hanson, San Francisco, 1981-85, Archer & Hanson, San Francisco, 1985—. Served with USN, 1942-45. Decorated Bronze Star. Mem. ABA, Am. Bar Found. (life), Am. Law Inst. (life). Republican. Home: 3110 Bohemian Hwy Occidental CA 95465-9113 Office: Mauka Tower Ste 2920 737 Bishop St Honolulu HI 96813-3201

ARCHER, ROBERT PATRICK, psychologist, educator; b. Newark, Mar. 17, 1949; s. Robert Sinclair Henderson Archer and Mildred Elizabeth Keasey; m. Linda Ruben, Mar. 17, 1984; 1 child, Elizabeth. BA, U. South Fla., 1971, MA, 1973, PhD, 1977. Diplomate Am. Bd. Clin. Psychology. Asst. prof. psychiatry Med. U. S.C., Charleston, 1977-78; assoc. prof., project dir. Fla. Mental Health Inst., U. South Fla., Tampa, 1978-82; assoc. prof. Ea. Va. Med. Sch., Norfolk, 1982-87, prof., vice chair dept. psychiatry and behavioral scis., 1987—, interim chair dept. psychiatry and behavioral scis., 1994-97, assoc. dean health professions, 1997-99, Frank Harrell Redwood disting. prof., 2000. Author: Using the MMPI with Adolescents, 1987, MMPI-A: Assessing Adolescent Psychopathology, 1997; editor Assessment, 1993, Jour. Personality Assessment, 1992. Recipient Walter G. Klopfer award Soc. Personality Assessment, 1988, Disting. Rschr. award Assn. Med. Sch. Profs. Psychology, 1994. Fellow APA; mem. Am. Bd. Assessment Psychology (bd. dirs. 1997—), Assn. Med. Sch. Psychologists (bd. dirs. 1996), So. Deans Health Professions Programs, Ea. Va. Med. Sch. Health Svcs. (bd. dirs. 1998—), Cruising Club Va. Mem. Soc. Of Friends. Avocations: sailboat racing, civil war history. Home: 619 Mowbray Arch Norfolk VA 23507 Office: Eastern Va Med Sch Hofheimer Hall 825 Fairfax Ave Norfolk VA 23507 Fax: (757) 446 5918. E-mail: archerrp@evms.edu.

ARCHER, RONALD DEAN, chemist, educator; b. Rochelle, Ill., July 22, 1932; s. Don Adam and Irma Cecil (Olson) A.; m. Joyce Hilder Carlson, Jan. 31, 1954; children: Paul Dean, Lynn Sue, Sharon Jean, Julie Anne. BS, Ill. State U., 1953, MS, 1954; PhD, U. Ill., 1959. Tchr. Larson Jr. High Sch., Elgin, Ill., 1954; asst. prof. U. Calif., Riverside, 1959-63, Tulane U., New Orleans, 1963-65, assoc. prof., 1965-66, U. Mass., Amherst, 1966-70, prof. chemistry, 1970-99, prof. emeritus, 1999—, head chemistry dept., 1977-83. Vis. prof. Tech. U. Denmark, 1972, U. Vienna, 1987; research scientist Naval Research Lab., Washington, spring 1980; cons., 1960-63, 64-70, 72—; chief chemistry reader advanced placement program, Ednl. Testing Service, 1985-88. Contbr. chem. articles to research jours. Served with U.S. Army, 1954-56. Grantee USAF, Rsch. Corp., NSF, Am. Chem. Soc., NIH, Army Rsch. Office, Office Naval Rsch.; recipient Alumni Achievement award Ill. State U., 1989. Fellow AAAS; mem. Am. Chem. Soc. (chmn. Conn. Valley sect. 1979, councilor 1981—, chmn. com. on edn. 1987-89, nominating and election com. 1990-94, coun. policy com. 1996-98, com. on econ. profl. affairs 1999-2000, chair, 2000, exec. com. divsn. chem. edn. 1995-98, chair-elect, chair, past chair divsn. chem. edn. 1996-98, chair adv. bd. gen. chem. curriculum project 1997—, com. on com. 2001—, sci. com. 2001—), Internat. Union Pure and Applied Chemistry, New Eng. Assn. Chemistry Tchrs., Sigma Xi, Phi Lambda Upsilon. Lutheran. Home: 19 Lantern Ln Amherst MA 01002-3222 Office: U Mass Dept Chemistry Grad Rsch Towers # A Amherst MA 01003-9336 E-mail: archer@chem.umass.edu. *Nothing surpasses the joy in the eyes of a student who has just synthesized a new chemical compound, especially if it has unique properties or may benefit the human endeavor.*

ARCHER, SARAH ELLEN, public health and humanitarian assistance consultant; b. Chgo., Dec. 7, 1938; d. H. Ross and Helen Emily (Wason) A. BS, Ind. U., 1960; MPH, U. Mich., 1964; DrPH, U. Calif., Berkeley, 1973. RN, 1960. Pub. health nurse Near East Christian Coun. Refugee Work, Jerusalem, Jordan, 1960-61, Marion County Health Dept., Indpls., 1962-63; instr. nursing W.Va. U., 1964-67; supervising public health nurse Santa Clara County Health Dept., San Jose, Calif., 1967-69; prof. U. Calif., San Francisco, 1972-84; maternal child health, nutrition and nursing cons. WHO, Dhaka, Bangladesh, 1985-90; tng. advisor German Govt. Tech. Assistance GTZ, Dhaka, 1990-94; emergency assessment maternal-child health needs Internat. Med. Corps, Luanda, Angola, 1994, med. coord. and country dir. Kigali, Rwanda, 1994-95; v.p. Shamitar, Inc., Indpls., 1995-98; vis. prof. cmty. health nursing U. Indpls., 1998. Rsch. cons. Royal Australian Nursing Fedn., Melbourne, 1976, 82; curriculum cons. Coll. of Nursing Australia, Melbourne, 1976-82; mentor, external PhD program Fielding Inst., Santa Barbara, Calif., 1975-81, founding trustee Nursing Dynamics Corp., Mill Valley, Calif., 1973-81; Humanitarian assistance and pub. health cons. Northrup Grumman Info. Techs., U.S. Mil., Herndon, Va., 1998—; vis. faculty Joint Forces Staff Coll., Norfolk, Va., 1999—, Command and Gen. Staff Coll., Ft. Leavenworth, Kans., 1999—, USAF Spl. Ops. Univ., Hurlburt Field, Fla., 2001—; humanitarian assistance cons. African Crisis Response Initiative, brigade tng. Senegal, Kenya, 2000—; health assessment cons. Internat. Med. Corps, Kosovo, Fed. Rep. Yugoslavia, 1998; cons. to dir. Divsn. of HIV/STD Ind. State Dept. of Health, Indpls., 1999; cons. fetal and infant mortality program Marion County Health Dept., Indpls., 1999; cons. program planning and evaluation Ind. Primary Health Care Assn., 2000; cons. tng. planning and evaluation U.S. Army SFOR MND(N) Bosnia-Herzegovina, 2000—, U.S. Army KFOR3B, Kosovo, 2001—; vis. fellow Hudson Inst., Indpls., 2001—; adj. fauclty, Sch. of Pub. Health, Ind. Univ., 2001—. Author: Implementing Change in Communities, 1984, Community, Health Nursing Patterns, 1976, 79, 85 (Book of Yr. 1976, 79), Nurses: A Political Force, 1982; contbr. chpts. to books and articles to profl. jours. Vol. disaster field rep. Indpls. chpt. Am. Red Cross, 1998—; vol. Indpls. Red Cross and nat. ARC, ARC Disaster Svcs. Human Resources Sys. Recipient Pearl McIver Pub. Health Nursing award, ANA, 1982. Fellow APHA (exec. bd. 1978-81, chair 1980-81, Creative Achievement award 1978), Coll. of Nursing Australia, Royal Soc. for Health, Acad. of Nursing, Ind. Pub. Health Assn. (legis. com. 1998—), Global Health Coun., Women in Def., Women in Internat. Security; mem. ACLU, Amnesty Internat. (Ptnr. of Couscience 2000—). Avocations: classical music, opera, history, sports. Home and Office: 3910 Rue Renoir Indianapolis IN 46220-5577 E-mail: drsearcher@aol.com.

ARCHER, STEPHEN HUNT, economist, educator; b. Fargo, ND, Nov. 30, 1928; s. Clifford Paul and Myrtle Mona (Blair) A.; m. Carol Rosa Mohr, Dec. 29, 1951 (div. Feb. 1971); children: Stephen Paul, Timothy William, David Conrad; m. Lana Jo Urban, Sept. 23, 1972 (dec. Mar. 2003). BA, U. Minn., 1949, MS, 1953, PhD, 1958; postdoctoral student (Ford Found. grantee), U. Calif. at Los Angeles, 1959-60. Mgr. trader J.M. Dain Co., Mpls., 1950, account exec., 1952-53; instr. econs. U. Minn., Mpls., 1954-56; asst. prof. fin. U. Wash., Seattle, 1956-60, assoc. prof., 1960-65, prof., 1965-73, chmn. dept. fin., bus. econs. and quantitative methods, 1966-70; dean Grad. Sch. Adminstrn. Willamette U., Salem, Oreg., 1973-76, 83-85, prof., 1976-79, Guy F. Atkinson prof., 1979-96. Fulbright sr. lectr. Bocconi U., Milan, Italy, 1982; v.p. Hinton, Jones & Co., Inc., Seattle, 1969-70; cons. Wash. Bankers Assn., 1971-72, Weyerhaeuser Co., 1971, Bus.-Econs. Adv. & Research Inc., 1969-77, State of Oreg., 1984, 86, 88, 91; vis. prof. Manchester Bus. Sch., Manchester, Eng., 1990-91, Aomori (Japan) Pub. coll., 2000-01. Author: Introduction to Mathematics for Business Analysis, 1960, Business Finance: Theory and Mgmt, 1966, rev. edit., 1972, The Theory of Business Finance, 1967, 2d rev. edit., 1983, Portfolio Analysis, 1971, rev. edit., 1979, Introduction to Financial Management, 1979, rev. edit., 1983, Cases and Readings in Corporate Finance, 1988; editor Jour. Fin. and Quantitative Analysis, 1966-70, Economic Perspectives, Economica Aziendale, Jour. Bus. and Entrepreneurship. Served with USNR, 1950-52. Mem.: Phi Beta Kappa, Beta Gamma Sigma.

ARCHER, WARD, JR., advertising executive; Grad., Rhodes Coll. CEO Archer/Malmo Advt. Inc., Memphis, 1991—. Chmn. Goals for Memphis, Shelby State C.C. Found.; bd. dirs. Memphis Race Rels. and Diversity Inst., The Ch. Health Ctr., Memphis Arts Coun., Memphis Mag., Memphis Flyer. Recieved 100 Addys Am. Advt. Fedn., Silver Medal. Office: Archer/Malmo Advt Inc 65 Union Ave Ste 500 Memphis TN 38103

ARCHER, WILLIAM REYNOLDS, JR., (BILL ARCHER), lobbyist, former congressman; b. Houston, Tex., Mar. 22, 1928; s. William Reynolds and Eleanor M. (Miller) A.; m. Sharon Sawyer; children: William Reynolds III, Richard M., Sharon, Elizabeth, Barbara. BBA, LLB with honors, U. Tex., Austin. Bar: Tex. Pvt. practice law; pres. Uncle Johnny Mills, Inc.; dir. Heights State Bank, Houston; councilman, mayor pro-tem Village of Hunters Creek, 1955-62; mem. Tex. Ho. of Reps., 1966-70, U.S. Congress from 7th Tex. dist., Washington, 1971-2000; lobbyist Noble Drilling Services and Weathorford Int., Tex., 2002—; sr. policy analyst Price Waterhouse Coopers LLP, DC, 2001—. Former mem. Joint Com. on Taxation, Rep. Policy Com., Rep. Leaders Task Force on Health; bd. dirs. Clark-Bardes Holdings Inc. Bd. dirs. Houston Soc. Prevention Cruelty to Animals; past chmn. Rep. Study Com. Task Force on Regulatory Reform, Rep. Leadership's Econ. Task Force; mem. Rep. Leadership Task Force on Health, Nat. Commn. on Social Security Reform, 1982. Served with USAF, 1951-53. Recipient numerous svc. and honor awards, Taxpayer's Best Friend award Nat. Tax Payers Union, Taxpayer's Hero award Citizen Against Govt. Waste; named Most Respected Congressman from Tex., Tex. Bus. mag., Watchdog of the Treasury Nat. Associated Bus. Republican. Office: Price Waterhouse Coopers LLP 1301 K St NW Ste 800W Washington DC 20005-3333

ARCHER-SORG, KAREN S. secondary school educator; b. Ft. Wayne, Ind., Dec. 19, 1957; d. Paul Walter and Betty Irene (Harmon) Archer; m. Joseph Henry Sorg, Apr. 8, 1977; children: Joseph Henry II, Levi Paul. AA, Purdue U., 1987; BA, Ind. U., 1995. Cert. grantsmanship, Calif. Rsch. asst. Ind. U., Ft. Wayne, 1987-89; coord. Gov.'s Commn. for a Drug-Free Ind., Ft. Wayne, 1989—. Staff Regional Adv. Bd., Ft. Wayne, 1989-97; mem. grants commn. Parks Bd., Ossian, Ind., 1990-97; mem. Stop Child Abuse and Neglect, Ft. Wayne, 1995-97. Past pres., co-founder No. Wells Soccer Club, Inc., Ossian, 1986-96; cons. Jr. Achievement, Ft. Wayne, 1994—; speaker Wells County Citizen's Against Drugs, Bluffton, 1993-96; vol. Smoke-Free Ind., Ft. Wayne, 1995—, schs. and town of Ossian, 1989-97; mem. Friends of Libr., 1999. Recipient Appreciation award Ossian Fire Dept., 1993, Norwell Comm., Ossian, 1994, Dept. of Mental Health, Indpls., 1997. Mem. Wells County Citizens Against Drug Abuse.

ARCHEY, MARY FRANCES ELAINE (ONOFARO), academic administrator, educator; b. Elkins, W Va. Sept. 15, 1947; d. Ross and Carmela Gallo Onofaro; m. Rick Archey. BA in Social Sci. Edn., U. Pitts., 1968; MEd in Social

Sci. Edn., Indiana U. of Pa., 1969; EdD in Higher Edn. Adminstrn. and Counseling, WVa. U., 1981; Profl. Cert. in Human Resource Devel., Pa. State U., 1996. Cert. nat. counselor 1984. Asst. prof. sociology West Liberty State Coll., Wheeling, W.Va., 1969—72; dean of students W. Va. Northern C.C., Wheeling, W.Va., 1972—85; asst. dean instrn. C.C. Allegheny County South Campus, West Mifflin, Pa., 1986—96; dean bus. and acctg. C.C. of Allegheny County, Pitts., 1996—99; dean arts and sci. C.C. of Allegheny County-South Campus, West Mifflin, Pa., 1999—, Adj. instr. bus., 1988. Adj. instr. bus. C.C. of Allegheny County-South Campus, West Mifflin, Pa., 1988—. Ctrl. Pa. regl. dir. U. Pitts. Alumni Assn., 2001—; past pres., current chair nominations com. U. Pitts. Alumnae Coun., 1998—; vol food packager Greater Pitts. Food Bank, Duquesne, 1995—; vol. tester, interviewer Greater Pitts. Literacy Coun., 1987—96. Fellow: The Ed. Policy and Leadership Ctr. (fellow 2002—03); mem.: ASTD, AAUW, Am. Coll. Personnel Assn., Am. Assn. Higher Edn. (life), Am. Counseling Assn., St. Elizabeth's Women's Club, Phi Lambda Theta, Phi Delta Gamma (v.p. 2000—), Beta Sigma Phi (svc. chairperson 1987—, Order of the Rose 1994), Delta Kappa Gamma-Alpha Phi Chpt. (past pres. 1996—, newsletter editor 1996—). Democrat. Roman Catholic. Avocations: reading, gardening. Home: 333 Old Clairton Rd Pittsburgh PA 15236 Office: CC of Allegheny -South Campus 1750 Clairton Rd West Mifflin PA 15122 Personal E-mail: marchey@ccac.edu

ARCHIBALD, GEORGE, reporter; b. Newmarket, Eng., 1944; BA in Polit. Sci. and History, Old Dominion U., 1967. Editl. writer, columnist Ariz. Republic, Phoenix, 1971—73; congrl. aide Washington, 1973—75, 1978—81; assoc. staff Ho. Appropriations Com., 1979—81; dep. asst. sec. edn. Washington, 1981—82; nat. corr. Washington Times, 1982—93, 1995 ; editor, gen. mgr. The Warren Sentinel, Front Royal, Va., 1993—95; investigative reporter Washington Times, 1995—; assoc. prof. Washington Grad. Journalism Ctr., Regent U., 2000—. Press sec., legis. asst. Rep. John B. Conlan, 1973—75; adminstrv. asst. Rep. Eldon Rudd, 1977—78; exec. dir. Am. Legis Exch. Coun., Washington, 1976. With USAF, 1967—71. Office: Washington Times 3600 New York Ave NE Washington DC 20002-1996 E-mail: g_archi@yahoo.com.

ARCHIBALD, JAMES KENWAY, lawyer; b. Mass., Mar. 29, 1949; s. John Lawrence and Jean (Kenway) A.; m. Joanne Mary Ricciuti, Aug. 16, 1975; children: Kathryn, John. BA, Johns Hopkins U., 1971; JD, U. Md., 1975. Bar: Md. 1975, D.C. 1985, U.S. Dist. Ct. Md. 1976, U.S. Ct. Appeals (4th cir.) 1978, U.S. Supreme Ct. 1979, U.S. Ct. Appeals (9th cir.) 1984, Maine 1998. Assoc. Venable, Baetjer and Howard, Balt., 1975-83, ptnr., 1983—. Co-author: Pleading Causes of Action in Maryland, 1990, Model Witness Examinations, 1997. Chmn. bd. trustees Md. State Colls. and Us., 1984-86; trustee Johns Hopkins U., 1997-2000; bd. dirs. Roland Park Country Sch., Inc., Balt., 1989-94; pres. Homeland Assn., Inc., Balt., 1990. Recipient Disting. Svc. award Litigation Sect. Md. State Bar, Md., 1981. Mem. ABA (litigation sect., co-chair com. 1987-2002), Internat. Assn. Def. Counsel, Def. Rsch. Inst. (Exceptional Performance award 1989, Md. state chair 1989-93), Md. Assn. Def. Trial Counsel (pres. 1988-89), Johns Hopkins Alumni Coun. (v.p. 1996-98, pres. 1998-2000), Johns Hopkins Second Decade Soc. (nat. chair 1989-91), Am. Law Inst. Home: 13037 Jerome Jay Dr Cockeysville MD 21030-1523 Office: Venable Baetjer & Howard 1800 Mercantile Bank Bldg 2 Hopkins Plz Ste 2100 Baltimore MD 21201-2982 E-mail: jkarchibald@venable.com.

ARCHIBALD, NOLAN D. household and industrial products company executive; b. Ogden, Utah, June 22, 1943; m. Margaret Hafen, June 8, 1967. AA, Dixie Coll., 1966; BS, Weber State Univ., 1968; MBA, Harvard U., 1970. Exec. v.p., gen. mgr. Sno Jet, Inc. div. Conroy, Inc., Burlington, Vt., 1970-77; sr. v.p., and pres. non-foods cos. Beatrice Foods, Chgo., 1977-85; chmn., pres., chief exec. officer The Black & Decker Corp., Towson, Md., 1985—. Former All Am. basketball player. Named one of 10 Most Wanted Execs in U.S., Fortune Mag.; recipient Six Best Mgrs. in U.S., Bus. Week Mag. Avocation: theater.

ARCHIBALD, REGINALD MAC GREGOR, physician, chemist, educator; b. Syracuse, N.Y., Mar. 2, 1910; s. Eben Henry and Minnie (Archibald) A.; m. Evelyn Stroh, June 12, 1948; children: Ruth, Lawrence. BA, U. B.C., 1930, MA, 1932; PhD, U. Toronto, Ont., Can., 1934, MD, 1939. Tchr., rsch. asst. U. B.C., 1930-32; tchg. and rsch. asst. U. Toronto, 1932-33, fellow pathol. chemistry, 1933-35; intern pathology Hosp. for Sick Children, Toronto, 1937, surgery, 1938, medicine, 1939; intern Toronto Gen. Hosp., 1939-40; fellow divsn. med. scis. NRC, 1940-42; asst. resident physician Rockefeller Inst. Hosp., 1941-46; assoc. Rockefeller Inst. Med. Rsch., 1946, mem., 1948—; prof. Rockefeller U., 1955-80, prof. emeritus, 1980—; sr. physician Rockefeller Hosp., 1955-80. Prof. biochemistry Sch. Hygiene and Pub. Health Johns Hopkins U., 1946-48; mem. adv. bd. Hosp. of Rockefeller U., 1992-93. Mem. editorial bd.: Jour. Biol. Chemistry, 1948-58, Jour. Clin. Endocrinology and Metabolism, 1952-60, Child Development, 1954-56; adv. bd.: Analytical Chemistry, 1957-60. Mem. Am. Chem. Soc., Am. Soc. Biol. Chemists, Harvey Soc., Med. and Chirug. Faculty Md., Endocrine Soc., Soc. Rsch. in Child Devel., Brit. Biochem. Soc., Lawson Wilkins Soc. Pediatric Endocrinology, Soc. Adolescent Medicine, Nat. Acad. Clin. Biochemistry, N.Y. Met. Pediatric Endocrine Soc., Internat. Assn. for Adolescent Medicine, Explorers Club, Sigma Xi. Achievements include medical research in pediatric endocrinology and biochemistry; development of clinical laboratory methods; study of influence of hormones on enzymes, problems of physical growth and maturation of children. Home: Apt 1810 211 Second St NW Rochester MN 55901

ARCHIBEQUE, CHARLENE PAULLIN, music educator; b. Mt. Sterling, Ohio, July 15, 1935; d. Howard Samuel and Roberta Mae (Miller) Paullin; 1 child, Melissa. BME, U. Mich., 1957; MA, San Diego State Coll., 1965; DMA, U. Colo., 1969. Tchr. San Diego Unified Sch. Dist., 1957-69; dir. San Jose (Calif.) State U. Choraliers, 1970—. Cons., guest lectr. many univs.; conductor choirs in 44 states and Can. Contbr. articles to profl. jours. Dir. chorus San Jose Symphony, 1970-2000, bd. dirs. 1993-2001. Named Woman of Vision Career Ctr., Disting. Alumni U. Colo., 1986, Woman of Achievement in Arts San Jose Mercury News and Women's Fund, 1998; recipient Pen award, 1996, numerous others. Mem. Am. Choral Dirs. Assn. (state pres. 1971-73, nat. chair 1973-75), Music Educators Nat. Conf., Internat. Choral Fedn. Avocations: travel, reading, cooking, entertaining. Home: 11511 Summit Wood Rd Los Altos Hills CA 94022-4512 Office: Sch of Music and Dance San Jose State U 1 Washington Sq San Jose CA 95192-0095 E-mail: chara@pacbell.net.

ARCHIE, CAROL LOUISE, obstetrician and gynecologist, educator; b. Detroit, May 18, 1957; d. Frank and Mildred (Barmore) A.; m. Edward Louis Keenan III, Mar. 7, 1993. BA in History, U. Mich., 1979, postgrad. in Pub. Health Adminstrn., 1979-83; MD, Wayne State U., 1983. Diplomate Am. Bd. Ob-Gyn., Am. Bd. Maternal-Fetal Medicine. Resident ob-gyn. Wayne State U., Detroit, 1983-87; fellow in maternal fetal medicine UCLA, 1987-89, asst. prof. ob-gyn., 1989-97, asst. prof. dept of cmty. health scis., 1995-97, assoc. prof. ob-gyn. and cmty. health scis., 1997—; dir. maternal fetal medicine Northridge (Calif.) Med. Ctr., 2000—01. Cons. Office Substance Abuse Prevention, Washington, 1989—, NIH, Bethesda, Md., 1990—, RAND, 1995—; residency coord. UCLA Ctr. of Excellence, 2001—. Peer reviewer jours. Obstetrics and Gynecology, 1989—, Am. Jour. Pub. Health, 1994—, Am. Jour. Obstetrics and Gynecology, 1993—; contbr. chpts. to books. Internal rev. bd. Friends Med. Rsch., 1991—99; residency coord. UCLA Sch. Medicine Ctr. of Excellence; bd. dirs. Matrix Inst. on Addictions, L.A., 1993—; bd. dirs., vice chair Calif. Advs. for Pregnant Women, 1993—98; bd. dirs., asst. v.p. med. svcs. Venice (Calif.) Family Clin., 1994—98, v.p. svcs., 1998—2002, chair bd. dirs., 2002—. Clin. Tng. grantee UCLA, 1993-99; recipient Faculty Devel. award Berlex Found., 1992. Fellow ACOG; mem. AMA, APHA, Soc. Perinatal Obstetricians, Royal Soc. of Medicine (Eng.), Assn. Profs. of Gynecology and Obstetrics. Office: Dept Ob-gyn UCLA Sch Medicine Rm 22-132 10833 Le Conte Ave Los Angeles CA 90095-3075 E-mail: carchie@mednet.ucla.edu.

ARCHULETA, KEITH ANTHONY, entrepreneur, business and management consultant; b. Denver, Mar. 13, 1955; s. Willie M. and Judith Ruth (Archuleta) Suggs; m. Iris Curtis, May 27, 1995; 1 child, Dorian. BA in Comm., BA in African and African Am. Studies, Stanford U., 1978; MA, U. San Francisco, 1992. Founder, bus. mgr. Stanford Black Media Inst., 1976; dir. So. Africa Media Ctr., San Francisco, 1979-80; program coord. Student Arts at Stanford (Calif.), 1982-84; asst. dir. Stanford Residential Edn., 1984-88; founder/dir. Black Cmty. Svcs. Ctr., Stanford, 1987-92; exec. dir. Oakland (Calif.) Youth Chorus, 1993; project adminstr. Arts Edn. Funders Collaborative, San Francisco, 1994-99; site adminstr. Young African Am. Achievers Program, San Francisco, 1995-97; interim exec. dir. LEAP...Imagination in Learning, San Francisco, 1996, Oakland Asian Cultural Ctr., Oakland, 1998; founder, CEO Ur At Work, Inc., 1999—2001; exec. dir. East County Bus.-Edn. Alliance, 2000—, CASA Contra Costa Ctr. Cash County, 2001—. Founder/pres. Emerald Consulting, Antioch, Calif., 1992—; mem. adv. bd. CIIS MBA Program, San Francisco, 1994-97; mem. bd. devel./mktg. chair LEAP...Imagination in Learning, San Francisco, 1995-97; mem. bd. emeritus Theatre Works, 1992-; rev. panelist Arts Coun. Santa Clara County, San Jose, Calif., 1996-97, NEA, Washington, 2001-02; bd. dirs. Micro Credit Loan Fund, Inc., Regional Tng. Inst. Author: (play) Their Spirits are Free, 1982; prodr., editor (ednl. video) Song for Melvin Truss, 1986. Fellow Calif. State Legislature, Sacramento, 1978-79; vol. Crossroads Africa, Liberia, West Africa, 1979, San Francisco Sch. Vols., 1995-99; founder Kuumba Arts Ensemble, 1979, East Palo Alto Youth Theatre Project, 1985; congrl. dist. coord./del. Jesse Jackson for Pres., Santa Clara County, Calif., 1984, 88. Mem. ASCD, Calif. Alliance Arts Edn., Calif. Assn. Non-Profits, PowerPac, Co-Op Am. Bus. Network, Fellowship Cos. Christ Internat., Bus. Social Responsibility (founding mem.), Antioch Christian Ctr., Am. Assn. Christian Counselors, Youth for Christ (mem. nat. adv. bd. 1997-99), Antioch C. of C., Nat. Alliance of Bus. Avocations: poetry writing, theatre, music, cinema, travel. Office: 1883 Mt Conness Way Antioch CA 94531-7492 E-mail: emeraldk@aol.com.

ARCIA, LUIS ALFREDO, artist; b. Caracas, Venezuela, Nov. 19, 1953; arrived in U.S., 1982; s. Francisco Graciela Arcia and Sofia Rosales; m. Nancy Lee Bardes; 1 child, James Bardes. Graphic design cert., Simon Bolivar U., Caracas, 1975; fine arts degree, Cristobal Rojas Art Sch., Caracas, 1979; student, Parsons Sch. Design, 1984; fine arts cert., Art Students League, 1985. Billboard designer Vallas C.A., Caracas, 1975—77; painter, designer Karl Mann Assocs., N.Y.C., 1985—92; muralist, designer Modeworks Inc., N.Y.C., 1994—. Exhibitions include. Recipient Artist Fellowship award, N.Y. Found. for the Arts, 2000, Concordia Fellowship award, 2000, Scholarship award, Young Artist Biennial, 1981. Achievements include development of device that allows an inexpensive polaroid camera to take pictures using the illumination of an electronic flash outside of the camera, or any other group of electronic flashes, or similar arrangement. Home: 457 Saint Pauls Ave Staten Island NY 10304 E-mail: alfredoarcia@hotmail.com.

ARCILLA, DEMETRIO BALLARES, JR., health facility administrator, rehabilitation services professional, writer, genealogist; b. Philippines, July 2, 1934; arrived in U.S., 1974; s. Demetrio F. Arcilla, Sr. and Justa M. Ballares; m. Juanita R. Arcilla; 1 child, Jeandell R. AA, Ateneo U., 1956; BS in Bus. Adminstrn., U. of the East, Manilla, Philippines, 1960. Acct. clk. Nat. Shipyard & Steel Corp., Manilla, 1956—58; internal auditor Manila (Philippines) Music Ctr., Inc., 1958—64; admin. Philrock, Inc., Manilla, 1964—74; chief bookkeeper Electroplating Co., Chgo., 1974—77; bookkeeper Bank of Am., Houston, 1977—79; acct. Kerr Steamship Co., Inc., Houston, 1979—85; pres. Adult & Children Rehab. Ctr., Houston, 1987—. Author: Pictoral Roster of Arcilla Clan-USA/Canada, 2000, Genealogy of Arcilla Clan-International, 2002; contbr., articles to newspapers. Co-coord. Feed the Hungry Ops. TAPP, Inc., 1998; founder BICOL USA, Houston, 1984—; chmn. White Cane Fund Raising, Houston; active Tex. Asian Rep. Caucus, Houston, 1989—; bd. trustees CIA Charitable Found., Chgo., 2000—. Mem.: Bicol Nat. Assns. Am. (v.p. 1986—88, adviser 1988—90), Tex. Assn. Philippine Physicians Alliance, Inc. (pres. 1995, 1998), Assn. Profl. Genealogists, Nat. Geneal. Soc., Tex. Med. Assn. Alliance, Harris County Med. Soc. Alliance, Fil-Am. Coun. South Tex., Catanduanes Internat. Assn. (v.p. 1991—, vol. med. and surg. missions 1993, 2002), Houston Fil-Am. Lion's Club (v.p., dir. 1987—96). Avocations: travel, dancing, genealogy, gardening, movies. Home: 5630 Auden St Houston TX 77005-2008 Office: Adult & Children Rehab Ctr PO Box 270301 Houston TX 77277-0301

ARCILLA, JUANITA R. physical rehabilitation physician; b. Manila City, Phillippines, June 24, 1942; d. Eliseo Rivera and Dominga Dimla; m. Denny B. Arcilla Jr., Mar. 25, 1973; 1 child, Jeandell R. BA in English, U. St. Tomas, Manila City, Phillipinnes, 1966; MD, Far Eastern U., Manila City, Phillipinnes, 1970. Lic. physician Pa., Tex., R.I. Rsch. assoc. Northwestern U., Chgo., 1975—77, U. Tex., Houston, 1977—80; resident in phys. medicine and rehab. La. State U., New Orleans, 1980—81, Baylor Coll. Medicine, Houston, 1981—83; fellow in pediat. rehab. Tex. Children's Hosp., Houston, 1983—84; staff physiatrist Profl. Rehab. Outpatient Svcs., Pitts., 1985—86; clin. dir. Phys. Handicap Offender Program, Jester III, Tex. Dept. Correction, Hunsville, Tex., 1986—87; cons. Tex. Dept. of Mental Health and Mental Retardation (MHMR), Richmond, 1987; med. cons. Phys. Handicap Offender Program, Jester III, Tex. Dept. Corrections, 1987—89; med. dir. Richmond State Sch., Richmond, 1987—97; med. staff Tex. Dept. of Mental Health & Mental Retardation (TDMHMR), Richmond, 1997—. Clin. instr. Baylor Coll. Medicine, Houston, 1981—83; asst. prof. U. Tex., Galveston, 1987—; faculty position appt. Tex. A&M U., 1988—94; med. dir. Adult & Children Rehab. Ctr., Houston, 1987—; med. cons. Total Care Med. Clinic, Houston, 1994—; designated Phys. with Tex. Dept. Worker Compensation Comm., Austin, 1994—; WC patient's phys. of Richmond State Sch., Richmond. Contbr. articles, (Academic Scholarship Award, 2002). Med. mission vol. Catanduanes Internat. Assn. Inc., 1993, Catanduanes Internat. Assoc. Inc., 2002; mem. fund raising Tex. Asian Rep. Caucus, Houston, 1989—. Named Outstanding Career Woman Yr., IC Metro Houston, Inc., 1996; fellow, United Cerebral Palsy Rsch. Edn. Found., 1983—84. Mem.: Am. Acad. Phys. Medicine and Rehab., Internat. Rehab. Medicine Assn., Am. Cong. Rehab. Medicine, Harris County Med. Soc., Tex. Med. Assn., Tex. Assn. Phillipinnes Physicians Inc. (pres. 1997—98, past v.p., coord. Feed the Hungry Opn. 1998, plaques for charity work 1997, 1998). Roman Catholic. Avocations: gardening, cooking, home decorating, traveling, crocheting, winner of Trophy 1st. of Tango Compet.. Office: Adult & Children Rehab Ctr PO Box 270301 Houston TX 77277-0301

ARCINIEGA, TOMAS ABEL, university president; b. El Paso, Tex., Aug. 5, 1937; s. Tomas Hilario and Judith G. (Zozaya) Arciniega; m. M. Concha Ochotorena, Aug. 10, 1957; children: Wendy H. Heredia, Lisa Gannon, Judy Shackleton, Laura. BS in Tchr. Edn., N. Mex. State U., 1960; MA, U. N. Mex., 1966, PhD, 1970; postdoc., Inst. for Ednl. Mgmt., Harvard U., 1989. Asst. dean Grad. Sch. U. Tex.-El Paso, 1972-73; co-dir. Southwestern Schs. Study, U. Tex.-El Paso, 1970-73; dean Coll. Edn. San Diego State U., 1973-80; v.p. acad. affairs. Calif. State U., Fresno, 1980-83, pres. Bakersfield, 1983—. Prof. ednl. adminstrn. and supervision U. N.Mex., U. Tex.-El Paso, San Diego State U., Calif. State U., Fresno, Calif. State U., Bakersfield; cons. in edn. to state and fed. agys., instns.; USAID advisor to Dominican Republic U.S. Dept. State., 1967-68; dir. applied rsch. project U. N.Mex., 1968-69, dep. chief party AID Project, Colombia, 1969-70; cons. in field. Author: Public Education's Response to the Mexican-American, 1971, Preparing Teachers of Mexican Americans: A Sociocultural and Political Issue, 1977; co-author: Chicanos and Native Americans: The Territorial Minorities, 1973; guest editor: Calif. Jour. Tchr. Edn., 1981; editor Commn. on Hispanic Underrepresentation Reports, Hispanic Underrepresentation: A Call for Reinvestment and Innovation, 1985, 88. Trustee emeritus Carnegie Corp. N.Y.; trustee Ednl. Testing Svc., Princeton, N.J., The Aspen Inst.; bd. dirs. Math., Engring., Sci. Achievement, Berkeley, Calif.; mem. bd. dirs. Air U., Hispanic Scholarship Fund; mem. Am. Coun. on Edn.; founding mem., trustee Tomas Rivera Policy Inst.; dir. Civic Kern Citizens Effective Local Govt.; mem. adv. bd. Beautiful Bakersfield; advisor Jr. League Bakersfield. Vis. scholar Leadership Enrichment Program, 1982; recipient Legis. commendation for higher edn. Calif. Legislature, 1975-78, Meritorious Svc. award Am. Assn. Colls. Tchr. Edn., 1977-78, Meritorious Svc. award League United L.Am. Citizens, 1983, Svc. award Hispanic and Bus. Alliance for Edn., 1991, Pioneer award Nat. Assn. Bilingual Edn., 1994; named to Top 100 Acad. Leaders in Higher Edn. Change Mag., 1978, Top 100 Hispanic Influentials Hispanic Bus. Mag., 1987, 97. Mem. Am. Ednl. Rsch. Assn. (editl. com. 1979-82), Am. Assn. State Colls. and Univs. (bd. dirs.), Hispanic Assn. Colls. and Univs. (bd. dirs.), Assn. Mexican Am. Educators (various commendations), Am. Assn. Higher Edn. (instl. rep.), Western Coll. Assn. (past pres.), Rotary, Stockdale Country Club, Bakersfield Petroleum Club. Democrat. Roman Catholic. Home: 2213 Sully Ct Bakersfield CA 93311-1560 Office: Calif State U 9001 Stockdale Hwy Bakersfield CA 93311-1022 *Ensuring the right of every American youngster to a first-rate public education has been a driving interest in my life. I consider myself extremely fortunate in having had numerous opportunities to become involved in meaningful efforts to ensure that basic right in our country.*

ARCOS, CRESENCIO S. ambassador; b. San Antonio, Nov. 10, 1943; m. Patricia Cordova; 2 children. BA, U. Tex., 1966; MA, Johns Hopkins U., 1973. Various pub. and cultural affairs positions, Leningrad, USSR, Sao Paulo, Brazil; consulate gen. Leningrad, Russia; various pub. and cultural affairs positions Am. Embassy, Lisbon, Portugal, from 1973, counselor pub. affairs Tegucigalpa, Honduras, 1980-85; dep. dir. Nicaraguan Humanitarian Assistance Office, Dept. State, Washington, 1985-86, dep. coord. Latin Am. and Caribbean pub. diplomacy, 1986-87, dep. asst. sec. state for Cen. Am., 1988-89; coord. pub. diplomacy White House Office Communications and Planning, Washington, 1987-88; amb. to Honduras, Am. Embassy, Tegulcigalpa, 1990-93; sr. dep. asst. sec. state for internat. narcotics and crime Dept. State, 1993-95; v.p. for L.Am. and Can. AT&T Corp, IPA, Coral Gables, Fla., 1995—2002; Dir. Internat. Affairs Dept. Homeland Security, 2003—. Mem. White House Pres.'s Fgn. Intelligence Adv. Bd., 1999-2003. Mem. Hispanic Coun. on Internat. Rels., Washington; bd. dirs. Caribbean Latin Am. Action, Coun. of the Americas, N.Y.C., Pan Am. Devel. Found.; adv. com. Fla. Internat. Univ. Latin Am. Carribean Ctr.; bd. visitors Zamorano Agr. Sch., Honduras; dir. United Negro Coll. Fund Inst. Internat. Pub. Policy; bd. dirs. Fla. Foster Care Rev., 1999-02; mem. corp. adv. bd. Pacific Coun. on Internat. Policy; mem. corp. bd. Cuban-Am. Nat. Coun. Decorated Orden de Morazan (Honduras); recipient awards USIA, Superior Honor awards State Dept.; Regents' fellow U. Calif., 1998-99. Mem. Coun. Fgn. Rels., Am. Fgn. Svc. Assn., Coun. of Ams. (bd. dirs.), Interam. Dialogue, Pacific Coun. Internat. Policy. (mem. corp. adv. bd.), Pan Am. Devel. Found. E-mail: arcoscs@yahoo.com.

ARCOT, PRAKASH KUMAR B, engineer, consultant; s. Bashyam Sarangapani and Shantha Arcot. Masters, Okla. State U., Stillwater Oklahoma, 1993—94. Professional Engineer, Minn., 1997, Certified Energy Manager, IEE, 1995. Sr. design engr. Fischtner Consulting Engineers, Chennai, India, 1988—93; rsch. engr. Okla. State U., Stillwater, Okla., 1993—94. Sr. software engr. Siemens Power Systems and Control, Minneapolis, Minn., 1995—2001; consulting engr. (cockpit avionics upgrade) United Space Alliance, Houston, 2002—. Author: (ieee paper) Screening Technique for Optimally Locating Phase Shifters in Transmission Systems (Selected as Top Ten Finalist, 1995). Fellow Govt. of India Merit Scholar, Govt. of India, 1984 - 1988. Mem.: IEE (Sr. Mem.). Achievements include research in Optimally Locating Phase Shifters in Power Systems; development of Software Architecture for Connecting Real Time Systems with Business Applications (Enterprise Integration); Object Oriented Architecture for Real Time Systems; Senior Member IEE; Government of India Merit Scholar. Personal E-mail: prakashkumar_a@yahoo.com.

ARCURI, LEONARD PHILIP, elementary education educator; b. Bklyn., Apr. 28, 1947; s. Leonard James And Elizabeth Eleanor (Jaeger) A.; m. Lillian Campo, Aug. 11, 1979. BA, St. John's U., Jamaica, N.Y., 1969; MS, St. John's U., 1974; profl. diploma, C.W. Post, Greenvale, N.Y., 1980. Sci. educator St. Agnes Parish Sch., Bklyn., 1969-73; narcotics coord. Dist. 32 Drug Prevention Program, Bklyn., 1973-74; common branches tchr. P.S. 86 K, Bklyn., 1974-75; narcotics coord. Dist. 32 Drug Prevention Program, Bklyn., 1975-77; sci. educator P.S. 123 K, Bklyn., 1977—. Tutor biology Empire State Coll., SUNY, N.Y.C., 1988-89; instr. sci. Coll. New Rochelle, N.Y., 1988-89; instr. camping St. John's U. Sch. Continuing Edn., Jamaica, 1989-91; del. to Assembly of United Fedn. Tchrs., 1996—. Pres. Greater Ridgewood (N.Y.) Hist. Soc., 1983-84; com. commr. Boy Scouts Am., (Queens, N.Y.), N.Y.C. 1979-80; mem. nat. coun. Boy Scouts Am., Tex., 1979-80; scout master troop 154, Boy Scouts Am., Goldens Bridge, N.Y., 1994—. Recipient Energy Conservation Achievement award Dept. of Gen. Svcs. City of N.Y., 1983, Silver Beaver, 1980. Mem. Elem. Sch. Sci. Assn. N.Y., Planetary Soc., Astron. Soc. of the Pacific, Nat. Sci. Tchrs. Assn., Kiwanis. Democrat. Roman Catholic. Avocations: canoeing, hiking, camping, flyfishing. Office: PS 123 K 100 Irving Ave Brooklyn NY 11237-2952

ARCUS, SAM GEORGE, social worker, educator, writer; b. Bklyn., Oct. 19, 1921; s. Nathan Louis and Mollie (Srulowitz) Arcus; m. Adele Rosenthal, Jan. 27, 1946; children: Norman Louis, Rochelle Linda Arcus/Ting. B.Social Sci., CCNY, 1947; MSW, Columbia U., 1949. Supr. Pride of Judea Children's Home, Bklyn., 1942—44; casework counselor Jewish Family Svc., N.Y.C., 1949—50; program dir. Jewish Cmty. Ctr., Albany, NY, 1950—52, YM-YWHA, Elizabeth, NJ, 1952—53; asst. dir. Jewish Cmty. Ctr., Houston, 1953—56; exec. dir. Jewish Cmty. Alliance, Jacksonville, Fla., 1956—57; area dir. Niles Twp. Jewish Cmty. Ctr., Skokie, Ill., 1957—61, exec. dir. Dallas, 1961—66, exec. dir. North Shore Marblehead, Mass., 1966—79, exec. dir. Tucson, 1979—86; coord. Ct. Visitor's Program, Superior Ct., Tucson, 1986—89; coord. long-term care advocacy program, Ariz. ombudsman program Pima Coun. on Aging, Tucson, 1989—. Faculty Albany Tchrs. Coll., NY, 1950—52; field work supr. Columbia U., Elizabeth, NJ, 1952—53; faculty sociology U. Houston, 1953—55; field work supr. Lady of Lake Coll., San Antonio, 1962—65; instr. Bishop Coll., Dallas, 1963—65; field work supr. Brandeis U./Heller Sch. Communal Svc., Waltham, Mass., 1967—69; part-time faculty North Shore C.C., Beverly, Mass., 1970—73; overall supr. field work students Salem State Coll., 1973—74, asst. prof., 1974—79; field work supr. Ariz. State U. Sch. Social Work, Tucson, 1981—86, field work superior, 1987—93. Author: Deja Views of An Ag'ng Orphan, 2000, Journeys, 2002; author: (editor) HNOH: Memories of Orphanage Life, 2001; author: Handbook for Volunteers in LTC Ombudsman Program, 1998; contbr. An Orphan Has Many Parents, 1999; contbr. numerous articles to profl. jours.; editor: alumni newsletter. Life mem. Jewish Cmty. Ctr.; mem. Jewish Hist. Soc. of So. Ariz. Recipient Ward medal in sociology, CCNY, 1947. Mem.: Columbia U. Alumni Assn., CCNY/Hunter Coll. Alumni Assn. Jewish. Avocations: reading, walking, classical music. Office: PIMA Coun on Aging 8467 E Broadway Tucson AZ 85710

ARD, HAROLD JACOB, library administrator; b. Herrick, Ill., Aug. 26, 1940; s. Jacob S. and Hazel E. (Taylor) A.; m. Erma Chapman, Jan. 30, 1960 (div. June 1974); children— Teri Ann, Mark Alan. BS in Edn, Ill. State U., 1962, MS in Psychology, 1964; M.L.S., Rosary Coll., River Forest, Ill., 1968. Tchr., materials cons. Decatur (Ill.) Pub. Schs., 1962-64; head librarian Barrington (Ill.) Pub. Library, 1964-68; exec. librarian Arlington Heights (Ill.) Meml. Library, 1968-72; library system dir. Jackson (Miss.) Met. Library System, 1972-77; assoc. dir. Rowland Med. Library, U. Miss. Med. Ctr., Jackson, 1978-84; mgr. bus., sci. and tech. units Fort Worth Pub. Libr., 1985-91; mgr. Wedgwood Libr., Ft. Worth, 1991-94; dir. S.W. Regional Libr., Ft. Worth, 1994-97; ret., 1997; part-time instr. U. Tex., Arlington, 2001—. Owner Antiques, Etc., Arlington; cons., lectr. in field. Mem. ALA, Tex. Library Assn., Med. Library Assn., Beta Phi Mu. Clubs: Rotary. Methodist. Home: 1125 Clara St Fort Worth TX 76110-1026 E-mail: hard730939@aol.com.

ARD, KENNETH PAUL, music educator; s. Mabel Loretta and Angus James Ard. Master of Musical Arts (MMA), (MusM), U. of So. Miss., 1977. Adj. prof. Grossmont Coll., El Cajon, Calif., 1988—, Southwestern Coll., Chula Vista, Calif., 1991—99. Jazz choral dir. Southwestern Coll., Chula Vista, Calif., 1996—99. Composer: (musical theater) The Delta Queen. V.p. Music teachers' Assn. of Calif., 1995—96. Mem.: Music Teachers' Assn. of Calif. (Calif. plan chair 2000—02). Democrat-Npl. Science Of Mind. Avocations: travel, exercise, cycling, swimming.

ARDAI, CHARLES E. online services executive; b. N.Y.C., Oct. 25, 1969; s. Tibor and Vera Ardai. BA, Columbia U., 1991. Mktg./subsidiary rights assoc. Davis Publs., Inc., N.Y.C., 1986-91; sr. v.p. D.E. Shaw & Co., L.P., N.Y.C., 1992—; pres. Juno Online Svcs., L.P., N.Y.C., 1995—, pres. & CEO, 2000—. Editor: Great Tales of Madness and Themalabre, 1990, Kingpins, 1992, Futurecrime, 1991, High Adventure, 1992; contbr. articles, revs. and stories to profl. publs. Mem. Phi Beta Kappa. Office: Juno Online Svcs 1540 Broadway New York NY 10036-4039

ARDANS, ALEXANDER ANDREW, veterinarian, laboratory director, educator; b. Ely, Nev., June 6, 1941; s. Jean Baptiste and Eleanora (Campbell) A.; m. Janice Gae Sanford, Dec. 23, 1961; children: Tamara Marie, Stephanie Marie, Melanie Alexandra, Angela Rosanne, Jeanette Alison. Student, U. Nev.,

1959-61; BS, U. Calif., Davis, 1963, DVM, 1965; MS, U. Minn., St. Paul, 1969. Instr. Colo. State U., Ft. Collins, 1965-66, U. Minn., St. Paul, 1966-69; asst. prof., Sch. Vet. Medicine U. Calif., Davis, 1969-74, assoc. prof., 1974-80, prof., 1980—, chmn. dept. medicine, 1983-87; dir. Calif. Animal Health and Food Safety Lab Sys., Davis, 1987—. Recipient Outstanding Tchr. award U. Calif.-Davis Sch. Vet. Medicine, 1970, 73, Alumni award Sch. Vet. Med. U. Calif. Davis, 2000. Mem. Nat. Acad. Practitioners, AVMA, Am. Assn. Vet. Lab. Diagnosticians (Pope award 2000), Calif. Vet. Med. Assn., Conf. Rsch. Workers in Animal Disease. Republican. Roman Catholic. Avocations: swimming, fishing, hunting. Office: Univ Calif Sch Vet Medicine CAHFS Davis CA 95617

ARDASH, GARIN, mechanical engineer; b. Detroit, July 14, 1963; s. Berge and Lucy Alice (Souldourian) A. BSME, U. Mich., 1986, MME, 1988. Grad. rsch. asst. U. Mich. Coll. Engring., Ann Arbor, 1986-87, Los Alamos (N.Mex.) Nat. Lab., 1987; analysis engr. Naval Reactors Facility, Idaho Falls, Idaho, 1989-92, rsch./analysis engr. materials tech. dept., 1992-94; sr. rsch./analysis engr. materials tech. dept. Bettis Atomic Power Lab. Bechtel Bettis Inc., West Mifflin, Pa., 1994—2001, sr. analysis and devel.engr. refueling engring. org., 2001—. U. Mich. Coll. Engring. fellow, 1986-87; State Mich. Coop. scholar, 1982-83. Mem. ASTM, AAAS, ASME, Internat. Legion Intelligence, Photog. Soc. Am., Acad. Sci. and Art of Pitts. (photog. sect.), Mensa, Pitts. South Soccer Assn. Avocations: soccer, photography, skiing, chess. Home: 700 Penn Center Blvd #202 Pittsburgh PA 15235-5912 Office: Bettis Atomic Power Lab REO M/S 36/EE PO Box 79 West Mifflin PA 15122-0079 E-mail: garinard7@netscape.net.

ARDEHALI, ABBAS, physician, surgeon; b. Tehran, Iran, Sept. 24, 1959; s. Ali and Masoumeh (Toti) A.; m. Mitra Mogharabi Ardehali, Jan. 15, 1994; children: Leila Jasmine, Sara Ashley. BA cum laude, Rutgers U., 1981, MS, 1982; MPH, U. Calif., Berkeley, 1990; MD magna cum laude, Emory U., 1986. Diplomate Am. Bd. Surgery, Am. Bd. Internal Medicine, Am. Bd. Thoracic Surgery, Nat. Bd. Med. Examiners. Intern U. Calif., San Francisco, 1986-87, resident dept. medicine, 1987-89; surg. intern UCLA, 1990-91, resident dept. surgery, 1991-92, 93-94, chief resident dept. surgery, 1994-95, chief resident divsn. cardiothoracic surgery, 1995-97; asst. prof. surgery UCLA Med. Ctr., 1997—. Contbr. articles to profl. jours. Recipient Golden Apple Tchg. award UCLA Sch. Medicine Class of 1995, Sandoz Pharm. award, 1986, Rutgers Grad. scholar, 1981. Fellow: ACS; mem.: Soc. Thoracic Surgeons, Internat. Soc. Heart and Lung Transplantation, AIChE, ACP, Alpha Omega Alpha, Phi Beta Kappa, Phi Sigma Iota. Office: UCLA Med Ctr/Cardiothor Surg CHS62-232 10833 Leconte Ave Los Angeles CA 90095-0001 E-mail: aardehali@mednet.ucla.edu.

ARDELT, MONIKA, sociologist, educator; b. Wiesbaden, Germany, Apr. 29, 1960; arrived in U.S., 1988; d. Manfred Ardelt, Waltraud Ardelt; m. Dietmar H. Kaul, Sept. 1, 1990; children: Michelle Kaul-Ardelt, Gabriel Kaul-Ardelt. Diploma in sociology, Johann Wolfgang Goethe U., Frankfurt/Main, Germany, 1987; PhD, U. N.C., 1994. Asst. prof. sociology U. Fla., Gainesville, 1994—2001, assoc. prof. sociology, 2001—. Contbr. articles to profl. jours. Fellow Brookdale Nat. fellow, Brookdale Found., 1999. Mem.: Am. Sociol. Assn., Soc. for the Study of Human Development, Gerontol. Soc. Am. Office: Univ Fla PO Box 117330 Gainesville FL 32611-7330 Office Fax: 352-392-6568. Business E-Mail: ardelt@soc.ufl.edu.

ARDEN, BRUCE WESLEY, retired computer scientist, retired engineering educator; b. Mpls., May 29, 1927; s. Wesley and Clare Montgomery (Newton) A.; m. Patricia Ann Joy, Aug. 25, 1951; children: Wayne Wesley, Michelle Joy. Student, U. Del., 1944; BS in Elec. Engring., Purdue U., 1949; postgrad., U. Chgo., 1949; MA, U. Mich., 1955, PhD, 1965. Detail engr. Allison div. Gen. Motors Corp., Indpls., 1950-51; asst. prof. dept. computing and communication scis. U. Mich., Ann Arbor, 1965-67, assoc. prof., 1967-70, prof., 1970-73, chmn. dept., 1971-73, from research asst. to assoc. dir. Computing Facilities, 1951-73; prof., chmn. dept. elec. engring. and computer sci. Princeton U., 1973-85, Arthur Le Grand Doty prof. engring., 1981-86; prof. elec. engring., computer sci., dean engring. and applied sci. U. Rochester, 1986-94, vice provost computing, 1992-94, William F. May Prof. Engring., 1993-95, dean emeritus, 1994—; William F. May Prof. Engring. Emeritus, 1995—. Vis. prof. U. Grenoble, France, 1971-72; guest prof. Siemens Research, Munich, Germany, 1983, also cons.; cons. to Gen. Motors Corp., Ford Corp., Westinghouse Co., RCA, Xerox Data Systems, IBM.; mem. sci. council USRA Inst. for Computer Applications in Sci. and Engring., 1973-79, 82-88; mem. sci coun. USRA Inst. Advanced Computer Sci., 1982-88; chmn. com. on anti-ballistic missile data processing Nat. Acad. Sci., 1966-71; mem. panel Inst. Computer Sci. and Tech., 1980-86; mem. acad. adv. council Wang Inst., 1978-87; mem. study sect. NIH, 1985-88; reviewer Guggenheim Found., 1985-91. Author: An Introduction to Digital Computing, 1963; (with K. Astil) Numerical Algorithms: Their Origins and Applications, 1970; editor: What Can Be Automated?, 1980. Served with USNR, 1944-46, 49-50. Fellow AAAS; mem. IEEE (sr.), Assn. for Computing Machinery, Univs. Space Research Assn. (bd. dirs. 1982-88), Sigma Xi, Tau Beta Pi, Eta Kappa Nu.

ARDEN, EUGENE, retired university provost; b. N.Y.C., June 25, 1923; s. Harry and Gussie (Shevach) A.; m. Sandra E. Rose, July 11, 1948; children: Stacey, Jonathan. BA, NYU, 1943; MA, Columbia U., 1947; PhD, Ohio State U., 1953. Mem. faculty Ohio State U., Columbus, Queen's Coll., Hofstra U., 1947-56; from asst. prof. to prof., chmn. dept. English and humanities div. C.W. Post Coll., Greenvale, N.Y., 1956-62, dean, 1962-64; dean grad. faculties L.I. U., 1964-70, dean Conolly Coll., 1970-71, exec. dean Bklyn. Ctr., 1971; vice chancellor, dean acad. affairs U. Mich., Dearborn, 1972-89, provost, 1989-91, ret., 1991. Editor: Boca Chase Newsletter, 1995—; contbr. articles to profl. jours., mags. Bd. dirs. Mid-Island YM and YWHA, 1962-64; mem. nat. exec. com. Hillel Founds.; asso. chmn. civil liberties com. Jewish Community Council, Met. Detroit. Served with AUS, 1943-46, ETO. Mem. AAUP (editor Academe jour. 1991-93), B'nai Brith (pres. Ctrl. Nassau lodge 1966-68). Home: 18102 Clear Brook Cir Boca Raton FL 33498-1943

ARDEN, SHERRY W. publishing company executive; b. N.Y.C., Oct. 18, 1930; d. Abraham and Rose (Bellak) Waretnick; m. Hal Marc Arden (div. 1974); children: Doren, Cathy; m. George Bellak, Oct. 20, 1979. Student, Columbia U. Publicity dir. Coward-McCann, N.Y.C., 1965-67; producer Allan Foshko Assoc., ABC-TV, N.Y.C., 1967-68; sr. v.p., pub. William Morrow & Co., N.Y.C., 1968-85, pres., pub., 1985-89; owner Sherry W. Arden Lit. Agy., 1990—. Mem. Assn. Am. Pubs. (dir.) Clubs: Pubs. Lunch.

ARDERY, PHILIP PENDLETON, lawyer; b. Lexington, Ky., Mar. 6, 1914; s. William Breckenridge and Julia (Spencer) A.; m. Anne Stuyvesant Tweedy, Dec. 6, 1941; children: Peter Brooks (dec.), Philip Pendleton, Jr., Joseph Lord Tweedy, Julia Spencer. AB, U. Ky., 1935; JD, Harvard U., 1938; MBA, U. Louisville, 1957. Bar: Ky. 1938. Practice law, Frankfort, 1938-40, 45-50, Louisville, 1952—; ptnr. Frost Brown Todd, 1972—. Sec. Ky. Aero. Commn., 1946-48; commr. Jefferson County, 1958-61 Author: Bomber Pilot: A Memoir of World War II, 1978, Heroes and Horses, Tales of the Bluegrass, 1996; also articles. Bd. dirs. Frazier Rehab. Ctr., 1953-93, Schizophrenia Found., Ky., 1981—, Thomas D. Clark Found., 1994—, Nat. Alliance Rsch. in Schizophrenia and Depression, 1985-92, Norton Hosp. Found., 1985-94, Ky. Mental Health Assn., 1985—, Jewish Hosp. Healthcare Svcs., 1986—, Ky. Shakespeare Festival, 1989-90, Ky. Humanities Coun., 1989-94; pres. Ky. Heart Assn., 1955, chmn. bd., 1956; incorporator, dir. Ballet Español, 1984—; chmn. bd. Am. Heart Assn., 1966-69; dep. Episcopal Gen. Convs., 1970, 73, 76, 79; mem. exec. com. Ky. Hist. Soc., 1983-95; trustee U. of South, 1977-80, Episcopal Theol. Sem. in Ky., 1985-90; sec. Ky. Horse Park Found., 1985—. Col. USAAF, 1940-45, col. USAF, 1950-52, maj. gen. USAFR, ret., 1974—. Decorated Silver Star, D.F.C. (2), Air medal (4); Croix de Guerre with palm (France) Mem. ABA, Ky. Bar Assn., Louisville Bar Assn., Soc. Cin., Order First Families of Va. (Burgess), Pendennis Club, Filson Club (bd. dirs. 1986-96), Phi Beta Kappa. Democrat. Episcopalian. Home: 448 Swing Ln Louisville KY 40207-1444 Office: 3200 Providian Ctr Louisville KY 40202-2873

ARDITTI, FRED D. economist, educator; b. N.Y.C., Jan. 30, 1939; s. David A. and Marie (Ben Nathan) A.; children: Elizabeth Marie, Anne Sarah, David Frederick. BS in Elec. Engring., MIT, 1960, MS in Indsl. Mgmt., 1962, PhD in Econs., 1966. Economist Rand Corp., Santa Monica, Calif., 1965-67; lectr., asst. prof. fin. U. Calif., Berkeley, 1967-71; from assoc. prof. to prof. fin. U. Fla., Gainesville, 1971-77, Walter J. Matherly chair fin. and econs., 1974-80, chmn. dept. econs., 1977-80; v.p. research, chief economist Chgo. Merc. Exchange, 1980-82; pres. GNP Fin. Inc., 1982-86, GNP Commodities Inc., 1984-86, Drexel, Burnham, Lambert Quantitative Asset Mgmt. Group, Chgo., 1986-89; fin. cons. Chgo., 1989—; prof. fin. DePaul U., Chgo., 1990-97; sr. exec. v.p. for planning and devel. Chgo. Merc. Exch., 1997-2000; prof. fin. DePaul U., Chgo., 2000—. Vis. prof. Hebrew U., 1973, U. Toronto, 1976-77, U. Chgo., 1981-83, 90. Author: Derivatives: A Comprehensive Resource for Options, Futures, Interest rate Swaps and Mortgage Securities, 1996; contbr. articles to profl. jours., chpts. in books. NSF fellow; Ford Found. research grantee; NDEA fellow; other fellowships. Jewish. E-mail: farditti@wppost.depaul.edu.

AREEN, GORDON E. finance company executive; b. Chgo., Feb. 10, 1918; s. Eric G. and Tillie S. (Nyberg) A.; m. Pauline J. Payberg, June 28, 1942; children: Judith Carol, Patricia Ann, Richard Gordon. Grad., Sch. Commerce, Northwestern U., 1940; LLD (hon.), Alma Coll., 1989. C.P.A., Ill. Acct. Arthur Andersen & Co. (C.P.A.s), 1945-46, Allstate Ins. Co., Chgo., 1946-47; asst. comptr. to exec. v.p. Assoc. Investment Co., South Bend, Ind., 1947-64; pres., dir., CEO Chrysler Fin. Corp., 1964-80, chmn. bd., CEO, dir., 1980-81; v.p. Chrysler Corp., 1974-81; pres., dir. Chrysler Ins. Co., 1964-81; pres., CEO, dir. Internat. Harvester Credit Corp., Chgo., 1981-84, chmn. bd., CEO, dir., 1984; v.p. Internat. Harvester Co., Chgo., 1981-84; dir. Onset BIDCO Inc., Farmington Hills, Mich., 1988-94, vice chmn. bd., 1989-94. Trustee Alma (Mich.) Coll., chmn. bd., 1981-85, vice chmn. bd., 1986-87, pres., 1987-88; past pres. Jr. Achievement S.E. Mich.; v.p., dir. Detroit Swedish Council, Inc., 1987-90; pres. bd. trustees Kirk in the Hills Presbyn. Ch., 1987-88. Served to maj. U.S. Army, 1940-45. Mem. Am. Inst. C.P.A.s, Alpha Kappa Psi, Clubs: Masons. Republican. Home: 1729 Haggin Grove Way Carmichael CA 95608-5962 E-mail: gareen@aol.com.

AREEN, JUDITH CAROL, law educator, university dean; b. Chgo., Aug. 2, 1944; d. Gordon Eric and Pauline Jeanette (Payberg) A.; m. Richard M. Cooper, Feb. 17, 1979; children: Benjamin Eric (dec.), Jonathan Gordon AB, Cornell U., 1966; JD, Yale U., 1969. Bar: Mass. 1970, D.C. 1972. Program planner for higher edn. Mayor's Office City of N.Y., 1969-70; dir. edn. voucher study Ctr. for Study Pub. Policy, Cambridge, Mass., 1970-72; mem. faculty Georgetown U., Washington, 1971—, assoc. prof. law, 1972-76, prof., 1976—, prof. cmty. and family medicine, 1980-89, assoc. dean Law Ctr., 1984-87; dean, exec. v.p. for law affairs Georgetown U, Washington, 1989—. Gen. counsel, project coord. Office Mgmt. and Budget, Washington, 1977—80; spl. counsel White House Task Force on Regulatory Reform, Washington, 1978—80; cons. NIH, 1984, NRC, 1985; bd. dirs. Kroll, Inc. Author: Youth Service Agencies, 1977, Cases and Materials on Family Law, 4th edit., 1999, Law, Science and Medicine, 1984, 2d edit., 1996. Mem. Def. Adv. Com. Women In Svcs., Washington, 1979-82; trustee Cornell Univ., 1997-2001. Woodrow Wilson Internat. Ctr. for Scholars fellow, 1988-89, Kennedy Inst. Ethics Sr. Rsch. fellow, Washington, 1982—. Mem. ABA, D.C. Bar Assn., Am. Law Inst. E-mail: areen@law.georgetown.edu.

AREGOOD, RICHARD LLOYD, editor; b. Camden, N.J., Dec. 31, 1942; s. Lloyd Samuel and Ruby Odell (Trousdale) A.; m. Barbara Sue Wittenberger, Oct. 6, 1962 (div. June 1978); children: Laurie, Christopher; m. Doris Joan Sampieri, Apr. 21, 1979 (div. July 1992); children: Deborah, David, Jennifer, William Sampieri; m. Kathleen Shea, Feb. 20, 1993; 1 child, James. BA in English, Rutgers U., 1965. Reporter, editor Burlington County Herald, Mount Holly, N.J., 1964-65; reporter Burlington County Times, Willingboro, N.J., 1965-66, Phila. Daily News, 1966-71, features editor, 1971-73, news editor, 1973-74, editor editorial page, 1975-95, dep. sports editor, 1976; editor the editl. page The Star Ledger of Newark (N.J.), 1995—. Co-author: Beyond Argument: A Handbook for Editorial Writers, The Journalist's Craft: A Guide to Writing Better Stories. Pres. local 10 Newspaper Guild, Phila., 1978-79, v.p., 1973-77. Recipient Pulitzer prize for editorial writing, 1985, Walker Stone award Scripps-Howard Newspapers, 1993; inducted into Rutgers Hall of Disting. Alumni, 1993. Mem. Am. Soc. Newspaper Editors (dir. 1996-2002, disting. writing award 1984, 90, 94), Nat. Conf. Editl. Writers. Episcopalian. Office: The Star Ledger Star Ledger Pla Newark NJ 07102-1200 E-mail: raregood@starledger.com.

ARELLA, ANN MARIETTA, music educator, vocalist; b. Montclair, N.J., Jan. 29, 1951; d. Peter John and Evelyn Elizabeth (De Carlo) Arella; m. William John Wallace, Feb. 9, 1974 (dissolved May 1983); children: Ryan Wallace, Shannon Wallace. MusB, Ind. U., Bloomington, 1973; student, Manhattan Sch. Music, N.Y., 1975; grad. cert., William Patterson U., N.., 1983; MA, New Jersey City Univ., N.J., 1991; postgrad., Shenanaoah Univ., Va., 2002—. Tchr. remedial reading & math Indep. Child Study Teams, Jersey City, 1983—86; tchr. choral music Lodi (N.J.) Bd. of Edn., 1986; singer Sacred Heart Ch., Suttern, NY, 1990—95, pianist, 1990—95; ch. music dir. Immaculate Conception, Mahwah, NJ, 1995—99; pvt. piano & voice tchr. Mahwah, NJ, 1998—2002. Ch. musician, 1974—99. Singer: Ridgewood Gilbert & Sullivan Opera Co., 1985—89; singer: (operatic soloist) Opera Festival di Roma, 2000; performer: Teotro Verdi, 1999. Fellow, Shenandoah Conservatory of Music, 2001. Mem.: NEA, Lodi Edn. Assn. (chmn. 1989—93, membership com. 1989—93, adj. rep. 1987—). Republican. Roman Catholic. Avocations: golf, weight training, decorating. Home: 1211 Sycamore Ln Mahwah NJ 07430 Office: Lodi Bd Edn S Main & Hunter Sts Lodi NJ 07644 E-mail: arella201@aol.com.

ARENA, ALBERT A. museum director; b. Waltham, Mass., Nov. 12, 1929; s. John Giovanni and Jennie (Inferrera) A.; m. Jean Marie MacDonald, Dec. 29, 1935; children: Albert A. Jr., Andrew A., Arthur A. BS, Mass. Maritime Acad., 1952. Licensed Chief Marine Engr. Marine engr. Gulf Oil Co., N.Y.C., 1952, Farrell Lines, Inc., Bklyn., 1952-54; naval engr. officer USS New Jersey, Norfolk, Va., 1954-56; engr. Commonwealth of Mass., various locations, 1957-59, Harvard U., Roxbury, Mass., 1960; marine engr. SS America, N.Y.C., 1960-62; boiler and machine inspector Factory Mutual Ins., Norwood, Mass., 1963-70; assoc. prof. Mass. Maritime Acad., Buzzards Bay, Mass., 1970-72; engr. instr. Raytheon Co., Lexington, Mass., 1973-74; chief stationary engr. Allied Maintenance Corp., Boston, 1974-80; museum dir. Waltham (Mass.) Museum, 1971—. Producer, narrator This Was Waltham for Waltham Cable Access TV, 1989—. Recipient Ship Safety Achievement award Am. Merchant Marine Inst., 1962, Citation of Svc. for efforts associated with Waltham Mus. Mass. Ho. of Reps., 1994. Roman Catholic. Home: 17 Noonan St Waltham MA 02453-4212 Office: Waltham Mus 196 Charles St Waltham MA 02453-4206

ARENA, BRUCE, professional soccer coach; b. Brooklyn, N.Y., Sept. 21, 1951; m. Phyllis Arena; 1 child, Kenny. Student, Nassau (N.Y.) C.C., 1969-71; BS in Bus., Cornell U., 1971-73. Asst. lacrosse coach, asst. soccer coach Cornell U., Ithaca, N.Y., 1973-76; head soccer coach U. Puget Sound, Tacoma, Wash., 1976-78; head soccer coach, asst. men's lacrosse coach U. Va., Charlottesville, 1978-95; head coach DC United, Washington, 1995-98, U.S. Nat. Soccer Team, Chgo., 1998—. Mem. U.S. nat. teams in both soccer and lacrosse and competed professionally in both sports; past chmn. ACC soccer coaches, ISAA Divsn. I nat. poll; "A" coaching lic. from U.S. Soccer Fedn.; mem. NCAA Divsn. I soccer com., 1989-95. Named ACC Coach of Yr., 1979, 84, 86, 88, 89, 91, South Atlantic Region Coach of Yr., 1982, 83, 87, nat. Coach of Yr. by Lanzera, 1993. Inducted into Cornell Athletic Field Hall of Fame, 1986, Long Island Lacrosse Hall of Fame, 1990. Head coach U.S. under-23 nat. team which will compete in 1996 Olympics. Achievements include career record of 295-58-32 (.808) in 18 yrs. at U. Va., leading U. Va. to NCAA titles in 1989, 91, 92, 93, 94, taking U. Va. to 6 or the last 7 NCAA semi-finals and 8 straight quarter finals, directing U. Va. to 15 straight NCAA tournament appearances (longest active streak in U.S.), Major League Soccer Cup Championships, 1996, 97, U.S. Open Cup Championship, 1996. Office: US Soccer 1801 S Prairie Ave Chicago IL 60616-1319

ARENA, KELLI, news correspondent; b. Bklyn., N.Y., Dec. 17, 1963; d. Melvin Mullins and Mary Ann (Scafa) Tracy. BFA, NYU, 1985. Prodr. various shows CNN, N.Y.C., 1985-89, prodr. spl. reports, 1988-89, line prodr., 1989-90, supervising prodr., 1990-92, exec. prodr. London, 1992, news editor N.Y.C., 1992-93, reporter, anchor, 1993—. Youth dir. St. George's Ch., N.Y.C., 1989-93. Recipient Peabody award U. Ga., 1987, Cable Ace award, 1987, Gold award Houston Internat. Film Festival, 1987, Nat. Headliner award Atlantic City Press Club, 2002, Emmy award for Sept. 11th coverage, CNN, 2002; named Topten Fin. Journalist Jour. Fin. Reporting, 1989-92; named Best Corr. N.Y. Festivals, 2002. Mem. Soc. Am. Bus. Editors and Writers, Internat. Womens Media Found. Office: CNN 820 1st St NE Washington DC 20002-4243 E-mail: kelli.arena@turner.com.

ARENAL, JULIE (MRS. BARRY PRIMUS), choreographer; Tchr. Herbert Berghof Studio; asst. on tng. program Lincoln Center Repertory Theatre. Dancer with cos. of Anna Sokolow, Sophie Maslow, John Butler, Jack Cole, Jose Limon; choreographer: Marat/Sade for, Theatre Co. of Boston, Harvard U. Loeb Theatre, Municipal Theatre, Atlanta, Hair, on Broadway (Most Original Choreographer of Year award Sat. Rev. 1968), also London; dir., choreographer Hair, Stockholm (Best Dir.-Choreographer of Year award 1969); choreographer, dir. Isabel's a Jezebel; choreographer: Indians on Broadway, Fiesta for Ballet Hispanico, 1972, 20008 1/2, Boccaccio, 1975, A Private Circus, 1975, Free to Be You and Me, 1976, The Referee, 1976, El Arbito, 1978; choreographer for San Francisco Ballet, Nat. Ballet de Cuba, (film) King of the Gypsies, Great Expectations, Fur. Friends, 1980, Mistress, 1991, Once Upon a Time in America, Houston Grand Opera Co., Porgy and Bess, 1995, Great Expectations, 1997; dir., choreographer (stage) Funny Girl, Tokyo, 1979-80; dir. N.Y. Express Hip Hop Dance Co., commd. by Spoleto Festival of the Two Worlds, N.C. and Italy; toured 7 cities in People's Republic of China. N.E.A. grantee for A Puerto Rican Soap Opera, Ballet Hispanico, 1973, Oreg. Shakespeare Festival, 1997, Porgy and Bess City Opera, N.Y.C. Opera, 2000, Am. Family PBS TV Series, 2002.

ARENAS, ANDREA TERESA, academic administrator; b. Milw. d. Juan Selerno Arenas and Laverne Lowry; children: Olivia, Victoria. PhD in Edn. Adminstrn., U. Wis., 1991. Asst. v.p. U. Wis. Sys. Adminstrn., Madison, 1999—. Office: U Wis Sys Adminstrn 780 Regent St Ste 305 Madison WI 53715 Fax: 608-262-9701. E-mail: tarenas@uwsa.edu.

ARENBERG, IRVING KAUFMAN KARCHMER, fund manager, strategist; b. East Chicago, Ind., Jan. 10, 1941; s. Harry and Gertrude (Field) Kaufman; divorced; children: Daniel Kaufman, Michael Harrison, Julie Gayle. BA in Zoology, U. Mich., Ann Arbor, 1963; MD, U. Mich., 1967. Diplomate Am. Bd. Otolaryngology. Intern Chgo. Wesley Meml. Hosp., 1967-68; resident Barnes and Allied Hosps., St. Louis, 1969-74; asst. prof. surgery U. Wis., Madison, 1976-80; chief otolaryngology VA Hosp., Madison, 1976-80; CEO Ear Ctr. PC, Englewood, Colo., 1989—96; chmn. bd., CEO IntraEar, Neurobiometrix Inc., Inc., 1994—99; pres., CEO, chmn. Arenberg and Assocs. Ltd., LLC, 2000—. Dir., founder Internat. Meniere's Disease Rsch. Inst., Denver, 1971—; guest of honor 39th Chinese Nat. ENT Congress, Taipei, 1985, U. Antwerp, 1995, West German ENT Soc., 1996; vis. scientist Swedish Med. Rsch. Coun., 1975-76; vis. prof. U. Mich., Ann Arbor, 1988, 94, St. Mary's Hosp. and Med. Sch., London, 1988, U. Verona (Italy) Med. Sch., 1989, U. N.C., Chapel Hill, 1989, U. Wurzburg (Germany) Med. Sch., 1989, 90, 92, U. Ark., Little Rock, 1990, 95, U. Innsbruck, Austria, 1991, U. Sydney, Australia, 1992, U. Tex., Dallas, 1993. Editor: Meniere's Disease, 1983, Inner Ear Surgery, 1991, Dizziness and Balance Disorders, 1993; assoc. editor AMA Archives of Otolaryngology, 1968-81; mem. editorial bd. Am. Jour. Otology, 1978-91, Head and Neck Surgery Jour., 1992—; guest editor Otolaryngologic Clinics N.Am., 1980, 83, Neurologic Clinics N.Am., 1990; editor Inner Ear Surgery, 1991; mem. rev. bd. Rev. de Laryngologie et Otology (France), 1984—; contbr. over 400 articles to profl. peer-reviewed jours. Recipient Pietro Caliceti prize and Gold Medal Honor award U. Bologna, Italy, 1983, Spl. Tchr. Investigation Tng. award NIH, 1970-1975; fellow Barnes and Allied Hosps., 1968-69, 75, NIH, 1971-76, U. Uppsala-Royal Acad. Hosp., Sweden, 1975-76; grantee NIH, 1971-77, Deafness Rsch. Found., 1971-73. Fellow ACS, Am. Acad. Otolaryngology; mem. AMA, Am. Neurotology Soc., N.Y. Acad. Scis., Colo. Otologic Rsch. Ctr. (pres., bd. dirs. 1980-88), Internat. Meniere's Disease Rsch. Inst. (founder, dir. 1971—), Assn. Rsch. in Otolaryngology, Barany Soc., Triological Soc., Politzer Soc., Prosper Meniere Soc. (founder, exec. dir. 1981-99), Acoustical Soc. Am., Ogura Soc., Sigma Xi. Achievements include 10 U.S. and fgn. patents in field. Avocations: skiing, golf, biking, tennis. Office: Arenberg and Assocs Ltd LLC 22 Ludlam Ave Bayville NY 11709

ARENBERG, JONATHAN WILLIAM, engineer; b. Denver, Jan. 6, 1961; s. Sheldon Ira and Janet Estelle (Rubin) A. BS in Physics, UCLA, 1983, MS in Engring., 1985, PhD in Engring., 1987. Cons. Pan Heuristics, Marina del Rey, Calif., 1985-87; staff physicist Hughes Aircraft Co., El Segundo, Calif., 1982-89; sr. project engr. TRW Space and Tech., Redondo Beach, Calif., 1989—. Patentee in field; contbr. articles to profl. jours. Founding dir. Santa Monica (Calif.) High Sch. Alumni Assn., 1989—; bd. dirs., chmn. Friends of the Santa Monica Pub. Libr., 1989—; com. mem., past chmn. UCLA Alumni Scholarship, Dist. III-1, 1988—. Edward Dickson scholar, UCLA Alumni Assn., 1979, Regents scholar, UCLA, 1979; recipient Hughes Aircraft Masters and Doctoral fellowship, Hughes Aircraft Co., L.A., 1983, 85, Nat. Powerlifting Champion, 1990, 91, 92, 93, 95, 96. Mem. IEEE, Sigma Pi Sigma (v.p. 1982-83), Eta Kappa Nu, Sigma Xi. Avocations: cooking, reading, brewing beer, powerlifting.

ARENBERG, JULIUS THEODORE, JR., retired accounting company executive; b. Chgo., May 29, 1923; s. Julius Theodore and Ellen A. (Foran) A.; m. Jean E. Young, June 19, 1948; children— Robert, Thomas, Mary, James, Michael, Douglas. BS in Acctg, U. Ill., 1947. C.P.A., Ill. With Arthur Andersen & Co. (C.P.A.'s), Chgo., 1947—, partner, 1962—, head fin. services div., 1975—; chmn. C.P.A. adv. com. Nat. Assn. Ins. Commrs., 1974-75. Mem. faculty Bank Adminstrn. Inst. Sch., U. Wis., 1966-69, Nat. Installment Credit Sch., U. Chgo., 1965-70 Mem. Lombard (Ill.) Elementary Bd. Edn., 1960-66, pres., 1962-66. Served with USNR, 1943-46. Mem. Am. Inst. C.P.A.'s (chmn. com. ins. acctg. and auditing 1966-73), Ill. Soc. C.P.A.'s. Clubs: St. Charles Country, Bay Hill, Isleworth Golf. Roman Catholic. E-mail: payde369@aol.com.

AREND, ANTHONY CLARK, international relations educator; b. Balt., Oct. 24, 1958; s. Paul Joseph and Cora Allen (Clark) A. BSFS magna cum laude, Georgetown U., 1980; MA, U. Va., 1982, PhD, 1985. Rsch. asst. U. Va. Sch. Law, Charlottesville, Va., 1981-84, sr. fellow, 1985-86; professorial lectr. dept. govt. Georgetown U., Washington, 1986, asst. prof., 1988-93, assoc. prof., 1993-2000, chair main campus exec. faculty, 1997-2001, prof., 2000—, v.p. main campus faculty senate, 2001—. Vis. asst. prof. Pa. State U., Harrisburg, 1987, Georgetown U., 1987—88; co-dir. Inst. for Internat. Law and Politics. Author: Pursuing a Just and Durable Peace: John Foster Dulles and International Organization, 1988, Legal Rules and International Society, 1999; co-author: International Law and the Use of Force: Beyond the United Nations Charter Paridigm, 1993; editor: The United States and the Compulsory Jurisdiction of the International Court of Justice, 1986; co-editor: The Falklands War: Lessons for Strategy, Diplomacy and International Law, 1985, International Rules: Approaches from International Law and International Relations, 1996; mem. bd. advisors Va. Jour. Internat. Law, 1992—; contbr. chpts. to books, articles to profl. jours. Chmn. adminstrv. coun. Severn United Meth. Ch., 1984-89, lay leader, 1990—; gov. bd. govs. Georgetown U. Alumni Assn., 2001—. Margaret Nils Butler Meml. DACOR fellow, 1980-81, Richard M. Weaver fellow, 1982-83, Lassen fellow, 1983-84, Philip Francis du Pont fellow, 1983-84. Mem. Am. Soc. Internat. Law, Georgetown U. Alumni Assn. (bd. govs. 2001—), Phi Beta Kappa. Democrat. Avocations: golf, squash. Home: 1301 33rd St NW Apt 1 Washington DC 20007-2850 Office: Georgetown U Dept Govt Washington DC 20057-0001 E-mail: arenda@georgetown.edu.

AREND, WILLIAM PHELPS, medical researcher; b. Utica, N.Y., Aug. 24, 1937; s. Ralph Wilcox and Frances Elizabeth (Clapp) A.; m. Ann Elizabeth Manes, June 5, 1964; children: Thomas Clapp, Christopher Austin, Jeffrey Phelps. BA, Williams Coll., 1959; MD, Columbia U., 1964. Intern U. Wash., Seattle, 1964-65, residency, 1965-66, 68-69, fellow, 1969-71, asst. prof. medicine, 1971-75, assoc. prof. medicine, 1975-81; prof. medicine U. Tex. Health Scis. Ctr., Houston, 1981-82, dir. divsn. rheumatology, 1981-82; prof. medicine, microbiology and immunology U. Colo. Health Scis. Ctr., Denver, 1983—, head divsn. rheumatology, 1983—2000; Scoville endowed prof. rheumatology, 1993—. Chief arthritis sect. VA Hosp., Seattle, 1971-80; vis. scholar Corpus Christi Coll., 1980-81, Cambridge U. Editor Arthritis Rheumatism, 1995-2000; assoc. editor Jour. Clin. Immunology, Jour. Immunology, Jour. Clin. Investigation, 1993-95; contbr. numerous articles to profl. jours. Mem.

exec. coun. Hall of Life, Denver Mus. Natural History; mem. adv. coun. NIAMS, NIH, 1995-98. Lt. comdr. USPHS, 1966-68. Guggenheim Found. fellow, 1980-81; recipient Novartis-ILAR Rheumatology prize, 1997, Hawley prize for rsch. Arthritis Found., 1998. Fellow AAAS, ACP; mem. Assn. Am. Physicians, Am. Soc. Clin. Investigation, Am. Assn. Immunologists, Am. Coll. Rheumatology (bd. dirs. 1991-94), Western Assn. Physicians, Western Soc. Clin. Investigation (councilor 1976-79), Henry Kunkel Soc., Phi Beta Kappa. Episcopalian. Achievements include discovery and patent for interleukin-1 receptor antagonist. Office: U Colo Health Scis Ctr 4200 E 9th Ave Denver CO 80220-3706

ARENDALL, CHARLES STEVEN, management consultant, educator; b. Warrington, Lancashire, Eng., Aug. 3, 1955; arrived in U.S., 1956, permanent resident; s. Charles Lewis and Pamela (Read) Arendall; m. Elizabeth Ann Kern, Dec. 13, 1980 (div. Apr. 3, 1984); m. Vivian Elizabeth Taylor, May 2, 1985; children: Dena Elizabeth, Charles Henry II. BBA U. Memphis, 1977; MBA, U. Memphis, 1980; PhD, U. Tenn., 1986. Mgr. territory Burroughs Corp., Memphis, 1977—79; grad. tchg. asst. U. Tenn., 1980—84; asst. prof. La. State U., Baton Rouge, 1985—88; mng. ptnr. Qualimetrics, Inc., Maryville, Tenn., 1987—90; asst. prof. Union U., Jackson, Tenn., 1990—93, assoc. prof., 1993—97, prof., dir. MBA program, 1997—. Cons. stats process control Qualimetrics, Maryville, Tenn., 1982—87; cons. job safety Jaws Offshore, Baton Rouge, 1985—87; cons. total quality Jackson (Tenn.) Gen. Hosp., 1992—. Contbr. articles to profl. jours. Fellow Found. La. State U., 1986. Mem.: So. Mgmt. Assn., Decision Scis. Inst. (presenter 1990—), Acad. Mgmt. (reviewer, session pres. 2002). Episcopalian. Avocations: camping, golf, hiking, skiing, water skiing. Home: 195 S Rembert St Memphis TN 38104 Office: Union Univ 2735 Hacks Cross Rd Germantown TN 38138 Office Fax: 901-759-1197. E-mail: sarendal@uu.edu.

ARENDS, HERMAN JOSEPH, insurance company executive; b. 1945; M of Math., Mich. State U., 1967. Tchr. Laningsburg (Mich.) H.S., 1967-72; chmn., CEO Auto Owners Ins. Co., Lansing, Mich., 1972—. Office: Auto Owners Insurance Co 6101 Anacapri Dr Lansing MI 48917-3994

ARENOWITZ, ALBERT HAROLD, psychiatrist; b. N.Y.C., Jan. 12, 1925; s. Louis Isaac and Lena Helen (Skovron) A.; m. Betty Jane Wiener, Oct. 11, 1953; children: Frederick Stuart, Diane Helen. BA with honors, U. Wis., 1948; MD, U. Va., 1951. Diplomate Am. Bd. Psychiatry, Am. Bd. Child Psychiatry. Intern Kings County Gen. Hosp., Bklyn., 1951-52; resident in psychiatry Bronx (N.Y.) VA Hosp., 1952-55; postdoctoral fellow Youth Guidance Ctr., Worcester, Mass., 1955-57; dir. Ctr. for Child Guidance, Phila., 1962-65, Hahnemann Med. Service Eastern State Sch. and Hosp., Trevose, Pa., 1965-68; dir., tng. dir. Child and Adolescent Psychiat. Clinic, Phila. Gen. Hosp., 1965-67; asst. clin. prof. psychiatry Jefferson Med. Coll., Phila., 1974-76; exec. dir. Child Guidance and Mental Health Clinics, Media, Pa., 1967-74; med. dir. Intercommunity Child Guidance Ctr., Whittier, Calif., 1976—. Cons. Madison Pub. Schs., 1957-60, Dane County Child Guidance Ctr., Madison, 1957-62, Juvenile Ct., Madison, 1957-62; clin. asst. prof. child psychiatry Hahnemann Med. Coll., Phila., 1966-74; asst. clin. prof. psychiatry U. Wis., Madison, 1960-62, clin. asst. prof. psychiatry, behavioral scis. and family medicine U. So. Calif., L.A., 1976—; mem. med. staff Presbyn. Intercommunity Hosp., Whittier, 1976—. Pres. Whittier Area Coordinating Coun., 1978-80; chmn. ethics com. Presbyn. Intercommunity Hosp. Flight officer, navigator USAF, 1943-45. Decorated Air medal, POW medal. Fellow Am. Psychiat. Assn., Am. Acad. Child Psychiatry; mem. AAAS, Los Angeles County Med. Assn., So. Calif. Psychiat. Soc., So. Calif. Soc. Child Psychiatry, Phila. Soc. Adolescent Psychiatry (pres. 1967-68), Peace Sci. Soc. Avocations: study of violence and aggression, ethnic travels, ethnic folk music, photography. Office: Intercommunity Child Guidance Ctr 8106 Broadway Ave Whittier CA 90606-3118

ARENS, JAMES F. anesthesiologist, educator; b. Hamel, Minn., Apr. 20, 1934; s. Frederick and Aurelia (Boldwe) Arens; m. Ann Gardner, Aug. 8, 1986; children from previous marriage: Patricia, James F. MD, Creighton U., Omaha, 1959. Diplomate Am. Bd. Anesthesiology. Commd. officer USAF, advanced through grades to capt.; intern Tripler Army Med. Ctr., Honolulu, 1959—60; resident Charity Hosp., New Orleans, 1960—62; ret. USAF, 1966; dir. anesthesia Ochsner Clinic, New Orleans, 1967—72; prof., chmn. anesthesiology U. Miss. Med. Ctr., Jackson, 1972—77; prof., chmn. dept. anesthesiology U. Tex. Med. Br., Galveston, 1977—99, dir. surg. operating and acute care support services, 1977—, med. dir. respiratory therapy dept., 1980—81, exec. dir. operating room, 1977—99; prof., chmn. dept. anesthesiology MD Anderson Cancer Ctr., Houston, 1999—. Chmn., sec. Joint Com. on Critical Care Medicine, 1982—. Mem.: Am. Soc. Anesthesiologists (pres. 1988), Soc. Acad. Anesthesia Chmn. (pres. 1979), Am. Bd. Med. Specialities (pres. 1996—98), Am. Coll. Anesthesiology. Roman Catholic. Home: 7900 N Stadium Dr Apt 117 Houston TX 77030-4418 Office: U Tex MD Anderson Cancer Ctr PO Box 42 Houston TX 77001-0042

ARENS, NICHOLAS HERMAN, bank executive; b. N.Y.C., Apr. 24, 1937; s. Nicholas and Sarah (Woods) A.; m. Eileen M. Casey, Jan. 27, 1960; children: Nicholas Jr., Steven, Cynthia, Linda. BBA, Pace U., 1969; postgrad., U. Wis., 1974. Audit officer Morgan Bank, N.Y.C., 1970-77, asst. auditor, 1978-80; chief auditor Algemene Bank Nederland, N.Y.C., 1981, sr. v.p., 1982-84; auditor Nat. Bank Kuwait, N.Y.C., 1984, mgr. ops. div., 1985-88, mgr. human resources/adminstrn. divsn., 1988-99, exec. mgr. human resources/adminstrn. divsn., 1999—. Served with U.S. Army, 1958-60. Mem. Council on Internat. Banking. Home: 95 Kime Ave North Babylon NY 11703-3316 Office: Nat Bank Kuwait 299 Park Ave New York NY 10171-0002

ARENSON, GREGORY K. lawyer; b. Chgo., Feb. 11, 1949; s. Donald L. and Marcia (Terman) A.; m. Karen H. Wattel, Sept. 4, 1970; 1 child, Morgan Elizabeth. BS in Econs., MIT, 1971; JD, U. Chgo., 1975. Bar: Ill. 1975, U.S. Dist. Ct. (no. dist.) Ill. 1975, N.Y. 1978, U.S. Dist. Ct. (so. and ea. dists.) N.Y. 1978, U.S. Supreme Ct. 1985, U.S. Ct. Appeals (2nd cir.) 1987, U.S. Dist. Ct. (ctrl. dist.) Ill. 1995, U.S. Ct. Appeals (7th cir.) 1997. Assoc. Rudnick & Wolfe, Chgo., 1975-77, Schwartz, Klink & Schreiber P.C., N.Y.C., 1977-81, ptnr., 1982-87, Proskauer, Rose, Goetz & Mendelsohn, N.Y.C., 1987-93, Kaplan Fox & Kilsheimer LLP, N.Y.C., 1993—. Mediator U.S. Dist. Ct. (so. dist.) N.Y., 1993—; mem. MIT Corp., 1997—2002; mem. corp. devel. com. MIT, 1994—, mem. alumni/ae fund bd., 1989—, chair, 1994—96; mem. adv. bd. Fed. Discovery News, 1999—. Co-editor: Federal Rules of Civil Procedure, 1993 Amendments, A Practical Guide, 1994; contbr. articles to profl. jours. Mem. ABA, N.Y. State Bar Assn. (comml. and fed. litigation sect., chair com. on discovery 1989-97, chair com. fed. procedure 1997—), N.Y. Bar Found., Assn. Bar City N.Y. Home: 125 W 76th St Apt 2A New York NY 10023-8334 Office: Kaplan Fox & Kilsheimer LLP 805 3d Ave New York NY 10022-7513

ARENSON, NATHAN, retired radiologist; b. N.Y.C., 1912; MD, N.Y. Med. Coll., 1937. Intern Metro Hosp., N.Y.C., 1937-39; resident radiology Hines VA Hosp., Chgo., 1940, Va. Hosp., Roanoke, 1940-41; assoc. radiologist Watts Hosp., Durham, N.C., 1945-47, Touro Infirm, New Orleans, 1947-48; chief radiologist Sacred Heart Hosp., Pensacola, Fla., 1948-75; radiologist chmn. West Fla. Regional Med. Ctr., Pensacola, ret. Recipient Gold medal Fla. Radiology Soc., 1992. Fellow Am. Coll. Radiology; mem. AMA, Am. Coll. Nuc. Medicine, Radiol. Soc. N.Am. E-mail: narenson@aol.com.

ARENSTEIN, WALTER ALAN, environmental scientist; b. N.Y.C., Apr. 17, 1955; s. Fred and Evelyn (Eckhaus) Arenstein; m. Gina Lilia Facca, June 6, 1993. BA in Human Ecology, Ramapo Coll. N.J., Mahwah, 1976; MA in Environ. and Urban Studies, CUNY, 1978; postgrad., U. Calif., Irvine. Cert. tchr. cmty. coll. ecology Calif., registered environ. assessor Calif., qualified environ. profl. Inst. Profl. Environ. Assoc. mem. profl. staff S.W. Regional Lab. for Ednl. Rsch. and devel., Orange County, Calif., 1979-80; mgr. L.A. Children's Mus., 1981-82; city coun. aide City of Irvine, Calif., 1983-86; pres. Writrac Cons., N.Y.C., 1983—; instr. U. Calif., Irvine, 1985-87; cons. Rand Corp., Santa Monica, Calif., 1988; staff specialist South Coast Air Quality Mgmt. Dist., L.A., 1989-91; air pollution control officer Placer County Air Pollution Control Dist., Auburn, Calif., 1992-94; sr. scientist Midwest Rsch. Inst., Kansas City, Mo., 1994-95. Instr. environ. sci. Scott C.C., Davenport, Iowa, 1997—; program coord. environ. tng. ctr., instr. environ. sci. Kirkwood C.C., 1997—2000; instr. natural sci. So. Vt. Coll., 2003—. Contbr. articles to profl. jours. Organizer, spkr. Earth Day Activities, N.Y., Calif., 1970—90; mem. Calif. uniform Air Quality Tng. Task Force, 1989—. Recipient Cert. of Appreciation, Placer County Econ. Devel. Bd., 1993. Mem.: AAAS, Air and Waste Mgmt. Assn. (chair pub. inof. com. 1993—, vice-chair transp. divsn.), Calif. Air Pollution Control Officers Assn. (bd. dirs. 1993—94), Assn. Environ. Profls. Avocations: tennis, computers, camping, music. E-mail: warenstein@hotmail.com.

ARENT, ALBERT EZRA, retired lawyer; b. Rochester, N.Y., Aug. 25, 1911; s. Hyman J. and Sarah (Weller) A.; m. Frances Feldman, Nov. 23, 1939; children: Stephen Weller, Margery Arent Safir. AB, Cornell U., 1932, LL.B., 1935. Bar: N.Y. 1935, D.C. 1945. Rsch. asst. N.Y. State Law Revision Commn., 1934; atty. U.S. Bur. Internal Revenue, 1935-39; spl. asst. to Atty. Gen. U.S., 1939-44; chief trial atty. Alien Property Unit, U.S. Dept. Justice, 1942-44; pvt. law practice specializing in taxation; ptnr. firm Arent, Fox, Kintner, Plotkin and Kahn and (predecessor firms), Washington, 1944-86; counsel, 1986—2003; lectr. taxation Am. U., 1948-52; prof. taxation Georgetown Law Sch., 1951-73; ret. Also lectr. tax subjects before Practising Law Inst., NYU, U. Chgo. tax insts., Am., Fed., various local and state bar assns.; prosecuted leading fgn. agt. registration act cases, World War II.; chmn. adv. coun. Cornell Law Sch., 1979-82 Contbr. articles to legal publs. Vice pres. Jewish Cmty. Coun. of Greater Washington, 1953-57, pres., 1957-61; chmn. Commn. on Social Action of Reform Judaism, 1973-77; chmn. Cornell Law Sch. Fund, 1975-77; mem. steering com. Nat. Urban Coalition, 1970-77, mem. exec. com., 1970-72; mem. governing bd. and exec. com. Common Cause, 1970-72; bd. dirs. Overseas Edn. Fund of LWV, 1961-79; vice chmn. Nat Jewish Cmty. Rels. Adv. Coun., 1967-70, chmn., 1970-73; vice chmn. Conf. Pres.'s Major Jewish Orgns., 1970-73; trustee Cornell U., 1978-83, trustee emeritus, 1983— ; 1st v.p. Washington Hebrew Congregation, 1978-80; v.p. United Jewish Appeal Fedn. Greater Washington, 1979-81. Recipient Stephen S. Wise medallion award Nat. Capital chpt. Am. Jewish Congress, 1965, Vicennial medal Georgetown U., 1971, Humanitarianism award B'nai Brith, 1975, Disting. Alumnus award Cornell U. Law Sch., 1982, award for outstanding svc. Overseas Edn. Fund, 1983, Disting. Svc. award Washington Lawyers Com. for Civil Rights Under Law, 1987, Judge Learned Hand award Am. Jewish Com., 1991. Mem. ABA, Am. Law Inst., Fed. Bar Assn., D.C. Bar Assn., Telluride Assn., Phi Beta Kappa, Phi Kappa Phi. Home: 6620 Boca Del Mar Dr Apt 608 Boca Raton FL 33433-5718

ARESKOG, DONALD CLINTON, retired chiropractor; b. Bklyn., Aug. 6, 1926; s. Andrew Albert and Jennie Margaret (Dickson) A.; m. Julia Catherine Koskela, May 15, 1954. D Chiropractic, Logan Coll., St. Louis, 1950; Philosopher of Chiropractic, Atlantic States Chiropractic Coll. Ret., 1989; pvt. practice, 1952-56, Wappingers Falls, N.Y., 1956-61, Poughkeepsie, N.Y., 1961-89; retired, 1989. Bd. govs. Atlantic States Chiropractic Coll., Bklyn., 1954; research in field. Developer technique for removal of mental aberrations. Mem. Am. Chiropractic Assn. (speakers bur. 1964), Ednl. Rsch. Soc., Internat. Basic Rsch. Inst., Internat. Platform Assn., Wappingers Falls C. of C. (treas. 1959), Toastmasters. Achievements include developing a technique to create peak experiences known as "the flow", 1995, technology for pure being, 1999, technology to create whole brain thinking, 2000, removal of all energy breaks, 2003. Home: 330 SE 20th Ave Apt 514 Deerfield Beach FL 33441-5181

ARESTY, JEFFREY M. lawyer; b. Framingham, Mass., Dec. 31, 1951; s. Victor Joseph and Pola (Granek) A.; m. Ellen Louise Gould, Aug. 15, 1976; children: Joshua, Abigail, Joanne. BA, Johns Hopkins U., 1973; JD, Boston U., 1976, LLM in Taxation, 1978, LLM in Internat. Banking, 1993. Bar: Mass. 1977, D.C. 1982. Tax specialist Coopers & Lybrand, Boston, 1976-78; assoc. Meyers, Goldstein & Crossland, Brookline, Mass., 1978-79; ptnr. Crossland, Aresty & Levin, Boston, 1979-87, Aresty & Levin, Boston, 1987-91, Aresty Internat. Law Offices, Boston, 1992—. Cons. editor Tax Shelter Investment Rev., 1981-85. Recipient Disting. Achievement award Boston Safe Deposit and Trust, 1976, Grad. Banking Alumni Achievement award Boston U. Law Sch., 1993. Mem. ABA (membership chmn. 1981-84, coun. 1985-91, vice chmn. computer divsn. 1985-90, reporter e lawyering 1999—, chmn. internat. interest group 1992-96, chmn. internat. negotiations task force 1992-96, chmn. Mass. membership com. 1985-91, internat. law sect., chair law practice com. 1995-98, co-editor ABA Guide Internat. Bus. Negotiations 1994-2000, prodr. ABA/AT&T CD-Rom on Cross-Cultural Comm. 1997, chmn. task force on e-commerce, 2002—), Am. Bar Found. (standing com. tech. and info. systems 1998-99, pub. bd. gen. practice 1998—), Mass. Bar Assn. (bd. dels., exec. com. 1981-83, chmn. law practice sect. 1983-85), Mass. Bar Found. Home: 35 Three Ponds Rd Wayland MA 01778-1732 Office: Aresty Internat Law Offices Bay 107 Union Wharf Boston MA 02109 E-mail: jaresty@cyberspaceattorney.com.

AREY, WILLIAM GRIFFIN, JR., former government official; b. Shelby, N.C., Feb. 18, 1918; s. William Griffin and Catherine (Roberts) A.; m. Louise Turner Craft, Mar. 7, 1942 (dec. 1988); children: William Griffin III, John G. C.; m. Jean Getman, July 13, 1991. AB, U. N.C., Chapel Hill, 1939. Pub., editor Cleveland Times Pub. Co., Shelby, 1941-48; pub. affairs officer U.S. Dept. State, Bogota, Colombia, 1948-51, Panama, Republic of Panama, 1951-53; pub. rels. officer Panama Canal Co., Balboa Heights, C.Z., 1954-62; with U.S. Travel Svc., U.S. Dept. Commerce, Washington, 1963-76, dir. travel promotion, 1963-67, dep. dir., 1967-70, exec. officer, 1970-73, exec. dir., 1973-76; asst. exec. v.p. Nat. Trust Hist. Preservation, 1976-81, corp. sec., 1981-83, ret., 1987. 1st lt. USAAC, 1942-45. Recipient Silver medal Commerce Dept., 1973. Mem. Pub. Rels. Soc. Am., Internat. Union Ofcl. Travel Orgns. (v.p.), pacific Area Travel Assn. (dir.), Sigma Nu, Nat. Press Club, Cosmos, Rotary. Methodist. Home: Wintergreen Resort RR 1 Box 563 Roseland VA 22967-9204 Home (Winter): The Cypress Bay Club 6 Hadley Lane Hilton Head Island SC 29926

ARFSTEN, DEBRA J, music educator; d. Gordon C and Jean D Arfsten. BA, St. John's Coll., Winfield, KS, 1981—83; MA, Concordia U., Seward, NE, 1989—90; postgrad., Colo. State U., Ft. Collins, CO, 2000—. Director of Christian Education Concordia U., Seward, NE, 1991. Dir. of music Lamb of God Luth. Ch., Humble, Tex., 1990—96, Mt. Calvary Luth. Ch., Phoenix, Ariz., 1996—97, St. John's Luth. Ch. & Sch., Chaska, Minn., 1997—99; dir. of sch. music Immanuel Luth. Ch. & Sch., Loveland, Colo., 1999—. Dir. of Christian edn. intern supr. Concordia U., Irvine, Calif., 1997—97. Cmty. life builder Luth. Ch.-Mo. Synod, St. Louis, 1992. Lutheran. Avocations: travel, outdoors, photography.

ARGETSINGER, CAMERON R. lawyer; b. Youngstown, Ohio, Mar. 1, 1921; s. James Cameron and Louise May (Williams) A.; m. Jean Rose Sause, July 26, 1941; children: James Cameron II, Louise B. (Mrs. Thomas J. Kanaley), Michael R., Marya J. (Mrs. Arthur B. Smith Jr.), Margretta E., Peter O., Robert C., Samuel W., Philip R. AB, Youngstown U., 1951; JD, Cornell U., 1954. Bar: N.Y. 1954, U.S. Dist. Ct. (we. dist.) N.Y. 1977, U.S. Dist. Ct. (no. dist.) N.Y. 1980, U.S. Supreme Ct. 1958. Pvt. practice, Watkins Glen, NY, 1955—70; exec. dir. Sports Car Club of Am., Inc., Denver, 1971-77; ptnr. Lape & Argetsinger, Montour Falls, N.Y., 1977-80; pvt. practice law Montour Falls, 1980—2002; pres. Internat. Motor Racing Rsch. Ctr., Watkins Glen, 2002—. Commr. Internat. Motor Sports Assn., Inc., Tampa, 1985-92. Founder, race dir., exec. dir. Watkins Glen Grand Prix and U.S. Grand Prix, Watkins Glen, 1948-70. 2d lt. U.S. Army, 1942-45. Recipient Woolf Barnato trophy Sports Car Club of Am., Inc., 1948, Best Organized World Championship Grand Prix, Grand Prix Drivers Assn., London, 1965. Mem. NRA, N.Y. Bar Assn. (ho. dels. 1981-82, 96-97), Schyler County Bar Assn. (pres. 1980-83). Republican. Presbyterian. Avocations: books, guns and hunting, cars. Office: 610 S Decatur St Watkins Glen NY 14891 Mailing: PO Box 215 Burdett NY 14818-0215 E-mail: cra@racingarchives.org.

ARGIRION, MICHAEL, editor; b. Chgo., May 2, 1940; s. Gus and Angela A.; m. Sherrie Berlant, Feb. 10; children: Carrie, Glen. Student, DePaul U., 1958-59, Northwestern U., 1959-60, U. Chgo., 1961-62. Copy editor Chgo.'s Am., 1959-68, wire editor, 1969; news editor Chgo. Today, 1970-71, Sunday and features editor, 1971-74; asst. Sunday editor Chgo. Tribune, 1974-75, features editor, 1975-79, asst. mng. editor features, 1979-81, asst. mng. editor news editing, 1981-82, exec. news editor, 1982-83, assoc. editor, 1983; editor Tribune Media Services, 1984, v.p., editor, 1985-93. Co-creator internationally syndicated newspaper word puzzle Jumble, That Scrambled Word Game, 1994—. Editor: History of Your World, 1969. Served with U.S. Army, 1962. Mem. Legacy Club Alaqua Lakes.

ARGIRIS, ATHANASSIOS, oncologist, researcher; b. Athens, Oct. 7, 1966; s. Stavros and Anna Argiris; m. Nektaria Koulaki. MD, Athens Med. Sch., 1990. Diplomate Am. Bd. Internal Medicine. Resident in radiation oncology Areteion U. Hosp., Athens, 1992—94; resident in internal medicine Beth Israel Med. Ctr., N.Y.C., 1994—97; fellow in hematology-oncology Yale U., New Haven, 1997—2000; attending physician Northwestern Meml. Hosp., Chgo., 2000—; asst. prof. medicine Northwestern U., Chgo., 2000—. Head & neck core com., thoracic core com. Ea. Oncology Coop. Group, 2002—. Recipient Young Investigator award, Am. Assn. Cancer Rsch., 2000. Mem.: AMA, ACP, Am. Soc. Clinical Oncology.

ARGIROPOULOS, KATHLEEN O'NEILL, lawyer; b. Washington, July 31, 1948; d. Thomas Grover O'Neill and Elizabeth Jean (Nesbit) O'Neill Berry; m. John George Argiropoulos, July 10, 1976. BA, Mary Wash. Coll of U. Va., 1970, JD, George Washington U., 1973. Bar: D.C. 1973, Temporary Emergency Ct. Appeals 1976, U.S. Ct. Appeals (D.C. cir.) 1978, U.S. Supreme Ct. 1979. Staff atty. Consumer Product Safety Commn., Bethesda, Md., 1973-74; asst. v.p. law, sec. Air Transport Assn. Am., Washington, 1974-84; v.p., gen. counsel, sec. Airlines Reporting Corp., Washington, 1985—; dir. Washington Met. Area Corp. Counsel Assn. (1984—, treas. 1986—). Contbr. chpts. to book. Mem. ABA (standing com. on aeronautical law 1982, taxation com. 1983-84, forum com. on air and space law 1983—, bus. law 1985—). Home: 4741 Rock Spring Rd Arlington VA 22207-4241 Office: Airlines Reporting Corp 1709 New York Ave NW Washington DC 20006-5206

ARGRAVES, HUGH OLIVER, poet, artist, playwright; b. Decatur, Ill., July 7, 1922; s. Wendell Oliver and Helen E. (Sax) A. Student, Beloit (Wis.) Coll., 1937. Retired. Author: Collected Poetry, 1960; contbr. poems to publs.; playwright: Osbert, 1978, The Great Depression, 1978, Greenwich Village, 1979, Hugh Oliver Argraves-Inferno, 1979, The Twenties, 1980, 2 One Act Plays, 1980, King Lear adaption, 1981, Skeleton Play, 1984, London Blitz-1941, 1984, Last Train to Berlin, 1985; 40-yr. retrospective Scuggi Gallery, Rockford, 1997; featured video The Great Depression; various group shows include Lynn Kottler Galleries, 1961, 66, Ahda Artz Galleries, N.Y.C., 1962-66, Ligoa Duncan Gallery, 1968; represented in permanent collection Mus. Modern Art, N.Y., Rockford Art Mus. Served with U.S. Army, 1943-46. Recipient Jessica Holt award, 1997. Republican. Presbyterian. Home and Office: Apt 502 111 W State St Rockford IL 61101

ARGUE, DON HARVEY, college president, minister; b. Winnipeg, Man., Can., July 12, 1939; came to U.S., 1948; s. Andrew Watson and Hazel Bell (May) A.; m. Patricia Jean Opheim, Sept. 23, 1961; children: Laurie, Lee, Jonathan. BA, Cen. Bible Coll., Springfield, Mo., 1961; MA, Santa Clara U., 1967; EdD, U. of the Pacific, 1969; postdoctoral study, Gordon-Conwell Theol. Sem., 1990, Regent Coll., Vancouver, Can., 1990. Ordained to ministry Assemblies of God, 1964. Pastor 1st Assembly of God, Morganville, Calif., 1965-67; dean of students/men Bethany Coll., Santa Cruz, Calif., 1967-69; asst. prof., dean of student life, dean of students Evangel Coll., Springfield, 1969-74; dean, v.p. North Cen. Bible Coll., Mpls., 1974-79; pres. North Ctrl. Bible Coll., Mpls., 1979—2002, Northwest Coll., 1998—. Gen. presbyter Assemblies of God, Springfield. Recipient Decade of Growth award Christianity Today, 1990. Mem. Nat. Assn. Evangs. (1st v.p.), Soc. for Pentecostal Studies (pres.), Rotary. Home: PO Box 579 Kirkland WA 98083-0579 Office: NW Coll 5520 108th Ave NE Kirkland WA 98033

ARHANGEL'SKII, ALEXANDER VLADIMIROVICH, mathematician, researcher; b. Moscow, Russia, Russia, Mar. 13, 1938; arrived in U.S., 1990, permanent resident, 1993; s. Vladimir Alexandrovich and Maria Pavlovna Arhangel'skii; m. Ol'ga Konstantinovna Razduvaeva, May 11, 1959; children: Tatyana Arhangelskaya, Vladimir. Ph D and DSc (Math), Moscow U., Moscow, Russia, 1961. Asst. prof. Moscow U., 1961—64, assoc. prof., 1964—69, prof., 1970—2000. Expert in topology (prof.) Unesco Project, Islamabad U., Pakistan, 1972—75; prof. Ohio U., Athens, OHIO, 1993—2002. Author: (book) Foundations of General Topology in Problems and Exercises, 1974, Topological Function Spaces, 1992. Grantee, NSF, 1994-1997. Office: Dept Math Ohio Univ 321 Morton Hall Athens OH 45701 Office Fax: 740-593-9805. Business E-Mail: arhangel@bing.math.ohiou.edu.

ARIAN, EYAL, mathematician; b. Rehovoth, Israel, July 23, 1962; came to the U.S., 1993; s. Asher and Shoshana Arian; m. Einat Arian, Sept. 21, 1992; children: Morelle, Yuval. BS in Physics and Math., Hebrew U., Jerusalem, 1987; MS in Physics, Tel Aviv U., 1990; PhD in Applied Math., Weizmann Inst., Rehovoth, 1994. Staff scientist Inst. Computer Applications in Sci. and Engring., NASA, Hampton, Va., 1994-99; asst. prof. dept. math. Ohio U., Athens, 1999—2001; applied mathematician The Boeing Co., Seattle, 2001—. E-mail: eyalarian1@netscape.net.

ARIARAJAH, S. WESLEY, educator, former clergyman, church administrator; b. Jaffna, Sri Lanka, Dec. 2, 1941; s. Ponniah David and Grace Annalukshimi (Sinnappu) S.; m. Christine Shyamala Chinniah, Dec. 7, 1953; children: Sudharshini, Niroshini, Anushini. BSc, Madras Christian Coll., India, 1963; BD, United Theol. Coll., Bangalore, India, 1966; ThM, Princeton (N.J.) Seminary, 1972; M. Phil., U. London, 1974, PhD, 1987. Ordained to ministry Methodist Ch. Minister Meth. Ch. of Sri Lanka, Jaffna, 1966-68; lectr. Theol. Coll. Lanka, Pilimatalawa, Sri Lanka, 1969-71; chmn. North and East Dist. Meth. Ch., Jaffna, 1974-81; program staff WCC program on Dialogue with People of Living Faiths, Geneva, 1981-83; dir. World Council Chs. program on Dialogue with People of Living Faiths, Geneva, 1983-91; dep. gen. sec. World Coun. Chs., Geneva, 1991—97; prof. Drew U., Madison, N.J., 1997—. Author: Dialogue, 1980, The Bible and People of Other Faiths, 1986, Hindus and Christians: A Century of Protestant Ecumenical Thought, Currents of Encounter Series, Vol. 5, 1991, Did I Betray the Gospel-The Letters of Paul and the Place of Women, Risk Series, 1996, Not Without My Neighbor-Issues in Interfaith Dialogue, W.C.C., 1998; contbr. articles to profl. jours. Home: Grand Saconnex 5 chemin de Taverney CH-1218 Geneva Switzerland Office: Drew U Sch Theology 36 Madison Ave Madison NJ 07940 E-mail: wariaraj@drew.edu.

ARIAS, INOCENCIO F. diplomat; b. Albox, Spain, Apr. 20, 1940; married; 3 children. Degree in law, U. Complutense, Madrid. Mem. Spanish Diplomatic Svc., 1967—; dir. Diplomatic Info. Office Spain Fgn. Ministry, 1980-82, 85-88, 1996-97, undersec., 1988-91, state sec. internat. cooperation and Iberamerican affairs, 1991-93; permanent rep. of Spain UN, 1997—. Mem. session European Coun., NATO summit, 1997.; mem. conf. on environ. and devel. UN, 1992; participant 4 Iberoamerican summits, Mid. East summit, Madrid, 1991. Contbr. articles to profl. publs. Gen. dir. Real Madrid Soccer Club, 1993, 95. Office: Permanent Rep Spain UN 823 UN Plaza 345 E 46th St Fl 9 New York NY 10017-3004

ARIAS, OMAR S. economist; b. Bani, Dominican Republic, Mar. 10, 1972; life ptnr. Mabel Martinez. M in econ., U. of Ill. at Urbana-Champaign, 1995, PhD in econ., 1993. Economist World Bank, Washington, 1998—99. Contbr. articles to prof. jours. and books. Exec. dir. Group of Dominican Professionals in Washington-DC, Washington, 2001—02. Recipient Jr. Profl., Inter-American Devel. Bank, 1999. Mem.: Econometric Soc., Latin Am. Econ. Assn. Avocation: chess. Home: 2038 S 6th St Arlington VA 22204 Office: Inter-American Development Bank 1300 New York Avenue, NW Washington DC 20577 Office Fax: 202 623 3299.

ARIAS SANCHEZ, OSCAR, former president of Costa Rica; b. Sept. 13, 1940; Law and econs., U. Costa Rica, 1967; M in Polit. Sci., U. Essex, Eng., 1974. Prof. U. Costa Rica, 1969-72; minister nat. planning Republic of Costa Rica, 1972-77; rep. Legis. Assembly, Costa Rica, 1978-82; pres. Republic of Costa Rica, 1986-90. Internat. sec. Nat. Liberation Party, 1975, gen. sec., 1979-81, v.p. bd. dirs. Cen. Bank of Costa Rica, 1970-72, dir., 1972-77; bd. dirs. Tech. Inst., Costa Rica, 1974-77; mem. Nat. Coun. Univ. Rectors, 1974-77; bd. dirs. Internat. U. Exch. Fund, Switzerland, 1976; mem. internat. adv. coun. Inst. Internat. Studies; participant numerous profl. confs. and seminars throughout the world. Author: Grupos De Presión En Costa Rica, 1970 (Essay's Nat. Award, 1971), Quién Gobierna En Costa Rica, 1976. Latin American Democracy, Independence and Society 1977, Roads for Costa Rica's Development, 1977, New Ways for Costa Rican Development, 1980. Mem. adv. coun. Stockholm Internat. Peace Rsch. Inst., The Inn at The Carter Ctr., Internat. Press

Svc., UNCED, Internat. Peace Acad., The Interaction Coun., The Commn. on Global Govts., Inst. Internat. Studies Stanford U. Recipient Nobel Peace prize, 1987, Martin Luther King Peace prize, 1987, Prince of Asturias award, 1988, Co-recipient Liberty medal Phila., 1991. Office: Arias Found Peace & Human Progress Apdo 8-6410-1000 San José Costa Rica

ARIEFF, ALLEN IVES, physician; b. Chgo., Sept. 30, 1938; BS in Math. and Chemistry, U. Ill., 1960; MS in Physiology, MD, Northwestern U., 1964. Intern Phila. Gen. Hosp., 1964-65; resident SUNY, Bklyn., 1967-68; renal fellow U. Colo., Denver, 1968-69; rsch. and edn. assoc., clin. investigator Wadsworth VA Med. Ctr., L.A., 1970-74; asst. prof. medicine, rsch. scientist UCLA Med. Ctr., 1971-74; asst. prof. medicine, dir. hemodialysis U. Calif. VA Med. Ctr., San Francisco, 1975-76, assoc. prof. medicine, dir. nephrology sect., 1976-83, prof. medicine, chief clin. nephrology, 1983-86, prof. medicine, dir. rsch. & edn. geriatrics, 1986—. Cons. and spkr. in field. Author: 6 books; contbr. . Fellow: ACP; mem.: Soc. Neurosci., Internat. Soc. Nephrology, We. Soc. Clin. Rsch., We. Assn. Physicians, Assn. Am. Physicians, Am. Soc. Bone and Mineral Rsch., Am. Soc. Clin. Investigation, Am. Soc. Neurochemistry, Am. Physiol. Soc., Am. Diabetes Assn., Am. Fedn. Med. Rsch., Am. Soc. Nephrology. Office: Penthouse 9400 Brighton Way Ph Beverly Hills CA 90210-4712

ARIENS, KARLA RAE, library director; b. Tremonton, Utah, July 3, 1966; d. Paul Elias and Lorna May Adams; m. Thaddeus William Ariens, Mar. 17, 1988; children: Talia Louise, Tori May, Terese Claire. BS in Elem. Edn., Utah State U., 1988. Tchr. asst. Children's Home, Logan, Utah, 1988-89; music specialist Hilltop Sch., Logan, Utah, 1988-89; chpt. I aide Adams Elem. Sch., Logan, Utah, 1989-90; gifted/talented specialist Cache County Sch. Dist., Logan, Utah, 1989-90; libr. dir. Brookville (Ind.) Town-Twp. Libr., 1991—2002. Sec. Franklin County Cmty. Network Com., Brookville, 1995. Mem. Lds Ch. Avocations: music, cooking, reading, piano, singing.

ARIETI, JAMES ALEXANDER, classics educator, writer; b. N.Y.C., May 12, 1948; s. Silvano and Jane (Jaffe) A.; m. Barbara Ann Mapes, May 23, 1976; children: Samuel Abraham, Ruth Sophia. BA, Grinnell Coll., 1969; MA, PhD, Stanford U., 1972. Asst. prof. Stanford (Calif.) U., 1972-74, Pa. State U., University Park, 1974-75, Cornell Coll., Mt. Vernon, Iowa, 1975-77; prof. dept. classics Hampden-Sydney (Va.) Coll., 1978—. Author: Love Can Be Found, 1975, Longinus on the Sublime, 1985, Interpreting Plato: The Dialogues as Drama, 1991, Discourses on the First Book of Herodotus, 1995, The Scientific and the Divine: Conflict and Reconciliation from Ancient Greece to Today, 2003; editor: Hamartia, 1983; contbr. articles to profl. jours. Woodrow Wilson fellow, 1969; NEH fellow, 1977-78. Mem. Am. Philol. Assn., Classical Assn. Middle West and South, Classical Assn. Va., Phi Beta Kappa, Phi Alpha Theta, Eta Sigma Chi. Jewish. Home and Office: Hampden Sydney Coll PO Box 746 Hmpden Sydney VA 23943-0746

ARIF, MOHAMMED, education educator; b. Gorakhpur, India, June 8, 1974; s. Abu Bashar and Bilquees Bano. BS in Mech. Engring., Jamia Millia Islamia, New Delhi, India, 1996; MS in Indsl. Engring., U. of Ctrl. Fla., 1998, PhD, 2002. Grad. rsch. asst. U. of Ctrl. Fla., Orlando, 1996—2001, instr. (gta), 2001—02; asst. prof. bus. adminstrn. Carthage Coll., Kenosha, Wis., 2002—. Fellow Walt Disney World, Lake Buena Vista, Fla., 1999—2001. Author presented papers at confs. on prodn. and ops. mgmt. Efficiency improvement Habitat for Humanity, Plains, Ga., 1997—98. Scholar Merit Fellowship, U. of Ctrl. Fla., 2001. Mem.: Am. Prodn. and Inventory Control Soc. Office: Carthage Coll 2001 Alford Park Dr Kenosha WI 53140

ARIK, BAHA ENGIN, engineering executive; b. Turgutlu, Manisa, Turkey, June 4, 1956; came to U.S., 1974; s. Mustafa Fethi and Nevzer (Ulug) Arik; m. Leyla Gucer, May 6, 1962; children: Yasemin, Meral, Erol. BA in Econs., BSME, Brown U., 1979; MS in Engring., PhD in Engring., Harvard U., 1986. Mech. engr. and economist MIGROS, Zurich, Switzerland, 1978; tchg. asst. Brown U., Providence, 1977-79; rsch. asst. Inst. Exptl. Fluid Mechanics, Goettingen, Fed. Republic of Germany, 1979, Von Karman Inst., Rhode-St.-Genese, Belgium, 1980-81; systems engr. Dantec Electronics, Inc., Allendale, NJ, 1986-87, sr. product applications specialist, 1987-88, mgr. software devel. Mahwah, NJ, 1989-91, v.p., 1990-99, corp. bus. devel. mgr., 1999—2001, mgr. simulation dept., 2000—01; exec. v.p. splty. fiberoptics OZ Optics Ltd., Mt. Arlington, NJ, Canada, 2001—; exec. v.p. Viosense Corp., Pasadena, Calif., 2001—. Rsch. asst. Harvard U., Cambridge, Mass., 1981-86, teaching fellow, 1982-85; lectr. numerous colls., bus. seminars, and confs. worldwide. Author: Classical Approach to Modern Fluid Mechanics, 1988. Recipient Belgian Govt. prize, Von Karman Inst., Rhode-St.-Genese, Belgium, 1981. Mem. ASTM, Am. Phys. Soc., Evelyn Wood Reading Dynamics Inst., Sigma Xi. Avocations: swimming, traveling, classical and new age music, photography, gardening. Home: 3105 Heavenly Ridge St Thousand Oaks CA 91362-1179 Office: 36 S Chester Ave Pasadena CA 91106-3105 Office Fax: 626-432-1996. E-mail: arik@viosense.com.

ARIKER, SHANTI ALICE, lawyer; b. Lafayette, Ind., Mar. 1, 1968; d. Theodore Fishman and Ernestine Stevenson. BA, U. Mass., 1991; JD, U. Va., 1995. Bar: N.Y. 1995, Calif. 1998, Wis. 2002. Assoc. Cadwalader, Wickersham and Taft, N.Y.C., 1995-97, Brobeck, Phleger and Harrison, San Francisco, 1997-98; mng. atty., assoc. gen. counsel E*Trade Group, Inc., Menlo Park, Calif., 1998-2000; sr. dir. legal affairs Logictier, Inc., 2000—01; assoc. Reinhart, Buerner & Van Deuren, Milw., 2002—. Mem. Israeli Def. Forces, 1986-88. Mem. ABA. Jewish. Office: Reinhart Boerner Van Deuren 1000 N Water St Box 2965 Milwaukee WI 53201-2965

ARING, MONIKA, education economist, consultant, researcher; b. Gablonz, Germany, Mar. 14, 1945; d. Heinrich G. and Gisela Ilse (Zelder) Kosmahl; m. Roomet Joost Aring, June 19, 1965; children: Antje, Emily. BA, Bklyn. Coll., 1972; MPA, Harvard U., 1989. Dir. Pro Portsmouth Inc., Portsmouth, N.H., 1976-80; cons. Monika Aring Assocs., Portsmouth, 1980-88; v.p. pub. rels. Internt. Hotels, Portsmouth, 1980-82; v.p. mktg. Am. Leadership Forum, Denver, 1989-91; dir. Inst. for Edn. and Employment, Edn. Devel. Ctr. Inc., Newton, Mass., 1991-96, dir. CTr. for Workforce Devel., 1996—; exec. dir. Ctr. Edn. and Tng. Employment Ohio State U., Columbus, Ohio, 2002—. Project dir. Options for a New Downtown, Portsmouth, 1976-78, N.H. Blue Ribbon Commn. on Edn. and Employment, 1986-88; advisor Edn. Commn. of U.S., 1999—; mem. UNESCO Forum on Lifelong Learning, 1999; tech. advisor U.S Dept. Edn., 1995; keynote spkr. Asian Pacific Econ. Commn., 1999. Author: Global Best Practice in Workforce Development, 1996, also other studies. Social entrepreneur/cons. N.H. Coun. for Humanities, 1977, Somersworth (N.H.) Children's Festival, 1980, Asia Devel. Bank, 1999, U.S. AID, Peru, India, Africa, 1997. Recipient Mayor's award City of Portsmouth, 1978, Leadership award C. of C., 1980; guest of German Parliament, Bonn, 1993. Mem. Knowledge Navigators Found. Avocations: outdoor sports, music, designing, foreign languages (german, russian, french, spanish). Home: 234 Reinhard Ave Columbus OH 43206-2617 E-mail: monikakaring@yahoo.com.

ARIS, JOHN LYNNWOOD, lawyer; b. Ann Arbor, Mich., Dec. 5, 1965; s. Leslie Lynnwood and Virginia Baldwin A.; m. Lana Marie Howe, Sept. 2, 1995; children: Mark Benjamin, Amy Lynne, Ashley Marie. BA in Econs., Coll. William and Mary, 1988; JD, U. Mich., 1991. Bar: Pa. 1991, U.S. Dist. Ct. (ea. dist.) Pa. 1992, U.S. Ct. Appeals (3rd cir.) 1993. Assoc. Duane, Morris LLP, Phila., 1991—2002, Lowenthal & Abrams, P.C., Bala Cynwyd, Pa., 2002—. Mem. Vols. for Indigent, Phila., 1991-96; home meeting leader Living Word Cmty., Phila., 1994-95, 1997-99. Mem.: Pa. Trial Lawyers Assn. Avocations: Bible, tennis, softball, trumpet. Office: Lowenthal & Abrams PC 555 City Line Ave Ste 440 Bala Cynwyd PA 19004

ARIS, ROBERT M, physician, researcher; b. Jacksonville, Fla., Jan. 31, 1958; s. Harry and Edna Aris; 1 child, Patrick H. MD, Vanderbilt U., 1980—84. Lic. med. doctor NC, 1993. Asst. prof. of medicine UCSF, San Francisco, 1990—93; assoc. prof. of medicine UNC at Chapel Hill, 1993—. Dir., lung transplantation program UNC at Chapel Hill, 1996—2002. Contbr. articles to profl. jours. Mem.: Am. Thoracic Soc. (assoc.). Office: U of NC CB # 7020 Pulmonary Division Chapel Hill NC 27599 Home Fax: 919-966-7013; Office Fax: 919-966-7013. E-mail: aris@med.unc.edu.

ARIS, RUTHERFORD, applied mathematician, educator; b. Bournemouth, Eng., Sept. 15, 1929; came to U.S., 1955, naturalized, 1962; s. Algernon Pollock and Janet (Elford) A.; m. Claire Mercedes Holman, Jan. 1, 1958. B.Sc. (spl.) with 1st class honours in Math, London (Eng.) U., 1948, PhD, 1960, D.Sc., 1964; student, Edinburgh (Scotland) U., 1948-50; D.Sc. (hon.), U. Exeter, 1984, Clarkson U., 1985; DEng honoris causa, U. Notre Dame, 1990; Ch.M., fellow, Inst. Math. Appications, 1992; D Engring. honoris causa, Tech. U., Athens, Greece. Tech. officer Billingham div. I.C.I. Ltd., 1950-55; research fellow U. Minn., 1955-56; lectr. tech. math. Edinburgh U., 1956-58; mem. faculty U. Minn., 1958—, prof. chem. engring., 1963—, Regents' prof., 1978-96, Regents prof. emeritus, 1996—. O.A. Hougen vis. prof. U. Wis., 1979; Sherman Fairchild Disting. scholar Calif. Inst. Tech., 1980-81; cons. to industry, lectr., 1961—; IXth Centennial lectr. in chem. engring. U. Bologna, 1988; mem. Inst. for Advanced Study, Princeton, 1994. Author: Optimal Design of Chemical Reactors, 1961, Vectors, Tensors and the Basic Equations of Fluid Mechanics, 1962, reprint edit., 1989, Discrete Dynamic Programming, 1964, Introduction to the Analysis of Chemical Reactors, 1965, Elementary Chemical Reactor Analysis, 1969, reprint edit., 1990, (with N.R. Amundson) First-Order Partial Differential Equations with Applications, 1973, reprint 1999, (with W. Strieder) Variational Methods Applied to Problems of Diffusion and Reaction, 1973, The Mathematical Theory of Diffusion and Reaction in Permeable Catalysts, 1975, Mathematical Modelling Techniques, 1978, 2d edit., 1994, Chemical Engineering in the University Context, 1982; co-editor: Springs of Scientific Creativity, 1982, An Index of Scripts for E.A. Lowe's Codices Latini Antiquiores, 1982, (with Amundson and Rhee) First-order Partial Differential Equations, Vol. I Theory and Applications of Single Equations, 1986, Vol. II Theory and Applications of Systems of Quasilinear Hyperbolic Equations, 1986, 2d edit., 2002, Explicatio Formarum Litterarum*The Unfolding of Letterforms, 1990, (with K. Alhumaizi) Surveying A Dynamical System: The Gray/Scott Reaction In A Two-Phase Reactor, 1995, Mathematical Modeling--A Chemical Engineer's Perspective, 1999. Recipient E. Harris Harbison award for disting. teaching, 1969, Alpha Chi Sigma award Am. Inst. Chem. Engrs., 1969, Chem. Engring. lectr. award Am. Soc. Engring. Edn., 1973, Damköhler medal Deutsche Vereinigung fur Chemie und Verfahrenstechnik, 1991, Richard E. Bellman Control Heritage award Am. Automatic Control Coun., 1992, N.R. Amundson award Internat. Symposium on Chem. Reaction Engring., 1998; sr. rsch. fellow NSF, 1964-65, Guggenheim fellow, 1971-72. Fellow Am. Acad. Arts and Scis., Inst. Math. and Applications, Instn. of Chem. Engring. (hon), mem. NAE, Soc. Nat. Philosophy, Soc. Indsl. and Applied Math., AIChE (R.H. Wilhelm award 1975, Inst. lectr. 1997, Founders award 1999), Mediaeval Acad. Lutheran. Office: Univ Minn Dept Chem Engring & Materials Sci Minneapolis MN 55455 E-mail: raris@umn.edu.

ARISON, MICKY, cruise line company executive, sports team executive; b. Tel Aviv, June 29, 1949; Student, U. Miami. Reservations mgr. Carnival Corp., 1974-76, v.p. passenger traffic, 1976-79, pres., CEO, 1979-90, chmn., CEO, 1990—; managing gen. ptnr. Miami Heat, Miami. Mng. gen. ptnr. Miami Heat. Office: Carnival Cruise Lines Inc 3655 NW 87th Ave Miami FL 33178-2428

ARISS, DAVID WILLIAM, SR., real estate developer, consultant; b. Toronto, Ont., Can., Nov. 29, 1939; s. William H. and Joyce Ethel (Oddy) A.; m. Lillie Ariss, Jan. 26, 1962 (div. 1989); m. Debra Ann Nocciolo, Nov. 17, 1990 (div. 1998); children: Katherine Joyce, David William Jr., Dylan William. BA, Claremont Men's Coll., 1961. Lic. real estate broker. Real estate broker Coldwell Banker, Torrance, Calif., 1971-75; v.p. The Lusk Co., Irvine, Calif., 1975-77; pres. DAL Devel. Co., Corona, Calif., 1977-84; mng. dir. Calif. Commerce Ctr. at Ontario, Ontario, Calif., 1984—. Chmn. Inland Empire Econ. Coun., Ontario, Calif., 1991-92; pres., adv. com. Chaffey Coll., Ontario, 1989; apptd. Calif. World Trade Commn., 1993, 95, 97. Maj. USMC, 1961-70, Vietnam. Decorated Silver Star, Disting. Flying Cross, two Purple Hearts, numerous Air medals. Mem. Urban Land Inst., Nat. Assn. Fgn. Trade Zone, Nat. Assn. Indsl. and Office Parks. Republican. Avocations: skiing, music, reading. Office: PIB Realty Advisors 4375 E Lowell Unit J Ontario CA 91761 Fax: (909) 390-6706. E-mail: daveariss@earthlink.net.

ARISTEI, J. CLARK, lawyer, educator; b. Washington, Sept. 6, 1948; s. Jerome and Eleanor Ruth (Clark) A. AA, L.A. Harbor Coll., 1968; BA cum laude, Calif. State U., Long Beach, 1971; JD, U. San Diego, 1975. Bar: Calif. 1975, U.S. Dist. Ct. (so. dist.) Calif. 1975, U.S. Dist. Ct. (cen. dist.) Calif. 1979, U.S. Dist. Ct. (ea. dist.) Calif. 1993, U.S. Dist. Ct. (no. dist.) N.Y. 1996, U.S. Ct. Appeals (7th cir.) 1997. Pvt. practice, San Diego, 1975; assoc. Bennett Olan Law Office, Beverly Hills, Calif., 1976-77, Fogel, Feldman, Kingler, Ostrov & Klevens, L.A., 1977-92, Kananack, Murgatroyd, Baum & Hedlund, L.A., 1993-94; shareholder Baum, Hedlund, Aristei et al, L.A., 1994—. Adj. prof. law U. West L.A., 1986-97, faculty libr. com., 1995-97. Lectr. in field. Mem. faculty libr. com. U. West L.A., 1995-97. Recipient Am. Jurisprudence award in Constl. Law, 1973, Nat. Air Disaster Found. Safety award, 2002. Mem. State Bar Calif., Consumer Attys. Calif., Consumer Atty. Assn. L.A., L.A. County Bar Assn. Avocations: architecture, bicycling. Office: Baum Hedlund Aristei Guilford & Schiavo 12100 Wilshire Blvd Ste 950 Los Angeles CA 90025-7107 E-mail: caristei@baumhedlundlaw.com.

ARISTIDOU, ARISTOS ANDREA, bioprocess company executive; b. Limassol, Cyprus, July 12, 1964; s. Andreas and Maria Aristidou; m. Pirjo Raikkala; children: Andreas, Alexandros. BSChE, Rice U., 1989, PhD in Chem. Engring., 1994. Bioprocess physiology leader Nat. Tech. Rsch. Ctr. VTT, Espoo, Finland, 1997—2001; quantitative physiology leader Cargill Dow LLC, Minnetonka, Minn., 2001—. Postdoctoral rsch. assoc. MIT, Cambridge, Mass., 1994—97. Author: Metabolic Engineering: Principles & Methodologies. Nat. del. of Finland European Fedn. Biotech., Helsinki, 1997—2001, mem. working party bioreactor performance, 1997—2001. Staff sgt., 1983—85, Cyprus mil. Recipient Outstanding Acad. Achievement award, Hellenic Profl. Soc. of Tex., 1990; Fullbright scholar, Cyprus-Am. Scholarship Program, 1985—89. Mem.: AAAS (assoc.), AIChE (AIChE) (assoc.), Soc. Indsl. Microbiology (assoc.), Am. Soc. Microbiology (assoc.), N.Y. Acad. Scis. (assoc.), Am. Chem. Soc. (assoc.). Achievements include patents for genetic engineering of yeasts for biotechnological applications. Home: 7909 Kingsview Ln N Maple Grove MN 55311 Office: Cargill Dow LLC 15305 Minnetonka Blvd Minnetonka MN 55345 Personal E-mail: aristidou@attbi.com. E-mail: aristos_aristidou@cargilldow.com.

ARKANI-HAMED, NIMA, physicist; b. Houston, Tex. PhD, UC Berkeley, 1993—97. Rsch. assoc. SLAC, Menlo Pk., Calif., 1997—99; prof. of physics UC Berkeley, 1999—2002, Harvard U., 2002—. Packard Found. fellow, David and Lucille Packard Found., 2000—, Sloan fellow, Alfred P. Sloan Found., 2000—02. Achievements include development of the theory of large extra dimensions of space, in collaboration with Savas Dimopoulos and Gia Dvali, to explain the extraordianry weakness of gravity relative to the other forces of nature. Office: Jefferson Laboratory of Physics Harvard U Cambridge MA 02138

ARKEEN, SOLOMON JAE, forensic counselor; b. Port Arthur, Tex., Feb. 21, 1961; s. Sol and Patsy (Vanorsdale) Arkeen; life ptnr. Charles Drake. Degree in social psychology, Park Coll., 1998. Diplomate Nat. Assn. Forensic Counselors; cert. hypnotherapist, alcohol and drug counselor, criminal justice specialist, additions counselor. Lead therapist Correctional Rehab. Svcs., Austin, Tex., 1990-98; adminstrv. dir. Nast, Arkeen & Assocs., Austin, 1998—. Mem. substance abuse adv. bd. Waterloo Counseling Ctr., Austin, 1995; cons., trainer parole divsn. Tex. Dept. Criminal Justice, Austin, 1990—. Contbr. mental health column to Tex. Triangle News, 1993-95. Bd. dirs. Cornerstone Cmty. Ctr., Austin, 1995; mem. Tex. Human Rights Campaign for Lesbi-Gay Polit. Caucus, Austin, 1992—. Mem. Nat. Assn. Alcohol and Drug Abuse Counselors, Tex. Assn. Alcohol and Drug Abuse Counselors, Tex. Assn. Sex Offender Treatment. Democrat. Jewish. Avocations: journalism, art. Office: Nast Arkeen & Assocs 8307 Shoal Creek Blvd Austin TX 78757-7525 E-mail: jaester@aol.com.

ARKHIPOVA, IRINA R. biologist; b. Moscow, Aug. 14, 1960; arrived in U.S., 1991; d. Robert G. Arkhipov and Natalia B. Livanova; m. Sergei V. Pokrovski, Mar. 7, 1981; 1 child, Andrew Pokrovski. BS/MS, Moscow State U., 1983; PhD, Inst. Molecular Biology, Moscow, 1986. Rsch. scientist Inst. Molecular Biology, Moscow, 1986—90; postdoctoral fellow U. Edinburgh, Scotland, 1990—91, Harvard U., Cambridge, Mass., 1991—94, rsch. assoc., 1994—2000, staff scientist, 2000—. Author: Drosophila Retrotransposons, 1995; contbr. articles to profl. jours. Fellow, The Wellcome Trust, London, 1990—91; grantee rsch. planning grant, NSF, 1996—97. Mem.: Genetics Soc. Am. Home: 65 Virginia Rd Waltham MA 02453 Office: Harvard Univ Dept Molecular Cellular Biology 7 Divinity Ave Cambridge MA 02138

ARKILIC, GALIP MEHMET, mechanical engineer, educator; b. Sivas, Turkey, Mar. 10, 1920; came to U.S., 1943, naturalized, 1960; s. Sabir Mehmet and Zahra Fatima (Hocazade) A.; m. Ann A. Bryan, Mar. 31, 1956. BME, Cornell U., 1946; MS, Ill. Inst. Tech., 1948; PhD, Northwestern U., 1954. Registered profl. engr., Va. Mech. engr. Miehle Printing Press and Mfg. Co., Chgo., 1948-49, analyst, 1954-56; research and devel. engr. Mech. and Chem. Industries, Turkey, 1949-52; asst. prof. Pa. State U., University Park, 1956-58; assoc. prof. dept. civil engring. George Washington U., Washington, 1958-63, prof. engring. and applied sci., 1963—, prof. emeritus, 1990—, chmn. dept. engring. mechanics, 1966-69, asst. dean, 1969-74. Contbr. articles to sci. jours. Vice pres. Courtland Civic Assn., Arlington, Va., 1965-66; pres. Am. Turkish Assn., Washington, 1967-71. Served to 2d lt. Turkish Army, 1939-41 Recipient Disting. Leadership award Am. Turkish Assn., 1972; Recognition of Service award Sch. Engring. and Applied Sci., George Washington U., 1976, Spl. Appreciation award Engring. Alumni Assn., George Washington U., 1990; Air Force Office of Sci. Research grantee, 1963-69 Mem. ASME, AAUP, Am. Acad. Mechanics, Math. Assn. of Am., Am. Math. Soc., Wash. Soc. Engrs., Sigma Xi. Clubs: George Washington U. (Washington). Home: 8403 Camden St Alexandria VA 22308-2111 Office: George Washington Univ Sch Of Engringand Applied Sc Washington DC 20052-0001 E-mail: gmarkilic@aol.com.

ARKIN, L. JULES, lawyer; b. NYC; s. Joseph and Mildred (Neidenberg) A.; m. Sandra Rauthbord (div. 1983); children: Richard, Gary; m. Shirley Feldman. Student, Emory U., 1946-48; LLB, U. Miami, 1952. Bar: Fla. 1952. Ptnr. Meyer, Weiss, Rose, Arkin, Shampanier, Ziegler & Barash, PA, Miami Beach, Fla., 1954-85, Therrel Baisden & Meyer Weiss, 1985-96; pres., dir. Fin. Fed. Savs and Loan Assn. Dade County, 1980-84. Past chmn. adv. bd. City of Miami Beach Social Svcs.; past pres., past chmn. Found. Jewish Philanthropies, Greater Miami Jewish Fedn.; bd. dirs. Hebrew Immigration Aid Soc., Coun. Jewish Fedns.; life trustee, past v.p. bd. Mt. Sinai Hosp. Greater Miami, past pres. sustaining bd. fellows. Lt. comdr. USNR, 1948-54. Recipient Pres.'s Leadership award Greater Miami Jewish Fedn., 1967, Silver Medallion award NCCH, 1979; named Outstanding Civic Leader of Miami Beach, Civic League Miami Beach, 1971. Mem. ABA, Fla. Bar Assn., Dade County and Miami Beach Bar Assn., Miami Beach C. of C. (trustee, past pres., past mem. bd. govs.), Greater Miami C. of C. (bd. govs.), Masons, Kiwanis, Westview Country Club (Miami; pres.). E-mail: jules@thearkins.com.

ARKIN, MICHAEL BARRY, lawyer, arbitrator, writer; b. Washington, Jan. 11, 1941; s. William Howard and Zenda Lillian (Liebermann) A.; children and stepchildren: Tracy Renee, Jeffrey Harris, Marcy Susan, Chatom Callan, Michael Edwin, Samuel Hopkins, Brandon Maddox, Jessica Remaley, Brandi Remaley, Casey Remaley; m. Laura Dorene Haynes, Aug. 16, 1998. AA, George Washington U., 1961; BA in Psychology, U. Okla., 1962, JD, 1965. Bar: Okla. 1965, U.S. Ct. Claims 1968, U.S. Supreme Ct. 1968, Calif. 1970, U.S. Tax Ct. 1970, U.S. Ct. Appeals (3d, 5th, 6th, 9th, 10th cirs.) 1970, U.S. Dist. Ct. (cen. dist.) Calif. 1970, U.S. Dist. Ct. (so. dist.) Calif. 1970, U.S. Dist. Ct. (ea. dist.) Calif. 1987. Trial atty. tax divsn. U.S. Dept. Justice, 1965-68, appellate atty., 1968-69; ptnr. Surr & Hellyer, San Bernardino, Calif., 1969-79; mng. ptnr. Wied, Granby Alford & Arkin, San Diego, 1979-82, Lorenz Alhadeff Fellmeth Arkin & Multer, San Diego, 1982, Finley, Kumble, Heine, Underberg, Manley & Casey, San Diego, 1983; pvt. practice Sacramento and San Andreas (Calif.), 1984-86; ptnr. McDonough Holland & Allen, Sacramento, 1986-87; pvt. practice San Andreas, Calif., 1987—; chief counsel Calaveras County Child Protective Svcs., 1996—2002; hearing officer Calif. Spl. Edn. Hearing Office, McGeorge Sch. Law, U. Pacific, 2002—. Judge pro-tem Calaveras County (Calif.) Consol. Cts., 1999-2002. Author: History of the Bench and Bar of Calaveras County California, 1997—. Bd. dirs. San Bernardino County Legal Aid Soc., 1971-73, sec., 1971-72, pres., 1973; mem. Calaveras County Adv. Com. on Alcohol and Drug Abuse, 1985-94, pres., 1991-92; treas. Calaveras County Legal Assistance Program, 1987—; trustee Calaveras County Law Libr., 1987-98; bd. dirs. Mark Twain Hosp. Dist., 1990-2003, treas., 1994—; mem. Calaveras County Rep. Ctrl. Com., 1990-92, 94-96; Calaveras County chmn. Wilson for Gov., 1994. Named to Hon. Order of Ky. Cols., 1967. Mem. ABA, Calif. Bar Assn. (Wiley F. Manuel pro bono pub. svc. award 1991), San Diego County Bar Assn., San Bernardino County Bar Assn. (bd. dirs., sec.-treas. 1973-75, pilot drug abuse program 1970), Calaveras County Bar Assn. (bd. dirs., v.p. 1988-90, pres. 1990-95), Am. Arbitration Assn. (arbitrator 1987—). Jewish. Home: 10675 Kate Vincent Ct Nevada City CA 95959 Office: McGeorge Sch Law U of Pacific 3200 5th Ave Sacramento CA 95817 E-mail: markin2500@aol.com.

ARKIN, STANLEY S. lawyer; b. L.A., Feb. 28, 1938; s. Jerome and Lillian (Rogo) A.; m. Suzanne Arkin, Mar. 3, 1963; children: Adam Arkin, Alexander Arkin, Anthony Arkin. AB, U. So. Calif., 1959; JD cum laude, Harvard U., 1962. Bar: N.Y. 1964, Calif. 1977, D.C. 1982. Sr. ptnr. Stanley S. Arkin, P.C., N.Y.C., 1969-90, Chadbourne & Parke, N.Y.C., 1990-93, Arkin Kaplan, LLP (formerly Arkin Kaplan & Cohen LLP), N.Y.C., 1994—; chmn. Arkin Group LLC (pvt. intelligence agy.), 2000—. Author: (with Matthew Bender) Business Crime, 1982, (with Matthew Bender) Hi Tech Crimes, 1989; columnist, contbr. articles to newspapers and profl. jour. With JAGC U.S. Army, 1962—68. Fellow Am. Coll. Trial Lawyers; mem. Coun. on Fgn. Rels., Phi Beta Kappa. Office: Arkin & Kaplan LLP 590 Madison Ave 35th Fl New York NY 10022

ARKING, LUCILLE MUSSER, nurse, epidemiologist, nursing administrator; b. Centre County, Pa., Jan. 26, 1936; d. Boyd Albert and Marion Anna (Merryman) Musser; m. Robert Arking, May 8, 1959; children: Henry David, Jonathan Jacob. RN, Episcopal Sch. Nursing, 1958; BSN, U. Pa., 1968; MSN, Wayne State U., 1986, postgrad., 1991—96. Psychiat. rsch. nurse Boston City Hosp., 1958; hosp. supr. Phila. Psychiat. Ctr., 1959-61; pub. health nurse Cmty. Nursing Svc., Phila., 1961-64; DON Green Acres Nursing Ctr., Phila., 1966-67; head nurse U. Va., Charlottesville, 1967-68; asst. DON U. Ky., Lexington, 1968-70; asst. dir. nursing edn. Rio Hondo Hosp., Downey, Calif., 1973-75; DON Bellwood Hosp., Bellflower, Calif., 1974-75; nurse epidemiologist Henry Ford Hosp., Detroit, 1975-84, dir. hosp. epidemiology, 1984-89, sr. clin. epidemiologist, 1990-94; v.p. clin. svcs. Great Lakes Rehab. Hosp., Southfield, Mich., 1994-96; adminstr. Cadillac Nursing Ctr., Detroit, 1997-99; exec. dir. St. Anthony Nursing Care Ctr., Warren, Mich., 1999—2001; with office of internat. affairs Pusan (South Korea) Nat. U., 2001; with St. James Nursing Ctr., Detroit, 2002—. Lectr. drug abuse Fountain Valley, Calif., 1970-75; instr. Santa Ana Coll., 1971-73. Contbr. articles to profl. jours. Co-founder Parents and Friends Learning Disabilities Orgn., 1968-70; dean leader Cub Scouts, Fountain Valley, 1968-75; bd. dirs. Wellness Networks, Detroit, 1982-86; mem. Mich. Gov. AIDS Task Force, 1985-86, Mich. Med. Soc. AIDS Task Force, 1986. Women's Club of Centre County scholar, 1954-58; grantee Cmty. Nursing Svc. Ednl., 1963-64; USPHS nursing trainee, 1965. Mem. APHA (mem. epidemiology sect. 1975-99), ANA, Mich. Nurses's Assn. (AIDS task force 1987-89, HIV adv. com. 1989-90), Assn. Practitioners Infection Control, Sci. Rsch. Soc., Assn. Women in Sci., Sigma Xi. Home: 4705 Stoddard Dr Troy MI 48085-3504

ARKY, RONALD ALFRED, medical educator; b. New Brunswick, N.J., June 26, 1929; s. Eugene and Ida (Glick) A.; m. Marie Mahoney, Sept. 14, 1963. AB, Cornell U., Ithaca, N.Y., 1951; MD, Cornell U., N.Y.C., 1955. Intern Bellevue Hosp., N.Y.C., 1955-56; resident N.Y. VA Hosp., 1958-60; fellow Thorndike Meml. Lab., Boston City Hosp., 1961-63; dir. diabetes clinic Boston City Hosp., 1966-71; Charles S. Davidson prof. medicine Harvard U. Med. Sch., Cambridge, Mass., 1984—. Chmn. dept. medicine Mt. Auburn Hosp., 1971-93; pres. Assocs. Program for Dirs. Internal Medicine, 1990-91; chief diabetes sect. Brigham and Women's Hosp., Boston, 1996—. Fellow AAAS; Master ACP, Peabody Soc. Harvard Med. Sch.; mem. Am. Diabetes Assn. (pres. 1979-80), Am. Soc. Clin. Investigation, Endocrine Soc., Am. Clin. Climatol. Soc. Office: Francis W Peabody Soc Harvard Med Sch 260 Longwood Ave Boston MA 02115-5701

ARLACCHI, PINO, protective services official; b. Gioa Tauro Marina, Feb. 21, 1951; Degree in Sociology, U. Trento, 1973. Expert criminologist, 1984-86; v.p. Italian Parliamentary Commn. on Organized Crime, 1987-91; cons. Bicameral Parliamentary Inquiry Commn., 1991, v.p., 1996; prof. U. Calabria;

dep. Dem. Party of the Left; mem. Justice Commn.; Senator Dem. Party of the Left, 1996-97; dir. Office Drug Control and Crime Prevention UN, 1997—. Vis. prof. Columbia U., N.Y.C. Contbr. articles to profl. jours. Named Hon. Pres. Giovanni Falcone Found. Office: UN Internat Drug Control Program Vienna Internat Ctr POB 500 1400 Vienna Austria

ARLEDGE, CHARLES STONE, former aerospace executive, entrepreneur; b. Bonham, Tex., Oct. 20, 1935; s. John F. and Mary Madeline (Jones) A.; m. Barbara Jeanne Ruff, June 18, 1966; children: John Harrison, Mary Katherine. BS, Stanford U., 1957, MS (Standard Oil Co. Calif. scholar 1958), 1958, MBA, 1966. Engr. Shell Oil Co., Los Angeles, 1958-64; with Signal Cos., La Jolla, Calif., 1966-86, v.p., 1970-79, group v.p., 1979-83, sr. v.p., 1983-86; v.p. Aerojet Gen. Corp., La Jolla, Calif., 1986-90; ptnr. Signal Ventures, 1990—. Mem.: California; La Jolla Beach and Tennis. Republican. Presbyterian. Home: PO Box 957 Rancho Santa Fe CA 92067-0957 Office: 777 S Pacific Coast Hwy Ste 107 Solana Beach CA 92075-2623

ARLEDGE, ROONE, television executive; b. Forest Hills, N.Y., July 8, 1931; m. Gig Shaw, May 21, 1994; children: Elizabeth Ann, Susan Lee, Patricia Lu, Roone Pinckney. BA, Columbia Coll., 1952; LHD (hon.), Boston U.; LLD (hon.), Wake Forest U. Prodr. network sports, Wide World of Sports ABC-TV, 1960—61, v.p. charge sports, 1964—68; pres. ABC Sports, Monday Night Football, 1968—85, ABC News, Nightline, 1977—98; group pres. ABC News and Sports, 1985—90; exec. prodr. all ABC sports programs, including 10 Olympic games, 1968; pres. ABC News, chmn., from 1998. Bd. dirs. Coun. Fgn. Rels., ESPN, Arts & Entertainment Network, History Channel; dean's coun. Harvard U. JFK Sch. of Govt. Creator ABC's Wide World of Sports, 1961, NFL Monday Night Football, 1970, ABC's World News Tonight, Nightline, 20/20, This Week with David Brinkley, PrimeTime Live, Viewpoint, Turning Point, Capital to Capital, World News This Morning, World News Now, Day One, responsible most tech. and editl. innovations in sports coverage. Mem. Pres.'s Coun. on Physical Fitness; pres. Com. Meml. Sloan Kettering Hosp.; bd. visitors Columbia Coll.; chmn. sports com. Pres.'s Coun. on Physical Fitness; trustee Columbia U. Served U.S. Army, 1953—54. Named Man of Yr., Nat. Assn. Program Execs.; named to TV Acad. Arts and Scis. Hall of Fame, 1990, U.S. Olympic Hall of Fame, 1990, Nat. Assn. Broadcasters Hall of Fame, 1994; recipient 36 Emmy awards, 4 George Foster Peabody awards, 2 Christopher awards, Broadcast Pioneers award, Gold medal, Internat. Radio and TV Soc., 1983, Disting. Svc. to Journalism Honor medal, U. Mo., John Jay Disting. Profl. Svc. award, Columbia U., Lifetime Achievement award, TV Critics Assn., Disting. Achievement award, U. So. Calif. Journlism Assn., Founders award, Acad. TV Arts and Scis. Inst., Grand Prix Montreux TV award, Olympic Order medal, Internat. Olympic Com., Grand prize, Cannes Film Festival. Mem.: Portmarnock Golf Club (Dublin), Castle Pines Golf Club, Winged Foot Golf Club, Deepdale Golf Club, Nat. Golf Links Am., Shinnecock Hills Golf Club, Royal and Ancient Golf Club. Died Dec. 5, 2002.

ARLEN, JENNIFER HALL, law educator; b. Berkeley, Calif., Jan. 7, 1959; d. Michael John and Ann (Warner) A.; m. Robert Lee Hotz, May 21, 1988; children: Michael Arlen Hotz, Robert Arlen Hotz. BA, Harvard U., 1982; JD, NYU, 1986; PhD in Econs., NYU, 1992, 1992. Bar: N.Y. 1987, U.S. Ct. Appeals (11th cir.) 1987. Summer clk. U.S. Dist. Ct. (ea. dist.) N.Y., Bklyn., 1984; summer assoc. Davis Polk & Wardwell, N.Y.C., 1985; law clk. U.S. Cir. Judge, 11th cir., Savannah, Ga., 1986-87; asst. prof. law Emory U., Atlanta, 1987-91, assoc. prof. law, 1991-93; prof. law U. So. Calif., L.A., 1994—2002, Ivadelle and Theodore Johnson prof. law and bus., 1997—2002; prof. law NYU, 2002—. Vis. prof. law U. So. Calif., 1993, Calif. Inst. Tech., winter, 2001, Yale U., 2001—02; dir. U. So. Calif. Ctr. in Law, Econs. and Orgn., 2000—02; mem. acad. bd. NYU Ctr. in Law and Bus., 2003—. Olin fellow U. Calif. Sch. Law, Berkeley, 1991. Mem. ABA, Am. Assn. Law Schs. (chair remedies sect. 1994, chair elect 1993, mem. exec. com. 1990-91, 95, chair torts sect. 1995, chair-elect 1994, treas. 1991, sec. 1992-93, exec. com. bus. assns. sect. 1995-96, 2000—, chair law and econ., sect. 1996, chair-elect law and econs. sect. 1995, chair 1996), Am. Law and Econ. Assn. (bd. dirs. 1991-93, program com. 1999), Am. Econ. Assn., Order of Coif, Am. Law Inst. Democrat. Office: NYU Law Sch 40 Washington Square S New York NY 10012

ARLEN, MICHAEL J. writer; b. London, Dec. 9, 1930; s. Michael and Atlanta (Mercati) A.; m. Ann Warner, 1957 (div. 1971); children— Jennifer, Caroline, Elizabeth, Sally; m. Alice Albright Hoge, 1972; stepchildren— Alicia, James Patrick, Robert Hoge. Grad., St. Paul's Sch., Concord, N.H., 1948, Harvard U., 1952; LLD (hon.), Colby Coll., 1984. Reporter Life mag., 1952-56; contbr., TV critic The New Yorker mag., 1957-82; juror Columbia U.-Dupont awards for broadcast journalism, 1969-72, 78-80; faculty Bread Loaf Writers Conf., 1980. Bd. dirs. Nat. Arts Journalism Program. Author: Living-Room War, 1969, Exiles, 1970, An American Verdict, 1973, Passage to Ararat, 1975, The View from Highway 1, 1976, Thirty Seconds, 1980, The Camera Age, 1981, Say Goodbye to Sam, 1984. Recipient award for television criticism Screen Dirs. Guild, 1968; Nat. Book award for contemporary affairs, 1976; Le Prix Brémond, 1976 Mem. Authors Guild (exec. coun.), PEN Am. Ctr., Knickerbocker Club, Century Assn., Harvard Club of N.Y.

ARLIDGE, JOHN WALTER, retired utility company executive; b. Rochester, N.Y., Feb. 4, 1933; s. Harold Wesley and Grace Edith (Kempshall) A.; m. Sandra Marie Koswar, Feb. 4, 1955; children: James William, Edward John. BS, L.A. State Coll., 1962. Registered profl. engr., Calif., Nev., Utah. Comm. sys. engring. design and purchase City of L.A., 1961-62, power sys. resource planning R & D, 1962-74; asst. to v.p. Nev. Power Co., Las Vegas, 1974-82, v.p. resource planning and power dispatch, 1982-89, sr. v.p. govt. affairs, 1989-93; v.p., dir. Nev. Electric Investment Co., Las Vegas, 1982-89; cons. on energy resources and regulation, Las Vegas, 1995—. Advisor electric-lignite sector Ministry Indusry and Trade, Warsaw, Poland, 1992-95; mem. Nev. Engr.'s Adv. Com. on Geothermal Devel., 1974-76, Nev. Solar Energy Devel. Adv. Group, 1976-86; mem. energy task force WEST, 1972-84, mem. energy engring. planning com., 1978; mem. advanced energy sys. divsnl. com. Electric Power Rsch. Inst., 1973-92; mem. Western Utility Group on Fed. Land, 1977; mem. endangered species subcom., rail issues group Edison Elec. Inst., 1977; cons. on air, land and water Western Regional Coun., 1977; mem. Nev. adv. bd. U.S. Bur. Land Mgmt., 1975-77, mem. adv. coun. Las Vegas dist., 1980-92; mem. rsch. adv. bd. U. Nev.; trustee Corp. Devel. Sci. Tech. Nev. Contbr. articles on energy resources to various publs. Mem. Nev. adv. bd. Nature Conservancy; mem. Sec. Energy's Nat. Coal Coun., 1988-93. With USMC, 1950-54. Mem. IEEE, Geothermal Resources Coun. (dir.), utility Coal Gasification Assn. (chmn.), Internat. Solar Energy Assn., Nat. Coal Coun. (advisor to sec. energy), Pacific Coast Elec. Assn., So. Nev. Off-Road Vehicle Assn., Slurry Transp. Assn. (dir. 1979), Masons.

ARLING, BRYAN JEREMY, internist; b. Mpls, Dec. 10, 1944; s. Leonard Swenson and Marion (Schroeder) A.; m. Donna Dickson; children: Elissa, Jeremy, Timothy. BA summa cum laude, U. Minn., 1965; MD, Harvard U., 1969. Diplomate Am. Bd. Internal Medicine. Intern Stanford Affiliated Hosp., Calif., 1969-70, resident in internal medicine, 1970-71; spl. asst. to adminstr. health sci. mental health adminstrn. USPHS, Rockville, Md., 1971-73; instr., chief resident medicine George Washington U. Hosp., Washington, 1973-74, asst. prof. medicine, 1974-77; pvt. practice Washington, 1977—; clin. prof. medicine George Washington U., 1988—, Georgetown U., Washington, 1997—. Adminstrv. bd. Chevy Chase United Meth. Ch.; mem. devel. com. Maret Sch., 1985-98, trustee, 1991-98, v.p., 1994-98; question relevance reviewer Am. Bd. Internal Medicine, 1991-92, com. on certifying and recertifying exam., 1992-93. Named One of Best Doctors in Town, Washington Mag., 1986, 95, 99, One of Best Pediatricians and Internists, 1987, Top Internist by other doctors, 1993, Best Doctors in Am., 1994-95, 1996. Fellow ACP; adv. coun. on med. ed., Harvard Med. Sch., 2003-; mem. AMA, Am. Soc. Internal Medicine, DC Med. Soc., Acad. Medicine (mem. exec. com. 1995—), Acad. of Sci. of Washington DC (v.p. 2001—), Smithsonian Assocs., Friends of Kennedy Ctr., Harvard Club Washington, Nat. Trust for Hist. Preservation, Friends of Nat. Zoo, Common Cause, ACLU, Physicians for Social Responsibility, Columbia Country Club, Bahamas Air-Sea Rescue Assn. Home: 3803 Taylor St Bethesda MD 20815-4117 Office: 2440 M St NW Ste 817 Washington DC 20037-1404 *1. Good medicine is more thoroughness than brilliance.2. The sickest body is smarter than the brightest doctor.3. Learn as though you'll never die - live as though you'll die tomorrow.*

ARLING, DONNA DICKSON, social worker; b. Jersey Shore, Pa., July 8, 1945; d. Eugene Robert and Helen (Bardo) Dickson; m. Bryan Jeremy Arling, Aug. 28, 1969; children: Elissa, Jeremy, Timothy. BS, Pa. State U., 1967; MSW, Smith Coll., 1969; PhD, Clinical Social Work Inst., Wash., DC, 2003. Bd. cert. diplomate in clin. social work; cert. social worker, Md.; cert. ind. clin. social worker, D.C. Clin. social worker N. County Mental Health Ctr., Palo Alto, Calif., 1969-71, VA Hosp., Washington, 1971-77; pvt. practice clin. social work Washington, 1978—. Mem. Nat. Assn. Social Workers, Greater Washington Soc. Clin. Social Work, Smith Coll. Sch. Social Work Alumni Assn. (nat. exec. com. 1979-82, Washington exec. com. 1976-86). Home: 3803 Taylor St Chevy Chase MD 20815-4117 Office: 1015 33rd St NW Washington DC 20007-3523

ARLINGHAUS, SANDRA JUDITH LACH, mathematical geographer, educator; b. Elmira, N.Y., Apr. 18, 1943; d. Donald Frederick and Alma Elizabeth (Satorius) Lach; m. William Charles Arlinghaus, Sept. 3, 1966; 1 child, William Edward. AB in Math., Vassar Coll., 1964; postgrad., U. Chgo., 1964-66, U. Toronto, Ont., Can., 1966-67, Wayne State U., 1968-70, MA in Geography, 1976; PhD in Geography, U. Mich., 1977. Vis. instr. math. U. Ill., Chgo., 1966; vis. asst. prof. geography Ohio State U., Columbus, 1977-78, lectr. math., 1978-79, Loyola U., Chgo., 1979-81, asst. prof. math., 1981-82; lectr. math. and geography U. Mich., Dearborn and Ann Arbor, 1982-83; founding dir. Inst. Math. Geography, Ann Arbor, 1985—; pres. Arlinghaus Enterprises, Ann Arbor, 1998—. Guest lectr. U. Chgo., 1979, 87, 2000-01, U. Calif., 1979, Syracuse U., 1991, U. No. Iowa, 1991; guest lectr. U. Mich., Ann Arbor, 1983, 90-93, adj. prof. math. geography, population-environ. dynamics Sch. Natural Resources and Environ., 1994—, adj. prof. Coll. Architecture and Urban Planning, 1997, 2001—; cons. Transp. Rsch. Inst., Coll. Architecture, 1985-86, Coll. Edn., 1992, Cmty. Sys. Found., 1993—; prodr. Ann Arbor Cmty. Access TV, 1988-90; dir. spatial analysis divsn. Cmty. Systems Found., 1996—, dir. fellowship tng. divsn., 1996—; co-founder Arlinghaus Enterprises, 1997, pres. 2000-02, mgr., 2003—. Author: Down the Mail Tubes: The Pressured Postal Era, 1853-1984, Essays on Mathematical Geography, 1986, Essays on Mathematical Geography-II, 1987, An Atlas of Steiner Networks, 1989, Essays on Mathematical Georgraphy-III, 1991; co-author: Population-Environment Dynamics, Sectors in Transition, 1992 and later editions through 1998, Mathematical Geography and Global Art, 1986, Environmental Effects on Bus Durability, 1990, Fractals in Geography, 1993, Graph Theory and Geography: An Interactive View, Ebook 2002, Wiley; founder, editor, co-author Solstice, 1990—, Image Interactive Atlases, Image Game Series, Image Discussion Papers, Internat. Soc. Spatial Scis., 1995—; author, editor-in-chief Practical Handbook of Curve Fitting, 1994; co-author, editor-in-chief Practical Handbook of Digital Mapping: Terms and Concepts, 1994; editor-in-chief Practical Handbook of Spatial Stats., 1995; editor internat. monograph series; reviewer Mathematical Reviews, 1992—; contbr. articles, book reviews to profl. jours. in field of geography, psychology, math., biology, history, philately. Mem. City of Ann Arbor Planning Commn., 1995-2003, sec., 1997-2002, chair, 2002-2003, vice-chmn., 2003; mem. City of Ann Arbor Environ. Commn., 2000-2003; bd. dirs., chmn. Bromley Homeowners Assn., Ann Arbor, 1989-93, pres., 1990-93, 95-96; mem. ordinance revisions com. City of Ann Arbor, 1996-2003, mem. master planning com., 2002-03; bd. dirs. World Jr. Bridge Championships, Ann Arbor, 1990-91, Dolfins Inc., 1993-96; artist Math. Awareness Week, Lawrence Tech. U., 1988; trustee Cmty. Sys. Found., 1995-2001; co-vice chair citizens adv. com. NE Ann Arbor master plan revision, 1999-2000; adv. bd. City of Ann Arbor Police Dept. Neighborhood Watch, 2001—. Recipient Cmty. Svc. award, City of Ann Arbor, 1999. Fellow Am. Geog. Soc. (rep. search com. for curator of collection in Golda Meir Libr. U. Wis.-Milw. Libr. 1993-94); mem. AAAS, Am. Math. Soc., Math. Assn. Am., Assn. Am. Geographers, Internat. Soc. Spatial Scis. (founder), N.Y. Acad. Scis., Engring. Soc. Detroit, Regional Sci. Assn. Achievements include discovery of exact fractal characterization of the geometry of central place theory and its electronic interpretation; alignment of earth marking sculptures to solstices and equinoxes in Minnesota, Washington, Alaska, New Brunswick, Canada, and USSR; creator of one of world's first refereed electronic journals; creator of applications of chaos theory in geography and population environment dynamics, maps for major international projects for Syria and Pakistan. Office: U Mich Sch Natural Resources Ann Arbor MI 48109

ARLOOK, IRA ARTHUR, non-profit association executive; b. N.Y.C., Apr. 7, 1943; s. George G. and Shirley (Meyers) A.; m. Karen Beth Nussbaum, July 9, 1978; children: Gene, Jack, Eleanor. BA, Tufts U., 1964; MA in History, Stanford U., 1966; PhD in Pub. Policy, Union Inst., 1978. Asst. prof. Cleve. State U., 1975-80; exec. dir. Ohio Pub. Interest Campaign, Cleve., 1976-93, Citizen Action, Cleve., Chgo. and Washington, 1980-97. Exec. dir. New Economy Comms., 1998—. Woodrow Wilson Nat. fellow, 1965, NSF fellow, 1980. Mem. Citizens for Tax Justice (pres. 1980-97), Nat. Conf. Alternative State and Local Pub. Policies (bd. dirs. 1976-80), Citizen Labor Energy Coalition (bd. dirs. Washington 1978-90), Nat. Campaign Against Toxic Hazards (bd. dirs. 1983-87). Avocations: sports, music. Office: New Economy Comm 1320 18th St NW 5th fl Washington DC 20036-1811 E-mail: ira@neweconomy.org.

ARLOW, ARNOLD JACK, advertising agency executive, artist; b. Bklyn., Sept. 29, 1933; s. Louis and Sylvia (Spitzberg) A.; m. Phyllis Banschick, Apr. 20, 1958 (div. 1990); children: Susan, Noah; m. Susan Gray, Nov. 22, 1992. B.F.A., Cooper Union, 1954. Art dir. N.Y. Times, 1958-61, Altman Stoller Advt., N.Y.C., 1961-65, Daniel & Charles Advt., N.Y.C., 1965, McCaffrey McCall Advt., N.Y.C., 1965-66; partner, creative dir. Martin Landey, Arlow Advt., N.Y.C., 1966-80; exec. v.p., creative dir. Geers Gross Advt., 1980-83; cons. communications industry, 1983-84; exec. v.p., creative dir. TBWA Advt., 1984-94; ptnr., creative dir. Margeotes, Fertitta & Ptnrs., N.Y.C., 1994—2003; creative cons., painter Amagansett, NY, 1998—99; sr. v.p., dir. luxury mktg. Berenter Greenhouse & Webster, N.Y.C., 2000—01. Tchr. design Wagner Coll., Staten Island, 1964-69 Alumni trustee Cooper Union, 1982-85. Served with USAF Res., 1961-66. Recipient Augustus Saint-Gaudens award for profl. achievement in art Cooper Union, 1995; Fulbright-Hays grantee Paris, 1954-55; Kelly award MPA for Absolut Vodka Campaign, 1988, 90. Democrat. Jewish. Home: 31 W 12th St New York NY 10011-8500 E-mail: arniearlow@aol.com.

ARLOW, JACOB A. psychiatrist, educator; b. N.Y.C., Sept. 3, 1912; s. Adolph A. and Ida (Feldman) A.; m. Alice Diamond, Oct. 31, 1936; children: Michael Saul, Allan Joseph, Seth Martin. BS, N.Y. U., 1932, MD, 1936; Grad., N.Y. Psychoanalytic Inst., 1947. Diplomate: Am. Bd. Neurology and Psychiatry. Rotating intern Harlem Hosp., N.Y.C., 1936-38; resident neuropsychiatrist USPHS Hosp., Ellis Island, N.Y., 1938-39; resident psychiatrist Kings County Hosp., Bklyn., 1939, asst. psychiatrist mental hygiene clinic, 1941; asst. resident neurologist Montefiore Hosp., Bronx, N.Y., 1940-41, asst. neurologist, 1942-44; resident psychiatrist N.Y. State Psychiat. Inst. and Hosp., N.Y.C., 1940-41; cons. psychiatrist Pride of Judea Children's Home, Bklyn., 1940-45; pvt. practice N.Y.C., 1942-92; lectr. N.Y. Psychoanaltyic Inst., 1948-50; instr. neurology Columbia Coll. Phys. and Surg., 1942-44, instr. psychiatry psychosomatic service of psychoanalytic clinic for tng. and research, 1947-51, John B. Turner vis. prof. psychiatry, 1967-68; research asso, instr. psychiatry Presbyn. Hosp.-Columbia Med. Center, 1944-51; clin. asst. prof. psychoanalytic medicine State U. N.Y. Coll. Medicine at N.Y.C., 1952-55, clin. assoc. prof., 1955-62, clin. prof., 1962 79, NYU, N.Y.C., 1979—, mem. faculty Ctr. Psychoanlytic Tng., N.Y.C.; prof. emeritus Albert Einstein Coll. Medicine, N.Y.C.; pvt. practice part-time N.Y.C., 1984—, Great Neck, N.Y., 1984—. Faculty N.Y. Psychoanalytic Inst., 1956— ; vis. prof. psychiatry La. State U. Sch. Medicine, 1969-70, Mt. Sinai Sch. Medicine, N.Y.C., 1972-73; vis. scholar Freud chair Hebrew U., Jerusalem, April, 1985; cons. Hillside Hosp., Glen Oaks, N.Y., 1989—. Author: Legacy of Sigmund Freud, 1956, (with Charles Brenner) Psychoanalytic Concepts and the Structural Theory, 1964, Psychoanalysis: Clinical Theory and Practice, 1991; editor: Selected Writings of Bertram D. Lewin; editor-in-chief Psychoanalytic Quar., 1970-79; mem. editl. bd. Psyche. Vice pres. Great Neck (L.I.) Coop. Sch.; trustee, sec. N.Y. Psychoanalytic Inst., 1956-59. Recipient Centennial award as Alumnus of Decade 1940-49, N.Y. State Psychiat. Inst., Heinz Hartmann award, 1980; Lenox Hill Disting. Clinicians award, 1980; Vexillarius Excellentae award Pride of Judea Mental Health Ctr., Mary Sigourney award Am. Coll. Psychoanalysts 1990, Henry Loughlin award 1991. Mem. APA, Am. Psychoanalytic Assn. (pres. 1960-61, chmn. COPE 1962-66, bd. editors journ. 1958-60, chmn. bd. profl. standards 1967-70, Jour. award 1988); mem. Internat. Soc. Study of Time (coun.), Am. Psychiat. Assn., Psychosomatic Soc., N.Y. Psychoanalytic Inst. (pres. 1966-68), Internat. Psycho-Analytic Assn. (treas., v.p. 1961-69). Address: 94 Wildwood Rd Great Neck NY 11024-1223

ARMACOST, MARY-LINDA SORBER MERRIAM, former academic administrator, consultant; b. Jeannette, Pa., May 31, 1943; d. Everett Sylvester Calvin and Madeleine (Case) Sorber; m. E. William Merriam, Dec. 13, 1969 (div. 1975); m. Peter H. Armacost, July 10, 1993. Student, Grove City Coll., 1961-63; BA, Pa. State U., 1963-65, MA, 1965-67, PhD, 1967-70; HHD (hon.), Carroll Coll., 1991; LLD (hon.), Wilson Coll., 1994. Rsch. assoc. Pa. State U., University Park, 1970-72; asst. prof. speech Emerson Coll., Boston, 1972-79, dir. continuing edn., 1974-77, spl. asst. to pres., 1977-78, v.p. adminstrn., 1978-79; asst. to pres. Boston U., 1979-81; pres. Wilson Coll., Chambersburg, Pa., 1981-91, Moore Coll. Art and Design, Phila., 1991-93; sr. fellow Office of Women in Higher Edn. Am. Coun. on Edn., 1994—; interim pres. Moore Coll. Art and Design, Phila., 1998-99; pres. emerita, 2000. Adj. prof. U. Pa. Grad. Sch. Edn., 2003; cons. Govt. Edn. and Secondary Edn. Act Title III, Alameda County, Calif., 1968. Bd. govs. New Eng. chpt. NATAS, 1980-81; bd. dirs. Sta. WITF, Inc., Harrisburg, Pa., 1982-91, chmn. bd., 1988-91; bd. dirs. Chambersburg Hosp., 1984-89, vice chmn. bd., 1987-89; bd. dirs. Elderhostel, 1997—; vice-chmn., 2000—; trustee Monmouth U., N.J., 1994-99, Sta. WHYY-FM-TV, Phila., 1992-93, Boston Zool. Soc., 1980-81, Arts Boston, 1979-81, Scotland Sch. Vets. Children, Pa., 1984-90, Randolph-Macon Woman's Coll., Lynchburg, Va., 2001—; bd. dirs. Fla. Orch., 1993 97, co chair edn. com., 1995-97, mem. exec. com., 1995-97; mem. exec. com. Found. for Ind. Colls., 1989-91, WEDU-TV, 1998—, chair planning com., mem. exec. com., 1998—; pres. Chambersburg Area Coun. Arts, 1988-90; chmn. higher edn. com. Gen. Assembly Presbyn. Ch., 1987-90; elder Falling Spring Presbyn. Ch., 1988-90; fellow Am. Coun. Edn., 1977-78, commn. on govtl. rels., 1985-89, commn. on women, 1992-93; mem. exec. com. Pa. Assn. Colls. and Univs., 1984-90, mem. exec. com. Assn. Presbyn. Colls. and Univs., 1983-88, pres., 1986-87; mem. edn. adv. com. John S. & James L. Knight Found., 1998-2000. Recipient Disting. Alumna award Pa. State U., 1984, Disting. Dau. of Pa., 1986, Athena award Chambersburg C. of C., 1988, Outstanding Alumnae award Sch. Dist. Jeannette, 1991. Mem.: Phi Kappa Phi. E-mail: mlsma@cs.com.

ARMACOST, MICHAEL HAYDEN, research institution executive, ambassador; b. Cleve., Apr. 15, 1937; s. George H. and Verda Gay (Hayden) A.; m. Roberta June Bray, Mar. 7, 1959; children: Scott, Timothy, Christopher. BA, Carleton Coll., 1958; postgrad., Friedrich Wilhelms U., 1959; MA, Columbia U., 1961, PhD, 1965. Assoc. prof. govt. Pomona Coll., Claremont, Calif., 1962-70, Wig Disting. prof., 1966; mem. policy planning staff State Dept., Washington, 1969-72; spl. asst. to ambassador Am. Embassy, Tokyo, 1972-74; mem. policy planning staff State Dept., Washington, 1974-77; sr. staff mem. NSC, Washington, 1977-78; dep. asst. sec. def. internat. security affairs Dept. Defense, 1978-80, prin. dep. asst. sec. East Asian and Pacific affairs, 1980-82; ambassador to Philippines, 1982-84; under sec. for polit. affairs, 1984-89; ambassador to Japan, 1989-93; disting. sr. fellow, vis. prof. Stanford U., 1993-95; pres. The Brookings Instn., 1995—. Author: The Politics of Weapons Innovation, 1969, The Foreign Relations of United States, 1969, Friends or Rivals ? The Insider's Account of U.S.-Japan Relations, 1996. Recipient Superior Honor award State Dept., 1976, Disting. Civilian Svc. award Def. Dept., 1980, Presdl. Disting. Svc. award, 1987, 89; White House fellow, 1969-70; Sec.'s award State Dept., 1988. Mem. Coun. on Fgn. Rels., Am. Acad. Diplomacy. Office: Brookings Institution 1775 Massachusetts Ave NW Washington DC 20036-2103 E-mail: marmacost@brookings.edu.

ARMACOST, PETER HAYDEN, academic administrator; b. N.Y.C., July 12, 1935; s. George Henry and Verda Gay (Hayden) A.; m. Suzanne Lee Sadosky, June 22, 1957 (dec. Feb. 1991); children: Martha Hayden, David Keys, Sarah Jane, Rebecca Ann; m. Mary-Linda Merriam, July 10, 1993. BA, Denison U., 1957; PhD, U. Minn., 1963. Dean students, chmn. dept. psychology Augsburg Coll., Mpls., 1959-65; program dir. Assn. Am. Colls., Washington, 1965-67; pres., prof. psychology Ottawa U., (Kans.), 1967-77; pres. Eckerd Coll., St. Petersburg, Fla., 1977—2000, pres. emeritus, 2000—; sr. adviser Coun. Ind. Colls., 2001—; pres., prin. Forman Christian Coll., 2002—. Author materials in field. Chmn. Kansas City (Mo.) Regional Coun. Higher Edn., 1972-74; pres. Am. Bapt. Chs. U.S., 1974-75, So. Univ. Conf., 1997; bd. dirs. United Way of Pinellas County, 1995—. Recipient Disting. Alumnus citation Denison U.; Woodrow Wilson fellow; Danforth fellow; named to Tampa Bay Bus. Hall of Fame, 1999. Mem. Assn. Am. Colls. (bd. dirs.), Am. Coun. Edn., Nat. Assn. Student Pers. Adminstrs. (bd. dirs. divsn. rsch., publs. and conf. chmn. Disting. Svc. award), Assn. Ind. Colls. Kans. (pres. 1970-72), Young Pres. Orgn. (chmn. Fla. chpt. 1983-84), So. Assn. of Colls. and Schs. (appeals com.), Am. Assn. Higher Edn., Soc. Values in Higher Edn., Nat. Assn. Ind. Coll. and U. Pres., Fla. Assn. Colls. and Univs. (pres. 1989-90), Ind. Colls. and Univs. Fla. (sec. 1984-86, treas. 1986-88, vice chmn. 1990-91, chmn. 1991-93), Coun. Ind. Colls. (bd. dirs. 1993—, sec. exec. com.), Nat. Assn. Ind. Colls. and Univs. (bd. dirs. 1995-98), Suncoast C. of C. (chmn. 1984-85), Pinellas Econ. Devel. Coun. (bd. dirs. 1989—), Fla. Coun. of 100, St. Petersburg C. of C. (bd. dirs. 1995—), St. Petersburg Yacht Club, Suncoasters Club, Rotary, SunTrust Bank of Tampa Bay (bd. dirs. 1983—), Blue Key, Phi Beta Kappa, Omicron Delta Kappa, Pi Gamma Mu, Psi Chi. Republican. Home: 555 5th Ave NE #914 Saint Petersburg FL 33701 Office: Eckerd Coll 4200 54th Ave S Saint Petersburg FL 33711-4744

ARMACOST, ROBERT LEO, management educator, former coast guard officer; b. Balt., July 17, 1942; s. Leo Mathias and Margaret Virginia (Ruth) A.; m. Susan Marie Danesi, Jan. 16, 1965 (div.); children: Robert Leo, Andrew Paul, Kathleen Erin; m. Julia Johanna Agricola Pet, Apr. 17, 1999. BS with honors, USCG Acad., 1964; MS, USN Postgrad. Sch., 1970; DSc in Ops. Rsch., George Washington U., 1976. Engring. officer USCG Cutter Mendota, Wilmington, N.C., 1964-66; ops. officer USCGC Cook Inlet, Portland, Maine, 1966-68; ops. rsch. analyst, ops. planning staff USCG Hdqrs., Washington, 1970-75, planning officer, aids to navigation divsn., 1976-78, comdr. Coast Guard Group Milw., 1978-81; comdg. officer USCG Marine Safety Office, Milw., 1981-84, capt. of port, 1981-84, officer in charge of marine inspection, 1981-84, ret., 1984. Instr. computer sci. Milw. Area Tech. Coll., 1982-83; asst. prof. mgmt. sci. Marquette U., Milw., 1984-91, assoc. prof. mgmt. sci., 1991; asst. prof. ops. rsch. U. Ctrl. Fla., 1991-96, assoc. prof. ops. rsch., 1996—, IE Grad. Program Coord., dir. office of univ. analysis and planning support, 2000—. Contbr. articles to profl. jours. Pres. Md. Right to Life, 1976-78; active Milw. Pastoral Coun., 1984-89, vice chmn., 1986-87, chmn., 1987 88; bd. dirs. Nicholet H.S. Found., 1986-88. Named Outstanding Civic Vol., Bowie, Md., 1976, nat. finalist White House fellow, 1977—78; recipient USCG commendation award, 1972, 1974, 1978, 1981, 1984. Mem. Ops. Rsch. Soc. Am. (com. 1983-94, chmn. 1990-94, fin. com. 1993-94), Math. Programming Soc., Decision Scis. Inst., Inst. Ind. Engrs. (v.p. tech. networking), Inst. Ops. Rsch. and Mgmt. Scis. (chair membership com. 1995-96, fin. com. 1995-97, dir. at large 1995-97, bd. dirs. 1995-97). Roman Catholic. Home: 602 Shorewood Dr Unit 402 Cape Canaveral FL 32920-5082 Office: U Ctrl Fla Univ Analysis and Planning Support Orlando FL 32826-3207 E-mail: armacost@mail.ucf.edu.

ARMACOST, SAMUEL HENRY, bank executive; b. Newport News, Va., Mar. 29, 1939; s. George Henry and Verda Gae (Hayden) A.; m. Mary Jane Levan, June 16, 1962; children: Susan Lovell, Mary Elizabeth. BA, Denison U., 1961; MBA, Stanford U., 1964. With Bank of Am. NT & SA, San Francisco, 1961-81, v.p. mgr. London br., 1972-74, sr. v.p., mgr. San Francisco, 1975-77, exec. v.p. Europe, Middle East and Africa div. London, 1977-79, exec. v.p., cashier San Francisco, 1979-81; pres., chief exec. officer Bank of Am. and Bank Am. Corp., San Francisco, 1981-86; chmn., chief exec. officer Bank of Am., San Francisco, 1986-87; mng. ptnr. Merrill Lynch and Co., San Francisco, from 1987; mng. dir. Merrill Lynch Capital Markets, San Francisco, 1988-90; ptnr. Weiss Peck & Greer, San Francisco, Calif., 1990—. Bd. dirs. Chevron Corp. Bd. dirs. The Failure Group, The James Irvine Found., Calif. Acad. Scis. Mem. Bus. Coun., Bus. Roundtable, Bohemian Club, Pacific Union Club, San Francisco Golf Club, Augusta (Ga.) Nat. Golf Club. Republican. Presbyterian. Office: Weiss Peck & Greer 555 California St Ste 4760 San Francisco CA 94104-1502

ARMAINGAUD, FRANCK, engineer; b. Marseille, France, July 3, 1939; s. Maurice Armaingaud and isabelle Marguerite Lourde-Rocheblave; m. Claude Alice Heer, May 25, 1963; children: Patrick, Yves, Agnes. Baccaloreat, Lycee Toulon, France, 1959. Field engr. and European support, Switzerland, France, Tunisia, Belgium, 1962-73; tng. mgr. Burroughs, France, Europe, 1973-75, internat. product mgr., 1975-77, internat. tng. mgr., 1977-79; country svc. mgr. Burroughs, Columbia and Equador, Bogota, 1979-80, Data Gen., France, 1980-81; gen. mgr. SFR/Ins., Monaco, 1981-83; country svc. mgr. Prime

Computer, France, 1983-85, country sales mgr., 1985-87; v.p. svc. South Europe ICL, Paris, France, 1987-89; pres. ICL-Sorbus, Europe, London, 1994-97; v.p. Jane Pannier, Marseille, 1998—2001. Mem. AFSMI (chmn., pres. 1992), Lions Club (pres. 2000-01). Avocations: gardening, sailing.

ARMALY, MANSOUR F(ARID), ophthalmologist, educator; b. Shefa Amer, Palestine, Feb. 25, 1927; came to U.S., 1955, naturalized, 1965; s. Fareed M. and Fadwa M. (Bahouth) A.; m. Aida Makdisi, July 2, 1950; children: Raya, Fareed. BA, Am. U., Beirut, 1947, MD, 1952; M.Sc., U. Iowa, 1957. Diplomate: Am. Bd. Ophthalmology. Intern Am. U. Hosps., Beirut, Resident, 1952-55; research fellow U. Iowa, 1955-57, instr., 1957-58, asst. prof. ophthalmology, 1958-60, asso. prof., 1960-66, prof., 1966-70; prof., chmn. dept. ophthalmology George Washington U. Med. Center, 1970-97; prof. emeritus, 1997—. Cons. in field; Univ. prof. U. Paraguay. Contbr. articles to profl. publs.; mem. editorial bd.: Investigative Ophthalmology, 1969-73, Ophthalmology Digest, 1971— ; asso. editor: Archives Ophthalmology, 1970. Decorated knight Order of Cedars, Lebanon; recipient Alumni Gold Medal Am. U. Beirut; NIH grantee, 1957-69, 58-75, 58-63, 63-73, 68-73; Nat. Eye Inst. grantee, 1972, 73-76, 74-76 Fellow ACS, Internat. Coll. Surgeons; mem. AMA (Knapp award 1968, Hektoen Silver medal 1969, Merit award 1976), Am. Acad. Ophthalmology, Assn. for Research in Vision and Ophthalmology (Fight for Sight award 1966), Am. Ophthalmol. Soc., Internat. Glaucoma Com., Internat. Glaucoma Congress (Ann. Achievement award 1979), Pan Am. Glaucoma Soc. (pres. 1983-87), French Ophthalmologic Soc., Introcular Lens Implant Soc., Internat. Eye Found. Office: 2150 Pennsylvania Ave NW Washington DC 20037-3201

ARMAN, ARA, civil engineering educator; b. Istanbul, Turkey, Sept. 12, 1930; came to U.S., 1955; s. Hayg and Mary Ann (Papazian) A.; m. Claudia Catherine Carr, Nov. 30, 1963; children— Eric H., Michell M. BSC.E., U. Tex., 1955, MSC.E., 1956. Dist. lab. engr. La. Dept. Transp., Baton Rouge, 1956-60; sr. v.p. GEC, Inc., Baton Rouge, 1998—; soil design engr. La. Dept. Transp., Baton Rouge, 1960-63; asst. prof. civil engring. La. State U., Baton Rouge, 1963-67, assoc. prof., 1967-70, prof., 1970-76, asst. dir. engring. research, 1965-76, chmn. dept. civil engring., 1976-80, assoc. dean Coll. Engring., 1980-87; dir. La. Transp. Rsch. Ctr., Baton Rouge, 1987-90; v.p., prin. Woodward Clyde Cons., Baton Rouge, 1990-98. Chair La. Bd. Registration for Profl. Engrs. and Land Surveyors, 1985-90, mem., 1987-93. Contbr. numerous articles on geotech. engring. to profl. jours. Active civic, county and parish assns. Mem. ASCE, ASTM, Nat. Acad. Scis., Transp. Research Bd., La. Engring. Soc., Am. Rd. and Transp. Builders Assn., Internat. Geotextiles Soc. (chmn. com. on rsch.). Internat. Soc. for Soil Mechanics and Found. Engring., Sigma Xi, Tau Beta Pi, Phi Kappa Phi. Mem. Armenian Apostolic Ch. Home: 1148 Verdun Dr Baton Rouge LA 70810-4683 Office: PO Box 84010 Baton Rouge LA 70884-4010

ARMAND, SUSANNE MARIE, pharmaceutical products executive; b. Houston, Jan. 20, 1952; d. Edward and Alice Ruth (Brown) A.; m. Ken Coleman Stevenson, Jan. 9, 1971; children: Jaime Susanne, Ken Coleman II. AAS in Biotech. summa cum laude, Kingwood Coll., 1994; student, Tex. A&M U., 1969-72. Cert. electrologist, Tex. Office mgr. Scientific Time Sharing, Spring, Tex., 1975-77; electrologist Tomball (Tex.) Electrolysis, 1984-86; owner, v.p. Stevenson Enterprises, Spring, Tex., 1986-98; metrology specialist, quality control scientist Aronex Pharms. Inc., The Woodlands, Tex., 1994-99; quality control supr. Mill Biopharm., Inc., The Woodlands, 1999-2000; quality mgr., quality improvement process mgr. Internat. Isotopes Inc., Denton, Tex., 2000—01; quality cons. Alcon Labs, Abbott Labs, 2001—02; quality control lab. mgr. PharmaFab, 2002—; QC mgr. PharmaFab, Inc., 2002—. Marathon runner Leukemia Soc. Fund Raiser, Houston, 1999; competitive runner Susan Koenig Breast Cancer Fund Raiser, Oklahoma City, 1999, Gulf Assn. of the Athletics Congress, 1982-99. Recipient Aronex Chmn.'s award Aronex Pharms. Inc., 1997. Mem. Am. Soc. for Quality. Republican. Methodist. Avocations: rollerskating, calligraphy, long distance running, cake decorating. Home: 4129 Double Oak Dr Bedford TX 76021 Office: 2300 Valley View Ln Ste 230 Farmers Branch TX 75234

ARMAN GELENBE, DENIZ, concert pianist; b. Ankara, Turkey, Oct. 8, 1944; came to U.S., 1962; d. Abdul Kerim and Ayse Mediha (Raif) A.; m. Erol Gelenbe, June 8, 1968; 1 child, Pamir Emre. Student, Eastman Sch. Music, 1962-64; MusB, Juilliard, 1967, MusM, 1968; postgrad., U. Mich., 1970-71. Founder, artistic dir., prof. piano Paris U., 1979-90; founder, artistic dir. Arman Ensemble, N.C., 1994—, Arman Ensemble, Arman Trio, Paris, 1994—. Vis. assoc. prof. piano U. Ctrl. Fla., Orlando, 1998—; dir. summer music program, Normandy, France, 1999—; artist in residence, assoc. prof. piano U. Ctrl. Fla., Orlando, 2001—. Musician (recitals): Carnegie Weill Hall, Salle Gaveau, Nat. Gallery Art, Tonhalle, Wigmore Hall, Concerts de Midi; musician: (soloist) Ensemble Orchestral Paris, New Japan Philharm., Ankara Presdl. Symphony Orch., Presdl. Symphony Orch., N.C. Symphony; musician: (CD) with Haydn Quartet, 1994, 2000, Arman Ensemble, 1996, Arman Trio, 2000. Emerging Artist grantee, Durham, N.C., 1984. Mem. Chamber Music Am., Coll. Music Soc. Avocations: painting, reading, walking. Office: Univ Ctrl Fla Dept Music PO Box 161354 Orlando FL 32816-1354 E-mail: arman@dur.mindspring.com.

ARMANIOS, ERIAN ABDELMESSIH, aerospace engineer, educator; b. Cairo, July 6, 1950; arrived in U.S., 1980; s. Abdelmessih Armanios; m. Mahera S. Philobos, May 2, 1980; children: Daniel, Laura. BS in Aero. Engring., Cairo U., 1974, MS in Aero. Engring., 1979; PhD in Aerospace Engring., Ga. Inst. Tech., 1985. Teaching asst. U. Cairo, 1974-79, asst. lectr., 1979-80; grad. rsch. asst. Ga. Inst. Tech., Atlanta, 1980-84, rsch. engr. I, 1985-86, asst. prof., 1986-91, assoc. prof., 1991-97, prof., 1997—. Cons. Bell Helicopter Textron Inc., Ft. Worth, 1984-85, Rolls-Royce Inc., Atlanta, 1989-95, Allison Engine Co., Indpls. 1995-96, Guided System Techs., 1991-92; judge Ga. Sci. and Engring. Fair, Atlanta, 1987; judge space sci. student program NASA, Atlanta, 1988-98, Internat. Sci. and Engring. Fair, 1998-2003; dir. Ga. Space Grant Consortium, 1991—; adv. bd. Ctr. Excellence in Sci., Engring. and Math., Morehouse Coll., 1997—. Editor: Interlaminar Fracture of Composites, 1989, Fracture of Composites, 1996, Composite Materials: Fatigue and Fracture, 6th vol., 1997; editl. bd. Jour. Composites Tech. and Rsch., 1992-99, editor-in-chief, 2000—; mem. editl bd. Jour. of Nat. Tech. Assn., 1995—; contbr. articles to profl. jours.; patentee in field. Recipient Tchg. Excellence award Ctr. for Enhancement of Tchg. and Learning, Amoco Found., 1990, Outstanding Paper award Jour. Aerospace Engring., 1990, Sigma Xi Outstanding PhD Thesis Advisor award, 1991, 98, Jr. Faculty award, 1991, Ga. Inst. Tech. Faculty Rsch. award 1996, Outstanding Tchr. award, 1999, Sci. Application Internat. Corp. cert. of award, 1990, 95, 97, Regents Tchg. Excellence award, 2000, Wayne W. Stinchcomb Meml. award, 2002. Fellow AIAA (assoc.); mem. ASTM (com. on high modulus fibers and composites 1988); Am. Soc. for Composites, Am. Helicopter Soc. (com. on structures and materials). Office: Ga Inst Tech Sch Aerospace Engring Atlanta GA 30332-0001

ARMBRECHT, THOMAS JEFFREY DEXTER, foreign language educator, writer, critic; b. Rumford, Maine, Apr. 9, 1970; s. Thomas Henry and Cheryl Dexter (Morrill) A. BA, Middlebury Coll., 1992; MA, Brown U., 1995, PhD, 1999. Tchg. asst. Brown U., Providence, 1993-99; instr. Antik Langs., Istanbul, Turkey, 1999; asst. prof. Colby Coll., Waterville, Maine, 2000; cons. Ency. Britannica, Chgo., 2000—02; TV screenwriter Hofmann & Voges Entertainment, Munich, 1997—; asst. prof. Coll. William & Mary, Williamsburg, Va., 2000—03, U. Wis., Madison, Wis., 2003—. Contbr. articles to profl. jours. Mem. Virginians for Justice, Richmond, Va., 2000. Grantee Coll. William & Mary, 2001, Mellon Found., 1998; Kenyon Dissertation fellow Brown U., 1998; tchg. fellow Academie de Paris, 1996. Mem. MLA, Ctr. Internat. de Documentation Marguerite Yourcenar, Phi Beta Kappa, Pi Delta Phi. Avocations: theatre, travel, cooking, skiing, yoga. Office: Coll William & Mary PO Box 8795 Williamsburg VA 23187 E-mail: txarmb@wm.edu.

ARMBRECHT, WILLIAM HENRY, III, retired lawyer; b. Mobile, Ala., Jan. 13, 1929; s. William Henry and Katherine (Little) A.; m. Dorothy Jean Taylor, Sept. 1, 1951; children— Katherine Handley, William Taylor, Alexander Paterson. BS, U. Ala., 1950, JD, 1952. Bar: Ala. 1952, U.S. Supreme Ct. 1972. Assoc. Inge, Twitty, Armbrecht & Jackson, Mobile, 1952-56; ptnr. Armbrecht, Jackson, McConnell & DeMouy, Mobile, 1956-65, Armbrecht, Jackson & DeMouy, Mobile, 1965-75, Armbrecht, Jackson, DeMouy, Crowe, Holmes & Reeves, Mobile, 1976-94, Armbrecht, Jackson, DeMouy, Crowe, Holmes & Reeves, LLC, 1994-96. Served to 1st lt. JAGC, AUS, 1952-54. Mem. ABA, Ala. Bar Assn. (chmn. grievance com. 1973-74, chmn. sect. corp. banking and bus. law 1976-78), Mobile Bar Assn., Mobile Area C. of C. Found. (bd. dirs. 1990-92), Southeastern Corp. Law Inst. (mem. planning com. 1967-96), Phi Delta Phi, Delta Kappa Epsilon Episcopalian. Home: 600 Fairfax Rd E Mobile AL 36608-2931

ARMBRISTER, DOUGLAS KENLEY, surgeon; b. Emory, Va., Feb. 20, 1934; s. Victor Stradley and Naomi Lucile (Byrd) A.; m. Nancy Sheri Douglas, Apr. 30, 1960 (div. Sept. 1995); children: Valere Lynn, Victor Kenley, Christopher Douglas, Karen Leigh; m. Barbara Ann Atwell, Sept. 9, 2000. BA in English/German, BS in Chemistry/Biology, Emory and Henry Coll., 1955; MD, U. Va., 1959, MS in Surg. Rsch., 1962. Diplomate Am. Bd. Surgery. Intern in surgery U. Va., 1959-60, resident in surgery, 1960-62, 64-67; pvt. practice Marion, Va., 1967—. Regional adv. group Va. Regional Med. Program, 1971; subarea coun. chmn. Health Systems Agy.; bd. dirs. Va. Health Quality Ctr.; pres. Smyth County Cmty. Hosp. Med Staff, 1973, chair surg. svcs., 1978—. Bd. visitors Emory and Henry Coll., 1982—. Capt. USAF, 1962-64. Fellow Am. Col. Surgeons: mem. Va. Surg. Soc. (malpractice review panel mem. 1972—), Med. Soc. Va. (review bd. dirs. 1985-95), Southwest Va. Med. Soc., Muller Surg. Soc., Nat. Eagle Scout Assn., Blue Key Nat. Honor Soc. (pres. 1953). Methodist. Avocations: tennis, classical music, singing, piano. Office: 592 Radio Hill Rd Marion VA 24354-4224

ARMBRISTER, TREVOR, journalist, author; b. Norwalk, Conn., Dec. 4, 1933; s. Geoffrey Campbell and Mary Kemball (Minor) A.; m. Dubos Middleton, Aug. 3, 1958 (div. Sept. 1980); children: Robertson, Alec; m. Judith Anne Cass, June 8, 1985. BA, Washington and Lee U., 1956. Account exec. J. Walter Thompson Co., Washington and N.Y.C., 1958-62; staff writer, bur. chief Saturday Evening Post, N.Y.C. and Washington, 1962-69; sr. staff editor Readers Digest, Washington, 1970-99, contbg. editor, 1999—2003. Author: A Matter of Accountability, 1970, Act of Vengeance, 1975, (with others O Congress, 1972; ghostwriter Presdl. memoir A Time to Heal, 1979. Founder, pres., chmn. Christmas in Apr., Washington, 1982; co-founder, pres., chmn. Christmas in Apr. U.S.A., Washington, 1988-91. Served to 1st lt. U.S. Army, 1956-58. Recipient Community Svc. award, 1985, Journalism award Big Bros./Big Sisters, Phila., 1986, others. Mem. Cosmos Club. Avocation: photography. Office: 6670 Hillandale Rd Chevy Chase MD 20815 E-mail: armbris@aol.com.

ARMBRUSTER, PAULA, child mental health educator, university director; b. N.Y.C., June 30, 1935; d. William and Anna Bertha Armbruster; children: K. Levni, Elif-Lale A., Murat A. Student, Smith Coll., Geneva, 1954—55; BA, U. Conn., 1956, MSW, 1974; MA, Yale U., 1964. Intelligence analyst Nat. Security Agy., Washington, 1956—62; Nat. Def. Act fellow Yale U., New Haven, 1962—66; clin. instr. social work Yale Child Study Ctr., Sch. Medicine, Yale U., New Haven, 1974—80, assoc. clin. prof., 1980—, dir. social work tng., 1984—, dir. outpatient svcs., 1985—. Fellow Pierson Coll., Yale U., 1976—; assoc. project dir. HEW tng. grant, asst. prof. residence U. Conn. Sch. Social Work, West Hartford, 1979-80; mem. adv. coun. U. Conn. Sch. Social Work, So. Conn. State U. Sch. Social Work; Johnson Wax fellow, vis. prof. U. Surrey, Eng., 1984. Author, editor works in field. Founder The Neighborhood Place, New Haven; founder, bd. dirs Leadership, Edn. Athletics in Partnership for Youth of Conn.; dir. children's programs Yale Behavioral Health, 1997; nat. steering coun. Habitat for Humanity Mental Health Partnership; rep. of the Nat. Assn. Social Worker to the Nat. Consortium on Children's Mental Health Svcs., Washington, sec., 1994—96, pres., 1996—98; chmn. regional adv. coun. Conn. Dept. Children and Youth Svcs., chmn. regional adv. couns.; bd. dirs. YWCA, New Haven, Sylvan House, VISTA, New Haven Dept. Edn. Sch. Based Clinics Bd., Arts Coun., New Haven, New Haven Land Trust; mem. Yale Sch. Medicine Adv. Com. on Sch. Based Clinics, adv. faculty, Yale Child Study Ctr.; mem. manage care/med. oversight coun. Conn. Legis., chair quality assurance, 1995—; nat. task force managed care implementation U. Pa.; nat. task force Sch. Bd. Mental Health Svcs. U. Pa.; expert adv. panel Office Adolescent Medicine; bd. dirs. New Haven Colony Hist. Soc., Inst. for Victims of Trauma, Summerbridge, New Haven; cons. Save the Children Found., Robert Wood Johnson Found., Bur. Maternal & Child Health, Substance Abuse and Mental Health Svcs. Adminstrn. Mem.: NASW (sec. Conn. chpt.), Conn. Soc. Clin. Social Work, Nat. Acad. Cert. Social Workers, Mory's Assn., New Haven Lawn Club, Yale Club N.Y.C., Yale Club New Haven. Office: Yale Child Study Ctr 230 S Frontage Rd New Haven CT 06519-1124

ARMELLINO, MICHAEL RALPH, retired asset management executive; b. Jersey City, Jan. 30, 1940; s. Ralph Michael and Florence (Arturo) A.; m. Patricia Ann Beckett, Mar. 3, 1963; children: Tracy, John, Joseph, Peter. BS in Econs., U. Pa., 1961; MBA, NYU, 1963. Chartered Fin. Analyst. Jr. analyst F.I. DuPont, N.Y.C., 1963-64; transp. analyst Standard & Poors, N.Y.C., 1964-67, Goodbody & Co., N.Y.C., 1967, Lord, Abbett & Co., N.Y.C., 1967-69; sr. transportation analyst Goldman, Sachs & Co., N.Y.C., 1970-90, dir. rsch., 1984-88, ptnr. in charge rsch., 1989-90; chmn., chief exec. officer Goldman, Sachs Asset Mgmt., 1991-94; ret. ptnr. GS & Co., 1995—. Mem. N.Y. Stock Exch. (allied); bd. dirs., chmn. strategic planning com. Canadian Nat. Ry. Bd. Mem. bd. overseers Stern Sch. Bus. NYU, 1994—, exec. com.; trustee Peddie Sch., 1996—, chmn. investment com., fin. com., exec. com. Mem. Benjamin Franklin Soc., U. Pa. Alumni Assn., Soc. Airline Analysts (pres. 1983-84). Roman Catholic. Home: 9 Sigtim Dr Little Falls NJ 07424-2422

ARMENAKAS, ANTHONY EMMANUEL, aerospace educator; b. Mytilene, Greece, Aug. 23, 1924; came to U.S., 1946; s. Emmanuel Anthony and Efterpe (Sakis) A.; m. Stella Dimitri Petroutsa, Jan. 3, 1950 (dec. Jan. 1988); children: Alexandra Daphne, Noel Anthony, Melina Cybel. BSCE, Ga. Inst. Tech., 1950; MSCE, Ill. Inst. Tech., 1952; PhD in Applied Mechanics, Columbia U., 1959. Registered profl. engr., N.Y., N.J., Greece. Instr. Ill. Inst. Tech., Chgo., 1950-52; sr. structural engr. Edwards Kelcey and Beck Cons. Engrs., Newark, 1952-54; ptnr. Rynar Armenakas and McCann Cons. Engrs., Newark, 1954-59; lectr. civil engring. CUNY, N.Y.C., 1954-57; assoc. prof. civil engring. Cooper Union for the Advancement Sci. and Art, N.Y.C., 1958-65; prof. engring. sci. U. Fla., Gainesville, 1965-67; prof. aerospace Poly. U., Bklyn., 1967—; Fulbright lectr. to Greece, 1972-73, 73-74; prof., dir. Inst. Structural Analysis, Nat. Tech. U., Athens, Greece, 1977-84. Vis. prof. divsn. engring. Brown U., Providence, 1964-65; cons. Vector Engring., Springfield, N.J., 1954-59; rsch. cons. Poly. Inst., Bklyn., 1962-67, Northwestern U., Evanston, Ill., 1962-65; pres. Stress-Optics, Inc., Queens, N.Y., 1970-72; bd. dirs. Greek r.r.s, 1978-80; vice-chmn. bd. dirs. Greek agy. for design and rsch. earthquake protection, 1989-92. Author: Free Vibrations of Circular Cylindrical Shells, 1969, Tensor Analysis for Engineers, 1974, Classical Structure Analysis-A Modern Approach, 1988, Modern Structural Analysis-The Matrix Method Approach, 1991; patentee in field; contbr. articles to profl. jours. Chmn. bd. dirs. Poulos Philanthropic Found., Athens, Greece. Fellow ASCE, ASME. Avocation: photography. Home: 52 Clark St Brooklyn NY 11201-2402 also: Kifissou 3A Xalandri Attica 15234 Athens Greece Office: Polytechnic Univ 333 Jay St Brooklyn NY 11201-2990

ARMENAKAS, NOEL ANTHONY, medical educator; b. Orange, N.J., Sept. 29, 1958; s. Anthony E. and Stella P. (Petroutsa) A.; m. Macrene R. Alexiades, Oct. 26, 1996; children: Sophie Stella, Anthony Emmanuel. MD, U. Athens, Greece, 1985. Diplomate Am. Bd. Urology. Intern surgery Lenox Hill Hosp., N.Y.C., 1985-86; resident surgery Monmouth Med. Ctr., Long Branch, N.J., 1986-87; resident urology Lenox Hill Hosp., N.Y.C., 1987-91; fellow trauma and reconstructive surgery U. Calif., San Francisco, 1991-92, clin. instr. dept. urology, 1991-92; clin. instr. dept. surgery Cornell U. Med. Coll., N.Y.C., 1992-94; clin. asst. prof. dept. urology Cornell U. Med. Sch., N.Y.C., 1994—2002, clin. assoc. prof. dept. urology, 2002—. Mem. oper. rm. com. Lenox Hill Hosp., 1990, outpatient clinic com., 1993—; mem. ChubbHealth Physician Adv. Panel, 1994-2000; mem. scholarship com. Hellenic Med. Assn.; attending staff San Francisco (Calif.) Gen. Hosp., 1991-92; dir., physician-in-charge Outpatient Urologic Clinics Lenox Hill Hosp., 1992—; attending staff N.Y. Presbyn. Hosp., N.Y.C., 1992—, Lenox Hill Hosp., N.Y.C., 1992—; lectr. in field. Contbr. chpts. to books and articles to profl. jours. Fellow ACS; mem. Internat. Soc. Urology, Am. Assn. Clin. Urologists, Am. Urol. Assn., Hellenic Med. Assn., Soc. for Urology and Engring., Soc. Genitourinary and Reconstructive Surgeons, N.Y. Acad. Medicine. Avocations: skiing, tennis, traveling. Office: New York Urological Assocs 880 5th Ave New York NY 10021-4951 E-mail: drarmenakas@nyurological.com.

ARMENANTE, PIERO M. chemical engineering educator; b. Avezzano, Aquila, Italy, June 2, 1953; came to U.S., 1979; s. Euclide and Maria (Antonini) A.; m. Annemarie Aigner, Oct. 21, 1983. Laurea in chem. engring., U. Rome, 1977; PhD in Chem. Engring., U. Va., 1983. Rsch. asst. Internat. Inst. for Applied Systems Analysis, Laxenburg, Austria, 1978, U. Lund (Sweden), 1978-79; engring. specialist UN Indsl. Devel. Orgn., Vienna, Austria, 1979-87; process engr. Farmitalia Carlo Erba, Milan, Italy, 1985-87; asst. prof. N.J. Inst. Tech., Newark, 1984-91, assoc. prof., 1991-93, prof., 1993-2000, disting. prof., 2000—. Cons. UN Indsl. Devel. Orgn., Vienna, 1978-86; mem. com. on rev. and evaluation of Army chem. stockpile disposal program NRC, 1998—; dir. N.E. Hazardous Substance Rsch. Ctr., 1999—; presenter in field. Author: Contingency Planning for Industrial Emergencies, 1991; author: (with others) Risk Assessment and Risk Management for the Chemical Process Industry, 1991; editor: Biotechnology Applications in Hazardous Treatment, 1989; contbr. articles to profl. jours.; author reports; peer reviewer Chem. Engring. Sci., Can. Jour. Chem. Engring., Biotech. Progress, Chem. Engring. Communications. V.p. North Am. Mixing Forum, 1990—. Grantee NSF, 1991, 95, EPA, 1989-90, 91-93, Exxon Edn. Found., 1991, Schering-Plough, Inc., 1992-93, Hazardous Substance Mgmt. Rsch. Ctr., 1988-95, Ctr. for Mfg. Engring. Sys., Schering-Plough, Inc., 1990, 90-91, 98-2003. Industry/Univ. Coop. Ctr. for Hazardous Substance Mgmt., 1986-89. Mem. AIChE (chmn. North Jersey sect. 1992-93), Am. Soc. Engring. Edn., N. Am. Mixing Forum, Order of the Engr., Sigma Xi, Tau Beta Pi. Office: Dept Chem Engring Chemistry Environ Sci NJIT Newark NJ 07102 E-mail: armenante@adm.njit.edu.

ARMENDARIZ, TONY, federal agency administrator; BS, Trinity U.; JD, St. Mary's U.; M Comparative Law, So. Meth. U.; postgrad., U. Catolica Andres Bello, Caracas. Gen. coun. U. System South Tex.; mem. Fed. Labor Rels. Authority, Washington, 1989—97, 2001—. Office: FLRA 607 14th St NW Washington DC 20424-0001

ARMENTROUT, DEBRA CATHERINE, neonatal nurse practitioner; b. Grand Forks, N.D., Mar. 26, 1953; d. Howard and Delores (Wilhelmi) Armentrout. BSN, U. N.D., 1975; MSN, U. Tex. Health Ctr., Houston, 1985. RN, Tex. Staff nurse Turner Newborn ICU, Hermann Hosp., Houston, 1975-79, 80-83; staff nurse, charge nurse newborn ICU/pediatrics Rogue Valley Meml. Hosp., Medford, Oreg., 1979-80; neonatal transport nurse Turner Newborn ICU, Hermann Hosp., Houston, 1981-86, 88-90, clin. nurse specialist, 1986-88; staff nurse nurseries and pediatrics Sierra Vista Regional Med. Ctr., San Luis Obispo, Calif., 1988; instr. clin. pediat. U. Tex. Health Ctr., Houston, 1990-94, asst. prof. pediatrics, 1994—, coord. neonatal nurse practitioner, 2000—. Clin. asst. prof. gen. instrn. Sch. Nursing U. Tex.; presenter in field. Contbr. articles to profl. publs. Mem. Nat. Assn. Neonatal Nurses (corr. mem. spl. interest group advanced practice role com., sec. practice com. 1990-94), Acad. Neonatal Nurses, Houston Area Assn. Neonatal Nurses (sec. 1993-94, pres. 1995), Sigma Theta Tau. Office: 6431 Fannin St Ste 3218 Houston TX 77030-1501 E-mail: Debra.C.Armentrout@uth.tmc.edu.

ARMENTROUT, PETER BRUCE, chemistry educator; b. Dayton, Ohio, Mar. 13, 1953; s. Harry Martin and Lorraine (Johnson) A.; m. Mary Ann White, Aug. 6, 1983; children: Matthew Martin, Patricia Christine, Erin Irene. BS, Case Western Res. U., 1975; PhD, Calif. Inst. Tech., 1980. Postdoctoral fellow Bell Telephone Labs., Murray Hill, N.J., 1980-81; asst. prof. chemistry U. Calif., Berkeley, 1981-87; assoc. prof. chemistry U. Utah, Salt Lake City, 1987-89, prof. chemistry, 1989-98, Disting. prof. chemistry, 1998—, chair, 2001—. Mem. editl. bd. Internat. Jour. Mass Spectrometry, 1987—, Jour. Cluster Sci., 1989-95, Current Topics in Ion Chemistry and Physics, 1991—, Organometallics, 1999-2001. Named Presdl. Young Investigator, NSF, 1984; Dreyfus Found. grantee, 1981, tchr.-scholar, 1988; A.P. Sloan fellow, 1986. Fellow AAAS, Am. Phys. Soc.; mem. Am. Chem. Soc. (mem. editl. bd. Jour. 1996-2001), Am. Phys. Soc., Am. Soc. Mass Spectrometry (mem. editl. bd.). Office: U Utah 315 S 1400 E Rm 2020 Dept Chemistry Salt Lake City UT 84112 E-mail: armentrout@chem.utah.edu.

ARMERDING, HUDSON TAYLOR, retired college president, consultant; b. Albuquerque, June 21, 1918; s. Carl Armerding and Eva May Taylor; m. Miriam Lucile Bailey, Dec. 26, 1944; children: Carreen, Taylor, Paul, Miriam, Jonathan. AB, Wheaton Coll., 1941; AM, Clark U., 1942; PhD, U. Chgo., 1948; DD (hon.), Gordon-conwell Sem., 1972, Reformed Episcopal Sem., 1990; LLD (hon.), Houghton Coll., 1973; HumD (hon.), John Brown U., 1983; STD (hon.), Greenville Coll., 1976; LittD (hon.), Asbury Coll., 1977, Colo. Christian U., 2000. Prof. Wheaton (Ill.) Coll., 1946-48, 61-82; provost Wheaton (Ill.) U., 1963-65, pres., 1965-82; prof. Gordon Coll., Wenham, Mass., 1948-49, 50-61, dean, acting pres., 1950-61. V.p. Quarryville (Pa.) Presbyn. Retirement Cmty., 1982-99; min-at-large Officers Christian Fellowship, Englewood, Colo., 1979-2003; chmn. Site Acquisition Com., Batavia, Ill., 1975; pres. Nat. Assn. of Evangelicals, Wheaton, 1970-72; chmn. World Evangelical Fellowship, Wheaton, 1974-80. Comdr. USN, 1942-46, USNR, 1946-66. Recipient Excellence in Leadership award Officers Christian Fellowship, 2001. Mem. Am. Legion, Mil. Officer Assn., Naval Inst. Republican. Presbyterian. Avocations: travel, walking, camping, reading. Home: 16 Fairway Dr Quarryville PA 17566 Office: Quarryville Presbyn Retirement Cmty 625 Robert Fulton Hwy Quarryville PA 17566

ARMES, WALTER SCOTT, vocational school administrator; b. Okmulgee, Okla., May 15, 1939; s. Ralph E. Armes; m. Jean Hopkins, June 5, 1965; children: Christina M., Rebecca J. BS in edn., Ohio No. U., 1960; MS, Ind. State U., Terre Haute, 1966; postgrad., Ohio State U. Cert. supt., prin., social studies tchr., Ohio. Tchr. social studies Holmes Liberty Sch. Dist., Bucyrus, Ohio, 1960-63, Painesville Twp. Schs., 1963-64, Weathersfield Twp. Sch. Dist., Mineral Ridge, Ohio, 1964-68, Eastland Career Ctr., Groveport, Ohio, 1968-97; dir. Eastland Vocat. Sch. Dist., Groveport, 1993—97; supr. Licking County Vocat. Sch., Newark, Ohio, 1998—2002; adj. faculty Ashland (Ohio) U., 2003—. Co-founder Franklin County Tchrs. Ctr.; adj. faculty Ashland U., 2003; exec. bd. Met. Edn. Coun. Chmn. Whitehall City Bd. Zoning and Bldg. Appeals; active C. Ray Williams Presch. Adv. Com.; pres. Whitehall City Bd. Edn.; adv. com. Ohio H.S. Athletic Assn. Track and Field; ofcl. USA Track and Field. Mem. Nat. Assn. Secondary Sch. Prins., Ohio Assn. Track and Field and Cross Country Ofcls., Track Registry Ctrl. Ohio, Ohio Sch. Bd. Assn., Am. Sch. Bds. Assn., Phi Delta Kappa. Home: 4010 Etna St Columbus OH 43213-2317

ARMEY, DOUGLAS RICHARD, investment consultant; b. Fresno, Calif., Oct. 23, 1948; s. Wilbur Rutter and Mildred (Broadbent) A.; m. Jennifer Louise Armey, Sept. 23, 1972; children: Laura Elizabeth, Andrew Douglas. AA, Fresno (Calif.) City Coll., 1969; BS summa cum laude, Calif. State U., Fresno, 1971; MA, Mennonite Brethren Sem., Fresno, 1976. Ordained to ministry, Ch. of Brethren, 1973. Intern pastor The Peoples Ch. of Fresno, 1972-73; founding chaplain Fresno County Juvenile Hall, 1973; pres. Precision Parts Distbrs., Inc., Fresno, 1973-80, Rutter Armey Engine Co., Inc., Bakersfield, Calif., 1980-88; sr. pastor Fresno Ch. of the Brethren, 1988-97; investment cons., 1997—. Radio broadcaster Fresno Fellowship of Christian Athletes/KIRV Radio, 1987-96. Contbr. articles to profl. jours. and mags. Bd. dirs. Fresno Youth for Christ, 1985-87, Fellowship of Christian Athletes, 1999—2003. Mem. Nat. Assn. Evangelicals, Rotary, Sigma Alpha Epsilon. Republican. Ch. of the Brethren. Avocations: martial arts, snow skiing, tennis, sailing. Office: 6475 N Palm Ave Ste 101 Fresno CA 93704-1020

ARMEY, RICHARD KEITH (DICK ARMEY), former congressman; b. Cando, N.D., July 7, 1940; s. Glen Forest and Marion (Gutschlog) A.; m. Susan Byrd; children: Kathryn, David, Scott A., Chip, Scott Oxendine. BA, Jamestown Coll., N.D., 1963; MA, U. N.D., 1964; PhD, U. Okla., Norman, 1969. Mem. econs. faculty U. Mont., 1964-65; asst. prof. West Tex. State U., 1967-68, Austin Coll., 1968-72; assoc. prof. North Tex. State U., 1972-77, chmn. dept. econs., 1977-84; mem. U.S. Congress from 26th Tex. dist., Washington, 1985—2002; former mem. edn. and labor com.; chmn. ho. rep. conf. com., 1992-94; former mem. joint economic com.; majority leader, 1995—. Author: Price Theory, 1977, The Freedom Revolution, 1995, The Flat Tax-A Citizen's Guide to the Facts on What it Will Do For You, Your Country, and Your Pocketbook, 1996. Republican.

ARMFIELD, DIANA MAXWELL, artist, educator; b. Ringwood, Eng., June 11, 1920; d. Joseph Harold Armfield and Gertrude Mary Uttley; m. Bernard Dunstan, 1949; 3 children. Student, Slade Sch. Art, Ctrl. Sch. Arts and Crafts,

London. Tchr. Byam Shaw Sch. Art, 1959-89. Artist in residence, Perth, Australia, 1985, Jackson, Wyo., 1989. One-woman shows include Browse & Darby, London, 1979-2000, 03, Royal Acad. Friends Rm. Gallery, 1995, Royal Cambrian Acad., 2001, Albany Gall, Cardiff, 2001, Albany Gallery, Cardiff, 2002, also in U.S., Australia, The Netherlands; author: (books) Mitchell Beazley Pocket Guide to Painting in Oils, Mitchell Beazley Pocket Guide to Drawing, The Art of Diana Armfield (Julian Halsby); represented in pub. collections at Yale Ctr. for Brit. Art, Govt. Eng., Faringdon, Mercury Asset Mgmt., Lancaster City, Victoria and Albert Mus. Commr. HRH Prince of Wales, Reuters, Contemporary Art Soc. Wales, Natural Trust. Mem. Royal Acad. Art, New English Art Club (hon. ret.), Royal W. of Eng. Acad., Royal Cambrian Acad. (hon.), Pastel Soc. (hon.), Royal Watercolor Soc. Avocations: music, gardening. Address: 10 High Park Rd Kew Richmond Surrey TW9 4BH England

ARMIGER, GENE GIBBON, telecommunications executive, consultant; b. Balt., Oct. 17, 1931; s. Edward Gibbon and Irene Juliet (Peppler) A.; m. Cynthia Clare Carroll, Feb. 14, 1954 (div. 1971); children: Karen Lee, Scott Andrew; m. Dorothy Sue Looney, Feb. 17, 1979. Archtl. student, U. Md., 1951-52, Md. Inst., 1956-58. Cert. lic. capt. USCG. Project engr. Cook Electric Co., Chgo., 1958-62, U.S. Underseas Cable Corp., Washington, 1962; gen. mgr. sales/mktg. Superior Cable Corp., Hickory, N.C., 1963-74; dir. sales/mktg. No. Telecom Inc., Nashville, 1974-76, Porta Systems Inc., Syosset, N.Y., 1976-78; founder/chief exec. officer Armiger & Assocs. Inc., Ft. Worth, Tex., 1978-86; v.p. Richard Thomas & Assocs., Chgo., 1986-88, Suttle Armiger Telecom, Hector, Minn., 1988-90; cons. Telecom. Cons., Ft. Worth, 1990—. Mem. FCC Telecom Industry Ad-hoc com. Washington, 1979-87. Contbr. articles to profl. jours. Bd. dirs. US Telecom. Industry Assocs., Washington, 1985-87; mem. Ft. Worth Airpower Coun. Sgt. U.S. Army, 1951-61, Korea. Mem. Am. Mgmt. Assn., U.S. Power Squadron, USCG Aux., Tel. Pioneer Assn., Ind. Tel. Pioneer Assn. (v.p. 1968-69), Va. Yacht Club, Petroleum Club, Ridglea Country Club, Shriners, Roayl Order of Jesters. Republican. Episcopalian. Avocations: deep water sailing, golf, tennis, snow skiing, hunting. Home: 5330 Collinwood Ave Fort Worth TX 76107-3634

ARMINANA, RUBEN, academic administrator, educator; b. Santa Clara, Cuba, May 15, 1947; came to U.S., 1961; s. Aurelio Ruben and Olga Petrona (Nart) A.; m. Marne Olson, June 6, 1954; children: Cesar A. Martino, Tuly Arminana. AA, Hill Jr. Coll., 1966; BA, U. Tex., 1968, MA, 1970; PhD, U. New Orleans, 1983; postgrad. Inst. of Applied Behavioral Scis., Nat. Tng. Labs., 1971. Nat. assoc. dir. Phi Theta Kappa, Canton, Miss., 1968-69; dir. ops. and tng. Inter-Am. Ctr. Loyola U., New Orleans, 1969-71; adminstrv. analyst City of New Orleans, 1972, adminstrv. analyst and orgnl. devel. and tng. cons., 1972-78; anchor and reporter part time STA. WWL-TV, New Orleans, 1973-81; v.p. Commerce Internat. Corp., New Orleans, 1978-83; exec. asst. to sr. v.p. Tulane U., New Orleans, 1983-85, assoc. exec. v.p., 1985-87, v.p., asst. to pres., 1987-88; v.p. fin. and devel. Calif. State Poly U., Pomona, 1988-92; pres. Sonoma State U., 1992—. TV news cons., New Orleans, 1981-88; lectr. Internat. Trade Mart, New Orleans, 1983-89, U.S. Dept. Commerce, New Orleans. Co-author: Hemisphere West-El Futuro, 1968; co-editor: Colloquium on Central America-A Time for Understanding, Background Readings, 1985. Bd. dirs. Com. on Alcoholism and Substance Abuse, 1978-79, SER, Jobs for Progress, Inc., 1974-82, Citizens United for Responsive Broadcasting, Latin Am. Festival Com.; dir. bd. advisors Sta. WDSU-TV, 1974-77; mem. Bus. Govt. Rsch., 1987-88, Coun. Advancement of Support to Edn.; mem. League of United Latin Am. Citizens, Mayor's Latin Am. Adv. Com., Citizens to Preserve the Charter, Met. Area Com., Mayor's Com. on Crime. Kiwanis scholar, 1966, Books scholar, 1966. Mem. Assn. U. Related Rsch. Prks., L.A. Higher Edn. Roundtable, Soc. Coll. and U. Planning, Nat. Assn. Coll. and U. Bus. Officers Coun., Am. Econ. Assn., Assn. of Evolutionary Econs., Am. Polit. Sci. Assn., AAUP, Western Coll. Assn. (pres. 1994-95), Latin Am. C. of C. (founding dir. New Orleans and River Region 1976-83), Cuban Profl. Club, Phi Theta Kappa, Omicron Delta Epsilon, Sigma Delta Pi, Delta Sigma Pi. Democrat. Roman Catholic. Avocation: mask collecting. Office: Sonoma State U 1801 E Cotati Ave Rohnert Park CA 94928-3609 E-mail: ruben.arminana@sonoma.edu.

ARMINAS, SCOTT ARNOLD, chemist, poet, writer; b. SI, NY, Feb. 12, 1960; s. Henry Arnold and Josephine Antoinette Arminas; m. Mariá Basora-Ruiz, Sept. 12, 1987. At, Rutgers U., 1978—79, at, 1997. Chemist Revlon Rsch. Ctr., Edison, NJ, 1987—2001. Author: Sojourn on Eternity's Edge, 2003. Vol. firefighter Middletown Twp. Fire Dept., Port Monmouth, NJ, 1983—86. Nominee Emily Dickenson award, The Amherst Soc., 1991; recipient Golden Poet award, World of Poetry, Sacramento, 1990, 1991. Mem.: Soc. Cosmetic Chemists, Nat. Rifle Assn., KC. Roman Catholic. Achievements include patents in field. Avocations: scuba diving, music, gymnastics, pen collecting. Home: 67 Citadel Dr Jackson NJ 08527

ARMINGTON, THOMAS C. mathematician, educator; b. Buffalo; s. James E. and Diane W. Armington; m. Maria Medrano; 1 child, Mercedes. MA, Univ. of Del., Newark, Delaware, 1992; BA, Stockton State Coll., Pomona, NJ, 1985; AS, Mercer County Cmty. Coll., West Windsor, NJ, 1983. Math. instr. Mercer County Cmty. Coll., West Windsor, NJ, 1985—87; acad. coun. The State Coll. of NJ, Ewing, NJ, 1987—89; rsch. asst. Univ. of Del., Newark, Del., 1989—91; math. specialist Independence Cmty. Coll., Independence, Kans., 1993—96; first yr. studies prof. Slippery Rock Univ., Slippery Rock, Pa., 1997—2000; math. prof. Felician Coll., Lodi, NJ, 2000—. Chair Math. Spl. Interest Network, Nat. Assoc. for Devel. Ed., Findlay, Ohio, 2000—03. Editor: (booklet) Best Practices in Devel. Math., 2000. Recipient Outstanding Svc. Award, Nat. Assoc. for Devel. Ed., 2002. Mem.: Nat. Assoc. for Devel. Ed. (chair 2002). Achievements include Nominated for Who's Who Among Am. Authors (1992), undergraduate math. and fgn. lang. awards (1983). Avocations: backpacking, running. Home: PO Box 199 Metuchen NJ 08840 Office: Felician Coll 262 So Main St Lodi NJ 07644

ARMISTEAD, KATHERINE KELLY (MRS. THOMAS B. ARMISTEAD III), interior designer, travel consultant, civic worker; b. Apr. 14, 1926; d. Joseph Anthony and Katherine Arnold (Manning) Kelly; m. Thomas Boyd Armistead III, Nov. 29, 1952. Grad., Finch Jr. Coll., 1946. Cert. travel cons. Editor news Sta. WOR, N.Y.C., 1946—51; with Dumont TV, 1951—52; editor Social Svc. Rev., L.A., 1956—57; interior designer L.A., 1963—; travel cons. Gilner Internat. Travels, Beverly Hills, Calif., 1980—. Mem. editl. bd. Previews Mag., 1984—87. Pres. Jrs. Social Svc., L.A., 1962—64; nat. chpt. chmn. Assoc. Alumnae of Sacred Heart, 1960—66; pres. Las Floristas, 1967—68; coord. Jr. Mannequin Assisteens, Assistance League So. Calif., 1971—72; pres. docent coun. L.A. County Mus. Art, 1976—77, pres. decorative arts coun., 1977—80, chmn. Am. Antiques Conf., 1979—81, mem. costume coun., mem. past pres.' coun., 1981—, mem. capital gifts campaign com.; bd. dirs. L.A. Orphanage Guild, 1970—. Recipient Eve award, Assistance League So. Calif. Mem.: Inst. Cert. Travel Agts., Am. Soc. Travel Agts., Lady Grand Cross Equestrian Order of the Holy Sepulchre of Jerusalem, Bel Air Garden Club, Birnam Wood Golf Club. Republican. Roman Catholic.

ARMISTEAD, THOMAS BOYD, III, television and film producer; b. St. Louis, Feb. 18, 1918; s. Thomas Boyd and Alice Townsend (Jones) A; m. Katherine Kelly, Nov. 1952; children: Katherine Armistead Roark, Thomas Boyd IV. BA, Amherst Coll., 1939; B of Theater Arts, 1941; M of Theater Arts, State Theater of Calif., 1942. Producer, dir. Don Lee Mutual, Hollywood, Calif., 1945; dir., dept. head, instr. direction State Theater of Calif., Pasadena, 1946-50; TV dir. live Sta. KTTV, Hollywood, 1948-50; assoc. producer Bing Crosby Enterprises, Inc., Hollywood, 1951-52; owner, producer, dir. Pickwick Pictures, Hollywood, 1953; film producer, dir. J. Walter Thompson, New York City and Hollywood, 1954-58; producer, dir. TV and film for various studios including Screen Gems, Filmways, Paramount, Hollywood, 1959-62; v.p. executive producer Don Fedderson Prodns., Hollywood, 1962-64; producer, dir. various film cos., ABC TV film, Hollywood, 1964—. Producer, dir. TV film and commls.; dir. first full length live dramatic show produced on TV. With USAF, 1940—45. Recipient Christopher award Action for Children's TV Achievement award, 1979; 3 film works disply Mus. Moving Images, London. Mem.: NATAS (founding mem., edn. com.), AIA, Dirs. Guild Am. (TV Coun. awards com.), Birnam Wood Golf Club. Republican. Roman Catholic. Avocations: photography, raising orchids, remodeling houses. Home and Office: Armistead Assocs 2142 Century Park Ln # 206 Los Angeles CA 90067

ARMISTEAD, WILLIS WILLIAM, university administrator, veterinarian; b. Detroit, Oct. 28, 1916; s. Eber Merrill and Josephine Brunell (Kindred) A.; m. Martha Sidney Clark, Sept. 17, 1938 (dec. 1964); children: Willis William, Jack Murray, Sidney Merrill; m. Mary Wallace Nelson, 1967. D.V.M., Tex. A&M Coll., 1938; M.Sc., Ohio State U., 1950; PhD, U. Minn., 1955. Diplomate: hon. diplomate; Am. Coll. Veterinary Surgeons, Am. Coll. Veterinary Preventive Medicine. Pvt. practice veterinary medicine, 1938—40; instr. Sch. Veterinary Medicine Tex. A&M U., 1940—42, asst. prof. to prof. Sch. Veterinary Medicine, 1946—53, dean Sch. Veterinary Medicine, 1953—57; dean Coll. Veterinary Medicine Mich. State U., East Lansing, 1957—74; dean Coll. Veterinary Medicine, U. Tenn., Knoxville, 1974—79, chmn. strategic planning adv. com., 1988—89; v.p. agr. U. Tenn. System, 1979—87. Collaborator animal diseases and parasite rsch. divsn. Dept. Agr., 1954-65; cons., adviser commn. veterinary edn. of South So. Regional Edn. Bd., 1953-56; mem. gov.'s sci. adv. bd., 1958-60; nat. cons. to Air Force Surgeon Gen., 1960-62; mem. adv. coun. Inst. Lab. Animal Resources, NRC, 1962-66; pres. Assn. Am. Veterinary Med. Colls., 1964-65, 73-74, Spl. award, 1983; veterinary med. resident investigators selection com. U.S. VA, 1967-70; veterinary medicine rev. com. Bur. Health Professions Edn. and Manpower Tng., HEW, 1967-71; mem. Nat. Bd. Veterinary Med. Examiners, 1970-74; mem. adv. panel for veterinary medicine Inst. Medicine, NAS, 1972-74; mem. bd. agr. and renewable resources NRC, 1976-77; 1st Allam lectr. Am. Coll. Veterinary Surgeons, 1972; Conti Meml. keynote lectr. Ariz.-Calif.-Nev. Veterinary Conf., 1994; mem. curriculum com. Oak Ridge Inst. Continued Learning, 1998-2001. Contbg. author: Canine Surgery, rev. edit, 1957, Canine Medicine, rev. edit, 1959; editor: The N.Am. Veterinarian, 1950-56, Jour. Veterinary Med. Edn, 1974-80; assoc. editor: Jour. Am. Animal Hosp. Assn., 1964-70; contbr. tech. articles to profl. jours. Bd. dirs. Tenn. Farm bur. Fedn., 1979-87, Tenn. Coun. Coops., 1982-87, Tenn. 4-H Club Found., 1979-87, Tenn. Agrl. Hall of Fame, 1979-87; mem. Tenn. State Soil Conservation Com., 1979-87; mem. Southwide adv. com. So. Agribus. Forum, 1979-87; mem. adv. bd. Clarence Brown Theater, U. Tenn., 2000-02. Maj. Vet. Corps AUS, 1942—46. Recipient Meritorious Svc. award Selective Svc. System, 1972; hon. alumnus Mich. State U., 1972; recipient Disting. Alumnus award Coll. Vet. Medicine, Tex. A&M U., 1980, 75th Anniversary Achievement award Tex. A&M U. Coll. Vet. Medicine, 1991; named V.P Emeritus, U. Tenn., 1987—. Mem. AAAS, U.S. Animal Health Assn., Am. Vet. Med. Assn. (pres. 1957-58, award 1977), Tex. Vet. Med. Assn. (pres. 1947-48), Mich. Vet. Med. Assn. (trustee Edn. and Sci. Trust 1970-74), Fedn. Assns. Schs. of Health Professions (pres. 1975), Tenn. Vet. Med. Assn. (Lifetime Achievement award 1995), Inst. Medicine of NAS, N.Y. Acad. Scis., Rotary (pres. 1987-88), Sigma Xi, Phi Kappa Phi, Alpha Zeta, Phi Zeta, Omega Tau Sigma (nat. Gamma award Ohio State U. 1962), Phi Eta Sigma, Gamma Sigma Delta, Omicron Delta Kappa. Lodges: Rotary. Episcopalian. Home: 1101 Cherokee Blvd Knoxville TN 37919-7852 E-mail: barmistead@msn.com.

ARMITAGE, KENNETH BARCLAY, biology educator, ecologist; b. Steubenville, Ohio, Apr. 18, 1925; s. Albert Kenneth and Virginia Ethel (Barclay) A.; m. Katie Lou Hart, June 5, 1953; children: Karole, Keith, Kevin BS summa cum laude, Bethany Coll., W.Va., 1949; MS, U. Wis.-Madison, 1951, PhD, 1954. Instr. U. Wis.-Green Bay, 1954-55; instr. U. Wis.-Wausau, 1955-56; asst. prof. biology U. Kans., Lawrence, 1956-62, assoc. prof., 1962-66, prof., 1966-96, William J. Baumgartner disting. prof., 1987-96, chmn. dept. systematics & ecology, 1982-88, dir. environ. studies program, 1976-82, dir. exptl. and applied ecology program, 1974-94, prof. emeritus, 1996—. Vis. prof. U. Modena, Italy, 1989; mem. com. examiners Grad. Record Exam. Biology Test, 1986-92, chmn., 1988-92; sr. investigator Rocky Mountain Biol. Lab., Gothic, Colo., 1962—, trustee, 1969-86, pres. bd. trustees, 1985-86; cons. Vancouver Island Marmot Recovery Program. Author: (lab. manual) Investigations in General Biology, (with others) Principles of Modern Biology; contbr. articles to profl. jours.; co-editor: Holarctic Marmots as a Factor of Biodiversity, 3d Internat. Marmot Conf. proceedings; mem. editl. bd.: Ethology, Ecology and Evolution, 1989—, Ibex Jour. Mountain Ecology, 1994—, Oecologia Montana, 1996—; sci. editor: Die Murmeltiere der Welt. Pres. Douglas County chpt. Zero Population Growth, 1969-71; bd. dirs. Children's Hour, Inc., Lawrence, 1969-70; v.p. Mt. Oread Hist., Lawrence, 1998—. Recipient Antarctic medal NSF, 1968, Edn. Service award U. Kans., 1979, Alumni Achievement award Bethany Coll., 1989. Fellow AAAS, Animal Behavior Soc.; mem. Am. Soc. Naturalists (treas. 1984-86), Am. Inst. Biol. Scis. (mem. task force for 90s), Ecol. Soc. Am., Am. Soc. Zoologists, Am. Soc. Mammalogists (C. Hart Merriam award 1997), Orgn. Biol. Field Stations (v.p. 1986-87, pres. 1988-89), Sigma Xi, Phi Beta Kappa, Beta Beta Beta, Gamma Sigma Kappa. Avocations: stamp collecting, gardening, natural history, western history. Home: 505 Ohio St Lawrence KS 66044-2245 Office: U Kans Dept Ecology & Evolutionary Biology Lawrence KS 66045-7534 E-mail: marmots@ukans.edu.

ARMITAGE, RICHARD LEE, federal government official; b. Boston, Apr. 26, 1945; s. Leo Holmes and Ruth H. Armitage; m. Laura Alice Samford, Apr. 15, 1968; children: Beth, Lee, Jenny, Paul. BS, U.S. Naval Acad. Naval ops. coordinator Def. Attache Office, Saigon, Vietnam, 1973-75; cons. Dept. Def., Washington, 1975-76, 1975-76; ptnr. Agt.-Export, Bangkok, 1976-78, 1976-78; adminstrv. asst. to U.S. Senator Robert Dole Washington, 1978-79; self-employed cons. Fairfax, Va., 1979-80; fgn. policy advisor Reagan for Pres. campaign, Washington, 1980; trans. advisor U.S. Govt., Washington, 1980-81; asst. sec. def. East Asia Dept. Def., Washington, 1981-83, asst. sec. def. internat. security affairs, 1983—89; presidential spec. negotiator for Philippines mil. bases Washington, 1989—92; ambassador NIS, Soviet Union, 1992—93; pres. Armitage Assoc., 1993; dep. sec. state Dept. State, Washington, 2001—. Served to lt. USN, 1967-73, Vietnam. Mem. Assn. Asian Studies Republican. Roman Catholic. Office: US Dept State Office of Secy 2201 C St NW Washington DC 20520

ARMITAGE, SHELLEY SUE, American studies educator; b. Ft. Worth, June 17, 1947; d. Robert Allen and Dorothy Mae (Dunn) A. BA, Tex. Tech. U., 1969, MA, 1971; PhD, U. N.Mex., 1983. Asst. prof. English Tarrant County Jr. Coll., Ft. Worth, 1971-78; lectr. Am. lit. Skidmore Coll., Colo. Inst., Adirondacks, 1977, 78; assoc. prof. Am. lit. West Tex. State U., Canyon, 1983-89; prof. Am. studies U. Hawaii, Honolulu, 1990-96; prof. cultural studies U. Memphis, 1993; chair women's studies U. Tex., El Paso, 1996-2001, Roderick Chair, 1995. Sr. Fulbright U., Nova Lisboa, Portugal, 1990; disting. Fulbright chair of lit. U. Warsaw, 2000; Fulbright sr. specialist U. Lodz, Poland, 2002. Author: John Held Jr., 1987 (N.Y. Times Notable Book), Kewpies and Beyond: Rose O'Neill, 1994 (Eudora Welty prize.U. Press Miss., 94), Women's Work: Cultural Essays, 1995, The Journals of Peggy Pond Church, 2001 (Border Books prize), Reading Into Photography, 1981. Cons. Oldham County Hist. Commn., Vega, Tex.; referee Praxis, El Paso; exec. dir. N.Mex. NEH, Albuquerque, 1985. Recipient Women Artists and Writers award Rockefeller found., 1985, Internat. Women's Studies award Ford Found., 1997, award NEH, 1999, U. Oreg., 1974, U. N.Mex., 1979, Emily Toth Prize Pop Culture Assn., Am. Studies Assn.; Women's Studies Confs., Costa Rica, Warsaw, Cuba, 2000-01, Nature and Society NEH U. Ill., 1999. Mem. Am. Studies Assn., We. History Assn., MLA, Soc. Photographic Educators. Methodist. Avocations: naturalist, photographer, documentary film consulting, organic farming. Home: PO Box 524 Vega TX 79092 Office: U Tex English Dept 500 W University Ave El Paso TX 79968

ARMITAGE, THOMAS EDWARD, library director; b. Torrington, Wyo., Dec. 11, 1946; s. Ross Eugene Armitage and Mary Kathleen (Donley) Wieland; m. Linda Lou Theisen, May 23, 1987; children: Anne, Nicholas, Rachel. AA in History, Santa Barbara (Calif.) C.C., 1971; BA in History, Kans. State U., Pittsburg, 1973; MLS, U. Mo., 1974. Asst. dir. Ottumwa (Iowa) Pub. Libr., 1975-77; libr. dir. Ft. Dodge (Iowa) Pub. Libr., 1977-86, Cedar Rapids (Iowa) Pub. Libr., 1987—. With USN, 1967-69. Mem. ALA, Iowa Libr. Assn., Iowa Urban Pub. Libr. Assn. (pres. 1999—, sec. 1995-98), Linn County Libr. Assn. (v.p. 1993—), Linn County Libr. Consortium (sec. 1995—), Rotary, Greater Cedar Rapids C. of C. Office: Cedar Rapids Pub Libr 500 1st St SE Cedar Rapids IA 52401-2002

ARMON, CARMEL, neurologist; b. Oct. 30, 1954; MD, MSc, Technion-Israel Inst. Tech., Haifa, 1980; MHS in Biometry, Duke U., 1993. Diplomate in Neurology Am. Bd. Psychiatry and Neurology, Am. Bd. Clin. Neurophysiology, Am. Bd. Electrodiagnostic Medicine. Resident in neurology Mayo Clinic, Rochester, Minn., 1984-89; clin. neurophysiology fellow Duke U. Med. Ctr., Durham, N.C., 1989-91; med. dir. EEG Lab. and Epilepsy Ctr. Loma Linda (Calif.) U., 1991—, dir. ALS Patients' Clinic, 1991—, dir. Neurol. Clin. Rsch. Ctr., 1994—, asst. prof. neurology, 1991-94, assoc. prof., 1994-99, prof. neurology, 1999—. Contbr. more than 50 articles to profl. jours., chpts. to books. Office: Coleman Pav Rm 11108 11175 Campus St Loma Linda CA 92350-1700

ARMOR, JOHN N. chemical company scientist and research manager; b. Phila., Sept. 14, 1944; s. Lloyd N. and Cornelia Armor; m. Connie B. Korzuch, Dec. 17, 1966; children: Kimberly, Gregory, Jennifer. BS in Chemistry, Pa. State U., 1966; PhD, Stanford U., 1970. Asst. prof. chemistry Boston U., 1970-74; group leader Allied Signal Corp., Morristown, N.J., 1974-85; prin. rsch. assoc. Air Products and Chems. Inc., Allentown, Pa., 1985—; head corp. catalysis rsch. ctr. Air Products, 1999—. Chmn. Inorganic Gordon Rsch. Conf., New London, N.H., 1988; gen. chmn. 2d World Congress on Environ. Catalysis. Editor-in-chief CATTECH, 2001—; editor Applied Catalysis, 1987-96; mem. editl. bd. Jour. Natural Gas Chemistry, Japanese Catalysis Surveys, Jour. Catalysis, others; contbr. more than 110 articles to profl. jours. Recipient Houdry award for excellence in applied catalysis, N. Am. Catalysis Soc., 1997, 2001, E. V. Murpee award, Am. Chem. Soc. Mem. AIChE, Am. Chem. Soc. (organizer symposium on environ. catalysis 1993), The N.Am. Catalysis Soc. (bd. dirs., treas. 1993-2001, pres. 2001—), Catalysis Club Phila. (award for Excellence in Catalysis 1995), Catalysis Club N.Y. (bd. dirs.). Achievements include more than 50 patents. Home: 1608 Barkwood Dr Orefield PA 18069-8923 Office: Air Products & Chem Inc 7201 Hamilton Blvd Allentown PA 18195-1526 E-mail: Cbarmor@enter.net., armorjn@APCI.com.

ARMOUR, CHRISTOPHER E. physician; b. Phenix City, Ala., Nov. 1, 1959; s. John Henry Crowder III and Mildred Louise (Perry) A.; m. Jacqueline Lyles Armour, Dec. 16, 1984; children: Jonathan R., Kristen M. BS, U. Ga., Athens, 1982; MD, Morehouse Sch. Medicine, Atlanta, 1987. Diplomate Am. Assn. Family Physicians. Physician Welstar divsn. Promina Health Care Sys., Kennesaw, Ga., 1995—, Southside Med. Ctr., 2003—. Physician Parkway Med. divsn. HCA Physican Svc., Mableton, Ga. Democrat. Baptist. Avocation: reading. Home: 2725 Thornbury Way College Park GA 30349-7119 Office: 5701 Mableton Pkwy Ste 2A Mableton GA 30126

ARMOUR, GEORGE PORTER, lawyer; b. Bryn Mawr, Pa., June 10, 1921; s. Charles Joseph and Florence (Eagle) A.; m. Isabel Blondet, Nov. 22, 1958; children: Luis O., Carlos O. BA, Temple U., 1943, JD, 1949. Bar: Pa. 1949, N.Y. 1969, Calif. 1975. Assoc. Bennett & Bricklin, Phila., 1949-59; atty. Atlantic Richfield Co., 1959-83; gen. atty. Phila., 1965 68; assoc. gen. counsel Phila., N.Y.C., L.A., 1968-78; dep. gen. counsel L.A., 1978-83; pvt. practice law, 1983—. Chmn. Internat. and Comparative Law Ctr., Southwestern Legal Found., Dallas, 1980-82. Mem. Assocs. Calif. Inst. Tech., 1981—; mem. Soc. of Fellows Huntington Libr. and Art Gallery, San Marino, Calif., 1982—. With USAAF, 1943-46. Mem. ABA, Calif. Bar Assn., Valley Hunt Club (Pasadena). Republican. Episcopalian. Home and Office: 481 S Orange Grove Blvd Apt 4 Pasadena CA 91105-1798

ARMOUR, JAMES LOTT, lawyer; b. Jackson, Tenn., May 19, 1938; s. Quintin and Frances (Breeden) A.; m. Nancy Stokes Johnson, Mar. 17, 1962; 1 son, John Lawson. BA, Vanderbilt U., 1961, LLB, 1964; LLM, So. Meth. U., 1967. Bar: Tenn. 1964, Tex. 1965, U.S. Supreme Ct. 1967, N.Y. 1969, Okla. 1972. Assoc. firm Turner Rodgers Winn Scurlock & Terry, Dallas, 1965-67; internat. atty. Mobil Corp., N.Y.C. and London, 1967-71, Phillips Petroleum Co., Bartlesville, Okla., 1971-74; asst. gen. counsel Conoco, Inc., Stamford, Conn., 1974-83; ptnr. firm Locke Liddell & Sapp LLP, Dallas, 1984-2001; pvt. practice James L. Armour Atty. at Law, Dallas, 2001—. Mem. adv. bd. oil and gas SW Legal Found., chair, 1996-99; mem. Dallas Com. on Fgn. Rels.; former mem. alumni bd. Vanderbilt Law Sch. Mem. ABA, Assn. of Bar of City of N.Y., State Bar Tex., Dallas Bar Assn., Petroleum Club, Phi Delta Phi, Kappa Sigma. Episcopalian. Home: 4541 Belfort Pl Dallas TX 75205-3618 Office: Law Offices of James L Armour 325 N Saint Paul St Ste 2460 Dallas TX 75201-3864 Fax: 214 999 0603. E-mail: jlarmour@jlarmourlaw.com.

ARMOUR, MAYA LYNNE, lawyer; b. Lancaster, Calif., July 8, 1959; d. Paul Arthur and Maria Louise Armour. BA, UCLA, 1981; JD (with honors), U. Calif., San Francisco, 1986. Bar: Calif. 1986, N.Y. 1989. Law clk. to judge U.S. Dist. Ct. DC, 1986-88; assoc. Dewey, Ballantine, Bushby, Palmer & Wood, N.Y.C., 1989-92; prin. Law Offices Maya Armour, San Francisco, 1995—; commr. pro tem San Francisco Superior Ct., 2000—; judge pro tem San Mateo Superior Ct., 1993—2002. Dir. Telegraph Hill Dwellers, 2000—, Telegraph Hill Neighborhood Ctr., 2002—. Mem. Thurston Soc. Office: PO Box 2884 San Francisco CA 94126

ARMS, GARY D. English literature educator; b. Waterloo, Iowa, May 18, 1951; s. Luverne DeWitt Arms and Wilma Toops; m. Carol Susan Arms; children: Joseph, David. BA, U. No. Iowa, 1981; PhD, U. Iowa, 1990. Adj. prof. Iowa State U., Ames, 1990-92; asst. prof. Clarke Coll., Dubuque, Iowa, 1992-99, assoc. prof., 2000—, chmn. English dept., 2001—. Author: (novels) Mythology Smart Jr., 1997, Spelling Smart Jr., 2000 (Parents Guide award 2000), (play) The Arranged Marriage, 1998. Pres. Dubuque Fine Arts Players, 1997—. Home: 1686 Lawndale Dubuque IA 52001 Office: Clarke Coll Dubuque IA 52001 E-mail: garms@clarke.edu.

ARMSTRONG, AGNES ROSE FINGERLIN, musicologist; d. Lewis Michel and Lois Crannell Payne Fingerlin; children: Rebecca Anne Harris, Brenda Sue Goodknight, Scott Dennis. BA in Performance, SUNY, 1974; MS in Music Edn., Coll. St. Rose, 1983; MA in Musicology, NYU, 1994, PhD, 2003. Organist, choirmaster Third Ref. Ch., Albany, NY, 1965—71, St. John's Luth. Ch., Altamont, 1972—2003, Helderberg Ref. Ch., Guilderland, 1975—; tchr. music theory Guilderland Ctrl. Sch., 1987—. Contbr. articles to profl. jours.; musician (producer): (cd audio recording) Guilmant Noels opus 60, Victorian Christmas at Round Lake; editor: (organ music score) Vepres des Vierges by Ernest Chausson. Recipient Tricentennial Hymn First prize, City of Albany, 1986; fellow, NYU, 1994—99. Mem.: N.Y. State Music Tchrs. Assn. (organ and harpsichord chair), Assn. Aristide Cavaille-Coll, Reed Organ Soc., Organ Hist. Soc. (grantee 1987, 1993), Am. Guild Organists (dean, regional convener), Delta Epsilon Sigma. Achievements include research in 19th-Century Organ Music, Organists, Organs. Avocations: travel, antiques, cats. Home: 168 Main St PO Box 19 Altamont NY 12009-0019 Home Fax: 518-861-5370. Personal E-mail: agnesrosea@aol.com.

ARMSTRONG, ALAN LEIGH, lawyer; b. L.A., Apr. 25, 1945; s. Don Leigh and Barbara Caroline (Hayes) A.; m. Margie Jean Lehner, July 1, 1972; children: Don Leigh, Mark Leigh. BA, U. Calif., Riverside, 1967; JD, Western State U., Fullerton, Calif., 1984. Bar: Calif. 1984, U.S. Dist. Ct. (cen. dist.) Calif. 1985, U.S. Ct. Appeals (9th cir.) 1985, U.S. Tax Ct. 1987, U.S. Dist. Ct. (so. dist.) Calif. 1995, U.S. Dist. Ct. (no. and ea. dists.) Calif. 2002, U.S. Supreme Ct. 1988. Physicist USN, Pomona, Calif., 1967-74, engr. Seal Beach, Calif., 74-93; pvt. practice Alan Leigh Armstrong, Atty. At Law, Huntington Beach, Calif., 1985—. Adj. prof. law Trinity Law Sch., 1992—. Lay reader St. James Episcopal Ch., Newport Beach, Calif., 1991—; vestryman St. Joseph's Episcopal Ch., Buena Park, Calif., 1985-88; cubmaster Boy Scouts Am., Huntington Beach, 1988-92, asst. scoutmaster, 1992-94, com. chair, 1994-97, com. mem. 1998—. Mem. Christian Legal Soc. Republican. Avocations: sailing, automatic musical instrument collecting. Office: Alan Leigh Armstrong Atty At Law 18652 Florida St Ste 225 Huntington Beach CA 92648-6007 E-mail: alan@alanarmstrong.com.

ARMSTRONG, ALEXANDRA, financial advisor; b. Washington, Sept. 26, 1939; d. Rhoda Elizabeth (Forbes) Armstrong; m. Jerry J. McCoy, 1994. BA in History, Newton (Mass.) Coll. Sacred Heart, 1960. Cert. fin. planner, 1997. Exec. sec. Ferris & Co., Washington, 1961—66, registered rep., 1966—77; sr. v.p. Julia Walsh & Sons, Washington, 1977—83; pres. Alexandra Armstrong Advisors Inc., Washington, 1983—91; chmn. Armstrong, Welch & MacIntyre Inc., Washington, 1991—2000, Armstrong, MacIntyre & Severns, Inc., Washington, 2001—. Bd. experts Boardroom Reports, 1987—. Author: On Your Own: A Widow's Passage To Emotional and Financial Wellbeing, 1993, 3d edit., 2000. Mem. Washington Jr. League, 1961—; vice chmn. Nat. Coun. Friends of Kennedy Ctr., Washington, 1987-91; pres. Nat. Capital coun. Boy Scouts Am., 1999-2000, chmn., 2000-01; mem. bd. visitors Sch. Bus. Georgetown U., 1988-91; v.p. programs Internat. Women's Forum, 1991-93, v.p.

membership 1997-99, dir. IWF leadership found., 2001-; bd. dirs. Reading is Fundamental, 1993—, treas. 2000-2003; chmn. Found. Fin. Planning, 1999-2000, bd. dirs., 2001—. Named Bus. Woman of Yr. Washington Bus. and Profl. Women's Club, 1978; recipient award of excellence for commerce Boston Coll. Alumni Assn., 1985, Woman Who Makes a Difference award Internat. Women's Forum, 1992, Silver Beaver award Boy Scouts Am., 1991, Loren Dutton award, Internat. Assn. Registered Fin. Cons., 2003, Beta Gamma Sigma chpt. honoree Georgetown U., 1992. Mem. Internat. Assn. for Fin. Planning (bd. dirs. 1980-87, chmn. emeritus, pres. 1986-87), Nat. Assn. Investment Clubs (columnist monthly mag. 1978—, Disting. Svc. award 1993), Nat. Assn. Securities Dealers (bus. conduct com. dist. 10 1986-89, vice chmn. 1988-89), Nat. Assn. Women Bus. Owners (pres. Capital Area chpt. 1980-81), D.C. Estate Planning Coun., Econ. Club (Washington D.C.), Cosmos Club (Washington, D.C.), Econ. Club, (N.Y.C.), Fin. Planning Assn. (Lifetime Achievement award 2001), Nat. Capital Gift Planning Coun. D.C. Republican. Roman Catholic. Home: 3560 Winfield Ln NW Washington DC 20007-2368 Office: 1155 Connecticut Ave NW Ste 250 Washington DC 20036-4314 E-mail: aarmstrong@amsindc.com.

ARMSTRONG, ANNE LEGENDRE (MRS. TOBIN ARMSTRONG), former ambassador, corporate director; b. New Orleans, Dec. 27, 1927; d. Armant and Olive (Martindale) Legendre; m. Tobin Armstrong, Apr. 12, 1950; children: John Barclay, Katharine, Sarita A. Hixon, Tobin and James L. (twins). BA in English, Vassar Coll., 1949. Co-chmn. Rep. Nat. Com., 1971-73; counsellor to U.S. Pres., 1973-74; U.S. amb. to Gt. Britain and No. Ireland, London, 1976-77; chmn. adv. bd. Ctr. for Strategic and Internat. Studies (formerly affiliated with Georgetown U.), 1981-87, chmn. bd. trustees, 1987-99; chmn. exec. com., 1999—; chmn. Pres.'s Fgn. Intelligence Adv. Bd., 1981-90. Commn. on Integrated Long Term Strategy, 1987; adv. coun. GM Corp., 1998. Bd. regents Smithsonian Instn., 1978-94, emeritus, 1994; bd. overseers Hoover Instn., 1978-97; co-chmn. Reagan-Bush Campaign, 1980; bd. regents Tex. A&M U., 1997-03; U.S. Commn. on Nat. Security/21st Century, 1999-2001. Recipient Gold Medal award for disting. svc. to humanity Nat. Inst. Social Scis., 1977, Rep. Woman of Yr. award, 1979, Texan of Yr. award, 1981, Presdl. Medal of Freedom award, 1987, Golden Plate award Am. Acad. Achievement, 1989; named to Tex. Women's Hall of Fame, 1986. Mem. English-Speaking Union (chmn. 1978-80), Coun. Fgn. Rels., Am. Assocs. of Royal Acad. Trust (trustee 1985—, vice-chmn. 1990), Gov.'s Task Force on Homeland Security, Alfalfa Club, Capitol Hill Club, Phi Beta Kappa. Republican.

ARMSTRONG, C. MICHAEL, communications company executive; b. Detroit, Oct. 18, 1938; s. Charles H. and Zora Jean (Brooks) A.; m. Anne Gossett, June 17, 1961; children: Linda, Julie, Kristy. BS in Bus. Econs, Miami U., Oxford, Ohio, 1961; grad., Dartmouth Inst., 1976; LLD (hon.), Pepperdine U., 1997, Loyola Marymount U., 1998. With IBM Corp., 1961-92, dir. systems mgmt. mktg. div., White Plains, N.Y., 1975-76, v.p. market ops. East, 1976-78, pres. data processing divsn., 1978-80, v.p., asst. group exec. plans and controls, data processing product group, 1980-83, v.p., group exec., 1983-84, sr. v.p., group exec., 1984-92, also pres., until 1988, pres., dir. gen. World Trade Europe/Middle East/Africa, 1987-89, chmn. World Trade Corp., 1989-92; chmn., CEO Hughes Aircraft Co., L.A., 1992-93, GM Hughes Electronics (now Hughes Electronics Corp.), 1993—97, AT&T, N.Y.C., 1997—. Mem. GM Pres. Coun.; bd. dirs. Travelers Corp., Hartford, Conn., The Times-Mirror-Co., L.A.- Citigroup; mem. supervisory bd. Thyssen-Bornemisza Group; chmn. Pres.'s Export Coun., The White House, 1994—. Trustee Johns Hopkins U., chmn. adv. bd. Johns Hopkins Med. Sch.; mem., CEO bd. of adv. U. So. Calif. Bus. Sch.; mem. bus. adv. coun. Miami U.; mem. Coun. on Fgn. Rels., Nat. Security Telecomm. Adv. Com., Def. Policy Adv. Com. on Trade (DPACT); adv. bd. Yale Sch. Mgmt.; vice-chmn. World Affairs Coun., L.A.; chmn. Sabriya's Castle of Fun Found.; bd. trustees Carnegie Hall. Mem. Calif. Bus. Roundtable. Office: AT&T Corp Corp Hdqs 32 Avenue of the Americas New York NY 10013-2412

ARMSTRONG, DANIEL WAYNE, chemist, educator; b. Ft. Wayne, Ind., Nov. 2, 1949; s. Robert Eugene and Nila Louise (Koeneman) A.; m. Linda Marilyn Todd, June 11, 1972; children: Lincoln Thomas, Ross Alexander, Colleen Victoria. BS, Washington and Lee U., 1972; MS in Chem. Oceanography, Tex. A&M U., 1974, PhD in Chemistry, 1977. Prof. Bowdoin Coll., Brunswick, Maine, 1978-79, Georgetown U., Washington, 1980-83, Tex. Tech. U., Lubbock, 1983-87; Curators' disting. prof., head ctr. environ. sci. and tech.; head dept. analytical chemistry U. Mo., Rolla, 1987-2000; Caldwell prof. chemistry Iowa State U., 2000—. Bd dirs. Advanced Separations Techs., Whippany, NJ; Moreton lectr. Millsaps Coll., 2001, R.A. Welch lectr., 2002. Host Univ. Forum Radio Show, Washington, 1981-83; writer, host weekly radio show We're Sci. Nat. Pub. Radio, 1993—; author film, radio shows; contbr. articles to profl. publs.; patentee in field. Recipient Tchg. Excellence award U. Mo., 1985, 88-89, 92, 94, Faculty Excellence award U. Mo., 1988-89, Martin medal, 1991, EAS Chromatography award, 1990, Isco award, 1992, Presdl. award, 1993, Perkin Elmer award, 1994, R&D 100 award R&D Mag., 1995, Benedetti-Pichler award Am. Microchem. Soc. 1996, Helen M. Free award, 1998, CLDG Merit award, 2001, Weber medal, 2001, Kenneth A. Spencer award, 2002, Chirality medal, 2003; named Disting. Scholar Hope Coll., 1999, Spencer award for agr. and vood chemistry, 2002; grantee Rsch. Corp., 1979, Petroleum Rsch. Fund, 1979, 91, NSF, 1981; Rsch. grantee Whatman Corp., 1981, Dept. Energy, 1984, 87, 91, 94, Dow Chem., 1985-90, NIH, 1986, 91, 95, 2000, EPA, 1995, Shell Co., 1989-92. Fellow Am. Assn. Pharm. Scientists; mem. Am. Chem. Soc. (49th Midwest award for chemistry 1993, award in chromatography 1999), Slovak Pharm. Soc. (hon.), Sigma Xi, Phi Lambda Upsilon. Office: Iowa State U Dept Chemistry Gilman Hall Ames IA 50011 E-mail: sec4dwa@iastate.edu.

ARMSTRONG, DAVID LIGON, psychiatrist; b. Ontario, Calif., May 5, 1927; s. John Awdry and Ruth (Harrison) A.; m. Mary Meredith, Mar. 30, 1953 (dec. Feb. 1997); children: Meredith Armstrong Richey, Paul, Adelaide Armstrong Butler. BS in Plant Sci., U. Calif., Berkeley, 1949; PhD in Genetics, U. Calif., Davis, 1956; MD, Creighton U., 1972. Diplomate Am. Bd. Psychiatry, Am. Bd. Neurology. Dir. rsch. Armstrong Nurseries, Inc., Ontario, Calif., 1953-68; resident in psychiatry U. Calif., Irvine, 1972-75; staff psychiatrist Met. State Hosp., Norwalk, Calif., 1975—. Pres. med. staff Met. State Hosp., Norwalk, 1985-88, 97—. Patentee new varieties roses and peaches. Pres. West End United Fund, Ontario, 1958-60, Chaffey Young Reps., Ontario and Upland, Calif., 1958-60, West End Coun. Cmty. Svcs., Ontario, 1960-64; chmn. Rep. Ctrl. Com., San Bernardino County, Calif., 1960-62. With USNR, 1945-46. Mem. State Employed Physicians Assn. (pres. 1984-86), Sigma Xi, Alpha Zeta. Republican. Avocations: politics, travel, gardening. Home: 2809 E Hillside Ave Orange CA 92867-8413 Office: Met State Hosp 11401 Bloomfield Ave Norwalk CA 90650-2096 Fax: 562-651-5714. Personal E-mail: DavidArmstrong22@SBCglobal.net. Business E-Mail: darmstro@dmhmsh.state.ca.us.

ARMSTRONG, DAVID MICHAEL, biology educator; b. Louisville, July 31, 1944; s. John D. and Elizabeth Ann (Horine) A.; children: John D., Laura C. BS, Colo. State U., 1966; MA in Teaching, Harvard U., 1967; PhD, U. Kans., 1971. From asst. prof. to prof. natural sci. U. Colo., Boulder, 1971-85, prof. ecology and evolutionary biology, 1993—, assoc. chair, 1997-99; sr. scientist Rocky Mountain Biol. Lab., Gothic, Colo., 1977, 79; resident naturalist Sylvan Dale Ranch, Loveland, Colo., 1984—; acting dir. Univ. Mus., 1987-88, dir., 1989-93. Cons. ecologist. Author: Distribution of Mammals in Colorado, 1972, Rocky Mountain Mammals, 1975, 87, Mammals of the Canyon Country, 1982; co-author: Mammals of the Northern Great Plains, Mammals of the Plains States, Mammals of Colorado. Mem. non-game adv. council Colo. Div. Wildlife, 1972-76, Colo. Natural Areas Council, 1975-80. Mem.: Colo. Wildlife Fedn. (bd. dirs. 2000—02), The Nature Conservancy (trustee Colo. chpt. 1989—99, 2002—, chair 1996—98), Rocky Mountain Biol. Lab. (trustee 1979—83), Southwestern Assn. Naturalists (editor 1976—80), Am. Soc. Mammalogists (editor 1981—87). Avocations: draft horses, conservation activities, writing. Office: U Colo EPO Biology PO Box 334 Boulder CO 80309-0334 E-mail: mausmann@aol.com., david.armstrong@colorado.edu.

ARMSTRONG, DONALD, biochemistry, pathophysiology educator; b. Hamilton, Ont., Can., July 20, 1933; came to U.S., 1933; s. Alfred George and Dorothy Emma (Burden) A.; m. Christine Marie Medieros, June 13, 1954; children: Donald, David, Dennis, Sandra, Kenneth, Elizabeth. BS, San Diego State U., 1957; MS, U. Colo., 1969; EdD, Tulsa U., 1974; PhD, U. Oslo (Norway) Med. Sch., 1980; DSc, Charles U. Med. Sch., Prague, Czech Republic, 1990. Instr. San Diego State U., 1960-62; chief rsch. assoc. U. Oreg., Portland, 1963-70; instr. U. Colo. Med. Ctr., Denver, 1967-70, Tulsa C.C., 1970-74; chief clin. chemist Hillcrest Med. Ctr., Tulsa, 1970-74; asst. prof. U. Colo., Denver, 1974-81; assoc. prof. U. Fla. Med. Ctr., Gainesville, 1981-86; prof., chmn. Kuwait U., 1986-90, SUNY, Buffalo, 1990-95, prof., 1995—; rsch. prof. U. Fla. Vet. Med. Coll., 2000-2001, prof. emeritus, 2001—; pres. Oxidative Stress Assocs., Inc., 2002—. Cons. VA Hosp., Ft. Lyon, Colo., 1975—81, Al-Amiri Tchg. Hosp., Kuwait, 1986—90, Bioxytech Inc., Paris, 1994—96, Receptogen Inc., Seattle, 1995—96, Oxigene, Inc., Boston, 1999—2001, Insite Vision, Inc., Palo Alto, 2000—01, Santen Pharm. Ltd., Japan, 2000—, Alcon Labs., Inc., Dallas, 2000—01; mem. sci. adv. bd. Nat. Inst. on Aging, Bethesda, Md., 1985—86, Internat. Assn. for Exptl. and Clin. Ocular Pharmacology and Pharm., 1997—, ZeptoMetrix Corp., 1999—; spl. fgn. vis. prof. Japanese Ministry Higher Edn., 1996, 2000; vis. prof. Showa U. Sch. Medicine, Japan, 1996—; adj. prof. U. Fla. Coll. Vet. Medicine, 1986—2001; pres. and CEO Oxidative Stress Assoc., Inc., 2003—. Editor: (books) Ceroid-Lipofuscinosis, 1982, Free Radicals in Molecular Biology Aging, and Disease, 1984, Effects of Age and Environment on Vision, 1991, Free Radicals in Diagnostic Medicine, 1994, Free Radical and Antioxidant Protocols, 1998, Oxidative Stress Biomarkers and Antioxidant Protocols, 2002, Ultrastructure and Molecular Biology Protocols for Oxidants and Antioxidants, 2002; reviewer: Jour. Investigative Ophthal. Visual Sci., 1990—, Jour. Biochemica Biophysica Acta, 1994—, Am. Jour. Vet. Med. Assn., 2001, Exp. Eye Rsch., 2001, editor-in-chief: Jour. Clin. Lab. Sci., 1992—96, Redox Rev. Chmn. North Fla. Lions Eye Bank, Gainesville, 1983—85; pres. Lions Sight and Hearing Found., 1984—85; trustee Lions Club Internat., Gainesville, 1984—86; chmn. United Way, Gainesville, 1985; pres. Am. Aging Assn., 1984—85; chmn. grad. rsch. edn. com. SUNY Sys. Adminstrn., 1995—98; rsch. prof. Nat. Pigmentosa Found., 1975—78. Rsch. grantee State of Kuwait, 1987-90, Am. Heart Assn., 1992-94,; recipient Rsch. Career Devel. award NIH, 1978-83, Exch. Scientist award NSF/Czechoslovak Acad. of Sci., Prague, 1983, 86, Sr. Scientist award Japan Soc. for Promotion of Sci., 1985, Omicron Sigma award Am. Assn. of Clin. Lab. Scientists, 1994; Norwegian Marshall Fund scholar, 1981, other awards. Fellow Assn. Clin. Scientists; mem. Am. Assn. Clin. Chemists, Assn. for Rsch. in Vision and Ophthalmology, Am. Aging Assn. Avocations: art, hunting, tennis. E-mail: donnchrisb@aol.com.

ARMSTRONG, DOUGLAS DEAN, journalist; b. Wichita, Kans., Mar. 12, 1945; s. H. Glenn and Emma F. (Starkey) A.; m. Paige Prillaman, Jan. 3, 1967 (div. Sept. 1982); children: David Douglas, Christine Elizabeth; m. Mary Alyce Dooley, Mar. 8, 1987; children: Patrick Glenn, Gillian Marie. BA, U. Minn., 1967. Entertainment writer Milw. Jour. Sentinel, 1967-72, editl. writer, 1972-74, consumer writer, 1974-81, movie critic, 1981-95, bus. writer, 1995-2000, personal fin. columnist, 1995-2000. Guest lectr. U. Wis., Milw., 1982-89; movie reviewer WISN-TV, Milw., 1984-85; movie critic WKTI-FM, Milw., 1989-97; pres. Lexington Software Corp., 1996—. Contbr. short fiction to Ellery Queen's Mystery Mag., Alfred Hitchcock's Mystery Mag., Boys' Life. Recipient Pub. Interest award Ctr. for Pub. Representation, 1978. Mem. Mystery Writers Am., Milw. Press Club. Avocations: video, piano, golf. Office: PO Box 170374 Milwaukee WI 53217-8031

ARMSTRONG, EDWARD BRADFORD, JR., oral and maxillofacial surgeon, educator, naval officer; b. Teaneck, N.J., Sept. 24, 1928; s. Edward Bradford and Ruth Elizabeth (Fippinger) A.; AB, U. Pa., 1950; DDS, N.Y.U., 1954; m. Dusanka Vladimirovna Jakovljevic, Nov. 5, 1960; children: Edward Bradford, III, James B., Hugh B. Commd. lt. j.g. U.S. Navy, 1954, advanced through grades to capt. 1971; intern oral surgery Roosevelt Hosp., N.Y.C., 1958, assoc. attending oral surgery, 1959—, attending oral surgeon out-patient dept., 1959—, chmn., moderator Oral Surgery Staff Confs., 1963-70; resident Carle Hosp., Urbana, Ill., 1959; assoc. attending oral surgeon Flower and Fifth Ave. hosps., N.Y.C., 1960-78; asst. attending oral surgeon Hackensack (N.J.) Hosp., 1963-65; adminstrv. officer Naval Res. Dental Co. 3-2, 1965-68, exec. officer, 1968-71, comdg. officer, 1971-73; comdt.'s rep. 3d Naval Dist., Naval Acad., 1972-78, 3d Naval Dist for Dentistry, 1973-75, group staff officer for dentistry and medicine, 1973-75, Ready Res. Unit 502, 1975-77, VTU 0207, 1977-79, ret., 1979; assoc. clin. prof. oral surgery N.Y. Med. Coll., 1963-93; adj. assoc. clin. prof. oral surgery Columbia U. Sch. Dentistry, 1973-89; chmn. bd. E. & R. Armstrong, Inc., Albany, N.Y., 1966-77; pres. Edward B. Armstrong, P.C., N.Y.C., 1979-90; dir. Songtime, Inc., Boston; dir., mem. exec. com. PGP Internat. Corps, Inc. Bd. dirs., trustee Christian Mission Farms of Paraguay, Inc., 1974-84; pres., trustee Central Bible Chapel, Palisades Park, N.J.; area rep., ann. giving U. Pa., 1960-68; Blue and Gold officer Naval Acad. Admissions Com.; sec. bd. dirs., trustee Boys' Club of N.Y. Health Svcs., Inc. Diplomate Am. Bd. Oral Surgery. Fellow N.Y. Acad. Dentistry (sec., dir., pres. 1979-80), Am., Internat. Colls. Dentists (life), Am. Coll. Oral and Maxillofacial Surgeons (founding), Am. Dental Soc. Anesthesiology (hon. life); mem. ADA (life, 1st dist. life), Am. Assn. Oral and Maxillofacial Surgeons (life, N.J. rep. Ho. of Dels. 1963-65), N.Y. Soc. Oral Surgeons (life, chmn. audit and budget com. 1972-79), First Dist. Dental Soc. (life), N.Y. Dental Soc., Bklyn. Dental Soc., Yokosuka Dental Soc. (hon.), Assn. Mil. Surgeons U.S., Mil. Order World Wars, Naval Res. Assn. (life), Union League (chmn. art com. 1973-76, bd. govs. 1974-77, 82-84, v.p. 1977-80, 85-88), Met. Club (bd. gov. 1992-96, 98-2002), N.Y.C., U. Pa. Club, U. Pa. Club of Met. N.J. (dir. 1982—), Acacia, Xi Psi Phi, Psi Omega (hon.), Delta Sigma Delta. Mem. Plymouth Brethren Ch.

ARMSTRONG, EDWIN ALAN, lawyer; b. Atlanta, June 20, 1950; s. Carl Edwin and Betty (Hawkins) A.; m. Marlene Bryant, Aug. 12, 1978. BA, Berry Coll., 1972; JD, Emory U., 1976. Bar: Ga. 1976, U.S. Dist. Ct. (no. dist.) Ga. 1977, U.S. Ct. Appeals (5th cir.) 1981, U.S. Ct. Appeals (11th cir.) 1982, U.S. Supreme Ct. 1989, U.S. Dist. Ct. (so. dist.) Ga., U.S. Ct. Appeals (4th cir.), U.S. Ct. Appeals (D.C. cir.) 1992, U.S. Ct. Appeals (6th cir.) 1992, U.S. Dist. Ct. (mid. dist.) Ga 1992. Atty. Flynt Jud. Cir. Pub. Defenders Office, McDonough, Ga., 1976-77; assoc. Neely, Neely & Player, Atlanta, 1977; pvt. practice, Atlanta, 1977-79, 81—; assoc. Stolz, Shulman & Loveless, Atlanta, 1979-81. Contbr. articles to profl. jours. Mem. ABA (forum com. on air and space law, tort and ins. practice sect.), ATLA, Atlanta Bar Assn., Decatur-DeKalb Bar Assn., State Bar Ga. (chmn. aviation law sect. 1998—), Ga. Trial Lawyers Assn., Nat. Transp. Safety Bd. Bar Assn. (founding, com. legis. and regulatory activity 1989—, editor newsletter 1991-92), Lawyer-Pilots Bar Assn. Episcopalian. Avocation: flying. Home: 4098 Northlake Creek Cv Tucker GA 30084-3416 E-mail: alan@alanarmstronglaw.com.

ARMSTRONG, EDWIN RICHARD, lawyer, publisher, editor; b. Chgo., Sept. 25, 1921; BA, Knox Coll., 1942; JD, Northwestern U., 1948. Ptnr. Reimers & Armstrong, 1949-55; assoc. Friedman & Friedman, 1957-62; ptnr. Friedman, Armstrong & Donnelly, 1962-78, Armstrong & Donnelly, Chgo., 1978—. Home: 860 N Lake Shore Dr Apt 17M Chicago IL 60611-1788 Office: 77 W Washington St Ste 515 Chicago IL 60602-2802

ARMSTRONG, ELIZABETH G. medical educator; d. Kurt C. and Marie E. Guether; m. Thomas R. Armstrong; children: Thomas K., Gregory R. BS, Cornell U., Ithaca, NY, 1968; M.A.T., Harvard U., 1970; PhD, Boston Coll., 1974; Dr. med. h.c. (hon.), Lund (Sweden)U., 2000. Instr. U. Ala., Huntsville, 1970—71; asst. prof. U. Hartford Coll. of Ednl. and Allied Services, Harvard, Conn., 1973—78, SUNY, Stony Brook, NY, 1980—84; lectr. in med. edn. Harvard Med. Sch., Boston, 1990—96, assoc. prof. in pediat. (med. edn.), 1996—. Dir. Harvard-Macy Inst., Boston, 1994—; core curriculum mem. China med. bd. Inst. Internat. Med. Edn., New York, NY, 2000—. Contbr. articles. Prin. Investigator, Josiah Macy Jr. Found., 1994-2001, Decision Resources, 1998 - Present, FIPSE - US EU Med. Edn. Exch., 1997-2000. Office: Harvard Med Internat 1135 Tremont St Ste 940 Boston MA 02120 Office Fax: 617-535-6442. E-mail: earmstrong@hms.harvard.edu.

ARMSTRONG, FLOYD DANIEL, pediatric psychologist; b. Albemarle, N.C., Feb. 7, 1956; s. Mack Monroe and Frances Marie (Dean) A.; m. Kim Virginia Wehunt, Aug. 5, 1978; children: Matthew Daniel, Timothy Michael. AA, Brevard Coll., 1976; BA, Duke U., 1978; MA, So. Meth. U., 1980; PhD, W.Va. U., 1985. Diplomate Am. Bd. Profl. Psychology. Asst. prof. U. Miami, Fla., 1985-94, assoc. prof., 1994-2000, prof., 2000—, assoc. chair pediat., dir. Mailman Ctr. for Child Devel., 1999—. Chair neuropsychology com. Coop. Study Sickle Cell Diseas, Nat. Heart Lung Blood Inst., 1989-2000; chair psychology discipline com. Pediat. Oncology Group, Nat. Cancer Inst., 1990—; chair pediat. bioethics com. Jackson Children's Hosp., Miami, 1994—; chair psychology com. Children's Oncology Group, 2000—. Contbr. articles to profl. jours. Recipient Ryan White Title I grant NIH, 1993-2002; rsch. grantee Am. Cancer Soc., 2003—. Fellow APA, Divsn. Clin. Psychology; mem. Soc. Behavioral Medicine, Divsn. Health Psychology, Assn. for Advancement of Behavior Therapy, Soc. Pediat. Psychology (mem.-at-large 1994-97, pres. 1999). Methodist. Avocations: golf, music, rock climbing. Home: 8221 SW 133rd St Miami FL 33156-6631 Office: Univ Miami Sch Medicine PO Box D-820 Miami FL 33101-6820 E-mail: darmstrong@miami.edu.

ARMSTRONG, F(REDRIC) MICHAEL, retired insurance company executive, consultant; b. Wichita, Kans., Dec. 20, 1942; s. Frederick Dale and Virginia Pauline A.; m. Patricia R. Latif, Dec. 13, 1976 (div. 1996). BSEE, MIT, 1964; MBA, Stanford U., 1966. Mgr. capital appropriations Trans World Airlines, N.Y.C., 1966-69; corp. planner Transam. Corp., San Francisco, 1969-70; v.p. Transam. Film Svc., Salt Lake City, 1970-73, also bd. dirs.; v.p. fin. Europe Transam. Airlines, Madrid, Spain, 1973-75, v.p. planning and info. svcs. Oakland, Calif., 1975-77; exec. v.p. fin. Budget Rent a Car Corp., Chgo., 1977-83, also bd. dirs.; exec. v.p., chief adminstrv. officer Transam. Ins. Group, L.A., 1983-93, also bd. dirs.; pres. Century Indemnity Co., Century Reinsurance Co., L.A., 1995-96, also bd. dirs. Bd. dirs. Melia Internat. Hotels, Panama, The Canadian Surety Co., Ins. Value Added Network Service, River Thames Ins. Co., London, Fairmont Fin. Inc., Mason-McDuffie Ins. Svc., Inc., The Completion Bond Co. Mem. adv. coun. Pierce Coll. E-mail: marmstrong@alum.mit.edu.

ARMSTRONG, GENE LEE, systems engineering consultant, retired aerospace company executive; b. Clinton, Ill., Mar. 9, 1922; s. George Dewey and Ruby Imald (Dickerson) A. m. Lael Jeanne Baker, Apr. 3, 1946; children: Susan Lael, Roberta Lynn, Gene Lee. BS with high honors, U. Ill., 1948, MS, 1951. Registered profl. engr., Calif. With Boeing Aircraft, 1948-50, 51-52; chief engr. astronautics divsn., corp. dir. Gen. Dynamics, 1954-65; chief engr. Def. Sys. Group TRW, Redondo Beach, Calif., 1956-86, pvt. cons. sys. engring., 1986; pres., CEO Armstrong Sys. Engring. Co, Westminster, Calif., 1986—. Mem. NASA Rsch. Adv. Com. on Control, Guidance & Navigation, 1959-62 Contbr. chpts. to books, articles to profl. publs. 1st lt. USAAF, 1942-45 Decorated Air medal; recipient alumni awards U. Ill., 1965, 77 Mem. Am. Math. Soc., AIAA, Nat. Mgmt. Assn., Am. Def. Preparedness Assn., Masons. Home: 5242 Bryant Cir Westminster CA 92683-1712 Office: Armstrong Sys Engring Co 5242 Bryant Cir Westminster CA 92683

ARMSTRONG, GREG L. oil company executive; BS, Southeastern Okla. State U., 1980. Formerly with Price Waterhouse; from various positions to sr. v.p./ CFO, pres./COO, now pres./CEO Plains Resources, Inc., 1981—. Office: Plains Resources Inc 500 Dallas St Ste 700 Houston TX 77002-4804

ARMSTRONG, HAMILTON REED, sculptor, educator; b. Greenwich, Conn., June 6, 1937; s. Noel Armstrong and Constance Malley; m. Roxolana Luczakowsky, May 22, 1960; children: Andrew, Gregory, Nicholas, Alexander. BSA, Pa. Acad. Fine Arts, Phila., 1960. Dir. Magi Art Ctr. Cath. U. Am., Washington, 1982—85; dir. fine arts The Heights Sch., Potomac, Md., 1985—; prof. fine arts Internat. Cath. U., Notre Dame, 1992—. Sculpture, Hon. Dag Hamarskold, 1968, H.M. Juan Carlos of Spain, 1975, H.H. John Paul II, 2002. Dir. Albanian Cultural Heritage Found., 1981—. Named Grand Officer, Order of Skenderbeg, 1998. Mem.: Fellowship of Cath. Scholars. Roman Catholic. Home: 4274 Rockland Rd Front Royal VA 22630

ARMSTRONG, HENRY CONNER, former Canadian government official, consultant; b. Winnipeg, Man., Can., June 16, 1925; s. William Arthur Laird and Archena May (Conner) A.; m. Barbara Fay Jackson, May 20, 1950; children: Barbara E., Nancy M., Scott J. B.Sc. in Metall. Engring., Queen's U., Kingston, Ont., 1949; MBA (Kresge fellow), U. Toronto, 1954; diploma in indsl. adminstrn. (Alcan fellow), Internat. Mgmt. Inst., Geneva, Switzerland, 1958. Various sales and marketing positions Aluminum Co. of Can., Ltd., 1954-64; commodity officer Dept. Trade and Commerce, Ottawa, Ont., 1964-66; comml. counsellor Canadian Embassy, Washington, 1966-74; chief research and planning div., resource industries and constrn. br. Dept. Industry, Trade and Commerce, Ottawa, Ont., Can., 1974-75; dir. minerals and metals div. Dept. Energy, Mines and Resources, Ottawa, Ont., 1975-81, exec. dir. internat. minerals, 1981-82, mgr. spl. projects, 1982-83; counsellor (metals, minerals and energy) Can. High Commn., Canberra, Australia, 1983-86; counsellor (commercial) Can. Embassy, Washington, 1986-89; pvt. practice cons. Ottawa, 1989—. Served with RCAF and Royal Navy Fleet Air Arm, 1944-45. Mem. Assn. Profl. Engrs. Ont., Canadian Inst. Mining and Metallurgy, Am. Soc. for Materials. Mem. United Ch. of Can. Home and Office: 2159 Delmar Dr Ottawa ON Canada K1H 5P6

ARMSTRONG, HENRY JERE, judge, lawyer; b. Dothan, Ala., Mar. 5, 1941; s. Henry Jordan and Lillian (Taylor) A.; m. Jeanne Bachmann, June 3, 1963; children: April Heather, Ashley Brooke. BA, U. Ala., Tuscaloosa, 1964, JD, 1966; postgrad., JAGs Sch., Charlottesville, Va., 1972-73; grad., Armed Forces Staff Coll., 1978. Bar: Ala. 1966, D.C. 1974, Va. 1984, U.S. Ct. Mil. Appeals 1967, U.S. Supreme Ct. 1972. Commd. 2d lt. U.S. Army, 1964, advanced through grades to col., 1983; def. counsel, prosecutor Ft. Ord., Calif., 1967-68; chief criminal law, chief civil law, mil. judge Ft. Shafter, Hawaii, 1968-72; chief legis. br. criminal law divsn. Dept. Army, Washington, 1973-75, exec. asst. to JAG, 1975-77; staff judge adv. 2d inf. divsn. Korea, 1978-79; exec. officer U.S. Army Trial Def. Svc., Falls Church, Va., 1979-82; exec. officer litigation divsn. Dept. Army, Washington, 1982-84, ret., 1984; counsel to chief Immigration Judge of U.S., 1984-86; judge, asst. chief immigration judge U.S. Dept. Justice, 1986-97, dep. chief immigration judge, 1997—. Profl. responsibility adv. com. dept. Army; guest lectr. on ethics and def. advocacy U.S. Army Europe Continuing Legal Edn. seminars; faculty Nat. Judicial Coll., Reno, Nev.; adv. bd. Nat. Fgn. Lang. Ctr. Johns Hopkins U. Contbr. articles to profl. jours. Elder Grace Presbyn. Ch., Springfield, Va. Decorated MSM (Meritorion Service medal) with 2 oak leaf clusters, ACM (Army Commedation medal), Legion of Merit; Fellow Inst. for Ct. Mgmt., Nat. Ctr. for State Cts., Williamsburg, Va.; named hon. Ky. Col., 1982. Mem. Ala. State Bar Assn., DC Bar Assn., Va. State Bar Assn., Assn. Trial Lawyers Am., Fed. Bar Assn., Judge Advs. Assn. (bd. dirs.), Kappa Sigma Alumni Assn., Phi Alpha Delta. Home: 8208 Little River Tpke Annandale VA 22003-2305

ARMSTRONG, JACK GILLILAND, lawyer; b. Pitts., Aug. 10, 1929; s. Hugh Collins and Mary Elizabeth (Gilliland) A.; m. Ellen Lee Gliem, June 10, 1951 (dec.); children: Thomas G., Elizabeth Armstrong Pride; m. Elizabeth Lacewell White, Mar. 27, 1993. AB, U. Mich., 1951, JD, 1956. Bar: Pa. 1956, Mich. 1956, U.S. Supreme Ct. 1968, Fla. 1981. Assoc. Buchanan, Ingersoll, Rodewald, Kyle & Buerger, Pitts., 1956-65; ptnr. Buchanan, Ingersoll, P.C., Pitts., 1965-90, counsel, 1990-94, of counsel, 1995, Rothman Gordon, P.C., 1996—. Dir. SSS Mgmt. Corp., Greer, S.C.; trustee Union Dale Cemetery, 1972—, pres., 1992-95. Dir. Sigma Nu Ednl. Found., 1998-2001. Lt. U.S. Army, 1951-53. Mem. Pa. Bar Assn. (real property, probate, and trust law sect., mem. coun. 1981-84, treas. 1985, vice chmn. probate divsn. 1986-88, chmn. 1988-89, tax law sect.), Fla. Bar (real property, probate and trust law sect., tax sect.), Allegheny County Bar Assn. (probate and trust law), Palm Beach County Bar Assn., Estate Planning Coun. Pitts., Am. Coll. Trust and Estate Counsel (Pa. state chmn. 1990-95), Am. Coll. Tax Counsel, U. Mich. Alumni Assn. (Disting. Alumni Svc. award 1981), Order of Coif, Duquesne Club, Univ. Club (pres. 1988-89), St. Clair Country Club, Town Club Jamestown, The Little Club, Delray Beach Club, Chautauqua Golf Club, Pine Tree Golf Club, Masons, Shriners, Jesters, Phi Alpha Delta, Sigma Nu. Home: Dorchester # 6N 200 N Ocean Blvd Delray Beach FL 33483 E-mail: jgarmstrong@rothmangordon.com.

ARMSTRONG, (ARTHUR) JAMES (ARTHUR ARMSTRONG), educator, consultant, lecturer, writer; b. Marion, Ind., Sept. 17, 1924; s. Arthur J. and Frances (Green) A.; m. Sharon Owen, Apr. 8, 2000; children from previous marriages: Eve Stoughton, Allison, James, Teresa, John, Rebecca Putens, Leslye Armstrong Hope. AB, Fla. So. Coll., 1948; BD, Candler Sch. Theology, Emory U., 1952; DD, Fla. So. U., 1960, DePauw U., 1965; LHD, Ill. Wesleyan U., 1970, Dakota Wesleyan U., 1970, Westmar Coll., 1971, Ind. Ctrl. U., 1982, Emory U., 1982. Ordained to ministry Meth. Ch., 1948. Minister in Fla., 1945-58; sr. minister Broadway Meth. Ch., Indpls., 1958-68; bishop United Meth. Ch., Dakotas area, 1968-80, Ind. area, Indpls., 1980-83; exec. v.p. conflict

resolution firm, Washington, 1984-87; vis. prof. preaching and social ministries Iliff Sch. Theology, Denver, 1985-91; sr. min. 1st Congl. Ch., Winter Park, Fla., 1991-99; exec. dir. Ctr. on Dialogue and Devel., Denver, 1984-96. Adj. prof. Rollins Col., 1992—, South Fla. Ctr. Theol. Studies, 1999—; instr. Christian Theol. Sem., Indpls., 1961-68; del. 4th Gen. Assembly, World Coun. Chs., 1968, 6th Gen. Assembly, 1983; pres. Nat. Coun. Chs., 1982-83; pres. bd. ch. and soc. United Meth. Ch., 1972-76, chmn. com. for peace and self devel. of peoples, 1972-76, pres. Commn. on Religion and Race, 1976-83; exec. v.p. Pagan Internat., 1982-87. Author: The Journey That Men Make, 1969, The Urgent Now, 1970, Mission: Middle America, 1971, The Pastor and the Public Servant, 1972, United Methodist Primer, 1973, 77, Wilderness Voices, 1974, The Nation Yet To Be, 1975, Telling Truth: The Foolishness of Preaching in a Real World, 1977, From the Underside, 1981, Feet of Clay, on Solid Ground, 2002; contbg. author: The Pulpit Speaks on Race, 1966, War Crimes and the American Conscience, 1970, Rethinking Evangelism, 1971, What's a Nice Church Like You Doing in a Place Like This?, 1972, The Miracle of Easter, 1980, Preaching on Peace, 1982, Ethics and the Multi-National Enterprise, 1986, The Best of the Circuit Rider, 1987, Prayerfully Pro-Choice, 1999. Vice-chmn. Hoosiers for Peace, 1968; mem. Ind. State Platform Com. Democratic Party, 1968, Nat. Coalition for a Responsible Congress, 1970. With USNR, 1942. Recipient Disting. Svc. award, Indpls. Jr. C. of C., 1959. Mem. Fla. Coun. Chs. (pres. 1996-97), Ctrl. Fla. Interfaith Alliance (co-chair 1994-96). Methodist.

ARMSTRONG, JAMES FRANCIS, III, educator; b. Penn Yan, N.Y., Mar. 17, 1945; s. James Francis Armstrong Jr. and Frances (Grady) Armstrong-Barden. BA in Eglish Edn. cum laude, Hobart-William Smith, 1983; cert., Kellogg Inst., 1989. Cert. English tchr.; cert. devel. educator. English tchr. Penn Yan Jr. High Sch., 1984-85; learning specialist Community Coll. of Finger Lakes, Geneva, N.Y., 1986-87, dir. learning ctr. and libr., 1987—. G.E.D. instr. Bd. of Coop. Ednl. Svcs., Stanley, N.Y., 1986-87. Singer/musician (album) Feels Like Spyders, 1975; author: The Asexuals, 2001, Subsect, 2002; contbr. articles to profl. jours.; film maker for Kodak, 1970. Avocation: musician. Office: Finger Lakes C C 361 Main St Geneva NY 14456-2601

ARMSTRONG, JANE BOTSFORD, sculptor; b. Buffalo; d. Samuel Booth and Edith (Purse) Botsford. Student, Middlebury Coll., 1939-40, Pratt Inst., 1940-41, Art Students' League, 1962-64. One-man shows include Frank Rehn Gallery, N.Y.C., 1973, 1971, 1975, 1975, Columbus (Ohio) Gallery Fine Arts, 1972, Columbia (S.C.) Mus. Art, 1975, 1972, Johnson Gallery, Middlebury Coll., 1973, Mary Duke Biddle Gallery for Blind N.C. Mus. Art, 1974, J.B. Speed Art Mus., Louisville, 1975, Buffalo State U., 1975, Marjorie Parr Gallery, London, 1976, Ark. Art Center, 1977, Dallas Mus. Fine Art, 1978, Wichita (Kans.) Art Mus., 1978, 1982, Wadsworth Athenuem, 1979, Foster Harmon Gallery Am. Art, 1979, 1981, 1992, Washington County (Md.) Mus. Fine Arts, Hagerstown, 1979, Chautauqua (N.Y.) Nat. Exhbn. Am. Art, 1980, Southeastern Center Contemporary Art, Winston-Salem, N.C., 1980, Rollins Coll., Winter Park, Fla., 1981, The Sculpture Center, N.Y.C., 1981, Sid Deutsch Gallery, 1983, Boca Raton (Fla.) Mus., 1983, Burchfield Ctr., Buffalo, 1985, Glass Art Gallery, Toronto, 1985, Schiller-Wapner Galleries, N.Y.C., 1987, St. Gaudens Gallery, St. Gaudens Nat. Hist. Site, 1988, Middlebury Coll., Vt., 1988, Grand Cen. Art Galleries, N.Y.C., 1989, Nat. Arts Club, invited retrospective, 1996, exhibitions include USIA, Europe, 1975—76, Artists of Am., Denver, 1981, 1982, 1983, 1984, 1985, 1986, 1987, 1988, 1990, 1991, 1992, 1993, 1994, 1995, 1996, 1998, 1999, 2000, Fleischer Mus., Scottsdale, Ariz., 1999—2000, Gt. Am. Artists, Cin., 1997, 1998, So. Vt. Ctr. for the Arts, Manchester, Vt., 2001, Nat. Sculpture Soc., 1975—2000, represented, numerous acad., indsl., pub. and pvt. collections. Recipient Pauline Law prize Allied Artists Am., 1969, 70, Porton award, 1981, Gold medal, 1976, Ralph Fabri medal of honor, 1978, Chaim Gross Found. award, 1980, Helen Apen Oehler Meml. award, 1988, Meiselman award, 1993, cert. merit NAD, 1973, Coun. Am. Artists' Socs. prize Nat. Sculpture Soc., 1973, gold medal of honor Knickerbocker Artists, 1986, Elliott Liskin Meml. award, 1991, Alumni Achievement award Middlebury Coll., 1993, Disting. Woman Status Buffalo (N.Y.) Sem., 1999. Fellow Nat. Sculpture Soc. (bronze medal 1976, 78, Tallix Foundry award 1985, Percival Dietsch prize, 1986, Proskauer prize 1995, mem. coun. 1997-2002), Nat. Sculpture Soc. (bd. 1994-1999); mem. Nat. Arts Club (gold medal 1968, 69, 71, Best in Show award 1973, Edith W. MacGuire award 1975, plaque of honor 1977, Alexander Saltzman award 1983, Exhbn. Com. award 1990, invited retrospective exhibit 1996), Audubon Artists (medal of honor 1972, Vincent Glinsky Meml. award 1992, gold medal 1994), Allied Artists Am., Nat. Assn. Women Artists (Charles N. Whinston Meml. prize 1973, Anonymous Meml. prize 1979, Elizabeth S. Blake prize 1980, Amelia Peabody award 1985, Freelander-Sawyer Meml. award 1993). Studio: 25 Swan Lane Manchester Center VT 05255-9223

ARMSTRONG, KAREN LEE, special education educator; b. Schenectady, N.Y., Dec. 6, 1941; d. William James and Rita Mae (Peabody) Safford; m. John Edward Armstrong, July 14, 1962; 1 child, Lori Ellen. BA in English, SUNY, Albany, 1963, MS in Spl. Edn., 1986. Tchr. English Ballston Lake High Sch., Burnt Hills, N.Y., 1963-66; tchr. spl. edn. Oak Hill Sch., Scotia, N.Y., 1975-88, Schenectady City Schs., 1988—; mem. policy bd. Ctr. Profl. Edn., 2001—. Mem. curriculum coun., lead tng. sessions Schenectady Schs., 1988—; mem. Shared Decision Making Team, 1994—, spl. edn. del. to China, U.S. del. to South Africa, 1995; lectr. in field of behavior mgmt. V.p. bd. edn. Oak Hill Sch., mem. bd. edn., 2001—. Mem. Coun. for Exceptional Children, Coun. for Children with Behavioral Disorders., Amnesty Internat. (founding Schenectady br.), Adirondack Mountain Club. Sufi. Avocations: hiking, camping, gardening. E-mail: armstrongk@schenectady.k12.ny.us.

ARMSTRONG, KENNETH, lawyer; b. Washington, June 25, 1955; s. Henry Kenneth and Ann (Bauman) A.; m. Deborah Baumgartner, Feb. 18, 1984 (div. Dec. 1993); 1 child, Caitlin; m. Trina Blandford-Hader, July 22, 1995. BA, Clark U., 1976; JD, Am. U., 1979. Bar: Md. 1979, D.C. 1980, U.S. Dist. Ct. Md. 1980, U.S. Dist. Ct. D.C. 1981. Assoc. Donahue, Ehrmantraut & Montedonico, Rockville, Md., 1979-83, ptnr., 1984-87, Armstrong, Donohue, Ceppos & Voughan, Rockville, Md., 1987—. Author: (with others) Medical Malpractice in Maryland, 1987. Fellow Internat. Acad. Trial Lawyers, Am. Coll. Trial Lawyers; mem. Am. Bd. Trial Advocates, Bar Assn. D.C., Bar Assn. of Montgomery County, Md. Bar Assn., Am. Inns of Ct. (Montgomery County chpt. master 1991-96). Democrat. Roman Catholic. Home: 13412 Cleveland Dr Rockville MD 20850-3603 Office: Armstrong Donohue Ceppos & Vaughan 204 Monroe St Ste 101 Rockville MD 20850-4434 E-mail: karmstrong@adclawfirm.com.

ARMSTRONG, LANCE, professional cyclist; b. Plano, Tex., Sept. 18, 1971; m. Kristin Richard, May 8, 1998; 3 children. Profl. cyclist Motorola Team, 1990—. Author: (book) It's Not About the Bike: My Journey Back to Life, 2001, Every Second Counts, 2003. World Road-Racing Champion, 1993; U.S. Profl. Champion, 1993; Triathlete Rookie of the Year, 1988; winner Tour DuPont, 1995; winner 19 out of 21 Tour de France, 1999; Sports Illustrated Man of the Yr., 2002;Associated Press Male Athlete of the Yr., 2002; overall winner, Tour de France, 1999-2003. Achievements include being a former swimmer and triathlete. Office: Capital Sports Ventures 803 Pressler St. Austin TX 78703-5129 also: Lance Armstrong Found. PO Box 161150 Austin TX 78716-1150*

ARMSTRONG, LARRY DON, activist, association administrator; b. Severy, Kans., Jan. 7, 1936; s. Lawrence Edward and Eartha Elizabeth (St. John) A.; m. Gloria Rose Southards, Nov. 23, 1962; children: Lawrence David, Craig Curtis. Student, Glendale Coll., 1953-54, L.A. State U., 1955, Calif. Inst. Tech., 1955, Chgo. Tech. Inst., 1965, Hutchinson C.C., 1992-95, Colo. State U., 1993-94. Painter McKenzie Autobody, 1957-72, Bottomley Cadillac & Olds, 1972-79, Nelson Body Factory, 1979-89; dept. mgr. Collins Industries, 1989-95; ret., 1995. Mem. Fedn. Metal Detector and Archaeol. Clubs (nat. alliance liaison 1997-98, pres. North Ctrl. chpt. 1998-99, rsch. dir., bd. dirs. 1997-03, Spl. Presdl. award 1997, Pres.'s award 1999, alliance liaison 2000-03), World Wide Assn. Treasure Searchers (bd. dirs. 2003—), People for the U.S.A. (Bull Fighter award 1998), Blue Ribbon Coalition, Am. Metal Detectors Assn. (fed. land dir. 2003—), Kappa Omicron Delta. Avocations: reading, treasure hunting, research, writing. Home: 117 E Forest Ave South Hutchinson KS 67505

ARMSTRONG, LEONA MAY BOTTRELL, retired counselor, educator; b. Rochester, Ill.; Aug. 14, 1930; d. Vernon Sampson Bottrell and Leonia Ruth (Meeks) Cooper; m. Bryce Glenn Armstrong, June 11, 1950 (div. 1975); children: Steven Lee, Rebecca Sue, Paul Bryce, (twins) Kevin John and Brian Mark. BS, U. Indpls., 1952; MS, U. Wis., 1967. Tchr., Dayton, Ohio, 1952-55; sch. counselor Oshkosh, Verona, West Allis, Wis., 1967-88; pvt. practice as counselor, astrologer, tchr. Milw., 1988-95; ret., 1995. Reiki master Reiki Healers Internat., 1992; guest spkr. in area of parapsychology and metaphysics U. Minn., U. Wis., Milw., other schs., 1980—; spkr. World Peace Program, Milw., 1987. Ecumenical spkr. United Ch. Women, 1966. Named Outstanding Sr. Woman, Philalethea Lit. Soc., 1952, one of Outstanding Personalities in Midwest, AAUW and Profs. at U. Wis.-Oshkosh, 1968. Mem. Nat. Coun. for Geocosmic Rsch. Home and Office: 4514 67th St Kenosha WI 53142-1602 E-mail: leonaarmstrong@acronet.net.

ARMSTRONG, LINDA JEAN (GENE ARMSTRONG), writer, artist; b. L.A., Feb. 23, 1947; d. Charles Fred and Mary Eugenia (Gentry) Keck; m. Alden Arthur Armstrong, July 28, 1966; 1 child, Amy Alice. BA, Calif. State Coll., 1969. Tchr. elem. sch. L.A. Unified Sch. Dist., 1970-86; writer, artist, 1986—. Author: Early Tigers, 1995, Tanya's Desert Star, 1997; adaptor: Winnie the Pooh, The Blustery Day, 2002, Pooh Helps Out, 2002, The Honey Tree, The Big Honeypot Rescue, 101 Dalmations Puppy Parade, 101 Dalmations II, The Little Mermaid: The Big Baby, The Lion King, 2002; author: Algebra at School. Grade 4 & Grade 5, 2003, Ancient Mesopotamia, 2002. Fellow Woodstock (N.Y.) Sch. Art, 1993. Mem. Soc. Children's Book Writers and Illustrators. Home: PO Box 3151 Grand Junction CO 81502-3151 E-mail: lindararm@earthlink.net.

ARMSTRONG, LLOYD, JR., university official, physics educator; b. Austin, Tex., May 19, 1940; s. Lloyd and Beatrice (Jackson) A.; m. Judith Glantz, July 9, 1965; 1 son, Wade Matthew. BS in Physics, MIT, 1962; PhD in Physics, U. Calif., Berkeley, 1966. Postdoctoral physicist Lawrence Berkeley (Calif.) Lab., 1965-66, cons., 1976; sr. physicist Westinghouse Research Labs., Pitts., 1967-68, cons., 1968-70; research asso. Johns Hopkins U., 1968-69, asst. prof. physics, 1969-73, assoc. prof., 1973-77, prof., 1977-93, chmn. dept. physics and astronomy, 1985-87, dean Sch. Arts and Scis., 1987-93; provost, sr. v.p. for acad. affairs U. So. Calif., L.A., 1993—, prof. physics, 1993—. Assoc. rsch. scientist Nat. Ctr. Sci. Rsch. (CNRS), Orsay, France, 1972—73; vis. fellow Joint Inst. Lab. Astrophysics, Boulder, Colo., 1978—79; program officer NSF, 1981—83, mem. adv. com. for physics, 1985—87, mem. visitors com. physics divsn., 1991; chmn. com. atomic and molecular scis. NAS/NRC, 1985—88, mem. bd. physics and astronomy, 1989—96; mem. adv. bd. Inst. for Theoretical Physics, Santa Barbara, 1992—96, chmn., 1994—95, Inst. Theoretical Atomic and Molecular Physics, Cambridge, Mass., 1994—97, Rochester Theory Ctr. for Optical Sci. and Engring., 1996—98, 1997—98; mem. Coun. on Fgn. Affairs, 2000—. Author: Theory of Hyperfine Structure of Free Atoms, 1971; contbr. articles to profl. jours. Bd. dirs. So. Calif. Econ. Partnership, 1994—2000, Calif. Coun. on Sci. and Tech., 1994—, Pacific Coun. on Internat. Policy, 1996—. NSF grantee, 1972-90; Dept. Energy grantee, 1975-82 Fellow Am. Phys. Soc. Office: U So Calif Office Provost University Park Los Angeles CA 90089-0001

ARMSTRONG, MICHAEL DAVID, investment banker; b. Bronxville, N.Y., May 7, 1955; s. Frank and Dorothy Armstrong; m. Deborah Jane Lauderdale, 1984. BA, Washington and Lee U., 1977; MBA, Coll. William and Mary, 1982. Account exec. Austin Kelley Adv., Atlanta, 1977-80; sr. assoc. 1st San Francisco Corp., Foster City, Calif., 1983-88, Bankers Trust Co., Atlanta, 1988-90; gen. mgr. Gimborn U.S., Atlanta, 1990-93; pres. PNI Co., Atlanta, 1994—. Mem. Atlanta Hist. Soc., Atlanta Bot. Gardens; trustee Washington and Lee U. Mem. Mu Beta Psi. Avocations: skiing, golf, swimming, reading, travel.

ARMSTRONG, NEAL EARL, civil engineering educator; b. Dallas, Jan. 29, 1941; m. Nancy L. Weinerth; 5 children. BA, U. Tex., 1962, MA, 1965, PhD, 1968. Research engr. Engring. Sci., Inc., 1967-68; asst. office mgr., cons. san. engring., 1968-70; mgr. Washington Research and Devel. Lab., 1970-71; assoc. prof. civil engring. U. Tex., Austin, 1971-79, prof., 1979—, assoc. chmn. dept. 1989-96, assoc. dean acad. affairs Coll. Engring., 1996—. Mem. ASCE, Water Environ. Fedn. (Svc. award 1976, 84, 96, 2003), Am. Acad. Environ. Engrs. (diplomate), Internat. Water Assn., Estuarine Rsch. Fedn. (v.p. 1975-77), Am. Soc. Engring. Edn. Office: U Tex Dept Civil Engring Austin TX 78712

ARMSTRONG, ORVILLE, judge; b. Austin, Tex., Jan. 21, 1929; s. Orville Alexander and Velma Lucille (Reed) A.; m. Mary Dean Macfarlane; children: Anna Louise Glenn, John M., Paul Jefferson. BBA, U. Tex., Austin, 1953; LLB, U. So. Calif., 1956. Bar: Calif. 1957, U.S. Ct. Appeals (9th cir.) 1958, U.S. Supreme Ct. 1980. Ptnr. Gray, Binkley & Pfaelzer, 1956-61, Pfaelzer, Robertson, Armstrong & Woodard, L.A., 1961-66, Armstrong & Lloyd, L.A., 1966-74, Macdonald, Halsted & Laybourne, L.A., 1975-88, Baker & McKenzie, 1988-90; judge Superior Ct. State of Calif., 1991-92; assoc. justice ct. appeal State of Calif., 1993—. Lectr. Calif. Continuing Edn. of Bar. Served with USAF, 1946-49. Fellow ABA, Am. Coll. Trial Lawyers; mem. State Bar Calif. (gov. 1983-87, pres. 1986-87), L.A. County Bar Assn. (trustee 1971-72), Chancery Club (pres. 1988), Calif. Club. Baptist. Office: 300 S Spring St Los Angeles CA 90013-1230

ARMSTRONG, PHILLIP DALE, lawyer; b. Waukegan, Ill., Mar. 27, 1943; s. James Leonard and Bernice Frances (Nader) A.; m. Leila Robson; children: Leonard Hart, Theodore Nader, Leila VIII. BS in Chem. Engring., U. Mo., 1966; JD, Gonzaga U., 1978; LLM, U. Mo., Kansas City, 1979. Bar: N.D. 1979, U.S. Dist. Ct. N.D. 1979, U.S. Dist. Ct. Ariz. 1991, U.S. Tax Ct. 1980, U.S. Ct. Appeals 1983, U.S. Supreme Ct. 1984. Mktg. trainee Dow Chem. Co., Midland, Mich., 1966-68; chem. engr. Clark Oil and Refining, Hartford, Ill., 1968-70; life guard, pool attendant, pool mgr. various hotels and condominiums, Miami Beach, Fla., 1970-75; assoc. McCutcheon Law Firm, Minot, N.D., 1979-81; sole practice Minot, 1981—, Mandan, N.D., 1995—; founder, pres. Producers Oil & Gas Corp., 1992—. Trustee in bankruptcy for chpts. 7, 12, and 13, N.W. and S.W. divs. Dist. of N.D., 1980-95; founder Armstrong Oilwell Ops., 1996. Mem. ABA, N.D. Bar Assn., Nat. Assn. Bankruptcy Trustees, Am. Bankruptcy Inst., Exch. Club (Minot), Phi Kappa Psi (pres. 1965). Republican. Episcopalian. Home: 1006 Valley View Dr Minot ND 58703-1642 Office: Armstrong Law Firm 12 Main St S Minot ND 58701-3871

ARMSTRONG, RICHARD STOLL, minister, educator, writer, poet; b. Balt., Mar. 29, 1924; s. Herbert Eustace and Elsie Davis (Stoll) A.; m. Margaret Childs, Jan. 31, 1948; children: Ellen, Richard, Andrew, William, Elsie. BA, Princeton U., 1947; MDiv, Princeton Theol. Sem., 1958; DMin, Christian Theol. Sem.-Indpls., 1978; doctoral, Temple U., 1962-68. Ordained to ministry Presbyn. Ch., 1958. Pastor Oak Lane Presbyn. Ch., Phila., 1958-68; dir. devel. Princeton (N.J.) Theol. Sem., 1968-71, v.p. devel., 1971-74, prof. ministry and evangelism, 1980-90, prof. emeritus, 1990—; pastor 2d Presbyn. Ch., Indpls., 1974-80. Life trustee Fellowship Christian Athletes, Inc., Kansas City, Mo., 1979—; mem. ch. mins. adv. bd. Christian Theol. Sem., 1975-80; bd. dirs. Nat. Conf. Christians and Jews, Ind., 1975-80, Ind. Inter-Religious Commn. on Human Equality, 1975-80. Author: The Oak Lane Story, 1971, Service Evangelism, 1979, The Pastor as Evangelist, 1984, The Pastor-Evangelist in Worship, 1986, Faithful Witnesses, 1987, The Pastor-Evangelist in the Parish, 1990, Enough, Already!, 1993, Now, That's A Miracle!, 1996, Faithful Witnesses MiniCourse, 1997, If I Do Say So Myself, 1997, Are you Really Free?, 2002; contbg. composer Carmina Princetonia, 1968; contbg. author: Westminster Dictionary of Christian Theology, 1983, The New Dictionary of Pastoral Studies, 2002. Bd. dirs. Indpls. Symphony Orch., 1978-80; trustee Am. Boychoir Sch., 1980—; trustee McDonogh Sch., Md., 1980-90; mem. adv. com., divsn. for contextual ministry Vista U., South Africa; mem. Nat. Coun. Presbyn. Men, 1995-98; Lt. (j.g.) USN, 1942-46. Recipient Disting. Svc. award Fellowship of Christian Athletes, 1965, Branch Rickey Meml. award, 1974, Alumni Svc. award Princeton Theol. Sem., 1974, Outstanding Svc. award Nat. Conf. Christians and Jews, 1980, Robert L. Peters award Princeton U., 1990; named Man of Week, Princeton Town Topics, 1957, 68. Mem. Presbytery of New Brunswick (v.p.), Acad. for Evangelism Theol. Edn. (pres. 1989-91, Jour. editor 1991-97, Charles Grandison Finney award 1997), Presbyn. Writers' Guild, Poetry Soc. Am., Gallup Internat. Inst., Phila. A's Hist. Soc. Presbyterian. Home: 2118 Windrow Dr Princeton NJ 08540 Office: Princeton Theol Sem PO Box 821 Princeton NJ 08542-0803 E-mail: richard.armstrong@ptsem.edu.

ARMSTRONG, RICHARD WILLIAM, bank executive, management consultant; b. Phila., June 18, 1932; s. Richard Mervyn and Elvina (Burns) A.; m. Barbara Robbins, Sept. 5, 1959; children: Richard W. Jr., James M. AB cum laude, Harvard U., 1954; MA, Johns Hopkins U., 1959. Disarmament specialist AEC, Washington, 1960—62; fin. mgr. NASA and OEO, Washington, 1962—67; Nat. Inst. Pub. Affairs fellow Princeton U., 1967—68; dep. mgr. Head Start, Washington, 1969-70; corp. budget dir. Chase Manhattan Bank, N.Y.C., 1970-78, chief fin. and adminstrv. officer real estate fin. bus., 1978-84, chief fin. and adminstrv. officer comml. sector, 1984-89, chief fin. and adminstrv. officer real estate fin. sector, 1989-91; mgmt. cons. N.Y.C., 1992—. Prin. Coun. for Excellence in Govt., 1992—. Mem. audit com. Madison (N.J.) Presbyn. Ch., 1981; trustee, fin. officer Bethesda (Md.) Congl. Ch., 1965-67; mem. N.J. Harvard Schs. and Scholarship Com., 1983-88; bd. dirs. Family Svc. of Morris County, N.J., 1998. Lt. USN, 1954-57. Avocations: sailing, swimming, travel, genealogy. Home and Office: 10 Pomeroy Rd Madison NJ 07940-2619

ARMSTRONG, ROBERT BEALL, physiologist, educator; b. Hastings, Nebr., Nov. 13, 1940; s. Edwin Ollis and Elena (Beall) A.; m. Ingrid Elizabeth Vaiculenas, Apr. 9, 1966; children: Edwin John, Andrew Niel, Sarah Elizabeth. BA, Hastings Coll., 1962; MS, Wash. State U., 1970, PhD, 1973. Asst. prof. biology Boston U., 1973—78; assoc. prof. physiology Oral Roberts U., Tulsa, Okla., 1978—81, prof. physiology, 1981—85; prof. U. Ga., Athens, 1985—90, rsch. prof., 1990—92; Omar Smith prof. health and kinesiology Tex. A&M U., College Station, 1992 , Omar Smith chair, 1995—, disting. prof., 1995—, dept. head, 1992—97, 2000—02. Assoc. zoology Harvard U., Cambridge, Mass., 1977-87, external examiner Nat. U. Singapore, 1984-85; rsch. com. Am. Heart Assn., Athens, 1987-89. Assoc. editor Med. Sci. Sports Exercise, Indpls., 1985-87; contbr. articles to Jour. Applied Physiology, Am. Jour. Physiology. NSF fellow, 1970-73; grantee NIH, 1975-97, Am. Heart Assn., 1981-89, NASA, 1997-2000. Fellow Am. Coll. Sports Medicine (trustee 1986-88); mem. Am. Physiol. Soc. Office: Tex A & M U Dept Health & Kinesiology College Station TX 77843-0001 E-mail: rb-armstrong@hlkn.tamu.edu.

ARMSTRONG, R(OBERT) DEAN, entertainer; b. Serena, Ill., July 2, 1923; s. Francis Robert and Viola D. (Thompson) A.; m. Ardith Roberta Taylor, Jan. 10, 1943; 1 child, Larry Dean. Grad. high sch., Serena, Ill.; student, Joliet (Ill.) Conservatory of Music, 1942. Host Dean Armstrong Show Sta. KOLD-TV, Tucson, 1953-75; leader, owner Ariz. Dance Hands, Tucson, 1946—. Served with U.S. Mil., 1943-45, ETO, PTO. Recipient Jefferson award Am. Inst. for Pub. Svc., 1992; inducted into Tucson Area Music Assn. Hall of Fame, 1994. Mem.VFW, Tucson Musicians Assn. (meritorious svc. award 1981), VFW, Western Music Assn. (charter mem.), Profl. Western Music Assn. Lodges: Elks, Eagles. Democrat. Methodist. Home and Office: 4265 N Avenida Del Cazador Tucson AZ 85718-7005 E-mail: Azdanchans@aol.com.

ARMSTRONG, ROBERT STEVENSON, JR., sales executive; b. Pitts., Aug. 14, 1954; s. Robert Stevenson and Mary Moreland (Coleman) A.; m. Alberta Louisa Scafuro, June 22, 1982; children: Kathryn Ballyreagh, Robert Stevenson III, Meredith Scafuro. AB, Wittenberg U., 1976. Asst. mgr. Minn. Fabrics, Inc., Washington, 1976-78; sales engr. K.J. Lesker, Inc., Pitts., 1979-82, sale regional mgr., 1982-83; pres. Telesis High Vacuum, Inc., Dallas, 1983—. Bd. dirs. Potomac Scientific, Silver Spring, Md., United Mercantile Co., Pitts. Chmn., coord. John Anderson for Pres., Pitts., 1980. Mem. Instrument Soc. Am., Am. Vacuum Soc., Material Rsch. Soc., Pi Kappa Alpha. Republican. Presbyterian. Office: Telesis High Vacuum Inc PO Box 835240 Richardson TX 75083-5240

ARMSTRONG, ROBIN LOUIS, physics educator; b. Galt, Ont., Can., May 14, 1935; s. Robert Dockstader and Beatrice Jenny (Grill) S.; m. Karen Elisabeth Feilberg Hansen, July 8, 1960; children: Keir Grill, Christopher Drew. BA, U. Toronto, Ont., 1958, MsC, 1959, PhD, 1961; DSc (hon.), U. N.B., Can., 2001. Rutherford Meml. fellow Oxford (Eng.) U., 1961-62; mem. faculty U. Toronto, 1962, prof. physics, 1971-90, adj. prof. physics, 1990-98, prof. emeritus, 1998—, chmn. dept., 1974-82, dean Faculty of Arts and Sci., 1982-90; pres. U. N.B., Fredericton, St. John, 1990-96, prof. physics, 1990-96, rsch. prof. physics, 1996-2001, Wilfrid Laurier U. spl. advisor to the pres., 1997-2000. Pres. Can. Inst. Neutron Scattering, 1986-89; founding dir. Can. Inst. Advanced Rsch., 1981-82, mem. rsch. coun., 1982-2000; mem. coun. Nat. Sci. and Engring. Rsch. Coun., 1991-97 mem. exec., 1992-97, v.p., 1994-97; mem. Atomic Energy Can. Ltd. R&D Adv. Com., 1999—. Co-author: Mechanics, Waves and Thermal Physics, 1970, Electromagnetic Interaction, 1973; contbr. articles to profl. jours. Recipient Commemorative medal for 125th Anniversary of Can. Confedn., 1992, Designated Visitante Distinguido U. Cordoba, Argentina, 1987. Fellow Royal Soc. Can.; mem. Can. Assn. Physicists (v.p. 1989-90, pres. 1990-91, Herzberg medal 1973, medal for achievement 1990), Can. Assn. Physics, Internat. Soc. Magnetic Resonance Medicine. Home: Unit 707 95 Price Arthur Ave Toronto ON Canada M5R 3P6 Office: U Toronto Dept Physics 60 St George St Toronto ON Canada M5S 1A7 E-mail: robinl.armstrong@sympatico.ca.

ARMSTRONG, RODNEY, librarian; b. Atlanta, Mar. 5, 1923; s. Harold Rodney and Mary Blair (Armstrong) A.; m. Katharine Price Cortesi, June 14, 1969; children: Louise Spencer Barton, Robert Knowlton. BA, Williams Coll., 1948; MS, Columbia U., 1950; HHD (hon.), U. Liberia, 2000. Libr. Phillips Exeter (N.H.) Acad., 1950-73; dir., libr. Boston Athenaeum, 1973-97, dir. and libr. emeritus, 1997—. N.E. assoc. Sotheby's. Pres., trustee Trustees For Edn. in Liberia, 1974—. Decorated Purple Heart; Benjamin Franklin fellow Royal Soc. Arts, 1974 Fellow Am. Acad. Arts and Scis., Soc. Antiquaries, Pilgrim Soc. (trustee); mem. ALA (life), N.H. Libr. Assn. (past officer, bd. dirs.), Am. Antiquarian Soc., Colonial Soc. Mass., Mass. Hist. Soc., Manuscript Soc. (bd. dirs., past pres.), New Eng. Hist. Geneal. Soc. (pres. 1977-82), Century Assn. (N.Y.C.), Grolier Club (N.Y.C.), Odd Volumes Club (pres. 1979-83). Home: Penthouse F 65 E India Row Boston MA 02110-3311 Office: Sothebys 67 1/2 Chestnut St Boston MA 02108-1121

ARMSTRONG, SUSAN J. academic administrator; b. Richmond, Mo., Jan. 21, 1958; d. Frank R. and Jean E. Stonner; m. Michael L. Armstrong. BA in Bus. Adminstrn., William Jewell Coll., 1983; MBA, Rockhurst U., 1987. Fin. aid sec. William Jewell Coll., Liberty, Mo., 1980—83, fin. aid specialist, 1983—84, dir. of fin. aid and scholarship svcs., 1984—2002. Freelance writer Target Mktg., Inc., Liberty, 1996—2002; adminstrv. adv. com. MOSTARS (Coordinating Bd. for Higher Edn.), Jefferson City, Mo., 2001—03; editl. bd. mem. Nat. Assn. of Student Fin. Aid Adminstrs., Washington, 1999—2002; fed. issues chair Midwest Assn. of Student Fin. Aid Adminstrs., Indpls., 2000—. City councilwoman City of Liberty, 1989—93. Recipient Exceptional Svc. award, Liberty Rotary Club, 2000. Mem.: Mo. Assn. of Student Fin. Aid Pers. (pres. 1987—88, Twenty-Year Svc. award 2000), Nat. Assn. of Student Fin. Aid Adminstrs., Midwest Assn. of Student Fin. Aid Adminstrs. (Twenty-Year Svc. award 2000), Sertoma. Avocations: golf, writing, deer hunting. Office: William Jewell Coll 500 College Hill Liberty MO 64068 Business E-Mail: armstrongs@william.jewell.edu.

ARMSTRONG, TERRY LEE, publishing executive, carpenter; b. Elgin, Nebr., Dec. 23, 1949; s. Lou Elvin and Donna Mae (Riggs) A.; m. Christine Angelina Alvarez, Nov. 15, 1991; 1 child, Rebecca Leigh. AA, San Antonio Coll., 1977. V.p. ArmWel, Inc., San Antonio, 1980-89; editor, pub. Lone Stars Mag., San Antonio, 1990—; carpenter San Antonio Indep. Sch. Dist., San Antonio, 1992—. Author: Wordweavers, 1992 (Hon. award), World of Poetry, 1992 (Golden Poet), Wordsmith, 1992 (Spl. Honor); editor, pub. Poet's Market, 1992. Recipient 1st pl. Nat. Libr. Poetry, 1990-91; named Poet of the Month Poetry of the People, 1990, Poet of the Yr. Poetry Break Jour., 1991.

ARMSTRONG, THEODORE MORELOCK, financial executive; b. St. Louis, July 22, 1939; s. Theodore Roosevelt and Vassar Fambrough (Morelock) A.; m. Carol Mercer Robert, Sept. 7, 1963; children: Evelyn Anne, Robert Theodore. BA, Yale U., 1961; LLB, Duke U., 1964. Bar: Mo. 1964. With Miss. River Transmission Corp. and affiliated cos., 1964-85; corp. sec. Mo. Pacific Corp., 1971-75, River Cement Co., 1968-75; asst. v.p. Miss. River Transmission Corp., 1974-75, v.p. gas supply, 1975-79, exec. v.p., 1979-83, pres., chief exec. officer, 1983-85; exec. v.p. Natural Gas Pipeline of Am., 1985; sr. v.p. fin. and adminstrn., chief fin. officer Angelica Corp., St. Louis, 1986—. Bd. dir. UMB Bank of St. Louis, Gen. Am. Capital Co. Bd. dirs., past pres. Boys and Girls Town Mo.; past pres. Tenn. Soc. St. Louis; mem. St. Louis County Boundary

Commn.; former alderman City of Frontenac; bd. dirs., past pres. Ctrl. Inst. for Deaf. Mem. Mo. Bar Assn., Bellerive Country Club, Saint Louis Club (bd. dirs.), Yale Club (St. Louis, N.Y.C.), Phi Alpha Delta. Republican. Presbyterian. Home: 43 Countryside Ln Saint Louis MO 63131-3310 Office: Angelica Corp 424 S Woods Mill Rd Chesterfield MO 63017-3406 E-mail: tarmstrong@angelica.com.

ARMSTRONG, THOMAS NEWTON, III, art and garden specialist; b. Portsmouth, Virginia, July 30, 1932; s. Thomas Newton, II and Mary Saunders (Tabb) A.; m. Virginia Whitney Brewster, May 18, 1963; children: Thomas Newton IV, Whitney, Eliot, Amory. Attended, Cornell U., 1950-54, Art Students League, summer 1953, Inst. Fine Arts, NYU, 1965-67. Pers. coord., asst. to chmn. bd. Stone & Webster, Inc., N.Y.C., 1957-65; curator, assoc. dir. Colonial Williamsburg, Abby Aldrich Rockefeller Folk Art Collection, Williamsburg, Va., 1967-71; dir. Pa. Acad. Fine Arts, Phila., 1971-73, Whitney Mus. Am. Art, 1974-90, dir. emeritus, 1990—; dir. Andy Warhol Mus., Pitts., 1993-95. Dir., vice chmn. The Garden Conservancy; mem. selection com. Henry Luce Found., Inc.; dir. Nat. Bldg. Mus.; cons. Sotheby's. Garden com. Winterthur, N.Y.C.; trustee N.Y. Sch. Interior Design, N.Y.C.

ARMSTRONG, WALLACE DOWAN, JR., data processor; b. Los Angeles, Feb. 9, 1926; s. Wallace Dowan and Vina Edith (Kreinbring) A.; 1 son: Erik Bentung. BS cum laude, U. So. Calif., 1951; postgrad., U. Oslo (Norway), 1955. Supr. accounting Ramo Wooldridge Corp., 1955-60; mgr. programmers, systems analyst Aerospace Corp., El Segundo, Calif., 1960-80, mgr. bus. systems, 1980—. Mem. Common Cause, Handgun Control, Inc. With USMCR, 1944-46, sgt., 1951-53, WWII, PTO, Korea. Mem. Data Processing Mgmt. Assn., Marine Corp. Assn., Am. Legion, VFW, 2d Amphibius Tractor Assn. Home: 25713 Crest Rd Torrance CA 90505-7022 Office: Aerospace Corp 2350 E El Segundo Blvd El Segundo CA 90245-4691

ARMSTRONG, WILLIAM ALLEN, mathematician, educator, textbook writer; b. St. Mary's, Ohio, Aug. 10, 1964; s. Alfred L. and Mabel Frances Armstrong; m. Lisa Marie Riblet, Aug. 25, 1990; children: Austin, Dylan. Bachelors, Ohio State U., 1988; masters, 1991. Undergraduate tchg. asst. Ohio State U., Columbus, 1986—88, grad. tchg. asst., 1988—91; prof. math. Phoenix Coll., Ariz., 1991—94, Lakeland Cmty. Coll., Kirtland, Ohio, 1994—. Author (book) Brief Calculus, 2000, 2003, Finite Mathematics, 2003, College Mathematics, 2003. Baseball coach Mentor Baseball League, Mentor, Ohio, 1998—; football coach Mentor Youth Football Assn., 2002—. Office: Lakeland Cmty Coll 7700 Clocktower Dr Kirtland OH 44094

ARMSTRONG, WILLIAM TUCKER, III, lawyer; b. Houston, Nov. 13, 1947; s. William Tucker Jr. and Jess (Nettles) A.; m. Nancy Bayliss Armstrong, Feb. 18, 1978; children: Will, Anne, Daniel. BA, Am. U., 1969; JD with honors, U. Tex., 1972. Bar: Tex. 1972, U.S. Ct. Appeals (5th cir.) 1972, U.S. Dist. Ct. (so. & we. dists.) Tex. 1978, U.S. Ct. Appeals (11th cir.) 1982, U.S. Ct. Appeals (D.C. cir.) 1983. Staff counsel for inmates Tex. Dept. Corrections, Huntsville, 1972-73; assoc. Foster, Lewis, Langley, Gardner & Banack, San Antonio, 1973-76, shareholder, 1976-96, Langley & Banack, 1996—. Active South Tex. Leukemia Soc., bd. dirs., 1989-92. Mem. Tex. State Bar Assn. (mem. coun. sch. law sect. 1985-87), Tex. Coun. Sch. Attys. (dir. 1999-2001, v.p. 2002-03), San Antonio Longhorn Club (pres. 1993-94), San Antonio Tex. Exes (pres. 1995-96), Oak Hills Country Club (dir. 1998-2001). Methodist. Avocation: golf. Office: Langley & Banack Inc 745 E Mulberry Ave Ste 900 San Antonio TX 78212-3141 E-mail: warmstrong@langleybanack.com.

ARMSTRONG-LAW, MARGARET, school administrator; b. Fargo, ND, Jan. 21, 1931; d. Theron L. and Besse Ross Armstrong; m. Robert Harold Law, Sept. 6, 1952 (div. Oct. 1964); children: William Robert, Anne Elizabeth Law Buckingham, Amy Catherine Law Burman. BS in English, N.D. State U., 1952, MS Secondary Sch. Adminstrn., 1974; postgrad., UCLA, Moorhead State U., 1984, Mich. State U., 1985; Cert., Harvard Prin.'s Sch., London, 1986. Cert. tchr., ednl. adminstr. Tchr. Agassiz Jr. High, 1963—66, Ben Franklin Jr. High, 1969—71, North HS, Fargo, ND, 1971—74, asst. prin., 1974—78; secondary head Taipei Am. Sch., Taiwan, 1978-87, Vienna Internat. Sch., Austria, 1987-90; dir. Internat. Sch. Amsterdam, The Netherlands, 1990-97; internat. ednl. cons., 1998—. Prof. devel. com. European Coun. Internat. Schs., London, chmn. bd., 1994-96; mem. No. European Coun. Internat. Schs., head coun., 1990-97; spkr. in field. Author: (booklet, film) Future: The Quality of Life, 1975; contbr. articles to profl. jours. Adv. bd. Coll. Arts, Humanities and Social Scis., N.D. State U., 1998—; pres. Fargo-Moorhead Opera Bd., 1999—2001; chmn. bd. Christian edn. Plymouth Congl. Ch., Fargo, 1998—99, mem. coun., 1988—99, vice chair women's fellowship bd., 1999; chair pres. adv. bd. Minn. State U., Moorhead, 2003; bd. dirs. Trollwood Performing Arts Sch., 2002. Recipient Bd. Dirs. award for Extraordinary Svcs. European Coun. Internat. Schs., Promotion of Internat. Edn. award, 1996; named hon. mem. for disting. svcs., European Coun. Internat. Schs., 1997; scholarship named in her honor by bd. govs. Internat. Sch. Amsterdam, 1997—. Mem. AAUW, LWV, ASCD, Assn. Advancement Internat. Edn., Am. Assn. Sch. Adminstrs., Am. Women's Club/Amsterdam, Am. C. of C., Rotary (bd. dirs. 1993-94, program chair 1993-94, v.p. 1994-96, pres. 1995-96/Amsterdam), World Future Soc., World Peace Com. (The Hague, Netherlands), De Amsterdamschekring Club, Phi Kappa Phi. Democrat. Congregationalist. Avocations: chinese brush painting, music, reading, tennis, interior decorating.

ARNALL, ROBERT ESRIC, physician, medical administrator; b. Griffin, Ga., Feb. 14, 1931; s. Paul Esric and Dolly (Henderson) A.; m. Sarah Maxwell, Jan. 18, 1933; children: Dana Kathryn, Robert Maxwell. BA, Emory U., 1953, MD, 1957. Diplomate Am. Bd. Pediatrics, Am. Bd. Med. Mgmt. Intern Atlanta VA Hosp., 1957-58; resident in pediat. Grady Meml. Hosp., Atlanta, 1958-60; chief resident Eggleston Hosp. for Children, Atlanta, 1960; med. dir. The Children's Hospital of S.W. FL, 2001—; med. dir., sys. v.p. Lee Meml. Health Sys., Ft. Myers, 1983-99; pvt. practice pediatrics Atlanta, 1960-64; pvt. practice Ft. Myers, 1964-84; ret., 2000. Instr. pediat. Emory U., Atlanta, 1960-64; attending physician Eggleston Hosp. for Children, 1960-64, Grady Hosp., 1960-64; dir. continuing med. edn. Lee Meml. Hosp., Ft. Myers, 1987-99, pres. med. staff, Ft. Myers, 1973-74, sys. v.p. physician integration, 1995-99; med. dir. Children's Hosp. S.W. Fla., Ft. Myers, 2001—; adv. bd. Lee Meml. Children's Hosp. Bd. dirs. Health Start, Ft. Myers, 1990-96, Goodwill Industries, Ft. Myers, 1989—, Edison-Ford Estates, 1991-99, Healthy Start Dist. 8 Coalition, Children's Hosp. Found., 2000—; past bd. dirs. Edison Pageant of Light, pres.; past bd. dirs. Edison Festival of Light, Children's Home Soc., United Way of Lee County, Lee County Assn. Retarded Citizens, Easter Seal Soc., Nat. Found. March of Dimes, Cmty. Coord. Coun.; co-chmn. Healthy Start Regional Perinatal Network; mem. Childrens Hosp. Devel. Bd. With U.S. Army Res., 1960-68. Recipient Disting. Svc. awards Ft. Myers H.S., 1980, Lee County Sch. Bd., 1983, Fla. H.S. Athletic Assn., 1991; named to Ft. Myers H.S. Hall of Fame Emerald Club, 2000. Fellow Am. Acad. Pediat. (subsect. adolescent medicine, past chmn. sch. health com. Fla. chpt.); mem. AMA (del. to hosp. med. staff sect. 1991-96, chmn. Southeastern Caucus 1994-96), Vol. Hosps. of Am. (task force on alternative delivery systems, task force on quality initiative, physician adv. bd., coun. med. dirs.), Fla. Med. Assn. (del. 1987-95, dist. rep. Coun. on Hosp. Med. Staffs 1989-93, vice chmn. 1991-93, chmn. 1993-95, chmn. governing coun. Organized Med. Staff sect. 1995-96, PRO com. 1991-95, long range planning com. 1995-96), Fla. Hosp. Assn. (quality assurance com.), Lee County Med. Soc. (chmn. sch. health adv. com. to Lee County sch. bd., chmn. sports medicine com. 1980-93, 99-2000), Emerald Club, Rotary (past bd. dirs.), Alpha Omega Alpha. Republican. Methodist. Avocation: golf. Home: 1324 Longwood Dr Fort Myers FL 33919-1821 Office: Children's Hosp SW Fla Health Pk Fla PO Box 2231 Fort Myers FL 33902 E-mail: arnalll324@aol.com.

ARNAUD, SANDRA, financial advisor; b. Arnaudville, La., July 6, 1945; d. Clarence and Nola (Artigue) A.; children: Andrea, Geralyn. Attended, U. Southwestern La. Cert. fin. planner. Bus. mgr. Schexnaider Farms, Arnaudville, 1969-81; fin. planner Apex Investors Corp., Lafayette, La., 1981-86, IDS Fin. Svcs., Ft. Myers, Fla., 1986; acct. exec. Securicorp., Inc., Ft. Myers, 1986-88; mgmt. cons. Profl. Strategies, Houston, 1988-89; fin. cons. Shearson Lehman Bros., Houston, 1989-93; fin. advisor IM & R, Raymond James, Houston, 1993—. Developer, prodr. ednl. program on retirement planning and mng. retirement plan distbns.; tchr. retirement planning program for various colls. and chem., aerospace and mfg. cos. in Houston area. Contbr. fin. articles to Bay Area Times newspaper, Houston. Featured in Wall Street Transcript. Mem. Internat. Bd. Standards and Practices for Cert. Fin. Planners. Avocations: cooking, gardening, travel. Office: Raymond James Fin Svcs Inc Ste 102 1550 W Bay Area Blvd Friendswood TX 77546-2666

ARNDT, CYNTHIA, educational administrator; b. N.Y.C., Sept. 27, 1947; d. Charles Joseph and Pura Maria (Rios) A. BA, Hunter Coll., 1971, MA, 1975; profl. diploma in adminstrn., Fordham U., 1981. Adminstrv. asst. to asst. registrar Hunter Coll., N.Y.C., 1968-69; cataloguer asst. Finch. Coll. Libr., N.Y.C., 1974; tchr. N.Y. Bd. Edn., N.Y.C., 1974-82; bilingual coord. Jr. High. Sch. 143, 1982-89; asst. prin. IS 164, 1989-93; project dir. Elem. Schs. in Restructuring Bilingual Sci., 1993-96; supr.-in-charge IS 136, 1996-97; asst. prin. Mott Hall, 1997—. Reviewer Booklist, 1981. Mem. Am. Artist Soc., Hispanic Am. Hist. Soc., Nat. Council Social Studies, N.Y. State Assn. Curriculum Devel., Puerto Rican Edn. Assn., N.Y. State Assn. Bilingual Edn., Assn. Curriculum Devel., Kappa Delta Pi, Phi Delta Kappa. Democrat. Roman Catholic. Home: 110 W 90th St Apt 4C New York NY 10024-1209

ARNDT, JAMES EDWARD, music educator, musician; s. James William and Janice Eileen Arndt; m. Maureen Lynn Wellen, June 3, 1989. B in Music Edn., U. Wis., Eau Claire, 1985. Teacher Certificate Wis., SD, Wyo., Iowa. Band dir. Selby pub. schools, Selby, SD, 1985—87, Kuemper Cath. schools, Carroll, Iowa, 1987—91, Converse county schools, Douglas, Wyo., 1991—93, Benton cmty. schools, Van Horne, Iowa, 1993—. Band mem. Cedar Rapids Municipal Band, Jazz Vanguard Collective, Clear Lake Municipal Band. Scoutmaster Boy Scouts, Blairstown, Iowa, 1993—; ambulance svc. Blairstown, Iowa, 2000—; city councilman, 2001—03. Recipient Wood Badge, Boy Scouts, 1993, Eagle Scout, 1977. Mem.: Iowa Bandmasters Assn., Nat. Bandmasters Assn., Music Educators Nat. Conf., Lions. Lutheran. Avocations: model railroading, fly fishing. Home: Po Box 315 Blairstown IA 52209-0315 Office: Benton commity schools 400 First Street Van Horne IA 52364

ARNDT, JANET S. state legislator; b. Providence, May 23, 1947; m. Kenneth G. Arndt; 4 children. AB, Gordon Coll., 1968; MEd, Boston U., 1970; student, U. Mass., 1998—, CAGS, 2002; EdD, U. Mass. Amherst, 2003. N.H. state rep. Dist. 27, Rockingham, 1992—2002; mem. children, youth and juvenile justice com. N.H. Ho. of Reps., mem. const. and statutory rev. com.; specialist counselor Early Childhood, 1987—; chmn. election law com., 1997—2002. Asst. prof. Gordon Coll., 1995—, N.H. Tech. Coll., 1997—2001, adj. prof., 2001—. Mem. Friends of the Libr. of Windham, chmn., 1991-92; active Girl Scouts Am., publicity chairperson; scholarship chmn. Nat. Order of Women Legislators; exec. bd. Rockingham County; events chairperson Nesmith Libr.; mem. edn. task force ALEC, mem. ch. early childhood task force; mem. nat. coun. of state legislators Coun. of State Govt.; chair Rockingham County Register of Deeds, 1996-02. Recipient M. Carter award for Outstanding Libr. Svc., 1995; named Leader of Yr. Windham Girl Scouts, 1995. Mem. N.H. Order Women Legislators, Gordon Coll. Alumni Coun. Address: NH House of Reps 8 Crestwood Rd Windham NH 03087-1429

ARNDT, MELVIN C. writer; b. Lenhartsville, Pa., Oct. 8, 1925; s. Charles Elwood Arndt, Helen Mae Arndt; m. Melba Mae Heffner; children: Dale C., Chris D. Grad., DeVry Tech. Inst., Chgo., 1950; student, Fla. So. Coll., 1979; grad., Bert Rogers Sch. Real Estate, Lakeland, Fla., 1984. Owner A and M Electronics, Kutztown, Pa., 1950—58; supr., foreman Charles Arndt, Lenhartsville, Pa., 1958—67; sales rep. Securities United Republic Investment Co., Harrisburg, Pa., 1967—68; supr. region United Republic Life Ins., Harrisburg, 1968—70; dir. state sales Americana Investment Co., Columbus, Ohio, 1970—72; sr. dir. state sales Americana Life Ins. Co., Columbus, 1972—77; dir., v.p. United Sun Life Ins. Co., Lakeland, Fla., 1977—84, broker real estate, 1988, mgr. property, 1988—2001; ret., 2001. Author: The PI Conspiracy, 2001. Ptnr. Foxstar Partnership, Mulberry, Fla., 1990—2002; mem. Cmty. Band; dir. Merchants Assn., Kutztown, Pa. With U.S. Army, 1944—46. Mem.: Free and Accepted Masons Vaux Lodge #406. Republican. Presbyterian. Avocations: fishing, painting. Home: 4955 Colonnades Club Blvd Lakeland FL 33811

ARNDT, RICHARD TALLMADGE, writer, consultant; b. Phila., Oct. 28, 1928; s. Howard Wilcox Arndt and Eleanor (Shaw) Branigan; m. Edith Robichon (div. 1964); children: Skyler-Jennifer Arndt-Briggs, Matthew Wilcox; m. Dorothy Serlin (div. 1973); children: Daniel Serlin, Sarah L. Piazza; m. Lois W. Roth (dec. 1986). BA, Princeton U., 1949, postgrad., 1971-72; PhD, Columbia U., 1959. Instr., asst. prof. French Columbia U., N.Y.C., 1953-61; cultural attaché U.S. embassies, Beirut, 1961-63, Colombo, Sri Lanka, 1963-66, Tehran, Iran, 1966-71, Rome, 1974-78, Paris, 1978-80; dir. policy and plans Bur. Ednl. and Cultural Affairs, U.S. Info. Agy., 1980-83; cultural coord. Near East/So. Asia, USIA, Washington, 1983-85; dep. dir. L.Am., dir. youth and student programs Bur. Ednl. and Cultural Affairs Dept. State, Washington, 1972-74; diplomat-in-residence, dir. mid-career study dept. govt. U. Va., Charlottesville, 1986-89; bd. dirs. Fulbright Assn., Washington, 1986-92, v.p., 1986-89, pres., 1989-91; U.S. rep. Ctr. for Am. Studies, Rome, 1997—. Adj. prof. George Washington U., 1993—95; mem. faculty div. psychopolitics Ctr. Study Mind and Human Interaction, Charlottesville, 1988—; chmn. bd. Lois W. Roth Endowment, Washington, 1986—; bd. mem Americans for UNESCO, 1992—2002, pres., 2002—. Prin. editor: The Fulbright Difference, 1948-92, Transaction, 1993; contbr. articles to profl. jours. Bd. advisors Toda Inst., Hawaii, 1997—; chmn. Com. to Save Ancient Tyre, 1999—. Fulbright fellow U. Dijon, France, 1949-50, USIA mid-career fellow, 1971-72; recipient USIA Merit award, 1963, 66, 71. Mem. Internat. Soc. for Edn., Cultural and Sci. Interchange (pres. 1986-89), Coun. Internat. Programs, (1986-95, v.p. 1991-95, adv. coun. 2000—), Nat. Peace Found. (bd. dirs. 1991, chmn. 1992-95, chmn. adv. coun. 1995—, Peace Builder award 2002), Am. Iranian Coun. (bd. advisors), Cosmos Club. Avocations: music, cultural diplomacy, political culture, theatre, history. Home: 1870 Wyoming Ave NW Washington DC 20009-1883 E-mail: DickArndt1@aol.com.

ARNELL, GORDON EDWIN, real estate development company executive; b. Calgary, Alta., Feb. 19, 1935; m. Reta; children: Patrick, Kevin, Paul, Dana. BA, U. of Alta., 1956; LLB, 1957. Called to bar, Alta., 1958. Lawyer, 1958-70; v.p. Allarco Devel. Ltd., 1970-73; pres. Seaboard Life Ins. Co. also North West Trust Co., 1973-75; exec. v.p. Oxford Devel. Group Ltd., 1975-80; pres. Dover Pk Deve. Corp. Ltd., 1980-84; exec. v.p. corp devel. Trizec Corp. Ltd., 1984-86; pres. c.o.o. Trilea Centres Inc., 1986-87, pres., CEO, 1987-88, Carena Devels. Ltd., from 1988; now chmn. Brookfield Properties, Toronto. Mem. Can. Bar Assn., Alta. Law Soc. Office: Brookfield Properties Corp 181 Bay St Ste 4440 Toronto ON Canada M5J 2T3

ARNELL, RICHARD ANTHONY, radiologist; b. Chgo., Aug. 21, 1938; s. Tony Frank and Mary Martha (Oberman) Yaki; m. Paula Ann Youngberg, June 28, 1964; children: Carla Ann, Paula Marie, Paul Anthony. BA, Grinnell Coll., 1960; MD, U. Iowa, 1964. Diplomate Am. Bd. Radiology, Am. Bd. Nuclear Medicine. With Innc., 1968—, v.p., 1970-78, sec., 1978-90, pres., 1990—93, trustee pension profit plan, 1979-2000; pres. Moline Radiology Assocs., S.C., 1990-93, Advanced Radiology, S.C., 1993-2001, Advanced Radiology Assocs., LLC, 2000—01, Advanced Radiology Diagnostic Ctrs., LLC, 2000—01. Mem. staff Luth. Hosp., Moline, 1968-88, dir. continuing mem. edn. prog. for physicians, 1979-83, bd. dirs., 1977-83; mem. staff Moline Pub. Hosp., 1968-88, Hammond Henry Dist. Ill., Geneseo, Ill.; mem. staff United Med. Ctr., 1989-92, chmn. radiology dept., 1992-94, mem. med. dir. radiology dept., 1992-99; pres. Moline Radiology Assocs., Inc., 1990-93; mem. med. staff Mercer County Hosp., 1994—, Ill. Hosp., 1995—, Trinity Med. Ctr., 1992; trustee Midstate Found. for Med. Care, 1975-79, mem. exec. com., 1976-79; v.p. Quad City HMO Health Plan, 1979; clin. lectr. U. Iowa. Pres. Moline Mgmt. Assocs., Inc., 1990—; chmn. mng. com. Metro MRI Ctr., LLC. Ltd. Ptnrshp. Supt. Sunday Ch. Sch. St. John's Ch., Rock Island, Ill., 1974-79, mem. ch. cabinet, 1975-76; del. Chs. United of Scott and Rock Island counties, Ill., 1977; mem. nat. exec. com. Augustana Coll., Rock Island, 1977-81; assoc. chmn. profl. div. United Way, 1985; bd. dirs. Luth. Hosp. Found., 1981-84, pres., 1982-84; bd. dirs. Quad Cities Health Care Resources, Inc., 1984-88; chmn. Luth. Health Care Found., 1984-88, United Health Care Found., 1989-91. Recipient David Theophillus trophy for outstanding athlete Grinnell Coll., 1960, Dr. of Distinction award Rock Island Med. Soc. Alliance, 1998. Mem. Am. Coll. Radiology, Ill. Radiol. Soc., Am. Coll. Nuclear Medicine, Soc. Nuclear Medicine, AMA, Ill. Med. Soc. (ho. of dels., 1974-79), Rock Island County Med. Soc. (exec. com. 1974-79, peer rev. com. 1975-79), Iowa-Ill. Ctrl. Med. Soc. (pres. 1978), Ctrl. Ill. Med. Assn. (v.p. 1977, pres. 1978), Ind. Physicians Assn. Western Ill. (dir. 1984-86, v.p. 1985, pres. 1986), World Med. Assn., Am. Coll. Med. Imaging, Short Hills Country Club. Office: 615 Valley View Dr Ste 101 Moline IL 61265 E-mail: rarny@aol.com.

ARNELL, WALTER JAMES WILLIAM, engineering educator, consultant; b. Farnborough, Eng., Jan. 9, 1924; arrived in U.S., 1953, naturalized, 1960; s. James Albert and Daisy (Payne) Arnell; m. Patricia Catherine Cannon, Nov. 12, 1955; children: Sean Paul, Victoria Clare, Sarah Michele. Aero. Engr., Royal Aircraft Establishment, 1946; BSc, U. London, 1953, PhD, 1967; MA, Occidental Coll., L.A., 1956; MS, U. So. Calif., 1958. Lectr. Poly. and Northampton Coll. Advance Tech., London, 1948-53; instr. U. So. Calif., L.A., 1954-59; asst. prof. mech. engring. Calif. State U., Long Beach, 1959-62, assoc. prof., 1962-66, prof., 1966-71, chmn. dept. mech. engring., 1964-65, acting chmn. divsn. engring., 1964-66, dean engring., 1967-69, rschr.; affiliate faculty dept. ocean engring. U. Hawaii, 1970-74; adj. prof. systems and insdl. engring. U. Ariz., 1981—; pres. Lenra Assocs. Ltd., 1973—; chmn., project mgr. Hawaii Environ. Simulation Lab., 1971-72. Contbr. articles to profl. jours. Trustee Rehab. Hosp. of the Pacific, 1975—78. Fellow: Ergonomics Soc.; mem.: AAUP, AIAA, IEEE Sys. Man and Cybernetics Soc., Human Factors and Ergonomics Soc., Soc. Engring. Psychology sect., Am. Psychol. Assn. Soc., Royal Aero. Soc., Pi Tau Sigma, Phi Kappa Phi, Tau Beta Pi, Alpha Pi Mu, Psi Chi. Home: 4491 E Fort Lowell Rd Tucson AZ 85712-1106

ARNESEN, TORE OLAV, structural engineer, inventor; b. Boston, Aug. 18, 1946; s. Egil and Olga (Tveekrem) A.; m. Sandra Louise Skyles, June 22, 1974. BS in Archtl. Engring., U. Wyo., 1972; MSCE, U. Nebr., 1974. Registered profl. engr., Colo., Wyo., Nebr., N.Mex., N.Y., La. Engr. Severud & Assocs., Inc., N.Y.C., 1974-75, Leo A. Daly Co., Omaha, 1975-78; project engr. Dana-Larson-Roubel & Assocs., Omaha, 1978-80; supr. engr. Gibbs & Hill, Inc./Dravo Corp., Omaha, 1980-82, chief structural engr. Denver, 1982-85; prin., pres. Arnesen & Assocs., Inc., Broomfield, Colo., 1985—. Vice chmn. Broomfield Constnr. and Rev. Bd., 1987-99. Contbr. articles to various publs.; co-author code standards for air supported structures and tensioned membrane structures ASCE-Nat. Bur. Standards. Mem. ASCE (co-author standard for peer rev. of civil engring. projects 1994), Cons. Engrs. Coun. Colo. (hon. mention 1989), Am. Concrete Inst., Internat. Assn. Concrete Repair Specialists, Rotary (bd. dirs. Broomfield chpt. 1989-91, pres. 1991-92), ABET Edn. Evaluator for Accreditation of Engring. Programs (1995—). Achievements include patent in thermo-vacuum structure. Home: 1330 Bellaire St Broomfield CO 80020-1327 Office: 7050 W 120th Ave Ste 206 Broomfield CO 80020-7604

ARNESON, GEORGE STEPHEN, manufacturing company executive, management consultant; b. St. Paul, Apr. 3, 1925; s. Oscar and Louvia Irene (Clare) A.; children: George Stephen, Deborah Clare, Diane Elizabeth, Frederick Oscar. BS in Marine Transp., U.S. Mcht. Marine Acad., 1945; BEE, U. Minn., 1949. Certified mgmt. cons. Sales engr. Hubbard & Co., Chgo., 1949-54; cons. Booz, Allen & Hamilton, Chgo., 1954-57; mgr. mktg. cons. services, dir. mktg., plant mgr. Borg-Warner Corp., Chgo., 1957-60; asst. gen. mgr., then v.p., gen. mgr. Delta-Star Electric div. H.K. Porter Co., Inc., Pitts., 1960-63, v.p., gen. mgr. elec. divs., 1963-65; v.p. mktg. Wheeling Steel Corp., 1965-66; pres., chief exec. officer Vendo Co., Kansas City, Mo., 1966-72, also dir., chmn. exec. com.; pres., chmn. Dun-Lap Mfg. Co., Newton, Iowa, 1973-77; pres. Arneson & Co., Overland Park, Kans., 1974—. Contbr. articles on mgmt. cons., bus. valuation and appraisal of mgmt. to profl. jours. Chmn. adv. bd. Kans. Dept. Corrections, Topeka, 1980-92. Lt. (j.g.) USNR, 1943-46. Recipient Outstanding Alumnus award U.S. Mcht. Marine Acad., 1968, Past Dir. award Automatic Merchandising Assn. Mem. Phi Gamma Delta (life), Alpha Phi Omega (life). Clubs: Masons, KT, Shriners. Presbyterian. Home: 3031 Shrine Park Rd Leavenworth KS 66048-4806 E-mail: georgearneson@yahoo.com.

ARNESON, JAMES HERMAN, lawyer; b. Winona, Minn., June 15, 1952; s. Herman Orlando and Vivian Agnes (Beardmore) A.; m. Ruth Helen Zimmerman, Sept. 2, 1979; children: Aaron Karl, Laura Rachel. BS, U. Wis., Eau Claire, 1974; JD, U. Mo., Kansas City, 1979. Bar: Mo. 1979, U.S. Dist. Ct. (we. dist.) Mo. 1979. Claims adjuster Crawford & Co., Columbia, Mo., 1974-76; assoc. Woolsey & Fisher, Springfield, Mo., 1979-82, Buck, Bohm & Stein, Kansas City, Mo., 1982-83, Shughart, Thompson & Kilroy, Kansas City, 1983-87, Sherman, Wickens, Lysaught & Speck, Kansas City, 1987-88; with Zimmerman Tree Svc., Lakeworth, Fla., 1988-89; of counsel Miller & Sanford, Springfield, 1993-98; atty. Law Office James H. Arneson, Springfield, 1998—. Adj. prof. law U. Mo., Kansas City, 1986-88, Drury Coll., 1993, S.W. Mo. State U., 1998—; mem. Springfield/Greene County Environ. Adv. Bd., 1992-98. Mem. youth com. Beth Shalom Synagogue, Kansas City, 1984, mem. memorialization com., 1985, vice chmn. legal com., 1986-87, chmn. legal com., 1987, bd. dirs., 1986; bd. dirs. Midwest Trauma Soc., Kansas City, 1987—, United Hebrew Congregation, treas. 1990, v.p., 1991-93; mem. Leadership Springfield, 1996—. Victor Wilson scholar, 1979. Mem. Mo. Bar Assn. (editor Cts. and CLE Bull., vice chmn. environ. and energy law sect. 1990), Greene County Bar Assn. (chair environ. law com. 1990-93), Multiple Sclerosis Soc. (bd. dirs Ozarks br. 1998), Sierra Club (legal chmn. Ozark chpt. 1981-83, coord. polit. edn. 1986—, chmn. Thomas Hart Benton group 1982-85), Springfield C. of C. (govt. rels. com., environ. subsect. 1990—, chmn. 1996—), Phi Alpha Delta. Office: 2103 E Sunshine St Springfield MO 65804-1816

ARNESON, WALLACE AGGERGAARD, JR., surgeon; b. Sioux Falls, S.D., Apr. 23, 1948; BA, Carleton Coll., 1970; MD, Harvard U., 1974. Intern U. Mich. Hosp., Ann Arbor, 1974-75, resident gen. surgery, 1975-80; staff surgeon St. Joseph Mercy Health Sys., 1980—. Clin. instr. U. Mich. Hosp., 1982—, clin. asst. prof., 2000—. Mem. ACS, Frederick Coller Soc., Midwest Surgical Soc., Ctrl. Surgery Assn. Office: PO Box 974 Ann Arbor MI 48106-0974

ARNET, WILLIAM FRANCIS, lawyer; b. St. Louis, Mo., Mar. 13, 1948; s. Aloysius Richard and Grace Marie (Luenebrink) A.; m. Judith Ann Wissmann, June 13, 1970; children— Christina, Matthew, Benjamin. B.A. in Polit. Sci., S.E. Mo. State U., 1970; J.D., U. Mo.-Columbia, 1970-73. Bar: Mo. 1973, U.S. Dist. Ct. (we. dist.) Mo. 1975, U.S. Ct. Appeals (8th cir.) 1975, U.S. Supreme Ct. 1977. Asst. atty. gen. State of Mo., Jefferson City, 1973-81, 81-84; legis. aide Sen. John Danforth, Washington, 1981; counsel U. Mo., Columbia, 1984—. Contbr. to law rev., 1971-73. Mem. Mo. Bar Assn., Order of Coif, Roman Catholic. Home: 2205 Topaz Dr Columbia MO 65203-1445 Office: U Mo 227 University Hall Columbia MO 65211-3020

ARNETT, EDWARD MCCOLLIN, chemistry educator, researcher; b. Phila., Sept. 25, 1922; s. John Hancock and Katherine Williams (McCollin) A.; m. Sylvia Gettmann, Dec. 10, 1970; children: Eric, Brian; stepchildren: Elden, Byron, Colin Gatewood. BS, U. Pa., 1943, MS, 1946, PhD, 1949. Rsch. dir. Max Levy & Co., Phila., 1949-53; asst. prof. Western Md. Coll., Westminster, 1953-54, 1954-55; assoc. prof. chemistry U. Pitts., 1957-61, assoc. prof., 1961-64, prof., 1964-80; R.J. Reynolds prof. Duke U., Durham, N.C., 1980-92, prof. emeritus, 1992—. Vis. lectr. U. Ill., 1963; vis. prof. U. Kent, Canterbury, Eng., 1970; dir. Pitts Chem. Info. Ctr., 1967-70; mem. adv. bd. Petroleum Research Fund, 1968-71, 1990-93; mem. com. on chem. info. NRC, 1969-71. Contbr. 200 articles to sci. jours. DuPont fellow, 1948-49, rsch. fellow Harvard U., Cambridge, Mass., 1955-57, Guggenheim fellow, 1968-69, Mellon Inst. adj. sr. fellow, 1964-80, Inst. Hydrocarbon Chemistry sr. fellow, 1980. Fellow AAAS; mem. Am. Chem. Soc. (James Flack Norris award 1977, Pitts. award Pitts. chpt. 1976, Petroleum Chemistry award 1985), Nat. Acad. Scis., The Chem. Soc., Sigma Xi, Phi Lambda Upsilon. E-mail: narnett@chem.duke.edu.

ARNETT, RITA ANN, social services administrator, consultant; b. Des Moines, Aug. 8, 1952; d. Roy Gardner and Rita Elizabeth A.; m. John Nick Allar, Aug. 5, 1990; children: Ebeneezer Shay, Hanii Shay, Eli Allar. BA cum laude, Ft. Lewis Coll., 1982. Editor Dolores Archael. Project, Colo., 1982-86; dir. Sunrise Youth Shelter Ute Mt. Ute Tribe, Towaoc, Colo., 1986-92; dep. dir. planning, devel. and compliance Aliviane NO-AD, Inc., El Paso, Tex., 1993—2002; owner Echelon Group, Inc., El Paso, Tex., 2001—; COO Echelon Group, El Paso, Tex., 2002—. Bd. dir. Rio Bravo Interfaith Pastoral Coun., El Paso; cons. St. Elizabeth's Hosp., Washington, 1999, Life Mgmt. Ctr., El Paso, 1996, West Care Found., Las Vegas, Nev., 2002-current; cons. Heritage Ranch Inst., Deming, N.Mex., 2002-current. Grantee Ctr. for Substance Abuse Treatment, 1993, 96, 99, 2000-02, Ctrs. for Disease Control and Prevention, 1997-2000, Ctr. for Substance Abuse Prevention, 1999-2002, Health and

Human Svc., 1987-93, 92-95, 94-97, Tex. Commn. Alcohol and Drug Abuse, 1993—, Tex. Dept. Health, 1993—, Tex. Dept. Protective and Regulatory Svcs., 1997—, Tex. Dept. Criminal Justice, 1995—, Tex. Workforce Commn., 2001-02, Grantee: DeKalb County, Ga., 2003; USfish & Wildlifef Svc., 2003, Bur. Indian Affairs, 1991—, Gates Found., 1990, Colo. VOCA Bd., 1987, 88-93, 91-93, Colo. Divsn. Youth Svc., Dekalb County, Ga. Democrat. Roman Catholic. Avocations: weight training, bicycling, gardening. Home: 4530 River Walk Las Cruces NM 88007 Office: 6114 Escondido El Paso TX 79912

ARNETT, RONALD CHARLES, communication educator; b. Ft. Wayne, Ind., Mar. 10, 1952; s. Arlo Guy and Dorothy Alice (Hennisa) A.; m. Mildred R. Bittinger, Jan. 30, 1972; children: Adam Geoffrey, Aimee Gabrielle. BS, Manchester Coll., 1974; MA, Ohio U., 1975, PhD, 1978; MDiv, Bethany Theol. Sem., 1983. Asst. prof., dir. basic comm. St. Cloud (Minn.) U., 1977-84; chair dept. comm. and rhetorical studies Marquette U., Milw., 1984-87; dean, v.p., prof. comm. Manchester Coll., North Manchester, Ind., 1987-93; chair dept. comm. and rhetoric studies Duquesne U., Pitts., 1993—, chair affiliate depts. comm. and English, 1997—2001. Mem. various coms. Duquesne U., Pitts., 1993—. Author: Dialogic Education, 1992, Communication and Community, 1986, Dwell in Peace, 1980; editor: The Reach of Dialogue, 1994, Communication In An Age of Diversity, 1996, Dialogic Civility in a Cynical Age--Community, Hope and Interpersonal Relationships, 1999. Mem. adminstrv. bd. Ingomas Meth. Ch., Pitts., 1993; 2nd vice pres., Religious Comm. Assn., 2000; bd. dirs. On Earth Peace, Md., 1994; mem. North Manchester Aquatic, 1991-93, assoc. bd./ch. bd., 1985-88; vice chmn. Peace and Conflict Commn., 1993. Recipient Ohio U. Alumnus award, 1996, Article of the Yr., Religious Comm. Assn., 1999. Mem. Ea. Comm. Assn., Nat. Comm. Assn. (chmn. ethics com. 1988). Avocation: camping. Office: Duquesne U Dept Comm & Rhetoric Studies Pittsburgh PA 15282-0001 E-mail: arnett@duq.edu.

ARNEY, JAMES DOUGLAS, forestry biometrics consultant; b. Hoquiam, Wash., Dec. 9, 1941; s. James Dennis and Martha (Wylam) A.; m. Jo Ann Joyce Loehrke, Febr. 14, 1991; children: Michael, BettiJean. BS in Forest Mgmt., U. Mont., 1965; MS in Forest Mensuration, Oreg. State U., 1968, PhD in Forest Biometrics, 1971. Forest mensurationist U.S. Forest Svc. Expt. Sta., Portland, 1965-66; rsch. scientist Canadian Forestry Svc., Victoria, B.C., 1970-72; rsch. mgr. Weyerhaeuser Co., Centralia, Wash., 1973-80; mgr. forest dept. Reid, Collins & Assocs., Vancouver, B.C., 1980-81; rsch. forester Potlatch Corp., Lewiston, Idaho, 1982-84; forestry cons. Applied Biometrics, Spokane, Wash., 1985-88, Mason, Bruce & Girard, Inc., Portland, 1989-94, Forest Biometrics, St. Regis, Mont., 1995—. Mem. Soc. Am. Foresters, Wc. Forestry Assn. Avocations: hiking, snow skiing, pacific nw history, golf, scuba diving. Home: 53 Trestle Creek Rd Saint Regis MT 59866-9709 Office: Forest Biometrics 53 Trestle Creek Dr Saint Regis MT 59866 E-mail: jdarney@forestbiometrics.com.

ARNEZ, NANCY LEVI, educational leadership educator; b. Balt., July 6, 1928; d. Milton Emerson Levi and Ida Barbour (Rusk) Levi Washington. AB, Morgan State Coll., 1949; MA, Columbia U., 1954, EdD, 1958. Tchr. English Druid Jr. H.S., Balt., 1949-52, Houston Jr. H.S., Balt., 1952-57; asst. to admissions officer Tchrs. Coll., Columbia U., N.Y.C., 1957-58, grad. asst., 1957; head dept. English Cherry Hill Jr. H.S., Balt., 1958-62; assoc. prof., dir. student teaching Morgan State Coll., Balt., 1962-66; co-founder Cultural Linguistic Early Childhood Follow Through Approach; prof., asst. dir./dir. Ctr. for Inner City Studies, Northeastern Ill. U., Chgo., 1966-74; prof., assoc. dean, acting dean Sch. Edn. Howard U., Washington, 1974-80, chmn. dept. ednl. leadership, 1980-86, prof., 1980-93, prof. emeriti, 1993—. Author: Partners in Urban Education: Teaching the Inner City Child, 1973, The Struggle for Equality of Educational Opportunity, 1975, Administrative Issues in the Implementation of the Response to Educational Needs Project, 1979, The Besieged School Superintendent, 1981, School Based Administrator Training, 1982; mem. editorial bd.: Phi Delta Kappan, 1975-80, Jour. Negro Edn., 1975-80, Black Child Jour., 1980— ; contbr. articles to profl. jours. State treas., mem. exec. com. Md. State council UN Children's Fund, 1965; founder Operation Champ, Balt, 1965; mem. adv. bd. Better Boys Found., Chgo., 1966-74, Mus. African-Am. History, 1969; state chmn. Right to Read, Washington, 1973-80; treas. Com. to Elect Douglass Moore to City Council, 1982. African Am. Inst. grantee, 1974, Spencer Found. grantee, 1976; AAUW grantee, 1977. Mem. Am. Assn. Sch. Adminstrs. (editorial bd. 1982), Assn. for Study of Afro-Am. Life and History, African Am. Heritage Assn., African Am. Writers Guild, Nat. Alliance Black Sch. Educators, D.C. Alliance Black Sch. Educators (pres. 1986-88), Phi Delta Kappa. Presbyterian. Home: 3122 Cherry Rd NE Washington DC 20018-1612

ARNHEIM, LOUISE A, marketing professional; d. Falk K. and Marian L. (Lambie) Arnheim. BA Polit. Sci., Duke U., Durham, NC, 1975—78; MA Exec./Legis./Regulatory Mgmt., George Wash. U., Washington, DC, 1985—87. Sr. mktg. mgr. Equals Three Comm., Beth., Md., 1999—; comm. mgr. Oceania, Inc., Falls Ch., Va., 1998—99; founder The Clerestory Group, Falls Ch., Va., 1995—99; sr. program officer NRC, Washington, 1994—95; telecom. policy specialist Arnold & Porter, Washington, 1991—94; sr. analyst Shooshan & Jackson, Washington, 1987—91; nightly news rschr. NBC News, Washington, 1980—83; asst. to correspondents CBS News, Washington, 1978—80. Mem., bd. of directors Huntington's Disease Soc. of Am., Wash. Metro Area Chpt., Fairfax, Va., 1996—, Am. Women in Radio & TV, Wash., DC Chpt., Washington, 1990—95. Author: (article) Telephony, Infrastructure Fin., (articles) Security Mgmt. Mag.; author: (co-author) (article) Communications Lawyer; editor (co-editor): (book) A Health Care Agenda for the States; author (co-author): (monograph/report) Pub. Broadcasting; editor: (report) Electronic Highways: Providing the Telecommunications Infrastructure for Pennsylvania's Econ. Future, (conference report) Higher Ed. and the NII; author: (newspaper article) Washington Post, 1982, (co-author) Article, Family Practice Mgmt., (feature articles) Computing Rsch. News, (book chapters) Telemedicine Sourcebook; editor (co-editor): (book) A Health Care Agenda for the States. Recipient Phi Beta Kappa, Summa cum laude, Duke U., 1978, Pi Sigma Alpha, Nat. Honor Soc. for Polit. Sci., 1978, Pi Alpha Alpha, Nat. Honor Soc. for Pub. Adminstrn., The George Wash. U., 1987, Director's Cert. of Appreciation, Dir., Agy. for Healthcare Rsch. and Quality, US HHS, 2002, Apex award for Best Rewrite, 2003. Avocations: music, architecture, art, dancing.

ARNHOLT, PHILIP J. biologist, educator; b. Danville, Ill., May 16, 1940; s. George Robert and Josephine Julia Arnholt; m. Karen Lenore Bartel; children: Mark Allen, Laura Lea. BS in Edn., Ea. Ill. U., 1963, MS in Edn., 1967; PhD, U. Nebr., 1971. Tchr. biology Dixon (Ill.) H.S., 1963—67, LaSalle-Peru H.S., LaSalle, Ill., 1967—68; prof. biology Concordia U., Mequon, Wis., 1971—2000, faculty laureate, 2000—. Lutheran. Avocations: photography, golf, hunting, fishing. Home: 10910 San Marino Dr Mequon WI 53092 Office: Concordia U 12800 N Lake Shore Dr Mequon WI 53097 E-mail: philip.arnholt@cuw.edu.

ARNICK, JOHN STEPHEN, lawyer, legislator; b. Balt., Nov. 27, 1933; s. John and Josephine (Gaillardo) A. BS, U. Balt., 1956; LLD, U. Balt. Law Sch., 1961. Bar Assn. U.S. Marine Corps., 1956-59; magistrate Balt. County, 1966-67; del. Md. Gen. Assembly, Annapolis, 1967-79, 87-94, 1994—; atty. pvt. practice, Balt., Md., 1962—; del. Md. Gen. Assembly, Annapolis, 1983—. Mem. Twin Dist. Dem. Club, Battle Grove Dem. Club, Sons of Italy. Mem. Ea. Balt. C. of C., Moose Lodge, New 7th Dem. Club, South East Dem. Club. Democratic. Roman Catholic. Home: 7918 Diehlwood Rd Baltimore MD 21222-3316 Office: 6914 Holabird Ave Baltimore MD 21222-6914

ARNO, JOSEPH PETER, physician, cosmetic surgeon; b. Phila., May 30, 1932; AB, U. Pa., 1954; MD, U. Heidelberg, Germany, 1963. Sci. rschr. Biol. Abstracts, Phila., 1963-65, Hoffman LaRoche, Nutley, N.J., 1965-66; sci. and clin. rschr. Merck Sharp & Dohme, Rahway, N.J., 1967-70; clin. rschr. Novartis Corp., Summit, N.J., 1970-72; intern Muhlenberg Hosp., Plainfield, N.J., 1972-73; resident Robt. Wood Johnson U. Hosp., New Brunswick, N.J., 1973-74, St. Luke's-Roosevelt, N.Y.C., 1975-76, St. Barnabas Hosp., Bronx, N.Y., 1980-81, Luth. Med. Ctr., Bklyn., 1981-82, Woodhull Med. Ctr., Bklyn., 1982-83; attending physician emergency medicine Brookdale U. Hosp., Bklyn., 1986-94, Bklyn. Hosp., 1994-96; pvt. practice, 1984—. Pharm. rsch. investigator. Contbr. to med. lit. Avocations: antique cars, dogs, horses. Office: Williamsburg Commons 10 Aver Ct East Brunswick NJ 08816-1860

ARNOLD, ADRIAN KING, state representative; b. Paris, Ky., Apr. 27, 1932; m. Delma Arnold; children: Lanny, Jeffrey, Eric. Student, Morehead State U. Owner Tobacco & Cattle Farm, 1950—2000. Past pres. Montgomery County Farm Bur. With U.S. Army, 1953—55. Mem.: VFW. Democrat. Office: Capitol Annex Rm 332 B Frankfort KY 40601*

ARNOLD, ALBERT JAMES, foreign language educator; b. Ballston Spa, N.Y., Nov. 8, 1939; s. Albert J. and Florence Emily (Cleveland) A.; m. Josephine Diane Valenza, June 8, 1963; 1 child, Elizabeth. AB, Hamilton Coll., 1961; MA, U Wis. Madison, 1964, PhD, 1968; cert French lang., lit., U. Paris, 1960. Instr. romance langs. Hamilton Coll., Clinton, N.Y., 1961-62; from asst. to prof. French U. Va., 1966—, chair com. comparative lit., 1974-79, 1986-89, co-chair comparative programs in literature and culture, 1989-95; dir. New World Studies, 1991-92. Vis. exch. prof. U. de Paris III, 1981; external examiner Queensland U., Australia, 1986, U. West Indies, 1991—, NYU, 1991, Yale U., 1994; external assessor French dept. U. West Indies, 1995, 2002-03; coord. com. on comp. lit. hist. Internat. Comp. Lit. Assoc., 1992-2001; mem. internat. adv. bd. New West Indian Guide, 1992—; spkr., cons. in field. Author: Paul Valéry, 1970, Sartre, 1973, Césaire, 1981, 90, Camus, 1983; gen. editor Caraf Books, 1987-93; editor New World Studies, 1992—, Plantation Soc. in the Ams., 1999—; contbr. articles to profl. jours. ACLS fellow, 1975-76; NEH fellow Nat. Humanities Ctr., 1989-90; Fulbright fellow, 1995-96; trans. grantee NEH, 1991-92; grantee U. Va., 1969, 70, 72, 75-76, 78, 80, 81-82, 86, 95-96, 2001-02, Camargo Found., 1981-82, 86, 2001, Va. Found. Humanities, 1992, 94; Queensland U. fellow, Australia, 1995. Mem. Phi Beta Kappa. Democrat. Avocations: gardening, photography, birding. Home: 310 E Beverley St Staunton VA 24401-4327 Office: U Va Dept French PO Box 400770 Charlottesville VA 22904-4770 E-mail: aja@ntelos.net., aja@virginia.edu.

ARNOLD, ANDREW, medical researcher, physician; MD, Harvard Med. Sch. Cert. Endocrinology and Metabolism Am. Bd. of Internal Medicine. Murray-Heilig Chair in Molecular Medicine Univ. of Conn. Sch. of Medicine, Farmington, Conn. Physician (over 125 articles in med. science). Recipient Fuller Albright award, Am. Soc. for Bone and Mineral Rsch., Outstanding Investigator award, Am. Fedn. for Med. Rsch., 1995, Gerald D. Aurbach award, The Endocrine Soc., 2001. Office: Univ of Conn Health Ctr 263 Farmington Ave Farmington CT 06030-3101

ARNOLD, ANDREW ALLEN, management consultant; b. Memphis, Aug. 18, 1947; s. George and Laura Arnold; m. Edith F. McCollister; children: Rachel Ivey, Danielle Rossi. BBA, Memphis State U., 1975; MBA, Rushmore U., 2000; PhD, Rushmore Univ., 2002. Prodn. mgr. Kellwood Mfg., Calhoun City, Miss., 1975—76; plant mgr. Elk Brand Mfg., Hopkinsville, Ky., 1976—78; chief cons. Alexander Proudfoot Co., Chgo., 1978—82; dir. of materials MacGregor Golf Co., Albany, Ga., 1982—84; sr. project mgr. Pricewaterhouse-Coopers LLP, Fairfax, Va., 1984—2002; pres. Arnold Bus. Consulting, Peachtree City, Ga., 2002—. Author: Excellence Unlimited: Ten Keys to Building and Sustaining Peak Performance in Any Business or Government Organization, 2002. Served with USN, 1968—72. Scholar, Firestone Tire & Rubber Co., 1965. Mem.: Am. Prodn. and Inventory Control Soc. (chpt. pres. 1982—84). Avocations: golf, travel. Home: 429 Holly Grove Church Rd Peachtree City GA 30269 Office Fax: 770-631-0710. Business E-Mail: aarnold@arbuco.com.

ARNOLD, BARBARA EILEEN, state legislator; b. North Adams, Mass., Aug. 3, 1924; d. Lester Flemming and Sarah (Van Hagen) Smith; m. William E. Arnold, Dec. 5, 1946; children: Wynn, Jeffrey, Gayle, Christopher. BA in Psychology, U. Mass.; postgrad., Keene State Coll. Spl. edn. tchr. Easter Seal Rehab. Ctr., Manchester, NH, 1967-74; state legislator NH, 1982-95; Rep. floor leader Ho. of Reps., 1989-95; mem. N.H. Coun. Vocat. Tech. Edn., 1986-95, State and Fed. Rels. Commn.; chmn. Manchester Rep. Del.; comm. chmn. Wayn Means, 1992—95. Sec. N.E. State Coun. Vocat. Edn.; mem. adv. bd. Greater Manchester Federated Women's Club; adv. bd. edn. N.H. Dept. Corrections; mem. adv. coun. adult rehab. Easter Seal Soc., NH, 1990—; state adv. com. Vocat. Child Care Programs, 1993—95; mem. com. for children, families, social svcs. Nat. Conf. of State Legislatures; bd. registration City of Manchester, 1999—; Manchester chmn. Dole for Pres. campaign, 1995, Gov. Judd Gregg for U.S. Senate, 1992; chair Manchester Rep. Com., 1993—95, George W. Bush for Pres., Manchester, 1999; chmn. Manchester Rep. Com., 1992—95; chmn. Manchester Sen. John E. Sununu Campaign, 2002; past mem. vestry, registered lay leader, mem. diocesan commn., del. gen. conv. Episcopal Ch.; bd. dirs. ARC, 1975—96, chmn. bd. dirs., 1977—80. Mem. Nat. Order Women Legislators, Nat. Fedn. Rep. Women, N.H. Kappa Kappa Gamma Alumni Assn. (pres. 1990-91). Address: 374 Pickering St Manchester NH 03104-2744

ARNOLD, BARRY RAYNOR, philosophy educator, medical ethicist, minister, counselor; b. Mooresville, N.C., Sept. 29, 1951; s. Adrian Leicester and Cleo Agnes (Fisher) A.; m. Margaret Elizabeth Morelock, Aug. 15, 1984. AB cum laude, Davidson Coll., 1973; MDiv magna cum laude, Emory U., 1976, PhD, 1986. Ordained to ministry Presbyn. Ch.; cert. Christian clin. counselor Am. Counseling Assn.; lic. mental health counselor, Ind. Min. various parishes, Ga., Fla., 1976—; instr. religion, assoc. chaplain The Lovett Sch., 1980-82; prof. Andrew Coll., Cuthbert, Ga., 1983-84; asst. prof. to prof. and honors prof. U. West Fla., Pensacola, 1986—2002, acting chmn. dept. philosophy/religion, 1997—, chmn. dept. interdisciplinary humanities, philosophy, relig., 2000—, exec. dir. Univ. Office for Applied Ethics, 2000—, joint prof. biology and philosophy divsn. life and health scis., 2003—; prof. Bioethics and Philosophy, dir. Ctr. for Health Care Ethics U. West Fla./Sacred Heart Hosp., Pensacola, 2003—, dir. Ctr. for Health Care Ethics, 2003—; pvt. practice clin. counseling, Pace, Fla., 1996—. Counselor Pace Counseling Ctr., 1996-97; spkr. in field. Author: The Pursuit of Virtue, 1989; editor: Essays in American Ethics, 1992; gen. editor (11 vols.) The Reshaping of Psychoanalysis, 1992-2002; assoc. editor Explorations: Jour. Adventurous Thought, 1999—; contbr. articles to profl. jours. Bd. dirs. Sacred Heart Hosp., Pensacola, Bapt. Hosp.; pres., bd. dirs. Assn. for Retarded Citizens, Albany, Ga., 1978—79; bioethicist, bd. dirs. West Fla. Regional Med. Ctr., Pensacola, 1990—2003, Bapt. Hosp., 2003—, Sacred Heart Hosp., 2003—. Recipient Disting. Tchg. award UWF and Fla. State Legislature, 1988, 90, 95; Award for Disting. Contbn., Honors Program UWF, 2002; fellow Rice U., 1973-75, Emory U., 1975-76, 79-82, U. Glasgow, 1976. Fellow: Am. Coll. Counselors (cert. Christian clin. counselor, chair examiners for cert.), Am. Assn. Integrative Medicine (diplomate, nat. bd. dirs., chair nat. bd. 2002—03), Am. Bd. Child Mental Health Providers; mem.: ACA, Assn. for Cognitive Behavioral Therapists (cert. cognitive forensic therapist, cert. anxiety disorders specialist), So. Soc. Philosophy and Psychology, Am. Acad. Religion, Internat. Thomas Merton Soc., Rotary (sgt.-at-arms 1982—83), Phi Beta Kappa, A£D (hon.), Alpha Epsilon Delta, Phi Kappa Phi (sec. 1988). Democrat. Avocations: antique cards, antique cars, birdwatching. Home: 5820 Kirkland Dr Milton FL 32570-8251 Office: Univ West Fla 11000 University Pkwy Pensacola FL 32514-5750 E-mail: barnold@uwf.edu.

ARNOLD, CECIL BENJAMIN, former small business owner; b. Bryantsville, Ky., Jan. 23, 1927; s. Walter Tribble and Ella Mae (Hagan) A.; m. Billie Jean Watkins, July 25, 1947; children: Mary Adrianne Davis, Cecil Benjamin Jr. Student, Heidelburg (Fed. Republic of Germany), 1945. Farmer, Lancaster, Ky., 1947-50; grocery store owner, 1950-54; ins. agt. Commonwealth Life Ins., Lancaster, Ky., 1954-57; pres. Cecil Arnold Real Estate, Lancaster, Ky., 1957—; agt. Arnold & Boone Ins., Lancaster, Ky., 1957-81; owner Arnold's Furniture, Inc., Lancaster, Ky., 1971-90; ret., 1992. Chmn. Lancaster-Garrard Indsl. Authority, 1993—, ret. 2000. Pres. Lancaster-Garrard Indsl. Devel., 1984-90; mem. Exec. Com. Dem. Orgn., Lancaster, 1965-75; bd. dirs. Ky. Ins. Guaranty Bd., 1972-75; mem. Ky. legis. rsch. com. for revision of Commonwealth of Ky. Ins. Law, 1969-70; dir. Garrard County Habitat for Humanity, Lancaster, Ky., 1995-99. Served with U.S. Army, 1945-47, ETO. Mem. Nat. Assn. Realtors, Ky. Assn. Realtors, Ky. Assn. Profl. Ins. Agts. (pres. 1968-69, bd. dirs. 1963-72, Mr. Chmn. award 1970, Mr. Profl. Agt. 1972, Profl. Agt. of Yr. 1975-76), Nat. Assn. Profl. Ins. Agts. (bd. dirs. 1972-80, v.p. 1979-80, Profl. Agt. of Yr. 1976-77), Dix River Bd. Realtors (pres. 1972), Nat. and Ky. Assn. Auctioneers, Lancaster-Garrard C. of C. (pres. 1966-68), Ky. Ins. Dept. (Ins. Svc. award 1969, 73; Special Recognition award 1975), Rotary (pres. 1966-68). Democrat. United Methodist. Avocations: basketball, golf, genealogy. Home: 1015 Danville Rd Lancaster KY 40444-2019 E-mail: c.b.arnold@worldnet.att.net.

ARNOLD, CHARLES BURLE, JR., psychiatrist, writer; b. Seattle, Aug. 13, 1934; s. Charles Burle and Ruth Helene (Hadley) A.; m. Sarah J. Slagle, Dec. 16, 1972; children: Geoffrey, Christopher, Jonathan. BS cum laude, U. Puget Sound, 1956; MD, CM, McGill U., 1960; MPH, U. N.C., 1965. Diplomate: Am. Bd. Preventive Medicine. Intern U. Wash. Hosp., Seattle, 1960-61, resident, 1961; physician Peace Corps, Bolivia, Washington, 1961-64; asst. prof. health adminstrn., assoc. Carolina Population Center, U. N.C., Chapel Hill, 1965-69; asst. prof. Albert Einstein Coll. Medicine, Bronx, N.Y., 1969-72; prof. public adminstrn. and clin. assoc. prof. preventive medicine NYU, N.Y.C., 1972-83, adj. prof. pub. adminstrn., 1983—; med. dir., med. rels. Met. Life Ins. Co., 1983-91, v.p. med. rels., 1991-93; psychiat. resident North Shore Univ. Hosp., Manhasset, N.Y., 1993-96, chief resident, 1995-96; pvt. practice of psychiatry, 1996-99; attending psychiatrist Augusta (Maine) Mental Health Inst., 1999—2002. Lectr. cmty. health Mt. Sinai Med. Sch., N.Y.C.; lectr. preventive medicine Downstate Med. Soc., SUNY, 1986-92; dir. Mahoney Inst. Health Maintenance, Am. Health Found., 1975-83, v.p. rsch., 1978-83, cons., 1983-86; chair Hitchcock Weekday Sch. Bd., 1986-92; chmn. Worksite Smoking subcom. N.Y. State Commn. on Smoking or Health, 1991-93; psychiatrist Drop-In Ctr., Ctr. Urban Cmty. Svcs., West Harlem, 1996-98; asst. attending psychiatrist N.Y. Presbyn. Hosp. Westchester Divsn.; dir. Open Arms Clinic; asst. clin. prof. psychiatry Cornell Med. Coll., 1998-2000. Editor, mem. exec. coun.: Transactions of Am. Acad. Ins. Medicine, 1988-93; assoc. editor Preventive Medicine Jour., 1975-83, sr. assoc. editor, 1983-85; editor Advances in Disease Prevention, 1981-83; editor-in-chief Statis. Bull., 1983-93; contbr. articles to profl. jours. Milbank Faculty fellow, 1967-74; OEO grantee, 1968-74; Population Council grantee, 1971-75; Health Research Council N.Y.C. grantee, 1972-75; Nat. Cancer Inst. grantee, 1975-83; Nat. Heart, Lung and Blood Inst. grantee, 1977-83; HEW Office Health Promotion grantee, 1978-80 Fellow Am. Coll. Preventive Medicine (pres. 1977-78); mem. N.Y. Acad. Medicine (com. on pub. health 1988—, vice chmn. 1992, chmn. 1993), Health Ins. Assn. Am. (chair com. on prevention and pub. health policy 1989-92). Home: PO Box 479 Topsham ME 04086-0479

ARNOLD, CRAIG ANTHONY (TONY ARNOLD), law educator; b. Montreal, Que., Can., May 22, 1965; came to U.S., 1968; s. Lloyd Edison and Shirley Ann (Gossett) A.; m. Donna Jean Higdon, June 17, 2000. BA with highest distinction, U. Kans., 1987; JD with distinction, Stanford U., 1990. Bar: Mo. 1990, U.S. Ct. Appeals (10th cir.) 1990, Tex. 1992, U.S. Dist. Ct. (we. dist.) Tex. 1992, U.S. Ct. Appeals (5th cir.) 1993. Law clk. to James K. Logan, U.S. Ct. Appeals for 10th Cir., Olathe, Kans., 1990-91; assoc. Matthews & Branscomb, P.C., San Antonio, 1991-95; vis. prof. U. P.R. Sch. of Law, 1995; tchg. fellow Stanford Law Sch., 1995-96; from asst. prof. Law Sch. to prof. Chapman U., Orange, Calif., 1996—2002, prof., 2002—; dir. Ctr. for Land Resources, 1999—; E. George Rudolph disting. vis. prof. law U. Wyo. Coll. Law, 2003. Adj. faculty Trinity U., 1995. Co-author: Beyond Litigation: Case Studies in Water Rights Disputes, 2002; exec. editor (jour.) Stanford Law and Policy Rev., 1988—90; contbr. articles to profl. jours. Organizer, chmn. Jefferson Bicentennial Meeting on Constn., Lawrence, Kans., 1987; mem. Willie Velasquez Book Fund Com., San Antonio, 1992; ordained deacon First Presbyn. Ch., San Antonio, 1994-95, worship leader, 1994-95, strategic planning com., 1994-95, leader classes and Bible studies, 1992-95; co-leader, participant Mission trips to Mex. and Kenya; bd. dirs. Good Samaritan Ctr.; bd. dirs. Fedn. Ecuménica Fe y Accion, San Antonio, 1992-95, Lawyers Com. for Civil Rights Immigrant and Refugee Rights Project, 1993-95; adv. bd. careers in law program North Orange County Regional Occupl. Program, 1998-99; adv. bd. Raymond Nichols League of Former Student Leaders, U. Kans., 1999—; commr. City of Anaheim Planning Commn., 1999—2002, chmn., 2001-2002; ordained elder Trinity United Presbyn. Ch., 2001—. Recipient Time Mag. Achievement award, Prof. of Yr. award Student Bar Assn., 2000; Harry S Truman scholar Truman Scholarship Found., 1985; Rosemary Ginn fellow Mortar Board Nat. Found., 1987; Hagman conf. scholar UCLA Land Use Law and Planning Conf. Mem. ABA, State Bar Tex. (Pro Bono Coll.), Phi Beta Kappa. Avocations: hiking, running, horseback riding, basketball. E-mail: caarnold@chapman.edu.

ARNOLD, DALE ROBERT, farm bureau association executive; b. Mt Vernon, Ohio, Dec. 20, 1959; s. James Francis and Diana Marie (Cornell) A.; m. Lori Ann Fisher, June 5, 1982; children: Mallory, MacKenzie, Madison. BS in Comm., Ohio Dominican U., 1982. Tchr. St. Francis De Sales H.S., Columbus, Ohio, 1982-85; orgn. dir. Ohio Farm Bur. Fedn., Columbus, 1985-89, dir. adult edn., 1989-92, regional supr., 1992-95, dir. commodity and mktg. info., 1995-98—; exec. dir. Ohio Land Improvement Assn., 1995—, Ohio Christmas Tree Assn., 1999—. Bd. dir. Energy Svcs.; mem. adv. bd. People's Travel Svc., Inc., Columbus, 1989-92, Ohio Biotech. Devel., 1989-92, Am. Elec. Power, Ohio, 1999; mem. adv. bd. customer choice program devel., Columbia Gas of Ohio, 1997—; mem. pub. benefits adv. bd. Ohio Dept. Devel., 2002, mem. Ohio Biomass Task Force, 2002; mem. consumer choice bd. Vectron Energy Delivery of Ohio, 2002--; bd. dirs. Green Energy of Ohio. Contbr. articles to Buckeye Farm News, 1989-92. Cub, den, pack master, Boy Scouts of Am., St. Francis Coun., Newark, Ohio, 1995—. Democrat. Roman Catholic. Office: Ohio Farm Bur 2 Nationwide Plz Columbus OH 43218-2383

ARNOLD, DAVID ALAN, surgeon; b. Sioux City, Iowa, Apr. 10, 1946; s. Allen and Mary Jean (Harjehausen) A.; m. Lana Beth Carlson, Sept. 11, 1971; children: Chad, Carl, Wade, Craig. BS, Morningside Coll., 1968; DO, Kirksville Coll. Osteo. Med., 1972. Diplomate Am. Bd. Osteo. Surgeons, Am. Bd. Hyperbaric Medicine. Intern Osteo. Hosp. of Maine, Portland, 1972-73; emergency rm. physician Bridgton (Mass.) Community Hosp., 1973; sr. med. officer Naval Air Sta., S. Weymouth, Mass., 1974-76, sr. flight surgeon, 1974-76; resident Des Moines (Iowa) Gen. Hosp., 1976-80; pvt. practice gen. surgery Davenport, Iowa, 1980—; med. dir. Trinity Ctr. for Wound Care and Hyperbaric Medicine, Davenport, Iowa, 1995—; chmn. dept. surgery Davenport Med. Ctr., 1996; chief staff Trinity Med. Ctr., Davenport, 2000. AMCCOM flight surgeon Rock Island (Ill.) Arsenal, 1986; founder Midwest Hernia Inst., Davenport, 1980—. Capt. USNR, 1990-91, Desert Shield/Desert Storm. Decorated Commendation medal Iowa Nat. Guard, Meritorious Svc. medal; named Flight Surgon of Yr., U.S. Army, 1984. Fellow Am. Coll. Osteo. Surgeons; mem. AMA, Am. Osteo. Assn., Iowa Med. Soc., Scott County Osteo. Soc., Scott County Med. Soc. Avocations: hunting, fishing, camping, backpacking, cross country skiing. Office: 1351 W Central Park Ave Ste 430 Davenport IA 52804-1854 also: Trinity Ctr Wound Care & Hyperbaric Med 3801 N Marquette St Davenport IA 52806-5538 E-mail: info@davidarnaldo.com.

ARNOLD, DAVID JOHN, marketing educator, consultant; b. Hornchurch, Essex, Eng., Dec. 26, 1955; came to U.S., 1992; s. Albert Edward and Margaret Ann Arnold; m. Megan Eileen Brown, Sept. 9, 1978; children: Katherine, Thomas. BA, U. London, 1978; MBA, City U., London, 1988; DBA, Harvard U., 1996. Editor, mktg. mgr. Mitchell Beazley, London, 1978-83; program dir. Ashridge Mgmt. Coll., Berkhamsted, Eng., 1983-92; prof. mktg. Harvard Bus. Sch., Boston, 1996—. Author: The Handbook of Brand Management, 1992. Office: Harvard Bus Sch Morgan Hall Soldiers Fld Boston MA 02163-1317 E-mail: darnold@hbs.edu.

ARNOLD, DEBORRAH ANN, human services director; b. Elkins, W.Va., June 1, 1950; d. Lawrence Arnold and Sybil Dumire. ADN, Broome Community Coll., 1977; BSN, MSN, SUNY, Syracuse, 1987. Cert. clin. nurse specialist. Community health nurse Broome County Health Dept., Binghamton, N.Y., 1977-81, supr. home health aides, 1981-82, coord. employee health svcs., 1982-86; dir. profl. svcs. Kimberly Quality Care, Binghamton, N.Y., 1987-91, div. dir. clin. svcs. Vestal, N.Y., 1991-93; quality assurance mgr. Olsten Kimberly Quality Care, Vestal, N.Y., 1993-96; clin. ops. edn. specialist Olsten Health Svcs., Endicott, N.Y., 1996-97, clin. ops. specialist, 1997-99; third party liability specialist Gentiva Health Svcs., 2000—.

ARNOLD, DONALD SMITH, chemical engineer, consultant; b. Cuyahoga Falls, Ohio, Sept. 14, 1920; s. Elton Dewey and Esther Anna (Schmid) A.; m. Eleanor Ann Webster, July 9, 1944; children: Ann A., Jane D., Elaine S., Dale F., David W., Douglas E. BSChemE, Ohio State U., 1942, MSChemE, 1947, PhD in Chem. Engring., 1949. Profl. engr., Ohio, Calif., Okla. Asst. prof., instr. dept. chem. engring. N.C. State U., Raleigh, 1947-53; head chem. dept. Nat. Lead Co. of Ohio, Fernald, 1953-59; head high energy fuels sect. Am. Potash & Chem. Corp., Henderson, Nev., 1959, mgr. Trona rsch. Trona, Calif., 1959-67, dir. cen. engring. L.A., 1967-69; from engring. specialist to sr. tech.

advisor Kerr-McGee Corp., Oklahoma City, 1969-91; pvt. cons. Bethany, Okla., 1991—. Mem. tech. com. Fractionation Rsch. Inc., 1981-84. Contbr. articles to profl. jours. Mem. County Svc. Area Com., Trona, Calif., 1960-62; assoc. advisor Explorer Post, Boy Scouts Am., Trona, 1960-64; mem. gen. coun. Washita Presbytery, Oklahoma City, 1979-80; mem. session Calvin Presbyn. Ch., 1998—, chmn. stewardship and missions com., 1999—; mem. budget and rev. com. Indian Nations Presbytery, 2001—. 2nd lt., 1st lt. US Army C.E., 1942-46, PTO, ETO. Named Disting. Alumnus Ohio State U. Coll. Engring., 1970. Fellow AIChE (Okla. trisectional meeting chmn. 1993, 95, com. mem. Design Inst. for Phys. Property Data, sect. vice-chmn 1998, sect. chmn. 1974, 99), Am. Inst. Chemists; mem. AAAS, NSPE, Am. Chem. Soc. (sect. chmn. 1962, 86), Am. Inst. Mining and Metall. Engrs., Am. Soc. for Engring. Edn., Okla. Soc. Profl. Engrs., Metall. Soc., Armed Forces Def. Preparedness Assn., Assn. Ind. Info. Profls., Nat. Def. Indsl. Assn., Sigma Xi, Tau Beta Pi, Phi Lambda Upsilon.. Achievements include patent in field. Home and Office: 2005 N Briarcliff Ave Bethany OK 73008-5656

ARNOLD, DONNA F. business educator; b. Charlotte, N.C., Aug. 16, 1947; d. Billy Lewis and Lily Frances (Wentz) Ferguson; m. Harvey Eugene Arnold, Feb. 3, 1979; 1 child, Sherry Lynne. BS in Fin., Fla. State U., 1982, MBA, 1983, postgrad. Fin. cons. Ferguson Acctg., Ft. Pierce, Fla., 1982-83; account exec., broker Merrill Lynch, Ft. Pierce, Fla., 1983-85; prof. Indian River C.C., Ft. Pierce, Fla., 1985—; endowed chair Fin. Mgmt., 2002—. Treas., bd. dirs. Treasure Coast Deaf Svc. Ctr., Port St. Lucie, Fla., 1993-96; mem. Jud. Nominating Com., Port St. Lucie, 1992-95. Mem. AAUP (pres. local chpt.), Delta Epsilon Chi (Advisor of Yr. 1997). Home: 8007 Plantation Lakes Dr Port Saint Lucie FL 34986-3014 Office: Indian River CC 3209 Virginia Ave Fort Pierce FL 34981-5541 E-mail: darnold@ircc.edu.

ARNOLD, DOUGLAS NORMAN, mathematician; b. N.Y.C., Apr. 30, 1954; s. Justin Bruce and Bernice Shirley (Goertzel) A.; m. Maria Carme Torrescassana Calderer, Aug. 3, 1985; 1 child, Clara Maria. BA, Brown U., 1975; MS, U. Chgo., 1976, PhD, 1979. Asst. prof. math. Dept. Math. U. Md., College Park, 1979-84, assoc. prof., 1984-89, prof., 1989-90; prof. math. Pa. State U., University Park, 1989-95, disting. prof. math., 1995—2001; dir. inst. math. and applications U. Minn., 2001—, prof. math, 2001—. Contbr. numerous articles to profl. jours. NATO fellow, 1982-83; NSF rsch. grantee, 1981—; recipient 1st Internat. Sacchi-Landriani prize, Acad. Scis. & Letters, Lombardy Inst.,1990. Mem. Am. Math. Soc., Soc. for Indsl. and Applied Math., Internat. Soc. for Interaction Mechanics and Math., Phi Beta Kappa, Sigma Xi. Home: 12120 54th Ave N Minneapolis MN 55442-1847 Office: Inst Math and Its Applications Univ Minn 400 Lind Hall 207 Church St SE Minneapolis MN 55455

ARNOLD, ELIZABETH BROWN, poet, educator; b. Jacksonville, Fla., June 5, 1958; d. William Edwin Jr. and Barbara (Horne) A BA, Oberlin Coll., 1981; MA in English, U. Chgo., 1984, PhD in English, 1990; MFA in Poetry, Warren Wilson Coll., Asheville, N.C., 1996. Vis. prof. U. Mont., Missoula, 1989-90; adj. prof. U. North Fla., Jacksonville, 1992-93; fellow in poetry Yaddo, Saratoga Springs, N.Y., 1995; Lannon fellow in poetry Fine Arts Work Ctr., Provincetown, Mass., 1997-98; tchg. fellow Warren Wilson Coll., Asheville, 1998-99; Bunting fellow in poetry Radcliffe Inst. Advanced Study, Cambridge, Mass., 1999-01; asst. prof. poetry U. Md., College Park, 2001—. Robert Frost fellow in poetry Breadloaf Writers Conf., 2002. Editor (novel) Insel (by Mina Loy), 1991; author: (book of poetry) The Reef, 1999. Recipient WhitingWriters award, 2002—03; fellow, Bread Loaf Writers Conf. Mem. Associated Writing Programs, Poetry Soc. Am. Home: # 203 1811 Vernon St NW Washington DC 20009

ARNOLD, ELLEN HOLT, continuing care retirement community administrator; b. Jamestown, N.Y., Jan. 3, 1943; d. Everett W. and Segrid Lindbeck Holt; m. Richard B. Arnold, June 20, 1964; children: Catherine Arnold Mayone, Barbara Arnold Potena. BA in Econs./Math., Bucknell U., 1964. Cert. fund raising exec. Blood svc. coord. ARC, Williamsport, Pa., 1978-82, exec. dir., 1982-84, Allied Arts Fund, Harrisburg, Pa., 1984-88; dir. annual giving Lebanon Valley Coll., Annville, Pa., 1988-91, dir. devel., 1991-97; v.p. devel. The Brethren Home Fedn., New Oxford, Pa., 1997-99, v.p. instnl. adv., 1999—. Bd. dirs. Penn Laurel Girl Scout Coun., 2002—. Recipient Hemlock award Hemlock Girl Scout Coun., 1991, Cmty. Svc. award Pine Run Grange, 1979; named Amb. of Yr. Lebanon C. of C., 1991. Mem.: Nat. Com. Planned Giving, Assn. Health Care Philanthropy, Nat. Soc. Fundraising Execs. (chair CEU rev. bd. 1996—2000, bd. dirs. ctrl. Pa. chpt., pres. 1993—94, v.p. 1991—92, treas. 1987—90, Fundraiser of Yr. 2000), Hanover Area C. of C. (human svc. com. 1997—), Kiwanis (Pa. Kiwanis Fdn., club pres. 1999—2000, lt. gov. Pa. divsn. 13S 2001—02). Avocations: travel, reading, needlework. Office: Brethren Home Found PO Box 128 2990 Carlisle Pike New Oxford PA 17350-9582

ARNOLD, ELLIOTT O. (BILL ARNOLD), secondary school educator; b. Oregon City, Oreg., Sept. 19, 1945; s. Curtis Frank Arnold and Margaret Louise (Miller) Olson; m. Sharon Lee Owens, July 19, 1945; children: Curtis Edgar, John Paul. BA, Ouachita Baptist U., Arkadelphia, Ark., 1967; BS in Edn., U. Ark., Fayetville, 1969; M in Guidance and Counseling, U. Ark., Little Rock, 2003. Nat. cert. tchr. elem., secondary Ark. H.S. tchr., coach McCall Sch. Sr. H.S., Tallulah, La., 1970—75; tchr. math., sci. Strong Jr. H.S., Marianna, Ark., 1980; tchr., counselor, K-12 De Vall's (Ark.) Bluff, 1981—. Pres. U.S Jaycees, Madison Parish, La. Petty officer USNR, 1960—63. Named Ark. Young Republican, 4th Cong. Dist. Rep. Orgn., 1962; recipient Speaking award, Nevada Jaycees, Carlin, Nev., 1970. Mem.: VFW, Am. Legion, Kiwanis Internat. (pres. 1980—85). Avocations: fishing, golf, sports, coaching youth. Home: PO Box192 De Valls Bluff AR 72041 Office: DeVall's Bluff Pub Schs Ash & Sycamore 70E De Valls Bluff AR 72041 Home Fax: 870-998-7195. E-mail: earnold868@aol.com.

ARNOLD, ERIC DANIELL, budget analyst, security supervisor; b. Raleigh, N.C., Sept. 12, 1970; s. Earl Marvin Dunston and Mary Ann Arnold-Dunston; 1 child, Aarica. BA, N.C. Ctrl. U., Durham, 1993; MPA, N.C. Ctrl. U., 1998. Sr. materials/receiving clk. OMG Ams., Inc., Research Triangle Park, N.C., 1993-99; budget analyst Office Mgmt. and Budget City Hall, Kansas City, Mo., 1999—; security supr. mid-Atlantic region Guardsmark Security, 2002—. Vol. David Price for Congress campaign, Cary, N.C., 1998; vol. intern Register of Deeds, Durham, 1991-92. Grad. Students Assn. scholar, 1998. Mem. Am. Soc. Pub. Adminstrn., Nat. Contract Mgmt. Assn. (scholar 1998), Internat. City/County Mgmt. Assn., Doric Lodge #28, Kappa Alpha Psi, Phi Alpha Alpha. Democrat. Baptist. Avocations: singing, basketball, running, bowling, mentoring. Office: Sprint c/o Guardsmark Security 14111 Capital Blvd Wake Forest NC 27587 E-mail: earnold47@hotmail.com.

ARNOLD, ERNEST WOODROW, minister; b. White Springs, Fla., Mar. 20, 1914; s. Turner Benjamin and Frances Essie (Wise) A.; m. Mildred Virginia Thomas, Jan. 26, 1945; children: Ernest Woodrow Jr., Cheryl Ruth Arnold Daves. BA magna cum laude, Furman U., 1943; BD, New Orleans Bapt. Theol. Sem., 1948; ThD, Luther Rice Sem., 1965. Ordained to ministry So. Bapt. Conv., 1942. Pastor East Pk. Bapt. Ch., Greenville, S.C., 1950-54, Brentwood Bapt. Ch., Charleston, S.C., 1955-58, Bethel Bapt. Ch., Shelby, N.C., 1958-72, Catawba Bapt. Ch., Rock Hill, S.C., 1972-75, 1st Bapt. Ch., Bostic, N.C., 1975-81, Lily Meml. Bapt. Ch., Shelby, 1987—. Mem. faculty Luther Rice Sem., 1968-76. Author: Truth: Tried and Tested, 1996. With USMC, 1934-38. Recipient commendation USMC, 1935; New Orleans Bapt. Theol. Sem. fellow, 1948-50. Home: 117 Ken Daves Rd PO Box 715 Boiling Springs NC 28017-0715 E-mail: Gospel@connectu.net. *Life can be a circle or it can be a line of movement to never ending joy and peace, accompanied by achievement, fulfillment and faith in God, the Eternal One.*

ARNOLD, FRED ENGLISH, lawyer; b. Mexico, Mo., May 10, 1938; s. Charles P. and Mary E. (Blackman) A.; m. Dorothy P. Offutt, Dec. 31, 1966 (div. Aug. 2002); children: Jane E., Charles P. III, Susan J. AB, Harvard U., 1960, LLB, 1963. Bar: Mo. 1963, U.S. Dist. Ct. (ea. dist.) Mo. 1964, U.S. Supreme Ct. 1966. Assoc. Thompson Coburn LLP, St. Louis, 1964-70, ptnr., 1971—. Trustee KETC/Channel 9, 2002—. Trustee Mary Inst., St. Louis, 1981-87, v.p., 1985-86; bd. dirs. Repertory Theatre of St. Louis, 1982-88; bd. dirs. Whitfield Sch., St. Louis, 1990-96, pres., 1991-93, Arts & Edn. Coun. Greater St. Louis, 1991-97, vice chmn., 1996-97; adv. com. Jordan Charitable Found., St. Louis, 1975—; bd. curators Ctrl. Meth. Coll., Fayette, Mo., 1997—. Mem. ABA, Am. Coll. Real Estate Lawyers, Noonday Club, (bd. govs. 2003—), The Racquet Club. Democrat. Methodist. Home: 750 S Hanley Rd Unit 190 Saint Louis MO 63105 Office: Thompson Coburn LLP One US Bank Plz Saint Louis MO 63101-1693 E-mail: farnold@thompsoncoburn.com.

ARNOLD, G. DEWEY, JR., accountant; b. Montgomery, Ala., Jan. 30, 1925; s. G. Dewey and Janie Esther (Terry) A.; m. Dorothy Louise Wenger, Dec. 4, 1954; children: Susan O., G. Dewey III. BA in Econs, U. of South, 1949; postgrad. in acct., U. Tenn. C.P.A., Pa., D.C., Md. With Aladdin Industries, Inc., Nashville, 1949-50; with Price Waterhouse, 1950—, ptnr., 1961—; ptnr. in charge Washington office Price Waterhouse & Co., 1965-76, mem. policy com., 1975-80, regional mng. ptnr., 1976-85; exec. dir. Nat. Commn. on Fin. Fraud, 1985-87; sr. v.p. Audit-Intelsat., 1987—. Instr. acctg. Robert Morris Sch. Acctg., 1952-53; lectr., course dir. mgmt. acctg. Inst. Mexicano de Administracion de Negocias, A.C., 1958-64; bd. dirs. Washington Bd. Trade, 1973-75; mem. audit adv. com. Sec. Navy, 1972-75 Bd. dirs. Jr. C. of C., 1954-55; trustee Fed. City Coun., 1966—; bd. dirs. Greater Washington Ednl. TV Assn., Inc., 1970-82, Minority Contractors Ctr., 1972-74, Redskins Found., 1973—; D. C. Mcpl. Rsch. Bur., 1974-76, Wolf Trap Found., 1975-90; chmn. bd. trustees Landon Sch., 1974-79; vice chmn. D.C. Bicentennial Commn., 1971-75. Served with USNR, 1943-45. Mem. AICPA, D.C. Inst. CPAs, Nat. Assn. Accts., Md. Inst. CPAs, Am. Arbitration Assn., Chevy Chase Club, Burning Tree Club, Pine Valley Golf Club, Rolling Rock Club, John's Island Club. Office: Intelsat Global Svcs Corp Box 1B 3400 International Dr NW Washington DC 20008-3006 E-mail: dewey.arnold@intelsat.com.

ARNOLD, GARY HOWARD, film critic; b. Princeton, Ind., Aug. 22, 1942; s. Charles Howard and Ferris (Smith) A.; m. Sue Datz, Dec. 29, 1967; children—Pauline, Jane, Esther. Student, NYU, 1959-60, U. Calif., Berkeley, 1960-63. Film critic Diplomat mag., 1966; film critic, reporter Ind. Film Jour., 1968-69; film critic Washington Post, 1969-84; co-host weekly TV commentary show The Moviegoing Family, 1985-90; arts critic The Connection, Reston, Va., 1987-89; movie critic The Washington Times, Washington, 1989—. Home: 5133 1st St N Arlington VA 22203-1207 Office: The Washington Times 3600 New York Ave NE Washington DC 20002-1996 E-mail: gsarnold@erols.com.

ARNOLD, GEORGE LAWRENCE, retired advertising company executive; b. Kansas City, Mo., Sept. 30, 1942; s. James Robert and Mary Virginia (Ellington) A.; m. Mary Antoinette Turrin, Dec. 31, 1964; children: Margery, Matthew, Molly, Sara. BJ magna cum laude, U. Tex., 1965, MA cum laude, 1966. Advt. and pub. relations trainee Gen. Electric Co., Phila., 1966; advt. asst. Dallas Power & Light Co., 1967-70; dir. comm. Continuum Co. Inc., Austin, Tex., 1970-73; pres. Evans/Dallas Inc., Dallas, 1977-99; ret., 1999. Bd. dirs. Evans Group, Inc., Salt Lake City, operating com. Salt Lake City. Bd. dirs. United Way Met. Dallas, 1978, Lone Star council Camp Fire, Dallas, 1978-84. Recipient Silver Anvil award Pub. Relations Soc. Am., 1980, Gold Effie award Am. Mktg. Assn., 1981. Mem. Tex. Pub. Rels. Assn. (bd. dirs. 1978-80, 92-97, pres. 1998, Silver Spur award 1979, 85, 2003), Dallas Advt. League (pres. 1981). Democrat. Roman Catholic. Home: 912 Kneese Rd Fredericksburg TX 78624-7057

ARNOLD, GEORGIANNE LEE, pediatric geneticist, clinical researcher; d. George Luzerne and Helen Jane Arnold. MD, SUNY Health Sci. Ctr., Syracuse, 1982—86. Cert. Biochemical Genetics and Clinical Genetics Am. Bd. Med. Genetics, 1993, Pediatrics Am. Bd. Pediat., 1989. Asst. prof. pediat. U. Ark. Med. Sciences, Little Rock, 1991—94; assoc. prof. pediat. and genetics U. Rochester Sch. Medicine and Dentistry, NY, 1994—. Fellow: Am. Coll. Med. Genetics. Achievements include research in Clinical research in genetics and inborn errors of metabolism. Office: Univ Rochester Sch Medicine 601 Elmwood Dr Box 777 Rochester NY 14642

ARNOLD, GLORIA MALCOLM, artist, educator; b. Covington, Ga., July 16, 1945; d. George Clifford and Mildred Sarah (Johnson) Malcolm; m. John Edward Arnold, Feb. 12, 1966; 1 child, Troy Chandler Arnold. BS in Edn., U. Ga., 1966. Self-employed artist, tchr., Lee, Mass., 1984—. Executed mural Sweet Brook, 1990; contbr. Best Flower Painting 2, 1999, Best of Wildlife Art 2, 1999, Art of the Animal Kingdom Exhbn., 2000-01; contbr. articles to profl. publs. Mem. Lee Cultural Coun., 1990-98, 2000-01; v.p. Pittsfield (Mass) Art League, 1987-89. Recipient Silver medal Nat. Parks Acad. Arts, 1996, Top 100, 1999, 1st in Oils award Internat. Nature Fine Arts Competition, 1998, Purchase prize Colonie Art League Nat. Exhbn., Bennington Ctr. for the Arts, 2000; named to Top 200 Arts for the Pks., 2001, 02,03; named one of Women Artist of the West Fifth Juried Competition, Wy, 2003, Barns and Farms Nat. Juried Exhibition, Barnsite Art Studio and Gallery, WI, 2003 Fellow Am. Artists' Profl. League; mem. Oil Painters Am. (award of excellence 1997, signature mem.), Copley Soc. Boston, North Shore Arts Assn. (James G. Saunders Meml. award 1997), Acad. Artists Assn. (coun. mem.), Kent Art Assn. (v.p. 1994-96, bd. dirs. 1994-99). Internat. Exhibition on Animals in Art, Louisiana State U. Sch. of Veterinary Med., Baton Rouge, 2003.

ARNOLD, GORDON B. social science educator; b. 1954; married; 2 children. BA, Clark U., 1976; MLS, U. R.I., 1982; PhD, Boston Coll., 1994. Libr. Goodnow Libr., Sudbury, Mass., 1980-87; libr. dir. Montserrat Coll. Art, Beverly, Mass., 1987-91, asst. dean, 1989-94, assoc. dean, 1994-97, assoc. prof. social sci., 1994—2002, prof. liberal arts, 2002—. Rsch. assoc. New England Resource Ctr. Higher Edn., U. Mass., Boston, 1991-96; adj. rsch. assoc. Ctr. Policy Analysis U. Mass., Dartmouth, 1995-2000; adj. lectr. Boston Coll., Chestnut Hill, 1999-2001, 2003. Author: Politics of Faculty Unionization, 2000; contbg. author: Revitalizing General Education in a Time of Scarcity, 1997; co-author: (chpt.) Handbook of the Undergraduate Curriculum, 1996. Mem. Am. Polit. Sci. Assn., Am. Soc. Assn., Boston Coll. Alumni (higher edn. coun. 1998-2002). Office: 23 Essex St # 26 Beverly MA 01915-4508

ARNOLD, HANS RICHARD, neurosurgeon; b. Nordhausen, Germany, Apr. 12, 1938; s. Erich H. and Hildegard (Noack) A.; m. Heike Renken, Apr. 4, 1964; children: Rüdiger, Martin. MD, Med. Sch. Erfurt, 1960, Dr.med., 1965; PhD, Hamburg, 1982. Resident Erfurt, Germany, 1961-67, surgeon, 1967, neurosurgeon, 1970, Hamburg, Germany, 1973-86; head of dept. U. Hosp., Lübeck, Germany, 1986—; pres. U. Luebeck, 1999—2002. Med. dir. U. Hosp. Luebeck, 1995-99. Contbr. articles to profl. jours. Mem. German Soc. Neurosurgery (pres. 1998-2000), German Neurosurg. Soc., Brazilian Neurosurg. Soc. (corr. mem.). Avocations: history, fine arts, chess. Office: Dept Neurosurgery Ratzeburger Allee 160 23538 Lübeck Germany

ARNOLD, HENRI, cartoonist; b. Bethlehem, Pa. s. Samuel Max and Dora (Schnur) A.; m. Harriet Chefetz, Feb. 14, 1980; children by previous marriage— Nora Sally, Ned Michael. Student, Cooper Union, 1946. Editorial/sports cartoonist Bridgeport (Conn.) Sun. Herald; cartoonist weekly humor page Chgo. Tribune, 1955-65; art dir. Chgo. Tribune-N.Y. News Syndicate, Inc., N.Y.C., 1957-77. Lectr. in field. Creator: This Man's Army, N.Y. Sun. News, 1954-64, Meet Mr. Luckey, N.Y. Daily News, 1991—; writer, cartoonist for Ching Chow, 1977—; producer Jumble, That Scrambled Word Game, 1960—; illustrator: The ABCs of Golf (by Tommy Armour), 63 vols. of Jumble, That Scrambled Word Game, 1962—, Super Jumble Puzzle Book, 1991, Jumble for Kids Book, 1992. Mem. Nat. Cartoonists Soc., Palm-Aire Country Club.

ARNOLD, J. KAREN, lawyer; b. Cleveland, Miss. B in Music Edn., James Madison U., 1969; M in Music, U. Cin., 1971; JD, U. Pitts., 1983. Bar: Pa. 1983, U.S. Dist. Ct. (we. dist.) Pa. 1983, Va. 1990, U.S. Supreme Ct. 1995, U.S. Dist. Ct. (mid. dist.) Pa. 1996; cert. Emergency Med. Technician, Pa. Music tchr. Russell Co. Pub. Schs., Lebanon, Va., 1971-72, Laurel (Del.) Pub. Schs., 1972-73, Pitts. Pub. Schs., 1973-77; paralegal Nernberg & Laffey, Pitts., 1977-80; pvt. practice Pitts., 1983-86; asst. pub. defender Centre County Pub. Defender's Office, Bellefonte, Pa., 1987-88; child abuse prosecutor Centre County Dist. Attys. Office, Bellefonte, 1988—. Arbitrator Allegheny County Ct. Common Plea, Pitts., 1984-87; spkr. Pa. Optometric Assn., Harrisburg, Pa., 1993; class presenter Pa. State U., State Coll., 1997—. Notes and comments editor U. Pitts. Law Rev., 1982-83. Vol. ambulance svc. B.E.M.S., Bellefonte, 1993—; vol. organist various chs., State Coll., 1990—. Full Performance scholar U. Cin., 1969-71. Mem. Nat. Dist. Atty. Assn., Pa. Dist. Attys. Assn., Pa. Bar Assn., Centre County Bar Assn., PDAI Child Abuse Prosecutors Coalition (facilitator trial adv. course 1994). Office: Centre County Dist Attys Office Fl 4 Courthouse Bellefonte PA 16823

ARNOLD, J. KELLEY, U.S. magistrate judge; b. Lewiston, Idaho, Oct. 3, 1937; m. Diane Louise Jenkins. Student, Wash. State U., 1955-58; LLB, U. Idaho, 1961. Bar: Wash. 1961. Dep. pros. atty. Pierce County, 1963-64; atty., 1965-82; judge Wash. Superior Ct. Pierce County, Tacoma, 1982-94; magistrate judge for western Wash., U.S. Dist. Ct., Tacoma, 1994—. With U.S. Army, 1961-63. Office: US Dist Ct 1717 Pacific Ave Rm 3409 Tacoma WA 98402-3234 E-mail: kelley_arnold@wawd.uscourts.gov.

ARNOLD, J(AMES) BARTO, III, marine archaeologist; b. San Antonio, Jan. 9, 1950; s. J. Barto Jr. and Wilnora (Barton) A.; children: Kathryn, Julia, Jessica. BA cum laude, U. Tex., 1971, MA, 1973. Rsch. asst. Tex. Archeol. Rsch. Lab. U. Tex., Austin, 1970-72; asst. state marine archaeologist Tex. Antiquities Com., Austin, 1972-75; state marine archaeologist Tex. Hist. Com., Austin, 1975-97; dir. Tex. ops. Inst. of Nautical Archaeology, Tex. A&M U., College Station, 1997—. Cons. NOAA, 1977-91, Nat. Trust Hist. Preservation, Washington, 1979-90, Congl. Office Tech. Assessment, Washington, 1986; mem. Md. Gov.'s Adv. Com. on Marine Archaeology, Annapolis, 1987-90; mem. history area com. nat. park sys. adv. bd. U.S. Dept. Interior, 1994-95; dir. La Salle Shipwreck Project, 1995-96, Confederate Blockade-Runner Denbigh Shipwreck Project, 1997—. Co-author: Nautical Archaeology of Padre Island, 1978, Documentary Sources for the Wreck of the New Spain Fleet of 1554, 1979 (Presidio La Bahaia 1979), others; Plenum series editor Underwater Archaeology, 1995—; contbr. articles to profl. jours. Recipient Achievement award for Hist. Preservation Dept. Interior, 1980. Mem. Soc. Profl. Archaeologists (cert.; sec.-treas. 1987-89, Spl. Achievement award 1990), Soc. Hist. Archaeology (pres. 1993), Tex. Archeol. Soc., Archaeol. Inst. Am., Explorers Club, Phi Beta Kappa. Methodist. Avocations: stamp collecting, science fiction. Office: Tex A&M U Inst Nautical Archaeology PO Drawer HG College Station TX 77841-5137 E-mail: barnold@tamu.edu.

ARNOLD, JAMES LEONARD, lawyer; b. Bronx, N.Y., Sept. 4, 1946; s. Leonard Anthony and Veronica Ann (Van Dien) A., (div.); children: David James, Katherine Marie. AB, Georgetown U., 1960, JD, U. Va., 1971. Vice pres., gen. counsel The Nat. Legal Research Group Inc., Charlottesville, Va., 1971-82, Hadron Inc., Fairfax, Va., 1982—, pres., chief exec. officer, 1990—. Mem. Am. Corp. Counsel Assn., Va. Bar, D.C. Bar, N.Y. Bar, Washington Met. Corp. Counsel Assn. Republican. Roman Catholic. Home: Quailsar Farm 1890 Calusa Ct Marco Island FL 34145-4207

ARNOLD, JAMES PHILLIP, religious studies educator, history educator; b. Greenville, S.C. s. David Lee and Vera Irene (Wilson) A. MA in Am. History, U. Houston, 1979; MA in Religious Studies, Rice U., 1984, PhD in Religious Studies, 1991. Instr. Am. History U. Houston, 1972-76; instr. religion Rice U., Houston, 1976-81; instr. ch. history, biblical studies, homiletics Houston Grad. Sch. Theology, 1984-86; instr. religion and history, exec. dir. The Reunion Inst., Houston, 1986—. Pres. Living History Studies, Inc., Houston, 1993—; counselor families divided by religious cult issues; advisor to FBI on Branch Davidian crisis, Waco, Tex., 1993, Freeman crisis, 1996. Dir. Fine Arts Found., Houston, 1987—; founder Religion-Crisis Task Force, 1994. Rice U. fellow, 1980-91, U. Houston fellow, 1972-76; Tex. Com. for Humanities grantee, 1979. Mem. Am. Acad. Religion, Soc. Biblical Lit. Avocations: air-hockey, archaeology. Office: Reunion Inst 5508 Chaucer Dr Houston TX 77005-2632 E-mail: reunion@blk.box.com.

ARNOLD, JAMES RICHARD, chemist, educator; b. New Brunswick, N.J., May 5, 1923; s. Abraham Samuel and Julia (Jacobs) A.; m. Louise Clark, Oct. 11, 1952; children: Robert C., Theodore J., Kenneth C. AB, Princeton U., 1943, MA, 1945, PhD, 1946. Fellow Inst. Nuclear Studies, U. Chgo., 1946-47, faculty, 1948-55; NRC fellow Harvard U., 1947-48; faculty chemistry Princeton U., 1955-58; assoc. prof. chemistry U. Calif., San Diego, 1958-60, prof., 1960-92, Harold C. Urey prof., 1983-92, chmn. dept. chemistry, 1960-63. Assoc. Manhattan Project, 1943-46; dir. Calif. Space Inst., 1980-89, interim dir., 1996-97; prin. investigator Calif. Space Grant Consortium, 1989—; mem. various bds. NASA, 1959—; space sci. bd. NAS, 1970-74, com. on sci. and pub. policy, 1970-77. Mem. editl. bd. Ann. Rev. Nuclear Chemistry, 1972, Revs. Geophysics and Space Physics, 1972-75, Moon, 1972—; contbr. articles to profl. jours. Pres. Torrey Pines Elem. Sch. PTA, 1964-65; pres. La Jolla Democratic Club, 1965-66; nat. council World Federalists-U.S.A., 1970-72. Recipient E.O. Lawrence medal AEC, 1968, Leonard medal Meteoritical Soc., 1976, Kuiper award Am. Astron. Soc., 1993; asteroid 2143 named Jimarnold in his honor, 1980; Guggenheim fellow, India, 1972-73. Mem. Nat. Acad. Sci., Am. Acad. Arts and Scis., Internat. Acad. Astronautics, Am. Chem. Soc., AAAS, Fedn. Am. Scientists, World Federalist Assn. Office: U Calif San Diego Dept Chemistry Code 0524 La Jolla CA 92093 E-mail: jarnold@ucsd.edu.

ARNOLD, JANET NINA, health care consultant; b. Poughkeepsie, N.Y., Apr. 23, 1933; d. Paul Dudley and Pauline Katherine (Board) Bartram; m. Robert William Arnold, Dec. 19, 1954; children: Paul Dudley, Janet Elizabeth. AB cum laude, Vassar Coll., 1955; postgrad. Sch. Med. Tech., Albany Med. Coll., 1955-56; MS in Microbiology cum laude, Vassar Coll., 1963; MHSM, Webster Coll., 1981. Rsch. asst., med. technologist H. Aird Boswell, M.D., Troy, NY, 1956-59; tchg. supr., adminstrv. cons. Vassar Bros. Hosp., Poughkeepsie, 1959-69; adv. to med. lab., lectr. med. mycology Vassar Coll., Poughkeepsie, 1961-66; asst. adminstr., lab. mgr. Boulder (Colo.) Meml. Hosp., 1975-80; cons. hosp. planning Mercy Med. Ctr., Denver, 1981-82; clin. lab. dir./adminstr. Humana, Denver, 1982-85, cons. health care mgmt., 1982-85, MRI, 1985—. Ptnr., 1988; cons. health care mgmt. Humana, Inc., 1982-96, Columbia/HCA Health Sys., 1992-96; pres. Arnold and Assocs., 1988—; ptnr. InterExec (divsn. MRI), 1994—; acad./adminstrv. cons. U. Guam, Vassar Coll., Boulder Cmty. Hosp., Humana Int., 1990-97, others; adj. faculty Vassar Coll.; sec., bd. dirs. Sanitas Fed. Credit Union, 1977-78, pres., 1979-82; teaching fellow Vassar Coll., 1961-63, unrestricted fund chmn., 1989-96, co-chair major gifts, 2002—. Assoc. editor Am. Jour. Med. Tech., 1980-88; contbr. articles to profl. jours. Contbr. NMC, 1988-92. NSF rsch. fellow, 1960-62. Mem. Am. Acad. Microbiology, Soc. for Gen. Microbiology, Am. Soc. Med. Technologists, Colo. Pub. Health Assn., Soc. Women Environ. Profls., Med. Mycological Soc. of the Ams. Republican. Episcopalian. Home: 4195 Chippewa Dr Boulder CO 80303-3610

ARNOLD, JAY, retired engineering executive, educator; b. Balt., Jan. 1, 1936; s. Otto Joseph and Margaret (Flannery) A.; m. Harriet Mary Metzbower, July 4, 1959; children: Kelly Marie Arnold Wood, Philip Driscoll Arnold, Michael Flannery Arnold. Student, Yale U., 1958—59; BS, Loyola Coll., Balt., 1965; MBA, Loyola Coll., Potomac, Md., 1977; postgrad., George Washington U., 1980-81, Berlitz Inst., Washington, 1987-90, U. So. Fla., 1994-95. With real times sys. IBM, Kingston, NY, 1962—64, Washington, 1964—65, software and systems engring. positions including mgt. NASA's Manned Space Program Houston, 1965—68; with FAA's Air Traffic Control, Atlantic City, 1968—73, FSD Advanced Tech., Bethesda, Md., 1973—78; vis. IBM prof. Morgan State U., Balt., 1978—79; planner of automation strategy Fed. Systems div. IBM, Gaithersburg, Md., 1979—81; sr. mgr. systems design depts. USAF Data Systems Modernization Fed. Systems divsn. IBM, Gaithersburg, 1981—83, sr. mgr. systems design depts. FAA Advanced Automation System, 1983—87; dir. network mgmt. and control Comsat Systems divs. Comm. Satellite Corp., Clarksburg, Md., 1987—88, sr. dir. Deutsche Fernmelde Satellite program, 1988—90, sr. dir. MOSCOM program, 1990, sr. dir. engring. advanced systems, 1991—93; program dir. computer tech. St. Petersburg (Fla.) Jr. Coll., 1993—97. Speaker, instr. and lectr. in field, tchr., entrepreneurial acad. Greater St. Petersburg C. of C., 1996-98; substitute tchr. Buckeye Valley HS, Buckeye Valley Middle Sch., Del. Joint Vocat. Schs., Del.-Union Counties Alternative Schs., 2001—. Caregiver Frederick County Hospice, 1984-87; club leader Frederick County 4-H, 1975-80; pres./v.p. Frederick County Sheep Breeders Assn., 1983-84; chmn. bd. govs. Am. Bouviers Des Flandres Club, 1981-82; active Suncoast Tiger Bay, 1994-98, Leadership St Pete Alumni, 1995-2000, Leadership Tampa Bay Alumni, 1997-2000; mem. Am. Legion, 1999—; asst. football coach/head coach track and field, asst. coach golf Buckeye Valley Mid. Sch. and HS, Del., Ohio, 2000—. With USAF, 1958-62, Korea, 1960-61. Recipient Parenting award Future Farmers of Am., 1978-80, Award for Advancement of Human Rights UN Assn., 1984; named Alumni of Yr. Mt. St.

Joseph Coll. H.S., 1989. Mem. AARP, St. Petersburg Yacht Club, St. Petersburg Sail and Power Squadron. Roman Catholic. Avocations: farming, golf, personal computing, boating. Home: 62 Glengary Dr Delaware OH 43015-7610 E-mail: jarnoldoh@hotmail.com.

ARNOLD, JEAN ANN, health science facility administrator; b. Coronado, Calif., Nov. 17, 1948; d. Scott Crittenden Daubin and Barbara Jean (Spooner) Annowada; m. Lonnie Lea Arnold, July 14, 1973; children: Danielle Louise and Casey Jean (twins). Student, Santa Barbara City Coll., Calif., 1966-67, U. Wyo., Laramie, 1968-69; BS in Allied Health Scis./Health Svcs. Adminstrn., Weber State U., 1995. Registered Technol., Llc. Technol., Calif., Wash. Staff technol. x-ray Mt. Auburn Hosp., Cambridge, Mass., 1971-72, Victor Valley Hosp., Victorville, Calif., 1972-74, Fairfield Hosp., Calif., 1974-76; chief technol. Oakridge Med. Group, Roseville, Calif., 1976-78; staff technol. radiation therapy U. Cancer Ctr., U. Hosp., Seattle, 1979-84; staff technol. Providence Med. Ctr., Seattle, 1984; relief technol. UCSD Med. Ctr., San Diego, 1984-85; staff technol. Scripps Meml. Hosp., La Jolla, Calif., 1984-87, dir. radiation oncology, 1987—95; mgr. radiation oncology Deaconess Med. Ctr., Spokane, 1995—98, St. Alphonsus Regional Med. Ctr., Boise, Idaho, 1999—. Clin. coord., instr. San Diego Radiation Therapy Tech. Edn. Program. Producer Video, Occpl. Radiation Safety 1988. Mem. Soc. for Radiation Oncology Adminstrs., Calif. Soc. Radiologic Technologists, Am. Soc. Radiologic Technologists, Am. Registry Radiologic Technologists (job analysis adv. com., radiation therapy exam. com., item writer Therapy Tech.). Republican. Baptist.

ARNOLD, JEANNE ELOISE, anthropologist, educator; b. Cleve., 1955; d. Lawrence Fred and Marybelle Eloise Arnold. BA, U. Mich., 1976; MA, U. Calif., Santa Barbara, 1979, PhD, 1983. Prof. anthropology U. No. Iowa, Cedar Falls, 1984-88, UCLA, 1988—, assoc. dir. Inst. Archaeology, 1988-99. Vis. instr. anthropology Rice U., Houston, 1981; vis. prof. anthropology Oreg. State U., Corvallis, 1983-84; sr. archaeologist Infotec Rsch., Inc., Sonora, Calif., 1986-87; cons. in field. Author 4 books; contbr. more than 45 articles and revs. to profl. jours. and over 25 chpts. to books. Rsch. grantee NSF, 1988-91, 95-99, 98—; Rsch. and Ednl. grantee UCLA and Santa Barbara, 1977—. Mem. Soc. Am. Archaeology, Soc. Calif. Archaeology, Cotsen Inst. Archaeology (mem. editorial bd. 1988—), Sigma Xi, Phi Beta Kappa. Avocations: photography, cinema, collecting ethnographic arts. Office: UCLA Dept Anthropology Box 951553 Haines Hall Los Angeles CA 90095-1553

ARNOLD, JEFFREY, Internet company executive; m. Meg Arnold. Student, U. Ga. Founder, chmn., CEO Quality Diagnostic Svcs., 1994; founder, chmn. bd., CEO WebMD; CEO Healtheon/WebMD. Office: Healtheon/WebMD Corp 400 Lenox Bldg 3399 Peachtree Rd NE Atlanta GA 30326-1120

ARNOLD, JEROME GILBERT, lawyer; s. Edward F. and Annastacia (Thielen) A.; m. Judith Lindor, Dec. 18, 1971; children: Thomas, Mark, John, Jason, Maria. BS, U. Minn., 1964; LLB, U. N.D., 1967. Bar: Minn. 1967, S.D. 1967, U.S. Dist. Ct. S.D. 1967, U.S. Dist. Ct. Minn. 1973, U.S. Ct. Appeals (8th cir.) 1986. Law clk. U.S. Dist. Ct., Aberdeen, S.D., 1967-68; asst. city atty. City of Duluth, Minn., 1968-69; asst. county atty. St. Louis County, Duluth, 1969-70, chief criminal prosecutor, 1970-71; spl. asst. to county atty. County of Carlton, Minn., 1971; ptnr. Hunt & Arnold, Duluth, 1971-86; U.S. atty. U.S. Dist. Ct. Minn., Mpls., 1986-91; ptnr. Larson, Husby, Brodin & Arnold, Duluth, Md., 1992-93; compensation judge State of Minn., 1993—. Mem. adv. com. Supreme Ct. Appointments, St. Paul, 1980; chmn. selection com. 6th Jud. Dist., Duluth, 1978-83. Chmn. St. Louis City (Minn.) Bd. Adjustment, 1978-82; Rep. nominee 8th Congl. Dist. Minn., 1974; mem. state steering com. Reagan for Pres., 1976, 80, 84. Mem. Fed. Bar Assn. (bd. dirs. 1986-91), Minn. Bar Assn. Roman Catholic. Avocations: fishing, hunting.

ARNOLD, JOHN DAVID, management counselor, catalyst; b. Boston, May 14, 1933; s. Israel and Edith (Gordon) A.; children by previous marriage: Derek, Keith, Craig; m. Diane Summers, Sept. 1994. BA cum laude in Social Rels., Harvard U., 1955. Prodn. supr., dealer svc. mgr. Arnold Stretch Mates Corp., Boston, 1957-59; asst. dir. manpower and orgn. devel. Polaroid Corp., Waltham, Mass., 1959-63; dir. internat. ops. Kepner-Tregoe & Assocs., Princeton, N.J., 1963-68; pres. John Arnold ExecuTrak Sys. Inc., Boston, 1968—. Merger integration catalyst, conflict resolution/prevention counselor, conf. leader numerous firms; speaker in field; bd. dirs. World Music. Author: Make Up Your Mind, 1978, The Art of Decision Making, 1978, Shooting the Executive Rapids, 1981, How To Make the Right Decisions, 1982, Trading Up-A Career Guide: How To Get Ahead without Getting Out, 1984, How To Protect Yourself Against a Takeover, 1986, The Complete Problem Solver! A Total System of Competitive Decision Making, 1992, When the Sparks Fly: Resolving Organizational Conflict, 1993; contbr. articles to popular mags. Bd. dirs., exec. com. Orange County Philharm. Soc., 2001. 1st lt. US Army, 1955-57. Mem.: Orange County Philharmonic Soc. (bd. dirs.). Office: John Arnold ExecuTrak Sys 32031 Point Pl Laguna Beach CA 92651-6862 Fax: 949-499-7608. E-mail: chimo7@cox.net.

ARNOLD, JOHN FOX, lawyer; b. St. Louis, Sept. 17, 1937; s. John Anderson and Mildred Chapin (Fox) Arnold; m. Martha Ann Freeman, June 29, 1963 (div. Oct. 1993); children: Lisa A. Galena, Laura Wray, Lynne A. Binder, Lesli Johnston; m. Ann Ruwitch, Mar. 3, 2003. AB, U. Mo., 1959, LLB, 1961. Bar: Mo. 1961, U.S. Dist. Ct. (ea. dist.) Mo. 1961, U.S. Ct. Appeals (8th cir.) 1961, U.S. Supreme Ct. 1971. Ptnr. Green, Hennings, Henry & Arnold, St. Louis, 1963-70; mem. Lashly & Baer, P.C., St. Louis, 1970—, chmn., 1987—. Mem. St. Louis County (Mo.) Charter Revision Com., 1968; chmn. St. Louis County Bd. Election Commrs., 1981—86; chmn. bd. dirs. Downtown St. Louis Inc., 1996—98, Downtown St. Louis Partnership, Inc., 1997—99; chmn. bd. overseers Lindenwood U., 1992—93, bd. dirs., 1993—95. Lt. USAR, 1961—63. Recipient citation of merit U. Mo. Law Sch., Columbia, 1984. Fellow Am. Bar Found.; mem. ABA (mem. house of dels. 1986-90), Bar Assn. Met. St. Louis (pres. 1975-76), Mo. Bar (pres. 1984-85), Nat. Conf. Commrs. on Uniform State Laws (drafting com. Securities Act, Partnership Act, article 2 sales, 2A leases and 8 investment securities of Uniform Comml. Code), Am. Law Inst. Republican. Office: Lashly & Baer 714 Locust St Saint Louis MO 63101 1699 E mail: jfarnold@lashlybaer.com.

ARNOLD, KAREN L. writer, consultant; b. East Chicago, Ind., July 2, 1945; d. Glenn T. and Lillian (Helding) Bovard; m. Gary G. Arnold, Dec. 16, 1967; children: Sara, Jenny, Emily. BA, No. Ill. U., 1967; MA, U. Md., 1983, PhD, 1994. Poet-in-residence Montpelier Cultural Arts Ctr., Laurel, Md., 1985—2000; scholar, lectr. NEH and Howard County Libr. Sys., Columbia, Md., 1988—; lectr., discussion moderator Balt. City Libr. Sys., 1994—; lectr., discussion moderation Montgomery County Libr. Sys., Rockville, Md., 1993—, Prince George's County Libr. Sys., Adelphi, Md., 1988—, Frederick (Md.) County Libr. Sys., 1998. Vis. prof. U. Lund, Sweden, 1997; writing workshop leader, cons. Montpelier Cultural Arts Ctr., Laurel, Md., 1982—; adj. faculty, vis. prof. U.S. Naval Acad., Annapolis, 1988-90, 97-98; pres., mem. adv. bd. Montpelier Cultural Arts Ctr., Laurel, Md., 1983-94. Author: Border Crossings, 1997; editor: Impetus III, 1988, Montpelier Plus 4, 1988. Vol. workshop leader Prince George's County Schs., Laurel, 1974 83, Howard County Schs., Columbia, Md., 1983—. Fellow Am. Scandinavian Found., 1998, Am. Women's Club in Sweden, 1997-98, Soc. for Advancement Scandinavian Studies, 1988; recipient Outstanding Arts Conf. award Mid-Atlantic Recreation Assn., 1984. Avocations: beach time, visits to maine coast, embroidery. Home and Office: 12213 Green Shoot Ct Columbia MD 21044-2891 E-mail: grshtct@aol.com.

ARNOLD, KEVIN DAVID, psychologist, educational researcher; b. Massilon, Ohio, Jan. 7, 1957; s. Jack Olen and Arlene Adele (Harrold) A.; m. Melissa Wervey. BS, Grace Coll., 1979; MA, Ohio State U., 1981, PhD, 1983; advanced cert., Ctr. for Cognitive Therapy, N.Y., 1994, Atlanta Ctr. Cognitive Therapy, 1994. Fellow and diplomate Am. Bd. Med. Psychotherapists; diplomate in behavioral psychology Am. Bd. Profl. Psychology; lic. psychologist, Ohio, Wis.; listed divorce mediator Franklin County (Ohio) Ct. Common Pleas. Grad. rsch. assoc. Ohio State U., Columbus, 1980-83, rsch. assoc., 1983-84, prin. investigator deaf and blind project, 1984-92, asst. dir. Ctr. Spl. Needs Populations, 1988-93, asst. prof., 1988-92; psychologist Columbus, 1991—. Dir. Ctr. for Cognitive and Behavioral Therapy Greater Columbus, 1995—; founder, CEO, Ohio Proficiency Test Rev., Inc., 1990—95; v.p. Englefield & Arnold Pub., 1995—2001; bd. dirs. Am. Bd. Behavioral Psychology; v.p., work sample coord.; mem. Ohio State Bd. of Psychology, 2003—; sec.-treas., dir. wine tastings Tastings By the Glass, Inc. Co-author: Passing the Ohio Proficiency Test, 1993, Passing the Ohio Ninth Grade Proficiency Test, 1996, Passing with Honors on Ohio's 12th Grade Proficiency Tests, 2000, Passing the Ohio Graduation Test, 2001, Show What You Know on the 7th Grade WASL, 2001, Show What You Know on the 10th Grade WASL, 2001, (test) Social Behavior Assessment Inventory, 1992; contbr. chapters to books, articles. Fundraiser Ohio Dem. gubernatorial campaign, 1989-90; twp. coord. Grass Roots campaign Tiberi Rep. U.S. Congl. Campaign, 2000; co-chair Franklin County (Ohio) Parenting Coord. Project, 2000—; mem. Ohio State Bd. of Pyschology. Deaf and Blind Ctr. grantee U.S. Dept. Edn., 1984-94, 99—, Sch. Psychology grantee, 1987-93, Evaluation Intervention Teams Ohio Dept. Edn. grantee, 1988-93, Drop-out Cost Study Ctr. Labor Rsch. grantee, 1990-91, Parent Satisfaction Study Ohio Devel. Disabilities Planning Coun. grantee, 1989-90, Tchr. Competency Survey Study grantee, 1992-93. Fellow: Am. Bd. Med. Psychotherapists, Am. Acad. Behavioral Psychology (pres.); mem.: APA (del. state leadership conf.), Ohio State Bd. Psychology, Acad. Family and Conciliatory Cts., Nat. Coun. Family Rels., Soc. Personality Assessment, Soc. Rsch. in Child Devel., Am. Psychology-Law Soc., Ctrl. Ohio Psychol. Assn., Am. Assn. Mental Retardation, Ohio Psychol. Assn. (former mem. cont. edn. com., trustee, former chmn. publs. com., former co-editor Ohio Psychologist, past pres., mem. exec. com. cont. edn. com., mem. fin. com., publs. coun., former fin. officer), Acad. Family Mediators, Assn. for Advancement of Behavior Therapy, Am. Pscyhol. Soc. Avocation: wine collecting. Office: CCBT 2121 Bethel Rd Ste D Columbus OH 43220-1804 E-mail: kda1757@earthlink.net.

ARNOLD, KRISTIN ANNE, chemist; b. Abington, Pa., Aug. 14, 1961; d. John E. and Jane E. (Sulzbuch) A.; m. Anthony M. Viscariello, July 5, 1986; children: Michael, Kristina. BA in Chemistry, La Salle U., 1983; PhD, U. Miami, Fla., 1988. Sr. rsch. chemist Monsanto, St. Louis, Mo., 1988-90, rsch. specialist, 1990-93, team leader, 1993; sr. rsch. scientist Ecogen, Langhorne, Pa., 1993-94, formulations mgr., 1994-95; mgr. formulations FMC, Princeton, N.J., 1995-97; dir. formulations Faulding/Purepac, Elizabeth, N.J., 1997-2001, sr. dir. product devel., 2001—. Contbr. over 20 articles to Jour. Am. Chem. Soc., Tetrahedron Letters, Pesticide Sci., EP, Pure Applied Chemistry, Jour. Organic Chemistry, others; also presentations at sci. meetings. Mem. Am. Chem. Soc. Office: Alpharma 200 Elmora Ave Elizabeth NJ 07202-1106

ARNOLD, LARRY KEITH, major general United States Air Force; m. Linda Smith; 2 children. BA in Polit. Sci., Wake Forest U., 1964; disting. grad., Squadron Officer Sch. USAF, 1972; MBA, Auburn U., 1977; student, Air War Coll., 1984; student Nat., Internat. Security Mgmt., Kennedy Sch Govt Harvard U., 1994; postgrad., Air Command and Staff Coll., 1977. Commd 2d lt. USAF, 1965, advanced through grades to maj. gen., 1998; fighter pilot 390th Fighter Squadron USAF, Da Nang Air Base, Republic Viet Nam, 1966-67; student combat crew tng., F-106 tng. USAF, Perrin and Tyndall AFBs, Tex., Fla., 1967-68, pilot instr. Langley AFB, Va., 1968-72, Tyndall AFB, Fla., 1972-73; instr., pilot tng. officer Air Nat. Guard, Atlantic City Airport, N.J., 1973-76, cmmdr., 1977-83, dep. comdr. ops. Fighter Interceptor Group, 1984-86; air nat. guard advisor to comdr. Air Univ and faculty mem. Air War Coll., Maxwell AFB, Ala., 1986-88; comdr. 147th fighter interceptor group Air Nat. Guard, Ellington AFB, Tex., 1988-89; asst. dir. readiness support Air Nat. Guard Readiness Ctr., Andrews AFB, Md., 1989-92; comdr. Air Nat. Guard Readiness Ctr., asst. dir. Air Nat. Guard Nat. Guard Bur. Pentagon, Washington, 1994-97; vice comdr. First Air Force, Tyndall AFB, 1997; comdr. 1st Air Force Air Combat Command, Tyndall AFB, Fla., 1997—. Decorated Legion of Merit, Disting. Flying Cross with oak leaf cluster, Meritorious Svc. medal with oak leaf cluster, Air medal with 14 oak leaf clusters, Air Force Commendation medal, Air Force Achievement medal, Combat Readiness medal with 3 oak leaf clusters, Republic of Vietnam Gallantry Cross with one device, Vietnam Armed Forces Honor medal, Republic of Vietnam Campaign medal, Vietnam Svc. medal with two bronze stars, others. Office: 1st Air Force Office Pub Affairs Tyndall AFB FL 32403-5428

ARNOLD, LEE, library director, archivist; b. Waukegan, Ill., Oct. 18, 1959; s. Louis Douglas and Verona Christina (Lemke) A. BA cum laude, Edgewood Coll., Madison, Wis., 1982; M of Libr. and Info. Sci., U. Wis., Milw., 1987; M of Liberal Arts, Temple U., 2000. Sales support mgr. Marshall Field and Co., Milw., Wis., 1982-88; asst. univ. libr. for adminstrv. svcs. Princeton (N.J.) U., 1988-92; tchr. English., Berlitz Schs. Lang., Princeton, 1990-92; dir. of libr. Hist. Soc. of Pa., Phila., 1992—. Contbr. articles to profl. jours.; numerous book reviews and presentations in field. Mem. Delta Epsilon Sigma. Democrat. Roman Catholic. Avocations: reading, travel, outdoors. Office: Hist Soc PA 1300 Locust St Philadelphia PA 19107-5661

ARNOLD, LESLIE ANN, special education educator; b. St. Louis, Mo., Oct. 20, 1953; d. Eugene L. and Louisa French (Gale) A. BS, Central State U., 1975, MEd, 1981. Cert. spl. edn., learning disabilities, mental retardation tchr., Kans. Tchr. level III educable mentally handicapped Unified Sch. Dist. 345, Topeka, 1976-82; tchr., specialist mentally retarded and occupationally handicapped Sch. Dist. 619, Wellington, Kans., 1982-87; coord. vocat. options level IV educable mentally handicapped Wellington Unified Sch. Dist. 353, Wellington, Kans., 1987—; area adminstr. Sangamon Area Spl. Edn. Dist., Springfield, Ill., 2002—. Coord. spl. edn. Wellington Unified Sch. Dist., 1995-98, dir. spl. edn., 1998, dir. spl. svcs., Poplar Bluff, Mo., 2000-02; cons. in field. Grantee Vocat. Rehab., 1992-95, Kansas Transition Network, 1994-98, Charter Sch., 1997; Access to Gen. Edn. grantee Positive Behavioral Intervention Strategies,(PBIS), 2001, Sangamon Area Spl. Edn. Dist. (SASED) Area Admin.

ARNOLD, MARGARET MORELOCK, music specialist, educator, performer; b. Craig AFB, Ala., May 12, 1959; d. William Daniel Morelock and Margaret Haynie Morelock Stapleton; m. Barry Raynor Arnold, Aug. 15, 1984. B of Music Edn., U. Montevallo, 1981; MEd in Music, U. South Ala., 1996. Cert. tchr. Fla., Ala. Tchr. music Staley Mid. Sch., Americus, Ga., 1981-82, Eastview Elem. Sch., Americus, Ga., 1982-84; tchr. music/mass prep. St. Thomas More Schs., Pensacola, Fla., 1984-85; tchr. music W.H. Rhodes Elem., Milton, Fla., 1985—; realtor Century 21, Richardson, Fla. Pvt. voice instr., Americus, 1981-84, Milton, 1989—; guest condr. Santa Rosa All-County Chorus, Milton, 1989, 95, Santa Rosa Celebrates the Arts, 1986—. Asst. dir. arts festivals, 1993—; singer (soprano, soloist): Gulf Coast Chorale, Singfest, Inc., The Choral Soc. Pensacola; dir.: (band) Change of Command, 2003. Dir. elem. chorus performing for Santa Rosa Convalescent Ctr., Milton, 1985—, Whiting Field, 2003, Live at the Capital, Tallahassee, 1986, Santa Rosa Celebrates the Arts, 1986-, Ptnrs. in Edn.-K-Mart and City of Milton and WEAR-TV, 1990—. Recipient Young Artist Competition S.E. Regional award Nat. Assn. Tchrs. of Singing, S.E. region, 1993; winner State of Ala. Young Artist competition, 1993; Computer Software grant Santa Rosa Ednl. Found., 1994. Mem. NEA, Music Tchrs. Nat. Assn., Nat. Assn. Realtors, Fla. Assn. Realtors, Santa Rosa Profl. Educators, Music Educators Nat. Conf., Pensacola (Fla.) Music Tchrs. Assn., Delta Kappa Gamma (music chair 1988-94), Kappa Delta Pi, Phi Kappa Phi. Presbyterian. Avocations: walking, gardening, volunteer for nursing home. Home: 5820 Kirkland Dr Milton FL 32570-8251 Office: WH Rhodes Elem 5563 Byrom St Milton FL 32570-3822 Business E-Mail: arnoldm@santarosa.k12.fl.us.

ARNOLD, MARSHA DIANE, writer; b. Kingman, Kans., July 7, 1948; d. Eugene Willard Krehbiel and Elsie Irene (Lippincott) Raymond; m. Frederick Oak Arnold, Jan. 25, 1970; children: Amy Marie, Calvin Diedrich Oak. BA in English cum laude, Kans. State U., 1970. Cert. secondary English tchr., Kans., standard elem. tchr., Calif. Eligibility worker Dept. Social Svcs., San Mateo, Calif., 1970-71, San Rafael, Calif., 1971-79, Calif. Children Svcs., Dept. of Health, San Rafael, 1979-81; kindergym tchr. Calif. Parenting Inst., Petaluma, 1981; writer children's books, columnist Sebastopol, Calif., 1985—; tchr.'s aide Twin Hills Sch. Dist., Sebastopol, 1991-94. Spkr. in field. Author: Heart of a Tiger, 1995 (Jr. Lib. Guild selection 1995, 1997-98 Show Me Readers Award Master List, Internat. Reading Assn. Children's Disting. Book award 1996, Young Hoosier Book Award selection, Houston Chronicle Best Book of '95 Christmas Roundup), Quick, Quack, Quick, 1996, The Bravest of Us All, 2000; contbr. columns, stories and articles to mags. Animal care vol. Boyd Mus. Sci., San Rafael, 1974-75, Calif. Marin Mammal Rehab. Ctr., Marin County, Calif., 1976; v.p. PTA, Sebastopol, 1985. Recipient Best Local Columnist award Calif. Newspaper Pubs. Assn., 1986, 87, 93, Marion Vannett Ridgway award for outstanding first published picture book for children by an author or illustrator, 1996. Mem. Soc. Childrens' Book Writers and Illustrators, Phi Kappa Phi, Kappa Delta Pi. Avocations: scuba diving, travel, nutrition. Home: 350 Mcgregor Ln Sebastopol CA 95472-5375

ARNOLD, MAXWELL, adveristing executive, writer; b. San Francisco, Feb. 18, 1919; s. Max Arnold and Lela Klein; m. Patricia Arnold, Oct. 6, 1950; children: Jane, Caroline, Oliver. AB, Stanford U., 1948. Mng. dir. The Hawthorne Inn, Gloucester, Mass., 1948-52; v.p., creative dir. Guild, Bascom & Bonfigli, San Francisco, 1953-68, Dancer-Fritzgerald-Sample, San Francisco, 1968-70; pres., chmn. The Maxwell Arnold Agency, San Francisco, 1970-85; sr. v.p. Cole & Weber, San Francisco, 1985-86; owner Arnold & Underwood, San Francisco, 1986—. Cons. Nat. Acad. Arts and Sci., Washington, 1978, Fed. Trade Commn., Washington, 1978. Author: (short stories) Never Hit a Cripple, 1948, The Cannibal Pot, 1950. Mem. Am. Assn. Adv. Agencies (bd. govs. 1980-82), Cercle de L'Union (bd. dirs. 1982—). Democratic. Jewish. Avocations: surf fishing, bicycling. Office: Arnold & Underwood 20 Lerida Ct Portola Valley CA 94028 E-mail: arnoldand@earthlink.net.

ARNOLD, MORRIS SHEPPARD, judge; b. Texarkana, Tex., Oct. 8, 1941; BSEE, U. Ark., 1965, LLB, 1968; LLM, Harvard U., 1969, SJD, 1971; MA (hon.), U. Pa., 1977, JD (hon.), 1986; LLD (hon.), U. Ark., Little Rock, 1968, U. Pa., 1985. Tchg. fellow law Harvard U., 1969-70; from asst. prof. to prof. Ind. U. Law Sch., 1971-76, prof., 1976-77, dean, 1985; prof. law, history U. Pa., 1977-81; Ben J. Altheimer disting. prof. law U. Ark., Little Rock, 1981-84; judge U.S. dist. Ct. (we. dist.) Ark., Ft. Smith, 1985-92, U.S. Cir. Ct. (8th cir.), 1992—. Vis.fellow commoner Trinity Coll., Cambridge U., 1978; v.p., dir. office of the pres. U. Pa., 1980—81; vis. prof. Stanford (Calif.) U. Law Sch., 1985. Author: Old Tenures and Natura Brevium, 1974, Yearbook 2 Richard II, 1378-79, 1975, On the Laws and Customs of England, 1980, Unequal Laws Unto a Savage Race, 1985, Select Cases of Trespass from the King's Courts, 1307-1399, 2 vols., 1985, 1987, Arkansas Colonials, 1986, Colonial Arkansas 1686-1804: A Social and Cultural History, 1991, The Rumble of a Distant Drum: Quapaws and Old World Newcomers, 1673-1804, 2000, Arkansas: A Narrative History, 2002. Chmn., Rep. party State of Ark., 1983; gen. counsel, Rep. party Ark., 1982, chmn., 1983; bd. dirs. Nature Conservancy of Ark., 1982—87, Ark. Arts Ctr., 1981—84. Decorated chevalier Ordre Palmes Acad., France; recipient Porter Literary prize, 2001, Worthen Literary prize, 2001, Ragsdale prize, 2001; Frank Knox fellow, Harvard U./U. London, 1970—71, Mus. Sci. Natural History fellow, 1986. Fellow: Am. Soc. Legal History (hon.; pres. 1981—85); mem.: Am. Antiquarian Soc., Country Club of Little Rock, Union League Club of Phila., Athenaeum Club London. Office: US Cir Judge 600 W Capital Ave Rm 208 Little Rock AR 72203-2060

ARNOLD, NANCY KAY, writer; b. Kalamazoo, Mich., May 9, 1951; d. Byron Lyle and Ada (Doorlag) Arnold; m. Louis Scott Hubert, May 5, 1989 (div. Jan. 29, 2002). BFA in Painting, Western Mich. U., 1983, postgrad., 1985-86. Writer Advanced Systems & Designs, Inc., Farmington Hills, Mich., 1987—89; pres., owner TechWrite, Kalamazoo, 1989—2002; writer Northrop Grumman IT, 2002—. Writer Northrop Grumman IT, 2002—. Author: (poetry) Tetragonal Pyramids, 1982; exhibited in group shows, Kalamazoo, 1983, Western Mich. U., 1982, 85. Mem. AAUW, NAFE, Kalamazoo County C. of C., Humane Farming Assn. Am. People for Ethical Treatment of Animals. Libertarian. Avocations: bicycling, skiing, reading, piano, singing. Office: PO Box 481 Oshtemo MI 49077-0481

ARNOLD, P. A. special education educator; b. Toledo; d. Mattie Spear; m. Earl E. Arnold. BA, BS, David Lipscomb Coll., 1960; MA, Wayne State U., 1962; MS, Nova U., 1986. Cert. spl. edn., psychology, speech, mental retardation, emotional disturbance, Bible, Fla. Tchr. dactyology, interpreter for deaf, 1960—; tchr. Hobbs (N.Mex.) Mcpl. Schs., 1981-82; tchr. spl. edn. City Systems, Rockford and Warren, Mich., 1960-67; dir. Four-County Ctr. Handicapped, Ark., 1977-81. Dir. model project ACTION; Project TREE Tech. Resources in Exceptional Edn.; conf. presenter in fields. Author: Instructor, Light for Deaf, 1992, Ol' Time Preacher Man, 1995, Little Red Schoolhouse, 1998, Trapezoid of Children, 1999. Bd. dirs., deaf advisor Hearing Soc. Volusia County; mem. project TREE-Tech. Resources in Exceptional Edn.-Tech. Exceptional Edn.-SY 2000, Dept. Edn., Fla. State U. Ctr. Ednl. Tech. Grantee Pub. Welfare, Nat. Gardening Assn., FUTURES, Newspapers in Edn. Mem. NEA, ARC, ASCD, Volusia Ednl. Assn., Fla. Edn. Assn., Coun. for Exceptional Children, Am. Assn. on Mental Deficiency, Nat. Assn. Deaf.

ARNOLD, PERI ETHAN, political scientist; b. Chgo., Sept. 21, 1942; s. Joseph Evon and Eve (Jacobs) A.; m. Beverly Ann Kessler, Aug. 22, 1965; children: Emma, Rachel. BA, Roosevelt U., Chgo., 1964; MA, U. Chgo., 1967, PhD, 1972. Lectr. Roosevelt U., Chgo., 1966-68; instr. polit. sci. Western Mich. U., Kalamazoo, 1970-71; asst. prof. polit. sci. U. Notre Dame, Ind., 1971-76, assoc. prof. govt., 1976-86, prof. of govt. and internat. studies, 1986; chair dept. govt., 1986-92. Compton vis. prof. of world politics Miller Ctr., U. Va., 1993-94; dir. Hesburgh Program in Pub. Svc., 1995-2001; dir. Notre Dame Semester in Washington, 1997-2001. Author: Making the Managerial Presidency, 1986 (Louis Brownlow Book award 1987), 2nd rev. ed., 1998; mem. editl. bd. Am. Jour. Polit. Sci., 1991-94, Polity, 1995—, Presdl. Studies Quar., 1997—; co-editor Jour. of Policy History, 1987-88; mem. editl. adv. bd. Hughes Leadership Series, Tex. A&M U. Press, 1999—; contbr. articles to profl. jours. and edited vols. Bd. dirs. South Bend Hebrew Day Sch., Mishawaka, Ind., 1985—88; chair Cmty. Rels. Coun. of Jewish Fedn. of St. Joseph Valley, South Bend, Ind., 1990—94; mem. acquisitions com. Snite Mus. Art, Notre Dame, Ind., 1994—99; trustee Congregation Beth El, South Bend, 1994—2000, sec., exec. com., 2000—02; bd. dirs. Jewish Fedn. of St. Joseph Valley, 1999—2002, v.p., 2001—03. Recipient Spl. Presdl. award U. Notre Dame, 1993, Marshall Dimock award Am. Soc. Pub. Adminstrn., 1996; grantee Am. Coun. Learned Socs., 1974; rsch. grantee Herbert Hoover Libr. Assn., 1993-94; Ford Found. fellow, 1978-81. Mem. Am. Polit. Sci. Assn. (program chmn., exec. com. presidency sect.), Midwest Polit. Sci. Assn., The Cliff Dwellers Club (Chgo.). Democrat. Jewish. Avocations: literature, music, drama. Home: 1419 E Colfax Ave South Bend IN 46617-3307 Office: U Notre Dame Dept Polit Sci Notre Dame IN 46556 E-mail: peri.e.arnold.1@nd.edu.

ARNOLD, PETER GORDON, communications consultant; b. Newton, Mass., Jan. 25, 1943; s. Israel Isaac and Edith (Gordon) A.; m. Kirsten Ellen Arnold, July 25, 1966 (div. 1979); 1 child, Jeremy Gordon; m. Margery Loewenberg, July 27, 1980; 1 child, Jessica Beth. BA, U. Mich., 1966; MA, U. So. Calif., 1969. Writer, producer Universal Studios, Hollywood, Calif., 1969-70; exec. v.p. Cameo Pictures, Hollywood, 1971-72; devel. writer Calif. Inst. Tech., Pasadena, 1973; dir. spl. projects Occidental Coll., Los Angeles, 1974-75; exec. dir. Hugh O'Brian Youth Found., Los Angeles, 1976; pres. Peter Arnold Assocs., Boston and Dallas, 1977—. Author: Lady Beware, 1973, Emergency Handbook, 1980 (Literary Guild selection 1980), Job and Career Building, 1980, Packaging Your House for Profit, 1986 and seven other books. Office: 1 Hollis St Ste 350 Wellesley MA 02482-4682 also: 2401 Internet Blvd Ste 115 Frisco TX 75034 E-mail: parnold@parnold.com.

ARNOLD, PHILIP BRUNO, physician; b. New Haven, Conn., Aug. 14, 1941; s. Hermann Bruno and Elizabeth Abbott (Wood) A.; m. Alison Stahl Richter, July 17, 1965; children: Stefan Bruno, Adam Frederick. BA, Yale U., 1963; MD, Tufts U., 1967. Intern Maine Med. Ctr., Portland, 1967-68; resident in physical medicine and rehab. Letterman Army Med. Ctr., San Francisco, 1968-71; dir. Gaylord Hosp., Wallingford, Conn., 1973-77, Danbury (Conn.) Hosp., 1977-84; dir. rehab. medicine Newington (Conn.) Childrens Hosp., 1984-96; v.p. med. affairs A Rehab. Corp., Newington, 1996-98; pvt. practice Meriden, Conn., 1998—2001. Contbr. chpt. to book. Maj. U.S. Army, 1968-73. Home: 131 Beecher Rd Woodbridge CT 06525-2011 Office: 30 Hazel Terr Ste 20 Woodbridge CT 06525 Fax: 203-389-7485.

ARNOLD, RALPH LEO, III, valuation analyst, consultant; b. Butte, Mont., Oct. 22, 1949; s. Ralph L. Jr. and Annie B. (Baker) A. BS in Acctg., Calif. State U., Hayward, 1973. Auditor Calif. State Controller's Office, San Francisco, 1973—76, chief auditor, 1976—79; assoc. Holton Accountancy Corp., 1979—83; sr. valuation analyst Willamette Mgmt. Assocs., Portland, Oreg., 1983—92; valuation cons. Arnold & Olds, LLC, 1992—2000; prin. Columbia Fin. Advisors, Inc., 2000—. Instr. Portland State U., 1986-87. Contbr. chpt. to

book, articles to profl. jours. Mem. Am. Soc. Appraisers (accredited sr. appraiser, pres. 1987-88), Fin. Analysts Fedn., Inst. Mgmt. Accts. Office: Ste 650 720 SW Washington St Portland OR 97205-3508

ARNOLD, RICHARD SHEPPARD, federal judge; b. Texarkana, Tex., Mar. 26, 1936; s. Richard Lewis and Janet (Sheppard) Arnold; m. Gale Hussman, June 14, 1958 (div.); children: Janet Sheppard, Arnold Hart, Lydia Palmer, Arnold Turnipseed; m. Kay Kelley, Oct. 27, 1979. BA summa cum laude, Yale U., 1957; LLB magna cum laude, Harvard U., 1960; LLD, U. Ark., 1992, U. Richmond, 1998. Bar: Ark. 1960, D.C. 1961. Pvt. practice, Washington, 1961—64, Texarkana, Ark., 1964—74; law clk. to justice Brennan U.S. Supreme Ct., 1960—61; assoc. Covington & Burling, 1961—64; ptnr. Arnold & Arnold, 1964—74; legis. sec. Gov. of Ark., 1973—74, staff coord., 1974; legis. asst. Senator Bumpers of Ark., Washington, 1975—78; judge U.S. Dist. Ct. (ea. and we. dists.) Ark., 1978—80, U.S. Ct. Appeals (8th cir.), Little Rock, 1980—2001, chief judge, 1992—98; sr. judge, 2001—. Part-time instr. U. Va. Law Sch., 1962—64; mem. Ark. Constl. Revision Study Commn., 1967—68; chair spl. redaction rev. panel Jud. Conf. of the U.S., 2000—; vice chair Com. on the Jud. Br., 2001—; disting. vis. prof. law So. Meth. U. Law Sch., 2001. Case editor: Harvard Law Rev., 1959—60; contbr. articles to profl. jours. Gen. chmn. Texarkana United Way Crusade, 1969—70; pres. Texarkana Cmty. Chest, 1970—71; mem. vis. com. Harvard Law Sch., 1973—79, U. Chgo. Law Sch., 1983—86, 1994—97; mem. Com. on Legis. Orgn., 1971—72; trustee U. Ark., 1973—74; chmn. budget com. Conf. of U.S., 1987—96; del. Dem. Nat. Conv., 1968, Ark. Constl. Conv., 1969—70; candidate for Congress 4th Dist. Ark., 1966, 1972; chmn. rules com. Ark. Dem. Com., 1968—74, mem. exec. com., 1972—74. Recipient Award of the Women Lawyers' Assn. of Greater St. Louis, 1998, Edward J. Devitt Disting. Svc. to Justice award, 1999, Meador-Rosenberg award, Standing Com. on Fed. Jud. Improvements of the ABA, 1999. Fellow: Am. Bar Found.; mem.: Jud. Conf. U.S. (exec. com. 1992—98), Am. Law Inst. (coun.), Cum Laude Soc., Phi Beta Kappa. Episcopalian. Office: 600 W Capitol Ave Ste 208 Little Rock AR 72201-3321 also: Thomas F Eagleton US Cthse 111 S 10th St Rm 26 325 Saint Louis MO 63102

ARNOLD, RINEE' STEPHEN, petroleum engineer; b. Dallas, July 22, 1951; s. Jesse Daniel and Betty Ruth (Rougeau) A.; m. Betty Lou Waggoner Arnold, July 31, 1976; children: Joshua Heath, Heather Dawn. BS in Petroleum Engring., Hamilton U., 1992, MS in Petroleum Engring., 1998. Supr. Otis Engring. Corp., Lake Charles, La., 1973-79; v.p. Pressure Control Inc., Longview, Tex., 1979-81; dist. mgr. Schlumberger, Lake Charles, 1981-91; v.p. Slickline Electronics Inc., New Iberia, La., 1991-97; field svc. mgr., electronics/explosives Stric-Lan Cos. Corp., Lafayette, La., 1997-99; sr. field support engr. Micro-Smart Systems, Inc., Houston, 1999-2000; ops. mgr. Wood Group Ops., Broussard, La., 2000-01; supr. Barnett Wireline, Youngsville, La., 2001—. Mem. La. State Police Explosive Adv. Coun., Baton Rouge, 1996—; instr., explosive safety course, Houston, 1996—. Contbr. articles to profl. jours. With USMC, 1970-73. Mem. Soc. Petroleum Engrs., Internat. Soc. Explosive Engrs. Avocations: martial arts, boating, flying, motorcycles. Home: 3581 Hwy 383 Kinder LA 70648-5004 E-mail: SEAWOLF@centurytel.net.

ARNOLD, ROBERT LLOYD, investment broker, financial advisor and planner; b. Seattle, June 18, 1952; s. Vern Lloyd and Ruth Francis (Bruty) A. Student, Bellevue Coll., Wash., 1971-72; BS magna cum laude, U. Wash., 1975; MS, Yale U., 1977. Lic. fed. securities agt.; CFP. Group leader U.S. Govt., Miramonte, Calif., 1977-78, economist Walla Walla, Wash., 1978-79; gen. mgr. Full Value Roofing, Bellevue, 1979-81; transp. mgr. N.W. Hydra-Line, Inc., Seattle, 1981-83; owner Fairfields, Seattle, 1982—; sr. fin. advisor Waddell & Reed, Inc., Bellevue, 1983—. Coord. Charles Givens Found., Seattle, 1984-85, 88-90; lectr. Comty. Sch., Seattle, 1984-91; guest spkr. Kiwanis, Puyallup, Wash., 1985; seminar leader Chgo. Title Ins. Co., Seattle, 1985-90. Guest spkr. Fin. Strategies, KVI AM Radio, 2002—. Fund raiser ARC, Seattle, 1984-85; chmn. fin. com. Unity Ch. of Seattle, 1988-90. Grantee Bloedel Found., 1973-74, Bishop Soc. grantee, 1974-75; fellow Yale U., 1975-77. Mem. Rainier Club (reciprocity com. 1994—, young Rainiers com. 1994-95, arts and libr. com. 1996-98), Seattle Delta Group (life, chmn. 1985-87), Letip Internat. Eastside (v.p. 1996, pres. 1996), Inglewood Beach Club (trustee 1996-2000, v.p. 1996, pres. 1996-2000), Bellevue Master Mind (pres. 1996-97), Rolls Royce Owners Club Pacific N.W. Region (trustee 2002--, treas. 2002--), Rotary, Xi Sigma Pi (treas. 1974-75). Republican. Avocations: fishing, exploring ghost towns, classic cars. Office: 11811 NE 1st St Ste 301 Bellevue WA 98005-3033

ARNOLD, ROBERT MORRIS, banker; b. Seattle, June 6, 1928; s. Lawrence Moss and Grace Elizabeth (Heffernan) A.; children: Grace Allen Arnold, Lauren McLellan Gorter. BA in Fin. and Bus. Adminstrn., Yale U., 1951; grad., Pacific Coast Sch. Banking, 1963. With Seattle-1st Nat. Bank, 1951, 1955—, v.p., 1965-73, mgr. nat. accounts dept., 1969-73, sr. v.p., mgr. corp. bus. devel., 1973-99, also bd. dirs. Bd. dirs. Seafirst Corp. Bank of Am. Bd. dirs. Centrum Found., Fred C. Hutchinson Cancer Rsch.; trustee Poncho; bd. dirs., exec. com., fin. com. Seattle Art Mus., also mem., joint founder its Contemporary Art Coun. Officer USNR, 1951-55. Mem. Am. Inst. Banking, Mcpl. League Seattle, Yale Assn. Western Wash., Newcomen Soc. (treas. Pacific N.W. com.), Seattle Golf Club, Seattle Tennis Club, Seattle Yacht Club, University Club (Seattle), Bohemian Club (San Francisco), Thunderbird Golf Club (Palm Springs, Calif.), O'Donnell Golf Club (Palm Springs), Mission Hills Country Club (Palm Springs). Home: 1535 Parkside Dr E Seattle WA 98112-3719 Office: 1001 4th Ave Ste 4710 Seattle WA 98154-1198 also: 50 Hilton Head Dr Rancho Mirage CA 92270-1607

ARNOLD, RONALD HENRI, nonprofit organization executive, consultant; b. Houston, Aug. 8, 1937; s. John Andrew and Carrie Virginia (Henri) A.; m. Phoebe Anne Trogdon, Oct. 12, 1963 (dec. Feb. 1974); 1 child, Andrea; m. Janet Ann Parkhurst, Aug. 8, 1974; stepchildren: Andrea Wright, Rosalyn Wright. Tech. publ. Boeing Co., Seattle, 1961-71; cons. Northwoods Studio, Bellevue, Wash., 1971—; exec. v.p. Ctr. for Def. of Free Enterprise, Bellevue, 1984—. Advisor Nat. Fed. Lands Conf., 1988-92. Author: James Watt and the Environment, 1981, Ecology Wars, 1987, The Grand Prairie Years, 1987; author: (with Alan Gottlieb) Trashing the Economy, 1993; author: Politically Correct Environment, 1996, Ecoterror, 1997, Battered Communities, 1998, Undue Influence, Power to Hurt, 2000, Trust Us, 2002; editor: Stealing theNational Parks, 1987; contbg. editor: Logging Mgmt. mag., 1978—81, We. Conservation Jour., 1974—81. Recipient Editorial Achievement award Am. Bus. Press, 1981. Mem. AFTRA, Forest History Soc. Republican. Avocation: music. Home: 12605 NE 2nd St Bellevue WA 98005-3206 E-mail: rarnold@eskimo.com.

ARNOLD, ROY GARY, academic administrator; b. Lyons, Nebr., Feb. 20, 1941; m. Jane Kay Price, 1963; children: Jana Lynn Hoffman, Julie Kay Salvi. BS with distinction, U. Nebr., 1962; MS, Oreg. State U., 1965, PhD in Food Sci. and Tech., 1967. Research and devel. project leader Fairmont Foods Co., Omaha, 1962-63; asst. prof. food sci. and tech. U. Nebr., Lincoln, 1967-71, assoc. prof., 1971-74, asst. dir. resident instrn., 1971-72, acting dir. resident instrn., 1972-73, prof., 1974-87, head dept. food sci. and tech., 1973-79, coordinator food protein research group, 1975-79, dean, dir. agrl. expt. sta., 1980-82, vice chancellor inst. agr. and natural resources, 1982-87; dean Coll. Agrl. Scis. Oregon State U., Corvallis, 1987-91, provost, exec. v.p., 1991-2000; exec. assoc., dean Coll. Argl. Scis., Corvallis, 2000—. Del., devel. com. Imo (Nigeria) State U., 1981; mem. Ralston Purina Grad. Food Sci. Fellowship com., 1976-78, rev. team dept. food sci. U. Ill., 1979, adminstrv. site visit com. to Mid-Am. Internat. Agriculture Consortium Agy. for Internat. Devel. Morocco project, 1983, exec. com. agr. 2001 com. U. Nebr. Bd. Regents, 1982-83; program chmn. corn and sorghum industry research conf. Am. Seed Trade Assn., 1985. Mem. editorial bd. Jour. Dairy Sci., 1976-82, Jour, Agrl. and Food Chemistry, 1978-81; contbr. numerous articles to profl jours.; patentee in field. Mem. adminstrv. bd. St. Mark's United Meth. Ch., Lincoln, 1975-78, chmn. long range planning com., 1977-78, chmn. bldg. com. 1978-82. Grantee Nutrition Found., FDA, Nebr. Soybean Bd., Am. Soybean Assn. Research Found., Am. Egg Bd; Gen. Foods fellow, 1963-66. Fellow AAAS; mem. Inst. Food Technologists (nat. orgn. chmn. forward planning subcom. of exec. com. 1976-79, expert panel food safety and nutrition 1979-82, chmn. 1980-81, nominations and elections com. 1981-83, exec. com. 1985-88, 93-96, pres.-elect 1993-94, pres. 1994-95, William V. Cruess award 1980, Carl R. Fellers award 1998; Ak-Sar-Ben sect. past treas., sec., chmn.-elect, chmn. nat. councilor), Nat. Assn. Colls. and Tchrs. Agr., Univ. Assn. Adminstrv. Devel. (exec. com. 1973-74, 76-77, pres. 1978-79), MidAm. Internat. Agrl. Consortium (bd. dirs. 1982-87, chmn. 1986-87), N. Cen. Adminstrv. Heads Agr. (chmn.-elect 1985-86), Nat. Assn. State Univs. and Land Grant Colls. (divsn. agr. coun. adminstrv. heads agr. exec. com. 1985-87), Coll. Agr. Alumni Assn. (v.p. 1977-79), Innocents Soc. (pres. 1961-62), Sigma Xi (Nebr. chpt. sec. 1979-81), Phi Kappa Phi, Alpha Zeta, Gamma Sigma Delta (Nebr. chpt. past treas., sec., v.p., pres., Merit Tchg. award 1975), Phi Tau Sigma, FarmHouse Frat. (Doane award Nebr. chpt. 1962). Clubs: Crucibles (Lincoln). Office: Oreg State Univ 126 Strand Ag Hall Corvallis OR 97331-8521

ARNOLD, RUTH ANN, elementary education educator; b. Lebanon, Pa., June 3, 1955; d. Earl Edwin and Joan Marie (Meyer) Rittle; m. Elijah Joseph Arnold III, July 17, 1976; 1 child, Nathan Joseph. BS, Lebanon Valley Coll., 1977; MEd, Millersville U., 1982, MEd, 2002. Cert. reading recovery tchr. Elem. reading specialist, reading recovery tchr. Palmyra (Pa.) Area Sch. Dist., 1980—. Vol. Local 4-H Club, Lebanon, Pa., 1973-98; organist, choir dir. Tulpehocken United Ch. of Christ, Richland, Pa., 1982-95. Mem. Internat. Reading Assn., Keystone State Reading Assn., Lebanon-Lancaster Reading Coun., Reading Recovery Coun. North Am. Avocation: music.

ARNOLD, RUTH SOUTHGATE, librarian; b. Cin., Oct. 2, 1950; d. Roger Frederick Arnold and Harriet Hendershot Wolf Arnold; m. Louis Dolive; children: Caroline Elizabeth Dolive, William Arnold Dolive. BA, Eckerd Coll., 1972; MSLS, Simmons Coll., 1977. Cert. libr. Va. Info. specialist Warner-Eddison Assocs., Inc., Cambridge, Mass., 1977—79; asst. dir. Augusta County Libr., Fishersville, Va., 1979—81; tech. svcs. libr. Staunton (Va.) Pub. Libr., 1987—91, dir., 1991—. Mem. ednl. com. Woodrow Wilson Birthplace, Staunton, 1998—2002; sec. Staunton (Va.) Downtown Devel. Assn., 2001—02, v.p., 2003—. Named Woman of the Yr., Staunton Bus. & Profl. Women's Orgn., 1997; fellow Paul Harris, Rotary, 1995. Mem.: ALA, Va. Pub. Libr. Dirs. Assn. (sec., regional rep. 1997—2002), Va. Libr. Assn. (2d v.p. 2000—01), Staunton Rotary Club (pres. 1998—99). Presbyterian. Avocations: singing, dancing. Office: Staunton Pub Libr 1 Churchville Ave Staunton VA 24401 Office Fax: (540) 332-3906. Business E-Mail: arnoldrs@ci.staunton.va.us.

ARNOLD, SANDRA RUTH KOUNS, photographer; b. Cleburne, Tex., Jan. 20, 1941; d. Wyatt Allen and Ethel Louise (Gandillon) Kouns; m. William Patrick Arnold, Feb. 27, 1960; children: Allyson Arnold House, Lynn Ann Workman. Student, Hill Coll., Cleburne, Tex., 1975, 78-79. 95, Richland Coll., Dallas, 1986, 94, Sam Houton State U., 1996, 97, 2001; profl. cert., Tex. Sch. Profl. Photography. Lic. realtor Tex., cert. photographer Profl. Photographers Assn., Nat. Profl. Photographers Assn. Decorator, owner Baileys Home Improvements, Cleburne, 1971-77; realtor Red Carpet and Holliday Assocs., Cleburne, 1979-98; pub./patient rels. Meml. Hosp., Cleburne, 1982-86; mktg./patient rels. staff, asst. coord. Walls Regional Hosp., Cleburne, 1986; mktg. mgr. Harris Meth. Health System, Ft. Worth, 1986-88; mktg./physician recruiting dir. Kimbro Med. Ctr., Cleburne, 1988-92; profl. photographer, 1996—; antique shop owner My Favorite Things, 1995-98. Owner, v.p. A&A Plastic Co., 1969-98; vocalist weddings, theaters, and chs., Cleburne, 1959—. Contbr. articles to profl. jours. Established Area Alzheimer Support Group, Cleburne, 1984, Cleburne Women's Tennis League; coord., cons. Adopt-A-Sch./Cleburne Schs., 1984—; mem., actress Carnegie Theater; active Johnson County Hist. Commn., PTA; vol. Johnson County Meml. Hosp., 1972—96; ARC; established crime watch neighborhood program, 1998; vol. mus. entertainment for hosp. patient; active St. Mark Meth. Ch., Cleburne. Named one of Outstanding Women of S.W., 1979. Mem.: Cleburne C. of C., Heritage Assembly (charter), Women's Forum, Beta Sigma Phi (pres., Woman of Yr. 1963, 1981). Avocations: music, genealogy, travel, antiques, yoga, music, genealogy, travel, antiques. Home and Office: PO Box 63 Cleburne TX 76033-0063

ARNOLD, STANLEY NORMAN, manufacturing consultant; b. Cleve., May 26, 1915; s. Morris L. and Mildred (Stearn) A.; m. Barbara Anne Laing, Aug. 31, 1946; 1 child, Jennifer Laing BS in Econs., U. Pa., 1937. Co-founder, exec. v.p. Pick-N-Pay Supermarkets, Cleve., 1937-51; exec. v.p., dir. Cottage Creamery Co., Cleve., 1937-51; dir. sales promotion div. Young & Rubicam, N.Y.C., 1952-58; founder, pres. Stanley Arnold & Assocs., Inc., N.Y.C., 1958—. Cons. Ford Motor Co., United Airlines, Gen. Electric, Nat. Cash Register, IBM, Philip Morris, Am. Express, Bank of America, DuPont, Goodyear, Quaker Oats, Readers Digest, Continental Can, Hunt Foods, Moet-Hennessy, Seagram, Pan Am, Chrysler Corp., Pillsbury, Coca Cola, Gen. Mills, Lever Bros., Exxon, Arco, Hallmark, others; mem. adv. bd. Bank of Palm Springs div. Bank of Calif. subs. Mitsubishi Corp., 1989—; vis. exec. prof. Freeman Sch. Bus., Tulane U., 1998—. Author: Tale of the Blue Horse, 1968; Magic Power of Putting Yourself Over with People, 1961; I Ran Against Jimmy Carter, 1977. Syndicated daily columnist, 1943-48. Architect of plan to install new office of v.p. in White House. Contbr. articles to profl. jours. Pres. Ind. Sch. Fund of N.Y.C., 1960-66; mem. fund raising com. U.S. Olympic Team, 1984. Founding mem. Nat. Businessmen for Humphrey, 1968, Nat. Citizens for Humphrey, 1968; candidate for Dem. nomination for v.p. U.S., 1972; chmn. White House Libr. Fund Raising Com., 1961-63; corp. sponsor for The Rose as Nat. Flower, 1983-86; nat. chmn. Golf's Tribute to Ike, 1980; mem. Clinton adv. com., 1991-92. Recipient Sales Exec. award Sales Exec. Club N.Y., 1965; Wisdom award of Honor Wisdom Soc., 1979 Mem.: Les Amis D'Escoffier, Doubles, Dutch Treat (N.Y.C.); 7 Lakes Country, La Quinta Country, Racquet, Tennis, Indian Wells Racquet, Desert Riders, La Quinta Fishing, Oasis Water Park (Palm Springs, Calif.); Balboa Bay (Newport Beach, Calif.), Outrigger Canoe Club of Honolulu. Home: 162 Desert Lakes Dr Palm Springs CA 92264-5521 also: 2895 Kalakaua Ave Honolulu HI 96815-4003 also: 375 Park Ave New York NY 10152-0002 Office: 162 Desert Lakes Dr Palm Springs CA 92264-5521

ARNOLD, STEPHEN PAUL, investment professional; b. San Antonio, Mar. 26, 1957; s. Francis Andrew and Charlene (Tyler) A.; m. Kenzie Lou Box, Dec. 16, 1978; children: Stephen Kameron, Kalen Lou. BS in Agrl. Econs., Tex. A&M U., 1979. Rsch. specialist Employee's Retirement System of Tex., Austin, 1982-84, adminstr. of spl. programs, 1984-85, dir. of spl. programs, 1985-87, asst. investment officer, 1987-91, investment portfolio mgr., 1991-94; strategist and portfolio mgr. Bluestone Investments, 1994-96; v.p., trust investment officer San Antonio, Tex.-Norwest Bank Tex., N.A., San Antonio, 1997-99; sr. v.p. instnl. svcs. Southwestern Capital Markets, San Antonio, 2000—. Mem. Tex. Econ. Forum, Austin, 1989-92; adv. bd. Internat. Bus. Forum, N.Y.C. Del. Tex. Rep. Party, Austin, 1980-86. Named to Outstanding Young Men of Am., 1983. Mem. Austin Investment Assn., Fin. Analyst Assn., Capitol City A&M Club, Former Student Assn./Tex. A&M. Baptist. Avocations: reading, parenting, coaching junior major baseball, coaching baseball all-stars. Home: 25110 Summit Cove San Antonio TX 78258-1930 Office: Southwestern Capital Markets 140 E Houston Ste 201 San Antonio TX 78205-

ARNOLD, THOMAS IVAN, JR., state legislator; b. Paterson, N.J. s. Thomas Ivan and Marjorie Lewis (Eccles) A.; m. Barbara Jane Phinney, July 25, 1953 (dec. June 1985); children: Thomas I., Barbara J., Edward H., Patricia J., Peter S., Dennis L., Nancy L., Richard B., Susan D., Charles P. ME, Stevens Inst. Tech., Hoboken, N.J., 1950, MS, 1954; PhD, U. Wexford, 1986. Registered profl engr., N.H. Asst. to quality mgr. Curtiss-Wright Corp., Wood Ridge, NJ, 1950-58; mgr. corp. quality control ops. Sanders Assocs., Inc., Nashua, NH, 1958-67; mgr. quality assurance RCA Corp., Burlington, Mass., 1967-72; mgr. product assurance and quality control Compugraphic Corp., Wilmington, Mass., 1972-81; mgr. quality assurance GE, Burlington, 1981-91; state rep. dist. 46 N.H. Gen. Ct., 1992—, vice chair com. on election laws, 1997-98, mem. com. on sci., tech. and energy, 1999—2000, mem. com. on sci. tech. and energy, 2003—, mem. com. on children and family law, 1999—. Moderator Sch. Dist., Brookline, 1960—, Town of Brookline, 1976—, selectman, 1968-69; chmn. Zoning Bd. Adjustment, Brookline, 1970-82; chmn. Rep. town com.; mem. N.H. State Rep. Com., 1999—; mem. EMT Brookline Vol. Ambulance, 1976-86; mem. N.H. Indsl. Heritage Commn., 1995-96. With USAAF, 1946-47. Mem.: NRA, Soc. for Quality (sect. chmn. 1964), GO N.H., Mensa, Order of Daedalians. Republican. Episcopalian. Avocations: fixing things, wood working. Home: 10 Milford St Brookline NH 03033-2446 Office: NH House State House Concord NH 03301 E-mail: TIArnold@yahoo.com.

ARNOLD, W. H. (DUB ARNOLD), state supreme court chief justice; b. Arkadelphia, Ark., May 19, 1935; m. Betty Earlene Aud; three children. BA, Henderson State U., 1957; LLB, Ark. Law Sch., 1962. Dep. prosecuting atty. Clark County, Ark., 1965-66; prosecuting atty. 8th Jud. Dist., State of Ark., 1969-72; chmn.hief justice Ark. Workers Compensation Commn., 1973-77; prosecuting atty. 9th Jud. Dist. East, State of Ark., 1981-90; mcpl. judge Clark County, 1979-80; cir./chancery judge 9th Jud. Dist. East, State of Ark., 1991-96; chief justice Ark. Supreme Ct., 1997—. Law educator Ouachita Bapt. U., Arkadelphia, Ark., 1975-76, Ark. Law Enforcement Acad., 1990, Garland County C.C., 1993; lectr. Ark. Prosecuting Atty.'s Assn., 1988. Office: Justice Bldg 625 Marshall St, 120 Justice Building Little Rock AR 72201-1052*

ARNOLD, WILLIAM EDWIN, health advocate, consultant; b. Charleston, SC, Aug. 13, 1938; s. Edwin Gustaf and Sara Louise (Hitchcock) A. BA, Yale U., 1960. Pres. Dixon & Rippel, Inc., Saugerties, N.Y., 1965-70; v.p. Taj Enterprises Ltd., 1965-67, Bellern Rsch. Corp.; pres. Dixon & Rippel divsn., Saugerties, 1970-75; v.p H & G Industries, Inc.; pres. World Brushworks, Inc., 1982-84; v.p. CFO Optimax III, Inc., N.Y.C., 1983-84; mng. dir. Brush Trading, Ltd., 1983-87; pres. Chestnut Holdings Ltd., 1985-91; part-time mng. dir. Cassi Properties, 1984—; pres. Computerworx, Inc., Washington, 1999—. Pres. Swan Holding Ltd., 1985-88. Bd. dirs. ARCS, 1991-92; chair Dutchess County AIDS Consortium, 1989-95; chmn. Dutchess County HIV Health Svcs. Planning Coun., 1995-96; bd. dirs. ARCS Cmty. Educator, 1989-91; pres. Hudson AIDS Cmty. Progress, Inc., 1992-94; exec. dir. Title II Nat. AIDS Coalition, 1994-95; CEO Title II Cmty. AIDS Nat. Network, Washington, 1995—; chair ADAP Working Group, Washington, 1995—; sec.-treas. AIDS Empowerment and Treatment Internat., Washington, 2002—. 1st lt. U.S. Army, 1961-63. Mem.: Res. Officers Assn., Yale Club (Washington). Home: 1755 Seaton Pl NW Washington DC 20009-2625 Office: 1775 T St NW Washington DC 20009-7124 E-mail: weaids@aol.com.

ARNOLD, WILLIAM HOWARD, retired nuclear fuel executive; b. Jefferson Barracks, Mo., May 13, 1931; s. William Howard and Elizabeth Welsh A.; m. Josephine Routheau, June 13, 1952; children: William, Frances, Edward, David, Thomas. AB, Cornell U., 1951; AM, Princeton U., 1953, PhD, 1955. Registered profl. engr., Pa. Sr. engr. comml. and atomic power Westinghouse Elec. Corp., Pitts., 1955-61, program mgr. Nerva project, 1962-68, engring. mgr. pressurized water reactor div., 1971-72, gen. mgr. pressurized water reactor div., 1972-78, gen. mgr. nuclear internat. div., 1979-80, gen. mgr. AESD div. Madison, Pa., 1981-86; mgr. Westinghouse Def. Ctr., Balt., 1968-70; v.p. engring. and devel. Westinghouse Hanford Co. (subs. Westinghouse Elec. Corp.), Richland, Wash., 1987-89; pres. La. Energy Svcs., 1989-96, ret., 1996. Contbr. articles to profl. jours.; patentee in field. Fellow AAAS, Am. Nuclear Soc.; mem. Nat. Acad. Engring. (elected), Am. Phys. Soc., Sigma Xi.

ARNOLD, WILLIAM MCCAULEY, lawyer; b. Waco, Tex., May 3, 1947; s. Watson Caulfield and Mary Rebecca Arnold; m. Karen Axtell, May 17, 1980; children: Margaret McCauley, William Axtell. BA, Duke U., 1969; JD, U. Tex., 1972. Bar: Tex. 1973, Va. 1975, D.C. 1977, Md. 1983, U.S. Dist. Ct. (ea. dist.) Va. 1975, U.S. Ct. Appeals (4th cir.) 1977, U.S. Ct. Claims 1977, U.S. Supreme Ct. 1978. Spl. atty. U.S. Dept. Justice, Newark, 1973-75; asst. county atty. County of Fairfax, Va., 1975-78; ptnr. Cowles, Rinaldi & Arnold, Ltd., Fairfax, 1978-95, McCandlish & Lillard, Fairfax, 1995—. Instr. No. Va. C.C., Alexandria. Pres. Clifton Betterment Assn., Va., 1979-81; chmn. Clifton Planning Commn., 1980-85, mem. Clifton Town Coun., 1985—; bd. dirs. Clifton Gentlemen's Social Club, 1981-84. Mem. ABA, Va. State Bar Assn., Fairfax County Bar Assn., Va. Trial Lawyers Assn., Associated Builders and Contractors. Office: McCandlish & Lillard PC 11350 Random Hills Rd Ste 500 Fairfax VA 22030-6044 E-mail: marnold@mccandlaw.com.

ARNOLD, WILLIAM PARSONS, JR., retired internist; b. Waterbury, Conn., May 10, 1922; s. William Parsons and Dorothy Amanda (Granniss) A.; m. Mildred Opal Beleu, Oct. 27, 1948; children: Susan Emerson Arnold Brainerd, Jane Elizabeth Arnold Pittari. BS, Yale U., 1943; MD, Columbia U., 1946. Diplomate Am. Bd. Med. Examiners. Intern St. Luke's Hosp., N.Y.C., 1946-47, resident in medicine, 1949-51, chief resident in medicine, 1951-52; pvt. practice Middlebury, Conn., 1952-89. Attending physician medicine Waterbury (Conn.) Hosp., 1952-89; assoc. attending physician St. Mary's Hosp., Waterbury, 1952-89; dir. health Middlebury (Conn.) Dept. Health, 1954—; sch. physician Region 15 Elem. Schs., Middlebury, 1955-92; asst. med. examiner Conn. State M-E Office, Middlebury, 1956-84; surgeon Middlebury Vol. Fire Dept. and Middlebury Police Dept., 1964—. Capt. U.S. Army Med. Corps, 1947-49, ETO. Recipient John N. Lewis Founders award Waterbury Vis. Nurse Assn., 1988. Mem. AMA, ACP, Conn. State Med. Soc., New Haven County Med. Assn., Waterbury Med. Assn. Republican. Congregationalist. Avocations: western riding, rodeos. Home: 142 White Deer Rock Rd Middlebury CT 06762-1314

ARNOLD, WILLIAM THOMAS, software developer, chemist; b. N.Y.C., Oct. 6, 1948; s. Herbert S. and Miriam Arnold. BS in Chemistry, Carnegie-Mellon U., 1970; MS in Chemistry, Fla. State U., 1976; postgrad. in enology, U. Calif., Davis, 1977-78. Winemaker Smothers Winery, Santa Cruz, Calif., 1978-85; consulting enologist Stag's Leap Wine Cellars, Napa, Calif., 1985-87; winemaker, gen. mgr. Domaine Laurier Vineyard, Forestville, Calif., 1987-88; sr. chemist U.S. Treasury Dept., San Francisco, 1990-97; prin. William Arnold Consulting, Walnut Creek, Calif., 1997—. Lectr., U. Calif., Santa Cruz, 1998; instr., Fed. Law Enforcement Tng. Ctr., Glynco, Ga., 1992-93; extension instr. computer sci. U. Calif., Berkeley, 2000—. Author: (computer programs) Standard Curve Pro & Chemical Databases, 1997—, Technicell 80 Stock-Market Program, 1999; contbr. articles to profl. jours. Sgt., USAF, 1971-74, Washington. Recipient Gold medal for comml. cabernet sauvignon, Sonoma (Calif.) Harvest Fair, 1982, Gold medal for comml. gewurztraminer, L.A. County Fair, 1981. Mem. Assn. Ofcl. Analytical Chemists Internat. (pres. Pacific region 1997-98), Am. Soc. Enology and Viticulture (mem. tech. projects com. 1992-97). Office: W Arnold Consulting 1240 Walker Ave Apt 209 Walnut Creek CA 94596-4829 Fax: 510-938-7280.

ARNOLD, WINNIE JO, retired mental health nurse, nursing administrator; b. Cromwell, Okla., May 21, 1929; d. Robb Henry and Luella (Odom) Boatman; widowed; children: Linda, Cherie. BSEd, Okla. U., 1962; ADN, Amarillo Coll., 1974; BSN, St. Joseph's Coll., 1977. RN, Tex. Charge nurse Northwest Tex. Hosp., Amarillo; staff nurse, team leader High Plains Bapt. Hosp., Amarillo; adminstr. Healthcare Svcs., Amarillo; dir. nurses Tex. Dept. Corrections, Amarillo, 1989-97. Vol. ARC. Recipient Vol. award ARC, 1989, Pilot Club, 1989. Mem. Am. Kidney Found., Women's Bus. Assn. (Bus. Woman of Yr. 1989). Home: 216 Ramada Trl Amarillo TX 79108-1128 E-mail: wjatexan@msn.com.

ARNOLD-OLSON, HELEN B. nonprofit consultant; b. Cedar Rapids, Iowa, Sept. 22, 1948; d. Duane Arnold Sr. and Henrietta Dows; m. Edward R. Krieger Jr., May 23, 1970 (div. Aug. 1974); m. Reuben I. Olson, July 2, 1982; 1 child, Andrew R. Olson. B in Music cum laude, Cornell Coll., 1970. Office mgr. Irving R. Zimmerman Co., Chgo., 1973-75; loan officer comml. and residential Banco Mortgage Co., Chgo., 1975-77, 79-82; asst. v.p., mgr., mortgage lending Olympic Savings & Loan Assn., Berwyn, Ill., 1977-79; underwriter, cons. Fed. Housing Adminstrn., Chgo., 1976-83; co-owner, pres. and exec. chef Hawkeye Nut Co., Cedar Rapids, 1983-87; pres. Dows Farms, Inc., Cedar Rapids, 1987-96; dir. devel. YWCA of Cedar Rapids and Linn County, 1996—2000; pres. Green Light, LLC, Arnold-Olson Assocs., Hel's Kitchen, 2000—; nonprofit cons. Bd. dirs. The Dows Cos., Cedar Rapids, Cedar Rapids Airport Commn. Bd. dirs., co-chair capital campaign endorsement The History Ctr., Cedar Rapids, 1996—; v.p., bd. dirs. Friends of the Zoo, Cedar Rapids, 1997—; bd. dirs. Kingston Hill Home for Aged Women, Cedar Rapids, 1998—. Recipient Leadership for Five Seasons award Cedar Rapids Area C. of C., 1996. Mem. AAUW, Assn. Fund Raising Profls., Iowa Women's Found., Variety Club of Iowa (bd. dirs., past chair, Sunshine award 1999), Rotary. Presbyterian. Avocations: cooking, traveling. Home: 3840 Bever Ave SE Cedar Rapids IA 52403-4366 Office: Arnold-Olson Assocs 3840 Bever Ave SE Cedar Rapids IA 52403 E-mail: HBAO48@aol.com.

ARNON, BARUCH, pianist, educator; b. Novi Sad, Yugoslavia, Aug. 26, 1931; came to U.S. 1962; s. Alexander and Vera (Berl) A.; m. Drora Schreiber, Aug. 9, 1960. AB in Piano, Pedagogue, Israel Acad. Music, Tel Aviv, 1960; MusB, The Julliard Sch., 1964, MS, 1965. Faculty Israel Acad. Music, 1960-62, The Juilliard Sch., N.Y.C., 1971—; artistic dir. Musica da Camera, Westchester, N.Y., 1972-80. Recitals, chamber music concerts, U.S. and Israel. Avocations: reading, gardening, travel. Home: 14 Wynmore Rd Scarsdale NY 10583-7263 Office: The Juilliard Sch Lincoln Ctr New York NY 10583

ARNON, STEPHEN SOULÉ, epidemiologist, research scientist; b. Oakland, Calif., Oct. 14, 1946; s. Daniel I. and Lucile S. Arnon; m. Joyce M. Meissinger, Aug. 24, 1985; children: Eric, Christina. AB, Harvard U., 1968, MPH, 1972, MD, 1973. Lic. physician Calif. Resident physician U. Colo. Hosps., Denver, 1973—75; med. epidemiologist Ctrs. for Disease Control, Atlanta, 1975—76, Berkeley, Calif., 1976—77; founder, chief infant botulism treatment and prevention program Calif. Dept. Health Svcs., Berkeley, 1977—. Contbr. articles and book chpts. to profl. publs. Bd. dirs. Orinda (Calif.) Pks. and Recreation Found., Orinda, 1992—. Lt. comdr. USPHS, 1975—77. Recipient Jens Aubrey Westengard and John Houghton Taylor scholarships, Harvard Med. Sch., 1968—73. Fellow: Am. Coll. Epidemiology, Infectious Disease Soc. Am. Achievements include creation and development of orphan drug Botulism Immune Globulin Intravenous (Human) for treatment of infant botulism; research in orphan drug development; medical and public health management of botulinum toxin if used as bioweapon. Office: Calif Dept Health Svcs 850 Marina Bay Pkwy Richmond CA 94804

ARNONE, MICHAEL JOHN, state legislator, dentist; b. Red Bank, N.J., Sept. 10, 1932; m. Barbara Covert, 1956; children: John Stephen, Suzanne, Mark Raymond, Paul Xavier, Michael David. Student, Seton Hall U.; DDS, Temple U., 1958. Pvt. practice dentistry, 1961—; mem. from dist. 12 N.J. State Assembly, 1989—, chmn. local govt. and housing com., 1992—. Chmn. Red Bank Zoning Bd., 1969; councilman City of Red Bank, 1970-73, mayor, 1979-90; mem. Monmouth County Rep. Exec. Com. Mem. KC, Elks. Home: 258 Broad St Red Bank NJ 07701-2003 Office: 244 Broad St Red Bank NJ 07701-2003*

ARNONE, SAMUEL FRANK, music educator, consultant; b. Canonsburg, Pa., Apr. 14, 1951; s. Philip Guytano and Phyllis Ann Arnone; m. Jayne Lynn Arnone, June 15, 1974; children: Philip Anthony, Samuel Nicholas. BS Music Edn., Clarion U., Clarion, Pennsylvania, 1973. Music educator Hughesville H.S., Hughesville, Pa., 1984—, Lock Haven H.S., Lock Haven, Pa., 1973—82. Consulting Arnone Consulting, Lock Haven, Pa., 1982—84. Mem.: Rotary Club, Elks, Sons of Italy, Phi Deta Kappa, Phi Beta Mu. Home: 26 Woodlan Dr Lock Haven PA 17737 Personal E-mail: sarnone2@adelphia.net.

ARNOTT, HOWARD JOSEPH, biology educator, university dean; b. Los Angeles, Mar. 9, 1928; s. Andrew Hugh and Evelyn Leonore (Donnelly) A.; m. Wanda Jean Cross, Jan. 28, 1950; children: John Joseph, Catherine Jean Arnott-Thornton, Susan Leonore Arnott Garrett, Virginia Anne Arnott Scott. AB, U. So. Calif., 1952, MS, 1953; PhD, U. Calif., Berkeley, 1958. Asst. prof. biology Northwestern U., Evanston, Ill., 1958-64; assoc. prof. dept. botany U. Tex., Austin, 1965-68, prof., 1968-72, acting chmn. dept., 1970-71; prof., chmn. dept. biology U. So. Fla., Tampa, 1972-74; dean Coll. Sci. U. Tex., Arlington, 1974-90, prof. biology, 1974-91, Ashbel Smith prof. biology, 1991-96, dir. Ctr. for Electron Microscopy Coll. Sci., 1984—, Jenkins Garrett prof., 1996—. Vis. mem. dept. biology Tex. A&M U., 1971-75; cons. Ency. Brit. Films, NASA, Alcon Labs., Frito-Lay; bd. dirs. Ft. Worth Nature Ctr., 1985-91; chmn. 2nd Gordon Conf. Calcium Oxalate, 1989, main spkr. 4th Conf., 1993; vis. prof. Purdue U., 1990-91; Bessey lectr. Iowa State U., 1993. Advisory editor: Protoplasma; Contbr. articles, abstracts to sci. jours., chpts. to books. With USN, 1946-48. Recipient award for disting. and continued research U. Tex. at Arlington, 1984; postdoctoral fellow U. Tex., NIH, 1964-65; NSF grantee, 1963-65, NIH grantee, 1989. Mem. Am. Soc. Plant Physiology, Bot. Soc. Am., Mycol. Soc. Am., Microscopy Soc. Am., Tex. Soc. Microscopy (hon., pres. 1988-89), Sigma Xi (bd. dirs. S.W. region 1984-91), Phi Sigma.

ARNOTT, ROBERT DOUGLAS, investment company executive; b. Chgo., June 29, 1954; s. Robert James Arnott and Catherine (Bonnell) Cameron; children: Robert Lindsay, Sydney Allison, Richard James. BA, U. Calif., Santa Barbara, 1977. V.p. Boston Co., 1977—84; pres., chief exec. officer TSA Capital Mgmt., L.A., 1984—87; v.p., strategist Salomon Bros. Inc., N.Y.C., 1987—88; mng. ptnr. First Quadrant Corp., Morristown, N.J., Pasadena, Calif., and London, 1988—96, Pasadena, London, Boston, 1996—2002; chmn. First Quadrant L.P., 2002—; chmn., CEO Rsch. Affiliates, LLC, 2002—. Mem. chmn.'s adv. coun. Chgo. Bd. Options Exch., 1989-94; bd. dirs. Internat. Faculty in Fin.; mem. product adv. bd. Chgo. Mercantile Exch., 1990-96; vis. prof. UCLA, 200103. Editor: Asset Allocation, 1988, Active Asset Allocation, 1992, Handbook of Equity Style Management, 1997, Fin. Analysts Jour., 2003—; mem. editorial bd. Jour. of Investing, 1990—, Jour. Portfolio Mgmt., 1984—2003, Jour. Wealth Mgmt., 1997—; contbr. articles to profl. jours. and chpts. to books. Mem. Inst. Internat. Rsch. (adv. bd. 1990—), Assn. for Investment Mgmt. and Rsch., Inst. Quantitative Rsch. in Fin., Toronto Stock and Futures Exch. (adv. coun. 1992—). Avocations: motorcycling, astrophotography, billiards, sommelier, travel. Office: 1st Quadrant LP 800 E Colorado Blvd Ste 900 Pasadena CA 91101-2141

ARNOULD, RICHARD JULIUS, economist, educator, consultant; b. Rochelle, Ill., Nov. 18, 1941; s. Elliott and Blanch (Colwell) A.; m. Carol Foster, Aug. 27, 1960; children: Debra, Laura. BS, Iowa State U., 1963, MS, 1965, PhD, 1968. Instr. Iowa State U., Ames, 1963-65; asst. prof. econs. and bus. adminstrn. U. Ill., Champaign, 1967-72, assoc. prof., 1973-82, prof., 1982—2003, prof. emeritus, 2003—, dir. Coll. Rsch. Office, 1995-96, assoc. dean for acad. affairs, Coll. Commerce and Bus. Adminstrn., 1979-87, prof. econs., Coll. Medicine, 1984—, adj. prof. Inst. of Govt. and Pub. Affairs, 1987—, dir. Program in Health Econs., Mgmt. & Policy, 1989—, head dept. econs., 1996—2003. Acting dir. Exec. Devel. Ctr., part-time 1982, 84, mem. Med. Scholars Steering Com., active numerous other univ., coll. and dept. coms.; rsch. economist pricing and competition grp., USDA, 1965-67; vice chmn. Dept. Econs., U. Ill., 1970-73; vis. economist Econ. Policy Office, U.S. Justice Dept., 1973-74; regional economist U.S. Comptroller of Currency, 1976-79; vis. rsch. prof. Duke U., 1977-78; vis. rsch. scholar York (Eng.) U.; cons. Carle Found., chmn. bd., 1989-91; mem. Gov.'s Task Force on Health Care Reform, 1992-95; cons. Auditor Gen. State of Ill., GAO, Health Care Financing Adminstrn., Anti-trust div. U.S. Justice Dept., ABA, AMA, Prepaid Legal Svcs. Inst., others; bd. dirs. First Busey Trust & Investment Co.; expert witness numerous law firms; speaker profl. meetings. Author: Extra Territorial Application and Effects of Certain U.S. and Canadian Laws, 1978, (monograph) Blue Shield Fee Setting in the Physicians' Service Market: A Theoretical and Empirical Analysis, (pamphlets) Diversification and Profitability Among Large Food Processing Firms, USDA, 1970, (with R. Resek) A Comparative Cost Study of Staff Panel and Participating Attorney Panel Prepaid Legal Service Plans, ABA, 1982; editor spl. issue Quar. Rev. of Econs. and Bus., 1990, also book chpts. and revs.; co-editor: (with R. Rich and W. White) Competitive Approaches to Health Care Reform, 1993; contbr. numerous articles to profl. jours. Bd. dirs. City Bank Champaign, First Basey Trust and Investment Co.; trustee Carle Found., 1981-93, chmn. fin. com., 1982-86, chmn. bd., 1989-91; elder 1st Presbyn. Ch., Champaign; mem. Gov.'s Task Force on Health Care Reform; mem. U.S. Govt. Study of Econ. Underpinning of Vaccine Markets. Brookings Inst. Econ. Policy fellow, 1973; recipient Outstanding Service award, U.S. Justice Dept., 1974; grantee Internat. Bur. Edn., 1979, Carle Found., 1982-83, Grad. Research Bd., 1983-86; named Outstanding Tchr. U. Ill. various yrs. Mem. Am. Econ. Assn., So. Econ. Assn., Internat. Health Econs. Assn., Midwest Econ. Assn. Avocation: golf. Office: U Ill 1206 S 6th St Champaign IL 61820-6978 E-mail: rarnould@uiuc.edu.

ARNOVE, ROBERT FREDERICK, education educator; b. Chgo. s. Isadore and Julie (Zeplowitz) A.; m. Toby Strout; 1 child, Anthony Keats BA, U. Mich., 1969; MA, Tufts U., 1961; PhD, Stanford U., 1969. Vol. tchr. Peace Corps, Venezuela, 1962-64; Ford Found. edn. advisor Bogota, Colombia, 1969-71; prof. comparative edn. Ind. U., Bloomington, 1969—, Ind. U.-Hangzhou, People's Rep. China, 1983; vis. prof. Stanford U., McGill U. Edn. cons. to Latin Am. ministries and agys.; dir. Overseas Study Program of Ind., Purdue, and Wis. univs. in Madrid, 1989—; USIA Exch. scholar, Ryazan, Russia, 1996, Yaounde, Cameroon, 1997, Salamanca, Spain, 2001; UNESCO-chair vis. scholar U. Palermo, Buenos Aires, 1997-2003; adv. prof. Hong Kong Inst. Edn. Author, editor, co-editor: Student Alienation, Educational Television, Education and American Culture Comparative Education, Philanthropy and Cultural Imperialism, Education and Revolution in Nicaragua, National Literacy Campaign: Historical and Comparative Perspectives, Emergent Issues in Education: Comparative Perspectives, Education as Contested Terrain: Nicaragua 1979-93, 1994, Comparative education: The Dialectic of the Global and the Local, 1999, 2003; prodr. (documentary) Alternative Public Schools, 1978, Asi Fue: Election Time Nicaragua, 1984; contbr. articles to profl. jours. Citizens Party candidate for U.S. Congress, 8th dist. Ind., 1982 Fulbright grantee, India, 1982; Fulbright lectr. Fed. U. Bahai, Brazil, 1995; Fulbright sr. scholar U. Iberoamericana, Dominican Republic, 2003. Mem. Comparative and Internat. Edn. Soc. (pres. 2001, hon. fellow), Latin Am. Studies Assn., Am. Ednl. Rsch. Assn. Phi Beta Kappa. Office: Ind U Sch Edn Bloomington IN 47405 E-mail: arnove@indiana.edu.

ARNOVITZ, BENTON MAYER, editor; b. Butler, Pa., July 21, 1942; s. Paul and Miriam (Shapiro) A. AB, Cornell U., 1964; MA, NYU, 1969; grad., U.S. Army Command and Gen. Staff Coll., 1982; grad. Nat.Security Mgmt. Program, Nat. Def. U., 1986. Editor Macmillan Pub. Co., N.Y.C., 1966-73; sr. trade editor Chilton Book Co., Radnor, Pa., 1973-76; exec. editor Stein and Day Pubs., Briarcliff Manor, N.Y., 1976-85, v.p., 1984-85; ind. editorial svcs., 1985-89, 91-93; editorial dir. Scarborough House Pubs. div. BookCrafters, Peekskill, N.Y., 1989-91; dir. acad. pubs. U.S. Holocaust Meml. Mus., Washington, 1994—. Contbr. articles to scholarly jour. and newspapers. Trustee Field Libr. Inc., 1985-94, Westchester Libr. Sys., 1992-94; mem. Spirit of Raoul Wallenberg Humanitarian award selection com. Am. Swedish Hist. Mus. Capt. U.S. Army, 1964-66, 70; lt. col. USAR. Mem. Alpha Phi Delta. Home: 13439 Overbrook Ln Bowie MD 20715-1159 Office: 100 Raoul Wallenberg Pl SW Washington DC 20024-2126

ARNOWITT, RICHARD LEWIS, physics educator, researcher; b. N.Y.C., May 3, 1928; s. Leon and Belle (Feinberg) A.; m. Young In Rhee, Apr. 21, 1961; children: Michael Paul, Myron Philip. BS, MS, Rensselaer Poly. Inst., 1948; PhD, Harvard U., 1953. Rsch. assoc. Radiation Lab. U. Calif., Berkeley, 1952-54; mem. Inst. Advanced Study, Princeton, N.J., 1954-56; asst. prof. Syracuse (N.Y.) U., 1956-59, assoc. prof., 1959-62; prof. Northeastern U., Boston, 1962-86, Tex. A&M U., College Station, 1986-88, disting. prof. physics, 1988—, dir. Ctr. Theoretical Physics, 1986-95, head dept. physics, 1987-93. Contbr. over 200 articles to profl. jours. Fellow Guggenheim Found., 1975-76. Fellow Am. Phys. Soc. (Dannie N. Heineman prize 1994, Burgess chair high energy physics 1997—). Office: Texas A & M U Dept Physics College Station TX 77843-4242 E-mail: arnowitt@physics.tamu.edu.

ARNSTEIN, PAUL MICHAEL, nurse practitioner, pain specialist, educator; b. Boston, Aug. 29, 1956; s. Saul and JoAnne (Willens) A.; m. Honor Arnstein, Oct. 2, 1982; children: Eric Daniel, Cody Aaron. BSN, St. Louis U., 1979; MSN, U. Utah, 1984; PhD, Boston Coll., 1997. Nurse practitioner Garfield Meml. Hosp., Panquitch, Utah, dir. nursing, 1982-86; clin. nurse specialist Concord (N.H.) Hosp., 1986-94; rsch. fellow Boston Coll., 1994-97, 1998—; nurse practitioner, pain cons. Concord Hosp. and Dartmouth-Hitchcock Clinic Sys., 1997—. Pres. N.H. Cancer Pain Initiative, 1990—95; nurse practitioner Deaconess Hosp. Pain Program, 1995—; investigator for pain rsch.; asst. prof. Boston Coll., 1998—. Contbr. chpts. to books, articles to profl. jours. Mem.: ANA (cert., clin. nurse specialist, med.-surg. nurse, cert. AANP, cert. FNP), New Eng. Pain Assn. (pres. 1999—2001), Am. Soc. Pain Mgmt. Nurses (dir. 2001—). Home: 12 Oxalis Way Concord NH 03303-3428

ARNSTEIN, WALTER LEONARD, historian, educator; b. Stuttgart, Germany, May 14, 1930; arrived in U.S., 1939, naturalized, 1944; s. Richard and Charlotte (Heymann) A.; m. Charlotte Culver Sutphen, June 8, 1952; children: Sylvia, Peter. BSS., CCNY, 1951; MA, Columbia U., 1954; PhD, Northwestern U., 1961; postgrad., U. London, Eng., 1956-57. Asst. prof. history Roosevelt U., Chgo., 1957-62, assoc. prof., 1962-66, prof., acting dean grad. div., 1966-67; prof. history U. Ill., Urbana, 1968-98, LAS Jubilee prof. history, 1989-98, prof. history and LAS Jubilee prof. history emeritus, 1998—, chmn. dept., 1974-78, assoc. Ctr. for Advanced Study, 1972-73. Vis. assoc. prof. history Northwestern U., 1963—64; vis. fellow Clare Hall, Cambridge U., 1982; hon. fellow U. Edinburgh, 1989. Author: The Bradlaugh Case: A Study in Late Victorian Opinion and Politics, 1965, 2d edit., 1984, Britain Yesterday and Today, 1966, 8th edit., 2001, Protestant Versus Catholic in Mid-Victorian England, 1982, (with the late William B. Willcox) The Age of Aristocracy, 3d edit., 1976, 8th edit., 2001. Queen Victoria, 2003; editor: The Past Speaks: Sources and Problems in British History Since 1688, 1981, 2d edit. 1993; editor: Recent Historians of Great Britain, 1990; bd. editors The Historian, 1976-2000, Am. Hist. Rev., 1982-85, Albion, 1988-93; mem. bd. advisers: Victorian Studies, 1966-75; contbr. articles profl. jours. Vice chmn. Ill. Humanities Council, 1983-84. Served with AUS, 1951-53, Korea. Fulbright scholar, 1956-57; Fellow Am. Council Learned Socs., 1967-68 Fellow Royal Hist. Soc.; mem. Am. Hist. Assn., Brit. Hist. Assn., N.Am. Conf. Brit. Studies (exec. com. 1971-76, v.p. 1993-95, pres. 1995-97), Midwest Conf. on Brit. Studies (pres. 1980-82), Midwest Victorian Studies Assn. (pres. 1977-80), Phi Beta Kappa, Phi Alpha Theta. Home: 804 W Green St Champaign IL 61820-5017 Office: U Ill Dept History 309 N Gregory Hall 810 S Wright St Urbana IL 61801-3644 E-mail: warnstei@uiuc.edu.

ARNT, GEORGIA LEE, psychiatric social worker; b. Poughkeepsie, NY, Nov. 5, 1940; d. George and Virginia Kelley Christopher; m. John Harold Arnt, Dec. 6, 1959; children: Laura Lee, Cheryl Lee, Christopher Douglas. BA in Social Work cum laude, Fairleigh Dickinson U., 1973; MSW., Rutgers U., 1978. Cert. social worker, N.Y.; cert. sch. social worker, N.J.; cert. psychoanalytic psychotherapist Inst. Mental Health Edn.; lic. marriage and family therapist, N.J.; lic. clin. social worker, N.J. Social worker Div. Youth and Family Services State of N.J., Hackensack, 1974-75; social worker Fair Lawn (N.J.) Public Schs., 1978-80; guidance counselor, social worker Wyckoff (N.J.) Public Schs., 1980-82; psychoanalytic psychotherapist N.J. Center Psychotherapy, Englewood, 1981—. Instr. Midland Park Waldwick (N.J.) Adult Sch., 1982-86, Fair Lawn Adult Sch., Paramus Community Sch., 1983; psychotherapist Women's Counseling and Psychotherapy Service, 1982, Marriage and Family Counseling Svc., 1983. Columnist Suburban News, 1983-84. Mem. Nat. Assn. Social Workers, N.J. Soc. Clin. Social Workers, Am. Bd. Examiners in Clin. Social Work, Am. Assn. Marriage and Family Therapy, Acad. Cert. Social Workers, Am. Orthopsychiat. Assn. Unitarian Universalist. Home: 520 Linwood Ave Ridgewood NJ 07450-3556 E-mail: georgia@optonline.net.

ARNTSEN, ARNT PETER, engineer, consultant; b. Hvaler, Norway, Oct. 23, 1921; s. Arnt Peter and Helene Oleane (Helgesen) A.; m. Margot Petra Nilsen, Oct. 24, 1953; children: Tom David, Carol Ann, John Frederick. Registered profl. engr., Mass. Engr., Westinghouse Research Center, Pitts., 1962-64; sr. engrng. scientist RCA Corp., Burlington, Mass., 1964-89; cons., 1989-96, ret., 1996. Patentee in field. Home and Office: 9 Lincoln Ave Manchester MA 01944-1119

ARNTSON, AMY ELLEN, artist, art educator; b. Frankfort, Mich., Mar. 24, 1947; d. Otto and Marguerite (Johnson) A. BFA, Mich. State U., 1969; MFA, U. Wis., Milw., 1981. Art dir., photographer, designer, Ohio, Okla., Ky., Wis., 1970-81; prof. art dept. U. Wis., Whitewater, 1982—, interim assoc. dean Coll. Arts, 1990-91. Art dept. chair U. Wis., Whitewater, 1991-96; artist in residence Isle Royale Nat. Park, 1998, Voyageurs Nat. Park, 1998; presenter in field. Author: Graphic Design Basics, 1987, 4th edit., 2003; exhibited in solo and group shows including Royal Coll. Art, London, 1992, Wustum Mus., Racine, Wis., 1992-93, 95, 96, 97, 99, Wright Art Mus., Beloit (Wis.) Coll., 1993, 95, 98, The Adirondacks Nat. Exhbn. Am. Watercolors, N.Y., 1993, Watercolor USA, Springfield Art Mus., 1996, 4th Internat. Symposium on Elec. Arts, Mpls. Coll. Art and Design, 1993, Soc. Illustrators, Otis Coll., L.A., 1993, Fla. State U. Gallery and Mus., Tallahasee, 1994, 5th Internat. Symposium on Elec. Arts, Helsinki, Finland, 1994, NGO Forum Internat. Conf. on Women, Beijing, 1995, Peltz Gallery, Milw., 2000, Walkers Point Ctr. for Arts, 2000, 02, Madison Art Ctr. Triennial, 2002, others. Recipient Addy award Am. Advt. Fedn., 1983, Watercolor Wis. award Wutsum Mus., 1984, 95, 96, Juror's Choice award Midwest Photography Competition, 1988, Artist in Residency award Exptl. TV Ctr., Oswego, N.Y., 1989, Seymour Chwast award Design Milw., MIAD, 1992, Cert. of Merit award Soc. of Illustrators, 1993, Joseph A. Marino Purchase award Wustum Mus. Permanent Collection, 1999; grantee U. Wis., Whitewater, 1985-86 88-89, 94, 97. Mem. Midwest Watercolor Soc., Coll. Art Assn., Found. in Art and Theory Edn., Women's Caucus for Art, Graphic Design Eductor's Assn., Ctr. for Photography at Madison. Home: N6475 Shorewood Hills Rd Lake Mills WI 53551-9724 Office: Art Dept U Wis-Whitewater Whitewater WI 53190 E-mail: arntsona@uwwvax.uww.edu.

ARNTSON, PETER ANDREW, lawyer; b. Washington, May 23, 1938; s. Paul Lee and Mary Ellen (Garrigan) A.; m. Colette Rousseau, July 11, 1962; 1 child, Eric Paul. BA, U. Va., 1960, JD, 1965; LLM in Taxation, Georgetown U., 1971; postgrad., U.S. Army War Coll., 1982. Bar: Va. 1965, U.S. Supreme Ct. 1973. Assoc., then ptnr. Phillips, Kendrick, Gearheart & Aylor, Arlington, Va., 1965-75; ptnr. McCandlish, Lilliard, Church & Best, Fairfax, Va., 1975-84, Miles & Stockbridge, Fairfax, 1984-95, McCandlish & Lillard, Fairfax, 1995—. Chmn. com. on taxation Va. State Bar, 1978; dep. commr. accts. County of Fairfax, 1994—. Chmn. bd. dirs. No. Va. Am. Heart Assn., 1978; bd. dirs. Benedictine Sch. Exceptional Children, Ridgely, Md., 1985—, Arlington Cmty. Found., 1992-96, No. Va. Cmty. Found., 1991—; mem. exec. coun. Nat. Capital Area coun. Boy Scouts Am., 1993—; founder, pres. Wakefield Ednl. Found., 1986—; trustee Claude Moore Charitable Found. 1st lt. U.S. Army, 1960-62, col. AUS, ret. Mem. ABA, Va. Bar Assn., Fairfax Bar Assn., Assn. U.S. Army, Rotary. Methodist. Home: 4047 27th Rd N Arlington VA 22207-5237 Office: McCandlish & Lillard 11350 Random Hills Rd Ste 500 Fairfax VA 22030-6044

ARO, ANTS GUSTAF, manufacturing executive; b. Tallinn, Estonia, Oct. 13, 1925; arrived in U.S., 1950; s. Jakob Oskar and Agnes Aro; m. Cornelia Victoria Aro; 1 child, Linda Veronica. BBA, Western Res. U., 1952; BS in Engring., Case Inst. Tech., 1954. Engr., mgr. factories Firestone-U.S. & U.K., Akron, Ohio, Des Moines, Decatur, Ill., Wrexham, Wales, 1954—67; pres., CEO Firestone-Australia, Sydney, 1968—71; dir. mfg. Firestone-Europa, Rome, 1972—73; pres., CEO Firestone Sweden, Viskafors, Sweden, 1974—77; mgr. engrng. and new bus. Firestone Tire & Rubber, Akron, 1978—89; v.p. project engrng. Krupp Rubber Machinery Inc., Kent, Ohio, 1990—98, v.p., gen. mgr., 1998—2000, mgmt. cons., 2000—01, Thyssen-Keupp, Hamburg, Germany, 2000—02. Advisor to prime min. Estonian Govt., Tallinn, 1989—91. Mem.: ASME, Beta Alpha Psi, Phi Beta Kappa. Republican. Lutheran. Avocations: travel, skiing, reading, gardening, bridge. Home: 1477 Rowles Dr Akron OH 44313 Office: Krupp Rubber Machinery Inc 1010 W Main St Kent OH 44240

ARO, GLENN SCOTT, environmental and safety executive; b. Balt., Jan. 18, 1948; s. Raymond Charles Sr. and Elizabeth Virginia (Coppage) A.; m. Marlene Rose Lefler, Jan. 8, 1972 (div. June 1987); children: Vincent Wade, Marlena Irene; m. Rosie Ann Lucero, Nov. 22, 1994. BS in Mech. Engring., Gen. Motors Inst., Flint, Mich., 1972; MBA in Fin., Wayne State U., 1980. Registered environmental assessor, Calif. From engr. to supr. GM, Detroit, Balt., L.A., 1966-84; environ. specialist New United Motor, Fremont, Calif., 1984-86; environ. engrng. mgr. Def. Systems FMC Corp., San Jose, Calif., 1986-89; cons./exec. sales rep. Gaia Systems, Menlo Park, Calif., 1990; corp. environ. & safety mgr. Ampex Corp., Redwood City, Calif., 1990-92; gen. ops. mgr. Hughes Environ. Systems, El Segundo, Calif., 1992-98; corp. EHS and ethics mgr. Hughes Electronics Corp., El Segundo, Calif., 1998—2001; prin. GS Aro & Assocs., Auburn, Calif., 2002—. Lectr. colls. and seminars Environ. Regulatory Issues, 1988—. Author: Developing a National Environmental Policy in a Global Market, 1989; contbd. articles to profl. jours. Panel mem. Toxics Awareness Project, San Francisco, 1989—; com. mem. Environ. Working Group, Sacramento, 1986-88. Mem. Peninsula Indsl. & Bus. Assn. (bd. dirs., v.p. 1988-91). Republican. Roman Catholic. Avocations: running, reading, travel, baseball, basketball. Home: 117 Palmyra St Auburn CA 95603

ARON, EVE GLICKA SERENSON, personal care industry executive; b. NYC, Sept. 5, 1937; d. Max and Edith (Gitelson) Serenson; m. Joel Edward Aron, Dec. 13, 1964; children: Jennifer, Joshua, Eric. BS, CCNY, 1958; MS, Yeshiva U., 1960; MBA with honors, Iona Coll., 1985. Med. technician Albert Einstein Coll. Medicine, Bronx, NY, 1959-60; chemist Strasenburgh labs., Belleville, NJ, 1961-63, Roche Labs., Nutley, 1963-67; sr. chemist Pantene Labs. div. Roche, 1967-69; mgr. R&D Combe Inc., White Plains, NY, 1978-85, assoc. dir. R&D, 1985-95, dir. tech., 1995—2002; tech. cons. to personal care industry Ft. Myers, Fla., 2002—. Dir. Vagisil Women's Health Ctr. (website), 2000-2002. Contbr. articles to profl. jours. Tutor Literacy Vols. of Am.; resident dir., bd. dirs. Sevilla Condo Assn. Mem.: NOW, Soc. Cosmetic Chemists (sec. Conn. chpt. 1989—90, chair 1992, chpt. advisor 1993, hospitality/membership chair 1994—96, program com. co-chair 1997, employment chair 1999—2002), Am. Chem. Soc. (legis. action network). Avocations: golf, walking, swimming. Home and Office: 10504 Sevilla Dr Apt 201 Fort Myers FL 33913 E-mail: ejaron@earthlink.net.

ARON, MARK G. lawyer, transportation executive; b. Hartford, Conn., Jan. 27, 1943; s. Samuel H. and Florence A.; m. Cindy Sondik, June 1, 1966; 1 child, Samantha. BA summa cum laude, Trinity Coll., 1965; LL.B., Harvard U., 1968. Bar: Va., Mass., D.C. Asst. prof. law Osgood Hall Law Sch., York U., Toronto, 1968-70; assoc. Goulston & Storrs, Boston, 1970-71; atty., asst. gen. counsel then dep. gen. counsel U.S. Dept. Transp., Washington, 1971-81; asst. gen. counsel CSX, Richmond, Va., 1981-83, gen. counsel spl. projects, 1983-85; sr. v.p. corp. svcs. Chessie System R.R., Balt., 1985-86; sr. v.p. law and pub. affairs CSX Corp., Richmond, 1986-95, exec. v.p. law and pub. affairs, 1995—2001, vice chmn., 2001—. Trustee Va. Union U.; bd. dirs. Va. Literacy Found. Mem. Va. Bar Assn., Mass. Bar Assn., D.C. Bar Assn., Bethesda Country Club. Office: CSX Corp Ste 560 National Pl 1331 Pennsylvania Ave NW Washington DC 20004 E-mail: aron@csx.com.

ARON, MOHIT, software engineer; b. Pathankot, Punjab, India, July 14, 1973; s. Anil Kumar and Manjula Aron. PhD, Rice U., 1995—2000. Rsch. asst. Rice U., Houston, 1995—2000; prin. software engr. Zambeel Inc., Fremont, Calif., 2000—02; software engr. Google, Inc., Mountain View, Calif., 2003—. Mem. program com. 2001 USENIX Ann. Tech. Conf., Boston, 2001. Mem.: ACM. Home: 114 Brenton Ct Mountain View CA 94043 Personal E-mail: aron@google.com.

ARON, PETER ARTHUR, charitable foundation executive, private investor; b. Memphis, May 26, 1946; s. Jack R. and Jane (Baerwald) A.; m. Erika Maria Kostron, Mar. 11, 1972; children: Heather Jane, Holly Frances. BA, Tulane U., 1969. Asst. v.p. J. Aron & Co., Inc., N.Y.C., 1965-83; v.p., treas. Lafayette Enterprises, Inc., N.Y.C., 1983—; pres. Ridgefield, Inc., Thibodaux, La., 1998—; pres., exec. dir. J. Aron Charitable Found., N.Y.C., 1974—. Bd. dirs. William B. Reily Co., New Orleans, The Standard Cos., Inc., New Orleans; bd. dirs., sec. J. Aron & Co., Inc., New Orleans, 1988—; trustee FTI Funds, Pitts., 1995-2001. Editor: Aspiration and Perseverance, 1984. Chmn. emeritus bd. trustees South Street Seaport Mus., N.Y.C., 1987-99; chmn. emeritus bd. dirs. Avon (Conn.) Old Farms Sch., 1975—; trustee Lenox Hill Hosp., N.Y.C., 1975—. FTI Funds, Pitts., 1995-2001; vice chmn. Tulane U., New Orleans, 1981-96; hon. life trustee The Asia Soc., N.Y., 1997—; trustee Village of Kings Point, N.Y., 1999—, Manhattan Eye, Ear and Throat Hosp., N.Y., 2000—; trustee Woods Hole Oceanographic Instn., Mass., 2002—; pres. South St. Seaport Mus. Found., 2001—. 1st lt., U.S. Army, 1970-71, Vietnam. Decorated Bronze Star; recipient Pub. Svc. award Nat. Neurofibromatosis Found., N.Y.C., 1994, Disting. Trustee award United Hosp. Found., N.Y.C., 1995, Tulane U. Disting. Alumnus award, 2000; named Man of Yr., Cystic Fibrosis Found., 1998. Mem. Asia Soc. Galleries Friends (past chmn.), Conferie Chevalier du Tastevin New Orleans. Avocations: yachting, asian art, scuba diving.

ARON, ROBERTO, lawyer, writer, educator; b. Mendoza, Argentina, Nov. 1, 1915; s. David and Catalina (Trostanetzky) A.; m. Catalina Berstein, May 1, 1940 (dec. Oct. 1965); children: Jaim, Sylvia, Daniel; m. Eva Coriat, Dec. 14, 1968; stepchildren: Sonia, Aileen (twins). BA in Law, U. Chile, 1943; LLM in Internat. Law, NYU, 1977, LLM in Corp. Law, 1979, M in Hebrew and Judaic Studies, 1995. Bar: Israel 1960. Sr. ptnr. Aron and Cia, Santiago, Chile, 1943-57, Arón, Tamir and Arón, Tel Aviv, 1960—. Adj. tchr. NYU, 1983; lectr. Tel Aviv U., 1985—, bd. govs., 1982; vis. prof. faculty of law U. Chile, 1991; bd. dirs. Otzar Itiashvut Hayeudim Bank, Tel Aviv; mem. Israeli del. to UN, 1975; participant Oxford Trial Advocacy Program. Co-author: How To Prepare Witnesses for Trial, 1985, Trial Communications Skills, 1986, Cross-Examination of Witnesses, 1989, Impeachment of Witnesses, 1990. Mem. Nat. Inst. Trial Advocacy (participant workshops on teaching trial advocacy Harvard Law Sch.), Advocates Assn., Assn. Trial Lawyers Am. Avocations: golf, pipe collecting. Home: 985 5th Ave Apt 12A New York NY 10021-0142 Office: Arón and Stern 7 ABA Hillel St Ramat-Gan 52522 Israel E-mail: aronbob@aol.com.

ARONIN, LEWIS RICHARD, metallurgical engineer; b. Norwood, Mass., Aug. 4, 1919; s. Samuel and Celia (Acoff) A.; B.S., M.I.T., 1940; m. Natalie Eleanor Wolfson, June 19, 1947; children— Marlene Aronin Sigel, Terry Aronin

Dubow. Asst. to research dir. Waltham Watch Co. (Mass.), 1940-48; staff mem. M.I.T. Metall. Project, Cambridge, 1949-54; mgr. research and devel. dept. Nuclear Metals, Inc., Concord, Mass., 1954-65; cons. Kennecott Copper Corp., Lexington, Mass., 1966-67; materials engr. Army Materials Tech. Lab., Watertown, Mass., 1967-90; pvt. cons. advanced materials devel., 1990—. Registered profl. engr., Mass. Mem. AIME, Am. Soc. Metals, AIAA, Soc. Advancement Materials and Process Engrng. (treas. Boston chpt. 1976-89), Engrng. Socs. New Eng. (dir. 1984-87), Sigma Xi. Lodges: Lions, Masons. Research and publs. on nuclear materials, radiation effects, beryllium, refractory materials, and advanced structural composites; patentee in field. Home and Office: 20 Ingleside Rd Lexington MA 02420-2522

ARONOFF, DONALD MATTHEW, mental health facility administrator; b. Red Bank, N.J., Jan. 19, 1949; s. Milton and Frances (Webber) A.; m. Carol Sena, June 1, 1979 (div. Jan. 1982); m. Sandra Rockwell, July 3, 1983. BA, New Coll., 1970; MA, West Ga. Coll., 1973. Lic. clin. social worker, nursing home adminstr., Ga. Coord. stds. and licensure Ga. Divsn. of Mental Health, Atlanta, 1974-76; dir. Columbus (Ga.) Area Mental Health/Mental Retardation Program, 1976-82; exec. dir. So. Hills Counseling Ctr., Jasper, Ind., 1982—; v.p. Trillium Corp., 1999—. Adj. prof. U. So. Ind., Evansville, 1995. Book rev. editor Human Services in the Rural Environment, 1989-90, Spencer County Leader, 1996-98, Spencer County Jor. Dem., 2000-2001. Bd. dirs. Metro Columbus Urban league, 1980-81, Lincolnland Econ. Devel. Corp., 1996-2002; pres. Santa Claus Town Bd., Ind., 1996-98, Leadership Spencer County, 1996-99; trustee Spencer County Cmty. Found., 2000—; vice chmn. Cmty. Found. Alliance, 2002—. Mem. Jasper C. of C. (bd. dirs. 1986-88), Kiwanis (bd. dirs. Jasper chpt. 1982-94), Santa Claus Optimist Club. Office: So Hills Counseling Ctr PO Box 769 Jasper IN 47547-0769 E-mail: daronoff@psci.net.

ARONOFF, MARK H. linguistics educator, writer, consultant; b. Montreal, Que., Can., Jan. 9, 1949; came to U.S., 1970; s. Moses and Grace (Rosenberg) A.; m. Frances A. Kelley, Jan. 16, 1976; children: Catherine, Peter, Ruth. BA, McGill U., 1969; PhD, MIT, 1974. Asst. prof. linguistics SUNY, Stony Brook, 1974-80, assoc. prof., 1980-85, prof., 1985—, assoc. provost, 1998—2001, dep. provost, 2001—. Author: Word Formation, 1976, Morphology by Itself, 1993; editor Language, The Jour. of the Linguistic Soc. Am., 1995-2001. NEH fellow, 1980, 93, Am. Inst. Indian Studies fellow, India, 1987. Fellow: AAAS (chair sect. 2, 2004); mem.: Linguistic Soc. Am. (pres.-elect 2004), Sigma Xi. Office: SUNY Dept Linguistics Sbs S 211 Stony Brook NY 11794-0001 E-mail: mark.aronoff@stonybrook.edu.

ARONOFF, MICHAEL STEPHEN, psychiatrist; b. Phila., Aug. 5, 1940; s. William Richard and Reva (Miller) A.; m. Carol R. Aronoff, Nov. 27, 1966; m. Dara Welles Aronoff, June 17, 1984; children: Amanda Susan, Jessica Ann. BA, Haverford Coll., 1962; MD, U. Pa., 1966; radiation biophysics cert., NIH, 1967; psychoanalysis cert., Columbia U., 1976. Diplomate Am. Bd. Forensic Examiners; cert. Am. Bd. Psychiatry and Neurology, Am. Bd. Forensic Psychiatry, Qual's Forensic Psychiatry. Intern medicine U. Chgo., 1966-67; staff assoc. NIMH, Bethesda, Md., 1967-69; resident psychiatry Columbia U., NYSPI, N.Y.C., 1969-72, chief resident, 1971-72; rsch. adminstr. unit for volitional disorders NYSPI, 1972-74; chief psychiat. outpatient svcs. Lenox Hill Hosp., N.Y.C., 1976-79, dir. rsch. dept. psychiatry, 1988, attending physician, sr. med. staff, 1976—; clin. prof. psychiatry NYU Med. Ctr., N.Y.C., 1995—. Adj. assoc. prof. psychiatry N.Y. Med. Coll., Valhalla; radio talkshow host WFAS, White Plains, N.Y. Author: Sleep and Its Secrets: The River of Crystal Light, 1991; host, assoc. editor The Elderly; contbr. 2 book chpts, 50 articles to profl. jours.; host, assoc. editor 2 PBS TV series on elderly; commentator Courtroom TV Network, 1997-2003; co-host PBS TV Calling for Health. Pres. Black Lake Assn., White Lake, N.Y., 1989-99, bd. dirs., 1999-2002. Lt. comdr., surgeon USN/USPHS, 1967-69. Fellow APA (Falk fellow 1970, chmn. pub. affairs NYCDB, cons., sec. NYCDB 1999-2000), Am. Coll. Psychoanalysts, Am. Acad. Psychoanalysts (bd. trustees 1996-99), The Pacific Rim Coll. of Psychiatrists; mem. Am. Pain Soc. (charter), N.Y. Soc. for Ericksonian Psychotherapy and Hypnosis (past exec. v.p.). Jewish. Avocations: photography (fantascenes), martial arts. Office: 60 Riverside Dr # 16E New York NY 10024-6171

ARONOFF, MYRON JOEL, anthropologist, educator, political scientist, educator; b. Kansas City, Mo., Mar. 1, 1940; s. Harry J. and Rebecca (Copaken) A.; m. Hendrika Elizabeth Liedermooy, Dec. 21, 1962; children: Miriam S., Yael S. Student, Northwestern U., 1958-60; BA, Miami U., Oxford, 1960-62; MA in Polit. Sci., UCLA, 1963, PhD in Polit. Sci., 1976; PhD Anthropology, Manchester U., 1969. Tchg. asst. UCLA, 1962-65; rsch. fellow Manchester (Eng.) U., 1965-69; vis. lectr. Tel Aviv U., Ramat Aviv, Israel, 1969-70, lectr., 1970-73, sr. lectr., 1974-75, assoc. prof., 1976-77, Rutgers U., New Brunswick, N.J., 1977-81, prof., 1982-90, prof. II, 1990—. Fellow in residence Netherlands Inst. Advanced Study, Wassenaar, Holland, 1974-75, 96-97; vis. prof. U. Cape Town, South Africa, 1988. Author: Frontiertown, 1974, Power and Ritual in the Israel Labor Party, 1977, rev. and expanded 1993, Israeli Visions and Divisions, 1989, The Spy Novels of John le Carré: Balancing Ethics and Politics, 1999; editor: Polit. Anthropology, 1980-95; assoc. editor: Transaction/SOCIETY, 1984-88. Grantee Soc. Sci. Rsch. Coun. 1969-71, Ford Found., 1972-73, Am. Coun. Learned Soc., 1982-83. Mem. Am. Polit. Sci. Assn., Am. Anthropol. Assn., Assn. Polit. and Legal Anthropology (pres. 1985-87), Assn. Israel Studies (pres. 1985-87), Internat. Union Anthropol. and Ethnol. Scis. (v.p. 1993-2003). Democrat. Jewish. Avocations: cross-country skiing, kayaking, listening to jazz. Office: Rutgers U Douglass Campus New Brunswick NJ 08901-1411 Home: 52 Shady Brook Ln Princeton NJ 08540-4152 E-mail: aronoff@polisci.rutgers.edu.

ARONOVICH, ILYA, small business owner; b. Leningrad, USSR, June 18, 1972; s. Yakov I. and Marina Aronovich. BA, Rutgers U., 1995; JD, Fordham U., 2001. Dir. eastbound ocean traffic Unitrans-P.R.A. Co., Inc., Fair Lawn, N.J., 1995-96; v.p. new product devel. and fin. IBK Corp., East Brunswick, N.J., 1996-97; pres., owner Cyweb Inc., East Brunswick, 1998—; rsch. asst., dir. death penalty project Fordham U. Sch. Law, N.Y.C., 1999-2000. Summer assoc. Gibney, Anthony & Flaherty, LLP, N.Y.C., 2000; law clk. to hon. Milton Pollack sr. dist. judge U.S. Dist. Ct. (so. dist.) N.Y., 2001—02; pres. Cyweb Holdings Inc., 2002—. Assoc. editor Fordham Fin., Securities and Tax Law Forum, 1999-2000; first editor-in-chief Fordham Jour. Corp. and Fin. Law, 2000-2001. Mem.: Fordham Jour. Corp. and Fin. Law Alumni Assn., Lambda Sigma Upsilon (pres. 1998—2000, mem. law com. North Am. interfraternity conf. 2001—02). Jewish. Avocations: world travel, playing classical piano, dancing mambo and salsa, spending time with friends and loved ones. Office: Lambda Sigma Upsilon Frat PO Box 645 Hoboken NJ 07030-0645 Fax: 212-636-6204. E-mail: iaronovich@hotmail.com.

ARONOW, EDWARD, psychologist, educator; b. Dec. 22, 1945; s. Hyman and Gertrude (Bakst) A.; m. Anna Aronow; children: David, Rebecca. BA in Psychology, CUNY, 1967; MA in Psychology, Fordham U., 1969, PhD in Clin. Psychology, 1973. Psychology trainee VA, N.Y.C., 1968-72; prof. psychology Montclair (N.J.) State U., 1972—; sr. clin. psychologist St. Vincent's Hosp., N.Y.C., 1972-79; clin. psychologist Verona, N.J., 1974—. Author: Rorschach Content Interpretation, 1976, A Rorschach Introduction: Content and perceptual Approaches, 1982, The Rorschach Technique, 1994, A Practical Guide to the TAT, 2001. Fellow Am. Bd. of Assessment Psychology; mem. APA, Ea. Psychol. Assn., N.J. Psychol. Assn., Soc. Personality Assessment. Office: 69 Forest Ave Verona NJ 07044-1217

ARONOW, INA GLORIA BRODY, journalist; b. Chgo., July 3, 1937; d. Meyer and Mildred (Paretzky) Brody; m. Wilbert S. Aronow, Sept. 20, 1958; children: Michael S., Janice S. BA, U. Chgo., 1959; MA in English, Calif. State U., Long Beach, 1974. Cert. secondary tchr., N.Y., Calif. English tchr. Harrison Tech. High Sch., Chgo., 1959-61; freelance writer for Weekend sect. Ind. Press-Telegram, Long Beach, 1978-82; intern, freelance contbr. L.A. Times, 1979-83; staff writer Mag. of the Midlands Omaha World-Herald, 1983-84; feature editor, news and feature writer Riverdale Press, Bronx, N.Y., 1984-85; staff writer Gannett Westchester Rockland Newspapers, 1986-88; freelance corr. N.Y. Times, N.Y.C., 1988-96. Journalism tchr., newspaper advisor Woodlands H.S., Hartsdale, N.Y., 1994-97, New Rochelle (N.Y.) H.S., 1997—. Pres. LWV, Long Beach, Calif., 1975-77; comm. dir., bd. dirs. LWV Westchester County; prodr., host LWV New Rochelle (N.Y.) cable programs. Mem. Nat. Writers Union. Jewish. Home: 23 Pebbleway Rd New Rochelle NY 10804-3914

ARONOW, SAUL, radiological physicist, consultant; b. N.Y.C., Oct. 4, 1917; s. Abraham and Minnie (Mirel) Aronow; m. Alice Pearlman, Feb. 12, 1942; children: Victor A, Frederick D, David B, Nathan J, Louise G, Jessie P Kravette. BEE, Cooper Union, 1939; PhD, Harvard U., 1953. Registered profl engr, Mass, cert. radiological physicist. Engr. Harvey Radio Labs., Cambridge, Mass., 1946-49; med. physicist Mass. Gen. Hosp., Boston, 1953-81; clin. engr. Project Hope, Jamaica, W.I., 1981-83; treas., chmn. bd. Tech. in Medicine, Inc., Holliston, Mass., 1972—, FDA, Winchester, Mass., 1976—2002. Adj prof Northeastern Univ, Boston, 1975—95; instr MIT, Cambridge, 1969—83. Editor: (book) The Fallen Sky, 1963. Mem Newton Dem City Comt. Served to 1st lt Signal Corps U.S. Army, 1942—46. Recipient Gano Dunn Medal, Cooper Union Inst Technology, 1981; fellow NSF, Harvard Univ, 1950, Fulbright, Danmarks Tekniske Hojskole, 1969. Fellow: IEEE; mem.: Harvard Musical Asn, Soc Nuclear Med, Newton Recycling Comt, Nat Fire Protection Asn (mem standards coun 1983—89), Asn Advancement Med Instrumentation (dir 1979—82), Am Asn Physicists in Med, Folk Song Soc Greater Boston. Jewish. Avocations: hiking, folk music. Home and Office: 86 Crofton Rd Newton MA 02468-2115

ARONOW, WILBERT SOLOMON, physician, educator; b. N.Y.C., Oct. 30, 1931; s. Simon and Bella (Safrin) A.; m. Ina Gloria Brody, Sept. 20, 1958; children: Michael Steven, Janice Susan. BS, Queens Coll., 1953; MD, Harvard U., 1957. Diplomate Am. Bd. Internal Medicine. Intern Michael Reese Hosp. and Med. Ctr., Chgo., 1957-58, resident, 1958-61; practice medicine specializing in internal medicine and cardiology; cardiologist, chief Noninvasive Cardiovascular Lab., Long Beach (Calif.) VA Hosp., 1964-72, chief cardiovascular diseases, 1973-82, asst. chief medicine for rsch., 1975-80; asso. prof. medicine U. Calif., Irvine, 1972-75, prof. medicine, 1975-82, prof. cmty. and environ. medicine, 1975-82, prof. pharmacology and therapeutics, 1976-82, vice chief cardiovascular divsn., chief cardiovascular rsch., 1974-82; prof. medicine, chief cardiovascular rsch. Creighton U., Omaha, 1982-84; chief Cardiology Clnic Westchester Med. Ctr./N.Y. Med. Coll., Valhalla, N.Y., 2001—. Vis. prof. U. Tex. Southwestern Med. Sch., Dallas, 1976, U. Man., 1979, U. Toronto, 1979, Tex. Tech U. Sch. Medicine, Lubbock, 1983, U. Medicine and Dentistry of N.J.-Rutgers Med. Sch., 1983; vis. prof. geriat. U. Rochester Sch. Medicine, 1999; cons. cardiology Orange County Med. Ctr., 1968—82; staff cardiology svc. St. Joseph Hosp., Omaha, 1982—84, cons. FDA, 1970—77, mem. ad hoc sci. ad. coms., 1970—72, mem. cardiovascular and renal adv. com., 1973—76; cons. U. Calif. Project Clear Air, 1970, Calif. Air Resources Bd., 1973, 78, 79, 80, EPA, 1973, 1978—83, dept. drugs AMA, 1974, 78, 81, 93, NIH, 1976, 80, West German Dept. Health, 1978, U.S. Dept. Justice Law Enforcement Assistance Adminstrn., 1978, NHLBI, 1979, FTC, 1980, 81, Dept. Health and Environ. Scis., State of Mont., 1980, Nat. Ctr. Health Stats., 1981; cons. and chmn. spl. rev. com. Nat. Cancer Inst., 1980; cons. and mem. subcom. on smoking Am. Heart Assn., 1980—83; med. dir. Hebrew Hosp. Home, 1984—2001; cons. in medicine Albert Einstein Coll. Medicine, 1990—2001, State of N.Y. Dept. of Health Office of Pub. Health, 1986, 93, 94; adj. prof. geriat. and adult devel. Mt. Sinai Sch. Medicine, 1992—; clin. prof. medicine N.Y. Med. Coll., 2001—; chief cardiology clinic Westchester Med. Ctr./N.Y. Med. Coll., 2001—; cons. Health Resources and Svcs. Adminstrn., 2003. Contbr. Served to capt., M.C. AUS, 1961-63. Fellow: ACP, Soc. Geriatric Cardiology (chmn. program com. 1993—, bd. dirs. 1994—2000), Coun. Clin. Cardiology of Am. Heart Assn., Gerontol. Soc. Am., Am. Geriatrics Soc., Am. Coll. Cardiology, Am. Coll. Chest Physicians (gov. So. Calif. 1977—83, vice chmn. coronary disease sect. 1978—79, chmn. coronary disease sect. 1979—81, mem. exec. coun. 1979—81, chmn. forum on cardiovasc. disease 1980—81, sec. coun. on govs. 1981—82, vice chmn. gov.'s coun.); mem.: Orange County Heart Assn. (dir. 1979—81), Long Beach Heart Assn. (dir. 1972—75), Assn. VA Cardiologists (pres. 1975—77), Am. Fedn. Med. Rsch., Am. Soc. Clin. Pharmacology and Therapeutics (chmn. cardiovasc. and pulmonary diseases sect. 1973—74, 1975—77), Phi Beta Kappa. Jewish. Home: 23 Pebbleway Rd New Rochelle NY 10804-3914 Office: Westchester Med Ctr/NY Med Coll Cardiology Divsn Macy Pavilion Valhalla NY 10595 E-mail: wsaronow@aol.com. *Concern for the public health as well as for individual patient care has been the motivating force behind my medical research, teaching, and patient care. Performing work in a very careful, scientific fashion, being honest, being helpful and supportive to others, working very hard and efficiently, and being true to my principles of conduct has contributed to my success.*

ARONOWITZ, JULIAN, management consultant; b. N.Y.C., June 27, 1949; s. George and Sophie (Bailin) A. Cert. in Computer Programming, NYU, 1980; BBA, CUNY, 1989. Data analyst Bunker Ramo, N.Y.C., 1974-76; mktg. rep. Cen. Hosiery Sales Co., Inc., N.Y.C., 1977-87; project asst. dept. mgmt. Baruch Coll./CUNY, 1988, 1990; computer instr. adult edn. program Norwood Triangle, Bronx, N.Y., 1989-92; computer profl. Bob Malmet Enterprises, Bronx, 1985-96; bus. advisor N.Y.C., 1991-97; Beta tester Expansion Systems, Fremont, Calif., 1992—2001; project leader Jay Miner Soc., Inc., N.Y.C., 1998-99. Resource for Software Mag., N.Y.C., 1991—; instr. Amiga Users' Group of N.Y., 1995—; demonstrator Users' groups and other orgns., N.Y.C.; adj. lectr. Lehman Coll. CUNY, Bronx, 1998—. Columnist: BUG News; author: (tutorials) File for BBS's, Files for Disk Libraries. Exec. trustee U.S. Assn. Evening Students, N.Y.C., 1983-86; exec. v.p. Com. for Equality in Edn., N.Y.C., 1988. Regents scholar N.Y. State Dept. Edn., 1967, others. Mem. IEEE Computer Soc., Assn. Computing Machinery, Amiga Users' Group of N.Y., Bronx Users' Group (v.p. 1991—), Westchester Amiga Users' Group, Knights of Pythias (past dep. grand chancellor), Royal-Hartman Lodge (knight, Man of Yr. 1993, 97). Jewish. Avocations: swimming, drawing, billiards, walking. Home: 3390 Wayne Ave Apt G52 Bronx NY 10467-2454

ARONS, BERNARD S. psychiatrist, educator, health services director; Grad., Oberlin Coll.; MD, Case Western Res. U. Psychiatrist, adminstr., instr. psychiat. residents St. Elizabeths Hosp. NIMH, Washington, dir. Dixon implementation office, 1980, chief clin. advisor, dir. med. nursing, psych. social work; assoc. dir. mental health fin. NIMH; legis. asst. to chair Health Subcom. Ways and Means Com., Washington; dir. Ctr. Mental Health Svcs. U.S. Dept. Health and Human Svcs., Washington, 1993—. Advisor to Mrs. Tipper Gore Office of V.P. U.S.; instr. Ctr. Mental Health Inc., Washington; clin. prof. psychiatry Georgetown U. Office: NIH/NIMH 6001 Executive Blvd Rm 8218 MSC 9669 Bethesda MD 20892-9669

ARONS, IRVING J. technology consultant, writer; b. Malden, Mass., July 17, 1935; s. Maurice Bernard and Carrie (Kaden) Arons; m. Elinor Ruth Marder, Mar. 2, 1958; children: Lori Gale Coocen, Robin Lynn. BS in Chemistry, U. Mass., 1957; postgrad., Northeastern U., Boston, 1959-61. Chemist refinery tech. lab. Gulf Oil, Phila., 1957-59; chemist container and closure sealant lab. Dewey and Almy div. W.R. Grace, Cambridge, Mass., 1959-63; adhesive chemist exploratory devel. lab. United Carr Inc., Cambridge, Watertown, Mass., 1963-69; founder, mgr. ophthalmic and med. laser cons. group Arthur D. Little, Inc., Cambridge, 1969-94; ret., 1994. Founder, mgr. dir. Spectrum Cons., 1990—; pub. Exec. Laser Briefing, 1995—. Editor: (newsletter) Tech. and Product Devel. News, 1988-90; columnist Vision Monday, 1987-90, Ophthalmology Mgmt., 1989-91, Ocular Surgery News, 1991—; contbr. editor Med. Laser Report, 1993—; contbr. Med. Laser Industry Outlook for Med. and Healthcare Marketplace Guide, 1990—, MedPro Month newsletter, 1990—; contbr. articles to profl. jours. 1st lt. U.S. Army, 1958. Fellow Am. Soc. Lasers in Medicine and Surgery; mem. Soc. for Biomed. Optics, Soc. Photo-Optical Instrument Engrs. Achievements include 11 patents including an all-plastic pencil, method for manufacturing plastic eyeglass frames, improved firefighters glove, erasable ball point pen ink, others. Home and Office: 4 Harvard St Peabody MA 01960-1304 E-mail: iarons@erols.com.

ARONS, MARVIN SHIELD, plastic and hand surgeon; b. Derby, Conn., Feb. 13, 1931; m. Moira Fitzsimmons, 1952 (dec. 1988); children: Kathryn Barry, Mark David, Jeffrey Alan, Megan Fitzsimmons; m. Gloria Whiston McLennan, 1992. BS, Yale U., 1952; DMD, Harvard U., 1955; MD, U. Md., 1957. Diplomate Am. Bd. Plastic Surgery. Intern in straight surgery Duke U. Hosp., Durham, N.C., 1957-58, jr. resident in surgery, 1958-59; clin. assoc. head and neck surgery Nat. Cancer Inst. NIH, Bethesda, Md., 1959-61; sr. resident in surgery Georgetown U. Hosp., Washington, 1961-62; resident, chief resident in plastic surgery U. Tex. Medical Br., Galveston, 1962-65, instr. plastic and maxillofacial surgery, 1964-65; clin. instr. plastic surgery Med. Sch. Yale U., New Haven, Conn., 1965-68, clin assoc. plastic surgery, 1968-70, asst. clin. prof. plastic surgery, 1970-78, assoc. clin. prof. plastic surgery, 1978-89; clin. prof. plastic surgery $D, $D, 1989—; attending staff plastic surgery Hosp. St. Raphael, New Haven, 1965—; chief sect. plastic surgery Hosp. of St. Raphael, New Haven, 1974-99; attending staff plastic surgery Yale-New Haven Hosp., 1965—; attending plastic surgeon VA Hosp., West Haven, Conn., 1965—. Cons. plastic surgery Laurel Heights Hosp., Shelton, 1965-85, Bur. Vocat. Rehab. State of Conn., 1967—, cons. in hand surgery Worker's Comp. Commn., 1965—; cons. in hand surgery Worker's Comp. Bd. Fed. Dist. New Eng., 1989—; vis. prof. plastic surgery U. Tex. Med. Br., Galveston, 1977, Sch. Medicine Washington U., 1978, Health Sci. Ctr. Coll. Medicine SUNY, 1995; presenter in field. Contbr. numerous articles to profl. jours. Bd. trustees Hosp. St. Raphael Found., 1975-90, Hopkins-Day Prospect Hill Sch., 1978-80; chmn. physician gifts United Way New Haven, 1984-85, co-chmn., 1997-98; bd. permanent officer Yale Med. Sch., 1989—; bd. dirs. Ind. Practice Assn. Hosp. St. Raphael, 1986-90, New Haven Jewish Cmty. Coun., 1968-75, Congregation B'nai Jacob, Woodbridge, 1972-74. Fellow Am. Cancer Soc., 1963-64, 64-65; recipient award Am. Acad. Dental Medicine, 1957. Fellow Saybrook Coll. (assoc.); mem. Am. Assn. Hand Surgery, Am. Assn. Plastic Surgeons, Am. Cleft Palate Assn., ACS, Am. Soc. Maxillofacial Surgeons, Am. Soc. Plastic and Reconstructive Surgeons, Am. Soc. Peripheral Nerve, Conn. Soc. Plastic and Reconstructive Surgeons, Conn. State Med. Soc., Lipoplasty Soc. N.Am., New Eng. Soc. Plastic and Reconstructive Surgeons, New Haven Med. Assn., New Haven County Med. Assn., Singleton Surg. Soc., U. Md. Med. Alumni Assn. (regional v.p. 1991-92), Yale Cancer Ctr. (assoc.), Blocker-Lewis Plastic Surgery Soc. (pres. 1990-91), New Haven Colony Hist. Soc. (bd. dirs. 1992—, v.p. 1997—), Woodbridge Country Club (bd. dirs. 1971-74), Friends of Am. Art at Yale, Yale Golf Club, Qunnipiack Club, Sigma Xi. Home: 66 Hunting Hill Rd Woodbridge CT 06525-1929 Office: 205 Orchard Med Ctr 330 Orchard St New Haven CT 06511-4417 E-mail: garons@smet.net.

ARONSKY, AMY JILL, physician; b. Englewood, N.J., May 20, 1966; BA, Brandeis U., 1989; DO, Phila. Coll. Osteo. Medicine, 1993. Diplomate in internal medicine, pulmonary diseases and critical care medicine, sleep medicine Am. Bd. Internal Medicine. With Peace Health Med. Group, Longview, Wash. Fellow, Med. Coll. Pa.

ARONSON, ARTHUR LAWRENCE, retired veterinarian, toxicologist, educator, pharmacologist; b. Mpls., Aug. 24, 1933; s. Arthur Theodore and Thorene (Elfstrand) A.; m. Marilyn Ann Lundeen, Sept. 15, 1956; children: Brenda Louise, Mark Theodore, Luann Marie. BS, U. Minn., 1955, DVM, 1957, PhD, 1963; MS, Cornell U., 1959. Asst. prof. pharmacology Cornell U., 1964-67, assoc. prof., 1967-71, prof., 1971-80; prof., head dept. anatomy, physiol. sci., and radiology Coll. Vet. Medicine, N.C. State U., Raleigh, 1980-99; prof. emeritus, 1999—. Mem. com. biologic effects atmospheric pollutants NRC; mem. vet. medicine adv. com. FDA.; mem. U.S. Pharmacopeia Adv. Panel Vet. Medicine; chmn. com. recognition of pain and distress in lab. animals, Inst. Lab. Animal Resources, NAS, 1988. Co-editor Jour. Vet. Pharmacology and Therapeutics, 1992-99. Mem. Friends of Scandinavia, Carl Larsson Vasa Lodge; pres. Wake County Literacy Coun., 1997-99; vol. mentor Communities in Sch. of Wake County, 1999—; dir. N.C. State U. Women's Club English conversation classes, 2000—. Mem. AVMA (chmn. coun. on biologic and therapeutic agts. 1986-87), Am. Soc. Pharmacology and Exptl. Therapeutics, Soc. Toxicology (animals in rsch. com.), N.C. Soc. Toxicology (pres. 1985-86), Am. Acad. Vet. Pharmacology and Therapeutics (pres. 1987-89), Am. Coll. Vet. Clin. Pharmacology (pres. 1993-95), Wake County Literacy Coun. (bd. dirs. 1991-2003, pres. 1997-99), Sigma Xi, Phi Zeta. Lutheran. Home: 1213 Glendale Dr Raleigh NC 27612-4772 E-mail: art-marilyn@earthlink.net.

ARONSON, CARL EDWARD, pharmacology and toxicology educator; b. Providence, Mar. 14, 1936; s. Carl Ivar and Ruth (Workman) A.; m. Marjorie Peck Boutelle, Dec. 17, 1960; children— Linda J., Kristen L. AB, Brown U., Providence, 1958; PhD, U. Vt., Burlington, 1966; MA, U. Pa., Phila., 1973. Asst. prof. pharmacology U. Pa. Sch. Medicine, Phila., 1971-75, assoc. prof. pharmacology, 1975-92; asst. prof. pharmacology and toxicology dept. animal biology U. Pa. Sch. Vet. Medicine, Phila., 1971-73, head labs. of pharmacology and toxicology, 1972-86, assoc. prof. pharmacology and toxicology, 1973-96; retired to emeritus status, 1996; instrument specialist, dept. chemistry Haverford (Pa.) Coll., 1996—. Editor Veterinary Pharmaceuticals and Biologicals, 1978-79, 80-81, 82-83, 85-86; contbr. chpts. to books, articles to profl. jours. Active local sch. dist. coms. and other civic assns. Served to 1st lt. USAFR, 1958-65. Recipient Norden award for disting. tchg. U. Pa. Sch. Vet. Medicine, 1982, Legion of Honor, Chapel of the Four Chaplains, 1984. Fellow: Am. Acad. Vet. and Comparative Toxicology, Am. Acad. Vet. Pharmacology and Therapeutics (newsletter editor 1982—2001, pres. 1983—85, Svc. award 1994, L.E. Davis Career Achievement award 2001); mem.: AAUP, Am. Soc. Pharmacology and Exptl. Therapeutics, Bay Region Mariners Sailing Assn. (treas. 1981—83, vice commodore 1986, commodore 1987), The Haven Yacht Club (charter), Masons, Sigma Xi. Lutheran. Avocations: sailing, photography, woodworking. Office: Haverford Coll Dept Chemistry 370 Lancaster Ave Haverford PA 19041-1392

ARONSON, DAVID, artist, retired art educator; b. Shilova, Lithuania, Oct. 28, 1923; came to U.S., 1929, naturalized, 1931; s. Peisach Leib and Gertrude (Shapiro) A.; m. Georgianna B. Nyman, June 10, 1956; children: Judith, Benjamin, Abigail. Certificate, Boston Mus. Sch., 1946; LHD (hon.), Hebrew Coll., 1993. Instr. painting Boston Mus. Sch., 1943-54; prof. art Boston U., 1962-89, chmn. div., 1954-62, chmn. painting dept., 1962-89, prof. emeritus, 1989—. Contbr. articles to profl. jours.; one man shows include Niveau Gallery, N.Y.C., 1945, 56, Mus. Modern Art, N.Y.C., 1946, Boris Mirski Gallery, Boston, 1951, 59, 64, 69, Downtown Gallery, N.Y.C., 1953, Nordness Gallery, N.Y.C., 1960, 63, 69, Rex Evans Gallery, LA, 1961, Long Beach (Calif.) Mus., 1961, Westhampton (N.Y.) Gallery, 1961, J. Thomas Gallery, Provincetown, Mass., 1964, Zora Gallery, LA, 1965, Hunter Gallery, Chattanooga, 1965, Kovler Gallery, Chgo., 1966, Bernard Danenberg Galleries, N.Y.C., 1969, 72, Pucker Gallery, Boston, 1976, 78, 86, 90, 94, 99, Phila. Mus. Judaica, 1990, Louis Newman Gallery, LA, 1977, 81, 84, 86, 89, 92, Sadye Bronfman Art Ctr., Montreal, Que., Can., 1982, Horwitch Newman Gallery, Scottsdale, Ariz., 1995, 96, MB Modern Gallery, N.Y., 1997, Alter & Gil Gallery, L.A., 1999; Sp. Galerie Yoram GIL, LA, 2002. group shows include N.Y. World's Fair, 1964-65, Bridgestone Gallery, Tokyo, Royal Acad. London, Mus. Modern Art, Paris, Palazzo Venezia, Rome, Congresse Halle, Berlin, Charlottenborg, Copenhagen, Palais Des Beaux Arts, Brussels, Smithsonian Instn., 1965, retrospective exhbns. include Rose Mus., Brandeis U., Waltham, Mass., 1978, Jewish Mus., N.Y.C., 1979, Nat. Mus. Am. Jewish History, Phila., 1979, So. Middlesex U., South Dartmouth, Mass., 1983, Mickelson Gallery, Washington, 1985; represented in permanent collections Art Inst. Chgo., Va. Mus. Fine Arts, Richmond, Bryn Mawr Coll., Brandeis U., Tupperware Mus., Orlando, Fla., Decordova Mus., Lincoln, Mass., Mus. Modern Art, Atlanta U., Atlanta Art Assn., U. Nebr., Krannert Art Mus. U. Ill., Whitney Mus. Am. Art, Colby Coll., U. N.H., Portland Mus. Art, Maine, Corcoran Gallery Art, Washington, Munson Williams Proctor Art Inst., Ithaca, N.Y., Boston Mus. Fine Arts, Smithsonian Instn., Washington, Milw. Art Inst., Pa. Acad. Fine Arts, Johnson Found., Racine, Wis., Worcester (Mass.) Art Mus., Brockton (Mass.) Mus. Art, Longy Sch. Music, Cambridge, Mass., Boston U., Jewish Community Ctr., Boston, Nat. Acad. Design, N.Y., Joseph Hirschhorn Collection, Hebrew Coll., Newton, Mass., David and Alfred Smart Mus., U. Chgo., Two-Ten Found., Boston, Pa. State U. Mus. Art, Syracuse (N.Y.) U., Beth Israel Hosp., Boston Mass. Guilford Coll. U. N.C., Greensboro Campus, U. Judaism, LA, Fine Arts Ctr., Cheekville, Tenn., Skirball Mus., L.A., Herbert F. Johnson Mus. Art, Cornell U., others; sculpture commns. Container Corp. Am., 1963, 65, Reform Jewish Appeal, 1980, Combined Jewish Philanthropies, 1981, Temple Beth Elohim, Wellesley, Mass., 1982, Brandeis U. Library, Waltham, Mass., 1983, Brandeis U. Berlin Chapel, 1996. Recipient 1st Judges prize Inst. Modern Art, Boston, 1944, 1st Popular prize, 1944; Choice Friends of Art Art Inst. Chgo., 1946; Purchase prize Va. Mus. Fine Arts, 1946; Travelling fellow Boston Mus. Sch., 1946; Grand prize Boston Arts Festival, 1952, 54; 2d prize, 1953; 1st prize Tupperware Art Fund, 1954, cert. of merit for sculpture NAD, 1990; grantee in art Nat. Inst. Arts and Letters, 1958; Purchase prize, 1961, 62, 63; purchase prize Pa. Acad. Fine Arts, also other purchase prizes; Samuel F.B. Morse Gold medal NAD, 1973; Isaac N. Maynard prize NAD, 1975; Joseph S. Isidor gold medal NAD, 1976; Guggenheim fellow, 1960; Adolph and Clara Obrig prize NAD, 1968, Academician NAD, 1970. Home: 137 Brimstone Ln Sudbury MA 01776-3200

ARONSON, DONALD ERIC, professional services firms consultant, value added tax consultant; b. Boston, Feb. 24, 1934; s. Harry and Nathalie A.; m. Margery Roth, Sept. 27, 1955 (dec. 1981); children: Nancy, Helaine; m. Joan Gelman, Jan. 12, 1986 AB, Dartmouth Coll., 1955; MBA, Columbia U., 1959. CPA, N.Y., N.J. Mem. audit and tax staff Arthur Young & Co., N.Y.C., 1959-63, tax mgr., 1963-68, tax ptnr., 1968-72, office mng. ptnr. Saddle Brook, N.J., 1972-80; dir. mktg. Arthur Young, N.Y.C., 1980-89; dir. tax mktg. Ernst & Young, N.Y.C., 1989-92; prin., profl. svcs. firms cons. Aronson/Heintz Assocs. LLC, N.Y.C., 1995—; value added tax recovery advisor, cons. and prin. VATAmerica, L.P., N.Y.C. and Princeton, NJ, 1993—. Asst. prof. acctg. Upsala Coll., East Orange, N.J., 1963-65; asst. prof. Columbia U. Grad. Sch. Bus., N.Y.C., 1966-67; acctg. adv. bd. Columbia U. Grad. Sch. of Bus., N.Y.C., 1981-89; assoc. prof. bus. NYU, 1992-97; cons. and lectr. in field. Contbr. articles to bus. and profl. jours. Served to 1st lt. USAF, 1955-57 Recipient Montgomery prize Columbia U. Grad. Sch. Bus., 1959; award N.Y. Soc. C.P.A.s, 1959 Mem. AICPA, N.Y. State Soc. CPAs, N.J. Soc. CPAs (trustee 1975-78). Democrat. Jewish. Avocations: tennis, skiing, boating. Office: Ste 6D 2 W 67st New York NY 10023

ARONSON, EDGAR DAVID, venture capitalist; b. N.Y.C., June 17, 1934; s. Aaron Solomon and Ida Claire (Minevitch) A.; m. Nancy Carol Pforzheimer, Dec. 23, 1956; children: Edgar David Jr., Alison C., Edith S., Peter Borrah. AB, Harvard U., 1956, MBA, 1962. Successively trainee, asst. cashier, v.p. 1st Nat. Bank of Chgo., 1962-67; v.p. Republic Nat. Bank of N.Y., 1968; trainee Salomon Bros., N.Y.C., 1968 69, ltd. partner, 1970, v.p., 1971-72, gen. partner, 1972-79; mng. dir. Salomon Bros. Internat. Ltd., London, 1971-76; chmn. bd. Dillon, Read Internat., 1979-81; pres. EDACO, Inc., 1981—2002. Bd. dirs. APL N.V., Curacao, Petrogas Ltd., Hong Kong, MidAmEnergy Holdings Pte., Inc., Omaha, H.L. Oakes & Co., Inc., Panama, Hertford Internat., N.V., Curacao. Author: (with others) New Old World, 1962, Response to Change, 1963. Trustee Lesley Coll., Cambridge, Mass., 1981-84, South St. Seaport Mus., N.Y., 1996-2002, Marine Mil. Acad., Harlingen, Tex.; bd. dirs. Carl and Lily Pforzheimer Found., N.Y.C.; founder Nat. Mus. U.S. Marine Corps. 1st lt. USMCR, 1956-60, maj. FMF ret. res. Mem. Marine Corps Res. Officers Assn., 1st Marine Divsn. Assn., The Cruising Assn. (U.K.), Mensa, N.Y. Yacht Club, Bass Harbor Yacht Club (Maine), Harvard Club N.Y.C., Royal Cork Yacht Club, Royal Nova Scotia Yacht Squadron, Eire, The Brook (N.Y.C.), Annabel's (London). Office: 551 Fifth Ave Rm 512 New York NY 10176-0599

ARONSON, ESTHER LEAH, retired foundation administrator, psychotherapist; b. Bklyn., Sept. 8, 1941; d. Nathan and Nellie (Borack) Aronson; m. Joel Allen Bernstein, Sept. 8, 1967 (div. Jan. 1978). BA, Bklyn. Coll., 1965; MA, New Sch. for Social Rsch., N.Y.C., 1982; MSW, NYU, 1984, PhD, 1996. LCSW. Resource cons. N.Y.C. Human Resources Adminstrn., 1965-82; counselor Fordham-Tremont Cmty. Mental Health Ctr., Bronx, 1982-83, South Beach Psychiat. Ctr., Bklyn., 1983-84; social worker Alfred Adler Clinic, N.Y.C., 1984-85; pvt. practice clin. social work psychotherapist N.Y.C., 1986—; program developer Emanu-El Midtown YM-YWHA, N.Y.C., 1987-88, dir. ret. adult divsn., 1988—2001. Lectr. Am. Mus. Natural History, N.Y.C., 1978. Contbr. Mem.: NAFE, Soc. for Pub. Health Edn., N.Y. State Soc. Clin. Social Work Psychotherapists, Inc., Am. Orthopsychiat. Assn., Inc., Kappa Delta Pi, Phi Delta Kappa. Avocation: collecting Middle Eastern and East Indian art. Home: 2 Fifth Ave Apt 31 New York NY 10011

ARONSON, HOWARD ISAAC, linguist, educator; b. Chgo., Mar. 5, 1936; s. Abe and Jean A. BA, U. Ill., 1956; MA, Ind. U., 1958, PhD, 1961. Asst. prof. Slavic langs. and lit. U. Wis., Madison, 1961-62; asst. prof. Slavic linguistics U. Chgo., 1962-65, asso. prof. depts. slavic langs. and lit. and linguistics, 1965-73, prof., 1973—2002, chmn. dept. linguistics, 1972-80, prof. emeritus, 2002—, chmn. dept. Slavic langs. and lits., 1983-91, 2000-01. Editor: Annual of the Society for the Study of Caucasia, 1989—. Mem. Am. Assn. Advancement Slavic Studies, Am. Assn. Tchrs. Slavic and East European Langs. Jewish. Home: 415 W Aldine Ave Apt 7B Chicago IL 60657-3601 Office: U Chgo Dept Slavic Langs and Lit Chicago IL 60637 E-mail: hia5@mac.com.

ARONSON, JAN, artist, educator; b. New Orleans, Dec. 19, 1949; d. Bernard J. and Merle (Wiener) A.; m. Edgar Miles Bronfman Sr., Sept. 2, 1993. BA, U. New Orleans, 1971; MFA, Pratt Inst., 1973. Instr. New Orleans Mus. Art, 1973-74, Dillard U., New Orleans, 1974-76; asst. prof. Ethan Allen C.C., Manchester, Vt., 1978-81; instr. So. Vt. Art Ctr., Manchester, 1978-81, Stratton (Vt.) Mountain Sch., 1981; artist N.Y.C., 1986—. Adj. faculty Pratt Manhattan Ctr., N.Y.C., 1988, 89; asst. prof. Ethan Allen C.C., Manchester, 1977-81; tutor external degree program Johnson (Vt.) State Coll., 1976-85; creator, tchr. art program Pub. Sch. 198, Manhattan, N.Y., 1992-94. One-woman shows include Bienville Gallery, New Orleans, 1976, Henri Gallery, Washington, 1978, Park McCullough Ho., North Bennington, Vt., 1979, Weston (Vt.) Playhouse Art Gallery, 1979, Green Mountain Coll., Poultney, Vt., 1979, So. Vt. Art Ctr., Manchester, 1979, U. New Orleans, 1980, 1985, Christine Price Gallery, Castleton, Vt., 1981, McKissick Mus., Columbus, S.C., Helio Galleries, N.Y.C., 1988, Stuart Kingston Gallery, Wilmington, Del., 1991, 2002, Anne Reed Gallery, Ketchum, Idaho, 1994, 1995, 1999, Winston Wachter Fine Art, N.Y.C., 1996, 1998, 2000, 2001, Hahn Gallery, Phila., 1997, Thomas J. Walsh Art Gallery, Fairfield, Conn., 1999, Bayly Art Mus., U. Va., Charlottesville, 2000, 2001, Makor Ctr., N.Y.C., 2000, M3/Studio, Miami, Fla., 2000, 2001, UN, 2001, Geneva, 2001, KGS2, Katonah, N.Y., 2002, Ochi Gallery, Ketchum, Idaho, 2003; artist (group shows) San Diego Watercolor Soc., 1980, Moonbrook Gallery, Rutland, Vt., 1981, Phyllis Needleman Gallery, Chgo., 1982, Brattleboro (Vt.) Mus., 1982, AVA Gallery, Hanover, N.H., 1983, Stratton (Vt.) Art Festival, 1981, 1982, 1983, 1984, 1985, Helio Galleries, 1988, Art Unltd. Gallery, Key West, Fla., 1989, Anne Reed Gallery, 1992, 1993, 1995, 1996, 1997, 1999, Hollis Taggart Gallery, N.Y.C., 1994, Boise Art Mus., 1994, Renee Fotouhi Gallery, N.Y.C., 1995, Marguerite Oestreicher Gallery, New Orleans, 1993, Winston Wachter Fine Art, 1997, 1998, 1999, 2000, Gallery 54, N.Y.C., 1997, Ctrl. Fine Arts, 1998, Discovery Mus., Bridgeport, Conn., 2000, numerous others, (permanent collections) U. Va. Art Mus, New Orleans Mus. Art, Fairfield U., Estee Lauder, Eiteljorg Mus. Western and Indian Art, UN Watch of the World Jewish Congress, U.S. Mission, Vt. Coun. Arts, Isidore Newman Sch., Vt. County Store Art Collection, pvt. collections; contbr. articles to mags. Bd. visitors U. New Orleans; nat. adv. panel Contemporary Art Ctr., New Orleans; bd. mem. Mus. U. Va.; bd. dirs. Skowhegan Sch., N.Y.C. Grantee Vt. Coun. Arts, 1981-82. Mem. Nat. Assn. Women Artists, Artists Equity. Jewish. Avocations: swimming, tennis, cycling, hiking, reading.

ARONSON, JASON, publisher; b. Minn., Jan. 25, 1928; s. Louis and Mollie (Weiner) A.; div.; 1 child, Jane; m. Joyce Kraus. BA, U. Minn., 1949, MD, 1953. Resident in psychiatry U. Minn. Hosps., 1954-57; asst. psychiatrist Harvard Med. Sch. and Mass. Gen. Hosp., 1959-64; editor-in-chief Internat. Jour. Psychiatry, 1962-70; pres. Jason Aronson Pubs. Inc., Northvale, N.J., 1964—. Capt. U.S. Army, 1957-59. Fellow Am. Psychiat. Assn. Office: Jason Aronson Inc 230 Livingston St Northvale NJ 07647-1731

ARONSON, JAY RICHARD, economics educator, researcher, academic administrator; b. N.Y.C., Aug. 26, 1937; s. Lester and Rose (Hacken) A.; m. Judith Libby Klein, Sept. 13, 1959; children: Sarah, Miriam, Anne. AB, Clark U., 1959, PhD, 1964; MA, Stanford U., 1961. Asst. prof. econs. Worcester Poly. Inst. (Mass.), 1961-65, Lehigh U., Bethlehem, Pa., 1965-68, assoc. prof., 1968-72, prof., 1972—, dir. Martindale Ctr. for Study Pvt. Enterprise, 1980—, William L. Clayton prof. bus. and econs., 1984—. Vis. scholar U. York (Eng.), 1973, hon. prof., 1996-; cons. Internat. City Mgmt. Assn.; commr. Pa. Pension Fund Study Commn. Author: books including (with J. Hilley) Financing State and Local Governments, Public Finance; editor: books including (with E. Schwartz) Management Policies in Local Government Finance, 1975, 3d edit., 1987; contbr. articles to profl. publs. Recipient Lindback award Lehigh U., 1968; recipient Stabler award Lindback award, 1974; Rockefeller fellow, 1959-61; named hon. fellow Clark U., 1962; grantee Ford Found., 1971-72, 76-77, HEW, 1978-79, Scaife Found., 1982; Fulbright research scholar, 1991, 96. Mem.: Roya Econ. Soc., Am. Fin. Assn., Nat. Tax Assn., Am. Econ. Assn. Democrat. Jewish. Home: 1804 Jennings St Bethlehem PA 18017-5235 Office: Lehigh U Dept Economy Bethlehem PA 18015

ARONSON, JUDITH, clinical social worker; b. Chgo., Nov. 26, 1953; d. Robert and Theodora Selma (Sachs) A.; m. Marc Hilton, Dec. 19, 1981; children: Leon Hilton, Ezra Hilton. BA magna cum laude, U. Ill., 1975; MA, U. Chgo., 1977. Lic. clin. social worker; diplomate Am. Bd. Social Work. Social worker St. Joseph's Home for Children, Mpls., 1977-79; social worker to social work supr. United Charities, Chgo., 1979-88; pvt. practice, Chgo. and Evanston, Ill., 1988—. Mem. adv. com. YWCA-North Shore Shelter for Battered Women, Evanston, 1988-90; humn rights monitor Children's Rights Internat., Guatemala, 1989; bd. dirs. Unity Nursery Sch., Evanston, 1987-89; leader Jr. Gt. Brooks; co-founder, bd. dirs. Chgo. Friends of Peace Now, Chgo., 1980-84. Mem.: Ill. Soc. Clin. Social Work, Phi Beta Kappa. Jewish. Office: 636 Church St Ste 409 Evanston IL 60201-4580

ARONSON, KRISTIN JANINA, philosopher, educator; b. Norwalk, Conn., Sept. 28, 1945; d. Herbert Leon and Janina (Urbanowicz) A. BA, Ohio State U., Columbus, 1967; MA, Ohio State U., 1971, PhD, 1983. Instr. philosophy U. Conn., Waterbury, 1973-74; lectr. philosophy/speech Middlesex C.C., Middletown, Conn., 1974-91; asst. prof. philosophy U. Hartford, Conn., 1988, Ctrl. Conn. State U., New Britain, 1989-91, We. Conn. State U., Danbury, 1993—. Adj. prof. philosophy Cen. Conn. State U., 1976-93, St. Joseph Coll., Hartford, 1988; nat. poetry contest judge Conn. Poetry Soc., 1991, 98, Milford Arts Coun., 1998, Chem. Injury Info. Network, 1999. Author: To Eat Flesh They Are Willing: Are Their Spirits Weak? Vegetarians Who Return to Meat, 1996; guest editor: Conn. River Rev., 1999, assoc. editor, 1991-92; contbr. poetry to literary jours.; playwright: Pointed Questions, 1978, The Butterfly Net, 1980, Bending the Bow, 1985; actress in various roles, 1973-93. Recipient Perpetual Pendulum award, Clockwork Repertory Theater, 1991, Animals and Soc. Course award, Humane Soc. U.S., 2001; grantee, Ohio Humanities, 1978; rsch. grantee, Conn. State U./AAUP, 1998, others. Mem. Ecol. Health Orgn. (bd. dirs.), Conn. Poetry Soc., N.Am. Vegetarian Soc., Phi Beta Kappa. Avocations: backpacking, canoeing, mountain climbing, drawing. Office: Dept Philosophy/Humanistic We Conn State U/181 White S Danbury CT 06810

ARONSON, LOUIS VINCENT, II, manufacturing executive; b. Newark, Jan. 18, 1923; s. Alexander H. and Leona L. (Lazarus) A.; m. Joan Barbara Fisch, Nov. 2, 1945; children: James Richard, Robert A., Kathryn Ann, Diane Barbara. BS, U.S. Naval Acad., 1945. Methods engr. Ronson Corp., Newark, 1947-48, supr. prodn. control, 1948-50, v.p. charge material procurement, 1950-52, v.p. charge ops., 1952-53, pres., 1952—, also bd. dirs. Bd. dirs. NCCJ. Served as ensign USN, 1945-47. Mem. U.S. Naval Acad. Athletic Assn Home: PO Box 9 Oldwick NJ 08858-0009 Office: Ronson Corp PO Box 6707 Somerset NJ 08875-6707

ARONSON, LUANN MARIE, actress; b. Ithaca, N.Y., Nov. 18, 1964; d. Arthur Lawrence and Marilyn Ann (Lundeen) A. MusB, Ithaca Coll., 1986; MusM, Southern Meth. U., Dallas, 1988. Appeared as Guenevere in the Nat. Tour of Camelot, 1991; originated the role of Betty Schaefer in the workshop prodn. of Sunset Boulevard at Andrew Lloyd Webber's Sydmonton Festival, London, 1992; features soloist in the Music of Andrew Lloyd Webber, Radio City Music Hall, N.Y.C., 1992; as Maria in the Far East Tour of the Sound of Music, 1992; as Christine Daaé on Broadway in Phantom of the Opera, N.Y.C., 1992-94; as Christine Daaé in the Internat. Tour of The Phantom of the Opera, 1995; as Marian Paroo in The Music Man, 1997, 2000; as Laurie in Oklahoma!, 1997, 2000; as Sharon in Master Class, 1999, as Aldonza in Man of La Mancha, 1999; participant Encores Series City Ctr., 1998. Recipient Outstanding Young Alumni award Ithaca Coll. Alumni Assn., 1994; Blossom Music Festival scholar, 1988, Tanglewood Summer Music Festival scholar, 1986. Mem. Actor's Equity Assn.

ARONSON, MARC, artist; b. Seattle, June 26, 1948; s. Leonard and Marian (August) A.; m. Sue Elizabeth Steiner, June 28, 1971; 1 child, Elliot. BA, Western Wash. U., Bellingham, 1971; MA, NYU, 1989, postgrad., 1989—. Represented by nextmonet.com. One-man shows Warren Benedek Gallery, N.Y.C., 1974, Synagogue for the Arts, N.Y.C., 2002; exhibited in group shows Seattle Art Mus. Pavilion, 1971, U. Denver Sch. Art, 1975, Orgn. Ind. Artists Fed. Courthouse, Bklyn., 1977, Aldrich Mus. Contemporary Art, Ridgefield, Conn., 1978, Foster White Gallery, Seattle, 1980, Rensselaer Poly. Inst., Troy, N.Y., 1980, Sci. Mus. Tokyo, 1985, Embellishment of Statue of Liberty Barneys N.Y., 1986, Island Introductions Galveston (Tex.) Arts Ctr., 1990, Art of N.E. USA Silvermine Guild Arts Ctr., New Canaan, Conn., 1991, Nat. Midyear Exhbn. Butler Inst. Am. Art, Youngstown, Ohio, 1991, Am. 500 Centro Cultural Recoleta, Buenos Aires, 1992, The Emerging Collector, N.Y.C., 1992, Art of Northeast USA Silvermine Guild Arts Ctr., New Canaan, Conn., 1993, Butler Inst. Am. Art, Youngstown, Ohio, 1994, Washington Sq. East Galleries, N.Y.C., 1995, Art of Northeast USA Silvermine Guild Arts Ctr., New Canaan, Conn., 1996, Nat. Competition Finalists' Exhibition Provincetown, Art Assn. and Museum, 1998, S.I. (N.Y.) Biennial Juried Art Exhibition, 1998, 2001, Art of N.E. Silvermine Guild Arts Ctr., New Canaan, Conn., 1999, 2001, Provincetown (Mass.) Art Assn. and Mus., 2000, represented in permanent collection Time Warner Inc.; featured in New American Paintings, 1997. Nat. Endowment for Arts fellow, 1976, N.Y. Found. Arts fellow, 1980. Mem. Kappa Delta Pi. Jewish. Avocation: racquetball. E-mail: Durango7@earthlink.net.

ARONSON, MARGARET RUPP, school psychologist; b. Lewistown, Pa., Dec. 12, 1921; d. Frederick Augustine and Claire S. (Schellenberg) Rupp; m. Morton Jerome Aronson, Oct. 31, 1948; children: Eris L. Aronson Renczenski, Frederick Rupp, Scott Charles. BA, Pa. State U., 1942, MS, 1943; JD, St. John's U., 1986. Nat. cert. sch. psychologist. Clin. psychologist Inst. Pa. Hosp., Phila., 1943-48, Georgetown Hosp., Washington, 1948-50; ind. cons. Patchogue (N.Y.) Pub. Schs., 1986-96, Luth. Ministries, Queens and Nassau County, N.Y., 1996—. Editor Winter Olympics Pindar Press, 1980-82. Mem. Met. Golf Assn., Phi Beta Kappa, Phi Kappa Phi, Psi Chi. Avocation: golf. Home: Windsor Gate, Great Neck NY 11020

ARONSON, MARK BERNE, retired attorney, consumer advocate; b. Pitts., Aug. 24, 1941; s. Richard J and Jean (DeRoy) Aronson; children: Robert M., Andrew A., Michael D. BS in Econs., U. Pa., 1962; JD, U. Pitts., 1965. Pvt. practice law, Pitts., 1965-90; sr. ptnr. Behrend & Aronson Law Firm, Pitts., 1967-80, Behrend, Aronson & Morrow Law Firm, Pitts., 1980-83; pres. Current Concepts Corp., Pitts., 1992-2000. Real estate broker, 1972—94; cons. to attys., 1991—2002; pvt. consumer adv., 1991—2002. Trustee Pitts. Child Guidance Found., 1987—90; mem. Pitts. Coun. Edn., 1986—89; pres. Cmty. Day Sch., Pitts., 1982—84, Rodef Shalom Jr. Congregation, 1970—71; trustee Rodef Shalom Congregation, Pitts., 1979—87, Rodef Shalom Jr. Congregation, 1967—71, Brotherhood, 1990—92, 2000—01. Master: Masons; mem.: Am Arbitration Asn (mem nat panel arbitrators), Tau Epsilon Rho (chancellor Eta chpt 1964—65). Republican. Jewish. Address: Ste 506-507 Churchill Mansions 2525 Greensburg Pike Pittsburgh PA 15221-3691 E-mail: sue4spam@aol.com.

ARONSON, MICHAEL ANDREW, editor; b. Bklyn., Apr. 27, 1939; s. Jesse Besthoff and Marcia (Sacks) A. BA, Johns Hopkins, 1960. Asst. dir. Ind. U. Press, Bloomington, 1966-69; London editor U. Chgo. Press, 1970, sci. editor, 1971-73; editor-in-chief Johns Hopkins U. Press, Balt., 1973-78; sr. editor social scis. Harvard U. Press, Cambridge, Mass., 1978—. Office: Harvard U Press 79 Garden St Cambridge MA 02138-1423

ARONSON, NORMAN LEONARD, publishing executive, consultant; b. Washington, June 7, 1924; s. Herman and Bertha Martha (Miller) A.; m. Marcia Ross Rosey, Mar. 29, 1952 (dec. Nov., 1989); children: Susan Elizabeth Aronson Baratta, John Michael. BS in Bus. and Pub. Adminstrn., Georgetown U., 1947, JD, 1949. V.p. Esquire Mag., N.Y.C., 1951-75; publisher Univ. Comms., Rahway, N.J., 1975-76; advt. dir. Signature Mag., N.Y.C., 1976-82; pres. Best Publs. Inc., N.Y.C., 1982-86; CEO Musculoskeletal Transplant Found., Little Silver, N.J., 1986-88; editor, publisher "Q" Physicians Guide to Quality, Princeton, N.J., 1988—. Entrepreneur, investor founder, pres. The Kings Ct. Restaurants, Princeton, N.J., Charlottesville, Va., Bostons Restaurant, Trenton, N.J., 1977-80; pres. The Svc. News Stands, Pentagon Bldg., Washington, 1965-75; cons. Universal Press Syndicate, Kansas City, Mo., 1988-89, Target Mktg., Kansas City, 1988—; ptnr. Medcom Ptnrs., 2001—. Publisher The Book of Bests, 1983-84. Lt. j.g. US Navy, 1942-46 PTO. Recipient Lone Sailor award, U.S. Navy, Washington, 1990. Mem. The Nassau Club (Princeton, N.J.), Univ. Club (N.Y.). Avocations: wine, cooking.

ARONSON, PETER SAMUEL, medical scientist, physiology educator; b. Bklyn., Feb. 3, 1947; s. Harry and Sydelle (Pincus) A.; m. Marie Louise Landry, Sept. 25, 1977; children: Paul L., William L. AB, U. Rochester, 1967; MD, NYU, 1970; MA (hon.), Yale U., 1987. Diplomate Nat. Bd. Med. Examiners, Am. Bd. Internal Medicine (subspeciality Nephrology). Intern and resident in internal medicine U. N.C. Sch. Medicine, Chapel Hill, 1970-72; clin. assoc. Gerontology Rsch. Ctr., NIH, Balt., 1972-74; fellow in nephrology Yale U. Sch. Medicine, New Haven, 1974-77, asst. prof. medicine and physiology, 1977-81, assoc. prof. medicine and physiology, 1981-87, prof. medicine and cellular and molecular physiology, 1987—, C.N.H. Long prof. internal medicine, 1995—2002. Chief sect. nephrology Yale U. Sch. Medicine, New Haven, 1987-2002; established investigator Am. Heart Assn., 1981-86. Mem. editl. bd. Am. Jour. Physiology, 1982-86, 87-90, 96-2000, Kidney Internat., 1990-94, Jour. Biol. Chemistry, 1995-2000; cons. editor Jour. Clin. Investigation, 1993-98; contbr. rsch. articles to profl. jours. With USPHS, 1972-74. Recipient Solomon Berson Med. Alumni Achievement award NYU, 1996. Fellow: AAAS; mem.: Soc. Gen. Physiologists, Internat. Soc. Nephrology, Am. Heart Assn. (exec. com. coun. on the kidney 1986—90), Am. Soc. Nephrology (Young Investigator award 1985, Homer Smith award 1994, councillor 2002—), Am. Soc. Clin. Investigation (councillor 1986—88, editl. com. 1993—98), Am. Physiol. Soc., Am. Fedn. Med. Rsch., Am. Assn. Physicians (editl. bd. Proc. 1997—99), Salt and Water Club (sec. 1985—87), Alpha Omega Alpha, Phi Beta Kappa. Office: Yale School of Medicine Dept of Medicine/Nephrology PO Box 208029 New Haven CT 06520 8029

ARONSON, RONALD, humanities educator, writer; b. Detroit, Mich., Oct. 31, 1938; s. Saul Aronson and Helen Emmer Aronson; m. Phyllis Ann Milberg, June 26, 1960; children: Pamela Judith, Nina Ellen. BA, Wayne State U., Detroit, MI, 1960; MA, Brandeis U., Waltham, MA; 1965, 1968; PhD, Brandeis Univ., Waltham, MA, 1965—68; LLD (hon.), U. of Natal, Durban, South Africa, 2002. Prof. of interdisciplinary studies Wayne State U., Detroit, Mich., 1984—. Rsch. fellow U. Coll. London, London, 1983—84; spl. projects editor Sartre Studies Internat. (jour.); vis. lectr. U. of Natal, Durban, South Africa, 1987; chair North Am. Soc. for Sartre Studies, 1991—94; com. on internat. rels. Am. Philos. Assn., 1992—95; editor Sartre Studies Internat., 1995—2000; pres. Wayne State U. Acad. of Scholars, 2001—02. Author: (book) Camus & Sartre: The Story of a Friendship and the Quarrel that Ended It, After Marxism; editor: (Jean-Paul Sartre, author) Truth and Existence, Sartre Alive; author: Stay out of Politics! A Philosopher Views South Africa, Sartre's Second Critique, The Dialectics of Disaster, Jean-Paul Sartre - Philosophy in the World; co-producer (with Judith Montell) (documentary film) One Man in His Time. Cmty. adv. panel Detroit Pub. TV, Detroit, 1998—2003; mem. bd. Dem. Socialists of Am., New York, NY, 1997—2001. Fellow, Am. Coun. of Learned Societies, 1983—84; grantee Film Grant, Mich. Coun. of Humanities, 1999-2002. Mem.: Phi Beta Kappa. Home: 10524 Elgin Huntington Woods MI 48070 Office: Wayne State University 5700 Cass Rm 2426 Detroit MI 48202 Office Fax: 313-577-8585. E-mail: ac7159@wayne.edu.

ARONSON, STANLEY MAYNARD, physician, educator; b. NYC, May 28, 1922; s. Eliuh and Lena (Hassner) A.; m. Betty Ellis, June 3, 1947; children: Susan, Lisa, Sarah. BS, CCNY, 1943; MD, NYU, 1947; MA, Brown U., 1971; MPH, Harvard U. Sch. Pub. Health, 1981. Diplomate: Am. Bd. Pathology., Am. Bd. Neuropathology. Resident Bellevue Hosp., Sydenham Hosp., Meml. Sloan-Kettering Ctr. for Cancer., NYC, 1946-51; fellow Mt. Sinai Hosp., NYC, 1951-54; faculty Columbia Coll. Physicians and Surgeons, 1951-54; prof. pathology, asst. dean SUNY, Bklyn., 1954-70; prof. med. sci., dean medicine Brown U., 1970-81, Univ. prof. med. sci., 1981-87, dean medicine emeritus, 1987—. Dir. labs. Kings County Hosp. Center, Bklyn., 1965-70; pathologist-in-chief Miriam Hosp., Providence, 1970-75; vis. prof. cmty. medicine Dartmouth Coll. Med. Sch., 1982— ; lectr. Yale Sch. Medicine, 1964-65; lectr. pathology Tufts U. Sch. Medicine, 1978— ; profl. lectr. Bklyn. Health Ctr., SUNY, 1970—; cons. physician neuropathology Jewish Chronic Disease Hosp., Bklyn., 1951—, NIH, 1962—, RI Hosp., Roger Williams Hosp., Meml. Hosp., Miriam Hosp., Providence VA Hosp., Butler Hosp., Providence, RI Med. Ctr., Luth. Med. Center, NYC Author: (with B.W. Volk) Cerebral Sphingolipidoses, 1962, Inborn Disorders of Sphingolipid Metabolism, 1966, Sphingolipids, Sphingolipidoses and Allied Disorders, 1972, (with A. Sahs and E Hartman) Guidelines for Stroke Care, 1976; (with Adachi and Hirano) The Pathology of the Myelinated Axon, 1985, Tapestry of Medicine, 1999, Worms, Germs and Wayward Physicians, 2000, Smallpox in Colonial America, 2002, (with R. Shield), Aging in Today's World, 2003; also numerous articles; mem. editorial bd. Jour. Submicroscopic Cytology, Jour. Neuropathology and Exptl. Neurology; editorial bd., editor-in-chief RI Med. Jour.; weekly columnist Providence Jour.-Bull. Commr. US Commn. Control of Huntington's Disease, 1976-79; chmn. Legis. Commn. Dementia Related to Aging; vice chmn. RI Bd. of Med. Licensure and Discipline, 1993-2003; pres. Hospice RI, 1989—, Interfaith Health Care Ministries, 1989-91; mem. Nat. Adv. Commn. on Multiple Sclerosis, 1973-74, NIH Perinatal Rsch. Commn., Joint Commn. on Stroke Facilities, med. adv. bd. Nat. Multiple Sclerosis Soc., Dysautonomia Found., Nat. Tay-Sachs Assn., Nat. Fund for Med. Edn.; trustee Finch Univ. Health Sci., Chgo.; cons. for internat. epidemiology programs The Rockefeller Found., 1990—; chmn. bd. trustees Jewish Home for Aged, RI, 1993-94; pres. Shalom Housing for Elderly, 1993-94. With US Army, 1942-46. Inductee R.I. Hall of Fame, 1997. Mem. AMA, Am. Neurol. Assn., Am. Assn. Neuropathology (pres. 1971-72), NY Acad. Medicine, Am. Acad. Neurology, Am. Assn. Pathologists and Bacteriologists, Internat. Soc. Neuropathology, Assn. Am. Med. Coll., NY Neurol. Soc., Am. Pub. Health Assn., Am. Osler Soc., Am. Coll. Epidemiology, Nat. Acad. Sci. (com. on nutrition in med. edn. 1983-85, com. on dietary guidelines implementation 1988-90). Achievements include research on genetics, epidemiology, pathology and diagnostic features of cerebral degenerative diseases, population dynamics, pathology and epidemiology of cerebral vasc. disease and organic dementia. Home: 26 Elm St Rehoboth MA 02769-0136 Office: Brown U Office Med Affairs Providence RI 02912-0001

ARONSON, VIRGINIA L. lawyer; b. Bremerton, Wash., June 4, 1947; BA, U. Chgo., 1969, MA, 1973, JD, 1975. Bar: Ill. 1975. Ptnr. Sidley Austin Brown & Wood, Chgo. Staff mem. U. Chgo. Law Review, 1974—75; mem. exec. & mgmt. com. Sidley Austin Brown & Wood. Contbr. articles to profl. jours. Mem. Am. Coll. Real Estate Lawyers, Chgo. Mortgage Atty.'s Assn., Chgo. Fin. Exchange, The Chgo. Network (dir. Chgo. ctrl. area com., Chgo. Pub. Edn. Fund). Office: Sidley Austin Brown & Wood Bank One Plz 10 South Dearborn St Chicago IL 60603

ARONSON-FRIEDMAN, AMY ILENE, education educator; b. Shreveport, La., Oct. 5, 1963; d. Irwin Leon and Barbara Sue (Ginsburg) Aronson; m. Ido Friedman, Dec. 22, 1990. BA, George Washington U., 1985; MA, Middlebury Coll., 1986, Ga. So. U., 1992; PhD, Temple U., 2000. Cert. tchr. Pa. Instr. Ga. So. U., Statesboro, 1982—91; tchg. asst. Temple U., Phila., 1994—99; asst. prof. No. Ga. Coll. & State U., Dahlonega, 1999—2000, Valdosta State U., 2002—. Adv. bd. So. Conf. on Lang. Tchg., Atlanta, 2002—. Scholar, Fulbright, Chile, Argentina; Travel grant, Valdosta State U., 2002—03. Avocations: horseback riding, travel, yoga. Home: 124 Brandywine Rd Savannah GA 31405 Office: Valdosta State Univ Dept Modern & Classical Lang Valdosta GA

ARONSTEIN, MARTIN JOSEPH, law educator, lawyer; b. N.Y.C., Jan. 25, 1925; s. William and Mollie (Mintz) A.; m. Sally K. Rosenau, Sept. 18, 1948 (dec.); children: Katherine Aronstein Porter, David M., James K. BE, Yale U., 1944; MBA, Harvard U., 1948; LLB, U. Pa., 1965. Bar: Pa. 1965. Bus. exec., Phila., 1948-65; assoc. firm Obermayer, Rebmann, Maxwell & Hippel, Phila., 1965-67, partner, 1968-69; assoc. prof. law U. Pa., 1969-72, prof., 1972-78; counsel firm Ballard, Spahr, Andrews & Ingersoll, Phila., 1978-80, partner, 1980-81; prof. law U. Pa., 1981-86, prof. emeritus, 1986—; of counsel firm Morgan, Lewis & Bockius, Phila., 1986-95. Contbr. articles to law revs.; mem. Permanent Editorial Bd. Uniform Comml. Code, 1978-80, counsel, 1980-87, counsel emeritus, 1987—. Served with USN, 1943-46. Mem. Am. Law Inst., ABA (reporter com. on stock certs. 1973-77, chmn. subcom. on investment securities 1982-84), Phila. Bar Assn., Order of Coif, Sigma Xi, Tau Beta Pi. Home: The Fountains at Logan Sq E Two Franklin Town Blvd 2213 Philadelphia PA 19103

AROUH, JEFFREY ALAN, lawyer; b. N.Y.C., May 2, 1945; s. Isaac E. and Jean J. (Halfon) A.; m. Karen Ann Wieder, Feb. 1, 1969; children: Russell Andrew, Ilonne A. BA, U. Mich., 1966; JD cum laude, NYU, 1969. Bar: N.Y.

1970; sr. cert. relocation profl. Assoc. Gilbert, Segall and Young, N.Y.C., 1969-74, ptnr., 1975-2001, Holland & Knight LLP, N.Y.C., 2001—. Spkr. in field. Editor NYU Law Rev., 1969; contbr. articles to legal publs. Recipient Founders Day award NYU. Mem.: ABA (bus. law sect. com. on corp. compliance), N.Y. State Bar Assn., Assn. Bar City N.Y., Employee Relocation Coun. (pub. policy com.), Order of Coif, Hampshire Country Club, Ibis Golf and Country Club. Home: 3 Ridgeway Rd Larchmont NY 10538-1123 Office: 195 Broadway Fl 23 New York NY 10007

AROWOSAFE, MUYI, education educator; b. Ikere Nig, Ekiti, Jan. 1, 1953; arrived in U.S., 1979; s. Peter Arowosafe and Phebean Adekogbba; m. Donna Schumacher, June 3, 1992 (div. Oct. 3, 1994); children: Joshua, Patrick, Yinica, Lola. MBA, Lincoln Univ., Jeff City, Mo., 1983; MEd, Fla. A & M Univ., Coll. Sta., 1987; EdM, Fla. State Univ., Tallahassee, Fla., 1992; PhD, Tex. A & M Univ., Coll. Sta., 1998. Dir. distance edn. Prairie View A & M, Prairie View, Tex., asst. prof.; dir. tng. Tex. A & M., Coll. Sta.; asst. dir. Fla. A & M. Univ., Tallahassee. Mem.: Tex. Educators, Nigerian Union (pres.). Home: 8226 Sotedad Dr Houston TX 77083

ARPESELLA, PIETRO, actor, writer; b. Bologna, Emilia Romagna, Italy, Jan. 26, 1964; s. Marco Arpesella and Tullia Turchi. M in Bus. & Fin., Bocconi U., Italy, 1987. Mergers & aquisitions fin. analysis Merrill Lynch, N.Y.C., 1987—89; dir. of merchant banking Can. Imperial Bank Of Commerce, Milan, 1989—91; assoc. mng. dir. The Grand Hotel of Rimini, Rimini, Italy, 1991—92; actor, 1992—. Host, performer (TV series) Cult Network Italia, N.Y.C.; dubbed : (films) Life is Beautiful; leading role (films) Karma Police; actor: (films) Business Sense; (plays) Life & Me...What A Couple!, (theatre);, author plays; actor: (plays); (TV series) Port Charles, Vivere, Spin City; (plays) Marriage Proposal, The Congress of the Birds; contbr. articles to profl. jours. Recipient Spl. Jury prize, N.Y. Internat. Ind. Film & Video Festival, 2000. Address: 1335 N Citrus Ave Los Angeles CA 90028 Home Fax: 310-943-1475. Personal E-mail: Pietro33@aol.com.

ARPEY, GERARD J. air transportation executive; b. July 26, 1958; m. Lisa Arpey; 3 children. BA, U. Tex., 1980; MBA, 1982. FAA multi-engine pilots license. Fin. analyst Am. Airlines, 1982, mng. dir. airline profitability analysis, mng. dir. fin. analysis and fleet planning, mng. dir. fin. planning, v.p. fin. planning and analysis, 1989-92, sr. v.p. planning, 1992-95, sr. v.p. fin. and planning, 1995—99; CFO AMR Corp. and Am. Airlines, exec. v.p. ops., 2000—02, pres., COO, 2002—03, pres., CEO, 2003—. Bd. dirs. The SABRE Group Holdings, Inc., AMR Investment Svcs., Inc. Avocation: private pilot. Office: AMR Corp Maildrop 5621 PO Box 619616 Dallas TX 75261-9616*

ARPINO, GERALD PETER, performing company executive; b. Staten Island, N.Y., Jan. 14, 1928; s. Luigi and Anna (Santanastasio) A. Student, Wagner Coll., PhD (hon.), 1980; student ballet under Mary Ann Wells, student modern dance under May O'Donnell and Gertrude Shurr. Dancer Ballet Russe, 1951-52; co-founder Joffrey Ballet, 1956, dancer, to 1962, former assoc. artistic dir., now artistic dir., resident choreographer, until 1990; with faculty Joffrey Ballet Sch. N.Y.C., from 1953, now artistic dir., 1988—, assoc. dir., 1988—, prin. choreographer, 1988—. Bd. dirs. Dance Notation Bur., Dancers in Transition; mem. adv. coun. to dept. dance Calif. State U., Long Beach, also mem. Disting. Artists Forum. Choreographer ballets including Incubus, 1962, Viva Vivaldi!, 1965, Olympics, Nightwings, both 1966, Cello Concerto, Arcs and Angels, Elegy, all 1967, Secret Places, The Clowns, Fanfarita, A Light Fantastic, 1968, Animus, The Poppet, 1969, Confetti, Solarwind, Trinity, all 1970, Reflections, Valentine, Kettentanz, all 1971, Chabriesque, Sacred Grove on Mount Talmalpais, both 1972, Jackpot, 1973, The Relativity of Icarus, 1974, Drums, Dreams on Banjos, 1975, Orpheus Times Light 2, 1976, Touch Me, 1977, Choura, L'Air d 'Esprit, Suite Saint-Saens, all 1978, Epode, 1979, Celebration, 1980, Ropes, Partita for Four, Sea Shadow, Diverdissement, 1980, Light Rain, 1981, Round of Angels, 1982, Italian Suite, Quarter-Tones, 1983, Jamboree (commd. by City of San Antonio) Adv. Sportsmedicine Edn. & Rsch. Found., L.A.; mem. adv. com. N.Y. Internat. Festival of the Arts; mem. nat. adv. coun. ITI/USA Internat. Ballet Competition; mem. hon. com. The Yard Benefit-Vineyard Celebration, 1989; mng. dir., bd. dirs. Found. for Joffrey Balllet, Inc. Served with USCG, 1945-48. Recipient Dancemagazine award, 1974, Bravo award San Antonio Performing Arts Assn., 1984, Disting. Achievement award Nat. Orgn. Italian-Am. Women, 1987, Tiffany award Internat. Soc. Performing Arts Adminstrs., 1989, Outstanding Artistic Achievement award Staten Island Coun. on Arts, 1990, Ammy award Am. Express Corp. Office: Joffrey Ballet Chgo 70 E Lake St Fl 1300 Chicago IL 60601-5917

ARP LOTTER, DONNA, venture capitalist, investor; b. Henrietta, Tex., Dec. 17, 1950; d. T.S. Jr. and Coy Lee (Howard) Grimsley; m. Bruce D. Lotter, Feb. 18, 1984; children: Brandon, Collin. BS, Midwestern State U., 1975, MS in Counseling, 1979. Sales rep. Burroughs-Wellcome Co., Fort Worth, Tex., 1978-79; sales mgr. Procter & Gamble Co., Dallas, 1979-84; pres. Arp-Lotter Investments, Colleyville, Tex., 1984—; mayor City of Colleyville, Tex., 1999—. Prin. DBL Investments, Inc.; sec., officer KCB Corp., Inc.; bd. dirs. Landmark Bank. Mem. adv. bd.: Philanthropy in Tex. mag. Chmn., trustee Baylor Hosp., Grapevine, Tex., 1998; bd. dirs. Am. Cancer Soc., North Tex. Commn., Am. Heart Assn., BRIT, 2003, Tarrant Co. Coll. Found.; adv. bd. Tex. Bank, 2002; bd. govs. N.E. Arts Coun.; city councilperson, City of Colleyville, 1996-98, mayor (pro tem.). 1997-98, mayor, 1999—; mem. exec. com. Ft. Worth Opera Assn.; bd. dirs. Casa Manana Teatro; officer Mayor's Coun. Tarrant County; bd. regents Midwestern State U. Named Alumnus of Yr., Midwestern State U., 1995, Colleyville Citizen of Yr., 2002; Hardin scholar, 1975; recipient Legacy of Women award Am. Heart Assn., 1995, Vol. of Yr. award, Colleyville, 1996, State of Tex. Local Leader award, 1998; voted Most Influential Female of Tarrant County, Tex., 1997, 98, 99, 2000, Woman of Influence award Tarrant County Women's Ctr., 2001, U.S. Inspiring Woman award Gen. Mills Corp., 2001, Disting. Woman award Northwood U., 2003. Mem. Bus. Profl. Womens Club, Nat. Assn. Women Bus. Owners, Colleyville C. of C. (pres. 1995). Republican. Baptist.

ARPS, DAVID FOSTER, electronics engineer; b. Napoleon, Ohio, July 28, 1948; s. Fred B. and Melba Lavern (Harrison) A.; m. Vickie Lee Westrick, Mar. 19, 1982; children: Derek, Elizabeth. BS in Astronomy, Case Inst. Tech., 1970; MAT in Physics, Bowling Green State U., 1975; MS in Atmospheric Physics, U. Nev., Reno, 1977. Cert. secondary edn. and community coll. tchr. Astronomy instr. U. Toledo, Ohio, 1970; physics tchr. Napoleon (Ohio) High Sch., 1970-74; teaching asst. Bowling Green (Ohio) State U., 1974-75; rsch. fellow Desert Rsch. Inst., Reno, 1975-78; mech. engr., physicist Naval Air Warfare Ctr., Aircraft Div., Indpls., 1978-84, elec. engr., failure analyst, 1984-96; elec. engr. component specification Def. Supply Ctr., Columbus, Ohio, 1996—. Astronomical rschr. Ritter Obs., U. Toledo, Ohio, 1970; solar radiation rschr. Desert Rsch. Inst., Reno, 1975-78. Mem. PTA, Mt. Comfort (Ind.) Elem., 1989-95; asst. coach Mt. Comfort (Ind.) Elem. Sports, 1992-95; coach Youth Softball, Pickerington, Ohio, 1998; active Pickertington PTO, local sch. music boosters, acad. boosters. Recipient Rsch. fellowships Desert Rsch. Inst., Reno, 1975-78. Mem. Sigma Pi Sigma. Methodist. Achievements include numerous technical reports on component failure analysis and x-ray microanalysis; defense specification preparing activity for fiber optic, electron tube, and microwave components. Home: 13314 Princeton Ln Pickerington OH 43147-8324 Office: Defense Supply Ctr PO Box 3990 Columbus OH 43216-5000 E-mail: david.arps@dla.mil.

ARQUIT, KEVIN JAMES, lawyer; b. Ithaca, N.Y., Sept. 11, 1954; s. Gordon James and Nora (Harris) A. BA cum laude, St. Lawrence U., 1975; JD cum laude, Cornell U., 1978. Bar: Ohio 1978, N.Y. 1980, U.S. Dist. Ct. (so. and ea. dists.) N.Y. 1980, U.S. Dist. Ct. (we. dist.) N.Y. 1983, U.S. Dist. Ct. (no. dist.) Calif. 1983, U.S. Ct. Appeals (3d cir.) 1983, U.S. Dist. Ct. (no. dist.) N.Y. 1985, U.S. Ct. Appeals(2d cir.) 1985, U.S. Supreme Ct. 1989. Assoc. Arter & Hadden, Cleve., 1978, Fish & Neave, N.Y.C., 1978-83, Harris, Beach & Wilcox, Rochester, N.Y., 1983-86; atty. advisor to chmn. FTC, Washington, 1986-87, chief staff, 1987-88, gen. counsel, 1988-89; dir. Bur. Competition, Washington, 1989-92; ptnr., dep. chmn., head Clifford Chance US LLP Antitrust Practice Group, N.Y.C., 1992—2002; ptnr. STB, 2003—. Republican. Roman Catholic. Office: Simpson Thacher & Bartlett 425 Lexington Ave New York NY 10017-3954 E-mail: karquit@stblaw.com.

ARQUIT, NORA HARRIS, retired music educator, writer; b. Brushton, N.Y., June 30, 1923; d. Samuel Elton George and Esther Cecelia (Gillen) Harris; m. Gordon James Arquit, Nov. 12, 1948; children: Christine Elaine Arquit, Kevin James Arquit, Candace Susan Arquit-Martel. BS in Music Edn., Ithaca Coll., 1945, MS, 1962; postgrad., St. Lawrence U., 1946-47, 74, Cornell U., 1970-71, N.Y. State Coll., Potsdam, 1973. Cert. aerospace edn. with techicians rating. Music dir., band dir., tchr. N.Y. and N.J. State Schs., 1945—80. Guest conductor U.S. Air Force Band, Washington, U.S. Navy Band, Washington, various massed bands in U.S.A., Canada, Europe; dir., coord. St. Lawrence County ann. High Sch. Band Day, 1973-2001; past supvr. Coll. Student Practice Tchrs., N.Y.; mem. Mid-States Commn. Secondary Schs. and Colls. Evaluations. Author: Before My Own Time and Since, 1978, From Hamlet to Cold Harbor, 1989, Our Lyon Line, 1993, The History of the New York State, Society of the National Society of the Daughters of the American Colonists, 1994. Past ajudicator h.s. and coll. band contests; past dir., coord. ann. St. Lawrence County Band Day; past capt. aux. USAF Civil Air Patrol; past John Philip Sosa bd. dirs. rep. to Hall of Fame enshrinement of Sousa. Named Dist. Band Master Am., First Chair Am.; recipient Letter of Commendation for People to People Diplomacy for work with student band groups, Embassy at the Hague, Europe, honored for 39 yrs. of svc. on Band Day, St. Lawrence County, 2002. Mem.: AAUW (past divsn. meeting rep.), Women Band Dirs. Nat. Assn. (past nat. pres., Silver Baton), N.Y. State Ret. Tchrs. Assn., N.Am. Band Dirs. Coordinating Coun. (pres. 1978, past nat. v.p.), Am. School Band Dirs. Assn. (emeritus mem. 1980, N.Y. state chmn. 2003—, past chmn. internat. band com., past nat. and state ofcr., honored nat. covention 2003, Dist. Bandmaster Am. award), Internat. Assn. U. Women, Colonial Daughters of the XVIIC (chpt. councillor 1988-91, past. mem. coms.), Soverign Colonial Soc., Soc. New England Women, De Schilpen Soc. (Holland), Kings County Hist. Soc. Nova Scotia, Daughters of Union Vets., N.Y. Ct. Assts. of Nat. Soc. Women Descendents of Ancient and Honorable Artillery Co. (past state officer, corr. sec., com. chmn.), Denison Soc., Daughters Am. Colonists (N.Y. state regent 1991—94, hon. state regent, life 1994), Soc. Colonial Dames of Seventeenth Century (past state officer, past state pres, registrar), Colonial Daughters Seventeenth Century (Atlantic Coast chmn. 2000—, nat. com. chmn. 2000— 2000—, past pres.), Daus. Colonial Wars, DAR (life; hon. regent Cayuga chpt., past state com. chmn., state genealogical chmn., hon. N.Y. state regent), Soc. Magna Charta Dames and Barons, Plantagenet Soc., Colonial Order of The Crown (Charlemagne), Soc. Sons and Daus. of the Pilgrims, Soc. U.S. Daughters 1812 (past pres., past Onondaga chpt. pres., past state ofcr.), Soc. Daughters of Founders & Patriots of Am. (past pres., past state pres., registrar), Soc. Sons and Daughters of Colonial Wars, Soc. New England Women, De Schilpen Mus. Soc. Netherlands, Nat. State Regents Club (nat. com chmn. 1994—97, atlantic sect.chmn genealogy 2003—), Summit N.J. Club (past mem. spl. panel), Nat. Fedn. Music Club (past mem. editl.com.), State Officers Club, Ithaca Music Club (past pres.), Delta Omicron. Avocations: writing, photography, research. Home: 130 Christopher Cir Ithaca NY 14850-1702

ARRARTE, EDUARDO R. travel agency executive; b. Guayaquil, Ecuador, July 6, 1924; arrived in Peru, 1944; s. Eduardo Arrarte and Rosa Salame; m. Irma Fiedler, May 8, 1948; children: Ana Maria, Eduardo, Jose Luis, Carlos Alberto, Maria Rosa. Pres. Lima Tours, Peru, 1946-91, chmn. bd. dirs., 1991—. Pres. Patronato de Lima, 1989-2002. Office: Lima Tours PO Box 4340, Belen 1040 Lima Peru

ARRATHOON, LEIGH ADELAIDE, medievalist, editor, writer, educator; b. N.Y.C., Nov. 30, 1942; d. Henry and Peggy Elkin; m. Raymond Arrathoon, June 10, 1967. Cours de vacances, U. de Genève, L'Université de Lausanne, L'Université de Lille à Boulogne sur Mer, 1961-63; AB in French and Spanish, Hunter Coll., 1963; MA in French, Stanford U., 1966, MA in Spanish, 1968; MA in Medieval French Lit., PhD in Medieval French Lit., Princeton U., 1975. Mem. UN Secretariat, N.Y.C., 1963-64; tchg. asst. Stanford U., 1964-66; tchr. Convent of Sacred Heart, Menlo Park, Calif., 1966-67; asst. prof. Spanish Rider Coll., Trenton, N.J., 1970-71; pub. editor-in-chief Solaris Press, Troy, Idaho, 1975-80, Rochester, Mich., 1980-86; pres. Solaris Press II, 1986—; pres., advt./mktg. A.D. Images, Inc., 1986-96; pres. Paint Creek Press, 1996—; v.p. John J. Davio, Rochester, Mich., 1996—. Enrichment tchr. French and creative writing Rochester Pub. Schs., 1996—; facilitator French and ESL PALS Internat., 1997—2000; asst. prof. French Oakland C.C., Auburn Hills, Mich., 1998—; vis. prof. French Oakland U., 1985. Author: Men and Women Who Changed the World: The Henry Ford Story, 1997, The First Birdmen: The Wright Brothers, 1997, Motown, 1999, Great Places: Jody's Michigan Adventures, Vol. I, Frankenmuth, Vol. II, Holland, Mich., Vol. III, Mackinac Island, 1997, reprinted and revised in full color, 3 vols., 1999, Michigan's Upper Penninsula, Vol. IV, Detroit, Vol. V, Northwest Michigan, Vol. VI, Greenfield Village, Vol. VII, 1999, (hist. novel) Magical Adventures in Michigan, 2003, Summer of the Bear, 2000, Eagle from the Dawn, 2001; contbg. editor: The Craft of Fiction: Essays in Medieval Poetics, 1984; editor, transl.: The Lady of Vergi, 1984; contbg. editor: Chaucer and the Craft of Fiction, 1986; contbr., articles to profl. jours. Scholar Centre d'Art Dramatique, 1957; univ. fellow Princeton U., 1969-70. Mem. MLA, Medieval Acad. Am., Courtly Lit. Soc., Sigma Delta Pi, Alpha Gamma Delta.

ARREOLA, JOHN BRADLEY, b. San Fernando, La Union, Philippines, Mar. 20, 1935; came to U.S., 1950; naturalized, 1960; s. Juanito Antonio and Catalina (Bacalzo) A.; m. Judith Anne Hughes, June 26, 1965; children: Bradley, Christopher. Student, Hartnell Coll., Salinas, Calif., 1950-52; BA, San Jose State Coll., 1955. Cert. real estate appraiser; cert. internat. financier; CFP. Statistician O'Connor Hosp., San Jose, Calif., 1955-60; tax cons. Arreola-Comita & Assocs., San Jose, 1960-63; cost acct. Granger & Assocs., Palo Alto, Calif., 1963-64; mgr. cost acctg. Gen. Micro-Electronics, Santa Clara, Calif., 1964-65; chief acct. Kaiser Engrs., Calif. and Venezuela, 1965-67; comptr. Aluminio del Caroni, S.A. (Reynolds Alumnium subs.), Caracas, Venezuela, 1967-78; bus. cons. Venezuela and U.S., 1978-83; pres. Arreola, Hughes & Co. Inc., Sarasota, Fla., 1983—; CEO, pres. MAP Fin. Group of Cos., Inc., Sarasota, 1985-92; pres. J&J Enterprises, Sarasota, 1992—2001; sr. v.p. High Mark Fin. Svcs., 2002—. Mem.: Fin. Planning Assn., Internat. Assn. Fin. Planning (pres. Sarasota chpt. 1988—89), Sarasota Ski Club, Tournament Players Club PGA at Prestancia. Republican. Roman Catholic. Avocations: golf, snow skiing, photography, football, baseball. Home: 3900 Torrey Pines Blvd Sarasota FL 34238-2833

ARRIETA, MARCIA, poet, editor, publishing executive, educator; b. Santa Monica, Calif., Aug. 24, 1952; d. Cecil and Dora Teresa (Ramos) A.; m. Kevin Timothy Joy, June 10, 1978; children: Matthew Kevin, Brendan Yeats, Dylan James. BA, UCLA, 1975; MFA, Vt. Coll., 1999. Lic. profl. clear tchg. credential, Calif. Tchr. English L.A. Unified Sch. Dist., 1985—; editor, publ. Indefinite Space, Pasadena, Calif., 1992—. Participant The Frost Place, Franconia, N.H., 1993; leader poetry workship, tchr. Pasadena (Calif.) Citywide Arts Program, 1991-92. Contbr. poems to The Midwest Quar., Cold Mountain Rev., Am. Writing, Minotaur, Small Pond, 88, Perceptions, Pacific Rev., The? WHY? Project, Heaven Bone, Poetry Salzburg Rev., Psychopoetica, Riverrun, Abraxas, Atticus Rev., Tight, Tinfish, West/Word, Bogg, Elf, Big Scream, Generator, So To Speak, Yefief, Juxta, Lost and Found Times, Atelier, Plainsongs, Hyphen, Tin Wreath, Pacific Coast Journal, NRG, Gestalten, others. Grantee Literary Arts Pasadena City Arts Commn., 1991; recipient Literary Arts award Pasadena Arts Coun., 1993. Mem. PEN, Calif. Poets in the Schs., Am. Fedn. Tchrs., Assoc. Writing Program. Avocations: travel, gardening, hiking, art. Office: Indefinite Space PO Box 40101 Pasadena CA 91114-7101

ARRIGO, CINDY JO, biochemist, researcher; d. Robert Eugene and Judith Ann Martin; m. Philip Joseph Arrigo; children: Philip Joseph Robert, Michael David. BS, N.J. City U., 1996; PhD, U. Medicine and Dentistry of N.J., 2002. Rschr. biochemistry N.J. Med. Sch., Newark, 1996—; adj. prof. biology N.J. City U., Jersey City, 1998—. Cons. biochemistry, grant devel. N.J. Med. Sch. Contbr. articles to profl. jours. Airman 1st class USAF, 1979—81, Ramstein AFB, Germany. Recipient Stanley S. Bergen Jr. M.D. medal of excellence, U. Medicine and Dentistry N.J., 2002. Mem.: NPA, AAAS, N.Y. Acad. Sci. Achievements include research in structure function analysis of Mycobacterium tuberculosis DNA polymerase I. Office: NJ Med Sch PO Box 1709 185 S Orange Ave Newark NJ 07101-1709 Office Fax: 973-972-5594. Personal E-mail: joarrigo@aol.com. E-mail: arrigoci@umdnj.edu.

ARRIGO, JAN ELIZABETH, photographer, writer; b. New Orleans, La., July 23, 1960; d. Joseph and Ruth Arrigo. BA, Loyola U., 1979—82. Italian Language Centro Fiorenza, Florence, Italy, 1994. Pres. Forest Sales and Distbg., Inc., New Orleans, 2002—. Author: New Orleans, The American Art Book, The Jean Lafille National Park and Preserve Explore Book; photography, New Orleans Museum of Art's Underexposed (2nd Pl. Photographer, 2003); pro-dr.(curator): (group show) Surreal New York, Soho Photo, (traveling exhibition) The Sweet and Sour Animal Book Traveling Show. Mentor Big Bros., Big Sisters, NYC, 2000—02; vol. Bellevue Hosp., New York, NY, 2001—02; docent The Internat. Ctr. of Photography, NYC, 1997—2000; panelist William Faulkner Words and Music Festival, 2002. Mem.: Greater New Orleans Photographic Soc., New Orleans Press Club, Arts Coun. New Orleans, Editl. Freelance Assn.

ARRIGO, ROBIN JEAN SEMPEY, piano educator, accompanist; b. Miami, Fla., Jan. 11, 1962; d. Edward James and Jean (Packman) Sempey; m. John Joseph Arrigo, July 23, 1988; children: Alyssa, Angela, Amanda. MusB in Piano Performance, Fla. State U., 1984, M Music Edn., 1987; D of Musical Arts in Accompanying and Chamber Music, U. Miami, 1998. Tchr. piano South Dade Sr. H.S., Homestead, Fla., 1987-88, Camden Mid. Sch., Kingsland, Ga., 1988-89; pvt. tchr. piano, Fernandina Beach, Fla., 1989-92; artist-in-residence Dreyfoos Sch. Arts, West Palm Beach, Fla., 1993-95; adj. prof. piano Palm Beach Atlantic Coll., West Palm Beach, 1995—. Accompanist Fla. Philharm. Chorus, Ft. Lauderdale, 1996, Fla. Grand Opera, Miami, 1996; judge Pathfinder Scholarship Competition, West Palm Beach, 1999. Co-editor: The Mendelssohns: Their Music in History, 1999; featured soloist WXEL's Ovation South Fla.; soloist Even Song, Internat. Pianist Parade, Faculty Showcase Gala, others; performances include Palm Beach Atlantic U. Symphony, Liszt, Hungarian Fantasy Concerto; rehearsal accompanist and collaborative artist with tenor, John Matz and Roberta Peters, soprano. Mem. Music Tchrs. Nat. Assn., Am. Coll. Musicians. Avocations: painting, raising her children. E-mail: robinja@aol.com.

ARRILLAGA, MARIA, foreign language educator; b. Mayagüez, P.R. m. Joseph M. Gutierrez; 1 child, María Ana McDonough. BS, St. Louis U., 1961; MA, NYU, 1966; postgrad., U. Dijon, France, 1976; PhD magna cum laude, U. P.R., 1987. Typist, translator, interpreter St. Luke's Hosp., 1962-63; Spanish tchr. Yeshiva Rabbi Samson Raphael Hirsch, N.Y.C., 1965-66, O. Henry Sch., N.Y.C., 1966-67; recreational dir. 1 Spy Health Program Beth Israel Hosp., N.Y.C., 1967-68; Spanish instr. SEEK program CUNY, N.Y.C., 1968-69; substitute tchr. Onteora H.S., Woodstock, N.Y., 1969-70; instr. art and music of P.R. N.Y.C. Tech. Coll., Bklyn., 1970-71; writer Dept. Edn. Press, Hato Rey, P.R., 1971-73; Spanish prof. Coll. Gen. Studies U. P.R., Río Piedras, 1973—2001, ret., 2001. Vis. prof. York Coll., CUNY, Queens, 1993-94, adj. prof. Spanish CUNY Coll.Tech., 2002-03. Author (poetry): Life in Time, 1974; author: New York in the Sixties, 1976, Cascade of Sun, 1977, Poems 747, 1977; Freshness, 1981; author (novel): Mañana Valentina, 1995; author: (collected poetry anthology) Yo soy Fili Melé (Hon. mention PEN, Puerto Rico, 1999); contbr. articles to profl. jours. Recipient First prize Inst. Puerto Rican Lit., 1981, Inst. Bus. Adminstrn., P.R. Jr. Coll., Mayagüez, 1982, 84, Luis Lloréns Torres award Puerto Rican Acad. of the Spanish Lang., 19987, medal of honor Josefina Romo Arregui Meml. Found. for Contbn. to Lit., N.Y., 1990. Home: 140 Charles St Apt 8E New York NY 10014-6515 E-mail: mariarrillaga@yahoo.com.

ARRINGTON, CAROLYN RUTH, education consultant; b. May 20, 1942; d. Robert Ray and Grace Dotson; m. Wayne Vernon Arrington; children: Kevin Ray, Kemp Gray, Korey shay, Wayne, Kimberly. AA, Ohio Valley Coll., 1962; BA, Fairmont State Coll., 1964; MA, W.Va. U., 1966, EdD, 1994. Cert. pub. sch. adminstr., 1993. Tchr. Greenbrier Bd. Edn., Lewisburg, W.Va., 1964-68; supr. Mason County Bd. Edn., Point Pleasant, W.Va., 1968-70; media specialist Kanawha County Bd. Edn., Charleston, W.Va., 1970-71; asst. dir., dir., asst. divsn. chief W.Va. Dept. Edn., Charleston, 1971-89, asst. state supt. schs., 1989-98; v.p. Arrington Assocs., Inc., 1998—. Edn. and bus. cons.; inspirational motivational spkr. Author numerous poems and children's books; developer workshop materials. Bd. dirs. YWCA, Charleston, 1988-91. Recipient medal of merit Edn. Ohio Valley Coll.; SEA fellow U.S. Dept. Edn., 1984. Mem. Assn. Ednl. Comm. and Tech. (pres. 1979-80, Edgar Dale award 1975, Spl. Svc. award 1982), Wva. Ednl. Media Assn. (pres. 1975-76). Office: Arrington Assocs Inc PO Box 3912 Charleston WV 25339-3912 E-mail: Warrington@charter.net.

ARRINGTON, HAROLD M. obstetrician; b. Detroit, Mich. s. Robyn James Arrington, Irene (Vonciel) Arrington. BS, Adrian Coll., 1968; MD, U. Mich., 1972. Diplomate Am. Bd. Ob-Gyn. Resident ob-gyn Wayne State U. Hosps., Detroit, 1972—76; ob-gyn Detroit, 1976—. Col. Army Nat. Guard, 1972—. Fellow: Internat. Coll. Surgeons, Am. Coll. Ob-Gyn. Office: 3800 Woodward Ave Ste 502 Detroit MI 48201

ARRINGTON, HARRIET ANN HORNE, historian, biographer, researcher, writer; b. Salt Lake City, June 22, 1924; d. Lyman Merrill and Myrtle (Swainston) Horne; m. Frederick C. Sorensen, Dec. 22, 1943 (div. Dec. 1954); children: Annette S. Rogers, Frederick Christian, Heidi S. Swinton; m. Gordon B. Moody, July 26, 1958 (div. Aug. 1963); 1 child, Stephen Horne; m. Leonard James Arrington, Nov. 19, 1983. BS in Edn., U. Utah, 1957. Cert. tchr., Utah, Ga. Supr. surg. secs. Latter-day Saints Hosp., Salt Lake City, 1954-58; tchr. Salt Lake City Schs., 1957-58, Glynn County Schs., Brunswick, Ga., 1958-59, 60—; from med. sec. to office mgr. Dr. Horne, Salt Lake City, 1962-83; tchr. Carden Sch., Salt Lake City, 1973-74, women's history rschr., biographer. Mem. Utah Women's Legis. Coun.; co-establisher, bd. dirs. Arrington Archives, Utah State U.; spkr. hist. and women's confs. Author: (essays) Heritage of Faith, 1988, Worth Their Salt, 1997, Nearly Everything Imaginable: The Everyday Life of Utah's Mormon Pioneers, 1999; contbg. author (biographies) Encyclopedia of Women in American History, 1999, Pioneer Women of Faith and Fortitude, 1999, Encyclopedia of Utah History, 1999. Dist. chmn. Utah Rep. Com., 1972-76; mem. art com. Salt Lake City Bd. Edn.; chmn. art exhibit Senator Orrin Hatch's ann. Utah Women's Conf., 1987; past pres. L.D.S. Women's Relief Soc., Twin Falls, cultural refinement and/or spiritual living tchr., Alaska, Ga., Utah, Idaho; chmn. Utah Women Artists' Exhbns., AAUW, Utah divsn., 1986-87, Springville Mus. of Art. Nominated Pres. Ronald Reagan's Vol. Action award Utah Women Artists' Exhbn., 1987; recipient resolution of appreciation Utah Arts Coun., 1989, Friends of the Humanities award Utah State U., 1995. Mem.: NSDAR (nat. vice chmn. Women in Am. History 2000—04), DAR (regent 1998—2000, Utah State DAR bd. historian 2000—02, Princess Timpanogos Utah Chpt., 1st vice-regent Princess Timpanogos), AAUW (Utah state cultural refinement chmn., cert. of appreciation 1988), Old Main Soc. Utah State U., Cannon-Hinckley History & Dinner Club, Classics Club (v.p. 2003—), Xi Alpha (past pres. alumni chpt.), Chi Omega. Avocations: art, writing, cooking, art, writing, gourmet cooking, needle-point. Home and Office: 2236 S 2200 E Salt Lake City UT 84109-1135 E-mail: harrietarrington@aol.com.

ARRINGTON, JAMES HENRY, journalist; b. Longview, Tex., Sept. 20, 1969; s. James H. and Teresa L. Arrington. AA, Kilgore (Tex.) Coll., 1992; BS, U. Tex., Tyler, 1994, MA in Interdisciplinary Studies, 1995. Editor The Light and Champion, Center, Tex., 1999-2001; reporter Jackson Ind., Jonesboro, La., 2001—. Freelance writer, Tyler, 1995-99. Named Journalist of Yr., North and East Tex. Press Assn., 1999. Mem.: Nat. Soc. Newspaper Columnists, La. Press Assn., Jonesboro-Hodge Lions Club (officer 2002—03). Democrat. Episcopalian. Avocations: reading, writing, skiing, sports. Home: 1115 S Hudson Ave Jonesboro LA 71251 E-mail: irishink@hotmail.com.

ARRINGTON, JOHN LESLIE, JR., lawyer; b. Pawhuska, Okla., Oct. 15, 1931; s. John Leslie and Grace Louise (Moore) A.; m. Elizabeth Anne Waddington, 1956 (div.); children: Elizabeth Anne, John Leslie III, Winifred L., Katherine M.; m. Linda Vance, 1972. Grad., Lawrenceville Sch., 1949; AB, Princeton U., 1953; JD, Harvard U., 1956, LLM, 1957. Bar: Okla. 1956, U.S. Supreme Ct. 1960. Assoc. Arrington, Kihle, Gaberino & Dunn and predecessor firms, Tulsa, 1957-61, ptnr., 1961-93, chmn., CEO, 1994-96; gen. counsel ONEOK, Inc., 1997-98; of counsel Gable & Gotwals, Tulsa, 1998—. Chmn. bd. dirs. Woodland Bank of Tulsa, 1979-94. Prin. draftsman Okla. Supreme Ct. rules governing disciplinary proceedings, 1980-81; bd. dirs. Tulsa County Legal Aid Soc., 1965-70, pres. 1967-70; bd. dirs. Tulsa Family Mental Health Ctr., 1982-89. Named Outstanding Young Man, Tulsa Jaycees, 1963 Mem. ABA,

Tulsa County Bar Assn. (Young Lawyer award 1962, pres. 1970, Pres.'s award 1984, Professionalism award 1993), Okla. Bar Assn. (mem. profl. responsiblity commn. 1977-84, vice chmn. 1983-84, Disting. svc. award 1984, Golden Gavel award 1985, Pres.'s award 1991, Masonic award for ethics 1995), So. Hills Country Club (Tulsa), Princeton Club (N.Y.C.). Republican. Episcopalian. Home: 2300 Riverside Dr Unit 3E Tulsa OK 74114-2402 Office: 100 W 5th St Ste 1000 Tulsa OK 74103-4293

ARRINGTON, LAVARR, football player; b. June 20, 1978; 1 child, Keeno Lamoni. Attended, Penn State Coll. Profl. football player Washington Redskins, 2000—. With Washington Redskins Leadership Coucil's Fields for Tomorrow program. Finalist Lombardi Trophy, Football News Nat. Defensive Player of Yr. award; recipient Pigskin Club Oxley award, 2002, Chuck Bednarik award, Dick Butkus award, Bronko Nagurski award. Office: 21300 Redskin Park Dr Ashburn VA 20147 Personal E-mail: 703-478-8900.

ARRINGTON, MICHAEL BROWNE, foundation administrator; b. Chgo., Mar. 24, 1943; s. W. Russell and Ruth Marian (Browne) A.; m. DeEtta Jane Watson, Dec. 15, 1966 (div. 1969); m. Trudi Jeanne Robertson, Dec. 4, 1971 (div. 1992); children: Jennifer Lorraine, Patrick Browne. AA, Kendall Coll., Evanston, Ill., BA in Polit. Sci., U. Ill. Adminstrv. asst. to Senate Majority Leader State of Ill., Springfield, 1966-67; dir. pub. affairs Union League Club of Chgo., 1967-68; exec. dir. South Loop Improvement Orgn., Chgo., 1968-69; pres., chief exec. officer The Arrington Found., Chgo., 1979—, Arrington Travel Ctr., Inc., Chgo., 1969-99, Recon Mgmt Svcs., Evanston, Ill., 1999—. Mem. Nat. White House Conf. Travel and Tourism, Disting. Entrepreneurship Bd., U. Ill., Chgo. Bd. dirs. Robert R. McCormick Chgo. Boys & Girls Club, 1982—, Friends of Prentice Hosp., Chgo., 1986—; mem. chancellor's adv. bd. U. Ill., Chgo. Cpl. USMC, 1962-64. Named finalist Entrepreneur of Yr., 1989, 1990, Man of Yr., Ill. Vietnam Vets Leadership Program, 1993; named to Hall of Fame, Nat. Assn. Trade and Tech. Schs., 1988, Entrepreneurship Hall of Fame, 1994; recipient Excellence in Phys. Fitness award, USMC, 1962, Significant Contbn.. to Dental Health award, Ill. Dental Health Soc., 1967, Alumni Achievement award, U. Ill., 2001. Mem. World Pres.'s Orgn., Econ. Club of Chgo., Chgo. Club, Westmoreland Country Club, 100 Club Cook County, Chief Execs. Orgn. Republican. Episcopalian. Avocations: golf, boating, skiing, scuba diving. Office: Recon Mgmt Svcs Inc 929 Edgemere Ct Evanston IL 60202-1428 E-mail: arringtonusa@ameritech.net.

ARRINGTON, REBECCA CAROL, occupational health nurse; b. Longmont, Colo., Apr. 14, 1948; d. Theodore Victor Anderson and Lucinda Beth Panabaker; m. Charles Arthur Keeran, Aug. 2, 1968 (div. 1973); m. C. R. Arrington, Oct. 30, 1982. RN, St. Mark's Sch. Nursing, Salt Lake City, 1970; BS in Profl. Arts, St. Joseph's Coll., Standish, Maine, 1993. RN Okla. Recovery rm. nurse McArthur Pk. Med. Ctr., Irving, Tex., 1976-77; claims analyst Blue Cross/Blue Shield, Dallas, 1977-78, 78-79; staff RN Parkland Meml. Hosp., Dallas, 1978; occupl. health nurse City of Tulsa, 1979—, wellness coord., 1984—, mgr. occupl. health, 1997. Ind. assoc. Mannatech, 1998; privacy officer HIPAA, 2003. Mem.: ANA, Tulsa Area Assn. Occupl. Health Nurses (mem. nominating com. 1988—90, treas. 1990—93, pres. 1993—94), Okla. Nurses Assn., Am. Assn. Occupl. Health Nurses. Republican. Baptist. Avocations: sewing, crafts, fishing, camping. Office: City of Tulsa 1145 S Utica Ave Ste 453 Tulsa OK 74104-4041 E-mail: ambrosia@familynet.net., barrington@ci.tulsa.ok.us.

ARRINGTON, RICHARD, JR., former mayor; b. Livingston, Ala., Oct. 19, 1934; AB, Miles Coll., 1955; MS, U. Detroit, 1957; PhD in Zoology, U. Okla., 1966. Asst. prof. Miles Coll., 1957-63, prof., 1966-70; exec. dir. Ala. Ctr. for Higher Edn., 1970-79; mayor City of Birmingham, Ala., 1979-99. Counselor Miles Coll., 1962-63, dir. summer sch., acting dean, 1966-67, dean, 1967-70. Mem. Birmingham City Council, 1971-79.

ARROL, ROBERT N. family physician; b. Kokomo, Ind., Nov. 19, 1939; BS, Tulane U., 1962, MD, 1964. Diplomate Am. Bd. Family Practice. Intern Decatur-Macon County Hosp., Decatur, Ill., 1964-65; pvt. family practice Arcola, Ill., 1965-66, 68—; city health officer, 1972—; chmn. dept. family practice Covenant Hosp., Urbana, 1997. Clin. assoc. Sch. Basic Medicine Scis.-U. Ill. Med. Sch., 1974—76, clin. instr., 1976—89; plant physician Equistar, 1988—99; coroner's physician Douglas County, Ill., 1989—; courtesy staff Covenant Hosp., Urbana-Champaign, Ill., Sara Bush Lincoln Health Ctr., Mattoon-Charleston, Ill., emeritus, 1999. Mem. Bd. Edn., Arcola, 1971-77, sec., 1975-76. Capt. USAF, 1966-68. Fellow Am. Acad. Family Physicians; mem. AMA, Ill. State Med. Soc., Douglas County Med. Soc. (pres. 1975, 76, 81, 82, 88, 97, 98, 99). Republican. Office: 126 S Locust St Arcola IL 61910-1714

ARROM, SILVIA MARINA, history educator; b. New Haven, Aug. 26, 1949; d. Jose Juan and Silvia (Ravelo) A.; m. David R. Oran, Dec. 30, 1972; children: Christina Alexandra, Daniel David. BA, Bryn Mawr (Pa.) Coll., 1971; PhD, Stanford (Calif.) U., 1978. Asst. prof. history Yale U., New Haven, 1977-84; assoc. prof. history Ind. U., Bloomington, 1987-91; Jane's prof. Latin Am. studies Brandeis U., Waltham, Mass., 1991—, dir. Latin Am. studies, 1991—. Author: La Mujer mexicana ante el divorcio eclesiástico (1800-1857), 1976, The Women of Mexico City, 1790-1857, 1985 (hon. mention Bolton prize 1986), Containing the Poor: The Mexico City Poor House 1774-1871, 2000; (with Servando Ortoll) Riots in the Cities: Popular Politics and the Urban Poor in Latin America, 1765-1910, 1996; co-editor: (with M.E. Brown and D. Sadlier) New Research: Latin American Women's Studies, 1991; mem. editl. bd. Latin Am. Rsch. Rev., Hispanic Am. Hist. Rev., SIGNS: Jour. Women in Culture and Soc., Secuencia: Revista de Historia y Ciencias Sociales, Anuario Mexicano de Historia del Derecho, Signos Históricos, Women's History Review; contbr. articles to profl. jours. Fgn. Area fellow Social Sci. Rsch. Coun./Am. Coun. Learned Socs. rsch. grant, 1981, Morse fellow Yale U., 1983-84, NEH fellow for univ. tchrs., 1988-89, Bunting Inst. fellow Radcliffe Coll., 1991, Am. Coun. Learned Socs. fellow, 1997. Mem. New Eng. Coun. Latin Am. Studies (pres. 1997), Boston Area Consortium on Latin Am. (dir. 1992—), Am. Hist. Assn., Com. on Latin Am. History, Latin Am. Studies Assn., Coordinating Com. on Women in History. Office: Brandeis U History Dept MS 036 Waltham MA 02454-2728 E-mail: arrom@brandeis.edu.

ARRONS-LANE, MARION JEAN, artist, educator; b. N.Y.C., July 8, 1928; d. Herman Arrons and Anita Gordon; m. Sidney Lane, Dec. 26, 1953 (div. Dec. 1988); children: Spencer G. Lane, George D. Lane. Student, Pratt Inst., Bklyn. Mus. Art Sch.; BA in Art Edn., William Paterson U., 1976; MFA, Rutgers U., 1978. Adj. prof. Bergen C.C., Paramus, N.J., 1979-85; part-time tchr., therapist Manhattan Psychol. Ctr., N.Y.C., 1986-99, acting curator Bergen County Mus., Paramus, 1971. One-woman and group exhbns. include Bklyn. Mus., 1958 (award), Montclair Mus., 1960, 65 (awards), Jersey City Mus., 1965, 66, State Mus., Trenton, N.J., 1968, 70, Bergen County Mus., 1972, Nat. Assn. Women Artists Annual 1973, Kraushaar Gallery, N.Y., 1974, Rockland County Ctr. for Arts, 1975, Pleaides Gallery, N.Y., 1976, 78, 98, Rutgers U. Newark, Paul Robeson Ctr., 1980, Rutgers U., New Brunswick, 1982, Edward Williams Coll., N.J., 1980, 82, 99, Women's Caucus for Art, N.Y., 1982, Hunterdon Art Ctr., N.J., 1983, City Without Walls Gallery, 1984, Noyes Mus., N.J., 1984, Newark Mus., 1961, 64, 85, Glassboro State Coll., 1985, Jersey State Coll., 1985, Ramapo Coll., N.J., 1985, Fair Lawn Libr., N.J., 1986, Pavillion Gallery Meml. Hosp., 1986, Women's Caucus for Art, NYU Grad. Sch., 1986, Monmouth Mus., N.J., 1988, William Carlos Williams Ctr. for Arts, 1990, William Paterson Coll. N.J., 1992, 94, Kerygma Gallery, 1993, Fourteen Sculptors Gallery, N.Y., 1995, 96, Kerygma Gallery, N.J., 1995, Nabisco Corp. Hdqrs., N.J., 1995, Westbeth Gallery, N.Y., 1996, Westbeth Gallery, 2000, La Mama La Galeria, N.Y., 1996, Broome St. Gallery, N.Y., 1996, numerous others; represented in permanent collections at Bloomfield Coll., Bergen County Mus., also many corp. and pvt. collections. Fellow N.J. State Coun. on Arts, 1983, 88, Edward Albee Found., 1983; Robert Florsheim Art Fund grantee, 2000, Resid Valparaiso Found., 2002. Avocations: photography, hiking, ballet. Home: 55 Bethune St # D351 New York NY 10014-2010 E-mail: mjlaneart@aol.com.

ARROTT, PATRICIA GRAHAM, artist, art instructor; b. Pitts., July 27, 1931; d. George Patterson and Helen (Gilleland) Graham; m. Anthony Schuyler Arrott, June 6, 1953; children: Anthony Patterson, Helen Graham, Matthew Ramsey, Elizabeth. BFA in Painting and Design, Carnegie-Mellon Univ., 1954; postgrad., Nat. Acad. Design, N.Y.C., 1985-87, Art Students League, 1980-91. Cert. tchr. art, Pa. Instr. children's ceramics Handcraft House, Vancouver, B.C., Can., 1970-72; courtroom artist Vancouver, B.C., Can., 1972-73; pvt. portrait artist Vancouver, N.Y.C., 1975—; instr. Art Students League, N.Y.C., 1993-99. Group shows include Nat. Acad. Design Ann. Exhbn., 1990, 92, 94, Cork Gallery, Lincoln Ctr., N.Y.C., 1991, Pen & Brush Club, N.Y.C., 1988-98, Silver Point Etc. traveling exhbn., 1992-93; represented by Eleanor Ettinger Gallery, N.Y.C., 1997—. Recipient Helen M. Loggie Prize, 1990, and cert. of merit, 1994, Nat. Acad. Design; recipient Emily Nicholas Hatch award Pen & Brush Club, 1989-91, Elizabeth Morse Genius award, 1988, 90, 93, 95, others. Mem. Art Student's League (life; mem. bd. 1989-92, women's v.p. 1991-92), Am. Fine Arts Soc. (mem. bd. 1991-92), Mayflower Soc. (life), Kappa Kappa Gamma (life). United Presbyterian.

ARROW, KENNETH JOSEPH, economist, educator; b. N.Y.C., Aug. 23, 1921; s. Harry I. and Lillian (Greenberg) Arrow; m. Selma Schweitzer, Aug. 31, 1947; children: David Michael, Andrew. BS in Social Sci., CCNY, 1940; MA, Columbia U., 1941, PhD, 1951, DSc (hon.), 1973; LLD (hon.), U. Chgo., 1967, CUNY, 1972; LLD (hon.), Hebrew U. Jerusalem, 1975, U. Pa., 1976, Washington U., St. Louis, 1989, Harvard U., 1999; D. Social and Econ. Scis. (hon.), U. Vienna, Austria, 1971; LLD (hon.), Ben-Gurion U. of the Negev, 1992; D. Social Scis. (hon.), Yale, 1974; D (hon.), Université René Descartes, Paris, 1974, U. Aix-Marseille III, 1985, U. Cattolica del Sacro Cuore, Milan, Italy, 1994, U. Uppsala, 1995, U. Buenos Aires, 1999; D (hon.), U. Cyprus, 2000; Dr.Pol., U. Helsinki, 1976; MA (hon.), Harvard U., 1968; DLitt, Cambridge U., Eng., 1985; LLD (hon.), Harvard U., 1999; PhD (hon.), Tel Aviv U., 2001. Rsch. assoc. Cowles Commn. for Research in Econs., 1947—49; asst. prof. econs. U. Chgo., 1948—49; acting asst. prof. econs. and stats. Stanford, 1949—50, assoc. prof., 1950—53, prof. econs., stats. and ops. rsch., 1953—68; prof. econs. Harvard, 1968—74, James Bryant Conant univ. prof., 1974—79; exec. head dept. econs. Stanford U., 1954—56, acting exec. head dept., 1962—63, Joan Kenney prof. econs. and prof. ops. rsch., 1979—91, prof. emeritus, 1991—. Economist Coun. Econ. Advisers, U.S. Govt., 1962; cons. RAND Corp.; Fulbright prof. U. Siena, 1995; vis. fellow All Souls Coll., Oxford, 1996; overseas rsch. fellow Churchill Coll., Cambridge, 1963—64, Cambridge, 1970, Cambridge, 73, Cambridge, 86. Author: Social Choice and Individual Values, 1951, Essays in the Theory of Risk Bearing, 1971, The Limits of Organization, 1974, Collected Papers, Vols. I-VI, 1983—85; co-author: Mathematical Studies in Inventory and Production, 1958, Studies in Linear and Nonlinear Programming, 1958, Time Series Analysis of Inter-industry Demands, 1959, Public Investment, The Rate of Return and Optimal Fiscal Policy, 1971, General Competitive Analysis, 1971, Studies in Resource Allocation Processes, 1977, Social Choice and Multicriterion Decision Making, 1985. Capt. U.S. Army, 1942—46. Recipient Alfred Nobel Meml. prize in econ. scis., Swedish Acad. Scis., 1972, Kempé de Feriet medal, 1998, medal, U. Paris, 1998; fellow Social Sci. Rsch. fellow, 1952, Ctr. for Advanced Study in the Behavioral Scis., 1956—57, Churchill Coll., Cambridge, Eng., 1963—64, 1970, 1973, 1986, Guggenheim, 1972—73. Fellow: AAAS (chmn. sect. K 1983), Am. Fin. Assn. (mem. coun. 1990—93), Internat. Soc. Inventory Rsch. (pres. 1983—90), Am. Econ. Assn. (exec. com. 1967—69, pres. 1973, John Bates Clark medal 1957), Inst. Math. Stats., Am. Acad. Arts and Scis. (v.p. 1979—81, 1991—93), Econometric Soc. (v.p. 1955, pres. 1956), Am. Statis. Assn.; mem.: NAS/Inst. of Medicine, Game Theory Soc., Brit. Acad. (corr.), Pontifical Acad. Social Scis., Soc. Social Choice and Welfare (pres. 1991—93), Western Econ. Assn. (pres. 1980—81), Finnish Acad. Scis. (fgn. hon.), Inst. Ops. Rsch. and Mgmt. Sci. (pres. 1963, chmn. coun. 1964, Von Neumann prize 1986, Fellows' award), Am. Philos. Soc., Internat. Econs. Assn. (pres. 1983—86). Office: Stanford U Dept Econs Stanford CA 94305-6072 Fax: 650-725-5702. E-mail: arrow@stanford.edu.

ARROWSMITH, NANCY, journalist; b. Oxford, Eng., Nov. 19, 1950; arrived in U.S., 1950; d. William Ayres and Jean Reiser Arrowsmith; 1 child, Anna Eleonore. Student, U. Calif., Santa Cruz, 1967—69, U. Vienna, Austria, 1977—79. Translator from German and Italian, Bisbee, Ariz., 1972—; lectr. on gardening and environ. issues, 1985—; founder, dir. Noah's Ark, Schiltern, Austria, 1989—97, Kraut & Rueben, Organic Gardening Mag., Munich, 1984—89; faculty dept. fgn. lang. U. Ariz., 2003—. Advisor Seedsavers Exchange, Decorah, Iowa, 1994—; garden advisor Lower Austrian Govt., St. Poelten, 1990—96. Author: A Field Guide to the Little People, 1997, Die Welt der Naturgeister, 1994, Das Grosse Buch der Naturgeister, 2002, Chemical Free Spot Removal, 1986, Household Tips for Kitchen, House and Laundry, 1985, List of Austrian Vegetable Varieties, 1994, History of our Family, 2002; editor: Kraut & Rüben, 1984—89; translator: Seed to Seed, 1995, Agrobiodiversität und Pflanzengenetische Ressourcen, 2001. Recipient 2d place Journalism Conservation award, Lower Austrian Govt., 1989, Ford Conservation award, Ford Conservation Found., 1991, Cultural Award for conservation for life work, Lower Austrian Govt., 1996. Home: PO Box 1707 Bisbee AZ 85603

ARROYO MARROQUIN, ROMARICO, former federal official; b. Tulancingo, Hildago, Mex., Dec. 13, 1942; married. BA in Civil Engring., Nat. Autonomous U.; MA in Sci., Stanford U. Chief analysis Ctr. Calculation, Sec. Hydraulic Resources, 1966; asst. dir. Nat. Tourism Fund, 1973-76, dir., 1976-77; adv. to undersec. Min. Housing Pub. Credit, 1977-78; undersec. basic industry Sec. Mines, Inter-State Industry, 1982-87; dir. gen. United Shipyards, 1987-91; dep. dir. gen. Hydraulic, Urban and Indsl. Infrastructure, 1991-94; undersec. Agr. and Livestock, 1995-98; sec. Agr., Livestock and Rural Develop., 1998—2000. Office: Partido Revolutionario Inst Col Buenavista Insurgentes Norte No 59 Edif 2 06359 Mexico

ARSENAULT, SAMANTHA, Olympic athlete; b. Salem, Mass., Oct. 11, 1981; d. Edward and Jeanne Arsenault. Student, U. Ga. Swimmer U. Mich., 2000—01. Recipient Gold medal 4 x 200-meter freestyle (team) Sydney Olympics, 2000; 2d pl. 200-meter freestyle U.S. spring nats., 1999, 3d pl. 100-meter and 200-meter freestyle U.S. summer nats., 1999; first internat. title win, 200m free, World Cup Paris, 2000 Office: USA Swimming 1 Olympic Plz Colorado Springs CO 80909-5746

ARSENEAU, JAMES CHARLES, physician; b. Syracuse, N.Y., Aug. 29, 1942; s. James Howard and Glenna Carolyn (Worth) A.; m. Jane Macy, July 2, 1966; children: Marc, David. AB, Syracuse U., 1964; MD, Albany Med. Coll., 1968. Intern and resident in medicine Strong Meml. Hosp., Rochester, N.Y., 1968-70, fellow in med. oncology, 1973-74; clin. assoc. med. br. Nat. Cancer Inst., Bethesda, Md., 1970-73; asst. prof. medicine U. Rochester, 1974-80, assoc. prof. medicine, 1980-83; head med. oncology unit Rochester Gen. Hosp., 1974-83; clin. assoc. prof. medicine Albany Med. Coll., 1985—; ptnr. Albany Regional Cancer Ctr., 1983—. Pres. med. staff St. Peter's Hosp., Albany, N.Y., 1993-95, bd. dirs., 1997—. Author numerous chpts. in textbooks; contbr. articles to profl. jours. Sr. Asst. Surgeon USPHS, 1970-73. Mem. Am. Soc. Clin. Oncology, Albany County Med. Soc. (exec. com. 1993—), Am Radium Soc., Upstate N.Y. Soc. Med. Oncology/Hematology (pres. 1994—), Gynecologic Oncology Group (chmn. devel. therapeutic com. 1980—), Wolfert's Roost Country Club, Zeta Psi, Alpha Omega Alpha (pres. 1966-67). Avocations: reading, writing, chess, tennis, golf, skiing. Home: 205 Graffunder Dr Albany NY 12204-1301 Office: Albany Regional Cancer Ctr 317 S Manning Blvd Ste 330 Albany NY 12208-1774

ARSHAD, ABRAR MEHMOOD, physician; b. Karachi, Pakistan, Dec. 18, 1963; came to U.S., 1992; Student, D.J. Sindh Govt. Sci. Coll., Karachi, 1979-81; MBBS, Dow Med. Coll., Karachi, Pakistan, 1989. Intern Civil Hosp., Karachi, Pakistan, 1989-90, resident, 1990-91, SUNY, Buffalo, 1992-95, asst. clin. instr. internal medicine, 1992-99; internist, gastroenterology cons. Assocs. Pulmonary and Critical Care Med., Bowling Green, Ky., 1999—2002, Logan Physician Practice, 2002—. Gastroenterology fellow SUNY Buffalo, 1995-97, Infectious Diseases fellow, 1997-99. Mem. ACP, Am. Gastroenterological Assn. Office: 1621 Nashville St Ste 103 Russellville KY 42276 E-mail: abrarma@yahoo.com.

ARSHAD, M. KALEEM, psychiatrist; b. Islam Garh Gujrat Dist, Punjab, Pakistan, Nov. 8, 1955; came to U.S., 1981; s. Amir and Rasool (Bibi) Bakhsh; m. Jameela Yasmeen, Nov. 26, 1982; 1 child, Nadeem Sohail. FSc, Govt. Nat. Coll., Karachi, Pakistan, 1973; MBBS, Dow Med. Coll., Karachi, 1981. Diplomate Am. Bd. Psychiatry and Neurology, Am. Bd. Forensic Medicine, Am. Bd. Geriatric, Forensic and Addiction Psychiatry. House officer psychiatry Dow Med. Coll. and Civil Hosp., 1981, Provident Hosp., Inc., Balt., 1983-85; resident in psychiatry Tex. Tech U. Health Scis. Ctr., El Paso, 1985-88; resident in internal medicine Tulane U. Med. Ctr., New Orleans, 1988-89; program dir. admission svcs. East La. State Hosp., Jackson, 1989; med. dir. Metairie (La.) Ctr. Psychotherapy, 1990-91; med. dir., pres. med. staff Meth. Psychiat. Pavillion, New Orleans, 1991-2001; med. dir. Meth. Behavior Resources, New Orleans, 1992-2001; regional med. ctr. Mental Health Network, Metairie, La., 2001—; psychiat. med. dir. Am. Internat. Home Health Care; dir. Sr. Behavioral Health Ctr., New Orleans, 2001—. Pvt. practice cons. First pres., founder Anjamane Nawjawanane Ahle Sunnat, Karachi, 1980, pres. Pakistan Muslim Student Fedn., Dow Med. Coll., 1979-80. Recipient Dr. Jacob Schut Achievement award, 1988. Mem. Am. Psychiat. Assn. (resident rep. 1987), Dow Med. Coll. Alumni Assn. (regional councilor 1989-90, sec.-treas. 1997-98, pres.), Assn. Pakistani Physicians N.Am. (pres. So. chpt. 1993-95), Dow Alumni Assn. N.Am. (pres. 1999-2000). Moslem. Avocations: fishing, swimming, golf. Home: 133 Chateau St Michel Dr Kenner LA 70065-2037 Office: Ste 5A 10555 Lake Forest Blvd New Orleans LA 70127 Fax: 504-244-3530. E-mail: KaleemArshadMD@aol.com.

ARSHAM, HOSSEIN, operations research analyst; b. Mashhad, Iran, Mar. 28, 1947; came to U.S., 1978; s. Gholam Reza and Habebeh (Babai) A.; m. Elaheh-Naaze Khoshghadam, Dec. 20, 1984; 1 child, Aryana. BSc in Physics, Arya-Mehr U. Tech., Tehran, Iran, 1971; MSc, Cranfield Inst., Eng., 1978; DSc, George Washington U., 1982. Cert. info. scientist, specialized in strategic decision making. Postdoctoral rschr. Internat. Water Resources Inst., Washington, 1982-83; prof. U. Balt., 1983—, Harry Wright disting. rsch. prof. mgmt. sci. and stats., chair dept. mgmt. scis., 1996—; rsch. prof. Info. Systems Rsch. Ctr., Balt., 1996—. Faculty advanced studies Calif. Nat. U., 1991—; faculty adv. bd. Western Govs. U., 1999; faculty cons. Kennedy-Western U., 1995—; mem. exec. adv. coun. Internat. Soc. for Theory and Application of Multi-Objective Decision Analysis; tech. lectr. Bethlehem Steel Co., Balt., 1983-84; sci. cons. in field. Editor InterStat: Stats. on the Internet, Ops. Rsch. category for the Netscape Open Directory, Jour. of Interdisciplinary Math.; sr. assoc. editor Computational Stats. and Data Analysis and Jour. Environ. Dynamics; mem. editl. bd. IEEE Ednl., Tech. and Soc. Jour., Jour. of End User Computing, Jour. Environ. Dynamics, Internat. Jour. Ops. and Quantitative Mgmt.; mem. editl. bd. Ednl. Tech. and Soc. Jour.; mem. internat. sci. com. Advances in Intelligent Data Analysis, 1997—, Internat. Symposium on Adaptive Systems, 1999—; contbr. articles to profl. jours. Commn. on Office Lab. Accreditation grantee, 1993, NSF grantee, 1995; recipient Black & Decker Corp. Rsch. award, 1987, 88, 98, Excellence in Rsch. award U. Sys. Md., 2000. Fellow Royal Statis. Soc., Operational Rsch. Soc., Inst. Combinatorics and Applications, World Innovation Found.; mem. AAAS, IEEE, Am. Math. Soc., Internat. Assn. Math. and Computer Modeling, Internat. Forecasting Soc., Am. Statis. Assn., Assn. for Computing Machinery, Digital Equipment Computer Users Soc., Info. Resources Mgmt. Assn., Math. Assn. Am., London Math. Soc., Inst. for Ops. Rsch. and Mgmt Scis., Soc. Indsl. and Applied Math., Soc. for Info. Mgmt., N.Y. Acad. Scis., Internat. Soc. for Theory and Application of Multi-Objective Decision Analysis (exec. adv. coun.), Beta Gamma Sigma, Omega Rho. Achievements include research in statistics, applied probability, discrete-event systems simulation, and mathematical programming and modeling. Office: U Balt 1420 N Charles St Baltimore MD 21201-5720 E-mail: harsham@ubmail.ubalth.edu.

ARSHT, EDWIN DAVID, physician; b. Phila., Oct. 6, 1929; BA in Zoology, Swarthmore Coll., 1951; MD, Jefferson Med. Coll., 1955. Diplomate Am. Bd. Family Practice; cert. med. dir./long term care. Intern Frankford Hosp., Phila., 1956; resident in gen. practice Mountainside Hosp., Montclair, N.J., 1959; pvt. practice Springfield, Pa., 1959-94; dir. med. edn. Delaware County Meml. Hosp., Drexel Hill, Pa., 1960-90, chief allergy, 1970-2000, chmn. dept. family practice, 1976-86, Riddle Meml. Hosp., Media, Pa., 1993-95; med. dir. HM Nursing Home, Springfield, 1965—. Author: Psychological Approaches to Family Practice, 1979. Chmn. commn. on med. edn. Pa. Acad. Family Practice, 1970—82. Capt. U.S. Army, 1956—58. Fellow Am. Acad. Family Physicians; mem. Delaware County Acad. Family Practice (pres. 1960-85). Home and Office: 611 W Woodland Ave Springfield PA 19064-1633 Office: Harlee Manor Nursing Home 463 W Sproul Rd Springfield PA 19064-2198

ARTEAGA, HAROLD AUGUSTINE, lawyer; b. San Francisco, Dec. 21, 1952; s. Augustine Jesus and Rosa Minar (Morales) A.; m. Doriliz Tovar, Sept. 3, 1967; children: Rebeca, Joshua, Michelle, Gabriel. BS in Polit. Sci., U. Santa Clara, Calif., 1976; JD, U. Calif., Berkeley, 1980; MBA in Internat. Bus., U. Miami, 1999. Atty. enforcement divsn. SEC, 1982-86; gen. counsel PAMCO Securities, Encino, Calif., 1986-88; ptnr. Casterline & Agajanian, L.A., 1988-93; sr. v.p., gen. counsel HBO Latin Am., Caracas, Venezuela, 1993-97; exec. v.p. HBO Latin Am. Media Svcs., Miami, Fla., 1995-97; of counsel Shook, Hardy & Bacon, Miami, 1999—. Mem. Calif. State Bar, Internat. Bar Assn., Fla. State Bar Assn. Office: Shook Hardy & Bacon 201 S Biscayne Blvd Ste 2400 Miami FL 33131-4313

ARTEST, RON, professional basketball player; Profl. basketball player Chicago Bulls, 1999-2001, 2002—, Indiana Pacers, 2001—02. Office: Chicago Bulls 1901 W Madison St Chicago IL 60612-2459

ARTHER, RICHARD OBERLIN, polygraphist, educator; b. Pitts., May 20, 1928; s. William Churchill Sr. and Florence Lind (Oberlin) A.; m. Mary-Esther Wuensch, Sept. 12, 1951; children: Catherine, Linda, William III. BS, Mich. State U., 1951; MA, Columbia U., 1960. Chief assoc. John E. Reid and Assocs., Chgo., 1951-53, dir. N.Y.C., 1953-58; pres. Sci. Lie Detection, Inc., N.Y.C., 1958—2003, chmn., 2003—; pres. Nat. Tng. Ctr. Polygraph Sci., N.Y.C., 1958—. Author: Interrogation for Investigators, 1958, The Scientific Investigator, 1964, 7th edit., Arther Polygraph Reference Guide, 1964—, 8th edit.; editor Jour. Polygraph Sci., 1966—. Fellow Acad. Cert. Polygraphists (exec. dir. 1962—), Am. Polygraph Assn. (founding mem.), Am. Assn. Police Polygraphists (founding mem., Polygraphist of Yr. 1980), N.Y. State Polygraphists (founder), N.J. Polygraphists (founder). Office: Sci Lie Detection Inc 200 W 57th St Ste 1400 New York NY 10019-3211

ARTHUR, ANDREW REISER, lawyer; b. Towson, Md., Feb. 17, 1966; s. Rodney Samuel and Mary Louise Arthur; m. Tara Sky Woodward, May 27, 1995; 1 child, Jefferson Finnburr. BA, U. Va., 1988; JD, George Wash. U., 1992. Bar: Ct. Appeals Md. 1992, U.S. Dist. Ct. Md. 1993, U.S. Ct. Fed. Claims 1994. Atty. advisor U.S. Dept. Justice, Exec. Office for Immigration Rev., Office of the Chief Adminstrv. Hearing Officer, Falls Church, Va., 1992—94; asst. dist. counsel U.S. Immigration and Naturalization Svc., San Francisco, 1994—98, Balt., 1998—99, assoc. gen. counsel Washington, 1999—2001; counsel Ho. Reps. Com. on the Judiciary, Washington, 2001—; acting chief nat. security law divsn. Gen. Counsel's Office, U.S. Immigration and Naturalization Svc., Washington, 2001—01. Mem. Congl. Legis. Staff Assn., Washington, 2002—. Bd. dirs. George Washington U. Law Sch. Alumni Assn., 1997—2002. Mem.: Quarterback Club Charities Balt., Phi Delta Phi. Republican. Roman Catholic. Office: House Com on the Judiciary Room B-370B Rayburn House Office Bldg Washington DC 20515

ARTHUR, CHARLES GEMMELL, IV, accountant; b. St. Louis, Jan. 28, 1965; s. Charles Gemmell III and Mary Elizabeth (Senes) A.; m. Denise Renee Dougherty, June 13, 1987. BSBA in Acctg. and BS in Econs., S.E. Mo. State U., 1987; MBA in Internat. Studies, Lindenwood Coll., 1990. CPA. Fiscal analyst McDonnell Douglas Corp., St. Louis, 1987-90, sr. acct., 1990-93, sr. spl. acct., 1993-97; sr. spl. bus. analyst Boeing Co., St. Louis, 1997-99, sr. specialist sys. analyst, 1999-2000. Recipient U.S. Congl. Gold medal for svc., achievement and initiative, 1987. Mem. Mensa. Methodist. Avocation: Tae Kwon Do. Home: 13192 Weatherfield Dr Saint Louis MO 63146-3656

ARTHUR, GREER MARTIN, maritime container leasing firm executive; b. Champaign, Ill., Feb. 15, 1935; s. Greer Martin and Olive Loretta (Simard) A.; m. Veronica Lattman, Nov. 30, 1968; children: Alexandra, Vincent, Tanya, Greer III. BA, Lafayette Coll., 1956; JD, Columbia U., 1961. Bar: N.Y. 1961. Acct. exec. tng. program Young & Rubicam, 1957-58; firm assoc. Havens, Wandless, Stitt & Tighe, N.Y.C., 1961-62; mgmt. cons. McKinsey & Co., 1962-67; asst. to v.p. internat. Scovill Mfg. Co., Waterbury, Conn.; internat. market mgr. Scovill France, Paris; market mgr. Hamilton Beach div. Scovill, Waterbury, 1967-69; pres., CEO SSI Container Corp., subs. Itel Corp., San Francisco, 1969-73; founder, chmn., pres., CEO, dir. Trans Ocean Ltd., San Bruno, Calif., 1973-96. Founder, dir., bd. dirs. Inst. Internat. Container Lessors, 1970—73, dir., 1977—96, pres., 1989—90, 1994—96; bd. dirs. Telogy Corp.,

Menlo Park, Calif.; chmn. bd. dirs. Trans Ocean Distbn., Ltd., Southampton, England. Treas., trustee Phillips Brooks Sch., Menlo Park, Calif., 1980-83; bd. dirs. Nat. Alzheimer's Assn., 1994—, San Francisco Opera, 1999—; with Lafayette Coll. Nat. Coun., 1981-83. Mem.: Young Pres. Orgn., World Pres. Internat., World Trade (San Francisco), Chief Exec. Orgn. World Presidents Orgn. (No. Calif. chpt. chmn. 1991—92, bd. dirs. 1994—99, 1990—91), Sharon Heights Golf Club, Lahontan Golf Club (Lake Tahoe), Lake Tahoe Yacht Club, Bankers Club, Family Club. Office: Trans Ocean Distribution 2105 Woodside Rd Woodside CA 94062

ARTHUR, JETT CLINTON, retired chemist; b. Hemphill, Tex., May 31, 1918; s. Jett Clinton Arthur and Anna Alice Smith; m. LaVerne Pitts Arthur, June 2, 1941 (dec. Nov. 30, 1997); children: Martha Stitsinger, Clinton Arthur, Laura Porter. BA in Chemistry, S.F. Austin State U., Nacogdoches, Tex., 1939; MA in Chemistry, U. Tex., 1946. Registered profl. engr., La. Rsch. chemist USDA So. Regional Rsch. Ctr., New Orleans, 1941—43, 1946—49, rsch. chemist in charge, 1949—66, chief rsch. chemist, 1966—79. Cons., Metairie, La., 1979—; organizer numerous nat. and internat. meetings. Contbr. articles to profl. jours.; editor 6 books. Worked with youth Boy Scouts Am., local and nat. parent-tchr. orgns. Lt. comdr. USNR, 1943—46. Recipient award, Alpha Chi, grants in field. Fellow: AIChE (com. chmn. 1969—, award New Orleans sect.); mem.: ACS (divsn. chmn., emeritus mem. bd. cell divsn. 1994—, Herty medal Ga. sect., So. Chemist award, S.W. Regional award, Anselme Payen Cellulose award), Chem. Heritage Found., Am. Acad. Environ. Engring., Sigma Xi. Democrat. Methodist. Achievements include patents in field; research in nuclear radiation, free radical and graft copolymerization reactions of cotton fibers to increase textile values; natural product research: cellulose, protein, enzyme. Avocations: chess, outdoor activities, sports, theology. Home and Office: 3013 Ridgeway Dr Metairie LA 70002

ARTHUR, JEWELL KATHLEEN, dental hygienist; b. Bloomington, Ind., Apr. 12, 1947; d. Gerald E. and Wilma Kathleen (McDonald) Beyers; m. Leland Stanley Arthur, Sept. 21, 1968; children: Sherri Kay, Brian Lee. AS in Dental Hygiene, Ind. U., 1968. Lic./registered dental hygienist. Infection control mgr., dental hygienist Office Dr. Thomas Watkins, DDS, Bloomington, Ind., 1990—. Spkr., presenter in field. Vice-chmn. precinct Rep. Com., Batholomew, 1987-98; chmn. Aids Com. Columbus, 1988-98, vice chair City of Columbus Bd. Zoning Appeals, 1989-93, Bartholomew County Pers. Adminstrn. Com., 1993—; councilwoman Batholomew County Coun., Columbus, Ind., 1993—; chmn. AIDS Com., Columbus, 1988-98. Mem. Am. Assn. Ret. Persons, Am. Dental Hygienists Assn. (liaison 1989—, Disting. Svc. award 1994), Ind. Dental Hygienists Assn. (pres. 1986-87, del. 1991—, Cmty. Svc. award 1991, Outstanding Dental Hygienists of Yr. award 1991), Ind. Pub. Health Assn. (chair legislation 1986-89), Driftwood Valley Dental Hygienists Assn. (trustee 1989-91, 98—), Assn. Ind. Counties, DAR-Joseph Hart, Order Eastern Star. Republican. Methodist. Avocations: antiques, pottery, old toys, music. Home: 1800 Clover Ct Columbus IN 47203-3615

ARTHUR, JOHN MORRISON, retired utility executive; b. Pitts., Aug. 17, 1922; s. Hugh Morrison and Anna Matilda (Crowe) A.; m. Sylvia Ann Martin, June 19, 1948; children: William Robert, John Martin, Andrew Scott. BEE, U. Pitts., 1944, MEE, 1947. With Duquesne Light Co., Pitts., 1944-87, asst. to chmn. bd. and pres., 1966-67, pres., 1967-68, chmn. bd., chief exec. officer, 1968-83, chmn. bd., pres., 1983-85, chmn. bd., 1986-87, ret., 1987. Trustee emeritus U. Pitts. With AUS, 1942-43. Mem. Duquesne Club, Montour Heights Country Club, Rolling Rock Club. E-mail: jmaama@stargate.net.

ARTHUR, LINDSAY GRIER, retired judge, author, editor; b. Mpls., July 30, 1917; s. Hugh and Alice (Grier) A.; m. Jean Johansen, Sept. 19, 1940; children: Lindsay G., Mollie K., Julie A. AB, Princeton U., 1939; postgrad., Harvard U., 1939-40; LLB, JD, U. Minn., 1946. Bar: Minn. 1946, U.S. Dist. Ct. Minn. 1948, U.S. Supreme Ct. 1964. Lawyer Nieman, Bosard & Arthur, Mpls., 1946-54; alderman Mpls. City Coun., 1951-54; judge Mcpl. Ct., Mpls., 1954-61; chief judge juvenile divsn. Dist. Ct., Mpls., 1961-79, 87-93, judge felony, civil divsn., 1979-83, chief judge mental health divsn., 1983-87; mediator, 1987—. Arbitrator civil and family cts., 1991—. Author: Minnesota Practice, 1974, Juvenile Case Law, 1980, Twin Cities Uncovered, 1996, A Manual for Mediators, 1995; editor Digest of Juvenile and Family Law, 1983-93; contbr. articles to profl. jours. Bd. dirs. Nat. Ctr. State Cts., Williamsburg, 1974-77, Metro YMCA, Mpls. area, 1981-85; chmn. trustees Bethlehem Luth. Ch., 1979-80. Lt. USNR, 1942-45, PTO. Mem. Nat. Coun. Juvenile Ct. Judges (pres. 1972-73, Jud. scholar 1985—), ABA (disabilities com. 1984-89), Am. Law Inst. (advisor divorce law 1989-93). Avocation: writing. Home: 431 Prairie Center Dr # 323 Eden Prairie MN 55344 E-mail: lgasr@earthlink.net.

ARTHUR, MARGARET FERNE, nurse, insurance paramedic; b. Green Sulphur Springs, W.Va., Mar. 12, 1948; d. John Noel Ford and Violet Pansy Ayers; m. Dwight Ellis Harris, Dec. 31, 1967 (div.); children: Daniel Ellis, Naomi Ruth Okes, David Nathaniel; m. Rev. Harry Earle Arthur, Jr., Mar. 29, 1985. Student, Bluefield Coll., 1992, Concord Coll., 1993, W.Va. No. C.C., New Martinsville, 1998. LPN. LPN Raleigh Gen. Hosp., Beckley, W.Va., 1980-83, South Ga. Med. Ctr., Valdosta, 1983-84, Wythe County Cmty. Hosp., Wytheville, Va., 1984-86, St. Luke's Hosp., Bluefield, W.VA., 1984-89, Bluefield Regional Med. Ctr., 1986-97, Sistersville (W.Va.) Gen. Hosp., 1997, Reynolds Meml. Hosp., Glendale, W.Va., 1997—99. V.p. Dist. 22 LPN Assn. W.Va., 1977-79, pres., 1979-83, acting pres. Dist. 26, 1990-93; rev. panel mem. Nat. Coun. State Bds. Nursing, Chgo., 1998. Mem. Nat. Assn. for Practical Nurse Edn. and Svc. Methodist. Avocation: reading. Home: PO Box 5373 3910 Grand Central Ave Vienna WV 26105 E-mail: ncd00804@mail.wvnet.edu.

ARTHUR, MICHAEL ELBERT, lawyer, financial advisor; b. Seattle, Oct. 9, 1952; s. Theodore E. and Gladys L. (Jones) A.; m. Claire C. Meeker, Dec. 23, 1974; children: Christine, Conor, Austin. BA, U. Calif., Santa Barbara, 1974; JD, Stanford U., 1977. Ptnr. Miller Nash LLP, Portland, Oreg., 1977—2001; fin. advisor Spence Partners at UBS Fin. Svcs., Portland, 2001—. Trustee Chiles Found. Home: 13535 NW Lariat Ct Portland OR 97229-7001 Office: UBS Financial Svcs 805 SW Broadway Ste 2600 Portland OR 97205-3365 E-mail: mike.arthur@ubs.com.

ARTHUR, PAUL KEITH, electronic engineer; b. Kansas City, Mo., Jan. 14, 1931; s. Walter B. and Frieda J. (Burckhardt) A.; m. Joy N. Lim, Apr. 26, 1958; children: Gregory V., Lia F. Student, Ohio No. U., 1947, Taylor U., Upland, Ind., 1948-49; BSEE, Purdue U., 1956; postgrad., N.Mex. State U., 1957-58. Registered profl. engr., N.Mex.; cert. army acquisition profl.; cert. Naval engring. duty officer, Navy material profl. With White Sands Missile Range, N.Mex., 1956—; electronic engr. field engring., group missile flight surveillance office, 1956-60; chief field engring group, 1960-62; project engr. Pershing Weapon Sys. Army Missile Test and Evaluation Directorate, 1962-74; chief high altitude air def. projects br., 1974-82; chief air def. materiel test divsn., 1982-91; dep dir. Materiel Test Directorate, 1991-95; dir., 1995-98; exec. dir. Nat. Range, 1998-99; dep. comdr. White Sands Test Ctr., 1999—2001, comdr., 2001—03; dep. to comdg. gen. tech. divsn. White Sands Missile Range, 2003—. Mem. N.Mex. Spaceport Commn., 1994-95, Southwest Regional Space Task Force, Metro Planning Orgn.; past pres. missile range pioneer group; bd. dirs. Dagupan Electric Corp. of the Philippines. Author numerous plans and reports on weapon systems test and evaluation and topics in naval engring. Chmn. adminstrv. bd. Meth. Ch., 1992-95. Served with USN, 1949-53, USNR, 1954-87, rear adm. and sr. engring. duty officer, 1984-87. Decorated Legion of Merit, Meritorious Svc. medal, Navy Achievement medal, Mil. Order St. Barbara, others. Mem. AIAA (past vice chmn.), Internat. Test and Evaluation Assn., Am. Def. Preparedness Assn. (past pres.), Assn. Old Crows, Naval Res. Assn., Res. Officers Assn. (pres. 1983-85), United Vets. Coun. (chmn. 1984-85), Am. Soc. Naval Engrs., Naval Inst., Navy League, Surface Navy Assn., Assn. U.S. Army, Purdue U. Alumni Assn. (past pres.), N.Mex. State U. Alumni Assn., Mesilla Valley Track Club, Bujutsukan Acad. Martial Arts. Home: 2050 San Acacio St Las Cruces NM 88001-1570 Office: White Sands Test Ctr White Sands Missile Range NM 88002 E-mail: arthurpk@wsmr.army.mil.

ARTHUR, THOMAS HAHN, theater educator, director; b. Chgo., 1937; s. Maxwell Arthur and Josephine Edith (Hahn) A.; m. Carolyn Ruth Dry (div. 1967); 1 child, Michael Dry; m. Ellen Mary Sharkey, Mar. 28, 1968 (div. 1976); children: Adam Stephen, Benjamin Douglas; m. Kathleen Alden Giles, Dec. 28, 1976; 1 child, Robert Kenneth. BS, Northwestern U., 1959; MA, Ind. U., 1969, PhD, 1973. Promotion dir. Graphic Arts Buyer Mag., Chgo., 1960-63; publicity supr., actor Court Theatre, U. Chgo., 1963, 64; teaching asst. Ind. U., Bloomington, 1965-68; co-founder, dir., publicity mgr. Ind. Summer Repertoire Theatre, Ind. U., Bloomington, 1966; asst. prof. theater Ill. State U., Normal, 1969-73; adj. lectr. theater history Ill. Wesleyan U., Bloomington, 1972-73; prof. theater, head dept. theatre and dance James Madison U., Harrisonburg, Va., 1973-94; dir. Sch. Theatre and Dance, 1994-95. Artistic dir. The Dinner Theatre, James Madison U., 1977, 82, 85, 88, 91, 92, 93; radio interviewer BBC, 1981, 84; acad. specialist USIA, South Africa and Finland, 1989, Hungary, 1994; cons. USIA, Naples, Italy, 1996; individual lectr. Am. Theatre, U. East Anglia, Richmond, Eng., Brit. Inst. Florence, Italy, 1990, Internat. Fedn. Theatre Rsch., Tel Aviv, 1996, Dhaka, Bangladesh, 1997, Ahmedabad, India, 1997, Ankara, Turkey, 1997, Nicosia, Cyprus, 2000, Honolulu, Hawaii, 2002, Olympia, Greece, 2003; program evaluator Nat. Assn. Schs. Theatre, 1990—; guest dir., actor Sweet Briar Coll., Amherst, Va., 1972-73; reaffirmation com. evaluator So. Assn. Colls., 2002—. Author: See You at the Movies: The Autobiography of Melvyn Douglas, 1986; contbg. editor Dramatics mag., 1979-84; contbr. interviews, articles, revs. and poetry to various mags. and jours.; dir. TV vignettes for NEH grant, 1979-80; prodr. Am. Coll. Theatre Festival prodn. Sizwi Bansi is Dead, Kennedy Ctr., Washington, 1992; dir. Am. Coll. Theatre Festival prodn. Carriage, Kennedy Ctr., 1998; dir. Shakespeare Festival, Williamsburg, Va., 1998; dir. Tex. Shakespeare Festival, 1999, Harrow Prodns., Va., 2000, Bigfork (Mont.) Summer Theatre, 2001, Other: Playworks, Chgo., 2001. Mem. Gov.'s Commn for 200th Aniv. of Constn., Richmond, 1983-84. NDEA fellow in Am. studies, 1965-68; grantee So. Ednl. Communications Assn., 1980. Mem. Assn. Internat. du Theatre a l'Université, Am. Studies Assn., Assn. Theatre in Higher Edn., Comm. Assn. Am., Soc. Theatre Rsch., Nat. Assn. Schs. of Theatre (chmn. com. on nominations 1995, chmn. com. on ethics 1996—), Internat. Fedn. Theatre Rsch., Southeastern Theater Conf., Va. Theatre Assn. (v.p. 1983-84, chair theatre divsn. 1991-95). Avocations: reading, travel. Home: 298 Campbell St Harrisonburg VA 22801-4014 Office: James Madison U Dept Theatre And Dance Harrisonburg VA 22807-0001 E-mail: arthurth@jmu.edu.

ARTHUR, WALLACE, physicist, educator; b. N.Y.C., Nov. 22, 1932; s. Adolph and Helen (Beckerman) Heimlich; m. Lois Shiller, Jan. 17, 1960; children: David A., Edward S., Stephen D. BEE, NYU, 1957, PhD, 1962. Asst. rsch. scientist Cosmic Ray Project NYU, N.Y.C., 1957—61; lectr. Rutgers U., Newark, 1961—62; asst. prof., prof. Physics Fairleigh Dickinson U., Teaneck, NJ, 1962—98, prof. emeritus, 1998—. Author: Mechanics, 1969. Cpl. U.S. Army, 1952—54. Mem.: N.Y. Acad. Scis., Sigma Xi. Democrat. Home: 9-6 Kingson Ln Medway MA 02053

ARTHUR, WILLIAM LYNN, environmental/political program director; b. Spokane, Wash., May 22, 1954; s. Robert Cyril and Mabel Mildred (Collison) A.; m. Debora Lee Donovan, Feb. 2, 1975; children: Kathleen, Jonathan. BA in Econs., Wash. State U., 1976, postgrad., 1982-83. Rsch. asst. Wash. State U., 1976-77; project mgr. Ctr. Environ. Understanding, Cheney, Wash., 1977-78; program dir. Wash. Energy Extension Svc., Spokane, 1978-79; econs. instr. Spokane Falls Community Coll., 1977-81; economist, cons. Biosystems Analysis Inc., Spokane, 1983; assoc. N.W. rep. Sierra Club, Seattle, 1983-87, N.W. rep., 1987-91, N.W./Alaska regional dir., 1992—, also mem. nat. wildlands campaign com. Chmn. bd. N.W. Conservation Act Coalition, Seattle, 1982-83; adv. com. N.W. Renewable Resources Ctr., Seattle, 1987-91; cons. energy workshops N.W. Regional Found., Spokane, 1982; mem. exec. com. Save Our Wild Salmon Coalition, 1991-95 (bd. dirs. 1999—); mem. adv. com. Inland Empire Pub. Lands Coun., 1990-2000; mem. steering com. Campaign for the Northwest, 1998-2000. Chmn., mem. city commn. Environ. Quality Commn., Pullman, Wash., 1976-77; bd. di rs. Ryegrass Sch., Spokane, 1978-81; conservation rep. Internat. Mountain Caribou Tech. Com., 1978-81; bd. dirs. Wash. Citizens for Recycling, Seattle, 1980-82; chair Wash. State Environmentalists for Clinton/Gore Com., 1992, 96; environ. rep. N.W. Forest Conf. convened and chaired by Pres. Clinton, Apr. 2, 1993; mem. steering com. on No Initiative 164 Coalition, 1995; mem. Wash. State Steering Com. to Re-elect Clinton/Gore, 1996; mem Wash. State steering com. Gore for Pres., 1999-2000; chair Wash. State Environmentalists for Gore Com., 2000; mem. exec. com. Alaska Def. Initiative, 2001—; founding mem. WildPAC, 2000. Recipient Michael McCloskey award, Sierra Club, 2003. Avocations: hiking, rafting, fishing, playing guitar. Office: Sierra Club NW Office 180 Nickerson St Ste 202 Seattle WA 98109-1631

ARTHURS, HARRY WILLIAM, legal educator, former university president; b. Toronto, Ont., Can., May 9, 1935; s. Leon and Ellen (Dworkin) A.; m. Penny Milnes, June 22, 1974. BA, U. Toronto, 1955, LLB, 1958; LLM, Harvard U., 1959; LLD (hon.), Sherbrooke, Brock Law Soc. Upper Can., McGill U.; D.Litt. (hon.), Lethbridge U. Prof. Osgoode Hall Law Sch., York U., Toronto, Ont., 1961-95, dean, 1972-77, pres. univ., 1985-92; univ. prof. York U., 1995—. Chief adjudicator Pub. Svc. of Can., 1967-68; assoc. Can. Inst. Advanced Rsch., 1995-98; arbitrator, mediator. Author various books and articles on labor law, legal history, adminstrv. law and legal edn. to profl. jours. Vice pres. Can. Civil Liberties Assn., 1964-76, pres., 1976-77; mem. U.A.W. Pub. Rev. Bd., 1967-77; vice chmn. Ont. Ednl. Relations Commn., 1976-77; chmn. S.S.H.R.C. Study on Legal Research and Edn. in Can., 1980-83; bencher Law Soc. Upper Can., 1979-83; mem. Econ. Council Can., 1978-81; bd. mem. Rights and Democracy, 1999—. Officer Order of Can., 1989; mem. Order of Ont., 1995. Fellow: Royal Soc. Can. (Killam Prize in the Soc. Scis. 2002). Home: 11 Hillcrest Pk Toronto ON Canada M4X 1E8 Office: York Univ Dept of Law 4700 Keele St Toronto ON Canada M3J 1P3

ARTIGLIERE, RALPH, lawyer, educator, judge; b. Morristown, NJ, Mar. 1, 1947; s. Fiore Joseph and Mary (Bolcar) A.; m. Gale Anderson, June 14, 1969; children: William Michael, Adam Robert. BS in Engring., U.S. Mil. Acad., 1969; JD, U. Fla., 1977. Bar: Fla. 1977, U.S. Dist. Ct. (mid. dist.) Fla. 1978, U.S. Ct. Appeals (11th cir.) 1981, U.S. Dist. Ct. (no. dist.) Fla. 1984, cert.: mediator 2000. Project mgr. Ryder System, Inc., Miami, Fla., 1974—75, cons. Gainesville, Fla., 1975—77; atty. Holland & Knight, Lakeland, Fla., 1977—81, Lane, Trohn, Clarke, Bertrand & Williams, Lakeland, Fla., 1981—91, Anderson & Artigliere, Pa., Lakeland, Fla., 1991—2001; cir. judge 10th Jud. Cir. Fla., Bartow, 2001—. Mem. jury instrn. com. Fla. Supreme Ct., Tallahassee, 1990-99, 2003—; aj. prof. U. South Fla., Tampa, 1991-92; instr. legal writing U. Fla. Law Sch., Gainesville, 1976-77. Author: (chpt.) Florida Forms of Jury Instruction, 1990, Drafting and Using Jury Instructions in Civil Cases, 1998. Pres. Santa Fe HS Bd., Lakeland, 1985; chmn. 10th Cir. Jud. Nominating Commn., Polk County, Fla., 1985-86; bd. dir. Polk Pub. Mus., Lakeland, 1987-89, United Cerebral Palsy of Polk County, Lakeland, 1980-82. Capt. US Army, 1969-74, Vietnam. Decorated Bronze Star, Air medal with "V"; recipient Fla. Bar Pro Bono award Fla. Supreme Ct., 1982. Master: Am. Inns of Ct.; fellow: Am. Coll. Trial Lawyers; mem.: FBA, ABA, Polk County Trial Lawyers Assn. (pres. 1998—99), Fla. Bar (cert. civil trial lawyer 1993—, chmn. CLE com. 1996—97, mem. bd. legal specialization and edn.com. 1996—98, mem. bd. legal specialization and edn. com. 2000—), Order of Coif, Phi Kappa Phi. Republican. Avocations: fly fishing, retriever field training. Office: Polk County Courthouse 255 N Broadway Bartow FL 33830

ARTSCHWAGER, RICHARD ERNST, artist; b. Washington, Dec. 26, 1923; s. Ernst and Eugenia (Brodsky) A.; m. Elfriede Wejmelka, 1947 (div. 1970); 1 child, Eva; m. Catherine Kord, 1972 (div. 1989); m. Molly O'Gorman (div. 1993); children: Clara, Augustus; m. Ann Sebring, 1995. AB, Cornell U., 1948; pupil of Amedee Ozenfant, N.Y.C., 1949-50. One-man shows include Leo Castelli Gallery, N.Y.C., 1965, 67, 72, 73, 75, 76, 78, 79, 89, 91, Kunstverein, Hamburg, Germany, 1979, Albright-Knox Art Gallery, Buffalo, 1979, Inst. Contemporary Art, U. Pa., Phila., 1979, La Jolla (Calif.) Mus. Contemporary Art, 1980, Mus. Contemporary Art, Houston, 1980, Mary Boone Gallery, N.Y.C., 1983, 86, 90, 93, 94, 97, Kunsthalle, Basel, Switzerland, 1985, Van Abbe Mus., Eindhoven, Netherlands, 1985, Whitney Mus. Retrospective, 1988 (travelled to San Francisco Mus. Modern Art, Mus. Contemporary Art, L.A., Palacio de Velasquez, Madrid, Spain, Mus. Nat. d'Art Moderne, Ctr. Georges Pompidou, Paris, Stadtische Kunsthalle, Dusseldorf, Fed. Republic Germany), Mus. Fine Arts, Boston, 1992, Kunstnernes Hus, Oslo, 1992, Portikus, Frankfurt, 1993, Fondation Cartier, Paris, 1994; mus. and gallery shows include Documenta IV, 1967, V, 1972, VII, 1982, VIII, 1987, IX, 1992, Kassel, Germany; outdoor sculpture commns. include Battery Park City, N.Y.C., 1984-88, Gen. Mills Corp. Hdqrs., Mpls., 1988, Elvehjem Mus. Art, Madison, Wis., 1990-91; represented in permanent collections Mus. Modern Art, N.Y., Whitney Mus., Centre Georges Pompidou, Paris, Emily Fisher Landau Found., N.Y., San Diego Mus. Contemporary Art, Mus. Ludwig, Cologne, Germany, Detroit Art Center, Met. Mus., N.Y.C., Walker Art Ctr., Mpls., Wadsworth Athenaeum, Conn., Rotterdam (Netherlands) Mus., Basel Mus., also pvt. collections; contbr. articles to profl. jours. With U.S. Army, 1944-46. Address: PO Box 12 Hudson NY 12534-0012

ARTZ, FREDERICK JAMES, diversified manufacturing company executive; b. Pitts., Dec. 28, 1949; s. Ray Edison and Jean Elizabeth (McClurg) A.; m. Donna Marie Moschella, Dec. 16, 1977; children: James Randall, BrieAnn Elizabeth. BS in Adminstrn. and Mgmt. Sci., Carnegie Mellon U., 1972; MBA, U. Pitts., 1973. Indsl. engr. Spang and Co., Butler, Pa., 1973-74; retail buyer Sun Drug div. Spang Stores, Butler, 1974-79, internal auditor, 1979-82, acctg. mgr., 1982-88, treas., 1988—. Bd. dirs. Spang & Co. Mem. Beta Gamma Sigma. Office: Spang & Co PO Box 11422 111 Zeta Dr Pittsburgh PA 15238-0422

ARTZ, JOHN CURTIS, lawyer; b. Columbus, Ohio, Mar. 4, 1946; s. Curtis Price and Kathryn Lucille (Risley) A.; m. Nancy Eileen Jones, Apr. 5, 1969; children: John Curtis Jr., Alexander Hardie, Kathryn Cullen. BA disting. mil. grad., Allegheny Coll., 1968; JD magna cum laude, U. S.C., 1976. Bar: Pa. 1976, U.S. Dist. Ct. (we. dist.) Pa. 1976, U.S. Ct. Appeals (3d and 6th cirs.) 1996, U.S. Supreme Ct. 1980. From assoc. to ptnr. Eckert Seamans Cherin & Mellott, Pitts., 1976-94; shareholder, dir. Polito & Smock, P.C., Pitts., 1994—. Adj. asst. prof. Grad. Sch. Pub. Health U. Pitts., 1988-92; instr. Robert Morris U., Pitts., 1998—; presenter Nat. Safety Coun., Western Pa. Safety Coun., Assn. of Iron and Steel Engrs., Pa. Bar Inst., Allegheny County Bar Assn., Pitts. Human Resources Assn., Butler Human Resources Assn., Westmoreland Human Resources Assn. Inst. SMC Bus. Couns., Constrn. Fin. Mgmt. Assn., Pa. Inst. CPAs, Western Pa. Cmty. Accts., YWCA Mid-Atlantic Regional Coun. Notes editor U. S.C. Law Rev., 1975-76; contbr. articles to profl. jours. Dir. Jr. Achievement S.W. Pa., Pitts., 1994—, vice-chair adminstrn., 1998—. Capt. USAF, 1968-73. Recipient Bronze Leadership award Jr. Achievement S.W. Pa., 1993. Fellow Allegheny County Bar Found.; mem. ABA (com. on occupl. safety and health law 1981—), Soc. for Human Resource Mgmt., Pa. Bar Assn. (com. on legal ethics and profl. responsibility 1987-94), Pitts. Human Resources Assn. (treas. 1997, sr. profl. human resources 1998—), Order of Wig and Robe, Omicron Delta Kappa. Office: Polito & Smock PC 444 Liberty Ave Ste 400 Pittsburgh PA 15222-1237 E-mail: jartz@politolaw.com.

ARTZT, ALICE JOSEPHINE, classical guitarist, writer; b. Phila., Mar. 16, 1943; d. Maurice Gustav and Harriett S. (Green) A.; m. Bruce Lawton. BA, Columbia U., 1966. Tchr. guitar Mannes Coll. Music, N.Y.C., 1966-69; classical guitarist touring worldwide, 1969—; tchr. Trenton (N.J.) State U., 1977-80; co-founder Alice Artzt Guitar Trio, 1989. Author: The Art of Practicing, 1978, Rhythmic Mastery, 1997; editor: The GFA International Guitarists' Cookbook, 1986; contbr. numerous articles to profl. jours.; musician: (albums) Variations, Passacaglias & Chaccones, Virtuoso Romantic Guitar, American Music of the Stage and Screen. Recipient various Critics' Choice awards. Mem. Guitar Found. Am. (chmn. bd. dirs. 1986-91), N.Y. Classical Guitar Soc. Avocations: travel, hi-fi, researching Chaplin films. Home: 51 Hawthorne Ave Princeton NJ 08540-3803 E-mail: Guitartzt@aol.com.

ARUM, ROBERT, lawyer, sports events promoter; b. N.Y.C., Dec. 8, 1931; s. Samuel and Celia (Baumgarten) Arum; m. Barbara Mandelbaum, July 2, 1960 (div. 1977); children: John, Richard, Elizabeth; m. Sybil Ann Hamada, Dec. 18, 1977 (div. 1991); m. Lovee Hazan Du Boef, Sept. 14, 1991. BA, NYU, 1953; JD cum laude, Harvard U., 1956. Bar: NY 1956. Atty. firm Root, Barrett, Cohen, Knapp & Smith, N.Y.C., 1956—61; asst. U.S. atty., chief tax sect. U.S. Atty.'s Office, So. Dist. N.Y., 1961—64; ptnr. firm Phillips, Nizer, Benjamin, Krim & Ballon, N.Y.C., 1964—72, Arum & Katz, N.Y.C., 1972—79; chmn. Top Rank, Inc.; Promoter Ali-Frazier Super Fight II, 1974, Evel Knievel Snake River Canyon Jump, 1974, Ali-Norton World Heavyweight Championship, 1976, Monzon-Valdez World Middleweight Championships, 1976, 1977, Ali-Spinks Championships, 1978, Leonard-Duran Championships, 1980, 1989, Top Rank/ESPN Boxing Series, 1980—, Arguello-Pryor Championship, 1983, Moore-Duran Championship, 1983, Hagler-Duran Championship, 1983, Hagler-Hearns Championship, 1985, Hagler-Leonard Superfight Championship, 1987, Leonard-Hearns "The War" Championship, 1989—91, Holyfield-Foreman World Heavyweight Championship, 1991, Holyfield-Holmes World Heavyweight Championship, 1992, Foreman/Morrison Heavyweight Championship, 1993, De la Hoya/Whitaker, 1997, De la Hoya/Chavez, 1996, 1998, De la Hoya/Quartey, 1999, De la Hoya/Trinidad, 1999, De la Hoya/Mosely, 2000, Morales/Barrera, 2002, De la Hoya/Vargas, 2002. Named to Boxing Hall of Fame, 1999. Mem.: Friars Club. Home: 36 Gulf Stream Ct Las Vegas NV 89113-1354 Office: 3980 Howard Hughes Pkwy Las Vegas NV 89109-0992 E-mail: erroa@aol.com.

ARUMUGAM, SIVAKUMAR, gastroenterologist; b. Colombo, Sri Lanka, Oct. 15, 1951; s. Velupillai Sinnathamby and Gnanaratnam (Vaithilingam) A.; m. Linges Sivakumar, Aug. 29, 1984; children: Niranjan, Nirushan, Angiela. MBBS, U. Ceylon, 1975. Diplomate Am. Bd. Internal Medicine, Am. Bd. Gastroenterology. Physician Dept. of Health, Sri Lanka, 1975-81, Nat. Health Svcs., U.K., 1981-86; internal medicine resident Sisters Hosp., Buffalo, N.Y., 1986-89; gastroenterology fellow SUNY, Buffalo, 1989-92; gastroenterologist Las Vegas, 1992—. Mem. invasive com. Desert Springs Hosp., Las Vegas, 1995—. Govt. postgrad. grant Govt. of Sri Lanka, 1981-84. Fellow ACP; mem. Royal Coll. Physicians, Am. Coll. Gastroenterology, Am. Gastroenterol. Assn. Hindu. Avocations: music, watching sports. Office: Ste 206 98 E Lake Mead Henderson NV 89015

ARUNASALAM, VICKRAMASINGAM (WILLIE), retired physicist; b. Mathagal, Jaffna, Sri Lanka, Aug. 26, 1935; arrived in U.S., 1958, naturalized, 1973; s. Sithamparapillai and Sithamparam Vickramasingam; m. Saradamani Sivagnanasundaram, Mar. 23, 1968 (dec. Dec. 21, 1997); 1 child, Sharmila. BS, U. of Ceylon, Colombo, Ceylon, 1957; MS, U. of Mass., 1960; PhD, MIT, 1964. Asst. lectr. U. of Ceylon, Colombo, Sri Lanka, 1957—58; instr. U. of Mass., Amherst, Mass., 1960—60; from rsch. assoc. to prin. rsch. physicist Princeton (N.J.) U., 1964—80, prin. rsch. physicist, 1980—96; vis. prof. William Paterson U., Wayne, NJ, 1997—97; adj. prof. Rider U., Lawrenceville, NJ, 1999—99; assoc. editor Physics Essays, Hull, Canada, 1992—. Contbr. 105 articles to profl. jours. Fellow: Am. Phys. Soc. (sr.); mem.: N.Y. Acad. of Scis. (past mem.), Sigma Xi. Achievements include research in Plasma Physics and Controlled Thermonuc. Fusion, Quantum Theory, Quantum Electrodynamics, Cosmology, Foundations of Physics, Particle Physics, Condensed Matter Theory, and Quantum Statis. mechanics. Home: 50 Windsor Drive Princeton Junction NJ 08550-1641 Office: Plasma Physics Lab Princeton University Princeton NJ 08543 Personal E-mail: williearunasalam@hotmail.com. E-mail: arunasalam@mail.com.

ARUNDEL, JOHN HOWARD, financial consultant; b. Washington, June 4, 1965; s. Arthur W. and Margaret C. (McElroy) A.; married; 1 child. BA in Polit. Sci., Duke U., 1988; MA in Internat. Econs., Johns Hopkins U., 1995. Registered fin. cons. Reporter, trainee The New York Times, N.Y.C., 1988-90; bur. chief States News Svc., Washington, 1991-92; corr. The Washington Post, Kuwait City, Kuwait, 1991; v.p. Smith Barney Citigroup, Washington, 1996—. Bd. mem. Va. Film Found.; bd. dirs. The Kennedy Ctr. Camelot Circle, Washington, 1995—. Author: The Student Guide to Duke, 1988, While America Slept, 2003; contbr. articles to profl. jours. Mem. Nat. Press Club. Democrat. Episcopalian. Home: 412 Queen St Alexandria VA 22314-2621 Office: Smith Barney Citigroup 1850 K St NW Ste 900 Washington DC 20006-2222

ARUZA, ALBERT FRANCIS, consulting firm executive; b. Stamford, Conn., July 4, 1941; s. Albert Francis Sr. and Olga Barbara Aruza; m. Dorothy M. Aruza, Oct. 14, 1963 (div. June 1995); children: Christine D., Amanda F.; m. Florence Caroline Aruza, June 29, 1996. Student, Duke U., 1959-63. Asst. chemist Am. Cyanamid, Stamford, 1963-65; recruiter JBM Corp., Stamford, Conn., 1968-70; office mgr. Sanford Rose Assocs., 1970-71; cons. JBM Corp., N.Y.C., 1971-73; v.p. BFL Assocs., N.Y.C., 1973-87; pres. LDA Assocs., N.Y.C., 1987-91; sr. mng. ptnr., COO Cornell Group Internat. Cons. Inc., Newburgh, N.Y., 1991—. Asst. chemist Am. Cyanamid, Stamford, 1963-65. Patentee in field. Bd. dirs. Mid. Hope Fire Co., Newburgh, 1996—. Cpl. USMC,

1966-68. Mem. Powelton Club, Union League Club, Grand Haven Club, Duke Alumni Assn., Duke Athletic Assn., Washington Duke Club. Avocations: golf, tennis, boating, racquetball, softball. Office: Cornell Group Internat Cons Inc 1 Corwin Ct Newburgh NY 12550-5159 E-mail: aaruza@hvc.rr.com., aaruza@cornellinternational.com.

ARVAY, NANCY JOAN, lawyer; b. Pitts., Aug. 27, 1952; d. William John and Cornelia (Prince) A. BA in History, Duke U., 1974; postgrad., Columbia U., 1974-75; JD, U. S.C., 1999. Polit. and internat. comm. specialist U.S. Senate Fgn. Rels. Com., Washington, 1975-77; broadcast media rels. rep. Am. Petroleum Inst., Washington, 1977-79, Chevron U.S.A., San Francisco, 1979-82, coord. electronic news media rels., 1982-85; sr. media rels. rep. Chevron Corp., San Francisco, 1985-87; dir. pub. rels. Fireman's Fund Corp., Novato, Calif., 1987-89; v.p., ptnr. The Resource Group, San Francisco, 1989-91; pres. Arvay, Moore & Buchanan, Washington, 1991-95, Columbia, SC, 1996—99; pvt. practice law, 1999—. Pub. affairs advisor to C. Everett Koop, M.D.; lectr. Dept. Interior-Park Service, Beckley, W.Va., 1983; chmn. pub. rels. Internat. Oil Spill Conf., Washington, 1984-85. Author, coordinator: Research Studies in Business and the Media, 1980-83; contbg. author This Is Public Relations, 1985. Founding mem. San Francisco chpt. Overseas Edn. Group; mem. pub. relations com. World Affairs Council San Francisco. Mem. Pub. Rels. Soc., Radio/TV News Dirs. Assn. (assoc.), San Francisco Women in Bus. Office: 8000 Farrow Rd Columbia SC 29203-3244

ARVESON, RAYMOND GERHARD, retired state official; b. Jamestown, N.D., May 11, 1921; m. Adelaide Arveson; children: Raymond, Susan Aden, John. BA, Mayville State U., 1942; MA, U. Minn., 1948; EdD, U. Calif., Berkeley, 1962. High sch. prin. Pub. Schs., Alamo and Langdon, N.D., 1942-44; supt. Langdon (N.D.) Pub. Schs., 1944-45, Leeds (N.D.) Pub. Schs., 1945-57; counselor, social sci. tchr. Hayward (Calif.) Union High Sch., 1957-58; dean of boys Tennyson High Sch. and Hayward Union High Sch., 1958-59, vice prin., 1958-59, prin., 1960-63; asst. supt. Hayward (Calif.) Union Sch. Dist., 1963-68; supt. Hayward (Calif.) Unified Sch. Dist., 1968-76, Mpls. Pub. Schs., 1976-80, East Baton Rouge (La.) Parish Pub. Schs., 1980-87, East Feliciana Parish Pub. Schs., 1989-90; asst. supt. acad. programs La. Dept. Edn., Baton Rouge, 1991, state supt. edn., 1991-96; ret., 1996. Bd. dirs. Operation Upgrade, S.W. Ednl. Devel. Lab., La. Edn. TV Authority, La. Sch. for Math., Sci. and Arts, La. Drug Policy, La. Children's Cabinet; co-chmn. bd. dirs. Satellite Ednl. Rsch. Consortium; co-project dir. La. Systemic Initiatives Program; bd. trustees La. Tchrs. Retirement System; mem. supts. adv. coun. State Bd. Elem. and Secondary Edn.; active Coun. Chief State Sch. Officers, Govs. Cabinet. Mem. joint adv. bd. Baton Rouge Gen. Hosp.; bd. dirs. Baton Rouge Symphony, La. Youth Orch., Playmakers, Crime Stoppers, Fairview Hosp., Tau Ctr.; trustee La. Arts and Scis. Coun., Our Lady of Lake Coll., pres. bd.; mem. visitation com. and bd. dirs. United Way, also ednl.hmn.; mem. standing com. for rsch. and analysis Am. Luth. Ch.; mem. tchr. edn. coun. La. State U.; and numerous others; mem. La. LEARN Commn. Recipient State Farmer award La. Assn. Future Farmers Am., Boss of Yr. award Am. Bus. Women's Assn. Mem. NEA (life), Am. Assn. Sch. Adminstrs. (emeritus), Nat. Sch. Bds. Assn. (mem. liaison com.), Nat. Speech Assn. (pres. debate and discussion divsn.), Nat. Soc. Study of Edn., Nat. PTA, La. Assn. Sch. Execs. (Outstanding Educator award), La. Assn. Sch. Supts. (bd. dirs.), Far West Lab. Ednl. Rsch. and Devel. (bd. dirs.), Assn. Supervision and Curriculum Devel. (bd. dirs.), Large City Schs. Supts. Assn. (pres.), PTA (hon. life), Baton Rouge C. of C. (mem. edn. com.) Horace Mann League, Phi Delta Kappa, Lambda Delta Lambda. Avocations: golf, tennis, camping, fishing, gardening.

ARVESON, WILLIAM BARNES, mathematics educator; b. Oakland, Calif., Nov. 22, 1934; s. Ronald Magnus and Audrey Mary (Hichens) A.; m. Lee A. Kaskutas. BS in Math, Calif. Inst. Tech., 1960; MA, UCLA, 1963, PhD, 1964. Benjamin Peirce instr. Harvard U., 1965-68; lectr. dept. math. U. Calif., Berkeley, 1968-69, assoc. prof., 1969-74, prof., 1974—, Miller rsch. prof., 1985—86, 1999—2000. Author: An Invitation to C*-algebras, 1976, A Short Course in Spectral Theory, 2001; assoc. editor: Duke Math. Jour, 1975-86, Jour. of Operator Theory, 1977-87, editor, 1987—; contbr. articles to math. jours. Served with U.S. Navy, 1952-55. John Simon Guggenheim fellow, 1976-77 Mem. Am. Math. Soc. (assoc. editor bulletin 1988-91), Edinburgh Math. Soc. (assoc. editor proceedings 1989—). Office: U Calif Dept Math Berkeley CA 94720-0001

ARVIDSON, ROBERT BENJAMIN, JR., geneticist, consultant; b. Lafayette, Ind., June 10, 1920; s. Robert Benjamin Sr. and Ollie Blanche (Ice) A.; m. Rose Janet Gaylord, Sept. 2, 1943 (dec. 2000); children: Cheryl R., James R., Kay E. BSA, Purdue U., 1942, MS, 1950. Poultry genetics staff Hy-Line Internat. Divsn. Pioneer Hi Bred Internat., Des Moines, 1947-50; dir. rsch. Hy-Line Internat., Des Moines, 1951-79, ret., 1979. Cons. World Bank, Washington, 1979-80. Precinct committeeman Rep. Party, Des Moines, 1970. Capt. Q.M.C., U.S. Army, 1942-46. Mem. World Poultry Sci. Assn., Poultry Sci. Assn., Kiwanis (pres. 1979). Methodist. Avocations: golf, fishing, gardening, dahlia growing. Home: 5921 Winwood Dr Apt 232 Johnston IA 50131

ARVIO, SARAH, poet; b. Phila., Apr. 3, 1954; d. Raymond Paavo Arvio and Cynthia Mallory. MFA in Poetry, Columbia U., 1983. Contbr. poems to numerous mags. including The New Yorker, Yale Review, Massachusetts Review, Paris Review; translator (poems) Ships Afire, 1988, Daimon, 1992, (documentary film) Azul, 1988. Recipient B.F. Connors prize, 1997, Frederich Boch prize, 2000, Prix de Nome, 2003. Home and Office: 314 E 9th St # 1 New York NY 10003-7918

ARVIZU, DAN ELIAB, mechanical engineer; b. Douglas, Ariz., Aug. 23, 1950; s. Walter and Ella (Rodriguez) A.; m. Patricia Ann Brady, Feb. 23, 1980; children: Joshua, Angela, Elizabeth, Kayley, Tecia. BSME, New Mexico State U., 1973; MSME, Stanford U., 1974, PhD in Mech. Engring., 1981. Mfg. engring. asst. Texas Instruments, Dallas, 1969-72; mem. tech. staff Bell Telephone Labs., Denver, 1973-77; mem. solar thermal tech. staff Sandia Nat. Labs., Albuquerque, 1977-81, mem. solar photovoltaic tech. staff, 1981-86, supr. photovoltaic cell rsch., 1986-88, mgr. tech. transfer, 1988-91, dir. tech. transfer, 1991-93, dir. adv. energy tech., 1993-97, dir. materials and process scis., 1997-98; v.p. energy, environment and sys. group CH2M Hill, 1998-2000, sr. v.p. tech., 2001—, chief technology officer for energy, environment and sys. bus., 2002—. Mem. tech. transfer steering com. Nat. Ctr. for Mfg. Scis., Ann Arbor, Mich., 1992; mem. tech. transfer mgrs. adv. bd. Nat. Tech. Transfer Ctr., Wheeling, W.Va., 1992—96; mem. commercialization adv. bd. Solar II Power Plant, Barstow, Calif., 1996—96; mem. adv. bd. U. Tex.-El Paso model Inst. Excellence Program, 1995—; chmn. indsl. adv. bd. ME Acad. N.Mex. State U., 1995—99, bd. dirs.; mem. com. to rev. DOE's renewable energy tech. program NRC, 1998—2000; mem. corp. adv. bd. Colo. Sch. Mines, 1999—; mem. nat. adv. bd. for Hispanic engr. nat. achievement award conf. HENAAC, 1999—, bd. dirs., 2000—; mem. indsl. adv. group U. Tex. El Paso Coll. Engring., 1999—; mem. nat. coal coun. Dept. Energy, 1999—; adv. group G8 Task Force Renewable Energy, 2000—01; mem. Army Sci. Bd. Dept. of Def., 2001—; adv. Divsn. Engring. and Physical Sci. Comm. Nat. Acad. of Engring., 2001—; bd. adv. Greater Metro Denver Salvation Army, 2000—; mem. com. to review Dept. Energy concentrating solar power tech. NRC, 2002—; chair blue ribbon panel on sci. and engring. workforce diversity Coun. on Competition. Contbr. articles to profl. jours. Recipient Sel. Hispanic Engr. Nat. Achievement award Exec. Excellence, 1996; named Disting. Engring. Alumnus N.Mex. State U., 1988, 96, Ingeniero Eminente, 1990, Outstanding Achievement award Hispanic Alliance for Career Enhancement, 1997, named Rising Star in Sci. Albuquerque Tribune newspaper, 1989, One of top 20 Hispanic Scientists and Engrs. in Am., Hispanic Engr. Mag., 1998, One of Most Important Hispanics in Am. in Tech. and Bus., Hispanic Mag., 2003. Mem. ASME (solar standards com. 1981-83, nat. lab. tech. transfer com. 1990-93), IEEE, IEEE Electronic Device Soc. (adminstrv. com. 1986-91), Am. Soc. Material Internat., Tech. Transfer Soc. Achievements include leadership of national laboratory negotiating teams that resulted in Department of Energy policy changes to improve U.S. Goverment/ Industry partnership agreements, management of research effort that developed 30 percent solar to electric conversion efficiency solar cell, and development of Sandia National Laboratory's technology transfer center including development of policy, maturation of technology, and formal partnerships between industry and laboratories. Office: CH2M Hill Energy Environment and Sys Bus Group 6060 S Willow Dr Greenwood Village CO 80111-5142 E-mail: darvizu@ch2m.com.

ARVYSTAS, MICHAEL GECIAUSKAS, orthodontist, educator; b. Vilnius, Lithuania, Dec. 18, 1942; arrived in U.S., 1949, naturalized, 1961; s. Mykolas and Antanina (Kleiza) Arvystas; m. Jane Grannis, 1969 (div. 1978); m. Mary Ruth Buchness, Nov. 2, 1992. BA, Colgate U., 1965; DMD, Tufts U., 1969. Cert. Columbia U., 1973, diplomate Am. Bd. Orthodontics. Chief orthodontic sect. Morrisania City Hosp., Bronx, NY, 1973—76; dir. orthodontics ctr. for cranio facial disorders and cleft palate ctr. Montefiore Hosp. and Med. Ctr., 1973—; chief orthodontic sect. North Ctrl. Bronx Hosp., 1976—83; clin. prof. N.J. Dental Sch., Newark, 1974—, dir., lectr. undergrad. and postgrad. students, 1974—. Lectr. in field; vis. prof. Albert Einstein Coll. Medicine, Bronx. Author (with others): (Book) Orthodonic Management of Agenesis and Other Complexitues: An Interdisciplinary Approach to Functional Aesthetics, 2003; contbr. articles to profl. jours., chpts. to books. Capt. Dental Corps USAF, 1969—71. Mem.: ADA, Am. Acad. Esthetic Dentistry (orgn. com. mem. greater N.Y. meeting), N.Y. Acad. Dentistry, Northeastern Soc. Orthodontists, Am. Assn. Orthodontists, Dental Soc. N.Y.C., N.Y. County Dental Soc. (bd. dirs.), Sigma Xi, Colgate U. Alumni Assn., Orthodontic Alumni Soc. Columbia U., Tufts U. Dental Alumni Assn. Office: 24 Washington Sq N New York NY 10011-9168

ARYA, SATYA PAL, meteorology educator; b. Mavi Kalan, Dist Meerut, India, Aug. 24, 1939; came to U.S., 1965. BE (Civil), U. Roorkee (India), 1961, ME (Civil), 1964; PhD, Colo. State U., 1968. Asst. engr. Irrigation Dept., Lucknow, India, 1961-62; lectr. U. Roorkee, 1963-65; rsch. asst. Colo. State U., Ft. Collins, 1965-68, rsch. assoc., 1968-69; rsch. asst., assoc. prof. U. Wash., Seattle, 1969-76; assoc. prof. N.C. State U., Raleigh, 1976-81, prof. meteorology, 1981—, acting head MEAS dept., 1982-83. Vis. prof. Indian Inst. Tech., Delhi, 1983-84. Author: Introduction to Micrometeorology, 1988, 2d edit., 2001, Air Pollution Meteorology and dispersion, 1999; contbr. sci. articles to jours. of atmospheric scis., applied meteorology, fluid mechanics, others. Fellow AAAS, Am. Meteorol. Soc.; mem. Am. Geophys. Union. Achievements include research in atmospheric sciences, applied meteorology, environmental fluid mechainics, micrometeorology and air pollution. Office: NC State U Dept Marine Earth & Atmosphe Raleigh NC 27695-8208 E-mail: sparya@unity.ncsu.edu.

ARYSTANBEKOVA, AKMARAL KHAIDAROVNA, diplomat; b. Alma-Ata, Kazakhstan, May 12, 1948; came to U.S., 1991; d. Khaidar Arystanbekov and Sharbanu Bekmanovna Nurmuhamedova. BA in Chemistry, Kazakh State U., Alma-Ata, 1971, PhD in Chemistry, 1975. Mem. faculty Kazakh State U., Alma-Ata, 1975-78; chief dept., sec. Ctrl. Com. Kazakh Komsomol, Alma-Ata, 1978-83; dpe. chmn. Kazakh Friendship Soc., Alma-Ata, 1983-84, chmn., 1984-89; min. fgn. affairs Ministry Fgn. Affairs, Alma-Ata, 1989-91; permanent rep., amb. Permanent Mission of Republic of Kazakhstan to UN, N.Y.C., 1992—99. Mem. Supreme Coun. Kazakh SSR, Alma-Ata, 1985-90, Presidium of Supreme Coun. Kazakh SSR, Alma-Ata, 1987-90. Recipient awards Supreme Coun. USSR, Moscow, 1970, 81. Avocations: classical music (opera), playing the piano. Home and Office: Permament Mission of Kazakhstan to UN 866 U N Plz Rm 586 New York NY 10017-1822

ARZOUMANIAN, LINDA LEE, early childhood educator; b. Madison, Wis., Apr. 29, 1942; d. James Arthur Luck and Rosemary M. (Peacock) Engstrom; children: Stephan, Aaron. BS, Stout State U., Menomonie, Wis., 1964; MEd, Ohio U., Athens, 1969; EdD, Nova U., 1994. Cert. tchr. vocat., secondary, cmty. coll., Ariz. Residence hall asst. Ohio U., Athens, 1965-67; quality control supr. Advalloy, Inc., Palo Alto, Calif., 1967; tchr. adult edn. Eau Claire (Wis.) Pub. Sch., 1964-65; patient svc. dietitian Camden Clark Meml. Hosp., Parkersburg, W.Va., 1970; adminstr. pre-sch. Fishkill (N.Y.) Meth. Nursery Sch., 1976-84; substitute tchr. Tucson Unified Sch. Dist., 1987; tchr. pre-sch. Tanque Verde Luth. Presch., Tucson, 1988-89; cons., early childhood ednl. curriculum specialist Tucson Unified Sch. Dist., 1988-93; instr. Ctrl. Ariz. Coll., 1990-98, Prescott Coll., 1991-92; dist. moderator Sch. Cmty. Partnership Coun., Tucson, 1988-90; dir. child and family svcs. in prevention, early intervention and treatment in sys. managed care CODAC Behavioral Health Svcs., Tucson, 1990-99, dir. mgmt. info. sys., 1999, dir. cmty. svcs., 1999-2000; supt. of schs. Pima County, 2000—. Mem. supts. adv. cabinet Tucson Unified Sch. Dist., 1988-89, mem. curriculum and instrn. coun., 1989-90, spl. edn. pre-sch. adv. com., 1989-91, info. tech. bond rev. com., 1989—, sex edn. curriculum adv. com., core curriculum com., 1988-90, 2000 com., 1988-89, and various others; nat. child devel. assoc. adv./field adv., nat. child devel. assoc. rep. Nat. Assn. for Edn. of Young Children; grantswriter Comstock Found.; validator early childhood programs for Nat. Acad. Early Childhood Programs; appt. Ariz. State Bd. Edn., 2002. Mem. Dutchess County Child Devel. Com., Poughkeepsie, N.Y., 1979-81; advancement chmn. troop 1968 Boy Scouts Am., Tucson, 1986, com. person troop 194, 1986-89; mem. joint com. on site based decision making Tucson Unified Sch. Dist./Tucson Edn. Assn., 1989-98; life mem. Ariz. PTA; mem. Early Childhood Edn. Coun. Consortium; mem. mgmt. com. Healthy Families of Pima County; commr. Met. Edn. Commn.; mem. Pima County Youth Coun., Greater Tucson Strategic Planning for Econ. Devel. Mem.: AAUW, Ariz. Sch. Bds. Assn., Am. Assn. Edn. Svc. Agys., Tucson Assn. Edn. Young Children (past pres.), Nat. Assn. Edn. Young Children, Tucson Rep. Women, Pima County Supt. and Governing Bd. Collaborative, Tucson Hispanic C. of C., Tucson Met. C. of C., So. Ariz. Forums on Children and Families, Cath. Cmty. Svc. (bd. dirs.). Avocations: basketmaking, quilting, hiking, gardening, cooking. Home: 8230 E Ridgebrook Dr Tucson AZ 85750-2442 Office: 3100 N 1st Ave Tucson AZ 85719-2513 : 130 W Congress Tucson AZ 85701

ARZOUMANIDIS, GREGORY G. chemist; b. Thessaloniki, Greece, Aug. 16, 1936; came to U.S., 1964, naturalized, 1976; s. Gerasimos and Sophia A.; m. Anastasia Anastasopoulos, Jan. 2, 1966; children: Sophia, Alexis. BS in Chemistry, MS in Chemistry, U. Thessaloniki, 1959; PhD in Inorganic Chemistry, U. Stuttgart, (Germany), 1964; MBA, U. Conn., 1979. Research assoc. MIT, 1964-66; research chemist Monsanto, Everett, Mass., 1966-69; sr. research chemist Am. Cyanamid Co., Stamford, Conn., 1969-72, Stauffer Chem. Co., Dobbs Ferry, N.Y., 1972-79; research assoc. Amoco Chem. Co., Naperville, Ill., 1979-94, Argonne (Ill.) Nat. Lab., 1995-96; with Oakwood Cons., 1996—. Inventor comml. catalysts for polypropylene plastics, new processes; patentee (U.S. and fgn.); prin. co-inventor Amoco supported polypropylene catalyst; contbr. articles to profl. jours. Served to 2d lt. Greek Army, 1959-61. Recipient acad. award Govt. of W.Ger., 1963, Presdl. award Amoco Chem. Co., 1990. Mem. AAAS, Am. Chem. Soc., Sigma Xi Greek Orthodox. Home: 7 S 610 Carriage Way Naperville IL 60540 E-mail: greg@arzou.net.

ARZUBE, JUAN ALFREDO, bishop; b. Guayaquil, Ecuador, June 1, 1918; came to U.S., 1944, naturalized, 1961; s. Juan Bautista and Maria (Jaramillo) A. BS in Civil Engring, Rensselaer Poly. Inst., 1942; BA, St. John's Sem., 1954. Ordained priest Roman Catholic Ch., 1954; asso. pastor St. Agnes Ch., Los Angeles, Resurrection Ch., Los Angeles, Ascension Ch., Los Angeles, Our Lady of Guadalupe Ch., El Monte, Calif.; aux. bishop, vicar gen. Diocese L.A., Los Angeles, 1971-93; episcopal vicar for Spanish speaking Los Angeles, 1973—. Mem. nat. bishops coms. Ad Hoc Com. for Spanish Speaking; chmn. Com. for Latin Am. Recipient Humanitarian award Mexican Am. Opportunity Found., 1978, John Anson Ford award Los Angeles County Commn. Human Relations, 1979 Roman Catholic. Home: Nazareth House 3333 Manning ave Los Angeles CA 90064 E-mail: arzube@aol.com.

ASAAD, KOLLEEN JOYCE, special education educator; b. West Union, Iowa, July 13, 1941; d. Leonard Henry and Catherine Adelade (Bishop) Anfinson; children: Todd, Robin, Tara, Jason. BA in Elem. Edn., Upper Iowa U., 1961; MA in Spl. Edn. and Adminstrn., U. Cin., 1973. Elem. tchr. Fredericksburg (Iowa) Elem. Sch., 1961-62, Tyler Sch., Cedar Rapids, Iowa, 1962-64, Oasis Sch., 29 Palms, Calif., 1964-69, Longfellow Sch., Waterloo, Iowa, 1969-70; spl. edn. tchr. Fairview Sch., Cin., 1970-77; learning disabilities tchr. Lincoln Sch., Portsmouth, Ohio, 1977-78; dir. spl. edn. Vermilion Assn. for Spl. Edn., Danville, Ill., 1978-94; dir. edn. Swann Spl. Care Ctr., Champaign, Ill., 1994-97, ret., 1997. Mem. Govtl. Rels. Com., Ill. Coun. for Exceptional Children, Jacksonville, Ill., 1992. Bd. mem. Crosspoints, Danville, Catlin Music Boosters, pres. Named Best Adminstr., Regional Supt. of Schs., 1991. Mem. Coun. for Exceptional Children, Coun. for Adminstrs. of Spl. Edn., Ill. Adminstrs. of Spl. Edn., Assn. for Persons with Severe Handicaps, Exec. Club. Lutheran. Avocations: reading, aquacise. Home: 122 Mapleleaf Dr Catlin IL 61817-9646

ASADI, ANITA MURLENE, business educator; b. Kirksville, Mo., Feb. 2, 1948; d. James Murl and Norma Waneva (Schillie) Wallace; m. Asad Asadi, Feb. 25, 1972; children: Soraya, Ali. BS in Bus. Edn., N.E. Mo. State U., 1970, MA, 1971. Grad. asst. N.E. Mo. State U., Kirksville, 1970-71; instr. bus. edn. Muscatine (Iowa) C.C., 1971-76; mem. faculty St. Ambrose U., Davenport, Iowa, 1977-83; instr. adminstrv. and office support programs Scott C.C., Davenport, 1977—. Adminstrv. asst. Stanley, Lande, Coulter & Pearce, Muscatine, 1971-74; cons. Rock Island (Ill.) Arsenal, 1983-85; writer Sci. Rsch. Assocs. a.k.a. SRA/Pergamon, Chgo., 1987-88, Paradigm Pub. Internat., Eden Prairie, Minn., 1989—. Author: (textbook) Stenoscript ABC Shorthand, 1989; mem. editorial bd. Answer Book, Illinois Legal Handbook; contbr. articles to profl. jours. Mem Pres. Club Rep. Nat. Com., 1990, Talent Identification Program Parent/Alumni Network, Duke U., Durham, N.C., 1989-90, Scott County Family YMCA, Davenport, 1984-90. Recipient Bus. Edn. award, 1990, Disting. Svc. and Scholarship award IBEA, 1990, Chancellor's award, 1991, Phebe Sudlow award Quad Cities Encouragement Bd., 1991; named Outstanding Postsecondary Bus. instr., IBEA, 1991. Mem. NAACP, NEA, Am. Careers and Tech. Edn., Iowa Am. Careers and Tech. Edn., Bus. Profl. Educators Iowa, Iowa Bus. Edn. Assn., Office Automation Network, Assn. Info. System Profl., Bus. Profl. Am., Iowa Women Edul. Leadership, Internat. Soc. Bus. Educators, Iowa Bus. Edn. Assn. (pres. 1999-00), Delta Pi Epsilon. Avocations: Mideast artifacts, Am. antiques, music boxes, reading autobiographies. Home: 5075 Crestview Heights Dr Bettendorf IA 52722-5626 Office: Scott CC 326 W 3d St Davenport IA 52801-1201 E-mail: asadi4@aol.com.

ASADI, ROBERT SAMIR, insurance company executive; b. Salt Lake City, Dec. 21, 1953; s. Abdul-Aziz and Wilma (Craig) A.; m. Karen Lee Schenk, June 16, 1990; children: Scott, Ryan. BS, U. Wyo., 1986; MEd, No. Ariz. U., 1994. Cert. tchr. and adminstr. Tchr., coach Cactus HS, Glendale, Ariz., 1986-89, Holbrook HS, Ariz., 1989-91; tchr., adminstrv. asst., coach Agua Fria Union HS South, Avondale, Ariz., 1991-94; prin. Agua Fria Union HS-North, Goodyear, Ariz., 1994-98, Millennium HS, Goodyear, Ariz., 1998-2001; mgr. Horace Mann Ins. Co., Tempe, Ariz., 2001—03, Agy. mgr., 2003—. Active West Valley Fine Arts Coun., Avondale, 1995-96, Leadership West II, Avondale, 1995-96; bd. dir. Leadership West, 2000—. Mem.: ASCD, Nat. Assn. of Ins. and Fin. Adv., Nat. Assn. of Secondary Sch. Prin., Ariz. Sch. Adminstrs., Tri City West C. of C. Avocations: computers, golf, backpacking, spectator sports. Home: 9139 W Evans Dr Peoria AZ 85381-3784 Office: Horace Mann Insurance 6101 S Rural Rd #109 Tempe AZ 85283 E-mail: basadi@cox.net.

ASAKAWA, TAKAKO, dancer, dance teacher, director, choreographer; b. Toyko, Feb. 23, 1939; came to U.S., 1962; d. Kamenosuke and Chiaki Asakawa. Student, Tokyo schs., 1962-91. Prin. dancer Martha Graham Dance Co., N.Y.C., 1962-76, 81—; dancer Alvin Ailey, 1968-69, Pearl Lang, 1967, Lar Lubovitch, 1974-80. Guest tchr. at numerous schs. and univs. throughout world, including Moscow Culture Exch. Program, Martha Graham Sch., Juilliard Sch.; co-founder Asakawalker Dance Co.; dir. Paris Opera Ballet Co., Am. Ballet Theater, Het Nationale Ballet in Amsterdam and various univs. throughout world. Performed all major roles in GRaham reperatory throughout world, including Paris Opera House, Covent Garden; Broadway and TV performances include Eliza in The King and I, Bell Tel. Hour. Named Legendary Woman of Am., St. Vincent's Hosp. Mem. Am. Guild Musical Artists Home and Office: 20 W 64th St Apt 29-E/F New York NY 10023-7180

ASARCH, ELAINE, interior designer, anthropologist; b. Des Moines, Nov. 4, 1944; d. Morris and Rose (Sherman) Feintech; m. Richard Asarch, Aug. 17, 1965; children: Deborah, Chad, Jonathan, Adam, David. BA, U. Iowa, 1966; postgrad., U. Colo., 1992—. Tchr. spl. edn. Univ. Hosp. Schs., Iowa City, 1966-69; tchr. Raleigh Hill Elem. Sch., Portland, Oreg., 1969; learning therapist Psychol. & Guidance Ctr., Devner, 1974; interior designer Sipple/Asarch Design, Denver, 1981-83, Elaine Asarch Design Assocs., Englewood, Colo., 1983—. Dir., prodr. documentary on domestic violence; contbr. articles, photographs to Better Homes and Garden, 1980. Mktg. chmn. Jr. League of Denver, 1985-87; mem. com. Rose Found., Denver, 1997—; Pres., chmn. women's campaign Allied Jewish Fedn. of Denver, 1990-93; chmn. cmty. rels. com., 1994-96; mem. steering com. Harvard Womens Studies in Religion, 1994-99; founder Cmty. Help and Abuse Info. Agy. Recipient Ann. award, Yeshiva Toras Chaim, Denver, 1994, Tree of Life award, Herzl Day Sch., Denver, 1997, Golda Meir award, Allied Jewish Fedn. Colo., 2001. Mem. Am. Soc. Interior Designers (cert.). Achievements include research in relationship between environment and healing with relationship to medical practices. Home: 1000 E Tufts Ave Englewood CO 80110-5931

ASARI, EIKICHI, information sciences educator, researcher; b. Fonto, Karafuto, Japan, Feb. 10, 1929; s. Shoukichi and Kiku (Kotaki) A.; m. Satsuko Yamada, June 13, 1959; 1 child, Kimie Grad., Military Scis. and Tech. Acad. Imperial Army of Japan, 1945; 1st class radio engr. (hon.), Ministry Telecom. of Japan, 1952; attended sci. : math. and computer sci., Hokkaido U., Sapporo, Japan, 1959-61, Polytech. Nippon Telegraph and Pub. Corp., Tokyo, 1964. Radio engr. Nippon Telegraph and Tel. Pub. Corp., Sapporo, 1951-64, mem. mgmt. staff, 1964-69; assoc. prof. Tokai U., Sapporo, 1969-88, Hokkaido Tokai U., Sapporo, 1988-92; prof. info. scis. Hokkaido Coll. Arts and Scis., Ebets, 1993-97. Part-time lectr. info. scis. Nat. Otaru U. Commerce, 1970-97, Sapporo Polytech. of Nippon Telegraph and Telephone Pub. Corp., Hokkaido, 1970-85, Rakuno Gakuen U., Ebets, 1997-99. Editor, author: Encyclopedia of Operations Research, 1974-75, Encyclopedia of hokkaido,1979-81; contbr. articles to profl. publs.; inventor complete solution and applications of renewal theory, 1967, microwave propagation in precipitation, 1974, theory of countermeasures for cold damage of rice cultivation in subpolar climate dists., 1973-77, weather forecast method by meteorological noises, 1989, ski resort radiosys., 1989-90 (govt. prize 1992). Commr. com. distbn. in Hokkaido, Ministry Transp., 1975-76; chmn. com. optimazization of rice cultivation in Hokkaido, Hokkaido Govt., 1977-78; chmn. com. establish planning Hokkaido teleport Hokkaido Inst. Future Advancement, 1985-86; chmn. com. ski resort radio systems Ministry Post and Telecom., 1989-90, detection of clear air turbulences, 1999. Technical corp. telecom. Imperial Army Japan, 1945-46. Recipient award of merit of cold dist. devel. Civil Assns. Dist. Devel., Hokkaido, 1991, award of merit for radio sci. devel. Hokkaido br. Ministry Post and Telecom., 1992, fellow Operations Rsch. Soc. of Japan, 1995. Mem. IEEE, UNESCO, N.Y. Acad. Scis., Hokkaido/Mass. Soc., The Planetary Soc., Ops. Rsch. Soc. Japan (councilor 1970-92), Inst. Electronics and Communication Engrs. Japan, Cold Dists. Agrl. Sci. Soc. Ministry Agriculture, Forest and Fishery of Japan. Avocations: travel, photography, mysteries and science fiction, history of wars research. Home and Office: Shinkawa 2-Jo 2-chome Kita-ku Sapporo 001-0922 Japan Personal E-mail: asarie@d2.dion.ne.jp .

ASATO, YUKIO, molecular geneticist, educator; b. Waipahu, Hawaii, Jan. 19, 1934; s. Kame and Kama Asato; m. Sue A. Asato, June 22, 1969; children: April Asato-Harr, Lynn Hannan. BA, U. Hawaii, 1957, MA, 1966, PhD, 1969. Rsch. assoc. Ames Rsch. Ctr. NASA, Mountain View, Calif., 1969-71; prof. U. Mass., Dartmouth, 1971-96, prof. emeritus, 1996—. Contbr. sci. articles to profl. jours. With U.S. Army, 1957-60. Mem. AAAS, Am. Soc. Microbiology, Genetic Soc. Am. Avocations: classical guitar, bonsai, golf.

ASBELL, FRED THOMAS, health industry association executive; b. Birmingham, Ala., May 23, 1948; s. George Thomas and Dorothy Elizabeth (Wood) A. BS in Bus. Adminstrn., Jacksonville State U., 1973. Dir. sales Gulf Hills Inn, Ocean Springs, Miss., 1974 76; dir. sales The Read House, Chattanooga, 1976-77; adminstrv. asst. U.S. Rep. Clay Shaw, Washington, 1981-83; dep. polit. dir. Republican Nat. Com., Washington, 1983-84; dir. com. service Nat. Republican Congressional Com., Washington, 1984-85; exec. asst. to sec. U.S. Dept. Labor, Washington, 1985-87; exec. asst. to chmn. Dole for Pres. Com., Washington, 1987-88; cons. The Brock Group (formerly William Brock Assocs.), Washington, 1988-89; v.p. Am. Viewpoint Inc., Alexandria, Va., 1989-90; cons. The Brock Group, Washington, 1993; pres. Friends of Bill Brock for U.S. Senate, Inc., Annapolis, 1993-94, Internat. Mobile Comm., Inc., Bethesda, Md., 1994-97; exec. dir. U.S. Census Monitoring Bd., Suitland, Md., 1998-2001; dir. strategic initiatives Health Industry Group Purchasing Assn., Washington, 2002—. Baptist. Home: 141 12th St NE Apt 15 Washington DC 20002-6457 Office: Health Industry Group Purchasing Assn Ste 1200 1100 Wilson Blvd Arlington VA 22209 Personal E-mail: FredA2817@aol.com.

ASBURY, ARTHUR KNIGHT, neurologist, educator; b. Cin., Nov. 22, 1928; s. Eslie and Mary (Knight) Asbury; m. Carolyn Holstein, May 17, 1980; children from previous marriage: Dana, Patricia Knight, William Francis. Grad., Phillips Acad., Andover, Mass., 1946; student, Stanford, 1947—48; BS, U. Ky., 1951; MD, U. Cin., 1958; MA (hon.), U. Pa., 1974. Diplomate FRCP, London, 2002. Intern in medicine Mass. Gen. Hosp., Boston, 1958—59, resident, 1959—63, fellow, 1963—65, staff neurologist, 1965—69; chief neurology San Francisco VA Hosp., 1969—74; prof. dept. neurology U. Pa., Phila., 1974—, chmn. dept. neurology, 1974—82, Van Meter prof. neurology, 1983—97; acting dean, exec. v.p. U. Pa. Sch. Medicine, 1988—89, vice dean for rsch., 1990—93, vice dean for faculty affairs, 1993—97, interim dean, 2000—01; tchg. fellow Harvard Med. Sch., 1958—65, instr., 1965—68, assoc., 1968—69; assoc. prof. neurology U. Calif. at San Francisco, 1969—73, vice-chmn., 1969—74, prof., 1973—74. Mem. nat. adv. neurol. disease & stroke coun. NIH, 1990—93; hon. prof. med. scis. Hebei Med. Coll., China, 1995. Sr. editor: Blue Books of Practical Neurology, 1980—, assoc. editor: Archives of Neurology, 1975—76, Annals of Neurology, 1976—81, chief editor:, 1985—93, mem. editl. bd.: Muscle and Nerve, 1977—89, Neurology, 1981—85, Jour. Neuropathology and Exptl. Neurology, 1981—83, Jour. Neurol. Scis., 1989—2001; contbr. chpts. to med. textbooks, articles to med. jours. V.p., bd. dirs. Forest Retreat Farms Inc., Carlisle, Ky., 1970—92. With U.S. Army, 1951—53. Recipient Daniel Drake medal, U. Cin., 1988, IS Ravdin Master Clinician award, U. Pa., 1999, Lindback Tchg. award, 2000; grantee, UPHS, 1967—93, Muscular Dystrophy Assn., 1974—82. Fellow: AAAS, Royal Coll. Physicians London, Am. Acad. Neurology (v.p. 1977—79); mem.: Coll. Physicians of Phila. (pres.-elect 2002—), World Fedn. Neurology (v.p. 1989—93, chair rsch. group on neuromuscular diseases 2001—), Assn. Univ. Profs. Neurology (pres. 1980—82), Assn. Brit. Neurologists (hon.), European Neurol. Soc. (hon.), Soc. Neurosci., Am. Assn. Neuropathologists (v.p. 1983—84), Am. Neurol. Assn. (councillor 1976—81, pres. 1982—83, hon. 1995), Inst. Medicine. Home: 408 S Van Pelt St Philadelphia PA 19146-1233 Office: U Pa Hosp Dept Neurology 3400 Spruce St Philadelphia PA 19104-4283

ASCENSÃO, JOÃO LUIS AFONSO, physician, researcher; b. Maputo, Mozambique, July 6, 1948; arrived in U.S., 1974; s. Joáo F. A. and Maria (Almeida) A.; m. Vivian Pereyra, June 27, 1993; children: Joáo André, Vítor Luís. MD, U. Lisbon Sch. Medicine, 1972, PhD, 1980. Resident U. Hosp. St. Mary, Lisbon, Portugal, 1972-74; immunology fellow Meml. Sloan-Kettering Cancer Ctr., N.Y.C., 1974-76; internal medicine resident U. Minn. Hosps., Mpls., 1977-78, hematology oncology fellow, 1979-81, instr., 1981-82, asst. prof., 1982-84; assoc. prof., assoc. dir. BMT program N.Y. Med. Coll., Valhalla, 1984-89; assoc. prof., dir. BMT program U. Conn. Health Sci. Ctr., Farmington, 1989-92; prof. medicine, pathology, microbiology and immunology U. Nev. Sch. Medicine, Reno, 1992—2002; prof. medicine George Washington U. Sch. Medicine, Washington, 2002—. Adv. bd. mem. Calif. Cancer Ctr., Modesto, 1992—; bd. mem. Nev. Am. Cancer Soc., Reno, 1992—. Editor: Regulation of Erythropoiesis, 1987, Molecular Biology of Hemopoiesis, 1988, Molecular Biology of Erythropoiesis, 1989. Portugal Sci. Found. fellow Ministry of Edn., 1974-75, Charles H. Revson Found. fellow, 1984-86; recipient Young Investigator award NIH, 1991-94. Fellow: ACP; mem.: Am. Assn. Immunology, Clin. Immunology Soc., European Soc. Med. Oncology, Internat. Soc. Exptl. Hematology (councillor), Am. Assn. Cancer Rsch., Am. Soc. Clin. Oncology, Am. Soc. Hematology. Avocations: photography, cooking, reading, collecting corkscrews. Office: George Washington Univ Divsn Hematology/Oncology 2150 Penn Ave NW 3-428 Washington DC 20002 E-mail: jascensao@mfa.gwu.edu.

ASCENZI, JOHN C. writer, editor; b. Phila., Oct. 31, 1950; s. Louis C. Ascenzi and Julia E. Warga; m. Carol S. Tenneriello, June 9, 1984; children: Martina Tenneriello, Arlo. BA, U. Pa., 1972; MS, Drexel U., 1987. Sci. instr. Franklin Inst. Sci. Mus., Phila., 1979—89; writer, editor Allegheny Health, Edn. and Rsch. Found., Phila., 1989—98; med./sci. writer Children's Hosp. Phila., 1998—. Editor: (physicians' newsletter) Pediatric Rounds, 1994 (Gold winner, Healthcare Advt. Awards, 1996), Children's Doctor, 1999. Vol. VISTA/ACTION, Bronx, NY, 1973—74; chair pub. rels. Playground-Raising Project, Phila., 2001—02; participant reciprocal youth project Am. Friends Svc. Com., San Juan, PR, 1974—75; writer, editor Comty. Newspaper, Phila., 1978—81. Mem.: Am. Med. Writers Assn., Nat. Assn. Sci. Writers. Democrat. Avocations: astronomy, music. Office: Children's Hosp Phila 34th & Civic Center Blvd Philadelphia PA 19104 Business E-Mail: ascenzi@email.chop.edu.

ASCH, ARTHUR LOUIS, investment company executive; b. N.Y.C., July 4, 1941; s. Alexander and Esther W. A.; m. Anita S.; children: Michael, Lisa. BS in Econ., U. Pa., 1963. Fin. analyst Schlumberger Ltd., N.Y.C., 1966-68, Colt Industries Inc., N.Y.C., 1968-69; chmn. bd. Rexx Environ. Corp (previously Oak Hill Sportswear Corp.), N.Y.C., 1969-2000; presl Anniston Affiliates, Inc., N.Y.C., 2000—. Bd. dirs. Nassau County chpt. Assn. for Help Retarded Children, Brookville, N.Y., 1987—. Office: Anniston Affiliates Inc 445 Park Ave 6th Fl New York NY 10022-2606

ASCHAUER, CHARLES JOSEPH, JR., corporate director, former company executive; b. Decatur, Ill., July 23, 1928; s. Charles Joseph and Beulah Diehl (Kniple) A.; m. Elizabeth Claire Meagher, Apr. 28, 1962; children: Karen A. Vorwald, Thomas Arthur, Susan A. Baisley, Karl Andrew. BBA, Northwestern U., 1950; certificate internat. bus. adminstr., Centre d'Etudes Industrielles, Geneva, Switzerland, 1951. Prin. McKinsey & Co., Chgo., 1955-62; v.p. mktg. Mead Johnson Labs. div. Mead Johnson & Co., Evansville, Ind., 1962-67; v.p., pres. automotive group Maremont Corp., Chgo., 1967-70; v.p., group exec. Whittaker Corp., Los Angeles, 1970-71; v.p., pres. hosp. products div. Abbott Labs., North Chicago, Ill., 1971-76, v.p., group exec., 1976-79, exec. v.p., dir., 1979-89, ret., 1989. Bd. dirs. Solar Comm., Naperville, Ill. Lt. Supply Corps, USNR, 1951-55. Mem.: Shadow Wood Country Club, Sunset Ridge Country Club, Econs. Club Chgo., Univ. Club Chgo.

ASCHBACHER, JAMES CARL, artist, consultant; b. Evanston, Ill., Oct. 9, 1951; s. Frederick Edward and Helen Jane A.; m. Lisa Jensen, Sept. 17, 1978. Grad. h.s., Winnetka, Ill., 1969. Founder Artist for Books, Santa Cruz, Calif., 1993; co-founder SoHo Beach Art Group, Santa Cruz, 1993-94; chmn. art com. Chaminade Conf. Ctr., Santa Cruz, 1993-94, mem. open studios com. Santa Cruz Cultural Coun., 1995—. Executed mural Santa Cruz, 1998, 2001; poster art Nat. Libr. Week, 1999, Nat. Dance Week, 2000; art donor wall Freedom Libr., Calif., 2000, Hestwood County Park, Santa Cruz, Calif., 2002, Highlands County Park, Ben Lomond, Calif., 2002. Home and Office: 1345 Dougmar Dr Santa Cruz CA 95062 E-mail: james@aschbacherart.com.

ASCHER, BERNARD, economist; b. Bklyn., Dec. 7, 1933; s. Nelson Nathan and Ida (Buchwald) A.; m. Elinor Hirsch, Aug. 12, 1956; children: Scott, Ruth, Mark. BA in Econs., Bklyn. Coll., 1956; MBA in Internat. Trade, CUNY, 1962. Asst. traffic mgr. Aero-Sea Shipping Corp., N.Y.C., 1950-57; mem. export traffic staff Continental Grain Co., N.Y.C., 1959-60; asst. export mgr. Jack Liss & Sons Co., N.Y.C., 1960-62; commodity analyst U.S. Tariff Commn., Washington, 1962-65; sr. economist import policy staff U.S. Dept. Commerce, Washington, 1965-70, dir. legis. and tariff analysis, 1970-71, dir. indsl. products div., 1971-76, dir. Office Import Programs, 1976-78; dir. sectoral trade monitoring div. Office Internat. Sectoral Policy, Washington, 1978-81; dir. svc. industry affairs Office U.S. Trade Rep., Washington, 1981—. Instr. econs. U. Balt., 1966-70, Dept. Agr. Grad. Sch., Washington, 1985-86; adj. prof. George Mason U., 2000—. Contbr. articles to profl. jours. Active Forest Knolls Boys Club, Silver Spring, 1966-77; pres. Forest Knolls Pool, Silver Spring, 1971. Mem. Am. Econ. Assn., Beta Gamma Sigma. Home: 811 Caddington Ave Silver Spring MD 20901-1108

ASCHER, JAMES JOHN, pharmaceutical executive; b. Kansas City, Mo., Oct. 2, 1928; s. Bordner Fredrick and Helen (Barron) A.; m. Mary Ellen Robitsch, Feb. 27, 1954; children: Jill Denise, James John, Christopher Bordner Student, Bergen Jr. Coll., 1947-48, U. Kans., 1946-47, 49-51. Rep. B.F. Ascher & Co., Inc., Memphis, 1954-55, asst. to pres. Kansas City, Mo., 1956-57, v.p., 1958-64, pres., 1965—2001, chmn. bd., 2001—. Bd. dirs. Childrens Cardiac Ctr., 1964-70, pres., 1968-70; mem. cen. governing bd. Children's Mercy Hosp., 1968-80; bd. dirs. Jr. Achievement of Middle Am., 1970-90, pres., 1973-76, chmn., 1979-81; edn. chmn. Young Pres.'s Orgn. 6th Internat. Univ. for Pres., Athens, 1975. 1st. lt. inf., U.S. Army, 1951-53, Korea Decorated Bronze Star, Combat Infantryman's Badge Mem.: VFW, Consumer Health Care Products Assn., Am. Mgmt. Assn. (pres.'s assn.), Chief Execs. Orgn., World Pres.'s Orgn., Lenexa City C. of C., Indian Hills Country Club, Kansas City Club, Lotos Club, N.Y. Athletic Club, Mercury Club, Delta Chi. Home: 6706 Glenwood St Shawnee Mission KS 66204-1451 Office: 15501 W 109th St Lenexa KS 66219-1307

ASCHER, MARK LOUIS, legal educator; b. Junction City, Kans., Sept. 23, 1953; s. Martin Louis and Bertha May (Clark) A.; m. Kerry Elizabeth Muldowney, Feb. 6, 1982. BA, Marquette U., 1975; MA, Kans. State U., 1977; JD, Harvard U., 1978; LLM in Taxation, NYU, 1981. Bar: N.Y. 1979, Fla. 1980, Ariz. 1982. Assoc. White & Case, N.Y.C., 1978-82; assoc. prof. U. Ariz., Tucson, 1982-86, prof., 1986-2000; Sylvan Lang Prof. in Law of Trusts U. Tex., Austin, 2000—. Vis. prof. U. Tex., Austin, 1986, NYU, 1988, U. Colo., Boulder, 1989, Cornell U., 1990, U. Miami, 1995, U. Mo., 1997, U. San Diego, 1999. Author: Federal Income Taxation of Trusts and Estates, 1988, 2d edit., 1996; co-author: (with Ferguson and Freeland) Federal Income Taxation of Estates, Trusts and Beneficiaries, 2d edit., 1993, 3d edit., 1998, (with Clark, Lusky, Murphy and McCouch) Gratuitous Transfers, 4th edit., 1999; editor: Scott on Trusts, 1992—; contbr. articles to profl. jours. Served with USAF, 1971-73. Fellow Am. Coll. Trust and Estate Counsel (acad.); mem. Am. Law Inst. (adviser Restatement (3d) of Trusts). Office: U Tex Sch Law 727 E Dean Keeton St Austin TX 78705-3224 E-mail: mascher@mail.law.utexas.edu.

ASCHER, NANCY LOUISE, surgeon; b. Detroit, Mar. 15, 1949; d. Meyer S. and Beckie (Berger) A.; m. John. P. Roberts, Dec. 10, 1992; children: Becky, John. AB, U. Mich., 1970, MD, 1974; PhD, U. Minn., 1985. Instr. surgery U. Minn., Mpls., 1982-85, staff surgeon, dir. liver transplant, 1982-87, assoc. prof., 1987; prof. surgery U. Calif., San Francisco, 1988—, chief transplant svc., 1989—, prof., vice chmn., 1993—99, chmn., dept. surg., 1999—. Presenter in field. Contbr. articles to profl. jours. Schering scholar, 1979; recipient Koret Israel prize, 1993. Fellow Am. Coll. Surgeons (surg. forum com.); mem. AMA, AAAS, Am. Assn. Immunologists, Am. Soc. Transplant Surgeons (publs. and programs com., edn. com., chair edn. com., councilor-at-large, sec., pres 2001-2002), Am. Surg. Assn., Calif. Med. Assn., Minn. Surg. Soc. (scholar 1982), Mpls. Surg. Soc., San Francisco Med. Soc., Internat. Transplantation Soc. (sec. local orgn. com.), Soc. U. Surgeons, Soc. Clin. Surgery, Surg. Biology Club, Acad. Medicine Task Force, Pacific Coast Surg. Soc., Live Transplant Soc., Inst. Medicine, Phi Beta Kappa, Phi Kappa Phi, others. Office: U Calif Box 0780 505 Parnassus Ave San Francisco CA 94122-2722

ASCHER, RICHARD ALAN, lawyer; b. June 3, 1945; s. Richard Oscar and Bernice (Spiegel) Ascher; m. Barbara Haberman, May 22, 1967; children: Jonathan Colin, Andrew David. BA, SUNY, Buffalo, 1967, JD, 1970. Bar: Calif. 1991. Staff atty. Legal Aid Soc., Queens, NY, 1970—73; ptnr. Ascher & Goldstein, Queens, 1973—83, Ascher & Novitt, Queens, 1983—90. Counsel Assemblyman L. Stavisky, Albany, NY, 1974—75, Assemblyman I. Lafayette, Albany, 1976—90. Counsel, bd. dir. Jackson Heights Cmty. Devel. Corp., Queens, NY, 1980—82; pres. Queens Ind. Democrats, 1976; mem. lawyers com. Hart Presdl. Campaign, 1984; chmn. Com. to Make Watergate Perfectly Clear, Queens, 1973—74. Mem.: Criminal Cts. Bar Assn., Queens County Bar Assn., JFK Dem. Club (Jackson Heights chpt.) (exec. bd. 1987). Jewish.

ASCHER, ROBERT, anthropologist, educator, archaeologist, educator, film producer; b. N.Y.C., Apr. 28, 1931; s. Alfred and Claire (Eliscue) A.; m. Marcia Alper, Mar. 10, 1956 PhD, UCLA, 1960. Prof. Grad. Sch. Dept. Theatre, Film and Dance Cornell U., Ithaca, NY, 1960—2003, prof. emeritus, 2003—. Fieldwork in Turkey, Mex., Eng., Peru, U.S., Israel, 1960—. Co-author: Mathematics of the Incas, 1997; contbr. articles to Anthropology and Humanism Quar., Sci., History of Sci., Visual Anthropology, other profl. jours.; filmmaker: Cycle: An Australian Myth, 1984-86, Bar Yohai: In Celebration of a Visionary, 1987-88, Blue: A Tlingit Odyssey, 1989-91, The Golem, 1992-95. Office: Cornell Univ Dept Anthropology 726 University Ave Ithaca NY 14850-3914 E-mail: ra27@cornell.edu.

ASCHERMAN, JEFFREY ALAN, plastic and reconstructive surgeon; b. Erie, Pa., Mar. 19, 1962; s. Herbert Stanley and Dorothy Rose A.; m. Corinne Fortunee Rouah, June 9, 1988; children: Jeremy, Benjamin, Jonathan, Sarah. Student, Am. U. Paris, 1983; BA, Harvard U., 1984; MD, Columbia U., 1988. Diplomate Am. Bd. Plastic Surgery. Resident in gen. surgery Columbia-Presbyn. Med. Ctr., N.Y.C., 1988-91, rsch. fellow, 1991-92, resident in plastic surgery, 1992-94; fellow in craniofacial and pediat. plastic surgery Hôpital Necker-Enfants Malades, Paris, 1994-95; instr. clin. surgery Columbia U., N.Y.C., 1995-97, asst. prof. surgery, 1998—. Assoc. adj. N.Y. Eye and Ear Infirmary, N.Y.C., 1995-2001, adj. surg., 2001—; asst. attending physician N.Y. Presbyn. Hosp., N.Y.C., 1995—; adj. asst. prof. surgery Cornell Univ., 2002—. Patentee palatal distractor; contbr. articles to profl. jours. Active local synagogues Kehilath Jeshurun, N.Y.C., 1996—. Palatal Distraction Rsch. grantee Columbia U., 1996, Plastic Surgery Edn. Found., 1997; Cranial Ossification Rsch. grantee Columbia U., 1997; Retention Suture Rsch. grantee Columbia U., 1998; Hydroxyapatite Resin Rsch. grantee Columbia U., 1999; Cranial bone rsch. grantee, 2000, Cranial Reossification Rsch. grantee, 2001, Wound Healing Rsch. grantee, 2002. Mem. AMA, ACS, Am. Soc. Plastic and Reconstructive Surgeons, Am. Cleft Palate-Craniofacial Assn., Am. Soc. for Aesthetic Plastic Surgery, Am. Soc. Peripheral Nerve, Med. Soc. State N.Y., N.Y. County Med. Soc., N.Y. Regional Soc. Plastic and Reconstructive Surgery, Plastic Surgery Rsch. Coun., No. Soc. Plastic Surgeons, Alpha Omega Alpha. Republican. Avocations: downhill skiing, tennis, travelling. Office: Columbia-Presbyn Med Ctr 161 Fort Washington Ave New York NY 10032-3713 E-mail: jaa7@columbia.edu.

ASCHHEIM, EVE MICHELE, artist, educator; b. NYC, Aug. 30, 1958; d. Emil and Lydie Aschheim. BA, U. Calif., Berkeley, 1983; MFA, U. Calif., Davis, 1987. Asst. prof. Occidental Coll., L.A., 1990, Sarah Lawrence Coll., Bronxville, N.Y., 1994-97. Vis. critic Md. Inst. Coll. Art, Balt., 1998-2000; lectr. Princeton (N.J.) U., 1991, 93, 98, 2000, sr. lectr., 2001—, dir. visual arts program, 2003—. One-woman shows include Stefan Stux Gallery, 1997, Galerie Rainer Borgemeister, Berlin, 1999, 2001, Galleri Magnus Åklundh, Lund, Sweden, 1999, Galerie Benden and Klimczak, Cologne, Germany, 1999, U. Mass. Gallery, Amherst, 2003; group exhbns. include Sackler Mus., Cambridge, Mass., 1997, Kunstmuseum Winterthur, Switzerland, 1998, Akademie der Künste, Berlin, 1998, Fonds régional d'art contemporain de Picardie and Museé de Picardie Amiens, 1997, Parrish Mus., L.I., N.Y., 1999, Stark Gallery, N.Y.C., 1999, U. Calif., San Diego, 1999, Landesgalerie Oberosterreich, Linz, Austria, 1999, Pratt Gallery, N.Y.C., 1999, So. Meth. U., 2000, N.Y. Studio Sch., 2000, Hunter Coll. Leubsdorf Gallery, N.Y.C., 2000, Maier Mus., Lynchburg, Va., 2000, Tucson Art Mus., 2000, Mus. Contemporary Art, Miami, 2001, D.A.A.D. Galerie, Berlin, U. Art Mus. Calif. State U., Long Beach, 2001, Colby Coll., 2002, N.Y. Hist. Soc., 2002, O.S.P. Gallery, Boston, 2002, Black and White Gallery, Bklyn., 2003, U. Mass., Amherst, 2003; represented in permanent collections at Fogg Mus., Nat. Gallery, Washington, N.Y. Hist. Soc., Hamburger Bahnhof, Berlin, M.O.C.A., Miami; artist (catalog) Eve Aschheim Paintings and Drawings, 1999, Eve Aschheim Drawings, 2003. Recipient Rosenthal award AAAL, 1997; fellow NEA, 1989, Pollock-Krasner Found., 1990, 2001, NY Found. for Arts, 1991, 2001; grantee Elizabeth Found., 1997. Mem. Am. Abstract Artists. E-mail: easchh@aol.com.

ASCHHEIM, JOSEPH, economist, educator; b. Hanover, Germany, May 28, 1930; s. Max and Sarah (Pfeffer) A.; married; 1 child. AB with highest honors, U. Calif. at Berkeley, 1951; A.M. (Charles H. Smith scholar), Harvard U., 1953, PhD (Thayer scholar, Willard scholar), 1954. Mem. faculty Johns Hopkins U., 1956-63; mem. faculty George Washington U., Washington, 1963-2001, prof. emeritus, 2001. Dir. rsch., econ. advisor to gov. Ctrl. Bank Kenya, 1971-72; faculty advisor D.C. univs. consortium U.S. Naval Res. Officers Tng. Corps Unit, 1984-2001; affiliated scholar Ctr. for Study of Ctrl. Banks, NYU Sch. of Law, 1995—. Author books and numerous articles in profl. jours.; editorial bd. So. Econ. Jour, 1960-63, Atlantic Econ. Jour, 1973— . Served with AUS, 1954-56. Ford Found. Faculty Research fellow. Mem. Am. Econ. Assn., Atlantic Econ. Soc. (v.p. 1973-76), Royal Econ. Soc., Phi Beta Kappa. Jewish. Office: PO Box 3758 Washington DC 20027

ASCHKINASI, DAVID JAY, lawyer; b. N.Y.C. BA, Brandeis U., 1972; JD, U. Colo., 1976. Bar: Colo. 1976, U.S. Dist Ct. Colo. 1976, U.S. Ct. Appeals (10th cir.) 1982. Sole practice, Boulder, Colo., 1976-77; asst. atty. gen. State of Colo., Denver, 1977-83; pvt. practice Denver, 1983-84; div. counsel U.S. West Info. Systems, Denver, 1984-87; atty. U.S. West Comms., Denver, 1988—; corp. counsel Qwest Comms., Denver, 2000—. Mem. ABA, Colo. Bar Assn., Denver Bar Assn., Am. Corp. Counsel Assn. Office: Qwest Communications 1801 California St Ste 3800 Denver CO 80202-2610

ASCHOFF, LAWRENCE MICHAEL (MICK ASCHOFF), computer information scientist; b. N.Y.C., Feb. 14, 1950; s. Edward William and Marie Louise (Marshall) A. BA in Art History, U. Fla., 1971; MBA in Fin., NYU, 1984, advanced profl. cert. in computer applications and info. systems, 1988. Sales rep. VIP Fabrics, N.Y.C., 1978-81; asst. to v.p. mktg. RAM Data, N.Y.C., 1981-82; sales agt. Equitable Life Assurance Soc., N.Y.C., 1982; programmer/analyst Drexel Burnham Lambert, N.Y.C., 1984-86, sr. programmer/analyst, 1986-88, project leader, 1988-89, project mgr., asst. v.p., 1989-90; officer, project mgr. retail banking systems Manufacurer's Hanover Trust, N.Y.C., 1990-92; asst. v.p. retail banking Chem. Bank (merger with Mfr. Hanover Trust), N.Y.C., 1992-95; v.p. project mgmt. competency ctr. retail banking systems Nat. Consumer Svcs. Chase Manhattan Bank (merger with Chem.), N.Y.C., 1996-2000; dir. GITSSO Program Mgmt. Office AXA Global I.T. Org., N.Y.C., 2000—01; dir. program mgmt. office AXA Technology Svcs., 2002—. Treas. Saunders Owners of Queens, Ltd., 1989-91, 2002-, pres., 1991-2000. Clin. assoc. Suicide and Crisis Prevention Ctr., Gainesville, Fla., 1972; mem. pres.'s coun. U. Fla., 1992—. Mem. Mensa, Phi Beta Kappa (sec. L.I. Alumni Assn. 1985-87, pres. 1987-93), Alpha Lambda Delta. Democrat. Avocations: travel, fitness, history, amusement parks, arts & sciences. Office: AXA Technology Svcs 30 Rockefeller Plz Fl 20 New York NY 10112-2099

ASCOLESE, MICHAEL J. corporate communications executive; AB in English, St. Peter's Coll., Jersey City, N.J., 1968. Reporter Bayonne (N.J.) Times, 1968; gen. assignment and beat reporter Star Ledger, Newark, 1972-79, asst. city editor, 1979-81, bus. and fin. editor, 1981-83; press rep. AlliedSignal, Inc., Morris Twp., N.J., 1983-86, media rels. mgr., 1986-88, pub. rels. dir., 1988-92, corp. comm. dir., 1992-94; dir. pub. rels. Price Waterhouse, 1994-98; dir. comms. PricewaterhouseCoopers, N.Y.C., 1998—. Bd. dirs. Voluntary Action Ctr., 1987-91, Am. Diabetes Assn., N.J., 1988-90, Morris Ctr. YMCA, 1992-98. Vol. U.S. Peace Corps, 1968-72; mem. Internat. Assn. Bus. Communicators, N.Y. Fin. Writers Assn., Pub. Rels. Soc. Am., Office: Pricewaterhouse-Coopers 101 Hudson St Jersey City NJ 07302-3915 E-mail: mike.ascolese@us.pwcglobal.com.

ASCONE, TERESA PALMER, artist, educator; b. Cortland, N.Y., Nov. 1, 1945; d. Lawrence Henry and Bernice Rosella (Holcomb) Palmer; m. Michael Wayne Ascone, Oct. 15, 1965; 1 child, Michael Palmer. Student, Alaska Meth. U., Alaska Pacific U., U. Alaska. Painter/tchr. Alaska Pacific U., Anchorage, 1989-91, U. Alaska, 1992; pvt. tchr. watercolor Anchorage, 1992—; owner Alaskan Portfolio, 1981—; tchr. U. Alaska, Anchorage, 1992—, dir. Ultimate Watercolor Acad., 1998-2001. Juried shows include Alaska State Fair, 1979-80, Fur Rendezvous Juried Show, 1979, 80, All Alaska Juried Show, 1981, 84, 85, 90, Alaska Watercolor Soc. juried show, 1981, 83, 85, 86, 87, 88, 89, 90, 91, April in Paris juried exhibit at Capt. Cook Hotel, 1982, 83, 84, 87, Featured Artist, 1986, Watercolor Fairbanks, 1989, Women Artist of West 1st Ann. Internat. Show, 1990; one women shows include Anchorage Mcpl. Librs., 1980, 82, NBA Heritage Libr., 1986, Alaska Pacific U., 1989, Chitose City Hall, Chitose, Hokkaido, Japan, 1990; represented in permanent collection Alaska Pacific U., Raymond P. Atwood Collection, Lincoln, Nebr.; cover artist Arctic Horizons Mag., 1986, Alaska Horizons Mag., 1986, U. Alaska Anchorage Summer Sessions Catalog, 1997; subject of TV spl., 1988; developer, patentee original design, manufacture & mktg. The Ultimate Palette, 1993; author: We're All Artists: Watercolor for Everyone, 1994; Painting Pleasure: Adventures in Watercolor, 1999; editor, publisher Hot Press Mag., 1994; illustrator: Things in the Sky, 1995; contbr. articles to profl. publs. Mcpl. commr. Anchorage Sister Cities Commn., 1991-93. Recipient Vol. of Yr. Caverly Sr. Ctr., 1986, various art show awards to date; works chosen as ofcl. gifts to cities of Inchon, Korea and Magadan, Russia and Whitby, Eng. from city of Anchorage. Mem. Alaska Watercolor Soc. (v.p. 1983),Athena Soc. Avocations: writing, reading, skating, dancing.

ASENSI, GUSTAVO, advertising executive, filmmaker; b. Vitoria, Spain; came to the U.S., 1992; s. Gustavo Asensi. Student, Sch. Dramatic Arts, Madrid, 1983, Sch. Cinematography, 1983. Copywriter Delvico Bates, Madrid, 1985-86, J. Walter Thompson, Madrid, 1986-87; creative dir. HDM, Madrid, 1987-89; exec. creative dir., v.p. Publinsa, Madrid, 1989-92; sr. v.p., exec. creative dir. Font & Vaamonde Advt., N.Y.C., 1993-94, mng. ptnr., CCO, 1994—. Recipient Bronze medal Festival San Sebastian, 1990, Silver medal, 1991, Gold medal Houston Internat. Film Festival, 1995, 96, Bronze medal, 1995, Gold medal Charleston Internat. Film Festival, 1995, Grand award, 1995, Gold Clio award, 1995.

ASH, DOROTHY MATTHEWS, civic worker; b. Dresden, Germany, Nov. 10, 1918; came to U.S., 1924; d. Kurt Horst and Ana Matthesius; m. Harry A. Ash, Apr. 13, 1941 (dec. June 1981); children: Fredrick Curtis, Dorothea Ash Linklater. Dancer, 1933-40; treas. Inheritance Abstractors Inc., Chgo., 1949-70; reporter Miami (Fla.) Sun Post, 1983; reporter, columnist Social Mag., Miami, 1984—. Chmn. Miss Universe Pageant, 1983-85; cruise chmn. Miami U., 1984, mem. Pres.'s Club, 1983. Pres. Big Bros. and Big Sisters, 1982-83; founding mem. World Sch. of Arts, 1985—; founding Notable Douglas Gardens 1988; Pres.'s Club U. of Miami, 1989; founding and bd. mem. Cancer Link Rsch., 1990; mem. Bd. Animal Welfare; active Project: Newborn, Am. Cancer Soc., March of Dimes, chmn. quest for the best, 1988-92, winner celebrity gourmet gala, 1988, leading lady 1998; active Children's Resource, Erase Diabetes, founding and bd. mem. 1990, Cerebral Palsy Found., Theatre Arts League, Linda Ray Infant Ctr., Miami City Ballet, Am. Ballet; bd. dirs. Greater Miami Opera, 1975—, Leading Ladies, Inc. 1997; pub. rels. vol. Miami Heart Inst., 1988—; com. mem. Miami Beach (Fla.) Beautification Program, 1984; mem. bd. Miami Mayor's Ad Hoc Com., 1984; mem. com. Challenger Seven Meml., 1988; active Cousteau Soc.; numerous others. Named Woman of Yr., Big Bros. and Big Sisters, Miami, 1981, Best Dressed, Am. Cancer Soc., 1981, Outstanding Humanitarian and Civic Leader, Mayor City of Miami, 1985, Woman of the Yr., Project: New Born, 1985, Miss Charity, Biscayne Bay Hosp., 1986, Queen of Hearts, Miami Children's Hosp., 1988, Leading Lady, March of Dimes, 1998; recipient Shining Star award Bon Secours Hosp., 1993, Patron Recognition award Mia Heart Rsch. Inst., 1993, Goddess of Love award Villa Maria Hosp., 1995, Shining Angel, 2000, Star of the Century award Miami Heart Rsch. Inst., 2000, Miracle Maker award Big Bros./Big Sisters, 2001, Salute to Dorothy Ash, Mia Heart Inst., 2002. Mem. Miami Internat. Press Club. Avocations: reading, writing, painting. Home: 10245 Collins Ave Bal Harbour FL 33154-1407 Home (Summer): 330 W Diversey Pky Apt 2209 Chicago IL 60657-6231

ASH, FAYOLA FOLTZ, musician, music educator; b. Lansing, Mich., Feb. 24, 1926; d. Leroy Stewart and Emily (Proctor) Foltz; m. Major McKinley Ash Jr., Sept. 2, 1947; children: George McKinley, Carolyn Marguerite, Thomas Edward, Jeffrey Leroy. Student, Shorter Coll., 1947-48; MusB magna cum laude, Mich. State U., 1948, grad. studies, 1950; MA in Organ Performance, Ea. Mich. U., 1985; pvt. piano studies with Helen Roberts Sholl and Maurice Dumesnil, pvt. organ studies with Helen Roberts Sholl, Charles Sheldon, Hans Vollenweider, Mary Ida Yost. Ind. keyboard soloist and accompanist various artists, Mich., Ga., Ariz., and Switzerland, 1936—; pvt. tchr. piano, Mich., Ga., 1938-96; tchr. Atlanta Pub. Schs., 1949-51; pvt. tchr. organ Ann Arbor and Chelsea, Mich., 1983-2000. Organist various chs., Mich. and Ga., 1945-82, 1st United Meth. Ch., Chelsea, Mich., 1982-95, Mich. and Ariz., 1995—; jr. choir dir. Westminster Presbyn. Ch., Ann Arbor, Mich., 1964-72; adult choir dir., various churches, 1967-97, docent to pub. schs. Phoenix Symphony Aux., 1996—; lectr. hymnology, Mich., Ariz., 1995—; preforming mem. Audrey's Angels, Ariz., 2002--. Recipient Grace Sponberg scholar Ea. Mich. Univ., 1985. Mem.: Phoenix Symphony Aux. (pub. sch. docent 1996—, bd. dirs. 1999—2001), Music Tchrs. Nat. Assn. (cert.), Mich. Music Tchrs. Assn. (cert.), Am. Guild Organists (chmn. nat. conv. com. 1982, sub dean Ann Arbor chpt. 1985—86, joint mem. Ann Arbor and Phoenix chpts. 1999—), Ann Arbor Area Piano Tchrs. Guild (hon.; pres. 1971—73, lectr. 1975—96, tchr.), Phi Kappa Phi, Tau Sigma, Mu Phi Epsilon (treas. Ann Arbor chpt. 1989—92, co-pres. Ann Arbor chpt. 1992—94, officer Phoenix chpt. 1999—2001, joint mem. Ann Arbor and Phoenix chpts.). Avocation: bird watching. : 6621 E Kelton Ln Scottsdale AZ 85254 E-mail: mmash@umich.edu.

ASH, FREDERICK MELVIN, retired manufacturing company executive; b. Columbus, Ohio, June 15, 1941; s. Melvin Edward and Ida Belle (Berry) A.; m. Karen Persichetti, Apr. 7, 1979; children: Jason, Carrie. Student, U. Cin., 1959-61; BS, BA, Ohio State U., 1963; MBA in Mgmt., Rutgers U., 1982. Staff acct. chem. plastics divsn. Gen. Tire & Rubber Co., Akron, Ohio, 1963-65; office mgr., 1965-67; acctg. mgr., 1968; controller Newcomerstown, Ohio, 1968-70; Lawrence, 1971-73; plant mgr., 1974-76; v.p. film, 1977; pres. Gen Tire & Rubber Plastic Film Co., Jeannette, 1977-78; bus. dir. plastics Tenneco Chems., Inc., Piscataway, 1978-80; gen. mgr. plastics, 1980-82; v.p., gen. mgr. plastics Nuodex, Inc., Edison, N.J., 1982-84; v.p. mkgt. and sales Am. Maize Products, 1985-89; v.p. ops., 1990-92; pres. ingredients divsn., 1993-95; pres., comml. dir. Cerestar USA, Inc., 1995-99. Bd. dirs. Oceanboy Farms, Inc., 2002—. Adv. Jr. Achievement, Akron, 1965; mem. budget com. Merrimack Valley United Fund, Lawrence, 1973-74, budget com. chmn., 1975, campaign chmn., 1976, dir., 1975-76; bd. dirs. Tradewinds Rehab Ctr., Lakeshore Devel. Coun., United Way of Westmoreland County, 1977-78, Lake Area United Way, NW Ind. Fourm, Olympia Fields/Flossmoor United Way, 1985, pres., 1986-87. U.S. Rubber scholar, 1961-63; recipient Pace Setter award Ohio State U., 1963. Mem. Nat. Assn. Accts., Soc. Plastics Industry (vice chmn. film gorup), Ind. Mfrs. Assn. (mem. bd. dirs.), Corn Refiners Assn. (bd. dirs.), Westmoreland County C. of C., Ohio State U. Alumni Assn., Rutgers U. Alumni Assn., Village 2 Homeowners Assn. (v.p.), Sea Chase Condominium Assn. (bd. dirs.), Masons, Scottish Rite, Sigma Chi, Beta Gamma Sigma. Republican. Home: 95136 Captains Way Amelia Island FL 32034-4386

ASH, HIRAM NEWTON, graphic designer; b. Paterson, N.J., Dec. 9, 1934; s. Newton Briton Todd and Ellen Sproule (Bowman) A.; m. Marilyn Ruth Robinson, 1957 (div. 1972); children: Erica Robinson, Jennifer Hamilton; m. Susan Main Humes. Student, Hobart Coll., 1952-56, Columbia U., 1956-58; BFA Sch. Art & Architecture, Yale U., 1960. Graphic designer Styling div. GM Tech. Ctr., Warren, Mich., 1959; art dir. N.W. Ayer & Sons, Phila., 1960-61; graphic designer George Nelson & Co., N.Y.C., 1961-62; ptnr. Ash/Reller Assocs., N.Y.C., 1962-63; pres. Hiram Ash, Inc., N.Y.C., 1963-70; prin. Hiram Ash, Colebrook, Conn., 1970—; founder, proprietor private press Ice Island Press, Colebrook, Conn., 1993—. Asst. in instrn. Sch. Art and Arch., Yale U., New Haven, Conn., 1959-60; adj. instr. graphic design Cooper Union, N.Y.C., 1965-67; designer TriVers Exhbn. Systems, 1964; designer numerous album covers Caedmon Records, N.Y.C., 1960s; designer theatre posters Rugoff Theatres, N.Y.C., 1960s; designer set and program graphics Pub. Broadcast Lab. of NET, Ford Found., 1966-67; designer signature trademark and graphics implementation Am. Shakespeare Theatre, Stratford, Conn., 1980; mktg. and product devel. cons. Indian jewelry Zuni Community Action Program, Zuni Pueblo, N.Mex., 1967-68. Designer numerous books; work presented in Graphis Anns., Indsl. Design, Trademarks & Symbols of the World, Trade Marks U.S.A. Chmn. Colebrook Town Hall/Fire House Bldg. com., 1988-91. Recipient Design and Printing for Commerce and 50 Books of Yr. awards Am. Inst. Graphic Arts, N.J. Art Dirs. Club awards. Mem. Fine Press Book Assn., Am. Printing History Assn., Printing Hist. Soc., Letterpress Guild of New England, Typophiles, Colebrook Hist. Soc. (pres. 1987-90, bd. dirs. 1993-96), Colebrook Land Conservancy, Inc. (trustee 1991—), Conn. Trust for Hist. Preservation, Millbrook Music Assembly, Sandanona Harehounds, Book Club Calif. Republican. Episcopalian. Avocations: antiquarian and private press book dealer, photography, beagling. Address: PO Box 309 61 Church Hill Rd Colebrook CT 06021-1007

ASH, J. MARSHALL, mathematician, educator; b. N.Y.C., Feb. 18, 1940; s. Barney and Rosalyn (Hain) A.; m. Alison Igo, Nov. 24, 1977; children: Michael A., Garrett A., Andrew A. SB, U. Chgo., 1961, SM, 1963, PhD, 1966. Joseph Fels Ritt instr. Columbia U., N.Y.C., 1966-69; asst. prof. math. DePaul U., Chgo., 1970-72, assoc. prof., 1972-74, prof., 1975—. Vis. prof. Stanford U., 1977. Author: Studies in Harmonic Analysis, 1976; contbr. articles to profl. jours. George Westinghouse fellow, 1961, NSF fellow, 1962-66. Mem. AAUP, Am. Math. Soc., Math. Assn. Am., Sigma Xi. Home: 662 Maple St Winnetka IL 60093-2312 Office: De Paul U Math Dept Chicago IL 60614 E-mail: mash@math.depaul.edu.

ASH, LAWRENCE ROBERT, public health educator, administrator; b. Holyoke, Mass., Mar. 5, 1933; s. Lawrence Clifton and Alice (Sartini) A.; m. Luana Lee Smith, Aug. 4 1960; 1 child, Leigh I. BS in Zoology, U. Mass., 1954, MA in Zoology, 1956; PhD in Parasitology, Tulane U., 1960. Asst. parasitologist U. Hawaii, Honolulu, 1960-61; instr. Tulane U., New Orleans, 1961-65; med. parasitologist South Pacific Commn., Noumea, New Caledonia, 1965-67; asst. prof. pub. health UCLA Sch. Pub. Health, 1967-71, assoc. prof., 1971-75, prof., 1975-94, chmn. dept., assoc. dean, 1979-84, prof. emeritus, 1994—. Panelist U.S. Panel on Parasitic Diseases, U.S.-Japan Program, Washington, 1972-78, chmn., 1978-84; cons. Naval Med. Rsch. Unit # 2 Taipei, China, Manila, 1970-80. Sr. author: Atlas of Human Parasitology, 1980, 4th rev. edit., 1997, Parasites: A Guide to Laboratory Procedures and Identification, 1987; co-author: Parasites in Human Tissues, 1995. NIH grantee, 1970-84. Fellow Royal Soc. Tropical Medicine and Hygiene; mem. Am. Soc. Tropical Medicine and Hygiene (councilor 1974-77), Am. Soc. Parasitologists (councilor 1972-75, 88-92, v.p. 1982-83). Home: 10400 Northvale Rd Los Angeles CA 90064-4332 Office: UCLA Sch Pub Health Los Angeles CA 90095-0001 E-mail: larryash@ucla.edu.

ASH, MAJOR MCKINLEY, JR., dentist, educator; b. Bellaire, Mich., Apr. 7, 1921; s. Major McKinley Sr. and Helen Marguerite (Early) A.; m. Fayola Foltz, Sept. 2, 1947; children: George McKinley, Carolyn Marguerite, Jeffrey LeRoy, Thomas Edward. BS, Mich. State U., 1947; DDS, Emory U., 1951; MS, U. Mich., 1954; Doctoris Medicine Honoris Causa, U. Bern, 1975. Instr. sch. dentistry Emory U., Atlanta, 1952-53; instr. U. Mich., Ann Arbor, 1953-56, asst. prof., 1956-59, assoc. prof., 1959-62, prof., 1962—, chmn. dept. occlusion, sch. dentistry, 1962-89, dir. stomatognathic physiology lab., sch. dentistry, 1969-89, dir. TMJ/oral facial pain clinic, sch. dentistry, 1983-89, Marcus L. Ward prof. dentistry, 1984-89, prof. emeritus, rsch. scientist emeritus, 1989—; cons. N.E. Regional Dental Bd., 1988-92. Vis. prof. U. Bern, 1989, U. Tex., San Antonio, 1990-98; pres. Basic Sci. Bd., State of Mich., 1962-74; cons. over the counter drugs FDA, Washington, 1985-89. Author, co-author 70 textbooks, 1958—; editor 4 books; contbr. over 190 articles to profl. jours. Served to tech. sgt. Signal Corps, U.S. Army, 1942-45, ETO. Grantee, Nat. Inst. Dental Rsch., 1962—85. Fellow Am. Coll. Dentists, Internat. Coll. Dentists, European Soc. Craniomandibular Disorders, European Soc. Oral Physiology; mem. AAAS, Am. Dental Assn. (cons. coun. on dental therapeutics 1982—, cons. coun. sci. affairs 1993—), N.Y. Acad. Scis., Washtenaw Dist. Dental Soc. (pres. 1963-64), Phi Kappa Phi. Presbyterian. Avocations: photography, birdwatching. Office: U of Mich Sch of Dentistry Ann Arbor MI 48109 E-mail: mmash@umich.edu.

ASH, ROY LAWRENCE, business executive; b. Los Angeles, Oct. 20, 1918; s. Charles K. and Fay E. (Dickinson) A.; m. Lila M. Hornbek., Nov. 13, 1943; children— Loretta Ash Danko, James, Marilyn Ash Hanna, Robert, Charles. MBA, Harvard, 1947. Chief fin. officer Hughes Aircraft Co., 1949-53; co-founder Litton Industries, Inc., Beverly Hills, Calif., 1953-72, dir., 1953-72, pres., 1961-72; chmn. Pres.'s Adv. Coun. on Exec. Orgn., 1969-71; asst. to Pres. U.S.; dir. Office Mgmt. and Budget, Washington, 1973-75; chmn. bd., chief exec. officer AM Internat., 1976-81. Co-chmn. Japan-Calif. Assn., 1965-72, 80-81; mem. vis. com. Harvard U. Kennedy Sch. Govt., 1992—; mem. Bus. Roundtable, 1977-81. Vice chmn. Los Angeles Olympic Organizing Com., 1980-85, chmn. fin. com.; trustee Calif. Inst. Tech., 1967-72, Com. for Econ. Devel., 1970-72, 75— ; dir. Los Angeles World Affairs Council, 1968-72, 78—, pres., 1970-72; chmn. adv. council on gen. govt. Rep. Nat. Com., 1977-80; chmn. L.A. Music Ctr. Opera Assn., 1988-93. From pvt. to capt. Army Air Corps, 1942-46. Mem. C. of C. U.S. (bd. dirs. 1979-85, chmn. internat. policy com. 1979-85). Clubs: Bel Air Country, Harvard, California (Los Angeles). Office: Ste 1600 1900 Avenue Of The Stars Los Angeles CA 90067-4407

ASH, STEPHEN R. nephrologist; b. Kansas City, Mo., Sept. 22, 1945; s. Robert Morton and Dorothy Fife Ash; m. Marianne Yeager, Aug. 24, 1969; children: Emily Louise Morin, Sarah Elizabeth. BS in Physics, Northwestern U., 1967; MD, U. Kans., 1971. Nephrologist Arnett Clinic, Lafayette, Ind., 1975—; dir. dialysis Greater Lafayette Health Sys., Lafayette, 1975—. Chmn., dir. R&D HemoCleanse, Inc. and Ash Med. Sys., Inc., Lafayette, 1983—; dir. R&D Renal Solutions, Inc., Pitts., 2000—; adj. assoc. prof. Purdue U., West Lafayette, Ind., 1980—. Contbr. chapters to books, articles to profl. jours.; numerous patents in field. Fellow: ACP; mem.: Am. Soc. Diagnostic and Interventional Nephrology (pres., editor-in-chief), Am. Soc. Artificial Internal Organs (program chmn.). Office: HemoCleanse Inc 3601 Sagamore Pky North Lafayette IN 47904 Office Fax: 765-742-4823. E-mail: sash@hemocleanse.com.

ASH, THOMAS PHILLIP, superintendent of schools; b. East Liverpool, Ohio, June 4, 1949; s. Bobby and Elizabeth Ann (Ludwig) A.; m. Nancy Elizabeth Gauron, June 8, 1951; children: Megan Elizabeth, John Gauron. BS in Edn., Bowling Green (Ohio) State U., 1971; MS in Edn., Youngstown (Ohio) State U., 1974. Tchr. East Liverpool City Schs., 1971-73, project coord., 1973-78, asst. supt., 1978-84, supt., 1984-99, Mid-Ohio Ednl. Svc. Ctr., 2000—. Bd. dirs. Ctrl. Fed. Savs. & Loan, Columbiana County Mental Health Assn.; chmn. Lincoln Way Spl. Edn. Resource Ctr., 1988-89, 93-94; treas. Richland County Youth and Family Coun., 2000—. Mem. exec. coun. Columbiana County Boy Scouts Am., 1989-91, Morrow County Workforce Investment Bd., 2000—; pres. East Liverpool Area United Way, 1990-92; mem. State Supt. Adv. Commn. for Spl. Edn., 1993-95. Recipient Disting. Alumni award East Liverpool High Sch. Alumni Assn., 1987, Ohio Adminstr. of Yr. award Ohio Ednl. Libr. and Media Assn., 1990. Mem. Am. Assn. Sch. Adminstrs., Buckeye Assn. Sch. Adminstrs. (pres. 1999-2000), East Liverpool Area C. of C. (bd. dirs. 1985-2000, Outstanding Educator award 1982, Disting. Svc. award 1982). Office: Mid-Ohio Educational Svs Center 1495 W Longview Ave Ste 202 Mansfield OH 44906

ASH, WILLIAM JAMES, geneticist, educator; b. Nov. 3, 1931; s. William and Anna Marie (Ruegg) A.; m. Gertrude Louise Kehm, June 15, 1953 (dec. June, 6, 2001); children: Annalee M., Barbara A. (dec.), William J., Jr., James J., Lydia A. BS, Cornell U., 1953, MS, 1958, PhD, 1960. Grad. rsch. asst. Cornell U., Ithaca, N.Y., 1955-59, rsch. geneticist, 1959-64; dir. rsch. Crescent Corp., Aquebogue, N.Y., 1964-65; asst. prof. W.Va. U., Morgantown, 1965-66; prof. St. Lawrence U., Canton, N.Y., 1966-81, Kuwait U., Arabian Gulf, 1976-78; program officer NSF, Washington, 1979-81; mem. sr. staff U.S.-Saudi Joint Commn., Riyadh, Saudi Arabia, 1982-83; pres. Adv. Assocs. Internat., Westhampton, N.Y., 1981-94; prof. SUNY, Stony Brook, 1985-91, prof. emeritus, 1991—. Contbr. articles to profl. jours. Comdr. Peconic Bay Power Squadron, Riverhead, N.Y., 1986-88; scoutmaster Boy Scouts Am., Canton, 1967-69; coach U.S. Amateur Ice Hockey Assn., Canton, 1970-75. Capt. U.S. Army, 1953-65. Recipient Travel award Cornell U., 1963, Travel award NSF, 1983; NSF grantee, 1970-72, 79-81. Fellow Am. Dermatoglyphics Assn.; mem. Cape Lookout Sail and Power Squadron Club, Alpenverein Club, Sigma Xi, Beta Beta Beta. Roman Catholic. Republican. Avocations: sailing, gardening, photography, travel, amateur radio, genealogy, celestial navigation. Home: 3507 Canterbury Rd New Bern NC 28562-7703 E-mail: bash@pamlico.net.

ASHANTI, BARON JAMES, poet, educator; b. N.Y.C., Sept. 5, 1950; s. Gladys Carroll Foxhall, David Lancaster Foxhall; life ptnr. Mary Beithe Chow, May 31, 1999; m. Brenda Cummings, Sept. 8, 1979; children: Marcus, Nova. Grad., Evander Childes H.S., Bronx, N.Y., 1964. Exec. asst. Marie Brown Assoc., N.Y.C., 1987—90; tchr., adminstr. Frederick Douglass Creative Arts Ctr., N.Y.C., 1988— 98; founder, pres. The Brilliance Factory, N.Y.C., 1990—. Tchr. Tchrs. & Writers Collaborative, N.Y.C., NY, 1995—. Author: Nubiana, vol. I, 1977, Nova, 1990, numerous poems (Killeen prize, 1982). Polit. organizer Afrikan Peoples Party, Phila., 1969—80. Sgt. USMC, 1967—71, Viet Nam. Grantee, Pen Writers, 1985. Mem.: Renaissance Writers Guild (co-founder), Black Writers Union (co-founder), Acad. Am. Poets. Avocations: archery, drawing, shaolin gung-fu, travel, photography. Home: 274 W 140th St New York NY 10030 Personal E-mail: briliancefactory@aol.com.

ASHBACH, DAVID LAURENCE, internist, nephrologist; b. Chgo., Nov. 17, 1942; s. Sol Henry and Lila Mae A.; AB, Knox Coll., 1964; MS, Case Western Reserve U., 1969, MD, 1970; Diplomate Am. Bd. Internal Medicine; m. Arlene Rosenthal Nov. 28, 1963; children: Barbara, Deborah, Robert. Intern, Presbyterian-St. Luke's Hosp., Chgo., 1970-71, resident, 1971-73, fellow in nephrology, 1973-75; practice medicine specializing in nephrology, Hammond, Ind., 1975—; pres. Nephrology Specialists P.C.; mem. staffs St. Margaret's Hosp., Hammond, Ind., Meth. Hosp., Gary, Ind., St. Anthony's Hosp., Crown Point, Ind.; asst. clin. prof. medicine Ind. U.; asst. prof. health sci. Purdue U; pres.- elect, 1995, bd. dirs; past pres. Meth. Hosp., Gary; pres. Nat. Kidney Found. Ind. affiliate, Comprehensive Renal Care Inc.; bd. dirs. Regional Organ Bd. Ill. Mem. Nat. Kidney Found. Ind., A.C.P., Am. Internat. Socs. Nephrology, Ind. Hosp. & Health Assn. (bd. dirs.), R.O.B.I. (bd. dirs.). Jewish. Home: 20457 Ithaca Rd Olympia Fields IL 60461-1341 Office: 222 Hohman Ave Hammond IN 46320-1965 also: 4802 Broadway Gary IN 46408-4509

ASHBAUGH, NANCY GOULD, writer, performing arts educator; b. Charlotte, N.Y., June 9, 1952; d. William Edward Gould and Daisy Artelli Hartley. Student, So. Oreg., 1972-74, Oreg. State U., 1975, U. Nev., 1976. Part-time instr. creative writing U. Nev.; dance instr. Author: (novels) Notorious among the People, 1978, Turn Left or Be Killed, 1980, Juno. 1987. (radio play series) Story of Bill Abrams, 1979, also short stories. Nat. Endowment Arts grantee. Home: 3667 Twain Cir Las Vegas NV 89121

ASHBERY, JOHN LAWRENCE, language educator, poet, playwright, art critic; b. Rochester, N.Y., July 28, 1927; s. Chester Frederick and Helen Ashbery. Grad., Deerfield Acad., 1945; BA, Harvard U., 1949; MA, Columbia U., 1951; postgrad., NYU, 1957—58; DLitt (hon.), Southampton Coll. of L.I.U., 1979, U. Rochester, Harvard U. Copywriter Oxford U. Press, N.Y.C., 1951—54, McGraw Hill Book Co., N.Y.C., 1954—55; art critic European edit. N.Y. Herald Tribune, Paris, 1960—65; Paris corr. Art News, 1964—65, exec. editor, 1965—72; prof. English Bklyn. Coll., 1974—90, Disting. prof., 1980—90, Disting. emeritus prof., 1990; Charles P. Stevenson Jr. prof. langs. and lit. Bard Coll., 1990—; editor quar. rev. Art and Lit., Paris, 1964—67; art critic Art Internat., Lugano, Switzerland, 1961—62; editor Locus Solus, Lans-en-Vercors, France, 1960-62; poetry editor Partisan Rev., 1976—80; art critic New York Mag., 1978—80, Newsweek, 1980—85; Charles Eliot Norton prof. poetry Harvard U., 1989—90; conducted spl. rsch. on life and work of Raymond Roussel. Author: Turandot and Other Poems, 1953, Some Trees, 1956, The Poems, 1960, The Tennis Court Oath, 1962, Rivers and Mountains, 1966, Selected Poems, 1967, Three Madrigals, 1968, Sunrise in Suburbia, 1968, Fragment, 1969, The Double Dream of Spring, 1970, The New Spirit, 1970, Three Poems, 1972, The Vermont Notebook, 1975, Self-Portrait in a Convex Mirror, 1975, Houseboat Days, 1977, As We Know, 1979, Shadow Train, 1981, A Wave, 1984, Selected Poems, 1985, April Galleons, 1987, Flow Chart, 1991, Hotel Lautréamont, 1992, And the Stars Were Shining, 1994, Can You Hear, Bird, 1995, Wakefulness, 1998, (plays) The Heroes, 1952, The Comprimise, 1955, The Philosopher, 1963, Three Plays, 1978, (poetry) Girls on the Run, 1999, Your Name Here, 2000, As Umbrellas Follow Rain, 2001, Chinese Whispers, 2002; author: (with James Schuyler) (novels) A Nest of Ninnies, 1969, represented in numerous anthologies; contbr. articles to periodicles;, author verse set to music. Named Lit. Lion, N.Y. Pub. Libr., 1984, Poet of Yr., Pasadena City Coll., 1984; recipient Yale Series of Younger Poets prize, 1955, Harriet Monroe Poetry award, Poetry Mag., 1963, Civic and Arts Found. prize, Union League, 1966, award, Nat. Inst. Arts and Letters, 1969, Shelley award, Poetry Soc. Am., 1973, Pulitzer prize, 1976, Nat. Book award, 1976, Nat. Book Critics Circle award, 1976, Jerome J. Shestack Poetry award, Am. Poetry Rev., 1983, Bollingen prize in poetry, Yale U. Libr., 1985, Lenore Marshall poetry prize, The Nation, 1985, Common Wealth award in lit., MLA, 1986, Creative Arts award, Brandeis U., 1989, Ruth Lilly Poetry prize, Poetry Mag. and Modern Poetry Assn. and Am. Coun. for Arts, 1992, Robert Frost medal, Poetry Soc. Am., 1995, Grand prize, Biennales Internat. Poetry, Belgium, 1996, Bingham Poetry prize, Boston Rev. Books, 1998, Walt Whitman Citation of Merit, State of N.Y., N.Y. State Writer's Inst., 2000, Medal for Achievement in the Arts, Signet Soc. Harvard U., 2001, Phi Beta Kappa Poet award, Harvard U., 1979; grantee, Poet's Found., 1960, 1964, Ingram Merrill Found., 1962, 1972; scholar Fulbright scholar, U. Montpellier, France, 1955—56, Rennes, France, 1956—57; Guggenheim fellow, 1967, 1973, Rockefeller Found. fellow, 1979—80, Wallace Stevens fellow, Yale U., 1985, McArthur Found. fellow, 1985—90. Fellow: Acad. Am. Poets (chancellor 1988—99, Wallace Stevens award 2001); mem.: Am. Acad. Arts and Scis., Am. Acad. Arts and Letters (Gold medal 1997). Office: c/o Georges Borchardt Inc 136 E 57th St New York NY 10022-2707 Address: Dept Langs and Lit Bard Coll PO Box 5000 Annandale On Hudson NY 12504-5000

ASHBROOK, ARTHUR GARWOOD, JR., economist, educator; b. Pitts., Jan. 30, 1921; s. Arthur Garwood and Theodora Arlene (Hoerle) A.; m. Cecilia Garcia Rodriguez, June 20, 1964; children: Marina-Yolanda, Alexandra. BS, Haverford Coll., 1941; PhD, MIT, 1947. Asst. prof. econs. Duke U., Durham, N.C., 1947-51; sr. economist Office of Price Stabilization, Charlotte, N.C., 1951-53; asst. prof. econs. Carnegie Inst. Tech., Pitts., 1953-54; sr. economist CIA, Washington, 1954-82, part-time contract economist, 1983—. Disting. vis. prof. econs. U.S. Naval Acad., Annapolis, 1976-77. Contbr. articles to profl. jours. Sgt. U.S. Army Air Corps, 1943-45. Mem. Am. Econs. Assn. Avocations: personal journal writing, Haverford alumni affairs. Home: 2925 39th St NW Washington DC 20016-5404

ASHBROOK, KATE JESSIE, charitable organization director; b. London, Feb. 1, 1955; d. John Benjamin and Margaret (Balfour) A. BSc with honors, Exeter (Eng.) U. Gen. sec. Open Spaces Soc., Eng., 1984—. Editor Open Space mag., 1984—. Mem. Ramblers' Assn. (chmn. 1995-98, EC mem. 1982—), Dartmoor Preservation Assn. (pres. 1995—), Coun. for Nat. Parks, vice-chmn. 1998—, chmn. 2003, Countryside Agy. (bd. dir. 1999—). Office: Open Spaces 25A Bell St Henley-on-Thames RG9 2BA England

ASHBURN, ANDERSON, magazine editor; b. Winston-Salem, N.C., Aug. 24, 1919; s. Arthur Lee and Nonnie Mae (Boyles) A.; m. Sue Shermer, Aug. 4, 1941; children: Kit (Mrs. Robert Champlin), Terri (Mrs. Robert Higgins), Edward Lee. BSE, U. Mich., 1940. Editor Mich. Technic, Ann Arbor, 1939-40; assoc. editor Tool Engr., Detroit, 1940-41; asst. editor Am. Machinist (McGraw-Hill Publs. Co., now Penton Pub.), N.Y.C., 1942, assoc. editor, 1946-54, mng. editor, 1955-64, chief editor, 1965-87, editor emeritus, 1987—; chief editor Product Engring., N.Y.C., 1970-71. Mem. mfg. studies bd. NRC Dir., past pres. Asbury Terr. Housing Devel. Fund; trustee Am. Precision Mus.; treas. Meth. Ch. of Tarrytown. Recipient Jesse H. Neal Editorial Achievement awards, 1966, 68, 71, 76, 78, Nat. Mag. award Columbia Grad. Sch. Journalism, 1969, Crain award Am. Bus. Press, 1st McGraw-Hill Disting. Editorial Career award, 1987. Fellow Soc. Mfg. Engrs. (bd. dirs. 1993-94, Disting. Contbns. award 1985); mem. ASME, Soc. Automotive Engrs. (past v.p., chmn. mfg. activity), Am. Soc. Mag. Editors (chmn. 1973-75), Computer and Automated Sys. Assn., Dutch Treat Club (N.Y.C.), Kappa Sigma, Tau Beta Pi. Home and Office: 45 Highland Ave Tarrytown NY 10591-4204

ASHBURN, ROY, state senator; b. Bakersfield, Calif., Mar. 21, 1954; m. Diane Ashburn; children: Shelley, Shannon, Stacey, Suzy. BA in Pub. Adminstrn., Calif. State Univ., Bakersfield, 1983; postgrad., Coll. Sequoias. Owner Roy Ashburn Signs, 1969—72; field rep. Supr. LeRoy Jackson, 1972—77; dist. rep. Congressman William Thomas, 1979—83; supr. Kern County, 1984—; mem. Calif. State Assembly, 1996—2002; mem. dist. 18 Calif. State Senate, Sacramento, 2002—. Mem. Appropriations Com., Health and Human Svcs. Com.; vice-chair Pub. Employees and Retirement Com.; mem. Revenue and Taxation Com., Transp. Com. Republican. Roman Catholic. Mailing: State Capitol Rm 2068 Sacramento CA 95814 Office: 5001 California Ave Rm 105 Bakersfield CA 93309*

ASHBY, FLORENCE HELEN, mathematics educator; b. Crawfordsville, Ind., Mar. 18, 1935; d. James Chester and Florence Muriel (Smith) A. BME, Fla. State U., 1957; MS, Purdue U., 1959. Field cons. Kappa Alpha Theta, Evanston, Ill., 1961-62; systems analyst IBM Corp., Bethesda, Md., 1964-66; prof. math., mathematician Montgomery Coll., Rockville, Md., 1966—. Mem. Montgomery County Hist. Soc., Rockville, 1974—, Peerless Rockville Preservation Soc., 1980—. Mem. Assn. for Women in Maths., Am. Math. Assn. for Two Yr. Colls., Nat. Coun. Tchrs. of Maths., Am. Math. Soc., Math. Assn. Am., AAUP, Kappa Alpha Theta Alumni Assn. (pres. Washington chpt. 1978-80, 90-93), Sigma Alpha Iota (found. trustee 1994-2000). Mem. Christian Ch. Avocations: photography, travel, reading. Office: Montgomery Coll 51 Mannakee St Rockville MD 20850-1101

ASHBY, FRANKLIN CHARLES, JR., business executive, author; b. Rockville Centre, N.Y., Feb. 20, 1954; s. Franklin Charles and Janet Mary (Rauscher) Ashby; m. Rita Sandra Birzkalns, June 26, 1993; 1 child, Daniel Matthew Ashby. BA, Hofstra U., 1976; MBA, N.Y. Inst. Tech., 1984; MA, Columbia U., 1987; Grad. Cert., Columbia Bus. Sch. Exec. Prog., 1987; PhD, American U., UK, 1994. V.p. & chief ed. officer Dale Carnegie & Assocs., Inc., NY, 1984—98, corporate spokesperson, 1996—98; pres. Manchester Training, Inc., 1998—2000; exec. v.p. Manchester Ptrns. Internat., Inc., 1998—2000; head Modis U., 1999—2000; incoming pres. The Chubb Inst., 2000; pres. The Leadership Capital Group LLC, 2000—. Dep. U.S. Marshal (WAE), 1975—80; radio talk show host, Career Clinic, 1986—87; doctoral dissertation adv. U. Southern Miss., 2002—03, U. Mo., 2002—. Author: Contemporary Approaches to Organizational Development and the Improving of Productivity, 1994, World Class, 1995, Revitalize Your Corporate Culture, 1999; author: (foreword) The Complete Idiot's Guide to Team Building, 1999, The Complete Idiot's Guide to Human Resource Management, 2002, The Complete Idiot's Guide to Managing People, 2003; co-author: Embracing Excellence, 2001, Back on Track, 2004; author/editor Effective Leadership Programs, 1999. Chmn. PONSI Bus. Adv. Bd., Am. Coun. on Educ., 1990-93; Comn. on Educ. Credit and Credentials, 1993-98; co-chmn. Comn. on Corporate Development, 1997; designated world's #1 Dale Carnegie instructor, 1984-1998; executive producer, Carnegie Refresher Series, 1986-1997; acting pres., Columbia U. Alumni Asn. (L.I. Region), 1992; chmn. Long Island Colls. & Univs. Comt., 1984-86; Bd. Dirs. Manchester Partners Internat., Inc., 1998-2000, Performance Resources Organization, Inc., 1998-99, Coalition for Fair Broadcasting, Inc., 1987-92, Advancement for Commerce & Industry, Inc., 1986-92, North Shore Montessori Sch., 2002-2003; tryout, New York Mets, Shea Stadium, 1976. Lutheran. E-mail: fashby1@optonline.net.

ASHBY, JEFFREY S. astronaut; BS in Mech. Engring., U. Idaho, 1976; MS in Aviation Systems, U. Tenn., 1993; grad., Naval Test Pilot Sch., Naval Fighter Weapons Sch. Commd. ensign USN, advanced through grades to capt.; commdg. officer Strike Fighter Squadron 94; astronaut NASA, Houston, 1999. Decorated DFC, 4 Navy Air medals, 2 Navy Commendation medals, Navy Achievement medal. Achievements include logged over 7,000 flight hours; 1,000 aircraft carrier landings; logged over 600 hours in space; pilot STS-100 Endeavour (2001); pilot STS-93 Columbia; commander STS-112 Atlantis. Avocations: skiing, soaring, backpacking, fly fishing. Office: Astronaut Office/CB NASA Johnson Space Ctr Houston TX 77058

ASHBY, NORMA RAE BEATTY, journalist, beauty consultant; b. Mont., Dec. 27, 1935; d. Raymond Wesley Beatty; m. Shirley Carter Ashby, Sept. 5, 1964; children: Ann, Tony. BA, U. Mont., Missoula, 1957. Reporter Helena Ind. Record, 1953-56; picture dept. Life mag., N.Y.C., 1957-58; picture rschr. MD Med. Newsmag., N.Y.C., 1959-61; prodr., hostess TV Show Today in Mont., Sta. KRTV, Great Falls, 1962—84; editor Noon News, Sta. KRTV, 1984—88; beauty cons. Mary Kay Cosmetics, Inc., 1988—. Freelance journalist, 1988—. Author: What Is a Montanan?, 1971, Montana Woman, 1977, Montanans, 1982; scriptwriter: Last Chance Gulch, 1964, Gentle Giants, 1969, Our Latchstring is Out, 1979, Paris Gibson, 1983, Martha, Pioneer Woman, 1984, Great Falls Centennial, 1984, First Ladies of Montana, 1986, Anuka, Montana's Island Home, 1986, North American Indian Days, 1987, Missiles of October, 1987, scriptwriter (with Norma Ashby): First Ladies of Montana, 1996, scriptwriter: The Chief and the Celebration, 2001; co-author: Symbols of Montana, 1989. Co-chmn. Cascade County Bicentennial Com., Gt. Falls, 1974—76, Gt. Falls Centennial Com., 1982—84; festivals chmn. Cascade County 89ers, 1987—89; coord. Mont. Statewide Bell Ringing Project, 1989; chair Mont. Jefferson awards; coord. Mont. Statehood Centennial Bell award, 1990—; co-host Children's Miracle Network Telethon, 1989—94; co-chmn. Cascade County Courthouse Centennial Celebration, 2002—03; organizer Bluegrass on the Bay, 2003—; scriptwriter Gov. Joseph K. Toole, Mont., 2002; deacon 1st Prebyn. Ch., 1999—2001; elder 1st Presbyn. Ch.; bd. dirs. Mont. Physicians Svc., Helena, 1980—87; founder, mem. steering com. C. M. Russell Auction, Gt. Falls, 1969—2003; co-chair com. Silver Anniversary Celebration Cascade County Hist. Soc., 1996—97, bd. dirs. Named Hon. Mem., Blackfeet Tribe, Browning, Mont., 1981, Tribune Most Influential Woman in Great Falls, 1984, Mont. TV Broadcaster of the Yr., 1985; recipient TV Program of the Yr. award, Greater Mont. Found., 1982—, Comm. and Leadership award, Mont. Toastmasters Internat., 1983, Preservation award, Cascade County Hist. Soc., 1994. Mem.: AWRT (pres. Mont. Big Sky chpt. 1967, founder, Cert. of Commenda-

tion 1982), Broadcast Pioneers, Great Falls Advt. Fedn. (dir. Silver medal 1980), Women in Comms. (pres. Great Falls chpt. 1988—90, founder), Nat. Lewis and Clark Trail Heritage Found., PEO Club. E-mail: norma@in-tch.com.

ASHBY, RICHARD JAMES, JR., bank executive, lawyer; b. Lancaster, Pa., Aug. 18, 1944; s. Richard James and Gloria Marie (Mayer) A.; m. Claire Lundberg, July 1, 1967; children: Douglas R., Elizabeth, Brian J. AB, Wittenberg U., 1966; JD, Ohio State U., 1969. Bar: Pa. 1969, Ohio 1969. Assoc. Arnold Bricker Beyer & Barnes, Lancaster, 1969-71; trust officer First Nat. Bank Strasburg (Pa.), 1971-73, v.p., 1973-78, Fulton Bank, Lancaster, 1978-80, sr. v.p., 1980-86, exec. v.p., 1986-91; chmn., pres., CEO Lafayette Bank, Easton, Pa., 1991-98; chmn, pres., CEO Fulton Bank, Lancaster, Pa., 1999—. Vice chmn. Lehigh Valley Econ. Devel. Corp., 1995-98. Author: Profitability in Community Bank Trust Department, 1977. Mem. adv. bd. Pa. Joint State Govt. Commn., Harrisburg, 1984—; mus. dir. Lancaster Red Rose Chorus, 1976—91; pres. Parish Resource Ctr., Lancaster, 1984—2002, Northampton C.C. Found., 1991—98, 1994—96, State Theatre, Easton, 1991—98, 1993—94, Easton Hosp., 1991—98; dir. Valley Health Found., 1992—99, Northampton County Devel. Corp., 1994—99, LeHigh Valley Partnership, 1993—98; commr. Manheim Twp., Lancaster County, 1988—92; bd. dirs. United Way of Lancaster County, 2002—, Fulton Opera House, 2002—, Lancaster C. of C., 1999—2002; bd. dirs., vice chmn. Two Rivers C. of C., 1993—99. Staff sgt. U.S. Army, 1970—76. Recipient George Beneman Meml. award Ohio State U. Coll. Law, Columbus, 1969, Am. Spirit Honor medal Army & Navy Vets Aux., Ft. Ord, Calif., 1970 Mem.: Pa. Bankers Assn., Am. Bankers Assn., Lancaster Bar Assn., Pa. Bar Assn., Lancaster Country Club, Hamilton Club. Republican. Lutheran. Avocations: barbershop quartet singing, golf, fishing. Office: 1 Penn Sq Lancaster PA 17602-2853

ASHCOM, JOHN M. sales executive, general management executive; b. Pitts., Apr. 7, 1945; s. John M. and Mary Grace (Herron) A. BSBA, Youngstown (Ohio) State U., 1969. Mgr. comm. Rockwell Internat., Pitts., 1972-77; dir. comm. Litton Industries, N.Y.C., 1977-78; dir. mktg. and comm. Republic Steel-LTV, Canton, Ohio, 1979-86; gen. mgr. Hanel Storage Systems, Pitts., 1986-92; sr. assoc. Green Assocs., Pitts., 1992-93; v.p. mktg. ACCU-Sort Systems Inc., Telford, Pa., 1993-94; owner JM Assoc., Quakertown, Pa., 1994—; divsn. mgr. TherMax divsn. Kooltronic Inc., Hopewell, N.J., 1994-96, nat. sales mgr. Versa Conveyor-Tompkins Industries, Columbus, Ohio, 1996-98; prin. sales, mktg. and bus. planning cons. JM Assocs., 1998—. Editor: Republic Profiler mag., 1979-84, Water Journal mag., 1972-78, Gas Line mag., 1972-78. Mem. Soc. Mfg. Engrs., Material Handling Inst., Am. Mgmt. Assn., Bus./Profl. Advertisers. Clubs: Clan Donald, Pitts. Republican. Avocations: golfing, reading, biking. Home: 2045 Clover Mill Rd Quakertown PA 18951-2142 E-mail: j_ashcom@hotmail.com.

ASHCRAFT, CHARLES OLIN, business educator; b. Kiowa, Kans., June 22, 1936; s. Olin N. and Esther Pauline (Young) A.; m. Letha May Bray, June 2, 1963; children: Farrah Elaine, Kyle Bray. BBA, Phillips U., 1958, MEd, 1965; postgrad., Air War Coll., 1977; diploma, Command & Gen. Staff Coll., 1975. Cert. tchr., Alaska, residential specialist. Tchr. Anchorage High Sch., 1958-61, East Anchorage (Alaska) High Sch., 1961-65; sch. adminstr. Ursa Maj. Elem. Sch., Ft. Richardson, Alaska, 1965-68, Arcturus Jr. High Sch., Ft. Richardson, 1965-73; instr. Anchorage Community Coll., 1959-73, Bartlett High Sch., Anchorage, 1973-90, rifle coach, 1980-90. Mem. adj. faculty Command & Gen. Staff Coll., Ft. Leavenworth, Kans., 1990—. Mem. Rep. Dist. 16, Anchorage, 1986-90; scoutmaster Western Alaska coun. Boy Scouts Am., 1976-80; post advisor Explorer Scout Post, Anchorage, 1980-91. Col. USAR, 1958-91. Recipient Silver Beaver award Western Alaska Boy Scouts Am., 1984; named to U.S. Army Inf. Officer Candidate Sch. Hall of Fame, 1991. Mem. NEA (life), NRA (life), Nat. Guard Assn. of U.S. (life), Res. Officers Assn. (life), Mil. Order of World Wars (life), F&AM Glacier Lodge (PM96), Pioneers for Ala. Igloo #15, Al Aska Shrine Temple, Royal Ct. Jesters Polarcourt, Scottish Rite, Orient of Alaska, Red Cross Constantine, Masons, Anchorage Yorkrite Coll. (past gov.), Prudential Jack White Real Estate. Republican. Methodist. Avocations: snow skiing, competition shooting and coaching. E-mail: cashcraft@alaskalife.net.

ASHCRAFT, NANCY OLSON, mining engineer; b. Charleston, W.Va., Nov. 8, 1959; d. Robert Edward and Jean Wadsworth Olson; m. Randy Ashcraft, Nov. 28, 1987; children: Kelly, Anna. BS in Mining Engring., Pa. State U., 1982. Cert. OSHA hazard tng. Lab. tech. R&P Coal Co., 1980; with Iselin Prep. Co., Homer City, Pa., 1981; chemist Sohio-Aft, Bridgeport, NJ, 1984; mining engr., chemist S.E. Coal Co., Isom, Ky., 1984—89; sr. lab. technician York Corp., Elyria, Ohio, 1996—97, asst. engr., 1997—99, engr., 1999—2000; staff engr. Carrier Corp., Indpls., 2001—. Internat. com. for sound and vibration York Corp., 2001—. Musician Christ the King Ch., North Olmsted, Ohio, 1994—2001, former editor; asst. diving coach Heritage Christian Sch., Indpls., 2002. Named Outstanding Young Woman of Am., 1984. Home: 4591 Abbey Dr Carmel IN 46033

ASHCROFT, JOHN DAVID, attorney general; b. Chgo., May 9, 1942; m. Janet Elise; children: Martha, Jay, Andrew. B cum laude, Yale U., 1964; JD, U. Chgo., 1967. Bar: Mo., U.S. Supreme Ct. Assoc. prof. S.W. Mo. State U., Springfield, 1967-72; pvt. practice Springfield, 1967-73; state auditor State of Mo., 1973-75, asst. atty. gen., 1975-77, atty. gen., 1977-84, gov., 1985-92; atty. Suelthaus and Kaplan P.C., 1993-94; U.S. senator from Mo., 1995-2001; U.S. atty. gen. U.S. Dept. Justice, 2001—. Mem. commerce, sci. and transp. coms., aviation subcom., comm. subcom., chmn. consumer affairs, fgn. commerce & tourism subcom., mfg. and competitiveness subcom., mem. fgn. rels. com., European affairs subcom., Near Ea. & South Asian affairs subcom., Western Hemisphere Peace Corps subcom., mem. jud. com., chmn. constitution, fedn. and property rights subcom.; mem. Presdl. Adv. Coun. Intergovtl. Affairs, The Pres.'s Export Coun.; nat. chmn. Edn. Commn. States, 1987-88, Jud. Com., Subcom., chmn. constn.; chmn. Nat. Govs. Assn. Task Force on Coll. Quality, 1985, Nat. Govs. Assn. Task Force on Adult Literacy; co-chair Renewal Alliance. Gospel singer: records include In the Spirit of Life and Liberty, The Gospel According to John; author: Lessons from a Father to a Son, 1998, (with wife) College Law for Business, 7th, 8th, 9th, 10, 11th edits., It's the Law, 1979-91; contbr. articles to profl. jours. Chmn. Task Force on Adult Literacy, Task Force on College Quality Nat. Gov.'s Assn., 1991; chmn. Rep. Gov.'s Assn., 1990; co-chmn. Rep. Platform Com., 1992. Recipient Nat. Sheriffs Assn. award, 1996; named Christian Statesman of Yr., 1996. Mem. ABA (ho. of dels.), Mo. Bar Assn., Cole County Bar Assn., Nat. Assn. Attys. Gen. (pres. 1980-81, chmn. budget com., exec. com., Wyman award 1983), Nat. Govs. Assn. (vice chmn. 1990, chmn. 1991-92, chmn. Pres.'s Commn. on Urban Families 1992). Republican. Mem. Assembly Of God Ch. Office: US Dept Justice 950 Pennsylvania Ave NW Washington DC 20530*

ASHCROFT, NEIL WILLIAM, physics educator, researcher; b. London, Nov. 27, 1938; m., 1961; 2 children BSc, U. New Zealand, 1958, MSc with honors, 1960; PhD, U. Cambridge, 1964; DSc (hon.), Victoria U., Wellington, New Zealand. Sci. rsch. coun. sr. fellow Cavendish Lab. U. Cambridge, Eng., 1973-74, vis. fellow Clare Hall, 1973-74; assoc. theoretical physics Cornell U., Ithaca, N.Y., 1965-66, from asst. prof. to assoc. prof., 1966-75, prof. physics, 1975—, Horace White Chair of Physics, 1990, various adminstrv. and acad. coms., dir. Lab. of Atomic and Solid State Physics, 1979-84; dep. dir. Cornell High Energy Synchrotron Source, Ithaca, N.Y., 1978-97; dir. Cornell Ctr. for Materials Rsch., Ithaca, 1997-2000. Chaire municipale Joseph Fourier U., Grenoble, France, 1989-93, 2000—; sci. cons. Los Alamos Nat. Lab., 1976-94; adv. com. High Flux Beam Reactor, Brookhaven, 1984-90; sci. cons. Lawrence Livermore Nat. Lab., 1985—; chmn. Gordon Rsch. Conf. on Rsch. at High Pressure, 1986—, trustee 1988-92, chmn. bd. trustees, 1991—; liasion rep. Nat. Rsch. Coun. Rev. Panel on Materials, Am. Phys. Soc. div. of Condensed Matter Physics Physics; vis. com. Brookhaven Nat. Lab., 1986—; Gordon Godfrey vis. prof. U. New South Wales, Australia, 1988; mem. rsch. briefing panel on high temperature superconductivity NAS, adv. panel solid state div. Oak Ridge Nat. Lab.; Erskine fellow Canterbury U., New Zealand, 1990, Ehrenfest lectr. U. Leiden, The Netherlands, 1991; Faraday bicentennial lectr. Electrochem. Soc., 1991; mem. solid state scis. com. NRC, 1993-96. Co-author: Solid State Physics, 1975; mem. editl. bd. Jour. of Physics, 1988-94, The Phys. Rev., 1996—, Australian Jour. of Physics, 1997—; contbr. numerous articles to profl. jours. Fellow Royal Soc. guest fellow, 1984—85, overseas fellow, Churchill Coll., Cambridge U., 1984—85, 2001—, Erskine fellow, Canterbury U., 1990; Guggenheim fellow, 1984—85. Fellow AAAS, Am. Phys. Soc., Royal Soc. New Zealand (hon.); mem. Assn. Internat. pour L'Avancement de la Recherche et de la Technologie Aux Hautes Pressions (exec. com. 1995-99, Bridgman prize 2003), Nat. Acad. of Sci. Office: Cornell U Clark Hall Ithaca NY 14853-2501 E-mail: mwa@ccmr.cornell.edu.

ASHCROFT, RICHARD CARTER, investment company executive; b. East Orange, N.J., Sept. 6, 1942; s. Herbert and Grace Alberta (Schwalb) A.; m. Gail P. Cook, Sept. 12, 1964 (div. May 1, 1981); children: Janet Lynn, Scott Carter; m. Marlene Ann Krueger, Jan. 23, 1982. BA in Econs., Grove City Coll., 1964; postgrad., U. Rochester, 1964-66. Asst. controller Schlegel Corp., Rochester, N.Y., 1972-73; adminstrv. mgr. Schlegel Tenn., Inc., Maryville, Tenn., 1973-74, controller, 1975-76, controller, asst. treas., 1977-79; group fin. dir. Schlegel U.K. Ltd., Leeds, Eng., 1979-80; corporate mgr. acctg. Schlegel Corp., Rochester, N.Y., 1980-83; controller, chief fin. officer Sugardale Foods, Inc., Canton, Ohio, 1983-86; pres., dir. Rotek, Inc., Aurora, Ohio, 1986-88; corporate controller Nesco, Inc., Cleve., 1988—; pres. Ashcroft Assocs. Inc., 1989—; also chmn., 1993-98; pres. Interim Settlement Funding Corp. Fin. chmn. St. Luke's Episc. Ch., Fairport, N.Y., 1983; chmn. Girls Clubs Am., Maryville, Tenn., 1978, treas., 1977. Mem. Prestwick Country Club (Uniontown, Ohio). Republican. Presbyterian. Avocations: golf, travel, reading, swimming, history. Home: 98 Jefferson Dr Hudson OH 44236-2110 E-mail: interimdick@altel.net.

ASHDOWN, MARIE MATRANGA (MRS. CECIL SPANTON ASHDOWN JR.), writer, lecturer; b. Mobile, Ala. d. Dominic and Ave (Mallon) Matranga; m. Cecil Spanton Ashdown Jr., Feb. 8, 1958; children: Cecil Spanton III, Charles Coster; children by previous marriage: John Stephen Gartman, Vivian Marie Gartman. Degree, Maryville Coll. Sacred Heart, Springhill Coll. Feature artist, women's program dir. daily program Sta. WALA, WALA-TV, Mobile; v.p., dir. Met. Opera Guild, N.Y.C., opera instr. in-svc. program, 1970-80, Marymont Coll., N.Y.C., 1979-85; exec. dir. Musicians Emergency Fund, Inc., N.Y.C., 1985—. Internat. adv. coun. Van Cliburn Found., 1998—; cons. No. Ill. U. Coll. Visual and Performing Arts, 1985—; lectr. in field. Author: Opera Collectables, 1979, contbr. articles to profl. jours. Recipient Extraordinary Svc. award March of Dimes, Medal of Appreciation award Harvard Bus. Sch. Club NYC, Cert. Appreciation, Kiwanis Internat., Arts Excellence award NJ State Opera, Cipario award, Albanese Puccini award Lincoln Ctr., 2002. Mem. AAUW, Nat. Inst. Social Scis., Com. for U.S.-China Rels. Avocations: collecting art, antique ceramics and porcelains, bookbinding. Home: 25 Sutton Pl S New York NY 10022-2456 Office: Musicians Emergency Fund Inc PO Box 1256 New York NY 10150-1256

ASHE, AARON MATTHEW, sales professional; b. Miami, Fla., Sept. 13, 1971; s. Leslie Drue and Cheryl King Ashe; m. Lisa Rainey, July 10, 1999. BA in Comm., George Mason U., 1993. Account exec. Cable Networks Inc., McLean, Va., 1994-99; sales mgr. Nat. Cable Comm., Chevy Chase, Md., 1999—. Office: Nat Cable Comm 5454 Wisconsin Ave # 625 Chevy Chase MD 20815 Fax: 301-951-2650. E-mail: aaron_ashe@spotcable.com.

ASHE, ARTHUR JAMES, III, chemistry educator; b. N.Y.C., Aug. 5, 1940; s. Arthur James and Helen Louise (Hawelka) A.; m. Penelope Guerard Vaughan, Aug. 25, 1962; children: Arthur J., Christopher V. BA, Yale U., 1962, MS, 1965, PhD, 1966; postgrad., Cambridge U., 1962-63. Asst. prof. chemistry U. Mich., Ann Arbor, 1966-71, assoc. prof., 1971-76, prof., 1976—, chmn. dept., 1983-86, prof. macromolecular sci. and engring., 2000—. Vis. scientist Phys. Chemistry Inst., U. Basle, Switzerland, 1974 Mem. editorial avd. bds. profl. jours, 1984—. Alfred P. Sloan fellow, 1972-76 Mem. Am. Chem. Soc. Office: U Mich Dept Chemistry Ann Arbor MI 48109 E-mail: ajashe@umich.edu.

ASHE, BERNARD FLEMMING, arbitrator, educator, lawyer; b. Balt., Mar. 8, 1936; s. Victor Joseph Ashe and Frances Cecelia (Johnson) Flemming; m. Grace Nannette Pegram, Mar. 23, 1963; children: Walter Joseph, David Bernard. BA, Howard U., 1956, JD, 1961. Bar: Va. 1961, D.C. 1963, Mich. 1964, N.Y. 1971. Tchr. Balt. Pub. Schs., 1956-58; atty. NLRB, Washington, 1961-63; asst. gen. counsel Internat. Union United Auto Workers, Detroit, 1963-71; gen. counsel N.Y. State United Tchrs., Albany, 1971-96, arbitrator, 1996—. Mem. adj. faculty Cornell Sch. Indsl. and Labor Rels., Albany div., 1981, 87, Fordham U. Law Sch., 1996-00, Roger Williams U. Law Sch., 1996-98. Contbr. articles on labor and constnl. law to profl. jours. Bd. dirs. Urban League Albany, 1979-85, 1st v.p., 1981-85; trustee N.Y. Lawyers Fund for Client Protection, 1981—, Adelphi Univ., Garden City, N.Y., 1997—. Recipient Nat Weinberg award, Wayne State U., Detroit, Mich., 2001. Fellow Am. Bar Found. (life), Coll. Labor and Employment Lawyers (emeritus); mem. NAACP (Thurgood Marshall Justice award 2000), ABA (chmn. sect. labor and employment law sect. 1982-83, consortium on legal svcs. and the pub. 1979-84, commn. on pub. understanding about the law 1987-91, mem. standing com. on group and prepaid legal svcs. 1996-97, ho. of dels. 1985-96, 97-2003, nominating com. 1988-91, chair drafting com., 1998-2000, bd. govs. 1991-94, exec. com. 1993-94, accreditation com. sect. legal edn. and admission to the bar 1994-98, chmn. standing com. on group and prepaid legal svcs. 1996-97, sr. lawyers divsn. coun. 1994-2000, standing com. on client protection 1998-2001, advisor commn. on judiciary in 21st century 2002-03, editl. bd. 2003—), Am. Law Inst., Nat. Bar Assn., Am. Arbitration Assn. (bd. dirs. 1982-98, Whitney North Seymour Sr. medal 1989), N.Y. State Bar Assn., Albany County Bar Assn.

ASHE, KATHY RAE, special education educator; b. Bismarck, N.D., Oct. 24, 1950; d. Raymond Charles and Virginia Ann (Mason) Lynch; m. Barth Eugene Olson, Aug. 11, 1973; 1 child, William Raymond; m. Fredrick A. Ashe, Aug. 5, 1994. BS, U. N.D., 1972, MS in Spl. Edn., 1987. Cert. elem. tchr. with spl. edn. credential, N.D. Instr. Grafton State Sch., N.D., 1972-74; tchr. spl. edn. Grand Forks Sch. Dist., N.D., 1974—. Bd. dirs. Agassiz Enterprises; mem. RAD com. Valley Jr. High; mem. transition governing bd., Region IV. Mem. spl. needs recreation program Grand Forks Park Bd., 1973—76; mem. Spl. Olympics Area Mgmt. Team, 1984—90; mem. region IV Low Incident Behavior Grant Com.; co-chair, vol. coord. Greater Grand Forks Soccer Club Tournament, 2000, 2001; bldg. rep. Grand Forks Edn. Assn., 2000—04; bd. dirs. Assn. Retarded Citizens, Devel. Homes, Inc., N.D. Sch. Blind Found., pres., 1997—. Named N.D. Tchr. of Yr., Coun. Chief State Sch. Officers, 1981. Mem. AAUW (pres. 1998-2000), Delta Kappa Gamma (sec. 1984-86, pres. 1990-94), Alpha Phi (alumni pres. 1984-86, 90-91, alumni treas. 1995—), Phi Delta Kappa. Republican. Roman Catholic. Avocations: sporting events, civic work, cross stitch, bowling, golf. Home: 3208 Walnut St Grand Forks ND 58201-7665 E-mail: ashekathy@hotmail.com.

ASHE, REID, publishing executive; b. 1948; Student, MIT. With Tech. Rev., Boston, 1971-72; asst. editor Washington (N.C.) Daily News, 1972-73; reporter, editl. writer, editl. page editor Jackson (Tenn.) Sun, 1973-84, exec. editor, 1974-78, editor, pub., pres., 1978-84; gen. exec. Knight-Ridder Inc., 1984; CEO Viewdata Corp. (a subsidiary of Knight-Ridder Inc.), 1984-87; pres., pub. The Wichita (Kans.) Eagle, 1987-96, Tampa Tribune, 1996—2001; pres. & COO Media General, 2001—. Office: Media General 333 Franklin St Richmond VA 23219

ASHENFELTER, DAVID LOUIS, reporter; b. Toledo, Oct. 20, 1948; s. Duaine Louis and Betty Jean A.; m. Barbara Ann Dinwieddie, Feb. 22, 1974. BS in Edn., Ind. U., 1971. Reporter Kokomo Morning Times, Ind., 1966-67, Bloomington Daily Herald-Telephone, Ind., 1968-69, Bloomington Courier-Tribune, 1970-71, Detroit News, 1971-82, Detroit Free Press, 1982—. Recipient Disting. Svc. award Soc. Profl. Journalists, 1981, 83, 85, Pulitzer prize for meritorious pub. service Columbia U., 1982, Silver Gavel award ABA, 1986, Worth Bingham Prize, 1986, and more than 40 local, state and nat. newswriting awards; named to Mich. Journalism Hall of Fame. Mem. Sigma Chi. Office: Detroit Free Press 600 W Fort St Detroit MI 48226-2706 E-mail: ashenf@freepress.com.

ASHER, AARON, editor, publisher; s. Samuel and Henny (Meyer) A.; m. Linda Wofsey, Oct. 11, 1956; children— Rachel, Abigail. BA with honors, U. Chgo., 1949, MA, 1952. Mem. editorial staff Alfred A. Knopf, Inc., N.Y.C., 1956-58; exec. editor Meridian Books, Inc., N.Y.C., 1958-64; sr. editor Viking Press, Inc., N.Y.C., 1964-69; dir. gen. book dept. Holt, Rinehart and Winston, Inc., N.Y.C., 1969-74; editor in chief Macmillan Pub. Co., Inc., N.Y.C., 1974; editor in chief, v.p. Farrar, Straus and Giroux, Inc., N.Y.C., 1975-81; exec. editor Harper & Row, N.Y.C., 1981-86; pub. Grove Press, N.Y.C., 1986-89, Grove Weidenfeld, N.Y.C., 1989-90, Aaron Asher Books, Harper Collins, N.Y.C., 1990-93; pub. cons., editor, translator, 1993—. Served with AUS, 1953-55. Home and Office: 201 W 86th St New York NY 10024-3349 E-mail: asher10024@hotmail.com.

ASHER, BETTY TURNER, academic administrator; b. Booneville, Ky., Oct. 19, 1944; BA, Ea. Ky. U.; MA, Western Ky. U.; EdD, U. Cin. Sr. assoc. vice provost U. Cin., 1978-80; assoc. vice chancellor acad. affairs Minn. State U. System, 1981-82; v.p. student affairs Ariz. State U., Tempe, 1982-89; pres. U. S.D., Vermillion, 1989-1996, Bus., Industry Tng., Destin, Fla., 1997—. Office: Bus and Industry Tng 898 Highway 98 E Destin FL 32541-2700 E-mail: bettyasher@cox.net.

ASHER, J. WILLIAM, education and psychology educator; b. Gary, Ind., Apr. 12, 1927; s. Floyd Gaylord and Ruth Ann (Williams) A.; m. Katherine Collyer, Apr. 10, 1955 (dec. July 1995); children: William Collyer, Ruth Ann Asher-Lynch, James Conover, Christopher Harrigan; m. Dorothy Davidson, Nov. 7, 1998. BA, DePauw U., 1950; MS in Psychology, Purdue U., 1951, PhD, 1955; postgrad., Harvard U., 1964-65. Cert. psychologist, Ind. Rsch. coord. U.S. Office Edn., Washington, 1956-60; prof. ednl. rsch. U. Pitts., 1960-66; prof. ednl. studies and psychol. scis. Purdue U., West Lafayette, Ind., 1966—2003. Pvt. practice psychology, West Lafayette; mem. com. NRC. Author: Educational Research and Evaluation Methods, 1976; co-author: Composition Research: Empirical Designs, 1988, Educational Research, 1995; also over 100 articles. Postdoctoral fellow, 1964-65. Fellow AAAS, Am. Psychol. Assn. (pres. div. ednl. psychology); mem. Am. Ednl. Rsch. Assn., Nat. Assn. Gifted Children, Sigma Xi, Phi Delta Kappa. Office: Purdue U Ednl Studies BRNG West Lafayette IN 47907 E-mail: asher@purdue.edu.

ASHER, JAMES EDWARD, forestry consultant, engineer, arborist, forensic expert; b. July 22, 1931; s. John Edward and Dorothy (Ingraham) A.; m. Marilyn Lee Struebling, Dec. 28, 1953; children: Lynne Marie, Laure Ann. Student, Pasadena City Coll., 1949-50; BS, Oreg. State U., 1954. Cert. continuing forestry edn. Soc. of Am. Foresters; registered profl. forester, registered profl. engr., Calif.; lic. pest control advisor, pest control applicator, Calif. With U.S. Forest Svc., San Bernardino (Calif.) Nat. Forest, summers 1950-53, forester, 1956-57; prin. James E. Asher, ACF, Cons. Forester, 1967—. Capt., bn. chief, asst. chief, fire prevention officer Crest Forest Fire Protection Dist., Crestline, Calif., 1960-69, chief, 1969-71; forester Big Bear divsn. Golden State Bldg. Products, Redlands, 1972, timber mgr., 1972-74; mem. profl. foresters exam. com. Calif. Bd. Forestry, 1978-90, vice chmn., 1982-90; mem. Calif. Bd. Forestry Resolution of Gratitutde, 1990—; mem. Calif. Forest Pest Control Coun.; mem. Forest Adv. Com., 1982—; chmn. Profl. Foresters Ad Hoc Task Force, 1983-90; presenter in field. Author: (with others) A Technical Guide for Community and Urban Forestry in Washington, Oregon and California; contbr. numerous articles to profl. jours. Vol. firewarden State of Calif., 1967—; mem. adv. com. Range Mgmt. Program, 1986-90; chmn. Tree Conservation Subcom., 1st Dist. Suprs. Ad Hoc Com. on Soil Erosion and Sediment Control, County of San Bernardino, 1984—; forensic expert witness. With AUS, 1954-56. Recipient Cert. of Merit, Nat. Fire Protection Assn., San Bernardino Mountains Assn., Resolution of Commendation, County Bd. Suprs., Forester of Yr. award So. Calif. sect. So. Am. Foresters, 1977, Superior Continuing Forestry Edn. accomplishment Soc. Am. Foresters, 1996, others. Mem. Internat. Soc. Arboriculture (cert. arborist 1988—), So. Calif. Assn. Foresters and Fire Wardens (exec. com. Inland Empire chpt. 1999—), Soc. Am. Foresters (cert., chmn. licensing and ethics com. So. Calif. sect., chmn. So. Calif, 1983), Assn. Cons. Foresters, Internat. Soc. Arboriculture, Calif. Urban Forests Coun., Calif. Agrl. Prodn. Cons. Assn., Pesticide Applicators Profl. Assn., Masons, San Bernardino Mountains Land Trust (spl. advisor 2000—), Mountain Rim Firesafe Coun. (chmn. tech. adv. com. 1999—), Tau Kappa Epsilon. Presbyterian. Office: PO Box 2326 Lake Arrowhead CA 92352-2326 E-mail: marilynjimasher@aol.com., foresterjimasher@aol.com.

ASHER, JERRY L. retired government agency administrator; b. Houston, Nov. 28, 1941; s. Wayne B. and Norma Faye (Morgan) M.; m. Beverly E. Herrin, Dec. 19, 1969 Idec. Dec. 1986); children: Debra Elizabeth, David Everett. BA in Polit. Sci., Georgetown U., 1963; MA in Pub. Adminstrn., U. Utah, 1965. Cert. tchr. Fiscal liaison dir. U.S.-U.K. Harrier Aircraft Project, London, 1977-80; fgn. mil. sales analyst Office of Sec. of Def., Washington, 1980-85; budget examiner U.s. Office Mgmt. and Budget, Washington, 1985-97; ret., 1997. Project budget and adminstrv. officer U.s. Naval Material Command Hdqrs., Washington, 1968-77. Author, editor: King Cotton's Lords and Ladies: A Dream Remembered, 1989. Mem. passenger rels. adv. bd. Met. Transit Authority of Houston, 1997—. Mem. English Speaking Union, Houston Forum. Episcopalian. Avocations: travel, reading, religious education. Home: 2401 Lazy Hollow Dr Apt 113 A Houston TX 77063

ASHER, KATHLEEN MAY, communications educator; b. Vassar, Mich., Aug. 19, 1932; d. Thomas Henry and Jessie (Smith) Pierce; m. Donald William Asher, July 17, 1957; children: David Kevin, Diane Kerri. BS, Ctrl. Mich. U., 1956, MA, 1967. Cert. fundraiser Williamsburg Devel. Inst., cert. QTM trainer. Tchr. speech and theater Standish (Mich.) Pub. Schs., 1956-58, Vassar (Mich.) Pub. Schs., 1959-67; prof. speech, adminstr. Mott C.C., Flint, Mich., 1967-89; assoc. prof. speech Palm Beach C.C., Lake Worth, Fla., 1990—2001, fundraiser, 1991-95, faculty polit. action chairperson, 1996-97, faculty emeritus, 2001. Cons. in speech, Flint, Mich., 1973—89; cons. quality total mgmt.; cons. in comms. and mgmt., Lake Worth, Fla., 2001—. Pres. Homeowner Assn., Lake Worth, 1993—95, legal chair, 2003; mem. Vassar Zoning Bd.; officer City Coun.; chair Tuscola County Dem Com., 1975—85; del., whip Dem. Conv. and Rules Com., 1976; del. Fla. Dem. Conv., 1999. Mem. United Faculty Palm Beach C.C. (chpt. pres.), Fla. Tchg. Profession, NEA, Nat. Collegiate Hons. Coun. (collegiate 1991-95), Mich. Women's Studies Assn. (pres. 1974-75), C.C. Humanities Assn., Phi Theta Kappa (leadership prof.). Presbyterian. Avocations: percussion, reading, golf, bowling, biking. Home: 4713 Rainbow Dr Lake Worth FL 33463-3610 Office: Palm Beach CC 4200 Congress Ave Lake Worth FL 33461-4705 E-mail: profashl@directvinternet.com.

ASHFORD, ALFRED ROBERT, internist; b. N.Y.C., NY, June 26, 1948; s. Alfred Cleotha and Janice Eulalia Ashford; m. Velvie Anne Pogue; children: Alfred, Adrienne. MD, Georgetown U., 1975. Cert. internal medicine. Chief hematology-oncology Harlem Hosp. Ctr., N.Y.C., 1990—2001, dir. medicine, 2000—. Prof. clin. medicine Columbia U. Coll. Physicians and Surgeons, N.Y.C., 1999—. Bd. dirs. ea. divsn. Am. Cancer Soc., N.Y.C., 2001—. Named Am.'s Leading Black Drs., Black Enterprise Mag., 2001. Fellow: ACP. Avocations: fly fishing, cooking. Office: Harlem Hosp Ctr 506 Lenox Ave New York NY 10037

ASHFORD, JOHN EDWARD, communications executive; b. Kansas City, Sept. 7, 1949; s. Volney Clinton and Zelma Elizabeth (Zahn) A.; m. Carolyn Kay Marquette, Aug. 11, 1973 (div. 1983); m. Vivian Elaine Riefberg, May 7, 1988; children: James Valeri, Katherine Alina. BA, Mo. Valley Coll., 1971, LittD (hon.), 2002; MPA, Harvard U., 1991. Announcer Sta. KMMO-KMFL-FM, Marshall, Mo., 1968-71; sr. analyst Mo. State Records Service, Jefferson City, 1971-72; adminstrv. asst. Mo. Sec. of State Office, Jefferson City, 1972-75, Office Congressman Jerry Litton, Washington, 1975-76; staff asst. Office Sen. Thomas F. Eagleton, Washington, 1976-77; pres. Campaigns, Inc., Jefferson City, 1977-80; sr. v.p. Reese Communications Cos., Inc., Arlington, Va., 1980-89; pub. affairs cons. Hawthorn Group, Alexandria, Va., 1989—, founder, chmn., 1992—, CEO, 1992—2002. Trustee Mo. Valley Coll., Marshall, 1973-88; bd. dirs. Lyceum Theatre, Arrow Rock, Mo., 1973-85. Mem. Am. Assn. Polit. Cons., Internat. Churchill Soc., Nat. Press Club, Harvard Club. Democrat. Methodist. Office: Hawthorn Group 1199 N Fairfax St Alexandria VA 22314-1437

ASHHURST, ANNA WAYNE, foreign language educator; b. Phila., Jan. 5, 1933; d. Astley Paston Cooper and Anne Pauline (Campbell) Ashhurst; m. Ronald G. Gerber, July 22, 1978. AB, Vassar Coll., 1954; MA, Middlebury Coll., 1956; PhD, U. Pitts., 1967. English tchr. Internat. Inst. Spain, Madrid, 1954-56; asst. prof. Juniata Coll., Huntingdon, Pa., 1961-63; asst. prof. Spanish dept. Franklin and Marshall Coll., Lancaster, Pa., 1968-74, acting chmn. Spanish dept., 1972, convenor, fgn. lang. council, 1972-74; assoc. prof. dept. modern fgn. langs. U. Mo., St. Louis, 1974-78. Author: La literatura hispano-

americana en la crítica española, 1980. Mem. Welcome Wagon of Lancaster, Pa., 1968-70, 71-74 Fulbright-Hays grantee, Colombia, S.Am., summer 1963; Ford Humanities fellow, summer 1970; Mellon fellow, 1970-71 Mem. AAUW (pres. Ferguson-Florissant br. 1989-91, 95-98, chmn. St. Louis area interbranch coun. 1992-94, chair environ. task force Mo. 1992-95, local arrangements chair for Mo. state conv. 1997, Woman of Distiction award 1998), Internat. Inst. in Spain, Instituto Internacional de Literatura Iberoamericana, Am. Assn. Tchrs. Spanish and Portuguese. Home: 2105 Barcelona Dr Florissant MO 63033-2805

ASHKENAZY, VLADIMIR DAVIDOVICH, concert pianist, conductor; b. Gorky, USSR, July 6, 1937; s. David and Evstolia (Plotnova) A.; m. Thorunn Johannsdottir, Feb. 25, 1961; children— Vladimir Stefan, Nadia Liza, Dimitri Thor, Sonia Edda, Alexandra Inga. Student, Cen. Music Sch., Moscow, Moscow Conservatory; studies with, Sumbatyan, Lev Oborin. Condr., music dir. Royal Philharm. Orch., London, 1987-95; prin. guest conductor Cleve. Orch., 1987-94; music dir. Deutsches Symphonie Orchester (formerly Radio Symphony Orch.), Berlin, 1989-99; music. dir. Czech Philharm. Orch., 1998—. London debut, London Symphony Orch. under George Hurst, later solo recital, Festival Hall, 1963, recs., concerts throughout world. Music dir. Czech Philharm. Orch., Prague, 1998. Co-recipient Tchaikovsky Piano Competition award, Moscow, 1962; recipient 2d prize, Internat. Chopin Competition, Warsaw, 1955, Gold medal, Queen Elizabeth Internat. Piano Competition, Brussels, 1956, Grammy awards, 1973, 1978, 1981, 1985, 1987, 1999. Office: care Harrison/Parrott Ltd 12 Penzance Pl London W11 4PA England

ASHKIN, MICHAEL, artist; b. Morristown, N.J., 1955; BA, U. Pa., 1977; MA in Mid. East Langs. and Cultures, Columbia U., 1980; MFA in Painting and Drawing, Sch. Art Inst. Chgo., 1993. One-man shows include Peter Miller Gallery, Chgo., 1992, 1994, Bronwyn Keenan Gallery, N.Y., 1996, Feigen Inc., Chgo., 1996, Galerie Jousse Seguin, Paris, 1997, Andrea Rosen Gallery, N.Y.C., 1998, exhibited in group shows at Peter Miller Gallery, Chgo., 1992, Sch. Art Inst. Chgo., 1993, Gallery 2, Sch. Art Inst. Chgo., 1994, 450 Gallery, N.Y.C., 1995, Andrea Rosen Gallery, 1996, Rosenberg Gallery, Hofstra U., Hempstead, N.Y., 1997, Kerlin Gallery, Dublin, Ireland, 1997, Mus. Contemporary Art, Miami, Fla., 1997, New Mus. Contemporary Art, N.Y.C., 1997, Turner & Runyon, Dallas, 1998, Saatchi Gallery, London, 1998, Four Walls Gallery, Bklyn., 1998, others, S.E. Ctr. Contemporary Art, Winston-Salem, 1999. Recipient award, The Pollock-Krasner Found., Inc., 1997; fellow Hon. Pres. fellow, Columbia U., 1978; scholar Full Merit scholar, Sch. Art Inst. Chgo., 1991—93. Office: care Andrea Rosen Gallery 525 W 24th St New York NY 10011-1104

ASHKINAZY, LARRY ROBERT, dentist; b. N.Y.C., Feb. 12, 1952; s. Philip and Kate (Scherer) A. BS, Bklyn. Coll., 1973; DDS, NYU, 1976. Cert. Nat. Bd. Dental Examiners. Gen. dental practice residency Cabrini Health Care Ctr., 1977; pvt. practice dentistry N.Y.C., 1977—. Pres., founder Doctors Who Care; assoc. attending dentist Cabrini Healthcare Ctr., 1984—, assoc. attending in implantology, 1983—86; postgrad. instr. Inst. for Grad. Dentists, 1981—82; guest lectr. various pub. and profl. edn. instns.; health and sci. corr. Sta. WWOR-TV. Author: Dentistry, 1982; contbr. articles to profl. jours.; mem. editorial bd. Internat. Congress Oral Implantologists newsletter, 1982; various radio and TV appearances; patentee in field; trademarks Bionic Tooth, Tooth Plant. Health care providor Drs. with a Heart, N.Y.C., 1987; health care spokesman Jr. League, N.Y.C., 1978, Community Fair, N.Y.C., 1983; founder Doctors Who Care. Recipient Cert. of Appreciation Greater N.Y. Dental Meeting, 1981, 87, Cert. of Appreciation NYU Dental Ctr., 1981. Fellow Acad. Gen. Dentistry, Acad. Dentistry Internat., Acad. Implants and Transplants, Am. Endodontic Soc., Internat. Congress Oral Implantologists; mem. Am. Dental Assn. (cert. appreciation 1980), Am. Acad. Oral Medicine, Internat. Analgesia Soc., 1st Dist. Dental Soc. (oral health clinician 1978, speakers bur. subcom-.chmn. 1984pub. and profl. relations com. 1982), Am. Prosthodontic Soc., Sociedad Venezolana de Implantodontologos, Am. Acad. Implant Dentistry (chmn. sci. exhibit com., 1984, edn. com. 1984, library cm. 1984, membership com. 1983, N.Y. chmn. 1983 ann. meeting and world assembly. Dentistry Alumni, Alpha Omega. Clubs: Greater N.Y. Implant Study (pres. 1981—). Home and Office: 200 Central Park S New York NY 10019-1415

ASHLEIGH, CAROLINE, art and antiques appraiser; BA, Worcester (Mass.) Coll., 1973; cert. in appraisal studies, NYU, 1994. Profl. lectr. on connoisseurship; appraiser Home and Garden TV; edn. dept. staff Cranbrook Art Mus., Bloomfield Hills, 1997—; columnist Detroit Monthly Mag., 1988—; edn. dept. staff Detroit Inst. Art, 1988—; regional rep. William Doyle Auctioneers, N.Y.C., 1997—2000; columnist Detroit Legal News, 1998—. Appraiser Chubbs Antique Roadshow, WGBH-TV, Boston, 1996—; cons. Southeby's; lectr. in field. Columnist: Antiques Roadshow Insider, Mich. Bar Jour., Detroit Monthly, 1995—96, Hour Detroit mag.; subject of feature presentations N.Y. Times, Art and Antiques, Detroit Free Press, Antique Trader Mag., others. Mem. Appraisers Assn. Am. (bd. cert.; Midwest regional rep.), Detroit Inst. Arts, Cranbrook Art Mus. Home: 800 E Lincoln St Birmingham MI 48009-1784

ASHLEMAN, IVAN RENO, II, health care executive, lawyer; b. Kansas City, Mo., June 9, 1940; s. Ivan Reno and Ellen Lorraine (Fisher) A.; m. Susan Haase, July 25, 1986; children: Brian Eugene, Michael Scott. B.S., U. Nebr., 1963, J.D., 1963. Bar: Nev. 1963, U.S. Dist. Ct. Nebr. 1963, U.S. Dist. Ct. Nev. 1964, U.S. Tax Ct. 1975, U.S. Ct. Appeals (9th cir.) 1968, U.S. Supreme Ct. 1975. Sole practice, Las Vegas and Reno, Nev., 1966-69; ptnr. Davis, Cowell & Bowe, San Francisco and Las Vegas, 1969-80, Ashleman & Clontz, Las Vegas, 1982-83, Raggio, Ashleman, Wooster, Clontz & Lindell, Las Vegas and Reno, 1981, Ashleman, Evans & Kelly, 1987-88; pvt. practice, Reno, 1988—; Clark County dep. dist. atty., Las Vegas, 1964-66; pres. Ins. Services, Inc., 1983—; bd. dirs., pres. Geriatric Health Resources, Inc.; pres., bd. dirs. Sierra Health Care Mgmt. Assocs., Inc. Contbr. articles to profl. jours. Chmn. Nev. Bd. Museums and History, Carson City; exec. bd. dirs., treas. Nathan Adelson Hospice, Las Vegas, 1981—; pres. Young Dems. of Las Vegas, 1970; bd. dirs. Sparks Family Hosp., 1980-83, Spring Valley Community Hosp., 1980—; mem. Nev. Homebuilders. Mem. ABA, Am. Judicature Soc., Nev. Bar Assn., Nebr. Bar Assn., Washoe County Bar Assn., Clark County Bar Assn., So. Nev. Arbitration Assn., Indsl. Relations Reps Assn., Am. Acad. Med. Adminstrs., Reno C. of C. Episcopalian. Clubs: Las Vegas Country, Hualapai (Las Vegas). Home: 485 Gonawabie Crystal Bay NV 89402 Office: 1661 E Flamingo Rd Ste 5A Las Vegas NV 89119-5291

ASHLER, PHILIP FREDERIC, international trade and development advisor; b. N.Y.C., Oct. 15, 1914; s. Philip and Charlotte (Barth) A.; m. Jane Porter, Mar. 4, 1942 (dec. 1968); children: Philip Frederic, Robert Porter, Richard Harrison; m. Elise Barrett Duvall, June 21, 1969; stepchildren: Richard Edward Duvall, Jeffries Harding Duvall. BBA cum laude, St. Johns Coll., 1935; MBA, Harvard U., 1937; grad., Indsl. Coll. Armed Forces, 1956; ScD, Fla. Inst. Tech., 1969; LLD (hon.), U. West Fla., 1969; postgrad., U. Oxford, Eng., 1988, 89, 91. Enlisted USMCR, 1932; commd. ensign USN, 1938, advanced through grades to rear adm., 1959; served in Normandy invasion France; served in; dir. Office Small Bus., Dept. Def., Washington, 1948-49; mem. joint staff Joint Chiefs Staff, 1957-59; ret., 1959; dir. devel. Pensacola Jr. Coll., 1960-68; vice chancellor adminstrn. State Univ. System Fla., 1968-70, exec. vice chancellor, 1970-75; treas., ins. commr., fire marshal State of Fla., 1975-76, sec. of commerce, 1977-79; pres. Philip F. Ashler & Assos., Tallahassee, 1979—; chmn. bd. Cambridge Community Care, Inc., Tallahassee, 1981-86, Circle Seven Internat., Tampa, 1988-91. Past dir. Fidelity Guaranty Life Ins. Co., Balt., U.S. Fidelity & Guaranty Co., 1st Fla. Bank N.A., Tallahassee; sec., dir. Fringe Benefits Mgmt. Co., Tallahassee, 1987—; mem. Fla. Edn. Council, 1967-68; commr. from Fla. Edn. Commn. States, 1967-68; mem. U.S. Dept. Commerce Dist. Export Council, 1978-92; chmn. bd., dir. Fla. Internat. Vol. Corps., 1988-90; mem. legis. adv. council So. Regional Edn. Bd., 1966-68; mem. Fla. Bd. Ind. Colls. and Univs., 1971-75, mem. adv. council for mil. edn., 1980-85; bd. advisors Ctr. Profl. Devel., Fla. State U., 1988-96; chmn. Fla. Civil Def. Adv. Council, 1966-69; mem. Fla. Council Internat. Devel., 1973-92, vice chmn., 1979-80, chmn., 1980-82, chmn. emeritus, 1990—; mem. Select Council on Post High Sch. Edn., 1967-68; chmn. Fla. Med. Liability Ins. Commn., 1975-76, Fla. Task Force on Auto and Workers Compensation, 1975-76; mem. Yugoslavia Adv. Council, 1976-87, InterAm. Congress on Psychology, Bogota, Colombia, 1974, NATO Advanced Sci. Inst., W.Ger., 1973; guest lectr. U. Belgrade, Yugoslavia, 1973; adviser econ. devel. to gov. Fla., 1977-78; mission leader Japan/S.E. U.S. Assn., Tokyo, 1977; trustee Fla. Council on Econ. Edn., 1979-81; mem. services policy adv. com. Office of U.S. Trade Rep., Exec. Office of Pres., Washington, 1980-85; mem. Republic of China/U.S.A. Econ. Council, 1979-92. Mem. Fla. Ho. of Reps., 1963-68; chmn. bd. dirs. Fla. Heart Assn., 1969-71; bd. dirs., treas. Internat. Cardiology Found.; bd. dirs. Tallahassee Meml. Hosp., Easter Seal Soc., 1963-68; bd. dirs., mem. exec. com. Am. Heart Assn., 1971-77, Internat. Cardiology Fedn., Geneva, 1975-77; founding chmn. Tallahassee Symphony Orch., 1981-82; trustee So. Ctr. Internat. Studies, Atlanta, 1988-91; mem. adv. bd. Fla./China Inst., Miami, Fla./Japan Inst., Tampa, Fla./Brazil Inst. Decorated Bronze Star with Combat V, Korean Presdl. citation; recipient Internat. Distinguished Service award Kiwanis Internat., 1965; Distinguished Service award Am. Heart Assn., 1965, 71; Distinguished Achievement award, 1975; Legislative award St. Petersburg Times, 1967 Mem. Fla. Med. Malpractice Joint Underwriting Assn. (chmn. bd. govs. 1975-76), Nat. Assn. Ins. Commrs. (vice chmn. exec. com. 1976), Internat. C. of C. (U.S. coun. 1979-87), U.S. S.E./Japan Assn. (chmn. 1981-83), S.E. U.S./Korea Econ. Coop. Coun. (bd. dirs.), Capital Tiger Bay Club (chmn. bd. dirs.), Govs. Club (bd. govs. 1989-93, v.p. for fin. 1992-93, bd. govs. 1994-96, treas. 1996), Econ. Club Fla. (chmn. 1987-90, chmn. emeritus 1991—), Masons (32 degree), Shriners, Rotary, Kappa Delta. Episcopalian (lic. lay eucharistic minister). Home: 2115 E Randolph Cir Tallahassee FL 32308 also: 11 Riad Sultan Kasbah Tangier Morocco Office: Fringe Benefits Mgmt Co PO Box 1878 Tallahassee FL 32302-1878 E-mail: ashler@worldnet.att.net.

ASHLEY, ELLA JANE (ELLA JANE RADER), medical technologist; b. Dewitt, Ark., Mar. 6, 1941; d. Clayton Ervin and Emma Mae (Coleman) Funderburk; m. Albert Ashley, Sept. 27, 1957 (div. Nov. 1962); 1 child, Cynthia Gayle. Student, Westark Community Coll. Cert. clin. lab. technologist, clin. lab. scientist. Lab. asst. U. Ark. Med. Ctr., Little Rock, 1966-67; lab. technician II, rschr. in lithium carbonate Ark. State Hosp., Little Rock, 1967-68; staff technologist Cooper Clinic, Ft. Smith, Ark., 1969-71; asst. chief technologist Lab. of Am. (Labcorp), Ft. Smith, 1972—, ops. mgr., 1997—2003; ret. Lab. of America (Labcorp), 2003. Mem. profl. adv. panel Med. Lab. Observer, 1976—. Research in lithium carbonate. Mem.: Am. Soc. Med. Tech. Methodist. Avocations: travel, theater, concerts, painting. Home: 1310 S Houston St Fort Smith AR 72901-7271

ASHLEY, HOLT, aerospace scientist, educator; b. San Francisco, Jan. 10, 1923; s. Harold Harrison and Anne (Oates) A.; m. Frances M. Day, Feb. 1, 1947 (wid.). Student, Calif. Inst. Tech., 1940-43; BS, U. Chgo., 1944; MS, MIT, 1948, ScD, 1951. Mem. faculty MIT, 1946-67, prof. aero., 1960-67; prof. aeros. and astronautics Stanford U., Palo Alto, Calif., 1967-89, prof. emeritus, 1989—. Spl. rsch. aeroelasticity, aerodynamics; cons. govt. agys., rsch. orgns., indsl. corps.; dir. office of exploratory rsch. and problem assessment and div. advanced tech. applications NSF, 1972-74; mem. sci. adv. bd. USAF, 1958-80, rsch. adv. com. structural dynamics NASA, 1952-60, rsch. adv. com. on aircraft structures, 1962-70, chmn. rsch. adv. com. on materials and structures, 1974-77; mem. Kanpur Indo-American program Indian Inst. Tech., 1964-65, governing bd. Nat. Rsch. Coun., 1988-91; AIAA Wright Bros. lectr., 1981; dir. Rann Inc. Co-author: Aeroelasticity, 1955, Principles of Aeroelasticity, 1962, Aerodynamics of Wings and Bodies, 1969, Engineering Analysis of Flight Vehicles, 1974. Recipient Goodwin medal M.I.T., 1952; Exceptional Civilian Service award U.S. Air Force, 1972, 80; Public Service award NASA, 1981; named one of 10 outstanding young men of year Boston Jr. C. of C., 1956; recipient Ludwig-Prandtl Ring, West German DGLR, 1987, Spirit of St. Louis Medal, ASME, 1992. Fellow AIAA (hon., assoc. editor jour., v.p. tech. 1971, pres. 1973, Structures, Structural Dynamics and Materials award 1969), Am. Acad. Arts and Scis., Royal Aero. Soc. (hon.); mem. AAAS, NAE (aeros. and space engring. bd. 1977-79, mem. coun. 1985-91), Am. Meterol. Soc. (profl., 50th Ann. medal 1971), Phi Beta Kappa, Sigma Xi, Tau Beta Pi. Home: 475 Woodside Dr Woodside CA 94062-2375

ASHLEY, JAMES MACGREGOR, management consultant; b. Little Falls, N.Y., July 29, 1941; s. Robert Cudworth and Vivien Arlene (McCaughan) A.; m. Jane Staszewski, Apr. 20, 1995; children: Christopher Robert, Kimberly Dawn. BA, U. Miami, 1964. Program dir. Sta. VUNC Radio, Okinawa, Japan, 1965-67; photographer Sta. WOKR-TV, Rochester, N.Y., 1968-70; film dir. Sta. WVNY-TV, Burlington, Vt., 1969-71; mng. dir. Champlain Coun. Holiday Magic Dist., Burlington, 1971-72; sales mgr. MAICO Hearing Aid Ctr., Burlington, 1972-77; buyer IBM, Burlington, 1978-83, internat. contract cons. Boca Raton, Fla., 1983-87, mgr., 1987—; pres. Procurement Arts Internat., Boca Raton, 1988—. Co-author: Handbook of Buying and Purchasing Management, 1992; author: International Purchasing Handbook, 1998, numerous quick study guides for colls. and univs. Capt. U.S. Army, 1964-67. Mem. ASTD (past pres.), Am. Mgmt. Assn. (past faculty), Am. Purchasing Soc. (exec. bd.), Inst. Mgmt. Cons. (past v.p.). Episcopalian. Avocation: uscg aux. Home and Office: 744 NE 12th Ter Boynton Beach FL 33435-3272

ASHLEY, JAMES PATRICK, lawyer; b. Terre Haute, Ind., May 5, 1953; s. Cornelius Ellis and Ruth LaVerne A.; m. Lisa Ann Larsson, Aug. 2, 1975; children: Alison Elisabeth, Amanda Suzanne. BSBA, Ill. State U., 1975; JD, Drake U., 1991. Bar: Minn. 1991; U.S. Dist. Ct. Minn. 1992; U.S. Ct. Appeals (8th cir.) 1993. Claim supr., claim examiner and claim rep. Ill. Employers Ins. of Wausau, River Forest, Ill., 1976-80; casualty claim mgr. Brotherhood Mut. Ins. Co., Fort Wayne, Ind., 1980-88; law clk. Hanson, McClintock & Riley, Des Moines, 1989-91; assoc. Chadwick, Johnson & Condon, Mpls., 1991-96; shareholder Chadwick & Assocs., Chanhassen, Minn., 1996-99; trial atty. Allstate Ins. Co., Edina, Minn., 1999—. Recipient acad. scholarship Drake Law Sch., Des Moines, 1989. Roman Catholic. Avocations: reading, winemaking. Home: 12771 Gerard Dr Eden Prairie MN 55346-3129 Office: Allstate Ins Co 7401 Metro Blvd Ste 510 Edina MN 55439-3033 E-mail: jpalal@msn.com.

ASHLEY, JOHN BRYAN, software executive, management consultant; b. Lake Charles, La., Dec. 1, 1955; s. John Nathaniel and Anne Lee (Baker) A.; m. Peggy Anne Daly, Mar. 21, 1988; children: John B. Jr., Robert Lee, Elizabeth Anne. BS, MS in Econs., La. Tech. U., 1977. Mktg. rep. IBM, Shreveport, La., 1978-81, acct. mgr., 1981-84, product mgr. Rochester, Minn., 1984-88, product mktg. mgr. Atlanta, 1988-93; v.p. mktg., founding ptnr. Distbr. Solutions Internat., Alpharetta, Ga., 1993-95; dir. strategic alliances Infinium Software, Inc., Hyannis, Mass., 1995-97, also London, Paris, Singapore, mng. dir. Europe, Mid. East, Africa, 1996-97, v.p. bus. devel., 1997-99; sr. v.p. mktg. bus. devel. Infinium eBus. Group, 1999-2000; v.p. strategic alliances Talus Solutions, 2000; v.p. global alliances Manugistics Group, 2000; dir. IBM Alliance Ariba Inc., Alpharetta, 2001—02; v.p. strategic/global alliances DWL Inc., Atlanta, 2002—. Cons. to IBM Corp., USA, 1993, IBM Europe, Paris, 1994, 95, Russian Fedn., 1995; market cons. to European Software Vendors, 1994, 95. Del. Ga. State Rep. Party, 1992-93, Cobb Rep. Party, 1992-93. Mem. Sons of Confederate Vets., Colonial Williamsburg Found., Haig Point Club, Kappa Sigma (pres.). Presbyterian. Avocations: wine, African safaris, oriental arts, horticulture, equestrian/dressage. Home: 4750 Talleybrook Dr NW Kennesaw GA 30152-5484 Office: DWL Inc 115 Perimeter Center Pkwy Atlanta GA 30046 E-mail: ashleyfam@msn.com.

ASHLEY, LOIS A. retired university reference librarian; b. Detroit, Aug. 1, 1942; d. S. Elbert and Gertrude B. Hobson; m. Melvin Allen Ashley, June 27, 1964 (dec. Nov. 1996); children: Scott E., Paul D., Craig R. AA, William Tyndale Coll., Farmington Hills, Mich., 1989, BA in Humanities, 1991; MS in LS, Wayne State U., 1993. Spl. corr. Mich. Blue Shield, Detroit, 1963-68; reservation agt. United Airlines, Dearborn, Mich., 1968-70; asst. Office of Records and Registration William Tyndale Coll., 1989-91; grad. rsch. asst. Wayne State U., Detroit, 1992-93; reference libr. U. Detroit Mercy, 1993-99; adj. Oakland C.C., 2000—. Organist Gracious Savior Luth. Ch., 2000—; mem. Friends of the Detroit Pub. Libr.; founding chair ret. mem. roundtable Mich. Libr. Assn., 2001. Recipient scholarships. Mem. ALA (Black Caucus), AAUW, Assn. Coll. and Rsch. Librs., Mich. Libr. Assn., Nat. Coun. Negro Women, Founders Soc. Detroit Inst. Arts, Women of the Evang. Luth. Ch. in Am., Beta Phi Mu, Delta Epsilon Chi. Mem. Evang. Luth. Ch. in Am. Home: 19934 Mark Twain St Detroit MI 48235-1607

ASHLEY, LYNN, educator, consultant, administrator; b. Rock Island, Ill., Nov. 18, 1920; d. Francis Ford and Cleo Marguerite (Monahan) Haynes; m. Edward Messenger Ashley, Aug. 16, 1946; children: Edward Jr., Ann Rice, Rebecca Pocisk, William. BS in Social Psychology, Union Inst., Cin., 1978; MEd., U. Cin., 1979, EdD, 1985. Clk. Lumberman's Mutual Casualty Co., Chgo., 1940-41; account asst. Quaker Oats Co., Chgo., 1941-43; riveter Douglas Aircraft Co., Chgo., 1943-44; organizer, dir. Forest Park Youth Ctr., Forest Park, Ohio, 1967-73; staffing coord. Presbytery of Cin., 1973-78; grad. teaching asst. U. Cin., 1978-84; pres. Nat. Corrective Tng. Inst., Cin., 1979—85. Adj. faculty, mem. undergrad. studies bd. Union Inst., 1986—; cons., trainer Hamilton County Probation Dept., Warren County Juvenile Ct., 1987—, Allen County Juvenile Ct., Worth Ctr., Allen County, field rep. Spkr., adv. women vets. to schs. and orgns.; mem. Cin.-Harare, Zimbabwe Sister Cities Assn., 1989—, Ohio Gov.'s Adv. Com. on Women Vets., 1993—99; with Women in Mil. Svc. for Am. Councilwoman City of Forest Park, 1981—85, organizer cmty. rels. coun., 1983. With WAC, 1944—46. Recipient in Recognition award Forest Park City Coun., 1985, In Appreciation award Union Inst., 1987, Recognition award AMVETS, U. Cin., 1993, award Commonwealth of Ky., 1989; inducted into Ohio Vets. Hall of Fame, 1999. Mem. Am. Corrections Assn., Nat. Assn. Corrective Tng. Affiliates (pres. 1987), Women's Army Corp Vet. Assn. (selected rep. to dedication of Dale Inst. of Politics), Assn. Family and Conciliatiion Cts., Am. Probation and Parole Assn. Avocations: photography, foreign travel, computers, camping, fishing. Office: Nat Corrective Tng Inst 811 Hanson Dr Cincinnati OH 45240-1921

ASHLEY, PERRY JONATHAN, journalism educator; b. West Lebanon, Ind., May 1, 1928; s. Terrell Garner and Viola Ethel (Whitmer) A.; m. Lita Grey Cochran, Nov. 29, 1952; children: Jonathan Edward, Richard Douglas. AB in Journalism, U. Ky., 1956, MA in Polit. Sci., 1966; PhD in Journalism, So. Ill. U., 1968. Instr. Sch. Journalism U. Ky., Lexington, 1956-65; teaching assoc. Sch. Journalism So. Ill. U., Carbondale, 1965-67; prof. Coll. Journalism and Mass Comm. U. S.C., Columbia, 1967-93, interim dean Coll. Journalism, 1985-86, assoc. dean, 1986-92, disting. prof. emeritus, 1993—. Dir. Ky. Scholastic Press Assn., U. Ky., 1956-65; dir. media rsch. Coll. Journalism, U. S.C., 1970-90; dir. S.C. Scholastic Press Assn., U. S.C., 1971-74; cons.on audience analysis S.C. Ednl. TV System, 1969-72. Editor: Newspaper Publishing in South Carolina, 1980, American Newspaper Journalists, 1873-1900, 1983, American Newspaper Journalists, 1901-1925, 1984, American Newspaper Journalists, 1926-1950, 1984, American Newspaper Journalists, 1690-1872, 1985, American Newspaper Publishers, 1951-1990, 1993. Mem. Gov.'s Safety Coun., Commonwealth of Ky.; mem. East Richland Pub. Svc. Commn., Columbia, 1972-79, chmn., 1973-77; trustee Richland County Sch. Dist. 2, Columbia, 1981-87, chmn., 1985. Cpl. U.S. Army, 1950-52, Germany. Named Nation's Outstanding Yearbook Adviser Nat. Coun. Coll. Publs. Advisers, 1964. Mem. Am. Journalism Historians Assn. (program chmn., bd. dirs. 1988-91), Assn. Edn. in Journalism and Mass Comm., Soc. Profl. Journalists (Disting. Campus Chpt. Adviser 1982), Alpha Delta Sigma, Kappa Tau Alpha, Alpha Epsilon Rho, Phi Alpha Theta, Psi Sigma Alpha, Omicron Delta Kappa. Independent. Presbyterian. Avocations: miniaturist, travel, reading, amateur photography, gardening, backyard birdwatching. Home: 3747 Greenleaf Rd Columbia SC 29206-3362

ASHLEY, RAYMOND WELDON, writer; b. Muenster, Tex., Aug. 27, 1942; s. Noble Preston and Velma Modene (Reed) A.; m. Cecilia Mackie Boyd, Dec. 19, 1964; children: Gregory Wayne, Audrey Rae, Laura Nell. BA, U. North Tex., 1963, MA, Mich. State U., 1970; postgrad., U. Nebr., Omaha, 1973-75; MA in English, Midwestern State U., 2000, MA in History, 2003. Commd. 2d lt. USAF, 1963, advanced through grades to lt. col., 1980, various positions in comm., resource mgmt., logistics, 1987; tchr. social studies St. Jo (Tex.) H.S., 1992; adult edn. instr. Region IX Edn. Svcs. Ctr., Wichita Falls, Tex., 1994-95. Spkr. in field. Author (videotape) Victor Guriev, Profile of a Soviet Officer, 1977, Tsar and Commissar, A History of Russia 862-1945, 1978; author: Old School Scholastics, A History of Education in Saint Jo, Texas, 1872-1922, 1995; writer Saint Jo Tribune, Nocona and Bowie News, Wichita Falls Times-Record News, 1991-96. Reporter Illinois Bend (Tex.) Civic Assn., 1991-93; trustee Illinois Bend Cemetery Assn., 1996—, Illinois Bend Civic Assn., 1998—. Decorated Bronze Star, Meritorious Svc. Medal with 2 oak leaf clusters, Air medal, Air Force Commendation medal with 2 oak leaf clusters, Air Force Achievement medal; honor medal 1st class (Vietnam); Ten Films scholar U. North Tex. Philosophy Club, 1962-63, merit scholar Midwestern State U., 1996-98, 2002-03. Mem. Ret. Officers Assn., Montague County Hist. Commn., Tex. State Hist. Assn., West Tex. Hist. Assn., Masons, Phi Alpha Theta. Avocations: landscaping, researching local history, gardening, reading. Home and Office: PO Box 430 Saint Jo TX 76265-0430

ASHLEY, RENEE, writer, creative writing educator, consultant; b. Palo Alto, Calif., Aug. 10, 1949; BA in English with honors, BA in French, BA in World and Comparative Lit., San Francisco State U., 1979, MA, 1981. Instr. creative writing West Milford (N.J.) Cmty. Sch., 1983-85; creative writing instructor, cons. artist residencies Rockland Ctr. for Arts, West Nyack, N.Y., 1985—; mem. MFA in Creative Writing faculty Fairleigh Dickinson U., 2001—. Author: Salt, 1991 (Brittingham prize in Poetry 1991), The Various Reasons of Light, 1998, The Revisionist's Dream, 2001, Someplace Like This, 2003; contbr. to anthologies including Touching Fire: Erotic Writings by Women, 1989, What's a Nice Girl Like You?, 1992, Breaking Up Is Hard to Do, 1994, Dog Music, 1996, (textbook) Writing Poems, 1995; contbr. to American Voice, Antioch Rev., Harvard Rev., Kenyon Rev., Poetry. Fellow N.J. State Coun. Arts, 1985, 89, 94, Yaddo, Saratoga Springs, N.Y., 1990, McDowell Colony, Peterborough, N.H., 1993-94, NEA, 1997-98; grantee Poets and Writers, Inc., 1986, N.Y. State Coun. Arts, 1986; recipient Washington prize in poetry Word Works, Inc., 1986, Lit. Excellence award, Kenyon Review, 1990, 92, Pushcart prize, 2000. Mem. MLA, Acad. Am. Poets, Poetry Soc. Am. (Ruth Lake Meml. award 1987, Robert H. Winner award 1989). E-mail: reneea@verizion.net.

ASHLEY, SHARON ANITA, pediatric anesthesiologist; b. Goulds, Fla., Dec. 28, 1948; d. John H. Ashley and Johnnie Mae (Everett) Ashley-Mitchell; m. Clifford K. Sessions, Sept. 1977 (div. 1985); children: Cecili, Nicole, Erika. BA, Lincoln U., 1970; postgrad., Pomona Coll., 1971; MD, Hahnemann Med. Sch., Phila., 1976; M in Pub. Health, UCLA, 2000. Diplomate Am. Bd. Pain Mgmt., Am. Bd. Anesthesiologists. Intern pediatrics Martin Luther King Hosp., L.A., 1976-77, resident pediatrics, 1977-78, resident anesthesiology, 1978-81, mem. staff, 1981—; assoc. dean grad. med. edn. Charles Drew U. Medicine and Sci., 2002—. Named Outstanding Tchr. of Yr., King Drew Med. Ctr., Dept. Anesthesia, 1989, Outstanding Faculty of Yr., 1991. Mem. Am. Soc. Anesthesiologists, Calif. Med. Assn., L.A. County Med. Soc., Soc. Regional Anesthesia, Soc. Pediatric Anesthesia. Democrat. Baptist. Avocations: reading, crocheting, sailing. Office: Martin Luther King Hosp 12021 Wilmington Ave Los Angeles CA 90059-3099

ASHLEY, WILLARD WALDEN C., SR., minister; b. N.Y.C., Nov. 16, 1953; s. Will and Clara (Peterkin) Ashley; m. Veronica Lamb, June 1975 (div. Sept. 1976); 1 child, Willard W.C. Ashley Jr.; m. Diane Theresa Manning, Sept. 29, 1979 (div. June 21, 2001). AAS, Fashion Inst. Tech., N.Y.C., 1974; BA, Montclair (N.J.) State Coll., 1981; MDiv, Andover Newton Sch. Theol., 1984, D Ministry, 1992. Ordained to ministry Am. Bapt. Ch., 1982. Seminarian First Bapt. Ch., Tewksbury, Mass., 1981-82; pastor New Hope Bapt. Ch., Portsmouth, N.H., 1982-84; asst. dean students, dir. recruitment Andover Newton Theol. Sch., Newton, Mass., 1984-86; pastor Monumental Bapt. Ch., Jersey City, N.J., 1986-96; founder Abundant Joy Bapt. Ch., Jersey City, 1996—; pastoral psychotherapy resident Blanton-Peale Counseling Ctr., N.Y.C., 1996-00; chmn. Abundant Joy Cmty. Devel. Corp., 1999—; COO Norwood Securities Cons., Columbia, Md., 2001—. Mem. Am. Bapt. Statement of Concerns Com., 1988—90; co-chmn. Interfaith Cmty. Orgn., Jersey City, strategy team, 1988—95, Indsl. Areas Found., Nat. Leaders Team, 1991—92; assoc. prof. NY Theol. Sem., 1992—2001, prof. Blanton Peale pastoral studies program, 1999—2001; assoc. prof. Drew Theol. Sem., 1995—98, Auburn Sem., 1998—99; dir. exec. svcs. Haris & Rothenberg Internat., 1999—2002; coord. pastoral care Barnert Hosp., Paterson, NJ, 1994—97; psychotherapist Montclair Counseling Ctr., Upper Montclair, NJ, 1998—2002; staff psychotherapist Riverside Ch., N.Y.C., 2000—; program dir. spiritual care for the care giver N.Y. Disaster Recovery Interfaith. Preacher weekly radio program WNJR, Hillside, N.J., 1987-92; contbr. Men of Color Study Bible, 2002. Bd. dirs. Visiting Homemakers of Hudson, Jersey City, 1988-93, YMCA of Jersey City, 1989-93; bd. regents St. Peter's Coll., 1995-99. Recipient Montclair State Coll. award, 1981, H. Otherman Smith Preaching award, 1984, Citation, Phi Delta Kappa, 1989, Appreciation award, Alpha Kappa Alpha, 1990, Humanitarian award, Nat. Conf. Christians and Jews. Mem. Am. Assn. Pastoral Counselors, Am. Group Psychotherapists Assn., Am. Assn. Marriage and Family Therapists,

Clin. Pastoral Edn., Ministers Coun. Am. Bapt. Ch., Blanton Peale Alumni Assn. (pres. 2002-), North N.J. Missionary Bapt. Assn. Home: 7000 Boulevard E # 48F Guttenberg NJ 07093 Office: Abundant Joy Bapt Ch 46 Fairview Ave Jersey City NJ 07304 also: 475 Riverside Dr Ste 725 New York NY 10115 E-mail: wwca@aol.com.

ASHLEY-FARRAND, MARGALO, lawyer, mediator, private judge; b. N.Y.C., July 26, 1944; d. Joel Thomas and Margalo (Wilson) Ashley; m. Marvin H. Bennett, Mar. 5, 1964 (div. June 1974),; children: Marc, Aliza; m. Thomas Ashley-Farrand, Dec. 11, 1981. Student, UCLA, 1962-63, U. Pitts., 1972-74; BA cum laude, NYU, 1978; JD, Southwestern U., 1980. Bar: D.C. 1981, Md. 1981, Calif. 1983, U.S. Dist. Ct. (ctrl. and no. dists.) Calif. 1984; cert. family law specialist Calif. State Bar. Pvt. practice law, Washington, 1981-82; ptnr. Ashley-Farrand & Smith, Glendale, Calif., 1983-87; pvt. practice law, 1987-95; pvt. practice, 1995—; v.p. Legal Inst. Fair Elections, 1995—; settlement officer L.A. Mcpl. Ct., 1990—99. Judge pro tem L.A. Mcpl. Ct., 1989-99, L.A. Superior Ct., 1993—. Convenor, pres. East Hills chpt. NOW, 1972-74, mem. Pa. state bd., 1972-74, pres. Hollywood chpt. 1974-75, mem. bd. N.Y.C. chpt. 1975-78; convenor, coord. L.A. Women's Coalition for Better Broadcasting, 1974-75; Dem. nominee Calif. State Assembly, 1994; convenor, coord. Shades of Culture Women's Club, 2000—. Themis soc. scholar, 1980; named one of Outstanding Young Women of Am., 1980. Mem. ABA, ACLU, NOW, NWPC, League of Conservation Voters, Calif. Women Lawyers, Women Lawyers Assn. L.A., L.A. County Bar Assn., Pasadena Interracial Women's Club (pres. 1993-94). Office: 215 N Marengo Ave Fl 3 Pasadena CA 91101-1504

ASHLEY-IVERSON, MARY E. retired librarian; b. L.A., Oct. 30, 1947; d. Curtis Lee Gosey and Allie Mae Sheppard-Gosey; m. Billy G. Ashley Sr., Nov. 14, 1965 (dec. Apr. 17, 1995); children: Billy G. Ashley Jr., Dexter Arnett(dec.); m. Willis Iverson Sr., July 6, 1997. Grad., Centennial H.S., Compton, Calif., 1965. Libr. asst. Crenshaw H.S., L.A., 1982—84; libr. clk. Stuttgart (Ark.) Pub. Libr., 1992—99; ret., 1999. Chmn. Records Preservation Com., Stuttgart-DeWitt, 2000—; rec. sec. Stuttgart Civic League, Stuttgart, 1988—91; mem. Wall of Tolerance Nat. Com. for Tolerance, 2001; bd. dirs. There Is Hope, Humphrey, Ark., 1995—, Resource Ctr. Aging, Stuttgart, 2000—. Recipient Dedicated Cmty. Svc. award, Modern Woodman Am., 1993. Mem.: NAACP. Democrat. Baptist. Avocations: coins, antiques, crystal. Home: 301 W Taft Stuttgart AR 72160-2600

ASHLINE, GEORGE LAWRENCE, education educator; s. Lawrence Clayton and Edith Katherine Ashline; m. Patricia Marie Bosley, May 15, 1999. BS, St. Lawrence U., 1985—89; PhD, U. of Notre Dame, 1989—94. Asst. prof. of math. Truman State U. (formerly N.E. Mo. State U.), Kirksville, 1994—95, St. Michael's Coll., Colchester, Vt., 1995—2000, assoc. prof. of math., 2000—. Ap calculus faculty cons. The Coll. Bd., N.Y.C., 1997—2002; instr. Vt. Math. Initiative, Burlington, 2001—. Treas. KC, Winooski, Vt., 1997—2002. Fellow Fees for three nat. conferences partially funded, Project NExT (New Experiences in Tchg.), sponsored by the Math. Assn. of Am., 1996-1997. Mem.: Delta Epsilon Sigma (coll. chpt. pres. 2002—03), Phi Beta Kappa. Roman Catholic. Avocations: hiking, basketball, bicycling. Office: St Michael's Coll 1 Winooski Pk Colchester VT 05439 E-mail: gashline@smcvt.edu.

ASHMAN, ALICIA KONINSKA, civic activist; b. Syracuse, N.Y., July 18, 1923; d. Edward and Stanislawa (Tomaszewska) Koninski; m. Hubert C. Ashman, Apr. 28, 1945; children: Wanda Lorain, Alice Barbara, Philip Richard, Martha Jane. RN, Kings County Sch. Nursing, Bklyn., 1945. Nurse eye dept. Mayo Clinic, Rochester, Minn., 1945-47; alderwoman City of Madison, Wis., 1968-77, coun. pres., 1974. Served on more than 30 civic coms., including parks, welfare, libr., re-devel., equal opportunities, housing, others. Co-founder 10th Dist. Assn., Regent Neighborhood Assn. Capital Cmty. Citizens, 1960s, Dane County Aux. Med. Soc.; mem. State of Wis. Environ. Coun., 1978-80, LWV, Dane County, 1948—; pres. bd. trustees Madison Pub. Libr., 1969-75, 1989-96; trustee South Cen. Libr. Sys., 1992-2002. Recipient Capital Community Citizen Orchid award 1970, cert. of appreciation Wis. Legis. Coun., 1976, LWV, Dane County, Inc., 1995, cert. of recognition Women's Issues and Affirmative Action Office, 1977, The Madison Equal Opportunities Commn., 1983; Alicia Ashman Pedestrian Overpass dedicated in her name, City of Madison, 1979; Trustee of Yr. South Ctrl. Libr. System, 1994; Alicia Ashman Branch Library named in her honor, 1999; named to All-Century List, City of Madison, 1999. Avocations: travel, reading, gardening, sewing.

ASHMAN, CHARLES H. retired minister; b. Johnstown, Pa., June 1, 1924; s. Charles H. Sr. and Flora A.; m. Frances Marie Bradley, July 12, 1946; children: Kenneth W., Judy Ashman Fairman, Karl W. BA cum laude, Westmont Coll., 1947; MDiv magna cum laude, Grace Theol. Seminary, Winona Lake, Ind., 1950. Ordained to ministry Grace Brethren Ch., 1950. Sr. pastor Grace Brethren Ch., Rittman, Ohio, 1950-55, Phoenix, 1955-62, Winona Lake, Ind., 1962-89, pastor emeritus, 1989—; asst. coord. Fellowship of Grace Brethren Chs., Winona Lake, Ind., 1979—. Prof. Grace Theol. Sem., 1969-89. Mem. Nat. Fellowship Grace Brethren Ministers (pres. 1984, Pastor of Yr. 1989, moderator nat. conf. 1973-74), Kiwanis (pres. 1991-92). Home: 1531 S Cherry Creek Ln Warsaw IN 46580-7691 Office: Fellowship Grace Brethren PO Box 386 Winona Lake IN 46590-0386 E-mail: charlesashman@fgbc.org.

ASHMAN, MARTIN C. federal judge; b. 1931; m. Betty Ashman; two children. JD, DePaul U., 1953. Bar: Ill. 1953, U.S. Supreme Ct. 1959. Atty. Ashman & Jaffe, 1954-70, Martin C. Ashman, Ltd., 1970-87; commr. Ill. Ct. Claims, 1974-87; corp. counsel Village of Morton Grove, Ill., 1977-87; cir. judge domestic rels. divsn., law divsn. State of Ill., 1987-95; magistrate judge U.S. Dist. Ct. (no. dist.) Ill., 1995—. Vol. Legal Svcs. Found., Chgo. Recipient Spl. Tribute award Ill. Coun. Against Handgun Violence; Outstanding Svc. to Legal Profession award, DePaul U. Law Sch., 2001. Mem. ABA, Fed. Bar Assn., Fed. Magistrate Judges Assn., Ill. State Bar Assn., Decalogue Soc. Lawyers, Chgo. Bar Assn. (Cert. of Appreciation). Office: US Dist Ct 1366 Dirksen Bldg 219 S Dearborn St Chicago IL 60604-1800

ASHMEAD, ALLEZ MORRILL, speech, hearing, and language pathologist, orofacial myologist, consultant; b. Provo, Utah, Dec. 18, 1916; d. Laban Rupert and Zella May (Miller) M.; m. Harvey H. Ashmead, 1940; children: Harve DeWayne, Sheryl Mae Harames, Zeltha Janeel Henderson, Emma Allez Broadfoot. BS, Utah State U., 1938; MS summa cum laude, U. Utah, 1952, PhD summa cum laude, 1970; postgrad., Idaho State U., Oreg. State Coll., U. Denver, U. Utah, Brigham Young U., Utah State U., U. Washington, U. No. Colo. Cert. secondary edn., remedial reading, spl. edn., learning disabilities; cert. ASHA clin. competence speech pathology and audiology; profl. cert. in orofacial myology. Tchr. pub. schs., Utah, Idaho, 1938-43; speech and hearing pathologist Bushnell Hosp., Brigham City, Utah, 1943-45; sr. speech correctionist Utah State Dept. Health, Salt Lake City, 1945-52; dir. speech and hearing dept. Davis County Sch. Dist., Farmington, Utah, 1952-65; clin., field supr. U. Utah, Salt Lake City, 1965-70, 75-78; speech pathologist Box Elder Sch. Dist., Brigham City, 1970-75, 78-84. Teaching specialist Brigham Young U., Provo, 1970-73; speech pathologist Primary Children's Med. Ctr., Salt Lake City, 1975-77; pvt. practice speech pathology and orofacial myology, 1970-88; del. USSR Profl. Speech Pathology seminar, 1984, 86; participant numerous internat. seminars. Author: Physical Facilities for Handicapped Children, 1957, A Guide for Training Public School Speech and Hearing Clinicians, 1965, A Guide for Public School Speech Hearing Programs, 1959, Impact of Orofacial Myofunctional Treatment on Orthodontic Correction, 1982, Meeting Needs of Handicapped Children, 1975, Relationship of Trace Minerals to Disease, 1972, Macro and Trace Minerals in Human Metabolism, 1971, Electromotive Potential Differences Between Stutterers and Non-stutterers, 1970, Learning Disability, An Educational Adventure, 1969, New Horizons in Special Education, 1969, Developing Speech and Language in the Exceptional Child, 1961, Parent Teacher Guidance in Primary Stuttering, 1951, numerous others; contbr. research articles to profl. jours. Student Placement chair Am. Field Service, Kaysville, Utah, 1962-66; ednl. del. Women's State Legis. Council, Salt Lake City, 1958-70; chairwoman fund raising Utah Symphony Orch., Salt Lake City, 1970-71; sec., treas. Utah chpt. U.S. Council for Exceptional Children, 1958-62, membership com. chair, 1962-66, program com. chair, 1966-68 Recipient Scholarship award for Higher Edn. U. Utah, Salt Lake City, 1969; Phi Kappa Phi scholar, Delta Kappa Gamma scholar, 1968; rsch. grantee Utah Dept. Edn., 1962. Mem. NEA, Utah Ednl. Assn., Am. Speech, Lang. Hearing Assn. (life, continuing edn. com. 1985, Ace award for Continuing Edn. 1984), Western Speech Assn., Internat. Assn. Orofacial Myology (life, bd. examiners, Sci. Contribution award 1982), Utah Speech, Hearing and Lang. Assn. (life, sec., treas. 1956-60), AAUW (Utah state bd. chair status of women 1959-62, Kaysville br. 1957-60, bd. dirs. Kaysville-Davis br. 1987-92, chair internat. rels. 1987-91, chair cultural interests Kaysville-Davis br. 1991-92), Delta Kappa Gamma (state scholarship award 1968, del. Woman's State Legis. Coun. 1958-70, profl. affairs chair 1963-67, tchr. of yr. award 1978), AAUW (bd. dirs. internat. rels. Kaysvile-Davis br., 1988-91), Daus. Utah Pioneers (parliamentarian Kaysville 1980-92, historian 1974-80, lesson leader 1992-95, capt. 1996-98), Soroptimists (charter, bd. dirs. 1954-56, pres. Davis County chpt. 1965-69, Rocky Mountain regional bd. dirs. 1965-70, cmty. svc. award 1968, pub. svc. award 1970), Sigma Alpha Eta, Theta Alpha Phi, Psi Chi, Zeta Phi Eta, Phi Kappa Phi. Republican. Mem. Lds Ch. Avocations: international travel, reading, boating, sports, fine and performing arts. Home: 719 E Center St Kaysville UT 84037-2138

ASHMUS, KEITH ALLEN, lawyer; b. Cleve., Aug. 19, 1949; s. Richard A. and Rita (Petti) A.; m. Marie Sachiko Matsuoka, Dec. 15, 1973; children: Emmy Marie, Christopher Todd. BA in Policy Sci., Mich. State U., 1971, MA in Econs., 1972; JD, Yale U., 1974. Bar: Ohio 1974, Calif. 1991, U.S. Dist. Ct. (no. dist.) Ohio 1975, U.S. Dist. Ct. (no., so. and cen. dists.) Calif. 1991, U.S. Dist. Ct. (so. dist.) Ohio 2000, U.S. Ct. Appeals (6th cir.) 1975, U.S. Supreme Ct. 1980. Assoc. Thompson Hine & Flory LLP, Cleve., 1974-82, ptnr., 1982—2000, ptnr.-in-charge Cleve. office, 1996-99, dept. chmn., 1999-2000; founding ptnr. Frantz Ward LLP, Cleve., 2000—. Mediator/arbitrator Am. Arbitration Assn. Comml. Employment Panels, 1995—. Co-author: Public Sector Collective Bargaining: The Ohio System, 1984. Trustee cmty. arts Baycrafters, Bay Village, Ohio, 1981-84, Hospice Coun. No. Ohio, 1982-84, Inst. for Personal Health Skills, Cleve. 1985-90; trustee Coun. Smaller Enterprises, 1990-96, 98—, 1st vice chmn., 2000-2001, chmn., 2001--; trustee Village Found., 1997—, Vocat. Guidance Svcs. 1999-2002, Youth Opportunities Unltd., 2000—, Cleve. Saves, 2001—; sec. George W. Codrington Charitable Found., 1994-2000; chmn. job placement for older persons Skills Available, Cleve., 1980-87; gov.'s appointee to Health Care Quality Adv. Coun., 1996; mem. adv. bd. Greater Cleve. Salvation Army, 1997—, treas., 2000-01, vice chmn., 2001—. Named one of Outstanding Vols. award Nat. Hospice Orgn., 1982, Vol. of Yr. Vocat. Guidance and Rehab. Services, 1985, 86. Mem. ABA, State Bar Calif., Ohio State Bar Assn. (coun. dels. 1995—, bd. govs. 1998-2001, pres. 2003), Cleve. Bar Assn. (trustee 1985-88, 98-2001, chmn. labor law sect. 1983-84), Def. Rsch. Inst., Pub. Sector Labor Rels. Assn. (exec. com. 1989-93). Avocations: golf, fishing. Office: Frantz Ward LLP 55 Public Sq 19th Fl Cleveland OH 44113-1999 E-mail: kashmus@frantzward.com.

ASHRAF, ELIZABETH ANN, pharmaceutical company executive; b. Troy, N.Y., July 2, 1947; d. Samuel S. and Rose (Earley) Basen; m. Mirza Khalil Ashraf, Feb. 14, 1976; children: Danial, David. BA in Biology, Coll. St. Rose, 1969; MS in Pharmacology, St. John's U., Queens, N.Y., 1976, PhD in Pharmacology, 1981. Rsch. biologist Microscopy for Biol. Rsch., Albany, N.Y., 1969-71; rsch. scientist N.Y.U., N.Y.C., 1973-74; rsch. coord. Winthrop Labs., N.Y.C., 1974-76; supr. Sterling Drug Inc., N.Y.C., 1976-78; sr. dir. med. comm. Ives Labs., N.Y.C., 1978-86; sr. dir. med. comms. Wyeth Consumer Healthcare, Madison, 1986—. Fellow Am. Med. Writers Assn. (sec. 1987-88, Past Pres.' award Met. chpt. 1981-82, 88-89); mem. Am. Soc. for Reproductive Medicine, Rho Chi. Roman Catholic. Avocations: travel, literature.

ASHTON, BETSY FINLEY, broadcast journalist, author, lecturer; b. Wilkes-Barre, Pa., May 13, 1944; d. Charles Leonard Hancock Jones and Margaretta Betty (Hart) Jones Layton; m. Arthur Benner Ashton, Nov. 5, 1966 (div. 1972); m. Robert Clarke Freed, May 18, 1974 (div. 1981); m. Jacob B. Underhill III, Oct. 17, 1987. BA, Am. U., 1966; postgrad., Corcoran Sch. Art, 1968; postgrad. in fine arts, Am. U., 1969-71; student in painting, Corcoran Sch. Art, 1968. Tchr. art Fairfax County (Va.) Pub. Schs., 1967-70; reporter, anchor Sta. WWDC, Washington, 1972-73, Sta. WMAL-AM-FM, Washington, 1973-75; corr. Sta. WTTG-TV, Washington, 1975-76, Sta. WJLA-TV, Washington, 1976-82; consumer corr. CBS News and Sta. WCBS-TV, N.Y.C., 1982-86; sr. corr. Today's Bus., 1986-87; personal fin. contbr. CBS Morning Program, 1987, Lifetime Cable TV, 1988—; anchor FNN Money Talk, 1989; exec. editor Great Giving, 2000—. Bd. dirs. Lowell E. Mellett Fund for a Free and Responsible Press, Washington, 1979-82; courtroom artist numerous trials, Washington, 1978-81. Reporter TV news report Caffeine, 1981 (AAUW award 1982); reporter spot news 6 P.M. News, 1979 (Emmy award); author: Betsy Ashton's Guide to Living on Your Own, 1988. Concert master of ceremonies Beethoven Soc., Washington, 1979-82. Recipient Laurel award Columbia Journalism Rev., 1984, Outstanding Alumna award Am. U., 1985, Outstanding Media award Am. U., 1986, Best Consumer Journalism citation Nat. Press Club, 1983. Mem. AFTRA, NATAS, Author's Guild, Newswomen's Club N.Y., Soc. Profl. Journalists (pres. N.Y. chpt. 1994, 2000, Washington chpt. 1980-81, bd. dirs. N.Y. chpt. 1989—, co-chair 2004 nat. conv.), Friends of Thirteen (bd. dirs. 1995—), Sigma Delta Chi Found. (bd. dirs. 1996—), Alpha Chi Omega (v.p. chpt. 1964-66). Avocations: painting, drawing, golf.

ASHTON, DORE, author, educator; b. Newark; d. Ralph N. and Sylvia (Ashton) Shapiro; m. Adja Yunkers, July 8, 1952 (dec. 1983); children—Alexandra Louise, Marina Svietlana; m. Matti Megged, 1985. BA, U. Wis., 1949; MA, Harvard U., 1950; PhD honoris causa, Moore Coll., 1975, Hamline U., 1982; attended, Minn. Coll. of Art, 2002. Asso. editor Art Digest, 1951-54; asso. critic N.Y. Times, 1955-60; lectr. Pratt Inst., 1962-63; head humanities dept. (Sch. Visual Arts), 1965-68; prof. Cooper Union, 1968—. Art critic, lectr., dir. exhbns. in arts; mem. adv. bd. John Simon Guggenheim Found, Dedalus Found. Author: Abstract Art Before Columbus, 1957, Poets and the Past, 1959, Philip Guston, 1960, The Unknown Shore, 1962, Rauschenberg's Dante, 1964, Modern American Sculpture, 1968, Richard Lindner, 1969, A Reading of Modern Art, 1970, Pol Bury, 1971; Cultural Guide for New York, 1972; Picasso on Art, 1972, The New York School: A Cultural Reckoning, 1973, A Joseph Cornell Album, 1974, Yes, But, A Critical Biography of Philip Guston, 1976, A Fable of Modern Art, 1980, American Art Since 1945, 1982, About Rothko, 1983, Jacobo Borges, 1984, 20th Century Artists on Art, 1985, Out of the Whirlwind, 1987, Fragonard in the Universe of Painting, 1988, Terence La Noue, 1992, Noguchi East and West, 1992, Ursula van Rydingsvard, 1995, The Delicate Thread: Teshigahara's Life in Art, 1997, À Rebours: La Rebellión Informalista, 1999, The Black Rainbow: The Work of Fernando de Szyszlo, 2003, The Walls of the Heart: The Work of David Rankin, 2001, William Tucker, 2001; also monographs; co-author: (with Denise Browne Hare) Rosa Bonheur, A Life and Legend, 1981; co-editor: Redon, Moreau, Bresdin, 1961; N.Y. contbg. editor Studio Internat, 1961-74, Opus Internat, 1968-74, XXième Siècle, 1955-70; assoc. editor Arts, 1974-92; contbr. to: Vision and Value series (Gyorgy Kepes), 1966, The New Art Anthology (Gregory Battcock), 1966. Adv. bd. Guggenheim Found. Recipient Mather award for art criticism Coll. Art Assn., 1963, Art Criticism prize St. Louis Art Mus., 1988; Guggenheim fellow, 1964; Graham fellow, 1963; Ford Found. fellow, 1960; Nat. Endowment for Humanities grantee, 1980 Mem. Internat. Assn. Art Critics, Phi Beta Kappa. Home: 217 E 11th St New York NY 10003-7302 Office: Cooper Union Advancement Sci and Art 41 Cooper Sq New York NY 10003-7136

ASHTON, HARRIS JOHN, business executive; b. Elizabeth, NJ, June 21, 1932; s. Earle S. and Dorothy (Black) A.; m. Angela Murphy, Oct. 20, 1962; children: Kelly Elizabeth, Victoria Catherine. BA, Yale U., 1954; LLB, Columbia U., 1959. Bar: NY 1960. Assoc. Breed, Abbott & Morgan, 1959-62, Lovejoy, Wasson, Lundgren & Huppuch, 1962-64; partner Lovejoy, Wasson, Lundgren & Ashton, 1964-75, of counsel, 1975-81; pres., chief adminstrv. officer Gen. Host Corp., 1967-69, chmn., pres., chief exec. officer, 1970-97. Bd. dir. Bar-S Foods Co., of 49 Franklin Templeton Group of Funds. Bd. dir. Madison Square Boys and Girls Club; trustee Greenwich Acad., 1977-81, Miss Porter's Sch., 1981-85, United Cerebral Palsy Rsch. and Ednl. Found., Inc.; mem. bd. visitors Columbia U. Sch. Law, 1982—, Yale New Haven Hosp., 1990-95; bd. overseers Inst. for Civil Justice, 1999, 2002. Mem. Yale Club (NYC), Blind Brook Club, Stanwich Club, Cypress Point Club, Bohemian Club.

ASHTON, MARK ALFRED, lawyer; b. July 18, 1944; s. Alfred Jackson and Margarette Carolyn (Green) A.; m. Linda Diane Stroud, May 15, 1971; children: Kathryn, Hillary, Courtney. BBA, U. Okla., 1966; JD, 1969. Bar: Okla. 1969, U.S. Dist. Ct. (we. Dist.) Okla. 1969, U.S. Ct. Appeals. (10th cir.) 1970, D.C. Ct. Appeals 1970, U.S. Supreme Ct. 1973. Assoc. Rhoads, Ashton, Johnson & Schacher & Lawton, Okla., 1969-72; ptnr. Ashton and Ashton, Lawton, 1972-73; ptnr., pres. Ashton, Ashton, Wisener and Munkacsy, Inc., Lawton, 1975—. Mem. com. apptd. by Okla. Supreme Ct. to write civil instrn. manual for all trial judges, 1978—; lectr. continuing legal edn. of bar; mem. Okla. Supreme Ct. Com. on Media in the Courtroom, 1978; commr. Okla. Jud. Nominating Commn., 1983-89; chmn., 1987; bd. dirs. Okla. Attys. Mutual Ins. Co., 1995—, exec. com., 1995—. Co-editor: Okla. Bar Assn. Desk Manual, 1976; editor: The Advocate, 1997—; contbr. articles on law to profl. jours. Mem. Comanche County Democratic party; 4th congl. dist. Okla. del. Dem. Nat. Conv., 1984, 2000; mem. Centenary United MEth. Ch., Lawton; chmn. City of Lawton Personnel Bd., 1975-80; past. chmn. Okla. chpt. Common Cause. Served to capt. Judge adv. Gen. USAF, 1969-72. Mem. Okla. Bar Assn. (lawyers ins. com. 1979, del. to ho. of dels. 1974, chmn. pub. info. com. 1982, 83, assoc. editor jour. 1983-87, editor, 1988-89; named Outstanding performance 1976, Golden Gavel award 1982, disting. svc. award 1988), SW Okla. Legal Inst. (pres. 1976), Okla. Trial Lawyers Assn. (pres. 1978, 87, bd. dirs. 1975-82, edn. chmn. 1976, pres., 1978, 87), ABA, Am. Trial Lawyers Assn., Okla. Bar Prof. Liability Co. (liability ins. com. 1979—, bd. dirs. 1979—, c.p. 1979-85, chmn. bd. 1985-87), Phi Delta Phi. Avocations: backpacking, photography. Home: 1618 NW 34th St Lawton OK 73505-3814 Office: Ashton Wisener & Munkacsy PC 711 SW C Ave Lawton OK 73501-4311

ASHTON, MARK RANDOLPH, lawyer; b. Abington, Pa., Sept. 10, 1955; s. Frank E. and Charlotte (Wagenbaur) A. BA in Internat. Affairs, George Washington U., 1977; JD, John Marshall U., 1980. Bar: Pa. 1980. Law clk. to Hon. Mason Avrigian Ct. of Common Pleas of Montgomery County, Norristown, Pa., 1980-81; assoc. Abrahams & Loewenstein, Norristown, 1982-87; dept. chmn. Riley, Riper, Hollin & Colagreco, 1987-90; ptnr. Fox, Rothschild, O'Brien & Frankel, Exton, Pa., 1990—. Mem. Montgomery Bar Assn. (bd. dirs. 1985-87), Chester County Bar Assn. (chmn. family law sect. 1988-90), Wissahickon Valley Hist. Soc. (former pres.), D.J. Freed Am. Inn of Ct. (former pres.). Republican. Episcopalian. Home: 413 Stratford Ave Collegeville PA 19426-2553 Office: Fox Rothschild O'Brien & Frankel 760 Constitution Dr Ste 104 Exton PA 19341-1149

ASHTON, RICHARD M. federal lawyer; BA, JD, Catholic U. Lawyer honors program FDIC, 1974-76; staff atty. Fed. Res. Bd., 1976-82, asst. gen. counsel, 1982-85, assoc. gen. counsel, 1985—. Office: Federal Reserve System Board Members Office 20th & C Sts NW Ofc Washington DC 20551-0001

ASHTON, RICK JAMES, librarian; b. Middletown, Ohio, Sept. 18, 1945; s. Ralph James and Lydia Marie (Thornbery) A.; m. Marcia K. Zuroweste, Dec. 23, 1966; children: Jonathan Paul, David Andrew. AB, Harvard U., 1967; MA, Northwestern U., 1969, PhD, 1973; MA, U. Chgo., 1976. Instr., asst. prof. history Northwestern U., Evanston, Ill., 1972-74; curator local and family history Newberry Libr., Chgo., 1974-77; asst. dir. Allen County Pub. Libr., Ft. Wayne, Ind., 1977-80, dir., 1980-85; city libr. Denver Pub. Libr., 1985—. Mem. Ind. Coop Libr. Svcs. Authority, 1980-85, pres., 1984-85; cons. NEH, Nat. Ctr. Edn. Stats., Northwestern U. Office Estate Planning, Snowbird Leadership Inst., Houston Pub. Libr. Author: The Life of Henry Ruiter, 1742-1819, 1974, The Genealogy Beginner's Manual: A New Edition, 1977, Stuntz, Fuller, Kennard and Cheadle Ancestors, 1987 (with others) Trends in Urban Library Management, 1989, Intelligent Library Buildings, 1999. Bd. dirs. Cmty. Coordinated Child Care, Evanston, 1972-74, Three Rivers Montessori Sch., Ft. Wayne, 1977-80; bd. dirs., sec. Allen County-Ft. Wayne Hist. Soc., 1977-83; trustee Iliff Sch. Theology, 2000—; conscientious objector. Recipient Old City Hall Hist. Svc. award, 1985, Phil Milstein award Denver AIA, 1998; NDEA fellow, 1967-69, Downtown Denver award, 1996, 97, Bonfils-Stanton Found. award in arts and humanities, 2003; Woodrow Wilson fellow, 1971-72. Mem. ALA, Colo. Libr. Assn. (Libr. of Yr. 2000), Colo. Alliance Rsch. Librs. (pres. 1987-88, sec. 1993-95, chmn. 1995-2000), Urban Librs. Coun., Cactus Club. Home: 217 S Jackson St Unit A Denver CO 80209-3132 Office: Denver Pub Libr 10 W 14th Avenue Pkwy Denver CO 80204-2731 E-mail: rashton@denver.lib.co.us.

ASHTON, ROBERT W. lawyer, foundation administrator; b. Memphis, Jan. 26, 1937; s. Robert Wilson and Ina Louise A.; m. Jean Isabel Willoughby; children: Katherine, Susanna, Emily, Isabel. BA, U. Mich., 1960; LLB, Vanderbilt U., 1964. Bar: N.Y. 1965. Assoc. Beekman & Bogue, N.Y.C., 1964-73, ptnr., 1973-81, Gaston Snow Beekman & Bogue, N.Y.C., 1981-89, counsel, 1989-91; atty. pvt. practice, N.Y.C., 1991—. Exec. dir. The Bay Found., 1977—, Josephine Bay Paul and C. Michael Paul Found., 1977-87; bd. dirs. St. Matthew's & St. Timothy's Neighborhood Ctr., N.Y.C., 1973-2001, Josephine Bay Paul and C. Michael Paul Found., 2001—, Marine Biol. Lab., Woods Hole, Mass., 1980-89, coun. visitors, 2000--; bd. dirs. Alumni Bd. Vanderbilt Law Sch., 1980-88, The Fund for Artists Colonies, 1983-90, Orch. St. Luke's, N.Y.C., 1988—, Millay Colony for Arts, Austerlitz, N.Y., 1994-2002. Mem.: Assn. Bar of City of N.Y., Century Assn., Estate Lawyers Club. Democrat. Home: 300 W 108th St New York NY 10025-2757 Office: 17 W 94th St New York NY 10025-7116

ASHTON, TAMARAH M. special education educator, consultant; b. Toledo, Dec. 5, 1961; d. Harold Leroy and Patricia Marie (Casto) Ashton; m. John G. Coombs, Feb. 11, 1989; 1 child, Rebecca Marie. MusB, Western Mich. U., 1984; MS, San Diego State U., 1988, MA, 1990; PhD, Claremont Grad. U., 1997. Cert. tchr., Calif. Asst. project dir. San Diego State U., 1994-98; asst. prof. dept. of spl. edn. Calif. State U., Northridge, 1998—2003, assoc. prof. dept. of spl. edn., 2003 . Cons. in field. Mem. Coun. for Learning Disabilities. Mem. Coun. for Exceptional Children, Phi Kappa Phi, Pi Lambda Theta. Avocation: needlework. Home: 28721 W Highland C Castaic CA 91384-3080 E-mail: tamarah.ashton@csun.edu.

ASHTON, THOMAS WALSH, investment banker; b. Rochester, N.Y., May 11, 1929; s. Charles Edward and Marie Margaret (Walsh) A.; m. Frances E. Hickey, May 16, 1953 (div. 1977); children: Lucy M. Van Atta, Mary B. Ashton Anders, Monica H., William T; m. Mary K Joy, Dec. 20, 1978 (dec. 1997); m. Carolyn B. Richardson, Jan. 26, 2002. BS, U.S. Mil. Acad., 1952; MBA, Harvard U., 1957. Assoc. corp. fin. Eastman Dillon Union Securities, N.Y.C, 1957-61, gen. ptnr., 1967-69; asst. v.p. Harris Upham & Co., N.Y.C., 1961-67; v.p. duPont Glore Forgan, Inc., N.Y.C., 1971-73; sr. v.p. ABD Securities Corp., N.Y.C., 1973-75; fin. cons. Am. Cancer Soc. of N.Y.C., East West Group Inc. Chmn. Peninsular Investments, Treasure Island, Fla., 1977-87; cons. Dept. Commerce, 1971; chmn. Ashton Investments, Inc., 1987—. Chmn. parents's coun. Smith Coll., 1974-76. With AUS, 1946-48, 52-55. Mem. Soc. Harvard Engrs. and Scientists (gov. 1974-75), West Point Soc. N.Y. (dir. 1971-75), Army and Navy Club (Washington), Ponte Vedra Inn and Club. Republican. E-mail: tashton749@aol.com.

ASHUTOSH, KUMAR, pulmonologist, educator; b. Darbhanga, Bihar, India, Feb. 14, 1940; arrived in US, 1968; s. Baldeva and Shiva Kumari Narayan; m. Sabita P. Prasad, June 6, 1966; children: Anu, Ishan. MD, Darbhanga Med. Coll., 1965, MB BS, 1962; I Sc in intermediate sci., HPD Jain Coll., Arrah, Bihar. Diplomate Am. Bd. of Internal Medicine, pulmonary diseases Am. Bd. of Internal Medicine. Assoc. prof. SUNY Upstate Med. Ctr., Syracuse, NY, 1981—91; staff phycian VA Med. Ctr., Syracuse, 1974—; med. officer Govt. of Bihar, Jaynagar, 1965—68; attending physician SUNY U. Med. Ctr., Syracuse, 1974—; chief pulmonary disease VA Med. Ctr., Syracuse; prof. of medicine SUNY Upstate Med. U., Syracuse, 1991—. Chmn. peer rev. com. VA Med. Ctr., Syracuse, 2000—, chmn. critical care com., 1994—, dir. ICU, 1989—96, med. dir. respiratory care, 1978—; presenter in field. Contbr. articles to profl. jours. Treas. Darbhanga Med. Coll. Alumni Assn.; bd. dirs. India Cmty Cultural and Religious Ctr., Syracuse, 2000—02; bd. of directors Hindu Temple of CNY, Syracuse, 1998—2002; pres. India Cmty Cultural Ctr., Syracuse, 1986—88. Recipient rsch. grant, Am. Heart Assn., 1980, Baesselar Assocs., 1984, GENETECH, 1986. Fellow: Am. Coll. of Chest Physicians (ad hoc cons. reviewer 1980—), ACP; mem.: Am. Thoracic Soc. (clin. problems com.). Achievements include research in Pulmonary Hypertension, Respiratory Failure, Chronic Obstructive Pulmonary Disease; Angiotensin Converting Enzyme, Aerobic Fitness. Avocations: tennis, literature. Office: VA Med Ctr 800 Irving Ave Syracuse NY 13210 Personal E-mail: kumar.ashutosh@med.va.gov. E-mail: kumar.ashutosh@med.va.gov.

ASHVIL-BIBI, SIGALIT, musician, artist; b. Kutaissi, Georgia, Apr. 28, 1952; came to U.S., 1983; BA, Acad. Music, Tbillissi, USSR, 1973; studied with Mordechai-Misha Dzanashvili, 1973-83; cert., N.Y. Acad. Art, 1993. Mem. staff Mus. Beit Ha'Omamin, Jerusalem, Mus. Yad Le Banim, Hulon, Israel, Yeshiva U. Mus., N.Y.C., The White House, Washington. One-man shows include The White House, Washington, 1981, 96, Queens "Y", N.Y., 1996, 97, 98, 99, 00, Chassidic Art Inst., Bklyn., 2000, Bklyn.-Queens (N.Y.) Conservatory of Music, 2001; exhibited in group shows at Bklyn. Mus., 1989, Yeshiva U. Mus., N.Y.C., 1991-92, Creative Alternative Gallery, Bklyn., 2001-02, Jerusalem, Israel, 2003; exhbn. and concert Guatemala Ctrl. America, 2002. Recipient Gold Medal award 6th Internat. Festival Between Musicians, USSR, 1968. Mem. Asn Israeli Artists (bd. dirs. 1979), Am. Artist Profl. League, Judaic Art. Home: 11001 62nd Dr Apt 2C Forest Hills NY 11375-1201 E-mail: ashvilart@aol.com.

ASHVO-MUÑOZ, ALIRA, language educator; arrived in U.S., 1962; d. Fernando de los Santos Muñoz Venereo and Enriqueta Díaz-Laurent Gonzalez; m. Juan Carlos Lira-Melzi, Jan. 15, 1983 (div. June 1986). BA in Archaeology, U. Tex., 1982, MA in Anthropology, 1989, MA in Spanish, 1992, PhD, 1999. Rschr. U. Tex., Austin, 1990—92, lang. instr., 1992—98; asst. prof. Coll. of N.J., Ewing, 1999—2000, Villanova (Pa.) U., 2000, Temple U., Phila., 2001—, Scholar, Gale Group, 2001. Avocations: art, early music, textiles. Office: Temple U Anderson Hall Philadelphia PA 19122

ASHWORTH, BRENT FERRIN, lawyer; b. Albany, Calif., Jan. 8, 1949; s. Dell Shepherd and Bette Jean (Brailsford) Ashworth; m. Charlene Mills, Dec. 16, 1970; children: Amy, John, Matthew, Samuel(dec.), Adam, David, Emily, Luke, Benjamin. BA, Brigham Young U., 1972; JD, U. Utah, 1975. Bar: Utah 1977. Asst. county atty. Carbon County, Price, Utah, 1975-76; assoc. atty. Frandsen & Keller, Price, Utah, 1976-77; v.p. legal affairs, sec., gen. counsel Nature's Sunshine Products, Provo, Utah, 1977—. Bd. dirs., gen. counsel Carbon County Nursing Home, Price, 1976—77; mem. Provo Landmarks Commn., 1997—2002, chmn., 2002—, co-chair sesquicentennial com., 1998—99; active Provo Libr. Bd., 2000—03, chmn., 2003—, Utah County Cancer Crusade Com., 1981—83, Provo LCOC Arts subcom., 1998—99; pres. Desert Village Spani Fork, Utah, 1988—90; gen. counsel Brigham Young Acad. Found., 1995—2001; founder, chmn. George E. Freestone Boy Scout Mus., Provo, 2000—; exec. bd. Utah Nat. Pk. coun. Boy Scouts Am., 2000—; city councilman, planning commn. Payson City, Utah, 1980—82, mayor pro tem, 1982; bd. dirs. ARC, Utah County chpt., 1988—94, Springville Mus. Art, 1998—2001, Celebration Health Found., 1999—, Provo Sch. Dist. Found., 2001—. Mem.: ATLA, SAR (pres. Utah County chpt. 1989—90, state chpts. 1st v.p. 1990—91, state soc. pres. 1991—92, chancellor 1992—94), ABA, Am. Corp. Counsel Assn. (sec. intermountain chpt. 1990—91), Utah State Bar Assn., Southeastern Utah Bar Assn. (sec. 1977), Sons Utah Pioneers, Emily Dickinson Soc. Utah (pres. 1995—97), Kiwanis Club (v.p. 1995—96, pres. 1997—98, lt. gov. Utah Idaho dist. 2001—02), Phi Eta Sigma, Phi Kappa Phi. Home: 1377 Cambridge Ct Provo UT 84604-4178 Office: Natures Sunshine Products PO Box 1000 Spanish Fork UT 84660-0901

ASHWORTH, DAVID J. management consultant, power company executive; Grad. in cons. engring. and mgmt., Manchester Coll., England, 1965; MBA with highest distinction, Case Western Res. U., 1988; mgmt. technology cert., U. Mich., 1992; grad., U. Pa., 1995. Sr. project controls engr., contract adminstr. Bldg. Design Partnership, England, 1970-77; assoc. project mgr. Dielschneider Assocs., Oreg., 1978-80; sr. cost engr., lead field cost engr. Bechtel Power Co., Mich., 1981-84; sr. project control sys. engr. Consumers Power Co., Mich., 1984-85; project mgr. Toledo Edison, Ohio, 1985-89; sr. rsch. devel. and demonstration coord. Centerior Energy, Ohio, 1989-92, bus. and tech. applications mgr., 1992-93, resource and bus. planning mgr., 1993-95; sr. mgr. bus. devel. Centerior Enterprises, Ohio, 1995-97; dir. bus. devel. FirstEnergy Ventures, Ohio, 1997-2000; v.p. Bay Shore Power Co., Stow, Ohio, 2000—03. Mem. Beta Gamma Sigma. Address: 520 Wheatfield Dr Aurora OH 44202-8034 Fax: 330-384-5033. E-mail: djashworth@aol.com.

ASHWORTH, DENISE MARCHANT, retired landscape architect; b. Langrick, Eng., Apr. 6, 1917; came to U.S., 1946; d. Gerald Marchant and Ella (Brand) Davis; divorced; children: Ella Marchant Ashworth Ingraham, Sarah Elizabeth Marchant Ashworth Flavell. MS summa cum laude, U. Conn., 1975, MS, 1977; MLA, U. Ga., 1978. Asst. landscape architect U.S. Forest Svc., Cleveland, Tenn., 1979-84, zone landscape architect Greeneville, Tenn., 1984-86, other resources asst. forest landscape architect Jackson, Miss., 1986-90; owner, operator Hilltop House Bed & Breakfast, Greeneville, 1990—2002. Pres. Magnolia Garden Club, Cleveland, 1985-86. Recipient Outstanding Job Performance award U.S. Forest Svc., 1988, Sustained Outstanding Job Performance award, 1989. Mem. Am. Soc. Landscape Archs., Soc. Am. Foresters, U. Tenn. Arboretum Soc., Tenn. Native Plant Soc., Audubon Soc., Westside Garden Club, Meadow Rose Garden Club (pres. 1989-90), Tenn. Conservation League (Tenn. Forest Conservationist award 1995), Toastmasters (pres. Jackson 1988-89, area bd. govs. dist. 43 1989, dist. 63 1990-91). Democrat. Episcopalian. Avocations: hiking, travel, detective novels, gardening. Home and Office: 113 Nanci Ln Apt 4 Greeneville TN 37743 E-mail: ashworth@greene.xtn.net.

ASHWORTH, KENNETH HAYDEN, public affairs specialist; b. Abilene, Tex., Feb. 24, 1932; s. Harold Laverne and Mae Beatrice (Grote) A.; m. Emily Yaung; children: Rodney Brian, Karen Grace. BA, U. Tex., 1958, PhD, 1969; M. Pub. Adminstrn., Syracuse U., 1959. Asst. commr. Tex. Higher Edn. Coordinating Bd., Austin, 1965-69, commr. higher edn., 1976-97; vice chancellor for acad. affairs U. Tex. System, Austin, 1969-73; exec. v.p. U. Tex. at San Antonio, 1973-76. Vis. prof. govt. and pub. affairs U. Tex., Austin, 1997—, Tex. A &M U., College Sta., 1997—. Author: Scholars and Statesmen, 1972, American Higher Education in Decline, 1979, (with Norman Hackerman) Conversations on the Uses of Science and Technology, 1996, Caught Between the Dog and the Fireplug or How to Survive Public Service, 2001. Served with USN, 1951-55. Mem. Philos. Soc. Tex., Phi Beta Kappa, Phi Delta Kappa, Phi Kappa Phi, Pi Sigma Alpha. Clubs: Town and Gown. Democrat. Unitarian Universalist. Home: 7616 Rustling Rd Austin TX 78731-1365 Office: U Tex LBJ Sch Pub Affairs PO Box Y Austin TX 78713-8925 also: Tex A&M U Bush Sch Govt And Pub Svc College Station TX 77843-0001

ASHWORTH, LAWRENCE NELSON, retired bank executive; b. Richmond, Va., Mar. 17, 1942; s. Durwood Ormond and Lillian Annie (Thomas) A.; m. Sandra Miller, Aug. 3, 1962; children: Christopher Sean, Matthew Todd. BBA, Marshall U., 1964; MBA, U. Richmond, 1980. Buyer Houdaille Industries, Huntington, W.Va., 1964-65, factory acct., 1965-68, asst. div. contr. Frankenmuth, Mich., 1968-70; dir. fin. planning Carlton Industries, Richmond, 1970-72; v.p. fin., co-founder TransAm Co., Richmond, 1972-76; asst. v.p. Signet Bank, Richmond, 1976-78, v.p., divsn. v.p., 1978-90, sr. v.p., unit mgr., 1990-91, sr. v.p., divsn. mgr., 1991-98; ret., 1998. Cons. in field. Author: (with others) Handbook of Bank Accounting and Finance, 1989. Pres. Tuckahoe Little League, Richmond, 1981, bd. dirs., 1976-83, coach, mgr., 1976-80; bd. dirs. Tuckahoe Sports, Inc., Richmond, 1984-94, sr. v.p., chief lending officer The Bank of Richmond, 2002—. Mem. Nat. Comml. Fin. Assn. (dir., mem. exec. com.), Turnaround Mgmt. Assn., Hermitage Country Club, Downtown Club, Am. Inst. Bankers. Avocations: golf, skiing, travel, reading, woodworking.

ASHWORTH, RONALD BROUGHTON, health facility executive, accountant; b. San Francisco, Apr. 19, 1945; s. Robert William and Tracy Marie (Parks) A.; m. Carol Lynn Heaps, Oct. 2, 1970; 1 dau., Christina Ann. B.B.A., U. Mo.-Columbia, 1967, M.A., 1968. C.P.A., Mo., N.C., Ill., La. With Peat Marwick Mitchell & Co., 1968—91, ptnr., 1975—91, in charge St. Louis Office health care practice, 1975-77, nat. dir. health care practice, 1978—91, Chgo., 1979—91, exec. v.p., COO, Sisters of Mercy Health System, 1991-99, pres., CEO, 1999-. Bd. dirs. Chgo. Lung Assn., Mid-Am. chpt. ARC. Recipient Haskins and Sells award, 1967; Fin. Execs. Inst. award, 1967; Alpha Kappa Psi scholar, 1967. Mem. Healthcare Fin. Mgmt. Assn., Am. Inst. C.P.A.s, Fedn. Am. Hosps., Am. Hosp. Assn., Ill. Soc. C.P.A.s. Clubs: Tavern, Medinah Country, Country Club of Mo. Office: Sisters of Mercy Health System 2039 North Geyer Road Saint Louis MO 63131

ASIAIE, REZA, research scientist; b. Tehran, Iran, July 18, 1962; s. Hassan-Ali Asiaie and Halimeh Hadizadeh; m. Baktanoush Parnian, Nov. 29, 2002. BA, Calif. State U., Fresno, 1985, MS, 1988, Ohio State U., 1991, PhD, 1995. Rsch. chemist Am. Cyanamid Co., Princeton, NJ, 1998—99; prin. scientist Roche Molecular Sys., Inc., Belleville, NJ, 1999—. Postdoctoral rschr. Yale U., New Haven, 1996—98. Contbr. articles to rsch. publs. Mem.: AAAS (hon.), Am. Ceramic Soc. (assoc.), Am. Chem. Soc. (assoc.), Phi Lambda Upsilon. Achievements include development of Siliceous Monolithic Column with Sintered Porous Packing for Capillary Electrochromatography and Micro-HPLC. Avocations: tennis, travel, skiing. Office: Roche Molecular Sys Inc 11 Franklin Ave Belleville NJ 07109 Office Fax: 973-235-8929. E-mail: reza.asiaie@roche.com.

ASIJA, S(ATYA) PAL, lawyer; b. Leiah, India, Apr. 26, 1942; came to U.S., 1967; naturalized, 1972; s. Chander Bhanu and Radha Bai (Chugh) P.; m. Madeline Rich Magill, June 1, 1974 (dec. June 1982); m. Terry Aguilar, July 15, 1989. Grad., IERE (Lond), Southampton, Eng., 1964; postgrad. diploma, U. Wales, Cardiff, 1967; MBA, U. Dayton, 1970; JD, No. Ky. U., 1974. Bar: U.S. Patent Office 1974, U.S. Supreme Ct. 1978, Conn. 1983, U.S. Ct. Appeals (fed. cir.) 1984. Supr. electronics AEC Radiation Lab. U. Notre Dame, Ind., 1967-68; rsch. and devel. systems engr. NCR, Dayton, Ohio, 1968-71; systems analyst Police Dept., Dayton, 1971-73; exec. dir. MINCIS, State of Minn., St. Paul, 1974-76; systems engr. Sperry Univac, Eagan, Minn., 1977-80; sr. mem. tech. staff ITT, Shelton, Conn., 1980-84; cons., avionics engr. Sikorsky Aircraft, Div. United Technologies Corp., Stratford, Conn., 1985-88; pvt. practice law Shelton, Conn., 1988—. Advisor Computer Users Legal Reporter, Westport, Conn., 1984—, Yale Sci. Park Legal Clinic, New Haven, 1984—; mem. on-line faculty U. Phoenix, 1996—. Author: 4 books; editor newsletter Chasette, 1972; contbr. articles to profl. jours.; 6 patents, 4 trademarks. Inventor Swiftanswer, 1977 (3d pl. award 1977), Magicfold, 1976 (2d pl. award 1976). Candidate for Minn. Ho. of Reps., 1976; capt. CAP, 1979-80. Named to Hall of Fame Engring., Sci. and Tech., 1990. Mem. ABA, IEEE (sr.), Am. Arbitration Assn. (panelist 1972—), Internat. Bar Assn., Minn. Computer Soc. (pres. 1977), Toastmasters (able toastmaster 1972, pres. 1972). Republican. Mem. Lds Ch. Home and Office: 7 Woonsocket Ave Shelton CT 06484-5536 Fax: 203-924-9956. E-mail: pal@ourpal.com.

ASKA, WARABÉ (TAKESHI MASUDA), artist, writer; b. Kagawa, Japan, Feb. 3, 1944; arrived in Can., 1979; s. Satoru and Miyoko (Fujimoto) Masuda; m. Keiko Inouye, Oct. 17, 1979; children: Yohyoh, Mari, Kohta. Student, Takamatsu Technol. Sch., Kagawa, 1963. Founder, pres. Ad House, Tokyo, 1964-78. Apptd. jury Gov.-Gen.'s Lit. Awards, 1993. Exhibited in group shows at UNESCO Exhbn., Tokyo, 1966, one-man shows include Konohana Gallery, 1972, Mitsukoshi Gallery, Takamatsu, 1973; author: Discovering Japan in Eighty Days, 1973; one-man shows include Madden Gallery, London, 1975; author: A Midsummer Night's Dream, 1976, Ma Vlast and Harry Janos, 1977; one-man shows include Tokai Gallery, Nagoya, Japan, 1978, Madden Gallery, London, 1982, Gustafsson Gallery, Toronto, 1982, Shayne Gallery, Montreal, 1984, Colborn Lodge, Toronto, 1984, exhibited in group shows at Biennale of Graphic Design, Brno, 1984, Biennale of Illustrations Exhbn., Bratislava, 1985, Soc. Graphic Designers Can., 1985, Market Gallery, Toronto, 1985, one-man shows include Art Emporium, Vancouver, 1986, exhibited in group shows at Biennale of Graphic Design, Brno, 1988, one-man shows include Royal Can. Acad. Arts, 1991, Mitsukoshi Gallery, Takamatsu, 1995, Isetan Art Gallery, Tokyo, 1995, Art Gallery Fushimi, Nagoya, 1995, Maruzen Art Gallery, Tokyo, 1995, Mitsubishi Trust Bank, Takamatsu, 1995, Art Gallery Mississauga, 1996, exhibited in group shows at Internat. Book Design Exhbn., Leipzig, 1985, Illustrators Exhbn., Bologna, 1986, Biennale of Illustrations Exhbn., Barcelona, 1986, Bratislava, 1987, Vancouver Art Gallery, 1988, Glendon Coll., Toronto, 1989, Internat. Book Design Exhbn., 1989, Can. at Bologna, 1990; illustrator: Seasons, 1990 (Gold award Studio Mag); Exhibited in group shows at Biennale of Illustrations Exhbn., Bratislava, 1991, Biennale of Graphic Design, Brno, 1992, Biennale of Illustrations Exhbn., Barcelona, 1992, Internat. Biennal, Belgrade, Yugoslavia, 1992, Illustrators Exhbn., Bologna, 1992, Tehran Internat. Biennale Illustrations, Iran, 1993, Represented in permanent collections Imperial Family Japan, Hino Diesel Ltd., Tokyo, Corp. of the Coll. of the City of Toronto, Osborne Coll.; illustrator: Aska's Animals, 1991; Represented in permanent collections Toronto Pub. Libr., NTT Docomo, Shikoku, City of Kumamoto, Seitoku U., Matsudo; author: Dandelion Puffs, 1981; illustrator: Aska's Birds, 1992 (First prize Teheran Inst. Biennale); author: P-yororo O-yororo, 1982, Who Goes to the Park, 1984 (City of Toronto Book award, 1985), Who Hides in the Park, 1986 (Honor award Internat. Book Design Exhib.); illustrator: Aska's Sea Creatures, 1994; one-man shows include Onoda Pub. Libr., Yamaguchi, 1995, exhibited in group shows at Biennale of Graphic Design, Brno, 1996; illustrator: Lulie the Iceberg, 1998; one-man shows include Mitsukoshi Gallery, Takamatsu, 1999, Hokkoku Shinbun Hall, Kanazawa, 1999, Living Arts Ctr., Mississanga, 1999, UNICEF House Gallery, NY, 1998, Mitsukoshi Gallery, Osaka, 2000; illus. with Her Imperial Highness Princess Takamodo & UNICEF: Wonderful Life, 2000; one-man shows include Port of Nagoya Pub. Aquarium, 2000, Mitsukoshi Gallery, Sapporo, 2000, Heartful Takefu, Fukui, Japan, 2000, Seitoku U., Matsudo, 2000, Kariya City Art Mus., Aichi, 2000, Artspot Matsudo, 2000, Daimaru Mus., Tokyo, 2000, Tsuruya Gallery, Kumamoto, 2000, Renison Coll., Waterloo, 2002, Imaginature-Poems for the Earth, 2003, one-man shows include Renison Coll., Waterloo, 2002, Japan Found., Toronto, 2003, Imaginature - Poemes for the Earth, Harmony - Poems for the Earth, 2003. Shintoist. Avocations: driving, swimming. Address: 26 Formula CRT Etobicoke ON Canada M9B 6L4

ASKANAS-ENGEL, VALERIE, neurologist, educator, researcher; b. Poland, May 28, 1937; came to U.S., 1969, naturalized, 1975; d. Marian and Leontyne Hornik; m. W. King Engel; 1 dau., Eve Monique Kerr. MD, Warsaw Med. Sch., Poland, 1960, PhD, 1967; Doctor honoris causa, U. d'Aix-Marseille, France, 1987. Rotating intern Univ. Hosp. Warsaw Med. Sch., 1960-61, resident in neurology, 1961-64, fellow in neuromuscular diseases, 1964-65; asst. prof. neurology Warsaw Med. Sch., 1965-69; assoc. mem. Inst. Muscle Diseases, N.Y.C., 1969-73; asst. prof. NYU Med. Sch., 1973-77; sr. investigator NIH, Bethesda, Md., 1977-81; prof. neurology and pathology U. So. Calif., L.A., 1981—; co-dir. Neuromuscular Ctr. at Hosp. Good Samaritan, 1981—, Muscular Dystrophy Assn. Clinic, 1981—, The Jerry Lewis ALS Clin. and Rsch. Ctr., 1988—. V.p. 6th Internat. Congress on Neuromuscular Diseases, 1986, 7th, 1990, 8th, 1994; vis. prof. internat. congresses, Europe, S.Am., Can., Far East; hon. lectr. Royal Coll. Physicians and Surgeons, 1999. Contbr. numerous articles, chpts., abstracts to med. publs.; sr. editor: (book) Inclusion-Body Myositis and Myopathies, 1998; assoc. editor Acta Neuromyologia, 2002—. Recipient Dean's prize for outstanding rsch., 1967, NIH Merit award, 1999—, Gaetano Conti Gold Medal for Basic Rsch., Napoli, 1999; Premio Associazione Stampa Medica Italiana Di Giurnal ItalianaIsmo Medico, 1980; grantee NIH, 1974-77, 83—, NIH Merit award, 1999—, Muscular Dystrophy Assn., 1969-77, 81—. Fellow Am. Acad. Neurology, L.A. Acad. Medicine; mem. Soc. for Neurosci., Am. Neurol. Assn., d'Honneur de la Soc. Francaise de Neurologie, Am. Soc. Cell Biology, Am. Assn. Neuropathology, Histochem. Soc., Uruguayan Neurological Assn. (hon. mem.), L.A. County Med. Assn., Polish Neurol. Assn. (hon.). Home: 527 S Arden Blvd Los Angeles CA 90020-4737 Office: U So Calif Neuromuscular Ctr Good Samaritan Hosp 637 Lucas Ave Los Angeles CA 90017-1912

ASKENASE, PHILIP WILLIAM, medicine and pathology educator; b. Bklyn., June 7, 1939; s. Irving and Hilda Askenase; m. Marjorie Dopkin, June 21, 1967; children: Hilary, Isabel. BA in Physics magna cum laude, Brown U., 1961; MD cum laude, Yale U., 1965. Diplomate Am. Bd. Internal Medicine, Am. Bd. Allergy and Immunology. Intern, asst. resident in medicine Boston City Hosp., 1965-67; clin. assoc. arthritis and rheumatism sect. Nat. Inst. Arthritis and Metabolic Disease, NIH, 1957-59; Brit. Am. Heart fellow of Am. Heart Assn., London Hosp. Med. Coll., 1969-70; postdoctoral trainee in inflammatory diseases Yale U. Sch. Medicine, New Haven, 1970-71, asst. prof. medicine, 1971-75, assoc. prof., 1975-82, assoc. prof. pathology, 1981-82, prof. medicine and pathology, 1982—, chief sect. clin. immunology dept. medicine, 1985—. Attending physician Yale-New Haven Hosp., 1971—, West Haven (Conn.) VA Hosp., 1971—; vis. scientist immunoparasitology div. Nat. Inst. Med. Rsch., London, 1977-78; lectr. biology Yale U., 1981—, vis. prof. molecular immunology unit, 1991; hon. rsch. fellow tumor immunology unit dept. zoology Univ. Coll., London, 1984-85; mem. Yale Comprehensive Cancer Ctr., 1987—; ad hoc reviewer numerous med. jours; vis. prof., Woods Hole, Mass., 1980-84; mem. U.S.-Israel Binat. Sci. Found., 1982—, Med. Rsch. Coun. Can., NSF, Netherlands Cancer Found., Wellcome Truste, London, Med. Rsch. Coun., London, Can. Med. Rsch. Coun.; mem. adv. bd. spl. program in tropical diseases WHO; mem. pathology-A/study sect. NIH, 1976, mem. immunol. scis. study sect., 1983-87, ad hoc mem. allergy and immunology study sect. NIH, 1987-89 Mem. editl. bd. Jour. Clin. Immunology, 1983—88, Jour. Allergy and Clin. Immunology, 1980-85, Clin. and Diagnostic Lab. Immunology, 1983—; assoc. editor Jour. Immunology, 1976082; mem. editl. adv. bd. Jour. Molecular and Cellular Immunology, 1983—; contbr. over 200 articles, abstracts and revs. to med. jours., chpts. to books. Laurens Hammond grantee for cancer rsch., 1975-77, grantee NIH, 1987—. Fellow Am. Acad. Allergy; mem. AAAS, Am. Assn. Immunologists (membership com. 1978-82), Am. Assn. Physicians, Am. Fedn. Clin. Rsch., Am. Rheumatism Assn., Am. Soc. Clin. Investigation, Am. Soc. Tropical Medicine and Hygiene, Am. Thoracic Soc., Brit. Soc. Immunology, Clin. Immunology Soc., Collegium Internat. Allergoium, Conn. Allergy Soc., Histamine Rsch. Soc. N.Am., Reticuloendothelial Soc., Serotonin Soc., Skin. Pharmacology Soc., Soc. Investigative Dermatology, Interurban Clin. Club, Polish Acad. Arts and Scis. (fgn. corr.), Phi Beta Kappa, Alpha Omega Alpha. Office: Yale U Sch of Medicine PO Box 208013 333 Cedar St New Haven CT 06510-3289

ASKER, JAMES ROBERT, magazine editor; b. Louisville, 1952; BA, Rice U., 1974. Reporter, columnist Houston Post, 1974—88; freelance reporter, 1988—89; mng. editor Electronic Bus., 1989—95; space tech. editor Aviation Week & Space Tech., Washington, 1989—95, Washington bur. chief, 1995—, mng. editor, 2003—. Recipient Knight Sci. Journalism fellow, MIT, Cambridge, 1987—88. Office: Aviation Week & Space Tech 1200 G St NW Ste 900 Washington DC 20005-3814 E-mail: asker@aviationweek.com, jim_asker@yahoo.com.

ASKEW, WILLIAM EARL, chemist, educator; b. Maysville, N.C., Aug. 31, 1943; s. Carl Lee and Sally Chinese (Pope) A. BA in Chemistry, U. N.C., 1965; MA in Biology, East Carolina U., 1968; PhD in Biophys. Sci., U. Houston, 1973. Rsch. assoc. Baylor Coll. Medicine, Houston, 1973-77, Vets.' Hosp., Houston, 1973-77; instr. chemistry Houston C.C. Sys. N.W., 1977—, chair phys. scis. dept., 2000—. With U.S. Army, 1968-70. Mem. Am. Chem. Soc., Am. Acad. Sci., Tex. Jr. Coll. Tchrs. Assn., 2-Yr. Chemistry Soc. Office: Town and Country Ctr 1010 W Sam Houston N Houston TX 77043-5008

ASKEY, RICHARD ALLEN, mathematician, educator; b. St. Louis, June 4, 1933; s. Philip Edwin and Bessie May (Yates) Askey; m. Elizabeth Ann Hill, June 14, 1958; children: James, Suzanne. BA, Washington U., St. Louis, 1955; MA, Harvard U., 1956; PhD, Princeton U., 1961. Instr. in math. Washington U., St. Louis, 1958-61; instr. U. Chgo., Chgo., 1961-63; asst. prof. U. Wis., Madison, 1963-65, asso. prof., 1965-68, prof., 1968-86, Gabor Szego prof., 1986-95, John Bascom prof., 1995—2003, prof. emeritus, 2003—. Author: (book) Orthogonal Polynomials and Special Functions, 1975; author: (with G. E. Andrews and R. Roy) Special Functions, 1999; editor: Theory and Application of Special Functions, 1975, Collected Papers of Gabor Szego, 1982. Fellow Guggenheim, 1969—70. Fellow: AAAS, Am. Acad. Arts and Scis., Indian Acad. Sci. (hon.); mem.: Soc. Indsl. and Applied Math., Math. Assn. Am., Nat. Acad. Sci., Am. Math. Soc. Home: 2105 Regent St Madison WI 53726-3941 Office: U Wis Van Vleck Hall Madison WI 53706

ASKEY, THELMA J. federal agency administrator; b. Lakehurst, N.J. BA, Tenn. Tech. U., 1970; postgrad., George Washington U., Am. U. Press asst. Rep. John Duncan, 1972-74; editor The Nat. Rsch. Coun. Marine Bd., 1974-76; asst. minority trade counsel Ho. Com. Ways and Means, 1976-79, minority trade counsel, 1979-94; staff dir., subcommitttee on trade Ho. Com. on Ways and Means, 1995-98; commr. U.S. Internat. Trade Commn., Washington, 1998—2000; dir. Trade and Development Agency, Arlington, Va., 2001—. Office: Trade and Devopement Agency Off of Dir 1621 N Kent St Arlington VA 22209-2131

ASKIN, FRANK, law educator; b. Balt., Jan. 8, 1932; s. Abraham and Rose (Mervis) A.; m. Marilyn Klein, Aug. 6, 1960; children: Andrea Marcy, Jonathan Michael, Daniel Simon; 1 son from previous marriage, Steven. BA, CCNY, 1966; JD, Rutgers U., 1966. Bar: N.J. 1966, N.Y. 1983, U.S. Dist. Ct. (ea. dist.) N.Y., U.S. Ct. Appeals (2d, 3d cirs.), U.S. Supreme Ct. 1971. Journalist N.Y. Post, Bergen Record, Newark Star-Ledger; disting. prof. law Rutgers Law Sch., Newark, 1975—. Vis. prof. U. Hawaii Law Sch., 1975; spl. counsel edn. and labor com. U.S. Ho. of Reps., 1976-77, cons. govt. ops. com., 1989-92; gen. counsel ACLU, 1976—. Author: Defending Rights: A Life in Law and Politics, 1997; co-editor: Enforcing Fair Housing Laws, 1970; contbr. articles to profl. jours. Nat. bd. dirs. ACLU, 1968—, sec., 1971-75, gen. counsel, 1976—; del. Dem. Nat. Conv., 1980, 88; Dem. candidate 11th dist. U.S. Ho. of Reps., N.J., 1986—. Named one of Best Lawyers in America, Woodward & White. Mem. Soc. Am. Law Tchrs. (treas. 1974-75). Office: Rutgers Law Sch 123 Washington St Newark NJ 07102-3192

ASKIN, RICHARD HENRY, JR., entertainment company executive; b. Flushing, N.Y., Feb. 11, 1947; s. Richard H. and Anne Margaret A.; children: Jennifer Leigh, Michael Richard. BA in Econs., Rutgers Coll., 1969; MA in Comm., U. Tex., 1971; MBA in Fin., Fordham U., 1976. Acct. exec. CableRep, Inc., N.Y.C., 1973-74, WNBC-TV Nat. Broadcasting Co., N.Y.C., 1974-75, NBC-TV, NBC, N.Y.C., 1975-76; sales mgr. KNBC-TV, L.A., 1976-79, dir. sales, 1979-85; v.p. domestic sales Fries Distbn. Co., L.A., 1985-86, sr. v.p. distbn., 1986-87; pres. TV The Samuel Goldwyn Co., L.A., 1987-96; pres., CEO Tribune Entertainment Co., L.A., 1996—. Decorated Army Commendation medal; Alcoa fellow, 1969-70. Mem. ATAS (bd. govs. TV exec. br., vice chmn., bd. dirs. 2001—), Hollywood Radio and TV Soc. (bd. dirs.), Advt. Industry Emergency Fund (former pres.), Entertainment Industry Coun. (trustee), Nat. Assn. TV Program Execs. (bd. dirs.), Alpha Rho Alumni Assn., Chi Psi. Home: 1520 Aldercreek Pl Westlake Village CA 91362-4211 Office: Tribune Entertainment 5800 W Sunset Blvd Los Angeles CA 90028-6607

ASKIN, WALTER MILLER, artist, educator; b. Pasadena, Calif., Sept. 12, 1929; s. Paul Henry and Dorothy Margaret (Miller) A.; child from previous marriage, Nancy Carol Oudegeest; m. Elise Anne Doyle, Apr. 17, 1993. BA, U. Calif.-Berkeley, 1951, MA, 1952; postgrad., Ruskin Sch. Drawing and Fine Art, Oxford. Asst. curator edn. Legion of Honor Mus., San Francisco, 1953-54; prof. art Calif. State U., Los Angeles, 1956-92; pub. Nose Press, Pasadena, Calif., 1984—; vis. artist Pasadena Art Mus., 1962-63, U. N.Mex., 1972, Calif. State U.-Long Beach, 1974-75, Cranbrook Acad. Art, Mich., 1978, Ariz. State U., Tempe, 1979, Art Ctr. Athens Sch. Fine Arts, Mykonos, Greece, 1973, Kelpra Studio, London, 1969, 73. Chief reader Advanced Placement Program Ednl. Testing Service, 1982-85; chmn. visual arts panel Art Recognition and Talent Search Nat. Found. Advancement in Arts-Commn. on Presdl. Scholars; mem. advanced placement studio art examinaton com. Coll. Bd., 1985-96, chmn., 1992-96; mem. Commn. of Future of Advanced Placement Program, The Coll. Bd., 1999-2001; mem. acad. coun. Coll. Bd., 1989-94, chair arts adv. com., 1987-93; adj. prof. Ariz. State U., 1986-90; artist-in-residence Ragdale Found., Lake Forest, Ill., 1986, John Michael Kohler Art Ctr., Sheboygan, Wis., 1987, Hambidge Ctr. for Arts & Sci., Georgia, 1991, Vt. Studio Colony, 1988; co-dir. 1st Internat. Conf. on Humor in Art, Chateau de la Bretsche, Brittany, France, 1989, 92; spkr., juror nat. travel show So. Graphics Coun. Conf., Ohio U., Athens, 1998; artist-in-residence U. Dallas, 2001; vis. prof. Ariz. State U., Tempe, 2001; invited artist 12 lithos Hullaballoo in Winter in collaboration with Wayne Kimball, Brigham Young U., 2001; historian art alumni group U. Calif., Berkeley, 2001—. Numerous exhbns. including one-man shows, Kunstlerhaus, Vienna, Austria, 1981, Santa Barbara Mus. Art, 1966, Hellenic-Am. Union, Athens, Greece, 1973, Hank Baum Gallery, San Francisco, 1970, 74, 76, Ericson Gallery, N.Y.C., 1978, Abraxas Gallery, Calif., 1979, 80, 81, Fla. State U., Tallahassee, 1988, Lizardi/Harp Gallery, Pasadena, 1988, 91, 95, L.A. Valley Coll., 1989, U. Dallas, 2001; one-man shows Brigham Young U., 2002, Calif. State U., Channel Islands, 2002; one-man traveling show U.S. Info. Agy., Yugoslavia, 1985-86, 15th Internat. Biennale of Prints and Drawings, Taipei Mus. Art, 1998; Pasadena's choice exhbn., Armory Ctr. for Arts, 1991, Contemporary Art in Pasadena, 1960-74, Norton Simon Museum, 1999, Taipei Fine Arts Mus., 1999, Gertrude Herbert Art Inst., Ga., 1999, Schafler Gallery, Pratt Inst., Bklyn., 1999, Kittredge Gallery, U. Puget Sound, Tacoma, Wash., 1999, Cmty. Visual Art Assn., Jackson Hole, Wyo., 1999, Wayland Bapt. U., Plainview, Tex., 1999, From Paris to Pasadena exhbn. Norton Simon Mus., 2000, Artists Do Opera exhbn. Brand Libr., Glendale, Calif., 2001, print and drawing exhbn. Bradley U., Peoria, Ill., 2000, others; author: A Briefer History of the Greeks, 1983, Another Art Book to Cross Off Your List, 1984, Modern Manifesto Match Game, 1998, Hideous Headlines, 1998, Womsters and

Foozlers, 1998, On Becoming an Artist, 1999, (calendar) Man, Dog, Bone Artists' Calendar; contbr. articles to profl. jours. and mags. Trustee Pasadena Art Mus., 1963-68; bd. dirs. Los Angeles Inst. Contemporary Art., 1978-81, Pasadena Gallery Contemporary Arts; bd. govs. Baxter Art Gallery, Calif. Inst. Tech., 1980-86; bd. dirs. The Calif. Artist, Book Program, 1985-2000; dir. The Visual Humor Project, 1989—. Recipient Outstanding Prof. award Calif. State U., 1973, Artists award Pasadena Arts Council, 1970, award 61st ann. exhbn. N.W. Watercolor Soc., 2001, Past Pres.' award 80th ann. exhbn. Nat. Watercolor Soc., 2000, Purchase prize 3d nat. print biennial Frederick R. Weisman Mus., Mpls., 2001; named Disting. Alumnus, Pasadena City Coll.; Ruth G. Jansen Edn. Meml. grantee, grantee Pasadena Arts Commn., 1990; also over 50 awards in competitive exhbns. art. Mem.: So. Graphics Coun., L.A. Printmaking Soc. (pres. 2002—, founding mem.), Nat. Watercolor Soc. (1st v.p. 1960), Coll. Art Assn. Am. Home and Office: PO Box D South Pasadena CA 91031-0120 *What can we do today that has any kind of meaning and value? We can search for a means to escape from conventions, from ordinariness, and from the limitations of everyday existence. We can help create the emergent fiction that is the world we live in. We can regenerate the key myths and archetypes so that life doesn't seem worth living unless one is on the side of the liberating and transformative. We can learn to play again - to not know what we are looking for, to break through the ice of habit, to know what it means to be truly alive and to experience the specialness of even the most ordinary things. We can find the god within, inspiration, magic, once again be visionaries, bring peace. The real joy is in making a better, more calm, more serene, more alive, more playful, more energized, more focused, more directed, more life filled existence for the time we're here.*

ASKINS, ARTHUR JAMES, accountant, finance management and auditing executive; b. Dec. 2, 1944; s. William J. and Rita M. (O'Brien) A.; m. Nancy E. Paulsen, Apr. 28, 1979. BS, LaSalle U., 1967; MA, Rider Coll., 1971. Cert. of specialization hospitality acctg. and mgmt. Am. Hotel and Motel Assn.; CPA, Pa., N.J.; cert. fraud examiner, hotel adminstr. Tchr. Cardinal Dougherty H.S., Phila., 1967-70; pvt. practice acctg., 1967—. Recipient cert. of Commendation Twp. of Abington, Pa., 1967, Disting. Svc. award Cmty. Accts., Phila., 1982, Superstar award Resorts Internat. Casino-Hotel, 1982, Brotherhood award NCCJ, Atlantic City, 1982, Mgmt. award Resorts Internat. Casino Hotel, 1986 1st Mgrs. award Resort Internat. Casino-Hotel, 1986, Outstanding Vol. Svc. award Big Bros./Big Sisters, 1987. Mem. AICPA, Nat. Assn. Accts. (nat. bd. dirs. 1983-85, pres. South Jersey Shore chpt. 1979-81, Cmty. Affairs award Suburban N.E. Phila. 1978), Inst. Internal Auditors (bd. dirs. 1984-89, audit com. 1979-83), N.J. Soc. CPAs, Pa. Inst. CPAs, Greater Mainland C. of C., Nat. Assn. Cert. Internat. Fraud Examiners, Internat. Assn. Hosp. Accts. Republican. Roman Catholic. Home: 915 Onondaga St Lewiston NY 14092 Office: The Seneca Nation of Indians Seneca Gaming Authority 360 Rainbow Blvd Niagara Falls NY 14302 Fax: 716-754-4105.

ASKINS, BILLY EARL, education educator, consultant; b. Burkburnett, Tex., Dec. 28, 1930; s. Sidney Earl and Nellie Alice (Johnson) A.; m. Sydney Loraine Gamblin, Feb. 21, 1954; 1 child, Dewayne Earl. BS, East Tex. State U., 1953; MEd, Midwestern U., 1959; EdD, U. North Tex., 1967. Instr., edn. specialist Sheppard Tech. Tng. Ctr., Wichita Falls, Tex., 1955-65; asst. dir. tchr. adminstrn. U. North Tex., Denton, 1965-66; tchr. Ft. Worth Pub. Schs., 1966-67; from asst prof. to prof. Tex. Tech. U., Lubbock, 1967-77, assoc. dean Coll. Edn., 1978-90, prof. edn., 1991—. Cons. to univs., fedn. edn. labs., state edn. svc. ctrs., pub. schs., state prisons schs., schs. of nursing, community colls., state bar assns., and pvt. agys., 1980—; presenter at profl. confs. Contbr. to profl. publs. 1st lt. USAF, 1953-55, lt. col. Res. to 1981. Mem. Am. Ednl. Rsch. Assn., Assn. Tchr. Educators (Disting. Maj. Prof. award 1982), Nat. Staff Devel. Coun., Tex. Staff Devel. Coun. (bd. dirs. 1989-92), Tex. Assn. Tchr. Educators (exec. bd. 1987-89), Internat. Rotary Club, Order Ky. Cols. Avocations: photography, fly fishing, travel. Home: 5214 28th St Lubbock TX 79407-3508 Office: Tex Tech U PO Box 41071 Lubbock TX 79409-1071

ASKINS, NANCY ELLEN PAULSEN, training and organizational development professional; b. St. Paul, Nov. 2, 1948; d. Charles A. and Stasia (Sawicki) Paulsen; m. Arthur J. Askins, Apr. 28, 1979. BS in Home Econs., U. Cin., 1970, BS in Edn., 1971, MEd, 1972; postgrad., SUNY-Buffalo, 1974-76, Temple U., 1976, Walden U., 1988-92; student, Inst. Fin. Edn., 1982-85; cert. in mgmt., Am. Mgmt. Assn./Monmouth Coll., 1984. Cert. gaming supr. Edn. Inst. Am. Hotel and Motel Assn.; cert. strategic planning facilitator; cert. quality mgr. Asst. aquatic supr. Cin. Recreation Commn., 1969-72; student affairs adminstr. U. Cin., 1970-72; mem. faculty student affairs adminstrn. Tex. Luth. Coll., 1972-73; mem. faculty, student affairs adminstr. SUNY-Geneseo, 1974-76; student affairs adminstr. Temple U., 1976-78; tchr. drug awareness coord. Adams Sch. Harlandale Sch. Dist., San Antonio, 1973-74; career life ins. agt., fin. planning cons. Phoenix Mut. Life Ins. Co., Phila., 1978-81; registered rep., securities agt. Phoenix Equity Planning Corp., Phila., 1980-81; owner Paulsen-Askins Fin. Svcs., Somers Point, N.J., 1980-81; mem. women's task force Phoenix Cos., 1980-81; tng. svcs. coord. Collective Fed. Savs. & Loan Assn., Egg Harbor City, N.J., 1981-82, asst. v.p., tng. dir., 1982-84; tng. mgr. Shore Meml. Hosp., Somers Point, N.J., 1984-86, wellness instr., 1984-89, dir. ednl. devel., 1986-89; dir edn. svcs. Holy Cross Hosp., Ft. Lauderdale, Fla., 1990-91, dir. cmty. and vol. svcs., 1991-94, part-time instr. wellness program, 1991-94; v.p. tng. and assoc. devel. Grand Casino, Biloxi, 1994-96; tng. svcs. coord. Gulf Coast Bus. Svcs., Gulfport, Miss., 1996-98; quality mgr. Hollywood Casino Resort/Tunica, Robinsonville, Miss., 1998—. Adj. prof. bus. and social scis. Atlantic C.C. Coll., Mays Landing, N.J., 1986-89; facilitator Assertiveness Tng. Group, Interpersonal Comms. Group, orgnl. and leadership devel. seminars and cons.; owner, exec. corp. cons. Askins Tng. and Cons., 1981—; mem. bd. examiners Malcolm Baldridge Nat. Quality Award, 2001, Pres.'s Quality Award, 2000, Tenn. Quality Award, 2000, Miss. Quality Award, 1999, 2000; instr. Inst. Fin. Edn., 1982-85, Ednl. Inst., Am. Hotel ad Motel Assn., 1999—; workshop presenter and spkr. in field; items writer Cert. Quality Improvement Assoc. Agy. chmn. United Way Campaign, Phila., 1979, 80; bd. dirs. South Jersey Regional Theater, 1983-86, chmn., 1983-84; active ann. Muscular Dystrophy Telethon, Phila.; active Girl Scouts U.S., 1956-74, 84—; mem. Parish coun., parish enrichment com., 1984-88, cantor St. Joseph Roman Cath. Ch., Somers Point, 1979-89; mem., lector Christ the King Cath. Ch., Southaven, Miss., 1998—; chmn. com. Women's Club St. Luke's Cath. Ch., Coconut Creek, Fla., 1992-94, parish coun., 1993-94; bd. dirs. Holly Shores Coun. Girl Scouts U.S., 1984-85; host fgn. exch. students Am. Scandinavian Student Exch. Program, 1985-87; mem. Somers Point Bd. Edn., 1986; mem. Libr. Adv. Bd. City of Margate, Fla., 1991-94, fundraising chmn., vice chmn., chmn. Recipient Brotherhood-Sisterhood Achievers award NCCJ, 1985, Rising Star award, 1997, Gold Dir. award, 1998 Carlson Learning Co., Minn.; named Biloxi Career Woman Bus. Profl. Women/Lighthouse of Biloxi, 1995, Women of Achievement Woman of Yr. Bus. Profl. Women Clarksdale, Coahoma County, Miss., 1999. Mem. N. Miss. chap. Am. Hotel & Motel Assn. (charter pres. 1999), Bus. and Profl. Women Robinsonville, Miss. (charter pres. 1999-2000), Bus. and Profl. Women Clarksdale (legis. com. chair, 1998-2000), Bus. and Profl. Women Lighthouse of Biloxi, Miss. (v.p. membership, newsletter ed., young careerist chair, chair 1997 Nat. Bus. Women's Week, selected Biloxi Career Woman, 1995, Bus. and Profl. Women Miss. (state 2d v.p., state membership chair, 1996-97, state legis. chair, 1999-20000, Greater Camden Assn. Life Underwriters (chmn. Life Ins. Week for South Jersey 1978-79, bd. dir. 1979-81, pub. rels. chmn. 1979-81, chmn. state edn. 1981), Am. Soc. for Quality (features editor Competitive Advantage quality divsn. 2000—), Am. Soc. Tng. and Devel. (treas. S. Jersey chpt., nat. dir. savs. and lending industry group 1983-84, hosps. and healthcare industry group 1984-86, nat. conf. speaker 1984-94, sec. Greater Broward/Ft. Lauderdale chpt, 1991, pres.-elect 1992, pres. 1993, nat. dir.-elect 1990-91, dir. 1991-92, Interfaith Trainers Cons. Network), Am. Hosp. Assn., Am. Soc. Health Edn. and Tng., Am. Mgmt. Assn., Fla. Soc. Healthcare Edn. and Tng., Greater Mainland C. of C. (v.p., treas., membership coord. 1979-89, Pres. award 1983), U. Cin. Alumni of Greater Phila. Area (pres. 1980-89), Greater Ft. Lauderdale C. of C. (diplomat 1992-93, edn. com. 1993-94), Alliance/The Women's Network (bd. dir. 1983-84), Rotary Internat., Rotary of Gulfport, MS, Rotary of Robinsonville, MS (sect. 1999, newsletter ed. 1998-99, pres.-elect 1999-2000, pres. 2000-2001), Rotary Dist. 6800 (chairperson, long range planning com. 1999-2001, mem. group study exch. com. 1999-2000, youth study exch. com. 1999-2000, chmn. matching grants com. 2001-2002). Democrat. Home: PO Box 445 915 Onondaga St Lewiston NY 14092 E-mail: quality4u@earthlink.net., nancyaskins@hwcc-tunica.com.

ASKINS, WALLACE BOYD, manufacturing company executive; b. Chgo., June 2, 1930; s. Wallace Fay and Evelyn Mae (Baker) A.; m. Trieste M. Olivieri, May 20, 1954 (div. Sept. 23, 1994); 1 child, Justin Wallace. BA, Lake Forest (Ill.) Coll., 1952; JD with honors, John Marshall Law Sch., Chgo., 1961. Bar: Ill. 1961; CPA, Ill. Sr. accountant Ernst & Young (CPAs), Chgo., 1952-55; controller, house counsel Nat. Lock Co., Rockford, Ill., 1955-65; asst. corp. controller Xerox Corp., Stamford, Conn., 1965-77; exec. v.p., chief fin. officer White Motor Corp., Cleve., 1977-81, chmn. bd., chief exec. officer, 1981-84; exec. v.p., chief fin. officer Armco Inc., Parsippany, N.J., 1984-92, also bd. dirs. Bd. dirs. Trump Hotel and Casino Resorts, Inc. Mem. ABA, AICPA, Ill. Soc. CPA's, N.Y. Soc. CPA's, Ill. Bar Assn. Home: 153 Indian Dr Greentown PA 18426-9021 Fax: (570) 887-0693. E-mail: walgator@aol.com.

ASKLAND, ANDREW, academic administrator, educator; b. New York, NY, Aug. 16, 1951; PhD, U. of Colo., 1989—95. Dir., ctr. for the study of law, sci. and tech. Ariz. State U. Coll. of Law, 1999—. Office: Arizona State U Coll of Law PO Box 877906 Tempe AZ 85287-7906 E-mail: sandy.askland@asu.edu.

ASKOV, EUNICE MAY, adult education educator; b. St. Louis, Nov. 20, 1940; d. David Hull and Marjorie Jane (Gutgsell) Nicholson; m. Warren Hopkins Askov, Jan. 22, 1967; children: David, Karen. BA in English, Denison U., 1962; MA in English, U. Wis., 1966, PhD in Curriculum and Instrn., 1969. English and reading tchr. Rich Twp. High Sch., Park Forest, Ill., 1962-64; reading svc. reading specialist U. Wis., Madison, 1965-66, project asst. Wis. R & D Ctr. for Cognitive Learning, 1966-67, rsch. assoc., 1969-72, lectr. dept. curriculum and instrn., 1968-69; coord. adult basic edn. programs U. Wis. Extension, 1966-67; remedial reading specialist Lincoln Jr. High Sch., Madison, 1966; adult basic edn. tchr. Madison Vocat., Tech. and Adult Schs., 1967-68; asst. prof. elem. edn. Minn. State U., Bemidji, 1972-74; assoc. prof. Pa. State U., University Park, 1974-79, prof. edn., 1980—2001, disting. prof., 2001—. Presenter seminars on adult edn., Germany, 1986, 93; cons., speaker in field; mem. editorial bd. Jour. Ednl. Rsch., Adult Edn. Quarterly, Adult Basic Edn., Am. Reading Forum Yearbook; mem. steering com. Adult Literacy and Tech.; mem. panel nat. work group on cancer and literacy Nat. Cancer Inst.; organizer, coord. Pa. State Coalition for Adult Literacy; mem. adv. coun. Nat. Coalition for Literacy. Contbr. articles to profl. publs. Fulbright sr. scholar, 1983; Literacy Leader fellow Nat. Inst. for Literacy, 1994-95; recipient Alumni Achievement award U. Wis.-Madison Sch. of Edn., 1994, Career Achievement award Pa State Coll. Edn.; Disting. fellow Flinders U. Inst. Internat. Edn., Australia, 1998. Mem. Am. Assn. Adult and Continuing Edn. (chair, mem. various coms., bd. dirs.),Commn. Profs. of Adult Edn., Am. Edn. Rsch. Assn., Am. Reading Forum, Internat. Reading Assn. (chair, mem. various coms.), Keystone State Reading Assn., Mid-State Literacy Coun. (bd. dirs., pers. com., long range planning com.), Mid-State Reading Coun. (pres.), Pa. Assn. Adult and Continuing Edn., Phi Beta Kappa, Phi Delta Kappa. Democrat. Methodist. Avocations: travel, aerobics, hiking, reading. Office: Pa State U Inst for Study Adult Lit 200 Rackley Bldg University Park PA 16802-3202 E-mail: ena1@psu.edu.

ASLAM, SYED, chemist, research; b. Patna, Bihar, India, Dec. 25, 1938; came to the U.S., 1970; s. Syed Abdul Aziz and Bibi Rakeya Khatoon; m. Shahnaz Ahmad Aslam, Mar. 13, 1967; children: Faiz, Amir, Shazia. BS with honors, Patna U., 1959, MS in Chemistry, 1961, Ea. Mich. U., 1973; cert. in Infra Red Spectroscopy, Bowdoin Coll., 1980. Cert. lab. analyst Mich. Water Pollution Control Assn. Lectr. chemistry Magadh U., Patna, 1961-69; rsch. asst. Ea. Mich. U., Ypsilanty, 1971-73; rsch. assoc. Detroit Med. Ctr., 1973-76; chemist County of Wayne Dept. Pub. Works, Wyandotte, MIch., 1976-92, asst. lab. dir., 1992—. Cons. Alfa Tech. Svcs., Trenton, Mich., 1989-91. Author: Elements of Organic Chemistry, 1965; inventor in field. Pres. Assn. Indian Muslim, Canton, Mich., 1993-2001. Mem. Water Environment Fedn. Avocations: gardening, hunting, woodworking, glass blowing. Home: 1212 Mill Brook Rd Canton MI 48188-5088 Office: County of Wayne Dept Environment 797 Central St Wyandotte MI 48192-7307 E-mail: aslamsyed@hotmail.com.

ASLAN, MADALYN, writer, educator; d. George Vincent Shea and Donna Marie Todd. BA with honors, U. London, 1984; BA, Cornell U., 1987; MFA, Sarah Lawrence Coll., 1991. Lectr. Coll. Psychic Studies, London, 2001—. Author: What's Your Sign? A Cosmic Guide for Young Astrologers, 2002, Madalyn Aslan's Jupiter Signs, 2003; actor: (TV series) The Martian Chronicles, 1980; (films) D.H. Lawrence. Recipient full undergrad. scholarship, Cornell U., 1984—87, full grad. fellowship, Sarah Lawrence Coll., 1989—91. Mem.: NCGR, Nat. Campaign for Tolerance (life; founder), AFA (life).

ÅSLUND, ANDERS, economist; b. Karlskoga, Sweden, Feb. 17, 1952; s. Ivan and Ingrid (Åblad) Å. BA, U. Stockholm, Sweden, 1976; MSc, Stockholm Sch. Econs., 1976; PhD, U. Oxford, England, 1982. Second sec. Swedish Embassy, Kuwait, 1977-78; first sec. Swedish Permanent Delegation, Geneva, 1982-84, Swedish Embassy, Moscow, 1984-87; rsch. scholar Kennan Inst. Advanced Russian Studies, Washington, 1987-88; prof., dir. Stockholm Inst. E. European Econs., Stockholm Sch. Econs., 1989-94; sr. assoc. Carnegie Endowment for Internat. Peace, Washington, 1994—. Fellow World Econ. Forum, Geneva, 1991—; adj. prof. Georgetown U., Washington, 2002—. Author: Private Enterprise in Eastern Europe, 1985, Gorbachev's Struggle for Economic Reform, 1989, 91, Post-Communist Economic Revolutions: How Big a Bang?, 1992, How Russia Became a Market Economy, 1995, Building Capitalism: The Transformation of the Former Soviet Bloc, 2002; co-author: Getting It Wrong; editor 10 books on Soviet, post-Soviet and Russian econ. affairs. Sr. econ. advisor to Russian Govt., 1991—94, Ukrainian Govt., 1994—97; pres. Akaev Kyrgyz Republic, 1998—. Mem. Cosmos Club (Washington). Office: Carnegie Endowment Internat Peace 1779 Massachussetts Ave Washington DC 20036

ASMA, LAWRENCE FRANCIS, priest; b. Waukegan, Ill., Oct. 21, 1947; s. Francis Victor and Isabelle Amelia (Recktenwald) A. BA in English, U. Wis., Whitewater, 1969; MA in English, Ill. State U., 1974; MA in Scripture magna cum laude, De Andreis Sem., 1982, MDiv, 1983. Ordained priest Roman Cath. Chr., 1983. Dir. spritual formation Cardinal Glennon Coll., St. Louis, 1983-85, instr. theology dept., 1983-85; chaplain St. Vincent's Div. DePaul Health Ctr., St. Louis, 1985—. Bd. dirs. Rosati Stabilization Ctr., St. Louis, 1988-94; vice chmn. Rosati Stabilization Ctr., 1990-94; advisor Explorers, 1991-92. Local religious superior Congregation of the Mission, 1994-99; chaplain Knights Columbus, 1996—. With USNR, 1970-72, Vietnam. Mem. Assn. Profl. Chaplains (bd. cert.), Cath. Biblical Assn., Congregation of Mission, Sigma Tau Delta. Avocations: ornithology, photography, drawing. Office: DePaul Health Center 12303 De Paul Dr Bridgeton MO 63044-2588 E-mail: fr_larry_asma@ssmhc.com.

ASMAR, LAILA MICHELLE, lawyer; b. Laurel, Miss., July 23, 1957; d. Mitchell and Marie Jeannette Asmar. BS in BA, U. So. Miss., 1979; JD cum laude, So. Tex. Coll. Law, Houston, 1985. Bar: Tex. 1985; CPA, Tex., Miss.; bd. cert. estate planning and probate lawyer; cert. mediator; cert. arbitrator N.Y. Stock Exch. and Nat. Assn. Securities Dealers. Acct. Peat Marwick Mitchell, Jackson, Miss., 1979-80, Houston Oil Internat., Houston, 1980-81; tax analyst Tenneco Inc., Houston, 1981-84; assoc. atty. Clark Thomas Winters & Newton, Austin, Tex., 1985-87; fin. cons. Linscomb & Williams, Houston, 1988-89; pvt. practice law, Houston, 1989—. Guest expert The Ron Stone Show, Sta. KPRC-TV, Houston, 1990-92, guest reporter Morning News, 1992. Co-author of ABA pub.: Federal Income Taxation of Life Insurance, 1989; contbr. articles to profl. jours. Trustee Theater Under Stars, Houston, 1989-91. Mem. Tex. Bar Assn. Republican. Episcopalian.

ASMUS, JOHN FREDRICH, physicist; b. Pasadena, Calif., Jan. 20, 1937; s. William F. and Eleanor E. (Kocher) A.; m. Barbara Ann Flaherty, Feb. 23, 1963; children— Joanne M., Rosemary H. BSEE, Calif. Inst. Tech., 1958, MSEE, 1959, PhDEE and Physics, 1965. Head optical systems dept. Aero Geo Astro Corp., Alexandria, Va., 1960-64; head laser dept. Gulf Gen. Atomic, San Diego, Calif., 1964-69; research staff Inst. Def. Analyses, Arlington, Va., 1969-71; v.p., bd. mem. Sci. Applications, Inc., Albuquerque, 1971-73; lectr. U. Calif., Davis, 1974, research physicist, co-founder art and sci. center San Diego, 1973—. Co-dir. JASON nat. laser program study Office of Pres. of U.S., 1971; cons. in field; mem. adv. group on electron devices Smithsonian Assocs.; featured cable, PBS TV documentaries, 1975—; conf. lectr. San Diego, 1999. Contbr. sci. articles to profl. jours.; patentee metallic vapor laser, embedded pinch laser, plasma pinch annealing system, chemical decontamination with ultraviolet; introduced laser, ultrasonic and computer image enhancement techniques to art conservation, introduced laser cleaning to the field of paleontology, and revealed new features (necklace and mountain pentimenti, 1978)of da Vinci's Mona Lisa; restored Cremona Cathedral, Calif. State Capital, White House mural, Washington, Arches Nat. Pk. Pictograph, Venice Ducal Palace Sculpture, office of Galileo in U. Padova using laser radiation; development of laser-robotic technique for the decontamination of the Hanford nuclear weapons facility of the U.S. Dept. of Energy; laser, flashlamp and pinchlamp systems for depainting stealth aircraft and decontaminating the JET TOKAMAK thermonuclear fusion reactor, Culham Laboratory, United Kingdom; laser system for branding bowhead whales at a distance. Recipient Rolex Laureate for Enterprise award for restoration Xian terra cotta warriors Montres Rolex SA, Geneva, 1990, Best Scholarly Article award Soc. for Tech. Com., 1988; named George Eastman lectr. Optical Soc. Am., 1994; winner IBM Supercomputing Competition for Image Enhancement of Mona Lisa, 1989; Schlumberger fellow, 1959-60, Tektronix fellow, 1960-61, Getty fellow, 1989, Oberlin Coll. fellow, 1990, Explorers Club fellow, 1997; decorated knight of Holy Sepulchre of Jerusalem, 1993. Mem.: Soc. Photo-Optical Instrumentation Engrs., Venice Soc., Nat. Trust Hist. Preservation, Am. Inst. Conservation, IEEE, Internat. Inst. Conservation of Hist. and Artistic Works, Lasers for the Conservation of Artworks (sci. bd. mem., hon. pres.), Bay Area Art Conservation Guild, Tau Beta Pi, Sigma Xi. Home: 8239 Sugarman Dr La Jolla CA 92037-2222 Office: IPAPS 0360 U Calif San Diego 9500 Gilman Dr La Jolla CA 92093-5004 E-mail: jfasmus@ucsd.edu. *The lessons and adventures that pervade our stories are manifestations of God's grace.*

ASMUSSEN, J. DONNA, retired educational administrator, researcher, artist; b. Woonsocket, R.I., Aug. 22, 1951; d. John E. and Marion Annette (Fanning) A. BS in Edn., R.I. Coll., 1974, MEd, 1984; student in Elem. Edn. and Visual Arts, U. Maine; spl. student Visual Arts, Colby Coll. Spl. edn. tchr. Lincoln Sch. Dept., RI, 1971—78, diagnostician, 1978—85; tchr. spl. edn. Maine Sch. Adminstrv. Dist. 36, Livermore Falls, 1985—89, composite rm. tchr., cons., 1989—90; dir. spl. svcs. Maine Sch. Adminstrv. Dist. 34, Belfast, 1990—95; cons. State Dept. Edn., Augusta, 1995—2000; visual artist, 2000—. Author: Soon to Be Reality: High Standards for All, 1999, School Reform: Achieving Enduring Change, 1999; artist (paintings) numerous pvt. collections. Home: PO Box 426 Oakland ME 04963-0426 E-mail: artjourneys@aol.com.

ASMUSSEN, NILS WIRENFELDT, pharmaceutical executive; b. Copenhagen, Jan. 12, 1938; s. Robert Wirenfeldt and Grethe (Abildgaard) A.; m. Marianne Bang, July 8, 1967; 1 child, Nicolai. BA, Østersøgades Gymnasium, Copenhagen, 1957; PhB, Copenhagen U., 1960; postgrad., Brunel U., Eng., 1982. Med. dir. Boehringer Ingelheim, Copenhagen, 1967-73; area med. dir. Searle, Copenhagen, 1973-79; regional med. dir. Ciba-Geigy, Copenhagen and Basel, Switzerland, 1979-83; regulatory dir. Europe Abbott, Paris, 1983-85; med. dir. Upjohn, Copenhagen, 1985-93; pres., med. dir. Wirenfeldt Asmussen, Denmark, 1993—. Cons. Medi-Lab, Copenhagen, 1994-2001; mem. com. Medicines Industry Assn. Denmark, 1985-93. Bd. dirs. Royal Guards Soc., Copenhagen, 1963, Gentofte Med. Lab., 1970; mem. Danish Salmon Found., Copenhagen, 1997. Guardsman Danish Royal Guards, 1962-63. Fellow Royal Soc. Medicine; mem. Am. Coll. Clin. Pharmacology, Royal Yacht Club. Avocations: hunting, skiing, sports fishing, yachting.

ASMUTH, GRETCHEN, law librarian, records manager; b. Stamford, Conn., 1954; BA, U Conn., 1977; MSLS, Cath. U. Am., 1983. Dir. libr. and records svcs. Preston Gates Ellis & Rouvelas Meeds LLP, Washington, 1982—. Mem. Am. Assn. Law Librs., Am. Records Mgmt. Assn. Presbyterian. Office: Preston Gates et al 1735 New York Ave NW Washington DC 20006-5209

ASNER, GLEN R. historian; b. Perth Amboy, N.J., Feb. 26, 1970; s. Joseph and Diane Asner. BA, U. Wis.; MS, Carnegie Mellon U., 1997, PhD, 2003. Rsch. analyst Wis. Fedn. Tchrs., Madison, 1995—96, Sci. and Engring. Assoc., Washington, 2002—. NSF grad. rsch. fellow Carnegie Mellon U., Pitts., 1996—99; Henry belin Du Pont fellow Hagley Mus. and Libr., Wilmington, Del., 2000, rsch. cons., 2001—02; Guggenheim fellow Nat. Air and Space Mus., Wash., 2000—01; spkr. in field. Grantee, NSF, 1999—2000; John E. Rovensky fellow in Econ. and Bus. History, Econ. History Assn., 1999—2000. Mem.: Am. Hist. Assn., Bus. History Conf., Soc. History of Tech.

ASNER, MARIE A. classical musician; b. St. Cloud, Minn., Feb. 28, 1948; d. Emil C. and Minnie A. (Anderson) Black; m. Aug. 18, 1973. BS, St. Cloud State U., 1972, MS, 1969; PhD, Columbia Pacific U., 1986. Supr. music Mpls. Sch. Sys., 1972-78; reviewer entertainment Jour. Herald, Shawnee, Kans., 1981—. Reviewer entertainment Wed. Mag., Kansas City, Mo., 1989-2000, 50 & Better Mag. 2000-2003, Metro Voice,, 1999—; chmn. Trinity Fine Arts Com., Mission, Kans., 1992-96. Composer (piano) Caroling with Bach, 1987, Tenebrae: Lenten Service, 2000; author (poetry collection) Secret Place, 1989, Man of Miracles, Man of Miracles II, Inquiring Mind, (with Rochelle Holt) The Tree of Life, Angels, Jesus of Nazareth; mem. adv. bd. Kansas City Film Soc., Potpourri Publs., Prairie Village, Kans. Recipient Grand prize in writing Kansas City Christian Writers Network Conf., 1998, Mini-fellowship in Poetry, Kans. Arts Commn., 2003. Mem. Internat. Women's Writing Guild, Am. Guild Organists (endowment fund publicity 2000-02), Poets and Writers, Nationally Cert. Tchrs. Music, Women in the Film Industry, Kansas City Christian Writers Network, Kansas City Film Critics Cir. Home: PO Box 4343 Overland Park KS 66204-0343

ASOKAN, UNISA, information professional; b. Augusta, Ga., May 8, 1969; d. S.K. and Kathleen (McGuirk) A. BA, NYU, 1991; MLS, San Jose State U., 1993. Libr. Printed Circuit Builders, Inc., Santa Clara, Calif., 1991-93; tech. writer Atre Assocs., Port Chester, N.Y., 1992-94; dir. info. svcs. Fin. World Mag., N.Y.C., 1994-96; rsch. libr. The Atlanta Jour. Constn., 1997—. Editor Fifth Planet Press, Atlanta, 1992—; bd. dirs. Eyedrum Inc., Atlanta, vice chair Eyedrum, Inc. Author: Non-Prophet, 1994, Pillow in the Kitchen, 2000. Recipient Youth Leadership award Congl. Youth Leadership Coun., 1987. Mem. ALA, Spl. Librs. Assn.

ASOMOZA, MIGUEL A. researcher, educator; b. Medero, Mex., Sept. 14, 1935; arrived in U.S., 1982; s. Miguel and Consuelo (Bosque) Asomoza; m. Martha A. Zozaya, Apr. 22, 1960 (div. July 1971); children: Miguel A., Martha; m. Hylda A. Asomoza, Dec. 30, 1976; 1 child, Paulo E. MD, Uamaulipas Autonomous U., Tampico, Mex., 1959; degree in indsl. security systems, Nat. Autonomous U. Mex., Mexico City, 1962; DSa, Nat. Poly. Inst., Mexico City, 1974, DSc, 1980. CEO PEMEX, Petroleos Mexicanos, Mexico City, 1959—79; prof., rschr. Nat. Poly. Inst., Mexico City, 1980—82, dir. adminstrv. rsch. ctr., 1982—84; med. mgr. PEMEX, Mexico City, 1985—86; rschr. U. Tex. Pan-Am., Edinburg, 1987—88; rschr., cons. Technol. Inst. Reynosa, Mexico, 1995—. Contbr. articles to profl. jours. Fellow: Masons; mem.: Am. Tolerance Assn., ACLU. Republican. Central Christian Church. Achievements include introduction of new variables in labor model design and industrial production in a non-linear model. Home: 4908 N 9th St McAllen TX 78504 Office: Technol Inst Ave Tecnologico s/u Reynosa Mexico E-mail: maasomoza@msn.com.

ASONGU, JANUARIUS JINGWA, information technology executive;, U.S., 1997; s. Nicholas Jingwa Asongu and Monique Nkeng; m. Christine Nkwayep Ngangsic, Dec. 1, 2000; children: Maria Yorkzah Ngangsic-Asongu children: Jude Jingwa Ngangsic-Asongu. PhB, Pontifical Urban U., Rome, 1993; cert. in mass. comm., U. Lagos, Nigeria, 1995; Diploma in Latin, Diploma in Greek, St. Thomas Aquinas Maj. Sem., Bambui, The Southern Cameroons, 1992; PhD, Pacific Western U., Hawaii, 1998; MS in Info. Tech., cert. CIO officer, U. Md., Adelphi, 2002; cert., Fed. CIO U., Washington, 2002. CEO Global Thrust Comm., Inc., Hyattsville, Md., 1999—; exec. dir. US-So. Cameroons Found., Inc., Hyattsville, 1999—; journalist various publs., Houston, 1997—99. Author: The Problem of National Unity in Cameroon, 1993, The Media & Nationalism: The Case of the Southern Cameroons (Nuffield Press Fellowship, 1998), Challenging Tyranny, 2003; editor: Houston Chronicle (AFPF, 1997), (mag.) Telecom Bus. (Telecom Profl. of the Yr., 1999), (online mag.) Global Tech. Trends; contbr. articles to profl. publs. Comm. commr. So. Cameroons Provisional Adminstrn., Washington, 2001—02. Named Best African Journalist in the US, Assn. of African Publishers, 1998; fellow, Alfred Friendly Press, 1997, Nuffield Press fellowship, Wolfson Coll., Cambridge U., 1998. Achievements include research in Southern Cameroons. Home: 6200 Brightlea Dr Lanham MD 20706 Office: Global Thrust Comm Inc 6475 New Hampshire Ave #620 Hyattsville MD 20783 Personal E-mail: asongu@yahoo.com.

ASP, WILLIAM GEORGE, librarian; b. Hutchinson, Minn., July 4, 1943; s. George William and Blanche Irene (Mattson) A. BA, U. Minn., 1966, MA, 1970; postgrad., U. Iowa, 1972-75. Dir. East Cen. Regional Libr., Cambridge, Minn., 1967-70; asst. prof. Sch. Libr. Sci. U. Iowa, 1970-75; dir. Minn. Office Libr. Devel. and Svcs., St. Paul, 1975-96, Dakota County Libr., Eagan, Minn., 1996—. Mem. Nat. Coun. Quality Continuing Edn. for Info., Libr. and Media Pers., 1979-85; bd. dirs. Bakken Libr. Electricity and Life, Mpls.; vice chmn. White House Conf. on Libr. and Info. Svcs. Task Force, 1980-81, chmn., 1982, mem. adv. com., 1989-91; pres. Continuing Libr. Edn. Network and Exch., 1986-87. Mem. Minn. Regional Network Bd., 1992-96. Mem. ALA (mem. coun. 1985-88, 00-02), Minn. Libr. Assn., Chief Officers State Libr. Agys. (chmn. 1979-80), Minn. Ednl. Media Orgn., Minn. Assn. Continuing and Adult Edn., Assn. Specialized and Coop. Libr. Agys. (pres. 1989-90), Am. Field Svc. Home: 4137 42nd Ave S Minneapolis MN 55406-3530

ASPEDON, MARY D. education educator; b. Tulsa, Nov. 8, 1941; d. Hercel L. and Lavina S. Robinson; m. Arden R. Aspedon, May 5, 1989; 1 child, Crista Lyn DePinto. BS in Elem. Edn., U. Kans., 1963, MS in Spl. Edn., 1971; PhD, U. Nebr., 1990. Cert. sch. supt., elem. prin., dir. spl. edn., k-12 spl. edn. tchr. Elem. prin. Millard Pub. Schs., Omaha, 1981—87; dir. student svcs. Kearney Pub. Schs., Nebr., 1987—89; spl. edn. coord. Lincoln Pub. Schs., 1989—93; supt. Francis Howell Sch. Dist., St. Charles, Mo., 1993—95, Ladue Sch. Dist., St. Louis, 1995—99; exec. dir. The Miriam Found., St. Louis, 1999—2000; asst. prof. Southwestern Okla. State U., Weatherford, 2000—. Ednl. cons., 1985—; exec. bd. mem. Edn. Equity Coalition, St. Louis, 1995—99; lectr. in field. Contbr. Vol. Ann. Art Fair, Weatherford, 2001—, Humane Soc., Weatherford, 2001—, Relay for Life, 2000—. Named Tchr. of the Yr., Kans. Jaycees, 1970; grantee Ednl. Rsch. grantee, Southwestern Okla. State U., 2001—03. Mem.: Mo. Assn. Curriculum and Supervision (pres. 1999—2000), Am. Assn. Sch. Adminstrs., Kappa Delta Pi (chpt. counselor 2002—). Home: 2100 Ryan Dr Weatherford OK 73096 Office: Southwestern Okla State Univ 100 Campus Dr Weatherford OK 73096

ASPEN, MARVIN EDWARD, federal judge; b. Chgo., July 11, 1934; s. George Abraham and Helen (Adelson) A.; m. Susan Alona Tubbs, Dec. 18, 1966; children: Jennifer Marion, Jessica Maile, Andrew Joseph. BS in Sociology, Loyola Univ., 1956; JD, Northwestern U., 1958. Bar: Ill. 1958. Individual practice, Chgo., 1958-59; draftsman joint com. to draft new Ill. criminal code Chgo. Bar Assn.-Ill. Bar Assn., 1959-60; asst. state's atty. Cook County, Ill., 1960-63; asst. corp. counsel City of Chgo., 1963-71; pvt. practice law, 1971; judge Cir. Ct. Cook County, Ill., 1971-79; judge ea. divsn. U.S. Dist. Ct. (no. dist.) Ill., Chgo., 1979-95, chief judge, 1995—2002. Edward Avery Harriman adj. prof. law Northwestern U. Law Sch.; past chmn. new judges, recent devels. in criminal law, and evidence coms. Ill. Judicial Conf., past chmn., adv. bd. Inst. Criminal Justice, John Marshall Sch. Law; past mem. Ill. Law Enforcement Commn., Gov. Ill. Adv. Commn. Criminal Justice, Cook County Bd. Corrections; past chmn. assoc. rules com. Ill. Supreme Ct., com. on ordinance violation problems; past vice chmn. com. on pattern jury instrns. in criminal cases; lectr. at judicial confs. and trial advocacy programs nationally and internationally; planner, participant in legal seminars at numerous schools including Harvard U., Emory U., U. Fla., Oxford U. (Eng.), U. Bologna, Nuremberg (Germany) U., U. Cairo, Egypt, U. Zimbabwe, U. Malta, U. The Philippines, U. Madrid; past mem. Georgetown U. Law Ctr. Project on Plea Bargaining in U.S., spl. faculty NITA advanced Trial Advocacy Program introducing Brit. trial techniques to experienced Am. litigators, spl. faculty of ABA designed to acquaint Scottish lawyers with modern litigation and tech.; frequent faculty mem. Nat. Judiciary Coll., Fed. Judicial Ctr., U. Nev. (Reno), Nat. Inst. for Trial Advocacy, Colo.; bd. dir. Fed. Judicial Ct., past chair dir. search com.; past mem. Judicial Conf. Com. on Adminstrn. of the Bankruptcy System, Trial Bar Implementation Com. on Civility of the 7th Fed. Cir.; mem. Northwestern U. Law Bd. Co-author Criminal Law for the Layman-A Citizen's Guide, 2d edit., 1977, Criminal Evidence for the Police, 1972, Protective Security Law, 1983; contbr. over two dozen articles to legal publs. Past mem. vis. com. Northwestern U. Sch. Law, chmn. adv. com. for short courses (post law sch. ednl. program), mem. law bd.; past mem. vis. com. U. Chgo. Law Sch.; mem. vis. com. No. Ill. U. Sch. Law; organizer, past pres. Northwestern Univ. Sch. of Law chpt. Amincourt Program U.S. Judicial Conf; past mem. Cook County Bd. Corrections, John Howard Assn.; active CEELI programs in Bulgaria and Yugoslavia Ford Found. Jud. Tng. Program in China. With USAF, 1958-59; trustee Am. Inns Ct. Recipient Nat. Ctr. Freedom of Info. Studies award, Ctr. for Pub. Resources award, Merit award Northwestern U. Alumni Assn., Herbert Harley award Am. Judicature Soc.; named Person of Yr. Chgo. Lawyer, 1995. Mem. Am. Bar Found. (bd. dirs.), Judicature Soc. Ill. (past chmn. coms.), Chgo. Bar Assn. (bd. mgrs. 1978-79, past chmn. criminal law com., past bd. editors Chgo. Bar Record, mem. commn. on criminal justice. coms. on cont. legal edn., devel. of law, civil disorder and others), Ill. State Bar Assn. (past chmn. pub. rels., corrections, fair trial/free press, criminal law coms., mem. others), Northwestern U. Law Alumni Assn. (past pres., Merit award), ABA (co-chair, sec. of litigation Inst. for Trial practical task force, mem. standing com. on fed. jud. improvements, pres. ABA mus., mem. bd. Am. Bar Fedn., past mem. ABA bd. govs., mem. house dels., past chmn. exec com., mem. bd. editors ABA Jour.), Nat. Conf. Fed. Trial Judges (past mem. coun. sect., past chmn. exec. com. litigation, past chmn., coun. sect. criminal justice, mem. edn. bd. sect. criminal justice mag., past co-chmn. liason jud. com. sect. litigation, mem. jury comprehension study com., ho. dels., standing com. fed. jud. improvements, co-chmn. sect. litigation Inst. Trial Practice Task Force), Am. Inns Ct. Office: US Dist Ct 2578 US Courthouse 219 S Dearborn St Chicago IL 60604-1800 E-mail: aspen@ilnd.uscourts.gov.

ASPENBERG, GARY ALAN, personnel and labor relations professional; b. Darby, Pa., Jan. 13, 1945; s. Albert Alexander and Edith Ellen (Ware) A.; m. Vicki Ann Carlson, Oct. 15, 1979; children: Carla Fay Lynn, Derek Alan. BA, Drew U., 1967, MA, 1972. Asst. pers. dir. Woodhull Med. Group, Bklyn., 1986, dir. pers. and labor rels., 1987-98, exec. dir. pers., labor. rels. and adminstrn., 1998—. Author: Bus Poems, 1993. Avocation: poet. Home: 323A E 89th St New York NY 10128-5007 Office: Woodhull Med Group 760 Broadway Brooklyn NY 11206-5317 E-mail: gaspenberg@aol.com.

ASPER, LEONARD, communications executive; Pres., CEO CanWest Global Comms. Corp., Winnipeg, Canada, 1991—. Office: CanWest Comm Corp 3100 TD Ctr 201 Portage Ave Winnipeg MB Canada

ASPERO, BENEDICT VINCENT, lawyer; b. Newton, N.J., Sept. 3, 1940; s. Umberto S. and Rose (Cerreta) A.; m. Sally Hennen, June 26, 1971; children: Benedict Vincent, Alexander Morgan. AB, U. Notre Dame, 1962, JD, 1966. Bar: N.J. 1970, N.Y. 1982, D.C. 1983, U.S. Dist. Ct. N.J. 1970, U.S. Supreme Ct. 1981. Assoc., then ptnr. Meyers, Lesser & Aspero, Sparta, N.J., 1971-76; atty. Benedict V. Aspero, Sparta and Morristown, N.J., 1976-82; ptnr. Broderick, Newmark, Grather & Aspero, Morristown, 1982-89, Courter, Kobert, Laufer, Purcell & Cohen, 1989-91; prin. Benedict V. Aspero, Esq., P.C., 1992—. Mem. adv. bd. Summit Bank, First Morris Bank. Trustee Harding Twp. Civic Assn., Loyola Retreat House, 1992—99, Craig Sch., 1985—, pres. bd., 1992—2002. Mem. ABA, N.J. Bar Assn., Morris County Bar Assn., Sussex County Bar Assn., Sorin Soc., Morristown Club, Essex Hunt Club. Republican. Roman Catholic. Office: 222 Ridgedale Ave PO Box 1573 Morristown NJ 07962-1573 E-mail: bvatty@GTI.net.

ASPINALL, CASSANDRA LOUISE, social worker, researcher; b. Seattle, Wash., Feb. 18, 1959; d. Ronald Leslie and Carolyn Irene Chard; m. Robert Thornton Aspinall, Aug. 12, 1980; children: Anthony Thornton, Timothy Michael, Simon Douglas. MA Soical Work, U. Wash., Seattle, Wash., 1987. Lic. Independent Social Worker Wash., 1992. Med. social worker Childrens Hosp. and Regional Med. Ctr., Seattle, 1988—2002, U. Wash. Med. Ctr., Seattle, 1987—. Mem.: Am. Cleft Palate and Craniofacial Assn., NASW. Office: Children's Hosp and Medl Ctr PO Box 5371 MS 6F-3 Seattle WA 98105 E-mail: cassandra.aspinall@seattlechildrens.org.

ASPINALL, MARA GLICKMAN, marketing and general management professional; b. N.Y.C., Aug. 14; d. Alvin and Betty Glickman. BA, Tufts U., 1983; MBA, Harvard U., 1987. Assoc. First Boston Corp., N.Y.C., 1986; cons. Bain & Co., Inc., Boston, 1987-90; dir. mktg., client svcs. Hale and Dorr LLP, Boston, 1990-97; v.p. corp. devel. Genzyme Corp., Cambridge, Mass., 1997-2000; pres. Genzyme Pharms., Cambridge, 1997—, Genzyme Emerging Techs., 2000-01, Genzyme Genetics, Framingham, 2001—; chmn. bd. DentaQuest Ventures, 2002—. Bd. dirs. Delta Dental Plan Mass., 2000—, Tufts U., Coll. of Citizenship and Pub. Svc., 2000—; mem. biotech project adv. group Radcliffe Pub. Policy Inst. Mem. editl. bd.: Rainmaker's Quar., 1996. Chmn. Am. Cancer Soc., Mass., 1996-99; bd. dirs. Arts Boston, 1996-1999, Dana-Farber Cancer Inst., Boston, 1998—; dir. Success by 6 Leadership Coun., United Way, 1998-99; co-chmn. Early Edn. for All, 2001—. Recipient Woman of Vision award Mass. Prevent Blindness Assn., 1995, Pinnacle award for Emerging Exec. of Yr. Greater Boston C. of C., 1997; named among Forty under Forty Top Bus. Execs., Boston Bus. Jour., 1999, Ten Outstanding Young Leaders Boston Jaycees, 1999, Acad. of Women Achievers YWCA, 1999. Mem. Nat. Assn. Law Firm Mktg. (pres. New Eng. 1992-94), Assn. Tufts Alumnae (pres. 1988-90, 92-94, alumni trustee rep. bd. trustees), Harvard Bus. Sch. Assn. (chairperson reunion com.), Harvard Bus. Sch. Network for Women (dir. 1995-98), WGBH Corp. Exec. Coun. (dir. 1997-99), The Children's Mus. Boston (trustee 1996—), Greater Boston C. of C. (bd. dirs. 1999—). Office: Genzyme Corp 1 Kendall Sq Cambridge MA 02139-1562

ASPINWALL, DAVID CHARLES, lawyer, insurance company executive; b. Denver, Apr. 15, 1955; s. Darrell David and Gwendolyn Beth (Skeels) Aspinwall; m. Inez Bussey Merritt, Dec. 5, 1981; children: Courney Merritt, Johnathan Westbrook. BA, Denver U., 1977, JD, 1980. Bar: Colo. 1980. Mem. Dunn, Crane & Burg, Denver, 1980—81, Michael S. Burg, P.C., Denver, 1981—83, Burg & Aspinwall, P.C., Denver, 1983—88; v.p. counsel, chief compliance officer Gt. West Life & Annuity Ins. Co., Greenwood Village, Colo., 1988—. Mem. class action working group ACLI, 1995—2000; mem. faculty, life ins. litig. ALIABA; mem. legal adv. com. Employment Retirement Income Security Act, 1998—2001; mem. adv. work group AAHP, 2001—; instr. in field. Mem. auction underwriting com. St. Anne's Episc. Sch., 1988—89; pre-marital facilitator Christ Episc. Ch., 1988—94; pres. Sundance Pride, 1987—90. Mem.: Internat. Claims Assn. (mem. law com. 1990—93, panel mem. law com. presentation ann. conv. 1992), Colo. Bar Assn., Def. Rsch. Inst., Arapahoe County Bar Assn., Phi Beta Kappa. Republican. Office: Great West Life & Annuity Ins Co 8525 E Orchard Rd Ste 200 Greenwood Village CO 80111-5097 E-mail: david.aspinwall@gwl.com.

ASPLIN, EDWARD WILLIAM, retired packaging company executive; b. Mpls., June 25, 1922; s. John E. and Alma (Carlbom) A.; m. Eleanor Young Rodgers, Oct. 20, 1951; children— Sarah L., William R., Lynn E. BBA, U. Minn., 1943; postgrad., U. Mich., 1947-48, Wayne State, 1949-50, Rutgers U. Sch. Banking, 1957-59. Cost accountant Nat. Bank Detroit, 1947-50; asst. v.p. adminstrn. Northwest Bancorp., Mpls., 1950-59; v.p. mktg. Northwestern Nat. Bank, Mpls., 1959-67; chmn. Bemis Co., Inc., Mpls., 1967-88. Advisor Opportunity Ptnrs., Inc.; hon. bd. dirs. Mpls. YMCA, Minn. Hist. Soc.; adv. bd. dirs. U. Minn. Cancer Adv. Bd. Mem. Woodhill County Club, Mpls. Club.

ASPLUNDH, CHRISTOPHER B. tree service company executive; b. Aug. 26, 1939; BS, U of Penn. With Asplundh, Willow Grove, Pa., 1963—, v.p., 1966, pres., 1992-2001, CEO, chmn., 2001—, also bd. dirs. Office: Asplundh Tree Expert Co 708 Blair Mill Rd Willow Grove PA 19090-1784*

ASPNES, DAVID ERIK, physicist, educator; b. Madison, Wis., May 1, 1939; s. Erik A. and Anita L. (Knabe) A.; m. Edna Joyce Hall, Jan. 27, 1964 (dec. 1996); children: James D., Gary E., Ann K.; m. Cynthia Jean Ball, July 26, 1997. BSEE, U. Wis., 1960, MSEE, 1961; PhD, U. Ill., 1965. Postdoctoral rsch. assoc. U. Ill., Urbana, 1965-66, Brown U., Providence, 1966-67; mem. tech. staff Bell Labs., Murray Hill, N.J., 1967-83; sr. scientist Max-Planck-Inst., Stuttgart, Fed. Republic Germany, 1976-77; dist. mgr. Bellcore, Red Bank, N.J., 1983-92; prof. physics dept. N.C. State U., 1992-99, Disting. Univ. prof. physics, 1999—. Bd. dirs. Therma-Wave, Inc. Contbr. more than 400 articles to Phys. Rev., Applied Optics, Thin Solid Films and other jours.; U.S. editor Applied Surface Sci., 1996-2001. Recipient Sr. Scientist award Alexander von Humboldt Found., 1976-77, John Yarwood medal Brit. Vacuum Coun., 1993, Max Planck Rsch. Award for Internat. Coop., 1997, Outstanding Rsch. award N.C. State U. Alumni Assn., 1997. Fellow AAAS, Am. Phys. Soc. (councillor divsn. condensed matter physics 1996-99, exec. coun. 1998-99, Frank Isakson prize 1996), Optical Soc. Am. (Wood prize 1987), Am. Vacuum Soc. (chmn. electronic materials and processing divsn. 1982-83, chmn. electronics materials and processing divsn. internat. Union Vacuum Sci., Techniques and Applications 1986-89, bd. dirs. 1991-92, trustee 2001—, Medard W. Welch award 1998), Soc. Photo-Optical Instrumentation Engrs.; mem. IEEE, Nat. Acad. of Scis., Materials Rsch. Soc., Alexander von Humboldt Assn. Am., Sigma Xi. Mem. Lds Ch. Achievements include discovery and development of reflectance-difference spectroscopy and low-field electroreflectance; development of spectroscopic ellipsometry with applications to process control; contributions to solid-state physics including 3rd derivative interpretation of low-field electroreflectance, ordering of the lower conduction bands of GaAs, elucidation of the kinetics of crystal growth by organometallic chemical vapor deposition, virtual-interface theory. Office: NC State U Physics Dept Raleigh NC 27695-8202 E-mail: aspnes@unity.ncsu.edu.

ASSAEL, ALYCE, artist; b. N.Y.C., Dec. 12, 1938; d. Joseph and Betty (Abrams) Friedman; m. Henry Assael, Aug. 19, 1961; children: Shaun, Brenda. Grad., Parsons Sch. Design, 1960; BS, NYU, 1960, M in Am. Folk Art, 1985. Window designer Henri Bendel, N.Y.C., 1960; interior store designer Macy's, N.Y.C., 1960-62; interior showroom designer Glenn of Mich., N.Y.C., 1962-63; illustrator for fashion catalogs and promotion pieces, N.Y.C., 1962-63; fine artist paintings and photographs, N.Y.C., 1964-70. Exhibited works in solo shows U. Pa., Phila., 1975, Ann Harper Gallery, Amagansett, N.Y., 1995; group shows at Louise Himmelfarb Gallery, Southampton,. N.Y., 1980, M.J. Green Gallery, Bridgehampton, N.Y., 1980, Guild Hall Mus., East Hampton, N.Y., 1997, 98, 99, 2001; curator, catalog author Singular Visions show. Mem. Guild Hall Mus., Mus. Modern Art, Mus. Am. Folk Art, Queens Mus., Mus. of Women in the Arts. Avocations: photography, theatre, film.

ASSAEL, HENRY, marketing educator; b. Sofia, Bulgaria, Sept. 12, 1935; s. Stanley Isaac and Anna (Behar) A.; m. Alyce Friedman, Aug. 19, 1961; children: Shaun Eric, Brenda Erica. BA cum laude, Harvard U., 1957; MBA, U. Pa., 1959; PhD, Columbia, 1965. Asst. prof. mktg. Sch. Bus. St. John's U., Jamaica, N.Y., 1962-65; asst. prof. mktg. Hofstra U., Hempstead, N.Y., 1965-66; prof. mktg. Stern Sch. Bus. NYU, 1966—, chmn. dept., 1979-91. Cons. AT&T, N.Y. Stock Exchange, Nestle Co., Inc., CBS. Author: Educational Preparations for Positions in Advertising Management, 1966, The Politics of Distributive Trade Associations: A Study in Conflict Resolution, 1967, Consumer Behavior and Marketing Action, 1981, 6th edit. 1998, Marketing Management: Strategy and Action, 1985, Marketing: Principles and Strategy, 1990, 2d edit., 1993, Marketing: Core Concepts, 1998, Consumer Behavior: A Strategic Approach, 2003; editor: A Century of Marketing, 33 vols., 1978, Early Development and Conceptualization of the Field of Marketing, 1978, History of Advertising, 40 vols., 1985; contbr. numerous articles to profl. jours. Mem. Am. Mktg. Assn., Assn. Consumer Research. Office: 44 W 4th St New York NY 10012-1106

ASSAEL, LEON A. dean, educator; Student, Harvard U. Resident Vanderbilt U. Med. Ctr., Nashville; dean, prof. U. Ky., 1997—. Office: Chandler Med Ctr 800 Rose St Lexington KY 40536

AS-SALAAM, JAMAAL (WILLIAM LOUIS WILLIAMS JR.), poet, film producer, writer; b. Albany, N.Y., Apr. 20, 1955; s. William Louis Williams Sr. and Helen Virginia Williams-Smith; m. Veronica Foster, June 20, 1980 (div. June 1985); children: Qwinde, Shani O.; m. Arlene Hooks (div. Sept. 1992); 1 child, Jamar Williams; m. Terisita Ann Lopez; 1 child, Mieko O. Lopez. Student, SUNY, Purchase, 1972-76, U. No. Colo., 1984-86, Nat. U., Encino, Calif., 1990-92, Calif. Arts Partnership, 1995-98. Cert. Microsoft cert. sys. engr. Ednet Career Inst., Microsoft software trainer, Microsoft cert. profl., A+ cert. computer svc. technician. Track laborer Burlington No. R.R., 1978-85; computer specialist Denver Pub. Schs., 1980-86; Saks cons. Tom Hopkins Sales Tng., Denver, 1984-86; tech. support Telepoetics, L.A., 1988-94; computer technician L.A. County Schs., Bellflower, Calif., 1987-94; video editor Calif. Arts Comty. Ptnrs., L.A., 1994-99; rschr. Sales, Inc., Beverly Hills, Calif., 1996-97; ind. prodr. Lightland Prodns., L.A., 1999—. Freelance prodr. Mile High Cable Co., Denver, 1983-86; radio announcer Sta. KUVO, Denver, 1984-85. Author: (anthology) Portraits of Life, 1997 (Editors Choice award), (chapbook) Facing East, 1995; actor: (TV) Naked Truth, General Hospital, also comml. and theatrical prodns.; dir., writer, prodr.: (film) Leimert Park, 1996; (theatre) New Age Perspective, The Muse; (video) Poetry 101, Leimert Park: Unlocking the Pyramid, Coming Full Circle, 2002; dir., writer: (theatre) Persona Suite, Kwanzaa Adatation; dir., prodr.: (video) History Revisited. Vol. Inner City Cultural Ctr., 1989-95; founding mem. Denver Black Arts Theater Co., 1980-85; mem. Win/Win Bus. Forum, Denver, 1984; vol., mem. Telepoetics, L.A., 1994; vol. L.A. In Support of Gang Truce, 1996; mem. Black Radical Congress, 1999. Recipient Calif. Arts Comty. Project award Calif. Inst. of Arts, 1996, 98, 1st prize Upstate Photography, Albany, N.Y., 1973. Mem. Black Radical Congress. Buddhist. Avocations: reading, sports, swimming, conga, martial arts, art restoration. Home and Office: PO Box 111072 Aurora CO 80042-1072 E-mail: jamaal21@hotmail.com.

ASSANE, DJETO, finance educator; b. Gagnoa, Cote d'Ivoire, Apr. 6, 1955; arrived in U.S., 1980; s. Nicolas Assane and Heleine Adjehi; m. Jeanne Assane, May 23, 1985; children: Corine, Manuela Rita. BA, U. Abidjan, Coté d'Ivoire, 1980; MA, U. Colo., 1982, PhD, 1988. Vis. asst. prof. U. Nev., Las Vegas, 1988—93, asst. prof., 1994—2000, assoc. prof., 1990—. Roman Catholic. Avocations: swimming, hiking. Office: U Nev-Las Vegas Dept Econs Las Vegas NV 89154-6005 Office Fax: 702-895-1354. E-mail: assane@ccmail.nevada.edu.

ASSANI, IDRIS, mathematician, educator; s. Layissou Assani and Berthe Parbey; m. Rosalie Akouele Abbey-Assani; 1 child, Nadjib. DSc, D 3d cycle, U. Pierre and Marie Curie, Paris, 1986. Postdoctoral fellow U. Toronto, Toronto, Canada, 1986—88; asst. prof. U. N.C. Chapel Hill, 1988—95, assoc. prof., 1995, prof., 1996—. Prin. investigator NSF, Washington, 1989—97, prin. investigator/project dir., 2000—01; mem. faculty coun. U. N.C.-Chapel Hill, 1998—2000, FITAC com. in instrnl. tech., numerous coms., math. dept.; mem. panel rev. math. program Howard U., Washington, 2002; vis. faculty numerous univs. France, Eng., Spain, U.S. Contbr. articles to profl. jours.; author: book, 2003. Recipient IBM -Jr. devel. award, U. N.C.-Chapel Hill, 1989, IBM -FITAC -Instrnl. Tech. award, 2000—01. Mem.: Am. Math. Soc. (reviewer 1993—2003, com. acad. freedom tenure and employment security 2000—03). Office: U NC Phillips Hall Cameron Ave Chapel Hill NC 27599-3250 Home Fax: 919-968-8731; Office Fax: 919-962-9620. Personal E-mail: idrona@bellsouth.net. E-mail: assani@email.unc.edu.

ASSELIN, JOHN THOMAS, lawyer; b. Manchester, Conn., May 13, 1951; s. Oliver Joseph and MaryRose Mildred (Dondero) A.; children: Jessica Lynn, Kristina Anne. BA, U. Conn., 1973, JD, 1976. Bar: Conn. 1976, U.S. Dist. Ct. Conn. 1976. Pvt. practice, New London, Conn., 1976—. Lectr. Practicing Law Inst. N.Y., Profl. Edn. Systems Inc. Author: Connecticut Workers' Compensation Practice Manual, The Trial Handbook for Connecticut Lawyers; contbr. articles to profl. jours. Served Conn. gov. Thomas J. Meskill, U.S. Rep. Robert Steele. Grantee Deerfield Found. Mem. ABA (lectr.), Conn. Bar Assn. (exec. com. civil justice sect.), Assn. Trial Lawyers Am., Conn. Trial Lawyers Assn. (bd. govs. 1981—), Phi Beta Kappa, Phi Kappa Phi, Pi Sigma Alpha. Roman Catholic. Avocations: horses, team penning. Office: 190 Governor Winthrop Blvd New London CT 06320-6633 Address: 38 Granite St New London CT 06320

ASSELTA, NICHOLAS, state legislator; b. 1951; m. Nancy Small. Grad., Cumberland County Coll., Frederick Mil. Acad., Rider Coll., Glassboro State Coll. State assemblyman dist. 1, N.J., 1995—. Mem. tourism and gaming com., sr. citizens and social svc. com., N.J. Commn. on Aging N.J. State Assembly; adj. faculty Atlantic C.C., 1978-81, head baseball coach, 1978-81; basketball coach Vineland High Sch., 1985-87; mktg. and comml. print dir. Times Graphics, Inc. Gannett Co. Mem. Vineland (N.J.) Planning Bd., Vineland Environ. Com., Vineland Hist. Antiquarian Soc., Newcomb Hosp. Found., 1992-93, Vineland Bd. Edn., 1993—. Office: Sun Nat Bank Bldg 226 W Landis Ave Ste 3 Vineland NJ 08360-8145*

ASSENSOH, AKWASI BRETUO, historian, educator; b. Dunkwa-on-Offin, Ghana, Apr. 1, 1946; s. Opanin Kwabena Assensoh and Abena Amoatemaah; m. Yvette Marie Alex, May 7, 1994; children: Gloria, Philip, Sam, Kwadwo, Livingston Alex; m. Irenita Benbow, 1980 (div. 1993); children: Rose-Abena, Akwasi Bretuo Jr. Diploma in Journalism, advanced diploma in Mass Comm. and Journalism, Sch. Journalism and TV, Frilsham, Eng., 1967; BA in History and Polit. Sci., Dillard U., 1981; MA in History, NYU, 1982, PhD in History, 1984. Sub-editor The Pioneer, Kumasi, Ghana, 1969—70, Monrovia, Liberia, 1970—72; editor-in-chief Daily Listener, Saturday Chronicle, Sunday Digest, 1969—70; mng. editor Internat. Observer Mag., New Orleans, 1980—81; assoc. editor African Commentary Jour., Amherst, Mass., 1990; vis. asst. prof. history Stanford U., Palo Alto, Calif., 1988—89; assoc. editor, dir. rsch. King Papers Project, Stanford U., Palo Alto, Calif., 1989—90; vis. scholar Emory U., Atlanta, 1989—90; assoc. prof. history So. U., Baton Rouge, Ind. U., Bloomington, 1995—2000, prof. history, 2001—; contbg. editor West Africa Mag., London, 2003—. Invited lectr. in field; editl. bd. Internat. Abraham Lincoln Jour., 2000—, Jour. 3d World Studies, 1988—, Africa and the World, London, 1987—88. Author: African Military History and Politics: Coups and Ideological Incursions, 1900-Present, 2001, African Political Leadership: A Comparative Study of Jomo Kenyatta, Julius K. Nyerere, and Kwame Nkrumah, 1998, Rev. Dr. Martin Luther King, Jr., and America's Quest for Racial Integration, 1986, Kwame Nkrumah of Africa: His Formative Years and the Shaping of his Nationalism and Pan-Africanism, 1935-1948, 1990, Essays on Contemporary International Topics, 1986, Africa in Retrospect, 1985, An Overview of Political Risk Reporting in Africa: The Liberian Example, 1985, Polygamy in the Ashanti Tribe of Ghana; a Histo-Political Overview, 1984, (historical novel) Black Woman, An African Story, 1980, (3-act play) Campus Life, 1986, Kwame Nkrumah: Six Years in Exile, 1966-1972, 1978; contbr. chapters to books, albums and revs. to profl. jours., mags. and newspapers; participant numerous TV and radio programs, various countries, 1978—99. Assoc. min. 2d Bapt. Ch., Bedford, Ind., 1998—, acting pastor, 1999—; bd. trustees Bethel AME Ch., 1996—97; sec./treas. Rev. Livingston Alex Partnership Found. Fellow NEH, 2000, others; grantee Spencer Found. rsch. conf., 2000; Fulbright-Hays faculty fellow, Asia, 1986. Mem.: PEN, Assn. Third-World Studies (pres. U.S. chpt. 2003—), Royal African Soc. Gt. Britain and Commonwealth, Internat. Fedn. Journalists, Am.-Scandinavian Found. N.Y., African Studies Assn., Nat. Geographic Soc. Am., So. Hist. Assn., Am. Hist. Assn., Smithsonian Instn. (assoc.), NYU Alumni Assn., Dillard U. Nat. Alumni Assn. (life), Press Club of New Orleans, Rosicrucians, Masons, Alpha Phi Alpha. Baptist. Office: Indiana U Box 1933 Bloomington IN 47402

ASSIE-LUMUMBA, N'DRI T. Africana studies educator; b. Potossou, Ivory Coast, 1952; d. Kouassi and Yaha (Kokora) Assie. Studnet, U. Abidjan, Ivory Coast, 1970-71; BA, U. Lyon, France, 1972; MA, U. Lyon, 1975; postgrad., U. Laval, Que., Can., 1976; PhD, U. Chgo., 1982. Rchr. U. Abidjan, 1975-76; postdoctoral fellow U. Houston, 1982-83; tchr., adminstr. U. Benin, CIRSSED, Lome, Togo, 1983-88; vis. Bard Coll., Annandale, N.Y., 1989, Vassar Coll., Poughkeepsie, N.Y., 1989-90; resident fellow Internat. Inst. for Ednl. Planning, Paris, 1990; dep. dir. Pan African Studies and Rsch. Ctr., Abidjan, 1996—; prof. Africana studies Cornell U., Ithaca, N.Y., 1991—. Cons. UNESCO, Paris, 1989, 94, UN Devel. Program, N.Y.C., 1997, 99, Forum for African Women, Nairobi, Kenya, 1997, Rockefeller Found., N.Y.C., 1999. Author: Les Africaine dans la politique, 1996; editor Jour. Comparative Edn., 1998—. Ford Found. fellow, 1991; Fulbright sr. rsch. felow, 1991-92; Rockefeller Found. grantee, 1996-97. Mem. AAUW, Assn. African Women for R&D (exec. com.), Comparative and Internat. Edn. Soc., Coun. for Devel. of Social Sci. Rsch. in Africa, Cornell Inst. for Social and Econ. Rsch., Pi Lambda Theta. Avocations: music (jazz, modern, african and classical), physical exercise, modern african dance, reading. Office: Cornell U Africana Studies 310 Triphammer Rd Ithaca NY 14850-2519

ASSINI, VINCENT PAUL, financial executive; b. Newark, Dec. 1, 1950; s. Vincent A. and Jean L. (Di Pietro) A.; m. Elisabeth Schmidt, May 2, 1979. BSBA, U. Fla., 1972. CPA, N.Y. Contr. Ingersoll-Rand, Vienna, 1976-81; mgr. planning OTIS, Paris, 1982-86, dir. fin. Munich, 1987-90; divsn. contr. J.I. Case, Paris, 1990-92; divsn. gen. mgr. Alusuisse-Lonza, Singen, Germany, 1993-96; CFO, Leica AG, St. Gallen, Switzerland, 1996-98. Bd. dirs. Leica Microsys., Wetzlar, Germany, Leica Geosys., Heerbrugg, Switzerland. Mem. AICPA, Swiss Fin. Execs. Home and Office: 4321 Dewey Dr New Port Richey FL 34652-3114

ASSINK, NELLIE GRACE, agricultural executive; b. Yakima, Wash., July 5, 1920; d. Martin Gilde and Grace Byl; m. George H. Assink, July 9, 1943 (dec. Nov. 1982); children: Macile Assink Zais, Jon Martin. BA, tchr.'s diploma in music and piano, Whitman Coll./Conserv. Music, 1942; postgrad., U. Wash. and Cen. Coll., 1944, 59. Gen. cert., Wash.; cert. supr. music. English tchr., libr. Mabton (Wash.) H.S., 1943-45; libr. Wide Hollow Sch., Yakima, 1948-49; English tchr., libr. Lower Naches (Wash.) Sch., 1960-80; pres. Assink Acres, Inc., Naches, 1982—. Ch. organist Meml. Bible Ch., Yakima, 1946-82; chmn. Christian Edn. Bd., 1981-82; bd. dirs., sec. Yakima County Farm Bur., 1985-99; libr. Meml. Bible Ch., Yakima, 1960—. Mem. Naches Union Irrigation Dist. (sec. 1993—), Yakima County Farm Bur. (past sec. 1997), Lower Naches Women's Club (pres. 1984-86, 2000-02), Yakima Music Club, Ch. Librs.-N.W. (past pres.). Republican. Avocations: genealogy, photography, classical piano. Home: 681 N Gleed Rd Naches WA 98937 Office: Assink Acres Inc 681 N Gleed Rd Naches WA 98937

ASSOIAN, RICHARD KENNETH, molecular biologist, educator; PhD, U. of Chgo., 1981. Prof. Univeristy of Pa., Philadelphia, Pa., 1998—; assoc. prof. U. of Miami Sch. of Medicine, Fla., 1992—98; asst. prof. Columbia U., New York, NY, 1886—1992; staff fellow Nat. Cancer Inst./NIH, Bethesda, Md., 1983—86, post-doctoral fellow, 1981—83. Editor Jour. of Cell Sci.; assoc. editor Molecular Biology of the Cell. Recipient Basil O'Conner Scholar award, Mar. of Dimes; grantee Established Investigator, Am. Heart Assn., NYC Affiliate. Mem.: Am. Soc. for Cell Biology. Office: Univ of Pa Sch of Med 3620 Hamilton Walk Philadelphia PA 19104-6084

ASSOUAD, MARIO, internist, nephrologist; b. Aleppo, Syria, Oct. 2, 1967; came to U.S., 1990; s. Jean and Saloua Denise (Akel) A. MD, U. Aleppo, 1990. Diplomate Am. Bd. Internal Medicine with subspecialty in nephrology. Intern U. Nev. Sch. Medicine, Reno, 1992-93, resident in internal medicine, 1993-95; fellow in nephrology Baylor Coll. Medicine, Houston, 1995-97, asst. prof., 1997—. Presenter 5th Internat. Congress Cancer Chemotherapy, Paris, 1995, 18th Internat. Med. Conv., Syria, 2001. Contbr. articles to med. jours. Fellow ACP; mem. AMA, Am. Soc. Nephrology, Arab Am. Med. Assn., Renal Physicians Assn. Roman Catholic. Home: # 110 7447 Cambridge Houston TX 77054 Office: 1130 Earle St # 121G Houston TX 77030-5008

ASSUNTO, RICHARD ANTHONY, human resources specialist; b. New Haven, Conn., Nov. 15, 1942; s. Joseph and Anne Maude. BA, Biola U., 1970; MBA, U. Hartford, 1987. Exec. dir. Youth For Christ, 1970-72; host 700 Club, WHCT, 1970-71; mgr. life issue Aetna Life Ins., Hartford, Conn., 1973-81, mgr. payroll, 1981-89, mgr. purchasing, 1989-92; mgr. payroll Allied Signal, Tempe, Ariz., 1992-94; dir. human resources adminstrn. Norrell Corp., Atlanta, 1994-97; sr. mgr. Andersen Consulting, Atlanta, 1997-99, KPMG, 2000; pres. Tull Fields Consulting, 2000—01; sr. mgr. AG Consulting, 2001—02. Chmn. United Way Aetna Life Ins., 1983; treas. Hill Ctr., Hartford, 1983—85; bd. dirs. Cowboy Artists Am. Mus., 1999—. With USAF, 1961—65. Mem.: Am. Soc. Payroll Mgrs., Am. Payroll Assn. (pres. 1983—85, v.p. 1993—94, Comm. award 1989, Spkrs. award 1989, 1992, 1996). Avocations: bicycling, swimming, basketry, golf.

ASTAIRE, CAROL ANNE TAYLOR, artist, educator; b. Long Beach, Calif., Aug. 26, 1947; d. John Clinton and Carolyn Sophie (Wright) Taylor; m. Frederic Astaire, Jr., Feb. 14, 1971; children: John Carroll, Johanna Carolyn. BFA, UCLA, 1969; grad. summer studies, Salzburg Summer Sch., Klessheim, Austria, 1969; cert. secondary sch. tchr., Calif. State U., Long Beach, 1971; postgrad., Calif. Polytechnic State U., San Luis Obispo, 1986-87. Cert. secondary sch. tchr. Calif. Tchr., tutor, cons. art edn. San Luis Coastal Unified Sch. Dist., San Luis Obispo, 1980-89. Author: (book) Left Handed Poetry from the Heart, 1983; Represented in permanent collections Yergeau Musée Interant. Art, Montreal, Can., Travis AFB Mus., Calif., Huntington Libr. Founder, trustee San Luis Coastal Unified Sch. Dist./Found. Arts Art Core, 1988—92; mem. adv. coun. Coastal Cmty. Edn. and Svc., San Luis Obispo, 1989—92; screening com. UCLA Alumni Scholarship, 1993—95; mem. archtl. needs assessment com. Art Ctr., San Luis Obispo. Recipient Nat. finalist, Kodak Internat. Newspaper Snapshot award, 1993, 1st pl. black and white photo award, Ann. Visions 99 Photography Group, Visions 2001/Ctrl. Coast Photog. Soc., 2001, 1st pl., B/W Visions, 2001. Mem.: Ctrl. Coast Photog. Soc. (two 1st place black-and-white photo awards), Ctrl. Coast Watercolor Soc., Oil Pastel Acrylic Group Brushstrokes (hon. mention 1994), San Luis Obispo Art Coun., Fine Arts Coun., San Luis Obispo Art Ctr., Nat. Mus. Women in Arts. Republican. Episcopalian. Avocations: classical ballet, architectural design, swimming, ocean kayaking, reading.

ASTE, MARIO ANDREA, foreign language educator; b. Carloforte, Italy, Jan. 11, 1943; came to U.S., 1966; s. Stefano and Francesca A.; m. Dorothy Elaine Balbirer, June 6, 1970; children: Stephen Robert, Marie Francesca, Kristina Elizabeth. BSEE, Tech. Inst., Cagliar, Italy, 1963; BA in Philosophy, Philos. Inst., Torino, Italy, 1966; MA in Italian, Cath. U. Am., 1969, PhD, 1971, MA in Spanish, 1978. Prof., chmn. langs. U. Mass., Lowell, 1971—2003. Bd. dirs. Internat. Inst., Lowell, pres., 1980—99. Author: La Narrativa Di Luigi Pirandello, 1979, Two Novels of Pirandello: An Essay, 1979, Grazia Deledda: Ethnic Novelist, 1989, They Came in Hope, 1995; editor: Technology Industry Labor and the Italian American Communities, 1997, Greece and Italy: Ancient Roots New Beginnings, 2003. Housing rev. bd. City of Lowell, 1981-84; pastoral fin. coun. St. Michael Parish, Lowell, 1987—. Teaching fellow Cath. U. Am., Washington, 1967; NEH grantee Stanford U., 1979, Princeton U., 1983, Cath. U., 1988. Mem. MLA (chair exec. com. 20th century Italian lit. divsn. 1996-97), Am. Assn. Tchrs. Italian (exec. bd. 2000—), Am. Assn. Italian Studies (jour. editor 1989-98, mng. editor 1998-2001), Am. Italian Hist. Assn. (exec. bd. 1992—, treas. 1997-99, pres. 2000-02), Mass. Soc. Prof. (pres. 1988-2003), N.E. Modern Lang. Assn. (exec. bd. 1998—2002, exec. bd. for Italian and Spanish 2000—), K.C. Democrat. Roman Catholic. Avocations: Italian folk life festivals, soccer, scouting. Home: 115 Reservoir St Lowell MA 01850-2244 Office: U Mass 1 University Ave Lowell MA 01854-5009

ASTER, RUTH MARIE RHYDDERCH, business owner; b. Cleve., Aug. 15, 1939; d. Roy William and Ruth Marie (Teckmeyer) Rhydderch; m. Ferdinand Aster, Nov. 23, 1963; children: Anneliese Ruth Aster Wilt, Christian Josef Roy. Student, Cooper Sch. Art, 1956-57; BS, Kent State U., 1962. Art tchr. North Olmsted (Ohio) Jr. and Sr. H.S., 1962; art dept. chmn. Andrews Sch. for Girls, Willoughby, Ohio, 1963-64; co-owner, treas. Aster Cabinet Shop, Chesterland, Ohio, 1963—; co-owner, v.p., treas. Ferdl Aster Ski Sch., Chesterland, 1964—; owner, v.p., sec., treas. Ferdl Aster Ski Shop, Chesterland, 1972—; owner, v.p., advt. designer, fashion buyer, tour advisor Ferdl Aster Sport Ctr., Chesterland, 1985—. Chmn. region IV U.S. Ski Assn., Colorado Springs, Colo., 1980—84, Alpine ofcl., 1983—88; ski racing coach U.S. Ski Coaches Assn., Park City, Utah, 1980—89, Fedn. Internat. Ski, Bern, Switzerland; adv. bd. First County Bank, Chesterland, 1992—2000; adv. coun. U.S. Postal Svc., Chesterland, 1993—2000; v.p., bd. mem. in charge of zoning2002 Lake Cardinal Timbering Corp. Exhibited paintings and photographs to various shows, 1963—. Creator blind ski program Cleve. Sight Ctr., 1969; trustee Chesterland (Ohio) Hist. Found., 1985—, past pres., past v.p., past treas.; past chair, vice chair Chester Twp. Zoning Commr., 1987—; life friend Geauga West Libr., 1989—, bd. dirs., historian; dir. history ARC, Cleve., amb., 1999—; bd. dirs. Geauga County Libr. Found., 1998—; bd. dirs., mrm. mktg. com. Geauga County Coun. for Arts and Culture, 2002—. Mem.: North Ea. Ohio Ski Retailers Assn. (bd. dirs. 1987—), Kent State U. Alumni Pvt. Sector Bus. Alliance, Chesterland C. of C. (past pres., v.p., treas., trustee 1985—, sec. to exec. bd. 2001—, Bus. Person of Yr. 1993), Internat. Platform Assn., Cmty. Improvement Corp. Geauga County (re-orgn. com., nominating com., trustee 1990—), Kent State U. Alumni Assn. (life), Chester Study Club (past v.p., pres. 1997—), Gamma Delta, Alpha Psi Omega, Chi Omega. Lutheran. Avocations: reading, hiking, hunting, collecting classic autos and historic homes. Office: Ferdl Aster Ski Shop 8330 Mayfield Rd Chesterland OH 44026-2520 E-mail: fasterskier@prodigy.net.

ASTI, ALISON LOUISE, lawyer; b. Phila., July 25, 1954; d. Andrew Paul and Elsie Aileen (Sincavage) A. BA, Duke U., 1975, MA in Pub. Fin., 1976; JD, U. Md., 1979. Bar: Md. 1979. Assoc. Gordon, Feinblatt et al, Balt., 1979-86, ptnr., 1986-90; gen. counsel Md. Stadium Authority, 1990—. Presenter Nat. Confs. on Sports Facility Fin. Chair editl. bd. The Daily Record, 1998—. Mem. Gov. Glendening's Task Force on Jud. Nominating Com., 1995; mem. U. Md. Law Sch. Bd. Vis., 1997—; pres. Gibson Island County Sch. Parents Assn., 1996-98; pres. Met. Bar Caucus, 1999-2000; mem. sect. coun. Nat. Conf. Bar Presidents, 2000-03. Recipient Md.'s Top 100 Women Warfield's Bus. Record, 1996. Fellow Am. Bar Found.; mem. ABA (ho. of dels. 1995-98), Md. Bar Assn. (bd. govs. 1986-88, 95-97, 2003—), Bar Assn. Balt. City (pres. 1994-95), Md. State Bar Found. (pres. 1999-2001), Balt. Women's Bar Assn. Md. (pres. 1986-87), Balt. City Bar Found. (pres. 1994-95). Avocations: water sports, running, skiing, horseback riding, photography. Home: 527 Sylview Dr # A Pasadena MD 21122-5523 E-mail: ala@mdstad.com.

ASTIGARRAGA, JOSE I(GNACIO), lawyer; b. Havana, Cuba, July 20, 1953; came to U.S., 1960, naturalized 1974; AA with honors, Miami Dade Community Coll., 1973; BBA summa cum laude, U. Miami, 1975; JD magna cum laude, 1978. Bar: Fla. 1978, U.S. Dist. Ct. (so. dist.) Fla. 1979, U.S. Dist. Ct. (mid. dist.) 1988, U.S. Ct. Appeals (5th and 11th cir.) 1981, U.S. Supreme Ct. 1990. Chief bailiff Dade County Juvenile and Family Ct., Miami, Fla., 1972-74; law clk.-bailiff 11th Jud. Cir., Miami, 1974-77; with firm Steel, Hector & Davis, Miami, 1978-84, ptnr., 1984—; adj. faculty U. Miami Sch. Law, Coral Gables, Fla., 1980-81; cons. World Bank; mem. U.S. del. Org. Am. States 6th Conf. on pvt. internat. law; Little Havana Activities and Nutrition Ctrs. of Dade County, Inc., 1987-94, NAFTA adv. comm. on the resolution of private commercial disputes, 1994-96; mem. panel arbitrators Comml. Arbitration and Mediation Ctr. for Ams., 1996; founder Latin Am. users coun. London Ct. Internat. Arbitration. Co-author: Secured Lenders Beware: Particular Issues Affecting Secured Lenders, 1993; adminstrv. hearing officer Dade County Sch. Bd., Miami, 1982-90; bd. dirs. Miami Children's Hosp., 1985-88, also chmn. quality assurance com., mem. fin. com.; bd. dirs. Miami Children's Hosp. Rsch. Inst., Inc., 1986-87, chmn. nominating com.; bd. dirs. Dade County Beacon Coun. Inc., 1985-95, Miami Coalition, Inc., 1988-94; mem. exec. com., chmn. schs. task force, 1988-90; trustee Fla. Internat. U. Found., 1988—. Named Harvey T. Reid scholar U. Miami Sch. Law, 1975-78, Leonard T. Abess scholar, U. Miami, 1974-75; recipient Up and Comers Law award Price Waterhouse and South Fla. Bus. Jour., 1988. Mem. ABA (com. on comml. fin. svcs., Uniform Comml. Code com., com. bus. bankruptcy 1990—, Internat. Bar Assn. (com. arbitration, insolvency), Am. Arbitration Assn. (panel on commercial fin. disputes 1994—), Am. Law Inst. (adv. transnat. insolvency project 1997), Fla. Bar Assn. (bus. law sect., sec. civil procedure rules com. 1979-84, bankruptcy UCC com. 1998—, (teach bankruptcy seminar 1992, 94), Dade County Bar Assn. (commr. jud. campaign practices commn. 1986-87), Cuban-Am. Bar Assn., Bankruptcy Bar Assn. (v.p. 1992-94), U. Miami Sch. Law Alumni Assn. (bd. dirs. 1981-88), Greater Miami C. of C. (bd. govs. 1985-86, group chmn. econ. devel. sect. 1986-87). Office: 200 S Biscayne Blvd Fl 41 Miami FL 33131-2310

ASTILL, KENNETH NORMAN, mechanical engineering educator; b. Westerly, R.I., July 16, 1923; s. John Henry and Mabel Nellie (Robotham) A.; m. Hazel Patricia Lamb, Apr. 10, 1948; children: Kenneth John, Robert Michael. BS, U. R.I., 1944; MA in Engring., Chrysler Inst. Engring., 1946; MS, Harvard U., 1953; PhD, MIT, 1961. Lab engr. Chrysler Corp., Detroit, 1944-47; prof. mech. engring. Tufts U., Medford, Mass., 1947-91, assoc. dean engring., 1980-88, prof. emeritus, 1991—. Mem. energy facilities siting coun. Commn. of Mass., 1989-92; mng. dir. U. Rsch. Engring. Assn., 1989—1997; cons. Sylvania Electric Co., Natick Labs., Kaye Instruments, C.S. Draper Labs.; vis. fellow U. Leeds, 1976, U. Sussex, 1983. Author: (with B. Arden) Numerical Algorithms, 1970, Elementary Experiments in Mechanical Engineering, 1971, (with others) Laboratory Demonstrations in Heat Transfer and Fluid Mechanics, 1968. Trustee Charles River Mus., 1992-2003. Recipient Ralph R. Teeter award Soc. Automotive Engrs., 1981; NSF fellow, 1968 Fellow ASME (life, chmn. Boston sect. 1981-82); mem. AAUP, Am. Soc. Engring. Edn., Engring. Soc. New Eng. (bd. dirs. 1982-87), Sigma Xi, Tau Beta Pi. Home: 72 Yale St Winchester MA 01890-2331 Office: Tufts U Anderson Hall Medford MA 02155

ASTILL, ROBERT MICHAEL, credit manager; b. Winchester, Mass., Apr. 11, 1960; s. Kenneth Norman and Hazel Patricia (Lamb) A. BA in Psychology and Polit. Sci., Merrimack Coll., 1982. Credit mgr. Kazmaier Internat., Concord, Mass., 1983-90; cons. Astill Group, Winchester, Mass., 1990-92; credit mgr. Internat. Ice Cream, Boston, 1992-93; corp. credit mgr. New Eng. Frozen Foods, Southborough, Mass., 1993-97; mgr. spl. credit and collection activities Garelick Farms-Lynn divsn, Dean Foods GTL LLC, Lynn, Mass., 1997—. Mem. New Eng. Steamship Found., 1997—, trustee, 2001—; bd. dirs. Friends of Winchester (Mass.) Libr., 1990—94. Mem. Nat. Assn. Credit Mgrs. (chmn. exec. bd. wholesale provision 1992-97, sec. exec. bd. restaurant and inst. group 1995-2000, bd. dirs. 1999—), Merrimack Coll. Alumni Assn. (class chair 1990-2000), Psi Chi. Roman Catholic. Avocations: photography, music, travel. E-mail: bob_astill@deanfoods.com., rastill@aol.com.

ASTIN, JOHN ALEXANDER, musician, researcher; b. Lexington, Ky., Aug. 28, 1959; s. Alexander William and Helen Stavridou Astin; m. Katherine Trueblood Astin, June 24, 1990; 1 child, Erin Trueblood. PhD, U. of Calif., Irvine, CA, 1993—97. Author: (academic textbook) Control Therapy: An integrated approach to psychotherapy, health, and healing; composer: (musical recording) Remembrance, Reflections. Mem. Cmty. Music Sch., Santa Cruz, 2002—02. Mem.: APA.

ASTLER, VERNON BENSON, surgeon; b. Wyoming, Ohio, Sept. 5, 1925; s. Vernon Wolfert and Blanche (Benson) A.; m. Louise Menge, Aug. 9, 1949 (div.); children: Kim Louise, Kristy Lee, Douglas Vernon; m. Diane Rosacker, Dec. 31, 1969 (div.); m. Frances Croft, Mar. 21, 1991. Student, Miami U., Oxford, Ohio, 1943-45; MD, Temple U., 1949; MS, U. Mich., 1953. Diplomate Am. Bd. Surgery, Am. Bd. Bariatric Medicine. Intern Univ. Hosp. Ann Arbor, Mich., 1949-50, resident, 1950-57; practice medicine specializing in surgery, Boynton Beach, Fla., 1958-90, Asheville, NC, 1995—. Mem. hon. staff Bethesda Hosp., Boca Raton Hosp.; past mem. Fla. Bd. Med. Examiners, pres., 1971-73. Past mem. Fla. Coun. of 100. With M.C., U.S. Army, 1953-55. Fellow: ACS, Southeastern Surg. Congress, Coll. Physicians Phila.; mem.: AMA, Frederick A. Coller Surg. Soc., Fla. Med. Assn. (life; gov. 1971—84, pres. 1975—76), Am. Soc. Bariatric Physicians (AMA del.), Am. Hosp. Assn. (com. on physicians 1974—76), Asheville Country Club, Orange Park (Fla.) Country Club, Kiwanis, Shriners, Masons, Am. Legion, Sigma Nu, Phi Chi. Office: Bariatric Clinic 1220 Hendersonville Rd Asheville NC 28803-1903 Fax: 828-277-0567.

ASTMAN, BARBARA ANN, artist, educator; b. Rochester, N.Y., July 12, 1950; d. George William and Bertha Dinah (Meisel) A.; m. Noel Robert Harding, Feb. 23, 1977 (div. 1983); m. Joseph Anthony Baker, Aug. 29, 1984; children: Amy Astman Baker, Laura Astman Baker. A degree, RIT, 1970; grad., Ont. Coll. Art, Toronto, 1973. Prof photography dept. Ont. Coll. Art and Design (formerly Ont. Coll. Art), Toronto, 1975—; prof. York U., Toronto, 1978-80, 86. Lectr. in field. Solo exhbns. include Baldwin St. Gallery Photography, Toronto, 1973, Ryerson Photo Gallery, Toronto, 1974, Nat. Film Bd. Can., Ottawa, 1975, S.A.W. Gallery Inc., 1976, The Sable-Castelli Gallery Ltd., Toronto, 1977, 79-84, 86, 88, 90, The Jean Marie Antone Gallery, Annapolis, Md., 1979, Whitewater Gallery, North Bay, Ont., Bruce Art Gallery, Canton, N.Y., 1980, The Mendel Art Gallery, Saskatoon, Sask., 1981, The So. Alberta Art Gallery, Edmonton, Alta., 1981, The Art Gallery Peterborough, Ont., 1982, Galerie du Musee, Musee du Quebec, 1986, Ctr. d'Animation et de Diffusion de la Photographie, Quebec, 1986, Thunder Bay Art Gallery, Ont., 1992, The Robert McLaughlin Gallery, Oshawa, Ont., 1993, McIntosh Gallery, London, Ont., 1994, Gallery Stratford, Stratford, Ont., 1994, Art Gallery of Hamilton, 1995;, The Edmonton Art Gallery, Edmonton, Alberta, The Kamloops Art Gallery, Kamloops, B.C., 1996—, Jane Corkin Gallery, 1997, 99, 2001, 2003; group exhbns. include Lamkin Camerawork Gallery, San Francisco, 1975, Art Gallery Ont., Toronto, 1975, 80, 84, 93, Rochester (N.Y.) Meml. Art Gallery, Montreal Mus. Fine Arts, 1975, Harbourfront Art Gallery, Toronto, 1977, 80, The Sable-Castelli Gallery Ltd., 77, 81, Anna Leonowens Gallery, Halifax, N.S., 1977, London (Ont.) Regional Art Gallery, 1978, 83, Edmonton (Ont.) Art Gallery, 1978, The Winnipeg Art Gallery, 1979, Everson Mus., Syracuse, N.Y., 1979, Galerie Luca Polazzoli, Milan, 1979, H.F. Johnson Mus. Art, Ithaca, N.Y., 1979, George Eastman House, Rochester, N.Y., 1979, The Hamilton (Ont.) Art Gallery, La Galerie Powerhouse, Montreal, 1981, YYZ Gallery Toronto, 1982, Forum des Halles, Paris, 1985, Graves Art Gallery, Sheffield, U.K., 1985, San Diego Art Ctr., 1986, Hallwalls Gallery, Buffalo, 1986, La Galerie des Arts Lavalin, Montreal, 1988, Pro Mus. Contemporary Art, Finland, 1988, The Kamloops (B.C.) Art Gallery, 1989, The Koffler Gallery, Toronto, 1990, Art Gallery of Peterborough, Ont., 1992, Art Gallery of Hamilton, Ont., 1993, Southern Alberta Art Gallery, Lethbridge, 1994; Art Gallery Hamilton, Gallerie Arts Tech., Montreal, P.Q., Basel Art Fair, Basel, Switzerland, 1998, Chgo. Art Fair, 1999, Nat. Gallery Can., Ottawa, Ont., 2000, Can. Mus. Contemporary Art, North York, Ont., 2000, Can. Mus. Contemporary Photography, Ottawa, 2000, 2001, Nat. Gallery Can., Ottawa, Art Gallery Hamilton, Ont., 2001, Kitchener-Waterloo Art Gallery, Ont., 2001, Art Base, 2002, Base Chgo. Art Fair, 2002, Toronto Photgraphers Workshop, 2002, Confedn. Art Ctr. Art Gallery, Prince Edward Island, 2003, Art Gallery of Bishop's U., Que., 2003; public collections include Agnes Etherington Art Ctr., Kingston, Ont., Art Gallery Hamilton, Art Gallery Ont., Toronto, Bibliotheque Nationale, Paris, The Gallery/Stratford, The Nickle Arts Mus., Calgary, Alta., The Robert McLaughlin Gallery, Oshawa, The Winnipeg Art Gallery, Victoria and Albert Mus., London; also involved with other pub. art projects. Coord. Colour Xerox Artists' Program, Visual Arts Ont., Toronto, 1977-83; bd. dirs. Art Gallery at Harbourfront, Toronto, 1983-85; apptd. mem. City of Toronto Pub. Art Commn., 1986-89; mem. curatorial team WaterWorks Exhbn., Toronto, 1988; chmn. Toronto Arts Awards, Visual Arts Jury, 1988; bd. dirs. Arts Found. of Greater Toronto, 1989-92. Mem.: Royal Can. Acad. Arts. Office: 23 Alcina Ave Toronto ON Canada M6G 2E7 Address: Jane Corkin Gallery 179 John St Toronto ON Canada M5T 1X4

ASTON, EDWARD ERNEST, IV, dermatologist; b. Jersey City, Jan. 14, 1944; m. Kirsten Anita. B.A., U. Md.-College Park, 1968; M.D., U. Md.-Balt., 1969. Diplomate Am. Bd. Dermatology. Intern, Orange County Med. Ctr., Orange, Calif., 1969-70; resident U. Calif.-Irvine-Orange County Med. Ctr., 1971-74; practice medicine specializing in dermatology Fullerton Med. Clinic of Dermatology, Calif., 1974—; part-time assoc. clin. prof., U. Calif. irvine, 2002-. Office: 301 W Bastanchury Rd Ste 220 Fullerton CA 92835-3424

ASTON, PETER GEORGE, music educator, composer, conductor; b. Birmingham, Eng., Oct. 5, 1938; s. George William and Elizabeth Oliver (Smith) A.; m. Elaine Veronica Neale, Aug. 13, 1960; 1 child, David Philip. ARCM, Royal Coll. of Music, London, 1958; GBSM, Birmingham (Eng.) Sch. Music, 1960; FTCL, Trinity Coll. of Music, 1961; DPhil, U. York, Eng., 1970. Lectr. in music U. York, 1964-72, sr. lectr., 1972-74; prof., head music U. East Anglia, Eng., 1974-98, profl. fellow, 1998-2001, emeritus prof. music, 2001—. Musical dir. The Tudor Consort, Eng., 1958-65, English Baroque Ensemble, 1968-70; prin. condr. Aldeburgh Festival Singers, Eng., 1975-88; artistic dir. Norwich Festival of Contemporary Ch. Music, 1981—; guest condr., cons. Sacramento Area Bach Festival, 1993—, Incontri Corali Internat. Choral Festival, Alba, Italy, 1996, Schola Cantorum Gedanensis, Poland, 1999; chmn. Royal Sch. Ch. Music Norfolk Area, 1998—. Composer numerous choral and orchestral works, ch. anthems and svcs., chamber music works, opera; author: The Music of York Minster, 1972; co-author: Sound and Silence, 1970, German edit., 1972, Italian edit., 1979, Japanese edit., 1982, Music Theory in Practice, 3 vols., 1992-93; editor various compositions by 16th and 17th century composers, including The Collected Works of George Jeffreys. Lay canon Norwich Cath., 2002—. Fellow Curwen Inst. (hon.), Guild of Ch. Musicians (hon.), Royal Sch. Ch. Music (hon.), Royal Soc. of Arts (hon.); mem. Royal Coll. Music (hon.), Ea. Arts Assn. (chmn. music panel 1976-81), Trianon Music Group (pres. 1984-96), Norfolk Assn. for Advancement of Music (chmn. 1991-94, pres. 1994-2000), Guild Ch. Musicians (chmn. acad. bd. 1996—). Mem. Ch. Of Eng. Avocations: bridge, cricket, travel, detective fiction. Office: U East Anglia Sch of Music Norwich NR4 7TJ England E-mail: p.aston@uea.ac.uk.

ASTOR, DAVID WARREN, journalist; b. Bronx, Mar. 29, 1954; s. Harold Milton and Thelma (Oppenberg) A.; m. Kathy Barbara Kattenburg, Jan. 12, 1985 (div.); 1 child, Maggie Elizabeth. BA in English, Rutgers U., 1976; MS in Journalism, Northwestern U., 1978. Rutgers corres. New York Times, N.Y.C., 1974-76; reporter Red Bank Register, Shrewsbury, N.J., 1976-77, Passaic (N.J.) Herald-News, 1978; assoc. editor, sr. editor Mktg. Communications Mag., N.Y.C., 1978-83; sr. editor Editor & Pub. Mag., N.Y.C., 1983—. Avocations: reading, guitar-playing, bicycling, baseball, cartooning. Office: Editor and Publisher 770 Broadway New York NY 10003-9595 E-mail: dastor@editorandpublisher.com.

ASTORE, WILLIAM JOSEPH, historian, dean; b. Brockton, Mass., July 14, 1963; s. Julius Anthony and Helen Louise (Wilder) Astore; m. Christine Faith Mach, Dec. 30, 1989. BS, Worcester Poly. Inst., 1985; MA, Johns Hopkins U., Balt., 1991; PhD, U. Oxford, Eng., 1996. Assoc. prof. and dir. internat. history USAF Acad., Colorado Springs, Colo., 1998—2002; assoc. provost and dean of students Def. Lang. Inst. Fgn. Lang. Ctr., Presidio of Monterey, Calif., 2002—. Contbr. articles to profl. jours., chapters to books. Lt. col. USAF, 2002—02, Presidio of Monterey. Mem.: History Sci. Soc., Brit. Soc. for the History of Sci., Soc. for Mil. History, Pi Tau Sigma, Tau Beta Pi. Roman Catholic. Avocations: hiking, tennis, reading. Home: 698 Madison St Monterey CA CA 93940 Office: AFELM Bldg 624 1759 Lewis Rd Ste 238 Monterey CA 93944-5006 Office Fax: 831-242-6495. E-mail: william.astore@monterey.army.mil.

ASTORGA, ALICIA MARGARITA, retired librarian; b. Havana, Cuba, Feb. 22, 1947; d. Rene Andres and Alicia C. Albacete; m. Maurice Astorga, June 24, 1967; children: Leslie Ann, Maurice Michael. BA, Corpus Christi State U., 1976; MLS, Drexel U., Phila., 1980. Sch. libr. Pa., Del., Tex. Libr. Internat. Reading Assn., Newark, Del., 1981-82; head libr. Incarnate Word Acad., Corpus Christi, Tex., 1983-86; dir. librs. Ursuline Acad., Wilmington, Del., 1987—98; head libr. Unionville HS, Kenneth Square, Pa., 1998—2000; ret., 2000. DuPont Co. grantee, 1991. Mem.: ALA, Beta Phi Mu.

ASTRIAB, STEVEN MICHAEL, army officer; b. Pitts., Mar. 10, 1952; s. Steven Leonard and Anna (Popivchak) A.; m. BettyLou Elaine Gimmi, Dec. 27, 1975. BA in Psychology, Washington and Jefferson Coll., 1974; MSW in Manpower Planning, W.Va. U., 1976; grad., Commd. & Gen. Staff Coll., 1985. Commd. 2d lt. U.S. Army, 1974, advanced through grades to lt. col., 1992; div. social work officer 1st Cav. Div., Ft. Hood, Tex., 1976-77, med. platoon leader, then med. co. comdr. 15th med. bn., 1977-79; med. ops. officer 1st Cav. Div. Hdqs., Ft. Hood, Tex., 1979-81; chief M.C. procurement Office Army Surgeon Gen., Washington, 1982-85; chief combat medicine Office Project Mgr. Saudi Arabian Nat. Guard, Riyadh, 1985-88; pers. officer 62 Med. Group, Ft. Lewis, Wash., 1988-90; asst. chief staff for med. civil and mil. ops. 3d U.S. Army (Army Cen. Command), Riyadh, 1990-91; med. ops. officer Hdqrs. I Corps, Ft. Lewis, 1991-93; chief med. plans for S.W. Asia Hdqs. 3d U.S. Army, Atlanta, 1993-95, chief coalition integration for S.W. Asia, 1995-96; chief med. plans and intelligence S.W. Asia Hdqrs. 3d U.S. Army, 1996; sr. med. and fgn. mil. sales advisor U.S. Mil. Tng. Mission for Saudi Arabia, Riyadh, 1996-98; chief of ops. Divsn., exec. officer Pacific Regional Med. Command, 1998-2000; dep. surgeon U.S. Army Pacific, 2000—01, ret., 2001; project mgr. Eagle Group Internat. Ltd., Kosovo, 2001—03; proposal coord., mgr. Eagle Group Internat. Inc., 2003; project mgr. emergency exercise program Ga. DPH, 2003—. Assoc. faculty Ctr. Excellence for Disaster Mgmt. and Humanitarian Assistance, 1999—. Author: Vendetta: Military Med. Peace Operations in Kosovo, 2003. Decorated Legion of Merit, Bronze Star medal, Def. Meritorious Svc. medal, Meritorious Svc. medal (7), Joint Svc. Commendation medal, Army Commendation medal (2), Joint Meritorious Unit award, Nat. Def. Svc. medal (2), S.W. Asia Campaign medal (3), Armed Forces Expeditionary Medal, liberation of Kuwait medal (Saudi Arabia), Liberation of Kuwait medal (Kuwait). Mem.: Order Mil. Med. Merit. Republican. Baptist. Avocations: running, weight training, computer applications. E-mail: SAstriab@aol.com.

ASTRUP, JENS LEO, retired civil engineer; b. Plentywood, Mont., Sept. 21, 1934; s. Jens Legend and Dagmar (Jensen) Astrup; m. Susanne Elizabeth Laime, Nov. 25, 1967 (div. Nov. 1985); children: Moriah Ann, Jens Aaron. BS, N.D. State U., 1956; MBA, Keller Grad. Sch. Mgmt., 1983. Registered profl. engr., Ill.; patent agt. Civil engr. City of Chgo. Dept. Urban Renewal, 1964—65, Harza Engring. Co., Chgo., 1965—69; city engr. City of Williston, ND, 1969—70; civil and resident engr. Bauer Engring., Inc., Chgo., 1970—71; civil and structural sr. engr. Brown and Root, Inc., Chgo., 1971—82; project engr. Lester B. Knight & Assocs., Chgo., 1983—85, Comstock Engring., Inc., Oak Brook, Ill., 1985—86; sr. civil engr. Allen Engring. Co., Villa Park, Ill., 1986—88; project engr. Globetrotters Engring. Corp., Chgo., 1988—92; sr. civil engr. Clark Dietz, Inc., Chgo., 1993—94. Mem.: ASCE, Am. Pub. Works

Assn. N.D. (past state sec. 1969—70), Ill. Soc. Profl. Engrs. (state v.p. 1979—80, chmn. state activities com. 1976—77, chpt. pres. 1977—78). Lutheran. Home: 1117 Briarbrook Dr Wheaton IL 60187-8657 E-mail: leoa2@juno.com.

ASTUCCIO, SHEILA MARGARET, educational administrator; b. Biddeford, Maine, Apr. 24, 1943; d. James T. III and Margaret H. (Cameron) Rollinson; m. Joseph Kevin Astuccio, Aug. 22, 1976 (dec. Apr. 1992); children: James M., Sheila E. BS in Edn., Salem (Mass.) State Coll., 1968, MEd, 1975; cert. advanced grad. studies, Lesley Coll., Cambridge, Mass., 1983. Cert. elem. tchr. and prin., supr., dir., Mass.; cert. instrnl. tech. grades K-12. Elem. educator Hood Elem. Sch., Lynn, Mass., 1968-79; tchr. grades 3 and 4 Lynn (Mass.) Pub. Schs., comp. coord., facilitator, 1981-84, tchr. academically talented, 1979-81, 84-85, computer program specialist, 1986-87, computer implementation team leader, MIS dir., 1987-98; adminstr. IS/MIS, 1998—; owner operator Pilot Imaging Computer Imaging, Lynn, Mass., 1991-92. Tchr. adult edn. North Shore C.C., 1982-87; part-time real estate broker, 1979—; part-time mktg. cons. IDN, 1993-95; presenter Beijing Dist. Edn. Bur., 2001; presenter in field. Mem. Chpt. II adv. coun., 1979-83; nat. grad. alumni rep. Lesley Coll., 1984-85; chair Mayor's Computer Adv. Com., 1985-86; participant Educators in Industry GE/Salem State Coll., 1983; People to People Amb. to China, 2000, 2001; sec.-gen. United Cult. Convention, 2001—. Recipient Educators in Industry cert., 1983, Novell Netware Adminstr. and Sys. Installation/Configuration certs., 1994-95, Letters of Commendation Mass. Dept. Edn., 2000, 2001. Mem. ASCD, AAUW, NAFE, NSBA, DECUS, PEI Nat. Users Group, New Eng. Pentamation Users Group, Boston Computer Soc. Office: Data Center LVTI 80 Neptune Blvd Lynn MA 01902-4570 E-mail: astuccios@lynnschools.org., astuccio@attbi.com.

ASTUTO, PHILIP LOUIS, retired Spanish educator; b. N.Y.C., Jan. 5, 1923; s. Salvatore and Anna (Insalaco) A.; m. Natella M. Digia, July 4, 1953; children: Philip, Anne Marie. BA, St. John's U., 1943; MA, Columbia, 1947; PhD, Columbia U., 1956. Mem. faculty St. John's U., 1947-89, prof. Spanish, 1958-89, prof. emeritus, 1991—, dir. Latin Am. studies, 1957-60, chmn. dept. modern fgn. langs., 1961-65. Participant Prof.-Student Summer Seminar, sponsored State Dept., 1950; OAS research fellow, Quito, Bogota, 1973-74 Contbr. articles to profl. jours. Mem. coll. coun. SUNY, Farmingdale, 1988-98. 1st lt., inf. AUS, 1943-46, ETO. Recipient Pietas medal St. John's U., 1977, Faculty Outstanding Achievement medal, 1986 Mem. Am. Assn. Tchrs. Spanish and Portuguese, Am. Hist. Assn., Assn. Latin Am. Studies, MLA, Nat. Acad. History of Ecuador (fgn. corr.) Home: 11 Steuben Dr Jericho NY 11753-1414

ASTWOOD, WILLIAM PETER, psychotherapist; b. N.Y.C., May 18, 1940; s. Henry Kenneth and Rose Margit (Eastby) A.; m. Sharon Lisa Sprung, June 10, 1979; 1 child, Jesse Jack. BA, CUNY, 1962; MA, NYU, 1967, PhD, 1975. Case worker, supr. dept. social services City N.Y., 1964-67; community orgn. trainer Block Communities, Inc., N.Y.C., 1967-68; field rep. Office Econ. Opportunity, N.Y.C., 1968-70, U.S. Dept. Health, Edn., Welfare, N.Y.C., 1970-71; pvt. practice Bklyn., 1971—; dir. family therapy div. DiMele Ctr. for Psychotherapy, N.Y.C., 1990—. Bd. dirs. South Beach Psychiat. Ctr., Bklyn., 1976-78, N.Y. Group for Comprehensive Family Therapy, Mineola, 1988—; exec. bd. Met. Ctr. for Psychotherapy, N.Y.C., 1969-72. Co-author: Practicing Psychotherapy, 1980. Exec. bd. Social Service Employees Union, N.Y.C., 1965-67. Staff sgt. USANG, 1963-69. Mem. N.Y. Acad. Scis., Assn. for Humanistic Psychology, Am. Assn. Marriage and Family Therapy (clin.). Home: 394 Atlantic Ave Brooklyn NY 11217-1703 Office: 150 Remsen St Brooklyn NY 11201 E-mail: Bastwood@aol.com.

ASWAD, DANA WILLIAM, biochemist, educator; b. Schenectady, N.Y., Nov. 12, 1947; s. William N. and Marjorie G. Aswad; m. Angelika Skaidrite Rozitis, May 16, 1981; children: Alexandra, Andrea. BA in Chemistry, Wesleyan U., 1969; PhD, U. Calif., Berkeley, 1974. Postdoctoral fellow UCLA, 1974-77, Yale Med. Sch., New Haven, 1977-80; from asst. prof. to assoc. prof. U. Calif., Irvine, 1980-92, prof., 1992—. Cons., 1988—; mem. neurol. sci. study sect. grant rev. NIH, Bethesda, Md., 1988-89. Author: Deamidation and Isoaspartate Formation in Peptides and Proteins, 1995; contbr. articles to profl. jours.; mem. editl. bd. Jour. Biol. Chemistry, 1999—; patentee in field. Judge Orange County (Calif.) Sci. Fair, 1992-2000; vol. pilot Angel Flight W., Santa Monica, Calif., 2000. Rsch. grantee NIH, 1981—, Rsch. Career Devel. award, 1981-86. Mem. AAAS, Am. Soc. Biochemistry and Molecular Biology. Republican. Avocations: skiing, private pilot. Office: U Calif Irvine 3205 McGaugh Hall Irvine CA 92697-3900 Office Fax: 949-824-8551. E-mail: dwaswad@uci.edu.

ATAIE, ATA JENNATI, oil products marketing executive; b. Mashad, Iran, Mar. 15, 1934; came to U.S., 1957, naturalized, 1969; s. Hamid Jennati and Mohtaram (Momeni) A.; m. Judith Garrett Bush, Oct. 7, 1961; children: Ata Jennati, Andrew J. BS in Agr., Fresno State U., 1964; BA in Econs., San Francisco State U., 1966. Mktg. exec. Shell Oil Co., Oakland, Calif., 1966-75; pres. A.J. Ataie &Cos., Danville, Calif., 1975—, Am. Value Inc., 1976—. 2d lt. Iranian Army, 1953. Mem. Nat. Petroleum Retailers Assn. Democrat.

ATAL, BISHNU SAROOP, retired speech research executive; b. Kanpur, Uttar Pradesh, India, May 10, 1933; came to U.S., 1961; s. Jagannath Prasad and Lakshmi Devi (Lakshmi) A.; m. Kamla Atal, July 3, 1959; children: Alka, Namita. BS with honors, U. Lucknow, India, 1952; elec. engring. degree, Indian Inst. Sci., Bangalore, 1955; PhD in Elec. Engring., Poly. Inst. Bklyn., 1968. Sr. rsch. asst. Indian Inst. Sci., Bangalore, 1955-56, lectr., 1957-60; sr. rsch. fellow Cen. Elec. Engring. Rsch. Inst., Pilani, Rajasthan, India, 1960-61; mem. tech. staff AT&T Bell Labs., Murray Hill, N.J., 1961-85, head acoustics rsch., 1985-90, head speech rsch., 1990-97; tech. dir. AT&T Labs., Florham Park, NJ, 1997—2002. Contbr. articles to various publs. Fellow Acoustical Soc. Am., IEEE (Acoustics, Speech and Signal Processing Sr. Tech. Achievement award 1975, ASSP Sr. award 1980, Centennial medal 1984, Morris N. Liebman Meml. Field award 1986); mem. NAE, NAS. E-mail: batal@bishnu.net.

ATAMIAN, CHARLES, oncologist, surgeon; b. Whitinsville, Mass., Feb. 9, 1925; s. Karope and Sarah (Garebedian) A.; m. Helen Germagian A., Sept. 13, 1947; children: Carol, Jill, Jan, Cheryl. Student, Clark U., 1942-43, Holy Cross Coll., 1943-44; MD, Boston U., 1948. Diplomate Am. Bd. Surgery. Intern surgery Worcester (Mass.) City Hosp., 1948-49; resident surgeon Down State Med. Ctr., Brooklyn, N.Y., 1949-51, Meml. Ctr. Cancer, N.Y.C., 1953-57; pvt. practice Springfield, 1957-91; surg. staff Bay State Med. Ctr., Springfield, 1957-91; ret., 1992; dir. cancer program Mercy Hosp., Springfield, 1970-91, dir. surgery, 1976-80, chief of staff, 1982-84; rsch. scientist U. Mass., Amherst, 1995—. Lectr., cons. Oncology Inst., Yerevan, Armenia, 1992, 93, 94. With USN, 1944; capt. USAF, 1951-53. Fellow Am. Coll.Surgeons. Avocations: study russian, armenian, french, german and greek. Home: 341 Converse St Longmeadow MA 01106-1708

ATAMIAN, SUSAN, nurse; b. Cambridge, Mass., Sept. 14, 1950; d. Raymond H. and Alice (Chakerian) A. BA, Simmons Coll., 1972, MS, 1995. RN, Mass.; cert. infection control. Staff nurse Mass. Gen. Hosp., Boston, 1972-74, pvt. duty nurse, 1975-76, staff nurse, 1976-77, rsch. study nurse, 1977-80, instr. nursing, 1982-84, sr. rsch. study nurse, 1984-87, dir. clin. rsch. nurse group, 1985-90, infection control nurse, 1988-90, infection control nurse clinician, 1990-92, coord., clin. rsch., vascular surg. div., 1992-99, individual assignments/spl. projects staff, 1999—2001, infection control practitioner, 2001—; staff nurse Kimberly Nurses, Orange, Calif., 1982. Cons. nutrition and liver diseases, McGaw Labs., Santa Ana, Calif., 1980-81; chmn. faculty devel. libr. com. Shepard Gill Sch., Boston, 1983-84; mem. rsch. nurses forum, Mass. Gen. Hosp., 1992—. Class agt. 1972 Simmons Coll., 1972, 86-97, mem. com. alumnae fund, 1987-89, reunion com., 1990-2002, com. on classes, 1991-92, class of 1972 reunion fund chair, 1991-92, chmn. class of 1972 reunion fund 1996-97, v.p. Class of 1972, 1997--, mem. travel and edn. com., 2002—. Mem.: ANA, Coun. Armenian Am. Nurses (v.p. 2002—), Assn. for Practitioners in Infection Control and Epidemiology, Rsch. Nurses Forum Mass. Gen. Hosp., Mass. Nurses Assn., Soc. for Vascular Nursing, Am. Nurses Found. Century Club, Simmons Coll. Alumnae Assn. (edn. and travel com. 2002—), Simmons Club Boston (bd. dirs. 1988—90, v.p. 1990—92, co-chmn. boutique 1992—94, mem. nominating com. 1994—95), Sigma Theta Tau, Simmons Coll. Nursing Honor Soc. Mem. Armenian Apostolic Ch. Avocations: travel, reading, knitting. E-mail: satamian@partners.org.

ATANG, CHRISTOPHER, humanities educator; b. Oct. 30, 1938; arrived in U.S.A., 1963; s. Martin Atang and Martina Awah Atang; m. Jackie Atang, July 29, 1972; 1 child, Azie. BS, U. Wis., 1966; diploma in Edn., Heriot Watt U., 1969; MS, Ind. State U., 1973; PhD, Iowa State U., 1994. From vis. prof. to assoc. chmn. Tex. So. U., Houston, 1994—99, assoc. chmn., 1999—2000; from assoc. prof. to prof. Anderson (S.C.) Coll., 2000—02, prof., 2002—. Student tchr. supr. Anderson (S.C.) Pub. Schs., 2000—. Author: A Breach of Trust, 1996, ADEPT PD for Teaching in SC, 2001; contbr. Mentor Homeland Pk. Elem. Sch., Anderson, SC, 2001—. Mem.: Am. Assn. Coll. Profs., Phi Delta Kappa. Avocations: tennis, aerobics, walking, jogging. Office: Anderson College Box 1113 316 Boulevard Anderson SC 29621 Fax: 864-231-2854. E-mail: catang@ac.edu.

ATCHESON, RICHARD, editor; Exec. editor Modern Maturity Am. Assn. Retired Persons, Washington. Office: Am Assn Retired Persons 601 E St NW Washington DC 20049-0001

ATCHESON, SUE HART, business educator; b. Dubuque, Iowa, Apr. 12; d. Oscar Raymond and Anna (Cook) Hart; m. Walter Clark Atcheson (div.); children: Christine A. Hischar, Moffet Zoe, Claye Williams. BBA, Mich. State U.; MBA, Calif. State Poly. U., Pomona, 1973. Cert. tchr. and adminstr. Instr. Mt. San Antonio Coll., Walnut, Calif., 1968-90. Bd. dirs. faculty assn. Mt. San Antonio Coll., mem. acad. senate, originator vol. income tax assistance; spkr. in field; lectr. in bus. mgmt. Calif. State Poly. U., Pomona, 1973—75; cons., trainer Joint Venture between Mt. San Antonio Coll. and County of Los Angeles Dept. Pub. Social Svcs., summer, 2001. Author: Fractions and Equations on Your Own, 1975. Charter mem. Internat. Commn. on Monetary and Econ. Reform; panelist infrastructure funding reform, Freeport, Ill., 1989. Mem. Cmty. Concert Assn. Inland Empire (bd. dirs.), Scripps Coll. Fine Arts Found., Recyclers Club (pres. 1996). E-mail: sueatch@bigsky.net.

ATCHISON, JOSEPH EDWARD, pulp and paper industry consultant; b. Barnum, W.Va., Dec. 25, 1914; s. Edward Washington and Frederica Catherine (Kerns) A.; m. Frances Julia Winebrinier, July 3, 1951 (dec. Apr. 1965); m. Betty Jeanne Pugh, May 30, 1968; children: Leah, Robert, Scott (dec.), Kevin (dec.). BSCE, La. State U., 1938; MS in Pulp & Paper Tech., Inst. Paper Chem., 1940, PhD in Pulp & Paper Tech., 1942. Tech. dir. John Strange Paper Co., Menasha, Wis., 1946-48; chief pulp & paper br. Marshall Plan, Washington, Paris, 1948-52; mill mgr., project dir. Portarican Paper Products, Inc., San Juan, P.R., 1952-53; v.p., sr. v.p. Parsons & Whittemore, Inc., N.Y.C., 1953-67; pres., owner Joseph E. Atchison Cons., Inc., N.Y.C., 1968-97, Atchison Cons., Inc., Sarasota, Fla., 1997—. Spkr. internat. confs. *Dr. Atchison has specialized in the utilization of all types of non-wood plant fibers for the manufacture of pulp and paper and of all types, including newsprint. These fibers include sugar cane bagasse, wheat straw, rice straw, reeds, grasses, bamboo, cotton linters, He has developed appropriate processes for utilizing these raw materials and assisted many companies, in the developing countries, who do not have adequate wood, to design and build pulp and paper mills, based on whatever raw materials they had available. He has provided technical services in some 50 different countries. Enabling many countries to establish pulp and paper industries, based on using these raw materials, especially in wood-poor countries.* Author: Waste Paper Recycling, 1972, Kenaf for Paper Pulp, 1976, contbr. more than 150 articles to profl. jouors. Lt. col. U.S. Army, 1942-46. Decorated DSM Bronze Star with oak leaf cluster; named to Paper Industry Internat. Hall of Fame, 1997; named Man of Quarter, In Paper Internat., 1999. Mem. TAPPI (Gunnar Nicholson Gold medal 1996), Internat. Soc. Sugar Cane Technologists. Presbyterian. Avocations: tennis, fitness, dancing, travel, theater. Fax: 941-371-7637.

ATCHISON, RICHARD CALVIN, trade association director; b. Altadena, Calif., Aug. 4, 1932; s. Floyd and Clara (Warwick) A.; m. Mildred Platt, Jan. 24, 1957; children: Tracey, Hayley. BS, UCLA, 1958. Salesman, product mgr. Lever Bros., N.Y.C., 1958-61; group product mgr., then regional sales mgr. Purex Corp.; pres. Van Camp Seafood Co. div. Ralston Purina Co., 1965-81; pres. Mitsubishi Foods (USA) Inc., 1981-91; exec. dir. Am. Tuna Boat Assn., San Diego, 1991-93; pres. Internat. Bus. Cons., 1993—. With USAF, 1952-56.

ATCHISON, RODNEY RAYMOND, retired lawyer, arbitrator; b. Hanford, Calif., Nov. 14, 1926; s. Clyde Raymond and Velma May (Watts) A.; m. Evaleen Mary McFadden, June 27, 1948; children: Cathlin Atchison, Susan Barisone, Kerry Atchison, Brian. Student, San Jose State Coll., 1946-49; JD, U. Santa Clara, 1952. Bar: Calif. 1953, U.S. Dist. Ct. (all dists.) Calif. 1953, U.S. Ct. Appeals (9th cir.) 1953, U.S. Supreme Ct. 1971. Assoc. Mullen & Filippi, Attys., San Francisco, 1953-55; dep. county counsel Santa Clara Calif. County Counsel, San Jose, 1955-57; city atty. City of Mountain View, Calif., 1957-62, City of Santa Cruz, Calif., 1962-90; pres. Atchison, Anderson, Hurley & Barisone, Profl. Law Corp., Santa Cruz, 1980-96; of counsel Atchison Barisone & Condotti, Profl. Law Corp., Santa Cruz, 1996, Law Offices of Rodney R. Atchison, 1996-2001. Arbitrator Am. Arbitration Assn., San Francisco, 1970—. Pres. Rotary Club Mountain View, Calif., 1961-62, Santa Cruz (Calif.) County Bar Assn., 1973. With USNR, 1944-46. Mem. ABA, Santa Cruz Rotary Club, Elks Lodge (life). Roman Catholic. Avocations: skiing, travel, golf. E-mail: r.atchison@sbcglobal.net.

ATCHLEY, CURTIS LEON, mechanical engineer; b. Lexington, Okla., June 3, 1940; s. Curtis Marvin and Hazel (Franks) A.; m. Barbara Ann Bryant, Feb. 14, 1976; children: Jeffrey Allen, Eric Andrew. BSME, U. Okla., 1970. Engr. Halliburton Oil Svc. Co., Enid, Okla., 1970-71, Tinker AFB, Midwest City, Okla., 1971-79; supervisory gen. engr. Lajes AFB, Azores, Portugal, 1979-80; gen. engr. Hdqrs. USAFE, Ramstein AFB, Fed. Republic Germany, 1980-82, Hdqrs. Air-Edn. and Tng. Command, Randolph AFB, 1985-99; ret., 1999; mem. staff Air Force Civilian Pers. Ctr., Randolph AFB, Universal City, Tex., 1983-85. U.S. and fgn. patentee in solar tech., U.S. patentee for light intensifying device for cameras and telescopes. Mem. Dem. Nat. Com., 1996-2003. Sgt. USAF, 1964-68. Mem. Amnesty Internat. (freedom writer), Internat. Soc. Poets (life, charter), Nashville Song Writers Assn., Broadcast Music Inc. Avocations: golf, skiing, camping, backpacking, swimming. Home: 7531 Oriental Trl San Antonio TX 78244-2400

ATCHLEY, RAYMOND DEVAL, technology company executive; b. Blackfoot, Idaho, Apr. 15, 1915; s. Claude Deval and Marie Himmelgarn Atchley; m. Virginia Gifford, Jan. 26, 1946; 1 child, Susan Virginia. BSME, MIT, 1951; bus. cert., UCLA, 1966. Chief tool designer, co-founder Rohr Aircraft, San Diego, 1939-41; design engr. USN Underwater Sound Lab., San Diego, 1942-46; assoc. rsch. engr. MIT Dynamic Analysis and Control Lab., Cambridge, Mass., 1946-51; v.p. engring. Midwestern Instruments Inc., Tulsa, 1951-54; owner, pres. Raymond Atchley, Inc., West Los Angeles, Calif., 1954-59; gen. mgr. Raymond Atchley divsn. Am. Brake Shoe, West Los Angeles, 1959-63; cons. aerospace divsn. Abex Corp., Oxnard, Calif., 1964-65; pvt. practice cons., 1966-68; pres. Deval Industries, Inc., West Los Angeles, 1969-84, Atchley Controls, Inc., Canoga Park, Calif., 1985-90; sr. tech. advisor fluid controls divsn. BW/IP Internat., Inc., Van Nuys, Calif., 1991-94; sr. tech. advisor E-Sys. Raytheon, West Los Angeles, 1996-97, Salt Lake City, 1995-96; cons., 1998—. Patentee pressure control valve for hydraulic actuator, end effector, component locating apparatus, electrical component testing apparatus, coating apparatus, writing surface and temporary eraseable ink composition for marking thereon, electro-hydraulic servovalve, others. Cpl. USMC, 1933-37. Mem. MIT Alumni Assn., UCLA Alumni Assn. Republican. Avocations: photography, fishing, sports cars, computers. Home: 3470 Mandeville Canyon Rd Los Angeles CA 90049-1020

ATCITTY, FANNIE L. elementary school educator, education educator; b. Shiprock, NM, Dec. 4, 1952; d. John and Betty Martin Lowe; m. Eugene Ronald Atcitty, Apr. 22, 1972 (dec. May 10, 2000); children: Antoinette, Ronald. BEd, Ea. N.Mex. U., 1978; M in Curriculum and Instrn., Doane Coll., 1997; M in Ednl. Leadership, Doane Coll., 2002. Elem. tchr. Central Consolidated Sch. Dist. 22, Shiprock, N.Mex., 1979—. Adj. instr. early childhood edn. program N.Mex. Highland U., Las Vegas, 1997—2002; adj. instr. edn. and tchr. prep. program Diné Coll., Shiprock, N.Mex., 1997—2002; profl. standards commn. mem. N.Mex. State Dept. Edn., Santa Fe, 2000—, tchr. assessment rev. panel, 1993—99, nat. coun. for accreditation of tchr. edn., 1997—. Contbr. poetry to lit. publs. Edn. chairperson Shiprock (N.Mex.) Cmty. Planning Commn., 1994—96; vice chair San Juan County Dem. Party, Farmington, 1998—2001; chairperson Cmty. Gov. Planning Bd., Shiprock, N.Mex., 1995—98; U.S Presdl. elector N.Mex., 1996. Recipient Golden Apple Found. award, Golden Apple Found. N.Mex., 2001. Mem.: Internat. Reading Assn., Am. Assn. Sch. Adminstrs., Las Amigas Women's Club. Democrat. Avocations: reading, walker, community events, gardening. Home: PO Box 3320 Shiprock NM 87420 Office: Mesa Elementary Sch PO Box 1803 Shiprock NM 87420

ATES, J. ROBERT, lawyer; b. New Orleans, Sept. 12, 1945; s. Loten Arthur Jr. and Eugenia Lea (Carpenter) A. BA, Tulane U., 1967; JD, Loyola U., New Orleans, 1972. Bar: La. 1973, U.S. Dist. Ct. (ea., mid. and we. dists.) La., U.S. Ct. Appeals (5th cir.), U.S. Supreme Ct., Colo. 1990. Prof., chmn. sci. dept. East Jefferson High Sch., Metairie, La., 1967-72; law clk. to judge La. Ct. Appeals (4th cir.), New Orleans, 1972-73; assoc. Kierr, Gainsburgh, Benjamin, Fallon & Lewis, New Orleans, 1974-78, ptnr., 1979-87, Gainsburgh, Benjamin, Fallon, David & Ates, New Orleans, 1987-94; prin. J. Robert Ates, A Profl. Law Corp., New Orleans, 1994-95, Ates & Assocs., A Profl. Law Corp., New Orleans, 1996—. Lectr. in field; mem. adj. law faculty and skills faculty, Continuing Legal Edn. Programs, Tulane U., Loyola Law Schs. Mem. ATLA, FBA, La. Bar Assn. (vice chmn. civil law sect. 1986-87, chmn. 1987—, sec., treas. 1985—, chmn. pub. rels. and edn. com. 1987—, mem. ho. of dels. 1987-94, bd. govs. 1993—, gen. sec. and editor La. Bar Jour. 1993-95), Orleans Bar Assn., Jefferson Bar Assn., La. Trial Lawyers Assn. (pres.'s adv. com.), Soc. Am. Law Tchrs., Am. Soc. Law and Medicine. Democrat. Baptist. Avocations: photography, snow skiing, water skiing, hunting, fishing. Home: 29 Turnberry Dr La Place LA 70068-1617 Office: Ates & Assocs A Profl Law Corp 4004 Magazine St Ste A New Orleans LA 70115-2762

ATESOGLU, H. SONMEZ, economist, educator; s. I. Ethem and Yegane Atesoglu; m. Jane Bentz; children: Aylin, Suzan, Filiz, Deniz. BS, Mid. East Tech. U., Ankara, 1967; MA, U. Pitts., 1968, PhD, 1972. Instr., asst. prof. Mid. East Tech. U., Ankara, 1972—73; economist Internat. Monetary Fund, Washington, 1975—77; mem. acad. planning bd. Turkish Mil. Academies, Nat. Security Coll., Istanbul, 1974—75; Fulbright rsch. prof. Inst. World Econs., Kiel (Germany) U., 1987—88; asst. to assoc. prof. econs. Clarkson U., Potsdam, NY, 1977—95, prof. econs., 1996—; lectr. dept. econs. San Diego State U., 2001. Contbr. articles to profl. jours. Second lt. Turkish Army, 1973—75. Named Tokten Cons. at Bilkent U., Turkey, UN Devel. Program in Turkey, 1991; fellow, U. Chgo., Grad. Sch. Bus., 1980; grantee, Fulbright Program, Inst. Internat. Edn., 1987—88; Ford Found. Econ. Demography fellow, U. Pitts., 1967—68, Tech. Cooperation fellow, O.E.C.D., 1968—72. Mem.: Am. Econ. Assn. Achievements include research in empirical testing of the effects of defense spending on growth; the balance-of-payments contrained growth model; and the Simple Keynesian and Monetarist models. Avocations: international relations and security studies, music, reading. Office: Clarkson Univ School of Business Potsdam NY 13699-5795 Office Fax: 315-268-3810. E-mail: atesoglu@clarkson.edu.

ATHANASIAN, EDWARD ARAM, surgeon; b. Huntington, N.Y., Apr. 5, 1962; s. Aram and June Lorette Athanasian; m. Susan Eileen Athanasian, May 19, 1996; children: Christian, John Andrew. AB, Harvard U., 1984; MD, Columbia U., 1986. Diplomate Am. Bd. Orthopedic Surgery; cert. in hand surgery. Surgery intern Beth Israel Hosp./Harvard, Boston, 1988-89; resident in orthopedic surgery Hosp. for Spl. Surgery, N.Y.C., 1989-93; fellow in hand/micro surgery Mayo Clinic, 1993-94; fellow orthopaedic oncology Meml. Sloan-Kettering Cancer Ctr., 94-95; asst. attending surgeon Hosp. for Spl. Surgery, N.Y.C., 1995—; clin. affiliate Sloan Kettering Cancer Ctr., N.Y.C., 1995—; asst. prof. Cornell U. Med. Coll., N.Y.C., 1999. Author: (with others) Greens Operative Hand Surgery, 1999.

ATHANASIOU, ROBERT BYRON, physician, psychologist; b. Danbury, Conn., Mar. 16, 1940; m. Barbara Bardeen, Jan. 27, 1962; children— William Robert, Kenneth Robert. B.S. in Elec. Engring., Rensselaer Poly Inst., 1962, MS in Psychology, 1965; PhD in Social Psychology, U. Mich., 1969; MD, Albany Med. Coll., 1977. Diplomate Am. Bd. Emergency Medicine. Asst. engr., spl. asst. to gen. mgr. N.Y. Telephone Co., Patchogue, 1962-64; asst. prof. psychology Johns Hopkins U., Balt., 1969-72, asst. prof. psychiatry, 1972-73, instr. ob-gyn, 1972-73; pvt. practice, Albany, 1973; vis. asst. prof. sociology SUNY, Albany, 1976-77, adj. rsch. assoc. dept. psychology, 1982-95; intern Albany Med. Ctr. Hosp., 1977, resident in ob-gyn, 1978; staff physician emergency dept. Samaritan Hosp., Troy, N.Y., 1978-81, dir. emergency dept., 1982-85; med. dir. Rensselaer Poly. Inst., Troy, 1985— ; adj. asst. prof. psychiatry Albany Med. Coll., 1979-81; mem. Regional Emergency Med. Services System Hudson Mohawk Valley, Inc., 1981-85; chmn. emergency med. services com. Rensselaer County, N.Y., 1982-85. Contbr. articles to profl. jours. Fellow Inst. Advanced Study Rational Therapy, 1974— . Fellow Am. Coll. Emergency Physicians; mem. Am. Psychol. Assn., Am. Coll. Emergency Physicians, AMA, Johns Hopkins Med. and Surg. Assn., Am. Assn. Sex Educators, Counselors and Therapists. Office: Health Service Rensselaer Poly Instit Troy NY 12180

ATHANASSIOU, NICHOLAS, education educator; b. Athens, Greece, May 17, 1946; s. Athanassios Nikolaos Athanassiou and Athena Tsouderou; m. Jeanne Marie McNett. PhD, U. of S.C., 1990—95. Prof. Northeastern U., 1995—. Home: 33 Garvey Rd Framinham MA 01701 Office: Northeastern U Coll of Bus Admnstrn Boston MA 02115 Personal E-mail: n.athanassiou@attbi.com.

ATHAS, GUS JAMES, lawyer; b. Chgo., Aug. 6, 1936; s. James G. and Pauline (Parhas) A.; m. Marilyn Carres, July 12, 1964; children: Paula C. Vlahakos, James G., Christopher G. BS, U. Ill., 1958; JD cum laude, Loyola U., Chgo., 1965. Bar: Ill. 1965, U.S. Dist. Ct. (no. dist.) Ill. 1965, U.S. Ct. Appeals (7th cir.) 1970. With Isham, Lincoln & Beale, Chgo., 1965-69; group gen. counsel, asst. sec. ITT, Skokie, Ill., 1969-87; assoc. gen. counsel Itel Corp., Chgo., 1987; sr. v.p., gen. counsel, sec. Eagle Industries, Inc., Chgo., 1987-97; exec. v.p. adminstrn., gen. counsel, sec. Falcon Bldg. Products, Inc., Chgo., 1994-99; sr. v.p., gen. counsel Great Am. Mgmt. and Investment, Inc., Chgo., 1995-97; ptnr. Stamos & Trucco, Chgo., 2000—. Contbr. articles to profl. jours. 1st lt. U.S. Army, 1958-62. Mem. ABA, Am. Corp. Counsel Assn., Ill. Bar Assn., Chgo. Bar Assn. Greek Orthodox. Home: 1240 Hawthorne Ln Downers Grove IL 60515-4503 Office: Stamos & Trucco 30 W Monroe Ste 1600 Chicago IL 60603

ATHERTON, CHARLES HENRY, federal commission administrator; b. Kingston, Pa., June 24, 1932; s. Thomas Henry and Mary A.; m. Mary Bringhurst Davis, Dec. 15, 1967; children: Sarah Scott, Thomas Henry, Charles Henry. BA summa cum laude, Princeton U., 1954, MFA, 1957. Registered architect, D.C. Asst. sec. Fine Arts Commn., Washington, 1960-64, sec., adminstrv. officer, 1964—. Trustee Nat. Child Rsch. Ctr., 1975-79; v.p. Washington Hist. Soc.; bd. dir. Hist. Am. Bldg. Survey Found., Navy Art Found.; mem. Citizens Commemorative Coin Adv. Com., 1994-2003; bd. dirs. Henrich House Found., 2003—. Lt. (j.g.) USNR, 1957-60. Lt. (j.g.) USNR, 1957—60. Recipient Martin Luther King Leadership award D.C. Pub. Libr. Sys., 1992, Centennial medal Washington chpt. AIA, 1993, lifetime achievement award: Comm. of 100 on the Federal City. Mem. Potomac Boat Club, Cosmos Club. Home: 3127 Newark St NW Washington DC 20008-3344 Office: Fine Arts Commn 401 F St NW Washington DC 20001-2614 E-mail: chatherton@cfa.gov.

ATHERTON, FLORA CAMERON, civic worker, former foundation executive; b. Waco, Tex.; d. William Waldo and Helen Emelyn (Miller) Cameron; m. Holt Atherton; children— Ike Simpson Iampmann, III, Megan Cameron Kampmann. Dir., mem. exec. com. Certain-Teed Corp., 1971-78; exec. com. San Antonio World's Fair, 1968; mem. Pres.'s Mission to Latin Am., 1969; U.S. del. Inter-Am. Commn. Women, 1969-72; mem. citizens stamp adv. commn. U.S. Postal Service, 1969-71; cons. Bur. Inter-Am. Affairs, Dept. State, 1972-75; vice chmn. exec. com. Tex. Republican Party, 1968-69; del. Rep. Nat. Conv., 1960, 64, alt. del., 1968, sec. platform com., 1960; mem. Rep. Nat. Fin. Com., 1965—, pres., chmn. 1976-78; past pres. KAMKO Found.; trustee Trinity U., San Antonio, 1965—, chmn., 1976-78; trustee Sweet Briar Coll., 1969-78; mem. Pres.'s Commn. German-Am. Tricentennial, 1983-84; bd. dirs.

San Antonio Art Inst., 1984—, mem. nat. council Met. Opera. Mem. San Antonio Jr. League, Colonial Dames Am. Home: 315 Westover Rd San Antonio TX 78209-5653 Office: 5701 Broadway St Ste 106 San Antonio TX 78209-5722

ATHERTON, LEONARD JAMES ARCHIBALD, musician, conductor; b. Harrow, Middlesex, Eng., Oct. 25, 1941; arrived in U.S., 1982; s. James William and Peggy (Haines) Atherton; m. Susan Frances Goldie, June 26, 1982; children: Malcolm, Patricia. BA with honors, U. Oxford, Eng., 1963, MA, 1967; Doctoral Equivalency, Ball State U., 1982. Assoc. Royal Coll. Music, licentiate Royal Acad. Music. Music dir. Nat. Symphony Orch., LaPaz, Bolivia, 1964—66; dir. chorus U. Pa., Phila., 1968—71; music dir. Niagara Symphony Orch., St. Catharines, Canada, 1972—80, Greater Boston Youth Symphony Orch., 1980—82; music dir. emeritus Muncie (Ind.) Symphony Orch., 2003—, music dir., 1982—2003; dir. orch. Ball State U., Muncie, 1982—. Dir. Boston U. Young Artists Vocal Program, Tanglewood, Mass., 1979—86; guest condr. Minn. Orch., St. Paul Chamber Orch., Balt. Symphony Orch., Sakai Opera, Japan, Osaka (Japan) Coll. Opera Orch., Taipei (Taiwan) Met. Symphony Orch., Century Orch., Osaka. Recipient Ricordi prize, Guildhall Sch. Music, London, 1964, Watney-Sargent award, 1967, Sagamore of Wabash award, Gov. Ind., 2003. Episcopalian. Home: 3201 W Beechwood Ave Muncie IN 47304 Office: Ball State Univ Sch Music Muncie IN 47306

ATHERTON, WILLIAM, actor; b. New Haven, July 30, 1947; s. Robert Atherton Knight and Myrtle (Robison) Raymond; m. Bobbi Goldin, Dec. 8, 1980. BFA, Carnegie-Mellon U., 1969. Film appearances include The Sugarland Express, The Day of the Locust, The Hindenburg, Looking for Mr. Goodbar, Real Genius, Ghostbusters, No Mercy, Die Hard, Die Hard 2: Die Harder, Grim Prairie Tales, Oscar, The Pelican Brief, Frank and Jesse, Biodome; stage appearances include title roles in The Basic Training of Pavlo Hummel and Suggs (Drama Desk award, Outer Circle Critics award, two Obie nominations, Theatre World award), role of Ronnie in original prodn. of House of Blue Leaves, Kennedy Ctr. prodn. The Scarecrow, Misalliance. Broadway prodn. The American Clock, The Caine Mutiny Court Martial; TV appearances include mini-series Centennial, The House of Mirth, Tomorrow's Child; series The Equalizer; numerous other made-for-TV movies; also actor, singer in musical comedies; song theme song What'll I Do? in movie The Great Gatsby

ATIBA, JOSHUA OLAJIDE O. internist, pharmacologist, oncologist, educator, philanthropist; b. Enugu, Nigeria, July 6, 1956; s. Joseph Ojo and Abigail Olayo A.; m. Stella N. Mordi, June 26, 1981; children: April, Annamarie, Joseph. MD, U. Lagos, Nigeria, 1979; MHA, St. Mary's Coll., 1999. Diplomate Am. Bd. Internal Medicine, Am. Bd. Oncology. Rotating intern Ahmadu Bello U. Tchg. Hosp., Kaduna, Nigeria, 1979-80; resident in internal medicine Lagos U. Tchg. Hosp., 1981-83; fellow in med. oncology Cancer Control Agy., Vancouver, B.C., Can., 1988-90; fellow in clin. pharmacology Stanford U. Med. Ctr., Palo Alto, Calif., 1983-86; pvt. practice Irvine, Calif. Dir. clin. investigation U. Calif., Irvine, 1991-95; mem. U. Calif. Irvine Med. Ctr., Orange, North Bay Med. Ctr., Fairfield, Calif., Vaca Valley Hosp., Vacaville, Calif.; asst. prof. medicine, pharmacology U. Calif., Irvine; med. dir. N. Bay Hosp., 1997-99; pres. NOAH Med. Svc. Corp.; med. dir. NOAH, Inc.; rancher Med. dir. North Bay Hospice, Fairfield, Calif.; pres. Newport Oncology and Healthcare Found. Fellow Royal Coll. Physicians Can.; mem. ACP, AMA, Am. Fedn. for Clin. Rsch., Am. Soc. of Clin. Pharmacology and Therapeutics, Am. Soc. Clin. Oncology, Calif. Med. Assn., Solano County Med. Soc. (sec./treas., pres.-elect, pres.), Physician Peer Rev. Orgn. (dir.), KC (knight 1997). Republican. Roman Catholic. Office: PO Box 1631 Suisun City CA 94585-4631 E-mail: jatiba@pol.net.

ATILGAN, TIMUR FAIK, structural engineer; b. Adana, Turkey, July 15, 1943; arrived in U.S., 1972; s. Faik Ahmet and Sacide (Togman) Atilgan; m. Gulsum Z. Kuzuoglu, Dec. 7, 1977 (div. 1980); m. Mirat Gurol, July 20, 1992 (div. 2002). BS in Civil Engring., Aegean U., Izmir, Turkey, 1967; MS in Structural Engring., U. Md., 1979. Registered profl. engr., Va. Civil engr. NATO/Infrastructure Dept., Ankara, Turkey, 1970-72; structural engr. Bendix Field Engring., Columbia, Md., 1977-79; sr. design engr. Northrop Svcs. Inc., NASA, GSFC, Greenbelt, Md., 1979-82; sr. antenna engr. COMSAT Gen. Corp., Washington, 1982-83; sr. structural engr. OAO Corp., Greenbelt, 1983-84; engring. specialist PRC-Kentron, Inc., Hampton, Va., 1984-86; prin. engr. Fairchild Space Co., Greenbelt, 1986-91; sr. engr. Def. Systems, Inc., McLean, Va., 1991-94; sr. staff engr. Astro Space divsn. Lockheed Martin, Valley Forge, Pa., 1995-98; sr. prin. engr. Canada-France-Hawaii Telescope Corp., Kamuela, Hawaii, 1999-2000; sr. staff engr. Lockheed Martin Corp., Moorestown, N.J., 2001—. Mem.: AIAA (sr.). Avocations: music, reading, swimming, cinema. Office: Lockheed Martin NE & SS Moorestown NJ 08057 E-mail: tatilgan@netzero.net

ATIQUZZAMAN, MOHAMMED, engineering educator; b. Dhaka, Dhaka, Bangladesh, June 6, 1959; married. MSc, U. Manchester, U.K., 1984; PhD, U. Manchester, 1987. Cert. engineering, 1982. Lectr. LaTrobe U., Melbourne, Australia, 1992—95; sr. lectr. Monash U., Melbourne, Australia, 1995—97; assoc. prof. U. Dayton, Ohio, 1997—2000, U. Okla., Norman, 2001—. Sr. tech. editor IEEE Comm. Mag., N.Y.C., 1998—2000; mem. editl. adv. bd. Computer Comm. Jour., Amsterdam, Netherlands, 1998—; assoc. editor Real Time Imaging Jour., N.Y.C., 2000—. Author: Performance of TCP/IP over ATM networks, 1990; mem. editl. bd. Telecom. Systems Jour., 1998. Recipient Infrared Avionics Signal Distbn. award, NASA, 2001, SCTP over Long Bandwidth Delay Product Networks award, 2001, Quality of Svc. for Real-Time Applications over Next Generation Data Networks award. Mem.: IEEE. Office: Univ of Oklahoma 200 Felgar St El 159 Norman OK 73019-6151

ATIYAH, SIR MICHAEL FRANCIS, mathematician; b. London, Apr. 22, 1929; s. Edward Selim and Jean (Levens) A.; m. Lily J. Brown, July 30, 1955; children: John (dec.), David, Robin. BA, Trinity Coll., Cambridge, 1952, PhD, 1955; DSc (hon.), Bonn, 1968, U. Durham, 1977, Trinity Coll., Dublin, 1983, U. Chgo., 1983, Cambridge (Eng.) U., 1984; others. Fellow Trinity Coll., Cambridge, 1954-58, 97—, hon. fellow, 1976-97, master, 1990-97; hon. prof. sch. math. U. Edinburgh, Scotland, 1997—; lectr., fellow Pembroke Coll., Cambridge, 1958-61, hon. fellow, 1983. Commonwealth Fund fellow Princeton, 1955-56, prof. Inst. Advanced Study, 1969-72; reader Oxford U., 1961-63, Savilian prof. geometry, fellow New Coll., 1963-69, hon. fellow, 2000; Royal Soc. rsch. prof., fellow St. Catherine's Coll., 1973-90, hon. fellow, 1991; dir. Isaac Newton Inst. for Math. Scis., Cambridge, Eng., 1990-96; chancellor Leicester U., 1995—; pres. Pugwash Confs. Sci. and World Affairs, 1997-2002. Author: K-Theory, 1966, Commutative Algebra, 1969; contbr. articles to math. jours., also collected works, 1987. Decorated knight; recipient Fields medal Internat. Congress Mathematicians, Moscow, 1966, DeMorgan medal London Math. Soc., 1980, Feltrinelli prize Accademia Nazionale dei Lincei, 1982, King Faisal Found. Internat. prize for sci., Saudi Arabia, 1987, Order of Merit, 1993, Royal medal, 2003. Fellow Royal Soc. (pres. 1990-95, Royal medal 1969, Copley medal 1988), Royal Soc. Edinburgh (hon.), Royal Instn. (hon.), Royal Acad. Engring. (hon.), Acad. Med. Scis. (hon.), Faculty Actuaries (hon.), Internat. Math. Union (exec. co 1966-74), Math. Assn. (pres. 1981), London Math. Soc. (pres. 1975-77); mem. Nat. Acad. Scis. U.S.A. (fgn.), Leopoldina Acad. (fgn.), Am. Acad. Arts and Scis. (fgn.), Swedish Royal Acad. (fgn.), Academie des Scis. (fgn.), Royal Irish Acad. (fgn.), Am. Philos. Soc. (fgn., Benjamin Franklin medal 1993), Third World Acad. Scis., Indian Nat. Sci. Acad. (fgn.), Chinese Acad. Sci. (hon. prof.), Ukrainian Acad. Scis. (fgn.), Venezuelan Acad. Sci., Australian Acad. Sci., Russian Acad. Sci., Georgian Acad. Sci., Accademia Nazionale dei Lincei, Norwegian Acad. Sci. and Letters, Spanish Royal Acad. of Sci., Order Andres Bello, Order Cedars of Lebanon. Office: U Edinburgh Sch Math James Clerk Maxwell Bldg Mayfield Rd Edinburgh EH9 3JZ Scotland E-mail: atiyah@maths.ed.ac.uk.

ATKIN, EDITH, artist, poet; b. Washington, Nov. 12, 1921; d. Phillip and Sylvia Hirschel; m. Irwin Symour; children: Shron Welch, Joan Atkin Winewriter. Student, Md. Coll. Art & Design, 1973-79, Strayers Bus. Coll., Alice Kilbaum's Coll. Music. Group exbhns. at Lynn Kottler Galleries, N.Y.C., Gudowsky Gallery, Silver Spring, Md., Akademia Raymond Duncan, Paris, Ligoa Duncan, N.Y.C., Salon Surindependants, Paris; represented in numerous pvt. collections. Recipient award for creative achievement Holly Daly Herman Palm Beach Galleries, 1984. Mem. Nat. Tobacco Distbrs. Assn., Bnai Brith Women's Assn. Jewish.

ATKIN, GARY EUGENE, lawyer; b. Salt Lake City, Oct. 7, 1946; s. Henry Eugene and Dolores Heckman (Dykes) A.; m. Marsha Selin, June 12, 1967; children: Kathryn Dawn, Kenneth Eugene. BS in Acctg., U. Utah, 1967, JD, 1970. Bar: Utah 1970, U.S. Dist. Ct. Utah 1970, U.S. Ct. Appeals (10th cir.) 1978, U.S. Supreme Ct. 1978. Assoc. Rawlings, Roberts & Black, Salt Lake City, 1970—74; assoc. counsel Utah State Legislature, Salt Lake City, 1974—79; ptnr. Gustin, Adams, Kesting & Liapis, Salt Lake City, 1979—81, of counsel, 1981—82; ptnr. Atkin & Anderson, Salt Lake City, 1982—91; sr. ptnr. Atkin & Assocs., Salt Lake City, 1992—. Mem. Assn. Trial Lawyers Am., Fed. Bar Assn., Utah Trial Lawyers Assn. (bd. dirs. 1980-90, pres. 1984-85). Avocation: announcer. Home: 4498 Adonis Dr Salt Lake City UT 84124-3923 Office: Atkin & Assocs 311 S State St Ste 380 Salt Lake City UT 84111-5215

ATKIN, J MYRON, science educator; b. Bklyn., Apr. 6, 1927; s. Charles Z. and Esther (Jaffe) A.; m. Ann Spiegel, Dec. 25, 1947; children— David, Ruth, Jonathan. BS, CCNY, 1947; MA, NYU, 1948, PhD, 1956. Tchr. sci. Ramaz High Sch., N.Y.C., 1948-50; tchr. elem. sch. sci. Great Neck (N.Y.) pub. schs., 1950-55; prof. sci. edn. Coll. Edn., U. Ill., Urbana, 1955-79, assoc. dean, 1966-70, dean, 1970-79; prof. Sch. Edn., Stanford (Calif.) U., 1979—, dean, 1979-86. Cons. OECD, Paris, Nat. Inst. Edn.; mem. edn. adv. bd. NSF, 1973-76, 84-86, vice-chmn., 1984-85, sr. advisor, 1986-87; mem. Ill. Tchr. Certification Bd., 1973-76; Sir John Adams lectr. U. London Inst. Edn., 1980, vis. scholar com. scholarly commn. Nat. Acad. Scis., People's Republic China, 1987; math. sci. edn. bd. NRC, 1985-89, nat. com. sci. edn. standards and assessment, 1992-96, com. on sci. edn. K-12, 1996-2002, vice chair, 1998, chair, 1999-2002; invited lectr. Nat. Sci. Coun., Taiwan, 1989—; resident Rockefeller Found., Bellagio Ctr., 1999; nat. assoc., Nat. Acads. of Sci., 2001-. Author children's sci. textbooks. Served with USNR, 1945-46. Fellow: AAAS (v.p. sect. Q 73 1974); mem.: NAS (assoc.), Am. Ednl. Rsch. Assn. (exec. bd. 1972—75, chmn. govt. and profl. liaison com.), Coun. Elem. Sci. Internat. (pres. 1969—70), Sigma Xi (chmn. com. on sci., math. and engring. edn.). E-mail: atkin@stanford.edu.

ATKIN, LAWRENCE RONALD, computer software engineer; b. Cleve., May 20, 1946; m. Ann M. Wasserman, Apr. 24, 1988; children: Katrina, Keegan. BS in Indsl. Engring., Northwestern U., 1969, MS in Computer Sci., 1975. Application analyst Control Data Corp., Hinsdale, Ill., 1969-71; sys. programmer Northwestern U., Evanston, Ill., 1971-76; programmer Health Info. Svcs., Evanston, Ill., 1976-77; cons. Evanston, Ill., 1977-90, 92-95; dir. tech. Odesta Corp., Northbrook, Ill., 1990-92; software arch. Helix Techs., Prospect Heights, Ill., 1995-97; cons., 1997—. Recipient Fredkin prize Am. Assn. for Artificial Intelligence, 1977, Allen Newell award for rsch. excellence, 1998. Mem. Assn. for Computing Machinery. Achievements include co-author of Chess 4.9, which won 13 trophies in 13 national and international computer chess tournaments, 1970-80. Home and Office: 3300 Grant St Evanston IL 60201-1830

ATKIN, LOUIS PHILLIP, recycling business executive; b. Rochester, N.Y., Apr. 18, 1951; s. Morris and Etta (Korpeck) A.; m. Jodi Rosenshein. Student, Am. Coll. Paris, 1970-71; BA, George Washington U., 1973; MA, U. So. Calif., 1977. Asst. editor Alan Landsburg Prodns., L.A., 1977-78; pres. Louis Phillip Holdings, Inc., Rochester, 1991—; Genesee Scrap & Tin Baling Corp., Inc. Pres. Atkin's Waste Materials, Inc., Rochester, 1990—, Pathways of Rochester, Inc., 1993—, Personal Pathways Inc., 1999—. Producer (with others), Jewish Community Fedn., documentary, 1982, Flights of Fancy, 1980; producer stage play Paradoxical Effects, 1987; writer, producer (play aired on Cable TV): Paradoxical Effects; writer, dir. Ceremony of Carols, 1974; scriptwriter, photographer, Posters of the First World War, 1983, exhibitor of posters, 1983. Interviewer Holocaust Com., Rochester, 1984; mem. Rochester Mus. and Sci. Ctr., 1985—, Meml. Art Gallery, GEVA Angels Repertory Contributors, 1985, Landmark Hist. Soc., Rochester, 1985, Nat. Trust for Hist. Preservation; mem. citizens' adv. com. Solid Waste for Monroe County; bd. dirs., exec. com. Jewish Home of Rochester; bd. dirs. Jewish Cmty. Ctr., 2000-03. NEH grantee, 1979, LIFT grantee N.Y. State Coun. Arts, 1987. Mem. Dramtists Guild (assoc.), World Pres.' Orgn., George Eastman Ho., U. So. Calif. Cinema Alumni Assn. Avocations: collecting World War I posters and political cartoon art, photography, writing. Office: 80 Steel St Rochester NY 14606-2112

ATKIN, RUPERT LLOYD, retired engineer; b. June 7, 1918; BSME, Ohio State U., 1941, DSc (hon.), 1979. Chief engr. Kelsey-Hayes Co., Romulus, MI, 1958-64; dir. engr. Mich. div. TRW Inc., Sterling Hts., MI, 1964-71, dir. engr. automotive worldwide Cleveland, 1971-76, v.p. engr., 1976-83. Mem. Nat. Acad. Engring. Home: 15191 Ford Rd Apt 617 Dearborn MI 48126-4656

ATKINS, BRUCE ALEXANDER, lawyer; b. Newport News, Va., July 3, 1948; s. Alexander and Clara Belle (Parker) A.; children: Alexandra Patrice, Brandon Jarod; m. Marilyn S. Richardson, Apr. 10, 1991. BA with high honors, Hampton Inst., 1969; JD, U. Va., 1976. Bar: Ga. 1976, Tex. 1979, U.S. Ct. Appeals (4th and 5th cirs.) 1977, U.S. Ct. Appeals (11th cir.) 1981, U.S. Dist. Ct. (no. dist.) Ga. 1977, U.S. Dist. Ct. (so. dist.) Tex. 1982, U.S. Dist. Ct. (no. dist.) N.Y. 1983. Atty. Gulf Oil Corp., Atlanta, Houston, 1976-85; assoc. gen. counsel TransAmerican Natural Gas Corp., 1985-86; sr. assoc. Wood, Lucksinger & Epstein, 1986-88; pvt. practice Houston, 1988—. Vis. prof. Nat. Urban League, Tex. and La., 1981-84; chmn. creditors commn. Continental Airlines, Inc., Houston, 1984, Hill Petroleum Co., Houston, 1984. Mem. editl. bd. Tex. Collections Manual; contbr. articles to profl. jours. Conf. faculty U. Houston Law Found. Capt. U.S. Army, 1969-73. Earl Warren Legal Tng. fellow Earl Warren Found., 1973-76. Mem. Houston Bar Assn., Houston Lawyers Assn., Raveneaux Club (Spring, Tex.). Episcopalian. Home: 5707 Lookout Mountain Dr Houston TX 77069-2618 Office: Bruce A Atkins Atty at Law Ste 249 13700 Veterans Meml Dr Houston TX 77014-1026 E-mail: attyatkins@aol.com.

ATKINS, CARL J. conductor, educator; DMA, Eastman Sch. Music. Adj. asst. prof. music Eastman Sch. Music, Rochester, N.Y., conductor Symphonia Wind Ensemble. Office: The Eastman Sch of Music U Rochester Rochester NY 14627

ATKINS, CLAYTON H. family physician, epidemiologist, educator; b. Beech Grove, Ind., Nov. 12, 1944; s. Amos H. Atkins and Edythe E. (Dale) Heneghan; m. Carole A. Kirlin, Aug. 2, 1974; children: Brenda M. Spencer, Craig N., Angela C. AB in Chemistry, Ind. U., Bloomington, 1965, MAT in Chemistry, 1967; MD, Ind. U., Indpls., 1969; BS in Math. summa cum laude with highest honors, Butler U., 1980. Diplomate Am. Bd. Family Practice. Rotating intern Meth. Hosp. Ind. Inc., Indpls., 1969-70; pvt. practice Greenwood, Ind., 1970-94; mem. active staff family practice dept. St. Francis Hosp. and Health Ctrs., 1970—, hosp. epidemiologist, 1989—2002, with med. exec. com., 1993-96, pres. med. staff, 1995, mem. exec. mgmt. com., 1995-96; pvt. practice associated with St. Francis Med. Group, Indpls. and Beech Grove, Ind., 1995—. Mem. courtesy med. staff family practice dept. Cmty. Hosp. South, Indpls., 1970—; instr. NSF math. for high sch. tchrs. Ind. U., Bloomington, 1966-67; instr. microbiology Ind. Ctrl. Coll. (now U. Indpls.), 1968; adj. asst. prof. Butler U. Coll. Pharmacy, Indpls., 1991-95; mem. Ops. Coun. St. Francis Med. Group, 1998-99, Mgmt. Coun. 1999-2000. Lt. col. M.C., USAFR, 1971-77, 91—. Fellow Am. Acad. Family Physicians; mem. AMA, Ind. State Med. Assn., Inpls. Med. Soc., Assn. for Practitioners in Infection Control and Epidemiology, Soc. for Hosp. Epidemiology in Am., Math. Assn. Am., Sigma Xi, Phi Kappa Phi, Phi Delta Kappa, Alpha Epsilon Delta, Phi Lambda Upsilon, Phi Eta Sigma, Mu Alpha Theta. Avocations: astronomy, cosmology, mathematics, gardening, mountain hiking. Home: 7610 W Banta Woods Dr Bargersville IN 46106-8740 Office: 8778 Madison Ave Ste 200 Indianapolis IN 46227-7202

ATKINS, DALE MORRELL, retired physician; b. Somerset, Colo., Jan. 20, 1922; s. James Perry and Lura May (Morrell) A.; m. Loretta Ilene Davidson, June 20, 1943 (dec.); children— Loretta, Linda, Peter, John. BA, U. Colo., 1943, MD, 1945, MS, 1953. Intern Mass. Meml. Hosp., 1945-46; resident medicine Colo. U. Sch. Medicine, 1948-50, resident urology, 1950-53; pvt. practice genitourinary surgery Denver, 1953-96. Mem. bd. regents U. Colo., 1963-74 Served to capt., M.C. AUS, 1946-48. Mem. Phi Beta Kappa. Home: 3860 S Dahlia St Denver CO 80237-1004

ATKINS, ERNEST EUGENE, chemist, retired; b. Nellis, W.Va., Mar. 14, 1926; s. Everett Jefferson and Etta Mae Atkins; m. Edna Myrtle Atkins, Aug. 13, 1948; children: Sandra Ellen, Thomas Ernest Eugene, Bonnie Lianne. Student, Ind. U., 1946-48; BA, U. Louisville, 1957; MS, Murray State U., 1977. Lab. technician B.F. Goodrich, Louisville, 1948-54, chemist, 1955-67, chief chemist Calvert City, Ky., 1967-84, ret., 1984. Cons., Paducah, Ky., 1984—; committeeman NSF, Washington, 1972, Chlorine Inst., N.Y.C., 1980; trainer, NRA. Author chem. listing U.S. Pharmacopia, 1980; contbr. articles to profl. jours. Mem. bd. police commrs. Town of Clarksville, Ind., 1963-67. With USN, 1943-46. Mem. Am. Chem. Soc. (chmn. 1971, Indsl. Chemist of Yr. Ky. Lake sect. 2000), Am. Soc. for Quality (chmn. 1982), Masons, Scottish York Rite (knight York cross of honor), Royal Order of Scotland. Democrat. Methodist.

ATKINS, HOWARD IAN, bank executive; b. N.Y.C., Feb. 12, 1951; s. Maurice and Gertrude Atkins; m. Vivian Leslie Katz; children: Jacqueline, Naomi. BS in Math., CCNY, 1972; MS in Econs., Ohio State U., 1974. Fin. analyst Chase Manhattan Bank, N.Y.C., 1974-78, global funding coord., 1978-80, global funding exec., 1980-82, area treasury exec., Europe, 1982-86, portfolio and funding exec., 1986-88, corp. treas., 1988—91, sr. v.p., 1991—96; v.p., CFO New York Life, 1996—2001; CFO Wells Fargo, San Francisco, 2001—. Treas. Blackstone Coop. Assn., N.Y.C. Mem. Bankers Assn. for Fgn. Trade (Washington), N.Am. Corp. Treasurers. Jewish. Avocations: tennis, skiing, chess. Office: New York Life 420 Montgomery St San Francisco CA 94163

ATKINS, JEANNINE CATHERINE, writer; b. Montclair, N.J., July 14, 1953; d. David Pierre and Marjorie Atkins. BA, U. Mass., 1980; MA, U. N.H., 1982. Author: Aani and The Tree Huggers, 1995, Mary Anning and The Sea Dragon, 1999, Becoming Little Women, 2001, Wings and Rockets: The Story of Women in Air and Space, 2003.

ATKINS, JOHN, concert pianist, voice teacher; b. Kilmichael, Miss., Dec. 4, 1938; s. Luther O'Neil and Carolyn Holmes (Applewhite) A. MusB, Chgo. Mus. Coll., 1960; pvt. studies, Julliard Sch. Music and Chgo. Mus. Coll.; grad. gemology, Gemological Inst. Am., 1990. Ind. concert pianist, worldwide, 1956—, V.p. Valhalla Prodns., Inc., N.Y.C., 1979—; cons. Warner Bros., Los Angeles, N.Y.C., 1985-86, Goldcrest Films, London, 1985-86. Profl. solo debut New Orleans Philharm. Symphony Orch., 1956, N.Y.C. solo debut Philharm. Hall, 1965; touring concert pianist worldwide; TV appearances include The Tonight Show, Dick Cavett, Good Morning America; premiered new works of numerous composers including Krenek, Puccini, Dallapiccola; collaborations with numerous singers including Jan Peerce, Renata Scotto; recs. on Angel, Columbia, CRI, Mercury labels; internat. voice tchr. with pupils in numerous major opera houses including Met. Opera, Bolshoi; editor: (chamber music) Sonata for Violin and Piano, 1966. Recipient 1st prize Music Festival of the South Competition, 1956, Brit. Film Inst. award, 1986. Mem. The Bohemians, Acad. Maison Internat. Des Intellectuels. Republican. Episcopalian. Avocations: bodybuilding, collecting modern and Asian art, rare gems, tng. Doberman pinschers.

ATKINS, LAURA JANE, music educator; b. Richmond, Ind., Oct. 5, 1975; s. James William and Shirley Louise West Mitchell; m. Douglas John Atkins, June 20, 1998; 1 child, Booker Doulas. MusB cum laude, Wheaton Coll. Conservatory of Music, 1998; MusM, Miami U., 2002. Piano tchr. pvt. instrn., Dayton, Ohio, 1998—2003; grad. asst. Miami U., Oxford, Ohio, 2000—02; applied piano instr. Sinclair Cmty. Coll., Dayton, Ohio, 2002—03; group piano instr. Ctrl. State U., Wiberforce, Ohio, 2002. Worship band mem. Far Hills Cmty. Ch., Dayton, Ohio, 2001—03, parking lot ministry coord., 2002—03. Recipient Concerto Competition 3rd Pl. prize, Richmond Symphony Orch., 1994, Concerto Competition 1st Pl. prize, 1992. Mem.: Dayton Music Club, Ohio Music Teachers Assn., Pi Kappa Lambda. Christian. Avocations: recorder, piano, gardening. Home: 328 E Dorothy Lane Dayton OH 45419

ATKINS, PAUL S. commissioner; AB, Wofford Coll., 1980; JD, Vanderbilt U. Sch. of Law, 1983. Bar: NY, Fla. Commr. US SEC, Washington, 2002—; exec. asst. Chmn. of SEC, Richard C. Breeden, Washington, 1990—94; counsellor Chmn. of SEC, Arthur Levitt, 1990—94. Mem.: Phi Beta Kappa. Office: 450 Fifth St NW Washington DC 20549*

ATKINS, PETER ALLAN, lawyer; b. N.Y.C., June 29, 1943; m. Lorraine Marilyn Feuerstadt, Apr. 3, 1966; children: Aileen Debra, Karen Jennifer. BA magna cum laude, CUNY, 1965; LLB cum laude, Harvard U., 1968. Bar: N.Y. 1969. Assoc. Skadden, Arps, Slate, Meagher & Flom LLP, N.Y.C., 1968—74, ptnr., 1975—. Mem. dean's adv. bd. Harvard Law Sch.; bd. dirs. A Better Chance, Inc. Contbr. articles to profl. jours. Mem.: ABA, Assn. of Bar of City of N.Y., N.Y. State Bar Assn. Office: Skadden Arps Slate Meagher & Flom LLP 4 Times Sq Fl 46 New York NY 10036-6595 E-mail: patkins@skadden.com.

ATKINS, RICHARD BART, film, television producer; b. Paterson, N.J., May 11, 1951; s. S. Stephen and Alice B. (Stein) A.; m. Joanna Pang; 1 child, David. AB in Polit. Sci., Princeton U., 1973. With Cadence Industries, N.Y.C., 1973-74; mgr. TV program devel. Benton & Bowles, N.Y.C., 1977-79, mgr. daytime programming, 1980; v.p. prodn. Telecom Entertainment, N.Y.C., 1981-83; pres. Atkins Pictures Inc./A-Films, Florham Park, N.J., 1984—. Programming and prodn. cons. Hearst Entertainment, Whittle Communications, D'Arcy Masius Benton & Bowles, King World Prodns., 1989-91, Quartier Latin, Paris, 1992, TeleVest, 1997-98. Prodr. (TV films) Shocktrauma, 1982, Murder in Coweta County, 1983, The Gift of Love: A Christmas Story, 1983, Trapped in Silence, 1986; exec. in charge prodn. About Sarah, 1998, Christmas in America, 1990; prodr., writer (videocassette) Knowing Childbirth, 1985; prodr., writer (feature film) Forced March, 1989; producer: (feature film) Asunder, 2000; dir. (documentary) Mongolia, 1995; author: Method to the Madness: Hollywood Explained, 1975, (musical plays) Getting to Know You, 1994, 97, In the Mirror, 1995, 98, Independence, 1996. Mem. Friar's Club, Princeton Club. Jewish. Avocations: golf, computers. Home and Office: A-Films 149 Ridgedale Ave Florham Park NJ 07932-1708 E-mail: datk@aol.com.

ATKINS, ROBERT ALAN, lawyer; b. N.Y.C., Apr. 30, 1944; s. David Atkins and Tabbie Crystal Sas; m. Carol Anne Pierson, Dec. 26, 1966 (div. Aug. 1975); children: Laura, Christopher; m. Mari Beth Loria, May 21, 1982 (div. July 1998); children: Sascha, Jordan. BS in Philosophy cum laude, CUNY, 1964; MA in Philosophy, U. Calif., Berkeley, 1967, PhD, 1973, JD, 1979. Bar: Calif. 1980, U.S. Dist. Ct. (no. dist.) Calif. 1980, U.S. Dist. Ct. (cen. dist.) Calif. 1985. From instr. to assoc. prof. philosophy Antioch Coll., Yellow Springs, Ohio, 1968-75; asst. Gordon Lapides, San Francisco, 1979-80; assoc. Erickson, Beasley & Hewitt, San Francisco, 1980-85; pvt. practice Berkeley, 1986—. Prof. Union Grad. Sch., San Francisco, 1975—; lectr. U. Calif., Berkeley, 1983-88, sch. law New Coll. Calif., 1983-86. Contbr. articles to profl. jours. Commr. Berkeley Citizens Budget Rev. Commn. 1985-87; mem. adv. bd. U.S.-China Edn. Inst. 1981-86, steering com. Bay Area Lawyers's Alliance for Nuclear Arms Control 1982-84, chmn. symposium com., internat. com.; trustee, sec. Ann Martin Ctr. 1982-84; commentator on pub. affairs for radio sta. WYSO, Yellow Springs, 1971-73, producer children's show 1974-75; mem. adminstrv. coun. Antioch Coll., 1973-75, chmn. humanities area, mem. Chancellor's Cabinet, 1974-75; mem. Union Grad. Sch. Coun., 1979-84. Recipient Am. Jurisprudence award, U. Calif., Berkeley, 1979; Ford Found. grantee, 1969. Mem. Order of Golden Bear. E-mail: ratkins700@aol.com.

ATKINS, RONALD RAYMOND, lawyer; b. Kingston, N.Y., Mar. 8, 1933; s. A. Raymond and Charlotte S. A.; m. Mary-Elizabeth Empringham, June 23, 1956; children: Peter Herrick, Timothy Barnard, Suzanne Elizabeth. BS in Econs., U. Pa., 1954; JD, Columbia U., 1959. Bar: N.Y. 1959. Assoc. Pell, Butler, Curtis & LeViness, N.Y.C., 1959-61, ptnr., 1962-67; ptnr. Bisset & Atkins, N.Y.C., 1967—, also Greenwich, Conn., 1982—; also of counsel Davidson, Dawson & Clark, LLP, N.Y.C.; mem. vis. com. Dept. Medieval Art and Cloisters, Met. Mus. Art.; mem. Coun. of Friends, NYU, Inst. Fine Arts; trustee Mianus Gorge Preserve, Inc., chmn., 1984-94, Westmoreland Sancutary. 1st lt. U.S. Army, 1954-56. Fellow Frick Collection, Pierpont Morgan Libr.; mem. ABA, N.Y. State Bar Assn., Assn. Bar City N.Y., Medieval Acad. Am., Coll. Art Assn., Assn. Art History, Internat. Ctr. Medieval Art. Republican.

Episcopalian. Club: University (N.Y.C.), Grolier Club (N.Y.C.), Field Club (Greenwich, Conn.), U. Pa. Club (N.Y.C.), Greenwich (Conn.) Croquet Club. Home: Hobby Hill Farm Mianus River Rd Bedford NY 10506 also: 777 North St Greenwich CT 06831-3105

ATKINS, THOMAS HERMAN, lawyer; b. Richmond, Va., Jan. 13, 1939; s. J. Herman Jr. and Elizabeth S. (Lowdermilk) A.; m. Karin-Heide Bach, Feb. 15, 1964; children: Tanja Alexandra, Tiffany Nichole. BA, U. Richmond, 1960; JD, U. Va., 1963. Bar: Va. 1963, U.S. Dist. Ct. (ea. dist.) Va. 1970, U.S. Ct. Appeals (4th cir.) 1970, Ohio 1972. Ptnr. Stallard, Levit & Atkins, Richmond, 1969-70; assoc. May, Garrett & Miller, Richmond, 1970-72; assoc. counsel Cooper Tire & Rubber Co., Findlay, Ohio, 1972-76; from asst. to assoc. counsel ARMCO Inc., Middletown, Ohio, 1976-86, assoc. counsel Parsippany, N.J., 1986-90; assoc. gen. counsel Ebasco Svcs. Inc., N.Y.C., 1990-95, Raytheon Engrs. & Constructors, Princeton, N.J., 1995-2000, Washington Group Internat., Inc., Princeton, N.J., 2000—. Maj. U.S. Army, 1963-69. Mem. Internat. Bar Assn., Va. Bar Assn., Ohio Bar Assn., Masons (sr. warden 1972), Phi Beta Kappa, Omicron Delta Kappa. Republican. Presbyterian. Avocations: scuba diving, travel, photography. Home: 31 Warren Cutting Chester NJ 07930-2728 Office: Washington Group Internat Inc 510 Carnegie Ctr Princeton NJ 08540-6249 E-mail: karinatkins@att.net., thomas.atkins@wgint.com.

ATKINS, THOMAS JAY, lawyer, missionary and pastor; b. Detroit, Apr. 21, 1943; s. Robert Alfred and Dorothy Irene Atkins. BS in Applied Math. and Physics, Rensselaer Poly. Inst., 1965, MS in Engring., 1967; JD, UCLA, 1979; postgrad., Harvard Law Sch., 1979; MBA, UCLA, 1983; MDiv, MB Bibl. Sem., 2000. Bar: Calif. 1979; ordained minister Am. Bapt. Chs.-USA, 2002. Ctr. for Advanced Studies, Gen. Electric Co., Washington (DC), Santa Barbara, Calif., 1967—70; prin. Cen. Valley Distbrs., Visalia, Calif., 1970—, Thomas Jay Atkins, P.C., Sacramento, 1979—, Calif. Merc. Inc., Tulare, Calif., 1980—, United Motors, San Jose, Fresno and Sacramento, Calif., 1986—; sr. cons. ptnr. Atkins Group, LLP, L.A., N.Y.C., London, Paris, 1989—. Founder Atkins Devel. Corp. (formerly Atkins Real Estate Corp.), L.A., 1985; chmn. bd. dirs., World Parts Corp., San Francisco; chmn. bd. dirs. Students Internat., Antigua, Guatemala and Jaracoba, Dominican Republic, 1996—. Recipient rsch. commendation NASA, 1969 Mem. ABA, Am. Mgmt. Assn., UCLA Alumni Assn. (bd. dirs. 1991—), Santa Barbara Yacht Club, Visalia Country Club, Regency Club of L.A., Visalia Racquet Club. Republican. Home: Badger Hill Ranch 363 Valley View Dr Exeter CA 93221-9798 Office: PO Box 3744 Visalia CA 93278-3744 also: 969 Hilgard Ave Ste 1007 Los Angeles CA 90024-3079 E-mail: tjatkins@arilion.com.

ATKINS, VICTOR KENNICOTT, JR., investment banker; b. Seattle, Feb. 8, 1945; s. Victor Kennicott and Elizabeth (Tanner) A. AB, Harvard U., 1967, MBA, 1972. Assoc. Blyth Eastman Dillon & Co., N.Y.C., 1972-75, v.p., 1976-78, 1st v.p., 1978-79, E.F. Hutton & Co., N.Y.C., 1979-81, sr. v.p., 1981-84; pres. Covington Ptnrs., 1984-85, Equity Income Ptnrs. Capital Corp., Southampton, 1987-94, also bd. dirs.; chmn. Polaris Industries Capital Corp., Southampton, 1987-94, also dir.; pres., dir. Am. Nat. Security Inc., Omaha, 1992-95. Internat. adv. bd. Laidlaw Holdings, Inc., N.Y.C., 1995-96; prin. Stone Pine Cos, Denver; dir. European e-Commerce Ltd., London. Lt. USNR, 1967-70, Vietnam. Decorated Bronze Star, Cross of Gallantry Republic of Vietnam. Mem. The Brook Club (N.Y.C.), Southampton Club, Nat. Golf Links, Pacific Union Club (San Francisco), Bohemian Club (San Francisco), Meadow Club of Southampton, The Valley Club (Montecito). Home: PO Box 310 Boyeson Rd Southampton NY 11969-0310 Office: 33 Flying Point Rd Ste 219 Southampton NY 11968-5276

ATKINS, WALTER J. electrical engineer; BSEE, Howard U., 1965; MSEE, U. Ill., 1971, PhD in Elec. Engring., 1977. Divsn. dir., chief engr. Tracor Applied Scis., 1986—87; chief scientist advanced govt. programs Hughes Space and Comm. Co., L.A., 1987—88, program mgr. def. satellite comm. sys., 1988—90, program mgr. milstar program, 1991—91, dir. continuous measurable improvment, 1991, dir. product assurance and total quality, 1992—94, gen. mgr., bus. unit leader, 1994—. Mem. Army Sci. Bd., Va. Named Black Engr. of Yr in profl. achievement category, 1991; recipient Air Force Meritorious Svc. medal, USAF, 1982, 1984, Def. Meritorious Svc. medal, 1986. Mem.: AIAA, IEEE (sr.), AFCEA. Office: SAAL-ASB 2511 Jefferson Davis Hwy Arlington VA 22202-3911 Address: Hugges Space and Comm Co PO Box 92919 Los Angeles CA 90009

ATKINS, WILLIAM ALLEN, academic administrator; b. St. Louis, Sept. 19, 1934; s. William Allen and Nancy Lou (Hunter) A.; m. Joan Markmann, Feb. 6, 1954 (div. Feb. 25, 1977); children: Andrew Bennett, Stephen Hunter; m. Maxine Stegman, Apr. 6, 1977. BA, U. Denver, 1955; MA in Edn., Washington U., 1958; CAS, Harvard U., 1962, EdD, 1965. Cert. Supt., N.Y., Mass., Vt. Elem. tchr. Univ. (Mo.) City Pub. Schs., 1956-61; asst. supt. Williamstown (Mass.) Pub. Schs., 1963-65; supt. Rutland (Vt.) Pub. Schs., 1965-68; mgr. Gen. Learning Corp., Washington, 1968-71; assoc. dean Hofstra U. Sch. Edn., Hempstead, NY, 1971-77; exec. dir. Sexton Ednl. Ctr., Massapequa, NY, 1977-82; dir. Queensborough C.C., Bayside, NY, 1982-85; exec. dir. S.I. Continuum of Edn., Inc., 1985-90; asst. dean Nassau C.C., Garden City, NY, 1990-92, v.p., 1992-93, exec. asst. to pres., 1993-95, assoc. dean for acad. affairs, 1995—2001, acting dean of instrn., 2001—02, dean instrn., 2002—. Adj. prof. in field; edn. dir. Episcopal Diocese L.I., Garden City, 1973-77; pres. N.Y. State Coun. for Resource Devel., 1994-96; dir. region II Coun. Resource Devel., 1996-98, also bd. dirs. Co-author: Developing An Educationally Accountable Program, 1973. Chair United Way, Garden City, 1972—77; bd. dirs. St. Mary's and St. Paul Episcopal Schs., Garden City, 1973—77, Rutland (Vt.) Hosp., 1965—68, Urban League L.I., 1994—2002; v.p. fin. Northgate Homeowners Assn., 1993—2000; treas. Wantagh Jewish Ctr., v.p., 1995—97. Recipient Faculty Disting. Svc. award Hofstra U., 1977, Internat. Reading Assn., 1987, Presdl. award L.I. Univ., 1989, Disting. Kappan award, 1989. Mem. NEA, Am. Assn. Sch. Adminstrs., Coun. for Resource Devel., Kappa Delta Pi (faculty sponsor 1971-77), Phi Delta Kappa (pres. 1989-90). Democrat. Jewish. Avocations: reading, photography, travel, golf. Home: 8 Northgate Ct Melville NY 11747-3046 E-mail: atkinsw@ncc.edu.

ATKINS, WILLIAM AUSTIN, SR., (BILL ATKINS), former state legislator; b. Tate, Ga., Aug. 16, 1933; s. Austin and Gladys Atkins; m. Jennifer Lee Atkins; children: Chip, Paige;stepchildren: Stacy, Justin. BS in Pharmacy, Mercer U., 1954. Former owner Atkins Pharmacy, Smyrna, Ga.; mem. Ga. Ho. of Reps., 1982-94, mem. appropriations, regulated beverages and industry coms.; dir. Drugs and Narcotics Agy. State of Ga., 1994—. Past chair Cobb County Joint House and Senate Legis. Delegation; past chmn. Ga. State Bd. Pharmacy. Leader, vocalist Bill Atkins Band. Adminstrv. bd. 1st United Meth. Ch.; bd. dirs. Mercer U. Sch. Pharmacy; governing bd. Brawner Hosp., 1993-96; long-range planning bd. Smyrna Hosp., 1993-96. With U.S. Army, 1955—57. Recipient Appreciation plaque Ga. div. Am. Cancer Soc., 1991, Legislator of Yr. Friendship award Personal Care Homes of Ga., 1991, Liberty Bell award Cobb County Bar Assn., 1991, Pharmacist of Yr. in Ga. award, Phi Delta Chi, 1978, One of a Kind award Cobb Clean Commn., 1992, Meritorious Svc. award Mercer U., So. Sch. Pharmacy, 1992, others. Mem. Ga. Pharm. Assn. (award for dedication and svc. to profession of pharmacy 1986, Cmty. Svc. award 1997, Bowl of Hygiea award 1997), Ga. Pharmacists Assn. (past bd. dirs.), Ga. Assn. Chiefs of Police, 7th Dist. Pharmacists Assn. (past pres.), Atlanta Metropol, Cobb C. of C., Moose (named Mr. Cobb County 1993), Nat. Sheriff's Assn. Home: 4719 Windsor Dr SW Smyrna GA 30082-4465

ATKINSON, A. KELLEY, insurance company executive; b. Tulsa, Okla., July 7, 1947; s. Milton A. Atkinson and Helen G. Brower; m. Patricia L. Morton, June 28, 1969 (dec. 1991); children: Gregory, Brent; m. Pamela A. Bender, Feb. 14, 1993. BS, Tex. Christian U., 1969; MBA, Ariz. State U., 1972. Sales rep. Mallinckrodt, Inc., Saint Louis, 1972-73, assoc. product mgr., 1973-74, regional sales mgr., 1974-76, mgr. market rsch. & data systems, 1976-77; mgr. product mktg. Intermedics, Inc., Freeport, Tex., 1977-79, dir. mktg., 1979-82, v.p. mktg., 1982-83; pres., COO Neuro Systems, Inc., Garland, Tex., 1983; pres. BoMed Mfg., Irvine, Calif., 1984; pres., CEO Physicians Health Plan Utah, Salt Lake City, 1984-87, United Health Care Ga., Atlanta, 1987-98, v.p. asst. projects, 1998—. Pres. Ga. Assn. HMOs, Atlanta, 1989, 94-96; adj. prof. Mercer U., Atlanta, 1990-92. Treas. Windward Cmty. Svcs. Assn., Alpharetta, Ga., 1995-96. Avocations: computer science, fly fishing. Office: United Healthcare Ga 2970 Clairmont Rd NE Ste 300 Atlanta GA 30329-4415

ATKINSON, ANN LENNETTE, mortician; b. Washington, Dec. 9, 1949; d. Samuel and Alma (Zimmerman) Williams; m. Oct. 6, 1968 (div. 1980); children: Lois, Jonathan, Crystal, Thomas; m. Melvin Atkinson, Feb. 4, 1985. AA in Mortuary Sci., Fayetteville Community Coll., N.C., 1982; BA in Elementary Edn., U. D.C., 1990; MA in Psychology, Cambridge U., 1998; PhD in Metaphysics and Sci., 2002. Lic. mortician, N.C. Mortician Colvin Funeral Home, Fayetteville, NC, 1979—82; tchr. Forsyth Cen. Coll., Winston-Salem, 1982-83; autopsy asst. Vets. Hosp., Washington, 1984—2000; receptionist Temporary Resources, Washington, 1986-87; micro-photographer Library of Congress, Washington, 1987-88; tchr. D.C. Pub. Schs., 1988-89; pres., coordinator Restorative Svcs., Suitland, Md., 1988—; tchr. phys. sci. Wilson County Sch. Sys., NC. Author: Unlock the Myths about the Funeral Industry, 1988; contbr. articles to profl. jours. Vol. tax asst. IRS, 1988; mem. Missionary Soc., N.C. Club First Bapt. Ch. With U.S. Army, 1974-75. Recipient Golden Poet award. Mem. Nat. Funeral Dirs. Assn., Am. Legion, Nat. Poetry Soc., Darden Alumna Assn., Sigma Phi Sigma. Democrat. Baptist. Avocations: tennis, reading, writing, poetry, french cooking. Home: 704 Cemetery St Wilson NC 27893

ATKINSON, ARTHUR JOHN, JR., pharmacologist, educator; b. Chgo., Mar. 22, 1938; s. Arthur John and Inez (Hill) Atkinson; m. Mary Jo Yunker, May 12, 1984. AB in Chemistry, Harvard U., 1959; MD, Cornell U., 1963. Intern, asst. resident medicine Mass. Gen. Hosp., Boston, 1963-65; chief resident, Howard Carroll fellow medicine Passavant Meml. Hosp., Chgo., 1967-68; fellow clin. pharmacology U. Cin., 1968-69, asst. prof. pharmacology, 1969; vis. scientist dept. toxicology Karolinska Inst., Stockholm, 1970; from asst. prof. to assoc. prof. medicine and pharmacology Northwestern U., Chgo., 1970—76, prof., 1976-94; corp. v.p. clin. devel. and med. affairs Upjohn Co., 1994-95; v.p. clin. R&D and worldwide clin. pharmacology Pharmacia & Upjohn, Inc., 1995-96; adj. prof. pharmacology Ctr. for Drug Devel. Sci., Georgetown U., 1996—. With NIH, USPHS, 1965—67; sr. advisor clin. pharmacology to dir. clin. ctr. NIH, 1998—; vice chair safe medication use expert com. U.S. Pharmacopeia, 2000—. Recipient Faculty Devel. award in clin. pharmacology, Pharm. Mfrs. Assn., 1970—72, award of excellence in clin. pharmacology, 2002; scholar Burroughs Wellcome, 1972—77. Master: ACP; mem.: Assn. Am. Physicians, Am. Soc. Clin. Pharmacology and Therapeutics (pres. 1995—96, Rawls Palmer award 1983), Am. Soc. Pharmacology and Exptl. Therapeutics (Harry Gold award 1989), Chgo. Yacht Club, Alpha Omega Alpha. Home: 5000 Battery Ln Apt 204 Bethesda MD 20814-2655 E-mail: aatkinson@cc.nih.gov.

ATKINSON, BARBARA F. dean, medical educator, academic administrator; b. Mpls., Oct. 19, 1942; MD, Jefferson Med. Coll., Thomas Jefferson Univ., 1974. Diplomate Am. Bd. Anatomic and Clin. Pathology, Am. Bd. Cytopathology. Intern Hosp. U. Pa., Phila., 1974—75, resident in pathology, 1975—78; mem. faculty U. Kans., Kansas City; dir. resident program U. Kans. Med. Ctr., Kansas City. Assoc. scientist Wistar Inst. Anatomy and Biology, 1983—87; mem. staff dept. pathology Hosp. of U. Pa., 1978—87, dir. cytopathology, 1978—87, med. program dir. Sch. Cytotech., 1978—86; chmn. dept. pathology and lab. medicine Med. Coll. Pa., 1987—94; dir. Delaware Valley Regional Lab. Svcs., Med. Coll. Hosps. and St. Christopher's Hosp. for Children, 1991—96; chmn. dept. pathology and lab. medicine Med. Coll. Pa. and Hahnemann U., 1994—96; trustee Am. Bd. Pathology, 1992—95, pres., 1998—. Mem. editl. bd. Lab. Investigation, 1988—94, Modern Pathology, 1990—94, Human Pathology, 1992—94, manuscript reviewer Cancer, Diagnostic Cytopathology, Modern Pathology, 1988—94, abstract rev. bd. U.S. and Can. Acad. Pathology, 1989—92, rev. panel Am. Soc. Clin. Pathology Abstract, 1991—96; contbr. articles, chapters to books. Bd. dirs., treas. Laennec Soc. Phila., 1979—81; bd. dirs. Thyroid Soc. Phila., 1982—84; exec. com., bd. dirs. Med. Coll. Pa., 1994—96; bd. trustees Hahnemann U., 1994—96. Recipient Golden Apple Tchg. award for excellent sci. tchg., 1994; grantee, NIH, 1985—88, Takeda-Abbott R&D, 1989—94, NIA, 1991—94. Fellow: ASIM, Coll. Am. Pathologists; mem.: NAS (mem. Inst. Medicine), U.S. and Can. Acad. Pathology, Am. Soc. Clin. Pathology (Janet M. Glasgow Meml. scholarship 1974), Am. Soc. Cytopathology. Office: U Kans Med Ctr 3901 Rainbow Blvd Kansas City KS 66130-7410

ATKINSON, BILL, artistic director; Studied with various tchrs., N.Y.C. Founder, artistic dir. Dallas Met. Ballet, 1965—; founder Etgen-Atkinson Ballet Sch., 1960—. Performer: (ballets) Royal Winnipeg Ballet, Ballet AAA, Dallas State Fair Musicals, Jacobs Pillow Dance Festival, (Broadway plays) My Fair Lady, Oh Captain, Happiest Girl in the World. Mem.: S.W. Regional Ballet Assn. (membership chmn.). Office: Dallas Met Ballet 6815 Hillcrest Ave Dallas TX 75205-1308

ATKINSON, BRUCE EARL, clinical psychologist, christian counselor; b. Seattle, Sept. 10, 1946; s. Thomas Earnest Jr. and La Zelle Simcox Swensson Atkinson; m. Barbra Ann, Apr. 26, 1971; 1 child, Amanda Catherine. BA, Beloit Coll., Wis., 1968; MS, Ill. State U., Normal, 1976; MA in theology, Fuller Theol. Sem., Pasadena, Calif., 1985; PhD of clin. psychology, Fuller Sch. Psychology, Pasadena, Calif., 1987. Lic. Psychologist, Ga. Case worker and therapist Boys Town Mo., St. James, 1977-1981; clinician and student supr. Covenant House, Pasadena, 1981-1985; trainee psychol. assessment Kaiser Permanente Mental Health Ctr., L.A., 1983-1984; doctoral intern The Cmty. Assistance Program for Srs., Pasadena, 1984-1985, The Pasadena Cmty. Counseling Clin., 1985-1986; psychol. examiner The Christian Psychol. Ctr., Memphis, 1987-1989; sr. clin. psychologist Oasis, Inc., Atlanta, 1989—; clin. supr. The Psychological Studies Inst., Atlanta, 1992—. Adj. faculty Psychol. Studies Inst. Contbr. articles to profl. jours. Sgt. U.S.A.F.M.C., 1969-73. Mem. Nat. Register Health Svc. Providers in Psychology, Christian Assoc. for Psychol. Studies, Mental Health Assn. Ga. Episcopalian. Avocations: gardening, fishing, college sports, science fiction. Office: Oasis Inc 1655 Phoenix Blvd Ste 4 College Park GA 30349-5550 E-mail: oasisc2@aol.com.

ATKINSON, DONALD D., SR., real estate broker; b. Hutchinson, Kans., Aug. 22, 1933; s. Theodore Sherman and Florence Marie (Morris) A.; m. Barbara Clara, Apr. 22, 1954; children: Sheryl Lynn, Donald D., Jr., Richard Lee. AA, Chaffey Jr. Coll., Alta Loma, Calif., 1965-71; BABA, San Bernadino State U., 1973-79. Telegrapher Santa Fe Railroad, San Bernardino, Calif., 1951-79; maintenance supr. Kaiser Steel Corp., Fontana, Calif., 1980-81; real estate salesman Acacia Realty, Fontana, 1981-83, Am. Pacific, Colton, Calif., 1983-86; ins. sales office mgr. State Farm Ins., Fontana, 1986-87; real estate sales office mgr. 5th Ave. Realty, Fontana, 1987-88, A&B Realty, Fontana, 1988-92, real estate broker, 1992—. Control and regulate trash, taxis, tow trucks, Bur. Franchise, City of Fontana, 1982-88. Sgt. U.S. Army, 1953, Korea. Mem. Nat. Assn. Realtors Property Mgmt. (founding), Bus. Devel. Assn., Realty Investment Assn. Calif., San Bernardino Valley Bd. Realtors. Republican. Avocations: gun collecting, shooting, fishing, skiing. Office: PO Box 2343 Fontana CA 92334-2343

ATKINSON, GORDON, chemistry educator; b. Bklyn., Aug. 29, 1930; s. John and Margaret (Barrie) A.; m. Betty Lou Dilmore, Apr. 1, 1976; children: Alan Gordon, Gwyneth, Valerie. BS in Chemistry, Lehigh U., 1952; PhD in Phys. Chemistry, Iowa State U., 1956. Instr chemistry U. Mich., Ann Arbor, 1957-61; asst. prof. U. Md., College Park, 1961-64, assoc. prof., 1964-67, prof., 1967-71; prof. chemistry U. Okla., Norman, 1971—, chmn. dept. chemistry, 1971-74; dean Grad. Coll., 1974-79, vice provost for research adminstrn., 1974-79. Cons. in field.; Fulbright prof. Copenhagen U., 1967-68 Author: Reactions and Reason, 1973; Contbr. articles to profl. jours. Recipient Excellence in Teaching award U. Md., 1963, Regent's award for research U. Okla., 1983 Fellow N.Y. Acad. Sci., Am. Inst. Chemists; mem. Am. Chem. Soc., AAAS, AAUP, Sigma Xi, Phi Beta Kappa, Tau Beta Pi, Phi Kappa Phi, Phi Lambda Upsilon, Kappa Sigma. Democrat. Unitarian-Universalist. Home: 1419 Greenbriar Dr Norman OK 73072-6858 Office: Okla U Dept Chemistry 620 Parrington Oval Norman OK 73019-3050

ATKINSON, HAROLD WITHERSPOON, utilities consultant, real estate broker; b. Lake City, S.C., June 12, 1914; s. Leland G. and Kathleen (Dunlap) A.; m. Pickett Rancke, Oct. 6, 1946; children: Henry Leland, Harold Witherspoon. BSEE, Duke U., 1934; MS in Engring., Harvard U., 1935. Registered profl. engr., Mass. Various postitions in sales, engring. Cambridge Electric Light Co., Mass., 1935-39, 46-73, asst. mgr. power sales dept., 1946-49, gen. mgr., 1957-73, dir., 1959-84, exec. v.p., 1972-73. Mgr. Pee Dee Electric Membership Corp., Wadesboro, N.C., 1939-46; gen. mgr. Cambridge Steam Corp., 1951-73, v.p., 1959-73, dir. 1955-84. Chmn. Cambridge traffic bd., 1962-73; pres. Cambridge Ctr. Adult Edn., 1962-64; v.p. Cambridge Mental Health Assn.; chmn. allocations com. Greater Boston United Cmty. Svcs., 1971-72; chmn. Cambridge Commn. Svcs., 1955-56; adv. bd. Cambridge Coun. Boy Scouts Am.; mem. corp. chmn. camping com. Cambridge YMCA, 1964-71; chmn. Cambridge chpt. ARC, 1969-71; trustee of trust funds Town of Harrisville, N.H., 1976-83; treas. North Myrtle Beach Citizens Assn., 1982-84. Served from pvt. to capt. AUS, 1942-45. Mem. IEEE (sr.), Mass. Soc. Profl. Engrs., Elec. Inst. (pres. 1971), Harvard Engring. Soc., Cambridge C. of C. (pres. 1957-58), Newcomen Soc. N.Am., Cambridge Boat (treas. 1962-65), Cambridge Club (pres. 1972-73), Bay Tree Golf Club, Plantation Club, Civitan (pres. Wadesboro 1940-41), Rotary (pres. Cambridge club 1959-60, former v.p. North Myrtle Beach, S.C. club), Phi Beta Kappa, Tau Beta Pi, Pi Mu Epsilon. Home: Covenant Towers Apt 409W 5001 Little River Rd Myrtle Beach SC 29577 E-mail: HaroldHALW@aol.com.

ATKINSON, JAMES BLAKELY, writer, editor; b. Honolulu, Nov. 24, 1934; s. Edward Clay and Gertrude (Blakely) A.; m. Starr Koester, Sept. 10, 1960 (dec. Oct. 1978); 1 child, Andreas Edward; m. Gretchen A. Holm, June 28, 1980; stepchildren: Nils, Katrina. AB in History, Swarthmore Coll., 1956; MA in Am. Lit. with honors, Columbia U., 1961, PhD in Comparative Lit. with distinction, 1968. Tchr. English Coll. Benjamin Franklin, Orléans, France, 1958-59; thcr. French, English and Am. history St. David's Sch., N.Y.C., 1960-62; asst. prof. English Dartmouth Coll., Hanover, N.H., 1966-73, Earlham Coll., Richmond, Ind., 1973-78; mem. core faculty Capital U., Dayton, Ohio, 1978-79; asst. prof. English Rutgers U., Camden, N.J., 1979-87; vis. scholar dept. Romance langs. U. Pa., 1987-89; ind. scholar, 1989—. Author: Machiavelli: The Prince, 1976; co-author: Machiavelli, The Complete Comedies, 1985, Machiavelli and His Friends: Their Personal Correspondence, 1996, Footprints of the Past, 1996, Machiavelli, Discourses on Livy, 2002, Guicciardini, Considerations of Discourses, 2002; contbr. articles to profl. jours.; translator. Pres. Cornish (N.H.) Hist. Soc., 1992—. With inf. U.S. Army, 1956-58. Mem. AAUP, MLA, Renaissance Soc. Am. Democrat. Mem. Soc. Of Friends. Avocations: hiking, gardening, art and antiques. Home: 117 Town House Rd Cornish NH 03745-4639 E-mail: atholm@valley.net.

ATKINSON, JANET E. lawyer; b. Detroit, Apr. 30, 1945; d. A.K. and Billie Dorothy Atkinson; m. Robert Joseph Kestell, Aug. 18, 1966 (div. Dec. 1992); children: Jeanette, Elizabeth, Robert, Katherine, Richard. BA, U. Wis., 1967; MLS, U. Md., 1972, JD, 1996. Libr. asst. Madison (Wis.) Pub. Libr., 1967-68; libr. Prince Georges (Md.) County Schs., 1972-74; real estate investor Kent County, Md., 1976-93, Washington, 1979; propr. Creative Cookery, Chestertown, Md., 1979-83; law clk. Shapiro & Olander, Balt., 1996-97; sr. assoc. Ctr. for Support of Families, Chevy Chase, Md., 1996—. Author: (with others) Year 2000 Family Law Update, 1999; contbr. articles to profl. jours. Chair Internat. Orgn. Family Rights Group, Washnigton, 1998-99; bd. dirs. Montgomery County NOW, Md., 1999—; mem. adv. bd. Divorce Roundtable, Montgomery County, 1999—. Mem. ABA (internat. com. chair family law sect. 1999—), Md. Bar Assn., Montgomery County Bar Assn., Women's Bar Assn. Roman Catholic. Office: Ctr for Support of Families 4 Leland Ct Chevy Chase MD 20815-4906 E-mail: jatkinson@thecsf.com.

ATKINSON, JEFF JOHN FREDERICK, law educator, lawyer, writer; b. Mpls., Nov. 12, 1948; s. Frederick Melville Atkinson and Patricia Atkinson Farnes; m. Janis Pressendo, Dec. 22, 1982; children: Tara, Abigail, Grant, Kelsey. BS, Northwestern U., 1974; JD summa cum laude, DePaul U., 1977. Bar: Ill. 1977, U.S. Ct. Appeals (7th cir.) 1977, U.S. Dist. Ct. (no. dist.) Ill. 1978, U.S. Supreme Ct 1982. Editor, reporter various Chgo. area newspapers and radio stas., 1967-71; assoc. Jenner & Block, Chgo., 1977-80; pvt. practice Evanston, Wilmette and Chgo., 1980—. Vis. prof., instr. Loyola U. Law Sch., Chgo., 1982-91; adj. prof. DePaul U. Coll. Law, Chgo., 1991—; spl. govt. employee and pvt. sector advisor U.S. State Dept., 1997—; prof.-reporter Ill. Jud. Conf., 1989—. Author: Modern Child Custody Practice (2 vols.) 1986, 2d edit., 2000, Am. Bar Assn. Guide to Family Law; contbr. articles on criminal, family, constl. law, health law and ethics to various publs. Elected bd. v.p. Avoca Sch., 1999-2001, sec., 2002—. Mem. ABA (chmn. child custody com. 1983-84, 86-87, 89-92, mem. editl. bd. Family Advocate 1988-96, mem. publs. devel. bd. 1984-89, mem. task force on needs of children 1983-85, chmn. rsch. com. 1987-88, advisor to Nat. Conf. Commrs. on Uniform State Laws 1994—, Merit awards 1984, 86-94, 2000), ACLU (bd. dirs. Ill. div. 1972-74), Ill. Bar Assn., Am. Health Lawyers Assn., Northwestern U. Coll. Alumni Assn. (v.p. 1987-89). Home: 3514 Riverside Dr Wilmette IL 60091-1050 E-mail: jatkin747@aol.com.

ATKINSON, LAWRENCE RUSH, IV, (RICK ATKINSON), journalist; b. Munich, Nov. 16, 1952; s. Larry Rush and Margaret Jean (Howe) A.; m. Jane Ann Chestnut, May 12, 1979; children: Rush, Sarah. BA, East Carolina U., 1974; MA, U. Chgo., 1975. Reporter Pittsburg (Kans.) Morning Sun, 1976-77, The Kansas City (Mo.) Times, 1977-83, The Washington Post, 1983—85, dep. nat. editor, 1985—87, investigative reporter, 1989—91, Berlin corr., 1993—95, asst. mng. editor, 1996—. Author: (novels) The Long Gray Line, 1989, Crusade, 1993, An Army At Dawn, 2002. Recipient Pulitzer prize, 1982, Livingston Award for internat. reporting, 1983, John Hancock Award for Excellence, 1989, George Polk Award for nat. reporting, 1990, PEN special citation for nonfiction, 1990, Pulitzer prize, 2003, numerous other journalism awards. Office: Washington Post 1150 15th St NW Washington DC 20071-0002*

ATKINSON, PERRY, political organization administrator; Chair Oreg. Rep. Party, Beaverton, 1999—. Office: Oreg Rep Party PO Box 789 Salem OR 97308-0789 also: Oregon Rep Party 570 Liberty St Ste 200 Salem OR 97301 Fax: 503-587-9244.

ATKINSON, RICHARD CHATHAM, university president; b. Oak Park, Ill., Mar. 19, 1929; s. Herbert and Margaret Atkinson; m. Rita Loyd, Aug. 20, 1952; 1 dau., Lynn Loyd. Ph.B., U. Chgo., 1948; PhD, Ind. U., 1955. Lectr. applied math. and stats. Stanford (Calif.) U., 1956—57, assoc. prof. psychology, 1961—64, prof. psychology, 1964—80; asst. prof. psychology UCLA, 1957—61; dep. dir. NSF, 1975—76, acting dir., 1976, dir., 1976—80; chancellor, prof. cognitive sci. U. Calif., San Diego, 1980—95; pres. U. Calif. Sys., 1995—. Author: (with Atkinson, Smith and Bem) Introduction to Psychology, 13th edit., 2000, Computer Assisted Instruction, 1969, An Introduction to Mathematical Learning Theory, 1965, Contemporary Developments in Mathematical Psychology, 1974, Mind and Behavior, 1980, Stevens' Handbook of Experimental Psychology, 1988. Served with AUS, 1954—56. Guggenheim fellow, 1967; fellow Ctr. for Advanced Study in Behavioral Scis., 1963; recipient Distinguished Research award Social Sci. Research Council, 1962. Fellow APA (Disting. Sci. Contbn. award 1977, Thorndike award 1980), AAAS (pres. 1989-90), Am. Psychol. Soc. (William James fellow 1985), Am. Acad. Arts and Scis.; mem. NAS, Soc. Exptl. Psychologists, Am. Philos. Soc., Nat. Acad. Edn., Inst. of Medicine, Cosmos Club (Washington), Explorer's Club (N.Y.C.). Home: 70 Rincon Rd Kensington CA 94707-1047 Office: U Calif Office Pres 1111 Franklin St Oakland CA 94607-5201 E-mail: richard.atkinson@ucop.edu.

ATKINSON, RICHARD LEE, JR., internal medicine educator; b. Petersburg, Va., May 15, 1942; s. Richard Lee and Ruth (Scarborough) A.; m. Susan Stayner Hume, Aug. 13, 1966; children: Catherine Crane, Barbara Hill, Deborah Gildea. BA, VA Mil. Inst., 1964, MD, Med. Coll. Va., 1968. Liaison endocrinologist Vanderbilt U., Nashville, 1973-74; adj. asst. prof. UCLA, 1975-77; asst. prof. internal medicine U. Va. Sch. Medicine, Charlottesville, 1977-83; assoc. prof. internal medicine U. Calif., Davis, 1983-87; prof. internal medicine Ea. Va. Med. Sch., Norfolk, 1987-93; assoc. chief staff for rsch. VA Med. Ctr., Hampton, Va., 1987-93; prof. medicine and nutritional scis., dir. Beers-Murphy Clin. Nutrition Ctr. U. Wis., Madison, 1993—2002; emeritus prof. medicine and nutritional scis. U. Wis., Madison, 2002—; dir. Obesity Inst. Medstar Rsch. Inst., Washington, 2002—. Mem. nutrition study sect. NIH, 1991-95, chair, 1993-95. Contbr. articles to profl. jours. Maj. U.S. Army, 1970—74. Mem. N.Am. Assn. Study Obesity (pres. 1990-91), Am. Soc. Clin. Nutrition, Am. Obesity Assn. (pres. 1995—). Home: 7211 Park Terrace Dr Alexandria VA 22307 Office: Obesity Inst Medstar Rsch Inst 100 Irving St NW Rm EB 4109 Washington DC 20010 E-mail: rla7@medstar.net.

ATKINSON, SUSAN D. producing artistic director, theatrical consultant; b. Phila., May 23, 1944; d. Joseph A. and Josephine (Mierley) Davis; m. Robert Atkinson, 1971 (div. 1986). BA, Juniata Coll., 1966; postgrad., San Francisco State Coll., 1968-69, U. Calif., Berkeley, 1968-69. Dir. Am. Conservatory Theatre, San Francisco, 1967-72; guest dir. Berkeley Repertory Theatre Co., 1968-69; dir. Marin Shakespeare Festival, Marin County, Calif., 1968-69; producing artistic dir. Repertory Theatre Co. Bucks County, Doyleston, Pa., 1980-86, Bristol (Pa.) Riverside Theatre, 1986—; guest dir. Grove Shakespeare Festival, 1992. Bd. dirs. Pa. Coun. on the Arts, Harrisburg, Pa., 1989—. Mem. Soc. Stage Dirs. and Choreographers (cert.). Office: Bristol Riverside Theatre PO Box 1250 Bristol PA 19007-1250

ATKINSON, WILLIAM JAMES, JR., retired cardiologist; b. Mobile, Ala., July 4, 1917; s. William J. and Gertrude (Smith) A.; m. Glenda E. Street, Oct. 29, 1949; children: Glenda Street, Regina Creswell, William James III. BA cum laude, Amherst Coll., 1939; MD, U. Pa., 1943; MS in Internal Medicine, St. Louis U., 1949. Diplomate Am. Bd. Internal Medicine, Am. Bd. Cardiovasc. Disease. Intern Phila. Gen. Hosp., 1943—44; resident in medicine St. Louis City Hosp., 1946—48; resident in cardiology St. Louis U., 1948—49; pvt. practice specializing in internal medicine/cardiology Mobile, Ala., 1949—. Chief cardiac clinic Mobile City Hosp., 1950-60; electrocardiographer Mobile Infirmary, 1949-92, Providence Hosp., 1949-75; cardiologist Diagnostic and Med. Clinic, 1949-92; mem. staff U. South Ala. Med. Ctr. Hosp., Mobile Infirmary, Providence Hosp.; chmn. bd. Diagnostic and Med. Clinic P.A., 1973-92; clin. assoc. prof. medicine U. Ala., 1964-89; clin. assoc. prof. medicine U. South Ala., 1973-92; ret.; life counselor Med. Assn. State of Ala. Capt. M.C., AUS, 1944-46. Decorated Bronze Star; recipient 4 Battle Stars, Combat Med. medal. Fellow ACP, Am. Coll. Cardiology, Am. Coll. Chest Physicians; mem. AMA, Am. Heart Assn., Ala. Heart Assn. (pres. 1955, chmn. bd. 1956), Am. Soc. Clin. Pharmacology and Therapeutics, Rotary, Mobile Country Club, Mobile Yacht Club. Republican. Episcopalian. Home: 3965 Byronell Ct Mobile AL 36693-5502

ATLAS, DAVID, meteorologist, research scientist; b. Bklyn., May 25, 1924; s. Isadore and Rose (Jaffee) A.; m. Lucille Rosen, Sept. 26, 1948; children: Joan Linda, Robert Fred. BSc, NYU, 1946; MSc, MIT, 1951, DSc in Meteorology, 1955. Chief weather radar br. Air Force Cambridge Research Labs., Bedford, Mass., 1948-66; prof. meteorology U. Chgo., 1966-72; dir. atmospheric tech. div. Nat. Center for Atmospheric Research, Boulder, Colo., 1972-73, dir. nat. hail research expt., 1974-75; dir. lab. for atmospheric sci. Nasa Goddard Space Flight Ctr., Greenbelt, Md., 1977-84, disting. vis. scientist, 1988—; sr. research assoc. dept. meteorology U. Md., 1985-87; disting. vis. scientist Jet Propulsion Lab. Calif. Inst. Tech., 1984-92. Chmn. panel on remote atmospheric probing, also mem. com. on atmospheric scis., NAS, 1975-82, mem. on modernization of the Nat. Weather Svc., 1996-99—; mem. weather radar beyond NEXRAD, 2001-02; vis. scientist Coop. Inst. for Marine and Atmospheric Scis., U. Miami, 1988-99. 1st lt. USAAF, 1943-46. Recipient Loeser award Air Force Cambridge Research Labs., 1957, O'Day award, 1964; Robert M. Losey award AIAA, 1966; NASA Outstanding Leadership medal, 1982; Presdl. Meritorious Sr. Exec. award, 1983; NSF sr. postdoctoral fellow Imperial Coll., London, Eng., 1959-60 Fellow Am. Meteorol. Soc. (councilor 1961-64, 72-74, Meisinger award 1957, assoc. editor publs. 1957-74, pres. 1975, Cleveland Abbe award 1983, Remote Sensing award 1991, Carl Gustav Rossby medal 1996, hon. 2001), Am. Geophys. Union, Am. Astron. Soc., Royal Meteorol. Soc. (Symons Meml. medal 1989), AAAS (chmn. atmospheric and hydrospheric scis. sect. 1986); mem. NAE, Internat. Radio Sci. Union (pres. inter-union commn. on radio meteorology 1969-72). Achievements include invention of weather radar devices. E-mail: datlas@alum.mit.edu.

ATLAS, ERNEST, physician; b. N.Y.C., Sept. 24, 1935; s. Eugene and Mary (Klein) A.; m. Barbara Phyllis Frank, Sept. 9, 1957 (div. Aug. 1996); children: David, Jennifer, Ian; m. Bonnie Gail Hyland, May 30, 1998. AB, Columbia Coll., 1957; MD, Albert Einstein Coll. Medicine, 1961. Cert. Am. Bd. Internal Medicine, Am. Bd. Infectious Disease. Intern in medicine Bronx Mcpl. Hosp., 1961-62; resident in medicine U. Wash., Seattle, 1965-67; fellow in infectious diseases King County Hosp., Seattle, 1967-68; staff physician Delaware Valley Hosp., Walton, N.Y., 1968-70; chief sect. infectious diseases Norwalk (Conn.) Hosp., 1970—; asst. clin. prof. Yale U., New Haven, Conn., 1975—. Lectr. medicine Chgo. Med. Sch., 1985—; cons. in field. Fellow Am. Coll. Physicians. Avocations: skiing, sailing, gardening. Home: 23 Brookside Pl Redding CT 06896 Office: Norwalk Med Group 40 Cross St Norwalk CT 06851-4647

ATLAS, JAMES ROBERT, editor, writer; b. Chgo., Mar. 22, 1949; s. Donald and Nora (Glassenberg) A.; m. Anna O'Conor Sloane Fels, Aug. 2, 1975; children: Amelia Eyre, William Easton. BA, Harvard U., 1971; postgrad. (Rhodes scholar), Oxford (Eng.) U., 1971-73. Staff writer Time, N.Y.C., 1977-78; asst. editor N.Y. Times Book Rev., N.Y. Times, 1978-81; assoc. editor Atlantic Monthly, 1981-85; contbg. editor Vanity Fair, N.Y.C., 1985-87; asst. editor N.Y. Times Mag., 1987-97; staff writer The New Yorker, 1997-99. Gen. editor Penguin Lives. Author: Delmore Schwartz: The Life of an American Poet, 1977, The Great Pretender, 1986; (novel) Battle of the Books, 1992, Bellow: A Biography, 2000; contbr. articles to various nat. mags. Home: 40 W 77th St New York NY 10024-5128 Office: Atlas Books 65 East 55th St New York NY 10022

ATLAS, JAY DAVID, philosopher, consultant, linguist; b. Houston, Tex., Feb. 1, 1945; s. Jacob Henry and Babette Fancile (Friedman) A. AB summa cum laude, Amherst (Mass.) Coll., 1966; PhD, Princeton (N.J.) U., 1976. Mem. common rm. Wolfson Coll., Oxford, Eng., 1978, 80; vis. fellow Princeton U., 1979; rsch. assoc. Inst. for Advanced Study, Princeton, 1982-84; vis. lectr. U. Hong Kong, 1986; prof. Pomona Coll., Claremont, Calif., 1989—, chair dept. linguistics and cognitive sci., 2002—03, Peter W. Stanley Prof. philosophy and linguistics, 2003—. Sr. assoc. Jurecon, Inc., L.A.; lectr. 2d European Summer Sch. in Logic, Lang. and Info., 1990; examiner U. Edinburgh, Scotland, 1993, U. Groningen, The Netherlands, 1991, 93-97, vis. rsch. prof., 1995; vis. prof. UCLA, 1988-95, Max. Planck Inst. for Psycholinguistics, Nijmegen, The Netherlands, 1997. Author: Philosophy Without Ambiguity, 1989, Logic, Meaning, and Conversation, 2003; contbr. to PC Laptop Computer Mag., 1994, articles to profl. jours. Mem. Am. Philos. Assn., Linguistic Soc. Am. Office: Pomona Coll 551 N College Ave Claremont CA 91711-4410 E-mail: jatlas@alumni.princeton.edu.

ATLAS, LIANE WIENER, writer; b. N.Y.C. d. Louis and Frances (Ferne) Wiener; m. Martin Atlas, Mar. 5, 1944 (dec. Mar. 1997); children: Stephen Terry, Jeffrey L. AB, Vassar Coll., 1943; postgrad., Johns Hopkins U., 1953-55. Cert. fin. planner. Fgn. affairs officer Dept. State, Washington, 1962-68; sr. economist U.S. Commerce Dept., Washington, 1968-75, U.S. Treasury Dept., Washington, 1975-79, Riggs Nat. Bank, Washington, 1980-82; v.p. Fintapes Inc., Washington, 1984-87, pres., 1987-95; freelance writer Washington, 1995—. Mem. U.S. delegation UN Econ. Orgns., N.Y.C., Geneva, 1963, 64, 68, 79. Author: Middle East Financial Institutions, 1977, (audio cassettes) What Every Wife Should Know, 1986, rev., 1992, Financial Planning for Divorce, rev. edit. 1992; freelance writer Changing Times and other mags., 1982-87. Treas. Entertaining People/Washington Home, 1986—90, Smithsonian Craft Show, 1993—95, Smithsonian Women's Com., 1996—97; mem. Kennedy Ctr. Cirs. Bd., 1999—. Fellow in econs. Johns Hopkins U., Balt., 1954-55; recipient Cert. of Appreciation U.S. Treasury Dept., Washington, 1977. Mem.: Washington Ind. Writers, Inst. CFPs, Vassar Club of Washington. Avocations: print collecting, travel, tennis. Home: 2254 48th St NW Washington DC 20007-1035

ATLAS, NANCY FRIEDMAN, judge; b. N.Y.C., May 20, 1949; BS, Tufts U., 1971; JD, NYU, 1974. Bar: N.Y. 1975, U.S. Dist. Ct. (so. and ea. dists.) N.Y. 1975, U.S. Ct. Appeals (2nd cir.) 1975, U.S. Dist. Ct. (so. dist.) Tex. 1982, U.S. Ct. Appeals (5th cir.) 1982, U.S. Dist. Ct. (no. dist.) Tex. 1989. Law clk. to Hon. Dudley B. Bonsal U.S. Dist Ct. (so. dist.) N.Y., 1974-76; assoc. Webster & Sheffield, 1977-78; asst. U.S. atty. So. Dist. N.Y., 1979-82; shareholder Sheinfeld, Maley & Kay, P.C., Houston, 1982-95, also bd. dirs.; judge U.S. Dist. Ct. Tex., Houston, 1995—. Lectr. numerous programs CLE. Mng. editor NYU Ann. Survey Am. Law, 1973-74; contbr. numerous articles to profl. jours. Chair Tex. Higher Edn. coord. Bd., 1992-95; mem. Tex. Coun. Workforce and Econ. Competitiveness, 1993-95. Fellow: ABA Found., Houston Bar Assn., State Bar Tex.; mem.: FBA, ABA (co-divsn. dir. litigation sect. 1996—98, co-chair ADR com. 1994—95, mem. coun. 1998—2001, bus. and litigation joint task force on bankruptcy practice 1994—98), Am. Law Inst., Houston Bar Found. (trustee), Phi Beta Kappa. Office: US Courthouse 515 Rusk St Ste 9015 Houston TX 77002-2605

ATLAS, SCOTT JEROME, lawyer; b. Austin, Tex., Jan. 15, 1950; s. Morris and Rita Jean (Willner) A.; m. Nancy Ellen Friedman, Mar. 26, 1983; 2 children. BA magna cum laude, Yale U., 1971; JD with honors, U. Tex., 1975. Bar: Tex. 1975, U.S. Dist. Ct. (so. dist.) Tex. 1976, U.S. Ct. Appeals (5th cir.) 1976, U.S. Supreme Ct. 1979, U.S. Ct. Appeals (11th cir.) 1981, U.S. Dist. Ct. (we, no. and ea. dists). Law clk. to judge U.S. Ct. Appeals (5th cir.), Austin, 1975—76; assoc. Vinson & Elkins, Houston, 1976—82, ptnr., 1982—. Mem. bd. visitors U. Tex. Law Sch., 1982-90; mem. Chancellors Coun. U. Tex., exec. com., 2001-; mem. Com. of 125, U. Tex., Austin, 2003--; lectr. numerous law schs. and legal orgns. Chancellor, Coif, editor-in-chief Tex. Law Rev.; contbr. numerous articles to profl. jours. Founding pres. Houston Shakespeare Festival, 1980-82; v.p., co-founder Tex. Lyceum Assn. Inc., 1983-85; exec. com. Alley Theatre, Houston, 1983—, ex-officio, 1989—; bd. dirs. ADL S.W. Region, 1998—, exec. com., 1999-, v.p., 2001—; past bd. dirs. Tex. Opera Theatre, Cultural Arts Coun. of Houston, Young Audiences Houston, others; county coord. U.S. Sen. Lloyd M. Bentsen, 1987-92; mem. adv. com. Law Firm Pro Bono Project, 1991-, chmn., 1997-2001. Named One of Outstanding Young Houstonians, Jaycees, 1984-85, One of Outstanding Young Tex. Exes, Tex. Ex-Students Assn., 1989, Outstanding Young Lawyer in Houston, Houston Young Lawyers Assn., 1984, Azteca Civil Rights award, Lulac Dist. XVIII, 1993, Lawyer of the Yr., Mexican-ABA Tex., 1996, spl. recognition for contbns. to cross-border relationships Tex.-Mex. Bar Assn., 1997, Pub. Interest award Tex. Law Fellowship, 1998, ADL Karen Susman Jurisprudence award, 2002. Fellow Houston Bar Found. (founder, life), Tex. Bar Found. (life), Am. Bar Found. (life); mem. ABA (chmn. litig. sect. 2002-03, chmn. appellate practice com. litigation sect. 1985-89, coun. mem. litigation sect. 1989-92, exec. com. 1992-96, standing com. on pro bono and pub. svc. 1995-98, co-chair strategic planning implementation task force litigation sect. 1996-97, dir. divns. litigation sect. 1997-98, co-chair fed. practice task force litigation sect. 1998-2000, liaison to civil adv. com. jud. conf. on rules of practice and procedure 1998-2000, planning com. mem. London 2000 meeting 1996-2000, working group on UCITA 2001-2002, task force on advocacy for the assn. and profession 2002-2003, Pro Bono Publico award 1986), State Bar Tex. (jud. selection funding com. 1985-87, liaison with law schs. 1988-90, legal aid to indigent com. 1986, numerous coms. 1986-87), Alliance for Jud. Funding (bd. dirs. 1992-95, 2003—), Tex. Law Rev. Assn. (past pres., bd. dirs. 1977-95, Leon Green award 1997), U. Tex. Ex-Students Assn. (exec. coun. 1992-98), Houston Bar Assn. (vol. lawyers program bd. 1998-2000), Houston U. Tex. Ex-Students Assn. (bd. dirs. 1991-92), Yale U. Alumni Club (class sec. 1991-96, coun. 1986-87, local dir. 1982-89, 90-91). Avocations: golf, books. Office: Vinson & Elkins LLP 1001 Fannin St Ste 2300 Houston TX 77002-6760 E-mail: satlas@velaw.com.

ATLAS, TERRY, journalist; b. Washington, 1952; BA in Econs. and Polit. Sci., U. Rochester, 1974. Energy reporter Chgo. Tribune, Washington, 1978—83, Washington corr., 1983—86, chief diplomatic corr., Washington bur., 1986—97, Washington news editor, 1997—99; asst. mng. editor (nation and world) U.S. News & World Report, Washington, 1999—. Named Bagehot fellow, Columbia U., 1976—77. Office: 1050 Thomas Jefferson St NW Washington DC 20007-3837

ATLASS, THEODORE BRUCE, lawyer, educator; b. Chgo., June 2, 1951; s. Ralph Louis Atlass and Opal Jeanne Collins. BSBA, U. Denver, 1972; JD, DePaul U., 1975; LLM, U. Miami, Coral Gables, Fla., 1976. Bar: Colo. 1975, U.S. Tax Ct. 1976, U.S. Supreme Ct. 1982. Shareholder Theodore B. Atlass, P.C., Denver, 1976-83, Atlass Profl. Corp., Denver, 1986—; ptnr. Welborn, Dufford, Brown & Tooley, Denver, 1983-85. Lectr. Colo. Soc. CPAs, 1977—, Coll. Law U. Denver, 1976—. Chmn. Advanced Estate Planning Symposium U. Denver, 1982—; bd. dirs. St. Joseph Hosp. Found., Denver, 1982-97, Colo. Ballet, Denver, 1985-92. Fellow Am. Coll. Tax Counsel, Am. Coll. Trust & Estate Counsel (Colo. state chair 1996-2001; fiduciary income tax com. chair 1997-2000); mem. Denver Estate Planning Coun. (pres. 1991-92), Denver Tax Assn. (pres. 1985), Centennial Estate Planning Coun. (pres. 1993-94). Republican. Presbyterian. Office: Atlass Profl Corp Ste 100 3665 Cherry Creek North Dr Denver CO 80209-3712

ATREYA, SUSHIL KUMAR, planetary-space science educator, astrophysicist; b. Apr. 15, 1946; came to U.S., 1966, naturalized, 1975; s. Harvansh Lal and Kailash Vati (Sharma) A.; 1 child, Chloë E. ScB, U. Rajasthan, India, 1963, MSc, 1965; MS, Yale U., 1968; PhD, U. Mich., 1973. Rsch. assoc. physics U. Pitts., 1973-74; asst., then assoc. rsch. scientist U. Mich., Ann Arbor, 1974-78, ast. prof., 1978-81, assoc. prof. atmospheric sci., 1981-87, prof. atmospheric and space sci., 1987—, dir. planetary sci. lab. Assoc. prof. U. Paris, 1984-85, vis. prof., 2000, 01; vis. sr. rsch. scientist Imperial Coll., London, 1984; mem. sci. and exptl. team Cassini-Huygens Probe to Saturn-Titan, Galileo Jupiter Probe, Nozomi Japanese Mars Mission, Mars Express Mission, Russian Mars '96 and Soviet Phobos projects, Voyager spacecraft missions to the giant planets, Comet Rendezvous/Asteroid Flyby, 1986-92, and SpaceLab I; guest observer/investigator on Hubble Space Telescope, Internat. Ultraviolet Spectrometer and Copernicus Orbiting Astron. Obs.; mem. sci. working groups NASA, Jet Propulsion Lab., European Space Agy. Author: Atmospheres and Ionospheres of the Outer Planets and their Satellites, 1986; editor: Planetary Aeronomy and Astronomy, 1981, Outer Planets, 1989, Cometary Environments, 1989, Origin and Evolution of Planetary and Satellite Atmospheres, 1989; contbr. numerous articles to books and profl. jours. Recipient NASA award for exceptional sci. contbns. Voyager Project, 1981, NASA Group Achievement award for Voyager Ultraviolet Spectrometer Investigations, 1981, 86, 90, NASA Group Achievement awards for Galileo Probe Mass Spectrometer experiment, and for Significant Outstanding Contbns. to the Galileo Probe and Orbiter to Jupiter, Excellence in Rsch. award U. Mich. Coll. Engring., 1995. Mem. AAAS, Internat. Assn. Meteorology and Atmospheric Scis. (pres. commn. planetary atmospheres and their evolution 1987-95, sec. 1983-87), Am. Geophys. Union (assoc. editor Geophys. Rsch. Letters jour. 1986-89), Internat. Astron. Union, Am. Astron. Soc., Internat. Acad. Astronautics (academician 1993—). Office: Space Rsch Bldg Univ Mich Ann Arbor MI 48109-2143

ATSADA, CHAIYANAM, diplomat; Rep. to UN Govt. of Thailand, N.Y.C., 1997—. Office: Permanent Mission Thailand to UN 351 E 52nd St New York NY 10022-6302

ATTAL, GENE (FRED EUGENE ATTAL), hospital executive; b. Oct. 6, 1947; s. Sam Arthur and Olga (Johns) A.; m. Marsha Ablah, July 26, 1970; children: Christopher, Allison, Anne. BJ with spl. honors, U. Tex., 1970; MS, Columbia U., 1972. Pub. rels. exec. Westinghouse Electric Corp.; sr. v.p. fund devel. Seton Healthcare Network, 1975—; pres. Seton Fund, Austin, 1975—. Mem. faculty U. Tex. Recipient Telstar Excellence in Comm. award, annually, 1978-81, Arthur W. Page award U. Tex., 1986; NDEA fellow in langs. U. Tex., 1968-69, Internat. fellow Columbia U., 1972. Mem. Am. Soc. Hosp. Pub. Rels. (regional dir.), Assn. Healthcare Philanthropy (internat. bd. dirs., chair bd. dirs. 2000-01), Tex. Soc. Hosp. Pub. Rels. (pres. 1981), Barton Creek Country Club. Greek Orthodox. Home: 1201 Constant Springs Dr Austin TX 78746-6615 Office: 1201 W 38th St Austin TX 78705-1006

ATTAWAY, FRITZ EDWARD EDWARD, lawyer; b. Detroit, July 12, 1946; s. Bert Frederick and Lorraine Marie (Distler) Attaway; m. E. Pembrooke Cartwright, June 18, 1976. BA, Coll. of Idaho, 1968; JD, U. Chgo., 1973. Bar: Idaho 1973, DC 1978, US Dist. Ct. Idaho 1973, US Ct. Appeals (DC cir.) 1979, US Supreme Ct. 1978. Atty., adv. FCC, Washington, 1973—75; counsel Motion Picture Assn. Am., Washington, 1976—78; v.p., counsel, 1978—; mem. US Trade Rep. Svc. Policy Adv. Com.; Bd. dir. and officer Am. Copyright Council, 1986. Served spl. forces U.S. Army, 1968—70. Mem.: Fed. Comm. Bar Assn., Motion Picture Export Assn. Am. (v.p.). Republican.

ATTEBERY, LOUIE WAYNE, English language educator, folklorist; b. Weiser, Idaho, Aug. 14, 1927; s. John Thomas Attebery and Tressie Mae (Blevins) Attebery Miller; m. Barbara Phyllis Olson, Dec. 31, 1947; children: Bobby Lou, Brian Leonard. BA, Albertson Coll. of Idaho, 1950; MA, U. Mont., 1951; PhD, U. Denver, 1961. Tchr. Middleton (Idaho) H.S., 1949-50, Payette (Idaho) H.S., 1951-52, Nyssa (Oreg.) H.S., 1952-55, East H.S., Denver, 1955-61; prof. English Albertson Coll. Idaho, Caldwell, 1961-99, holder Eyck-Berringer chair English, 1987-98, acting acad. v.p., 1983-84; pres. West Shore Press, 1998—. Vis. fellow Harvard U., Cambridge, Mass., 1993-94. Author: The College of Idaho, 1981-91, A Centennial History, 1991, Sheep May Safely Graze: A Personal Essay on Tradition and A Contemporary Sheep Ranch, 1993, The Most of What We Spend, 1998, Albertson College of Idaho: The Second Hundred Years, 1999, J.R. Simplot: A Billion the Hard Way, 2000; editor: Idaho Folklife: Homesteads to Headstones, 1985; editor Northwest Folklore, 1985-91; gen. editor U. Idaho Northwest Folklife series, 1991—. Trustee Idaho Hist. Soc., 1984-91, Albertson Coll. Idaho, 2003—. With USN, 1945-46. Bruern fellow, U. Leeds, Eng., 1971—72. Mem. Western Lit. Assn. (exec coun. 1964-65), Assn. Lit. Scholars and Critics, 1995—. Methodist. E-mail: lattebery@albertson.edu.

ATTENBOROUGH, BARON RICHARD SAMUEL, actor, producer, director, goodwill ambassador; b. Cambridge, England, Aug. 29, 1923; s. Frederick Attenborough; m. Sheila Beryl Grant Sim; 3 children. Leverhulme scholar to Royal Acad. Dramatic Art, 1941 (Bancroft Medal); DLitt (hon.), U. Leicester, 1970, U. Kent, 1981, U. Sussex, 1987; DCL (hon.), U. Newcastle, 1974; LLD (hon.), Dickinson Coll., 1983; DLit (hon.), Am. Internat. U., 1994; DLitt (hon.), Cape Town, 2000. Fleming Meml. lectr. R.T.S., 1989; Cameron Mackintosh vis. prof. of theatre Oxford U., 1996; pro-chancellor U. Sussex, 1970-98, chancellor 1998—. First stage appearance as Richard Miller in Ah, Wilderness, Intimate Theatre, Palmers Green, 1941; Ralph Berger in Awake and Sing, Arts (West End debut), 1942; The Little Foxes, Piccadilly, 1942; Brighton Rock, Garrick, 1943. Joined RAF 1943; seconded to RAF Film Unit for Journey Together, 1944; demobilised, 1946. Returned to stage in The Way Back (Home of the Brave), Westminster, 1949; To Dorothy a Son, Savoy, 1950, Garrick, 1951; Sweet Madness, Vaudeville, 1952; The Mousetrap, Ambassadors, 1952-54; Double Image, Savoy, 1956-57, St. James's, 1957; The Rape of the Belt, Piccadilly, 1957-58; film appearances: In Which We Serve (screen debut), 1942; School for Secrets, The Man Within, Dancing With Crime, Brighton Rock, London Belongs to Me, The Guinea Pig, The Lost People, Boys in Brown, Morning Departure, Hell is Sold Out, The Magic Box, Gift Horse, Father's Doing Fine, Eight O'Clock Walk, The Ship That Died of Shame, Private's Progress, The Baby and the Battleship, Brothers in Law, The Scamp, Dunkirk, The Man Upstairs, Sea of Sand, Danger Within, I'm All Right Jack, Jet Storm, SOS Pacific; The Angry Silence (also co-prod.), 1959; The League of Gentlemen, 1960; Only Two Can Play, All Night Long, 1961; The Dock Brief, The Great Escape, 1962; Seance On a Wet Afternoon (also prod., Best Actor, San Sebastian Film Festival and Brit. Film Acad.), The Third Secret, 1963; Guns at Batasi (Best Actor, Brit. Film Acad.), 1964; The Flight of the Phoenix, 1965; The Sand Pebbles (Hollywood Golden Globe), 1966; Dr. Dolittle (Hollywood Golden Globe), The Bliss of Mrs. Blossom, 1967; Only When I Larf, 1968; The Last Grenade, A Severed Head, David Copperfield, Loot, 1969; 10 Rillington Place, 1970; And Then There Were None, Rosebud, Brannigan, Conduct Unbecoming, 1974; The Chess Players, 1977; The Human Factor, 1979, Jurassic Park, 1992, Miracle on 34th St., 1994, The Lost World, 1997, Elizabeth, 1998, The Passer, (voice), 1998, Puckoon, 2002; producer: Whistle Down the Wind, 1961; The L-Shaped Room, 1962; producer, dir.: Oh! What a Lovely War (16 Internat. Awards including Hollywood Golden Globe and BAFTA UN Award), 1968; dir.: Young Winston (Hollywood Golden Globe), 1972; A Bridge Too Far (Evening News Best Drama Award), 1976; Magic, 1978; producer, dir.: Gandhi (8 Oscars, 5 Brit. Acad. TV and Film Artists Awards, 5 Hollywood Golden Globes, Dirs.' Guild of Am. Award for Outstanding Directorial Achievement), 1980-81, Cry Freedom (Berlinale Kamera, BFI award tech. achievement), 1987, Chaplin, 1992, Shadowlands, 1992 (Alexander Korda award for outstanding Brit. film of yr., BAFTA), In Love and War, 1997, Grey Owl, 1998; publications: In Search of Gandhi, 1982, Richard Attenborough's A Chorus Line (with Diana Carter), 1986, Cry Freedom, A Pictorial Record, 1987; actor: Light Keeps Me Company (Europe), 2000, TheRailway Children, 2000 (TV), Joseph and the Amazing Technicolor Dreamcoat, 2000. Goodwill amb. UNICEF, 1987—; mem. Brit. Actors' Equity Assoc. Council, 1949-73, Cinematograph Films Council, 1967-73, Arts Council of Great Britain, 1970-73; formed Beaver Films with Bryan Forbes, 1959, Allied Film Makers, 1960; dir. Chelsea Football Club, 1969-82, life v.p., 1993—; dir. Young Vic, 1974-84; chmn. The Actor's Charitable Trust, 1956-88, pres., 1988—; chmn. European Script Fund, 1988-96, hon. pres., 1996—, Combined Theatrical Charities Appeals Council, 1964-88, pres., 1988—; chmn. Brit. Acad. TV and Film Artists (v.p. from 1971-94, chmn. trustees, 1970—), 1969-70, Royal Acad. Dramatic Art, mem. council 1963—, chmn., 1972—, Capital Radio, 1972-92, life pres., 1992—, Help a London Child, 1975—; trustee King George V Fund for Actors and Actresses, 1973—; chmn. U.K. Trustees Waterford-Kamhlaba Sch., Swaziland (gov. 1987—), 1976—, Duke of York's Theatre, 1979-92, Brit. Film Inst., 1981-92, Goldcrest Films & TV, 1982-87, Com. of Inquiry into the Arts and Disabled People, 1983-85, Channel Four TV (dep. chmn. 1980-86), 1987-92, Brit. Screen Adv. Council, 1987—; Gov. Nat. Film Sch., 1970-81, 96, hon. pres. 96; pres. Muscular Dystrophy Group of Great Britain (v.p. 1962-71), 1971-96, hon. pres. 1996—; pres. The Gandhi Found., 1983—, Brighton Festival, 1984-95, Brit. Film Yr., 1984-86; trustee Tate Gallery, 1976-82, 94-96, Tate Found., 1986—, Found. Sport and Arts, 1991—; pres. Arts for Health, 1989—, Gardner Centre Arts, Sussex U., 1990—; gov. Motability, 1977—; patron Kingsley Hall Community Ctr., 1982—; R.A. Centre Disability & Arts, Leicester, 1990—. Decorated Commander Brit. Empire, 1967, Knighted 1976; recipient Evening Std. Film award, 40 yrs. svc. to Brit. Cinema, 1983, Praemium Imperiale award, 1998, Martin Luther King Jr. Peace Prize, 1983, Padma Bhushan, India, 1983, award of merit for humanitarianism in film making, European Film awards, 1988, Shakespeare prize Outstanding Contbn. European culture, 1992; named Commandeur, Ordre des Arts et des Lettres, France, 1985; Chevalier, Order de la Legion d'Honneur, France, 1988; named Freeman of City of Leicester, 1990; named fellow Kings Coll. London, 1993; named Baron, Life Peer of Long Borough of Richmond upon Thames, 1993; recipient hon. fellowship U. Wales, Bangor, 1997, Manchester Poly., 1994, Kings Coll., 1993. Fellow BAFTA, Brit. Film Inst.; mem. Garrick Club, Beefsteak Club. Avocations: collecting paintings and sculpture, listening to music, watching football. Home: Old Friars Richmond Green Surrey England Office: Richard Attenborough Prodns Twickenham Studio Saint Margaret's Middlesex TW1 2AW England*

ATTERBURY, ROBERT RENNIE, III, retired lawyer; b. Englewood, N.J., July 11, 1937; s. Robert Rennie Jr. and Beatrice May (Tether) A.; m. Lynda Duer Smith, Sept. 14, 1963; children: Stockton Ward, Kendall C. B. BA, U. Pa., 1960, LLB, 1963. Bar: N.Y. 1963, Ill. 1966. Assoc. Donovan, Leisure, Newton & Irvine, N.Y.C., 1963-66; atty. Caterpillar Tractor Co., Peoria, Ill., 1966-73; sr. atty. Caterpillar Overseas S.A., Geneva, Switzland, 1973-78; gen. atty. Caterpillar Tractor Co., Peoria, 1978-83; assoc. gen. counsel Caterpillar Inc., Peoria, 1983-91, v.p., sec., gen. counsel, 1991—2002. Mem. planning com. Ray Garrett Jr. Corp. and Securities Law Inst., Chgo.; mem. steering com. Civil Justice Reform Group; mem. adv. bd. Southwestern Legal Found., Internat. and Comparative Law Ctr.; mem. adv. coun. Asia/Pacific Ctr. for Resolution of Internat. Bus. Disputes, San Francisco, corp. exec. bd., gen. counsel roundtable; mem. Mfrs. Alliance Law Coun. I., Arlington, Va., 1992-98, vice chair, 1998-99, chair, 1999; mem. The Forum for U.S.-European Union Legal-Econ. Affairs, Boston, large law dept. coun.; mem. corp. counsel com. Nat. Ctr. for State Cts.; mem. adv. bd. Georgetown U. Law Ctr. Corp. Cousel Inst.; dir. Ill Equal Justice Found.; trustee Eureka Coll. Bd. dirs. Lakeview Mus. Arts and Scis., 1995—98, vice chmn., 1998—99, chmn., 1999—2001; bd. dirs., sec. Lakeview Mus. Found.; bd. dirs. Prairie State Legal Svcs. Mem. SAR, Am. Judicature Soc. (dir. 1998), Am. Corp. Counsel Assn., Am. Soc. Corp. Secs., Assn. Gen. Counsel, Country Club Peoria (dir.), Rotary.

ATTIA, ALAN LAWRENCE, physician; b. N.Y.C., June 29, 1963; BA, Wesleyan U., 1985; MD, Columbia U., 1990. Diplomate Am. Bd. Internal Medicine, Am. Bd. Gastroenterology. Intern St. Lukes Roosevelt Hosp. Ctr., N.Y.C., 1990-91, resident, 1991-93, fellow, 1993-95, assoc. staff, 1995—; dir. med. info. St. Luke's Roosevlet Hosp. Ctr., N.Y.C., 2000—; assoc. staff Columbia P&S, 1995—. Office: 350 W 58th St New York NY 10019-1804 E-mail: lattia@slrhc.org.

ATTIG, JOHN CLARE, secondary education educator, consultant; b. Chgo., Apr. 2, 1936; s. Clare McKinley and Elsie Bertha (Nagel) A.; m. Harriet Jane Rinehart, June 13, 1959; children: Laura, Victoria. BA, DePauw U., 1958; MA, U. Chgo., 1961. Cert. tchr., Calif. Social studies tchr. Lyons Twp. H.S., LaGrange, Ill., 1961-65, Henry Gunn H.S., Palo Alto, Calif., 1965-72, 78-98;

univ. faculty assoc. Simon Fraser U., Burnaby, Canada, 1972-73; social studies tchr. Jordan Jr. H.S., Palo Alto, 1973-75, Cubberley Sr. H.S., Palo Alto, 1975-78. Lectr., demonstrator, pub. simulation games for classes in history and govt. various univs. and sch. dists. in U.S. and Can. Author: College in Three Years: Stop Wasting Time and Money, 2002, numerous simulation games; contbr. numerous articles to profl. jours. With USAR, 1958-64. NEH fellow, 1983, 87, 89, Tchr. fellow St. Andrews U., Scotland, 1993. Mem. NEH (project dir. Masterworks Seminar 1991), Western History Assn. Methodist. Avocations: travel, reading, wine. E-mail: jnhattig@efn.org.

ATTIYEH, RICHARD EUGENE, economics educator; b. Bklyn., Oct. 8, 1937; s. Semeer Mathew and Dorothy (Krentz) A.; m. Jessica Falikman, July 20, 1958; children: Michael Richard, Amy Lauren, Gregory Moss. BA, Williams Coll., 1958; PhD, Yale U., 1966. Staff economist Pres.'s Council of Econ. Advisers, Washington, 1961-62; asst. prof. econs. Stanford U., Palo Alto, Calif., 1962-64, Yale U., New Haven, 1964-67; from assoc. prof. to prof. U. Calif.-San Diego, La Jolla, 1967—, dean grad. studies and research, 1982-94, vice chancellor for rsch., dean grad. studies, 1994—, interim sr. vice chancellor acad. affairs, 1996-97. Mem. Grad. Record Examinations Bd., 1987-92, chmn., 1990; bd. dirs. Coun. Grad. Schs., 1990-93, chmn., 1992. Mem. Am. Econ. Assn., Assn. Grad. Schs. (pres. 1996), Calif. Biomed. Rsch. Assn. (bd. chmn. 1997-99), Calif. Soc. for Biomed. Rsch. (treas. 1998-99). Office: U Calif San Diego Office Grad Studies La Jolla CA 92093 E-mail: rattiyeh@ucsd.edu.

ATTLESON, ADRIANA LEE, mathematics educator; d. Rodney and Irene Vellinga; m. Sjur Richard Attleson, June 15, 1968; children: Ross, Ryan, Laura. BA in Math Edn., U. No. Iowa, 1967; MS in Higher Edn., Iowa State U., 1985. Cert. Iowa Dept. Edn. Math. tchr. jr. high sch. Walled Lake (Mich.) Cmty. Schs., 1967—68, Mason City (Iowa) Cmty. Schs., 1968—70; instr. math. North Iowa Area C.C., Mason City, 1981—. Elder 1st Presbyn. Ch., Mason City, 2000—02. Avocations: reading, quilting. Home: 30 Kentucky Ct Mason City IA 50401 Office: N Iowa Area CC 500 College Dr Mason City IA 50401 Business E-Mail: attleadr@niacc.edu.

ATTOLE, MARY BERTHA, writer; b. Lafayette, La., Dec. 12, 1958; d. Antoine and Elia Guillory Attole. Student, So. U., Baton Rouge, La., 1976—80. Tchr.'s aide Glendale Elem., Eunice, La., 1980—82; mem. staff Fred's Dept. Store, Eunice, 1983—85, John's IGA Grocery Store, Eunice, 1985—88. Author: My Brother's Keeper, 2001. Vol. So. Poverty Law Ctr.'s Civil Rights Meml. Visitors Ctr. Walle of Tolerance, St. Matilda Cth. Ch., Eunice, 1991—. Mem.: Alpha Mu Gamma. Democrat. Roman Catholic. Avocations: reading, genealogy, comedy, classic television, pets. Home: 310 N Martin Luther King Dr Eunice LA 70535

ATTRIDGE, DANIEL F. lawyer; b. Washington, Oct. 4, 1954; s. Patrick and Teresa A.; m. Anne Asbill, Aug. 23, 1980; children: James, William, and Thomas. BA magna cum laude, U. Pa., 1976; JD cum laude, Georgetown U., 1979. Bar: D.C. 1980, U.S. Dist. Ct. D.C. 1980, U.S. Ct. Appeals (D.C. cir.) 1980, U.S. Supreme Ct. 1983, U.S. Dist. Ct. Md. 1985, U.S. Ct. Appeals (fed. cir.) 1985, U.S. Ct. Appeals (2d.cir.) 1987, U.S. Ct. Claims 1988, U.S. Ct. Appeals (4th and 6th cirs.) 1990, U.S. Ct. Appeals (8th cir.) 1997, U.S. Ct. Appeals (1st cir.) 2000. Law clk. to judge Oliver Gasch U.S. Dist. Ct. D.C., Washington, 1979-80; assoc. Kirkland & Ellis, Washington, 1980-85, ptnr., 1985—. Faculty Nat. Inst. Trial Advocacy, 1991—. Exec. editor Georgetown U. Law Jour., 1978-79. Fellow Am. Bar Found.; mem. ABA (vice chmn. antitrust sect. Sherman Act sect. 2 com. 1999-2002), D.C. Bar Assn. (bd. govs. 1996-99, co-chair litigation sect. 1993-96). Roman Catholic. Home: 1249 Cherry Tree Ln Annapolis MD 21403-5023 Office: Kirkland & Ellis 655 15th St NW Fl 12 Washington DC 20005-5793 E-mail: daniel_attridge@kirkland.com.

ATTRIDGE, RICHARD BYRON, lawyer; b. Atlanta, Oct. 14, 1933; s. Archibald Angus and Katherine Elizabeth (Babb) A.; m. Florence Law, Dec. 14, 1963; children: Anne Habersham, Elizabeth Barnes, R. Byron Jr. BA, Princeton U., 1955; LLB, Emory U., 1961. Bar: Ga. 1960. Ptnr. King & Spalding, Atlanta, 1960—. Chmn. State Bd. of Bar Examiners, Ga., 1978-83. Vice chmn. Cmty. Rels. Com., Atlanta, 1968-73; various local charities; vestry Episc. Ch. 1st lt. U.S. Army, 1956-57. Fellow Am. Coll. Trial Lawyers; mem. ABA, State Bar Ga. (bd. govs. 1974-83), Atlanta Bar Assn. (pres. 1971-72), Lawyers Club Atlanta, Capital City Club (bd. dirs. 1989—), Piedmont Driving Club. Avocations: hunting, fishing, tennis. Home: 2820 Habersham Rd NW Atlanta GA 30305-2959 Office: King & Spalding 191 Peachtree St NE Ste 40 Atlanta GA 30303-1740

ATTWOOD, DAVID THOMAS, physicist, educator; b. N.Y.C., Aug. 15, 1941; s. David Thomas and Josephine (Banks) A.; divorced; children: Timothy David, Courtney Catherine, Kevin Richard; m. Linda Jean Geniesse, Aug. 3, 1991. BS, Hofstra U., 1963; MS, Northwestern U., 1964; D Engring. Sci., NYU, 1972. Physicist Lawrence Livermore Nat. Lab., Livermore, Calif., 1972-83, Lawrence Berkeley Nat. Lab., Berkeley, Calif., 1983—; sci. dir. Advanced Light Source, 1985—88; prof. in residence dept. elec. engring. and computer sci. U. Calif., Berkeley, 1989—, founding chair applied sci. and tech. PhD program. Founder Ctr. for X-Ray Optics, Lawrence Berkeley Lab., 1983; assoc. dir. NSF EUV Sci. Tech. Ctr., 2003—. Author: Soft X-Rays and Extreme Ultraviolet Radiation: Principles and Applications, 1999; editor: (with B.L. Henke) X-Ray Diagnostics, (with J. Bokor) Short Wavelength Coherent Radiation, (with F. Zernike) Extreme Ultraviolet Lithography, (with W. Meyer-Ilse and T. Warwick) X-Ray Microscopy; reviewer numerous sci. jours.; contbr. numerous articles to profl. publs. Fellow: Optical Soc. Am.; mem.: AAAS, Am. Phys. Soc. Achievements include research on x-ray optics and microscopy, extreme ultraviolet lithography, synchrotron radiation, partially coherent x-rays, and laser-plasma interactions. Office: Lawrence Berkeley Nat Lab Ctr X-ray Optics Berkeley CA 94720

ATTYGALLE, ATHULA BUDDHAGOSHA, chemist, researcher; b. Galle, Sri Lanka, June 3, 1950; came to U.S., 1989; s. Peter and Chandra (Wijesekera) A.; m. Miho Yamakawa; children: Suneth, Anjali. BSc, U. Ceylon, Sri Lanka, 1975; MSc, U. Sri. Lanka, 1977; postgrad. diploma, Tokyo Inst. Tech., 1979; PhD, U. Keele, Eng., 1983. Rsch. fellow U. Erlangen, Germany, 1984-87, 88-89; vis. asst. prof. U. Houston, 1987-88; vis. assoc. prof. Cornell U., Ithaca, NY, 1989-90, sr. rsch. assoc., 1990—2001, dir. mass spectrometry facility, 1992—2001; prof. chemistry Stevens Inst. Tech., Hoboken, NJ, 2001—. Patentee in field. U.S. Agy. for Internat. Devel. grantee, 1992-96. Fellow Alexander von Humboldt Found.; mem. Am. Chem. Soc. Home: 113 Coy Glen Rd Ithaca NY 14850-5009 Office: Stevens Inst Tech Dept Chemistry and Chem Biology Castle Point on Hudson Hoboken NJ 07030 E-mail: aattygal@stevens-tech.edu.

ATWATER, JOHN BANCROFT, physician; b. Ocean, N.Y., Aug. 25, 1929; s. Reginald Meyers and Charlotte Martin (Penfield) A.; m. Leah Janet Cannon, May 24, 1954 children: Andrew, Richard, David. BA, Oberlin Coll., 1951; MD, Yale U., 1955; MPH, Johns Hopkins U., 1959, Dr PH, 1960. Intern in pediatrics Yale-New Haven Hosp., 1955-56; resident in pub. health Md. State Dept. Health, 1956-57; city health officer City of Trenton (N.J.), 1960-62; city health dir. City of New Haven (Conn.), 1962-73; pub. health dir. Washtenaw County, Ann Arbor, 1973-89. Adj. prof. health U. Mich., Ann Arbor, 1973-90; UN vol. Sierra Leone, West Africa, 1992-94; cons. in field. Fellow Am. Pub. Health Assn. (sect. chmn. 1971), Rotary (Paul Harris fellow). Avocation: biking. Home: 1132 Aberdeen Dr Ann Arbor MI 48104-2812 E-mail: jbatwater@compuserve.com.

ATWATER, JULIE DEMERS, critical care nurse; b. Santa Maria, Calif., Aug. 29, 1945; d. Julian G. and Luella M. (Drown) Demers; m. Roy Michael Atwater, Jan. 29, 1977; children: Michael J. Kawecki, Joel M. LPN, Fanny Allen Sch. for Practical Nursing, Winooski, Vt., 1967; ADN, Weber State Coll., Ogden, Utah, 1982, BS in Allied Health, 1987, BSN, 1989. Lic. practical nurse, Vt., Mass., N.H., RN Utah, CCRN, cert. trauma nurse, ENPC. Practical nurse Brattleboro (Vt.) Meml. Hosp.; practical nurse ICU, Cooley Dickerson Hosp., Northampton, Mass., Cheshire Meml. Hosp., Keene, N.H.; clin. nurse ICU/CCU Evanston (Wyo.) Regional Hosp., 1978-87; clin. nurse VA Hosp., Salt Lake City, 1985-87; critical care nurse McKay Dee Hosp., Ogden, Utah, 1978-92, level IV nurse, 1989-92, clin. head nurse ICU, 1992-95, critical care svc. line shift coord., 1995-97, emergency rm. nurse, 1997—. Com. mem. ICU and Heart Right Group, mem. ICU adv. com. and critical care re-engring. com., 1992-95, organized move to new hosp. location com., 2002, organ donor liason, 1982—, trauma com., 1982-97, express admit pilot program, 2000-01, staff nurse, mgmt. team, 2002—, hosp. ethics com., 1998-. Recipient Utah Critical Care Nurse of Yr. award, 1991; named Emer. Room Nurse of Yr., 2000. Mem. AACN, No. Utah AACN, Emergency Nurses Assn. Home: 3191 S 3500 W Taylor UT 84401-9624 E-mail: Juliedka@aol.com.

ATWATER, MARY MONROE, science educator; b. Roswell, N.Mex., July 26, 1947; d. John C. and Helen (Wallace) Monroe; children: Helena A., Jonathen A. BS magna cum laude, Meth. Coll., 1969; MA, U. N.C., 1972; PhD, N.C. State U., 1980. Nat. sci. coord. Fayetteville (N.C.) State U., 1975-77; teaching asst. dept. maths. and sci. N.C. State U., Raleigh, 1977-79, rsch. asst., 1977-79; assoc. dir. N.Mex. State U., Las Cruces, 1980-83; asst. prof., program dir. sci., maths., tech. edn. Atlanta U., 1984-87, assoc. prof. and program dir. sci., math., tech. edn., 1987; asst. prof. dept. sci. edn. U. Ga., Athens, 1987-92, assoc. prof. dept. sci. edn., 1993-97, prof., 1997—. Vis. assoc. prof. Cornell U., 1993; adj. prof. Atlanta U., 1987-88; mem. rev. com. NSF, 1993, cons., 1994, Harvard-Smithsonian Ctr. Astrophysics, 1993, N.Y. Biology Network Workship, 1993, ABT Assocs., Inc., 1993, NSF, U.S. Dept. Edn.; mem. adv. com. World Book Publ., 1993; presenter at numerous convs., speaker in field. Co-editor Multicultural Edn.: Inclusion of All, 1994; contbr. chpts. to books; contbr. numerous articles to profl. jours. Cons. Sci. Edn. in Mich. Schs., 1990-91; elem. sci. curriculum guide project Ga. Dept. Edn., 1988-90; judge numerous internat., state, local sci. fairs, 1978-96. Recipient Herbert Lehman Edn. Fund award, 1965, NSTA OHAUS award for innovations in four-yr. coll. tchg., 1990, Coll. Edn. and Psychology Disting. Alumnus award N.C. State U., 1996, Top Minority Women in the Scis. award Nat. Tech. Assn., 1998, African-Am. Phenomenal Women award African-Am. Profl. Women of Athens Area, 1999; numerous rsch. grants; Lily Tchg. fellow, 1989; inducted into Acad. Top Women Sci. & Engring. Nat. Tech. Assn., 1998 Fellow AAAS; mem. ASCD, Am. Chem. Soc., Am. Edn. Rsch. Assn., Assn. Edn. Tchrs. in Sci., Assn. Tchr. Edn., Ga. Sci. Tchrs. Assn. (pres.), Nat. Assn. Multicultural Edn., Nat. Assn. Rsch. in Sci. Tchg., Southeastern Assn. Edn. Tchrs. in Sci., South African Assn. for Rsch. in Math. and Sci. Edn., Phi Beta Delta, Phi Delta Kappa (Warren Finley Rsch. award 1996). Office: U Ga 212 Alderhold Hall Athens GA 30602-7126

ATWATER, PHYLLIS T. municipal administrator; b. Memphis, Nov. 4, 1947; d. Jeff D. and Thelda E. A.; m. John R. Ernst, Dec. 28, 1972. BA, Vassar Coll., 1968; MA, Boston U., 1970; postgrad., New Sch. Soc. Rsch., N.Y.C., 1974-82. Lectr. math. Tufts U., Medford, Mass., 1970-72; instr. math. higher edn. program Boston Model Cities Adminstrn., 1970-74, coord. program, 1971; instr. econs. SUNY, Old Westbury, N.Y., 1977-82; dep. dir. adminstrn. and fin. Divsn. Solid Waste Mgmt., Commonwealth of Mass., 1984-88; pres. and chief operating officer Recoverable Resources/R2B2, Inc., Bronx, N.Y., 1989-91; dir. divsn. waste N.Y. State Dept. Environ. Conservation, 1992-93, regional dir., 1993-95; pvt. practice computer svcs. cons., 1995-99; data adminstr. N.Y.C. Dept. Employment, N.Y.C., 1999—2002, assoc. commr. for info. tech. and adminstrn., 2002—03; assoc. commr. N.Y. Dept. Small Bus. Svcs., 2003—. Assoc. Recycling Adv. Coun., EPA, Washington, 1990-93; vice chair Manhattan Solid Waste Adv. Bd., N.Y.C., 1991-92. Mem. founding bd. advisors N.Y. Feminist Art Inst., N.Y.C., 1979—81; bd. advisors The Labor Inst., N.Y.C., 1985—97, West Harlem Environ. Action Inc., N.Y.C., 1996—99; founder, pres., bd. dirs. Inst. for Labor and the Cmty., N.Y.C., 1997—; sec. bd. dirs. O.R.E., Inc., N.Y.C., 1998—; bd. dirs. Scenic Hudson, Inc., Poughkeepsie, NY, 2001—. Ford Found. fellow Nat. Fellowship Fund, 1975-78, Danforth Found., 1980-82.

ATWATER, TONY, provost,dean, educator; b. Nashville, Mar. 11, 1952; s. Herman and Lonnie May A.; m. Beverly Laverne Roberts, Dec. 20, 1980. AAS in Radio and TV Prodn., Va. Western Cmty. Coll., 1972; BA in Mass Media Arts, Hampton U., 1973; PhD in Comm., Mich. State U., 1983. Prof. journalism Mich. State U., East Lansing, 1983-91; dept. chmn. Rutgers U., New Brunswick, N.J., 1991-95; assoc. v.p. Univ. Toledo, Ohio, 1995-99; dean profl. studies Northern Ky. U., Highland Heights, 1999-2001; provost Youngstown (Ohio) State U., 2001—. Asst. dir. Mich. State U. Honors Coll., East Lansing, 1988-91; bd. trustee Northwest Ohio Pub. TV Found., Toledo, 1997-99; bd. dirs. Covington (Ky.) Ednl. Found., 2000-01. Mem. editl. bd. Jour. of Broadcasting and Electronic Media, 1996-2000. Expert panel mem. Gov.'s Taskforce Youth and Substance Abuse, Lexington, Ky., 2000-01; mem. Leadership Cin., 2000-01. Mich. State U. doctoral fellow 1979, Tchg. fellow The Poynter Inst., 1990, Univ. Adminstrn. fellow Univ. Conn., Storrs, 1994, postdoctoral fellow Ford Found., U. Mich., 1988; rsch. grantee NSF, Toledo, 1988-89. Mem. Internat Comm. Assn., Assn. Edn. Journalism and Mass Comm. (pres. 1992-93), Am. Assn. Higher Edn., Broadcast Edn. Assn., Soc. Profl. Journalists, Phi Kappa Phi. Avocations: international travel, theater, public speaking. Office: Youngstown State U Tod Hall One Univ Plz Youngstown OH 44555 E-mail: tatwater@ysu.edu.

ATWATER, VERNE STAFFORD, finance educator; b. Pitts., Aug. 22, 1920; s. Verne L. and Priscilla (Brodeur) A.; m. Evelyn Lowe, May 29, 1943; children: Lynda Mary Atwater Pyfrin, Louise Christine Atwater Cross. BA, Heidelberg Coll., 1942; MBA, Harvard U., 1943; PhD, NYU, 1961; LHD, Heidelberg Coll., 1989. Asst. prof. bus. adminstrn. Syracuse U., 1946-50; asst. to chmn. bd. N.J. Bank, Paterson, 1950-56; dir. adminstrn. Ford Found., 1956-61; rep. Argentina/Chile, 1961-63; dir. Latin Am. and Caribbean Program, 1963-64, v.p., 1964-68; pres. Westinghouse Learning Corp., N.Y.C., 1968-71; chmn., chief exec. officer Central Savs. Bank, N.Y., 1971-81; prof. fin. Lubin Grad. Sch. Bus., Pace U., N.Y.C., 1981-90, vice dean, 1984-86, prof. emeritus in residence, 1990-2001. Bd. dirs. Hudson City Bancorp.; mem. Nat. Commn. on Electric Fund Transfers, 1975—77, Pres.'s Task e on Career Devel., 1967—68, N.J. Housing Fin. Agy., 1966—70. Chmn. bd. trustees Heidelbeg Coll., 1982-89; chmn. Woodlawn Cemetery, 1994-98, James T. Lee Found. Lt. USNR, 1943-46. Mem. Arcola Country Club (dir., Paramus, N.J.), Univ. Club (N.Y.C.). Home: PO Box 1176 232 Boston Post Rd Amherst NH 03031-1176

ATWELL, CONSTANCE WOODRUFF, health services executive, researcher; b. Jan. 27, 1942; AB with high honors in psychology, Mount Holyoke Coll., 1963; MA, UCLA, 1965, PhD, 1968. Asst. prof. psychology Pitzer Coll., Claremont (Calif.) Grad. Sch., 1967-72, assoc. prof. psychology, 1972-77, prof. psychology, 1977-78; grants assoc. div. of rsch. grants NIH, Bethesda, Md., 1978-79; chief, Office of Clin. Applications of Vision Rsch. Nat. Eye Inst., NIH, Bethesda, 1979-88, asst. chief, Strabismus, Amblyopia and Visual Processing Br., 1980-81, chief, Strabismus, Amblyopia and Visual Processing Br., 1981-92, dep. assoc. dir. Extramural and Collaborative Programs, 1988-92; assoc. dir. for extramural rsch. Nat. Inst. Neurol. Disorders and Stroke, Bethesda, 1992—, acting dep. dir., 1997-98. Rsch. proposal reviewer for the Nat. Found. March of Dimes, Nat. Inst. of Disability and Rehab. Rsch., Nat. Soc. to Prevent Blindness, U.S. Dept. Edn., NIH office of Program Planning and Evaluation, co-chair adv. com. women's health issues; mem. exec. com. Fed. Demonstration Partnership; mem. various adv. bds., exec. coms. and rsch. projects, co-chair improving peer rev. reinvention com. Contbr. articles to profl. publs. Reader for Recording for the Blind, 1973-78; trustee Claremont Collegiate Sch., 1975-77; chmn. guidance adv. com. Cabin John Jr. High Sch., 1980-81, exec. com., 1980—, pres. parent tchrs. assn., 1981-82; mem. exec. com. Winston Churchill High Sch. PTA, 1982-85. Recipient Nat. Merit scholarship, 1959-63; named Sara Williston scholar, Mary Lyon scholar. Mem. AAAS, Soc. for Neurosci., Assn for Women in Sci., Phi Beta Kappa, Sigma Xi. Office: Ninds Ste 3309 6001 Executive Blvd Bethesda MD 20892-9531 E-mail: ca23c@nih.gov.

ATWELL, NEDRA WHEELER, education educator, consultant; b. Louisville, Ky., Sept. 24, 1950; d. James Riley and Elsie Parsley Skaggs; m. Charles William Atwell, Aug. 10, 2000; children: Donald Wheeler, Jonathan Wheeler. BA in hist. and psychology, Western Ky. U., 1972, MA in exceptional child edn., 1988; EdD in ednl. leadership, Vanderbilt U., 1995. Cert. dir.special edn. U. Ky., Lexington, 1989, Ky. Standard Cert. for Tchrs. of Exceptional Children. LBD tchr. New Providence Sch., Clarksville, Tenn., 1972—75; prin. and ednl. therapist Rivendell America, Bowling Green, 1986—88; area program cons. Ky. Dept. Edn., Frankfort, 1988—90; dir. profl. devel. consortia Ky. Valley Ednl. Consortia, Hazard, 1990—97; special edn. faculty Alice Lloyd Coll., Pippa Passes, Ky., 1994—97; adj. grad. faculty Morehead State U., Ky., 1996—97; dir. tchr. edn., assoc. prof. Va. Intermont Coll., Bristol, 1997—2000; assoc. prof., personnel preparation grant coord. Radford U., Va., 2000—02; assoc. prof. special instrnl. programs, exceptional edn. Western Ky. U., Bowling Green, 2002—. Co-editor Tchr. Educators Jour. ATE-VA; copy editor Southeast Regional Assn. Tchr. Educators Jour., editl. bd. Author: (book) KVEC Principal Institute 1, 1992, KVEC Principal Institute 2, 1993, Affective Data Interpretation, 1993, Beans, Buses, and Basketball, 1993, Building School Communities for All, 1994, Change Process, 1995, The Instructional Leader's Primer in Systems Thinking, 1995, SMART: Science and Math Appalachian Regional Teachers Instructional Manual, 1996, Implementing School Centered Decision-Making, 1996, HEART: Humanities Education Appalachian Regional Teachers Integrated Curriculum Guide, 1996, Kentucky and Missouri School Improvement Models, 1997, Lighting Strikes Twice, 1997, Troubled Students and School, 1999. Mem.: Ky. Inst. Women Sch. Adminstrn. (mentor), Southeast Regional Assn. Tchr. Educators, Am. Assn. Tchr. Educators, Va. Assn. Tchr. Educators (exec. bd., editl. bd.), Nat. Staff Devel. Coun., Am. Coun. Rural Special Edn., Coun. Exceptional Children, VA Declaration (editor), Coun. Children Behavioral Disorders, VA Fedn. (past pres.), Coun. Exceptional Children, VA Fedn. (past pres.), Ky. Reading Assn., Internat. Reading Assn., Am. Ednl. Rsch. Assn., Am. Assn. U. Women, Appalachian Studies Assn., Phi Delta Kappa (v.p. membership, Radford U. chpt.). Office: Western Ky U 1 Big Red Way Bowling Green KY 42101

ATWELL, ROBERT HERRON, higher education executive; b. Washington, Pa., Jan. 26, 1931; s. R. Boice and Elsie (Herron) A.; m. Suzanne Fogg, Apr. 22, 1989; children by previous marriages: Mary, Robert, John, Nancy, Carl, Catherine, Cynthia. BA, Coll. Wooster, 1953; MA in Pub. Adminstrn, U. Minn., 1957. Budget examiner U.S. Bur. Budget, Washington, 1957-60; fiscal economist, loan officer U.S. Devel. Loan Fund, Dept. State, 1960; budget examiner, program analyst for higher edn. and med. research programs U.S. Bur. Budget, 1961-62; program planning officer, asst. chief Cmty. Mental Health Ctrs. br. NIMH, HEW, 1962-65; vice chancellor for adminstrn. U. Wis., Madison, 1965-70; pres. Pitzer Coll., Claremont, Calif., 1970-78; v.p. Am. Coun. Edn., 1978-84, pres., 1984-96, pres. emeritus, 1996—. Chmn. coun. Claremont Coll., 1971—72; pres. Ind. Colls. So. Calif., 1974—75; trustee Eckerd Coll., Collegis Corp., Edn. Mgmt. Corp., Argosy U. With AUS, 1953-55. Home: 447 Bird Key Dr Sarasota FL 34236-1805

ATWOOD, CASEY, race car driver; b. Aug. 25, 1980; Race car driver Ray Evernham, 2001, Ultra Motorsports, Mooresville, NC, 2001—. Named Champion, Busch Series, 1999. Office: Ultra Motorsports 222 Raceway Dr Mooresville NC 28115

ATWOOD, DONNA ELAINE, financial manager, retired; b. Sewickley, Pa., Apr. 17, 1933; d. Donovan E. and Hazel Marie (Rush) Oelschlager; m. G. Richard Atwood, Oct. 22, 1955; children: Stephen Parker Atwood, Elaine Alden Atwood Henderson. BS in Commerce and Fin., Grove City Coll., 1955. Acctg. clk. 1st Nat. Bank, Coraopolis, Pa., 1949; asst. libr. Coraopolis Pub. Library, 1949—51; acctg. asst. Aluminum Co. of Am., Pitts., 1951—55; sec. to dean Grad. Sch. Indsl. Adminstrn. Carnegie Mellon U., Pitts., 1955—56; fin. sec., acct. Third Presbyn. Ch., Pitts., 1956—65; fin. mgr., acct. Dominical Sisters of the Sick Poor, Ossining, NY, 1972—92; ret. Mother advisor Internat. Order Rainbow for Girls N.Y., 1980—83, state chmn., 1985—, mem. state adv. bd., 1987—, gen. chmn. Grand Assembly com., 1987—93; sec. Internat. Order for Rainbow Girls N.Y., 1997—; pubs. chmn. Ossining Woman's Club, 1965—69, pres., 1969—71, house mgr., 1971—72; yearbook chmn. AAUW, Chappaqua, NY, 1964; sec. Internat. Order Rainbow for Girls N.Y., NY, 1997—; gen. chmn. grand assembly Internat. Order Rainbow for Girls, NY, 1987—93; treas. trustees Pleasantville United Meth. Ch., 1980—83, mem. pastor parish rels. com., 1989—91, sec. United Meth. Women, 1993—96, auditor, 1988—, mem. choir, 1980—. Mem.: DAR (chpt. libr. 1957, state page 1957—68), Women Descs. of Ancient and Honorable Arty. Co., Huguenot Soc., Daus. Am. Colonists (state page 1957—76, chpt. sec. 1961—64, nat. page 1968—79, state chmn. Golden Acorns and Pages 1970—73, nat. chmn. Golden Acorns and Pages 1973—79, state rec. sec. 1976—79, state chmn. pages 2000—03, state marshal 2003—), Colonial Dames XVII Century, Order Ea. Star (past matron 1962—63, grand Esther 1991, past matron 1996, chmn. com. 1997, trustee 1997—2002). Home: 21 Redwood Ln Briarcliff Manor NY 10510 E-mail: GRAtwood@aol.com.

ATWOOD, EDWARD CHARLES, economist, educator; b. N.Y.C., Dec. 2, 1922; s. Edward Charles and Bertha Margaret (Moloney) A.; m. June Matilda Ruschmeyer, Mar. 30, 1946; children— Edward Terrell, Jeffrey Terrell. AB, Princeton U., 1946, MA, 1950, PhD in Econs, 1959. Teaching fellow U. Buffalo, 1946-47; part-time instr. Princeton U., 1948-50; instr. Denison U., 1950-52; from asst. to assoc. prof. Washington and Lee U., 1952-60, dean students, 1961-69, dean Sch. Commerce, 1969-86. Lewis W. Adams Prof. of Econs., 1986-93, prof. econs. emeritus, 1993—. Econ. cons. Bankers Trust Co., N.Y.C., 1956; economist Gen. Electric Co., 1960-61; tchr. courses Am. Inst. Banking, Va. Sch. Banking, 1957-59; co-chmn. Va. Council Higher Edn. Bus. Adminstrn. Task Force, 1985-86; dir. United Va. Bankshares/Rockbridge, Lexington; vis. prof. Tamkang U., Taiwan, Fall, 1986; vis. fellow U. Coll., Oxford U., Spring, 1987. Pres. Rockbridge Area Housing Corp., 1974-75; trustee Lawrenceville Fathers Assn; mem. Southbury-Middlebury Scholarship Fund, 2000-2001; mem. Waterbury Found., 2001—; deacon United Ch. Christ, Southbury, 2001—. Served with USNR, 1942-46. Mem. Am. Assembly Collegiate Schs. Bus. (initial accreditation com., continuing accreditation com. 1969-86), Am., So. econ. assns., Am. Bankers Assn (selection com. 1973-74), Beta Gamma Sigma, Omicron Delta Kappa, Omicron Delta Epsilon. Congregationalist. Home: 389B Heritage Vlg Southbury CT 06488-1717

ATWOOD, GLENN ARTHUR, engineer, educator; b. Rock Rapids, Iowa, Oct. 24, 1935; s. Elmer Henry and Clara Marie (McCrory) A.; m. Mary Ellen Ensminger, Aug. 28, 1955; children: Ruth Marie, John Aaron, Robert Mark. BSChemE, Iowa State U., 1957, MS, 1959; PhD, U. Wash., 1963. Registered profl. engr., Ohio. Process engr. Exxon Rsch. and Engring., Flornam Park, N.J., 1962-65; asst. prof. U. Akron, Ohio, 1965-70, assoc. prof., 1970-77, prof., 1977-83, asst. dean, 1983-85, assoc. dean, 1985-88, acting dean coll. engr., 1988-89; R&D dir. Midwest Ore Processing Co., Inc., Plainville, Ind., 1990—95; prof. emeritus U. Akron, Ohio, 1990—. Cons. Knapp Foundry, Akron, Firestone Co. Patentee in field. Founder, officer Marriage Encounter United Meth. Ch., Ohio, 1977-89; pres., vice chmn. United Cerebral Palsy, 1966-77, trustee 1970-74. Mem. ASEE, NSPE, Am. Inst. Chem. Engrs., Sigma Xi, Tau Beta Phi. Home: 939 Devonwood Dr Wadsworth OH 44281-8859 Office: 939 Devonwood Dr Wadsworth OH 44281-8859

ATWOOD, HAROLD ASHLEY, retired historian; b. Antioch, Ill., Dec. 18, 1921; s. Charles and Elaine (Pritchard) A.; m. Georgia Elnora Christlieb, Aug. 21, 1954. BA, U. Ill., 1948; MA, U. Wis., 1950; MLS, Western Mich. U., 1976. Tchr. Benton Harbor (Mich.) H.S., 1952-72; adminstrv. asst. hist. preservation City of Benton Harbor, 1979-80; history cons. Benton Harbor Area Schs., 1989-91. Home: 234 Searles Ave Benton Harbor MI 49022-5431

ATWOOD, HOLLYE STOLZ, lawyer; b. St. Louis, Dec. 25, 1945; d. Robert George and Elise (Sauselle) Stolz; m. Frederick Howard Atwood III, Aug. 12, 1978; children: Katherine Stolz, Jonathan Robert. BA, Washington U., St. Louis, 1968; JD, Washington U., 1973. Bar: Mo. 1973. Jr. ptnr. Bryan Cave, St. Louis, 1973-82, ptnr., 1983—2001, mem. exec. com., 1995-2000, of counsel, 2002—. Bd. dirs. St. Louis coun. Girl Scouts U.S., 1976-86; trustee John Burroughs Sch., St. Louis, 1983-86. Mem. ABA, Met. St. Louis Bar Assn., Washington U. Law Sch. Alumni Assn. (pres. 1983-84). Clubs: Noonday (St. Louis) (bd. govs. 1983-86). Office: Bryan Cave One Metropolitan Sq 211 N Broadway Saint Louis MO 63102-2733 E-mail: hsatwood@bryancave.com.

ATWOOD, JAMES R. lawyer; b. White Plains, N.Y., Feb. 21, 1944; s. Bernard D. and Joyce Rose Atwood; m. Wendy Fisler, Aug. 22, 1981 (div.); children: Christopher Charles, Carl Fisler; m. Nancy A. Udell, Oct. 6, 2001. BA, Yale U., 1966; JD, Stanford U., 1969. Bar: Calif. 1969, D.C. 1970. Law clk. to judge U.S. Ct. Appeals, L.A., 1969-70; law clk. to Chief Justice Warren Burger U.S. Supreme Ct., 1970-71; mem. Covington & Burling, Washington, 1971-78, ptnr., 1977-78, 81—. Dep. asst. sec. for transp. affairs U.S. Dept. State, Washington, 1978-79, dep. legal adviser, 1979-80; acting prof. Law Sch. Stanford U., 1980 Author: (with Kingman Brewster) Antitrust and American Business Abroad, 2nd edit, 1981. Mem. bd. visitors Law Sch. Stanford U.,

1995-97. Mem. ABA, Am. Soc. Internat. Law, D.C. Bar Assn. Home: 8020 Greentree Rd Bethesda MD 20817-1304 Office: Covington & Burling 1201 Pennsylvania Ave NW Washington DC 20004-2401

ATWOOD, JOHN BRIAN, dean; b. Wareham, Mass., July 25, 1942; s. Ellsworth Savary and Bernice Anita (Perkins) A.; m. Susan Johnson, Aug. 3, 1991; children: John, Deborah, Michelle. BA, Boston U., 1964; postgrad., Am. U., 1970, LLD (hon.), 1995. Mgmt. intern Nat. Security Agy., Washington, 1964-66; fgn. service officer U.S. Dept. State, Washington, 1966-71; legis. asst. to Senator Thomas F. Eagleton, 1971-77; dep. asst. sec. for congl. relations U.S. Dept. State, Washington, 1977-79, asst. sec., 1979-81; dean, profl. studies and acad. affairs Fgn. Service Inst., Washington, 1981-82; v.p. Internat. Reporting and Info. Systems, Washington, 1982—; exec. dir. Dem. Senatorial Campaign Com., Washington, 1982-84; pres. Nat. Dem. Inst. for Internat. Affairs, Washington, 1985-93; adminstr. U.S. AID, Washington, 1993-99; pres. Citizens Internat., Boston, 1999—2002; prof. Harvard U., Cambridge, Mass., 1999—; dean Hubert H. Humphrey Inst. Pub. Affairs U. Minn., Mpls., 2002—. Mem. Coun. Fgn. Rels., UN Assn. Bd. dirs. Nat. Dem. Inst., Freedom House, World Peace Found., African-Am. Inst., Acad. Ednl. Devel. Recipient Harvard Prize Book award, 1959. Mem. Boston U. Alumni Assn. Office: Hubert H Humphrey Inst for Public Affairs 300 Humphrey Ctr 301 19th Ave Minneapolis MN 55455 E-mail: jbatwood@hhh.umn.edu.*

ATWOOD, JOYCE CHARLENE, curriculum and instruction administrator, consultant; b. Chillicothe, Ohio, Apr. 29, 1943; d. Pearl and Blanche (Martindill) Workman. BS in Edn., Ohio U., 1965, MEd, 1969; postgrad., Ohio State U., 1976-88, Ashland U., 1992-97. Cert. tchr., supr., adminstr. 4th-6th grade tchr. Chillicothe (Ohio) City Schs., 1965-73, K-3d grade reading tchr., 1973-86, tchr. leader reading recovery, 1986-88, asst. prin. mid. sch., 1988-89, adminstrv. asst., 1989—, asst. supt. for curriculum and instrn., 1993—. Cons. study skills for mgmt. in industry Pickaway-Ross Joint Vocat. Sch., Chillicothe, 1984-88; mem. Child Care Adv. Bd., Portsmouth (Ohio), 1993— Sec., v.p. Big Bros. and Sisters, Ross County, 1989-93; mem. Walnut St. Ch. Staff Parish, Chillicothe, 1991-94, 99—; coord. Area Artist Series, Ross County, 1989—; edn. chairperson Ross County Area Labor Mgmt., 1990—; mem. Interagy. Childcare Vocat. Choir; bd. dirs. YMCA, 2002—. Named to Ross County Women's Hall of Fame, Ross County C. of C., 1993; recipient North Ctrl. Accredition award, 2002; George Washington U. Partnership award, 2002. Mem. ASCD (Ohio Creative Staff Devel. award 1997), Internat. Reading Assn., Nat. Assn. Edn. Young Children, Buckeye Assn. Sch. Adminstrs., Ohio Assn. for Curriculum Devel. (Staff Devel. Creative award 1997), Bus. and Profl. Women Assn., Altrusa, Kiwanis, Phi Delta Kappa. Methodist. Avocations: reading, gardening. Home: 10 Overlook Dr Chillicothe OH 45601-1925 E-mail: jatwood@mailgsu.k12.oh.us.

ATWOOD, MARGARET ELEANOR, writer; b. Ottawa, Ont., Can., Nov. 18, 1939; d. Carl Edmund and Margaret Dorothy (Killam) A. BA, U. Toronto, 1961; AM, Radcliffe Coll., 1962; postgrad., Harvard U., 1962-63, 65-67; LittD (hon.), Trent U., 1973, Concordia U., 1980, Smith Coll., Northampton, Mass., 1982, U. Toronto, 1983, U. Waterloo, 1985, U. Guelph, 1985, Mt. Holyoke Coll., 1985, Victoria Coll., 1987, Univ. de Montréal, 1991, McMaster U., 1996; LLD (hon.), Queen's U., 1974. Lectr. in English U. B.C., 1964-65, Sir George Williams U., 1967-68, U. Alta., 1969-70; asst. prof. English York U., Toronto, 1971-72; writer-in-residence U. Toronto, 1972-73, U. Ala., Tuscaloosa, 1985. Berg Chair NYU, 1986; writer-in-residence Macquarie U., Australia, 1987, Trinity U., San Antonio, 1989. Author: (poetry) Double Persephone, 1961, The Circle Game, 1967, The Animals in That Country, 1968, The Journals of Susanna Moodie, 1970, Procedures for Underground, 1970, Power Politics, 1973, Poems for Voices, 1970, You Are Happy, 1975, Selected Poems, 1976 (Am. edit. 1978), Selected Poems, 1966-84, 1990, Margaret Atwood Poems, 1965-75, 1991, Two-Headed Poems, 1978, True Stories, 1981, Interlunar, 1984, Selected Poems II: Poems Selected and New, 1976-1986, 1986, Morning in the Burned House, 1995; (novels) The Edible Woman, 1969 (Am. edit. 1970), Surfacing, 1972, (Am. edit. 1973), Lady Oracle, 1976, Life Before Man, 1979, Bodily Harm, 1981, The Handmaid's Tale, 1985, Cat's Eye, 1988 (City Toronto Book award 1989, Coles Book of the Yr. 1989, Can. Booksellers Assn. Author of the Yr., 1989, Book of the Yr. award Found. for Advancement of Can. Letters, Periodical Marketers Can., 1989, Torgi Talking Book award 1989), The Robber Bride, 1993 (award for Fiction Can. Authors Assn., 1993, Trillium award for Excellence in Ont. Writing 1993, Regional Commonwealth Lit. award), Alias Grace, 1996 (Giller Prize 1996, Medal of Honor for Literature, Nat. Arts Club 1997), The Blind Assassin, 2000 (The Booker Prize 2000); (short stories) Dancing Girls, 1977, Bluebeard's Egg, 1983, Murder in the Dark, 1983, Wilderness Tips, 1991 (Trillium award 1992, Book of the Yr. award Periodical Marketers of Can., 1992), Good Bones, 1992; (juvenile) Up in the Tree, 1978, Anna'a Pet, 1980, For the Birds, 1990, Princess Prunella & the Purple Peanut, 1995; (non-fiction) Survival: A Thematic Guide to Canadian Literature, 1972, Second Words: Selected Critical Prose, 1982, Strange Things: The Malevolent North in Canadian Literature, 1995 Recipient E.J. Pratt medal, 1961, Pres.'s medal U. Western Ont., 1965, YWCA Women of Distinction award, Gov. Gen.'s award, 1966, 1st pl. Centennial Commn. Poetry Competition, 1967, Union Poetry prize Chicago, 1969, Bess Hoskins prize of Poetry Chicago, 1974, City of Toronto Book award, 1977, Can. Booksellers Assn. award, 1977, award for short fiction Periodical Distbr. Can., 1977, St. Lawrence award for Fiction, 1978, Radcliffe Grad. medal, 1980, Molson award, 1981, Internat. Writer's prize Welsh Arts Council, 1982, Book of Yr. award Periodical Distbrs. of Can. and Found. for Advancement Can. Letters, 1983, Los Angeles Times Fiction award, 1986, Gov. Gen.'s Lit. award, 1986, Ida Nudel Humanitarian award, 1986, Toronto Arts award, 1986, Arthur C. Clarke award for Best Sci. Fiction, 1987, shortlisted for Ritz Hemingway prize, Paris, 1987, Commonwealth Lit. Prize regional award, 1987, 94, Silver medal for Best Article of Yr. Council for Advancement and Support of Edn., 1987, Nat. Mag. award 1st prize, 1988, Sunday Times award for literary excellence, YWCA Women of Distinction award 1988, Centennial medal Harvard U., 1990, John Hughes prize Welsh Devel. Bd., 1992, Commemorative medal 125th Anniversary of Can. Confedn., 1992, Trillium award for excellence in Ont. writing, 1995; Guggenheim fellow, 1981; decorated companion Order of Can., 1981, Order of Ont., 1990; named Woman of Yr. Ms. Mag., 1986, Humanist of Yr., 1987, Chevalier de l'Ordre des Arts et des Lettres, 1994. Fellow Royal Soc. of Can., Am. Acad. Arts and Scis. (fgn. hon. lit. mem. 1988). Address: care Oxford U Press 70 Wynford Dr Don Mills ON Canada M3C 1J9

ATWOOD, MARY SANFORD, writer; b. Mt. Pleasant, Mich., Jan. 27, 1935; d. Burton Jay and Lillian Belle (Sampson) Sanford; B.S., U. Miami, 1957; m. John C. Atwood, III, Mar. 23, 1957. Author: A Taste of India, 1969. Mem. San Francisco/N. Peninsula Opera Action, Hillsborough-Burlingame Newcomers, Suicide Prevention and Crisis Center, DeYoung Art Mus., Internat. Hospitality Center, Peninsula Symphony, San Francisco Art Mus., World Affairs Council, Mills Hosp. Assos. Mem. AAUW, Suicide Prevention Aux. Republican. Club: St. Francis Yacht. Office: 40 Knightwood Ln Hillsborough CA 94010-6132 E-mail: jazperkhat@mindspring.com.

ATWOOD, RAYMOND PERCIVAL, JR., lawyer; b. Ossining, N.Y., June 25, 1952; s. Raymond Percival and Berniece Lucille Atwood; m. Theresa Carol Goeken, Aug. 13, 1977; children: Shannon, Heather, Sarah, Raymond III, Jennifer. BS, U. Nebr., 1972, JD, 1974; cert. Trial Advocacy, Hastings Coll. Law U. Calif., San Francisco, 1978; Advanced Trial Advocacy, Harvard U. Law Sch., 1988. Bar: Nebr. 1975, U.S. Dist. Ct. Nebr. 1975, U.S. Bankruptcy Ct. 1975, Mo. 1978, U.S. Ct. Appeals (8th cir.) 1979. Agy. legal counsel Nebr. Workmen's Compensation Ct., Lincoln, 1975-77; staff counsel Hartford Ins. Co., Kansas City, Mo., 1977-78; ptnr. McCord, Janssen & Atwood, Lincoln, 1978-80, Healey, Wieland, Kluender, Atwood, Geier & Bartle, Lincoln, 1980-92, Healey and Wieland, Lincoln, 1992-2000; pres. Atwood and Assocs. Law Firm, P.C., LLC, Lincoln, 2000—. Educator Lincoln Sch. Commerce, Nebr., 1978-81; bd. dirs. legal studies Lincoln Sch. Commerce, Nebr., 1979-81; educator U. Nebr. Coll. Law, Lincoln, 1982—; legal seminar lectr., 1976—. Contbr. articles to profl. jours. Organizer United Way, Lincoln, 1975-77; campaign chmn. Larson for Legislature, Lincoln, 1984. Mem. ABA, Nebr. Order Barristers, Nebr. Assn. Trial Attys., Assn. Trial Lawyers Am., Nebr. State Bar, Delta Theta Phi. Unitarian Universalist. Office: Atwood and Assocs Law Firm PC LLO 1133 H St Lincoln NE 68508

ATZ, SARAH J. music educator; b. Hillsdale, MI, Oct. 20, 1957; BA, Judson Coll., Elgin, Ill., 1980; MA cum laude, U. Louisville. Cert. tchr. Ky. Music tchr. Oswego (Ill.) Sch. Dist., 1981; band tchr. Dundee (Ill.) Sch. Dist., 1982; tchr., music/chorus Jefferson County Pub. Schs., Louisville, 1988—93; handbell dir. First Bapt. Ch., Elgin, Ill., 1980—82, Peter's Creek Bapt. Ch., Library, Pa., 1984—87, St. Paul's Episc. Ch., Louisville, 1988—89. Office: Carrithers Middle Sch 4320 Billtown Rd Louisville KY 40299

AU, MARY LEE, school system administrator; b. West Chester, Pa., June 17, 1931; d. James and Lau Shee (Fong) Lee; m. Markley Lee Au, June 24, 1956. BS in Elem. Edn., West Chester State U., 1953; MA in Elem. Edn., George Washington U., 1968; student, U. So. Calif., 1975-76. Cert. elem. and middle sch. adminstr., Md. Tchr. West Chester Sch. Dist., 1953-59, Marple Newton, Pa., 1959-62, Montgomery County Pub. Sch., Md., 1962-68; asst. prin. Roling Terr. Elem. Sch., Tacoma Park, Md., 1989-91; acting asst. prin. Wyngate Elem. Sch., Bethesda, Md., 1990-91; acting prin. Oakland Terr. Elem. Sch., Kensington, Md., 1991, asst. prin., 1991—2003, Thurgood Marshall Sch., 1994—99; cons. LA Assocs. Human Resources. Mem. undergrad. affairs com., mem. curriculum devel. Am. U., Washington, 1968-79; adv. multicultural curriculum devel. U. So. Calif., 1977; tchr. certification advisor to Md. state supt. Md. State Dept. Edn., 1979-85; pres., dir. L.A. Assocs. Cons. for Human Resources, 1977—, diversity trainer, 1999—; coord. tchr. tng. ctr. Am. U./Montgomery County (Md.) Pub. Schs.; pers. recruiter Montgomery County Pub. Schs. Author: Chronology of Asian Pacific American History, 1979-94. Deacon Bradley Hills Presbyn. Ch., 2003—. Named one of the Women of the 80's, Ms. Mag., Asian-Chinese Am. historian "Write Women Back Into History" project by Nat. Women's Project. Mem. ASCD, Nat. Assn. Elem. Sch. Prins., NAACP, Md. Assn. Elem. Sch. Adminstrs., Asian Pacific Am. Heritage Coun. (co-founder 1979—, nat. treas. 1990-91, nat. pres. 1998—), Orgn. Chinese Ams. (nat. pres. 1980, v.p. ednl., social, and cultural program 1975), Actors Guild. Avocations: golf, vocal music, interior decorating, jewelry designing. Home: 8800 Fox Hills Trl Potomac MD 20854-4211

AUBERJONOIS, RENÉ MURAT, actor; b. N.Y.C., June 1, 1940; s. Fernand and Laura (Murat) A.; m. Judith Helen Mihalyi, Oct. 19, 1963; children: Tessa Louise, Rémy-Luc. BFA, Carnegie-Mellon U., 1962. Tchr. acting U. Calif. at Berkeley, San Francisco State U., Julliard Sch.; bd. dirs. Calif. Theatre Council, Calif. State U. Summer Sch. of the Arts; mem. artistic advancement panel NEA, bd. dirs. Calif. State Summer Sch. Arts. Actor: (films) M*A*S*H, 1969, Brewster McCloud, 1970, McCabe and Mrs. Miller, 1970, Pete N' Tillie, 1972, Images, 1972, The Hindenberg, 1973, King Kong, 1976, Eyes of Laura Mars, 1978, Where the Buffalo Roam, 1980, 3:15, 1985, Walker, 1987, My Best Friend is a Vampire, 1987, Police Academy V, 1988, The Feud, 1989, The Little Mermaid, 1989, Star Trek: The Undiscovered Country, The Ballad of Little Jo, 1993, Batman Forever, 1995, Los Locos, 1997, Burning Down the House, 1997, Snide and Prejudice, 1997, Cats Don't Dance, 1997, Inspector Gadget, 1999, The Patriot, 2000, (repertory theatre): Arena Stage, 1962—65, A.C.T., 1965—68, B.A.M. Rep., 1976—77, Mark Taper Forum, 1980—83, : (Broadway plays) Fire!, 1968, Coco, 1970, The Good Doctor, 1974 (Tony nomination), Tricks, 1972, Break a Leg, 1979, Big River, 1985 (Tony award, Tony nomination); (films) Every Good Boy Deserves Favor, 1986, metamorphosis, 1989; contbr. (Tony nomination); actor(star TV series): Benson, 1980—86 (Emmy nomination); creator role Odo, shape shifter on Star Trek, Deep Space Nine; actor: (TV appearances) Ashenden (mini-series), Los Language of Cranes (BBC and PBS), 1983, Chicago Hope, 1999, The Memoirs of Sally Hemmings, Geppetto, 2000, The Practice, 2000 (Emmy nomination), Frasier, 2000, Judging Amy; dir.: Marblehead Manor (TV); actor(dir.): Star Trek: Deep Space Nine (TV).

AUBERTIN, MADELINE KATHERINE, retired nursing educator, medical/surgical nurse, mental health services professional; b. Detroit, May 16, 1930; Grad., Providence Hosp. Sch. Nursing; BS in Nursing Edn., Mercy Coll., 1951; MEd, Wayne State Coll., 1955. RN, Mich. Staff nurse Vets. Hosp., Dearborn, Mich., 1951-58; staff nurse, nursing educator St. John's Hosp., St. Louis, 1960-64; staff nurse U. Mich., Ann Arbor, 1965-66; instr., staff nurse Harper Hosp., Detroit; insvc. dir., nursing instr. Holy Cross Hosp., Detroit, 1966-68; insvc. instr., dir. Grace Hosp., Detroit, 1968-72; nursing instr. Wayne County Community Coll., Detroit, 1972-96; ret., 1996. Mem. ARC, Detroit, 1962-92, Am. Heart Assn., Southfield, Mich., 1962-92, Assn. for Learning Disabilities, Farmington, Mich., 1972-92, Nat. League of Nursing, Detroit, 1962-92. Democrat. Roman Catholic. Avocations: singing, church choir, sewing, reading. Home: 9576 Winston Redford MI 48239-1660 E-mail: Madge246@aol.com.

AUBERY, STEPHEN ROYSTON EDMUND, film producer; b. Kingston Upon Hull, Yorkshire, Eng., July 4, 1951; came to U.S., 1964; s. Gerald Royston and Doreen (Stevens) A.; m. Rose Marie Marks, Feb. 23, 1973 (div. Dec. 1991); children: Suzanne Marie, Julia Dawn, Wendy Lynn, Katrina Rose; m. Tamara Phizacklea, Oct. 4, 1994 (div. May 2000); m. Cheryl Curran, Dec. 28, 2002. Student, U. Utah, 1968-70, Brigham Young U., 1974-75. Sound dept. mgr. Brigham Young U. Motion Picture Studio, Provo, Utah, 1972-76; film prodr., ptnr. Linton Prodns., Salt Lake City, 1976-79; prodr., gen. ptnr. Seven Star Pictures, Salt Lake City, 1979-82; news editor KUTV Inc., Salt Lake City, 1982-84; film prodr., mgr. LDS Audiovisual, Salt Lake City, 1984-94; film prodr. Challenger Schs., Salt Lake City, 1994—95; film prodr., owner Encore Prodns., Salt Lake City, 1995-96; film prodr. Mountain Prodns., Inc., Draper, Utah, 1997-99, Mark Phillips Phвитms & Telephision, L.A., 1999-2000; film prodr., owner flixnpix.com, L.A., 2000—02; dir. mktg., video prodr. ACS State and Local Solutions, Austin, Tex., 2001—. Film dept. instr. U. Utah, Salt Lake City, Brigham Young U., Provo; mgr., lead singer, guitarist Tapestry top 40 soft rock dance band, 1980-97. Co-author, prodr., cinematographer (screenplay, book, feature motion picture) Knocking at Heaven's Door, 1980; film prodr. (internat. film) Temple Open House, 1992 (Telly award 1993); film prodr., dir. (ednl. film) Phonics Fun, 1993 (two Telly awards 1994); prodr., dir. (motivational film) From Thoughts to Things, 1997 (Telly & Communicator award 1997), prodr., dir., dir. photography, editor, Undercover Stings, Learning Channel, 1999, The Jer-Z Games, Disney Channel, 2000, K-9 Cops-The Learning Channel, 2000, Bridges to Freedom, 2000, First Impressions, 2000 (Videographer Excellence award and Communicator award and Cindy Award 2001); author, contbg. editor Super 8 Filmaker Mag., 1975-80. Bd. dirs. World Firefighters Assistance League, Salt Lake City. Mem. Internat. TV Assn., Soc. Motion Picture and TV Engrs. (presenter tech. paper L.A. conv. 1974-80, cert. presentation 1995), Media Comm. Insternat. Avocations: vocal performing, playing guitar, computers. Office: ACS Inc 515 Congress Ave Ste 1400 Austin TX 78701-3516 Fax: 512-479-7010. E-mail: stephen.aubery@acs-inc.com.

AUBIN, BARBARA JEAN, artist; b. Chgo., Jan. 12, 1928; d. Philip Theodore and Dorothy May (Chapman) A. BA, Carleton Coll., 1949; B Art Edn., Sch. Art Inst. Chgo., 1954, M Art Edn., 1955. Lectr. Centre D'Art & Haitian Am. Inst., Port-Au-Prince, Haiti, 1958-60; asst. prof. Sch. Art Inst. Chgo., 1960-67, Loyola U., Chgo., 1968-71; lectr. Calumet Coll., Hammond, Ind., 1971-75; prof. art Chgo. State U., 1971-91; ret., 1991. Vis. prof., artist Wayne State U., Detroit, Mich., 1965; vis. artist St. Louis C.C., Forest Park, Mo., 1980-81, U. Wis., Green Bay, 1981; co-curator Art for the Next Millennium Kimo Theatre Gallery, Albuquerque, 1997; spkr. and exhibiting artist, Womens's Caucus For Art Regional Conf./Exhibition, 1999. One-woman shows include Countryside Arts Ctr., Arlington Heights, Ill., 1954, 87, Avant Arts Gallery, Chgo., 1954, Riccardo's Restaurant and Gallery, Chgo., 1956, Evanston (Ill.) Twp. H.S., 1958, Centre d'Art, Port-au-Prince, Haiti, 1960, Chgo. Pub. Libr., 1960, Chgo. Acad. Fine Arts, 1965, Oxbow Summer Sch. Fine Arts, 1965, Lewis Towers Gallery, Loyola U., Chgo., 1970, Chgo. State U., 1971, 74, 85, North River Cmty. Gallery, Northeastern Ill. U., Chgo., 1974, Ill. Arts Coun., Chgo., Crossroads-Jr. Mus., Art Inst. Chgo., 1976, Fairweather Hardin Gallery, Chgo., 1978, 80, 85, 90, U. Wis., 1981, Illini Union Gallery, U. Ill., Urbana, 1986, Artemisia Gallery, Chgo., Katerina's, Chgo., 2002; exhibited in group shows at Art Inst. Chgo., 1960, 78, 80, 85, 89, Vanderpoel Art Assn., Beverly Art Ctr., Chgo., 1992, Ancient Echoes, Chgo., 1992, Renaissance Ct., Chgo. Cultural Ctr., 1993, 2001, 2002, Artemisia Gallery, Chgo., 1994, Art Place Gallery, Chgo, 1994, Chgo. State U., 1994, Chgo. Women's Caucus for Art, 1994, 98, 2000, Eastern Ill. U., Charleston, 1991, 1993-2001, ARC Gallery, Chgo., 1995, 97, N.Mex. Art League, Albuquerque, 1996, Mirage Gallery, Albuquerque, Barrington Arts Coun., 1997, Meridian Ctr., Washington, 1997, Chgo. Women's Caucus for Art No. Ill. U., 1998, Springfield Art Mus., Mo., 1999, (Patron Purchase award), Beacon St. Gallery, Chgo., 1999, DeKalb (Ill.) Area Women's Ctr., 1999, Mini-Millennium Women's Caucus For Art Nat. Gallery, 2000, Eastern Ill. U., Charleston, Ill., 2000-01, Chgo. Cultural Ctr., 2001-02; represented in permanent collections at Art Inst. Chgo., Ill. State Mus., Ball State Mus., Calumet Coll., Hammond, Ind., Shimer Coll., Waukegon, Ill., Kemper Group Collection, Long Grove, Ill., State of Ill. Bldg., Chgo., Seyfarth, Shaw, Fairweather & Geraldson, Washington, Ernst & Ernst, Chgo., Foote, Cone & Belding, Chgo., U.S. League of Savs. and Loans, Chgo., Northside Industries, Chgo., Keck, Cushman, Mahin & Cate, Chgo., Gould, Inc., Rolling Meadows, Ill., First Nat. Bank Chgo., Internat. Mineral and Chem., Skokie, Ill.; reporter Women Artists News, 1977, 80, 83-86. V.p. Midwest region Womens Caucus for Art, Chgo., 1982-88; founding mem. local chpt. Chgo. Women's Caucus for Art, 1973, bd. dirs., 2002, 2003; bd. dirs. Chgo. Artists' Coalition, 1992-94. Recipient George D. Brown Fgn. Travel fellow Sch. Art Inst. Chgo., 1955-56; Art grant Fulbright fellow, 1958-60, Huntington Hartford Fedn. grant, 1963, Project Completion grant Ill. Arts Coun., 1978-79, Chgo. Cultural Ctr., 2002, CAAPS grant, 2002. Mem. Arts Club Chgo., Chgo. Artists' Coalition, Chgo. Womens Caucus for Art. Home: The Hallmark 2960 N Lake Shore Dr #405 Chicago IL 60657-5645

AUBREY, JAMES REYNOLDS, English educator; b. Kittanning, Pa., Dec. 3, 1945; s. Samuel Moss and Alice (Reynolds) A.; m. Marilyn Sue Awbrey, June 8, 1968 (dec.); children: Sarah Elizabeth, Meredith Anne. BS, USAF Acad., 1968; MA, Northwestern U., 1973; PhD, U. Wash., 1979. Commd. 2d lt. USAF, 1968, advanced through grades to lt. col., 1984; ret., 1989; intelligence briefer Hq. Mac, 1970-72; chief of intelligence 42ECS, 8TFW, RAF Upper Heyford, 1983-86; prof. English USAF Acad., 1973-76, 79-83, 86-89; prof. English, Met. State Coll., Denver, 1989—. Author: John Fowles, 1991, John Fowles and Nature, 1999.

AUBURN, NORMAN PAUL, university president; b. Cin., May 22, 1905; s. Joseph and Huldah A.; m. Kathleen Montgomery, June 28, 1930 (dec. 1974); children: Ames Auburn Latta, Richard, Mark, David Bruce; m. Virginia Kirk, Jan. 4, 1977. AB, U. Cin., 1927, postgrad., 1927-28, 34-35, LLD, 1952, Parsons Coll., 1945, U. Liberia, 1959, U. Akron, 1971; DSc, U. Tulsa, 1957; LittD, Washburn U., 1961; LHD, Coll. of Wooster, 1963; DCL, Union Coll., 1979. Editor Cin. Constructor, 1928-33; asst. mgr. Asso. Gen. Contractors of Am., 1928-33, publicity mgr. Allied Constrn. Industries, 1930-33; exec. sec. U. Cin. Alumni Assn., 1933-36; editor Cin. Alumnus, 1929-36; asst. dir., asst. prof. Evening Coll., U. Cin., 1936-38; assoc. prof. U. Cin., 1938-40, acting dean, 1940-41, dean and prof., 1941-43, dean of univ. adminstrn., clk. bd. dirs., 1943-51, v.p., 1943-51, acting pres., 1949; exec. dir. U. Cin. Research Found., 1943-51; pres. U. Akron, 1951-71, pres. emeritus, cons., 1971—2003. Acting pres. Council Fin. Aid to Edn., N.Y.C., 1957-58, bd. dirs., 1957-71; spl. asst. univ. relations AID, U.S. State Dept., 1965-66, cons., 1966—2003; cons. Acad. Ednl. Devel., Inc., N.Y.C., 1965-70, sr. v.p., dir. institutional ops., 1971-89, sr. v.p., emeritus, 1989-2003; acting pres. Poly. Inst., Bklyn., 1973, Stephens Coll., Columbia, Mo., 1974-75, Cedar Crest Coll., Allentown, Pa., 1977-78, Union Coll., Schenectady, N.Y., 1978-79; acting chancellor Union U., Albany, N.Y., 1978-79; sr. v.p., provost Widener U., Chester, Pa., 1979-82; acting pres. Salem Coll., W.Va., 1982-83, Lincoln U., Jefferson City, Mo., 1987-88; spl. asst. to pres. for planning W.Va. U., Morgantown, 1983-86; chmn. Univ. Council on Edn. for Pub. Responsibility, 1965-66; dir. Great Lakes Megalopolis Research Project, 1968-74; vice chmn. Am. Council Edn., 1963-64, dir., 1969-72; bd. dirs. First Fed. Savs. and Loan Assn., Akron, 1963, chmn., 1973-2003; bd. dirs. Charter One Fin., Cleve., 1988-2003, Charter One Bank, 1988-2003, 1st Nat. Bank Akron, emeritus; hon. pres. Lane Theol. Sem., Cin., 1990-2003. Contbr. articles to ednl. jours. Bd. dirs. Akron Gen. Hosp., U. Akron Devel. Found., 1967-2003; trustee Greater Akron Musical Assn., 1967-2003; trustee, sec. Lane Theol. Sem., Cin., 1945-2003, hon. pres., 1990-2003; trustee Ohio Coll. Assn., pres., 1960-61; mem. Air Force ROTC Adv. Panel to Dept. USAF, 1960-64; mem. exec. com. Ohio Research and Devel. Bd., 1962-65; pres. Herman Muehlstein Found., 1965-2003; mem. U. Cin. Endowment Fund Assn. Recipient Bert A. Polsky Humanitarian award Akron Cmty. Found., 1997, Judge Harold K. Stubbs Emeriti award for lifetime of disting. svc. African Meth. Episcopal Ch., 2000. Fellow AAAS; mem. Assn. Am. Colls. (vice chmn. commn. coll. adminstrn. 1965-68), Am. Soc. Engring. Edn., Am. Assn. State Colls. and Univs. (chmn. com. on internat. programs 1970-71), Assn. Univ. Evening Colls. (pres. 1944), Assn. Urban Univs. (pres. 1955-56, sec.-treas. 1956-65), Newcomen Soc., Cincinnatus Soc., Summit County Hist. Soc. (trustee 1975-80), Queen City Assn., Alpha Kappa Psi, Phi Alpha Delta, Lambda Chi Alpha, Omicron Delta Kappa, Scabbard and Blade. Clubs: Rotary (pres. Cin. 1950-51, Akron 1958-59), Commonwealth (Cin.), Univ. (N.Y.C., Columbus, Ohio), City, Portage Country (Akron), Lago Mar Beach (Ft. Lauderdale, Fla.). Presbyterian. Home: Akron, Ohio. Died July 21, 2003.

AUCELLA, LAURENCE FRANK, counseling administrator, educator; b. Waterbury, Conn., July 24, 1959; s. Louis Joseph and Julia Janet A. BA, Anna Maria Coll., Paxton, Mass., 1982; MEd, Boston Coll., 1984; EdD, U. Bridgeport (Conn.), 1997; MS, So. Conn. State U., 1996. Lic. profl. counselor/gifted sch. counselor. Counselor Morris Found., Waterbury, 1984-86; adj. faculty Tunxis C.C., Farmington, Conn., 1991, So. Conn. State U., New Haven, 1992-96, Albertus Magnus Coll., New Haven, 1998—; Mattatuck C.C., Waterbury, 1985-90; disability specialist Western Conn. State U., Danbury, 1997—; ednl. counselor Waterbury Adult Edn., 1986—; counselor Rotella Magnet Sch., Waterbury, 2001—. Mem. Ctr. for Blood Rsch., Boston, 1999—. Contbr. articles to profl. jours. Moderator (election official) City of Waterbury, 1995—; city coord. United Way, 1988 (Cmty. Spirit Award 1988); pres. La Casa Bienvenida, Waterbury, 1987—. Recipient Impact 99 Blessing Award Hispanic chs. of Waterbury, 1999, Riverfront Preservation Award Riverfront Preservation Soc., Rock Hill, Conn., 1999; named an Outstanding Young Man of Am. Jaycees, 1985-88. Mem. Am. Counseling Assn., Am. Statis. Assn., Am. Advance of Sci., Conn. Counseling Assn., Kiwanis (treas. 1991-94, Treas. award 1994), Phi Delta Kappa. Republican. Roman Catholic. Avocations: collecting books, history books, books on U.S. presidents, immigration. Home: 90 Oakleaf Dr Waterbury CT 06708-3633 Office: Rotella Magnet Sch 380 Pierport Rd Waterbury CT 06705

AUCH, WALTER EDWARD, securities company executive; b. Detroit, Apr. 12, 1921; s. Fred J. and Beatrice H. (Higgins) A.; m. Patricia H.; children: Walter Edward, Timothy R., Terrance H. Student, Albion Coll., also U. Detroit, 1939-42, Cornell U., 1959. Stockbroker William C. Roney & Co., Detroit, 1946-55; sr. partner Bache & Co., N.Y.C., 1955-64, Paine, Webber, Jackson & Curtis, N.Y.C., 1964-70; pres. Nat. Securities & Research Corp., N.Y.C., 1970-72; exec. v.p. duPont, Glore, Forgan, Inc., N.Y.C., 1972-73; pres. duPont Walston, Inc., 1973-74; sr. exec. v.p. Paine, Webber, Jackson & Curtis, N.Y.C., 1974-79; chmn., chief exec. officer Chgo. Bd. Options Exchange, 1979-86, cons., 1987—. Bd. dirs. Smith Barney Concert Series Fund, Smith Barney Trak Fund, Advisors Series Trust, Nicholas/Applegate Funds, Banyan Land Trust, Semele Group, Inc., UBS Funds. Trustee Hillsdale Coll., Ariz. Heart Inst. With USAAF, 1942-45. Mem. Bond Club N.Y., Bond Club Chgo., N.Y. Stock Exch. Club, Chgo. Club, Greenwich Country Club, Paradise Valley Country Club (Scottsdale), Crystal Downs Country Club (Crystal Lake, Mich.), Sigma Chi. Address: 2700 Crystal Dr Crystal Lake Beulah MI 49617 *When I was a boy, my grandfather advised me to "live every day in such a way that the line behind the hearse gets longer." I've tried hard to follow that advice.*

AUCHINCLOSS, LOUIS STANTON, writer; b. Lawrence, N.Y., Sept. 27, 1917; s. Joseph Howland and Priscilla (Stanton) A.; m. Adele Lawrence, Sept. 1957; children: John, Blake, Andrew. Student, Yale U., 1939; LLB, U. Va., 1941; LittD, NYU, 1974, Pace U., 1979, U. of the South, 1986. Bar: N.Y. bar 1941. Assoc. Sullivan & Cromwell, 1941-51, Hawkins, Delafield & Wood, N.Y.C., 1954-58, ptnr., 1958-86. Author: The Indifferent Children, 1947, The Injustice Collectors, 1950, Sybil, 1952, A Law for the Lion, 1953, The Romantic Egoists, 1954, The Great World and Timothy Colt, 1956, Venus in Sparta, 1958, Pursuit of the Prodigal, 1959, The House of Five Talents, 1960, Reflections of a Jacobite, 1961, Portrait in Brownstone, 1962, Powers of Attorney, 1963, The Rector of Justin, 1964, Pioneers and Caretakers, 1965, The Embezzler, 1966, Tales of Manhattan, 1967, A World of Profit, 1968, Motiveless Malignity, 1969, Second Chance, 1970, Edith Wharton, 1971, I Came As a Thief, Richelieu, 1972, The Partners, A Writer's Capital, 1974, Reading Henry James, 1975, The Winthrop Covenant, 1976, The Dark Lady, 1977, The Country Cousin, 1978, Persons of Consequence, 1979, Life, Law and Letters, 1979, The

House of the Prophet, 1980, The Cat and the King, 1981, Watchfires, 1982, Exit Lady Masham, 1983, The Book Class, 1984, Honorable Men, 1985, Diary of a Yuppie, 1986, Skinny Island, 1987, The Golden Calves, 1988, Fellow Passengers, 1989, The Vanderbilt Era, 1989, The Lady of Situations, 1991, False Gods, 1992, Three Lives, 1993, Tales of Yesteryear, 1994, The Style's The Man, 1994, Collected Stories, 1994, The Education of Oscar Fairfax, 1995, The Man Behind the Book, 1996, LA Gloire, 1996, The Atonement, 1997, The Anniversary, 1999, Her Infinite Variety, 2000, Woodrow Wilson, 2000, Theodore Roosevelt, 2002, Manhattan Monologues, 2002. Trustee emeritus Josiah Macy, Jr., Found.; chmn. Mus. City of N.Y. Lt. USNR, 1941-45. Mem. AAAL (pres. emeritus), Assn. Bar City N.Y., Century Assn. Episcopalian. Home: 1111 Park Ave New York NY 10128-1234*

AUCH YELLIN, BARBARA ANN, musician; d. Mary Lorinda McGlinn and Willard David Auch, Hilda Jean Carpenter; m. Jack David Yellin, May 2, 1982; 1 child, Michelle Elizabeth Yellin. MusB, CSUN, Northridge, Calif., 1969—75; MusM for Fgn. Piano, Conservatory of Santa Cecilia, Rome, Italy, 1976—78. Music instr. Yamaha Music Sch., Los Angeles, Calif., 1979—83; piano instr. self-employed, Los Angeles, Calif., 1983—2000, Santa Monica, Calif., 1983—2000; piano accompanist Free Lance, Santa Monica, Calif., 1998—, Los Angeles, Calif., 1998—. Composer Self;children's Music, Los Angeles, Calif., 1995—. Girl scout leader Girl Scouts of Am., Santa Monica, Calif., 1997—2002. Fellow Rotary Fellowship, Rotary Clubs of Am., 1975-1977; scholar Music, Bank of Am., 1978. Mem.: Calif. Assoc. of Prof. Music Teachers (treas. 1987—89), Music Teachers Assn. of Calif. (assoc.; treas. 1994—96), Sigma Alpha Iota (life), Pi Kappa Lambda (hon.). D-Conservative. Avocations: swimming, gourmet cooking, traveling. Home and Office: 1714 Stoner Ave unit 8 Los Angeles CA 90025 Home Fax: 310-820-0029. Personal E-mail: barbara.yellin@verizon.net.

AUCLAIR, LOUISE A. education educator; b. Somersworth, N.H., Feb. 25, 1941; d. Alphonse J. and Alice M. (Chretien) A. BA in English and Elem. Edn., Notre Dame Coll., 1968; MEd in Reading, Salem State Coll., 1973; PhD in Higher Edn., Boston Coll., 1990. Mem. Sisters of Holy Cross, 1958—. Elem. sch. tchr. New Bedford (Mass.) Schs., 1960-61, Nashua and Rochester (N.H.) Schs., 1963-70; elem. sch. prin. Suncook and Nashua, N.H., 1970-74; reading specialist Rochester Cath. Sch., 1974-75, Nashua Cath. Sch., 1975-80; grad. divsn. chair Notre Dame Coll., Manchester, N.H., 1981-87, 90-91, dean edn., 1991-95, prof. edn., 1995—2002; dean faculty edn. Regina Assumpta Coll., Cap Haitien, Haiti, 1995—; assoc. prof. edn. Rivier Coll., Nashua, NH, 2002—. Author: Ideas for Teachers from Teachers, 1983, Historical Development of Departmental Leadership in American Higher Education, 1990. Mentor College Bound program Boston Coll., Chestnut Hill, Mass., 1988-90; usher Palace Theater, Manchester, 1995—. Named Moreau Disting. Svc. Prof., Notre Dame Coll., 1995. Mem. Internat. Reading Assn., New Eng. Reading Assn., Granite State Reading, Assn. Supervision and Curriculum Devel., Phi Delta Kappa (v.p. 1982-84, pres. 1984-85, coll. rep. 1985-87, 90—2001, historian 1995-2001), Alpha Sigma Nu. Roman Catholic. Avocations: reading, travel, sewing. Home: 68 Mammoth Rd Londonderry NH 03053-4024 Office: Rivier Coll 420 Main St Nashua NH 03060-5086 E-mail: lauclair@rivier.edu.

AUCUTT, RONALD DAVID, lawyer; b. St. Paul, Dec. 28, 1945; s. Howard Lewis and Eleanor May (Malcolm) A.; m. Grace Diane Kok, Apr. 3, 1976; children: David Gerard, James Andrew. BA, U. Minn., 1967, JD, 1975. Bar: Minn. 1975, D.C. 1976, Va. 1978, Tex. 1999, U.S. Supreme Ct. 1978, U.S. Tax Ct. 1980, U.S. Dist. Ct. D.C. 1980, U.S. Ct. Appeals (D.C. cir.) 1980, U.S. Ct. of Claims 1980, U.S. Claims Ct. 1982, U.S. Ct. Appeals (fed. cir.) 1982, U.S. Dist. Ct. (ea. dist.) Va. 1986, U.S. Ct. Appeals (4th cir.) 1986. Assoc. Miller & Chevalier, Chartered, Washington, 1975-81, ptnr., 1982-98, McGuireWoods LLP, McLean, Va., 1998—. Mem. bd. advisors IRS Practice Alert, N.Y.C., 1987-93; adj. prof. Sch. Law U. Va., 1998—; mem. adv. com. Philip E. Heckerling Inst. on Estate Planning U. Miami, 1999—. Mem. bd. advisors Jour. Taxation Exempt Orgns., 1989-2000, Bus. Entities, N.Y.C., 1999—; mem. editl. bd. Estate Planning, N.Y.C., 1993—, mem. adv. bd. Tax Mgmt. Estates, Gifts, and Trusts Jour., 1999—; editl. adv. bd. Bus. Valuation Update, Portland, Oreg., 1999—; contbr. articles to profl. publs. Orgn. Security and Coop. in Europe internat. observer Bulgarian Parliamentary Election, 1997; sec.-treas. Miller and Chevalier Charitable Found., Washington, 1980—82, pres., 1993—97; bd. dirs. Coun. for Ct. Excellence, Washington, 1993—99, Advocates Internat., Fairfax, Va., 1997—2000, vice chmn., 1999—2000; mem. adv. bd. Trinity Law Sch., Santa Ana, Calif., 1998—2001; bd. visitors U. Minn. Law Sch., 1998—; bd. regents Trinity Internat. U., Deerfield, Ill., 2000—; bd. dirs. Evang. Free Ch. Am., Mpls., 1986—92, vice moderator, chmn. bd. dirs., 1993—95, moderator, 1995—97. Lt. USN, 1970—73. Fellow: Am. Coll. Trust and Estate Counsel (bd. regents 1996—, chmn. bus. planning com. 1997—2000, sec. 1999—2000, treas. 2000—01, v.p. 2001—02, pres.-elect 2002—03, pres. 2003—), Am. Coll. Tax Counsel, Am. Bar Found.; mem.: ABA (chair taxation sect., com. on estate and gift taxes 1986—88, vice chmn. com. on govt. submissions 1989—91, liaison to sect. real property, probate and trust law 1990—, chmn. com. on govt. submissions 1991—93, coun. 1993—97, vice chair com. ops. 1998—2000), Christian Legal Soc., Internat. Acad. Estate and Trust Law (exec. coun. 2000—, academician), U. Minn. Law Alumni Assn. (bd. dirs. 1998—), Met. Club Washington. Home: 3417 Silver Maple Pl Falls Church VA 22042-3545 Office: McGuireWoods LLP 1750 Tysons Blvd Ste 1800 Mc Lean VA 22102-4215 E-mail: raucutt@mcguirewoods.com.

AUDET, HENRI, retired communications executive; b. Montreal, Que., Can., Aug. 7, 1918; s. Victor F. and Alice (Turgeon) A.; m. Marie Labelle, June 24, 1950; children: Louis, François, Denise, Bernard, Geneviève. BA, BA in Sci., U. Montreal; DSc (hon.), U. Montreal Poly., 2000; MSEE, MIT; DSc (hon.), U. Que., 1979. Staff CBC, 1945-47, engr.-in-charge Montreal dist., 1948-52, regional engr. Que., spl. TV com., 1953-57; pres. TV St. Maurice Inc., 1957-72, La Belle Vision, Inc., 1973, TV St. François, Inc., 1974-76; chmn., CEO Cogeco Inc., 1976-93, chmn. bd. dirs., 1993-96, Cogeco Cable, Inc., 1993-96; chmn. emeritus, ret., 1996. Chmn. bd. Publ. Dumont Inc., 1988, TV de l'Est du Can., 1982; pres. Cogeco Devel. Fund, 1992-96. Past chmn. Que. U., Trois Rivières, Com. Trifluvien des Concerts Symphonique de Que., Cultural Ctr.; past dir. Symphonic Concerts Que., Ctr. Hospitalier Ste.-Marie; active Festivals de Musique Que., Counseil des gouverneurs associès des U. Montreal, bd. govs. Fondation U. Ctr. Que., 1989; mem. hon. coun. Montreal Symphonic Orch.; pres. Fondation du Theatre du Rideau Vert, Fonds du Patrimoine de la paroisse St-Viateur d'Outremont. Decorated Order of Can.; recipient Prix de comm. Govt. of Que., 1989, Prix Mérite, Assn. Anciens de Poly., 1991; named to honors list Can. Cable TV Assn., 1994. Mem. l'ACRTF (Can. French lang. broadcasters, pres. 1962-64, Grand Prix 1987), IEEE, Can. Assn. Broadcasters (pres. 1971, Golden Ribbon award 1989), Engring. Inst. Can. (past dir.), Hall of Fame of the Canadian Assn. Broadcasters, Broadcast Execs. Soc., Found. Des Ingenieurs du Quebec (bd. dirs.), Hydro-Quebec (bd. dirs.), Can. Acad. Engring, Order of Egrs., Can. C. of C., Que. C. of C., Montreal C. of C., Montreal Bd. Trade, Thelma Finlayson Soc., Mount-Royal Club, St. Denis Club, St. Maurice Yacht Club, Laviolette Club, Radisson Club, Ki-8-Eb Golf Club, Club des Ambassadeurs de la CEDIC, Pres. Club. Roman Catholic. Avocations: travel, sailing, arts, photography. Home: 169 Maplewood Ave Outremont, Que QC Canada H2V 2M6 Office: Cogeco Inc 1 Pl Ville Marie Ste 3636 Montreal QC Canada H3B 3P2

AUDET, PAUL ANDRE, retired newspaper executive; b. Quebec, Can., Mar. 14, 1923; s. Sylvio and Rose Aimee (Cloutier) A.; m. Michele Richard, Sept. 13, 1947; children: Francine, Andre, Marc. D. Honoris Causa (hon.), U. Québec, 1985. Newspaper reporter L'Evenement Jour., 1942-44; staff writer The Canadian Press, 1944, asst. mng. editor, 1945-48, sales and sales mgr. printing dept., 1948-54; advt. dir. Le Soleil Quebec, 1955-74; pres., gen. mgr., 1974-88. Past pres. Edimedia, Inc., Que. Opera Co. Named hon. col. Les Voltigeurs de Que. Regt. Mem. Ordre des Chevaliers de Meduse, Garrison Club, Order of Can. Roman Catholic. *Whatever you do or you are, try to be the best. Somehow, some day, someone is bound to find out and you will be rewarded accordingly.*

AUER, JAMES MATTHEW, art critic, journalist; b. Neenah, Wis., Dec. 2, 1928; s. Matthew George and Charlotte Agnes (Friedland) A.; m. Marilyn Mills, Feb. 1, 1964; 1 son, Charles William. BA, Lawrence Coll., Appleton, Wis., 1950. With accounting dept. George Banta Co., 1950-51; reporter Twin City News-Record, 1953-56, asst. to editor, 1957-60, news editor, 1960-61; asst. Sunday editor Appleton Post-Crescent, 1960-65, Sunday editor, 1965-72; art critic Milw. Jour., 1972—. Author: The Spirit is Willing, 1960; plays: The City of Light, 1961, Tell It to Angela, 1971; motion pictures: The Magic World of Patrick Farrell, 1978, The Bohrod Touch, 1984, An Artist's Vision: Born on the Stone, 1986, Olgivanna Lloyd Wright: A Partner to Genius, 1993, In Your Face: The Distorted World of John Kascht, 1994, Etched in Acid: Warrington Colescott, 1998. Presiding officer Attic Theatre, Inc., 1959-62; pres. Friends of Bergstrom Art Center, 1967-68; mem. Neenah Municipal Mus. Found., Inc. Recipient Pres.'s award Wis. Heart Assn., 1969 Mem. Am. Assn. Sunday and Feature Editors (pres. 1972-73), State Hist. Soc. Wis. (award of merit 1962), Soc. Profl. Journalists, Milw. Press Club, Phi Kappa Tau. Congregationalist. Home: 1849 N 72nd St Wauwatosa WI 53213-2353 Office: Milw Jour Sentinel 333 W State St Milwaukee WI 53203-1305 E-mail: jauer@onwis.com. *Art is not a luxury or a frill. It is a quality-of-life issue. That is why I have spent so much of my life enjoying, collecting and writing about it.*

AUER, MANFRED STEFAN, structural biologist, biochemist; b. Gottmadingen, German, Dec. 25, 1966; came to U.S., 1998; s. Werner and Elisabeth (Ritter) A.; m. Michaela Liedtke, July 9, 1969; 1 child, Natasha Sophie. Diploma in Biochemistry, U. Hannover, Germany, 1993; PhD, U. Frankfurt, Germany, 1998. Vis. scientist Johns Hopkins U., Balt., 1993; fellow European Molecular Biology Lab., Heidelberg, Germany, 1993-97, Max Plank Inst. of Biophysics, Frankfurt, 1997-98; rsch. assoc. Skirball Inst., NYU Med. Ctr., N.Y.C., 1998—, Rockefeller U., N.Y.C., 1998—2002, rsch. assoc. Lab. Sensory Neurosci., 2002—. Contbr. articles to profl. jours. Cusanuswerk fellow, 1989-93, Human Frontier Sci. Program fellow, 1998-2000, Jane Coffin Childs Meml. fellow, 2000-2002; recipient Otto-Hahn award Max-Planck Soc., 1999. Mem. AAAS, Biophys. Soc., Harvey Soc. Avocations: soccer, painting, travel. Office: Lab Sensory Neurosci Rockfeller Univ 1230 York Ave New York NY 10021

AUERBACH, ALAN JEFFREY, economist, educator; b. N.Y.C., Sept. 27, 1951; s. William and Tess (Kasper) A.; m. Gay Cameron Quimby, June 25, 1978; children: Ethan, Andrew. BA, Yale U., 1974; PhD, Harvard U., 1978. Asst. prof. dept. econs. Harvard U., Cambridge, Mass., 1978-82, assoc. prof., 1982-83; assoc. prof. dept. econs. U. Pa., Phila., 1983-85, prof., 1985-94, chmn. dept., 1988-90, prof. Sch. Law, 1990-94; Robert D. Burch prof. of tax policy and pub. fin. U. Calif., Berkeley, 1994—, chmn. dept., 2001—02. Author: The Taxation of Capital Income, 1983 (David A. Wells prize); co-author: Dynamic Fiscal Policy, 1987, Macroeconomics: An Integrated Approach, 1995, Generational Accounting Around the World, 1999; editor: Corporate Takeovers, 1988, Mergers and Acquisitions, 1988, Fiscal Policy: Lessons from Economic Research, 1997; co-editor: Handbook of Public Economics, Vol. I, 1985, Vol. II, 1987, Vol. III, 2002, Vol. IV, 2002, Demographic Change and Fiscal Policy, 2001; editor jour. Econ. Perspectives, 1995-96. Fellow Am. Acad. Arts and Scis., Econometric Soc.; mem. Am. Econ. Assn. (exec. com. 1992-94, v.p. 1999), Phi Beta Kappa. Home: 110 El Camino Real Berkeley CA 94705-2823 Office: U Calif Berkeley Dept Econs 549 Evans Hall Berkeley CA 94720-3880 E-mail: auerbach@econ.berkeley.edu.

AUERBACH, ANDREW B, polymer engineer, chemist; s. Isidor and Geraldine Auerbach; m. Diane L. Shapass, June 11, 1972; children: Meredith, Lee. BS - Chemistry, Bklyn Coll., 1968; MBA -Mktg., Rutgers U., Newark, NJ, 1979; PhD - Polymer Chemistry, CUNY, 1974. Registered Patent Agt. U.S. Patent and Trademark Office Dept. Commerce, 1994. Group leader ITT Rayonier, Whippany, NJ, 1974—81; devel. assoc. Ticona Divsn. of Celanese, Summit, NJ, 1981—. Course dir. Ctr. for Profl Advancement, East Brunswick, NJ, 1992—2002. Patentee in field. Fellow: Soc. Plastics Engineers (Best Paper in Divsn. 1994); mem.: Am. Chem. Soc. Home: 23 Orchard Ln Livingston NJ 07039 Office: Ticona Divsn Celanese 90 Morris Ave Summit NJ 07901 Personal E-mail: daauerbach@msn.com. E-mail: andy.auerbach@ticona.com.

AUERBACH, ANITA L. clinical psychologist; b. Flushing, N.Y., Dec. 23, 1946; d. Ben and Gussie (Zuckerman) Weiss; m. Steven Miles Auerbach, May 25, 1969. BA cum laude, SUNY, Buffalo, 1968, MA, 1970; PhD (N.Y. State Regents fellow 1970-72), George Washington U., 1977. Diplomate Am. Bd. Med. Psychotherapists, Internat. Acad. Behavioral Medicine. Chief rsch. Youth Crime Control Project D.C. Dept. Corrections, 1970-74; intern clin. psychology No. Va. Tng. Ctr., Fairfax, 1974-75, staff psychologist, then chief psychol. svcs., 1975-79; pvt. practice clin. psychology Commonwealth Psychol. Assocs., McLean, Va., 1979—, dir., 1979—, pres., 1979—; asst. clin. prof. psychology George Washington U. Lectr. Washington Tech. Inst., 1972-74, George Mason U., 1978—82; asst. clin. prof. psychology George Washington U., 2003—; cons. in field. Contbr. articles to profl. jours. Mem. adv. bd. World Children's Choir, 2000—02; mem. family edn. project Joseph P. Kennedy Jr. Found., 1977—79; mem. regional appeals bd. No. Va. Pub. Sch. Sys., 1977—79; mem. adv. bd. Value Options Behavioral Health, 2001—. Recipient N.Y. State Scholar Incentive award, 1969. Mem. APA, Am. Soc. Clin. Hypnosis (approved cons.), Va. Acad. Clin. Psychologists, Va. Psychol. Assn., No. Va. Soc. Clin. Psychologists, Washington Soc. Study Clin. Hypnosis, Psi Chi, Alpha Lambda Delta. Office: 1479 Chain Bridge Rd Mc Lean VA 22101-5730

AUERBACH, BOB SHIPLEY, librarian; b. N.Y.C., Dec. 14, 1919; s. Leo and Gertrude Anne (Shipley) A.; m. Mary Carson, July 13, 1954 (div. Mar. 1976); children: Hopi, Jennine. BA, NYU, 1948; MA in Libr. Sci., Vanderbilt U., 1956. Asst. libr. Shepherd Coll., Shepherdstown, W.Va., 1956-57, Coll. Steubenville (Ohio), 1957-58; libr. Tecumseh High Sch, New Carlisle, Ohio, 1958-59, Urbana (Ohio) Coll., 1959-61; dir. Capital Libr. Svc., Greenbelt, Md., 1961-72; reference libr. U. D.C., Washington, 1972-87; libr. World Hunger Edn. Svc., Washington, 1988-91; retired, 1991—. Chair Peoples Party Md., 1972-73, Md. Green Party, 1998-2001; mem. Green coun. Green Nat. Com., Lawrence, Mass., 1995-97; chair Greenbelt Greens, 1990-2001, Socialist Discussion Group, Washington, 1975—; mem. Nat. Com. Socialist Party, 1991-95, alt. mem. nat. com., 1995-97, nat. com. mem., 1997-99; mem. state com. Md. Green Party, 2001—. Mem. ALA, AAUP, Am. Polit. Sci. Assn., Washington Independent Writers Assn. Avocations: stamp collecting, button collecting. Home: 14 X Ridge Rd Greenbelt MD 20770 E-mail: bauerbach1@aol.com.

AUERBACH, ERNEST SIGMUND, lawyer, company executive, writer; b. Berlin, Dec. 22, 1936; s. Frank L. and Gertrude A.; m. Jeanette Taylor, 1990; 1 child, Hans Kevin. AB, George Washington U., 1958, JD, 1961; postgrad., U.S. Army Gen. Staff Coll., 1975. Bar: D.C. 1962, Pa. 1978. Atty. So. Ry. Co., Washington, 1961-62; commd 1st lt. U.S. Army, 1962, advanced through grades to col.; served in Germany, Vietnam, Pentagon; div. counsel Xerox Corp., Stamford, Conn., 1970-75; mng. atty. NL Industries, Inc., N.Y.C., 1975-77; from asst. to assoc. gen. counsel, staff v.p. INA Corp., Phila., 1977-79; sr. v.p. INA Svc. Co., 1979-82; sr. v.p., chief of staff INA Internat., 1982-83; pres. internat. life and group ops. CIGNA Worldwide Corp. div. CIGNA Corp., 1984-89; mng. dir. Crusader Life Ins. PLC, Reigate, Eng., 1984-86, chmn., 1986-89; pres., COO N.Y. Life Worldwide Holding, Inc., N.Y.C., 1989-90; pres., CEO Paperless Claims, Inc., N.Y.C., 1991-92; dir. gen. Seguros Azteca Ins. Co., Mexico City, 1992-93; sr. cons. Anderson Consulting, Mexico City, 1993-95; sr. v.p. United Ins. Cos., Inc., Irving, Tex., 1995-97, also pres., CEO student ins. divsn., 1996-97, pres., CEO ins. group, 1997; pres., COO Software Testing Assurance Corp., N.Y.C., 1998; pres., CEO Tesin Corp., N.Y.C., 1998—2001, chmn., bd. dirs., 2002; sr. v.p. Strickland Group, N.Y.C., 2001—03; v.p. ALICO, 2003—. Mem. adv. bd. revbox.com, 1998—2001. Author: Joining the Inner Circle: How To Make It As A Senior Executive, 1990; contbg. author: The Wall St. Jour. on Mng., 1990; contbr. articles to legal, fin., news, and def. jours. Mem. Am. Coun. on Germany, 1980-2000; computer sys. tech. adv. com. Dept. Commerce, 1974-76; mem. bd. adv. dirs. Salvation Army, Mexico City, 1993-94; commr. bd. adjustment City of Coppell, Tex., 1996-97. Ret. col. USAR, 1985. Decorated Legion of Merit with oak leaf cluster, Bronze Star. Mem. Westchester-Fairfield Corp. Counsel Assn. (founding officer 1973-78), Audubon Soc. (pres., bd. dirs. Greenwich chpt. 1999-2002, bd. dirs. Conn. chpt. 2002—), Univ. Club, Nat. Arts Club (N.Y.C.), Army and Navy Club (Washington chpt.). Home: 150 Southwoods Terr Southbury CT 06488 E-mail: colauerbach@earthlink.net.

AUERBACH, JEROLD S. university educator; b. Phila., May 7, 1936; s. Morry M. and Sophie (Soloff) A.; m. Susan H. Levin, May 16, 1982; children: Shira, Rebecca; children from previous marriage Jeffrey, Pamela. BA, Oberlin Coll., 1957; MA, Columbia U., 1959, PhD, 1965. Lectr. Queens Coll. CUNY, 1964-65; asst. prof. Brandeis U., Waltham, Mass., 1965-71, Wellesley (Mass.) Coll., 1971-72, assoc. prof., 1972-77, prof., 1977—. Vis. scholar Harvard Law Sch.; Fulbright lectr. Tel Aviv U., 1974-75. Author: Labor and Liberty, 1966, Unequal Justice, 1976, Justice Without Law?, 1983, Rabbis and Lawyers, 1990, Jacob's Voices, 1996, Are We One?, 2001. Guggenheim Meml. Found. fellow, 1974-75; fellow NSF, 1979-80, NEH, 1986-87, 91-92. Office: Wellesley Coll 106 Central St Wellesley MA 02481-8268 E-mail: jsauerbach@attbi.com.

AUERBACH, JOSEPH, lawyer, educator, retired; b. Franklin, N.H., Dec. 3, 1916; s. Jacob and Besse Mae (Reamer) A.; m. Judith Evans, Nov. 10, 1941; children: Jonathan L., Hope B. Pym. AB, Harvard U., 1938, LLB, 1941. Bar: N.H. 1941, Mass. 1952, U.S. Ct. Appeals (1st, 2d, 3d, 5th, 7th and D.C. cirs.), U.S. Supreme Ct. 1948. Atty. SEC, Washington and Phila., 1941-43, prin. atty., 1946-49; fgn. service staff officer U.S. Dept. State, Dusseldorf, W. Ger., 1950-52; ptnr. Sullivan & Worcester, Boston, 1952-82, counsel, 1982—; lectr. Boston U. Law Sch., 1975-76, Harvard Bus. Sch., Boston, 1980-82, prof., 1982-83, Class of 1957 prof., 1983-87, prof. emeritus, 1987—; prof. Harvard Extension Sch., 1988, 91-95. Bd. dirs. Nat. Benefit Life Ins. Co., N.Y.C. Author: (with S.L. Hayes, III), Investment Banking and Diligence, 1986, Underwriting Regulation and Shelf Registration Phenomenon in Wall Street and Regulation, 1987, also chpt. to book, papers and articles in field. Trustee Mass. Eye and Ear Infirmary, Boston, 1981—, chmn. devel. com., 1985-88, chmn. nominating com., 1993-94; mem. adv. bd., former chmn. devel. com. Am. Repertory Theatre, Cambridge, Mass., 1985—; bd. dirs., past pres. Friends of Boston U. Librs., 1972—; past v.p., bd. dirs. Shakespeare Globe Ctr., N.A., 1983-90; overseer New Eng. Conservatory of Music, 1992-98, mem. fin. com.; bd. dirs. English Speaking Union, Boston, 1995-98; chair 1938 Harvard Pres. Assn.; active Harvard Coll. Fund, Harvard Law Sch. Fund. Decorated Army Commendation medal; recipient Disting. Svc. award Harvard Bus. Sch., 1996, Disting. Teaching award 1993, Exemplary Svc. award Harvard Extension Sch., 1995. Mem. ABA, Mass. Bar Assn., Boston Bar Assn., Harvard Mus. Assn., St. Botolph Club, Harvard Club N.Y.C., Shop Club, Downtown Club. Home: 300 Boylston St Apt 512 Boston MA 02116-3923 Office: Sullivan & Worcester 1 Post Office Sq Ste 2300 Boston MA 02109-2129 also: Harvard Bus Sch Cumnock Hall Rm 300 Boston MA 02163

AUERBACH, MARSHALL JAY, lawyer; b. Chgo., Sept. 5, 1932; s. Samuel M. and Sadie (Miller) A.; m. Carole Landsberg, July 3, 1960; children: Keith Alan, Michael Ward Student, U. Ill.; JD, John Marshall Law Sch., 1955. Bar: Ill. 1955. Sole practice, Evanston, Ill., 1955-72; ptnr. in charge matrimonial law sect. Jenner & Block, Chgo., 1972-80; mem. firm Marshall J. Auerbach & Assocs., Ltd., Chgo., 1980—. Mem. faculty Ill. Inst. Continuing Legal Edn. Author: Illinois Marriage and Dissolution of Marriage Act, enacted into law, 1977; Historical and Practice Notes to Illinois Marriage and Dissolution of Marriage Act, 1980-88; contbr. chpts. to Family Law, Vol. 2 Fellow Am. Acad. Matrimonial Lawyers; mem. Ill. State Bar Assn. (chmn. family law sect. 1971-72), ABA (vice-chmn. family law sect. com. for liaison with tax sect. 1974-76) Home and Office: Marshall J Auerbach & Assoc Ltd 30 N La Salle St Ste 3400 Chicago IL 60602

AUERBACH, PAUL IRA, lawyer; b. N.Y.C., Dec. 30, 1932; s. Joseph and Fannie (Steingard) A.; children: Stuart Andrew, Beth Royce. LLB, Bklyn. Law Sch., 1954; CLU, Am. Coll., 1980, ChFC, 1982. Bar: N.Y. 1955, Fla. 1991, U.S. Dist. Ct. (so. and ea. dists.) N.Y., U.S. Dist Ct. (so. dist.) Fla. 1991. Trial counsel Cosmopolitan Mutual Ins. Corp., N.Y.C., 1955-57, Hertz Corp., N.Y.C., 1957-59; ptnr. Brent, Phillips, Auerbach & Dranoff, Rockland, N.Y., 1959-63; prin. Paul I. Auerbach, Atty. at Law, N.Y.C. and Bronx, 1963-97, Palm Beach Gardens, Fla., 1990—. Founder Young Dem. Com., Bronx, 1955-60; committeeman Rep. Com., South Orangeton, N.Y., 1970-76. Mem.: KP, Rotary (chmn. drug prevention com. 1970—74), ABA, Nat. Acad. Elder Law Attys., Internat. Assn. Fin. Planners, Planned Giving Coun. of Palm Beach County, Tax Inst. of Palm Beach County, Fla. Bar Assn., Palm Beach County Bar Assn., North Palm Beach County Bar Assn. (pres. 1999—2000), Bronx Bar Assn. (chmn. criminal law com. 1990—91), N.Y. State Bar Assn., Masons. Avocations: tennis, gourmet food, golf. Home: 11215 Curry Dr Palm Beach Gardens FL 33418 E-mail: piaesq@yahoo.com.

AUERBACH, SEYMOUR, architect; b. N.Y.C., May 28, 1929; s. Nathan and Jennie (Norman) A.; m. Alyce Kelly, Oct. 21, 1963 (div. 1977); children: Kalin Marie Hyman, Alison Kelly; m. Patricia Sullivan, July 31, 1985 (div. 1991). B.Arch., Yale U., 1951. Asso. firm Satterlee & Smith (Architects), Washington, 1955-59; partner Cooper & Auerbach (Architects), Washington, 1960-69, Walton, Madden, Cooper & Auerbach (Architects), Washington, 1970-71; prin. Offices Seymour Auerbach (Architect), Washington, 1971—. Pres. Kamak Enterprises, Inc., sole propr. for patent commercialization; developer, architect Battery Subdiv., Washington, Buck's Knoll Farm, Yellow Spring, W.Va.; prof. architecture Cath. U. Am., 1960-99; cons. construction failures, 1982—. Prin. works include Nat. Visitor Ctr., Washington, campus plan and dormitories, Georgetown U., Olam Tikvah Synagogue, Fairfax, Va., Brith Sholom Synagogue, Bethlehem, Pa., resort cmtys., Rehoboth Beach, Del., campus for Bowling Brook prep; patentee in unrelated fields. Bd. mgrs. Chevy Chase Village, Md., 1973-77, vice chmn. bd., 1976-77; mem. archtl. adv. panel Union of Am. Hebrew Congregations. With C.E. U.S. Army, 1951-54. Decorated knight honor and merit Imperial Russian Order St. John of Jerusalem; recipient award excellence in architecture Met. Washington Bd. Trade, 1964, Papal Benemerenti medal, 1994, Rsch. Ctr. award Georgetown U., 1964; winner award competition for design of Copley Plaza, Boston, 1967, award for excellence in arch. Wash. Bd. Trade, 1964; William Wirt Winchester fellow, 1951. Fellow AIA (1st award for excellence in design Potomac Valley chpt. 1964); mem. AAUP, Soc. Archtl. Historians, Guild Religious Architecture, Cosmos Club Washington, Yale Club Washington. Republican. Jewish. Home and Office: 115 Hesketh St Chevy Chase MD 20815-4222 *I consider it to be of the highest calling to be involved in the improvement of man's physical environment: not only his shelter, but also his public environment and the implements he uses. In this context I have held architecture to be an Applied, rather than a Fine, Art. I consider it to be a higher calling to be a designer than to be an architect and I find the greatest of personal pleasure in solving individual problems of design for man, by myself, without regard to "style", and without regard to political or other irrelevant considerations.*

AUERBACH, STANLEY IRVING, ecologist, environmental scientist, educator; b. Chgo., May 21, 1921; s. Abraham and Carrie (Friedman) A.; m. Dawn Patricia Davey, June 12, 1954; children: Andrew J., Anne E., Jonathan B., Alison M. BS, U. Ill., 1946, MS, 1947; PhD, Northwestern U., 1949. Instr., then asst. prof. Roosevelt U., Chgo., 1950-54; assoc. scientist, then scientist health physics divsn. Oak Ridge (Tenn.) Nat. Lab., 1954-59, sr. scientist, sect. leader, 1959-70, dir. ecol. sci. divsn., 1970-72, dir. environ. scis. divsn., 1972-86, sr. rsch. advisor, 1986-90; adj. prof. ecology U. Tenn., 1965-90; adj. rsch. prof. radiation ecology U. Ga., 1964-90. Mem. U.S. exec. com. Internat. Biol. Program, co-chmn. program coord. com., dir. deciduous forest biome project, 1969-74; mem. exec. com. Sci. Adv. Bd. U.S. EPA, 1986-92; adv. com. Sci. and Tech. NSF, 1989-91; environ. adv. bd. U.S.C.E., 1989-93; mem. NAS Adv. Com. on Rsch. to Sec. Agr., 1969-70, NAE Power Plant Siting Program Commn., 1970-71, mem. bd. energy studies, 1974-77, chmn. com. on energy and environ., 1974-77, chmn. environ. studies bd., 1983-86, mem. com. on phys. scis., math. and resources, 1982-83, mem. com on natural resources, 1979-82; chmn. archtl. rev. com. Oak Ridge Nat. Lab., 1971-84; mem. ecol. adv. bd. Bur. Reclamation; mem. NAS-NAE Bd. on Energy Studies, 1974-77; mem. C.E. bd. environ. cons. Tenn.-Tombigbee Waterway, 1975-86; mem. ad hoc com. on transuranic burial ERDA (Dept. Energy, 1976-78; mem. Pres.' Spl. Com. on Health and Environ. Effects of Increasing Coal Utilization, 1977-78, Resources for the Future Rsch. Adv. Com., 1978-81; mem. commn. natural resources NRC, 1979-81; mem. adv. coun. Water Resources Rsch. Ctr. U. Tenn., 1980-91; mem. NAS-NRC Com. on Bldg. an Environ. Mgmt. Sci. Program for DOE, 1996-97. Ecology editor Environ. Internat., 1979-94; mem. adv. bd. Environ. and Exptl. Botany, 1967-92; mem. bd. editors Radiation Rsch., 1975-77. 2nd lt. AUS, 1942-44. Recipient Dist. Assoc. award U.S. Dept. Energy, 1987, Comdr.'s award U.S. Dept. Army, 1990. Fellow AAAS; mem. Am. Inst. Biol. Scis. (bd. govs.), Soc. Zoology (chmn. ecology div.), Am. Soc. Agronomy, Brit. Ecol. Soc., Health Physics Soc., Entomol. Soc. Am., Soc. Systematic Biology, Ecol. Soc. Am. (chmn. com. radioecology 1963-65, sec. 1964-69, chmn. fin. com. 1969, pres. 1971-72, Disting. Service award 1985), Internat. Union Radioecology (pres. 1984-87, mem. of honour 1991), Sigma Xi (pres. Oak Ridge br. 1972-73, chmn. admissions 1980-82), Alpha Epsilon Pi. Achievements include research on ecology centipedes, radioecology and

radioactive waste disposal; on environmental behavior of radionuclides and ecosystem analysis; pioneer in large scale interdisciplinary ecological research with emphasis on ecosystem processes. Home: 3314 West End Ave Apt 202 Nashville TN 37203-0916 E-mail: stanauer@icx.net.

AUERBACH, STUART CHARLES, development loan fund administrator, journalist; b. N.Y.C., Oct. 28, 1935; s. Jack and Betty (Segnes) A.; m. Lena F. Lee, Sept. 29, 1995. BA, Williams Coll., 1957. Reporter Berkshire Eagle, Pittsfield, Mass., 1957-60, Miami (Fla.) Herald, 1960-66; reporter, then sci.-med. corr. Washington Post, 1966-76, Middle East corr., 1976-77, legal corr., columnist, 1977-79, South Asia corr., 1979-83, econ. corr., 1983-93, health corr., 1995-97; chmn. bd. Media Devel. Loan Fund, Washington, 1996-97, dir. devel., trustee, 1997—. Recipient Pub. Service award Nat. Kidney Found., 1973; certificate commendation Am. Acad. Family Physicians, 1976 Mem. Nat. Assn. Sci. Writers (Sci.-in-Society award 1976), Coun. on Fgn. Rels. Clubs: Nat. Press, Fed. City (Washington); Overseas Press (N.Y.C.); Delhi Gymkhana. Home: 2812 28th St NW Washington DC 20008-4110 Office: Media Devel Loan Fund 2812 28th St NW Washington DC 20008-4110 E-mail: auers@aol.com.

AUERBACHER, MARY JANE, church organist; b. Alhambra, Calif., Sept. 21, 1922; d. Alvah Jasper McConnel and Mamie Estelle Ruhe; children: Alice, Eleanore, Julia. BA, U. Redlands, 1944, MusB, 1947. Tchr. 1st grade Migratory Camp, Indio, Calif., 1944—45; founder Valley Pre. Sch. (accredited CAIS, WASC), Redlands, Calif., 1958; tchr. music Valley Prep. Sch., Redlands, 1960—76; organist, choir dir. several chs., San Bernadrino, 1976—. Dean Am. Guild Organists, Redlands, 1980; pres. Spinet, 1986. Author: Devotions, 1995. Bd. dirs. Valley Prep. Sch., 1976—2001; pres. Am. Bapt. Women, Redlands, 1981—83, 1990—92. Named Gifr Honor, AAUW, Redlands, 1984, Woman of Yr., City of Redlands, 1986; recipient Grail award, Knights of Round Table, 1988. Mem.: Redlands Cmty. Music Assn. Baptist. Avocations: birdwatching, hiking, reading. Home: 121 Sierra Vista Dr Redlands CA 92373 Office: Christ the King Luth Ch 1505 Ford St Redlands CA 92373

AUERBACK, SANDRA JEAN, social worker; b. San Francisco, Feb. 21, 1946; d. Alfred and Molly Loy (Friedman) Auerback. BA, U. Calif., Berkeley, 1967; MSW, Hunter Sch. Social Work, 1972. LCSW. Clin. social worker Jewish Family Services, Bklyn., 1972-73, clin. social worker Hackensack, N.J., 1973-78; pvt. practice psychotherapy San Francisco, 1978—; dir. intake adult day care Jewish Home for the Aged, San Francisco, 1979-91. Mem.: NASW (bd. dirs. Bay Area Referral Svc. 1983—87, chmn. referral svc. 1984—87, state practice com. 1987—91, rep. to Calif. Coun. Psychiatry, Psychology, Social Work and Nursing 1987—95, chmn. 1989, regional treas. 1989—91, v.p. cmty. svcs. 1991—93, chmn. 1993, chair Calif. polit. action com. 1993—95, v.p. profl. stds. com. 2000—02, cert.), Mental Health Assn. San Francisco (trustee 1987—95). Home: 1100 Gough St Apt 8C San Francisco CA 94109-6638 Office: 450 Sutter St San Francisco CA 94108-4206

AUFDERHEIDE, ARTHUR CARL, pathologist; b. New Ulm, Minn., Sept. 9, 1922; s. Herman John and Esther (Sannwald) A.; m. Mary Lillian Buryk, Jan. 26, 1946; children: Patricia Ann, Tom Paul, Walter Herman. MD, U. Minn., 1946; DSc (hon.), Coll. of St. Scholastica, 1983. Chief dept. pathology Mpls. VA Hosp., 1952-53, St. Mary's Hosp., Duluth, Minn., 1953-57; chief dept. pathology Sch. Medicine U. Minn., Duluth, 1970-87, dean Sch. Medicine, 1974-75, dir. paleobiology lab. Sch. Medicine, 1977—. Mem. Plaisted Polar Expdn., 1968; rsch. cons. anthropology lab. U. Colombia, Bogota, 1989—, Pigorini Mus., Rome, 1988, Archeol. Mus. of Tenerife, Canary Islands, 1989-90; chmn. sci. com. Cronos Rsch Project, Santa Cruz, Tenerife, 1991—. Author: Cambridge Ency. Author: Scientific Study of Mummies 2002 Human Paleopathology, 1998; co-editor: Paleopathology, 1991; author: (documentary film) Copper Eskimo, 1970; contbr. numerous articles to profl. publs. Chmn. civil com. to devel. a degree-granting med. sch., Duluth, 1988. Capt. U.S. Army, 1947-49. Fellow AAAS; mem. Paleopathology Assn., N.Y. Acad. Scis. Democrat. Lutheran. Achievements include research in soft tissue paleopathology. Home: 4711 Colorado St Duluth MN 55804-1512 Office: U Minn 10 University Dr Duluth MN 55812-2403

AUFHAUSER, DAVID, federal agency administrator; married; 3 children. Grad., Wesleyan U.; degree, Harvard U.; JD, U. Pa. Bar: Pa. 1977, D.C. 1978. Lawyer Williams and Connolly LLP, Washington, 1977—2001; gen. counsel U.S. Dept. Treasury, Washington, 2001—. Mem. steering com. Civil Justice Reform Task Force; gen. counsel credentials com. Rep. Convention; mem. legal adv. group Rep. House Leadership Conf. Mem.: Phi Beta Kappa. Republican. Office: US Dept Treas Gen Counsel 1500 Pennsylvania Ave NW Washington DC 20220

AUFSES, ARTHUR H(AROLD), JR., surgeon, medical educator; b. N.Y.C., Feb. 8, 1926; s. Arthur Harold and Beatrice (Hauser) A.; m. Harriet Whitman, Dec. 28, 1947; children: Arthur Harold III, Carolyn Aufses Blashek. Student, Columbia U., 1942-43; BS, Union Coll., 1944; MD, Columbia U. Coll. Physicians and Surgeons, 1948. Diplomate Am. Bd. Surgery. Intern Presbyn. Hosp., N.Y.C., 1948-49, resident in surgery, 1950-51, 53-54, Mt. Sinai Hosp., N.Y.C., 1954-56; practice medicine specializing in surgery N.Y.C., 1956-97; prof. Mt. Sinai Med. Ctr., N.Y.C., 1974—; chmn. dept. surgery Mt. Sinai Sch. Medicine, N.Y.C., 1974-96, L.I. Jewish Med. Ctr., 1971-74; prof. surgery SUNY-Stony Brook, 1971-74; surgeon-in-chief Mt. Sinai Hosp., N.Y.C., 1974-96. Contbr. articles to med. jours. Bd. dirs. 92d St. YMHA, 1974—. 1st lt. U.S. Army, 1951-53. Recipient Jacobi medallion Mt. Sinai Med. Ctr., 1979; recipient Gold Headed Cane award Mt. Sinai Med. Ctr., 1982 Fellow ACS (2nd v.p. 1996-97), Am. Surg. Assn. (2nd v.p. 1995-96), Am. Coll. Gastroenterology (pres. 1986-87), Assn. of Program Dirs. Surgery (pres. 1989-91), N.Y. Acad. Medicine; mem. Soc. Surg. Oncology, Am. Gastroent. Assn., N.Y. Surg. Soc. (pres. 1979-80), Soc. Surgery Alimentary Tract, Brazilian Coll. Surgeons, Chilean Congress Surgeons, Portuguese Soc. Gastroenterology. Jewish. Home: 1185 Park Ave New York NY 10128-1308 Office: Mt Sinai Sch Medicine Box 1077 1 Gustave L Levy Pl New York NY 10029-6500

AUGELLI, JOHN PAT, geographer, educator, writer, consulant, rancher; b. Celenza, Italy, Jan. 30, 1921; s. Pat John and M. Antoinette (Iacaruso) A.; divorced; children: John, Robert. BA, Clark U., 1943; MA, Harvard U., 1949, PhD, 1951. Teaching fellow Harvard U., Cambridge, Mass., 1948—49; from asst. to assoc. prof. geography U. P.R., Rio Piedras, 1949—51; assoc. prof. U. Md., College Park, 1952—61; prof. U. Kans., Lawrence, 1961—70, 1971—91; prof. geography, dir. Ctr. Latin Am. Studies U. Ill., Champaign-Urbana, 1970—71. Lectr., travel cons. Mediterranean and Latin Am. cruises, 1991-95; mem. Bd. Fgn. Scholarships, Washington, 1967-70; cons. Nat. Geographic Soc., Washington, 1984-87; del. U.S. Acad. Scis., New Delhi, 1968; sec. Coun. of Inter-Am. Affairs, Washington, 1959-60. Author: Carribean Lands, 1965, Puerto Rico, 1973, Middle America, 3d edit., 1989; cons.: (atlas) World & North America, 1984; contbr. 76 articles to profl. jours. Served to lst lt. U.S. Army, 1943-46, PTO, Res., 1949-51. Recipient Fulbright research grant, 1982. Fellow Am. Geog. Soc.; mem. Assn. Am. Geographers (sec. 1966-69), Latin Am. Studies Assn. (pres. 1969), Nat. Council Geographic Edn. (master tchr. 1979), Conf. of Latin Americanist Geographers (outstanding contbn. to research and teaching award 1982). Democrat. Roman Catholic. Avocations: travel, fishing. Address: 35 Mediterranean Blvd E Port Saint Lucie FL 34952-8557

AUGENBRAUM, HAROLD, library director, editor; b. N.Y.C., Mar. 31, 1953; s. Samuel and Ada (Baker) A.; m. Carla S. Scheele, Sept. 23, 1989; 1 child, Audrey Baker Scheele. BA, Boston U., 1976. Tchr. English as fgn. lang., Barcelona, Spain, 1976-79; with United Way, N.Y.C., 1980-81; fundraising cons., 1982-84; dir. external affairs Brookdale Ctr. on Aging, N.Y.C., 1984-87; assoc. dir. for external affairs Mus. City N.Y., 1987-89; dir. Merc. Libr. N.Y., N.Y.C., 1990—. Bd. dirs. Asian Am. Writers Workshop, 1999—, co-dir., Nat. Steinbeck Centennial, 2001-03. Editor: Latinos in English, 1992, Bendíceme, America, 1993, Growing Up Latino, 1993, The Latino Reader, 1997, U.S. Latino Literature: A Critical Guide for Students and Teachers, 2000; transl.: Chronicle of the Narávez Expedition, 2002. Mem. bd. N.Y. Coun. for Humanities, N.Y.C., 1993-98, vice chmn., 1996. Grantee NEH, 1992, 95, 96, 2000, 2001-2002. Mem. Proust Soc. Am. (pres. 1997—). Office: Merc Libr NY 17 E 47th St New York NY 10017-1920 E-mail: harold@mercantilelibrary.com.

AUGENSTEIN, BRUNO W. research scientist, researcher; b. Germany, Mar. 16, 1923; came to U.S., 1927, naturalized, 1935; s. Wilhelm C. and Emma (Mina) A.; m. Kathleen Greenlaw, May 27, 1950; children: Karen, Eric, Christopher. Sc.B. in Physics and Math, Brown U., 1943; MS in Aero, Calif. Inst. Tech., 1945. Supr. N.Am. Aviation Co., 1946-48; asst. prof. Purdue U., 1948-49; Navaho project leader, 1948; sr. scientist Rand Corp., 1949-58; ICBM project leader, 1952-56; chief scientist satellite programs; dir. planning Lockheed Missiles & Space Co., 1958-61; spl. asst. for reconnaisance and intelligence, dep. dir. intelligence activities Office Sec. Def., 1961-65; now cons.; rsch. adviser Inst. Def. Analyses, 1965-67; v.p. research Rand Corp., Santa Monica, Calif., 1967-71, chief scientist, 1971-72, resident cons., 1972—, sr. scientist, 1976—, emeritus scientist, 1995—, corp. scholar emeritus, 2001—. Cons., NAS, Bur. Budget, 1965—, Nat. Bur. Standards, 1971—, Xerad, Inc., 1972—, Dept. Navy, NSF, NASA, 1973—, Dept. Def., 1978—, Hi Tech Investment Mgmt., Inc., 1983; chmn. naval health systems rev. com. Office Sci. Tech. Policy, 1975—, cons., 1978—; v.p. rsch., bd. dirs. Spectravision, Inc.; bd. regents, asst. chmn. Nat. Libr. Medicine, HEW, 1967-73; mem. NAS computer sci. com. Nat. Bur. Standards, 1971-79, chmn., 1973-76; chmn., editor, Internat. Conf. on Antiproton Sci. and Tech., 1987; initiated Dept. Def. program on micro air vehicles, 1992. Guest contbr., editor Chaos, Solitons and Fractals Jour., 1995, 99. Recipient Distinguished Pub. Service award for reconnaisance and intellignece direction Dept. Def., 1965 Mem. Am. Inst. Physics, AIAA, AAAS, IEEE, Math. Assn. Am., Am. Nuclear Soc., Philosophy of Sci. Assn., N.Y. Acad. Scis., Beta Theta Pi. Home: 1144 Tellem Dr Pacific Palisades CA 90272-2244 Office: 1700 Main St Santa Monica CA 90401-3208

AUGHENBAUGH, DEBORAH ANN, mayor, retired educator; b. Bklyn., Oct. 15, 1922; d. James R. and Alice Lillian (Walsh) Donecho; m. William Irving Hopwood, Mar. 31, 1946 (dec. July 1966); 1 child, William James; m. Kenneth Merle Aughenbaugh, Oct. 20, 1973 (dec. Sept. 1997). BS, Towson (Md.) State Coll., 1952; MS, Shippensburg (Pa.) U., 1967. Cert. elem. tchr., guidance counselor, Md. Tchr. Balt. City Pub. Schs., 1952-54, St. John's Cath. Ch., Frederick, Md., 1960-63, Frederick County Bd. Edn., Frederick, 1963-84; mem. city coun. City of Burkittsville, Md., 1971-74, 80-83, mayor, 1986-95; ret., 1995. Mem. Gov.'s Policy Com. on Edn., 1994-95, Frederick County Bd. Edn., 1995-2002, v.p., 2000-01; mem. Md. Assn. Bds. of Edn. legis. com., 1995-97, 98-99. Chmn. Burkittsville Planning and Zoning Commn., 1969-79; mem. Frederick Recycling Com., 1989-91; mem. Frederick Solid Waste Adv. Bd., 1991-93; mem. Frederick County Bd. of Edn., 1995-2002, v.p., 2000-01; mem. Frederick County Park and Recreation Com.; mem. legis. com. Md. Assn. Bd. Edn., Nat. Bd. Edn., 1998—; mem. Frederick County Future Growth and Sch. Schedule Adv. Com. Mem. Frederick County Ret. Sch. Personnel (pres.-elect), Md. Mcpl. League (pres. Frederick County chpt. 1992, state legis. com. 1985-95, chair 1992-93, bd. dirs. 1985-95), Nat. League Cities (human devel. com. 1991-95), pres. elect retired Frederick County Public Sch. Employees. Democrat. Avocations: reading, travel, crocheting. Home: PO Box 408 Burkittsville MD 21718-0408

AUGOUSTIDES, JOHN GEORGE THEMISTOCLES, cardiothoracic anesthesiologist, educator; b. Cape Town, South Africa, May 31, 1967; came to U.S., 1994; s. Themistocles Alexander and Marina (Yamoyany) A. MB CHB, U. Cape Town, 1990. Diplomate Am. Bd. Anesthesiology; cert. in perioperative echocardography. Residency in family practice, Cape Town, Pt. Elizabeth, South Africa, 1991-94; resident in internal medicine Grad. Hosp., Phila., 1994-95; resident in anesthesia U. Pa., Phila., 1995-98, cardiothoracic anesthesia fellow, 1998-99, clin. asst. prof., 1999—. Author: (book chpts.) Echocardiography Atlas, 1999, (CD-Rom chpt.) Cardiothoracic Anesthesia, 1999; guest reviewer (mag.) Anes. and Analgsia, 2002, 03, Anesthesiology, 2003. Recipient Anesthesiology medal S. African Soc. Anesthetists, Physicians Recognition award, AMA, 2002. Mem. Am. Soc. Anesthesiologists, Soc. Cardiovascular Anesthesiologists, Hellenic Med. Soc. of Greater Phila. (founding, treas. 1997, 98), European Soc. Anesthesiologists, Internat. Anes. Rsch. Soc. Greek Orthodox. Avocations: film, impressionist art, swimming, tennis, theology. Office: Hosp U Penn Dept Anesthesia 3400 Spruce St Philadelphia PA 19104 E-mail: yiandoc@hotmail.com.

AUGSBURGER, AARON DONALD, clergyman; b. Elida, Ohio, Dec. 21, 1925; s. C.A. and Estella R. (Shenk) A.; m. Martha L. Kling, June 5, 1948; children: Phyllis Augsburger Ressler, Patricia Augsburger, Don Richard. BA, Mennonite Coll., 1949; MRE, Ea. Bapt. Sem., Phila., 1956; DEd, Temple U., 1963. Ordained to ministry Mennonite Ch., 1951. Mem. pers. and student svcs. coms. Mennonite Bd. Missions and Charities, 1954-70; pastor students, tchr. Christian edn. Ea. Mennonite Coll., Harrisonburg, Va., 1958-64; asst. dean Goshen (Ind.) Sem., 1964-65; pastor, bishop North Goshen (Ind.) Mennonite Ch., 1965-70; tchr. psychology Goshen (Ind.) Coll., 1965-66; pastor Park View Mennonite Ch., Harrisonburg, 1974-80; prof. Ea. Mennonite Sem., 1980-89; pastor Bahia Vista Mennonite Ch., Sarasota, Fla., 1989-96; dir. pastoral care Mennonite Home, Lancaster, Pa., 1996—. Author: Creating Christian Personality, 1966, A Pattern for Living, 1993; editor: Marriages That Work, 1984, Reshaping Your Marriage, 1996. Guidance counselor Bethany Christian High Sch., Goshen, 1966-68, supr., 1968-70; moderator Gen. Assembly of Mennonite Chs., 1971-73. Home: 1632 College Ave Harrisonburg VA 22802-5541

AUGSBURGER, JAMES JAY, ophthalmology educator; b. Bluffton, Ohio, June 21, 1948; m. Emma Augsburger, June 18, 1972; children: Jay, Amy, Bret. BS, Heidelberg Coll., 1970; MD, U. Cin., 1974. Diplomate Am. Bd. Ophthalmology, Nat. Bd. Med. Examiners. Prof., chmn. dept. ophthalmology U. Cin., 1999—. Recipient Golden Plaque Retinal Fellows of Wills Eye, Phila., 1999, Silver Tray, Residents of Wills Eye Hosp., 1999. Mem. Alpha Omega Alpha. Office: U Cin Dept Ophthalmology PO Box 670527 Cincinnati OH 45267-0527 E-mail: jaugie1@aol.com.

AUGUR, MARILYN HUSSMAN, distribution executive; b. Texarkana, Ark., Aug. 23, 1938; d. Walter E. and Betty (Palmer) H.; m. James M. Augur, Dec. 29, 1962; children: Margaret M. Hancock, Elizabeth H. Taylor, Ann Louise Hardaway. BA, U. N.C., 1960; MBA, So. Meth. U., 1989. Pres. North Tex. Mountain Valley Water, Dallas, 1989—. Bd. dirs. Camden News Pub. Co., Little Rock. Trustee Hussman Found., Little Rock, 1991—, U. Tex. Southwestern Med. Found., 1993—, Nat. Jewish Hosp., 1993—2000, Marilyn Augur Family Found., Dallas, 1991—; bd. dirs. Baylor Health Sys. Found., 1992—, chmn., 1995; bd. dirs. Tate Lectr. Series, 1994—2000; mem. adv. bd., Salvation Army, 1996-, chmn. William Booth Soc., 1999-2000; mem. Tex. Bus. Hall Fame, 1992—98, exec. com., 1994—95; mem. Dallas Citizens Coun., 1994—; exec. com., bd. dirs. Dallas County C.C., 1995—98; exec. com. Dist. Found., 1995—; bd. mem. Dallas Helps, 1995—99, Charter 100, 1998—2001, Baylor Oral Health Found. Bd., 1998—2001; mem. exec. bd. So. Meth. U. Dedman Law Sch. & Cox. Bus. Sch., 1998—; bd. dirs. Children's Health Care Sys. Found., 1998—, Dallas County C.C. Mem. Dallas Country Club, Crescent Club, Dallas Women's Club, Beta Gamma Sigma. Episcopalian. Avocations: travel, skiing, trekking. Office: North Tex Mountain Valley Water 3131 Turtle Creek Blvd Ste 1000 Dallas TX 75219-5439

AUGUST, GILBERT PAUL, physician; b. N.J., Sept. 18, 1936; m. Bernice Ide, Apr. 27, 1938; children: Sharon Michal, Lauren Joelle. BS, CCNY, 1958; MD, NYU, 1962. Diplomate in pediatrics and pediatric endocrinology Am. Bd. Pediatrics. Intern, then resident in pediat. Bellevue Hosp., N.Y.C., 1962-65; pediatric endocrinologist Children's Nat. Med. Ctr., Washington, 1969—; prof. pediatrics George Washington U., Washington, 1983—. Contbr. articles to med. jours. Mem. Lawson Wilkins Pediatric Endocrine Soc., Endocrine Soc., Soc. for Pediatric Rsch., Am. Pediatric Soc. Office: Children's Nat Med Ctr 111 Michigan Ave NW Washington DC 20010-2916 E-mail: gaugust@cnmc.org.

AUGUST, JUNE, artist, educator; b. Warren, Ohio, 1957; d. Fred and Maria Susan Homec; children: Trillium Hinton. BFA, N.Y.U., 1979; postgrad., U. N.H., 1979—88; MFA, Tufts U.; Mus. Sch., 1996; postgrad., Tokyo U., 2002—. Art prof. Stratham (N.H.) Sch., 1983—. Lectr. in field. Artist: Target III, Biennial Portland Mus., 1998, Red Banners, Waino Aaltonen Mus., Finland, 1996, Museo d'Art Conte, Brazil, 1999, Target II, Gallery, Cologne, Germany, 1998, others; one-woman shows include O'Farrell Gallery, Brunswick, Maine, 1999, Fondazione Adolph Carmine, Florence, Italy, 1999, 68 Elf Gallery, Koln, Germany, 1998, Flemish Min., Kasterlee, Belgiu, 1998, others; exhibited in group shows at Museo d'Art Moderna, Rio de Janeiro, Brazil, 1999, Norsk Internat. Print Triennale, Fredrikstad, Norway, 1999, German Internat. Grafik Triennal, Frechen, Germany, 1999, O Mio Dolce Ardor-Ableben, Orangerie Köln Gallery, Cologne, 2000, Westbrook Coll., Maine, 2000, Judith Dielammer Gallery, Grevenbroich, Germany, 2001, Gallery Winds, Tokyo, Japan, 2002, Tokyo Nat. U. Art/Music Gallery, 2002, Cascade Performance Ctr., Tokyo, 2002, Flemish Ministry of Culture, 2003, Boston Arts Festival, 2003, Edinburgh Festival, 2003others; works represented at Galerie Michele Broutta, Paris, O'Farrell Gallery, Brunswick; represented in permenant collections Royal Mus. Art, Antwerp, Belgium, Boston Pub. Libr., Singapore, Malaysia, Belgium, others. Active fundraiser Aids Action Com., Boston, 1994-99; contbr. Medici Soc. scholarship, Boston, 1991-99, 2002; artist Polit. Art. vs. War, U.S., Europe, Mid. East, 1992-2002. Recipient Frans Masereel Flemish Min. of Culture, Kasterlee, Belgium, 1995, 97, 99, 2001, 2003, Fulbright to France, 1992, to Japan, 1997, Cite Internat. des Arts award French Min. of Culture, Paris, 1991-2001, 2003, award Finnish Union of Artists, Turku, 1993, 95, award CAGE, Cin., 1995, rsch. fellow Japanese art, culture, printmaking award Tokyo Nat. Univ. Fine Arts, 2001-2002, others. Achievements include work in sculpture, installation, painting and printmaking with internat. shows and awards. Home: PO Box 160 North Hampton NH 03862-0160

AUGUST, ROBERT OLIN, journalist; b. Ashtabula, Ohio, Oct. 6, 1921; s. Frank and Lillian (Olin) A.; m. Marilynn Eccles, Sept. 23, 1943; 1 dau., Alison. BA, Coll. Wooster, 1943. With Cleve. Press, 1946-82, staff sports dept., 1950—, covered profl. football, 1953-58, exec. sports editor, 1957-58, sports editor, 1958-64, sports columnist, 1964-67, sports columnist, sports editor, 1967-79, gen. columnist, asst. to editor, 1979-81, assoc. editor, 1981-82; sports editor Lake County News-Herald, 1982-89. Sports columnist 4 Ingersoll newspapers, 1982— ; nationally syndicated columnist Wiser Side of 60 Universal Press Syndicate, 1982-86. Author: Fun and Games, 2001, And The Wiser Side of 60, 2002. Served from ensign to lt. (j.g.) USNR, 1943-46. Recipient Cleve. Newspaper Guild awards, 1958, 61, 81, 82, 83; inducted into Cleve. Journalism Hall of Fame, 1988. Mem. Sigma Delta Chi (Disting. Svc. award 1981). Home: 1140 Hedgecliff Dr Wooster OH 44691-3088

AUGUST, ROBERT WILLIAM, designer, educator; b. Chgo., Mar. 31, 1944; s. Benjamin R. and Lillian (A.) A.; m. Lois J. Yoder, Feb. 19, 1977; children: Kristen J., Michael M. BA, L.I. U., 1970; MA, Nat.-Louis U., 1995. USNR, 1966-70; pres. Design Agy. Inc., Chgo., 1976-77; pres., chief exec. officer Expocom Inc., Elgin, Ill., 1977—. Elected to bd. edn. Sch. Dist. U-46, Elgin, 1989-93. Mem. Chgo. Conv. and Tourism Bur., North Suburban Assn. Commerce and Industry. Avocations: gardening, historical restoration work, arts, personal computers, amateur astronomy. E-mail: rwaugust@msn.com.

AUGUST, RUDOLF See SCHLOEMANN, ERNST

AUGUSTA, JUDITH WOOD, librarian; b. Apr. 29, 1940; BA, Wellesley Coll., 1962; MLS, So. Conn. State U., 1994. Adminstrv. asst. Joint Ctr. for Urban Studies of Harvard and MIT, Cambridge, Mass., 1966-72; indexer Rsch. Publs. Inc., Woodbridge, Conn., 1980-90; head libr. Derby (Conn.) Neck Libr., 1994—. Sec., bd. dirs. Valley Arts Coun.; corporator Hewitt Hosp. Co-chair Healthy Valley/Valley Coun. for Health and Human Svcs., 2002—. Recipient Healthy Valley Vol. award 1999, Conn. Post Woman of Substance award, 2000. Mem.: Derby Hist. Soc. (bd. dirs.). Office: 307 Hawthorne Ave Derby CT 06418-1122 E-mail: laughter@ix.netcom.com.

AUGUST-DEWILDE, KATHERINE, banker; b. Bridgeport, Conn., Feb. 13, 1948; d. Edward G. and Benita Ruth (Miller) Burstein; m. David deWilde, Dec. 30, 1984; children: Nicholas Alexander, Lucas Barrymere. AB, Goucher Coll., 1969; MBA, Stanford U., 1975. Cons. McKinsey & Co., San Francisco, 1975-78; dir. fin. Itel Corp., San Francisco, 1978-79; sr. v.p., CFO PMI Group, San Francisco, 1979-85, pres., CFO, 1988-91; CEO, pres. First Republic Thrift & Loan of San Diego, 1988-96; exec. v.p. First Republic Bank, San Francisco, 1987—, sr. v.p., chief fin. officer, 1985-87, COO, 1996—. Mem. policy adv. bd. Ctr. for Real Estate and Urban Econs., U. Calif., Berkeley, 1987—2000; bd. dirs. First Republic Bank, Trainer, Wortham & Co., Inc. Bd. dirs. San Francisco Zool. Soc., 1993-2001, vice-chair, 1995-2000; trustee Carnegie Found., 1999—, Town Sch. for Boys, San Francisco, 1999—; mem. adv. coun. Stanford U. Grad. Sch. Bus., 2003—. Mem. Women's Forum (bd. dirs.), Bankers Club, Belvedere Tennis Club, Villa Taverna. Home: 2650 Green St San Francisco CA 94123-4607 Office: First Republic Bank 111 Pine St San Francisco CA 94111-5602

AUGUSTINE, CYNTHIA H. lawyer; BA, Sarah Lawerence Coll., 1979; JD, Rutgers Law Sch., 1982. Bar: N.J., N.Y. Lawyer Pitney, Hardin, Kipp & Szuch, 1982, Times Co., 1986-93; ptnr., employment law Sabin, Bermant & Gould LLP, 1993—; sr. v.p., human resources New York Times Co., N.Y.C., 1998—. Bd. dirs. Urban Pathways. Mem. ABA. Office: The New York Times Co 1120 Aves Americas 8th fl New York NY 10036

AUGUSTINE, JEAN, member of parliament; b. Grenada, 1937; BA, U. Toronto, Ont.; MEd, LLD (hon.), U. Toronto. Elem. sch. prin. Met. Toronto Separate Sch. Bd.; chair bd. dirs. Met. Toronto Housing Authority; mem. Can. Parliament for Etobicoke-Lakeshore, 1993—. Past Parliamentary sec. to Prime Minister, vice chair ministerial task force on social security reform; mem. former chair standing com. on fgn. affairs and internat. trade, standing com. on citizenship and immigration; vice chair standing com. on human resources devel, mem. standing com. on human rights and status of persons with disabilities Ho. of Commons. Bd. dirs. Harbourfront, Cath. Children's Aid Soc., Can. Adv. Coun. on Status of Women, Ont. Jud. Coun., Urban Alliance on Race Rels., Grenada Assn., Metro Action Com. on Pub. Violence Against Women and Children, Etobicoke Social Devel. Coun.; mem. Toronto Mayor's Task Force on Drugs, Metro Toronto Drug Abuse Prevention Task Force, Toronto Crime Inquiry, 1991; former chair women's caucus Nat. Liberal Caucus, Ont. Caucus Comm. Com., Social Policy Sub-Com. on Housing. Recipient Vol. award and pin Govt. Ont., Caribana Achievement award, Bob Marley award, Kay Livingstone award, Women of Distinction award YWCA, Women on the Move award Toronto Sun, Can. Black Achievement award 1994. Mem. Can. Assn. for Parliamentarians on Population and Devel. (founder, chair), Nat. Sugar Caucus (chair, sec. state multiculturalism status of women, 2002). Office: Ho of Commons 433 W Block Ottawa ON Canada K1A 0A6

AUGUSTINE, JEROME SAMUEL, merchant banker; b. Racine, Wis., May 7, 1928; s. Lester Samuel and Pearl (Hilker) A.; m. Camilla Sewell, Feb. 7, 1953; children: Theodore Samuel Purnell, Julia Sewell Augustine Marshall, Elizabeth Stroebel Augustine Burgoyne. AB cum laude, Harvard U., MBA, 1952. Cons. Scudder, Stevens & Clark, Boston, 1952-56; founder, treas., dir. Vencap, Inc., Boston, 1956-58; treas., dir. Consumer Products, Inc., Boston, 1956-58; founder, treas., dir. Microsonics, Inc., Hingham, Mass., 1956-58; treas., dir. Capitol Mgmt. Corp., Boston, 1956-58; cons. Kidder, Peabody & Co., Boston, 1958-64; pres. Cosmos Am. Corp., N.Y.C., 1964-66; founder, pres., dir. Cosmos Securities Corp., 1965-70, Cosmos (Bahamian) Ltd., Nassau, 1964-70; mng. dir. J. Samuel Augustine & Co., Ltd., Toronto, Ont., Can., 1966—. 1st v.p. Van Alstyne, Noel & Co., N.Y.C., 1973-74; v.p. Wright Investors' Svc., Bridgeport, 1974-87, sr. v.p., 1987-92; pres. Kredietbank (Belgium) Global Asset Mgmt., Stamford, 1992-94. Trustee Low-Heywood Sch.; trustee The Augustine Family Charitable Trust. Named to Washington Hall of Fame, 1986. Mem. Boston Fin. Rsch. Assocs. (gov. 1960-64, v.p. 1963-64), New Eng. Amateur Rowing Assn. (past pres.), Union Boat Club, Harvard Club, Noroton Yacht Club, Royal Canadian Yacht Club, Ox Ridge Hunt Club, Centaur Polo Club, Royal Ascot Polo Club, East India Club (London). Anglican. Office: Ste F24 122 St Patrick St Toronto ON Canada M5T 2X8 Fax: 416-932-9825. E-mail: augustco@hotmail.com.

AUGUSTINE, NORMAN RALPH, organization executive, educator; b. Denver, July 27, 1935; s. Ralph Harvey and Freda Irene (Immenga) A.; m. Margareta Engman, Jan. 20, 1962; children: Gregory Eugen, René Irene. BSE magna cum laude, Princeton U., 1957, MSE, 1959; DEng (hon.), Rensselaer Poly. Inst., 1988; DSc (hon.), U. Colo., 1989; ED (hon.), Western Md. Coll., 1990; DEng (hon.), U. Md., 1992; D Aerospace Mgmt. (hon.), Embry Riddle U., 1992; DEng (hon.), Stevens Inst., 1993; HHD (hon.), Wheeling Jesuit Coll., 1994; DSc (hon.), SUNY, 1994; DEng (hon.), U. Ctrl. Fla., 1995, Worcester Polytech., 1996; LHD (hon.), U. Denver, 1996, Georgetown U., 1997, Trinity Coll., 1997; DEng (hon.), U. Ariz., 1997; LLD (hon.), Duke U., 1997; DEng

(hon.), Milw. Sch. Engring., 1998. Rsch. asst. Princeton U., 1957-58; program mgr., chief engr. Douglas Aircraft Co., Inc., Santa Monica, Calif., 1958-65; asst. dir. def. rsch. and engring. U.S. Govt., Office of Sec. Def., Washington, 1965-70; v.p. advanced systems Missiles and Space Co., LTV Aerospace Corp., Dallas, 1970-73; asst. sec. army The Pentagon, Washington, 1973-75, undersec. army, 1975-77; v.p. ops. Martin Marietta Aerospace Corp., Bethesda, Md., 1977-82, pres. Martin Marietta Denver Aerospace Co., 1982-85, sr. v.p. info. systems, 1985, from pres., COO to chmn., CEO, 1986-95, also bd. dirs.; pres. Lockheed Martin Corp., Bethesda, 1995-96, pres., CEO, 1996-97; lectr. (rank of prof.) Princeton U., 1997—; former chair. American Red Cross, Washington. Chmn. exec. com. Lockheed Martin Corp., Bethesda, Md., 1998—; bd. dirs. Phillips Petroleum Co., Procter & Gamble Co., New Am. Schs. Devel. Corp.; cons. office Sec. of Def., 1971—. Exec. Office Pres., 1971-73, Dept. Army, Dept. Air Force, Dept. Navy, FAA, Dept. Energy, Dept. Transp.; mem. USAF Sci. Adv. Bd.; chmn. Def. Sci. Bd., Exel Comm., 1997—; mem. NATO Group Experts on Air Def., 1966-70, NASA Rsch. and Tech. Adv. Coun., 1973-75, chmn. Space Sys. and Tech. Adv. Bd., 1985-89; mem. Chief of Naval Ops. Exec. Bd., 1989-92; chmn. def. policy adv. com. on trade, 1988-91, 93—; lectr. Princeton U., 1997—. Author: Augustine's Laws; co-author: The Defense Revolution, 1990, Augustine's Travels, 1997; mem. adv. bd. Jour. Def. Rsch., 1970—; assoc. editor Def. Systems Mgmt. Rev., 1977-82; mem. editorial bd. Astronautics and Aerospace. Trustee Johns Hopkins U., Princeton U., MIT; mem. bd. govs. Colonial Williamsburg, 1996—; chmn. White House/NASA Adv. Com. on Future of U.S. Space Program, 1991, Nat. Security Telecomm. Adv. Com., U.S. Antarctic Program Rev. Com., 1996-97; nat. program evaluation com., coun. v.p. Boy Scouts Am., pres., 1993—; chmn. ARC; mem. Pres.'s Com. of Advisors on Sci. and Tech. Recipient Meritorious Svc. medal Dept. Def., 1979, 5 Disting. Civilian Svc. medals Dept. Def., Nat. Engring. award Am. Assn. Engring. Socs., 1991, Am. Acad. Achievement Golden Plate award, 1995, James Madison medal Princeton U., 1995, Blumenthal award Johns Hopkins U. Sch. Engring., 1996, Gold Eagle award Soc. Am. Mil. Engrs. Acad. of Fellows, 1996, Ralph Coates Roe medal ASME, 1996, M. Eugene Merchant Mfg. medal, 1997, Nat. Medal of Technology, 1997; named Personality of Yr., Flight Internat. Aerospace, 1996. Fellow IEEE (Founders' award 1996), AIAA (hon., bd. dirs. 1978-85, pres. 1983-84, Goddard medal 1988), Am. Astron. Soc., Am. Helicopter Soc. (dir. 1974-75), Royal Aero. Soc.; mem. NAE (chmn. 1994—, Arthur M. Bueche award 1991), Am. Acad. Arts and Scis., Internat. Acad. Astronautics, Assn. U.S. Army (pres. 1980-84, chmn. 1990—, George C. Marshall medal), Nat. Security Indsl. Assn. (Forrestal medal 1988), Indsl. Coll. Armed Forces (Eisenhower award 1990), Armed Forces Comm. and Electronics Assn. (Sarnoff medal 1990), Nat. Space Club (Goddard Trophy 1991), Rotary (Nat. Space Trophy 1992), Planetary Soc. (bd. dirs.), Phi Beta Kappa, Sigma Xi, Tau Beta Pi. Presbyterian. Office: Lockheed Martin Corp 6801 Rockledge Dr Bethesda MD 20817-1877 also: Amer Red Cross Nat Hdqs Bldg 17th & D St NW Washington DC 20006

AUGUSTINE, ROSEMARY, vocational counselor, writer; b. Millville, N.J., Sept. 2, 1950; d. Ernest and Rose (O'Brien) A. Adminstrv. Cert., Peirce Coll., Phila., 1969. Exec. sec. Wheaton Industries, Millville, N.J., 1969-71; sec. Sports Conf. USAF, Ramstein, Germany, 1973; vocat. rehab. sec. Leesburg (N.J.) State Prison, 1974-75; adminstrv. asst. 20th Century Fox Film Corp., L.A., 1976-79; asst. to CFO Minoco So. Corp., L.A., 1980-82; divsn. adminstrv. mgr. Integrated Resources, Denver, 1982-86; mgr. investor rels. Intercap Monitoring, Denver, 1987-90; writer, publisher, owner Blue Spruce Publ. Co., Denver, 1991—; career coach, author pvt. practice, Denver, 1990—. Trainer Career Transition Ctrs., Colo., 1994—; founder www.careeradvice.com., 1996—. Author: Facing Changes in Employment, 1995, How to Live and Work Your Passion (and still earn a living), 2000, (newsletter) Career StrateGems, 1991—. Assoc. mem. Colo. Women's Leadership Coalition, Denver, 1995—; weekly facilitator Career Connection Network, Denver, 1996—. Recipient 1st pl. writing and design Small Bus. Rev., Denver, 1993. Mem. Denver Bus. Women's Network (bd. dirs., newsletter editor, 1995-96), Colo. Ind. Publs. Assn. (bd. dirs., pub. rels. 1995-96), Internet C. of C., Am. Soc. Tng. and Devel. Avocations: walking, hiking, biking, fishing. Office: Blue Spruce Pub Co Inc PO Box 24938 Denver CO 80224-0938

AUGUSTINI, MICHAEL CHARLES, lawyer; b. Denver, Sept. 28, 1967; m. Hope Hall, Nov. 18, 1995. BA, Bowdoin Coll., Brunswick, Maine, 1989; JD, U. Maine, 1995. Bar: Maine 1995, U.S. Ct. Appeals (1st cir.) 1996, D.C. 1996. Law clk. U.S. Ct. Appeals, 1st Cir., Bangor, Maine, 1995-96; assoc. Arnold and Porter, Washington, 1996—. Office: Arnold and Porter 555 12th St NW Washington DC 20004-1206

AUGUSTINUS, NORMAN THEODORE, inventor, writer; b. Detroit, Feb. 15, 1960; AAS, BS, Ferris State U., 1987. Writer, prodr., dir. numerous TV commls. Inventor Toy Flying Saucer, Swamp Love, 2002; author: Leonard; appeared in : TV commls., numerous stage plays. Commr. candidate City of Tarpon Springs, Fla., 2002. Personal E-mail: naugustinus@yahoo.com.

AUGUSTYN, FREDERICK JOHN, JR., librarian; b. Stamford, Conn., Aug. 4, 1951; s. Fred John and Helen Josephine (Bienkowski) A. BA, Boston U., 1973; student, U. Wis., 1973-77; MA, MLS, U. Md., 1983, PhD, 1996. Tchg./rsch. asst. dept. history U. Md., College Park, 1979-83; libr. Libr. of Congress, Washington, 1984—. Congl. Constituent tour guide, 1992—. Book reviewer Libr. of Congress, Choice. Mem. ALA, Am. Hist. Assn., Am. Assn. State and Local History, Orgn. Am. Historians, Popular Culture Assn., Phi Alpha Theta, Beta Phi Mu. Avocations: political campaign collectibles, sport history, popular culture, linguistics. Home: 7800 Hanover Pky # 301 Greenbelt MD 20770-2620 E-mail: faug@loc.gov.

AUH, YANG JOHN, librarian, educational administrator; b. Chulla Namdo, Korea, Mar. 18, 1934; came to U.S., 1962, naturalized, 1971; s. Sam Hyuck and So Yae (Suh) A.; m. Karen Kyung-ja Kim, Mar. 11, 1969; 1 child, Alice Kim. BA, Chung-ang U., 1957; MA in LS, Western Mich. U., 1964; Cert. in Libr. Adminstrn. Devel., U. Md., 1973; Cert. in Advanced Librarianship, Columbia U., 1975; Cert. in Mgmt., Clarkson U., 1978; MBA, St. John's U., 1979; postgrad., NYU, 1996, Oxford (Eng.) U., 1997. Asst. libr. Korean Nat. Libr., Seoul, 1957; tech. svcs. libr. Korean Mil. Acad. Libr., Seoul, 1958-61; asst. libr. Branch County Libr., Coldwater, Mich., 1964; head union catalog L.I. U. Librs., Greenvale, N.Y., 1965-68; head catalog dept., tech. svcs. coord. Wagner Coll. Libr., S.I., N.Y., 1968-71, libr. dir., 1972-84, dir. Libr. and Learning Resources Ctr., 1984-2000; dir. Internat. Exch. program Wagner Coll., S.I., N.Y., 2000—; vis. prof. Chung-Ang U., Seoul, 2000—; pres. Highland Realty Mgmt., 1984—; dean internat. study & program Daebul U., Mokpo, Republic of Korea, 2001—. Evaluator, Commn. Higher Edn., Middle States Assn. Colls. and Schs., 1984; trustee Am. Friends of Chung-ang U., 1979—, vis. prof., 2000—; dean internat. study and program Daebul U., Mokpo, Korea, 2001—; life dep. gov., bd. govs. Am. Biographical Inst., Inc., Raleigh, N.C., 1998—; adv. coun. Internat. Biographical Ctr., Cambridge, Eng., 1999—. Fellow, HEW, 1973, 1978. Mem. ALA, N.Y. State Libr. Assn., Korean Libr. Assn., N.Y. Librs. Club, Omicron Delta Kappa (chpt. adminstrv. mem. 1995). Office: Wagner Coll Horrmann Libr One Campus Rd Staten Island NY 10301-4428

AUKAMP, ANN WALKLEY NORTH, social worker, consultant, small business owner; b. Ann Arbor, Mich., Feb. 7, 1944; d. Edward David and Mary Emile (Yntema) North; m. Donald Richard Aukamp, Jan. 25, 1964; 1 child, Elizabeth Ann. BS, U. Ill., 1966; MSW, NYU, 1978; cert., U. Md., 1983. Lic. clin. social worker, Md.; bd. cert. diplomate in clin. social work. Social worker Montgomery County Dept. Social Svcs., Rockville, Md., 1978-81; program mgr. Md. Dept. Human Resources, Balt., 1981-84, spl. asst., rsch. and planning, 1984-88; dir. profl. affairs NASW, Inc., Silver Spring, Md., 1988; founding co-owner Inst. for Mgrs. and Profls., Silver Spring, 1989-90; assoc. Loss Counseling Ctr. of Washington, 1989-91; pvt. practice Silver Spring, Md., 1990—. Mem., sec., chmn. Md. Bd. Social Work Examiners, Balt., 1990-95. Sec. Valley Brook Citizens Assn., Silver Spring, 1989-91. Mem. NASW (treas. Greater Washington 2001-03), Soc. for Clin. Social Workers, Assn. for Employee Assistance Program Practitioners, Am. Soc. for Clin. Hypnosis. Avocations: travel, photography, potting, weaving, reading. Home: 319 Valley Brook Dr Silver Spring MD 20904-2948 Office: Clin & Cons Svcs 319 Valley Brook Dr Silver Spring MD 20904-2948 also: 5454 Wisconsin Ave Ste 1435 Chevy Chase MD 20815 E-mail: aauka@tellatlantic.net.

AUKER, TODD ALAN, ophthalmologist, surgeon; b. Nyskyona, N.Y., Mar. 8, 1958; s. Raymond B. Auker and Nancy Beth Armittage; m. Karin Alison Corfee, Dec. 22, 1984; children: Kirstin, Julia, Ryan. BA, U. Calif., Santa Barbara, 1981; MD, U. Calif., San Francisco, 1985. Lic. Calif., 1986, Mo., 1988, diplomate Am. Bd. Ophthalmology. Eye physician and surgeon The Permanente Med. Group, Walnut Creek, Calif., 1991—2001; founder, dir. Acker Eye Inst., Pleasanton, Calif., 2001—. Fellow: Am. Soc. Cataract and Refractive Surgeons, Am. Acad. Ophthalmology; mem.: Kaiser-Permanente Ophthalmology Soc. (pres. 1997), East Bay Ophthalmology Soc. (pres. 1996). Avocations: mountaineering, bicycling, skiing. Home: 629 Camino Amigo Danville CA 94526-2306 Office: Auker Eye Inst 2324 Santa Rita Rd Pleasanton CA 94566

AUKLAND, DUNCAN DAYTON, lawyer; b. Delaware, Ohio, July 6, 1954; s. Merrill Forrest and Elva Sampson (Dayton) A.; m. Diane Sue Clevenger, Aug. 7, 1982. BA, Va. Polytech. Inst., 1978; JD, Capital U., 1982. Bar: Ohio 1982, U.S. Dist. Ct. (so. dist.) Ohio 1982. Legal intern Ohio EPA, Columbus, 1982, staff atty., 1982-83, legal cons., 1983; sole practice Columbus, 1983-90; judge adv. USNG, Columbus, 1990—. Atty. Clean Up and Recycling Backers of Clintonville, Columbus, 1983-89; deacon Overbrook Presbyn. Ch., Columbus, 1986-89. With JAGC, USAR, 1984-90. Mem. Ohio Bar Assn., Va. Poly. Alumni Assn. Cen. Ohio (pres. 1984-85), Ohio Gamma Alumni Corp. (trustee 1983-88, 91-95). Republican. Avocations: golf, home repairs. Home: 5789 Crescent Ct Worthington OH 43085-3804 Office: Ohio Adj Gen's Dept Attn: AGOH-JA 2825 W Dublin Granville Rd Columbus OH 43235-2789 E-mail: duncan.aukland@tagoh.org.

AUKOFER, FRANK ALEXANDER, journalist; b. Milw., Apr. 6, 1935; s. Herbert Anselm and Wanda Mary (Kaminski) A.; m. D. Sharlene Talatzko, Aug. 6, 1960; children: Juliann Navarrete, Matthew P., Becky Hawryluk, Joseph J. BA in Journalism, Marquette U., 1960; Fellowship Cert., Northwestern U., 1967. With The Milw. Jour. Sentinel (merger The Milw. Jour., Sentinel), 1960-2000; with Washington Bur. The Milw. Jour. Sentinel, 1970-2000, bur. chief; ret., 2000. Writer syndicated column on automobiles DriveWays, 1985—; automobile columnist Artists & Writers Syndicate, Scripps Howard News Svc. With USAF Res., 1952-60. Recipient Byline award for lifetime achievement in journalism Marquette U., 1992, Profl. Merit award Marquette U., awards from Wis. Press. Assn., Milw. Press Club, Soc. Profl. Journalists; Vis. Profl. Freedom Forum First Amendment scholar Vanderbilt U., 1994-95. Mem. Nat. Press Club (pres. 1978, bd. dirs. bldg. corp., Corr. award), Nat. Press Found. (pres., chmn. bd. 1980-85, bd. dirs.), Soc. Profl. Journalists, Standing Com. Corr. U.S. Congress (sec. 1976), Washington Automotive Press Assn. (pres. 1987-88), Gridiron Club Washington. Roman Catholic. Home: 6325 Beachway Dr Falls Church VA 22044

AULBACH, GEORGE LOUIS, retired real estate company executive; b. York, Pa., July 9, 1925; s. George A. and Mary N. (Goulden) Aulbach; m. Gertrude Frisby, June 24, 1949; children: Jeanne, Cynthia, Patricia, Kathleen, Barbara. BSCE, Villanova U., 1945. Registered profl. engr., Pa., Ga. Field engr., estimator, chief engr., project mgr., exec. v.p R.S. Noonan, Inc., York, Pa., 1946-63; pres., CEO R.S. Noonan, Inc. & Noonan Engring. Corp., York, Pa., 1963-72; pres. systems bldg. divsn. McCrory-Sumwalt, Columbia, SC, 1972-76; pres., CEO Laing Properties, Inc., Atlanta, 1976-90; ret., 1990. Adv. bd. dirs. Bank South, Atlanta; vice-chmn., dir. Cath. Continuing Care Retirement Cmtys., Inc.; adv. bd. Ga. Tech. Rsch. Inst.; dir., treas. York, Pa. Meml. Osteo. Hosp., 1966—72; pres. York ABC Corp., 1966—72. Bd. dirs. Northside Hosp. Found., Cath. Housing Initiative; trustee So. Tech. Found.; cons. non-profit corp. developing affordable housing; chmn. sch. implementation com. Cath. Archdiocese of Atlanta, chmn. fin. com.; vice chmn. Cath. Continuum Care Com. Lt. (j.g.) USN, 1943—46. Decorated Knight Comdr. St. Gregory Vatican. Roman Catholic. E-mail: imdutchman@citcom.net.

AULD, BERNIE DYSON, civil engineer, consultant; b. Austin, Tex., Oct. 5, 1958; s. George Ernest and Lois Ann (Justillian) A.; m. Cynthia Lynn Smith, June 15, 1985 (div.); children: Jamie Meredith, Kirsten Marlee, Lucas Austin; m. Elizabeth Ann Claxton, Jan. 1, 2000. BSCE, Lamar U., 1982; MSCE, U. Tenn., 1992. Registered civil engr., Ky., Ala., S.C., Ark., Miss., Tenn., Ga., Fla. Civil engr. City of San Angelo, Tex., 1982-84, Arlington (Tex.) Engring. Co., 1984-85; civil project mgr. Barge, Waggoner, Sumner & Cannon, Nashville, 1985-89; civil dept. mgr. Lockwood Greene Engrs., Nashville, 1989-92; pres. BA Engring., Nashville, 1992—. Athletic scholar Lamar U., 1977-82. Mem. ASCE, Engrs. Assn. Nashville (pres. 1993). Home and Office: 4825 Trousdale #213 Nashville TN 37220

AULD, DAVID STUART, biochemist, educator; b. Newton, N.J., Jan. 8, 1937; s. William Auld and Jessie Cummings Riddel; m. Loretta Frances Patricia, Sept. 2, 1961; children: Cynthia Ann, Douglas Stewart. BS, Lehigh U., 1960, MS, 1962; PhD, Cornell U., 1966. Assoc. staff in medicine Brigham & Women's Hosp., Boston, 1966—; assoc. in biol. chemistry Harvard Med. Sch., Boston, 1969-70, from asst. to assoc. prof. biol. chemistry, 1970-83, assoc. prof. pathology, 1983—. Bd. tutors biochem. scis. Harvard U., 1977—, asst. chmn., 1983-84, bd. editors Biochemistry 1980—, ABB 1994—. Contbr. over 175 articles and revs. to profl. publs. Achievements include research in mechanism of zinc metalloenzymes; categorizing zinc sites in proteins; developed specialized methods for kinetic analysis of intermediates in catalysis & conversion of substrate to products based on radiationless energy transfer; designed low-temperature stopped-flow. Home: 29 Railroad Ave Bedford MA 01730-2100 Office: Harvard Med Sch One Kendall Sq Cambridge MA 02139 E-mail: david_auld@hms.harvard.edu., auld@fas.harvard.edu.

AULD, FRANK, psychologist, educator; b. Denver, Aug. 9, 1923; s. Benjamin Franklin and Marion Leland (Evans) A.; m. Elinor James, June 29, 1946 (dec. June 1990); children— Mary, Robert, Margaret; m. Elinor Leah Levine, Dec. 8, 1996. AB, Drew U., 1946; MA, Yale U., 1948, PhD, 1950. Cert. psychologist, Mich., Ont. Instr. psychology Yale U., New Haven, 1950-52, asst. prof., 1952-59; asso. prof. Wayne State U., Detroit, 1959-61, prof., 1961-67, dir. clin. psychology tng. program, 1960-66; prof. U. Detroit, 1967-70, dir. psychol. clinic, 1967-69; prof. U. Windsor, Canada, 1970—91, prof. emeritus, 1992—. Cons. in field. Author: Steps in Psychotherapy, 1953, Scoring Human Motives, 1959, Resolution of Inner Conflict, 1991; contbr. articles to profl. jours. Chmn. Dearborn (Mich.) Community Council, 1962; mem. adv. com. on coll. work Episcopal Diocese Mich., 1962-71. Recipient Alumni Achievement award Drew U., 1965 Fellow Am. Psychol. Assn. (evaluation com. 1961-66); mem. Can. Assn. U. Tchrs., Can., Mich. psychol. assns., Ont. Psychol. Assn. (edn. and tng. bd. 1976-91, Lifetime Achievement award 1998), Conn. State Psychol. Soc. (pres. 1958), Soc. Psychotherapy Research, Phi Beta Kappa, Sigma Xi. Office: U Windsor Dept Psychology Windsor ON Canada N9B 3P4 E-mail: frankauld@aya.yale.edu.

AULD, JAMES S. educational psychologist; Grad., U. Nebr. Cert. sch. counselor, profl. counselor. Dir. testing, asst. prof.; K-12 dir. guidance; kindergarten-12 dir. psychol. svcs. Author: Real Personality. Mem. APA, AACD, ASCD, Can. Psychol. Assn., Nebr. Profl. Counselors, Gold Key, nat. Disting. Svc. Registry for Counselors, Phi Delta Kappa. Office: PO Box 6228 Lincoln NE 68506-0228

AULD, ROBERT HENRY, JR., biomedical engineer, educator, consultant, author; b. Akron, Ohio, Sept. 19, 1942; s. Robert Henry Sr. and Elsie Mae (Rollans) A.; children: Sheila Kay, Jason Craig; stepson: Christopher William Weiss. BSBA, Biomed. Engr., U. San Francisco, 1978. Registered profl. egnr., calif.; cert. clin. engr. Reg. svc. mgr. scientific products div. AHSC, Sunnyvale, Calif., 1963-68; founder, gen. mgr. Lab. Instrument Svc., Campbell, Calif., 1968-77; nat. mgr. Biomed. Svcs. Group Pilot Project Honeywell, Inc., Denver, 1977-79; internship Stanford U. Med. Ctr., 1976, UCSF, 1978; profl. engr. Robert Auld Enterprises, San Jose, Calif., 1979-86; dir. clin. engring. St. Louis Reg. Med. Ctr., 1987-89; engring. mgr. Robert Auld Engring.-West, Imperial, Mo., 1989—, biomedical engr. cons. Santee, Calif., 1989—; nat. svc. mgr. R.C. Network, Cleveland, OH, 1990-99; expert examiner State of Calif. Bd. Registration for Profl. Engrs., Sacramento, 1995-99. Seminar dir. ASMT, Phoenix AZ., 1968-79; instrument workshop seminar coordinator, Stanford U. Med. Ctr., 1980-84; engring. advisor St. Louis Reg. Career Access Ctr., 1987-89, U. Mo., Rolla and St. Louis. Author: The Clone Factory (A True Story About Police), 1992; contbr. articles to profl. jours. Del. at large Rep. Legion of Merit, Imperial, MO., 1990-93; apptd. hazardous waste com., State of Mo., 1988-90. With USN, 1959-61. Recipient Disting. Leadership award Am. Biographical Inst., Raleigh, N.C., 1988, 94, Golden Spike award, Calif., 1986. Mem. N.Y. Acad. Scis., IEEE, Am. Soc. Hosp. Engrs., NSPE, Mo. Soc. Profl. Engrs. (chmn. 1988-89, chmn. minority Math Counts pilot project 1987-89), Order Demolay (life). Republican. Achievements include development of device for equilibrating gases in a liquid or blood for measurement of gases in blood; patent pending for dual halogen colormetric light source; Innovator "Single Source Service", "Parts Banks" for Clinical Equipment for Health Care Facilities. Home: 3526 Fairmount Ave Apt 1006 San Diego CA 92105-3492 Office: Robert Auld Engring West 3526 Fairmont Ave Ste 1006 San Diego CA 92105-3492 E-mail: robertauld@juno.com., redwood2c2@aol.com.

AULETTA, JOAN MIGLORISI, construction company executive, mortgage and insurance broker; b. July 23, 1940; d. Angelo George and Ann (Passa) Miglorisi; m. E.V. Auletta, Oct. 5, 1958; children: Ann, Vincent, George, Jeanne. ABS, Bklyn. C.C., 1957. Owner, mgr. Auletta Realty, 1947-76, E&J Pancake House, L.I., N.Y., 1947-76; office and fin. mgr. Larchwood Constrn. Co., Farmingville, N.Y., 1976-77; prodn. mgr. Lawlor Industries, Holtsville, N.Y., 1977-79; real estate and fin. adv. Family Home Improvement Corp., Queens Village, N.Y., 1979-81; co-owner Total Home Constrn. Co., N.Y.C., 1981-86; owner, mgr. Century 21, Echo Hills Realtors Inc., Miller Place, N.Y., 1987-92, Auletta Realty, 1989—, Tone-O-Matic, 1988-89; owner, mgr. comml. property, 1970—. Bd. dirs. Multiple Listing Svc. of L.I., 1986-91, L.I. d. Realtors, 1986-92, Fin. Dept. Waste Industry, 1992-99. Mem. Miller Pl.-Mt. Sinai C. of C. (pres. 1988-90). Roman Catholic. Home: 7901 NW 83d St Tamarac FL 33321 E-mail: jma6715@hotmail.com.

AULETTA, KEN, writer, columnist; b. Bklyn., 1942; BA in History, SUNY, Oswego, 1963; MA in Polit. Sci., Syracuse U., 1965. Polit. columnist Daily News, N.Y.C., 1977—93; comm. columnist New Yorker mag., N.Y.C., 1993—. Author: Three Blind Mice: How the TV Networks Lost Their Way, Green and Glory on Wall Street, The Highwaymen: Worries of the Information Superhighway, others. Office: The New Yorker 4 Times Sq New York NY 10036-6561

AULL, ELIZABETH BERRYMAN, real estate development executive; b. Independence, Mo., 1951; d. Homer Hayter and Mary Elizabeth (Wulfert) A. AA, Christian Coll., 1971; BS, U. Mo., 1973; master gardener, U. Mo. ext., Columbia, 1996; grad., Econ. Devel. Inst., 1992. With Mo. Senate Staff and Dept. Revenue, Jefferson City, 1973-74; adminstrv. asst. B. State Devel. Agy., St. Louis, 1974-76, Bingham Sketches, Inc., St. Louis, 1976; rate/routing analyst Mo. Pacific R.R., St. Louis, 1976-78; sr. property mgmt. specialist Burlington No. Inc., St. Louis, Springfield, Mo., 1978-87; dir., prop. mgmt. Glacier Park Co. subs. Burlington No., Inc., 1987-88; indsl. devel. mgr. Burlington No. R.R., Omaha, 1989-91, with Ft. Worth, 1991-95; indsl. and market devel. exec. Bd. dirs. Indpendence Ctr., St. Louis, 1982-83, Mental Health Assn. Greater St. Louis, 1982-83, Mental Health Assn. of Ozarks, Springfield, 1983-87; mem. Jr. League St. Louis, 1980-83, Jr. League Springfield, 1984-88, Jr. League, Omaha, 1989-92, Jr. League Ft. Worth, 1992—; chmn. bldg. subcom. Ozark Food Harvest Springfield Coun. of Chs., 1987-88; pres. Greater St. Louis Area Christian (Columbia) Coll. Alumni Assn., 1981-83; greeting card chmn. UNICEF Com. S.W. Mo., 1997. Named one of Outstanding Young Women Am., 1978, 80, 81. Mem. DAR, Dau. Am. Colonists, Colonial Dames 17th Century, Celtic Soc., German, Austrian and Swiss Soc., Friends of the Springfield Art Mus. Republican. Avocations: travelling, art, herb gardening, genealogy. Home: 2391 E Wayland St Springfield MO 65804-3332

AULL, JAMES STROUD, retired bishop; b. Winnsboro, S.C., Mar. 3, 1931; s. Luther Bachman and Ruth (Bull) A.; m. Virginia Kloeppel, Aug. 9, 1958; children: Diane, James Jr. (dec.), Virginia Ruth. AB magna cum laude, Newberry Coll., 1953; MDiv cum laude, Luth. Theol. So. Sem., Columbia, S.C., 1960; M in Systematic Theology, Luth. Sch. Theology, Chgo., 1970; PhD, Duke U., 1971; DD (hon.), Newberry Coll., 1988. Ordained to ministry United Luth. Ch. in Am., 1961. Pastor St. Timothy Luth. Ch., Camden, S.C., 1961-62; instr., staff mem. Luth. Theol. So. Sem., Columbia, S.C., 1962-79; sec. S.C. Synod, Luth. Ch. in Am., Columbia, 1979-87, bishop, 1988-96; ret., 1996. Author: Obey My Voice: a Form Critical Study of Selected Prose in the Book of Jeremiah", 1971. Trustee Newberry Coll., 1972-96, sec., 1977-82; trustee Luth. Home, White Rock, S.C., 1988-96, Lutheridge/Lutherock Ministries, Inc., 1988-96; bd. dirs. divsn. for edn. Evang. Luth. Ch. Am., Chgo., 1988-91, mem. ch. coun., 1991-96, bd. trustees, bd. pensions, 1997-2003; mem. adv. bd. Lowman Home, 2003—. Mem. Soc. Bibl. Lit., Rotary (bd. dirs. 1987-90, pres. 1996-97). Lutheran. Home: PO Box 608 White Rock SC 29177-0608 E-mail: jimaull3@aol.com.

AULT, ETHYL LORITA, special education educator, consultant; b. Bklyn., May 30, 1939; d. Albert Nichols Fadden and Marion Cecil (Corrigan) Snow; (div.); children: Debra Marie Ault Butenko, Milinda Lei Jones, Timothy Scott. BS, Ga. State U., MEd, 1976, cert. in spl. edn. 6th yr., 1984. Tchr. spl. edn. Butts County Sch. System, Jackson, Ga., 1972-73, Rockdale County Sch. System, Conyers, Ga., 1973-75, lead tchr., 1975-77; cons. spl. edn. Newton County Sch. System, Covington, Ga., 1977-79; curriculum specialist spl. edn. La Grange (Ga.) Sch. System, 1979-83, dir. spl. edn., 1983-94, dir. accredited studies curriculum, 1994—, dir. student svcs., 1995—; collaboration process trainer State of Ga., 1990—, dir. student svcs./spl. program, 1996-2000; fine arts cons. Troup County Schs., 2001—. Instr. La Grange Coll., 1984-97, assoc. prof., 1997—; mem. Tchr. Competency Testing Commn., Atlanta, 1988—, Task Force Documentation and Decision Making, Atlanta, 1988—. Contbg. editor: (manual) Mainstream Modification Handbook, 1989. Chairperson Jud. Adv. Panel, LaGrange, 1988; bd. dirs. Crawford Tng. Ctr. Adv. Panel, La Grange, 1985—; pres. West Ga. Youth Coun. Bd., La Grange, 1980—; mem. State Adv. Panel for Spl. Edn.; bd. dirs. Troup County Hist. Soc., 1999—; mem. State of Ga. Task Force on Alt. Edn., 1998—. Mem. Coun. Exceptional Children, Ga. Assn. Edn. Leaders, Ga. Assn. Curriculum and Instrn. Supervision, Ga. Coun. Adminstrs. Spl. Edn. (v.p. 1988—, pres.-elect 1989, pres. 1992—, Gifted State Task Force 1994—), La Grange Women's Club (v.p. 1989—), Profl. Assn. Ga. Spl. Educators (Adminstr. of Yr. 1993), Ga. Supporters of the Gifted, Nat. Assn. for Gifted Edn., Ga. Assn. for Gifted Students (pres.-elect 2000-2001), Kiwanis Club LaGrange (pres. elect 1999-2000, pres. 2000-01), Phi Delta Kappa (pres. 2000-2001), Lafayette Soc. Arts (bd. dirs., v.p.). Democrat. Episcopalian. Avocations: swimming, fishing, walking, gardening. Home: 441 Gordon Cir Lagrange GA 30240-2621 Office: LaGrange Coll Board St Lagrange GA 30240

AULT, JAMES MASE, bishop; b. Sayre, Pa., Aug. 24, 1918; s. Tracey Everett and Bessie (Mase) A.; m. Dorothy Mae Barnhart, Dec. 22, 1943; children: James Mase, Kathryn Louise, Elizabeth Ann, Christopher John (dec.). AB magna cum laude, Colgate U., 1949; BD magna cum laude, Union Theol. Sem., N.Y.C., 1952, STM, 1964; postgrad., St. Andrews U., Scotland, 1966; DD, Am. U., Washington, 1968; LLD (hon.), Albright Coll., 1973, Ohio Wesleyan U., 1973; DHL (hon.), Drew U., 1986; LHD (hon.), Allegheny Coll., 1987. Ordained to ministry Meth. Ch. as deacon, 1951, as elder, 1952. Tool engr. Ingersoll-Rand Co., 1936 42; pastor Meth. Ch., Preston, N.Y., 1946-49, Carlton Hill Meth. Ch., East Rutherford, N.J., 1951-53, Meth. Ch., Leonia, N.J., 1953-58, First Meth. Ch., Pittsfield, Mass., 1958-61; dean students, asso. prof. practical theology Union Theol. Sem., N.Y.C., 1961-64, prof. practical theology, dir. field edn., 1964-68; dean, prof. pastoral theology Theol. Sch., Drew U., Madison, N.J., 1968-72; bishop Phila. area United Meth. Ch., 1972-80, bishop Pitts. area, 1980-88, bishop Wyo. conf., 1990; prof. contemporary ministries Theol. Sch. Drew U., Madison, N.J., 1988-91, interim dean Theol. Sch., 1990-91; sec. council of bishops United Meth. Ch., 1980-84, pres. council bishops, 1986-87. Mem. governing bd. Nat. Coun. Chs. of Christ in U.S.A., 1981-84; mem. central com. World Coun. Chs., 1981-91; mem. exec. com. World Meth. Coun., 1981-88. Author: Responsible Adults for Tomorrow's World, 1962. Mem. sr. exec. ecumenical seminar Hartford Theol. Sem. and the Lilly Endowment, 1989-92; chair U.S. Bossey com. World Coun. Chs., 1994-98. Lt. U.S. Army, 1942-46. Faculty fellow Am. Assn. Theol. Schs., 1965-66. Mem. AAUP, Acad. Polit. and Social Sci., Phi Beta Kappa. Methodist. Home: 1 Amoskegan Dr Brunswick ME 04011-9524 E-mail: jmaorda@gwi.net.

AULT, JEFFREY MICHAEL, investment banker, commodities trader; b. Norfolk, Va., Jan. 20, 1947; s. Frank Willis and Helen Blake (Hamner) A.; m. Lesley Linda Ault; 1 child, Jeffrey Franklin. BS, U. Calif., San Diego, 1974; postgrad., U. San Diego, 1975-84, Word of Faith Bible Inst., Dallas. Ordained to ministry Fedn. Gen. Assemblies Internat., 1988. Dir. nat. bus. devel.

Mayflower, San Diego, 1970-75; dir. nat. accounts Aero-Mayflower Transit Co., Alexandria, Va., 1976-78; v.p. Mchts. Mgmt. Co., Washington, 1976-78; v.p. mktg. Stevens Van Lines, various states, 1978-80; exec. v.p. Fla. Am. Van Lines Inc., Tampa, 1980-84; pres. Victory World Trade Corp., Washington, 1984-85; chmn., CEO Maranatha Van Lines, Inc., Tampa, 1984-90; exec. dir. Swords Into Plowshares, France, Russia, Vietnam, U.S.; pres., CFO Scheherazade Internat. Asset Mgmt. Ltd., Genesis Global Fin. Group, Ltd.; pres., CEO Red Star Oil and Petrochems. Ltd. Pres. Ea. Star Trading Co., Minsk, Belarus; v.p., sr. ptnr. Noord Prince Mchts. Bank, Curacao; trustee Gold-Lyon Trust, The Bear Trust, Vaduz, Leichtenstein. Mem. U.S. Senate Trust, Hillsborough County Republican Party; sustaining mem. Rep. Nat. Com. Sgt. USMC, 1966-72, Vietnam. Mem. DAV, Am. Legion, Aircraft Owners and Pilots Assn., U. Calif. at San Diego Alumni Assn., First U.S. Marine Div. Assn., USMC Combat Corrs. Assn., Mensa. Home: PO Box 811 18026 Lindawoods St Odessa FL 33556-4713 Office: PO Box 811 Tampa FL 33601-0811 also: Flat 142 Samarkandsky Bulvar 15/1 Moscow Russia E-mail: MaxxBruno@aol.com.

AUMANN, R. KARL, state official, lawyer; b. Balt., May 17, 1960; s. Frederick Carl and Marjorie Patterson (Rue) A.; m. Susan Langley Mueller, Sept. 20, 1986. BA, Loyola Coll., Balt., 1982; JD, U. Balt., 1985. Bar: Md. 1986, U.S. Dist. Ct. Md. 1986. Assoc. Power and Mosner PA, Towson, Md., 1986-88, MIles & Stockbridge, Balt., 1988—; sec. of state State of Md., Annapolis, 2003—. Mem. Republican State Cen. Com., Baltimore County, 1986—. Mem. ABA, Md. State Bar. Assn., Baltimore County Bar Assn., Balt. City Bar Assn., SAR. Roman Catholic. Avocation: travel. Office: State Ho Office Sec State Annapolis MD 21401*

AUMILLER, DAVID, nuclear engineer; b. Lewistown, Pa. m. Tammi Aumiller. BSME, U. Pa., 1991; MS in Nuc. Engring., Pa. State U., 1993, PhD in Nuc. Engring., 1996. Sr. engr. Bechtel Bettis, Inc., West Mifflin, Pa., 1996—2001, prin. engr. West Mifflin, Pa, Pa., 2001—. Contbr. articles. Office: Bechtel Bettis Inc Zap 34L PO Box 79 West Mifflin PA 15122

AUNE, ADONICA SCHULTZ, education educator, consultant; d. Lloyd James Schultz and Margaret Estelle Gulbranson; m. Robert Dale Aune, Jan. 1, 2001; children: Shane David Seaver, Jerod Keith Seaver, Travis Adonis Seaver. PhD, U. of N.D., 1994. Instructional Tech. U. of Minn., 2002. Lectr. Little Hoop C.C., Ft. Totten, ND, 1991; English expert Hefei U. of Tech., China, 1994; asst. prof. Christian Invention Computer Coll., Seoul, 1996; English tchg. cons. China Airlines, Taipei, Taiwan, 1997—99; adj. prof. U. of Minn., Crookston, 2000—02, U. of N.D., Grand Forks, 2002—. Dir.: (performance) Milk Dreams (Cmty. Theatre, 2003). Recipient Hatton Cmty. Theatre Hall of Fame, 2000. Mem.: Internat. Literacy and Edn. Rsch. Network (assoc.). Achievements include research in Aviation Ambiguity. Avocations: golf, bicycling, travel, swimming, writing. Home: 815 40th Ave S #K143 Grand Forks ND 58201 Office: Box 7169 U of ND Grand Forks ND 58201 Personal E-mail: adonica.schultz@und.nodak.edu.

AUNE, DEBRA BJURQUIST, lawyer; b. Rochester, Minn., June 13, 1956; d. Alton Herbert and Violet Lucille (Dutcher) Bjurquist; m. Gary ReMine, June 6, 1981 (div. June 1993); children: Jessica Bjurquist ReMine, Melissa Bjurquist ReMine; m. David Aune, Jan. 1, 1995. BA, Augsburg Coll., 1978; JD, Hamline U., 1981. Bar: Minn. 1981. Assoc. Hvistendahl & Moersch, Northfield, Minn., 1981-82; adjuster Federated Ins. Cos., Owatonna, 1982-84; advanced life markets advisor Federated Life Ins. Co., Owatonna, 1984-87; mktg. svcs. advisor Federated Ins. Cos., Owatonna, 1987-89, 2d v.p., corp. legal counsel, 1989-92, v.p. gen. counsel, 1992-95, 1st v.p., gen. counsel, 1996-99; ind. cons., 1999—. Mem. Hamline Law Rev., 1979-80. Pres. Owatonna Ins. Women, 1983-84; charter commr. City of Owatonna, 1992—. Mem. ABA, Minn. State Bar Assn., 5th Dist. Bar Assn., Steele County Bar Assn. (sec. 1986-87, v.p. 1987-88, pres. 1988-89), Assn. Life Ins. Counsel, Alliance Am. Insurers (legal com. 1989—). Lutheran. Office: Federated Ins Cos 121 E Park Sq Owatonna MN 55060-3046

AUNG-THWIN, MICHAEL ARTHUR, history educator; b. Rangoon, Burma, 1946; BA, Doane Coll., 1969; MA, U. Ill., Urbana, 1971; PhD, U. Mich., 1976. Asst. prof. Asian history Elmira (N.Y.) Coll., 1980-87; assoc. prof. history No. Ill. U., DeKalb, 1987-95, dir. Ctr. S.E. Asian Studies, 1987-95; prof. Asian Studies U. Hawaii, Honolulu, 1995—. Vis. prof. Cornell U., 1981; vis. scholar Ctr. for S.E. Asian Studies, Kyoto, Japan. Contbr. articles to profl. jours. NEH fellow, 1977-80. Mem. Assn. for Asian Studies (bd. dirs. 1980-83, mem. S.E. Asia Coun.), Burma Studies Found. (sec.-treas.). Office: U Hawaii Sch Hawaiian Asian Studies 1890 E West Rd Honolulu HI 96822-2318 E-mail: aungthwin@hawaii.edu.

AUPING, MICHAEL G. curator; b. Portland, Oreg., Oct. 17, 1949; s. Jack Louis and Jane (Hammel) A.; m. Patricia Contreras, Aug. 22, 1974; children: Alicia Contreras, Jonathan Contreras. AA, Santa Ana Coll., 1969; BA, Calif. State U., Fullerton, 1971; MA, Calif. State U., Long Beach, 1975. Editor #1 Powell Libr. UCLA, 1975-77; assoc. curator Univ. Art Mus., Berkeley, Calif., 1977-80; head of curatorial, curator 20th century art Ringling Mus. Art, Sarasota, Fla., 1980-84; chief curator Albright-Knox Art Gallery, Buffalo, 1984-93, Modern Art Mus. of Ft. Worth, 1993—. Instr. art history Citrus Coll., Azusa, Calif., summer, 1977, San Francisco Art Inst., spring, 1978; adj. lectr. U. Calif., Santa Barbara, fall, 1977, U. Buffalo, 1988—89; guest curator Artist's Space, NY, 1988; panelist mus. aid program N.Y. State Coun. on Arts, 1988—89, Fed. Adv. Com. for Internat. Exhbns., NEA and Rockefeller Found., 1992—; curator Whitney Biennial, 2000; cons. commr. Am. Pavilion 1990 Venice Biennale, Italy; mem. adv. com. Intermus. Conservation Lab., CARE Pub., Art in Pub. Places, Met.-Dade area, 1984—, The Bush Found., St. Paul, 1985; cons. L.A. County Dept. Parks Cultural Arts sect., 1973; grant panelist mus. programs spl. exhbns. NEA, Washington, 1985; panelist, on-site evaluator Artists Orgn., N.Y.C., 1983; visual arts panelist Divsn. Cultural Affairs State of Fla., Tallahassee, 1980, Tallahassee, 81. Author: Francesco Clemente, 1985, Jenny Holzer, 1992, Drawing Rooms: Jonathan Borofsky, Sol LeWitt, Richard Serra, 1994, Arshile Gorky: The Breakthrough Years, 1995, Tatsuo Miyajima: Big Time, 1996, Susan Rothenberg Paintings, 1996, Georg Baselitz: Portraits of Elke, 1997, Agnes Martin/Richard Tuttle, 1998, House of Sculpture, 1999, Natural Deceits, 2000, Philip Guston Retrospective, 2003; TV appearances including CBS Sunday Morning, 1988; mng. editor L.A. Inst. Contemporary Art Jour., 1976-77; contbr. articles to profl. jours.; organizer exhbns. Office: Modern Art Mus 3200 Darnell St Fort Worth TX 76107

AURAND, CHARLES HENRY, JR., music educator, educator; b. Battle Creek, Mich., Sept. 6, 1932; s. Charles Henry and Elisabeth Dirk (Hoekstra) A.; m. Donna Mae Erb, June 19, 1954; children: Janice, Cheryl, Sandra, Charles III, William. MusB, Mich. State U., 1954, MusM, 1958; PhD, U. Mich., 1971. Cert. tchr., Mich., Ohio. Asst. prof. music Hiram Coll., Ohio, 1958-60; dean, prof. music Youngstown State U., 1960-73; dean No. Ariz. U., Flagstaff, 1973-88, prof. music, 1988-94, prof. emeritus, 1994—. Chmn. Ariz. Alliance for Arts Edn., 1974-77; solo clarinetist Flagstaff Symphony; solo, chamber music and orch. musician, 1973-86; fine arts cons. Miami U. of Ohio, 1982 Author: Selected Solos, Methods, 1963; solo clarinetist Sonora Winds, 2002—. Elder Presbyn. Ch., 1965; chmn. Boy Scouts Am., Coconino dist., 1974-78; bd. dirs. Ariz. Com. Arts for the Handicapped, 1982-88, Flagstaff Symphony Orch., 1973-85, Flagstaff Festival of Arts, 1973-89, Sedona Chamber Mus. Soc., 1989-99, Sedona Med. Ctr., 1998-2002, Civic Orch. Tucson, 2003—; conf. dir. Internat. Clarinet Soc., 1991; pres. Citizens for an Alt. Route, 1995-98; mem. Ariz. Town Hall, 1996—; bd. dirs. Sedona Med. Ctr. Found., 1998-2002; mem. Ariz. Town Hall, 1996-2002; solo clarinet Sonora Winds, 2002—. 1st lt. USAF,1955-57 Recipient award of merit Boy Scouts Am., 1977; cert. appreciation John F. Kennedy Ctr. Performing Arts, 1985. Mem. Am. Assn. Higher Edn., Ariz. Humanities Assn., Music Educators Nat. Conf., State Adminstrs. of Music Schs. (chmn. 1971-73), Internat. Clarinet Soc./ClariNetwork Internat. (conf. dir. 1991), No. Ariz. U. Retirees Assn. (pres. 1997-98), SAR (pres. No. Ariz. chpt. 2000-02, pres. Ariz. Soc. 2003—), Kiwanis (pres. 1984-85). Republican. Presbyterian. Avocations: golf, tennis, bridge. Home: 37738 S Hill Side Dr Tucson AZ 85739-2221

AURBACH, HERBERT ALEXANDER, sociology educator; b. Cleve, Aug. 6, 1924; s. Nate and Sara (Munitz) A.; m. Rebecca Rachel Blumenfeld, Nov. 2, 1952 (dec. July 1999); children— Jacquelyn Aurbach Scheidlinger, Seth Jacob. BS, Western Res. U., 1948; PhD, U. Ky., 1960. Asst. rural sociologist Miss. State Coll., 1954-55; asst. prof. sociology and research asso. N.C. State Coll., Raleigh, 1955-57; research dir. Pitts. Commn. Human Relations, 1957-61; rsch. assoc., asst. prof. sociology U. Pitts., 1961-66; assoc. prof. edn. and sociology Pa. State U., 1966-70; prof. sociology Buffalo State Coll., 1970-93, chmn. dept. sociology, 1970-74, prof. emeritus, 1993—. Assoc. dir. Nat. Study Am. Indian Edn., 1968-69 Author: (with Estelle Fuchs) The Status of American Indian Education, 1970; Assoc. editor: Social Problems, 1966-74; Contbr. profl. jours. Bd. dirs. Citizens Commn. Criminal Justice, Buffalo and Erie County, 1972-74, Anti-Defamation League of B'nai B'rith, Buffalo, 1971-75, Coun. of Sr. Citizens Clubs of Buffalo and Erie County, 1997-01; co-chair adult edn. com. Temple Shaarey Zedek, Buffalo, 1995—, bd. trustees, 1998—, fin. sec., 2002—; mem. sr. svcs. adv. bd. Town of Amherst, 1997-2000. Decorated Air medal with 4 clusters; recipient N.Y. State/United Univ. Professions Excellence award, 1991; fellow So. Fellowship Fund, 1956-57. Mem. Soc. Study Social Problems (sec. 1965-69, treas. 1966-74, exec. officer 1975-86, v.p. 1987-88, chair bylaws com. 1988—2002, chair youth, aging and life course divsn. 1993-94, chair Lee Founders award com. 1999-2000), Am. Assn. Ret. Persons/VOTE (27th congl. dist. coord. 1993-95), Nat. Coun. Sr. Citizens (Amherst chpt. v.p. 1997-98, pres. 1998-99). Home: 120 Meyer Rd Apt 413 Amherst NY 14226-1013

AURBACH, ROBERT MICHAEL, lawyer, consultant, photographer; b. Chgo., Mar. 12, 1952; s. Arthur B. and Helen T. Aurbach; m. Elizabeth Cervantes, Aug. 7, 1994; children: Elyse Louise, Rebecca Michelle. BA summa cum laude, Boston U., 1974; JD, Cornell U., 1979; postgrad., U. N.Mex., 1992, 98. Bar: N.Mex. 1979, U.S. Dist. Ct. N.Mex. 1979, U.S. Ct. Appeals (10th cir.) 1979, U.S. Supreme Ct. 1984. Assoc. Montgomery & Andrews, P.A., Santa Fe, 1979-80; asst. dist. atty. 1st Jud. Dist. Atty.'s Office, Santa Fe, 1980-84; exec. dir. N.Mex. Adminstrv. Office of Dist. Attys., Santa Fe, 1984-89; sr. assoc. U. N.Mex. Inst. Criminal Justice, Albuquerque, 1989-90; pvt. practice law Santa Fe, 1989-90; gen. counsel N.Mex. Workers' Compensation Adminstrn., Albuquerque, 1990—. Cons. Navajo Nation Workers' Compensation Task Force, Windowrock, Ariz., 1993-97, U.S. V.I. Workers Compensation Adminstrn., Charlotte Amalie, 1992-93; chmn. Children's Justice Act Adv. Group, Albuquerque, 1989; instr. N.Mex. Law Enforcement Acad., Santa Fe, 1985-90; del. to working group on cross border workers' compensation issues Secretariat, Commn. on Labor Coop., N.Am. Agreement of Labor Coop., 1997—; cons. Small Bus. Regulatory Fairness Enforcement Act, lead govt's rep. Western Gov.'s Assn. regarding OSHA proposed std. on ergonomics. Author: (handbook) Peace Officer Prosecutions, 1985. Mem. bar coun. Disciplinary Bd. of N.Mex. Supreme Ct., 1979—; mem. com. Unauthorized Practice of Law Com., 1991-97; bd. dirs. Albuquerque Met. Crimestoppers, 1994-95; docent Albuquerque Aquarium; mediator Albuquerque Met. Ct. Mediation Program, bd. dir. N.M. DWI Resource Ctr., 2002—. Mem. Internat. Assn. Indsl. Accident Bds. (legal editor jour. 1997—, co-chair coverage and compliance com. 1998-99, chair taskforce on tribal sovereignty 1999-2000, chair standing regulation and enforcement coms. 2000-02, editor IAIABC jour. 2002-, lectr. Workers' Compensation Coll. 2002--), So. Assn. WCA, Western Assn. Workers Compensation Bds., Phi Beta Kappa. Avocations: golf, scuba diving, fishing. Home: 819 Suzanne Ln SE Albuquerque NM 87123-4502 Office: NMex Workers Compensation 2410 Centre Ave SE Albuquerque NM 87106-4190 E-mail: rmaurbach@aol.com., robert.aurbach@state.nm.us.

AURELL, JOHN KARL, lawyer; b. Tulsa, Sept. 26, 1935; s. George E. and Maxine (Reagor) A.; m. Jane Brevard Collins, Oct. 1, 1960; 1 child, Jane B. BA, Washington and Lee U., 1956; LLB, Yale U., 1964. Bar: Fla. 1964, D.C 1971, U.S. Dist. Ct. (no., mid. and so. dists.) Fla., U.S. Ct. Appeals (5th and 11th cirs.), U.S. Supreme Ct. Gen. counsel to Gov. State of Fla., Tallahassee, 1979-80; ptnr. Ausley & McMullen, 1994—2002, sr. counsel, 2002—. Mem. Fed. Jud. Nominating Commn. Fla.; chmn. No. Dist. Fla., 1993—97; bd. dirs. Z-Tel Techs., Inc. Mem. exec. com., v.p. Yale Law Sch. Assn., 1975-80; mem. Orange Bowl Com. 1st lt. U.S. Army, 1956-57. Fellow Am. Bar Found., Internat. Soc. Barristers, Am. Coll. Trial Lawyers; mem. ABA, Fla. Bar Assn. (bd. govs. young lawyers sect. 1966-71), Am. Law Inst., Gov.'s Club, Exch. Club, Yale Club (N.Y.C.), Econ. Club Fla. (chmn. 1997-98), Capital City Country Club. Democrat. Home: 1225 Live Oak Plantation Rd Tallahassee FL 32312-2509 Office: Ausley & McMullen PO Box 391 Tallahassee FL 32302-0391 E-mail: jaurell@ausley.com.

AURILIA, ANTONIO, physicist, educator; b. Napoli, Italy, May 14, 1942; came to U.S., 1967, naturalized, 1993; s. Clemente and Assunta (Ligesto) A.; m. Elizabeth Christine Adams, Dec. 1, 1972; children: Darius Matthew, Alexandra Rebecca. Laurea in Physics, U. Naples, Italy, 1966; PhD in Physics, U. Wis., Milw., 1970. Postdoctoral fellow dept. physics U. Alta., Edmonton, 1970-72; rsch. assoc. dept. physics Syracuse (N.Y.) U., 1972-74; rsch. scientist Internat. Ctr. Theoretical Physics, Trieste, Italy, 1974-75, Nat. Inst. Nuclear Physics, Trieste, 1975-86; prof. dept. physics Calif. State Poly. U., Pomona, 1986—. Mem. Am. Phys. Soc., Am. Assn. Physics Tchrs., N.Y. Acad. Sci., Sigma Xi. Democrat. Roman Catholic. Achievements include research in theoretical physics. Office: Calif State U Dept Physics 3801 W Temple Ave Pomona CA 91768-2557

AURILIA, CHRISTINE MARIE, administrative assistant; b. Bklyn., Mar. 23, 1962; d. Anthony Neil and Christina Mary (Chernega) A. BA in Journalism, Rutgers U., 1984. Editorial asst. Marvel Entertainment Group, N.Y.C., 1985-87, adminstrv. asst., 1987-96. Sponsor Futures for Children, Albuquerque, 1988--, Childreach, 1996-97; active Am. Friends of the Royal Shakespeare Co., London, 1985, Amnesty Internat., 1990, Oxfam Am., 1991, Greenpeace, 1991; supporter Colonial Williamsburg Found., 1994. Avocations: reading, writing, theatre, film, music.

AURIN, ROBERT JAMES, entrepreneur; b. St. Louis; m. Kathryn L. Engel, 1998. B in Journalism, U. Mo., 1965. Copywriter Leo Burnett Co., Chgo., 1971-72, Young & Rubicam, Inc., Chgo., 1972-73; from copywriter to v.p., creative dir. Foote, Cone & Belding, Inc., Chgo., 1973-79; exec. v.p., dir. creative services Grey-North Inc., Chgo., 1979-82; pres. Robert Aurin Assocs., Chgo., 1982—; owner ROMAR Investments Co., Chgo., 1984-99. Exec. creative dir. DraftWorldwide, Inc., 1996-99. Served to lt. USN, 1965-70, Vietnam.

AURNER, ROBERT RAY, II, oil company, auto diagnostic, restaurant franchise and company development executive; b. Madison, Wis., Mar. 24, 1927; s. Robert Ray and Kathryn (Dayton) A.; m. Phyllis Barrett, 1951 (div. 1966); children: Sheryl, Roxanne, Kathryn, Suzanne, Robert III; m. Deborah Marion Lucas, Jan. 31, 1976 (div. 1999); children: William Lucas, Christopher Ray. AA, Monterey Peninsula Coll., 1949; BA, Calif. State U. Fresno and Occidental Coll. Eagle Rock, 1950; postgrad., U. Calif., Berkeley, Duquesne U., Pitts. Lic. in real estate, Calif., Pa., N.Y.; registered investment advisor. Announcer Radio Sta. WSUI, Iowa City, 1946-48; featured celebrity Cowboy Bob, William Randolph Hearst Radio Sta. WISN-CBS, Milw., 1950-51; sr. sales supr. Shell Oil Co., San Francisco, 1952-60; dir. devel. ctrl. Calif. coast svc. sta. Gulf Oil Corp., 1960-67; ea. divsn. mgr. ops. Sunray DX Oil Co. (merger Sunoco), Tulsa, 1967-72; mgr. site devel. franchising Milex Auto Diagnostic Franchise, Inc., Plymouth Meeting, Pa., 1972-74; mgr. real estate store devel. Pitts. divsn. Atlantic & Pacific Tea Co. Supermarkets, 1974-77; real estate adminstr. store devel. N.E. U.S. region Steak and Ale - Bennigan's Restaurant divsn. Pillsbury Cos.; real estate mgr. N.Y. and Phila. regions Burger King Corp. restaurant divsn. Pillsbury Cos., N.Y., N.J., Pa., Del., 1977-87; real estate mgr. Ky. Fried Chicken and Pizza Hut divsns. Pepsico, Inc., Metro SMSA, N.Y.C., 1987-89; nat. dir. real estate, store devel. Nathan's Famous Coney Island Hot Dog Restaurants, Inc., N.Y.C., 1989-90; ret., 1990. Founder, chmn. bd. dirs., pres., CEO Bristlecone Trading and Devel., Inc., Carmel, Calif.; pres., CEO Aurner and Assocs. Resource Devel. & Project Mgrs., Carmel, 1987—, chmn. bd. dirs., 1990—; tower devel. mgr. So. N.J. Nextel Wireless Telecom. Corp., N.J., 1994-95; founder Trader Bob, Inc., Carson City, Nev., 1997; career counselor U.S. Coast Guard Acad. and Pub. Affairs. Officer and flotilla comdr. Flotilla 64 C.G. Aux., Coast Guard Sta., Monterey, Calif., 2000—03; divsn. chmn. Nat. Safe Boating Week USCG Aux., 2000—03. With USN, 1944—46, PTO. Named to Hon. Order Ky. Col., Gov. of Ky., Commodore in Okla. Navy Gov. of Okla. Mem.: Navy League Monterey Peninsula, Carmel Valley (Calif.) C. of C. (bd. dirs., sec. 1999—2003), USS Yellowstone Assn. (USNR), Pacheco Club of Monterey, Monterey Peninsula Yacht Club, Buccaneer Club (past pres. N.Y. and Conn.), Rotary Club of Monterey, Monterey Elks, Sigma Alpha Epsilon. Republican. Episcopalian. Avocations: golf, precious metals connoisseur, civil war buff. Office: Aurner & Assocs Inc PO Box 222135 Carmel CA 93922-2135 also: Bristlecone Trading & Devel Carmel CA 93923 also: Trader Bob Inc 251 Jeanell Dr Ste 3 Carson City NV 89703-2129 Office Fax: 831-626-3747. E-mail: TraderBob2@aol.com.

AUSBROOKS, CARRIE Y. BARRON, education educator, researcher; d. Sib Bruce and Claudia Faye Fitzgerald Barron; m. Kevin Gerard Ausbrooks, Dec. 5, 1953. AAS, Tarrant County Coll., Tex., 1974; BBA, U. of North Tex., 1983, MEd, 1984, PhD, 1996. Secondary Bus. Composite Tex. Edn. Agy., 1983, Vocational Occpl. Orientation Tex. Edn. Agy., 1985, Vocational Data Processing Tex. Edn. Agy., 1986, Mid-Management Tex. Edn. Agy., 1990, Computer Literacy State Bd. of Edn.,Tex., 1985, cert. Office Automation Profl. Office Automation Soc., Internat., 1986, Instructional Leadership Tng. U. of North Tex., 1990. Bus. computer sci. instr. Ft. Worth Ind. Sch. Dist., 1983—87, vocat. academic coord., 1987—91, dir., prin., 1991—96; asst. prof. U. of North Tex., Denton, 1996—2003, U. of Tex., Arlington, 2003. Cons. North Hills Sch., Irving, Tex., 1996, Tex. Ctr. for Ednl. Rsch., Austin, 1997; design team mem. Tex. Ctr. for Ednl. Tech., Tex. Assn. for Sch. Administrators, Denton, Austin, 1998. Author: (book chpts.) Texas Public School Organization and Administration. Spkr. Kiwanis Club, Ft. Worth, 1996, Las Colinas Assn., Tex., 1997; corp. breakfast spkr. North Hills Sch., Irving, Tex., 1996. Recipient Grad. Student Rsch. Seminar in Ednl. Adminstrn., Am. Ednl. Rsch. Assn., 1996. Mem.: World Affairs Coun. of Greater Ft. Worth (exec. bd., sec. 1994—97), ASCD, Am. Mgmt. Assn., Am. Ednl. Rsch. Assn., Edn. Law Assn., Delta Pi Epsilon (exec. bd., pres., v.p., corr. sec. 1985—88), Phi Delta Kappa. Avocations: photography, martial arts, writing, physical conditioning, reading. Office: U Tex at Arlington PO Box 19227 Arlington TX 76019-2841 Office Fax: 817-272-2530.

AUSBY, KENNETH LAVON, criminologist; b. Evergreen, Al, Mar. 27, 1960; s. Richard Carter and Dot (Ausby) Floyd; m. Aretha Tidmore, Oct. 25, 1996; children: Gerard, Markia, Alexandra, Vincent. BS, Al A&M U, Normal, AL, 1983; MS, Auburn U, Montgomery, Al, 1995—. Sgt. invest. Evergreen Police Dept., Evergreen, Ala., 1983—94; jailer/dispatcher Conecult Co.-sheriff dept., Evergreen, Ala., 1994—95; invest. Dist. Atty., Evergreen, Ala., 1995—. Pres. Hillcrest HS Band Booster, 2001—; mem. Conecuh County Juvenile Justice Coord. Coun. Mem.: Ala. Arson Prevention Task Force, Ala. Psychological Assn., Ala. Police Officers Assn., Internat. Narcotics Officers Assn., Assn. Profl. Police Investigator, New Beulah Baptist Church, Fraternal Order of Police Lodge #19. Avocation: basketball. Home: 403 Perryman St Evergreen AL 36401 Office: District Attorney PO Drawer 860 Evergreen AL 36401

AUSHERMAN, LARRY PRICE, lawyer; b. July 1, 1952; B in Gen. Studies, U. Kans., 1974; M in Natural Resources, U. Mich., 1978; JD, U. N.Mex., 1979. Bar: N.Mex. 1979. Shareholder Modrall, Sperling, Roehl, Harris & Sisk, Albuquerque, 1979—. Mem. ABA (past chair SONREEL hard minerals com.), N.Mex. State Bar Assn. (past chair sect. natural resources, energy and environ. law), Nature Conservancy (trustee, past chmn. N.Mex. chpt.). Office: Modrall Sperling Roehl Harris & Sisk 500 4th St NW Ste 1000 Albuquerque NM 87102-2186

AUSLANDER, MARC ALAN, computer scientist; b. Bklyn., May 12, 1942; s. David and Mildred Auslander; m. Rochelle Judith Griffithskig, July 5, 1963; children: Kyra Joan, Joel Edward. AB, Princeton U., 1963. Programmer IBM, Cambridge, Mass., 1963-68; mem. rsch. staff IBM T.J. Watson Rsch. Ctr., Yorktown Heights, N.Y., 1968-91; fellow IBM, Yorktown Heights, 1991—. Inventor in field. Fellow IEEE, Assn. Computing Machinery; mem. NAE, Shattemnc Yacht Club. Jewish. Avocations: sailing, bridge, reading. Office: IBM T J Watson Rsch Ctr PO Box 218 Yorktown Heights NY 10598-0218

AUSMAN, JAMES I. neurosurgeon, educator; b. Milw., Dec. 10, 1937; s. Donald C. and Mildred G. A.; m. Carolyn R. Ausman, June 30, 1960; children: Elizabeth, Susan. BS, Tufts U., 1955—59; MD, Johns Hopkins U., 1959—63; MA, SUNY-Buffalo, 1964; PAD, George Washington U., 1969. Cert. Bd. cert. neurosurgery 1974. Asst. prof. neurosurgery and pharmacology U. Minn., 1972—; chmn. dept. neurosurgery Henry Ford Hosp., Detroit, 1978—; prof. neurosurgery U. Mich., Ann Arbor, 1978—; prof., head dept. neurosurgery U. Ill., Chgo., 1991—2001, prof. neurosurgery, 2001—. Bd. dirs. Somanetics Corp., Detroit, 1993—. Editor: (jour.) Surg. Neurology, 1994—. Lt. col. USPHS. Mem.: Columbian Neurosurgery Soc. (hon.), Turkish Neurosurgery Soc. (hon.), French Speaking Neurosurgery Soc. (hon.), Argentine Neurosurgery Soc. (hon.), Brazil Neurosurg. Soc. (hon.), German Neurosurg. Soc. (hon.), Peru Neurosurg. Soc. (hon.), Japan Neurosurg. Soc. (hon.). Home: 70-950 Fairway Dr Rancho Mirage CA 92270

AUSMAN, ROBERT K. surgeon, research executive; b. Milw., Jan. 31, 1933; s. Donald Charles and Mildred (Shafrin) A.; m. Christine McCann, 1992. Ed., Kenyon Coll., 1953; MD, Marquette U., 1957. Damon Runyon cancer fellow U. Minn., 1958-61; dir. Health Research Inc. Roswell Park Meml. Inst., 1961-69; dep. dir. Fla. Regional Med. Assn., 1969-70; v.p. clin. research Baxter Travenol Labs., 1970-82, pres. advanced devel. group, 1982-90; pres. Mildon Corp., 1985—, Citation Pub. Co., 1991—. Clin. prof. surgery Med. Coll. Wis., 1972—. Named Outstanding Young Man in N.Y. Buffalo Evening News, 1966, Citizen of Year, 1967 Mem.: Am. Assn. Cancer Rsch., Am. Soc. Clin. Oncology, Masons. Home: PO Box 3538 Long Grove IL 60047 Office: Willow Valley Rd Long Grove IL 60047

AUSNEHMER, JOHN EDWARD, lawyer; b. Youngstown, Ohio, June 26, 1954; s. John Louis and Patricia Jean (Liguore) A.; m. Carole Marie Ausnehmer; children: Jill Ellen, Amber Layne. BS, Ohio State U., 1976; JD, U. Dayton, 1980. Bar: Ohio 1980, U.S. Dist. Ct. (no. dist.) Ohio 1981, U.S. Ct. Appeals (6th cir.) 1984, U.S. Supreme Ct. 1984. Law clk. Ohio Atty. Gen., Columbus, 1978, Green Schiavoni, Murphy, Haines & Sgambati Co., L.P.A., 1978; assoc. Dickson Law Office, Petersburg, Ohio, 1979-85; sole practice Youngstown, 1984—. Asst. pros. atty. Mahoning County, Ohio, 1986-89, 92—. Mem.: Columbiana County Bar Assn., Mahoning County Bar Assn., Cleve. Acad. Trial Attys. Ohio, Ohio State Bar Assn., Ohio Acad. Trial Lawyers, Moning Valley Soccer Club (rep. 1982—84), Phi Alpha Delta. Democrat. Roman Catholic. Home: 51 S Shore Dr Boardman OH 44512-5926 Office: PO Box 3965 120 Marwood Cir Youngstown OH 44513-3965

AUSPITZ, JOSIAH LEE, writer, consultant; b. Phila., Feb. 5, 1941; s. Herman Jacob Auspitz and Gabriella (Hartstein) Auspitz-Labson; m. Katherine Holahan, Oct. 10, 1965; children: Rachel Berthe, Benjamin Adam. BA, Harvard U., 1963; postgrad., Oxford (Eng.) U., 1963-64. Rsch. dir. Pres.'s Adv. Coun. on Exec. Orgn., 1969-70; tutor in govt. Harvard U., Cambridge, Mass., 1969-73; dir. philosophy program Sabre Found., Cambridge, 1978—, founder sci. assistance book donation project, 1986. Cons. computer firms dealing in data analysis and natural lang. processing, 1995—. Contbr. chpts. to books, articles to profl. jours., newspaper, mags. Mem. Davis Sq. Task Force, Somerville, Mass., 1974—; bd. dirs. Sabre Found., 1969—, Michael Oakeshott Assn., 1999—. Marshall scholar, 1963-64; fellow NEH, 1975-76, Internat. Rsch. Exch. Bd., 1986-87, 88, Earhart Found., 1996—. Mem. Coun. on Fgn. Rels., Com. for Study of Am. Electorate, Learned Soc. Praxiology (hon. charter mem.), Ripon Soc. (nat. pres. 1969-71). Republican. Jewish. Home: 17 Chapel St Somerville MA 02144-1901

AUST, JOE BRADLEY, surgeon, educator; b. Buffalo, Sept. 8, 1926; s. Joe Bradley and Edith (Derby) A.; m. Constance Ann MacMullin, June 18, 1949; children— Jay Bradley, Bonnie Jean, Barbara Ann, Linda Lee, Mary Louise, Tracey Roberta. MD, U. Buffalo, 1949; MS in Physiology, U. Minn., 1957, PhD in Surgery, 1958. Diplomate: Am. Bd. Surgery, Am. Bd. Thoracic Surgery. Intern U. Minn. Hosps., 1949-50, resident, 1950-58; scholar Am. Cancer Soc. U. Minn., 1957-62, mem. faculty, 1957-66, prof. surgery, 1964-66; prof. surgery, chmn. dept. U. Tex. Med. Sch., San Antonio, 1966-96, prof. dept. surgery, 1996—. Cons. Minn. State Prison, 1958-62, Anoka State Hosp., 1962-65, Brooke Army Med. Hosp., 1967—, Wilford Hall USAF Hosp., 1967—, Audie Murphy Meml. VA Hosp., 1973— ; nat. cons. to surgeon gen. USAF, Washington, 1975-78 Served with M.C. USNR, 1950-52. Fellow ACS; mem. Am. Surg. Assn., Western Surg. Assn., So. Surg. Assn., Cen. Surg. Assn., Soc. U. Surgeons, Soc. Head and Neck Surgeons, Am. Assn. Cancer Rsch., Soc. Surg. Oncology, San Antonio Surgical Soc., Am. Assn. Cancer Edn., Halsted

Soc., Soc. Clin. Oncology, Transplantation Soc., Sigma Xi, Alpha Omega Alpha, Phi Ch. Achievements include spl. research cancer immunity, regional cancer chemotherapy, shock, homotransplantation. Office: U Tex Med Sch 7703 Floyd Curl Dr San Antonio TX 78284-6200

AUST, STEVEN DOUGLAS, biochemistry, biotechnology and toxicology educator; b. South Bend, Wash., Mar. 11, 1938; s. Emil and Helen Mae (Crawford) A.; m. Nancy Lee Haworth, June 5, 1960 (dec.); children: Teresa, Brian. BS in Agr., Wash. State U., 1960, MS in Nutrition, 1962; PhD in Dairy Sci., U. Ill., 1965. Postdoctoral fellow dept. toxicology Karolinska Inst., Stockholm, 1966; N.Z. facial exzema sr. postdoctoral fellow Ruakura Agrl. Research Ctr., Hamilton, 1975-76; mem. faculty dept. biochemistry Mich. State U., East Lansing, 1967-87, prof., 1977-87, assoc. dir. Ctr. for Environ. Toxicology, 1980-85, dir. Ctr. for the Study of Active Oxygen, 1985-87; dir. biotech. ctr. Utah State U., Logan, 1987-91, prof. chem. biochemistry, 1987—. Dir. basic rsch. and tng. program Super Fund Nat. Inst. Environ. Health Scis., 1988-96; mem. toxicology study sect. NIH, 1979-83; mem. environ. measurements com., mem. sci. adv. bd. EPA, 1980-83; mem. toxicology data bank, mem. peer rev. com. Nat. Libr. Medicine, 1983-85; mem. Mich. Toxic Substance Control Commn., 1979-82, chmn., 1981-82; pres., founder Intech One-Eighty Corp., North Logan Utah, 1993-99, pres. 1999—; mem. adv. panel for metabolic biochemistry program NSF, 1998; mem. EPA/DOE/NSF/ONR Joint Program on Bioremediation, 1998. Contbr. articles to profl. jours. Recipient Nat. Rsch. Svc. award NIH, USPHS, Dupont Sci. and Engring. award, 1988, Alumni Achievement award Wash. State U., 1998, Univ. Outsatanding Grad. Mentor award, 2003; named D. Wynne Thorne Rschr. of Yr., 2003; NRC facial eczema fellow Ruakura Agrl. Rsch. Ctr., Hamilton, New Zealand, 1975, Gov.'s medal sci. and tech., 2002. Fellow Acad. Toxicology Scis., Oxygen Soc.; mem. Am. Soc. Biol. Chemists, Am. Soc. Pharmacology and Exptl. Therapeutics, Soc. Toxicology, Am. Chemical Soc., Am. Soc. Microbiology. Office: Utah State U Biotech Ctr Logan UT 84322-4705 also: Intech One-Eighty Corp PO Box 6218 North Logan UT 84341-6218 E-mail: sdaust@cc.usu.edu.

AUSTAD, VIGDIS, computer software company executive; b. Utica, N.Y., Sept. 26, 1954; d. Helge and Viola Austad. BS in Econs., U. Pa., 1981; postgrad., NYU, 1982-84. Cert. employee benefit specialist. Asst. to pres. Almet, Inc., Bernardsville, N.J., 1973-81; mgr. info. systems Buck Consultants, Inc., N.Y.C., 1981-86; v.p. mktg. Cascade Techs. Inc., N.Y.C., 1986-88, pres., chief exec. officer, 1988—. Treas., dir. Cascade Techs., Inc., 1985—; bd. dirs. Beacon Global Solutions, Inc., Somerset, N.J. Contbr. articles to profl. publs. Recipient scholarship, U. Pa., Phila., 1979-81. Mem. Info. Tech. Assn. Am., N.Y. Software Assn. (bd. dirs. 1994-95), Internat. Found. Cert. Employee Benefit Specialists, N.J. Software Industry Assn. (legis. com.), Cert. Employee Benefit Specialists (found. dir. 1986-88). Republican. Lutheran. Avocations: scuba diving, skiing, biking, racquetball. Office: Cascade Techs Inc 1075 Easton Ave Ste 11-256 Somerset NJ 08873

AUSTAN, FRANK ACOSTA, clinician, educator; b. Medellin, Colombia, Apr. 29, 1951; arrived in U.S., 1959; s. Guillermo Austan and Lillian Acosta; m. Joan Robin Pliner, July 14, 1974; children: Lara Nicole, Jason Michael. AB, Univ. Miami, Coral Gables, Fla., 1980; MSc, Nova Southeastern Univ., Ft. Lauderdale, Fla., 1983. Lic. Bd. Medicine, Fla., Pa., Nat. Bd. for Respiratory Care, 1978. Dir., respiratory care Berlin West Jersey Hosp., Berlin, NJ, 1986—99, Temple Univ. Hosp. & Med. Sch., Phila., 1999—. Asst. prof. Miami-Dade Cmty. Coll., Miami, Fla., 1980—82; sr. instr., dept. medicine Hahnemann Med. Coll. & Hosp., Phila., 1983—86; clin. instr. Univ. Medicine and Dentistry, Newark, 1992—. Contbr. articles to profl. jour. Mem.: Am. Coll. Chest. Physicians, Am. Thoracic Soc., Am. Assoc. Respiratory Care (Respironics Fellowships Prize 2000). Democrat. Achievements include Contrb. to med. lit. via Heart & Lung Jour., Am. J clin. hypnosis in the clin. area of ventilator weaning, treatment of asthma and chronic obstructive pulmonary disease, artery puncture pain reduction. Office: Temple Univ Hosp & Med Sch 3401 N Broad St Philadelphia PA 19140-5103

AUSTEN, K(ARL) FRANK, internist, educator; b. Akron, Ohio, Mar. 14, 1928; s. Karl and Bertle (Jehle) Austen; m. Joycelyn Chapman, Apr. 11, 1959; children: Leslie Marie, Karla Ann, Timothy Frank, Jonathan Arthur. AB, Amherst Coll., 1950; MD, Harvard U., 1954. Intern in medicine Mass. Gen. Hosp., 1954—55, asst. resident, 1955—56, sr. resident, 1958—59, chief resident, 1961, asst. in medicine, 1962—63, asst. physician, 1963—66, chief pulmonary unit, 1964—66, also cons. in medicine; practice medicine, specializing in internal medicine, allergy and immunology, 1962—66; USPHS postdoctoral research fellow Nat. Inst. Med. Research, Mill Hill, London, 1959—61; asst. in medicine Harvard Med. Sch., 1961, instr., 1961—62, asso. in medicine, 1962—64, asst. prof., 1965—66, assoc. prof., 1966—68, prof., 1969—72, Theodore B. Bayles prof., 1972—; physician-in-chief Robert B. Brigham Hosp., Boston, 1966—80; chmn. dept. rheumatology and immunology Brigham and Women's Hosp., Boston, 1980—95, dir. lab. inflammation and allergic disease rsch. sect., 1995—. Mem. fellowship subcom. Arthritis Found., 1968—71, chmn., 1971; mem. coun. Infectious Disease Soc. Am., 1969—71; mem. arthritis tng. grants com. Nat. Inst. Arthritis and Metabolic Diseases, NIH, 1970—73; NHLB adv. coun., 1994—; mem. directing group, task force on immunology and disease Nat. Inst. Allergy and Infectious Diseases, 1972—73; bd. dirs. Arthritis Found., 1972—75, chmn. manpower study com., 1972—73, chmn. rsch. com. Multipurpose Arth. Ctr., 1972—76; chmn. rsch. com. Med. Found., Inc., 1972—76; mem. Am. Bd. Allergy and Immunology, 1973—78, Nat. Commn. on Arthritis and Related Musculoskeletal Diseases, 1975—76, Allergy and Immunology Rsch. com., NIAID, 1975—79, chmn., 1976—79; chmn. nomenclature com. Internat. Union Immunol. Socs., 1983—; mem. adv. com. to the dir. NIH, 1986—90, mem. nat. heart, lung and blood adv. com., 1966—80. Mem. editl. bd.: Arthritis and Rheumatism, 1968—81, Proc. of Transplantation Soc., 1968—82, Jour. Infectious Diseases, 1969—79, Jour. Exptl. Medicine, 1971—, Immunol. Comm., 1972—85, Clin. Immunology and Immunopathology, 1972—89, Proc. of NAS, 1978—83, Clin. and Exptl. Immunology, 1978—88, Internat. Jour. Immunopharmacology, 1984, Advances in Immunology, 1985—, Advances in Pharmacology, 1989—; contbr. articles to profl. jours. Trustee Amherst Coll., 1981—. Capt. M.C. U.S. Army, 1956—58. Recipient Warren Alpert Found. prize, 1999. Mem.: ACP, NAS (chmn. sect. on med. microbiology and immunology 1983—86), Internat. Soc. Immunopharmacology (pres. 1994), Internat. Assn. Allergology and Clin. Immunology, Fedn. Am. Soc. Exptl. Biology, Am. Acad. Allergy and Immunology (exec. com. 1970—72, sec. 1977—80, pres. 1981), Assn. Am. Physicians (recorder 1978—84, pres. 1989—90), Am. Acad. Arts and Scis., Transplantation Soc., Am. Rheumatism Assn., Am. Soc. Clin. Investigation, Brit. Soc. Immunology, Am. Assn. Immunologists (pres. 1977—78), Am. Soc. Exptl. Pathology, Am. Soc. Pharm. and Exptl. Therapeutics, Inst. Medicine, Interurban Clin. Club. Office: BWH Dept Rhem & Allergy Smith Bldg 55 Francis St Boston MA 02115-6105

AUSTEN, W(ILLIAM) GERALD, surgeon, educator; b. Akron, Ohio, Jan. 20, 1930; s. Karl and Bertl (Jehle) Austen; m. Patricia Ramsdell, Jan. 28, 1961; children: Karl Ramsdell, William Gerald Jr., Christopher Marshall, Elizabeth Patricia. BS, MIT, 1951; MD, Harvard U., 1955; HHD (hon.), U. Akron, 1980; DSc (hon.), U. Athens, Greece, 1981; DSc (hon.), U. Mass., 1985, Northeastern Ohio U. Coll. Medicine, 1996. Diplomate Am. Bd. Surgery, Am. Bd. Thoracic Surgery. Intern, then resident surgery Mass. Gen. Hosp., Boston, 1955—61, chief surg. cardiovascular rsch. unit, 1963—69, chief surgery, 1969—97, surgeon-in-chief, 1989—97, surgeon-in-chief emeritus, 1997—; surgeon clinic surgery Nat. Heart Inst., 1961—62; CEO, pres. Mass. Gen. Physicians Orgn., Boston, 1994—98, CEO, chmn., 1998—99, chmn., 1999—2000, hon. trustee, chmn. emeritus, 2000—. Assoc. in surgery Harvard Med. Sch., 1963—65, assoc. prof. surgery, 1965—66, prof. surgery, 1966—74, Edward D. Churchill prof. surgery, 1974—; mem. residency review com. surgery Accreditation Coun. Grad. Med. Edn., 1988—93. Author, editor : med. textbooks; contbr. articles to profl. jours. Mem. corp. MIT 1972-, life mem. corp., 1982-, mem. exec. com. corp., 1986-98; trustee John S. and James L. Knight Found., 1986-, vice chmn., 1991-96, chmn., 1996-; bd. dirs. Found. Biomed Rsch., 1988-; trustee Mass. Eye and Ear Infirmary, 1991-, Ptnrs. HealthCare System Inc., 1994-97, Mass. Gen. Hosp., 1997-99, Dana Farber/Ptnrs. Cancer Care Inc., 1999-, North Shore Medical Center, 2000—; hon. trustee Mass. Gen. Hosp., 1999-. Markle scholar, 1963-68. Fellow AAAS, Royal Coll. Surgeons Eng. (hon.), Am. Acad. Arts & Scis.; mem. NAS Inst. Medicine, Am. Heart Assn. (pres. 1977-78), Am. Surg. Assn. (sec. 1979-84, pres. 1985-86), Am. Assn. Thoracic Surgery (v.p. 1987-88, pres. 1988-89), Am. Bd. Surgery (mem, bd. 1969-74, sr. 1974—), Am. Bd. Thoracic Surgery (bd. dirs. 1984-90), ACS (regent 1982-91, chmn. bd. regents 1989-91, pres. 1992-93), Assn. Acad. Surgery (pres. 1970), Soc. Univ. Surgeons (sec. 1967-70, pres. 1972-73), New Eng. Cardiovascular Soc. (pres. 1972-73), Mass. Heart Assn. (pres. 1972). Home: 330 Beacon St Apt C66 Boston MA 02116-1190 Office: Mass Gen Hosp BUL 3 Boston MA 02114-2696

AUSTER, CAROL JEAN, sociology educator; b. Bloomington, Ind., Mar. 2, 1954; d. Donald and Nancy Eileen (Ross) Auster; m. Stanley A. Mertzman; children: Lauren Jean, Lisa Amy. AB in Social Rels., Colgate U., 1976; MA in Sociology, Princeton U., 1979, PhD in Sociology, 1984. Instr. sociology Franklin and Marshall Coll., Lancaster, Pa., 1981-84, asst. prof., 1984-88, assoc. prof., 1988-96, prof., 1996—, acting chair dept., 1982-83, chair dept., 1988—91, 1999—2004. NSF rsch. assoc. N.H. Coll., Manchester, 1974, Hampshire Coll., Amherst, Mass., 1975; cons. dept. planning Lancaster (Pa.) Gen. Hosp., 1984—. Author: The Sociology of Work: Concepts and Cases, 1996; contbr. articles, revs. to profl. jours. N.Y. State Regents scholar Colgate U., 1976; Princeton U. fellow, 1977-80; Rockefeller Found. grantee U. Ill., 1979-80, Alfred P. Sloan Found. grantee, 1993-96. Mem.: AAUP (dist. VII rep. to nat. coun. 1986—89, com. F. on confs. 1986—92, memberships grants com. 1987—89, 2d v.p. 1990—92, chair com. B. on ethics 1994—2000), So. Sociol. Soc., Ea. Sociol. Soc., Sociologists for Women in Soc., Soc. for Study Social Problems, Am. Sociol. Assn. (com. on employment 1994—96). Office: Franklin and Marshall Coll Dept Sociology Lancaster PA 17604

AUSTER, PAUL, writer; b. Newark, Feb. 3, 1947; s. Samuel and Queenie (Bogat) A.; m. Lydia Davis, Oct. 6, 1974 (div. 1979); 1 child, Daniel; m. Siri Hustvedt, June 16, 1981; 1 child, Sophie. BA, Columbia U., 1969, MA, 1970. Lectr. Princeton (N.J.) U., 1986-90. Author: (poetry) Unearth, 1974, Wall Writing, 1976, Fragments From Cold, 1977, Facing the Music, 1980, Disappearances: Selected Poems, 1988, (non-fiction) White Spaces, 1980, The Invention of Solitude, 1982, The Art of Hunger, 1982, expanded edit., 1992, Why Write, 1996, Translations, 1997, Hand to Mouth, 1997, The Red Notebook, 2002; author: (with Sam Messer) The Story of My Typewriter, 2002; author: (fiction) City of Glass, 1985, Ghosts, 1986, The Locked Room, 1986, In the Country of Last Things, 1987, Moon Palace, 1989, The Music of Chance, 1990, Leviathan, 1992, Mr. Vertigo, 1994, Timbuktu, 1999, The Book of Illusions, 2002, Oracle Night, 2003, (films) Smoke, 1995 (Ind. Spirit award, 1996), Blue in the Face, 1995, Lulu on the Bridge, 1998; editor: The Random House Book of Twentieth-Century French Poetry, 1982, I Thought My Father was God and Other True Tales from NPR's National Story Project, 2001. Decorated officier de l'Ordre des Arts et des lettres (France), Prix Médicis Etranger; fellow, Nat. Endowment for the Arts, 1979, 1985. Mem. PEN. Office: care Carol Mann Agy 55 5th Ave New York NY 10003-4301

AUSTERLITZ, HOWARD, electronics engineer, writer; b. Brooklyn, N.Y., Dec. 21, 1952; s. Julius and Esther (Olshansky) A.; m. Kiel Stuart, June 20, 1977. BS, SUNY, 1973. Rsch. engr. dept. physics SUNY, Stonybrook, 1975-77, instr. dept. materials sci., 1981-86; engr. Bunker Ramo, Westlake Village, Calif., 1977-79; r & d engr. Eaton Corp., Melville, N.Y., 1979-81; applications engring. mgr. ERG, Ronkonkoma, N.Y., 1986-87; sr. design engr. OCG Technology, Farmingdale, N.Y., 1987-89; sr. project engr. Cybex, Ronkonkoma, N.Y., 1989-95; sr. electronics engr. RVSI, Hauppauge, N.Y., 1995-2001, Cosense Inc., Hauppauge, 2001—02; with Parker Hannifin, Smithtown, NY, 2002—. Cons. in field. Author: Data Acquisition Techniques Using PCs, 1991, 2d edit., 2002; mng. editor: Keystrokes, 1989-95; contbr. articles to profl. jours. Mem. IEEE, DEC Users Soc. (steering com. 1983-85). Office: Parker Aerospace ESD 300 Marcus Blvd Smithtown NY 11788 Business E-Mail: hausterlitz@parker.com.

AUSTERMAN, DONNA LYNNE, Spanish language educator; b. Colorado Springs, Colo., Aug. 5, 1947; d. Herman Raymond Ogg and Shirley (Cooper) Price; m. Thomas Lanham Brown, Jan. 26, 1966 (div. Jan. 1972); 1 child, Thomas Roy; m. Randy Lynn Austerman, Nov. 25, 1972; 1 child, Michael Neil. Student, Washburn U., 1965-67; BS, Pittsburg State U., 1970, MS, 1971; postgrad., U. Kans., 1980, U. Okla., 1983, Okla. State U., 1990. Cert. tchr. (life), Mo., std. tchr., Okla. Tchr. Spanish, English Liberal (Mo.) R-2 Schs., 1970-72, Unified Sch. Dist. 346, Mound City, Kans., 1972-74, Nowata (Okla.) Pub. Schs., 1983-86; tchr. Spanish Bartlesville (Okla) Sch. Dist. # 30, 1986—2001. Steering com. mem. North Ctrl. Assn., 1993—2001. Mem. NEA, ASCD, Am. Assn. Tchrs. Spanish and Portuguese, Nat. Staff Devel. Coun., Okla. Edn. Assn., Okla. Fgn. Lang. Tchrs. Assn., Bartlesville Edn. Assn., Bartlesville Fgn. Lang. Coun., Bartlesville Profl. Improvement Com. (chmn. mid-h.s. staff devel. com.). Avocations: travel, swimming, country and western dancing, old movies, reading. Home: 170 Desert Inn Way Colorado Springs CO 80921

AUSTILL, ALLEN, dean emeritus; b. Newton, Mass., June 22, 1927; s. William E. and Anna (Pifer) A.; m. Joan Mildred Sellery, June 4, 1950; children: Randolph Allen, Christopher Scott, Lara Anne. BA, U. Chgo., 1948, MA, 1951; LHD (hon.), New Sch. Social Rsch., 1987. Research asso. Council State Govts., Chgo., 1951-52; mem. faculty, dir. admissions and placement St. Johns Coll., 1953-55; dir. student housing U. Chgo., 1955-57; tchr., dean students SUNY-Stony Brook, 1957-61; cons. Ford Found., Middle East, Amman, Jordan, 1962; mem. faculty, asso. dean New Sch. Social Research, 1962-64, dean, 1964-79, v.p. acad. affairs and exec. dean, 1979-82, dean, 1982-87, chancellor, 1987-89. Cons. Chatham Coll., 2000, Corcoran Gallery Coll., 2003; cons. title I Higher Edn. Act, State N.Y.; mem. council academic fellows Shimer Coll., 1971-80; mem. N.Y. Regents Adv. Task Force for Adult Edn., 1972-77, chmn., 1976-77; chmn. bd. dirs. Harpers Mag. Found., 1988—; bd. dirs. Ednl. Mgmt. Network, 1985-95; chmn. vis. com. Am. Mus. Natural History, 1990. Author: (with others) Higher Education in the Forty-Eight States, 1952; Summary of State Legislation and Elections (with others), 1953. Pres. Friends of Cresskill Libr., 1969-71; mem. vis. com. continuing edn. Harvard U., 1977-83; mem. Boston Ctr. for Adult Edn., 1990—, chair bd. trustees, 1991-95. With AUS, 1945-46. Home: 6 Hammersmith Dr Saugus MA 01906-4168 E-mail: aaustill@comcast.net.

AUSTIN, ANN SHEREE, lawyer; b. Tyler, Tex., Aug. 25, 1960; d. George Patrick and Mary Jean (Brookshire) A. BA cum laude, U. Houston, 1983; JD, South Tex. Coll., 1987. Bar: Tex. 1987, U.S. Dist. Ct. (no. dist.) Tex. 1988, U.S. Ct. Appeals (5th cir.) 1989, U.S. Dist. Ct. (we. dist.) Tex. 1990, U.S. Ct. Appeals (D.C. cir.) 1992, U.S. Supreme Ct. 1992, U.S. Dist. Ct. (ea. dist.) Tex. 1993. With First City Ops. Ctr., Houston, 1980-85; law clk. Lipstet, Singer, Hirsch & Wagner, Houston, 1985-86, Pizzitola, Hinton & Sussman, Houston, 1986-87; briefing atty. Hon. Hal M. Lattimore Ct. Appeals, 2d Jud. Dist., Ft. Worth, 1987-88; assoc. Cantey & Hanger, Ft. Worth and Dallas, 1988-93, Smith, Ralston & Russell, Dallas, 1993-94, Russell, Austin & Henschel, Dallas, 1994-95; pvt. practice Arlington, 1995-96; prin. Landau, Omahana & Kopka, Ltd., Dallas, 1996-97; asst. city atty. City of Dallas, 1997—2002; atty. Law Offices of W. Blake Hyde, 2002—. Tchr. Project Outreach State Bar of Tex., 1992. Author: Personnel Rules, Park & Recreation Department; co-author Annual Meeting of Invited Attorneys, Construction Law; chpt. editor: Cases and Materials on Civil Procedure, 1987. Mem. Ft. Worth Hist. Preservation Soc., com. mem., 1992; fundraiser Prevention of Child Abuse in Am., 1988—, Women's Haven. Mem. Tex. Young Lawyers Assn. (jud. rev. com. 1990, women in the profession com., profl. ethics and grievance awareness com. 1992-94), Dallas Bar Assn. (jud. com. 1992-94, ethics com. 1999-01, cmty. involvement com., employment law sect. CLE com. 1999-2000), Dallas Assn. Young Lawyers, Dallas Women's Bar Assn., Ft. Worth Tarrant County Young Lawyers Assn. (treas. 1989-90, dir. 1989, Teen Ctr., co-chair Adopt-A-Sch. program, chair CLE program), Tarrant County Women's Bar Assn., Am. Inns. of Ct. Methodist. Avocations: walking, reading, sky diving. Office: Law Offices of W Blake Hyde Ste 490/LB11 1301 E Collins Blvd Richardson TX 75081

AUSTIN, ARTHUR DONALD, II, lawyer, educator; b. Staunton, Va., Dec. 2, 1932; s. George Milnes and Mae (Eichner) A.; m. Irene Clara Wittenberg, June 12, 1960; 1 son, Brian Carl. BS in Commerce, U. Va., 1958; JD, Tulane U., 1963. Bar: Va. 1964, D.C. 1970. Asst. prof. Coll. of William and Mary, Williamsburg, Va., 1963-64, Bowling Green State U., Ohio, 1964-66; asst. prof. law Cleve. State U., 1966-68; prof. law Case Western Res. U., Cleve., 1968-70, 72-78, Edgar A. Hahn prof. jurisprudence, 1978—. Atty. Dept. Justice, Washington, 1970-71 Author: Antitrust: Law, Economics, Policy, 1976, Complex Litigation Confronts the Jury System, 1984, The Empire Strikes Back: Outsiders and the Struggle Over Legal Education, 1998; contbr. articles to law revs. Served with U.S. Army, 1952-54. Decorated Bronze Star medal with V, Purple Heart. Home: 1174 Stony Hill Rd Hinckley OH 44233-9538 Office: 11075 East Blvd Cleveland OH 44106-5409

AUSTIN, BERIT SYNNOVE, small business owner, central services specialist; b. Oslo, July 22, 1938; came to U.S., 1957; d. Johan Andreas and Astrid (Bjerke) Irgens; m. William Paul Austin, Dec. 22, 1961 (div. 1978); children: Lisa Christine, Paul Erik, Ivar Jon; m. Berit Synnove Funnemark, Feb. 20, 2000. AA, Saddleback Coll., 1984, AS, 1988. Accounts payable clk. Dynatech Corp., Santa Ana, Calif., 1976-78; accounts payable acct., jr. buyer/Kardex Brunswick Corp., Costa Mesa, Calif., 1978-81; fin. clk. Fluor Corp., Irvine, Calif., 1981-84; warehouse asst. Saddleback Coll., Mission Viejo, Calif., 1984—, instr. Norwegian lang. Owner, cons. Home Prescription, Lake Elsinore, Calif., Mission Viejo, 1984—. Mem. Sierra Country Club, Sons of Norway Fraternal Internat. Soc. (historian 1972, publicity dir. 1973, asst. soc. dir. 1974, social dir. 1992, cultural dir. 1994, pres. 1996). Republican. Lutheran. Avocations: gardening, bicycling, cross-country skiing, travel. Home: PO Box 4013 Mission Viejo CA 92690-4013 Office: Home Prescription PO Box 4013 Mission Viejo CA 92690-4013 E-mail: baustin7@yahoo.com.

AUSTIN, CLAUDE LIDELL, retired surgeon; b. Winona, Miss., Jan. 4, 1919; s. Luther Barksdale Austin and Cora Claudine Carter; m. Elizabeth Hightower, Sept. 2, 1944 (dec. Mar. 1990); children: Larry, Richard; m. Merry Cobb Lowry, Feb. 1, 1991. BA, U. Miss., 1940, BS, 1944; MD, Jefferson Med. Sch., 1946. Pvt. practice, Hattiesburg, Miss., 1947—91; ret., 1992. Pres. med. staff Hattiesburg Hosp., 1969—80; established vol. med. office and ongoing med. care Home of Grace, 1997—. Pres. Belle Fontaine Beach Assn., Ocean Springs, Miss., 1995; bd. dirs. Rotary Club, Hattiesburg, 1947. Fellow: Internat. Coll. Surgeons; mem.: AMA, Miss. State Med. Assn. Republican. Methodist. Avocation: deep sea fishing. Home: 7601 Belle Fontaine Dr Ocean Springs MS 39564-8490 Office: Home of Grace 14200 Jericho Rd Ocean Springs MS 39565

AUSTIN, DANFORTH WHITLEY, newspaper executive; b. Hutchinson, Kans., Sept. 21, 1946; s. Whitley and Mary Frances (Danforth) Austin; m. Gail Ellen Davenport, Sept. 2, 1967; children: Stephen D., Richard D. BS, U. Kans., 1968. Staff reporter The Wall St. Jour., Dallas, Detroit, 1970—76, spl. writer N.Y.C., 1976—78, news editor, 1978, bur. chief Pitts., 1978—83, from asst. to deputy nat. editor N.Y.C., 1984—86, spl. reports editor, 1986—87; dir. corp. rels. Dow Jones and Co. Inc., N.Y.C., 1987—89; dir. circulation Wall St. Jour., Barron's, Princeton, N.J., 1989-95; v.p. circulation Wall St. Jour., 1992—95, v.p., gen. mgr., 1995—2002; v.p. Dow Jones & Co. Inc., 2002—. Vice chmn. Ottaway Newpapers Inc., Campbell Hall, NY, 2002—03, chmn., CEO, 2003—. Trustee William Allen White Found., U. Kans., Lawrence, 1996—; sr. warden St. Peter's Episcopal Ch., Brentwood, Pa., 1981; lay reader Episcopal Diocese of Pitts., 1981—83, Diocese of Newark, 2001—; vestryman St. George's Episcopal Ch., Maplewood, NJ, 1985—88; bd. dirs. Episcopal Ch. Found., N.Y.C., 2002—. Sgt. U.S. Army, 1968—70, Vietnam. Decorated Bronze Star, Air medal. Mem.: N.Y. Newspaper Pubs. Assn. (bd. dirs. 2000—02), Soc. Profl. Journalists, Kappa Sigma. Home: 51 Joanna Way Short Hills NJ 07078-3206 Office: Ottaway Newspapers Inc 97 Rt 416 PO Box 401 Campbell Hall NY 10916 Business E-Mail: dan.austin@dowjones.com.

AUSTIN, DANIEL WILLIAM, lawyer; b. Springfield, Ill., Feb. 24, 1949; s. Daniel D. and Ruth A. (Ahrenkiel) A.; m. Lois Ann Austin, June 12, 1971; 1 child, Elizabeth Ann. BA, Millikin U., 1971; JD, Washington U., 1974. Bar: Ill. 1974, U.S. Dist. Ct. (cen. dist.) Ill. 1979, U.S. Ct. Appeals (7th cir.) 1980, U.S. Supreme Ct. 1980, U.S. Tax Ct. 1986. Assoc. Miley & Meyer, Taylorville, Ill., 1974-78; ptnr. Miley, Meyer & Austin, Taylorville, 1978-81; prin. Meyer, Austin & Romano P.C., Taylorville, 1981—, Meyer, Austin, Romano & Paisley, P.C., Taylorville. Pres. United Fund, Taylorville, 1980, Christian County YMCA, Taylorville, 1983-85, St. Vincent Meml. Hosp. Found., 1998—. Named one of Outstanding Young Men Am., 1985, Outstanding Citizen of City of Taylorville, 1993. Mem. ABA, Ill. Bar Assn., Christian County Bar Assn., Order of Barristers. Clubs: Taylorville Country (pres. 1985). Democrat. Presbyterian. Avocations: golf, photography. Home: 14 Westhaven Ct Taylorville IL 62568-9064 Office: Meyer Austin Romano & Paisley PC 210 S Washington St Taylorville IL 62568-2245

AUSTIN, DAVID GEORGE, dentist; b. Dayton, Ohio, Sept. 11, 1951; s. Donald Edward and Mary Josephine (Thompson) A.; m. Mary Allene Allen, Dec. 23, 1977; children: Jonathon David, Jennifer Mary. BA, Ohio Wesleyan U., 1973; DDS, Ohio State U., 1977; MS, U. Med. Dentistry N.J., 1992. Diplomate Am. Bd. Orofacial Pain, Am. Acad. Pain Mgmt. Sr. assoc. dentist Dr. Deeds and Assocs., Inc., Columbus, Ohio, 1980-82, clinic dir., 1982-85; gen. practice dentistry Columbus, 1981-88; fellow TMJ/Orofacial Pain Ctr. Univ. Med. Dentistry N.J., 1988-90; clin. asst. prof. neurology Coll. Medicine Ohio State U., Columbus, 1992-98, asst. dir. dept. neurology headache clinic, 1994-98. Dental cons. Franklin County Dept. Human Svcs., Columbus, 1982-88; bd. dirs. Found. Pedodontique d'Haiti, Port-au-Prince; pres. Brineserve, Inc., Columbus, 1985-88; adj. assoc. prof. Coll. Dentistry Ohio State U., 1986-88; chmn. Coll. Dentistry Almni Assn. Class Reunion Ohio State U., 1997. Patents in apparatus/method for processing oil well brine, 1988; in apparatus and method for measuring human mandibular movement, 1990; in apparatus and method for craniovertebral imbalance and headache during sleep, 1992. Mem. pub. rels. com., chmn. cmty. ctr. project Upper Arlington Leadership Program, 1999; bd. dirs. Upper Arlington Friend of the Arts, 2002—; pres., founder Vol. Health Svcs. Found., Columbus, 1982—. Capt. U.S. Army, 1977-80. Mem.: ADA (Fgn. Vol. Svc. award 1988), U. Med. Dentistry N.J.-TMJ Alumni Soc., Columbus Dental Assn. (spkrs. bur. 1982—88, pub. rels. coun. 1984—88, vice chmn. radio com. 1985—88), Ohio Oil and Gas Assn., Ohio Dental Assn. (alt. del. 1994—96, 1998, 2002—, Humanitarian of Yr. 1986), Ohio Headache Assn., Am. Acad. Pain Mgmt., Am. Assn. for Study of Headache, Am. Acad. Orofacial Pain (bd. dirs. 2000—, splty. status com., chmn. external rels. com., chmn. found. com.), Am. Pain Soc., Ohio Xi Psi Phi Alumni Assn. (pres. 2001—), Sigma Xi, Xi Psi Phi (pres. Kappa chpt. 1976—77). Home: 3600 Olentangy River Rd Ste C5 Columbus OH 43214-3437 Office: 3600 Olentangy River Rd Ste C5 Columbus OH 43214-3437

AUSTIN, DAVID MAYO, social work educator; b. New Haven, June 9, 1923; s. Ralph Vernon and Helen Howe (Mayo) A.; m. Zuria Farmer; Clayton Mayo, Judith Ann, Paul Farmer. BA, Lawrence Coll., 1943; MS Social Adminstrn., Western Res. U., 1948; PhD, Brandeis U., 1969. Cert. social worker, Tex. Group worker U. Settlement, Cleve., 1948-51; assoc. neighborhood svcs. United Community Svcs. Met. Boston, 1951-54; planner, exec. dir. Spl. Youth Program, Roxbury, Mass., 1953-56; exec. sec. group work coun. Welfare Fedn. Cleve., 1957-61; planning dir. Greater Cleve. Youth Svcs. Planning Commn., 1961-63; assoc. dir. planning and rsch. Community Action Youth Cleve., 1963-64; lectr. Sch. Applied Social Scis. Case Western Res. U., Cleve., 1964-65, Florence Heller Grad. Sch. for Advanced Studies in Social Welfare Brandeis U., Waltham, Mass., 1968-71, assoc. prof., 1971-73; prof. Sch. Social Work U. Tex., Austin, 1973-2001, Bert Kruger Smith Centennial prof., 1987-98, acting dean, 1991-92, emeritus, 2001. Vis. prof. Coll. Social Work U. Tenn., Knoxville, 1985-86, cons., 1979; vis. scholar Nelson Rockefeller Coll. Pub. Affairs and Policy, SUNY, Albany, 1986; chmn. state adv. bd. Mass. Dept. Pub. Welfare, Boston, 1970-73; chmn. task force on social work rsch. NIMH, 1988-91; cons. Hogg Found. for Mental Health, Austin, 1989; chmn. adv. coun. Hogg Found. for Mental Health, 1994-96; external reviewer Sch. Social Work Rutgers U., New Brunswick, N.J., 1985; vis. com. Mandel Sch. Applied Social Scis., Case Western Res. U., Cleve., 1993-96. Author: (with others) Organization and the Human Services: Cross-Disciplinary Reflections, 1981, (monograph) A History of Social Work Education, 1986, The Political Economy of Human Service Programs, 1988, A Report on Progress in the Development of Research Resources in Social Work, 1998, Human Services Management, 2002; mem. editl. bd. Social Work, 1983-89; interim co-editor Jour. Applied Behavioral Sci., 1988-89; contbr. articles to profl. jours., publs. including Ency. of Social Work. Bd. dirs. Unitarian Universalist Svc. Com., Boston, 1983-88. Sgt. U.S. Army, 1943-46. Named Alumnus of Yr. Sch. Applied Social Scis. Case Western U., 1980; fellow NIMH, 1965-68; named Outstanding Grad. Tchr. U. Tex. at Austin, 1989. Mem. Acad. Cert. Social Workers (cert.), NASW (bd. dirs.

1963-66, chmn. human rights commn. 1964-67, pres. award Excellence Social Work Rsch. 1992, Tex. chpt. lifetime achievement award 2000), Coun. on Social Work Edn. (ho. dels. 1975-78, 79-82, ednl. planning commn. 1979-82, significant lifetime achievement award 1997), Am. Pub. Welfare Assn. (bd. dirs. 1980-82), Am. Soc. Pub. Adminstrn., Nat. Conf. Social Welfare (bd. dirs. 1980-83), Phi Beta Kappa, Phi Kappa Phi. Office: U Texas Sch of Social Work Austin TX 78712

AUSTIN, ERIK, physician, osteopath; b. Gold Beach, Oreg., Nov. 22, 1975; s. Frank Austin and Margo (Blount) Johnson. AAS, Edmonds CC, Lynnwood, Wash., 1992; BS with distinction, U. Wash., 1993, postgrad., 1994; DO, Coll. Osteo. Medicine Pacific, Pomona, Calif., 2001; MPH, Harvard U., 2003. Mem. med. team Internat. Med. Svc. Commn., Tanzania, 1995; pres. Am. Bd. Nutritional Medicine, 1996—2001; clin. fellow in occupl. and environ. medicine Johns Hopkins U. Hosp., 2003—. Rsch. affiliate dept. otolaryngology Harvard Med. Sch., 1997—2000. Pres. med. ethics soc. Western U. Health Sci., 1996—98. Recipient Physicians Recognition award, AMA, 2001, Weyuker award, Osteo. Physicians and Surgeons Calif., 1998; Policy Promotions grantee, AMA, 1996, Geriat. scholar, Summer Geriat. Inst., Boston U. Med. Ctr., 1998. Mem.: Am. Osteo. Assn. (Burnett Rsch. award 1997), Sigma Sigma Phi, Phi Theta Kappa. Home: 517 N 137th St Seattle WA 98133-7412

AUSTIN, ERLE HARRIS, pediatric cardiac surgeon; b. Portsmouth, Va., July 29, 1948; s. Erle H. and Flora Waller (Dunham) A.; m. Scott Dabney Austin, July 24, 1976; children: Christopher, Hunter, Waller, Jonathan. MD, Harvard U., 1974. Diplomate Am. Bd. Surgery, Nat. Bd. Med. Examiners, Am. Bd. Thoracic Surgery. Intern Duke U., Durham, N.C., 1974-75, resident, 1975-76, 78-85; assoc. prof. East Carolina U., Greenville, N.C., 1985-89, dir. pediatric cardiac surgery, 1985-89, chief cardiac surgery, vice chmn., 1988-89, prof. surgery, 1989, U. Louisville, 1989—; chief cardiovascular surgery Kosair Children's Hosp., Louisville, 1989—; pvt. practice Louisville, 1989—. Contbr. chpts. to textbook: Surgery of the Chest, 1995. Grantee Kosair Children's Hosp., 1995, WHAS Crusade of Children, 1996. Mem. ACS, Am. Heart Assn., Internat. Soc. Heart Transplantation, So. Surg. Assn., Loiusville Pediatric Soc., Louisville Surgery Soc., David C. Sabiston MD Surg. Soc. Avocation: snow skiing. Home: 3000 Woodside Rd Louisville KY 40222-5963 Office: UCSA 201 Abraham Flexner Way Louisville KY 40202-3841

AUSTIN, GLENN, retired pediatrician, medical researcher; b. Richmond, Calif., July 5, 1921; s. Albert Buckley Austin and Laura Roxanne Lakamp; m. Olive Edna Thomas; children: Carla, Linda, Glenn L., Starr. AB, U.C. Berkeley, 1943; MD, Stanford, 1952. Instr. parisitology U.S. Army, San Antonio, 1945; Pub. Health bacteriologist State of Calif., Berkeley, Calif., 1946; gen. practice Mine Worker's Union, Harlan County, Ky., 1952—54; chief resident O.P. Clin. Cin. Children's Med. Ctr., Cin., 1954—56; pvt. practice Los Altos, Calif., 1956—2000. Exec. dir. Nat. Fedn. Pediat. Soc., 1955—60; pres. Family Med. Clinical El Camino, Mt. View, Calif., 1993—2000, Calif. Primary Care Network, Los Altos, Calif., 1995—99. Author: The Parents guide to Child Raising, 1978, The Parents Medical Manual, 1978, Love and Power- Parent and Child, 1988, 2nd, edit., 1993, Grandparenting for the 90's, 1990, An Innovative Proposal for the Health Care Financing System of the United States, 2003; contbr. articles to profl. jour. Alt. del. centra Com. Rep., Santa Clara, Calif., 1998—2000; del. Calif. Med, Assoc., 1995, AMA, 1960—62. Recipient Santa Clara County Med. Soc. award for Outstanding Contbn. in Cmty. Svc., Cert. of Honor, Am. Acad. of Pediat. Republican. Presbyn. Home: 10506 8W Forest Ridge Pl Beaverton OR 97007

AUSTIN, GRANT WILLIAM, real estate appraiser; b. Toronto, July 15, 1954; m. Joanne; 1 child, Kelly Rae. BA summa cum laude, York U., 1983; MS, U. St. Thomas, 2003. Cert. gen. appraiser, Fla. Pres. Am. Valuation, Inc., Ft. Lauderdale, Fla., 1998—. Expert witness. Author: Calculator Skills for the HP 19B, 1995, The Property Owner's Guide to Condemnation, 1998. Mem.: Assn. Eminent Domain Profls. (v.p., dir. 1994—95), Market Rsch. Soc., Appraisal Inst. (chair pub. rels. com. 1995—97), Lambda Alpha Internat. (pres. 1997—99). Avocations: golf, tennis. E-mail: amervalu@bellsouth.net.

AUSTIN, H(ARRY) GREGORY, lawyer; b. N.Y.C., Mar. 18, 1936; s. Harry Gregory and Pauline (Moore) A.; m. Deanna Ruth Anderson, Nov. 28, 1970; children: Sabrina Elizabeth, Harry Gregory III, Anne Catherine. BE, Yale U., 1957, postgrad., 1958; JD, U. Mich., 1961; LLD (hon.), Lincoln U., 1976. Bar: Colo. 1961, U.S. Supreme Ct. 1974. Assoc. Holland & Hart, Denver, 1962—73, ptnr., 1977—2001, of counsel, 2002—; gen. counsel SBA, Washington, 1973—75; solicitor, gen. counsel U.S. Dept. Interior, Washington, 1975—77. Trustee Colo. Legal Aid Found., Denver, 1984-91, chmn., 1988-91; bd. dirs. Children's Hosp., Denver, 1985-97; mem. adv. com. Colo. Sec. State, 1996—. 1st lt. USAR, 1957-64. Fellow Am. Bar Found.; mem. Am. Law Inst., Colo. Bar Assn. (chmn. bus. entities subsect. bus. law sect. 1987-89, vice chmn. bus. law sect. 1989-91, chmn. 1991-93, chmn. partnership laws com. 1993—), Denver Bar Assn., Metro Denver C. of C. (bd. dirs., sec. 1995-97). Republican. Office: Holland & Hart LLP 555 17th St Ste 2900 Denver CO 80202-3979 E-mail: gaustin@hollandhart.com.

AUSTIN, HARRY GUIDEN, engineering and construction company executive; b. Belton, Tex., Dec. 10, 1917; s. Harry Guiden and Emma Lena (Brown) A.; m. Elizabeth Ann Heard, Aug. 31, 1940; children— Lucy Ann, Elizabeth Austin Page, Catherine Austin Wyatt. BS in Elec. Engring, Tex. A&M Coll., 1938; MBA, Harvard U., 1940; H.H.D., Wiley Coll. Registered profl. engr., Tex. With Pan Am. Airways, Miami, Fla., 1940-41; elec. engr. Brown Shipbldg. Co., Houston, 1941-45; with Brown & Root, Inc., Houston, 1945—, v.p., 1960-65, sr. v.p., 1965-68, sr. group v.p., 1968-70, exec. v.p. engring. and constrn., 1970-78; also dir.; pres. Hael, Inc., Houston, 1978—. Mem. Tex. A&M Geosci. Coun. Bd. dirs. Retina Rsch. Found. Mem. NSPE, IEEE, Mus. Fine Arts, Petroleum Club, Houston Country Club, Rive rhill Country Club (Kerrville, Tex.). Methodist. Home: 267 Pine Hollow Ln Houston TX 77056-1501 Office: Hael Inc 267 Pine Hollow Houston TX 77056-1501

AUSTIN, JACOB (JACK AUSTIN), Canadian government official; b. Calgary, Alta., Can., Mar. 2, 1932; s. Morris and Clara Edith (Chetner) A.; m. Natalie Veiner Freeman, Apr. 2, 1978; children: Edith Clare, Sharon Jill, Barbara Joan. BA, LLB, U. B.C.; LLM, Harvard U.; postgrad., U. Calif., Berkeley; ScD in Social Sci., U. East Asia. Bar: B.C. 1958, Yukon 1966. Chief of staff to prime minister, 1974-75; dep. minister energy, mines and resources, 1970-74; mem. Senate, 1975—; minister of state, 1981-82; minister of state for social devel., 1982-84. Mem. Vancouver Club, Rideau Club. Liberal. Jewish. Home: 3439 Point Grey Rd Vancouver BC Canada V6R 1A6 Office: The Senate Victoria Bldg Rm 304 Ottawa ON Canada K1A 0A4

AUSTIN, JOAN KESSNER, mental health nurse; b. Tell City, Ind., Sept. 24, 1944; d. Edward E. and Dorothy A. (Ziegelgraber) Kessner; m. David Ross Austin, Dec. 18, 1965; 1 child, Janet Lynn. Diploma, Deaconess Hosp., Evansville, Ind., 1965; BS in Nursing, Tex. Woman's U., 1975; MS in Nursing, Ind. U., 1978, DNS, 1981. Clin. instr. Tex. Woman's U., Denton, Tex.; prof. Ind U., Indpls. Contbr. articles for profl. jours. Grantee Nat. Inst. Neurol. Disorders and Stroke. Fellow Am. Acad. Nursing; mem. Epilepsy Found. Am. (profl. adv. bd. 1987-95), Inst. Medicine. Home: 3040 N Ramble Rd W Bloomington IN 47408-1052

AUSTIN, JOHN DAVID, retired financial executive; b. Memphis, Jan. 16, 1936; s. Thomas L. and Vela M. (Davis) Austin; m. Dorothy Clemans, Dec. 31, 1959 (div.); children: Laura Jan, David John; m. Marilyn C. Brewster, Nov. 2, 1985; 1 child, Christopher Brewster. BBA, Ga. State U., 1961. Acct. Price Waterhouse & Co., Atlanta, 1961—64, sr. tax acct. Miami, 1964—67; audit mgr. N.C. Nat. Bank Corp., Greensboro, 1968, v.p., gen. auditor Charlotte, 1969—73; sr. v.p., dir. corp. planning 1st Nat. Bank Mobile, Ala., 1973—74; sr. v.p. Southeast Nat. Bank. Pa., Malvern, 1974—75, exec. v.p., 1975—83, acting pres., CEO, 1978—80; sr. v.p. Va. Fed. Savs. and Loan, Richmond, 1984, exec. v.p., 1985, pres., also bd. dirs., 1986—88; exec. v.p. and CEO, also bd. dirs. Citizens Fed. Savs. & Loan, Salisbury, NC, 1988—90; self employed Marietta, Ga., 1990—91; v.p., CFO Atlanta Cutlery Corp, Conyers, Ga., 1991—96, COO, 1993—96, ret. Former pres. United Arts Coun. of Rowan; former bd. dirs. Chester County Mental Health/Mental Retardation Bd., The Chester Group, Del. County Econ. Devel. Com., Del. County Cmty. Coll. Found., St. John's Hosp. With U.S. Army, 1957—59. Home: 1303 Spring Gate Cir Woodstock GA 30189-5489

AUSTIN, JOHN DELONG, judge; b. Cambridge, N.Y., May 31, 1935; s. John DeLong and Mabel Cowles (Bascom) A.; m. Marcia Kay Behan, Aug. 15, 1969 (dec.); children: John DeLong, Susan Behan. AB, Dartmouth Coll., 1957; postgrad., u. Minn., 1959; JD, Albany Law Sch., 1969. Bar: N.Y. 1970. Editl. dir. Glens Falls (N.Y.) Times, 1960-66; sole practice Glens Falls, 1970-79; law asst. Warren County Judge and Surrogate, 1975-79, N.Y. State Supreme Ct., 1980-84; judge Warren County Family Ct., NY, 1984-99, Warren County Ct. and Surrogate's Ct., 1999—2003. Instr. Adirondack Comm. Coll., Glens Falls. Editor New Eng. Hist. and Geneal. Register, 1970-73; contbr. hist. and geneal. articles to various periodicals. Councilman Town of Queensbury, N.Y., 1969-71, supr., 1972-74; budget officer Warren County, N.Y., 1974; mem. N.Y. State Local Govt. Records Adv. Coun. With U.S. Army, 1958-60. Recipient Adminstrv. Law prize Albany Law Sch., 1969. Fellow Am. Soc. Genealogists; mem. N.Y. State Bar Assn., Warren County Bar Assn., Mohican Grange, Elks. Republican.

AUSTIN, JOHN NORMAN, classics educator; b. Anshun, Kweichow, China, May 20, 1937; s. John Alfred and Lillian Maud (Reeks) A. BA, U. Toronto, 1958; MA, U. Calif.-Berkeley, 1959, PhD, 1965. Vis. lectr. Yale U., New Haven, 1971; asst. prof., then assoc. prof. UCLA, 1966-76; Aurelio prof. Greek Boston U., 1976-78; prof., chmn. dept. classics U. Mass., Amherst, 1978-80; prof. classics U. Ariz., Tucson, 1980—, acting dean humanities, 1987-88, head dept. classics, 1995—2000, prof. emeritus, 2000—. Vis. prof. Leeds U., 1999. Author: Archery at the Dark of the Moon, 1975, Meaning and Being in Myth, 1990, Helen of Troy and Her Shameless Phantom, 1994; editor: (with others) The Works of John Dryden, vol. III; sr. editor Calif. Studies Classical Antiquity, vols. VI and VII. Jr. fellow Ctr. for Hellenic Studies, 1968-69, J.S. Guggenheim Found. fellow, 1974-75 Episcopalian. Home: 3200 NE 36th St #1216 Fort Lauderdale FL 33308 E-mail: normana764@aol.com.

AUSTIN, JOHN RILEY, surgeon, educator; b. St. Louis, Feb. 19, 1960; s. Thomas L. and Barbara (Riley) A.; m. Sara Beth Goehringer, May 16, 1987; children: Claire Frances, Emily Grace, John Michael. BS with highest honors, U. Wyo., 1982; MD, U. Utah, 1986. Diplomate Am. Bd. Facial Plastic and Reconstructive Surgery, Am. Bd. Otolaryngoly, Nat. Bd. Med. Examiners. Surg. intern U. So. Calif., L.A. County Med. Ctr., L.A., 1986-87, resident otolaryngology, head and neck surgery dept., 1987-91; fellow in head and neck surg. oncology M.D. Anderson Cancer Ctr. M.D. Anderson Cancer Ctr. U. Tex., Houston, 1991-92; asst. surgeon, clin. instr. U. Tex., Houston, 1992-93; asst. prof., asst. surgeon M.D. Anderson Cancer Ctr. U. Tex., Houston, 1993-95, clin. asst. prof., 1995—; adj. asst. prof. dept. otorhinolaryngology/comm. disorders Baylor Coll. Medicine, 1993-95. Otolaryngologic cons. dept. infectious diseases U. So. Calif., 1988-91; mem. utilization com. M.D. Anderson Cancer Ctr., U.Tex., 1993-95, mem. laser com., 1993-95; presenter in field. Cons. editor Head and Neck, Laryngoscope, Otolaryngology-Head and Neck Surgery, Cancer, 1993—, Archives of Otolaryngology; contbr. articles to profl. jours. Mem. Graduate Edn. com. U. Tex., 1994. Fellow ACS, Am. Acad. Otolaryngology (human resource com.), AMA, Am. Acad. Facial Plastic and Reconstructive Surgery (mem. publs. com.), Tex. Med. Assn. (mem. physician oncology edn. program 1993—, mem. com. cancer 1993—), M.D. Anderson Assocs., Soc. Univ. Otolaryngologists, N.Am. Skull Base Soc., Tex. Assn. Otolaryngology, Sir Charles Bell Soc. (founding), Travis County Med. Soc. (jour. com.), Salerni Collegium, Phi Kappa Phi, Phi Beta Kappa, Sigma Nu. Methodist. Avocations: photography, fishing, golfing, skiing, reading. Office: 3705 Medical Pkwy Ste 310 Austin TX 78705-1028

AUSTIN, JOYCE CAROLINE, cake decorator, artist; b. Bussum, Netherlands, Nov. 3, 1943; came to U.S., 1956; d. Antonie C. and Lida J. Schatborn; divorced; children: Cynthia, Cameron. AA, Fresno City Coll., 1964; BA, Fresno State U., 1967. Artist freelance, Merced, Calif., 1987-94; cake decorator Anna's Fairview Bakery, Santa Barbara, Calif., 1994-95, Vons Co., Santa Barbara, 1995—; painter pet portraits, 2002—. Recipient Discovery award Art of Calif. mag., 1993. Mem. Pastel Soc. Am. (award 1991), Soc. Western Artists (signature mem.), Pastel soc. West Coast (signature mem.). Avocations: showing cats in cat shows, painting, reading. Home: 333 Old Mill Rd Spc 147 Santa Barbara CA 93110-4486 E-mail: Joyceaustin@aol.com.

AUSTIN, JUDY ESSARY, scriptwriter; b. Jackson, Tenn., Apr. 7, 1948; d. Hershel Dee and Elizabeth Sue (Rhodes) Essary; m. James Michael Austin, July 4, 1965; children: James Allan Austin, Julia Ann Austin Barr. AS, DeKalb Coll., 1988; BA in Communications and Journalism, Mercer U., 1989. Retail mgr. Bankers Note, Atlanta, 1980-84, Le Chocolat Elegant, Atlanta, 1984-85; student asst. student affairs DeKalb Coll., Dunwoody, Ga., 1987-88; asst. art dir. Sportime, Atlanta, 1990-92; writer, prodr. CAMA, Atlanta, 1993-94; freelance scriptwriter Atlanta, 1994—. Bd. dirs. Second Wind Orgn., Dekalb Coll., Dunwoody, 1987-88. Scholar Am. Bus. Womens Assn., 1987. Mem. Women in Communications, NAFE, Phi Kappa Phi. Avocations: photography, reading, flying, fishing, writing. Home: 3133 Raymond Dr Atlanta GA 30340-1826 E-mail: jaustin@bigzoo.com.

AUSTIN, LEONARD GEORGE, mineral engineer; b. London, Oct. 5, 1929; arrived in U.S., 1957; s. Albert William and Charlotte Ada (Freeth) A.; m. Penelope Ann Dahl, Dec. 10, 1951 (div. 1980); children: Mark R., Timothy L., Stuart R.; m. Sofia Francisca Barraneche, Apr. 15, 1983. BSc, London U., 1951; PhD, Pa. State U., 1961. Chemist South Eastern Gas Bd., London, 1952-54; fuel engr. Cen. Elect. Generating Bd., London, 1954-57; asst. prof. fuel tech. Pa. State U., University Park, 1961, assoc. prof., 1961-66, prof. fuels sci., 1966-67; prof. chemical engr. N.C. State U., 1967-68; prof. materials sci. Pa. State U., 1968-77, prof. fuels & mineral engr., 1977-89, prof. emeritus, 1989—. Editorial bd. jour., Powder Tech., Netherlands, 1980-88, Particle Characterization, Germany, 1984-92; numerous cons. activities, 1958—. Co-author: Process Engineering of Size Red, 1984, Diseno y Simulacion de Circuitos de Molienda, 1994; contbr. articles to profl. jours. Recipient Gaudin award Soc. Mining Engrs., 1983, Nicholls award Joint Engring. Soc., 1987. Achievements include international reputation in the field of crushing and grinding for the power, mining and chemical industries. Office: Pa State U 115 Hosler Bldg University Park PA 16802-5000

AUSTIN, MARIE A. academic administrator; d. Raymond F. and Etta Lucy Keck; m. Robert C. Keck, Aug. 1, 1970; children: Jessica Megal Austin-Kassabian, Jennifer Robin. MS, Syracuse U., 1997. Faculty, adminstr. U. South Fla., Tampa, Fla., 1997—2001; exec. dir. first yr. experience programs U. Ark., Fayetteville, 2001—. Author: The Successful University Experience (Award of Appreciation, 2001). Councilperson Town Bd., Volney, NY, 1982—92. Scholar Comm. scholar, Syracuse Advt. Club, 1989. Mem.: NASPA (assoc.). Office: University of Arkansas Maple Street Santa Ana CA 92701 E-mail: maustin@uark.edu.

AUSTIN, MICHAEL CHARLES, insurance company executive; b. Syracuse, N.Y., Dec. 7, 1955; s. Harold Ernest and Helen (Sanderson) A.; m. Patricia Farrell, Aug. 12, 1978; 1 child, Bryan Michael. AA in Liberal Arts, Mohawk Valley Community Coll., 1974; BA in English, SUNY, Oswego, 1976. Dir. pub. rels. United Way of Greater Utica, N.Y., 1976-79; asst. mgr. advt. and pub. relations Utica Nat. Ins. Group, 1979-81, asst. dir. corp. communications, 1981-89, dir. corp. communications, 1989—; v.p. Utica (N.Y.) Mut. Ins. Co., 1997. Adj. faculty Mohawk Valley Community Coll., Utica, 1982. Contbr. articles to profl. jours. Bd. dirs. United Cerebral Palsy Found., Utica, 1987—, pres., 1992-95, 98-99, Mohawk Valley Chamber, 1998-2002, Utica Safe Schs., 2003—; pres. bd. trustees Mohawk Valley C.C. Found., 1990-95; chmn. Mohawk Valley Stop-DWI, Utica, 1994-99; Mohawk Valley Coun. on Alcoholism, Utica, 1987-93, United Way, Utica, 1982. Recipient Alumni Merit award Mohawk Valley C.C., 1989, Honor Roll award SUNY Alumni, 1996, STOP-DWI Cmty. Svc. award 1997; named Caring Person of Yr., United Cerebral Palsy, 2001; named Outstanding New Yorker Jaycees, 1994. Mem. Ins. Consumer Affairs Exch., Ins. Mktg. Comm. Assn., Utica C. of C. (bd. dirs. 1998—), Mohawk Valley Advt. Club (pres. 1989-90, dir. 1982-93, awards excellence, Ad Person of Yr. 1992, 95), Syracuse Ad Club, Mohawk Valley Ad Club, Profl. Ins. Comm. Am., Mohawk Valley C. of C. (named to Hall of Fame, 2003). Roman Catholic. Avocations: photography, comic book collecting, autograph collecting. Office: Utica Nat Ins Group 180 Genesee St Utica NY 13502-4324

AUSTIN, PHILIP EDWARD, university president; b. Fargo, N.D., 1942; s. William and Angelyn A.; children: Patrick William, Philip James. BS, N.D. State U., 1964, MS, 1966; MA, Mich. State U., 1968, PhD, 1969; hon. doctorate, Autonomous U. Guadalajara, Mexico, N.D. State U., U. Ala. Economist U.S. Office of Mgmt. and Budget, Washington, 1971-74; dep. asst. sec. HEW, Washington, 1974-77, acting asst. sec., 1977; dir. doctoral program in edn. policy George Washington U., Washington, 1977-78; v.p. for acad. affairs, prof. econs. and fin. Bernard Baruch Coll., N.Y.C., 1978-84; pres., prof. econs. Colo. State U., Fort Collins, 1984-89; chancellor U. Ala. System, Tuscaloosa, 1989-96; pres. U. Conn., Storrs, 1996—. Served with U.S. Army, 1969-71. Decorated Bronze Star. Office: U Conn Office of the Pres 352 Mansfield Rd Storrs Mansfield CT 06269-2048

AUSTIN, ROBERT BRENDON, civil engineer; b. West Point, N.Y., Aug. 10, 1956; s. Thomas and Margaret Ann (Hart) A. BS, U. Conn., 1979; M Civil Engring., U. Tex., Arlington, 1992. Registered profl. engr., Tex., La., Colo., Ga., Fla., S.C., Conn. Resident engr. Stone & Webster Engring. Corp., Dallas, 1979-94; rsch. assoc., instr. U. Tex., Arlington, 1990-95; city engr. City of Arlington, 1994-95; tech. dir. Nat. Precast Concrete Assn., Indpls., 1995—2000; mgr. engring. New Basis, 1998—2001; constrn. mgr. DMJM & Harris, 2001—. Contbr. articles to profl. jours. Recipient Constrn. Innovation award Stone & Webster Engring., Boston, 1987. Mem. ASCE, NSPE, ASTM, Am. Concrete Inst., Constrn. Specifications Inst. Address: 1154 Woodtick Rd Wolcott CT 06716-2125 also: 1154 Woodtick Rd Wolcott CT 06716-2125

AUSTIN, ROBERT CLARKE, naval officer; b. Cleve., Sept. 5, 1931; s. Clarke Albert and Margaret Jane (Richardson) A.; m. Joyce Ann Bisese, Apr. 22, 1957; children— Susan Lynn, James Holden, Robert Clarke, Cecelia Ann. BS, U.S. Naval Acad., 1954; MS in Physics, Naval Postgrad. Sch., 1963. Enlisted U.S. Navy, 1948, commd. ensign, 1954, advanced through grades to rear adm., 1980; commdg. officer USS Finback, 1968-72; comdr. Submarine Devel. Group Two, 1974-76; commdg. officer Naval Submarine Sch., 1976-78; chief of staff submarine force U.S. Atlantic Fleet, 1979-80; dep. dir. for internat. negotiations for Plans and Policy Directorate, Joint Chiefs of Staff, Pentagon, Washington, 1981-82; chief naval tech. tng., 1982-86; supt. Naval Postgrad. Sch., 1986-89; ret. USN, 1989; pres. Austin Assocs., Inc., Alexandria, Va., 1989-97. Decorated Def. Superior Service Medal, Legion of Merit with 4 gold stars, Meritorious Service medal, others. Mem. Sigma Xi. Episcopalian.

AUSTIN, ROBERT DANIEL, b. Fort Polk, La., Feb. 6, 1962; s. Robert Dekalb and Sylvia Caylor Austin; m. Laurel Cecelia Mohs; 3 children. PhD, Carnegie Mellon U., 1994; MS, Northwestern U., 1986; BA, BS, Swarthmore Coll., 1984. Mgr. Ford Motor Co., Dearborn, Mich., 1986—96; prof. Harvard Bus. Sch., Boston, 1997—. Fellow tech. coun. Cutter Consortium, Arlington, Mass., 2000—. Author: Measuring and Managing Performance in Organizations, 1996, Creating Business Advantage in the Information Age, 2002, Corporate Information Strategy and Management, 2003, Artful Making: What Managers Need to Know About How Artists Work, 2003. Recipient Phi Beta Kappa award, 1984, Tau Beta Pi award, 1984. Mem.: INFORMS, IEEE, Performance Mgmt. Assn. Methodist. Avocations: reading, baseball.

AUSTIN, ROBERT EUGENE, JR., lawyer; b. Jacksonville, Fla., Oct. 10, 1937; s. Robert Eugene and Leta Fitch A.; children: Robert Eugene, George Harry Talley; m. Carolyn Rhea Songer. BA, Davidson Coll., 1959; JD, U. Fla., 1964. Bar: Fla. 1965, D.C. 1983, U.S. Supreme Ct. 1970; cert. in civil trial law Nat. Bd. Trial Advocacy. Pvt. practice law, 1965—. Asst. state atty., 1972; mem. Jud. Nominating Commn. and Grievance Com. 5th Dist. Fla.; gov. Fla. Bar, 1983; trustee U. Fla. Law Ctr.; mem. com. on std. jury instns. Fla. Supreme Ct. Chmn. Lake Dist. Boy Scouts Am.; asst. dean Leesburg Deanery Diocese Cen. Fla.; trustee Fla. House, Washington, U. Fla. Law Ctr., 1983—, chmn., 1988-90. Mem. Acad. Fla. Trial Lawyers, Am. Arbitration Assn., Am. Law Inst., Nat. Inst. Trial Advocacy, Lake County Bar Assn., Roscoe Pound Am. Trial Found., Kappa Alpha, Phi Delta Phi. Democrat. Episcopalian. Home: PO Box 490200 Leesburg FL 34749-0200 Office: 1321 Citizens Blvd Ste C Leesburg FL 34748-3946 E-mail: reajr@aust-pep.com.

AUSTIN, ROBYN MICHELLE, development administrator, speech professional; b. Black Mountain, NC; d. Robert Austin and Iva Gragg; m. Anthony J. Panepinto. BA, U. Ariz., Tucson, 1983; MA, No. Ariz. U., Flagstaff, 2000. Cmty. rels. specialist CODAC, Tucson, 1994—97; devel. officer U. Ariz., 2003—. Cert. trainer True Colors, 2000—. Author: (book) Life Chimes: A Collection of Simple TRuths, 2002. Pres. bd. dir. YWCA of Tucson, 2001—03; vol. SAMLTE, Tucson, 2002—. Recipient Copper Letter award, Mayor of Tucson, 1994, YWCA Woman on Move award, YWCA of Tucson, 1996.

AUSTIN, ROY L. ambassador; b. Kingstown, St. Vincent & The Grenadines, Dec. 19, 1939; m. Glynis Josephine Sutherland; 3 children. BA in Sociology, Yale U., 1968; MA in Sociology, Univ. Wash., 1972; PhD in Sociology, U. Wash., 1973. Faculty mem. sociology dept. Pa. State U., 1972—2001; U.S. amb. to Trinidad and Tobago, 2001—. Mem.: Am. Soc. Criminology, Caribbean Studies Assn., Am. Sociol. Assn. Office: DOS Amb 3410 Port of Spain Pl Washington DC 20521*

AUSTIN, SAM M. physics educator; b. Columbus, Wis., June 6, 1933; s. A. Wright and Mildred G. (Reinhard) A.; m. Mary E. Herb, Aug. 15, 1959; children: Laura Gail, Sara Kay. BS in Physics, U. Wis., 1955, MS, 1957, PhD, 1960. Rsch. assoc. U. Wis., Madison, 1960; NSF postdoctoral fellow Oxford U., Eng., 1960-61; asst. prof. Stanford U., Calif., 1961-65; assoc. prof. physics Mich. State U., East Lansing, 1965-69, prof., 1969-90, univ. disting. prof., 1990-2000, univ. disting. prof. emeritus, 2000—, chmn. dept., 1980-83, acting dean Coll. Natural Sci., 1994, assoc. dir. Cyclotron Lab., 1976-79, rsch. dir., 1983-85, co-dir., 1985-89, dir., 1989-92. Guest Niels Bohr Inst., 1970; guest prof. U. Munich, 1972-73; sci. collaborator Saclay and Lab. Rene Bernas, 1979-80; vis. scientist Triumf-U. B.C., 1993-94; invited prof. U. Paris, Orsay, 1996; mem. grant selection com. for sub-atomic physics, NSERC (Can.), 1996-99; mem. com. on nuc. physics NRC, 1996-99; mem. steering com. Nuc. Physics Summer Sch.; mem. internat. adv. com. and exec. com. NSF Joint Inst. for Nuc. Astrophysics, 2003—. Author, editor: The Two Body Force in Nuclei, 1972, The (p,n) Reaction and Nucleon-Nucleon Force, 1980; editor Phys. Rev. C, 1988-2002, Virtual Jour. Nuclear Astrophysics; assoc. editor Atomic Data and Nuc. Data Tables, 1990—. Fellow NSF, 1960-61, Alfred P. Sloan Found., 1963-66; recipient Mich. Assn. of Governing Bds. Disting. Prof., 1992. Fellow AAAS (chair nominating com.), Am. Phys. Soc. (vice chmn. nuc. physics divsn. 1981-82, chmn. 1982-83, exec. com. 1983-84, 86-89, coun. 1986-89, coun. exec. com. 1987-88, panel on pub. affairs 1996-98); mem. APS, Sigma Xi (Sr. rsch. award 1977). Achievements include research in nuclear physics, nuclear astrophysics and nitrogen fixation. Home: 1201 Woodwind Trl Haslett MI 48840-8994 Office: Mich State U Nat Supercondr Cyclotron Lab East Lansing MI 48824 E-mail: austin@nscl.msu.edu.

AUSTIN, SANDRA IKENBERRY, nurse educator, consultant; b. Lexington, Va., Dec. 22, 1941; d. William Peters and June Virginia (Blackwell) Ikenberry; m. Joseph M. Austin, Apr. 10, 1965; children: Joseph M. Jr., Susan C., Christopher M. BSN, U. Va., 1963; MSN, U. Calif., L.A., 1967; EdD, U. Mass., 1997. RN, Mass. Pub. health nurse Dept. Health, Waynesboro, Va., 1963-64; instr. U. Va., Charlottesville, 1964-65; staff nurse Santa Monica (Calif.) Hosp., 1965-66; faculty nursing Boston U., 1968-69, Quinsigamond C.C., Worcester, Mass., 1969-70, Fitchburg (Mass.) State Coll., 1973-96; assoc. prof. nursing Framingham (Mass.) State Coll., 1997—; project dir., sr. health edn. cons. HealthCo Consulting Inc., Shrewsbury, Mass., 1996—. Mem. Shrewsbury Town Meeting, 1992—95; chair steering com. Framingham State Coll. Nursing Honor Soc., 1998, faculty counselor/advisor, 1999, pres., 1999—2002. HBO and Co. Nurse scholar, 1995. Mem.: Assn. Critical Care Nurses, Nat. League Nursing (awards com. 1999—2001), Assn. Women's Health, Obstet. and Neonatal Nurses, Am. Ednl. Rsch. ASsn., Sigma Theta Tau (Epsilon Beta edn. chair 1993—95, Rho Phi chpt. pres. 2002—, rsch. grant 1996), Pi Lambda

Theta. Republican. Congregationalist. Avocations: computer multimedia production, reading, walking. Home: 100 Harrington Farms Way Shrewsbury MA 01545-4081 Office: Framingham State Coll Nursing Dept Framingham MA 01701

AUSTIN, SANDRA J. small business owner; b. Clarkburg, W.Va., May 1, 1956; d. Mary Paden Austin Ford; adopted children: Michael Renwick, Reginald Renwick. Grad., Va. Learning Inst. Sch. of Massage, Falls Church, Va., 2000. Police cadet Met. Police D.C., Washington, 1974—77, police officer, 1977—91, drivers tng. instr., 1990—91, police detective, 1991—2000; ret.; massage therapist, owner Sanctus, Burke and Dumfries, Va., 2001—. Instr. percussion Boys and Girls Club, Washington, 1980—82; percussionist Met. Police D.C. Choir, 1980—82; founder Blue Angels Female Flag Football Team, 1996; percussionist gospel choir Howard U., 1974—77. Named Police Officer of the Yr., Kiwanis, 1989, Policewoman of the Yr., Women's Aux. Club, 1989, Uniformed Narcotic Officer of the Yr., Coun. of God, 1989. Mem.: FOP (union rep. 1987—93). Avocations: softball, basketball, football, writing, crafts. Office: Sanctus Day Spa/Massage 9554 Old Keene Mill Rd #F Burke VA 22015

AUSTIN, SANDRA JENELLE, school librarian, language educator; b. Ashdown, Ark., Mar. 31, 1958; d. Farce Desoto and Vester Alice Christopher; m. Glen Thomas Austin, July 26, 1986; children: Alicia Laverne, Glen Thomas Jr. EdB summa cum laude, U. Ark., 1980, MA, 1982; MLS, Tex. Women's U., 2000. Cert. tchr. Tex. Tchr. French, libr. Ark. HS, Texarkana, 1982—92; libr. Tex. HS, Texarkana, 1992—2002, tchr. French, libr., 2002—. Mem. tech. task force Texarkana Ind. Sch., Tex., 2000—. Mem. literacy coun. Miller County, Ark., 2001, Bowie County, Tex., 2001; sec. bd. dirs. Texarkana Mus. Sys., Tex., 2003—. Mem.: ALA (staff reporter Chgo. 2001—, sec. distance learning interest group Chgo. 2002—), Tex. Libr. Assn., Libr. and Info. Tech. Assn., Kappa Delta Pi, Beta Phi Mu. Avocation: gardening. Office: Texarkana Ind Sch Dist 4241 Summerhill Rd Texarkana TX 75503

AUSTIN, SCOTT RAYMOND, lawyer; b. Newark, Ohio, Jan. 14, 1956; s. Frank W. and Donna J. (Essig) A.; m. Jilise B. Bushling, May 27, 1989; children: Alec Steven, Luke William. BS summa cum laude, Ohio U., 1979, MBA, 1981; JD, Georgetown U., Washington, 1984. Bar: Fla. 1984, U.S. Dist. Ct. (so. dist.) Fla. 1986, U.S. Dist. Ct. (mid. dist.) Fla. 1991, U.S. Ct. Appeals (11th cir.) 1995, U.S. Supreme Ct. 2001. Law clk. Nat. Assn. Broadcasters, Washington, 1982-83; assoc. atty. Ruden, Barnett et al., Ft. Lauderdale, Fla., 1984-92; ptnr. Houston & Shahady, P.A., Ft. Lauderdale, 1992-97, English, McCaughan & O'Bryan, P.A., Ft. Lauderdale, 1997—2000, Bilzin, Sumberg, Dunn et al, Miami, 2000—01, Adorno & Zeder P.A., Boca Raton, 2001—03, Arnstein & Lehr, W. Palm Beach, Fla., 2003—. Sr. editor, mem. exec. editl. bd. Law and Policy in Internat. Bus., 1983-84; contbr. articles to profl. jours. Mem. ABA (mem. corp., banking and bus. law sect., chmn. revisions com.), Fed. Bar Assn., Fla. Bar Assn., Palm Beach County Bar Assn. (chair corps. and securities com.), Georgetown Club (pres. 1994—), Beta Gamma Sigma. Avocations: computer programming, music, hockey. Office: Arnstein & Lehr 515 N Flagler Dr Ste 600 West Palm Beach FL 33401

AUSTIN, SUSAN REBECCA, librarian, writer, storyteller; b. Harrisburg, Pa., Jan. 23, 1945; d. Paul Leighty and Margaret Erna (Keim) A. BS in Library Edn., Kutztown (Pa.) State U., 1966; MS in Library Sci., Villanova (Pa.) U., 1967; MEd, Temple U., 1971; PhD, U. Pa., 1989. Cataloger, instr. West Chester (Pa.) State U., 1967-69; libr., media coord. St. James/Msgr. Bonner High Sch., Chester and Drexel Hill, Pa., 1969-72, 73-76; librarian elem. div. Am. Sch. in London, 1972-73; asst. prof. Applachian State U., Boone, N.C., 1976-78; librarian Upper Darby (Pa.) High Sch., 1980-81; asst. prof. Kutztown State U., 1981-82; learning materials specialist Sabold Elem. Sch., Springfield, Pa., 1984—. Freelance storyteller, 1980—. Contbr. articles to profl. jours. Mem. NEA, Pa. State Edn. Assn., Nat. Assn. for the Preservation and Perpetuation of Storytelling. Republican. Methodist. Avocations: traveling, gardening, music, photography, sailing. Home: 3701 Columbia Court Way Newtown Square PA 19073-1064 Office: Sabold Elem Sch Thomson Ave & Baltimore Springfield PA 19064

AUSTIN-GARRISON, MARTHA A. education educator, researcher; d. Buck and Martha Smallcanyon Austin; m. Edward R Garrison, May 27, 1978; children: Nanibaa' A Garrison, Bijiibaa' K Garrison, Edward Austin Garrison II. MA in edn., Ariz. State U., 1999—2002. Faculty Dine Coll., Shiprock, N.Mex., 1990—. Rsch. project dir. Navajo Ethno-Medical Ency. Project, Kayenta, Ariz., 1975—80. Sec. Kayenta Cmty. Sch., Inc., Kayenta, Ariz., 1978—80; mem. Navajo Health Authority, Window Rock, Ariz., 1978—82; sec. Kayenta Rsch. Associates, Inc, Kayenta, Ariz., 1980—2003. Scholar Edward Sapir scholarship, 1995 Summer Linguistics Inst. at UNM, 1995. Mem.: Ariz. State Wide Health Coordinating Coun., State Health Planning Adv. of Ariz. Coun., Kayenta Rsch. Associates, Inc (assoc.). Home: P O Box 1950 Kayenta AZ 86033 Office: Dine College P O Box 580 Shiprock NM 87420 Personal E-mail: maustin@dinecollege.edu. E-mail: maustin@dinecollege.edu.

AUSTIN-SEYMOUR, MARY M. radiation oncologist; b. Indiantown Gap, Pa., Dec. 8, 1952; m. Ronald Seymour; children: Kristin, Mark. BA in Math., St. Olaf Coll., Northfield, Minn., 1974; MD, U. Chgo., 1978. Diplomate Nat. Bd. Med. Examiners, Am. Bd. Radiology with subspecialty in therapeutic radiology. Intern Northwestern U., Chgo., 1978-79, resident, 1979-81, Stanford (Calif.) U., 1981-83; instr. Harvard U., Boston, 1984-86, asst. prof., 1986-88, U. Wash. Med. Ctr., Seattle, 1988-91, assoc. prof., 1991—2002, vice chair radiation oncology, 1999—, Wootton prof. radiation oncology, 2002—. Office: Univ of Wash Med Ctr Dept Radiation Oncology Box 356043 Seattle WA 98195-6043

AUSTIN-THORN, CYNTHIA KAY, religious organization administrator, poet; b. Dallas, Feb. 24; d. Kenneth and Anita E. Fujii; m. George Austin, Dec. 20, 1978 (dec. July 1990); 1 child, Christopher; m. Kenneth Thorn, July 3, 1994 (dec. Aug. 1999). AAS, El Centro Coll., Dallas, 1987. Sr. accounts payable clk. Plymouth/Poco Shops, N.Y.C.; mgr. Funky Things, Huntington Beach, Calif.; with select inventory mgmt. office Joske's Dept. Store, Dallas; sec., receptionist George E. Austin Piano Tech., Dallas; owner, writer, design creator Son of Dust Creations, Dallas; active The Road to Damascus Ministries, Dallas. Contbg. poet: (anthologies) A Muse to Follow, 1996 (Editor's Choice award 1996), A Tapestry of Thoughts, 1996 (Editor's Choice award 1996), (cassettes) The Sound of Poetry, 1996, 97 (named 1 of 10 best poets 1996, 97), Searching for Soft Voices, 1997. Mem. choir 1st Family Ch., Dallas, 1996-97, 99, 2000, 2002. Recipient cert. of achievement 1st Family Ch., 1996. Republican. Avocations: creative writing, song writing, singing in church plays, intercessory prayer, ministering to others. Home and Office: Apt B 10410 Lone Tree Ln Dallas TX 75218-3008

AUSTON, DAVID HENRY, former academic administrator, electrical engineer, educator; b. Toronto, Ont., Can., Nov. 14, 1940; arrived in U.S., 1963; BS, U. Toronto, 1962, MS, 1963; PhD, U. Calif., Berkeley, 1969. Rsch. physicist GM, Santa Barbara, Calif., 1963—66; tech. staff AT&T Bell Labs., Murray Hill, NJ, 1969—82, head dept., 1982—87; former prof. Columbia U., N.Y.C., chmn. elec. engring. dept., 1990, dean sch. engring. and applied sci., 1991—94; provost Rice U., Houston, 1994—99; pres. Case Western Res. U., Cleve., 1999—2002, Kavli Found. and The Kavli Inst., Oxnard, Calif. Author 1 book; contbr. scientific papers. Fellow: IEEE (Quantum Elecs. award 1990, Morris E. Leeds award 1991), Am. Phys. Soc., Am. Acad. Arts and Scis., Optical Soc. Am. (R.W. Wood prize 1985); mem.: NAE, Nat. Acad. Scis. Achievements include patents in field of 7. Office: The Kavli Inst 1801 Solar Dr Ste 250 Oxnard CA 93030

AUSTRIA, STEVE, state legislator; BA in Polit. Sci., Marquette U. Mem. Ohio Ho. Reps. from 76th dist., Columbus, 1998-2000, Ohio Senate from 10th dist., Columbus, 2001—. Recipient Great Am. Family of the Yr. award Reagan Adminstrn. Mem. KC (Family of the Yr. award), Miami Valley Mil. Affairs Assn., Ohio Twp. Assn., Beavercreek C. of C., Fairborn C. of C., Xenia C. of C., Rotary. Office: Rm # 034 Senate Bldg Columbus OH 43215

AUSTRIAN, ROBERT, physician, educator, department chairman; b. Balt., Apr. 12, 1916; s. Charles Robert and Florence (Hochschild) Austrian; m. Babette Friedmann Bernstein, Dec. 29, 1963; stepchildren: Jill Bernstein, Toni Bernstein. AB, Johns Hopkins U., 1937, MD, 1941; DSc (hon.), Hahnemann Med. Coll., 1980, Phila. Coll. Pharmacy and Sci., 1981, U. Pa., 1987; DSc (hon.), SUNY, 1996. Diplomate Am. Bd. Internal Medicine. House officer Johns Hopkins Hosp., 1941—50, asst. dir. med. out-patient dept., 1951—52; assoc. prof. medicine, then prof. medicine SUNY Coll. Medicine, 1952—62; John Herr Musser prof., chmn. rsch. medicine U. Pa. Sch. Medicine, 1962—86, prof. emeritus, chmn. emeritus, 1986—. Attending physician Hosp. U. Pa.; Tyndale vis. lectr. and prof. Coll. Medicine U. Utah, 1964; spl. rsch. on infectious diseases, bacterial genetics; mem. Meningococcal Infections Commn., 1964—72, Commn. on Acute Respiratory Disease, 1965—72, Commn. Streptococcal and Staphylococcal Diseases, 1970—72, Armed Forces Epidemiol. Bd.; cons. surg. gen. U.S. Army R&D Command, 1966—69; mem. subcom. streptococcus and pneumococcus Internat. Com. Bacteriol. Nomenclature; mem. allergy and immunology study sect. Nat. Inst. Allergy and Infectious Diseases, 1965—69, mem. bd. sci. counselors, 1967—70, chmn., 1969—70; mem. WHO Expert Adv. Panel Acute Bacterial Diseases, 1979—2001. Mem. editl. bd.: Jour. Bacteriology, 1964—69, Am. Rev. Respiratory Diseases, 1963—66, Bacteriol. Rev., 1967—71, Jour. Infectious Diseases, 1969—74, Antimicrobial Agents and Chemotherapy, 1972—86, Infection and Immunity, 1973—81, Revs. of Infectious Diseases, 1979—89, Vaccine, 1983—, guest editor: Drugs and Aging, 1999. Trustee Johns Hopkins U., 1963—69. Capt. M.C. U.S. Army, 1943—46. Recipient U.S. Typhus Commn. medal, 1947, Albert Lasker Clin. Med. Rsch. award, 1978, Phila. award, 1979, Willard O. Thompson award, Am. Geriatric Soc., 1981, Lifetime Sci. award, Inst. Advanced Studies in Immunology and Aging, 1997, Pasteur Merieux MSD award, 1st Internat. Symposium on Pneumococci and Pneumococcal Diseases, 1998, Maxwell Finland award for sci. achievement, Nat. Found. for Infectious Diseases, 2001. Master: ACP (James D. Bruce Meml. award 1979); fellow: AAAS (chmn. sect. on med. scis. 1975), Am. Acad. Microbiology, N.Y. Acad. Scis.; mem.: NAS, Johns Hopkins Soc. Scholars, Infectious Disease Soc. Am. (pres. 1971, Maxwell Finland lecture award 1974, Bristol award 1986), Coll. Physicians Phila. (pres.-elect 1986, pres. 1988—89, Meritorious Svc. award 1980, Disting. Svc. medal 1997), Phila. County Med. Soc. (Strittmatter award 1979), N.Y. Acad. Medicine (sec. sect. microbiology 1961—62), Am. Assn. Immunologists, Balt. Med. Soc., Inst. Medicine, Am. Fedn. Clin. Rsch., Harvey Soc., Soc. Exptl. Biology and Medicine, Am. Philos. Soc., Am. Soc. Microbiology (v.p. N.Y. br. 1961—62), Am. Clin. and Climatol. Assn. (pres. 1984), Am. Soc. Clin. Investigation, Assn. Am. Physicians, 14 W. Hamilton St. Club (Balt.) (Balt.), Interurban Clin. Club (pres. 1970), Omicron Delta Kappa, Alpha Omega Alpha, Sigma Xi, Phi Beta Kappa. Office: U Pa Sch Medicine Dept Rsch Medicine 522 Johnson Pavilion Philadelphia PA 19104-6088

AUSUBEL, HILLEL, librarian; b. N.Y.C., Nov. 25, 1924; s. Herman and Lillian Leah (Leff) A.; m. Lucille Whintrop, June 19, 1949; children: Joan Ellen, Carol Ruth, Lawrence Marc. BA, Yale U., 1947; MA, Columbia U., 1948, MS in Libr. Svc., 1949, PhD in Music, 1953. Cert. pub. and sch. librarian, N.Y. Librarian Bklyn. Pub. Libr., 1949-50, Queens Pub. Libr., Jamaica, N.Y., 1954-63, Mt. Vernon (N.Y.) Schs., 1963-66, New Rochelle (N.Y.) Pub. Libr., 1968-89; head librarian N.Y. Coll. Music, N.Y.C., 1966-68; adj. librarian Queens (N.Y.) Coll., 1996-2000. Music book reviewer Libr. Jour., 1980-89; pvt. music tchr., 1945—. Composer various works for piano, voice and chamber music. Bd. dirs. Dems. for New Politics, Flushing, N.Y., 1990—. Mem. Ret. Educators & Profls., Queens Oratorio Soc. (trustee 1982-90). Democrat. Jewish. Avocations: music, gardening. Home: 46-10 216th St Bayside NY 11361

AUTEN, ARTHUR HERBERT, history educator; b. Cleve., Dec. 25, 1936; s. Herbert and Gladys Perry (Sessions) A.; m. Patricia Ann Kichak, June 5, 1971; children: David Arthur, Daniel Joseph. AB magna cum laude, Case Western Res. U., 1959, MA, 1960, PhD, 1965; cert. ednl. mgmt., Harvard U., 1972, CAS, 1977. Instr., asst. prof. history Westminster Coll., New Wilmington, Pa., 1963-66; asst. prof. history Colo. State U., Ft. Collins, 1966—69; v.p. planning, devel. and evaluation, dean Arts & Scis., U. Guam, Agana, 1970—76; pres. Alliance Coll., Cambridge Springs, Pa., 1977-81; acad. dean Coll. Basic Studies, U. Hartford, West Hartford, Conn., 1981-87, prof. history, 1987—2002. Sec. Pa. region 9/10 HIgher Edn. Planning Coun., 1979—80; vis. scholar Grad. Sch. Edn., Harvard U., 1988, prof. emeritus, 2002. Author: Critical Thinking Exercises for Western Civilization Courses, 1993, Readings in the History of Western Civilization: From the Dawn of Civilization to Columbus, From Columbus to Napoleon, From Napoleon to the Space Age, 1996; adv. editor Ann. Edits.: Am. History, 12th edit., 1993, 13th edit., 1995, 14th edit., 1997, 15th edit., 1999, 16th edit., 2001, 17th edit., 2002, Ann. Edits.: Western Civilization, 6th edit., 1991, 7th edit., 1993, 8th edit., 1995, 9th edit., 1997, 10th edit., 1999, 11th edit., 2001, 12th edit., 2002, World Civilization: A Brief History, 2d edit., 1993, 3d edit., 1998, A History of Civilization, 9th edit., 1995, Discovering the Western Past, 3d edit., 1995, Sources of the West, 3d edit., 1996. Cmty. devel. assistance com. City/Colls./Bus. Partnership, Meadville, Pa., 1980; mem. ednl. svcs. for cmty. devel., Guam Terr., 1972-76; spkr., events planner Kiwanis, Cambridge Springs, Pa., 1978-81; mem. Nat. Trust for Hist. Preservation. Recipient Hon. Membership pin, Polish Nat. Alliance, 1980, Cmty. Svc. citation, Mayor of Meadville, 1980, Ann. Svc. award, Gov. of Guam, 1976, Hon. Jagiellonian U. pin, Internat. Student Exch., 1979, Outstanding Educators Am. award, 1972, Tchg. Excellence designation, 1969; scholar U. Hartford scholar in humanities, 1997. Fellow: Phi Beta Kappa; mem.: New Eng. Hist. Assn., Am. Hist. Assn., Nat. Coun. Social Studies, Nat. Assn. Devel. Edn. (presenter, chair nat. conf. 1987, 1989—91, chmn. profl. interest group 1989—94, presenter, chair nat. conf. 1993, 1997, Dean's Recognition award 1986, cert. appreciation 1990, 1991, 1992), Orgn. Am. Historians (life Recognition award 1992), Mystic Seaport Mus. Am. and the Sea, Colonial Williamsburg Found., Phi Delta Kappa, Chi Omicron Gamma. Avocations: travel, theater, chess, model railroading, reading. Home: 17 Peddler Dr Windsor CT 06095-1748

AUTEN, DAVID CHARLES, lawyer; b. Phila., Apr. 4, 1938; s. Charles Raymond and Emily Lillian (Dickel) A.; m. Suzanne Crozier Plowman, Feb. 1, 1969; children: Anne Crozier, Meredith Smedley. BA, U. Pa., 1960, JD, 1963. Bar: Pa. 1963. Ptnr. Reed Smith LLP (and predecessors), Phila., 1963—. Author articles in field. V.p. N.E. Cmty. Mental Health Ctr., 1971-72; vice chmn. alumni ann. giving U. Pa., 1975-77, 81-82, chmn., 1982-84, trustee, 1977-80, 83-88; pres. Gen. Alumni Soc., 1977-80; chmn. Benjamin Franklin Assocs., 1975-77, 81-82, bd. overseers Sch. Arts and Scis., 1983-96; trustee U. Pa. Health Sys., 1995—. Pa. Medicine, 2002-, Springside Sch., 1985-88, v.p., 1987-88; pres. Soc. of Coll., 1975-77; v.p. Assn. Reps. for Educated Action, 1971-79; bd. mgrs. Presbyn.-U. Pa. Med. Ctr., 1980—, vice chmn., 1983-85, 88-95, chmn., 2002--; trustee Presbyn. Found. for Phila., 1986—, vice chm., 1996-98, chm., 1998—; bd. mgrs. Phila. City Inst., 1981—, treas., 1990-99; bd. dirs. Kearsley Home, 1974-2002, treas., 1990-96, chmn., 1996-2002; bd. mgrs. St. Peter's Sch., 1975-88, pres., 1978-79; bd. dirs. Greater Phila. Internat. Network, 1989-94, Com. of Seventy, 1990-2003, Courtland Found., Del Pres Health Care Inc., New Courtland Elder Svs., chmn., 1998—; mem. econ. devel. com. Greater Phila. First Corp.; rector's warden Christ Ch., Phila., 1996-2001. Mem. ABA, Pa. Bar Assn. (vice chmn. real property sect. 1985-87, chmn. 1987-88), Am. Land Title Assn., Phila. Bar Assn. (vice chmn. young lawyers sect. 1971-72), Juristic Soc. (pres.), Am. Coll. Real Estate Lawyers, Interfrat. Alumni Coun. U. Pa. (pres. 1970-74), French Am. C. of C. (bd. dirs. 1989—), Phi Beta Kappa, Theta Xi (pres. 1974-76, chmn. found. 1977-86), Rittenhouse Club (pres. 1979-82), Union League (bd. dirs., v.p., pres. 1993-94, chmn. Lincoln Found. 1996-2002), Fourth St. Club (bd. dirs. 1998-2000), Phila. Club. Episcopalian (vestryman). Home: 120 Delancey St Philadelphia PA 19106-4303 Office: Reed Smith LLP 2500 One Liberty Pl Philadelphia PA 19103

AUTEN, GEORGE ROBERT, JR., civil engineer; b. Charlotte, N.C., July 22, 1956; s. George Robert and Jean Barnette Auten; m. Grace Conley McCall, July 8, 1979; children: Graham, Taylor, Michael. BS in Indsl. Engring., N.C. State U., 1978, MS in Indsl. Engring., 1985; postgrad., George Washington U., 1991-95. Registered profl. engr., Nebr., N.C. Commd. 2d lt. USAF, 1978, advanced through grades to lt. col., 1994; chief environ. and contract planning 51 Civil Engr. Squadron, Osan Air Base, Korea, 1983-84; chief engr. force mgmt. divsn. Hdqr. Strategic Air Command, Offutt AFB, Nebr., 1984-89; mil. constrn. program mgr. Office of USAF Civil ENgr., Washington, 1990-92; mil. asst. Dep. Asst. Sec. Air Force, Washington, 1992-95; comdr. base civil engr. 437 Civil ENgr. Squadron, Charleston AFB, S.C., 1995-97, 375 Civil Engr. Squadron, Scott AFB, Ill., 1997-99; founder, pres. Atriax, PLLC, Architects & Engrs., Hickory, NC, 2000—. Recipient Engr. of Yr. award Charleston Engrs. Jt. Coun., 1996. Mem. Inst. Indsl. Engrs. (sr.), Soc. Am. Mil. Engrs. (past pres., v.p. 1996-99). Avocations: sports, hiking, biking, running. Home: 307 41st Avenue Pl NW Hickory NC 28601-9028 Office: PO Box 5277 10 21st Ave NW Ste 197 Hickory NC 28603-5277 E-mail: auteng@aol.com.

AUTERI, ROSE MARY PATTI, school system administrator; b. N.Y.C., June 6, 1928; d. Francesco and Stefana (Patti) A. BS, Hunter Coll., 1950; MA, Columbia U., 1962; EdD, Nova-Southeastern U., 1975; postdoctoral, Columbia U., 1976-77. Tchr. Howell Rd Sch., Valley Stream, N.Y., 1951-58, asst. prin., 1958-64; prin. Centennial Ave Sch., Roosevelt, N.Y., 1964-69, Northside Sch., Levittown, N.Y., 1969-83, Abbey Ln. Sch., Levittown, 1983-89; adminstr. in charge elem. schs. Levittown Pub. Schs., 1989-90; prin. Abbey Ln. Sch., Levittown, 1990—2000. Bd. trustees Nassau Cmty. Coll. Mem. Nassau County Youth Bd.; coord. Nassau County Mentoring Program; trustee Sacred Heart Roman Cath. Ch., Merrick. Recipient Disting. Prin. award State of N.Y., 1988, 89, Disting. Svc. award Nat. PTA, Pathfinder award for edn. Town of Hempstead, 2002; named Italian Am. Woman of Yr., Consortium L.I. Italian Am. Orgns., 1990, Woman of Yr. Societa Scarese D Am., 1998. Mem. Am. Assn. Sch. Adminstrs., Nat. Assn. Elem. Sch. Prins., Nat. Assn. Supervision and Curriculum Devel., Nassau County Elem. Prins. Assn. (pres.), L.I. Assn. Supervision and Curriculum Devel. (bd. dirs.), N.Y. State Assn. Devel., Am. Assn. Electroencephalographic Technologists, Am.-Italian Hist. Assn. (sec. 1988—, pres., editor L.I. regional chpt.). Home: 1816 Thomas St Merrick NY 11566-2652 E-mail: ROmpAut@aol.com.

AUTHEMENT, RAY P. college president; b. Chauvin, La., Nov. 19, 1929; s. Elias Lawrence and Elphia (Duplantis) A.; m. Barbara B. Braud, June 1, 1950; children: Kathleen Elizabeth, Julie Ann. BS, U. Southwestern La., 1950; MS, La. State U., 1952; PhD, 1956. Instr. La. State U., Baton Rouge, 1952-56; asso. prof. McNeese State Coll., Lake Charles, La., 1956-57, U. Southwestern La., 1957-59, prof. math., from, 1959, acad. v.p., 1966-73, pres., 1973—. Vis. prof. U. N.C., Chapel Hill, 1962-63 Mem. Downtown Devel. Com. Lafayette, 1972—; commr., mem. exec. com. Lafayette Econ. Devel. Authority, 1988—; mem. La. Bicentennial Commn., 1973, Lafayette Bicentennial Commn., 1973, Econ. Devel. Com., Lafayette, 1973, Sch. Bd. Fatima Parish, Lafayette, 1963-65; bd. dirs. United Way, 1973, U. Southwestern La. Found., 1967, Gulf South Rsch. Inst., 1985-91; trustee Lafayette Gen. Hosp., 1981—; mem. bd. advisers John Gray Inst., 1982-91, St. Joseph Sem., 1967; mem. Commn. Colleges So. Assn. Colls., 1981-83; bd. dirs. Lafayette Health Ventures, Inc., 1989—, Enterprise Ctr. of La., Inc., 1990—, Affiliated Blind of La., Inc., 1991—, La. Patrnership for Tech. and Innovation, 1989—, chmn., 1993; chmn. Acadiana Navigation Channel Task Force, 1990—. Named Outstanding Citizen of Acadiana Internat. Rels. Assn. Acadiana, 1991; recipient Lafayette Civic Cup award, 1991. Mem. AAAS, Lafayette C. of C. (dir. 1983—), Blue Key, Phi Kappa Phi, Kappa Mu Epsilon, Sigma Pi Sigma, Phi Kappa Theta. Roman Catholic. Home: PO Drawer 41008 USL Station Lafayette LA 70504 Office: U Southwestern La Office Pres USL Drawer 41008 University Ave Lafayette LA 70504-1008

AUTIN, DIANA MARIE THERESE KATHERINE, lawyer, educator; b. Golden Meadow, La., Sept. 16, 1954; d. Alphonse Adam and Lorraine (Leydecker) A.; m. W. Keith Hefner, Sept. 15, 1979; children: Peter Richard, Elena Lorraine, Emilia Lee Autin-Hefner. BA, U. Mich., 1974, JD, 1977. Bar: Mich. 1977, U.S. Dist. Ct. (ea. dist.) Mich. 1978, N.Y. 1982. Atty. Transp. Employees Union, Ann Arbor, Mich., 1977-79; atty., asst. dir. Downtown Welfare Adv. Ctr., N.Y.C., 1979-81; exec. dir. Fund Open Info. Accountability, Inc., N.Y.C., 1981-84; dep. gen. counsel N.Y.C. Bur. Labor Services, 1984-87; exec. dir. Statewide Parent Advocacy Network, Newark. Adj. prof. Indsl. Labor Relations Sch. Cornell U.; apptd. mem. Mich. Ad Hoc Com. Juvenile Justice, Ann Arbor, 1978. Author: Young People and Law, 1979, Segregated and Second-Rate: Special Education in New York, 1992; also articles. Named Woman to Watch in the 1980's, Mademoiselle Mag., 1982, Advocate of the Yr. N.Y. State Commn. on the Quality of Care for the Mentally Disabled, 1993; Leadership fellow Advocacy Inst., 1994, Wasserstein Pub. Interest fellow Harvard Law Sch., 1993-94. Mem. Assn. Trial Lawyers Am., N.Y. Trial Lawyers Assn., N.Y. Bar Assn. (chair edn. health and early childhood subcom., mem. edn. com.), Nat. Lawyers Guild (cons. 1984). Home: 9 Lexington Ave Montclair NJ 07042-4501 Office: SPAN 35 Halsey St 4th Fl Newark NJ 07102

AUTIN, NANCY PELLERIN, secondary school educator; b. Franklin, La., July 23, 1948; d. Althamus E. and Lucille Pellerin; m. I. Joseph Autin; children: David C., Kate M. BS, Loyola Univ. New Orleans, New Orleans, 1971; MED, Univ. New Orleans, New Orleans, 1985, PhD, 2001. Asst. prin., math dept. chair, supr. of instrn., math. tchr. Brother Martin H.S., New Orleans, 1977—2001; prin. St. Mary's Dominican H.S., New Orleans, 2001—. V.p. St. Dominic Sch. Bd., New Orleans, 1986—89. Contbr. articles. Recipient Outstanding Doctoral award, Univ. New Orleans, 2001, Outstanding Tchr. award, Univ. Chgo., 1999, Brother More Schaeffer Faculty award, Brother Martin H.S., 1993. Mem.: So. Assn. of Sch. and Coll., Nat. Assn. of Sec. Sch. Prin., Am. Edn. Rsch. Assn., Am. Math. Assn. of two yr. colls., Nat. Coun. of Math., Assn. for Supr. and Cirriculm Devel., Phi Delta Kappan. Avocations: interior decorating, travel. Office: St Mary's Dominican HS 7701 Walmsley Ave New Orleans LA 70125

AUTREY, KATHY W. social worker; b. Ashland, Ky., Apr. 19, 1953; d. James Greeley and Jo Ann (Sparks) Walker;m., Henry Louis, Autrey, Jr. BA with distinction, U. Ky., 1978; MS with honors, Ea. Ky. U., 1994. Tng. supr. Blue Grass Assn. for Retarded Citizens, Lexington, Ky., 1971-75, Bur. Vocat. Rehab., Lexington, Ky., 1976-77; social worker Ky. Dept. for Social Svcs., Lexington, Ky., 1978-79, field office supr., 1979-85, social work/domestic violence prog. specialist, conf. coord. Frankfort, Ky., 1985-97, tng. instr., 1987—; assoc. dir. univ. tng. consortium project Ea. Ky. U., Richmond, Ky., 1997—. Instr. Ky. Sheriff's Acad., 1986-92; cert. instr. domestic violence Ky. State Police, 1995—; cert. instr. Levington Fayette div. police, 1981-87, 90-91; cons., trainer for social svc., 1983—; mem. adv. bd. Assn. for Older Kentuckians, 1989-93; mem. Ky. Law Enforcement Tng. Project, 1989-91; mem. Atty. Gen. Task Force on Domestic Violence Crime, 1991-93, Legis. Task Force on Domestic Violence, 1994-95; coord. 1st Nat. Teleconf. on Domestic Violence and Family Preservation Svc., 1994; mem. Gov. Coun. Domestic Violence, 1996-97; staff facilitator Nat. Coll. Dist. Atty. domestic violence conf., 1995; mem. Domestic Violence Jud. Edn. Planning Com., 1995-96; asst. course dir., presenter Nat. Coll. Dist. Atty., 1997, 98; cons. in field. Contbr. articles to profl. jour. Ad hoc grant com. Violence Against Women Act, 1995. Recipient Outstanding Svc. award Lexington Fayette div. of Police, 1984, Ky. Sheriff's Acad. Hon. Grad., 1989, tributes, 1986-88, Outstanding Kentuckian award Gov. Martha Layne Collins, 1987, Outstanding Young Am. Women award, 1987, Outstanding Victim Adv. award Lexington Urban County Govt., 1990, Outstanding Victim Advocacy award Ky. Victims' Coalition, 1993, Outstanding Svcs. Recognition Senate Ky. Gen. Assembly, 1995, Ky. Comm. Women, 1996, Exemplary Svc. award Ky. Dept. for Social Svcs., 1997; named Ky. Col., 1985, 96, Outstanding Alumni, Ea. Ky. U. Coll. Law Enforcement, 1996. Mem. Ky. Domestic Violence Assn. (homicide-suicide task force 1990-94), Ky. Law Enforcement Coun. (cert.). Democrat. Avocations: reading, music, boating.

AUTRY, ALAN, mayor, actor, former professional football player, film company executive; b. Shreveport, La., 1952; m. Kimberlee Autry; children: Lauren, Heather, Austin. Attended, U. of the Pacific. Mayor City of Fresno, Calif., 2001—; founder & pres. Dirt Road Prodns.; quarterback Green Bay Packers. Office: 2600 Fresno St 2nd Fl Fresno CA 93721 E-mail: mayor@fresno.gov.*

AUTRY, CAROLYN, artist, art history educator; b. Dubuque, Iowa, Dec. 12, 1940; d. William Tilden and Vela (Laseman) A.; m. Peter Elloian, May 27, 1966; 1 dau., Cybele Justine. BA, U. Iowa, 1963, MFA, 1965. Instr. art, art history Baldwin-Wallace Coll., Berea, Ohio, 1965-66; adj. assoc. prof. art history dept. art Ctr. for Visual Arts U. Toledo, 1966-2001. Artist-in-residence Sch. Arts in France, Lacoste, 1984, 87, adj. instr. in printmaking, 1987. Exhbns. include San Francisco Mus. Art, 1973, Oakland Mus., 1975, Santa Barbara Mus., 1975, U. Mo., 1975, Ljubljana Internat. Biennial, 1975, 81, 87, Internationale Grafik Biennale, Frechen, W. Ger., 1976, Biella, Italy, 1976, Genoa, Italy, 1976, Leverkusen, Fed. Republic Germany, 1977, Phila. Mus. Art, 1980, 97, Visual Arts Ctr., Anchorage, Alaska, 1980, U. Louisville, 1981, U. Dallas, 1981, Grunwald Ctr. Graphic Arts, UCLA, 1981, Ohio State U., 1982, Belle Arts & Graphic Inc., Nyack, N.Y., 1982, Mus. Arts and Sci., Macon, Ga.,

1983, U. Tenn., Knoxville, 1983, Pratt Graphics Ctr., NYC, 1983, Calif. State Coll. San Bernardino, 1983, Am. Embassy Cultural Ctr., Belgrade, Yugoslavia, 1983, Taipei Fine Arts Mus., 1983, 85, 87, 89, 91, 95, Museo Arte Contemporaneo, Ibiza, Spain, 1984, Drake U., 1985, Fla. State U., 1985, Irvine (Calif.) Fine Arts Ctr., 1986, Inter-graphic Internat., East Berlin, 1984, 87, Met. Mus. Art Ctr., Coral Gables, Fla., 1987, Fifth Internat. Graphic Exhbn., Catania, Italy, 1988, Korean Cultural Svc. Gallery, L.A., Walker Hill Gallery, Seoul, Korea, and Korean Embassy Cultural Ctr., Paris, 1989, Barbican Art Centre, London, Salford (Gt. Britain) Mus., Mead Gallery, U. Warwick, Coventry, Gt. Britain, Brighton and Poly. Gallery, Brighton, Gt. Britain, 1989, Internat. Exhbn. Prints, Kanagawa, Japan, 1989, 90, 95, 97, Gallery Fine Arts Ctr. Seoul, 1989, Nat. Exhbn. Prints, Ringling Sch. Art and Design, Sarasota, Fla., 1990, Internat. Impact Art Festival, Kyoto City Mus., Japan, 1990, 91, 92, 93, 94, Ohio Drawing and Printmaking Invitational, Upper Arlington, 1991, Fondation Mona Bismarck, Paris, 1991, Fine Arts Assn. Gallery, Hanoi, Republic of Vietnam, 1991, Prints Internat., 1992, Silvermine Guild Arts Ctr., New Caanan, Conn., 1993, Taejon (Korea) Expo Graphic Art, 1993, Soc. Am. Graphic Artists 65th Nat., N.Y.C., 1993, Architecture in Contemporary Print Making, Boston Archtl. Ctr., 1994, Am. Inst. Architecture, Washington, 1994, U. N.H., 1995, Midwest Select, South Bend Regional Mus. of Art, Ind., 1994, Triton Mus., Santa Clara, Calif., 1995, Mansfield (Ohio) Art Ctr., 1995, 20th Harper Nat. Exhbn., Macomb, Ill., 1996, Hunterdon Art Ctr., Clinton, N.J., 1996, Soc. Am. Graphic Artists 66th Nat. Print Exhbn., Hanover, N.J., 1997, Internat. Print Triennial, Cracow, Poland, 1997, Fla. Printmakers 9th Ann. Nat. Print Exhbn., Jacksonville, 1997, 11th Ann. Nat. Print Exhbn., 2000, Institut Franco-Américain, Rennes, France, 1997, Prized Impressions, Internat. Exhbn. of Prints, Phila. Mus. of Art, 1997, Nat. Print Exhbn., Calif. State Univ. Chico, 1997, 22d nat. Print Biennal Silvermine Guild Arts Ctr., Conn., 1998, Counterpoint Exhbn. Hill Country Arts Found., Tex., 1998, 99, 2000, Printmakers 98, Pittsburgh Ctr. for the Arts, Penn., 1998, U. Hawaii, Hilo, 2000, 13th Ann. McNeese Nat. Works on Paper Exhbn., McNeese State U., Lake Charles, La., Baton Rouge (La.) Gallery, 2000, Printwork 2K, 2000, The 7th Ann. Nat. Juried Exhbn., Barrett Art Ctr., Poughkeepsie, N.Y.C., 2000, 1st Biennial Nat. Print Competition, No. Ariz. U., Flagstaff, 2002, Internat. Print exhib. invitational, Minsk, Belarus, 2002, Soc. Am. Graphic Artists 69th Nat. Exhbn. Arts Student League, NY, 2002, Interior/Exterior Landscapes, U. Wyo., Laramie and U. Dallas, Irving, Tex., 2002, 23d Nat. Print Exhbn. Art Link Contemporary Art Gallery, Ft. Wayne, Ind., 2003, L.S. Printmakers Soc. Juried Membership Exhbn., Brawd Libr. Art Galleries, Glendale, Calif., 2003, Boston Printmakers Juried N.Am. Print Exhbn., 1971-81, 86-87, 2003; Boston Printmakers Juried North American Print Exh. 1971-1981, 1986-1987, 2003, and others; represented in permanent collections Libr. of Congress, Phila. Mus. Art, Worcester Art Mus., Mount Holyoke Coll., U. Colo., Bradley U., Calif. State U., San Diego, Ga. State U., U. S.D., U. N.D., U. Louisville, St. Lawrence U., U. Dallas, Hunterdon Art Ctr., Clinton, N.J., Fitchburg (Mass.) Mus., Duxbury (Mass.) Art Complex, Elvehjem Mus. Art U. Wis.-Madison, Inst. per la Cultura E L'Arte, Catania, Italy, Lakeview Mus. Arts and Scis., Peoria, Ill., Nat. Mus. Fine Arts, Hanoi. Recipient Boston Printmakers N.Am. Print Exhbn. award 1971, 79, 80, 81, 87, Pennell award Libr. Congress, 1971, 75, Phila. Print Club awards, 1972, 75, 79, Wesleyan Coll. Internat. award of merit, 1980, Anne Steele Marsh award Hunterdon Art Ctr., Clinton, N.J., 1991, Bradley U. Nat. award, 1991, Friends of the Janet Turner Gallery Nat. Exhbn. award Chico State U., Calif., 1995, Exhbn. award 16th Nat. Print Exhbn., Artlink, 1996, Exhbn. award 17th Nat. Print Exhbn., 1997, Counterpoint, 2000, Nat. Exhbn. award The Hill Country Arts Found., 2000; Ford Found. grantee, 1961-63, Ohio Arts Coun. grantee, 1979, 90, Yale-Norfolk Summer Sch. Art and Music scholar, 1962. Mem. Boston Printmakers (Louis Black award 1971), L.A. Printmakers Soc., Soc. Am. Graphic Artists (Jo Miller award 1985, Phillip Monteith award 1986), Calif. Soc. Printmakers, Coll. Art Assn. Am., The Print Club of Albany, N.Y. (Ledyard Logswell, Jr. Meml. prize 1995), Phi Beta Kappa. Address: 26114 W River Rd Perrysburg OH 43551-9128

AUTRY, PHILIP EARL, music educator, musician; b. Humboldt, Tenn., Apr. 9, 1965; s. Max E. and Evelyn Mayo Autry. BS, David Lipscomb U., 1987; MA, Middle Tenn. State U., 1989; D. Musical Arts, U. Okla., 1996; Program Cert., Russian Piano Inst. of Internat. Fine Arts Inst., Moscow, 1998, Russian Piano Inst. of St. Petersburg Conservatory, 1999. Independent studio tchr. Pvt. Piano Studio, 1987—2002; asst. prof. music Angelo State U., San Angelo, Tex., 1996—2001; assoc. prof. music, chair dept. music Fisk U., Nashville; solo performer, orch. pianist Tenn. Discussion leader Nat. Conf. on Keyboard Pedagogy, Oak Brook, Ill., 2001. Contbr. articles to profl. jours., Hymnal. Mem.: Music Tchrs. Nat. Assn. (South-Ctrl. Divsn. Competition chair 1995—2001), Phi Kappa Phi, Pi Kappa Lambda, Phi Mu Alpha Sinfonia. Office: 1000 17th Ave N Nashville TN 37208-3045 Business E-mail: PAutry@fisk.edu.

AUVENSHINE, ANNA LEE BANKS, school system administrator; b. Waco, Tex., Nov. 27, 1938; d. D.C. and Lois Elmore Banks; B.A., Baylor U., 1959, M.A., 1968, Ed.D., 1978, postgrad., 1989—, Colo. State U., 1970-71, U. No. Colo., 1972; m. William Robert Auvenshine, Dec. 21, 1963; children— Karen Lynn, William Lee. Tchr. math. and English, Lake Air Jr. High Sch., Waco Ind. Sch. Dist., 1959-63, Ranger (Tex.) Ind. Sch. Dist., Ranger High Sch., 1964, Canyon (Tex.) Ind. Sch. Dist., Canyon Jr. High Sch., 1964-66; instr. English, Baylor U., 1963; tchr. math. Canyon Ind. Sch. Dist., Canyon High Sch., 1968-70; tchr. math. and English, St. Vrain Sch. Dist., Erie (Colo.) High Sch., 1970-71; tchr. English and reading Thompson Sch. Dist., Loveland (Colo.) High Sch., 1971-72; instr., reading program dir. Ranger Jr. Coll., 1972-84, chmn. humanities div., 1978-82; tchr. math. Hillsboro High Sch., 1984-85, adminstr. Hillsboro Ind. Sch. Dist., 1985-92. Trustee, Ranger (Tex.) Ind. Sch. Dist., 1979-84, v.p. bd. trustees, 1980-82, pres., 1982-84; community chmn., publicity chmn., troop leader Ranger Girl Scout Assn., 1974-77; sec. Eastland County Heart Assn., 1975-77; ch. sch. supt. First United Meth. Ch., Ranger, 1979-81, organist, 1974-77, mem. adminstrv. bd., 1979 84; assoc. program dir. community and tech. colls. and fed. projects, equity dir. Tex. Higher Edn. Coordinating Bd., Austin, 1992—. Mem. Internat. Reading Assn., Assn. Supervision and Curriculum Devel., Western Coll. Reading Assn., Tex. Assn. Sch. Adminstrs., Tex. Assn. Gifted and Talented, Tex. Jr. Coll. Tchrs. Assn. (cert. of appreciation 1979, mem. profl. devel. com. 1974-79, vice chmn. 1976-77, mem. resolutions com. 1979-80), Ranger PTA (parliamentarian 1978-79), Ranger Jr. Coll. Faculty Orgn. (pres. 1980-81), Baylor Alumni Assn. (life, bd. dirs. 1988-94), director, Baylor Alum. Assn., 1988-92, Delta Kappa Gamma (pres. Beta Upsilon chpt. 1978-80, pres. Gamma Delta chpt. 1986—, achievement award 1980). Methodist. Clubs: 1947 (pres. 1977-78) (Ranger); Baylor Bear (Waco). Home: 1107 E Walnut St Hillsboro TX 76645-2637 Office: Texas Higher Edn Coordinating Bd PO Box 12788 7745 Chevy Chase Dr Bldg 5 Austin TX 78752-1508

AUWARTER, BRIAN WILLIAM, sculptor; b. Greene, N.Y., Mar. 22, 1950; s. Frederick Alvin and Mildred Louise (Hill) A.; m. Kathryn Maureen Hendrick, Aug. 16, 1972 (div. Apr. 1999); children: Tyler, Tessa. BS in Edn., SUNY, Buffalo, 1974. Tchr. Ballston Spa (N.Y.) Schs., 1974—; owner Design Mill, 1999—. Design dir. AdROC, Gansevoort, N.Y., 1998—. Exhibited in group shows at Schenectady (N.Y.) Mus., 1981-2001, Munson-Williams-Proctor Mus. Art, Utica, N.Y., 1982, 88, Rice Gallery, Albany (N.Y.) Inst. History and Art, 1984, 89, 95, 98, Corp. Woods, Albany, 1986, Burlington County Coll., Pemberton, N.J., 1989-91, Hyde Mus. Art, Glens Falls, N.Y., 1977-90, Contemporary Artist Ctr. Gallery, North Adams, Mass., 1994, Center Galleries, Albany, 1999, Nat. Historic Trust at Chesterwood, Stockbridge, Mass., 1983, 90, 95, 2002, Saratoga County Arts Coun. Gallery, 2000, 01.

AUWERS, STANLEY JOHN, motor carrier executive; b. Grand Rapids, Mich., Mar. 22, 1923; s. Joseph T. and Cornelia (Moelhoek) A.; m. Elizabeth Kruis, Apr. 6, 1946; children— Ellen (Mrs. William Northway), Stanley John, Thomas. Student, Calvin Coll., 1940-41; BBA, U. Mich., 1943. C.P.A., Mich. With Ernst & Ernst, Detroit, 1943-51; controller Interstate Motor Freight System, Grand Rapids, Mich., 1951-61, v.p., controller, 1961-65, v.p. finance, 1965-69, exec. v.p., 1969-72; also dir.; pres. Transam. Freight Lines, Detroit, 1973—. Chmn. cost com. Mich. Trucking Adv. Bd. to Mich. Pub. Service Commn., 1958-63; mem. citizens com. to study Mich. tax structure advisory Mich. Ho. Reps., 1958 Mem. Am. Motor Carriers Central Freight Assn. (gov. regular common carrier conf.), Mich. Motor Carriers Central Freight Assn. (v.p., gov.), Tax Execs. Inst., Am. Inst. C.P.A.s, Trucking Employers. Presbyterian. Home: 3099 Lakeshore Dr Douglas MI 49406 Office: 3684 28th St SE Grand Rapids MI 49512-1606

AUXENTIOS, clergyman; b. June 28, 1953; BA in Religion, Princeton U., 1976; Lic. Theol., Ctr. for Traditionalist Orthodox Studies, 1986; ThD, Grad. Theol. Union, Berkeley, Calif., 1992. Ordained as rasophore monk, then hierodeacon Old Calendar Greek Orthodox Ch., 1976, hieromonk, 1977, great schema, 1986, oikonomos, 1989, archimandrite, 1989, titular bishop of Photiki, 1991. Co-dir. Ctr. for Traditionalist Orthodox Studies, 1987—. Author: (with Chrysostomos and Akakios) Contemporary Eastern Orthodox Thought: The Traditionalist Voice, 1982, (with Chrysostomos and Ambrosios) Scripture and Tradition, 1982, (with Chrysostomos) The Roman West and the Byzantine East, 1988, The Holy Fire, 1991; translator: (with Chrysostomos) The Future Life According to Orthodox Teaching (Constantine Cavarnos), 1988, The Monastic Life (Met. Cyprian of Oropos and Fili), 1988; (with others) The Evergetinos: A Complete Text, Vol. I of the First Book, 1988, Vol. II, 1990; editor Orthodox Tradition, 1989—; contbr. articles to profl. jours. Greek Orthodox. Address: St Gregory Palamas Monastery Etna CA 96027-0398

AUXER, CATHY JOAN, elementary school educator; b. Chambersburg, Pa., May 16, 1951; d. Pat and Joan Irene Wedo; m. Jeffrey Lynn Auxer, Aug. 21, 1971 (dec. Aug. 23, 1996); 1 child, Jeffrey Lynn Auxer Jr. BS in Edn., Shippensburg State U., 1974; MEd, Shippensburg U., 1978. Cert. tchr. Pa., Md. 1st grade tchr. Mooreland Elem. Sch., Carlisle, Pa., 1975—2000, Worcester Prep. Sch., Berlin, Md., 2000—. Cons. Apple Learning Interchange, Berlin, 2001—. Co-author: (pamphlet) Whole Language, 1981; author: (lessons online) Computer Learning Found., 2000—01. Recipient 2d pl. award for lesson plan, Computer Learning Found. Tchrs., 2001. Mem.: Internat. Reading Assn., Eastern Shore Reading Coun. Home: 18 Carriage Ln Berlin MD 21811 E-mail: occookiemd@aol.com.

AVADHUT, HITENDRANANDAACARYA, spiritual counselor, yoga teacher; b. Raigarh, India, Jan. 24, 1968; s. Shouki Lal and Shanti Devi Gupta. BA, Guru Ghasidas U., Bilaspur, India, 1988. Sec. Renaissance Universal Anada Marga, Dallas, 1992—. Avocations: music, poetry. Home: 3157 CR 1670 Willow Springs MO 65793 Office: Renaissance Universal 2355 Trellis Pl Richardson TX 75081 E-mail: hitendrananda@hotmail.com.

AVAKIAN, HELEN ROSS, musician, educator; b. Wilmington, Del. d. Peter and Barbara (Loveland) Avakian; m. Terry Doyle Champlin, Aug. 10, 1991. BMusic, Hunter Coll., CUNY, 1985, MMusic, 1987. Music dept. tutor Hunter Coll., N.Y.C., 1985-86; guitar instr., mgr. Musical Assocs., Bedford, N.Y., 1987-98; guitar instr. Dutchess C.C., Poughkeepsie, N.Y., 1996—; flamenco dance accompanist Bard Coll., Annandale-on-Hudson, N.Y., 1993—; classical/flamenco guitarist, folk/pop singer and guitarist Music Splties., Milton, N.Y., 1987—. Adj. instr. Shenandoah Conservatory, Shenandoah U., Winchester, Va., 1998-99; songwriter Highwater Music, Pleasant Valley, N.Y., 1992—. Composer/performer: recs. A Hudson Valley Christmas Compilation, 1997, Helen Avakian, 1993, Helen Avakian Live at the Rosendale Street Festival, 1999, Vanishing Point, 2000, music video Mistletoe Blues, 1998, composer: recs. Musikos Peripatos: Classical Guitar Duos with Terry Champlin, 2002; composer: Ho Ho Ho Spice Christmas Compilation. Benefit performer Hudson River Housing, Grace Smith Home for Battered Women, others. Winner in song contest Cityfolk, 1989, others; named Favorite Acoustic Act, Rhythm and News Mag., 1997, 99, 2001, 03, Favorite Recording Rhythm and News Mag., 2001, 03; Esther Hoffman scholar, 1985. Mem. Am. Fedn. Musicians, Am. Soc. Composers and Performers. Avocations: reading, storywriting. Office: Highwater Music PO Box 1571 Pleasant Valley NY 12569-1571 E-mail: info@helenavakian.com.

AVAKIAN, LAURA ANN, academic administrator; b. DeSoto, Mo., July 6, 1945; d. Edward Ernest and Elizabeth (Gamel) McClary; m. Stephen Avakian, Dec. 30, 1969. BA, U. Mo., 1967; MA, Northwestern U., 1968. Instr. Sacramento (Calif.) State Coll., 1968-69; tchr. English Hathaway Brown Sch., Cleve., 1969-73; pers. profl. Huron Rd. Hosp., Cleve., 1974-76, dir. human resources, 1978-80; dir. employment Cleve. Clinic Found., 1976-78; sr. v.p. human resources Beth Israel Deaconess Med. Ctr., Boston, 1980-96, Beth Israel Deaconess Med. Ctr. and Care Group, Boston, 1996—; v.p. human resources Mass. Inst. Tech., 1999—. Bd. dirs. ArQule, Inc., Wellspring. Assoc. editor Yearbook of Healthcare Management, 1990, 91, 92, 93. Mem. Mayor's Commn. on Comparable Worth, Boston, 1989-90; trustee Pine Manor Coll., 1997—; trustee Wellspring, Inc., 2003—. Mem. Am. Soc. Healthcare Human Resources Adminstrn. (bd. dirs. 1989-93, Pres. Leadership award 1989, Lit. award 1992, pres. 1994-95, Disting. Svc. award 1997, Mentoring award 2001), Soc. Human Resource Mgmt. (Profl. Excellence award 1996), Mass. Health Care Human Resources Assn. (pres. 1987-88), N.E. Human Resources Assn. (bd. dirs. 2003—). Avocation: crossword puzzle construction. Office: Mass Inst Tech 77 Mass Ave # E19-239 Cambridge MA 02139-4301 E-mail: lavakian@mit.edu.

AVAKOFF, JOSEPH CARNEGIE, medical consultant, law consultant; b. Fairbanks, Alaska, July 15, 1936; s. Harry B. and Margaret (Adams) Avakoff; m. Teddy I. Law, May 7, 1966; children: Caroline, Joe E., John. AA, U. Calif., Berkeley, 1956, AB, 1957; MD, U. Calif., San Francisco, 1961; JD, Santa Clara U., 1985. Bar: Calif. 1987; diplomate Am. Bd. Surgery, Am. Bd. Plastic Surgery. Physicist U.S. Naval Radiol. Def. Lab., San Francisco, 1957, 59; intern So. Pacific Gen. Hosp., San Francisco, 1961-62; resident in surgery Kaiser Found. Hosp., San Francisco, 1962-66; resident in plastic surgery U. Tex. Sch. Medicine, San Antonio, 1970-72; pvt. practice specializing in surgery Sacramento, 1966-70; pvt. practice specializing in plastic surgery Los Gatos and San Jose, Calif., 1972-94; cons. to med. and legal professions, 1994—. Clin. instr. Sch. Medicine U. Calif., Davis, 1967—70; chief dept. surgery Mission Oaks Hosp., Los Gatos, 1988—90; chief divsn. plastic surgery Good Samaritan Hosp., San Jose, 1988—91; expert med. reviewer Med. Bd. Calif., 1995—2001; spl. cons. Calif. Dept. Corps., 1997—2002; presenter numerous med. orgns. Contbr. articles to profl. jours. Mem. San Jose Adv. Commn. Health, 1975—82; bd. govs. San Jose YMCA, 1977—80. Mem.: AMA, Union Am. Physicians and Dentists, Santa Clara County Med. Assn., Santa Clara County Bar Assn., Calif. Med. Assn., Phi Beta Kappa, Phi Eta Sigma. Republican. Presbyterian. Avocations: music, photography, computer programming. Home: 6832 Rockview Ct San Jose CA 95120-5607

AVALLE-ARCE, JUAN BAUTISTA, Spanish language educator; b. Buenos Aires, May 13, 1927; came to U.S., 1948; s. Juan B. and Maria Martina Avalle-Arce; m. Constance Marginot, Aug. 20, 1953 (dec. 1969); children: Juan Bautista, Maria Martina, Alejandro Alcantara; m. Diane Janet Pamp, Aug. 30, 1969 (div.); children: Maria la Real Alejandra, Fadrique Martín Manuel. AB, Harvard U., 1951, MA, 1952, PhD, 1955; LittD (hon.), U. Castilla-La Mancha, Spain. Tutor, Harvard U., 1953-55; asst. prof., then assoc. prof. Spanish, Ohio State U., 1955-62; prof. Spanish, Smith Coll., Northampton, Mass., 1962-66, Sophia Smith prof. Hispanic studies, 1966-69; William Rand Kenan, Jr. prof. Spanish, U. N.C., Chapel Hill, 1969-85; prof. Spanish U. Calif., Santa Barbara, 1985—, chmn. dept. Spanish and Portuguese, 1991-95, dir. Summer Inst. Hispanic Langs. and Culture, 1991—, José Miguel de Barandiarán prof. Basque studies, 1993—. Vis. scholar Univ. Ctr. Ga., 1972, lectr., 1961—, Univ. Ctr. Va., 1976; vis. prof. U. Salamanca, 1982, 84, 86, 88, U. Málaga, 1987, 90, 91, U. della Tuscia (Italy), 1988, Sophia U. (Japan), 1988, Kyoto U. Fgn. Affairs, 1988, U. Cuyo, U. Buenos Aires, 1989, Alcalá de Henares, 1995; vis. Hillyer Prof. Humanities U. Nev., Reno, 1996; Eccles scholar State U. Utah, 2003, Garner vis. scholar, 2003; PhD program evaluator N.Y. State Bd. Regents; cons. Coun. Grad. Schs. in U.s.; reader Nat. Humanities Ctr., Govt. Found. for 5th Centennial of Discovery of Am., Spain; cultural corr. Radio Nacional de España; ofcl. guest Euskadiko Erradio, Spain, 1988-89. Author: Conocimiento y vida en Cervantes, 1959, La novela pastoril española, 1959, 2d enlarged edit., 1974, La Galatea de Cervantes, 2 vols., 1961, 2d rev. edit., 1987, Gonzalo Fernández de Oviedo, 1962, 2d edit., 1989, El Inca Garcilaso en sus Comentarios, 1961, Deslindes cervantinos, 1961, Three Exemplary Novels, 1964, Bernal Francès y su Romance, 1966, El Persiles de Cervantes, 1969, Los entremeses de Cervantes, 1969, Don Juan Valera y Morsamor, 1970, El cronista Pedro de Escavias Una vida del Siglo XV, 1972, Suma cervantina, 1973, Narradores hispanoamericanos de hoy, 1973, Las Memorias de Gonzalo Fernández de Oviedo, 2 vols., 1974, El Peregrino en su patria de Lope de Vega, 1973, Nuevos deslindes cervantinos, 1974, Temas hispánicos medievales, 1975, Don Quijote como forma de vida, 1976, Dintorno de una època dorada, 1978, Cervantes, Don Quixote, annotated critical edit., 2 vols., 1978, rev. and enlarged edit., 1995, Cervantes, Novelas ejemplares, annotated edit., 3 vols., 1982, Lope de Vega, Las hazañas del Segundo David, 1984; La Galatea de Cervantes: 400 Años Despuès, 1985, Garci Rodriguez de Montalvo: Amadís de Gaula, 2 vols., 1985, Amadís de Gaula: El primitivo y el de Montalvo, 1991, Lecturas, 1987, Gonzalo Fernández de Oviedo, Batallas y quinquagenas, 1989, Garci Rodriguez de Montalvo Amadis de Gaula, 2 vols., 1991, Cancionero del Almirante don Fadrique Euriquez, 1993, Enciclopedia Cervantina, 1995, Poesía completa de Jorge de Montemayor, 1996, La épica colonial, 2000, Una obra olviera de Gonzalo Fernandez de Ovideo, 2003. Trustee Teutonic Order of the Levant, Marqués de la Lealtad. Recipient Bonsoms medal Spain, 1961; Guggenheim fellow, 1961; grantee Am. Coun. Learned Socs., 1965, 68; grantee NEH, 1968, 1978-80; grantee Am. Philos. Soc., 1961, 67; recipient Susan Anthony Potter Lit. prize, 1951; Centro Gallego Lit. prize, 1947; Diploma of Merit, Universitá delle Arti, Italy; named Grand Companion, Societé Internationale de la Noblesse Héréditaire. Sr. fellow Southeastern Inst. Medieval and Renaissance Studies; hon. fellow Soc. Spanish and Spanish Am. Studies; fellow Colegio Mayor Arzobispo D. Alonso de Fonseca of U. Salamanca; mem. MLA, Acad. Lit. Studies, Am. Acad. Rsch. Historians Medieval Spain, Academia Argentina de Letras, Anglo Am. Basque Studies Soc., Cervantes Soc. Am. (pres. 1979—), Ctr. for Medieval and Renaissance Studies, UCLA (assoc.), Soc. de Bibliofilos Espanoles, Modern Humanities Rsch. Assn., South Atlantic MLA, Asociación de Cervantistas (bd. mem.), Assn. Internac. de Hispanistas, Renaissance Soc. Am. (nat. del. to exec. coun. 1971), Real Sociedad Vascongada de Amigos del Pais, Centro de Estudios Jacobeos, Inst. d'Etudes Medievales, Inst. de Lit. Iberoamericana, Hispanic Soc. Am., Acad. Lit. Studies (charter), Mediaeval Acad. Am., Real Academia de Buenas Letras de Barcelona, Instituto Internacional de Literatura Iberoamericana, Sovereign Mil. Teutonic Order of the Levant (bailiff, knight grand cross, Grand Prior, Grand Priory of the U.S.), Harvard Club. Clubs: Triangle Hunt (Durham) (gentleman Whipper-in); U. N.C. Polo, Combined Training Events Assn. Home: 4640 Oak View Rd Santa Ynez CA 93460-9331 Office: U Calif 4323 Phelps Hall Santa Barbara CA 93106

AVALOS, HECTOR IGNACIO, language educator; b. Nogales, Sonora, Mexico, Oct. 8, 1958; s. Magdalena Avalos Bernal and Ignacio Arizmendi; m. Cynthia Dee Schultz, May 8, 2000. PhD, Harvard U., 1991. Carolina minority postdoctoral fellow U. N.C., Chapel Hill, 1991—93; assoc. prof. Iowa State U., Ames, 1993—. Dir. U.S. Latino studies program Iowa State U., Ames. Author: (book) Illness and Health Care in the Ancient Near East: The Role of the Temple in Greece, Mesopotamia, and Israel. Exec. dir. sci. exam. of religion com. Coun. for Secular Humanism, Amherst, NY, 1997. Independent. Avocations: travel, music, debate. Home: 3604 Grand Ave Ames IA 50010 Office: Iowa State Univ 402 Catt Hall Ames IA Office Fax: 515-294-0780. E-mail: havalos@iastate.edu.

AVANT, GAYLE, political science educator; b. Mercedes, Tex., Aug. 23, 1940; s. George Clarence and Winnie Lela (Bagley) A.; m. Patricia Kay Coalson, Sept. 1, 1970; children— Samantha, Celia. B.A., U. Tex., 1962; M.A., U. N.C., 1965, Ph.D., 1969. Devel. Officer AID/State Dept., Washington, 1966-68; asst. prof. Miami U., Oxford, Ohio, 1968-70; assoc. prof. polit. sci. Baylor U., Waco, Tex., 1970—; vis. prof. Inst. Brit. and Am. Studies, U. Oslo, Norway, 1993; vis. prof. polit. sci., sr. lectr. U. Ballarat, Australia, 1996-97. Editor: Foundations of Citizenship, 1990. Dir. Baylor Washington Program, 1985-92; mem. Am.-Thai Found. Bd., 1993—. Mem. Centex Pub. Adminstrn. Assn. (program chmn. 1991-93), S.W. Social Sci. Assn., Nat. Coun. Social Studies, Tex. Coun. for Social Studies, Am. Polit. Sci. Assn. Baptist.

AVANT, GRADY, JR., lawyer; b. New Orleans, Mar. 1, 1932; s. Grady and Sarah (Rutherford) A.; m. Katherine Willis Yancey, Feb. 23, 1963; children: Grady M., Mary Willis Yancey. BA magna cum laude, Princeton U., 1954; JD, Harvard U., 1960. Bar: N.Y. 1961, Ala. 1962, Mich. 1972. Assoc. Bradley, Arant, Rose & White, Birmingham, Ala., 1961-63; assoc., ptnr. Long, Preston, Kinnaird & Avant, Detroit, 1972-87; ptnr. Dickinson, Wright, Moon, Van Dusen & Freeman, Detroit, 1988-94; sr. v.p. investment banking North Am. Capital Advisors, Inc., Bloomfield Hills, Mich., 1995-96; pvt. practice Grosse Pointe, Mich., 1996—2001, Birmingham, Ala., 2001—. Contbr. articles to legal jours. Served to lt. USMC, 1954-57. Mem. ABA (bus. law sect., fed. regulation of securities com.), State Bar of Mich. (coun. sect. antitrust law 1978-85, chmn. sect. 1983-84, bus. law sect.), Detroit Com. on Fgn. Rels. (exec. com. 1979—2001, chmn. 1986-88), Mountain Brook Club, Knickerbocker Club, Princeton Club of Mich. (pres. 1976-77, 94-95). Episcopalian. Home and Office: 13 Cross Creek Dr Birmingham AL 35213

AVANT, ROBERT FRANK, physician, educator; b. Chisholm, Minn., 1937; m. Betty Jensen, Dec. 28, 1962; children: Paul, Gregory, Todd. MD, U. Minn., 1963. Intern San Bernardino, Calif. County Hosp., 1963-64; chief of family practice Glenwood Hills Hosp., 1970-71, chief of staff, 1972; dir. family practice residency North Meml. Hosp., Mpls., 1973-77; asst. prof. dept. family practice and cmty. health U. Minn., 1973-77; chmn. dept. family medicine Mayo Clinic, Rochester, Minn., 1977-91, assoc. prof. family medicine, 1977-84; prof. family medicine Mayo Med. Sch., Rochester, 1984-93; Sanders prof. primary care Mayo Clinic, Rochester, 1986-93; chmn. dept. family medicine Mayo Clinic Jacksonville, 1991-93; dep. exec. dir. Am. Bd. Family Practice, Lexington, Ky., 1991-97, exec. dir., 1998—2002, sr. exec., 2003—. Capt. MC, USAF, 1964-66. Office: Am Bd Family Practice 2228 Young Dr Lexington KY 40505-4219

AVARD, JOSEPH L. mathematician, educator; b. Carleton, Okla. s. Joseph Samuel and Ada Irene Avard; children: Steven, Samuel, Nathan, Alan, Jamie. BS, Southeastern State Coll., 1961; MS, Okla. State U., 1965, EdD, 1967. Statis. analysis specialist Standard Oil of Jersey Rsch. Prodn. Lab., Tulsa, 1957—58; space flight rschr. Douglas Aircraft Corp., El Segundo, Calif., 1958—60; programming studies/rschr. Sys. Devel. Corp., Santa Monica, Calif., 1960—61; rschr. NASA, Boston, 1967—70; math. prof. N.E. La. U., Monroe, 1967—89; prof. math. So. Ark. U., Magnolia, 1989—, chmn. math. dept., 1989—93. Mem.: Soc. Indsl. and Applied Math. Avocation: flying airplanes. Home: 6003 Pleasant Ln Texarkana TX 75503 Office: So Ark U SAU Box 9357 Magnolia AR 71753

AVARD, STEPHEN LEWIS, finance educator; b. Chgo., Feb. 16, 1940; s. William Richard and Helen M. (Gundy) A.; m. Bonnie J. Fulford, Sept. 1, 1962; children: Margaret, Stephen Jr., Jean. BA, Northwestern U., 1961; MBA, Tex. A&M U., Commerce, 1976; PhD, U. North Tex., 1983. CFA, 1987. Asst. city mgr. City of Highland Park, Ill., 1961-64; treas., asst. hosp. adminstr. Sherman (Tex.) Cmty. Hosp., 1964-69; hosp. cons. and zone supr. Tex. State Dept. Health, Austin, 1969-71; real estate broker John King Realtors, Sherman, 1971-73; pres. Miracle Gardens of Tex., Sherman, 1973-79; sec., gen. mgr. Med. Mart, Inc., Sherman, 1979-83; prof. fin. Tex. A&M U., Commerce, 1983—, head dept. econs. and fin. dept., 1995—. Co-author (monographs): Feasibility Study for a Graduate Program in Health Care Administration, 1984, Accounting for the Non-Accounting Manager, 1984, Overview of the Petroleum Industry, 1983, 89, 98; contbr. articles to refereed profl. jours. and conf. procs., including Jour. Banking and Fin. (Top Six Best Articles, bd. editors Rsch. Mgmt. jour., 1983). Grad. fellow Gulf Oil, Inc., 1982. Mem.: Dallas Soc. Fin. Analysts, Fin. Execs. Inst. (mem. Dallas chpt. 1988—), Assn. Investment Mgmt. and Rsch. (cons. 1999), Rotary Internat. Avocation: sailing. Home: 1111 Western Hills Sherman TX 75092-5523 Office: Tex A&M U Econs-Finance Dept Commerce TX 75429 E-mail: steve_avard@tamu-commerce.edu.

AVARY, ROGER ROBERTS (FRANK BRAUNER), film director, producer, writer; b. Flin Flon, Manitoba, Canada, Aug. 23, 1965; s. Edwin Roberts and Brigitte (Bruninghaus) A. Student, Art Ctr., Pasadena, Calif., 1985-88. Writer D'Arcy, Masius, Benton & Bowles, L.A., 1989-90, J. Walter Thompson, L.A., 1990—. Writer: (film) 99 Days, 1991, (with Mario Puzo) The Lorch Team, 1992; writer, dir. (film): Killing Zoe, 1994 (Yubari Internat. Film Festival Best Film award, 1994, Mystfest Best Film award, 1994, Mystfest Critics prize, 1994, Cannes Prix Tres Spl. Best Film award, 1994), True Romance, 1993; exec. prodr. (film): The Last Man, 1999; writer, prodr., dir. (film): The Worm Turns, 1993, The Rules of Attraction (screenplay), 2002; co-exec. prodr. (film): Boogie Boy, 1997; co-writer (film): Pulp Fiction, 1994 (L.A. Film Critics Assn. Best Screenplay award, 1995, N.Y. Film Critics Cir. Best Screenplay award, 1995, Boston Soc. Film Critics Best Screenplay award, 1995, Nat. Soc. Film Critics Best Screenplay award, 1995, Chgo. Soc. Film Critics Best Screenplay award, 1995, BAFTA Best Screenplay award, 1995, Acad. award best screenplay 1995), Hatchetman, 1995, (children's book) Marshall's Dreams, 1991,

(music video) for the group The Go Go's song The Whole World Lost Its Head, 1994; writer, dir., prodr. (TV movie) Mr. Stitch, 1995, Odd Jobs, 1997; actor: Phantasm IV: Oblivion, 1998 Office: Creative Artists Agy Care Rob Paris 9830 Wilshire Blvd Beverly Hills CA 90212-1804*

AVDEEF, THOMAS, lawyer; b. NYC, Dec. 16, 1940; s. Alexis and Marie Ann Avdeef; m. Lucille Arlene Cardwell, May 8, 1965; children: Christine, Rachel, Andrea. AA, Orange Coast Coll., 1968; BA, Long Beach State U., 1971; JD, Am. Coll. Law, Anaheim, Calif., 1978. Bar: Calif. 1979, U.S. Dist. Ct. (ctrl. dist.). Calif. 1980, U.S. Dist. Ct. (so. dist.) Calif. 1994, U.S. Dist. Ct. (ea. dist.) Calif. 1995, U.S. Dist. Ct. (no. dist.) Calif. 2001, U.S. Supreme Ct. 1986. Officer Santa Ana (Calif.) Police Dept., 1964-69; investigator Orange County Dist. Atty. Office, Santa Ana, 1969-81, dep. dist. atty., 1981-91; pvt. practice Orange, 1991—. With USN, 1959-63. Mem. Am. Legion, Elks, Moose. Republican. Roman Catholic. Avocations: golf, fishing. Office: Law Offices of Thomas Avdeef 158 N Center St Orange CA 92866-1502

AVED, BARRY, retail executive, consultant; b. Mpls., Mar. 27, 1943; s. Alick Leonard and Marna Claire (Sandon) A.; m. Marlys Sandra Drentlaw, Sept. 3, 1961; children: Andrea Aved Stewart, Nicole Aved Badeau, Danielle, Rachelle. Grad. high sch., Mpls., 1961. Buyer Dayton Hudson Co., Mpls., 1963-72; v.p. Ltd. Stores, Columbus, Ohio, 1972-82; pres. Id, Inc., Green Bay, Wis., 1982-86; pres., CEO Brooks Fashion Stores, N.Y.C., 1986-89; pres. Ormond Stores, Inc., North Bergen, N.J., 1989-90; pres., CEO Lerner N.Y., N.Y.C., 1991-95; prin. Aved Cons., Lakeville, Minn., 1995-99, 2001—; pres. Tarrant Apparel Group, 1999-2000, Aved Cons., 2000—. Pres. Tarrant Apparel Group, 1999-2000. Avocations: swimming, fishing, reading.

AVEDISIAN, ARCHIE HARRY, community organization executive; b. Binghamton, N.Y., June 22, 1928; s. Harry and Charlotte (Charkjian) A.; m. Gloria Ann Rogers; children: Debra Ann, Anthony Joseph. BS in Edn., SUNY, Cortland, 1951; MA in Orgn. and Adminstrn., NYU, 1954, postgrad. Phys. dir. Jamestown Boys Club, N.Y.C., 1951-53; program dir. Flatbush Boys Club, Bklyn., 1953-56; exec. dir. Boys Clubs of East St. Louis, Ill., 1956-59, Columbia Park Boys Club, San Francisco, 1959-60, Santa Rosa Boys Clubs, Calif., 1960-67, Boys Clubs of Seattle and King County, 1967-72; pres., CEO Boys and Girls Clubs of Greater Washington, D.C., 1972-95, Archie Avedisian & Co., Montgomery Village, Md., 1998—; mem. rels. specialist Washington Area New Automobile Dealers Assn., 2001—. Cons. Boys Clubs of Am. tng. program, 1974-75; tchr. Montgomery Coll., 1998-2000; mem. rels. specialist Washington Area New Automobile Assn., 2001—. Chmn. Seattle-King County Youth Commn., 1967-72, Congress for Community Programs, Santa Rosa, 1964, Calif. Youth Authority Sch. for Girls, 1961-66; United Way of Am., Washington, San Francisco, East St. Louis, Seattle, 1957—; bd. govs. Congress for Community Progress, East St. Louis, 1958; active President's Commn. on White House Fellowships, 1993, D.C. Bar Assn. Anti-Drug Coalition, 1993, Inst. of Internat. Edn. Met. Washington Consortium on Alcohol and Drug Abuse, 1992, Nat. Partnership Alcohol and Drug Abuse, 1986—, Greater Washington Billy Graham Crusade Adv. Com., 1986, Met. Washington Bd. Trade, 1973—, Montgomery County Employment Devel. Commn., 1978-82, Sonoma County Community Action Council, 1969, Govs. Conf. on Youth, Sonoma County, 1965, Gen. Plan Program, Santa Rosa, 1964. Recipient Disting. Svc. award Jr. C. of C., 1958, various gov. commd. awards, 1970-73, various United Way Am. awards, 1974-79, H. Roe Bartle Am. Humanities Recruiting award, 1979, Cmty. Svc. award Sales and Mktg. Execs. of Met. Washington, 1985, Chmns. award Greater Washington Soc. Assn. Execs., 1986, Cmty. Leadership award FBI Dirs., 1990, Alumni award SUNY, Golden Links award Bd. of Trade, Disting. Alumni award SUNY, Cortland; named one of Outstanding Young Men Am., 1965; named Outstanding Young Man of Yr., East St. Louis, 1958, Businessman of Day, Santa Rosa, 1967; presented key to San Francisco, 1959; Archie and Gloria Avedisian Ednl. Scholarship Fund established in his name, Boys and Girls Clubs. Mem. NAACP, Boys Clubs Profl. Assn. (numerous local and nat. offices 1953—), Boys Clubs Am. (numerous local and nat. offices 1951—), Nat. Soc. Fund Raisers (mem. membership com.), Greater Washington Soc. Assn. Execs. (chmn. various coms.), Am. Soc. Assn. Execs., Internat. Platform Assn., Ctr. for Devel. and Population Activities, Inst. Internat. Edn., D.C. C. of C. (various com. memberships, mem. bd. dirs. 1985—), Upper Montgomery County C. of C., 1986—, Jr. League of Washington Community (mem. adv. bd. 1991—). Clubs: Washington, D.C. Touchdown, Montgomery Village Golf (Gaithersburg, Md.), Tam O'Shanter Country (Bellevue, Wash.). Lodges: Rotary (pres.-elect, pres.), Elks, Lions. Republican. Roman Catholic. Home and Office: 9832 Meadowcroft Ln Montgomery Village MD 20886-1337

AVEDON, RICHARD, photographer; b. N.Y.C., May 15, 1923; s. Jack and Anna (Polonsky) A.; m. Dorcas Nowell, 1944; m. Evelyn Franklin, Jan. 29, 1951; 1 child, John. Student, Columbia U., 1941-42; studied with Alexey Brodovitch, Design Lab. New Sch. for Social Rsch., N.Y.C., 1944-50; DSc (hon.), Royal Coll. Art, London, 1989, Parsons Sch. Design, N.Y.C., 1994, Kenyon Coll. Staff photographer Jr. Bazaar, 1945-47, Harper's Bazaar, 1945-65; photographer French collections, 1947-84; staff photographer, editor Theatre Arts, 1952-53; staff photographer Vogue mag., 1966-90; first staff photographer The New Yorker, 1992—. Visual cons. for film: Funny Face, Paramount Studios, 1957; conducted master class in photog. (with Marvin Irael), Avedon studio, 1967 Author: (comments by Truman Capote) Observations, 1959, (text by James Baldwin) Nothing Personal, 1964, (intro. by Harold Rosenberg) Portraits, 1976, (essay by Harold Brodkey) Avedon Photographs, 1947-1977, 1978, In the American West, 1985, The Sixties, 1999, Made in France, 2001; author spl. bicentennial edit. Rolling Stone mag. The Family, 1976; editor: Diary of a Century (photographs by Jacques Henri Lartigue), 1970, (with Doon Arbus) Alice in Wonderland: The Forming of a Company, The Making of a Play, 1973, An Autobiography, 1993, (essays by Jane Livingston, Adam Gophik) Evidence: 1944-94, 1994; photographs in permanent collections: Smithsonian Instn., Met. Mus. Art, N.Y.C., Mus. Modern Art, N.Y.C., Amon Carter Mus., Fort Worth, San Francisco Mus. Modern Art, Mus. Fine Arts, Houston, Victoria and Albert Mus., London, Nat. Portrait Gallery, Washington, Nat. Portrait Gallery, London, Ctr. for Creative Photography U. Ariz., Tucson, Kunstaus Zurich, Switzerland, Kunstaus, Basel, Switzerland, Andreas Reinhart Found., Winterthur, Switzerland; one-man retrospective exhbn. Smithsonian Instn., Washington, 1962, Mpls. Inst. Arts, 1970, Univ. Art Mus., Berkeley, Calif., 1980, Whitney Mus. Am. Art, 1994; one-man shows: Mus. Modern Art, 1974, Marlborough Gallery, 1975, Met. Mus. Art, N.Y.C., 1978, Amon Carter Mus., 1985, Corcoran Gallery of Art, Washington, DC, San Francisco Mus. Modern Art, Art Inst. Chgo., Phoenix Art Mus., Inst. Contemporary Art, Boston, The High Museum, Atlanta, 1985, Installation Brandenburg Gate, Carnegie Mus. of Art, Pitts., 1991; group shows include: Mus. Modern Art, 1955, Met. Mus. Art, 1959, 60, 63, 67, Musée Réattu, Arles, France, 1965, N.Y. World's Fair, 1965-66, Fogg Art Mus., Cambridge, Mass., 1967, Mus. Modern Art, N.Y.C., 1964, 65, 69, Expo '70, Osaka, Japan, 1970, Whitney Mus. Am. Art, 1974, Corcoran Gallery Art, Washington, 1985, Nat. Gallery Art, Washington, 1989; photographed civil rights movement in the South, 1963, anti-war movement across U.S., 1969, Vietnam, 1971, Am. Working Class, 1978-84; exhibitions: In the American West, Kunstmuseum Wolfsburg, Germany, 2001, Made in France, Fraenkel Gallery, San Francisco, Calif., 2001, The Metropolitan Mus. Art, N.Y.C., 2002-. With USMC, 1942-44. Recipient highest achievement medal awards Art Dirs. Show, 1950—; voted one of world's ten greatest photographers Popular Photography, 1958; citation of dedication to fashion photography Pratt Inst., 1976; Nat. Mag. award Visual Excellence, 1976; Pres.'s fellow RISD, 1978; Chancellor's citation U. Calif., Berkeley, 1980; named to Hall of Fame Art Dirs. Club, 1982; Photographer of Yr., Am. Soc. Mag. Photographers, 1985; Best Photog. Book of Yr. award Maine Photog. Workshop, 1985; Dir. of Yr., Adweek mag., 1985; Comml. Dir. of Yr. award of excellence Eastman Kodak, 1985; Lifetime Achievement award Coun. Fashion Designers Am., 1989; Internat. Photography prize Erna and Victor Hasselblad Found., 1991; Master of Photography award Internat. Ctr. Photography, 1993, Prix Nadar Bibliotheque Nationale, 1994, Humanitarian award Mental Health Assn., N.Y.C., 1996, Lifetime Achievement award Columbia U. Grad. Sch. of Journalism, 2000, Berlin Photography prize Deutsches Centrum for Photography, 2000, inducted into The Am. Acad. of Arts and Sci., 2001. Office: Richard Avedon Studio 407 E 75th St New York NY 10021-3102 Fax: 212-327-4340., 212-439-0793.

AVELLA, JOHN THOMAS, educational administrator; b. Passaic, N.J., June 23, 1957; s. John T. and Margaret Louise (Watson) Avella; m. Jane Marie Myers; children: Katelyn Mary, Shaylyn Clare. BS in Spl. Edn., Trenton State Coll., 1981; MA in Ednl. Adminstrn., Georgian Ct. Coll., 1986; EdD, Nova Southeastern U., 1999. Tchr. Lacey Twp. (N.J.) Bd. Edn., 1982-88; supr. Union City Edn. Svcs. Commn., Westfield, N.J., 1988-89; prin., asst. supt. Monmouth Ocean Edn. Svcs. Commn., Freehold, N.J., 1989—. Mem. Nat. Assn. Sch. Adminstrs. Avocations: sports, music. Office: 100 Tornillo Way Ste 1 Asbury Park NJ 07712-7520

AVELLA, JOSEPH RALPH, university executive; b. N.Y.C., Nov. 13, 1942; s. Salvatore Ralph and Bianca (Artoni) A.; m. Elizabeth Theresa Eberhardt, Aug. 12, 1967 (div. May 1991); children: Edward Jay, James Joseph. BS in Chemistry, Rensselaer Poly. Inst., 1964; MA, Cath. U. Am., 1992, PhD, 1995; MBA, Capella U., 2001. Mgr. Md. ops. The Great Atlantic and Pacific Tea Co., Inc., 1978-83; program mgr. Honeywell Fed. Sys., Inc., McLean, Va., 1984-86, mgr. integration svcs., 1987-89; dep. dir. mobilization Office of Sec. Def., Washington, 1990-92, dir. internat. programs, 1992-93; sr. fellow global strategy program Potomac Found., McLean, 1995-98; prof. and acad. dean Am. Mil. U., Manassas, Va., 1995-98. Cons. Masi Rsch. Cons., Inc., Washington, 1995-97; exec. sec. NATO Forces Com., Brussels, Belgium, 1992-94; seminar moderator U.S. Naval War Coll., Newport, R.I., 1989-91; pres. Delphic Consulting Inc., 1998; exec. v.p. Capella U., 1998—. Contbr. articles to profl. jours. With USNR, 1970-95. Recipient Achievement award No. Va. Navy League, 1989, Cert. of Appreciation Sec. of Navy, 1986, 88, Award of Appreciation U.S. Naval Sea Cadet Corps, 1986. Mem. Am. Polit. Sci. Assn., Ctr. for Study of Presidency (contbg. author), U.S. Strategic Inst., Assn. Naval Aviation (past chpt. sec.), Navy League of U.S. (former mem. bd. dirs.), U.S. Naval Inst. (contbg. author), Pi Sigma Alpha. Office: Capella Univ 222 S 9th St 20th Fl Minneapolis MN 55402 Home: 313 Pine Glen Way Englewood FL 34223 E-mail: javella@aol.com.

AVENDAÑO, FAUSTO, language educator, writer; b. Culiacan, Mex., June 5, 1941; s. Alfonso Diaz and Maria Luisa Avendaño; m. Evelia Salas, June 23, 1968 (div. Aug. 1994); children: Nadia, Sofia, Laura; m. Jocelyn Alivio, Apr. 23, 1999; 1 child, Adrian. BA, Calif. State U., San Diego, 1967; MA, U. Ariz., 1969, PhD, 1973. Prof. Spanish, Portuguese and French Calif. State U., Sacramento, 1973—. Translator Profl. Translators, Sacramento, 1974—; dir. overseas programs Calif. State U., Sacramento; editor Internat. Jour. Hispanic Lit. Explicacion de Textos Literarios. Author: El Sueño de Siempre, 1996 (Fuentes Mares award, 1995), Salazar's Gold, 2000. Served U.S. Army, 1963—65, Hawaii. Grantee Gulbenkian Found., Lisbon, Portugal, 1975; Fulbright fellow, Toulouse, France, 1983, Ford Found. fellow, 1971—72. Mem.: Escritores del Nuevo Sol. Avocation: travel. Office: Calif State U Dept Fgn Langs 6000 J St Sacramento CA 95831

AVENDANO, GARY FIDEL, cardiologist, internist; b. Butte, Mont., Sept. 19, 1960; s. Graciano Calderon and Trifonia Valenzuela Avendaño; m. Beverly Gorosin Cornel-Avendano; 1 child, John Andrew Philippe. BS, U. Santo Tomas, Manila, the Philippines, 1979; MD, U. Santo Tomas, 1983. Diplomate Am. Bd. Internal Medicine, Am. Bd. Internal Medicine with subspecialty in cardiovascular diseases. Postdoctoral rsch. fellow Emory U. Sch. Medicine, Atlanta, 1988—90; resident in internal medicine U. Medicine and Dentistry of N.J., Newark, 1990—93, fellow in cardiology, 1993—96; fellow in interventional cardiology Newark-Beth Israel Med. Ctr., 1996—97; sr. ptnr. Cardiovascular Interventionalists of Ctrl. Jersey, East Brunswick, 2001—. Capt. USAR, 1985. Recipient Nat. Rsch. Svc. award, NIH, 1988—90. Mem.: Am. Coll. Cardiology. Roman Catholic. Home: 22 Deputy Minister Dr Colts Neck NJ 07722 Office: Cardiovascular Interventionalists Ctrl Jersey 575 Cranbury Rd East Brunswick NJ 08816 E-mail: gavendano@pol.net.

AVENI, ANTHONY JOSEPH, lawyer, educator; b. Cleve., Aug. 1, 1938; s. Vincent James and Antoinette Elizabeth (Finelli) A.; m. Marie-Terese Sweeney, Aug. 22, 1964; children: Karen Marie, James Vincent, Laura Ann. BSCE, U. Notre Dame, 1961; MSCE, Stanford U., 1962; JD, Cleve.-Marshall Law Sch., 1966. Bar: Ohio 1966, U.S. Dist. Ct. (no. dist.) Ohio 1969. Ptnr. Sweeney & Aveni, Painesville, Ohio, 1966-75; assoc. Milburn, Cannon, Stern & Aveni, Painesville, Ohio, 1975-80; ptnr. Cannon, Stern, Aveni & Loiacono, Co. LPA, Painesville, Ohio, 1980—. Instr. real estate law Lakeland C.C., Mentor, Ohio, 1970—; lectr. in field. Mcpl. law dir. City of Eastlake, 1975, City of Mentor-on-the-Lake, 1983-88; asst. law dir. City of Willowick, 2000—; bd. atty. Lake County Assn. Realtors, mentor, 1982—; bd. dirs. Western Res. Counseling Svc., Painesville, 1968—; chmn., prof. div. United Way Lake County, 1978; county chmn. March of Dimes, Cleve., 1973. Mem.: Ohio State Bar Assn. (bd. govs. real property sect.), Lake County Bar Assn. (chmn. real property com., pres. 1995—96), Madison Country Club, Gyro-We. Res. Club (pres. Painesville chpt. 1973—74), K.C. Roman Catholic. Avocations: golf, fishing. Office: Cannon Stern Aveni & Loiacono LPA 41 E Erie St Painesville OH 44077-3947 E-mail: aaveni@csalawgroup.com.

AVENIA, RONALD JOSEPH, ophthalmologist; b. Bklyn., July 30, 1950; s. Joseph Vincent and Jeanette Mary (Racinski). BA, NYU, 1971; MD, Georgetown U., 1975. Diplomate Am. Bd. Ophthalmology. Pvt. practice Bloomsburg (Pa.) Hosp., 1979—. Fellow Am. Acad. Ophthalmology (Physicians Recognition award 1982-98); mem. AMA, Pa. Med. Soc. (Excellence award 1999-02), Columbia County Med. Soc., Antiques and Collectibles Dealer Assn. Avocations: photography, scuba diving, antiques. Office: 410 Glen Ave Ste 302 Bloomsburg PA 17815-1200 E-mail: rjavenia@aol.com.

AVENT, CHARLES KIRK, medical educator; b. Memphis, Oct. 27, 1939; s. C. Harold and Emily Schoolfield (Wallace) A.; m. Rosalie Phillips Adams, Aug. 16, 1962 (div. Mar. 1981); children: Emily Wallace, Mary Adams Avent Mezera; m. Nancee Ruth Neel, Dec. 17, 1983; 1 child, Clayton B. Neel. BA, Vanderbilt U., 1961; MD, Harvard Med. Sch., 1965. Diplomate Am. Bd. Internal Medicine. Resident in medicine Univ. Hosp., Birmingham, 1965-68; fellow in infectious disease U. Washington, Seattle, 1968-70; from instr. medicine to prof. U. Ala. Sch. Medicine, Birmingham, 1970—2002, prof. medicine emeritus, 2002—; med. dir. of disease control Jefferson County Dept. of Health, Birmingham, Ala., 2003—. Dir. med. clerkships U. Ala. Sch. Medicine, Birmingham, 1981-2002, title IX coord., 1976-78. Author: Medicine for Mountaineering, 1992. Mem. Am. Coll. Physicians, Infectious Disease Soc. Am., Phi Beta Kappa, Alpha Omega Alpha. Office: Jefferson Co Dept Health Box 2648 Birmingham AL 35202-2648

AVENT, RAYMOND RICHARD, JR., civil engineering educator; b. Newport News, Va., Nov. 16, 1941; s. Goley Marlette and Raymond Richard A.; m. Sandra Kay French, Feb. 1, 1962; children: Raymond III, Mark, Courtney Rahm. BSCE, N.C. State U., 1965, MSCE, 1968, PhD, 1969. Asst. prof. Ga. Inst. Tech., Atlanta, 1969-75; assoc. prof. Miss. State U., Starkville, 1975-82; prof. La. State U., Baton Rouge, 1982—, chmn. dept. civil & environ. engring., 1990-98. Pres. Structural Damage Control, Inc., Baton Rouge, 1991—. Author: Heat-Straightening Repair of Damaged Steel Bridges, 1998; contbr. articles to profl. jours. Fellow Am. Soc. Civil Engring.; mem. Am. Concrete Inst., Am. Soc. Engring. Edn. Avocations: skiing, basketball, golf, tennis. Home: 13524 Mary Edith Pl Baton Rouge LA 70809 Office: La State U Dept Civil & Environ Engr Baton Rouge LA 70803 Fax: 225-578-8652. E-mail: ceaven@eng.lsu.edu.

AVENT, SHARON L. HOFFMAN, manufacturing company executive; b. St. Paul, Feb. 7, 1946; Student, Hamline u., St. Paul. With Smead Mfg. Co., Hastings, Minn., 1965—, pres., CEO, 1998—. Office: Smead Mfg Co 600 Smead Blvd Hastings MN 55033-2219

AVERBACH, DAVID JOEL, surgeon; b. Paterson, N.J., 1935; AB, U. Pa., 1957, MD, 1961. Diplomate Am. Bd. Surgery. Intern Monmouth Med. Ctr., Long Branch, N.J., 1961-62, resident in surgery, 1962-66; pvt. practice Atlantic Surgical Group, 1968—. Mem. staff Monmouth Med. Ctr., Long Branch; assoc. attending physician Jersey Shore Med. Ctr., Neptune; assoc. clin. prof. Hahnemann U., Phila. With U.S. Army, 1966-68, Vietnam. Mem. ACS, AMA, Monmouth County Med. Soc. Office: Atlantic Surg Group PA 255 Monmouth Rd Oakhurst NJ 07755 E-mail: daverbach@msn.com.

AVERBUCH, MARK STEPHEN, internist; b. Nashville, Sept. 16, 1948; s. Gerald and Blossom (Davis) A.; m. Shelley Elizabeth Snyder, June 6, 1981; children: Jared, Cutler. Student, Emory U., 1966-69; MD, Tulane U., 1973. Diplomate Am. Bd. Internal Medicine. Intern in internal medicine Vanderbilt U., Nashville, 1973-74, resident in internal medicine, 1974-76; pvt. practice Nashville, 1976—2001; assoc. clin. prof. medicine Vanderbilt U. Sch. Medicine, 2001—. Former mem. physicians adv. bd. Blue Cross, Chattanooga; cons. in field. Former trustee Ensworth Sch., Nashville, 1989-92. Fellow ACP; mem. Tenn. Med. Assn., Nashville Acad. Medicine. Avocations: snow skiing, fishing, golf. Office: 5606 Brookwood Pl Nashville TN 37205-1472 E-mail: doctormod@aol.com.

AVERCH, HARVEY ALLAN, economist, educator, academic administrator; b. Denver, Dec. 18, 1935; s. Louis and Gussie (Weiner) A.; m. Barbara Ann Duvall, July 5, 1962; children: Elizabeth, Caroline. AB. summa cum laude (Univ. scholar), U.Colo., 1957; PhD (Univ. fellow, Ford Found. fellow), U. N.C., 1962. Sr. staff economist Rand Corp., Santa Monica, Calif., 1961-71; dir. Div. Social Systems and Human Resources, Research Applications Directorate, NSF, Washington, 1971-74, dep. asst. dir. for analysis and planning, 1974-75, acting asst. dir. for sci. edn., 1975-76, asst. dir. for sci. edn., 1976-77, asst. dir. sci., technol. and internat. affairs, 1977-82, sr. staff assoc. Office of Dir., 1985-89; prof. pub. adminstrn., acting dir. Fla. Internat. U., 1989-90, prof., dir., 1990-94, prof., 1994—. Mem. faculty UCLA, 1963-64, Calif. Inst. Tech., 1967, Rand Grad. Inst., 1970-71; vis. prof. policy scis. and econs. U. Md.-Baltimore County, 1982-85, adj. prof. policy scis. and econs., 1985—. Author: Behavior of the Firm Subject to Regulatory Constraint, 1962, Asymmetry and Arms Control: Some Basic Considerations, 1963, (with M. Lavin) Simulation of Decision-Making in Crisis: Three Manual Gaming Experiments, 1964, (with F. Denton and J. Koehler) A Crisis of Ambiguity: Political and Economic Development in the Philippines, 1970, The Matrix of Policy in the Philippines, 1971, (with others) How Effective is Schooling: A Critical Review and Synthesis of Research Findings, 1972, How Effective is Schooling: A Critical Review of Research, 1974, A Strategic Analysis of Science and Technology Policy, 1985, Applied Social Science, Policy Science, and The Federal Government, 1987, Measuring The Cost-Efficiency of Basic Research Investments, 1987, Exploring the Cost-Efficiency of Basic Research Funding in Chemistry, 1989, Policy Research for the University Research System, 1989, Private Markets and Public Interventions, 1990, The Political Economy of R&D Taxonomies, 1991, Practice of Research Evaluation in the United States, 1991, Evaluation of Projects and Portfolios, 1992, Systematic Use of Expert Judgment, 1994, Evaluation of Urban Model, 1997, The Rhetoric of War: Language, Argument and Policy During the Vietnam War, 2002; chief co-editor Policy Studies Rev., 1990—; contbr. articles to profl. jours. Chmn. U.S./Israel Binat. Sci. Found., 1979. Recipient Meritorious Service award NSF, 1973, Disting. Service award, 1977 Mem. Phi Beta Kappa. Office: Fla Internat U Sch Policy & Mgmt PCA 362C Miami FL 33199 E-mail: averchh@fiu.edu., averchh@bellsouth.net.

AVERILL, BRUCE ALAN, chemistry educator; b. Bucyrus, Ohio, May 19, 1948; s. Kenneth L. Averill and Mildred (Reid) Krug; m. Patricia Ann Eldredge, Aug. 23, 1986; children: Lindsay Patricia, Alan Eldredge, Ryan Eldredge. BS, Mich. State U., 1969; PhD, MIT, 1973. Asst. prof. chemistry Mich. State U., East Lansing, 1976-81, assoc. prof. chemistry, 1981-82, U. Va., Charlottesville, 1982-88, prof. chemistry, 1988-94; prof. biochemistry U. of Amsterdam, 1994-2001; disting. univ. prof. chemistry U. Toledo, 2001—. Mem. biophysics adv. panel NSF, Washington, 1985-88; mem. faculty forum for sci. rsch. U. Va., Charlottesville, 1984-88; group leader protein rsch. and coord. chemistry working parties Dutch Found. Chem. Rsch., 1995-2001, mem. exec. com. protein rsch. working party, 1996-99. Acquisitions editor ChemTracts-Inorganic Chemistry, 2002—; contbr. more than 140 articles to sci. jours. A.P. Sloan fellow, 1981-83; recipient creativity award NSF, 1991. Mem. AAAS, Am. Soc. Biochemistry and Molecular Biology, Am. Chem. Soc., Royal Soc. Chemistry, Soc. Biol. Inorganic Chemistry, Sigma Xi. Office: U Toledo Dept Chemistry 2801 W Bancroft Rd Toledo OH 43606-3390 E-mail: baa@utoledo.edu.

AVERILL, ELLEN CORBETT, secondary education science educator, administrator; b. Milledgeville, Ga. d. Felton Conrad and Vivian Iris (Brookins) Corbett; m. George Edmund Averill, July 31, 1971; 1 child, John Conrad. BS, U. Ga., 1966, MS, 1971; teaching cert., Columbus Coll., 1979, EdS, 1994. Grad. teaching asst. U. Ga., Athens, 1966-68; tchr. sci. Decatur (Ga.) City Schs., 1971-72; tchr. sci., chair dept. Kendrick High Sch., Columbus, Ga., 1980—. Rsch. asst. Caretta Rsch. Project, Savannah (Ga.) Sci. Mus., 1985, NEWMAST, Kennedy Space Ctr., 1986; rsch. assoc. Inhalation Toxicology Rsch. Inst., Albuquerque, summer, 1990; instr. sci. Gov.'s Honor Program Valdosta State Coll., summer, 1991, Woodrow Wilson Biotechnology Inst., Princeton, N.J., 1993. Contbr. articles to newspapers, jours.; inventor The Wrap-All, 1992. Mem. Nat. Sci. Tchrs. Assn. (program com., regional conf. 1993), Nat. Assn. Biology Tchrs. (Outstanding Biology Tchr. 1990-91), Ga. Sci. Tchrs. Assn. (dist. VI rep. 1988-90, secondary rep. 1990-91, pres.-elect 1991-92, pres. 1992-93, conf. coord. ann. conf. 1992, Dist. VI Sci. Tchr. of Yr. 1995), Coalition for Excellence in Sci. Edn. (orgnl. com. 1992-93), Ga. Sci. Tchrs. Edn. Found. (chair 1994-98), Valley Area Sci. Tchrs. (charter, pres.-elect 1996-97, pres. 1997-98), Muscogee Area Literacy Assn. (treas. 1992-93), Phi Delta Kappa (PDK Tchr. of Yr. 1992, v.p. 2002-), Delta Kappa Gamma Edn. Soc. Unitarian-Universalist. Avocations: procelain art, gardening, amateur radio operator. Home: 126 Waterway Dr Cataula GA 31804-4407 Office: Kendrick High Sch 6015 Georgetown Dr Columbus GA 31907-4698 E-mail: eaverill@ldl.net.

AVERILL, JAMES REED, psychology educator; b. San Francisco, Nov. 29, 1935; s. Dupree Reed and Rosalie (Diamond) Averill. BA, San Jose U., 1959; PhD, UCLA, 1966. Psychologist U. Calif.-Berkeley, 1966-71; mem. faculty U. Mass., Amherst, 1971—, prof. psychology, 1976—. Served with U.S. Army, 1954-57. Fulbright fellow W. Germany, 1959-60 Mem. APA, Am. Psychol. Soc., Internat. Soc. for Rsch. on Emotion. Office: U Mass Dept Psychology Amherst MA 01003

AVERILL, THOMAS FOX, writer, educator; b. Berkeley, Calif., Apr. 30, 1949; s. Stuart Carson and Elizabeth (Walter) A.; m. Jeffrey Ann Goudie, Jan. 31, 1974; children: Eleanor Goudie-Averill, Alexander Goudie-Averill. BA, U. Kans., 1971, MA, 1974; MFA, U. Iowa, 1976. Prof. English, writer-in-residence Washburn U., Topeka, 1980—. Mem. editl. bd. Kans. State Hist. Soc., Topeka, 1990—, Ctr. Gt. Plains Studies, Emporia, 1992—. Author (short stories) Passes at the Moon, 1985 (Coffin award 1985), Seeing Mona Naked, 1989 (Smith award 1991), (edited essays) What Kansas Means to Me, 1990, (novels) Secrets of the Tsil Café, 2001, The Slow Air of Ewan MacPherson, 2003. Radio commentator Sta. KANU, Lawrence, 1991—. Recipient Roberts Writing award Roberts Found., 1989, O. Henry award Anchor Doubleday, 1991, Humanities Horizon award Kans. Humanities Coun., 1992, Gov.'s Arts award Kans. Arts Commn., 1993. Fellow Ctr. for Kans. Studies; mem. Associated Writing Programs. Democrat. Avocations: gardening, bagpiping, cooking. Home: 322 SW Greenwood Ave Topeka KS 66606 Office: Washburn U English Dept Topeka KS 66621

AVERS, CARL DENNISON, computer engineer; b. Keyser, W.Va., Feb. 3, 1942; s. Carl Edward and Sarah (Dennison) A.; m. Mary Anne (Nancy) Konski, May 9, 1981. BSEE, W.Va. U., 1964, MSEE, 1965. Registered profl. engr. W.Va. Staff engr. IBM FSD, Gaithersburg, Md., 1965-75, sr. engring. mgr. Gaithersburg, Md., Manassas, Va., 1976-84; dir. planning IBM Fed. Systems Co., Gaithersburg, 1984-86, mgr. image sys. devel., 1987-90, mgr. internat. programs Bethesda, Md., 1990-93, dir. W.Va. programs, 1993-95, Loral/Lockheed-Martin, Bethesda, 1995-96; consulting engr. Palmyra, Va., 1996—. Mem. Engring. Accreditation Commn., Balt., 1995-2000. Bd. dirs. W.Va. Spl. Olympics, Parkersburg, 1993-98; mem., past chair bd. visitors W.Va. U. Coll. Engring., Morgantown, 1988—; v.p. bd. advisors Potomac State Coll., Keyser, W.Va., 2000—; pres./CFO Potomac Highlands Symphony Orch., Keyser, 1998—. Named Inaugural Mem. Elec. & Computer Engring. Acad. Disting. Alumni, W.Va. U., 1989; named to Legion of Honor, Edward Kelley Soc., 1990; named Disting. West Virginian, Gov. W.Va., 1996; recipient Alumni Achievement award Potomac State Coll., 1998. Fellow IEEE (sr., tng. coord. com. engring. accreditation 1992—, Disting. Svc. award 2001), Accreditation Bd. for Engring. and Tech.; mem. Am. Radio Relay League (life), Quarter Century Wireless Assn. (life), W.Va. U. Alumni Assn. (life, pres. Nat. Capital Area chpt. 1999-2001), Mineral County C. of C., Golden Horseshoe Soc.

(founder, exec. dir. 1996—), Rotary (Keyser bd. dirs.), Tau Beta Pi, Eta Kappa Nu. Lutheran. Achievements include inventor of signal insertion and conferencing in a resonant transfer integrated time division switching and frequency division multiplexing communication system. Home and Office: 7 Lakeview Cir Palmyra VA 22963 E-mail: denny@avers.net.

AVERSA, DOLORES SEJDA, educational administrator; b. Phila., Mar. 26, 1932; d. Martin Benjamin and Mary Elizabeth (Esposito) Sejda; m. Zefferino A. Aversa Jr., May 3, 1958; children: Dolores Elizabeth, Jeffrey Martin, Linda Maria. BA, Chestnut Hill Coll., 1953. Owner Personal Rep. & Pub. Rels., Phila., 1965-68; ednl. cons. Franklin Sch. Sci. and Arts, Phila., 1968-72; pres., owner, dir. Martin Sch. Bus., Inc., Phila., 1972—. File reader, cons. for ct. reporting and travel tng. Southwestern Pub. Co., 1990; mem. ednl. planning com. Ravenhill Acad., Phila., 1975-76. Active Phila. Mus. ARt, Phila. Drama Guild; mem. Met. Opera Guild, 2002, 8th Ward Rep. Exec. Com. Mem.: Lower Bucks County C. of C., Am. Soc. Travel Agts. (sch. divsn., nat. educators com., sec. Del. chpt., edn. chmn., PAC chmn. 1997—), Hist. Soc. Pa., World Affairs Coun. Phila., Phila. Hist. Soc., Pa. Sch. Counselors Assn., Am. Bus. Law Assn., Pa. Bus. Edn. Assn., Nat. Bus. Edn. Assn., Andrea Doria Survivor Assn., Chestnut Hill Coll. Alumnae Assn. (sec. class '53), Phila. Orch., Am.-Italy Soc., Met. Opera Guild, Stone Harbor Golf Club. Roman Catholic. Home: 2111 Locust St Philadelphia PA 19103-4802 Office: 2417 Welsh Rd Philadelphia PA 19114-2213 E-mail: msb-aversa@erols.com.

AVERY, BRUCE EDWARD, lawyer; b. Boonville, N.Y., Aug. 16, 1949; s. Edward Cecil and Marian Alma (Pierce) A.; m. Margaret Calvert, June 21, 1969; children: Sarah, Prudence. BA in Sociology, Polit. Sci., Hobart Coll., 1971; JD, U. Louisville, 1976. Bar: Ky. 1976, U.S. Ct. Mil. Appeals 1977, U.S. Army Ct. Mil. Rev. 1984, U.S. Supreme Ct. 1984, Md. 1992, D.C., 1993, U.S. Ct. Vet. Appeals 1992, U.S. Dist. Ct. Md. 1993. Commd. capt. U.S. Army, 1976, advanced through grades to maj., 1983; rschr. U.S. Army Rsch. Inst., Ft. Knox, Ky., 1972-76, atty., 1976-77, U.S. Army, Camp Zama, Japan, 1977-80, U.S. Army Recruiting, Ft. Meade, Md., 1980-83, U.S. Army Claims Svc., Ft. Meade, 1984-87, U.S. Armed Forces Claims Svc., Seoul, Korea, 1987-89; chief claims V Corps, Frankfort, Germany, 1989-91; pvt. practice Rockville, Md., 1991—. Mem. Ft. Knox Bd. Edn., Ky., 1975-76. Mem. ABA, ATLA, FBA, D.C. Bar, Md. State Bar, Ky. Bar Assn. Office: 51 Monroe St Ste 1509 Rockville MD 20850-2414 E-mail: bavery@compuserve.com.

AVERY, DONALD HILLS, metallurgist, educator, ethnographer; b. Hartford, Conn., May 7, 1937; s. Charles Raymond and Loma Ellinor (Mulholland) A.; m. Marianna Pinchot, Dec. 3, 1994; children: Jon Weymouth, Nathaniel Caleb, Jessica van Voast. Student, Loomis Inst., 1951-55; BS, MIT, 1959, ScD, 1962; MA, Brown U., 1969. Lic. profl. engr.; lic. pvt. dectective. Pres. Strathmore Research Co., Cambridge, Mass., 1961-69; dir. research Armor Flite Group, Rangely, Maine, 1973-83; pres. A.T.S. Cons. Engrs., 1980—; dir. A.P.C. Engrs., East Providence, R.I., 1977-82; asst. prof. M.I.T., 1962-66, Brown U., 1966-69, asso. prof., 1969-74, prof. engring., 1974-97, prof. emeritus, 1997—. Vis. scholar, prof. U. Capetown, 1974, 76, 79, 82, 83; vis. fellow Yale U. Sch. Forestry, New Haven, 1995; vis. prof. Wharton Sch. U. Pa., 1999-01. Contbr. articles to profl. jours.; patentee in field. NSF fellow, 1959-62; Ford fellow, 1965; rsch. scholar Tanzania, 1976, 79; rsch. scholar Malawi, 1982, 83 Mem. AIME (Metall. Soc.), AAAS, AAU, Am. Soc. Metals (past chmn. R.I., Howe medal 1965), Soc. Plastics Engrs., Soc. Automotive Engrs., Hist. Metall. Soc., History Sci. Soc., Soc. History Tech., Hope Club, Explorers Club, Athenaeum, Barrington Yacht Club, Kasungu Farmers. Home: 142 Toandos Rd Quilcene WA 98376-9687 Office: Brown U Div Engring Providence RI 02912-0001

AVERY, JAMES STEPHEN, oil company executive; b. Cranford, N.J., Mar. 24, 1923; s. John Henry and Martha Ann (Jones) A.; m. Joan Avery; children: Sheryl Ann, James Stephen. BA, Columbia U., 1948, MA, 1949. Pub. relations rep. Esso Standard Oil Co. (named changed to Exxon Co. U.S.A.), N.Y.C., 1956-63; coordinator community relations Humble Oil and Refining Co. (named changed to Exxon Co. U.S.A.), N.Y.C., 1963-68; mgr. pub. relations Exxon Co., Pelham, N.Y., 1968-71; mgr. pub. affairs Exxon Co. U.S.A., 1971-83, pub. affairs cons., 1983-86, ret. Vice-chmn., chmn. adv. com. to Vice Pres.'s Task Force on Youth Motivation, 1966-69; chmn. Union County (N.J.) Coordinating Agy. for Higher Edn., 1968-81; nat. vice-chmn. ann. campaigns United Negro Coll. Fund, 1962, 63, 64; trustee N.Y. and N.J. State Councils Econ. Edn., 1974-86, N.Y. State Traffic Coun., 1974-81, Coun. Mcpl. Performance, 1983-86; vice chmn. Phila. Regional Intro. to Minorities to Engring. and Other Sci-Math. Based Professions, 1986-95; bd. dirs. N.J. State Bd. Higher Edn.'s Opportunity Fund, 1988—, assistance bd., 1993-99; mem. N.J. Higher Edn. Student Assistance Authority; trustee Lincoln U., Pa., 1994-2002. With AUS, 1942-46. Named one of 100 most influential blacks in Am. Ebony Mag., 1973 Mem. Nat. Assn. Market Devel. (pres. 1964-66, chmn. bd. 1967), Omega Psi Phi (Grand Basileus 1970-73) Baptist. Home: 389B Orrington Ln Monroe Township NJ 08831

AVERY, JAMES THOMAS, III, lawyer, management consultant; b. Richmond, Va., July 21, 1945; s. James Thomas Jr. and Hester Vail (Kraemer) A.; m. Nancy Carolyn Hoag, June 22, 1968; children: James Thomas IV, Carolyn Sears, John Dolph II. AB magna cum laude, Princeton U., 1967; MBA, JD, Harvard U., 1975. Bar: Mass. 1975, U.S. Dist. Ct. Mass. 1975, U.S. Ct. Appeals (1st cir.) 1975. Assoc. Choate, Hall & Stewart, Boston, 1975-79; dir. Cambridge (Mass.) Research Inst., 1979-85; pres. The Avery Co., Boston, 1985—; prin. Symmetrix, Inc., Lexington, Mass., 1992-94; pres./CEO PHH Fantus Cons., Inc., Hunt Valley, Md., 1995-97. Bd. dirs. Boston Pub. Co. Treas. All Saints Ch., Brookline, Mass., 1976-78; vestryman Ch. of Redeemer, Chestnut Hill, Mass., 1985-89. Capt. U.S. Army, 1967-71, Vietnam. Decorated Bronze Star, Air medal. Mem. ABA, Phi Beta Kappa. Clubs: Somerset, Harvard, The Second (trustee, sec. 1980-91) (Boston); Brookline Thursday. Republican. Episcopalian. Avocations: tennis, golf, skiing.

AVERY, JOHN ORVAL, lawyer; b. Idaho Falls, Idaho, June 25, 1951; s. Orval Eames and Lucile (Wheeler) Avery; m. Betty Rae Bird, May 15, 1970 (div. May 2, 1997); children: Jonathon Mark, Christopher John, Shelly Ann, Charles B., Tracie Lee, Jacqueline, Stphanie, Alex; m. Melodee Morgan, Mar. 18, 2000. Assoc. in Bus., Ricks Coll., 1971; BS in Acctg., Brigham Young U., 1973; JD, U. Idaho, 1985. Atty. intern Idaho Legal Aid Clinic, Moscow, 1984-85; dep. prosecuting atty. Bingham County Dep. Atty.'s Office, Blackfoot, Idaho, 1985-86; assoc. atty. Moss & Luke P.A., Blackfoot, 1985-86, Jenkins Law Office, Idaho Falls, 1986-89; ptnr. Cooper Wetzel Avery & Lee P.A., Idaho Falls, 1989—. Mem. Ea. Idaho Falls Estate Planning Coun., Idaho Falls, 1993—2001. Bd. dirs. Bonneville Joint Sch. Dist. 93, 1993—2002, chmn., 1996—2002. Mem.: Idaho State Bar Assn. Republican. Mem. Lds Ch. Avocations: skiing, sailing, golf, hiking, horseback riding. Office: Cooper Wetzel Avery & Lee PA 770 S Woodruff Ave Idaho Falls ID 83401-5285

AVERY, KEITH WILLETTE, artist, educator; b. Lansing, Michigan, Dec. 3, 1921; s. Norton Louis and Ruby Mae (Willette) A.; m. Carol Joyce (Haddan), Oct. 10, 1946; children: Carleton Louis, David Keith, Jane Ellen (Avery)Gray. BS, N. Mex. State U., 1955, LittD (hon.), 1986. Cert. secondary edn. tchr., N.Mex., Ariz., and Mich. Horse trainer, exhibitor A.B. Johnson Chevrolet Co., Grand Rapids, Mich., 1946-47; ranch foreman, horse trainer Lazy U Ranch, Bartlesville, Okla., 1949-50, Mill Iron Lazy 3 Ranch, Carrizozo, N.Mex., 1950-51; artist N.Mex. State U., Las Cruces, 1951-55; instr. and calf roping coach Judson Sch., Scottsdale, Ariz., 1955-59; instr. Lowell High Sch., Mich., 1961-74; artist and horseman Springer, and Roswell, N.Mex., 1974—. Dir. alumni rels., N. Mex. State U., Las Cruces, 1959-60. Author: Ridden Hard and Put Up Wet, 1990; Campfire Echoes, publ. fully funded scholarships at N. Mex. State U. in agrl. and home econ., 1994; (biography) Trails of a Wanderer, 1995. Served in U.S. Air Force, 1942-46. Recipient Champion Working Stock Horse, Nat. Horse Show Assn., Chgo., 1946; Gold, Silver, and Bronze medals, Phippen Invitational Art Show, Prescott, Ariz., 1978; Stetson Hat Award, Tex. Cowboy Artists Gold Medal Exhibit, San Angelo, Tex., 1983; Best of Show Painting Award, S.W. Regional Art Show Roswell, 1982; Govenor's Award of Excellence and Achievement in the Arts as the dean of N.Mex. cowboy poets and premier painter of the working cowboy, 1994; rep. N.Mex. Cowboy Poetry gathering, Nat. Endowment for the Arts, Elko, Nev., 1986; all poetry to archives Cowboy Hall of Fame, Oklahoma City, 2002; painting to Frank Phillips Found., Woolaroc Mus., Bartesville, Okla., 2002. Republican. Methodist. Home: 2809 S Graves Rd Roswell NM 88203-9024

AVERY, MARY ELLEN, pediatrician, educator; b. Camden, N.J., May 6, 1927; d. William Clarence and Mary (Miller) Avery. AB, Wheaton Coll., Norton, Mass., 1948, DSc (hon.), 1974; MD, Johns Hopkins U., 1952; DSc (hon.), Trinity Coll., 1976, U. Mich., 1975, Med. Coll. Pa., 1976, Albany Med. Coll., 1977, Med. Coll. Wis., 1978, Radcliffe Coll., 1978; MA (hon.), Harvard U., 1974; LHD (hon.), Emmanuel Coll., 1979, Northeastern U., 1981, Russell Sage Coll., 1983, Meml. U., Newfoundland, 1993; DHL, Johns Hopkins U., 1999; LLD, Queen's U., Kingston, Ont., 2000. Intern Johns Hopkins Hosp., 1953—54, resident, 1954—57; rsch. fellow in pediat. Boston, 1957—59, Balt., 1959—69; assoc. prof. pediat. Johns Hopkins U., 1964—69; prof., chmn. dept. pediat. McGill U. Med. Sch., 1969—74; Thomas Morgan Rotch prof. pediat. Harvard U. Med. Sch., Boston, 1974—97, prof. emerita, 1997—; physician-in-chief Montreal Children's Hosp., 1969—74, Children's Hosp. Med. Ctr., Boston, 1974—85. Mem. Med. Rsch. Coun. Can.; mem. study sect. NIH, 1968—71, 1984—88. Author: The Lung and Its Disorders in the Newborn Infant, 4th edit., 1981; author: (with A. Schaffer) Avery's Diseases of the Newborn, 7th edit., 1998; author: (with H.W. Taeusch and R. Ballard) ; author: (with G. Litwack) Born Early, 1984; author, editor: (with L. First) Pediatric Medicine, 1988, 2d edit., 1994, also articles; mem. editl. bd.: Pediatrics, 1965—71, Am. Rev. Respitory Diseases, 1969—73, Am. Jour. Physiology, 1967—73, Jour. Pediatrics, 1974—84, Medicine, 1985, Johns Hopkins Med. Jour., 1978—82, Clin. and Investigative Critical Care Medicine, 1990—96, New Eng. Jour. Medicine, 1990—95. Trustee Wheaton (Mass.) Coll., 1965—85, Radcliffe Coll., Johns Hopkins U., 1982—88. Recipient Mead Johnson award in pediatric rsch., 1968, Trudeau medal, Am. Thoracic Soc., 1984, Nat. Medal of Sci., NSF, 1991, Marta Philipson award, Karolinska Inst., Stockholm, 1998; scholar Markle in med. scis., 1961—66. Fellow: NAS (mem. coun. 1997—), AAAS (dir. 1989, pres. 2002—), Royal Coll. Physicians of Edinburgh, Am. Acad. Arts and Scis., Am. Acad. Pediat., Internat. Pediatric Assn. (standing com. 1986—89); mem.: Am. Pediatric Soc. (pres. 1990), Royal Coll. Pediat. and Child Health (hon.), Inst. Medicine (coun. 1987, Walsh McDermott award 2000), Soc. Pediatric Rsch. (pres. 1972—73), Am. Physiol. Soc., Can. Pediatric Soc., Alpha Omega Alpha, Phi Beta Kappa. Address: 300 Longwood Ave Boston MA 02115-5724 Office: Children's Hosp 300 Longwood Ave # HU432 Boston MA 02115-5737

AVERY, PAT MCGRATH, writer; b. Ottawa, Kans., Dec. 3, 1940; d. Gerald William McGrath and Esda Faye Sink; m. Everett Avery; children: Christopher, Mark. BA, Colo. Coll., Colorado Springs, CO, 1962; MA, U. Mo. Kans. City, Kansas City, MO, 1971. Educator Hickman Mills Schools, Kansas City, Mo., 1969—82; pvt. practice Prime Time, Inc., Belton, Mo., 1982—92; writer WSA Corp., Shawnee, Kans., 1990—; pub. River Rd. Press, Kimberling City, Mo., 1997—. Author: The Aged Tree Stands Proud, Letters From Korea, Tommy's War. Mem.: Pubs. Mktg. Assn., Pubs. Assn. of the South, Small Pubs. Assn. N.Am., Ozark Writers League, Mo. Writers Guild. Achievements include publisher of several books including How High Can You Fly, sponsor of annual poetry contests. Office Fax: 417-739-2251. E-mail: patmcgrathavery@excite.com., riverroadpress@yahoo.com.

AVERY, ROBERT DEAN, lawyer; b. Youngstown, Ohio, Apr. 23, 1944; s. Donald Carson and Alta Belle (Simon) A.; m. Ann Mitchell Lashen, May 16, 1993; 1 child from previous marriage: Benjamin Robert. BA, Northwestern U., 1966; JD, Columbia U., 1969. Bar: Ohio 1971, Calif. 1973, Ill. 2001. Law clk. to Hon. Robert P. Anderson US Ct. Appeals 2d Cir., NYC, 1969-70; assoc. lawyer Jones Day, Cleve., 1970-74, LA, 1974-76, ptnr., 1977-98, adminstrv. ptnr., 1990-92, ptnr. Chgo., 1999—. Editor: Columbia Law Rev., 1968-69. Harlan Fiske Stone Scholar. Home: 45 E Division St Chicago IL 60610-2316 Office: Jones Day 77 W Wacker Dr Chicago IL 60601-1662 E-mail: rdavery@jonesday.com.

AVERY, ROBERT NEWELL, sculptor; b. May 22, 1940; s. Robert Newell and Margaret (Andrews) A.; m. Karen Lissol, Aug. 27, 1963 (div. 1978); 1 child, Robert Walter; m. Amanda Fair Jones, May 5, 1979; 1 child, Melinda Hopkins. BFA, Calif. Coll. Arts and Crafts, Oakland, 1962; postgrad., Coll. of San Mateo, Calif., 1969-70, Coll. of Redwoods, 1975-76. Freelance comml. artist, Mendocino, Calif., 1971-75; exec. dir. Mendocino Art Ctr., Inc., 1975-79; proprietor Missing Link Prodns., Mendocino, 1979-93; mng. dir. Mezzanine Gallery at Daly's, Ft. Bragg, Calif., 1986-87, 91-93; exec. dir. Staunton/Augusta Art Ctr., Staunton, Va., 1995-96; proprietor Avery Studio Gallery, Staunton, 1996—. Art dir. The Mendocino Rev., 1983-91; judge Sonoma County Fair, Santa Rosa, Calif., 1977; auctioneer many arts/ednl./polit. events; art dir. The Mendocino Rev. #3, 1975; disc jockey Radio Sta. KMFB-FM, Mendocino, 1971-73, KJAZ-FM, Berkeley, Calif., 1960-61; lead player (play) The Great American Desert, 1975, Candida, 1977, Mousetrap, 1978, Rain, 1979, The Real Inspector Hound, 1984; prodr.: Twin Peaks (stage play), 1985; host interviewer: Art View, 1987-89, The Now and Then Show, 1985-91; prodr., programmer radio show: Odd Bob Comedy Show, KZYX-FM, 1989-90. Contbr. articles, photographs, illustrations to profl. jours.; columnist The Mendocino Daily Planet, 1972-73, The Mendocino Beacon, 1975-79, The New Settler Interview, 1986, Mendocino Grapevine, 1977-82; illustrator: The House that Jack Built; one man shows include Winona Gallery, Mendocino, 1990, Stock Exch. Deli, Waynesboro, Va., 1995, Augusta County Libr., Fishersville, Va., 1996; group shows include Mendocino Art Ctr., 1986, 1990, 91-93, Mayhew Wildlife Gallery, Mendocino, 1986-93, Mezzanine Gallery, Ft. Bragg, 1986-88, Caspar Studios Gallery, 1990, Shenandoah Valley Art Ctr., Waynesboro, Va., 1994-95, Beverley St. Studio Sch., Staunton, Va., 1995, Jordan Gallery, Charlottesville, Va., 1995, Lynchburg Fine Arts Ctr., 1995, Augusta Art Ctr., 1997, others Master of ceremonies 4th of July Parade, Mendocino, 1976-93; judge Bodega Bay Fisherman's Festival Ann. Arts Show, 1976; chmn. art acquisition com. Augusta Hosp. Corp., 1997; mem. founding bd. Mendocino Performing Arts Co., Inc.; past pres. Mendocino Cmty. Land Trust, Inc.; trustee Mendocino Unified Sch. Dist., 1973-77, pres., 1977; past dir. Mendocino Bus. and Profl. Coun.; mem. citizen's adv. coun. Coll. of the Redwoods, 1979-80; mem. exec. com. Calif. Arts Coun., Rural Arts Svcs., 1978-79; trustee Mendocino Art Ctr., Inc., 1980-85, chmn. citizen's adv. com., 1991, hon. life mem. Recipient numerous sculpture awards various art assns. Mem. Assn. of Sci. Fiction Artists, Internat. Sculpture Commn. Home and Office: 4855 Morris Mill Rd Swoope VA 24479-2323 E-mail: avery@ntelos.net.

AVERY, STEPHEN NEAL, playwright, author; b. Hot Springs, Ark., Mar. 20, 1955; s. Leo A. Avery and Dedette Carol (Miles) Andree; m. Kathleen Annette Twin, Sept. 7, 1979. Free-lance reporter Hot Springs Sentinel-Record and New Era, 1970-73. Author: Hungry: 3 Plays, 1991, Because, 1991, Insidious, 1992, Burning Bridges, 1999. With USN, 1973-77. Mem.: Nat. Campaign for Tolerance, Drama League, Theatre Comms. Group, Authors League of Am., Dramatists Guild Inc., Nat. Mus. Women in the Arts, Nat. Trust for Hist. Preservation, Habitat for Humanity Internat., Rep. Nat. Com. Pres. Club. Avocation: museum and gallery exhbns.

AVERY, WILLIAM HINCKLEY, physicist, chemist; b. Ft. Collins, Colo., July 25, 1912; s. Edgar Delano and Mabel Abbey (Gordon) A.; m. Helen Wallace Palmer, July 18, 1938; children— Christopher, Patricia (Mrs. W. Randolph Bartlett, Jr.). AB, Pomona Coll., 1933; AM, Harvard, 1935, PhD in Phys. Chemistry, 1937. Postdoctoral research asst. infrared spectroscopy Harvard, 1937-39; research chemist Shell Oil Co., St. Louis, Houston, 1939-43; head propulsion div. Allegany Ballistics Lab., Cumberland, Md., 1943-46; cons. in physics and chemistry Arthur D. Little Co., Cambridge, Mass., 1946-47; profl. staff mem. Applied Physics Lab., Johns Hopkins Univ., Laurel, Md., 1947-73, asst. dir. exploratory devel., 1973-78, dir. ocean energy programs, 1978-89, ret., 1989. Mem. various coms. DOD, NASA, NRC, Nat. Acad. Scis.; Nat. Acad. Engring., 1955— ; mem. tech. adv. bd. panel on SST environ. research Dept. Commerce, 1971; mem. subcom. AEC, Pres.'s Energy Report, 1973 Author: Renewable Energy from the Ocean: A Guide to OTEC, 1994; contbr. articles to profl. jours. Recipient C.N. Hickman award, 1951, Presdl. certificate of merit, 1948, Naval Ordnance Devel. award, 1945, IR 100 award, 1979, Sir Alfred Egerton award, 1972, William H. Avery Propulsion Rsch. Lab. established in his honor Johns Hopkins U., 1989, renamed William H. Avery Advanced Tech. Devel. Lab., 1996. Fellow AIAA (tech. dir. 1968-71); mem. AAAS, Hydrogen Energy Assn., Am. Chem. Soc., Combustion Inst. (dir. 1960-80, Sir Alfred C. Egerton Gold medal 1971), Marine Tech. Soc., Internat. Hydrogen Energy Inst., Cosmos Club (Washington), Phi Beta Kappa. Home and Office: 60 Daley Ter Orleans MA 02653-3318

AVERYT, GAYLE OWEN, retired insurance executive; b. Montgomery, Ala., Oct. 13, 1933; s. Edwin Franklin and Asenath Pratt (Murfee) A.; m. Margaret Rosborough Finlay, June 15, 1963; children: Caroline Elliott, Margaret McQueen, Elinor Finlay. BS cum laude, Davidson Coll., 1955; MBA, Harvard U., 1958; D Pub. Svc. (hon.), U. S.C., 1989. Chmn. bd. Colonial Cos., Inc., Columbia, S.C., 1970-93. Bd. dirs. UNUM Cor., 1993-99; bd. dirs., treas. Palmetto Bus. Forum, 1977-94;. mem. S.C. Ins. Commn., 1976-84, S.C. State Ports Authority, 1994-99. Trustee Davidson Coll., N.C., 1980-84; pres. S.C. Orch. Assn., 1986-88. Recipient Order of Palmetto State of S.C., 1994, Disting. Alumnus award Davidson Coll., 1997—; named Business Man of Yr. S.C. C. of C., 1989, Man of the Decade Columbia Met. Mag.; inducted into S.C. Bus. Hall of Fame, 1998. Mem. Phi Beta Kappa. Home: 1717 Greene St Columbia SC 29201-4014 Office: Colonial Cos Inc 1200 W Colonial Life Blvd Columbia SC 29210-7646

AVESON, MARTHA CARALYN, pharmaceutical company executive; m. Russell Edward Aveson, Sept. 19, 1981. AS, Essex County Coll., 1974; BA, Rutgers U., 1976; MA, Montclair State U., 1983. Lab. technician Airwick Products, Teterboro, N.J., 1977-79; chemist SmithKlineBeecham, Parsippany, N.J., 1979-84; chemist II Shulton Toiletries, Inc., Clifton, N.J., 1984, Church and Dwight, Inc., Princeton, N.J., 1985-86; rsch. scientist Whitehall-Robins, Inc., Hammonton, N.J., 1986-92; sr. rsch. scientist/sr. clin. supplies assoc. Bayer Corp., Morristown, N.J., 1992-99. Patentee in field. Mem. Internat. Soc. Pharm. Engrs., Am. Chem. Soc. Avocations: snow skiing, hiking. Home: 5193 E Baseline Rd Belgrade MT 59714 E-mail: MTAveson@aol.com.

AVGERAKIS, GEORGE HARRIS, film director; b. Trenton, N.J., Feb. 5, 1949; m. Maria Rosa Pastorelli, June 1977; children: Stephanie Luisa, Alexander Thomas. BA, U. Md., 1971; diploma, London Film School, 1972. Film editor Mai Harris, London, 1973-75; copywriter Pace Advt., N.Y.C., 1972-73; art dir. Fritzsche-Dodge and Olcott, N.Y.C., 1975-77; producer Grey Advt., N.Y.C., 1977-79; pres., art dir. Varistaff Inc., N.Y.C., 1979-80; mgr. TV ctr. Nabisco Brands Inc., East Hanover, N.J., 1980-81; v.p., creative dir. Avekta Prodns. Inc., N.Y.C., 1981—. Prodr., dir. (TV shows) My Craft...My Life, PBS, Ripley's Believe It or Not, ABC, Living Room, Russia, 1995, (home videos) Liquid Assets, 1995, (corp. profile series) Jerry Lewis-Celebrity Cooking, Masthead: The People of Time Inc. Magazines, [illegible] The People of PSE&G, segments of CNBC's The Money Club, The People of Mikasa, also nat. commls. for Investor's Bus. Daily, Fidelity Investor, animator Mind, Body and Sports, animator, graphic designer Horatio Alger awards, PBS, tradeshow designer JVC, Vinten, HP, NAB and COMDEX; author: Desktop Video Studio Bible, 2002, Digital Animation Bible, 2003. Mem.: Masons. Avocations: flying, sailing. Office: Avekta Prodns Inc 145 E 48th St Apt 17C New York NY 10017-1257 E-mail: george@avekta.com.

AVGERIS, GEORGE NICHOLAS, lawyer; b. Chgo., Apr. 18, 1939; s. Charles and Theodora (Thouas) A.; m. Demetra Datsopoulos, Nov. 19, 1967; children: Charles Christopher, Theodora Demetra. BA, North Cen. Coll., 1961; JD, U. Ill., 1964. Bar: Ill. 1964. Assoc. John R. Collis, Hinsdale, Ill., 1964-67, Sweeney & Riman, Chgo., 1967-69; pvt. practice Hinsdale, 1969—. Mem. Ill. State Bar Assn., Ill. Trial Lawyers Assn., Assn. Trial Lawyers Am., Chgo. Bar Assn., DuPage County Bar Assn. (lectr. seminars, chmn. med. legal com., civil practice com.). Republican. Greek Orthodox. Avocations: children, reading, baseball. Home: 801 S County Line Rd Hinsdale IL 60521-4728 Office: 29 E 1st St Hinsdale IL 60521-4182 E-mail: gavgeris@earthlink.net.

AVI, (AVI WORTIS), author; b. N.Y.C., Dec. 23, 1937; s. Joseph and Helen (Zunser) Wortis; children: Shaun Wortis, Kevin Wortis; m. Linda Wright; stepchildren: Katie Spina, Robert Spina, Jack Spina. BA, U. Wis., 1959, MA, 1962; MS in Libr. Sci., Columbia U., 1964. Staff mem. Lincoln Ctr. Libr. of Performing Arts, N.Y.C., 1962-70, Lambeth Pub. Lib., London, 1968; asst. prof., humanities libr. Trenton (N.J.) State Coll., 1970-86; writer, 1968—. Dir. workshop Young People's Fiction, Ill. Wesleyan U. Writers Conf., 1983, course in children's lit., 1986; tchr. course in writing for Children, UCLA Extension, 1987, course in aesthetics and ideology of children's lit., Simmons Coll., Boston, 1987, course in history of children's lit. Simmons Coll., 1988, course The Writers's Achievement, Simmons Coll., spring 1990; condr. more than 2000 workshops and seminars with children, parents and educators in U.S. and abroad. Author: Things That Sometimes Happen, 1970, Snail Tale, 1972 (One of Best Books of Yr. Brit. Book Coun. 1973), No More Magic, 1975 (Spl. award Mystery Writers Am. 1975), Captain Grey, 1977, Emily Upham's Revenge, 1978 (Spl. award Mystery Writers Am. 1979, Book of Month PCRRT, 1978), Encounter at Easton, 1980 (Christopher award 1980), The History of Helpless Harry, 1980 (Book of the Month PCRRT 1980), Man from the Sky, 1980 (IRA Children's Choice 1980), A Place Called Ugly, 1981, Who Stole the Wizard of Oz, 1981, Sometimes I Think I Hear My Name, 1982, Shadrach's Crossing, 1983 (Spl. award Mystery Writers Am. 1983), Devil's Race, 1984 (ALA Best Books Hi-Lo 1984), The Fighting Ground, 1984 (O'Dell award 1984, ALA Notable Book, One of Best Books for Young Adults 1984, Notable Children's Trade Books in Social Studies 1984, Jefferson Cup award Honor Book Va. Libr. Assn. 1985, Book of the Month PCRRT 1984), Wolf Rider, 1986 (named One of Best Books for Young Adults, ALA 1986, N.Y. Pub. Libr. 1986, One of Best Books of the 80s, Booklist 1989,, Recommended Book for Reluctant Readers 1986, Va. Young Readers award 1990), Romeo and Juliet—Together (and Alive!)—at Last, 1987 (LA/YASD Recommended Book for Reluctant Readers, 1988, IRA Children's Choice 1988, named One of Best Books of Yr., Bank St. Coll. Children's Book Com., Wis. Children's Book Ctr. 1988), Something Upstairs, 1988 (Rhode Island award 1991, named One of Best Books of Yr. Libr. Congress 1989), The Man Who Was Poe, 1989, (named One of Best Books of Yr., N.Y. Pub. Libr. 1989, Notable Children's Book, NCTE 1990, One of Best Books of Yr., Libr. Congress 1990), The True Confessions of Charlotte Doyle (IRA Children's Choice award 1990, Lopez Meml. Found. award 1990, Golden Kite award Soc. Children's Book Authors 1991, named One of Best Books of Yr., Child Study Assn. 1990, Notable Childrn's Trade Book in the Lang. Arts 1990, N.Y. Pub. Lib. Best Books for Teens 1990, Editors' Choice, Booklist 1990, ALA Notable Book, 1990, YASD Best Books for Young Adults 1991, Newbery Honor Book 1991), Nothing But the Truth, 1991, (Newbery Honor Book, 1992, Horn Book-Boston Globe award Honor Book, 1992, ALA Notable Book, 1992, named One of Best Books of Yr.-Hornbook, SLJ, 1991, YASD Best Books for Young Adults, 1992, Pub. Weekly Best Books of 1991, Am. Booksellers Children's Choice List, 1992, Best Books for Teens, N.Y. Pub. Libr., 1992, Notable Nat. Coun. Social Studies/Children's Book Council, 1991, Blue Ribbon Book Bulletin of Ctr. Children's Books), Windcatcher, 1991, Who Was that Masked Man, Anyway?, 1992, Blue Heron, 1992, City of Light, City of Dark, 1993, The Bird, The Frog and the Light, 1994, The Barn, 1994, Tom, Babette & Simon, 1995, Poppy, 1995, Beyond the Western Sea, 1996, Crispin: The Cross of Lead, (Newbery Medal Winner 2003); contbr. articles to jours. in field. Mem.: Authors Guild. Home: 859 S York St Denver CO 80209-4646

AVIAN, BOB, choreographer, producer; b. N.Y.C., Dec. 26, 1937; s. John Hampar and Esther (Keleshian) Avedisian. B.F.A., Boston U., 1959. Dancer, 1959-68; danced in: West Side Story, Broadway, 1960, Funny Girl, Broadway, 1964-65, assoc. choreographer, dir., Michael Bennett Prodns., N.Y.C., 1967-89, choreographer-producer, 1975—; Broadway prodns. include: Henry, Sweet Henry, 1967, Promises, Promises, 1968, Coco, 1969, Company, 1970, Follies, 1971, Twigs, 1971, Seesaw, 1973, God's Favorite, 1974, A Chorus Line, 1975 (Tony award for best choreography 1976, Los Angeles Drama Critics award for best choreography 1977), Ballroom (Tony award for best choreography 1979, Drama Desk award for choreography 1979); choreographer (London premieres): Follies, 1987, Miss Saigon, 1989, Sunset Boulevard, 1993 (Tony nomination, 1995), Martin Guerre, London, 1996 (Laurence Olivier award for best choreography 1996), Putting It Together, 1999, The Witches of Eastwick, 2000; prodr.Dreamgirls, 1981.

AVIL, RICHARD DANIEL, JR., lawyer; b. Phila., Nov. 28, 1948; s. Richard Daniel and Elizabeth (McGinley) A.; m. Karen Mudry, May 27, 1972; children: Sierra Soo, Brier Sung, Winston Richard. BEE, Villanova U., 1970; JD, Cornell U., 1974. Law clk. U.S. Dist. Ct. Northern Dist. N.Y., 1974-75, 75-76, U.S. Ct. Appeals Second Cir., N.Y.C., 1976-77; assoc. Jones Day, Cleve., 1977-83, ptnr., 1984-91, Washington, 1991—. Speaker in field. Mem. Energy Bar Assn. Home: 10850 Patowmack Dr Great Falls VA 22066-3032 Office: Jones Day 51 Louisiana Ave NW Washington DC 20001-2113 E-mail: rdavil@jonesday.com.

AVILA, CARLOS ALBERTO, physics researcher, inventor; b. Arecibo, P.R., May 7, 1950; s. Manuel Antonio Avila and Natalia Rivera; m. Gladys Esther Rivera, Feb. 9, 1973; children: Carlos Jr., Rolando, Elias, David. BEd in chemistry, NYU, 1976, BA, 1978, MEd in sci. edn., 1986; BAW in chemistry and gen. sci., Inter Am. U., P.R., 1988; MA in sci. edn., NYU, 1992. Tchr. of sci. Dept. Edn., P.R., 1976-86, tchr. chemistry lab., 1992-93; rschr. physics dept. U. P.R., 1993—; pres., owner EBINC-CINCE, Inc. Spanish cmty. svcs. staff Dept. Edn., Penns Grove, N.J., 1982-83; substitute tchr. Dept. Edn., Meml. H.S., 1983-84; owner, pres. CINCE. Songwriter Man Should Understand, others; author: Space is Not Empty - It is the 5th State of the matter, Modifying Einstein Equation, Universe Not Expanding. With U.S. Army, 1991-92. Nominee Nobel Prize in Physics, Internat. Peace prize. Mem. Nat. Sci. Assn., IP&R Inventors and Pub./Rsch. Corp. (recipient Internat. Personality of Yr., Cambridge, Eng., others), Am. Fedn. Tchrs., Puerto Rico Fedn. Tchrs. Achievements include invention of Thermoelectric battery and power plant using the same; developer of Avila's Singunification Theory; developer of a new technology in antigravity to put anybody in orbit with no need of chemical polluted fuels, theory called antigravitational equilibrium; developer of the idea of vehicles that can move in the Earth's atmosphere as transportation vehicles using the antigravitational equilibrium between gravity force, centripetal force-moving in synchronization with the earth rotation; proposed the atmosphere energy levels of flight, in which technology of the future uses the virtual reality and the concept of energy levels in the electrous clouds of the atoms, the microsm and the macrocosm are the same concepts, therefore if the electrons rotate around the atom nucleus at different energy levels, in the same way, vehicles can fly at different altitudes over the earth's surface (atmosphere) between each sphere of the atmosphere; developer of the idea that space is not empty, not a vaccuum, it is the fifth state of matter; proposed that the planets do not exist, are not real, are optical illusions; proposed that the space or the universe does not expand, it rotates around the huge hole in the center of the universe; the original matter that formed the Big Bang Universe is not expanding, it rotates around its center; the universe reproduces itself, the universe is xy and xx; the dark matter is xy and stars and black holes are xx which is the process of reproduction, births and death of stars. Home and Office: PO Box 14 Angeles PR 00611-0014 also: 40150 Friar Tuck Trl Zephyrhills FL 33540-7702

AVILA, JOHN SANTOS, agricultural pilot; b. Turlock, Calif., Jan. 31, 1958; s. John Santos Avila and Erlene Doris Thomas. Student, Coll. of the Sequoias, Visalia, Calif., 1987—. Lic. comml. pilot, FAA; cert. vector control technician, State Calif. Circulation dist. supr. Tulare (Calif.) Advanced-Register, 1977-80; with The Fresno Bee, Tulare, 1980-90; agrl. pilot, ground educator Calif. Agrl. Aeronautics, Tulare, 1990-94; vector control technician, pilot Tulare Mosquito Abatement Dist., 1991—. Bd. dirs. Tulare Police Dept. Citizen complaint Rev. Bd., 1997—, Visalia Cmty. Tennis Assn., 2003—; instr. tennis City of Tulare Youth Instrnl. Program, 2000—. Mem. Calif. Agrl. Aircraft Assn., Tulare Tennis Club (treas. 1997—). Republican. Roman Catholic. Avocations: tennis, softball, music, bike riding. Home: 1397 East Westminster Ave Tulare CA 93274 E-mail: johnavila@aol.com.

AVILA, LIDIA D. school administrator; b. Phoenix; d. Pete A. and Elvira (Duarte) A. B.A. in Edn., M.A. in Edn., 1968; Ed.D., Ariz. State U., 1981. Cert. elem. tchr., counselor, adminstr. Successively tchr., counselor, coordinator, Phoenix, 1958-73, prin., 1973-75; adult edn. tchr., Tempe, Ariz., 1966-68; fed. project reader cons., Phoenix, 1968-72; prin. Glendale Elem. Sch. Dist. (Ariz.), 1976—88; prin. Tucson, 1988-91, Phoenix, 1991—; textbook cons. Active Robert A Taft Inst. Govt., 1981; del. Inter-Club Council Women's Orgn. Greater Phoenix area; bd. dirs. YWCA, 1968-70; mem. steering com. 1st US-China Ednl. Conf, Beijing, 1997. Baylor U. Leadership/Mgmt. Inst. grantee 1980; NDEA grantee, UCLA Inst. Linguistics, Manila, Philippines, 1968. Mem. AAUW (state pres., mem. edn. found. panel), Am. Bus. Women's Assn. (Woman of Yr. 1982), Assn. Supervision and Curriculum Devel., Nat. Assn. Elem. Sch. Prins. (participant nat. fellows program), Delta Kappa Gamma, Phi Delta Kappa. Office: 5810 N 49th Ave Glendale AZ 85301

AVILDSEN, JOHN GUILBERT, film director; b. Oakpark, IL, Dec. 21, 1935; s. Clarence John and Ivy (Guilbert) A.; m. Tracy Brooks Swope, Feb., 1987; children: Anthony Guilbert, Jonathan, Bridget Emily Margaret. Student, NYU, 1955. Advt. mgr. Vespa Motor Scooters, 1959. Asst. dir. Greenwich Village Story, 1961; prodn. mgr.: Mickey One, 1964; 2d unit dir.: Hurry Sundown, 1964; with Muller, Jordan & Herrick Indsl. Films, 1965-67; dir. photography Out of It, 1967; dir. films Turn on to Love, 1967, Sweet Dreams, 1968, Guess What We Learned in School Today, 1969, Joe, 1970, Cry Uncle, 1971, Save the Tiger, 1972, Inaugural Ball, 1973, W.W. and the Dixie Dancekings, 1974, Rocky, 1976 (Acad. award for best direction, Directors Guild of Amer. award, 1976), Slow Dancing in the Big City, 1978, The Formula, 1980, Neighbors, 1981, A Night in Heaven, 1983, The Karate Kid, 1984, Happy New Year, 1985, The Karate Kid II, 1986, For Keeps, 1987, The Karate Kid III, 1989, Lean on Me, 1989 (Image award NAACP), Rocky V, 1990, The Power of One, 1992, 8 Seconds, 1994; prodr., dir. documentary film Traveling Hopefully, 1982 (Acad. nomination for best documentary). Served with U.S. Army, 1959-61. Mem. Dirs. Guild Am., Motion Picture Photographers Union, Motion Picture Editors Union. Office: care United Talent Agy Dan Aloni 9560 Wilshire Blvd Fl 5 Beverly Hills CA 90212-2401

AVILES, ALICE ALERS, psychologist; b. N.Y.C; d. Jose Oscar and Pauline (Irizarry) Alers; m. Jose A. Aviles, Aug. 13, 1954 (div. Oct. 1981); children: Jeffrey (dec.), Brian, Gregory; m. Clifford M. Goldman, June 29, 1997. BS magna cum laude, SUNY, Oswego, 1955; MA, Queens Coll., 1978; PhD, Yeshiva U., 1984; postdoctoral diploma in psychoanalysis and psychotherapy, Adelphi U., 1991. Lic. psychologist, N.Y. Tchr. elem. schs., Spring Valley, N.Y., 1955, Erlangen (Fed. Republic Germany) Am. Sch., 1955-56, Uniondale, N.Y., 1956, Freeport, N.Y., 1957-58, Island Park, N.Y., 1973-75; psychology clk. Fifth Ave. Ctr. for Counseling and Psychotherapy, N.Y.C., 1978-80; psychology intern St. Vincent's Hosp. and Med. Ctr., N.Y.C., 1980-81; psychologist Kingsboro Psychiat. Ctr., Bklyn., 1981-84; psychologist to assoc. psychologist South Beach Psychiat. Ctr., Bklyn., 1984-86; pvt. practice Valley Stream, N.Y., 1985—. From staff psychologist to sr. psychologist Luth. Med. Ctr., Bklyn., 1986-95; cons. Beach Terrace Care Ctr., Long Beach, N.Y., 1995-97; mem. adv. com. Hispanic Counseling Ctr. of Family Svc. Assn. of Nassau County, Hempstead, N.Y., 1978-80; cons. Nassau County Extended Care Ctr., Hempstead, 1997-99, Resort Nursing Home, Far Rockaway, N.Y., 1998-2000, Woodmere (N.Y.) Rehab. and Health Care Ctr., 1999-2000. Ford found. grad. fellow, 1978-81. Mem. APA, N.Y. State Psychol. Assn., Nassau County Psychol. Assn. (mem. pvt. practice com. 1992-93), Adelphi Soc. Psychoanalysis and Psychotherapy. Office: 10 Valley Ln E North Woodmere NY 11581-3629

AVILEZ, VICTORIA MARIE, lawyer; b. Flint, Mich., Apr. 9, 1962; d. John Richard and Brenda Jean (Mitrage) Stevens; m. R. Antonio Avilez, Aug. 24, 1996. BA in History, Alma (Mich.) Coll., 1984; JD, Ariz. State U., Tempe, 1991. Bar: Ariz., 1991, U.S. Dist. Ct. Ariz., U.S. Ct. Appeals (9th cir.). Reporter The Ariz. Republic, Phoenix, 1984-88; assoc. Snell & Wilmer LLD, Phoenix, 1991-97, Ryley, Carlock & Applewhite, Phoenix, 1998-99; ptnr. Cross, Meda & Avilez, Phoenix, 1999 . Mem. Fed. Bar Assn. (bd. mem., sec. Phoenix 1999—, chair bankruptcy practice and procedures com. 1998-99), Maricopa County Bar Assn. (bd. mem. 1995-99, pres. young lawyers divsn. 1997). Office: Cross Meda & Avilez PLC 411 N Central Ave Ste 700 Phoenix AZ 85004-2140 E-mail: vmavilez@uswest.net.

AVINS, STYRA, musician, writer; b. Bronx, N.Y. d. William and Suzanne Avins; m. Josef Eisinger, June 24, 1963; children: Alison, Simon. BA, CCNY, 1959; postgrad., Juilliard Sch., 1958-59; MM, Manhattan Sch. Music, 1963. Solo cellist Seoul Symphony, 1959-60; cellist Am. Symphony, N.Y.C., 1966-68, N.Y. City Opera Orch., N.Y.C., 1967-68, Young Audiences, Wyndham Ensemble, N.Y.C. and N.J., 1970-85, Cameo Trio, N.Y.C., 1982-86, Queens Symphony, N.Y., 1981—. Adj. prof. music history Drew U., Madison, N.J., 1995—; artistic exec. dir. Cmty. Chamber Concerts, N.Y. and N.J., 1982-88. Author: Johannes Brahms: Life and Letters, 1997 (Royal Philharm. Soc. award 1998); contbr. articles to profl. jours. Trustee Hunterdon Land Trust Alliance, Sargentsville, N.J., 1998—; at-large officer Musconetcong Mountain Conservancy, Hampton, N.J., 2002--; mem. adv. sch. bd. com. Bethlehem Township Sch. Bd., N.J., 1998-99; agrl. liaison to county agrl. bd. Bethlehem Township Gov. Body, 1997—. Mem. Am. Musicol. Soc., Am. Brahms Soc. (trustee), Assoc. Fedn. Musicians (Local 802), The Bohemians, Violoncello Soc. N.Y., Phi Beta Kappa. Jewish. Avocation: open space preservation activities. Office: 197 W Houston St New York NY 10014

AVISE, JOHN CHARLES, geneticist, educator; b. Grand Rapids, Mich., Sept. 19, 1948; s. Reginald Dean and Edith Dorothy (Johnson) A.; m. Joan Marie Yanov, Dec. 24, 1979; 1 child, Jennifer Ann. BS, U. Mich., 1970; MA, U. Tex., 1971; PhD, U. Calif., Davis, 1975. Asst. prof. U. Ga., Athens, 1975-79, assoc prof., 1980-84, prof., 1985—. Author: Molecular Markers, Natural History and Evolution, 1994, The Genetic Gods: Evolution and Belief in Human Affairs, 1998, Phylogeography: The History and Formation of Species, 2000, Captivating Life: A Naturalist in the Age of Genetics, 2001, Genetics in the Wild, 2002; contbr. articles to profl. jours. Recipient William Brewster Meml. award Am. Ornithologists' Union, 1997 Mem. AAAS, NAS. Avocations: nature study, sports. Office: Univ of Ga Dept of Genetics Athens GA 30602 E-mail: avise@arches.uga.edu.

AVISON, DAVID, photographer; b. Harrisonburg, Va., July 13, 1937; s. Charles and Kathryn (Driver) A.; July 10, 1973. Sc.B., MIT, 1959; PhD, Brown U., 1966; MS, Ill. Inst. Tech., 1974. Tchr. photography Columbia Coll., 1970-86; owner, operator Avison Photo Products. Exhibitions include Mus. Contemporary Photography, Chgo., 1973-76, 80, 81, 84-89, 95, 97, 98, Art Inst. Chgo., 1977, 78, 79, 80, 81, 82, 83, 84, 89, Grey Art Gallery, NYU, 1977, Dittmar Meml. Gallery, Northwestern U., 1974-76, 78, Crocker ARt Gallery, Sacramento, 1978, Block Gallery, Northwestern U., 1984, Burden Gallery, N.Y.C., 1985, Macintosh Mus., Scotland, 1985, Photography Archives U. Louisville, Ky., 1988, Chgo. Hist. Soc., 1989, Mesa (Ariz.) SW Mus., 1989, Davenport Mus. Art, 1992, Contemporary Arts Ctr., Cin., 1993, Musée des Beaux Arts, Reims, France, 1994, Addison Gallery Am. Art, Andover, Mass., 1998, Taken by Design: Photographs from the Inst. of Design 1937-1971, Art Inst. Chgo., San Francisco Mus. Modern Art, Phila. Mus. Art, 2002-03; represented in permanent collection, Mus. Modern Art, Art Inst. Chgo., Mus. Fine Art, Boston, Internat. Mus. Photography at George Eastman House, Rochester, N.Y., Dallas Mus. Fine Arts, Hallmark Collection, Kansas City, Mo., Exchange Bank, Chgo., Mus. Contemporary Photography, Chgo., Ball State U. Gallery, Muncie, Ind., No. Ill. U. Sven Parson Gallery, DeKalb. Photographers fellow NEA, 1977; Focus Infinity Fund grantee, 1987-88; recipient Time-Life Search for Photog. Talent award 1974. Studio: 300 Summer St Ste 58 Boston MA 02210-1115

AVIV, JONATHAN ENOCH, otolaryngologist, educator; b. NYC, Aug. 24, 1960; s. David Gordon and Rena (Rod) A.; m. Robin Kiam, Nov., 1998; children: Caleigh Kiam, Nikki Claire, Blake Victor. BA, Columbia U., 1981, MD, 1985. Diplomate Am. Bd. Otolaryngology, Nat. Bd. Med. Examiners. Resident dept. surgery Mount Sinai Med. Ctr., N.Y.C., 1985-87, resident dept. otolaryngology, 1987-90, fellow microvascular surgery, 1990-91; prof., dir. divsn. laryngology, med. dir. voice and swallowing ctr. Coll. Physicians and Surgeons, Columbia U., N.Y.C., 1991—. Co-founder AP Healthcare, L.L.C., Surgery 411. Contbr. articles to profl. jours., numerous book chpts. Fellow Am. Soc. Head and Neck Surgery; mem. AMA, ACS (faculty), Am. Acad. Otolaryngology, Am. Acad. Facial, Plastic and Reconstructive Surgery, Am. Broncho-Esophagological Assn. (v.p. 2001-03), Am. Laryngological Assn., N.Am. Skull Base Soc., N.Y. Head and Neck Soc., N.Y. Laryngological Soc. (pres. elect), Triological Soc. Achievements include development of and a patent for method and device to endoscopically measure sensory discrimination in throat and voice box. Office: Columbia-Presbyn Med Ctr Dept Otolaryngology 630 W 168th St New York NY 10032-3702 Business E-Mail: jea10@columbia.edu.

AVNET, JONATHAN MICHAEL, motion picture company executive, film director; b. Bklyn., Nov. 17, 1949; m. Barbara Brody; children: Alexandra, Jacob, Lily. BA, Sarah Lawrence Coll., 1971; postgrad., U. Pa., 1967-69; student, Conservatory for Advanced Film Studies, 1972-73. Reader United Artists, L.A., 1974; dir. creative affairs Sequoia Pictures, L.A., 1975-77; pres. Tisch/Avnet Prodns., L.A., 1977-85; chmn. Avnet/Kerner Co., L.A., 1985—. Pres. Allied Communications, Inc. Dir., producer: (motion pictures) Fried Green Tomatoes (3 Acad. award nominations, 3 Golden Globes, Writers Guild Gladd best feature film award), The War; producer, writer, dir. (TV series) Call To Glory, 1984-85 (Golden Reel award), Between Two Women (1 Emmy award); producer, exec. producer: (motion pictures) Risky Business, Men Don't Leave, Less Than Zero, When a Man Loves a Woman, Mighty Ducks(all three), Deal of the Century, Miami Rhapsody, Three Musketeers, and others; exec. producer: (movies of the week) The Burning Bed (8 Emmy nominations), Silence of the Heart, Heatwave (4 Cable Ace awards, including Best Picture), Do You Know the Muffin Man, No Other Loved, others. Trustee L.A. County Opera. Am. Film Inst. fellow. Mem. Am. Film Inst., Dir.s Guild of Am., Writers Guild of Am., Acad. Motion Pictures Arts and Scis., Producers Caucus. Avocations: basketball, skiing, biking.

AVRAHAM, REGINA, retired secondary education educator; b. Ludenscheid, Germany, Aug. 15, 1935; Came to U.S., 1937. d. Joseph and Feiga (Press) Artman; m. Josef Esa Abraham, Mar. 12, 1962; children: Randi Beth, Jesse Richard. BS, City Coll., N.Y.C., 1955. Elem. tchr. N.Y. Bd. Edn., 1955-63, tchr., 1963-91; sci. cons., prin. writer N.Y.C. Bd. Edn. Sci. Curriculum, 1996—. Sci. and health magnet tchr. Bd. Edn., N.Y., 1987-91; presenter and cons. in field. Author: Our Founding Sisters, 1976, Readings in Life Science, 1986, Readings in Physical Science, 1986, The Downside of Drugs, 1988, Substance Abuse Treatment and Prevention, 1988, The Circulation System, 1989, The Digestive System, 1989, The Reproductive System, 1989; prin. writer Sci.-Lit. Connection, N.Y.C. Bd. Edn., 1996, contbg. writer, cons. A Study in Role Models, 1997, The Multiple Intelligences, 1998; contbg. editor: Celebrating the Century, 1999, Reading and Writing Connections, 2000, Celebrating Diversity, 2001; project coord., contbg. writer, editor, cons. Promoting Excellence through Best Practices, 2002. Woodrow Wilson fellow, 1989; named Tchr. of Yr., Bklyn. Sch. Bd., 1987. Mem. United Fed. Tchrs. Democratic. Avocations: theatre, opera, crossword puzzles, cats, N.Y. Mets. Home: 2218 Avenue P Brooklyn NY 11229-1508

AVRAM, HENRIETTE DAVIDSON, librarian, government official; b. N.Y.C., Oct. 7, 1919; d. Joseph and Rhea (Olsho) Davidson; m. Herbert Mois Avram, Aug. 23, 1941; children: Lloyd, Marcie, Jay. Student, Hunter Coll., N.Y.C., George Washington U.; ScD (hon.), So. Ill. U., 1977; DLitt (hon.), Rochester Inst. Tech., 1991; DSc (hon.), U. Ill., 1993. Systems analyst, methods analyst, programmer Nat. Security Agy., 1952-59; systems analyst Am. Rsch. Bur., 1959-61, Datatrol Corp., 1961-65; supervisory info. systems specialist Libr. of Congress, Washington, 1965-67, asst. coord. info. systems, 1967-70, chief MARC Devel. Office, 1970-76, dir. Network Devel. Office, 1976-80, dir. processing systems, network and automation planning, 1980-83, asst. libr. for processing svcs., 1983-89, assoc. libr. Collection Svcs., 1989-92; ret. Libr. Congress, 1992; chmn. network adv. com. Libr. of Congress, Washington, 1981-92, chmn. emerita network adv. com., 1992—. Chair subcom. 2 sectional com. Z39 Am. Nat. Standards Inst., 1966-80, RECON Working Task F, 1968-73, Internat. Rels. Round Table, 1986-87, subcom. 4 working group 1 on character sets Internat. Orgn. for Standardization, 1971 80; lectr. sch. of info. and libr. sci. Cath. U. Am., Washington, 1973-80, com. mem. strategies for 80's, 1980-81; bd. visitors libr. and learning resources com., 1980; mem. internat. standards coord. com. Info. Sys. Standards Bd., 1983-86; del. to U.S. nat. com. UNESCO/Gen. Info. Program, 1983; chair internat. rels. com. Nat. Info. Standards Orgn., 1983-92. Bd. editors: Jour. Library Automation, 1970-72; contbr. articles to profl. jours. Recipient Superior Svc. award Libr. of Congress, 1968, Margaret Mann citation, 1971, Fed. Woman's award, 1974, Achievement award ALA/Libr. Info. Tech. Assn., 1980, Meritorious Svc. award ANSI, 1992, Disting. Exec. Svc. award Fed. Govt., 1990; co-recipient Rsch. Libr. of Yr. award Assn. Coll. and Rsch. Libr. Acad., 1979. Fellow Internat. Fedn. Libr. Assns. and Instns. (chair working group on content designators 1972-77, chair profl. bd. 1979-81, mem. program mgmt. com. 1983-90, mem. exec. bd. 1983-87, 1st v.p. 1985-87); mem. ALA (bd. dirs., past pres. info sci. and automation div., John Ames Humphrey Forest Press award 1990, Melvil Dewey award 1981, Lippincott award 1988, Hon. Membership award 1997), Am. Soc. Info. Sci. (spl. interest group on libr. automation and networks 1965), Spl. Librs. Assn. (Recognition award 1990), Assn. Libr. and Info. Sci. Edn. (Libr. of Congress disting. svc. award 1992), Assn. Bibliog. Agys. Gt. Britain, Australia, Can. and U.S. (del. 1977—). Home: 44041 Fieldstone Way California MD 20619-2097 E-mail: havram@erols.com.

AVRAM, MORRELL M. nephrologist, educator, consultant; b. N.Y.C., Nov. 11, 1929; m. Maria G. Kunzle; children: Rella Marie, Marc Robert, Eric Michael, Mathew Mendel, David Keith. BS, L.I. U., 1951, DS (hon.), 1988; MD, U. Geneva, 1959. Intern L.I. Coll. Hosp., Bklyn., 1959-60, chief resident, 1962-63, fellow in nephrology, 1963-64, chief hemodialysis lab., 1964—, first dir. renal clinic, 1966—, first chief div. nephrology, 1970—, chief renal clin. rsch. lab., 1987—; clin. prof. SUNY, Bklyn., 1979—; cons. in field. Cons. Southampton Hosp., Univ. Hosp., SUNY, Cath. Med. Ctr.—Bklyn./Queens; vis. physician Kings County Med. Ctr., N.Y.C., 1964—; founder, dir. The Bklyn. Kidney Ctr., 1971—; vis. prof. numerous univs. including U. Conn., U. Ariz., SUNY, Johns Hopkins U., Harvard U., UCLA, univs. in Beijing, Rio de Janeiro, Tel Aviv, Cairo; speaker in field. Author: Parathyroid Hormone in Kidney Disease, 1980, Prevention of Kidney Disease and Long-Term Survival, 1982, Protenuria, 1985; (with C. Giordano) Ambulatory Peritoneal Dialysis, 1990; contbg. author numerous books; mem. editorial bd. Nephron, 1978—, Clin. Nephrology, 1981—, Dialysis and Transplantation, 1980—, Jour. Geriatric Nephrology and Urology, 1990—, Internat. Jour. Artificial Organs, 1978—, Internat. Jour. Pediatric Nephrology, 1980, Jour. Diabetic Complications, 1987, Hypertension, 1975-77, Urology Times, 1974-84; reviewer various publs.; contbr. numerous articles to profl. jours. Chmn. med. adv. bd. Nat. Kidney Found. N.Y./N.J., Inc., 1982-87, med. adv. bd. mem. 1999; founding mem. Am. Soc. Hypertension, 1986—; bd. dirs., exec. com. World Affairs Coun., 1989—; bd. mem. St. Luke's Roosevelt Hosp. Ctr., L.I. Coll. Hosp., Pianofest; co-chmn. bd. dirs. World Affairs Coun., Southampton, N.Y.; active numerous community and svc. orgns. With U.S. Army, 1951-53, Korea. Clin. rsch. trng. fellow L.I. Coll. Hosp., 1968—, Nat. Kidney Found. fellow L.I. Coll. Hosp., 1969—; recipient Lester Hoenig award Nat. Kidney Found., 1984. Fellow ACP; mem. AMA, AAAS, Am. Soc. Nephrology, Am. Soc. for Internal Organs (editor Transactions XXXIII 1987), Internat. Soc. Nephrology, Internat. Soc. Artificial Internal Organs, Bklyn. Acad. Medicine, Am. Anthropol. Soc., N.Y. Acad. Scis., N.Y. Soc. Nephrology (pres. 1977-78), Renal Network N.Y. (pres. 1978-79). Home: 115 Remsen St Brooklyn NY 11201-4212 Office: LI Coll Hosp Div Nephrology Atlantic Ave Brooklyn NY 11201-5526

AVRIT, RICHARD CALVIN, defense consultant, career officer; b. Tilamook, Oreg., Feb. 18, 1932; s. Roy Calvin and Mary Louise (Morgan) A.; m. Alice Jane Tamminga, July 10, 1959; 1 dau., Tamra Jane. BS in Engring, U.S. Naval Acad., 1953; MS in Engring. Electronics, U.S. Naval Postgrad. Sch., 1960; postgrad., U.S. Naval War Coll., 1971-72. Commd. ensign U.S. Navy, 1953, advanced through grades to rear adm., 1979; served weapons dept. U.S.S. George K. Mackenzie, 1953-54; ops. dept. U.S.S. Willis A. Lee, 1954-57; comdg. officer U.S.S. Sumner County, 1960-63; project officer, staff of comdr. Operational Test and Evaluation Force, Key West, Fla., 1963-66; exec. officer U.S.S. Berkeley, 1966-68; ops. officer, AAW project officer Comdr. Cruiser Destroyer Florilla Nine, 1968-70; comdg. officer U.S.S. Sellers, 1970-71; mil. asst. for surface guns and missiles to asst. dir. Ocean Control Directorate, Def. Research and Engring., Office Sec. of Def., 1972-76; comdg. officer U.S.S. Harry E. Yarnell, 1976-78; chief of staff, comdr. Naval Surface Force U.S. Atlantic Fleet, 1978-79; project mgr. for Saudi Naval Expansion Program, Naval Material Command, Washington, 1979-82; dir. navy logistics plans Office Chief of Naval Ops., Washington, 1982-84; cons. Info. Spectrum, Inc., 1984-88; pres. Mil. Data Corp., Arlington, Va., 1989-91; small bus. cons., 1992—. Decorated D.S.M., Legion of Merit (3), Bronze Star with Combat V, Meritorious Service Medal (2). Mem. Naval Inst., IEEE. Methodist. Home: 4839 Keswick Ct Dumfries VA 22026-1084 Office: 1254 W Cedar Ave Denver CO 80223-1728 E-mail: dick-a-keswick@att.net.

AWACHIE, PETER IFEACHO ANAZOBA, chemistry educator, research chemist; b. Umunnachi, Anambra, Nigeria, Aug. 31, 1952; came to U.S., 1994; s. Ifejika Okonkwo and Juliana Uluji (Malobi) A.; m. Miriam Nwaka Akudu, Dec. 23, 1988; children: Ifeanyichukwu Onefolu, Chisom Ogonna, Tochukwu Onyedikachi, Ifeacho Ifejika, Ngozi Nwaka. BSc, U. Nigeria, Nsukka, 1978; PhD, U. Nigeria, 1986. Tutor chemistry State Edn. Commn., Enugu, Nigeria, 1979-89; rsch. assoc. U. Nigeria, Nsukka, 1982-89, asst. prof., 1989-94; rsch. fellow Shaman Pharms., Inc., South San Francisco, Calif., 1994-95. Resource person Raw Materials R & D coun., Lagos, Nigeria, 1992—; rsch. assoc. Internat. Orgn. Chemistry in Devel., 1992—; faculty rep. Senate of U. Nigeria, 1993-94. Discovered organic reaction mechanism, 1990. Tchr., mentor Nat. Youth Svc. Corps, Lagos, 1978-79; co-founder Grad. Students' Union U. Nigeria, Nsukka, 1982, chmn. Kwame Nkrumah Hall, 1982-83. Rsch. grantee Stiftung Volkswagenwerk, Hannover, Germany, 1991; grad. scholar Fed. Ministry of Edn., Nigeria, 1982-84. Mem. AAAS, Am. Chem. Soc., Soc. Free Radical Rsch. (assoc. editor 1992), Nigerian Soc. Pharmacognosy. Roman Catholic. Avocations: jogging, reading, hiking, classical music. Home: 417 Valley Hill Rd SW Apt K8 Riverdale GA 30274-2773 Office: Tetrahedron Labs Inc PO Box 741295 Riverdale GA 30274 E-mail: apusimalobi@hotmail.com.

AWAIS, GEORGE MUSA, obstetrician, gynecologist; b. Ajloun, Jordan, Dec. 15, 1929; arrived in U.S., 1951; s. Musa and Meha (Koury) A.; m. Nabila Rizk, June 24, 1970 AB, Hope Coll., 1955; MD, U. Toronto, 1960. Diplomate Am. Bd. Obstetrics and Gynecology. Intern U. Toronto Hosps., Ont., Can., 1960-61, resident in obstetrics and gynecology, 1961-64, chief resident, 1965, Harlem Hosp., Columbia U., N.Y.C., 1966; asst. obstetrician and gynecologist Cleve. Met. Gen. Hosp., 1967, assoc. obstetrician and gynecologist, 1969; instr. obstetrics and gynecology Case Western Res. U., Cleve., 1967-70, asst. obstetrician and gynecologist MacDonald House, 1970, asst. prof., 1970, asst. clin. prof. dept. reproductive biology, 1971, asst. obstetrician and gynecologist Univ. Hosps., 1971; mem. staff, dept. gynecology Cleve. Clinic Found., 1971-91. Chmn. dept. ob-gyn. King Faisal Specialist Hosp. and Rsch. Ctr., Riyadh, 1975-76; cons. panel mem. Internat. Corr. Soc. Obstetricians and Gynecologists, 1971; emeritus staff Cleve. Clinic Found., 1991; pres. Task Force on Humanitarian Aid and Relief Inc., 1997. Contbr. articles to publs. in field, papers, reports to confs., TV appearances, Saudi Arabia Named Grand Officer of Order of Independence His Majesty King Hussein of Jordan, 1992. Fellow ACS, Am. Coll. Obstetricians and Gynecologists, Royal Coll. Surgeons Can.; mem. AMA, AAAS, Am. Infertility Soc., Arab Am. Med. Assn. (pres. 1991—, chmn. humanities relief 1996), Acad. Medicine of Cleve. Office: Cleve Clinic Found Emeritus Office EE/40 9500 Euclid Ave Cleveland OH 44195-0001 E-mail: emeritus@ccf.org.

AWAN, AHMAD NOOR, civil engineer; b. Chakwal, Punjab, Pakistan, June 2, 1942; came to U.S., 1969; s. Ghulam Hussain and Sayada Awan; m. Nargis Parveen Janjua, Dec. 24, 1972; children: Monazza, Shujah, Noureen, Farah. BSc in Civil Engring., U. Engring., Lahore, Pakistan, 1965; MS in Civil Engring., U. Pa., Phila., 1971; grad. project mgmt. program, Poly. Inst. N.Y., 1976. Registered profl. engr., N.Y., N.J., Pa. Civil engr. Water & Power Devel. Authority of Govt. Pakistan, Lahore, 1965-66; project resident engr., cons. Govt. Libya, El Beida, 1966-68; sr. structural engr. Stone & Webster Enging. Corp., N.Y.C., 1971-79; sr. project mgr., mgmt. cons. U.S. Army C.E. Middle East, Saudi Arabia, 1979-83; sr. engr. project Port Authority of N.Y. and N.J., N.Y.C., 1985—. Mem. internat. roster of experts in fields of engring., constrn. bldg., fin. and contracts and tenders Habitat, UN Centre for Human Settlements, 1980. Recipient Exceptional Svc. award Port Authority N.Y. and N.J. Mem. ASCE, Am. Concrete Inst. Achievements include development of computerized project management system for U.S. Army Corps of Engineers for 10 billion dollar super construction project; managed major restoration team after New York World Trade Center bombing, 1993. Home: 6 Silver Hollow New Brunswick NJ 08902-2600 E-mail: aawan@optonline.net.

AWASTHI, VIDYA NIDHI, accounting educator; b. Jhansi, India, July 8, 1955; BSc, Meerut (India) U., 1974, MA, 1976; MBA, Calif. State U., Fresno, 1984; PhD, U. Wash., 1988. CPA, Wash., cert. mgmt. acct., cert. in fin. mgmt. Bank officer State Bank of India, Kanpur, 1976-82; tchg. assoc. U. Wash., Seattle, 1984-88; asst. prof. Santa Clara (Calif.) U., 1988-96, Seattle U., 1996-99, assoc. prof. Contbr. articles to profl. jours. Mem. Am. Acctg. Assn., Inst. Mgmt. Accts., Mensa. Office: Seattle U 900 Broadway Seattle WA 98122-4340

AWSUMB, ROBERT ARDIN, lawyer; b. St. Paul, Minn., Nov. 26, 1959; s. Roger Leonard Awsumb and Paula Ann Downs. BA, U. Minn., 1982; JD magna cum laude, William Mitchell Coll. Law, St. Paul, 1986. Bar: Minn. 1986. Assoc. atty. Rider, Bennett, Egan & Arundel, Mpls., 1986—91; pres., founding ptnr. Rambow & Awsumb, Bloomington, Minn., 1991—98; founder, chief mgr. R.A.

Awsumb & Assocs., St. Paul, 1998—. Adj. prof. William Mitchell Coll. Law, 1993—; mediator Minn. Supreme Ct., St. Paul, 1994—. Avocations: camping, fishing, travel. Office: RA Awsumb & Assocs 2010 Landmark Towers 345 Saint Peter St Saint Paul MN 55102-1211 E-mail: raawsumb@mediate.com.

AWTREY, JIM L. sports association executive; b. Oakland, Calif., Nov. 18, 1943; s. Hal G. and Betty D. (Kieff) A.; m. Jeannie M. Scott, Feb. 8, 1968; children: Jena, Julie, Justin. BABA, U. Okla., 1966. Asst. profl. Okla. City Country Club, 1966-69, Siwanoy Country Club, Bronxville, N.Y., 1968-69; profl. golfer PGA Tour, 1970-71; coach, gen. mgr. Univ. Golf Club, Norman, Okla., 1972-77; head Heritage Hills Golf Club, Claremore, Okla., 1977-80, Dornick Hills Golf Club, Ardmore, Okla., 1980-82; gen. mgr. The Trails Golf Club, Norman, 1982-86; mgr. tournament ops. PGA, Palm Beach Gardens, Fla., 1986-87, exec. dir., CEO, 1987-88, chief exec. officer, pres., exec. dir., 1988—. Sec.-treas., pres. South Cen. sect. PGA, 1975-76, co-vice chmn. rules com, 1984-86, co-vice chmn. jr. golf, 1985-86, vice chmn. info. svcs., 1987, vice chmn. tournament 1987; head coach golf team U. Okla., Norman, 1972-77. Mem. Econ. Coun., Palm Beach, Fla., 1989-92; bd. dirs. Fellowship Christian Athletes, Palm Beach Gardens, 1989-92. Recipient Golf Profl. of Yr. award South Ctrl. PGA, 1977, Horton Smith award, 1979. Republican. Methodist. Avocation: fishing. Office: PGA 100 Avenue of Champions PO Box 109601 Palm Beach Gardens FL 33410-9601

AX, EMANUEL, pianist; b. Lvov, Poland, June 8, 1949; s. Joachim and Hellen (Kurtz) A.; m. Yoko Nozaki, Nov. 23, 1974; 2 children. Student of Mieczyslaw Munz, Juilliard Sch. Music; BA, Columbia U. Appeared as soloist Chgo., Los Angeles, Phila., Rochester, Seattle, St. Louis and London, Philharm. orchs., N.Y. Philharm., Israel Philharm., Pitts. Symphony; recitalist (with Yo-Yo Ma) Avery Fisher Hall, Carnegie Hall, N.Y.C., festival at Tanglewood, Hollywood Bowl and Ravinia; toured extensively in C.Am. and S.Am., performed in joint recital (with violinist Nathan Milstein), extensive tours, Europe, Japan; with major orchs.; also recs. Winner Arthur Rubinstein Internat. Competition 1974, Avery Fisher prize 1979; recipient Young Concert Artist's Michaels award 1975; 4 Grammy awards Office: care ICM Artists 40 W 57th St New York NY 10019-4001 or: care Harold Holt Ltd 31 Sinclair Rd London W14 ONS England

AXCELL, DOUGLAS NORMAN, business consultant, minister; b. Southend-on-Sea, Essex, Eng., Jan. 13, 1934; s. Frank Norman and Evelyn Ida (Giles) A.; m. Nora Ellen Tree, Aug. 3, 1957 (div. 1972); children: Ruth Ellen, Joy Evelyn; m. Janita Dianne Lines, June 21, 1980. BDiv with honours, Knightsbridge U., Denmark, 1992; Bus. Mgmt. Diploma, Ford Mktg. Inst. Cert. road transport engr., transport adminstr. Apprentice Malcolm Motors, Leigh-on-Sea, Eng., 1949-55; technician RAF, U.K., Gibraltar, Africa, 1955-57; foreman Abbott Motors, Leigh-on-Sea, Eng., 1957-66; svc. mgr. Harpurs of Letchworth, Eng., 1966-69; depot mgr. Charles King, Bedford, Eng., 1969-73; group svc. mgr. Welch & Co., Bristol, Eng., 1973-75; gen. mgr. Mohsin Haider Darwish, Sultanate of Oman, 1975-88; cons. on Arab bus. affairs, 1988—; min. Javea (Spain) Internat. Bapt. Ch., 1988—99. Deacon, Ferndale Bapt. Ch., Southend-on-Sea, 1957; lay asst. pastor Westcliff Free Ch., Westcliff-on-Sea, 1961; lay pastor Rochford (Eng.) Bapt. Ch., 1964; itinerant preacher Bunyan Ch. Soc., Bedford, 1967-72; chorister and gospel singer, 1957—.; moderator Scunthorpe (Eng.) Baptist Ch., 2002—. Mem. Inst. Road Transport Engrs., Inst. Transport Adminstrn. Avocations: singing, european history, theology, photography, target shooting. Home: Charis, 6 Eccles Ct Wrawby Lincolnshire DN20 8TD England E-mail: dangard@beeb.net.

AXE, JOHN RANDOLPH, lawyer, financial executive; b. Grand Rapids, Mich., Apr. 30, 1938; s. John Jacob and Elizabeth Katherine (Lynott) A.; m. Linda Sadlier Stroh, June 1, 1989; children from previous marriage: Catherine, Peter, Meredith, Sara, Jay. stepchildren: Suzanne Stroh, Greg Stroh. AB, U. Mich., 1960; LLB, Harvard U., 1963. Bar: Mich. 1964. Ptnr. Dickinson, Wright, McKean, Cudlip, Detroit, 1972-80, Martin, Axe, Buhl & Schwartz, Bloomfield Hills, Mich., 1981-82, Axe & Schwartz, Bloomfield Hills, 1983-85, Dykema, Gossett, Spencer, Goodnow, Detroit, 1985-89; prin. John R. Axe and Assocs., Detroit, 1989—2000; shareholder Axe & Ecklund, P.C., Detroit, 2001—. Pres. Mcpl. Fin. Cons., Inc., Detroit, 1982—; adj. prof. Wayne State U. Law Sch., 1992—. Mem. Mich. Higher Edn. Assistance Authority, Lansing, Mich., 1977-83. Served to lt. USNR, 1965-69. With USNR, 1965—69. Mem. Nat. Assn. Bond Lawyers (steering com. 1981-83, 86, bd. dirs. 1987-90), Mich. Assn. County Treas. (gen. counsel 1977-88), Downtown Assn. Club (N.Y.C.), Doubles Club (N.Y.C.), Mill Reef Club (Antigua). Office: Axe & Ecklund PC 21 Kercheval Ave Ste 360 Grosse Pointe Farms MI 48236-3633

AXEL, BERNARD, finance executive; b. Bklyn., May 23, 1946; s. Joseph and Irene (Rosen) A.; m. Tobie Reznik, Sept. 3, 1995. BS, U. Ala., 1967; grad., Am. Inst. Banking, 1970. Asst. cashier, comptroller Nat. Bank of Commerce (formerly Am. Nat. Bank), Birmingham, Ala., 1967-72; supr. internat. travel Travel Anywhere, Birmingham, 1972; acctg. and purchasing agt. U.S. Dept. Justice, Texarkana, Tex., 1972-74; mgr. Styslinger Realty, Birmingham, 1974-75; pres. Christian's Inc., Birmingham, 1975-92, Christian's Tutwiler, Inc., Birmingham, 1992-98; mgr. Tucker Cos., Tuscaloosa, Ala., 1998—; v.p. Tucker Fin. Co., Tucker Title Co., Tuscaloosa, 1998—; v.p., COO Tucker Fin. Co., 2001—. Gourmet chef Top of Morning show Sta. WVTM-T-V, Birmingham, 1991—, Good Day Ala. WBRC-TV, Birmingham, 1996—. Contbr. recipes to mags. Judge March of Dimes Gourmet Gala, Birmingham, 1986, Miss Ala.-U.S.A. Pageant, 1990, 91, Miss Teen Ala., 1992; mem. gov.'s staff State of Ala., Montgomery, 1968-70, mem. lt. gov.'s staff, 1980-84; bd. dirs. Temple Beth El, 1969-72; mem. adv. bd. U. Ala. Sch. Restaurant Hospitality Mgmt., 1989—, chmn. adv. bd., 1992—. Awarded Key to City of Birmingham, Ala., 1991. Mem. Nat. Restaurant Assn. (cert. foodsvc. mgmt. profl., mem. adv. bd. polit. action com. 1987-98, state chmn. 1993-98, bd. dirs. 1996-98), Am. Culinary Fedn. (bd. dirs. Birmingham chpt., medal 1986, Appreciation award 1991), Ala. Restaurant and Food Svc. Assn. (bd. dirs. 1983-98, pres. 1990-92, trustee self-ins. fund 1994-96, Restaurateur of Yr. 1992, Polit. Eagle award 1994), Birmingham-Jefferson County Restaurant Assn. (bd. dirs. 1981-83, 89-98, Restaurant Operator of Yr. 1995), Birmingham-Jefferson Restaurant Assn. (pres. 1995), Chaine des Rotisseurs (L'Order Mondial des Gourmets Degustateurs 1989, coord. culinaire south ctrl. 1996-97), Les Disciples d'Auguste Escoffier Assn. Gastronomique, Commanderie des Cordon Bleus France. Republican. Avocations: travel, cooking. Home: 1716 Dauphine Dr Tuscaloosa AL 35406-3070 Office: Tucker Cos 3302 Mcfarland Blvd E Tuscaloosa AL 35405-2424

AXELRAD, JEFFREY, lawyer; b. Uniontown, Pa., July 29, 1942; s. Louis M. and Leila (Husin) A.; children: Michelle G., Douglas R. BS, Carnegie Inst. Tech., 1964; JD cum laude, Northwestern U., 1967. Bar: Ill. 1967, D.C. 1969, U.S. Ct. Appeals (2d, 3d, 5th, 6th, 8th, 10th, 11th and D.C. cirs.), U.S. Supreme Ct. Trial atty. Dept. Justice, Washington, 1967-75, chief info. and privacy sect., 1975-77, chief torts sect., 1977-78, dir. torts br., 1978—. Mem. Fed. Bar Assn. Home: 4601 N Park Ave Apt 217 Chevy Chase MD 20815-4530 Office: Dept Justice PO Box 888 Washington DC 20044-0888 E-mail: ja729@aol.com.

AXELROD, EMILY H. urban planner; d. Granger F. and Virginia S. Hill; m. Ronald H. Axelrod, Nov. 26, 1976; children: David Farwell, Melissa Winslow. BA, U. Calif., Santa Cruz, 1968; MA in city planning, Harvard Grad. Sch. of Design, 1976. Sr. planner dept. planning City of San Francisco, 1968—74; cons. Benjamin Thompson & Assoc., Cambridge, Mass., 1984—89; sr. planner Fleet Ctr. Devel. Team, Boston, 1989—95; dir. Rudy Bruner Award, Cambridge, Mass., 1995—. Home: 26-B Shepard St Cambridge MA 02138 Office: Bruner Fdn 130 Prospect St Cambridge MA 02139

AXELROD, GLEN SCOTT, publishing company executive, pet product company executive; b. Newark, Nov. 4, 1953; s. Alan Robert and Janet Lee Axelrod; m. Jennifer Anderson, June 24, 1979; children: Jason Aaron, Daniel Jay. BA in Biology, Rutgers U., 1975; MSc in Zoology/Ichthyology, Rhodes U., Grahamstown, South Africa, 1978. Rschr. in phylogenetics Rhodes U. and Mus. Comparative Zoology, Harvard U., 1978-79; asst. to pres., sr. editor TFH Pubs., Inc., Neptune City, N.J., 1979-81; asst. to prin. Six Star Cablevision Group, Englewood, N.J., 1981-82; exec. v.p. Breckenridge Devel. Corp., Wayne, N.J., 1985-92; pres., CEO Design Svcs., Riverdale, N.J., 1992-95; pres. GJA Prodn. Corp., Mahwah, N.J., 1982—; exec. v.p. TFH Pubs., Inc., Neptune City, 1996-97, pres., CEO, 1997—. Bd. dirs. TFH Pubs., Inc. Exec. editor zool. mags.; patentee in field; contbr. articles to profl. jours. Trustee, treas. Deerhaven Assn., Mahwah, 1990-97. Fellow The Zool. Soc. London (sci.), Masons. Achievements include taxonomic description of new Pisces species. Office: TFH Publications Inc One TFH Plz 3d & Union Neptune City NJ 07753

AXELROD, JONATHAN GANS, lawyer; b. N.Y.C., Oct. 23, 1946; s. Arthur and Rosalind (Gans) Axelrod; m. Carol Jean Zachary, Jan. 16, 1983; children: Zachary Arthur, Tristan Gans. AB, Dartmouth Coll., 1968; JD, Columbia U., 1971; LLM in Labor Law, George Washington U., 1975. Bar: N.Y. 1971, D.C. 1975. Trial atty. App. Ct. Br. NLRB, 1971-74; asst. gen. csl Ea. Conf. Teamsters, 1974-80; ptnr. Beins, Axelrod, Osborne, Mooney & Green, Washington, 1980-96, Beins, Axelrod, Kraft, Gleason & Gibson, P.C., Washington, 1996—. Contbr. articles to profl. jours. Mem. ABA, D.C. Bar Assn. (co-chmn. sect. on labor law 1985-89, steering com. 1990-91). Office: Beins Axelrod Kraft Gleason & Gibson PC 1717 Massachusetts Ave NW Washington DC 20036-2001 E-mail: jaxelrod@bakgg.com.

AXELROD, JULIUS, pharmacologist, researcher; b. N.Y.C., May 30, 1912; s. Isadore and Molly (Leichtling) Axelrod; m. Sally Taub, Aug. 30, 1938; children: Paul Mark, Alfred Nathan. BS, CCNY, 1933; MA, NYU, 1941, DSc (hon.), 1971; PhD, George Washington U., 1955, LLD (hon.), 1971; DSc (hon.), U. Chgo., 1965, Med. Coll. Wis., 1971, Med. Coll. Pa., 1974, U. Pa., 1986, Hahnemann U., 1987; LLD (hon.), CCNY, 1972; PhD (hon.), U. Panama, 1972, U. Paris (Sud), 1982, Ripon Coll, 1984, Tel Aviv U., 1984; DSc (hon.), McGill U., Montreal, 1989. Chemist Lab. Indsl. Hygiene, 1935—46; rsch. assoc. 3d NYU rsch. divsn. Goldwater Meml. Hosp., 1946—49; assoc. chemist sect. chem. pharmacology Nat. Heart Inst., NIH, 1949—50, chemist, 1950—53, sr. chemist, 1953—55; acting chief sect. pharmacology Lab. Clin. Sci. NIMH, 1955, chief sect. pharmacology, 1955—84, guest worker Lab. Cell Biology, 1985—; scientist emeritus NIH, 1996. Otto Loewi Meml. lectr. NYU, 1963; Karl E. Paschkis Meml. lectr. Phila. Endocrine Soc., 1966; NIH lectr., 67; Nathanson Meml. lectr. U. So. Calif., 1968; James Parkinson lectr. Columbia U., 1971; Wartenberg lectr. Am. Acad. Neurology, 1971; Arnold D. Welch lectr. Yale U., 1971; Harold Carpenter Hodge Distinguished lectr. toxicology U. Rochester, 1971; Bennett lectr. Am. Neurol. Assn., 1971; Harvey lectr., 71; Mayer lectr. MIT, 1971; Disting. Prof. Sci. George Washington U., 1972; Salmon lectr. N.Y. Acad. Medicine, 1972; Eli Lilly lectr., 72; Mike Hogg lectr. U. Tenn. 1972; Fred Schueler lectr. Tulane U., 1972; others; vis. scholar Herbert Lehman Coll. CUNY, 1973; professorial lectr. George Washington U., 1959—; panelist U.S. Bd. Civil Svc. Examiners, 1958—67; rsch. adv. com. United Cerebral Palsy Assn., 1966—69; mem. psychopharmacology study sect. NIMH, 1970—74; mem. Internat. Brain Rsch. Orgn.; rsch. adv. com. Nat. Found.; vis. com. Brookhaven Nat. Lab., 1972—76; bd. overseers Jackson Lab., 1974—88. Editl. bd. Jour. Pharmacology and Exptl. Therapeutics, 1956—72, Jour. Medicinal Chemistry, 1962—67, Circulation Rsch., 1963—71, Currents in Modern Biology, 1966—72, mem. editl. adv. bd. Communication in Behavioral Biology, 1967—73, Jour. Neurobiology, 1968—77, Jour. Neurochemistry, 1969—77, Jour. Neurovisceral Relation, 1969, Rassegna di Neurologia Vegetativa, 1969—, Internat. Jour. Psychobiology, 1970—75, hon. cons. editor Life Scis., 1961—69; co-author: The Pineal, 1968; contbr. articles to profl. jours. Recipient Meritorious Rsch. award, Assn. Rsch. Nervous and Mental Diseases, 1965, Gairdner award disting. rsch., 1967, Nobel prize in Med. Physiology, 1970, Alumni Disting. Achievement award, George Washington U., 1968, Superior Svc. award, HEW, 1968, Disting. Svc. award, 1970, Claude Bernard professorship and medal, U. Montreal, 1969, Disting. Svc. award, Modern Medicine mag., 1970, Albert Einstein award, Yeshiva U., 1971, medal, Rudolf Virchow Med. Soc., 1971, Myrtle Wreath award, Hadassah, 1972, Leibniz medal, Acad. Sci. East Germany, 1984, Salmon medal, N.Y. Acad. Medicine, Bristol-Myers award for disting. rsch. in neurosci., 1989, Thudicum medal, Brit. Biochem. Soc. (lectr.), 1989, Gerard medal, Soc. Neurosci., 1991. Fellow: AAAS, Am. Soc. Neuropsychopharmacology, Am. Acad. Arts and Scis.; mem.: NAS, Deutsche Academie Naturfoucher (East Germany), Am. Philos. Soc., German Pharmacol. Soc. (corr.), Am. Neurol. Assn. (hon.), Inst. Medicine (sr.), Am. Psychopathol. Assn. (hon.), Royal Soc. London (fgn. mem.), Am. Soc. Pharmacology and Exptl. Therapeutics (Torald Sollmann award 1973), Am. Chem. Soc., Sigma Xi. Home: 10401 Grosvenor Pl Rockville MD 20852-4646 Office: NIH Dept Health Edn & Welfare 9000 Rockville Pike Rm 3a-15 Bethesda MD 20892-0003

AXELROD, LEAH JOY, tour company executive; b. Milw., Sept. 7, 1929; d. Harry J. and Helen Janet (Ackerman) Mandelker; m. Leslie Robert Axelrod, Mar. 10, 1951; children: David Jay, Craig Lewis, Harry Besser, Garrick Paul, Bradley Neal, Nell Anne. BS, U. Wis., 1951. Creative drama specialist Highland Park (Ill.) Parks and Recreation Dept., 1962-82; program specialist Pub. Libr., Highland Park, 1972-82; ednl. cons. Bd. Jewish Edn., Chgo., 1973-80; children's edn. specialist Jewish Cmty. Ctr., Chgo., 1975-82; tour cons. My Kind of Town Tours, Highland Park, 1975-79, pres., 1979—. Co-owner Tours at the Mart, 1992-95. Editor: Highland Park: All American City, 1976; co-author: Highland Park By Foot or By Frame, 1980, Highland Park: American Suburb, 1982; co-editor: Adventures in Highland Park, 2001. Founding mem., v.p. Highland Park Hist. Soc., pres., 1987—94, past pres., 1994—; bd. dirs. Ill. State Hist. Soc., 1989—, exec. bd. dirs., 1999—; founder, bd. dirs. Chgo. Jewish Hist. Soc., 1975—, Team Ill., 1999, sec., 2001—03; exec. com., adv. bd. Apple Tree Theatre Co., assoc. bd. pres., 2001—; active Highland Park Hist. Preservation Commn.; pres. B'nai Torah Sisterhood, 1982—84; Bd. dirs. Midwest Zionist Youth Commn.; bd. dirs. Highland Park Hist. Soc., 1996—, Friends Jens Jensen, 1995—99. Mem. Nat. Assn. Women Bus. Owners, Am. Theatre Assn., Ill. Theatre Assn. (dir. creative dramatics 1977-79), Hadassah Club (Highland Park chpt.), Chgo. Area Women's History Conf. Bd., Coun. for Ill. History. Home: 2100 Linden Ave Highland Park IL 60035-2516 E-mail: tourtime@worldnct.att.net.

AXELROD, LEONARD, court administrator; b. Oct. 27, 1950; s. Morris and Doris S. A. BA, Ind. U., 1972; MPA, U. So. Calif., 1974; JD, Hamline U., 1982. Asst. dir. Ind. Jud. Ctr. Ind. U. Sch. Law, Indpls., 1974-76; cons. Booz, Allen & Hamilton, Washington, 1976-77; staff assoc. Nat. Ctr. State Cts., St. Paul, 1977-82; ptnr. Ct. Mgmt. Cons., Mpls., Va., 1982-87, Friedman, Farrar & Axelrod, Mpls., 1984-86; prin. Ct. Mgmt. Cons., Mpls., 1987-94; sec., treas. CMC Justice Svcs., Inc., Mpls., 1994—95; project mgr. Legal Rsch. Ctr., Mpls., 1996-97; ct. adminstr. U.S. Bankruptcy Ct., Mpls., 1997—. Cons. Ctr. Jury Studies, Vienna, Va., 1979-82, Calif. Atty. Gen., 1972-73, Control Data Bus. Advisers, Mpls., 1982-88; adj. prof. Coll. Mgmt., Met. State U., 1998—; arbitrator BBB, 2002—. Author: North Dakota Bench Book, 1982; contbr. articles to profl. jours.; assoc. editor Law Rev. Digest, 1982. Mem. presdl. search com. Hamline U., 1980-81; reporter Minn. Citizen Conf. on Cts., 1980; appointed to The Petrofund Bd., 1994. Samuel Miller scholar, 1981. Mem. ABA, ASPA, So. Calif. Soc. Pub. Adminstrn., Booz, Allen & Hamilton Alumni (pres. Minn. 1980), The Brandeis Soc. (exec. dir. Mpls. 1980), U. so. Calif. Midwest Alumni (exec. bd. Chgo. 1974), Phi Alpha Alpha, Phi Alpha Delta. Office: US Bankruptcy Ctt Dist of Minn 316 Robert St N Ste 200 Saint Paul MN 55101-1241 E-mail: mnusb@juno.com.

AXELROD, LLOYD, endocrinologist, diabetologist, educator; b. Bklyn., July 29, 1942; s. Louis E. and Sadie Rachel (Katz) A.; 1 child, Catherine Louise. AB, Princeton U., 1963; MD, Harvard U., 1967. Diplomate Am. Bd. Internal Medicine, endocrinology, diabetes and metabolism. Intern in medicine Peter Bent Brigham Hosp., Boston, 1967-68, jr. resident in medicine, 1968-69, rsch. fellow endocrinology, 1969-70, asst. in medicine, 1970-72; resident in medicine Mass. Gen. Hosp., Boston, 1970-71, clin. and rsch. fellow in medicine, 1971-72, chief resident in medicine, 1973, asst. in medicine, 1974-78, asst. physician, 1979-80, assoc. physician, 1981-89, physician, 1989—, chief James Howard Means firm, 1989—; chief med. unit Mass. Eye and Ear Infirmary, Boston, 1977-85. Instr. medicine Harvard Med. Sch., 1973-76, asst. prof. medicine, 1976-83, assoc. prof. medicine, 1983—; chmn. spl. rev. group Nat. Inst. Arthritis, Diabetes and Digestive and Kidney Diseases NIH, 1984-85; staff com. on ethics and stds. practice Mass. Gen. Hosp., 1989-94, ad hoc com. on informed consent, 1989-95, pharmacy com. 1985-90, tng. program com., med. svcs., 1989—, tchg. and tng. com., med. svcs., 1997-, com. mem., instr. primary care program, 1974-88; chief's com. Mass. Eye and Ear Infirmary, 1977-85, patient care com., 1977-85, planning com., 1977-85, other coms.; standing com. on alumni fellowships Harvard Med. Sch., 1980-97; chmn. Harvard Med. Sch. bicentennial com. Mass. Eye and Ear Infirmary, 1981-83; preceptor New Pathway Project in Gen. Med. Edn. Harvard Med. Sch., 1986-88; cons. U.S. Atty., Dept. Justice, 1999, 2003, State of Calif. Dept. of Justice, 2001; lectr. in field. Co-author: (with others) Pineal Tumors, 1977, Human Health and Disease, 1977, Handbook of Drug Therapy, 1979, Textbook of Rheumatology, 1981, 4th rev. edit., 1993; Reviews on Endocrine Related Cancer, 1981, Conn's Current Therapy, 36th edit., 1984, Pathophysiology The Biological Principles of Disease, 2d edit., 1985, Anti-inflammatory Steroid Action: Basic and Clinical Aspects, 1989, Principles and Practice of Endocrinology and Metabolism, 1990, 3d rev. edit., 2001, Joslin's Diabetes Mellitus, 13th edit., 1994, Endocrinology, 4th edit., 2001, Endocrinology Mebabolism Clin. N.Am., 2003; editor Endocrinology Rounds, 2002—; mem. editl. bd. Diabetes, 1988-90; contbr. articles to profl. jours. Mem. U.S. Del. to China, 1975; mem. Mass. Gen. Hosp. Del. to China, 1979; mem. Guangdong com. of Mass. fgn. bus. coun. Commonwealth of Mass., 1981-82; adv. coun. Gov. Michael S. Dukakis on Mass.-Guangdong Friendship Agreement, 1984-88; diabetes guidelines work group Diabetes Control Program, Dept. Pub. Health Commonwealth of Mass., 2001, 03. Daland fellow for rsch. in Clin. Medicine Am. Philos. Soc., 1974-77. Fellow ACP; mem. Am. Diabetes Assn., Am. Fedn. Med. Research, N.Y. Acad. Scis., The Endocrine Soc., AAAS, Fuller Albright Soc. Harvard Med. Sch., Phi Beta Kappa, Alpha Omega Alpha. Achievements include discovery prostacyclin prodn. by adipose tissue, regulation of lipolysis by prostaglandins in adipose tissue and role of prostacyclin in pathogenesis of hemodynamic complications of diabetic ketoacidosis; and description of insulin-like growth factor II(IGF-II) in pathogenesis of tumor-induced hypoglycemia; scholarly contributions on glucocorticoid therapy. Office: Mass Gen Hosp Diabetes Unit Fruit St Boston MA 02114-2620

AXELROD, NORMAN N(ATHAN), technical planning and technology application consultant; b. N.Y.C., Aug. 26, 1934; s. Louis E. and Sadie (Katz) A.; m. Victoria Ann Grant, Mar. 21, 1975; children: Lauren Grant, Brian George. AB, Cornell U., 1954; postgrad., U. Paris, France, 1958; PhD in Optics and Physics, U. Rochester, 1959. Aerospace scientist NASA, Goddard Space Flight Ctr., Washington, 1959-60; rsch. fellow U. London, 1960-61; asst. prof. U. Del., 1961-65; mem. tech. staff Bell Labs., Murray Hill, N.J., 1965-72; prin. Axelrod Assocs., N.Y.C., 1972—. Bd. dirs. World Resources Devel. Corp., Input-Output Tech., Inc.; mem. adv. bd. Del. Dept. Edn., 1963-64; participant vis. scientist program Am. Inst. Physics, 1963-64; cons. Met. Mus. Art, N.Y.C., 1969-72; advisor to White House, 1969-70, French Ministry Nat. Def. and War, 1971, Am. Consumer Products, Inc., Bausch & Lomb, Calor plc, Compuscan, Corning, CPC, Dalen, Finnegan, Henderson et al, GE, Gen Probe, Honeywell, IBM, ITT, Internat. FiberCom, Gen-Probe, Konishiroku, Johnson & Johnson, Labatt, Lear Siegler, Lockheed Martin, Medtronic, Recognition Equipment Inc., Perkin-Elmer, Sharp, Proctor & Gamble, Sensar, Teradyne, Timken Co., Unilever Rsch., Wall St. Jour., Wheatland Tube, Woodgrain Millwork; guest cons. Marine Biol. Lab., Woods Hole, Mass., 1993—. Editor: Optical Properties of Dielectric Films, 1968; book reviewer, cons. John Wiley & Sons, 1965-68, Rheinhold-Van Nostrand, 1968-70, Pergamon Press, 1969-70; contbr. articles to profl. jours. Patentee in field. Boldt scholar; recipient Fortune 500 Corp. award for tech. contbn., 1990; grantee NATO, NSF, Office of Naval Rsch. Fellow AAAS; mem. IEEE, Am. Phys. Soc., Am. Optical Soc., Soc. Mfg. Engrs. (cert. by stature as CMfgE in machine vision), Del. Acad. Sci., N.Y. Acad. Sci., Electrochem. Soc., Sigma Xi, Sigma Pi Sigma, Pi Mu Epsilon. Home: 445 E 86th St New York NY 10028-6433 Office: Norman Axelrod Assocs 121 W 27th St Ste 601 New York NY 10001-6207 E-mail: naxelrod@axelrodassociates.com.

AXELSON, CHARLES FREDERIC, retired accounting educator; b. Chgo., Apr. 24, 1917; m. Dorothy L. Jepson, July 23, 1940 (dec. Oct. 1994); children: Linda Axelson Masters, Fred, Lorraine Axelson Gresty; m. Marion I. Murray, Mar. 11, 1995. AB, MBA, U. Chgo., 1937. Staff acct. Lybrand, Ross Bros. & Montgomery, Chgo., 1938-41; with U.S. Gypsum Co., Chgo., 1941-70, asst. controller, 1946-52, controller, 1952-60, controller, asst. treas., 1960-70; v.p. controller Libby, McNeill & Libby, Chgo., 1970-78; v.p., chief fin. officer Lawry's Foods, Inc., Los Angeles, 1978-82; prof. acctg. U. So. Calif., Los Angeles, 1982-85; vis. lectr. Darling Downs Inst. Advanced Edn., Toowoomba, Queensland, Australia, 1985; lectr. acctg. Calif. State Poly. U., Pomona, 1985-92; lectr. emeritus, 1992. Lectr. acctg. Northwestern U., 1946-53; bd. dirs. Air Conditioning Co., 1982-96; bd. dirs. Goodwill Industries So. Calif., 1982—. Trustee emeritus Nat. Louis U.; bd. dirs. Ability First (formerly Crippled Children's Soc. So. Calif.), chmn., 1986-89, vice-chmn., 1990-99. Named to Calif. Poly. Acctg. Hall of Fame, 1996; named Lipton Vol. of Yr., 1997. Mem. AICPA, Fin. Execs. Inst. (past dir. L.A. chpt., past pres. Chgo. chpt., past nat. dir., past v.p. Midwestern area), Phi Delta Theta. Clubs: Town Hall (Los Angeles). Presbyterian. Home: 888 S Orange Grove Blvd # 2-w Pasadena CA 91105-1790 *Whatever successes I've had - business and personal - can be traced to self-discipline, a good education, a reputation for integrity, much reading, good health, outside interests to offset business pressures and lots of advance planning.*

AXELSON, JOSEPH ALLEN, professional athletics executive, publisher; b. Peoria, Dec. 25, 1927; s. Joseph Victor Axelson and Florence (Ealen) Massey; m. Malcolm Rae Smith, Oct. 7, 1950 (dec.); children: David Allen, Mark Stephen, Linda Rae. BS, Northwestern U., 1949. Cert. judge Kansas City Barbeque Soc. Sports info. dir. Ga. So. U., Statesboro, 1957-60, Nat. Assn. Intercollegiate Athletics, Kansas City, Mo., 1961-62; tournament dir. Bowling Proprs. Assn. Am., Park Ridge, Ill., 1963-64; asst. exec. sec. Nat. Assn. Intercollegiate Athletics, Kansas City, Mo., 1964-68; exec. v.p., gen. mgr. Cin. Royals Profl. Basketball Team, Cin., 1969-72; mgr. Cin. Gardens, 1970-72; pres., gen. mgr. Kansas City Kings Profl. Basketball Team, Kansas City, Mo., 1972-79, 82-85, Sacramento Kings Profl. Basketball Team, 1985-88, exec. v.p., 1988-90; pres. Arco Arena, Sacramento, 1985-88; exec. v.p. Sacramento Sports Assn., Arco Sports Complex, 1988-90, Profl. Team Publs., Inc., Stamford, Conn., 1991-92; pub. Between The Vines Newsletter, 1993—. Exec. v.p. ops. NBA, N.Y.C., 1979-82, chmn. competition and rules com., 1975-79; trustee Naismith Basketball Hall of Fame; co-host The Sports Page, Sta. KFMB-AM, San Diego, 1994-97. Author: Basketball Basics, 1987. Mem. Emil Verban Meml. Soc., Washington. Capt. Signal Corps. AUS, 1949-54. Named Nat. Basketball Exec. of Yr. The Sporting News, St. Louis, 1973, Sportsman of Yr., Rockne Club, Kansas City, 1975; recipient Annual Dirs. award Downtown, Inc., Kansas City, Mo., 1979, Nat. Assn. Intercollegiate Athletics Frank Cramer Nat. Svc. award, 1983, Man of Yr. award Sacramento (Calif.) C. of C., 1986, Sacramento Bus. Cmty. award, 1986; named to Ga. So. U. Sports Hall of Fame, 1990. Mem. Am. Philatelic Soc., Soc. for Am. Baseball Rsch., Phi Kappa Psi, Morse Telegraph Club, Inc. Republican. Presbyterian.

AXELSON, LINDA RAE, event planning specialist; b. Statesboro, Ga., May 22, 1959; d. Joseph Allen and Malcolm Rae (Smith) Axelson; m. Aug. 29, 1981 (div. Feb. 1989). BA in Spanish, Baker U., 1981. Acct. Lois A. Brozey, CPA, San Diego, 1981-82; bus. mgr. San Diego Chicken, Inc., 1983; discount brokerage mgr. Union Bank and Trust, Bartlesville, Okla., 1984; bus. mgr. ARCO Arena, Sacramento, 1985-86, box office mgr., 1987-91, San Diego Sports Arena, 1991-92, Arrowhead Pond of Anaheim, Calif., 1993-96; asst. contr. Stamford Ctr. for the Arts, 1997-98, box office mgr., 1999—2000; events mgr. Allied Domecq Spirits and Wine N.Am., 2001—. Cons. Dor Chargin Boxing Prodns., L.A., 1987—. Recipient scholarship Baker Univ., 1981. Mem. Alpha Chi Omega (sch. com. chmn. 1981), Sigma Delta Pi, Alpha Mu Gamma. Republican. Presbyterian. Avocation: collector of mystery novels and miniatures. Home: 230 B Ave Coronado CA 92118-1970 Office: 355 Riverside Ave Westport CT 06880

AXENSON, THERESA J. physicist; b. Moscow, Idaho, June 3, 1971; d. N. Richard and Charlene Marie Acrndon; m. Steven A. Mumford. BS in Chemistry, U. Rochester, 1993; PhD in Chemistry, U. So. Calif., 1997. Physicist Sci. and Tech. Corp., Hampton, Va., 1998—. Presenter at confs. Contbr. articles to profl. jours. Bausch & Lomb fellow, 1989-93. Mem.: Optical Soc. Am., Am. Chem. Soc., Soc. Photo-optical Instrumentation Engrs. Avocation: tomiki aikido. Home: 730 Harpersville Rd Newport News VA 23601-1634 Office: Sci and Tech Corp NASA Langley Rsch Ctr 5 N Dryden St Hampton VA 23681-2109 E-mail: t.j.axenson@larc.nasa.gov.

AXFORD, ROY ARTHUR, nuclear engineering educator; b. Detroit, Aug. 26, 1928; s. Morgan and Charlotte (Donaldson) A.; m. Anne-Sofie Langfeldt Rasmussen, Apr. 1, 1954; children: Roy Arthur, Elizabeth Carole, Trevor Craig Charles. BA, Williams Coll., 1952; BS, Mass. Inst. Tech., 1952, MS, 1955, Sc.D., 1958. Supr. theoretical physics group Atomics Internat., Canoga Park,

Calif., 1958-60; assoc. prof. nuclear engring. Tex. A&M, 1960-62, prof., 1962-63; assoc. prof. nuclear engring. Northwestern U., 1963-66; assoc. prof. U. Ill., Urbana, 1966-68, prof., 1968—. Cons. Los Alamos Nat. Lab., 1963—. Vice-chmn. Mass. Inst. Tech. Alumni Fund Drive, 1970-72, chmn., 1973-75; sustaining fellow MIT, 1984. Recipient cert. of recognition for excellence in undergrad. teaching U. Ill., 1979, 81; Everitt award for teaching excellence, 1985. Mem. ASME, Am. Nuclear Soc. (Excellence in Undergrad. Teaching award 1990, 95, 97, 99, 2002, Disting. faculty Alpha Nu Sigma 1991), SAR (sec.-treas. Piankeshaw chpt. 1975-81, v.p. chpt. 1982-3, pres. chpt. 1984-86), Kiwanis (charter life patron fellow 1992), Sigma Xi, Tau Beta Pi, Phi Kappa Phi. Home: 2017 S Cottage Grove Ave Urbana IL 61801-6353

AXILROD, STEPHEN HARVEY, global economic consultant, economist; b. N.Y.C., June 21, 1926; s. Jacob James and Pearl (Feltenstein) A.; m. Katherine Podolsky, July 1, 1950; children: Peter, Emily Axilrod Hildner, Richard. Student, So. Meth. U., 1943-44; AB magna cum laude, Harvard U., 1948; MA, U. Chgo., 1950, postgrad., 1951-52. Assoc. dir. div. research and statistics Fed. Res. Bd., Washington, 1970-73, advisor to bd. govs., 1973-76, staff dir. for monetary and fin. policy, 1976-86; economist domestic fin. Fed. Open Market Com., Washington, 1974-78, economist, 1978-81; staff dir., sec. Fed. Open Market Commn., Washington, 1981-86; vice chmn. Nikko Securities Internat., N.Y.C., 1986-94; cons. internat. orgns. and ctrl. banks on policy ops., 1994—; cons. global econs. and markets pvt. practice, 1994—. Advisor Brookings Panel on Econ. Activity, Washington, 1986-89; mem. investment com. Japan Soc.; mem. adv. coun. Cul. Bank of Oman, 1993-99. Contbr. articles on monetary policy, credit and securities markets, transformation of policy ops. and markets in emerging countries and related matters to books, newspapers, mags. and profl. jours. With USN, 1944-46. Mem. Phi Beta Kappa. Avocations: flute, tennis, reading, hiking, poetry.

AXINN, DONALD EVERETT, real estate investor and developer, poet, writer; b. N.Y.C., July 13, 1929; s. Michael and Ann (Schneider) A. AB, Middlebury Coll., 1951, LittD (hon.), l989; MA, Hofstra U., 1975, LLD (hon.), 1991; LittD (hon.), So. Vt. Coll., 1989; LHD (hon.), SUNY, Farmingdale, 1996; LHD (hon), Adelphi U., 2003. Founder, owner Donald E. Axinn Co., Jericho, L.I., NY, 1958—; dir. Farrar, Straus & Giroux, Inc., N.Y.C., 1971-94; assoc. dean Hofstra U. Liberal Arts and Scis., Hempstead, NY, 1971-72; also dir. Inst. Arts.; chmn., mem. Nassau County Fine Arts Commn., 1970-73; mem. Gov.'s Task Force on Cultural Life and Arts, 1975—. Trustee N.Y. Ocean Scis. Labs., Montauk, N.Y., 1969-71, Waldemar Cancer Rsch. Inst., Woodbury, N.Y., 1966-68, North Shore U. Hosp., 1980-91, N.Y. State Nature and Hist. Preserve Trust, 1978-83, Nassau County Mus., 1980-83; trustee Hofstra U., 1970, 72—, sec., 1973-74, vice chmn., 1974—; trustee emeritus The Nature Conservancy, 1990—, chmn. Long Island chpt., 1997—; bd. dirs. Pro Arte Symphony Orch., 1967-70, N.Y. Quar. Poetry Rev. Found., Inc., 1969—, Eglevsky Ballet Co., Outward Bound, Inc.; v.p. bd. dirs. Leukemia Soc.; treas. Interfaith Nutrition Network, 1984-85, bd. of trustees, Nassau Heritage, 2001-. Author: Sliding down the Wind, 1978, The Hawk's Dream and Other Poems, 1982, Against Gravity, 1986, The Colors of Infinity, 1990, Spin, 1992, Dawn Patrol, 1992, The Latest Illusion, 1995, The Ego Makers, 1998, Change as a Curved Equation, 2002; producer, film, Spin, 2003. Trustee Nassau Heritage, 2001—. Recipient archtl. design and community enhancement awards L.I. Assn. and Plainview C. of C., 1962-70, Brotherhood award NCCJ, 1977, Humanitarian award Am. Jewish Com., l978, Interfaith Nutrition Network, l989, hon. award Beta Gamma Sigma, 1978, L.I. Disting. Leadership award, l979, Estabrook award Hofstra U., l987; Tennessee Wiliams fellow in poetry Bread Loaf, 1979, Long Island Assn. Humanitarian of the Year award, 2003. Mem. PEN, Nat. Pilots Assn., Poets and Writers, Aircraft Owners and Pilots Assn., L.I. Early Fliers Club, Poetry Soc. Am. (bd. govs. 1987-95), Acad. of Am. Poets (bd. dirs. 1996—), L.I. Regional Econ. Devel. Coun., Poets House, Middlebury Coll. Alumni Assn. (v.p., adv. bd. 1978), Players Club (N.Y.C.), Sands Point Country Club (L.I.), Old Westbury Racquet Club (N.Y.), Delta Upsilon. Achievements include designing, developing Long Island Office Park, Engineers Hill Indsl. Parks, Montvale Office Park, The Ellipse at Garden City, Montvale III, Montvale IV, Meadow Hill Office Plz. Office: 131 Jericho Tpke Jericho NY 11753-1060 *A wonderful characteristic of this great democracy of ours is the right to fail— which is, of course, the opportunity to succeed. As we pursue some goal, especially a noble one, we learn about the aspects and degrees of success or failure. The aspiration, therefore, becomes a worthwhile endeavor in itself.*

AXINN, GEORGE HAROLD, rural sociology educator; b. Jamaica, N.Y., Feb. 1, 1926; s. Hyman and Celia (Schneider) A.; m. Nancy Kathryn Wigsten, Feb. 17, 1945; children: Catherine, Paul, Martha, William. BS, Cornell U., 1947; MS, U. Wis., 1952, PhD, 1958. Editorial asst. Cornell U. Geneva, N.Y., 1947; bull. editor U. Md., College Park, 1949; chmn. dept. rural communication U. Del., Newark, 1950; mem. faculty Mich. State U., East Lansing, 1953—, assoc. dir. coop. extension service, 1955-60; coordinator U. Nigeria program, 1961-65, prof. agrl. econs., 1970-85, prof. resource devel., 1985-95, prof. emeritus, 1996—, asst. dean internat. studies and programs, 1964-85; pres., exec. dir. Midwest Univs. Consortium for Internat. Activities, Inc., 1969-76, 1969-76. FAO rep. to Nepal, 1983-85, India and Bhutan, 1989-91; cons. World Bank, 1973-74, Ford Found., 1968, UNICEF, 1978, FAO, 1974, 87, 89, Govt. of India, 1988; vis. prof. Cornell U., Ithaca, N.Y., 1958-60, U. Ill., Urbana, 1969-70 Author: Modernizing World Agriculture: A Comparative Study of Agricultural Extension Education Systems, 1972, New Strategies for Rural Development, Rural Life Associates, 1978, FAO Guide Alternative Approaches to Agricultural Extension, 1988, Collaboration in International Rural Development - A Practitioner's Handbook (with Nancy W. Axinn), 1997; contbr. articles to various publs. Served with USNR, 1944-46. Recipient Outstanding Alumni award Cornell U. Coll. Agrl. and Life Sci., 1993; W.K. Kellogg Found. fellow, 1956-57. Home: 280 E Morning Sun Ct Tucson AZ 85704-6945 E-mail: axinn@msu.edu.

AXINN, STEPHEN MARK, lawyer; b. N.Y.C., Oct. 21, 1938; s. Mack N. and Lili H. (Tannenbaum) A.; m. Stephanie Chertok, May 12, 1963; children: Audrey, David, Jill. BS, Syracuse U., 1959; LLB, Columbia U., 1962. Bar: N.Y. 1962, U.S. Supreme Ct. 1962. Assoc. Cahill & Gordon, N.Y.C., 1963-64, Malcolm A. Hoffman, N.Y.C., 1964-66, Skadden, Arps, Slate, Meagher & Flom, N.Y.C., 1966-69, ptnr., 1970-97, Axinn, Veltrop & Harkrider LLP, N.Y.C., 1997—. Lead counsel WorldCom-Spring major investigation and litigation antitrust divsn. U.S. Dept. Justice, 1999-2000; adj. prof. Law Sch. NYU, 1981-83, Law Sch. Columbia U., 1983-85. Author: Acquisitions Under H-S-R, 1980; contbr. articles to profl. jours. Chmn. lawyers div. United Jewish Appeal, N.Y.C., 1985-87; mem. exec. com., treas. Jewish Theol. Sem. Am., 1984-96; mem. bd. visitors Columbia Law Sch., 1993-98; mem. adv. panel on environ. crimes by orngs. U.S. Sentencing Commn., 1992-94. Capt. U.S. Army, 1965-68. Mem. ABA (council antitrust sect. 1983-85), N.Y. State Bar Assn. (chmn. antitrust sect. 1982-83). Office: Axinn Veltrop & Harkrider LLP 1370 Ave of the Americas New York NY 10019-6708 E-mail: sma@avhlaw.com.

AXON, DONALD CARLTON, architect; b. Haddonfield, NJ, Feb. 27, 1931; s. William Russell Sr. and Gertrude L. (Ellis) A.; m. Rosemary Smith, Sept. 1952 (div. Oct. 1967); children: Donald R., James K., Marianne Axon Flannery, Darren H., William R. II; m. Janice Jacobs, Mar. 16, 1968; stepchildren: Jonathan Lee, Elise Marie. BArch, Pratt Inst., 1954; MS in Arch., Columbia U., 1966. Registered architect, NY, Pa., Calif. Designer, drafter Keith Hibner, Assoc., Hicksville, NY, 1954-56; designer Charles Wood, Riverhead, NY, 1956-59; architect, prin Donald C. Axon, Assoc., Wantaugh, NY, 1959; ptnr. Bailey-Axon & Assoc., Long Beach, NY, 1960-66; project mgr. Caudill Rowlett Scott, Houston, 1966-69; in-house arch. Kaiser Permanente Hosp., LA, 1969-75; dir. med. facilities Daniel Mann Johnson Mendenhall, LA, 1975-78, Lyon Assoc., LA, 1979-80; pres. Donald C. Axon, FAIA, Inc., LA, 1980—. Tchr. bldg. sci. program U. So. Calif., 1978-82; lectr. in field; profl. advisor dept. architecture U. Tex., 1968-69; advisor to chmn. Sch. Architecture Rice U., Houston, 1968-69; profl. dir. Future Architect Am., 1965-66. Mem. Crestwood Hills Assn., bd. dir. 1971-75, pres., 1973-75, archtl. rev. com., 1987—; bd. dir. Brentwood Community Fedn., 1973-75, v.p., 1974-75. Recipient LA Beautiful award KPH Norwalk Hosp. Fellow AIA Royal Soc. Health, Health Facilities Inst., Am. Coll. Healthcare Arch. (founding fellow),(Calif. regional bd. dir. 1987-89, mem. various subcoms., chair steering com. 1980, liaison 1991—, bd. dir. L.A. chpt. 1983-84, pres. 1986, chair com. on architecture for health 1974, chair health facilities com. Calif. coun. 1975, Disting. Svc. citation 1992), mem. Am. Soc. Healthcare Engr., Archtl. Found. LA (founding, v.p. 1985-89, pres. 1989-90), Internat. Conf. Bldg. Ofcl., Am. Hosp. Assn., Forum for Health Care Planning (bd. dir. 1982—, pres. 1993-94). Office: 24302 Carlton Ct Laguna Niguel CA 92677-3718 Fax: 949-360-8114. E-mail: donaxon@aol.com.

AXTELL, CLAYTON MORGAN, JR., lawyer; b. Deposit, N.Y., Aug. 4, 1916; s. Clayton Morgan and Olive Aurora (Vosburgh) A.; m. Margaret Williamson Ritchie, Apr. 24, 1943 (dec. 2000); children: Margaret R. Axtell Stevenson, Clayton Morgan III, Karen R. Axtell Arnold, Susan R. Axtell. AB, Cornell U., 1937, JD, 1940. Bar: N.Y. 1940, U.S. Dist. Ct. (no. dist.) N.Y. 1941, U.S. Supreme Ct. 1964. Assoc. Hinman, Howard & Kattell, Binghamton, N.Y., 1940-48, ptnr., 1948—. Former mem. adv. bd. First-City Nat. Bank, Binghamton; bd. dirs. Farmers Nat. Bank, Deposit, N.Y., First City Nat. Bank, Binghamton. Pres. N.Y. State Sch. Bd. Attys., Albany, 1962-63, Broome County Bar Assn., Binghamton, 1967-68, Conrad and Virginia Klee Found.; mem. N.Y. State Rep. Com., Binghamton, 1988-93. 1st lt. US Army, 1942-46 ETO. Decorated Bronze Star U.S. Army, 1945, Croix de Guerre, Govt. of France, 1945; recipient Disting Svc. award U.S. Jr. C. of C., 1942; named Young Man of Yr. Binghamton Jr. C. of C., 1949. Mem. ABA, N.Y. State Bar Assn., Hillcrest -Port Dick Kiwanis (past pres.), Binghamton Club. Republican. Lutheran. Home: 1338 Chenango St Binghamton NY 13901-1539 Office: Hinman Howard & Kattell 80 Exchange St Binghamton NY 13901-3490

AXTELL, JAMES LEWIS, history educator; b. Endicott, N.Y., Dec. 20, 1941; s. Arthur James Axtell and Laura (England) Levinsky; m. Susan Carol Hallas, Aug. 31, 1963; children: Nathaniel Harsen, Jeremy England. BA, Yale U., 1963; PhD, U. Cambridge, Eng., 1967. Asst. prof. Yale U., New Haven, Conn., 1966-72; assoc. prof. Sarah Lawrence Coll., Bronxville, N.Y., 1972-75; vis. prof. Northwestern U., Evanston, Ill., 1977-78; prof. Coll. of William and Mary, Williamsburg, Va., 1978—, William R. Kenan Jr. prof. of humanities, 1986—. Author: The Educational Writings of John Locke, 1968, The School Upon a Hill, 1974, The European and the Indian, 1981, The Invasion Within, 1985 (prize, 1985, 2 prizes, 1986), After Columbus, 1988, Beyond 1492, 1992, The Indians' New South, 1997, The Pleasures of Academe, 1998, Natives and Newcomers, 2001; editor: The Indian Peoples of Eastern America, 1981; contbr. articles to profl. jours. in field. Recipient Outstanding Faculty award Va. State Coun. Higher Edn., 1988; NEH fellow, 1975-77, 86, 92, J.S. Guggenheim Meml. Found. fellow, 1981-82, Am. Coun. Learned Socs. fellow, 1987. Mem. Soc. Am. Historians, Am. Soc. for Ethnohistory (pres. 1988-89), The Champlain Soc., Am. Hist. Assn., Orgn. Am. Historians, Colonial Soc. Mass., Pilgrim Soc, Mass. Hist. Soc. Democrat. Avocation: book collecting. Home: 109 Walnut Hills Dr Williamsburg VA 23185-3426 Office: Coll of William & Mary Dept History Williamsburg VA 23187-8795 E-mail: jlaxte@wm.edu.

AXTELL, ROBERT LEA, economist; b. Warsaw, NY, June 24, 1960; s. Robert McKune and Paula Ann Axtell; m. Roxanne Constantino, Oct. 2, 1993; children: Emma, Elizabeth, Robert. PhD, Carnegie Mellon U., 1992. Author: Growing Artificial Societies: Social Science from the Bottom Up, 1996. Mem.: Econometric Soc., Am. Geophys. Union, Soc. for Computational Econs., Assn. for Computing Machinery, Am. Econ. Assn. Office: The Brookings Inst 1775 Massachusetts Avenue NW Washington DC 20036

AXWORTHY, LLOYD, Canadian government official; b. North Battleford, Sask., Can., Dec. 21, 1939; s. Norman Joseph and Gwen Jane A.; m. Denise Ommanney, Aug. 3, 1984; 1 child, Stephen. BA, U. Winnipeg; MA, PhD, Princeton U. Min. employment and immigration Canada, 1980-83, min. responsible for status of women, 1980-81, min. transp., 1983-84; critic on internat. trade Official Opposition, 1984-88; critic Liberal Caucus Com. on External Affairs and Nat. Defense, 1988—; vice chmn. Standing com. on External Affairs and Internat. Trade, 1991—; dir. U. Rsch. Inst, assoc. prof.; min. human resources devel., western econ. diversification Canada, 1993-96; min. fgn. affairs Canadian Govt., Ottawa, 1996—. Elected to various positions. Office: House of Commons Rm 418-N Centre Block Ottawa ON Canada K1A 0A6

AYAD, JOSEPH MAGDY, retired psychologist; b. Cairo, May 21, 1926; arrived in U.S., 1949, naturalized, 1961; s. Fahim Gayed and Victoria Gabour (El-Masri) Ayad; m. Widad Fareed Bishai, May 29, 1954; children: Fareed Merritt, Victor Maher, Michael Joseph, Mona Elaine. BA in Social Scis., Am. U., Cairo, 1946; MA in Clin. Psychology (Univ. scholar), Stanford U., 1952; PhD in Clin. Psychology (Univ. scholar), U. Denver, 1956. Trans. Hoover Inst. War and Peace, Stanford U., 1950—51; asst. to chief psychologist Colo. Psychopathic Hosp., 1952—54; cons. Child Guidance Clinic, State Dept. Pub. Welfare, Denver, 1953—56; cons. psychologist Dept. Pub. Welfare, State of Tex., 1957—72, Dept. Insts., Social and Rehab. Svc., State of Okla., 1960—72, N.Mex. Dept. Pub. Welfare, 1960—72; lectr. Fitzsimmons Army Hosp., Denver, 1953—54; vis. psychologist State Dept. Pub. Welfare, Child Guidance Clinic, Pueblo, Colo., 1953—54; staff psychologist Cons. Psychol. Svc., Denver, 1956—57, High Plains Neurol. Ctr., Amarillo, Tex., 1973—2002; pres. JMA Cattle Co., Amarillo, 1973—2002; v.p., treas. Filigon Inc., Amarillo, 1962—75, pres., 1976—2002; ret., 2002. Mem. profl. adv. bd. Amarillo Mental Health Assn., 1968—69. Contbr. articles to profl. jours. Mem. Amarillo Child Welfare Bd., 1961—63; area chmn. U. Denver Fund Raising Campaign, 1963; mem. profl. adv. bd. St. Paul's Meth. Ch. Sch. for Children with Learning Disabilities, Amarillo, 1969—70. Recipient Grad. Sr. award in philosophy, Am. U. at Cairo, 1946. Mem.: APA, Calif. Psychol. Assn., Tex. Psychol. Assn., Potter-Randall County (Tex.) Psychol. Soc. (pres. 1974), Am. Assn. Marriage and Family Therapists, Internat. Assn. Applied Psychology, Am. Psychol. Soc., Amarillo Country Club. Presbyterian. Home: 4239 Erik Ave Amarillo TX 79106-6008 Office: High Plains Neurological Ctr 2301 W 7th Ave Amarillo TX 79106-6601

AYADI, OLUSEGUN FELIX, finance educator; b. Erinje, Ondo, Nigeria, Mar. 7, 1956; came to the U.S., 1987; s. Thompson Morayo and Dorcas Metele Ayadi; children: Olufemi, Olukemi, Olusegun Jr. BS in Banking and Fin., U. Lagos, Nigeria, 1980; MS in Fin., U. Lagos, 1983; PhD in Fin., U. Miss., 1991. Lectr. U. Lagos, 1980-87; asst. prof. Lemoyne-Owen Coll., Memphis, 1991-92, Savannah (Ga.) State U., 1992-94, acting dean, 1993; assoc. prof. Fayetteville (N.C.) State U., 1994-97, prof. fin., 1997—2001, Jesse H. Jones Sch. Bus., Tex. So. U., Houston, 2001 , Tex. So. U., 2001—. Assoc. grad. faculty Ga. So. U., Statesboro, 1992-94; vice chair, Faculty Senate, Fayetteville State U., 1999-2000, chair, 2000-01. Author: Modern Commerce in West Africa, 1995; guest editor Managerial Fin., 1996-98; contbr. numerous articles to profl. jours. Cons. Jr. Achievement, Savannah, 1992-94, Cumberland County Planning Com., Fayetteville, 1996-97; adv. bd. mem. Savannah Youth Entrepreneur, 1993-94; spkr. C. of C., Savannah, 1992, Cumberland County Schs., Fayetteville, 1995, 98. Recipient Positive Image award Pee Dee Newspaper Group, Greenville, S.C., 1996; named Tchr. of Yr., Sch. Bus. and Econs., Fayetteville State U., 1998-99, 2001-02; Nissan fellow in fin. Nissan Corp./Ednl. Testing Svc./Historically Black Colls. and Univs., Chgo., 1994. Mem. Am. Fin. Assn., Am. Acad. Econs. and Fin., Assn. for Global Bus., Fin. Mgmt. Assn., Ea. Fin. Assn., Nat. Assn. African Am. Studies (N.C. state chair 1995-2001, Tex. state chair 2001—). Avocations: reading, tennis, fishing, traveling, watching television. Office: Tex So Univ Jesse H Jones Sch Bus 3100 Cleburne Ave Houston TX 77004 Business E-Mail: ayadl_fo@tsu.edu.

AYALA, FRANCISCO JOSÉ, geneticist, educator; b. Madrid, Mar. 12, 1934; came to U.S., 1961, naturalized, 1971; s. Francisco and Soledad (Pereda) A.; m. Hana Lostakova, Mar. 8, 1985; children by previous marriage: Francisco José, Carlos Alberto. BS, Universidad de Madrid, 1954, D. honoris causa, 1986; MA, Columbia U., 1963, PhD, 1964; D. honoris causa, Universidad de León (Spain), 1982, Universidad de Barcelona, Spain, 1986, U. Athens, Greece, 1991, U. Vigo, Spain, 1996, U. Islas, Baleares, Spain, 1998, U. Valencia, Spain, 1999, U. Bologna, Italy, 2001, U. Vladivostok, Russia, 2002. Research assoc. Rockefeller U., 1964-65; asst. prof. Providence Coll., 1965-67, Rockefeller U., 1967-71; assoc. prof. to prof. genetics U. Calif., Davis, 1971-87, disting. prof. biology Irvine, 1987-89, Donald Bren prof. of Biol. scis., 1989—, univ. prof., 2003—. Bd. dirs. basic biology NRC, 1982-91, chmn., 1984-91, mem. commn. on life scis., 1982-91; mem. nat. adv. coun. Nat. Inst. Gen. Med. Scis.; mem. exec. com. EPA, 1979-80; mem. adv. com. directorate sci. and engring. edn. NSF, 1989-91; mem. nat. adv. coun. for human genome rsch. NIH, 1990-93; mem. Pres. com. advisors sci. and tech., 1994-2001. Author: Population and Evolutionary Genetics, 1982, Modern Genetics, 1980, 2d edit., 1984, Evolving: the Theory and Processes of Organic Evolution, 1979, Evolution, 1977, Molecular Evolution, 1976, Studies in the Philosophy of Biology, 1974. Recipient medal Coll. de France, 1979, Mendel medal Czech Republic Acad. Scis., 1994, Hon. Gold medal Acad. Nat. dei Lincei, Rome, 2000, U.S. Nat. Medal of Sci. award 2001; Guggenheim fellow, Fulbright fellow. Fellow AAAS (Sci. Freedom and Responsibility award 1987, bd. dirs. 1989-93, pres.-elect 1993-94, pres. 1994-95, chmn. of bd. 1995-96, chmn. com. on health of sci. enterprise 1991—, mem. nat. coun. for sci. and edn. for phase II, project 2061 1990—); mem. NAS (sect. population biology evolution and ecology chmn. 1983-86, councillor 1986-89, bd. dirs. Nat. Acad. Corp. 1990—), Am. Acad. Arts and Scis., Am. Soc. Naturalists (sec. 1973-76), Genetics Soc. Am., Am. Genetic Assn. (hon. life, Wilhelmine E. Key award), Ecology Soc. Am., Am. Philos. Soc., Soc. Study Evolution (pres. 1979-80), Royal Acad. Scis. Spain (fgn. mem.), Russian Acad. Natural Scis. (fgn. mem.), Mex. Acad. Scis. (fgn. mem.), Acad. Nat. dei Lincei (Rome) (fgn.), Sigma Xi (William Proctor prize 2000, pres.-elect 2003—). Home: 2 Locke Ct Irvine CA 92612-4034 Office: U Calif Dept Ecology & Evolution Irvine CA 92697-0001 E-mail: fjayala@uci.edu.

AYALA, ISAAC BEN, musician; b. N.Y.C., N.Y., Jan. 17, 1969; s. Gilbert James Ayala and Eleanor (Pasler) Soper. Cert., Hebrew Arts Sch., N.Y.C., 1987; B in Music, Oberlin Conservatory of Music, 1991. Pianist Cunard's Queen Elizabeth II, 1989; composer, music dir. The Swing Mikado Karamu House Theater Co., Cleve., 1992; asst. condr. The Harlem Nutcracker Donald Byrd Dance Co., N.Y.C., 1997—2000; pianist (jazz) Quincy Jones, N.Y.C., L.A., Paris, 2000—; pianist James Spaulding Quintet LIve: Blues Up and Over, 2002. Guest The Letterman Show, Theatre de Champs Elysées, France, L.A. Philharm.; guest condr. Lake Charles Symphony Orch. with Preservation Hall Jazz Band, 2003. Composer (instrumental work): Monk You, 2000; composer: (film) Quincy Jones: In The Pocket--PBS Am. Masters Series, 2001. Scholar B'nai Brith Scholarship, 1987, United Fedn. Tchrs. Scholarship, 1987. Mem.: Musicians Union (Local 802) (jazz com. 1997—). Avocation: Avocations: golf, tennis, current events.

AYALA, JOHN, librarian, dean; b. Long Beach, Calif., Aug. 28, 1943; s. Francisco and Angelina (Rodriguez) Ayala; m. Patricia Marie Dozier, July 11, 1987 (dec. Jan. 19, 2001); children: Juan, Sara; m. Gloria Ann Aulwes, Dec. 28, 2003. BA in History, Calif. State U., Long Beach, 1970, MPA, 1981; MLS, Immaculate Heart Coll., L.A., 1971. Library paraprofl. Long Beach Pub. Library, 1963-70; librarian L.A. County Pub. Libr., 1971-72, Long Beach City Coll., 1972-90, assoc. prof., 1972-90, pres. acad. senate, 1985-87; dean, Learning Resources Fullerton (Calif.) Coll., 1990—, evening/weekend supr., 1997—99, adminstr. study abroad program, 2000—. Chmn. Los Angeles County Com. to Recruit Mexican-Am. Librs., 1971-74; mem. acad. senate Calif. Cmty. Colls., 1985-90; pres. Latino Faculty/Staff Assn., NOCCD, 1993-2000. Editor Calif. Librarian, 1971. Served with USAF, 1966-68, Vietnam. U.S. Office Edn. fellow for library sci., 1970-71. Mem. ALA (com. mem. 1971—, Melvil Dewey award com. 1998—), Calif. Libr. Assn., REFORMA Nat. Assn. to Promote Spanish Speaking Libr. Svc. (founding mem., v.p., pres. 1973-76), Arnul Fo Trejo Libr. of the Yr. Award 2001, from Reforma,CSULB, (Alumni Assn. (treas., 2003—). Democrat. Roman Catholic. Office: Fullerton College Library 321 E Chapman Ave Fullerton CA 92832-2011

AYALA, ORLANDO, information technology executive; BA in Mgmt. Info. Sys. Various positions NCR Corp., Dayton, Ohio, 1981—91; from sr. dir. Latin Am. region to group v.p. Microsoft, Redmond, Wash., 1991, group v.p. Office: One Microsoft Way Redmond WA 98052-6399

AYAN, ONER, emerging markets manager; b. ISTANBUL, Turkey, Mar. 17, 1973; s. OMER EROL AYAN, ULKU AYAN. MA, NEW YORK UNIVERSITY, NEW YORK, 2001—03. VP-TURKISH EQUITIES AUERBACH GRAYSON COMPANY, NEW YORK, NY, 1998—2000; MANAGER-EMERGING MARKETS RAYMOND JAMES & ASSOCIATES, NEW YORK, NY, 2000—. TECHNICAL ANALYSIS TEACHING MARMARA UNIVERSITY, ISTANBUL, Turkey, 1996—98. Mem.: AIMR. Office: RAYMOND JAMES & ASSOCIATES 250 PARK AVE, FL 2 New York NY 10177 Business E-Mail: onerayan@yahoo.com.

AYAS, KAREN, management consultant, educator; b. Istanbul, Turkey, Aug. 23, 1962; Immigrated to Israel, The Netherlands, US; d. Max Ayas; m. Didier Sabag, Aug. 21, 1985 (div. Aug. 1993); 1 child, Lior; m. Atilla Habip, Apr. 24, 1997. BSc, Technion, Israel, 1985, MSc, 1988; PhD, Erasmus U., The Netherlands, 1997. Asst. rschr. Technion, Israel, 1985-88; dep. human resource dir. Rambam Med. Ctr., Israel, 1988-90; human resource dir. Wolfson Med. Ctr., Israel, 1990-92; fellow rschr. Rotterdam Sch. Mgmt., 1992-96; sr. cons. Bus. Mgmt. Group, The Netherlands, 1996-97; asst. prof. Erasmus U., Rotterdam, 1997; prin. Ripples Inst., 1998. Lectr. Babson Coll., 2001. Author: To the Desert and Back, 2003; Design for Learning for Innovation, 1997; author, editor: Orgl. Learning, 1996; assoc. editor Reflections: The Sol Jour. on Learning Knowledge and Change; contbr. chpt. to books, numerous articles to profl. jour. Basketball coach NAA. Avocations: swimming, jazz dancing, classical music, theater, basketball. Home and Office: 80 High Rock Ter Chestnut Hill MA 02467-2654 E-mail: kayas@attbi.com.

AYASO, MANUEL, artist; b. Coruna, Galicia, Spain, Jan. 1, 1934; came to U.S., 1947, naturalized, 1955; s. Jose and Dolores (Dios) A.; m. Lucia Rivas, May 2, 1959; children: Monica, Jose Luciano. Student, Newark Sch. Fine and Indsl. Art, N.J., 1953-56. One-man shows include Cober Gallery, N.Y.C., 1961—68, Forum Gallery, 1970—74, Ft. Worth Art Ctr., 1964, SUNY-Oswego, 1965, Witt meml. Mus., San Antonio, 1967, Casa de Galicia, Madrid, Spain, 1994, N.Y. Armory, 1995, Casa da Parra, Santiago de Compostela, Spain, 1997, exhibited in group shows at 22d Biennial Internat. Watercolor Exhbn., Bklyn. Mus., 1963, U. Mex., Mexico City, 1963, Exhibit Contemporary Am. Artists, Nat. inst. Arts and letters, 1962—71, Whitney Mus. Am., 1963, Vatican Exhibit Contemporary Am. Spiritual Art, Rome, 1976, The Fine Line: Drawing with Silver in Am., 1985—86, Objects and Drawings from the Sanford M. and Diane Besser Collection, 1992—93, Casa da Cultura, Riveira La Coruna, Museo Valleinclan Puebla del Caraminal, La Coruna, 2001, retrospective exhbn., Fundacion Museo del Grabado, Artes, Riveira, Spain, 2002—03. Served with U.S. Army, 1956-58. Recipient St. Paul Gallery and Sch. Art Purchase award, 1961; Tiffany Found. Award, 1962; Ford Found. grantee, 1964; recipient Nat. Inst. Arts and Letters Childe Hassam Purchase award, 1971, hon. mention 2d Ann. Int. Exhibit of Miniature Art, Del Bello Gal, Toronto, Can., 1987. Mem. Nat. Geog. Soc., Smithsonian Instn., Whitney Mus. Am. Art, N.J. State Mus. Roman Catholic. Address: 12 Vincent Pl Verona NJ 07044-3022

AYCOCK, HUGH DAVID, steel manufacturing company executive; b. Lilesville, N.C., 1930; married. With Nucor Corp., Charlotte, N.C., 1954—, div. shop supt., 1955-57, div. sales mgr., 1957-63, div. gen. mgr., 1963-84, v.p., 1965-84, pres., 1984-91, also bd. dirs.; v.p. Nucor Steel SC div. Nucor Corp., 1965-84; pres., chmn. & CEO Nucor Copr., Charlotte, NC, 1999—. Bd. dirs. Bowater Inc. With USN, 1950 54. Office: Nucor Corp 2100 Rexford Rd Charlotte NC 28211-3484

AYDEDE, MURAT, education educator; b. Ankara, Turkey, Aug. 18, 1961; s. M. Ali Yavuz and Nuran Fatma Aydede; m. Sema Kutay, Feb. 2, 1982; 1 child, Derya. PhD, U. of Md., 1986—93. Vis. scholar Stanford U., 1993—94; cons. Xerox Palo Alto Rsch. Ctr., Palo Alto, 1993—94; asst. prof. U. of Chgo., 1994—2001. Contbr. articles to scholarly jours. Fellowship, Chgo. Humanities Ctr., 1998—99. Mem.: Am. Philosophil Assn. Achievements include research in consciousness, pain, cognition. Office: University of Florida Philosophy Dept PO Box 118545 Gainesville FL 32611-8545 Office Fax: 352-392-5577.

AYDELOTTE, MYRTLE KITCHELL, retired nursing administrator; b. Van Meter, Iowa, May 31, 1917; d. John J. and Larava Josephine (Gutshall) Kitchell; m. William O. Aydelotte, June 22, 1956; children: Marie Elizabeth, Jeannette Farley. BS, U. Minn., 1939, MA, 1947, PhD, 1955; postgrad., Columbia U. Tchrs. Coll., 1948. Head nurse Charles T. Miller Hosp., St. Paul, 1939—41; surg. tchg. St. Mary's Hosp. Sch. Nursing, Mpls., 1941—42; instr. U. Minn., 1945—49; dir., dean State U. Iowa Coll. Nursing, 1949—57, prof., 1957—62; assoc. chief nurse VA Hosp. Rsch. for Nursing, Iowa City, 1963—64, chief nursing rsch., 1964—65; prof. U. Iowa Coll. Nursing, 1964—76, 1982—88; exec. dir. Am. Nurses Assn., 1977—81; ret., 1988. Dir. nursing U. Iowa Hosps. and Clinics, 1968—76; mem. sci. adv. bd. Ctr. Health Rsch. Wayne State U.,

1972—76, Inst. Medicine, 1973—; cons. U. Minn., 1970, 82, 90, U. Rochester, 1971, U. Mich., 1970, 73, U. Colo., 1970—71, U. Hawaii, 1972—73, Ariz. State U., 1972, U. Nebr., 1972—73. Contbr. articles to profl. jours.; mem. editl. bd.: Nursing Forum, 1969—72, Jour. Nursing Adminstrn., 1971. Mem., v.p. Iowa City Libr. Bd., 1961—67; mem. Johnson County Bd. Health, 1967—70; mem. adv. com. family living courses Iowa City Bd. Edn., 1970—72. Served with Nurse Corps. U.S. Army, 1942—46. Mem.: Am. Acad. Nursing, Inst. Medicine, Am. Nurses Assn., Sigma Theta Tau (rsch. com. 1968—72). Home: 1570 East Ave Apt 106 Rochester NY 14610

AYER, DONALD BELTON, lawyer; b. San Mateo, Calif., Apr. 30, 1949; m. Anne Norton; children: Christopher, Alison BA in History with great distinction and honors, Stanford U., 1971; MA in History, Harvard U., 1973, JD cum laude, 1975. Bar: Calif. 1975, D.C. 1978. Law clk. to Judge Malcolm R. Wilkey U.S. Ct. Appeals D.C. Cir., 1975-76; law clk. to Justice William H. Rehnquist, U.S. Supreme Ct., Washington, 1976-77; asst. U.S. atty. criminal div. No. Dist. Calif., San Francisco, 1977-79, in charge San Jose office, 1978-79; assoc. Gibson Dunn & Crutcher, San Jose, Calif., 1979-81; U.S. atty. Eastern Dist. Calif., Sacramento, 1982-86; prin. dep. solicitor gen. Dept. Justice, 1986-88; ptnr. Jones, Day, Reavis & Pogue, Washington, 1988—, 1990—; dep. atty. gen. U.S. Dept. Justice, Washington, 1989-90; adminstrv. ptnr. Jones, Day, Reavis & Pogue, Washington, 1991-93, chair gov. disputes sect., 1993-96, chair. pro bono com., 2003—. Mem. Calif. State Bar Fed. Cts. Commn., 1983-86; mem. exec. com. 9th Cir. Jud. Conf., 1983-85; mem. Atty. Gen.'s Adv. Com. of U.S. Attys., 1986; publs. com. U.S. Supreme Ct. Hist. Soc., 1991—. Articles editor Harvard U. Law Rev., 1974-75; contbr. articles to legal jours. Pres. Stanford Young Reps., 1970-71; mem. vestry St. Mary's Episc. Ch., 1987-90; bd. dirs. Langley Non-Profit Housing Corp., 1990-98; mem. Fed. City Coun., 1991-93; mem. adv. com. State and Local Legal Ctr., 1992—; trustee Potomac Sch., McLean, Va., 1994-2000; bd. dirs. Am. Rivers, Inc., 1997—, treas., 1998—; bd. advisors Supreme Ct. Inst. of Georgetown U., 1999—. Fellow Am. Bar Found. (life); mem. ABA (litigation sect., task force on internat. criminal ct. 1991-94), Am. Bar Found., Am. Acad. Appellate Lawyers (mem. com. 1997-2002), Am. Law Inst., D.C. Bar Found. (adv. bd. 1992—), Calif. State Bar, D.C. Bar Assn. (ct. funding com. 2000-01), NYU Inst. Jud. Adminstrn. (bd. dirs. 2000—), Edward Coke Am. Inn of Ct. Office: Jones Day Reavis & Pogue 51 Louisiana Ave NW Washington DC 20001

AYER, RAMANI, insurance company executive; BS, Indian Inst. Tech., Bombay; MS in Chem. Engring., D in Chem. Engring., Drexel U. With The Hartford, Hartford, Conn., 1973—, asst. sec., staff asst. to chmn. and chief exec., 1979-83; v.p. HartRe, 1983-86; pres. Hartford Specialty Co., 1986-89; sr. v.p. The Hartford, 1989-90, exec. v.p., 1990-91; pres., COO property-casualty ops. Hartford Fire Ins. Co., 1991-97; chmn., CEO, pres. The Hartford Fin. Svcs. Group, Inc., 1997—. Past chmn. Ins. Svcs. Office; bd. dirs. Ins. Info. Inst.. Trustee Mark Twain House, Hartford, Conn.; chmn. Metro Hartford Regional Econ. Alliance; bd. dirs. Hartford Hosp.; trustee Drexel U.; mem. Bus. Roundtable. Mem. Am. Ins. Assn. (bd. dirs., past chmn. task force catastrophic issues, past vice chmn. spl. bd. com. workers compensation), Am. Inst. Property and Liability Underwriters (trustee), Ins. Inst. Am. (trustee). Office: Hartford Plz 60 Asylum Ave Hartford CT 06105-3840

AYERS, ANNE LOUISE, small business owner, consultant, counselor; b. Albuquerque, Oct. 22, 1948; d. F. Ernest and Gladys Marguerite (Miles) A. BA, Kans. U., 1970; MEd, Seattle Pacific U., 1971. Staff cons. in student devel. Cen. Wash. State U., Ellensburg, 1971-72; dir. Aerospace Def. Command Resident Edn. Ctrs. for N.D. and Mont. Chapman U., Orange, Calif., 1972-74; instr. psychology Hampton (Va.) U., 1973-75; edn. svc. specialist Gen. Ednl. Devel. Ctr., Fort Monroe, Va., 1975-77; edn. specialist U.S. Army Transp. Sch., Ft. Eustis, Va., 1977-79, Nat. Mine Health and Safety Acad., Beckley, W.Va., 1979-89; edn. svcs. specialist NASA Hdqrs., Washington, 1989-96; ret., 1996. Pres. Appalachian Love Arts, Martinsburg, W.Va., 1983—; tchr. undergrad. and grad. evening classes in psychology, 1972-74; program mgr. NASA Tchr. Resource Ctr. Network Program; sub. counselor Berkeley County, W.Va.. Inventor decorative pen/thermometer holder/corsage, psychedelic jewelry process. Mem. Nat. Soc. Inventors, Nat. Assn. Women Deans Adminstrn. and Counselors, Internat. Soc. Photographers, Alumnus of Growing Vision (Century in Edn. award), Mayflower Soc. Methodist. Avocations: travel, collecting gems and shells, coin collecting, rock and fossil collecting, oboe and clarinet. Home and Office: 480 Tanbridge Dr Martinsburg WV 25401-4695

AYERS, BENJAMIN C. finance educator; BS summa cum laude, U. Ala., Tuscaloosa, 1986, M in Tax Acctg., 1987; PhD, U. Tex., 1996. CPA Ala., 1988. Tax mgr. KPMG, Tampa, Fla., 1987—91; contract mgr. Complete Health, Inc., Birmingham, Ala., 1991—92; asst. prof. U. Ga., Athens, 1996—2001, assoc. prof., 2001—. Mem. editl. bd.: The Acctg. Rev., 1999—, Jour. Am. Taxation Assn., 2000—, Acctg. Horizons, 2001—; contbr. articles to profl. jours. Recipient Acctg. Achievement award, Ala. Soc. CPA's, 1986; fellow Lily Tchg. fellow, U. Ga., 1997—99; Alumni Leadership scholar, U. Ala., 1983, C&BA Entrepreneurial scholar, 1984—85, Arthur Young & Co. scholar, 1985, William A. Tate scholar, 1986, Chester Knight Meml. scholar, 1986, Coopers & Lybrand scholar, U. Tex., 1992—93, Arthur Andersen scholar, 1993—94, C. Aubrey Smith Acctg. Edn. scholar, 1994—96, grad. fellow, U. Ala., 1986—87, Grad. Sch. Competitive Entrance fellow, U. Tex., 1992—93, Doctoral fellow, AICPA, 1992—94, KPMG, 1993—94, Deloitte & Touche, 1994—96, Doctoral Consortium fellow, Am. Acctg. Assn., 1995, Sanford Rsch. fellow, Terry Coll. Bus., 1999, 2000, 2001, 2002, 2003, Tax Rsch. grantee, Ernst & Young, 1997. Mem.: Nat. Tax Assn., Am. Tax Assn., Am. Acctg. Assn., Alpha Lambda Delta, Phi Eta Sigma, Beta Gamma Sigma, Omicron Delta Kappa. Office: Univ Ga 255 Brooks Hall Athens GA 30602-6252

AYERS, HARRY BRANDT, editor, publisher, columnist; b. Anniston, Ala., Apr. 8, 1935; s. Harry Mell and Edel Olga (Ytterboe) A.; m. Josephine Ehringhaus, Dec. 9; 1 child, Margaret. BA in History, U. Ala., Tuscaloosa, 1959; LHD (hon.), U. Ala., Birmingham, 1994, U. Ala., 1994. Polit. writer The Raleigh (N.C.) Times, 1959-61; corr. Bascom Timmons Bur., Washington, 1961-63; mng. editor The Anniston Star, 1963-69, editor, pub., 1969—. Chair Consolidated Publ. Co., 1998—; commentator Pub. Radio, NPR "Morning Edition." Mem. adv. bd. Inside Story, Pub. Broadcasting System, N.Y.C., 1981-85; co-editor: You Can't Eat Magnolias, 1972; co-author: A Bicentennial Portrait of the American People, U.S. News Books, 1976, Inaugural Book President Carter, 1977, Dixie Dateline, 1983; frequent contbr. to internat. and nat. newspapers. Trustee Talladega (Ala.) Coll., 1972-89, Wooster Sch., Danbury, Conn., 1989-90, Century Found., 1985—, Ctr. for Excellence in Govt., 1985-88, Am. Com., Internat. Press Inst., Vienna, 1985—; bd. dirs. So. Ctr. for Internat. Studies, Atlanta, 1979—, Bd. Fgn. Scholarships, Washington, 1981-84; mem. adv. bd. Am. Ditchley Found., London; mem. Coun. Fgn. Rels., N.Y.C., 1983—; bd. dirs. Inter-Am. Press Assn., Miami, 1992-93; chmn. UN Day Ala., 2000. Named Disting. Journalism Grad., U. Ala., 1967; recipient Human Rels. award Am. Jewish Com., 1977, Green Eyeshade award Soc. Profl. Journalists, 1985, Editl. Leadership award, Soc. Newpaper Editors, 2003; named to Ala. Acad. Honor, 1991; fellow Nieman Found., Harvard U., 1968, sr. fellow Gannett Ctr., Columbia U., 1989; inductee Hall of Fame, U. Ala. Sch. Comm., 2000, Tutwiler dist. svc. award, 2002, Lifetime achievement award, Ala. Press Assn., 2003 Mem. Ala. Press Journalism Found. (founding pres. 1969), Am. Soc. Newspaper Editors (Editl. Leadership award 2003), So. Newspaper Pubs. Assn. (dir. 1981-84), Century Assn. N.Y.C., Met. Club Washington, The Summit Club Birmingham. Democrat. Episcopalian. Home: 1 Booger Holw Anniston AL 36207-6805 Office: Anniston Star PO Box 189 Anniston AL 36202-0189

AYERS, JANICE R. social service administrator; b. Idaho Falls, Idaho, Jan. 23, 1930; 1 child, Thomas. MBA, U. So. Calif., 1952, MA, 1953. Gen. mgr. Tamasha Town and Pvt. Country Club, Anaheim, Calif.; asst. to dir. gen. svcs. Disneyland, Anaheim; state dir. Mental Retardation Assn., Las Vegas, Nev.; exec. dir., chief exec. officer 13-County Retired Sr. Vol. Program, Carson City, Nev. Cons. in field. Contbr. articles to profl. jours. Mem. Pub. Rels. Soc. Am., Nat. Assn. RSVP Dirs., Women in radio and TV, AAUW, Optimist Club, Las Vegas Club. Home: 1624 Karin Dr Carson City NV 89706-2626

AYERS, JEFFREY DAVID, lawyer; b. Grant, Nebr., Nov. 30, 1960; s. William D. and Lela R. (Gilmore) A.; m. Shelly Jo Dodds, June 11, 1988; children: Sydney Elizabeth, Bailey Anne. BS, Graceland U., 1982; MBA, JD, U. Iowa, 1985. Bar: Mo. 1985. Assoc. Stinson, Mag & Fizzell, Kansas City, Mo., 1985-88, Bryan, Cave, McPheeters & McRoberts, Kansas City, 1989-92; ptnr. Blackwell Sanders Peper Martin LLP, Kansas City, Mo., 1992-95, mng. ptnr. London, 1996-99; sr. v.p., gen. counsel and corp. sec. Aquila Mcht. Svcs., Inc., Kansas City, 1999—2002; v.p., assoc. gen. counsel GE Employers Reinsurance Corp., Overland Park, Kans., 2003—. Mayor City of Lake Tapawingo, Mo., 1993-96. Trustee Little Blue Valley Sewer Dist., 1994-95. Democrat. Mem. Cmtys. of Christ. Office: GE Employers Reinsurance Corp 5200 Metcalf PO Box 2991 Overland Park KS 66201-1391 E-mail: jayers@kc.rr.com.

AYERS, KATHY VENITA MOORE, librarian; b. Amherst, Tex., Jan. 15, 1946; d. Charles Edward and Jean (Willman) Moore; children: Suzanne Flanary, Charles Flanary. BA, U. Ill., 1972, MLS, 1974. Cert. profl. libr., N.Mex.; cert. tchr., N.Mex. Dir. children's libr. Hayner Pub. Libr., Alton, Ill., 1974-76; dir. Ruidoso (N.Mex.) Pub. Libr., 1978-80; libr. media specialist Horgan Libr., N.Mex. Mil. Inst., Roswell, 1985-93; libr. N.Mex. Sch. Visually Handicapped, Alamogordo, 1993—. Workshop presenter Lewis & Clark Regional Libr. Systems, Ill., 1975; outreach programer Hayner Pub. Libr., 1974-76; del. Pre-White Ho. Conf., State of N.Mex., 1991. Contbr. articles to newspapers and profl. jours. Bd. dirs. Alton Symphony, 1975; mem. Altrusa, Ruidoso, 1979-84, Friend of Roswell Pub. Libr.; sec. Ruidoso Summer Festival, 1979; bd. dirs. Supts. Adv. Bd., Roswell, N.Mex., 1987-89; pres. Friends of Libr., Ruidoso, 1980-83, Parent Advocacy for Gifted Edn., 1990-92; v.p. Sunset PTA; bd. dirs. N.Mex. Libr. Found., 1992—; mem. State Task Force on Sch. Librs., 1999. Recipient Svc. award, Altrusa, 1979, Sunset PTA, 1989. Mem. N.Mex. Libr. Assn. (libr. devel. com., ednl. tech. roundtable vice chair 1991, chair elect 1992, co-chair state conv. local arrangements 1990-91, 2d v.p. 1993-94, 1st v.p. 1994-95, pres. 1995-96, Libr. Leadership award 2001), N.Mex. Acad. and Rsch. Librs. (vice chair 1992, pres. 1993), N.Mex. Taskforce for Sch. Librs., Kiwanis (bd. dirs. 1990-92). Avocations: travel, stained glass, music, hiking. Office: White Mountain Intermediate 201 White Mountain Dr Ruidoso NM 88345

AYERS, RICHARD WAYNE, electrical company official, writer, journalist; b. Atlanta, Aug. 23, 1945; s. Harold Richard and Martha Elizabeth (Vaughan) A.; m. Nancy Katherine Martin, Aug. 9, 1969. BBA, Ga. State Coll., 1967; MBA, Ind. U., 1969. Specialist mktg. comm. tech. GE Co., Schenectady, N.Y., 1969-70, copywriter lamp divsn. Cleve., 1970-73, supr. distbr. advt. & sales promotion, 1973-75; supr. comml. & indsl. promotional programs GE Lighting Bus. Group, 1975-79, mgr. comml. & indsl. market distbr. and promotional programs, 1979-87, mgr. comml. & indsl. comm., 1987-91, mgr. mktg. comms., 1992—2000; reporter, feature writer Tampa Bay newspapers, 2000—. Lectr. in field. Author: Winning Through Promotion, 1987, 93, 96, Cleveland and The Western Reserve, 2000, Ohio's Lake Erie Vacationland, 2000; St. Petersburg: The Sunshine City, 2001, Tampa Bay's Gulf Beaches, 2002. Dir.-at-large Ga. Young Reps., 1966-67. Recipient Best Indsl. Promotion award Advt. Age, 1974, Incentive Showcase award Nat. Premium Sales Exec. Assn., 1975, 76, 87, 91, Gold Key award Nat. Assn. Incentive Mktg., 1976, 77, 87, Golden Communicators award Factory mag., 1976, Leader award Direct Mktg. Assn., 1983, Top prize Am. Lighting Assn., 1990, 91, 92, 95, 96, 97, 98, Addy award Am. Advt. Assn., 1992, Gold Tower award Bus. Mktg. Assn., 1998, ProComm award, 1998. Mem. Elfun Soc., Blue Key, Delta Sigma Pi, Beta Gamma Sigma. Home: 2900 Gulf Blvd #304 Belleair Beach FL 33786

AYHAN, HAYRIYE, educator; b. Istanbul, Turkey, May 21, 1969; arrived in U.S., 1991; d. Osman and Bahire Ayhan; m. Anand Srinivasa. Bachelor's, Bogazici U., Istanbul; Master's, PhD, Tex. A&M U. Asst. prof. Ga. Inst. Tech., Atlanta, 1995—2002, assoc. prof., 2002—. Contbr. articles to profl. jours. Recipient Career award, NSF, Washington, 2002. Mem.: INFORMS (sec./treas. Applied Probability Soc. 1999—). Home: 3569 Duberry Ct Atlanta GA 30319 Office: Sch ISyE Ga Tech 765 Ferst Dr Atlanta GA 30332-0205

AYITTEY, GEORGE BILLY NII, economics educator, consultant, researcher; b. Tarkwa, Ghana, Oct. 13, 1945; came to U.S., 1981; s. Augustus Armah and Comfort (Asare) A. BSc in Econ., U. Ghana, 1969; MA in Econ., U. Western Ont., 1971; PhD in Econ., U. Man., 1981. Lectr. econ. U. Man., Winnipeg, Canada, 1975-81; asst. prof. econ. Wayne State Coll., Nebr., 1981-84; assoc. prof. econ. Bloomsburg U., Pa., 1984-90, Am. U., Washington, 1990—. Cons. World Bank, Washington, 1988; nat. fellow Hoover Instn., Stanford (Calif.) U., 1988-89; columnist African Letter, Toronto, The Continent, Washington. Author: Indigenous African Institutions, 1991, Africa Betrayed, 1992; contbr. articles to newspapers. Heritage Found. Bradley scholar, 1989-90. Mem. Am. Econ. Assn. Avocations: jogging, swimming, reading, writing, dancing. Home: 6936 Hamilton Ct Lorton VA 22079-1211 Office: Am U Dept Econs 4400 Massachusetts Ave NW Washington DC 20016-8003

AYLESWORTH, JULIE ANN, writer, personal care industry executive; b. Cin., Apr. 11, 1953; d. Robert Dean and Evelyn Jane (Francis) A. BA in Drama with honors, Vassar Coll., Poughkeepsie, N.Y., 1975. Adminstrv. asst. Gruber Realty Co., Cin., 1986-87, Gruber Design & Mktg., Cin., 1987-89. Radio broadcaster Radio Reading Svcs., Cin., 1980-81; job counselor Joy Ctr., Cin., 1980-81; consumer activist Marlowe House, Cin., 1984-86; dramatic coach Marlowe House, Cin., 1984-86; mem. Nightwriters, Highland Heights, Ky., 1986-88. Actress play Man of La Mancha, 1969; writer, dir. one-woman show Artist of the Woman as A Young Portrait, 1974; author: Quiet Times and Quotations, Vols. 1-16, 1979-84, Power Times, Vols. 1-25, 1984-89, Luna, Lazarus and Love, 1983, Of Her Own Free Will: A Schizophrenic Succeeds, 1990; songwriter Color me Country, 2001, Land That I Love, 2002, Ain't No Place Like Cincinnati, 2001, There is a Light, 2002; contbr. articles to profl. jour. Telephone vol. Telecare, Cin., 1990; sch. crossing guard Cin. Police, 1978-80. Recipient Recognition award Joy Ctr., Cin., 1981, Merit award Radio Reading Svcs., Cin., 1981, Golden Poet awards World of Poetry, Editors Choice Award, Internat., Soc. of Poets, 1990-2002, Mem. Willing, Enabled Consumers are Needed (pres. 1984-86), founder an owner, Jesus' Art House, 1986-present. Republican. Avocations: cello, horticulture, zoological, reading, investing. Home and Office: 1673 Cedar Ave #405 Cincinnati OH 45224-2851

AYLESWORTH, OWEN ROY, firefighter; b. Appleton, Wisc., Jan. 21, 1926; s. Frederick Donovan and Adeline Louise Minnie (Hauert) A.; m. Mary Hildred Horton, Aug. 23, 1946 (div. Sept. 1949); children: Sheldon Roy, Earl Lynn; m. Mary Corrine Patti Gray, Dec. 26, 55 (div. Nov. 1964); 1 child, Nancy Denise. AA, Santa Barbara City Coll., 1973. Fireman City of Santa Barbara, Calif., 1950-56, alarm operator, 1956, fire engr., 1956-62, fire capt., 1962-69, 76-79, fire tng. officer, 1969-76, acting fire batallion chief, 1976. Webmaster, Aylesworth.net; dir. v.p., pres. City Employee's Assn., 1961-69; coord. fire sci. Santa Barbara City Coll., 1969-74, instr. 1972-74. Author, editor: Caleb Sheldon Aylesworth His Descendents, 1963, 82, Hauert Family Genealogy, 1965, 73. Instr. advanced first aid and emergency care ARC; cardiopulmonary resustation instr. Am. Heart Assn.; life mem. Santa Barbara Fireman's Relief Assn., 1952-64, v.p. 1964-66. With U.S. Navy, 1944-47. Mem. Calif. State Fire Tng. Officers Assn. (life), Calif. Firefighters Assn. (life, state conf. del. 1955-61), Santa Barbara High Sch. Alumni Assn. (life, bd. dirs. 1974-76, treas. 1976-94, sec. 1994-96, exec. sec. 2000—, dir. membership 1996—, Disting. Alumnus award 1993). Avocations: genealogy, research, woodworking, aesthetometry, metal sculpture. Home: 621 W Arrellaga St Santa Barbara CA 93101 E-mail: olenug@aol.com.

AYLING, HENRY FAITHFUL, writer, editor, consultant; b. Bklyn., Dec. 30, 1931; s. Albert Edward John and Mina Campbell McCurdy (Lindsay) A.; m. Julia Corinne Gornto, 1954; children: Campbell, Eben, Corey, Harry, Faith. BA, Grinnell Coll., 1953; MA, Columbia U., Calif. State U., Carson, 1984; 2 grad. teaching certs., Calif. State U., Carson, 1985. Asst to registrar Columbia U., N.Y.C., 1958-59; supr. crew scheduling Pan Am World Airways, Jamaica, N.Y., 1959-62, supr. payload control, 1963-65; mgr. crew scheduling Seabd. World Airlines, Jamaica, 1962-63, 65-68, mgr. system control, 1968-80; mgr. ops. control Flying Tiger Line, 1980-84; instr. English, ESL Long Beach (Calif.) City Coll., 1984-85; mng. editor IEEE Expert, IEEE Computing Futures IEEE Computer Soc., Los Alamitos, Calif., 1985-90, editorial dir. Computer Soc. Press, 1990-93; writer, editor, cons., 1993—. Mem. editorial bd. Expert Mag., 1986-90, CamAm Programming Inc., 1987-88; columnist Mag. Design and Prodn. mag., 1988-89; contbr. articles to profl. mags. and tech. books; contbr. poetry to various mags. and anthologies. Bd. dirs. Playa Serena Home Owners Assn., Playa Del Rey, Calif., 1983-85. Recipient Maggie awards Western Publs. Assn., 1988-89, IEEE Computer Soc. Golden Core award, 1997. Avocations: music, fine arts. Home and Office: 78291 Allegro Dr Palm Desert CA 92211-1894 E-mail: Jcayling@msn.com.

AYLSWORTH, ROBERT REED, lawyer; b. Evansville, Ind., Oct. 24, 1953; s. Robert Earl and Loraine L. (Simmons) A.; m. Carolyn Sue Cundiff, Mar. 5, 1976; children: Beth Anne, Benjamin Reed. BS, U. So. Ind., 1975; JD magna cum laude, Ind. U., Indpls., 1979. Bar: Ind. 1979, U.S. Dist. Ct. (so. dist.) Ind. 1979, U.S. Ct. Appeals (7th cir.) 1992. Assoc. Phillips and Long, Boonville, Ind., 1979-82; dep. pros. atty. Warrick County-2d Jud. cir., Boonville, Ind., 1980-93; atty. pvt. practice, Boonville, Ind., 1982-93; judge Warrick Superior Ct. #2, Ind., 1993—. Mem. ABA, Ind. State Bar Assn., Warrick County Bar Assn. (pres. 1983), Evansville Bar Assn., Brooks Inns of Ct. Office: 1 County Sq Ste 380 Boonville IN 47601-1813

AYLWARD, RONALD LEE, lawyer; b. St. Louis, May 30, 1930; s. John Thomas and Edna (Ketcherside) A.; m. Margaret Cecilia Hellweg, Aug. 10, 1963; children: Susan Marie Jotte, Stephen Ronald, Carolyn Ann Dolan. AB, Washington U., St. Louis, 1952, JD, 1954; student, U. Va., 1955. Bar: Mo. 1954, Ill. 1961, U.S. Supreme Ct. 1968. Assoc. Heneghan, Roberts & Cole, St. Louis, 1958-59; asst. counsel Olin Corp., East Alton, Ill., 1960-64; asst. gen. counsel INTERCO, Inc., St. Louis, 1964-66, asso. gen. counsel, mgr. law dept., 1966-69, asst. sec., 1966-74, gen. counsel, 1969-81, mem. operating bd., 1970-92, v.p., 1971-81, mem. exec. com., dir., 1975-92, exec. v.p., 1981-85, vice chmn. bd. dirs., 1985-92; chmn., pres. Aylward & Assocs., Inc., St. Louis, 1992—. Mem. dist. export coun. U.S. Dept. Commerce, 1974-77; dir., mem. exec. com. Boatmen's Nat. Bank St. Louis, 1982-91, trust estates com., 1982-85, chmn. audit com., 1986-91; bd. dirs. Boatmen's Bancshares, Inc., mem. audit com., 1984-91, mem. compensation com., 1986-91; trustee Maryville U., 1989-92, chmn. bd., 1991-92. Trustee St. Louis Coun. World Affairs, sec., 1977—84; chmn. lay bd. DePaul Health Ctr., 1979—81; mem. exec. com. lay bd., 1981—89; mem. lay adv. bd. Chaminade Coll. Prep. Sch., 1980—84, chmn. bd. trustees, 1981—84; mem. lay bd. Acad. of the Visitation, 1981—85; bd. dirs. Cath. Charities of St. Louis, 1994—2001, vice chmn., 1995—97, chmn., 1997—99; mem. coun. Archdiocesan Devel. Appeal, 1994—97, chmn., 1996—97, vice chmn., 1995—97, mem. exec. com., 1995—97, chmn. rev./planning com., 1995—96, chmn., 1996—, hon. life mem.; mem. fin. coun. Archdiocese of St. Louis, 1995—98, mem. investment com., 1995—97; bd. dirs. St. Louis chpt. Nat. Found. March of Dimes, 1974—84, sec., 1976—78, chmn., 1979—82; bd. dirs. Cardinal Ritter Inst., 1975—90, chmn. pers. com., 1986—90; bd. dirs. St. Louis chpt. ARC, 1977—82, Linda Vista Montessori Sch., 1975—77, BBB Greater St. Louis, 1978—81, YMCA Greater St. Louis, 1981—2001, adv. dir., 2001—, NCCJ, 1992—93; bd. dirs. Carindal Glennon Children's Hosp., 1991—96, mem. exec. com., 1992—96, bd. dirs. Found., 1996—2001, dir.emeritus, 2001—; bd. dirs., fin. United Way Greater St. Louis, 1986—2001; mem. investment com. St. Louis Cmty. Found., 1993—95. With U.S. Army, 1955—58. Recipient of Order of St. Louis's King, Archdiocese of St. Louis. Mem.: NAM (taxation com. 1970—76, pub. affairs com. 1973—76, govt. ops./expenditures com. 1973—78), St. Louis Bar Assn., Mo. Bar Assn., Am. Soc. Corp. Secs. (pres. St. Louis regional group 1972—73), Am. Footwear Industries Assn. (nat. affairs vice chmn. 1970, chmn. 1971—75), Am. Apparel Mfrs. Assn. (bd. dirs. 1983—85), Assoc. Industries Mo. (bd. dirs. 1973—80, exec. com. 1974—80, 2d v.p. 1974—76, pres. 1976—78), St. Louis C. of C. (legis. and tax com. 1966—74, vice-chmn. 1970—71), Bellerive Country Club, Mo. Athletic Club, Rotary (bd. dirs. St. Louis Club 1976—79), Bellerive Country Club (bd. dirs. 1981—84), Order of St. Louis King, Knights of Holy Sepulcher, Knights of Malta, Delta Theta Phi (dist. chancellor Mo. 1970—79, pres. St. Louis Alumni 1963). Home: 55 Muirfield Saint Louis MO 63141-7372 Office: Aylward and Assoc Inc 55 Muirfield Ct Saint Louis MO 63141 Fax: 314-434-6528. *Having something to achieve is the essence of my career. Continuing to set higher goals throughout life has made it both interesting and rewarding.*

AYMAN, IRAJ, educational consultant; b. Tehran, Feb. 9, 1928; came to the U.S., 1978; s. Abbas and Lagha (Hamidi) A.; m. Lily Ahy; children: Roya, Saba, Rama. BA, Tehran U., 1949; EdD, Edinburgh U., 1952; PhD, U. So. Calif., 1957; postgrad., Harvard U., 1963. Cert. tchr. Assoc. prof. applied psychology, dir. Pers. Mgmt./Rsch. Ctr. U. Tehran, Iran, 1957-70; prof., chair psychology dept. Nat. U. Tchr. Edn., Tehran, 1963-70; dir. Inst. Ednl. Studies, Tehran, 1963-70; pres. Nat. Inst. Psychology, Tehran, 1970-80; rsch. assoc. U. Chgo., 1979-83; regional edn. advisor Asia and Pacific UNESCO, Bangkok, 1983-87, chief tng. ednl. pers. Paris, 1987-88; dir. internat. programs Human Resource Inst., Westport, Conn., 1979-83; founder, dir. Landegg Acad., Wienacht, Switzerland, 1988-94; dir. Inst. Internat. Edn., St. Gallen, Switzerland, 1988-94; internat. cons. Internat. Edn. Systems, L.A., 1994-96; dean Wilmette (Ill.) Inst., 1995—. Program evaluation cons. IIT, 1975—; vis. prof. grad. colls. edn. & mgmt. scis. UCLA, 1974-75; vis. prof., Ford Found.; cons. grad. colls. edn. and pub. adminstrn. U. Philippines, Mania, 1965-67; dir. inst. edn. Nat. Tchr. Edn. U., Tehran, 1960-63; mgmt. tng. advisor Pakistan Internat. Airline, Karachi, 1969-70; faculty Capella U., 1996—; acad. bd. Pacific Rim Inst. for Devel. and Edn., 1999; adv. coun. Ctr. for Global Integrated Edn., 2003. Author, co-editor: Personnel Administration, 1955; author: Merit Rating, 1958; gen. editor: Educational Psychology, 1960; author, editor: A New Framework for Moral Education, 1993; co-editor: Transition to Global Society, 1993. Cons. UN Devel. Program, N.Y.C., Sri Lanka, 1993; exec. sec., coord. Internat. Dialogue on Transition to Global Soc., Switzerland, 1989-94; cons. Activity Ctr. for Edn., Beijing, 1988—; commr. of audit Eastern Regional Orgn. for Pub. Adminstrn., Manila, 1962-82. Specialist grantee Govt. of U.S., 1963, U.K. Tech. Cooperation Dept., 1962, USAID, 1955-57. Fellow Chinese Assn. Local Edn. Annals (sr., advisor Coun. Edn.- Bus. Partnership 1995—); mem. Am. Ednl. Rsch. Assn., Religious Edn. Assn. (exec. bd. 1994-2000), Am. Psychol. Assn., Internat. Assn. Ednl. Assessment (v.p. 1975-82), Internat. Test Commn. (pres. 1978-82), Internat. Assn. Applied Psychology (pres. divsn. 1978-82), Internat. Union Sci. Psychology (adminstrv. coun. 1960-90). Avocations: mountaineering, swimming, stamp collecting, hiking, chess playing. Home: 5715 S Kenwood Ave Apt 3N Chicago IL 60637-1742 E-mail: iayman@usbnc.org.

AYNES, RICHARD L(EE), law educator; b. Dayton, Ohio, June 12, 1949; s. Carl D. and B. Louise (Burton) A.; m. Kathleen H. Szokan, Aug. 20, 1971; children: Jennifer Elizabeth, Jeffrey Alexander. BS, Miami U., Oxford, Ohio, 1971; JD, Cleve.-Marshall Coll. Law, 1974. Bar: Ohio 1975, U.S. Supreme Ct. 1979. Inter, atty. Cleve. Legal Aid, 1974-75; law clk. 8th Dist. Ohio Ct. Appeals, Cleve., 1975-76; faculty U. Akron (Ohio) Law Sch., 1976—, assoc. dean, 1984-93, interim athletic dir., 1993-94, prof. John F. Seiberling Constl. Law Chair, 1995, dean, 1995—. Trustee Western Res. Legal Svcs., Medina, Summit and Portage Counties, Ohio, 1982-93; chmn. Mayors Task Force on Mcpl. Campaign Fin., 1998; racial fairness implementation task force Ohio Supreme Ct., 2000-02. U. Akron fellow, 1980. Mem. ABA (amicus com. criminal justice sect. 1982-88, cons. victims com. 1982-83, reporter spl. com. on evaluation jud. performance 1982-84, questionnaire com. 1999—). Office: Univ Akron Law Sch Akron OH 44325-2901 E-mail: raynes@uakron.edu.

AYOUB, ASHRAF S. engineering educator; b. Cairo, Oct. 20, 1967; s. Salah E. Ayoub and Amira A. Nekola. PhD, U. Calif., Berkeley, 1999. Post doctoral fellow Stanford U., Calif., 1999—2000; asst. prof. U. S. Fla., Tampa, 2001—. Mem.: ASCE (assoc.), Fla. Engring. Soc., Earthquake Engring. Rsch. Inst., Am. Concrete Inst. Office: University of South Florida 4202 E Fowler Ave Tampa FL 33620 Office Fax: 813-974-2957. E-mail: aayoub@eng.usf.edu.

AYOUB, AYOUB BARSOUM, mathematician, educator; b. Cairo, May 22, 1931; came to U.S., 1975, naturalized, 1997; s. Barsoum Ayoub and Linda (Naguib) Rizk; m. Germaine Hozayen Saad, Feb. 5, 1972; children: Sameh, Mariane. BSc in Math., Ain-Shams U., Cairo, 1951; MA in Math., Temple U., Phila., 1977, PhD in Math., 1980. Tchr. Tawfikia High Sch., Cairo, 1951-55; instr. Ain-Shams U., Cairo, 1955-75; teaching asst. Temple U., Phila., 1975-77, rsch. asst., 1977-80, vis. asst. prof., 1982-83; asst. prof. Ain-Shams U., Cairo, 1980-82; asst. prof. math. Pa. State U., Abington, 1983-90, assoc. prof., 1990-97, prof., 1997—, coord. math. dept., 1992-94. Referee Math. Mag., Coll. Math. Jour., Math & Computer Edn. Jour., Pi Mu Epsilon Jour.; reviewer Math. Tchr.; contbr. articles to profl. jours. Chmn. United Way Campaign, Pa. State, Ogontz Campus, 1990. Mem. Math. Assn. Am., Nat. Coun. Tchrs. Math., Am.

Math. Assn. Two-Yr. Colls., Pa. State Math. Assn. Two-Yr. Colls., Pa. Coun. Tchrs. Math., Assn. Math. Tchrs. N.Y. State. Avocation: travel. Office: Pa State U Abington Coll Abington PA 19001 E-mail: aba2@psu.edu.

AYOUB, PAUL JOSEPH, lawyer; b. Boston, Nov. 4, 1955; s. Joseph and Eleanore Ayoub; m. Jane Cronin; 1 child, Elizabeth. BA magna cum laude, Brown U., 1978; JB, Boston Coll., 1982. Bar: Mass. 1982, U.S. Dist. Ct. Mass. 1984, U.S. Ct. Appeals (1st cir.) 1984, U.S. Tax Ct. 1986. Assoc. Gaston & Snow, Boston, 1982-90, ptnr., 1990-91, Peabody & Arnold, Boston, 1991—2002, vice mng. ptr., 2000—02; ptnr. Nutter, McClennen & Fish LLP, 2002—. Mem. mgmt. com. Peabody & Arnold, Boston, 1997—2002. Chair alumni ann. fund Noble and Greenough Sch., Dedham, Mass., 1988—90, mem. capital campaign com., 1992—96, mem. alumni steering com., 1998—, mem. grads. coun., 2001—; mem. adv. com. to exec. bd. St. John of Damascus Ch., Dedham, 1995—98, exec. mgmt. bd., 1997—; mem. devel. com. Park Sch., Brookline, Mass., 1998—2001; co-chair Alumni Ann. Fund, 1998—2001; vice-chair graduates assn., 2003—; bd. dirs. St. Jude Children's Rsch. Hosp., Memphis, 1992—; chmn. legal com. Mem.: Mortgage Bankers Assn. Am. (legal affairs com. 1996—), Mass. Conveyancers Assn., Mass. Bar Assn., Boston Local Devel. Corp., Boston C. of C. (bd. dirs. 2000—, devel. and govt. affairs com.). Office: Nutter-McClennen & Fish,LLP 155 Seaport Blvd Boston MA 02210-3339

AYOUB, ROULA G. artist; b. Monrovia, Liberia, Mar. 4, 1964; arrived in U.S., 1982; B in Interior Design, U. Nebr., 1985; M in Interior Design and Fine Art, Fla. State U., 1988. Exhibitions include Art Deco, Beirut, 1998, 1999, State of the Art Gallery, 1998, 1999, 2000, 2001, 2002, Fine, Ctrl. Dist., 1998, 1999, Zouk Michael, 1998, Index, Dubai (United Arab Emirates) World Trade Ctr., 1998, 1999, 2000, Solemar-Kaslik, Jounieh, Lebanon, 1998, Artuel, Phoenicia Intercontinental Hotel, Beirut, 2000, 2001, Artexpo, Miami, Fla., 2000, Artexpo N.Y., N.Y.C., 2000, Exposition d'Art Plastique, Beirut, 2001, French & Francophine Fine Art, Dubai, 2001, Art Contemporain, Beirut, 2002, Blue Fig, Amman, Jordan, 2002, Artsud, Phoenicia Intercontinental Hotel, Beirut, 2002, Burkholder Gallery, Lincoln, Nebr., 2002, 2003, 24th Annual Invitational, BryanLGH, Lincoln, 2002, The Parade of Homes, 2003, Farra Design, Mkalles-Dekwaneh, Lebanon, 2003, many others, Represented in permanent collections Le Meridien Hotel, Dubai, Esteban, N.Y.C. Home: Bldg P-77 6100 Vine St Lincoln NE 68505

AYRES, BRENDA ANN, literature educator; b. York, Pa., Jan. 17, 1953; d. Charles L. and Norma J Ayres. PhD, U. So. Miss., Hattiesburg, 1992. Assoc. prof. Mid. Ga. Coll., Cochran, 1993—. Author: (scholarly book) Dissenting Women in Dickens' Novels: Subversion of Domestic Ideology, 1998, Frances Trollope and the Novel of Social Change, 2002, Silent Voices: Forgotten Novels by Victorian Women Writers, 2003, The Emperor's Old Groove: Decolonizing Disney's Magic Kingdom, 2003. Vice-chair Cochran-Bleckley County Arts Alliance, Ga., 2002—03. Recipient Outstanding Tchr. award, South Atlantic Assn. of Depts. of English, 1995, award, Ga. Coun. Tchrs. of English, 1997. Mem.: MLA (assoc.), Victoria ListServ (corr.), So. Conf. of Brit. Studies (assoc.). Office: Mid Ga Coll 1100 Second St SE Cochran GA 31014 Office Fax: 478-934-3517. E-mail: bayres@mgc.edu.

AYRES, JANICE RUTH, social services administrator; b. Idaho Falls, Idaho, Jan. 23, 1930; d. Low Ray and Frances Mae (Salem) Mason; m. Thomas Woodrow Ayres, Nov. 27, 1953 (dec. 1966); 1 child, Thomas Woodrow Jr. (dec.). MBA, U. So. Calif., 1952, M in Mass Comms., 1953. Asst. mktg. dir. Disneyland, Inc., Anaheim, Calif., 1954-59; gen. mgr. Tamasha Town & Country Club, Anaheim, Calif., 1959-65; dir. mktg. Am. Heart Assn., Santa Ana, Calif., 1966-69; state exec. dir. Nev. Assn. Mental Health, Las Vegas, 1969-71; exec. dir. Clark Co. Easter Seal Treatment Ctr., Las Vegas, 1971-73; mktg. dir., fin devel. officer So. Nev. Drug Abuse Coun., Las Vegas, 1973-74; exec. dir. Nev. Assn. Retarded Citizens, Las Vegas, 1974-75; assoc., cons. Don Luke & Assocs., Phoenix, 1976-77; program dir. Inter-Tribal Coun. Nev., Reno, 1977-79; exec. dir. Ret. Sr. Vol. Program, Carson City, Nev., 1979—. Chair sr. citizen summit State of Nev., 1996; apptd. Nev. Commn. Aging Gov. Guinn, 2001; presenter in field. Bd. suprs., Carson City, Nev., 1992—; commr. Carson City Parks and Recreation, 1993—; obligation bond com., legis. chair Carson City; bd. dirs. Nev. Dept. Transp., 1993; active No. Corp. for Nat. and Cmty. Svc. by Gov., 1994, V&TRR Commn., 1993, chair, 1995; vice-chair, chair pub. rels. com., bd. dirs. Hist. V&TRR Bd.; chair PR Cmty./V&RR Commn. Nev. Home Health Assn.; appointed liaison Carson City Sr. Citizens Bd., 1995; chair summit Rural Nev. Sr. Citizens, Carson City; pres. No. Nev. R.R. Found., 1996—; chair Tri-Co-R.R. Commn., 1995, Gov.'s Nev. Commn. for Corp. in Nat. and Comty. Svc., 1997—, pres., 1998, Carson City Pub. Transp. Commn., 1998—; Carson City Commn. for Clean Groundwater Act, 1998—; chairperson Celebrate Svc. Conf. Americore, 2000; appointed by Gov. of Nev. Commn. on Aging, 2001—; appointed by Nev. Gov. new Nev. Commn. to Restructure the Historic V&T R.R., 2002—; mem. Nev. Commn. on Aging, 2001—; apptd. rep. of gov. to Nev. Commn. Recruitment V&T RR, 2002. Named Woman of Distinction, Soroptimist Club, 1988, Oustanding Dir. of Excellence, Gov. State of Nev., 1989, Outstanding Nev. Women's Role Model, Nev. A.G., 1996, Woman of Distinction, Carson Valley Optimist, 2002, Nev.'s Outstanding Older Worker for Experience-Works, 2002, Oldest CEO in Nev., 2002, Outstanding Nev. Pvt. Citizen, Nev. Gov. Guinn, 2003, Outstanding Dir., Vol. Action Ctr., J.C. Penney Co., invitee to White Ho. for outstanding contbns. to Am.; recipient Gold award, Western Fairs Assn., 2000, Woman of Distinction award, Soroptimist, 2003, Carson City Optimist, 2003, Nat. Optimist Conv., Reno, Nev., 2003, Outstanding Contbn. to Success of Women in Bus., Carson Valley Sorpotomists. Mem.: AAUW, Nat. Assn. RSVP Dirs. (pres. 2003), Internat. Assn. Bus. Commentators, No. Nev. Railroad Found. (pres. 1996—), Am. Soc. Assn. Execs., Nev. Assn. Transit Svcs. (bd. dirs., legis. chmn.), Nev. Fair and Rodeo Assn. (pres.), Nat. Soc. Fund Raising Execs., Women in Radio and TV, Pub. Rels. Soc. Am. (chpt. pres.), Internat. Platform Assn., Am. Mktg. Assn. (bd. dirs. 1999—), Am. Mgmt. Assn. (bd. dirs.), Nat. Women's Polit. Caucus, Nev. Women's Polit. Caucus. Home: 1762 Montelena Ct Carson City NV 89703-8376 Office: Ret Sr Vol Program 501 E Caroline St Carson City NV 89701-4054

AYRES, JAYNE LYNN ANKRUM, community health nurse; b. Reed City, Mich., Oct. 12, 1944; d. Quinten Wayne and Marshia Agetha (Crum) Ankrum; m. James Anthony Lane, May 4, 1963 (div. Jan. 1975); children: Linda, Michele, Julie; m. Ronald Francis Ayres, Apr. 16, 1977 (div. Sept. 1997). ADN, Manatee C.C., Bradenton, Fla., 1975. RN Fla., Ga. Staff nurse med.-surg., cardiac, oncology and float team Sarasota (Fla.) Meml. Hosp., 1975—77; nursing supr. Upjohn Healthcare Svcs., Sarasota, 1981—85; staff nurse Devereux Found., Kennesaw, Ga., 1986—89; staff nurse, supr. Vis. Nurse Health Sys., Metro, Atlanta, 1989—97; health clinic nurse Equifax, Atlanta, 1996—97; entertainer JPM Prodn. Co., 1996—97; adv. bd. Waldrop Personal Care, Inc., 1998—. Mem. adv. subcom. Waldrop Personal Care, Inc., 1998—. Vol. ARC, M.U.S.T., Ministries Health Clinic for Homeless, Marietta, Ga., Summer Olympic Games, Atlanta, 1996; Vol. East Pasco Med. Ctr., Zephyrhills, Fla., 2003. Mem. Am. Legion (hon.), Fla. Nurses Assn. (hon.), Beta Sigma Phi. Achievements include invention of the syringe filling monitor. Address: 36745 Kimela Ave Zephyrhills FL 33542

AYRES, JUDITH ELIZABETH, federal agency administrator; b. Akron, Ohio, Sept. 3, 1944; d. William Hanes and Mary Helen (Coventry) A.; m. John Woolfolk Burke, III, June 17, 1978; 1 child, Elizabeth Coventry Ayres. BA, Miami U., Oxford, Ohio, 1966; postgrad., Internat. Christian U., Mitaka, Japan, 1968; MPA, Harvard U., 1980. With U.S. Dept. Interior, 1972-78, communication-legis liaison person, 1974-78; cons. San Francisco, 1978-82; regional adminstr. EPA, San Francisco, 1983-88; prin. William D. Ruckelshaus Assocs., San Francisco, 1988-89, The Environ. Group, San Francisco, 1989—; asst. adminr. int. affairs EPA, Washington, 2001—. Lectr., speaker in field. Contbr. articles to numerous publs. Del. Republican. Nat. Conv., 1988; bd. dirs. Women's Leadership Fund, Kennedy Sch. Govt., Harvard U.; mem. bd. Conservationists for Bush; co-chmn. Bush for Pres., Marin County, Calif., 1988, Calif. Conservationists for Bush, 1988. Mem. Women's Forum West, Harvard Club, Lambda Alpha. Republican. Avocations: music, natural history, skiing, sculling. Office: EPA Int Affairs 1200 Pennsylvania Ave NW MC 2610R Washington DC 20460 Office Fax: 202-565-2407.

AYRES, MARY ELLEN, government official; b. Spokane, Wash., June 23, 1924; d. Frank H. and Marion (Kellogg) A. Student, U. Wash., 1942-43; BA, Stanford U., 1946; postgrad., Am. U., 1960. With Henry von Morpurgo, Advt., 1946-47; reporter Wenatchee Daily World, Wash., 1947-50, Washington Post, 1950-51; with U.S. Fgn. Service, Dept. State, 1950-51; mem. editorial staff Changing Times, 1952-61; editor Family Guide, Kiplinger Washington Editors, 1958-61, Bur. Labor Stats., Manpower Adminstrn., U.S. Dept. Labor, 1962-67; pub. info. specialist Bur. Indian Affairs, U.S. Dept. Interior, 1967-75; writer-editor Bur. Labor Stats., 1975—. Tchr. newsletter class Dept. Agriculture Grad. Sch., 1975-89, editing style and technique class, 1987-89; past treas. Govt. Info. Orgn. Mem. publicity com. Nat. Capitol YWCA, 1982-83; dir. Wenatchee High Sch. Scholarship Found., 1988-95. Mem. Nat. Assn. Govt. Communicators (founding treas., dir. 1975-80, 89-91, chmn. Blue Pencil Contest 1987, nat. capital chpt. treas. 1989), Nat. Press Club (Washington), Washington Athletic Club (Seattle), Am. News Women's Club, Am. Econ. Assn., Stanford U. Alumnae Assn., Kappa Kappa Gamma. Episcopalian. Home: 2400 Virginia Ave NW Apt C802 Washington DC 20037-2657 Office: Bur Labor Stats 2 Massachusetts Ave NE Washington DC 20212-0022 Fax: (202) 691-7890. E-mail: ayres_m@bls.gov.

AYRES, MARY JO, professional speaker, writer, composer; b. Aberdeen, Miss., Jan. 27, 1953; d. Walter Stephen and Sarah Louise (Pearson) Peugh; m. William Stanley Ayres, June 28, 1975; children: Elizabeth, Will. BS, Miss. State U., Starkville, 1974; MEd, Delta State U., 1993. Tchr. Greenville (Miss.) Pub. Schs., 1974-75, Leland (Miss.) Acad., 1975-77, Leland United Meth. Child Devel. Ctr., Leland, 1984-91, chmn. bd. dirs., 1993—; profl. speaker Natural Learning, Leland, 1987—. Author: Happy Teaching and Natural Learning, 1992, Natural Learning from A-Z, 1997; prodr. cassette and CD 32 Natural Learning Songs from A-Z (Parent's Choice award), More Natural Learning Songs from A-Z (Parent's Choice award), Natural Learning Fun Songs (Parent's Choice award), Ms. Magnolia Puppet; contbr. articles to profl. jours. Mem. Assn. for Childhood Edn. Internat., Miss. Early Childhood Assn., So. Assn. for Children Under Six, So. Early Childhood Assn., Miss. Reading Assn., Internat. Reading Assn. Avocation: tennis. Home and Office: 103 Sycamore St Leland MS 38756-3136 E-mail: nlearn@naturallearning.com.

AYRES, PAUL ERDMAN, artist; b. Detroit, Apr. 13, 1921; s. Harry Erdman and Bessie Marie (Friedman) A.; m. Marianne Elizabeth Kuhn, May 29, 1944 (dec. Sept. 1995); children: Martha, Jeffrey, Christopher. DVM, Mich. State U., 1943; student, Oakland C.C., Rochester, Mich., 1981-83, Coll. of Charleston, S.C., 1983-91. Lic. DVM, Mich. Tech. asst. Parke Davis & Co., Detroit, 1944-53, mgr. vet. dept. Rochester, Mich., 1953-74, mgr. lab., 1974-76; mgr. indsl. hygiene dept. Parke Davis & Co., divsn. Warner Lambert Co., Rochester, 1976-83. Pres. Lowcountry Artists Ltd., Charleston, 2001—. One-man shows include Lowcountry Artists, Ltd., Charleston, 1984—; represented in numerous pvt. collections. Pres. Cmty. Chest, Oakland Twp., Mich., 1962-65; bd. dirs. Print Studio South, Charleston, 1994-96; treas., bd. dirs. Charleston Artists Guild, 1987-90. Roman Catholic. Avocation: sailing. Home and Office: 1161 Shadow Lake Cir Apt A Mount Pleasant SC 29464-9060

AYRES, ROBERT MOSS, JR., retired university president; b. San Antonio, Sept. 1, 1926; s. Robert Moss and Florence (Collett) A.; m. Patricia Ann Shield, Sept. 10, 1955; children: Robert Atlee, Vera Patricia. Student, Tex. Mil. Inst., 1944; BA, U. of the South, 1949, DCL, 1974; postgrad., Oxford (Eng.) U., 1949; MBA, U. Pa., 1952. With Kidder, Peabody & Co., Phila., N.Y.C., 1950-52; with Dittmar & Co., San Antonio, 1952-53; pres., dir. Russ & Co., Inc., San Antonio, 1953-73; sr. v.p., dir. Rotan Mosle Inc., San Antonio, 1973-77; pres. U. South, Sewanee, Tenn., 1977-88, pres. emeritus, 1988—; past pres. So. Univ. Conf.; chmn. So. Coll. and Univ. Union. Former allied mem. N.Y. Stock Exch., Am. Stock Exch.; bd. dirs. Rail Tex. Corp., Howell Corp., James Avery Craftsman. Past pres. Assn. Alumni U. of South; past pres. bd. dirs. Bexar County chpt. ARC; past pres. bd. trustees Tex. Mil. Inst.; trustee, past chmn. bd. regents U. of South; trustee Brother's Bro. Found.; mem. exec. coun. Episcopal Ch., 1976-82, also mem. nat. and world mission com., dir., past pres. St. Mary's Episcopal Ctr.; mem. Commn. on Ministry Com. Diocese of Tex.; past bd. dirs. Inst. European Studies, Presiding Bishop's Fund World Relief, Alfalit, Internat.; vol. exec. dir. Vol. in Mission, 1976; bd. dirs. Inst. of Servant Leadership, Soc. Promotion of Christian Knowledge/U.S.A., Salvation Army, Episcopal Hist. Soc. With USN, 1944-46; lt. Res. 1949-60. Mem. San Antonio Soc. Fin. Analysts (past pres.), Securities Industries Assn. (past mem. governing coun.), Investment Bankers Assn. Am. (past chmn. Tex. group), Nat. Assn. Securities Dealers (past mem. dist. com.) Young Pres. Orgn., Order of Alamo, Tex. Cavaliers, Argyle, Am. Soc. Order of St. John, Sigma Alpha Epsilon. Episcopalian (mem. exec. bd. diocese W. Tex.; vestryman). Clubs: San Antonio German, San Antonio Country. Home: 5705 Scout Island Cv Austin TX 78731-3386

AYRES, ROBERT UNDERWOOD, environmental economics and technology educator; b. Plainfield, N.J., June 29, 1932; s. John Underwood and Alice Conrow (Hutchinson) A.; m. Leslie Wentz, June 26, 1954; 1 dau., Jennifer Leigh. BS in Math., U. Chgo., 1954; MS in Physics, U. Md., 1956; PhD, U. London, 1958. Rsch. assoc. Hudson Inst., Croton-on-Hudson, N.Y., 1962-67; vis. scholar Resources for Future, 1967-68; v.p., dir. Internat. Research & Tech. Corp., Washington, 1968-76, Delta Research Corp., Arlington, Va., 1976—; prof. engring. and pub. policy Carnegie-Mellon U., 1979-92. Chmn. bd. Variflex Corp., Pitts., 1969-87; cons. in field; mem. tech. and water com. Nat. Acad. Scis., 1971, new transp. systems and tech. com., 1971—, strategic and critical materials com., 1971-72, com. steel rsch., 1978, com. alts. for reduction chlorofluorocarbon emissions, 1979; mem. com. on engring. edn. Nat. Acad. Engring., 1984; dep. program leader, project leader Internat. Inst. Applied Systems Analysis, 1986-90; prof. environ. econs., Sandoz prof. environ. mgmt., dir. Ctr. for Mgmt. Environ. Resources, INSEAD, Fontainebleau, France, 1992-2000, prof. emeritus, 2000—; Jubilee prof. Chalmers Inst. Tech., Sweden, 2000-01; vis. prof. Inst. for Advanced Study, UN U., Tokyo, 2000-02. Author: Technological Forecasting and Long Range Planning, (with others) Economics and the Environment, 1971, Alternatives to the Internal Combustion Engine, 1972, Resources, Environment and Economics, 1978, Uncertain Futures, 1979, Robotics: Applications and Social Implications, 1983, The Next Industrial Revolution: Reviving Industry Through Innovation, 1984, CIM: Revolution in Progress, 1991, Information, Entropy and Progress: A New Evolutionary Paradigm, 1994, (with L.W. Ayres) Industrial Metabolism, 1994, Industrial Ecology: Closing the Materials Cycle, 1996, Turning Point: An End to the Growth Paradigm, 1998, (with L.W. Ayres) Accounting for Resources 1: Materials and Waste, 1998, 2, The Life Cycle of Materials, 1999; co-editor: (with L.W. Ayres) Handbook of Industrial Ecology, 2001, (with L.W. Ayres and Rode) Life Cycle of Copper, 2003; assoc. editor Energy, 2001—contbr. articles to profl. jours. Fellow World Econ. Forum 1994); mem. Am. Econ. Assn., Internat. Soc. Ecology Econs. (Boulding Meml. prize 2002), Internat. Soc. Indsl. Ecology (Outstanding Rsch. prize 2003). Office: INSEAD Fontainebleau 77305 France

AYRES, STEPHEN MCCLINTOCK, physician, educator; b. Elizabeth, N.J., Oct. 29, 1929; s. Malcolm B. and Florence M. A.; m. Dolores Kobrick, June 11, 1955; children— Stephen (dec. May 1998), Elizabeth, Margaret. BA, Gettysburg Coll., 1951; MD, Cornell U., 1955. Intern N.Y. Hosp., N.Y.C., 1955, resident, 1958-61; dir. cardio-pulmonary lab. St. Michael's Hosp., Newark, 1961-63, St. Vincent's Hosp. and Med. Center, N.Y.C., 1963-73; physician-in-chief St. Vincent Hosp., Worcester, Mass., 1973-75; prof., chmn. dept. internal medicine St. Louis U. Med. Center, 1975-85; dean Med. Coll. Va., Richmond, 1985-93; dean emeritus, dir. office internat. health program Med. Coll. Va./Va. Commonwealth U., Richmond, 1993—. Author: Care of the Critically Ill, 3d edit., 1988; co-author: Textbook of Critical Care, 1988, Nutritional Support of the Critically Ill, 1988; editor: Major Issues in Critical Care Medicine, 1984; contbr. articles to profl. jours. Chmn. bd. Found. for Critical Care, 1985—. Served with M.C., U.S. Army, 1956-58. Fellow A.C.P., Am. Coll. Cardiology, Am. Coll. Chest Physicians; mem. Soc. Critical Care Medicine (pres. 1979-80), Am. Lung Assn., Assn. Am. Physicians, Am. Soc. Clin. Investigation. Home: 5103 Cary Street Rd Richmond VA 23226-1644 Office: Med Coll Va PO Box 565 Richmond VA 23218-0565

AYRES, TED DEAN, lawyer, academic counsel; b. Hamilton, Mo., July 14, 1947; m. Marcia Sue Busselle; children: John Corbett, Jackson Frazer, Joseph Dean. BSBA, Ctrl. Mo. State Coll., 1969; JD, U. Mo., 1972. Bar: Mo. 1972, U.S. Dist. Ct. (we. dist.) Mo. 1972, U.S. Ct. Appeals (8th cir.) 1977, U.S. Supreme Ct. 1977, Colo. 1984, U.S. Dist. Ct. Colo. 1984, U.S. Ct. Appeals (10th cir.) 1984, Kans. 1987. Law clk. to presiding justice Mo. Supreme Ct., Jefferson City, 1972-73; ptnr. Stubbs & Ayres, Chillicothe, Mo., 1973-74; atty. Southwestern Bell Tel. Co., St. Louis, 1974-76; counsel U. Mo., Columbia, 1976-84; gen. counsel U. Colo., Boulder, 1984-86, Kans. Bd. Regents, Topeka, 1986 92, gen. counsel, dir. govtl. rels., 1992-96; acting pres. Pitts. State U., 1995; gen. counsel, assoc. to pres. Wichita (Kans.) State U., 1996—2002, interim dir. Edwin A. Ulrich Mus. Art, 1999-2000, v.p., gen. counsel, 2002—, dir. equal employment opportunity, 2003—. Adj. asst. prof. coll. bus. adminstrn. U. Colo., Denver, 1984-85, adj. assoc. prof., 1985-86; spl. asst. atty. gen. State of Colo., 1984-86, State of Kans., 1986—; presenter region II conf. Assn. Coll. Unions Internat., U. Mo., Rolla, 1983; spkr. Soc. Colo. Archivists, U. Colo., Boulder, 1985; adj. prof. Washburn U., Topeka, 1989; adj. prof. kinesiology and sport studies Wichita State U., 1999—. Contbr. articles to profl. jours. Active adv. com. Boone County (Mo.) Cmty. Svcs.; mem. com. social concerns Mo. United Meth. Ch., 1979-81, supervisory com. Mothers' Morning Out program, 1980-84; adminstv. bd., com. on fin. and stewardship 1st United Meth. Ch., Topeka, 1989-91, family life coun., 1994-95; trustee Mid-Mo. chpt. Nat. Multiple Sclerosis Soc., 1981-84; mem. bd. mgrs. Topeka YMCA-Downtown Br., 1991-96, fedn. coun. Indian Guides program, 1988-91; treas. pack 175 Cub Scouts, 1990-95; bd. dirs. Innovative Tech. Enterprise Corp., 1991-94, S.W. Youth Athletic Assn., Inc., 1994-96, Friends of Topeka Zoo, 1995-2000, Wichita Tech. Corp., 1997—, Wichita State U. Hist. Preservation Commn., 1998—, parents coun. Truman State U., 1997-99. Curator scholar, 1969-70, Omar E. Robinson scholar, 1970-71, John M. Dalton Ednl. Trust scholar 1971-72. Mem. Mo. Bar Assn., Nat. Assn. Coll. and Univ. Attys. (chairperson Southwestern region 1979-81, bd. dirs. 1985-88, com. mem. 1979—, del. and presenter numerous CLE workshops), U. Mo. Alumni Assn. (life). Home: 2820 Tallgrass St Wichita KS 67226-1815 Office: Wichita State Univ 203 Morrison Hall Wichita KS 67260-0001 E-mail: ted.ayres@wichita.edu.

AYROVAINEN, ROBERT MICHAEL, music educator; b. Amityville, N.Y., Nov. 27, 1964; s. Martin J. and Florence T. Ayrovainen. BA in Music Edn., SUNY, Potsdam, 1986; MA in Jazz Studies, CUNY, 1991. Cert. sch. dist. adminstrn. Band dir. Hauppauge (N.Y.) Sch. Dist., 1986—. Jazz ensemble dir. Hauppauge Sch. Dist., 1991—; performing musician. Vol. Care and Share Not for Profit Orgn., Hauppauge, 1994—2002. Mem.: Music Educators Nat. Conf., Suffolk County Music Educators Assn., NY State United Tchrs. Avocations: outdoors, running, reading, music. Office: Hauppauge Mid Sch 600 Townline Rd Smithtown NY 11788 E-mail: ayrovainenr@netscape.com.

AYSCUE, EDWIN OSBORNE, JR., lawyer; b. May 21, 1933; s. Edwin Osborne and Grace Elizabeth (Fields) A.; m. Emily Mizell Urquhart, Aug. 17, 1957; children: Grace Thompson, E. Osborne, Emily Hassel, Margaret Certain. Grad. cum laude, Phillips Acad., Andover, Mass., 1951; AB in Polit. Sci., U. N.C., Chapel Hill, 1954; LLB with honors, U. N.C., 1960. Bar: N.C. 1960, U.S. Supreme Ct. 1979. Mem. Helms Mulliss & Wicker, PLLC (and predecessor firms), Charlotte, 1960—. Mem. Civil Justice Reform Act Com., Western Dist. N.C., 1991-95. Editor-in-chief: N.C. Law Rev., 1959-60; contbr. articles to profl. jours. Bd. dirs. Legal Svcs. of So. Piedmont, 1983-85, Legal Svcs. of N.C., 1984-85, 88-94; sr. warden Christ Episcopal Ch., 1990-91; U.S. Supreme Ct. Hist. Soc., 1999-2003; trustee St. Mary's Sch., Raleigh, N.C., 2000—; bd. vis. U. N.C. Chapel Hill, 2000— . Lt. USNR, 1955-57. Fellow: Am. Coll. Trial Lawyers (pres. 1998—99), Am. Bar Found. (life); mem.: ABA (ho. of dels. 1991—95, standing com. fed. judiciary 2001—), People's Republic of Cuba Legal Exch. (chair 2001), People's Republic of China Legal Exch. (chair 1987), Anglo-Am. Legal Exch. (co-chair 1999—2000), Am. Judicature Soc. (bd. dirs. 1985—89), Mecklenburg County Bar (pres. 1980—81), N.C. State Bar, N.C. Bar Assn. (pres. 1984—85, Gen. Practice Hall of Fame), 4th Cir. Jud. Conf., Nat. Conf. Bar Pres., U. N.C. Chapel Hill Law Alumni Assn. (pres. 1999—2000), Order of Coif, Order Golden Fleece, Charlotte Country Club, Phi Beta Kappa. Democrat. Episcopalian. Office: Helms Mulliss & Wicker PLLC PO Box 31247 Charlotte NC 28231-1247

AYUB, YACUB, financial consultant; b. Bombay, May 14, 1944; s. Ayub and Aziza Abbas; children: Murtaza, Marzia. MBA, U. Karachi, Pakistan, 1966. CPC, CEP. Rep. officer United Bank of Pakistan, Tehran, 1966-73; calling officer Bank Credit and Commerce Internat. (Iran Arab Bank), Tehran, 1974-78; audit officer Bank Credit and Commerce Internat., London, 1978-79, mgr. br. ops. Panama City, Panama, 1979-83, mgr. mktg. and bus. devel. N.Y.C., 1983-88; fin. cons. Investment & Mgmt. Cons. Inc., Holmdel, 1988—2002; morgage cons. Residential & Comml., 2002—. Fellow Life Underwriters Tng. Coun. Republican. Home: 1001 Plaza Dr Woodbridge NJ 07095 E-mail: ayubm@aol.com. *Perseverance, hard work, faith and hope are the true ingredients to success. Add to it honesty and trust which leads to great achievements in business and life.*

AYUS, JUAN CARLOS, nephrologist; b. Buenos Aires, Feb. 25, 1941; came to U.S., 1973; s. Jose and Matilde A.; m. Linda Maria Giudici; children: Sebastian, Mariana. BS, Nat. Coll., 1959; MD, U. Buenos Aires, 1967. Diplomate Am. Bd. Internal Medicine, Am. Bd. Nephrology. Resident in internal medicine U. Buenos Aires, 1968-71, fellow in nephrology, 1971-72; resident in internal medicine U. Mass., Worcester, 1973-74, U. Minn., Mpls., 1974-75; fellow in nephrology U. Calif., San Francisco, 1975-77; chief renal svc. Ben-Taub Regional hosp., Houston, 1977-84; from assoc. prof. to prof. medicine Baylor Coll. Medicine, Houston, 1984—2001; prof. medicine U. Tex. Health Sci. Ctr., San Antonio, 2001—. Recipient Gold Insignia, Spanish Soc. Nephrology, 1999. Fellow ACP; mem. Lat. Am. Soc. Nephrology (sec.-treas. 1993-96, v.p. 1996-99), Argentine Soc. Critical Care (founder). Home: 1967 Haddon St Houston TX 77019-5762 E-mail: carlosayus@yahoo.com.

AYYUB, BILAL M. civil engineering educator, researcher, executive; b. Shweikeh, Tulkaram, Palestine, Jan. 5, 1958; came to U.S., 1980; s. Mohammed S. and Thuraya Ayyub; m. Deena L. Ziadeh, June 27, 1987; children: Omar, Rami, Samar, Ziad. BSCE, U. Kuwait, 1980; MSCE, Ga. Inst. Tech., 1981, PhD, 1983. Registered profl. engr., Md. Asst. prof. dept. civil engring. U. Md., College Park, 1983-88, assoc. prof., 1988-93, prof., 1993—, gen. dir. Ctr. for Tech. and Sys. Mgmt.; pres. BMA Engring. Inc., Md., 1988—; CEO, Decide-Now.com, Inc., 2000—. Cons. prof. Carderock divsn. of Naval Surface Warfare Ctr., USN; cons. USCG, Groton, Conn., 1987-90, USN, Crystal City, Va., 1990—, ASME, Washington, 1990—, Internat. Monetary Fund, Washington, 1993, Chevron Rsch. and Tech. Corp., Richmond, Calif., 1992-94, U.S. Army Corps. of Engrs., Washington, 1994—; mem. adv. bd. to internat. jours. and Naval Engrs. Jour., 1989—; gen. chmn. Internat. Symposium on Uncertainty Modeling and Analysis, 1990, 93, 95; dir. Ctr. for Tech. and Sys. Mgmt. Editor: Analysis and Management of Uncertainty, 1992, Uncertainty Modeling and Analysis, 1995, Uncertainty Modeling in Finite Element, Fatigue and Stability of Systems, 1997, Uncertainty Modeling in Vibration, Control and Fuzzy Analysis in Structural Systems, 1997, Uncertainty Modeling and Analysis in Civil Engineering, 1998, Uncertainty Modeling and Analysis in Engineering and the Sciences, 1997; editor: (textbooks) Numerical Methods for Engineers1995, Probability, Statistics and Reliability for Engineers, 1997, Elicitation of Expert Opinions for Uncertainty and Risks, 2001; conbr. over 350 articles to profl. jours. Recipient Cert. of Appreciation, U.S. Army C.E., 1995; grantee, NSF, 1985—92, Md. State Hwy. Adminstrn., 1986—90, USN, 1990—95, U.S. Army C.E., 1994—95. Fellow ASCE (Outstanding Rsch. Oriented Paper award 1988, Edmund Friedman award 1989, Walter L. Huber Civil Engring. Rsch. award 1997, chmn. reliability of offshore structures com. 1993-96, assoc. editor Jour. Structural Engring., mem. com. on fatugue and fracture reliability, mem. tech. adminstrv. com. on structural safety and reliability 1993-96), Soc. Naval Archs. and Marine Engrs. (chmn. panel on design procedure and philosophy of the hull structures com., Jour. Ship Rsch. com.), ASME (polit. action com. 1990—, risk-based tech. rsch. com.); mem. IEEE (sr), NRC (working groups of marine bd.), Am. Soc. Naval Engrs. (life, Jimmie Hamilton award 1986, 93, 2000, chmn. naval engrs. jour. com.), Am. Concrete Inst., Am. Acad. Mechanics, N.Am. Fuzzy Info. Processing Soc. (K.S. Fu award 1995, gen. chmn. ann. conf. 1995), Computer Soc. Achievements include risk and uncertainty analysis in engineering, design guidelines for posttensioned composite bridges, general guidelines for risk-based inspection, structural reliability assessment using variance reduction techniques, uncertainty modeling and analysis in engineer-

ing, fuzzy logic in civil engineering, reliability-based design of marine structures, reliability assessment and reliability-based design of navigation structures. Office: U Md Dept Civil & Environ Engr College Park MD 20742-0001

AZAD, ABUL KASHEM MOHAMMOD, engineer; b. Dhaka, Bangladesh, Jan. 1, 1959; s. Monazzir Ali and Meherunnessa Khanam; m. Sabira Azad, Sept. 9, 1988; 1 child, Tanjiv. BS, U. Dhaka, 1984, MS, 1987; PhD, U. Sheffield, Eng., 1994. Asst. engr. Atomic Energy Ctr., Bangladesh, 1978—81, 1985—87, jr. engr., 1982—84; lectr. U. Dhaka, 1987—88; rsch. fellow U. Portsmouth, England, 1996—2001; asst. prof. dept. tech. No. Ill. U., DeKalb, 2001—. Recipient Chancellor's award U. Dhaka, 1986; rsch. fellow U. Sheffield; Commonwealth scholar, England, 1988-94. Mem. IEEE, IEE (assoc.), ISA (sr.). Avocation: travel. Office: Dept Tech No Ill Univ Coll Engring & Engring Tech Dekalb IL 60115 Home: 611 Hill St Apt #6 Sycamore IL 60178 E-mail: azad@ceet.niu.edu.

AZAD, GM SALAM, engineer, researcher; BS, Bangladesh U. of Engring. & Tech., Dhaka, 1991, MS, 1993, Prairie View A&M U., 1996; PhD, Tex. A&M U., 2000. Lectr. Bangladesh U. of Engring. & Tech., Dhaka, 1991—93, asst. prof., 1993—95; rsch. asst. Tex. A&M U., Coll. Sta., 1995—2000; project engr. Tech. Devel. Group, Inc., Shawnee, Okla., 2000; advanced engr. Siemens Westinghouse Power Corp., Orlando, 2001—. Vis. lectr. Cost & Mgmt. Accountants of Bangladesh, Dhaka, 1993—95. Author: (rsch. article) ASME Jour. Turbomachinery, ASME Jour. of Heat Transfer, AIAA Jour. of Thermophysics and Heat Transfer, Internat. Jour. of Enhanced Heat Transfer, Internat. Jour. of Rotating Machinery, Jour. of the Institution of Engineers' Bangladesh, Jour. of NOAMI, Bangladesh; reviewer Internat. Jour. of Heat and Fluid Flow. Scholarship, Hazi Muhsin Trust Fund, 1978, Edn. Bd., Bangladesh Govt., 1982—91, Bangladesh U. of Engring. & Tech., 1987—91, Grant, State of Tex. LoanSTAR program, 1995—96, NASA Lewis Rsch. Ctr., 1996—2000. Mem.: ASME (assoc.). Achievements include research in Developed squealer tip geometry for gas turbine blades that reduce tip leakage and thermal load. Avocations: fishing, travel.

AZADEH, MOHAMMAD, electrical engineer, researcher; b. Tehran, Iran, June 4, 1965; s. Mohammad Javad Azadeh and Farideh Nourbakhsh. BS, Tehran U., 1990; MS, Portland State U., 1995; PhD, U. Wash., 2000. Rsch. asst. Portland State U., Oreg., 1992-95, U. Wash., Seattle, 1995-2000; sr. design engr. Luminent Inc., Chatsworth, Calif., 2000—. Presenter in field. Contbr. articles to profl. jours. Mem. IEEE, Optical Soc. Am.

AZANK, ROBERTO, artist; b. Buenos Aires, Nov. 3, 1955; came to U.S., 1979; s. Neazi and Dora Margarita (Estevez) A.; m. Monika Schifler, Oct. 20, 1990; 1 child, Rudi Vinicius. Student, U. Arch., Buenos Aires, 1975-78. One-man shows include Marcos J. Alegria Sch. Fine Arts, P.R., 1991, Consulate Gen. of Argentina, N.Y.C., 1997, Lizan Tops Gallery, East Hampton, N.Y., 1998, Albers Fine Arts, Memphis, 1998, Albert White Gallery, Toronto, Can., 1998, Hooks-Epstein Galleries, Houston, Tex., 1998, Brewster Arts Limited, N.Y.C., 1999, Addison-Ripley Fine Art, Washington D .C., 1999, 2003, Byron Cohen Gallery, Kansas City, Mo., 2000, Albert Einstein U., N.Y.C., 1999, Eleonore Austerer Gallery, San Francisco, 2001, 2002, 2003, Palm Springs, Calif., 2003, Gomez Gallery, Balt., 2001, Bachelier-Cardonsky Gallery, Kent, Conn., 2001, 2003, Austerer-Crider Gallery, Palm Springs, Calif., 2002, Ctr. of Earth Gallery, Charlotte, N.C., 2003; group exhbns. include Olympia and York Gallery, N.Y., 1991, Galaxy Gallery, Miami Beach, Fla., 1990, SUNY, Albany, 1993, Ramis Barquet Gallery, Miami, 1997, N.Y. Arts Mag. 2d City-wide Biennial, 1997, Mulligan Shanoski Gallery, San Francisco, 1998, Elite Fine Art, Miami, 1998, Art Miami, '98, 1998, Lyons. Wier Gallery, Chgo., 1998, Artspace/Va. Miller Gallery, Miami, 1998, Meredith Kelly Fine Arts, Santa Fe, 1998, 2000, 02, 03, Kougeas Gallery, Boston, 1999, William Havu Gallery, Denver, 1999, Art Miami, 2000, Palm Springs Art Fair, Eleonore Austerer Gallery, 2000, Art Miami, 2001, Palm Springs Art Fair, 2001, Ctr. of Earth Gallery, Charlotte, N.C., 2002; represented by Robert Miller Gallery, N.Y., Addison-Ripley Gallery, Washington, Artspace/Virginia Miller Gallery, Miami, Eleonore Austerer Gallery, San Francisco and Palm Springs; works featured in publs. including N.Y. Arts Mag., New Am. Painting, Waterfront Week, Kansas City Star, The Washington Post, Miami Herald, Palm Springs Life; included in pub. collections at Washington Convention Ctr., Am. Express Fin. Advisors, Spring Telecomms., also pvt. collections. Avocations: classical music, astronomy, chess. Office: Roberto Azank Studio 8 Watch Hill Rd New Paltz NY 12561-2705 E-mail: RobertoAzank@mac.com.

AZAR, ALEX M., II, federal agency administrator; Grad., Dartmouth Coll., Yale U. Bar: U.S. Dist. Ct. D.C., U.S. Dist. Ct. Md., U.S. Ct. Appeals Md., U.S. Ct. Appeals (D.C. cir.), U.S. Ct. Appeals (4th cir.), U.S. Supreme Ct. Clk. Assoc. Justice Antonin Scalia Supreme Ct. U.S.; clk. Judge J. Michael Luttig U.S. Ct. Appeals 4th Cir.; assoc. Kirkland & Ellis, Washington; assoc. ind. counsel Whitewater Investigation; ptnr. Wiley, Rein & Fielding, Washington; gen. counsel Dept. HHS, Washington, 2001—. Office: Dept HHS Gen Counsel 200 Independence Ave SW Washington DC 20201

AZAR, FRED S. biomedical engineer, researcher; BEE, McGill U., 1993; MS in BioEngring., Ecole Centrale Paris, 1994; PhD, U. Pa., 2001. Registered profl. engr., Pa. Med. imaging R&D Royal Victoria Hosp., Montreal, 1993, GE Med. Sys., Buc, 1994; rsch. scientist Montreal Neurol. Inst., 1994—95; breast cancer imaging rschr. U. Pa., Phila., 1995—2001; biomed. engring. cons. Sarnoff Corp., Princeton, 2002; biomed. engring. scientist Siemens Corp., Princeton, NJ, 2002—. Contbr. articles to profl. publs. Fellow Dean's fellow, U. of Pa., 1995—96, Bus. Towne fellow, U. Pa., 1996—2000, Academic fellow, U. of Pa., 1998. Mem.: IEEE (life bioengring. paper award 2000), Engring. Medicine Biology Soc., IEEE Computer Soc., Am. Soc. Therapeutic Radiology Oncology (assoc.). Achievements include research in deformable 3D model of the breast for predicting mechanical deformations during interventional medical procedures. Personal E-mail: fredazar@alumni.upenn.edu.

AZARNOFF, DANIEL LESTER, pharmaceutical company consultant; b. Bklyn., Aug. 4, 1926; s. Samuel J. and Kate (Asarnow) A.; m. Joanne Stokes, Dec. 26, 1951; children: Rachel, Richard, Martin. BS, Rutgers U., 1947, MS, 1948; MD, U. Kans., 1955. Asst. instr. anatomy U. Kans. Med. Sch., 1949-50, rsch. fellow, 1950-52, intern, 1955-56, resident, Nat. Heart Inst. research fellow, 1956-58, asst. prof. medicine, 1962-64, assoc. prof., 1964-68, dir. clin. pharmacology study unit, 1964-68, assoc. prof. pharmacology, 1965-68, prof. medicine and pharmacology, 1968, dir. Clin. Pharmacology-Toxicology Ctr., 1967-78, Disting. prof., 1973-78, also prof. medicine, 1965-67, pres. Sigma Xi Club, 1968-69, clin. prof. medicine, 1982-96, prof. medicine, 1996—; Nat. Inst. Neurol. Diseases and Blindness spl. trainee Washington U. Sch. Medicine, St. Louis, 1958-60; asst. prof. medicine St. Louis U. Sch. Medicine, 1960-62; sr. v.p. worldwide R&D, G.D. Searle & Co., Skokie, 1978; pres. Searle R&D, Skokie, 1979-85, Azarnoff Assocs., Inc., Evanston, Ill., 1986-87, D.L. Azarnoff Assocs., So. San Francisco, Calif., 1987—; prof. pathology, clin. prof. pharmacology Northwestern U. Med. Sch., 1978-85; sr. v.p. clin. regulatory affairs Cellegy Pharms., San Francisco, 1998—; commr. Nat. Commn. on Orphan Diseases, 1985-87; chmn. bd. dirs. Alpha RX Corp., South San Francisco, Calif., 1992-94; clin. prof. med. Stanford U. Sch. Med., 1998—2002. Professorial lectr. U. Chgo., 1978-86; dir. Second Workshop on Prins. Drug Evaluation in Man, 1970; chmn. com. on problems of drug safety NRC-NAS, 1972-76; chmn. bd. dirs. Oread, Inc., Lawrence, Kans., 1998-99; CEO Cibus Pharms., Burlingame, Calif., 1996-97; cons. numerous govt. agys.; chmn. bd. dirs. Cibus Pharm., Inc., 1996-97. Editor: Devel. of Drug Interactions, 1974-77, Yearbook of Drug Therapy, 1977-79; series editor: Monographs in Clin. Pharmacology, 1977-84; mem. editl. bd. Drug Investigation, Brit. Jour. Clin. Pharmacology, Clin. Pharmacol. Therapy, Clin. Pharmacokinetics, Clin. Drug Investigation, 1989—, others. Served with U.S. Army, 1945-46. Recipient Ginsburg award in phys. diagnosis U. Kanas. Med. Ctr., 1953, Outstanding Intern award, 1956, Ciba award for gerontol. rsch., 1958, Rectors medal U. Helsinki, 1968, Nathanial T. Kwit Meml. Disting. Svc. award Am. Coll. Clin. Pharmacology, 2002; named Disting. Med. Alumnus, U. Kans. Coll. Health Sci., 1995; John and Mary R. Markle scholar, 1964, William N. Creasy vis. prof. clin. pharmacology Med. Coll. Va., 1975; Bruce Hall Meml. lectr. St. Vincents Hosp., Sydney, 1976, 7th Sir Henry Hallett Dale lectr. Johns Hopkins U. Med. Sch., 1978; Fulbright scholar Karolinska Inst., Stockholm, 1968. Fellow ACP, N.Y. Acad. Scis., Am. Assn. Pharm. Scientists (Rsch. Achievement award in clin. scis. 1995), AAAS (chmn. elect pharm. sect. 2001, chmn. pharm. divsn. 2002-03); mem. AMA (vice chmn. coun. on drugs 1971-72, editl. bd. jours.), Am. Soc. Clin. Nutrition, Am. Nutrition Instn., Am. Soc. Pharmacology and Exptl. Therapeutics (chmn. clin. pharmacology divsn. 1969-71, mem. exec. com. 1966-73, 78-81, del. 1975-78, bd. publ. trustees), Am. Soc. Clin. Pharmacology and Therapeutics (Oscar B. Hunter Meml. award 1995), Am. Fedn. Clin. Rsch., Brit. Pharmacol. Soc., Ctrl. Soc. Clin. Rsch., Royal Soc. for Promotion Health, Inst. Medicine of Nat. Acad. Scis., Soc. Exptl. Biology and Medicine (councillor 1976-80), Internat. Union Pharmacologists (sec. clin. pharmacology sect. 1975-81, internat. adv. com. Paris Congress 1978), GPIA (blue ribbon com. on generic medicine 1990), Sigma Xi. E-mail: dazarnoff@earthlink.net.

AZAROFF, LEONID VLADIMIROVITCH, physics educator; b. Moscow, June 19, 1926; came to U.S., 1939, naturalized, 1945; s. Vladimir Ivanovitch and Maria Yulievna (Odlen) A.; m. Carmen Wade, Mar. 9, 1946 (div. July 1968); m. Beth Sulzer, Mar. 4, 1972; children: David, Richard, Lenore. BS cum laude, Tufts Coll., 1948; PhD, MIT, 1954. Research physicist Armour Research Found., Chgo., 1953-54, sr. scientist, 1954-57; asso. prof. metall. engring. Ill. Inst. Tech., Chgo., 1957-61, prof., 1961-66; prof. physics, dir. Inst. Material Sci., U. Conn., Storrs, 1966-92. Guest physicist Brookhaven Nat. Lab., 1961, 62, 64; vis. prof. U. Mass., 1978—79, 1985—86; cons. Owens-Ill., Philips Electronics, Hilger-Watts, Inc.; U.S. del. Internat. Union Crystallography, tchg. commn., 1963—69; bd. dirs. Conn. Product Devel. Corp.; pres. Conn. Acad. Sci. and Engring., Hartford, 1976—82; transl. editor Am. Inst. Physics, N.Y.C., 1958—99. Author 8 books, including X-Ray Diffraction and X-Ray Spectroscopy, 1973, Physics Over Easy, 1996; also articles. With AUS, 1944-46. Recipient ofcl. citation Conn. Gen Assembly, 1982, 91. Fellow Am. Phys. Soc. (cons. editor), Mineral. Soc. Am.; mem. AAAS (dir.), IEEE (sr.), Am. Soc. Engring. Edn., Conn. Acad. Sci. and Engring. (pres. 1976-82), Am. Crystallographic Assn., Am. Inst. Mining Engrs., Am. Inst. Electronic Engrs., Internat. Union Physics, Internat. Union Crystal Growth, Sigma Xi, Phi Kappa Phi (pres. Medford Mass. chpt. 1947-48), Sigma Pi Sigma. Republican. Russian Orthodox. Home: 5555 Heron Point Dr Naples FL 34108-2708 Office: U Conn Inst Materials Sci PO Box 136 Storrs Mansfield CT 06268-0136 E-mail: leeazaroff@cs.com. *I have always adhered to the principle that anything worth doing at all is worth doing as well as possible. Therefore, I select very carefully the tasks to undertake.*

AZAROW, KENNETH S. surgeon; s. Arnold Paul Azarow and Sheila Cateraccio; m. Judith Joan Hylinski, June 12, 1983; children: Katherine Eleanor, Elizabeth Eva, Samantha Lillian. MD, USUHS, 1983—87. Pediatric Surgery Am. Bd. of Surgery, 1998, General Surgery Am. Bd. of Surgery, 1993. Pediatric surgeon & tchg. chief, gen. surgery Madigan Army Med. Ctr., Tacoma, 2000—; assoc. prof. of surgery Uniformed Svcs. U., Bethesda, Md. LTC Army M.C., Madigan Army Med. Ctr. Fellow: ACS; mem.: Assn. of Program Directors in Surgery, Assn. of Academic Surgeons, Soc. of U. Surgeons, North Pacific Surg. Assn., Can. Pediatric Surg. Assn., Am. Pediatric Surg. Assn. Office: Madigan Army Med Ctr MCHJ-SGY Tacoma WA 98431

AZARYAN, ANAHIT VAZGENOVNA, biochemist, researcher; b. Yerevan, Armenia, Jan. 9, 1950; came to U.S., 1991; d. Vazgen Kh. and Dazy T. (Mirzoyan) A.; m. David B. Akopian, Jan. 30, 1981; 1 Child, Tigran. MD, Med. Sch., Yerevan, 1972; PhD, Inst. Molecular Biology, Moscow, 1979; Dr. Sc., Inst. Biochemistry, Yerevan, 1988. Prin. investigator Inst. Biochemistry, Yerevan, 1980-84, head proteolysis group, 1984-90; Fogarty rsch. program vis. scientist Nat. Inst. Child Health and Human Devel./NIH, Bethesda, Md., 1991; rsch. assoc. dept. biochemistry Uniformed Svcs. U. Health Scis., Bethesda, 1992-94, sr. rsch. scientist dept. pharmacology, 1994-99; dep. dir. clin. rsch. Tech. Resources Internat., Inc., Bethesda, 2000—. Author: Brain Peptide Hydrolases and Their Biological Functions, 1989; contbr. articles to Jour. Biol. Chem., Neurochem. Rsch., Jour. Neurosci. Rsch., others. Recipient fellowship Martin Luther U., Halle, Germany, 1983, fellowship N. Kline Inst. Psychiat. Rsch., N.Y.C., 1988, Travel award Internat. Soc. Neurochem.-FIDIA, Washington, 1991; Fogarty Internat. Ctr. Rsch. fellow, 1991. Mem. Internat. Soc. for Neurochemistry, European Soc. for Neurochemistry, Am. Soc. for Neuroscience, N.Y. Acad. Scis. Achievements include characterization of ATP-Ubiquitin-dependent protease in brain proves the existence of cytosolic ATP-Ub-dependent proteolysis pathway in that tissue; characterization of YAP3, a novel yeast aspartic protease and chromaffin granule convertases PC1/PC2 involved in the activitation of prohormones and proneuropeptides. Office: Tech Resources Internat Inc 6500 Rock Spring Dr Ste 650 Bethesda MD 20817 E-mail: aazaryan@tech-res.com.

AZER, SAMY AZIZ, gastroenterologist, medical educator; b. Cairo, Mar. 28, 1953; s. Aziz Azer and Sania Sedrak; m. Mary Azer; children: Sarah, Diana. B in Medicine and Surgery, Ain Shams U., Cairo, 1977, M in Medicine, 1983; MEd, U. New South Wales, 1993; PhD, U. Sydney, 1995; postgrad. in Pub. Health, U. NSW, 1997. Resident in internal medicine Govt. of Health, Egypt, 1979-80, cons. in medicine, 1983-84, 1984-89; vis. med. officer Ain Shams U. Hosps., 1980-83; postdoctoral fellow U. Kans. Med. Ctr., 1994; sr. lectr. in med. edn. U. Melbourne, Australia, 1999—, dir. problem-based learning tng. program faculty medicine, dentistry and health scis., 2001—. Cons. NIHS, Australia, 1995; lectr. spkrs. bur. ACG, Australia, 1996; instr. pathology and grad. med. program, faculty medicine U. Sydney, 1997, sr. lectr. in med. edn., 1998—99; mem. assessment working group, new curriculum com., faculty of medicine, dentistry and health scis. U. Melbourne. Co-author: Our Children, 1987; writer med. column El-Telegraph, Australia, 1996-97; contbr. chpts. to books, articles to profl. jours. Mem. ch. coun. Fairfield Anglican Chs., Australia, 1994, 95; elder Presbyn. Ch. of Australia, South Yarra, Victoria, 2002. Scholar Ministry of Edn., Egypt, 1968-71, undergrad. scholar, 1972-77, postgrad. scholar U. Sydney, 1993-94. Fellow Am. Coll. Gastroenterology, Royal Soc. of Health; mem. U. New South Wales Union (life), Gastroenterol. Soc. Australia, Am. Assn. for Study Liver Disease, Am. Coll. Gastroenterology. Presbyn. Avocations: painting, soccer, history of medicine. Office: FEU Faculty of Medicine U Melbourne Dentistry & Health Scis Parkville VIC 3052 Australia E-mail: s.azer@medicine.unimelb.edu.au., azer2000@optusnet.com.au., samy@unimelb.edu.au.

AZINFAR, FATEMEH, financial analyst, writer, finance educator; b. Tehran, Iran, Mar. 30, 1965; arrived in U.S., 1979; d. Hassan Azinfar and Helen Bauer Chehregosha. BA, UCLA, 1988; PhD, Harvard U., 1999. Tchg. fellow UCLA, 1988—90, Harvard U., Cambridge, Mass., 1993—98; editor Rehavard, L.A., 2000—02; fin. analyst World Fin. Group, L.A., 2002—. Fellow Ctr. Cultural Studies Harvard U., Cambridge, 1991—99. Author: (book) Doubt and Dissent in the Literary Tradition of the Medieval, 1999, Nationalism, Philosophy & Modernism, 2001, A Battle with Life, 2003. Active Dem. regional campaigns, Cambridge, 1995—97. Ford Found. fellow, Harvard U., 1994—95, 1994—96. Fellow: Harvard Club N.Y. Avocations: reading, swimming, tennis, photography, bicycling. Home: 1211 N Columbus Ave #202 Glendale CA 91202 Office: World Fin Group 26 E Colorado Blvd Ste 1 Pasadena CA 91105 Home Fax: 818-548-8060. Personal E-mail: fazinfar@mailstation.com.

AZIZ, KHALID, petroleum engineering educator; b. Bahawalpur, Pakistan, Sept. 29, 1936; came to U.S., 1952; s. Aziz Ul and Rshida (Atamohammed) Hassan; m. Mussarrat Rizwani, Nov. 12, 1962; children: Natasha, Imraan. BS in Mech. Engring., U. Mich., 1955; BSc in Petroleum Engring., U. Alta., 1958, MSc in Petroleum Engring., 1961; PhD in Chem. Engring., Rice U., 1966. Jr. design engr. Massey-Ferguson, 1955-56; various position to asst. prof. petroleum engring. U. Alta., 1960-62; various positions, chmn. bd. Neotech. Cons. Ltd., 1972-85; mgr., dir. Computer Modelling Group, Calgary, Alta., 1977-82; various positions to chief engr. Karachi (Pakistan) Gas Co., 1958-59, 62-63; various positions to prof. chem. and petroleum engring. U. Calgary, 1965-82; hon. prof., 1994—2001; prof. petroleum engring. dept. Stanford (Calif.) U., 1982—, assoc. dean rsch. Sch. Earth Scis., 1983-86, chmn. petroleum engring. dept., 1986-91, 94-95, Otto N. Miller prof. in earth scis., 1989—. Co-author: Flow of Complex Mixtures in Pipes, 1972, Petroleum Reservoir Simulation, 1979; contbr. articles to profl. jours. Recipient Diploma of Honor, Pi Epsilon Tau, 1991; Chem. Inst. Can. fellow, 1974, Killam Resident fellow U. Calgary, 1977. Mem. AIME (hon.), European Assn. Geoscientists and Engrs., European Acad. Scis., Soc. Petroleum Engrs. (disting. mem., Ferguson award 1979, Reservoir Engring. award 1987, Lester C. Uren award 1988, Disting. Achievement award for Petroleum Engring. Faculty 1990, hon. mem. 1996), Nat. Acad. Engring., Russian Acad. Natural Scis. (fgn.), European Acad. of Sci.. Moslem. Achievements include rsch. in multiphase flow of oil/gas mixtures & steam in pipes & wells, multiphase flow in porous media, reservoir simulation (black-oil, compositional, thermal, geothermal), natural gas engring., hydrocarbon fluid phase behavior. Office: Stanford U Dept Petroleum Engring Stanford CA 94305-2220

AZIZKHAN, RICHARD GEORGE, pediatric surgeon, educator; b. London, Aug. 10, 1953; came to U.S., 1964; s. Reza George and Helga Marianne (Behnke) A.; m. Geralyn Brindisi; children: Richard Anthony, Kathryn Marie, Christine Elizabeth Ann, Aaron Brindisi. BS with honors, Dickinson Coll., Carlisle, Pa., 1972; MD, Pa. State U., 1975; PhD (hon.), Tuzla U., 2000. Diplomate in gen. surgery and pediat. surgery Am. Bd. Surgery. Resident in surgery U. Va., Charlottesville, 1976-78, 80-83; rsch. fellow in pediat. surgery Harvard Med. Sch. Boston Children's Hosp., 1978-80; fellow in pediat. surgery Johns Hopkins Univ., Balt., 1983-85; chief pediat. surgery U. N.C., Chapel Hill, 1985-93; surgeon-in-chief Child Hosp., Buffalo, 1993-98; prof. surgery and pediats. SUNY, Buffalo, 1993-98; surgeon-in-chief Children's Hosp. Med. Ctr., Cin., 1998—; prof. surgery and pediats., vice chair dept. surgery U. Cin., 1998—. Surg. adv. bd. Smith, Kline, Beecham, Phila., 1990-95; dir. pediat. surgery tng. program U. Cin., 1998—, founder hemangioma and vascular malformation treatment ctr. Cin. Childrens Hosp., 2001. Author: Congenital Malformations: Prenatal Diagnosis and Management, 1990, A Geneology of Pediatric Surgery of North America, 1997; co-author: Operative Pediatric Surgery, 2003; contbr. over 115 articles to profl. jours. Recipient Upjohn Achievement award U. Va. Sch. Medicine, 1981, Hugh J. Warren Tchg. award, 1983, Battle Disting. Excellence in Tchg. award U. N.C. Sch. Medicine, 1988, Disting. Alumnus award Pa. State U., 1995; Schering scholar ACS, 1982; SmithKline & French fellow ACS, 1986. Fellow ACS, Am. Acad. Pediats. (chair program com. 1995, surg. sect. exec. com. 1997—, chair surg. sect. 2001-02), Am. Pediat. Surgery Assn. (program com. 1990-93, bd. govs. 1998—), Pa. State U. Alumnae Assn. (life); mem. Assn. of Acad. Surgery (exec. coun. 1986-89), Alpha Omega Alpha. Roman Catholic. Achievements include research of heparin in the growth of new blood vessels (angiogenesis); development of novel technique utilizing fiberoptic laser to treat bronchial stenosis in infants. Office: Childrens Hosp Med Ctr 3333 Burnet Ave Cincinnati OH 45229-3026 E-mail: richard.azizkhan@cchmc.org

AZRAEL, JUDITH ANNE, educator; b. Balt., July 28, 1938; d. Maurice and Altie A.; m. Herbert Greenberg, Dec. 20, 1960; children: Denise, Jeffrey. BA, U. Wis., 1959; MFA, U. Oreg., 1974. Tchr. U. Oreg., Eugene, 1973. Vis. writer Western Wash. U., Bellingham, 1978-80. Author 4 vols. of poetry; contbr. poems, short stories and essays to mags. Recipient Helene Werlitzer Found. award, Taos, N.Mex., 1973; nominated Pushcart prize, 1999. Avocations: travel, hiking, reading.

AZRIELANT, AYA, jewelry manufacturing executive; b. Israel; Came to U.S. 1981. m. Ofer Azrielant; 3 children. BA in Fine Arts and Lit., Haifa U.; postgrad. in film-making, London. Designer, owner Aya Azrielant, N.Y.C. Avocation: collector of modern art. Office: Andin International Inc 609 Greenwich St New York NY 10014-3683 Fax: 212-886-6006.

AZRIN, NATHAN HAROLD, psychologist, educator; b. Boston, Nov. 26, 1930; s. Harry and Esther (Alper) A.; m. Victoria Behar Besalel, Jan. 25, 1953; children— Rachel, Michael, David, Richard. BA cum laude, Boston U., 1951, MA, 1952; PhD, Harvard U., 1956. Mem. faculty So. Ill. U., Carbondale, 1958-80, prof. rehab., 1959-80; rsch. dir. Anna (Ill.) Mental Health Ctr., 1958-80; prof. Nova Psychol. Clinic, Nova U., Ft. Lauderdale, Fla., 1980-87, Nova Southeastern U., Ft. Lauderdale, 1980—. Author: Token Economy, 1968, Toilet Training in Less than a Day, 1974, Toilet Training the Retarded, 1973, Habit Control, 1977, Job Club, 1980, Finding a Job, 1982. Editor psychol. jours. Served with AUS, 1956-58. Mem. Am. Psychol. Assn. (pres. div. 25 1963, ann. award applications in psychology 1975), Fla. Assn. Behavior Analysis (pres.), Midwestern Psychol. Assn. (pres.), Assn. Advancement Behavior Therapy (pres., Lifetime Achievement award 1997), Midwestern Analysis of Behavior Assn. (pres.) Home: 5151 Bayview Dr Fort Lauderdale FL 33308-3433 Office: Nova Southeastern U 3301 College Ave Fort Lauderdale FL 33314-7796

AZZARONE, CAROL ANN, marketing executive; b. Jersey City, Aug. 1, 1946; d. Paul Buglione and Catherine (DellaFave) LiCalsi; m. Dominick L. Azzarone, May 13, 1967 (div. 1989); children: Anthony Paul, Kathryn Ann. AA, Bergen C.C., 1982; BA, Ramapo Coll., 1984. Editl. asst. McGraw-Hill, Inc., N.Y.C., 1964-69; real estate agt. Auburn Realty, Inc., Bergenfield, N.J., 1975-80, Weichert Realty, Morris Plains, N.J., 1975—; pub. rels. coord. Ridgefield (N.J.) Bd. Edn., 1982-84; mktg. dir. Spa Lady Corp., Fairfax, Va., 1984-86, Newson Fitness, Morristown, N.J., 1986-88; creative dir. Publ. Corp., Morristown, 1988-90; advt. dir. Ronton Advt., Union, N.J., 1990-98; mktg. v.p. Dynamic Tech. Group, Inc., Parsippany, N.J., 1998—. Adv. bd. N.J. Tech. Coun., 2001—03; cons. in field; spkr. in field. Editor (newsletters) Ridgefield Sch. News, 1982-84, Cliffside Park Sch. News, 1984-85, The Grapevine, 1985-86. Mem. adv. bd. N.J. Tech. Coun. N.J. Bell scholar N.J. Bell Corp., 1980, Bergen Community Coll. Alumni scholar, 1981. Mem. NOW, NAFE (First Place award of excellence 1996, Jersey award), Advt./Pub. Rels. Assn., NJ Advt. Club, Phi Theta Kappa. Democrat. Roman Catholic. Avocations: cross country skiing, horseback riding, biking, reading. Office: Dynamic Tech Group Inc 1055 Parsippany Blvd Parsippany NJ 07054-1230

AZZI, JENNIFER L. basketball player; b. Oak Ridge, Tenn., Aug. 31, 1968; d. James and Donna Azzi. Diploma, Stanford U., 1990. Basketball player Arvika Basket, Sweden, 1995—96, Viterbo, Italy, Orchies, France, San Jose Lasers, 1996—99, Salt Lake City Starzz, 1999—. Mem. Nat. Women's Basketball Team. Named Al-Pac 10 1st team, 1988, 1989, 1990, MVP, NCAA Final Four, 1990, NCAA West Region, 1990, Naismith Nat. Player Yr., 1990; recipient gold medal, Goodwill Games, 1994, World Championship Qualifying team, 1993, U.S. Olympic Festival West Team, 1987, 2 gold medals, World Championship and Goodwill Games, 1990, bronze medal, Pan Am. Games, 1991, World Championship team, 1994, Wade Trophy, 1990, Kodak All-Am. 1st team, 1989, 1990, gold medal, U.S. Olympic Team, 1996. Office: 301 W South Temple Salt Lake City UT 84101

AZZOLI, VAL, music company executive; Co-chmn., co-CEO Atlantic Recording Corp., N.Y.C. Office: Atlantic Group 1290 Avenue Of The Americas New York NY 10104-0101

AZZOLINA, DAVID SEAN, librarian; b. East Orange, N.J., May 22, 1957; s. Alexander and Helen (Fitzpatrick) A. BA, U. Pa., 1978, MA, 1991, PhD, 1996; MS, Columbia U., 1979. Social sci. libr. Rice U., Houston, 1980-82; ref. libr. Johns Hopkins U., Balt., 1982-86, U. Pa., Phila., 1986—, adj. prof. English, 1997—. Mem. adv. bd. Lesbian Gay Bisexual Ctr. U. Pa. Author: Tale Type and Motif Indexes, 1987, The Circle Always Grew: Folklore and Gay Identity 1945-1960, 1996; contbr. (book) Guide to Reference Books, 11th edit., 1997; reviewer various jours. Democrat. Episcopalian. Home: 256 S 44th St Philadelphia PA 19104-2944 Office: University of Pennsylvania Library 3420 Walnut St Philadelphia PA 19104-3411 E-mail: azzolina@pobox.upenn.edu., davidazzolina@hotmail.com.

AZZOLINA, JOSEPH, state legislator, grocery executive; b. Newark, June 26, 1926; Student, Drew U.; BS, Holy Cross Coll., 1946; postgrad., NYU. Pres. Food Circus Supermarkets, Inc., Middletown, N.J.; chmn. bd. Foodtown, Capdebret, N.J.; mem. N.J. State Senate, 1972-73; mem. from dist. 13 N.J. State Assembly, 1966-71, 86-88, 91-2001. Chmn. N.J. State Rep. Conv., 1967. Capt. USN, ret. Named Man of Yr., Deborah Hosp., Italian Tribune News, St. Joseph's Coll., Legislator of Yr., Freeholder Assn., 1971. Mem. VFW, Am. Legion, Navy League, Middletown C. of C., Monmouth County Rep. Club, Lions. Address: 1 Arin Park Bldg STe 102 1715 Highway 35 Middletown NJ 07748-1867*

BAAB, CARLTON, advertising executive; COO, CFO CKS Ptnr., Cupertino, Calif., 1994-98; COO & CFO RemarQ Communities, San Jose, CA, 1999—. Mem. bd. dirs., Peoplesoft, 1999— Office: RemarQ Communities 55 S Market St Ste 1080 San Jose CA 95113-2386

BAACH, MICHAEL L. internist; b. Ft. Wayne, Ind., Sept. 21, 1963; m. Suzanne Michelle LeClear, Oct. 22, 1994; children: William Richard, Elizabeth LeClear. BA in Chemistry, Northwestern U., 1986; MD, Ind. U., Indpls., 1991. Diplomate Am. Bd. Internal Medicine. Intern Ind. U. Med. Ctr., 1991-92, resident, 1992-95; mem. staff Cmty. Hosp. Indpls., 1995—; pvt. practice, 1995—. Mem. ACP-Am. Soc. Internal Medicine, AMA, Ind. Med. Assn., Indpls. Med. Soc. Office: Parkside Internal Medicine 13050 Parkside Dr Ste 210 Fishers IN 46038-8235 Fax: (317) 588-2244.

BAACK, PAULA D. music educator; b. Omaha, Nebr., June 13, 1949; d. Paul and Wilma J. Teigeler; m. Robert A. Morris, May 10, 1969 (div. Oct. 1979); m. L. Thomas Baack, July 26, 1980; 1 child, Paul R. BS, U. Nebr., 1971, MusM, 1973. Cert. lifetime tchg. Nebr., Cmty. Coll. Tchr. Ariz. Dir. choral Lincoln Pub. Schs., Nebr., 1971—97; dir. choral, voice coach Scottsdale C.C., Ariz., 1998—. Asst. prof. U. Nebr., Lincoln, 1995—97. Named Nat. Anthem Singer for Phoenix Coyotes Hockey Game. Mem.: Nebr. Choral Dirs. Assn. (exec. bd. 1995—97), Nebr. Music Educators Assn. (exec. bd. 1993—95). Republican. Avocations: bicycling, singing, dancing. Home: 11083 E Oberlin Way Scottsdale AZ 85262 Office: Scottsdale Cmty Coll 9000 E Chaparral Rd Scottsdale AZ 85256*

BAADE, HANS WOLFGANG, legal educator, law expert; b. Berlin, Dec. 16, 1929; s. Fritz and Edith (Wolff) Baade; m. Anne Adams Johnston; children: Friedrich James, Hans Alastair. BA, Syracuse U., 1949; JD, Kiel U., Germany, 1951; LLB, LLM, Duke U., 1955; diploma, Haue Acad. Internat. Law, 1956. Assoc. Inst. Internat. Law, Kiel, Germany, 1955—60; assoc. prof. law Duke U., 1960—64; prof. law, 1964—70, U. Toronto, 1970—71; Hugh Lamar Stone prof. civil law U. Tex., Austin, 1971—; arbitrator internat. comml. matters; dir. Am. Soc. Comparative Law. Editor: (novels) Law and Comparative Problems, 1961—66; contbr. articles. Recipient Hon. Fellow Faculty of Law, U. Edinburgh /Scotland, 1997. Mem.: German Yr. Book Internat. Law (editorial sec. 1956—60), Am. Jour. Comparative Law (bd. editors 1960), Internat. Acad. Comparative Law (assoc. mem.), Am. Arbitration Assn. (nat. panel arbitrators). Home: 6002 Mountainclimb Dr Austin TX 78731-3822 Office: U Tex Sch Law Austin TX 78705

BAAR, JAMES A. public relations and corporate communications executive, author, consultant, internet publisher, software developer; b. N.Y.C., Feb. 9, 1929; s. A.W. and Marguerite R. B.; m. Beverly Hodge, Sept. 2, 1948; 1 son, Theodore Hall. AB, Union Coll., Schenectady, 1949. Washington corr. UPI, also other wire service burs. and newspapers, 1949-59; sr. editor Missiles and Rockets mag., 1959-62; mgr. various news bur. ops. Gen. Electric Co., 1962-66; mgr. European Mktg. Communications Ops., 1966-70; pres. Gen. Electric subs. Internat. Mktg. Communications Cons., 1970-72; sr. v.p., dir. public relations Lewis & Gilman, Inc., Phila., 1972-74; exec. v.p. Creamer Dickson Basford, Inc., 1974-78; pres. Creamer Dickson Basford-New Eng., 1978-83; sr. v.p./mgr. Northeast region Hill & Knowlton, Inc., Boston, 1983-84; v.p. communications Computervision Corp., 1984-86; sr. v.p. Gray & Co. Pub. Communications and gen. mgr. Gray & Co., N.Y., 1986-87; exec. v.p., worldwide dep. dir. advanced tech. practice Hill & Knowlton, Inc., 1987-90; pres., mng. cons. Omegacom, Inc., Boston, 1990—. Cons. internet publishing, software developer and strategic comms. cons., 1990—. Author: Polaris, 1960, Combat Missileman, 1961, Spacecraft and Missiles of the World, 1962, The Great Free Enterprise Gambit, 1980, The Careful Voters Dictionary of Language Pollution, 1999, Spinspeak II--The Dictionary of Language Pollution, 2003, author numerous articles and short stories; editor: The Spinspeak Letter, 2003. Bd. overseers New Eng. Conservatory Music. Mem. Nat. Investor Relations Inst., Pub. Relations Soc. Am., Counselors Acad., Internat. Pub. Relations Assn., Chi Psi, Nat. Press Club, Overseas Press Club, English Speaking Union (bd. dirs. Boston), Univ. Club (Providence). Republican. Roman Catholic. Office: 24 Thayer St Providence RI 02906-1021 E-mail: jimbar@omegacom.com.

BAAR, JOHN GREENFIELD, II, school educator; b. New Haven, Sept. 10, 1952; s. William Henry and Katherine Baar; m. Janet Gail Hansa, July 9, 1988. BA, U. of the South, 1975; MS, U. Ill., Chgo., 1980, MS in Tchg. Math., 1998; MEd, U. Ill., Urbana, 1991. Youth dir. Emmanuel Ch., La Grange, Ill., 1976—85; sci. instr. Evanston (Ill.) Twp. High Sch., 1981—82, Butler Sch., Oak Brook, Ill., 1982—, asst. prin., 1999—, cross country coach, 2003—. Varsity boys basketball coach, 1981-99, girls soccer coach, 1984-2002; cons. Dupage County Curriculum Com., Wheaton, Ill., 1990-91. Pres. Westchester (Ill.) Place Assn., 1988-91; advisor IMSA Leadership Conf., Aurora, Ill., 1990-91, Fermi Lab. Edn. Ctr., Batavia, Ill., 1990-92, DuPage Drug Edn. Com., Wheaton, Ill., 1988; v.p. Oak Brook Civic Assn., 1996-97, pres. 1997-2002; chmn. Oak Brook Police and Fire Commn., 2003—; mem. blue ribbon panel Family Recreation Ctr., Oak Brook Pak Dist., 1994; mem. Aquatic Ctr. Adv. Coun., 1997. Recipient Quest for Excellence in Chemistry award NSF, 1986, award of Excellence, Ill. Math. and Sci. Acad., 1991. Mem. NAESP, Ill. Sci. Tchrs. Assn., NSTA, Oak Brook Edn. Assn., Ill. Assn. Elem. Sch. Prins. Episcopalian. Avocations: golf, alpine skiing, canoeing. Home: 3 Brighton Ln Oak Brook IL 60523-2323 Office: Butler Sch 2801 York Rd Oak Brook IL 60523-2334 E-mail: jbaar@mail.butler53.com.

BAAS, JACQUELYNN, museum consultant, art historian; b. Grand Rapids, Mich., Feb. 14, 1948; BA in History of Art, Mich. State U.; PhD in History of Art, U. Mich. Registrar U. Mich. Mus. Art, Ann Arbor, 1974-78, asst. dir., 1978-82; editor Bull. Museums of Art and Archaeology, U. Mich., 1976-82; chief curator Hood Mus. Art, Dartmouth Coll., Hanover, N.H., 1982-84, dir., 1985-89, U. Calif. Berkeley Art Mus. and Pacific Film Archive, Calif., 1989-99, emeritus dir., 1999—; program dir. Awake: Art and Buddhism, 1999—. Cons. in field; organizer exhbns.; ind. art historian, program dir. Awake: Art & Buddhism in Am. Contbr. articles and essays to jours. and books. Mem. Coll. Art Assn. Am. Address: 1442 A Walnut St PMB 434 Berkeley CA 94709

BAASAN, RAGCHAA, diplomat; b. Ulaanbaatar, Mongolia, Nov. 19, 1943; d. Tumer and Demberel (Tsendsuren) Ragchaa; m. Jamsran Gendendaram, Sept. 1967; children: Enhbat, Enhtsetseg, Enhtuvshin. Diploma, Moscow Inst. Fgn. Langs. Asst. officer Ministry of External Rels., Ulaanbaatar, 1967-69; diplomat Mongolian Embassy in India, New Delhi, 1969-74; attache Ministry of External Rels./Asian Dept., Ulaanbaatar, 1974-78, 2d sec., 1981-83, Mongolian Embassy, Kabul, Afghanistan, 1978-81, Embassy Mongolia, New Delhi, 1983-88; 1st sec., counsellor Ministry External Rels., Ulaanbaatar, 1988-97; 1st sec., polit. Embassy Mongolia, Washington, 1997—. Decorated Polar Star Order (Mongolia); recipient Honor of Svc. award Govt. of Mongolia, 1991/ Buddhist. Avocations: reading, analysing, knitting, cooking. Home: XI Region SA Apt 26 Ulaanbaatar Mongolia Office: Embassy of Mongolia 2833 M St NW Washington DC 20007-3712 E-mail: Baasan@aol.com.

BABA, MARIETTA LYNN, business anthropologist, university administrator; b. Flint, Mich., Nov. 9, 1949; d. David and Lillian (Joseph) Baba; m. David Smokler, Feb. 14, 1977 (div. 1982); 1 child, Alexia Nicole Baba Smokler. BA with highest distinction, Wayne State U., 1971, MA in Anthropology, 1973, PhD in Phys. Anthropology, 1975; MBA, Mich. State U., 1994. Asst. prof. sci. and tech. Wayne State U., Detroit, 1975-80, assoc. prof. anthropology, 1980-88, prof., 1988—, spl. asst. to pres., 1980-82, econ. devel. officer, 1982-83, asst. provost, 1983-85, assoc. provost, 1985-89, dir. internat. programs, interim assoc. dean Grad. Sch., 1988-89, assoc. dean Grad. Sch., 1989-90, acting chair dept. anthropology, 1990-92, chair dept. anthropology, 1996-2001; dean, prof. anthropology Mich. State U. Coll. Social Sci., East Lansing, 2001—. Program dir. transformations to quality orgns., dir. social, behav., and econ. scis. NSF, 1994—96; evolution rschr. Wayne State U., 1975—82; cons. GM Rsch. Labs., 1988—92, Electronic Data Sys., 1990—93, McKinsey Global Inst., 1991; rsch. contractor GM/EDS, 1990—94; lectr. nat. and internat. symposia, profl. confs. Adv. for editor orgnl. anthropology: American Anthropologist, 1990-93; issued letters patent for method to map joint ventures and maps produced thereby; contbr. numerous papers and abstracts to tech. jours.; patentee in field. Mem. State Rsch. Fund Feasibility Rev. Panel, 1982—84; mem. adv. panel on tech. innovation and U.S. trade U.S. Congl. Office Tech. Assessment, 1990—91, mem. panel on electronic enterprise, 1993—94; active Leadership Detroit Class IV, 1982—83; dir. Mich. Tech. Coun. (S.E. divsn.), 1984—85. With USAF, 1992—94. Job Partnership Tng. Act grantee, 1981-90, NSF grantee, 1982, 84-85, 99-01. Fellow Am. Anthrop. Assn. (bd. dirs. 1986-88, exec. com. 1986-88, del. to Internat. Union Anthrop. and Ethnol. Sci. 1990-94, chair global commn. anthropology 1993-98), Nat. Assn. Practice Anthropology (pres. 1986-88), Soc. Applied Anthropology, Phi Beta Kappa, Sigma Xi (Morton Fried award 1991), Beta Gamma Sigma.

BABAILOV, IGOR V. artist, educator; b. Glazov, Russia; s. Valery and Rosa Babailov; m. Mary Babailov; children: Nikita, David Knecht, Maksim Knecht, Maurice Knecht, Daniel Robin Knecht. Cert. and diploma, Prep. Sch. Fine Art, Glazov, 1979; fine arts diploma, H.S. diploma, Surikov Coll. for Fine Arts, Moscow, 1983; MFA, Surikov Acad. for Fine Arts, Moscow, 1990; 3rd Generation Student of I. Repin, Surikov Acad. Fine Arts, Moscow. Cert. living master The Art Renewal Ctr. - Living Masters/Mus., 2003. Bd. dirs. Igor Babailov Inst. Realism, Shoreham, NY; co-author, dir. The Am. Hist. Panorama Project, N.Y.C., 2003—. Featured artist (book) Contemporary Russian Realists, The World of Igor Babailov; exhibitions include Painting Presentation, Harvard Univ., Boston Mass., 2000, Ctrl. Armed Forces Mus., Russia, 2001, one-man shows include Oglivy's Ltd. (Benefit), Montreal, 1999. Recipient First Prize Winner - Ann. Graphic Works Competition, Surikov Acad. Fine Arts, Moscow, 1989, Outstanding Achievement award in Portrait Painting - Nat. Portrait Seminar, Am. Artist Mag., 1993, Grand Prize Winner - Internat. Competition, Am. Soc. Portrait Artists, 1994, Merit award Realism 97 Internat. Art Competition, Realism Mag., 1997, Hon. Mention, Portrait Competition, Internat. Artist Mag., 2001, Portrait Competition, The Artist's Mag., 1999. Mem.: Can. Soc. Portrait Artists, Can. Inst. Portrait Artists, Am. Soc. Portrait Artists, Portrait Soc. Am., Portrait Inst. N.Y.C. (charter). Personal E-mail: babailov@optonline.net.

BABAR, RAZA ALI, industrial engineer, utility consultant, futurist, management educator, marketing strategist, author, publisher; b. Shujabad, Punjab, Pakistan, May 29, 1947; arrived in U.S., 1972; s. Syed Mohammad Ali Shah and Syeda Hafeeza (Gilani) Bukhari; m. Sufia K. Durrett, July 23, 1974 (div. 1983); children: Azra Yasmeen, Imran Ali, Amenah Andaleep; m. Syeda Afshan Gilani, Aug. 23, 1983; children: Abdullah Ali, Hammad Ali, Omaima Ali, Mustafa Ali. Pre Engring. student, Govt. Coll., Lahore, Pakistan, 1965; BS in Mining Engring., U. Engring. and Tech., Lahore, 1969; MS in Indsl. Engring., Wayne State U., 1978; postgrad., Detroit Coll. Law, 1982; postgrad. U.S. Econ. Outlook Conf., U. Mich., 1977-84. Engr., planner Bukhari Elec. Concern, Multan, Pakistan, 1969-70; mgr. mining ops. Felezzate Yazd Co., Iran, 1970-72; salesman Great Books, Inc., Chgo., 1972-73; field underwriter N.Y. Life Ins. Co., 1972-73; indsl. engr. Ellis/Naeyaert Assocs., Inc., Warren, Mich., 1973-74; grad. asst. dept. indsl. engring. and ops. rsch. Wayne State U., Detroit, 1974-75; prin. engr., work leader project svcs. divsn. Generation Constrn. Dept., Detroit Edison Co., 1975-79; tech. advisor Ministry of Prodn., Govt. Pakistan, Islamabad, 1979-80; chmn. dept. bus. adminstrn. Zakariya U., Multan, Pakistan, 1980-83; prin. engr. project controls Enrico Fermi 2 Detroit Edison Co., 1981-82, supr. Fermi 2 rate case task force, 1982-84, spl. projects engr. planning, 1984-88; mgr. econ. support svc. Syndeco, Inc., 1985-88; market planner Detroit Edison Co., 1988-89, sr. mktg. strategist, 1989-90. Dir. global rsch. and intelligence, 1990-92, project dir. bus. customer satisfaction, new products and svcs. rsch., 1992-93, dir. demand side mgmt., 1993-95, dir. customer energy solutions, 1995-96, dir. ethnic mktg., 1996-98, dir. svc. ctr. oper., 1998-2001, mgr. mktg. and sales, 2001—; nat. tech. adv. bd. E-Source; vis. prof. Grad. Sch. Bus. Adminstrn., Wayne State U., 1987—; bd. trustees Asian and Mid. Ea. Am. Coalition; bd. dirs. Asian and Mid. Ea. Am. Forum. Author rsch. papers and articles, presentations in field. Founder Fedn. Engring. Assns. Pakistan, 1969; pres. acad. staff assn., mem. chancellor's com. Zakariya U., Pakistan, 1980-81; pres. Pakistan Cultural Group, Detroit, 1975-76, Pakistan Students Assn., 1975-76; bd. dirs. Detroit Islamic Libr., 1976-77; mem. Econ. Outlook Conf., U. Mich., Ann Arbor, 1977-84, Rep. Presdl. Task Force Honor Roll, Rep. Nat. Com.; charter mem. Rep. Congl Task Force, Rep. Presdl. Legion Merit; vol. planning advisor Cmty. Tng. and Devel. Orgn., Beginning Experience and Mich. Tng. and Resource Ctr.; tchg. cons. applied econs. Jr. Achievement; vol. cons. Detroit Area Agy. on Aging; industry rep. U. Mich. Global Citizenship Program; mem. adv. com. bus. and internat. edn. program Mott C.C.; bd. dirs. Wayne County Foster Care Rev. Bd.; mem. adv. panel Office Tech. Assessment U.S. Congress; mem. bd. dirs. Asian Am. Ctr. for Justice, 1998—; founder Asian and Mid. Eastern Am. Forum, 1996, bd. dirs.; founding mem. Asian & Middle Eastern Cmty Coalition, 1998, trustee; bd. dirs. IAATRADE U.S.A., 1998—. Recipient Pride of Performance medal Engring. U. Pakistan, 1967; Acad. Merit scholar Detroit Coll. Law, 1982. Mem. IEEE, Am. Mgmt. Assn., Am. Mgmt. Assn. Internat., Econ. Club Detroit, Am. Inst. Indsl. Engrs., Am. Assn. Cost Engrs., Engring. Soc. Detroit, ESD Profl. Activities Coun. (co-chmn. civic affairs com., emerging techs. com.), Pakistan Engring. Congress, Pakistan Inst. Mining Engrs., Am. Assn. MBA Execs., Assn. Muslim Scientists and Engrs., Assn. Muslim Social Scientists, Internat. Platform Assn., Islamic Soc. N.Am., Am. Moslem Soc., Islamic Cultural Inst., Islamic Assn. Mich. (chmn. Islamic edn. com., mem. editl. bd. Muslim News), Tanzeem-e-Islami Pakistan and N.Am., Pakistan Assn. of Am., Internat. Assn. Bus. Communicators (bd. dirs., chmn. multicultural communicators com.), Soc. Competitor Intelligence Profls. (steering com.), Assn. Energy Svcs. Profls., Assn. Demand Side Mgmt. Profls., World Future Soc., Internat. Dist. Energy Assn., Bldg. Owners and Mgrs. Assn. Avocations: reading, writing, public speaking, sports, travel. Home: 627 Weybridge Dr Bloomfield Hills MI 48304-1083 Office: Ste 205 661 Plum St Detroit MI 48201 E-mail: babarr@dteenergy.com.

BABATUNDE, EMMANUEL DEBO, education educator; b. Imeko, Ogun, Nigeria; PhD, Oxford Univ., Eng., 1985. Prof., dir. of honors program Lincoln Univ., Pa. Found. of Lincoln Univ. summer Inst. of Sci. Tech., & Work Ethics Lincoln Univ., 1996. Mem.: Oxford & Cambridge Alumni of Pa. Avocations: squash, tennis. Home: 701 Crossan Rd Newark DE 19711 Office: Lincoln Univ Lincoln University PA 19352

BABAUTA, JUAN NEKAI, governor; b. Saipan, No. Mariana Islands, Sept. 7, 1953; s. Santiago Miyasaki and Carmen (Nekai) B. BS, MA, Ea. N.Mex. U., 1976; MS, U. Cin., 1979. Health planner TTPI Dept. Health Services, Saipan, 1977; dep. exec. dir. State Health Planning and Devel. Agy., Saipan, 1979; exec. dir. Saipan, 1980-86; senator No. Marianas Commonwealth Legislature, Saipan, 1986—90; resident rep. to U.S. Commonwealth of No. Mariana Islands, 1990—2002, governor, 2002—. Co-chmn. 902 Covenant Negotiation team; instr. No. Marianas Coll., Saipan, 1986. Chmn. bd. regents No. Marianas Coll., 1982-83, 84-86; chmn. Bd. Edn., Saipan, 1982-83, 84-86; mem. Med. Profession Licensing Bd., Saipan, 1983-86, Nat. State Bd. Edn., Saipan, 1982-86. Mem. Phi Kappa Phi. Republican. Roman Catholic. Avocation: reading. Office: Office of the Governor Caller Box 10007 Capitol Hill Saipan MP 96950*

BABAYANS, EMIL, financial planner; b. Nov. 9, 1951; arrived in U.S., 1969; s. Hacob and Jenik (Khatchatourian) B.; m. Annie Ashjian. BS, U. So. Calif., 1974, MS, 1976. CLU; cert. fin. planner. Pres. Babtech Internat., Inc., Sherman Oaks, Calif., 1975—85; sr. ptnr. Emil Babayans & Assocs., Woodland Hills, Calif., 1985—. Mem.: Million Dollar Round Table, Am. Soc. CLU and Chartered Fin. Cons., Internat. Assn. Fin. Planners, Inst. Cert. Fin. Planners, Nat. Assn. Life Underwriters, Am. Mgmt. Assn. Armenian Orthodox. Office: 21700 Oxnard St Ste 1100 Woodland Hills CA 91367 7574

BABAYEV, DJANGIR ALI IKRAM, physicist, researcher; b. Baku, Azerbaijan, July 10, 1930; arrived in U.S., 1992; s. Ali Ikram Melik Bakhish Babayev and Rugiya Jahangir Babayeva; m. Sevil Yusuf Huseinova; 1 child, Rauf Djangir. B.Engring., Moscow Inst. Physics and Engring., 1953; PhD in Physics and Math., Inst. Problems of Mechanics, USSR Acad. Scis., Moscow, 1962; Dr.Engring. Scis., Inst. Cybernetics, Acad. Scis. of Ukraine, Kiev, 1974. Engr. aerodynamics diploma, Moscow Inst. Physics and Engring., 1954; cert. sr. fellow scientist, computational math. diploma USSR High Attestation Bd., 1963, prof. computerized mgmt. and control sys. diploma USSR High Attestation Bd., 1984. Engr., sr. engr., lead engr. Ctrl. Inst. Aero-Hydrodynamics, Moscow, 1954—62; dep. dir. of inst., dir. dept. ops. rsch. Inst. Cybernetics, Acad. Scis. of Azerbaijan, Baku, 1962—92; mem. tech. staff U.S. West Advanced Technologies, Boulder, Colo., 1992—2000; sr. rsch. scientist Cox Assocs., Inc., Denver, 2000—. Prof. computational math. Baku State U., 1970—77; prof. computational math., optimization theory and methods Azerbaijan State Oil Acad., 1977—85; prof. math. methods of econs. Azerbaijan State U. Econs., 1985—92; supr. PhD dissertations on ops. rsch. Inst. Cybernetics of Azerbaijan Acad. Scis., 1972—92; on info. and comm. tech. UN Devel. Programs, N.Y.C., 2002—. Mem. editl. bd. Internat. Jour. Applied and Computational Math., 2001—; contbr. :, translator books. Recipient State Prize of Azerbaijan on Sci. and Tech., Azerbaijan, 1984, prize for outstanding applications of ops. rsch. in mng. bus., Ops. Rsch. Soc. Am., 1994. Mem.: Lofti Zade Internat. Acad. Modern Scis. Achievements include development of nonlinear theory of the delta wing on supersonic flow; patents for on methods and systems of solving different classes of management problems in communication industry. Home: 4834 MacIntosh Pl Boulder CO 80301 Office: Cox Associates Inc 503 Franklin St Denver CO 80218-3623

BABB, ALBERT LESLIE, biomedical engineer, educator; b. Vancouver, B.C., Can., Nov. 7, 1925; came to U.S., 1948, naturalized, 1954; s. Clarence Stanley and Mildred (Gutteridge) B.; m. Marion A. McDougall; children— Eugene Matthew, Philip Leslie, Christine Louise. BASc., U. B.C., 1948; MS, U. Ill., 1949, PhD, 1951; student Internat. Sch. Nuclear Sci. and Engring., Argonne Nat. Lab., 1956, 57. Chem. engr. Nat. Research Council Can., 1948; research engr. Rayonier, Inc., 1951-52; faculty U. Wash., Seattle, 1952—, chmn. nuclear engring. group, 1957-65, prof. chem. engring., 1960—, acting chmn. dept. chem. engring., 1985, dir. nuclear reactor labs., 1962-72, prof. nuclear engring., 1965-91, prof. emeritus nuclear engring. and chem. engring., 1991—, chmn. dept. nuclear engring., 1965-81, acting chmn. dept. nuclear engring., 1984-86, adj. prof. bioengring., 1985-91; v.p. rsch. Meridian Med. Corp., Seattle, 1991—. Del. Japan-U.S. Seminar on Nuclear Engring. Edn., 1974; lectr. hemodialysis engring. USSR Ministry of Health, Moscow, 1976; lectr. biomed. engring. Norwegian Nephrological Soc., Oslo, 1980; lectr. hemodialysis engring. Kuratorium für Hemodialyse, Münster, Germany, 1980, Clinique Iser, Munich, Germany, 1980, Mcpl. Hosp., Hvidovre, Denmark, 1980, State Hosp., Copenhagen, 1980; mem. Assembly Engring., NRC, Com. Transp. Plutonium by Air, cons. med. engring., 1952— Contbr. chpts. to books, profl. jours. Trustee Pacific Sci. Center Found., mem. exec. com., 1973-80. Recipient citation Wash. Joint Legis. Com. Nuclear Energy, 1968, Disting. Teaching award Coll. Engring. U. Wash., 1987, Clyde Shields Disting. Svc. award N.W. Kidney Found., 1992, U. Ill. Alumni Achievement award, 1993, tchg. excellence award Aspen Tech. Inc., 1999, Am. Engr. Specifying award for excellence in design artificial kidney systems, 1970, Nat. Kidney Found. Pioneer award, 1982, Sigma Xi award, 1982; named Engr. of Yr. Wash. State Profl. Engrs. Assn., 1969; recipient Aspen Tech. U. Tchg. Excellence award, 2000. Fellow Am. Inst. Chemists, Am. Inst. Chem. Engrs. (Engr. Distinction award), Am. Nuclear Soc. (v.p. 1982-83, chmn. 1983-84), Am. Inst. Med. and Biol. Engring.; mem. NAS (chmn. com. on future devel. nuclear power 1990, mem. Inst. Medicine), NAE (memberships com.), Engrs. Joint Coun., Am. Soc. Engring. Edn. (chmn. nuclear engring. divsn. 1965-66), Internat. Soc. Artificial Organs, Am. Soc. Artificial Internal Organs, European Dialysis and Transplantation Assn., Inst. Medicine, Biomed. Engring. Soc., Sigma Xi, Tau Beta Pi, Pi Mu Epsilon, Alpha Chi Sigma. Clubs: U. Wash. Pres.', Wash. Athletic. Presbyterian. Achievements include co-inventing continuous central artificial kidney system for low cost treatment in centers, also co-inventor automatic artificial kidney system for overnight unattended hemodialysis of patients in homes, and techniques for early diagnosis of cystic fibrosis in children using a nuclear reactor; formulated dialysis index for prescribing minimum adequate treatment for patients undergoing hemodialysis; co-inventor, dir. design and devel. extracorporeal system for treatment of sickle cell anemia; co-developer computerized wearable insulin pump for diabetics; patentee systems for stblzn. of structures in permafrost, also field of artificial kidney, artificial pancreas, and respiratory diagnostics. Home: 3237 Lakewood Ave S Seattle WA 98144-7229

BABB, FRANK EDWARD, lawyer, executive; b. Maryville, Mo., Dec. 22, 1932; s. Dale Victor and Esther (Hull) B. BS, Northwest Mo. State U., Maryville, 1954; LL.B., Harvard U., 1959. Ptnr. McDermott, Will & Emery, Chgo., 1959-90, of counsel, 1991—; chmn. AF Ptnrs., Tucson, 1991—. With CIC U.S. Army, 1954-56. Mem. Univ. Club Chgo., Am. Alpine Club.

BABB, HAROLD, psychologist, educator; b. Mosheim, Tenn., Sept. 4, 1926; s. Ray Edward and Mary Louise (Brown) B.; m. Marjorie Craig Leask (Sept. 27, 1947); children: Patricia Craig, Barbara Lou, David Edward. BA, Wayne State U., 1950; MA, Ohio State U., 1951, PhD, 1953. Asst. prof., assoc. prof., chmn. dept. psychology Coe Coll., 1953-58; prof., chmn. dept. psychology Hobart and William Smith Colls., 1958-63; NIH, NIMH exec. sec., grants specialist, 1963-64; prof., chmn. dept. psychology U. Mont., Missoula, 1964-71; prof. psychology SUNY-Binghamton, 1971-95, prof. emeritus, 1995—, chmn. dept., 1971-74. Contbr. articles on psychology to profl. jours. Served with USNR, 1944-46. NIMH research grantee, 1960-62; NSF research grantee, 1968-69 Fellow Am. Psychol. Assn., Am. Psychol. Soc.; mem. AAAS, AAUP, Ea. Psychol. Assn., Midwestern Psychol. Assn., Psychonomic Soc., Sigma Xi Home: RR 1 Box 1957 Stanley Lake Rd Friendsville PA 18818 E-mail: hbabb@epix.net.

BABB, JAMES RONALD, editor, writer; b. Lenoir City, Tenn., June 18, 1949; s. Walter Everett and Katherine Marie Stocksdale B.; m. Linda Hayes Greene Babb, March 4, 1949; 1 child: Ethan. Grad., Lenoir City Schs., 1955-66. Lobster fisherman, Belfast, Maine, 1975-81; editor Internat. Marine Divsn. McGraw-Hill, Rockport, Maine, 1987-94, The Lyons Press, N.Y.C., 1994-97, Gray's Sporting Jour., Augusta, Ga., 1997—. Cons. Marine Books Divsn., W.W. Norton and Co., N.Y., 1995-97. Author: River Music: A Flyfisher's Four Seasons, 2001, Crosscurrents: A Flyfisher's Progress, 1999. With USN, 1966-69. Avocations: fly fishing, gardening, cooking.

BABB, JOSEPH DOLBY, physician; b. Columbus, Ohio, Apr. 16, 1939; s. Joe A. and Dorothe (Dolby) B.; m. Anne Tanner Hammerlund, Sept. 2, 1969 (div. Apr. 1985); children: Elizabeth Anne, Peter Dolby; m. Margo Tregenza, Oct. 6, 1990. BA magna cum laude, Kenyon Coll., Gambier, Ohio, 1961; MD, Johns Hopkins U., 1966. Diplomate in internal medicine and cardiovascular diseases Am. Bd. Internal Medicine; cert. physician, Pa., Conn., N.C. Intern Mass. Gen. Hosp., Boston, 1966-67, resident in internal medicine, 1967-68, clin. and rsch. fellow, 1970-72; teaching fellow Harvard Med. Sch., Boston, 1970-72; asst. prof. med. cardiology Pa. State U. Sch. Medicine, Hershey, 1972-76, assoc. prof., 1976-80; chief of cardiology Bridgeport (Conn.) Hosp., 1980-95; clin. assoc. prof. medicine (cardiology) Yale U., New Haven, 1980-95; prof. medicine (cardiology) East Carolina U. Sch. Medicine, Greenville, 1995—. Bd. dirs., pres. Alcohol and Drug Dependency Coun., Westport, Conn., 1987-95. Maj. U.S. Army, 1968-70, Vietnam. Fulbright fellow, Utrecht, Netherlands, 1961-62. Fellow Am. Coll. Cardiology (gov. 1987-90, 2002—), Am. Heart Assn. (coun. clin. cardiology), Soc. Cardiac Angiography and Intervention (trustee 1993-99, pres. 2001-02), Coalition of Cardiovasc. Orgns. (pres.-elect). Avocations: fishing, hiking. Home: 3804 Charleston Ct Greenville NC 27834-7667 Office: East Carolina U Sch Med PCMH Teaching Annex Rm 352 Greenville NC 27858-4354

BABB, RALPH W., JR., banker; b. Sherman, Tex., Feb. 4, 1949; s. Ralph Wheeler and Billie Margaret (Odneal) B.; m. Barbara Louise Alexander, Aug. 30, 1970; children: Dana P., Derek R. BS in Acctg., U. Mo., Columbia, 1971. CPA, Mo. Audit mgr. Peat, Marwick, Mitchell & Co., CPA's, St. Louis, 1971-78; contr., sr. v.p. Mercantile Bancorp. Inc., St. Louis, 1978-83, treas., sr. v.p., 1979-83, CFO, exec. v.p., 1983-94, vice chmn., 1987-95; vice-chmn., CFO Comerica, Inc., Detroit, 1995—2002, chmn., pres., CEO, dir., 2002—; pres., CEO, dir. Comerica Bank, Detroit, 2002—. Mem. Fin. Execs. Inst. (pres. St. Louis chpt. 1986-87). Methodist. Office: Comerica Inc PO Box 75000 Detroit MI 48275-0001

BABB, ROBERTA JOAN, educational administrator; b. East Chicago, Ill., Jan. 5, 1944; d. Joseph A. and Katherine Phillips; m. Donald L. Babb, July 30, 1966; children: Sasha M., Holly S. BS in Edn., Ind. U., 1966; postgrad., De Paul U., 1972-73. Tchr. East Chicago Pub. Schs., 1969-70, Hammond (Ind.) Pub. Schs., 1966-68, 70-71; head tchr. The Lab Sch., Washington, 1968-69, 74-79; co-founder, dir. Creme de le Creme, Houston, 1982—. Scholar Ind. U., PTA. Mem. Nat. Child Care Assn., Tex. Lic. Child Care Assn; bd. dirs. Crem dela Creme Inc., Denver.

BABB, WYLIE SHERRILL, college president; b. Greenville, S.C., Aug. 20, 1940; s. J. Wylie and Sally P. B.; m. Linda Witmer, June 30, 1963; children: Corinne, Michelle, David. BA in History, Post Coll., 1963; Th.M., Dallas Theol. Sem., 1967; PhD in Ednl. Adminstrn, U. Pitts., 1979. Ordained to ministry Scottsdale, Ariz., 1967; pastor Bible Ch., 1967-71; dean acad. affairs Lancaster (Pa.) Bible Coll., 1971-76; dean faculty Moody Bible Inst., Chgo., 1976-79;

pres. Phila. Coll. Bible, 1979—. Speaker, cons. in field. Mem. Am. Assn. Higher Edn., Doctoral Assn. Educators, Am. Assn. Bible Colls. (pres.), Lower Bucks County C. of C., Middle States Assn. Commn. for Higher Edn., Phi Delta Kappa. Home: 805 S Pine St Langhorne PA 19047-2924 Office: Phila Coll Bible Langhorne Manor 200 Manor Ave Langhorne PA 19047-2943

BABBEL, DAVID FREDERICK, finance and insurance educator; b. Salt Lake City, Apr. 12, 1949; s. Frederick William and June (Andrew) Babbel; m. Mary Jane Benson, Aug. 27, 1975; children: Tara Nicole, Elise Kiera, Karisa Rose, Tyson Frederick. BA, Brigham Young U., 1973; MBA, U. Fla., 1975, PhD, 1978; MA (hon.), U. Pa., 1986. Prof. of fin. U. Calif., Berkeley, 1978—85; prof. fin. and ins. U. Pa. Wharton Sch., Phila., 1985—. V.p. Goldman, Sachs & Co, New York, NY, 1987, cons.; pres. A/L Technology, Bryn Mawr, Pa.; cons. IBM, Chase, MMC, World Bank, Verizon, Morrison-Knudson, Aetna, GE Capital, Met Life, 1978—; pres. Brazil Mission LDS Ch., 2002—. Author: 6 books on fins and ins; contbr. articles to profl jours. Pres. Brasilia, Brazil Mission of L.D.S. Ch., 2002—. Fellow Fulbright, 1976—77. Republican. Mem. Lds Ch. Office: Wharton Sch U Pa 303 Colonial Penn Ctr Philadelphia PA 19104 *Any idea, without at least some element of absurdity, is probably not worth further consideration.*

BABBITT, BRUCE EDWARD, former federal official, lawyer; b. June 27, 1938; m. Hattie Coons; children— Christopher, T.J. BS magna cum laude, U. Notre Dame; MS, U. Newcastle, Eng., 1962; LL.B., Harvard U., 1965. Bar: Ariz. 1965. Assoc. Brown and Bain, Phoenix, 1965-74; atty. gen. State of Ariz., Phoenix, 1975-78, gov., 1978-87; ptnr. Steptoe & Johnson, Phoenix; sec. U.S. Dept. Interior, Washington, 1993-2001; of counsel, environ. dept. Latham & Watkins, Washington, 2001—. Mem. President's Commn. on Accident at Three Mile Island, 1979-80; chmn. Nuclear Safety Oversight Com., 1980-81, Western Govs.' Policy Office, 1982; mem. Adv. Commn. on Intergovtl. Relations, 1980-84; chmn. task force on fed. budget deficit Roosevelt Ctr. for Am. Policy Studies, 1984; chmn. Nat. Groundwater Policy Forum, 1984— Author: Color and Light: The Southwest Canvases of Louis Akin, 1973, Grand Canyon: An Anthology, 1978 Trustee Dougherty Found.; candidate for Dem. Party nomination for Pres. of U.S. Recipient Thomas Jefferson award Nat. Wildlife Fedn., 1981, spl. conservation award Nat. Wildlife Fedn., 1983 Mem. Nat. Govs. Assn. (chmn. subcom. on water resources), Democratic Govs. Assn. (chmn. 1985) Democrat. Office: Latham & Watkins 555 Eleventh St NW Ste 1000 Washington DC 20004-1304

BABBITT, SAMUEL FISHER, retired university official; b. New Haven, Feb. 22, 1929; s. Theodore and Margaret (Fisher) B.; m. Natalie Zane Moore, June 28, 1954; children: Christopher Converse, Thomas Collier, Lucy Cullyford. BA, Yale U., 1953, MA, 1957, PhD, 1965; LLD (hon.), Hamilton Coll., Clinton, N.Y., 1968. Asst. dean Yale Coll. Grad. Sch., New Haven, 1953-57, 63-66; dean of men Vanderbilt U., Nashville, 1957-62; chief coll. and univ. liaison Office Pub. Affairs, U.S. Peace Corps, Washington, 1962-63; pres. Kirkland Coll., Clinton, N.Y., 1966-78; v.p. program planning and resources Meml. Sloan-Kettering Cancer Ctr., N.Y.C., 1979-83; v.p. devel. Brown U., Providence, 1982-90, sr. v.p. The Campaign, 1990-93, sr. advisor to pres. for Far Eastern Affairs, 1993-96. Mem. N.Y. State Commn. on Civil Rights, 1968-76. Author: The 49th Magician, 1966; producer: (film) The Eyes of the Amaryllis, 1981. Pres., bd. dirs. Sandra Feinstein-Gamm Theatre; v.p. bd. The Pawtucket Armory Assn. With inf. U.S. Army, 1948-51, Korea. Decorated Silver Star. Mem. Century Assn. (N.Y.C.). Democrat. E-mail: sambabb1@cox.net.

BABBY, ELLEN REISMAN, education administrator; b. Montreal, Que., Can., Oct. 21, 1950; came to U.S., 1973; d. Mark Reisman and Rose Gutwillig (Reisman); m. Lon Scott Babby, June 17, 1973; children— Kenneth Robert, Heather Lynn. Student, McGill U., 1968-70; BA, Beaver Coll., 1972; MA, Lehigh U., 1973, Yale U., 1976, M.Phil., 1977, PhD, 1980. Tchr. elem. schs. to coll. levels; instr. resident assoc. program Smithsonian Instn., Washington, 1980-82; exec. dir. Assn. for Can. Studies in U.S., Washington, 1982-92; with Nat. Fgn. Lang. Ctr. Johns Hopkins U., Washington, 1992-94; sr. dir. planning and devel. Nat. Assn. Fgn. Student Affairs Assn. Internat. Educators, Washington, 1995-99; v.p. Am. Coun. On Edn., Washington, 1999—. Author: Play of Language and Spectacle: A Structural Reading of Selected Texts by Gabrielle Roy, 1986. Contbr. articles on Quebec lit. to profl. jours. Mem. Assn. for Can. Studies in U.S., Am. Soc. Assn. Execs., Nat. Soc. Fund Raising Execs., Yale Alumni (del. 1989-92). Office: Am Coun On Edn One Dupont Cir #800 Washington DC 20036 E-mail: ellen@babby.com.

BABBY, LON S. lawyer; b. Bklyn., Feb. 21, 1951; BA, Lehigh U., 1973; JD, Yale U., 1976. Bar: Conn. 1976, D.C. 1977, U.S. Supreme Ct. 1981, U.S. Claims Ct., 1986; cert. agt. Nat. Basketball Players Assn., Nat. Football League Players Assn. Law clk. to Hon. M. Joseph Blumenfeld Dist. Conn., 1976-77; mem. Williams & Connolly, Washington, 1977—. Adj. faculty George Washington U. Law Sch., 1991-92. Editor Yale Law Jour., 1974-76; contbr. articles to profl. jours. Trustee Naismith Meml. Basketball Hall of Fame, 2002—. Mem. ABA, D.C. Bar, Conn. Bar Assn., Phi Beta Kappa, Omicron Delta Kappa. Office: Williams & Connolly 725 12th St NW Washington DC 20005-5901 E-mail: lbabby@wc.com.

BABCOCK, CATHERINE EVANS, artist, educator; b. Rydal, Pa, Feb. 23, 1924; d. William Wayne and Marion (Waters) Babcock; m. Douglas Paul Torre, May 28, 1977; 2 stepchildren. Diploma, Sarah Lawrence Coll., 1942; BFA, Temple U., 1944, MFA, 1948. Tchr. Rudolf Steiner Sch., 1949; tchr. jr. high sch. Stratford, Conn., 1959-63; tchr. elem. art Locust Valley Primary and Elem. Sch., 1963-68; instr. Darien Cmty. Ctr., 1975-81; art tchr. Rowayton Arts Ctr., Conn., 1979—, also bd. mem. Rec. sec. Portrait painter; artist to Sea Svc. (USCG and USN); equestrian artist Fairfield Hunt Club Show's Benefit Horse Show, 1993; watercolor tchr. Darien Cmty. Assn., 1993-94. Illustrator: Atheneum, 1968 (libr. award), Cutaneous Cryosurgery (Douglas Torre), 1978, rev., 1979; translator: Undertow (Finn Havrevold), 1968; painter, mural for Babcock Surg. Wards, Temple U. Hosp., Phila., 1944; designer display Cryosurgery of Skin Cancer, Dallas, 1979 (Gold award); author: Biography in American References, 1989, (poem) Vikings Habitat, The National Library of Poetry, River of Dreams, 1994, Poetic Voices of America, 1995, Best Pastels, 1996, Chips and Chirps of Verses, 1998; exhbns. include internat. miniature shows Fine Arts Club, Washington, 1984, New Canaan Soc. for the Arts, 1988, 93, Grand Nat. Salmagundi Club, St. Petersburg Mus., Fla., Degas Pastel Soc., New Orleans, 1990-95, Mus. of Art, New Orleans, 1990, (portrait of husband) NY Hosp., Amb. Ernst Jaakson Mus. in Tallin, Estonia, 2001, Portrait of Sr. Ambassador of UN painted in 1997, kept in his NYC office, is now in mus. in ESTONIA, 2001; Cert. of Excellence from Miniature fSpc. (MSPG) of Washinton DC for portrait of a firefighter, 2002. Recipient awards including 10 USCG awards, Am. Acad. Dermatology Art Shows, 2 award, Rowayton Arts Ctr., 1993—94, Best Poems award, Nat. Libr. Poetry, 1996, Amherst Soc. award, Sparrowgrass Soc. award, cert. appreciation, USCG, 1971—82, Naval Sta. of N.Y., 1981, 1st prize, Rowayton Art Ctr., 2000, USCG award, Alexander Hamilton Custom House, 2000. Mem. Internat. Soc. Poets (lifetime, Merit award 1997, medal 1997, Silver cup 2003), Met. Portrait Inst., Conn. Pastel Soc., Pastel Soc. Am. (cert. of merit), USCG Art Program (ofcl. artist), COGAP artist, 1999, London Diplomatic Acad., 2001. Congregationalist. Home and Office: 122 Rowayton Ave Norwalk CT 06853-1409

BABCOCK, CHARLES LUTHER, classics educator; b. Whittier, Calif., May 26, 1924; s. Robert Louis and Margarette Estelle (Fuller) B.; m. Mary Ayer Taylor, Aug. 6, 1955; children: Robert Sherburne, Jennie Rownd Chapman, Jonathan Taylor. AB in Latin, U. Calif., Berkeley, 1948, MA in Latin, 1949, PhD in Classics, 1953. Asst. in classics U. Utah, Salt Lake City, 1949-50; instr. classics Cornell U., Ithaca, N.Y., 1955-57; acting. instr. Stanford U., Calif., summer 1956; asst. prof. classical studies U. Pa., Phila., 1957-62, assoc. prof., 1962-66, asst. dean, vice dean of coll., 1960-62, 62-64, acting dean, spring 1964; prof. classics Ohio State U., Columbus, 1966-92, prof. emeritus, 1992—, chmn. dept., 1966-68, 80-88, dean coll. of Humanities, 1968-70. Prof.-in-charge summer sch. Am. Acad. in Rome, 1966, resident in classical studies, 1986, acting Mellon prof.-in-charge sch. classical studies, 1988-89, chmn. adv. coun. sch. classical studies, 1992-94; Latin exam. com. Advanced Placement Program, 1967-74, chmn., 1972-74; prof.-in-charge Intercollegiate Ctr. Classical Studies, Rome, 1974, chair mng. com., 1975-82; scholar in residence Hope Coll., 1993. Co-author: Aspects of Roman Civilization, 1980; contbr. articles on Latin lit. (especially Horace), Latin epigraphy, Roman civilization. Served to capt. inf. U.S. Army, 1943-47, ETO. Univ. fellow in classics U. Calif., Berkeley, 1951-53; Fulbright scholar in classics, Rome, 1953-55. Fellow Am. Acad. in Rome (trustee 1981-83, trustee emeritus 1994—); mem. Am. Philol. Assn. (bd. dirs. 1968-72), Classical Assn. of Mid. West and South (Ovatio award 1982, pres. 1977-78), Vergilian Soc. Am. (pres. 1975-76), Assn. Depts. Fgn. Langs. (pres. 1986), Archeol. Inst. Am., Ohio Classical Conf., Phi Beta Kappa (pres. Epsilon of Ohio 1969-70), Phi Kappa Phi, Phi Sigma Kappa (former pres. U. Calif., regional dep. 1949-51), Scabbard and Blade Club (Pa., hon.), Philomathean Soc. (hon.), Greater Columbus Latin Club. Home: 973 Lynbrook Rd Columbus OH 43235-3307 Office: Ohio State U Dept Greek & Latin 230 N Oval Mall Columbus OH 43210-1319 E-mail: babcock.2@osu.edu.

BABCOCK, CHARLES WITTEN, JR., lawyer; b. Kansas City, Mo., Dec. 6, 1941; s. Charles W. and Esther L. (Marcy) B.; m. Sharon K. Chamberlain, June 26, 1976; children: David, William, Susan, Stephen. BA with honors, U. Mo., 1963; JD, Harvard U., 1966. Bar: Mo. 1966, Mich. 1971. Judge advocate USMC, various locations, 1966-69; assoc. Blackwell, Sanders, Kansas City, 1969-71; staff atty. Gen. Motors Corp., Detroit, 1971—. Contbr. articles to profl. jours. Bd. dirs. Mothers Against Drunk Driving, 1992-99, nat. chmn., 1996-98. Avocation: amateur radio. Home: 917 Grand Marais St Grosse Pointe MI 48230-1867 Office: Gen Motors Corp PO Box 33122 Detroit MI 48232-5122

BABCOCK, HOPE SMITH, counselor, educator, program designer; b. Attleboro, Mass., July 3, 1941; d. Ezra Sheldon and Virginia (Fernandez) Smith; m. Robert C. Miner, June 20, 1959 (div. Oct. 1973); children: Eric, Robert, Jonathan, William, Garret; m. John A. Bucciarelli Jr., June 20, 1975 (dec. Aug. 1981); m. Richard B. Babcock, Nov. 8, 1997. AA, Brevard C.C., Cocoa, Fla.; BA, U. Ctrl. Fla., Orlando; MA, MHC, Webster U., Merritt Island, Fla. Cert. clin. hypnotherapist; lic. real estate agt. Fla., domestic violence intervention specialist. Coord. suicide prevention jr./sr. high schs. Mental Health Assn., Rockledge, Fla., 1985-86; program designer, intervention arbitrator, instr. Juvenile Justice Ct. Alternatives, 1986-91; program designer, specialist, counselor, tchr. life skills Dept. Corrections-Probation/Parole Svcs., Cocoa, 1990—; counselor, tchr. Brevard County Jail, Sharpes, Fla., 1993-96; coord. parents, children, divorce Brevard County Ct. Sys., 1995-98; substance abuse counselor, life skills tchr. Alco-Rest Rehab. Ctr., Cocoa, 1997-2001. Cons., advisor Probationers Ednl. Growth Program, Cocoa, 1995—; bd. dirs. Turning Point Rehab. Ctr., Rockledge, 1996—98; domestic violence interventions svcs. facilitator Family Counseling Ctr., Rockledge, 2001. Program designer, implementer, arbitrator Juvenile Alternative Svcs. Program, 1985-91, Brevard County Mentoring Program, Merritt Island, 1999, Cmty. Crisis Response Team, 2002. Named J.C. Penney's Cmty. Vol. of Yr., 1993; recipient numerous awards of recognition. Avocations: real estate investing, international travel, interior crafts and decorating. Home: 4560 Horse Shoe Bnd Merritt Island FL 32953-7900

BABCOCK, JAMES WILLIAM, geotechnical engineer; b. Rochester, N.Y., Jan. 17, 1953; s. Joseph William and Lillian M. Babcock; m. Janet Marie Perich, Aug. 6, 1977; children: Gregory James, Kevin George. AAS, SUNY, Alfred, 1973; BSCE, Clarkson U., 1975; MSCE, U. Pitts., 1979. Registered profl. engr., Fla., 1980. Sr. project mgr. Ardaman & Assoc., Inc., Orlando, Fla., 1975—79; structural engr. Dravo Corp., Pitts. Mem.: ASCE.

BABCOCK, JO, artist, educator; b. St. Louis, Feb. 24, 1954; s. Boyd Leon and Shirley Lynn (Hamm) B.; m. Kitty Costello, May 25, 2003. Student, UCLA, 1975; BFA, San Francisco Art Inst., 1976, MFA, 1979. Color printer Rolling Stone mag., San Francisco, 1976, Outside mag., San Francisco, 1977; cameraman 1st Calif. Press, San Francisco, 1977-80; electrician Bros. Electric, San Francisco, 1984-89; assoc. prof. San Francisco Art Inst., 1989-93; exhibit designer Levi Strauss & Co., 1989—. One-man shows include Zwinger Gallery, Berlin, 1987, Marcuse Pfeiffer Gallery, N.Y.C., 1988, Artspace, San Francisco, 1989, Visual Studies Workshop, Rochester, N.Y., 1990, Ctr. for the Arts, San Francisco, 1995, Oakland (Calif.) Mus., 1997, Kyle Roberts Gallery, San Francisco, 1992, Addison Gallery Am. Art, Andover, Mass., 1997, Chgo. Art Inst., 1982, CEPA, Buffalo, 1988, others; exhibited in group shows at Friends of Photography Gallery, Carmel, 1976, Sao Paulo (Brazil) Bienal, San Francisco Mus. of Modern Art, 1989, Rena Bransten Gallery, San Francisco, 1991, Oliver Art Ctr., CCAC, 1991, Lieberman & Saul, N.Y., 1991, Tampa Mus. Art, 1992, San Jose Mus. Art, 1992, Palm Springs Desert Mus., 1993, 100 Years of Landscape Art in the Bay Area, M.H. de Young Mus., San Francisco, 1995, Bay Area Landscapes, 1995, The Alternative Mus., N.Y., 1981, Wooster St. Gallery, N.Y., 1981, Living Mus., Rejkjavik, Iceland, 1983, 10 on 8, N.Y., 1983, Windows on White, N.Y., 1984, Public Image, N.Y., 1984, Otis Parsons Gallery, L.A., 1985, Hotel Project, Oakland, Calif., 1986, Roanoke (Va.) Mus. Fine Art, 1988, Ctr. for contemporary Arts, Santa Fe, 1988, Artists at the Rock, Alcatraz, Calif., 1988, others; represented in permanent collections at San Francisco Mus. Modern Art, Bklyn. Mus., Newport Harbor Art Mus., Lightwork, Syracuse, N.Y., La Biblioteque, Avignon, France, San Francisco Pub. Libr., San Francisco Arts Commn., George Eastman House, Rochester, N.Y., Nat. Collection, Smithsonian Instn., others. Grantee City of Oakland, 1985, N.Y. State Coun. on Arts, 1988, Nat. Endowment for Arts, 1990. Mem. Primitive Hunting Soc. Avocation: building pinhole cameras. Studio: 378 San Jose Ave Apt B San Francisco CA 94110-3700 E-mail: jobabcock@webtv.net.

BABCOCK, JONATHAN PAUL, music educator, conductor; b. Binghamton, NY, July 15, 1969; s. William Richard and Dorothy Jean Babcock; life ptnr. Danton Bankay, July 21, 2001. MusB, SUNY, Potsdam, 1991, MusM, 1993; D Mus. Arts, U. Hartford, 2003. Music tchr. Mt. Sinai(NY) Union Free Sch. Dist., 1992—98; doctoral fellow U. of Hartford, Conn., 1998—2001; artistic dir. Gay Gotham Chorus, N.Y.C., 1999—; instr. Bklyn Coll., CUNY, 2001—. Asst. condr. Conn. All-State Chorus, Hartford, 2000; condr. All Nassau County Chorus, Massapequa, NY, 2001, Westechester County Area All State Chorus, 2002. Conductor of world premiere (choral composition) Three Metrical Psalms by Arthur Frackenpohl, 1997; dir.: (choral/orchestral composition) David and Jonathan (by Stefan Weisman), 2001 (Young Composer's Award, 2001), (conductor of World Premiere) (choral composition in memory of sept. 11) Rejoice in Jerusalem! by Mark Miller, 2001, No Words (by Paul Moraver), 2003. Mem.: Chorus Am., Am. Choral Directors Assoc., NY State Sch. Music Assoc. (major orgn. adjudicator 1999—), Music Educators' Nat. Conf. Democrat. Methodist. Office: Conservatory of Music Brooklyn College 2900 Bedford Ave Brooklyn NY 11210 Personal E-mail: jbabcock715@yahoo.com. E-mail: jbabcock@brooklyn.cuny.edu.

BABCOCK, KEITH MOSS, lawyer; b. Camden, N.J., Aug. 5, 1951; s. William Strong Jr. and Dinah Leslie (Moss) B.; m. Jacquelyn Sue Dickman, Aug. 16, 1975; children: Michael Arthur, Max William. AB, Princeton U., 1973; JD, George Washington U., 1976. Bar: S.C. 1977, U.S. Dist. Ct. S.C. 1977, U.S. Ct. Appeals (4th cir.) 1977, U.S. Supreme Ct. 1980. Staff atty. S.C. Atty. Gen.'s Office, Columbia, 1977-78, state atty., 1978-79, asst. atty. gen., 1979-81; ptnr. Barnes & Austin, Columbia, 1981-82, Austin & Lewis, Columbia, 1982-84, Lewis, Babcock & Hawkins, Columbia, 1984—. Mem. civil justice adv. com. for dist. S.C., 1991-94; mem. S.C. Bd. Bar Examiners, 2001—. Bd. dirs. Columbia Jewish Community Pre-Sch., 1984, chmn., 1985-86; bd. dirs. Columbia Jewish Community Ctr., 1986-88. Mem. ABA, S.C. Bar Assn. (chmn. prof. resp. com. 1985-86), Richland County Bar Assn., Princeton Alumni Assn. of S.C. (v.p. 1980-86, 88-89, pres. 1990-93, 96-98), George Washington U. Law Sch. Alumni Assn. (bd. dirs. 1983-87), Summit Club, Spring Valley Country Club (Columbia). Democrat. Episcopalian. Home: 233 W Springs Rd Columbia SC 29223-6912 Office: Lewis Babcock & Hawkins 1513 Hampton St Columbia SC 29201-2928 E-mail: kmb@lbhlaw.com.

BABCOCK, LYNDON ROSS, JR., environmental engineer, educator; b. Detroit, Apr. 8, 1934; s. Lyndon Ross and Lucille Kathryn (Miller) B.; m. Betty Irene Immonen, June 21, 1957; children— Lyndon Ross III, Sheron Lucille Babcock Fruehauf, Susan Elizabeth Babcock Williams, Andrew Dag BSChemE, Mich. Tech. U., 1956; MSChemE, U. Washington, 1958, PhD in Environ. Engring., 1970. Registered profl. engr., Ill. Chem. engr. polymers Shell Chem. Co., Calif., N.J., N.Y., 1958-67; assoc. prof. environ. engring., geography, pub. health U. Ill., Chgo., 1970-75, prof. environ. engring., geography, pub. health, 1975-90, prof. emeritus, 1990—, dir. environ. health scis. program Sch. Pub. Health, 1978-79, dir. environ. and occupational health scis. program Sch. Pub. Health, 1979-84, assoc. dean Sch. Pub. Health, 1984-85. Cons. WHO, 1985, Interam. Devel. Bank, 1990-91, Environ. Secretariat Fed. Dist., Mexico City, 1995-97; USA coord. air quality project for Gestión de la Calidad del Aire, Mexico City, 1986-92; environ. cons./lectr. Tech. Instns., Mexican Secretariat of Pub. Edn., 1993-95; vis. prof. El Colegio de Mexico, Mexico City, 1996-2000. Mem. editorial bd. The Environ. Profl., 1979-90; contbr. environ. articles to profl jours.; patentee plastics composition and processing. Bd. dirs. Chgo. Lung Assn., 1981-92. Fulbright lectr., Turkey and India, 1975-76, Mexico, 1986-87, 1992-93; fed. and state environ. research and ednl. grantee Mem. Air and Waste Mgmt. Assn. (chmn. Lake Michigan sect. 1977-78), League Am. Bicyclists, Chicagoland Bicycle Fedn. (v.p. 1985-86). Office: U Ill Sch Pub Health EOHS MC922 2121 W Taylor St Chicago IL 60612-7260 E-mail: lyndonrb@comcast.net.

BABCOCK, MARGUERITE LOCKWOOD, addictions treatment therapist, educator, writer; b. Jacksonville, Fla., Jan. 1, 1944; d. Allen Seaman and Emilie (Lockwood) B. BA in Art History, Am. U., 1965; M Counselor Edn., U. Pitts., 1982. Lic. profl. counselor, Pa.; cert. addictions counselor Pa., nat. cert. counselor, master's addiction counselor (nat.). Addictions therapist South Hills Health Sys., Pitts., 1978-81; addiction therapist, clin. supr., clin. dir. Alternatives- Turtle Creek Mental Health/Mental Retardation/D&A Ctr., Pitts., 1981-86; addictions therapist, coord. Ligonier Valley Treatment Ctr., Stahlstown, Pa., 1986—88; addictions clin. supr., unit dir. Ctr. for Substance Abuse Mon-Yough, McKeesport, Pa., 1988-96; quality assurance Mon-Yough, McKeesport, 1996-97; clin. supr. Sojourner House, Pitts., 1997-2000; co-founder, addictions cons. consortium Outcomes Builders, 2000—. Adj. instr. in addictions courses Seton Hill Coll., Greensburg, Pa., 1989-91, C.C. Allegheny County, West Mifflin, Pa., 1989-91, Pa. State U., McKeesport, 1993—; pvt. trainer, writer, Acme, Pa., 1985—; ind. info. profl. in addictions, 2003—. Co-author, co-editor: Challenging Codependency: Feminist Critiques, 1995; mem. editl. bd. Jour. Tchg. in Addictions, 2000—; contbr. articles to profl. jours. Fellow Andrew Mellon Found., 1966-68, NSF, 1967. Mem.: Alpha Lambda Delta, Phi Kappa Phi. Avocation: website designer. Home and Office: RR 1 Box 138 Acme PA 15610-9712 E-mail: allele@lhtc.net.

BABCOCK, MICHAEL WARD, economics educator; b. Bloomington, Ill., Dec. 10, 1944; s. Bruce W. and Virginia (Neeson) B.; m. Virginia Lee Brooks, Aug. 4, 1973; children: John, Karen. BSBA, Drake U., 1967; MA in Econs., U. Ill., 1971, PhD in Econs., 1973. Tchg. asst. U. Ill., Urbana, 1968, 71, rsch. asst., 1972; prof. econs. Kans. State U., Manhattan, 1972—. Cons. Santa Fe, Burlington No., and Union Pacific R.R., Brotherhood of Maintenence Way, United Transp. Union, Kans. Dept. Transp., Kans. Dept. Agr., U.S. Dept. Agr., Kans. Dept. Commerce. Gen. editor Jour. Transp. Rsch. Forum; contbr. articles to profl. jours., newspapers, mags. Apptd. to Kans. Govs. R.R. Working Group to Evaluate Class I R.R. Mergers, 1995, 96, 2000. With U.S. Army, 1969-71. Recipient A.T. Kearney award Transp. Rsch. Forum, 1987, 89, UPS Found. award, 1990, Edgar S. Bagley award Kans. State U., 1989, 93, 97, 03, Outstanding Rsch. in Agrl. Transp. award Burlington No. R.R., 1994, Rail-Tex. Corp. award Transp. Rsch. Forum, 1997, Sr. Faculty award for rsch. excellence in social sci. Kans. State U., 1998; grantee U.S. Army C.E., 1978-79, USDA, 1978-79. 80-82, 84-85, 96-97, 2000, Kans. Dept. Agr., 1987, Kans. Wheat Commn., 1989, 92, 93, Midwest Transp. Ctr., 1989, 92, 93, Kans. Dept. Transp., 1991—, Mid-Am. Transp. Ctr., 1995, 96. Mem. Am. Assn. Agrl. Economists, Missouri Valley Econ. Assn., Mid-Continent Regional Sci. Assn., So. Regional Sci. Assn., Transp. Rsch. Forum (gen. editor Jour.), Transp. Rsch. Bd., Coun. Logistics Mgmt., So. Econs. Assn., Western Econs. Assn., Beta Gamma Sigma, Omicron Delta Epsilon. Home: 720 Harris Ave Manhattan KS 66502-3614 Office: Kans State U Dept Econs Manhattan KS 66506

BABCOCK, PETER HEARTZ, professional sports executive; b. Bangor, Maine, May 12, 1949; s. Bernard Roland and Jeanne Sargent (Heartz) B.; m. Yolanda Marie Cava; children: Amy, Katherine. BA, Ariz. State U., 1971, MA, 1976. Tchr., coach Glendale Union High Sch. Dist., Phoenix, 1972-80; asst. coach San Diego Clippers, 1980-82, dir. player pers., 1982-83, v.p. basketball ops., 1983-84; dir. player pers. Denver Nuggets, 1984-85, dir. basketball ops., 1985-86, v.p. basketball ops., 1986-87, pres., gen. mgr., 1987-90; v.p., gen. mgr. Atlanta Hawks, 1990—2003. Mem. competition and rules com., dir. Chgo. pre-draft camp NBA, 1985—, mem. steering com., 1995—; mem. USA Basketball Sr. National Team Com., 1995—. Mem. bd. addiction rsch. and treatment svcs. U. Colo. Med. Sch., 1986—, vis. mem. dept. psychiatry, 1989—; mem. bd. Adopt-A-Sch., Denver Pub. Schs., 1985-89; adv. bd. Big Bros., Denver, 1985—, Kops N Kids, 1987—; exec. com. Cmtys. for Drug Free Colo., Denver, 1987—; pres. NET Found./Charitable Fundraising, 1987-90; mem. Mayor's Coun. on Phys. Fitness, 1987-90; bd. dirs. Ga. Alliance for Children, 1996—, Yes! Atlanta, 1990—, Atlanta Urban League. Recipient Golden Apple award Atlanta Pub. Schs., 1996; named Outstanding Sports Personality of Ga., Spl. Olympics, 1992. Mem. Atlanta Tip Off Club (mem. nat. adv. bd. 1990—). Episcopalian. Avocations: jogging, weight-lifting, swimming, reading. Office: Atlanta Hawks S Tower 1 Cnn Ctr NW Ste 405 Atlanta GA 30303-2762 *Learn to respect others for their differences rather than to discriminate due to those differences. Tolerance, acceptance, and understanding are necessary for us to grow as human beings.*

BABEL, DEBORAH JEAN, social worker, paralegal; b. Fulton, N.Y., Oct. 12, 1959; d. Sheldon Rowell and Mary Jane (Dimon) Ford; m. Charles Jacob Babel III, Sept. 7, 1984 (seperated); children: Casandra Jane, Stefan Michael (dec.). BA in Acctg., Aurora (Colo.) C.C., 1981; BS in Social Wk., U. Boulder, 1982, MS in Social Work, 1984; cert., Denver Paralegal Inst., 1995. Cert. respite care for abused children; paralegal cert. Denver Paralegal Inst., 1986. Acct. Dale Conklin and Assocs. CPA Firm, Englewood, Colo., 1981-84, Beechcraft Aviation Inc., Denver, 1985-92; pres., founder The Parents Help Network, Aurora, 1993—. Adv. Adoptive Families of Am., Mpls., 1989—, Colo. Coalition for Children, Denver, 1989—, Fedn. of Families for Childrens Mental Health, Alexandria, Va., 1989—; parent rep. N.Am. Coun. on Adoptable Children. Contbr. articles to profl. jours. Mem. NAFE, NASW, Nat. Com. on the Prevention of Child Abuse, Attachment Disorder Parents Network (v.p. 1988—, Parent Advocacy award 1989), N.Am. Coun. on Adoptable Children (Warmline and Parent Advocate). Democrat. Roman Catholic. Avocations: adoption and foster care legislation, abuse and neglect issues in children, swimming, crafts, spending time with children. Home and Office: # 11 324 Ridgeway St Sylva NC 28779-5496

BABEL, RAYONIA ALLEEN, retired librarian, educator; b. Herrin, Ill., Sept. 5, 1935; d. Hubert Ray and Mabel Alleen (Manning) Vaughn; m. Jerald Lee Babel, Sept. 5, 1954 (div. 1973); children: Thomas, Carl, Penny, Heidi, Krista. Student, Milliken U., 1953-55; BA in Edn., No. Ill. U., 1970, MA in Libr. Sci., 1971. Cert. tchr., Ill. Head ref. svcs. Aurora (Ill.) U., 1971—2000; ret., 2000. Precinct committeeman Dems. of Kane County, 1973-78; treas. Charlemagne on the Fox Questers, 1991-93; sec. Restorations of Kane County. Mem. Libras, Inc. (v.p. 1991-92, pres. 1992-93). Methodist. Avocations: reading, miniatures, needlework. Home: 623 Katherine St Saint Charles IL 60174-3734

BABER, WILBUR H., JR., lawyer; b. Dec. 18, 1926; s. Wilbur H. and Martha Corinne (Allen) Baber. BA, Emory U., 1949; postgrad., U. NC, 1949—50, U. Houston, 1951—52; JD, Loyola U., New Orleans, 1965. Bar: La. 65, Tex. 66. Sole practice, Hallettsville, Tex., 1966—. Trustee Raymond Dickson Found. With U.S. Army. Mem.: ASCE, ABA, Tex. Surveyors Assn., Tex. Bar Assn., La. Bar Assn., Rotary. Methodist. Office: PO Box 294 Hallettsville TX 77964-0294

BABIARZ, FRANCIS STANLEY, lawyer; b. Wilmington, Del., Feb. 23, 1948; s. John Edward and Adele Frances B.; m. Joyce Elaine Pierson. BA with honors, U. Del., 1970; JD cum laude, U. Mich., 1973; LLM, Temple U., 1976. Bar: Del. 1973. Atty. Biondi & Babiarz, P.A., Wilmington, 1974—79, Morris, Nicholas, Arsht & Tunnell, Wilmington, 1979—84, Biggs & Battaglia, Wilmington, 1984—88, Manta & Welge, Wilmington, 1998—99; dir. legal affairs Family Ct. State of Del., 1999-2000, dep. bank commr. for supervisory affairs, 2000—. Sec. Del. State Bd. Accountancy, 1977—80. Staff mem. U. Mich. Jour. Law Reform, 1971-73. Served to Capt. USAR. Mem. Del. State Bar Assn. (profl. guidance com.), Am. Hort. Soc., Pa. Hort. Soc., Phi Beta Kappa, Phi Kappa Phi. Democrat. Roman Catholic. Office: 555 E Loockerman St Dover DE 19901-3779 Fax: 302-739-3609. E-mail: fbabiarz@state.de.us.

BABICH, BABETTE E. philosophy educator, writer; b. N.Y.C., Nov. 14, 1956; d. Robert Joseph and Barbara Jane (Alstead) B.; m. William Strongin (div.); m. Tracy B. Strong. BA, SUNY, Stony Brook, 1980; MA, Boston Coll., 1981, PhD, 1987. Vis. asst. prof. Denison U., Granville, Ohio, 1987-88; asst. prof. Marquette U., Milw., 1988-89; prof. Fordham U., N.Y.C., 1989—. Adj.

rsch. prof. Georgetown U., Washington, 1994—. Author: Nietzsche's Philosophy of Science, 1994; editor: From Phenomenology to Thought, Errancy, and Desire, 1995, Nietzsche and the Sciences, 2 vols., 1999, Hermeneutic Philosophy of Science, Van Gogh's Eyes, and God, 2002; exec. editor: New Nietzsche Studies, 1996—. Recipient Fulbright fellowship Fulbright Commn., Tubingen, Berlin, Germany, 1984-85, Belgium Am. fellowship Belgium Am. Ednl. Found., 1985-86; named Fulbright prof. Fulbright Commn., Tubingen, 1991-92. Mem. Am. Philos. Assn., Soc. for Phenomenology and Existential Philosophy, Nietzsche Soc. (exec. sec. 1997—). Jewish. Home: 825 W 187th St New York NY 10033-1225 Office: Fordham Univ 113 W 60th St New York NY 10023-7484

BABICH, MICHAEL WAYNE, chemistry educator, educational administrator; b. Milw., Sept. 23, 1945; s. Michael S. and Helen (Obradovic) B.; m. Cynthia Ann Charusch, July 1, 1973; children: Jessica R., Ashley E. BS in Chemistry, U. Wis., 1967; PhD in Chemistry, U. Nev., 1974. U.S. Dept. Energy postdoctoral fellow Iowa State U., Ames, Iowa, 1974-76; vis. asst. prof. Ohio Wesleyan U., Delaware, Ohio, 1976-77, U. Del., Newark, 1977-78; asst. prof. chemistry Fla. Inst. Tech., Melbourne, 1978-81, assoc. prof., 1981-86, prof., 1986—, head dept. chemistry, 1987—. Co-chmn. biochemistry program Fla. Melbourne, 1987—. Contbr. articles to profl. jours. Mem. Space Coast Sci. Ctr., Melbourne, Brevard Art Ctr. and Mus., Melbourne; bd. dirs. Joint Ctr. for Advanced Therapy and Biomed. Rsch. NDEA fellow HEW, Reno, 1968-72; rsch. grantee NSF, 1980, 82, Fla. Solar Energy Ctr., 1987-99. Fellow Am. Inst. Chemists; mem. Am. Chem. Soc. (petroleum rsch. fund rsch. grantee 1984-86, Outstanding Chemist Orlando sect. 1995), Am. Crystallographic Assn., Coun. for Chem. Rsch. (chmn. sci. edn. com., bd. govs.), EauGallie Yacht Club (Indian Harbour Beach, Fla. chpt.), Internat. Confederation of Thermal Analysis, N.Am. Thermal Analysis Soc., Sigma Xi. Avocations: tennis, golf, travel. Office: Fla Inst Tech Dept Chemistry 150 W University Blvd Melbourne FL 32901-6982

BABIK, DENNIS ALLEN, social worker, consultant; b. Johnstown, Pa., Sept. 6, 1943; s. Stephen Edward and Bernice Ann (Britz) B.; m. Esther Rebecca Rosenbaum, Jan. 18, 1992 (div. Feb. 1996). BS, U. Pitts., 1967; MSW, Marywood U., 1972; PhD, NYU, 1991. Cert. expert in traumatic stress Am. Acad. Experts in Traumatic Stress; lic. social worker Pa., N.Y., Tex., R.I.; cert. Article 81 court evaluator. Med. caseworker John Kane Hosp., Pitts., 1967, 70; psychiat. social worker Dutchess County Dept. Mental Hygiene, Poughkeepsie, N.Y., 1972-83; clin. dir. Veterans Coalition, Beacon, N.Y., 1986-93; pvt. practice social work Rhinebeck and Newburgh, N.Y., 1981-96; clin. supr. Riceland Reg. Mental Health Authority, Rosenberg, Tex., 1997-98; behavior specialist Alternative Cmty. Resource Program, Johnstown, Pa., 2000—; pvt. practice specializing in victims of trauma, 2000—. Program cons. N.Y. State Dept. Correctional Svcs., Albany, 1985-93; mem. nat. adv. coun. U.S. Jaycees, Tulsa, 1976-78; adj. instr. Dutchess County Cmty. Coll., Poughkeepsie, 1972-82; presenter, facilitator workshops, 1975-90. Contbr. to book: Incoming, 1998; contbr. articles to newspapers, profl. jours. With U.S. Army, 1967-69. Decorated Bronze Star; named Outstanding Young Man Am., U.S. Jaycees; recipient Disting. Svc. Cross, 1968, Outstanding Achievement award, U.S. Jaycees. Fellow: N.Y. State Soc. Clin. Social Workers; mem.: APA, Am. Acad. Experts in Traumatic Stress, Internat. Soc. Traumatic Stress Studies, The Menninger Soc., Nat. Assn. Social Workers, Mid-Hudson Valley Multiple Sclerosis Soc. (adv. bd. 1980—83, Red Cross nat. disaster team 2001), Ft. Bend County C. of C., Vietnam Vets. of Am. Roman Catholic. Achievements include development of and direction of a therapeutic program to assess and treat traumatized incarcerated veterans within N.Y. State correctional system. Avocations: reading, music, hiking, jogging, outdoor sports. Home: 1202 Virginia Ave Johnstown PA 15906

BABIN, CLAUDE HUNTER, history educator; b. Baton Rouge, Feb. 6, 1924; s. Ventress Victor and Essie (Bond) B.; m. Barbara Ann Murphy, Dec. 29, 1947; 1 son, Claude Hunter. BA, La. State U., 1945; MA, U. Wis., 1946; PhD, Tulane U., 1954; LLD, Hendrix Coll., 1965. Instr. history U. Miami, Fla., 1946-49; grad. fellow Tulane U., 1949-54; asst. prof., asso. prof., then prof. history Ark. A. and M. Coll., Monticello, 1954-60, acad. dean, 1960-62, pres., 1962-71; chancellor U. Ark. at Monticello, 1971-77, prof. history, 1977-92, chancellor, prof. emeritus, 1992—. Ford fellow, 1951-52 Mem. Am. Hist. Assn., Ark. Hist. Assn., Ark. Farm Bur. Fedn., Drew County Hist. Soc., Kappa Sigma, Phi Alpha Theta, Pi Sigma Alpha. Democrat. Methodist. Home: 135 Ross Ave Monticello AR 71655-4249

BABIN, REGINA-CHAMPAGNE, artist, educator, consultant; b. New Orleans, La, July 17, 1956; d. Eddie Anthony and Martha Ann (Bergeron) Champagne; m. Terry Lynn Babin, Apr. 25, 1981; children: Jonathan Paul, Michelle Elizabeth. BA with high honors, Nicholls State U., 1978, postgrad., 1992-96. Pvt. portraitist, Houma, La., 1972—; freelance artist, musician, writer So. Portraits, Plus, Houma, 1981—; bank teller Raceland Bank and Trust, Larose, La., 1979-80; sch. tchr. Lockport Christian, La., 1979-80; bank teller Nat. Bank Commerce, Kenner, La., 1980-81; free-lance author Terrebonne Enhancement Commn., Houma, 1985—; art instr. Genesis Alternative HS, 1996—2003, Lisa Pk. Elem., 2003—. Artist-in-residence, tour guide Terrebonne Hist. and Cultural Soc., Houma, 1981-85; founding chairperson Houma (La.)-Terrebonne Community Band, 1984-85; gallery dir. Terrebonne Fine Arts Guild, Houma, 1985-86; founding bd. dirs. Houma (La.)-Terrebonne Arts & Humanities Coun., 1985-87. Author, composer: (books with music) Pistoche, 1985, Santa's Prayer, 1991, The J.A.M. Adventure, 1994, (anti-drug packet with music tape) Just Say No To Drugs, 1989 (Nat. Jr. Aux. award 1990, South La. Alcohol and Drug Abuse Coun. 1990). Art/Music demonstrater Terrebonne Parish Libr., St. Charles Parish Libr., 1980—90; art program designer, instr. YMCA, Houma, 1981—87; artist, docent musician Southdown Mus., Houma, 1981—87; hurricane aid vol. ARC, Houma, 1986; summer camp art tchr. Girl Scouts, 2000—. Recipient Cert. Honor/Svc. award South La. Alcohol and Drug Abuse Coun., Houma, 1989, 1st prize in painting, 1st prize in drawing Gonzalez Art Assn., 1991; named to Nicholls State U. Hall of Fame, 1978-2001; Geneseis High Tchr. of the yr., HS Tchr. of the Yr. Award, Terrebonne Parish, 2001. Mem. ALA, Internat. Reading Assn., Nat. Mus. Women in Arts (charter mem., supporter), Terrebonne Fine Arts Guild, Terrebonne Hist. and Cultural Soc., Houma Jr. Aux. (life). Republican. Avocations: music, art, people, literature. Home and Office: So Portraits Plus 107 Willard Ave Houma LA 70360-7554

BABIN, STEVEN MICHAEL, atmospheric scientist, researcher; b. Lawton, Okla., Sept. 6, 1954; s. Cleveland Victor Jr. and Delys Lilian (Lowry) B.; m. Pamela Gail Nee, June 23, 1990; 1 child, Heather Rebecca. BS in Engring. Physics spl. distinction, U. Okla., 1976; MD, U. Okla., Oklahoma City, 1980; MSEE, U. Pa., 1983; MS in Meteorology, U. Md., 1994, PhD in Meteorology, 1996. Diplomate Am. Bd. Med. Examiners. Assoc. instr. pathology and lab. medicine U. Pa. Hosp., Phila., 1980-82; sr. engr. Applied Physics Lab. Johns Hopkins U., Laurel, Md., 1983—. Presenter in field. Contbr. articles to profl. jours. Engring. scholar Frontiers Sci. Found., 1972, Spl. scholar Nat. Merit Found., 1972. Mem. IEEE (sr.), Am. Meteorol. Soc., Am. Geophysics Union (life), Am. Mensa (life), Union Radio-Sci. Internat., Sigma Xi, Tau Beta Pi, Alpha Epsilon Delta, Phi Eta Sigma. Achievements include investigation of meteorological effects on microwave propagation in the marine boundary layer; design and development of data acquisition and analysis software in use on helicopters, rocketsondes, buoys, etc.; development of optical waveguide pH sensor; design and creation of working proportional counter for exo-electron research. Office: John Hopkins U Applied Physics Lab Johns Hopkins Rd Laurel MD 20723-6099

BABINEAU, ANNE SERZAN, lawyer; b. Jersey City, Dec. 16, 1951; d. Joseph Edward and Mary (Golding) Serzan; m. Paul A. Babineau, Apr. 7, 1973; children: John Regis, Matthew Paul. BA, Coll. New Rochelle, 1973; JD, Seton Hall U., 1977. Bar: N.J. 1977, N.Y. 1983, U.S. Ct. Appeals (3d cir.) 1984. Staff atty. rate counsel div. N.J. Dept. Pub. Adv., Newark, 1977-78; assoc. Wilentz, Goldman & Spitzer, P.C., Woodbridge, N.J., 1979-85, ptnr., 1985—. Trustee N.J. Future. Mem. ABA, N.J. State Bar Assn. (former chair pub. utility sect.), Urban Land Inst. Roman Catholic. Office: Wilentz Goldman & Spitzer PO Box 10 90 Woodbridge Ctr Dr Ste 900 Woodbridge NJ 07095-1142

BABINGTON, CHARLES MARTIN, III, lawyer; b. St. Louis, Mar. 15, 1944; s. Charles Martin Jr. and Sarah Elizabeth (Karraker) B.; m. Ann Baker, July 6, 1974; children: Martin, Anthony, Liza. AB, Dartmouth Coll., 1965; JD, U. Mich., 1968; LLM in Tax, Washington U., St. Louis, 1975. Bar: Mo. 1968, U.S. Dist. Ct. (ea. dist.) Mo. 1968, U.S. Ct. Appeals (8th cir.) 1973, U.S. Ct. Claims 1974, U.S. Tax Ct. 1975. Judge adv. USAF, Beale AFB, Calif., 1968-72; assoc. Thompson & Mitchell, St. Louis, 1972-77, ptnr., 1978-95; of counsel Thompson Coburn, 1996-98; ret., 1999. Bd. dirs., sec. St. Louis Steam Train Assn., 1986-2002; bd. dirs. Ecumenical Housing Prodn. Corp., 1992-97. Capt. USAF, 1968-72. Mem. Mo. Bar Assn. (mem. staff benefits com. 1979-96), Univ. Club St. Louis (bd. dirs. 1994-98, sec. 2002—). Republican. Episcopalian. Avocations: steam locomotive restoration, photography. Home: 25 Warson Ter Saint Louis MO 63124-1680 E-mail: cbabing3@swbell.net.

BABISH, CHARLES A., IV, aerospace engineer; b. Kettering, Ohio, May 15, 1964; s. Charles A. Babish, III and Gail A. Babish. BS in Aerospace Engring., Ohio State U., 1986; MS in Mech. Engring., U. Dayton, 1990. Aerospace engr. Wright-Patterson Air Force Base, Ohio, 1986—. Mem.: Am. Inst. Aeronautics and Astronautics (sr.). Republican. Avocations: volleyball, skiing. Home: 1573 Dale Ct Dayton OH 45432-2501 Office: Wright Patterson Air Force Base 1981 Monahan Way Bldg 12 Wright Patterson Afb OH 45433-7205

BABITZKE, THERESA ANGELINE, health facility administrator; b. Madison, Ill., Dec. 19, 1925; d. Victor Joseph and Angela (Ziolkowski) Sobolewski; m. Douglas Christ Babitzke, May 2, 1953; children: Charlotte, Mary Ann, Rose Marie, Helen. Student, Quincy Coll., 1943; diploma, St. John's Sch. Nursing Edn., Springfield, Ill., 1949; student, U. Ill., Chgo., 1970; BA, St. Francis Coll., 1973; MA in Geronology summa cum laude, Sangamon State U., 1982. Co-founder, admin. dir. Mayslake Village, Oakbrook, Ill., 1962, St. Paschal's Infirmary, Oakbrook, 1962; night supr. Godair Home, Hinsdale, Ill., 1958-72; DON King Bruwaert House, Hinsdale, 1973-76; head nurse Mt. Sinai Hosp., Chgo., 1976-82; DON Rosary Hill Home, Justice, Ill., 1989—. Election judge Rep. Com. DuPage County, 1953-98, 2003; mem. adv. bd. Gower Grade Sch., 1973-76; mem. adv. com. Burr Ridge Marriot Brighton Gardens Assisted Living, 1996—. Named Ill. Nurse of Yr. of the Midwest, 1981, Catholic Woman of Yr. 1962, St. Mary's Ch., Joliet, Ill. Mem. Downers Grove and Suburban Nurses Club (pres. Downers Grove chpt.), U. of Ill. Gerontology, Forty and Eight, Premier Nurse Ill., Am. Legion Aux., Sigma Phi Omega (Eta chpt. U. Ill.). Roman Catholic. Avocations: travel, bicycling, doll collecting, reading.

BABIUK, LORNE ALAN, virologist, immunologist, research administrator; b. Canora, Sask., Can., Jan. 25, 1946; s. Paul and Mary (Mayden) Babiuk; m. Betty Lou Carol Wagar, Sept. 29, 1973; children: Shawn, Kimberley. BSA, U. Sask., Saskatoon, 1967, MSc, 1969, DSc, 1987; PhD, U. B.C., Vancouver, 1972. Postdoctoral fellow U. Toronto, Ont., Can., 1972-73; asst. prof. We. Coll. Vet. Medicine, Saskatoon, Sask., 1973-75, assoc. prof., 1975-79, prof., 1979—; assoc. dir. rsch. Vet. Infectious Disease Orgn., Saskatoon, 1984-93, dir., 1993—. Cons. Molecular Genetics, Mpls., 1980—84, Genentech, San Francisco, 1981—84, Ciba Geigy, Basel, Switzerland, 1984—91; Can. rsch. chair in vaccinology. Contbr. Recipient award, Can. Soc. Microbiology, 1990, Am. Vet. Immunology, 1992, Xerox-Can. Forum, 1993, Emerging Sci. and Tech. award for innovation, 1995, Pfizer award in animal health, 1998, Nat. Merit award, 1998, Bill Snowden Meml. award, 2000. Fellow: Royal Soc. Can., Infectious Disease Soc. Am. (Can. Rsch. chair in vaccinology 2001); mem.: Internat. Soc. Antiviral Rsch., Soc. Gen. Microbiology, Can. Soc. Microbiology, Am. Soc. Virology, Am. Soc. Microbiology, Internat. Soc. Interferon Rsch. Achievements include 17 patents in field. Home: 245 East Pl Saskatoon SK Canada S7J 2Y1 Office: Vet Infectious Disease Orgn 120 Veterinary Rd Saskatoon SK S7N 5E3 Canada S7N 5E3 E-mail: babiuk@sask.usask.ca.

BABKO-MALYI, SERGEI VLADIMIROVITCH, process engineer, researcher; b. Kazan, Russia, Nov. 19, 1960; s. Vladimir Grigoevich and L'ubov' Alexandrovna Babko-Malyi; m. Olga Borisovna Rodina, Nov. 15, 1983; children: Daniel, Ekaterina. MSc in Chem. Engring., Leningrad Lensovet Inst. Tech., St. Petersburg, Russia, 1985; MSc in Applied Physics, Rutgers U., 1996. Rsch. engr. Ioffe Physico-Tech. Inst., St. Petersburg, 1984-92; rsch. asst. Rutgers U., Newark, 1994-96; sr. process engr. MSE Tech. Applications, Inc., Butte, Mont., 1996—2001; staff engr. Plasma Sol Corp., Hoboken, NJ, 2001—. Contbr. articles to profl. jours.; patentee method and apparatus for extraction of contaminants from a gas. Assoc. Western Univs. fellow, 1996-97; recipient Recognition award Assoc. Western Univs., 1997. Mem. IEEE, AIAA. Avocation: music. Home: 164 South Ln West Windsor NJ 08550 Office: Plasma Sol Corp 614 River St Hoboken NJ 07030 Fax: 201-216-5427. E-mail: sbabko-malyi@plasmasol.com.

BABLER, WAYNE E. lawyer, retired telephone company executive; b. Orangeville, Ill., Dec. 8, 1915; s. Oscar E. and Mary (Bender) B.; m. Mary Blome, Dec. 27, 1940; children: Wayne Elroy Jr., Marilyn Anne Monson, Sally Jane Sperry. BA, Ind. Cen. Coll., 1935; JD, U. Mich., 1938; LLD, Ind. Cen. U., 1966. Bar: Mich. 1938, N.Y. 1949, Mo. 1955, Wis. 1963, U.S. Supreme Ct. 1963. Assoc. Bishop & Bishop, Detroit, 1938-42, ptnr., 1945-48; atty. AT&T, 1948-55; gen. solicitor Southwestern Bell Tel. Co., St. Louis, 1955-63, v.p., gen. counsel, sec., 1965-80, ret., 1980; v.p., gen. counsel Wis. Tel. Co., Milw., 1963-65. Bd. dirs., chmn. St. Louis Soc. Crippled Children; bd. dirs. St. Louis Symphony Soc. Mem. ABA (chmn. pub. utility sect. 1978-79), Fed. Communications Bar Assn., Mo. Bar Assn., Delray Dunes Country Club, Ocean Club. Home: 19 Holly Dr Boynton Beach FL 33436-5534

BABLER, WAYNE E., JR., lawyer; b. Detroit, Apr. 29, 1942; s. Wayne E. and Mary E. (Blome) B.; m. Patricia A. Ward, Feb. 5, 1972; children: Dean W., Anne E. BA, Wittenberg U., 1964; JD, U. Wis., 1967. Bar: Wis. 1967, U.S. Ct. Appeals (7th cir.) 1971, U.S. Supreme Ct. 1980, U.S. Dist. Ct. (ea. and we. dists.) Wis., 1967, U.S. Dist. Ct. (ctrl. and no. dists.) Ill. 1987, U.S. Dist. Ct. (ea. and we. dists.) Mich. 1990; U.S. Ct. Appeals (9th and 10th cirs.) 1981, U.S. Ct. Appeals (D.C. cir.), 1983. Assoc. Quarles, Herriott, Clemons, Teschner & Noelke, Milw., 1971-74, Quarles & Brady, Milw., 1974-76, ptnr., 1976—. Rep. of chief justice Wis. Supreme Ct. to Wis. Jud. Compensation Com., 1983-84. Author: (with others) Business and Commercial Litigation in Federal Court, 1998; Rsch. editor Wis. Law Rev., 1966-67, Antitrust, Federal Civil Litigation, State Civil Litigation. Mem. U. Wis. Benchers Soc.; campaign cabinet United Performing Arts Fund, Inc., Milw., 1977-78, bd. dirs. Milw. Bar Found., 1976-79, treas., 1977-78; bd. dirs. Wis. Bar Found., 1983-2000, pres., 1985-87; bd. dirs. Legal Aid Soc. Milw., 1997—. With JAGC, USN, 1967-71. Fellow: Wis. Law Found., Am. Coll. Trial Lawyers (state chair 2002—), Am. Bar Found.; mem.: ABA (ho. of dels. 1984—96), Bar Assn. 7th Fed. Cir., Nat. Inst. Trial Advocacy Advocates, State Bar Wis. (bd. govs. 1983—87), Milw. Bar Assn. (bd. dirs. 1976—83, pres. 1981—82), Tripoli Country Club, Univ. Club, Order of Coif. Home: 1475 E Fairy Chasm Rd Milwaukee WI 53217-1433 Office: Quarles & Brady 411 E Wisconsin Ave Milwaukee WI 53202-4497 E-mail: web@quarles.com.

BABLIN, MARK EDWARD, security administrator, mortgage consultant; b. Amsterdam, N.Y., Oct. 30, 1949; s. Edward and Diane B.; m. Mediatrix Ferrer, Aug. 8, 1983 (div. May 1989); children: Francis, Michael, Alex. BS, Siena Coll., 1971; student, Albany State U., 1972. Real estate mgr. Kasow Estates, Phila., 1972-76; credit mgr. Pub. Fin. and Assoc. Fin., Montclair, N.J., 1976-84; security cons. Arboc Security, Reading, Pa., 1984-87; with chem. sales dept. HyTest Industry, Springfield, N.J., 1988-90; dir. corp. security Benjamin Moore/Ingersoll Rand, Woodcliff Lake, N.J., 1990—; mortgage sales cons. Mercury Mortgage, Fairfield, N.J., 1998—. Mem. N.J. Rep. State Com., Trenton, 1988—. Mem. N.J. Rep. Heritage Coun. (nat. vice chair 2000--, Ethnic Leader of Yr. 1989). Roman Catholic. Avocations: photography, travel, history, sports, literature. Home: 53 Linden St Millburn NJ 07041-2132 Office: Ingersoll Rand 200 Chestnut Ridge Rd Woodcliff Lake NJ 07677-7700

BABLITCH, WILLIAM A. state supreme court justice; b. Stevens Point, Wis., Mar. 1, 1941; BS, U. Wis., Madison, 1963, JD, 1968; MA, U. of Virginia, 1987. Bar: Wis. 1968. Pvt. practice law, Stevens Point, Wis.; mem. Wis. Senate, 1972-85, senate majority leader, 1976-82; justice Wis. Supreme Ct., Madison, 1983—; dist. atty. Portage County, Wis., 1969-72. Mem. Nat. Conf. State Legislators (exec. com. 1979) Office: Wis Supreme Ct PO Box 1688 Madison WI 53702-1688*

BABSON, IRVING K. publishing company executive; b. Tel Aviv, Apr. 15, 1936; came to U.S., 1940; s. Matthew and Miriam B.; m. Laurie Sher; children: Stacey B., Mia L., Christopher. BBA, CCNY, 1957; postgrad. NATD seminars, Harvard U., 1965. Dir. Tribune/Fox Cos., 1987-90; chmn. BMT Publs., Inc., Tulsa, 1989-91, Convenience Store News, U.S. Distbn. Jour., Gaming Bus. Mag., Smokeshop Mag., N.Y.C., Jour. Petroleum Mktg., N.Y.C.; mng. ptnr. Babson Capital Ventures, J.V., 1995—, Holdsworth Investments Inc., Belize, 1995—. Ptnr. Mag. Devel. Fund, Babson Family Investment, J.V., N.Y.C., Babson Capital, 1988. With AUS, 1956-57. Mem. Nat. Assn. Corp. Dirs. Clubs: Friars. Home: 19707 Turnberry Way Aventura FL 33180-2566

BABST, JAMES A. lawyer; b. New Orleans, Mar. 31, 1949; BA, Yale U., 1971; JD, Tulane U., 1976. Bar: La. 1976, U.S. Ct. Appeals (5th and 11th cirs.), U.S. Supreme Ct. Mem. Chaffe, McCall, Phillips, Toler & Sarpy, New Orleans. Bd. student editors Tulane Law Rev., 1974-76. Bd. trustees United Way, New Orleans, 1995—. Mem. ABA (ho. of dels. 1994—), La. State Bar Assn. (ho. of dels. 1983-95, sect. antitrust and trade regulation law 1991-93), La. State Law Inst. Coun., La. Jud. Coun. (complex litigation com. 1995—), Order of Coif. Office: Chaffe McCall Phillips Toler & Sarpy 2300 Energy Ctr 1100 Poydras St New Orleans LA 70163-1101

BABULA, WILLIAM, university dean; b. Stamford, Conn., May 19, 1943; s. Benny F. and Lottie (Zajkowski) B.; m. Karen L. Gemi, June 19, 1965; children: Jared, Joelle. BA, Rutgers U., 1965; MA, U. Calif., Berkeley, 1967, PhD, 1969. Asst. prof. English U. Miami, Coral Gables, Fla., 1969-75, assoc. prof., 1975-77, prof., 1977-81, chmn. dept. Eng., 1976-81; dean of arts and humanities Sonoma State U., Rohnert Park, Calif., 1981—. Author: Shakespeare and the Tragicomic Archetype, 1975, Shakespeare in Production, 1935-79, 1981; (short stories) Motorcycle, 1982, Quarterback Sneak, 1983, The First Edsel, 1983, Ransom, 1983, The Last Jogger in Virginia, 1983, The Orthodontist and the Rock Star, 1984, Greenearth, 1984, Football and Other Seasons, The Great American Basketball Shoot, 1984, Ms. Skywriter, Inc., 1987; (plays) The Fragging of Lt. Jones (1st prize Gualala Arts Competition, 1983), Creatures (1st prize Jacksonville U. competition 1987), The Winter of Mrs. Levy (Odyssey Stage Co., New Play Series 1988), Nat. Playwright's Showcase, 1988, Theatre Americana, 1990 (James Ellis award), Basketball Jones, Black Rep of Berkeley, 1988, West Coast Ensemble, Festival of One Acts, 1992, Mark Twain Masquers, 9th Ann. Festival One Act Plays, 1994 (2d Place award), The Last Roundup, 1991 (Odyssey Stage Co.); (novels) The Bombing of Berkeley and Other Pranks (1st prize 24th Ann. Deep South Writers' Conf. 1984), St. John's Baptism, 1988, According to St. John, 1989, St. John and the Seven Veils, 1991, St. John's Bestiary, 1994, St. John's Bread, 1999; contbr. articles to profl. pubs. and short stories to lit. mags. Mem. Shakespeare Assn. of Am., Dramatists Guild, Assoc. Writing Programs, Mystery Writers Am., Phi Beta Kappa. Office: Sonoma State U Sch Arts and Humanities Rohnert Park CA 94928

BABUTS, NICOLAE, French educator; b. Uzdin, Yugoslavia, Dec. 7, 1929; m. Florence Tamas, Sept. 3, 1960. BA in French and English, U. Toronto, Ont., Can., 1957; PhD in French, U. Mich., 1967. Tchg. fellow U. Mich., Ann Arbor, 1963-67; from asst. prof. to prof. French Syracuse (N.Y.) U., 1967-95, prof. emeritus, 1995—. Author: Dynamics of the Metaphoric Field, 1992, Baudelaire, 1997. Mem.: MLA. E-mail: nbabuts@twcny.rr.com.

BACA, JIM, former mayor; BSBA, U. N.Mex. Mayor City of Albuquerque, 1997—2001. Former dir. alcohol and beverage control State of N.Mex., press sec. to gov., commr. pub. lands; past asst. to mayor, gen. mgr. Rio Grande Conservancy Dist.; former dir. Fed. Bur. Land Mgmt.; nat. cons. pub. land and conservation issues. Served with USAF.

BACA, JOE, congressman; b. NM, Jan. 23, 1947; m. Barbara Baca; children: Joe Jr., Jeremy, Natalie, Jennifer. BS in Sociology, Calif. State U., L.A., 1971. Ptnr. Interstate World Travel, San Bernardino, Calif.; formerly with cmty. rels. divsn. GTE; spkr. pro tempore Calif. State Assembly, Sacramento, 1992-97, asst. spkr. pro tempore, spkr.'s fed. govt. liaison, mem. rules com., 1997-98; mem. rules com., vet. affairs com., pub. employment and ret. com., energy, utilities and comm. com., local govt. com., govtl. orgn. com. Calif. State Senate, 1998-99; mem. U.S. Congress from 42nd Calif. Dist., Washington, 1999—; mem. agriculture and sci. coms. U.S. Ho. Reps. Trustee San Bernardino Valley Coll. Dist., 1979—. With U.S. Army, 1966-68, Vietnam. Named Citizen of Distinction San Bernardino Area LWV, Kiwanian of Yr. Greater San Bernardino Kiwanis Club, Disting. Citizen Inland Empire Dist. Boy Scouts Am., Outstanding Legislator Calif. Rifle and Pistol Assn., VFW, 1994-95, Legislator of Yr. Am. Legion, Dept. Calif.; recipient Minority Male of Yr. award Greater Riverside Area Urban League. Democrat. Office: US Ho Reps 328 Cannon Ho Office Bldg Washington DC 20515-0543 also: 201 N E St Ste 102 San Bernardino CA 92401-1520*

BACA, JOSEPH FRANCIS, retired judge; b. Albuquerque, Oct. 1, 1936; s. Amado and Inez (Pino) Baca; m. Dorothy Lee Burrow, June 28, 1969; children: Jolynn, Andrea, Anna Marie. BA in Edn., U. N.Mex., 1960; JD, George Washington U., 1964; LLM, U. Va., 1992. Asst. dist. atty. 1st Jud. Dist., Santa Fe, 1965-66; pvt. practice Albuquerque, 1966-72; dist. judge 2d Jud. Dist., Albuquerque, 1972-88; justice N.Mex Supreme Ct., Santa Fe, 1989—2002, chief justice, 1995-97; ret., 2002. Spl. asst. to atty. gen. Office of N.Mex Atty. Gen., Albuquerque, 1966—71. Bd. dirs. State Justice Inst., 1994—, vice chmn., 1999—; Dem. precinct chmn. Albuquerque, 1968; del. N.Mex Constl. Conv., Santa Fe, 1969. Named one of 100 Most Influential Hispanics, Hispanic Bus. Mag., 1997, 1998; recipient Judge of the Yr. award, People's Commn. Criminal Justice, 1989, Quincentennial Commemoration Achievement award, La Hispanidad Com., 1992, Luchando pro la Justicia award, Mex. Am. Law Students Assn. U. N.Mex Law Sch., 1993, J. William Fulbright Disting. Pub. Svc. award, George Washington U. Alumni Assn., 1994, Recognition and Achievement award, Commn. Opportunities for Minorities in the Profession, 1992, others. Mem.: ABA, N.Mex Hispanic Bar Assn. (Outstanding Hispanic Atty. award 2000), Santa Fe Bar Assn., Albuquerque Bar Assn., Am. Jud. Soc. (bd. dirs. 1999—), Scribes (bd. dirs. 1998—), Am. Law Inst., N.Mex Bar Assn. (Outstanding Jud. Svc. award 1998, Disting. Jud. Svc. award 2002), Hispanic Nat. Bar Assn. (Lincoln-Juarez award 2000), Alumni Assn. (pres. 1980—81), KC, Kiwanis (pres. Albuquerque chpt. 1984—85, dep. grand knight 1968). Roman Catholic. Avocation: reading history.

BACALL, LAUREN, actress; b. N.Y.C., Sept. 16, 1924; m. Humphrey Bogart, May 21, 1945 (dec. 1957); children: Stephen, Leslie; m. Jason Robards, July, 1961 (div.); 1 son, Sam. Student pub. schs., Am. Acad. Dramatic Art. Actress in Broadway plays Franklin Street, 1942, Goodbye Charlie, 1959; motion picture actress, 1944—, film appearances include To Have and Have Not, 1945, Confidential Agent, 1945, The Big Sleep, 1946, Dark Passage, 1947, Key Largo, 1948, Young Man With a Horn, 1949, Bright Leaf, 1950, How To Marry a Millionaire, 1953, Woman's World, 1954, The Cobweb, 1955, Blood Alley, 1955, Written on the Wind, 1956, Designing Woman, 1957, The Gift of Love, 1958, Flame Over India, 1959, Shock Treatment, 1964, Sex and the Single Girl, 1965, Harper, 1966, Murder on the Orient Express, 1974, The Shootist, 1976, Health, 1980, The Fan, 1981, Tree of Hands, 1987, Appointment With Death, 1987, Mr. North, 1988, Misery, 1990, A Star for Two, 1991, All I Want for Christmas, 1991, Ready to Wear (Prêt-à-Porter), 1994, My Fellow Americans, 1996, The Mirror Has Two Faces, 1996 (Golden Globe award, 1997, SAG award, 1997), The Line King: Al Hirschfield, 1996, Le Jour et la Nuit, 1997, Diamonds, 1999, Dogville, 2002; appeared in Broadway play Cactus Flower, 1966-68, Applause, 1969-71 (Sarah Siddons award 1975); also road co., 1971-72, London co., 1972-73 (Tony award for best actress in a musical 1970); Broadway play Woman of the Year, 1981 (Tony award for best actress in a musical 1981, Sarah Siddons award 1983), Sweet Bird of Youth, 1983 (London, 1985, Australia, 1986, L.A., 1987; TV spl. The Paris Collections, 1968, Applause, 1973, A Commercial Break (Happy Endings), 1975; TV movies: Perfect Gentlemen, 1978, Dinner at Eight, 1989, The Portrait, 1992, A Foreign Field, 1993, From the Mixed Up Files of Mrs. Basil E. Frankweiler, 1995; author: Lauren Bacall By Myself, 1978, Lauren Bacall Now, 1994. Recipient Am. Acad. Dramatic Arts award for achievement, 1963, Standard award London Evening, 1973, Nat. Book award, 1979; decorated comdr. Order of Arts and Letters (France), 1995. Office: care Johnnie Planco William Morris Agy 1325 Avenue Of The Americas New York NY 10019-6026*

BACALOGLU, RADU, chemical engineer; b. Bucharest, Romania, July 21, 1937; came to the U.S., 1985; s. Dan and Elena (Lazarescu) B.; m. Ilze Irina Schiff, Aug. 29, 1963; 1 child, Radu Dan. MSChE, Poly. Inst., Romania, 1959, PhD in Organic Chemistry, 1968. Asst. prof. Poly. Inst., Timisoara, Romania,

1959-79, prof. chemistry, 1979-85; rsch. assoc. U. Calif., Santa Barbara, 1985-89; asst. prof. Rutgers U., New Brunswick, N.J., 1989-91; group leader R&D vinyl Witco Corp., Oakland, N.J., 1991-97, mgr. R&D vinyl Tarrytown, N.Y., 1997—. Dir. rsch. group of homogeneous and enzymatic catalysis Inst. Chem. Energetics, Bucharest, 1981-85. Author 2 books, more than 180 papers; contbr. articles to Rev. Roumaine Chemie, Tetrahedron, Spectrochimica Acta, Jour. Am. Chem. Soc. Phys. Chem. Polymer Degree Stabilization, others. Recipient 1st prize for scientific rsch. Ministry of Edn., Romania, 1965, G. Spacu award for rsch. in chemistry Romanian Acad., 1981. Mem. Am. Chem. Soc., N.Y. Acad. Scis., Soc. Plastic Engrs., AAAS. Achievements include 13 patents in organic chemistry; research in physical and synthetic organic chemistry, kinetic study of degradation and stabilization of polymers, especially polyvinyl chloride. Home: 27 Burlington Ct Hamburg NJ 07419-1320 Office: Witco 771 Old Saw Mill River Rd Tarrytown NY 10591-6716 E-mail: bacalra@cromptoncorp.com.

BACANI, NICANOR-GUGLIELMO VILA, civil and structural engineer, consultant; b. Dagupan City, Pangasinan, Philippines, Jan. 10, 1947; s. Jose Montero and Felisa (Vila) B.; m. Julie Bacani, June 24, 1972; children: Julinor, Jazmin, Joymita, Normina, Nicky, Noel.. BSCE, U. Philippines, 1968, M in Engring. Stuctures, 1973. Registered profl. engr., Philippines. Structural engr. FR Estuar, PhD. Assocs., Quezon City, Philippines, 1970-72; civil structural engr. BestPhil Cons., Dagupan City, 1972-73; engring. mgr. Supreme Structural Products, Inc., Manila, 1974; chief engr. Tecphil Cons., Quezon City, 1974-76; v.p. Erectors, Inc., Makati, Philippines, 1977-81; pres. NGV Bacani & Assocs., various locations, 1981—. Advisor, cons. Met. Manila Office of Commr. Planning, 1980-85; profl. lectr. U. Manila Grad. Sch., 1982-83; resource person Nat. Engring. Ctr. U.P., Quezon City, 1983—; cons. Geo. J. Fosdyke Assocs., L.A., 1985-86, Victor Constrn. & Devel., 1986-87, Stanley Assocs. Internat., 1988, H.A. Simons Internat., 1988-90, Azlon Devel. Corp., 1990—; pres. Mgmt. Design & Investment Co., 1987—; sr. structural cons. Seismic Engring. Ltd., 1990—; sr. cons. Davey Gibson Cons., 1991-92; pres. Bestphil Can., 1992—, Seismic Cons., 1993—; cons. Chemetics Internat., 1994—; sr. cons. Sturdy Engring. Corp., Wash., 1997—; pres. Bestphil Enterprises Internat., 2000—. Author: A Reference for Engineers and Builders, 1983. Mem. Internat. Assn. Bridge and Structural Engrs. Switzerland, Assn. Structural Engrs. Philippines (life, bd. dirs. 4 terms), U. Philippines Alumni Engrs. Assn. (life), Nat. Geog. Soc., Nature Conservancy. Avocations: guitar playing, choir, dancing. Office: 1104-29th St #4 Anacortes WA 98221

BACCIGALUPPI, ROGER JOHN, agricultural company executive; b. N.Y.C., Mar. 17, 1934; s. Harry and Ethel (Hutcheon) B.; m. Patricia Marie Wier, Feb. 6, 1960 (div. 1978); children: John, Elisabeth, Andrea; m. Iris Christine Walfridson, Feb. 3, 1979; 1 child, Jason. BS, U. Calif., Berkeley, 1956; MS, Columbia U., 1957. Asst. sales promotion mgr. Maco Mag. Corp., N.Y.C., 1956-57; merchandising asst. Honig, Cooper & Harrington, San Francisco and L.A., 1957-58, 1958-60, asst. dir. merchandising, 1960-61; sales rep. Blue Diamond Growers (formerly Calif. Almond Growers Exch.), Sacramento, 1961-64, mgr. advt. and sales promotion, 1964-70, v.p. mktg., 1970-73, sr. v.p. mktg., 1973-74, exec. v.p., 1974-75, pres., 1975-91; founder RB Internat., Sacramento, 1992—. Vice chmn., bd. dirs. Agrl. Coun. Calif., 1975-91; mem. consumer-prodr. com., adminstrn. com.; mem. U.S. adv. com. Trade Policy and Negotiations, 1983-2002; mem. U.S. adv. bd. Rabobank Nederlands, 1988-91; mem. Calif. World Trade Commn., 1993-2001; mem. adv. coun. Nat. Ctr. for Food and Agr. Policy Resources for Future, 1990-99. Vice chmn. Calif. State R.R. Mus. Found.; chmn. Cmty. Colls. Found.; vice chmn. Grad. Inst. Cooperative Leadership, 1986-87, chair, 1987-89; bd. dirs. Valley Vision, Inc., 1995-2003. With AUS, 1957. Mem. Calif. C. of C. (chmn. internat. trade com. 1988-94, bd. dirs. 1988—, vice chmn. bd. 1992-94, chmn. bd. 1995, Sacramento Host Com. (chmn. 1997, 98), Calif. for Higher Edn., Grad. Inst. Coop. Leadership (chmn., trustee), Grocery Mfrs. Am., Inc. (bd. dirs. 1988-91), Sutter Club. Office: RB Internat 777 Campus Commons Rd Ste 200 Sacramento CA 95825-8343

BACCINI, LAURANCE ELLIS, lawyer; b. Nov. 16, 1945; m. Tracey Judith Lane, Dec. 20, 1969; 1 child, Allyson Alexandra Lane. BS, Drexel U., 1968; JD, Villanova U., 1971. Bar: Pa. 71, U.S. Dist. Ct. (ea. dist.) Pa. 73, U.S. Ct. Appeals (3d cir.) 79. Law clk. to chief judge U.S. Dist. Ct. (ea. dist.) Pa., 1971—73; assoc. Schnader, Harrison, Segal & Lewis, Phila., 1973—78, ptnr., 1979—91, mem. exec. com., 1990—91; ptnr. Wolf, Block, Schorr and Solis-Cohen, 1991—2002, Klehr, Harrison, Harvey, Branzburg & Ellers LLP, Phila., 2002—. Spkr., faculty mem. on labor law Practicing Law Inst., N.Y.C.; trustee Phila. Bar Found., 1986—; bd. dirs. Interest on Lawyers Inst. Acct. Bd. Author: NLRA Supervisor's Handbook; assoc. editor: albums. Recipient Drexel One Hundred honor award, 1992. Mem.: ABA (former chmn. and dir. young lawyers divsn. 1981—82, ho. of dels. 1988—, chmn. long-range planning com., fed. jud. standards com., mem. editl. bd. The Labor Lawyer, young lawyers divsn. fed. practice com., jud. conf. for 3d cir.), Greater Phila. C. of C. (bd. dirs. 1988), Pa. Bar Assn., Phila. Bar Assn. (commn. on jud. selection, retention and evaluation 1978—79, bd. govs. 1978—, chmn. 1982, ho. of dels. 1983—, vice chancellor 1986, chancellor-elect 1987, chancellor 1988, chmn. exec. com. young lawyers sect., chmn. long range planning com.). Office: Klehr Harrison Harvey Branzburg & Ellers LLP 260 S Broad St Philadelphia PA 19102

BACEVICIUS, JOHN ANTHONY, V, (JOHN BACE), research executive; b. Chgo., Mar. 8, 1953; s. John Anthony IV and Mary Ann (Slazas) B.; m. Irene Joyce Rooney, Oct. 16, 1976; 1 child, John Anthony VI. BS in Psychology, Polit. Sci., Rockford Coll., 1975; MS in Journalism, Northwestern U., 1982; postgrad., The Union Inst. Accredited pub. rels. profl. Reporter, editor United Press Internat., Chgo., 1974-79; managing editor WCFL-AM, Mutual Broadcasting, Chgo., 1979-80; writer, editor WIND. Group W Westinghouse, Chgo., 1980-81; reporter, writer WBBM-AM, CBS News, Chgo., 1981-82; comms. advisor IBM Corp., Chgo., 1982—91; pres. J.A. Bace Comms., Inc., 1991—; dir. mktg., rsch. and industry rels. Technology Solutions Co., Chgo., 1995-97; v.p., dir. rsch. and knowledge assets Gartner, Inc., Chgo., 1997—. Asst. prof. Northwestern U., Evanston, Ill., 1988-92; mgr. media rels. Zenith Data Systems, 1992-93. Nat. Sea Explorer Boy Scouts Am. Com., Irving, Tex., 1986-95, recipient Quartermaster award, 1972, Silver Beaver award, 1990; Vigil honor, 1971. Gannett fellow, Northwestern U., 1981. Mem. NATAS, Pub. Rels. Soc. Am., Internat. Assn. Bus. Comms., U.S. Naval Inst., Publicity Club of Chgo., Soc. Profl. Journalists, Radio-TV News Dirs. Assn., U.S. Navy League (life). Roman Catholic. Avocations: backpacking, hiking, sailing, photography. Home: 252 W Washington Ave Lake Bluff IL 60044-2036 Office: Gartner Inc Sears Tower 233 S Wacker Dr Ste 1810 Chicago IL 60606 E-mail: john.bace@gartner.com.

BACH, BETTY JEAN, health services educator; b. Jackson, Ky., Dec. 25, 1952; d. Eugene Parker and Celeste White B. AA, Ea. Ky. U., 1975, BS, 1995; student, Ohio U., 1984, Morehead U., 1986. RN, Ky.; cert. ob-gyn. nurse practitioner, advanced RN practitioner; cert. family planning nurse practitioner. Staff nurse, nurse practitioner Breathitt County Health Dept., Jackson, Ky., 1975-80; sch. health nurse, health svcs. coord. Breathitt County Bd. Edn., Jackson, 1983-88; health svcs. instr. Breathitt Area Vocat. Edn. Ctr., Jackson, 1988—. Mem. NEA, Ky. Edn. Assn. Am. Vocat. Assn., Vocat. Assn. Kappa Delta Pi. Home: 13546 Hwy 30 E Rousseau KY 41366 E-mail: bbach28073@aol.com.

BACH, CYNTHIA, educational program director, writer; b. Oct. 28; BA in Art Edn., UCLA, 1955; MPA, U. So. Calif., 1978; LDS, Calif. Luth., 1993. Cert. gen. elem., spl. secondary art, and gen. jr. h.s. tchr. Staff asst. L.A. Unified Sch. Dist., 1976; rainbow tchr., gifted coord. Trinity Elem. Sch., L.A., 1978-81; field worker/in-svc. for parents and staff educator Hubbard Elem. Sch., Sylmar, Calif., 1981-90; student observer Liggett Elem. Sch., Panorama City, Calif., 1990-92; tng. tchr. Calif. State U. (Northridge)-Vena Sch., Arleta, Calif., 1992-93; pres. Comprehensive Learning Systems. Rsch. bd. advisors Am. Biograph. Inst., Inc. Author: Alternatives to Retail Marketing for Seniors (Bur. of Consumer Affairs); creator: (theological game) Might is the Wind. Lectr. Sr. Citizens Bur. Consumer Affairs, City Hall; past pres. local PTA; del. Children's Def. Fund Conf., 1998; sch. bd. mem. St. Martin-in-the-Fields Parish Sch.; mem. coun. bd. Amnesty Internat.; sponsor Christian Found. for Children and Aging; mem. Mus. of Tolerance, Alliance for Tolerance; co-founder scholarship fund for women ministers; ofcl. hostess rep. for vis. diplomats through the World Affairs Coun. City of Los Angeles; lay eucharistic min., 1998; established scholarship fund King's Sem. Ch. on the Way. Named 79 State Evaluation Mar Team-outstanding educator, Phi Alpha Alpha, Nat. Acad. Hon. Soc. Pub. Affairs Adminstrn., Order of Internat. Fellows Edn., Outstanding Woman of 20th Century, 2000, on Wall of Tolerance, Montgomery, Ala.; named to Nat. Divsn. Rsch. Bd. Advisors, Am. Biog. Inst.; recipient Spl. Recognition award, 21st Century Award for Achievement, Pres.'s Award of Merit as outstanding citizen in field of edn.; scholar, Nat. Art, Chouinard Art Inst. Mem. NAFE, AAUW, 1st Century Soc. UCLA, Nat. Mus. Women in Arts (assoc.), Phi Alpha Alpha. Avocations: reading, theology, old movies, writing, gardening. Home: 5140 White Oak Ave Apt 214 Encino CA 91316-2435

BACH, JAN MORRIS, composer, educator; b. Forrest, Ill., Dec. 11, 1937; s. John Nicholas and Anne (Morris) B.; m. Dalia Zakaras; children: Dawn, Eva. *His father, J.N. Bach, was born in 1913 and has been active as a Boy Scout volunteer for over sixty years, co-founding two wilderness camps in Minnesota and Ontario and serving as the chairman of the second one for twenty-four years; his hard work and dedication were recognized recently by the Ontario Names Board with a Canadian bay named "Bach Bay" in his honor. Dr. Bach's wife, Dalia, singer and actress, directed the choral program at the prestigious Illinois Mathematics and Science Academy for the last thirteen years.* MusB, U. Ill., 1959, MusM, 1961, MusD, 1971; postgrad., U. Va., Arlington, 1963-65, Yale U., summer 1960, Berkshire Music Ctr., summer 1961. Instr. music U. Tampa, Fla., 1965-66; prof. music No. Ill. U., DeKalb, 1966—2002, Presdl. Rsch. prof. Dekalb, 1982-86, Disting. Rsch. prof., 1986—; composer-in-residence Institut de Hautes Etudes Musicales, Montreux, Switzerland, 1976; editor for brass compositions M.M. Cole, Chgo., 1969-72. Mem. Ill. Arts Coun., 1986-89, Ind. Arts Coun., 1992. Composer: Skizzen, 1967, Woodwork, 1970, Eisteddfod, 1972, Turkish Music, 1968, Four Two-Bit Contraptions, 1971, The System, 1973, Dirge for a Minstrel, 1974, Three Choral Dances, 1975, Laudes, 1975, Piano Concerto, 1975, Three Bagatelles, 1978, Hair Today, 1978, The Happy Prince, 1978, My Wilderness, 1979, Student from Salamanca, 1979, Rounds and Dances, 1980, Horn Concerto, 1982, Helix, 1984, Escapade, 1984, Dompes & Jompes, 1986, Harp Concerto, 1986, Trumpet Concerto, 1987, A Solemn Music, 1987, Triptych, 1989, Euphonium Concerto, 1990, With Trumpet and Drum, 1991, Anachronisms String Quartet, 1991, People of Note, 1993, Concerto for Steelpan and Orchestra, 1994, The Last Flower, 1995, Pollations, 1995, Bassoon Concertino, 1996, Pilgrimage, 1997, Variations on a Theme of Brahms, 1997, Kimberly's Song, 1998, Dear God, 1998, NIU MIUSIC, 1999, In the Hands of the Tongue, 1999, The Duel, 1999, Songs of the Streetwise, 2000, Music for a Low Budget Epic, 2001, If Music be the Food of Love, 2001, Tuba Concerto, 2003, Choral Fanfare, 2003. Served with U.S. Army, 1962—65. Recipient BMI student composers 1st prize, 1957, Koussevitsky composition award, 1961, Harvey Gaul composition award, 1973, Mannes Opera award, 1973, Pulitzer prize nomination, 1973, 81, 82, 84, 92, SAI composition award, 1974, Excellence in Tchg. award No. Ill. U., 1978, choral composition award Brown U., 1978, Nebr. Sinfonia Chamber Orch. contest, 1979, N.Y.C. Opera contest, 1980; commns. include Tuba Brotherhood, 1977, Internat. Trumpet Guild, 1978, 86, Internat. Brass Congress, 1980, Greenwich Philharmonia, 1981, Orch. of Ill., 1982, NACWPI, 1982, Minot Symphony, 1984, Am. Brass Quintet-Chamber Music Am., 1988, Sacramento Symphony-N.C. Symphony, 1989, Camarata Singers, 1991, WFMT-Vermeer Quartet, 1991, Woodstock Chimes Fund, 1994, Ronen Chamber Ensemble, 1994, Stockholm Chamber Brass, 1994, Eileen Gress-N.C. Symphony, 1995, Elmhurst Symphony, 1996, Ramon Parcells, 1996, Palos Park Cmty. Chorale, 1997, Cantori of Hobart and William Smith Colls., 1998, Northern Ill. Children's Chorus, 1999, So. Bend Chamber Singers, 1999, Robert Sims, 1999, Regina H. Helcher, 2000, Jeff Nesseth, 2001, Jay Hunsberger-Fla. West Coast Symphony,2002, Gloria Musicae, 2003. Mem. Coll. Mus. Soc., Broadcast Music, Phi Eta Sigma, Phi Mu Alpha, Phi Kappa Phi, Pi Kappa Lambda., Omicron Delta Kappa E-mail: janbach@janbach.com.

BACH, JONATHAN P.G. political scientist; b. N.Y.C., Jan. 26, 1966; s. Robert and Suzanne Bach; m. Yukiko Koga. BA, U. Mass., 1988; MA, Syracuse U., N.Y., 1993; PhD, Syracuse U., 1997. Program officer Inst. for East-West Studies, N.Y.C., NY, 1988—90; postdoctoral rsch. fellow Harvard U., Cambridge, Mass., 1998; postdoctoral rsch. scholar Columbia U., N.Y.C., 1999—2002; core faculty New Sch. U., N.Y.C., 2002—. Author: Between Sovereignty and Integration: German Foreign Policy and National Identity after 1989, 1999; contbr. articles. Mem.: German Studies Assn., Internat. Studies Assn., Am. Polist. Sci. Assn.

BACH, JUDIT, music educator; arrived in U.S., 1990; d. Ivan Bach and Hedy; 1 child, Géza. MS, Eötvös Lóránd Sci. U., Budapest, 1987, U. Oreg., 1993, MusB, 1995; MusM, Ohio State U., 1997, postgrad. Grad. tchg. asst. music Ohio State U., Columbus, 1995—2000, grad. tchr. asst. math., 2000—, instr. music and piano Jefferson Acad. Music, 2002—, lectr. music and piano, 2003—. Mem. adj. faculty math. Columbus State C.C., 2002—; mem. adj. faculty music Ohio Wesleyan U., 2003—. Translator articles to profl. jours. V.p. Grad. Music Students Assn., Columbus, 2001—02; del. Coun. Grad. Students, Columbus, 2000—02. Recipient Grad. award for mus. excellence, Ohio Fedn. Music Clubs; presdl. fellow, Ohio State U., 2001—02. Mem.: Music Soc, Phi Kappa Lambda, Phi Kappa Phi.

BACH, ROBERT J. information technology executive; BA in Econ., U. N.C.; MBA, Stanford U. Fin. analyst Morgan Stanley & Co.; from product mgr. to sr. v.p. Microsoft, Redmond, Wash., 1988—98, sr. v.p. games divsn., chief Xbox officer, 1998—. Office: One Microsoft Way Redmond WA 98052-6399

BACH, STEVE CRAWFORD, lawyer; b. Jackson, Ky., Jan. 31, 1921; s. Bruce Grannis and Evelyn (Crawford) B.; m. Rosemary Husted, Sept. 6, 1947; children— John Crittenden, Greta Christine AB, Ind. U., 1943, JD, 1948; postgrad. Eastern studies, U. Mich., 1944, Nat. Trial Judges Coll., 1966, U. Minn. Juvenile Inst., 1967. Bar: Ky. 1948, Ind. 1948. Atty. Bach & Bach, Jackson, Ky., 1948-51; investigator U.S. CSC, Indpls., 1951-54; sole practice Mt. Vernon, Ind., 1954-65, 83—; judge 11th Jud. Circuit, Mt. Vernon, Ind., 1965-82; pres. Internat. Inst. for Youth, Inc., Mt. Vernon, 1985-90; sr. judge State of Ind., 1997—. Spl. overseas rep. Nat. Council Juvenile and Family Ct. Judges, 1983-86, bd. trustees, 1979-83; moderator Ind. Conf. Crime and Delinquency, Indpls., 1968; tchr. seminar on juvenile delinquency, Ind. Trial Judges Assn., 1969, del. Internat. Youth Magistrates Conf., Geneva, 1970, Oxford, Eng., 1974, Can., 1977; faculty adviser Criminal Law Inst., Nat. Trial Judges Coll., 1973; treas. Ind. Council Juvenile Ct. Judges, 1975, v.p., 1976, pres., 1978-79; bd. dirs. Jud. Conf., Ind. Jud. Ctr., 1978-79; faculty adviser Nat. Jud. Coll., 1978; mem. faculty Seminar for Inst. for New Judges, State of Ind., 1979. Pres. Greater Mt. Vernon Assn., 1958-59; past mem. Juvenile Justice divsn. Ind. Jud. Study Commn.; mem. Ind. Gov.'s Juvenile Justice Delinquency Prevention Adv. Bd., 1976-78, community adv. coun. Ind. U. Sch. Medicine, 1986-96. With intelligence Signal Corps, AUS, 1943-46. Mem. Nat. Coun. Juvenile Ct. Judges, Am. Legion, Ind. Bar Assn. (del.), Ind. Judges Assn. (mem. bd. mgrs. 1966-71), Masons, Elks, Kiwanis, Sigma Delta Kappa, Delta Tau Delta. Democrat. Methodist. Home and Office: 512 Walnut St Mount Vernon IN 47620-1862

BACH, THOMAS HANDFORD, lawyer, investor; b. Vineland, N.J., Dec. 25, 1928; s. Albert Ludwig and Edith May (Handford) B. AB, Rutgers U., 1950; LLB, Harvard U., 1956. Bar: N.Y. State bar 1957. Assoc. firm Hawkins, Delafield & Wood, N.Y.C., 1956—61, Reed, Hoyt, Washburn & McCarthy, N.Y.C., 1961—62; ptnr. Bach & Condren, N.Y.C., 1963—71, Bach & McAuliffe, N.Y.C., 1971—79, Stroock & Stroock & Lavan, N.Y.C., 1979—88, Sullivan & Donovan, N.Y.C., 1989—2000, of counsel, 2000—02, Sullivan, Donovan & Gentile, N.Y.C., 2002—; arbitrator Nat. Assn of Securities Dealers Reg., 2000—. Co-counsel N.Y. State Senate Housing and Urban Devel. Com., 1971; fiscal cons. N.Y.C. Fin. Adminstrn., 1967-70; asst. counsel State Fin. Com., N.Y. State Constl. Conv. of, 1967; del. U.S./Japan Bilateral Session, 1988, Moscow Conf. on Law and Bilateral Econ. Rels., 1990; spkr. Practicing Law Inst., Mcpl. Bond Workshop, N.Y., 1995-97. Contbr. articles to profl. jours.; co-author: A Guide to Certificates of Participation, 1991, the Handbook of Municipal Bonds, 1994. Mem. N.Y. State Commn. to Study Constl. Tax Limitations, 1974-75; chmn. subcom. Pub. Securities Assn., 1990-91; dir. Citizens Union of N.Y. Served with U.S. Army, 1951-53, 1st lt. U.S. Army, 1952-53, Japan. Mem. ABA (state and local govt., dispute resolution and internat. law. sects.), N.Y. State Bar Assn., Assn. of Bar of City of N.Y., N.J. Bar Assn., N.Y. Mcpl. Analysts Group (chmn. 1973-74), Mcpl. Forum of N.Y., Market Technicians Assn. (affiliate), Internat. Fin. Svcs. Vol. Corps. Episcopalian. Home: 4 E 89th St New York NY 10128-0636 also: 615 W Oak Rd Vineland NJ 08360-2262 Office: Sullivan Donovan & Gentile 20th Flr 40 Exchange Pl New York NY 10005

BACHARACH, BURT, composer, conductor; b. Kansas City, Mo., May 29, 1929; s. Bert and Irma (Freeman) Bacharach; m. Paula Stewart; m. Angie Dickinson (div.); 1 child, Lea Nikki; m. Carole Bayer Sager, Mar. 30, 1982 (div.); 1 child, Christopher Elton. Student, McGill U.; pupil Darius Milhaud at, New Sch. for Social Rsch.; pupil Henry Cowell at, Music Acad. West, Santa Barbara, Calif. Accompanist Vic Damone, 1952, Polly Bergen, Georgia Gibbs, Joel Gray, Ames Bros., Marlene Dietrich; now composer songs, film scores, stage musicals; frequent collaborator Carole Bayer Sager. Composer: Raindrops Keep Fallin' on My Head, Magic Moments, The Story of My Life, Don't Make Me Over, Walk on By, Trains and Boats and Planes, Close to You, Anyone Who Had a Heart, What the World Needs Now, I'll Never Fall in Love Again, Do You Know the Way to San Jose?, The Look of Love, One Less Bell to Answer, Alfie (Grammy award, 1967), Heartlight, Power, On My Own, Arthur's Theme, That's What Friends Are For (Grammy award, 1986), (film scores) The Man Who Shot Liberty Valence, 1962, Wives and Lovers, 1963, Send Me No Flowers, 1964, A House is Not a Home, 1964, Who's Been Sleeping in My Bed, 1964, What's New Pussycat?, 1965, Alfie, 1966, Promise Her Anything, 1966, After the Fox, 1966, Casino Royale, 1967, The April Fools, 1969, Butch Cassidy and the Sundance Kid, 1969 (Acad. awards, 1969), Lost Horizon, 1972, Together?, 1979, Arthur, 1981 (Acad. award), Night Shift, 1982, Best Defense, 1984, Baby Boom, 1987, Arthur 2: On the Rocks, 1988, Love Hurts, 1991, Fargo, 1996, Grace of My Heart, 1996, (TV series) Any Day Now, 1998—; composer music for play Promises, Promises, 1969 (Drama Desk award, 1968, Grammy award, 1969), recs. for A&M Records, Kapp Records; actor: The Bacharach-David Song Book, 1970. Served with AUS, 1950—52. Named (with David) Entertainers of Yr., Cue Mag., 1969; recipient 3 Acad. awards, 5 Grammy awards, 2 Emmy awards, Tony award.

BACHARACH, MELVIN LEWIS, retired venture capitalist; b. Oakland, Calif., May 14, 1924; s. Max and Ellen Mildred (LeValley) B.; m. Vera Patricia Mortimer, Aug. 20, 1950; children: Kimberly Bacharach Arnone, Craig Ronald. BCBA, U. Calif., Berkeley, 1948. With Levi Strauss & Co., 1948-70, v.p., then exec. v.p., 1973-79, pres. U.S. group, 1975-79, also bd. dirs., mem. exec. com.; pres., CEO Internat. Bus. Sponsors, Inc., 1979-86, also bd. dirs.; pres., CEO VMB, Inc., San Francisco, 1986-98, ret., 1998; mng. ptnr. Diamond View LP, San Francisco, 1973—. Bd. dirs. Internat. Bus. Sponsors, Inc., Above the Belt, Inc. Patentee in field. Served as pilot USNR, 1942-46, 51-53. Decorated Air medal. Mem. U. Calif. Bus. Adminstrn. Alumni Assn., Beta Gamma Sigma, Pi Lambda Phi. Clubs: Marine Meml., Mira Vista Country, Concordia Argonaut, Palm Valley Country, Avondale Golf Club.

BACHE, WILLIAM B. retired literature educator, editor, writer; b. Nanticoke, Pa., May 8, 1922; s. Thomas Cartwright Bache and Edith Davies; 1 child, Nancy Hutchinson. BA, Pa. State U., State Coll., Pa., 1947, MA, 1948, PhD, 1952. Instr. Eng. Pa. State U., 1952, Purdue U., West Lafayette, Ind., 1953, asst. prof., 1953—56, assoc. prof., 1956—62, prof., 1962—69. Editor: Modern Fiction Studies, 1956—92; author: (books) Design and Closure in Shakespeare, 1991, Shakespeare's Deliberate Art, 1996, On the Road to Innsbruck and Back, 2001. With U.S. Army, 1942—46, ETO. Meth. Avocations: poetry, walking, golf. Home: 616 Hillcrest Rd West Lafayette IN 47906-2350

BACHELDER, JOSEPH ELMER, III, lawyer; b. Fulton, Mo., Nov. 13, 1932; s. Joseph Elmer and Frances Evelyn (Gray) B.; m. Louise Este Mason, June 12, 1955; children: Louise Stewart Bachelder Alcock, Christina Cathryn Bachelder Dufresne, Hilary Houston. BA magna cum laude, Yale U., 1955; LLB, Harvard U., 1958. Bar: N.Y. 1959. Assoc. Mudge, Rose, Guthrie & Alexander, N.Y.C., 1958-67, McKinsey and Co., Inc., N.Y.C., 1967-69; ptnr. Satterlee and Stephens, N.Y.C., 1969-72, Leboeuf, Lamb, Lieby & MacRae, N.Y.C., 1972-80; founder, sr. ptnr. Law Offices Joseph E. Bachelder, N.Y.C., 1980—; chmn. The Bachelder Group, Inc., 1989—. Lectr. NYU Ann. Inst. on Fed. Taxation, 1972-74, Practicing Law Inst., 1977-80, 2000, Am. Law Inst., 1980, 97, 98, The Conf. Bd., 1986. Co-author, editor: Employee Stock Ownership Plans, 1979; columnist N.Y. Law Jour. 1977—; speaker Academia Symposia Stanford Law Sch., 1999, 2000, Northwestern U., Kellogg Sch. Bus., 1999, U. Del., 2000. Mem. Princeton Twp. (N.J.) Zoning Bd., 1981-82; trustee Concord (Mass.) Acad., 1986-92. Fellow Am. Coll. Tax Counsel; mem. ABA, N.Y. State Bar Assn., Assn. of Bar of N.Y.C. Clubs: The Down Town Assn. (N.Y.), Yale Club N.Y.; Bedens Brook (Princeton), Nassau (Princeton); Siasconset Casino (Nantucket, Mass.). Republican. Congregationalist. Home: 226 Constitution Dr Princeton NJ 08540-6712 Office: 780 3rd Ave New York NY 10017-2024

BACHELDER, ROBERT STEPHEN, minister; b. Middletown, N.Y., Nov. 2, 1951; s. Stephen and Dorothy Esther (Gunderson) B.; m. Beverly June Brandt, Sept. 17, 1977; children: Stephen, Elizabeth. AB, Dartmouth Coll., 1973; MDiv, Yale U., 1978. Ordained to ministry United Ch. of Christ, 1978. Money markets trader R.I. Hosp. Trust Nat. Bank, Providence, 1973-75; pastor United Ref. Ch., Pangbourne, Eng., 1978-79; min. 1st Congl. Ch., Shrewsbury, Mass., 1980-84; min. for mission and svc. Worcester (Mass.) Area Mission Soc., 1984—. Advisor to religious congregations for charitable giving. Author: Mystery and Miracle, 1983, Between Dying and Birth, 1983; contbr. chpts. to books, articles to profl. jours. Bd. dirs. Mass. Coun. of Chs., 1991—93, Worcester Interfaith, 1992—94, Worcester County Ecumenical Coun., 1992—96, Mass. Conv. Congl. Mins., 1983—85, Ctrl. Assn. Mass. Conf., United Ch. of Christ, 1983—, Worcester Coop. Coun., 1985—89, Accord: The Ctr. for Human Rels., 1991—93, Corx, Inc., 1993—, WCHR Securities, Inc., 1993—, Mass. Congl. Fund, 1999—, New Am. Cmty. Forum, 1995—97, Pakachoag Cmty. Music Sch., 1996—98, Congl. Christian Hist. Soc., 1997—, Worcester Pastoral Counseling Ctr., 1998—2000, Greater Worcester Cmty. Found. Exec. Com., 1998—, Colony Retirement Homes, 1998—, Worcester Area Campus Ministry, 1998—, Jeremiah's Hospice, 2000—, Accion Worcester, 2002—, United Way of Ctrl. Mass., 2000—; chair Bus. Advisory Coun Martin Luther King Jr. Bus. Empowerment Ctr., 1999—, bd. dirs., 1993—99; chair Capital Devel., 1996—2001; mem. City Mgr.'s Housing Task Force, 1990—92; distbn. com. mem. Fed. Emergency Mgmt. Agy., Ctrl. Mass., 1984—86, Housing Ind. Fund, 1989—92, Greater Worcester Cmty. Found., 1994—2000, chair, 1998—2000; bd. dirs. Higgins Armory Mus., 1993—2002, pres., 1997—99; v.p. Worcester Housing Partnership, 1991—93; pres. Habitat Worcester, 1984—86, Worcester Cmty. Loan Fund, 1986—90, Worcester Com. on Homelessness and Housing, 1988—91, Worcester Cmty. Housing Resources, 1993—95. Recipient award Pernet Family Svc., 1993, Outstanding Charitable Svc. award United Ch. of Christ, 1995, Nipmuc Women's Health Coalition award, 1999, Spirit in Art award, 2002, Exemplary Leadership award Nat. Conf. on Cmty. and Justice, 2002. Mem.: Worcester Com. on Fgn. Rels., United Ch. of Christ Ministers' Fellowship (pres. 1982—83), St. Wulstan Soc., Dartmouth Club of Ctrl. Mass. (pres. 1991—93). Home: PO Box 67 North Oxford MA 01537-0067 Office: Worcester Area Mission Soc 128 Central St Auburn MA 01501-2820 E-mail: wamsucc@bigplanet.com.

BACHENHEIMER, RALPH JAMES, merchant banker; b. Frankfurt, Germany, Jan. 24, 1928; came to U.S., 1946; s. Ferdinand and Louise (Felber) B.; m. Clare Conway (dec. Feb. 1991); children: Lisa Clare, Cara Conway; m. Brith Bore. Student, Coll. Marianum, Vaduz, Liechtenstein, Switzerland, U. Zürich, Switzerland, Columbia U. V.p. Iselin-Jefferson Co., Inc., N.Y.C., 1946-66; pres., chief exec. officer Indian Head Yarn Co., N.Y.C., 1966-69; v.p. Europe Internat. Standard Brands Inc., N.Y.C., 1970-71; corp. v.p. Genesco, Inc., Nashville, 1971-76; exec. v.p., dir. Corland Corp., N.Y.C., 1976-84; mng. dir. E. S. Jacobs & Co., N.Y.C., 1985-93, S.N. Phelps & Co., Greenwich, Conn., 1993-95; self-employed Greenwich, 1995—. Bd. dirs., past v.p. N.Y. Bd. Trade; bd. dirs. numerous corps. Founding mem. Rep. Nat. Senatorial Inner Cir., Washington; mem. Nat. Panel Arbitrators, N.Y.C. Named to Jaycees Hall of Fame, 1983. Mem. Vets. the 7th Regiment, Met. Club (N.Y.C., past gov.), Greenwich Country Club. Republican. Avocation: golf. Home and Office: 5 Hill Rd Greenwich CT 06830-4024

BACHER, JUDITH ST. GEORGE, executive search consultant; b. New Rochelle, N.Y., July 14, 1946; d. Thomas A. and Rose-Marie (Martocci) Baiocchi; m. Albert Bacher, Jan. 2, 1972; 1 son, Alexander Michael. BS,

Georgetown U., 1968; MLS, Columbia U., 1971. Rschr. Time mag., N.Y.C., 1968-71; librarian Mus. Modern Art, N.Y.C., 1971-72; cons. Informaco Inc., N.Y.C., 1972-74, Booz-Allen & Hamilton, N.Y.C., 1974-79; prin. Nordeman Grimm/MBA Resources, N.Y.C., 1979-96, Spencer Stuart, 1996—. Mem. White House Adv. Com. on Pers., Exec. Office of Pres., 1979-81. Mem. Assn. of Exec. Search Cons. (N.E. region chair 1994—), Internat. Assn. Corp. and Profl. Recruiters (bd. dirs. 1996-97), Phi Beta Kappa. Office: Spencer Stuart 277 Park Ave Fl 29 New York NY 10172-2998

BACHER, LUTZ, film, video and photography educator; b. Karlsruhe, Germany, May 2, 1941; came to U.S., 1965; s. Ludwig and Liselotte (Hauth) B.; m. Patricia Delores Stamp, Dec. 18, 1964; children: Brent, Burton, Dara. B of Commerce, U. Windsor, Can., 1964; MA, Wayne State U., 1976, PhD, 1984. Owner, mgr. LBJP Concert Agy., Detroit, 1964-74; freelance prodn. asst. Detroit, 1975-76; asst. dir. Roger Jackson Prodns., Detroit, 1976-78; instr. Wayne State U., Detroit, 1978-80; asst. prof. film, video, photography Robert Morris U., Coraopolis, Pa., 1981-97, assoc. prof., 1998—2002, prof., 2003—. Author: The Mobile Mise-en-Scene, 1978, Max Ophuls in the Hollywood Studios, 1996; writer, dir. Interstate Incident, 1972, Changes, 1973. Mem. Univ. Film-Video Assn., Soc. for Cinema Studies. Avocations: jazz, travel, swimming. Home: 4066 Sanlin Dr Coraopolis PA 15108-2877 Office: Robert Morris U Univ Blvd Moon Township PA 15108-1189 E-mail: bacher@rmu.edu.

BACHICHA, JOSEPH ALFRED, physician, educator; b. Rock Springs, Wyo. s. Alfred and Helen B. BA, Stanford U., 1977; MD, Boston U., 1982. Diplomate Am. Bd. of Ob-Gyn. Intern St. Luke's-Roosevelt Hosp., N.Y.C., 1982-83; resident in ob-gyn. Stanford U. Hosp., Palo Alto, Calif., 1983-86; pvt. practice Chgo., 1986-95; asst. prof. ob-gyn. U. Calif., San Francisco, 1996-97, assoc. prof., 1997-99; med. dir. Pacific Occupl. Health Med. Assocs., South San Francisco, 1999—2003; assoc. physician Kaiser Permanente, 2000—. Cons. WHO, UN Family Planning Assn.; asst. prof. Northwestern U., Chgo., 1986-95; Gen. Hosp., 1996-99, dir. student edn. dept. ob-gyn., 1998-99, dir. obstetrics, 1995-98; dir. Excelsior Group Health Care for Women and Children, San Francisco, 1995-98; dir. low-risk obstetrics, coord. undergrad. med. edn. Prentice Women's Hosp., Chgo., 1990-95; mem. Liaison Com. on Med. Edn.; physician, educator Carnegie Found., Ghana, 1989, Project Hope, Nicaragua, 1992. Contbr. articles to profl. jours. Mem. Chgo. Coun. Fgn. Rels. Grad. fellow Rotary Found., 1980; mem. Harvard Macy Scholars Inst., 1995. Fellow ACOG, Assn. Profs. Gynecology and Obstetrics, Internat. Coll. Surgeons, Royal Soc. Medicine; mem. AMA, APHA, Nat. Bd. Med. Examiners, Am. Assn. Maternal and Neonatal Health, Am. Fertility Soc., Chgo. Gynecol. Soc., San Mateo County Med. Soc., Stanford U. Alumni Assn., Boston U. Sch. Medicine Alumni Assn., Commonwealth Club Calif. Roman Catholic. Avocations: mystery books, cross country skiing, weight training, running, aerobics. Office: 27400 Hesperian Blvd Hayward CA 94545

BACHINI, PETER P. insurance company executive; b. White Plains, N.Y., Oct. 4, 1965; BS in Exercise Physiology, SUNY, Buffalo, 1987. Profl. svcs. coord. US Healthcare, Lake Success, N.Y., 1987-90; mgr. network devel. The Travelers, White Plains, N.Y., 1990-93; assoc. mgr. negotiations Prudential Ins. Co., Suffern, N.Y., 1993-95; regional contracting mgr. Blue Cross Blue Shield of N.C., Durham, 1995-98; v.p. network mgmt. and devel. Doctors Health Plan, Inc., Durham, 1999—; dir. provider networks Mid Atlantic Med. Svcs., Inc./Health Plans, Inc., Durham. Mem. Am. Coll. Healthcare Execs. (assoc.), Healthcare Fin. Mgmt. Assn., Acad. for Healthcare Mgmt.; mem. N.C. Hosp. Assn., Triangle Healthcare Execs. Forum. Republican. Roman Catholic. Home: 12028 N Exeter Way Raleigh NC 27613-7837 Office: MAMSI Health Plans 628 Davis Dr Ste 100 Durham NC 27713 E-mail: pbachini@mamsi.com.

BACHMAN, ARTHUR, lawyer; b. Phila., Nov. 18, 1947; s. Stanley Bachman and Ann (Rosen) Flashner; m. Linda Kay Moss, June 8, 1969; children: Helene, Allison. BBA, Temple U., 1969, JD, 1972, postgrad., 1980. Bar: Pa. 1972. Atty., advisor legis./regulations divsn. Office Chief Coun. IRS, Washington, 1972-76; assoc. Fox, Rothschild, O'Brien & Frankel, 1976-79; ptnr. Blank, Rome, Comisky & McCauley, Phila., 1979—. Instr. Am. Coll., 1986, 88, Temple U., 1988; lectr. Estate Planning Coun. Lehigh Valley, 1983, C. of C. of Cherry Hill, N.J., 1985, Nat. Conf. CPA Practitioners, 1988, Am. Soc. Pension Actuaries, 1988, Internat. Soc. Employee Benefit Specialists, 1991; guest speaker Harry S. Gross radio program Sta. WCAU, 1987, 88, 89. Co-author: (booklets) The REA's Joint and Survivor Annuity Rules--Coping with the Regulations, 1986, How to Defer Income with IRA's and Sec. 401(k) Plans, 1987, Evaluation of Probable Impact of Proposed Nondiscrimination Regs: An Interview with 8 Pension Experts, 1990, An Evaluation of the Proposed Regulations on Separate Lines of Business, 1991, ERISA: A Comprehensive Guide, 1991-97, A Second Look at Final Regulations on FICA and FUTA Tax on Non-Qualified Deferred Compensation; contbr. articles to jours., chpts. to books. Mem. Pa. Bar Assn. (lectr. 2001), Phila. Bar Assn., Am. Society Pension Actuaries Benefits Coun. Del. Valley (bd. dirs. 1997-2003, lectr. 2001), Phi Alpha Delta, Alpha Epsilon Pi, Beta Gamma Sigma. Office: Blank Rome Comisky et al Fls 10-13 One Logan Square Philadelphia PA 19103-2521

BACHMAN, CAROL CHRISTINE, trust company executive; b. Buffalo, Jan. 20, 1959; d. Christian George and Joan Marie (Fincel) B. Student, Grad. Inst. Internat. Study, 1979-80; AB, Smith Coll., 1981; grad., New Eng. Sch. Banking, 1987. Trust asst. BayBank Middlesex, Burlington, Mass., 1984-85, sr. trust asst., 1985-87, trust adminstr., 1987, trust officer, 1987-88; estate settlement specialist Bank of Boston, 1988-90, system cons., 1990, mgr. adminstrv. support svcs., asst. v.p., 1990-96; sr. sys. analyst Fleet Boston, Dedham, Mass., 1996-2000; asst. v.p. Webster Fin. Advisors, Waterbury, Conn., 2001—02; cons., 2002—. Office: Webster Fin Advisors Webster Plz Waterbury CT 06702 E-mail: ccbachm@yahoo.com.

BACHMAN, DAVID, neurologist, pediatric neurologist; b. Savannah, Ga., Apr. 22, 1944; s. Henry and Ilse Bachman; m. Bunnie Blanken; children: Eric (dec.), Kevin. BA, Harvard U., 1965; MD, Johns Hopkins U., 1969. Diplomate Am. Bd. Psychiatry and Neurology, Am. Bd. Pediat. Intern Pitts. Children's Hosp., 1969-70; resident in pediat. Johns Hopkins U., Balt., 1972-73, resident in neurology, 1973-76; pvt. practice Wilmington, N.C.; pres. Wilmington Health, 1993-2000. Officer USPHS, 1970-72. Office: Wilmington Health 1202 Medical Center Dr Wilmington NC 28401-7307

BACHMAN, DAVID CHRISTIAN, orthopedic surgeon; b. Peoria, Ill., Apr. 11, 1934; s. Leland Alvin and Elsie May (Springer) B.; m. Betty June Foster, Sept. 9, 1956; children: Lynne Allison, Laura Ailene. BA, Goshen Coll., 1958; MD, Northwestern U., 1962. Intern Cook County Hosp., Chgo., 1962-63; resident in orthopaedic surgery Northwestern U. Med. Sch., 1963-67; practice medicine specializing in orthopaedic surgery Chgo., 1967-80; practice specializing in ski injuries, 1980-93; with Mountain Med. Services, Telluride, Colo., 1982-87, Ouray Mountain Rescue Team, Inc., Ouray Med. Ctr., Ouray, Colo.; coroner Ouray County, Colo., 1982-93; mem. staffs Northwestern Meml. Hosp., Children's Meml. Hosp., Grant hosp., (all Chgo.), 1967-80, Montrose Meml. Hosp., Colo., 1984-93; med. cons. Western Area U.S. Postal Svc. Dir. Ctr. for Sports Medicine, Northwestern U. Med. Sch., 1978-80; team physician Chgo. Bulls, Nat. Basketball Assn., 1967-80; asst. prof. dept. orthop. surgery Northwestern U. Med. Sch., 1967-80; syndicated columnist on sports medicine Dr. Jock, 1976-90; cons. Western area U.S. Postal Svc., 1996-97; sr. area med. dir. Western Area U.S. Postal Svc., 1997-2002, Pacific Arae U.S. Postal Svc., 2002—. Author: (with Marilyn Preston) Dear Doctor Jock . . .The Peoples Guide to Sports and Fitness, 1980, (with others) The Diet That Lets You Cheat, 1983, (with Tod Bacigalupi) The Way it Was, 1990, (with Robert Pickering) The Use of Forensic Anthropology, 1996. Elder Presbyn. Ch., 1965—; rsch. assoc. anthropology dept. Denver Mus. Natural History, 1994-99. Mem. ACS, Am. Acad. Orthop. Surgery, Am. Orthop. Soc. for Sports Medicine, Phi Rho Sigma. Presbyterian. Home: 552 Shorebird Cir # 1101 Redwood City CA 94065 Office: 390 Main St San Francisco CA 94105

BACHMAN, DAVID M. ophthalmologist; b. Scranton, Pa., Aug. 10, 1951; s. Seymour W. and Natalie (Goodman) B. BA, Johns Hopkins U., 1973, MD, 1976. Resident in ophthalmology Stanford (Calif.) U. Hosp., 1977-80; fellow Nat. Eye Inst.-NIH, Bethesda, Md., 1980-82; pvt. practice ophthalmology Washington, 1982—. Sr. ophthalmic surgeon Washington Hosp. Ctr., Washington, 1982—; clin. instr. ophthalmology George Washington Hosp., Washington, 1990-98. Manuscript reviewer Archives of Ophthalmology; contbr. articles to profl. jours. Bd. dirs. Myasthenia Gravis Found., Washington, 1986—, Young Concert Artists, Washington, 1983—. Recipient Physician's Recognition award AMA, 1980, 83, 86, 93, 96, 2000. Fellow Am. Acad. Ophthalmology; mem. Washington Ophthalmol. Soc., Med. Soc. D.C. Jewish. Avocation: classical pianist. Office: 1133 20th St NW Ste B-150 Washington DC 20036-3424

BACHMAN, HENRY LEE, electrical engineer, engineering executive; b. Bklyn., Apr. 29, 1930; s. Solomon and Frances (Cortese) B.; m. Doris Engelhardt, Dec. 8, 1951; children: Steven, Diane, Lorraine. BEE, Poly. U., N.Y., 1951, MSEE, 1954; postgrad. Advanced Mgmt. Program, Harvard U., 1972. Engr., mgr. Wheeler Labs., Great Neck, N.Y., 1951-55, exec. v.p., dir., 1967-68, pres., dir., 1968-70; product line dir. BAE systems Marconi Aerospace Systems, Green Lawn, N.Y., 1970-72, v.p. quality assurance and logistics, 1973-75, v.p. quality assurance and customer svc., 1975-78, v.p. ops., 1978-84, v.p. engring., 1985-90, v.p. market planning, 1991, v.p. spl. projects, 1992-95, ret. v.p., 1996, dir. tech. mktg., 1996—. Chmn. L.I. Forum for Tech., 1985—86; cons. Rsch. Found. of State Univ. of N.Y., 2001—. Contbr. articles to profl. jours. Pres., bd. dirs. Friends of L.I. Mus. Sci. and Tech., 1994-96; bd dirs. Huntington Arts Coun., 1994-96; mem. Pres.'s Adv. Com. on Indsl. Innovation, 1979. Named Fellow and Disting. Alumnus Poly. Inst., N.Y., 1986; recipient Engring. Mgr. of Yr. award IEEE/Engring. Mgmt. Soc., 1985. Fellow AAAS, IEEE (Centennial medal 1984, Haradem Pratt award 1995, exec. v.p. 1984, treas. 1985, pres. 1987, pres. IEEE Found. 1994-99, v.p. projects 2000-2002, dir. 1986-2002, pres. emeritus 2003, 3d Millennium medal 2000); mem. Sigma Xi, Eta Kappa Nu, Tau Beta Pi. Avocations: sailing, opera, piano. Home: 5 Brandy Rd Cold Spring Harbor NY 11724-2401 Office: BAE Systems Mail Sta 1-30 Greenlawn NY 11740 E-mail: h.bachman@ieee.org.

BACHMAN, SISTER JANICE, healthcare executive; b. Coshocton, Ohio, Oct. 25, 1945; d. Edward Michael and Kathryn Elizabeth (Norris) B. Student, Ohio Dominican Coll., 1963-67; BS in Pharmacy, Ohio State U., 1971; MBA in Mgmt., Xavier U., 1976; MA in Christian Spirituality, Creighton U., 1989. Joined Dominican Sisters, 1963. Staff pharmacist St. George Hosp., Cin., 1971-73, dir. pharmacy svcs., 1973-76; instr. pharmacology and related courses Coll. Mt. St. Joseph, Cin., 1973-74; instr. pharmacology Sch. Nursing Bethesda Hosp., Cin., 1975; adminstrv. resident St. Joseph Hosp., Mt. Clemens, Mich., 1976-77, adminstrv. asst., 1977-78, asst. adminstr., 1978-79; corp. dir. religious programs St. Francis-St. George Hosp., Inc., Cin., 1979-80, asst. v.p. hosp. support svcs., 1980-82, v.p. therapeutic and diagnostic svcs., 1983-89; dir. exec. affairs Benedictine Health Sys., Inc., Duluth, Minn., 1989-90; vicaress Dominican Sisters St. Mary of the Springs, Columbus, Ohio, 1990-96. Editor: Guidelines for Developing an IV Admixture, 1976. Trustee Ohio Dominican Coll., 1980-96, mem. devel. com., 1984-94, physical facilities com., 1994-96; mem. radiologic tech. adv. bd. Xavier U., Cin., 1983-89; mem. MLT adv. bd. Coll. Mt. St. Joseph, 1983-85; trustee Program for Medically Underserved dba Health Moms and Babes, 1986-91, co-founder, chair, 1986-89; bd. dirs. Franciscan Health Sys. Cin., 1990-92; chmn. bd. dirs. Nazareth Towers, Columbus, 1990-94; bd. dirs. Dominican Acad., N.Y.C., 1990-95; trustee St. Mary of the Springs Montessori Sch., Columbus, 1990-95; trustee Milford (Ohio) Spiritual Ctr., 1993-99, vice chair, 1993-94, chair, 1994-98; mem. fin. com. Dominican Leadership Conf., 1994-96; bd. dirs. Westwood Civic Assn., Cin., 1979-86, past sec., past 1st v.p., past pres.; mem. steering com. Cong. Neighborhood Groups, Cin., treas., 1981-84; mem. planning divsn. bd. Cmty. Chest and Coun., Cin., 1981-88, chair single parent task force study, 1983-85; mem. rev. bd. City of Cin. Commercial/Indsl. Revolving Loan Fund, 1982-84; bd. dirs. Cin. Area Chpt. ARC, 1982-89, chair nursing and health com., 1983-87, bd. exec. com., 1987-89; bd. dirs. SW Ohio Residences, Cin., 1983-89, vice chair, 1984-87, chair, 1987-89; trustee Providence Fund, Franciscan Sisters of Stella, Niagara, N.Y., 1996—, C.G. Jung Assn. Ctrl. Ohio, co-chair program com., 1996-99; trustee La Casas (Ministry to Cheyenne and Arapaho Native Ams.), Canton, Okla., 1996, treas., 1997—. Recipient Cmty. Leadership award United Appeal and Cmty. Chest, 1985, 9th Ann. Living Faith award Columbus Met. Area Ch. Coun., 2000. Fellow Am. Coll. Healthcare Execs.; mem. Spiritual Dirs. Internat. Avocations: swimming, cross-country skiing, biking. Office: St Mary of the Springs 2320 Airport Dr Columbus OH 43219-2098 E-mail: janbachman@aol.com.

BACHMAN, JERALD GRAYBILL, psychologist, researcher; b. Harrisburg, Pa., Oct. 20, 1936; s. Jacob Clarence and Harriet Mathias Bachman; m. Virginia Ludy, Nov. 28, 1957; children: Terri Lynne Dyer, Steven Jerald, Jon Andrew. AB, Lebanon Valley Coll., 1958; MA, U. Pa., 1961, PhD, 1962. Rsch. asst. U. Pa., Phila., 1958-59, asst. instr., 1959-62; study dir. U. Mich., Survey Rsch. Ctr., Inst. for Social Rsch., Ann Arbor, 1962-67, sr. study dir., 1967-72, program dir., sr. rsch. scientist, 1972-98, disting. sr. rsch. scientist, 1998—. Mem. nat. adv. panel Nat. Ctr. for Ednl. Stats., Washington, 1982—; mem. com. on mil. performance NAS, Washington, 1983-89, mem. com. on youth population and mil. recruitment, 1999—. Author: (book series) Youth in Transition, 1967-78, The All-Volunteer Force, 1977, Smoking, Drinking, and Drug Use in Young Adulthood, 1997, The Decline of Substance Use in Young Adulthood, 2002; cons. editor Am. Jour. Sociology, 1983-85; contbr. chpts. to books and articles to profl. jours. NSF fellow, Washington, 1959, 60, 62. Mem. Am. Assn. for Pub. Opinion Rsch., Soc. for Psychol. Study Social Issues, Inter-Univ. Seminar on Armed Forces and Soc. Avocations: sailing, cross-country skiing, house renovation, hiking, traveling. Office: Inst for Social Rsch Univ Mich 426 Thompson St Ann Arbor MI 48104-2321 E-mail: jbachman@umich.edu.

BACHMAN, KENNETH LEROY, JR., lawyer; b. Washington, Aug. 24, 1943; s. Kenneth Leroy and Audrey Teresa (Torrence) B.; m. Sharon Abel, June 18, 1966; children— Laura Ann, Eric Kenneth. A.B. summa cum laude, Ohio U., 1965; J.D. cum laude, Harvard U., 1968. Bar: D.C. 1968, U.S. Ct. Appeals (D.C. cir.) 1971, U.S. Supreme Ct. 1981. Law clk. to judge U.S. Dist. Ct. So. Dist. N.Y., 1968-70; assoc. Cleary, Gottlieb, Steen & Hamilton, Washington, 1970-76, ptnr., 1976— . Mem. ABA. Contbg. editor Oil and Gas Price Regulation Analyst, 1978-83, Natural Gas Journal, 1983-85; contbr. articles to profl. jours. Home: 5332 Falmouth Rd Bethesda MD 20816-2915 Office: 1752 N St NW Washington DC 20036-2904

BACHMAN, RALPH WALTER, lawyer; b. Mpls., Sept. 16, 1944; s. Ralph W. and Marguerite L. (Curfman) B.; m. Mary K. Zakariasen, July 29, 1967; children— Melissa, Rachel, Matthew. B.A. summa cum laude, U. Minn., 1966; M.A., Oxford U., 1968; J.D., Stanford U., 1970. Bar: Minn. 1970. Assoc., Gray, Plant, Mooty, Mooty & Bennett, Mpls., 1970-71; ptnr. Broeker & Bachman, Mpls., 1971-76; dir. profl. conduct Minn. Lawyers Profl. Responsibility Bd., 1976-79; chief dep. Hennepin County Atty.'s Office, Minn., 1979-83; atty. Lindquist & Vennum, Mpls., 1983— ; adj. prof. U. Minn. Law Sch., 1980. Mem. ABA (com. on ethics and profl. responsibility 1980-83), Minn. State Bar Assn., Hennepin County Bar Assn. (pres. 1984-85). Office: Bachman's Inc 6010 Lyndale Ave S Minneapolis MN 55419-2289

BACHMANN, BILL, photographer; b. Pa., Mar. 4, 1946; s. Ernest Edward and Helen May (Himler) B. BS, Roberts Wesleyan Coll., Rochester, N.Y., 1967; MBA, NYU, 1971; postgrad., U. London, U. Calif., Berkeley, Rochester Inst. Tech., U. Pitts., Ft. Lauderdale Art Inst. Freelance comml. and advt. photographer, Miami, N.Y.C., Orlando, 1972—. Worked in over 140 countries worldwide; instr. photography Triangle Inst., 1992, S.E. Ctr. for Creative Arts, Daytona, 1990—; dir. TV comms. and co. videos; vis. instr. photography at several colls. and univs.; guest numerous TV programs, 1978—; lectr. in field, 1980—. Prin. works include Miami Herald, 1978-80, Fla. Tourism, 1982—, Sheraton Hotels, 1982—, Gen. Mills Restaurants, 1983—, Olive Garden, 1986—, Marriott Hotels, 1992—, Bahamas Tourism, 1984--, Radisson Hotels, 1986—, Grosvenor Hotels, 1988—, Revlon, 1991—, Harris Corp., 1993—, Sea Escape Cruises, 1988—, Century Club, 2000—, Regent China Tours, 1999—, Burger King, 1988—, Caribbean Travel & Life, 1990—, Fuji, 1990—, Far & Wide, 2000—, Nickelodeon, 1989—, Merv Griffin's Paradise Island, Bahamas, 1990—, Kodak Films, 1976—, McDonalds, 1987—, Stern Mag., 1987—, AAA, 1985—, Regal Boats, 1990—, Renaissance Cruises, 1996—, Universal Studios, 1990—, General Tours, 2002—, Citibank VISA, 1990—, Delta Airlines, 1991—, Am. Showcase, 1991—, Creative Black Book, 1994—, PepsiCo, 1994—, Hilton Hotels Internat., 1992—, NuSkin, 1995—, Pizza Hut, 1996—, Grey Poupon, 1995—, Atlantis Resort, 1996—, Arnold Palmer, 1996—, Home Depot, 1996—, Whale Cay, 1997—, Sandals Resorts, 1997—, People Mag., 1998—, Grand Circle Tours, 1999—, Sony, 2003—, Pitcom, 1999, Saga Holidays, 1999-2001, Regent China Tours, 1999—, Backstreet Boys, 2000, Cooper Tires, 2000—, Far & Wide, 2001, Brendan Tours, 2001--, SIKA, 2002--, Sony, 2003--, Venus Williams, 2003--, Reebok, 2003—; dir. TV comms. and videos, 1987—; author: Clicking the Shutter is the Easy Part, 1988, Introspective World, 1996, Welcome Back Berlin, 1990, Bali-Paradise in Indonesia, 1994, Shooting Figure Studies, 1990, Kathmandu, A Jewel Discovered, 1996, One Dream Too Many, 1989, Images of Women, 1997, Treasures of the Caribbean, 1992, China's Greatest Resource, It's Diverse People, 1997, Orlando-The City Beautiful, 1998, Traveling After Terrorism, 2002, Travel Hints for Photographers, 2003; photographer 295-Day Kodak World Photo Tour, 1992-95, Photo Pro Mag., 1991—; photgraphed over 800 mag. covers. Bd. dirs. Big Bros.; active Vols. in Action, 1989—. Named Photographer of Yr. Fla. Peoples Choice Awards, 1987, Photographer of Yr. Asia, 1993; recipient Addy awards, 1976—. Mem. One Club (bd. dirs. 1988—), Sales and Mktg. Execs. (bd. dirs., officer), Am. Soc. Media Photographers N.Y., Orlando C. of C. (pres.' club 1983—), Cen. Fla. Photographers Assn. (v.p., bd. dirs. 1983—), Fla. Motion Pictures and TV Guild, Heathrow Club (social dir. 1986—), Rotary. Republican. Methodist. Avocations: snow skiing, tennis, golf, writing. Home and Office: PO Box 950833 Lake Mary FL 32795-0833

BACHMANN, GLORIA ANN, physician, educator; b. Newark, N.J., Nov. 4, 1949; d. Paul Bachmann and Rose Detrolio; 1 child, Michael. BA, Rutgers U., 1970, MMS, 1972; MD, U. Pa., 1974. Diplomate Am. Bd. Ob-Gyn., Am. Bd. Med. Examiners. Resident in ob-gyn. Hosp. of the U. of Pa., 1974-78; instr. U. Medicine & Dentistry N.J./Robert Wood Johnson Med. Sch., New Brunswick, N.J., 1978-81, asst. prof. Robert Wood Johnson U. Hosp., New Brunswick, N.J., 1981-86, assoc. prof., 1986-92, prof., 1992—. Chief ob-gyn. Robert Wood Johnson U. Hosp., 1992—; dir. Women's Health Inst. Editl. bd. Maturitas, 1989—, Med. Crossfire, 1998, Managing Menopause, 1998—, Jour. of Reproductive Medicine, 1999—, Med. Aspects of Human Sexuality, 1989-92, OBG Mgmt., 1994—, Menopaul Mgmt., 1991-93, Obstetric Gynecology, 1990-94; contbr. chpts. to books and articles to profl. jours. Dir. Women's Wellness and Health Care Connection, New Brunswick, N.J., 1998—. Recipient Recognition award March of Dimes, 1982, 83, Planned Parenthood, 1987, 88, Award for Women's Health Edn. YMCA, 1984, Judge Advocate Gen. award Tri-State Metro, 1984, Lifetime Achievement award Middlesex County Commn. on the Status of Women, 1995, Women of Achievement award Del. Valley Girl Scouts, 1996. Fellow Am. Coll. Ob-Gyn. (Issue of the Yr. award 1988); mem. Am. Fertility Soc., Internat. Menopaušе Soc., Am. Med. Women's Assn. (Gender Equity Recognition 1994), N.J. Obs.-Gyn. Soc., N.Am. Menopause Soc., Acad. of Medicine of N.J., Phi Beta Kappa. Office: Robert Wood Johnson Med Sch Women's Health Inst 125 Paterson St Rm 2104 New Brunswick NJ 08901-1962 E-mail: gloria.bachmann@umdnj.edu.

BACHMANN, JOHN WILLIAM, securities firm executive; b. Centralia, Ill., Nov. 16, 1938; s. George Adam and Helen (Johnston) B.; m. Katharine I. Butler; children: John C., Kristene Ellen Bachmann Wright. AB, Wabash Coll., 1960; MBA, Northwestern U., 1962; LLD (hon.), Wabash Coll., 1990. Researcher Edward Jones, St. Louis, 1962-63, investment rep., 1963-70, gen. ptnr., 1970-80, mng. ptnr., 1980—. Bd. dirs. Am. Airlines, Inc. Trustee Wabash Coll., Crawfordsville, Ind., 1980—; chmn. bd. visitors Drucker Ctr. Claremont (Calif.) Grad. Sch., 1987—; past chmn., bd. dirs. Arts and Edn. Coun. Greater St. Louis; commr. St. Louis Art Mus.; past chmn. St. Louis Symphony Soc.; past chmn. St. Louis Regional Chamber and Growth Assn. Mem. Nat. Assn. Securities Dealers (past dist. chmn.), Securities Industry Assn. (bd. dirs., chmn. 1976-79), Securities Industry Found. for Econ. Edn. (chmn. trustees 1988-92), Civic Progress, U.S. C. of C. (vice chmn.), St. Louis Club, Bogey Club. Office: Edward Jones 12555 Manchester Rd Saint Louis MO 63131

BACHMANN, MICHELE, state legislator; m. Marcus Bachmann; 5 children. JD, Coburn Law; LLM, Coll. William and Mary. Mem. Minn. State Senate, 2000—, mem. capital investment com., edn. com., taxes com., E-12 edn. budget divsn. com., jobs, housing and cmty. devel. com., property tax budget divsn. com. Republican. Home: 1801 Johnson Dr Stillwater MN 55082 Office: 125 State Office Bldg 100 Constitution Ave Saint Paul MN 55155-1206 E-mail: sen.michele.bachmann@senate.leg.state.mn.us.

BACHMANN, RICHARD ARTHUR, oil company executive; b. Green Bay, Wis., Dec. 6, 1944; s. Richard Arthur and Anita Sidonia (Dohmeyer) B.; children: Richard A., Joseph E., Christina J.; m. Susan Dawn Minney, July 31, 1993. BBA, Wis. State U., 1967; MBA, U. Wis., 1968. Mgr. fgn. fin. Exxon Corp., N.Y.C., 1968-78; v.p., treas. Itel Corp., San Francisco, 1978-81; sr. v.p. fin. and adminstrn., chief fin. officer La. Land and Exploration Co., New Orleans, 1981-85, exec. v.p. fin. and adminstrn., chief fin. officer, 1985-97; pres., COO, 1995-97; pres., CEO, chmn. bd. Energy Ptnrs., Ltd., New Orleans, 1997—; also bd. dirs. La. Land and Exploration Co., New Orleans. Bd. dirs. Univ. Health Care Sys. Gov. Com., Penn Va. Corp., Superior Energy Svcs. Inc. Bd. dirs., mem. exec. com., sustaining membership com. chmn. New Orleans coun. Boy Scouts Am., 1984—, pres., mem. exec. bd., 1988-92, nat. bd. coun. fin. cabinet mem., chmn. supply com., 1990-92; bd. dirs. Audubon Park and Zool. Garden, Audubon Inst.-Aquarium of Ams., Covenant House, 1990—; bd. dirs., chmn. fin. oversight com. met. Arts Fund; bd. govs. Isadore Newman Sch., bd. dirs., 1990—; adv. bd. Summerbridge, 1989—. Office: Energy Partners Ltd 201 Saint Charles Ave Ste 3400 New Orleans LA 70170-1026

BACHMANN, WILLIAM THOMPSON, dermatologist; b. Orange, N.J., Mar. 21, 1940; s. George Kirsten and Agnes Mary (Cunningham) B.; m. Carolyn Emily Loeber, Dec. 28, 1961 (div. June 1971); children: John Kirsten, William Thompson; m. Judith Richmond, June 20, 1981; 1 stepchild, Julia Garriga. AB, Williams Coll., 1962; MD, Boston U., 1966. Diplomat Am. Bd. Internal Medicine, Am. Bd. Dermatology. Intern St. Francis Hosp., Hartford, Conn., 1966-67, resident, 1967-68, Yale New Haven (Conn.) Hosp., 1971-72, 72-74; dermatologist Westerly (R.I.) Hosp. Lt. comdr. USN, 1969-71. Fellow Am. Coll. Physicians, Am. Acad. Dermatology; mem. New England Dermatological Soc., R.I. Med. Soc., Yale Soc. Attendings in Dermatology (sr. attending mem.), Alpha Omega Alpha. Avocations: boating, photography. Office: 39 East Ave Westerly RI 02891-3113

BACHMEYER, STEVEN ALLAN, secondary education educator; b. Queens, N.Y., Feb. 8, 1945; s. Harold Frederick and Dorothy (Blackstone) B.; m. Mary Louise Bachmeyer, June 18, 1968; children: Steven Adam, Melanie Hope. AA, Miami Dade C.C., 1966; BEd in Indsl. Arts Edn., U. Miami, 1969; MS in Computer Edn. Tech., Barry U., 1995. Cert. tech. edn. Tchr. indsl. arts Miami Springs (Fla.) Jr. High Sch., 1969-73, dept. chmn., 1972-73; tchr. indsl. arts Hialeah-Miami Lakes Sr. High Sch., Hialeah, Fla., 1973-86, chmn. graphic arts, architecture and engring. drafting dept., 1986; instr. architecture and engring. drafting, tech. studies and aerospace tech. South Dade Sr. High Sch., Homestead, Fla., 1988-2000; part-time dir. Camp Adventure, Black Mountain, N.C., 1984-86, dir., 1986-88; chmn. tech. edn. dept. South Dade Sr. High Sch., Homestead, Fla., 1991—; vocat. dept. chmn. Felix Varela Jr. H.S., 2000—. Founder/exec. dir. Aerospace Edn. Alliance, 1997; dir. Tech. Concepts, Homestead, Fla., 1991—; instr. part-time dept. indsl. arts edn. U. Miami, Coral Gables, Fla., 1971-72; instr. part-time bldg. constrn. drawing and archtl. history dept. arch./bldg. constrn. Miami Dade C.C., 1980-84; writer curriculum framework aerospace tech. program Fla. State Dept. Edn., 1991; mem. equity com. South Dade Sr. H.S., 1989-90, mem. tchrs. as advisors steering com., 1989-91, mem. sch. based mgmt. team, 1990-91; mem. tech. com. for tech. edn. Fla. Dept. Edn., 1991, 92, 93, Fla. Tchr. Cert. Devel. Com., 1992-93; mem. state tech. com. Tech. Ed.; chmn. bd. Fla. Tech. Student Assn. and Found., Inc., 1993; demonstration tchr. Fla. Acad. Excellence in Teaching, Fla. Dept. Edn., 1993; part-time instr. Fla. Internat. Univ., 1996—; presenter blueprint workshop Fla. Dept. Edn., 1991, aerospace tech. curriculum project, Lakeland, Fla., 1993, aerospace tech. curriculum project Nat. Congress Aviation and Aerospace Edn., Orlando, Fla., 1993, Norfolk, Va., 1994, NASA Internat. Space Camp, Huntsville, Ala., 1993; workshop instr. Dade County Pub. Schs., 1993; adj. prof. dept. vocat./adult edn. U. South Fla., 1994, dept. vocat. edn., 1995; adj. prof. div. vocat. edn. Fla. Internat. U. Author: Aerospace Technology Curriculum Project--Principles of Aeronautics, 1991-93, Technology in Action Project Series, 1994, Parachutes Yesterday, Today, Tomorrow, 1993, Up From Clay A Beginners Guide to R/C, Space-Science and Technology Series, 1996; author The World of Comms. visual media, 1972, The World of Comms. audio visual media, 1973, An Introduction to Comms. Careers, 1974. Asst. supt. Dade County Youth Fair, 1990-95; supt. aerospace tech. divsn. Dade County Youth Fair, 1997; waterfront dir. McGregor-Smith Scout Reservation, Inverness, Fla.,

1981, program dir., 1982-83; cert. camp dir. Boy Scouts Am., cubmaster, scoutmaster, explorer advisor troop 124, Hollywood, Fla., 1980-86, scoutmaster troop 811, Old Fort, N.C., 1987-88; mem. sch. bd. Prince of Peace Luth. Ch./Sch. 2d lt. U.S. Army. Recipient Graphic Arts Tchr. Excellence award Kiwanis Club Miami, 1981, Tchr. Excellence award Dade County DAVACCE, 1990, Newsmast Honor award NASA, 1990, scholarship Fla. Assn. Ednl. Data Systems, 1991, Tchr. Excellence award Internat. Tech. Edn. Assn., Fla., 1993, Excellence in Aviation Edn. award Gen. Aviation Mfrs. Assn., 1993, Best Practice award Fla. Vocat. Assn., 1993, 94, Ednl. Profl. Excellence award Kelvin Found. Tech., 1994, Tandy Tech. scholar, 1993-94/nat. hon. mention, 2 nat. awards, 1997, 1 regional award, Regional Tchr. of the Yr., Dade County Pub. Schs., Fla., 1997, Janice M. Dwyer Aviation Edn. award Aircraft Distbrs. and Mfrs. Assn., 1998, Christa McAuliffe award Air Force Assn./Nat. Aerospace Tchr. of the Yr., 1998, A. Scott Crossfield award Civil Air Patrol-Crown Cir., 1998, Glenn Curtis award Greater Miami Aviation Assn., 2002. Mem. Am. Vocat. Assn., Fla. Aerospace Edn. Assn. (mem. exec. bd. 1993), Fla. Vocat. Assn. (presenter conf. 1991-94), Fla. Tech. Edn. Assn. (conf. presenter 1989-94, pres. region V 1989-91, bd. dirs. 1989-91, pres.-elect 1992, pres. 1993, Tchr. of Yr. finalist 1990, 1, 92, Tchr. of Yr. award 1993), Fla. Assn. Computers Edn., Dade County Tech. Edn. Assn., Internat. Tech. Edn. Assn. (presenter nat. conf. 1992, 93, 94, 95, scholarship 1992, Program Excellence award Fla. chpt. 1992, Tchr. Excellence award 1993), Internat. Soc. Tech. Edn., Tech. Student Assn. (event chmn. aerospace tech. nat. conf. 1991-95, Outstanding Advisor award Fla. chpt. 1990, chmn. adv. coun. 1990-92, dir. adv. tng. conf. 1990, presenter nat. conf. 1990-92, instr. profl. workshop 1992, state advisor Vocat. Student Orgn., 1993, region tchr. year, 1997), Aerospace Edn. Found., Assn. Ednl. Comm. and Tech. (divsn. interactive systems and computers), Am. Camping Assn. (advanced campcraft, tripmaster and campcraft instr. certs.), Am. Canoe Assn. (whitewater canoe instr.), Epsilon Pi Tau (pres. Alpha Omega chpt.). Democrat. Avocations: sailing, photography. Office: Felix Varela Sr HS 15255 SW 96th St Miami FL 33196-1200 Home: 34845 SW 187th Ct Homestead FL 33034-4538 E-mail: bach1@earthlink.net., sbachmeyer@varela.dadeschools.net.

BACHNER, BARBARA LAVERDIERE, artist; b. Waterville, Maine, Sept. 14, 1934; d. Thaddeus Eugene and Bernadette Arthemise (Vashon) LaVerdiere; m. Robert Lawrence Bachner, Mar. 22, 1959; 1 child, Suzanne Jouvé. BA in Fine Arts magna cum laude, NYU, 1968; student, Nat. Acad. Sch. Design, 1975-78, Art Students League, 1977-80, 82-84; MFA in Studio Art, Johnson State Coll., 1999. Lectr. Ulster County Art Assn., 1992, Woodstock Sch. Art, 1994, tchr., 1999—2000; co-curator Belmont Towbin Mus., Woodstock Artists Assn., 2002—; panelist Women on Men, Denise Bibro, 2000; juror in field. One-woman shows include Kleinert Arts Ctr., Woodstock, NY, 1992, exhibited in group shows at Pastel Soc. Am., NYC, 1978, 1980, one-woman shows include TAI Gallery, 1994, 1998, Fletcher Gallery, Woodstock, 1995, Pen and Brush, NYC, 1995, Woodstock Artist Assn., 1997, Pen and Brush, NYC, 1999, Julian Scott Meml. Gallery, Johnson State Coll., Johnson, Vt., 1999, exhibited in group shows at Five Towns Juried Show, Woodmere, N.Y., 1983, Nat. Arts Club, NYC, 1984, Woodstock Artists Assn., 1989—, Artists of Ulster County, Kingston, NY, 1989, Pen & Brush, NYC, 1990—, Springfield (Mo.) Art Mus., 1990, U. Tex., Tyler, 1991, A.I.R. Gallery, NYC, 1992, SUNY, New Paltz, 1992, Gallery Korea, NYC, 1993, CUNY, Bayside, 1994, Barrett House, Poughkeepsie, N.Y., 1994, Woodstock Sch. Art, 1994—, Nat. Arts Club, NYC, 1995, Krasdale Corp. Galleries, White Plains, N.Y., 1995—96, Nat. Assn. Women Artists, 1996, Harper Collins, NYC, 1996, SUNY, New Paltz, 1996, The Art Studio, Bearsville, NY, 1997, Woodstock Artists Assn., 1997, Cork Gallery, Lincoln Ctr., NYC, 1998, NY State Mus., Albany, 1998, Dist. Coun. 37, NYC, 1999; author: Behind Closed Eyes, 1999; Exhibited in group shows at Orensanz Found., NYC, 1999, Nat. Assn. Women Artists, 1999—2001, Schoharie County Art Assn., Cobbleskill, N.Y., 1999, Interfaith Ctr., NYC, 1999, Biennale Internat. Dell'Arte Contemporanea, Florence, Italy, 1999, LA Printmaking Soc., No. Hollywood, Calif., 1999—2001, Elements 2000 Ernest Rubenstein Gallery, NYC, 2000, Florence New York Orensanz Found., 2000, It's About Time Barrett Art Ctr., Poughkeepsie, N.Y., 2000, Utopia/Dystopia Kleinert Art Ctr./Byrdciffe, Woodstock, NY, 2000, Nat. Assn. of Women Artists, Balt., 2000, Attleboro Mus., Mass., 2000, Denise Bibro Fine Art, NYC, 2000, About Shoes Studio, D'Ars, Milan, 2001, Grounds for Sculpture, Hamilton NJ, 2001, one-woman shows include Studio Dars, Milan, Italy, 2001, exhibited in group shows at Lankershim Arts Ctr., N. Hollywood, Calif., 2001, Purdue U. Galleries, West Lafayette, Ind., 2001, Roessler Gallery, Ravensburg, Germany, 2002, Represented in permanent collections Texaco Corp., Houston, Printmaking Workshop, NYC, Kaatsbaan Internat. Dance Ctr., Tivoli, NY, Four Seasons Hotel Corp., Las Vegas, Nev., Nat. Assn. Women Artists, numerous pvt. collections, one-woman shows include Gallery @49, NYC, 2002, exhibited in group shows at A.I.R. Gallery, 2002; subject of articles: ; Exhibited in group shows at Denise Bibro Fine Art, NYC, 2002, one-woman shows include Lab. Inst. Merchandisisng, 2003, TAI Gallery, 2003, Internat. Works on Paper/William Whipple Art Gallery, SW State Univ./Marshall, Minn., 2003, Tai Gallery, 2003, exhibited in group shows at Denise Bibro Fine Art, 2002, Monique Goldstrom, NYC, 2003. Mem.: Monique Goldstrom, Ulster Arts Alliance, Woodstock Artists Assn. (exhbn. com. 1991—94, svc. in the arts dir., dir. 1992—95, trustee 1995—2002, exhbn. com. 1998—2002, Dan Gottschalk award 1991, Breth-Borkmann award 1995), Pen & Brush (co-chair graphics divsn. 1994—98, Solo Show award 1993, 1996), NY Artists Equity Assn., Coll. Art Assn., Women's Caucus Art, Nat. Assn. Women Artists (rec. sec. 1999—2000, Medal of Honor 1998, Elizabeth Stanton Blake meml. award 1998), Art Students League (life Concours award 1978, 1981, 1984, Merit scholar 1979, 1983). Avocations: music, theater, travel. Home: 25 Sutton Pl S Apt 19N New York NY 10022-2455 E-mail: blbachner@earthlink.net.

BACHNER, JOHN PHILIP, business consultant; b. Boston, Nov. 8, 1944; s. Barnard and Bertha (Bellar) B.; m. Patricia B. Gartenhaus, June 14, 1997. AB, Harvard U., 1966. Screenplay writer Screen Presentations Inc., Washington, 1967-68; account exec. Hoffman Assocs. Inc., Silver Spring, Md., 1968-71; pres. Bachner Communications Inc., Silver Spring, 1971—. Pres. Bachner Mgmt. Systems, 1973—; exec. v.p. Cons. Engrs. Coun. of Met. Washington, Silver Spring, 1971-96, Property Mgmt. Assn., Silver Spring, 1973-96, Washington Area Coun. Engring. Labs., Silver Spring, 1975-93; exec. v.p. ASFE, 1973—; pres., chmn. bd. Constrn. Industry Tech. Inc., Silver Spring, 1973—; pres. Most for the Lease, 1982—; v.p. Bachner R.E., 1985-97; exec. v.p. Mid-Atlantic Coun. of Shopping Ctr. Mgrs., 1986-93; exec. v.p. Inst. Profl. Practice, Silver Spring, 1988-94, Coll. Property Mgmt. Found., Silver Spring, 1988-96; pres. Cons. Engrs., Ednl. Found. Inc., 1990-99; exec. dir. Profl. Liability Agts. Network Inc., 1991-98, Mid-Atlantic Cancer Rsch. Found., Silver Spring, 1992-95, Internat. Found. Advancement of Thrombosis and Hematosis Rsch. Inc., Silver Spring, 1992-98, Calif. R.E. Inspection Assn., 1993-98, Metro Washington Heat Pump Assn., 1994-99; pres. Bus. Art and Graphics, 1993-97. Author: Marketing and Promotion for Design Professionals, 1977, Guide to Practical Property Management, 1991, Practice Management for Design Professionals, 1991, ASFE Contract Reference Guide, 3d edit., 1996, 3.1 edit., 1998, ECS Contract Reference Guide, 1997, 2nd edit., 1999, RA&MCO Contract Reference Guide, 1997, 2d edit., 2002, Derailed by Dispute, 2003; writer 25 motion picture screenplays; contbr. over 1500 articles to profl. publs., popular mags.; columnist, author contract reference guides, 1996-2000. Pres. Engrs.' Leadership Found., 1999—2003; bd. govs. Found. for Profl. Practice, 2001—. Home: 9206 Sterling Montague Dr Great Falls VA 22066-4002 E-mail: john@bachner.com.

BACHOP, WILLIAM EARL, JR., retired anatomist, zoologist; b. Youngstown, Ohio, Aug. 31, 1926; s. William Earl Sr. and Mary Agnes (Murray) B.; m. Annabelle Adams, Dec. 27, 1958; children: Alice Mary, Margaret Anne. BA, Western Res. U., 1950; MS, Ohio State U., 1958, PhD, 1963. Asst. prof. biology U. Omaha, 1963-65; postdoctoral fellow U. Wash., Seattle, 1965-69; asst. prof. zoology Clemson (S.C.) U., 1969-73; gross anatomy studentship Bowman Gray Med. Sch., Winston-Salem, N.C., 1973-74; asst. prof. anatomy Nat. Coll. Chiropractic, Lombard, Ill., 1974-77, assoc. prof. anatomy, 1977-81, prof. anatomy, 1981-96, prof. emeritus, 1996—, also acting chmn. dept. anatomy, 1974-76, chmn. dept. anatomy, 1976-86. Vis. scientist NSF, Omaha, 1963-65, Inst. Marine Scis., Morehead City, N.C., summer 1972; gen. anatomy examiner Bd. Chiropractic Examiners, Boulder, Colo., 1975-76; summer fellowship NSF, Columbia U., N.Y.C., 1960. Author: (chpt.) Early Embryology of Fish, 1974, Development of the Spine and Spinal Cord, 1995; contbr. articles to profl. jours. Served to cpl. U.S. Army, 1951-53. Recipient Nebr. Coop. grant NSF, 1964, Rsch. associateship U. Mich., 1964, Tuition scholarship NIH, 1973. Mem. Am. Assn. Anatomists, Am. Assn. Clin. Anatomists, Ill. State Acad. Scis. Achievements include research establishing that giant nuclei in yolk sac syncytium of oviparous teleostean embryos contains polyploid amounts of DNA; establishing that respiratory deficient strains of bakers yeast lacked elementary particles in their mitochondria. Home: 1133 S Finley Rd Apt 410 Lombard IL 60148-3872 Office: Nat Coll Chiropractic 200 E Roosevelt Rd Lombard IL 60148-4583

BACHRACH, EVE ELIZABETH, lawyer; b. Oakland, Calif., July 4, 1951; d. Howard Lloyd and Shirley B. AB cum laude, Boston U., 1972; JD with honors, George Washington U., 1976. Bar: D.C. 1976, U.S. Dist. Ct. D.C. 1976, U.S. Ct. Appeals (D.C. cir.) 1976. Assoc. Stein, Mitchell & Mezines, Washington, 1976-79; assoc. gen. counsel Cosmetic, Toiletry, and Fragrance Assn., Washington, 1979-85; v.p., assoc. gen. counsel, corp. sec., 1985-95; v.p., deputy gen. counsel, corp. sec. Consumer Healthcare Products Assn., Washington, 1995-98, sr. v.p., gen. counsel, sec., 1998—. Guest lectr. Am. U., Washington, 1986—, George Washington Nat. Law Ctr., Washington, 1986—, Cath. U. Law Sch., 1988— Contbr. articles to profl. jours. Vol. lawyer Legal Counsel for the Elderly, Washington, 1978—. Mem.: ABA (food and drug com., antitrust sect., adminstrv. law sect.), Food Drug Law Inst. (chmn. writing awards com. 1982—88, vice chmn. 1987—89, chmn. 1990, adv. bd. 1998—2002, bd. of dir. 2002—, bd. dirs., editl. adv. bd. Update Mag. 2002—, editl. adv. bd. Food Drug Law Jour.), Fed. Bar Assn. (chmn. food and drug com. 1986—90), D.C. Bar Assn. Avocation: classical pianist. Office: Consumer Healthcare Products Assn 1150 Connecticut Ave NW Washington DC 20036-4104

BACHRACH, HOWARD L. biochemist; b. Faribault, Minn., May 21, 1920; s. Harry and Elizabeth (Panovitz) Bachrach; m. Shirley F. Lichterman, June 13, 1943; children: Eve E., Harrison J. BA in Chemistry, U. Minn., 1942, PhD in Biochemistry, 1949. Research chemist synthetic rubber Jos. E. Seagram & Co., 1942; Research asst. explosives research lab. Nat. Def. Research Com. project Carnegie Inst. Tech., Pitts., 1942—45; research asst. U. Minn., Mpls., 1945—49; biochemist, foot-and-mouth disease mission USDA, Denmark, 1949—50; research biochemist virus lab. U. Calif-Berkeley, 1950—53; chief scientist, head biochem. and phys. investigation Plum Island Animal Disease Ctr., Greenport, NY, 1953—80, research chemist, advisor to dir., 1981—89, sci. collaborator, 1989—95. Charter mem. Sr. Exec. Svc. U.S. Govt., 1979; mem. viral and rickettsial grants subcom. Walter Reed Army Inst. Tsch., 1982—85; cons. Pan Am. Health Orgn., Brazil, 1981, Coop. State Res. Svcs. USDA, 1982—83, Assessment U.S. Congress, 1984—85, cons, 1988—89, Nat. Cancer Inst., 1984—87, Tex. A&M U. Inst. Bioscis. and Techs., 1987—89; Theobald Smith lectr. Am. Soc. Microbiology, 1981. Contbr. Named to USDA Agr. Sci. Hall of Fame, 1987; recipient Naval Ordnance Devel. award, 1945, Cert. of Merit, USDA, 1960, Disting. Svc. award, 1982, U.S. Presdl. citation, 1965, U.S. Sr. Exec. Svc. award, 1980, Newcomb Cleveland prize, AAAS, 1982, Nat. Award for Agrl. Excellence, 1983, Alexander von Humboldt award, 1983, Nat. Medal Sci., Pres. Ronald Reagan, 1983, ISI Citation Classics Publ., 1986. Fellow: N.Y. Acad. Sci.; mem.: Am. Soc. Virology, Am. Chem. Soc. (Kenneth A. Spencer medal 1983, 50 yr. mem. 1997), Am. Coll. Veterinary Microbiologists (hon.), Nat. Acad. Scis. U.S. (Nominated to Wisdom Hall of Fame 2000), Phi Lambda Upsilon, Gamma Alpha, Sigma Xi. Achievements include development of first purification and electron microscopic visualization of polio and foot-and-mouth disease viruses; subunit vaccines--protection of swine with a protein isolated from foot-and-mouth disease virus; reported first effective recombinant DNA cloned viral protein vaccine for use in animals or humans; described comparative molecular pathways of replication for all classes of animal and human viruses. Home: 355 Dayton Rd PO Box 1054 Southold NY 11971-0932 also: 10220 Andover Coach Cir Apt G2 Lake Worth FL 33467-8137 E-mail: howshy@aol.com.

BACHRACH, STEVEN MAURICE, chemistry educator; b. Chgo., Aug. 14, 1959; s. Joseph and Ruth Bachrach; m. Carmen Irma Nitsche, Nov. 23, 1984; 1 child, Dustin. BS, U. Ill., 1981; PhD, U. Calif., Berkeley, 1985. Dir.'s fellow Los Alamos (N.Mex.) Nat. Lab., 1985—87; prof. No. Ill. U., DeKalb, 1987—99; disting. prof. Trinity U., San Antonio, 1999—2002. Editor: (book) The Internet: A Guide for Chemists, 1996. Office: Trinity U 1 Trinity Pl San Antonio TX 78212 Business E-Mail: sbachrach@trinity.edu.

BACHTEL, ANN ELIZABETH, educational consultant, researcher, educator; b. Winnipeg, Man., Can., Dec. 12, 1928; d. John Wills. and Margaret Agnes (Gray) Macleod; m. Richard Earl Bachtel, Dec. 19, 1947 (dec.); children: Margaret Ann, John Macleod, Bradley Wills; m. Louis Philip Nash, June 30, 1978 (div. 1987). AB, Occidental Coll., 1947; MA, Calif. State U., L.A., 1976; PhD, U. So. Calif., 1988. Cert. life tchr., adminstr., Calif. Elem. tchr. various pub. and pvt. schs., Calif., 1947-50, 64-77; dir. emergency sch. aid act program, spl. projects, spl. art State of Calif., 1977-80; leader, mem. program rev. team Calif. State Dept. Edn., 1981-85; cons. Pasadena Unified Sch. Dist., 1981-85. Cons. Pasadena Unified Sch. Dist., 1981-86; tchg. asst., adj. prof. U. So. Calif.; cons., presenter in field. Editor: Arts for the Gifted and Talented, 1981; author Nat. Directory Programs for Artistically Gifted and Talented Students K-12; contbr. articles to profl. jours. Active legis. task forces; chair resource allocation com. City of Pasadena, 1982-90; mem. Pasadena-Mishima (Japan) Sister Cities Internat. Com., 1983—; asst. chair Pasadena-Jarvenpaa, Finland, 1990-92, chair, 1992-95; asst. chair Pasadena-Mishima, 1996-97; active L.A. World Affairs Coun., Bonita Unified Sch. Dist. Curriculum Coun., 1990-93, Dist. Task Force Fine Arts, 1990-93, Dist. Task Force Tech., 1990-93, Dist. Handwriting Task Force, 1993, Pasadena Hist. Soc., Pasadena Philharm. Com., Womens Com. Pasadena Symphony Assn.; deacon Pasadena Presbyn. Ch., 1989-92, elder, 1997-2000; vice-moderator Presbyn. Women, 2000—; bd. govs. Occidental Coll. Alumni Assn., 2000—. Emergency Sch. Aid Act grant, 1977-81; named to Bonita Unified Sch. Dist. Hall of Fame, 1990 91. Mem. World Coun. Gifted and Talented Children, Internat. Soc. Edn. Through Art, Nat. Art Educators Assn. (dels. assembly 1988-92), L.A. County Art Edn. Coun., Clan MacLeod Soc. (bd. dirs. So. Calif. chpt.), Phi Delta Kappa, Kappa Delta Pi, Pi Lambda Theta (pres. L.A. chpt. 1991-95, nat. rsch. awards com. 1989-91, chair 1991-95, co-pres. region V 1993-97, Ella Victoria Dobbs Nat. Rsch. award 1989, Outstanding Pi Lambda Thetan in region V 1993-95, Internat. by-laws com. 1999-2003), Assistance League Pasadena.

BACHUS, BENSON FLOYD, mechanical engineer, consultant; b. LeRoy, Kans., Aug. 10, 1917; s. Perry Claude and Eva Pearl (Benson) B.; m. Ruth Elizabeth Beck, May 31, 1942; children: Carol Jean Schueler, Bruce Floyd, Linda Ruth Gadway. Degree, Hemphill Diesel Sch., Chgo., 1937; student, Sterling Coll., 1937-39; BSME, Kans. State U., 1942; postgrad., Ohio State U., 1961, Stevens Inst., 1964; MBA, Creighton U., 1967. Registered profl. engr., Ariz., Ill., Nebr. Rschr., mech. engr. Naval Ordnance Rsch. Lab., Washington, 1942-43; jr. product engr. Western Electric Co., Inc., Chgo. and Eau Claire, Wis., 1944-46, sr. devel. engr. Chgo., 1946-56, devel. engr. Omaha, 1960-66; product engr. mgr. Century Electronics and Instruments, Inc., Tulsa, Okla., 1956-60; sr. staff engr. Western Electric Co. div. AT&T Techs., Phoenix, 1966-85; owner, pres. Bachus Industries, Phoenix, 1982—. Chmn. energy conservation AT&T Techs., Inc., 1973-85; advisor to student engrs. Ariz. State U., 1967-87. Patentee in field (9). Trustee Village of Westchester (Ill.), 1949-53; sec.-treas. Westchester Broadview Water Commn., 1949-53; Sunday Sch. supr. Westchester Cmty. Ch., 1949-56; vol. campaign worker, precinct committeeman, capt. Phoenix Rep. Party, 1986—. Named Westchester Family of Yr., Westchester Cmty. Ch., 1952; recipient Centennial medal Am. Soc. Engrs., 1979, Recognition and Appreciation award Sterling Coll., 1996; named to Kans. State U. Coll. Engring. Hall of Fame, 1995. Fellow ASME (state legis. coord. 1985-86, 88-93, treas. Ariz. sect. 1971-72, sec. 1972-73, vice-chmn. 1973-74, chmn. 1974-75, 50-Yr. Membership award, President's Dedicated Svc., Devotion, Leadership, Performance award 1992, Dedicated Svc. award 1993); mem. TAPPI, NSPE (Engr. of Yr. award 1979), Soc. Profl. Engrs. (editor mag. 1972-86), Ariz. Coun. Engring. and Sci. Assn., Am. Security Coun., Soc. Plastics Engrs., Weoma Sci. Club (pres. 1963-66), Tel. Pioneers Am., Order of Engrs., Elks, Airstream Wally Byam Caravan Club Internat. Trailer Club. Avocations: woodworking, hiking, fishing, tennis, writing. Home and Office: 5229 N 43d St Phoenix AZ 85018-1671 Fax: 602-840-0822. E-mail: bbachus@pol.net.

BACHUS, SPENCER T., III, congressman, lawyer; b. Birmingham, Ala., Dec. 28, 1947; m. Linda; children: Warren, Stuart, Elliott, Candance, Lisa. BA, Auburn U., 1969; JD, U. Ala., 1972. Atty., 1972—; state senator from Ala. 17th dist., 1982-83; state rep. from Ala. 46th dist., 1984—86; sr. ptnr. Bachus, Dempsey, Carson, & Steed; mem. U.S. Congress from 6th Ala. dist., 1993—; mem. com. banking and fin. svcs., com. trans. and infrastructure, com. vets. affairs. Vice chmn. Jefferson County Legis. Del. Mgr. Guy Hunt's Gubernatorial campaign, 1986; del. Rep. Nat. Conv., 1988; mem. Ala. Bd. Edn.; chmn. Ala. State Rep. Exec. Com., 1991. Served in USAR, 1969—71. Recipient Commr's. merit award as Outstanding Rep. Ala. Dept. Human Resources, 1986, Henry M. Somerville award U. Ala. Republican. Office: US Ho of Reps 442 Cannon Bldg Washington DC 20515-0106*

BACHUS, WALTER OTIS, retired army general, former association executive; b. Grand Saline, Tex., Oct. 27, 1926; s. Walter Harry and Gladys Marie Bachus; m. Helen Singer, Dec. 12, 1946; children: Bruce, Leslie. BSCE, Tex. A&M U., 1950; M in Indsl. Engring., NYU, 1957; grad., Army War Coll., 1968; grad. Advanced Mgmt. Program, Harvard U., 1973. Registered profl. engr., Tex., Wash., D.C. Officer Corps Engrs. U.S. Army, 1950, advanced through grades to brig. gen.; ret., 1978; exec. dir. Soc. Am. Mil. Engrs., Alexandria, Va., 1978-93, ret., 1993. Decorated D.S.M., Legion of Merit, Bronze Star, Army Commendation medal; recipient Sec. of Def. Pub. Svc. medal. Christian Scientist. Home: 3808 Great Neck Ct Alexandria VA 22309-2634

BACHYNSKI, MORREL PAUL, physicist; b. Bienfait, Sask., Can., July 19, 1930; s. Nick and Karolina (Bachynski) B.; m. Slava Krkovic, May 1959; children: Caroline Dawn, Jane Diane. B.Eng., U. Sask., 1952, M.Sc., 1953; PhD, McGill U., 1955; LLD (hon.), U. Waterloo, 1993; DSc (hon.), McGill U., 1994; LLD (hon.), Concordia U., 1997. Mem. sci. staff RCA Ltd., Montreal, Que., 1955-58, dir. microwave physics lab., 1958-65, dir. research, 1965-72, dir. research and devel. labs., 1972-75, v.p. research and devel., 1975-76; pres. MPB Technologies Inc., Pointe Claire, Que., 1976—; Scitec, 1974-75. Author: (with Johnston and Shkarofsky) The Particle Kinetics of Plasmas, 1968; contbr. Recipient David Sarnoff Gold medal, 1963, Prix Scientifique du Quebec, 1973, Can. Enterprise Devel. award, 1977, Prix PME Que., 1984, Medal of Achievement Can. Rsch. Mgmt. Assn., 1988, Can. awards for Business Excellence-Entrepreneurship, 1989, 90, Prix award Assn. Que. Dirs. Indsl. Rsch., 1991, Prix Lionel Boulet, 2001. Fellow IEEE, Am. Phys. Soc., Royal Soc. Can. (Thomas W. Edie medal 2003), Can. Aero. and Space Inst., Can. Acad. Engring.; mem. Can. Assn. Physicists (pres. 1968, medal of achievement 1984, Applied Physics medal 1995), Sci. Coun. Can., Engring. Inst. Can. (hon.). Home: 78 Thurlow Rd Montreal QC Canada H3X 3G9 Office: MPB Techs Inc 151 Hymus Blvd Pointe Claire QC Canada H9R 1E9 E-mail: m.p.bachynski@mpb-technologies.ca.

BACIGALUPE, GONZALO MANUEL, family therapist, educator; b. Santiago, Chile, Nov. 23, 1958; came to U.S., 1988; s. Pedro Raimundo and Flor Maria Bacigalupe; m. Antonieta María Bolomey, Oct. 13, 1959; 2 children: Bethania Constanza, Diego Andreas. BA in Psychology, Cath. U. Chile, Santiago, 1984, MA equivalent Psychologist, 1986; EdD in Marriage and Family Therapy, U. Mass., 1995. Lic. marriage and family therapist, Mass. Clin. dir. adolescent unit La Granja Cmty. Mental Health Ctr., Santiago, 1985-86; clin. staff mem. Family Therapy Inst. Santiago, 1985-87; psychologist, mental health supr. Protection for Youth Damaged by States of Emergency, Temuco and Valdivia, Chile, 1987-88; prof. U. Los Lagos, Osorno, Chile, 1987-88; teaching asst. U. Mass., Amherst, 1988-91; outreach family therapist Northampton (Mass.) Area Mental Health Svcs., 1989-90; clin. supr. Mass. Soc. for Prevention of Cruelty to Children, Holyoke, Mass., 1990-94; asst. prof. Sch. Social and Systemic Studies Nova Southeastern U., Ft. Lauderdale, Fla., 1994-96; asst. prof. Grad. Coll. of Edn. U. Mass., Boston, 1996—2002, dir. family therapy program, 2000—02, assoc. prof., 2002—; staff clinician trauma evaluation and intervention team Judge Baker Children's Ctr./Harvard Med. Sch., 1997-99. Adj. prof. La Araucania Coll., Temuco, 1987—88; cons. Roxbury Comprehensive Health Ctr., 1996—97; staff psychologist Judge Baker Children's Ctr. Harvard Med. Sch., 1997—99; assoc. con. L.Am. Consultancy Svcs., 1996—98; mem. faculty family therapy team Ctr. for Multicultural Tng. in Psychology, 1997—2000; Fulbright sr. rsch. scholar Autonomous U. Barcelona, Spain. Mem. editl. rev. bd.: Jour. Systemic Therapies, 1994—; co-editor, 2001—; mem. editl. bd.: Jour. Marital and Family Therapy, —, Jour. Trauma Practice, 1993—2001; mem. editl. bd. Jour. of Qualitative Rsch. in Psychology; overview book reviewer: Readings, 1993—2001; prodr.: (TV series) cable access ACTV, 1991—94; video prodn. coord. : MCTV, 1992. Bd. dirs. Coun. Contemporary Families, 2000—02. Fgn. student tuition scholar U. Mass., 1989-90; rsch. fellow Mauricio Gaston Inst. Latino Cmty. Devel. and Pub. Policy, 1998-99, Am. Assn. for Marriage and Family Therapy Coun. of Elections, 1999-2001, Fulbright Sr. scholar, 2004. Fellow: Chilean Soc. Clin. Psychology; mem.: APHA, APA, Acad. for Health Svcs. and Health Policy, Assn. for Family Therapy, Internat. Family Therapy Assn. (3d World Family Therapy Congress award 1991), Interam. Soc. Psychology, Chilean Psychol. Assn., Am. Soc. Cybernetics (Travel scholar 1990), Am. Assn. for Marriage and Family Therapy (chair elections coun. 2001, supr. and clin.), Latin Am. Studies Assn., Am. Family Therapy Acad. (bd. dirs. 2001—), Soc. for the Psychol. Study of Social Issues. Office: Univ Mass Boston Grad Coll Edn 100 Morrissey Blvd Boston MA 02125-3393 E-mail: gonzalo.bacigalupe@umb.edu.

BACIN, MARK STEPHEN, museum director, retired naval officer; b. Cleve., Mar. 20, 1953; s. Donald Patrick and Sylvia Eleanor (Venglarchik) B. BA in History, Miami U., Oxford, Ohio, 1975. Commd. ensign USN, 1975, advanced through grades to comdr., 1990; gunnery officer USS Steinaker DD-863, Balt., 1975-77; electronics officer USS Schofield FFG-3, San Diego, 1977-78; 1st lt. USS Schofield, 1978-79, auxs. officer, 1979-80; pre-commissioning chief engr. USS Copeland FFG-25, Long Beach, Calif., 1980-84; ship sys. officer Lamps MK III Fleet Introduction Team, San Diego, 1984-86; combat sys. readiness, tactics and rsch., devel. officer Commander-in-Chief Pacific Fleet, Pearl Harbor, Hawaii, 1986-88; exec. officer USS Halsey CG-23, San Diego, 1989-90, Naval Ship Weapons Sys. Engring. Sta., Port Hueneme, Calif., 1990-95; ret. USN, 1995; exec. dir. Ventura County Maritime Mus., Oxnard, Calif., 1996—. Decorated Meritorious Svc. medal, Navy Commendation medals (3), Navy Achievement medals. Mem. U.S. Naval Inst., Am. Legion, Navy League, VFW. Home: 1190 Say Rd Santa Paula CA 93060 Office: Ventura County Maritime Mus 2731 S Victoria Ave Oxnard CA 93035-2947

BACK, LLOYD H. mechanical engineer, researcher; b. San Francisco, Feb. 13, 1933; s. Uno and Elna (Norgard) B.; m. Carol Peterson, Dec. 17, 1955; children: Martin, Carla, Debra. BS, U. Calif., Berkeley, 1959, PhD, 1962. Supr. fluid dynamic, reactive processes and biomed. rsch. Jet Propulsion Lab./Calif. Inst. Tech., Pasadena, 1962-92; clin. asst. prof. medicine U. So. Calif., 1974-92. Cons. in field, 1992—; vol. faculty mem. Sch. Medicine, U. So. Calif., L.A., 1992—. Author book chpt. Sgt. U.S. Army, 1953-55, Korea. Recipient Exceptional Svc. award NASA, 1979. Fellow ASME (life; chmn. heat transfer divsn., tech. editor jour., Heat Transfer Divsn. Disting. Svc. award 1987, 50th Anniversary award 1988), AIAA (assoc.; assoc. editor jour.). Achievements include contributions to the understanding of fundamental aspects of fluid mechanics and heat transfer in rocket propulsion, fluid dynamics of blood flow through diseased arteries, and in other experimental and analytical investigations of laminar and turbulent flows. Home: 16 Rushingwind Irvine CA 92614-7409

BACK, ROBERT WYATT, investment executive, pharmaceutical company executive consultant; b. Omaha, Dec. 22, 1936; s. Albert Edward Jr. and Edith (Elliott) B.; m. Linaya Gail Hahn, Aug. 30, 1964; children: Christopher Frederick, Gregory Franklin. BA, Trinity Coll., 1958; postgrad., London Sch. Econs. and Polit., 1959-60, Harvard U., 1960-61; MA, Yale U., 1960. CLU; CFA; ChFC. Head trader, reinsurance rep., security analyst Lincoln Nat. Life Ins. Co., Fort Wayne, Ind., 1964-69; sr. investment analyst Allstate Ins. Co., Northbrook, Ill., 1969-72; investment adv. acct. mgr. Brown Bros. Harriman & Co., Chgo., 1972-74; asst. v.p., investment analyst Harris Trust & Savs. Bank, 1974-82; v.p. instnl. rsch. Prescott Ball & Turben, 1982-83, Blunt, Ellis & Loewi, Inc., 1983-84; v.p. instnl. equity sales Rodman & Renshaw, Inc., 1984-87; v.p. instnl. rsch. ins. Legg, Mason, Wood & Walker, Inc., 1987-89; mng. dir. instnl. dept. J.E. Liss & Co., 1989-92; sr. v.p., sales mgr. SNC Capital Mgmt., 1991—; CEO IPOSITE.COM Inc. Mng. dir. investor pub. rels. CCR Assocs. Contbr. numerous articles to profl. jours. Mem. long-range planning com. Adlai Stevenson H.S., Prairie View, Ill., 1980-82; chmn. investments Ill. Police Pension Fund Assn., Chgo., 1985-87; pres. Buffalo Grove Police Pension Fund, 1973-90; deacon Presbyn. Ch.; active Founding Coun. Nat. Edn. Access Fund, 1992; chmn. emeritus Biolipids Pharm. Corp., 1992; fund mgr.

AIDS/HIV Select Fund, 1992—. Capt. USAFR, 1961-64. Woodrow Wilson fellow Yale U., 1958, English-Speaking Union fellow London Sch. Econs., 1959, Russian Rsch. fellow Harvard U., 1960-61; subject of Superanalyst profile Crains Chgo. Bus., 1987. Fellow Fin. Analysts Fedn. (internat. del. 1974—), Assn. for Investment Mgmt. and Rsch.; mem. Inst. Chartered Fin. Analysts (sec., bd. dirs. Chgo. chpt. 1980-84, lectr.), Am. Coll. CLUs and Chartered Fin. Cons. (bd. dirs. 1986-87), Yale Club Chgo. (bd. dirs. alumni assn. del. 1972—, coord. grad. and profl. alumni), Yale Club Fort Wayne, 1964-1990, (pres., co-author, Yale In the Modern World: Bush/Clinton/Bush, Big Money and the Presidential elections, Trinity Club (mem. exec. com. Chgo. chpt. 1987-90), Wheaton AM Rotary Club (charter, Paul Harris fellow 1995), Phi Beta Kappa, Pi Gamma Mu. Republican. Avocations: skiing, international travel, homeland security. Home: 225 N Dorchester Ave Wheaton IL 60187-4707 Office: CCR Assocs 225 N Dorchester Ave Wheaton IL 60187-4707

BACKAS, JAMES JACOB, foundation administrator; b. Chgo., May 3, 1926; s. John and Ernestine (Harms) B.; m. Margot Wells Schutt, Dec. 1973; 1 dau., Amy Elizabeth. BA, Mich. State U., 1950; postgrad., U. Mich., 1953-54; MA, U. Iowa, 1960; ArtsD (hon.), Oklahoma City U., 1999. Teaching fellow U. Iowa, Iowa City, 1958-59, research fellow, 1959-60; mgr. Coll. div. Doubleday & Co., N.Y.C., 1962-66; mktg. dir. publs. Brookings Instn., Washington, 1966-69; mng. editor Am. Mus. Digest, N.Y.C., 1969; exec. dir. Md. State Arts Council, 1972-76; spl. cons. to chmn. Nat. Endowment for Arts, 1976-78; exec. dir. Am. Arts Alliance, 1978-80; mgmt. cons. Washington, 1980-82; exec. dir. So. Arts Fedn., Atlanta, 1982-84, D.C. Commn. on Arts and Humanities, Washington, 1984-86, Md. State Arts Coun., 1986—2001. Music critic Washington Star, 1966-76; lectr. music history Peabody Conservatory, Balt., 1970-73; mem., co-chmn. music adv. panel Nat. Endowment Arts, 1982-87. Contbr. numerous articles on arts administration to profl. and govt. publs. Mem. adv. bd. ESEA Title III, Md., 1972-76; mem. policy com. for cultural affairs Johns Hopkins U., 1974-76; mem. exec. bd. Nat. Assembly State Arts Agy.; bd. dirs. Nat. Pub. Radio, Kennedy Ctr., Community Fedn. Greater Balt., Mid-Atlantic Arts Fedn., 1987-2001. Mem.: AAUP, Music Critics Assn., Assn. Univ. Presses, Phi Mu Alpha. Home: 3315 Q St NW Washington DC 20007-2717 E-mail: jmbackas@aol.com.

BACKER, CARL LEWIS, pediatric cardiac surgeon, educator; b. Mpls., Apr. 29, 1955; s. Gordon L. and Arlene I. Backer; m. Julia Ford Backer, May 1, 1992; children: Charlotte, Annabelle, Ford. BA with honors, Northwestern U., Evanston, Ill., 1976; MD, Mayo Med. Sch., 1980. Diplomate Am. Bd. Surgery, Am. Bd. Thoracic Surgery. Asst. prof. surgery Northwestern U., Chgo., 1988-96, assoc. prof. surgery, 1996-99, prof. surgery, 2000—. Attending cardiovascular surgeon Children's Meml. Hosp., Chgo., 1988—. Editor: Arterial Switch, 1991, Coarctation, 1993, Pediatric Cardiac Surgery, 1994, 2003. Named to Wausau (Wis.) Hall of Fame, Wausau Sch. Dist., 1994; recipient Physician's Recognition award AMA, 1997. Fellow ACS, Am. Coll. Cardiology, Am. Assn. Thoracic Surgery, Soc. Thoracic Surgeons, Drs.' Mayo Soc., Internat. Soc. Heart and Lung Transplantation, Phi Beta Kappa. Avocations: skiing, sailing, tennis, golf. Office: Children's Surg Found 2300 N Childrens Plz Chicago IL 60614-3363 E-mail: c-backer@childrensmemorial.org.

BACKER, JOANNE ARLENE, case manager; b. St. Paul, Dec. 15, 1950; d. Clarence Frederick and Beatrice P. (Slavik) B. BA in Psychology, U. Minn., 1977, BA in German, 1979; MA in German, Northwestern U., 1981. Family caseworker Ramsey County Cmty. Human Svcs., St. Paul, 1983—; mem. reference staff St. Paul Pub. Libr., 1999—. Freelance writer; staff writer The Guitarist, 1990-93. Mem. Minn. Guitar Soc. (bd. dir. 1990—, v.p. 1994—), Soroptimists of Greater Twin Cities (v.p. 1996-2000, Juclje award, 2003), League Minn. Poets, Pyrotechnics Guild Internat. (cert. shooter 2000—), No. Lighters Pyrotechnics, Judge, Soroptomists of Greater Twin cities Women's Opportunity Awards, 2003. Avocations: playing classical guitar, community theater, writing fiction, textile designing. E-mail: pyrolass@yahoo.com.

BACKER, MATTHIAS, JR., obstetrician, gynecologist; b. St. Louis, Dec. 19, 1926; s. Matthias Henry Sr. and Louise (Jokisch) B.; m. Laverne Elizabeth Knapp, June 4, 1949 (dec. Oct. 15, 1992); m. Georgia Lynn Garrison, Apr. 28, 1997; children: Mary Kathryn, Matt III, Marilyn Ann, Mary Lou, Donald, Robert, Edward, Mary Susan, Mary Carol, Mary Patrice, Joseph, Brian, Denis. MD, St. Louis U., 1950. Diplomate Am. Bd. Ob-Gyn. (examiner 1986-93), Nat. Bd. Med. Examiners. Intern Nat. Naval Med. Ctr., Bethesda, Md., 1950-51; resident in ob-gyn St. Louis U. Hosps., 1951-54; practice medicine specializing in ob-gyn St. Louis, 1954-85; instr. ob-gyn St. Louis U. Sch. Medicine, 1954-60, sr. instr., 1960-63, asst. clin. prof., 1963-66, assoc. clin. prof., 1966-72, clin. prof., 1972-85, prof. ob-gyn., chmn. dept., 1985-92, prof. and chmn. emeritus, 1992—, dir. ob-gyn outpatient clinic, 1967-69, mem. com. faculty appointments and promotions, 1972-81, mem. exec. com. faculty, 1972-76, mem. faculty affairs com., 1975-78, dir. residency program, 1985-92; staff cons. tchg., rsch, patient care Naval Med. Ctr., San Diego; adj. prof. ob-gyn. Uniformed Svc. Univ. of the Health Scis., 1994—. Chief ob-gyn St. Joseph's Hosp., Kirkwood., 1959-62, St. Anthony's, St. Louis, Hosp., 1966-69; pres. St. Louis U. Hosps. Med. Staff, 1968-69; mem. governing bd. St. Louis U. Hosps., 1969-70; pres. med. and dental staff St. Anthony's Med. Ctr., 1984-85; lectr. Archdiocesan PreCana Council, 1955-58, Archdiocesan Sch. Commn., 1969-72; pres. Backer & Probst Inc., St. Louis, 1967-85. Contbr. numerous articles to profl. jours. Bd. dirs. St. Louis chpt. Am. Cancer Soc., 1970-76, Blue Shield Mo. Med. Svc., 1970-80; lector Our Lady of Providence Ch., St. Louis, 1969-92; guardian ad litem for unborn Mo. Supreme Ct., 1971. Served to rear adm. M.C., USNR, 1944-84. Decorated Legion of Merit, Dept. Def. Superior Service medal; recipient Backer award St. Louis U. High Sch., 1983. Fellow ACS, ACOG (Adm. Robert A. Ross award Armed Forces dist. 1993); mem. AMA, Mo. Med. Assn., St. Louis Med. Soc., Soc. Mil. Surgeons U.S., Ctrl. Assn. Obstetricians and Gynecologists, St. Louis Gynecol. Soc. (pres. 1969-70), Naval Res. Assn. (past pres. Spirit of St. Louis chpt.). Roman Catholic. Home and Office: 3903 California St Unit 5 San Diego CA 92110-2157 also: 101 Flamingo Dr Saint Louis MO 63123-1007 E-mail: mattbacker@aol.com.

BACKER, WILLIAM EARNEST, food products executive; b. Fulton, Mo., Dec. 3, 1922; s. William Earnest and Ida Lorraine (Smith) B.; m. Marjorie Jean Keller, Dec. 25, 1943; children: W. Dale, Vicki Lynn McDaniel, Carolyn Sue Cave. BA in Chemistry, Westminster Coll., 1943; postgrad., Wayne U., 1954. Chemistry lab. technician Delco Remy, Muncie, Ind., 1943—44; gen. mgr. Backer Potato Chip Co., Fulton, Mo., 1946—50, pres., CEO, 1957—88, chmn. of bd., 1988—; regional sales exec. A.P. Green Refractories, Mexico, Mo., 1950—51, salesman Detroit, 1951—53; test engr. Ford Motor Co., Dearborn, Mich., 1953—57. Patentee M39-20mm Cannon components, package machine components, socket holder, socket wrench sorter having Braille for the blind. Pres. Fulton C. of C., 1977, also bd. dirs., chmn. planning and zoning; v.p. adminstrn./product sales Great Rivers coun. Boy Scouts Am., Columbia, Mo., 1980-92, also current trustee; chmn. bldg. and grounds Westminster Coll., Fulton, 1990-91; chmn. nominating com. Children's Hosp., Columbia; established Fulton Visitor Ctr./Collector Vehicle Mus., 1996; founding bd. dirs. The Carpenter's Kids, 1999. Recipient Resolution, donation for bldg., Callaway County Commrs., Fulton, 1989, Disting. Eagle Scout award Nat. Eagle Scout Assn., 1995, Disting. Eagle Scout award Mo. Ho. of Reps., 1996, Excellence in Cmty. Svc. award Daughters of the Am. Revolution, 2000; named Disting. Indsl. Developer, Fulton Rotary, 1994. Mem. Kiwanis Internat. (lt. gov. Mo./Ark. divsns 1987-88), Fulton Kiwanis (pres. 1968, Kiwanian of Yr. 1984, 94), Kingdom of Callaway (pres.-elect 2003). Republican. Presbyterian. Avocation: collector of vintage automobiles. Home: PO Box 128 Fulton MO 65251-0128 Office: Backer Potato Chip Co One Industrial Rd Fulton MO 65251 E-mail: webacker@ktis.net.

BACKES, JACK ABRAHAM, application developer; b. Brestowatz, Yugoslavia, Oct. 4, 1939; arrived in U.S., 1952, naturalized, 1957; s. Josef and Magdalena Zellenkowitsch Backes; m. Faye Moore, 1964 (div. 1970); children: Trina, Bobbie, Susan; m. Irene Villalobos, 1971 (div. 1977). Grad., Mesa (Ariz.) C.C., 1968; student, Ariz. State U. Computer programmer. Amateur U.S. chess champion, 1993, 1995—97, 2001. With USMC, 1960—64. Avocations: dancing, writing. Home: PO Box 12777 San Diego CA 92112

BACKES, JOAN, artist, educator; b. Milw., Jan. 31, 1950; d. Gilbert Frances and Jeanne (Vogt) B.; m. Thomas Deeg Sills, June 14, 1975; children: Joseph Backes Sills, Elizabeth Backes Sills. BA, U. Iowa, 1972; MA, U. Mo., 1983; MFA, Northwestern U., Evanston, Ill., 1985. Adj. asst. prof. U. Mo., Kansas City, 1985-88; instr. Kansas City Art Inst., 1988-94; vis. prof. U. Chile, Santiago, 1994-95; adj. asst. prof. Brown U., Providence, 1997-2000; resident artist Nova Scotia Coll. Art and Design, Halifax, Can., 1999, Pori Coll. of Art, Finland, 2001. Adj. prof. Maine Coll. Art Grad. Program, 2000—; resident artist Aberdeen Art Mus., Scotland, 1986—87, Nat. Gallery, Reykjavik, Iceland, 1989, Edward Munch Studio Ekely, Oslo, 1991, Yellowstone (Wyo.) Nat. Park, 1992; artist-in-residence Ragdale Found., 1998—99, 2000, Hafnarborg Inst. Culture and Fine Art, 1998—99, 2000, 02; vis. artist Mass. Coll. Art Grad. Prgm., Portland, 2000—01, U. Mass./Dartmouth, 2001, Pori Coll. Art, Finland, 2001, Boston U., 2003, Hafnarborg Inst., Iceland, 2003; mem. selections com. Fulbright Sr. Scholar award. One-women shows include Aberdeen Art Mus., Scotland, 1987, Hafnarborg Art Mus., Iceland, 1991, 98, 2003, Dorry Gates Gallery, Kansas City, 1988, 90, 94, Tiverton, RI, 1995, 97, 2000, Museo de Arte Contemporaneo, Santiago, Chile, Mus. Contemporary Art, Santiago, 1996, Centro Cultural Recoleta, Buenos Aires, 1997, James Baird Gallery, St. Johns, Newfoundland, 1998, Nova Scotia (Can.) Coll. Art and Design, 1999, Braitmayer Art Ctr., Marion, Mass., 2000, Jan Weiner Gallery, Kansas City, Mo., 2001, Dartmouth Coll., Hanover, NH, 2002; exhibited in group shows at Chgo. Art Inst., 1990, Joslyn Art Mus., 1990, New Bedford (Mass.) Art Mus., 1997, 99, Museo de Arte Contemporaneo, Santiago, Chile, 1998, U. Mass., Dartmouth, 1999, Attleboro (Mass.) Art Mus., 2000, Wustum Mus. Fine Arts, Racine, Wis., 2000, Nelson-Atkins Art Mus., Kansas City, Mo., 2000, Nielsen Gallery, Boston, 2000, RISD-RI Found., Providence, 2000, Contemporary Mus. Balt., 2001, Block Mus., Northwestern U., 2001, RI Sch. Design, 2001, Wustum Mus. Fine Arts, Racine, Wis, 2001, 03, Newport(RI) Art Mus., 2002, Sotheby's, NYC, 2002 Virginia Lynch Gallery, Tiverton, RI, 2003, Borusan Found., Istanbul, Turkey, 2003; represented in permanent collections at Milw. Art Mus., Nelson-Atkins Mus., Kansas City, Aberdeen Art Mus., Scotland, Hafnarborg Art Mus., Wustum Mus. Fine Arts, Joslyn Art Mus., Omaha, Nova Scotia Coll. Art and Design, Halifax, Can., Embassy of the US in Iceland. Bd. trustees Ragdale Found.; mem. selections com. Fulbright Sr. Scholar Awards. Grantee Kans. Arts Commn./NEA, 1986, 92, Am.-Scandinavian Found., NY, 1991; Fulbright scholar 1994-95; recipient award Ragdale Found., 1998, 99, 2000, Fulbright/Hays award, 2003. Mem. Coll. Art Assn., Kansas City Artists Coalition, Phi Kappa Phi. Avocations: swimming, hiking, travel. Office: PO Box 100 Seekonk MA 02771-0100

BACKES, ORLIN WILLIAM, lawyer; b. Glenburn, N.D., May 11, 1935; s. Leonard P. and Irene G.(Keller) B.; m. Millie Jensen, Oct. 15, 1958; children—Brent, Jon, Mary, Paul. B.S., Minot State U., 1958; J.D., U. N.D., 1963. Bar: N.D. Faculty Max Pub. Sch., N.D., 1958-60; ptnr. McGee Law Firm, Minot N.D., 1963— ; dir. First Western Bank, Minot., dir. Integrity Mutual Fund Board; Mayor, City of Minot, 1994-98, fellow, Am. Coll. of Trial Lawyers; Advocate Am. Bd. of Trial Advocates. bd. regents Minot State U., 1981. Recipient Golden award Minot State U., 1984. Mem. Order of Coif, Minot C. of C. (pres. 1974). Roman Catholic. E-mail: obackes@mcgeelaw.com. Home: 948 13th Ave SE # 2 Minot ND 58701-2708 Office: McGee Law Firm Wells Fargo Bank Ctr Minot ND 58701

BACKHERMS, KATHRYN ANNE, parochial school educator; b. Cin., Aug. 19, 1955; d. Francis Walter and Mary Elizabeth (Healy) B. BA, Coll. Mount St. Joseph (Ohio), 1977; MusM, U. Cin., 1981. Cert. tchr., Ohio. Music specialist 1-8 St. Ursula Villa, Cin., 1977-79; choral music dir. McAuley High Sch., Cin., 1980-86; chairperson music dept. Coll. Mt. St. Joseph, 1986-89; music dir. St. Ursula Acad., Cin., 1989—. Mem. rev. teams area high schs. North Cent. Assn., Cin., 1987-89; presenter Archdiocesan In-Svc. Day, Cin., 1988; adjudicator Ohio Fedn. Music Clubs, Cin., Ohio Fedn. Music Clubs Collegiate Solo Auditions, Columbus, 1989. Composer: (musicals) Musical, 1973, Just Like Me, 1975, Take A Chance, 1976, Nothing Can Stop Us Now, 1979, Heaven Help Us, 1983, Some Things Never Change, 1984, The Real Me, 1985, Something Special, 1997, The Magic Touch, 2001. Recipient Tchr. award Greater Cin. Found., 1984; profl. devel. grantee St. Ursula Acad., 1997, 2000. Mem. Music Educators Nat. Conf., Mu Phi Epsilon (v.p. Cin. alumnae chpt. 1992-94), Kappa Gamma Pi (treas. Cin. alumnae chpt. 1988-89). Avocations: composing, playing instruments, pets, astronomy. Office: Saint Ursula Acad 1339 E McMillan St Cincinnati OH 45206-2180

BACKLUND, JAMES DAVID, psychology educator; b. Iron Mountain, Mich., Jan. 6, 1955; s. Adolph Matthew and Rena H. B.; m. Mary Sue Metor, June 5, 1981; children; Zachary, Maxwell. BS, No. Mich. U., 1982; MA, Western Mich. U., 1983. Instr. psychology Kirtland C.C., Roscommon, Mich., 1988-2001. With USAF, 1973-75. Mem.: Am. Psychol. Soc. Home: 2206 Deepwoods Dr Gaylord MI 49735

BACKMAN, GERALD STEPHEN, lawyer; b. N.Y.C., Apr. 16, 1938; s. Morris (dec. Dec. 2001) and Marion (London)(dec. Jan. 2003) B.; m. Susan Pergament, Sept. 3, 1961 (dec. May 1978); children: Jonathan A., Kenneth S.; m. Barbara Fried Kaynes, Nov. 3, 1979 (dec. Jan. 2003); children: Jonathan J. Kaynes, Adam R. Kaynes. BA, U. Pa., 1959; LLBcum laude, Harvard U., 1962. Assoc. Weil, Gotshal & Manges LLP, N.Y.C., 1962-70, ptnr., 1970—. House counsel The Associated Merchandising Corp., N.Y.C., 1965-68; lectr. N.Y.U., 1973, Irving Trust Co., N.Y.C., 1981-88; mem. Blue Ribbon Commn. on Audit Coms. of Nat. Assn. Corp. Dirs., also chair N.Y. chpt.; adj. prof. law Fordham U. Sch. Law, N.Y.C., 2000—; mem. Tri-Bar Opinion Com., 2000—. Bd. dirs. Hewlett-East Rockaway (N.Y.) Jewish Ctr., 1976-97, chmn. legal com., 1974-85, sec., 1980-82; bd. dirs. 25 E. 86th St. Corp., 1996-99. Mem.: ABA, Assn. Bar N.Y.C., N.Y. State Bar Assn. (trustee bus. law sect. 2000—03, chmn. securities regulation com. 2000—03), Am. Arbitration Assn. (arbitrator), Nat. Assn. Corporate Dirs. (chmn., pres. N.Y. chpt.), Masons. Republican. Jewish. Avocations: golf, skiing, tennis, fishing. Home: 25 E 86th St Apt 9G New York NY 10028-0553 Office: Weil Gotshal & Manges LLP 767 5th Ave New York NY 10153-0119 E-mail: Gerald.Backman@Weil.com.

BACKMAN, MELVIN ABRAHAM, English educator; b. Lynn, Mass., Feb. 12, 1919; s. David A. Backman and Sophie Berman; m. Dorothy Weisman, Dec. 23, 1946 (dec. Oct. 1962); children: Sherril Jo Backman Aaron, Maren Ruth (dec.); m. Lisbeth-Anne Niesz, June 27, 1971. BS, Bridgewater Tchrs. Coll., 1941; MA, Columbia Tchrs. Coll., 1947; PhD, Columbia U., 1960. Instr. English Richmond (Va.) Profl. Inst., 1948-51; prof. humanities Clarkson Coll. Tech., Potsdam, N.Y., 1953-67; prof. English C.W. Post Coll., L.I. U., Brookville, N.Y., 1967-89, prof. emeritus, 1989—. Author: Faulkner: The Major Years, 1966, (French translation) William Faulkner, 1968; contbg. author: Hemingway and His Critics, 1961, The Stoic Strain in American Literature, 1979. Staff sgt. USAAC, 1943-46, China, Burma, India. Avocations: reading, gardening. Home: 11 Northfield Rd Glen Cove NY 11542-1717

BACKSTEDT, ROSEANNE JOAN, artist; b. San Francisco, Dec. 15, 1941; d. Anthony and Tillie LaRocca; m. Lawrence Henry Backstedt, Aug. 9, 1964; 1 child, Simone Rose. Student, San Francisco Art Inst., 1960-64, U. Oreg., 1966-68, Aesthetic Realism Found., 1976—. Mem. Ceres Gallery, N.Y.C., 1991—. One-woman shows include Sullivan County Mus., Hurleyville, N.Y., 1972, Hansen Gallery, N.Y.C., 1973-77, The Viewing Rm., N.Y.C., 1978, Noho Gallery, N.Y.C., 1987, Ceres Gallery, N.Y.C., 1991—; group shows include Elysian Art Gallery, San Francisco, 1962-64, Portland Art Mus., 1969, Terrain Gallery, N.Y.C., 1979-85, 2000, Ligoa Duncan Gallery, N.Y.C., 1980, Krasdale Food Corp., Bronx, 1989, 91, 94, Z Gallery, N.Y.C., 1991, 92, World Trade Ctr., N.Y.C., 1991, Triplex Gallery, N.Y.C., 1992, Snug Harbor Cultural Ctr., S.I., N.Y., 1992, Lincoln Ctr., N.Y.C., 1994, Cedco Calendars, 1994-97, JCB Internat. Co., N.Y.C., 1996, Univ. Luth Ch., Harvard Square, Mass., 1996, Mills Pond Ho., St. James, N.Y., 1997, Artemisia Gallery, Chgo., 1997, Künstlerforum, Bonn, 1998, Orange County C.C., Middletown, N.Y., 1998, Soho 20 Gallery, N.Y.C., 1999, Kingsborough C.C., Bklyn., 1999, Caelum Gallery, N.Y.C., 2000-03, SUNY at Buffalo, 2000; presenter ART TALK, Aesthetic Realism Found., N.Y.C., 1998-01. Office: Ceres Gallery 547 W 27th St 2d Floor New York NY 10001

BACKUS, GEORGE EDWARD, theoretical geophysicist; b. Chgo., May 24, 1930; s. Milo Morlan and Dora Etta (Dare) B.; m. Elizabeth Evelyn Allen, Nov. 15, 1961 (div. 1971); children: Benjamin, Brian, Emily; m. Varda Esther Peller, Jan. 8, 1977 PhB, U. Chgo., 1947, BS in Math., 1948, MS in Math. and Physics, 1950, 53, PhD in Physics, 1956; D honoris causa, Inst. de Physique de Globe, Paris, 1995. Jr. mathematician Inst. for Air Weapons, Chgo., 1951-53; physicist Project Matterhorn, Princeton, N.J., 1957-58; asst. prof. math. MIT, Cambridge, 1958-60; assoc. prof. geophysics U. Calif. San Diego, La Jolla, 1960-62, prof. geophysics, 1962-94, rsch. prof. geophysics, 1994-99, prof. geophys. emeritus, 1999—. Mem. vist. com. Institut de Physique du Globe de Paris, 1987; co-chmn. Internat. Working Group on Magnetic Field Satellites, 1983-90; chair acad. senate U. Calif., San Diego, 1992-93. Contbr. articles to profl. jours. Guggenheim Found. fellow, 1963, 71; Royal Soc. Arts fellow, London, 1970 Fellow Royal Astron. Soc. (Gold medal 1986), Am. Geophys. Union (John Adam Fleming medal 1986); mem. NAS (com. on grants and fellowships Day Fund 1974-79, com. on sci. and pub. policy 1971-74), Académie des Sciences (France), Am. Phys. Soc., Am. Math. Soc., Math. Assn. Am., Soc. for Indsl. and Applied Math., Am. Geophys. Union. Avocations: skiing, swimming, bicycling, hiking, history. Office: IGPP U Calif San Diego La Jolla CA 92093-0225 E-mail: gbackus@ucsd.edu.

BACKUS, JOHN, computer scientist; b. Phila., Dec. 3, 1924; m. Una Stannard, 1968; children: Karen, Paula. BS, Columbia U., 1949, AM, 1950; D.Univ. (hon.), U. York, Eng., 1985; ScD (hon.), U. Ariz., 1988; D honoris causa, Université de Nancy 1, France, 1989; ScD (hon.), Ind. U., 1992. Programmer IBM, N.Y.C., 1950—53, mgr. programming rsch., 1954—59; staff mem. IBM T.J. Watson Rsch. Ctr., Yorktown Heights, NY, 1959—63; IBM fellow IBM Rsch., Yorktown Heights and San Jose, Calif., 1963—91; mgr. functional programming IBM Almaden Rsch. Ctr., San Jose, 1980—91; cons., 1991—. Mgr. Incest Info. Bay Area, 1992—2003. With U.S. Army, 1943—46. Recipient W. Wallace McDowell award, IEEE, 1967, Nat. Medal of Sci., 1975, Harold Pender award, Moore Sch. Elec. Engring., U. Pa., 1983, Achievement award, Indsl. Rsch. Inst., Inc., 1983. Fellow: Am. Acad. Arts and Scis.; mem.: NAE (Charles Stark Draper prize 1993), NAS, Assn. Computing Machinery (Turing award 1977). Achievements include system design of IBM 704, Fortran programming lang., Backus-Naur Form lang., function level programming; mem. design group ALGOL 60 lang. Home: 91 Saint Germain Ave San Francisco CA 94114-2129

BACKUS, JOHN KING, former chemical company research administrator; b. Buffalo, May 22, 1925; s. Arthur Osgood and Lois V. (King) B.; m. Marjorie North, June 18, 1950; children: David King, Lois Victoria, Laura North Scott, Ruth Ellen Grillo. BA in Chemistry and Math., Hamilton Coll., 1947; MS in Phys. Chemistry, Cornell U., 1950, PhD, 1952. Rsch. chemist Procter & Gamble Co., Cin., 1952-53; rsch. chemist, supr. Gen. Mills, Inc., Tonawanda, N.Y., 1953-61; rsch. specialist Mobay Corp. (now Bayer Corp.), Pitts., 1962-64, group leader, 1964-67, mgr. applications rsch., 1967-68, mgr. rsch. svcs., 1968-90; ret., 1990. Participant profl. confs. Patentee in field (3); contbr. articles to tech. jours. Chmn. bd. dirs. Bach Choir Pitts., 1969-70; bd. dirs. Western Pa. Safety Coun., 1975-90, mem. exec. com., 1983-90, chair safety and health conf., 1980; mem. Pitts. Concert Chorale, 1989-2000; mem. coun. First Luth. Ch., Pitts., 1978-80, 84-87, 92-93, pres., 1979; mem. coun. southwestern Pa. synod Evang. Luth. Ch. in Am., 1992-97, 2002—; co-pres. chpt. AFS Internat. Scholarships, 1972-75, host parent, 1969-70, 79; pres. H.S. Parent-Faculty Assn., 1970-71; advisor Explorer Post, 1967-68; chair corp. sect. United Way Western Pa., 1981-82; organizer, dir. Bayer Choir, 1978-90. With U.S. Army, 1944-46. Mem. Am. Chem. Soc. (environ. improvement com. 1990-95, chmn. elect Pitts. sect. 1992, chmn. 1993, dir. 1995—, chmn. elect chemists club group 2000, chmn. 2001-03), N.Y. Acad. Scis., AAAS, Soc. Plsatics Industry (chair tech. conf. of urethane divsn. 1977), Sigma Xi. Republican. Avocations: music, gardening, swimming. Home: 9441 Katherine Dr Allison Park PA 15101-2020 E-mail: mjbackus@worldnet.att.net.

BACKUS, KEVIN MICHAEL, minister; b. Holyoke, Mass., Oct. 27, 1956; m. Sharon Diane Marshall, Aug. 16, 1980. BA in Bibl. Lit., Shelton Coll., Cape Canaveral, Fla., 1978; MDiv, Faith Theol. Sem., Elkins Park, Pa., 1982; STM, Whitefield Theol. Sem., 1995, PhD in Bibl. Counseling, 1997. Cert. tchr. Bible, history, and langs., cert. sch. adminstr.; ordained to ministry Bible Presbyn. Ch., 1982. Asst. pastor Armor Bible Presbyn. Ch., Orchard Park, N.Y., 1977, Bible Presbyn. Ch., Grand Island, NY, 1978-80, assoc. pastor, 1982-99, sr. pastor, 1999—; stated supply pastor Calvary Bible Presbyn. Ch., Trenton, N.J., 1980-82; dir. devel. Faith Christian Sch., Collingswood, N.J., 1981-82; adminstr. Grand Island Christian Sch., 1986-92; adj. prof. Biblical counseling Western Ref. Sem., 1995—; dir. grad. Sch. biblican counseling Whitefield Theol. Sem., 1996—2001. Pres. Internat. Christian Youth, Collingswood, 1982-86; stated clk. Bible Presbyn. Ch.-Gen. Synod, 1989-95, chmn. interchurch rels., 1989—, moderator 64th Synod. Staff editor Christian Observer, 1994—; contbr. articles to profl. jours. Fellow Nat. Assn. Nouthetic Counselors (bd. dirs.); mem. Presbyn. Missionary Union (coun. mem. 1989—, exec. mem. 1989—, 2000-01, v.p. 1991-95, pres. 1996-98, v.p. 1998-2000, pres. 2000-02), N.Y. State Sunday Sch. Assn. (bd. dirs. 1994, cons. 1995). Office: Bible Presbyn Ch 1650 Love Rd Grand Island NY 14072-2311 *Two things I constantly underestimate in life: the depravity of man, and the grace of God. Thankfully sovereign grace is greater.*

BACKUS, ROBERT COBURN, biophysical chemist; b. Carroll, Iowa, Aug. 25, 1913; s. Roy Eugene and Ethel (Coburn) B.; m. Beverly Helen Torwelle, July 5, 1940; children: Byron Torwelle, Robley Dean. BS, Dakota Wesleyan U., 1937; MS in Biochemistry, U. Mich., 1944, PhD in Bacteriology/Immunology, 1951. Instr. field army sanitation, rsch. viral hepatitis Sch. Pub. Health (U.S. Army contracts), 1942-45; rschr. physics dept. U. Mich., Ann Arbor, 1946-50; rschr. Virus Lab. U. Calif., Berkeley, 1950-56; cons. rsch. grants, contracts Am. Cancer Soc., N.Y.C., 1957; rsch. grants adminstr. Nat. Cancer Inst.-NIH, Bethesda, Md., 1958-61. Nat. Inst. Allergy, Infectious Disease, NIH, Bethesda, Md., 1962-65; office of dir. NIH, Bethesda, Md., 1965-87, ret., 1987. Biophysicist U.S. Dept. Agrl. European Commn. Foot and Mouth Disease, Pirbright, Eng., 1951; staff Surgeon Gen.'s Ad Hoc Adv. Com. on Quarantine, Washington, 1967; staff HEW Tuskegee Syphilis Study Ad Hoc Adv. Panel, Washington, 1972-73; acting exec. sec. HEW Ethics Adv. Bd., 1978; bd. trustees Am. Type Culture Collection, 1962-68; mem. Civil Svc. Exam. Bd. for Health Scientist Adminstrn. Applicants, 1962-68. Contbr. articles to profl. jours. Mem. Electron Microscope Soc. Am. (bd. dirs. 1954-57), Sigma Xi (life). Achievements include electron microscopic counts of virus particles and determination of macromolecular weights; correlation of bacteriophage counts with infectivity; invention of field aligning capsule centrifugation; others. Home: 5305 Roosevelt St Bethesda MD 20814-1431

BACKUS, SUSAN, clinical social worker, educator; b. Dec. 18, 1943; d. Norman Lloyd and Mildred (Billington) Backus; children: Rebecca Sue, Joshua Allen. BS, Ind. U., 1965, MA, 1967; MSW, U. Denver, 1977; Cert. in Family Therapy, Smith Coll. Social Wk., 1984-85; PhD in Religious and Psychol. Studies, Illiff Sch. Theology/U. Denver, 1992. Lic. clin. social worker, Colo. Counselor II Human Svcs., Inc., Travelers Aid, 1978-79; sr. clinician Arapahoe Community Mental Health, 1979-81; sch. social worker Westminster Sch. Dist. #50, 1981-86; family edn. counselor and family therapist Jefferson Ctr. for Mental Health, 1987-89; pvt. practice Denver, 1983—. Practicum supr. Lesley Coll., Denver, 1988—91, instr., 1994—95; asst prof. St. Thomas Sem., Denver, 1992—95; assoc. prof. Regis U., Denver, 1995—. Schlessmann fellowship U. Denver, 1986-90. Mem. Nat. Orgn. Social Workers, Am. Assn. Pastoral Counselors (profl. affiliate), Am. Counseling Assoc. Episcopalian. Avocations: skiing, hiking, music, naturalist. Office: 777 Grant St Ste 304 Denver CO 80203-3534

BACON, A. SMOKI, television host; b. Brookline, Mass., Jan. 29, 1928; d. Alfred Leon and Ruth Dorothy (Burns) Ginepra; m. Edwin Conant Bacon, May 11, 1957 (dec. July 1974); children: Brooks Conant, Hilary Conant; m. Richard Francis Concannon, Oct. 13, 1979. Student, Art Inst. Boston, 1947; grad., Jackson Von Ladau Sch. Design, Boston, 1951. Pub. rels. cons., Boston, 1968—; pres. Bacon-Concannon Assocs., Boston, 1979-95; dir. craftsmobiles Summerthing Program, Boston, 1968-73; dir. exhibits Citifair, Boston, 1974; dir. Victorian exhibits Bicentennial Boston 200, 1975, dir. spl. events, 1976; cons. spl. events. Inst. Contemporary Art, 1977-78, Boston Tea Party Ship, 1978-79; fundraiser Mass. Assn. Mental Health, 1979; dir. promotions Met. Ctr., 1979; coord. grand finale celebration Boston Jubilee 350, 1979-80; coord. Elliot Norton Awards, 1983; pub. rels. Dyansen Gallery, Boston, 1987-88, French Speaking League, 1987; cons. spl. events Jordan Marsh, 1987; fundraiser, pub. rels. Boston Philharmonic, 1988; coord. 30th anniversary celebration Charles Playhouse, 1988; fundraiser Elliot Norton Awards, 1989; coord. benefit New Eng. Premiere of film Glory Afro-Am. Mus., 1990; pub. rels. cons. Boston Chamber Music Soc., 1990; pub. rels. Paul Sorota Gallery of Fine Arts,

1990-91; fundraising cons. Internat. Inst., 1991; pub. rels., fundraiser Brookline H.S. Sesquicentennial Celebration, 1992-93; co-host radio show Celebrity Time, 1980—; co-host TV show On the Town. Guest lectr. Boston U. Sch. Pub. Rels., 1979, ARC, 1987, Radcliffe Coll. 4'0'Clock Forums, 1989, publicity club Boston, ARC, YMCA, Boston U. Sch. Pub. Rels., Mass Polit. Women's Conf., Women's Italian Club, Brookline Rotary, Harvard Coll. Rotary Club; contbg. editor Design Times Mag. Social calendar editor Boston Tab Newspaper, 1987-90; contbg. editor Design Times Mag.; columnist BeaconHill News. Candidate Dem. State Rep., Mass., 1980; Bastille Day chmn. French Libr. Boston, 1994—; local adv. com. Nat. Trust for Historic Preservation; bd. dirs. Boston Lit. Hour; host parents com. Harvard Coll.; bd. dirs. Mugar Libr., Spl. Collections, 1994—; vis. com. Mus. Fine Arts, Eqyptian Dept., 1994—; bd. trustees Boston Arts Festival, 1960-63; bd. dirs., treas. Samaritans, Boston, 1974-84; art auction chairperson WGBH-Pub. Radio-TV, Boston, 1969-70; bd. dirs. Urban League Ea. Mass., Boston, 1975-85, Elders Living at Home Program, Boston City Hosp. Kids Fund ; former mem. numerous civic coms. Recipient Woman of Great Achievement award Cambridge Young Women's Assn., 1991, appreciation award The Samaritans, 1991, Leadership award Friends of the Pub. Garden, 1975; named One of Boston's 100 Female Leaders, Boston Mag., 1980, One of the Boston Area Schs. Notable Grad. List, 1994; Guest of Honor, Womens' City Club Ann. Dinner Dance, 1979; Honored Those who Help Keep Boston's Non-Profit Agencies Alive Horizons for Youth, 1972, Charitable and Civic Endeavors Boston Italian Women's Club, 1995; donated personal ofcl. documents Women's Time Capsule Schlesinger Libr. Radcliffe Coll., 1981. Mem. AAUW, Harvard Club Boston, Women's City Club. Democrat. Avocation: artistics graphics. Home: 94 Beacon St Ste 1 Boston MA 02108-3329 Office: Bacon Concannon Assocs 94 Beacon St Boston MA 02108-3329 Fax: (617) 523-1998. E-mail: SmokBacon@aol.com.

BACON, BRETT KERMIT, lawyer; b. Perry, Iowa, Aug. 8, 1947; s. Royden S. and Aldeen A. (Zuker) B.; m. Bonnie Jeanne Hall; children: Jeffrey Brett, Scott Michael. BA, U. Dubuque, 1969; JD, Northwestern U., 1972. Bar: Ohio 1972, U.S. Ct. Appeals (6th cir.) 1972, U.S. Supreme Ct. 1980. Assoc. Thompson, Hine & Flory, Cleve., 1972-80, ptnr., 1980-2000; founding ptnr. Frantz Ward, Cleve., 2000—. Spkr. in field. Author: Computer Law, 1982, 84. V.p. profl. sect. United Way, Cleve., 1982-86; pres. Shaker Heights Youth Ctr., Inc., Ohio, 1984-86; elder Ch. of Western Res., 1996—. Mem. Fedn. Ins. and Corp. Counsel, Bar Assn. Greater Cleve., Cleve. Play House Club (officer 1986-94, pres. 1991-93, pres. men's com. 1993-96), Pepper Pike Civic League (trustee and treas. 1994-97). Home: 33076 Woodleigh Rd Cleveland OH 44124-5257 Office: Frantz Ward LLP Ste 1900 55 Public Sq Bldg Cleveland OH 44114

BACON, BRUCE RAYMOND, physician; b. Amherst, Ohio, Nov. 7, 1949; s. Raymond Clifford and Cathryn E. (Fowell) B.; children: Jeffrey Dale, Laurie Katherine. BA in chem., Coll. Wooster, 1971; MD, Case Western Reserve U., 1975. Diplomate Am. Bd. Internal Medicine and Gastroenterology. Asst. prof. medicine Case Western Reserve U., Cleve., 1982-87, assoc. prof. medicine, 1987-88; assoc. prof. medicine, chief gastroenterology sect. La. State U., Shreveport, 1988-90; prof. internal medicine, dir. gastroenterology divsn. St. Louis U. Sch. Medicine, St.Louis, 1990—. Chair subspecialty bd. gasteroenterology Am. Bd. Internal Medicine, 1999—. Co-author: Essentials of Clinical Hepatology, 1993; co-editor: Liver Disease: Diagnosis and Management, 2000; contbr. numerous articles to profl. jours. Fellow ACP, Am. Coll. Gastroenterology, Am. Soc. Clin. Investigation; mem. Am. Assn. Study Liver Disease (pres.-elect 2003). Presbyterian. Avocation: photography. Office: St Louis U Health Sci Ctr 3635 Vista Ave PO Box 15250 Saint Louis MO 63110-0250

BACON, CAROLINE SHARFMAN, investor relations consultant; b. Ann Arbor, Mich., Aug. 27, 1942; d. Mahlon Samuel and Mary Patricia (Potter) Sharp; m. William Lee Sharfman, Sept. 5, 1964 (div. 1985); m. James Edmund Bacon, Nov. 4, 1989. BA with distinction, U. Mich., 1964; MBA, Columbia U., 1975. Assoc. Goldman, Sachs & Co., N.Y.C., 1975-80, v.p., 1980-83, Goldman Sachs Money Markets Inc., N.Y.C., 1983-90; sr. cons. investor rels. Burson-Marsteller, 1991; mng. dir. Johnnie D. Johnson & Co. Investor Rels., N.Y.C., 1992-95. Investor rels. cons. Mem. Phi Beta Kappa, Phi Sigma Iota, Beta Gamma Sigma. Episcopalian.

BACON, DONALD CONRAD, author, editor; b. Jacksonville, Fla., Jan. 15, 1935; s. Francis Herbert and Myrtis Ann (Gunter) B.; m. Barbara Lee Barnwell, June 22, 1957; children— Elizabeth, Jennifer (dec.). BS in Journalism, U. Fla., 1957. Staff writer Wall St. Jour., 1957-61; Congl. fellow, 1961-62; staff writer Washington Star, 1962-63; successively Congl. corr., White House corr., sr. corr. and columnist Newhouse News Service, 1963-75; asso. editor U.S. News & World Report mag., Washington, 1975-79, sr. editor, 1979-81, asst. mng. editor, 1981-88; sr. editor Nation's Business, 1988-89; project dir. Ency. of U.S. Congress, Washington, 1989-95; pres. Fund for the Study of Congress, 1989—. Author: Congress and You, 1969; co-author: The New Millionaires, 1961, Rayburn-A Biography, 1987 (Best Biography award Tex. Hist. Commn. 1987, Best Book award Washingtonian mag. 1987); co-editor: Encyclopedia of the United States Congress, 1995 (Best Reference Source Libr. Jour., 1995). Recipient (with others) Loeb award U. Conn., 1961; award for excellence in journalism Lincoln U., Jefferson City, Mo., 1977, Disting. Alumnus award, U. Fla. Coll. Journalism, 2001. Mem. Cosmos Club (Washington). Home: 3809 E West Hwy Chevy Chase MD 20815-5918 E-mail: donbacon@erols.com.

BACON, EDMUND NORWOOD, city planner; b. Phila., May 2, 1910; s. Ellis W. and Helen (Comly) B.; m. Ruth Holmes, Sept. 16, 1938 (dec. May 1991); children: Karin Ellis, Elinor Ruth, Hilda Holmes, Michael Comly, Kira, Kevin Norwood. B.Arch., Cornell U., 1932. Archtl. designer, Shanghai, China, 1934; with W. Pope Barney, architect, Phila., 1935; supr. city planning Inst. Research and Planning, Flint, Mich., 1937-39; mng. dir. Phila. Housing Assn., 1940-43; co-designer Better Phila. Exbn.; also sr. land planner Phila. City Planning Commn., 1946-49, exec. dir., 1949-70, also devel. coordinator, 1968-70; v.p. design devel. Mondev Internat. Ltd., 1972-87. Prof. adviser in Franklin D. Roosevelt Meml. Competition, 1959; adj. prof. U. Pa., 1950-87 Author: Design of Cities, 1967, rev. edit., 1974; prod.: Understanding Cities film series Rome: Impact of an Idea, Paris: Living Space, John Nash and London, The American Urban Experience, The City of the Future, 1983. Mem. Pres.'s Citizen's Adv. Com. Recreation and Natural Beauty, 1966-69; Trustee Am. Acad. in Rome, 1965-76. Recipient Art Alliance Phila. medal achievement, 1961, Man of Yr. award City Bus. Club Phila., 1962, Brown medal award Franklin Inst., 1962, R.S. Reynolds award for community architecture, 1976, Fairmount Park Art Assn. medal of honor, 1976, Gold medal Royal Instn. Chartered Surveyors, 1974, Chgo. Archtl. award, 1989, Sir Patrick Abercrombie prize Internat. Union Architects, 1990, Planning Pioneer award Am. Inst. Cert. Planners, 1993; Ford Found. travel fellow, 1959; Rockefeller fellow, 1963; Nat. Endowment for the Arts Disting. Designer fellow, 1987, emeritus fellow Urban Land Inst., 1989, Plym disting. professorship in architecture U. Ill. Fellow AIA (medal 1976), Am. Inst. Planners (Distinguished Service award 1971, Phila. award 1983, Penn Club award 1984) Address: 2117 Locust St Philadelphia PA 19103-4802

BACON, GEORGE EDGAR, pediatrician, educator; b. N.Y.C., Apr. 13, 1932; s. Edgar and Margaret Priscilla (Anderson) B.; m. Grace Elizabeth Graham, June 30, 1956; children: Nancy, George, John BA, Wesleyan U., 1953; MD, Duke U., 1957; MS in Pharmacology, U. Mich., 1967. Diplomate Am. Bd. Pediatrics, subsplty. Bd. Pediatric Endocrinology. Intern in pediatrics Duke Hosp., Durham, N.C., 1957-58; resident in pediatrics Columbia-Presbyn. Med. Ctr., N.Y.C., 1961-63; from instr. to prof. emeritus U. Mich., Ann Arbor, 1963—86, prof. emeritus, 1986—, chief pediatric endocrinology svc., dept. pediatrics, 1970-83, dir. house officer programs, dept. pediatrics, 1981-86, assoc. chmn. dept. pediatrics, 1983-86, mem. senate assembly, 1978-80; vice chmn. dir.'s adv. coun. Univ. Hosp., Ann Arbor, 1981-82; prof. pediatrics Tex. Tech U., Lubbock, 1986—90, chmn. dept., 1986—90, chmn. med. practice income plan, 1989; chief staff pediatrics Lubbock Gen. Hosp., 1986—90; dir. med. edn. and rsch. Butterworth Hosp., Grand Rapids, Mich., 1990-91, med. dir. dept. pediatrics, 1991—95; prof. pediatrics Mich. State U., East Lansing, 1990—95; pediatric endocrinologist Univ. Mich. Hosp., Ann Arbor, 1995—, Detroit Medical Ctr., Southfield, Mich., 1996—2001. Coord. profl. svc. C.S. Mott Children's Hosp., 1973-83, mem. exec. com. for clin. affairs, 1975-76, 77-79, assoc. vice chmn. med. staff, 1978-79; chmn. exec. com. Women's Hosp., Holden Hosp., Ann Arbor, 1973-82. Author: A Practical Approach to Pediatric Endocrinology, 1975, 3d edit., 1990; contbr. articles to profl. jours. Capt. U.S. Army, 1958-61. Fellow Am. Acad. Pediatrics (treas. Mich. chpt. 1983-86, alt.-at-large 1995-2001, coun. Tex. chpt. 1986-89, Pediatrician of Yr. Mich. chpt. 2002); mem. Am. Pediatric Soc., Pediatric Endocrine Soc. Home: 3911 Waldenwood Dr Ann Arbor MI 48105-3008 Office: U MIch Med Ctr Dept Pediatrics PO Box 718 Ann Arbor MI 48106-0718

BACON, GEORGE HUGHES, JR., retired systems analyst; b. Phila., Mar. 4, 1935; s. George Hughes Sr. and Alice Olive (Campbell); divorced; children: Christopher Scott, Melissa Anne Hinkle. BA in English Lit. and Music, Temple U., 1957; MS in Ednl. Adminstrn., U. Pa., 1968. Computer programmer 1st Pa. Bank, Phila., 1960-62; tchr. Bucks County, Pa., 1962-72; assoc. dir. Kranzley and Co., Cherry Hill, N.J., 1973-74; computer programmer Phila. Nat. Bank, 1975-77; cons. Sci. and Computer Tech. Inc., Malvern, Pa., 1978-79; lead systems analyst Ednl. Testing Svc., Princeton, N.J., 1979-86; cons. in field, 1986. Cons., lectr. computer literacy and software Abington (Pa.) Pub. Libr., 1983-84, Jenkintown (Pa.) Music Sch., 1984, Fudan U., Shanghai, China, 1985; invited lectr., sr. tech. advisor UN Devel. Program Jao Tong U., Shanghai, 1988. Vol. aide Mercer County Geriatric Unit, Lawrenceville, N.J., 1986, Holy Redeemer Hosp., Meadowbrook, Pa., 1988-98, Rydal Park Retirement Home, 1988—; cons. Abington Sch. Bd., 1989-98; tutor Abington Pub. Libr. Literacy Project, 1988; mem. headmaster's coun. Am. Boychoir, Princeton, 1987, Abington Presbyn. Ch. Mem. Temple U. Coll. Arts and Scis. Alumni Assn., U. Pa. Grad. Sch. Edn. Alumni Assn., Phila. Orch. Assn., Friends of Princeton U. Avocations: films, public television and radio, classical music, reading. Home: 1515 The Fairway Apt 331H Rydal PA 19046-1435

BACON, LEONARD ANTHONY, accounting educator; b. Santa Fe, June 10, 1931; s. Manuel R. and Maria (Chavez) Baca; m. Patricia Balzaretti; children— Bernadine M., Jerry A., Tiffany A. B.E., U. Nebr.-Omaha, 1965; M.B.A., U. of the Americas, Mexico City, 1969; Ph.D., U. Miss., 1971. CPA; cert. mgmt. acct., internal auditor. Commd. 2d lt. U.S. Army, 1951, advanced through grades to maj., 1964, served fin. and acctg. officer mainly Korea, Vietnam; ret., 1966; asst. prof. Delta State U., Cleveland, Miss., 1971-76; assoc. prof. West Tex. State U., Canyon, 1976-79; prof. acctg. Calif. State U., Bakersfield, 1979—; cons. Kershen Co. (now Atlantic Richfield Oil Co.), Canyon, 1979-80. Contbr. articles to profl. jours. U.S., Mex., Can., papers to profl. confs. Leader Delta area Boy Scouts Am., Cleveland, 1971-76; dir. United Campus Ministry, Canyon, 1976-79; min. Kern Youth Facility, Bakersfield, 1983—, Christians in Commerce, 1990—. Paratrooper Brazilian Army, 1955. Mem. Am. Acctg. Assn., Am. Inst. CPA's, Am. Assn. Spanish Speaking CPA's, Inst. Mgmt. Accts. (pres. Bakersfield chpt. 1981-82, Most Valuable Mem. award 1981), Am. Mgmt. Assn., Inst. Mgmt. Acctg., Calif. Faculty Assn., Acad. Internat. Bus., Inst. Internal Auditors, Inst. Cost Estimators and Analysts, Alpha Kappa Psi (Dedicated Service award 1979), Omicron Delta Epsilon, Beta Gamma Sigma. Clubs: Jockey (Rio de Janeiro). Lodges: Lions (v.p. Cleveland 1971-73), Kiwanis (v.p. 1974-79, A Whale of a Guy award, Cleveland 1975, Plaque of Appreciation, 1992-93). Office: Calif State U 9001 Stockdale Hwy Bakersfield CA 93311-1022

BACON, LOUIS ALBERT, retired consulting civil engineer; b. Champaign, Ill., Apr. 10, 1921; s. Harrison Waxler and Mabel Mae (Watson) B.; m. Clara Elizabeth Manny, Aug. 28, 1943; children: Robert Louis, David Kenneth, William Harrison. BSCE, U. Ill., 1943. Registered profl. engr., Ga., Ill.; registered structural engr., Ill. Wing designer Douglas Aircraft Co., El Segundo, Calif., 1943-44; structural designer C.A. Metz Engring. Co., Chgo., 1946-47; chief structural engr. Shaw, Metz & Dolio, architects-engrs., Chgo., 1947-53; chief structural engr., assoc. ptnr. Shaw, Metz & Assocs., Chgo., 1953-66; pres. P&W Engrs., Inc., cons., Chgo., 1966-74; v.p., head Atlanta div. Stanley Cons., Inc., 1974-76; v.p., dir. engring. div. Heery Internat., Inc., Atlanta, 1976-84, dir. mktg. to fed. govt., 1984-89; ret. Mem. planning com. City of Brookfield, Ill., 1951-54, mem. bd. local improvements, village trustee, 1954-59; mem. Glen Ellyn (Ill.) Environ. Protection Commn., 1971-74; pres. Ridgeview Neighborhood Civic Assn., Atlanta, 1980-82, sec.-treas. 1991—; chmn. Fulton County Developers Adv. Com., 1981; bd. dirs. Literacy Vols. Am.-Met. Atlanta, 1992-95, 1996-2002, pres., 1993-94; commr. Housing Authority Fulton County, 1995—2003, vice chmn., 1998-99, chmn., 1999-2003; vol. Habitat for Humanity, Atlanta, 1994-96; bd. dirs. Cancer Network St. Joseph's Hosp. Atlanta, 1995-99, 2003—; founder, chmn., Ga. Prostate Cancer Coalition, 1998—. With USNR, 1944-46. Recipient Outstanding Achievement award Engrs. of Met. Atlanta, 1980; named Engr. of Yr., Engrs. of Met. Atlanta, 1984 Fellow ASCE, Soc. Am. Mil. Engrs. (v.p. 1988-89), NSPE (life, dir. 1966-69, v.p. 1969-71, pres.-elect 1982-83, pres. 1983-84, divsn. chmn. profl. engrs. in pvt. practice 1971-72, Chmn.'s award profl. engrs. in pvt. practice 1972, PEPP award 1976, Disting. Svc. award 1993); mem. Ill. Soc. Profl. Engrs. (hon. mem., pres. 1964-65, Ill. award 1968), Ga. Soc. Profl. Engrs. (Pres.'s award Sandy Springs chpt. 1980, Engr. of Yr. award 1982), Engrs. Greater Atlanta (Engr. of Yr. 1984), U. Ill. Civil Engring. Alumni Assn. (pres. 1980-82, Disting. Alumnus award 1985), U. Ill. Alumni Assn. (Loyalty award 1985, Constituent award 1988), Chi Epsilon (hon.) Clubs: Dunwoody (Ga.) Country. Methodist. Home: 5240 W Kingston Ct NE Atlanta GA 30342-2129

BACON, LYDIA LEACH, human resources professional; b. Harrisburg, Pa., Nov. 9, 1948; d. Charles Franklin and Lorna Elizabeth (Rissinger) Leach; 1 child, Melahn Lyle; m. John Wallace Bacon, June 6, 2000. BS, Pa. State U., 1970. Flight attendant Pan-Am. World Airways, Miami, Fla., 1970-73, supr. in-flight services, 1974-80, relocation staff assoc., 1980-81, employee services staff assoc., 1981-82, affirmative action mgr., 1982-85, dir. system-wide EEO and affirmative action, 1986-87, dir. labor relations, 1987-92; dir. spl. projects The Beacon Coun., Miami, 1992-93; employee rels. rep. Am. Airlines, Miami, 1993-96, sr. human rels. rep., 1996-97, sr. human rels. specialist, 1997-98, counsel, 1998-99, counsel internat. employee rels., 2000—01, counsel arbitration unit, 2002—. Cons. Alert Security Systems, N.Y.C., 1987, Solar Reactor Techs., Miami, 1986-95; mem. Orgnl. Resource Counselors Equal Opportunity Group, 1981-86, Office Fed. Contracts Compliance Program Corp. Liaison, 1986-88; bd. dirs. Pan-Am. Mgmt. Club, 1983, 86, v.p., 1984, 87. Active Dade County Employ the Handicapped Com., 1981-85; mem. Pvt. Industry Council, 1985-86. Mem. Air Transport Assn. (human resources com.), Internat. Explorers Soc., Soc. for Human Resources Mgmt., Delta Gamma (social chmn.), Omicron Nu, Phi Kappa Phi. Republican. Avocations: hot air ballooning, golf, reading, skiing, boating. Office: Am Airlines 999 Ponce De Leon Blvd Coral Gables FL 33134-3000 E-mail: lydia.bacon@aa.com.

BACON, MARTHA BRANTLEY, small business owner; b. Wrightsville, Ga., Apr. 20, 1938; d. William Riley and Susie Mae (Colston) B.; m. Albert Sidney Bacon, Jr., Aug. 3, 1958 (dec.); children: Albert Sidney, III, Gregory Riley. BS, Ga. So., Statesboro, 1959; grad., Realtors Inst., 1959; Post Grad., U. Va., Charlottesville, 1978-80, Adrian Hall Interior Design, Savannah, Ga., 1984. Lic. real estate broker, Ga., Va. Tchr. Chatham Bd. Edn., Savannah, Ga., 1961; co-owner mgr. Two Kentucky Fried Chicken Restaurants, Charlottesville, Va., 1967-80; real estate broker Real Estate III, Charlottesville, Va., 1978-83, Landmark Realty, Statesboro, Ga.; tree farmer Johnson Co., Ga., 1980—; mgr., co-owner Restaurant, 1987-92; co-owner Plunderosa Antiques and Collectibles, Statesboro, Ga., 1993—. V.p. Bd. Realtors Statesboro Ga. 1985; regional franchise agt., owner Ice Cream Churn of South Ga.; mem. adv. bd. Ga. So. U. Sch. Edn., 2002—. Chmn. Jaycettes Gov. Columbus, Ga., 1962; vol. First Bapt. Ch. Pers. Com., Charlottesville, 1978, U. Va. Hosp., 1980-83; com. mem. Athletic Hall of Fame Ga. So. U.; mem. Ga. Forestry Stewardship, 1991—. Recipient Outstanding Sales award Real Estate III Co. Charlottesville 1980; named Outstanding Jaycette 1961, Jaycettes Gov. Columbus, 1962. Mem. AAUW, Charlottesville Restaurant Assn., Westchester Garden Club, Ga. Restaurant Assn., Ga. So. Univ. Alumni Bd., Ga. So. Symphony Guild, Ga. So. Univ. Athletic Boosters Club, Pilot Club, Evergeen Garden Club, Ga. (v.p.), Optimist (Statesboro essay chmn.), Baptist. Avocations: bridge, auctions, theatre. Home: 30 Golf Club Cir Statesboro GA 30458-9160

BACON, PHILLIP, geographer, author, consultant; b. Cleve., July 10, 1922; s. Hollis Phillip and Emma (Schneider) B.; m. Dorothy Willey, 1951 (div. 1980); children: Laura Bacon Fraser, Phillip Everett; m. Jane Lowrie, 1980 (dec. 1991); m. Sandra Sullivan, 1995. Cadet, The Citadel, 1940-42; AB, U. Miami, 1946; MA, George Peabody Coll. for Tchrs. (now Vanderbilt U.), 1951, EdD, 1955. Tchr. social studies, tactical officer Castle Heights Mil. Acad., Lebanon, Tenn., 1946-47; tchr. social studies, tactical officer Army and Navy Acad., Carlsbad, Calif., 1948-53; grad. asst. geography George Peabody Coll. for Tchrs. (now Vanderbilt U.), 1953-55; dean Grad. Sch., 1963-64; acting dir. Library Sch., 1964; asst. prof. geography U. Pitts., 1955-57; vis. asst. prof. geography Columbia U. Tchrs. Coll., 1956-57, assoc. prof., 1957-60, prof., 1960-63, 64-66; prof. geography and social studies edn. U. Wash., Seattle, 1966-71, co-dir. tri-univ. project in elementary edn., 1967-71; prof. geography U. Houston, 1971-85, chmn. dept., 1973-78, prof. geography and anthropology emeritus, 1985—. Instr. history George Peabody Coll. for Tchrs., summer 1951; vis. prof. geography U. Colo., 1961, U. Wash., 1965, 79; Jennings lectr., 1963; vis. scholar N.C. Central U., 1966; vis. lectr. geography U. Tex., 1966, NSF vis. scientist, 1970-72; Disting. vis. prof. social studies edn. and geography Seattle Pacific U., 1977, 78, 79, vis. prof., geographer-in-residence, Coll. of Edn., U. N.Mex., 1993-95; co-coord. N.Mex. Geog. Alliance, 1993-97; mem. editl. adv. bd. World Book Ency., 1965-84; bd. cons. World Book Atlas, 1965-70; cons. editor Golden Press, 1958-61; ednl. dir. Golden Book Inst. Knowledge, 1960-61; cons. book div. Time, Inc., 1960-69; cons. social sci. project Ednl. Research Council Am., 1962-70; mem. steering com. High Sch. Geography Project, 1965-70; cons. U.S. Office Edn., 1964-71; mem. Wash. Social Studies Adv. Commn., 1968-71; dir. Follett Social Studies Program, 1980-83, Allyn and Bacon elem. social studies program, 1983-85, dir. Summer Geography Inst., N.Mex. Geographic Alliance, 1993-97; social scis. cons. Harcourt Brace, 1985-2002, Holt, Rinehart and Winston, 1989-97; prof. geography grad. faculty U. Colo., Boulder, 1999-2000; geography cons. SWAP Project, Colo. Dept. Edn., 1998; curriculum cons. Author: Australia, Oceania, and the Polar Lands, 1961, North America, 1961, Children's Picture Atlas of the World, 1966, (with Norman Carls and Frank E. Sorenson) Knowing Our Neighbors in the United States and Canada, 1966, Regions Around the World, 1970, (with R.R. Boyce) Towns and Cities, 1970, (with others) The United States and Canada, 1970, (with P.V. Greco) The Story of Latin America, 1970, (with others) America: In Space and Time, 1976, Exploring Our World, 1982, (with Donald C. Fairweather) World Regions, 1983, (with James B. Kracht) Our World Today, 1983, (with M. Evelyn Swartz) Our State: California, 1983, World Geography, The Earth and Its People, 1989; editor: Focus on Geography, Key Concepts and Teaching Strategies, 1970; co-editor (with Lorrin G. Kennamer) Foundations of World Regional Geography Series, 1970; cons. editor: (with others) Life Pictorial Atlas of the World, 1961; mem. adv. bd.: (with others) Jour. of Geography, 1967-70, Social Edn., 1975-78; editl. dir.: (with others) Field Social Studies Program, 1972-73; co-dir.: (with others) Addison-Wesley Elementary Social Studies Program, 1973-80; ednl. cons. The American Nation, Reconstruction to the Present, 1986, The American Nation, Beginnings Through Reconstruction, 1986, Triumph of the American Nation, 1986, World History: People and Nations, 1990, The Story of America, 1994; sr. editl. advisor HBJ Social Studies, K-7, Landmark edits., 1988; geography cons. Harcourt Brace Elem. Social Studies Program Stories in Time, 1997, 2000, Chosen Places, 2000, A Very Personal History, 2002; contbr. articles to profl. jours., chpts. to books, yearbooks. Mem. adv. bd. Grad. Sch., U. Colo., 1987-93. With USNR, 1942-45. Recipient Teaching Excellence award U. Houston, 1975, 79, 80 Mem. NEA (life), Assn. Am. Geographers (coun. 1976-79, chmn. publs. com. 1976-78), Nat. Coun. for Geog. Edn. (life, pres. 1966, disting. svc. award 1974), Alaska Geog. Soc., Nat., Tex., N.Mex. (exec. bd. 1992-95), Social Studies Couns. (exec. bd. 1992-95), Vanderbilt U. Alumni Assn. (dir. 1979-83), Peabody Coll. Alumni Assn. (pres. 1981-83, Disting. Alumnus award 1986, alumni bd. 1994-95), Peabody Coll. Roundtable, Sigma Xi, Sigma Alpha Epsilon, Phi Delta Kappa, Kappa Delta Pi, Kappa Phi Kappa (life), Omicron Delta Kappa, Gamma Theta Upsilon, Pi Gamma Mu. Presbyterian. Home: 2718 Caribbean Dr Grand Junction CO 81506-1712 E-mail: Sanphil@aol.com.

BACON, ROBERT DALE, lawyer; b. Huntington, W.Va., July 31, 1952; s. Omar Albert and Margaret (Grow) B. BA, Stanford U., 1973; JD, U. Calif., Davis, 1976. Bar: Alaska 1977, Calif. 1977, D.C. 1978, U.S. Supreme Ct. 1981. Law clk. Alaska Supreme Ct., Anchorage, 1976-77; staff atty. U.S. Ct. Appeals, Washington, 1977-78; clk. appellate cts. Alaska Ct. Sys., Anchorage, 1978-84; asst. atty. gen. Office of Spl. Prosecutions and Appeals, Anchorage, 1984-90; sr. dep. Office of State Pub. Defender, Calif., 1990-97; pvt. practice Oakland, Calif., 1997—. Democrat. Unitarian Universalist. Office: 484 Lake Park Ave # 110 Oakland CA 94610-2730 E-mail: bacon2254@aol.com.

BACON, VICKY LEE, lighting services executive; b. Oregon City, Oreg., Mar. 25, 1950; d. Herbert Kenneth and Lorean Betty (Boltz) Rushford; m. Dennis M. Bacon, Aug. 7, 1971; 1 child, Randene Tess. Student, Portland Community Coll., 1974-75, Mt. Hood Community Coll., 1976, Portland State Coll., 1979. With All Electric Constrn., Milwaukie, Oreg., 1968-70, Lighting Maintenance Co., Portland, Oreg., 1970-78; svc. mgr. GTE Sylvania Lighting Svcs., Portland, 1978-80, br. mgr., 1980-83; div. mgr. Christenson Electric Co. Inc., Portland, 1983-90, v.p. mktg. and lighting svcs., 1990-91, v.p. svc. ops. and mktg., 1991—2000; CEO, owner Dryer Electric, Inc., 2002—. Chmn. Oreg. Ltd. Energy Com., 1993—; vice chmn. to labor commr. Oreg. State Apprenticeship Coun., 1996—. Mem. Energy Contractors Assn., Illuminating Engring. Soc., Nat. Elec. Contractors Assn. (bd. dirs. Oreg. Columbia chpt. 1997—), Nat. Assn. Lighting Maintenance Contractors, Elec. Contractors Assn., Office: Dryer Electric Inc PO Box 3514 Portland OR 97208-3514 E-mail: vlbacon@comcast.net.

BACON-SMITH, CAMILLE, educator, writer; b. Phila., July 13, 1949; d. John P. and Elizabeth Bacon; children: Erik, David. MA, U. Penn., 1985, PhD, 1989. Author: Enterprising Women, 1992, Eye of the Daemon, 1996, Face of Time, 1996, Eyes of the Empress, 1998, Science Fiction Culture, 1999, other titles under pseudonyms; editor Directions in Folklore. Avocation: theatre.

BACOT, JOHN CARTER, retired banking executive; b. Utica, N.Y., Feb. 7, 1933; s. John Vacher and Edna (Gunn) B.; m. Shirley Schou, Nov. 26, 1960; children: Elizabeth, Susan. AB, Hamilton Coll., Clinton, N.Y., 1955; LLB, Cornell U., 1958. Bar: N.Y. 1959. With firm Utica, 1959-60; with Bank of N.Y., N.Y.C., 1960—, pres., 1974-84, chief exec. officer, chmn., 1982-98, bd. dirs., 1992—; ret., 1998; non. exec. chmn. Foot Locker, 2001—. Bd. dirs. Home Life Ins. Co., Atlantic Reins. Co., Centennial Ins. Co., Bank of N.Y. Internat. Corp., Bank of N.Y. Co., Inc.; trustee Atlantic Mut. Ins. Co.; chmn. bd. trustees Hamilton Coll. Mem. Econ. Club N.Y., Pilgrims of U.S., Assn. Res. City Bankers, N.Y. State Bar Assn., Coun. on Fgn. Rels., Montclair Golf Club, Links Club, Union Club. Episcopalian.*

BACOT, MARIE, management consultant, researcher; b. Jackson, Miss., Oct. 2, 1942; d. James Peter and Marie (Moore) B. BA, Millsaps Coll., 1964; MEd, U. New Orleans, 1974, PhD, 1992. Tchr. Houston Ind. Sch. Dist., 1964-68, Jefferson Parish Sch. Bd., Gretna, La., 1968-86; dir. Ednl. Testing Assocs., New Orleans, 1982-86, Marie Bacot Innovation & Creativity Cons., New Orleans, 1987—. Presenter Acad. Mgmt., 1989, So. Mgmt. Assn., 1989, Decision Scis. Inst., 1990. Co-author chpt.: Understanding Students with High Incidence Exceptionalities: Categorical and Non-categorical Perspectives, 1991; contbr. articles to profl. jours. Recording sec. The New Orleans City Ballet, 1986-87; publicity chmn. book fair New Orleans Symphony Orch., 1986-87; spl. donor chmn. opera ball New Orleans Opera Assn. 1986-87; soloist, quartet/trio choir mem. Trinity Episcopal Ch., 1981-88. Mem. Ctr. for Rsch. in Applied Creativity, Creative Edn. Found., Acad. Mgmt., Am. Soc. for Quality Control. Republican. Episcopalian. Achievements include developer Bacot Orgnl. Learning and Innovation Scale (BOLIS), instrument used to assess orgns. Office: PO Box 15695 New Orleans LA 70175-5695

BACOW, LAWRENCE SELDON, academic administrator, environmental educator; b. Detroit, Aug. 24, 1951; s. Mitchell Leon and Ruth Wertheim Bacow; m. Adele Fleet, June 1, 1975; children: Jay, Kenneth. SB, MIT, 1972; JD, M in Pub. Policy, Harvard U., 1976, PhD, 1978. Bar: Mass. 1978. Asst. prof. law and environ. policy MIT, Cambridge, 1977-84, assoc. prof. law and environ. policy, 1984-90, dir. Ctr. for Real Estate, 1990-92, prof. law and environ. policy, 1992-97, Lee and Geraldine Martin prof. environ. studies, 1997—2001, chmn. faculty, 1995-97, chancellor, 1998—2001; pres. Tufts Univ., 2002—. Vis. assoc. prof. law Hebrew U., Jerusalem, 1981-82; rsch. assoc. Harvard Law Sch., Cambridge, 1982-88; vis. prof. Politecnico di Torino, Italy, 1990, U. Bari, Italy, 1991, Gabriela Mistral U., Santiago, Chile, 1992, 93, 94, 95, 97, Faculty Econs.-U. Amsterdam, The Netherlands, 1993-94; rsch. fellow The Tinbergen Inst., Amsterdam, 1993-94. Author: Bargaining for Job Safety and Health, 1980; co-author: (with M. O'Hare and D. Sanderson) Facility Siting and Public Opposition, 1982, (with L. Susskind and M. Wheeler)

Resolving Environmental Regulatory Disputes, 1983, (with M. Wheeler) Environmental Dispute Resolution, 1984. Mem. presdl. transition team Occupl. Safety and Health Adminstrn., 1977; mem. socio-econ. subcom. NAS Com. on Surface Mining and Reclamation, 1978-79; advisor Mass. Spl. Legis. Commn. on Hazardous Water, 1980; gubernatorial appointee Mass. Hazardous Waste Facility Site Safety Coun., 1980-83; Town Meeting mem., Arlington, Mass., 1981-83; advisor Israel Environ. Protection Svc., 1981-83; chair citizens adv. com. Mass. Water Resources Authority, 1989; exec. com. One Thousand Friends Mass., 1989-95; advisor Cross Israel Hwy. Commn., 1994-95; dir. MIT Hillel, Cambridge, 1995-98, Jewish Cmty. Housing for the Elderly, Brighton, Mass., 1995—; trustee Hebrew Coll., Brookline, Mass., 1999—, Wheaton Coll., Norton, Mass., 1999—, dir. Am. Coun. on Edn., 2003—. Recipient William S. Ballard award Am. Soc. Real Estate, 1991; adminstrn. fellow Harvard U., 1972-76, post-doctoral fellow Ford Found., 1977; Legal scholar Ctr. for Pub. Resources, 1985. Mem. Am. Acad. Arts and Scis., Mass. Bar Assn., Phi Beta Kappa. Jewish. Avocations: sailing, skiing, running. Office: Tufts University President's Office Ballou Hall Medford MA 02155 E-mail: bacow@tufts.edu.

BADAL, DANIEL WALTER, psychiatrist, educator; b. Lowellville, Ohio, Aug. 22, 1912; s. Samuel S. and Angelina (Jessen) Badal; m. Julia Lovina Cover, June 1939 (dec. May 1968); children: Petrina Badal Gardner, Julia Badal Graf, Peter C.; m. Eleanor Bosworth Spitler, Sept. 5, 1969 (dec. Feb. 1994). AB, Case Western Res. U., 1934, MD, 1937. Resident in medicine, neurology and psychiatry Peter Bent Brigham Hosp., Mass. Gen. Hosp., Boston City Hosp., 1937-41; fellow in psychiatry and neurology Harvard U., Boston, 1941-45; asst. prof. psychiatry Washington U., St. Louis, 1945; mem. faculty Sch. Medicine Case Western Res. U., Cleve., 1946—, assoc. clin. prof. emeritus psychiatry, 1983—; practice medicine specializing in psychiatry and psychoanalysis Cleve., 1955—2002; ret., 2002. Mem. faculty Cleve. Psychoanalytic Inst., 1975—. Author: Treatment of Depression and Related Moods, 1988, Treatment of Chronic Depression, 2003, Treating Chronic Depression--Psychotherapy and Medication, 2003; contbr. articles to profl. jours. Fellow NRC Office Sci. R&D, 1941—45. Fellow: Am. Psychiat. Assn. (cert. Excellence Tchg. 1999), Internat. Psychoanlytic Assn. (life); mem.: AMA, Cleve. Psychoanalytic Soc. (pres. 1963), Phila. Assn. Psychoanalysis, Am. Psychoanalytic Soc., Acad. Medicine Cleve., Cleve. Psychiat. Soc., Ohio Med. Assn. Home: Judson Pk Apt 312 2181 Ambleside Rd Cleveland OH 44106

BADALAMENT, ROBERT ANTHONY, urologic oncologist; b. Detroit, Mar. 20, 1954; s. Louis F. and Grace D. (Costello) B.; m. Providence F. Vitale, Nov. 9, 1980; children: Louis F., Peter P., Grace F. BS in Biology, So. Meth. U., 1976; MD, Emory U., 1980. Diplomate Am. Bd. Urology. Surg. intern Henry Ford Hosp., Detroit, 1980-81, surg. resident, 1981-82, urologic resident, 1982-85; fellow in urologic oncology Meml. Sloan Kettering Cancer Ctr., N.Y.C., 1985-87; asst. prof. Ohio State U., Columbus, 1987-92, assoc. prof., 1992-95, prof. Sch. Pub. Health, 1995—; mem. attending staff Arthur James Cancer Ctr., Columbus, 1990-95, Crittenton Hosp., Rochester Hills, Mich., 1995—. Contbr. chpt. to book, articles to profl. jours. Fellow ACS; mem. AMA, Soc. Urologic Oncology, Am. Cancer Soc. (bd. trustees Mich. divsn.). Office: Rochester Urology PC 1135 W University Dr Ste 420 Rochester Hills MI 48307-1893

BADALAMENTI, ANTHONY, financial planner; b. St. Louis, Apr. 1, 1940; s. Sebastino and Grace (Orlando) B.; 1 child, Annette Marie. BS in Acctg., Washington U., 1970. CPA, Mo.; registered investment advisor. Staff acct. Fischer & Fischer, CPAs, St. Louis, 1959-63; acct. McDonnell Aircraft Corp., St. Louis, 1963-65; asst. chief acct. Dempsey Tegler, Inc., St. Louis, 1965-66; contr. Cummins Mo. Diesel, Inc., St. Louis, 1966-67; sr. acct. Elmer Fox & Co., CPAs, St. Louis, 1967-71; pvt. practice St. Louis, 1972-94; fin. planner Asset Builders Fin. Planners, St. Louis, 1995—. Tchr. Meramec C.C., St. Louis, 1973-75. Mem. Mo. Soc. CPAs, Crestwood-Sunset Hills C. of C. (pres. 1980-81, Bus. Profl. Month award 1986, 91), Rotary (pres. Crestwood-Sunset Hills chpt. 1982-83). Republican. Roman Catholic. Avocations: basketball, softball, dancing. Home: 1865 Locks Mill Dr Fenton MO 63026-2662 Office: 4400 S Lindbergh Blvd Ste 3 Saint Louis MO 63127-1603

BADALAMENTI, ANTHONY FRANCIS, mathematician, researcher; b. Bronx, N.Y., Feb. 2, 1943; s. Charles Salvator and Carmella-Maria (D'Ambrosio) B.; m. Karolina V. Kungl. Nov. 30, 1968 (div.); 1 child, Paul Anthony. BS, Manhattan Coll., 1964; MS, Stevens Inst. Tech., 1967; PHD equivalent, Bell Tel. Labs., 1967; PhD, Poly. Inst. Bklyn., 1970. Mem. tech. staff Bell Telephone Labs., 1964-70; asst. prof. Fairleigh Dickinson U., 1970-72; mem. tech. staff Gen. Rsch. Corp., 1972-74; dir. revenue modeling and reporting Western Union Telegraph Co., 1974; rsch. scientist Rockland Rsch. Inst. (now Nathan Kline Inst. Psychiat. Rsch.), Orangeburg, N.Y., 1975—. Vis. scientist Nathan Kline Inst., 1993—; cons. in field. Author publs. on systems, psychoanalysis and artificial intelligence. Italian Charities Am. scholar, Bklyn. Poly. Inst. scholar. Mem. Am. Stats. Assn., Assn. Computing Machinery, Am. Math. Soc., Soc. Indsl. and Applied Math., Soc. Gen. Systems Rsch., N.Y. Acad. Scis., Am. Soc. Cybernetics, Soc. Psychoanalytic Psychotherapy, Bergen County Alumni Soc. Manhattan Coll. (v.p.). Home: 19 Crest St Apt 3B Westwood NJ 07675-3128 E-mail: afjb@ix.netcom.com.

BADALAMENTI, FRED LEOPOLDO, artist, educator; b. Long Island City, N.Y., June 25, 1935; s. Leopoldo and Concetta (Vitale) B.; m. Barbara J. Frankenfield, June 14, 1959; children: Katherine, Alexander, Frederick. Student, Pratt Inst., 1953-55, U. Alaska, 1957-58; BS, SUNY, New Paltz, 1961; MFA, Bklyn. Coll., 1967. Art tchr. Newburgh (N.Y.) Pub. Schs., 1960-63, Deer Park (N.Y.) High Sch., 1963-65; prof. emeritus Bklyn. Coll., 1967-92. Vis. prof. art, lectr. SUNY, Stony Brook, 1977-78, 80, 81, 83; dep. chmn. for studio art Bklyn. Coll., 1990-92, dep. chmn. for grad. art, 1972-89; dir. First St. Gallery, N.Y.C., 1978; adj. faculty art dept. Bklyn. Coll., 1992-93, Stony Brook U., 1993-99. One man shows include Suffolk Community Coll., 1971, First Street Gallery, 1973, 76, 80, 89, Nassau County Mus. of Fine Arts, 1987, St. Joseph's Coll., 1987, The Alfred Van Loen Gallery, South Huntington, N.Y., 1998; exhibited paintings and drawings of representational art in N.Y.C. and L.I., 1967—. With USAF, 1955-59. Bklyn. Coll. grad. fellow, 1965-67. Mem. Coll. Art Assn., AAUP. Avocations: travel, tennis, gardening. Home: 182 Lower Sheep Pasture Rd East Setauket NY 11733-1826

BADASH, LAWRENCE, science history educator; b. Bklyn., May 8, 1934; s. Joseph and Dorothy (Langa) B.; children: Lisa, Bruce. BS in Physics, Rensselaer Poly. Inst., 1956; PhD in History of Sci., Yale U., 1964. Instr. Yale U., New Haven, 1964—65, research assoc., 1965-66; from asst. to assoc. prof. U. Calif., Santa Barbara, 1966-79, prof. history of sci., 1979—2002, prof. emeritus, 2002—. Dir. summer seminar on global security and arms control U. Calif., 1983, 86, energy rsch. group, 1992, pacific rim program mem., 1993-95; cons. Nuclear Age Peace Found., Santa Barbara, 1984-90. Author: Radioactivity in Am., 1979, Kapitza, Rutherford, and the Kremlin, 1985, Scientists and the Development of Nuclear Weapons, 1995; editor: Rutherford and Boltwood, Letters on Radioactivity, 1969; Reminiscences of Los Alamos, 1943-45, 1980. Bd. dirs. Santa Barbara chpt. ACLU, 1971-86, 96—, pres., 1982-84, 96-98; nat. bd. dirs. Com. for a Sane Nuclear Policy, Washington, 1972-81; mem. Los Padres Search and Rescue Team, Santa Barbara, 1981-94. Lt. (j.g.) USN, 1956-59. Grantee, NSF, Cambridge, Eng., 1965-66, 69-72, 90-92, Am. Philos. Soc., New Zealand, 1979-80, Inst. on Global Conflict and Cooperation, Univ. Calif., 1983-87; J.S. Guggenheim fellow, 1984-85. Fellow AAAS (sect. mem. at large 1988-92), Am. Phys. Soc. (chmn. divsn. of history of physics 1988-89, exec. com. forum on physics and society 1991-93); mem. History of Sci. Soc. (founder West Coast chpt., chpt. bd. dirs. 1971-73, nat. coun. 1975-78). Democrat. Jewish. Avocation: backpacking. Office: Univ Calif Dept History Santa Barbara CA 93106-9410

BADDERS, REBECCA SUSANNE, military officer, educator, writer; b. Knoxville, Tenn., Jan. 6, 1962; d. John Albert and Tamara Elizabeth Badders. BA in Edn., U. Fla., 1984; MA in Edn., U. South Fla., Tampa and St. Petersburg, 1997; MSM in Bus., Troy State U., 2002. Cert. profl. tchr., Fla. Commd. ensign USN, 1984, advanced through grades to lt. comdr., 1995; oceanographic watch officer Naval Facility Brawdy, Wales, 1984-86; oceanographic officer antisubmarine warfare Comdr. Undersea Surveillance, Norfolk, Va., 1986-90; dept. head Readiness Tng. Facility, Dam Neck, Va., 1990-93; tchr. Pinellas County Schs., Largo, Fla., 1994-97; commanding officer Naval Weapon Sta. res. det., Charleston, S.C., 1995-97; exec. officer Naval Res. Ctr., Kearny, N.J., 1997-99, Earle, N.J., 1999-2000, Naval Res. Profl. Devel. Ctr., New Orleans, 2000—03; commanding officer Naval Res. Ctr., Columbia, SC, 2003—. Faculty rep. Pinellas County Tchrs. Assn., Largo, 1994-97. Author: Maddy and the Peek-A-Boo Moon, 1995. V.p., bd. dirs. Pilot Club Internat., Mid-Pinellas, Fla., 1993-99. Recipient Navy Achievement medal, 1990, 93, 96, Navy Commendation medal, 2000, Meritorious Svc. medal, 2003. Mem. Naval Res. Assn., Res. Officers Assn., Navy League of U.S., Coun. for Exceptional Children, U. Fla. Alumni Assn., U. South Fla. Alumni Assn., Troy StateAlumni Assn., LHS Alumni Assn., Internat. Order of Rainbow (worthy advisor, pres. 1975-82), Scabbard and Blade, Kappa Delta Pi. Republican. Episcopalian. Avocations: travel, computers, reading, gourmet cooking, arts. Office: 513 Pickens St Columbia SC 29201 E-mail: rbadders@aol.com.

BADDOUR, ANNE BRIDGE, pilot; b. Royal Oak, Mich. d. William George and Esther Rose (Pfiester) Bridge; m. Raymond F. Baddour, Sept. 25, 1954; children: Cynthia Anne, Frederick Raymond, Jean Bridge. Student, Detroit Bus. Sch., 1948-50; BA, Pine Manor Coll. Stewardess Eastern Airlines, Boston, 1952-54; instr. aero. Powers Sch., Boston, 1958; co-pilot, flight attendant Raytheon Co., Bedford, Mass., 1958-63; flight dispatcher, ferry Pilot Comerford Flight Sch., Bedford, 1974-76; adminstrv. asst., ferry pilot Jenney Beachcraft, Bedford, 1976; mgr., pilot Balt. Airways, Inc., Bedford, 1976-77; rsch. test pilot Lincoln Lab. Flight Test Facility MIT, Lexington, 1977-97. Aviation cons., corp. pilot Energy Resources, Inc., Cambridge, Mass., 1974-84; holder World Class speed records for single-engine aircraft; Boston to Goose Bay, Labrador, 1985, Boston to Reykjavik, Iceland, 1985, Portland, Maine to Goose Bay, 1985, Portland to Reykjavik, 1985, Goose Bay to Reykjavik, 1985, records for twin-engine aircraft: Sept Isles to Goose Bay, 1988, Mont Joll to Goose Bay, 1988, Presque Isle to Goose Bay, 1988, Millinocket to Goose Bay, 1988, Bedford to Goose Bay, 1988, Goose Bay to Narssassrag, Greenland, 1988, Narssassrag to Klevelevic, Iceland, 1988, Narssassrag to Reykjavik, 1988, Bedford to Narssassrag, 1988, Millinochet to Narssassrag, 1988, Presque Isle to Narssassrag, 1988, Bedford to St. John, 1991, Bedford to Charlottetown, 1991, Charlottetown to Kennebunk, 1991, Charlottetown to Portsmouth, 1991, Muncton to Bedford, 1991, St. John, to Kennebunk, 1991, St. John to Bedford, 1991, World Class Speed Records Single-Engine Aircraft, 1991, Bedford, Mass. to Sydney, Nova Scotia, Bedford, Mass. to Sydney, Nova Scotia to Beford, Mass., Portsmouth, New Hampshire to Sydney Nova Scotia to Portsmouth, Brunswick to Sydney Nova Scotia to Brunswick. Mem. campaign coun. Mus. Transp., Boston; mem. coun. assocs. French Libr. in Boston; commr. Commonwealth of Mass., Mass. Aero. Commn., 1979—83; trustee bd. adminstrn. Amelia Earhart Birthplace Mus., 1992—93; trustee Daniel Webster Coll., Nashua, NH, 1995—; v.p., trustee Friends of the Libr. Spl. Collections Boston U., 1997—; trustee Viscaya Mus., 2002—; bd. dirs. Smithsonian Nat. Air & Space Mus., 1998—, Cambridge Opera, 1977—79. Winner trophy Phila. Transcontinental Air Race, 1954, New Eng. Air Race, 1957, Clifford B. Harmon trophy Internat. Aviatrix, 1988; recipient Spl. Recognition award FAA, 1990; honoree Internat. Aviation Forest of Friendship, Atchison, Kans., 1991; named Pilot of the Year, New Eng. sect. Internat. Women Pilots Orgn./The Ninety-Nines, Inc., 1992. Mem.: DAR, Friends of Switzerland, Soc. Exptl. Test Pilots, U.S. Sea Plane Pilots Assn., Nat. Pilots Assn., Assn. Women Transcontinental Air Race, Bostonian Soc., Aircraft Owners Pilots Assn., Nat. Aero. Assn., Fedn. Aeronautique Internat., Ninety-Nines (New Eng. Safety trophy 1986), Fairchild Tropical Garden Club, Harvard Travellers Club, Boston Women's Travel Club, Chilton Club, Belmont Hill Club, Aero Club New Eng. (v.p. 1978—80, dir. 1978—2002). Home: PO Box 274 123 Old Town Rd Hancock NH 03449

BADDOUR, RAYMOND FREDERICK, chemical engineer, educator, entrepreneur; b. Laurinburg, NC, Jan. 11, 1925; s. Frederick Joseph and Fannie (Rizk) B.; m. Anne M. Bridge, Sept. 25, 1954; children: Cynthia Anne, Frederick Raymond, Jean Bridge. BS, U. Notre Dame, 1945; MS, Mass. Inst. Tech., 1949; ScD, 1951; D (hon.), St. Andrew's Coll., 1999. Asst. dir. Engring Practice Sch., Oak Ridge, 1948-49; asst. prof. Mass. Inst. Tech., 1951-57, assoc. prof., 1957-63, prof. chem. engring, 1963-89, Lammot du Pont prof. chem. engring., 1973-89, prof. emeritus, 1989—, also head dept., 1969-76; dir. Environ. Lab., 1970-76. Mem. Project Separation AEC, 1954; AIChE del. Mendeleev Conf. on Pure and Applied Chemistry, Moscow, 1959; lectr. Max Planck Insts., Germany, 1962; Shell lectr. Cambridge (Eng.) U., 1962; P.C. Reily lectr. Notre Dame U., 1964; Dr. Warren K. Lewis lectr., chmn. engring. MIT, 1998; mem. sci. adv. com. Gen. Motors Corp., 1971-82; co-founder, chmn. Abcor, Inc., Cambridge, Mass., 1963-72; dir. Raychem Corp., 1972-80; founder, chmn. Energy Resources Co., Inc. (ERCO), 1974-83; chmn. ERCO AG, 1980-83; co-founder dir. Amgen, Inc., 1980-97, Lam Rsch., 1980-82; co-founder BREH, Inc., 1983; co-founder, dir. SKB, Inc., 1984, MatTek Corp., 1985, BLW Corp., 1985, Enterprise Mgmt. Corp., 1985, Ascent Pediat., Inc., 1989-2001; cons. Mobil Chem. Co., NYC, 1963-84, U.S. Dept. Commerce, 1960-62, Freeport Minerals Co., NYC, 1976-83, Allied Chem. Co., 1980-81; bd. dirs. Scully Signal, 1996—; bd. dirs., chmn. Activ Biotics, Inc., 2001—; Warren K. Lewis lectr. chem. engring. MIT, 1998. Mem. corp. Boston Museum Sci.; mem. sci. and tech. adv. bd. Field Enterprises, Chgo. (World Book Ency.), 1966-68. United Engrs. and Constructors preceptorship, 1956; NSF sr. post-doctoral fellow, 1967-68; recipient honor award U. Notre Dame Coll. of Engring., 1976 Fellow Am. Inst. Chem. Engrs., Am. Inst. Chemists, Am. Acad. Arts and Scis., N.Y. Acad. Scis.; mem. AAAs, Am. Chem. Soc. Achievements include research publs. and patents in field.

BADDOURA, RASHID JOSEPH, emergency medicine physician; b. Beirut, Aug. 4, 1947; came to U.S., 1974; s. Joseph and Renée Baddoura; m. Rola Tohme, July 15, 1989; children: Joseph, Philip, Karen. BS, Am. U. Beirut, 1970, MD, 1974. Diplomate Am. Bd. Emergency Medicine (examiner 1984-89), Am. Bd. Internal Medicine, Am. Bd. Pulmonary Diseases. Intern Am. U. Med. Ctr., Beirut; resident in internal medicine St. Joseph's Hosp. & Med. Ctr., Paterson, N.J., 1974-76; fellow in pulmonary and critical care Duke U., 1976-79; dir. emergency dept. Meml. Hosp., Danville, Va., 1981-84; corp. med. officer, mem. med. adv. bd. Coastal Healthcare Group, Durham, N.C., 1981-86; assoc. dir. emergency dept. Valley Hosp., Ridgewood, NJ, 1986-90, dir. emergency dept., 1990—2000; ptnr., bd. dirs. Valley Emergency Assocs., 1986—, Valley Regional Emergency Group, 1999—; pres. Valley Emergency Assocs., 2002—. Mem. bd. Coastal Found. for Med. Edn., Durham, 1984-89; clin. asst. prof. emergency medicine Georgetown U., Washington, 1986-89. Fellow Am. Coll. Emergency Physicians, Am. Coll. Chest Physicians; mem. Am. Coll. Physician Execs. Avocations: hunting, fishing, philosophy, classical music. Office: Valley Hosp Dept Emergency Medicine Ridgewood NJ 07451

BADE, CARL AUGUST, retired secondary education educator; b. St. Louis, Dec. 6, 1924; s. Carl William and Lena Wilhelmina Christina (Gruendler) B.; m. Marie Hoefer, Sept. 11, 1954; children: Steven Carl, Paul Martin, David Edward. BS in Edn., Washington U., St. Louis, 1949, MA in Edn., 1951. Cert. secondary edn. tchr., Mo. Jr. H.S. tchr. Normandy (Mo.) Sch. Dist., 1949-51; youth assoc. Evangelical and Reformed Ch., Phila., 1951-52; cmty. outreach worker Zion Evangelical and Reformed Ch., St. Louis, 1952-54; assoc. dir. voluntary svc. Evangelical and Reformed Ch., Pottstown, Pa., 1954-61; co-dir. voluntary svc. United Ch. of Christ, Pottstown, Pa., 1961-74, dir. voluntary svc. N.Y.C., 1975-91; ret., 1991. Pres. Commn. on Voluntary Svc., N.Y.C., 1960-66, mem. exec. com. Christian Ministry in Nat. Pks., N.Y.C., 1991-2000; sec. Prisoner Visitation and Support, Phila., 1991-2001, treas., 2002—; bd. dirs. Waldensian Aid Soc., N.Y.C., 1985—. With U.S. Army, 1943-45. Democrat. Mem. United Ch. of Christ. Avocations: reading, world travel. E-mail: cmbade@talon.net.

BADEER, HENRY SARKIS, physiology educator; b. Mersine, Turkey, Jan. 31, 1915; came to U.S., 1965, naturalized, 1971; s. Sarkis and Persape Hagop (Koundakjian) B.; m. Mariam Mihran Kassarjian, July 12, 1948; children: Gilbert H., Daniel H. MD, Am. U., Beirut, Lebanon, 1938. Gen. practice medicine, Beirut, 1940-51; asst. instr. Am. U. Sch. Medicine, Beirut, 1938-45, adj. prof., 1945-51, asso. prof., 1951-62, prof. physiology, 1962-65, acting chmn. dept., 1951-56, chmn., 1956-65; research fellow Harvard U. Med. Sch., Boston, 1948-49; prof. physiology Creighton U. Med. Sch., Omaha, 1967-91, emeritus prof., 1991—, acting chmn. dept., 1971-72. Vis. prof. U. Iowa, Iowa City, 1957-58, Downstate Med. Center, Bklyn., 1965-67; mem. med. com. Azounieh Sanatorium, Beirut, 1961-65; mem. research com. Nebr. Heart Assn., 1967-70, 85-88. Author textbook Spanish translation; contbr. chpts. to books, articles to profl. jours. Recipient Golden Apple award Students of AMA, 1975, Disting. Prof. award, 1992; Rockefeller fellow., 1948-49; grantee med. research com. Am. U. Beirut, 1956-65 Mem. Internat. Soc. Heart Rsch., Am. Physiol. Soc., Internat. Soc. for Adaptive Medicine (founding mem.). Home: 2808 S 99th Ave Omaha NE 68124-2603 Office: Creighton U Med Sch 2500 California Plz Omaha NE 68178-0001 *My success seems to be related to having set a goal and persevering in achieving it; satisfaction in or enjoyment of the performance of my daily task no matter how mundane; and eagerness to learn from personal experience or the experience of others.*

BADEL, JULIE, lawyer; b. Chgo., Sept. 14, 1946; d. Charles and Saima (Hrykas) Badel. Student, Knox Coll., 1963-65; BA, Columbia Coll., Chgo., 1967; JD, DePaul U., 1977. Bar: Ill. 1977, U.S. Dist. Ct. (no. dist.) Ill. 1977, U.S. Ct. Appeals (7th and D.C. cirs.) 1981, U.S. Supreme Ct. 1985, U.S. Dist. Ct. (ea. dist.) Mich. 1989. Hearings referee State of Ill., Chgo., 1974-78; assoc. Cohn, Lambert, Ryan & Schneider, Chgo., 1978-80, McDermott, Will & Emery, Chgo., 1980-84, ptnr., 1985-2001, Epstein, Becker & Green, PC, Chgo., 2001—. Legal counsel, mem. adv. bd. Health Evaluation Referral Svc. Chgo., 1980-89; bd. dirs. Alternatives, Inc., Chgo. chpt. Asthma and Allergy Found., 1993-94, Glenwood Sch. Author: Hospital Restructuring: Employment Law Pitfalls, 1985; editor DePaul U. Law Rev., 1976-77. Mem. ABA, Chgo. Bar Assn., Labor & Employment Alliance for Women, Columbia Coll. Alumni Assn. (1st v.p., bd. dirs. 1981-86), Pi Gamma Mu. Office: Epstein Becker & Green 150 N Michigan Ave Ste 420 Chicago IL 60601-7353

BADEN, THOMAS JAMES, dermatologist; b. Coral Gables, Fla., Dec. 29, 1951; s. Thomas Benjamin and Helen (Threadgill) B.; m. Sandra Louise Bradley, June 22, 1974; children: Craig, Scott, Michael. AB in Chemistry, Duke U., 1973; MD cum laude, Emory U., 1977. Diplomate Am. Bd. Internal Medicine, Am. Bd. Dermatology. Internal medicine resident N.C. Meml. Hosp., Chapel Hill, 1977-80, dermatology resident, 1983-86; internist Toe Valley Med. Assn., Spruce Pine, N.C., 1980-83; dermatologist West Piedmont Dermatology Assn., Morganton, N.C., 1986—. Consulting dermatologist Western Carolina Ctr., Broughton Hosp., Morganton, 1986—; staff dermatologist Grace Hosp., Morganton, 1986—. Contbr. articles to profl. jours. Troop leader Boy Scouts Am.; deacon First Bapt. Ch., Morganton. Fellow ACP, Am. Acad. Dermatology, Am. Soc. Dermatology Surgeons; mem. AMA, Christian Med. Soc. Avocations: music, hiking, photography. Office: West Piedmont Dermatology 111 Foothills Dr Morganton NC 28655-5152

BADER, ALFRED ROBERT, chemist; b. Vienna, Apr. 28, 1924; came to U.S., 1947, naturalized, 1964; s. Alfred and Elizabeth Maria (Serenyi) B.; m. Isabel Overton, Jan. 26, 1982; children from previous marriage: David, Daniel. BS in Engring. Chemistry, Queens U., Can., 1945, BA in History, 1946, MS in Organic Chemistry, 1947, LLD (hon.), 1986; MA, Harvard U., 1949, PhD, 1950; DS (hon.), U. Wis.-Milw., 1980, Purdue U., 1984, U. Wis.-Madison, 1984, Northwestern U., 1990; D.Univ. (hon.), U. Sussex, Eng., 1989; DSc, U. Edinburgh, 1998, Glasgow U., 1999, Masaryk U., 2000. Rsch. chemist PPG Co., Milw., 1950-53, group leader, 1953-54; chief chemist Aldrich Chem. Co., Milw., 1954-55, pres., 1955-81, chmn., 1981-91; pres. Sigma-Aldrich Corp., 1975-80, chmn., 1980-91, chmn. emeritus, 1991-92; pres. Alfred Bader Fine Arts, Milw., 1991—. Author: Adventures of a Chemist Collector, 1995; patentee in field. Guest curator Milw. Art Mus., 1976, 89. Recipient Winthrop-Sears medal Chem. Industry Assn., 1980, J.E. Purkyne medal Acad. Scis., Czech Republic, 1994, Gold medal Am. Inst. Chemists, 1997, Boron USA award, 1997; named Entrepreneur of Year Research Dirs. Assn., 1980, Hon. Citizen, U. Vienna, 1995, Comdr. of the Brit. Empire, 1998. Fellow: Royal Soc. Arts, Royal Soc. Chemistry (hon.); mem.: Appraisers Assn. Am., Am. Chem. Soc. (award Milw. sect. 1971, Parsons' award 1995, named one of the top 75 disting. contbrs. to the chem. enterprise in the last 75 years 1998), Univ. Club (Milw.). Jewish. Office: Alfred Bader Fine Arts 924 E Juneau Ave Ste 622 Milwaukee WI 53202-2748 Fax: 414-277-0709. E-mail: baderfa@execpc.com.

BADER, CAL JOSEPH, JR., broadcast executive; b. Phila., Aug. 13, 1950; s. Cal Joseph and Elizabeth (Jones) Bader; m. Carol Kelly, Mar. 24, 1973 (div. 1980); 1 child, Robert Joseph. Student, Northampton County Community, Bethlehem, Pa., 1970. Sales rep., prog. dir., news dir. Sta. WCRV-Radio, Washington, 1972-76; afternoon drive show host Sta. WNOW-Radio, York, Pa., 1977; afternoon show host Sta. WKAP-Radio, Allentown, Pa., 1983-84; sales rep./announcer Sta. WQQQ-Radio, Easton, Pa., 1984-85, Sta. WLEV-Radio, Easton, 1985-88; sales rep./reporter Cellular One Traffic Bur., Allentown, 1988-89; news dir. Sta. WODE-FM, WEEX-AM, Easton, 1989-98, TBC Media, Phillipsburg, N.J., 1998; owner Baker Entertainment, Easton, Pa., 1999-2000; program dir., news dir. Sta. WGPA Sunny 1100, Bethlehem, Pa., 2001—; cons. Baker Consulting, 2001—. Radio mktg. and telecomms. cons.; fin. cons. for out-of-work mgmt. and execs. and sales reps.; franchise broker. Recipient N.Y. State Spot News Award, AP, 1973, Orson Wells award, Radio Advt. Bur., N.Y.C., 1988, Outstanding Contribution award, AP, Phila., 1990, 91, 92, 93, 94, 95; recipient award for Best Pub. Affairs Program or Series in Pa., 1996, Pa. Assn. Broadcasters. Democrat. Maronite Catholic. Avocations: coin collecting, fishing. Home: 710 Whitney Ave Easton PA 18045 Office: Baker Entertainment 710 Whitney Ave Easton PA 18045

BADER, DAVID MANSFIELD, education educator; b. Slayton, Minn., July 14, 1952; s. Jean Lyon and Margaret Mansfield Bader; m. Cathy Rogers Rogers, June 17, 1978; children: John Mansfield, William Lyon. BA, Augustana Coll., 1970—74; PhD, U. of ND, 1974—78. Asst., assoc., and full prof. Cornell U. Med. Coll., NYC, 1982—95; Gladys P. Stahlman prof. Vanderbilt U., Nashville, 1995—. Chair, stahlman cardiovasc. rsch. laboratories Vanderbilt U., Nashville, 1995—. Contbr. scientific papers. Recipient Hershl scholar, Hershl Found., 1988—93, Established Investigator, Am. Heart Assn., 1990—95, Commencement Spkr., Slayton H.S., 1991, Augustana scholar, Augustana Coll., 1974; Post-doctoral fellow, NIH, 1978—80, Am. Heart Assn., 1980—82. Mem.: Am. Heart Assn., Soc. of Devel. Biology, FASEB. Achievements include patents for Bves, a novel cell adhesion molecule; discovery of 8-12 novel heart-specific genes. Avocations: golf, athletics, reading, gardening. Office: Vanderbilt University 2220 Pierce Ave Nashville TN 37232 Office Fax: 615-936-3527. E-mail: david.bader@vanderbilt.edu.

BADER, DIEDRICH, actor; b. Alexandria, Va., Dec. 24, 1966; s. William and Gretta Bader; m. Duley Rodgers, 1998. Actor in feature film debut in dual role as twins Jethro and Jethrine in remake of tv series: The Beverly Hillbillies; actor (film): Teresa's Tattoo, 1994, Office Space, 1999, The Assassination File, Certain Guy, 1999, Couple Days...A Period Place, 2000, Jay & Silent Bob Strike Back, 2001, Kim Possible, 2002, Evil Alien Conquerors, 2002, (voices in films) Baby Blues, 2000, The Zeta Project, 2001, Lloyd in Space, 2001, Recess: School's Out, 2001, Ice Age, 2002, The Country Bears, 2002, Dead and Breakfast, 2003; (tv movies) Preppie Murder, 1989; (tv series): Danger Theatre, 1993, The Drew Carey Show, 1995—, Hercules, 1998; tv guest appearances include: 21 Jump Street, 1987, Fresh Prince of Bel-Air, 1990, Star Trek: The Next Generation, 1987, Cheers, 1982, Quantum Leap, 1989, Broken Badges, 1990, Flying Blind, 1992, Diagnosis Murder, 1993, Frasier, 1993, Gargoyles, 1994, Murphy Brown, 1988, Happy Hour, 1999; exec. prodr. Jimmy Scott: If You Only Knew, 2002. Office: 4000 Warner Blvd Burbank CA 91522*

BADER, GERALD LOUIS, JR., lawyer; b. St. Louis, Mar. 15, 1934; s. Gerald L. and Mabel A. (Stephens) B.; (div.); children: Gerald L. III, Stephanie, Cynthia, Carlie, Deborah; m. Barbara Anne Lien, June 2, 1979; children: Matthew Stephen, Mary Rachel. BA, Washington U., 1956; LLB, U. Mich., 1959. Bar: Colo. 1960, Mo. 1960, N.Y. 1961, U.S. Supreme Ct. 1972. Assoc. White & Case, N.Y.C., 1960-62, 64-65, Hodges, Silverstein & Harrington, Denver, 1965-68; pres. Bader and Assocs. P.C., Denver, 1969—. Sec. Denver Rep. Ctrl. Com., 1969-73; pres. Rocky Mountain Child Devel. Fedn., Denver, 1982-90; dir. Ctrl. City Opera House Assocs., Denver, 1984-2002, The Legal Ctr., Denver, 1992-98. 1st lt. U.S. Army, 1962-64. Republican. Roman Catholic. Avocations: golf, running, skiing. Office: Bader and Assocs LLC 14426 E Evans Denver CO 80014 Fax: 303-534-1701. E-mail: gbader@bader-associates.com.

BADER, JOHN MERWIN, lawyer; b. Wilmington, Del., June 29, 1919; s. Merwin Oldrin and Escelyn (Connell) B.; m. Constance Wulffaert, Dec. 27, 1944 (div. Oct. 1965); children: Andrew M., Mary Drakely Donley, Eileen Williams, Matthew J.; m. Anne S. Shane, Jan. 15, 1973 (dec. Jan. 5, 2003). BA, Villanova U., 1941; LLB, U. Pa., 1948. Bar: Del. 1948, U.S. Supreme Ct. 1956. Pvt. practice, Wilmington, 1948-56, 66-70; ptnr. Balick and Bader, Wilmington, 1956-59, Bader and Biggs, Wilmington, 1959-66, Bader, Dorsey & Kreshtool, Wilmington, 1970-81; pvt. practice Wilmington, 1981—88; of counsel Tomar,

O'Brien, Kaplan, Jacoby & Graziano, Wilmington, 1988—2001, Thomas S. Neuberger, PA, Wilmington, 2001—. Counsel Rep. State Com., Wilmington, 1975-85; mem. Ethics Commn., City of Wilmington, 1998-2001. 1st lt. U.S. Army, 1941-45. Mem. Del. Bar Assn. (v.p. 1969-71), ATLA (bd. govs. 1969-73, 75-80), Del. Trial Lawyers Assn. (pres. 1977-80), Elks, Kiwanis, Univ. and Whist Club (Wilmington). Home: 402 Rockwood Rd Wilmington DE 19802-1238 Office: 2 E 7th St Ste 302 Wilmington DE 19801

BADER, LORRAINE GREENBERG, textile stylist, designer, consultant; b. Bklyn., Sept. 5, 1930; d. Isidore and Sadie (Schreier) Greenberg; m. Martin Bader, June 24, 1950; children: Evan Ashley, Reid Scott, Wade. Student, Parsons Sch. Design, 1948-49. Textile stylist, dir. design, fashion and spl. creative projects, color coord. Cortley Fabrics Corp., N.Y.C., 1950-64, Avon Fabrics, N.Y.C., 1964-67, R.S.L. Fabrics Corp., N.Y.C., 1967-71; textile stylist, fashion dir. Shirley Fabrics Corp., N.Y.C., 1971-76; interior designer, decorator Lorraine Bader Interiors, Lawrence, N.Y., 1976-79; textile stylist, dir. design, fashion, and spl. projects, color coord. Lida Inc., N.Y.C., 1979-81; textile designer Fresh Paint, N.Y.C., 1981-87; textile designer for women's wear, children's wear, fabrics, sweaters, scarves, dinnerware, tablecloths, placemats and bedding for home furnishings Lorraine Bader Designs, Hackensack, N.J., 1987-97, owner, designer Boynton Beach, Fla., 1998. Scholar Parsons Sch. Design, 1948. Mem. The Fashion Group, Women in the Visual Arts. Avocations: painting all mediums, antiquing, interior decorating, faux decorative art.

BADER, ROBERT S. dermatologist; b. Queens, N.Y., June 14, 1968; BA, George Washington U., 1990, MD with distinction, 1994. Diplomate Am. Bd. Dermatology, lic. Fla., Ohio, N.J. Resident in internal medicine Yale-New Haven Hosp., New Haven, 1994—95; resident in dermatology Allegheny U. Hosps.-Hahnemann, Phila., 1995—98, chief resident in dermatology, 1997; fellow in dermatologic cosmetic surgery and Mohs' micrographic surgery Am. Acad. Cosmetic Surgery, Am. Soc. for Moh's Surgery, 1998—99; pvt. practice Ft. Lauderdale, Fla., 1999—2000; dermatologist RSB Dermatology, Inc., Deerfield Beach, Fla., 2000—. Active staff sect. dermatology, dept. medicine North Broward Hosp., Pompano Beach, Fla., 1999—; lectr., presenter in field. Contbr. articles to med. jours. Recipient Physician Recognition award, AMA, 1998. Fellow: Am. Soc. for Dermatologic Surgery, Am. Acad. Dermatology (Continuing Med. Edn. award 1998); mem.: Broward County Dermatol. Soc., Am. Soc. for Mohs Surgery. Achievements include research in evaluation of clinical margins of basal cell carcinoma; chronic necrotizing aspergillosis; aspergillus mastoiditis; acute pancreatitis. Office: Ste 204 1500 E Hillsboro Blvd Deerfield Beach FL 33441

BADER, ROBERT SMITH, biology, zoology educator and researcher; b. Falls City, Nebr., June 18, 1925; s. Ray Jay and Grace (Smith) B.; m. Joan Larson; children: Douglas, Jonathan, Eric, Joel. BS, Kans. State U., 1949; PhD, U. Chgo., 1954. From instr. to asst. prof. biology U. Fla., 1952-56; from asst. prof. to prof. zoology U. Ill., Urbana, 1956-68; prof. biology, dean Coll. Arts and Scis., U. Mo., St. Louis, 1968-83, rsch. prof., 1983-85; rsch. assoc. dept. history U. Kans., 1985-91. Adj. prof. history Kans. State U., 1986-91. With USNR, 1943-45. Achievements include research on Kansas history, prohibition history, Biblical theology. Home: 2165 Squirrel Rd Neosho Falls KS 66758-7122 E-mail: jlbader@terraworld.net.

BADER, RONALD L. advertising executive; b. 1951; With Amana (Iowa) Refrigeration, 1949-55, Gittens Co., Milw., 1955-60, Brady Co., Milw., 1961-70, Hoffman, York, Baker & Johnson, Milw., 1971-74, Bader Rutter & Assocs., Inc., Brookfield, Wis., 1975—, now pres, sec., treas., CEO. Office: Bader Rutter & Assoc Inc Bishop's Wood Ctr 13555 Bishops Ct Ste 300 Brookfield WI 53005-6231

BADER, WILLIAM ALAN, computer engineer; b. Bethlehem, Pa., Sept. 10, 1964; s. Morris and Sophie Karen B. BS in Computer Engring., Lehigh U., 1985, MSEE, 1986. Dir. rsch. and devel. Software Cons. Svcs., Nazareth, Pa., 1982—. Office: Software Cons Svcs LLC 630 Selvaggio Dr Ste 420 Nazareth PA 18064

BADER, WILLIAM BANKS, historian, foundation executive, former corporate executive; b. Atlantic City, Sept. 8, 1931; s. Edward L. and Celeste Bader (Burkard) B.; m. Gretta Lange, Dec. 19, 1953; children: Christopher, Katharine, John, Diedrich. BA, Pomona Coll., Claremont, Calif., 1953; MA, Princeton U., 1960, PhD, 1964. With Library of Congress, 1954-55; with Office Nat. Estimates, 1962-64; lectr. history Princeton U., 1964-65; with Dept. State, 1965-66, U.S. Senate Fgn. Relations Com., 1966-69; program officer, then European rep. Ford Found., 1969-73; program officer Office European and Internat. Affairs, Washington and; N.Y.C., 1973-74; fellow Woodrow Wilson Internat. Ctr. Scholars, 1974-75; dir. fgn. intelligence task force U.S. Senate, 1975-76; asst. dep. under sec. for policy Dept. Def., 1976-78; staff dir. U.S. Senate Fgn. Relations Com., 1978-81; v.p. SRI Internat.-Washington, Arlington, Va., 1981-87; sr. v.p. SRI Internat., Menlo Park, Calif., 1988-92; pres. Eurasia Found., Washington, 1992-96; with World Bank Group, Washington, 1996-97, Ctr. Strategic and Internat. Studies, 1997-98; asst. sec. of state ednl. and cultural affairs Dept. State, 1998—2001; with World Bank Group, Washington, 2001—02; v.p. Nat. Def. U., 2002—. Adj. prof. Georgetown U. Author: Austria Between East and West: 1945-1955, 1966, The U.S. and the Spread of Nuclear Weapons, 1968, The Taiwan Relations Act: A Decade of Implementation, 1989; also articles. Bd. dirs. Samuel H. Kress Found. Served as officer USNR, 1955-58, capt. Res. ret. Recipient Meritorious Service medal Dept. State, 1966, Sec. Def. medal for outstanding pub. service, 1979, Osterreichische Ehrenkreuz fur Wissenschaft und Kunst 1. Klasse (officer's cross), Republic of Austria, 1991. Mem. Council Fgn. Relations, Internat. Inst. Strategic Studies. Clubs: Cosmos (Washington). Roman Catholic. Office: Nat Def univ Ft Lesley J McNair 300 5th Ave Washington DC 20319-5066

BADER, W(ILLIAM) REECE, lawyer; b. Portland, Oreg., Oct. 31, 1941; s. William Lange and Phyllis Harriet (Cole) B.; m. Jean McCarty, Aug. 3, 1963 (div. 1993); children: Lawson R., Cole R.; m. Alicia Spatafore, June 14, 1998. BA, Williams Coll., 1963; JD, Duke U., 1966. Bar: D.C. 1967, Calif. 1969, U.S. Dist. Ct. D.C., U.S. Dist. Ct. (no., ctrl., ea. and so. dists.) Calif., U.S. Ct. Appeals (D.C., 2d, 3d, 7th, 9th and fed. cirs.), U.S. Tax Ct., U.S. Claims Ct., U.S. Supreme Ct. Law clk. to judge U.S. Ct. Appeals (D.C. cir.), Washington, 1966-68; assoc. Orrick, Herrington & Sutcliffe LLP, San Francisco, 1968-74, ptnr., 1974—. Mem. legal adv. bd. Hastings Law Ctr. Found., 1981-87; mem. securities disputes resolution com. Ctr. for Pub. Resources, 1990—; mem. nat. arbitration and med. com. NASDR, 1994-98; mem. ad hoc com. on ct. facilities and design U.S. Jud. Conf., 1969-72, mem. adv. com. on civil rules, 1982-87, mem. standing com. on rules of practice and procedure, 1987-90; lectr., panelist Practicing Law Inst., ABA Am. Law Inst., Internat. Franchise Assn., Calif. Electronic Assn., many others; arbitrator, mediator Nat. Assn. Securities Dealers Regulation Inc., 1979—, Am. Arbitration Assn., 1979—, N.Y. Stock Exch., 1984—, Nat. Futures Assn., 1985—, Pvt. Adjudication Found., 1987-96. Mem. editl. bd. Alternatives, 1991—; editor: Securities News, 1993-94, Securities Arbitration, 1999-, Private Securities Litigation Reform Act Reporter, 1996—; contbr. article to profl. jours. Trustee North Park Coll. and Theol. Sem., Chgo., 1984-89, sec., 1985-86, chmn., 1986-89. Fellow Am. Bar Found., Environ. Law Inst.; mem. ABA (litig., bus., natural resources, dispute resolution sects.), State Bar Calif. (litig., bus., environ. sects.), Securities Industry Assn. (compliance and legal divsn.), Futures Industry Assn. (compliance and legal divsn.), Bar Assn. San Francisco, D.C. Bar Assn. Avocations: collecting toy trains, squash, reading, travel. Home: 62 Lloyden Dr Atherton CA 94027-3834 Office: Orrick Herrington Sutcliffe LLP 1020 Marsh Rd Menlo Park CA 94025-1021 E-mail: wrbader@orrick.com.

BADERTSCHER, DAVID GLEN, law librarian, consultant; b. Morrow, Ohio, Jan. 31, 1935; s. Glen C. and Blanche (Cluff) Badertscher; m. Betty Jo Shafer, June 25, 1965. BS, Ind. State U., 1957, MS, 1962, Rosary Coll., 1967. Tchr. Rockville HS, Ind., 1957-59, Medinah Elem. Sch., Ill., 1961-63; libr. Elgin Acad., Ill., 1963-64; tchr. Beachwood HS, Ohio, 1964-65; libr. Chgo. Pub. Libr., 1965-66; circulation, asst. reference libr. U. Chgo. Law Sch., 1966-70; libr. Schiff Hardin Waite Dorschel & Britton, Chgo., 1970-73; exec. libr. Georgetown U. Law Ctr., Washington, 1973-78; dir. libr. Milbank, Tweed, Hadley & McCloy, N.Y.C., 1978-80; prin. law libr. N.Y. Supreme Ct., N.Y.C., 1980—. Cons. Urban Rsch. Corp., Chgo., 1970—73, Herner & Co., 1977—, R. R. Bowker & Co., 1981—91, Nat. Ctr. State Cts., 1992—96; advisor Computer Law Svc., 1972—82, EIS, 1978—; adj. prof. Baruch Coll., 1982—; bd. dirs. N.Y. Met. Reference and Rsch. Libr. Agy., chmn. bd. pers. com., 1989—93; mem. judges com. automation and tech. State of N.Y. Unified Ct. Sys., 1994—96. Contbr. articles to profl. jours. Mem. corp. adv. bd. Tech. Forum Internat., 1997—. With U.S. Army, 1959—61. Mem.: ABA (assoc.; mem. com. sci. and tech. criminal justice sect. 2000—), Assn. Info. Mgrs., Am. Soc. Info. Sci. (editor SIG/Law Newsletter 1975—79), Chgo. Assn. Law Librs. (pres., conf. chmn. 1970—72, mem. com. automation and tech. judges N.Y. 1994—96), Am. Assn. Law Librs. (chmn. com. automation, sci. devel. 1970—72, chmn. state, city, and county law librs. sect. 1989—90, mem. adv. com. law libr. jour. 1989—91, conv. grantee 1970), Medinah Tchrs. Assn. (pres. 1962—63). Home: 257 Orchard St Apt 8 Westfield NJ 07090-3130 Office: NY Supreme Ct 100 Centre St New York NY 10013-4308

BADERTSCHER, DORIS RAE, elementary education educator; b. Akron, Ohio, May 10, 1935; d. Ray and Doris Ada (Lee) Shanaberger; m. James Lee Badertscher, Feb. 2, 1958; children: Leslie, Lynn. BS, Kent State U., 1957; MS, Calif. State U., Dominguez Hills, 1987. Tchr. Marion (Ohio) City Schs., 1968—. Supr. Saturday sch., 1989-90; coach Odyssey Mind, 1984-85; chmn. Marion City Schs. divsn. Marion Art Fair, 1970; drama coach for 54 programs, 1968—, dir. make up, 1975-79. Author: (children's books) The Prying Princess, 1990, The Dragon Dilemma, 1990. Vol. Marion Gen. Hosp., 1970; mem. Marion Little Theatre, 1975-79, com. Teach-In Day, 1980, com. ednl. fair, 1990, Marion Women's Roundtable, 1987; coord. Black History Month, 1990; participant sexual assault and abuse prevention workshop, 1990, Jennings Scholar Alumni workshop, 1986; mem. Christian edn. com., deacon 1st Presbyn. Ch., Marion, 1986-88; founding mem. Guild One Grady Meml. Hosp., past pres., sec., 1986—; founder Kids for Grady Christmas News Paper; chair Right-to-Read Week, 1989-90; wedding coord., stewardship com. Emanuel Luth. Ch., 1996, bd. edn., chmn. of day care bd., 1997. Martha Holden Jennings scholar, 1980-81, Ohio Theatre Alliance scholar, 1984, 86; Career Exploration grantee, 1987; recipient Disting. Alumni award Cuyahoga Falls (Ohio) High Sch., 1991, Golden Apple Achiever award Ashland Oil Co., 1990. Mem. AAUW (pres. 1986-87, pres. 1993-94), Phi Delta Kappa, Alpha Gamma Delta, Alpha Psi Omega. Avocations: theatre, travel, knitting, reading, interior decoratin. Home: 1660 Westminster Rd Marion OH 43302-5854

BADGAIYAN, RAJENDRA D. medical educator, researcher; s. Shyam and Sundari Badgaiyan; 1 child, Ashutosh. MD, Gandhi Med. Coll., 1982. Lic. psychiatrist Harvard Med. Sch. Faculty Harvard Med. Sch., Boston, 1998—2002. Recipient BK Anand Rsch. prize, India, 1992, Solomon prize, Harvard Med Sch., 2002. Achievements include research in Nonconscious processing. Office: Harvard Med Sch Fruit St Boston MA 02145 E-mail: rajendra@wjh.harvard.edu.

BADGER, DAVID HARRY, lawyer; b. Indpls., June 16, 1931; s. David Henry and Mayme Pearl (Wright) B.; m. Donna Lee Bailey, June 24, 1954; children: David Mark, Lee Ann, Steven Michael. BEE, Rose Poly. Inst., 1953; JD, Ind. U., 1964. Bar: Ind. 1964, U.S. Dist. Ct. (so and no. dists.) Ind. 1964, U.S. Patent Office 1964, U.S. Ct. Customs and Patent Appeals 1971, U.S. Ct. Appeals (fed. cir.) 1982. Engr. GE, 1953-56, Ransburg Corp., Indpls., 1956-62; chief elec. engr. Rex Metal Craft, Inc., Indpls., 1963-64; patent counsel, corp. sec. Ransburg Corp., Indpls., 1964—76; legal counsel Ball Corp., Muncie, Ind., 1976-77; ptnr. Jenkins, Coffey, Hyland, Badger & Conard, Indpls., 1977-82; mng. ptnr. Brinks, Hofer, Gilson & Lione, Indpls., 1982-98. Contbr. articles to profl. jours.; patentee in U.S. and fgn. countries. With USN, 1953-55, lt. comdr. USNR. Named Hon. Alumnus Rose Hulman Inst. Tech., 1987. Mem. ABA (various coms.), IEEE, Ind. Bar Assn. (various coms.), Am. Intellectual Property Law Assn. (various coms.), Licensing Execs. Soc. (various coms.), Indpls. Bar Assn., Internat. Assn. Intellectual Property Law, Indpls. Jazz Club (bd. dirs. 1983-85, 95-97), Junto of Indpls. (bd. dirs. 1997-99). Home: 3524 Inverness Blvd Carmel IN 46032-9379 Office: Brinks Hofer Gilson & Lione 1 Indiana Sq Ste 1600 Indianapolis IN 46204-2045 E-mail: badger938@aol.com.

BADGER, PHILLIP CHARLES, agricultural engineer; b. Lodi, Ohio, Jan. 7, 1948; s. Clifford Russell and Helen Pauline (Fair) B.; m. Cheryl Lynn Baker, Aug. 14, 1971 (div. Feb. 1999); children: Brian, Scott, Mark; m. Bonnie Watkins, Aug. 14, 1999. BS in Agrl. Engring., Ohio State U., 1971, MS in Agrl. Engring., 1973; MBA, Vanderbilt U., 1993. Registered profl. engr., Ohio, Ala. Design engr. Ideanamics, Columbus, Ohio, 1972—74; rsch. assoc., project engr. Ohio State U. and Ohio Agrl. R & D Ctr., Wooster, 1975—78, ext. specialist, rsch. assoc., 1978—79; mgr. waste heat utilization project TVA, Muscle Shoals, Ala., 1979—80, mgr. small scale fuel ethanol project, 1980—82, mgr. fuel ethanol from non-woody cellulose program, 1982—84; mgr. Regional Biomass Energy program Dept. Energy, Muscle Shoals, 1984—, leader TVA biomass applications group, 1994—, leader mgr. regional biomass energy program, 1994—99; pres. Gen. Bioenergy, Inc., Florence, Ala., 1999—; pres., chief mgr. Renewable Oil Internat., Florence, 2000—, ROI Ala. Ops. LLC, Florence. Mem. biomass and waste energy com. Electric Power Rsch. Inst., Palo Alto, Calif., 1990—; mem. Renewable Energy and Efficiency Inst. Quality Control Bd., 1996—. Author: Conserving Energy in Ohio Greenhouses, 1979 (Am. Soc. Agr. Engrs. blue ribbon award 1979); mem. editl. bd. CIGR Electronic Jour.; contbr. articles to profl. jours. Bd. dirs. New Uses Coun., 1997—. Recipient Tech. Achievement award Dept. Energy, 1985, 96, 98, Outstanding Tech. Presentation award WATTec '89, 1989, Cert. of Environ. Achievement, Nat. Awards Coun. for Environ. Sustainability, 1994-99, Industry Leader award Fiber Fuels Inst., 1993. Mem. Am. Soc. Agrl. Engrs. (v.p. energy com. 1990-91, pres. 1991-92), Am. Solar Energy Soc., Am. Assn. Indsl. Crops, Internat. Solar Energy Soc., Nat. Mgmt. Assn., Am. Assn. Indsl. Crops, Biomass Energy Rsch. Assn. (bd. dirs. 1987—), New Uses Coun. (bd. dirs. 1997—), Coun. of Forest Engring., Coun. for Agrl. Sci. and Tech., Florence Exch. Club (bd. dirs. 1985-86). Office: Gen Bioenergy Inc Renewable Oil Internat ®LLC and ROI Ala Ops PO Box 26 Florence AL 35631-0026

BADGER, RONALD KAY, lawyer; b. Horton, Kans., Aug. 24, 1933; s. Clarence E. and Josephine L. (Rick) Badger; m. Janet L. Horner, Feb. 16, 1963; children: Hellen L. Badger Haag, Ronald K. Jr., Laura J. Badger Davis. BS in Bus., U. Kans., 1958, BS in Law, 1961, JD, 1968. Bar: Kans. 1961, U.S. Dist. Ct. Kans. 1961, U.S. Ct. Appeals (10th cir.) 1973, U.S. Supreme Ct. 1982, U.S. Ct. Claims 1990. Law clk. to Hon. Arthur J. Stanley Jr., U.S. Dist. Ct. Kans., Kansas City, 1961—62; spl. asst. to U.S. atty. for dist. of Kans., Dept. Justice, Topeka, 1962—64; assoc. Foulston & Siefkin, Wichita, Kans., 1964—66; atty. in contract adminstrn. Boeing Co., Wichita, 1966—68; pvt. practice Wichita, 1968—. Bd. dirs. Envision. Mem. bd. edtiors Kans. Bar Jour., 1966—82; contbr. articles to profl. jours. Bd. dirs. Wichita Symphony Soc., 1970—. Mem.: Fed. Bar Assn. (pres. Kans. chpt. 1978—80), Christian Legal Soc. (pres. Wichita chpt. 2001—03), Wichita Estate Planning Coun. (sec. 1996—97, pres. 1997—98), Wichita Bar Assn., Kans. Bar Assn., Lions (pres. Wichita chpt. 1984—85). Republican. Methodist. Office: 330 N Main St Wichita KS 67202

BADGER, SANDRA RAE, health and physical education educator; b. Pueblo, Colo., Nov. 2, 1946; d. William Harvey and Iva Alberta (Belveal) Allenbach; m. Graeme B. Badger, Oct. 9, 1972; 1 child, Jack Edward. BA in Phys. Edn., U. So. Colo., Pueblo, 1969; MA in Arts and Humanities, Colo. Coll., 1979; postgrad., Adams State U., Alamosa, Colo., 1980-91. Cert. tchr., secondary endorsement in health and phys. edn., Colo. Head women's swimming coach Mitchell High Sch., Doherty High Sch., Colorado Springs, Colo., 1969-90; head dept. health edn. Doherty High Sch., 1979-2000; asst. coach cross country and track, men and women, indoor and outdoor track men and women U. Colo., 1996—. Trainer student asst. program CARE, Colorado Springs, 1983—; trainer drug edn. U.S. Swim Olympic Tng. Ctr., Colorado Springs, 1988-89; coach in track and field, Colorado Springs, 1989, 91; cons. Assocs. in Recovery Therapy, 1989—; asst. instr. scuba diving, 1999; dir. Colo. Health, Fitness and Coaching Conf., 1999—; speaker in field. Author, editor: Student Assistant Training Manual, 1983-95. Bd. dirs. ARC, Colo. Springs, 1990-96, sec., 1991-92, mem. health and safety com., 1990-95; reviewer ARC/Olympic Com. Sports Safety Tng. Manual Handbook Textbooks; mem. comprehensive health adv. com. Dept. Edn., State of Colo., Denver, 1991. Recipient Svc. award ARC, 1985, Coach of Yr. award Gazette Telegraph, 1979, 84, CARE award State of Colo., 1988, others; Gamesfield grantee, 1985; Nat. Coun. on Alcoholism grantee, 1990; nominated Readers' Digest Tchr. of Yr., 1998-99. Mem. NEA, Colorado Springs Edn. Assn. Avocations: scuba diving, running, travel. Office: U Colo 1420 Austin Bluffs PO Box 7150 Colorado Springs CO 80933-7150

BADGEROW, JOHN NICHOLAS, lawyer; b. Macon, Mo., Apr. 7, 1951; s. Harry Leroy Badgerow and Barbara Raines (Buell) Novaria; m. Teresa Ann Zvolanek, Aug. 7, 1976; children: Anthony Thornton, Andrew Cameron, James Terrill. BA in Bus. and English with honors, Principia Coll., 1972; JD, U. Mo., Kansas City, 1975. Bar: Kans. 1976, U.S. Dist. Ct. Kans. 1976, U.S. Ct. Appeals (10th cir.) 1977, U.S. Ct. Appeals (4th cir.) 1979, U.S. Supreme Ct. 1982, U.S. Ct. Appeals (fed. cir.) 1985, U.S. Ct. Appeals (8th cir.) 1986, Mo. 1986, U.S. Dist. Ct. (we. dist.) Mo. 1986. Ptnr. McAnany, VanCleave & Phillips, P.A., Kansas City, Kans., 1975-85; ptnr.-in-charge Spencer, Fane, Britt & Browne, Kansas City, Mo. and Overland Park, Kans., 1986—. Chmn. ethics grievance com. Johnson County, 1988—; mem. Kans. Jud. Coun., 1995—, Kans. Bd. Discipline for Attys., 2000—, chmn. Ethics 2000 Commn., 2002—. Co-author: Kansas Employment Law, 1992, 2d edit., 2001; co-author, co-editor Kansas Lawyer Ethics, 1996. Co-chmn. Civil Justice Reform Act Commn., Dist. of Kans., 1995-96. Mem.: ABA, Earl O'Connor Am. Inn of Ct. (pres. 1996), Kans. Assn. Def. Counsel (age discrimination seminar), Lawyers' Assn. Kansas City, Kansas City Met. Bar Assn. (chmn. civil rights com.), Kans. Bar Assn. (employment seminar, bd. editors 1982—88, CLE com. 1989—95, ethics adv. opinion com. 1997—, Outstanding Svc. award 1995), Kans. Jud. Coun., Mission Valley Hunt Club (Stilwell, Kans.). Republican. Christian Scientist. Avocations: horseback riding, carpentry, reading. Office: Spencer Fane Britt & Browne 9401 Indian Creek Pkwy Ste 700 Shawnee Mission KS 66210-2038

BADGLEY, JOHN ROY, architect; b. Huntington, W.Va., July 10, 1922; s. Roy Joseph and Fannie Myrtle (Limbaugh) B.; m. Janice Atwell, July 10, 1975; 1 child, Adam; children by previous marriage: Dan, Lisa, Holly, Marcus, Michael. AB, Occidental Coll., 1943; MArch, Harvard U., 1949; postgrad., Internat. Ctr., Vincenza, Italy, 1959. Lic. Calif. Pvt. practice, San Luis Obispo, Calif., 1952-65; chief arch., planner Crocker Land Co., San Francisco, 1965-80; v.p. Cushman & Wakefield Inc., San Francisco, 1980-84; pvt. practice, San Rafael, Calif., 1984—. Insr. Calif. State U., San Luis Obispo, 1952-65. Bd. dirs. Ft. Mason Ctr., Angel Island Assn. With USCGR, 1942-54. Mem. AIA, Am. Arbitration Assn., Golden Gate Wine Soc. Home and Office: 1356 Idylberry Rd San Rafael CA 94903-1074 E-mail: jrbadgley@mindspring.com.

BADGLEY, THEODORE MCBRIDE, psychiatrist, neurologist; b. Salem, Ala., June 27, 1925; s. Roy Joseph and Fannie (Limbaugh) B.; m. Mary Bennett Wells, Dec. 30, 1945; children: Justice O'Neil, Jan Badgley, Mona Jean Covey, Jason Wells, James John, Mary Rose Bleier. Student, Occidental Coll., 1942-44; MD, U. So. Calif., 1949. Diplomate: Am. Bd. Psychiatry and Neurology. Intern Letterman Gen. Hosp., San Francisco, 1949-50, resident in psychiatry, 1950-53; commd. capt. M.C. U.S. Army, 1950, advanced through grades to lt. col., 1967; chief mental hygiene cons. service Ft. Gordon, Ga.; and asso. clin. prof. psychiatry and neurology Med. Coll. Ga., 1954-55; resident in neurology Walter Reed Gen. Hosp., Washington, 1955-57, asst. chief psychiatry service, 1957-59, chief psychiatry service, 1959-62, asst. chief dept. psychiatry and neurology, 1962-63, dir. edn. and tng. psychiatry, 1957-63; chief dept. psychiatry and neurology U.S. Army Gen. Hosp., Landstuhl, Germany, 1963-66; chief psychiatry outpatient dept. Letterman Gen. Hosp., 1966-67; ret., 1967; dir. Kern View Mental Health Center, Bakersfield, Calif., 1967-69; pvt. practice medicine specializing in med. and forensic neuropsychiatry Bakersfield, 1967-93; pres. Sans Doloroso Inst., Bakersfield, 1969-93. Lectr. community health service orgns., profl. confs., seminars. Contbr. articles to profl. jours. Fellow Am. Psychiat. Assn.; mem. Kern County Psychiat. Soc. (pres. 1972-93), Kern County Med. Soc. (pres. 1981).

BADHAM, JOHN MACDONALD, motion picture director; b. Luton, Eng., Aug. 25, 1939; came to U.S., 1945; s. Henry Lee and Mary Iola (Hewitt) B.; 1 child, Kelly MacDonald; m. Julia Laughlin, 1992. BA, Yale U., 1961, MFA, 1963. Assoc. producer Universal Studios, 1969-70; pres. Gt. Am. Picture Show; chmn. bd. JMB Films, Inc. Pres. Badham Co.; guest lectr. UCLA, Yale U., U. So. Calif., Amherst Coll. Assoc. producer TV movies Night Gallery, 1969, Neon Ceiling, 1970; assoc. producer, dir. TV movies The Senator, 1970 (Emmy award nomination 1971); dir. numerous episodes of The Bold Ones, others; motion pictures for TV include The Law (Emmy nomination 1974), 1974 (ARD reihe 'das film festival award 1975), Isn't It Shocking, 1973, Reflections of Murder, 1973, The Impatient Heart (Christopher award 1971), The Gun, (So. Calif. Motion Picture Council award 1974), The Godchild, 1974, Sorrow Floats, 1998; theatrical motion pictures include The Bingo Long Travelling All Stars and Motor Kings (NAACP image award nomination 1976), Saturday Night Fever, 1977, Dracula, 1979 (Grand prize 9th Internat. Sci. Fiction Festival of Paris, Best Horror Film award and, 1st George Pal Meml. award, both Acad. of Sci. Fiction Fantasy and Horror Films), Whose Life Is It Anyway, 1981, Blue Thunder, 1983, War Games (Best Dir., Acad. of Sci. Fiction Fantasy and Horror Films), 1983, American Flyers, 1985, Short Circuit, 1986, Stakeout, 1987, Bird on a Wire, 1989, The Hard Way, 1990, Point of No Return, 1993, Another Stakeout, 1993, Drop Zone, 1994, Nick of Time, 1995, Incognito, 1998, Floating Away, 1998, (TV) The Jack Bull, 1999, The Last Debate, 2000, My Brother's Keeper, 2002, Obsessed, 2002; exec. prodr. motion picture Rebound, 1996. Bd. dirs. Indian Spring Sch. Served with U.S. Army, 1963-64. Mem. Dirs. Guild Am., Am. Film Inst., Acad. Motion Picture Arts and Scis., Yale Drama Alumni Fund (chmn.). Office: c/o Jeff Berg, Nick Reed ICM 8942 Wilshire Blvd Beverly Hills CA 90211

BADIAN, ERNST, history educator; b. Vienna, Aug. 8, 1925; arrived in U.S., 1968; m. Nathlie A. Wimsett, 1950; children: Hugh I., Rosemary J. BA, U.N.Z., 1945, MA, 1946; BA, Oxford U., Eng., 1950, MA, 1954, PhD, 1956; LittD, Victoria U., Wellington, N.Z., 1962; DLitt (hon.), Macquarie Univ., 1993, U. Canterbury, Eng., 1999. Jr. lectr. classics Victoria U., England, 1947-48; asst. lectr., classics and ancient history U. Sheffield, England, 1952-54; lectr. classics U. Durham, England, 1954-65; prof. ancient history U. Leeds, England, 1965-69; prof. classics and history SUNY, Buffalo, 1969-71; prof. history Harvard U., Cambridge, Mass., 1971-82, John Moors Cabot prof. history, 1982-98, John Moors Cabot prof. history emeritus, 1998—. Vis. prof. universities, Colo., Oreg., Wash., South Africa, Heidelberg, Tel-Aviv, Western Australia, UCLA; Sather prof., U. Calif., Berkeley, 1976; vis. mem. Inst. Advanced Study, Princeton, fall 1980, fall 1992, Nat. Humanities Ctr., fall 1988, Kommission für Alte Geschichte, Munich, May 1989. Author: Foreign Clientelae, 264-70 B.C., 1958 (Conington prize Oxford U.), Studies in Greek and Roman History, 1964, Roman Imperialism in the Late Republic, 1967, Publicans and Sinners, 1972, From Plataea to Potidaea: Studies in the History and Historiography of the Pentecontaetia, 1993, Zöllner und Sünder, 1997; editor: Polybius, 1966, Ancient Society and Institutions, 1966, Sir Ronald Syme, Roman Papers vols. 1-2, 1979, Am. Jour. Ancient History, 1976-2001. Fellow Am. Coun. Learned Soc., 1972-73, 82-83, Leverhulme fellow, Eng., 1973, Guggenheim fellow, 1984, hon. fellow Univ. Coll., Oxford, Eng.; decorated Austrian Cross of Honor for Sci. and Art, 1999. Fellow Brit. Acad., Am. Acad. Arts and Sci., Am. Numismatic Soc.; hon. mem. Soc. Promotion Roman Studies; corr. mem. Austrian Acad. Sci., German Archeol. Inst.; fgn. mem. Finnish Acad. Sci.; mem. Am. Philol. Assn., Assn. Ancient Historians, Classical Assn. Can., U.K. Classical Assn., adv. Australian Soc. Classical Studies, Soc. Promotion Hellenic Studies, Virgil Soc., Intrnat. Assn. for Greek and Latin Epigraphy, Australian Soc. for Classical Studies. Office: Harvard U Robinson Hall Cambridge MA 02138

BADIK, ELEANORE, artist; b. Salem, Mass. d. Henry Luzinski and Rose Podgajski; m. Michael Badik, Nov. 1949 (dec. 1975); children: Michael, Tamara. Student, New England Conservatory, Boston, 1945-47. Pres. Las Vegas Art Mus., 1972-74; dir. gallery Paintings of World, Las Vegas, 1977-85; owner Galleria de Badik, Carmel, Calif., 1986-88. Exhbns. include George Mason U., 2000, Las Vegas Art Mus., 2000, 01 Mem. Nat. League Am. Pen Women (pres. 1976-78), Nev. Pastel Soc. (v.p. 2003), Gallery Guild U.Nev. Las Vegas (pres. 1969-71). Avocation: antiques. Home: 2717 Glencliff Dr Las Vegas NV 89134

BADIRU, ADEDEJI BODUNDE, industrial engineer; b. Lagos, Nigeria, Sept. 2, 1952; s. Sharafa Ola and Rukayat Abeni (Shabi) B.; m. Iswat Amori Onatolu, Sept. 25, 1975; children: Abi, Ade, Tunji. BS, Tenn. Tech. U., 1979, MS, 1981; PhD, U. Ctrl. Fla., 1984. Registered profl. engr. Prof. Sch. Indsl. Engring. Univ. Okla., Norman, 1985-2000, U. Tenn., Knoxville, 2000—. Cons. UN Devel. Program, Lagos, 1994. Author: Project Management in Manufacturing and High Technology Operations, 1996, Expert Systems Application in Engineering and Manufacturing, 1992, Industry's Guide to ISO 9000, 1995. Recipient Teetor

Educator award Soc. Automotive Engrs., 1988. Fellow Inst. Indsl. Engrs. (pres. Okla. City chpt. 1992-2000, Excellence award 1992). Avocations: painting, poetry. Home: PO Box 31304 Knoxville TN 37930-1304 Fax: 865-974-0588. E-mail: abadiru@utk.edu.

BADMAN, JOHN, III, real estate developer, architect; b. Kansas City, Mo., July 11, 1944; s. John II and Barbara (Smith) B.; m. Katherine Ballantine, May 12, 1984; children: Lindsay Cathryn, Barbara Smith, John IV. BA, Yale U., 1966, MArch, 1969, postgrad., 1969-70, M in Environmental Design, 1971. Registered architect, Conn.; real estate broker, Conn. Gen. mgr. S.J. Willy, Architects, New Haven, Conn., 1971-73; v.p. Schumacher & Forelle, Great Neck, N.Y., 1973-77, exec. v.p., 1986-87; dir. planning and devel. Dravo Engrs., N.Y.C., 1977-81; sr. v.p. Parsons, Brinckerhoff, Quade & Douglas, N.Y.C., 1981-86, also bd. dirs.; chmn., chief exec. officer Ballantine and Badman, Inc., Real Estate Developers, Greenwich, Conn., 1986—; sr. v.p. H.W. Lochner, Planners and Engrs., 1991—. Chmn. Conf. of Patriotic and Hist. Socs., N.Y.C., 1993—. Mem. Lacrosse all-Am. Team U.S. Intercollegiate Lacrosse Assn., 1966. Mem. AIA, Soc. Colonial Wars (coun. 1987—, chmn. exec. com. 1996—, gov. 1996—), The Pilgrims of the U.S., Colonial Order of the Acorn (chancellor 1997—), Baronial Order of the Magna Charta, Jamestown Soc., Nat. Coun. Archtl. Registration Bds. (cert.), New Eng. Soc. N.Y., Round Hill Assn., Mayflower Soc., Plymouth Com., Yale Club (N.Y.C.), Greenwich Country Club, Greenwich Polo Players Club, Adirondack League Club (Old Forge, N.Y.). Republican. Episcopalian. Home: 20 Mackenzie Gln Greenwich CT 06830-3421

BADO, KENNETH STEVE, automotive company administrator; b. Amherst, Ohio, Mar. 13, 1941; s. Steve and Hildegarde Paulene (Gutosky) B.; m. Linda Bonita Crabtree, May 30, 1962 (div. Oct. 1989); children: Bradley Steve, Cheryl Lynn Smith, John Robert; m. Polly Ann Steele, Nov. 28, 1989. Student, Ohio U., 1958-60, Lorain County Community Coll., 1960-62. Mfg. planning specialist Ford Motor Co., Lorain, Ohio, 1961-97; farmer Henrietta, Ohio, 1972—; owner, mgr. The Galleon, Lorain, 1986—. Leader Sub-System Group (Group Tng.), Lorain, 1987-92. Advisor Lorain County Steer Club (4-H), Lorain County, 1977-93, Henrietta Hazers Club (4-H), Lorain County, 1976-88. Mem. Am. Quarter Horse Assn., Ohio Quarter Horse Assn., Moose, Masons (32 degree), Scottish Rite Soc. Republican. Lutheran. Avocations: boating, fishing, horseback riding, computer work. Home: 12359 Baird Rd # 2 Oberlin OH 44074-9632 Office: The Galleon 4875 W Erie Ave Lorain OH 44053-1331 E-mail: Galleon@aol.com.

BADR, GAMAL MOURSI, legal consultant; b. Helwan, Egypt, Feb. 8, 1924; came to U.S., 1970; s. Ahmad Moursi and Aisha Morshida (Al-Alaily) B.; m. Fatima al-Zahraa Barakat, June 18, 1950; children: Hefni, Hussein. LLB, U. Alexandria, Arab Republic of Egypt, 1944, LLD summa cum laude, 1954; diploma in econs., U. Cairo, 1945, diploma in pvt. law, 1946. Asst. dist. atty. Mixed Cts. Egypt, Alexandria, 1945-49; from assoc. to ptnr. Vatimbella, Catzeflis, Garrana & Badr, Alexandria, 1949-63; legal advisor UN Congo Operation, Kinshasa, Congo, 1963-64; justice Supreme Ct. Algeria, Algiers, 1965-69; from mem. to dep. dir. legal dept. UN Secretariat, N.Y.C., 1970-84; legal advisor Mission of Qatar to UN, N.Y.C., 1984-94; advisor Mission of Saudi Arabia to UN, N.Y.C., 1998—. Permanent bur. mem. Pan-Arab Lawyers' Fedn., Cairo, 1959-61; adj. prof. law NYU, 1982-98; lectr. The Hague Acad. Internat. Law, 1984. Author: Agency, 1980, State Immunity, 1984; gen. editor Commercial Law of the Middle East; contbr. articles to profl. jours. Mem. Internat. Law Assn. (London), Am. Soc. Internat. Law, Am. Arbitration Assn. (panel of arbitrators), Am. Fgn. Law Assn. (v.p. 1985-87, 89-92), Egyptian-Am. Assn. (pres. 1987-90), Rotary (pres. Alexandria Club 1962-63). Moslem. Home: 18 Peter Lynas Ct Tenafly NJ 07670-1115

BADRA, ROBERT GEORGE, theology studies educator, humanities educator; b. Lansing, Mich., Dec. 8, 1933; s. Razouk Anthony and Anna (Paul) Badra; m. Maria Theresa Beer, Oct. 25, 1968 (div. 1973); m. Kristen Lillie Stuckey, Dec. 30, 1977 (div. 2001); children: Rachal Jennifer, Danielle Elizabeth Jane. BA, Sacred Heart Sem., 1957; MA, Western Mich. U., 1968; MDiv, St. John's Provincial Sem., 1985. Ordained priest Roman Cath. Ch., 1961. Mem. faculty Kalamazoo Valley CC, 1968—, prof. philosophy, religion and humanities, 1968—. Adj. prof. Nazareth Coll., 1985—91, Siena Heights U., 1993—; mem. faculty ministry formation Cath. Diocese Kalamazoo, 1999—. Bd. dirs. Kalamazoo Coun. Humanities, 1983—86, Van Buren Youth Camp, 1993—95, v.p. bd. dirs., 2002—. Recipient Edn. award, Exxon, 1996; grantee NEH, 1991—. Mem.: Assn. Religion and Intellectual Life. Office: Kalamazoo Valley CC PO Box 4070 Kalamazoo MI 49003-4070

BAE, FRANK S. H. law educator, law library administrator; b. Chung King, Szechuan, China, Dec. 19, 1941; came to U.S., 1967; s. Tse H. and Yu F. (Wang) B.; m. Anne Rita Donavan, March 15, 1975; children: Stephen, David, Marie, Elizabeth. LLB, Nat. Chung Shing U., Taipei, Taiwan, 1965; MCL, U. Miami, Fla., 1968; MS, U. Wis., 1970; JurD (hon.), New England Sch. Law, Boston, 1977. Dir. law libr. New England Sch. Law, 1970—, asst. prof. law, 1970-73, assoc. prof. law, 1973-74, prof. law, 1974—. Co-author: Searching the Law, 2nd edit., 1999. Mem. New England Law Libr. Consortium (bd. dirs.). Office: New Eng Sch Law Libr 154 Stuart St Boston MA 02116-5616

BAE, SEONGTAE, electrical engineer; b. Seoul, Republic of Korea, Apr. 10, 1968; s. Young-Sik Bae and Jum-Hong Kwon. PhD, U. Minn., 2002. Rsch. scientist Korea Inst. Sci. and Tech., Seoul, Republic of Korea, 1993—96; rschr. U. Minn. Ctr. Micromagnetics and Info. Tech., Mpls., 1998—2002. Contbr. numerous articles to profl. jours. Math. tchr. Buk-Boo Teenager Sch., Seoul, Republic of Korea, 1989—92. Recipient Excellent prize, Republic of Korea, 1991, Student Travel award, Internat. Conf., Japan, 2000, Young Rschr. award, 2000. Mem.: IEEE, Am. Physics Soc. Home: 1150 Cushing Cir #204 Saint Paul MN 55108 Office: Univ Minn EEsci bldg 4-174 200 Union St SE Minneapolis MN 55455 Office Fax: 612-625-4583. E-mail: sbae@ece.umn.edu.

BAECHTOLD, ROBERT LOUIS, lawyer; b. Jersey City, Dec. 18, 1937; s. Fred Jacob and Catherine (Lenning) B.; m. Henrietta Thelma Hornbaker, Jan. 24, 1959; children: Kathi Ann, Christina Lee, Theresa Lynn. BS, Rutgers U., 1958; JD summa cum laude, Seton Hall U., 1966. Bar: N.Y. 1967, N.J. 1971, Pa. 1994, U.S. Dist. Ct. (so. and ea. dists.) N.Y. 1967, U.S. Ct. Appeals (fed. cir.) 1971, U.S. Ct. Appeals (2d cir.) 1967. Rsch. chemist Am. Cyanamid Co., Bound Brook, N.J., 1958-62; patent agt. M&T Chems., Inc., Rahway, N.J., 1962-65; assoc. Ward, Haselton, Orme, McElhannon, Brooks & Fitzpatrick, N.Y.C., 1965-68, ptnr., 1969-71, Fitzpatrick, Cella, Harper & Scinto, N.Y.C., 1971—. Lectr. Am. Patent Law Assn., 1979, Practising Law Inst., 1981, 88, others; mem. adv. com. to Fed. Cir. Ct. Appeals, 1991-94. Contbg. author course handbook Practising Law Inst., 1981, 88; patentee chemistry field. Mem. Cranford (N.J.) Bd. Edn., 1970-73. Nat Starch Products scholar; Leopole Schepp Found. grantee, 1954-58. Mem. ABA, Am. Intellectual Property Law Assn. (com. chmn. 1981, bd. dirs. 1987-90), Fed. Cir. Bar Assn. (bd. dirs. 1997—, pres. 2002-), N.J. Patent Law Assn. (pres. 1978-80), N.Y. Intellectual Property Law Assn., N.Y. State Bar Assn., N.J. Bar Assn. Office: Fitzpatrick Cella Harper & Scinto 30 Rockefeller Plz New York NY 10112 E-mail: rbaechtold@fchs.com.

BAECKLER, VIRGINIA VAN WYNEN, librarian, writer; b. Englewood, N.J., June 18, 1942; d. Kenneth Gregg and Esther Grace (Thompson) Van Wynen; m. William W. Baeckler, Apr. 9, 1971; children— Gregg William, Sarah Angela. B.A., Cornell U., 1964, M.A., 1967; postgrad. Moscow State U. (USSR), 1967-69; M.L.S., Rutgers U., 1972. Head Slavic acquisitions Princeton U. Library, 1969-71; head Mercer County Library, Ewing, N.J., 1972-75; dir. Sources, Hopewell, N.J., 1975—; dir. Plainsboro (N.J.) Pub. Libr., 1991— . Author: Go, Pep and Pop!, 1976, PR for Pennies, 1978, Sparkle!, 1980, Storytime Science, 1986. Vol., tchr. YWCA of Princeton, N.J., 1979— . Mem. Nat. Sci. Tchrs. Assn., Alliance for Arts and Edu.,ALA, Ednl. Media Assn. (lobbyist). Democrat. Home: 26 Hart Ave Hopewell NJ 08525-1425

BAECKSTROM, MARIANNE, actuary; b. Stockholm, Mar. 16, 1925; came to U.S., 1959; d. Carl Emil Leonard and Anna Brita Marianne (Eastman) Liedstrand; m. Gosta Michael Baeckstrom, July 8, 1947; children: Christer Gustav, Monica Ann. BS, Stockholm U., 1948. Actuarial asst. Towers Perrin, Phila., 1950-65, actuarial supr., 1965-74, asst. mgr., 1974-79, mgr. actuarial ops., 1979-85, prin., 1976-85, outside cons., 1985-93; retired. Mem. Am. Swedish Hist. Mus. (bd. dirs. women's aux. 1995—2002), Swedish Colonial Soc., Swedish Women's Ednl. Assn., Vasa Order Am. Home: 1321 Carol Rd Meadowbrook PA 19046-2505 Home (Winter): 4310 Falmouth Dr Unit A 206 Longboat Key FL 34228-2318 E-mail: mbaeckstrom@aol.com.

BAEHMANN, SUSAN ELIZABETH, artist; b. Milw., May 16, 1945; d. Chester Reuben Smith and Dorothy Margaret (Meyer) Johnson; m. Dale Fredrick Baehmann, May 27, 1972; children: Edan Andrew, Hai Phan. BFA, U. Wis., 1978. Painting and drawing instr. U. N.C.-W., 1993-97; printmaking instr. St. John's Mus. Art, 1998-99. One-woman shows include Carroll Coll., Otteson Gallery, Waukesha, Wis., 1982-83, Bradley Galleries, Milw., 1982, 95, 91, The Fanny Garver Gallery, Madison, Wis., 1985, John Michael Kohler Art Ctr., Sheboygan, Wis., 1985, U. N.C., Wilmington, 1994; exhibited in group shows Artists of Southeastern N.C., St. John's Mus. Art, Wilmington, N.C., 1997, Art du Monde, 16 Gallery tour of Japan, 1990-91, Milw. Art Mus., 1988-89, Art Inst. Chgo., 1985, 87, also numerous others; represented in 60 permanent corp., pub. and ednl. collections; represented in pvt. collections throughout 8 countries; work pub. in Women in Print: Prints from 3M by Contemporary Women Printmakers, 1995. Recipient Milw. Arts Commn. Purchase award, 1982, 87, Wis. Painters and Sculptors award, 1982, Catherine Lorillard Wolfe Cert. of Merit, Nat. Arts Club, 1983, Exceptional Achievement awrd UWM Alumni Assn. Art Show, 1987, Best of Show N.C. Art Assn. Spring Show, 1992, Exhibitors Choice award Spoleto, Charleston, S.C., 1995, Best of Show Arts Coun. Lower Cape Fear, 1995, 1st Pl. Drawing and Printmaking Summerfair, 1997, 2d pl. award Telfair Mus. Art, 1997, Best of Show Atalaya, 1999. Democrat. Avocations: animal rescue work, horticulture. Home: 2616 Sapling Clr Wilmington NC 28411-6110 E-mail: artcatins@cs.com.

BAEHR, THEODORE, religious organization administrator, communications executive; b. N.Y.C., May 31, 1946; m. Liliana Milani, 1975; children: Theodore Peirce, James Stuart Castiglioni, Robert Gallatin, Evelyn Noelle. Student in French lit., U. Bordeaux and Toulouse, France, 1967; student English lit., Cambridge (Eng.) U., 1967; student German lit., U. Munich, 1968; BA in Comparative Lit., Dartmouth Coll., 1969; JD, NYU, 1972; postgrad. Inst. Theology, Cathedral St. John the Divine, 1978-80. Rsch. engr. Precision Sci. Co., Chgo., 1964-65; legal cons. firm Dandeub, Fleissig & Assocs., N.Y.C., 1970-71; law student asst. U.S. Atty.'s Office, so. Dist. N.Y., 1971-72; pres. Agape Prodns., N.Y.C., 1972-79, chmn. bd., 1979-82; exec. dir. Good News Comms., Inc., N.Y.C., 1978-80, chmn. bd., 1980—; pres. Episc. Radio-TV Found., Inc., Atlanta, 1981-82, Trinity Concepts, 1982; cons. media; dir. TV Center CUNY at Bklyn. Coll., 1979-80, 82—; pub. Movieguide Mag., 1985—. Episc. Communicators, 1981-84; exec. prodr. Ch.'s Presence at World's Fair, Knoxville, Tenn., 1982; dir. Am. Theater Actors, Episc. Comms. Author: Faith in God and Generals, 2003, What Shall We Watch Tonight, 2003, Frodo and Harry, 2003; editor (commentator): NYU Law Sch. newspaper, 1969—72, Contemporary Drug Problems, 1971—72, Atlanta Area Christian News; creator, coord. Communicate Workshops, 1979, creator, writer, editor Episc. Ch. Video Resource Guide and Episcopal Video/TV Newsletter, 1979; prodr.(dir., writer): (various TV and radio programs including) Movieguider®, Joy of Music, Perspectives, PBS, 1981—82, Religionwise on WGST, CBS, 1981— (Religion in Media award), Getting the Word Out, 1986, Hollywood's Reel of Fortune, 1991, The Media-Wise Family, 1998; dir.: Runaways (Chgo. Intercom Gold plaque and Religion in Media award, 1989); prodr.: In Their Own Words, Was It Love (Religion in Media award). V.p. Ctr. for TV in Humanities, 1982; chmn. bd. Christian Film & TV Commn., 1978—; bd. dirs. Nat. Religious Broadcasters, Celebrate Life, Religious Heritage of Am., Dorsey Theatre, Nat. Think Tank, Mission Am., Nehemiah Inst., Coalition on Revival; mem. steering com. Theol. Summit Conf.; bd. dirs. Am. Theatre of Actors, Nat. Council on Bible Curriculum in Pub. Schs., United Srs. Assn., Campus Renewal Ministries Nat. Broadcast Day of Prayer; bd. dirs., nat. adv. bd. United Srs. Assn. Recipient Pres.'s award, LifeNET, 1998, Eagle award, Nat. Religious Broadcasters, 2001. Mem. Mission Am., Bishop in Ind. Christian Chs. Internat, Nat. Press Club. Fax: (805) 383-4089. E-mail: movieguide@compuserve.com., Ted@TedBaehr.com.

BAENA, ROBERT BOB, interior designer; b. Bronx, N.Y., Aug. 24, 1930; s. Jacob and Luisa (Jaffe) B.; m. Rita R. Bejarano, July 15, 1951; children: Ellen R. Baena Youssef, Lisa R. Baena Horn, Andrea R. Baena Macdonald. Student, NYU, 1948-49, N.Y. Sch. Interior Design, 1952. V.p. Baena Decorators Inc., Bronx, 1948-68; pres. Baena Decorators Rockland Inc., Nanuet, N.Y., 1968-76, Robert B. Baena Inc., Spring Valley, N.Y., 1985-96; sales mgr. Lexington Manor, Ethan Allen Gallery, Nanuet, 1977-85, 20th Century Draperies Inc., N.Y.C., 1986-97; home design furnishings cons. Baers Furniture Co., Boca Raton, Fla., 1997—2000; furniture salesman Sears Homelife, Boca Raton, Fla., 2000—01; decorator Boca Raton, Fla., 2001—02. Mem.: Am. Interior Design Soc. (assoc.), Rotary (editor bull. Nanuet 1970, pres. 1980—81, fellow . 1986, v.p. Monsey, N.Y. chpt. 1989—90, pres. 1990—91, sec. 1992—95, mem. Delray Beach Sunrise 1997—, pres. 2000—01). Democrat. Jewish. Avocations: golfing, flying, poetry, photography. E-mail: bulletinbob@webtv.net.

BAENA, SCOTT LOUIS, lawyer; b. N.Y.C., Sept. 15, 1949; s. I. Alexander and Rose (Snofsky) B.; children: Jeffrey Lance, Brad Alexander. BBA in Acctg., Geogre Washington U., 1970, JD with honors, 1974. Bar: Fla. 1974. Ptnr. Helliwell, Melrose & DeWolf, Miami, Fla., 1974-79; mng. ptnr. Stroock & Stroock & Lavan, Miami, 1979-2000; founding ptnr. Bilzin Sumberg Baena Price & Axelrod, 2000—. Adj. prof. U. Miami Sch. of Law, 1983-89. Mem. Pres. Com. on Econ. Devel., 1970; pres. Coral Gables-Riviera Homeowners Assn., 1986; mem. Coral Gables Zoning and Planning Bd., Code Enforcement Bd., Hist. Preservation Task Force. Fellow Am. Bar Found.; mem. ABA (com. on comml. fin. svcs., corp., banking and bus. law sect. 1983—), Fla. Bar Assn. (chair bus. law sect. 1986-87, bd. govs.), Dade County Bar Assn. (bd. dirs. young lawyers div. 1977-79), Am. Law Inst. Jewish. Avocations: golf, horseback riding, woodworking. Office: Bilzin Sumberg et al Ste 2500 200 S Biscayne Blvd Miami FL 33131-2385 E-mail: sbaena@bilzin.com.

BAER, ADAM SCOTT, artist; b. Portchester, N.Y., Mar. 16, 1969; s. Stephen Samuel Baer and Linda Elaine (Kassed) Nieberg. BFA in Photography, SUNY, Purchase, 1992. Solo shows include Calif. Mus. Photography, Fifty One Fine Art Photography, Antwerp Belgium; exhibited in group shows PS1 Contemporary Art Ctr., N.Y., Neuberger Mus., N.Y., Paris Photo, Carrousel de Louvre, Paris; represented in permanent collections including The Art Mus. Princeton U., N.J., Calif. Mus. Photography, The Bklyn. Mus. Art. Mem. People for the Ethical Treatment of Animals, Greenwich, Conn., 1994—. Fellowship in photography J.S. Guggenheim Meml. Found., 1998, The Aaron Siskind Found., 1995, N.Y. Found. for the Arts, 1994. Mem. Sierra Club. Avocations: hiking, theater, arts and dance, music. Home: 270 Maple Rd Valley Cottage NY 10989-1424 E-mail: atomb@optonline.net.

BAER, BYRON M. state legislator; b. Pitts., Oct. 18, 1929; m. Linda Pollitt; children: David, Laura, Roger Pollitt, Lara Pollitt. Student, Cornell U. Mem. N.J. Gen. Assembly, Trenton, from 1972, asst. minority leader, 1986-93; mem. N.J. Senate, Dist. 37, Trenton, 1994—. Alt. del. Dem. Nat. Conv., 1984. Recipient Assemblyman of Yr. award N.J. Coun. Chs., Equal Justice medal Legal Svcs. Corp. and N.J. Bar Assn., Legislator of Decade award N.J. Tenants Orgn., 1981. Mem. Anti Defamation League, Nat. Assn. Jewish Legislators (sec. 1985-87), Nat. Consumer Congress (bd. dirs. 1973-76), Holocaust Meml. COm. Address: 125 State St Hackensack NJ 07601-5433*

BAER, HAROLD, JR., judge; b. N.Y.C., Feb. 16, 1933; s. Harold and Edna (Jacobus) B.; m. Suzanne Harris, Aug. 18, 1957; children: Elizabeth Jane, Linda Gail. Grad. magna cum laude, Hobart Coll., 1954; LLB, Yale U., 1957. Bar: N.Y. 1959, U.S. Dist. Ct. (so. dist.) N.Y. 1961, U.S. Ct. Appeals (2d cir.) 1961, U.S. Supreme Ct. 1964. Asst. U.S. atty., chief organized crime unit, U.S. Atty.'s Office for So. Dist. N.Y., N.Y.C., 1961-66, 1st asst. U.S. atty., chief criminal divsn., 1970-71; exec. dir. civilian complaint rev. bd. N.Y.C. Police Dept., 1966-67; ptnr. Guggenheimer & Untermyer, N.Y.C., 1968-70, 72-82; justice N.Y. State Supreme Ct., 1982-92; exec. jud. officer Jud. Arbitration and Mediation Svcs./Endispute, 1992-94; judge U.S. Dist. Ct. for So. Dist. N.Y., N.Y.C., 1994—. Mem. N.Y.C. mayoral com. alleged police corruption, 1993, 94. Contbr. articles to law jours. Mem. N.Y. State Bar Assn. (ho. of dels. 1977-89, 93-96), N.Y. County Lawyers Assn. (pres. 1979-81, bd. dirs., mem. exec. com.), Assn. Bar City N.Y. (criminal justice coun. 1980-82, judiciary com. 1993-94), Network Bar Leaders (founder, chmn. 1981-83), Assn. Justices N.Y.C. and N.Y. State (officer). Office: US Courthouse 500 Pearl St Rm 2230 New York NY 10007-1316

BAER, JOHN METZ, entrepreneur; b. Md., June 30, 1908; s. Adam Daniel and Leah Bertie (Metz) B.; m. Joan Cushwa, Oct. 16, 1976; children: John Metz, Deborah Ann. BS, Goshen Coll., 1932. Food distgn. cons.; pres. Profl. Arts Assocs. Inc., Greencastle (Pa.) Ice and Cold Storage Inc., Baer Packing Corp., Greencastle. Nat. Frozen Foods Assn. ofcl. rep. to 1st Internat. Foods Conf., Paris, 1950; participant numerous internat. food confs. Pres. Washington County Hosp., Hagerstown, 1958-60, Washington County Bd. Edn., 1962-68; bd. dirs. Am. Heart Assn. of Md.; trustee Hagerstown Jr. Coll.; chmn. United Way of Washington County; hon. mem. Greater Hagerstown Club; chmn. Hagerstown Parking Authority; bd. dirs. Md. Symphony Orch. Mem. Produce Mktg. Assn. (past pres.), Fountainhead Country Club, Hagerstown C. of C. (pres.), Assembly of Hagerstown, Rotary. Republican. Methodist. Home: 13217 Hillandale Rd Hagerstown MD 21742-2647 Office: 5 Public Sq Hagerstown MD 21740-5528 Fax: 301-739-0171. E-mail: ppoarts5211@juno.com.

BAER, JOHN RICHARD FREDERICK, lawyer; b. Melrose Park, Ill., Jan. 9, 1941; s. John Richard and Zena Edith (Ostreyko) B.; m. Linda Gail Chapman, Aug. 31, 1963; children: Brett Scott, Deborah Jill. BA, U. Ill., Champaign, 1963, JD, 1966. Bar: Ill. 1966, U.S. Dist. Ct. (no. dist.) Ill. 1967, U.S. Ct. Appeals (7th cir.) 1969, U.S. Ct. Appeals (DC cir.) 1975, U.S. Ct. Appeals (9th cir.) 1979, U.S. Supreme Ct. 1975. Assoc. Keck, Mahin & Cate, Chgo., 1966-73, ptnr., 1974-97; of counsel Sonnenschein Nath & Rosenthal LLP, Chgo., 1997-99, ptnr., 2000—. Mem. Ill. Atty. Gen.'s Franchise adv. bd., 1992-94, 96—, chair 1996—. Editor Commerce Clearing House Sales Representative Law Guide, 1998—; mem edtl. bd. U. Ill. Law Forum, 1964-65, asst. editor, 1965-66; contbg. editor: Commercial Liability Risk Management and Insurance, 1978. Mem. Plan Commn., Village of Deerfield (Ill.), 1976-79, chmn., 1978-79, mem. Home Rule Study Commn., 1974-75, mem. home rule implementation com., 1975-76. Mem. ABA (topics and articles editor Franchise Law jour. 1995-96, assoc. editor 1996-99, editor-in-chief The Franchise Lawyer 1999-2002, governing com. forum on franchising 2003—), Internat. Franchise Assn. (legal/legis. com. 1990—), Inter-Pacfic Bar Assn., Ill. Bar Assn. (competition dir. region 8 nat. moot ct. 1974, profl. ethics com. 1977-84, chmn. 1982-83, spl. com. on individual lawyers advt. 1981-83, profl. responsibility com. 1983-84, standing com. on liaison with atty. registration and disciplinary commn. 1989-93, spl. com. on ethics 2000 1999—), Internat. Bar Assn. Office: Sonnenschein Nath & Rosenthal LLP 8000 Sears Tower 233 S Wacker Dr Chicago IL 60606-6491 E-mail: jbaer@sonnenschein.com.

BAER, MICHAEL ALAN, political scientist, educator; b. Atlanta, Feb. 4, 1943; s. Kurt Arthur and Beulah (Mendelson) Baer; m. CHarlotte Glazer, Aug. 16, 1964; children: Daniel Noach, Naomi Aviva. BA, Emory U., 1964; MA, U. Oreg., 1966, PhD, 1968. Rsch. asst. Ctr. Advanced Study Ednl. Adminstrn., U. Oreg., 1964-68; faculty U. Ky., Lexington, 1968-90, prof. polit. sci. and pub. adminstrn., 1980-90, chmn. dept. polit. sci., 1977-81, dean Coll. Arts and Scis., 1981-90; polit. analyst WAVE-TV, Louisville; prof. polit. sci. Northeastern U., Boston, 1990-2000, provost, sr. v.p. acad. affairs, 1990-98; sr. v.p. for programs and analysis Am. Coun. on Edn., Washington, 1998—; dir. Ctr. for Policy Analysis, Washington, 1998-2000. Co-author: (book) Lobbying: Influence and Interaction in American State Legislatures, 1969; co-editor: Political Science in America, 1991; mem. editl. bd.: State and Local Govt. Rev., 1977—81; contbr. articles to profl. jours. Bd. dirs. Coun. Colls. Arts and Scis., 1983—89, pres., 1988; rec. sec. Bluegrass chpt. Ky. Assn. Gifted Edn., 1983—85; mem. Mayor's com. to establish Lexington Children's Mus., 1988—90, bd. dirs., 1990; mem. coun. Inter Univ. Consortium for Polit. and Social Rsch., U. Mich., 1988—94, chmn., 1990—92; bd. dirs. Congregation Ohavay Zion, Lexington, 1976—78, Ctrl. Ky. Jewish Assn., 1970—74, pres., 1973—74; bd. dirs. Ctrl. Ky. Civil LIberties Union, 1973—77, Bluegrass chpt. NCCJ, 1980—81, Jamaica Pond Assn., 1992—97. Fellow Leverhulme, 1974—75. Mem.: Nat. Capitol Area Polit. Sci. Assn. (bd. mem. 2001—03), Nat. Assn. Univ. and Land Grant Colls. (commn. on arts and scis. 1986—90, chmn. 1990), Ky. Conf. Polit. Sci., So. Polit. Sci. Assn. (chmn. nominating com. 1993—94, 1996), Brit. Politics Group (exec. coun. 1978—80), Midwest Polit. Sci. Assn. (exec. coun. 1980—83), Am. Polit. Sci. Assn. (endowed programs com. 1993—94, 1995—98, centennial celebration com. 2002—). Home: 4103 38th St NW Washington DC 20016-2217 Office: Am Coun on Edn 1 Dupont Cir NW Washington DC 20036-1110 E-mail: michael_baer@ace.nche.edu.

BAER, ROBERT J. transportation company executive; b. St. Louis, Oct. 25, 1937; s. Charles A. and Angeline Baer; m. Jo Baer, Aug. 27, 1960; children: Bob Jr., Angie, Tim, Cathy. BA, So. Ill. U., 1962, MS, 1964. Regional supr. div. recreation City of St. Louis, 1957-64; dep. dir. Human Devel. Corp., St. Louis, 1964-70; chief to staff to co. exec. St. Louis County Govt., 1970-74; exec. dir. Bi-State Devel. Agy., St. Louis, 1974-77; v.p., gen. mgr. United Van Lines Inc. and subs., Fenton, Mo., 1977-80, exec. v.p., 1980-82; pres. COO, 1982-95; CEO United Van Lines, Fenton, 1995—2002, Vanliner Ins. Co., Fenton, Total Transp. Svcs. Inc., Mayflower Transit, Fenton, 1995—2002, UniGroup Worldwide, Inc., Fenton, 1998—2002; pres., COO UniGroup Inc., Fenton, Mo., 1987—2002; pres. emeritus UniGroup, Inc., 2002—. Bd. dirs. Firstar-St. Louis. Pres. St. Louis Bd. Police Commn., 1984-89; chmn. St. Louis Regional Conv. and Sports Conv. and Sports Complex Authority, 1990-96; mem. Civic Progress, Inc., 1996—2002. Office: UniGroup 1 Premier Dr Fenton MO 63026-2989

BAER, ROBERT JACOB, retired army officer; b. Jamestown, Mo., Aug. 12, 1924; s. John William and Esther Elizabeth (Knipker) B.; m. Ann O'Hara, Dec. 31, 1948; children: John, Thomas, Stephen, Teresa. BS, U.S. Mil. Acad., 1947; grad., Army War Coll., 1967. Commd. 2d lt. U.S. Army, 1947, advanced through grades to lt. gen., 1977; service in ETO; staff div. chief Dept. Army, 1969-71; dir. devel. office Chief R & D, 1971-72; project mgr. XM-1 Tank Systems Tank Automotive Command, Warren, Mich., 1972-77; dep. comdr. Army Devel./Readiness Command, Alexandria, Va., 1977-80; ret., 1980; sr. v.p. XMCO, Inc., 1980-90; pvt. cons., 1990. Mem. U.S. Army Sci. Bd., 1982-88; dir. Western Design Howden Corp. Contbr. to mil. jours. Decorated D.S.M., Silver Star, Legion of Merit with oak leaf cluster, Def. Superior Svc. medal, Meritorious Svc. medal, Air Medal with 11 oak leaf clusters, Army Commendation medal with oak leaf cluster, Combat Inf. badge. Mem. U.S. Armor Assn. (past pres.), Assn. U.S. Army, German-Am. Bus. Assn. (mem. adv. bd.), Washington Inst. for SW Affairs, Kappa Alpha, Country Club of Fairfax. Roman Catholic. Home: 6213 Militia Ct Fairfax Station VA 22039-1325 E-mail: bobbaer@cox.net.

BAER, SUSAN M. airport executive; BA, Barnard College; MA, New York Univ. Gen. mgr. LaGuardia Airport, Flushing, N.Y., 1994-98, N.J. Airports, Newark, 1998—. Office: Newark Int & Teterboro Airports Conrad Rd, Bldg 1 Newark NJ 07114*

BAER, WALTER S. research executive; b. Chgo., July 27, 1937; s. Walter S., Jr. and Margaret S. (Mayer) B.; m. Miriam R. Schenker, June 18, 1959 (div. 1987); children: David W., Alan B.; m. Jeri Weiss, Oct. 23, 1988. BS, Calif. Inst. Tech., 1959; PhD (NSF fellow), U. Wis., 1964. Rsch. physicist Bell Telephone Labs., Murray Hill, N.J., 1964-66; White House fellow Washington, 1966-67; White House sci. adv. staff, 1967-69; cons. and sr. scientist RAND Corp., Santa Monica, Calif., 1970-81, dir. energy policy program, 1978-81; dir. advanced tech. Times Mirror Co., Los Angeles, 1981-89; deputy v.p. domestic rsch. RAND Corp., Santa Monica, Calif., 1990—. Cons. UN, maj. U.S. corps, 1970—; dir. Aspen (Colo.) Cable TV Workshop, 1972-73, L.A. Ednl. Partnership; pres. KCRW Found., Santa Monica, Calif.; adv. bd. Columbia U. Inst. Tele-Info., U.S. Com. for Internat. Inst. Applied Systems Analysis; dir. Am. Tng. Internat.; mem. gov. coun. on info. tech. State of Calif. Author: Interactive Television, 1971, Cable Television: A Handbook for Decisionmaking, 1973, also articles; editor: The Electronic Box Office, 1974, w/ RAND Cable Television Series, 1974; editorial bd.: Telecommunications Policy, 1976—, Internat. Ency. Communications. Mem. European Community Visitor, 1978. Recipient U. Wis. award for excellence in teaching, 1960; Preceptor award Broadcast Industry Conf., 1974— Fellow AAAS (chmn. Indsl. Sci. Sec.

1992-93); mem. IEEE (mem. com. on comm. and info. policy 1994—), Am. Phys. Soc., Internat. Inst. Communications, Sigma Xi. Office: RAND 1700 Main St Santa Monica CA 90401-3297

BAER, WERNER, economist, educator; b. Offenbach, Germany, Dec. 14, 1931; came to U.S., 1945, naturalized, 1952; s. Richard and Grete (Herz) B. 58776, CUNY, N.Y.C., 1953; MA, Harvard U., 1955, PhD, 1958; D honoris causa, Fed. U. Pernambuco, Brazil, 1988, New U. Lisbon, Portugal, 2000, Fed. U. Ceara, Brazil, 1993. Instr. Harvard U., 1958-61; asst. prof. Yale U., New Haven, 1961-65; asso. prof. Vanderbilt U., Nashville, 1965-69, prof., 1969-74; prof. econs. U. Ill., Urbana, 1974—. Vis. prof. U. São Paulo, Brazil, 1966-68, Vargas Found., Brazil, 1966-68; Rhodes fellow St. Antony's Coll., Oxford (Eng.) U., 1975 Author: The Brazilian Economy: Growth and Development, 5th edit., 2001, Privatization in Latin America, vol. 17, 1994, The Changing Role of International Capital in Latin America, 1998; co-author: (with P. Elosegui and A. Gallo) The Achievements and Failures of Argentina's Neo-Liberal Policies, 2002, (with J. Bang) Privatization and Equity in Brazil and Russia, 2002, (with E. Amann) Anchors Away: The Costs and Benefits of Brazil's Devaluation, 2003; co-editor: Latin America-Privatization, Property Rights and Deregulation, 1993, (with W. Maloney) Neo-Liberalism and Income Distribution in Latin America, 1997, (with W. Miles, A. Moran) The End of the Asian Myth, 1999, The State and Industry in the Development Process, 1999 (with E. Amann) Neoliberalism and it's Consequences in Brazil, 2002; contbr. articles to profl. jours. Decorated Order So. Cross (Brazil) Mem. Am. Econ. Assn., Latin Am. Studies Assn. Home: 1703 Devonshire Dr Champaign IL 61821-5901 Office: U Ill 1407 W Gregory Dr Urbana IL 61801-3606

BAER, WILLIAM HAROLD, business executive; b. Eatontown, N.J., Dec. 6, 1947; s. Irving and Martha Ann (Ruddy) B. BSBA, Waynesburg Coll., 1971. Pres. Baldinos, Inc., Fayetteville, N.C., 1976—, Rondout Country Club, Ltd., Accord, N.Y., 1979-81, W.H.B. Cons., Accord, N.Y., 1979-85, Baldinos Giant Jersey Subs., Inc., Hinesville, Ga., 1982—. With Baldinos Mgmt. Group, Ltd., Augusta, Ga., 1987—; pres. Baldinos of Atlanta, 1991; pres. Leisure Life Inc., Tinton Falls, N.J., 1980-87, Baldinos of Savannah, 1989—, Pro Active Enterprises, Inc., Savannah, Ga., 1986-89, bd. dirs., 1989; bd. dirs. Triumph Steel, Inc., Birmingham, Ala., 1992, vice chmn. Chmn. campaign March of Dimes, Liberty County, 1986-87; dir. Coastal Ga. March of Dimes, Savannah, 1986-92; mem. Forward Atlanta, 1992—, Atlanta Sports Coun., 1992—. 1st lt. USMC, 1971-75. Recipient Navy Achievement medal. Mem. Hinesville-Liberty County, Ga. C. of C. (bd. dirs. 1989-91), Atlanta C. of C., Coastal Racquet Club (pres. 1986-87, treas.-sec. Hinesville chpt. 1987—), Ga. Hospitality Travel Assn. (bd. dirs. 1999-2001). Home: 708 Robinson Farms Dr Marietta GA 30068-3277 Office: 760 Elaine St Hinesville GA 31313-4825 also: 3823 Roswell Rd Ste #204 Marietta GA 30062

BAER, WILLIAM J. lawyer; b. May 31, 1950; s. Joseph and Roses B.; m. Nancy Hendry; children: Michael Hendry, Andrew Hendry. BA, Lawrence U., 1972; JD, Stanford U., 1975. Bar: Wis., 1975, D.C., 1981, U.S. Ct. Appeals D.C., 1989, U.S. Supreme Ct. 1999. Trial atty. divsn. nat. advertising FTC, Washington, 1975-76, asst. to dir. bureau consumer protection, 1976-77, atty. advisor to chmn., 1977-78, asst. gen. counsel for legis., 1978-80; assoc. Arnold & Porter, Washington, 1980-83, ptnr., 1984-95; dir. Bur. of Competition FTC, Washington, 1995-99; ptnr., head antitrust practice group Arnold & Porter, Washington, 2000—. Contbr. articles to numerous publs. Trustee Lawrence U. Mem. ABA. Democrat. Avocations: tennis, golf. Office: Arnold & Porter 555 12th St NW Ste 810 Washington DC 20004-1200 E-mail: william_baer@aporter.com.

BAERG, RICHARD HENRY, podiatrist, surgeon; b. L.A., Jan. 19, 1937; s. Henry Francis and Ruth Elizabeth (Loven) B.; children from previous marriage: Carol Elizabeth, William Richard, Michael David, Brie Ann, Niccolo, Monica, Deven, Arianna, Mia. AA, Reedles Coll., 1956; BS, Calif. Coll. Podiatric Medicine, 1965, DPM, 1968, MSc in Foot Surgery, 1970; MPH in Med. Adminstrn., U. Calif., Berkeley, 1971; ScD (hon.), N.Y. Coll. Podiatric Medicine, 1980; LittD (hon.), Ohio Coll. Podiatric Medicine, 1984; postgrad. Sch. Edn. and Pub. Health, U. Mich., 1973—74; postgrad. Sch. of Bus. and Sch. of Edn., Harvard U., 1975. Diplomate Am. Bd. Podiatric Surgery (foot and ankle surgery), Am. Bd. Podiatric Orthopedics and Primary Podiatric Medicine (exec. dir. 1980-90), Am. Bd. podiatric Pub. Health (bd. dirs. 1980-89). Intern Highland Alameda County Gen. Hosp., Oakland, Calif., 1969; resident in surgery Calif. Podiatry Hosp. (Pacific Coast Hosp.), San Francisco, 1970; acad. dean N.Y. Coll. Podiatric Medicine, N.Y.C., 1971-74; v.p., dean Calif. Coll. Podiatric Medicine, San Francisco, 1974-76; chief podiatric medicine Los Angeles County-U. So. Calif. Med. Ctr., 1976-78; dir. So. Calif. Podiatric Med. Ctr., 1976-78; pvt. practice Beverly Hills, Calif., 1976-78; dean Finch U. Coll. Podiatric Medicine, Chgo., 1978-79; mem. spl. med. adv. group to sec. Dept. Vets. Affairs, Washington, 1976-79, dir. podiatric service, dept. medicine and surgery, 1979-84, acting dir., 1984-86; health resources adminstrn. cons. Dept. Health and Human Svcs., Washington, 1974-88; chief podiatry VA Med. Ctr., Loma Linda, Calif., 1984-89; dir. residency tng. Loma Linda Foot Clinic, 1990; exec. v.p., med. dir. Dr. Footcare Corp., Montclair, Calif., 1988-90; faculty podiatry U. N.C. Hosps., Chapel Hill, 1992—; clin. prof. Sch. of Podiatric Medicine Barry U., Miami, Fla., 1993—; clin. prof. Med. Sch., U. N.C., 1992—; staff podiatrist Morehead Hosp., Eden, N.C., 1997-2000. Mem. podiatric staff Chapel Hill Surg. Ctr., 1993—; chief of podiatry Umstead Hosp., Butner, N.C., 1997-2000, VA Med. Ctr., Huntington, W.Va., dir. residency tng. chief podiatry sect., 2000-02; assoc. clin. prof. Stanford U. Med. Sch., 1974-76; clin. prof. Temple U. Coll. Podiatric Medicine, 1979-86, Des Moines U. Medicine and Health Sci., 1984-; prof. dept. surgery Marshall U. Sch. Medicine, Huntington, W.Va., clin. prof. podiatric medicine and surgery Pikeville Coll. Sch. Osteopathic Medicine; pres. Baerg & Assocs.; cons. foot surgery, Las Vegas, 2002—; mem. podiatry adv. panel NAS Inst. Medicine, 1974; mem. bd. podiatric medicine Calif. Dept. Consumer Affairs, 1989-90, chmn. residency, edn. and hosp. inspection com. Contbg. author: (text) Podiatric Medicine and Public Health, 1987; mem. editl. bd. Jour. Podiatric Edn., Yearbook of Podiatric Medicine and Surgery, Mil. Medicine Jour.; contbr. over 30 articles to profl. jours., 3 chpts. to textbooks. With M.C. U.S. Army and USN, 1958-64. Mead-Johnson fellow, 1968-69. Fellow USPHS, Am. Podiatric Med. Assn. (com. on pub. health 1971-84, coun. podiatric edn. 1975-84, chmn. profl. edn. com. 1977-78, com. on hosp. 1980-85, Kenison award 1984, cert. appreciation 1990, com. on pub. health and preventive medicine), Am. Coll. Foot and Ankle Surgeons, Am. Coll. Foot & Ankle Orthopedics and Medicine (exec. dir. 1980-90), Acad. Ambulatory Foot Surgery; mem. APHA (governing coun. 1977-80, chmn. podiatric health sect. 1991-94, chmn. nominating com. 1994-96), Am. Acad. Podiatric Adminstrs. (exec. dir. 1990-91), Nat. Bd. Podiatric Med. Examiners (bd. dirs.), Assn. Podiatrists in Fed. Svc., Am. Assn. Colls. Podiatric Medicine (exec. com. 1973, pres. 1980-81), Assn. Mil. Surgeons U.S., Nat. Acads. of Practice (podiatric medicine 1985), N.C. Foot and Ankle Soc. (bd. dirs. ins. com. 1994-97, cons. 1997-2000, chmn. zone III 1994-97, rep. N.C. Health Care Reform Com. 1994-97), Coun. Med. Sch. Affiliated Podiatrists (bd. dirs., dir. region 10), N.C. Symphony Assn., Mason (Scottish Rite, 32 degree), Sigma Pi Epsilon, Pi Delta. Republican.

BAERMANN, DONNA LEE ROTH, real estate property executive, retired insurance analyst; b. Carroll, Iowa, Apr. 28, 1939; d. Omer H. and Mae Lavina (Larson) Real; m. Edwin Ralph Baermann, Jr., July 8, 1961 (dec. Aug. 1997); children: Beth, Bryan, Cynthia. BS, Mt. Mercy Coll., Ames, 1973; student, Iowa State U.-Ames, 1957-61. Cert. profl. ins. woman; fellow Life Mgmt. Inst. ins. agt. Luthern Mut. Ins. Co., Cedar Rapids, Iowa, 1973; home economist Iowa-Ill. Gas & Electric Co., Cedar Rapids, Iowa, 1973-77; supr. premium collection Life Investors Ins. Co. (now Aegon USA), Cedar Rapids, Iowa, 1978-83, methods and procedures analyst, 1987-94; pres., CEO Baermann Apts. Inc., 1992-94, owner, pres., 1992—. Mem. telecom. study group com. 1982-83, mem. productivity task force, 1984-94, TAB cert. facilitator, 2001—. Vol. Mercy Med. Ctr., Cedar Rapids, Iowa, 2002—; apptd. by Mayor and City Coun. Housing Bd. Appeals, Cedar Rapids, 2003. Mem. Internat. Platform Assn., Citizens Com. for Person with Disabilities, Nat. Assn. Ins. Women, Nat. Mgmt. Assn. (bd. dirs. Cedar Rapids chpt.), DAR, Knights of Malta (named Damsel of Ancient Order of St. John, N.Y.C.), Chi Omega. Republican. Presbyterian. Home: 361 Willshire Ct NE Cedar Rapids IA 52402-6922 E-mail: dlrbaer@worldnet.att.net.

BAERNSTEIN, ALBERT, II, mathematician, educator; b. Birmingham, Ala., Apr. 25, 1941; s. Albert and Kathryn (Wiesel) B.; m. Judith Haynes, June 14, 1962; children— P. Renée, Amy. Student, U. Ala., 1958-59; AB, Cornell U., 1962; MA, U. Wis., 1964, PhD, 1968. Instr. math. U. Wis., Whitewater, 1966-68; asst. prof. math. Syracuse U., N.Y., 1968-72; assoc. prof. math. Washington U., St. Louis, 1972-74, prof. math., 1974—. Fulbright sr. research scholar Imperial Coll., London, 1976-77 Mem. Am. Math. Soc., Math. Assn. Am. Office: Washington U Dept Math Saint Louis MO 63130

BAETZ, W. TIMOTHY, lawyer; b. Cin., Aug. 5, 1944; s. William G. and Virginia (Fauntleroy) Baetz. BA, Harvard U., 1966; JD, U. Mich., 1969. Bar: Ill. 1969, D.C. 1980. Assoc. McDermott, Will & Emery, Chgo., 1969-74, income ptnr., 1975-78, capital ptnr., 1979—2001. Mem. mgmt. com. McDermott, Will & Emery, 1987-92, 95-2001. With U.S. Army, 1969-75. Fellow Am. Coll. Trust and Estate Counsel. Episcopalian. Home: 940 Golfview Rd Glenview IL 60025-3116

BAETZHOLD, HOWARD GEORGE, English language educator; b. Buffalo, Jan. 1, 1923; s. Howard Kuster and Harriet Laura (Hofheins) B.; m. Nancy Millard Cheesman, Aug. 5, 1950; children: Howard King, Barbara Millard. Student, Brown U., 1940-43, MIT, 1943-44; AB magna cum laude, Brown U., 1944, A.M., 1948; PhD, U. Wis., 1953. Asst. dir. Vets. Coll., Brown U., Providence, 1947-48, dir., 1948-49, admissions officer, 1948-50; teaching asst. U. Wis.-Madison, 1950-51; asst. to assoc. dean Coll. Letters and Sci., 1951-53; asst. prof. English Butler U., Indpls., 1953-57, assoc. prof., 1957-67, prof. English, 1967-88, Rebecca Clifton Reade prof., 1981-88, Rebecca Clifton Reade prof. emeritus, 1988—, head dept., 1981-85. Vis. prof. U. Del., summer 1963. Author: Mark Twain and John Bull: The British Connection, 1970; co-editor: The Bible According to Mark Twain: Writings on Heaven, Eden and the Flood, 1995, paperback edit., 1996, Three Decades of Odes, 1997; contbr. articles to profl. jours., Dictionary Lit. Biography, Mark Twain Ency. Mem. OASIS (Older Adult Svcs. and Info. Sys.) adv. coun., 1996-2002, Indpls. Art Ctr., Indpls. Mus. Art. Named Sagamore of the Wabash, 1988; faculty fellow Butler U., 1957-58, 69-70, Butler U. fellow, 1986, 87, John S. Tuckey meml. rsch. fellow Elmira Coll. Ctr. for Mark Twain Studies at Quarry Farm, 1990—, Henry Nash Smith fellow, 2001--; grantee Am. Philos. Soc., 1967, Am. Coun. Learned Socs., 1958. Mem. AAUP (v.p. state com. 1955), MLA, Ind. Coll. English Assn. (exec. bd. 1983-85), Am. Lit. Assn., Mark Twain Cir. Am. (exec. com. 1987-88, hon. life mem. 1995), Am. Philatelic Soc., Greater Ind. Masters Swimming Assn., Indpls. Lit. Club (2d v.p. 1985-86, 1st v.p. 1987-88, 92-93, pres. 1993-94), Butler U. Odd Topics Soc., Ovid Butler Soc. (exec. com. 1998—), Delta Upsilon. Home: 6723 Riverview Dr Indianapolis IN 46220-1628

BAEZ, JOAN CHANDOS, folk singer; b. S.I., N.Y., Jan. 9, 1941; d. Albert V. and Joan (Bridge) B.; m. David Victor Harris, Mar. 1968 (div. 1973); 1 son, Gabriel Earl. Appeared in coffeehouses, Gate of Horn, Chgo., 1958, Ballad Room, Club 47, 1958-68, Newport (R.I.) Folk Festival, 1959-69, 85, 87, 90, 92, 93, 95, extended tours to colls. and concert halls, 1960s, appeared Town Hall and Carnegie Hall, 1962, 67, 68, U.S. tours, 1970—, concert tours in Japan, 1966, 82, Europe, 1970-73, 80, 83-84, 87-90, 93—, Australia, 1985; rec. artist for Vanguard Records, 1960-72, A&M, 1973-76, Portrait Records, 1977-80, Gold Castle Records, 1986-89, Virgin Records, 1990-93, Grapevine Label Records (UK), 1995-97, Guardian Records, 1995-97, European record albums, 1981, 83, award 8 gold albums, 1 gold single; albums include Gone From Danger, 1997, Rare, Live & Classic (box set), 1993, Dark Chords on a Big Guitar, 2003; author: Joan Baez Songbook, 1964, (biography) Daybreak, 1968, (with David Harris) Coming Out, 1971, And a Voice to Sing With, 1987, (songbook) An Then I Wrote, 1979. Extensive TV appearances and speaking tours U.S. and Can. for anti-militarism, 1967-68; visit to Dem. Republic of Vietnam, 1972, visit to war torn Bosnia-Herzegovina, 1993; founder, v.p. Inst. for Study Nonviolence (now Resource Ctr. for Nonviolence, Santa Cruz, Calif.), Palo Alto, Calif., 1965; mem. nat. adv. coun. Amnesty Internat., 1974-92; founder, pres. Humanitas/Internat. Human Rights Com., 1979-92; condr. fact-finding mission to refugee camps, S.E. Asia, Oct. 1979; began refusing payment of war taxes, 1964; arrested for civil disobedience opposing draft, Oct., Dec., 1967. Office: Diamonds & Rust Prodns PO Box 1026 Menlo Park CA 94026-1026

BAEZA, CHERYL ANNE, psychiatric social worker; b. Wichita, Kans., Aug. 6, 1946; d. Andrew and Verda Mae (Gilbreth) Washburn; m. Hector Baeza, Oct. 26, 1980; children from previous marriage: Patrick Daron, Jill Anne Vincent, Hannah. BA in English and Edn., U. Colo., 1969; MSW, U. So. Calif., 1978. Social worker Lanterman State Hosp., 1978-79, L.A. County Dept. Adoptions, 1979-83, Children's Home Soc., Santa Ana, Calif., 1983-84, Psychiat. Health Care, Orange, Calif., 1985-88, FHP, Fountain Valley, Calif., 1988-96; pvt. practice, 1996-99. Project dir. Ctr. Apptd. Spl. Advs., Orange, 1984-85, Western Youth Svcs., Garden Grove, Calif., 1985-88; field instr. U. So. Calif., L.A., 1986-95; adj. prof. Calif. State U., Long Beach, 1988-89; mem. Task Force, Child Sexual Abuse Network, Orange, 1987-88; conf. chair Alliance for Mentally Ill., Orange County, 1994-95, 96-97. Joint Honor scholar State of Colo., 1964-69; recipient McConnell Found. stipend, 1977-78, Master Field Instr. award U. So. Calif.; named Leadership Vol. of Yr., Pikes Peak Region, Chamber Non Profit Partnership, 2001, Vol. of Yr., Pikes Peak Mental Health, 2001. Mem.: Nat. Alliance for Mentally Ill (pres. 2000—02). Avocations: writing, needlework, travel.

BAFFONI, FRANK ANTHONY, biomedical engineer, consultant, internist; b. Cranston, R.I., Aug. 3, 1954; s. Anthony Frank and Margaret Rose (Mastrati) B. BChem, U. R.I., 1977; MD, Ross U., 1986. Diplomate Am. Bd. Internal Medicine. Intern, resident R.I. Hosp., Brown U.; biomed. engr. artificial internal organs Brown U., Providence, 1977-79; intern, resident R.I. Hosp., Providence, 1986-90; doctor internal medicine State of Conn., Southbury, 1990-93; pvt. practice Warwick R.I., 1993—; med. dir. Seracare, 2000—. Biomed. cons. Davol, Inc., Cranston, 1989-91; cons. Intellitech, 1990-95, Medicore, Hungary, 1988-90, COMED, U.S.S.R., 1988-90, EDL, Can., 1988-91; spl. adv. com. mem. Blue Cross/Blue Shield, Providence, 1994-95. Author: Situational Soloing-A Systematic Approach to Guitar Phrasing, 2d edit., 1985; patentee multiple phase acoustic systems. Mem. breast cancer com. Am. Cancer Soc., Providence, 1994-95; mem. state bd. HIV/AIDS Significant Exposure, Hartford, Conn., 1992-93. Mem. Am. Soc. Internal Medicine, Kent County Med. Soc. Avocations: music, computer art, computer animation, billiards. Office: 300 Toll Gate Rd Ste 304 Warwick RI 02886-4447

BAG, REMZI, nuclear medicine physician, internist, pulmonologist, critical care physician, transplant pulmonologist; b. Kastamonu, Turkey, Feb. 3, 1964; s. Mehmet Bag and Emine Dincer. MD summa cum laude, Gata Gulhane Med. Sch., Ankara, Turkey, 1988. Diplomate Am. Bd. Nuclear Medicine, Am. Bd. Internal Medicine, Am. Bd. Pulmonary and Critical Care Medicine. Dir. Infirmary of Mil. Colls., Istanbul, Turkey, 1989-91; resident in nuclear medicine Gata Gulhane Med. Sch., 1991-92, St. Vincent's Hosp., N.Y.C., 1992-94; resident in internal medicine Albert Einstein Coll. Medicine, Bronx, N.Y., 1994-97; fellow in pulmonary and cricital care Baylor Coll. Medicine, Houston, 1997-2000, asst. prof. medicine, 2000—; med. dir. lung transplant program Baylor Coll. Medicine/Meth. Hosp./St. Luke's Episcopal Hosp., Houston. Co-editor: Ozet Patoloji, 1990; contbr. articles to med. jours. Capt. Turkish Army, 1988-94. Mem. ACP (assoc.), Am. Thoracic Soc., Am. Coll. Chest Physicians, Turkish Soc. Nuclear Medicine, Turkish Am. Med. Assn. Avocations: travel, classical music, internet. Office: Baylor Coll Medicine Divsn Pulmonary Dis 6550 Fannin Smith Twr 1236 Houston TX 77030

BAGAJEWICZ, MIGUEL, engineering educator; b. Rosario, Argentina, Sept. 16, 1951; s. Roscislaw and Maria (Korabinski) B.; m. Patricia Iris Lara. Chemical engr., Universidad Nat. del Litoral, Santa Fe, Argentina, 1977; MS, PhD, Calif. Inst. Tech. Prof. U. Okla., Norman, 1995—, Samuel Roberts Found. Presdl. prof.; sr. devel. engr. Simulation Sci., Brea, Calif., 1993-95; rsch. assoc. UCLA, 1989-93; assoc. prof. Universidad Nacional del Litoral, Santa Fe, Argentina, 1980-89. Dir. Ctr. Engrng. Optimization, U. Okla. Author: (book) Design and Upgrade of Process Plant Instrumentation, 2000; contbr. articles to profl. jours. Office: CEMS U Okla 100 E Boyd St Rm T335 Norman OK 73019-1028 Fax: 405-325-5813. E-mail: bagajewicz@ou.edu.

BAGALE, JOHN R. music educator; b. Dallas, Tex., Nov. 30, 1954; s. Joseph E. and Arlene (Barbeau) Bagale; m. Moire I. Archer, Sept. 1, 1956; children: Adrian M., Peter R., Joseph B. MusM in Music Edn., Eastman Sch. Music, 1990; BS in Music Edn., Nazareth Coll., 1981. Cert. Music Tchr. K-12 State of N.Y., 1982. Instr. percussion Hochstein Music Sch., Rochester, NY, 1980—; music faculty Penfield Ctrl. Schools, Penfield, NY, 1992—, Monroe C.C., Rochester, NY, 1999—2000; music dir., dept. chair K-12 Harley Sch., Rochester, NY, 1983—90; music faculty Kendall Ctrl. Schools, Kendall, NY, 1990—92; adj. music faculty Finger Lakes C.C., Canandaigua, NY. Cons., tchr. tng. in music tech. Regional Sch. Districts, Monroe, Wayne Counties, NY, 1996—; multi-instrumental performer/composer, jazz and contemporary media, Rochester, NY, 1976—; pvt. instr. of percussion, music theory, composition and music tech., Rochester. Composer: (documentary, public television) Junkmen, (film documentary, national geographic) Submersable Vehicles, (theme and backround music, regional tv) Great Lakes Boater, 52 episodes, (national television advertisement) Sportscast 91' - TNN television, Better In Bahamas - Carnival Cruise Lines. Recipient Outstanding Music Educator, Rochester Philharm. Orch., 2002. Mem.: Music Educators Nat. Conf. Achievements include research in Presenter of workshops in curriculum design and studentscomposition at state and national music conferences, MENC and AOSA. Home: 40 Larchwood Dr Pittsford NY 14534 Office: Penfield High School 25 High School Dr Penfield NY 14526 Personal E-mail: johnbagale@earthlink.net.

BAGAN, MERWYN, neurological surgeon; b. Phila., Jan. 25, 1936; s. Frank and Shirley (Lindenbaum) B.; m. Carol Augusta Joseph, Nov. 14, 1964; children: Eric, Seth, Karin. AB, Dartmouth Coll., 1957; MD, Boston U., 1962, MPH, 1995. Diplomate Am. Bd. Neurol. Surgery. Neurol. surgeon Surg. Neurology Profl. Assn., Concord, N.H., 1970-93; chmn. Healthsource, Inc., Hooksett, 1985-97. Chmn., pres. Healthsource N.H., Concord, 1985-93; adj. asst. prof. clin. surgery (neurosurgery) Dartmouth Med. Sch., 1981-88; vis. prof. dept. surgery Tribhuvan U. Inst. Medicine, Kathmandu, Nepal, 1997-2000. Lt. comdr. USPHS, 1963-65. Recipient Disting. Alumnus award Boston U. Sch. Medicine, 1993, alumni award Boston U., 1999, Suprabal Gorkha Dakshina Bahu award, 2000. Fellow ACS; mem. AMA, Am. Assn. Neurol. Surgeons (pres. 1992-93, humanitarian award 2000), N.H. Med. Soc. (pres. 1983), Congress of Neurol. Surgeons (Disting. Svc. award 1990), Alpha Omega Alpha. Home: 173 School St Concord NH 03301-2568

BAGBY, GLEN STOVALL, lawyer; b. Memphis, Sept. 1, 1944; s. Steadman Thomas and Sarah Frances (Rhodes) B.; m. Terri Stovall; children: Sarah Jane, Elizabeth Anne. AB, Transylvania U., 1966; JD, U. Ky., 1969. Bar: Ky. 1969, U.S. Ct. Claims 1975, U.S. Tax Ct. 1972, U.S. Supreme Ct. 1972. Assoc. Brock & Brock, Lexington, Ky., 1969-71; ptnr. Brock, Brock & Bagby, Lexington, Ky., 1971-98, Woodward, Hobson & Fulton, Lexington, Ky., 1999—. Chmn. Bd. Constrn. Appeals, Bd. Rev., Lexington, 1979-81. Co-author: Kentucky Probate, 2000—. Bd. dirs. Julius Marks Home for Elderly, Lexington, 1975—88; vice chmn. Good Samaritan Hosp., Lexington, 1980—92; chmn. bd. trustees Ky. Conf. United Meth. Ch., 1993—96, chancellor, 1976—2001; bd. dirs. Magee Christian Edn. Found., 1989—, pres., 2002—. Fellow: Ky. Bar Found., Am. Coll. Trust and Estate Counsel; mem.: ABA, Blue Grass Estate Planning Coun. (pres. 1987—88), Fayette County Bar Assn., Ky. Bar Assn. (probate com. 1974—2000, ho. of dels. 1985—92), U. Ky. Alumni Assn., Lexington C. of C. Office: Woodward Hobson & Fulton 200 W Vine St Fl 5 Lexington KY 40507-1720

BAGBY, JOHN R. management consultant; b. Aurora, Mo., Mar. 3, 1919; BS, U. Ark., 1953, MS, 1956; PhD, Emory U., 1963. Scientist CDC, Atlanta, 1946-69; prof. Colo. State U., Ft. Collins, 1969-84; dir. Mo. Dept. Health, Jefferson City, 1984-90; mgmt. cons. Lohman, Mo., 1993—. Cons. planetary quarantine/protection NASA, 1966—; chmn. nat. adv. com. Energy Related Epidemiologic Rsch., 1993-2002; mem. Armed Forces Epidemiologic Bd., 1993-98.

BAGBY, JOSEPH RIGSBY, financial investor; b. Banner Elk, N.C., Aug. 23, 1935; s. Wesley Marion and Ila Paunee (Rigsby) B.; m. Martha Green, Jan. 1, 1965; 1 child, Meredith Elaine. Student, Fla. State U., 1955; BBA, U. Miami, 1959; MCR, Inst. Corp. Real Estate, West Palm Beach, Fla., 1977. Employee and supr. Miami Herald Pub. Co., 1953-63; rsch. and sales asst. Oscar Dolly Assocs., Miami, 1961-63; sales, appraising and property mgr. Jack Thomas Realty, Miami, 1963-65; dir. corp. real estate Burger King Corp., Miami, 1965-70; founder, pres. Internat. Assn. Corp. Real Estate Execs., Coral Gables, Fla., 1969-88; chmn. bd. trustees Nat. Assn. Corp. Real Estate Execs., Coral Gables, Fla., 1973-88, bd. dirs., 1971—; pres., founder Property Resources Corp. and 20 other investment cos., Miami and Palm Beach, 1970—. Founder merger and acquisition investment co., 1997; mem. businessman's adv. com. U.S. Postal Svc., Washington, 1984-88. Author: Real Estate Financing Desk Book, 1975, rev. edits. 1977, 81, Real Estate Directory, 1975. Pres. interfraternity coun. U. Miami (co-editor campus newspaper); mem., chmn. fin. com. St. Edward's Cath. Ch., Palm Beach, Fla., 1985-93. With U.S. Army, 1959-61. Named to Hall of Fame, Nat. Assn. Corp. Real Estate Execs., 1991. Mem. Nat. Assn. Location Analysts and Negotiators (founder), Internat. Corp. Real Estate Execs. Assn. (life hon. mem., bd. dirs. Corenet Global), Progress Club of Miami (co-founder), Optimist (founding mem. Miami Downtown club), Rotary (Harris fellow), Interfaith Cotillian (co-founder), Sigma Chi (pres. 1958), Alpha Kappa Psi. Democrat. Avocations: swimming, tennis. Home: 125 Brazilian Ave Palm Beach FL 33480-4221 Office: Property Resources Corp PO Box 3149 Palm Beach FL 33480-1349

BAGBY, MARTHA L. GREEN, real estate holding company executive, writer, publishing executive; b. West Palm Beach, Fla., June 17, 1937; d. Hampton and Louise (Lambert) Green; m. Joseph R. Bagby, 1966; 1 child, Meredith E, AA, Palm Beach Jr. Coll., 1957; AB, U. Miami, 1959; MA, Pa. State U., 1964. Tchr. journalism, english Palm Beach County, 1959—62; instr. journalism Pa. State U., 1962—63; city editor, writer Palm Beach News & Life, 1963—64; editor Alfred Hitchcock Mag., Riviera Beach, Fla., 1964; editor, supr. editl. svc., pub. rels. employee newspaper Nat. Airlines, Inc., Miami, Fla., 1965—73; corp. sec., chmn. bd. Property Resources Co., Palm Beach, Fla., 1971—. Life dir. CareNet Global, 2002—; Ill. franchisee Burger King Corp.; founder Internat. Health Awareness Assn.; lectr. journalism Dade, Palm Beach counties; instr. Barry Coll., Miami; pub. The Bagbys Health Digest, 1985—. Author: Stranglehold, 1977, The Complete Real Estate Dictionary, 1992, The Real Estate Financing Deskbook, 1979-90; author: (with others) The Complete Real Estate Book. Mem. exec. bd. Childbirth and Parent Edn. Assn., Miami. Mem.: Internat. Assn. Corp. Real Estate Execs. (founder, trustee, exec. editor, dir. life), Women in Comm. (pres.), Air Transport Assn. Am., Airline Editors Conf. (chmn.), S. Fla. Indsl. Chmn. Internat. Council Indsl. Editors, Fla. Pub. Relations Assn. Office: 125 Brazilian Ave Palm Beach FL 33480-4221

BAGDIKIAN, BEN HAIG, journalist, emeritus university educator; b. Marash, Turkey, Jan. 30, 1920; came to U.S., 1920, naturalized, 1926; s. Aram Theodore and Daisy (Uvezian) B.; m. Elizabeth Ogasapian, Oct. 2, 1942 (div. 1972); children: Christopher Ben, Frederick Haig; m. Betty L. Medsger, 1973 (div.); m. Marlene Griffith, 1983 AB, Clark U., 1941, LittD, 1963; LHD, Brown U., 1961, U. R.I., 1992. Reporter Springfield (Mass.) Morning Union, 1941-42; assoc. editor Periodical House, Inc., N.Y.C., 1946; successively reporter, fgn. corr., chief Washington corr. Providence Jour., 1947-62; contbg. editor Saturday Evening Post, 1963-67; project dir. study of future U.S. news media Rand Corp., 1967-69; asst. mng. editor for nat. news Washington Post, 1970-71, asst. mng. editor, ombudsman, 1971-72; nat. corr. Columbia Journalism Review, 1972-74; prof. Grad. Sch. Journalism U. Calif., Berkeley, 1976-90, dean, Grad. Sch. Journalism, 1985-88, prof. emeritus, Grad. Sch. Journalism, 1990—. Author: In the Midst of Plenty: The poor in America, 1964, The Information Machines: Their Impact on Men and the Media, 1971, The Shame of the Prisons, 1972, The Effete Conspiracy, 1972, Caged: Eight Prisoners and Their Keepers, 1976, The Media Monopoly, 1983, 6th edit., 2000, Double Vision: Reflections on My Heritage, Life and Profession, 1995; also pamphlets; contbr.: The Kennedy Circle, 1961; editor: Man's Contracting World in an Expanding Universe, 1959; bd. editors Jour. Investigative Reporters and Editors, 1980-88. Mem. steering com. Nat. Prison Project, 1974-82; trustee Clark U., 1964-76; bd. dirs. Nat. Capital Area Civil Liberties Union, 1964-66, Com. to Protect Journalists, 1981-88, Data Ctr., Oakland, Calif., 1990-97; pres. Lowell Mellett Fund for Free an Responsible Press, 1965-76; acad. adv. bd. Nat. Citizens Com. for Broadcasting, 1978—; judge Ten Most Censored Stories, 1976-98. Recipi-

ent George Foster Peabody award, 1951, Sidney Hillman Found. award, 1956, Most Perceptive Critic citation Am. Soc. Journalism Adminstrs., 1978, Career Achievement award Soc. Profl. Journalists, John and Catherine Zenger award, 1996, James Madison award ALA, 1998; named to R.I. Journalism Hall of Fame, 1992; fellow Ogden Reid Found., 1956, Guggenheim fellow, 1961-62. Mem. ACLU. Home: 25 Stonewall Rd Berkeley CA 94705-1414 *Personal philosophy: The most compelling principles in my life have been, in private life the pervasive need of love and trust in human relations, in public life dignity of the individual combined with devotion to the common good, in intellectual life a distrust of detachment from the human condition, and in journalism honesty and clarity.*

BAGG, CARTER DAVIS, architect, urban planner; b. Evanston, Ill., May 12, 1945; s. John Herbert and Dorothy Santee (Davis) B.; m. Sally Frances Brown, Aug. 1, 1980; children: Elliotte Carter, Sara Allyson. BArch, U. Calif., Berkeley, 1969; M in Environ. Planning, Ariz. State U., 1984. Registered arch., Ariz., Wash. Project mgr. Jack Kaufman, Phoenix, 1972-74; job capt. John S.M. Hamilton, Phoenix, 1974-76; project arch. Peter A. Lendrum, Phoenix, 1976-78; v.p. Kenneth S. Allison, Phoenix, 1978-81; planner-in-charge GSAS, Phoenix, 1981-83; asst. zoning adminstr. City of Chandler, Ariz., 1983-85; exec. v.p. Kenneth S. Allison & Assocs., Inc., Scottsdale, Ariz., 1985-88; bldg. project supr. Seattle Sch. Dist., 1988-91; archtl. cons. Office of Supt. Pub. Instrn., 1992-95, R & D analyst, 1996-97, N.W. Wash. regional facilities coord., 1998—, interim dir. sch. facilities and orgn. sect., 2000-01. Prin. works include masterplans for Andover Corp., Lone Mountain Shadows, Silver Creek Ctr. Chmn. Coronado Neighborhood Planning Com., Phoenix, 1981-83; mem. corp. bd. Neighborhood Housing Svcs., Phoenix, 1980-88; mem. Ctrl. Phoenix Streetscape Citizen Com., 1983; mem. sign ordinance rev. com. City of Phoenix, 1985-86, mem. design rev. task force, 1987-88, mem. bd. zoning adjustment, 1987-88; mem. land use com. South Rose Hill/Bridle Trails Neighborhood Assn., 1999—. With USAR, 1970-97. Mem. AIA, Am. Inst. Cert. Planners. Republican. Episcopalian. Home: 12819 NE 84th St Kirkland WA 98033-8011 Office: Old Capitol Bldg PO Box 47200 Olympia WA 98504-7200 E-mail: baggfamily@earthlink.net., cbagg@ospi.wednet.edu.

BAGG, ROBERT ELY, poet, educator, translator; b. Orange, NJ, Sept. 21, 1935; s. Theodore Ely and Elma Hague (White) B.; m. Sarah Frances Robinson, Aug. 24, 1957 (div. 1996); children: Theodore, Christopher, Jonathan, Melissa, Hazzard; m. Mary L. Bauman, July 27, 1996. AB, Amherst Coll., 1957; MA, U. Conn., 1961, PhD, 1965. Instr. English, U. Wash., Seattle, 1963-65; asst. prof., then prof. U. Mass., Amherst, 1965-96, chmn. dept. English, 1986-92; stage prodn. selection, U Utah. Lectr. Smith Coll., Northampton, Mass., 1967; assoc. prof. classics U. Tex., Austin, 1971; vis. artist Rome Am. Acad. Arts and Letters, 1980, 96; cons. in field. Author: (poems) Madonna of the Cello, 1961, The Scrawny Sonnets, 1973, Body Blows, 1988; translator: (Greek dramas) Hippolytos, 1973, The Bakkhai, 1977, Oedipus the King, 1982, Women of Trachis, 1993, Antigone, 2001. Recipient Prix de Rome Am. Acad. Arts and Letters, 1959; fellow Am. Acad. in Rome, 1958-59; vis. artist Ingram Merrill Found., 1961, 62, 63, 74, NEA, 1975, Guggenheim Found., 1980; Bellagio residency Rockefeller Found., 1999. Mem. MLA. Democrat. Avocation: golf. Home: 582 Pfersick Rd Shelburne Falls MA 01370-9590

BAGGER, RICHARD HARTVIG, lawyer; b. Plainfield, N.J., Mar. 27, 1960; s. Donald Hartvig and Elizabeth Claire (Broback) B.; m. Barbara Jane Laird, May 14, 1988; Katherine Bianca, Jennifer Anne, Meredith Skye. AB, Princeton U., 1982; JD, Rutgers U., 1986. Bar: N.J. 1986, U.S. Dist. Ct. N.J. 1986. Legis. aide N.J. Gen. Assembly, Trenton, 1979-82; mem. profl. staff Select Com. on Aging U.S. Ho. Reps., Washington, 1982-83; assoc. McCarter & English, Newark, 1986-91; asst. gen. counsel Blue Cross and Blue Shield of N.J., Inc., Newark, 1991-93; mgr. civic affairs Pfizer, Inc., N.Y.C., 1993-96, dir., state corp. affairs, 1996-99, nat. dir. state govt. rels., 1999—2002, v.p. govt. rels., 2002—03, sr. v.p. govt. rels., 2003—. Trustee N.J. Hist. Trust, Trenton, 1986-89, Westfield Found., 1995-2001, Overlook Found., 2001—; bd. govs. N.J. Hist. Soc., 1989-98. Editor, author Rutgers Law Rev., 1985-86. Mem. N. J. Gen. Assembly; councilman Town of Westfield, NJ, 1984—90; chmn. appropriations com., NJ; mem. N.J. Senate, 2002—03; Westfield Planning Bd., 1987—92; dist committeeman Union County Reps., Elizabeth, NJ, 1980—83, 1987. Episcopalian. Office: Pfizer Inc 235 E 42nd St New York NY 10017-5755 E-mail: rich.bagger@pfizer.com.

BAGGETT, ALICE DIANE, critical care nurse; b. Louisville, Dec. 27, 1964; d. Stanley Wayne and Pauline (Stearman) B. BSN cum laude, Spalding U., Louisville, 1988. Nurses aide Wesley Manor-Meth. Retirement Homes, Louisville, 1983—88, medication technician; staff nurse, charge nurse TCU, ICU nurse, relief house supr. Columbia Hosp.-Suburban, Louisville, 1988—2001; house supr. Norton Suburban Hosp., 2001—. Home: PO Box 85 Depauw IN 47115-0085

BAGGETT, DONNIS GENE, journalist, editor; b. Livingston, Tex., July 16, 1952; s. Sam Jr. and Mavis Baggett; children: Valerie Shaddix, David Shaddix. BA, Stephen F. Austin State U., 1973. Reporter, photographer East Tex. Eye, Livingston, Tex., 1973-74, co-editor, 1974; reporter Longview (Tex.) Morning Jour., 1974-75, East Tex. editor, 1975-76; reporter The Dallas Morning News, 1976, asst. night city editor, 1977, asst. state editor, 1977-82, state editor, 1982-94, asst. mng. editor, 1994-95; pub., editor The Eagle, Bryan-College Station, Tex., 1996—. Chmn. Tex. Agrl. Summit Exec. Com., 1997—98; bd. dirs. Brazos Valley Mus. Natural History, Am. Heart Assn.; bd. dirs., campaign chair Brazos Valley United Way, 2000; mem. adv. bd. Twin Cities Missions, 2001—. Mem.: Soc. Profl. Journalists, Tex. Press Assn. (dir.), Tex. Daily Newspaper Assn. (dir., v.p., chair assn. legis. adv. com.), Press Club of Dallas (sec. 1990—91, treas. 1991—92, pres. 1992—94). Methodist. Avocation: ranching.

BAGGETT, JAMES LAMAR, anatomy, physiology and microbiology educator; b. Memphis, June 25, 1952; s. James Lamar Baggett Sr.; m. Karen Louise Baggett, Dec. 28, 1990; children: Katherine Grace, Jonathan Daniel. AS, Jackson State C.C., 1973; BA, U. Miss., 1979; MS, U. So. Miss., 1986, PhD, 1993. Classroom tchr. Memphis City Schs., 1978-85; radiation safety officer U. So. Miss., Hattiesburg, 1985-90, NASA-Stennis Space Ctr., Pickyune, Miss., 1985-90; prof. Gulf Coast C.C., Gautier, Miss., 1990 . Sci. cons. Miss. Pub. Schs., 1986—. Contbr. articles to profl. jours. Category judge Miss. Sci. Fairs, 1986—; judge zoology divsn. Nat. Sci. Fairs, Biloxi, Miss., 1993. Named Top 2000 Scientist of 20th Century, 2000. Fellow Am. Assn. of Anatomist; mem. Human Anatomy and Physiology Assn., Miss. Acad. of Sci. (vice chmn. sci. edn. divsn.), Golden Key. Democrat. Avocations: golfing, astronomy, photography, guitar. Home: 9229 Pt Aux Chenes Ocean Springs MS 39564 Office: PO Box 100 Gautier MS 39553-0100

BAGGETT, REBECCA GAYE, academic advisor, poet; b. Wilmington, N.C., Nov. 25, 1957; d. Claude Nash Baggett and Lillian Anna Lebo; m. Elmer Lanier Clark, July 10, 1976; children: Morgan Rebecca Baggett-Clark, Emma Rachel Baggett-Clark. BA in Classical Langs., Salem Coll., 1980. Acad. advisor Ga. So. U., Statesboro, 1990—91, Albany (Ga.) State U., 1991—93; sr. acad. advisor U. Ga. Franklin Coll., Athens, 1993—. Author: (chapbook) Still Life with Children, 1996, Greatest Hits: 1981-2000, 2001. Democrat. Episcopalian. Avocations: gardening, reading. Home: 330 College Cir Athens GA 30605

BAGGETT, STEVEN RAY, lawyer; b. Fayetteville, Ark., July 3, 1963; s. Harold Ray and Norma June (King) B.; m. Amy Lynn Griggs, Jan. 2, 1999; 1 child, Lauren Michelle. BA, U. Ark., 1985; JD, So. Meth. U., 1988. Bar: Tex. 1988, U.S. Dist. Ct. (no. dist.) Tex. 1988, U.S. Ct. Appeals (5th cir.) 1992. Assoc. Thompson & Knight, Dallas, 1988-95, shareholder, ptnr., 1996—. Recipient Am. Jurisprudence awards Bancroft-Whitney Co., 1985-86. Mem. Tex. Bar Assn., Dallas Bar Assn. (spkrs. com. 1997—, state fair trial by jury com. 1998-2001, jud. com. 1999-2001, cmty. involvement com. 1999-2001, law in schs. and cmtys. com. 1999), Ark. U. Alumni Assn., So. Meth. U. Law Sch. Alumni Assn. (steering com.), Phi Beta Kappa. Avocations: weight training, running, ice skating, music. Office: Thompson & Knight 1700 Pacific Ave Ste 3300 Dallas TX 75201-4693 E-mail: baggetts@tklaw.com.

BAGGETT, W. MIKE, lawyer; b. Waco, Tex., Nov. 8, 1946; s. Bill R. and Jenna (Robertson) B.; m. Jo Kilpatrick, May 28, 1968; children: Carl, Cary. BBA, Tex. A&M U., 1968; JD cum laude, Baylor U., 1973. Bar: Tex. 1973. Law clk. Tex. Supreme Ct., Austin, 1973—74; assoc. Winstead, Sechrest & Minick, Dallas, 1974-79, shareholder, 1979—, chmn. and chief exec. officer, 1992—. Author: Texas Foreclosure: Law & Practice, 1983, Texas Practice Series West, 2nd edit., 2001, Real Estate Litigation, Texas Practice Guide West, 2002; co-author: Lender Liability Law and Litigation, 1989. Trustee Tex. A&M Found., 1989-98, chmn., 1992-93; mem. Joint Select Com. on Judiciary, 1988; bd. dirs. Tex. Higher Edn. Coordinating Bd., 1989-95, North Tex. Commn., Dallas Citizens Coun., State Fair of Tex., Southwestern Bell-SMU Athletic Forum; chmn. Dallas Ft. Worth Regional Sports Commn.; chmn., CEO, Cotton Bowl Athletic Assn. 1st lt. U.S. Army, 1968-71, Vietnam. Decorated Bronze Star. Master: Patrick E. Higginbotham Am. Inn Ct.; fellow: Am. Bd. Trial Advocates, The Ctr. for Am. and Internat. Law, Tex. Bar Found., Am. Bar Found., Dallas Bar Found. (chmn. and trustee); mem.: Tex. Supreme Ct. Reverse Mortgage Rules Com., Tex. Supreme Ct. Home Equity Loan Foreclosures Rules Com., Dallas Bar Assn. (pres. chmn., bd. dirs.), Tex. Bar Assn. (bd. cert. civil trial com. 1983, bd. dirs., adminstrn. justice com.), Baylor Law Sch. Alumni Assn. (pres., bd. dirs.), Assn. Former Students Tex. A&M U. (pres. 1988, Outstanding Alumni Coll. Bus. 1996, Disting. Alumni 1998), Ctrl. Dallas Assn. (chmn.), City Club, Royal Oaks Club. Methodist. Office: Winstead Sechrest & Minick 5400 Renaissance Tower 1201 Elm St Ste 5400 Dallas TX 75270-2199

BAGGOTT, BRENDA JANE LAMB, elementary educator; b. Augusta, Ga., Nov. 10, 1948; d. Morgan Barrett Jr. and Ollie Virginia (Toole) Lamb; m. John Carl Baggott, July 8, 1967 (div. Jan. 1998); children: Carla Baggott Walczak, John Carl Jr. Student, Truett McConnel Jr. Coll., 1966-67; BS in spl. Edn., Augusta Coll., 1974; postgrad., Southeastern La. U., 1976-77, U. New Orleans, 1977-78, U. Ctrl. Fla., 1987, 97—; MEd, Nova Southeastern U., 1997. Cert. spl. edn. tchr. in varying exceptionalities and mental handicaps, elem. tchr., coaching for Spl. Olympics, Fla. Spl. Olympics tchr. Copeland Elem. Sch., Augusta, Ga., 1973-74; spl. edn. tchr. Percy Julian Spl. Sch., Marrero, La., 1974-78; Spl. edn. resource tchr. Rosemary Mid. Sch., Andrews, S.C., 1978; spl. edn. tchr. Bynum Elem. Sch., Gerogetown, S.C., 1979, Ridgewood Park Elem. Sch., Orlando, Fla., 1979-97; reading recovery tchr. Rock Lake Elem. Sch., Orlando, 1997—2002; lab tchr. Read 180, 2002—. Curriculum coord. Percy Julian Spl. Sch., 1975-77; mem. state tchr. mentally handicapped exam validation team Inst. for Instnl. Rsch. and Practice, Fla. Dept. Edn., Tampa, 1990—. Coord. Orange County Spl. Olympics, Orlando, 1984-85, coach, 1974—. Mem. Coun. for Exceptional Children, Internat. Reading Assn., Orange County Reading Coun., Reading Recovery Coun. N.Am., Fla. Reading Assn. Democrat. Baptist. Avocations: directing children's choirs, coaching special olympics. Office: Rock Lake Elem Sch 408 N Tampa Ave Orlando FL 32805-1296

BAGLEY, CATHY LORRAINE, obstetrician, gynecologist; b. Bklyn., Apr. 17, 1961; BA, Dartmouth Coll., 1978-82; MD, Brown U., 1986. Diplomate Am. Bd. Ob-Gyn. Resident Cook County Hosp., Chgo., 1986-90; ob-gyn. Dept. HHS, Chgo., 1990-92; mem. staff The Hammond Clinic, Munster, Ind., 1992-93, St. Lawrence Hosp., Lansing, Mich., 1993-94; ob-gyn. Ctrl. City Ob/Gyn. Assocs., Inc., Macon, Ga., 1994—, pres., 1998—. Fellow Am. Coll. Ob-Gyn.; mem. AMA (Physicians Recognition award 1997). Avocations: tennis, jazz appreciation and promotion. Office: Ctrl City Women's Specialists PC 556-B 3d St Macon GA 31201-

BAGLEY, CHARLES FRANK, III, lawyer; b. Dec. 3, 1944; m. Kirsten L., Aug. 19, 1967; children: Charles F. IV, Gordon T. BA, Southwestern U., 1966; JD, Washington & Lee U., 1969. Judge advocates gen. ct. lt. U.S. Navy, 1969-74; ptnr. Campbell, Woods, Bagley, Emerson, McNeer & Herndon, 1974—. Pres. bd. dirs. tri state coun. Boy Scouts of Am., 1982-85; bd. dirs. Contact Huntington, Hospice Huntington, chmn. 1987-89; active Huntington Area C. of C., Enslow Park Presbyn. Ch. Fellow Internat. Soc. Barristers, West Va. Bar Found.; mem. ABA, Va. Bar Assn., W.Va. State Bar Assn. (bd. govs. 1986-93, pres. 1991-92), W.Va. Bar Assn. (exec. coun. 1986-95, pres. 1993-94), Def. Trial Coun. W.Va. (bd. govs. 1985-90), Cabell County Bar Assn. (pres. 1985-86), Internat. Assn. Ins. Coun., Def. Rsch. Inst., Inc. (state chmn. 1985-90). Address: 1123 12th Ave Huntington WV 25701-3423

BAGLEY, HUGHES ANDERSON, SR., retail executive, consultant; b. St. Louis, Dec. 13, 1924; s. William Jefferson and Ivy B. (Wells) B.; m. Marilyn Ann Blattner, May 5, 1945; children: Hughes A. Jr., Herbert F., Brett J., Mary Rebecca, Melissa Ann, Ellen E., Heidi M. BSBA, Wash. U., 1948. Beef mktg. exec. Royal Packing Co., St. Louis, 1949-56; merchandiser Kroger Co. Cin., St. Louis, Charleston, W.Va., 1956-58, Chgo., 1958-65, Columbus, Ohio, 1965-67; pres. Tradewell Supermarkets, Seattle, 1967-68; v.p. Bohack Corp., Bklyn., 1968-70; asst. pres. First Nat. Stores, Somerville, Mass., 1968-71; v.p. mktg. Iowa Beef Processors, Dakota City, Nebr., 1971-75, Spencer (Iowa) Foods, 1975-78; exec. v.p. Dubuque Packaging Co., 1978-79; ind. cons., 1979-84; dir. meat and deli Super-Valu Cub Foods Divsn., Stillwater, Minn., 1985-87; COO Cub Foods, Atlanta, 1987-88. Ind. cons. Xtra Divsn., 1988-89, Seaboard Farms, 1990, Beef Specialists of Iowa, Hartley, 1992, Ukrop Super Markets, Richmond, Va., 1993, Grupo Ganadero Indsl., Costa Rica, 1993, Berliner & Marx, Plume de Veau Veal, South Bend, Ind., 1997, Packerland, Green Bay, Wis., 1996; mem. Chgo. Mercantile Exch., 1971. Republican. Avocations: reading, studying industry trends, marketing. Home and Office: Hereford Trading Corp Consulting 22632 Grenoble Ave Sioux City IA 51108-8691 Fax: 712-252-5017.

BAGLEY, JAMES ROBERT, freelance writer; b. Valdosta, Ga., Dec. 7, 1946; s. Rayford Virdoe Bagley and Frances Cowart; m. Carol Ann Blackman, Dec. 17, 1972; children: James Brennan, Kimberly Ann. BS, Valdosta State U., 1975. Numerous positions including dep. sheriff, probation officer, 1975-85; clerical specialist Fla. Hwy. Safety Dept., Tallahassee, 1985-86; freelance writer, Tallahassee, 1986-89; security officer Mus. Fla. History, Tallahassee, 1989-93; cons. State Bd. Adminstrn., Tallahassee, 1994-95; freelance writer. Author: (poetry) The Star, 1977, The Alchemist, 1980, Soul-Speak from the Matrix, 1985, I Am No River Like Yesterday, 1995, (novels) Lustmords of Bithinsinia, 1995, Tetrarcha, 2000. With U.S. Army, 1966-69, Vietnam. Recipient cert. of appreciation Lions Club, Valdosta, 1977. Mem. Author's Guild, Acad. Am. Poets, 22nd Infantry Regiment Soc. Home and Office: 2317 Limerick Dr Tallahassee FL 32309-3508

BAGLEY, PHILIP JOSEPH, III, lawyer; b. Richmond, Va., Nov. 24, 1941; s. Philip Joseph Jr. and Louise (Bourne) B.; m. Sally Ann Twedell, Aug. 18, 1967; children: Elizabeth Bourne Faulkner, Anne Tunstall Twedell. BA, U. Richmond, 1963; LLB, U. Va., 1966. Bar: Va. 1966, U.S. Supreme Ct. 1972. Assoc. Troutman Sanders LLP, Richmond, 1970—74, ptnr., 1974—; v.p. Richmond Real Estate Group, 2002—03, pres., 2003—. Chmn. state adv. coun. Nat. Legal Svcs. Corp., Richmond, 1977-79; bd. dirs. Legal Svc. Corp. Va., 1978-86. Legal advisor Jr. League Richmond, 1977—; bd. dirs. Richmond Symphony, 1986-96, pres. 1992-94; bd. dirs. Richmond Eye and Ear Hosp., 1988—, pres. 1991-96; trustee Benedictine H.S., 1994-2002, pres., 1996-2002; bd. dirs. Carpenter Ctr. Performing Arts, 1995—, mem. exec. com., 1998—; bd. dirs., mem. exec. com. Va. Performing Arts Found., 2001—; bd. dirs. Richmond Renaissance, 2002—. Fellow Am. Law Found., Va. Bar Found.; mem. ABA (lectr. real estate financing com. 1984, title ins. com. 1987, leasing 1992, coun. real property, probate and trust law sect. 1993-98, sec. 1998-2000, vice-chair real property divsn. 2000-02, chair-elect 2002-03, chair 2003—), Am. Coll. Real Estate Lawyers (bd. govs. 1988-97, treas. 1991-93, v.p. 1993-94, pres. 1995-96), Anglo-Am. Real Property Inst. (bd. govs. 1995—), Coun. for Am.'s 1st Freedom (bd. govs. 1994-2000, pres. 1996-2000), Internat. Coun. Shopping Ctrs. (co-chair law conf. com. 1996-98), Va. Bar Assn., Richmond Bar Assn., Country Club Va., Commonwealth Club, Order of Coif, Phi Beta Kappa, Omnicron Delta Kappa. Roman Catholic. Office: Troutman Sanders LLP 1111 E Main St Richmond VA 23218-1122

BAGLEY, THOMAS STEVEN, private equity investor; b. Chgo., Oct. 25, 1952; s. James A. and Corinne M. (Catania) B.; m. Christine A. Elliott; 1 child, Derek Elliott Bagley. BA in Econs. cum laude, North Park Coll., Chgo., 1974; MBA in Fin., DePaul U., 1977. Mgr. contr. divsn. Continental Ill. Nat. Bank, Chgo., 1975-78, officer Clev. Office, 1978-81, asst v.p. Corr. Banking, 1981, v.p. mgr. Ill. & Wisc., 1981-84; v.p. area mgr. of Midwest Area of Leveraged Capital Group Citicorp North Am., Inc., Chgo., 1984-88; founder, mng. gen. ptnr. Pfingsten Ptnrs., Deerfield, Ill., 1989—. Founder, gen. ptnr. Chgo. Assocs. Internat., 1988-89; bd. dirs. Woodall Pub. Group, Inc., Hallcrest, Inc., Huebcore Comm., Inc., Am. Acad. Suppliers, Inc., Park Foods, L.P., Barjan Products, L.P., Norcraft Cos. LLC, Pfingsten Pub. LLC, Four Wheel Drive Hardware LLC. Blum Glover scholar, 1973-74. Mem. Union League Club of Chgo., Conway Farms Golf Club, Geneva Nat. Golf Club, Execs. Club Chgo., Econs. Club Chgo., Delta Mu Delta. Republican. Lutheran. Home: 1155 Ashlawn Dr Lake Forest IL 60045-1504 Office: Pfingsten Ptnrs Corporate 500 Centre 520 Lake Cook Rd Ste 375 Deerfield IL 60015-5632

BAGLEY, WILLIAM EVAN, application technology specialist; b. Marfa, Tex., Jan. 28, 1949; s. Cleon Lester Jr. and Alice Lucille (McKinney) B.; m. Cynthia Gail Keener, June 23, 1952; children: William Lester, Evan Blake, Jason Lee, Keri Lynn. BS in Entomology, Tex. A&M U., 1971. Extension entomologist Tex. Agrl. Extension Svc., Pecos, Tex., 1972-75; dir. R&D Stull Chem., San Antonio, 1975-87; product mgr. Wilbur Ellis Co., Fresno, Calif., 1987—. Mem. devel. coun. Tex. A&M U. Coll. of Agriculture. Mem. ASTM, Nat. Roadside Vegetation Mgmt. Assn., Nat. Agrl. Aviation Assn., Inst. of Liquid Atomization and Spray Systems, Am. Soc. of Agrl. Engrs., Entomological Soc. of Am., Southwestern Entomology Soc., Nat. Coalition Drift Minimization. Avocations: karate (3rd degree black belt), refereeing, Tae Kwon Do, racing pigeons. Home and Office: 4396 E Evans Rd San Antonio TX 78259-2202

BAGLEY, WILLIAM THOMPSON, lawyer; b. San Francisco, June 29, 1928; s. Nino J. and Rita V. (Thompson) Baglietto; m. Diane Lenore Oldham, June 20, 1965; children: Lynn Lorene, William Thompson, Walter William, Shana Angela, Tracy Elizabeth. AB, U. Calif., Berkeley, 1949, JD, 1952. Bar: Calif. 1953, U.S. Supreme Ct. 1967. Atty. Pacific Gas & Electric Co., 1952-56; assoc. Gardiner, Riede & Elliott, San Rafael, Calif., 1956-60; ptnr. Bagley Bernt & Bianchi, San Rafael, 1961-74; mem. Calif. Legis., 1961-74; chmn. Commodity Futures Trading Commn., Washington, 1975-79; ptnr. Nossaman, Guthner, Knox and Elliott, San Francisco, 1980—. Mem. Calif. Pub. Utilities Commn., 1983-86; mem. Calif. Transp. Commn., 1983-89, chmn., 1987-88. Bd. editors Calif. Law Rev., 1951-52. Bd. regents U. Calif., 1989-2002; bd. dirs. Nat. Futures Assn., Calif. Coun. Environ. and Econ. Balance, Edmund G. Brown Inst. Govtl. Affairs, L.A.; chmn. bd. Calif. Rep. League, 1980-82. Recipient Freedom of Info. award Sigma Delta Chi, 1970, Golden Bear award Calif. Pk. Commn., 1973; named Most Effective Assemblyman, Capitol Press Corps, 1969, Legislator of Yr., Calif. Trial Lawyers Assn., 1970, Alumnus of Yr., U. Calif. Alumni Assn., 2002. Mem. ABA, Calif. State Bar Assn., World Trade Club, Elks Club (life), Phi Beta Kappa, Alpha Tau Omega. Presbyterian. E-mail: wbagley@nossaman.com.

BAGLIO, VINCENT PAUL, engineering executive; b. Patchogue, N.Y., Feb. 18, 1960; s. Lorenzo and Nancy (Morello) B.; m. Katerina Barnova, Apr. 3, 2002. BS, Princeton U., 1982; MS, Poly. U., Bklyn., 1986; MBA, Hofstra U., 1993. Product mgr. integrated sys. and aerostructures sector Northrop Grumman Corp., Bethpage, N.Y., 1982-99; mgmt. cons. Beacon Cons. Svcs. Inc., 1999-2000; sr. mgr. bus. devel. Cubic Transp. Sys., Inc., N.Y.C., 2000—02; dir. engrng. Smiths Aerospace-Electronic Sys., L.I., NY, 2002—. Contbr. articles to profl. jours. Alumni schs. com. Princeton (N.J.) U.; chmn. Princeton Alumni Assn. of L.I. Mem. AIAA (tech. com. 1995-97), Soc. Automotive Engrs. (indsl. lectr. 1990-91), Internat. Coun. Aero. Scis. (program com. 1989-93), Friends Princeton Football. Avocations: golf, running. Office: Smiths Aerospace-Electronic Sys 1000 MacArthur Memorial Hwy Bohemia NY 11716 E-mail: vincent.baglio@smiths-aerospace.com.

BAGLOW, DAVID RICHARD, marine facility administrator; b. Manchester, Eng., May 14, 1939; s. Wilfrid Charles and Edith (May) B. Cert. heat engines/gas industry supply; cert. comms. engr. Engr. indsl. gas supply N.W. Gas Bd., Manchester, 1958-62; comms. engr. Cable & Wireless Ltd. various locations worldwide, 1962-74, Saigon, Vietnam, 1970-72; asst. mgr. The Moorings Ltd., Tortola, British Virgin Islands, 1974-75; mgr., v.p. W.I. Yacht Charter, Tortola, 1975-78; gen. mgr., v.p. Nanny Cay Marine Ctr., Tortola, 1978-80; ops. mgr. South Pacific Yacht Charter, Tonga, Tahiti, Logan, Utah, 1980-85; base mgr., rschr. The Moorings Ltd., Tortola, Tonga, Grenada, Bahamas, 1985-94; ops. mgr., co-dir. The Moorings Australasia Pty./Ltd., Sydney/Whitsunday Islands, Australia, 1994-2000. Author: Cruising Guide to Isles Sous le Vent Tahiti and Vava'u Islands of Tonga, Tonga Guide, 1980, Tahiti Guide, 1982. Avocations: yachting, music, yacht engineering research, reading nonfiction, travel. Home and Office: PO Box 6454 Ocean View HI 96737-6454 E-mail: baglowdavidr@aol.com.

BAGNALL, LINDSAY LOMAX, human resources specialist; d. Victor William and Jacqueline (Bryant) Lomax; m. Kent Alan Bagnall, May 4, 1985; children: Hannah Marie, Lydia Kent. BA, U. Mo., Rolla, 1976. Nat. accounts rep. Orkin Exterminating Co., Inc., Atlanta, 1977—78, customer svc. rep., 1978—80; supr. customer svc. Orkin Exterminating Co., Inc./Rollins, Inc., Atlanta, 1980—83; computer programmer, analyst Rollins, Inc., Atlanta, 1983—85; co-owner, v.p. human resources Kent Jewelry and Fine Gifts, Rolla, 1985—; computer programmer, analyst U. Mo., Rolla, 1986—88, asst. dir., asst. v.p., 1988—2002, exec. dir., exec. v.p., 2002—. Advisor juggling club U. Mo., Rolla, 2001—, advisor Panhellenic, 2003—. Vol. Ozark Actors Theater, Rolla, 1985—2003, Pub. Radio Sta. KUMR, Rolla, Mo., 1985—2003; mem. Arts Rolla!, 1990—2003, Friends of Rolla Pub. Libr., 1990—2003; vol. Mark Twain Elem. PTO, Rolla, Mo., 1995—2002; mem. Champions Rolla Edn., 1995—2003. Mem.: Coun. Advancement and Support Edn., Rolla Area C. of C., P.E.O. Internat. (rec. sec. 1997—99), Duston-Dustin Family Assn. (life), Coterie U. Mo.-Rolla (chair publicity 1999—2003, chair auditing 2000—03, initiation corr. sec. 2001—03), Phelps County Alumnae Panhellenic (treas. 1990—91, tel. chair 1990—91, chair scholarship com. 2000—01, co-chair cotillon 2000—02). Avocations: theater, art collecting, travel, reading. Home: 16541 State Route F Rolla MO 65401 Office: MSM-UMR Alumni Association Castleman Hall 1870 Miner Circle Rolla MO 65409-0650 Personal E-mail: bagnall@rigerner.missouri.org E-mail: lindsayb@umr.edu

BAGSHAW, BRADLEY HOLMES, lawyer; b. Salem, Mass., Mar. 26, 1953; s. James Holmes and Hope (Bradley) Bagshaw. AB summa cum laude, Bowdoin Coll., 1975; JD cum laude, Harvard U., 1981. Bar: Wash. 1981, U.S. Dist. Ct. (we. dist.) Wash. 1981, U.S. Dist. Ct. (ea. dist.) Wash. 1989, U.S. Ct. Appeals (9th cir.) 1989. Assoc. Helsell Fetterman, Seattle, 1981-88, ptnr., 1988—, mng. ptnr., 1991-97, ptnr., 1997—. Office: Helsell Fetterman 1325 4th Ave Ste 1500 Seattle WA 98101-2569 E-mail: bbagshaw@helsell.com.

BAGSHAW, JOSEPH CHARLES, molecular biologist, educator; b. Niagara Falls, N.Y., Sept. 2, 1943; s. Joseph Stanley and Nancy Jo (Pannabaker) Pash; children: Joseph Scott, Alan David. BA, Johns Hopkins U., 1965; PhD, U. Tenn., Oak Ridge, 1969. Research fellow Mass. Gen. Hosp., Boston, 1970-71; asst. prof. molecular biology Wayne State U., Detroit, 1971-77, assoc. prof., 1977-84; prof. biology and biotech. Worcester (Mass.) Poly. Inst., 1984—. Dir Worcester Consortium PhD Program Biomedical Sci, 1985—. Editor (with others): (book) Cell and Molecular Biology of Artemia Development, 1989. Fellow Predoctoral fellow, NSF; grantee Research, NIH, USDA. Mem.: AAAS, Am Soc Cell Biol, Am Soc Biochemistry and Molecular Biol. Office: Worcester Poly Inst Dept Biology/Biotech Worcester MA 01609 E-mail: jbagshaw@wpi.edu.

BAGSHAW, MALCOLM A. radiation oncologist, educator; b. Adrian, Mich., 1925; BA, Wesleyan U., 1946; MD, Yale U., 1950. Diplomate Am. Bd. Radiology. Surg. intern Grace-New Haven Hosp., 1950-51, resident in surg. pathology, 1951-52; resident in radiology U. Mich., 1953-56, clin. instr. radiology, 1955-56; instr. Stanford U., Palo Alto, Calif., 1956-59, asst. prof., 1959-62, assoc. prof., 1962-69, prof., 1969-92, Henry S. Kaplan-Harry Lebeson prof. emeritus, 1992—, dir. div. radiation therapy, 1960-92, chmn. radiology dept., 1972-86, chmn. radiation oncology dept., 1986-92. Resident etranger Inst. Gustave-Roussy, France, 1962-63; cons. radiation therapy VA Hosp., Palo Alto, Calif., 1960-92. Recipient Medal of Honor, Am. Cancer Soc., 1984, Told medal Nihon U. Sch. Medicine, Japan, 1984,Gold Medal award Am. Soc. for Therapeutic Radiology and Oncology, 1985, Disting. Alumnus award Wesleyan

U., 1996, Charles P. Kettering Gold medal Gen. Motors Co., 1996. Mem. AMA, Radiol. Soc. N.Am. (Gold medal 1999), Am. Coll. Radiology (Gold medal 2002). Office: 300 Pasteur Dr Palo Alto CA 94304-2203

BAGSTAD, KRISTIN KIM, pediatric nurse practitioner; b. Salina, Kans., Nov. 11, 1954; d. Richard William and Barbara Bee (Billings) Fry; m. Brian D. Bagstad Diploma in Nursing, St. Francis Hosp. Sch. Nursing, Wichita, Kans., 1975; BSN, Pitts. State U., 1979; MSN, U. Kans. Med. Ctr., 1987. cert. PNP. Staff nurse St. Francis Hosp., Wichita, Kans., 1975—76, charge nurse, 1976—78; staff nurse St. Joseph's Hosp., Kansas City, 1979—80, Wesley Med. Ctr., Wichita, Kans., 1981, charge nurse, 1981—82; nurse clin. Prime Health, Kansas City, 1982—87; clin. nurse specialist Children's Mercy Hosp., Kansas City, 1987—95, PNP, 1995—2000. Mem. affiliate faculty U. Mo., Kansas City, 1988-2000; mem. family ad. bd. Am. Lung Assn., Kansas City, 1987-94, mem. program com., 1992-97; coord. Asthma Camp Western Mo., 1987-96; lactation cons. Children's Mercy Hosp., Kansas City. Author, rschr.: Erikson's Developmental Milestones in Relation to a Chronic Immune Deficiency Syndrome, 1992; contbr. articles to profl. jours. Vol. nurse Turner House Children's Clinic, Kansas City, Kans., 1991-92, bd. dirs. Turner House, 1992-95. Mem. Nat. Assn. Pediat. Nurse Assocs. and Practitioners, Sigma Theta Tau. Episcopalian. Achievements include research on family functioning in families with children with chronic illness, specifically asthma.

BAGTZOGLOU, AMVROSSIOS C. civil engineering educator; b. Thessaloniki, Greece, Jan. 21, 1962; came to U.S., 1985; s. Christos and Zoe Bagtzoglou; m. Anna Dongari, Dec. 28, 1987; children: Christos and Yiannis (twins). Diploma in Civil Engring., Aristotle U. Thessaloniki, Greece, 1985; MS, Fla. Inst. Tech., 1987; PhD, U. Calif., Irvine, 1990. Registered profl. engr., Greece. Postdoctoral rsch. assoc. U. Calif., Irvine, 1990-91; rsch. engr. S.W. Rsch. Inst., San Antonio, 1991-93, sr. rsch. engr., 1993-96; asst. prof. civil engring. Columbia U., N.Y.C., 1997—2002; assoc. prof. civil engring. U. Conn., Storrs, 2002—. Assoc. editor Jour. of Groundwater, 1994-97, Jour. Water Resources Rsch., 1999—, Environ. Forensics, 2002—, Jour. Am. Water Resources Assn., 2003—; contbr. articles to profl. jours. Mem. ASCE, Internat. Assn. Hydrol. Scis., Nat. Groundwater Assn., Am Geophys. Union, N.Y. State Acad. Scis. Avocations: soccer, scuba diving, swimming. Office: U Conn Dept Civil and Environ Engring 261 Glenbrook Rd Unit 2037 Storrs CT 06269 2037 Home: 781 Higgins Rd Cheshire CT 06410- E-mail: Bagtzoglou@aol.com., acb@engr.uconn.edu.

BAGUISI, ALEXANDER, embryologist; b. Quezon City, Metro Manila, Philippines, Feb. 6, 1959; s. Federico and Purificacion Baguisi; m. Stella Marie Samaniego, Apr. 29, 1958; children: Kathrine Marie, Rosalyn Marie, Michael Alexander. MS, U. Coll. Dublin, Ireland, 1999. Rsch. embryologist TranXenoGen Inc., Shrewsbury, Mass. Contbr. Recipient Spl. Achievement award, UP Vanguard Inc., 1979, Gold Medal for target shooting, Armed Forces of the Philippines, 1978; scholar, UP Vanguard Inc., 1977—80. Achievements include invention of methods of cloning animals using the Induced Enucleation and the Telophase- II techniques to produce cloned mice and transgenic goats respectively; method for targeted germline production of birds using primordial germ cells. Method useful for avian transgenesis and conservation programs; research in avian pembryonjic germ cells can be transferred into the embryonic vasculature and contribute to somatic lineage formation of the different organs in syngeneic and allogeneic transplant recipients; hypothermic preservation and cryopreservation of animal embryos can be enhanced using antifreeze proteins and glycoproteins from polar dwelling fish; developed a triple fluorescent staining method to vitally identify live, necrotic and apoptotic cells simultaneously; first to clone the worlds first transgenic goats using somatic cell nuclear transfer. The first to have cloned two different species of animals using two novel techniques. Avocations: tennis, reading, travel, soccer. Office: TranXenoGen Inc 800 Boston Turnpike Shrewsbury MA 01545 Office Fax: 508-842-2786. E-mail: abaguisi@tranxenogen.com.

BAGWELL, JEFF (JEFFREY ROBERT BAGWELL), professional baseball player; b. Boston, May 27, 1968; Grad., Hartford Coll. With Boston Red Sox, 1989-90; first baseman Houston Astros, 1991—. Mem. Nat. League All-Star Team, 1994, 96. Recipient Nat. League Gold glove, 1994; named Ea. League MVP, 1990, Nat. League Rookie Player of Yr., Sporting News, 1991, Nat. League Rookie of Yr., Baseball Writers' Assn. Am., 1991, Nat. League MVP, 1994, Major League Player of Yr., Sporting News, 1994, First Baseman, Sporting News Nat. League All-Star Team, 1994, First Baseman, Sporting News Nat. League Silver Slugger Team, 1994. Office: Houston Astros PO Box 288 Houston TX 77001-0288

BAGWELL, KIM DIANE, accountant; b. Santa Ana, Calif., Apr. 26, 1957; d. Howard Vernon and Mary Louise (Countryman) Horner; m. Roger Odell Standridge, Jan. 7, 1978 (div. Aug. 1983); m. Rick Bagwell, July 27, 1996; 1 child, Kathelyn Hope. BSBA, Okla. State U., 1984; Cert. in Music Min., Bible Sch., Tulsa, 1993. CPA, Okla. Acct. Kerr-McGee Corp., Oklahoma City, 1980-82, Warren Petroleum Co., Tulsa, 1983, Occidental Petroleum Co., Tulsa, 1985-89, Phillips Petroleum Co., Bartlesville, 1990-92, Amoco Prodn. Co., Tulsa, 1994-96; owner Multinet Internat., 1988-96. Auditor Ernst & Young, Tulsa, 1984-85. Vol. med. missions team to Nigeria, 1990, Bulgaria, 1991, Latvia, 1993; mem. min. music Charismatic Ch. Mem. AICPAs, NAFE, Okla. Soc. CPAs, Nat. Assn. Accts., Toastmasters, Phi Kappa Phi, Beta Gamma Sigma, Beta Alpha Psi. Republican. Avocations: singing, performing in musicals, snow and water skiing, sailing, softball. Home: PO Box 686 Charleston IL 61920-0686

BAGWILL, JOHN WILLIAMS, retired pension fund company executive; b. Seattle, Aug. 9, 1930; s. John Williams and Amy (Munday) B.; m. Emily Bend Sedgwick, Dec. 28, 1953; children: John Williams III, David Sedgwick, Elizabeth Bagwill Komjathy. BA, Hamilton Coll., 1952; MBA, Harvard U., 1958. CFP. Asst. to pres. George O. Muir, Inc., N.Y.C., 1961-64; v.p. Fin. Instns. Retirement Fund, White Plains, N.Y., 1964-85, exec. v.p., 1985-87, pres., 1987-94; ret., 1994. Gov. Newport (R.I.) Health Care Corp., 1997; cons. long-term care issues, 1999—. Bd. dirs. Town Club New Castle, Chappaqua, N.Y., 1975-79, pres., 1978-79; alumni coun. Hamilton Coll., 1977-82, pres., 1980-82; trustee, treas. Newport Art Mus., 1997—. Mem. Newport Reading Rm. Episcopalian. E-mail: jbagwilljr@aol.com.

BAHAL, VISHAL, cardiologist; b. Ghaziabad, India, July 28, 1967; s. Prem Nath and Lata Bahal. BS in Biology with honors, Ursinus Coll., 1989; DO, Phila. Coll. Osteo. Medicine, 1993. Diplomate Am. Bd. Internal Medicine, Am. Osteo. Bd. Internal Medicine. House physician Nazareth Hosp., Mercy Haverford Hosp., 1995-97, Holy Redeemer Hosp., Meadowbrook, Pa., 1995-97, 99—; rotary internship U. Med. and Dentistry of N.J., Stratford, 1993-94; intern and resident in internal medicine Med. Coll. Pa.-Hahnemann U. Hosp., Phila., 1994-97; hospitalist ICU Vencor Hosp., Chgo., 1998-99; hospitalist CCU and postsurg. cardiac unit St. Francis Hosp., Evanston, Ill., 1997-99; cardiology fellow Deborah Heart and Lung Ctr., Browns Mills, NJ, 1999—2002; staff ICU/CCU phys. Hamilton Hosp., 2000—01; invasive cardiologist Chester County Hosp., West Chester, Pa., 2002—. Ho. physician Holy Redeemer Hosp., 1995—97, med. housestaff coord.; officer com. on interns and residents U. Medicine and Dentistry of N.J., 1993—94; med. technologist Temple U. Hosp., Phila., 1991—93. Active Social Vision of Mankind, 1994—. Mem.: ACP, AMA, N.J. Assn. Osteo Physicians and Surgeons, Am. Coll. Osteo. Internists, Am. Osteo. Assn., Am. Coll. Cardiology, Beta Beta Beta. Avocations: weightlifting, sports, boating, video movie production, flying. Home: 2 Elizabeth Ct Downingtown PA 19335

BAHAR, EZEKIEL, electrical engineering educator; U.S. citizen; s. Silas and Hannah Bahar; m. Ophira Rodoff; children: Zillah, Ruth Iris, Ron Jonathan. BS, Technion IIT, Haifa, Israel, 1958, MS, 1960; PhD, U. Colo., 1964. Instr. Technion, Haifa, Israel, 1960-62; rsch. assoc. U. Colo., Boulder, 1962-64, asst. prof., 1964-67; assoc. prof. U. Nebr., Lincoln, 1967-71, prof., 1971-80, Durham prof., 1981-89, George Holmes Disting. prof., 1989—, Univ. prof., 1999—, dir. program revs., 1981-83. Vis. prof. NOAA, Boulder, 1979; prin. investigator radio wave propagation in complex media, remote sensing, nanotechnology rsch., 1964--. Pres. faculty senate U. Nebr., Lincoln, 1980. Recipient Outstanding Rsch. and Creative Activities award U. Nebr., Lincoln, 1980, Scholarship citation U. Colo., Boulder, 1964 Fellow IEEE (life); mem. Internat. Union Radio Sci. (rep. 1978, 81, 84, 87, 90, 93, 96, 99, 2002). Avocation: swimming. Home: 2431 Bretigne Dr Lincoln NE 68512-1913 Office: U Nebr WSEC 218 N Lincoln NE 68588-0511 E-mail: ebahar1@unl.edu.

BAHARIEV, DIMITAR B. plant pathologist; b. Sousam, Bulgaria, June 6, 1939; arrived in U.S., 2002; s. Bahari A. Bahariev and Altunka Baharieva; m. Vasilka Baharieva, Mar. 19; children: Borislav, Albena Baharieva. MS in Viticulture and Hort., Higher Inst. of Agr. Plovdiv, Bulgaria, 1966; PhD in Agronomy, Plant Protection Inst., Kostinbrod, Bulgaria, 1980. Advisor agr. Ministry of Agr. and Food Industry, Sofia, Bulgaria, 1992; head dept. plant protection Maritsa Rsch. Inst. of Vegetable Crops, Plovdiv, 1994—, chmn. gen. assembly of scientists, 1994—. Mem. State New Variety Commn., Sofia, State Food and Drug Commn., Sofia; expert Arbitration Ct., Plovdiv. Contbr. ; author: books and brochures. Nominee Internat. Peace Prize, United Cultural Conv., 2002; named Man of the Yr., Am. Biog. Inst., 2001; recipient Gold medal, 4th Internat. Fair, Plovdiv. Mem.: AAAS, Union of Scientists of Bulgaria. Achievements include patents for in plant protection and plant breeding. Avocation: history. Home: 260 N West Ave Elmhurst IL 60126

BAHBAH, BISHARA ASSAD, editor, business executive, philanthropist; b. Jerusalem, Apr. 10, 1958; came to U.S., 1976; s. Assad R. and Filomene H. Bahbah; m. Heather Del Parsons, Sept. 24, 1983; children: Leila Jean, As'ad Victor, Jubran Ronald, Remzi Robert. BA, Brigham Young U., 1979; MA, Harvard U., 1981, PhD, 1983; cert., George Washington U., 1988. Editor-in-chief Al-Fajr Newspaper, Jerusalem, 1983-84; dir. United Palestinian Appeal, Washington, 1985-87; pres., chmn., CEO Internat. Mktg. and Fund Raising Assocs., Inc., Scottsdale, Ariz., 1987—2002; pres., CEO Ethnic Lists & Marketing, LLC, 2003—; editor-in-chief The Return Mag., Washington, 1988-90; exec. com. mem. Ctr. Policy Analysis on Palestine, Washington, 1990-96; assoc. dir. Middle East Inst., Kennedy Sch., Harvard U., 1992-96; pres., CEO TV Devel. Ptnrs., Inc., N.Y.C., 1997; regional rep. Middle East and Africa RSL COM and RSL Studios, N.Y.C., 1997-98; pres., CEO BHB Enterprises, Woodbridge, Va., 1998—2002, Holy Land Enterprises, Woodbridge, 1999-2000; pres. Eden Advisors, Mass., 1994—96. Vis. prof. Brigham Young U., Provo, Utah, 1985, adj. prof. polit. sci., 1985-90; sr. fellow Kennedy Sch. Govt. Harvard U., 1996-98; guest columnist The Arizona Republic, 2000—. Author: Israel and Latin America--The Military Connection, 1986; mem. adv. bd. Internat. Ency. Comm., 1984—. Chmn., bd. trustees Palestine Children's Relief Fund, U.S.A., 1999-2002; bd. dirs. Givat Haviva, U.S.A., Palestine Consultancy Group, Jerusalem: mem. Nat. Policy Coun., Arab Am. Inst., Washington; mem. Palestinian Del. to the Multi-Lateral Peace Talks on Arms Control and Regional Security, 1991-2000; bd. dirs. Ariz. Acad. Decathlon. Mem. Assn. Fundraising Profls., Direct Mktg. Assn. Washington. E-mail: imfra@cox.net.

BAHCALL, JOHN NORRIS, astrophysicist; b. Shreveport, La., Dec. 30, 1934; s. Malcolm and Mildred (Lazarus) Bahcall; m. Neta Assaf, Sept. 21, 1966; children: Ron Assaf, Dan Ophir, Orli Gilat. BA, U. Calif., 1956; MSc, U. Chgo., 1957; PhD, Harvard U., 1961; DSc (hon.), U. Pa., 2000; degree (hon.), U. Chgo., 2000; DSc, U. Notre Dame, 2001. Rsch. assoc. Ind. U., 1961—62; theoretical physicist, rsch. assoc., asst. prof., then assoc. prof. theoretical physics Calif. Inst. Tech., 1962—70; mem. Inst. Advanced Study, Princeton, NJ, 1968—70, prof. natural scis., 1971—, Richard Black prof. natural scis., 1997—. Mem. physics adv. panel NSF; mem.-at.large, large space telescope mgmt. and ops. working group NASA; chair Nat. Underground Sci. Lab. Com., 2001—. Co-author (with Field and Arp): The Redshift Controversy, 1973; author: Neutrino Astrophysics, 1989. Recipient Disting. Pub. Svc. medal, NASA, 1992, Nev. medal, 1994, Dannie Heineman prize for Astrophysics, Am. Inst. for Physics, 1994, U. Helsinki Award medal, 1996, U.S. Nat. medal of sci., 1998, medal Coll. de France, 1999, Berhard Lecture and Medal, Royal Swedish Acad. Scis., 2001; fellow, Sloan Found., 1968—71. Fellow: Am. Phys. Soc. (Hans Bethe prize 1998); mem.: NRC (chmn. Astronomy and Astrophysics Suvey Com. 1989—91), NAS, Am. Philos. Soc., Academia Europaea, Internat. Astron. Union (vice chair U.S. Nat. Com. 1996—98), Am. Astron. Soc. (pres.-elect 1989—90, pres. 1990—92, Helen B. Werner prize 1969, Russell prize 1999), Nat. Acad. Arts and Scis. Jewish. Office: Inst Advanced Study Sch Natural Scis Einstein Dr Princeton NJ 08540

BAHCALL, SAFI R. pharmaceutical executive; s. John N. and Neta A. Bahcall. PhD, Stanford U., 1995. Post-doctoral fellow, theoretical physics U. of Calif., Berkeley, 1995—97; cons. McKinsey & Co., N.Y.C., 1997—2001; CEO Synta Pharmaceuticals, Lexington, Mass., 2001—. Fellow, NSF, 1988—91, ARCS Fellowship, Stanford U., 1991—93, Miller Post-Doctoral Fellowship, U. of Calif. Berkeley, 1995—97. Office: Synta Pharmaceuticals 45 Hartwell Ave Lexington MA 02421

BAHIRI, SIMCHA, economist; b. N.Y.C., Aug. 24, 1927; arrived in Israel, 1950; s. Juda and Sarah (Rosenbaum) Breitbart; m. Anita Hudaly, Oct. 4, 1954 (div. Oct. 1978); children: Amos, Gidon, Kim; m. Doreen Belle Mirvish, Jan. 25, 1979 B Engring., Liverpool (Eng.) Coll. Tech., 1956; MSc, U. Birmingham, Eng., 1967, PhD, 1970. Recipient cert. Ford Found., 1966, Parapsychology Found., 1984, Armand Hammer Peace Found., 1985; chartered engr. Cons. Matmatica, Princeton, N.J., 1969-71; sr. lectr. Tel Aviv U., 1971-75, sr. rschr. Interdisciplinary Forecasting Ctr., 1980-85, dir. Bahiri Peace Econs., 1986—; mng. dir. Icarus Health Aids, Netanya, Israel, 1971-75; vis. prof. Rensselaer Poly. Inst., Troy, N.Y., 1979-80. Forecasting cons. Nat. Cement Co., Tel Aviv, 1972--; cons. Econ. Coop. Found., Tel Aviv, 1992-95; program specialist Instn. Adminstrn., Enugu, Nigeria, 1963-66. Author: Peaceful Separation or Enforced Unity, 1984; co-author: Peace Pays, 1993; contbr. articles to profl. jours. Co-chair Israel/Palestine Ctr. for Rsch. and Info., Bethlehem and Jerusalem, 1992—; founding bd. dirs. Palestine Israel Jour., Jerusalem, 1994—; trustee Internat. Ctr. for Peace in the Mid. East, Tel Aviv, 1984-97. With USN, 1945-46. Mem. Man, Nature and Law, Assn. Civil rights in Israel. Social Democrat. Jewish. Avocations: cartography, swimming, hiking, theater, music. Home and Office: 28 Hovevei Zion St Tel Aviv 63346 Israel E-mail: dervish_il@yahoo.com.

BAHL, ROY WINFORD, economist, educator, consultant; b. Miami, Fla., June 28, 1939; s. Roy Winford and Vista Lee (Becks) B.; m. Marilyn Seifried, Dec. 22, 1963; children: Renee, Alexandra, Martin, Ashley. BA, Greenville (Ill.) Coll., 1961; MA, U. Ky., 1963, PhD in Econs., 1965. Asst. prof. econs. W.Va. U., Morgantown, 1965-67; economist IMF, Washington, 1967-71; prof. econs. Syracuse (N.Y.) U., 1971-88, Maxwell prof. polit. economy, 1985-88; prof. econs. Ga. State U., Atlanta, 1988-96, dir. Policy Rsch. Ctr., 1988-96, dean Andrew Young sch. policy studies, 1996—. Bd. dirs. N.Y. State Energy Authority, Albany, 1979-87, Lincoln Found., Phoenix, 1986-93; mem. So. Growth Policies Bd., 1997—; cons. World Bank, Washington, 1971—. Author: Urban Public Finance in LDCs, 1992, Economic Growth and Fiscal Plan, 1992, Fiscal Policy in China, 1999; editor: The Jamaican Tax Reform, 1991. Recipient Fiscal medal Govt. of Philippines, 1986, Disting. Economist award State of Ky., 1989. Mem. Nat. Tax Assn. (pres. 1986), Am. Econs. Assn., So. Econs. Assn. (v.p. 1993). Democrat. Office: Ga State U Andrew Young Sch Policy Studies 35 Broad St Ste 602 Atlanta GA 30303-2302

BAHL, SAROJ MEHTA, nutritionist, educator; b. New Delhi, Apr. 4, 1946; came to U.S., 1972; d. L.D. and G.D. Mehta; m. Vishwa Mittar Bahl; children: Rahul, Ragini. BS in Home Sci., Delhi U., 1965, MS in Nutrition, 1967, PhD in Nutrition, 1973. Lectr. Lady Irwin Coll., New Delhi, 1970-71; instr. U. N.D., Grand Forks, 1972-74; from rsch. assoc. med. sch. to assoc. prof. dental sch. U. Tex., Houston, 1976—2002, assoc. prof. dental sch., 2002—. Program dir. Peace Corps, Houston, 1984. Author: Nutritional Management of the AIDS Patient; contbr. articles to profl. jours. Den leader Boy Scouts Am., Hosuton, 1983; mem. ednl. com. March of Dimes, Houston, 1986—; mem. exec. bd. Indo-Am. Charity Found. of Houston, 1995-98. Recipient several awards for tchg. excellence including John P. McGovern award, 1992, 95; named Outstanding Dietetic Educator Tex. Tex. Dietetic Assn., 1995; nominated for U.S. Prof. of Yr., 1993, 94. Mem. Am. Inst. Life Threatening Illness (assoc.), Soc. Nutrition Edn. (editor newsletter), Minority Faculty Assn. (pres. 1996-97), Vivekananda Vedanta Soc. (pres. 1993-1998). Avocations: painting, music, reading. Office: U Tex Dental Sch Rm B-37 6516 MD Anderson Blvd Houston TX 77025 E-mail: Saroj.M.Bahl@uth.tmc.edu.

BAHLER, GARY M. lawyer; BA, Houghton Coll., 1973; JD, Cornell U., 1976. Bar: N.Y. 1977. Sec., dep. gen. counsel Foot Locker, Inc. (formerly Venator Group, Inc.), N.Y.C., 1991-93, v.p., gen. counsel, sec., 1993-98, sr. v.p., gen. counsel, sec., 1998—. Office: Foot Locker Inc 112 W 34th St New York NY 10120

BAHLKE, CONRAD GEORGE, lawyer; b. Phila., Sept. 17, 1958; m. Roxane Orgill; children: Charlotte, Nolan. BA, Oberlin Coll., 1980; MBA, JD, U. Chgo., 1984. Bar: Mass. 1985, N.Y. 1988. Atty. Fed. Res. Bd., Washington, 1984-87; assoc. White & Case, N.Y.C., 1987-94; assoc., spl. counsel Schulte Roth & Zabel LLP, N.Y.C., 1994-2000; ptnr. Weil, Gotshal & Manges LLP, N.Y.C., 2000—. Contbr. articles to profl. publs. Trustee Oberlin (Ohio) Coll., 1980-83. Mem. ABA (com. on futures and derivative investments, chmn. subcom. 2000—), Assn. Bar City N.Y. (com. on futures regulation 1992-95, 96-99. 2000—, N.Y. County Lawyers' Assn. (banking law com., chmn. subcom. 1990-98), Phi Beta Kappa. Episcopalian. Avocations: art, music, travel, sports. Office: Weil Gotshal & Manges LLP 767 5th Ave New York NY 10153 E-mail: conrad.bahlke@weil.com.

BAHLKE, GEORGE WILBON, English language educator; b. Chgo., June 20, 1934; s. William Herbert and Agnes Louise (Wilbon) B.; m. Valerie Worth, Dec. 28, 1955 (dec. July 1994); children: Conrad George, Catherine Worth Bahlke Hornstein, Margaret Grey Bahlke Diskin; m. Felicity Isabel Colby, Feb. 22, 1998. AB, U. Chgo., 1953, MA, 1956; BA, Swarthmore Coll., 1955; PhD, Yale U., 1960. Instr. Mary Washington Coll., Fredericksburg, Va., 1958-60; asst. prof. Rutgers U., New Brunswick, NJ, 1960-61, Middlebury (Vt.) Coll., 1961-69; asst. prof., assoc. prof., then prof. Kirkland Coll., Clinton, NY, 1969—78; prof. English, Hamilton Coll., Clinton, NY, 1978—. Author: The Later Auden, 1970 (MLA Scholars Libr. award 1970), Critical Essays on W.H. Auden, 1991; contbr. articles to profl. jours., including Virginia Woolf Miscellany, D.H. Lawrence Rev. Recipient Outstanding Tchr. award Hamilton Coll. Class of 1962, 1992. Mem. MLA, D.H. Lawrence Soc., Virginia Woolf Soc. Democrat. Episcopalian. Office: 198 College Hill Rd Clinton NY 13323-1218 E-mail: gbahlke@aol.com.

BAHLMAN, DUDLEY RHODES, journalist; b. New Haven, Conn., June 10, 1953; s. Dudley Ward Rhodes and Jean Maxwell (Mitchell) B.; m. Arlene Marie Thomason, Dec. 10, 1983 (div. Dec., 1988), 1 child Jaycee Ann. BA, New Eng. Coll., 1977. Reporter, editor Troy (N.Y.) Times Record, 1977-86; editor Laurin Pub. Co., Pittsfield, Mass., 1986-88; comms. dir. Profit Ptnrs. in Mktg., Pittsfield, 1988-89; reporter The Berkshire Eagle, Pittsfield, 1989—. Mem. Soc. Profl. Journalists Home: 39 Sabin Dr Williamstown MA 01267 Office: The Berkshire Eagle 75 S Church St Pittsfield MA 01201-6166 E-mail: dbahlman@berkshireeagle.com.

BAHLMAN, WILLIAM THORNE, JR., retired lawyer; b. Cin., Jan. 9, 1920; s. William Thorne and Janet (Rhodes) B.; m. Nancy W. DeCamp, Mar. 21, 1953; children: Charles R., William Ward, Baker D. BA, Yale U., 1941, LL.B., 1947. Bar: Ohio 1947. Prin. Paxton & Seasongood, L.P.A., Cin., 1947-67, 73-88; ptnr. Paxton & Seasongood, Cin., 1954-67, Thompson Hine, LLP, Cin., 1989-94; prof. law U. Cin. Coll. Law, 1967-73, lectr., 1965-67, 73-77; ret., 1994. Served with USAAF, 1942-46. Mem. Am. Law Inst., ABA, Ohio State Bar Assn., Cin. Bar Assn. Office: Thompson Hine LLP 312 Walnut St Fl 14 Cincinnati OH 45202-4024

BAHMAN, MUJIBUR, engineer; b. Mathbaria, Bangladesh, Dec. 1, 1958; came to U.S., 1992; s. Abdul Hakim Howlader and Rowshonara Begum. MSME with honors, Kiev Inst. Civil Aviation Engr, Russia, 1983, PhD in Tech. Sci., 1987. Stuctural and design engr. Bangladesh Airlines, Dhaka, 1987-92; vis. rsch. scholar U. Mich., Ann Arbor, 1992-94; design engr. Meritor Automotive, Troy, Mich., 1998; vehicle devel. engr. Daimler Chrysler, Auburn Hills, Mich., 1998—. Contbr. articles to profl. jours. Mem.: ASME, AAAS, Math. Assn. Am. Avocations: reading philosophy, theory of aesthetics, methods of science. Home: 3019 W 13 Mile Rd Apt 214 Royal Oak MI 48073-2956 Office: Daimler Chrysler Corp CIMS # 484-14-01 800 Chrysler Dr Auburn Hills MI 48326-2757

BAHN, GILBERT SCHUYLER, retired mechanical engineer, researcher, novelist; b. Syracuse, N.Y., Apr. 25, 1922; s. Chester Bert and Irene Eliza (Schuyler) B.; m. Iris Cummings Birch, Sept. 14, 1957 (dec.); 1 child, Gilbert Kennedy. BS, Columbia U., 1943; MSME, Rensselaer Poly. Inst., 1965; PhD in Engring., Columbia Pacific U., 1979. Registered profl. engr., N.Y., Calif. Chem. engr. GE Co., Pittsfield, Mass., 1946-48, devel. engr. Schenectady, 1948-53; sr. thermodynamics engr. Marquardt Co., Van Nuys, Calif., 1953-54, rsch. scientist, 1954-64, rsch. cons., 1964-70; engring. specialist LTV Aerospace Corp., Hampton, Va., 1970-88, ret., 1988. Freelance rsch. FDR at Nadir, 1988-2000, Am. hist. demography, 2000—; mem. JANNAF performance standardization working group, 1966-83, Thermochemistry Working Group, 1967-72; propr. Schuyler Tech. Libr., 1952—. Author: Reaction Rate Compliation for the H-O-N System, 1968, Blue and White and Evergreen: William Byron Mowery and His Novels, 1981, Oliver Norton Worden's Family, 1982, Studies in American Historical Demography to 1850, Vol. 1, 1987, Overall Population Trends, Age Profiles, and Settlement, Vol. 2, 1987, The Wordens, Representative of the Native Northern Population, Vol. 3, 1994, Computerized Treatment and Statistical Evaluation of the 1790 Federal Census for the Northern Half of the State of New York, Vol. 4, 1999, Computerized Treatment and Statistical Evaluation of the 1790 Federal Census for the Southern Half of the State of New york, Vol. 5, 1999, Surname Counts and Given Name Counts in the 1790 Federal Census of New York, The Ancient Worden Family in America: A Story of Growth and Migration, 1988, FDR at Nadir: 1937 & 1938, 1993, Senator Alva B. Adams of Colorado, 1993, Senator Bennett Champ Clark of Missouri, 1993, Senator Walter F. George of Georgia, 1993, Senator Guy Mark Gillette of Iowa, 1993, Senator Augustine Lonergan of Connecticut, 1993, Senator Frederick Van Nuys of Indiana, 1993, Senator Patrick Anthony McCarran of Nevada, 1994, Senator Ellison D. Smith of South Carolina, 1995, Senator Millard E. Tydings of Maryland, 1996, Franklin D. Roosevelt's Appointments and Itineraries for the New Deal Years in Alphabetical Fashion, 1996, Infestation of Yankees: Reference Guide to Union Troops in Confederate Territory, 1998, American Place Names of Long Ago, 1998, One Man's Platform, 1998, Slaves and Nonwhite Free Persons in the 1790 Federal Census of New York, 2000, Franklin D. Roosevelt's Appointments and Itineraries for the War Years in Alphabetical Fashion, 2000, Worden Surname Census, 1640-1850, As of 2000, 2000, Four Novels: We Were All Men of Honor, Paul Adams, Hero?, "Need to Know," 2001, Vicky in Time: Alternative History of the Princess Royal, Victoria Adelaide Mary Louisa, 2002, The Worden Surname from Peter Worden of Yarmouth to 1850, 2002, The Long Life of Enos Warren, 2003, collected novels: Other Men's Dreams, Mother was a Faro Dealer, All the Winter of Our Sins, Red Red One, Plastic Cookies, Bottled Tea, Job Never Had it So Good, Certain Rules, Jasmine, Ambition, Christy and Joey and Five Long Years, 1940-1945, 2003; founding editor Pyrodynamics, 1963-69; procs. editor Kinetics, Equilibria and Performance of High Temperature Systems, 1960, 1963, 1967; contbr. articles to profl. jours. Air raid warden, 1941-43; active Boy Scouts Am., 1958-78. Capt. USAAF, 1943-46. Recipient Silver Beaver award Boy Scouts Am., 1970. Mem. ASME, Combustion Inst. (sec. western states sect. 1957-71), Soc. for Preservation Book of Common Prayer. Democrat. Episcopalian (Vestryman 1968-70). Achievements include discovery of free radical chemical species diboron monoxide, 1966. Home: 4519 N Ashtree St Moorpark CA 93021-2156

BAHNIUK, EUGENE, mechanical engineering educator; b. Weirton, W.Va., Mar. 10, 1926; s. Michael and Mary (Sikora) B.; m. Margaret J. Hilton, June 11, 1977; children— Douglas Eugene, Joy Ruth, Barbara Jane, Becky Lynn, David Robert BS, Case Inst. Tech., 1950, MS, 1961; PhD, Case Western Res. U., 1970. Registered profl. engr., Ohio. Devel. engr. Air Brake, Watertown, N.Y., 1950-54; project engr. Lear Corp., Elyria, Ohio, 1954-56; supr. Borg Warner Corp., Bedford Heights, Ohio, 1956-61; mgr. research and devel. Weatherhead Corp., Cleve., 1961-68; faculty Case Western Res. U., Cleve., 1970—, prof. mech. engring., 1972—. Contbr. articles to profl. jours.; patentee in field Served to 1st lt., inf. U.S. Army, 1944-46 NIH fellow, 1969-70, NSF fellow, 1968-69, NASA fellow, 1982 Fellow ASTM (award of merit 1988); mem. Am. Soc. Biomechanics, Internat. Soc. Ski Safety, Sigma Xi Home: 7629 Cairn Ln Gates Mills OH 44040-9738 Office: Case Western Reserve Univ Engring Dept Cleveland OH 44106

BAHR, BEVERLY KATHERINE, critical care nurse; b. St. Louis, Oct. 23, 1950; d. Leeds Brown and Ruth Katherine (Purzner) Berridge; m. Robert John Bahr, Jan. 12, 1980; children: Kris, Zach, Gabe. Diploma, Luth. Hosp. Sch. Nursing, St. Louis, 1971; BA, Stephens Coll., Columbia, Mo., 1975; BSN, St. Mary of the Plains, Dodge City, Kans., 1988; MS, Okla. U., 1993. CCRN, Cert. ACLS, ACLS instr. Staff nurse ICU Boone County Hosp., Columbia, Mo., 1971-73; staff nurse dialysis U. Mo. Med. Ctr., Columbia, 1973-74; staff nurse ICU/Critical Care Unit U. Mo. Med. Ctr./Boone County, Columbia, 1974-76; staff devel. coord. U. Mo. Med. Ctr., Columbia, 1976, head nurse cardiac cath lab., 1977-79; instr. Stephens Coll., Columbia, 1975-76; asst. head nurse med. ICU/Critical Care Unit Parkland Hosp., Dallas, 1977-78; head nurse cardiac rehab. Placentia (Calif.) Linda Hosp., 1980-82; staff nurse ICU Stillwater (Okla.) Hosp., 1986-90; staff nurse ICU float pool Okla. Meml. Hosp., Oklahoma City, 1989-92, transplant program mgr., coord., 1992-93, critical care instr., 1994-97, cardiovascular clin. nurse specialist, 1997—, cardiac rehab. coord., 1998—. Cons. Early Autumn Residential Care Home, Stillwater, 1991-92; coord., instr. ACLS Am. Heart Assn., Oklahoma City, 1988—; class alumni reporter Luth. Hosp. Sch. Nursing Alumni Assn., Stillwater, 1988, 92, 95. Isntr. Sunday Sch. Zion Luth. Ch., 1985-2001, midweek sch., 1985, chmn. bd. edn.; pres. Vet. Wives Aux., Stillwater, 1986-87. Mem. AACN (pres. Ctrl. Mo. chpt. 1975, membership chair 1994-96, program chmn. 1996-97, pres. elect 1997-98, pres. 1998-99), Grad. Nurse Assn. (sec. 1992), Sigma Theta Tau. Republican. Avocations: hiking, reading, biking, dancing. Home: 1119 Oakridge Dr Stillwater OK 74074-1111

BAHR, CARMAN BLOEDOW, internist; b. Middletown, Ohio, Mar. 24, 1931; d. Edwin Louis and Berneice Mae (Bacon) Bloedow; m. Walter Julien Bahr, Aug. 28, 1968 (dec. Sept. 1971). BA cum laude, Miami U., Oxford, Ohio, 1952; MD, Ohio State U., 1956; MS, U. Okla., 1996. Cert. diabetes educator, 1986, 92. Intern St. Luke's Hosp., Chgo., 1956-57; resident U. Okla. Health Sci. Ctr., 1957-60; assoc. prof. medicine Okla. Health Sci. Ctr., 1971-93, prof. emeritus, 1993. Fellow: ACP (Joslin 50 Yr. medal, cert. of achievement 2001); mem.: AMA (Physician's Recognition award 1976, 1979, 1982, 1985, 1988, 1991, 1994, 1998), Okla. Med. Assn., Am. Med. Women's Assn., Western Okla. Diabetes Educators, Am. Assn. Diabetes Educators, Am. Diabetes Assn. (chpt. pres. 1989, Robert Endress award 1985). Home: 5609 N Everest Ave Oklahoma City OK 73111-6729 Office: VA Med Ctr 921 NE 13th St Oklahoma City OK 73104-5007 E-mail: cbb2@cox.net.

BAHR, DONALD WALTER, retired chemical engineer; b. Chgo., Dec. 13, 1927; s. Walter James and Justine Antonia (Schwegler) Bahr; m. Mary Estelle Zieverink, Oct. 15, 1960; children: Donald Walter Jr., Susan Mary. BS ChemE, U. Ill., 1949; MSChemE, MS in Gas Tech., Ill. Inst. Tech., 1951. Registered Profl. Engr., Ohio. Aero rsch. scientist Lewis Flight Propulsion Lab. NASA, Cleve., 1951—54; chem. engr. GE Co., Cin., 1956—62, engring. mgr. Phila., 1962—68, GE Aircraft Engines, Phila., 1968—94. Vice chmn. jet engine fuels panel NASA Lewis Rsch. Ctr., Cleve., 1973—76. Contbr. articles to profl. jours. 1st lt. USAF, 1954—56. Named to Propulsion Hall of Fame for GE, 1995; recipient Outstanding Engring. Achievement award, GE Co., 1982. Fellow: ASME (combustion and fuels com. 1975—, vice chmn. combustion and fuels com. 1985—87, chmn.combustion and fuels com. 1987—89, Tom Sawyer award 1998, Aircraft Engine Tech. award 2003), AIAA (Air Breathing Propulsion award 1983); mem.: NAE, Coordinating Rsch. Coun. (aviation fuel, lubricant and other equpment com.), Gen. Aviation Mfrs. Assn. (environ. com.), Aerospace Industries Assn. (chmn. aircraft engine emissions com. 1971—95), Combustion Inst. (bd. advisors ctrl. states sect. 1986—, chmn. bd. advisors 1993—95, chmn. ctrl. states sect. 1995—97). Republican. Roman Catholic. Home: 6576 Branford Ct Cincinnati OH 45236-2212

BAHR, EHRHARD, Germanic languages and literature educator; b. Kiel, Germany, Aug. 21, 1932; came to U.S., 1956; s. Klaus and Gisela (Badenhausen) B.; m. Diana Meyers, Nov. 21, 1973; stepchildren: Gary, Timothy, Christopher. Student, U. Heidelberg, Germany, 1952-53, U. Freiburg, 1953-56; MS Ed. (Fulbright scholar), U. Kans., 1956-58; postgrad., U. Cologne, 1959-61; PhD, U. Calif., Berkeley, 1968. Asst. prof. German UCLA, 1968-70, assoc. prof., 1970-72, prof., 1972—, chmn. dept. Germanic langs., 1981-84, 93-98, chair grad. council, 1988-89. Author: Irony in the Late Works of Goethe, 1972, Georg Lukacs, 1970, Ernst Bloch, 1974, Nelly Sachs, 1980; editor: Kant, What is Enlightenment?, 1974, Goethe, Wilhelm Meister's Journeyman Years, 1982, History of German Literature, 3 vols., 1987-88; co-editor: The Internalized Revolution: German Reactions to the French Revolution, 1789-1989, 1992; commentary: Thomas Mann: Death in Venice, 1991; contbr. articles to profl. jours. Author: Irony in the Late Works of Goethe, 1972, Georg Lukacs, 1970, Ernst Bloch, 1974, Nelly Sachs, 1980; editor: Kant, What is Enlightenment, 1974, Goethe, Wilhelm Meister's Journeyman Years, 1982, History of German Literature, 3 vols., 1987-88, 2nd edit., 1998-99, The Novel as Archive: The Genesis, Reception and Criticism of Goethe's Wilhelm Meisters Wanderjahre, 1998; co-editor: The Internalized Revolution: German Reactions to the French Revolution, 1789-1989, 1992; commentary: Thomas Mann: Death in Venice, 1991; contbr. articles to profl. jours. Recipient Disting. Teaching award UCLA, 1970, Humanities Inst. award, 1972, summer stipend NEH, 1978 Mem. MLA, Am. Soc. 18th Century Studies, Am. Assn. Tchrs. German, Western Soc. 18th Century Studies, German Studies Assn. (pres. 1987-88), Pacific Ancient & Modern Lang. Assn., Lessing Soc., Goethe Soc. N.Am. (exec. sec. 1979-89, pres. 1995-97). Office: UCLA Dept Germanic Langs Los Angeles CA 90095-1539 E-mail: bahr@humnet.ucla.edu.

BAHR, HOWARD MINER, sociologist, educator; b. Provo, Utah, Feb. 21, 1938; s. A. Francis and Louie Jean (Miner) B.; m. Rosemary Frances Smith, Aug. 28, 1961 (div. 1985); children: Bonnie Louise, Howard McKay, Rowena Ruth, Tanya Lavonne, Christopher J., Laura L., Stephen S., Rachel M.; m. Kathleen Slaugh, May 1, 1986; children: Alden Keith, Jonathan Andrew, Dmitry Michael, Anton Hinckley. BA with honors, Brigham Young U., 1962; MA, U. Tex., 1964, PhD, 1965. Rsch. assoc. Columbia U., N.Y.C., 1965-68; vis. lectr., summer 1968; lectr. in sociology NYU, 1967-68, Bklyn. Coll., CUNY, 1967; assoc. prof. sociology Wash. State U., Pullman, 1968-73, prof., 1972-73, chmn. dept. rural sociology, 1971-73; prof. sociology Brigham Young U., Provo, Utah, 1973—; dir. Family Rsch. Inst., 1977-83; fellow David M. Kennedy, 1992, Virginia F. Cutler lectr., 1997; vis. prof. sociology U. Va., 1976-77, 84-85. Author: Skid Row: An Introduction to Disaffiliation, 1973, Old Men Drunk and Sober, 1974, Women Alone: The Disaffiliation of Urban Females, 1976, American Ethnicity, 1979, Sunshine Widows: Adapting to Sudden Bereavement, 1980, Middletown Families, 1982, All Faithful People: Change and Continuity in Middletown's Religion, 1983, Life in Large Families, 1983, Divorce and Remarriage: Problems, Adaptations and Adjustments, 1983, Social Science Research Methods, 1984, Recent Social Trends in the United States 1960-90, 1991, Dine' Bibliography to the 1990's, 1999; contbr. articles to profl. jours.; assoc. editor: Rural Sociology, 1978-83, Jour. Marriage and the Family, 1978-83. NIMH grantee, 1968-70, 71-73; NSF grantee, 1971-72, 76-80 Mem. Soc. Applied Anthropology, Rural Sociol. Assn., Nat. Coun. Family Rels. Mem. Lds Ch. Office: Brigham Young U Dept Sociology 842 SWKT Provo UT 84602 E-mail: hmbahr@byu.edu.

BAHR, JANE MARIE, writer, retired English educator; BS in English, U. Wis., River Falls, 1971; MST in English, U. Wis., Whitewater, 1978. English tchr. Whitewater (Wis.) H.S., 1973-82, Eau Claire (Wis.) Meml. H.S., 1985, Glenwood City H.S., summers 1990-91; freelance writer Wis. Regional Writers' Assn., 1985—, Wis. Fellowship of Poets, 1981—, Wis. Arts Bd. Grant, 1998. Author poems in numerous publs. including Wis. Poets' Calendars, Poetry Out of Wis. V, Free Verse, Poetry Motel, Wallpaper Broadside Series, Poesy and Sweet Pea Press, among others. WRWA Soar scholar Sch. of Arts, U. Wis., Madison, 1999.

BAHR, LAUREN S. publishing company executive; b. New Brunswick, N.J., July 3, 1944; d. Simon A. and Rosalind J. Bahr. Student, U. Grenoble, France, 1964; BA (Branstrom scholar); MA, U. Mich., 1966. Asst. editor New Horizons Pubs., Inc., Chgo., 1967, Scholastic Mags., Inc., N.Y.C., 1968-71; supervising editor Houghton Mifflin Co., Boston, 1971; product devel. editor Appleton-Century-Crofts, N.Y.C., 1972-74; sponsoring editor McGraw-Hill, Inc., N.Y.C., 1974-75; editor Today's Sec. mag., 1975-77; sr. editor Media Systems Corp., N.Y.C., 1978; sr. editor coll. dept. CBS Coll. Pub., N.Y.C., 1978-82, mktg. mgr. fgn. langs., dir. mktg. adminstrn., 1982-83; from dir. devel. coll. divsn. to pub. cons. Harper & Row, N.Y.C., 1983-91; v.p., editl. dir. Atlas Edits., Inc., N.Y.C., 1991-98; dir. publs. Bank St. Coll. Edn., N.Y.C., 1999—2000; mng. editor Inkwell Pub., N.Y.C., 2000—02; editl. dir. 4 Lakes Colorgraphics, 2002—. Democrat. Jewish. Home: 444 E 82nd St New York NY 10028-5903

BAHR, MORTON, trade union executive; b. Bklyn., July 18, 1926; s. Martin and Elizabeth B.; m. Florence Bahr, 1945; 2 children. Student, Bklyn. Coll., 1942-43. Pres. Local 1172 Communications Workers Am., 1954-58, Organizer Dist. 1, 1958-61, dir. N.Y. State, 1961-63, asst. to v.p. Dist. 1, 1963-69, now pres. Dir. Myasthenia Gravis Found, 1962—; trustee Maritime Port Coun. AFL-CIO, 1973—; mem. exec. coun. N.Y. State AFL-CIO, 1974 Office: Comm Workers Am 501 3rd St NW Washington DC 20001-2760

BAHRAINWALA, ABDUL HUSEIN, allergist, immunologist; s. Taher A and Munira T Bahrainwala; m. Parveen Mohsin Darbar, Dec. 10, 1997; 1 child, Nisreen. MBBS, Bombay U., T.N. Med Sch., 1988; MD, Bombay Univ, T.N.Med Scool, 1992. Cert. FCAAI Am. Coll. of Allergy, Asthma & Immunology, 2001. Dir. of allergy and asthma Children's Hosp. of Mich., 1990—; asst. prof of pediat. Wayne State Univ, Detroit, 1988—. Vice chief of staff Med. Ctr. of Manchester, Tenn., 1996—97; bd. mem. U. Pediatricians, Detroit, 2002—. Rsch. grant, CRCM, 2000, WOMC, FM 104.3 Christmas for kids, 2002. Achievements include research in tansplacental transmisssion of dust mite antigen; study of probiotics to prevent allergies. Avocations: travel, reading. Office: Children's Hosp of Mich 3901 Beaubien Blvd Detroit MI 48201

BAHRE, JEANNETTE, English language and literature educator, education educator, librarian, educational consultant and tutor; b. Darby, Pa., Dec. 28, 1948; d. Paul Florent and Jeanne (Shangraw) Gibson; m. Stephen Alan Bahre, May 14, 1974; children: Kimberly, Christian, Rachael. BA, Merrimack Coll., 1970; MEd, U. Ariz., 1979. Cert. experienced tchr., NH; English and social studies tchr., Mass. Tchr. Eng. and Social Studies, Mass., 1970—; libr. St. Augustine Sch., Andover, Mass., 1980-83, Beverly Sch. for Deaf, Mass., 1988-89; instr. No. Essex C.C., Haverhill, Mass., 1982-84, libr. evening svc., 1986-88; tchr., advisor Linton Hall Sch., Bristow, Va., 1985-86; lectr. George Mason U., Fairfax, Va., 1985-86; tchr., tutor Even Start: Family Lit. Project, Amesbury, Mass., 1990-93; Chpt. I tutor Seabrook Elem. Sch., NH, 1994-95; libr. So. Hampton Pub. Libr., NH, 1994—99. Summer seminar for tchr. Univ. N.H., N.H. Humanities Found., 1997; tchr. Family Scrapbooks program New England Found. Humanities, Lawrence, Mass., 1997; participantem. summer seminar for tchr. U. NH NHH Found., 1997, 2001. Editor Four Winds, adult student Lit. Jour., 1992-96. Grantee NEH, 1988. Home: PO Box 523 Amesbury MA 01913 Office: PO Box 523 Amesbury MA 01913

BAHRI, ABBAS, mathematician, educator; b. Tunis, Tunisia, Jan. 1, 1955; s. Mohamed El Hedi Bahri and Jalila Ben Othman; m. Diana Nunziante, June 18, 1991; children: Thouraya, Kahena, Salima, Mohamed El Hedi. PhD, Paris6, Paris, France, 1977—81; alumnus ENS Ulm, ENS Ulm, Paris, France, 1974—78; agregation de mathematiques, Paris, France, 1975. Tenured Professor Rutgers/ U of NJ., 1988. Asst. prof. Ecole Polytechnique, Paris, France (incl. Monaco), 1984—93; prof. Rutgers, The State U of NJ, New Brunswick, NJ, 1988—. Author: (research in mathematics, related books) Critical Points At Infinity (Fermat Prize in Math., 1988). Dir. Ctr. for Nonlinear Analysis, New Brunswick, NJ, 1988—2002. Achievements include research in Theory Of Critical Points At Infinity. Office: Rutgers University Dept of Mathematics New Brunswick NJ 08903

BAHRIM, CRISTIAN, physicist, educator; b. Bucharest, Romania, June 8, 1967; came to U.S., 1998; s. Corneliu and Elena Bahrim; m. Bogdana Mioara, June 28, 1967. BS, H.S. Math & Physics, Bucharest, 1985; MS, U. Bucharest, 1991; PhD, U. Paris XI, 1997. Rsch. asst. Nat. Inst. Lasers, Plasma and Radiation, Bucharest, 1991-97, prin. sci. rschr., 1998-99; rsch. assoc. J. R. MacDonald Lab. Kans. State U., Manhattan, 1998—2001; vis. asst. prof. dept. chemistry and physics Lamar U., Beaumont, Tex., 2001—. Contbr. articles to profl. jours. Scholar French Govt., 1992-96. Mem. Romanian Phys. Soc., French Optical Soc., Am. Phys. Soc., Am. Assn. Advancement Sci. Romanian Orthodox. Avocations: history, astronomy, biology, sports. Office: Lamar U Dept of Chem and Physics Beaumont TX 77710 E-mail: bahrimcx@hal.lamar.edu.

BAHUN, SANJA, literature educator, researcher; b. Zagreb, Croatia, Mar. 30, 1972; d. Dragutin Bahun and Gordana Les. BA in Gen. Lit., Belgrade U., Yugoslavia, 1998; MA in Comparative Lit., Rutgers U., 2003. Fellow Rutgers U., New Brunswick, NJ, 2000—02, tchg. asst., 2002—. Author: (book) Atomic Bomb, Pain, Laughter, Spaghetti, etc., 1994, To Icarus, with Love, 1998 (Best Young Poet of Yugoslavia, 1998). Recipient grad. sch. fellowship, Rutgers U., 2000—02. Mem.: MLA, Comparative Lit. Assn. Roman Catholic. Avocations: chess, music, films. Office: Rutgers U Comparative Lit 131 George St New Brunswick NJ 08901-1414

BAI, BIN, physicist, researcher; b. Kunming, China, July 24, 1964; came to U.S., 1990; s. Huanxin Bai and Peili Tang; m. Ying Shen, Dec. 21, 1990. BS, Nanjing (China) U., 1985, MS, 1988; PhD, Washington State U., 1997. Rsch. assoc. Inst. Acoustics, Academia Sinica, Beijing, 1988-90; rsch. asst. Washington State U., Pullman, 1991-97; test engr. Micron Electronics, Inc., Nampa, Idaho, 1997—. Panel organizer Internat. Test Conf., Atlantic City, N.J., 1999. Mem. AAAS, IEEE Computer Soc. (test and technology tech. coun.), Am. Phys. Soc., N.Y. Acad. Scis. Home: 5210 N Joe Robbie Ave Boise ID 83713-1254 E-mail: bai@micron.net.

BAI, YONG, engineering executive, educator; b. Jiang Xi, China, May 30, 1963; came to U.S., 1999; s. J. Bai and M. Liu; m. Hua Peng, Aug. 26, 1986; children: Lihua, Carl Junhua. PhD in Engring., Hiroshima (Japan) U., 1989. Rschr. CRC Rsch. Ctr., Osaka, Japan, 1989-90; postdoctoral fellow Danish Tech. U., Copenhagen, 1990-91, Norwegian Tech. U., Trondheim, 1991-92; sr. engr. Det Norske Veritas, Oslo, 1992-96; postdoctoral fellow U. Calif., Berkeley, 1994; mgr. advanced engring. JP Kenny, Stavanger, Norway, 1996-99; mgr. offshore tech. Am. Bur. Shipping, 1999—2001, Shell Oil Co., Houston, 2002 . Prof. U. Stavanger, 1997-2001. Contbr. articles to profl. jours. Norwegian Rsch. Coun. fellow, Oslo, 1991. Mem. Internat. Soc. Offshore and Polar Engrs. (com., chair), Internat. Conf. Offshore Mechanics and Arctic Engring. (com., chair, Best Paper award), Soc. Naval Architects and Marine Engrs., Internat. Congress Ship and Offshore Structures. Avocations: jogging, swimming, table tennis. Home: 3415 Hackberry Ct Spring TX 77388-2712 Office: Shell Internat E&P Inc 200 N Dairy Ashford Houston TX 77079-E-mail: yong.bai@shell.com.

BAICA, MALVINA FLORICA, mathematician, educator; b. Oravita, Banat, Romania, Nov. 3, 1942; came to U.S., 1968, naturalized, 1973; d. Adam and Cornelia (Stefan) Bunghiu; m. Adrian Baica, Sept. 14, 1963. BS in Math. and Physics, U. Timisoara, Romania, 1964, MS in Math., 1965, Ill. Inst. Tech., 1974; PhD in Math., U. Houston, 1980. Asst. prof. Western Ill. U., Macomb, 1978-80, Marquette U., Milw., 1980-81, Marshall U., Huntington, W.Va., 1981-83, Valparaiso (Ind.) U., 1983-84; assoc. prof. U. Wis., Whitewater, 1984-92, prof., 1992—. Contbr. articles to profl. jour.s on algebraic number theory and number theory. Recipient U. Wis. Excellence in Rsch. award, 1988. Mem. N.Y. Acad. Scis., Pi Mu Epsilon. Achievements include development of an algorithm in a complex field which turned out to be the Generalized Euclidean Algorithm used to approach unsolved problems in algebraic number theory and number theory; discovery of Baica's trigonometric identities; research in algebraic number theory and number theory. Home: 122 N Esterly Ave Whitewater WI 53190-1313

BAIER, EDWARD JOHN, former public health official, industrial hygiene engineer, consultant; b. Pitts., Apr. 1, 1925; s. Edward O. and Lucy M. Baier; m. Grace Cecelia McDonald, Jan. 15, 1947; children: Edward Michael, Grace Cecelia. BS, U. Pitts., 1946, MPH (fellow), 1955. Lic. indsl. hygienist Ill., cert. internat. hazard control mgmt. Hazard Control Mgr. Cert. Bd., hazardous materials mgmt. Inst. Hazardous Materials Mgmt., safety profl. Bd. Cert. Safety Profls. Chief indsl. hygiene sect. Dept. Health State of Pa., 1956-68, dir. divsn. occupl. health, 1968-71, Dept. Environ. Resources, 1971; dir. Bur. Mines and Occupl. Health and Safety, 1971-72; dep. dir. Nat. Inst. for Occupl. Safety and Health, HEW, Rockville, Md., 1972-78; corp. dir. indsl. hygiene and toxicology Diamond Shamrock Corp., Cleve., Dallas, 1978-82; dir. tech. support OSHA, Dept. Labor, 1982-89; cons. in occupl. and environ. health and safety, 1989—. Lectr. in field. Contbr. articles to profl. jours. Chmn. West Shore coun. Boy Scouts Am., 1970-71; sec. Upper Allen Twp. (Pa.) Sewer Authority, 1970-72. Fellow Am. Indsl. Hygiene Assn. (pres. 1975-76, Cummings Meml. award 1982, Edward J. Baier Tech. Achievement award 1984); mem. Am. Conf. Govt. Indsl. Hygienists (chmn. 1968-69), Am. Acad. Indsl. Hygiene (founder, pres. 1987-88), Indsl. Hygiene Roundtable (steward 1975-76), Inst. Hazardous Materials Mgmt. (cert. hazardous materials mgrs. bd. examiners 1991—, bd. dirs., vice chmn. 1993-2001, Disting. Diplomate award 2001), Nat. Am. Indian Safety Coun., N.Y. Acad. Scis., Pa. Soc. Profl. Engrs., Am. Bd. Indsl. Hygiene (bd. dirs. 1970-76). Roman Catholic.

BAIER, ELIZABETH DOMSIC, lawyer; b. Chicago Heights, Ill., Aug. 4, 1954; d. Joseph Thomas and Marguerite Charlotte Domsic; m. Donald Edward Baier, June 16, 1979. BA, Ind. U., 1976, JD, 1979. Bar: Ind. 1979, U.S. Dist. Ct. (so. dist.) Ind. 1979. Pvt. practice, Mt. Vernon, Ind., 1979—; exec. dir. United Way of Posey County, Mt. Vernon, 1982—. Mem. character and fitness com. Ind. Bd. Law Examiners, Indpls., 1988—. Mem., sec. of parish coun. St. Matthew Ch., Mt. Vernon, 1987-89; bd. dirs. Mt. Vernon 175th Birthday, Inc., 1990-94, Posey County Dem. Women's Club, pres. 1991-92, 98-99, 2003—; mem. Posey County Welfare to Work Local Planning Coun., Posey County Comty. Found. Recipient Young Careerist award Bus. and Profl. Women's Club, Mt. Vernon, 1980, Woman of Yr., 1985; named to Outstanding Young Women of Am., 1983; honoree as a Sagamore of the Wabash, Gov. of Ind., 2002. Mem. Optimists (bd. dirs. Mt. Vernon chpt. 1989-92), Ind. Bar Found. (mem. pro bono com. Dist. 13, Ind. 1999—), Posey County Bar Assn. (sec./treas. 1979-80), Ind. State Bar Assn., Posey County Hist. Soc., others. Democrat. Roman Catholic. Avocations: needlepoint, gardening, reading, rose growing. Office: 128 W 3d St PO Box 367 Mount Vernon IN 47620-0367

BAIER, ROBERT EDWARD, chemist, educator; b. Buffalo, Oct. 31, 1939; s. Harry Edward Baier and Florence Elizabeth (Manno) Militello; m. Corinne May Bongiovanni, Sept. 9, 1961; children: Valerie Ann, Anne Marie. BS in Engring. and Physics, Cleve. State U., 1962; PhD in Biophysics, SUNY, Buffalo, 1966. Registered profl. engr., Ohio, N.Y. Postdoctoral fellow NAS-NRC, Washington, 1966-68; rsch. physicist Cornell Aero. Lab., Buffalo, 1968-72; staff scientist Calspan Advanced Tech. Ctr., Buffalo, 1972-84; rsch. prof. biophys. scis. SUNY, Buffalo, 1983—, exec. dir. NSF Industry/U. Coop. Rsch. Ctr., 1988—; exec. dir. Ctr. for Advanced Tech. in Healthcare, Buffalo, 1985-89; prof., dir. biomaterials grad. program SUNY, 1998—. Mem. Soc. Biomaterials (mem. coun., sec.-treas., pres. 1974—). Home: 37 Rosedale Blvd Buffalo NY 14226-3347 Office: SUNY 110 Parker Hall Buffalo NY 14214-3007

BAIGIS, WENDY SUE, probation and parole officer; b. Bellefonte, Pa., Sept. 25, 1967; d. Andrew J. and Judith A. (Miga) Baigis; m. John R. Freas, Nov. 25, 1994. BS, West Chester U., 1989, MS, 1995. Rsch. asst. U. Pa., Phila., 1985-86; pub. safety officer West Chester (Pa.) U., 1987-90; probation and parole officer Chester County Adult Parole and Probation Dept., West Chester, 1989-92, probation and parole officer specialist, 1992—. Adj. faculty Chestnut Hill Coll., Phila., 1999—, Montgomery County C.C., Blue Bell, Pa., 2000—, Imaculata U., Malvern, Pa., 2002—, Temple U., Phila., 2003—. Mem.: Am. Soc. Criminology, Am. Correctional Assn., Acad. Criminal Justice Scis., Lambda Alpha Epsilon (nat. conf. coord. 1995).

BAIK-HAN, WON H. pediatrician, educator, pediatrician, consultant; b. Seoul, Jong Ro Gu, Republic of Korea, July 22, 1956; arrived in U.S., 1983; d. Hong In Baik and Ok Hee Chang; m. Muyol Han, Nov. 15, 1986; children: Jeffrey J. Han, Steven J. Han. MD, Ewha Woman's U., Seoul, 1981. Diplomate Am. Bd. Pediat. Intern Soon Chun Hyang U. Hosp., Seoul, Republic of Korea, 1981—82, resident in pediat., 1982—83; pediat. externship St. Elizabeth Hosp. Ctr., Youngstown, Ohio, 1983—84; vol. pediat. physician Flushing (N.Y.) Hosp. Med. Ctr., 1984—86, resident in pediat., 1986—89; fellow in allergy and clin. immunology St. Luke's/Roosevelt Hosp. Ctr., N.Y.C., 1989—91; clin. fellow in allergy & immunology and medicine Columbia U., N.Y.C., 1989—91; dir. pediat. allergy and immunology Flushing (N.Y.) Hosp. Med. Ctr., 1991—, dir. pediat. allergy and asthma clinic, 1991—, consulting physician medicine and pediat., 1991—, com. mem. pharmacy therapeutic com., 1999—. Dir. pediat. allergy Wyckoff Heights Med. Ctr., Bklyn., 1995—99; consulting physician pediat., allergy and immunology N.Y. Hosp. Queens, Flushing, 1997—2000; dir. pediat. allergy clinic Jamaica (N.Y.) Hosp. Med. Ctr., 2000—; asst. prof. pediat. Albert Einstein Coll. Medicine, Bronx, 1994—96, asst. clin. prof. pediat., 1999—; clin. asst. prof. pediat. Cornell U. Med. Coll., N.Y.C., 1997—99; regional spkr. allergy immunology Schering Plough Pharm. Co., NJ, 2001—. Author (with D.M. Rubin): Pediatric Emergency Medicine-Self Assessment and Review, 1994; author: (with A. Stock) Allergic & Immunologic Disease: Pediatric Emergency Medicine-Self Assessment and Review, 2nd edit., 1998. Consulting physician The Korean Am. Nail Assn. N.Y., Inc., Flushing, 1998—, The Korean Sr. Citizen Ctr., Corona, NY, 1999—. Recipient Presentation award for allergy and asthma, Soon Chun Hyang U. Hosp., Seoul, 1992, Physicians Recognition award, AMA, 1999—, Contbn. award for Korean Health Fair, Korean-Am. Nail Assn. N.Y., Inc., Flushing, 1999. Fellow: Am. Acad. Pediat.; mem.: Coalition for Asian Am. Children and Families (com. mem.), N.Y. Allergy, Asthma and Immunology Soc., Am. Acad. Allergy, Asthma and Immunology (Travel Grand award for rsch. project 1991), Hunter Coll. H.S. Korean-Am. Parents Assn. (pres. 2002—03). Avocations: drawing and painting, playing pingpong and tennis, singing, collecting coins, stamps and collectibles, collecting antiques. Office: 1st Fl 143-20 Sanford Ave Flushing NY 11355

BAIK-KROMALIC, SUE S. metallurgical engineer; b. Korea; m. Joseph. BS in Metall. Engring., Ohio State U. Project engr. Cummins Engine Co., Columbus, Ind; engring. staff, materials testing and devel. engr. Honda Am. Mfg., Inc., East Liberty, Ohio; trainer problem solving Honda Am., Inc., East Liberty, Ohio, new model project engr., leader tech. devel.; prodn. planning ops. and control; engring. coord. mfg. ops., cost & manpower resources control Honda of Am. Mfg., Inc., with ops. office gen. planning and control, asst. mgr. bus. mgmt. sys., staff engr. prodn. control. Guest spkr. Ohio State U., Columbus. Chmn. Opera Columbus Ball, 2003. Mem. ASM Internat. (Columbus chpt. awards chmn., chpt. devel. task force, sec., task force, membership devel. com., treas., chpt. coun., chair, vice-chair membership devel. com., chair membership devel. com., found. bd. trustees). Roman Catholic. Avocation: golf. Office: Honda of Am Mfg Inc Honda Ops Office 24000 Honda Pkwy Marysville OH 43040-9251

BAILAR, BARBARA ANN, statistician, researcher; b. Monroe, Mich., Nov. 24, 1935; d. Malcolm Laurie and Clara Florence (Parent) Dezendorf; m. John Francis Powell (div. 1966); 1 child, Pamela; m. John Christian Bailar; 1 child, Melissa. BA, SUNY, 1956; MS, Va. Poly. Inst., 1965; PhD, Am. U., 1972. With Bur. of Census, Washington, 1958-88, chief Ctr. Rsch. Measurement Methods, 1973-79, assoc. dir. for statis. standards and methodology, 1979-88; exec. dir. Am. Statis. Assn., Alexandria, Va., 1988-95; sr. v.p. for survey rsch. Nat. Opinion Rsch. Ctr., Chgo., 1995—2001. Instr. George Washington U., 1984-85, head dept. math. and stats. USDA Grad. Sch., Washington, 1972-87. Contbr. articles, book chpts. to profl. publs. Pres. bd. dirs. Harbour Sq. Coop., Washington, 1988-89. Recipient Silver medal U.S. Dept. Commerce, 1980. Fellow Am. Statis. Assn. (pres. 1987); mem. AAAS (chair sect. stats. 1984-85), Internat. Assn. Survey Statisticians (pres. 1989-91), Internat. Statis. Inst. (Pres.'s invited speaker 1983, v.p. 1993-95), Cosmos Club. E-mail: bbailar@health.bsd.uchicago.edu.

BAILAR, JOHN CHRISTIAN, III, retired public health educator, physician, statistician; b. Urbana, Ill., Oct. 9, 1932; married; 4 children. BA, U. Colo., 1953; MD, Yale U., 1955; PhD in Stats., Am. U., 1973. Intern U. Colo. Med. Ctr., Denver, 1955-56; field investigator, biometry br. Nat Cancer Inst., NIH, Bethesda, Md., 1956-62, head demography sect., 1962-70, dir. 3d nat. cancer survey, 1967-70, dep. assoc. dir. for cancer control, 1972-74; editor-in-chief JNCI, 1974-80; dir. research service VA, Washington, 1970-72; lectr. in biostats. Harvard U., Cambridge, Mass., 1980-87; prof. McGill U., Montreal, 1987-95, chair dept. epidemiology and biostats., 1993-95; sr. scientist Office Disease Prevention and Health Promotion, Dept. HHS, Washington, 1983-92; prof. dept. health studies U. Chgo., 1995-99, chair dept. health studies, 1995-98, assoc. faculty Harris Sch. Pub. Policy, 1999-2000, prof. emeritus, 2000—. Sr. scientist

health and environ. rev. divsn. EPA, 1980-83; lectr. epidemiology and pub. health Yale U., New Haven, Conn., 1958-83; mem. faculty math. and stats. USDA Grad. Sch., Washington, 1966-76; vis. prof. stats. SUNY, Buffalo, 1974-80; professorial lectr. George Washington U., Washington, 1975-80; cons. in biostats. and epidemiology Dana-Farber Cancer Inst., Boston, 1977-83; vis. prof. Harvard U., 1977-79; spl. appointment grad. faculty U. Colo. Med. Ctr., Denver, 1979-81; scholar in residence NAS, 1992-96, 2002—. Mem. editl. adv. bd. Cancer Rsch., 1968-72; statis. cons. New Eng. Jour. Medicine, 1980-91; mem. bd. editors New England Jour. Medicine, 1992—; contbr. numerous articles to profl. jours.; editor JNCI, 1974-80. John D. and Catherine T. MacArthur Found. fellow, 1990-95. Fellow AAAS (chair sect. U 2000—), Am. Coll. Epidemiology, Am. Statis. Assn. (chair-elect and chair biometric sect. 1979-81, founding chair sect. stats. and environment 1990); mem. Am. Med. Women's Assn. (hon.), Inst. of Medicine, Internat. Statis. Inst., Coun. Biology Editors (chair publishing policy com. 1983-89, pres.-elect, pres., past pres. 1986-89), Soc. Risk Analysis (founding chair Boston chpt. 1985-86). Office: Apt 8 2101 Connecticut Ave NW Washington DC 20008 E-mail: jcbailar@midway.uchicago.edu.

BAILE, CLIFTON A. biologist, researcher; b. Warrensburg, Mo., Feb. 8, 1940; s. Harold F. and Salome (Mohler) B.; m. Beth Lucile Hoover, Aug. 21, 1960; children: Christopher A., Marisa B. BS in Agr., Bus., Cen. Mo. State U., 1962; PhD in Nutrition, U. Mo., 1965; MA (hon.), U. Pa., 1979. NIH rsch. fellow Sch. Pub. Health Harvard U., Boston, 1964-66, from. instr. to asst. prof. Sch. Pub. Health, 1966-71; mgr. neurobiol. rsch. SmithKline Animal Health, Phila., 1971-75; from assoc. prof. to prof. Sch. Vet. Medicine U. Pa., Phila., 1975-82; disting. fellow, dir. R & D Monsanto Agrl. Co., St. Louis, 1982-95; adj. prof. nutrition Sch. Medicine Washington U., St. Louis, 1982-95; adj. prof. dept. animal sci. U. Mo., 1982-95; dist. prof. animal sci. and food and nutrition U. Ga., Athens, 1995—; Ga. Rsch. Alliance Eminent scholar Agrl. Biotech., Athens, 1996—; CEO, ProLinia, Inc., 1999—. Presenter in field. Contbr. over 275 articles to sci. publs. Rsch. fellow Ralston Purina, 1962-64, spl. postdoctoral fellow NIH, 1969; recipient Georgia Lamar Dodd award, 2002. Mem. Am. Soc. Animal Sci. (bd. dirs. 1990-93, animal growth and devel. award 1989), Am. Physiol. Soc., Am. Inst. Nutrition, Am. Dairy Sci. Assn. (Am. Feed Mgmt. award 1979), Soc. Neurosci., Endocrine Soc. Achievements include 17 patents in field; research in control and feed intake and regulation of energy balance. Office: U Ga 444 ADS Complex Athens GA 30602-2771 E-mail: cbaile@arches.uga.edu.

BAILEY, AMOS PURNELL, clergyman, syndicated columnist, author; b. Grotons, Va., May 2, 1918; s. Louis William and Evelyn (Charnock) B.; m. Ruth Martin Hill, Aug. 22, 1942 (dec. 1992); children: Eleanor Carol Bailey Harriman, Anne Ruth Bailey Page, Joyce Elizabeth Bailey Richardson, Jeanne Bailey Dodge-Allen; m. Betty Lou Sheffield, Mar. 5, 1994. BA, Randolph-Macon Coll., 1942, DD, 1956; BD, Duke U., 1948; ThM, Union Theol. Sem., 1957; postgrad., Ecumenical Inst., Jerusalem, 1977. Ordained to ministry United Meth. Ch., 1942; pastor Emporia, Va., 1938, Beulah UMC Ch., Richmond, Va., 1938-43, New Kent circuit, 1943-44, Oak Grove United Meth. Ch., Norfolk, Va., 1948-50, Grace United Meth. Ch., Newport News, 1950-54, Centenary Ch., Richmond, 1954-61; supt. Richmond dist. United Meth. Ch., 1961-67; sr. minister Reveille Ch., Richmond, 1967-70; assoc. gen. sec., div. chaplains Bd. Higher Edn. and Ministry United Meth. Ch., Washington, 1970-79; v.p. Nat. Meth. Found., 1979-82; interim minister Herndon Ch., 1985-86; pres., CEO Nat. Temple Ministries, Inc., Fredericksburg, Va., 1982—. Pres. S.E.J. and S.C.U. Comms., 1968-76; dir. Reeves-Parvin Co., 1978-85; v.p. Va. Conf. Bd. Missions, 1955-61, Meth. Commn. Town and Country Work, 1956-67; mem. Meth. Commn. on Higher Edn., 1960-70, Meth. Interbd. Coun., 1960-70; del. Southeastern Jurisdictional Conf., 1964, 68, Gen. Conf., 1964, 66, 68, 70, World Meth. Conf., London, 1966, Denver, 1970, Dublin, 1976, Rio de Janeiro, 1996; exec. com. Congress, 1987-88; fin. com. Nat. Ch. Growth Rsch. Ctr., 1986-89; frequent chaplain U.S. Senate, U.S. Ho. of Reps., Va. Gen. Assembly; mem. coun., exec. com., pres. comms. com. Southeastern Jurisdiction, 1968-76; pres. Joint Comms. Com., 1968-76; vice chmn. Ministry to Svc. Pers. in East Asia, 1972-79; mem. Commn. on Interpretation, Va. Conf. Bd. Ordained Ministry, 1974-82; participant Ednl. Study Mission to Eng., 1988. Author: Daily Bread, 1997, Daily Bread, The Second Slice, 1999; syndicated columnist Daily Bread, 1945— (50th Anniversary award 1995), syndicated radio devotional, 1945-69; condr. weekly radio counseling program The Night Pastor, 1955-69, Sunshine and Shadows, 1967-70; contbr. articles to profl. jours. Mem. exec. com. Va. Conf. Bd. Edn., 1968-72; mem. World Meth. Coun., Va. Commn. Aging; pres. adv. bd. Richmond Welfare Dept., 1956-68, Va. Conf. Bd. Ministry, Richmond Pub. Assistance Com., Richmond Coun. Alcoholism, Citizen Adv. Bd. Duke U. Comprehensive Cancer Ctr., 1995-01; group chmn. industry divsn. Richmond United Givers Fund, 1961; chmn. chaplains adv. coun. VA, Washington; bd. mgrs. Richmond YMCA, 1961-69; bd. dirs. Va. Meth. Advisers; trustee Randolph-Macon Coll., 1960-82, trustee emeritus, 1986; bd. visitors Duke Div. Sch., 1964-70; trustee So. Sem., 1961-76. With Chaplains Corps AUS, 1945-47. Recipient Disting. Alumni award, Duke Div. Sch., 2001; scholar A. Purnell Bailey Preministerial, Randolph-Macon Coll., 2002; Two Million Dollar scholar fund, 2002. Mem.: DAV (life), Duke Div. Alumni Assn. (pres.), Meth. Hist. Soc., Kiwanis, Kiwanis Club. Home: Apt 1312 12100 Chancellors Village Ln Fredericksburg VA 22407-6595 Office: PO Box 41296 Fredericksburg VA 22404-1296 *Life for me is rich and meaningful in a Christian commitment which allows a free and unfettered search for truth. Discipline of time and resources, the love of persons in my sphere of activity, a devoted family — all are part of the life I cherish daily.*

BAILEY, BARRY STONE, sculptor, educator; b. High Point, N.C., Oct. 21, 1952; s. Richard Junior and Dorothy (Harris) B. MFA, East Carolina U., 1978. Sculptor, New Orleans, 1980—; curator, visual arts coord. Contemporary Arts Ctr., New Orleans, 1980-82; curator La. World Expo., New Orleans, 1984; instr. La. State U., Baton Rouge, 1985; prof. U. Ga., Cortona, Italy, 1992, 96; asst. prof. Tulane U., New Orleans, 1989-93, assoc. prof., 1993—. Grantee: Sculpture grant for Italy, Ford Found., Cortona, Italy, 1977, NEA/So. Arts Found., 1987. Office: Tulane U Newcomb Art Dept - Sculpture New Orleans LA 70118 Business E-Mail: bailey@tulane.edu.

BAILEY, BEATRICE NAFF, researcher and educator in English; b. Roanoke, Va., July 7, 1957; d. Wesley W. Jr. and Angelia (Hunt) Naff; m. William Glenn Bailey, Nov. 5, 1994. BA in English, Longwood Coll., 1979; MA in Theology, Bethany Theol. Sem., 1981; EdD, Va Tech., 1987. Prof. Clemson (S.C.) U., 1991—, dir. Clemson Writing Project, 1993—. Author: Our Upcountry: Teachers and Students Write About Place, 2000, Literacy Clubs for At Risk Girls, 1988, (with others) Religious Schools and America, 1988, Planning Models Matter in English Education, 1989. Recipient A.L. Burruss Rsch. and Svc. award, 1991, Good Apple award SCCTE, 1998, Career Woman of Yr. award Easley Bus. and Profl. Women, 1998. Mem. Nat. Coun. Tchrs. English (Promising Researcher award 1988, Richard Meade rsch. award 1990), Nat. Conf. Rsch. English, Phi Delta Kappa (Rsch. award 1988). Avocations: golf, tennis, collecting nativity scenes. Office: Clemson U 401 Tillman Hl # B Clemson SC 29634-0001

BAILEY, BYRON JAMES, otolaryngologist, medical association executive; b. Okla. City, Apr. 5, 1934; s. Jay Gordon and Christine F. (Koehn) B.; m. Margaret Ann Whale, June 6, 1957; children: Michael Jon, Debra Lynn, James Grant, Jennifer Leigh, John Albert. BA, U. Okla., 1955, MD, 1959. Intern UCLA Med. Ctr., Los Angeles, 1959-60, resident in gen. surgery, 1960-61, resident, head and neck specialist, 1961-64, asst. prof., 1964-68; Wiess prof., chair dept. otolaryngology U. Tex., Galveston, 1968—. Treas. Am. Bd. Med. Specialties. Editor The Laryngoscope, 1994—. Chmn. Emergency Med. Svcs. Commn., Galveston, 1975-80. Recipient Mosher award Triological Soc., 1971, Harvey W. Wiley medal U.S. FDA, 1988. Mem. Am. Acad. Otolaryngology (pres. 1988-89), Am. Bd. Otolaryngology (pres. 1992-94), Am. Soc. Head and Neck Surgery (pres. 1992-93), Soc. Univ. Otolaryngologists (pres. 1976), Assn. Acad. Dept. Otolaryngology (pres. 1984), Am. Laryngol. Assn. (pres. 1993-94, DeRoaldes medal 1996, James Newcomb award 2001), Am. Bd. Med. Specialities (treas. 1993-97), Galveston C. of C. (v.p. 1978), Cosmos Club, Triological Soc. (v.p. 1997-98, Gold medal 2001), Nat. Assn. Physicians for the Environ. (pres. 1998-2000), Galveston County Med. Soc. (pres. 2001). Office: U Tex Med Br Dept Otolaryn 7104 JSA 301 University Blvd Galveston TX 77555-0521

BAILEY, CALVIN DEAN, audio engineer; b. Oklahoma City, May 13, 1955; s. Hoyle Dean and Clara Bell (Thomson) B. BS in Radio, TV and Film, Okla. State U., 1980. Rec. engr., producer CAM Sound Studios, Oklahoma City, 1972-75; announcer Sta. KVRO-FM, Stillwater, Okla., 1973-77; equipment conditioner, salesman Ford Audio & Acoustics, Oklahoma City, 1974-75; announcer, studio engr. Stas. KOCY and KXXY-FM, Oklahoma City, 1975-77; announcer, pub. svc. announcement dir., studio engr. Sta. KILE, Galveston, Tex., 1977-78; prodr. TM Country TM Comm. Inc., Dallas, 1978-84; prodn. dir., rec. engr. Sta. KVIL-FM, Dallas, 1985-95; prodn. dir. Sta. KDMX-FM, Dallas, 1995—; owner Dean Bailey Rec. Studio Svcs., 1997—; prodn. dir. Sta. KEGL-FM, Dallas, 1998—. Freelance audio engr. Dallas, 1980—; studio designer, engr. Loomis Prodns., Carrollton, Tex., 1986-90, J.H. Prodns., Dallas, Tex., 1981—, Specialists Internat. Inc., Dallas, 1981-85, The Voice Box, Arlington, Tex., 1981—. Recipient Spotlight award NWC Theatre, 1971, 72. Avocations: photography, skating, scuba. Home and Office: 10027 Church Rd Dallas TX 75238-1517 E-mail: dean@deanbaileyrecording.com.

BAILEY, CARLA LYNN, nursing administrator; b. Balt., June 4, 1957; d. Carlton L. and Helen P. (Wales) B. BSN, U. Md., Balt., 1979; MS in Health Sci., Towson (Md.) State U., 1987; PhD in Healthcare Mgmt., Century Brentwick U., 2000. Nurse clinician I, charge nurse, clin. nurse U. Md. Med. Systems, Balt., 1981—87; maternal transport coord. U. Md. Med. Systems Hosp., Balt., 1979—96; rsch. nurse Tokos Med. Corp., Balt., 1988—91; perinatal care coord. U. Md. Med. Systems/Hosp., 1993—99; perinatal programs dir., nurse adminstr. Md. Inst. Emergency Med. Svcs. Sys., 1999—. Mem. assoc. faculty U. Md. Sch. Nursing, 1993-95; mem. fetal and infant mortality rev. bd. Healthy Start; mem. State Commn. on Infant Mortality Prevention. Mem. Assn. Women's Health, Obstetric and Neonatal Nurses, Md. Nurse's Assn., Nat. Perinatal Assn., Md. Perinatal Assn. (bd. dirs., pres.).

BAILEY, CECIL DEWITT, aerospace engineer, educator; b. Zama, Miss., Oct. 25, 1921; s. James Dewitt and Matha Eugenia (Roberts) B.; m. Myrtis Irene Taylor, Sept. 8, 1942; children: Marilyn, Beverly. BS, Miss. State U., 1951; MS, Purdue U., 1954, PhD, 1962. Commd. 2d lt. USAF, 1944, advanced through grades to lt. col., 1965, pilot, 1944-56, sr. pilot, 1956-60, command pilot, 1960-67, asst. prof. Air Force Inst. Tech., 1954-58, assoc. prof., 1965-67, ret., 1967; assoc. prof. aero. and astronautical engring. Ohio State U., Columbus, 1967-69, prof., 1970-85, prof. emeritus, 1985—. Dir. USAF-Am. Soc. Engring. Edn. summer faculty research program Wright-Patterson AFB, Ohio, 1976-78 *In 1975, for the first time in the 200 year history of analytical mechanics, the direct analytical solution to time dependent, initial value dynamical systems was published in Foundations of Physics. An equation that was first called "The General Energy Equation" made possible these solutions. Potential functions were eliminated. The equation applies to systems that may be stationary or non-stationary, conservative or non-conservative, potential or non-potential, linear or non-linear. Many examples now abound in the literature. Successful papers on finite elements in time began to proliferate in the 1980's. In January 2002, a Philosophical paper was published in Foundations of Physics. In this paper it is shown that Euler and Lagrange required that the "action" integral vanish because of their belief in natures requirement of "minimum" energy. In 1834, Hamilton proved that the "action" integral does not vanish. One cannot have it both ways! Those who came after Hamilton chose to apply the theory of Euler and Lagrange to Hamilton's law and thereby reduced it to Hamilton's principle. In 1972, Dr. B.E. Gatewood, a professor at the Ohio State University, discovered that the disputed term, which occurs when the differential equation is derived from Hamilton's principle, is not zero. Hamilton was correct. Euler and Lagrange were in error. The error, by two of the greatest mathematicians who ever lived and its cause, is discussed in the January 2002 paper, the unifying laws of classical mechanics. No calculus of variations is involved because there is no requirement for maximum or minimum.* Contbr. articles to profl. jours., scientific papers. Mem. Soc. Exptl. Stress Analysis, Am. Soc. Engring. Edn., Am. Acad. Mechanics, Res. Officers (life), Ret. Officers Assn. (life), Am. Legion (life), Sigma Xi, Sigma Gamma Tau. Clubs: USAF Officers. Achievements include research in a unified theory of mechanics. The gen. energy law was first presented through NASA Grant NGR 36-008-197, April 1973, Application of the Gen. Energy Equation- A Unified Approach to Mechanics; proof that the gen. energy law is more gen. than Hamilton's "Law of Varying Action" is presented in Found. of Physics, vol. 32, Jan. 2002, pp. 159-176, The Unifying Laws of Classical Mechanics. Home and Office: 4176 Ashmore Rd Columbus OH 43220-4683 also: Dept Aerospace Engring Appl Mech Ohio State U Columbus OH 43210

BAILEY, CHARLES MICHAEL, clinical data analyst, pharmacist; b. Little Rock, Ark., Oct. 16, 1958; s. Norman Lester and Ann Louise Fox Bailey; m. Dana P. Shaw. BS in Pharmacy, U. Ark., 1983. Prin. investigator Biotech. Svcs., Inc., North Little Rock, Ark., 1993—94, quality assurance mgr., 1994—95, project mgr., clin. Data Analyst, 1995—. Sr. contbg. editor All About Jazz, 1997—. Mem.: Drug Info. Assn. Methodist. Avocations: reading, writing, music, fishing, hunting. Office: Biotech Svcs Inc 4610 W Commercial Dr North Little Rock AR 72116-7059 Office Fax: 501-753-5963.

BAILEY, CHARLES WALDO, II, journalist, author; b. Boston, Apr. 28, 1929; s. David Washburn and Catherine Ruth (Smith) B.; m. Ann Card Bushnell, Sept. 9, 1950; children: Victoria Britton, Sarah Tilden. Grad., Phillips Exeter Acad., 1946; AB magna cum laude, Harvard U., 1950. Reporter, Mpls. Tribune, 1950-54; reporter, corr. Washington bur. Mpls. Tribune, Des Moines Register, Look mag., 1954-67; chief Washington bur. Mpls. Tribune, 1968-72, editor, 1972-82, Mpls. Star and Tribune, 1982; Washington editor Nat. Pub. Radio, 1984-87. Mem. Standing Com. Corr., Washington, 1962-63; pres. White Ho. Corr. Assn., 1969-70. Author: Conflicts of Interest: A Matter of Journalistic Ethics, 1984, The Land Was Ours, 1991; co-author: (with Fletcher Knebel) No High Ground, 1960, Seven Days in May, 1962, Convention, 1964; contbr. to Candidates 1960, 1959, Exeter Remembered, 1965, The President's Trip to China, 1972, The Media and Foreign Policy, 1990. Trustee Carnegie Endowment for Internat. Peace, Henry L. Stimson Ctr. Mem. Coun. on Fgn. Rels., Gridiron Club, Cosmos Club. Home: 3001 Albemarle St NW Washington DC 20008-2102

BAILEY, CHARLES WILLIAM, management consultant, researcher; b. Mpls., May 26, 1932; s. Charles Nelson and Ruth Elthleen (Brower) B.; m. Anne G. Stultz (div. 1979); children: Charles R., George L., Dana R., William W., Jonathan D., Margaret R. BBA in Indsl. Rels. and Psychology, U. Minn., 1955. Orgn. analyst Duluth Missabe & Iron Range Railway, 1958-60, supr. orgn. planning, 1960-67; dir. safety Duluth (Minn.) Missabe and Iron Range Ry., 1967-86; pres. Bailey and Assocs., Duluth, 1986—. Cons. rail safety com. NRC, Washington, 1979-80; chmn. adv. com. masters program-indsl. safety U. Minn., 1976—. Author: Using Behavioral Techniques to Improve Safety Program Effectiveness, 1989; Inventor system for digital computer rec. of petroglyphs, 1991. Advisor Minn. Safety Coun., Mpls., 1982-86; bd. dirs., treas. Duluth Pub. Schs. Bd. of Edn., 1967-71. With U.S. Army, 1955-58, Korea. Mem. Nat. Safety Coun. (gen. chmn. r.r. sect. 1973-74), Assn. Am. R.R.s Washington (chmn. safety rsch. com. 1976-86), No. Lakes Archaeol. Soc. (sec., treas. 1988-91), Inst. for Study of Am. Cultures (researcher), Epigraphic Soc. (contbr.), Am. Rock Art Rsch. Assn., Kiwanis. Republican. Presbyterian. Office: Bailey and Assocs 530 N 40th Ave E Duluth MN 55804-2158 E-mail: cwbailey@duluth.infionline.net.

BAILEY, CHARLES-JAMES NICE, linguistics educator; b. Middlesborough, Ky., May 2, 1926; s. Charles Wise and Mary Elizabeth (Nice) B. AB in Classical Philology highest honors, Harvard U., 1950, MTh, 1955; DMin, Vanderbilt U., 1963; AM, U. Chgo., 1966, PhD, 1969. Faculty dept. linguistics U. Hawaii, Manoa, 1968-71, Georgetown U., 1971-73; prof. Technische U. Berlin, 1974-91, prof. emeritus, 1991—. Vis. prof. U. Mich., Ann Arbor, 1973, U. Witwatersrand, Johannesburg, 1976, U. Brunei, Darussalam, 1990; Forcheimer prof. U. Jerusalem, 1986; propr. Orchid Land Publs.; hon. col. Staff Gov. of Ky. Fellow: Internat. Soc. Phonetic Scis. (life), Netherlands Inst. Advanced Study (life); mem.: Internat. Palm Soc., So. Linguistica Europaea, N.Y. Acad. Scis., European Acad. Scis., Arts and Letters (corr.), AAAS, Am. Dialect Soc. (life), Linguistic Soc. Am. (life). E-mail: orlapubs@orlapubs.com.

BAILEY, CHIP, investment advisor, former state senator; b. Birmingham, Sept. 10, 1944; m. Angela Gaylord (Brown) B., June 8, 1985; children: Meredith, Christopher, Whitney. BA in Polit. Sci., U. Ala., 1966; Chartered Life Underwriter, Fin. Cons., Am. Coll. With fin. svs., 1968—; mem. Ala. State Senate, Montgomery, 1978-98; ptnr. Bailey, Espy & Lee, Inc., Dothan, Ala., 1990; intern dept. HUD-fed. govt., urban renewal rep. Former chmn. conservation and forestry com., agr. com., edn. com., fiscal responsibility and accountability com.; chairperson. Chmn. Ala. Commn. on Aging. Named Outstanding Legis., Mont. Advertiser and Capital Press Corp. Republican. Presbyterian. Avocations: fishing, backpacking. Home: 301 Redwood Ave Dothan AL 36303-3805 also: PO Box 6791 Dothan AL 36302-6791 Office: PO Box 6791 Dothan AL 36302-6791

BAILEY, CLAUDIA JEAN, retired professor, librarian, artist; b. Akron, Ohio, July 2, 1936; d. Lloyd Carl Lowe and Vergie P. Hively; m. Richard E. Bailey; children: Laurel Lynn Bailey-Wallace, Robert E. BA, Asbury Coll., 1960; MAL.S., U. Mich., 1966; MA, Ohio State U., 1970; BFA, U. R.I., 1992. Ref. libr. Columbus Pub. Libr., Columbus, Ohio, 1966—68; head journalism, acting head social work libr. Ohio State U., Columbus, Ohio, 1969—70; head fine arts libr. Bridgeport Pub. Libr., Bridgeport, Conn., 1970—72; head providence campus libr. CC of R.I., Providence, 1972—76, head Lincoln campus libr. Lincoln, RI, 1976—82, coord. ref./collection devel., 1982—87, ref. libr. Warwick, RI, 1987—97. Co-sponsored libr. concerts and art exhibits Bridgeport Pub. Libr., Bridgeport, Conn., 1971—72; chairperson, faculty sabbatical com. CC of R.I., Warwick, RI, 1979—80. Author: A Guide To Reference And Bibliography For Theatre Research, 1971, A Guide To Reference And Bibliography For Theatre Research., 2d edit., 1983. Scholar Grad. Libr. Sci., State Of Ohio, 1965-66, Scholar Grad., London Theatre Libraries, 1968. Mem.: NEA, Westbrook Fine Arts Assn., George Chelena Chorale. Liberal. Avocations: art collages, drawing, painting, singing, opera, theater. Home: 19483 N 90th Ln Peoria AZ 85382-8560

BAILEY, CRAIG BERNARD, lawyer; b. Camden, N.J., Aug. 20, 1952; s. Bernard Thomas and Nora Frances (DiDomenico) B. BA and BS, Bucknell U., 1975; JD, George Washington U., 1978. Bar: U.S. Patent Office 1977, D.C. 1978, Calif. 1984, U.S. Ct. Claims, U.S. Ct. Internat. Trade, U.S. Tax Ct., U.S. Ct. Mil. Appeals, U.S. Ct. Appeals (1st, 4th, 5th, 7th, 8th, 9th, 10th, D.C. and fed. cirs.), U.S. Supreme Ct. Law clk. to chief judge U.S. Ct. Appeals (fed. cir.), Washington, 1978-80; assoc. Brenner & Wray, Arlington, Va., 1980-83; patent atty. Hughes Aircraft Co., El Segundo, Calif., 1983-86; assoc. Fulwider, Patton, Lee & Utecht, L.A., 1986-89, ptnr., 1990—. Mem. ABA, L.A. Patent Law Assn., Tau Beta Pi. Office: Fulwider Patton et al Hughes Ctr 6060 Center Dr Tenth Fl Los Angeles CA 90045

BAILEY, DANIEL ALLEN, lawyer; b. Pitts., Aug. 31, 1953; s. Richard A. and Virginia (Henry) B.; m. Janice Abraham, Oct. 10, 1981; children: Jeffrey, Megan. BBA, Bowling Green State U., 1975; JD, Ohio State U., 1978. Bar: Ohio 1978, U.S. Dist. Ct. (so. dist.) Ohio 1978, U.S. Tax Ct. 1979. Ptnr. Arter & Hadden, Columbus, Ohio, 1978—2003, chair exec. com., 2000—03; mem. Baily Cavalieri LLC, Columbus, 2003—, chair bd. mgrs., 2003—. Co-author: Handbook for Corporate Directors, 1985, Liability of Corporate Officers and Directors, 7th edit., 2002. Bd. dirs. Columbus Met. Community Action Orgn., 1979-80, Franklin County Head Start, Columbus, 1979-80, Faith Luth. Ch., Whitehall, Ohio, 1985-90, Luth. Social Svcs. Cen. Ohio, 1991-2000, Concorde Counseling Svcs., 2000—. Mem. ABA, Ohio Bar Assn., Columbus Bar Assn., Phi Kappa Phi, Beta Gamma Sigma, Omicron Delta Kappa. Office: Bailey Cavalieri LLC 10 W Broad St Ste 2100 Columbus OH 43215-3422

BAILEY, DAVID NELSON, pathology educator, university official; b. Anderson, Ind., June 21, 1945; s. Omer Nelson and Louise Genevieve (Hurst) B. BS with high distinction, Ind. U., 1967; MD, Yale U., 1973. Diplomate Nat. Bd. Med. Examiners, Am. Bd. Pathology (Clin. and Chem. Pathology). Clin. fellow dept. lab. medicine Yale U., 1973-75; asst. resident specializing in clin. pathology Yale-New Haven Hosp., 1975-76, chief resident specializing in clin. pathology, 1976-77; asst. prof. pathology U. Calif., San Diego, 1977-81, assoc. prof. pathology, 1981-86, prof. pathology, 1986—, head div. lab. medicine, 1983-89, 94-98, acting chmn., 1986-88, chmn. dept. pathology, 1988—99, 2000—01; dir. toxicology lab. U. Calif. Med. Ctr., San Diego, 1977—, dir. clin. labs., 1982-99, interim vice chancellor for health scis., dean, 1999-2000, dep. vice chancellor for health scis., 2001—, dean for faculty/student matters, 2003—. Mem. editorial bd. Jour. Analytical Toxicology, 1979—, Clin. Chemistry Jour., 1983-93, Am. Jour. Clin. Pathology, 1991—; contbr. articles to profl. jours. Recipient Gerald T. Evans award Acad. Clin. Lab. Physicians and Scientists, 1993; Merit scholar Ind. U., 1963-65, Arthur R. Metz scholar, 1965-67. Mem. Calif. Assn. Toxicologists (pres. 1981-82), Acad. Clin. Lab. Physicians and Scientists (pres. 1988-89), Am. Assn. Clin. Chemistry, Am. Chem. Soc., Assn. Pathology Chmn. (sec.-treas. 1996-99), Phi Lambda Upsilon, Alpha Omega Alpha. Office: U Calif San Diego Sch Medicine 9500 Gilman Dr La Jolla CA 92093-0602 E-mail: dnbailey@ucsd.edu.

BAILEY, DAVID ROY SHACKLETON, classics educator; b. Lancaster, Eng., Dec. 10, 1917; came to U.S., 1968; s. John Henry Shackleton and Rosamund Maud (Giles) B.; m. Kristine Zvirbulis, 1994. BA, Gonville and Caius Coll., Cambridge, 1939, MA, 1943, Litt.D., 1958; Litt.D. (hon.), U. Dublin, 1984. Fellow Gonville and Caius Coll., 1944-55, praelector, 1954-55, dep. bursar, 1964, sr. bursar, 1965-68, Univ. lectr. Tibetan, 1948-68; fellow, dir. studies in classics Jesus Coll., Cambridge, 1955-64; vis. lectr. classics Harvard U., 1963, prof. Greek and Latin, 1975-82, Pope prof. Latin lang. and lit., 1982-88, prof. emeritus, 1988—; prof. Latin U. Mich., Ann Arbor, 1968-75, adj. prof., 1989—. Vis. Andrew V.V. Raymond prof. classics SUNY, Buffalo, 1973-74; vis. fellow Peterhouse, Cambridge, 1980-81, Inst. For Advanced Study, Princeton U., 1986. Author: The Satapancasatka of Matrceta, 1951, Propertiana, 1956, Cicero's Letters, 10 vols., 1965-81, Cicero, 1971, Profile of Horace, 1982, Anthologia Latina I, 1982, Horatius, 1985, Cicero's Philippics, 1986, An Onomasticon to Cicero's Speeches, 1988, Ciceronis Epistulae, 4 vols., 1987-88, Lucanus, 1988, Quintilianus, Declamationes Minores, 1990, Martialis, 1990, Martial, 3 vols., 1993, Back From Exile, 1994, Homoeoteleuton in Latin dactylic poetry, 1994, Onomasticon to Cicero's Letters, 1995, Onomasticon to Cicero's Treatises, 1996, Selected Classical Papers, 1997, Cicero Letters To Atticus, 4 vols., 1999, Valerius Maximus, 2 vols., 2000, Cicero, Letters to Friends, 3 vols., 2001, Cicero, Letters to Quintus and Brutus, 2002, Statius, Silvae, 2003, Statius Thebaud, 2 vols 1904, others; contbr. articles on Oriental and classical subjects to profl. jours.; editor Harvard Studies in Classical Philology, 1978-84. Recipient Charles J. Goodwin award of merit, 1978; Nat. Endowment for Humanities fellow, 1980-81; Kenyon medal, Brit. Acad., 1985; hon. fellow Gonville and Caius Coll. Fellow Brit. Acad., Am. Acad. Arts and Scis.; mem. Am. Philos. Soc., Soc. for Promotion of Roman Studies (hon.).

BAILEY, DAWN MARIE, fund raising systems consultant; b. L.A., June 23, 1972; d. Dayton Dana and Pamela Jean Bailey. BS, U. So. Calif., 1994. Supr. Am. Tours Internat., L.A., 1993—96; donor recruiter ARC, L.A., 1996—98, devel. rep. nat. hdqrs. Washington, 1998—99; sr. cons. Blackbaud Inc., Chgo., 1999—. Mentor Am. Tours Internat., 1994-95. Vol. Rep. Party, L.A., 1992-96; grad. Riordan Vol. Leadership Devel. Program, L.a., 1995-96. Mem. Nat. Soc. Fund Raising Execs. Office: Blackbaud 2000 Daniel Island Dr Charleston SC 29492 E-mail: Dawn.Bailey@blackbaud.com.

BAILEY, DONOVAN, Olympic athlete; b. Manchester, Jamaica, Dec. 16, 1967; 1 child, Adrienna. Diploma in bus. adminstrn., Sheridan Coll. Named winner, World's Fastest Man Race, 1997, 2d pl., World Championships, Athens, 1997; recipient Silver medal in 100 and 200 Meters, Pan Am. Trials, 1991, Silver medal in 400 Meter Relay, Pan Am. Games, 1991, Silver medal in 100 Meters, Harry Jerome Classic, 1991, Bronze medal in 200 Meters, Can. Nat. Indoor Championship, 1992, Meeting der Spitzenklesse, Lindau, Germany, 1993, Silver medal in 100 Meters, Rendez-Vous MontrCal, 1993, Silver medal in 200 Meters, Can. Nat. Championships, 1993, Bronze medal in 100 Meters, 1993, Silver medal in 100 Meters, Jeux de la Francophonie, Paris, 1994, Gold medal in 4x100 Meter Relay, Commonwealth Games, 1994, Silver medal, Cominidad de Madrid, 1995, Lausanne Grand Prix Meeting, 1995, Bronze medal, Gateshead Games, 1995, Gold medal, Mutual Games, 1995, Internat. Quelle Fest in Narnberg, 1995, Ill. State Championships, 1995, Gold medal in 4x100 Meter Relay, World Outdoor Championships, Giteborg, Sweden, 1995, Bronze medal in 100 Meters, Atlanta Grand Prix, 1996, Gold medal in 100 Meters, Brazil Grand Prix, 1996, Can. Olympic Trials, 1996. Office: c/o Flynn Sports MGmt 606-1185 Eglinton Ave E Toronto ON Canada M3C 3C6

BAILEY, ELIZABETH ELLERY, economics educator; b. N.Y.C., Nov. 26, 1938; d. Irving Woodworth and Henrietta Dana (Skinner) Raymond; children: James L., William E. BA magna cum laude, Radcliffe Coll., 1960; MS, Stevens Inst. Tech., 1966; PhD, Princeton U., 1972; LLD (hon.), De Paul U., 1988. Successively sr. tech. aid, assoc. mem. tech. staff, mem. tech. staff, supr. econ. analysis group, rsch. head econs. rsch. dept. Bell Labs., 1960-77; commr. CAB, 1977-83, v.p., 1981-83; dean Grad. Sch. Indsl. Adminstrn. Carnegie-Mellon U., 1983-90;, 1990-91; John C. Hower prof. pub. policy and mgmt. Wharton Sch. U. Pa., Phila., 1991—. Vis. prof. Yale Sch. Ogn. and Mgmt., 1990-91; bd. dirs. Altria Group, CSX Corp., Tchrs. Ins. and Annuity Assn., Bancroft NeuroHealth; adj. asst., then assoc. prof. econs. NYU, 1973-77. Author: Economic Theory of Regulatory Constraint, 1973; editor: Selected Economics Papers of William J. Baumol, 1976; Deregulating the Airlines, 1985; bd. editors Am. Econ. Rev., 1977-79, Jour. Indsl. Econs., 1977-84. Founding mem., v.p. bd. trustees Harbor Sch. for Children with Learning Disabilities; trustee Princeton U., 1978-82, Presbyn. U. Hosp., 1984-91, Nat. Bureau Econ. Rsch., 1993—, Brookings Inst., 1988—, Catalyst, 1988-90, Am. Assembly Collegiate Schs. of Bus., 1987-90, Nat. Bur. Econs. Rsch., 1993—; mem. exec. coun. Fedn. Orgns. for Profl. Women, 1980-82; chmn. Com. on Status of Women in Econs. Profession, 1979-82; mem. corp. vis. com. Sloan Sch. Mgmt., MIT, 1982-85; mem. adv. bd. Brookings Inst., 1987—, Ctr. Econ. Policy Rsch., Stanford U., 1983—, MIT econs. dept., 1989—, Princeton econs. dept., 1989—. Recipient Alumni Recognition award Radcliffe Coll., 1988, Dirs.' Choice award Nat. Women's Econ. Alliance Found., 1990; Program Design Trainee award Bell Labs; Bell Labs grantee Princeton U., 1972. Mem. Am. Econ. Assn. (exec. com. 1981-83, v.p. 1985), Am. Assn. Collegiate Schs. Bus. (bd. dirs. 1987—), Beta Gamma Sigma. Home: 253 Mountwell Ave Haddonfield NJ 08033-3859 Office: U Pa Wharton Sch Steinberg Hall—Dietrich Hall Philadelphia PA 19104-6372

BAILEY, EXINE MARGARET ANDERSON, soprano, educator; b. Cottonwood, Minn., Jan. 4, 1922; d. Joseph Leonard and Exine Pearl (Robertson) Anderson; m. Arthur Albert Bailey, May 5, 1956. BS, U. Minn., 1944; MA, Columbia U., 1945; profl. diploma, 1951. Instr. Columbia U., 1947-51; faculty U. Oreg., Eugene, 1951—, prof. voice, 1966-87, coordinator voice instrn., 1969-87, prof. emeritus, 1987—; faculty dir. Salzburg, Austria, summer 1968, summer 1976. Vis. prof., head vocal instrn. Columbia U., summers 1952, 59; condr. master classes for singers, developer summer program study for h.s. solo singers, U. Oreg. Sch. Music, 1988—, mem. planning com. 1998-99 MTNA Nat. Convention. Profl. singer, N.Y.C.; appearances with NBC, ABC symphonies; solo artist appearing with Portland and Eugene (Oreg.) Symphonies, other groups in Wash., Calif., Mont., Idaho, also in concert; contbr. articles, book revs. to various mags. Del. fine arts program to Ea. Europe, People to People Internat. Mission to Russia for 1990. Recipient Young Artist award N.Y.C. Singing Tchrs., 1945, Music Fedn. Club (N.Y.C.) hon. award, 1951; Kathryn Long scholar Met. Opera, 1945 Mem. Nat. Assn. Tchrs. Singing (lt. gov. 1968-72), Oreg. Music Tchrs. Assn (pres. 1974-76), Music Tchrs. Nat. Assn. (nat. voice chmn. high sch. activities 1970-74, nat. chmn. voice 1973-75, 81-85, NW chmn. collegiate activities and artists competition 1978-80, editorial com. Am. Music Tchr. jour. 1987-89), AAUP, Internat. Platform Assn., Kappa Delta Pi, Sigma Alpha Iota, Pi Kappa Lambda. Home: 17 Westbrook Way Eugene OR 97405-2074 Office: U Oreg Sch Music Eugene OR 97403 *My chief goal in life is to realize my potentials through perfecting my innate talents and capabilities.*

BAILEY, FRED ARTHUR, history educator; b. Dumas, Ark., Mar. 28, 1947; s. Fred L. and Dorothy M. B.; m. Bonnie Mignon Pitt, Aug. 22, 1968; children: Amber McClendon, Alex, Stan. BA, Harding U., 1970; MA, U. Tenn., 1972, PhD, 1979. Assoc. prof. history Freed-Hardeman Coll., Henderson, Tenn., 1973-84; T.K. Ann prof. Am. history Johns Hopkins U./Nanjing U. Ctr. Chinese/Am. Studies, Nanjing, China, 1993-94; prof., chair dept. history Abilene (Tex.) Christian U., 1984—. Author: Class and Tennessee's Confederate Generation, 1987 (Book award 1988), William Edward Dodd: The South's Yeoman Scholar, 1997; contbr. articles to profl. jours. Mem. Orgn. of Am. Historians, So. Hist. Assn. Mem. Chs. of Christ. Home: 1400 Compere Blvd Abilene TX 79601 Office: Abilene Christian U 1600 Campus Ct Abilene TX 79699 Fax: 915-674-2369. E-mail: baileyf@acu.edu.

BAILEY, FRED COOLIDGE, retired engineering consulting company executive; b. Claremont, N.H., Oct. 5, 1925; s. Howard Perry and Helen Gare (Coolidge) B.; m. Mary Beecroft Cunningham, June 26, 1948; children: Susan Bailey Hunter (dec.), Stephen Coolidge, Elizabeth Bailey George. BS, MIT, 1948, MS, 1949. Registered profl. engr., Mass. Research engr. Caterpillar Tractor Co., Peoria, Ill., 1949-51; asst. tech. dir. com. ship structural design Nat. Acad. Scis., Washington, 1952-55; engr. Lessells & Assocs., Inc., Boston, 1955—65; pres. Teledyne Engring. Services, Waltham, Mass., 1965—86, chmn., 1986-87; group exec. Teledyne Inc., Waltham, Mass., 1983-87, cons., 1987-90, ret., 1990. Chmn. exec. com. Lexington Savs. Bank, 1989-94, chmn. bd. dirs., 1994-97; dir. Affiliated Cmty. Bancorp, 1995-98. Chmn. bd. Fire Commrs., Lexington, Mass., 1964—69; mem. Bd. Selectmen, 1969—78; trustee Cary Meml. Libr., Lexington, 1971—78, pres., 1972—77; trustee Symmes Hosp., Arlington, Mass., 1969—2001, mem. exec. com., 1977—89, v.p., 1978—80, pres., 1980—81; trustee Brookhaven at Lexington, 1986—, chmn. pres., 1994—96; chmn. Choates-Symmes Health Svcs., 1981—83; v.p. Charles River Mus. Industry, 1983—86, trustee, 1984—, pres., 1986—89. With USNR, 1944—46. Fellow Soc. for Exptl. Mechanics (pres. 1968-69, recipient Tatnall award 1974, hon. mem. 1992); mem. Soc. Naval Architects and Marine Engrs. (recipient Linnard prize 1972), ASME, Am. Welding Soc. Home: 48 Coolidge Ave Lexington MA 02420-1838

BAILEY, GARRICK ALAN, anthropologist, educator; s. Linus Eugene and Alma Townsend Bailey; m. Roberta Joan Glenn, Sept. 10, 1965. BA in History, U. Okla., 1963; MA in Anthropology, U. Oreg., 1968, PhD in Anthropology, 1970. Prof. anthropology U. Tulsa, 1968—. Mem. Indian health adv. com. Indian Health Svc., HEW, Washington, 1975—78; mem., com. to rev. Glen Canyon environ. studies NRC, Washington, 1993—96; mem., nat. Native Am. Graves Protection and Repatriation Act rev. com. Nat. Pk. Svc., Washington, 2000—. Author: Changes in Osage Social Organization: 1673 1906, 1973; co-author: Historic Navajo Occupation of the Northern Chaco Plateau, 1982, A History of the Navajo: The Reservation Years, 1986, Humanity:An Introduction to Cultural Anthropology, 1988; editor: The Osage and the Invisible World, 2002. Mem. Tulsa Indian Emphasis Program, 1975—78, Osage Tribal Mus., Pawhuska, Okla., 1993—96, Okla. Humanities Coun., Oklahoma City, 2000—02. Recipient Weatherhead Resident scholar, Sch. of Am. Rsch., Santa Fe, N.Mex, 1982—83, fellowship for Coll. Teachers and Ind. Scholars, Nat. Endowment for the Humanities, 1987—88; fellow, Smithsonian Instn., Washington, 1992. Fellow: Am. Anthrop. Assn.; mem.: Am. Soc. for Ethnohistory, Am. Ethnol. Soc. Office: U Tulsa 600 S College Tulsa OK 74104

BAILEY, HAROLD RANDOLPH, surgeon; b. Palestine, Tex., Jan. 20, 1943; m. Kelly Curry Bailey. BA in Biology summa cum laude, Rice U., 1964; MD, U. Tex., Dallas, 1968. Diplomate Am. Bd. Surgery, Am. Bd. Colon and Rectal Surgery. Intern straight surg. Parkland Hosp., Dallas, 1968 69; resident gen. surgery U. Tex. Med. Sch./Hermann Hosp., Houston, 1969-73; fellow colon and rectal surgery Ferguson-Droste-Ferguson Hosp., Grand Rapids, Mich., 1973-74; clin. faculty U. Tex. Med. Sch., Houston, 1974—, dir. residency tng. program colon and rectal surgery, 1984—, clin. prof. surgery, 1986—; clin. faculty Baylor Coll. Medicine, 1986—, clin. prof. surgery, 1999—. Assoc. examiner Am. Bd. Colon and Rectal Surgery, 1985—89, bd. dirs., 1989—97, chmn. exam. com., 1996—97, pres., 1996—97, sr. examiner, 1997—; chief staff Park Plaza Hosp., Houston, 1988—90. Bd. dirs. Am. Cancer Soc., Greater Houston unit, 1989-93, v.p., 1991-93, pres., 1993-95; mem. vestry Palmer Meml. Episcopal Ch., Houston, 1979-83, 84-86, chmn. fin. com., 1984-86; mem. fund coun. Rice U., Houston, 1993-95, class fund drive chmn. 1993-95). Recipient George Waldron award Hermann Hosp., 1970, Violet Keller award, 1973; named to Good Housekeeping mag. 400 Best Doctors in U.S., 1991, Good Housekeeping mag. Best Cancer Doctors in U.S., 1993; named Disting. Alumnus, Rice U., 2000. Fellow ACS (chmn. adv. coun. colon and rectal surgery 1996-2001, gov. 2002—), Internat. Soc. Univ. Colon and Rectal Surgeons (program com. 1986), Am. Soc. Colon and Rectal Surgeons (treas., exec. coun. 1993-99, pres. 1999-2000), Tex. Surg. Soc.; mem. AMA, Tex. Soc. Colon and Rectal Surgeons (pres. 1981, exec. sec. 1982-88), Soc. Am. Gastrointestinal Endoscopic Surgeons, Tex. Med. Assn., Tex. Soc. Gastrointestinal Endoscopy, Harris County Med. Soc., Houston Surg. Soc., Phi Beta Kappa, Alpha Omega Alpha. Office: Colon & Rectal Clinic 6550 Fannin St Ste 2307 Houston TX 77030-2723 E-mail: h.r.bailey@uth.tmc.edu.

BAILEY, HELEN MCSHANE, historian; b. Gardner, Kans., Oct. 17, 1916; d. Harry Cramer and Maude Ethel (Kramer) McShane; m. James Edwin Bailey, Feb. 23, 1946; children: James Edwin, Barbara Ann Bailey Crawford. BA, Bethany Nazarene Coll., 1938. Adminstrv. asst. Office Chief of Staff, U.S. Army, Washington, 1941-48; historian U.S. Army ofcl. history of World War II, U.S. Army, Washington, 1948-58; research asst. George C. Marshall Research Found., Washington, 1958-59; historian Orgn. Joint Chiefs of Staff, Dept. Def., Pentagon, Washington, 1968-87; cons., 1987—. Mem. Am. Hist. Assn., Soc. Historians of Am. Fgn. Relations, World War Two Studies Assn., Soc. History in the Fed. Govt. Republican. Lutheran. Home: 9451 Lee Hwy Apt 415 Fairfax VA 22031-1812

BAILEY, HENRY FRANKLIN, JR., lawyer; b. Buffalo, Wyo., May 10, 1953; s. Henry Franklin and Alma Oneita (Cotton) B.; m. Sandra Adele Shanor, Aug. 3, 1973; children— Brian, Jeffrey, Marcus, Douglas, Katherine. B.S. in Econs. with honors, U. Wyo., 1975, J.D. with honors, 1978. Bar: Wyo. 1978, U.S. Dist. Ct. Wyo. 1978, U.S. Ct. Appeals (10th cir.) 1978. Assoc. Loomis, Lazear, Wilson & Pickett, Cheyenne, Wyo., 1978-80, jr. ptnr., 1980-82, ptnr., 1982— ; instr. Summitt Bar Rev., Laramie, Wyo., 1980-83. Sr. editor Land and Water Law Rev., 1977. Bishop Ch. of Jesus Christ of Latter-Day Saints, Cheyenne, 1982— ; bd. dirs. Laramie County Community Coll. Booster Club, Cheyenne, 1978-80. Named Outstanding Young Man Am., U.S. Jaycees, 1980; Thurmond Arnold Law scholar, U. Wyo., 1975. Mem. ABA (trial practice com.), Wyo. Trial Lawyers Assn., Nat. Assn. R.R. Trial Lawyers (instr. 1982), Def. Research Inst., Def. Lawyers Assn. Wyo., Wyo. Bar Assn., Phi Kappa Phi, Beta Gamma Sigma. Club: Exchange (Cheyenne). Home: 5708 Blue Blf Cheyenne WY 82009-4419

BAILEY, HENRY JOHN, III, retired lawyer, educator; b. Pitts., Apr. 4, 1916; s. Henry J. and Lenore Powell Bailey Cahoon; m. Marjorie Jane Ebner, May 30, 1949 (dec. July 1998); children: George W., Christopher G., Barbara W., Timothy P. Student, U.S. Naval Acad., 1934-36; BA, Pa. State U., 1939; JD, Yale U., 1947. Bar: N.Y. 1948, Mass. 1963, Oreg. 1974. Ins. investigator Liberty Mut. Ins. Co., N.Y.C., 1941-42; atty. Fed. Res. Bank of N.Y., N.Y.C., 1947-55; asst. v.p. Empire Trust Co., N.Y.C., 1955-56; atty., legal dept. Am. Bankers Assn., N.Y.C., 1956-62; editor Banking Law Jour., Boston, 1962-65; asso. prof. law Willamette U., Salem, Oreg., 1965-69, prof., 1969 81, prof. emeritus, 1981—, adj. prof., 1981-83, scholar in residence, 1987; counsel firm Churchill, Leonard, Brown & Donaldson, Salem, 1981-85; vis. prof. sch. law U. Akron, 1983-84; vis. prof. coll. of law Fla. State U., 1984-85; vis. prof. sch. law Rutgers U., Camden, N.J., 1985-87. Cons., lectr. to bar and banking groups; lectr. Banking Sch. of South, Baton Rouge, 1972, 73, 75. Author: Brady on Bank Checks (The Law of Bank Checks), 1960, 3d edit., 1962, 4th edit., 1969, 5th edit., 1979, 6th edit., 1987 and periodic supplements, 7th edit. (with Richard B. Hagedorn), 1992, (with Richard B. Hagedorn) rev. edit. 2 vols., 1997, periodic supplements, Uniform Commercial Code Forms, 1963, (with Clarke and Young) Bank Deposits and Collections, 1972, UCC Deskbook: A Short Course in Commercial Paper, 1973, (with Robert D. Hursh) The American Law of Products Liability, 2d edit, 1984, (with William D. Hawkland) The Sum and Substance of Commercial Paper, 1976, 80, 88, Secured Transactions in a Nutshell, 1976, 2d edit., 1981, 3d edit. (with Richard B. Hagedorn), 1988, (with Richard B. Hagedorn) 4th edit., 2000, Oregon Uniform Commercial Code, 3 vols., 1983, 84, 86, 88, 2d edit. 3 vols., 1990, New 1990 Uniform Commercial Code: Article 3, and 4, periodic supplements; contbr. articles on sales, products liability, comml. paper and secured transactions to legal jours. 1st lt. USAAF, 1942-45; lt. col. Res.; ret. Mem. Am. Bar Assn. (chmn. subcom. on comml. paper 1965-66, 79-81), Am. Law Inst. (mem. editorial bd. The Practical Lawyer 1981-93, emeritus mem. editorial bd. 1993—), Oreg. State Bar, Lambda Chi Alpha. Republican. Roman Catholic. Office: Coll Law Willamette U Salem OR 97301

BAILEY, HERBERT SMITH, JR., retired publisher; b. N.Y.C., July 12, 1921; s. Herbert Smith and Viola (Howe) B.; m. Elizabeth M. Brown, June 26, 1943; children: John R., James C., Robin E., George W. AB, Princeton U., 1942, LLD (hon.), 1986; LHD (hon.), Yale U., 1976. Sci. editor Princeton U. Press, 1946-52, editor, 1952-54, dir., 1954-86; ret., 1986. Past bd. dirs. Nat. Enquiry into Scholarly Publ., Franklin Book Programs, Princeton Bank; past mem. adv. com. on tech. publs. AEC; bd. govs. Wesleyan U. Press; past mem. bd. visitors Duke U. Press; past chmn. sci. info. coun. NSF; vis. fellow Nat. Humanities Ctr., 1984; R.R. Bowker lectr., 1977; mem. publs. com. Am. Scientist. Author: The Art and Science of Book Publishing, 1970; contbr. articles to profl. jours. Past mem. Princeton Regional Bd. Edn.; past mem. and chmn. long range planning Princetown Twp. Bd. of Edn.; past commr. Commn. on Preservation and Access; bd. dirs. Triangle Opera. Lt. USNR, 1942-45. Mem. Am. Book Pubs. Coun. (past bd. dirs.), Assn. Am. Pubs. (past bd. dirs., Curtis Benajmin award for creative pub. 1987), Assn. Am. Univ. Presses (past bd. dirs. and pres.), Am. Philos. Soc. (mem. publs. and program coms.), Sigma Xi. Home: 6 Carolina Meadows Apt 302 Chapel Hill NC 27517-8525

BAILEY, HERTA LUISE, real estate broker; b. Duesseldorf, W. Ger., Apr. 26, 1938; came to U.S. 1962. d. Karl M. and Herta J. (Dietrich) Otto; m. Millard A. Knecht, Sept. 11, 1958 (div. 1970); children: G. Alan, Eileen K. Oravic, Christina L. Womack; m. Robert C. Bailey, Dec. 11, 1971. Student, U. Heidelberg, 1958. Lic. real estate broker Ala. Mgr. Walgreen's Food Dept., Columbus, Ga., 1970-72; supr. Shoney's Ent., Columbus, 1972-77; realtor Homefinder, Columbus, 1977-82, Land, Inc., Columbus, 1983—2000, SP7 Realtors, Columbus, 2000—. Real estate appraiser. Mem. Exec. Club Columbus, Million Dollar Club of Columbus Bd. Realtors, Sojourners of Columbus. Republican. Episcopalian. Avocations: horses, travel, reading, swimming. Home: # 2 Oliver Ct Columbus GA 31904 Office: SP7 Realty 4903 Armour Rd Columbus GA 31904

BAILEY, HUGH COLEMAN, university president; b. Berry, Ala., July 2, 1929; s. Coleman Costello and Susie (Jenkins) B.; m. Ahleida Joan Seever, Nov. 17, 1962; children: Debra Jane, Laura Joan. AB with honors, Samford U., 1950; MA, U. Ala., 1951, PhD, 1954. Instr. history and polit. sci. Samford U., 1953-54, asst. prof., 1954-56, assoc. prof., 1956-59, prof., 1959-75, chmn. dept., head div. social scis., 1967-70; dean Howard Coll. Arts and Scis., 1970-75; v.p. for acad. affairs Francis Marion U., Florence, S.C., 1975-78; pres. Valdosta (Ga.) State Univ., 1978—2002, pres. emeritus, 2002—. Mem. commn. colls. So. Assn. Colls. and Schs., 1974-75; v.p. Ala. Acad. Sci., 1968-69; pres. Ala. Writers Conclave, 1971-73 Author: John Williams Walker, 1964, 2003, Hinton Rowan Helper: Abolitionist-Racist, 1965, 2003, Edgar Gardner Murphy: Gentle Progressive, 1968, 2003, Liberalism in the New South, Southern Social Reformers and the Progressive Movement, 1969, America: The Framing of a Nation, 2 vols, 1975; Editorial bd.: Social Sci. Vice pres. Homewood City Bd. Edn., 1972-75; pres. Valdosta chpt. ARC, 2001-03; bd. dirs. Salvation Army; chmn. Valdosta Habitat's Jimmy Carter Work Project, 2003. Guggenheim fellow, 1963-64; Am. Council Learned Socs. fellow, 1965-66; recipient award merit Am. Assn. State and Local History, 1967 Fellow Royal Soc. Arts; mem. Valdosta C. of C., Pi Gamma Mu (trustee, nat. trustee-at-large 1969-71, nat. 1st v.p. 1978-84, pres. 1984-90), Kiwanis. Episcopalian. Home: 3224 Wildwood Plantation Circle Valdosta GA 31605-1031 Office: Valdosta State Univ 1500 N Patterson St Valdosta GA 31698-0001

BAILEY, JAKE SCHULTZ, volunteer, retired electrical engineer; b. Middlesboro, Ky., Dec. 29, 1927; s. Charles Wise and Mary Elizabeth (Nice) Bailey; m. Barbare Jean McClelland, Sept. 11, 1947; children: Linda Heguy, Mary Marjorie, Alan Curtis. BSEE, U. Ala., 1949; postgrad., U. Minn., 1958. Registered prof. engr., 7 ea. states. Engr. Memphis Light Gas & Water Divsn., 1949—52, Boeing Airplane Co., Wichita, Kans., 1952—54; part-time engr. Carl Green, Elec. Cons., Wichita, 1953—54; evaluation engr. design evaluation dept. aero divsn. Honeywell, Mpls., 1954—56, design engr. F-100 autopilot design group aero divsn. chmn. edn. com. Honeywell exec. forum, 1956—58; sr. electronics engr. Link divsn. Gen. Precision Inc., Binghamton, NY, 1958—59; systems exptl. engr. systems exptl. engring. missile and space dept. GE Co., Phila., 1960—61, mgr. exptl. methods and tech. spacecraft dept. King of Prussia, Pa., 1961—62, project systems engr. systems engring. spacecraft dept., 1962, sr. engr. Nimbus operational systems spacecraft dept., 1962—64, project systems engr., operational systems engring., 1964—65, systems engr. advanced simulation requirements re-entry systems dept., 1965—66, cons. engr. simulation engring. lab. re-entry systems dept., chmn. G.E. math. simulation workshop, 1966—70; pres. B&G Corp., Valley Forge, Pa., 1969—74; chief elec. engr. Zenith Engrs., Inc., Ardmore, Pa., 1974—75; sole proprieto Jake S. Bailey, P.E., Phoenixville, Pa., 1975—81; mgr. Elec. Engring. Archtl. Design Cons. Internat., Milan, 1981—82; chief elec. engr. Haines Lundberg Waehler, N.Y.C., 1982—83; elec. design engr. John D. Hollingsworth, Greenville, SC, 1984—87; design engr. on contract Michelin Tire, Greenville, 1987—92; ret., 1992. Author: (book) Relationships Without Entanglements, 1997; contbr. articles. Vol. S.C. Dept. Probation, Anderson, SC, 2000—; vol. Bible tchr. Mariner Nursing Care, Seneca, SC, 1992—; vol. fireman Vestal Fire Co., Vestal, NY, 1958—60. Lt. USNR, 1949—69. Named Vol. of the Yr., Mariner Health Care, S.C. Dept. Probation, Parole and Pardon Svcs. Mem.: IEEE (sr.), Loyal Order of Ky. Cols. Avocations: flying, private flying. Home: 1403 Leeward Rd Anderson SC 29625-5927 E-mail: lambb@statecom.net.

BAILEY, JAMES ANDREW, principal; b. Jackson, Tenn., Mar. 15, 1957; s. John Truman and Hazel (Cox) B.; m. Lisa McDaniel, June 13, 1992; children: Abby E., Amber N. AS, Jackson (Tenn.) State C.C., 1977; BS, Memphis State U., 1980; MA, Bethel Coll., 1989. Cert. tech. edn. instr. adminstrn. and supervision, Tenn. Indsl. arts instr. Kirby High Sch., Memphis, 1980-83; tech. edn. instr. Parkway Mid. Sch., Jackson, 1983-99; prin. South Elem. Sch., Pinson, Tenn., 1999—. Writing team mem. State Tenn. Tech. Edn. Curriculum Project, 1984-90; tech. edn. participant People to People/Citizen Amb. Program, People's Republic China, summer 1991. Co-author: Instructor's Guide to Metric 500, 1980; contbg. author: Production Technology, 1991. Chmn. Madison-Chester Assn. Bapt. Singles Coun., Jackson, 1990-91; mem. West Jackson (Tenn.) Bapt. Ch., dir., tchr. singles Sunday sch. Named Outstanding Young Man of Am., 1985, Indsl. Arts Advisor of Yr., Tenn. Indsl. Arts Students Assn., 1987, 2000 Notable Am. Men, 1994. Mem. NEA, Tenn. Edn. Assn. (Disting. Classroom Tchr. 1997), Am. Vocat. Assn., Jackson-Madison County Edn. Assn. (pres. 1998-99, exec. bd. 1995-99, 2002—, chmn. instruction and profl. devel. com. 1995-97, mem. legis. com. 1995-98), Tenn. Vocat. Assn. (Tech. Tchr. of Yr. 1989), Internat. Tech. Edn. Assn. (area rep. 1991-92), Tenn. Tech. Edn. Assn., West Tenn. Tech. Edn. Assn. (bd. mem. 1990-92). Avocations: tennis, spelunking, hunting, fishing. Home: 20 London Park Pl Jackson TN 38305-3547 Office: South Elem Sch 570 Stone Rd Pinson TN 38366-7914 E-mail: jabailey@jmcss.org.

BAILEY, JAMES STEPHEN, scientist; b. Paris, Tex. s. Hal Lee and Minnie Yvonne (Swint) Bailey. BSEE, U. Tex., Arlington, 1965, MSEE, 1968, PhD in Elec. Engring. and Physics, 1971; MS in Physics, So. Meth. U., Dallas, 1982. Registered profl. engr., Tex. Analog computer engr. Gen. Dynamics Corp., Ft. Worth, 1964—66, project engr., 1985—91; microwave rsch. engr. Collins Radio Co., Dallas, 1966—68; engring. specialist assigned to Gen. Dynamics Vought Corp., Dallas, 1973—76, engring. specialist, 1976—78, pvt. cons. Ft. Worth, 1983—85; scientist Rockwell-Collins Inc., Dallas, 1978—80; pvt. cons. Ft. Worth, 1982—83, 1989—. Fund raising, vol. tchr. local univs. Lt. col. USMC, 1971—94. Mem.: Sigma Xi, Sigma Pi Sigma, Eta Kappa Nu, Tau Beta Pi. Baptist. Achievements include research in baseband adaptive signal generation electronics, flight control design and simulation, communications; electronic warfare, antennas, weapons systesm. Avocations: hiking, scuba diving, flying, amateur radio. Home and Office: 4401 Bellaire Dr Ste 226 Fort Worth TX 76109-5180

BAILEY, JANET DEE, publishing company executive; b. Newark, Aug. 23, 1946; d. Richard and Mary Louise (Dee) Shapiro; m. John Frederick Bailey, May 9, 1971; children: Jason David, Juliana Dee. BA, U. Del., 1968; MBA, Pace U., 1981. Prodn. editor Prentice-Hall, Inc., Englewood Cliffs, N.J., 1968-70; dir. publs. Spl. Libraries Assn., N.Y.C., 1970-76; dir. mktg. services Knowledge Industry Publs., White Plains, N.Y., 1978-81, v.p., 1984-85; dir. inventory and contracts Macmillan Book Clubs, N.Y.C., 1981-84; group pub. Elsevier Sci. Pub. Co., N.Y.C., 1985-95, v.p. global mktg., 1996-99; v.p. STM books John Wiley & Sons, 1999—. Mem. Assn. Am. Publishers (chmn. jours. com., PSP exec. coun.), Soc. for Scholarly Publishing. Office: John Wiley & Sons Inc 605 Third Ave New York NY 10158

BAILEY, JEFFREY WAYNE, law enforcement educator, consultant; s. Willie Nmn and Emma Jean Bailey; 1 child, Ben. Student, Jefferson State, 1976—79, Jacksonville State, 1980; BS, Pacific Western U., 1986, MPA, 1988; PhD, Pickering U., Honolulu, 2001. Cert. peace officer stds. tng. Ala., peace officers stds. and tng. instr. Ala., medicolegal death investigator St. Louis Sch. Medicine, arson investigation Ala., advanced hostage negotiations U.S. Treasury. Dir. of security edn. (law related edn.) RETS Inst., Birmingham, Ala., 1985—91; forensic investigator Ala. Dept. of Forensic Scis., Montgomery, Ala., 1988—89; dep. sheriff Jefferson County Sheriff's Dept., Birmingham, 1989—; instr. Online Police Acad., 2000—. Cons. The Backup Corp., Couer de Alene, Idaho, 2001—, Know Gangs, Modesto, Calif., 2002—, News Orgns., Birmingham, 2000—. Author: (book) What is Going on in our Schools? An Examination of Crime in our Schools, 2000, Perspectives on Terrorism, 2002, (CD) Tactics: Prevention and Response to School Violence, 2001. Capt. Ala. State Def. Force, Birmingham, 2002. Named Dep. of Yr., Jefferson Co. Sheriff's Dept., 1992; recipient Silver Star, Nat. Assn. of Chiefs of Police, 1983, 94, 2003, Lifesaving award, USAF Aux., 1982, Commendation, Gov. Fob James, State of Ala., 1998, Vice-President Al Gore, 1998, Police Mus. Display, Carbo's Smoky Mountain Police Mus., 1979—, Competitive Shooting awards, Various, 1993—97, Police Olympic medals, Ala. Peace Officers Assn., 1992—94, Purple Heart award, Nat. Assn. Chiefs of Police, 2003. Mem.: State Guard Assn. of the U.S., Am. Criminal Justice Assn., Am. Soc. of Law Enforcement Tng., Am. Soc. of Criminology. Avocations: travel, visiting flea markets, antiques, research. Office: Jefferson County Sheriff's Dept 2200 8th Ave N Birmingham AL 35023 Office Fax: 205-379-2495. Personal E-mail: jba3034221@aol.com.

BAILEY, JOHN, cinematographer; b. Mo., Aug. 10, 1942; m. Carol Littleton, Mar. 11, 1972. Student, U. Santa Clara, Loyola U., U. So. Calif., U. Vienna. Cinematographer: (films) Premonition, 1972, End of August, 1974, Legacy, 1976, The Mafu Cage, 1978, Boulevard Nights, 1979, American Gigolo, 1980, Ordinary People, 1980, Honky Tonk Freeway, 1981, Continental Divide, 1981, Cat People, 1982, That Championship Season, 1982, Without a Trace, 1983, The Big Chill, 1983, Racing with the Moon, 1984, The Pope of Greenwich Village, 1984, Mishima: A Life in Four Chapters, 1985, Silverado, 1985, Crossroads, 1986, Brighton Beach Memoirs, 1986, Light of Day, 1987, Swimming to Cambodia, 1987, Tough Guys Don't Dance, 1987, The Accidental Tourist, 1988, My Blue Heaven, 1989, A Brief History of Time, 1990; (TV films) Battered, 1978, City in Fear, 1980; photographer, dir. : The Search for Signs of Intelligent Life in the Universe, 1990; dir.: (films) China Moon, 1991, Mariette in Ecstacy, 1995; photographer : Groundhog Day, 1992; In the Line of Fire, 1993; Nobody's Fool, 1994; Passion, 1995; Extreme Measures, 1996; As Good as it Gets, 1997; Living Out Loud, 1997; Always Outnumbered, 1998; The Out-of-Towners, 1998; For Love of the Game, 1999; Forever Mine, 1999; Via Dolorosa, 2000; NSYNC: Bigger Then Live, 2001; The Anniversary Party, 2001; The Kid Stay in the Picture, 2002; Divine Secrets of the YaYa Sisterhood, 2002; How to Lose a Guy in 10 Days, 2003. Mem.: Acad. Motion Picture Arts and Scis. (bd. govs.), Am. Soc. Cinematographers (v.p.). Office: United Talent Agy 9560 Wilshire Blvd Fl 5 Beverly Hills CA 90212-2400 also: Am Soc Cinematographers 1782 N Orange Dr Los Angeles CA 90028-4307

BAILEY, JOHN MARTIN, retired transportation planner, educator; b. Lakewood, Ohio, Feb. 23, 1928; s. Frank Moherman and Elma (Keener) B.; m. Dorothy Jane Stubbs, Apr. 9, 1960; children: Leslie Jane, Brian John. BA, Hiram Coll., 1949; MS, MIT, 1951; PhD, U. Va., 1959, postgrad., 1977-78. Aero. research scientist NASA, Cleve., 1951-55; mem. faculty dept. physics Beloit (Wis.) Coll., 1959-76; transp. planner Balt. Regional Coun. Govs., 1976-89, Md.-Nat. Capital Pk. and Planning Commn., 1989-95; ret., 1995. Sabbatical research Cambridge U., 1965-66; dir. Overseas Seminar in Quantum Physics, Copenhagen, Denmark, 1970 Author: Liberal Arts Physics, 1974. Mem. Am. Planning Assn., Transp. Research Bd. Episcopalian. Home: 9502 Good Lion Rd Columbia MD 21045-3948

BAILEY, JOSELYN ELIZABETH, physician; b. Pine Bluff, Ark. d. Joseph Alexander and Angeline Elaine (Davis) B. BMus., Manhattanville Coll., 1952; M Music Edn., Manhattan Sch. Music, 1954; MD, Howard U., 1971. Straight

med. intern Huntington Hosp., Pasadena, Calif., 1971-72, resident, 1972-74; fellow in nephrology Wadsworth VA Hosp., L.A., 1975-77; practice medicine specializing in internal medicine and nephrology, Torrance, Calif. Assoc. staff Torrance Meml. Hosp.; active Little Company of Mary Hosp.; attending staff Harbor Gen. Hosp.; clin. faculty dept. medicine UCLA; trustee Bay Harbor Hosp., 1982—. Mem ACP.

BAILEY, JUDITH IRENE, university official, consultant; b. Winston-Salem, N.C., Aug. 24, 1946; d. William Edward Hege Jr. and Julia (Hedrick) Hege; m. Brendon Stinson Bailey, Jr. June 8, 1968. BA, Coker Coll., 1968; MEd, Va. Tech., 1973, EdD, 1976; postgrad., Harvard U., 1994,, 1994—95. Tchr. Chariho Regional H.S., Wood River Junction, RI, 1969—70, Prince William County Pub. Schs., Woodbridge, Va., 1968—72; asst. prin. Osbourn H.S., Manassas, Va., 1973; secondary sch. coord. Stafford (Va.) County Schs., 1973—74; middle sch. coord. Stafford County Schs., 1975—76; human rels. coord. Coop. Extension Svc. U. Md., College Park, 1976—79; dep. dir. Coop. Extension Svc. U. D.C., Washington, 1980-88; asst. v.p., dir. Coop. Extension U. Maine, Orono, 1988—92, interim v.p. for rsch. and pub. svc., 1992—93, v.p. rsch. and pub. svc., 1993—95, v.p. acad. affairs, provost, 1995—97; pres. No. Mich. U., Marquette, 1997—2003, Western Mich. U., Kalamazoo, 2003—. Trustee Bronson Healthcare Group, Kalamazoo, 2003—; adj. prof. George Mason U., Fairfax, Va., 1978; grad. student adv. U. Md., 1979—80; spkr. and cons. in field; bd. trustees Kalamazoo Branson Healthcare Group, 2003—. Co-author: Contingency Planning for a Unitary School System; contbr. articles to profl. jours. Co-v.chmn. Lake Superior Cmty. Partnership, 1997—2003; bd. trustees Marquette (Mich.) Gen. Health Sys., 1998—2003; active Mich. Humanities Coun., 1999—2002, sec., treas., 2002—; bd. dirs. Pine Tree State 4-H Found., 1988—97, Maine Toxicology Inst., 1992—95, Bangor (Maine) Symphony Orch, 1991—97, Shorebank, 1997—. Recipient Disting. Alumni Achievement award, Coker Coll., 1998, Northwoods Woman Educator of Yr. award, 1999, Case V Chief Exec. Leadership award, 2002; fellow Susan Coker Watson fellow, 1967. Mem.: AAUW, Econ. Club Marquette County (bd. dirs. 1997—2003), Rotary, Epsilon Sigma Phi (sec. Mu chpt. 1987, v.p. 1988, State Disting. Svc. award), Phi Kappa Phi, Phi Delta Kappa. Republican. Avocations: cooking, hiking. Home: 1201 Short Rd Kalamazoo MI 49008 Office: Western Mich U Office of the President 1903 W Michigan Kalamazoo MI 49008 5202 E-mail: judi.bailey@wmich.edu.

BAILEY, JULIA NANCY, geneticist; b. Van Nuys, Calif., Aug. 13, 1965; d. David Bertram and Elizabeth Mary (Kiss) B. BSc with honors, Concordia U., Montreal, Que., 1988; PhD, Yale U., 1996. Rsch. asst. Yale U., New Haven, 1989-96; rsch. assoc. U. Miami, Fla., 1990-94; postdoctoral fellow UCLA, 1996-2000, rsch. fellow, 2000—. Contbr. articles to profl. jours. Yale U. fellow, 1989-96, NIMH fellow, 1996, CAN fellow 1998. Mem. Am. Soc. Human Genetics, Internat. Soc. Genetic Epidemiology, Soc. for Creative Anacronism, Am. Epilipsy Soc. Office: UCLA 760 Westwood Plz # 47421 Los Angeles CA 90095-8353

BAILEY, KATHERINE CHRISTINE, artist, writer; b. Glendale, Calif., Dec. 1, 1952; d. Carl Leonard and Anna Alice (Dzamka) Abrahamson; m. David Francis Bailey, Sept. 27, 1975. BA, Calif. State U., L.A., 1974, MA, 1975; PhD, U. N.Mex., 1982. Exhbns. include Miniature Painters Sculptors & Gravers Soc., Washington, Oil Pastel Assn. Internat., N.Y.C., Mont. Miniature Art Soc. Internat., many others; author: (novel) Brush With Death; also numerous short stories; participant in Cyberspace Exhbn. on internet. Recipient hon. mention in mixed media category Nat. Western Small Painting Show, Bosque Art Gallery, N.Mex., 1985, 2d pl. award in pastels, 1986, internat. award hon. mention Multi-Media Art Exhbn., Oil Pastel Assn., 1999, Gen. Pencil Co. and Pastel Jour. award, 2000, Charles Hughes award UPA/OPA Show, 2001; tuition fellow U. N.Mex., 1977; Alpha Gamma Sigma scholar, 1972. Mem. Oil Pastel Assn. (Cert. Merit awrad 4th Ann. Holiday Exhbn. 1994, Internat. Hon. Mention award Multi Media Exhibn. 1999), Nat. Mus. Women in Arts, Mont. Miniature Art Soc., Laramie Art Guild, N.W. Pastel Soc., Phi Kappa Phi, Alpha Gamma Sigma. Avocations: playing piano, photography, hiking. Home: PO Box 301 Daggett CA 92327-0301 E-mail: Katherine481@webtv.net.

BAILEY, KAY WOOD, management consultant; b. Wilmington, Del. m. Richard H. Bailey. Adminstr. prison arts program Del. Dept. Correction, Dover, 1986—2002; pres., founder A.B.C. Consulting, Smyrna, Del., 2002—. Founder, pub., editor Wyoming (Del.) Gazette, The Internat. Correctional Arts Network Jour. Past bd. mem. Del. Symphony, Grand Opera House. Named Del. Trailblazer of the Yr., Agenda of Del. Women, 1991, hon. African Am., Star Hill A.M.E. Ch., 1995, Del. Mother of the Yr., Del. Chpt. Am. Mothers, 1997, Del. Art Educator of the Yr., Art Educators Del., 2000, Del. Communicator of Achievement, Del. Press Assn., 2002; recipient She Knows Where She's Going award, Girls Inc., 1993, Nat. Communicator of Achievement, Nat. Fedn. Press Women, 2002—03. Home: 105 Front St Wyoming DE 19934-1123

BAILEY, KEITH E. petroleum pipeline company executive; b. 1942; married. BS, Mo. Sch. Mines, 1964. With Continental Pipe Line, 1964—66; with Yellowstone Pipeline, 1966, Continental Pipeline, 1966—73, William Pipe Line Co. Inc., Tulsa, 1973—83, past pres.; pres., chief oper. officer N.W. Ctrl. Pipeline Corp., Tulsa; past exec. v.p. fin. and adminstrn. The Williams Cos., Tulsa, pres., 1992; former chmn., pres., CEO The Williams Cos., Inc., Tulsa. Office: Williams Cos Inc 1 Williams Ctr Tulsa OK 74172-0140

BAILEY, KELLY FRANK, occupational health company executive; b. Havre, Mont., June 7, 1949; s. George William and Valeria Lucille (Novak) B.; m. Rebecca Vance, June 21, 1969 (div. Mar. 1976); 1 child, Jonathan Noel; m. Teresa Brewer, June 12, 1992; 1 child, Destin Mariah. BS in Chemistry and Human Biology, Lamar U., Beaumont, Tex., 1973. Cert. indsl. hygienist. Chief chemist Olin Corp., Beaumont, 1973-74; environ. chemist Celanese Chem. Co., Bay City, Tex., 1974-77; wastewater ind. cons. Bay City, 1975-78; tech. rep. Hercules Inc., Houston, 1978; plant indsl. hygienist Celanese Chem. Co., Houston, 1978-79; chem. divsn. indsl. hygienist Vulcan Chems. Co., Birmingham, Ala., 1979-84; corp. mgr. occupational health Vulcan Materials Co., Birmingham, 1984—. Chmn. safety and health com. Nat. Stone Assn., Washington, 1997-99; chmn., pres. Indsl. Health Coun., Birmingham, 1997—. Author: (booklet) Occupational Health Programs in Mining, 1997. Named Safety and Health Profls. of Yr., Nat. Stone Assn., Washington, 1993. Mem. Am. Indsl. Hygiene Assn., Am. Acad. Indsl. Hygiene, Ala. Am. Indsl. Hygiene Assn. (pres. 1982-83, apptd. mine safety and health rsch. adv. com.). Avocations: guitar, camping, canoing, fly fishing. Office: Vulcan Materials Co 1200 Urban Center Dr Birmingham AL 35242-2545 E-mail: bailey@vmcmail.com.

BAILEY, KENNETH D. sociology educator; b. San Angelo, Tex. s. Kenneth R. and Sherline Bailey; m. Jo Neil Evans, Sept. 21, 1963. PhD in Sociology, U. Tex., 1968. Prof. sociology UCLA, 1968—. Author: Methods of Social Research, 1978, Social Entropy Theory, 1990, Sociology and the New Systems Theory, 1994, Typologies and Taxonomies, 1994; assoc. editor Am. Sociol. Rev., 1974-76; contbr. over 100 articles to profl. jours. Sr. rsch. fellow Internat. Sys. Inst., La Jolla, Calif., 1984—. Mem. Soc. Study of Social Problems (bd. dirs. 1985-90, mem. permanent orgn. com. 1997—), Am. Sociol. Assn. (com. on profl. ethics 1997-2000), Internat. Sociol. Assn. (pres. rsch. com. sociocybernetics 1995-98), Internat. Soc. Sys. Scis. (sec.-treas. 1994-97, mem. editl. bd. Sys. Rsch. and Behavioral Sci. 1997). Avocations: travel, hiking, reading. Office: UCLA Dept Sociology 405 Hilgard Ave Los Angeles CA 90095 Fax: 310-206-9838. E-mail: kbailey@soc.ucla.edu.

BAILEY, KENNETH KYLE, history educator; b. nr. Coldwater, Miss., Dec. 3, 1923; s. John Parham and Ruby Ross (Allen) B.; m. Mary Lou Crain, Aug. 5, 1961. Student, Northwest Miss. Jr. Coll., 1941-42, 45-46; BA, Vanderbilt U., 1947, MA, 1948, PhD, 1953. Instr. social sci. Cumberland (Ky.) Coll., 1949-50; instr. social sci. N.M. Mil. Inst., 1952-53, asst. prof., 1953-55; instr. history Ind. U., 1955-56, Tex. Western Coll., 1956-57; asst. prof. North Tex. State Coll., 1957-58, La. State U., 1958-60; assoc. prof. history U. Tex., El Paso, 1960-63, prof., 1963-91, prof. emeritus, 1991—; chmn. dept. U. Tex. at El Paso, 1968-71, 74. Author: Southern White Protestantism in the Twentieth Century, 2d edit, 1968; bd. editors: Jour. So. History, 1975-79. Mem. City of El Paso Historic Landmark Commn., 1983-90, chmn., 1986-90; pres. El Paso Landmarks, Inc., 1992-96; mem. Pelzer Meml. Award Com., Orgn. of Am. Historians, 1965-69. With AUS, 1942-45. Social Sci. Research Council grantee, 1955; Guggenheim Meml. fellow, 1966-67 Mem. So. Hist. Assn. Presbyterian. Home: 3033 Federal Ave El Paso TX 79930-4307

BAILEY, LEE WORTH, philosophy and religion educator; b. West Palm Beach, Fla., Nov. 21, 1943; s. Harold Stallsworth and Anne Barbara (Kiss) B.; m. Anne Hetherington Brinton, June 15, 1974; children: Soren B., Rhiannon B. BFA, U. Ill., 1965; MDiv, Union Theol. Sem., N.Y.C., 1970; PhD, Syracuse U., 1983. Asst., assoc. prof. dept. philosophy and religion Ithaca (N.Y.) Coll., 1983—, chmn. dept., 1991-93. Co-author: Rudely Stamp'd, 1983, The Near-Death Experience: A Reader, 1996, An Anthology of Living Religions, 2000; contbr. articles and revs. to profl. jours. Mem.: Am. Acad. Religion. Democrat. Office: Ithaca Coll Dept Philosophy & Religion Ithaca NY 14850 E-mail: bailey@ithaca.edu.

BAILEY, LLOYD ROBERT SCOTT, publishing company executive, editor, historian; b. N.Y.C., Sept. 4, 1924; s. Lloyd Whitfield and Josephine (LaBree) B.; m. Margaret Jean Teets, Dec. 27, 1947; children: Margaret Buchanan, Douglass Whitfield. Student, Miami U., Oxford, Ohio, 1945-47, U. Cin. Coll. Law, 1947-50. Reporter Middletown (Ohio) Jour., 1939; asst. exec. Boy Scouts Am., Elmira, N.Y., 1952, dist. exec. Mineola, N.Y., 1952-54; pub. rels. counsel Ea. R.R. Pres. Conf., Carl Byoir & Assocs., 1954-60; dir. pub. rels. Am. Rocket Soc., N.Y.C., 1960-61; founding editor, pub. Automobile Quar. Publs. Inc., N.Y.C., 1962-86; pres. Princeton (N.J.) Pub. Inc., 1975—, Princeton Inst. for Hist. Rsch., 1976—. Mem. Devel. coun. Miami U., 1955-58; exec. v.p., bd. dirs. pub. rels. editor Antique Automobile Club Am., Hershey, Pa., 1957-65; bd. dirs. Greenwich Village Symphony, 1958-60; trustee Michael Sedgwick Trust, vice chmn. Nat. Motor Mus., Beaulieu Eng., 1984—, Weymss Meml. Trust, vice chmn. Stanway, Eng., 1991—. With USNR, 1941-45, PTO. Fulbright scholar, 1950; recipient Submarine Svc. commendation medal, Silver Anvil award Am. Pub. Rels. Soc., 1958, Thomas McKean award for hist. rsch., 1963; 65, Disting. Svc. award Boy Scouts Am., 1964, gold and silver medals Phila. Franklin Inst., 1971-72. Mem. U.S. Naval Inst., Nassau Club (Princeton), DKE, Yale Club, Masons (32d degree), Dayton, Ohio Consistory, Delta Kappa Epsilon, Phi Alpha Delta. Republican. Mem. Soc. Of Friends. Home: Whitfield House Wood Stanway Winchcombe Cheltenham GL54 5PG England Office: care Victor Walcoff 997 Lenox Dr Lawrenceville NJ 08648-2317

BAILEY, MARY BEATRICE, retired nursing information systems director; b. Pitts., Dec. 24, 1933; d. Harry Chantler and Beatrice Iseli (Koenig) B. Diploma in Nursing, Allegheny Gen. Hosp., Pitts., 1956; BSNE, Chatham Coll., Pitts., 1956; MSN, Duke U., Durham, 1967. Cert. nursing adminstr., advanced. Staff nurse, head nurse, nursing supr. Allegheny Gen. Hosp., Pittsburgh, 1956-60; nursing instr. pediatrics Duke U. Sch. Nursing, Durham, N.C., 1960-61; nursing instr. med. surg Rex Hosp. Sch. Nursing, Raleigh, N.C., 1962-63; nursing supr. Rex Hosp., Raleigh, 1964-71, patient care coord., 1972-86, clin. dir., 1987, dir. nursing info. system, 1987-95. Author: The Role of the Mother with her Hospitalized Child, 1966. Vol. Rn open door clinic, Raleigh, 1987-88, Meals on Wheels, Wake Co., 1996—, Raleigh Little Theatre, 1993—; mem. N.C. Coalition for Choice; elected N.C. Bd. of Nursing, 1991-93, 94-96. Named to The Great 100 N.C. Nurses, 1992. Mem. NOW, N.C. Coun. Women's Orgns., N.C. League for Nursing, N.C. Nurses Assn. (life, treas. 1977-79), Great 100 (charter treas. 1989), Zonta Club of Raleigh (charter treas.). Democrat. Episcopalian. Avocations: reading, theater, music, sports. Home: 311 Furches St Raleigh NC 27607-4015

BAILEY, MICHAEL KEITH, lawyer; b. Washington, Feb. 19, 1956; s. Alda Merrill and Joan (Moyers) B.; m. Linda Ann Braswell, Dec. 18, 1982; children: Julia Anne, David Allen. AB in Econs. and Polit. Sci., Coll. William and Mary, 1978; JD, Stetson U., 1981. Bar: Fla. 1981, U.S. Dist. Ct. (mid. dist.) Fla. 1982, U.S. Ct. Appeals (11th cir.) 1982, U.S. Supreme Ct. 1986. Assoc. Pitts, Eubanks, et al, Orlando, Fla., 1981-86; ptnr. Parrish, Bailey & Myers, P.A., Orlando, 1986-98, Bailey & Myers, P.A., Maitland, Fla., 1998—. Mem.: ATLA (charter, pres.'s club), ABA, Fla. Bar Bd. Ctr. (civil trial atty.), Nat. Bd. Trial Adv. (cert. civil trial advocate), Acad. Fla. Trial Lawyers (eagle patron), Orange County Bar Assn., So. Trial Lawyers Assn. Republican. Presbyterian. Office: Bailey & Myers PA 100 E Sybelia Ave Ste 120 Maitland FL 32751-4777 Home: 701 Lake Sue Ave Winter Park FL 32789-5807 E-mail: mbailey@baileymyers.com.

BAILEY, MICHAEL SCOTT, cardiovascular electrophysiologist; b. Kingsport, Tenn., Apr. 20, 1968; s. Roy Thomas and Phyllis Ann Bailey; 1 child, Chandler Madisen. BS, East Tenn. State U., 1992; MD, U. Tenn., Memphis, 1996. Diplomate Am. Bd. Internal Medicine. Internal medicine intern, resident U. Fla., Gainesville, 1996—99, fellow cardiovasc. diseases, 1999—2002, fellow cardiovasc. electrophysiology, 2002—03; cardiovasc. electrophysiologist Nashville Arrhythmia Cons., PC, 2003—. Shuttle support physician NASA, Cape Canaveral, Fla., 1997—. Republican. Achievements include research in cardiovascular effects of estrogen as it relates to arrhythmias. Avocations: flying, bicycling, coin collecting, scuba diving, weight training.

BAILEY, MICHAEL WALLACE, aerospace engineer; b. Shelby, Miss., Sept. 24, 1968; s. Wallace Bryant and Flossie Mae (Cobb) B.. BS in Aerospace Engrng. summa cum laude, Miss. State U., 1990. Sr. specialist engr. internat. space sta. program Boeing Co., Huntsville, Ala., 1990-97, 2000; sr. specialist engr. express rack program Internat. Space Sta., Boeing Co., Huntsville, Ala., 1998-99, sr. specialist engr. propulsion module program, 1999—. Mem.: Phi Kappa Phi, Tau Beta Pi. Baptist. Avocations: car restoration, racing, church.

BAILEY, NAN HUTCHINS, mathematician, educator; b. Tyler, Tex., July 2, 1952; d. Lemuel Conner and Martha (Hawes) Hutchins; m. Blake Henry Bailey, Nov. 1, 1984 (div. May 1998); children: Laura Elizabeth, Katherine Conner. Premier deg., Sorbonne U., 1972; BA in Math and French, Hollins U., 1974; MS in Math., George Mason U., 1977. Tchr. Math. London County Ind. Sch. Dist., Sterling Park, Va., 1974—75; tchr. h.s. Dept. Def., Okinawa, Japan, 1977—78; tchr. Math., French Carlsbad Ind. Sch. Dist., Carlsbad, Calif., 1979—81; tchr. Math. Crooked Oak Ind. Sch. Dist., Oklahoma City, 1981—83; instr. Math. U. Tex. Tyler, 1984—85, Tyler Jr. Coll., Tyler, 1987—94; tchr. Math. Tyler Ind. Sch. Dist., Tyler, 1997—. Bd. regents Tex. Women's U., Denton, 1992—98. Named Educator of Distinction, Coca Cola Found., 2002, Secondary Tchr. of Yr., Tyler Ind. Sch. Dist., 2002. Democrat. Presbyterian. Avocations: hiking, reading, pen and ink drawing, philosophy. Home: 800 Fox Cove Tyler TX 75703 Office: John Tyler High Sch 1120 NNW Loop 323 Tyler TX 75704

BAILEY, NANCY JOYCE, educator; b. Detroit, May 9, 1942; d. Thomas Hill and Margaret (McGrath) Rainey; m. Carl John Bailey, June 12, 1963 (dec. 1996); 1 child, John; m. Thomas Barthelemy, 2000. BA, Vanderbilt U., 1960; internat. exchange student, Stuttgart, Germany, 1960; postgrad., U. Mex., 1957, U. Santa Clara, 1975, George Washington U., 1979-80. Cert. early childhood edn. tchr., early childhood specialist. Hostess Brentwood (Tenn.) Country Club, 1960; adminstrv. aide U.S. Senate, Washington, 1966; sec. U.S. Ho. of Reps., Washington, 1971-74; tchr. D.C. Pub. Schs., 1961—2001; prin., owner Historic Hilltop House Hotel, Harpers Ferry, W.Va., 2001—; pres., owner Hilltop House Hotel, Restaurant and Conf. Ctr., Harpers Ferry, W.Va. Bd. dirs Cabvin Internat. Corp., 1985—, Helms Passive Imaging, Inc., 2001--; rep. Washington Tchrs. union, 1982-94; founder David Lipscomb U., Nashville, 1988; participant Internat. Tchr. Exch. Program, Korea, 1994; mem. Ednl. Delegation to China, 1996; mem. postgrad. program NIH, Bethesda, Md., 1996. Keyperson United Way Campaign, Washington, 1974-93; docent The White House, Exec. Office of the Pres., Washington, 1987—; vol. First Lady's Corr., The White House, Washington, 1990—, Social Sec.'s Office, East Wing, 1993, 98—, Office of First Lady, 1993; coord. Presdl. Youth Vol. Day, 1993; mem. Nat. Trust for Historic Preservation, 1990—, Friendship Force of Nat. Capital Area, 1993—, People to People Internat. of Nat. Capital Area, 1993—; mem. adv. bd. New Visions for Child Care, Inc., 1993; chair Local Schs. Restructuring Team, 1992-93; participant Internat. Tchr. Exch. Program, Korea, 1994; mem. exec. com. YWCA Internat. Fair, Washington, 1994; del. Internat. Women's Friendship Conf. World Peace, Washington, 1995; mem. World Affairs Coun., Washington, 1995—; mem. Internat. Policy Inst., Washington, 1997-2000, v.p. edn., 1998-2000; tchr. adv. panel Nat. Capital Children's Mus., Japan, 1998; mem. ARK Found. Mission to Africa, RUVU Project, Tanzania, 1997; mem. adv. bd. ARK Found. to Africa, 1999—; supr. mcpl. elections Orgn. for Security and Coop. in Europe Mission in Bosnia/Herzegovina, 1997, supr. presdl. elections out of country voters, Croatia, 1998; supr. mcpl. elections, Kosovo, 2000; supr. Kosovo Assembly elections, out of country voters, Montenegro, 2001; mem. Coun. of European Election Observation Mission in Kosovo, 2002; pres. Hilltop House Hotel, Harpers Ferry, W. Va., 2003—. Recipient Internat. Cooperation award Am. Fgn. Study Program, Am. Study Program, 1984-86, Am. Student Edn. Travel. Mem. Delta Group (mem. coun. 1989-92), Am. Fedn. Tchrs., Internat. Reading Assn., World Affairs Coun., Delta Kappa Gamma. Avocations: antiques, numismatics, flying, boating. Home: 6703 Lupine Ln Mc Lean VA 22101-1579 Office: Historic Hilltop House Hotel 400 E Ridge St PO Box 930 Harpers Ferry WV 25425

BAILEY, PHILIP SIGMON, JR., university official and dean, chemistry educator; b. Charlottesville, Va., Mar. 17, 1943; s. Philip Sigmon Bailey and Marie Jeanette (Schultz) Hatch; m. Christina Anne Wahl; children: Karl, Jennifer, Kristen, Michael. Student, Am. U., Cairo, 1961; BS in Chemistry, U. Tex., 1964; PhD, Purdue U., 1969. Asst. prof. chemistry Calif. Poly. State U., San Luis Obispo, 1969-73, prof., assoc. dean, 1973-83, prof. chemistry, dean Coll. Sci. and Math., 1983-89, v.p. acad. affairs. sr. v.p., 1989-90, dean, 1990—. Author: (lab texts) Experimental Chemistry for Contemporary Times, 1975, Organic Chemistry, 1978, (textbook) Organic Chemistry, 1978, 6th edit., 2000. Mem. Am. Chem. Soc., Alpha Chi Sigma. Home: 1628 Royal Way San Luis Obispo CA 93405-6334 E-mail: pbailey@calpoly.edu.

BAILEY, REEVE MACLAREN, museum curator; b. Fairmont, W.Va., May 2, 1911; s. Joseph Randall and Elizabeth Weston (Maclaren) B.; m. Marian Alvinette Kregel, Aug. 13, 1939; children— Douglas M., David R., Thomas G., Susan Helen. Student, Toledo U., 1929-30; AB, U. Mich., 1933, PhD, 1938. Instr. zoology Iowa State Coll. (now univ.), 1938-42, asst. prof., 1942-44; asst. prof. zoology U. Mich., 1944-50, asso. prof., 1950-59, prof., 1959-81, prof. emeritus, 1981—. Assoc. curator Mus. Zoology, 1944-48, curator, 1948—; rsch. assoc. Am. Mus. Nat. History, 1964—. Contbr. over 150 articles, bulls., revs. to profl. jours. on ichthyology and herpetology. Fellow Iowa Acad. Sci.; mem. Am. Soc. Ichthyologists and Herpetologists (editl. bd., v.p. 1954, pres. 1959, Robert H. Gibbs Jr. Meml. award 1995), Am. Fisheries Soc. (pres. 1974, hon. mem. 1979—, recipient Award of Excellence 1980, Meritorious Svc. award 1989, Justin W. Leonard award of excellence Mich. chpt. 1985), Am. Inst. Fisheries Rsch. Biologists (Outstanding Achievement award 1996), AAAS (coun. 1968-72), Ecol. Soc. Am., Soc. Study Evolution, Soc. Systematic Biologists, Soc. Limnology and Oceanography, Mich. Acad. Sci., Arts and Letters. Avocation: ichthyol. expdns. in U.S., Bermuda, Bolivia, Guatemala, Paraguay, Zambia. Home: 4001 Glacier Hills Dr Apt 325 Ann Arbor MI 48105-3652 Office: Univ Mich Museum Zoology Ann Arbor MI 48109 E-mail: reevemarian@yahoo.com.

BAILEY, RICHARD BRIGGS, investment company executive; b. Weston, Mass., Sept. 14, 1926; s. George William and Alice Gertrude (Cooper) B.; m. Rebecca C. Bradford, June 20, 1950 (div. Dec. 1974); children: Ann, Elizabeth, Richard, Rebecca; m. Anne D. Prescott, Dec. 14, 1974 (div. 1980); m. Anita S. Lawrence, Sept. 12, 1980 (div. 1990); 1 child, Alexandra; m. Nanette Sexton, Sept. 27, 1993. BA, Harvard, 1948, MA, 1951; postgrad., Grad. Sch. Bus. Adminstrn., 1966. Prodn. engr. C. Brewer & Co., Honolulu, 1951-53; prodn. engr. Raytheon Co., Waltham, Mass., 1953-54; security analyst Keystone Custodian Funds, Boston, 1955-59; industry specialist Mass. Investors Trust, 1959-69; v.p. Mass. Fin. Svcs., Co., Boston, 1969-77, pres., 1978-82, chmn., dir., 1982-91, ret., 1991. Chmn. Lincoln (Mass.) Fin. Com., 1966-68. Trustee Plimoth Plantation, Inc., Plymouth, Mass., Phillips Exeter Acad., Exeter, N.H., 1978-82, Handel and Haydn Soc. 2d lt. Signal Corps, AUS, 1944-46. Decorated Letter of Commendation. Mem. Somerset Club (Boston). Republican. Episcopalian. Address: c/o William F Kehoe Taylor Ganson & Perrin 160 Federal St Boston MA 02110

BAILEY, RICHARD WELD, English language educator; b. Pontiac, Mich, Oct. 26, 1939; s. Karl Deanor and Elisabeth Phelps (Weld) B.; m. Margaret Louise Bowman, 1960 (div. 1976); children— Eleanor Bowman (dec.), Charles Andrew Stuart; m. Julia Ruth Huttar, 1990; 1 child, Oceana Yi Huttar. Student, U. Edinburgh, Scotland, 1959-60; AB, Dartmouth Coll., 1961; MA, U. Conn., 1963, PhD, 1965. From asst. prof. English to assoc. prof. U. Mich., Ann Arbor, Mich., 1965-76, prof., 1976—, Fred Newton Scott Collegiate prof., 2002. Del. ACLS, 1996-2002. Author: Images of English, 1991, Nineteenth-Century English, 1996; Rogue Scholar: the Sinister Life and Celebrated Death of Edward H. Rulloff, 2003; editor: (with others) English Stylistics, 1968, Milestones in the History of English in America, 2002; Computing in the Humanities, 1982; Michigan Early Modern English Materials, 1975; English as a World Language, 1982, Literacy for Life, 1983, Dictionaries of English, 1987. Trustee Washtenaw C.C., Ann Arbor, 1974—, chair, 1985-95, 1999-2001; del. platform com. Nat. Dem. Conv., 1976; sr. warden St. Clare of Assisi Episcopal Ch., Ann Arbor, 1981-82, guild of scholars, NY, 1997—, pres., 2001—. Grantee NEH, 1971-75, 78, 85, 91-92, Ford Found., 1978-82; Inst. for Advanced Studies in the Humanities fellow, 1971 Mich. Linguistic Soc. (pres. 1975-76), Commn. on English Lang., Nat. Coun. Tchr. of English, Am. Dialect Soc. (exec. coun. 1980-84, v.p. 1985-87, pres. 1987-88), Dictionary Soc. N.Am. (exec. com. 1992-95, v.p. 1999-2001, pres. 2001-03), Assn. Computing in the Humanities (v.p. 1980-83), Am. Coun. Learned Soc. (del. 1996-2002), Flounders Club (Ann Arbor); The Athenaeum (London). Home: 1609 Cambridge Rd Ann Arbor MI 48104-3520 Office: U Mich Dept English Ann Arbor MI 48109-1003 E-mail: rwbailey@umich.edu.

BAILEY, RITA MARIA, investment advisor; b. Frankfurt, Germany; d. Ludwig and Gertrude (Cierniak) Fleischmann; m. William W. Bailey, Feb. 17, 1974; children: Anne Christine, Cynthia Patricia. BS in Psychology, Austin Peay U., 1975, MA in Psychology, 1977, postgrad., 1977-79. Cert. counselor, Tenn. Editor U.S. Army Spl. Warfare Inst., Ft. Bragg, N.C., 1967-74, edn. officer, 1979-82, Augsburg (Germany) Cmty. Ctr., 1982-85; pvt. practice counseling Leavenworth, Kans., 1985-90; pvt. practice investments, 1990—. Sr. investment advisor pvt. orgns., Washington, 1991—. Author: Extroversion and Introversion, 1978, Special Warfare Training Plan, 1981; author, editor tng. manual Foreign Small Arms, 1982. Dir. Energy Conservation Campaign, Clarksville, 1976; founder, dir. Women's Support Ctr., Leavenworth, 1986. Mem. Nat. Assn. Investors, Alpha Mu Gamma. Roman Catholic. Avocations: long distance swimming, gardening, german poetry.

BAILEY, ROBERT, JR., advertising executive; b. Kans. City, Apr. 27, 1945; s. Robert and Sarah (Morgan) B.; m. Rita Carol Burdinie, June 26, 1971; children: Rebecca, Sarah. AB, U. Kans., 1967; MA, Northwestern U., Ill., 1968; PhD, Northwestern U., 1972, MBA, 1979. Research supr. BBDO Chgo., 1973-78, v.p. research dir., 1978-82, sr. v.p., mktg. services dir., 1982-85, exec. v.p., rsch. and planning dir. Author: Radicals In Urban Politics, 1974; contbr. articles to profl. jours. Mem. Am. Mktg. Assn.. Office: BBDO Chgo 410 N Michigan Ave Ste 8 Chicago IL 60611-4273 E-mail: bob.bailey@bbdoch.com.

BAILEY, ROBERT A. child/adolescent psychiatrist; MD, Stanford U. Sch. of Medicine, 1976—80. Cert. General Psychiatry Am. Bd. of Psychiatry & Neurology, 1987, Child/Adolescent Psychiatry Am. Bd. of Psychiatry & Neurology, 1997. Internship Yale U., New Haven (Conn.) Med. Ctr., 1980—81; resident gen. psychiatry Stanford (Calif.) U. Med. Ctr., 1981—83; vice chair, dir. tng., divsn. of child & adolescent psychiatry U. of N.Mex Sch. of Medicine, Albuquerque, 1997—; chief of staff U. of N.Mex Health Sciences Ctr., Albuquerque, 2002—. Assoc. prof. psychiatry U. of N.Mex Sch. of Medicine, Albuquerque, 1999—. Mem.: Soc. of Professors of Child & Adolescent Psychiatry, Assn. for Academic Psychiatry (sect. chief, child/adolescent psychiatry 2002), Soc. for Rsch. in Child Devel., Am. Acad. of Child & Adolescent Psychiatry. Office: Psychiatry UNM-SOM 2400 Tucker Ave NE - 4th Fl Albuquerque NM 87131-5326

BAILEY, ROBERT C. opera company executive; b. Metropolis, Ill., Dec. 28, 1936; m. Sally McDermott, July 13, 1958. BA in Speech, U. Ill., 1958, MA in English, 1960; BM in Applied Voice, Eastman Sch. Music, 1965; MM in Applied Voice, New Eng. Conservatory Music, 1969. Music prodr. Nat. Pub. Radio, Washington, 1971-73, dir. cultural programming, 1973-75; mgr. Western Opera Theatre, San Francisco, 1975-79; instr. arts mgmt. Golden Gate U., San Francisco, 1977-82; cons. arts mgmt. San Francisco, 1980-82; gen. dir. Portland

Opera Assn., Oreg., 1982—; dir. Opera Am., 1995—2001. Cons. On-Site Program Nat. Endowment Arts, Washington, 1982—; judge Met. Opera Auditions, 1977—. Recipient Chevalier in the Order of Arts and Letters French Govt., 1999. Mem. Bohemian Club (San Francisco), City Club (Portland), Arlington Club, Rotary Club. Office: Portland Opera Assn Inc 1515 SW Morrison St Portland OR 97205-1814

BAILEY, ROBERT ELLIOTT, financial executive; b. Logansport, Ind., Mar. 29, 1932; s. Edwin William and Elizabeth Carolyn (Elliott) B.; m. Geraldine E. Hershberger, Jan. 31, 1954; children: Susan Elaine, Kathryn Jane. BS in Acctg., Ind. U., 1954; LLB, Tex. A&M U., Houston, 1962. CPA, N.Y. Ptnr. Arthur Andersen & Co., Chgo., 1958-72; exec. v.p., dir., CFO Damson Oil Corp., N.Y.C., 1972-82; exec. v.p., CFO ENI Cos., Seattle and Houston, 1982-85; exec. v.p., CFO, dir. Gearhart Industries, Inc., Ft. Worth, Tex., 1985-88; corp. fin. cons., 1988-91; chmn. fin. The Turner Corp., N.Y.C., 1991-93; sr. v.p., CFO Rotondo Cos., Avon, Conn., 1993-94; dir. fin. UCAR, Danbury, Conn., 1995-96, Tauck Tours, Inc., Westport, Conn., 1996-98. Capt. USAFR, 1958. Mem. AICPA, Tex. Bar Assn., N.Y. CPA Soc., Fla. CPA Soc. Home: #209 988 Boulevard of the Arts Sarasota FL 34236-4833

BAILEY, ROBERT SHORT, lawyer; b. Bklyn., Oct. 17, 1931; s. Cecil Graham and Mildred (Short) B.; m. Doris Furlow, Aug. 29, 1953 (dec. 2001); children: Elizabeh Jane Goldentyer, Robert F., Barbara A. Jongbloed. AB, Wesleyan U., Middletown, Conn., 1953; JD, U. Chgo., 1956. Bar: Ill. 1965, U.S. Dist. Ct. D.C. 1956, U.S. Supreme Ct. 1960. Atty. criminal divsn. U.S. Dept. Justice, 1956-61, asst. U.S. atty. No. dist. Ill., 1961-65; ptnr. LeFevour & Bailey, Oak Park, Ill., 1965-68; pvt. practice, Chgo., 1968—. Panel atty. Fed. Defender Program, 1965—. Mem. NACDL (faculty 1976-78, legis. chmn. 1976-78). Home: 17 Timber Trail Streamwood IL 60107-1353 Office: 53 W Jackson Blvd Ste 918 Chicago IL 60604-3607

BAILEY, ROY H. member of parliament; b. Dec. 16, 1928; m. Helen Bailey; 2 children. BEd, U. Saskatchewan, Can., 1964; BA, U. Regina, Can., 1969. Farmer, 1951—61; vice prin., v.p. Bengough Sch., 1961—71; mem. Legis. Assembly Saskatchewan, 1975—78; mem. 37th parliament House of Commons, Ottawa, Canada, 1997—. Vets. affairs critic for ofcl opposition House of Commons, mem. standing com. on environment, mem. standing com. on def. and vets. affairs, ofcl. opposition dep. critic for transport, 1997—2000, scrutiny of regulations com., 1997—98, ofcl. opposition dep. critic for agr., 1998—2000, dep. house leader for ofcl. opposition, 1998—99, procedure and house affairs com., 1998—99, caucus interim policy mgmt. com., 1998—99, mem. libr. of parliament com., 1999—2000. CEO, dir. edn. Eston-Elrose Sch. Divsn., 1971—82; Justice of the Peace Saskatchewan; exec. mem. Saskatchewan Sch. Trustees Assn., 1990—93; trustee Borderland Sch. Divsn., 1984—93. Avocation: hockey (referee). Office: House of Commons 250-180 Wellington Bldg Ottawa ON U1A 0A6 Canada also: # 2 405 Souris Ave Weyburn SK S4H 0C9 Canada

BAILEY, STEPHEN, history educator; b. Chgo., Apr. 4, 1939; s. Roland James Bailey and Zena Karras Sutherland; m. Susan Wood, Aug. 9, 1966; children: James, Andrew, Elisabeth. BA, U. Chgo., 1960, PhD, 1966. Prof. history Knox Coll., Galesburg, Ill., 1965—. Mem. acad. coun. Coll. Bd., N.Y.C., 1997-2000; cons. Javits Fellowship, U.S. Dept. Edn., Washington, 1987—; reader, table leader Ednl. Testing Svc., Princeton, N.J., 1980-93; grant cons. Joyce Found., Chgo., 1991-94; chmn. Coll. Bd. Midwestern Regional Coun., 2002-03; cons. North Ctrl. Assn. Contbr. more than 100 book revs. to Choice, 1977—. Vol. Galesburg Humane Soc., 1996—. Recipient Phillip Green Wright Tchg. prize Knox Coll., 1984. Democrat. Avocations: reading, gardening. Home: 1216 N Cherry St Galesburg IL 61401-1814

BAILEY, STEPHEN FAIRCHILD, museum director and curator, ornithologist; b. Stamford, Conn., Feb. 7, 1948; s. Edwin Montgomery and Frances (Sherman) B.; m. Karen Lynn Burtness, Aug. 18, 1971 (div. July 1987); divorced. BA in Biology magna cum laude, Beloit Coll., 1971; PhD in Zoology, U. Calif., Berkeley, 1978. Museum dir. and curator Pacific Grove Mus. of Natural Hist., Calif., 1992—. Collections mgr. for ornithology and mammalogy Calif. Acad. Scis., San Francisco, 1984-92; biological cons., 1979-92; adj. prof. biology San Francisco State U., 1986—; teaching Albany Adult Sch., Calif., 1979-85. Co-author Atlas of the Breeding Birds of Monterey County, 1993; co-author, photographer Audubon Society Master Guide to Birding 3 vols., 1983; regional editor Am. Birds, 1985-98; contbr. articles to profl. jours. Rsch. fellowship Christensen Rsch. Inst., Papua New Guinea, 1989. Mem. Am. Birding Assn. (elected), Ecological Soc. Am. (life), Am. Ornithologists Union, Cooper Ornithological Soc. (life), Pacific Seabird Group, Soc. Preservation of Natural Hist. Collections, Phi Eta Sigma, Phi Beta Kappa. Avocations: birding, travel, nature study, military history. Home: 830 Sunset Dr Apt J Pacific Grove CA 93950-4729 Office: Pacific Grove Museum Natural History 165 Forest Ave Pacific Grove CA 93950-2612

BAILEY, STEVEN R. cardiologist, researcher; b. San Antonio, Tex., Sept. 27, 1951; s. Raymond S. Bailey and Maxine Miller Mariam; m. Linda Craighill. BA, U. Oreg., 1973, MD, 1978. Diplomate Am. Bd. Interventional Cardiology, Am. Bd. Cardiovasc. Medicine, Am. Bd. Internal Medicine, lic. Nat. Bd. Med. Examiners. Asst. prof. medicine U. Tex. Health Sci. Ctr., San Antonio, 1989—92, asst. prof. radiology, 1992, assoc. prof. medicine and radiology, 1992—97, prof. medicine and radiology, 1997—; staff cardiologist Brooke Army Med. Ctr., Ft. Sam Houston, Tex., 1990—. Dir. interventional cardiology U. Tex. Health Sci. Ctr., San Antonio, 1989—, dir. cardiac catheterization labs., 1989—, dir. interventional cardiology fellowship program, 1990—. Contbr. articles to profl. jours. Chmn. Am. Heart Assn., San Antonio, 1996; bd. dirs. Habitat for Humanity, San Antonio. Lt. col. USAR, 1989—91. Named Shining Star, Univ. Health Sys., 2001; named one of Am.'s Top Drs., Castle Connolly Guide, 2001; recipient Internal Medicine Resident Rsch. award, Merck, 1981, William Wright Jr., M.D. award for cmty. svc., 1996. Mem.: Am. Coll. Cardiology (com. 2002, gov. Tex. chpt. 1997—99, bd. govs. task force on cardiovasc. econ. and practice, cardiac catheterization and intervention com.), Soc. Cardiac Angiography and Interventions, Soc. Cardiac Angiography, Am. Heart Assn. (bd. dirs. Tex. affiliate 1996—, pres.-elect San Antonio chpt. 1994—95, pres. 1995—96, v.p. cardiology soc. 1990—91, bd. dirs. San Antonio divsn. 1990—), Bexar County Med. Soc., Am. Soc. Artificial Internal Organs. Home: 3 Village Knoll San Antonio TX 78232 Office: U Tex Health Sci Ctr San Antonio 7703 Floyd Curl Dr San Antonio TX 78229-3900 Office Fax: 210-567-6960. Personal E-mail: srbailey@msn.com. E-mail: baileys@uthscsa.edu.

BAILEY, STEVEN SCOTT, operations research analyst; b. Ft. Benning, Ga., Dec. 9, 1948; s. Claude Esmond and Marietta (Tanzola) B.; m. Wendy Cropf, Dec. 10, 1988; 1 child, Michael. BS, U.S. Mil. Acad., 1970; MPA, U. Colo., Denver, 1977, MS, 1981; PhD, Colo. Sch. of Mines, 1989. Cert. prodn. and inventory mgmt. Commd. 2nd lt. U.S. Army, 1970, advanced through grades to lt. col., 1987; asst. prof. U.S. Mil. Acad., West Point, N.Y., 1981-84; ops. rsch. analyst Concepts Analysis Agy. U.S. Army, Bethesda, Md., 1984-86; asst. prof. Park Coll., Denver, 1986-89; ops. rsch. analyst RAND Corp., Santa Monica, Calif., 1989-92; rsch. analyst Ctr. for Naval Analyses, Alexandria, Va., 1992—97; dir. analysis COMUSNAVCENT, Bahrain, 1994—97; asst. prof. U. Bahrain, 1997—2003, Gulf U. Coll., 2002—03; adj. prof. Troy State U., 2003—. Instr. C.W. Post Coll., L.I. (N.Y.) U., 1982-84, Colo. Sch. Mines, Golden, 1988-89, UCLA Extension, 1990-91, CSUN, 1991-92, Amideast, 1996-98, U. Md., 1997-2003. Mem. Am. Prodn. and Inventory Control Soc., Inst. Mgmt. Sci., RAND Scuba Club (pres. 1989-92), Phi Kappa Phi. Avocation: scuba. E-mail: scottbailey70@fastmail.fm.

BAILEY, SUSAN MARY, editor, writer; b. Keene, N.H., Dec. 1, 1952; d. Howard A. and Margaret A. Bailey. BA in English Lit., U. N.H., 1974, MA in English Lit., 1976; MA in Creative Writing, Syracuse U., 1990. Living sect. editor Portsmouth (N.H.) Herald, 1985—87; composition tchr. Syracuse (N.Y.) U., 1988—90; arts editor, copy editor Idaho Mountain Express, Ketchum, 1990—96; children's libr. Cmty. Libr., Ketchum, 1996—99; arts editor Wood River Jour., Hailey, Idaho, 1999—. Author: The Kissing Beast, 1978, Lucky Accident, 1991 (nominated for Pushcart prize). Fellow creative writing fellow, Syracuse U., 1988, Ucross Found., 1991; scholar writers at work scholar, U. Utah, 1988. Mem.: Idaho Press Club (1st place edn. writing award 1995, 2d place humor column award 2001, 2002). Roman Catholic. Home: PO Box 1703 Sun Valley ID 83353 Office: Wood River Jour 11 E Bullion St Hailey ID 83333

BAILEY, THERESA L. director, consultant; d. George and Fammie Barnes Bailey, Albert, Sr. Evans; 1 child, Natasha N. BS, Alcorn State U., Miss., 1979, MS, 1994, PhD, Fla. State U., 2002—. Sec. Dept. of Fine Arts, Alcorn State U., Lorman, Miss., 1979—82; home health Adams County Health Dept., Natchez, Miss., 1982—83; gen. acct. The Piney Woods Country Life Sch., Miss., 1983—90; asst. to the v.p. for instl. advancement Tougaloo Coll., Miss., 1990—92, program adminstr., 1992—93; grants coord. Tuskegee U., Ala., 1993—95; assoc. in grants devel. Divsn. of Sponsored Rsch., Fla. A&M U., Tallahassee, 1995—2002, acting assoc. dir. sponsored rsch., 2002—. Pres., CEO TLB & Assocs.; cons. U. of Ark., Pine Bluff, 1997; instr., cons. Minority Health Professions Found., Atlanta, 1999; cons. Johnson C. Smith U., Charlotte, 1998, Miss. Valley State U., Itta Bena, Fla., 2000. Mem. Tallahassee Mus., 2003, Tallahassee Urban League, 2003; polit. campaign supporter, worker Charles Sheppard Campaign for State Govt., Lorman, Miss.; mem. Alcorn State U. Nat. Alumni Assn., Lorman, Miss. Mem.: AREA, Sisters of the Acad., Phi Delta Kappa, Nat. Coun. of Univs. Rsch. Administrs., Soc. of Rsch. Administrators (SRA) (mem. external rels. com. 1996—2000), Nat. Sponsored Programs Administrs. Alliance (chairperson membership com. 1997—2001). Democrat. Avocations: travel, reading, music, art, real estate. Office: Florida A&M U 400 Foote Hilyer Administrn Ctr Tallahassee FL 32307 Office Fax: 850-599-3952. Personal E-mail: tlbassociate@earthlink.net. E-mail: theresa.bailey@famu.edu.

BAILEY, THOMAS CHARLES, lawyer; b. Rochester, N.Y., Nov. 26, 1948; s. Charles George and Teckla Barbara (Driscoll) B.; m. Rosalie Stoll, Sept. 24, 1974; children: Leah Isabelle, Molly Driscoll, Elizabeth Rose. BA, Princeton U., 1970; JD, SUNY, Buffalo, 1974. Bar: N.Y. 1975, Fla. 1977. Assoc. Little & Burt, Buffalo, 1974-78, ptnr., 1978-80, Saperston & Day, PC, Buffalo, 1980-92; pvt. practice Buffalo, 1992-97; mem. Albrecht Maguire Heffern and Gregg PC, Buffalo, 1997-2000, Phillips, Lytle, Hitchcock, Blaine & Huber, LLP, Buffalo, 2000—. Bd. dirs., sec. Buffalo Therapeutic Riding Ctr. Inc., 1999-2001. Pres. St. Thomas Moore Guild, 1981; trustee Shea's O'Connell Preservation Guild, 1986-96, chmn., 1994; bd. dirs. Opera Niagara, Ltd., 1999—, pres., 2001-. Mem. ABA, N.Y. State Bar Assn. (exec. com. of real property law sect. 1994-2000), Fla. Bar Assn., Am. Assn. Franchisees and Dealers (fair franchising standards com.), Saturn Club (dean 2000), Princeton U. Alumni Assn. Western N.Y. (pres. 1990-91), Brookhaven Trout Club. Avocations: fly fishing, boating, horses. Office: Phillips Lytle et al 3400 HSBC Tower Buffalo NY 14203

BAILEY, THOMAS EVERETT, engineering company executive; b. Atlantic, Iowa, Mar. 30, 1936; s. Merritt E. and Clara May (Richardson) B.; m. Elizabeth Jane Taylor, Sept. 9, 1956; children: Thomas E., Douglas L., Steven W. BS, U. Iowa, 1959. Registered profl. engr., environ. assessor, expert witness. Engr. Calif. Dept. Water Resources, Sacramento, 1960-67; sr. engr. Calif. Water Quality Control Bd., San Luis Obispo, 1967-72; asst. div. chief, dir. water quality planning State Water Resources Control Bd., Sacramento, 1972-75, chief div. planning rsch., 1975-77, chief tech. support br., 1977-79; sr. tech. advisor Yemen Arab Republic, Sana'a, 1979-81; chief Calif. superfund program Calif. Dept. Health Svcs., Sacramento, 1982-86; prin., v.p. Kleinfelder Inc., Walnut Creek, Calif., 1986-92, also bd. dirs.; pres. Bailey Environ., Goodyear, Ariz., 1992-2000; ret., 2000. Cons. engr. Contbr. articles to profl. jours. Mem. San Luis County Obispo Rep. Ctrl. Com., 1969-72, vice-chmn., 1970-71, chmn., 1971-72; vice-chmn. bd. trustees Meth. Ch., San Luis Obispo, 1970-72; mem. Contra Costa County Hazardous Materials Com., 1988-89; chmn. bus. practices com. Hazardous Waste Action Coalition, 1991-93, bd. dirs., 1992-93; mem. Calif. Remedial Action Group, co-chmn., 1991-92. With U.S. Army, 1959-60. Office: 15434 W Piccadilly Rd Goodyear AZ 85338-8805 E-mail: teb4ejb@worldnet.att.net.

BAILEY, VICKY A. federal agency administrator; b. Indpls. BS, Purdue U.; postgrad., Ind. U., Indpls. Promotions dir. Glass Container divsn. Owens-Ill., Inc., Alton; asst. admissions officer Ind. U. Sch. Medicine; commr. Fed. Energy Regulatory Commn., 1993—2000; pres. PSI Energy, Inc., Ind., 2000—01; asst. secy. intl. affairs and domestic policy U.S. Dept. Energy, Washington, 2001—. Rep. to bd. trustees N.AM. Electric Reliability Coun.; mem. exec. com. Gt. Lakes conv. Mid-Am. Regulatory Commrs. Conf.; mem. Keystone Ctr. Energy Bd.; mem. Harvard Electricity Policy Group. Mem. Ind. Coun. for Econ. Edn.; active Boys and Girls Club of Indpls.; past pres. Indpls. Pub. Schs. Edn. Found., Ind. Humanities Coun., Nat. Coalition of 100 Black Women. Recipient Ind. Sagamore of the Wabash award. Mem. Nat. Assn. Regulatory Utility Commrs. (exec. and electricity coms.). Republican. Office: US Dept Energy Policy & Int Affairs 1000 Independence Ave SW Washington DC 20585-0001 Office Fax: 202-586-3047.

BAILEY, WILLIAM HARRISON, artist, educator; b. Council Bluffs, Iowa, Nov. 17, 1930; s. Willard Kendall and Marjorie Esther (Cheyney) Bailey; m. Sandra Stone, May 28, 1958; children: Ford Hamilton, Alix Brook. Student, U. Kans., 1948-51; BFA, Yale U., 1955, MFA, 1957; HHD (hon.), U. Utah, 1987; DFA (hon.), Adelphi U. Instr. art Yale U., New Haven, 1957-61, asst. prof., 1961-62, adj. prof., 1969-73, prof., 1973-79, Kingman Brewster prof., 1979-95, Kingman Brewster prof. emeritus, 1995—, dean Sch. Art, 1974-75; from asst. prof. to assoc. prof. Ind. U., 1962—68, prof., 1968-69. Mem. Nat. Coun. Arts, 1992—97. Exhibitions include Robert Schoelkopf Gallery, N.Y.C., 1968, 1971, 1974, 1979, 1982, 1986, 1990, 1991, Glleriea Il Gabbiano, Rome, 1985, 1989, 1993, 1997, John Berggruen Gallery, San Francisco, 1988, Andre Emmerich Gallery, N.Y.C., 1992, 1994, 1995, Alpha Gallery, Boston, 1998, Robert Miller Gallery, N.Y.C., 1999, 2003, Represented in permanent collections Mus. Modern Art, Whitney Mus., Hirshorn Mus., St. Louis Art Mus., Neu Galerie Der Stadt Aachen, Germany, Pa. Acad., Yale Art Gallery. With U.S. Army, 1951—53. Alice Kimball English Travelling fellow, 1955, Guggenheim fellow, 1965, Ingram Merrill fellow, 1975. Mem.: Academia di Belli Arti, Perugia, Acad. San Luca, Rome, Am. Acad. Arts and Letters, Nat. Acad. Design, Smithsonian Archives Am. Art (trustee), Tiffany Found. (bd. dirs.), Yaddo (mem. corp.). Office: Yale U Sch Art Dept Painting Printmaking New Haven CT 06520

BAILEY, WILLIAM HENRY, real estate appraiser; b. Kingsport, Tenn., Jan. 28, 1949; s. Fred M. and Ora Juanita (Barton) B.; m. Sharon Shanks, Nov. 17, 1973 (div.); 1 child, Allison Michelle; m. Penny S. Shoemaker, Dec. 26, 1983; children: Alexandra Amanda, William Henry. BS in Real Estate, East Tenn. State U., 1972. Salesman, auctioneer, appraiser C. Worley Richardson, Real Estate & Auction, Church Hill, Tenn., 1971-76; salesman, appraiser The Property Shop, Mt. Carmel, Tenn., 1976-78; broker, auctioneer, appraiser, owner Preferred Properties Realty & Auction, Mt. Carmel, 1978-81; appraiser, pres. W. Henry Bailey Appraisers, Mt. Carmel, 1981—; adj. prof. E. Tenn. State U., 2002—. Rep. pub. rels. com. Appraisal Inst., State of Tenn., 1990-92, chmn., 1997-99, mem. representing ETN, 2000—; del. Holston Meth. Conf., Lake Junaluska, N.C., 1991, mem. curriculum com., dept. fin. and econs. East Tenn. State U.. Pres., sec., treas. Church Hill (Tenn.) Housing Devel. Corp., 1973 ; mem. Planning Commn., City of Church Hill, 1975-77, alderman, 1975-77; pres. Carter's Valley Elem. Sch. PTSO, Church Hill, 1982; gov. appointed commr. Tenn. Real Estate Appraisal Commn., 1994-97; alderman City of Mt. Carmel, 1998—; mem., appraisal mem. Ea. Tenn./S.W. Va. Appraisal Com.; mem. Mt. Carmel Regional Planning Commn., 2002--; mem. adv. bd. econs. and fin. East Tenn. State U., 2002--. Named Ky. Col., Commonwealth of Ky., Frankfort, 1973. Mem. Soc. Real Estate Appraisers (pres. Tenneva chpt. 1986-87, co-chmn. legis. com. 1987-91, candidate guidance com. chmn. 1987-91, Appraiser of Yr. 1989, Gideon Internat. Jaycees (external v.p. Church Hill, Tenn. chpt. 1973-74), Masons, Shriners, Upper East Tenn. Appraiser Coalition (chpt. pres. S.W. Va. 1994, chmn. Tenn., Va. regional MLS appraisal com. 1994). Methodist. Avocations: teaching real estate, lay speaker in church, farming. Office: W Henry Bailey Appraisers 117 Commerce St Kingsport TN 37660-4348 Home: PO Box 2288 Kingsport TN 37662-2288

BAILEY, WILLIAM NATHAN, nutritionist, consultant; b. Thomasville, N.C., Nov. 30, 1955; s. Charlie Franklin and Bonnie Mae (West) B.; m. Joy Linda Wagner, June 10, 1978 (dec. Feb. 1987); m. Belinda Carol Church, Aug. 8, 1988; 1 child, Benjamin Franklin. BFA, U. N.C., Greensboro, 1978; MA, Life Christian U., 1996, PhD, 1997; ND, Trinity Coll. of Natural Health, 2003. Cert. natural health profl. Sr. programmer CIBA-GEIGY Corp., Greensboro, N.C., 1986-88, sr. system analyst, 1990-95; system mgr. N.C. A&T State U., Greensboro, 1988-90; cons. CIBA-GEIGY Corp., Greensboro, NC, 1995-96; sr. systems engr. BizNetz, Inc., Greensboro, 1996-97; engr. Ctr. for Creative Leadership, Greensboro, 1998—2002; acad. dean Life Christian U., Greensboro, NC, 1998—2002; owner Low Carb Nexus, High Point, NC, 1999—. Chmn. DECUS PI-LUG, Greensboro, 1987-88, 90-96, asst. chmn., 1988-89; cons. Ciba-Geigy Corp., 1995-96; prof. LCU, Greensboro campus, 1996—. Contbr. articles to profl. jours. Tchr. Faith & Victory Ch., Greensboro, 1988—. Mem. Am. Assn. Nutritional Cons., Internet Developers Assn., Piedmont Triad NT Users Group (chmn. 1997—), HTML Writers Guild. Republican. Office: Low Carb Nexus 2209 N Centennial St High Point NC 27265 E-mail: drbill@lowcarbsnexus.com.

BAILEY, WILLIAM RUFUS, lawyer, corporation executive; BA, Yale U, 1939; LLB, U Va., 1947. Bar: NY 1950, Ohio 1952. V.p. law Armco, Inc., Middletown, Ohio, 1974—77, sec., 1974—77, v.p., gen. counsel, 1968—74, counsel, 1964—68, asst. counsel, 1951—63, v.p., gen. counsel, sec., 1977—. Office: Armco Inc 703 Curtis St Middletown OH 45044-5812

BAILEY, WILLIAM WADDELL, writer, communications executive; b. Gordonsville, Va.; s. George W. and Phyllis K. (Kennon) B.; m. Rita Maria Fleischmann, Feb. 17, 1974. BA in Psychology, U. Miss., 1973; MA in Internat. Rels., U. So. Calif., 1985; disting. grad., Command and Gen. Staff Coll., 1987. Cert. software engr. Commd. 2d lt. U.S. Army, 1973, advanced through grades to lt. col., officer, 1973-82; software mgr. U.S. Govt., Augsburg, Germany, 1982-85, modernization mgr. Leavenworth, Kans., 1985-90, divsn. chief Arlington, Va., 1990-92, spl. exec., 1992-93; sr. advisor to pvt. orgns. Washington, 1993-97; pres. Writer's Ink, Fayetteville, N.C., 1997—; resident artist Urban Arts Prgm., 1998, Arts and Tech., 1999. Cons. Sierra Cybernetics, Yorba Linda, Calif., 1993—. Author, editor: 2004 Future Architecture, 1987, Modernization Plan, 1989; author: Desert Storm Lessons Learned, 1991; contbr. articles, stories and poems to mags. and jours. Mem. fundraising com. Hist. Mus., Fayetteville, 1981; mem. Arts Coun., 1996—. Decorated Legion of Merit. Avocations: astronomy, fencing.

BAILEY-STEIN, DEENA TAMARA, health care administrator; b. Haifa, Israel, June 13, 1947; came to U.S., 1960; d. Fred Ephraim and Devora (Glaser) Mansbacher; m. Wayne W. Bailey, Apr. 4, 1970 (div. 1977); 1 child, Devora Elyse; m. Randy Stein, Mar. 19, 1999. BS in Health Sci., U. Redlands, 1989; MHA, U. So. Calif., 1995. Mgr. dept. surgery Cedars-Sinai Med. Ctr., L.A., 1980-87, mgr. cardiovasc. intervention ctr., 1988-93; dir. Cardiology Mgmt. Svcs., 1993-94; adminstrv. resident UniHealth, Burbank, Calif., 1994-95; adminstrv. dir. UniHealth-Arroyo Seco Med. Group/Mgmt. Svcs., 1995—96; v.p., COO UniMed-Arroyo Seco Med. Group/Mgmt. Svcs., 1996—2000; dir. health svcs. Searchwest, Inc., L.A., 2001—02; v.p. bus. devel. JR Assocs., L.A., 2002—. Mem. Health Care Execs. So. Calif. (membership chair 2003—), Women in Health Adminstrn. (pres. 1993), Am. Coll. Cardiovasc. Adminstrs. (regional dir. 1990-92), U. So. Calif. Health Svcs. Adminstrs. Alumni Assn. (pres. 1996-97, v.p., chmn. mentoring program 1999-2001). Democrat. Jewish. Avocation: photography. Business E-Mail: deena@1jra.com.

BAILLIE, JAMES, humanities educator; b. Glasgow, Scotland, Feb. 18, 1957; arrived in U.S., 1990; s. James Baillie and Helen Mary Torley; m. Anne Marie Fuller, Oct. 14, 1994 (div. June 1999). MA with honors, U. Glasgow, 1979, PhD, 1989. Asst. prof. philosophy U. Portland, Oreg., 1990—95, assoc. prof., 1995—2002, full prof. philosophy, 2002—. Author: Problems in Personal Identity, 1993, Hume on Morality, 1999; editor: Contemporary Analytic Philosophy, 2003. Avocations: yoga, guitar, movies, literature. Office: Univ of Portland Dept Philosophy 5000 N Willamette Blvd Portland OR 97253

BAILLIE, JOAN M. chemical company official, biology educator; b. Manchester, N.H., Mar. 11, 1950; d. Robert Eugene and Doris Theresa (Dube) Nippert; m. Richard Douglas Baillie, Oct. 4, 1986. BA in Sci., Mt. St. Mary Coll., Hooksett, N.H., 1971; MA in Biology, East Carolina U., 1974. Microbiology technologist Becton Dickinson, Research Triangle Park, NC, 1974—76; mgr. quality control Bio Data Corp., Willow Grove, Pa., 1976—78; various positions to nat. accounts mgr. E.I. Du Pont, Wilmington, Del., 1978—89, DuPont cons. Ptnrs. in Sci. program Deepwater, NJ, 1993—. Program mgr. Straight at You WJIC, Salem, NJ, 1990—99; instr. biology Salem C.C., Carneys Point, NJ, 1997—2000, instr., dept. chair, 2001—; dir. Ctr. for Cmty. Edn. and Recreation, 1991—92; bd. dirs. Salem CC. Found., 1990—, chmn., 1993—98; bd. trustees Salem C.C., 1995—97. Bd. dirs. Salem County chpt. Am. Heart Assn., 1993-97, pres., 1993-95; founding mem. Friends of Pennsville Pub. Libr., 1991, trustee, 1995-97, pres., 1992-94; vol. coord. Salem County Health Heart Program, 1990-97; mem. panel for K-12 edn. Salem County Profl. Devel. Bd., 2000—; founding mem., mem. exec. com. Salem County 2000 Edn. Coun., 1991—; mem. exec. com. Goals 2000, Salem County, 1991—. Recipient Excellence award, N.J. Cmty. County Colls., 1992. Mem. Delta Kappa Gamma. Avocations: reading, paper crafts, travel, teaching art classes for children. Home: 2 Lenape Dr Pennsville NJ 08070 Office: E I DuPont Co Chambers Works Deepwater NJ 08023 E-mail: jbaillie@snip.net.

BAILLIE, RICHARD THOMAS, economist, educator; b. London, Feb. 14, 1948; came to U.S., 1979; s. Thomas Edward Baillie and Muriel Hervét Podmore; m. Anne Rosalind Waller, Nov. 2, 1974. BS, Middlesex U., London, 1970; MS, U. Kent, Canterbury, Eng., 1972; PhD, London Sch. Econs., 1978. Prof. Mich. State U., East Lansing, 1988-92, 93-98, A. J. Pasant prof., 1998—; prof. Georgetown U., Washington, 1992-93. Cons. Fed. Res. Bank Cleve., 1994—; vis. scholar Fed. Res. Bank St. Louis, 1994; part-time prof. U. London, 1999—. Grantee NSF, 1992, 93, 99; fellow Jour. Econometrics, 1997. Fellow Am. Statis. Assn.; mem. Econometric Soc., Am. Fin. Assn., Am. Econ. Assn. Avocations: travel, tennis, wine, film, cricket. Home: 1090 Whittier Dr East Lansing MI 48823 Office: Mich State U Dept Econ East Lansing MI 48824 E-mail: baillie@msu.edu.

BAILLIE-DAVID, SONJA KIRSTEEN, controller; b. Lac Megantic, Que., Can., Mar. 26, 1961; came to the U.S., 1964; d. Patrick Eugene and Erika (Bagdonowich) Baillie-David; m. Glenn Frank Skoff, Nov. 12, 1988; 1 child, Elaine Elise Skoff. AA, Joliet Jr. Coll., 1983; BBA, Coll. St. Francis, 1985; MBA in Entrepreneurship, DePaul U., 1992. CPA, Ill. Auditor Peat, Marwick Main, Chgo., 1985-87, Ill. Tool Works, Chgo., 1987-88, fin. analyst, 1988-89, fin. systems project mgr. Glenview, Ill., 1989-94; contr. U.S. Wire-Tie Systems, Woodridge, Ill., 1994-96, Pennysaver Publs., Inc., Tinley Pk., Ill., 1996-97, Littell Internat., Inc., Addison, Ill., 1997—2001, Opportunity Internat., Oak Brook, Ill., 2001—. Mem. Ill. CPA Soc., NAFE, Am. Mgmt. Assn. Roman Catholic. Avocations: underwater photography, refinishing antiques, scuba diving, underwater photography, travel, refinishing antiques, reading. Office: 2122 York Rd Ste 340 Oak Brook IL 60523-1996

BAILLIEUL, JOHN BROUARD, aerospace engineering and applied mathematics educator; b. Boise, Idaho, May 13, 1945; s. Paul Brouard and Geneva (Gillam) B.; m. Patricia Pfeiffer; children: Emily, Charlotte, John Paul. BA, U. Mass., Amherst, 1967; M in Math., U. Waterloo, Waterloo, Can., 1969; MS, Harvard U., 1973, PhD in Applied Math., 1975. Asst. prof. math. Georgetown U., Washington, 1975-79; sr. mathematician Sci. Systems, Inc., Cambridge, Mass., 1979-83; Vinton Hayes vis. scientist Harvard U., Cambridge, 1983-85; prof. aerospace and mech. engring. Boston U., 1985—, prof. mfg. engring., 1988—, prof. elec. and computer engring., 2001—, dir. div. engring. and applied sci., 1990-93, assoc. dean Coll. Engring., 1993—96, chmn. dept. mfg. engring., 1994-99, chmn. dept. aerospace/mech. engring., 1999—. Cons. Sci. Systems, Inc., Cambridge, 1985-87, AMD Corp., Stratford, Conn., 1986, Computational Engring., Inc., Laurel, Md., 1988-89; vis. sr. scientist Lab. for Info. and Decision Systems, MIT, 1991; chmn. dept aerospace/mech. engring., 1992-93. Author: Mathematical Control Theory, 1998; assoc. editor IEEE Transactions on Automatic Control, 1984—85, 1989—92, editor-in-chief, 1992—98; assoc. editor: IEEE Robotics and Automation Soc. newsletter, Bifurcation and Chaos in Applied Scis. and Engring.; mem. editl. bd. Procs. IEEE, Comm. in Info. and Systems, Robotics and Computer Integrated Mfg.; contbr. articles to profl. jours. U.S. Dept. Energy grantee, USAF Office Sci. Rsch. grantee Boston U., 1985—, NSF grantee; frequent grantee for study

nonlinear control theory and mechanics Fellow IEEE (mem. publs. bd., 3D Millennium medal 2000). Home: 105 Longmeadow Rd Belmont MA 02478-1709 Office: Boston U Aero Mech Engring 110 Cummington St Boston MA 02215-2407

BAILON, GILBERT, newspaper editor; From mem. staff to v.p., exec. editor Dallas (Tex.) Morning News, 1986—97, exec. editor, 1997—, v.p., 1997—. Mem.: Nat. Assn. Hispanic Journalists (past pres.). Office: The Dallas Morning News PO Box 655237 508 Young St Dallas TX 75202-4828*

BAILYN, BERNARD, historian, educator; b. Hartford, Conn., Sept. 10, 1922; s. Charles Manuel and Esther (Schloss) Bailyn; m. Lotte Lazarsfeld, June 18, 1952; children: Charles David, John Frederick. AB, Williams Coll., 1945; MA, Harvard U., 1947, PhD, 1953; LHD (hon.), Lawrence U., Bard Coll., Clark U., Yale U., Grinnell Coll., Trinity Coll., Manhattanvill Coll., Dartmouth Coll., U. Chgo., Coll. of William and Mary; LLD (hon.), Harvard U.; LHD (hon.), Pa. State U., Williams Coll.; LittD (hon.), Rutgers U., Fordham U., La Trobe U., Australia, Washington U., St. Louis. Mem. faculty Harvard U., Cambridge, Mass., 1953—, prof. emeritus, 1993—, editor in chief John Harvard Libr., 1962—70, Winthrop prof. history, 1966—81, Adams U. prof., 1981—93, dir. Charles Warren Ctr. for Studies in Am. History, 1983—94. Trevelyon lectr. Cambridge U., 1971, vis. prof.; mem. inst. advanced study Princeton U., 1980—81; sr. fellow Soc. Fellows Harvard U.; postt. prof. am. history, 1986—87; Pitt prof. Cambridge U., 1986—87; trustee Princeton U., 1989—94; fellow Dartmouth Coll., 1991; dir. Internat. Seminar on History of Atlantic World, 1995—. Co-author (with Lotte Bailyn): Mass. Shipping 1697-1714, A Statis. Study, 1959; author: New Eng. Merchants in the 17th Century, 1955, Edn. in the Forming of Am. Society, 1960, The Ideological Origins of the Am. Revolution, 1967 (Pulitzer prize, 1968, Bancroft prize, 1968), The Origins of Am. Politics, 1968, The Ordeal of Thomas Hutchinson, 1974 (Nat. Book award, 1975), The Peopling of Br. North Am.: An Intro., 1986, Voyagers to the West, 1986 (Pulitzer prize, Saloutos award Immigration History soc., Triennial Book award Soc. of the Cin.), Faces of Revolution, 1990, On The Tchg. and Writing of History, 1994, To Begin the World Anew, 2003; co-author: The Gt. Republic, 1977; editor: Pamphlets of the Am. Revolution 1750-1776, 1965, The Aplogia of Robert Keayne, 1965, The Debate on the Constn., 1993; co-editor: The Intellectual Migration, Europe and Am., 1930-1960, 1969, Law in Am. History, 1972, Perspectives in Am. History, 1967—77, 1981—86, The Press and The Am. Revolution, 1980, Strangers Within the Realm, 1990. With AUS, 1943—46. Recipient Robert H. Lord award, Emmanuel Coll., 1967, medal, Fgn. Policy Assn., 1998, Catton prize for lifetime achievement in writing of history, Soc. Am. Historians, 2000, Centennial medal, Harvard Grad. Sch. Arts and Scis., 2001; fellow, Christ Coll., Cambridge U.; Jefferson lectr., NEH, 1998, First Millenium lectr., White House, 1998. Fellow: Royal Hist. Soc. (corr.); mem.: Academia Europaea, Russian Acad. Scis., Mex. Acad. History and Geography, Brit. Acad., Mass. Hist. Soc., Am. Philos. Soc. (Thomas Jefferson medal 1993, Henry Allen Moe prize 1994), Nat. Acad. Edn., Am. Acad. Arts and Scis., Am. Hist. Assn. (pres. 1981). Home: 170 Clifton St Belmont MA 02478-2604 Office: Harvard U History Dept Cambridge MA 02138

BAILYN, LOTTE, psychology and management educator; b. Vienna, July 17, 1930; came to U.S., 1937; d. Paul Felix Lazarsfeld and Marie (Jahoda) Albu; m. Bernard Bailyn, June 18, 1952; children: Charles, John. BA in Math. with high honors, Swarthmore Coll., 1951; MA in Social Psychology, Harvard U., 1953, PhD in Social Psychology, 1956; PhD (hon.), U. Piraeus, Greece, 2000. Rsch. assoc. Grad. Sch. Edn., Harvard U., Cambridge, Mass., 1956-57, rsch. assoc. dept. social rels., 1958-64, lectr., 1963-67; instr. dept. econs. and social sci. MIT, Cambridge, 1957-58, rsch. assoc. Sloan Sch. Mgmt., 1969-70, lectr., 1970-71, from sr. lectr. to prof., 1971-91, T Wilson prof. mgmt., 1991—, chair MIT faculty, 1997-99; acad. visitor Imperial Coll. Sci., Tech. and Medicine, London, 1991, 1995, 2000; disting. vis. prof. Radcliffe Coll., 1995-97. Trustee Cambridge Savs. Bank, 1975-98; mem. adv. coun. Suffolk U. Mgmt. Sch., Boston, 1983-86; mem. sr. coun. Leadership Devel. Inst., Rutgers U., 1986-89; panel mem. NAS, NRC, Washington, 1988-90; mem. task force in career devel. and maintenance IEEE, Washington, 1982-90; vis. scholar Imperial Coll. Sci. and Tech., London, 1982, New Hall, Cambridge (Eng.) U., 1986-87; scholar-in-residence Rockefeller Found. Study and Conf. Ctr., Bellagio, Italy, 1983; vis. fellow U. Auckland, N.Z., 1984. Author: Mass Media and Children, 1959, Living with Technology, 1980, Breaking the Mold: Women, Men, and Time in the New Corporate World, 1993; co-author: Working with Careers, 1984, Relinking Life and Work: Toward a Better Future, 1996, Beyond Work-Family Balance: Advancing Gender Equity and Workplace Performance, 2002; mem. editl. bd. Jour. Engring. and Tech. Mgmt., Cmty., Work and Family; contbr. chpts. to books and articles to profl. jours. Trustee Radcliffe Coll., 1974-79, Cambridge Fin. Group, Inc., 1998—; bd. dirs. Families and Work Inst., 1995—, Cambridge Savings Bank, 1998—. Recipient Grad. Soc. medal Radcliffe Coll., 1998, Everett Cherrington Hughes award for careers scholarship Acad. of Mgmt., 2003. Fellow APA; mem. Acad. Mgmt., Am. Sociol. Assn. Home: 170 Clifton St Belmont MA 02478-2604 Office: MIT Sloan Sch Mgmt 50 Memorial Dr Cambridge MA 02142-1347

BAIMAN, GAIL, real estate broker; b. Bklyn., June 4, 1938; d. Joseph and Anita (Devon) Yalow; children: Steven, Susan, Barbara. Student, Bklyn. Coll., 1955-57. Lic. real estate broker, N.Y., Pa., Fla.; hypnotherapist, stress mgmt. cons.; firewalk instr. Pers.-pub. rels. dir. I.M.C., Inc., N.Y.C., 1970-72; pres., broker Gayle Baiman Assocs., Inc., N.Y.C., 1972-74; v.p., broker Tuit Mktg. Corp., Mt. Pocono, Pa., 1974-83; pres., broker Timeshare Sales, Inc., St. Petersburg/Orlando, Fla., 1983-98; founder, CEO Universal Rembrance U. Inc., 1998—. Author: Vacation Timesharing, A Real Estate, 1992. Mem. Am. Resort Developers Assn., Better Bus. Arbitration Assn., Internat. Resale Brokers Assn. (co-founder), Chmns. League, Better Bus. Bur. Arbitrators. E-mail: gbaiman@aol.com.

BAIN, C. RANDALL, lawyer; b. Greeley, Colo., Feb. 1, 1934; s. Walter Lockwood and Harriet Lucille (Stewart) B.; m. Joanne Berg, Aug. 4, 1956 (div.); children: Jennifer Harriet, Charles Alvin; m. Lois Jean Frazier, Feb. 1, 1973 (dec.); 1 child, Frazier; m. Anna Scalise, Dec. 16, 2000. BA, Yale U., 1955, LLB, 1960. Bar: Ariz. 1961, U.S. Dist. Ct. Ariz. 1961, U.S. Ct. Appeals (9th cir.) 1963, U.S. Supreme Ct. 1968, U.S. Ct. Appeals (fed. cir.) 1992. Ptnr. Brown & Bain, Phoenix, 1961—2003, pres., 1972-87, exec. v.p., 1987—, of counsel, 2003—. Bd. dirs. UDC Homes, Inc., Tempe, Ariz., 1974-95; adj. prof. of law Arizona State Univ. Sch. of Law, 2000-01. Trustee Phoenix Country Day Sch., 1983-94; chmn. bd. dirs. Ariz. Audubon, 2003—. Fellow Am. Bar Found., 2002—, mem. ABA, Ariz. Bar Assn. (chmn. fee arbitration com. 1982-86), Am. Law Inst., Yale U. Law Sch. Alumni Assn. (exec. com. 1982-85, 93-97), Audobon Soc. Ariz. (chmn. bd. dirs. 2003—). Office: Brown & Bain PA 2901 N Central Ave Ste 2000 Phoenix AZ 85012-2788

BAIN, CONRAD STAFFORD, actor; b. Lethbridge, Alta., Can., Feb. 4, 1923; came to U.S., 1946, naturalized, 1946; s. Stafford Harrison and Jean Agnes (Young) B.; m. Monica Marjorie Sloan, Sept. 4, 1945; children: Kent Stafford, Mark Alexander, Jennifer Jean. Grad., Am. Acad. Dramatic Art, 1948. Founder Actors Fed. Credit Union, 1962 Broadway appearances include Candide, 1957, Lost in the Stars, 1958, Hot Spot, 1963, Advise and Consent, 1961, Twigs, 1971, Uncle Vanya, 1973, On Borrowed Time, 1991; off-Broadway appearances include The Iceman Cometh, 1957, Hogan's Goat, 1966, Scuba Duba, 1967, The Kitchen, 1968, Steambath, 1969, The Dining Room, Pasadena Playhouse, 1991, On Borrowed Time, 1992, Ancestral Voices, 1999; film appearances A Lovely Way to Die, 1967, Who Killed Mary Whats er Name, 1968, Up the Sand Box, 1970, C.H.O.M.P.S, 1979, Child Bride of Short Creek, 1982, Postcards from the Edge, 1990; Pasadena Playhouse The Dining Room, 1991; co-star: (TV) Maude, 1971-78; star: (TV) Diff'rent Strokes, 1978-86, Mr. President, 1987—. Served with Canadian Army, World War II. Mem. Actors Equity Assn. (councilor 1962-76), ANTA West (dir. since 1977) Clubs: Players (N.Y.C.). Office: 1230 Chicory Ln Los Angeles CA 90049-1403 *I have come to realize that each job no matter how small must be an end in itself, and that each day of whatever character must be lived for that day, in all its fullness. Yesterday is gone, regret is a waste, and tomorrow is unknown.*

BAIN, DAVID HAWARD, writer; b. Camden, N.J., Feb. 23, 1949; s. David M. and Rosemary (Haward) B.; m. Mary Smyth Duffy, June 6, 1981; children: Mimi Aitken Duffy Bain, David Montrose Duffy Bain. BS, Boston U., 1971. Editorial asst. Alfred A. Knopf, Inc., N.Y.C., 1973-76; editor Stonehill Press, N.Y.C., 1976-77; editor Harmony Books Crown Pubs., Inc., N.Y.C., 1977-78; writer N.Y.C., 1978-87; mem. faculty Bread Loaf Writers' Conf., Middlebury, Vt., 1981-87, 2003; asst. editor New Eng. Rev., Middlebury, 1989—. Instr. creative writing Middlebury Coll., 1987—. Mem. editl. bd.: Bread Loaf Writers' Conf., 1987-88, 93-97, 2001—; author (with Mary Smyth Duffy): Whose Woods These Are: A History of the Bread Loaf Writers' Conference, 1993; author: Aftershocks, 1980; Sitting in Darkness: Americans in the Philippines, 1984 (Robert F. Kennedy award 1985), Empire Express: Building the First Transcontinental Railroad, 1999 (New Eng. Hist. Assn. Book award 2000), The College on the Hill, 1999, The Old Iron Road, 2003; co-prodr. (documentary) American Experience Transcontinental Railroad, 2003; contbr. articles to profl. jours. Grantee Mary Roberts Rinehart N.Y., 1979, Lebensburger Found., 1984, Wyndham Found., 1987; recipient PEN award N.Y. State Coun. on the Arts, 1983, Reader's Choice award Prairie Schooner mag., 1997. Fellow Soc. Am. Historians. Avocation: jazz piano playing. Home: 36 N Orwell Rd Orwell VT 05760-9760 Office: Dept English Middlebury Coll Middlebury VT 05753

BAIN, DIANE MARTHA D'ANDREA, clinical nurse specialist in critical care; b. Westfield, Mass., June 29, 1949; d. John Anthony and Eva Margaret (Gerulis) D'Andrea; m. John Kenneth, Sept. 24, 1972. AS with hons., Quinsigamond Community Coll., 1971; BS with high hons., Worcester State Coll., 1977; MS with highest honors, U. Mass., Worcester, 1987. Staff and asst. head nurse MICU and crit. care St. Vincent Hosp., Worcester, 1971-77; instr. St. Vincent Hosp. Sch. Nursing, 1977-79; nurse educator critical care U. Mass. Hosp., Worcester, 1979-87, clin. nurse specialist critical care, 1987-93; assoc. faculty U. Mass. Grad. Sch. Nursing, Worcester, 1987-93, Worcester State Coll., 1987-93. Presenter, lectr., cons. for regional orgns., agencies, and hosps. Reviewer for Applied Rsch. nursing jour., 1988-89; contbr. articles to profl. jours. Mem. AACN, Sigma Theta Tau, Iota Phi.

BAIN, DONALD KNIGHT, lawyer; b. Denver, Jan. 28, 1935; s. Francis Marion and Jean (Knight) B.; divorced; children: Stephen A., Andrew K., William B. AB, Yale U., 1957; LLB, Harvard U., 1961. Bar: Colo. 1961. From assoc. to ptnr. Holme Roberts & Owen, Denver, 1961-93, chmn. exec. com., 1988-90; ptnr. Holme Roberts & Owen LLP, Denver, 1993—; chmn. Colo. Rep. Com., 1993-97. Bd. dirs. Fairmount Cemetery Co.; mem. grievance com. Colo. Supreme Ct., 1975-80, chmn., 1980. Trustee Denver Pub. Libr. Friends Found., 1978—96, Denver Found., 1989—95, chmn., 1993—95; trustee Berger Found., 1994—96; trustee, chmn. Colo. Coun. on Arts, 1999—; trustee Human Svcs., Inc., 1970—81, chmn., 1979—80; trustee Colo. Humanities Program, 1975—78; mem. Denver Pub. Libr. Commn., 1983—91; active Rep. Nat. Com., Washington, 1993—97; candidate for mayor City of Denver, 1987, 1991; bd. dirs. Rocky Mountain Corp. Pub. Broadcasting, 1975—83, Downtown Denver, Inc., 1977—, Denver Metro C. of C., 1998—, BigHornAction.org, 1999—2003, Auraria Found., 1986—, Legal Aid Found., Colo., 1999—, Auraria Higher Edn. Ctr., 1978—89, chmn., 1986—89. Fellow Royal Geog. Soc., Am. Coll. Trial Lawyers, Explorers Club; mem. ABA, Colo. Bar Assn., Denver Bar Assn., Colo. Yale Assn. (pres. 1974-76), Assn. Yale Alumni (bd. govs. 1982-85), Selden Soc., Am. Antiquarian Soc., Internat. Wine and Food Soc., Confrerie des Chevaliers du Tastevin, Western Stock Show Assn., Cactus Club, Denver Country Club, Mile High Club, Denver Law Club, Grolier Club, Yale Club, Colo. Mountain Club, Capitol Hill CLub, Univ. Club (Denver). Republican. Avocations: antiquarian book collecting. Home: 1201 Williams # 13C Denver CO 80218 Office: Holme Roberts & Owen LLP 1700 Lincoln St Ste 4100 Denver CO 80203-4541 E-mail: baind@hro.com.

BAIN, JAMES ARTHUR, pharmacologist, educator; b. Langdon, N.D., May 22, 1918; s. James Hamilton and Mabel (Aldritt) B.; m. Eleanor Theo Hohaus, Dec. 5, 1947; children: Andrew J., Peter T. AA, Wayland Jr. Coll., 1938; BS, U. Wis., 1940, PhD, 1944. Research asst. McArdle Meml. Lab., U. Wis., 1940-44, Rockefeller fellow, 1946-47; research asso. U. Ill., 1947-50, asst. prof., then asso. prof., 1952-54; mem. faculty dept. pharmacology Emory U., 1954—, prof., 1954-89, chmn. dept., 1957-62, dir. div. basic health scis., 1960-76; exec. asso. dean Emory U. (Sch. Medicine), 1976-88, prof. emeritus, 1988—, cons. to dean, v.p., 1989-93. Cons. to govt., nat. agys., industry, 1954— Contbr. articles profl. jours. Mem. Am. Chem. Soc., Am. Soc. Pharmacology and Exptl. Therapeutics, AAAS. Home: 1800 Clairmont Lake # 518 Decatur GA 30033-4040

BAIN, MARISSA, social worker; b. Providence, Sept. 30, 1977; d. Bruce Alan and Laurie Eleanor Bain. BA, U. R.I., 1999; MSW, R.I. Coll., 2000. Cert. cmty. support prof. R.I. Social worker NRI Cmty. Svcs., Woonsocket, 1999—, program mgr., 2000—03. Vol. adv. Sexual Assault and Trauma Resource Ctr., Providence, 1997—99. Mem.: NASW, NOW (R.I. chpt.), Planned Parenthood Fedn. Am. Democrat. Home: 12 Oregon Ave North Providence RI 02911

BAIN, TRAVIS WHITSETT, II, manufacturing and retail executive; b. San Antonio, Mar. 4, 1934; s. Travis Whitsett and Zelma Gladys (Middleton) B.; m. Karlen Jo Bruner, May 30, 1957; children: Travis W. III, James Henry III. B in Chem. Engring., U. Tex., 1956; MBA, Harvard U., 1958. Mfg. supt. Tex. Instruments, Dallas, 1958-61; sr. assoc. McKinsey and Co., L.A. and Chgo., 1961-65; exec. v.p., COO Trend Line Corp., Jackson, Miss., 1965-81; pres., CEO W.E. Walker Stores, Inc., Jackson, 1981-86; CEO Sunbelt Nursery Group, Inc., Ft. Worth, 1986-87; investor, cons. Bain Assocs., Ft. Worth, 1987-88; pres. Jarman Shoe Co. div. Genesco Inc., Nashville, 1988-92, Bain Enterprises, Inc. dba Sandler Pools, Plano, Tex., 1993-99; chmn. Tex. Custom Pools, Inc., Plano, 1999—. Bd. dirs. Atmos Energy Corp., Dallas, 1988—, Tex. Commerce Bank, Ft. Worth, 1986-88, Delta Industries, Inc., Jackson, 1984—; chmn. bd. dirs. Master Pools Guild, 1997-99. Bd. dirs. New Stage Theatre, Jackson, 1980-86, Boy Scouts Am., Ft. Worth, 1986-88, Miss. Ballet Internat., Jackson, 1984-86; bd. dirs., exec. com. Nashville Ballet, 1989-92; mem. placement coun. Owen Sch. Mgmt. Vanderbilt U., Nashville, 1984-92; mem. adv. bd. CBA Found. U. Tex., Austin, 1987—. Mem. Dallas Exec. Assn. (pres. 1998-99). Republican. Presbyterian. Avocations: gardening, tennis, jogging, travel, scuba diving. Office: Tex Custom Pools Inc 4016 W Plano Pkwy Ste 100 Plano TX 75093-5696 Fax: 972-596-9460. E-mail: travkar@mail.airmail.net., tbain@texascustompools.com.

BAIN, WILLIAM DAVID, electronics systems technician, writer; b. Flint, Mich., Sept. 3, 1958; s. William David and Frances Geraldine B. Student, Jordan Coll., 1984-85. Theater mgr. asst. Northwest Theater, Flint, 1975-81, Commonwealth Theater, Denver, 1981-82; theater mgr., promotions asst. Towne Cinemas, Flushing, Mich., 1987-91; pvt. practice Flint, 1991—. Author: Oasis, 1995, Inspirational Collection, 1997, Tear Drops Fall Like Rain, 1997, Romantic Collection, 1997, Verses From The Heart, 1999. Mem. Comms. com. Democratic Party, 1994-98; delegate Democratic Party, 1996-98; elected exec. bd. trustees UAW, 1999—2002. Mem.: United Automobile, Aerospace, Agrl. Implement Workers, Jerry B. Jenkins Christian Writers Guild, Poetry Soc. Am., The Acad. Poets. Avocations: writing, nature photography, gardening, cookouts, political advocate for people. Home and Office: PO Box 70 Flushing MI 48433 E-mail: Author58@yahoo.com.

BAIN, WILLIAM DONALD, JR., lawyer, chemical company executive; b. Rochelle, Ill., July 1, 1925; s. William Donald and Gretchen (Kittler) B.; m. Pauline Thomas, Jan. 14, 1950 (dec. Nov. 1991); children: Elizabeth Kittler Zibart, Anne Alexander, Nancy Hemenway Cotè; m. Barrie Feighner, Mar. 30, 1996. BS in Econs, U. Pa., 1947; JD, Washington and Lee U., 1949. Bar: S.C. 1952. Mortgage loan field rep. Travelers Ins. Co., Hartford, Conn., Cleve.; Orlando, Fla., 1949-51; with Moreland-McKesson Chem. Co., Spartanburg, S.C., 1951-83, pres., 1965-83, also dir.; v.p., gen. mgr. McKesson Chem. Corp., San Francisco, 1982-84. Bd. dirs. Cote Color & Chem. Co., Inc., Spartan Comms. Corp., Tietex Corp.; co-founder, bd. dirs. Affiliated Chem. Group, Bermuda; ptnr. Triple B Ptnrs. Mem. Spartanburg Sch. Bd., 1958—72, chmn., 1963—72; trustee Converse Coll., 1968—92, chmn. bd., 1985—92; chmn. alumni bd. Washington and Lee U., 1979—82; trustee Hollins (Va.) Coll., 1992—98; bd. dirs. Mary Black Meml. Hosp., 1975—96, chmn., 1980—82; trustee Mary Black Found., 1996—2002; trustee, former chmn. Spartanburg County Found.; bd. dirs. Spartanburg Animal Shelter, 2002—; mng. dir. Bain Found. With USAAC, 1943—45. Mem. S.C. Bar Assn., Rotary. Republican. Presbyterian.

BAIN, WILLIAM JAMES, JR., architect; b. Seattle, June 26, 1930; s. William James and Mildred Worline (Clark) B.; m. Nancy Sanford Hill, Sept. 21, 1957; children: David Hunter, Stephen Fraser (dec.), Mark Sanford, John Worthington. BArch, Cornell U., 1953. Lic. 1st class architect, Japan, lic. architect in 18 states, Can., Guam, U.K. Consulting ptnr. NBBJ (formerly Naramore, Bain, Brady & Johanson), Seattle. Lectr. U. Wash., Seattle, mem. affiliate program steering com. Coll. Architecture and Urban Planning, 1969-71; lectr. Wash. State U., U. Wash., Cornell U.; organizer founding bd. dirs. Pacific N.W. Bank. Prin. works include U. Wash. South Campus, U.S. Pavilion at Expo '74 Worlds Fair, Honolulu Mcpl. Bldg., Two Union Square High-Rise Office Bldg., Four Seasons Olympic Hotel and Sun Mountain Lodge,, U.S. Courthouse, Seattle, Bagley Wright Theater and Paramount Theater renovation, Saitama Prefecture Demonstration Housing, Japan, Pacific Place Retail Complex, others. Bd. dirs. Corp. Coun. for Arts, 1989—, Arboretum Found., 1971-74; bd. dirs. Downtown Seattle Assn., 1980—, 1st vice-chmn., 1990-91, chmn., 1991-92; bd. dirs. Seattle Symphony Orch., 1974-87, pres., 1977-79; mem. adv. coun. Coll. Architecture, Art & Planning, Cornell U., 1987-91, 94—, vis. com. U. Washington, 1999—; archl. adv. to bd. dirs. Seattle Pub. Libr. Citizen's Adv. Bd., 1997. With C.E., U.S. Army, 1953-55. Recipient Cert. of Achievement Port of Whittier, Alaska, 1955, Disting. Alumnus award Lakeside Sch., 1985. Fellow AIA (pres. Seattle chpt. 1969, chmn. N.W. regional student profl. fund 1971, pres. Wash. coun. 1974, co-commn. Seattle centennial yr., Seattle medal 1997), N.W. Regional Archtl. Found. (pres. 1975); mem. Royal Inst. Brit. Architects, Japan Inst. Architects, Seattle C. of C. (bd. dirs. 1980-83), Urban Land Inst., Pacific Real Estate Inst., N.W. Forum, Am. Arbitration Assn. (comml. panel 1975—), L'Ogive Soc., Seattle Athletic Club, Seattle Tennis Club, Town Hall (bd. dirs. 2002—), Rotary (bd. dirs. 1970-72, svc. found. bd. 1976-80), Lambda Alpha Internat. (Robert Filly award 2003), Phi Delta Theta. Clubs: Rainier, Wash. Athletic, Tennis (Seattle); University, Columbia Tower (founding bd. dirs.). Episcopalian. Home: 2033 1st Ave Seattle WA 98121-2132 Office: NBBJ 111 S Jackson St Seattle WA 98104-2881

BAINBRIDGE, DONA BARDELLI, international marketing executive; b. Irvington, N.J., Feb. 27, 1953; d. Alfred Bainbridge and Dona Ellen (Self) Bardelli; m. Harry M. Bainbridge, May 23, 1981 (dec.); 1 child, Harry Michael. Cert. de Langue, Sorbonne U., Paris, 1974; BA, U. Ky., 1975; MA in Internat. Studies, Am. U., 1976, MSc in Econs. and Social Planning in Devel. Countries, London Sch. Econs. Rsch. assoc. Woodrow Wilson Internat. Ctr. for Vis. Scholars, Washington, 1976-77, World Bank, Washington, 1977-79; legis. asst. to Congressman Marc Lincoln Marks Washington, 1979-80; itnernat. trade analyst Internat. Trade Adminstrn. U.S. Dept. Commerce, Washington, 1980-82; internat. mgmt. cons. Coopers and Lybrand, 1982-86; v.p. Bankers Trust Co. Internat. Pvt. Banking, 1986-88; sr. mktg. dir. internat. svcs. BDO Seidman, N.Y.C., 1988-90; founder, pres. D.H. Bainbridge Assocs., 1990—. Chair nat. membership Am. Friends of London Sch. Econs., 1981-83, nat. bd. dirs., 1982-84, 94-96; chmn. mem. com.; mem. mktg. com., bd. dirs., vice chair Camp Sloane YMCA, Lakeville, Conn., 2000; chair Washington Com. Women's Studies in Religion program Div. Sch. Harvard U., 1996-98; trustee, co-chair capital campaign The Washington Episcopal Sch., Bethesda, Md., 1996-98; trustee The Town Hill Sch., Lakeville, Conn., 1999, N.W. Ctr. for Family Svcs., Lakeville, 2002; mem. adv. bd., chmn. White Plains Salvation Army, 1992-93; mem. bd. trustees Northwest Ctr. for Family Svcs., Lakeville, 2002. Mem. Soc. Internat. Devel. (D.C. chpt.), Bus. and Profl. Women's Clubs Am. (acad. scholar 1971), Nat. Press Club, Fin. Women's Assn. N.Y., Kiwanis. Democrat. Lutheran.

BAINBRIDGE, FREDERICK FREEMAN, III, architect; b. Charlottesville, Va., Sept. 15, 1927; s. Frederick Freeman and Cornelia Winston (Burnley) B.; m. Binki Baker, Jan. 6, 1948 (div. Nov. 1972); children— Burnley, Susan Winifred, Meriwether, Robin; m. Anna Bacon, Jan. 1976; 1 son, Nicholas Gordon. B.Arch., U. Va., 1950; M. Indsl. Design, Kansas City Art Inst., 1952. Asst. prof. Sch. Architecture Clemson (S.C.) U., 1952-55; asso. firm Toombs, Amisano & Wells (Architects), Atlanta, 1955-62; prin. firm Martin & Bainbridge, Atlanta, 1962-70, Bainbridge & Assos., 1970—. Southeastern project architect U. Ky. civil defense research project, 1964; vis. critic Ga. Inst. Tech., 1964-67 Chmn. archtl. rev. com. Atlanta Civic Design Commn., 1967— . Served with USNR, 1944-46. Recipient honor awards S. Atlantic Region AIA, 1964, 66, 68, 70; honor award prestressed Concrete Inst., 1967 Mem. AIA. Clubs: Fairington Golf and Tennis, Amelia Island Plantation; Farmington Country (Charlottesville, Va.). Home: Oldham Farm PO Box 317 Ivy VA 22945-0317 Office: 6795 Brandon Mill Rd NW Atlanta GA 30328-2028

BAINBRIDGE, JOHN SEAMAN, retired law school administrator, law educator, lawyer; b. NYC, Nov. 1, 1915; s. William Seaman and June Ellen (Wheeler) Bainbridge; m. Matharine Barker Garrett, Feb. 3, 1943 (div. July 24, 1968); 1 child, John Seaman; m. Elizabeth Kung-Ji Liu Bainbridge, May 13, 1978. BS, Harvard U., 1938; LLB, JD, Columbia U., 1941. Bar: NY 1941, Md 1946, US Dist. Ct./Md. 1946, US Supreme Ct. 1946, US Dist. Ct. (so. dist.)/NY 1948. Gen. practice law, Md., 1945—56, 1945—56; asst. dean Columbia U. Law Sch., 1956—65; assoc. dir. Internat. Fellows Program, 1960—62; asst. to pres. Columbia U., 1965—66; dir. Project on Staffing of African Instns. of Legal Edn. and Rsch., 1962—72; assoc. dir. Ctr. Adminstrn. of Justice, Wayne State U., Detroit, 1972—74; dir. planning Sch. Law, Pace U., Westchester County, NY, 1974—76; assoc. dean, dean, prof. law No. Ill. U. Coll. Law, Glen Ellyn, 1976—81; vis. prof., assoc. dean Del. Law Sch., Wilmington, 1981—82; dean, prof. law Touro coll. Sch. Law, Huntington, NY, 1982—85. Cons. Edward John Noble Found., 1959—61, Inst. Internat. Edn., 1962—67. Author: The Study and Teaching of Law in Africa, 1972. Lt. comdr. USNR, 1940—46. Mem.: ABA, African Law Assn. in Am., Inc., Peace Corps Lawyers Project, Sons of Revolution, Harvard (NYC). Sr Presbyn. Home: 102 Crosslands Dr Kennett Square PA 19348

BAINE, STUART ALLAN, cardiologist; b. N.Y.C., Dec. 22, 1952; BA in Biology, CUNY, Queens, 1973; MD, Wayne State U., 1977. Diplomate Am. Bd. Internal Medicine, Am. Bd. Cardiovasc. Diseases. Intern Maimonides Med. Ctr., Brooklyn, N.Y., 1977-78, resident internal medicine, 1978-80; fellow pulmonary medicine Med. Sch. Washington U., St. Louis, 1980-81; fellow in cardiology Lenox Hill Hosp., N.Y., 1983-85; cardiologist Delray (Fla.) Med. Ctr., Boca Raton (Fla.) Cmty. Hosp., Bethesda Meml. Hosp., Fla.; asst. prof. medicine U. S. Fla.; pvt. practice Delray Beach, Fla. Fellow Am. Coll. Cardiology; mem. ACP, So. Med. Assn., Fla. Med. Assn., Am. Soc. Internal Medicine, Palm Beach County Med. Assn. Office: 5258 Linton Blvd Ste 106 Delray Beach FL 33484-6529 Fax: 561-495-8276. E-mail: sabmdcvd@aol.com.

BAINE, WILLIAM BRENNAN, public health service officer, internist; b. Washington, Aug. 10, 1945; s. John Raymond and Alice (Brennan) B.; m. Martha Scott, Aug. 30, 1969; 1 child, Britton Alexander. AB, Princeton U., 1966; MD, Vanderbilt U., 1970. Diplomate Nat. Bd. Med. Examiners, Am. Bd. Internal Medicine, Am. Bd. Infectious Disease, Am. Bd. Internal Medicine Advanced Achievement in Internal Medicine; Added Qualifications in Geriatric Medicine. Intern, asst. resident in medicine Cleve. Met. Gen. Hosp., 1970-72; commd. lt. (j.g.) USPHS, 1990, advanced through grades to capt., 2000—; officer epidemic intelligence svc. Ctrs. Disease Control, Atlanta, 1972-74; med. epidemiologist Ctr. for Disease Control, Atlanta, 1977-81; resident in internal medicine Parkland Meml. Hosp., Dallas, 1974-75, attending physician, 1982-92; fellow in infectious disease U. Tex. Health Sci. Ctr., Dallas, 1975-77; asst. prof. internal medicine, microbiology U. Tex. Southwestern Med. Ctr., Dallas, 1981-88, assoc. prof. internal medicine, microbiology, 1988-92, clin. assoc. prof. internal medicine, 1992-95; infectious disease cons. Tex. Infectious Disease Assocs., 1992-95; pvt. practice, Leesburg, Va., 1995-96; sr. med. advisor Ctr. for Cost and Financing Studies Agy. for Health Care Policy and Rsch., Rockville, Md., 1996-98; sr. med. adv. Ctr. Outcomes and Effectiveness Rsch. Agy. for Health Care Rsch. and Quality, Rockville, 1998—. Guest Istituto Superiore di Sanitá, Rome, 1979-81; assoc. staff physician Presbyn. Hosp. Dallas, 1992-95; courtesy staff physician Garland Cmty. Hosp., 1992-95; staff physician Zale Lipshy U. Hosp., Dallas, 1989-92, Loudoun Hosp. Ctr., Lesburg, 1995-96; courtesy staff physician Reston (Va.) Med. Ctr., 1995-96. Contbr. articles to profl. jours. Vol. staff physician Cmty. Health Ctr., Loudoun County Health Dept., Leesburg, 1996—. Fellow ACP, Infectious Diseases Soc. Am., Am. Coll. Epidemiology; mem. Am. Fedn. Clin. Rsch. Episcopalian. Achievements include research in purification and characterization of phospholipase C

from Legionella pneumophila; epidemiologic implication of raw shellfish and seafood as vehicles for cholera in Italy. Office: Agy Healthcare Rsch and Quality Outcomes and Effectiveness 540 Gaither Rd Rockville MD 20850

BAINES, KEVIN HAYS, planetary scientist, astronomer; b. Norwalk, Conn., Feb. 11, 1954; s. Elliot A. and Martha Ellen (Ashcroft) B.; m. Jenine Bsharah, June 4, 1982; children: Emily Ansara, Christopher Lewis. BA, Amherst Coll., 1976; MA, Washington U., St. Louis, 1978, PhD, 1982. Resident rsch. assoc. NRC-JPL, Pasadena, Calif., 1982-84; rsch. scientist Jet Propulsion Lab. Calif. Tech. Inst., Pasadena, 1984—. Co-investigator Galileo Near-Infrared Mapping Spectrometer and Cassini Visual-Infrared Mapping Spectrometer expts. Contbr. articles to profl. jours. Flight dir. Aero Assn. Calif. Tech. Inst., 1986, 99--, treas., 1987-99. Virgil I. Grissom Astronaut fellow Washington U., 1976-79. Mem. AAAS (planetary scis. divsn.). Republican. Achievements include research in determination of vertical cloud/haze structures of Uranus and Neptune; role of asteroid-impact generated sulfuric gases on dinosaur extinctions; first to detect the spectrally-identifiable discrete ammonia ice clouds in Jupiter; determination of methane and ortho/para hydrogen above solar averages in Uranus and Neptune; near-infrared imagery and analysis of the cloud structures of Jupiter, Saturn and Titan from the Galileo and Cassini spacecraft; near-infrared imagery and spectroscopy of Venus surface; near infrared photometry of rings and satellites of Uranus and Saturn. Avocations: flight instructor (FAA cert.), multi-engine and single-engine aircraft, airline transport and rotorcraft pilot, scuba diving. Home: 778 Forest Green Dr La Canada Flintridge CA 91011 E-mail: kbaines@aloha.jpl.nasa.gov.

BAINS, DAVID RALPH, religious studies educator; b. Newport News, Va., July 5, 1971; s. George and Nancy Jane Cyrus B.; m. Martha Jean Anderson, July 15, 2000. BA, U. Va., 1993; AM, Harvard U., 1995, PhD, 1999. Asst. prof. religion Samford U., Birmingham, 1999—. Fellow Louisville Inst., 1998-99, Rhodes Consultation on the Future of Ch. Related Coll., 2000—. Mem. Am. Soc. Ch. History, Am. Acad. Religion, Hist. Soc. Episcopal Ch., Am. Hist. Assn., N.Am. Acad. Liturgy, Mercersburg Soc. (bd. dirs. 1998-2001), Phi Beta Kappa. United Methodist. Office: Samford U 800 Lakeshore Dr Birmingham AL 35229-2251 Fax: 205-726-2535.

BAINS, HARRISON MACKELLAR, JR., financial executive; b. Pasadena, Calif., July 8, 1943; s. Harrison MacKellar and Celeste Adele (Callahan) B.; m. Leslie E. Tawney, Mar. 7, 1970; children: Harrison MacKellar, III, Tawney Elizabeth. BA, U. Redlands, 1964; MBA, U. Calif., Berkeley, 1966. Asst. v.p. Citibank N.A., 1968-72; asst. treas. Richardson-Merrell Inc., 1972-76; v.p. treas. Nabisco Inc., East Hanover, N.J., 1976-81; sr. v.p., treas. Nabisco Brands, Inc., East Hanover, N.J., 1981-85; v.p., treas. RJR Nabisco, Inc., Winston-Salem, N.C., 1985-87; sr. v.p. Chase Manhattan Bank, N.Y.C., 1987-88; v.p., treas. Bristol-Myers Squibb Co., N.Y.C., 1988—2002, acting CFO, 2002, v.p., treas., 2002—. Mem. Fin. Execs. Inst., Food Safety Council (treas. 1980—) Office: Bristol-Myers Squibb Co 345 Park Ave New York NY 10154-0004

BAINTON, DENISE MARLENE, lawyer; b. Trenton, N.J., June 12, 1949; d. Milford C. and Anne M. (Docherty) Smith; m. Raymond Port McKinster, Dec. 26, 1987. MusB, U. Ariz., 1971, MusM, 1974, JD highest distinction, 1983. Bar: Ariz. 1983, U.S. Dist. Ct. Ariz. 1984, U.S. Ct. Appeals (9th cir.) 1985, U.S. Supreme Ct. 1988. Music tchr. Flowing Wells Pub. Schs., Tucson, 1971-80; piano instr. Pima Community Coll., Tucson, 1974-77; law clk. to judge U.S. Dist. Ct. Ariz., Phoenix, 1983-84; ptnr. DeConcini McDonald Yetwin & Lacy, Tucson, 1984—. Editor Ariz. Law Rev., 1982 83. Mem. Ariz. Bar Assn., Ariz. Bd. Psychol. Examiners, Pima County Bar Assn., Nat. Coun. Sch. Attys., Nat Assn. Coll. and U. Attys., Order of Coif. Office: DeConcini McDonald Yetwin & Lacy 2525 E Broadway Blvd Ste 200 Tucson AZ 85716-5300

BAINTON, DONALD J. diversified manufacturing company executive; b. NYC, May 3, 1931; s. William Lewis and Mildred J. (Dunne) B.; m. Aileen M. Demoulins, July 10, 1954; children: Kathryn C., Stephen L., Elizabeth A., William D. BA, Columbia U., 1952, postgrad., 1960. With The Continental Group, Inc., 1954-83, gen. mgr. prodn. planning, 1967-68, gen. mgr. mfg. Eastern divsn., 1968-73, gen. mgr. Pacific divsn., 1973-74, gen. mgr. Eastern divsn., 1974-75; v.p., gen. mgr. ops. U.S. Metal, 1975-76; exec. v.p., gen. mgr. CCC USA, 1976 78, corp. exec. v.p., pres. diversified ops., 1978-79, pres. Continental Can Co., 1979-81, Continental Packaging, 1981-83, exec. v.p., operating officer parent co., bd. dirs., 1979-83; chmn., CEO, dir. Viatech Inc., Syosset, N.Y., 1983-92; chmn., CEO Continental Can Co., Inc., Boca Raton, Fla., 1992-99; chmn., CEO, dir. Continental Can Co., Sunrise, Fla., 1999—. Bd. dirs. Viatech Inds., LLC. Bd. dirs. Columbia Coll. With USN, 1952-54, Korea. Mem. Inst. Applied Econs. (dir.), Milbrook Country Club (Greenwich, Conn.), Winged Foot Club (Mamaroneck, N.Y.), Union League Club (N.Y.C.), Royal Palm Yacht and Country Club (Boca Raton, Fla.). Republican. Roman Catholic. Office: Continental Container Corp 5001 N Hiatus Rd Sunrise FL 33351-8018

BAINTON, DOROTHY FORD, pathology educator, researcher; b. Magnolia, Miss., June 18, 1933; d. Aubrey Ratcliff and Leta (Brumfield) Ford; m. Cedric R. Bainton, Nov. 28, 1959; children: Roland J., Bruce G., James H. BS, Millsaps Coll., 1955; MD, Tulane U. Sch. of Medicine, 1958; MS, U. Calif., San Francisco, 1966. Postdoctoral rsch. fellow U. Calif., San Francisco, 1963-66, postdoctoral rsch. pathologist, 1966-69, asst. prof. pathology, 1969-75, assoc. prof., 1975-81, prof. pathology, 1981—, chair pathology, 1987-94, vice chancellor acad. affairs, 1994—. Mem. Inst. of Medicine, NAS, 1990—. NIH grant, 1978-98. Fellow AAAS, Am. Acad. Arts & Scis.; mem. FASEB (bd. dirs.), Am. Soc. for Cell Biology, Am. Soc. Hematology, Am. Soc. Histochemists and Cytochemists, Am. Assn. of Pathologists. Democrat. Mem. Soc. Of Friends. Office: Office of Acad Affairs U Calif San Francisco Med Scis Bldg Rm 115 San Francisco CA 94143-0001 E-mail: baintond@chanoff.ucsf.edu.

BAINTON, J(OHN) JOSEPH, lawyer; b. Long Branch, N.J., May 21, 1947; s. Robert L. and Elizabeth (Dowling) B.; 1 child, John Joseph Jr. BA, Kenyon Coll., 1969; JD, Rutgers U., Newark, 1973. Bar: N.Y. 1973. Assoc. Burke & Burke, N.Y.C., 1972-76; ptnr. Reboul, MacMurray, Hewitt, Maynard & Kristol, N.Y.C., 1976-89, Shea & Gould, N.Y.C., 1989-90, Whitman & Ransom, N.Y.C., 1991-92, Ross & Hardies, N.Y.C., 1993-98, Bainton McCarthy LLC, N.Y.C., 1998—. Contbr. articles to legal jours. Mediator Mandatory Mediation Program So. Dist. N.Y. Mem.: Nat. Inst. Trial Advocacy (faculty), Products Liability Adv. Coun., Internat. Anticounterfeiting Coalition (bd. dirs. 1986—92), Internat. Trademark Assn. (editor The Trademark Reporter 1976). Avocation: yacht racing. Office: Bainton McCarthy LLC 26 Broadway New York NY 10004 also: Bainton McCarthy LLC 3 Stamford Landing 46 Southfield Ave Stamford CT 06902 also: Bainton McCarthy LLC 320 Carleton Ave Central Islip NY 11722-4502

BAINUM, PETER MONTGOMERY, aerospace engineer, consultant; b. St. Petersburg, Fla., Feb. 4, 1938; s. Charles J. Bainum and Mildred (Trincher) Salyer; m. Carmen Cecilia Perez, Sept. 7, 1968; 1 child, David P. BS, Tex. A&M U., 1959; SM, MIT, 1960; PhD, Cath. U., 1967. Asst. engr. MIT Naval Supersonic Lab., Cambridge, Mass., 1959-60; sr. engr. Martin Co., Orlando, Fla., 1960-62, staff engr. IBM Fed. Systems Div., Bethesda, Md., 1962-65; sr. staff, aerospace engr., cons. Johns Hopkins U. Applied Physics Lab., Laurel, Md., 1965-69, 69-72; assoc. prof. Howard U., Washington, 1969—73, prof., 1973—90, disting. prof., 1990—2002, disting. prof. emeritus, 2003—. V.p. rsch., cons. WHF & Assocs., Bethesda, 1977-86; mem. NASA/PSN Tether Applications Simulation Working Group, 1987; lectr. various internat. univs., rsch. ctrs. and confs.; hon. vis. prof. Universidad Francisco Marroquin, Guatemala, 1991. Editor, co-editor 18 books, 1981-2002; author tech. reports and conf. procs.; contbr. numerous articles to profl. jours. Judge, D.C. Sci. Fair, Washington, 1973. Recipient Ralph R. Teetor award Soc. Automotive Engrs., 1971. Fellow: AAAS, AIAA (capital sect. cmty. action com. 1975—76, astrodynamics com. 3 terms, space transp. com. 1989—93), Brit. Interplanetary Soc., Am. Astronautical Soc. (v.p. internat. 1986—96, bd. dirs. 1996—, Brouwer award 1990, Spark M. Matsunaga Meml. award 2001); mem.: Internat. Astronautical Fedn. (materials and structures com. 1992—), Japanese Rocket Soc. (hon.), Internat. Acad. Astronautics, Sigma Xi. Office: Howard Univ Dept Of Mechanical Engr Washington DC 20059-0001 E-mail: pbainum@fac.howard.edu. *With a doctoral degree comes significant responsibilities: to search out truth scientifically, to safeguard it, and to apply it to the shaping of both private and public life.*

BAIR, BRUCE B. lawyer; b. St. Paul, May 26, 1928; s. Bruce B. and Emma N. (Stone) B.; m. Jane Lawler, July 19, 1952; children: Mary Jane, Thomas, Susan, Barbara, Patricia, James, Joan, Bruce, Jeffrey. BS, U. N.D., 1950, JD, 1952. Bar: N.D. 1952, U.S. Dist. Ct. N.D. 1955, U.S. Ct. Appeals (8th cir.) 1971, U.S. Supreme Ct. 1974. Assoc. Lord and Ulmer, Mandan, ND, 1955-57; ptnr. Bair, Bair, and Garrity, Mandan, 1957—2001, of counsel, 2002—. Spl. asst. atty. gen. N.D. Milk Mktg. Bd., 1967—; chmn. bd. Bank of Tioga, 1984-2003, also bd. dirs.; Rep. precinct committeeman, 1956-70, chmn. Morton County Rep. Com., 1958-62, mem. N.D. Rep. State Cen. Com., 1962-67; pres. sch. bd. St. Joseph's Cath. Ch., 1967-68; bd. dirs. Mandan Pub. Sch. Dist. #1, 1971-77; exec. com. Internat. Assn. Milk Control Agys., 1970-2000; bd. regents U. Mary, Bismarck, N.D., 1984—. 1st lt. JAG Corps USAF, 1952-55. Fellow: Am. Coll. Trust and Estate Counsel; mem.: ABA, N.D. Bar Assn., Am. Coll. Barristers (sr. counsel), Am. Legion, Elks, Rotary. Roman Catholic. Home: 901 3rd St NW Mandan ND 58554-2537 Office: 210 1st St NW Mandan ND 58554-3115

BAIR, DONNA MARLENE, medical laboratory administrator; b. Howard, Kans., Oct. 17, 1936; d. Ray Joe Stark and Mary Electa (Webster) Barnes; m. Donald Everett Bair, Dec. 21, 1958; children— Jerald David, Rayburn Webster. Student, Kans. State Tchrs. Coll., 1954 56; A.S. in Mgmt., Eastfield Coll., 1978; cert. med. technology, St. Francis Hosp., Wichita, Kans., 1957. Cert. med. technologist. Lab. supr. East Town Hosp., Dallas, 1970-78; adminstrv. dir. clin. lab. Mesquite Community Hosp. (Tex.), 1978—1985; lead med.technologist Quest Diagnostics, Irving, Tex, 1985-; . Mem. adv. bd. El Centro Coll., Dallas, 1978— . Mem. Am. Med. Technologists (Exceptional Merit nat. award 1983, Disting. Achievement nat. award 1979, jour. awards 1978, 79, 80, 81, 82, 83, del. nat. conv., program moderator nat. conv. 1979, 83), Tex. State Soc. Am. Med. Technologists (host seminars 1980, 82, 84, unification task force on nat. and state level, editor jour. 1978—1984), Republican. Lodge: Altrusa Internat. Home: 2224 Reynoldston Ln Dallas TX 75232-2336

BAIR, HARVEY EDWARD, polymer scientist; b. Williamsport, Pa., June 6, 1936; s. Kenneth LaRue Bair and Bernice Ester Hawk; m. Michaele B. Harner, June 7, 1958; children: Jeffrey S., Ann B. Pierson, Susan B. Eckna, Edward K. BA, Dickinson Coll., 1958; MS, Pa. State U., 1962. Rsch. tng. fellow Gen. Electric Rsch. Lab., Schenectady, NY, 1962—64; assoc. chemist The Johns Hopkins U. Applied Physics Lab., Silver Spring, Md., 1964—65; mem. of the tech. staff Bell Laboratories, Lucent Technologies (formerly AT&T), Murray Hill, NJ, 1965—2001; cons. OFS Fitel and Lucent Technologies, Murray Hill, NJ, 2001—02. 1st lt. Army Missile Corps, 1959—60, Philadephia Air Defense System. Fellow: North Am. Thermal Analysis Soc. (pres. 1984, Mettlar award 1987), Americal Phys. Soc.; mem.: Soc. of Plastics Engineers (Internat. award 2000, Internat. Engring./Tech. award 1998), Am. Chem. Soc. Achievements include Pioneered in the development of quantitative thermoanalytical techniques to assay polymers and commercial plastics; created a new process for assembling optoelectronic devices. Home: 20 Mountain View Dr Chester NJ 07930 Office: OFS Fitel 600 Mountain Ave New Providence NJ 07974 Personal E-mail: hebair@att.net. Business E-Mail: heb@lucent.com.

BAIR, ROYDEN STANLEY, retired architect; b. New Rochelle, N.Y., Jan. 21, 1924; s. Roy S. and Ruth Irene (Farmer) B.; m. Margaret Davis Powell, Sept. 7, 1946 (dec. July 1972); children: Katherine, David, Laurence (dec. 1990), Andrew, Matthew; m. Martha Ann Cooper, July 7, 1973. BS in Civil Engring., Purdue U., 1947; BArch, MIT, 1950. Registered architect, Tex, Fla.; registered profl. engr., Tex. Construction adminstrn. Skidmore, Owings & Merrill, Chgo., 1950-53; draftsman J.N. MacCammon, Dallas, 1953-56; sr. assoc. Harrell & Hamilton, Dallas, 1956-67; sr. architect Lloyd Morgan Jones, Houston, 1967-68; owner R.S. Bair, Architects, Houston, 1969-95; ptnr. Turner & Bair Architects, Houston, 1996—2002. Capt. U.S. Army, 1942-46, 51-53. Mem. AIA (fellowship 1988, pres. Houston chpt. 1982), Construction Specifications Inst. (nat. pres. 1979, fellowship 1972), Construction Scis. Rsch. Found. (v.p. 1980-87), Tex. Soc. Architects. Home: 9573 Doliver Dr Houston TX 77063-1010 E-mail: stanandmartha@houston.rr.com.

BAIR, SHEILA COLLEEN, federal agency administrator; b. Wichita, Kans., Apr. 3, 1954; d. Albert E. and Clara F. (Brenneman) B.; m. Scott Cooper; 1 child, Preston Carlos. BA in Philosophy, U. Kans., 1975, JD, 1978. Bar: Kans. 1979. Teaching fellow Sch. Law, U. Ark., Fayetteville, 1978-79; atty.-advisor HEW, Kansas City, Mo., 1979-81; legal and policy advisor Office of Senator Bob Dole, Washington, 1981-86; of counsel Kutak, Rock & Campbell, Washington, 1986-87; dir. rsch. Bob Dole for Pres., Kans., 1987-88; legis. counsel N.Y. Stock Exch., Washington, 1988-91; commr. Commodity Futures Trading Commn., Washington, 1991—, acting chmn., 1993; Asst Secy Financial Inst Dept Treasury, Washington, 2001—. Candidate U.S. Ho. of Reps. from 5th Kans. dist., 1990; mem. bd. govs. Sch. Law, U. Kans., 1990-93; bd. dirs. Women's Campaign Fund, 1991—. Mem. ABA. Democrat. Office: US Dept Treasury Financial Insts 1500 Pennsylvania Ave NW Washington DC 20220

BAIR, WILLIAM ALOIS, engineer; b. Bklyn., Aug. 13, 1931; s. Henry Auchu and Anna Margaret (Zidar) B.; m. Patricia Anne Doyle, July 23, 1955; children: William A. Jr., Joseph M. Student, Pa. State U., 1949-51; BS in Engring., U.S. Naval Acad., 1955; BS in Civil Engring., Rensselaer Poly. Inst., 1958; MS in Nuclear Engring., U. Calif., 1966; grad. advanced mgmt. program, Wharton Sch., 1987. Registered profl. engr., N.Y., N.J., Pa., Conn., Md., Del., Va., S.C., Ga., D.C. Commd. ensign USN, 1955, advanced through grades to comdr., 1969; with USN Civil Engr. Corps, 1957—77; ret. USN, 1977; project mgr. Ebasco Svc. Inc., Princeton, NY, 1977—85, Raytheon Engrs. & Constrn., N.Y.C., 1988—96; dir. program planning and devel. Ebasco Svcs. Inc., N.Y.C., 1985—88; pres. Bair Engring. Cons., 1996—. Appointed mem. spl. 3 man NATO tech. com. to evaluate effectiveness of European Airfield Phys. Protection Program to counter damage from attack by Warsaw Pact Nations, 1972-75. Author: Helium 3 Neutron Spectrometer, 1966; contbr. articles to profl. jours. Scoutmaster Boy Scouts Am., Rockville, Md., 1969-70; coun. mem. European br., Casteau, Belgium, 1971-75. Decorated Legion of Merit, Bronze Star with V, Joint Svc. Commendation medal, Vietnamese Cross of Gallantry, Vietnamese Medal of Honor 1st class. Fellow ASCE; mem. Am. Nuclear Soc., Soc. Am. Mil. Engrs., Am. Legion, VFW. Republican. Roman Catholic. Achievements include research and development of innovative processes/procedures for decontamination and demolition of contaminated radioactive structures. Home and Office: Bair Engring Cons 21 Lorrie Ln Princeton Junction NJ 08550-5112

BAIR, WILLIAM J. retired radiation biologist; b. Jackson, Mich., July 14, 1924; s. William J. and Mona J. (Gamble) B.; m. Barbara Joan Sites, Feb. 16, 1952; children: William J., Michael Braden, Andrew Emil. BA in chemistry, Ohio Wesleyan U., 1949; PhD in Radiation Biology, U. Rochester, 1954. NRC-AEC fellow U. Rochester, 1949-50, research asso. radiation biology, 1950-54; biol. scientist Hanford Labs. of Gen. Electric Co., Richland, Wash., 1954-56, mgr. inhalation toxicology sect., biology dept., 1956-65, Battelle Meml. Inst., 1965-68; mgr. biology dept. Pacific Northwest Labs., Richland, Wash., 1968-74, dir. life scis. program, 1973-75, mgr. biomed. and environ. research program, 1975-76, mgr. environ. health and safety research program, 1976-86, mgr. life scis. ctr., 1986-93, sr. advisor health protection rsch., 1993—2002; ret., 2002. Demonstrated toxicology of plutonium and carcinogenisis of radioactive particles in lung; lectr. radiation biology Joint Ctr. Grad. Study, Richland, 1955-75; cons. to adv. com. on reactor safeguards Nuclear Regulatory Commn., 1971-87; mem. com. on plutonium toxicology; subcom. inhalation hazards, com. pathologic effects atomic radiation NAS, 1957-64, ad hoc com. on hot particles of subcom. biol. effects ionizing radiation NAS-NRC, 1974-76, vice-chmn. com. on biol. effects of ionizing radiation, BEIR IV Alpha radiation, 1985-88, battlefield radiation exposure com., 1997-99; chmn. task force on biol. effects of inhaled particles Internat. Commn. on Radiol. Protection, 1970-79, com. 2 on permissible dose for internal radiation, 1973-93, chmn. task group on respiratory tract models, 1984-93; mem. Nat. Coun. on Radiation Protection and Measurements, 1974-92, hon. mem., 1992, com. on maximum permissible concentration of radionuclides for occupl. and nonoccupl. exposure, 1970-74, com. basic radiation protection criteria, 1975-92, chmn. ad hoc com. on hot particles, 1974, chmn. ad hoc com. internal emitter activities, 1976-77, com. on internal emitter stds., 1977-92; radiation adv. com. and sci. adv. bd. EPA, 1993-99. Author 200 books, articles, reports, chpts. in books. With AUS, 1943-46. Decorated Bronze Star; recipient E.O. Lawrence Meml. award AEC, 1970, cert. of appreciation AEC, 1975, Alumni Disting. Achievement citation Ohio Wesleyan U., 1986. Fellow AAAS (life), Health Physics Soc. (life, bd. dirs. 1970-73, 83-86, pres. elect 1983-84, pres. 1984-85, Disting. Sci. Achievement award 1991, Herbert H. Parker award Columbia chpt. 1998); mem. Radiation Rsch. Soc., Nat. Coun. Radiation Protection measurement (hon., Lauriston S. Taylor lectr. 1997), Soc. Exptl. Biology and Medicine (vice chmn. N.W. chpt. 1967-70, 74-75), Sigma Xi, Kiwanis (dir.). Home: 578 Clermont Dr Richland WA 99352-1966 Office: Battelle Pacific NW Labs PO Box 999 Richland WA 99352-0999

BAIRD, ALAN C. screenwriter; b. Waterville, Maine, Jan. 5, 1951; s. Chester A. and Beverly E. B. BA, Mich. State U., 1973. Pres. Souterrain Teeshirts, Nice, France, 1977-78; page NBC, N.Y.C., 1979-80; producer, dir. Random Prodns., Hollywood, Calif., 1981; writer, producer Preview STV, N.Y.C., 1982-83, Sta. KCOP-TV, Hollywood, 1983-84; writer Vidiom Prodns., Hollywood, 1985-95; screenwriter, 1995—. Author: ATS Operations, 1976, Writes of Passage, 1992, 9TimeZones.com, 1999; prodr. TV script Live at the Palomino, 1981; designer Screenwright Screenplay Formatting Software, 1985; writer TV scripts Night Court, 1986, 20/60, 1986, Golden Girls, 1986, Family Ties, 1986, Max Headroom, 1987, Dave's World, 1993, movie scripts Trading Up, 1988, Merlinsky, 1989, Eleven Thousand Virgins, 1994, The Fall in Budapest, 1997; play script Twisted Pair, 1998. Crisis counselor San Francisco Suicide Prevention, 1975; prodn. asst. March of Dimes Telethon, Hollywood, 1985; escort, host, vol. Verdugo Hills Hosp., 1994-96. Recipient Harvard Book prize Harvard U., Cambridge, Mass., 1969. Avocations: flying, running, scuba diving, parachuting, competitive driving.

BAIRD, BRIAN N. congressman; b. Chama, N.Mex., Mar. 7, 1956; m. Rachel Nugent. BS, U. Utah, 1977; MS, U. Wyo., 1980, PhD, 1984. Mem. faculty dept. psychology Pacific Luth. U., 1986—97; mem. U.S. Congress from 3d Wash. dist., 1999—; mem. transp. and infrastructure, sci., and budget. Cons. clin. psychologist St. Charles Med. Ctr., 1994-96. Author: The Internship Practicum Handbook, Are We Having Fun Yet?. Mem. APA, Wash. State Psychol. Assn. Democrat. Office: US Ho of Reps 1421 Longworth Ho Office Bldg Washington DC 20515-0001*

BAIRD, BRUCE ALLEN, lawyer; b. Cin., Mar. 26, 1948; s. William Wendell and Audrey (Geignetter) B.; m. Erica Borden, July 27, 1975 (div. 1993); 1 child, Jessica; m. Nicolette Adair Heidepriem, Sept. 17, 1993; 1 child, William. BA, Cornell U., 1970; JD, NYU, 1975. Spl. asst. to dep. atty. gen. U.S. Dept. Justice, Washington, 1975-76; law clk. to presiding judge U.S. Ct. Appeals (2d cir.), Brattleboro, Vt. and N.Y.C., 1976-77; assoc. Davis, Polk & Wardwell, N.Y.C., 1977-80; asst. U.S. atty. U.S. Attys. Office (so. dist.) N.Y., N.Y.C., 1980-86, dep. chief criminal div., 1986-87, chief narcotics unit, 1987, chief securities and commodities frauds unit, 1987-89; of counsel Covington & Burling, Washington, 1989-91, ptnr., 1991—. Editor in chief NYU Law Rev., 1974-75. Mem. ABA (co-chair securities and commodities fraud subcom. of white collar crime com. of criminal justice sect. 1994—), N.Y. State Bar Assn. (profl. jud. ethics com. 1982-89), Assn. of Bar of City of N.Y. (profl. jud. ethics com. 1979-82, 86-89), Fed. Bar Council, D.C. Bar Assn. Republican. Presbyterian. Home: 5404 Edgemoor Ln Bethesda MD 20814-1326 E-mail: bbaird@cov.com.

BAIRD, CHARLES BRUCE, lawyer, consultant; b. DeLand, Fla., Apr. 18, 1935; s. James Turner and Ethelyn Isabelle (Williams) B.; m. Barbara Ann Fabian, June 6, 1959 (div. Dec. 1979); children: C. Bruce Jr., Robert Arthur, Bryan James; m. Byung-Ran Cho, May 23, 1982; children: Merah-Iris, Haerah Violet. BSME, U. Miami, 1958; postgrad., UCLA, 1962-64; MBA, Calif. State U., 1966; JD, Am. U., 1971. Bar: Va. 1971, U.S. Dist. Ct. (ea. dist.) Va. 1971, D.C. 1973, U.S. Dist. Ct. D.C. 1973, U.S. Ct. Appeals (4th cir.) 1974, U.S. Supreme Ct. 1975. Rsch. engr. Naval Ordnance Lab., Corona, Calif., 1961-67; aerospace engr. Naval Air Systems Command, Washington, 1967-69; cons. engr. Bird Engring. Rsch. Assts., Vienna, Va., 1969-71; prof. Def. Systems Mgmt. Coll., Ft. Belvoir, Va., 1982; spl. asst. for policy compliance USIA Voice of Am., Washington, 1983-84. Cons. Booz, Allen & Hamilton, Inc., Bethesda, 1975-82, IBM, Bethesda, Md., 1984, Logistics Mgmt. Inst., McLean, Va., 1986-98, 2002—, TelcoExchange.com, 1998-2000, 2001; adj. prof. Fla. Inst. Tech., 1988. Contbr. articles to profl. jours.; inventor computer-based comm. systems for the gravely handicapped. Bd. govs. Sch. Engring. U. Miami, 1957; trustee Galilee United Meth. Ch., Arlington, Va., 1983-87. Mem. Va. Trial Lawyers Assn., Internet. Soc., Fed. Comm. Bar Assn., United We Stand Am. (founding mem.), Sigma Alpha Epsilon. Home and Office: 5396 Gainsborough Dr Fairfax VA 22032-2744

BAIRD, CHARLES FITZ, retired mining and metals company executive; b. Southampton, N.Y., Sept. 4, 1922; s. George White and Julia (Fitz) B.; m. Norma Adele White, Sept. 13, 1947; children: Susan Baird Creyke, Stephen White, Charles Fitz, Nancy Baird Harwood. AB, Middlebury (Vt.) Coll., 1944; grad., Advanced Mgmt. Program, Harvard, 1960; LLD, Bucknell U., 1976. With Standard Oil Co., N.J., 1948-65, dep. European fin. rep., 1955-58, asst. treas., 1958-62; dir. Esso Standard SA Française, 1962-65; asst. sec. for fin. mgmt. Dept. of Navy, 1966-67, undersec., 1967-69; v.p. fin. Inco Ltd., 1969-72, sr. v.p., 1972-76, vice-chmn., 1976-77, pres., 1977-80, chmn., CEO, 1980-87. Trustee CNA Corp., 1990—2002, chmn., 1992—97; past trustee Logistics Mgmt. Inst.; mem. Pres.'s Commn. on Marine Sci., Engring. and Resources, 1967—69, Nat. Adv. Commn. on Ocean and Atmosphere, 1972—74. Trustee Marine Corps U. Found., 1993—2002, Bucknell U., 1969—95, chmn. bd. trustees, 1976—82; bd. advisers Ctr. for Naval Analyses, 1991—96, Naval War Coll., 1970—74. Served to capt. USMC, 1950—51, 1943-46. Mem. Coun. Fgn. Rels., Chevy Chase Club (Md.), Maidstone Club (East Hampton, N.Y.), Bridgehampton Club (N.Y.). Home: 4423 Boxwood Rd Bethesda MD 20816-1817 Fax: 301-320-5274.

BAIRD, DAVIS W. philosophy educator; b. Boston, Apr. 12, 1954; s. Walter Scott and Mary Warren (Davis) B.; m. Linda Weingarten, June 10, 1982 (dec. June 1992); 1 child, Ian; m. Deanna Leamon, Apr. 11, 1994. BA, Brandeis U., 1976; MA, PhD, Stanford U., 1981. Vis. asst. prof. U. Ariz., Tucson, 1981-82; asst. prof. U. S.C., Columbia, 1983-88, chmn. dept. philosophy, 1992—, assoc. prof., 1988-01, prof., 2001—. Author: Inductive Logic, 1992, Thing Knowledge, 2003; editor: Heinrich Hertz, 1997; contbr. articles to profl. jours. Office: U SC Dept Philosophy Columbia SC 29208-0001 E-mail: db@sc.edu.

BAIRD, DONALD ROBERT, retired secondary school educator; b. Boise, Idaho, June 26, 1941; s. Donald Whitney and Pauline June (Cox) B.; m. Donna Colleen Karnes, Sept. 18, 1970; children: Patricia Colleen Baird Duffey, Diane Marie Baird Henry. BS, Coll. Idaho, 1963; MS, Boise State U., 1980. Advanced secondary teaching cert. Instr. NESEP USN, San Diego, summers 1969-75; tchr. South Jr. H.S., Boise, 1969-80, Capital H.S., Boise, 1980-2000; instr. BOOST USN, San Diego, summers 1984-89. Tchr. Boise State U., 1981-82; computer cons. Capital H.S., Boise, 1990-2000; dept. chmn. South Jr. H.S., Boise, student body advisor, 1975-76. Info. officer U.S. Naval Acad., Annapolis, Md., 1991—. Comdr. USN, 1963-66, res., 1967-89. Recipient Outstanding Educator award Acad. of Am. Educators, 1973. Mem. Nat. Coun. Tchrs. Math., Idaho Coun. Tchrs. of Math. (sec.-treas. 1983-85), Naval Res. Assn. (chpt. pres. 1985-89), Boise Edn. Assn. (rep.), Order of Demolay (chevalier 1959), Masons (Master # 39). Republican. Presbyterian. Avocations: tennis, golf, computers, chess, model ship building.

BAIRD, DOUGLAS GORDON, law educator, dean; b. Phila., July 10, 1953; s. Henry Welles and Eleanora (Gordon) B. BA, Yale U., 1975; JD, Stanford U., 1979; LLD, U. Rochester, 1994. Law clk. U.S. Ct. Appeals (9th cir.), 1979, 80; asst. prof. law U. Chgo., 1980-83, prof. law, 1984—, assoc. dean, 1984-87, Bigelow prof. law, 1988—, dean, 1994-99. Author: (with others) Security Interests in Personal Property, 1984, 2d edit., 1987, Bankruptcy, 1985, 3d edit., 2000, Elements of Bankruptcy, 1992, 3d edit., 2001; (D. Baird, R. Gertner, R. Picker) Game Theory and the Law, 1994. Mem. AAAS, Order of Coif. Office: U Chgo Sch Law 1111 E 60th St Chicago IL 60637-2776 E-mail: Douglas_Baird@law.uchicago.edu.

BAIRD, DOUGLAS JAMES, investment banker; b. Rochester, N.Y., Feb. 3, 1962; s. James David and Carol Agatha (Pascale) B.; m. Sarah Lee Stevenson, Dec. 12, 1987; children: David Harrington, Henry Stevenson, Roxanna Margaret. Diploma, Deerfield (Mass.) Acad., 1980; AB Dartmouth Coll., 1984; MBA, Amos Tuck Sch., Hanover, N.H., 1989. Fin. analyst pub. fin. group Merrill Lynch Capital Markets, N.Y.C., 1984-85, jr. assoc. internat. fin. group,

1985-86; assoc. equity transactions group Merrill Lynch Europe Ltd., London, 1986-87; assoc. mergers and acquisitions Merrill Lynch Capital Markets, N.Y.C., 1988, Alex. Brown & Sons, Balt., 1989-91, v.p. corp. fin. environ. svcs., 1991-93, mng. dir. equity capital markets, 1993-99; head U.S. equity capital mkts. Deutsche Bank Securities, Balt., 2000—. Mem. adv. bd. applied corp. fin. program U. Wis., Madison; mem. bd. advisors Ind. Securities Rsch., LLC; trustee Boys' Latin Sch. of Md.; bd. dirs. PACT: Helping Children with Spl. Needs; intern, White House Office of Media Relations and Planning, 1983. Mem. Yale Club of N.Y.C., Maryland Club, Webhannet Country Club, Balt. Country Club, Univ. Club. Republican. Episcopalian. Office: Deutsche Bank Securities 31 W 52d St New York NY 10019-

BAIRD, DUGALD EUAN, global technology services company executive; b. Aberdeen, Scotland, Sept. 16, 1937; came to U.S., 1979; s. Dugald and Matilda Deans (Tennant) B.; m. Angelica Hartz, May 24, 1961; children: Camilla N., Maiken E. MA in Geophysics, Cambridge U., 1960; LLD, Aberdeen U., 1995, Dundee U., 1998; DSc, Heriot-Watt U., 1999. Joined Schlumberger, 1960, various field assignments worldwide, 1979—86, chmn., CEO, 1986—. Office: Schlumberger Ltd 153 E 53 St New York NY 10022

BAIRD, EDWARD ROUZIE, JR., lawyer; b. Norfolk, Va., Aug. 29, 1936; s. Edward Rouzie and Eleanor Gray (Perry) B.; m. Nell McGlaughon, Oct. 8, 1967 (dec. Oct. 1973); 1 child, Eleanor Gray; m. Abby St. John Starke, Feb. 5, 1977; children: Abby St. John, Edward Rouzie V. BA, U. Va., 1960, LLB, 1967. Assoc. Baird, Creshaw & Ware, Norfolk, 1967—68; asst. dist. counsel U.S. Army C.E., Norfolk, 1968—73; asst. U.S. Atty. U.S. Atty.'s Office, Norfolk, 1973—77; sole practice Norfolk, 1977—82, 1999—; ptnr. Willcox & Baird, Norfolk, 1982—99. Served to lt. (j.g.) USN, 1960-63. Mem. Va. Bar Assn., Norfolk-Portsmouth Bar Assn., Soc. Cincinnati, Va. Club (Norfolk). Home: 1711 Cloncurry Rd Norfolk VA 23505-1717 Office: 210 Monticello Ave Norfolk VA 23510-2301

BAIRD, GEORGE, architecture educator; BArch with honors, U. Toronto, 1962; student, Univ. Coll., London, 1964—67; AM (hon.), Harvard U., 1994. Assoc. prof. architecture U. Toronto, 1968—75, prof. architecture, 1976—93, acting chmn. dept. architecture, 1983—85, chmn. program in architecture, 1985; prof. architecture Grad. Sch. Design Harvard U., 1993—96, dir. MArch I and MArch II programs Grad. Sch. Design, 1995—, G. Ware Travelstead prof. architecture Grad. Sch. Design, 1996—. Vis. design critic in architecture dept. architecture Grad. Sch. Design Harvard U., 1986—87, 1992—93; vis. design critic Sch. Architecture Gill U., 1987; Davenport vis. prof. architecture Yale U., 1993; lectr. in field. Author: The Space of Appearance, 1995; co-editor: Meaning in Architecture, English, French, and Spanish edits., 1968, Queues, Rendezvous, Riots: Questioning the Public in Art and Architecture, 1995; curator (exhbn.) Akademie der Kunst, Berlin, 1982, co-curator Banff Ctr. Arts, Alberta, 1992, prin. works include Urban Design for Lakeshore Neighborhood, Etobicoke, Ont., 1990, Master Plan and Bldg. Program, Cranbrook Ednl. Cmty., Bloomfield Hills, Mich., 1990, Additions and Alterations to Parliament St. Libr., Toronto, 1990, Cloud Gardens Pk., 1993, Spl. Needs Apt. Bldg., 1993, Butterfly Conservatory, Niagara Falls, Ont., 1996, Student Residence for U. Toronto, Mississauga, Ont., 1998, Mausoleum, Toronto, 2000, Mausoleums, Toronto and Vaughan, Ont., 2002; contbr. articles to profl. jours. and mags. Recipient Can. Arch. award for the Harborfront Pub. Open Space Sys., Toronto, 1985, Can. Arch. award for Elliot Lake Auditorium, Ont., 1986, Can. Arch. award for Cloud Gardens Pk., Toronto, 1991, award for architecture and design, Toronto Arts Found., 1992, Gov. Gen.'s award for architecture for Cloud Gardens Pk., Toronto, 1994, Can. Arch. award for Student Residence for U. Toronto, 1998, Can. Arch. award for Mausoleum, Toronto, 1999. Fellow: Royal Archtl. Inst. Can.; mem.: Ont. Assn. Archs. (da Vinci medal 2000). Office: Harvard Design Sch 207A Gund Hall 48 Quincy St Cambridge MA 02138*

BAIRD, JAMES ABINGTON, retired judge; b. Kirksville, Mo., Jan. 28, 1926; s. James Abington and Dorothy (LaGest) B.; m. Georgia Jane Suliburk, Mar. 29, 1948 (dec. Dec. 1999); children— James Abington III, Mary J.; m. Alice K. Barter, Dec. 2, 2002. BS, U. Mich., 1949; JD, U. Toledo, 1957. Bar: Ohio 1957. Sales rep. Fruehauf Trailer Co., Chgo., 1949-50; pres. Kaiser-Frazer dealership, Caro, Mich., 1950-51; sales rep. Warren-Teed Products Co., Toledo, 1951-52, Dictaphone Corp., Toledo, 1952-53; claims adjuster Nationwide Ins. Co., Toledo, 1953-57; since practiced in Toledo; judge Sylvania Ohio Municipal Ct., 1970-82. Chmn. Sch. Levy campaigns Sylvania Pub. Sch. System, 1968-69, candidate Sch. Bd., 1969. Served with USNR, 1944-46. Mem. ABA, Ohio Bar Assn., Toledo Bar Assn., Nat. Trial Attys. Assn., VFW, Am. Legion, U. Mich., U. Toledo alumni assns., Bowling Green Country Club, Sertoma, Rotary, Elks, Masons, Phi Delta Theta. Home: 85 Nottingham Cross Bowling Green OH 43402-9384

BAIRD, JAY WARREN, historian, educator; b. Toledo, July 1, 1936; s. Warren Austin and Helen Lucille Baird; m. Sally Eshelman Baird, Aug. 23, 1958; children: Lisa Jane, Bryan Eshelman, Stanford Davis. BA, Denison U., 1958; postgrad., Free U. Berlin, 1959; MA, Columbia U., 1960, PhD, 1966. Instr. history Stanford (Calif.) U., 1963—65; asst. prof. history Pomona Coll., Claremont, Calif., 1965—67; assoc. prof. Miami U., Oxford, Ohio, 1967—, full prof. history, 1975—. Vis. fellow Clare Hall, Cambridge, England, 1997, Selwyn Coll., Cambridge, 2002. Author: The Mythical World of Nazi War Propaganda, 1939-1943, 1974, To Die For Germany, 1990; editor: From Nuremberg to My Lai, 1972, Kultur und Staatsgewalt, 2003; contbr. articles to profl. jours. Mem.: Ohio Acad. History (Disting. Tchg. award 1996), German Studies Assn. (pres. 1993—95), Am. Hist. Assn. Republican. Presbyterian. Home: 11 Bull Run Oxford OH 45056 Office: Miami U Dept History 240 Upham Hall Oxford OH 45056

BAIRD, JOHN ABSALOM, JR., retired college official; b. Honolulu, Sept. 13, 1918; s. John Absalom and Helen (Bates) B. m. Virginia Walton, Mar 8, 1941 (dec. 1983); children: Suzanne W. Baird Perot, Linda Baird Woodruff, Barbara Baird Rogers; m. Clare A. Emmons, May 12, 1984 (dec. 1998). AB, Princeton U., 1940; postgrad., Johns Hopkins U., 1941. Asst. supt. Charles S. Walton Co., 1942-47, asst. sec. and dir., 1947-52, v.p., 1952-72; asst. pres. Ea. Bapt. Theol. Sem., Phila., Ea. Coll., St. Davids, Pa., 1952-61, v.p., 1961-88, advisor to pres., 1988—2002. Author: A Leap of Faith, 1972, The Whole Gospel for the Whole World, 1975, All Things Are Thine, 1976, Profile of a Hero, 1977, The Shining Fire, 1979, Horn of Plenty, 1982, Great House, 1984, Promises to Keep, 1989, More Than Knowledge, 1992, The Power of One, 1997, Inheritance of Value, 1999; contbr. articles to profl. jours. Trustee, v.p. Pa. Lupus Found.; v.p. Pa. Chpt. Lupus Found. Am., 1973—95; trustee Vol. Svcs. for the Blind, Phila., 1971—85, Ludington Libr., Bryn Mawr, Ralston House, Phila., 4th Bapt. Mission Found., 1976—80, Seaman's Ch., Phila.; v.p., bd. dirs. Am. Sunday Sch. Union, Phila., 1957—69; bd. dirs. Pa. United Theol. Sem. Found., Pitts.; bd. corporators, bd. dirs. Covenant Life Ins. Co., 1971—74; Phila. Main Line dist. chmn. Valley Forge coun. Boy Scouts Am., 1952—54, dist. commr., 1954—56; vice chmn. Main Line br. YMCA Greater Phila., 1947—63; mem. adv. bd. Phila. Inglis House, 1963—2003, Union League; chmn. bd. trustees Shipley Sch., Bryn Mawr, Pa., 1972—78; bd. dirs. Watchman Examiner Corp., N.Y.C., 1958—70, Am. Ednl. Film and Video Ctr., Std. Davids., Athenaeum, Phila., Beaumont Retirement Cmty. Recipient Freedom Founds. Honor medal, 1973. Mem.: Soc. Colonial Wars (gov. 1994—97), U.S. Naval Found., U.S. Naval Inst., Am. Coll. Pub. Rels. Assn., Am. Alumni Coun., Am. Bapt. Pub. Rels. Assn., Hist. Soc. Pa. (dir. 1992—2001), Order Fgn. Wars, Soc. of Cin. (pres. Del. 1972—75, sec. gen. 1977—83), Loyal Legion, Colonial Soc. Pa. (gov. 1994—97), S.R., English-Speaking Union, Am. Assn. Sem. Staff Officers (pres. 1966—68), Geneal. Soc. Pa. (dir. 1988—2003), Pa. Acad. Fine Arts, Am. Philatelic Soc., Am. Rose Soc., Merion Cricket Club (Haverford, Pa.), Right Angle Club, Penn Club. Republican. Presbyterian. Home: 74 Pasture Ln # 116 Bryn Mawr PA 19010-1766 Office: Ea Coll Off of Advisor to Pres Saint Davids PA 19087

BAIRD, JULIAN THOMPSON, JR., art dealer; b. Harlingen, Tex., Jan. 28, 1938; s. Julian Thompson and Faye Devilbiss Baird; m. Carol Friedell Baird (div. 1985); m. Elaine Fraser Baird, Jan. 9, 1986. AB magna cum laude, Harvard U., 1960, PhD, 1968; BA, Oxford (Eng.) U., 1962, MA, 1967. Assoc. prof. Boston U., 1967-80; pres. Baird Enterprises d/b/a Tree's Place, Orleans, Mass., 1981—. Lectr. Cape Mus. Fine Art, Old Lyme Acad. Art, St. Botolph Club, Boston, others. Contbr. articles to profl. jours. Mem. Orleans Charter Commn., 1989-90; pres. Orleans Bd. of Trade, 1983-84, Orleans Taxpayers Assn., 1985-87; fine wine charity auctioneer Cape Mus. Fine Arts, 1994-96. Recipient Spl. Distinction award Boston U. Alumni Assn., 1990. Mem. St. Botolph Club, Oxford and Cambridge Soc. Avocations: collecting art, wine and books, boating, gardening, computers, investing. Home: 4 Mayflower Cir PO Box 666 Orleans MA 02653-0666 Office: Tree's Place 62 Route 6A Orleans MA 02653-2411

BAIRD, LARRY DON, minister, nurse; b. Abilene, Tex., Sept. 23, 1949; s. Delmar Lee Baird and Frances Elizabeth Weathers; m. Mary Margaret Ledbetter, Dec. 22, 1970; 1 child, Shannon Kirk; 1 adopted child, Walter Dale. Student, San Diego State U., 1971-72, Cisco Jr. Coll., Clyde, Tex., 1977-78; diploma in nursing, Hendrick Meml. Hosp., Abilene, 1972-73. Ordained to ministry United Pentecostal Ch. Internat., 1973-84, Assemblies of Lord Jesus Christ, 1984. Pastor United Pentecostal Ch., Hamlin, Tex., 1979-82; residential dir. Tupelo (Miss.) Children's Mansion, 1982-84, campus dean, 1983-84; DON Valley View Care Ctr., Anson, Tex., 1990-91; unit dir. Hill Resources Inc., Abilene, Tex., 1992—. Asst. choir dir., musician, dir. and interpreter for deaf United Penecostal Ch., Abilene, 1984—; dir. Spirit of Freedom Alcoholic Ministries, 1984-95; pvt. nurse coord. Health Care Svcs., Abilene, 1984-85; sr. pastor Abundant Life Apostolic Ministries, Abilene, 1984—; dir. home missions Tex.-N.Mex. Distr. for Assemblies of Lord Christ Jesus Christ, 1986-91; bd. dirs. Blue Mountain (Miss.) Childrens Home; chaplain Am. Legion Post 57, Abilene, 2003—. Active various health support groups, Abilene, 1984—; chmn., mem. exec. bd. Abilene Coord. Coun., 1984-2003; chmn. adv. com. Home Cmty. Svc. Mental Health-Mental Retardation Program, Abilene, 1994-2003; dist. sec., treas. Assemblies of the Lord Jesus Christ, West Tex. N.Mex. dist., 2000—. Fellow Ministerial Alliance (pres. 1980-82). Republican. Home: 1918 Sayles Blvd Abilene TX 79605-6036 Office: Abundant Life Apostolic Ministries 741 S 11th St Abilene TX 79602-3852 *Life is like jig saw puzzle. Many pieces seem unnecessary, however, the true beauty is only seen at the time of completion, when all pieces fit perfectly together. It is finished—so also is a finished life in Christ.*

BAIRD, LAUREL COHEN, clinical nurse; b. Chgo., Dec. 1, 1943; d. Carl Eugene and Joan Adele (Arenz) Patterson; m. Sidney Henry Cohen, June 29, 1968 (div. Nov. 1981); children: Elizabeth Ann Cohen, David Arthur Patterson, Douglas Edward, Deborah Sue; m. Frederick Joseph Foti, Jan. 19, 1985 (div. June 1991) m. Jack W. Baird (Nov. 10, 2001). Diploma in nursing, Swedish Covenant, 1967; BS, Moody Bible Inst., 1976. RN, N.J., Md. Staff nurse Overlook Hosp., Summit, N.J., 1980-82; pub. health nurse Patient Care Svc., West Orange, N.J., 1982-83; hospice nurse The Hospice, Inc., Montclair, N.J., 1984-92; fin. svc. rep. Primerica Fin. Svcs., Duluth, Ga., 1985-89; coord. home care Vis. Nurse Assn. Essex Valley, East Orange, N.J., 1993-96; Medicare case mgr. Aetna US Healthcare Cmty. Outreach, Fairfield, NJ, 1996-99; on-site nurse Johns Hopkins Cmty. Physicians, 1999—2001, Sun Plus Home Care, Pleasant Hill, Calif., 2001; hospice nurse care mgr. Sutter VNA and Hospice, Pleasant Hill, 2002—. State coord. La Leche League, N.J., 1976-78; hospice vol. The Hospice, Inc., 1992-98; mem. MADD, Rep. Presdl. Task Force, 1989. Lt. (j.g.) USNR, 1967-69. Mem. Adoptees Liberty Movement Assn. (spokesman 1977-83), DAR. Republican. Presbyterian. Avocations: orchid culture, gardening, marathoning, speed walking, piano. Home: 303 Eastgate Lane Martinez CA 94553- E-mail: lolly1331@aol.com.

BAIRD, LEONARD LYNN, social scientist, educator, researcher, editor; s. Russel Thomas and Edith Isabel Baird; m. Rosanne Clark Baird, Oct. 19, 1962; children: William Russell, Diana Ragan. BA, U. Calif., LA, 1962, MA, 1965, EdD, 1966. Rsch. psychologist Am. Coll. Testing Program, Iowa City, 1966—69; sr. rsch. psychologist Ednl. Testing Svc., Princeton, NJ, 1969—83; prof. U. Ky., Lexington, 1983—94, Ohio State U., Columbus, 1994—; editor Jour. of Higher Edn., Columbus, 1994—. Editl. bd. Rsch. in Higher Edn., 1987—96. Author: (books) The Elite Schools, 1977; author: (and editor) Understanding Student and Faculty Life, 1980, Increasing Grad. Student Retention, 1993; contbr. chapters to books, articles to profl. jours. Recipient Sydney Suslow award for outstanding rsch., Assn. for Instl. Rsch., 1991, Sr. Scholar award, Am. Coll. Pers. Assn., 2003. Office: Ohio State Univ 301 Ramseyer Columbus OH 43210

BAIRD, MARIANN SAUNORUS, critical care clinical nurse specialist, administrator; b. Chgo., Dec. 15, 1953; d. John and Irene (Lameka) Saunorus; m. Thomas W. Baird, Sept. 10, 1983; 1 child, Rachel. BSN, Loyola U., Chgo., 1975; MSN, Emory U., 1982. Critical care RN, cert. advanced cardiac life support instr., Ga. Supr. surg. nursing Rush-Presbyn. St. Lukes Med. Ctr., Chgo., 1978—80; from staff nurse, clin. mgr. intensive care unit to case mgr. St. Joseph's Hosp., Atlanta, 1982—96, case mgr. depts. pulmonary and nephrology, 1996—2001; clin. assoc. faculty Emory U., Atlanta, 1996—; clin. nurse specialist for critical care and med.-surg. nursing St. Joseph's Hosp., Atlanta, 2001—. RN preceptor, ednl. staff Genentech, Inc., 1995-2002. Author several nursing textbooks; contbr. articles to profl. jours. Mem. med. supply com. Atlanta Com. for Olympic Games, 1994-96. Recipient Fed. traineeship Emory U., 1980-81; named one of Outstanding Young Women of Am., 1991. Mem. AACN (bd. dirs. Atlanta chpt. 1984-86), Soc. Critical Care Medicine, Am. Holistic Nurses Assn., Blue Key, Kappa Gamma Pi, Sigma Theta Tau. Office: 5665 Peachtree Dunwoody Rd NE Atlanta GA 30342-1701 E-mail: mbaird@sjha.org.

BAIRD, PATRICIA ANN, physician, educator; b. Rochdale, Eng. came to Can., 1955; d. Harold and Winifred (Cainen) Holt; m. Robert Merrifield Baird, Feb. 22, 1964; children— Jennifer Ellen, Brian Merrifield, Bruce Andrew BSc with gen. honors in biol. sci., McGill U., 1959, MD, CM, 1963; DSc (hon.), McMaster U., 1991; D Univ. (hon.), U. Ottawa, 1991; LLD (hon.), Wilfrid Laurier U., 2000. Intern Royal Victoria Hosp., Montreal, Que., Can., 1963-64; resident, fellow in pediat. Vancouver Gen. Hosp., B.C., Can., 1964-67; instr. pediat. U. B.C., Vancouver, 1968-72, from asst. prof. to prof., 1972-94, Univ. Killam Disting. prof., 1994—; head dept. med. genetics Grace Hosp., Vancouver, 1981-89, Children's Hosp., Vancouver, 1981-89, Health Scis. Centre Hosp., 1986-89. Med. cons. B.C. Health Surveillance Registry, 1977-90; chmn. genetics grants com. Med. Rsch. Coun., Ottawa, Ont., Can., 1982-87, mem. coun., 1987-90; mem. Nat. Adv. Bd. on Sci. and Tech. to Fed. Govt., 1987-91; mem. genetic predisposition study steering com. Sci. Coun. Can., 1987-90; chair Royal Commn. on New Reproductive Technologies, 1989-93; co-chair Nat. Forum Sci. and Tech. Couns., 1991; v.p. Can. Inst. for Advanced Rsch., 1991-2002, vice chmn. bd., 2002--; bd. dirs. Biomed. Rsch. Centre, 1986-89; bd. govs. U. B.C., 1984-90; temporary cons. WHO, 1999, 2000, 01, mem. human genetics ELSI planning group, 2000-02, mem. expert adv. panel on human genetics, 2002--. Contbr. articles to med. jours. Bd. govs. U. B.C., 1984-90. Decorated officer Order of Can., 2000, Order of B.C., 1992; recipient Commemorative medal for Confedn. of Can., 1992, Queen's Golden Jubilee medal, 2002. Fellow RCP Can., Royal Soc. Can., Can. Coll. Med. Geneticists (v.p. 1984-86); mem. Am. Soc. Human Genetics (chair nominating com. 1987-89), B.C. Med. Assn., Can. Med. Assn., Genetics Soc. Can., Genetic Epidemiology (adv. bd. 1991-94), Internat. Fedn. of Gyn. and Obs. (mem. ethics com. 1997-99). Avocations: skiing, cycling, music. Office: U BC Dept Med Genetics Vancouver BC Canada V6T 1Z3 Business E-Mail: pbaird@interchange.ubc.ca.

BAIRD, PENNY DRUE, interior designer; b. N.Y.C., July 19, 1951; d. Philip Robert and Terri Baird; m. Fred Deutsch, Dec. 31, 1991; children: Alexander Baird Deutsch, Benjamin Baird Deutsch, Philip Baird Deutsch;1 child, Adam Baird Alpert. BA, U. Rochester, 1973; PsychD, Yeshiva U., 1991. Pres. Dessins LLC, N.Y.C., 1982—. Archtl. Digest, 1997, 1998, 2000. Pres. City Meals on Wheels, N.Y.C., 1985—90; mem. women's com. N.Y. Hosp., N.Y.C., 1994—; mem. women's bd. Albert Einstein Coll. Medicine, N.Y.C., 1990—. Mem.: Phi Beta Kappa. Office: Dessins LLC 787 Madison Ave New York NY 10021

BAIRD, ROBERT DAHLEN, religious educator; b. Phila., June 29, 1933; s. Jesse Dahlen and Clara (Sonntag) B.; m. Patty Jo Lutz, Dec. 18, 1954; children: Linda Sue, Stephen Robert, David Bryan, Janna Ann. BA, Houghton Coll., 1954; BD, Fuller Theol. Sem., 1957; STM, So. Meth. U., 1959; PhD, U. Iowa, 1964. Instr. philosophy and religion U. Omaha, 1962-65; fellow Asian religions Soc. for Religion in Higher Edn., 1965-66; asst. prof. religion U. Iowa, Iowa City, 1966-69, assoc. prof., 1969-74, prof., 1974-2001, acting dir. Sch. Religion, 1985; Leonard S. Florsheim Sr. Eminent Scholar's chair New Coll., U. South Fla., Sarasota, 1988-89; dir., Sch. of Religion U. Iowa, Iowa City, 1995—2000, prof. emeritus, 2001—. Faculty fellow Am. Inst. Indian Studies, India, 1972, sr. fellow, 1992; vis. prof. Grinnell Coll., 1983; Goodwin-Philpot Eminent chair in religion, Auburn U., 2001—. Author: Category Formation and the History of Religions, 1971, 2d paperback edit., 1991, (with W.R. Comstock et al) Religion and Man: An Introduction, 1971, Indian and Far Eastern Religious Traditions, 1972; editor, contbr.: Methodological Issues in Religious Studies, 1975, Religion in Modern India, 1981, 2d edit., 1988, 3rd rev. edit., 1995, 4th edit., 2001, Essays in the History of Religion, 1991; editor, contbr. Religion and Law in Independent India, 1993; book rev. editor: Jour. Am. Acad. Religion, 1979-84; contbr. articles to profl. jours. Ford Found. fellow, 1965-66; U. Iowa Faculty Devel. grantee, 1979, 86, 92; Am. Inst. Indian studies sr. fellow, 1972, 92. Mem. Am. Acad. Religion, Assn. Asian Studies, N.Am. Assn. for the Study Religion. Democrat. Presbyterian. Office: U Iowa Sch of Religion Iowa City IA 52242 E-mail: robert-baird@uiowa.edu.

BAIRD, ROBERT DEAN, mission director; b. Hereford, Tex., Aug. 12, 1933; s. Kay and Maybelle (Witherspoon) B.; m. Margaret Ann Roberts, Aug. 27, 1953; children: Sandy, Deana Young. AA, Amarillo Jr. Coll., 1953; BTh., Bapt. Bible Coll., 1970, DD (hon.), 1986, Atlantic Bapt. Bible Coll., 1986. Ordained to ministry Bapt. Ch., 1969. Asst. pastor High St. Bapt. Ch., Springfield, Mo., 1969-72; missionary Bapt. Bible Fellowship Internat., Springfield, 1972-77, asst. mission dir., 1977-81; pastor Hallmark Bapt. Ch., Fort Worth, 1981-86; mission dir. Bapt. Bible Fellowship Internat., Springfield, 1986—. Mem. Internat. Conf. on World Evangelism (steering com. 1990—). Office: Bapt Bible Fellowship Inter PO Box 191 Springfield MO 65801-0191

BAIRD, THOMAS BRYAN, JR., retired lawyer; b. Newport News, Va., June 21, 1931; s. Thomas Bryan and Mary Florence (Rieker) B.; m. Mildred Katherine Clark, June 23, 1956; children: Sarah, Thomas Bryan III, William, Laura. BA, U. Va., 1952; LLB, U. Tenn., 1960. Bar: Tenn. 1964, Va. 1969, U.S. Dist. Ct. (we. dist.) 1970. With Stat Farm Ins., Knoxville, Tenn., 1960-68; asst. commonwealth atty. Wytheville, Va., 1969-71; commonwealth atty. Wythe County, 1972-98; prin. Thomas B. Baird, Jr. Trustee Simmerman Home for the Aged, 1972-83. Served with U.S. Army, 1953-55. Democrat. Presbyterian. Home: 875 N 18th St Wytheville VA 24382-1022

BAIRD, WILLIAM DAVID, retired anesthesiologist; b. Dallas, Feb. 17, 1927; s. John B. and Sue S. B.; m. Virginia Claye Sanders, June 27, 1948; children: Linda B. Moore, Cynthia B. Matthews, C. Sanders Baird, Ginger B. Stark, J. Davies Baird. BA, Rice Inst., Houston, 1949; MD, U. Tex., 1953. Diplomate Am. Bd. Anesthesiologists. Intern U. Tex. Med. Br. Hosps., Galveston, 1953-54, resident in anesthesiology, 1954-56, fellow, instr. anesthesiology, 1956-57; pvt. practice anesthesiology Garland, Tex., 1957-80; med. cons. Garland Cmty. Hosp., 1980-81, Branson & Misko, 1981-93. Clin. instr. U. Tex. SW Br., 1963-80; chief anesthesiology Garland Clinic and Hosp., 1957-75, Garland Meml. Hosp., 1975-78; exec. staff com. Meml. Hosp. Garland, 1975-78; adv. bd. Presbyn. Hosp. Dallas, 1969. Author: Some Descendants of John Baird, A Genealogy, 1997; editor, pub.: The 17th Sortie Newsletter of the 17th Bomb Group/Wing Reunion Assn. Precinct chmn. Rep. party, Garland, 1969-74; bd. dirs. Garland YMCA, 1972-74. Fellow Am. Coll. Anesthesiologists; mem. AMA, Am. Soc. Anesthesiologists, Tex. Med. Assn., Dallas County Med. Soc., Tex. Soc. Anesthesiologists, Dallas County Anesthesiology Soc., Dallas County Hist. Soc., Dallas County Pioneer Assn., Marauder Men of Metroplex, B-26 Marauder Hist. Soc. Republican. Avocations: genealogy, 17th bomb group history, farming, hunting, fishing.

BAIRD, ZOË, foundation president, lawyer; b. Bklyn., June 20, 1952; d. Ralph Louis and Naomi (Allen) B.; m. Paul Gewirtz, June 8, 1986; 2 children. AB, U. Calif., Berkeley, 1974, JD, 1977. Bar: Washington, 1979, Calif. 1977, Conn. 1989. Law clk. Hon. Albert Wollenberg, San Francisco, 1977-78; atty., advisor Office Legal Counsel U.S. Dept. Justice, Washington, 1979-80; assoc. counsel to Pres., The White House, Washington, 1980-81; assoc., then ptnr. O'Melveny & Myers, Washington, 1981-86; counsellor, staff exec. GE, Fairfield, Conn., 1986-90; v.p., gen. counsel Aetna Life & Casualty, Hartford, 1990-93, sr. v.p., gen. counsel, 1993-96; pres. Markle Found., N.Y.C., 1998—. Bd. dirs. Chubb Corp. Bd. dirs. James A. Baker III Inst. for Pub. Policy, Lawyers for Children Am., Brookings Inst., Save the Children. Mem. Am. Law Inst., Coun. on Fgn. Rels. Office: Markle Found 10 Rockefeller Plaza 16th Fl New York NY 10020-1903 E-mail: info@markle.org.

BAIRSTOW, FRANCES KANEVSKY, arbitrator, mediator, educator; b. Racine, Wis., Feb. 19, 1920; d. William and Minnie (DuBow) Kanevsky; m. Irving P. Kaufman, Nov. 14, 1942 (div. 1949); m. David Steele Bairstow, Dec. 17, 1954; children: Dale Owen, David Anthony. Student, U. Wis., 1937-42; BS, U. Louisville, 1949; student, Oxford U., England, 1953-54; postgrad., McGill U., Montreal, Que., Can., 1958-59. Rsch. economist U.S. Senate Labor-Mgmt. Subcom., Washington, 1950-51; labor edn. specialist U. P.R., San Juan, 1951-52; chief wage data unit WSB, Washington, 1952-53; labor rsch. economist Can. Pacific Ry. Co., Montreal, Canada, 1956-58; asst. dir. indsl. rels. ctr. McGill U., 1960-66, assoc. dir., 1966-71, dir., 1971-85, lectr., indsl. rels. dept. econs., 1960-72, from asst. prof. to assoc. prof. faculty mgmt., 1972—83, prof., 1983-85; lectr. Stetson Law Sch., Fla.; spl. master Fla. Pub. Employees Rels. Commn., 1985-97. Cons. Nat. Film Bd. Can., 1965—69; arbitrator Que. Consultative Coun. Panel Arbitrators, 1968—83, Ministry Labour and Manpower, 1971—83, United Air Lines and Assn. Flight Attendants, 1990—95, Am. Airlines and Transport Workers Union, 1997—98, State U. Sys. Fla., 1990—2003, FDA, 1996—98, Social Security Adminstrn., 1996—2003, Am. Airlines, 1997—, Tampa Gen. Hosp., 1996—, Cargo Internat. Airlines, 2001, Govt. of Fla. and Fla. State Police, 2002—, Bell South and Comm. Workers Am., 2003—, USAF at Warner Robins and AFGE, 2003—; mediator Can. Pub. Svc. Staff Rels. Bd., 1973—85, So. Bell Tel., 1985—, AT&T and Comm. Workers Am., 1986—; cons. on collective bargaining arbitration OECD, Paris, 1979. Contbg. columnist: Montreal Star, 1971—85. Chmn. Nat. Inquiry Commn. Wider-Based Collective Bargaining, 1978; dep. commr. essential svcs. Province of Que., 1976—81. Fulbright fellow, 1953—54. Mem.: Ctrl. Fla. Indsl. Rels. Rsch. Assn. (pres. 1999), Nat. Acad. Arbitrators (bd. govs. 1977—80, program chmn. 1982—83, v.p. 1986—88, nat. coord. 1987—90), Indsl. Rels. Rsch. Assn. Am. (mem. exec. bd. 1965—68, chmn. nominating com. 1977), Can. Indsl. Rels. Rsch. Inst. (mem. exec. bd. 1965—68). Home and Office: 1430 Gulf Blvd Apt 507 Clearwater FL 33767-2856

BAIRSTOW, RICHARD RAYMOND, retired lawyer; b. Waukegan, Ill., Sept. 26, 1917; s. Fred Raymond and Mildred (Wright) B.; m. Mary Kelley, Aug. 8, 1942 (dec. June 19, 1979); children: Kathleen Bairstow Young, Suzanne Bairstow Hicks, Mary Bairstow Neely; m. Agnes Macaitis Caldwell, July 22, 1980 (dec. July 22, 1995). AB, U. Ill., 1939, JD, 1947; postgrad., George Washington U., 1939-41. Bar: Ill. 1947, U.S. Dist. Ct. (no. dist.) Ill. 1964, U.S. Ct. Mil. Appeals 1963, U.S. SUpreme Ct. 1963. Assoc. Hall, Meyer & Carey, Waukegan, 1947-49; asst. state's atty. Lake County, Waukegan, 1949-53; ptnr. McClory & Bairstow, Waukegan, 1953-60, McClory, Bairstow, Lonchar & Nordigan, Waukegan, 1960-66; prin. Richard R. Bairstow & Assocs., Waukegan, 1966-98; ret., 1998. Dist. atty. Fox Lake Fire Protection Dist., Ingleside, Ill., 1948-98; adminstrv. law judge Ill. Dept. Revenue, Chgo., 1953-87. Bd. dirs. ARC, Lake County, 1947-73; mem., pres. Salvation Army, Waukegan, 1954-66; bd. dirs. Lake County Family YMCA, 1990-91. Col. U.S. Army, 1941-46, ETO, USAR, 1946-71, ret. U.S. Army Command and Gen. Staff Coll., 1965. Mem. ABA, Ill. Lake County Bar Assn., Assn. U.S. Army, Mil. Officers Assn. Am., Am. Legion, Glen Flora Country Club, Waukegan City Club, Elks, Delta Tau Delta, Phi Alpha Delta. Republican. Episcopalian. Home: 2122 Ash St Waukegan IL 60087-5033

BAISDEN, ELEANOR MARGUERITE, retired airline compensation executive, consultant; b. Bklyn., Nov. 7, 1935; d. Vernon McKee and Ethel Mildred (Cockle) Baisden. BA, Hofstra U., 1970. Clk. Trans World Airlines, N.Y.C., 1953-55, sec., 1955-64, compensation analyst, 1964-75, compensation mgr., 1975-85, dir. compensation and orgn. planning, 1985-88, dir. compensation and adminstrn., 1988-97; ret., 1997; owner, mgr. Embassy Estates Rental Properties, 1997—. Bd. dirs., treas. Weatherby Lake Improvement Co., 1997-2001. Mem. Airline Pers. Dirs. Conf. (pers. com. 1984-85), Airline Tariff Pub. Co. (pers. com. 1978-96), Nat. Fgn. Trade Coun. (compensation com. 1980-84), Internat. Pers. Assn. (co. rep. 1980-84), Mensa, Weatherby Lake Yacht Club (Mo.), BIG

Investment Club (treas. 1998-2001), Alpha Sigma Lambda (scholar 1965-66). Republican. Methodist. Avocations: boating, swimming, piano, travel. Home: 7818 NW Scenic Dr Kansas City MO 64152-1643

BAISLEY, ROBERT WILLIAM, music educator, educator; b. New Haven, Apr. 5, 1923; s. Joseph V. and Mary (Bergin) B.; m. Jean Shanley, July 30, 1955; children: Joan Ann, Susan Jean, Elizabeth Veronica. Mus.B., Yale U., 1949; MA, Columbia U., 1950. Tchr. Cherry Lawn Sch., Darien, Conn., 1950-51; dir. Neighborhood Music Sch., New Haven, 1951-56; asst. prof. piano, exec. officer Sch. Music Yale U., New Haven, 1956-65; prof. music Pa. State U., University Park, 1965-87, chmn. dept. music, 1965-79. Concert pianist in various concerts, recitals, radio and TV. Vol. United Fund, New Haven, 1951-65; rep. to Coun. of Social Agys., 1951-60; mem. adv. coun. Salvation Army, 1963-65; bd. dirs. Ctrl. Pa. Festival of Arts (pres. 1969-71). Served with AUS, 1942-45. Recipient cert. of merit Yale U., 1979 Mem. Coll. Music Soc., Yale U. Sch. Music Alumni Assn. (pres. 1979-82, 89-94, exec. com. 1977-97). Home: 454 Park Ln State College PA 16803-3207 Office: Pa State U Music Dept University Park PA 16802

BAITSELL, WILMA WILLIAMSON, artist, educator, lecturer; b. Palmyra, N.Y., July 5, 1918; d. Glen Hiram and Luetta (Newell) Williamson; m. Victor Harry Baitsell, Oct. 29, 1941; children: Corin Victor, Coby Allan, Corrine Luetta. BSE, SUNY, Oswego, 1957, MSE, 1964; postgrad., Iowa State Tchrs. Coll., Syracuse U., Ind. State U., Cooper Union, McGill U., Montreal, Western State U.; HHD, World U., 1982; PhD, U. Cambridge, Eng., 1981. Tchr. rural sch., 1939-41, Phoenix Central Sch., 1957-71, SUNY, Oswego, 1971-77; ret., 1977. Cons. area schs., Ford Found., 1965-68; art cons. N.Y. State Dept. Edn., summers 1968-70. Author: Creativity and Intelligence, 1965, Art for Campers, 1972, Crafts for Children, 1976, Christianity, Creativity and Democracy, 1978, Create or Destroy, Love or Hate, Peace or War, 1983; editor Summer Art mag., 1957-71. Chmn. Republican Twp. Com.; pres. Oswego County Women's Rep. Club; chmn. Sch. Bldg. and Orgn. Com., 1954; mem. ch. adminstrv. bd., 1948—, Ford Found. sci. and math. grantee, 1958-59; recipient 1st prize Mid-States Art Show, 1981, hon. mention for painting, Yamiguchi, Japan, 1981, 1st prize Am. Craftsman's Show, 1973. Mem. N.Y. State Ret. Tchrs. Assn. (life), Internat. Soc. Edn. Through Art, Oswego Art Guild (life), Nat. Ret. Tchrs. Assn., Oswego County and Scriba Hist. Soc. (life), SUNY Oswego Alumni Assn. (life), N.Y. State Grange, AAUW, DAR, Order Eastern Star (life). Methodist. Home and Office: 104 Whittemore Rd Oswego NY 13126-6613

BAITY, JOHN COOLEY, lawyer; b. South Bend, Ind., June 22, 1933; s. Roscoe Flake and Gladys Paula (Kline) B.; m. Patricia Ann Bowen, Nov. 9, 1985; children: Keith F., John C. Jr., Cheryl R., Michael P., Philip J., Mark A. AB, U. Mich., 1955, JD, 1958. Bar: Ill. 1958, N.Y. 1961, Calif. 1977, D.C. 1979. Assoc. Cravath, Swaine & Moore, N.Y.C., 1960-62, Donovan Leisure Newton & Irvine, N.Y.C., 1962-65, ptnr., 1966-83, Hunton & Williams, N.Y.C., 1983-84, Baity & Joseph, Los Angeles, 1984-86, Milbank, Tweed, Hadley & McCloy LLP, N.Y.C., 1986—. Gen. counsel U.S. Golf Assn., Far Hills, NJ, 1980—85. Chmn. fin. com., mem. coun. and exec. com. Union Internationale Contre le Cancer, 1995—; trustee Nat. Hypertension Assn., N.Y.C., 1981—91; bd. dirs. Am. Cancer Soc., Atlanta, 1983—87, 1990—2002, treas., 1994—98, vice chmn., 1998—99, chmn.-elect, 1999—2000, chmn., 2000—01. Mem. N.Y. State Bar. Assn., Calif. Bar Assn., Order of Coif, Phi Beta Kappa, Phi Kappa Phi. Office: Milbank Tweed Hadley & McCloy LLP 1 Chase Manhattan Plz Fl 46 New York NY 10005-1413 E-mail: jbaity@milbank.com.

BAIUL, OKSANA, clothing designer, former figure skater; b. Dnepropetrovsk, Ukraine, Nov. 16, 1977; d. Marina Baiul. Now clothing designer Oksana Baiul Collection. Skating tours include Champions on Ice, 1993, 94, 95, 96, 97, 98, The Great Skate II: Charity Event, 1995, Great Skate III, 1997, Nutcracker on Ice, 1995, CBS Spl.: Too Hot to Skate, 1995, 96, Sergei Grinkov: Celebration of a Life, 1996, CBS Spl.: Wizard of Oz on Ice, 1996, An Evening with Champions: Charity Benefit, 1997, 98, Fire on Ice: Charity Event, 1998, 75 Yrs. of Disney Magic, 1998, FTD Champions on Ice, 1999. Recipient 2d Pl. award women's figure skating European Championships, 1993, 1st Pl. award women's figure skating World Figure Skating Championships, 1993, Gold medal women's figure skating Olympic Games, 1994, 2d Pl. Nikon Championship, 1994, 4th Pl. Am. Skating Invitational, 1994, 2d Pl. Ice Wars Overall Team Results, 1995, 98, 2d Pl. Gold Championships, 1995, 2d Pl. Rock'n' Roll Championships, 1996, 1st Pl. Ice Wars Overall Team Results, 1997, 3d Pl. Skate TV Championships, 1998, among others. Office: Oksana Baiul Collection GO Enterprises 177 Main Street 395 Fort Lee NJ 07024

BAIZA, MARY PESINA, development management consultant; b. Mission, Tex., May 28, 1944; d. Patricio and Maria Cuevas (Gutierrez) Pesina; m. Eusebio Molina Baiza, Jan. 8, 1966; children: Julie Suzanne, Elizabeth. Cert. in Nursing, South Plains Coll., 1966; BS, Tex. Tech. U., 1984. Cons. Eastfield Coll., Mesquite, Tex., 1972-76; coord. Heath Sci. Ctr. Tex. Tech U., Lubbock, 1977-83; interior designer J.C. Penney, Lubbock, 1984-85; dir. Guadalupe Econ. Svc. Inc., Lubbock, 1985-87; coord. Cmty. Resource Group, Inc., Lubbock, 1988-99; mem. nat. drinking water adv. coun. EPA, 1999—. Dir. South Plains Assn. Govts., Lubbock, 1992; v.p. Christ the King Sch. Bd., 1981-83; mem. health edn. bd. St. Mary's of the Plains Hosp., 1988. Recipient Marble plaque City of Roaring Spring, 1990, Leadership Tex. Found. for Women award, 1992. Mem. Am. Mktg. Assn. (sec. 1983-90). Democrat. Roman Catholic. Avocations: jogging, choir. Home: RR 2 Box 1563 Post TX 79356-9400 Office: CRG Inc 1901 University Ave Lubbock TX 79410-1555

BAJAD SUNIL, UTTAMRAO, pharmacologist, researcher; b. Shendla, Maharashtra, India, Feb. 20, 1972; s. U.N. and Radha Bajad. M.Pharm., Ph.D., U. Inst. Pharm. Scis., Panjab U., Chandigarh, India, 2002. Sr. project fellow Regional Rsch. Lab (CSIR), Jammu, India, 1996—97, sr. rsch. fellow, 1997—2000, rsch. officer, 2000, rsch. assoc., 2000—02; rsch. assoc. dept. med. sci. Sch. Vet. Medicine U. Wis., Madison, 2002—. Recipient Khatib Gold Medal, Medley pharm. Ltd., 1994, U. Gold Medal, Amaravati U., G.P.Nair Award, Indian Drug Manufacturers Assn., Indian Pharm. Assn. Medal, Indian Pharm. Assn., Maharashtra Dr.; fellow Sr. Rsch. Fellowship, Coun. of Sci. and Indsl. Rsch., India, Rsch. Associateship; scholar Jr. Rsch. Fellowship, U. Grants commn., India. Mem.: Internat. Soc. Study of Xenobiotics. Achievements include 6 international research papers and one patent. Home: 209 Eagle Heights Apt # F Madison WI 53705 Personal E-mail: sbajad@yahoo.com. E-mail: bajads@svm.vetmed.wisc.edu.

BAJART, ANN M. ophthalmologist; b. N.Y.C., June 25, 1946; BA magna cum laude, Vassar Coll., 1968; MD, Harvard U., 1972. Resident Mass. Eye and Ear Infirmary, Boston, 1974-77; fellow pediatric ophthalmology Children's Hosp. Med. Ctr., Boston, 1977; pvt. practice Boston, 1978—; instr. ophthalmology Harvard Med. Sch., Boston, 1983—; asst. prof. ophthalmology Tufts U. Sch. Medicine, Boston, 1991—. Examiner Am. Bd. Ophthalmology; mem. admissions com. Harvard Med. Sch., 1988—. Fellow ACS; mem. Am. Acad. Ophthalmology, New Eng. Ophthalmol. Soc. Avocations: skiing, swimming, ballroom dancing. Office: Ophthalmic Cons Boston 50 Staniford St Ste 600 Boston MA 02114-2587 E-mail: ambajart@eyeboston.com.

BAJCSY, RUZENA KUCEROVA, computer science educator; b. Bratislava, Czechoslovakia, May 28, 1933; came to U.S., 1968; d. Felix and Marguita (Weisz) Kucerova; m. Sherman Frankel. PhD in Elec. Engrin., Slovak Tech. U., Bratislava, 1967; PhD in Computer Sci., Stanford U., 1972. Asst. prof. elect. engrin. Slovak Tech. U., 1967-68; rsch. scientist artificial intelligence lab. Stanford (Calif.) U., 1968-72; prof. computer science U. Pa., Phila., 1972—, chair computer and info. sci. dept., 1985-90, dir. Grasp Lab., 1985—; dir. Nat. Sci. Found., asst. dir. comp. sci. Washington, 1998—. Vis. scientist INRIA, France, 1979; vis. prof. U. Copenhagen, Denmark, 1984, 1988, U. Pisa, Italy, 1988; Forsythe lectr. Stanford U., 1989; cons. in field. Editor periodicals including Computer Vision. Fellow IEEE, Assn. Computing Machinery; mem. NAE, Inst. Medicine NAS.

BAJEK, FRANK MICHAEL, retired army officer, financial consultant; b. Chgo., July 4, 1950; s. Edward Joseph and Anna J. (Banik) B.; m. Renee Ann Kaspar, Aug. 1, 1981; children: David, Amanda, Erica. BBA, Loyola U., Chgo., 1972; MBA, Keller Grad. Sch. Mgmt., 1981. CPA, Ill.; cert. govt. fin. mgr., Assn. Govt. Accts. Asst. mgr. svc. auditing Aldens, Inc., Chgo., 1976-78, indsl. engr., 1978-79, internal auditor, 1979-80; field auditor Stewart-Warner Corp., Chgo., 1980-81; commd. 2d lt. USAR, 1972, advanced through grades to lt. col., 1992, ret., 1996; tax, fin. cons. Ill., 1989—; contr. Overland Bond and Investment Corp., 2000—. Adj. instr. acctg. Nat.-Louis U., 1994, Northwestern Bus. Coll., 1997-99, 2001—, Robert Morris Coll., 1998-99. Mem. AICPA, Am. Soc. Mil. Comptrollers, Ill. CPA Soc., Assn. Govt. Accts., Assn. Profls. in Bus. Mgmt. (cert. bus. mgr.). Roman Catholic. Office: 4701 W Fullerton Ave Chicago IL 60639-1817 E-mail: fmbajek@aol.com.

BAJOR, JAMES HENRY, musician, jazz pianist; b. Detroit, May 7, 1953; s. Henry Stanley and Irene (Hetmanski) B. Student, Wayne State U., 1976. Rec. artist Sugo Music, Half Moon Bay, Calif. Produced albums of own piano compositions: Awakening, 1987 (nominated for New Age solo acoustic Grammy award 1987), Gentle Images, 1988; appears regularly on radio and TV programs. Mem. ASCAP, NARAS. Office: PMB 114 34841 Mound Rd Sterling Heights MI 48310 E-mail: jim.bajor@comcast.net.

BAJSCY, RUZENA, computer engineer; MSEE, Slovak Tech. U., 1957, PhD, 1967; PhD in Artificial Intelligence, Stanford U., 1972. Asst. prof. dept. computer and info. sci. U. Pa., 1972—77, assoc. prof., 1977—84, prof., 1984—, chmn. dept. computer and info. sci., 1985—90, head GRASP Lab.; asst. dir. Directorate for Computer and Info. Sci. and Engring. NSF. Mem. rev. bd. computer sci. dept. Stanford U., 1997. Contbr. articles to profl. publs. Fellow: AAAI, IEEE; mem.: NAE, Computer Rsch. Assn. Women, Nat. Inst. Medicine. Office: U Pa Dept Computer Info Sci 200 S 33d St Philadelphia PA 19104-6389

BAJTAI, ATTILA, pathologist; b. Temesvar, Romania, July 12, 1933; came to Hungary, 1940; s. John and Louise (Csehalik) B.; m. Eva Toóth, Feb. 15, 1958; 1 child, Zoltán. MD, Med. Sch. Budapest, 1958. Asst. physician Town Coun. Hosp., Budapest, 1958-60; cons. Med. Sch. Budapest, 1960-68; cons., lectr., asst. prof. Postgrad. Med. Sch., Budapest, 1968-89; head dept. pathology Town Coun. Hosp., Budapest, 1989-2000, cons., 2000—. Profl. inspector pathology Capital of Budapest, 1992—. Contbr. articles to profl. jours., chpts. to books. Recipient Hungarian Med. medals (4), Batthyány-Strattmann award, 2000. Mem.: Internat. Acad. Pathology, Hungarian Soc. Gastroenterology, Hungarian Soc. Pathologists (sec.-gen. 1990—95). Avocations: music, records, philately, travel. Office: Uzsoki Mcpl Hosp Uzsoki u 29 H-1145 Budapest Hungary

BAJURA, RICHARD ALBERT, university administrator, engineering educator; b. Duquesne, Pa., Feb. 2, 1941; BSME, Notre Dame, 1962, MSME, 1964, PhD, 1967. Energy rsch. dir. W.Va. U., Morgantown, 1984-90; rsch. engr. Babcok & Wolcox R&D Ctr., Alliance, Ohio, 1967-68; postdoctoral rschr. Johns Hopkins U., Balt., 1968-69; prof. mech. engring. W.Va. U., Morgantown, 1969—, assoc. provost, 1990-94; dir. Nat. Rsch. Ctr. for Coal and Energy, 1994—. Editor: Polyphase Flow Transport Technology, 1980. Mem. ASME (v.p. basic engring. 1998-2001), Am. Soc. Am. Engring., Washington Coal Club (pres. 1999). Office: WVa U Nat Rsch Ctr for Coal & Energy PO Box 6064 Morgantown WV 26506-6064

BAJWA, SHAZIA, sociologist; b. Karachi, Sindh, Pakistan, Aug. 2, 1974; arrived in U.S., 1987; d. Manzur Ahmed and Shamsa Bajwa; m. Babur Ahmed, Aug. 3, 1997. cert. in women studies, BA in Sociology cum laude, postgrad., Fla. Atlantic U., 2000—. Spkr. in field. Mem.: NOW, Am. Sociol. Assn., Alpha Kappa Delta, Golden Key. Home: 888 E 96th St Apt 2-I Brooklyn NY 11236

BAJZER, ŽELJKO, scientist, educator; b. Zagreb, Croatia, Jan. 9, 1947; came to U.S., 1986; s. Marko and Marija Concetta (Spalatin) B.; m. Stefanija Kastelan, Jan. 2, 1955; children: Luka, Matej, Lucija, Marko David. BSc in Theoretical Physics, U. Zagreb, Croatia, 1970, MSc in Physics, 1974, PhD in Physics, 1980. Asst. scientist Rugjer Bošković Inst., Zagreb, Croatia, 1970-80, rsch. asst. prof., 1980-86, rsch. assoc. prof., 1986-95; sr. rsch. fellow Mayo Clinic and Found., Rochester, Minn., 1986-89, rsch. assoc., 1989-91, assoc. cons., 1991-92, sr. assoc. cons., 1992-97; cons., 1997—; assoc. prof. Mayo Med. Sch., Rochester, Minn., 1997—. Cons. physicist Dr. M. Stojanovic Clin. Hosp., Zagreb, 1977-80, 83-86. Editor: Procs. Internat. Conf. Applications of Physics to Medicine and Biology, 1982, 83; contbr. articles to profl. jours. Mem. Soc. for Mathematical Biology, Biophys. Soc., Internat. Fedn. of Nonlinear Analysts. Roman Catholic. Achievements include devel. of theory for quasifree scattering for Coulomb-like potentials; math. model of positive feedback in tumor growth; math. methods of analysis of fluorescence in proteins. Home: 1735 8th St SW Rochester MN 55902-0914 Office: Mayo Clinic and Found 200 1st St SW Rochester MN 55905-0002 E-mail: bajzer@mayo.edu.

BAKAL, CARL, writer, public affairs consultant, photojournalist; b. N.Y.C., Jan. 11, 1918; s. William and Esther (Tutelman) B.; m. Shirley Sesser, 1956; children: Stephanie, Emilie, Amy, Wendy. BS, CCNY, 1939; postgrad., Columbia, 1949. Advt. mgr. Fotoshop, N.Y.C., 1939-41; editor Fotoshop Almanac, 1939-41; assoc. editor, contbg. editor U.S. Camera, 1939-43; sales promotion mgr. Universal Camera Corp., 1941-43; editorial chief information control div. Mil. Govt., Germany, 1947-48; writer N.Y. Mirror, 1948-50; assoc. editor Coronet mag., N.Y.C., 1950-55; free-lance writer, photo-journalist, 1955—; editor Real, See mags., 1957-58; pub. affairs cons. U.S. Dept. Commerce, 1961-62; sr. assoc. Howard Chase Assos., N.Y.C., 1962-65; dir. mag. dept. Carl Byoir & Assocs., 1966-68; account supr. Anna M. Rosenberg Assocs., 1968-84; sr. v.p. Jack Raymond & Co., Inc., N.Y.C., 1984-86; pres. Carl Bakal Assocs., N.Y.C., 1986—. Guest lectr. photo-journalism U. Wis., 1953 Author: Filter Manual, 1953, How to Shoot for Glamour, 1955, The Right to Bear Arms, 1966, No Right to Bear Arms, 1968, Charity U.S.A, 1979; contbr. articles and photographs to publs. including McCall's, Redbook, Life, Reader's Digest, Harper's, Town & Country, Esquire, Good Housekeeping; contbr. to Ency. Photography, 1942, Treasury of Tips for Writers, 1965, Tools of the Writer's Trade, 1990; photojournalism columnist Writers Digest.; travel editor Sylvia Porter's Personal Fin. mag., 1984-86. Served to 1st lt. AUS, 1942-46, 51-52. Recipient 1st prize Popular Photography $25,000 picture contest, 1956. Mem. Author's Guild, Violoncello Soc., P.E.N., Am. Soc. Journalists and Authors (v.p. 1968), Dutch Treat Club, Nat. Coun. for Responsible Firearms Policy (founder, v.p.). Home and Office: 225 W 86th St New York NY 10024-3330

BAKALAR, JOHN STEPHEN, printing and publishing company executive; b. Lynn, Mass., Feb. 10, 1948; s. Leo and Ann Beatrice (Lepie) B.; m. Christine Lake Heilman, Sept. 24, 1972; children— Brooke Heilman, Jessica Heilman, Luke Heilman. BA, U. Pa., 1970; MBA, Stanford U., 1973. Investment mgr. First Chgo. Corp., Chgo., 1973-76; treas. Rand McNally & Co., Skokie, Ill., 1976-78, v.p. fin., treas., 1978-86, exec. v.p., 1986-93, pres., chief oper. officer, 1993-98. Dir. Racing Champions. Adv. bd., dir. Broader Urban Involvement and Leadership Devel., Chgo., 1976—; fellow Leadership Greater Chgo., 1987-88; trustee North Shore Country Day Sch. Found., Winnetka, Ill., 1997—. Mem. Econ. Club Chgo., Northmoor Country Club (Highland Park, Ill.), Country Club of the Rockies (Edwards, Colo.), Eagle Springs Country Club (Wolcott, Colo.). Home: 1760 Dale Ave Highland Park IL 60035-3303

BAKALOV, BOJKO, mathematician; b. Karlovo, Bulgaria, May 9, 1973; arrived in U.S.A., 1996; s. Nencho Bakalov and Maria Bakalova; m. Vesselina Rousseva. PhD, MIT, 2000. Asst. prof. NC State U., Raleigh, NC, 2003—. Contbr. articles to profl. jours. (Charles W. and Jennifer C. Johnson prize, 2000); author: (monograph) Lectures on Tensor Categories and Modular Functors. Recipient Miller Rsch. fellowship, Miller Inst. for Basic Rsch. in Sci., 2000—03. Mem.: Am. Math. Soc. Office: NC State Univ Dept Math Raleigh NC 27695 E-mail: bojko_bakalov@ncsu.edu.

BAKALOV, BOJKO NENTCHEV, mathematician; b. Karlovo, Bulgaria, 1973; s. Nencho B. Bakalov and Maria P. Bakalova. PhD, MIT, 2000. Miller rsch. fellow, dept. math. U. Calif., Berkeley, 2000. Author: Lectures on Tensor Categories and Modular Functors, 2001; contbr. articles to profl. jours. (Charles W. and Jennifer C. Johnson prize, 2000). Mem.: Am. Math. Soc. Office: U Calif Dept Math Berkeley CA 94720 Business E-Mail: bakalov@math.berkeley.edu.

BAKALY, CHARLES GEORGE, JR., lawyer, mediator; b. Long Beach, Calif., Nov. 15, 1927; s. Charles G. Sr. and Doris (Carpenter) B.; m. Patricia Murphey, Oct. 25, 1952; children: Charles G. III, John W., Thomas B. AB, Stanford U., 1949; JD, U. S.C., 1952. Assoc. O'Melveny & Myers, L.A., 1956-63, ptnr., 1963-94; mem. JAMS, L.A., 2000—. Mem. Commn. on Calif. State Govt. Orgn. and Economy, 1991-94, President's Nat. Commn. on Employment Policy, 1992-94; mem. 9th Cir. Jud. Conf. Lawyer Del. Ch., 1984-87, mem. indigent def. panel, 1992-94; chmn. Calif. Dispute Resolution Adv. Coun., 1987-88; pres. Dispute Resolution Svcs. Bd. Dirs., Calif. Dispute Resolution Coun. Author: (with Joel M. Grossman) Modern Law of Employment Relationships, 1983, 2d edit. 1989; contbr. chpts. to books. Capt. JAG, U.S. Army, 1952-56. Fellow Am. Coll. Trial Lawyers, Coll. Labor and Employment Lawyers, Internat. Acad. Mediators; mem. ABA (chmn. sect. labor and employment law 1981-82, sect. dispute resolution), L.A. County Bar Assn. (trustee, chmn. labor law sect. 1976-77, dispute resolution sect.), Lincoln Club (pres. 1989-91), Chancery Club, Valley Hunt Club (Pasadena, Calif.), Calif. Club (L.A.), Bohemian Club (San Francisco). Office: JAMS 350 S Figueroa St Ste 990 Los Angeles CA 90071-1102

BAKANOWSKY, LOUIS JOSEPH, visual arts educator, architect, artist; b. Conn., Oct. 8, 1930; s. Louis Joseph Bakanowsky and Alice (Sullivan) Derda; m. Marie A. Golas, Jan. 27, 1951; 1 child, Louis J., III. BFA, Syracuse U., 1957; MArch, Harvard U., 1961. Registered architect. Asst. prof. architecture Cornell U., Ithaca, N.Y., 1961; assoc. prof. Harvard U., Cambridge, Mass., 1963-71, prof. architecture, 1972—, prof. visual arts., 1975-97, Osgood Hooker prof. visual studies emeritus, 1997—, chmn. dept. visual and environ. studies, 1976-86. Dir. Carpenter Ctr. for Visual Arts, 1984-90; prin. Cambridge Seven. Assocs., 1962—. Prin. works include U.S. Pavillion for Expo '67, Montreal, Can., Henry DuPont Libr., Pomfret Sch., Conn., Columbia Sch., Rochester, N.Y., Rostropovich residence; (sculpture) Carl Siembab Gallery, Boston, 1958; represented in various pub. an pvt. collection. With USAF, 1951-53. Grantee Nat. Endowment Arts, 1979, 83, Graham Found. for Advanced Studies in Fine Arts, 1983. Fellow AIA (design awards 1967, 70). Office: Harvard U Carpenter Ctr for Visual Arts 24 Quincy St Cambridge MA 02138-3804

BAKEMAN, CAROL ANN, travel manager, singer; b. San Francisco; d. Lars Hartvig and Gwendolyne Beatrice (Zimmer) Bergh; m. Delbert Clifton Bakeman; children: Laurie Ann, Deborah Ann. Student, UCLA, 1954-62. Singer Roger Wagner Chorale, L.A. Master Chorale, 1964-86, The Wagner Ensemble, 1991—; libr. Hughes Aircraft Co., Culver City, Calif.; head econs. libr. Planning Rsch. Corp., L.A., 1961-63; corp. libr. Econ. Cons., Inc., L.A., 1963-68; head econs. libr. Daniel, Mann, Johnson & Mendenhall, archs. and engrs., L.A., 1969-71, corp. libr., 1971-77, mgr. info. svcs., 1978-81, mgr. info. and office svcs., 1981-83, mgr. adminstrv. svcs., 1983-96, sr. assoc., 1996-98, assoc. v.p., 1998—; travel mgr. AECOM Tech. Corp., 1996—. Assoc. v.p. Corp. Consol. Svcs., Inc., (divsn. AECOM), 1997—; pres., Creative Libr. Sys., L.A., 1974-83; libr. cons. ArchiSystems (divsn. SUMMA Corp.), L.A., 1972-81, Property Rehab. Corp., Bell Gardens, Calif., 1974-75, VTN Corp., Irvine, Calif., 1974, William Pereira & Assos., 1975; mem. office sys. and bus. edn. adv. bd. Calif. State U. Northridge, 1992. Mem. Assistance League, So. Calif., 1956-86, nat. auxilaries com., 1968-72, 75-78, nat. by-laws com., 1970-75, assoc. bd. dirs., 1966-76. Mem. AFTRA, SAG, Am. Guild Musical Artists, Adminstrv. Mgmt. Soc. (v.p. L.A. chpt. 1984-86, pres. 1986-88, internat. conf. chmn. 1988-89, internat. bd. dirs. 1988-90, internat. v.p. mgmt. edn. 1990-92), L.A. Master Chorale Assn. (bd. dirs. 1978-83), Wagner Ensemble (bd. dirs.), L.A. Bus. Travel Assn. (bd. dirs. 1995, sec. 1997, v.p. 1998, pres. 1999, past pres. 2000, bd advisor 2001-2002), Nat. Bus. Travel Assn. (nat. conv. seminar com. 1994-95, conv. vol. chmn. 1994, 2000, nat. conv. panelist 2001, 03, profl. svc. award 2001). Office: AECOM Travel Ctr Level C Ste 22 515 S Flower St Los Angeles CA 90071-2201 Business E-Mail: carolann.bakeman@ccsi.com.

BAKER, ALDEN, artist; b. Manhattan, N.Y., Jan. 10, 1928; d. Samuel Burtis Baker and Grace Whalley Higgins; m. Robert Oppenheim, Aug. 21, 1963 (dec. June 1986); 1 child, Jessica Oppenheim. Cert., Berkeley Secretarial Sch., 1948; student, Cape Sch. Art, summer 1957-63, Art Students League, N.Y.C., 1965-66. Reporter, ch. and sch. editor Montclair (N.J.) Times, 1951-53; publicity dir. Newark Mus., 1953-56; editor, pub. rels. dir. Assn. Jr. Leagues Am., N.Y.C., 1956-64. Pastel demonstrator, Xian, China, 1997. Exhbns. include Manhattan's Lincoln Ctr., LEver House, Salmagundi Club, Pen and Brush Club, Nat. Arts Club, Allied Artists Am., Catherine Lorillard Wolfe Art Club, Pastel Soc. Am., Hudson Valley Art Assn., The Queens, Bergen and Hammond Mus., Copley Gallery, Boston; curator: The Best of Pastel II, 1999; featured in Am. Artist Mag., 1995. Mem. Pastel Soc. Am. (bd. dirs. 1994-2000, signature, critiques chmn., bd. dirs., Mr. and Mrs. Andrew Giffuni award 1999), Pen and Brush, Inc. (chmn. pastel sect. 1997-2000, solo exhbn. award), Hudson Valley Art Assn., Am. Artist Profl. League (various awards), Art Ctr. N.J. (pres., newsletter editor, exhbn. chair), Salmagundi Club (Dianne Bernhard Gold medal 2000) Unitarian Universalist. Home: 100 Stone Hill Rd Apt P12 Springfield NJ 07081-2154

BAKER, ALTHEA ROSS, court hearing officer, lawyer, mediator, arbitrator, educator; b. San Francisco, Dec. 24, 1949; d. Vernon and Ethel Ross; m. Bruce Mitchell. BA in Psychology, Pepperdine U., 1970, MA in Clin. Psychology, 1974; JD, Loyola U., L.A., 1984. Bar: Calif. 1984, U.S. Dist. Ct. (cen. dist.) Calif. 1985, U.S. Ct. Appeals (9th cir.) 1985; lic. marriage, family and child counselor, Calif. Prof., chmn. dept. L.A. Mission Coll., 1975-89; pvt. practice law L.A., 1985—93. Marriage therapist Woodland Hills, Calif., 1976-84; mediator Dispute Resolution Svcs., Santa Monica, 1987-91; referee L.A. Superior Ct., 1993; staff atty. Harriet Buhai Family Law Ctr., L.A., 1988. Trustee L.A. C.Cs., 1989-2001. Mem. Los Angeles County Bar Assn., Women Lawyers L.A., Black Women Lawyers L.A., San Fernando Valley Marriage and Family Therapists (v.p. 1978), Calif. Fedn. Tchrs. Coll. Guild (exec. bd. local 1521, 1982-89, chief negotiator collective bargaining 1988-89). Democrat. Episcopalian. Office: 1903 Parkdale Pl La Canada CA 91011 Fax: 213 255-6154.

BAKER, ALTON FLETCHER, III, newspaper editor, publishing executive; b. Eugene, Oreg., May 2, 1950; s. Alton Fletcher Jr. and Genevieve B.; m. Wendy, Jan. 27, 1979; children: Benjamin A., Lindsay A. BA in Comms., Washington State U., 1972. Reporter Associated Press, 1972-79; asst. city editor The Register-Guard, Eugene, 1979-80, city editor, 1980-82, mng. editor, 1982-86, editor, 1986-87, editor, publisher, 1987—; pres. Guard Publishing Co., Eugene, 1987—. Pres. Cmty Newspapers, Inc., Portland. Pres. YMCA, Eugene, 1989, United Way of Lane County, Eugene, 1985-01, Eugene Festival Musical Theatre, 1990-94. Mem.: Oreg. Newspaper Pubs. Assn. (pres. 1999), Eugene Country Club (pres. 1999). Avocation: golf. Office: Guard Publishing Co 3500 Chad Dr Eugene OR 97408-7348

BAKER, ANITA DIANE, lawyer; b. Atlanta, Sept. 4, 1955; d. Byron Garnett and Anita (Swanson) B.; m. Thomas Johnstone Robison III, Sept. 26, 1995. BA summa cum laude, Oglethorpe U., 1977; JD with distinction, Emory U., 1980. Bar: Ga. 1980. Assoc. Hansell & Post, Atlanta, 1980-88, Kitchens, Kelley, Gaynes, Huprich & Shmerling, 1989-90; asst. gen. counsel NationsBank Corp., 1991-97; v.p., gen. counsel Adaris Corp., 1997-99; pvt. practice Atlanta, 1999—. Trustee Oglethorpe Univ. Mem.: Oglethorpe U., Stormy Petrel Bar Assn. (pres.), Ga. Assn. Women Lawyers, Atlanta Bar Assn., Ga. Bar Assn., Oglethorpe U. Nat. Alumni Assn. (pres.), Atlanta Hist. Soc., Pace Acad. Alumni Assn., Ga. Alliance of Private Clubs, Concourse Athletic Club, Omicron Delta Kappa, Alpha Chi, Phi Alpha Theta, Phi Alpha Delta, Order of Coif. Office: 1144 Canton St Ste 100A Roswell GA 30075 E-mail: dianebaker@adblaw.com.

BAKER, ARNOLD BARRY, economist; b. N.Y.C., Feb. 3, 1946; s. Max Michael and Sue (Feingold) B.; m. Wendy Glaus, 1990. BA in History, Va. Poly. Inst., 1968, MA in Econs., 1970, PhD, 1972. Spl. asst. to undersec. for monetary affairs U.S. Dept. Treasury, Washington, 1977-79, sr. cons. Atlantic Richfield Co., L.A., 1979-82; mgr. strategic planning Arco Oil & Gas Co., Dallas, 1983—86, dir. energy market analysis L.A., 1986-89, dir. pub. issues, 1989-94, dir. polit. econ. analysis, 1994-95; mgr. energy and critical infrastructure policy & planning Sandia Nat. Labs., Albuquerque, 1996—2001, chief economist, 2001—. Contbr. articles to profl. jours., chpts. to books. Mem. Nat. Assn. Bus. Econs., U.S. Assn. for Energy Econs. (pres. 2002), Internat. Assn. Energy Econs. Avocations: tennis, jogging. Office: Sandia Nat Labs PO Box 5800 Albuquerque NM 87185-0100

BAKER, AUGUSTUS L., JR., surgeon, retired; b. Dover, N.J., May 1, 1915; s. Augustus L. and Ellene (Dodge) B.; m. Eleanor Jean Black, Apr. 24, 1948; children: Karen, Susan, Augustus III, Adrienne, Eric. AB, Princeton U., 1936; MD, NYU, 1940. Diplomate Am. Bd. Surgery. Intern Mountainside Hosp.,

Montclair, N.J., 1940-41; resident in surgery French Hosp., N.Y.c., 1951-54; fellow in surgery Lahey Clinic, Boston, 1954-55; now ret., 1988. Alderman Town of Dover, 1956-60. With U.S. Army, 1941-47. Fellow ACS, Internat. Coll. Surgeons; mem. Med. Soc. N.J. (pres. 1980-81), Rotary Internat. (gov. dist. 4740 1987-88). Republican. Presyterian. E-mail: gusnd2a@aol.com.

BAKER, BERNARD ROBERT, II, lawyer; b. Toledo, Nov. 19, 1915; s. Joseph Lee and Grace (Baker) O'Neil; m. Elinor Shutts, Oct. 16, 1943; children: Bernard Robert III, Lynn Agnes. *Maternal grandfather, Bernard R. Baker, was a prominent merchant in the Toledo and Cleveland areas. He established specialty stores in their respective areas in 1893 and 1915. He treated his grandson, Bernard R. Baker II, as his son and provided him with guidance and educational opportunities for which he is eternally grateful.* AB, Kenyon Coll., 1936; JD, Harvard U., 1941. Bar: Ohio 1946. Practice in, Toledo, 1947—95; ptnr. Brown, Baker, Schlageter & Craig and predecessor firm, 1950-91, ret. Pres. B.R. Baker Co., 1946-60; dir. emeritus First Nat. Bank Toledo, First Ohio Bankshares (now Fifth Third Bank); ret. sec., dir. Toledo Blade Co., Blade Comm., Inc. *Bernard Baker's being elected a director of The First National Bank, of Toledo in 1948 and subsequently appointed to the Executive Committee and Chairman of the Trust Committie, resulted in a rewarding and interesting 37 years of service. During that period the bank was the first one in the Midwest to make installment auto loans and among the first to have an international department.* Regional vice chmn. U.S. Com. for UN, 1955-62; past pres. St. Vincent Hosp. Found., Toledo United Appeal, Toledo C. of C.; past trustee Med. Coll. Ohio at Toledo, Salvation Army, Toledo, Goodwill Industries, Toledo; trustee emeritus Rutherford B. Hayes Presdl. Ctr., Fremont, Ohio; past trustee Boys Clubs Toledo; past pres., trustee Med. Coll. Ohio Found., Toledo. Lt. comdr. USNR, 1940-45. Recipient Boys Club Bronze Keystone award, 1965, Disting. Citizen award Med. Coll. Ohio, 1986; named Toledo Outstanding Man of Year, 1948. Mem. ABA, English Speaking Union, Young Pres. Orgn., Harvard Club (N.Y.C.), Belmont Country Club, Carranor Hunt and Polo Club (Toledo), Bath and Tennis Club, Beach Club, Chevaliers du Tastevin, Old Guard Soc. (Palm Beach). Roman Catholic. Home: Apt 905 311 S Flagler Dr West Palm Beach FL 33401-5645

BAKER, BETTY LOUISE, retired secondary education educator; b. Chgo., Oct. 17, 1937; d. Russell James and Lucille Juanita (Timmons) B. BE, Chgo. State U., 1961, MA, 1964; PhD, Northwestern U., 1971. Cert. tchr. secondary and elem. grades 3-8 math., Ill. Tchr. math. Harper H.S., Chgo., 1961-70, Hubbard H.S., Chgo., 1970-94, also chmn. dept.; ret., 1994. Part-time instr. Moraine Valley C.C., 1982-83, 84-86, 94—; reader AP calculus exams. Ednl. Testing Svc. Contbr. articles to profl. jours. Cultural arts chmn. Hubbard Parents-Tchrs.-Students Assn., 1974-76, 1st v.p., program chmn., 1977-79, 82-84, pres. 1979-81; organist Hope Luth Ch., 1964-95, accompanist S.W. Luth. Chorus, 1987—; organist and choir dir. Faith Luth. Ch., Oak Lawn, 1995—. Univ. fellow, 1969-70. Mem. Nat. Coun. Tchrs. Math., Ill. Coun. Tchrs. Math., Chgo. Tchrs. Union, Nat. Coun. Parents and Tchrs. (life), Sch. Sci. and Math. Assn., Am. Guild of Organists, Luth. Collegiate Assn., Walther League Hiking Club, Met. Math. Club Chgo., Kappa Mu Epsilon, Rho Sigma Tau, Mu Alpha Theta (sponsors), Kappa Delta Pi, Pi Lambda Theta, Phi Delta Kappa. Home: 6330 Pine Ridge Dr Apt 1D Tinley Park IL 60477-4928 E-mail: bakermus@aol.com.

BAKER, BRIDGET DOWNEY, newspaper executive; b. Eugene, Oreg., Sept. 14, 1955; d. Edwin Moody and Patricia B.; m. Guy Dominique Wood, June 30, 1977 (div. Oct. 1981); m. Rayburn Keith Kincaid, June 27, 1987; stepchildren: Benjamin, Jacob. BA in English, French and Theatre, Lewis and Clark Coll., 1977; MA in Journalism, U. Oreg., 1985. Circulation dist. supr. The Register-Guard, Eugene, 1978-80, pub. relations coordinator, 1980-83, promotion dir., 1983-86, mktg. dir., 1986-88; corp. pub. rels. dir., 1989—. Bd. dirs. Guard Pub. Co., Eugene, Lane Met. Partnership, Arts Found. We. Oreg., chmn. 1997-99; pres. Baker Family Found., 1998—. Bd. dirs. Wilani Coun. Camp Fire, 1982-88, pres. bd. dirs., 1986-88; bd. dirs. Lane County United Way, 1982-88, community info. com. chairperson, 1982-84; chair planning com., 1987-88; bd. dirs. Eugene Opera, 1988-91, pres. bd. dirs., 1990-91. Recipient 1st pl. advt. award Editor and Pub. Mag., N.Y.C., 1984, also 1st pl. TV promotion, 1st pl. newspaper rsch. award, 1988, Best Mktg. Idea/Campaign award Oreg. Newspaper Pub. Assn., 1984, 85; named Woman of Yr., Lane County Coun. of Orgns., 1994. Mem. Internat. Mktg. Assn. (bd. dirs. Western region 1986-88, internat. bd. dirs. 1995—, 8 1st pl. Best in the West awards 1983-91), Pub. Rels. Soc. Am. (pres. Greater Oreg. chpt. 1995-96, Spotlight award 1986), Eugene C. of C. (bd. dirs. 1989-92), U. Oreg. Alumni Assn. (bd. dirs. 1990-93), Lane C.C. Found. (bd. dirs. 1995-97), Town Club (bd. dirs. 1995-97), Downtown Athletic Club, Eugene Yacht Club, Zonta Internat. (pres. Eugene Club 1994-96, area dir. 1997-98, lt. gov. Dist. 8, 1998-2000, gov. 2000-2002, internat. pub. rels. chair 2002—). Republican. Avocations: sailing, folk dance, outdoor activities, piano. Office: Guard Pub Co PO Box 10188 Eugene OR 97440-2188

BAKER, BRINDA ELIZABETH GARRISON, infectious disease nurse; b. Groveland, Ga., May 9, 1946; d. Archie and Nora Lee (Haynes) Garrison; m. Jerome Baker, Feb. 1970 (div. 1972); children: Katrina Lenyse Adams, Kelbert Lenard Adams. Student, Savannah (Ga.) State Coll., 1964-68; LPN, Savannah Tech. Sch., 1968; ADN, Armstrong State Coll., 1984, BSN, 1990. RN, Ga.; cert. provider BLS, Am. Heart Assn. LPN Candler Gen. Hosp., Savannah, 1968-72, staff nurse Cross Country Traveling Corps, 1990; LPN Ga. Regional Hosp., Savannah, 1972-74, sr. staff nurse, 1989-92; LPN St. Joseph Hosp., Savannah, 1974-84, staff nurse, 1984-90; sr. nurse, clinic supr. Chatham County Health Ctr., Savannah, 1992-95, clinic supr., 1995—. Part-time clin. instr. Armstrong State Coll., Savannah, 1991—. Mem. ANA, Ga. Nurses Assn., Assn. Nurses in AIDS Care. Democrat. Roman Catholic. Avocations: bowling, reading, gardening, music, sports. Home: 1307 E 71st St Savannah GA 31404-5735 Office: Chatham County Health Dept 2 Wheeler St Savannah GA 31405

BAKER, BRUCE EDWARD, orthopedic surgeon, consultant; b. Oswego, N.Y., Mar. 22, 1937; s. Elbert J. and Reatha (Hartranft) B.; m. Patricia Therese Gormel, Aug. 19, 1961; children: Brett, Clayton, Sean, Reatha. BSME, Syracuse U., 1959; MD, SUNY-Syracuse, 1965. Intern State U. Iowa, Iowa City, 1965-66, asst. resident, 1966-67; resident orthopaedics SUNY-Upstate Med. Ctr., Syracuse, 1969-72, NIH orthopaedic rsch. fellow, 1972-73, asst. prof. orthopaedic surgery, 1973-79, assoc. prof., 1979-86, prof., 1986-89. Dir. univ. sports medicine svc. divsn. dept. orthopaedic surgery 1980-89; team physician, dir. sports medicine athletic dept., Syracuse U., 1973-93, orthopaedic cons. Student Health Ctr., 1973-93, staff SUNY Hosp., Syracuse, 1973-89, Syracuse VA Hosp., 1973-89, A.C. Silverman Pub. Health Hosp., 1973-77, Crouse-Irving Meml. Hosp., 1973—; cons. in field. Contbr. numerous articles to profl. jours. Capt. USAF, 1967-69. Recipient AMA Physicians Recognition award, 1978, Bronze medal award Am. Roentgen Ray Soc., 1980, Gold medal award Sound Slide Prodn. Conditioning, 1977; Syracuse U. scholar, 1955; N.Y. State Regents scholar, 1955-59; USPHS grantee, 1973-74; Hendricks Research fund grantee, 1973-75; NIH grantee, 1974-76, 76-77. Fellow ACS, Am. Acad. Orthop. Surgeons; mem. AMA, Med. Soc. State N.Y., Onondaga County Med. Soc., Orthop. Rsch. Soc., Am. Coll. Sports Medicine, N.Y. Soc. Orthop. Surgeons, Royal Soc. Medicine, Internat. Soc. Arthroscopy, Knee Surgery and Orthop. Sports Medicine, Am. Orthop. Soc. Sports Medicine, European Soc. Sports Trauma, Knee Surgery and Arthroscopy, Arthroscopy Assn. N. Am. Office: 600 E Genesee St Ste 117 Syracuse NY 13202-3108

BAKER, BRUCE JAY, lawyer; b. Chgo., June 18, 1954; s. Kenneth and Beverly (Gould) B. Student, U. Leeds, Eng., 1974-75; BS, U. Ill., 1976; JD, Washington U., 1979. Bar: Ill. 1979, U.S. Dist. Ct. (no. dist.) Ill. 1984. Asst. atty. gen. antitrust divsn. State of Ill., Chgo., 1979-83; assoc. Mass, Miller & Josephson Ltd., Chgo., 1983-86; sr. counsel Discover Card Services Inc., Riverwoods, Ill., 1986-89; sr. legis. counsel Dean Witter Fin. Svcs. Group, Riverwoods, 1989-91; gen. counsel Ill. Commr. Banks and Trust Cos., Chgo., 1991-94; ptnr. Schiff Hardin & Waite, Chgo., 1994-99, of counsel, 1999-2001, Barak, Ferrazzano, Kirschbaum, Perlman & Nagelberg, Chgo., 2001—; sr. v.p., gen. counsel Ill. Bankers Assn., 1999—. Gen. editor Advising Illinois Financial Institutions, 2002; contbr. articles to profl. jours. Registered lobbyist Ill. Legislature, Springfield, 1985-91, 94—. Named Ill. State scholar, 1972. Mem. ABA (antitrust com., banking com., chmn. state banking law devels. task force 1998—), Ill. State Bar Assn. (comml. banking and bankruptcy sect.), Chgo. Bar Assn. (fin. insts. com.), Ill. Bankers Assn. (legis. counsel 1985-86, gen. counsel 1994—. Disting. Bank Counsel award 1991, 97). Office: Ill Bankers Assn 111 W Jackson Blvd Ste 910 Chicago IL 60604-3502 also: Barack Ferrazzano Et Al 333 W Wacker Dr Ste 2700 Chicago IL 60606 E-mail: bbaker@ilbanker.com.

BAKER, BRUCE ROY, retired art educator, artist; b. Syracuse, N.Y., July 18, 1937; s. Morse Roy and Gladys Irene (Hilton) B.; m. Helen Louise Butler, Apr. 16, 1965; children: Paul, Suzanne, Diana, Amy. BS in Art Edn., New Paltz Coll., 1959; MS in Art Edn., Syracuse U., 1966. Cert. tchr. N.Y. Tchr. art Catskill (N.Y.) Pub. Schs., 1959-62, Cortland (N.Y.) City Schs., 1964-66, Marcellus (N.Y.) Ctrl. Schs., 1966-92; pvt. practice artist, illustrator Marcellus, 1992—. Tchr. art Mex. (N.Y.) Acad., 1975-76. Works exhibited in group shows Artists of Ctrl. N.Y.-Munson-Williams-Procter Inst., Utica, 1969, N.Y. State Fair, Syracuse, 1973, 74, 75, Cooperstown (N.Y.) Ann., 1974; contbg. painter Leopold F. Landsberger, N.Y.C., 1979-86; contbg. illustrator Firestone Pub. Corp., Miami Lakes, Fla., 1982-2001, Spartacus/Centurian, Reno, 1983—, Quadriga Art, Inc., N.Y.C., 1993—; illustrator (book) Erotic Art of Bruce Baker, 1995; contbr. articles to profl. jours. With U.S. Army, 1962-64. Recipient Hon. Mention (sculpture) N.Y. State Fair, 1975. Avocation: reading. Home: 11 1st St Marcellus NY 13108-1114

BAKER, C. B. retired day care director, organizer, communicator; b. Ft. Wayne, Ind. d. James Edwin Doelling Sr. and Susie Mae Nutter; m. Gerald R. Baker, June, 1962 (div. 1966); 1 child, Erin Lee; m. Jeffrey E. Baker, June, 1967 (div. 1972); 1 child, Shannon Rae. Student, Internat. Bus. Coll., Ft. Wayne, 1961. Expeditor Wayne Fabricating, Ft. Wayne, 1971; county adminstr. Champaign (Ill.) County Bd., 1974-76; sec. WICD-TV, Champaign, 1976-77; dir. ops. 40 Plus of Colo., Inc., Denver, 1988, v.p., 1984-85, CEO, 1985-86; co-owner, CEO St. Anne's Extended Day Program and Day Care Program, Denver, 1986-89; self-employed organizer Denver, 1998—. CEO, editor The Village Voice newsletter, Savoy, Ill., 1974. Dir. Winfield Village Swimming Pool Com., Savoy, 1975; CEO, dir. Mich. Sugar Festival, Sebewaing, 1991. Mem. Am. Bus. Women's Assn., Colo. Women's C. of C. Avocations: reading, horseback riding, weights, walking.

BAKER, CAMERON, lawyer; b. Chgo., Dec. 24, 1937; s. David Cameron and Marion (Fitzpatrick) B.; m. Katharine Julia Solari, Sept. 2, 1961; children: Cameron III, Ann, John. Student, U. Notre Dame, 1954-57; AB, Stanford U., 1958; LLB, U. Calif., Berkeley, 1961. Bar: Calif. 1962, U.S. Dist. Ct. (so. dist.) Calif. 1962, U.S. Dist. Ct. (no. dist.) Calif. 1963, U.S. Ct. Appeals (9th) 1963. With Adams, Duque & Hazeltine, Los Angeles, 1961-62, Pettit & Martin, San Francisco, 1962-95, mng. ptnr., 1972-81, 84-87, exec. com., 1971-82, 84-88; with Farella, Braun & Martel, San Francisco, 1995—. Mayor City of Belvedere, Calif., 1978-79; owner Larkmead Vineyards, Napa Valley, Calif. Mem. ABA (sects. on bus. law and internat. law and practice), Calif. Bar Assn. (sect. bus., real property and internat. law), Bar Assn. San Francisco (bd. dirs. 1966, 72-73), Boalt Hall Alumni Assn. (dir. 1982-84), Bohemian Club, Tiburon Peninsula Club. Home: 38 Alcatraz Ave Belvedere CA 94920-2504 Office: Farella Braun & Martel LLP 235 Montgomery St San Francisco CA 94104-2902 E-mail: cbaker@fbm.com.

BAKER, CARL GWIN, research administrator; b. Louisville, Ky., Nov. 27, 1920; s. Edward Forrest and Naomi (Taylor) B.; m. Lois Eleane Oxsen, Mar. 24, 1949 (div. May 1975); children: Cathryn, Jeannette; m. Catherine Valerie Smith, May 23, 1975. AB in Zoology, U. Louisville, 1942, MD, 1944; MA in Biochemistry, U. Calif., Berkeley, 1949; DSc (hon.), U. Louisville, 1980. Lic. med. practice, Ky., Calif. Rsch. investigator Biochemistry Lab. Nat. Cancer Inst., NIH, Bethesda, Md., 1949-52, 53-55, staff grants and fellowships br., 1952-53, asst. to NIH assoc. dir., 1956-57, asst. dir., acting sci. dir., 1958-61, assoc. dir. program, 1961-67, sci. dir. etiology, 1967-69; dir. Nat. Cancer Inst., Bethesda, 1969-72; dir. program policy staff Health & Human Svcs. Adminstr., Rockville, 1975-76; med. dir. Ludwig Inst. Cancer Rsch., Zurich, Switzerland, 1977-85, ret., 1985; adj. instr. U. Md., College Park, 1989—. Mem. gov. coun. Internat. Agy. for Cancer Rsch., Lyon, France, 1969-72. Assoc. editor Jour. of the Nat. Cancer Inst., 1954-55; mem. editorial adv. bd. Cancer Jour., 1965-73; contbr. articles to jours. Biochemistry, Oncology, Mgmt. Sci. Del. State Bd. Edn., Annapolis, Md., 1957; mem. exec. com. adv. panel on health Am. Revolution Bicentenial Commn., Washington, 1970-72; v.p. 10th Internat. Cancer Congress, Houston, 1970. Asst. surgeon gen. USPHS, 1970—. Decorated PHS Meritorious Svc. medal; Jane Coffin Childs Fund fellow, 1946-48, Spl. fellow Nat. Cancer Inst., NIH, 1949. Mem. Am. Assn. Cancer Rsch. (bd. dirs. 1972-76), Am. Chem. Soc. (divsn. biol. chemistry, sec. 1955-57, councillor 1958-61), Am. Soc. Biochemistry and Molecular Biology, Soc. Exptl. Biology and Medicine, Cosmos Club, Sigma Xi, Alpha Omega Alpha, Phi Kappa Phi. Achievements include research in application of systems analysis and planning to strategic planning in medical research and laying the foundations for development of national cancer plan. Home: 19408 Charline Manor Rd Olney MD 20832-1044

BAKER, CARL TENEYCK, lawyer; b. Gloversville, N.Y., Jan. 15, 1951; s. Henry TenEyck and Virginia (Tasheff) B; m. Sandra A. Stoffolano, Oct. 12, 1975; children: Christopher T., Jessica A. BA, Cornell U., 1973; JD, Albany Law Sch., 1978. Bar: N.Y. 1979; U.S. Dist. Ct. (no. dist.) N.Y. 1979. Assoc. LaPann, Reardon, Fitzgerald & Firth, P.C., Glens Falls, N.Y., 1978-83; ptnr. LaPann, Reardon, Morris, Fitzgerald & Firth P.C., Glens Falls, N.Y., 1983-90, Fitzgerald, Morris, Baker & Firth P.C., 1990—. Pres. Estate Planning Coun. Northeastern N.Y., 1993-94; lectr. N.Y. State Bar Assn. Continuing Legal Edn. Contbg. author: (book) The New York Estate Tax; author course materials in field. Treas. Widowed Persons Svc., Glens Falls, 1984-97, pres., 1997-99; bd. govs., chmn. planned giving coun. Glens Falls Hosp., 1995—; active Glens Falls Hosp. Found., 1996—, v.p., 2003—; dir., vice-chair Compre-Care Inc., 1993-2000. Mem. ABA (real property, probate and trust law sect.), N.Y. State Bar Assn. (trusts and estates sect., chair com. on practice and ethics 1999-2001), Kiwanis (pres. Glens Falls chpt. 1985-86). Office: FitzGerald Morris Baker Firth PC 1 Broad St PO Box 2017 Glens Falls NY 12801-4301 E-mail: ctb@fmbf-law.com.

BAKER, CARLETON HAROLD, physiology educator; b. Utica, N.Y., Aug. 2, 1930; s. Harold George and Loretta (Darling) B.; m. Sara Frances Johnson, July 20, 1963; children: Elizabeth Ann, Janet Lee. BA, Utica Coll. of Syracuse U., 1952; MA, Princeton U., 1954, PhD, 1955. Asst. instr. Princeton (N.J.) U., 1952-54, asst. in research, 1954-55; asst. prof. Med. Coll. Ga., Augusta, 1955-61, assoc. prof., 1961-67, prof., 1967; prof. physiology and biophysics U. Louisville Health Scis. Ctr., 1967-71; prof., chmn. dept. physiology and biophysics U. South Fla. Coll. of Medicine, Tampa, 1971-92, dep. dean for research and grad. studies, 1980-82, prof surgery, physiology and biophysics, dir. surg. rsch., 1992-95; prof. emeritus U. South Fla., 1995—; rsch. prof. physiology U. S.C. Coll. Medicine, Columbia, 1994-2001. Rsch. com. mem. Am. Heart Assn., Louisville, 1969-71; rsch. com., bd. dirs. Am. Heart Assn. of Fla., Tampa, 1971-85; NIH program project site visit team, 1982-84, mem. LCME Accreditation Survey Team, 1980-81; cons. U. Louisville Grad. Sch., East Carolina U. Grad. Program. Editor: Microcirculatory Technology, 1986; mem. numerous editorial bds.; contbr. numerous articles in field. Pres. Augusta Choral Soc., 1963; v.p. Blount Rd. Homeowners Assn., Lutz, Fla., 1986-93; bd. dirs. Friends of Augusta. Grantee NIH, 1960-92, Am. Heart Assn., 1968-97; recipient Svc. awards Am. Heart Assn. Fla., 1974, 77, Disting. Scientist award U. South Fla. Coll. Medicine, 1981, Outstanding Artist/Scholar award Phi Kappa Phi, 1991, Dean's Citation U. So. Fla. Coll. Medicine, 1991, Founder award, 1992. Fellow: Am. Physiol. Soc. (fellow cardiovasc. sect. mem. com. 1982—85); mem.: Shock Soc. (mem. program coms.), European Microcirculatory Soc., Microcirculatory Soc., Torch Club Internat. Republican. Avocations: golfing, fishing. Home: 4039 Old Waynesboro Rd Augusta GA 30906-9254

BAKER, CAROL ANN, elementary school educator; b. Milw., Dec. 6, 1958; d. Alfred Walter and Gertrude Marian (Grabler) Krause; m. Donald Albert Baker, Aug. 11, 1984; 1 child, Caitlin Ann. BA in Psychology, Cardinal Strich Coll., 1982. Cert. tchr. grades kindergarten through 3rd, cert. tchr. spl. edn. grades kindergarten through 8th, Wis. Elem. tchr. St. Josaphat Sch., Milw., 1982-90; substitute tchr. Mukwonago Sch. Dist., 1997—. Mem. Psi Chi, Kappa Delta Pi (charter). Democrat. Roman Catholic. Avocations: needle crafts, fishing, gardening.

BAKER, CAROLYN, non-profit executive, fundraiser; b. Corona, Calif., Sept. 4, 1953; d. Earl Ross and Mary Louise (Stanley) Baker; children: Jaime Ann, Samuel Earl. BS in Liberal Arts, Ariz. State U., 1981; MA in Human Rels., No. Ariz. U., 1988. Sr. devel. officer Cedars-Sinai Med. Ctr., L.A., 2002—. Founder western music group Daus. of the Purple Sage, 1995. Avocations: hiking, gardening, painting. Office: 8700 Beverly Blvd Ste TSB-190 Los Angeles CA 90048

BAKER, CHARLES D. health insurance company executive; Past founder, co-dir. The Pioneer Inst.; past sec. health and human svcs., sec. adminstrn. and finance to former Gov. Mass. William Weld; past pres., CEO Harvard Vanguard Med. Assocs.; pres., CEO Harvard Pilgrim Health Care, Quincy, Mass., 1999—. Office: Harvard Pilgrim Healthcare 1600 Crown Colony Dr Quincy MA 02169-0913 also: 10 Brookline Pl W Brookline MA 02445-7295

BAKER, CHARLES DUANE, business administration educator, former management executive; b. Newburyport, Mass., June 21, 1928; s. Charles Duane and Eleanor (Little) B.; m. Alice Elizabeth Ghormley, 1955; children: Charles D., Jonathan G., Alexander K. AB, Harvard, 1951, MBA, 1955. With Westinghouse Electric Corp., Elmira, N.Y., 1955-57, Jersey City, 1957-61; v.p., treas. United Research, Inc., Cambridge, Mass., 1961-65; various positions through chmn., chief exec. Harbridge House, Inc., Boston, 1965-69, 72-83; prof. bus. adminstrn. Northeastern U., Boston, 1985—. Dep. under sec. U.S. Dept. Transp., Washington, 1969-70, asst. sec. policy and internat. affairs, 1970-71; under sec. U.S. Dept. HHS, Washington, 1984-85; presiding dir. Millipore Corp., 1986-87; adv. bd. dept. health policy Harvard Med. Sch.; chmn. McLean Heath Svcs. Inc. Author various studies dealing with mgmt. transp., health care, pub. policy. Mem. vis. com. Harvard U.; bd. dirs. Pioneer Inst. for Pub. Policy, Millipore Corp., Am. Med. Response, Inc.; trustee, chmn. McLean Hosp.; pres. Hall-Mercer Hosps.; trustee Harvard Med. Ctr., 1996-99; mem. Group Ins. Commn. Lt. (j.g.) USNR, 1946-48, 51-53. Recipient Award for Outstanding Achievement U.S. Govt., 1971 Mem. Pi Eta, Beta Gamma Sigma (Hon.). Clubs: Essex County; Harvard, Comml., Clover (Boston); E. India (London); Metropolitan (Washington). Republican. Congregationalist. Home: 81 Marmion Way Rockport MA 01966-1928 Office: Northeastern U 319 Hayden Hall 360 Huntington Ave Boston MA 02115-5000

BAKER, CHARLES LYNN, management consultant; b. Dallas, Mar. 17, 1934; s. Leonard Allan and Nellie (Boals) B.; m. Joan Heverly, June 1, 1968; 1 child, Annette Lynn. BS in Internat. Rels. summa cum laude, Syracuse U., 1967; MA in Polit. Sci. cum laude, Auburn U., 1975. Commd. USAF, advanced through grades to col., dep. inspector gen., 1975-80, retired, 1980; mng. ptnr. T.Z. Assocs., Balt., 1980-83; pres. McDermott Internat. Trading A.G., Zurich, 1983-88; mng. dir. McDermott Internat. Gen. Svcs., Hong Kong, Hong Kong, 1983-88; pres. Baker Assocs., Rancho Santa Fe, Calif., 1988—. Bd. dirs. T.Z. Assocs., Balt., Environ. Scis., San Diego, Broadleaf Industries, San Diego; adj. prof. U. Redlands Grad. Bus. Sch. Author: Strategic Planning, 1987. Pres. Redlands Ballet Co., 1987-89; chmn. Redlands Cultural Art Commn., 1988—. Mem. Am. C. of C. (v.p. Hong Kong br. 1984-86), Rotary (pres. Redlands chpt. 1989-90, bd. dirs. internat. chpt. in Hong Kong 1983-85), Pres.'s Assn. (chmn. 1988—), Calif. Cultural Arts Commn. Republican. Episcopalian. Avocations: golf, tennis, reading. Office: Baker Assocs 16047 Via Galan Rancho Santa Fe CA 92091-4014

BAKER, CHARLES STEPHEN, music educator; b. Cleve., July 25, 1942; s. LeRoy Williams and Nellie Angela (Burskey) B. BMus, Oberlin Coll. Conservatory, 1964; MA, Case Western Reserve U., 1967. Cert. music educator, Ohio. Tchr. music Madison Local Schs., Mansfield, Ohio, 1964-65, Wickliffe (Ohio) City Schs., 1967-96; pvt. clarinet instr., freelance clarinet performer Sch. of Fine Arts, Willoughby, Ohio, 1969—. Prin. clarinet, assoc. condr. Lakeland Civic Orch., Mentor, Ohio, 1972—. Recipient Disting. Svc. award Sch. of Fine Arts, 1992. Mem. NEA, Ohio Music Edn. Assn. (gen. music com. mem. 1972-99, 25 Yr. Svc. award 1991), Music Educators Nat. Conf. (N.E. region chair 1986-92, 94-98, all-state orch. chair 1990-92), Lake County Music Educators (sec. v.p., pres.), Ohio Edn. Assn., Am. Fedn. Musicians, U.S. Figure Skating Assn. Roman Catholic. Avocations: figure skating, photography, gardening, travel. Home: 5476 A Wildwood Ct Willoughby OH 44094-3261 E-mail: cbakermus@aol.com.

BAKER, CHESTER BIRD, agricultural economics educator; b. Mount Union, Iowa, Aug. 25, 1918; s. Herbert Victor and Florence Heston (Bird) B.; m. Virginia Hall, Sept. 11, 1942; children: Edwin C., Barbara C. (Mrs. John F. Chaney), Thomas H. Student, Iowa Wesleyan Coll., 1934-35; BS, Iowa State U., 1948; PhD, U. Calif., Berkeley, 1953. Asst. sec.-treas. Mount Pleasant Prodn. Credit Assn., Iowa, 1938-40; faculty Mont. State U., Bozeman, 1950-56, prof. agrl. econs., 1955-56; assoc. prof. U. Ill., Urbana, 1957-58, prof. agrl. econs., 1958-88, prof. emeritus, 1988—. J.S. McLean vis. prof. Ont. Agrl. U., 1961; cons. Western Agrl. Econs. Rsch. Coun., 1961, Midwest Rsch. Inst., 1962, Nat. Assn. Food Chains, 1964-66, Ill. Bankers Assn., 1969, Can. Task Force on Agriculture, 1967-69, Dept. Agriculture, 1963—, Ford Found., 1971, AID, 1973, Govt. of Australia, 1973, NAS, 1976; vis. lectr. numerous univs., U.S., Eng., Asia, Australia, Caribbean, Russia, Ukraine; disting. visitor Latrobe U., 1982. Author books and articles. With AUS, 1941-46. Travelling fellow Social Sci. Rsch. Coun., India, 1958; Fulbright-Hays sr. rsch. scholar U. Sydney, Australia, 1966-67, U. Melbourne, Australia, 1980-81; recipient Ernest H. Wakefield award, 1975, Paul A. Funk award, 1976; rsch fellow Australian Fedn. Res. Bank, U. Melbourne, 1973-74. Fellow: Am. Agrl. Econs. Assn. (life; dir., pres. 1984—85); mem.: Am. Econs. Assn., Alpha Gamma Rho, Gamma Sigma Delta. Presbyterian. Home: 10204 Oso Redondo NE Albuquerque NM 87111

BAKER, CHRISTOPHER CAMERON, surgeon; b. Boston, May 10, 1948; s. William Jessamin and Jean (Houghton) B.; m. Lynne Pearo; children: Jonathan, Katherine. BA, Williams Coll., Williamstown, Mass., 1970; MD, Harvard U., 1974. Diplomate in gen. surgery and in surg. critical care Am. Bd. Surgery; diplomate Nat. Bd. Med. Examiners. 1981surg. resident U. Calif., San Francisco, 1974; asst. prof. surgery Yale U. Sch. Medicine, New Haven, 1981-86, assoc. prof., 1986-89; dir. Trauma Ctr. Yale New Haven Hosp., 1982-89; prof. surgery U. N.C., Chapel Hill, 1989—, dir. trauma svc., 1989—, chief divsn. trauma, burns and critical care, 2000—. Exec. dir. N.C. Trauma Registry, N.C., 1991—; cons. Hwy. Safety Rsch. Ctr., N.C., 1993—; assoc. dir. Ctr. for Functional Gastrointestinal Disorders, Chapel Hill, 1994—. Grantee NIH, 1986-89, 91-2002; tchg. scholar U. N.C. Sch. Medicine, Chapel Hill, 1994-95. Fellow ACS (exec. coun. 1986-89); mem. Soc. Univ. Surgeons (sec. 1988-91, pres. 1992-93), Am. Assn. Surgery of Trauma, N.E. Med. Assn. Avocations: taekwondo (3d degree blackbelt), skiing. Office: U NC Sch Medicine Dept Surgery Cb # 7228 Chapel Hill NC 27599-7228

BAKER, CLARENCE ALBERT, SR., structural steel construction company executive; b. Kansas City, Kans., July 2, 1919; s. Earl Retting and Nancy Jefferson (Price) B.; m. Georgia Earlen Wibberding (dec. Apr. 1957); children: Clarence Albert, Jorgeann Baker Hiebert; m. Marjorie Ellen Yoakum, Mar. 19, 1959 (dec. Feb. 1981); stepchildren: Robert Beale, Barbara Anne Stegner (Mrs. Robert T. Kenney II); m. 2d, Katherine V. Cochran, Nov. 6, 1982. Student, Finley Engring. Coll., 1937-39, Kans. U., 1939-40, Ohio State U., 1967, 69. With Kansas City (Kans.) Structural Steel Co., 1937-48, shop supt., 1959-68, v.p., plant mgr., 1968-73, v.p. plant ops., 1973-76, v.p. engring., 1976-84, dir., 1969-84. Curriculum adv. Kansas City (Mo.) Met. Jr. Coll., 1971-72, Kansas City Vocat. Tech. Sch., 1973-84. Committeeman, Rep. Party, 1970-72; chmn. City of Mission (Kans.) Rep. Party, 1970-72; councilman, City of Merriam (Kans.), 1957-59; adv. bd. Wentworth Mil. Acad.; bd. dirs. Kansas City Jr. Achievement. With USNR, 1944-46. Mem. Am. Welding Soc. (pres. 1970-71, chmn. 1970-84, code com.), ASTM, Kans. Engring. Soc., Nat. Assn. Tax Profls. (enrolled agt. 1988—, IRS 1989—), Kansas City C. of C., Masons. Home: 7300 W 107th St Apt 416 Overland Park KS 66212-6604 Office: 21st and Metropolitan Sts Kansas City KS 66106 Fax: 913-901-8374.

BAKER, CORNELIA DRAVES, artist; b. Woodbury, N.J., Mar. 2, 1929; d. Carl Zeno and Cornelia (Powell) Draves.; m. Philip Douglas Baker, July 16, 1955; children: Brinton, Todd, Claudia, Samuel. Student, Ohio Wesleyan U., 1947-50, Goethe U., Frankfurt, Germany, 1950-52. Travel dir. Am. Youth Hostels, Inc., N.Y.C., 1953-57. Artist Cornelia Gallery, Kumamoto, Japan, 1990—; gallery dir. Presbyn. Ch., Franklin Lakes, N.J., 1988-97, Marcella

Geltman Gallery, New Milford, N.J., 1993-96; bd. dirs. Bergen Mus. Art and Sci., N.J., 1996-2000, corr. sec., mem. exec. com., 1999-2000. One-woman shows include Ramapo Coll., 1986, Shimada Mus., Kumamoto, 1990, Sekaikan Gallery, Tokyo, 1990, Am. Ctr., Fukuoka, 1990, Bergen Mus. Art and Sci., 1993, L'Atelier Inc. Gallery, 1994, N.Y. Theol. Sem., N.Y.C., 1996, The Gallery, Franklin Lakes, 1997, Office Congressman S.R. Rothman, Hackensack, N.J., 1997, Lee Hecht Harrison, Paramus, N.J., 1998, Willows Cafe, Ramsey, N.J., 2000; represented in permanent collections Bergen Mus. Art and Sci., Paramus, Beekley Internat. Skiing Fine Art and Graphics. Chair social problems com. Borough of Franklin Lakes Coun., 1973-76. Recipient Best of Show award Ringwood Manor Assn. of the Arts, 1987, Bergen Mus. Art and Sci., 1989, Emeriti award for excellence N.J. Ctr. for Visual Arts, 1989, Excellence cert. Internat. Art Competition, 1988, Women Making History in Arts award Bergen County, N.J., 1993, Crabbie award Art Calendar, 1994, Gold prize RISO Edn. Found., Japan, 1997, Artist Showcase award Manhattan Art Internat., 2000, merit award Salute to Women in Arts. 2000. Mem. Nat. Assn. Women Artists (printmaking jury chmn. 1992-94), Salute to Women in the Arts (pres. 1988-90), Mastodon Artists Soc. (life), Altrusa Club of Bergen County, N.J. Republican. Presbyterian. Avocations: skiing, traveling, tennis. Home: 293 Green Ridge Rd Franklin Lakes NJ 07417-2011 E-mail: pdbaker@optonline.net

BAKER, DANIAL EDWIN, director, consultant, pharmacy educator; b. Whitefish, Mont., May 25, 1955; s. Arby E. and Cathy Lee (Yarroll) B.; m. Patricia Samuelson, Aug. 28, 1976 (div.); 1 child, Kristin Nicole. B in Pharmacy, Wash. State U., 1978; PharmD, U. Minn., 1980. Lic. pharmacist, Wash. Instr. in pharmacology for respiratory therapist St. Paul Tech. Vocat. Inst., 1980; asst. prof. U. Okla., 1980-83, Wash. State U., Spokane, 1983-88, dir. Drug Info. Ctr., 1983—, assoc. prof., 1988-95, prof., 1995—, dir. clin. pharmacy programs, interim chmn. pharmacy dept., 1994-95, 96-97, dir. continuing edn., 1997—, assoc. dean clin. programs, 2002—. Drug formulary adv. com. divsn. med. assistance Wash. Dept. Social and Health Svcs., Olympia, 1990, chmn., 1990-92, cons. 1999—; cons. panel The Upjohn Co., Kalamazoo, 1990-93; adv. panel on drug info. sci. U.S. Pharmacopeial Conv., Inc., Rockville, Md., 1990-95; mem. Inst. for Safe Medication Practices, Inc., Huntington Valley, Pa., 1990—. Inst. Rev. Bd., Spokane, 1992-2002, Wash. State U., 1993-97; mem. adv. bd. Syntex Area Adv. Bd., Denver, 1994-96; cons., pharmacy and therapeutics com. Merck Health Solutions, Franklin Lakes, N.J., 1995—; pharmacy and therapeutics com. Whatcom Med. Bur., Bellingham, Wash., 1996-98. Sect. editor Rev. Gastroenterology Disorders, 2001—; asst. editor Hosp. Pharmacy, 2000—. Outdoor emergency care adminstr. Inland Empire region Nat. Ski Patrol, 1999—, sr. patrol, 1998—, instr., trainer, 1999—, asst. OEC supr. pacific N.W. divsn., 2001-; 49 degree North Chewelah, Wash., 1994—. Recipient Pharmacist Achievement award Merck Sharp and Dohme, 1993; named Outstanding Outdoor Emergency Care Instr. Inland Empire Region, Nat. Ski Patrol, 1999-2000, Pacific N.W. Divsn., 1999-2000, Outstanding Instr. Pacific N.W. Divsn., Nat. Ski Patrol, 1999-2000. Fellow Am. Soc. Cons. Pharmacists, Am. Soc. Hosp. Pharmacists; mem. Am. Assn. Colls. Pharmacy, Am. Coll. Clin. Pharmacy, Am. Pharm. Assn., Wash. Pharmacists Assn. (senator 1991-95, continuing edn. com. 1988—, award com. 1989-95, co-chmn. undergrad. affairs com. 1990-92, del. quinquinnel conv. 1987—, Pharmacist of Yr. award 1992), Wash. Soc. Hosp. Pharmacists (coun. edn. and manpower 1989-92, chmn. 1990-92, bd. dirs. 1989-93, pres. Spokane chpt. 1992-93), Wash. Pharmacy Coun. Republican. Avocations: skiing, snow shoeing, photography, cycling, kayaking. Office: Wash State U PO Box 1499 310 N Riverpoint Blvd Spokane WA 99210-1495 E-mail: bakerdan@wsu.edu.

BAKER, DANIEL RICHARD, computer company executive, consultant; b. Copenhagen, Mar. 19, 1932; came to U.S., 1936; s. Arthur and Molly (Needman) B.; m. June Ellin Nebenzahl, Oct. 2, 1960; children: David Charles, Jill Alison. Student, Tufts Coll., 1949-51; BA, Bklyn. Coll., 1957; postgrad, Fairleigh Dickinson U., 1961-64, Am. U., 1968-69; grad. Realtors Inst., U. Va., 1972. Math tchr. N.Y.C. Pub. Schs., 1958-59; computer programmer Sys. Devel. Corp., Paramus, N.J., 1959-61; programmer analyst ITT, Paramus, N.J., 1961-64; sr. mathematician Melpar Corp., Falls Church, Va., 1964-65; sys. analyst Wolf R & D Corp., Bladensburg, Md., 1965-66, Aries Corp., McLean, Va., 1966-68; sr. sys. analyst N. Am. Rockwell Corp., Roslyn, Va., 1968-70; pres. Data Assocs., Fairfax Station, Va., 1970—. Real estate broker. Group leader Dale Carnegie Sales Courses; vol. Ann. Fund Campaign Tufts Coll., 1976—. With AUS, 1954-55, vet. Korean War. Mem.: No. Va. Assn. Realtors Pioneer Club (25 Yr. Mem.), Va. Assn. Realtors (dir. 1977—80, 1983—97, Lifetime award 1992, 1994—2002), Nat. Assn. Realtors (No. Va. chpt. multilist com., edn. com., pub. rels. com., 5-yr. Million Dollar Sales Club award), Charles Tufts Soc., Silvanus Packard Soc., Washington Tufts Club (v.p. 1975). Office: Data Assocs 5622-G Ox Rd Fairfax VA 22039-1018 E-mail: ridem_cowboy@usa.com.

BAKER, DANIEL NEIL, physicist; b. Postville, Iowa, Nov. 10, 1948; s. Joseph N. and Alvira H. (Amundson) B.; m. A. Victoria Vaughan, Aug. 14, 1971. BA, U. Iowa, 1969, MS, 1973, PhD, 1974. Research aide dept. physics U. Iowa, Iowa City, 1967-69, grad. research asst., 1970-74, postdoctoral research assoc., 1974-75; research fellow Calif. Inst. Tech., Pasadena, 1975-78; mem. staff Los Alamos (N.Mex.) Nat. Lab., 1978-81, group leader, 1981-87; chief Lab. for Extraterrestrial Physics NASA, Goddard Space Flight Ctr., Greenbelt, Md., 1987-94; dir. Lab. for Atmospheric and Space Physics U. Colo., Boulder, 1994—. Chmn. data sys. users group NASA, Washington, 1982-90, tech. cons., 1985—, mem. space physics mgmt. and ops. com., adv. coun. Space Sci. and Applications, 1988-92, grand tour cluster mission study scientist, 1991-95, living with star mgmt. group, 2003—; mem. com. solar and space physics NAS, Washington, 1983-86, com. data mgmt. and computation, 1986-88, space studies bd., 1995-2001; co-chmn. adv. com. Tech. Applications Ctr. USAF, 1998—; mem. panel on long-term observations NRC, Washington, 1985-88, commn. D Sci. Com. on Solar-Terrestrial Physics, 1986-90, U.S. coordinating com. Solar Terrestrial Energy Program, 1988—, U.S. STEP project scientist, 1990-97, chair results, analysis, modeling phase (S-Ramp), 1997—2003, Geospace Environ. Modeling com. NSF, 1988-91; project sci. NASA small explorer program, prin. investigator NASA rocket program, numerous NASA ESA satellite missions in field; project sci. Internat. Solar-Terrestrial Physics POLAR Spacecraft Mission, 1992-94; U.S. rep. Internat. Assn. Geomagnetism and Aeronomy, 1996—; mem. internat. union geod and geophysics panel IGY, 2002—. Assoc. editor Geophys. Research Letters, Washington, 1986-88, Space Weather jour., 2003—; regional editor Jour. of Atmospheric and Solar-Terrestrial Physics, 1998—; mem. space tech. rev. bd. Los Alamos Nat. Lab.; contbr. numerous articles to profl. jours. Mem. external adv. com. Boston U. Ctr. for Space Rsch., 1989-94; mem. sci. vis. com. U. Md. Inst. Phys. Sci. and Tech., 1990-94; mem. external adv. com. Solar-Terrestrial Environ. Lab., Nagoya (Japan) U., 1995-97. NSF research fellow U. Iowa, 1970-74; grantee Inst. Geophys. and Planetary Physics U. Calif., 1980-89. Fellow Am. Geophys. Union (mem. natural hazards panel 1996—2000, pres.-elect space physics and aeronomy sect. 2000-02, pres. space physics and aeronomy sect. 2002—); mem. AAAS, Am. Geophys. Union (geomagnetism assessment panel 1987-88, sec. magnetospheric sect. 1988-90), Internat. Acad. Astronautics, Univs. Space Rsch. Assn. (chair coun. of instns. 1996-97), Sigma Xi. Avocations: jogging, creative writing, basketball, cinema.

BAKER, DAVID ALLEN, protective services official; b. Rockledge, Fla., Dec. 8, 1967; s. Charles and Betty Baker; m. Tammy Noah, Sept. 29, 2001; children: Jason, Victoria, Cheyenne. AA, Brevard C.C., Cocoa, Fla., 1994; BA in Criminal Justice and Pub. Adminstrn., MPA, U. Ctrl. Fla., 2001. Cert.: Fla. (police officer). Sgt. Cocoa Police Dept., 1995—2002. 1st sgt. Fla. N.G. U.S. Army, 1986—. Decorated medal of Valor Cocoa Police Dept. Mem.: ASPA, Fraternal Order Police (labor chmn. 2001—03), U. Ctrl.Fla. Alumni Assn., Pi Alpha Alpha. Office: Cocoa Police Dept 1226 W King St Cocoa FL 32926 Personal E-mail: dbaker7123.

BAKER, DAVID HIRAM, nutritionist, nutrition educator; b. DeKalb, Ill., Feb. 26, 1939; s. Vernon T. and Lucille M. (Severson) B.; m. Norraine A. Baker; children: Barbara G., Michael D., Susan G., Debora A., Luann C., Beth A. BS, U. Ill., 1961, MS, 1963, PhD, 1965. Sr. scientist Eli Lilly & Co., Greenfield, Ind., 1965-67; mem. faculty U. Ill., Champaign-Urbana, 1967—, prof. nutrition, dept. animal sci., nutritional biochemist, 1974—, dept. head, 1988-90. Author: Sulfur in Nonruminant Nutrition, 1977, Bioavailability of Nutrients for Animals, 1995; mem. editorial bd. Jour. Animal Sci., 1969-73, Jour. Nutrition, 1975-79, 89-99, Poultry Sci., 1978-84, Nutrition Revs., 1983-92; contbr. numerous articles to sci. jours. Chmn. bd. Champaign-Urbana Teen Challenge Drug Rehab. Program, 1977-80. Recipient Disting. Svc. award USDA, 1987; Univ. Scholar award, 1986; Nutrition Rsch. award, 1986; Am. Feed Mfrs., 1973; Merck award, 1977; Paul A. Funk award, 1977; H. H. Mitchell teaching award, 1979, 85; Broiler Rsch. award, 1983. Mem. Am. Soc. Animal Sci. (Young Scientist award 1971, Gustaf Bohstedt award 1985, Hoffman LaRoche award 1985, Morrison award 1994), Poultry Sci. Assn., Am. Soc. Nutritional Sci. (Borden award 1986, Dannon award 2003), Fedn. Am. Socs. Exptl. Biology, Sigma Xi, Phi Kappa Phi, Alpha Zeta, Gamma Sigma Delta. Home: 2609 Wadsworth Ln Urbana IL 61802-9403 Office: U Ill Nutrition Dept Urbana IL 61801 E-mail: dhbaker@uiuc.edu.

BAKER, DAVID REMEMBER, lawyer; b. Durham, N.C., Jan. 17, 1932; s. Roger Denio and Eleanor Elizabeth (Ussher) B.; m. Myra Augusta Mullins, Nov. 2, 1955 PhB, U. Chgo., 1949; BA, Birmingham-So. Coll., 1951; JD, Harvard U., 1954. Bar: Ala. 1954, NY 1963, U.S. Supreme Ct. 1972. Assoc. Cabaniss & Johnston, Birmingham, Ala., 1957-62, Chadbourne, Parke, Whiteside & Wolff, N.Y.C., 1962-66, ptnr., 1967-86, Jones, Day, Reavis & Pogue, N.Y.C., 1986-93, ret. ptnr., 1993—; ptnr. Afridi, Angell & Baker, N.Y.C., 1993-96, Gersen, Baker & Wood LLP, N.Y.C., 1997-98, Baker, Johnston & Wilson LLP, Birmingham and N.Y.C., 1998—2003; of counsel Haskell Slaughter Young & Rediker, LLC, Birmingham and N.Y.C., 2003—. Gen. counsel Econ. Club N.Y., 1977—; dir. HIEnergy Techs., Inc. Co-editor Due Diligence, Disclosures and Warranties in the Corporate Acquisition Practice, 1988, 2d edit., 1992; author articles and book chpts. Pres. N.Y. Legis. Svc., N.Y.C., 1975-98, chmn., 1998—; mem. adv. com. Ctr. for N.Y.C. Law, 2000—; sec., dir. Jr. Achievement of N.Y., 1973-99; dir. Jr. Achievement of Greater Birmingham, 1999—; trustee Birmingham-So. Coll., 1985—. With U.S. Army, 1954-57. Mem.: Musica Viva N.Y. (pres. 1994—96), Internat. Ins. Soc., N.Y. State Bar Assn. (exec. com. bus. law sect. 1987—89, exec. com. internat. law and practice sect. 1991—92, chmn. internat. investment and devel. com. 1991—92), Assn. Lloyd's Mems. (N.Am. adv. bd.), Internat. Law Assn., Internat. Bar Assn. (vice chmn. bus. orgn. com. 1986—90, rep. to U.S. mems. N.Y. area 1988—2000, chmn. com. on trusts for bus. 1990—94, prin. rep. to UN in N.Y. 1993—), Birmingham Bar Assn., Ala. Bar Assn., Assn. Bar City N.Y. (chmn. com. on state legis. 1968—70), Am. Fgn. Law Assn., Am. Law Inst., Am. Arbitration Assn. (nat. panel), ABA (liaison com. fin. acctg. stds. bd.), Birmingham Music Club, Met. Club N.Y.C., Harvard Club N.Y.C., Birmingham Athletic Club. Democrat. Unitarian Universalist. Avocation: bridge. Home: 1200 Beacon Pkwy E Apt 500 Birmingham AL 35209-1041 also: 315 E 72d St Apt 2-J New York NY 10021-4626 Office: Haskell Slaughter Young & Rediker LLC 1400 Park Pl Tower 2001 Park Pl N Birmingham AL 35203-2700 also: Fl 30 515 Madison Ave New York NY 10022 E-mail: drb@hsy.com.

BAKER, DAVID WARREN, earth scientist; b. Great Falls, Mont., Nov. 9, 1939; s. Roy Earnest Baker and Thora Leona Martin; m. Evelyn Elizabeth Herbstrith, 1962 (div. 1978); children: Erik Conrad, Andrew Craig, Paula Alicia. PhD, UCLA, 1969; MS in Natural Sci., Swiss Fed. Inst. Tech., 1964; BS, MIT, 1961. Consulting earth scientist, owner Little Belt Consulting Svcs., Monarch, Mont., 1984—; rsch. geologist Gulf R & D Corp., Pitts., 1976—83; asst. prof. U. Ill., Chgo., 1970—76. Cons. Export Bd. of Zambia, Lusaka, 1995—95, World Bank, Lusaka, 1995. Scoutmaster Boy Scouts Am., Oak Park, Ill., 1970—76, New Alexandria, Pa., 1976—82. Mem.: Tobacco Root Geol. Soc., Mont. Geol. Soc., Nat. Ctr. Sci. Edn., Geol. Soc. Am., Am. Geophys. Union. Unitarian. Achievements include first to Reconstructed plate tectonic history of Montana; research in Determined plate tectonic origin of Yogo Sapphire Deposit in Montana; first to Developed technique to analyze extremely deformed rock (mylonite) using X-rays and spherical harmonic analysis; Conducted field courses for Montana teachers on plate tectonic history of Montana. Home: PO Box 906 Monarch MT 59463 Office: Little Belt Consulting Services PO Box 906 Monarch MT 59463 E-mail: dbaker@3rivers.net.

BAKER, DAVID WESTON, education educator; b. Toronto, Can., Feb. 22, 1950; s. J. Weston and Mary K. Baker; m. Moruen R. Roberts, Nov. 25, 1972; children: Adam D.R., Emily M. AB, Temple Univ., Phila., 1970; MLS, Regent Coll., Vancouver, 1973; MPhil, Univ. London, London, Eng., 1976, DLD, 1982. Asst. prof. Betha Coll., St. Paul, 1979—80; Pastrol Staff Westminister Gospel Chapel, Barnby, 1981—83; sr. lectr. Univ. De Witwatersand, Johannesburg, 1983—85; assoc. prof. Univ. Durben, Durben, South Africa, 1985—86; prof. Ashland Theol. Sem., 1986—. Author: More Light on the Path, 1999; editor: Interpreting the Old Testament, 2001, The Face of Old Testament Study, 1999, Faith, Tradition and History, 1994; contbr. articles to profl. jour. Avocations: travel, reading. Office: Ashland Theol Sem 910 Ctr St Ashland OH 44805

BAKER, DENISE R. technical computer educator, consultant; d. Sandi D. Garrett and Lou M. Ray, Curtis W. Garrett (Stepfather) and Joyce M. Ray(Stepmother); m. Ralph A. Baker, Apr. 27, 1996; 1 child, Cody R. A.A.S. in Computer-Aided Drafting Tech., So. Tech. Coll., Little Rock, AR, 1986—88. Estimator Hanover Co., Houston, 1996—97; instr. ITT Tech. Inst. - Houston North, Houston, 1997—. Drafter/pub. rels. US Army Corps Engrs., Little Rock, 1986—88, Sudduth Engring., Little Rock, 1988—89; instr. So. Tech. Coll., Little Rock, 1989—90; drafter Harden Constructors, Houston, 1990—91; designer/drafter Wind Prodn. Systems, Houston, 1991—93; designer Hanover Co., Houston, 1993—96. Vol. drafter Habitat for Humanity, Houston, 2002—02. Mem.: Am. Soc. Engring. Edn. (assoc.), Nat. Trust Hist. Preservation (assoc.), Tex. Libr. Assn. (assoc.), Am. Design & Drafting Assn. (assoc.). Office: ITT Tech Inst Houston N 15621 Blue Ash Dr Ste 160 Houston TX 77090 Personal E-mail: drbaker@itt-tech.edu.

BAKER, DEXTER FARRINGTON, manufacturing company executive; b. Worcester, Mass., Apr. 16, 1927; s. Leland Dyer and Edith (Quimby) B.; m. Dorothy Ellen Hess, June 23, 1951; children: Ellen L., Susan A., Leslie A., Carolyn J. BS, Lehigh U., 1950, MBA, 1957. Sales engr. Air Products & Chem., Inc., Allentown, Pa., 1952-56, gen. sales mgr., 1956-57, mng. dir., 1957-64, chief exec. ops. in Europe, bd. dir., 1964-67, exec. v.p., 1967-78, pres., 1978-86, 90-91, chmn., pres., 1990-91, chmn., chief exec. officer, 1986-92, chmn. exec. com. bd. dir., 1992-98. Former chmn. investment policy US Trade Rep. Bd. assocs. Muhlenberg Coll.; trustee Harry C. and Mary M. Trexler Found. Served with USNR, 1945-46; with U.S. Army, 1950-52. Mem. AIChE, Am. Mgmt. Assn., Nat. Assn. Mfrs. (former chmn.), Theta Chi. Presbyterian (elder). Office: Air Products and Chems Inc 7201 Hamilton Blvd Allentown PA 18195-1501

BAKER, DIANE R.H. dermatologist; b. Toledo, Nov. 17, 1945; BS, Ohio State U., 1967, MD cum laude, 1971. Diplomate Am. Bd. Dermatology. Intern U. Wis. Hosp., Madison, 1971-72, resident in dermatology, 1972-74, Oreg. Health Sci. Ctr., Portland, 1974-76; pvt. practce, Portland, 1976—. Clin. prof. dermatology Oreg. Health Sci. U., 1986—; mem. med. staff Meridian Park Hosp., Tualatin, Oreg., 1981—; dir. Am. Bd. Dermatology, 1995—, v.p., 2001. Mem.: AMA (del. 1995—), Oreg. Dermatol. Soc., Am. Dermatol. Assn. (v.p. 2001), Am. Acad. Dermatology (v.p. 1990), Alpha Omega Alpha. Office: 1706 NW Glisan St Ste 2 Portland OR 97209-2225

BAKER, DINA GUSTIN, artist; b. Phila., Nov. 07; d. Albert Isadore Kevles and Rose Schwartz; m. John Calvin Gustin (dec. July 4, 1964); m. William Baker, Jan. 5, 1968. Student, Phila. Coll. Fine Arts, 1940, Barnes Found, 1942—46, Templer Tyler Sch. Fine Arts, 1943, Art Students League, 1945, Hayter Atelier 17, N.Y.C., 1945. One-woman shows include Roko Gallery, N.Y.C., 1963, Angeleski Gallery, 1965, Regensburg (Germany) Mus., 1974, Amerika House, Munich, 1974, Hamburg, Germany, 1974, Ingber Gallery, N.Y.C., 1976, 1978, 1980, 1982, Brigham Young U., Provo, Utah, 1983, Utah State U., Logan, 1983, Gracie Lawrence Gallery, Delray Beach, Fla., 1999, 2000, Ora Sorensen Gallery, Delray Beach, 2000—02, Represented in permanent collections Bergen Mus. Arts and Scis., Paramus, N.J., Rutgers U., Nelson Hall, Piscataway, N.J., NYU, N.Y.C., Gannet Found., Columbia U., Boca Raton (Fla.) Mus., exhibited in group shows at Guild Hall, East Hampton, N.Y., 1954, Art USA, N.Y.C., 1955, Acad Fine Arts, Phila., 1963, Nat. Acad. Design, N.Y.C., 1968, Lehigh U., Bethlehem, Pa., 1977, Montclair (N.J.) Art Mus., 1978, Parrish Mus., Southampton, N.Y., 1981, Ingber Gallery, N.Y.C., 1984, Bergen Mus. Arts and Scis., Paramus, N.J., 1984, Adlena Adlung Gallery, N.Y.C., 1991, Rutgers U., 1996, Gracie Lawrence Gallery, 1996, 1999, 2000, Ora Sorensen Gallery, 2000. Scholar, Phila. Coll. Fine Arts, 1940, Art Students League, 1945, Barnes Found., 1942—45. Mem.: Women in the Arts. Home: Bay Hill estates 11820 Blackwoods Ln West Palm Beach FL 33412

BAKER, DON R. musician; b. Edgerton, Ohio, Apr. 10, 1948; s. Virgil H. and Marilyn M. (Stryker) B. BA, Adrian Coll., 1970; EdM, Indiana U. of Pa., 1972; D of Mus. Arts, U. Ill., 1985. Cert. tchr., Mich. Instr. music Western Mich. U., Kalamazoo, 1972-76; instr. percussion Internat. Music Camp, Bottineau, N.D., 1973-74; instr. music U. N.C., Greensboro, 1978-83; instr. percussion Interlochen (Mich.) Ctr. for the Arts, 1979; freelance musician various orchs., mus., ballets, San Francisco, 1985—; instr. music Mt. Tamalpais Sch., Mill Valley, Calif., 1999—. Cons. various pub. schs., univs., Mich., N.C., Calif., 1972—. Author: Music of Lou Harrison, 1985; rec. artist: CRI, Ubres, Opus 1 labels, 1983—; editor, contbr. Instrumentalist, 1975-83; composer various pieces including Akanda, 1985. Area rep. Music in Our Schs. Day, Kalamazoo,1974; mem. AIDS Found. com., San Francisco, 1988. Mem. Percussive Arts Soc. (nat. bd. dirs. 1978-82, pres. N.C. chpt. 1980-82), Soc. for Ethnomusicol., Am. Fedn. Musicians, Phi Mu Alpha (Music award 1969, 70), Phi Kappa Lambda (hon.).

BAKER, DON ROBERT, chemist, inventor, writer; b. Salt Lake City, Apr. 6, 1933; s. Ralph H. and Ruth Eve (Thalmann) B.; m. Shirley May Nelson, Nov. 20, 1954 (dec. 1993); children: Robert, David, George, Barbara; m. Shirlee Ann Call, Sept. 17, 1994. AA, Sacramento City Coll., 1953; AB, Calif. State U., Sacramento, 1955; PhD, U. Calif., Berkeley, 1959. Sr. rsch. chemist Stauffer Chem. Co., Richmond, Calif., 1958-72, rsch. assoc., 1970-74, supr., 1974-85; sr. rsch. assoc. ICI Ams. Inc. Zeneca Ag Products, Richmond, 1985 97; cons. in chemistry and chem. safety, 1998—; corp. cons., bd. dirs. Berkeley Discovery, Inc., 1999—, CFO, 2001—. Lectr. family history topics. Editor: Agrochemical Discovery: Insect, Weed and Fungal Control, 2000; editor Calif. Chemists Alert, 1986-2000, Synthesis and Chemistry of Agrochems., 1987, 90, 92, 95, 98, 2001; contbr. articles to profl. jours.; holder 204 U.S. patents. Recipient Zeneca Patent award, 1996. Mem. Am. Chem. Soc. (chmn. Calif. sect. 1973, councilor 1971—, chmn. nat. divsn. profl. rels. 1980, coord. com. Calif. sects. 1970—, vice-chmn. agrochem. divsn. 1993, chmn. agrochems. divsn. 1995, bylaws chair agrochems. divsn. 1998—, nat. com. chem. health and safety 1999-2001, Walter Petersen award 1991, fellow award 1991, Internat. award for agrl. rsch. 1999), Orchid Soc. Calif. (pres. 1979-80), Oakland Family History Ctr. (libr. 1967—). Republican. Mem. Lds Ch. Avocations: orchid growing, mineralogy, genealogy. Office: 15 Muth Dr Orinda CA 94563-2805 Fax: 925-254-3721. E-mail: d.r.baker@sbcglobal.net.

BAKER, DONALD, lawyer, director; b. Chgo., May 28, 1929; s. Russell and Elizabeth B.; m. Gisela S. Carli, Oct. 6, 1960; children: Caryna, Andrew, Russell. Student, Deep Springs Coll., Calif., 1947-49; JDS., U. Chgo., 1954. Bar: Ill. 1955, N.Y. 1964. Ptnr. Baker & McKenzie, Chgo., 1955-94, ret., 1994; sec., gen. counsel, bd. dirs. Air South, Inc., Columbia, S.C., 1994-95. Bd. dirs. Trimedyne, Inc., Cardiomedics, Inc. Bd. dirs. exec. com. Mid-Am. Com., Chgo., 1980-94. Mem. ABA. Clubs: Michigan Shores (Wilmette, Ill.). E-mail: dbaker5727@aol.com.

BAKER, DONALD GENE, social sciences educator; b. Elgin, Ill., Feb. 16, 1932; s. Glenn O. and Helen K. Baker; m. Barbara L. Sands; 1 child, Catherine K. BA in Polit. Sci., Denver U., 1953; MA in Polit. Sci., Syracuse U., 1957, PhD in Social Scis., 1961. Asst. prof., dir. dept. Am. studies Skidmore Coll., Saratoga Springs, N.Y., 1959-64; assoc. prof., then prof. Southampton (N.Y.) Coll. of L.I. U., 1964—, dir. social scis. divsn., 1964-70. Cons. Peace Corps, Washington, 1964-67, N.Y. State Dept. Edn., Albany, 1964-66, AID, Washington, 1977-79; dir. Grad. Legis. Intern Program, Albany, 1962-67. Author: Politics of Race, 1975, Race, Ethnicity and Power, 1983. Cpl. U.S. Army, 1954-56. Rsch. fellow U. Rhodesia, 1976-78, U. Zimbabwe, 1981, Victoria U., New Zealand, 1993; assoc. rsch. fellow Yale U., 1992-93; rsch. grantee St. Antony's Coll., Oxford U., Eng., 1980-81, 86. Democrat. Avocations: travel, writing. Home: PO Box 701 Hampton Bays NY 11946-0607 E-mail: donald.baker@liu.edu.

BAKER, DONALD P. lawyer; b. L.A., Oct. 27, 1947; s. Albert G. and Janet C. Baker; m. Caroline E. BA magna cum laude, U. Redlands, 1970; JD, UCLA, 1973. Bar: Calif. 1973. Ptnr. Latham & Watkins, L.A., chair transp. practice group, 1991—. Dir. UCLA Pub. Interest Law Found., 1982-84, UCLA Alumni Assn., 1984-86, Japan Am. Symphony Assn. L.A., 1992-95; dir. Western Justice Ctr. Found., 1988—, pres., 1995—; trustee Claremont Grad. U., 2002—. Fellow ABA (numerous coms. and offices), Nat. Assn. Colls. and Univ. Attys., Star Bar Calif. (com. jud. nominees evaluation 1981-82), Internat. Bar Assn., L.A. County Bar Assn. (pres. 1986-87, numerous coms. and offices, Shothuck-Price Meml. award 1999), Barristers L.A. County Bar Assn. (pres. 1979-80, numerous coms. and offices), L.A. County Bar Found. (sec. 1983-84), Japan Am. Soc. So. Calif. (bd. dirs., v.p. 1992—)Chancery Club, Order of the Coif. Office: Latham & Watkins 633 W 5th St Ste 4000 Los Angeles CA 90071-2005

BAKER, DOUG W. history and humanities educator; b. Wausau, Wis., July 12, 1950; s. Lloyd Earl Baker and Geraldine Lee baker; m. Linda Sue Davis, July 26, 1987. BA in History, Andrews U, 1972; BA in Religion, Union Coll., Lincoln, Nebr., 1980; MA in History, U of Ctrl. Okla., 1990; D Min., Am. Christian Coll. and Sem., 1997. Prof. history and humanities Okla. State U, Okla. City, 1990—. Author: The Am. Journey: 1865 To The Present; contbr. articles. Adv. Young Dem., Okla. City, Okla., 2002—03. Recipient Dr. Doug Baker Day, Gov. Okla., 2000. Democrat. Avocations: writing, travel. Office: Oklahoma State Univ 900 N Portland Ave Oklahoma City OK 73107

BAKER, DUSTY (JOHNNIE B. BAKER JR.), professional baseball team manager; b. Riverside, Calif., June 15, 1949; Student, Am. River Coll. Player Atlanta Braves, 1968-75, L.A. Dodgers, 1976-83, San Francisco Giants, 1984, Oakland A's, 1985-86; coach San Francisco Giants, 1988-92, mgr., 1993—2002, Chgo. Cubs, 2002—. Mem. Nat. League All-Star Team, 1981-82. Recipient Silver Slugger award, 1980-81, Gold Glove, 1981; named to Sporting News All-Star Team, 1980. Office: Chgo Cubs Wrigley Field 1060 W Addison Chicago IL 60613-4397

BAKER, EDWARD KEVIN, retail executive; b. Chester, Ill., Nov. 25, 1948; s. Edward Louis and Betty Lou (Huch) B.; m. Janet Lynn Verbal, Oct. 26, 1967 (div. 1973); 1 child, Shawn Allen; m. Doris Mary Kubala, June 12, 1975; stepchildren: Jimmy Lee, Jennifer Lou Godard. Mgr. F.W. Woolworth Co., St. Louis, then Dallas, 1968-74; pres. Baker Mktg. Co., Dallas, 1974-76; mgr. E.B. Mott Co., Dallas, 1976-83; mkt. mgr. Michaels Stores Inc., San Antonio, 1983-86, dir. merchandising Irving, Tex., 1986-88, dir. mgmt. devel., 1988-89, v.p. ops., 1989-91; sr. v.p. ops., distbn. mktg. Silk Greenhouse Inc., Tampa, 1990-91; dir. ops. mdse. Crafts & More div. Ames Dept. Stores, Rocky Hill, Conn., 1991-92; pres. E.K. Baker Group, Inc., Treasure House Stores, Inc., Seattle, 1993—, chief oper. officer, bd. dirs. Bd. dirs. H. Mangelsen & Sons Inc., Omaha, Nebr., 1997—. Author The Edge 1988; producer (video) Framing Technique 1989; editor (video) Art Materials 1989. Mem. Southwest Craft & Hobby Assn. (bd. dirs. 1987-93), Am. Soc. Tng. Dirs., Art Materials Trade Assn., Am. Soc. Decorative Painters, Profl. Picture Framers Assn. Lutheran. Avocation: restoring antique furniture. E-mail: ekdbaker@cs.com.

BAKER, EDWARD L., JR., physician, science facility executive; b. Chattanooga, Nov. 18, 1946; s. Edward Lamar and Sue B. Baker; m. Pamela Taylor, June 21, 1969; children: Justin, Ryan, Lindsay. BA, Vanderbilt U., 1968; MD, Baylor U., 1972; MPH, Harvard U., 1979, MS, 1980. Diplomate Am. Bd. Internal Medicine, Am. Bd. Occupational Medicine. Commd. USPHS, 1974—, advanced through grades to rear adm., 1995, asst. surgeon gen.; asst. prof. Harvard U. Sch. Pub. Health, Boston, 1980-82, assoc. prof., 1982-85; asst. dir. Nat. Inst Occupl. Safety and Health Ctr. Disease Control, Atlanta, 1985-88, dep. dir. Nat. Inst. Occupl. Safety and Health, 1988-90, asst. surgeon gen., dir. Pub. Health Practice Program Office, 1990—. Bd. dirs. Internat. Commn. on Occupl. Health, 1986-92. Author, editor 100 sci. articles and book chpts. Fellow Am. Coll. Epidemiology; mem. APHA, Am. Coll. Occupl. and Environ. Medicine (authorship award 1988), Soc. Occupl. and Environ. Health, Royal Soc. Medicine (London, vis. fellow). Home: 755 Kirk Rd Decatur GA 30030-4529 Office: Ctr Disease Control Pub Health Practice Program Office (K36) 2877 Brandywine Rd Atlanta GA 30341-3724

BAKER, EDWARD MARTIN, engineering and industrial psychologist; b. Bklyn., Mar. 13, 1941; s. Harold H. and Paula B.; m. Shige Jajiki; 1 son, Evan Keith. BA, CCNY, 1962, MBA, 1964; PhD (Research fellow), Bowling Green State U., 1972. Human factors research engr. environ. and safety engring. staff Ford Motor Co., Dearborn, Mich., 1972-77, tech. tng. assoc. mgmt. and tech. tng. dept. Detroit, 1977-79, orgn. devel. cons., personnel and orgn. staff, 1979-81, statis. assoc., ops. support product quality office, 1981-83, statis methods mgr. Asia-Pacific and Latin-Am. automotive ops., 1983-87, dir. total quality planning, cons. and statis. methods corp. quality office, 1987—, dir. quality strategy and ops. support, 1990-92; sr. fellow Aspen Inst., Wye, Md., 1992-95. Mgmt. cons., 1993—. Author: Scoring a Whole in One, 1999; contbr. articles to profl. jours.; editorial referee: Jour. Quality Tech, 1974-75, 77-81. Trustee The W. Edwards Deming Inst., Washington, 1993—. Fellow Am. Soc. Quality (Brumbaugh award 1975, Craig award 1976, 79, 86, 88, Ishikawa medal 1995, Deming medal 1997).

BAKER, EDWIN MOODY, retired newspaper publisher; b. Cleve., Dec. 20, 1923; s. Alton Fletcher and Mildred Elizabeth (Moody) B.; m. Patricia Petersen, 1954 (dec. 1983); children: Bridget Baker Kincaid, Amanda Baker Barber, Jonathan; m. Marie Kottkamp Randall, 1984; stepchildren: Steven, Mark, Bruce Randall. BS in Bus. Adminstrn., U. Oreg., 1948. With Eugene (Oreg.) Register-Guard, 1948-88; successively advt. mgr., bus. mgr., gen. mgr., pub., pres. Guard Pub. Co., chmn. bd. Mem. exec. bd. Oreg. Trail Coun., Boy Scouts Am., 1953—, pres. 1960-61, chmn. Region XI, 1971, Area I (N.W.), pres., 1972, mem. nat. exec. bd., 1971-72, nat. adv. coun., 1972-82; trustee U. Oreg. Found., 1975-90, Lane C.C. Found. Bd.; bd. dirs. Oreg. Cmty. Found., 1982-90; Oreg. Hist. Soc., 1988-92; trustee Eugene Arts Found., 1980-85; campaign chair Eugene Performing Arts Ctr. campaign; pres. Oreg. Pacific Econ. Devel. Corp., 1984-85; 2d v.p. Eugene Springfield Mt. Ptnrship; mem. chmn. Kakegawa Sister City com., 1986-88; co-chmn. Birth to Three Capital Campaign, 1997; chmn. United Way Leadership, 1997-98; hon. co-chair Eugene Pub. Libr. Found. campaign for New Pub. Libr., 1999-2000. With AUS, WWII. Decorated Bronze Star, Purple Heart; recipient Silver Beaver award Boy Scouts Am., 1962, Silver Antelope, 1965, Pioneer award U. Oreg., 1982, Disting. Eagle Scout, 1982, Aubrey Watzig award Lewis and Clark Coll., 1988, MS Hope award for Oustanding Philanthropic Cmty. Svc. and Bus. Leadership, 2000; named Eugene First Citizen, 1983. Mem. Am. Newspaper Pus. Assn. (rsch. inst. lab. com. 1978-79), Oreg. Newspaper Pubs. Assn. (dir. 1982-90, pres. 1988-89), U. Oreg. Pres. Assocs., Nat. Assn. Fund Raising Execs. (vol. 1994, Oreg. chpt. Fund Raiser of Yr. 1993), Rotary, Eugene Country Club. Home: 2121 Kimberly Cir Eugene OR 97405-5821 Office: PO Box 10188-2188 Eugene OR 97401-3204

BAKER, EDWIN STUART, retired computer consultant; b. Ottumwa, Iowa, Feb. 14, 1944; s. Edwin Moore and Geraldine Vivian (Irby) B; m. Wilma Jeanne Parker, 1968 (div. 1970). Student, Whitman Coll., 1962-64; BS, Oreg. State U., 1978. Programmer agrl. engring. dept. Oreg. State U., Corvallis, 1977-78, rsch. asst., 1979-83, sr. rsch. asst., 1984-89; measurement standards specialist Oreg. Dept. Agr., Salem, 1990-93. Cons. in field. Mem. IEEE, Assn for Computing Machinery, Am. Legion, VFW, DAV, NRA, VFW, 59ers Svc. Club. Avocations: photography, horses. Home: PO Box 370 Lebanon OR 97355-0370 Office: Oreg Dept Agr Measurement Standards Divsn Salem OR 97310-0001 E-mail: esb@computer.org.

BAKER, EVA LEE, education educator, researcher; b. L.A., May 31, 1940; d. David Brainin and Janice Frances Funk; m. Peter S. Baker, July 27, 1960 (div. Oct. 2, 1978); children: Tristan Bickman, Christopher; m. Harold F. O'Neil, Sept. 15, 1984. BA in English, UCLA, 1963, MA in Edn., 1965, EdD, 1967. Peace Corps instr UCLA, 1965—67, asst. prof., 1968—72, assoc. prof., 1973—78, prof. edn., 1978—, dir. Ctr. for the Study of Evaluation, 1975—, co-dir. Nat. Ctr. for Rsch. on Evaluation, Stds. and Student Testing, 1985—, acting dean Grad. Sch. Edn. and Info. Studies, 1995—97; mem. profl. staff S.W. Regional Lab., 1967—68. Chair Stds. for Ednl. and Psychol. Testing, 1993—99, Bd. on Testing and Assessment, Washington, 2000—; mem. Adv. Coun. on Ednl. Stats., Washington, 2002; presenter in field; cons. in field. Editor (with M.C. Wittrock): Testing and Cognition, 1991; co-editor (with H.F. O'Neil Jr.): Technology Assessment in Software Applications, 1994, Technology Assessment in Education and Training, 1994; contbr. chapters to books, articles to profl. jours.; mem. editl. bd., spl. issue editor: Am. Jour. Edn., internat. adv. bd. mem.: Assessment in Education: Principles, Policy & Practice, mem. editl. bd.: Educational Assessment; editor: Educational Evaluation and Policy Analysis; mem. editl. bd.: The Education Researcher, Jossey-Bass, guest editor: Jour. Ednl. Rsch., mem. editl. bd.: Jour. Ednl. Psychology; co-editor: Jour. Learning & Evaluation. Grantee, L.A. Annenberg Met. Project, 1996—2000, Stuart Found., 1997—2000, 1998—2001, L.A. Unified Sch. Dist., 1995—2000, State of Wyo. Dept. Edn., 1999—2000, The Joyce Found., 1999—2000, others. Mem.: APA, Am. Ednl. Rsch. Assn., Nat. Coun. on Measurement in Edn., Am. Psychol. Soc.

BAKER, FAITH MERO, retired elementary education educator; b. Pitts., May 9, 1941; d. Vincent G. and Georgetta (Rothwell) Mero; m. Gerald A. Baker, Dec. 22, 1968; children: Jeremy D., Kara L. BA, Carlow Coll., Pitts., 1963; MEd, U. Pitts., 1965, postgrad., 1966-68. Cert. elem. and spl. edn. tchr., Pa. Tchr. sci. Pitts. Pub. Schs., 1963-64, tchr. spl. edn., 1968-87, tchr., primary sci. specialist, 1987-98; ret. Leader instrnl. team Fulton Acad., Pitts., 1988—; facilitator, tchr. Project Wild and project Aquatic Wild, Project Learning Tree, Pitts., 1988—; mem. leadership team Fulton Acad. for New Am. Schs.-area Sch. to Career. Leader Girl Scouts U.S.A., Monroeville, Pa., 1979-86; mem. Supts. Roundtable Gateway Schs., Monroeville, Pa., 1987-89. Mem.: AAUW (chair scholarship com Monroeville br. 1996—), Pa. Bus. and Profl. Women's Assn. (mem. polit. action com., pres. Monroeville 1987—88, bd. dirs. dist.3 1991—, mem. polit. action com., pres. Monroeville 1992—93), Pitts. Fedn. Tchrs. (bldg. steward 1968—98), U. Pitts. Alumni Assn. (asst. v.p. 1987—88, sec. 1989—91, alumnae coun. recording sec. 1998—2000), Delta Kappa Gamma, Alpha Delta Kappa (treas. 1992—99), Phi Delta Gamma (pres. 1982—84, regional coord. 1984—86, sec. Kappa chpt. 1986—90, nat. v.p. 1992—94, nat. pres. 1994—96, nat. treas. 1998—2000, chpt. 2d v.p. 1999—2000, 1st v.p. 2000—02, pres. 2002—). Democrat. Roman Catholic. Avocations: sewing, gourmet cooking, writing, short stories and poetry. Home: 102 Penn Lear Dr Monroeville PA 15146-4734 E-mail: fayze@adelphia.net.

BAKER, FLOYD WILMER, surgeon, retired army officer; b. Leavenworth, Kans., May 25, 1927; s. Floyd Winfield and Lolita Clare (Somers) B.; m. Darlene Marie Fulk, Apr. 10, 1949; children: Linda Marie, Diane Louise, Barbara Jayne. BA, U. Kans., 1950, MD, 1953; grad., Army Command and Gen. Staff Coll., 1964, Indsl. Coll. Armed Forces, 1967. Diplomate: Am. Bd. Surgery. Commd. 1st lt. U.S. Army, 1953, advanced through grades to maj. gen., 1980; intern Madigan Gen. Hosp., Tacoma, 1953-54; resident in gen. surgery Fitzsimons Army Hosp., Denver, 1955-59; dir. personnel and tng. Office of Surgeon Gen., 1970-71; comdg. gen. Brooke Army Med. Center, Ft. Sam Houston, Tex., 1974-78; Letterman Army Med Center, Presidio of San Francisco, 1978-81; chief surgeon U.S. Army, Europe; comdg. gen. U.S. Army 7th Med. Command, 1981-83, U.S. Army Health Services Command, Ft. Sam Houston, 1983-86; retired U.S. Army, 1986. Served with USNR, 1945-46. Decorated Legion of Merit (2), Meritorious Service medal, Army Commendation medal (3), Air medal (2), Disting. Service medal. Fellow Am. Coll. Physician Execs.; mem. AMA, Soc. U.S. Army Flight Surgeons. Republican. Baptist. Home and Office: 1413 Wiltshire Ave San Antonio TX 78209-6050 E-mail: fbaker1@satx.rr.com.

BAKER, FRANK C. (BUZZ BAKER), advertising executive; m. Terry Baker; 1 child, Scott. BA in History and Econs., postgrad., Harvard U. With Fletcher/Mayo Assocs., St. Joseph, Mo., 1976-81; pres. & mng. dir. Cedar Rapids unit, dir. acct. mgmt. Creswel Munsell Fultz & Zirbel, Cedar Rapids, Iowa, 1981-90, pres., CEO, 1990—2002; sr. cons. Alexander Marketing Svcs., Grand Rapids, Mich., 2002—. Bd. dirs. United Way, Hugh O'Brien Found., March of Dimes, Young Parent's Network. Named to Ad Fed Hall of Fame, 1991. Mem. Nat. AgriMktg. Assn., Cedar Rapids Advt. Fedn. Avocation: sports. Office: 277 Crahen Ave NE Grand Rapids MI 49546

BAKER, FREDERICK MILTON, JR., lawyer; b. Flint, Mich., Nov. 2, 1949; s. Frederick Milton Baker and Mary Jean (Hallitt) Rarig; m. Irene Taylor; children: Jessica, Jordan. BA, U. Mich., 1971; JD, Washington U., St. Louis, 1975. Bar: Mich. 1975, U.S. Dist. Ct. (we. dist.) Mich. 1980, U.S. Dist. Ct. (ea. dist.) Mich. 1981, U.S. Ct. Appeals (6th cir.) 1983, U.S. Supreme Ct. 1986. Instr. law Wayne State U., Detroit, 1975-76; research atty. Mich. Ct. Appeals, Lansing, 1976-77, law clk. to chief judge, 1977; asst. prof. T.M. Cooley Law Sch., Lansing, Mich., 1978-80; ptnr. Willingham & Cote, Lansing, 1980-86, Honigman, Miller, Schwartz & Cohn, Lansing, 1986—. Adj. prof. T.M. Cooley Law Sch., 1980—86, 1995—96, Detroit Coll. Law Mich. State U., East Lansing, 2001—. Author: Michigan Bar Appeal Manual, 1982; editor Mich. Bar Jour., 1984—; contbr. articles to profl. jours. Founder, pres. Sixty Plus Law Ctr., Lansing, 1978-87, bd. dirs., 1987—; mem. community adv. bd. Lansing Jr. League, 1983-90; co-founder, dir., sec.-treas. John D. Voelker Found., 1989—; bd. dirs. Lansing chpt. ACLU, 1997—, bd. dirs. Greater Lansing chpt., 1997-99; treas. Kehillat Israel, 1996-98; trustee Thoman Found., 2000—. Recipient Disting. Brief award T.M. Cooley Law Rev., 1988, 99. Fellow Mich. State Bar Found.; mem. ABA (Outstanding Single Project award 1980), Mich. Bar Assn. (vice chmn. jour. adv. bd. 1984-87, chmn. jour. adv. bd. 1987—, young lawyers sect. coun. 1980-84, grievance com. 1982-84, John W. Cummiskey award 1984), Ingham County Bar Assn. (Disting. Vol. award 2000). Clubs: Big Oak (Baldwin, Mich.). Unitarian Universalist. Avocations: photography, fishing, running, frisbee, squash. Home: 5127 Barton Rd Williamston MI 48895-9304 Office: Honigman Miller Schwartz & Cohn 222 N Washington Sq Ste 400 Lansing MI 48933-1800 E-mail: fmb@honigman.com.

BAKER, GARY HUGH, lawyer; b. Broken Arrow, Okla., Nov. 18, 1947; s. Theodore Roosevelt and Maxine Gladys (Smittle) Baker; m. Karen Louise DeLong, Aug. 29, 1970; 1 child, Katherine Elizabeth. BA with highest honors, U. Okla., 1970; JD, U. Chgo., 1973. Bar: Okla. 1973, U.S. Dist. Cts. (no., we. and ea. dists.) Okla. 1973, U.S. Ct. Appeals (10th cir.) 1975, Fla. 2001. With Conner, Winters, Ballaine, Barry & McGowen Assocs., Tulsa, 1973—79, ptnr., 1979—81, Baker & Hoster, 1981—97; dir. Crowe & Dunlevy, Tulsa, 1997—99, Legal Svc. Eastern Okla., Tulsa, 1980—84; gen. counsel 800 Travel Sys., Inc., 2001—02; mng. dir. Equus XI, LLC, 2002—. Mem. Citzen's coalition for Cmty. Devel., Tulsa, 1980. Mem.: Okla. Bar Assn. (banking com. 1981—), Tulsa County Young Lawyers Assn. (chmn. 1979), Tulsa County Bar Assn. (sec. 1981, Outstanding Young Lawyer award 1979). Office: 2101 Sussex Ct Palm Harbor FL 34683

BAKER, GEORGE CHISHOLM, engineering executive, consultant; b. Dartmouth, N.S., Can., Oct. 29, 1918; s. Clifford Lyall and Edith (Chisholm) B.; m. Ethel Marie Suzanne Humbert, Jan. 2, 1942; children: Alison Marie, Catherine Ann. Diploma, Royal Mil. Coll. Can., 1939, D Engring. (hon.), 1988; BA in Sci., Toronto U., 1946; D Engring. (hon.), Tech. Coll. N.S., 1987; DCL, Acadia U., 1993. Registered profl engr., Can. Pres. Kentville (N.S.) Pub. Co. Ltd., 1948-77; engr. Kentville Electric Commn., 1960-81; exec. v.p. Tidal Power Corp., Halifax, N.S., 1971-89; pres. G.C. Baker Engring. Ltd., Kentville, 1977—. Chmn. Cam Pubs. Ltd., New Glasgow, N.S., 1978-2002. Contbr. numerous articles to profl. pubs. Chmn. Acadia U. Inst., Wolfville, N.S., 1968-70; gov. Acadia U., Wolfville, 1979-92. Maj. Signal Corps Royal Can. Army, 1939-46. Decorated Order of Brit. Empire, Order of Can. Fellow Engring. Inst. Can., Can. Acad. Engring.; mem. IEEE (Centennial Gold medal). Office: G C Baker Engring Ltd 536 Main St Kentville NS Canada B4N 1L3

BAKER, GEORGE HAROLD, III, physicist; b. Cheverly, Md., Mar. 23, 1949; s. George Harold Jr. and Betty (Fost) B.; m. Donna Prillaman, Jun 21, 1975; children: Matthew C., Jeffrey P., Virginia E. BA, Western Md. Coll., 1971; MS, U. Va., 1974; PhD, USAF Inst. Tech., Dayton, Ohio, 1987. Teaching asst. U. Va., Charlottesville, 1971-73; physicist Harry Diamond Labs., Adelphi, Md., 1973-77, Def. Nuclear Agy., Alexandria, 1977-87, group leader, 1987-89, asst. for program devel., 1989-94; chief innovative concepts divsn., 1994-96; Def. Threat Reduction Agy. dir. Springfield (Va.) Rsch. Facility, 1996-99; sr. scientist Logicon, Alexandria, Va., 1999-2000; assoc. prof. James Madison U., 1999—, dir. Inst. for Infrastructure and Info. Assurance, 2002—03. Def. cons., 2000—. Contbr. articles to profl. jours. Tchr. Agape Christian Fellowship, Chantilly, Va., 1974-94, elder, 1994-2000; music and youth leader New Life Fellowship, Annandale, Va., 1979-83; canvasser Citizens for Sensible County Planning, Fairfax County, Va., 1989-2000. Fellow: Nuc. Electromagnetic Soc. (chmn. program com. 1984, co-chair non-proliferation and arms control underground focus group 1996—99, session chair 1998, chmn. nat. HPM conf. steering group 1999, session chair 2002, mem. nat. com. 2001—); mem.: IEEE (session chmn. 1987, 1992), Forum for Mil. Application of Directed Energy, Directed Energy Profl. Soc. (charter), Assn. Old Crows, Phi Delta Theta. Achievements include patent for optically coupled differential voltage sensor, 1976; co-developer sea-going nuclear EMP simulator concept, 1979; initiated Def. Nuclear Agy. EMP underground test program, 1983, High Power Microwave program, 1984, space nuclear power, 1994. Office: Coll Integrated Sci and Tech James Madison U MSC 4102 Harrisonburg VA 22807

BAKER, GEORGE R. insurance industry executive; Pres., CEO Reliance Group Holdings Inc., N.Y.C., 2000—. Office: Reliance Group Holdings Park Ave Plz 55 E 52d St New York NY 10055

BAKER, GEORGE S. federal official; b. Green's Harbour, Nfld., Can., Sept. 4, 1942; Chief clk., asst. clk., chief law clk., chief legis. libr. Nfld. Ho. Assembly, editor Hansard; elected mem. Ho. of Commons, 1974, chmn. standing com. on fisheries and oceans, mem. fin. com., trade and econs. affairs com., fisheries and forestry com., environment com.; parliamentary sec. Mins. Fisheries, Transp., Environment and Nat. Revenue; min. vets. affairs, sec. state Atlantic Can. Opportunities Agy., 1999. Past chmn. Atlantic Caucus; past mem. Exec. Caucus. Office: Min Vets Affairs 101 Colonel By Dr Ottawa ON Canada K1A OK2

BAKER, GEORGE WALTER, lawyer; b. N.Y.C., Apr. 25, 1948; s. George W. and Una (O'Reilly) B.; m. Susan Keane, Sept. 5, 1981; children: Jane, Thomas. BA, Columbia U., 1969, JD, 1973. Bar: Conn. 1973. Ptnr. Bentley Mosher & Babson, Stamford, Conn., 1973-94, Hawthorne Ackerly & Dorrance, New Canaan, Conn., 1994—. Atty. trial referee Superior Ct., 2000—. Host (TV series) New Canaan Roundtable, Channel 79. Councilman Town of New Canaan, 1989—; founder, dir. Laurel House, Inc., Stamford, Conn., 1983-93; mem. vestry St. Mark's Parish, New Canaan, Conn., 2003—. Mem. Conn. Bar Assn., New Canaan Rotary Club (pres. 1993-94). Democrat. Episcopalian. Avocation: playing the piano. Office: Hawthorne Ackerly & Dorrance 25 South Ave New Canaan CT 06840-5485 E-mail: GWBaker@aol.com.

BAKER, GORDON EDWARD, political science educator; b. Poughkeepsie, N.Y., Dec. 6, 1923; s. Gordon Denzil and Emma (Calhoun) B.; m. June Sharpe, Sept. 2, 1947; children: Jefferson, Leslie Marie. BA, Reed Coll., 1948; MA, U. Wash., 1949; postgrad., Brown U., 1950; PhD, Princeton U., 1952. Mem. faculty U. Calif., Santa Barbara, 1952—, prof. polit. sci., 1965-93, chmn. dept., 1965-71, prof. emeritus, 1993—. Dir. NEH seminars, 1979, 80; spl. cons., Calif., 1973, 91. Author: Rural Versus Urban Political Power, 1955, The Reapportionment Revolution, 1966; co-author: Free Government in the Making, 1985; contbr. chpts. in books and articles to profl. jours. Mem. 20th Century Fund Conf. Rsch. Scholars and Polit. Scientists in Legis. Apportionment, 1962. Served with AUS, 1943-46. Guggenheim fellow, 1969; Social Sci. Rsch. Coun. faculty rsch. fellow, 1962. Mem. Am. Polit. Sci. Assn. (coun. 1968-70, exec. com. 1968-69), Nat. Mcpl. League. Office: U Calif at Santa Barbara Dept Polit Sci Santa Barbara CA 93106

BAKER, GRANT CODY, civil engineering educator; b. Eugene, Oreg., May 16, 1956; s. Irwin Gerald and Louise (Powell) B.; m. Tina Louise Denton, Apr. 9, 1988; children: Jessica, Calvin, Benjamin. BSChemE, U. Wash., 1978; MS in Mining Engring., U. Alaska, 1983, PhD in Geophysics, 1987. Chem. engr. UOP, Chgo., 1978-79; comml. fisherman F/V Patricia Sue, Anchorage, 1979-80; asst. prof. mech. engring. U. Alaska, Fairbanks, 1988-94, asst. prof. civil engring. Anchorage, 1994—2002, assoc. prof. civil engring., 2002—. Author, pub. Edutech, Anchorage, 1992—. Author: Bridge to Engineering, 1993, FORTRAN Reference Programs, 1995, ANSI C Reference Programs, 1996, BASIC Reference Programs, 1996, ANSI C++ Reference Programs, 1998. Named Engring. Prof. of Yr., 1993, 94, 96, 97, U. Alaska student chpt. ASME, ASCE. Republican. Baptist. Avocation: walking with family. Home: PO Box 240986 Anchorage AK 99524-0986 Office: U Alaska 3211 Providence Dr Anchorage AK 99508-4614 E-mail: baker@alaska.net.

BAKER, HARRISON SCOTT, computer consultant; b. Marion, Ohio, Mar. 12, 1950; s. Stanley Wallace and Starling (Dixon) Baker. BA, BS, Fla. State U., 1972, 80; MBA, Embry-Riddle Aeronaut. U., 1986. MCSE, cert. computing tech. Computing Tech. Industry Assn., Cisco network assoc.; lic. radiotelephone with radar endorsement FCC. Mgr. Vincent Auto Parts, Inc., Marathon, Fla., 1972-78; maintenance supr. Ea. Air Lines, Inc., Miami, 1980-92; computer cons. Upper Sandusky, Ohio, 1992—. Author: Index to the Muster Rolls of PA in War of 1812, 1995, Early Settlers of Wyandot County, 1995; indexer: Obituaries in Upper Sandusky newspapers 1868-1911, 1994, Obituaries in Upper Sandusky newspapers 1912-1937, 1996, Obituaries in Upper Sandusky newspaper 1938-1958, 1997, Obituaries in Upper Sandusky newspapers 1959-1979, 1997, Journal of William Kennedy Beall, 1999, Civil War Soldiers Buried in Wyandot County, Ohio, 2000, Civil War Veterans Buried at the Ohio Veterans Home, 2001. Trustee Wyandot County Geneaol. Soc., 1995-2001. Mem. SAR (pres. Hancock chpt. 1995-96), IEEE Computer Soc., Assn. Computing Machinery, Soc. War of 1812 (Ohio pres. 1996-99), Sons of Union Vets. (camp sec. 1994-98, Dept. of Ohio signals officer 1999-2000, nat. chief of staff 2002—), Sons of Vets. Res. (capt., pub. info. officer 2000—), Sons of Union Vets. (nat. chief of staff, 2002—). Avocations: electronics, genealogy. Home: PO Box 411 Upper Sandusky OH 43351-0411 E-mail: hsbaker@udata.com.

BAKER, HELEN DOYLE PEIL, realtor; b. Los Angeles, June 26, 1943; d. James Cyril and Jacqueline (White) Doyle; m. Gary Edward Peil, Aug. 5, 1967 (dec. May 6, 1969); children: Andrea Christine, Kevin Doyle; m. Nathaniel W. Baker, Jr., Jan. 1, 1971 (div. July 23, 1983). AA, Santa Monica Coll., 1963; postgrad., U. Wash., 1963-64. Licensed real estate agent; cert. domestic violence counselor. Sales, mgmt. trainee Saks Fifth Ave., Beverly Hills, Calif., 1958-63; flight attendant Am. Airlines, Los Angeles, 1964-67; realtor, assoc. Stapleton Assocs., Honolulu, 1978-80; realtor Dolman Assocs. Inc., Kailua, Hawaii, 1980-87; loan rep. Honolulu Mortgage Co., Kailua, 1986-87; pres., owner, realtor Helen Baker Properties, Inc., Honolulu, 1987-93; v.p. Internat. Property Investment, Inc., Honolulu, 1993-94; owner Property Investment Internat., 1994—; loan officer Western Pacific Mortgage, Inc., 1999—. Pres. Global Listing Svc. Hawaii Inc., 1990-96. Dir. Kailua Community Coun., 1987-91; pres., v.p., sec. Aikahi Community Assn., Kailua, 1980-85; vol. Am. Cancer Soc., Heart Assn. Schs., Kailua, 1971-86; adv. spouse abuse shelter, 1995-98. Mem. C. of C., Windward Spouse Abuse Coalition, Rotary. Avocations: tennis, fitness workout, reading, travel, music. Office: Property Investment Internat PO Box 37066 Honolulu HI 96837-0066 E-mail: propinvst@hawaii.rr.com.

BAKER, HENRY S., JR., retired banker; b. Balt., June 10, 1926; s. Henry S. and Frances (Robinson) B.; m. Marian Stockton Towsend, June 12, 1948; children— Frances, Sandra, Stockton. BA, Johns Hopkins U., 1950; grad. with honors, Grad. Sch. Banking, Rutgers U., 1957. With Md. Nat. Bank, Balt., 1950-86, sr. exec. v.p., 1973-86. Chmn. Redwood Capital Mgmt. Co., AAA Md., Ins. Agy. Inc., 1983-90, Ind. Coll. Fund Md., 1984-89; v.p., bd. dirs. Manab Properties. Chmn. Md. chpt. Nature Conservancy, 1984-90; chmn. investment com. Kennedy Inst. for Handicapped Children, 1985-88, Episcopal Diocese Md., 1974-80; trustee, treas. Garrison Forest Sch., 1962-88, St. Paul's Sch. for Girls, 1968-77; pres. Jr. Achievement Met. Balt., 1971, Florence Crittenden Home, 1964-66; bd. dirs. Keswick, Home for Incurables, 1965, 1991, 1979; gen. campaign chmn. United Way Cen. Md., 1979. With USNR, 1944-46. Mem. Assn. Res. City Bankers, Md. Bankers Assn. (pres.), Md. State C. of C. (treas., dir.) Republican.

BAKER, HERMAN, medical educator, author; b. N.Y.C., Jan. 22, 1926; s. Harry and Fannie Baker; m. Shirley Levitz, Nov. 15, 1952; children: Elliott Robert, Joel Martin. BS, CCNY, 1946; MS, Emory U., 1948; PhD, NYU, 1956. Cert. specialist human nutrition Am. Bd. Nutrition. Research asst. Columbia U., N.Y.C., 1949-50; research assoc. Mt. Sinai Hosp., N.Y.C., 1950-60; assoc. prof. medicine N.J. Med. Sch., Jersey City, 1960-70, prof. medicine and preventive medicine Newark, 1970—. Contbr. over 280 articles on metabolic imbalances to profl. jours.; author: Clinical Vitaminology: Methods and Interpretation. Fellow: Am. Coll. Nutrition. Avocation: music. Home: 27 Wilk Rd Edison NJ 08837-2726 Office: NJ Med Sch Martland GB 159 65 Bergen St Newark NJ 07107-3001

BAKER, HERMAN DUPREE, lawyer; b. Statham, Ga., Apr. 18, 1928; s. William Grady and Mary O. (Gauntt) B.; m. Esther May Deal, May 17, 1953; children: Cynthia Jane Buchanan, Gloria Ann Baker Fondren, Joyce Hazel. AB, Mercer U., 1949, JD, 1952. Bar: Ga. 1965. Investigator U.S. Civil Svc. Commn., Augusta, Ga., 1953-59; asst. v.p. claims Pub. Savs. Ins. Co., Charleston, S.C., 1960-63; criminal investigator IRS, Atlanta, 1963-69, estate tax atty., 1969-76, appeals officer, 1976-86; pvt. practice probate and tax atty., 1986—. Chmn. fin. com., 1st Bapt. Ch., Decatur, Ga., 1982—. Served to comdr. USNR, 1945-46, PTO. Mem. Fed. Bar, State Bar Ga. Home: 2285 Winding Woods Dr Tucker GA 30084-3934 Office: 545 N McDonough St Ste 201 Decatur GA 30030 Fax: 404-377-8304. E-mail: hdbaker700@aol.com.

BAKER, HOLLIS MACLURE, furniture manufacturing company executive; b. Allegan, Mich., Apr. 27, 1916; s. Hollis Siebe and Ruth (MacClure) B.; m. Betty Jane Brown, Aug. 2, 1947; children: Tomelyn Ann, Susan MacClure. Student, U. Va., 1935-37. With Baker Furniture, Inc., Holland, Mich., 1938-40, 45-73, v.p., treas., 1959-61, pres., 1961-70, chmn. bd., 1970-73; v.p., gen. mgr. Grand Rapids Chair Co., Mich., 1959-61, pres., 1961-70. V.p., dir. Manor House, Inc., N.Y.C., 1958-70; pres. Boyne City R.R. Co., Mich., 400 Bldg. Corp., Palm Beach, Fla.; dir. Mich. Nat. Bank, Lansing, 1968-83, Am. Seating Co., Grand Rapids, 1973-83, Mich. Nat. Bank, Grand Rapids, 1959-84, Norton Gallery, Palm Beach, 1984-91. Author: A Brief History of Schloss Branzoll, 1975, A History of the Chateau de Caussade, 1980, A History of the Chateau de la Roque, 1985, Five Castles Are Enough, 1989. Bd. dirs. USCG Found., 1981-91. Lt. (s.g.) USNR, 1941-45. Mem. Nat. Assn. Furniture Mfrs. (dir.), Furniture Mfrs. Assn. Grand Rapids (dir., past pres 1970-84), Zeta Psi. Clubs: Brook (N.Y.C.), River (N.Y.C.), New York Yacht (N.Y.C.), Leash (N.Y.C.); Kent Country (Grand Rapids), University (Grand Rapids), Indian (Grand Rapids), Peninsular (Grand Rapids); Everglades (Palm Beach), Bath and Tennis (Palm Beach); Buck's (London). Episcopalian. Home: 301 Chapel Hill Rd Palm Beach FL 33480-4124 Office: 2220 Wealthy St Grand Rapids MI 49506

BAKER, HOWARD HENRY, JR., ambassador, former senator, lawyer; b. Huntsville, Tenn., Nov. 15, 1925; s. Howard Henry and Dora (Ladd) B.; m. Joy Dirksen, Dec. 22, 1951 (dec. 1993); children: Darek Dirksen, Cynthia; m. Nancy Landon Kassebaum, Dec. 7, 1996. Student, U. of South, Tulane U.; LLB, U. Tenn., 1949. U.S. senator from, Tenn., 1967-85; minority leader, 1977-81; majority leader, 1981-85; ptnr. Vinson & Elkins, Washington, 1985-87; chief of staff Office of the Pres. U.S., Washington, 1987-88; ptnr. Baker, Worthington, Crossley, Stansberry & Woolf, Knoxville, Tenn., 1985-87, 88-95, Baker, Donelson, Bearman & Caldwell, Washington, 1995—2000; amb. to Japan Tokyo, 2001—. Bd. dirs. Pennzoil Co.; chmn. bd. dirs. Cherokee Aviations; mem. internat. adv. bd. Barrick Gold Corp. Bd. regents Smithsonian Instn. Office: US Embassy 1--10-1 Akasaka Minato-ku Tokyo 107 Japan*

BAKER, IAN ARCHBALD, explorer, educator, writer, photographer; b. N.Y.C., Dec. 10, 1957; s. John Milnes and Virginia Lea Busser Baker. BA in Art History cum laude, Middlebury Coll., 1980; MA in English Lit., Oxford U., 1985; postgrad., Columbia U. Field work Explorer's Club N.Y., India, Sikkim, and Nepal, 1981-82; acad. dir. semester abroad programs Sch. Internat. Tng., Brattleboro, Vt., 1983-90; freelance writer, photographer, 1993—. Tour leader Smithsonian Instn., Boston Mus. Fine Arts, Distant Horizons; rsch. assoc. Found. Shamanic Studies; acad. advisor U. Wis., 1985-93; cons. Tibetan and Himalayan art Togendo Collection, Kyoto, Japan, 1990-92; founder Red Panda Expdns., Ltd., 1993—; leader rsch. expdns. in Namche Barwa-Tsangpo gorge region of Tibet, 1993-98. Author: The Tibetan Art of Healing with foreword by Dalai Lama, 1997, The Dalai Lamas' Secret Temple: Wall Paintings from the Lukhang with forword by the Dalai Lama, 2000, Celestial Gallery, 2000; co-author: Tibet: Reflections from the Wheel of Life with foreword by Dalai Lama, 1993; co-prodr. (documentary film) Buddhist Hunters of Tsangpo Gorge, 1998; contbr. writings and photography to mags., books in Holland, France, Germany, U.S., Britain. Nat. Merit fellow Columbia U., 1990; Presdl. scholar Bread Loaf Sch. English, Lincoln Coll., Oxford U., 1985; selected by Rolex Awards for Enterprise for explorator rsch. in field of Himalayan sacred geography, 1990, named one of seven explorers for the millennium, Natl.

Geographic Soc., 1999. Mem. The St. Nicholas Soc. N.Y., Colonial Lords of Manors in Am., The Explorers Club (Internat. fellow 1997, Rsch. grantee 1980). Achievements include leading Natl. Geographic Soc. expedition into Tsangpo Gorge's previously unexplored section and documented and measured 110' high falls that had previously been only subject of speculation. Named it Hidden Falls of Dorje Phagmo, 1998. Home: GPO Box 1373 Kathmandu Nepal Address: 85 Girdle Ridge Rd Katonah NY 10536-3814 Fax: 914-232-7306; 9771-423391., 914-232-7306. E-mail: ianbaker@mos.com.np.

BAKÉR, J. A., II, emeritus, executive management advisor and consultant, monetary architect, financial engineer; b. N.Y.C., Dec. 12, 1944; s. Leonard Ernest and Miriam Violet (Roché) B. Postgrad. in fin. svcs. mgmt., The Am. Coll., 1994—. ChFC, CLU, fin. planning advisor, property/casualty/liability field underwriter, comml. and personal lines; cert. instr., Monitor continuing and profl. edn.; cert. in advanced mgmt. Cons. mgr. Life Ins., N.Y.C., 1964-79; supr. Physician's Planning Group, Atty.'s Planning Svc., Bus. Planning Svcs., Profl. Svc. Corp., N.Y.C., 1979-81; chief satisfaction officer J A L B Enterprises, East Garden City, NY, 1980—91, emeritus, 1991—. Monitor N.Y. State continuing edn. program, 1996-, instr. continuing profl. edn. program, 1996-99, licensing courses, 1996-99. Bd. dirs. Medic Alert, Nassau County, N.Y., 1985-87; rep. The Living Bank, Houston; nominated mem.: Citizen Ambassador Program Internat. Recipient Cert. of Appreciation, VWF D.C., 2002. Fellow Life Underwriters Coun.; mem. Nat. Assn. Life Underwriters (emeritus, pres. Cortland N.Y. chpt. 1974-75, legis. chair 1972-74, v.p. pub. info. Nassau County 1980-87, instr. Bklyn. 1987-90, Queens 1991-92), Am. Automobile Assn., Am. Coun. Ind. Life Underwriters, Soc. Fin. Svc. Profls., N.Y.C. Life Underwriters Assn., Fraternal Order of Police, N.Y.C. Civil Svc. Ret. Employee Assn., Gen. Agts. Mgrs. Assn. Internat. (charter mem.), United Assn. Entrepreneurs N.Y.C., Jaycees (past dir.), Sovereign Mil. Order of Malta (pilgrim 1999), Am. Assn., Nat. Orgn. for Men, Smithsonian Inst. Assn. (nat. assoc.), The Srs. Coalition. Office: J A L B Enterprises PMB #2053 630 Olde Country Rd East Garden City NY 11531-9998

BAKER, JACK SHERMAN, architect, designer, educator; b. Champaign, Ill., Aug. 8, 1920; s. Clyde Lee and Jane Cecilia (Walker) B. BA with honors, U Ill., 1943, MS, 1949; cert., N.Y. Beaux Art Inst. Design, 1943. Aero engr., designer Boeing Aircraft, Seattle, 1943-44; assoc. Atkins, Barrow & Lasswith, Urbana, 1947-50; pvt. practice architecture Champaign, 1947—; mem. faculty U. Ill., Urbana, 1947—, prof. architecture, 1950-90, acting prof. emeritus, 1990—. Former mem. exec. com. Sch. Architecture, U. Ill.; hon. bd. dirs. Gerhart Music Festival, Guntersville, Ala., Stravinsky awards, Champaign, Conservatory of Cen. Ill.; hon. bd. dirs. Ruth Hindman Found., Huntsville, Ala., dir., performer personal performance loft space for Interaction of the Arts and Architecture, 1960—; participant U. Ill. Exploring the Arts course (Act-NCEA award), 1970—, campus honors program, 1995—; former mem. Chancellor's com. on graphic design and art acquisition and installation, former mem. adv. bd., designer of exhbn., Krannert Mus., U. Ill., engr. basic, Ft. Leonard Wood, Mo., topog. engr., Ft. Blevoir, Va. Exhibitions include watercolors, archtl. drawings and photography, Monograph and Retrospective Arch. Exhibit: "I" Space Gallery, Chgo., 1997, U. Ill. Temple Buell Arch. Gallery, 1998, Temple Buell Hall Gallery, 2000, Japanese House Drawings Exhibit, Krannert Art Mus., U. Ill., 1998; contbr. articles to numerous jours. and confs. Mem. U. Ill. Pres.'s Coun., U. Ill. Bronze Cir., 1986; mem. mus. bd. and affiliate World Heritage Mus.; former mem. adv. bd. Krannert Ctr. for Performing Arts, Assembly Hall U. Ill.; exhbn. designer World Heritage Mus., U. Ill. Served with U.S. Army, AFH, 1945-46, Caserta, Italy, ETO. Recipient "prix d'Emulation Societe des Architectes Diplomes par le Gouvernment" Beaux-Arts medal, 1942, cert. for dedicated and disting. svc., Nat. AIA Com. on Environ. and Design, 1955, Decade of Achievement award, World Heritage Mus., 1992, Art and Humanities award medal, 1981, Art and Humanities award and medal, 1982, Honor award for advancing profession architecture, CIC/AIA, 1983, Excellence in Edn. award and medal, IC/AIA, 1989, Heritage award, PACA, 1997, numerous other honors and design excellence awards in field, Recognition award, U. Ill. Found., 2001. Fellow: AIA (medal 1977), Nat. Coun. Archtl. Registration Bds. (cert.); mem.: Soc. Archtl. Historians, Ill. Coun./AIA, The Nature Conservancy, Nat. Resources Def. Coun., Gargoyle, Scarab, Cliff Dwellers Club (Chgo.), Alpha Rho Chi. Home: 71 1/2 E Chester St Champaign IL 61820-4149 Office: U Ill 117 Temple Hoyne Buell Hall 611 Taft Dr MC-621 Champaign IL 61820-6922

BAKER, JACK THOMAS, design engineer, environmental scientist, consultant; b. Nov. 7, 1924; s. George J. and Oneta L. Baker; m. Sylvia E. Tofte, July 1, 1971; children: Frances, Robert, Catherine, Cynthia, Christine, Jason, Justin. BS, U.S. Maritime Acad., 1945; ME, Stevens Inst. Tech., 1949. Design engr. Miller Mercurial Svcs., 1965—74; cons. design engr. Sebco Mfg. Co., Greenwich, N.Y., 1974—. V.p., gen. mgr. Universal Convection Corp., pres., chief exec. officer; cons. in field. Author articles on waste energy recovery. Achievements include patents for energy recovery and the environment.

BAKER, JAMES A. lawyer, former state supreme court justice; b. Evansville, Ind., Mar. 30, 1931; BBA, So. Meth. U., 1953, LLB, 1958. Bar: Tex. 1958, U.S. Dist. Ct. (no. dist.) Tex. 1958, U.S. Ct. Appeals (5th cir.) 1961, U.S. Ct. Appeals (11th cir.) 1981, U.S. Supreme Ct. 1980. Atty. Goldberg, Alexander and Baker, 1958-72, Weber, Baker and Allums, 1972-79; prin. Law Office of James A. Baker, 1979-86; judge U.S. Ct. Appeals (5th cir.), Dallas, 1986-95; justice Supreme Ct. of Tex., Austin, 1995—2002; atty. Hughes & Luce, LLP, 2002—. Lectr. State Bar of Tex. Profl. Devel. Program; guest lectr. So. Meth. U. Sch. Law, Dallas Bar Assn., El Centro Dalls C.C. Contbg. author Tex. Collection Manual, 1980. Fellow Tex. Bar Found., Dallas Bar Found.; mem. ABA (mem. task force on appellate delay reduction 1991-92), State Bar Tex., Dallas Bar Assn. (former chair bankruptcy and comml. law sect. 1974, bd. dirs. 1995), Coll. of State Bar Tex., Am. Judicature Soc., Inst. Judicial Adminstrn., William Mac Taylor Jr. Inn of Ct.*

BAKER, JAMES BARNES, architect; b. N.Y.C., Feb. 18, 1933; s. William Edgar and Violet (Twachtman) B.; children: Mary Morgan, James Edgar, Catriona Griswold, Frederick Alden; m. Rosemary Burgis, June 14, 1997 (dec. 2001). AB, Princeton U., 1954; M.Arch., Yale U., 1960. With firms Blake & Neski, N.Y.C., 1960-62, George Lewis, N.Y.C., 1962-63, Kahn & Jacobs, N.Y.C., 1963-61; ptnr. firm Baker & Blake, N.Y.C., 1964-72, Baker/Grinnell, N.Y.C., 1972-74; cons., 1974-77; dir. Llewelyn Davies Assocs., N.Y.C., 1976-78; pres. Tower Devel. Group Inc., Ohio, 1978-83, Park-Tower Devel. Co., Ltd., Bermuda, 1978-83, Springland Assocs. Inc., 1983-90; prin. Baker & Baker, Architects, N.Y.C., 1990—; pres. Tech. Panel Systems, 1992-93; mng. dir. William McDonough Archs., 1993-94, Forge Co., N.Y.C., 2002; chief exec. Forge Llewellyn, London, 2003. Vis. prof. Sch. Architecture, CUNY, 1964-89. Trustee Darrow Sch., Mt. Lebanon Shaker Village. Recipient design awards HUD, others. Fellow AIA (bd. dirs., design awards); mem. Am. Arbitration Assn., Holland Soc., St. Nicholas Soc., Squadron A. Home: North Family Forge PO Box 98 New Lebanon NY 12125-0098 also: 105-109 Strand London WC2R 0AA England

BAKER, JAMES EDWARD, city planner; b. San Antonio, Tex., Aug. 4, 1961; s. Jim and Dora Pitts B. BA, BBA, BFA, So. Meth. U., 1983; MS, Trinity U., San Antonio, Tex., 1995; MS, U. Tex., 1997; postgrad., U. Phoenix Online, 2001—. Tech. writer II JANA, Inc., San Antonio, 1985-86; adminstrv. asst. United Svcs. Automobile Assn., San Antonio, 1987-89; Brackenridge fellow Trinity U., San Antonio, 1993-95; HUD fellow U. Tex., Austin, 1995-97; city planner City of New Braunfels, Tex., 1997-2000; devel. planner City of Georgetown, Tex., 2000; sr. planner City of Dallas, Tex., 2001—. Mem. emerging leaders program Nat. Congress Cmty. Econ. Devel., 2001. With U.S. Army, 1989—93, with USAR, 1993—. Decorated Army Commendation medal (x3), Army Achievement medal (x3), Kuwait Liberation medal, Joint Svc. Achievement medal, Joint Meritorious Unit award. Mem. Am. Inst. Cert. Planners, Kiwanis, Prince Hall Freemasons, Delta Sigma Phi (pres. Lambda chpt. 1981-82). Avocations: outdoor photography, wing chun, weight ting. Office: City of Dallas Plan & Devel Bldg Inspect Divsn Rm 105 Dallas TX 75203-2632 E-mail: jebaker@mail.ci.dallas.tx.us.

BAKER, JAMES EDWARD SPROUL, retired lawyer; b. Evanston, Ill., May 23, 1912; s. John Clark and Hester (Sproul) B.; m. Eleanor Lee Dodgson, Oct. 2, 1937 (dec. Sept. 1972); children: John Lee, Edward Graham (dec. Aug. 1988). AB, Northwestern U., 1933, JD, 1936. Bar: Ill. 1936, U.S. Supreme Ct. 1957. Practice in, Chgo., 1936—; assoc. Sidley & Austin, and predecessors, 1936—48, ptnr., 1948—81; of counsel Sidley Austin Brown and Wood, 1981—93. Lectr. Northwestern U. Law Sch., 1951-52; nat. chmn. Stanford U. Parents Com., 1970-75; mem. vis. com. Stanford Law Sch., 1976-79, 82-84, Northwestern U. Law Sch., 1980-89, DePaul U. Law Sch., 1982-87. Served to comdr. USNR, 1941-46. Fellow: Am. Coll. Trial Lawyers (regent 1974—81, sec. 1977—79, pres. 1979—80); mem.: ABA, Soc. Trial Lawyers Ill., Chgo. Bar Assn., Ill. State Bar Assn., Bar Assn. 7th Fed. Cir., Northwestern U. Law Alumni Assn. (past pres.), Pauma Valley Country Club (Calif.), Lawyers Club (Chgo.), Univ. Club (Chgo.), John Evans Club (chmn. 1982—85, Northwestern U.), John Henry Wigmore Club (past pres.), Law Club (pres. 1983—85, Chgo.), Westmoreland Country Club (Wilmette, Ill.), Sigma Nu, Phi Lambda Upsilon, Order of Coif. Republican. Methodist. Home: 1300 N Lake Shore Dr Chicago IL 60610-2167 Office: Sidley Austin Brown & Wood Bank One Plz 10 S Dearborn St Chicago IL 60603

BAKER, JAMES GUY, health facility administrator; b. Corona, Calif., Oct. 28, 1955; s. James Asa and Rita Phillips Baker; m. Janet Claire Nichols, Dec. 29, 1979; 1 child, Sarah Elizabeth. BS in Chemistry, U. Okla., 1977, MS in Chemistry, 1978; MD, U. Okla., Oklahoma City, 1982; MBA, Houston Bapt. U., 1999. Cert. psychiatry Am. Bd. Psychiatry and Neurology, 1989, child and adolescent psychiatry Am. Bd. Psychiatry and Neurology, 1991. Child and adolescent psychiatrist, 1987—94; med. dir. adult mental health Mental Health Authority of Harris County, Houston, 1994—99; med. dir. Magellan Health Tex., Dallas, 1999—2000, Dallas Metrocare Svcs., 2000—02, CEO, 2002—. Contbr. articles to profl. jours. Named Exemplary Psychiatrist, Nat. Alliance for the Mentally Ill, 1999. Fellow: Am. Psychiat. Assn.; mem.: AMA, Am. Acad. Child and Adolescent Psychiatry. Office: Dallas Metrocare Svcs 1380 Riverbend Dr Dallas TX 75427 Office Fax: 214-630-3469. E-mail: jbaker@dallasmetrocare.com.

BAKER, JEAN HARVEY, history educator; b. Balt., Feb. 9, 1933; d. F. Barton and Rose (Lindsay) Hopkins Harvey; m. R. Robinson Baker, Sept. 12, 1953; children— Susan Dixon, Robinson Scott, Robert W., Jean Harvey. AB, Goucher Coll., Towson, Md., 1961; MA, Johns Hopkins U., Balt., 1965, PhD, 1971. Lectr., instr. history Notre Dame Coll., Balt., 1967-69; instr. history Goucher Coll., Balt., 1969, asst. prof. history, 1969-75, assoc. prof. history, 1975-78, prof. history, 1979-82, Elizabeth Todd prof. history, 1981—. Author: The Politics of Continuity, 1973, Ambivalent Americans, 1976, Affairs of Party, 1983, Maryland: A History, Mary Todd Lincoln: A Biography, 1986, The Stevensons: A Family Biography, 1995; co-author: Civil War and Reconstruction, 2002; editor: Md. Hist. Mag., 1979, Votes for Women: The Suffrage Battle Revisited, 2001. Am. Coun. Learned Socs. fellow, 1976, NEH fellow, 1982, Newberry Libr. fellow, 1991, Rockefeller Ctr. fellow, 1998; recipient Faculty Teaching prize Goucher Coll., 1979, Willie Lee Rose prize in Southern history, 1989. Mem. Orgn. Am. Historians, Am. Hist. Assn., Berkshire Conf. Women Historians, Phi Beta Kappa. Democrat. Home: 8717 Mcdonogh Rd Baltimore MD 21208-1021 Office: Goucher Coll History Dept Towson MD 21204 E-mail: jbaker@goucher.edu.

BAKER, JOANNE EVELYN, retired government official; b. Crucible, Pa., Dec. 1, 1933; d. George Joseph and Anna Leona (Kagle) Cormack; m. Warren Clair Baker, July 7, 1956 (dec. May 1968); m. James Lewis Wilson, June 2, 1970; (div. Sept. 1984); former stepchildren: James Lloyd, John Thomas, Charles Edward, Debra Ruth, Jeff Lee Wilson Cert. applied music, Waynesburg Coll., 1951. Various clerical positions including Exec. Offices Pres., Washington, 1951-66; supr. USN, Washington, 1966-71; pres., treas. Little Round Top Farm, Inc., Gettysburg, Pa., 1971-86; logistician USN-U.S. Army, Gettysburg, Pa., 1974—90, ret., 1990. Program mgr. electronic comm. end items and for Ship Alterations (SHIPALT), 1974-77, Ship Parts Control Ctr. (SPCC), Mechanicsburg, Pa., Army Stock Fund, program mgr., 1977-80, 84-90, chief consolidated property account (CPA), 1980-81, U.S. Army Garrison (USAG), Ft. Ritchie, Md.; insp. Office of Insp. Gen. 7th Signal Command, U.S. Army, Ft. Ritchie, Md., 1981-84; chief supply and svcs. divsn., 1984-89, chief plans and resources mgmt. divsn., 1989-90; logistics directorate USAG, Ft. Detrick, Frederick, Md.; mgmt. cons., 1991-. Author: Reflections, 1974 Bd. dirs. Adams County Mental Health Assn., Gettysburg, 1982-87 Recipient Sustained Superior Achievement award Dept. Navy, 1975, Dept. of Army 1986; named Outstanding Woman of Yr. Ft. Detrick, 1986, recipient Comdr.'s award, 1990. Mem. World Inst. of Achievement (life). Roman Catholic. Avocations: handwriting analysis, writing children's stories, ceramics, piano, studying self-improvement and psychology. Home: 5605 Shookstown Rd Frederick MD 21702-2704

BAKER, JOHN EDWARD, cardiac biochemist, educator; b. London, Eng., Dec. 12, 1954; arrived in U.S., 1984; s. Edward D. and Florence I. (Dobson) Baker; m. Mary E. Zurawski, Oct. 29, 1988; children: David J., Elizabeth A. BSc, Poly. Wolverhampton, Eng., 1977; PhD, St. Thomas' Med. Sch., London, 1984. Sr. biochemist Cen. Pathology Labs., London, 1977-78; rsch. asst. St. Thomas' Hosp. Med. Sch., London, 1978-84; rsch. fellow Med. Coll. Wis., Milw., 1984-86, vis. prof., 1986-87, asst. prof. cardiothoracic surgery, 1987-92, assoc. prof., 1992-99, assoc. prof. pediat. surgery, biochemistry, pharmacology, 1999-2001, prof., 2001—. Mem. peer rev. rsch. com. NIH, 2002—. Mem. editl. bd.: Am. Jour. Physiology, Heart and Circulatory Physiology; contbr. articles to profl. jours. Founder Heart Sci. Found., Ltd.; bd. dirs. Adelaide Banaszynski Sch. Piano Studies. Grantee, NIH, 1989, 1990, 1993, 1997, 2000, 2001, Culpeper Found., 1987, Ronald McDonald Children's Charities, 1989, 1991, Children's Hosp. Found., 1995. Mem.: Am. Heart Assn. (mem. peer rev. rsch. com. Wis. affiliate 1989—93, mem. peer rev. rsch. com. Northland affiliate 1999—2001, mem. coun. basic. sci., mem. Nat. Inst. of Health Study Sections 2002—). Methodist. Achievements include patents for method for sealing blood vessel puncture sites and method for coating intraluminal stents. Avocations: walking, music. Office: Med Coll Wis 8701 W Watertown Plank Rd Milwaukee WI 53226-3548 E-mail: jbaker@mcw.edu.

BAKER, JOHN I., III, communications educator; b. Denver, Jan. 4, 1961; s. John I. Jr. and Esther Ann (Austin) B.; m. Carol Jean Breninger, Mar. 15, 1986; children: Courtney Ann, John William. BA in Comm., U. No. Colo., 1983, MA in Speech Comm., 1984; MA in Journalism Mass Comm., Abilene Christian U., 1992; cert., Nat. Cath. Radio & TV Ctr., London, 1990. Salesman A.E. Meek Trunk and Bag Co., Denver, 1984-86; author, prodr., puppeteer The Magic Storybook (children's TV show) Bismarck (N.D.) Pub. Libr., 1994-97; children's theatre dir. Shade Tree Players, Bismarck, 1990-97; asst. prof. comm. U. Mary, Bismarck, 1988-97, York (Nebr.) Coll., 1997—, head dept. comms., chair div. humanities, 2000—. Author, prodr. (children's TV show) Bible Town, 1992; actor, dir. theatre various shows, 1987—. Bd. dirs. Cmty. Access TV, Bismarck, 1992-97, Yorkshire Playhouse, York, 1998—; mem. artistic com. Dakota Stage Ltd., Bismarck, 1992-97; Cub Scout leader Boy Scouts Am., 1998-2002; youth soccer coach, 2002—. Named Outstanding Faculty of Yr., U. Mary, 1991, inducted into Dakota Stage Wall of Fame, 2001; recipient Best News Package award, Greeley Press Club, 1983. Mem. Speech Comm. Assn., N.D. Speech and Theatre Assn. (Creative Artist of Yr. award 1997). Mem. Ch. of Christ. Avocations: guitar, theatre, back packing, hiking. Home: 1618 E 6th St York NE 68467-3315 Office: York Coll 1125 E 8th St York NE 68467 E-mail: jibaker@york.edu., storybook@navix.net.

BAKER, JOHN MILNES, architect; b. Port Jefferson, NY, Oct. 15, 1932; s. Alan Griffin and Lucy Hayden (Milnes) B.; m. Virginia Lea Busser (div. 1969); children: Ian Archbald, Jennifer Lea (Mrs. Christopher Warren); m. Elizabeth Jennings Morrison, Jan. 17, 1970; children: James Morrison, Hayden Sheffield. BA, Middlebury Coll., 1955; March, Columbia U., 1960. Designer, draftsman Sir Basil Spence, London, 1960-61; project mgr., later project architect Rogers & Butler, N.Y.C., 1962-64; project architect John A. Pruyn, AIA, N.Y.C., 1965-66; pvt. practice architecture N.Y.C., 1967-68, 75-79; ptnr. Manice & Baker, N.Y.C., 1968-74; pvt. practice architecture specializing in residential design Katonah, N.Y., 1979—. Pres. J.M. Baker Houses Inc.; lectr. New Sch. for Social Rsch., N.Y.C. Author: How to Build a House with an Architect, 1977, rev. edit., 1988, The Baker Family and the Edgar Family of Rahway, N.J. and New York City, 1972, American House Styles: A Concise Guide, 1994. Past trustee N.Y. Revels Inc.; past trustee Bedford Free Libr.; mem. Katonah Hist. Dist. Adv. Commn., Town of Bedford. Home designs included among Better Homes and Garden Top Ten Homes Plans, 1982; 3 designs selected by USIA for Design U.S.A., a traveling exhibit in USSR, 1989-90. Mem. AIA, Nat. Coun. Archtl. Registration Bds., Am. Arbitration Assn. (panel mem.), Soc. Archtl. Hists., St. Nicholas Soc. (past pres.), Holland Soc. N.Y. (past trustee), St. Andrews Soc., Colonial Lords of Manors in Am. (v.p.), New Eng. Soc., Order Founders and Patriots, Soc. Colonial Wars, Pilgrims, Corinthians, Coffee House, Squadron A, Century Assn. (N.Y.C.), Bellport Bay Yacht (Club past trustee), Bedford Golf and Tennis Club, Norwalk Yacht Club. Home: Rivendell Girdle Ridge Rd Katonah NY 10536 Office: 85 Girdle Ridge Rd Katonah NY 10536-3814 E-mail: jmbaker@bestweb.net.

BAKER, JOHN RUSSELL, utilities executive; b. Lexington, Mo., July 21, 1926; s. William Frederick and Flora Anne (Dunford) B.; m. Elizabeth Jane Torrence, June 16, 1948; children— John Russell, Burton T. BS, U. Mo., 1948, MBA, 1962. With Mo. Public Service Co., Kansas City, 1948—, treas., 1966-68, v.p. fin., 1968-71, sr. v.p., 1971-73, exec. v.p., 1973—, also dir. Lectr. fin. U. Mo.; vice-chmn. Aquila Inc., 1991—. Vice-pres. Mid-Continent coun. Girl Scouts U.S., 1981; mem. adv. coun. Sch. Acctg., U. Mo., Columbia. Recipient Outstanding alumnus award Sch. Adminstrn. U. Mo., Kansas City, 1965; citation of merit U. Mo., 1995. Mem. Tax Execs. Inst. (pres. Kansas City 1968), U. Mo. Sch. Adminstrn. Alumni Assn. (pres. 1965). Clubs: Kansas City. Republican. Methodist. Home: 205 NW Oxford Ln Lees Summit MO 64063-2118 Office: Aquila Inc 20 W 9th St Kansas City MO 64105-1704

BAKER, JOHN STEVENSON (MICHAEL DYREGROV), writer; b. Mpls., June 18, 1931; s. Everette Barrette and Ione May (Kadletz) B. BA cum laude, Pomona Coll., Claremont Colls., 1953; MD, U. Calif. at Berkeley and San Francisco, 1957. Writer, 1958—; book cataloger Walker Art Center, Mpls., 1958-59; editor, writer neurol. rsch. articles Louis F. Phillips Psychobiol. Rsch. Fund, Mpls., 1960-61. Contbr. articles and poetry to various publs. in Eng. and U.S.; author 65 pub. poems, 21 short essays and 10 sets of aphorisms. Donor numerous species of native plants and seeds to Minn. Landscape Arboretum, U.S. Nat. Arboretum and Arnold Arboretum, Harvard U., papers of LeRoi Jones and Hart Crane to Yale U., Brahms recs. to Bennington Coll., several others; pres. Mission Lakes Assn., Merrifield, Minn., 1989-90. Recipient Disting. Service award Minn. State Hort. Soc., 1976; Cert. of Appreciation U.S. Nat. Arboretum, 1978; property registered as a Minn. Natural Area Minn. chpt. Nature Conservancy, 1990 Mem. Ctr. for Plant Conservation, Nat. Audugon Soc., Nature Conservancy, Nat. Mus. Am. Indian, Nat. Trust for Hist. Preservation, Met. Opera Guild, Phi Chi, Nu Sigma Nu. Office: PO Box 16007 Minneapolis MN 55416-0007

BAKER, JUDITH ANN, retired computer technician; b. Junction City, Kans., Mar. 2, 1947; d. David Daniel and Mildred Elaine Bates; m. Jimmy Ray Baker, Oct. 8, 1972; 1 child, Jimmy Ray Baker, Jr. Student, East Ctrl. U., 1994—98; postgrad., Tulsa C.C., 1999—. Cert. travel and tourism Draughon Coll., 1988. ADA support group leader Multiple Sclerosis Assn. of Am., Tulsa, Okla., 1995—. Author poetry; editor: (newsletter) Ada MS Support Group. Mem.: Ada Writing Club. Avocations: writing, painting, crafts, decorating. Home: Rt 6 Box 2395 Ada OK 74820 Personal E-mail: ourplace@compworldnet.com.

BAKER, JULIE ANN, language educator; b. Lubbock, Tex., Aug. 29, 1973; d. David Michael and Susan Lynne Baker. PhD French Lit./Minor: Lang. Edn., Ind. U, Bloomington, IN, 1995—2002; MA; French Lit., Ind. U, Bloomington, IN, 1995—97; BA French and Comm., U of Mich., Ann Arbor, MI, 1991—95. Technology and Language Instruction Middlebury Coll./Vt., 2001. Assoc. instr. of french Ind. U., Bloomington, Ind., 1995—99; lectr. (lectrice) of English Université Marc Bloch (Strasbourg II), Strasbourg, France, 1999—2000; assoc. instr. of French Ind. U, Bloomington, Ind., 2000—02; dir., intensive lang. program in french U. of Richmond, Richmond, Va., 2002—; discussion moderator (animatrice) CUS: Communauté Urbaine de Strasbourg, Strasbourg, France, 1999—2000. Dir., summer study abroad U of Richmond, Richmond, Va., 2002—; reviewer NE Conf. on the Tchg. of Fgn. Languages (NECTFL), 2002—. Author: (thesis) The Childhood of the Epic Hero: A Study of the Old French Enfances Texts of Epic Cycles, (article/ conference proceedings) The Childhood of the Epic Hero: Representation of the Child Protagonist in the Old French Enfances Texts. Recipient Tchg. Excellence Recognition Award, Ind. U. Bd. of Trustees, 1997-1998, Grace P. Young Grad. Award for Excellent Scholarship in French Lit., Ind. U. Dept. of French and Italian, 1996-1997, Outstanding Tchg. Award, 1995-1996, FRITNET Prize for best Web-based materials devel., 2001-2002; grantee Andrew W. Mellon Stipend, Ctr. for Ednl. Tech., Middlebury Coll., 2001. Mem.: MLA, Fgn. Lang. Assn. of Va. (FLAVA). Office: University of Richmond Dept of Modern Languages & Literatures Richmond VA 23173 Office Fax: 804-287-6446. Personal E-mail: julbaker@yahoo.com. E-mail: jbaker@richmond.edu.

BAKER, JUNE FRANKLAND, poet; b. Schenectady, N.Y., May 27, 1935; m. David Addison Baker, July 6, 1962; children: Elizabeth Kelley, Ellen Rebecca. AB summa cum laude, SUNY, Albany, 1957; MA, U. Pa., 1958. Tchr. North Syracuse (N.Y.) High Sch., 1958—60, Skaneateles (N.Y.) High Sch., 1960—61; tchr., libr. Ctrl. Sch., Longmont, Colo., 1961—64; tchr. poetry Richland, Wash., 1986. Judge h.s. poetry contest Columbia Basin Coll., Pasco, Wash., 1981-85, Mid-Columbia Writers, Wash., 1996. Author of poems. Chmn. Citizens Adv. Coun. Marcus Whitman Sch., Richland, 1973-74; vol. Sacajawea Sch., Richland, 1975-78. Home: 614 Lynnwood Ct Richland WA 99352

BAKER, KATHERINE JUNE, elementary school educator, minister, artist; b. Dallas, Feb. 3, 1932; d. Kirk Moses and Katherine Faye (Turner) Sherrill; m. George William Baker, Jan. 30, 1955; children: Kirk Garner, Kathleen Kay. BS, BA, Tex. Women's U., 1953, MEd, 1979; cert. in religious edn., Meadville Theol. U., 1970; postgrad., North Tex. State U., 1987—; DD (hon.), Am. Fellowship Ch., 1981. Cert. elem. and secondary tchr., adminstr., Tex.; lic. and ordained min. Kingsway Internat. Ministries, 1991. Mgr. prodn. Woolf Bros., Dallas, 1953-55; display mgr. J.M. Dyer and Co., Corsicana, Tex., 1954; advt. artist Fair Dept. Store, Ft. Worth, 1954-56; artist, instr. Dutch Art Gallery, Dallas, 1960-65; dir. religious edn. 1st Unitarian Ch., Dallas, 1967-69; edn. dir. day care, tchr. Richardson (Tex.) Unitarian Ch., 1971-73; dir. camp Tres Rios YWCA, Glen Rose, Tex., 1975-76; dir. program of extended sch. instrn. Hamilton Park Elem. Sch. Richardson Ind. Sch. Dist., 1975-78, tchr. Dover Elem. Sch., 1979—80, tchr. Jess Harben Elem. Sch., 1980—92; founder ednl., editorial and arts/evang. assn. Submitted Ministries, Richardson, 1992—. Dir. Flame Fellowship Internat., 1987-94, state rep., 1994-99—, asst. state overseer (Tex.), 1999-2001, chaplain, 2002--. Contbr. articles to ch. newspaper, 1967-69; exhibited in group show at Tex. Art Assn., 1966; one-woman show Dutch Art Gallery - Northlake Ctr., Dallas, 1965. Advocate day care Unitarian Unicersalist Women's Fedn., Boston, 1975—76, mem. nominating com., 1976—77; cert. instr. aquatics program Arthritis Found. YMCA AFYAP, Plano Rehab. Hosp., 1997—99, Aquatics Inst. Oak Point Ctr., Plano, 1999—, Aquatics Inst. Fun Fit Crew, 2001—. Mem. NEA, ASCD, Nat. Coun. Social Studies, Tex. State Tchrs. Assn. (treas. Richardson chpt. 1984-85), Tex. Ret. Tchrs. Assn., Richardson Ret. Tchrs. Assn., Women's Ctr. Dallas, Sokol Athletic Ctr., Smithsonian Assn., Dallas Mus. Assn., Alpha Chi, Delta Phi Delta (pres. 1952-53), Phi Delta Kappa. Avocations: gospel and folk singing, guitar, volleyball, camping. Fax: 972-312-9295.

BAKER, KEITH LEON, lawyer; b. Columbus, Ind., Jan. 22, 1950; s. Richard Leon and Sarah Elizabeth (Wisehart) B. A.B., Princeton U., 1972; J.D., Syracuse U., 1975; LL.M. with highest honors, George Washington U., 1978. Bar: N.Y. 1976, D.C. 1976, Va. 2000, U.S. Ct. Appeals (D.C. cir.) 1983, U.S. Ct. Internat. Trade 1983. Asst. bank examiner U.S. Treasury Dept., N.Y.C., 1974; law clk. U.S. Dept. of Justice, Syracuse, N.Y., 1974-75; atty.-adviser GAO, Washington, 1975-78; atty.-adviser U.S. EPA, Washington, 1978-80; pvt. practice, Washington, 1980-99; ptnr. Barton, Baker, McMahon & Tolle, 1999—. Author: Small Business Financing, 1983; contbr. articles to profl. jours. Mem. ABA, Fed. Bar Assn., Nat. Contract Mgmt. Assn. Methodist. Home: 6645 Hawthorne St Mc Lean VA 22101-4423 Office: Barton Baker McMahon & Tolle The Madison Bldg Ste 440 1320 Old Chain Bridge Rd Mc Lean VA 22101

BAKER, KEITH MICHAEL, history educator; b. Swindon, Eng., Aug. 7, 1938; came to U.S., 1964; s. Raymond Eric and Winifred Evelyn (Shepherd) B.; m. Therese Louise Elzas, Oct. 25, 1961 (div. 1999); children— Julian, Felix. BA, Cambridge U., 1960, MA, 1963; postgrad., Cornell U., 1960-61; PhD, U. London, 1964. Instr. history and humanities Reed Coll., 1964-65; asst. prof. European history U. Chgo., 1965-71, assoc. prof., 1971-76, prof., 1977-89, master collegiate div. social scis., 1975-78, assoc. dean coll., 1975-78, assoc. dean div. social scis., 1975-78, chmn. commn. grad. edn., 1980-82; chmn. Council Advanced Studies in Humanities and Social Scis., 1982-86; prof.

European history Stanford U., 1989—, J.E. Wallace Sterling prof. in humanities, 1992—, chair dept. history, 1994-95; Anthony P. Meier family prof. humanities, dir. Stanford Humanities Ctr., 1995-2000, cognizant dean humanities, 2000—. Vis. assoc. prof. history Yale U., 1974; mem. Inst. Advanced Study, Princeton (N.J.), 1979-80; vis. prof., dir. studies Ecole des Hautes Etudes en Scis. Sociales, Paris, 1982, 84, 91; fellow Ctr. for Advanced Study in Behavioral Scis., Stanford (Calif.) U., 1986-87; vis. prof. UCLA, 1989; vis. fellow Clare Hall, Cambridge (Eng.) U., 1994; chair scholars com. Am. Com. on the French Revolution, 1989. Author: Condorcet: From Natural Philosophy to Social Mathematics, 1975, Inventing the French Revolution, 1990; prin. author: Report Commission on Graduate Education, U. Chgo., 1982; editor: Condorcet: Selected Writings, 1977, The Political Culture of the Old Regime: The Old Regime and the French Revolution, 1987, The Terror, 1994; co-editor Jour. Modern History, 1980-89, What's Left of Enlightenment?, 2001. Decorated chevalier Ordre des Palmes Académiques, 1988; NEH fellow, 1967-68, ACLS study fellow, 1972-73, Guggenheim fellow, 1979. Fellow AAAS; mem. Am. Hist. Assn. (com. on coms. 1991-94), Soc. French History Studies, Am. Soc. for 18th Century Studies (v.p. 1999, pres. 2000-01), Am. Philos. Soc. Office: Stanford U Dept History Stanford CA 94305 E-mail: kbaker@stanford.edu.

BAKER, KENDALL L. academic administrator; b. Clearwater, Fla., Nov. 1, 1942; s. Robert B. and Anne E. Baker; m. Tobin Ratliff McGough, Apr. 12, 1981; children: Kraig, Kris, John, Shannon, Brian. BA with honors, U. Md., 1963; MA, Georgetown U., 1967, PhD, 1969. Instr., Dept. Polit. Sci. U. Wyo., Laramie, 1967-69, asst. prof., 1969-73, assoc. prof., 1973-77, prof., 1977-82, chmn., 1979-82, asst. v.p. for Acad. Affairs, 1976-77; dean, Coll. Arts & Scis., Bowling Green State U., Ohio, 1982-87; v.p., provost No. Ill. U., DeKalb, 1987-92; pres. U. N. D., 1992-99, Ohio Northern U, 1999—. Cons. on survey research to various agys. and polit. candidates, 1967—; panel chmn. Rocky Mt. Social Sci. Conv. 1973, We. Social Sci. Conv., 1975, Council Colls. Arts and Scis., 1983, 86; guest participant study trip to Fed. Republic of Germany, 1977; election observer Fed. Republic of Germany, 1980. Author: The Wyoming Legislature: Lawmakers, the Public, and the Press, 1973; (with R. Dalton and K. Hildebrandt) Germany Transformed: Political Culture and the New Politics, 1981; contbr. articles on polit. sci. to profl. jours. Coach Laramie Soccer Assn., 1978-81. Mem. Am. Polit. Sci. Assn. (chmn. panel ann. conv. 1983), Midwest Polit. Sci. Assn. (chmn. panel ann. conv. 1985, 86), Conf. Group on German Politcs (exec. com. 1984-87, co-editor newsletter 1985-91), Phi Kappa Phi, Omicron Delta Kappa, Pi Sigma Alpha. Home: 920 West Lima Ada OH 45810 Office: President's Office 525 S Main St Ada OH 45810-1599 E-mail: k-baker@onu.edu.

BAKER, KENT ALFRED, broadcasting, publishing company executive; b. Sioux City, Iowa, Mar. 22, 1948; s. Carl Edmund Baker and Miriam M. (Hawthorn) Baker Nye. Student, Iowa State U., 1966-70. Editor Iowa State Daily, 1969-70; mem. U.S. Peace Corps., 1971-72; editor The Glidden (Iowa) Graphic, 1973-75; bur. chief The Waterloo (Iowa) Courier, Iowa, 1975; state editor The Des Moines Register, 1976-77; news dir. Sta. WQAD-TV, Moline, Ill., 1978; Sunday editor The Des Moines Sunday Register, 1979; news dir. Sta. KHON-TV, Honolulu, 1980-95; v.p., gen. mgr. KHON-TV, Honolulu, 1996-2000; pres. Baker Newspapers, 2000—. Pub. The Moville Record, 2000—. Mem. Hoover Libr. Assn., Iowa State U. Alumni Assn., Iowa Newspaper Assn., Iowa Hist. Soc. Office: The Moville Record 12 South Second St Moville IA 51039 E-mail: record@netins.net.

BAKER, KERRY ALLEN, management consultant; b. Selmer, Tenn., Sept. 21, 1949; s. Austin Clark and Betty Ann (Brooks) B.; m. Ellen Fleming. BIE, Ga. Inst. Tech., 1971; MBA, Ga. State U., 1973; JD, Memphis State U., 1987. With dept. law State of Ga., 1971-73; div. engr. N.W. Ga. div. Gold Kist Inc., Ellijay, 1977-80; sr. mfg. engr. Plough, Inc., Memphis, 1980-82, mgr. indsl. engring., 1983-86, supr. mfg. engr., 1986-90; plant bus. mgr. Clorox Co., Dyersburg, Tenn., 1990-95; ops. mgr. Huish Detergents, Inc., Dyersburg, 1995; exec. dir. Mgmt. Recruiters of Dyersburg, 1996-97; mgr. adminstrn. Gabriel Ride Products, Pulaski, Tenn., 1998-99; pres. Rock Ridge Ventures, Inc., Dyersburg, 1997—; contr. Mahle Motorsports, Inc., Fletcher, N.C., 2000—. Decorated Order of St. Barbara. Mem. Inst. Indsl. Engrs., Am. Prodn. and Inventory Control Soc., Scabbard and Blade, Masons, Phi Delta Phi. Methodist. Home: PO Box 87 Arden NC 28704-0087 Business E-Mail: kerry.baker@us.mahle.com. E-mail: kbaker151@earthlink.net.

BAKER, KRISTINA MARIE, family practice nurse practitioner; b. Oneida, N.Y., Sept. 27, 1968; d. Danny Dean Meyers and Roslie Mae Tallman. AS, Morrisville Agr. and Tech. U., 1989; BS, SUNY, Syracuse, 1997, MS, 2001. With SUNY Health Sci. Ctr. at Upstate Med. U., Syracuse, 1989—2001; RN Favority Nurses, Manhattan, NY, 2002—; nurse practitioner Maimonides Med. Ctr., Bklyn., 2002—. Nurse educator cons. neurosurgery St. Elizabeth Hosp., Utica, NY, 2000—01. Avocations: golf, exercising, reading. Office: Maimonides Med Ctr Dept Vascular Surgery 4802 Tenth Ave Brooklyn NY 11219

BAKER, LAUREN ALEXIS, psychology educator, aerial performer; b. Wutzberg, Germany, Feb. 2, 1973; came to U.S., 1974; d. James Samuel and Jacquelyn Claire Baker. BA in Psychology, Furman U., 1995; MA in Cognitive Psychology, Ga. State U., 2000, postgrad., 2000—. Counselor Hidden Lake Acad., Daholonega, Ga., 1995-96; rsch. asst. Ga. State U., Atlanta, 1996—, instr., 1998—; aerial performer 7-Course Theatre, Atlanta, 2000—. Mem. APA, Am. Psychol. Soc., Southeastern Psychol. Assn., So. Soc. Philosophy and Psychology, Comparative Cognition Soc., Psi Chi. Office: Ga State U Dept Psychology Atlanta GA 30303 E-mail: psylab@langate.gsu.edu.

BAKER, LAWRENCE ALAN, environmental engineer, researcher; b. Louisville, Ky., Mar. 30, 1951; s. Peter John and Marion Cornwell Baker; m. Nancy Ann Rodenborg, Dec. 15, 1951; children: Anna Katherine, Paul Lawrence. PhD, U. of Fla., 1979—84. Rsch. assoc. U. of Minn., 1984—92; asssitant prof. Ariz. State U., 1992—99; environ. cons. Baker Environ. Consulting, St. Paul, 1999—2002; tech. dir., synthesis and integration project Corvallis EPA Lab, Oreg., 1989—92; sr. fellow U. of Minn., 2001—. Assoc. editor Urban Ecosystems, United States; mem., Integrated Assessment Task Group Nat. Acidic Precipitation Assessment Program; project dir. Water in Arid Lands Initiative, Ariz. State U., United States. Editor: (book) Environ. Chemistry of Lakes and Reservoirs; contbr. scientific papers. Chmn. Human Health Subcommittee, Ariz. Comparative Environ. Risk Project, Phoenix, 1994—95. Recipient Best Tchr., Am. Soc. of Civil Engring., Ariz. Student Chpt., 1997, Governor's Recognition Award, Ariz. Governor's Office, 1995; Sommerfeld fellow, U. of Minn., 1981—82. Mem.: Am. Water Works Assn., Ecol. Soc. of Am., Nat. Assn. of Lake Mgmt., Am. Chem. Soc. Avocations: fishing, volleyball, weight training. Office: Water Resources Center U of Minnesota 173 McNeal Hall 1985 Buford Ave Saint Paul MN 55108 E-mail: baker127@umn.edu.

BAKER, LEE EDWARD, biomedical engineering educator; b. Springfield, Mo., Aug. 31, 1924; s. Edward Fielding and Oneita Geneva (Patton) B.; m. Jeanne Carolyn Ferbrache, June 20, 1948; children: Carson Phillips, Carolyn Patton. BEE, U. Kans., 1945; MEE, Rice U., 1960; PhD in Physiology, Baylor U., 1965. Registered prof. engr., Tex. Asst. prof. electrical engring. Rice U., Houston, 1960-64; asst. prof. physiology Baylor U. Coll. Medicine, Houston, 1965-69, assoc. prof., 1969-75; prof. biomed. engring. U. Tex., 1975-82, Robert L. Parker Sr. Centennial Prof. Engring., 1982-2000, prof. emeritus, 2000—. Co-author: Principles of Applied Biomedical Engineering, 1968, 3d edit., 1989; author, co-author scientific papers. Served to lt. USN, 1943-46, PTO, 1951-53. Spl. research fellow NIH, 1964-65. Fellow Am. Inst. Med. and Biol. Engring., Royal Soc. Medicine; mem. IEEE (sr.), Biomed. Engring. Soc. (sr.), Am. Physiol. Soc. Avocation: gardening. Office: Univ Tex ENS 610 Biomed Engring Program Austin TX 78712

BAKER, LEONARD MORTON, manufacturing company executive; b. Medford, Mass., Oct. 2, 1934; s. Abraham and Sarah B.; m. Ruth Lee Edelstein, June 15, 1958; children: Charles Harold, Andrew Mark, Douglas Jon. BS in Chemistry, Harvard U., 1956; PhD in Phys.-Organic Chemistry, MIT, 1960. With Union Carbide Corp., 1959-92, assoc. dir., then dir. rsch. and devel., 1969-77, v.p. rsch. and devel., 1977-80, v.p., gen. mgr. coatings materials div., 1980-82, v.p. splty. chems. div., 1982-84, corporate dir. tech., 1984-86, v.p. spltys. and services Bus. Group., 1986, corp. v.p. tech., 1986; sr. v.p. tech., chief tech. officer Praxair, Inc., Danbury, Conn., 1992—2002; cons. Tech. Planning and Assesment, 2003—. Bd. dirs. Rogers (Conn.) Corp. Exec. bd. Cornell Inst. Biotech.; mem. sci. adv. com. MIT; mem. materials sci. adv. bd., vis. com. U. Conn.; industry rep. Nat. Acad.-Industry Program, NRC; industry adv. panel NSF; mem. industry adv. bd. Presdl. Sci. Adv. Commn.; mem. sci. adv. bd. Conn. Coll.; active Nat. Industry Coun. for Sci. Edn., adv. bd. Coun. for Competitiveness Rsch. Devel. MIT fellow, 1956-57; NSF fellow, 1957-58; Sun Oil Corp. fellow, 1958-59 Mem. AICE, N.Y. Acad. Scis. (sci. policy com.), Am. Chem. Soc., Indsl. Rsch. Inst. (fed. sci. and tech. com.. pre-coll. edn. com., rsch. com.), Council Chem. Rsch. (gov. bd., univ./industry liaison com.), Soc. Chem. Industry, Dirs. Indsl. Rsch., Am. Mgmt. Assn. (rsch. and devel. council), Conn. Acad. Sci. and Engring., Sigma Xi. Home: 60 Lyons Plains Rd Westport CT 06880-1305 Office: Praxair Inc Old Ridgebury Rd Danbury CT 06817-0001

BAKER, LYNNE RUDDER, philosophy educator; b. Atlanta, Feb. 14, 1944; d. James Maclin and Virginia (Bennett) Rudder; m. Thomas B. Baker III, Feb. 1, 1969. BA, Vanderbilt U., 1966, MA, 1971, PhD, 1972; student, Johns Hopkins U., 1967-68. Asst. prof. philosophy Mary Baldwin Coll., Staunton, Va., 1972-76, Middlebury (Vt.) Coll., 1976-79, assoc. prof., 1979-84, prof., 1984-94, acting dean arts and humanities, 1982, chairperson humanities divsn., 1982-85, acting chairperson philosophy, 1986-87; prof. U. Mass., Amherst, 1989—, dir. philosophy grad. program, 1994—. Mem. panel to select summer seminars NEH, Washington, 1982, mem. panel to select fellows, 1989—90; Gifford lectr. U. Glasgow, Scotland, 2001. Author: Saving Belief: A Critique of Physicalism, 1988, Explaining Attitudes: A Practical Approach to the Mind, 1995, Persons and Bodies: A Constitution View, 2000; contbr. scholarly articles to profl. jours. Trustee Vanderbilt U., Nashville, 1969-70, mem. alumni bd. dirs., 1985-89. Mellon fellow, 1974, NEH fellow, 1983-84, Nat. Humanities Ctr. fellow, 1982-83, Woodrow Wilson Internat. Ctr. for Scholars fellow, 1988-89. Mem. Am. Philos. Assn. (program com. 1983, exec. com. 1992-95), Soc. for Philosophy and Psychology, Soc. Christian Philosophers (exec. com. 1992-95), Soc. Women in Philosophy, Phi Beta Kappa. Democrat. Episcopalian. Office: U Mass Dept Philosophy Amherst MA 01003

BAKER, MARIA LUISE, retired secondary school educator; b. Bad Reichenhall, Germany, Oct. 18, 1947; came to U.S., 1948; d. William and Maria Eleanore (Bauer) McStay; m. Clyde Norman Baker, July 29, 1969 (div. Jan. 1973). BA in Spl. Edn., Social Studies, U. No. Colo., 1969. Cert. tchr. secondary social studies/spl. edn. K-12. Tchr. spl. edn. Adams City H.S., Commerce City, Colo., 1969-76, 79-89, tchr. social studies, 1989—; tchr. spl. edn. Adams City Mid. Sch., Commerce City, 1976-79, mentor coord., 2002—03. Performance assistance team, mem. mentor program Adams County Sch. Dist. #14, 1990—; presenter insvcs. in field. Mem. Denver Mus. of Natural History, Denver Art Mus. Recipient Disting. Tchr. award/Colo., 1991-92, A-Plus Tchr. - Channel 4 (NBC), 1994; Title II mini-grantee, Title I grantee. Mem.: Am. Fedn. Tchrs. (v.p. 1979—82, pres. 1993—2001), Nat. Coun. for the Social Studies, Colo. Hist. Soc., Colo. Wildlife Fedn. Avocations: gardening, needlework. Office: Adams City High School 4625 E 68th Ave Commerce City CO 80022-2381 Business E-Mail: mbaker@acsd14.k12.co.us.

BAKER, MARK ALLEN, author, historian, consultant, graphologist; b. Binghamton, N.Y., Mar. 27, 1957; s. Ford William and Marilyn A. (Allen) B.; divorced; children: Aaron Anthony, Elizabeth Margaret, Rebecca Jeanne. BA, SUNY, Oswego, 1979. Computer operator Gen. Electric Corp., Liverpool, N.Y., 1980-81, tng. specialist, 1981-82; art dir. Genigraphics Corp., Liverpool, 1982-83, mgr. market rsch., 1983-85, exec. asst. to pres. and CEO, 1985-86, corp. bus. planner, 1986-90. Pvt. rschr., 1986—; historian Internat. Boxing Hall Fame; appeared in numerous pubs. such as USA Today and also on TV, incluidng VH-1. Author: Baseball Autograph Handbook, I and II, 1990, Team Baseballs, All Sport Autograph Guide, 1994, Complete Guide to Boxing Collectibles, 1995, Auto Racing, 1995, Collector's Guide to Celebrity Autographs, 1996, Rock and Roll Memorabilia, 1997, The Standard Guide to Collecting Autographs, 1999, Advanced Autograph Collecting, 1999, Collector's Guide to Celebrity Autographs, 2000, Sports Collectibles, 2001; contbr. articles to profl. jours. Lifetime donor mem. Baseball Hall Fame, Historian Internat. Boxing Hall of Fame. Mem. Am. Mgmt. Assn. (pres. 1985—), Assn. Computer Mfrs. (pres. 1985—), Assn. Med. Illustrators (corp. rep., pres. 1986—), Am. Assn. Individual Investors (pres. 1987—), Siggraph (pres. 1985—), Manuscript Soc. Avocations: forensic document analysis, literature, finance. Address: PO Box 160878 Altamonte Springs FL 32716-0878

BAKER, MARK BRUCE, lawyer, educator; b. Bridgeport, Conn., Dec. 27, 1946; s. Phillip and Lillian (Islovitz) Bader; m. Sandra Fay Wolf, June 9, 1968 (div. 1982); 1 dau. Rachel Barrett Bader; m. Nora Kay Mandell, Dec. 30, 1984; 1 dau. Lisa Anne Baker. BBA, U. Miami, Coral Gables, Fla., 1968; JD, So. Meth. U., 1974. Bar: Tex. 1974. Assoc. firm Herndon, Girand and Dooley, Dallas, 1974-76; ptnr. firm Pailet and Bader, Dallas, 1976-80; prof. internat. law U. Tex., Austin, 1980—; of counsel firm Bard and Groves, Houston, 1981-83; gen. counsel Embree Constrn. Group, Inc., Austin, Tex., 1987—2000; of counsel Goodall and Davison, Austin, 1991—. Chmn. bd. Embree Health Care Group, Inc. Contbr. articles to legal publs. Bd. dirs. Jewish Cmty. Coun. Austin, 1983-86, Big Bros./Big Sisters Program, 1999—, Vol. Svcs. of Children's Hosp. of Austin, 2003—. Recipient Outstanding Asst. Prof. award U. Tex., 1982, Outstanding Class Lectr. award, 1984, Tex. Excellence Tchg. award U. Tex. Alumni Assn., 1983. Mem. ABA, Union Internat. des Avocats, Am. Friends Wilton Park (sec.-treas. 1982-84), Tex. Bar Assn. (internat. law sect.), Austin Fgn. Trade Coun., Am. Bus. Law Assn. (internat. law sect., pres. 1990-91). Home: 406 Brookhaven Trl Austin TX 78746-5413 Office: Bldg 2 Ste 400 1250 Capital of Tx Hwy S Austin TX 78746 E-mail: m.baker@mail.utexas.edu.

BAKER, MARTI A(NN), privacy and compliance consultant; b. Indpls., Nov. 6, 1953; d. Donald A. Baker and Georgia Ann Pitcher; 1 child, Courtney Jo Allison. BSN, Ind. U., 1976, JD, 1988. Staff nurse, charge nurse various hosps., Ind., 1976-92; clin. instr. nursing Ivy Tech. State Coll., Bloomington, Ind., 1980, Evansville (Ind.) Sch. Practical Nursing, 1982; atty. Price & Shula, Indpls., 1989-90; chief nurse cons. Ind. State Dept. Health, Indpls., 1992-95, program dir. info. dispute resolution Office Legal Affairs, 1995-97; benefits mgr. employee benefit divsn. State Personnel Dept., State of Ind., 1997-98; asst. dir. divsn. organiational devel. Family & Social Svcs. Adminstrn., State of Ind., 1998-99; human resources cons. Cmty. Hosps. Indpls., 1999—2002, privacy and compliance cons., 2002—. Vol. Marion County Dem. Election, Perry Twp., 1992-99. Mem. Exec. Women in Health Care, Ind. Dem. Club, Alpha Chi Omega. Roman Catholic. Avocations: aviculture, camping, gardening, gourmet cooking, raising domestic livestock. Office: Cmty Hosps Indpls 1500 N Ritter Ave Indianapolis IN 46219 E-mail: mabaker@ecommunity.com.

BAKER, MARTIN WILLIAM, management consultant; b. Kingston, Surrey, Eng., Aug. 22, 1950; s. William French and Kathleen Audrey (Richards) B.; m. Elaine Rosemary France, July 27, 1973; children: Alexander Martin, Clare Jane. BSc, Holloway, London, 1973; PhD, Rutherford, Kent, Eng., 1980. Chatered mathematician. Engr. Brit. Post Office, London, 1968-73; exec. engr. Brit. Telecom., London, 1973-78; comms. cons. CAP Ltd., London, 1978-82; dir. tech. UNICOM, London, 1982-85; prin. cons. York Devel. and Rsch., Reigate, Eng., 1985—, Planning and Strategy Ltd., Reigate, 1988—, dir. advanced trading sys., 1989-96. Mng. dir. York Devel. and Rsch. Ltd., Reigate, 1985—, bd. dirs.; lectr. on money mgmt., computers in tech. analysis, risk and trading. Author: Expanding the Scope of Technical Analysis, 1988; contbr. series of articles to profl. pubs. Named Brain of Kent, Mensa Competition, 1975. Mem. Inst. Math. and Its Applications (assoc.), Soc. Tech. Analysts, Brit. Computer Soc., Malden and Dist. Soc. Model Engrs. (dir.). Office: York Devel & Rsch 22 Belmont Rd Surrey Reigate RH2 7EE England E-mail: martinwbaker@compuserve.com.

BAKER, MARVIN PALANGE, cardiologist, internist; b. Portsmouth, Va., Oct. 5, 1949; s. James Ellis and Aida (Palange) B.; m. Carmelita Donadi. BS, U. Autonoma, Jaliso, Mexico, 1970, MD, 1974. Diplomate Am. Bd. Nuclear Cardiology. Intern South Jersey Sch. Medicine, 1974-75; resident Prince George's Med. Ctr., 1975-76; fellow Rush-Presbyn. Med. Ctr., Chgo., 1978-80; chief dept. medicine, chmn. peer rev. Butler (Pa.) Meml. Hosp., 1994—, chair dept. cardiology, 2001—. Fellow Am. Coll. Cardiology, Am. Coll. Chest Physicians, Am. Soc. Nuclear Cardiology. Republican. Roman Catholic. Avocations: amateur radio, golf, audiophile, guns, scuba diving. Office: 165 Brugh Ave Ste 303 Butler PA 16001-6472 E-mail: marvinb@zbzoom.net.

BAKER, MARY EVELYN, retired librarian; b. Columbus, Ohio, May 8, 1912; d. Abram Jackson and Martha Maria (Dailey) Shoemaker; m. Richard Heinley Baker, Sept. 18, 1937 (dec.); children: Richard Shoemaker, David Guy. BA, Ohio State U., 1934; BS in Libr. Sci., Western Res. U., Cleve., 1935. Mem. staff libr. Ohio State U., Columbus, 1935-37, 38-44, 1955-74, part-time libr., 1955-66, adminstrv. asst. to the dir., 1958, serial cataloger, 1958-67, asst. reviser, sr. cataloger, 1967-68, head serial div. catalog dept., 1968-71, head catalog dept., 1971-74. Libr. com. First Congl. Ch., Columbus, 1941-97, libr. co-chmn., 1962-65, 74-75, libr. chmn., 1976-97; past mem. ALA, sec. serials sect., resources and tech. div., 1970-73. Den mother Boy Scouts Am., Columbus, 1953-58; libr. co-chmn. Friendship Village, Dublin, Ohio, 1981-97, chmn., 1997—. Mem. Ohioana Libr. Assn. (past chmn. various coms., life mem.), PEO (telephone chmn. chpt. V 1987—), DAR (Indians com.), Ohio State Univ. Women's Club (past pres.), Agrl. Circle (past pres.), Franklin Co-Ret. Tchrs. Assn. (life mem.), Ohio Ret. Tchrs. Assn. (life mem.), Ohio State Alumni Assn. (life mem.), Polar Bear Alumni Assn. Columbus North H.S. (life), Alumni Assn. Univ. Sch. (life), Ohio State U. Retirees Assn. (life, bridge chmn. 1984—), Ohio State U. Friends of the Librs., Ohio Hist. Soc., Worthington Hist. Soc. (life), Columbus Hist. Soc. (life), Ch. Women United of Columbus and Franklin County, Columbus Mus. Art, Columbus Zoo, Gypsies Travel Club, Motts Mil. Mus. (charter), Phi Mu (various offices including pres. active and alumni chpts.). Republican. Home: 6000 Riverside Dr Apt 233A Dublin OH 43017-1494

BAKER, MARY ALICE, communication educator, consultant; b. Stuart, Okla., Sept. 9, 1937; d. James Roy and Emma M. (Bird) B. BS, U. Okla., 1959, MA in Speech, 1966; PhD in Comm., Purdue U., 1983. Speech and debate tchr. SE High Sch., Oklahoma City, 1959-65; instr. Ea. Ill. U., Charleston, 1966-69; prof. Lamar U., Beaumont, Tex., 1966-75, 78—, dir. forensics, 1969-75, Regents' Merit prof., 1984, pres. faculty senate, 1986-88. Contbr. articles to profl. jours. Mem. R & D com. Nat. Coun. Tchr. Retirement Sys., 2003; trustee Tchrs. Retirement Sys. Tex., 1999—, chair ethcis com. David Ross fellow, 1977. Mem. Tex. Speech Comm. Assn. (regional rep. 1978-88), Nat. Comm. Assn. Am., Tex. Assn. Coll. Tchrs. (regional v.p. 1985-88, pres.-elect 1988-89, state pres. 1989-90, state bd. legis. liason 1997-99), Tex. Forensics Assn. (pres. 1974), Internat. Comm. Assn., Zeta Phi Eta, Alpha Delta Pi. Democrat. Episcopalian. Avocations: reading, politics, travel. Office: Lamar U Dept Communication Beaumont TX 77710

BAKER, MARY JANE, social worker; b. Watertown, Mass., Oct. 21, 1917; d. Lenox Stanley and Mary Angela (Rue) Karner; m. David Curtis Baker, Aug. 28, 1942; children: Peter Rue, Nancy Jewell Baker Aucella. AB, Tufts U., 1939; MSS, Simmons Coll., Boston, 1944. Caseworker Family Welfare, Fairfield, Conn., 1940-42; social worker Army Hosp., 1943-44; psychiat. social worker N.H. Program Alcohol and Drug Abuse, Berlin, North Conway, 1966-76; pvt. practice North Conway, 1976—. Avocations: gardening, piano. Home: Rt 16 Box 15 Jackson NH 03846 Office: Box 265 Intervale NH 03845

BAKER, MATTHEW EDWARD, state legislator; b. Westfield, Pa. m. Brenda Fitzsimmons, Nov. 17, 1990. AAS in Parlegal Studies, Corning C.C.; BS in Polit. Sci. and Law, Elmira Coll.; student, Mansfield U. Dist. legis. polit. aide 68th legis. dist. Pa. Ho. of Reps., 1979-91, mem. 68th legis. dist., 1992—. Past trustee and Sunday sch. tchr. 1st Bapt. Ch., Wellsboro, Pa.; mem. adv. bd. Pa. Coll.; past mem. adv. bd. paralegal program Corning C.C.; vice chmn. Pa. Gov.'s Com. on Employment People with Disabilities; mem. Tioga County Job Task Force, Pine Creek Hdqs. Protection Group; past pres. Wellsboro Area Food Pantry; trustee Guthrie Healthcare Sys.; chmn. Laurel Health Devel. Coun.; committeeman 2d ward Wellsboro Rep. Com. Recipient Vol. of Yr. award Gov. of Pa., 1991, Rural Health Legis. of Yr. award, 1998; named Legislator of Yr., Ctr. Rural Health Pa. State Coll. Mem. Pa. Farmers Assn., Tioga County Farmers Assn., Charleston Valley Grange, Rotary. Avocations: hunting, fishing, basketball, tennis, golf. Office: 74 Main St Wellsboro PA 16901-1504

BAKER, MELVIN, hospital pharmacy administrator; b. Cleve., Sept. 6, 1931; s. Barnet and Florence (Kleinman) B. BA In Biol. Scis., Ohio State U., 1954; BSc in Pharmacy, U. Toledo, 1959. Registered pharmacist, Ohio. Dir. pharmacy svcs. Richmond Heights (Ohio) Gen. Hosp., 1964-86; chief pharmacy svcs. City of Cleve. Dept. Pub. Health, 1999—. Cons. Greater Cleve. Hosp. Assn., 1966-86, A.K.A. Ctr. for Health Affairs. Recipient Cert. of Recognition, Greater Cleve. Hosp. Assn., 1976, 80, Cert. of Commendation, Legislature of State of Ohio, 1984. Mem. AMA (affiliate), Am. Pharm. Assn., Am. Soc. Health Sys. Pharmacists, Ohio Soc. Health Sys. Pharmacists, Cleve. Soc. Health Sys. Pharmacists (bd. dirs. 1980-86), No. Ohio Acad. Pharmacy (bd. dirs. 1978—), Masons, Scottish Rite, Shriners, Alpha Zeta Omega (pres. 1991-92, 98-99). Avocations: humor, storytelling, lecturing, comedy. Home: PO Box 24937 Cleveland OH 44124-0937

BAKER, MERL, engineering educator; b. Cadiz, Ky., July 11, 1924; s. Jesse F. and Argie (Coyle) B.; m. Emily Wilson, Sept. 14, 1946; children: Merl Wilson, Marilyn Ruth. BS in Mech. Engring., U. Ky., 1945; MS, Purdue U., 1948, PhD, 1952. Grad. asst. Purdue U., 1946-48; mem. faculty U. Ky., 1948-63, prof. mech. engring., 1955-63; exec. dir. Ky. Research Found., 1953-63; coordinator, dir. U. Ky. coop. programs with AID, 1956-63, exec. dir. research and relations with industry, 1957-63; dean U. Mo. Sch. Mines and Metallurgy, 1963; chancellor U. Mo., Rolla, 1964-73, spl. asst. to pres. statewide system, 1973-77; coordinator energy conservation program Oak Ridge Nat. Lab., 1977-79, energy mgmt. specialist, 1979-82; provost U. Tenn.-Chattanooga, 1982-85, prof. engring., 1985-97, dir. Ctr. for Career Enhancement, 1985-97; engring. cons. Lexington, Ky., 1997—. Recipient Disting. Alumnus award U. Ky., 1965, Disting. Engring. Alumnus award Purdue U., 1968; named Outstanding Mech. Engr., 1991; named to U. Ky. Engring. Hall of Distinction, 2003. Fellow Am. Soc. Engring. Mgmt. (bd. dirs.), Am. Soc. Engring. Edn.; mem. ASHRAE (award of merit tchg. 1959, chmn. edn. com. 1960-61, Disting. Svc. award 1971), NSPE (pres. Tenn. Soc. 1995-96), Ky. Acad. Sci., Newcomen Soc. N.Am., Cosmos Club (Washington), Blue Key, Scabbard and Blade, Sigma Xi, Phi Kappa Phi, Phi Eta Sigma, Tau Beta Pi, Pi Tau Sigma, Sigma Pi Sigma, Omicron Delta Kappa, Chi Epsilon, Rotary Club of Lexington. Home and Office: 1973 Blairmore Rd Lexington KY 40502-2432

BAKER, MICHAEL A. astronaut; b. Memphis, Oct. 27, 1953; s. Clyde E. and Baker; 2 children. BS in Aerospace Engring., U. Tex., 1975; grad. flight tng., Naval Air Sta. Chase Field, Beeville, Tex., 1977; grad., U.S. Naval Test Pilot Sch., 1981. Commd. ensign USN, 1978, advanced through grades to capt.; pilot USS Midway, Yokosuka, Japan; air wing landing signal officer Carrier Air Wing 30; pilot Carrier Suitability Br. of Strike Aircraft Test Directorate; instr. U.S. Naval Test Pilot Sch.; exch. instr. Empire Test Pilots Sch., Boscombe Down, England; mem. team for Shuttle Landing and Deceleration Systems, NASA, 1986—, with Shuttle Avionics Integration Lab., ascent, entry and orbit spacecraft communicator, flight crew ops. directorate rep. to Space Shuttle Program Office, dir. ops. Gagarin Cosmonaut Tng. Ctr., asst. dir. Johnson Space Ctr. for Human Space Flight Programs, Russia, astronaut, internat. space sta. program mgr. for internat. ops., 2001—. Mem. adv. com. dept. aerospace engring. U. Tex. Coll. Engring.; NASA Johnson Space Ctr. rep. to Russian Space Agy., Gagarin Cosmonaut Tng. Ctr., Mission Control Ctr.-Moscow, Energia Rocket and Spacecraft Corp., Krunichev State Sci. and Prodn. Space Ctr. Decorated DFC, Nat. Def. medal, 3 Navy Expeditionary medals; named Outstanding Univ. Tex. Alumni, 1993. Mem.: Nat. Aeronautic Assn., Assn. Space Explorers, Tailhook Assn., Assn. Naval Aviation, Soc. Exptl Test Pilots, VFW, Sierra Club. Achievements include 4 space flight; logged 965 hours in space; pilot on STS-43 Atlantis (Aug. 2-11, 1991) and STS-52 Columbia (Oct. 22-Nov. 1, 1992); mission comdr. STS-68 Endeavour (Sept. 30-Oct. 11, 1994) and STS-81 Atlantis (Jan. 12-22, 1997). Office: Astronaut Office/CB NASA Johnson Space Ctr Houston TX 77058

BAKER, MICHELLE LYNN, software designer; b. Missoula, Mont., Mar. 8, 1956; d. Blaine Lynwood and Margaret Neil (Davis) B.; m. Henry Etzkowitz; 1 child, Alexander. BA, SUNY, Purchase, 1980; MA, Columbia U., 1984, MS, 1985, MPhil, 1989. Pres. Intellinet, Inc., N.Y.C., 1992—; pres., CEO Umbanet Inc., 2000—. Cons. Econ. & Social Rsch. Coun., London, 1994, Ind. Schs. Multimedia Ctr., N.Y.C., 1994-95; exec. bd. N.Y. Software Ind. Assn. Patentee: pictorial user interface for electronic file systems; trouble ticket system for network management; adaptive fault diagnosis; author: Uncertainty on Artificial

Intelligence, 1991. Soccer coach Am. Youth Soccer Orgn., N.Y.C., 1994-98. Recipient Small Bus. Innovative Rsch. award NSF, 1994, 95, 97, Nat Inst. of Stds. and Tech. Advanced Tech. Program, 2002; IBM fellow Ctr. for advanced Studies, Toronto, Can., 1991 Mem. IEEE, Assn. Computing Machinery, N.Y. Software Industry Assn. (bd. dirs.). Avocations: soccer, yoga, swimming, biking, hiking. Office: Intellinet Inc 325 Riverside Dr New York NY 10025-4162 E-mail: michelle@umbanet.com.

BAKER, NADINE DIANE, writer; b. Jilo, W.Va., Sept. 3, 1948; d. Douglas and Bertha Evelyn (Adams) Dial; m. Ernest Wilson Holmes Jr., Sept. 3, 1964 (div. 1979); children: Deana Kay McGlamory, Ernest Wilson Holmes; m. Stone Dwayne Baker (dec. 1996). Cert. nursing asst., S.W. C.C., Richlands, Va., 1992. Cosmetologist Am. Hair Stylest Assn., 1977—80; nursing asst. NC, Va. and W.Va., 1989—97; freelance writer, poet W.Va. Poetry Soc., 2001—. Author: (poems) Mind and Spirit Unity I, 2002, Cooking in the Spirit, 2003; contbr. poems to lit. publs. Recipient cert. of recognition, Famous Poets Soc., 2000, hon. mention, W.Va. Poetry Soc., 2001. Baptist. Home: 45 Riverside Dr Apt 704 Welch WV 24801

BAKER, NANCY KASSEBAUM (NANCY KASSEBAUM), former senator, foundation official; b. Topeka, July 29, 1932; d. Alfred M. and Theo Landon; children: John Philip, Linda Josephine, Richard Landon, William Alfred; m. Howard Baker, 1996. BA in Polit. Sci, U. Kans., 1954; MA in Diplomatic History, U. Mich., 1956. Mem. Maize (Kans.) Sch. Bd., 1972-75; mem. Washington staff Sen. James B. Pearson of Kans., 1975-76; mem. U.S. Senate from Kans., 1979-96, mem. fgn. relations com., labor and human resources com., Indian Affairs com.; mem. com. fgn. rels., subcom. African affairs, 1980-96; mem. subcom. arts, edn. Arts & Humanities; mem. com. banking, housing & urban affairs, subcom. internat. fin. & monetary policy; former chmn. bd. trustees Robert Wood Johnson Found.; co-chair The Presdl. Appointee Initiative Adv. Bd., Brookings Inst., Washington. Mem. Kans. Press Women's Assn., Women's Assn. Instnl. Logopedics. Republican. Episcopalian. Office: Presdl Appointee Initiative 1720 Rhode Island Ave NW Ste 301 Washington DC 20036

BAKER, NATALIE MICHELE, child therapist; b. Kingston, Jamaica, Sept. 29, 1971; came to the U.S., 1977; d. Harold and Marylin Deidre Chlup. BA in Fine Art, BA in Psychology, U. Del., 1994; MS in Cmty. Counseling, Wilmington Coll., 1999. Lic. profl. counselor of mental health, cert. nat. counselor. Crisis counselor Family Svcs. of Cecil County, Elkton, Md., 1994-95; asst. mgr. residential group home Martin Luther Homes of Del., Newark, 1995; psychol. technician Healthcare Commons, Elkton, 1997-99; individual/group therapist Healthcare Commons, Inc., Carneys Point, N.J., 1998-2000, elem. sch. based therapist, 2000—. Cons. Healthcare Commons, Inc., Carneys Point, 1999. Mem. New Castle Hist. Soc. Mem. ACA. Office: Healthcare Commons Inc 500 Pennsville-Auburn Rd Carneys Point NJ 08069

BAKER, PAMELA, lawyer; b. Detroit, Apr. 6, 1951; d. William D. and Lois (Tukey) Baker; m. Jay R. Franke, June 10, 1972; children: Baker Eugene, Alexandra Britell. AB, Smith Coll., 1972; JD, U. Wis. Madison, 1976. Bar: Ill. 1976, Wis. 1976. Ptnr. Sonnenschein, Nath & Rosenthal, Chgo. Contbr. articles to profl. jour. Fellow Am. Coll. Employee Benefits Counsel (charter), Am. Bar Found.; mem. ABA (mem. employee benefits com. 1984—, chair-elect 1998-99, chair 1999-2000, mem. plan mergers and acquisitions com. 1985— mem. fed. regulation of securities com. 1989—, chair 1989-95), Ill. State Bar Assn. (sec. employee benefits sect. coun. 1989-90, vice chair 1990 91, chair 1991-92), Chgo. Bar Assn. (employee benefits com. 1978—, sec. 1984-85, vice chair 1985-86, chair 1986-87, fed. taxation com. 1980—, exec. coun. 1982-85). Office: Sonnenschein Nath & Rosenthal Sears Tower 233 S Wacker Dr Ste 8000 Chicago IL 60606-6491

BAKER, PATRICIA ANN, publishing executive; b. Englewood, N.J., Apr. 3, 1939; BA, St. Mary's Coll., 1961. Prodn. designer Little, Brown Pubs., 1961-63; mktg. & promotion dir. Sunset Books, 1963-68; design & prodn. mgr. Hoover Instn. Press, Stanford, Calif., 1981-89, exec. editor, 1989—. Office: Hoover Instn Press Stanford U Stanford CA 94305-6010

BAKER, PAUL RAYMOND, history educator; b. Everett, Wash., Sept. 28, 1927; s. Loren Robbins and Alma Irene (Ball) B.; m. Elizabeth O. Kemp, Feb. 11, 1972; 1 dau., Alice Elizabeth. AB, Stanford U., 1949; MA, Columbia U., 1951; PhD, Harvard U., 1960. Staff editor Ency. Americana, N.Y.C., 1952-55; instr., asst. prof. Calif. Inst. Tech., Pasadena, 1960-63; lectr. U. Calif.-Riverside, 1963-64, U. Oreg., Eugene, 1964-65; assoc. prof., then prof. history NYU, N.Y.C., 1965-99, emeritus prof., 1999—, dir. Am. civilization program, 1972-92. Mem. media panel NEH, 1978. Editor: Views of Society and Manners in America, 1963; gen. editor: American Problem Studies series, 40 vols., 1968—; author: The Fortunate Pilgrims, 1964, Richard Morris Hunt, 1980, Stanny: the Gilded Life of Stanford White, 1989; compiler: The Atomic Bomb, 1968, The Atomic Bomb, rev. edit., 1976; co-author: The American Experience, 5 vols., 1976, 79, (Spanish translation) Nueva Historia de los Estados Unidos, 1986; (with others) Master Builders, 1985, The Architecture of Richard Morris Hunt, 1986, (French translation) Richard Morris Hunt Architecte, The Italian Presence in American Art, 1860-1920, 1992, Henry Adams and His World, 1993, La Virtù e la Libertà, 1995. Mem. Glen Ridge Hist. Preservation Commn., 1994-96. Kennedy travel fellow Harvard U., 1958-59, NEH fellow, 1982. Mem. Am. Studies Assn. (pres. met. N.Y. chpt. 1968-69, Mary C. Turpie prize for outstanding contbns. to tchg. advisement and program devel. 1994), Orgn. Am. Historians, Victorian Soc. in Am., Phi Beta Kappa (v.p., pres. Beta of N.Y. 1966-70). Home: 90 Hillside Ave Glen Ridge NJ 07028-2212 Office: NYU Dept History 53 Washington Square South New York NY 10012-1098

BAKER, PAUL THORNELL, anthropology educator; b. Burlington, Iowa, Feb. 28, 1927; s. Palmer Ward Baker and Viola Isabelle (Thornell) Loughlin; m. Thelma Marion Shoher, Feb. 21, 1949; children: Deborah C., Amy L., Joshua S., Felicia B. Student, U. Miami, 1947—49; BA, U. N.Mex., 1951; PhD, Harvard U., 1956. Rschr. U.S. Army Q.M., Natick, Mass., 1952—57; asst. prof. anthropology Pa. State U., University Park, 1957—61, assoc. prof., 1961—65, prof., 1965—81, Evan Pugh prof. anthropology, 1981—87, Evan Pugh prof emeritus, 1987—, head dept., 1980—85. Sci. advisor Wenner-Gren Found., N.Y.C., 1980—83; mem. U.S. Commn. for UNESCO, 1982—84, exec. commn., 1983—84. Editor: Biology of Human Adaptability, 1966, Man in the Andes, 1976, Biology of High Altitude Peoples, 1978, The Changing Samoans, 1986; co-author (with G.A. Harrison, J.M. Tanner, D.R. Pilbeam): Human Biology, 1988. With U.S. Army, 1945—47. Decorated Yugoslavian Order of the Golden Star with Necklace; recipient Huxley medal, Royal Anthrop. Inst. Gt. Brit., 1982; fellow, Guggenheim Found., 1974—75; scholar Fulbright rsch. scholar, 1962. Fellow: Am. Anthrop. Assn. (assoc. editor jour. 1973—76); mem.: NAS, Internat. Union Anthropol. and Ethnol. Scis. (hon. life, v.p. 1988—93, sr. v.p. 1993—98), Internat. Assn. Human Biologists (pres. 1980—89, Franz Boas Disting. Achievement award), Human Biology Coun. (pres. 1974—77), Am. Assn. Phys. Anthropologists (pres. 1969—71, Charles R. Darwin Lifetime Achievement award 1993). Address: 337 Upton Pyne Dr Brentwood CA 94513-6458

BAKER, PAULINE HALPERN, political scientist, policy analyst; b. Jersey City, Aug. 9, 1941; d. Michael Harry and Dorothy (Dubilier) Halpern; m. Raymond W. Baker, Aug. 29, 1964; children: Deren James, Gayle Janice. BA, Rutgers U., 1962; MA, UCLA, 1963, PhD with distinction, 1970. Lectr. U. Lagos, Nigeria, 1965-72; internat. affairs fellow Rockefeller Found., N.Y.C., 1975-76; profl. staff mem. U.S. Senate Fgn. Rels. Com., Washington, 1977-81; rsch. scientist Battelle Meml. Inst., Washington, 1981-84; dir. PHB Assocs., Washington, 1984-85; sr. assoc. Carnegie Endowment for Internat. Peace, Washington, 1986-92, dir. South African meeting series; pres. Fund for Peace, Washington, 1996—. Profl. lectr., Sch. Advanced Internat. Studies, Johns Hopkins U., Washington, 1987-92; dep. dir. congressional program, The Aspin Inst., 1992—; cons., Rockefeller Found., Aspen Inst. Humanistic Studies, World Bank, AID, U.S. Dept. State, others. Author: Urbanization and Political Change: The Politics of Lagos, 1917-1967, 1974, Obstacles to Private Sector Activities in Africa, 1983, The Economics of Nigerian Federalism, 1984, The United States and South Africa: The Reagan Years, 1989; co-editor: African Armies: Evolution and Capabilities, 1986; contbr. articles to topical and gen. interest publs. Grantee NDEA, 1966, Rockefeller Found. Fellowship, 1975-76. Mem. African Studies Assn. (bd. dirs. 1987-89), Coun. Fgn. Rels., Am. Polit. Sci. Assn., Internat. Studies Assn. Home: 7300 Broxburn Ct Bethesda MD 20817-4754 Office: Fund for Peace 1701 K St NW Washington DC 20036

BAKER, PETER MITCHELL, laser scientist, educator, science administrator; b. London, July 18, 1939; s. George Edward and Clarice (Griffiths) Baker; m. Sunny Baker, Oct. 15, 1988; 1 child, Scott George. BSc in Physics with honors, London U., 1963. Sr. physicist Itek Corp., Lexington, Mass., 1966-69; sr. v.p. Micronetic Sys., Burlington, Mass., 1969-74; tchr. physics Hillcrest Sch., Nairobi, Kenya, 1975-77; pres. Quantrad Corp., Torrance, Calif., 1977-84, Ebtec Calif., Huntington Beach, 1985-88; exec. dir. Laser Inst. Am., Orlando, Fla., 1988—. Lectr. lasers UCLA Ext., 1986—88. Contbr. articles to profl. jours. Recipient CEO award for Outstanding Small Bus., 1982. Fellow: Laser Inst. Am. (pres. 1987); mem.: Engring. and Sci. Soc. Execs. (bd. dirs. 2000, v.p. 2003). Avocations: walking, tennis. Office: Laser Inst Am 13501 Ingenuity Dr Ste 128 Orlando FL 32826-3009 *My guiding principle is "Do What You Say".*

BAKER, PHILIP DOUGLAS, consultant, retired investment banker; b. Los Angeles, Mar. 19, 1922; s. J. Douglas and Alice (Brown) B.; m. Cornelia Draves, July 16, 1955; children: Brinton, Todd, Claudia, Samuel Baker. BS, UCLA, 1947; MBA, U. Calif., Berkeley, 1948. Assoc. Marshall Plan, Germany, 1948-52; with White, Weld & Co., Inc., N.Y.C., 1952-76, ptnr., 1960-72, sr. v.p., 1972-76; pres. Insts. of Religion and Health, 1978-81; cons. Nat. Exec. Service Corps, 1978—. Chmn. bd. Found. Religion and Health, 1982-86; adj. assoc. prof. Grad. Sch. Bus. Adminstrn., NYU, 1964-66. Trustee Valley Hosp., 1972-83, West Bergen Mental Health, 1998—; pres. Valley Health Services, 1987-94; pres.'s coun. Berea Coll., 1988—. Capt. USMCR, 1943-46. Decorated Purple Heart. Mem. Investment Bankers Assn. Am. (pres. 1971-72), Securities Industry Assn. (vice chmn. bd. 1972), Bond Club N.Y. Home: 293 Greenridge Rd Franklin Lakes NJ 07417-2011

BAKER, R. ROBINSON, surgeon; b. Balt., Dec. 30, 1928; s. Henry Scott and Frances (Robinson) B.; m. Jean Harvey, Sept. 12, 1953; children: Susan, Scott, Robert, Jean. AB, Johns Hopkins U., 1950, MD, 1954. Diplomate: Am. Bd. Surgery and Bd. Thoracic Surgery. Intern Johns Hopkins U., 1954-55; sr. asst. surgeon Nat. Heart Inst., 1955-57; asst. resident Johns Hopkins Hosp., 1957-58, resident, 1958-61, chief surg. resident, 1961-62; surgeon-in-charge Johns Hopkins Hosp. (Breast Clinic), 1970—, Johns Hopkins Hosp. (Oncology Center), 1976; prof. surgery Johns Hopkins U., 1967—, prof. oncology, 1975—, Warfield M. Firor prof. surgery, 1991—; mem. (Coop. Lung Cancer Detection Group), 1971—. Recipient grants Am. Cancer Soc., 1966-71, grants John A. Hartford Found., 1968-73, grants Upjohn Co., 1973, grants Sterling Winthrop Rsch. Inst., 1975—; named hon. fellow Royal Coll. Surgeons of Ireland. Fellow ACS, Royal Coll. Surgeons (hon.); mem. Soc. Univ. Surgeons, Am. Assn. Thoracic Surgery, So. Thoracic Surg. Assn., Soc. Head and Neck Surgeons, AMA, Am., So. Surg. Assns., Elkridge (Balt.) Club, Fishers Island (N.Y.) Club, Hay Harbor Club (Fishers Island). Home: 8717 Mcdonogh Rd Baltimore MD 21208-1021 Office: 600 N Wolfe St Baltimore MD 21287-0005

BAKER, REBECCA LOUISE, musician, music educator, consultant; b. Covina, Calif., Apr. 12, 1951; d. Allan Herman and Hazel Margaret (Maki) Flaten; m. Jerry Wayne Baker, Dec. 22, 1972; children: Jared Wesley, Rachelle LaDawn, Shannon Faith. Grad. high sch., Park River, N.D.; student, Trinity Bible Inst., 1968-69. Sec. Agrl. Stblzn. & Conservation Svc. Office, Park River, N.D., 1969; pianist, singer Paul Clark Singers & Vic Coburn Evangelistic Assn., Portland, Oreg., 1969-72; musician, singer Restoration Ministries Evangelistic Assn., Richland, Wash., 1972-80; musician, pvt. instr. Calvary Temple Ch., Shawnee, Okla., 1980-81; organist, choirmaster St. Francis Episcopal Ch., Tyler, 1984-87; co-founder, owner Psalmist Sch. of Music & Recording Studio, Whitehouse, 1983—; pianist/entertainer Willowbrook Country Club, Tyler, Tex., 1991—; pianist, vocalist Mario's Italian Restaurant, Tyler, 1994—. Pianist Garner Ted Armstrong, Tyler, 1986—; pianist, dir. Children's Choir, Calvary Bapt. Ch., Tyler, 1987—; pianist, entertainer Ramada Hotel, Tyler, 1988-90; pianist Whitehouse (Tex.) Sch. Dist. choirs, 1988—; accompanist Tyler Area Children's Chorale, 1988-90, Univ. Interscholastic League; pvt. instr. keyboard and vocal. Composer: Religious Songs (12 on albums), 1979; pianist, arranger, prodr., rec. artist 6 albums; editor, arranger: Texas Women's Aglow Songbook, 1987; editor Shekinah Glory mag., 1989—; developer improvisational piano course; star, prodr. weekly, nationally syndicated mus. religious programs for TV, 1995, 96, Proclaim His Glory, 1997—; played for receptions honoring Gov. George Bush, Tex. Senator Phil Gramm and Congressman John Bryant. Performer, spkr. many charitable, civic and religious orgns., Tex. and U.S. including AAUW, Kiwanis Clubs; co-founder Psalmist Mins. Internat., 1988—; founder, pres. Christian Music Tchr.'s Assn., 1991; worship leader Mayor's Prayer Breakfast, Tyler, 1994. Mem. Women's Aglow Fellowship (music dir., spkr., performer at retreats and tng. seminars). Republican. Full Gospel. Avocations: travel, reading, interior decorating, collecting. Home and Office: Psalmist Music & Recording PO Box 961 Whitehouse TX 75791-0961 E-mail: psalmistministries@netzero.com.

BAKER, RICHARD GRAVES, geology educator, palynologist; b. Merrill, Wis., June 12, 1938; s. Dillon James and Miriam Baker; m. Debby J.Z. Baker; children: Kristina Kae, James Dillon, Charity Ann. BA, U. Wis., 1960; MS, U. Minn., 1964; PhD, U. Colo., 1969. Asst. prof. geology U. Iowa, Iowa City, 1970-75, assoc. prof., 1975-81, prof., 1981—, chmn. dept., 1992-95, prof. botany, 1988-92, prof. biol. scis., 1992-2000, prof. emeritus, 2000—. Contbr. articles to profl. jours., chapters to books. Chmn. Iowa chpt. Nature Conservancy, Des Moines, 1981-82. Grantee NSF, 1984-86, 88-90, 94-97, NOAA, 1992-93; recipient Disting. Scientist award Iowa Acad. Sci., 2001. Fellow Geol. Soc. Am., Iowa Acad. Sci.; mem. AAAS, Am. Quaternary Assn., Ecol. Soc. Am. Office: Univ Iowa 121 Trowbridge Hall Dept Geosci Iowa City IA 52242-1319 Business E-Mail: dick-baker@uiowa.edu.

BAKER, RICHARD HUGH, congressman; b. New Orleans, La, LA, May 22, 1948; m. Karen Carpenter; children: Brandon, Julie. BA, La. State U., 1971. State rep. La. Dist. 64, former chmn. com. on transp., hwys. and pub. works, 1981-82, state rep.; mem. La. Ho. of Reps., 1972—86, 100th-106th Congresses from 6th La. Dist., 1987—; mem. transp. and infrastructure com. and vets. affs. com.; chmn. Banking & Fin. Svcs. subcom. on Capital Mkts., Securities and Govt. Sponsored Enterprises; also real estate broker. Republican. Methodist. Office: US Ho of Reps 341 Cannon House Offc Bldg Washington DC 20515-1806*

BAKER, RICHARD SOUTHWORTH, lawyer; b. Lansing, Mich., Dec. 18, 1929; s. Paul Julius and Florence (Schmid) B.; m. Kathleen E. Yull, 1956 (dec. 1964); m. Marina J. Vidoli, 1965 (div. 1989); children: Garrick Richard, Lydia Joy; m. Barbara J. Walker, 1997. Student, DePauw U., 1947-49; AB cum laude, Harvard, 1951; JD, U. Mich., 1954. Bar: Ohio 1957, U.S. Dist. Ct. (no. dist.) Ohio 1958, U.S. Tax Ct. 1960, U.S. Supreme Ct. 1971, U.S. Ct. Appeals (6th cir.) 1972. Mem. firm Fuller & Henry, and predecessors, 1956-91; pvt. practice Toledo, 1991—. Chmn. nat. com. region IV Mich. Law Sch. Fund, 1967-69, mem.-at-large, 1970-85. Bd. dirs. Assn. Harvard Alumni, 1970-73. Served with AUS, 1954-56. Fellow Am. Coll. Trial Lawyers; mem. ABA, Ohio Bar Assn., Toledo Bar Assn., Toledo Club, Harvard Club (pres. Toledo chpt. 1968-77), Capital Club, Phi Delta Theta, Phi Delta Phi. Office: 2819 Falmouth Rd Toledo OH 43615-2215

BAKER, RICK, make-up artist; b. Binghamton, N.Y., Dec. 8, 1950; s. Ralph B. and Doris (Hamlin) Baker; m. Elaine Parkyn (div. 1984); m. Silvia Abascal, Nov. 10, 1987. Spl. effects makeup artist on the following films Octaman, 1971, The Thing With Two Heads, 1972, Pirahna, 1972, Bone, 1972, The Exorcist, 1973, Schlock, 1973, Live and Let Die, 1973, Hell Up in Harlem, 1973, It's Alive, 1974, Death Race 2000, 1975, Black Caesar, 1975, Squirm, 1976, Food of the Gods, 1976, King Kong, 1976, Track of the Moonbest, 1976, Zebra Force, 1976, Kentucky Fried Movie, 1977, Star Wars, 1977, The Incredible Melting Man, 1978, It's Alive 2, 1978, The Fury, 1978, Tanya's Island, 1980, The Funhouse, 1980, The Incredible Shrinking Woman, 1981, An American Werewolf in London, 1981 (Acad. award Best Makeup), Videodrome, 1983, Greystoke: The Legend of Tarzan, Lord of the Apes, 1984, Starman, 1984, My Science Project, 1985, Cocoon, 1985, Ratboy, 1986, Captain Eo, 1986, Harry and the Hendersons, 1987 (Acad. award Best Makeup), Summer School, 1987, Missing Link, 1988, Coming to America, 1988, Gorillas in the Mist, 1988; co-prodr.: Gorillas in the Mist, 1988; Spl. effects makeup artist on the following films Gremlins 2; The New Batch, 1990; co-prodr.: Gremlins 2; The New Batch, 1990; Spl. effects makeup artist on the following films The Rocketeer, 1991, Ed Wood, 1994 (Acad. award Best Makeup), Wolf, 1994, Batman Forever, 1995, The Amazing Panda Adventure, 1995, Just Cause, 1995, The Nutty Professor, 1996 (Acad. awd. Best Makeup), The Frighteners, 1996, Escape from L.A., 1996, Men in Black, 1997 (Acad. awd. Best Makeup, 1997), Mighty Joe Young, 1998, Life, 1999, TV work includes (movies) The Autobiography of Miss Jane Pittman, 1974 (Emmy award Best Makeup), An American Christmas Carol, 1979, Something Is Out There, 1988, Body Bags, 1993, TV work includes (series) Davey and Goliath, 1960—65, Werewolf, 1987—88, Beauty and the Beas, 1987—90, designed spl. makeup effects for Michael Jackson's Thriller, 1983, The Klumps, How the Grinch Stole Christmas (Acad. awd. Best Makeup), Planet of the Apes. Office: IATSE Local 706 828 N Hollywood Way Burbank CA 91505-2831

BAKER, ROBERT EDWARD, lawyer, retired financial corporation executive; b. Albion, Mich., May 6, 1930; s. Robert Charles and Loretto A. (Barrett) B.; m. Mary Anne Mulcahy, Feb. 20, 1965. BBA, U. Mich., 1952, LLB, 1955. Bar: Mich. 1956. Atty. legal dept. Chrysler Corp., Detroit, 1955-64; with Chrysler Fin. Corp., Troy, Mich., 1964-90, also bd. dirs., v.p. corp. fin., 1970-80, v.p. fin., gen. counsel, 1980-85, vice chmn. bd., 1985-90; regional dir. Mich. Nat. Bank, 1978-90. Trustee Independence One Mut. Funds, Farmington Hills, Mich., 1990-2002. Trustee Comprehensive Health Svcs., Inc., 1972-99, chmn. bd., 1977-99; trustee, sec. Rose Hill Ctr., Inc., Holly, Mich., 1989—; trustee Sacred Heart Major Sem., Detroit, 1996—, chmn. fin. com., 2000—. With CIC, AUS, 1955-57. Recipient Disting. Service award Am. Fin. Services Assn., 1981 Mem. ABA, State Bar of Mich., Am. Assn. Sovereign Mil. Order of Malta, Orchard Lake Country Club, Dutch Settlers Soc. Albany. Roman Catholic. Home: 4327 Stoneleigh Rd Bloomfield Hills MI 48302-2157 E-mail: bobanne220@earthlink.net.

BAKER, ROBERT ERNEST, JR., retired foundation executive; b. Tuscaloosa, Ala., Oct. 17, 1916; s. Robert Ernest and Faye (Whitson) B.; m. Billye Louise Driskell, June 25, 1947; 1 son, Brent Driskell. BS in Indsl. Engring, U. Ala., 1939. Registered profl. engr., Tex. Indsl. engring., mgmt. and fin. cons., 1939-62; exec. adminstr., sec. Moody Found., Galveston, Tex., 1962-97; ret., 1997. Mem.: Arty. (Galveston). Presbyterian. Home: 6 Adler Cir Galveston TX 77551-5828

BAKER, ROBERT FRANK, molecular biologist, educator; b. Weiser, Idaho, Apr. 9, 1936; s. Robert Clarence and Beulah (Hulet) B.; m. Mary Margaret Murphy, May 29, 1965; children: Allison Leslie, Steven Mark. BS, Stanford U., 1959; PhD, Brown U., 1966. Postdoctoral rsch. assoc. Stanford (Calif.) U., 1966-68; asst. prof. dept. biol. scis. U. So. Calif., L.A., 1968-72, assoc. prof., 1972-83, prof., 1983—, dir. molecular biology div., 1978-80, mem. Comprehensive Cancer Ctr., 1984—. Vis. assoc. prof. Harvard U. Med. Sch., Boston 1975-76; mem. genetic study sect. NIH, Bethesda, Md., 1977-79, 82 Contbr. articles to profl. jours. Grantee NIH, NSF, 1968—. Mem. Am. Soc. Zoologists, Am. Soc. Microbiology, Sigma Xi. Avocations: amateur radio, electronics. Home: 607 Almar Ave Pacific Palisades CA 90272-4208 Office: U So Calif Dept Molecular Biology Mc 1340 Los Angeles CA 90089-0001

BAKER, ROBERT J(OHN), hospital administrator; b. Detroit, Feb. 2, 1944; s. Wesley Ries and Irma Louise (Richards) B.; m. Priscilla Horschak, Sept. 10, 1966; children: Scott, Katherine. BA, Kalamazoo Coll., 1966; MBA, U. Chgo., 1968. Adminstr. Indian Hosp., Sells, Ariz., 1968-70; asst. dir. U. Minn. Hosp., Mpls., 1970-73, assoc. dir., 1973-74, assoc. dir. ops., 1974-77, sr. assoc. dir., 1977; dir. U. Nebr. Hosp. and Clinic, Omaha, 1977-86; pres., chief exec. officer U. Health Sys. Consortium, Oak Brook, Ill., 1986—. Served with USPHS, 1968-70. Recipient Mary H. Bachmeyer award U. Chgo., 1968; Carl A. Erickson fellow, 1966 Mem. Council Teaching Hosps., Omaha-Council Bluffs Hosp. Assn. (pres. 1983) Office: U Health Systems Consortium 2001 Spring Rd Ste 700 Oak Brook IL 60523-1890

BAKER, ROBERT LEON, naval medical officer; b. Oak, Nebr., Feb. 7, 1925; s. Oscar E. and Ada Veru (Davis) B.; m. Rebecca Chandler, Dec. 12, 1956; children: Rebecca Ann, Jay Milton, Betsy Jean, Robert Leon, Bruce Chandler, Brenda Carole. BS in Liberal Arts, La. Poly. Inst., 1945; BS in Medicine, MD with highest honors, U. Ark., 1949; grad. program health systems mgmt., Harvard U. Grad. Sch. Bus., 1972. Diplomate: Am. Bd. Obstetrics and Gynecology. Apprentice seaman U.S. Navy, 1943, commd. lt. (j.g.), M.C., 1949, advanced through grades to rear adm., 1973; rotating intern Tripler Gen. Hosp., Honolulu, 1949-50; resident in obstetrics and gynecology U.S. Naval Hosp., Oakland, Calif., 1954; assigned U.S. and overseas as obstetrician-gynecologist; chmn. dept. obstetrics and gynecology Naval Hosp., Portsmouth, Va., 1969-72; med. aide Office Comdr. in chief, NATO, 1970-72; dir. grad. tng. and chmn. dept. ob-gyn. Naval Regional Med. Center, Oakland, 1973-75, comdg. officer Phila., 1975-77, Naval Aerospace and Regional Med. Center, Pensacola, Fla., 1977-79; chief ob-gyn. service Baxter Gen. Hosp., Mountain Home, Ark., 1980-82. Clin. prof. Va. Commonwealth U. Med. Sch., 1971—72; med. dir. Hospice of Ozarks, 1984—96. Contbr. articles to med. jours. Bd. dirs. Phila. YWCA, 1975-77, USO, Phila., 1976-77, Pensacola, Fla., 1978-80, Baxter County Regional Hosp., 1985-87, also various bds. tng. insts., 1980—; bd. dirs. Ctrl. Ark. Radiation Therapy Inst., 1990-96, 98—, chmn. adv. bd. Mountain Home, 1990—; pres. Baxter County chpt. Am. Cancer Soc., 1995-96; founding mem. Internat. Coll. Hospice/Palliative Care, 1995; mem. Make A Wish Found.; bd. dirs. Internat. Hospice Inst. and Coll., 1996-99. Decorated Legion of Merit, Meritorious Service medal, Navy Commendation medal; recipient Letters of Commendation Comdr. in Chief NATO, Sec. Navy; recipient Wish Team award for Ark., Make A Wish Found., 1996. Fellow: ACOG (chmn. armed forces dist. Navy sect. 1967—69, vice chmn. armed forces dist. 1971—74, asst. sec. 1977—79); mem.: AMA (del. 1976—77), Acad. Hospice Physicians (founding mem.), Ark. Med. Soc. (del. 1982—2002), Baxter County Med. Soc. (v.p. 1982—84), Assn. Mil. Surgeons U.S. (chpt. pres. 1973—74), Union League (Phila.), Phi Chi, Alpha Omega Alpha. Mem. Christian Ch. (Disciples Of Christ). Home: PO Box 44 Mountain Home AR 72654-0044 Office: 3763 Highway 5 S Mountain Home AR 72653-5944 *Time is critical for top management. It is divided into People time and Paper time. People time, almost invariably, must take precedence at any moment, but paper time still demands and must be accomplished. People time demonstrates concern. This perception by people of concern by management is the essential element of true leadership, and the essence of morale. One who can follow this precept while, at the same time completing paper work, is a top manager. This takes time.*

BAKER, ROBERT THOMAS, interior designer; b. Kansas City, Mo., Mar. 23, 1932; s. Robert Blume and Justina (Early) B. BA in Art, U. Mo., Columbia, 1954, MA in Interior Design, 1962; cert., Parsons Sch. Design, N.Y.C., 1958. Interior designer Edward Keith, Inc., Kansas City, Mo., 1958-60, 63-71, Nereoux Interiors, New Iberia, La., 1960-61, Bloomingdales, N.Y.C., 1962-63, Thomas Price Interiors, Kansas City, Mo., 1971-78; owner Robert Baker Interiors Inc., Kansas City, 1978-89; chmn. interior design dept. Au Marché, Inc., Kansas City, 1989; pres. Baker Design, Inc., Kansas City, 1989—. Mem. guidance com. Found. Interior Designer Edn. Research, 1972-82 Bd. visitors Found. Interior Design Edn. Research, 1984-90. Mem. adv. bd. Toy & Miniature Mus. Kansas City, 1985—; bd. govs., chmn. adv. bd. Hand-in-Hand, 1995—. With USAAF, 1954-57. Award of merit Mo.W./Kans. chpt., 1971 Fellow Am. Soc. Interior Designers (pres. Mo.W./Kans. chpt. 1966-72, 73-74, regional v.p. 1969-71, nat. gov. 1969-74) Presbyterian. Home and Office: 12801 Cherry St Kansas City MO 64145-1308 *As strange as it may sound in this day and age, I have always tried my best to treat my clients, my suppliers, my peers, and whomever I come in contact with, in the same manner that I hope they would treat me. Professionally, I have always tried to project my clients personality and interests so that the completed job reflects them and not me. To me, an interior is not a success if it winds up looking like the designer rather than the person, or persons, for whom it was designed.*

BAKER, ROBERT WOODWARD, airline executive; b. Bronxville, N.Y., Sept. 3, 1944; s. Richard Woodward and Dorothy Marilyn (Garett) B.; m. Martha Jane Hauschild, June 11, 1966; children: Richard Woodward, Robert Woodward, William Garrett, Suzanne. BA, Trinity Coll., 1966; MBA, U. Pa., 1968. Dir. ramp services Am. Airlines, Inc., N.Y.C., 1973-76, asst. v.p. mktg. adminstrn., 1976-77, v.p. so. div., 1977-79, v.p. freight mktg. Dallas-Ft. Worth

Airport, 1979-80, v.p. sales and advt., 1980-82, v.p. mktg. automation systems, 1982-85, sr. v.p. info. systems, 1985, sr. v.p. ops., 1985-89; sr. v.p. AMR Corp., 1985-89; exec. v.p. ops. Am. Airlines, Inc., 1989-2000, vice chmn., 2000—02, ret., 2002. Died Apr. 20, 2003.

BAKER, ROLAND JERALD, educator; b. Pendleton, Oreg., Feb. 27, 1938; s. Roland E. and Theresa Helen (Forest) B.; m. Judy Lynn Murphy, Nov. 24, 1973; children: Kristen L., Kurt F., Brian H. BA, Western Wash. U., 1961; MBA, U. Mich., 1968. Cert. purchasing mgr., profl. contract mgr. Asst. dir. purchasing and stores U. Wash., Seattle, 1970-75; mgr. purchasing and material control Foss Launch & Tug Co., Seattle, 1975-79; faculty Shoreline C.C., 1972-79, 98—, Pacific Luth. U., 1977-79, Edmonds C.C., 1974-79; chmn. educators group Nat. Assn. Purchasing Mgmt., Tempe, Ariz., 1976-79, exec. v.p., 1979-98; pres. Nat. Assn. Purchasing Mgmt. Svcs., Tempe, Ariz., 1989-95. Faculty Ariz. State U., Tempe, 1988-91; world bus. adv. Coun. Am. Grad. Sch. of Internat. Mgmt., Glendale, Ariz., 1994-98; adv. bd. blockbuy.com, Inc., 1999-01, Perfect.com., Inc., 2000—; exec. v.p. MyGroupbuy Inc., 2000—, also bd. dirs.; mem. faculty Shoreline C.C., Seattle, Wash., 1998—. Author: Purchasing Factomatic, 1977, Inventory System Factomatic, 1978, Policies and Procedures for Purchasing and Material Control, 1980, rev. edit., 1992. With USN, 1961-70, comdr. Res., 1969-91. Recipient Disting. Achievement award Ariz. State U. Coll. Bus., 1997; U.S. Navy postgrad. fellow, 1967. Mem. Purchasing Mgmt. Assn. Wash. (pres. 1978-79), Nat. Minority Supplier Devel. Coun. (bd. dirs.), Am. Prodn. and Inventory Control Soc., Nat. Assn. Purchasing Mgmt. (exec. v.p. 1979-97), Nat. Contract Mgmt. Assn., Internat. Fedn. Purchasing and Materials Mgmt. (exec. com. 1984-87, exec. adv. com. 1991-98). Office: Shoreline CC 16101 Greenwood Ave N Seattle WA 98133-5667

BAKER, RONALD JAMES, English language educator, university administrator; b. London, Aug. 24, 1924; s. James Herbert Walter and Ethel Frances (Miller) B.; m. Helen Gillespie Elder, Sept. 3, 1949; children: Ann, Lynn, Ian, Sarah, Katherine; m. Frances Marilyn Frazer; 1 son, Ralph Edward. BA, U. B.C., Can., 1951, MA, 1953; LLD (hon.), U. N.B., Can., 1970, Mt. Allison U., 1977, U. P.E.I., 1989, Simon Fraser U., 1990. Lectr. U. B.C., 1951-53, instr., 1953-54, 56-57, asst. prof., 1957-62, sec. Senate Com. Acad. Orgn., 1961-62, assoc. prof., 1962-63; prof. English Simon Fraser U., 1964-69, dir. acad. planning, 1964-65, head dept. English, 1964-68; first pres. U. P.E.I., Charlottetown, Can., 1969-78, univ. prof., 1979-91. Dir. Inst. Dept. Leadership, U. P.E.I., David MacDonald Stewart prof. Can. studies, 1988-91; disting. vis. prof. U. New Eng., Australia, 1984; mem. Acad. Bd. B.C., 1963-69, Joint Bd. Tchr. Edn. B.C., 1964-66; mem., chmn. various selection coms. including Can. Coun., 1971-77, Social Sci. and Humanities Rsch. Coun. Can. Nat. Def. Dept., 1981-98, Can. Radio-TV and Telecomm. Commn., 1982-87, and 25 others; bd. govs. N.S. Tech. Coll., Holland Coll., 1968-78, Killam Prize Com., 1984-87, Molson Prize Com., 1987-88; chair mil. and strategic studies com. Nat. Def. Can., 1989-98. Editor: The Faculty Handbook, 1960; author (with W. G. Hardwick): North Shore Regional College Study, 1965, Regional College Study: Delta, Langley, Richmond, Surrey, 1966; contbr. articles to profl. jours. Mem. interim coun. U. No. B.C., 1989-90; presiding officer Can. Citizen Ct., 1990-; vol. advisor First Nations Bands, Can. Exec. Svc. Orgn., 1984-. Served with RAF, 1943-47. Decorated Officer Order of Can., 1978; recipient Can. Centennial medal, 1967, Jubilee medal, 1977, Disting. Mem. award Can. Soc. Study of H.E., 1988, Can. 125 medal, 1992, Golden Jubilee medal, 2002; Humanities Rsch. Coun. Can. fellow, 1954, 55, grantee, 1968; Royal Soc. Can. fellow, 1954-56; Can. Coun. rsch. grantee, 1969. Mem. Assn. Univs. and Colls. Can. (dir. 1972-78), Assn. Atlantic Univs. (pres. 1976-78), Can. Soc. for Study Higher Edn. (v.p. 1974, pres. 1975-76, named Disting. Mem. 1988), Assn. Can. Univ. Tchrs. English (pres. 1967-68), Can. Linguistic Assn. (exec. 1966-67). E-mail: rjfbaker@hotmail.com.

BAKER, RONALD LEE, English educator; b. Indpls., June 30, 1937; m. Catherine Anne Neal, Oct. 21, 1960; children: Susannah Jill, Jonathan Kemp. BS, Ind. State U., Terre Haute, 1960; MA, Ind. State U., 1961; postgrad., U. Ill., 1963-65; PhD, Ind U., 1969. Instr. English U. Ill., Urbana, 1963-65; teaching assoc. Ind. U., Ft. Wayne, 1965-66; prof. English Ind State U., Terre Haute, 1966—, chmn. dept., 1980—; vis. lectr. U. Ill., 1972-73; vis. assoc. prof. Ind. U., Bloomington, 1975, vis. prof., 1978, 84. Author: Folklore in the Writings of Rowland E. Robinson, 1973, Hoosier Folk Legends, 1982, Jokelore, 1986, French Folklife in Old Vincennes, 1989, The Study of Place Names, 1991, From Needmore to Prosperity: Hoosier Place Names in Folklore and History, 1995, Homeless, Friendless, and Penniless: The WPA Interviews with Former Slaves Living in Indiana, 2000; (with others) Indiana Place Names, 1975. Fellow Am. Folklore Soc.; mem. MLA, Am. Name Soc. (v.p. 1981-82), Hoosier Folklore Soc. (pres. 1970-79, exec. sec.-treas. 1988-2000). Home: 3688 N Randall St Terre Haute IN 47805-9736 Office: Indiana State University Terre Haute IN 47809-9989 E-mail: ronbaker@indstate.edu.

BAKER, RONALD PHILLIP, service company executive; b. Kansas City, Mo., Feb. 15, 1942; s. Harry and Ruth Sarah (Bornstein) B.; m. Marilyn Gitterman, Dec. 27, 1964 (div. Dec. 1993); children: Kevin, Corey; m. Kendra F.; m. Dierdre Christensen, May 8, 1994. Student, U. Okla., 1960-63; BA in Sociology and Govt., postgrad., U. Mo., Kansas City, 1965. Acct. rep. Am. House and Window Cleaning Co., Kansas City, 1965-69; dist. ops. mgr. Am. Bldg. Services, Kansas City, 1969-72; pres. BG Maintenance Mgmt., Kansas City, 1972-86; chmn. bd. dirs. BGM Industries, Kansas City, 1987—. Bd. dirs. Flo Harris Supporting Found., Village Shalom. V.p. Jewish Cmty. Ctr., Kans. City, 1985—88, pres., 1989—90, Jewish Vocat. Svcs., Kans. City, 1985—88; v.p. Jewish Fedn. Greater Kans. City, 1992—93; bd. dirs. Village Shalom, 1998—2003; chmn., CEO search com. Village of Shalom, 2002, chmn. bd. dirs., 2003—; bd. dirs. Beth Shalom Synagogue, Kans. City, 1985—89, Flo Harris Supporting Found.; chmn. and CEO SEARCH com. Village Shalom, 2002; bd. dirs. Jewish Cmty. Ctrs. Assn., 1989—93, mem. exec. com., 1990—91; bd. dirs. Jewish Fedn. Greater Kans. City, 1986—92, Jewish Cmty. Found. Greater Kans. City, 1991—94, mem. strategic planning com., 1997; bd. dirs. Village Shalom. Mem. Bldg. Svc. Contractors Assn. Internat. (bd. dirs., chmn. seminars, conv. speaker, pres. club 1981-93, mem. edn. com. 1981-90, chmn. edn. com. 1989—, info. ctrl. com. 1985-93, chmn. ann. conv. 1988, exec. com. 1988—, treas. 1989, v.p. 1990-92, pres. 1994, chmn. fin. com. 1990, mem. exec. com., chair strategic planning task force 1989-90, chmn., CEO seminar com. 1997-99, strategic planning com. 1996—, govt. affairs com. 1996—), Bldg. Owners and Mgrs. Assn. Kansas City, Jewish Fedn. Kansas City (v.p. 1986-87, 91-93, co-chmn. fin. resources planning com., Young Leadership award 1981), Menninger Found. (pres. Topeka chpt. 1986—), Hallbrook Country Club, Sigma Alpha Mu, Delta Sigma Pi. Republican. Avocations: water sports, boating, snow skiing, running, reading. Office: BGM Industries 1225 E 18th St Kansas City MO 64108-1605

BAKER, ROSALYN HESTER, state senator; b. El Campo, Tex., Sept. 20, 1946; BA, Southwest Tex. State U., 1968; student, U. Southwestern La., 1969. Lobbyist, asst. dir. Govt. Rels. Nat. Edn. Assn., Washington, 1969-80; owner, retail sporting goods store Maui, Hawaii, 1980-87; legis. aide to Hon. Karen Honita Hawaii Ho. of Reps., Honolulu, 1987, mem., 1989-93, house majority leader, 1993, state senator Hawaii, 1993-98, majority leader, 1995-96; dir. office econ. devel. County of Maui, Hawaii, 1999—2002, chair health com., 2003—. Co-chair ways and means com., 1998; co-chair rules com. Hawaii State Dem. Conv., 1990, chair health com. 2003, resolutions com. 1994; mem. energy environ. com., trans., mil. affairs, govt. ops. com.; vice chmn. consumer protection and housing com. Del.-at-large Dem. Nat. Conv., 1984, 92, 96; mem. exec. com. Maui County Dem. Com., 1986-88; mem. Workforce Investment Bd.; former vice chmn. Maui Svc. Area Bd. om Mental Health and Substance Abuse; former unit pres. Am. Cancer Soc. Mem.: Maalaea Cmty. Assn., Kidei Cmty. Assn., West Maui Taxpayers Assn. (mem. Lahaina town action com.). Democrat. Home: PO Box 10394 Lahaina HI 96761-0394 Office: 200 S High St # 612 Wailuku HI 96793-2155

BAKER, ROY GORDON, JR., lawyer; b. San Antonio, June 19, 1953; s. Roy Gordon and Carolyn Blanch (Slinkert) Baker; m. Cynthia Lynn Lee, July 6, 1977; children: Teri Diane, Amanda Christine. BA magna cum laude, Pepperdine U., 1974; JD, U. Calif., San Francisco, 1977; LLM in Taxation, Golden Gate U., 1989. Bar: Calif. 1977, U.S. Dist. Ct. (no. dist.) Calif. 1977, U.S. Ct. Appeals (9th cir.) 1977, U.S. Dist. Ct. (ctrl. dist.) Calif. 1984, U.S. Tax Ct. 1984; accredited estate planner. Dep. atty. gen. Calif. Dept. Justice, San Francisco, 1977-79; atty., assoc. Stark, Stewart, Wells, Rahl, Field & Schwartz, Oakland, Calif., 1979-83, atty., ptnr., 1983-85, Walnut Creek, Calif., 1985-89, Field, Baker & Richardson, Walnut Creek, 1990-94; atty., ptnr., shareholder R. Gordon Baker, Atty. At Law, P.C., Walnut Creek, 1994—. Contbr. articles to profl. jours. Participant Leadership Contra Costa Walnut Creek C. of C., 1993. Mem.: ABA (taxation sect., real property, probate and trust law sect.), Ciable Valley Estate Planning Coun., Nat. Assn. Estate Planners and Counsels, Contra Costa County Bar Assn. (taxation sect., bd. dirs. 1993—, pres. 1994, 2001), State Bar Calif. (taxation sect., estate planning, trust and probate sect., bus. law sect., cert. specialist estate planning, trust and probate law). Avocations: fishing, gardening, sailing, canoeing. Office: R Gordon Baker Atty At Law PC 2033 N Main St Ste 750 Walnut Creek CA 94596-3728 E-mail: g_baker@pacbell.net.

BAKER, SARAH E. music educator, composer, writer; b. Parsons, Tenn., Sept. 17, 1943; d. Fred Sails and Grace Houston Baker. MusB, Union U, Jackson, TN, 1965; MA, Sonoma State U, Rohnert Park, CA, 1998; PhD, Union Institute, Cin, OH, 2002—. Lectr. Sonoma State U, Rohnert Park, Calif., 1997—. Dir. mentor svc. Songpeddler, 2001—. Prodr.(songwriter): (CD) Sarah Baker, 1990, (performer) (CD solo) Maybe Someday, 1993; composer: (songs) (String quartet) Inneracts, 2000—02 ($2000, 2002). Nominee Woman student leader, Sonoma State U, 1996; recipient Hughes, Union U, 1965; scholar Presdl. scholar, Sonoma State U, 1997. Mem.: Am. Soc. of Composers, Authors & Publishers (assoc.). Achievements include published article. Home: PO Box 577 Cotati CA 94931-0577

BAKER, SAUL PHILLIP, geriatrician, cardiologist, internist; b. Cleve., Dec. 7, 1924; s. Barnet and Florence (Kleinman) B. BS in Physics, Case Inst. Tech., 1945; postgrad., Western Res. U., 1946-47; M.Sc. in Physiology, Ohio State U., 1949, MD, 1953, PhD in Physiology, 1957; JD, Case Western Res. U., 1981. Intern Cleve. Met. Gen. Hosp., 1953-54; sr. asst. surgeon Gerontology Br. Nat. Heart Inst, NIH, now Gerontology Research Ctr., Nat. Inst. Aging, 1954-56; asst. vis. staff physician dept. medicine Balt. City Hosps. (now Francis Scott Key Hosp.) and Johns Hopkins Hosp., 1954-56; sr. asst. resident in internal medicine U. Chgo. Hosps., 1956-57; asst. prof. internal medicine Chgo. Med. Sch., 1957-62; assoc. prof. internal medicine Cook County Hosp. Grad. Sch. Medicine, Chgo., 1958-62; assoc. attending physician Cook County Hosp., 1957-62; practice medicine specializing in geriatrics, cardiology, internal medicine Cleve., 1962-70, 72-93; cons., 1993—. Head dept. geriatrics St. Vincent Charity Hosp., Cleve., 1964-67; cons. internal medicine and cardiology Bur. Disability Determination, Old-Age and Survivors Ins., Social Security Adminstrn., 1963—; cons. internal medicine City of Cleve., 1964—; medicare med. cons. Gen. Am. Life Ins. Co., St. Louis, 1970-71; cons. internal medicine and cardiology Ohio Bur. Worker's Compensation, 1964—; cons. cardiovascular disease FAA, 1973—; cons. internal medicine and cardiology State of Ohio, 1974—. Contbr. articles to profl. and sci. jours. Mem. sci. coun. Northeastern Ohio affiliate Am. Heart Assn.; former mem. adv. com. Sr. Adult div. Jewish Community Ctr. Cleve.; mem. vis. com. colls. Case Western Res. U.; former mem. com. older people Fedn. Community Planning Cleve. Fellow AAAS, Am. Coll. Cardiology, Gerontol. Soc. Am. (former Ohio regent), Am. Geriatrics Soc., Cleve. Med. Library Assn. (life); mem. Am. Physiol. Soc., AMA, Ohio Med. Assn., N.Y. Acad. Scis., Chgo. Soc. Internal Medicine, Am. Fedn. Clin. Research, Soc. Exptl. Biology and Medicine, Am. Diabetes Assn., Diabetes Assn. Greater Cleve. (profl. sect.), Am. Heart Assn. (fellow council arteriosclerosis), Nat. Assn. Disability Examiners, Nat. Rehab. Assn., Am. Pub. Health Assn., Acad. Medicine Cleve., Internat. Soc. Cardiology (council epidemiology and prevention), Am. Soc. Law and Medicine, Sigma Xi, Phi Delta Epsilon, Sigma Alpha Mu (past pres. Cleve. alumni club). Clubs: Cleve. Clinical (past sec.). Lodges: Masons (32 degree), Shriners. Home: PO Box 24246 Cleveland OH 44124-0246

BAKER, STANLEY BECKWITH, education educator; b. Mpls., Sept. 3, 1935; s. Stanley Forrest and Dorothy Ruth (Beckwith) B.; m. Barbara Ann Laufenburger, Aug. 17, 1957 (dec.); children: Susan Elizabeth, David Allen; m. Mary Esther Clark Martin, June 10, 2000. BA, Augsburg Coll., 1957; MA, U. Minn., 1963; PhD, SUNY, Buffalo, 1971. Lic. profl. counselor, N.C.; nat. cert. counselor. Tchr. social studies Spring Valley (Wis.) High Sch., 1957-63; tchr. history Janesville (Wis.) High Sch., 1963-66, sch. counselor, 1964-67, Parker High Sch., Janesville, 1967-69; asst. prof. edn. Pa. State U., University Park, 1971—74, assoc. prof. edn., 1974—84, prof. edn., 1984—94; prof., head dept. N.C. State U., Raleigh, 1994—2001, prof., 2001—. Office: NC State U PO Box 7801 Raleigh NC 27695-0001

BAKER, STEPHEN, advertising executive, author; b. Vienna, Apr. 17, 1923; s. Oscar and Renee (Lavesky) Bacher; 1 child, Stephen Scott. BA, William Jewell Coll.; postgrad., NYU, Art Students League. V.p., creative dir. Cunningham and Walsh, 1951-62; pres. Baker and Byrne, 1962-65; pres., dir. Mogul, Baker, Byrne & Weiss, N.Y.C., 1965-69, Baker Hartel, N.Y.C., 1969-72; pres. Stephen Baker Assocs., N.Y.C., 1974—. Prof. NYU, 1982-84, N.Y. Sch. Visual Arts, 1982-93. Creator "Let Your Fingers Do The Walking" for AT&T; columnist Advertising Age mag., Art Direction mag.; author 23 books including How to Live with a Neurotic Wife, How to Play Golf in the Low 120's, How to Live with a Neurotic Husband, How to Be Analyzed by a Neurotic Psychoanalyst, How to Get a Job Without Asking for It, Games Dogs Play, I Hate Meetings, 5001 Names for Cats, The Executive Mother Goose, How to Live with a Neurotic Cat, 1985, How To Live With A Neurotic Dog, How To Look Like Somebody In Business Without Being Anybody, Advertising Layout and Art Direction, Visual Persuasion: Effect Of Pictures On The Subconscious, An Art Director's Viewpoint, Systematic Approach To Advertising Creativity, 1979, Get-Around Guide To New York City, 1982, Advertiser's Manual, 1988, How to Live with a Neurotic Cat Owner, 1992, Me & My Cat, 1993. Nominated Art Dir. of Yr. Nat. Soc. Art Dirs., 1961, 63. Home: 5 Tudor City Penthouse 5 New York NY 10017-6853

BAKER, STEPHEN DENIO, physics educator; b. Durham, N.C., Nov. 30, 1936; s. Roger Denio and Eleanor Elizabeth (Ussher) B.; m. Paula Eisenstein, June 24, 1962; children: Hannah Hitzhusen, Sarah Topper. BS, Duke U., 1957; MS, Yale U., 1959, PhD, 1963. Lectr. physics Rice U., Houston, 1963-66, asst. prof., 1966-69, assoc. prof., 1969-73, prof., 1973—. Office: Rice Univ Dept Physics-MS 61 6100 Main St Houston TX 77005-1892

BAKER, STEPHEN MONROE, school system administrator; BA, Roanoke Coll., 1964; MS, Radford U., 1968; EdD, U. Va., 1976. Supt. Hanover County Pub. Schs., Ashland, Va., 1980-95; exec. dir. elem. and mid. sch. commn. So. Assn. Colls. and Schs., Decatur, Ga., 1995—. Chair Nat. Study Sch. Evaluation, 2000—; pres. Commn. on Internat. and Transregional Accreditation, 2002—. Named state finalist Nat. Supt. of Yr. award. Office: So Assn Colls & Schs 1866 Southern Ln Decatur GA 30033-4033 E-mail: sbimb@attglobal.net.

BAKER, STEPHEN R. physician; b. Bklyn., Mar. 22, 1942; s. Louis and Edith Helen (Kalm) B.; m. Marjorie Gilman, Sept. 18, 1971; children: Amelia, Elizabeth, Catherine, Nina. BA, Wesleyan U., Middletown, Conn., 1964; MD, Albert Einstein Sch. Medicine, 1968; MPhil, Columbia U., 1980. Staff radiologist Albert Einstein Coll. Medicine, Bronx, N.Y., 1972-73, 75-76; pvt. practice radiology Perth Amboy, N.J., 1976-78; staff radiologist Cabrini Hosp., N.Y.C., 1978-79; ast. dir. radiology Albert Einstein Coll. Medicine, 1980-86, acting chmn. radiology, 1986-90; chmn. radiology N.J. Med. Sch., Newark, 1990—, assoc. dean grad. med. edn., 2000—. Mem. exec. bd. Radiology Outreach Found., San Francisco, 1994-2002; bd.dirs. Children of Chernobyl, N.J., 1996-99. Author: 10 books; editor-in-chief Emergency Radiology, 2000—, asst. editor Am. Jour. Radiology, 1999—. Maj. U.S. Army, 1973-75. Mem. Am. Soc. Emergency Radiology (pres. 1994-95). Avocations: geography, history, softball, classical piano. Office: UMDNJ-NJ Med Sch Dept Radiology 150 Bergen St Newark NJ 07103-2406 E-mail: bakersr@umdnj.ed.

BAKER, STEVEN WRIGHT, lawyer; b. Pitts., Oct. 23, 1947; s. Donald E. and Janet (Zahniser) B.; m. Louise G. Burrell, Oct. 31, 1970; children: Sara, Beth, Chad. BA, Allegheny Coll., 1969; JD, U. Calif.-San Francisco, 1974. Bar: Calif. 1974, U.S. Dist. Ct. (no. dist.) Calif. 1974, U.S. Ct. Internat. Trade 1974. U.S. Ct. Appeals (fed. cir.) 1975. Assoc. Glad, Tuttle and White, San Francisco, 1974-78; part. Bellsey & Baker, San Francisco, 1978— . Contbr. articles to profl. jours. Served with U.S. Army, 1969-71. Mem. ABA (internat. law sect.), Am. Inst. Internat. Steel (customs counsel), Am. Soc. Internat. Law, San Francisco Bar Assn., Customs Brokers and Forwarders Assn. No. Calif. Home: 190 Ignacio Valley Cir Novato CA 94949-5517 Office: Bellsey & Baker 100 California St Ste 670 San Francisco CA 94111-4584

BAKER, STUART DAVID, lawyer; b. N.Y.C., July 2, 1935; s. Stuart and Edith (Kennelly) B.; m. Alixandra Fitzwilliam-Tate Collins, June 16, 1980; children from previous marriage— Stuart Richard, David Michael, Elisabeth Kendall BA, Hamilton Coll., 1957; LLB, Columbia U. Bar: N.Y. 1960. Assoc. Chadbourne, Parke, Whiteside & Wolff, N.Y.C., 1960-69, ptnr., 1969-85, Chadbourne & Parke, N.Y.C., 1985—, mem. mgmt. com., 1985-95, 96—. Exec. v.p. Purdue Frederick Co., Purdue Pharma L.P.; dir. Napp Pharm. Group Ltd. (UK), Mundipharma Labs. GmbH, Mundipharma AG (Switzerland); mem. supervisory bd. Mundipharma GmbH, Germany, 1994—. Vestryman St. Mary's Ch., Scarborough-on-Hudson, N.Y., 1967-76, sr. warden, 1974-76; chmn. zoning bd. appeals Town of Ossining, N.Y., 1968-78; mem. Coun. of Diocese of N.Y., 1974-79; bd. dirs. Legal Aid Soc., 1993-99; bd. trustees St. Peters Sch., 1975-99. Mem. N.Y. State Bar Assn., Conn. Bar Assn., Westchester County Bar Assn., Assn. Bar City of N.Y., Suffolk County Bar Assn., Internat. Bar Assn. (rapporteur), Inter-Am. Bar Assn., Union Internat. des Avocats, Swiss Am. C. of C., SAR, Sleepy Hollow Country Club, River Club (N.Y.C.), Netherlands Club (N.Y.C.), Water Mill Beach (N.Y.) Club (pres. 1991-96). Episcopalian. Avocations: fly fishing, tennis, golf, windsurfing. Home: 16 Sutton Pl New York NY 10022-3057 Office: Chadbourne & Parke LLP 30 Rockefeller Plz Fl 31 New York NY 10112-0129

BAKER, SUSAN MARIE VICTORIA, writer, artist; b. Phila., Pa., Aug. 30, 1961; d. John Joseph and Dorothy Phyllis (Dispensiere) Erdlen. BA in Liberal Arts/Comm., Rowan U., 1983; postgrad., U. of Arts, Phila. Ordained priestess. Published author, visual and performing artist. Art critic and healing artist. Author 3 books; songwriter (performed and published under name Chelsea Mann); art editor Avant mag., 1981; contbr. poetry to various publs.; composer numerous songs. Active animal rights and environ. activities; mem. Newport Cultural Arts Alliance, Sedona Arts Ctr. and Ascension Group. Recipient awards for poetry, creative writing.

BAKER, SUSAN P. public health educator; b. Atlanta, May 31, 1930; d. Charles Laban and Susan (Lowell) Pardee; m. Timothy Danforth Baker, June 23, 1951; children— Timothy D., David C., Susan L. AB, Cornell U., Ithaca, N.Y., 1951; M.P.H., Johns Hopkins U., Balt., 1968; ScD (hon.), U. N.C., 1998. Rsch. assoc. Office of Chief Med. Examiner, Balt., 1968-81; rsch. assoc. Sch. Hygiene and Pub. Health, Johns Hopkins U., Balt., 1968-71, asst. prof., 1971-74, assoc. prof., 1974-83, prof. health policy and mgmt., 1983—, assoc. chmn. dept. health policy and mgmt., 1997-99, joint appointment in environ. health scis., 1975—, joint appointment in pediatrics, 1983—, dir. Injury Prevention Ctr., 1987-88, co-dir., 1988—, acting head div. pub. health, 1988-90, joint appointment emergency medicine Sch. Medicine, 1991—. Vis. prof. U. Minn. Sch. Pub. Health, 1975-87; chmn. nat. rev. panel for nat. accident sampling sys. Dept. Transp., Washington, 1976-81; vice chmn. com. on trauma rsch. Nat. Rsch. Coun., Washington, 1984-85; mem. adv. com. on injury control CDC, 1989-95; mem. Armed Forces Epidemiol. Bd.; commr. West Latir Ditch Assn., N.Mex., 1990—; vis. lectr. in injury prevention Harvard Sch. Pub. Health, 1984-87; John T. Law meml. lectr. U. Calgary, Alta., 1984; expert panel Age 60 rule FAA, 1991-93; cons. and lectr. in field. Author: (monograph) Fatally Injured Drivers, 1970 (Prince Bernhard medal 1974), The Injury Fact Book, 1984, 2d edit., 1992, Saving Children: A Guide to Injury Prevention, 1991, Injury Prevention: An International Perspective, 1998; contbr. articles to books and articles to profl. jours. Recipient Charles A. Dana award for pioneering achievements in health, 1989, Johns Hopkins U. Disting. Alumnus award, 1996, Am. Public Health Assn. Excellence award, 1999. Fellow Am. Assn. Automotive Medicine (bd. dirs. 1971-76, pres. 1974-75, award of merit 1985, Abe Mirkin Svc. award 2002), Aerospace Med. Assn. (editl. bd. 1994-97); mem. APHA (governing coun. 1975-77, jour. bd. 1983-87, award for excellence 1999), Am. Trauma Soc. (bd. dirs., Disting. Achievement award 1981, Stone lectr. 1985), Am. Assn. for Surgery of Trauma (h on., Fitts oration award 1996), Phi Beta Kappa, Delta Omega. Office: Johns Hopkins U Sch Hygiene & Pub Health 624 N Broadway Baltimore MD 21205-1900

BAKER, SUZANNE MARTIN, artist, rancher; b. Mar. 6, 1939; d. Euclid and Josephine Sprague Martin; m. Gordon Calvin Baker, June 28, 1960; children: Brett, Owen Hoss, Jenny Baker Salazar. Self employed artist, Raymond, Calif., 1985—. Contbr. articles, paintings to profl. jours. Mem. Am. Women Artists, Calif. Art Club. Avocations: mountain climbing, hiking, horseback riding, interior design, building.

BAKER, SYLVIA HALLDORSON, music educator; d. Marvin Albert and Edith Marie (Kiesling) Halldorson; m. John Frank Baker, Aug. 25, 1960 (dec. Nov. 2000); children: Anne-Marie Fuhrmeister, M. Orien. AA in Music, Mesa Jr. Coll., Grand Junction, Colo., 1955—57; BMusEd, U. Colo., Boulder, 1957—60; studied, Eastman Sch. Music, Rochester, N.Y., 1961—62; MMus, U. Idaho, Moscow, 1963—65. Band dir. Emmett Pub. Schs., Idaho, 1960—61; band & string tchr. Bonner Co. Pub. Schs., Sandpoint, Idaho, 1961—62, band dir., choir dir., gen. music tchr. Potlatch, Idaho, 1962—63; sec., zoology dept. Wash. State U., Pullman, 1963—65; band dir. Whitman Co. Schs., Oaksdale, Wash., 1966—67; band dir., gen. music tchr. Plummer, Idaho, 1968—70; saxophone instr. Whitworth Coll., Spokane, Wash., 1969—, Gonzaga U., Spokane, Wash., 1989—; double reed tester Jones Double Reed Products, Spokane, Wash., 1999—. Musician pvt. music studio, 1961—: adjudicator Wash., Idaho, Mont. Prin. saxophonist Spokane Symphony, 1962—91, pit musician Spokane Civic Theater, 1972—99. Mem. allocations com. United Way, Spokane, Wash., 1987—89; mem. prayer ctr. Unity Ch., Spokane, Wash., 1981—99, dir. prayer ctr., 1986—99. Mem.: Music Educators Nat. Conf., Sigma Alpha Iota (v.p. history 2002—). Avocations: painting, reading, crocheting, knitting, hiking. Office: Whitworth Coll Music Dept 300 W Hawthorne Rd Spokane WA 99231 Business E-Mail: sbaker@whitworth.edu.

BAKER, THOMAS EDWARD, lawyer, accountant; b. Washington, July 24, 1923; s. John Thad and Angelina E. (Rappa) B.; m. Mildred M. Younglove. Dec. 26, 1944 (dec. May 1995); children: Jean Ann Baker Holland, Cindy Baker Goralewicz, Linda Hogan; m. Helen Draughon, Nov. 3, 1996. BS, JD, U. Okla., 1950. Bar: Okla. 1950; CPA, Okla. Pvt. practice, Oklahoma City, 1950; agt., spl. agt. IRS, 1951-53; ptnr. Shutler Baker Simpson & Logsdon, Kingfisher, Okla., 1953-79, Baker, Logsdon, Schulte & Gibson, Kingfisher, 1979—. Trustee U. Okla. Found., Inc., 1987-89. WithAUS, 1943-46. Mem. Am. Legion (past svc. officer), Elks, Rotary (pres. Kingfisher club 1957). Democrat. Mem. Christian Ch. (Disciples Of Christ). Home: 1211 Regency Ct Kingfisher OK 73750-4251 Office: Baker Logsdon Schulte & Gibson 302 N Main St Kingfisher OK 73750-2799

BAKER, THOMAS EUGENE, law educator; b. Youngstown, Ohio, Feb. 25, 1953; s. John M. and Helen Marie (Kish) B.; m. Jane Marie Schussler, June 15, 1974; 1 child, Thomas Athanasius. BS cum laude, Fla. State U., 1974; JD with high honors, U. Fla., 1977. Bars: Fla. 1979, U.S. Dist. Ct. (no. dist.) Tex. 1979, U.S. Supreme Ct. 1982, U.S. Ct. Appeals (5th cir.) 1979, U.S. Ct. Appeals (11th cir.) 1981. Law clk. to presiding judge U.S. Ct. Appeals (5th cir.) Ga., Atlanta, 1977-79; prof. law Tex. Tech. U., Lubbock, 1979-98, Alvin R. Allison prof., 1992-98; jud. fellow U.S. Supreme Ct., Washington, 1985-86, acting adminstrv. asst. to chief justice, 1986-87; James Madison chair constnl. law, dir. constnl. law ctr. Drake U. Law Sch., Des Moines, 1998—2002; mem. founding faculty Coll. of Law, Fla. Internat. U., Miami, 2002—. Mem. adv. bd. Am. Criminal Law Rev., Washington, 1981-85; standing com. rules and procedures U.S. Jud. Conf., 1990-95; vis. prof. U. Fla., 1994; Fulbright prof. U. Athens, Greece, 1993; bd. editors Preview U.S. Supreme Ct. Cases, 1991—. Author: Rationing Justice on Appeal: The Problems of the U.S. Court of Appeals, 1994, The Most Wonderful Work: Our Constitution Interpreted, 1996; author: (with T. Floyd) Can a Good Christian Be a Good Lawyer?, 1998; author: Federal Court Practice and Procedure: A Third Branch Bibliography, 2001; mem. editl. bd. Jour. Supreme Ct. History, 1991—93; contbr. articles to profl. jours.; author (with J. Williams): Constitutional Analysis in a Nutshell, 2003. Recipient Faculty Rsch. award Tex. Tech. U., 1996, 94, 83, Outstanding Law Prof. award, 1988, 89, Spencer A. Wells U. teaching award; SBA Pres.'s award Drake Law Sch., 2002; Justice Tom C. Clark fellow Jud. Fellows, 1986. Mem. ABA (various sects. and

coms.), Am. Law Inst. (elected), Am. Judicature Soc. (bd. dirs. 2000-02), Order of Coif. Byzantine Catholic. Avocations: pottery, racquetball. Office: Fla Internat U Coll Law University Park GL 496 Miami FL 33199 E-mail: thomas.baker@fiu.edu.

BAKER, THURBERT E. state attorney general; b. Rocky Mount, N.C., Dec. 16, 1952; m. Catherine Baker; children: Jocelyn, Chelsea. BA in Polit. Sci., U. N.C.; JD, Emory U., 1979. Mem. Ga. Ho. of Reps., 1988—90, asst. adminstrn. fl. leader, 1990—93, adminstrn. fl. leader, 1993—97; atty. gen. State of Ga., 1997—. Trustee Statewide Ga. Diabetes Bd., Ebenezer Bapt. Ch., Atlanta, DeKalb Coll. Found. Mem.: Nat. Med. Soc.-Emory U., DeKalb County C. of C. (bd. dirs.). Democrat. Office: Atty Gen Dept Law 40 Capitol Sq SW Atlanta GA 30334-9003*

BAKER, TIMOTHY DANFORTH, physician, educator; b. Balt., July 4, 1925; s. Frank and Alice Elizabeth (Chandler) B.; m. Susan Lowell Pardee, June 23, 1951; children: Timothy, David, Susan. BA, Johns Hopkins U., 1948, MPH, 1954; MD, U. Md., 1952. Intern U. Md. Hosp., Balt., 1952-53; resident pub. health N.Y. State Dept. Pub. Health, N.Y.C., 1953-56; health officer Syracuse, N.Y., 1958-59; asst. and acting chief health USAID, India, 1956-58; assoc. prof. Johns Hopkins U. Sch. Pub. Health, Balt., 1959-67, asst. dean, 1959-77, prof. internat. health, health svcs. adminstrn., and environ. health, 1967—, pres. faculty gen. assembly, 1987—, dir. Hubert H. Humphrey scholars program, 1987—. V.p., dir. Univ. Assocs., 1973-77; vis. prof. epidemiology U. Minn., 1976; dir. Intermed., 1982—; cons. health planning, med. edn., Brazil, Burma, Canada, India, Indonesia, Taiwan, Saudi Arabia, Kuwait, Ukraine, Viet Nam, Yunnan, China, Armenia, Greenland, Cuba, Russia, Md., Calif., D.C.; external examiner U. Singapore; vis. prof. Am. U., Armenia, 1999. Author: Health Manpower in a Developing Economy, Assessment of Health Status and Needs, International Health Perspectives; contbr. articles to profl. publs. First vice chmn. Balt. com. Republican party; del., nominating com. Republican party; bd. dirs., treas. Pan Am. Health Edn. Found. Served with USAF, 1943-45; USPHS, 1956-58. Recipient Disting. Grad. award Balt. Polytechnic Inst. Fellow AAAS (govs. commn. on minority health, task force on violence); mem. Am. Pub. Health Assn. (chmn. epidemiology sect., internat. health sect., Lifetime Achievement award 1994), Md. Med. Soc. (chmn. health manpower com., ho. of dels.), Md. Pub. Health Assn. (pres.), Balt. Med. Soc. (chmn. med. care com.), Omicron Delta Kappa, Delta Omega. Republican. Home: 4705 Keswick Rd Baltimore MD 21210-2322 Office: Johns Hopkins U Sch Hygiene 615 N Wolfe St Baltimore MD 21205-2103 E-mail: tbaker@jhsph.edu.

BAKER, TIMOTHY KEVIN, education educator; b. Fullerton, Calif., Apr. 16, 1958; s. Glen Rhodes and Lorraine Helen Baker. BA in Math. and Economics, Claremont McKenna Coll., 1976—80; MS in Ops. Rsch., U. of N.C., 1980—82; PhD in Mgmt. Sci., Ohio State U., 1989—94. Ops rsch. analyst Unocal, LA, 1982—84, DynCorp Meridian/B-K Dynamics, San Diego, 1984—86; sr. ops rsch. analyst United Technologies Advanced Mil. Systems, San Diego, Calif., 1986—89; grad. rsch. and tchg. asst., dept. of mgmt. sci. Ohio State U., 1989—94; assoc. cons. Simat, Helliesen, and Eichner, Cambridge, Mass., 1994—96; sr. ops rsch. analyst Six Continents Hotels, Atlanta, 1996—99; asst. prof., dept. of mgmt. and decision sciences Wash. State U., 1999—. Author: (jour. articles) Decision Sciences Jour., (conf. procs. articles) Decision Sciences Inst. Procs., (conf. procs.) Procs. of the Am. Control Conf., Procs. of the Joint Con. on Info. Sciences. Grantee Rsch. Funding, IXL Ctr. for Electronic Commerce, DuPree Coll. of Mgmt., Ga. Inst. of Tech., 1999. Mem.: Decision Sciences Inst., INFORMS. Home: 1650 Mowry Sq #313 Richland WA 99352 Office: Wash State U 2710 U Dr CIC 125N Richland WA 99352 Office Fax: 509-372-7512. E-mail: bakert@tricity.wsu.edu.

BAKER, TRACY MCKENZIE, family practice physician; b. San Antonio, Jan. 26, 1951; s. Owen Bruner and Sarah Louise (Perry) B.; m. Kathryn Lynette Nachbor, June 10, 1994; 1 child, Dawn Marie. BS, U. Fla., 1974; MA, Webster U., St. Louis, 1980; MD, U. Kans., 1992. Resident St. Francis Regional Med. Ctr., Wichita, Kans., 1992-95; family practice physician Wichita Clinic-Augusta (Kans.) br., 1995—. Mem. med. sci. com. Arthritis Found., Wichita, 1996-98; chmn. med. records com. Augusta Med. Complex, 1995—, pres. medical staff, 1998-99; med. dir. Valley Hope Drug and Alcohol Rehab. Program, Augusta, 1997-98. With USAF, 1974-86, maj., USAFR, 1986-99. Mem. AMA, Am. Assn. Family Practice, Gideons Internat. Republican. Baptist. Avocations: water skiing, snow skiing, hunting, horseback riding, scuba diving. Office: Whichita Clinic-Augusta 120 W Josephine Ave Augusta KS 67010-2037

BAKER, VICTORIA JEAN, anthropology educator; b. Austin, Tex., Aug. 20, 1945; d. Leonidas and Virginia Capps Baker; 1 child, Maurits Vlek. PhD, U. Leiden, The Netherlands, 1988. Tchr. Am. Internat. Sch. of The Hague, Netherlands, 1967—83; rschr. Leiden Inst. Devel. Studies and Consultancy Svcs. (LIDESCO), Leiden, 1986—87. Lectr. U. Leiden, Netherlands, 1986; prof. anthropology Eckerd Coll., St. Petersburg, 1988—2002. Author: (book) A Sinhalese Village in Sri Lanka: Coping with Uncertainty, 1998, The Blackboard in the Jungle: Education in Disadvantaged Rural Areas, 1988. Recipient Robert A. Staub Disting. Tchr. award, Eckerd Coll., 1997; grantee Rotary univ. tchg. grantee, 2001Rotary International, 2001; scholar Freeman Found. Student-Faculty grantee, 1998. Mem.: Fulbright Association (scholar 2000—01), Sigma Xi, Omicron Delta Kappa, Phi Beta Kappa. Avocation: travel. Home: 1244 Murok Way S Saint Petersburg FL 33705 Office: Eckerd Coll 4200 54th Ave S Saint Petersburg FL 33711 Office Fax: 727-864-7995. Business E-Mail: bakervj@eckerd.edu.

BAKER, VINCENT LAMONT, professional basketball player; b. Lake Wales, Fla., Nov. 23, 1971; Grad., Hartford U., 1993. Player Milw. Bucks, 1993—97, Seattle Supersonics, 1997—. Named NBA All Star, 1995—97; named to NBA All-Rookie First Team, 1994, All-NBA Third Team, 1996—97, All-NBA Second Team, 1997—98. Avocation: singing. Office: Boston Celtics Fleet Center One Fleet Center Place; Suite 200 Boston MA 02114

BAKER, WALTER ARNOLD, lawyer; b. Columbia, Ky., Feb. 20, 1937; s. Herschel T. and Mattie B. (Barger) B.; m. Jane Stark Helm, Apr. 24, 1965; children: Thomas Herschel, Ann Tate. AB magna cum laude, Harvard U., 1958, LLB, 1961. Assoc. Brown, Ardery, Todd & Dudley, Louisville, 1961-63; ptnr. Wilson, Baker, Herbert and Garmon, Glasgow, Ky., 1963-67; pvt. practice Glasgow, 1967-81, 83—; asst. gen. counsel Office Sec. Def., Washington, 1981-83; justice Supreme Ct. of Ky., Frankfort, 1996. Rep. Ky. Ho. of Reps., 1968-71, senator State of Ky., 1972-81, 89-96; active Ky. Coun. on Postsecondary Edn., 1997—. Lt. col. USAFR. Mem. Ky. Bar Assn., Barren County Bar Assn., Glasgow Rotary, Glasgow Golf and Country Club, Phi Beta Kappa. Republican. Presbyterian. Address: 917 S Green St Glasgow KY 42141-2086 Office: 213 S Green St Glasgow KY 42141-2643

BAKER, WARREN J(OSEPH), university president; b. Fitchburg, Mass., Sept. 5, 1938; s. Preston A. and Grace F. (Jarvis) B.; m. Carol Ann Fitzsimons, Apr. 28, 1962; children: Carrie Ann, Kristin Robin, Christopher, Brian. BS, U. Notre Dame, 1960, MS, 1962; PhD, U. N.Mex., 1966. Research assoc., lectr. E. H. Wang Civil Engring. Research Facility, U. N.Mex., 1962-66; assoc. prof. civil engring. U. Detroit, 1966-71, prof., 1972-79, Chrysler prof., dean engring., 1973-78, acad. v.p., 1976-79; NSF faculty fellow M.I.T., 1971-72; pres. Calif. Poly. State U., San Luis Obispo, 1979—. Mem. Bd. Internat. Food and Agrl. Devel., USAID, 1983-85; mem. Nat. Sci. Bd., 1985-94, Calif. Bus. Higher Edn. Forum, 1993-98; founding mem. Calif. Coun. on Sci. and Tech., 1989—; trustee Amigos of E.A.R.T.H. Coll., 1991-96; bd. dirs. John Wiley & Sons, Inc., 1993—; bd. regents The Am. Archtl. Found., 1995-97; co-chair Joint Policy Coun. on Agr. and Higher Edn., 1995—; mem. Bus.-Higher Edn. Forum, 2001—; bd. dirs. Westport Innovations, Inc., 2002—, Soc. Manf. Engrs. Edn. Found., 2001— Contbr. articles to profl. jours. Mem. Detroit Mayor's Mgmt. Adv. Com., 1975-76; mem. engring. adv. bd. U. Calif., Berkeley, 1984-96; bd. dirs. Calif. Coun. for Environ. and Econ. Balance, 1980-85, Soc. Mfg. Engrs. Edn. Found., 2001—; trustee Nat. Coop. Edn. Assn.; chmn. bd. dirs. Civil Engring. Rsch. Found., 1989-91, bd. dirs., 1991-94. Fellow Engring. Soc. Detroit; mem. ASCE (chmn. geotech. div. com. on reliability 1976-78, civil engring. edn. and rsch. policy com. 1985-89), NSPE (pres. Detroit chpt. 1976-77), Am. Soc. Engring. Edn., Am. Assn. State Colls. and Univs. (bd. dirs. 1982-84), Soc. Mfg. Engrs. Edn. (bd. dirs. 2002—). Office: Calif Poly State U Office of Pres 1 Grand Ave San Luis Obispo CA 93407 E-mail: presidentsoffice@calpoly.edu.

BAKER, WILLIAM, British literature educator; b. Shipston-on-Stour, Warwicks, Eng., July 6, 1944, came to U.S., 1989; s. Stanley and Mabel (Woolf) Baker; m. Rivka Frank, Oct. 16, 1969; children: Sharon, Karen. BA in English Studies with honors, U. Sussex, Brighton, Eng., 1966; MPhil in English, U. London, 1970, PhD in English, 1974. Cert. MLS/Loughborough U., Eng. Lectr. City Literary Inst., London, 1967-71, Ben Gurion U., Beer-Sheva, Israel, 1971-77, U. Kent, Canterbury, Kent, U.K., 1977-78; sr. lectr. West Midlands Coll., Walsall, U.K., 1978-85; housemaster Clifton Coll., Bristol, U.K., 1986-89; prof. No. Ill. U., DeKalb, 1989—, Presdl. rsch. prof., 2003—. Vis. prof. Pitzer Coll., Claremont Coll., Calif., 1981-82; mem. exec. com. Bibliography and Textual Studies, MLA, N.Y., 1996-99; coun. Bibliographical Soc. Am. Author: Literary Theories, 1996; author, editor: Scott: History of France, 1996, Twentieth-Century Bibliography and Texthead Criticism, 2000; editor: G.H. Lewes Letters, 3 vols., 1995, 1999, British Book Collectors, 3 vols., 1998—99, Letters of Wilkie Collins, 2 vols., 1999 (Choice Outstanding Acad. Book of Yr., 2000), Wilkie Collins's Library: A Reconstruction, 2002, George Eliot: A Bibliographical History, 2002, others, George Eliot - G.H. Lewes Studies, 1981—, Year's Work in English Studies, 2000—; adv. editor: New Dictionary National Biography, U.K. and Oxford, 1995—. Rsch. fellow Am. Philos. Soc., 1997, Bibliog. Soc. Am., 1995-96, Brit. Acad., 1979, 82, NEH, 2002—03. Mem.: Bibliog. Soc. Am. (rsch. com. 2003—), Internat. Assn. Univ. Profs. of English. Office: No Ill Univ Dekalb IL 60115 E-mail: wbaker@niu.edu.

BAKER, WILLIAM ARNOLD, lawyer; b. Boston, June 23, 1938; s. A. Richard and Doris (Anderson) B.; m. Faith Barnett, Apr. 13, 1963; children—Mary Louise, Margaret Gage. B.A., Williams Coll., 1960; J.D., U. Mich., 1964. Bar: R.I. 1965, N.H. 1966, U.S. Dist. Ct. R.I. 1965, U.S. Dist. Ct. N.H. 1966, U.S. Ct. Appeals (1st cir.) 1969. Assoc., Hinckley, Allen, Salisbury & Parsons, Providence, R.I., 1964-66; ptnr. Baker & Page, Lebanon, N.H., 1966-78, Baker & Hayes, Lebanon, 1980— . Mem. ABA, N.H. Bar Assn. (pres. 1983-84), R.I. Bar Assn. Address: 29 School St PO Box 524 Lebanon NH 03766-0524

BAKER, WILLIAM DUNLAP, lawyer; b. St. Louis, June 17, 1932; s. Harold Griffith and Bernice (Kraft) B.; m. Kay Stokes, May 23, 1955; children: Mark William, Kathryn X., Beth Kristie, Frederick Martin. AB, Colgate U., 1954; JD, U. Calif., Berkeley, 1960. Bar: Calif. 1961, Ariz. 1961, U.S. Supreme Ct. 1969. Practice in, Coolidge, 1961, Florence, 1961-63, Phoenix, 1963—; law clk. Stokes & Moring, 1960; spl. investigator Office Pinal County Atty., 1960-61, dep. county atty., 1961-63; partner McBryde, Vincent, Brumage & Baker, 1961-63; assoc. atty. Rawlins, Ellis, Burrus & Kiewit, 1963-65, partner, 1965-81; pres., atty. Ellis & Baker, P.C., 1981-84, Ellis, Baker, Lynch, Clark & Porter P.C., 1984-86, Ellis, Baker, Clark & Porter, P.C., 1986-89, Ellis, Baker & Porter, P.C., 1989-92, Ellis Baker & Porter Ltd., Phoenix, 1992-95, Ellis, Baker & Porter, P.C., Phoenix, 1995-99, Ellis & Baker, P.C., 1999—. Referee Juvenile Ct. Maricopa County Superior Ct., 1966-85 Contbr. articles to profl. jours. Mem. Gov.'s Adv. Coun., Phoenix, 1969-71, Ariz. Environ. Planning Commn., 1974-75; bd. dirs. Agri-Bus. Coun., 1978—, sec., 1978-82; pub. mem. State Bd. Accountancy, 1995—, sec., 1998-99, treas., 1999-2000, pres., 2000-02; mem. Nat. Assn. Bds. Accountancy, litig. com., 2001-, nominating com., 2002—, Nat. Assn. State Bds. Accountancy; spl. legal counsel Ariz. Com. Rep. Party, 1965-69, mem. exec. com., 1972-78; vice-chmn. Maricopa County Rep. Com., 1968-69, chmn., 1969-71; bd. dirs. San Pablo Home for Youth, 1964-72, pres., 1971; bd. dirs. Maricopa County chpt. Nat. Found. March of Dimes, 1966-71, campaign chmn., 1970; trustee St. Luke's Hosp., 1976-85, sec., 1978-82, chmn., 1982-85; bd. dirs. Luke's Men, 1971-80, pres., 1976-77; bd. dirs. Combined Health Resources, 1982-85, St. Luke's Health Sys., 1977-95, chmn., 1985-89; bd. dirs. St. Luke's Health Initiatives, 1995—, vice chair, 2000-02; bd. dirs., v.p. Ariz. Anglican Cursillo Movement, 1982-86; Western dist. layman rep. Nat. Episcopal Cursillo Com., 1996-98; regional v.p. Colgate Alumni Corp., 1977-82; vice chancellor Episcopal Diocese Ariz., 1970-96; sr. warden Christ Ch. of Ascension, 1983-86, 2001—; ch. atty. Episc. Diocese Ariz., 1996—. Served to 1st lt. USAF, 1954-57. Mem. ABA, Nat. Water Resources Assn. (co-chmn. task force on reclamation law 1990-97, resolutions com. 1990-93, chmn. state caucus 1993-99, chair water policy task force 2000—), Ariz. Bar Assn., Calif. Bar Assn., State C. of C. (bd. dirs. 1988-92), Maricopa County Bar Assn., Nat. Assn. State Bds. Accountancy, Flagstaff Golf Assn. (bd. dirs. 1992-93, 94-96, pres. 1994-95), Phoenix Country Club, Sigma Chi, Phi Delta Phi. Episcopalian. Home: 1627 E Cactus Wren Dr Phoenix AZ 85020-5550 Office: Ste 320 7310 N 16th St Phoenix AZ 85020 E-mail: wdb@ellisbaker.com.

BAKER, WILLIAM FRANKLIN, public broadcasting company executive; b. Cleve., Sept. 20, 1942; s. William Franklin and Rita Marie (Huebner) Baker; m. Jeannemarie Gelin, June 22, 1968; children: Christiane, Angela. BA in Comms. and Organizational Behavior, Case Western Res. U., 1965, MA in Comms. and Organizational Behavior, 1968, PhD in Comm., 1972; DSc St. John's U. (hon.), N.Y., 1981; LLD (hon.), St. Elizabeth Coll., 1995; DHL (hon.), L.I. U., 2000; PhD (hon.), New Sch. Univ., 2002, Seton Hall U., 2003. Exec. prodr. Sta. WEWS-TV, Cleve., 1971—75, asst gen. mgr., 1975—77; v.p., gen. mgr. Sta. WJZ-TV, Balt., 1977—78; pres. Group W. Prodns., Hollywood, Calif., 1978—79, Group W-TV, N.Y.C., 1979—81; chmn. Group W-TV Satellite Comm., N.Y.C., 1981—87; pres., CEO Sta. WNET, N.Y.C., 1987—. Bd. dirs. Playhouse Pictures Internat., PBS, Leitch Video Ltd., The Consumers Union, Rondale Press; owner Rudder Mag., Schneider Vineyards. Author: Down the Tube: An Insider's View of American Television, 1998; exec. prodr.: (films) The Face: Jesus in Art, 2001. Bd. trustees St. Elizabeth Coll., Intrepid Air-Space Mus.; vice chmn. N.Y. Arts, 1997; bd. dirs. Ea. Ednl. Network, Lowell Obs., Liberty Sci. Ctr., Lamont-Doherty Earth Obs. Named Culture Honoree, N.Y. Pops, 2003; recipient 8 Emmy awards, 2 Twyla M. Conway awards, Dupont Columbia Journalism award (2), Triscort award (2), 1991, Modern Lang. award, Iona Coll., 1991, Silver Cir. award, N.Y. TV Acad., Humanitarian award, So. Manhattan Arts Coun., 1999, Frank Knox Media medal, U.S. Navy League, 1999, Comm. honor, U. San Diego, Sarnoff citation, Radio Club Am., 2002. Fellow: Explorers Club (North Pole expedn. 1983, South Pole expdn. 1974, 1984, 1988, 1996); mem.: NATAS (exec. com., bd. internat. coun., pres. N.Y. chpt., Gabriel award for outstanding broadcaster 1998, trustees' award), Bd. Ctr. for Comm., Internat. Radio-TV Soc., Nat. Lighthouse Mus. and Ctr. Soc. (bd. dirs.), N.Y. Yacht Club. Roman Catholic. Home: 2 Highgate Rd Riverside CT 06878-2611 Office: 450 W 33rd St New York NY 10001-2603

BAKER, WILLIAM MORRIS, cultural organization administrator; m. Robin Baker. BA in History, U. Va., 1961. With FBI, 1965-87-89-91, asst. dir. criminal investigative divsn., ret., 1991; dir. pub. affairs CIA, 1987-89; sr. v.p., dir. worldwide anti-piracy Motion Picture Assn., Encino, Calif., 1991-94, pres., COO, 1994—. Spkr. in field; guest lectr. Ctr. for Internat. Affairs Harvard U., Fed. Exec. Inst. U. Va. 1st lt. USAF, 1962-65. Named Disting. Exec. by U.S. Pres. George Bush, 1990; recipient Disting. Intelligence medal CIA, 1989, Edmund J. Randolph award U.S. Atty. Gen.'s 40th Ann. Awards Ceremony, 1992, U.S. Marshals Star for lifetime achievement in law enforcement, 1992. Avocations: reading, running, sailing, skiing, cooking. Office: Motion Picture Assn 15503 Ventura Blvd Encino CA 91436-3103

BAKER, WILLIAM OLIVER, retired research chemist; b. Chestertown, Md., July 15, 1915; s. Harold May and Helen (Stokes) Baker; m. Frances Burrill, Nov. 15, 1941; 1 child, Joseph Burrill. BS, Washington Coll., 1935, ScD (hon.), 1957; PhD, Princeton U., 1938; ScD (hon.), Georgetown U., 1962, U. Pitts., 1963, Seton Hall U., 1965, U. Akron, 1968, U. Mich., 1970, St. Peter's Coll., 1972, Poly. Inst. N.Y., 1973, Trinity Coll., Dublin, Ireland, 1975, Northwestern U., 1976, U. Notre Dame, 1978, Tufts U., 1981, N.J. U. Medicine and Dentistry, 1981, Clark U., 1983, Fairleigh Dickinson U., 1983, Rockefeller U., 1990; DEng. (hon.), Stevens Inst. Tech., 1962, N.J. Inst. Tech., 1978; LLD (hon.), U. Glasgow, 1965, U. Pa., 1974, Kean Coll., N.J., 1976, Lehigh U., 1980, Drew U., 1981, Monmouth Coll., 1973, Clarkson Coll. Tech., 1974, Princeton U., 1993, Rutgers U., 1995. With AT&T Bell Labs., 1939—80, in charge polymer research and devel., 1948—51, asst. dir. chem. and metall. research, 1951—54, dir. research, phys. scis., 1954—55, v.p. research, 1955—73, pres., 1973—79, chmn. bd., 1979—80; retired. Bd. dirs. Gen. Am. Investors, Inc.; dir. Health Effects Inst., 1980—95; vis. lectr. Northwestern U., Princeton U., Duke U.; Schmitt lectr. U. Notre Dame, 1968; Harrelson lectr. N.c. State U., 1971; Herbert Spencer lectr. U. Pa., 1974; Charles M. Schwab Meml. lectr. Am. Iron and Steel Inst., 1976; NIH lectr., 58; Metall. Soc. Am. Inst. Mining Engrs./Am. Soc. Metals disting. lectr., 76; Miles Conrad Meml. lectr. Nat. Fedn. Abstracting and Indexing Svcs., 1977; Wulff lectr. MIT, 1979; Mayo Found. lectr., 80; Logue lectr., 81; Whitehead lectr. U. Ga., 1985; Lazerow lectr. U. Pitts., 1984; Taylor lectr. Pa. State U., 1984; other lectureships; cons. Office Sci. and Tech., 1977—81; mem. Princeton Grad. Coun., 1956—64; bd. visitors Tulane U., 1963—82; mem. commn. sociotech. systems NRC, 1974—78, also chmn. adv. bd. on mil. pers. supplies, 1964—78, mem. com. oh phys. chemistry of divsn. chemistry and chem. tech., 1963—70; also steering com. Pres.'s Food and Nutrition Study Commn. Internat. Rels. NAS-NRC, 1975; mem. panel on phys. chemistry Office Naval Rsch., 1948—51; past mem. Pres.'s Sci. Adv. Com., 1957—60; nat. sci. bd. NSF, 1960—66; past chmn. Nat. Sci. Info. Coun., 1959—61; mem. sci. adv. bd. NSA, 1959—76, cons., 1976—, Dept. Def., 1958—71; cons. to spl. asst. Pres. for sci. and tech., 1963—73; cons. Panel of Ops. Evaluation Group USN, 1960—62; mem. N.J. Bd. Higher Edn., 1967—94, exec. com., 1970—94, vice chmn., 1970—72, 1982—84; mem. liaison com. for sci. and tech. Libr. Congress, 1963—73; mem. Pres.'s Fgn. Intelligence Adv. Bd., 1959—77, 1981—90; chmn. diplomatic telecommunication systems policy bd. Dept. State, 1984—; chmn. Pres.'s Adv. Group Anticipated Advances in Sci. and Tech., 1975—76; vice chmn. Pres.'s Com. Sci. and Tech., 1976—77; bd. regents Nat. Libr. Medicine, 1969—73; bd. visitors Air Force Systems Command, 1962—73; mem. mgmt. adv. coun. Oak Ridge Nat. Lab., 1970—78; mem. Nat. Commn. on Librs. and Info. Scis., 1971—75, Commn. on Critical Choices for Ams., 1973—75, Nat. Cancer Adv. Bd., 1974—80, Nat. Commn. on Excellence in Edn., 1981—83, Nat. Commn. on Jobs and Small Bus., 1985—87, Nat. Commn. on Role and Future State Colls. and Univs., 1985—87; mem., vice chmn. Commn. on Sci. and Tech. N.J., 1985—; mem. Carnegie Forum on Edn. Sci. Tech. and The Economy, 1985—; co-chmn., nat. coun. on sci. and tech. edn. AAAS, 1985—; mem. adv. panel Inst. Materials Rsch. Nat. Bur. Stds., 1966—69; mem. Coun. Trends and Perspectives U.S. C. of C., 1966—74; chmn. tech. panels adv. to Nat. Bur. Standards NAS-NRC, 1969—78; mem. Nat. Coun. Ednl. Rsch., 1973—75; mem. energy R & Dadv. coun. Energy Policy Office, 1973—75; mem. Project Independence adv. com. Fed. Energy Adminstrn., 1974—75; mem. Gov.'s Com. to Evaluate Capital Needs N.J., 1974—75; mem. governing bd. Nat. Enquiry into Scholarly Communication, 1975—79; mem. adv. coun. N.J. Regional Med. Libr., 1975—; mem. Spl. Libr. Assn., 1985—, Fed. Emergency Mgmt. Adv. Bd., 1980—93, Gas Rsch. Inst. Adv. Bd., 1978—85; mem. adv. bd. N.J. Sci./Tech. Ctr., 1980—86; mem. sci. adv. bd. Robert A. Welch Found., 1968—; mem. vis. com. for chemistry Harvard U., 1959—72; mem. coun. Marconi Fellowships, 1978—; vis. com., divsn. chemistry and chem. engring. Calif. Inst. Tech., 1969—72; vis. com. on scis. and math. Drew U., 1969—; assoc. in univ. seminar on tech. and social change Columbia U., 1969—80; vis. com., dept. materials sci. and engring. MIT, 1973—76; bd. overseers Coll. Engring. and Ap1plied Sci. U. Pa., 1975—; bd. dirs. Coun. on Libr. Resources, 1970—, Clin. Scholar Program Robert Wood Johnson Found., 1973—76, Third Century Corp., 1973—76, EDUCOM, 1985—92; organizer labs. for numerous cos.; originator nat. tech. means of satellite survey Nat. Security Coun. Orgn. Fed. Telecommunications System ; co-sponsor Nat. Cancer Plan, Nat. Materials Program; co-founder Aerospace Corp., 1961, Health Effects Inst., 1980—95, N.J. Commn. on Sci. and Tech., 1985—. Contbr.,, ; editl. adv. bd. Jour. Info. Sci., past mem. adv. editl. bd. Chem. and Engring. News, hon. editl. adv. bd. Carbon, contbr. numerous articles to tech. jours. Trustee Urban Studies, Inc., 1960—78, Aerospace Corp., 1961—76, Carnegie-Mellon U., 1967—87; now trustee emeritus Princeton U., 1964—86, Fund N.J., 1974—, Harry Frank Guggenheim Found., 1976—, GM Cancer Rsch. Found., 1978—, Charles Babbage Inst., 1978—, Newark Mus., 1979—89; trustee Rockefeller U., 1960—90, chmn. emeritus, 1990—; trustee Andrew W. Mellon Found., 1965—90, chmn., 1975—90, chmn. emeritus, 1990—; chmn. Rockefeller U., 1980—90. Co-recipient Nat. medal Tech., 1985, Thomas Alva Edison Sci. medal, State of N.J., 1987, Nat. Materials Advancement award, Fedn. Materials Socs., 1987, Nat. medal of Sci., 1988; named one of 10 top scientists in U.S. industry, 1954; recipient Perkin medal, 1963, Honor scroll, Am. Inst. Chemists, 1962, award to execs., ASTM, 1967, Edgar Marburg award, 1967, Indsl. Rsch. Inst. medal, 1970, Frederik Philips award, IEEE, 1972, Indsl. Rsch. Man of Yr. award, 1973, Procter prize, Sigma Xi, 1973, James Madison medal, Princeton U., 1975, Mellon Inst. award, 1975, Soc. Rsch. Adminstrs. award for disting. contbns., 1976, von Hippel award, Materials Rsch. Soc., 1978, Fahrney medal, Franklin Inst., 1977, N.J. Sci./Tech. medal, 1980, Jefferson medal, N.J. Patent Law Assn., 1981, David Sarnoff prize, AFCEA, 1981, Vannevar Bush prize, Nat. Sci. Bd., 1981, Pres.'s Nat. Security medal, 1983, Baker medal, Security Affairs Support Assn., 1984, Disting. Svc. award, Nat. Assn. Gov. Bd., 1993, Philip Hauge Abelson prize, AAAS, 1995; fellow Harvard U., 1937—38, Procter, 1938—39. Fellow: Am. Acad. Arts and Scis., Franklin Inst., Am. Inst. Chemists (Gold medal 1975), Am. Phys. Soc.; mem.: NAE (Bueche prize 1986), NAS, Indsl. Rsch. Inst. (medal 1970), Inst. Medicine, Am. Philos. Soc., Am. Chem. Soc. (Priestly medal 1966, Parsons award 1976, Willard Gibbs award 1978, Madison Marshall award 1980), Dirs. of Indsl. Rsch., Princeton Club of Northwestern N.J., Chemists Club of N.Y. (hon.), Cosmos Club, Sigma Xi, Omicron Delta Kappa, Phi Lambda Upsilon. Achievements include patents for (13); research in semiconducting polymers; solid state structure of linear polymers-polyamides and polyester; influence of microstructure on mechanical and engineering properties of rubbers and plastics; development of polyethylene for cable sheathing and microwave dielectric; synthesis and properties of polymer carbon-pattents as resistor; microphonic and composite (fibrous) material; dynamic mechanics of polymers; relaxation times of dilute macromolecules. Office: c/o Rockefeller Univ 1230 York Ave New York NY 10021-6307*

BAKER, WILLIAM P. (BILL BAKER), former congressman; b. Oakland, Calif., June 14, 1940; m. Joanne Atack; children: Todd, Mary, Billy, Robby. Grad. in Bus. and Indsl. Mgmt., San Jose State Coll. Budget analyst State Dept. Fin., Calif.; assemblyman 15th dist. State of Calif., 1980-92; mem. of Congress from 10th Calif. dist., 1993-96; ptnr. Baker, Welch & Wiens, Alamo, Calif. Vice chmn. budget writing Ways and Means Com., 1984-91 Exec. v.p. Contra Costa Taxpayers Assn.; active Contra Costa County Farm Bur. With USCG Res., 1958-65. Republican. Office: Baker Welch & Wiens 3189 Danville Blvd Ste 200 Alamo CA 94507-1956

BAKER, WILLIAM PARR, lawyer; b. Balt., Sept. 5, 1946; s. George William and Jane (Parr) B.; m. Christine Corbett, Oct. 23, 1982; children: William Corbett, Brendan Parr, Laura Elizabeth. BA, St. Francis Univ., Loretto, Pa., 1968; JD, U. Md., 1971. Bar: Md. 1971, U.S. Dist. Ct. Md. 1972, U.S. Tax Ct. 1978, U.S. Supreme Ct. 1980, U.S. Ct. Appeals (4th cir.) 1982. Law clk. Md. Ct. Appeals, 1971-72; ptnr. Baker and Baker, PA and predecessors, Balt., 1972—. Civil case mediator Cir. Ct. for Balt. County; adj. prof. U. Md. Sch. Law. Contbr. articles to profl. jours. V.p. bd. dirs. Santa Claus Anonymous, 1973-76; bd. dirs. Balt. Assn. Retarded Citizens, 1981—. Mem. ABA, Md. Bar Assn., Bar Assn. Balt. City, Golfers Charitable Assn. (bd. dirs. 1989—), Am. Mensa, Balt. Country Club. Roman Catholic. Office: Baker and Baker PA 1000 Mercantile Trust Bldg 409 Washington Ave Baltimore MD 21204-4920

BAKER, WILLIAM THOMPSON, JR., lawyer; b. N.Y.C., Jan. 19, 1944; s. William Thompson and Elizabeth (Baird) B.; children: Alice Whetherly, Richard Cass, Heather Thompson. BA cum laude, Yale U., 1965; JD, U. Va., 1968. Bar: N.Y. 1968, U.S. Dist. Ct. (so. and ea. dists.) N.Y. 1969, U.S. Supreme Ct. 1990, U.S. Ct. Appeals (D.C. cir.), 1992. Assoc. Thelen, Reid & Priest (formerly known as Reid & Priest), N.Y.C., 1968-74, ptnr, 1975—, mng. ptnr., 1986-87, mem. exec. com., 1980-82, 86-91, chmn. exec. com., 1990-91. Chmn. or co-chmn. Utility/Energy Svcs. Group Dept., 1991—; chmn. legal com. Edison Electric Inst., 1997-99. Trustee Episcopal Sch. in City of N.Y., 1969-71, Chase Wildlife Found., 2003—; mem. bd. govs. The Hotchkiss Sch. Alumni Assn., 2003—. Mem. ABA (chmn. subcom. pub. utility law 1990—), New York County Lawyers Assn., Assn. Bar City N.Y., Union Club N.Y.C., Yale Club N.Y.C., N.Y. Anglers Club. Republican. Episcopalian. Avocations: fishing, fly tying, rod building, wood working.

BAKER, WILLIAM W. nonprofit company executive; b. Jamaica, N.Y., Nov. 29, 1963; s. William and Rosa; m. Robin Lisa Baker, Sept. 7, 1991. Student, Cornell U., 1981-87. Dir. rhetorical scholarship labs. Cornell U., Ithaca, N.Y., 1987-88; dir. debate Columbia U., N.Y.C., 1988-91, stragetic comms. officer, 1992-94; chief mgmt. officer Unitarian Universalist UN Office, N.Y.C., 1992-95; N.Am. coord. Internat. Assn. for Religious Freedom, N.Y.C., 1995-99; exec. dir., CEO Impact Coalition, N.Y.C., 1999—. Pres. Baker Cons. Svc., N.Y.C., 1993—; corp. adv. bd. Lakeside Faily and Children's Svcs., N.Y.C., 1992-97. Sr. editor periodical Window on the world, 1995-96; editor mag. Survey of Activities of Religious Non-Govtl. Ops, 1998, 2000. Assembly dist. leader

Dem. Party, Queens, N.Y., 1992; mem. focus group on religion Hague Appeal for Peace, N.Y.C., 1999. Recipient Will Baker Limited Prep. award in his honor Binghamton U., 1990, Don Brownlee award Cross Exam. Debate Assn., 1999, Glen Pelham award for nat. svc., 2001. Mem. Internat. Assn. for Religous Freedom (UN rep. 1996—, layout editor IARF World 1998, Svc. award 1999), N.Am. Interfaith Network (bd. dirs. 1997—), Nat. Soc. Fundraising Execs., Assn. for Fundraising Profls., Cornell Forensics Alumni Assn., Delta Sigma Rho. Democrat. Methodist. Avocations: bridge, chess, racquetball. Office: IMPACT Coalition 330 W 42d St Ste 2420 New York NY 10036

BAKER, ZACHARY MOSHE, librarian; b. Mpls., June 8, 1950; s. Michael Harry and Margaret Esther (Zanger) B. BA, U. Chgo., 1972; MA, Brandeis U., 1974; MA in LS, U. Minn., 1975. Head tech. svcs. Jewish Pub. Libr., Montreal, Que., Can., 1981-87; asst. libr. Yivo Inst. for Jewish Rsch., N.Y.C., 1976-80, assoc. libr., 1980-81, head libr., 1987-99; Reinhard family curator Judaica & Hebraica collections Stanford U. Librs., 1999—. Hist. cons. Que. Inst. Rsch. on Culture, Montreal, 1983; libr. cons. U.S. Holocaust Meml. Coun., Washington, 1984-85, Fla. Atlantic U., Boca Raton, 1994, Ariz. State U., Tempe, 1998. Contbg. author: From a Ruined Garden, 1983, 98; author, contbg. editor Toledot, 1978-82, Judaica Librarianship, 1983—; editor: Yiddish Catalog and Authority File of the Yivo Library, 1990. Crown fellow Brandeis U., 1973-74; travel and rsch. grantee Andrew W. Mellon Found., 1997, Lucius N. Littauer Found., 1990, 94, 96, 98/ Mem. ALA, Assn. Jewish Librs. (pres. 1994-96), Assn. for Jewish Studies, Coun. Archives and Rsch. Libr. in Jewish Studies (pres. 1998-02), Phi Beta Kappa, Beta Phi Mu. Avocations: map and atlas collecting, current events, travel. E-mail: zbaker@stanford.edu.

BAKER-GARDNER, JEWELLE, interior designer, business consultant; b. Ayden, N.C., May 23, 1925; d. Roland Ray and Helen Wingate (Jackson) Cannon; m. Paul Thomas Baker, July 25, 1956 (dec. 1963); children: Paula Jewelle Baker Bryan, Paul Thomas; 1 stepchild, Blanche Baker Miller; m. Fred Calvin Gardner, Apr. 19, 1969 (dec. May 1983); 1 stepchild, Angela Gardner Jones Hollowell. Student, Woods Bus. Sch., New Bern, N.C., 1942-45; BA, Am. Sch. Design, N.Y.C., 1948; BFA, U. N.C., Greensboro, 1950. Dept. head Navy Supply, Cherry Point, N.C., 1941-45; ptnr. Cannons Paint & Wallpaper Co., Ayden, 1945-70; exec. v.p. Baker Furniture Co., Kinston, N.C., 1950-63, pres., treas., 1963-69; operator Cannon Farms, Ayden, 1956—; with consumer program Drexel Co., 1965-66; owner Jewelle Baker Cons., Kinston, 1969—; v.p. Gardner Homes, Elizabeth City, N.C., 1972-81, CEO, 1982—; bus. cons. Gardner Constrn. Co., Kinston, 1975-81, chmn. bd. dirs., CEO, 1982—; bus. cons. Lenoir Plumbing & Heating Co., Kinston, 1975-81, chmn. bd. dirs., CEO, 1982—. Cons. Carolina Power & Light, 1963-65, N.C. Solar Energy Assn., 1977-79, Nutritional Therapy, Durham, N.C., 1979-81; lectr., 1950-63; del. U.S.-China Joint Session on Industry, Trade and Econ. Devel., Beijing, 1988. Columnist Ayden Dispatch and Greenville News Leader, 1940-56; prodr. Performer Baker's Commls., 1960-69. Mem. Devel. Auth. of Neuse River Coun. of Govts., 1984-85. Mem. C. of C. Kinston (bd. dirs., v.p., chmn. retail mchts. divsn.), So. Retail Furniture Assn., Nat. Retail Furniture Assn., N.C. Mchts. Assn., N.C. Farm Assn., Assn. Gen. Contractors Am., Cmty. Coun. for the Arts, Internat. Platform Assn., N.C. Zool. Assn., N.C. Art Soc., Kinston Country Club, Coral Bay Club, Pineknoll Golf and Country Club, Sea Water Marina Club. Democrat. Mem. Ch. Disciples Of Christ. Home: 1708 Elizabeth Dr Kinston NC 28504-3416 Office: Gardner Constrn Co PO Box 856 Kinston NC 28502-0856 E-mail: jewelle@coastalnet.com., jewellebaker@cox.net.

BAKER KNOLL, CATHERINE, lieutenant governor; b. Pitts. d. Nicholas James and Theresa Mary (May) Baker; m. Charles A. Knoll Sr. (dec.); children: Charles A. Jr., Mina B., Albert B., Kim Eric. BS in Edn., Duquesne U., 1952, MS in Edn., 1973. Dir. western Pa. region Safety Adminstrn. Dept. Transp., Pitts., 1971-79; exec. dir. community svc. Dept. of Adminstrn., Allegheny County, Pa., 1980-88; treas. Pa. Treasury Dept., Harrisburg, 1988—. Owner, operator pvt. bus. firm, Pitts., 1952-70. Mem. Pa. Dem. State Com., Pa. Fedn. Dem. Women, YMCA Bd., Pitts., Harrisburg, Duquesne U. Alumni Bd., Mom's House, Zontas Inc. Bd. Mem. Nat. Assn. State Treas., Women Execs. in State Gov., Coun. State Gov. (exec. com. ea. region). Roman Catholic. Office: Governor Office 225 Main Capitol Bldg Harrisburg PA 17120*

BAKER-ROELOFS, MINA MARIE, retired home economist, educator; b. Holland, Mich., Mar. 1, 1920; d. Thomas and Fannie (DeBoer) Baker; m. Harold Eugene Roelofs, Aug. 16, 1985; children: Howard, Donald, Ann. BS, Iowa State U., 1942, MS, 1946; postgrad., Ariz. State U., 1965, Ind. State U., 1968, 76. Dietitian Annville (Ky.) Inst., 1942-45; chmn., tchr. family and consumer scis. Cen. Coll., Pella, Iowa, 1946-85, ret., 1985. Mem. dean's grad. adv. coun. Iowa State U., Ames, 1955-56, coord. coop. plan, 1967-85. Editor: Dandy Dutch Recipes, 1991; co-editor: Pella Collectors Cookbook, 1982, A Taste of the World, 1992. Mem. com. Pell Hist. Soc. Recipient Career award Iowa State U. Coll. Family Consumer Sci., 2002; grantee Govt. Cross-Cultural, 1974, NEH, 1980. Mem. AAUW, Am. Assn. Family and Consumer Sci. (life), Iowa Assn. Family and Consumer Sci. (pres. 1953-55, sec. 1979-81, Disting. Svc. award 1985), Iowa Elder Hostel Tchr. Ctrl. Coll. Aux., PEO Sisterhood, Women's Social and Literary Club (pres. 1990-92). Republican. Mem. Reformed Ch. Avocations: photography, reading, crafts. Home: 229 Main St Pella IA 50219-2024

BAKHT, BAIDAR, civil engineer, researcher, educator; b. Delhi, India, Sept. 4, 1940; arrived in Can., 1973; s. Mukhtar and Anwar Jehan Chishti; m. Anita Das, Sept. 11, 1968; children: Natasha, Sacha. BSc in Engring. Aligarh (India) U., 1962; MSc, Imperial Coll., London, 1972; DSc, London U., 1990. Registered profl. engr., Ont., Can. Asst. engr. Heavy Engring. Corp., Ranchi, India, 1962-66; engr. Dept. Environ., London, 1967-73; prin. rsch. engr. Ministry Transp. Ont., 1974-97; pres. JMBT Stuctures Rsch., Inc., Toronto, Ont., 1997—. Adj. prof. civil engring. U. Toronto, U. Manitoba, 2000—. Co-author: Bridge Analysis Simplified, 1985, Bridge Analysis by Microcomputer, 1988, Soil-steel Bridges: Design and Construction, 1993, Bridge Engineering, Recent Innovations, 1994; Bridge Superstructures, New Developments, 1996; translator 16 books of Urdu poetry to English, 1985—; contbr. over 190 articles to profl. jours.; co-inventor unique deck slab of bridges, inventor of stressed-log bridge. Recipient Moisseif award ASCE, 1982, President's medal Road and Transp. Assn. Can., 1985, Profl. Engrs. Ont. Engring. medal, 1997. Fellow: Profl. Engrs. Ont. (Engring. medal 1996), Engring. Inst. Can. (Gzowski medal 1983), Can. Soc. for Civil Engring. (Pratley award 1988, 1994, Vance award 1996, award for outstanding contbn. to bridge engring. 2002), Instn. Engrs. (India) (cert. of merit 1990). Avocation: translating urdu poetry into english. E-mail: bbakht@rogers.com.

BAKHUIZEN, WILLEM ANTHONIE HENDRIK JOHANNES, civil engineer; b. Vlaardingen, The Netherlands, Apr. 25, 1945; arrived in Sweden, 1969; s. Martinus and Johanna K. (van Leeuwen) B.; m. Anita S.G. Lofman, Sept. 5, 1970; 1 child, Mattias H. BSc, HTS-Inst. Advanced Tech., Utrecht, 1967. Cert. cons. civil engr. Area mgr. Far East Viak Cons., Gothenburg, Sweden, 1969-83; mgr. offshore ops. Benima Engring., Gothenburg, 1983-87; pres. Hasselblad Engring. AB, Gothenburg, 1987-91, WB Geomap, 1991—. Survey cons. Ingenieros Consultadores Associados/Tunel S.A., Mexico City, 1973; cons. Food and Agr. Orgn. for Remote Sensing Project Mekong Delta-Ho Chi Minh City, 1987; chief surveyor Swedish Internat. Devel. Authority, Bai Bang, Vietnam, 1975-77. Active Nat. Swedish Devel. Authority, Stockholm, 1979. Fellow Remote Sensing Soc., Am. Soc. Photogrammetry; mem. Civil Engrs. Assn. Sweden, Chartered Land Surveyor Sweden. Office: WB Geomap Hantverksvagen 15 SE 43633 Askim Sweden E-mail: geomap@algonet.se.

BAKINOWSKI, CAROL ANN, journalist; b. Waterbury, Conn., Apr. 8, 1949; m. John McCormick. BA in English, U. Conn., 1971; MS in Journalism, Columbia U., 1975. Stringer UPI, Hartford, Conn., 1968-71; copy editor Hartford Courant, 1971-74, Wall St. Jour., 1975-76, Louisville Times, 1976-80; news design editor N.Y. Times, 1980—. Mem. Soc. News Design, Soc. Profl. Journalists. Office: NY Times 229 W 43d St New York NY 10036 E-mail: carolbak@nytimes.com.

BAKKE, DENNIS W. energy company executive; m. Eileen Bakke. MBA, Harvard U. With Fed. Energy Agy.; with Energy Productivity Ctr., Carnegie Mellon U.; founder, pres. & CEO The AES Corp., Arlington, Va., 1981—. Co-author: Creating Abundance-America's Least Cost Energy Strategy. Pres. Mustard Seed Found. Mem. Am. Gass Assn. (past dir.). Office: The AES Corp 1001 19th St N Arlington VA 22209-1722 Fax: 703-528-4510.

BAKKE, LUANNE KAYE, music educator; b. Rochester, Ind., Apr. 3, 1937; d. Lyman Dean and Anna Lorraine (Bull) Burkett; m. Ronald Roark (div. 1981); m. Jacques Roland Bakke, Feb. 24, 1988; 1 child, Kathleen Anne. BA, Calif. St. U., Northridge, 1977; MusM, Calif. State U., Fullerton, 1981. Instr. Calif. State U., Fullerton, 1979—81, City Coll. Chgo., Karlsruhe, Germany, 1985—86, Gadsden City Coll., Gadsden, Ala., 1986—87; pvt. practice piano & voice Lander, Wyo., 1995—. Music dir. Wood'N Ship Prodn., L.A., Calif., 1978—80; prodr. & dir. Off the Track Singers, L.A., 1975—77. Contbr. ; composer: (plays) The Adventure of Doraleen, 1981. Pres. Pomona Valley Music Tchrs. Assn., 1969; music dir. Anniston Cmty. Theater, Anniston, Ala., 1987—89; cmty. choir dir. Harmonic Jam, Granite Falls, Minn., 1992—95; creator Performing Arts in Miniature, 1997—. Recipient Frank Jones award for leadership in the arts, City of Anniston, 1986. Mem.: Music Tchrs. Nat. Assn., Pi Kappa Lambda. Republican. Avocations: scuba diving, hiking, care of animals. Home and Office: PO Box 514 Lander WY 82520 E-mail: jbakke@wyoming.com.

BAKKEN, DOUGLAS ADAIR, foundation executive; b. Breckenridge, Minn., Mar. 12, 1939; s. John and Marie (Folstad) B.; m. Jacquelyn Ann Nielsen, July 8, 1962; children: Amy Michelle, Wendy Kay. BS, N.D. State U., 1961; cert. archives adminstrn., Am. U., 1966; MA in History, U. Nebr., 1967. Archivist Nebr. State Hist. Soc., Lincoln, 1966-67; assoc. archivist Cornell U., Ithaca, N.Y., 1967-71; archivist adminstr. Anheuser Busch Cos., St. Louis, 1971-77; dir. archives and library Henry Ford Mus., Dearborn, Mich., 1977-83; exec. dir. Ball Bros. Found., Muncie, Ind., 1983—. Pres. Ind. Donors Alliance Found., 1993—; mem. Minn. Cultural Found., 1989—. Served to 1st lt. Intelligence Corps U.S. Army, 1962-64. Sagamore of the Wabash, 1992. Fellow Soc. Am. Archivists; mem. Muncie Rotary Club, Ind. Colls. of Ind., Sports and Hobby Devel. Group Inc., Ind. Donors Alliance (founding mem.) Republican. Lutheran. Home: 4801 N Everett Rd Muncie IN 47304-1092 Office: Ball Bros Found 222 S Mulberry St Muncie IN 47305-2802

BAKKEN, EARL ELMER, electrical engineer, bioengineering company executive; b. Mpls., Jan. 10, 1924; s. Osval Elmer and Florence (Hendricks) B.; m. Constance L. Olson, Sept. 11, 1948 (div. May 1979); children: Wendy, Jeff, Brad, Pam; m. Doris Jane Marshall, Oct. 21, 1982. BEE, U. Minn., 1948, postgrad. in elec. engring., DSc (hon.), 1988, Tulane U., 1988. Ptnr. Medtronic, Inc., Mpls., 1949-57, pres., 1957-74, chmn., CEO, 1974-76, founder, sr. chmn., 1976-85, sr. chmn., 1985-89, dir., 1989-94, founder, dir. emeritus, 1994—. Contbr. articles to profl. jours.; developer first wearable, external, battery-powered heart pacemaker. Pres., bd. dirs. Bakken Libr. and Mus. Electricity in Life, Mpls., 1975-94, v.p., 1994—; pres. North Hawaii Cmty. Hosp., 1990-2000, Five Mtn. Med. Cmty., Waimea, Hawaii, 1997—; vice chmn. Pavek Mus. Broadcasting, Mpls., 1989—; chmn. bd. dirs. Archaeus Project, Waimea, Hawaii, 1985—. Staff sgt. USAAF, 1942-46. Decorated royal officer Order of Orange-Nassau (Netherlands); recipient Minn. Bus. Hall of Fame award, 1978, Outstanding Achievement award U. Minn., Mpls., 1981, Med.-Tech. Outstanding Achievement award Wale Securities, 1984, Engring. for Gold award NASPE, 1984, Achievement award Sci. Mus. Minn., 1988, Govs. award Minn. Med. Alley Assn., 1988, Centennial medal Coll. St. Thomas, 1986; named Outstanding Minnesotan of Yr. Minn. Broadcasters Assn., 1988, Lifetime Achievement award Entrepreneur of the Yr. program, 1991, Entrepreneur of Yr. award Minn. Entrepreneur's Club, 1993, Spl. Svc. award Richard Smart Big Island Cmty. Achievement, Waimea, Hawaii, 1995, Am. Creativity Assn. Lifetime Creative Achievement award, 1996, Lifetime Achievement award Minn. High Tech. Coun., 1996, Am. Heart Assn. Heart Ball honoree, Hawaii, 1996, Found. Laufman-Greatbatch prize, 1998, Spl. award Cardiostim 98 XX Anniversary for Engrs. and Industry Founders, 1998, Honpa Hongwanji Mission of Hawaii Living Treasure of Hawaii award, 1998, Heart Inst. Innovator award, 1998, NASPE Pioneering award, 1999, Gold medal European Soc. Cardiology, 1999, Tex. Heart Inst. Innovator awrd, 1999, Outstanding Philanthropist of Yr., Nat. Philanthropy Soc., 2000, Russ prize Nat. Acad. Engring., 2001, Trailblazer award Scripps Ctr. for Integrative Medicine, 2002, others; named to Minn. Inventors Hall of Fame, 1995, Am. Heart Assn. West Hawaii Hall of Fame, 1998. Fellow IEEE (Centennial medal 1984, Eli Lilly award in med. and biol. engring. 1994), Bakken Soc., Instrument soc. Am., Am. Coll. Cardiology (hon.), Internat. Coll. Surgeons (hon.); mem. N.Am. Soc. Pacing and Electrophysiology (assoc., Disting. Svc. award 1985), Assn. Advancement Med. Instrumentation (Tex. Heart Inst. Innovator award 1998), Am. Antiquarian Soc., Minn. Med. Alley Assn. (bd. dirs. 1985-94), NAE, 1990—. Lutheran. Avocations: history of medical electrical technology, future studies, ballroom dancing. Office: Medtronic Inc MS LC110 710 Medtronic Pkwy Minneapolis MN 55432-5604

BAKKEN, GORDON MORRIS, law educator; b. Madison, Wis., Jan. 10, 1943; s. Elwood S. and Evelyn A. H. (Anderson) B.; m. Erika Reinhardt, Mar. 24, 1943; children: Angela E., Jeffrey E. BS, U. Wis., 1966, MS, 1967, PhD, 1970, JD, 1973. From asst. to assoc. prof. history Calif. State U., Fullerton, 1969-74, prof. history, 1974—, dir. faculty affairs, 1974-86. Cons. Calif. Sch. Employees Assn., 1976-78, Calif. Bar Commn. Hist. Law., 1985—; mgmt. task force on acad. grievance procedures Calif. State Univ. and Colls. Systems, 1975; mem. Calif. Jud. Coun. Com. Trial Ct. Records Mgmt., 1992-97. Author 7 books on Am. legal history; contbr. articles to profl. jours. Placentia Jusa referee coord., 1983. Russell Sag resident fellow law, 1971-72, Am. Bar Found. fellow in legal history, 1979-80, 84-85; Am. Coun. Learned Socs. grantee-in-aid, 1979-80. Mem. Orgn. Am. Historians, Am. Soc. Legal History, Law and Soc. Assn., Western History Assn., Calif. Supreme Ct. Hist. Soc. (v.p.), Phi Alpha Theta (v.p. 1994-95, pres. 1996-97). Democrat. Lutheran. E-mail: gbakken@fullerton.edu.

BAKKEN, JILL, Olympic athlete; b. Portland, Oreg., Jan. 25, 1977; Mem. U.S. Women's Bobsled Team, Lake Placid, NY, 1994—. Mem. Armed Forces World Class Athlete Program. With U.S. Army Nat. Guard. Finalist Sportswoman of Yr., Women's Sports Found., 1998; nominee Nat. Dial award, 1995; recipient Gold medal, Internat. Push Competition, Gotha, Germany, 1997, 1st pl., U.S. Sliding Sport Championships, Park City, 2000, Gold medal, 2002 Olympic Games, Salt Lake City, U.S. Olympic Spirit award, 2002. Address: US Bobsled and Skeleton Fedn PO Box 828 421 Military Rd Lake Placid NY 12946-0828

BAKKENSEN, JOHN RESER, lawyer; b. Pendleton, Oreg., Oct. 4, 1943; s. Manley John and Helen (Reser) B.; m. Ann Marie Dahlen, Sept. 30, 1978; children: Michael, Dana, Laura. AB magna cum laude, Harvard U., 1965; JD, Stanford U., 1968. Bar: Oreg. 1969, Calif. 1969, U.S. Dist. Ct. Oreg. 1969. Ptnr. Miller, Nash, Wiener, Hager & Carlsen, Portland, Oreg., 1968-99. Lawyer del. 9th Cir. Jud. Conf., San Francisco, 1980-82. Author: (with others) Advising Oregon Businesses, 1979, Arbitration and Mediation, supplement, 2000. Past bd. dirs. Assn. for Retarded Citizens, Portland; advisor Portland Youth Shelter House; mem. and counsel to bd. dirs. Friends of Pine Mountain Observatory, Portland. Mem. ABA (forum on constrn. industry), Am. Arbitration Assn., Oreg. State Bar, Oreg. Assoc. Gen. Contractors (legal com. 1991, counsel to bd. dirs. 1992), Arbitration Svc. Portland, Inc. (arbitrator), Multnomah Athletic Club. Avocation: astronomy.

BAKKER, THOMAS GORDON, lawyer; b. San Gabriel, Calif., Aug. 18, 1947; s. Gordon and Eva Marie (Hoekstra) B.; m. Charlotte Anne Kamstra, Aug. 1, 1969; children: Sarah, Jonathan. AB in History, Calvin Coll., Grand Rapids, Mich., 1969; JD, U. Mich., 1973. Bar: Ariz. 1973, U.S. Dist. Ct. Ariz. 1973, U.S. Ct. Appeals (9th cir.) 1973. Staff reporter Ariz. Criminal Code Revision Com., Phoenix, 1973-75; asst. atty. gen. State of Ariz., Phoenix, 1975-77; staff atty. div. 1 Ariz. Ct. Appeals, Phoenix, 1977-79; assoc. Burch, Cracchiolo et al, Phoenix, 1979-80; from assoc. to ptnr. Olson, Jantsch, Bakker, Phoenix, 1980—. Vice chmn. tort and ins. practice sect. Appellate Advocacy Commn., 1982-83; judge pro tem div. 1 Ariz. Ct. Appeals, 1985, 92. Served with U.S. Army, 1969-71. Fellow Ariz. Bar Found. (founding fellow); mem. Ariz. Bar Assn., Maricopa County Bar Assn., Am. Health Lawyers Assn., Def. Rsch. Inst., Ariz. Assn. Def. Counsel 163. Mem. Christian Reformed Ch. Avocations: reading, golf, aerobics, salt water fishing. Office: Olson Jantsch Bakker 7243 N 16th St Phoenix AZ 85020-5203 E-mail: TGB@OJBB.com.

BAKKO, ORVILLE EDWIN, retired health care executive, consultant; b. Kenyon, Minn., Oct. 10, 1919; s. Marcus and Caroline (Leding) B.; m. Norma Evelyn Cronquist, Sept. 25, 1951; children: Sandra Karen, Kristi Camille. BA, St. Olaf Coll., Northfield, Minn., 1941; M. in Hosp. Adminstrn., Northwestern U., 1948. Adminstrv. intern, resident U. Iowa Hosps., 1947-49; adminstrv. asst. Kadlec Hosp., Richland, Wash., 1949-50, asst. adminstr., then adminstr., 1950-56; asst. supt. Arroyo Del Valle Sanatorium, Livermore, Calif., 1956-60, Highland Hosp., Oakland, Calif., 1958-60; adminstr. Fairmont Hosp., San Leandro, Calif., 1960-82. Vis. scholar Agder Coll., Kristiansand, Norway, 1983-84. Author: The Administrative Internship—What Can the Field Contribute to the Program?, 1948, Administration of Group Clinics, 1949, Employee Safety Program, 1970, Survey of Medical Rehabilitation in Norway, 1984. Mem. Alameda County Work Safety Com., 1959-72; mem. med. svcs. adv. com. Chabot Coll., San Leandro, 1962-72; mem. dis. svcs. adv. com. area 1 Regional Med. Program, 1970-72; 2d v.p., bd. dirs. Wash. State Hosp. Assn., 1954-55; pres. S.E. Wash. Hosp. Coun., 1953-54; chmn. Tri-City Hosp. Coun., 1954-56; trustee Commn. on Accreditation Rehab. Facilities, 1974-76; mem. Internat. Hosp. Fedn., 1982-88. Capt. Med. Adminstrv. Corps, AUS, 1942-46, NATOUSA. Decorated officer Ordre du Nichan-Iftikhar (Tunisia). Fellow Am. Coll. Healthcare Execs. (life); mem. Am. Hosp. Assn. (life, governing coun. rehab. and chronic disease hosp. sect. 1972-77, chmn. 1976), Calif. Hosp. Assn. (mem. com. on continuing care and rehab. 1967-70), Assn. Western Hosps., Health Care Execs. No. Calif., East Bay Hosp. Conf. (exec. com. 1971-72), Richland Toastmasters Club (officer 1949-56), Los Rios Homeowners Assn. (bd. dirs., chmn. landscape com. 1994-96), Rotary (charter). Mem. Emmanuel Faith Comm. Ch. Home: 11887 Caminito Corriente San Diego CA 92128-4552

BAKLANOFF, ERIC NICHOLAS, economist, educator; b. Graz, Austria, Dec. 9, 1925; came to U.S., 1937, naturalized, 1943; s. Nicolas W. and Lucille (King) B.; m. H. Christina Janes, June 17, 1956 (div. June 1973); children: Nicholas, Tanya, Ana-Maria; m. Joy Driskell, June 6, 1982. Student, Antioch Coll., 1943-44; AB, Ohio State U., 1949, MA, 1950, PhD, 1958; postgrad. (Fulbright scholar), U. Chile, 1957, Harvard Grad. Sch. Bus. Adminstrn., 1959; postgrad. (NDEA postdoctoral fellow), U. Tex., summer 1963. Instr. econs. Ohio State U., 1957-58; asst. prof. La. State U., 1958-61, assoc. prof., 1961-62; prof. econs., dir. Latin Am. Studies Inst., 1965-68; assoc. prof. econs., dir. Grad. Center for Latin Am. Studies, Vanderbilt U., 1962-65; prof. econs., dean for internat. studies and programs U. Ala., 1969-73, bd. visitors rsch. prof. econs., 1974-92, rsch. prof. econs. emeritus, 1992—. Disting. vis. prof. Luther Coll. summer 1965; cons. Am. Council on Edn., USAF Inst., Pres.'s Southeastern Council on Latin Am. Studies, 1963-64, U.S. Dept. Edn., Centro de Estudios y Communicacion Economica, Am. Enterprise Inst. Pub. Policy Rsch., Fed. Rsch. divsn., Hispanic divsn. Libr. of Congress. Author: Expropriation of U.S. Investments in Cuba, Mexico and Chile, 1975, The Economic Transformation of Spain and Portugal, 1978, La Transformation Economica de Espana y Portugal: La economia del Fanquismo y de del Salazarismo, 1980; author: (with Jeffrey Brannon) Agrarian Reform and Public Enterprise in Mexico: The Political Economy of Yucatan's Henequen Industry, 1987; author: (with Edward H. Moseley) Competing for Latin American Markets: A Business Perspective on the Spanish-American War Centennial, 1999; author: (with others) Revolutionary Change in Cuba, 1971, Modern Brazil: New Patterns and Development, 1971, Background to Revolution: The Development of Modern Cuba, 1979, Yucatan: A World Apart, 1980, The Iberian-Latin America Connection: Implications for U.S. Foreign Policy, 1986, State Shrinking: A Comparative Analysis of Privatization, 1987, The Alabama Economy: Issues for the 1990s, 1990, Portugal: Ancient Country, Young Democracy, 1990, Portugal: A Country Study, 1994, Cuba in Transition, 2001; contbg. author: others, editor, contbg. author: The Shaping of Modern Brazil, 1969, New Perspectives of Brazil, 1966, Mediterranean Europe and the Common Market, 1976, Competing for Latin American Markets: A Business Perspective on the Spanish American War Centennial, 1999, The Handbook of Portuguese Studies, 1999, El Triángulo Económico: España-USA-America Latina, 2002; contbr. articles to profl. jours. Active Boy Scouts Am. Served with USNR, 1944-46, PTO. Decorated Knight of Grace, Hospitaler and Mil. Order St. Lazarus of Jerusalem, Malta obedience; named Outstanding Scholar U. Ala., 1980-81; fellow Ctr. Advanced Study Behavioral Scis., 1964-65; grantee U.S. Dept. State, Spain, 1974; rsch. fellow Andrew W. Mellon Found., 1987. Mem. Delta Chi, Beta Gamma Sigma, Sigma Delta Pi, Omicron Delta Epsilon, Phi Beta Delta. Eastern Orthodox. Office: U Ala PO Box 870224 Tuscaloosa AL 35487-0154

BAKOS, DANIEL FRANK, music educator, organist, composer; b. Hartford, Ohio, Mar. 9, 1945; s. Joseph and Katherine Elizabeth Bakos; m. Karen L Campbell, July 22, 1984 (div. Mar. 15, 1996); children: Joseph Richard Daniel, Daniel Anthony. B in Music, U. Cin., 1967, M in Music, 1969; PhD in Music Theory, Ohio State U., Columbus, Ohio, 1981. Music instr. Black Hill State U., Spearfish, SD, 1969—73; grad. asst. Ohio State U., Columbus, Ohio, 1973—75; prof. music State U. West Ga., Carrollton, Ga., 1975—. Organist Dallas First United Meth., Dallas, 1996—; organist/choir dir. Our Lady Cath. Ch., Carrollton, Ga., 1988—91; organist Carrollton First United Meth., Carrollton, Ga., 1976—88. Composer Don't Forget Me songs; contbr. articles Jazz Scales for Pianists. Dir. U. West Ga. Jazz Ensemble; province gov. 33 Phi Mu Alpha Sinfonia, Evansville, Ga., 1991—2002; province gov. Phi Mu Alph Sinfonia, Evansville, Ga., 1991—. Mem.: Internat. Assn. Jazz Educators, Music Educators Nat. Conf., Coll. Music Soc. Conservative-R. Presbyterian. Home: 252 Ruby Court Carrollton GA 30116-5401 Office: State University West Georgia Music Department Carrollton GA 30118-2210 Office Fax: 770-836-4472. E-mail: dbakos@westga.edu.

BAKRI, YOUNES NOAMAN, surgeon, oncologist, gynecologist; b. Amman, Jordan, Dec. 29, 1950; s. Noaman Ibrahim and Sadia Karim Bakri; children: Noaman, Nadine, Linda, Dina. PhD, U. of Alexandria, Alexandria, 1975. Board Certified Gynecologic Oncology Hussein Coll., Jordan, 1964, Board Certified Obstetrics/Gynecology Hussein Coll., Jordan, 1964. Prof. gynecology and dir. U. of SD, Sioux Falls, SD, 1994—97; educator Va. Med. Sch., Norfolk, Va., 1982, Thomas Jefferson U., Philadelphia, Pa., 1980. Dir. gynecologic oncology King Faisal Specialist Rsch. Ctr., Riyadh, Saudi Arabia, 1999. Recipient Photography Contest award, Wash. Post, 1993. Achievements include invention of Temponade Balloon For Treatment Of Obstetrical Hemorrhage. Office: Geisinger Health System 100 North Academy Danville PA 17822

BAKROW, WILLIAM JOHN, college president emeritus; b. Parson, Kans., Apr. 22, 1924; s. Leonard A. and Edith B.; m. Maree Bakrow (dec.); children: Bruce Wrigley, Caren Edith, Lance. BA, Brown U., 1948; MS, Ind. U., 1958, EdD, 1960; LLD (hon.), St. Mary Coll., Omaha, St. Ambrose U. Reporter Providence Jour., 1948-51; legis. corr. U.P., Albany, N.Y., 1951-56; dir. devel. U. Buffalo, 1956-59, Canisius (N.Y.) Coll., 1961-66; pres. Motorola Exec. Inst., Oracle, Ariz., 1966-73, St. Ambrose U., Davenport, Iowa, 1973—87, Montserrat Coll. Art, Beverly, Mass., 1988-89; ptnr. B & F Assocs., Rockport, Mass. Dir. Southeast Nat. Bank Moline, Ill., Sears Mfg. Co., Davenport., Mercy Hosp., Davenport, Handicapped Devel. Ctr., Davenport; Mem. Scott County Govtl. Study Commn., 1974— Mem. Illowa Council exec. bd. Boy Scouts Am., 1975— ; trustee Palmer Jr. Coll., Davenport, St. Katherine's-St. Mark's Sch., Bettendorf, Iowa, dir. Endicott Coll., Beverly, Mass., pres. Montserrat Coll. of Art, Beverly; mem. Rockport fin. com., Rockport planning bd., supt. schs. selection com.; bd. dirs. Iowa Handicapped Devel. Served with USNR, 1942-46. Home and Office: 4 Bayridge Ln Rockport MA 01966-1353

BAKSHI, SANJIV, internist; s. Amar Nath and Ram Chameli Bakhshi; m. Parampreet Kaur Kaur, June 12, 1964; children: Nayaab, Surya. MB, BChir, Govt. Med. Coll., Amritsar, Punjab, India, 1981. Diplomate Am. Bd. Internal Medicine, 2002. Ho. surgeon in ophthalmology Shri Guru Teg Bahadur Hosp., Amritsar, 1982—82, ho. physician in internal medicine, 1982—82; med. officer Punjab Civil Med. Svc., Amritsar, 1982—85, med. specialist, 1989—91, cardiologist Mohali, India, 1994—95; resident dept. internal medicine Post Grad. Inst. Med. Edn. and Rsch., Chandigarh, India, 1986—88, post doctoral fellow (sr. resident), cardiology, 1992—93; med. officer dept. cardiology Govt. Med. Coll., Amritsar, 1995—97, registrar (sr. resident) dept. cardiology, 1997—98, sr. lectr. dept. cardiology, 1998—2000; resident dept. internal medicine Wyckoff Heights Med. Ctr., Bklyn., 2000—02, chief resident internal medicine, 2002—. Med. officer cons. Punjab Civil Med. Svc., Amritsar, 1983—85, med. specialist, cons. in internal medicine, 1989—91, cardiology cons., Mohali, 1993—94; med. officer, cons. cardiology Govt. Med. Coll., Amritsar, 1996—97, registrar (sr. resident) dept. cardiology, 1997—98; pre-

senter in field. Contbr. articles to profl. jours. Mem.: ACP-Am. Soc. Internal Medicine (assoc.), Cardiol. Soc. India (life). Hindu. Achievements include research in natural history of 86 patients with hypertrophic cardiomyopathy; cardiac specific troponin T and C-reactive protein as prognostic markers in myocardial infarction; empirical use of Roxithromycin in acute myocardial infarction and subsequent cardiovascular events; genetic factors predisposing to atherosclerosis; gene therapy in coronary and peripheral artery disease. Avocations: chess, association football, cricket, badminton, table tennis. Home: 95-39 225th St Floral Park NY 11001 Office: Wyckoff Heights Med Ctr 374 Stockholm St Brooklyn NY 11237 Personal E-mail: sbakshi_cardio@yahoo.com. E-mail: sbakshi_cardio@yahoo.com.

BAKWIN, EDWARD MORRIS, banker; b. N.Y.C., May 13, 1928; s. Harry and Ruth (Morris) B. BA, Hamilton Coll., 1950; MBA, U. Chgo., 1961. With Nat. Stock Yards Nat. Bank, National City, Ill., 1953-55; with Mid-City Nat. Bank Chgo., 1955—2001, pres., 1962-72, chmn. bd., CEO, 1967—2001, Mid-City Fin. Corp., 1982—2001, Darling-Del. Corp., Chgo., 1972-86, Nat. Stock Yards Co., 1985-93; chmn. bd. MBFI, Chgo., 2001—. Mem. Chgo. Crime Commn. Adv. bd. U. Chgo., 1967—; bd. dirs. Duncan-Med. YMCA, 1963-72, Northwestern Meml. Hosp., 1980-88; bd. dirs. West Ctrl. Assn., 1962-67, pres., 1962-65; trustee Am. Mus. Fly Fishing, 1990—. With AUS, 1951-52. Mem. Am. Bankers Assn., Ill. Bankers Assn. (bd. govs. 1966-69), Explorers Club, Adventurers Club (Chgo.), Chgo. Yacht Club, Mid-Am. Club, N.Y. Yacht Club. Home: Apt 8207 175 E Delaware Pl Chicago IL 60611-1756 Office: MBFI Ste 612 801 W Madison St Chicago IL 60607

BALA, SRIRAM, research scientist; b. Singapore, Oct. 3, 1971; arrived in U.S., 1992; s. Balasubramanian Ramanadha and Saraswathy Vaidianathan. BS in Molecular Biology, U. Tex., 1996; MS in Recombinant DNA Tech., NYU, 2001. Crystallographic rschr. U. Tex., Austin, 1994—96, grader, tutor, 1996; content coord. Medlinx Interactive Inc., Westport, Conn., 1997—98; quality assurance engr., rschr. InterNova Corp., N.Y.C., 1998—2000; documentation specialist GiantBear Inc., N.Y.C., 2001; rsch. assoc. Lexicon Genetics Inc., The Woodlands, Tex., 2001—. Project coord. MedLinx Interactive Inc., Westport, 1997—98; website launch team mem. InterNova Corp., N.Y.C., 1998—2000; lead tech. writer, editor GiantBear Inc., N.Y.C., 2001; molecular genetics team mem. Lexicon Genetics, The Woodlands, 2001—. Vol. Stamford (Conn.) Hosp., 1997. Grantee, U. Tex., Austin, 1996; scholar, 1994. Mem.: AAAS, Am. Chem. Soc., N.Y. Acad. Scis., Am. Mensa, Phi Beta Kappa, Phi Kappa Phi, Golden Key. Avocations: reading, movies, sports, travel, fine dining. Office: Lexicon Genetics Inc 8800 Technology Forest Place The Woodlands TX 77381

BALABAN, AVRAHAM, literature educator, poet, writer; b. Kibbutz Hulda, Israel, Oct. 29, 1944; arrived in U.S., 1983; s. Yonah and Shprintza Balaban; m. Rachel Gil-Balaban, Oct. 10, 1992; children: Ron, Tal Dotan. PhD, Tel Aviv U., Tel Aviv, Israel, 1978. Vis. scholar Harvard U., Boston, 1983—84; asst. prof. of modern Hebrew lit. U. Mich., Ann Arbor, 1984—89; assoc. prof. of modern Hebrew lit. U. Fla., Gainesville, Fla., 1989—90, full prof. of modern Hebrew lit., 1991—, chair, dept. of African and Asian languages and literatures, 1996—2002. Author: (poetry) Poetry is Able, Tristan and Isolde: A Series of Love Poems (Prime Minister's Prize for Creativity, 1983), (literary scholarship) Meaning, Form and Rhetoric in Natan Alterman's Stars Outside (Talpir Prize for Lit. Scholarship, 1982), Between God and Beast, An Examination of Amos Oz's Prose, A Different Wave of Hebrew Fiction: Postmodernist Israeli Fiction, (a memoir) Shiva (Mourning), (literary scholarship) Mr. Molcho - An Examination of A.B. Yehoshua's Novles. Recipient Tchg. Incentive Award, U. Fla., 1994, Rsch. Devel. Award, U. Fla., 1990, 1992. Mem.: World Union of Jewish Studies, Nat. Assn. of Prof. of Hebrew, Assn. of Jewish Studies. Achievements include research in Skirball Fellowship, The Oxford Centre for Jewish Studies, Oxford, January-June 1995; Skirball Fellowship, The Oxford Centre for Jewish Studies, Oxford, January-June, 2000; Professorial Exellence Award, U. of Florida, 2000. Home: 3926 NW 29th Ln Gainesville FL 32606 Office: Univ Fla AALL 470 Grinter Hall POBox 115565 Gainesville FL 32611-5565 Home Fax: 352-335-4017; Office Fax: 352-392-1443. Personal E-mail: balaban@aall.ufl.edu. E-mail: balaban@aall.ufl.edu.

BALABANIAN, NORMAN, electrical engineering educator; b. New London, Conn., Aug. 13, 1922; s. Adam B. and Elizabeth (Seklemian) B.; m. Jean Tajerian, Aug. 16, 1947 (div. 1977); children: Karen J., Doris R., Gary N., Linda C.; m. 2d, Rosemary Lynch, Jan. 19, 1979. BSEE, Syracuse U., 1949, MSEE, 1951, PhD, 1954. From instr. to prof. Syracuse U., 1949-91, prof. emeritus, 1991—; mem. tech. staff Bell Labs., Murray Hill, N.J., 1956, IBM Devel. Lab, Poughkeepsie, N.Y., 1962; vis. prof. U. Calif., Berkeley, 1965-66; mem. UNESCO field staff Inst. Politecnico Nacional, Mexico City, 1969-70; Fulbright fellow U. Zagreb, Zagreb, Jugoslavia, 1974-75; acad. advisor Inst. Nat. d'Elec. et d'Elec., Boumerdes, Algeria, 1977-78; chmn. Dept. of Elec. & Computer Engring. Syracuse U., 1983-90. Vis. scholar MIT, 1990-95, Tufts U., 1990-95; courtesy prof. U. Fla., 1995—. Author: Network Synthesis, 1958, Fundamentals of Circuit Theory, 1961, Fourier Series, 1976, Ensenanza Programada en la Education Activa (in Spanish), 1974, Activne RC Mreze (in Serbo-Croatian), 1977, Electric Circuits, 1994; co-author: Linear Network Analysis, 1959, Electrical Network Theory, 1969, Electrical Science: Resistive Networks, 1970, Electrical Science: Dynamic Networks, 1973, Linear Network Theory, 1981, Digital Logic Design Principles, 2001; editor: Undergraduate Physics and Mathematics in Electrical Engineering, 1960, Electrical Engineering Education, 1961; editor (jour.) IEEE Transactions on Circuit Theory, 1963-65, (mag.) IEEE Technology and Society, 1979-86, 1993-95. Dist. commr. Dem. Party, Syracuse, N.Y., 1959-61; pres. Cen. N.Y. Civil Liberties Union, Syracuse, 1963-64, 79-80 (Civil Liberties award 1966); cong. candidate Liberal Party, People's Peace Party, Syracuse, N.Y., 1966. S/Sgt. Army AC, 1943-46. Recipient peace award Syracuse Peace Coun., 1966. Fellow AAAS, IEEE (life fellow, Centennial award 1984, Third Millenium medal 2000), IEEE Soc. Implications Tech. (v.p., pres. 1988-91); DK. mem. Am. Soc. for Engring. Edn. (life mem., pres. EE div. 1966-67), AAUP (pres. Syracuse U. chpt. 1964-65). Office: U Fla Dept ECE Gainesville FL 32611-6200 E-mail: balabanian@ece.ufl.edu.

BALACH, CLAUDIA ANN, director; d. John Casimir and Audrey Marie Szot; m. Kenneth John Balach, Mar. 7, 1987. EdD, Duquesne U., 2003. Nat. bd. cert. tchr. Nat. Bd. for Profl. Tchg. Stds. Sci. educator Quaker Valley Sch. Dist., Sewickley, Pa., 1997—2002; dir. of profl. devel. schs. Duquesne U., Pitts., 2002—. Office: Duquesne U 404 Canevin Hall Pittsburgh PA 15282 Office Fax: 412-396-5585. E-mail: balach@duq.edu.

BALADA, LEONARDO, composer, educator; b. Barcelona, Sept. 22, 1933; s. Jose and Lucia (Ibanez) B.; m. Monica McCormack, July 3, 1962 (div. 1977); 1 child, Dylan; m. Joan Winer, July 28, 1979. Profesorado de Teoria, Conservatory del Liceu, 1953; Profesorado de Piano, Conservatory Liceu, Barcelona, Spain, 1954; diploma in composition, Juilliard Sch. Music, 1960; postgrad., Mannes Coll. Music, 1961-62. Instr. Walden Sch., NYC, 1962-63; head dept. music UN Internat. Sch., NYC, 1963-70; prof. composition Carnegie-Mellon U., Pitts., 1970—, Univ. prof. Carnegie-Melon U., Pitts., 1990—. Mem. faculty Torroella de Montgri Internat. Music Course and Festival, Spain, 1991—. Composer-in-residence, Aspen (Colo.) Inst., 1970; guest composer, U. Tel Aviv, Israel, 1975, guest condr. various orchs.; collaborated with painter Salvador Dali, Nobel Prize laureate writer Camilo José Cela; composer numerous compositions including Guernica (premiered New Orleans Philharmonic), 1966 (CD New World Records), Sinfonia en Negro-Homenaje a Martin Luther King; commd. and premiered, Spanish Radio TV Symphony Orch., 1968 (CD Albany Records); Maria Sabina; oratorio, premiered, Carnegie Hall, 1970 (CD New World Records); Cumbres; premiered at Carnegie Hall, 1971 (CD Albany Records); Steel Symphony; premiered, Pitts. Symphony, 1972 (recorded by Lorin Maazel and Pitts. Symphony, New World Records); composer: commd. and premiered by Nat. Orch. Spain Auroris, 1973; Ponce de Leon, for narrator and orch., 1973, premiered by Jose Ferrer and, New Orleans Philharm. Symphony Orch., 1973, Concerto for Piano, Winds and Percussion, recorded CD on New World Records, 1974; commd. by, Carnegie-Mellon U. Alumni Assn., premiered at, Carnegie Hall, 1974, Homage to Casals and Homage to Sarasate, recorded on CD Albany Records, 1975, premiered by Pitts. Symphony, 1976, Cantata NO-RES recorded on CD Naxos Records, premiered by Barcelona Symphony Orch., Nat. Chorus of Spain, 1975 (City of Barcelona Composition prize 1976), Concertino for Castanets and Orch., world premier Philharmonia Orch. London, 1980, US premiere Phila. Orch., 1987; Fantasias Sonoras, recorded on CD Naxos Records, commd. by Pitts. Symphony Orch., 1987; composer chamber works Voces 1, for mixed chorus a capella, Tresis, 1971; commd. for guitar, flute and cello Composers Theatre Inc., premiered at, May Festival in NYC, 1973; composer Apuntes for guitar quartet, 1974 (Internat. Composition prize Ciudad de Zaragoza), premiered Zaragoza, 1974; solo compositions include Analogias, for guitar, 1968 (premiered by Narciso Yepes at Besançon Music Festival Elementalis), for organ, 1972 (premiered by Pitts. Symphony, 1982 Sardana), 1979; commd. by Nat. Endowment Arts, premiered by N.Y. Philharm., 1982 Quasi un Pasodoble, recorded on CD Albany Records 1981; premiered at Carnegie Hall, 1982 Concerto for Violin recorded on CD Naxos Records and Orch., 1982; commd. and premiered by Internat. Barcelona Music Festival, 1982 Hangman, Hangman recorded on CD Naxos Records (opera), 1982; grand opera in 2 acts, commd. by San Diego Opera Zapata, 1984; composer 2 act opera Christopher Columbus, commd. for 5th centennial of discovery of Am., premiere 1989, Teatro del Liceo, Barcelona, performed by tenor Jose Carreras and soprano Monserrat Caballé, The Town Greed, recorded on CD Naxos Records, 1997; composer Sinfonia Concertante for amplified guitar and orch. recorded on CD Albany Records, premiered by Narciso Yepes and Nat. Orch. Spain, 1987, Zapata: Images for Orch., world premier by Nat. Orch. Spain, Am. premier by Pitts. Symphony, 1987, music for strings and flute, premiered by Atlanta Virtuosi, 1987, Torquemada, recorded on CD New World Records, 1980, Divertimentos for recorded on CD Albany Records, string orchestra premiere Royal Coll. Music String Ensamble of London, 1991, Columbus: Images for recorded on CD Albany Records, Orch., 1992, Symphony #4 premiere Lausanne recorded on CD Albany Records, Chamber Orch., 1992, Celebration recorded on CD Naxos Records, premiere Prague Symphony, 1992, Escenas Borrascosas recorded on CD on New World Records, premiere by Nat. Orch. and Chorus of Spain, 1992, Music for Oboe and Orchestra recorded on CD New World Records, premiered by Lorin Maazel and the Pitts. Symphony, 1993 (recorded), Line and Thunder recorded on CD Naxos Records, premiere by Pitts. Symphony Orch., 1998, Shadows recorded on CD Naxos Records, premiere by Cin. Symphony Orch., 1995, Morning Music premiere by Julius Baker and CMU Philharmonic, 1995, Concerto Magico recorded on CD Naxos Records, for guitar and orchestra premiered by Angel Romero and Cin. Symphony Orch., 1997, Folk Dreams recorded on CD Naxos Records premiered by Nat. Symphony Orch. Ireland, 1998, Concerto Piano and Orchestra #3 premiered Berlin Radio Symphony Orchestra, 1999; Passacaglia recorded on CD Naxos Records, premier orchestra de Cadaques, 2000, Concerto Cello & Orchestra No. 2, recorded on CD Naxos Records, 2002, "Symphony N.5-American" 2003 Comm. & premiered by Pittsburg Symphony Orchestra also composer several ballets and songs; composer works for many soloists and conductors, including, Andrés Segovia, Nicanor Zabaleta, Alicia de Larrocha, Lorin Maazel, Maris Jansons Angel Romero, Narciso Yepes, music played by numerous orchs. at numerous festivals in U.S. and abroad, music recorded by Serenus Records, Louisville Orch. First Edit. Records, Deutsche Grammophon, Naxos Records, Albany Records, BASF, New World Records, over 100 works pub. by and G. Schirmer. Recipient B. Martinu prize in composition Mannes Coll. Music, 1962, Internat. Composition prize Cuidad de Zaragoza, 1974, Internat. prize City of Barcelona, 1975, 80, Nat. Music prize of Catalonia, 1993; Fundacion March fellow. Mem. ASCAP (awards), Am. Music Center, Hispanic Soc. Am. (corr.) Office: Carnegie-Mellon U Sch Music Pittsburgh PA 15213

BALAGURU, PERUMALSAMY, civil engineering educator; b. Tamil Nadu, India, Mar. 26, 1947; s. Perumal and Kengammal (Perumal) Ramasamy; m. Suryaprabha Venkatesalu, June 6, 1974; children: Balasoundhari, Balamuralee. BS with honors, U. Madras, Coimbatore, India, 1968; MS with distinction, Indian Inst. Sci., Bangalore, 1970; PhD, U. Ill., 1977. Assoc. lectr. U. Madras, 1970-73; asst. prof. Rutgers State U. N.J., Piscataway, 1977-82, assoc. prof., 1982-88, prof., 1988—2002, dist. prof., 2002—; program dir. Nat. Sci. Found., 2002—. Author: Fiber Reinforced Cement Composites, 1992; contbr. more than 20050 articles to profl. jours. Recipient Long Standing Contbrn. award, Internat. Ferrocement Soc. Fellow Am. Concrete Inst.; mem. ASCE. Office: Rutgers U 623 Bowser Rd Piscataway NJ 08854

BALAJI, K.C. urologist, researcher; s. K.C. and Vijaya Krishnaswamy; m. Shoba Charavarthy Mani, Apr. 4, 1991; children: Navin Charavarthy, Nandita Charavarthy. MB BS, Madras Med. Coll., India, 1986. Cert. med. dr. Indian Med. Coun., Am. Bd. Urology. Resident in urology U. Mass. Med. Ctr., Worcester, 1993—97; fellow in urol. oncology Meml. Sloan Kettering Cancer Ctr., N.Y.C., 1997—99; asst. prof., dir. urol. oncology So. Ill. U. Sch. Medicine, Springfield, 1999—2000; assoc. prof., dir. urol. oncology rsch. U. Nebr. Med. Ctr., Omaha, 2000—. Urol. oncologist U. Nebr. Med. Ctr., Omaha, 2000—. Actor, writer Tamil Plays - Amateur. Vol. Indian Assn. Nebr., Omaha. Fellow: Royal Coll. Surgeons Edinburgh; mem.: Am. Urol. Assn. Achievements include research in prostate cancer; robotic urological surgery. Office: U Nebr Med Ctr 982360 Omaha NE 68198-2360 Office Fax: 402-559-6529. E-mail: kcbalaji@unmc.edu.

BALAKRISHNAN, P.V. (SUNDAR), finance educator; s. P.B. and Lakshmi Venkatasubramanian; m. Shobana Srinivasan, Apr. 18, 1989; children: Tara, Maya, Lila. B. in Tech., I.I.T., 1976—81; M.S., U. Tex., Arlington, 1981—83; Ph.D., A.M., U. Pa., Phila., 1983—88. Asst. prof. Ohio State U., Columbus, 1988—94, Univ. Wash., Bothell, 1994—96, assoc. prof., 1996—, acting dir., bus. program, 1998—2000. Contbr. scholarly research. Fellow AMA Doctoral Consortium, Wharton Sch., Univ. Pa, 1986. Mem.: Beta Gamma Sigma. Achievements include first to introduce aritificial intelligence methodologies to marketing; research in business negotiations and new product marketing; development of software for negotiations and product designs. Office Fax: 425-352-5277. Personal E-mail: sundar@u.washington.edu.

BALAKRISHNAN, VENKATARAMANAN, statistician, educator; b. India; arrived in U.S., 1985; MS in Stats., PhD, Stanford U., 1992. Postdoctoral rschr. Inst. for Sys. Rsch., College Park, Md., 1993—94; asst. prof. Purdue U., West Lafayette, Ind., 1994—98, assoc. prof., 1998—2003, prof., 2003—. Author: (book) Linear Matrix Inequalities in System and Control Theory, 1994. Named Young Investigator, Office of Naval Rsch., 1997; recipient Pres. of India Gold Medal, Indian Inst. of Tech., Madras, India, 1985. Mem.: SIAM, IEEE. Office: Purdue U 465 Northwestern Ave West Lafayette IN 47907-2035 Office Fax: 765-494-6951. E-mail: ragu@ecn.purdue.edu.

BALANDIN, ALEXANDER A. electrical engineer, educator; b. Nizhny Novgorod, Russia, Apr. 30, 1968; came to U.S., 1993; s. Alexei A. and Tania A. (Ovechkin) B.; m. Maria P. Spitsin, Jan. 12, 1996. BS in Applied Math., Moscow Inst. Physics & Tech., 1989, MS in Applied Physics, 1991; MSEE, U. Notre Dame, 1995, PhD in Elec. Engring., 1996. Rsch. asst. dept. elec. engring. U. Notre Dame, Ind., 1993-96; rsch. assoc. dept. elec. engring. Quantum Device Lab. U. Nebr., Lincoln, 1996-97; rsch. engr. dept. elec. engring. Device Rsch. Lab. UCLA, 1997-99; asst. prof. dept. elec. engring. U. Calif., Riverside, 1999-2001, assoc. prof. dept. elec. engring., 2001—; dir. Nano-Device Lab., 2000—. Mem. AAAS, IEEE, Am. Phys. Soc., Am. Soc. Engring. Edn., Electrochem. Soc., Eta Kappa Nu. Office: Univ Calif Dept Elec Engring Riverside CA 92521-0425 E-mail: alexb@ee.ucr.edu.

BALANDRAN, STELLA VARONA, interpreter, lyricist, composer, writer; b. NYC, May 16, 1932; d. Rafael Patricio Garcia and Stella Ginorio; m. Ricardo Balandran; m. Emilio Varona; children: Charles Varona, Henry Varona, Emil Varona. Student, Middlesex C.C., Middletown, Conn., 1966—68, New Haven U., 1970—72, U. Davis, 1990—92; cert. paralegal, Napa Valley Coll., 1993. Cert. mediator Conflict Resolution and Rsch. Inst. Interpreter Meriden (Conn.) Police Dept. Ct., 1961—72; elderly specialist City of Meriden, 1972—74; mgr. Am. Cancer Soc., Vallejo, Calif., 1982—87; paralegal Solano County Legal Assistance, Vallejo, 1987—94; dir. Spanish Translations Lake County, Umatilla, Fla., 1997—; interpreter LanguageLine, Monterey, Calif., 2000—02. Composer: (Album) De Amantes A Extraños, 1987, (Album) Dare to Dream, 1991; author: (poetry) Am. Poetry Assn., World of Poetry, Nat. Libr. Poetry. Pres. Friends of the Libr., Umatilla, 1999—2000; bd. mem. Commn. on Aging, Meriden, 1972—74, Bd. Suprs. Affirmative Action Com., Solano County, Calif., 1992—93; pres. P.R. Rep. Club, Meriden, 1964—67; del. Dem. State Conv., Orlando. Named Disting. Poet, 1996; named to, Internat. Poetry Hall of Fame, 1996; recipient various awards, San Francisco Festival de la Cancion, 1986, 1987, 1988, 1989, 1990, 1992, 1998. Mem.: ASCAP, NARAS, Am. Soc. Composers, Authors, Pubs., Latin Assn. Rec. Arts and Scis. Roman Catholic. Avocation: volunteer English as Second Language Teacher . Office: Spanish Translations of Lake County 95 S Trowell Ave Umatilla FL 32784 Home Fax: 352-669-1848; Office Fax: 352-669-1848. Personal E-mail: EstelaBMus@CS.Com. Business E-Mail: EstelaBMus@CS.Com.

BALANIS, CONSTANTINE APOSTLE, electrical engineering educator; b. Trikala, Thessaly, Greece, Oct. 29, 1938; came to U.S., 1955; s. Apostolos G. and Erini (Vlahocostas) B.; m. Helen Jovaras, May 21, 1972; children: Erini, Stephanie. BSEE, Va. Poly. Inst., 1964; MEE, U. Va., 1966; PhDEE, Ohio State U., 1969. Electronics engr. NASA, Hampton, Va., 1964-70; asst. professorial lectr. George Washington U. Extension, Hampton, 1968-70; vis. assoc. prof. dept. elec. engring. W.Va. U., Morgantown, 1970-72, assoc. prof., 1972-76, prof., 1976-83; prof. dept. elec. engring. Ariz. State U., Tempe, 1983-91, Regents' prof., 1991—, dir. Telecommunications Rsch. Ctr., 1988-99. Cons. Motorola Inc., Scottsdale, Ariz., 1984-94, Loral Def. Systems, Litchfield Park, Ariz., 1986-88, Gen. Dynamics, Pomona, Calif., 1986-87, Naval Air Warfare Ctr., Patuxent River, Md., 1977-90, Naval Surface Warfare Ctr., Dahlgren, Va., 1985-86, Nat. Radio Astronomy Observatory, Green Bank, W.Va., 1972-74; Boeing, Seattle, 1996, Rockwell Internat., Cedar Rapids, Iowa, 1997. Author: Antenna Theory: Analysis and Design, 1982, 2d edit., 1997, Advanced Engineering Electromagnetics, 1989; patentee in field. Recipient Halliburton Best Researcher award W.Va. U., 1983, Russ award for Rsch., Ohio U., 1984, Teaching Excellence award Ariz. State U., 1988, also Outstanding Grad. Mentor award, 1996-97; grantee and contracts NASA, Army Rsch. Office, NSF, Office Naval Rsch., Dept. of Energy, Dept. of Transp., Naval Air Warfare Ctr., Naval Surface Warfare Ctr., Motorola Inc., Gen. Dynamics, Boeing Helicopter Sys., Sikorsky Aircraft, Rockwell Internat., Boeing Helicopters, IBM, 1972—. Fellow IEEE (Individual Achievement award region 6, 1989, Spl. Engring. Professionalism award Phoenix sect. 1992, Third Millennium award 2000); mem. Am. Soc. Engring. Edn., Sigma Xi, Phi Kappa Phi, Eta Kappa Nu, Tau Beta Pi. Avocations: golf, jogging, tennis, bowling. Home: 3154 E Encanto St Mesa AZ 85213-6110 Office: Ariz State U Dept Elec Engring Tempe AZ 85287-7206

BALANTEKIN, AKIF BAHA, physicist, educator; b. 1954; PhD, Yale U., 1982. Assoc. prof. physics U. Wis., Madison, Wis., 1989—92, prof. physics, 1992—. Named U.S. Presdl. Young Investigator, NSF, 1987; recipient Jefferson Cup, Martin Marietta Corp., 1986, Sr. Scientist award, Alexander von Humboldt Found., Germany, 1996—2001, Mid-Career Award, Wis. Alumni Rsch. Found., 1997, Sci. Prize, Turkish Sci. and Tech. Rsch. Coun., 2001; Japan Promotion of Sci. fellow, 1994. Fellow: Am. Phys. Soc. (chmn. nuclear physics 2003—04). Office: Univ Wis Dept Physics 1150 University Ave Madison WI 53706

BALAS, EGON, applied mathematician, educator; b. Cluj, Romania, June 7, 1922; came to U.S., 1967, naturalized, 1973; s. Ignat and Boriska B.; m. Edith Lovi, 1948; children: Anna, Vera. Diploma licenciae, Bolyai U., Cluj, 1949; D.Sc.Ec. summa cum laude, U. Brussels; D.U. in Math., U. Paris; PhD (hon.), U. Miguel Hernandez, Spain, 2002. Asso. prof. econs. Inst. Econ. Sci., Bucharest, 1949-58; analyst Designing Inst. Forestry and Timber Industry, Bucharest, 1959-64; head math. programming sector Center Math. Stats. of Romanian Acad., 1964-66; research mathematician Internat. Computation Centre, Rome, 1966; vis. prof. ops. research U. Toronto, 1967, Stanford U., 1967; Ford disting. research prof. Carnegie Mellon U., 1967-68; prof. indsl. adminstrn. and applied math. Carnegie-Mellon U., 1968—, univ. prof., 1990—, holder GSIA alumni chair, 1980—; Thomas Lord Prof. Ops. Rsch., 1997—. Vis. ops. rsch. analyst Fed. Energy Adminstrn., 1976; cons. NSF grantee, 1972—; vis. prof. Maths. Inst. Köln, 1980-81. Author: Will to Freedom: A Perilous Journey Through Fascism and Communism, 2000; assoc. editor: Ops. Rsch., 1967-96, Zeitschrift für Operations Research; adv. editor: Discrete Applied Math., Jour. Combinatorial Optimization; mem. editorial bd. Computational Optimization and Applications, Revue Française d'Automatique et Recherche Operationelle, Annals of Operations Research; editorial assoc.: European Jour. Operational Research; contbr. over 180 articles to profl. jours. Informs fellow, 2002; recipient Alexander von Humboldt Sr. U.S. Scientist award, 1980-81, John von Neumann Theory award, 1995, Euro Gold medal, 2001, Citation Classic, Current Contents, 1982. Mem. SIAM, Math. Programming Soc. (coun. 1989-92), Inst. Mgmt. Scis. (coun. 1972-75), Oper. Rsch. Soc., Inst. Operatives Rsch. and Mgmt. Scis. Achievements include research in math. programming, integer and disjunctive programming, combinatorial optimization, graphs, networks, crew scheduling, machine sequencing, energy models; devel. of scheduling system for steel rolling. Home: 136 Beechwood Ln Pittsburgh PA 15206-4526 Office: Graduate School of Industrial Adm Carnegie Mellon Univ Pittsburgh PA 15213 E-mail: eb17@andrew.cmu.edu.

BALAS, IRENE BARBARA, artist; b. Budapest, Hungary, Feb. 28, 1928; came to U.S., 1973; d. Sandor and Ilona (Udvardy) B.; m. Tom Elliot, July 30, 1974 (dec. May 1980). Studies with Karl Kaufmann and Hans Hoff, Vienna, Austria; B Degree, Budapest, 1943; MA in Art Therapy and Psychology, KunstAkad./Sigmund Freud Inst., Vienna, 1948. Cert. art therapist, psychoanalyst. Artist, 1974—. One-woman shows in Vienna, Paris, Munich, Madrid, Chile, Bolivia, Peru, Venezuela, Colombia, Haiti, N.Y., San Francisco, Miami and L.A.; represented in permanent collections Vatican, Mus. Atelier, other museums, and pvt. collections of Rockefeller, Henry Ford, Olga, Bruce Walker and others; commd. to paint History of Cuba in 7 paintings, 1990, Hungarian Hang Gliding Expdn. Around the World in 7 paintings for Mil. Mus. in Budapest, 1993; TV show hostess, 1977-78. Recipient Nat. prize of Austrian Painters, 1948. Home and Office: 1621 Collins Ave Apt 907 Miami FL 33139-3142

BALASA, FLORIN, software engineer, mathematician; b. Lupeni, Romania, July 19, 1956; came to U.S., 1995; s. Nicolae and Lucia V. (Marinescu) B. MSc in Computer Sci., Poly U., Bucharest, 1981; PhD in Computer Sci., Poly. U., Bucharest, 1994; MSc in Math., Bucharest U., 1990; PhD in Elec. Engring., Cath. U., Leuven, Belgium, 1995. Software engr. Computing Equipment Entreprise, Bucharest, 1981-83; sr. rschr., group leader R&D Inst. for Electronic Components, Bucharest, 1983-90; rschr. Interuniv. Microelectronics Ctr., Leuven, 1990-95; sr. design automation engr. Conexant Sys., Inc. (formerly Rockwell Semicondr. Sys.), Newport Beach, Calif., 1995-2000; asst. prof. dept. elec. engring. and computer sci. U. Ill., Chgo., 2000—. Co-author: Custom Memory Management Method: Exploration of Memory Organization for Embedded Multimedia System Design, 1998; contbr. articles to profl. jours. Recipient Career award, NSF, 2001. Achievements include patent for background memory allocation for multi-dimensional signal processing. Office: U Ill at Chgo Dept Elec Engring/Comp Sci 851 S Morgan St Chicago IL 60607-7042 E-mail: fbalasa@cs.uic.edu.

BALASA, MARK EDWARD, investment consultant; b. Petoskey, Mich., July 2, 1958; s. Edward S. and Mary N. (Wiklanski) B.; m. Laurel Marie Monaco, July 6, 1985; children: Bryant, Brett. AS, North Cen. Mich. Coll., Petoskey, 1978; BSBA, Cen. Mich. U., Mt. Pleasant, 1980; MA, Coll. Fin. Planning, Denver, 1992. CPA, Ill.; cert. fin. planner. Contr. Perfection Machinery Sales, Wheeling, Ill., 1981-87; investment cons. Elite Adv. Svcs., Schaumburg, Ill., 1987-89; investment cons., ptnr. Burton Investment Mgmt., Schaumburg, Ill., 1989-97, Balasa & Hoffman, Inc., Schaumburg, Ill., 1998-2001; ptnr. Balasa, Dinverno, Foltz & Hoffman, LLC, Schaumburg, Ill., 2001—. Tchr. Mundelein Coll., Chgo., 1988; mem. adv. fin. bd. TIAA-CREF Inst., N.Y. Mem. adv. bd. Jour. Retirement Planning; regular columnist CCH's Rtirement Planning Jour. Named One of Best 120 Planners for Physicians, Med. Econs. mag., 1998, 1999, 2000, 2002; named one of 200 Best Fin. Advisors in the Country, Worth mag., 1996, 1997, 1998, 1999, 2001, 2002, the Best 100 Fin. Advisors in the Country, Mutual Funds Mag., 2001. Mem. AICPA, Fin. Planning Assn. (v.p. 1990-91, pres. 1991-92, exec. com. 1992-93), Internat. Assn. Fin. Planning (pres. Chgo. chpt. 1992-93). Roman Catholic. Avocations: running, racquetball, chess. Home: 1219 N Lakeview Ct Palatine IL 60067-2086 Office: Balasa Dinverno Foltz Hoffman LLC 1920 Thoreau Dr N Ste 174 Schaumburg IL 60173-4151 E-mail: mbalasa@BD-FH.com.

BALASHOV, YURI V. philosophy educator; arrived in US, 1992; PhD, U. of Notre Dame, 1998. Asst. prof. of philosophy Moscow Inst. Physics and Tech., 1986—92, U. Ga., Athens, 1999—. Co-editor: (book) Philosophy of Science: Contemporary Readings; editor: Einstein Studies in Russia; contbr. articles to profl. jours. and scholarly books. Recipient Presdl. fellowship, U. Notre Dame, 1992—96, Postdoctoral fellowship, Rice U., 1998—99, Jr. Faculty grant, U. Ga.

Rsch. Found., 2000, Rsch. fellowship, Ctr. Humanities and Arts, U. of Ga., 2002—03. Mem.: Philosophy of Sci. Assn. (assoc.), Am. Philos. Assn. (assoc.). Achievements include research in philosophy of physics and contemporary analytic metaphysics. Office: U Ga Philosophy Dept 107 Peabody Hall Athens GA 30602-1627 Office Fax: 706-542-2839.

BALASI, MARK GEOFFREY, architect; b. Chgo., Feb. 29, 1952; s. Alfred Victor and Betty Lou (Biggs) B.; m. Barbara Jane Ritt, May 25, 1985; children: Geoffrey Adam, Maria Elizabeth. Student, Ecole-des-Beaux-Arts, Versailles, France, 1974-75; BS in Archtl. Studies, U. Ill., 1975; postgrad., U. Wis., 1986, 89, 92. Lic. architect, Ill., Mich., Ohio. Architect Davy McKee, Chgo., 1976-80, Perkins & Will, Chgo., 1980-82; prin. Hansen Lind Meyer Inc., Chgo., 1982-95; v.p. Phillips Swager Assocs., Naperville, Ill., 1995—2003, HDR Architecture, Inc., Chgo., 2003—. Lectr. Italian Nat. Ctr. Hosp. Bldg. and Technique. Editor: Balasi Archives, U. Iowa Librs. Spl. Collections; author: Sgt. Balasic WWI Album-Austro-Hungarian Army, 1996, Balasic Family Vaudeville Album, 1994; contbr.: (with Paul F. Stevens) Low Level Liberators in World War II, 1998; contbr. articles to profl. jours.; prin. works include Villa Schaefer, Mattoon, Ill., Nunamaker House, Mattoon, Mary Brown Stephenson Radiation Oncology Ctr., Zion, Ill. Active Hist. Preservation Commn., McHenry County, Ill. Mem. AIA (Nat. Coun. Archel. Registration Bds. cert.), Am. Soc. Hosp. Engring., Acad. Architecture for Health, Health Facility Inst., PB4Y Assn., U. Ill. Alumni Assn. Avocations: genealogy, entomology, travel. Office: HDR Architecture Inc 8550 W Bryn Mawr Ave Ste 900 Chicago IL 60631-3223 E-mail: mark.balasi@hdrinc.com.

BALASUBRAMANIAN, KRISHNAN, research scientist, educator; b. Bangalore, India, Apr. 10, 1956; s. Sankariyer Krishnan and Mennakshi Ramaiyaiyer; m. Gomathy Bala; children: Nila Bala, Sangeetha Bala. MA, The Johns Hopkins U., Balt., 1978; PhD, The Johns Hopkins U., 1980. Prof. and sr. scientist U. of Calif. Davis, Livermore, 2000—; Prof. emeritus Ariz. State U., Tempe, 2000—. Sr. scientist Lawrence Livermore Nat. Lab., Livermore, Calif., 2000—; Senior Scientist Lawrence Berkeley Nat. Lab, Berkeley, 2000—; adj. prof. computer sci. dept. Calif. State U.; mem. editl. bd. Jour. Math. Chemistry, N.Y.C., 1998—; former mem. adv. panel Airforce Office Sci. Rsrch.; mem. adv. bd. Dept. of Energy, Washington, 1999—. Author: (Books) Relativistic Effects in Chemistry, 1997 (Alfred P. Sloan Fellow, 1984); contbr. articles to Refereed Jours. (Camille & Henry Deyfus Teacher-Scholar award, 1985, Robert S. Mulliken lectr. award, 2003). Adv, Panel Nat. Acad. Scis., Washington. Recipient Camille and Henry Deyfus Tchr-Scholar award, 1985; grantee, Department of Energy, 1985—, NSF, 1985—. Mem.: N.Y. Acad. Scis., Math. Assn. Am., Internat. Math. Chemist Soc., Am. Phys. Soc., Alpha Chi Sigma, Phi Kappa Phi, Mathematical Association of America, American Physical Society, International Mathematical Chemistry Society, American Chemical Society. Office: Univ Calif Davis DAS Bldg 661, Hertz Hall Livermore CA 94550 Home Fax: 925-422-6810; Office Fax: 925-422-6810. Personal E-mail: kbala@ucdavis.edu. Business E-Mail: kbala@ucdavis.edu.

BALAY, ROBERT ELMORE, editor, reference librarian; b. Wichita, Kans., Oct. 6, 1930; s. Loren Elmore and Gladys Lois (Crites) B.; m. Harriette Shirley Anderson, Dec. 23, 1961; children— Christopher Loren, Anne Gladys, Jean Mary BA, Macalester Coll., 1952; MA, U. Minn., 1954; MS in Libr. Sci., Columbia U., 1959. Tech. writer Beech Aircraft Corp., Wichita, 1956-58; asst. librarian Grumman Aircraft Corp., Bethpage, N.Y., 1959-62, Gen. Precision, Little Falls, N.J., 1962-64; asst. sci. librarian Wayne State U., Detroit, 1964-68, adj. instr. library sci., 1966-67; head reference dept. Yale U. Library, New Haven, 1968-86; reference editor Choice mag., Middletown, Conn., 1986—. Author: Early Periodical Indexes, 2000; editor: Guide to Reference Books, 11th edit., 1996; contbr. articles to profl. jours. Served with U.S. Army, 1954-56 Democrat. Home: 97 Livingston St New Haven CT 06511-2411 Office: Choice Mag 100 Riverview Ctr Middletown CT 06457-3445 E-mail: rbalay@ala-choice.org.

BALBACH, STANLEY BYRON, lawyer; b. Normal, Ill., Dec. 26, 1919; s. Nyle Jacob and Gertrude (Cory) B.; m. Sarah Troutt Witherspoon, May 22, 1944; children: Stanley Byron Jr., Nancy Ann Fehr, Barbara Haines, Edith. BS, U. Ill., 1940, LLD, 1942. Bar: Ill. 1942, Fla. 1980, U.S. Ct. Appeals (7th cir.) 1961, U.S. Supreme Ct. 1950. Ptnr. Couchman & Balbach, Hoopeston, Ill., 1945-48, Webber & Balbach, Urbana, 1948-81, Balbach & Fehr, Urbana, 1981—. Nat. chmn. Jr. Bar Conf., 1955; bd. dirs. Atty.'s Title Guaranty Fund, Champaign, Ill. Author: Reverse Mortgages, 1997, The Lawyers Guide to Retirement: Serving a New Clientele in a Second Career in Real Estate, 1998. Capt. USAAF, 1942-45 (pilot). Mem. ABA (ho. of dels. 1956, lawyer title guaranty fund com., past mem. coun. law office practice and real property, probate and trust law sects.), LWV, Ill. State Bar Assn. (elder law com., Laureate of the Acad. Ill. Lawyers 2002), Am. Judicature Soc., Masons, Rotary, Phi Delta Phi, Alpha Kappa Lambda. Home: 1009 S Douglas Ave Urbana IL 61801-4933 Office: Balbach & Fehr Box 217 102 N Broadway Ave Urbana IL 61801-2705

BALBEKOV, VALERI I. physicist, researcher; b. Poushkin, Leningrad Region, Russia, Sept. 6, 1939; arrived in U.S., 1997, permanent resident, 2001; s. Ivan I. Balbekov and Olga I. Balbekova; m. Tatiana I. Mishenkova; 1 child, Olga. Master Degree in Physics, Moscow State U., Moscow, Russia, 1956—62; PhD in Physics, Phys. Inst. of USSR Acad. of Sci., Moscow, 1965. From jr. scientist to sr. scientist II Inst. for High Energy Physics, Protvino, Russia, 1965—2000; scientist II Fermi Nat. Accelerator Lab., Batavia, Ill., 2001—. Sr. lectr. Moscow State U., Russia, 1980—86; assoc. prof. Moscow Phy.-Tech. Inst., 1986—92; guest scientist Superconducting Supercollider Lab., Dallas, 1993—94, Fermi Nat. Accelerator Lab., Batavia, ILL., 1997—2001. Home: 742 Graham Rd North Aurora IL 60542 Office: Fermilab MS 231 PO Box 500 Batavia IL 60510 Office Fax: 630-840-6311. Personal E-mail: balbekov@aol.com. Business E-Mail: balbekov@fnal.gov.

BALBI, KENNETH EMILIO, environmental specialist, researcher; b. N.Y.C., Apr. 13, 1963; s. George Emilio and Blanca Amelia (Fonseca) B.; m. Julie Ann Lopez, Feb. 19, 1989; children: Danielle Elizabeth, Joshua Emilio. MD, U. Ctrl. del Este, Dominican Republic, 1985; BS, SUNY, Albany, 1989. Rsch. assoc. Montefiore Med. Ctr., NY, 1988-94; govtl. and instnl. cons. SCITEC Corp., Kennewick, Wash., 1994-95; dir. tng. and profl. svcs. U.S. Lead, Oyster Bay, NY, 1995-97; v.p., co-founder ANDO Internat., Bklyn., 1995—2002; dir. franchise ops. PRO-TECT Franchising Inc., Oyster Bay, NY, 1996-97; v.p. rsch. & design AIA Environ. Corp., Astoria, NY, 1997-99; pres. "E" The Solution, Inc., Douglaston, NY, 2002—. Contbr. articles to profl. jours. Mem. St. Michael's Hispanic Assn., Flushing, N.Y., 1991—, Cuban-Am. Assocs., Flushing, 1988—, Alliance to End Childhood Lead Poisoning, Washington, 1992—. Mem.: ASTM, AAAS, Nat. Environ. Health Assn., Am. Indsl. Hygiene Assn., United Internat. Med. Grads., NY Acad. Scis., InterAm. Coll. Physicians and Surgeons, Nat. Assn. for Search and Rescue. Roman Catholic. Home: 24015B Oak Park Dr Little Neck NY 11362 Office: "E" The Solution Inc PO Box 620790 Douglaston NY 11362 E-mail: KBalbi@aol.com.

BALBOA, MARCELO, professional soccer player; b. Cerritos, Calif., Aug. 8, 1967; s. Luis Balboa; m. Cindy Balboa. Grad., San Diego State U., 1988. Player U.S. Nat. Team, 1988—, San Diego Nomads, APSL, 1989, San Francisco Blackhawks, APSL, 1990—91, Colo. Foxes, APSL, 1992, Leon, Mex. 1st Divsn., 1995—96, Colo. Rapids, 1996—. Mem. U.S. World Cup Team, 1994—. Named MVP, World Cup, 1994, Colo. Rapids, 1997. Office: c/o Colo Rapids Ste 3350 555 17th St Denver CO 80202-3909 also: US Soccer Fedn 1801 S Prairie Ave # 1811 Chicago IL 60616-1319

BALCER, CHARLES LOUIS, college president emeritus, educator; b. McGregor, Iowa, May 23, 1921; s. Ludwig Frank and Iva (Vaughan) B.; m. Martha Elizabeth Belgum, Jan. 6, 1944; children— Mary Elizabeth, Mark Lewis, Beth Louise, Brian Charles. BS, Winona (Minn.) State Tchrs. Coll., 1942; MA, State U. Iowa, 1949, PhD, 1954; DHL (hon.), Augustana Coll., 2003. Tchr. Minn. and Iowa high schs., 1942-43, 46-47; instr. State U. Iowa, 1947-50; high sch. prin. Detroit Lakes, Minn., 1950-54; assoc. prof. speech St. Cloud (Minn.) State Coll., 1954-56, prof., acad. dean, 1958-64; prof. speech SUNY-Oswego, 1956-57; pres. Augustana Coll., Sioux Falls, S.D., 1965-80, pres. emeritus, 1980—, Disting. Service prof., 1980-95, interim chair edn. dept., 1999-00. Interim pres., CEO Good Samaritan Soc., 1997-98. Author: (with H. F. Seabury) Teaching Speech. Mem., bd. dirs. Evang. Luth. Good Samaritan Soc.; mem. Marquette Bank of S.D., Sioux Falls Symphony Assn. Served with AUS, 1943-46. Decorated knight 1st class Royal Order St. Olav, Norway). Mem. Speech Communication Assn. Am., Central States Speech Assn. (pres. 1954), NEA, Assn. Higher Edn., Delta Sigma Rho, Kappa Delta Pi, Phi Delta Kappa. Democrat. Home: 111 W 17th St # 115 Sioux Falls SD 57104-4901 E-mail: clbalcer@aol.com. *I have learned that the purpose of this earthly life is not happiness. It is to be useful, to be honorable, to be compassionate. It is to matter— to have it made some difference that you lived at all.*

BALCH, GLENN MCCLAIN, JR., academic administrator, minister, writer; b. Shattuck, Okla., Nov. 1, 1937; s. Glenn McClain and Marjorie (Daily) Balch; m. Diana Gale Seeley, Oct. 15, 1970; children: Bryan, Gayle, Wesley, John. Student, Panhandle State U., 1958-60, So. Meth. U., summers 1962-64; BS, S.W. State U., Okla., 1962; BD, Phillips U., 1965; JD, L.A. Coll. Law, 1969; MA, Chapman U., 1973, MA in Edn., MA in Psychology, Chapman U., 1975, MA in Sch. Counseling; PhD, Alliant Internat. U., 1978; postgrad., Claremont Grad. Sch., 1978-70, U. Okla., 1965-66. Ordained to ministry Meth. Ch., 1962. Sr. min. First Meth. Ch., Eakly, Okla., 1960-63, Calumet, Okla., 1963-65, Goodrich Meml. Ch., Norman, Okla., 1965-66, First Meth. Ch., Barstow, Calif., 1966-70, Brea United Meth. Ch., Fullerton, Calif., 1978-89; asst. dean Chapman U., Orange, Calif., 1970-76; v.p. Hope Internat. U., Fullerton, Calif., 1976-79; pres., CEO So. Calif. Inst., Fullerton, Calif., 1988-95; pres. Westmar U., Le Mars, Iowa, 1995-96; exec. v.p. Advance Cons. Network (name now Synergistics, Inc.), Rochester, N.Y., 1996—. Mental health cons. U.S. Army, 1969; edn. cons. USAF, 1974—75. Bd. dirs. Found. Internat. Cmty. Assistance, 1988—96. With USMC, 1956—57. Named Man of the Yr., Jr. C. of C., Bartow, 1969; recipient Eastern Star Religious Tng. award, 1963, 1964; Broadhurst fellow, 1963—65. Mem.: Nat. Assn. Sports Psychologists (diplomate), Calif. Assn. Family Therapists, Elks, Shriners, Masons, Rotary (pres. 1969—70, 1983—84, 1999—2000, dist. gov. 1987—88, 1988—89). Home: 39 Bowen Rd Churchville NY 14428-9737 Office: Synergistics Tng LLC 39 Bowen Rd Churchville NY 14428-9737 E-mail: glenn@synergisticstraining.com.

BALCH, HENRY H. surgeon, educator, retired; b. Asuncion, Paraguay, June 11, 1917; (parents Am. citizens); MD, U. Dublin, 1943. Diplomate Am. Bd. Surgery. Intern French Hosp., N.Y.C., 1944; resident in surgery Bellevue Hosp. Ctr., N.Y.C., 1944-48; mem. staff Sibley Meml. Hosp., Washington, clin. prof. surgery Georgetown U. NYU fellow, 1946-47; Markle scholar, 1948-53. Fellow ACS; mem. Am. Surg. Assn. Sc. Surgery Alimentary Tract, Soc. Univ. Surgeons, SIC.

BALCH, SAMUEL EASON, lawyer; b. Madison, Ala., Sept. 5, 1919; s. Joseph Austin and Clara Irene (Vaughn) B.; m. Elizabeth Gordon Brock, Apr. 17, 1943; children: Samuel Eason, Elizabeth Gordon Balch Lanier, Gene Austin Balch Limbaugh, Ann Warwick Balch Miano. BS in Commerce and Bus. Adminstrn, U. Ala., 1940; LLB, U. Va., 1948, JD, 1970. Bar: Va. 1947, Ala. 1948, U.S. Supreme Ct. 1960, U.S. Ct. Appeals (11th cir.) 1981, U.S. Ct. Appeals (5th cir.) 1965. Assoc. Martin, Turner & McWhorter, 1948; sr. ptnr. Balch & Bingham (and predecessor firms), 1962-89, of counsel, 1990—. Chmn. legal com. Edison Electric Inst., 1979-81, chmn. econs., pub. policy and strategic planning, exec. adv. com., 1986-88. Served to major AUS, 1941-46, ETO, PTO. Life fellow Am. Bar Found.; mem. ABA (mem. coun. pub. utility law, telecomms. and transp. sect.), Fed. Energy Bar Assn., Ala. Bar Assn., Birmingham Bar Assn., Newcomen Soc., Am. Judicature Soc., Farrah Law Soc., Mountain Brook Club, The Summit Club, The Club (Birmingham, Ala.), Kappa Sigma. Episcopalian. Home: 4227 Old Leeds Rd Birmingham AL 35213-3211 Office: PO Box 306 1710 6th Ave N Birmingham AL 35203-2015

BALCOM, ORVILLE, engineer; b. Inglewood, Calif., Apr. 20, 1937; s. Orville R. and Rose Mae (Argo) B.; children: Cynthia, Steven. BS in Math., Calif. State U., Long Beach, 1958, postgrad., 1958-59, UCLA, 1959-62. Engr. AiResearch Mfg. Co., 1959-62, 64-65; chief engr. Meditron, El Monte, Calif., 1962-64, Astro Metrics, Burbank, Calif., 1965-67; chief engr., gen. mgr. Varadyne Power Systems, Van Nuys, Calif., 1968-71; owner, chief engr. Brown Dog Engring., Lomita, Calif., 1971—. Patentee in field. Mem. IEEE Computer Group, Independent Computer Cons. Assn., Torrance Athletic Club. Home: 24521 Walnut St Lomita CA 90717-1260 Office: PO Box 427 Lomita CA 90717-0427

BALD, RONALD JAMES, military officer; b. Dover, N.J., Mar. 6, 1965; s. Ronald Alan Bald and Jeanette Ann Carlstedt; m. Wanda Hope Yates; 1 child, William. BS Civil Engring., USCG Acad., New London, Conn., 1987; MA Pub. Mgmt., U. Houston, 1995; postgrad., Tulane U. Deck watch officer/ops. officer U.S. Coast Guard Cutter Buttonwood, Galveston, Tex., 1987—89; adminstrv. officer/aids to nav. officer U.S. Coast Guard Group Galveston, Galveston, Tex., 1989—93; ops. officer USCG Vessel Traffic Svc. Houston/Galveston, Galena Park, Tex., 1993—96; supply officer U.S. Coast Guard Cutter Boutwell, Alameda, Calif., 1996—98; cmdg. officer U.S. Coast Guard Cutter Cushing, San Juan, PR, 1998—2000. Lt. comdr. (O-4) USCG, 1987. Recipient Coast Guard Commendation Medal, Seventh Coast Guard Dist., 1998—2000, Coast Guard Pacific Area, 1996—98, Eighth Coast Guard Dist., 1993—96, Coast Guard Achievement Medal, 1993, 1990—93, 1990—91, Commandant's Letter of Commendation, Coast Guard Group Galveston, 1993; Stiles scholar for maritime law, 2002—03. Mem.: ASPA, Tulane Law Sch.-Maritime Law Soc./Mil. Law Soc. Avocation: coaching youth athletics. Home: 103 Dublin Ct Slidell LA 70461-3923 Office: Eighth Coast Guard District Legal Office 501 Magazine St New Orleans LA 70130-3396 Personal E-mail: rhwbald@bellsouth.net.

BALDACCI, JOHN ELIAS, governor, former congressman; b. Bangor, Maine, Jan. 30, 1955; m. Karen Weston; 1 child, Jack. BA in History, U. Maine, 1986. With Momma Baldacci's Restaurant, Bangor; mem. Bangor City Coun., 1978-81, Maine State Senate, 1982-94, 104th-106th Congress from 2nd dist., 1994—2002; Governor, 2003—. Mem. agr. com. Maine State Senate, transp. com., regional whip North East. Democrat. Office: Office of the Governor #1 State House Station Augusta ME 04333-0001*

BALDASSANO, VINCENT J. artist; b. Staten Island, N.Y., Apr. 27, 1943; s. Vincent F. and Antonette Baldassano; m. Carole Ann Baldassano; children: Alexandre, Francesca. BA, Wagner Coll., 1964; MFA, U. Oreg., 1966. Asst. prof. fine arts Niagara County C.C., Sanborn, N.Y., 1966-74; ptnr., pres. A.J. Murray & Co., Inc., N.Y.C., 1974-83; owner, pres. Artpak Transport Ltd., N.Y.C., 1983-90; owner, dir. Sta. Gallery, Katonah, N.Y., 1990-96; mng. dir. No. Westchester Ctr. for Arts, Mt. Kisco, N.Y., 1996; gallery dir. Silvermine Art Ctr., New Canaan, Ct., 1997-2000. One-man exhbns. include J. Fields Gallery, N.Y.C., 1981, U. Wis., Superior, 1983, Jean Lumbard Fine Arts, N.Y.C., 1983, Marie Pellicone Gallery, South Hampton, N.Y., 1984, Jakob Kunsthandlung, Basel, Switzerland, 1986, Silvermine Galleries, New Caanan, Conn., 2001, Zimmerman-Saturn Gallery, Nashville, 1987, Anna Howard Gallery, Washington Depot, Conn., 1993, The Schoolhouse, Croton Falls, N.Y., Hammond Mus., 1996, Stamford (Conn.) Mus., 1997, Greenwich (Conn.) Academy, 1999, Inner Space Gallery, Mpls., 1999, Collabrative Concepts, Beacon, N.Y., 2001, others; group exhbns. include Deutsche Amerikanisches Inst., Regensburg, Germany, 1988, Olaf Clausen Gallery, N.Y.C., 1990, Butler Art Inst., Youngstown, Ohio, 1990, Noel Fine Arts, Bronxville, N.Y., 1994, No. Westchester Ctr. Arts, 1994, Carriage Barn Space, New Canaan, 1995, Gallery at the Courtyard, 1996, Housatonic Mus. Art, Bridgeport, Conn., 1995, 98, Soho 20 Invitational, N.Y.C., 1996, Vt. Coll. Art, Montpelier, 1996, Broome St. Gallery Invitational, N.Y.C., 1999, Mus. Cagnes sur Mer, France, 1998, Savannah (Ga.) Coll. Art & Design, 1997, Silvermine Galleries, 1999, The Silo, New Milford, Conn., 1998, Alan Stone Gallery, N.Y.C., 1977-81, 99, 2000, others; represented in pub. collections Savannah Coll. Art & Design, Burchfield Penney Mus., Housatonic Mus. Art, Hammond Mus., U. Oreg., Wagner Coll., Sacred Heart U., Westchester C.C., Norwalk C.C. Trustee Hammond Mus., North Salem, N.Y., 1998. Grantee N.Y. State Coun. Arts, 1975, 71, 99, Va. Ctr. Creative Arts, 1978; SUNY Painting fellow, 1969, 70, 71, 73. Mem. Silvermine Guild (artist mem.), N.Y. Artist Equity (artist mem.). E-mail: vincentbaldassano@hotmail.com.

BALDASSIN, MICHAEL ROBERT, secondary school educator; b. Tacoma, Wash., July 26, 1955; s. Robert Allen and Mary Lee (Hager) B.; Mary Katherine Hartman, Oct. 10, 1981; children: Jessica, Corrine, Beau, Kaylee. BS in Sociology, U. Wash., 1980. Profl. football player San Francisco 49ers, 1977-80; police officer Seattle Police dept., 1980-83, Oakland (Calif.) Police Dept., 1983-91; Wash. state dir. drug and alcohol Fellowship of Christian Athletes, Kansas City, Mo., 1991-92; tchr., head football coach Bellarmine Prep, Tacoma, 1992—. Bd. dirs. youth adv. Sparrow Found., Seattle, 1995—. Decorated Medal of Valor, Oakland Police Dept., 1985; named Coach of Yr. Nat. Football Found., 1996, Narrows League, 2000, Tacoma New Tribune, 2000; named Footbal Coach of Yr., 2003, Overbo Coach of Yr., 2003; inducted into Woodrow Wilson H.S. Athletic Hall of Fame, 2000 Avocation: guitar. Office: Bellarmine Preparatory High Sch 2300 S Washington St Tacoma WA 98405-1304

BALDAUF, KENT EDWARD, lawyer; b. Pitts., Feb. 6, 1943; s. Walter William and Esther Baldauf; m. Kathleen Dian Abels, June 10, 1967; children: Kent Edward Jr., Krista K., Kara K. BS in Metall. Engring., Carnegie Mellon U., 1964; JD, Cleve. State U., 1970. Bar: Pa. 1970, U.S. Patent and Trademark Office 1971, U.S. Ct. Appeals (Fed. cir.) 1990, U.S. Supreme Ct. 1977. Shareholder, v.p., dir. Webb Law Firm, Pitts., 1988—. Mem. ABA, Pa. Bar Assn., Allegheny County Bar Assn., Am. Intellectual Property Law Assn. (pres. 1998-99), Pitts. Intellectual Property Law Assn., Valley Brook Country Club, Duquesne Club. Office: The Webb Law Firm 436 7th Ave Pittsburgh PA 15219-1826

BALDI, STÉPHANE, education researcher, sociologist; b. Paris, Jan. 31, 1969; s. Georges and Marie-Claude (Gardan) B. BA, U. Mass., Boston, 1992; MA, U. Conn., 1993; PhD, Ohio State U., 1997. Cons. NRC, Washington, 1997; rsch. analyst Am. Insts. Rsch., Washington, 1997-99, sr. rsch. analyst, 1999; adminstr. Orgn. Econ. Coop. and Devel., Paris, 2000; sr. rsch. analyst Am. Insts. Rsch., 2000—02, prin. rsch. scientist, 2002—. Reviewer Am. Sociol. Rev., Work and Occupation, Ednl. Evaluation and Policy Analysis, Sociol. Forum, Am. Jour. Sociology, Sociol. Perspectives. Author: The American Sociologist, 1994, 2d edit., 1997, Scientrometrics, 1995, The Sociological Quarterly, 1995, Work and Occupations, 1997, American Sociological Review, 1998, International Education Indicators, 2000, What Democracy Means to Ninth Graders, 2001, Education Finance in G-7 Nations: An International Perspective, 2002, Outcome Assessment of the American Council of Young Political Leaders Program, 2002, Outcome Assessment of the Institute for Representative Government Program, 2003; contbr. articles to profl. jours. Recipient rsch. grant NSF, 1996; Fgn. Lang. Area Studies fellow U.S. Dept. Edn., 1995. Mem. Am. Sociol. Assn., Am. Ednl. Rsch. Assn. Office: Am Insts for Rsch 1000 Thomas Jefferson St NW Washington DC 20007-3835 E-mail: sbaldi@air.org.

BALDIGA, JOSEPH HILDING, lawyer; b. Woonsocket, R.I., Dec. 18, 1962; s. Robert S. and Lois E. (Wickstrom) B.; m. Mary P. Baldiga, June 9, 1990; children: Lucy Porter, Robert Kenneth. BA, Boston Coll., 1984, JD, 1987. Bar: Mass. 1987, U.S. Dist. Ct. Mass. 1988. Assoc. Peabody & Brown, Boston, 1987-88, Goodwin Procter & Hoar, Boston, 1988-94; ptnr. Mirick O'Connell, Worcester, Mass., 1994—. Trustee Dynamy, Worcester, 1997—, Chestnut St. Mktg. House Assn., Millville, Mass,. 1992—. Mem. Mass. Bar Assn., Boston Bar Assn. (co-chair bankruptcy sect. 2000—), Worcester Bar Assn., Am. Bankruptcy Inst., Comml. Law League, Turnaround Mgmt. Assn. Office: Mirick O'Connell 100 Front St Worcester MA 01608-1425 Fax: 508-791-8502. E-mail: jhbaldiga@modl.com.

BALDINI, LAURA FLYNN, lawyer; b. Hartford, Conn. d. Daniel Francis and Barbara Lois Flynn; m. Matthew Alfred Baldini, June 13, 1998. BA, Yale U., 1992; JD, Seton Hall U., 1996. Bar: Conn. 1997, N.Y. 1997, U.S. Dist. Ct. Conn. 1998. Trial prep asst. Dist. Attys. Office N.Y. County, N.Y.C., 1992-93; law clk. Morgan, Melhush, Monaghan, Arvidson, Abrutyn & Lisowski, N.Y.C., 1995-96; assoc. Chrenstein & Brown, N.Y.C., 1996-98, Updike, Kelly & Spellacy, Hartford, Conn., 1998—. Author: Insider's Guide to Teenage Tennis, 1996. Vol. Jr. Achievement, Hartford, 1998—. Recipient Gilbert Shepard award Yale Club Hartford, 1989. Mem. ABA, Conn. Bar Assn., N.Y. Bar Assn., Hartford Golf Club, Jr. League Hartford. Roman Catholic. Avocations: tennis, golf, gardening, community service. Office: Updike Kelly & Spellacy PC One State St Hartford CT 06123

BALDNER, KAREN A. artist, art educator; b. Baton Rouge, Nov. 9, 1952; d. Thomas and Gabriella Baldner. Student, Acad. Bildedenen Kunste, Munich, 1974-76; BFA in Printmaking, Ind. U., 1981, MFA in Printmaking with honors, 1986. Vis. asst. prof. U. Ark., Fayetteville, 1987-88, Ind. U. Hope Sch. Art, Bloomington, 1990-91, St. Mary's Coll. Md., St. Mary's City, 1992-93; asst. prof. Bucknell U., Lewisburg, Pa., 1988-90; assoc. prof. Herron Sch. Art, Indpls., 1998—. Pvt. tchr. paper and bookmaking, 1983—; condr. workshops in hand papermaking and book binding Coe Coll., Cedar Rapids, Iowa, 1986, Miami U., Oxford, Ohio, 1992, 94, Columbus (Ga.) State U., 1995, 2000, IAPMA Conf., Chgo., 2002, N.W. Ark. Sch. Sys., 1995-98; resident Ill. State U., Normal, 1997; artist-in-resident Ark. Arts Coun., 1995-96, 97-98; conf. presenter, lectr. in field. One-woman shows include Paper Press Gallery, Chgo., 1992, Artemesia Gallery, Chgo., 1992, 97, St. Mary's Coll., 1993, Soho 20 Gallery, N.Y.C., 1993, 94, 95, Northcutt Steele Gallery, Billings, Mont., 1996, Anne Kitrell Gallery, U. Ark., Fayetteville, 1997, Matrix Gallery, Sacramento, 1997, Mendelsohn Gallery, Bloomington, Ind., 1999, New Harmony Ind.Gallery, 2000, Indpls. Art Ctr., 2002; exhibited in group shows, 1991—, including Papermaking Mus., Düren, Germany, 1991, Gallery 451, Rockford, Ill., 1992, Spaces Gallery, Cleve., 1991, Gemeente Bibliothek, Rotterdam, The Netherlands, 1993, Lite Rail Gallery, Sacramento, 1993, Massillon (Ohio) Mus., 1994, Haggin Mus., Stockton, Calif., 1994, Soho 20 Gallery, 1994, 96, 97, 99, 2000, 01, 02, Evansville (Ind.) Mus. Arts and Scis., 1994, Columbia (Mo.) Coll., 1995, Matrix Gallery, 1995 (Best in Show award), Woman Made Gallery, Chgo., 1995, 96, 98, 2000, Fine Arts Ctr. Gallery, U. Ark., 1996, Katherine Nash Gallery, U. Minn., Mpls., 1996, Edna Carlsten Gallery, U. Wis., Stevens Point, 1997, Columbia Coll., Chgo., 1998, DePauw U., Greencastle, Ind., 1999, Mc Neese State U., Lake Charles, La., 2001, Ind. U., Kokomo, 2002, The Ctr. for Book Arts; represented in collections at Ind. U., Sch. Fine Arts Libr., Bloomington, Ind. U. Sch. Fine Arts, Artists Books Collection, Kinsey Inst., Ind. U. Fine Arts Collection, Bookarts Collection; work reviewed in various publs. Recipient Best of Show award No. German Photography Competition, 1987, merit award 50th Quad State Exhbn., Quincy (Ill.) Art Ctr., 2000; Kiel U. exch. scholar Ind. U., 1986-87; Fulbright travel grantee, Germany, 1986-87, faculty devel. grantee Bucknell U., 1989, grantee Ludwig Vogelstein Found., 1991-92, Nat. Endowment Arts grantee Mid Am. Arts Alliance, 1996, grantee Ind. Arts Commn., 2000; fellow Ark. Arts Coun. for Works on Paper, 1998; Creative Renewal Arts fellow, Indpls. Arts Coun., 2003. Mem.: The Ctr. for Book Arts, Internat. Assn. Papermakers, Mid.-Am. Coll. Arts Assn., Coll. Arts Coun., Friends of Dard Hunter, Soho 20 Gallery. Home: 629 N College Ave Bloomington IN 47404 E-mail: kambi@kiva.net.

BALDOCCHI, DENNIS DAVID, micrometeorologist; b. Antioch, Calif., Apr. 12, 1955; s. Evo Savario and Helen Marie (Marieni) B.; m. Nicole Marie Lepoutre, Nov. 24, 1984; 1 child, Ian McCully. BS, U. Calif., Davis, 1977; MS, N. Nebr., 1979, PhD, 1982. Biometeorologist ORAU, Oak Ridge, Tenn., 1983-86; physical scientist NOAA/ATDD, Oak Ridge, Tenn., 1996—99; acting assoc. prof. U. Calif. Berkeley, 1999—2002, prof. Biometeorology, 2002—. Vis. scientist U. Stockholm, 1990, Inst. Nat. Rsch. Agronomique, Bordeaux, France, 1996; mem. exec. bd. NASA Boreas Project, 1993—; mem. editorial bd. Agrl. Forest Meteorology, 1993—; mem. sci. panel Internat. Satellite Land-Surface Climatology Project, 1994—; mem. steering com. Trace Gas Network. Author: (12 chpts.) Scaling Physiological Processes: contbr. 120 articles to profl. jours.; mem. editl. bd. Plant, Cell and Environ., 1996—, Boundary Layer Meteorology, 1996—; subject editor Global Change Biology. RAISA fellow U. Tuscia, Viterbo, Italy, 1992-93, postdoctoral fellow ORAU, 1982. Mem. Am. Mateorological Soc. (Biometeorological com. 1990-93), Am. Geophys. Soc. (Editorial citation 1990). Avocations: soccer, hiking, tennis, reading. Home: 3908 Enos Ave Oakland CA 94619-2860 Office: Univ Calif Berkeley Dept Environ Sci Policy & Mgmt 151 Hilgard Hall Berkeley CA 94720 E-mail: baldocchi@nature.berkeley.edu.

BALDOCK, BOBBY RAY, judge; b. Rocky, Okla., Jan. 24, 1936; Grad., N.Mex. Mil. Inst., 1956; JD, U. Ariz., 1960. Bar: Ariz. 1960, N.Mex. 1961, U.S. Dist. Ct. N.Mex. 1965. Ptnr. Sanders, Bruin & Baldock, Roswell, N.Mex., 1960—83; adj. prof. Eastern N.Mex. U., 1962—81; judge U.S. Dist. Ct. N.Mex., Albuquerque, 1983—86, U.S. Ct. Appeals (10th cir.), 1986—2001, sr. judge, 2001—. Mem.: Chaves County Bar Assn., Ariz. Bar Assn., N.Mex. Bar Assn., Phi Alpha Delta. Office: US Ct Appeals PO Box 2388 Roswell NM 88202-2388

BALDRACHI, RYAN MICHAEL, psychologist; b. Bartlesville, Okla., Mar. 15, 1973; s. Michael and Susan (Black) B. BA in Psychology cum laude, U. Ark., 1998; MS in Clin. Psychology, Ohio U., 2002. Crisis line vol. N.W. Ark. crisis Intervention Ctr., Springdale, 1996—99; supported employment specialist Lifestyles Inc., Fayetteville, Ark., 1997—98; rsch. asst. Personality Assessment and Psychtherapy rsch. Lab., U. Ark., Fayetteville, 1996—2001, Psychotherapy rsch. Lab., Ohio U., Athens, 1999—. Sandra Lawson Taylor fellow Ohio U., 1999-01, Silo Adv. Coun. Undergrad. rsch. fellow, 1997, W.J. richards Meml. awardee, U. Ark., 1997. Mem.: ACLU, APA, Soc. for Personality Assessment, Internat. Rorschach Soc. Avocations: electronic music production, photography, film making. Office: Ohio Univ Dept Psychology 200 Porter Hall Athens OH 45701

BALDRIDGE, JANE L. graphic artist, fine artist; b. Stevens Point, Wis., Feb. 23, 1959; d. Ralph Bayard and Elizabeth (McIntosh) Baldridge; m. Mark Harrington Brown, Oct. 11, 1978 (div. 1982); m. David Cook, Dec. 27, 1986 (div. 1989); 1 child, Jason David Cook. Student, Calif. Inst. Arts, Valencia, 1977-78, Alfred Glassel Sch. Art, Houston, 1978-81. Artist, Tex., Calif., Mich., N.C., 1972—; owner The Village Gallery, Brooklyn, Mich.; salesperson, framer Fidler's Gallery, Wilmington, N.C.; asst. pub. Cape Fear Real Estate Directory, Wrightsville Beach, N.C.; owner, designer Artspeaks, Wilmington. Curator Arts Coun. Lower Cape Fear, Wilmington; tchr., lectr. in schs., Wilmington; advt. agy. cons. Exhibited in shows at Art Gallery Originals, Winston-Salem, N.C., Sea Pines Gallery, Hilton Head, S.C., Feast of the Pirates Art Show, Wilmington, N.C., St. John Mus., Wilmington, N.C., New Elements Gallery, Wilmington, New Eng. Art Inst., Boston, Women's Ctr. 10th Ann. Art Show, Chapel Hill, N.C., Piney Woods Art Festival, Wilmington, Fayetteville (N.C.) Mus. Art, Arts Festival, Dalton, Ga., Creative Resource Gallery, Wilmington, Art Mus., Mytrle Beach, S.C., Lincoln Ctr., N.Y.C., World Festival Paper, Kranj, Slovenia, numerous others; represented in collections at Merrill Lynch, Dean Witter Reynolds Inc., Landmark Homes, Inc., others. Mem. troop com. Boy Scouts Am., treas., 1998—. Recipinet Gold medal for Adams Cup (sailing, 1976, Gold medal for Art, Scholastic awards, 1974, Pres.'s award Calif. Inst. of the Arts, 1978, numerous awards for art; regional artist grantee, 1994, 2000. Mem. St. Johns Mus. Art, N.C. Coastal Fedn., Citizens Protecting Resources. Office: Artspeaks 8947 Shipwatch Dr Wilmington NC 28412-3537 E-mail: dolphinae@earthlink.net.

BALDRIGE, LETITIA, writer, management training consultant; b. Miami Beach, Fla. d. Howard Malcolm and Regina (Connell) B.; m. Robert Hollensteiner; children: Clare, Malcolm. BA, Vassar Coll., 1946; postgrad., U. Geneva, 1946-48; DHL (hon.), Creighton U., 1979, Mt. St. Mary's Coll., 1980, Bryant Coll., 1987, Kenyon Coll., 1990. Personal-social sec. to amb. Am. Embassy, Paris, 1948-51; intelligence officer Washington, 1951-53; asst. to amb. Am. Embassy, Rome, 1953-56; dir. pub. rels. Tiffany & Co., 1956-60; social sec. The White House, 1961-63; pres. Letitia Baldrige Enterprises, Chgo., 1964-69; dir. consumer affairs Burlington Industries, 1969-71; pres. Letitia Baldrige Enterprises, Inc., Washington, 1972—. Author: Roman Candle, 1956, Tiffany Table Settings, 1958, Of Diamonds and Diplomats, 1968, Home, 1972, Juggling, 1976, Amy Vanderbilt's Complete Book of Etiquette, 1978, Amy Vanderbilt's Everyday Etiquette, 1979, Entertainers, 1981, Letitia Baldrige's Complete Guide to Executive Manners, 1985, Letitia Baldrige's Complete Guide to a Great Social Life, 1987, Complete Guide to the New Manners for the '90s, 1990, New Complete Guide to Executive Manners, 1993, (novel) Public Affairs Private Relations, 1990, More Than Manners! Raising Today's Kids to Have Kind Manners and Good Hearts, 1997, In the Kennedy Style, 1998, Legendary Brides, 2000, A Lady, First, 2001, New Manners fr New Times, 2003. Mem. adv. bd. Woodrow Wilson House, Washington, Reading Is Fundamental, Malcolm Baldrige Nat. Quality Awards, Woodrow Wilson Nat. Fellowship Found. Republican. E-mail: lbaldrige@aol.com.

BALDUKAS, ANN-MARI PEIRCE, dean; d. Olav Kristian and Inger Johanne Ingebrigtsen; m. Nicholas Peter Baldukas, Aug. 31, 1985; children: Pamela Ann Patch, Shane Erik Peirce. BA, U. of Oslo, Norway, 1964; MA, U. of Utah, 1969; MBA, U. of Wis., 1987, PhD, 2001. English instr. N.C. State U., Raleigh, 1968—69, No. Ariz. U., Flagstaff, 1970—73, U. of Wis., Parkside, 1979—82; mktg. cons. Korndoerfer Corp., Racine, Wis., 1980—83; comm. specialist Wis. Energies, Racine, 1983—87; dean of instrn. Gateway Tech. Coll., Kenosha, Wis., 1987—. Consulting Korndoerfer Corp, Racine, Wis., 1980—83. Bd. mem. Bus. Edn. Co-op Adv. Com., Racine, Wis., 1999; mem. Racine Hist. Soc., Wis., 2001; pres. primary orgn. Kenosha, Wis., 1981—84; sec. Cmty. Action Agy., Racine, Wis., 1993—95; bd. mem. U. of Wis. Parkside Alumni Assn., Kenosha, 1993—96. Scholar, Nat. Def. Scholarship Found., 1967—68. Mem.: Wis. Assn. for Career and Tech. Edn. Avocations: hiking, reading. Office: Gateway Tech Coll 1001 S Main St Racine WI 53403

BALDWIN, ALLAN OLIVER, information scientist, higher education executive; b. Chgo., Apr. 10, 1948; s. Albert Oliver and Virginia Josephine (Stack) B.; m. Suzanne Balasty, Nov. 28, 1969 (div.); m. Janice Louise DiVito, Jan. 25, 1992; children: Steven, Jennifer, Jeremy, Matthew, Katherine. BS, U. Ill., Chgo., 1969; MBA, Keller Grad. Sch. Mgmt., 1982. Asst. systems mgr. U. Ill., Chgo., 1970-76, asst. dir. info. systems svcs., 1976-79, dir. hosp. info. svcs., 1979-86; dir. systems devel. Loyola U. Chgo., Maywood, Ill., 1986-88, asst. v.p. info. systems, 1988-90, acting v.p. info. tech., 1990-92, v.p. info. tech., 1992—2000; IT cons., 2000—. Chmn. parent human rels. com. Oak Park (Ill.)-River Forest High Sch., 1991. Mem. Coll. and Univ. Systems Engrs., Healthcare Info. Mgmt. Systems Soc., Med. Info. System Assn., EduCause. Home: 109A S Euclid Ave Oak Park IL 60302-2905 E-mail: abaldwi@mediaone.net.

BALDWIN, ALLEN ADAIL, lawyer, writer; b. St. Augustine, Fla., July 15, 1939; s. Larrie Paul and Bertha Mae (Capallia) B. BA, Brigham Young U., 1969; JD, So. U., Baton Rouge, 1975. Bar: Fla. 1975. Tchr. Putnam County Sch. Bd., Palatka, Fla., 1969-71; pvt. practice, Palatka, 1975—. Author: Tricks to Make the Angels Weep, 1986, Call It Not Heaven, 1991, Redeem Us From Virtue, 1992. Mem. Lds Ch. Avocations: reading, swimming, hiking. Office: 308 St Johns Ave Palatka FL 32177-4723

BALDWIN, BRUCE GREGG, botany educator, researcher; b. San Luis Obispo, Calif., Oct. 24, 1957; s. Robert Lee and Sally Louise (Elrod) B. BA in Biol. Scis. with honors, U. Calif., Santa Barbara, 1981; MS in Botany, U. Calif., Davis, 1985, PhD in Botany, 1989. NSF postdoctoral fellow U. Ariz., Tucson, 1990-92; asst. prof. dept. botany Duke U., 1992-94; curator Jepson Herbarium U. Calif., Berkeley, 1994—, asst. prof. in residence dept. integrative biology, 1994-98, assoc. prof. in residence dept. integrative biology, 1998-2000, assoc. prof. dept. integrative biology, 2000—. Mellon vis. scholar Rancho Santa Ana Bot. Garden, 1994. Contbr. articles to profl. jours. and books, reviewer; chief editor Jepson Flora project, 1994—. Recipient NSF Nat. Young Investigator award, 1994; Calif. Acad. Scis. fellow, 1999—. Mem. Am. Soc. Plant Taxonomists (publicity com. 1993—, coun. 2002—), Calif. Bot. Soc. (pres. 2000—). Achievements include research in plant systematics, phylogenetics, plant cytogenetics and chromosome evolution, plant speciation, California floristics, phytogeography, insular evolution. Home: 2408 Parker St Berkeley CA 94704-2812 Office: U Calif Berkeley Jepson Herbarium Dept Integrative Biology 1001 Valley Life Scis Bldg 2465 Berkeley CA 94720-2465

BALDWIN, C. ANDREA, JR., retired science educator; b. Chgo., May 18, 1927; s. C. Andrew Sr. and Lillian (Evans) B.; m. Claire Awkerman, July 10, 1954; children: Debbie, Judi. BA in Zoology, U. Tex., 1951; MA in Theology, Berkeley Bapt. Sem. of West, 1956, MDiv, 1961; postgrad., numerous colls., univs. Cert. elem. tchr., Calif., secondary tchr., Calif., Tex., Ill.; edn. adminstr., Calif., K-12 substitute and biology, Oreg. Sci. tchr. Brazosport Ind. Sch. Dist., Freeport, Tex., 1951-53; sustitute tchr. Chgo. Pub. Sch., 1953-54; child care and substitute tchr. Berkeley (Calif.) Pub. Sch., 1954-56; tchr. 7th and 8th grades Redwood City (Calif.) Elem. Sch., 1956-60; swimpool mgr. San Mateo County Parks/Recreation, 1957-64; 6th grade/jr. high biology/sr. high biology, geology tchr., coord. field biology Palo Alto (Calif.) Unified Sch. Dist., 1960-93; vice prin. Franklin-McKinley Sch. Dist., San Jose, Calif., 1970-71; Biology, 6-12th grade substitute Salem and Woodburn (Oreg.) Schs., 1993-2000; mem. faculty in ESL, Chemeketa C.C., 1997-2001. Founder, dir. pvt. summer ecology and field biology camp program-Summer Sci. Safaris, 1972-76; coord. sci. fairs Wilbur Jr. H.S. & Stanford Middle Sch. Contbr. articles to publs. Unit dir., counselor, mem. water safety staff YMCA, Chgo., Denver, Berkeley, Oakland, Calif.; counselor Chgo. Boys Club, 1945—56, Oakland Cath. Youth Orgn., 1945—56; pres. YMCA's Men's Club, Redwood City, 1967—69, Lorelei Homeowners Assn., Menlo Park, Calif., 1959—60; v.p. Hoover Elem. Sch. PTA, 1959—60; elected Sequoia United Sch. Dist. B.d; pres. Freeport Jr. High Sch. PTA, 1952—53, Senn High Sch. Crusaders Club, Chgo.; vol. YMCA, Chgo., Chgo. Boys' Clubs, Boy Scouts Am., ARC; candidate U.S. Congress, 1967; elder, chair mission com. Trinity Presbyn. Ch., San Carlos, Calif.; elder, mem. choir, various coms. 1st Presbyn. United Mission Advance; staff assoc. Carlmont Meth. Ch.; vol. asst. min. Woodside Rd. Cmty. United Meth. Ch., Redwood City, People's Assembly of God Ch., Salem, Oreg., 1st Bapt. Ch., Salem; mem. Men's Bible Fellowship Internat., Salem; elected trustee Redwood City Sch. Dist. Bd. Edn., 1961—69, pres., 1968—69; active com. against racism, various others Sequoia High Sch. Dist. Sgt. USAAF, 1945—47. Decorated Brevet 2nd Lt. Commn. U.S. Army, 1945; named Outstanding Citizen, Redwood City YMCA, 1968, Realtors, South San Mateo County, 1967; recipient Oak Leaf and Life Membership award Calif. PTA, 1959, 5 and 10 yr. Vol. pin ARC, Vol. pin Chgo. Boys' Club; nominated for Presdl. award for excellence in tchg., 1992; Chevron Corp. grantee, 1985. Mem. AAAS, NEA, Calif. Tchrs. Assn., Palo Alto Edn. Assn. (sch. rep., salary com.), Christian Educators Assn. Internat., Astron. Soc. Pacific, Earth Sci. Tchrs. Assn., Calif. Sci. Tchrs. Assn., Nat. Sci. Tchrs. Assn. (12th dist. dir. 1984-86, local leader 1993-97), Oreg. Sci. Tchrs. Assn., Nat. Assn. Biology Tchrs. Avocations: hiking, swimming, reading (especially biographies and mysteries), sudying religion, history, Spanish, science and anthropology.

BALDWIN, CALVIN BENHAM, JR., retired medical research administrator; b. Radford, Va., Dec. 22, 1925; s. Calvin Benham and Louise (Delp) B.; m. Elizabeth Buell, Mar. 10, 1951; children: Susan B., Sally C., Ann H. AB, U. N.C., 1949; postgrad., N.C., 1949-51; MPA, Harvard U., 1961. Research asst. Inst. Research Social Scis., Chapel Hill, N.C., 1949-50; methods examiner NIH, Bethesda, Md., 1953-55, budget examiner, 1955-57, adminstrv. officer, 1957-58, adminstrv. officer div. gen. med. sci., 1958-61; exec. officer Divsn. Gen. Med. Scis., Bethesda, Md., 1961-62, Nat. Inst. Child Health, Bethesda, Md., 1963-70, Nat. Cancer Inst., Bethesda, Md., 1970-80; assoc. dir. adminstrn. NIH, Bethesda, 1980-86. Mem. Montgomery County Econ. Coun., Rockville, Md., 1982—85, Bethany Beach (Del.) Town Coun., 1991—92, 1994—96; pres. Bethany Beach Landowners Assn., 1998—2002; mem. Bethany Beach Planning Commn., 1998—2002, 2000—02. Recipient W.A. Jump meritorious award HEW, 1960; recipient Superior Service award HEW, 1973 Mem. NIH Alumni Assn. (pres. 1995-97), Phi Beta Kappa Democrat. Unitarian Universalist. Home: 10705 Weymouth St Garrett Park MD 20896-0017

BALDWIN, CARLA SUZANN, psychologist; b. Bristol, Tenn., Sept. 21, 1954; d. Carl E. and Carolyn R. (Broce) Baldwin; m. Thomas E. May, June 29, 1986; 1 child, Hannah Baldwin-May. BA in Psychology summa cum laude, Cleve. State U., 1983, MA in Psychology, 1985. Lic. psychologist Pa. Psychologist PSI, Cleve., 1986-89, Shaler Area Sch. Dist., Glenshaw, Pa., 1990-95, Seneca Valley Sch. Dist., Harmony, Pa., 1995—2003, North Allegheny Sch. Dist., Pitts., 2003—. Contbr. Bd. dirs. Children's Meml. Fund, Pitts. Mem.: Nat. Assn. Sch. Psychologists (cert.), Gaia Circle, Psi Chi. Office: North Allegheny Sch Dist 200 Hillvue Ln Pittsburgh PA 16037

BALDWIN, CYNTHIA ANN, industrial hygienist; b. Fort Sill, Okla., Sept. 18, 1951; d. Arthur Roy Baldwin and Dolores Mae Hill. BS in Biology, Met. State Coll., Denver, 1973; MS in Environ. Health, Colo. State U., 1981. Cert. in comprehensive practice indsl. hygiene Am. Bd. Indsl. Hygiene, 1988. Clk. typist admissions and records Colo. State U., Ft. Collins, 1974-75, student coordinator, office supr. dept. microbiology, 1975-80, grad. research asst. dept. microbiology, 1980-81; indsl. hygienist Consultation div. Iowa Bur. Labor, Des Moines, 1981-84; dir. occupational health Amana (Iowa) Refrigeration, Inc., 1984-93, mgr. environ. health and safety, 1993-95; sr. project mgr. Beling Cons., Moline, Ill., 1995-97; sr. indsl. hygienist Pointer Environ. Inc., Cedar Rapids, Iowa, 1997—2002; sr. indsl. hygenist Terracon, Cedar Rapids, 2002—. Mem. adv. council U. Iowa Inst. Agrl. Medicine and Occupational Health, Iowa City, 1986-90. Mem. Am. Indsl. Hygiene Assn. (diplomate; pres. Iowa-Ill. sect. 1987-88), Am. Soc. Safety Engrs., Am. Conf. Govtl. Indsl. Hygienists (assoc.), Quad-City Engring. and Sci. Coun. (pres. 2000-01). Avocations: dance, needlework. Office: Terracon 5855 Willow Creek Dr SW Cedar Rapids IA 52404-4312 E-mail: cabaldwin@terracon.com .

BALDWIN, DANIEL FLANAGAN, mechanical engineer, researcher, educator; b. Fort Collins, Colo., Jan. 4, 1965; s. Lionel Vernon and Kathleen Baldwin; m. Kristen Jean Schamberger, Aug., 1989; children: Kelsey Rae, Patrick Flanagan, Christopher Glenn. BS in Engring. summa cum laude, Ariz. State U., 1988; MS, MIT, 1990, PhD, 1994. Engr. in tng., Ariz. Software analyst Colo. State U., Fort Collins, 1984, 85, rsch. asst., 1986; engring. intern Mitsubishi Electric Corp., Kamakura, Japan, 1987; Draper fellow C.S. Draper Lab., Cambridge, Mass., 1988-90; rsch. mgr. MIT, Cambridge, 1990-94; mem. tech. staff AT&T Bell Labs., Princeton, N.J., 1994-95; asst. prof. George W. Woodruff Sch. Mech. Engring. Ga. Inst. Tech., Atlanta, 1994—99; dir. Advanced Assembly Tech. Siemens Dematic Electronics Assembly Sys., Norcross, Ga., 2000—01, v.p., 2002—03; pres. Engent, Inc., Norcross, 2003—; assoc. prof. George W. Woodruff Sch. Mech. Engring. Ga. Inst. Tech., 2000—. Gen. chair 3d Internat. Advanced Tech. Workshop; tech. program chair for the 2d internat. advanced tech. workshop on low cost flip chip tech., Internat. Microelectronics and Packaging Soc., 1998; symposium organizer The Pacific RIM/ASME Internat. Intersoc. Electronic and Photonic Packaging Conf., 1997, 99; co-chair Pacific RIM/ASME Internat. Intersoc. Electronic and Photonic Packing Conf., 1999, symposium chair conf., 2001; gen. chair 4th Internat. Advanced Tech. Workshop on Flip Chip Tech., 2000. Referee Robotics and Computer-Integrated Mfg., 1992-94, ASME Jour. Sys. Dynamics and Control, 1996, Internat. Jour. Engring. Design and Automation, 1996, IEEE Transactions on Components, Packaging and Mfg. Tech., 1996—, Polymer Engring. and Sci.; contbr.: Computer-Aided Mechanical Assembly Planning, 1991; contbr. articles to IEEE Transactions in Robotics and Automation, Jour. Engring. Materials and Tech., Polymer Engring. and Sci., Jour. Japan Soc. of Polymer Processing, Rsch. in Engring. Design, Biomaterials, Internat. Jour. Microcircuits and Electronic Packaging, among others. Recipient Outstanding Rsch. Faculty of Yr. award, NSF Engring. Rsch. Ctr., 1996, 98, 2000, Milton C. Shaw Outstanding Young Mfg. Engring. award Soc. Mfg. Engrs., Best Paper award 2001 APEX Electronics Assembly Process Conf. and Exhbn., 2001. Mem. ASME (chair electric and electronic packaging divsn. MEMS packaging com., Outstanding Young Engr. award 1998), IEEE Components Pkg. and Mfg. Tech. (chair ICard pkg. assembly tech. com.), Am. Soc. Engring. Edn., Internat. Microelectronics and Packaging Soc., Surface Mount Tech. Assn. (bd. dirs.), Soc. Mfg. Engrs. (bd. advisors Assn. for Electronics Mfg.), Soc. Plastics Engrs., Sigma Xi, Pi Tau Sigma, Tau Beta Pi, Phi Kappa Phi. Achievements include patent for microcellular foamed materials using supercritical fluids; patent for processing microcellular/supermicrocellular plastics, patent for semiconductor devices having gallium amalgams on bumped leads; patents for injection molding of microcellular plastics; sheet extrusion of microcellular plastics; low-cost materials and processes for metallizing and bumping semiconductor devices; snap cure of underfill and flip chip interconnect of high I/O devices; patent pending for methods for application of polymer underfills onto bumped semi conductor wafers; research in advanced electronics packaging, advanced electronics manufacturing and assembly; materials processing, manufacturing system design; polymer processing, microelectronics manufacturing and assembly. Office: Ga Inst Tech George W Woodruff Sch Mech Engring Atlanta GA 30332-0405

BALDWIN, DAVID ALLEN, political science educator; b. Indpls., July 28, 1936; s. James Howell and Pearl Mabel (Fisher) B.; m. Marilyn Claire Austin, Aug. 10, 1957 (div. Sept. 1990); children: Sarah, Rebecca, Emily; m. Helen Virginia Milner, May 24, 1991. AB, Ind. U., 1958; MA, Princeton U., 1961, PhD, 1965; MA (hon.), Dartmouth Coll., 1978. Asst. prof. govt. Dartmouth Coll., Hanover, N.H., 1965-70, assoc. prof. govt., 1970-75, John S. Dickey Prof., 1975-80, prof. govt., 1980-85; prof. polit. sci. Columbia U., N.Y.C., 1985-89, Ira Wallach Prof., 1989—. Dir. Inst. of War and Peace Studies, Columbia U., 1987-94. Author: Foreign Aid, 1966, Economic Statecraft, 1985 (Kammerer award 1986), Paradoxes of Power, 1989, Economic Development and Foreign Policy, 1966; editl. bd. Internat. Orgn., 1984-97, Polit. Sci. quar., N.Y.C., 1989-94, Jour. Internat. Affairs, 1988—. Mem. Coun. on Fgn. Rels., N.Y.C., 1986—. 1st lt. U.S. Army, 1962-63. Recipient Moffat Econs. prize Ind. U., Bloomington, 1958, fellowships German Marshall Fund, Washington, 1982-83, Brookings Instn., Washington, 1964-65, Danforth Found., St. Louis, 1958-64. Mem. Am. Polit. Sci. Assn. (recipient Kammerer award 1986), Internat. Polit. Sci. Assn., Internat. Studies Assn., British Internat. Studies Assn., Acad. Polit. Sci., Phi Beta Kappa. Home: 450 Riverside Dr New York NY 10027-6801 Office: Inst of War & Peace Studies Columbia University 420 W 118th St New York NY 10027-7213

BALDWIN, DAVID SHEPARD, physician; b. Rochester, N.Y., Sept. 5, 1921; s. Jacob and Anna B.; m. Halee Morris, June 24, 1945; children— Neil, Andrew, Daniel, James. BA, U. Rochester, 1943, MD, 1945. Intern Barnes Hosp., St. Louis, 1945-46; resident in medicine Bellevue Hosp., N.Y.C., 1946-48; renal fellow in medicine and physiology N.Y.U. Sch. Medicine, 1948-50, mem. faculty, 1950—, prof. medicine, nephrology, 1972—. Attending physician Bellevue Hosp.; honorary attending physician N.Y.U. Hosp.; mem. med. adv. bd. coun. high blood pressure rsch. AHA. Author papers in med. jours., chpts. in books. Served as officer M.C. AUS, 1953-55. Mem. AHA, Harvey Soc., Am. Soc. Nephrology, Am. Soc. Clin. Investigation, Internat. Soc. Nephrology, N.Y. Soc. Nephrology (pres. 1974-75), N.Y. Heart Assn. Home: 333 E 69th St New York NY 10021-5560 Office: NYU Sch Medicine 550 1st Ave OBV CD679 New York NY 10016-6402 E-mail: david.baldwin@med.nyu.edu.

BALDWIN, DEANNA LOUISE, dietitian; b. Oklahoma City, Okla., Jan. 14, 1946; d. Jesse Burlin and Celena Mae (Robison) Smith; m. James Stephen Baldwin, Apr. 7, 1989; 1 child, Melissa. BS, Stephen F. Austin, 1985. Dietetic tech. Pasadena (Tex.) Bayshore Hosp., 1969-70; payroll clk. Seismic Computing Corp., Houston, 1971-72; restaurant mgr., mgr. trainer H. Salt Fish n' Chips, Pasadena, 1972-75; asst. food svc. dir. East Tex. Med. Ctr. Hosp., Tyler, 1990-92, 92—; sales woman Mary Kay Cosmetics, 1995—. Avocations: singing, sewing, cooking, crafts.

BALDWIN, DEWITT CLAIR, JR., physician, educator; b. Bangor, Maine, July 19, 1922; s. DeWitt Clair and Edna Frances (Aikin) B.; m. Michele Albre, Dec. 27, 1957; children: Lisa Anne, Mireille Diane. BA, Swarthmore Coll., 1943; postgrad. Div. Sch., Yale U., 1943-45, MD, 1949; DSc (hon.), North Eastern Ohio U. Coll. of Medicine, 2003. Diplomate Am. Bd. Med. Examiners, Am. Bd. Pediatrics, Am. Bd. Family Practice. Intern, then resident in pediatrics U. Minn. Hosps., Mpls., 1949-51; rsch. fellow Yale Child Study Ctr., New Haven, 1951-52; instr., asst. prof. pediatrics U. Washington Sch. Medicine, Seattle, 1952-57; resident in psychiatry Met. State Hosp., Waltham, Mass., 1957-58; chief resident in psychiatry Mass. Meml. Hosps., Boston, 1958-59; fellow in child psychiatry Boston City Hosp., 1959-61; asst. prof. pediatrics Harvard Med. Sch., Boston, 1961-67; prof., chmn. behavioral scis. and community health U. Conn. Health Ctr., Farmington, 1967-71; prof. chmn. behavioral scis. U. Nev. Sch. Medicine, Reno, 1971-73, dir. health scis. program, 1971-81, prof. psychiatry and behavioral scis., 1971-83, asst. dean rural health, 1977-83, prof. emeritus psychiatry and behavioral scis., 1983—; pres. Earlham Coll. and Earlham Sch. Religion, Richmond, Ind., 1983-84, Connor Prairie Pioneer Settlement Mus., Noblesville, Ind., 1983-84; dir. office edn. rsch. AMA, Chgo., 1985-88, dir. divsn. med. edn., rsch., info., 1988-91, scholar-in-residence, 1991—2002, sr. assoc. Inst. Ethics, 1991—2002, scholar-in-residence Accreditation Coun. for Grad. Med. Edn., 2002—; adj. prof. psychiatry and behavioral scis. Northwestern U. Med. Sch., Chgo., 1986—; adj. prof. med. edn. U. Ill. Coll. Medicine, Chgo., 1988-93; pres. Med. Edn. and Rsch. Assocs., Inc., Chgo., 1992—. Trustee Friends World Coll., Huntington, N.Y., 1980-83; bd. dirs. Nat. League Nursing, N.Y.C., 1981-83, Gt. Lakes Colls. Assn., 1983-84, Am. Rural Health Assn., 1985-87; mem. Nat. Bd. Med. Examiners, 1979-88, Nat. Adv. Coun. Nursing Tng., 1978-82; mem. coun. acad. socs. AAMC, Washington, 1987-94. Author: (with others) Behavioral Sciences and Medical Education, 1983, other books; author, editor: (with others) Interdisciplinary Health Care Teams in Teaching and Practice, 1981, Interdisciplinary Health Team Training, 1978; contbr. over 150 articles to scholarly publs. Recipient Rsch. Career Devel. award USPHS, 1961-67, Louis Gorin award in rural health, 1991, John P. McGovern award Health Scis., 1997; Commonwealth Fund fellow, 1951-52, Milbank Fund fellow, 1968, Rural Health fellow WHO, 1976. Mem. Assn. Behavioral Scis. and Med. Edn. (pres. 1978-79, 90-91), Nev. Bd. Oriental Medicine (pres. 1976-83). Democrat. Mem. Soc. Of Friends. Home: 1550 N Lake Shore Dr Chicago IL 60610 Office: Ste 2000 515 State St Chicago IL 60610 Business E-Mail: dbaldwin@acgme.org.

BALDWIN, DOROTHY LEILA, secondary school educator; b. Irvington, N.J., Feb. 28, 1948; d. Daniel Thomas and Lillian Frances (Wainright) B. BA, Kean Coll., Union, N.J., 1969, MA in Edn. and Humanities, 1971; EdD in Adminstrn. and Supervision, Seton Hall U., 1987, cert. reading specialist, 1979, cert. bus. adminstr., 1985. Tchr., reading coord. St. Paul Apostle Sch. Irvington, 1969-74; tchr. Summit (N.J.) Jr. High Sch., 1975-79; social studies coord. K-9, chmn. dept. 7-9 Summit Pub. schs., 1979-87; social studies supr. Livingston (N.J.) Pub. Schs., 1987; prin. Point Road Sch, Little Silver, N.J., 1987-89; dir. gifted edn. K-12 Clifton, N.J., 1989-90; prin. Sch. Two, Clifton, N.J., 1989-90, Deerfield Sch., Mountainside, 1990-92, Eisenhower Sch., Bridgewater-Raritan, N.J., 1992—. Adj. prof. Fairleigh Dickenson U., NJ; adj. prof. Montclair (N.J.) U.; adj. prof. Passaic County C.C., Morris County C.C.; tchr. adult and cmty. schs.; workshop coord.; cons. in field. Author books; contbr. articles to profl. jours. PTA scholar, 1965. Mem. ASCD, Nat. Assn. Elem. Sch. Prins., Nat. Coun. Social Studies, Am. Assn. Sch. Adminstrs., N.J. Assn. Elem. Sch. Prins., N.J. Prins. Ctr., Somerset County Assn. Elem. Sch. Prins., Phi Delta Kappa, Kappa Delta Pi. Home: 737 River Rd Chatham NJ 07928-1136 Office: Eisenhower Sch Bridgewater NJ 08807

BALDWIN, EDWIN STEEDMAN, lawyer; b. St. Louis, May 5, 1932; s. Richard and Almira (Steedman) B.; m. Margaret Kirkham, July 1, 1958; children: Margaret B. Dozler, Edwin S. Jr., Harold K. AB, Princeton U., 1954; LLM, Harvard U., 1957. Bar: Mo. 1957, U.S. Dist. Ct. (ea. dist.) Mo. 1957. Assoc. Teasdale, Kramer & Vaughan, St. Louis, 1957-64; ptnr. Armstrong Teasdale, LLP, St. Louis, 1965-97, of counsel, 1998—. Fellow Am. Coll. Trust and Estate Counsel, St. Louis Country Club, Noonday Club. Republican. Episcopalian. Avocations: golf, hunting, sailing. Office: Armstrong Teasdale LLP 1 Metropolitan Sq Ste 2600 Saint Louis MO 63102 2740 E mail: tbaldwin@armstrongteasdale.com.

BALDWIN, ELIZABETH ANN, academic administrator; b. Munich, Feb. 28, 1952; d. Charles Orley and Virginia Katherine Baldwin; m. David Eugene Bucher, Sept. 11, 1982 (div. Mar. 31, 2003); 1 child, Gabriel Baldwin Bucher. BS in Biology, SUNY, Cortland, N.Y., 1974; MS in Entomology, U. Ill., 1977; MA in Sci., Tech. and Pub. Policy, George Washington U., 1986. Sr. rsch. asst. in sci. and tech. policy Congl. Rsch. Svc., Washington, 1987—89; rsch. ethics officer Am. Psychol. Assn., Washington, 1989—93, legis. and fed. affairs officer, 1993—95, sr. legis. and fed. affairs officer, 1995—96; pub. policy mgr. Optical Soc. Am., Washington, 1996—2000; dir. fed. rels. U. Calif. Riverside, Washington, 2000—. Mem.: AAAS. Office: University of California Riverside 1608 Rhode Island Ave NW Washington DC 20036 Fax: 202-833-3963. E-mail: elizabeth.baldwin@ucr.edu.

BALDWIN, GEORGE CURRIDEN, physicist, educator; b. Denver, May 5, 1917; s. Harry Lewis and Elizabeth (Watson) B.; m. Winifred M. Gould, Apr. 27, 1952; children— George T., John E., Celia M. BA, Kalamazoo Coll., 1939; MA, U. Ill., 1941, PhD, 1943. Instr. physics U. Ill., Urbana, 1943-44; rsch. assoc. GE, Schenectady, N.Y., 1944-55, nuclear engr. Cin., 1955-57; reactor mgr. Argonne (Ill.) Nat. Lab., 1957-58; physicist Gen. Engring. Lab. GE, Schenectady, 1958-67; adj. prof. nuclear engring. and sci. Rensselaer Poly. Inst., Troy, N.Y., 1964-67, prof., 1967-77, prof. emeritus, 1977—; staff mem. Los Alamos (N.Mex.) Nat. Lab., 1975-87; vis. scientist, 1987-99; ret., 1987. Author: An Introduction to Nonlinear Optics, 1969; contbr. articles on nuclear and radiation physics to sci. publs. Councilman, Niskayuna, N.Y., 1965-69; mem. Zoning Bd., 1969-77. Recipient Disting. Alumnus award Kalamazoo Coll., 1987. Fellow Am. Phys. Soc.; mem. AAAS, Phi Beta Kappa, Sigma Xi, Phi Kappa Phi, Gamma Alpha. Achievements include discovery of nuclear giant dipole resonance; research on gamma-ray lasers; discovery of 1776 Escalante inscription. E-mail: geoc142857@corad.net.

BALDWIN, GEORGE KOEHLER, retired retail executive; b. Cedar Rapids, Iowa, Nov. 17, 1919; s. Nathan and Ada Lillian (Koehler) B. BBA, State U. Iowa, 1942. From office mgr. to mgr. Wapsie Valley Creamery, Cedar Rapids,

Iowa, 1946-60; treas., head payroll, accounts payable, sales audit dept. Armstrong's Inc., Cedar Rapids, 1960-87; also bd. dirs., treas. Armstrong's of Dubuque, Iowa, 1982-87; ret., 1987. Mem. adv. coun. Firstar Club, Firstar Bank, Cedar Rapids; theatre organist, 1961—. Composed and copyrighted for band Kinnick Stadium band march, 1992. Mem. Cedar Rapids Performing Arts Commn.; bd. dirs., pres. Cedar Rapids Cmty. Concert Assn.; pres. State U. of Iowa Concert Band, 1941-42; sec., treas., asst. conductor El Kahir Shrine Band of Cedar Rapids; bd. dirs. Cedar Rapids Stamp Club, 1997-2000; chmn. adminstrv. bd. Trinity United Meth. Ch., 1987-92, head usher and staff parish rels. com. chmn.; apptd. by mayor to Cedar Rapids Mcpl. Band Commn., 1994, vice chmn. 1998—; organist Paramount and Iowa theaters, Cedar Rapids. With U.S. Army, 1942-46, ETO. Decorated Bronze Star medal; named hon. Ky. Col.; George K. Baldwin day proclamation in his honor, Mayor of Cedar Rapids, Apr. 16, 1987. Mem. VFW, Cedar Rapids Consumer Credit Assn. (pres. 1968-69), Am. Theatre Organ Soc. (bd. dirs., treas. Cedar Rapids chpt.), Am. Legion, Rotary, Masons, Shriners (past pres. uniformed units), Rotary Svc. Club (chmn. fellowship com., sgt. of arms), State U. Iowa Pres.'s Club and Alumni Assn. Methodist. Home: 1017 F Ave NW Cedar Rapids IA 52405-2724 E-mail: baldwingeo@aol.com.

BALDWIN, GORDON BREWSTER, law educator, lawyer; b. Binghamton, N.Y., Sept. 3, 1929; s. Schuyler Forbes and Doris Ambeline (Hawkins) B.; m. Helen Louise Hochgraf, Feb., 1958; children: Schuyler, Mary Page. LLB, Cornell U., 1953; BA, Haverford Coll., 1950. Bar: N.Y. 1953, Wis. 1965. Pvt. practice, Rochester and Rome, N.Y., 1953-57; prof. law U. Wis., Madison, 1957-99, Evjue-Bascom profl. law, 1991-99, emeritus prof., 1999—, assoc. dean law, 1968-70, dir. officer edn., 1972-99; of counsel Murphy & Desmond, S.C., Madison, Wis., 1986-95. Chmn. internat. law U.S. Naval War Coll., 1963-64; Fulbright prof., Cairo, 1966-67, Tehran, Iran, 1970-71; lectr. State Dept., Cyprus, 1967, 1969, 1971; counselor internat. law U.S. Dept. State, Washington, 1975-76, cons., 1976-77; vis. prof. Chuo U., Tokyo, 1984, Giessen U., Fed. Republic Germany, 1987, 92, Thommasat U., Thailand, 1997; cons. U.S. Naval War Coll., 1961-65; chmn. screening com. on law Fulbright Program, 1974; mem. constl. law com. Multi-State Bar Exam, 1972-82; chmn. State Pub. Def. Bd., 1980-83, Wis. Elections Bd., 1991-96; cons., rep. Marshall Island Constn. Conv., 1990. Mem. Wis. Bd. Elections, 1991-95, Wis. Land Coun., 1998-2002, Wis. State Ethics Bd., 2000-2003. Ford Found. fellow, 1962-63 Fellow Am. Bar Found.; mem. AAUP (nat. coun. 1975-78, pres. Wis. conf. 1986-87), Bar Assn. (vice chmn. sect. on individual rights 1973-75), Fulbright Alumni Assn. (dir. 1979-82), Am. Law Inst., Order of Coif, Madison Club, Madison Lit. Club (pres. 1985-86, 2000-03), Univ. Club, Rotary (pres. Madison 1980, dist. gov. 1999-00), Phi Beta Kappa. Home: 3958 Plymouth Cir Madison WI 53705-5212 Office: U Wis 975 Bascom Mall Sch Law Madison WI 53706-1399 E-mail: gbaldwin@facstaff.wisc.edu.

BALDWIN, HAROLD SCOTT, pediatrician; b. Honolulu, Md., Dec. 22, 1954; MD, U. Va. Sch. Medicine, 1981. Diplomate Am. Bd. Pediat. Intern U. Rochester/Strong Meml. Hosp., NY, 1982—86, resident in pediat.; assoc. prof. Children's Hosp., Phila.; fellow in pediatric cardiology U. Iowa Coll. Med., Iowa City, 1986—90; prof. pediatrics, cell and devel. biology Vanderbilt U. Med. Ctr., Nashville; vice chmn. for lab. rsch. Vanderbilt Children's Hosp., Nashville. Recipient Established Investigator award, Am. Heart Assn., 1995. Office: Vanderbilt U Med Ctr D2220 Med Ctr North Nashville TN 37232 E-mail: scott.baldwin@vanderbilt.edu.

BALDWIN, HENRY FURLONG, banker; b. Balt., Jan. 15, 1932; s. Henry du Pont and Margaret (Taylor) B.; div.; children: Mary Stevenson, Severn Eyre. AB, Princeton U., 1954. With Merc.-Safe Deposit & Trust Co., Balt., 1956—2001; pres. Merc. Bankshares Corp. and Merc.-Safe Deposit & Trust Co., Balt., 1970-76, chmn., CEO, 1976-2001; chmn. Merc. Bankshares Corp., Balt., 2001—03. Bd. dirs. W.R. Grace & Co., Merc. Bankshares Corp., Merc. Safe Deposit & Trust Co., Wills Group, Inc., NASDAQ, Platinum Underwriters Holdings; mem. bd. govs. Nat. Assn. Securities Dealers, Inc. Trustee Johns Hopkins Hosp., chmn., 1989-94; trustee Johns Hopkins U., Marine Corps Heritage Found., Marine Corps U., Va. Hist. Soc. With USMC, 1954-56. Office: Merc Bankshares Corp PO Box 1477 Baltimore MD 21203-1477

BALDWIN, IRENE S. corporate executive, real estate investor; b. Didge City, Kans., Sept. 8, 1939; d. Albert A. McMichael and Eleanor L. (Johnson) McMichael McGrath; m. Miles Edward Baldwin, June 30, 1961. BS, Friends U., 1961. Dress designer, Wichita, 1959-61; social worker Sedgwick County, Kans., 1963-65; owner motel chain Kans., 1965—; comml. and agrl. real estate investor, 1971—. Owner motel chain, Kans., 1965—; comml. and agrl. real estate investor, 1971—; corp. sec.-treas. Baldwin, Inc., Kans., 1970—, fin. advisor, 1970—; pvt. practice fin. cons., Colby, Kans., 1975—; founder, advisor Charitable Found., Kans., 1980—; fundraiser various charitable orgns., 1982—; pvt. placement of homeless animals, Kans. and Nebr., 1965—; helped develop 1st artificial front leg for canines, 1985. Contbr. articles to profl. jours. Fundraiser various charitable orgns., 1982—; pvt. placement of homeless animals, Kans. and Nebr., 1965—. Avocations: horseback riding, hiking, travel, sewing, drawing. Address: 2320 S Range Ave Colby KS 67701-9056

BALDWIN, JAMES EDWARD, lawyer, city administrator; b. Grand Rapids, Mich., Sept. 9, 1956; s. Bradford James and Emily Gertrude Baldwin; m. Mary Margaret Roberts, Sept. 6, 1986; children: James Patrick, Catherine Elizabeth. BS, Western Mich. U., Kalamazoo, 1984; JD, U. Cin., 1992. Bar: Ohio. Mgr. human resources Gold Circle Stores, Columbus, Ohio, 1985-86; prodn. supr. Gen. Dynamics and Systems, Lima, Ohio, 1986-89; atty., sole practitioner, Cin., 1992—; dir. telecomms. City of Lebanon, Ohio, 1997—. Republican. Roman Catholic. Avocations: sports, history, travel. Home: 9036 Country View Ln Loveland OH 45140-1417 Office: City of Lebanon 50 S Broadway St Lebanon OH 45036-1777

BALDWIN, JAN LINSE, family practice physician; b. Eau Claire, Wis., Jan. 10, 1957; m. R. Larry Baldwin, Aug. 16, 1986. BA in Psychology, U. Minn., 1979, MD, 1983. Diplomate Am. Bd. Family Practice. Resident in family practice U. Wis., Appleton, 1983-86; physician Medford (Wis.) Clinic, 1986-91, Duluth Clinic, Hibbing, Minn., 1991—. Recipient cert. of appreciation Wis. Assn. Perinatal Care, 1989, Range Women's Advs. Annual Recognition award, 1997. Mem. AMA, Am. Acad. Family Physicians, Minn. Acad. Family Physicians (bd. dirs. 1992-94), Minn. Med. Assn., Minn. Women Physicians. Office: Duluth Clinic-Hibbing 730 E 34th St Hibbing MN 55746-2341

BALDWIN, JANICE MURPHY, lawyer; b. Bridgeport, Conn., July 16, 1926; d. William Henry and Josephine Gertrude (McKenna) Murphy; m. Robert Edward Baldwin, July 31, 1954; children: Jean Baldwin Grossman, Robert William, Richard Edward, Nancy Baldwin Kitsos. AB, U. Conn., 1948; MA, Mt. Holyoke Coll., 1950; postgrad., U. Manchester, Eng., 1950-51; MA, Tufts U., 1952; JD, U. Wis., 1971. Bar: Wis. 1971, U.S. Dist. Ct. (we. dist.) Wis. 1971. Staff atty. legis. coun. State of Wis., Madison, 1971-74, sr. staff atty., 1975-94; pvt. practice Madison, 1994—. Atty. adviser HUD, Washington, 1974—75, Washington, 1978—79. Fulbright fellow, 1950-51. Mem. AAUW, NOW, LWV (sec. 1996-99, v.p., 1999-2001, bd. dirs. Dane County 1996-2003, exec. com. 1997-2003), U.S. and Wis. Women's Polit. Caucus, Legal Assn. for Women (chmn. Marygold Meili award com. 1997-99), Wis. Bar Assn. (pres. govt. lawyers divsn. 1985-87, bd. govs. 1985-89, treas. 1987-89, participation of women in bar com. 1987-98, professionalism com. 1990-97, bd. bar examiners rev. 1990-94, law-related edn. com. 1992-95, govt. lawyers divsn. 1981—), Dane County Bar Assn. (legis. com. 1980-81, long range planning com. 1990-97, law for the pub. com. 1993-94), Wis. Women's Network, U. Wis. Univ. League, Older Women's League, Fulbright Assn. Home and Office: 125 Nautilus Dr Madison WI 53705-4329

BALDWIN, JASON HOLT, secondary school educator; b. Clarksville, Tenn., Oct. 6, 1974; s. William Elmo Baldwin and Faith Hancock Marshall; m. Alison Carmen Walker, Oct. 25, 1997; children: Joshua David, Kylie Delaney. BS English Secondary Edn., Appalachian State U., 1996; postgrad., U. N.C., Greensboro. Cert. English secondary edn. grades 9-12 N.C. Dept. Pub. Instrn. Asst. mgr., customer svc. rep. Blockbuster Video, Greensboro, NC, 1996—99; program tng. coord. Greensboro Youth Coun., Greensboro, NC, 1996—99; tchr. Guilford County Schs., Greensboro, NC, 1997—. Mem.: Guilford County Assn. Educators, N.C. Assn. Educators, Nat. Edn. Assn. Methodist. Avocations: reading, writing, using computers. Office: Weaver Edn Ctr 300 S Spring St Greensboro NC 27401-2343 E-mail: jhbaldwin@netmcr.com.

BALDWIN, JEFFREY KENTON, lawyer, educator; b. Palestine, Ill., Aug. 8, 1954; s. Howard Keith and Annabelle Lee (Kirts) B.; m. Patricia Ann Mathews, Aug. 23, 1975; children: Matthew, Katy, Timothy, Philip R. BS summa cum laude, Ball State U., 1976; JD cum laude, Ind. U., 1979. Bar: Ind. 1979, U.S. Dist. Ct. (so. dist.) Ind. 1979, U.S. Ct. Appeals (7th cir.) 1979, U.S. Dist. Ct. (no. dist.) Ind. 1984. Majority leader's staff Ind. Senate, Indpls., 1976; instr. Beer Sch. Real Estate, Indpls., 1977-78, Am. Inst. Paralegal Studies, Indpls., 1987—; dep. Office Atty. Gen., Indpls., 1979-81; mng. ptnr. Baldwin & Baldwin, Danville, Ind., 1979—. Agt. Nat. Attys. Title Assurance Fund, Vevay, Ind., 1983—; officer, bd. dirs. Baldwin Realty, Inc., Danville; conf. participant White House Conf. on Small Bus. (Ind. meeting 1994), congl. appointee, 1995; bd. dirs. Small Bus. Coun. Bd. dirs. Hendricks Civic Theatre, Inc.; organizer, Hendricks County Young Republicans, 1972; sec. Hendricks County Rep. Com., 1978-84; bd. dirs. Hendricks County Assn. for Retarded Citizens, Danville, 1982-86; cons. Hendricks County Right for Life, Brownsburg, Ind., 1984—; mem. philanthropy adv. com. Ball State U., Muncie, Ind., 1987—; judge Hendricks County unit Am. Cancer Soc., 1987; coordinator region 2 Young Leaders for Mutz, Indpls., 1987-88; cubmaster WaPaPh dist. Boy Scouts Am., 1988, S.M.E. chmn., 1988-89; steering com. Ind. Lawyers Bush/Quayle; founder, chmn. Christians for Positive Reform; candidate for Congress 7th Congl. Dist. of Ind.; del. to Annual Conf. South Ind. Conf. of United Meth. Ch., 1993, 95-98, 2000; host com. Midwest Rep. Leadership Conf., 1997; dist. coord. Hoosier Famiies for John Price for U.S. Senate; advisor John Price for Gov., 1999-2000; v.p. Danville Little League Baseball, 1998—. Recipient Presdl. award of honor Danville Jaycees, 1980; named hon. sec. State Ind., 1980. Mem. ABA, Ind. Bar Assn., Hendricks County Bar Assn., Indpls. Bar Assn., Internat. Platform Assn., Nat. Assn. Realtors, Ind. Assn. Realtors, Met. Indpls. Bd. Realtors (Hendricks County div.), Federalist Soc., Ind. Farm Bur., Nat. Fedn. Ind. Bus., Ind. C. of C., Danville C. of C. (sec. 1986), Moot Ct. Soc., Blue Key, Phi Soc. Methodist. Home: PO Box 63 Danville IN 46122-0063 E-mail: jbbfc@aol.com.

BALDWIN, JEFFREY NATHAN, pharmacy educator; b. Sidney, NY, Dec. 20, 1947; s. Reverdy Ernest and Helen Elizabeth (Humphrey) B.; m. Suzanne Marie Smith, Dec. 27, 1969; children: Paul Kevin, Gregory Michael. AS, Jamestown C.C., 1967; BS in Pharmacy summa cum laude, SUNY, Buffalo, 1970; DPharm, U. Ky., 1973. Lic. pharmacist Ky., Nebr. Resident in pharmacy U. Ky.-A.B. Chandler Med. Ctr., Lexington, 1970-73; pharmacy faculty U. Nebr. Med. Ctr., Coll. Pharmacy, Omaha, 1973—; med. faculty U. Nebr. Med. Ctr., Coll. Medicine, Omaha, 1977—. Pres., co-founder Nebr. Coun. for Continuing Pharm. Edn., Inc., Omaha, 1980-82. Author: (chpts.) Points of Light: A Guide for Assisting Chemically Dependent Health Professional Students, 1996; sect. editor: Applied Therapeutics: The Clinical Use of Drugs, 1995, 2001; contbr. 41 chpts. in books, 28 articles to profl. jours. Chmn. Nebr. Pharmacist Recovery Network, Lincoln, Nebr., 1988—; scout leader Mid Am. Coun., Boy Scouts, Omaha, 1983—, chair tng. com., 1997—98, trustee, 2000—, exec. com., 2001—; counselor Camp CoHoLo, Gretna, Nebr., 1985—98, 2000, 2002. Recipient Leadership award, McKesson, 1995. Fellow Am. Pharm. Assn. (Merit award 1995), Am. Soc. Health-Sys. Pharmacists (chair pediatric pharmacy spl. interest group 1977-78), Am. Assn. Colls. Pharmacy (chair substance abuse spl. interest group 1988-97, chair pharmacy practice sect. 1998-99), Nebr. Pharmacists Assn. (pres.-elect 1994-95, pres. 1995-96, chmn. bd. 1996-97, NARD Leadership award 1995) Avocations: travel, bicycling, backpacking, camping, whitewater rafting. Office: 982135 Nebr Med Ctr Omaha NE 68198-2135 E-mail: jbaldwin@unmc.edu.

BALDWIN, JOHN CHARLES, surgeon, researcher; b. Ft. Worth; BA summa cum laude, Harvard U., 1971; MD, Stanford U., 1975; MA Privatim (hon.), Yale U., 1989. Diplomate Am. Bd. Internal Medicine, Am. Bd. Surgery, Am. Bd. Thoracic Surgery. Fellow in medicine Harvard Med. Sch., Boston, 1975-77; fellow in surgery, resident in surgery Mass. Gen. Hosp., 1977-81; resident in cardiothoracic surgery Stanford (Calif.) U., 1981-82, chief resident cardiothoracic surgery, 1983, asst. prof., 1984-87; dir. heart-lung transplantation transplant rsch. lab. Stanford U., 1986-87; prof. surgery and chief cardiothoracic surgery Yale U., New Haven, 1988-94; cardiothoracic-surgeon-in chief Yale-New Haven Hosp.; DeBakey/Bard prof., chmn. Baylor Coll. Medicine, Houston, 1994-98; sr. attending physician, chief surg. svcs. Meth. Hosp., Houston, 1994-98; sr. attending physician, surgeon in chief Ben Taub Gen. Hosp., Houston, 1994; dean med. sch., v.p. health affairs Dartmouth Coll., 1998—. Bd. dirs. United Network Organ Sharing, 1984-87; mem. clin. rsch. com. ad hoc rsch. grant rev. Cystic Fibrosis Found.; trustee New Eng. Organ Bank, 1988; mem. solid organ transplant com. Blue Cross & Blue Shield of Conn., 1990-94; mem. sci. adv. bd. Alexion Pharms., Inc., 1991-94; bd. dirs. Baylor Coll. Medicine Healthcare, Inc.; mem. adv. bd. Donate Life Found.; mem. exec. faculty Baylor Coll. of Medicine, pres.'s coun.; bd. dirs. New England chpt. Transplant Recipients Internat. Orgn., 1992-94. Co-editor: Thoracic Surgery, Oxford Textbook of Surgery, 1989—; assoc. editor Jour. Applied Cardiology, 1985-92; editorial bd. Jour. Thoracic and Cardiovascular Surgery, 1990-97, Transplantation, 1990—, Transplantation Sci., 1992-95, Andromeda Interactive Ltd., The Cardiovasc. System Interactive Teaching Program, 1993—; contbr. numerous articles and book chpts. in field. Mem. Harvard Club Schs. Com., Harvard Coll. Fund, Harvard U. Undergrad. Admissions Interview Com.; fellow Timothy Dwight Coll. Yale U., Yale U. Art Gallery Assocs.; mem. appointments and promotions com. Sch. Medicine, Yale U., 1991-94, bd. dirs. Neighborhood Music Sch. New Haven., 1989-92; bd. overseers Harvard U., 1995—; bd. permanent officers Yale U., 1988-94. John Harvard scholar, 1969, 70, Wendell scholar Harvard U., 1969, Rhodes scholar Oxford U., 1971, Alumni scholar Stanford Sch. Medicine, 1974 ; medalist Gothenburg (Sweden) Thoracic Soc., 1985; recipient Medaille de la Ville de Bordeaux French Thoracic Soc., 1987, travelling lectureship, 1988, Master Tchr. award Cardiovascular Revs. & Reports, 1990; travelling fellow Australia and New Zealand chpt., ACS, 1989; traveling lectureship, 1989. Fellow ACP, ACS, Royal Coll. Surgeons (Eng., traveling lectr. 1989), Am. Coll. Angiology, Am. Coll. Cardiology (mem. transplantation com. 1991-94, chmn. task force cardiac donor procurement Bethesda Conf. 1992), Am. Coll. Surgeons (bd. govs. 1993-97), Am. Coll. Chest Physicians, Mass. Med. Soc.; mem. AMA, AAAS, Am. Assn. Thoracic Surgery (mem. com. grad. edn. thoracic surgery 1992-97, chmn. Evarts A. Graham Meml. Traveling Fellowship com. 1993-99), Am. Soc. Transplant Surgeons (com. on heart transplantation 1986-89, adv. com. in issues 1989—, chmn. subcom. on heart transplantation, physician payment reform commn. 1989-92), Nat. Heart, Lung and Blood Inst. (cons. divsn. extramural affairs rev. br. 1990—), Assn. Acad. Surgery, Am. Physiol. Soc., Am. Heart Assn. (mem. rsch. grant peer rev. subcom 1984-87, coun. circulation, cert. of appreciation for outstanding svc. 1986), Am. Surg. Assn., Am. Thoracic Soc., Am. Soc. Artificial Internal Organs, Am. Soc. Extracorporeal Tech., Am. Assn. Lab. Animal Sci., Am. Organ Transplant Assn., Am. Venous Forum, Internat. Soc. Heart and Lung Transplantation (chmn. program com. 1988), Internat. Assn. Cardiac Biol. Implants, Internat. Fedn. Surg. Colls., Internat. Soc. Cardiovasc. Surgery, Internat. Soc. Cardio-Thoracic Surgeons (pres. 1999), Internat. Soc. for Heart Rsch. (mem. Am. sect.), Internat. Soc. for Artificial Organs, Mediterranean Assn. for Cardiology and Cardiac Surgery, New Century Soc., Thoracic Surgery Found. for Rsch. and Edn., Norman E. Shumway Surg. Soc., New Eng. Surg. Soc., Pan Am. Med. Assn. (coun. on organ transplantation), North Am. Soc. Pacing and Electrophysiology, Societe Internat. de Chirurgie, Royal Soc. Medicine, Soc. Univ. Surgeons, Thoracic Surgery Dirs. Assn. (chmn. curriculum com. transplantation 1993-94), Transplantation Soc., Assn. Alumni of Magdalen Coll. Oxford U., Assn. Rhodes Scholars, Acad. Surg. Rsch., Assn. Surg. Edn., Assn. Program Dirs. in Surgery, Conn. Thoracic Soc., Harris County Med. Soc., Calif. Med. Assn., Calif. Thoracic Soc., Calif. Thoracic Soc. Respiratory Care Assembly, No. Calif. Cystic Fibrosis Found., So. Calif. Transplant Soc., Conn. Med. Soc., Conn. Soc. Am. Bd. Surgeons, Mass. Med. Soc., N.Y. Soc. Thoracic Surgery, Harvard Med. Alumni Assn. (assoc.), Soc. Crit. Care Medicine, Soc. Thoracic Surgeons, Southeastern Surg. Congress, Southern Surg. Assn., Southwestern Surg. Congress, Tex. Surg. Soc., Halsted Soc., Houston Surg. Soc. Soc. for Organ Sharing, San Francisco Surg. Soc., Santa Clara Med. Soc., Stanford Med. Alumni Assn., Stanford Club Conn., Harvard Clubs San Francisco, Peninsula, N.Y.C., So. Conn., Houston, Boston, Mory's Assn., New Haven Lawn Club, Inner Quad Stanford U., The Hasty Pudding Club - Inst. 1770, Quinnipiack Club, Forum World Affairs, Ambs. Roundtable, Oxford Soc., Phi Beta Kappa, others. Office: Dartmouth Coll Dartmouth Med Sch Office Dean 1 Rope Ferry Rd Hanover NH 03755-1404

BALDWIN, JOHN EDWIN, chemistry educator; b. Berwyn, Ill., Sept. 10, 1937; s. Francis Miller and Irville (Miller) B.; m. Anne Kruesi Nordlander, Sept. 23, 1961; children— Claire Miller, John Nordlander, Wesley Hale. AB summa cum laude, Dartmouth Coll., 1959; PhD, Calif. Inst. Tech., 1963. Mem. chemistry faculty U. Ill., 1962-68; prof. chemistry U. Oreg., Eugene, 1968-84; dean Coll. Arts and Scis., 1975-80; prof. chemistry Syracuse U., N.Y., 1984-2000, disting. prof., 2000—. Cons. Stauffer Chem. Co., Office Sci. and Tech., NIH; 150th anniversary vis. prof. Chalmers U., 1990. Author: Experimental Organic Chemistry, 1965, also articles.; Adv. bd.: Organic Reactions. Guggenheim fellow, 1967; Sloan fellow, 1966-68; recipient Sr. U.S. Scientist award Alexander von Humboldt Found., 1974-75, Syracuse Sect. award Am. Chem. Soc., 1997. Home: 5 Brattle Rd Syracuse NY 13203-2803

BALDWIN, JOHN WESLEY, history educator; b. Chgo., July 13, 1929; s. Edward N. and H. Gladys (McDaniel) B.; m. Jenny Jochens, Dec. 24, 1954; children: Peter, Ian, Birgit (dec.), Christopher. BA, Wheaton Coll., 1950; MA, Pa. State U., 1951; PhD, Johns Hopkins, 1956. Instr., then asst. prof. U. Mich., Ann Arbor, 1956-61; mem. faculty Johns Hopkins U., Balt., 1961—, prof. history, 1966—, Charles Homer Haskins prof. history, 1986—, prof. emeritus, 2001—; prof. e'tranger Coll. de France, 1984, 95. Author: The Medieval Theories of the Just Price, 1959, Masters, Princes and Merchants, 2 vols, 1970, The Scholastic Culture of the Middle Ages, 1971, City on the Seine: Paris under Louis IX, 1226-1270, 1975, The Government of Philip Augustus, 1986 (French transl. 1991), Les Registres de Philippe Auguste, 1992, The Language of Sex: Five Voices from Northern France Around 1200, 1994, (French translation) Les Languages de l'amour, 1997, Aristocratic Life in Medieval France: The Romances of Jean Renart and Gerbert de Montreuil, 1190-1230, 2000, Le Livre de Terres et de Revenues de Pierre du Thillay, 2002; editor (with Richard Goldthwaite) Universities in Politics: Case Studies from the Late Middle Ages and Early Modern Period, 1972. Decorated Chevalier de la légion d'honneur (France), Chevalier Ordre des Arts et des Lettres (France); Prix Litteraire Etats-Unis-France, 1992; Guggenheim fellow, 1960-61, 83-84, Howard fellow, 1960-61, Fulbright fellow, 1953-55, 65-66, Sr. fellow NEH, 1972-73, 90-91; grantee Am. Coun. Learned Socs., 1965-66. Fellow Medieval Acad. Am. (v.p. 1994, pres. 1996-97, Charles Homer Haskins medal 1990), Am. Acad. Arts and Scis., Brit. Acad. (corr.); mem. Soc. for French Hist. Studies, Royal Danish Acad. Scis. and Letters (fgn.), Am. Hist. Assn., Commn. Internat. de Diplomatique (hon.), Acad. Inscriptions et Belles Lettres (France) (assoc. fgn.), Société Nationale des Antiquaires de France (assoc. corr. fgn.). Office: Johns Hopkins U Dept Of History Baltimore MD 21218

BALDWIN, KATHRYN LEIGH, psychologist, educator, consultant; b. Madisonville, Ky., Nov. 15, 1972; d. George Mark and Linda Kay Sandidge; m. Jeffery Donald Baldwin, Dec. 13, 1997; 1 child, Tyler James. Ph.D., Ed.S., U. of Ky., Lexington, KY., 1997—2002; M.S., Ea. Ky. U., Richmond, KY., 1994—95; B.A., Western Ky. U., Bowling Green, KY., 1992—93. Psychologist KY. Asst. prof. Austin Peay State U., Clarksville, Tenn., 2001—; psychologist Logan County Pub. Schools, Russellville, Ky., 2002—; clin. psychology intern Jefferson Co. Internship Consortium, Louisville, Ky., 2000—01; sch. psychologist Fayette Co. Pub. Schools, Lexington, Ky., 1998—2000. Rsch. cons. Rosalynn Carter Inst. for Human Devel., Americus, Ga., 2002—02; student editl. bd. mem. Sch. Psychology Quar., 2000—01; rsch. asst. U. of Ky. Human Devel. Inst., Lexington, Ky., 1997—98. Presenter (tennessee conference) Practical Considerations for School Crisis Response Teams, (conference) 2000 Leading Teens in the New Millennium, co-author (article- alternate assessment practices) The Journal of Special Education, (multiple federal grant applications) Primary Prevention And Early Intervention. Bd. mem. New Beginnings Bluegrass, Inc., Lexington, Ky., 1999—2000. Recipient Golden Key Nat. Honor Soc., 1993-Present, Nat. Dean's List, 1991-1993. Mem.: NASP, APA. Home: 458 Bamburg Dr Clarksville TN 37040 Personal E-mail: leigh_psych@charter.net.

BALDWIN, LIONEL VERNON, retired university president; b. Beaumont, Tex., May 30, 1932; s. Eugene B. and Wanda (Wiley) B.; m. Kathleen Flanagan, Sept. 3, 1955; children: Brian, Michael, Diane, Daniel. BS, U. Notre Dame, 1954; SM, MIT, 1955; PhD, Case Inst. Tech., 1959. Rsch. engr. Nat. Adv. Com. Aeros., Ohio, 1957-59; unit head NASA, 1959-61; asso. prof. engring. Colo. State U., 1961-64; acting dean Coll. of Engring., 1964-65, dean and prof., 1966-84; pres. Nat. Tech. U., Fort Collins, 1984—2000; ret. Served to capt. USAF, 1955-57. Recipient award for plasma research NASA, 1964, Kenneth Andrew Roe award Am. ASsn. Engrin. Soc., 1996 Fellow Am. Soc. Engring. Edn. (chmn. engring. deans coun.); mem. ASME, IEEE, NSPE, Sigma Xi, Tau Beta Pi, Sigma Pi Sigma. Achievements include patentee apparatus for increasing ion engine beam density. Home: 1900 Sequoia St Fort Collins CO 80525-1540 E-mail: lionelvbld@attbi.com.

BALDWIN, MARIE HUNSUCKER, retired educator; b. Dallas, Dec. 22, 1923; d. Clyde Augustus and Charlotte (Moore) Hunsucker; m. Brewster Baldwin, Aug. 20, 1946 (dec. July 1992); children: Jean Baldwin McLevedge, David, Stephen, Christopher. BS in Edn., Tex. Tech. U., 1944; MFA in Writing, Norwich U., 1988. Tchr. Pub. Sch., Corpus Christi, Tex., 1944-45, Presbyn. Day Sch., Corpus Christi, 1945-46, Pub. Sch., Moriah, N.Y., 1964-66; field dir. Vt. Girl Scout Coun., Burlington, 1966-78; ret. Vice chair Vt. State Dem. Com., Montpelier, 1976-80; apptd. mem. Gov.'s Adult Edn. Coun., 1985-89; founder, pres. Vt. Caths. for Free Choice, 1989—; elected Justice of the Peace, Middlebury, Vt., 1989—. Mem. ACLU (bd. 1984-90), AAUW, LWV (founder, pres. 1952-56), Cath. Daus. Am., Bus. and Profl. Women. Avocations: creative writing, walking, reading.

BALDWIN, MARK ALAN, communications consultant, writer; b. Sheboygan, Wis., June 13, 1958; s. Robert Franklin and Lucille Bertha (Karsteadt) B. BA, U. Wis., La Crosse, 1980. Pub./client rels. specialist Cap-Rock-Walworth, Janesville, Wis., 1981-82; energy advisor Madison (Wis.) Gas & Electric, 1982-85; devel. specialist WHA-TV, Madison, 1985-89; devel. assoc., editor San Francisco AIDS Found., 1989-92; dir. found. rels. Sierra Club Legal Def. Fund, San Francisco, 1992-94; devel. dir. Marin Cons. Corps, San Rafael, Calif., 1995-96; dir. comms. Merritt Cmty. Capital Corp., Oakland, Calif., 1996—. Fundraising cons. Brothertown Indian Nation, Woodruff, Wis., 1980—. Author: (brochure) Winds of Change, 1987. Home: 1935 Clay St Apt 102 San Francisco CA 94109-3432 Office: Merritt Cmty Capital Corp 1736 Franklin St Ste 600 Oakland CA 94612-3423 E-mail: baldwin1@merrittcap.org.

BALDWIN, PETER ARTHUR, psychologist, educator, author, minister; b. Andover, Mass., Apr. 7, 1932; s. Alfred Graham and Katherine (Ashworth) B.; m. Carolyn Whitmore, Sept. 3, 1955; children: Sarah MacDonald Baldwin-Welcome, Judith Helen Baldwin-Gleason, Robert Henry. BA, Middlebury Coll., 1955; S.T.B., Boston U., 1959, PhD, 1964; student, New Coll., U. London, 1957-58. Lic. psychologist, N.H.; approved cons. in clin. hypnosis, Am. Soc. Clin. Hypnosis. Ordained to ministry Unitarian-Universalist Ch., 1959; pastor 2d Ch., Boston, 1955-57, in Dighton, Mass., 1958-62; religious counselor M.I.T., 1959-63; exec. dir. Liberal Religious Youth, Unitarian Universalist Assn., 1963-66; asst. prof. Crane Theol. Sch., Tufts U., 1965-67, Meadville Theol. Sch., U. Chgo., 1967-73; pastor All Souls 1st Universalist Soc., Chgo., 1971-73; assoc. prof. psychology New Eng. Coll., Henniker, N.H., 1973-74; vis. assoc. prof. psychology Colby-Sawyer Coll., New London, N.H., 1974-76; assoc. prof. dept. clin. psychology Antioch-New Eng. Grad. Sch., Keene, N.H., 1976—; pvt. practice, 1976—. Dir. Sr. High and Family Insts., Rowe, Mass., 1967-74; Nat. Edn. Conf. lectr. Williston Acad., 1967; Judy lectr., Omaha, 1970; invited speaker 5th Internat. Congress on Gestalt Therapy, Valencia, Spain, 1993. Recipient; Disting. Svc. Antioch New Eng. Grad. Sch., 1994, New Hampshire Psychological Assn., Margaret M. Riggs Disting. Contribution award, 1995. Fellow: ISDF, N.H. Psychol. Assn. (pres. 1980—81, 1988—90); mem.: APA, Unitarian- Universalists Mins. Assn., Liberal Religious Youth (life). Democrat. Home: 113 Pancake Hill Rd Gilmanton NH 03237 Office: Univ Assocs in Psychology 222 West St Keene NH 03431-2455

BALDWIN, RALPH BELKNAP, retired manufacturing company executive, astronomer; b. Grand Rapids, Mich., June 6, 1912; s. Melvin D. and Julie (Belknap) B.; m. Lois Virginia Johnston, Aug. 3, 1940; children: Melvin Dana

II, Pamela, Bruce Belknap. BS, U. Mich., 1934, MS, 1935, PhD, 1937, LLD (hon.), 1975; ScD (hon.), Grand Valley State U., 1989, Aquinas Coll., 1999. Asst. dept. astronomy U. Mich., 1935-36, U. Pa., 1937-38; instr. dept. astronomy Northwestern U., 1938-42; lectr. Adler Planetarium, Chgo., 1940-42; sr. physicist Applied Physics Lab. Johns Hopkins, Silver Spring, Md., 1942-46, cons. East Grand Rapids, Mich., 1946-47; acting supt. schs. East Grand Rapids, 1947; prodn. mgr. Oliver Machinery Co., Grand Rapids, 1947-56, dir., 1948-87, successively personnel dir., prodn. mgr., sec., 1949-56, v.p., 1956-70, pres., 1970-84, chmn. bd., 1984-87. Chmn. bd. Internat. Woodworking Machinery and Furniture Supply Fair-U.S.A., 1969-70, 77-78 Author: The Face of the Moon, 1949, The Measure of the Moon, 1963, The Moon— A Fundamental Survey, 1966, The Deadly Fuze: Secret Weapon of World War II, 1980, They Never Knew What Hit Them, 1999; contbr. articles to profl. jours. Recipient Presdl. Cert. of Merit, 1947, U.S. Naval Bur. Ordnance award, 1945, U.S. Army Chief of Ordnance award, 1945, Disting. Alumnus award U. Mich., 1967, Woodworking and Furniture Digest award Forest Products Rsch. Soc., 1973, J. Lawrence Smith medal Nat. Acad. Scis., 1979, G.K. Gilbert award Geol. Soc. Am., 1986, Disting. Alumni award Ctrl. H.S., Grand Rapids, Mich., 1997. Fellow AAAS, Am. Geophys. Union, Meteoritical Soc. (Leonard medal 1986, Barringer medal 2000), Am. Acad. Arts and Scis.; mem. Am. Astron. Soc., Royal Astron. Soc. Can. (hon.), Grand Rapids Mus. Assn., NAM (dir. 1963-64), Employers Assn. Grand Rapids (pres. 1960-64), Woodworking Machinery Mfrs. Assn. (pres. 1964-68). Home: 1757 Marsh Run Naples FL 34109 E-mail: drrbb@yahoo.com.

BALDWIN, ROBERT EDWARD, economics educator; b. Niagara Falls, N.Y., July 12, 1924; s. Gilbert and Margaret (Ostman) B.; m. Janice Murphy, July 31, 1954; children: Jean, Robert, Richard, Nancy. AB, U. Buffalo, 1945; PhD, Harvard U., 1950. Instr., then asst. prof. econs. Harvard, 1950-57; asso. prof., then prof. econs. UCLA, 1957-64; prof. econs. U. Wis. at Madison, 1964-97, F.W. Taussig research prof., 1974-97, Hilldale prof., 1982-97, prof. emeritus, 1997—, chmn. econ. dept., 1975-79. Chief economist Office Spl. Trade Rep. Exec. Office of President, 1963—64; vis. prof. Brookings Instn., Washington, 1967—68, U.S. Dept. Labor, 1975—76, World Bank, 1978—79; mem. adv. bd. Inst. Internat. Econs.; chmn. social systems Rsch. Inst., 1986—89; rsch. assoc. Nat. Bur. Econ. Rsch., 1982—, Ctr. Econ. Policy Rsch., 1994—97; chair panel on fgn. trade stats. NAS, 1989—91; mem. external adv. panel to dir. gen. World Trade Orgn., 2001—. Author: Economic Development and Export Growth, 1966, Nontariff Distortions of International Trade, 1970, Foreign Trade Regimes and Economic Development: The Philippines, 1975, The Inefficiency of Trade Policy, 1982, Polit. Econ. U.S. Import Policy, 1985, Trade Policy in a Changing World Economy, 1988; co-author: Economic Development, 1957, Disease and Economic Development, 1973, The Political Economy of U.S.-Taiwan Trade, 1997, Congressional Trade Votes: From NAFTA Approval to Fast-Track Defeat, 2000; mem. bd. editors Econs. and Politics, Jour. Asian Econs., Atlantic Econ. Jour., Pakistan Devel. Rev., World Economy; editor: Trade Policy and Empirical Analysis, 1984, Empirical Studies of Commercial Policy, 1991; co-editor: The Structure and Evolution of U.S. Trade Policy, 1984, Current U.S. Trade Policy Analysis, Agenda and Administration, 1986, Issues in US-European Community Trade Relations, 1988, The Uruguay Round and Beyond, 1991, Geography and Ownership as Bases for Economic Accounting, 1988. Written in his honor: (Ronald Jones and Anne Krueger, eds.) The Political Economy of International Trade, 1990. Fellow Am. Acad. Arts and Scis.; mem. Am. Econ. Assn., Internat. Trade and Fin. Assn. (pres. 1992), Midwest Econ. Assn. (pres. 1994), Coun. on Fgn. Rels., Conf. on Rsch. in Income and Wealth. Home: 125 Nautilus Dr Madison WI 53705-4329 E-mail: rebaldwi@facstaff.wisc.edu.

BALDWIN, ROBERT LESH, biochemist, educator; b. Madison, Wis., Sept. 30, 1927; s. Ira Lawrence and Mary (Lesh) B.; m. Anne Theodora Norris, Aug. 28, 1965; children: David Norris, Eric Lawrence. BA, U. Wis., 1950; D.Phil. (Rhodes scholar), Oxford (Eng.) U., 1954. Asst. prof., then asso. prof. biochemistry U. Wis., 1955-59; mem. faculty Stanford, 1959—, prof. biochemistry, 1964-98, prof. emeritus, 1998—, chmn. dept., 1989-94. Vis. prof. Collège de France, Paris, 1972, Tsinghua U., Beijing, 2002; mem. adv. panel biochemistry and biophysics NSF, 1974—76; mem. NIH study sect. molecular and cellular biophysics, 1984—88. Assoc. editor Jour. Molecular Biology, 1964-68, 75-79; mem. editorial bd. Trends Biochem. Sci., 1977-84, Biochemistry, 1984—, Protein Sci., 1992-97. Mem. award panel Searle Scholars, 1993—96, 1997—98; mem. adv. panel in biophysics Burroughs-Wellcome, 1995—2001. Recipient Wheland award in chemistry U. Chgo., 1995; Guggenheim fellow, 1958-59. Fellow Am. Biophysics Soc. (coun. 1977-81, Founder's award 1999); mem. NAS, Am. Soc. Biol. Chemists (Merck award 1999), Am. Chem. Soc., Am. Acad. Arts and Scis., Protein Soc. (coun. 1993-95, Stein and Moore award 1992). Home: 1243 Los Trancos Rd Portola Valley CA 94028-8125 Office: Stanford Med Sch Dept Biochemistry Beckman Ctr Stanford CA 94305-5307 E-mail: bbaldwin@cmgm.stanford.edu.

BALDWIN, SHAUN MCPARLAND, lawyer; b. Chgo., Oct. 19, 1954; BS, No. Ill. U., 1976; JD with distinction, John Marshall Law Sch., 1980. Bar: Ill. 1980, U.S. Dist. Ct. (no. dist.) Ill. 1980, U.S. Ct. Appeals (7th cir.) 1981. Assoc. McKenna, Storer, Rowe, White & Farrug, Chgo., 1980-86, Tressler, Soderstrom, Maloney & Priess, Chgo., 1986-87, ptnr., 1987—. Mem. ABA, Ill. Bar Assn., Def. Rsch. Inst. (chair ins. law com. 1996-98), Ill. Assn. Def. Trial Counsel (bd. dirs. 1996, amicus com. chair 1992—), Ill. Appellate Lawyers Assn. (bd. dirs. 1987-89), John Marshall Alumni Assn. (bd. dirs. 1982-86), Internat. Assn. Def. Trial Counsel (chair membership com. 1996-97, chair casualty ins. com. 1995-96), Profl. Liability Underwriting Soc. Office: Tressler Soderstrom Maloney & Priess 233 S Wacker Dr Ste 2200 Chicago IL 60606-6399 E-mail: sbaldwin@mail.tsmp.com.

BALDWIN, SUSAN OLIN, community service administrator; b. Battle Creek, Mich., Sept. 1, 1954; d. Thomas Franklin and Gloria Joan (Skidmore) Olin; m. James Patrick Baldwin, Sept. 15, 1979; children: Christopher Mark, David James. BA, Miami U., Ohio, 1976; JD, U. Cin., 1979. Bar: Ohio 1979, Mich. 1984. Assoc. editor Am. Legal Pub. Co., Cin., 1979-80; corp. atty. Hosp. Care Corp., Cin., 1980-84; legal counsel Peak Health Plan, Cin., 1984; assoc. Cook & Goetz, P.C., Bloomfield Hills, Mich., 1984-91, Pringle & Assocs., P.C., Farmington Hills, Mich., 1991-94; exec. dir. Calhoun County Econ. Devel. Forum, Battle Creek, 1994—2003; owner Am. Computer Svcs., Battle Creek, 2002—. Mem. steering com. Ctr. Workforce Excellence, 1994-96, Barriers to Employment, 1996—; bd. dirs. BC/Cal/Kal Inland Port Devel. Corp., The Forum for Greater Kalamazoo, 1995-2001, Calhoun County Health Improvement Program, 1998-99; mem. Battle Creek Cmty. Leadership Acad., 1996-97, Battle Creek Area Chamber of Commerce, 1998—, mem. adv. bd. 1998—, Southwest Mich. Healthplan Purchasing Alliance, 1998-2000; adv. bd. Starr Commonwealth Battle Creek Child Guidance Ctr., 1998—; mem. Cmty. Devel. Block Grant Coun., 1996-99. Contbr. articles to profl. jours. Pres. Hunter's Green Homeowner's Assn., Independence, Ky., 1982-83; chairwoman Safety Town Cmty. Project, 1993-95; v.p. fin. Jr. League Battle Creek, 1996-98; key communicator, Minges Brook PTA, 1993-2001, treas., 1994-96, 98-99; bd. mem. Vol. Ctr. Battle Creek, 1999—, Lakeview Sch. Dist. com. continuous improvement, 1999—, Battle Creek Cmty. Found. Philanthropic Devel. com., 1998—; chair South Ctrl. Mich. Jr. Achievement campaign, 1999, Calhoun County Crossroads Initiative, 1999-2002; mem. Blitz Build com. Habitat for Humanity, 1999; mem. Mayor's Commr. Compensation Commn., 1997—, capital campaign com.-making BC Green Leila Arboretum, 1999-2000; bd. dirs. Vol. Ctr., 2000—, sec., 2003. Mem. ABA, State Bar Mich., Ohio State Bar, Am. Businesswomen's Assn. (v.p. 1980-81, editor 1980), Battle Creek Area C. of C. (bd. mem. 1998—), Alpha Lambda Delta, Phi Alpha Delta, Birmingham Evening Newcomers Club (treas. 1986-87, pres. 1988). Office: 164 W Hamilton Ln Battle Creek MI 49015-4030

BALDWIN, TAMMY, congresswoman; b. Madison, Wis., Feb. 11, 1962; AB, Smith Coll.; JD, U. Wis. Pvt. practice as atty., 1989-92; Dane Country supr. Board of Supervisors, 1986-1994; mem. 78th dist. Wis. State Assembly, 1993-99; mem. U.S. Congress from 2d Wis. dist., Washington, 1999—; mem. budget com., judiciary com. Mem. NOW, ACLU, Wis. State Bar Assn., Internat. Network Lesbian and Gay Ofcls., Nat. Women's Polit. Caucus. Democrat. Office: 1022 Longworth Ho Office Bldg Washington DC 20515 also: 10 E Doty St Ste 405 Madison WI 53703-5103*

BALDWIN, WESLEY HALE BARRICK, music educator; b. Urbana, Ill., Sept. 15, 1966; s. John Edwin and Anne Nordlander Baldwin; m. Melisa Anne Barrick, June 6, 1998; 1 child, John Francis Barrick. BA, Yale Coll., 1987; MusM, New Eng. Conservatory, 1991; Mus D, U. Md., 1998. Sect. and prin. cellist New World Symphony, Miami Beach, Fla., 1991—95; cellist and founder Plymouth String Quartet, Miami Beach, 1991—96; artist in residence Fla. Internat. U., Miami, Fla., 1992—95; dir. Tenn. Cello Workshop, Knoxville, Tenn., 1999—; adj. regional auditions New World Symphony, Miami Beach, 2000—; faculty mentor Hot Springs Music Festival, Hot Springs, Ark., 1999—; resident musician Mich. City Chamber Music Festival, Mich. City, 2002—; asst. prof. of cello and chamber music U. Tenn., Knoxville, 1998—. Recipient 2nd Prize, Fischoff Chamber Music Competition, 1994, Prix Mercure, Semmering Musik Academie, 1994. Mem.: Am. Fedns. Musicians, Music Tchrs' Nat. Assn., Am. String Tchrs' Assn., Music Educator's Nat. Conf. Avocations: yoga, running. Home: 2214 Fisher Pl Knoxville TN 37920 Office: U Tennessee Sch of Music Knoxville TN 37996 Office Fax: 865-974-1941. Personal E-mail: wbaldwin@utk.edu.

BALDWIN, WILLIAM HOWARD, lawyer, retired foundation executive; b. Detroit, Feb. 21, 1916; s. Howard Charles and Ruth E. (Jensen) B.; m. Carol Lees, May 24, 1947; children: Susan, Jeffrey (dec.), Julie, Deborah. BA, Williams Coll., 1938; JD, U. Mich., 1941. Bar: Mich. 1941. Ptnr. Dykema Gossett, Detroit, 1970-77, of counsel, 1977—; chmn., trustee Kresge Found., Troy, Mich., 1963-87. Asst. U.S. prosecutor Nuremburg Trials, 1946. Served with USAAF, 1942-45, lt. col. (ret.). Mem. ABA, Mich. Bar Assn., Baker Hill Golf Club, Lake Sunapee Yacht Club. Republican. Episcopalian. also: PO Box 1308 New London NH 03257-1308 Home: 4620 Saint James Ave Vero Beach FL 32967-7336 E-mail: hbal@aol.com.

BALDWIN, WILLIAM LEE, economics educator; b. N.Y.C., Apr. 12, 1928; s. William Lee and Mildred (Karnes) B.; m. Marcia Diane Hurt, Aug. 18, 1956 (dec. 1989); children: Douglas Lee, Ellen Baldwin Faulkner; m. Marjorie Anne Sa'adah, July 13, 1991. BA, Duke U., 1951; MA, Princeton U., 1953, PhD, 1958. Instr., vis. asst. prof. Princeton U., 1952—56, 1961—62; instr., asst. prof., assoc. prof., prof. Dartmouth Coll., Hanover, N.H., 1956-84, John French prof., 1984—98; vis. prof. Thammasat U., Bangkok, 1968-70, 74-75; ret., 1998. Mem. spl. field staff Rockefeller Found., 1974-75; vis. researcher U. Sains Malaysia, 1979; cons. FTC, 1980; vis. prof. Budapest U. of Econs., 1991. Author: Antitrust and the Changing Corporation, 1961, The Structure of the Defense Market, 1955-64, 1967, (with S.D. Maxwell) The Role of Foreign Financial Assistance to Thailand in the 1980s, 1975, The World Tin Market: Political Pricing and Economic Competition, 1983, Market Power, Competition and Antitrust Policy, 1987; (with J.T. Scott) Market Structure and Technological Innovation, 1987; contbr. articles to profl. jours. Served with AUS, 1946-47. Brookings research prof., 1963-64 Mem. Am. Econ. Assn., Indsl. Orgn. Soc. (v.p. 1977-78), AAUP, ABA (assoc.), Phi Beta Kappa, Omicron Delta Kappa. Home: 7 Prospect St Hanover NH 03755-1906 Office: Dartmouth Coll Dept Econs Hanover NH 03755

BALDWIN, WILLIAM RUSSELL, optometrist, foundation executive; b. Danville, Ind., July 29, 1926; s. Edward Claire and Letha Verona (Russell) B.; m. Honey Esther Fisher, Aug. 16, 1947; children: Linda Marie Smith (dec.), Leslie Ann Baldwin Bloom. BS, Pacific U., 1949, OD, 1951, ScD (hon.), 1991; MS, Ind. U., 1956, PhD, 1964; LHD (hon.), New Eng. Coll., 1982; D.S. (hon.), SUNY, 1998; DS (hon.), Pa. Coll. Optometry, 2003. Pvt. practice, Beech Grove, Ind., 1951-54; dir. optometry clinic Ind. U., Bloomington, 1959-63; dean Coll. Optometry Pacific U., Forest Grove, Oreg., 1963-69; pres. New England Coll. Optometry, Boston, 1969-79; dean Coll. Optometry U. Houston, 1979-90; pres. River Blindness Found., 1990-96, chmn. bd. dirs., 1996—. Author: (with C.R. Schick) Corneal Contact Lenses, Fitting Procedures, 1962, (with others) The Refractive State of the Eye, 1969, Pediatric Optometry, 1988; editor Vision Science Symposium, Ind. U., 1988, (with others) Refractive Anomalies, 1991. Mem. exec. com. Rep. Ctrl. Com., Washington County, Oreg., 1963-69; chmn. arts, scis. divsn. Ind. Reps., 1962-63; chmn. Vellore India Hosp. Fund Drive, 1959-61; mem. men's adv. coun. Bloomington Hosp., 1959-63, bd. dirs. Am. Optom Found., 1998—. Recipient Alumni Svc. award Ind. U., 1977, Pacific U., 1995, Gold Medal award Beta Sigma Kappa, 1968, Lifetime Achievement award Prevent Blindness Am., 1995, Disting. Svc. award USPHA Vision Sect., 1998, Social Justice Action award New Eng. United Meth. Conf., 1999, Disting. Svc. award World Coun. Optometry, 2000; named Man of Vision Prevent Blindness Mass., 1994; Disting. scholar Nat. Acad. Practice, 1994, Disting. Svc. award, Vis. Section Am. Pub. Health Assn., 1998. Fellow AAAS, Am. Acad. Optometry (life, chmn. sect. on edn. 1984-87); mem. working group Nat. Rsch. Coun. Com. Vision of NAS, Am. Optometric Assn. (chmn. com. on rsch. 1964-69, chmn. task force on manpower 1968, Disting. Svc. award 1992), Assn. Schs. Colls. Optometry (pres. 1974-76, chmn. internat. optometric edn.), Tex. Soc. to Prevent Blindness (v.p. 1985-90), Nat. Soc. to Prevent Blindness Am. (bd. dirs. 1988-96, chm. 1st World Conf. on Optometric Edn. 1990), Optometric Rsch. Inst. (bd. dirs. 1995-2001), Rotary, Sigma Xi, Sigma Nu, Kappa Kappa Sigma.

BALDYGA, LEONARD J. retired diplomat, international consultant; b. Chgo., Mar. 19, 1932; s. Stanislaw J. and Frances T. (Gorzynski) B.; m. Joyce Brinkley, June 25, 1960; children: Natalya M., Sarah E. AA, J. Sterling Morton Coll., 1954; BS, So. Ill. U., 1959; M Internat. Affairs, Columbia U., 1962. City editor Marion (Ill.) Daily Rep., 1958-59; fin. writer Am. Banker, N.Y.C., 1959-61; overseas, 1963-78; dep. dir. Europe U.S. Info. Agy., Washington, 1979-81, dir., 1981-83, 92-94; minister, counselor Am. Embassy, Rome, 1983-88, New Delhi, 1988-91; sr. rsch. assoc. Washington, 1994—. Acting dir. Murrow Ctr. Tufts U. Fletcher Sch. Law and Diplomacy, Medford, Mass., 1991-92, adj. prof., 1991-92. Mem. editl. bd. Polish Ency. Britannica. Trustee St. Stephen's Sch., Rome, 1984-88; bd. dirs. Ptnrs. for Dem. Change, Washington, Pub. Diplomacy Coun., Sabre Found. Decorated Polish Order of Merit Republic of Poland, 1994, Commander's Cross, 2002; recipient Presdl. Disting. Svc. award White House, 1984, Edward R. Murrow award Tufts U., 1988, Presdl. Merit award White House, 1988. Home: 3622 Vacation Ln Arlington VA 22207-3820 Office: Internat Rsch/Exchs Bd 2121 K St NW Ste 700 Washington DC 20037

BALE, JUDITH R. health science association administrator; Dir., bd. on Global Health Inst. Medicine, Washington, 1998—. Office: Global Health IOM 2101 Constitution Ave NW Washington DC 20418-0007

BALÉE, WILLIAM L. anthropology educator; b. Ft. Lauderdale, Fla., Oct. 12, 1954; s. William Lockert Balée and Lorraine Kathryn Monahan; m. Pamela Van Rees, May 24, 1980 (div. Dec. 1986); m. Maria da Conceição Bezerra, Mar. 9, 1987; children: Nicholas, Isabel. BA with high honors, U. Fla., 1975; MA, Columbia U., 1979, MPhil, 1980, PhD, 1984. Assoc. rschr. ecology Museu Paraense Emílio Goeldi, Belém, Brazil, 1988-91, chair ecology, 1990-91; assoc. prof. anthropology Tulane U., New Orleans, 1991-98, prof., chair dept. anthropology, 1998-2001, prof. anthropology, 1998—. Adj. prof. anthropology CUNY, 1983-84, SUNY, Purchase, 1982; adj. prof. social scis. CUNY, 1983; adj. prof. sociology and anthropology Rutgers U., 1984; vis. assoc. prof. Ctr. for L.Am. Studies, U. Fla., 1990; fieldwork with forest peoples in Amazon of Brazil and Bolivia, 1980-97; acad. cons. Smithsonian Instn., 2000—. Author: Footprints of the Forest: Ka'apor Ethnobotany, 1994 (award Soc. Econ. Botany, 1996); editor: Advances in Historical Ecology, 1998, Jour. Ethnobiology, 1999—2002; mem. editl. bd.; 2002—; co-editor: Resource Management in Amazonia: Indigenous and Folk Strategies, Advances in Economic Botany, vol. 7, 1989, Hist. Ecology Series, 1998—; contbr. articles to profl. jours., chapters to books. Decorated officer Order of the Golden Ark (Netherlands), 1993; NY Bot. Garden fellow, 1984-88, Fulbright-Hays fellow, 1980-81, Newcomb Coll. fellow, 1992-94, Conselho Nacional de Desenvolvimento Tecnológico e Científico fellow, 1988-91; grantee OAS, 1981-82, Ford Found., 1989-90, Jessie Smith Noyes Found., 1990-91, World Wildlife Fund, 1991-92, 2003, Tulane U., 1992, Wenner-Gren Found., 1993-94 ; apptd. to 60th and 61st Coll. Disting. Lectrs., Sigma Xi, 1997-99; recipient Outstanding Book of Yr. award Soc. Econ. Botany. Fellow Am. Anthrop. Assn.; mem. Soc. Ethnobotanists (India), Soc. Ethnobiology, Soc. Anthropology of Lowland S.Am. (pres. 2002—), Soc. Etnobiologia e Etnoecologia, Phi Beta Kappa (pres. Alpha of La. 1997-98), Phi Kappa Phi. Office: Tulane U Dept Anthropology 1021 Audubon St New Orleans LA 70118-5238 E-mail: wbalee@tulane.edu.

BALENT, ANDREW, composer, musician; b. Washington, Pa., July 23, 1934; s. Andrew Balent and Margaret Maslanik; m. Roxie Merritt Balent, July 29, 1967 (dec.); m. Barbara Pryzbyla, July 21, 1956 (div. Mar. 1962); children: Laura, Andrew III, Matthew; m. Carole A. Hopkins, May 31, 2003. MusB, U. Mich., 1956, MusM, 1960. Music tchr. New Haven (Mich.) Pub. Schs., 1956—60; instrumental music tchr. Uttica (Mich.) Pub. Schs., 1960—62, Fitzgerald Pub. Schs., Warren, Mich., 1962—86; freelance composer Greenville, SC, 1970—; composer Carl Fischer LLC, N.Y.C., 1985—99. Composer, arranger, editor Warner Bros. Pub., N.Y.C., 1975—83; guest educator Volta Redonda, Brazil, 0200, Brazil, 2001, Brazil, 03. Composer over 500 publ. Home: 112 Cliff Ridge Drive Cleveland SC 29635

BALES, DOROTHY JOHNSON, violinist, educator; b. Ketchikan, Alaska, Aug. 31, 1917; d. Harry and Lillian Mae (Pierce) Johnson; m. Robert Freed Bales, Sept. 14, 1941. BA, U. Oreg., 1948; BMus, Boston U., 1950; postgrad., Marlboro Sch. Music, Inernat. d'Ete; student of Ivan Galamian, Gabriel Bouillon, Henryk Szeryng. Instr. violin New Eng. Conservatory, 1949-50, 85-99; tchr. violin Longy Sch. Music, Cambridge, Mass., 1950-58; violin and chamber music tchr., orch. dir. Winsor Sch., Boston, 1950-55; lectr. music Emmanuel Coll., Boston, 1961-69, 1974-78, 90-91, asst. prof., 1969-74; lectr. Northeastern U., Boston, 1975-78, 82-83; vis. assoc. prof. U. Mass., Amherst, 1978. Bd. dirs. Kodaly Ctr. of Am., 1988-89; solo concert tours throughout U.S., 1964-68; concerts in Paris, 1952, Salzburg, 1952, 56, 64, 72, Vienna, 1964, 72, Geneva, 1964, Saarbruken, Konstanz, 1984; contractor-concertmaster, Choral Art Soc., Scituate, 1953-86; concertmaster Ch. of the Advent, Boston, 1966-83. Assoc. artist tchr. N.J. String tchrs. Summer Conf., 1980-83; founder, music dir. Chamber of Music Soc. Cape Ann., 1960-62; bd. dirs. Young Audiences of Mass., 1986-89; workshop leader, 1993; violin soloist Waltham Symphony, 1995, Marlboro Orch., 1996, Salem Philharm., 1995; bd. dirs. Choral Art Soc., Scituate, Mass., 1978-87; concertmaster Marlborough Symphony, 1985-95; founder, artistic dir. Weston Chamber of Music, 1990-99; Author articles in the field. Grantee Ella Lyman Cabot Trust, 1956, Mass. Arts Coun., 1986, 89-92; winner N.W. Dist. Young Artists award Fedn. Music Clubs, 1939, Mus. Guild Boston Debut award, 1948. Mem. Am. String Tchrs. Assn. (pres. Mass. chpt., 1974-84, 94-96, chmn. nat. solo competition, 1981), Music Educators Nat. Conf., Am. Fedn. Musicians, Sierra Club, Audubon Soc., Nature Consevancy, World Wildlife Fedn. Episcopalian. Home: San Diego, Calif. Died July 14, 2002.

BALES, EDWARD WAGNER, consultant, former manufacturing executive; b. Chgo., Jan. 30, 1939; s. Edward Joseph and Esther (Wagner) B.; m. Barbara LaVarre, Nov. 26, 1960; children: Edward Joseph, Karen Mary, Kathryn Mary, Timothy Joseph. BEE, Ill. Inst. Tech., 1960; MBA, U. Chgo., 1969. Elec. engr. Motorola, Inc., Chgo., 1963-69, sales mgr., 1969-80, mgr. mktg. and client services, 1980-85; founder, dir. ops., chief of staff Motorola Univ., Chgo., 1985-90, dir. edn., external systems, 1990-97; pres. LTE Consulting Firm, 1997—. Mem. editorial bd. U.S. Gen. Acct. Office Jour. Mem. edn. coun. NSF; mem. edn. com. Nat. Conf. Bd.; vice chmn. edn. com. Bus. Industry Adv. Coun. to Orgn. Econ. Corp. and Devel.; pres. Mary Seat of Wisdom Ch. Bd., Park Ridge, Ill., 1980-83; trustee Nat. Sch. Bd. Assn. Found., Ray Graham Assn. for People with Disabilities, Actuarial Found., 1997—; mem. Nat. Rsch. Coun. Commn. on Work, Learning and Assessment. Lt. USN, 1960-63. Mem. Nat. Alliance of Bus. (mem. edn. com., bus./policy com.), Soc. Actuaries Found. (bd. trustees), Nat. Sch. Bd. Found. (bd. trustees). Republican. Roman Catholic. Avocations: photography, automobile repair. Office: LTE 916 S Lincoln Ave Park Ridge IL 60068-4513

BALES, FLOSSIE KATHLEEN, retired librarian, systems analyst; b. El Dorado, Kans., Sept. 4, 1938; d. Francis Justus and Flossie Mae (Smith) O'Reilly; m. Royal Eugene Bales, Apr. 16, 1960; children: David Scott, Elizabeth Laurel. B in Music Edn. magna cum laude, Wichita State U., 1960; MLS, U. Calif., Berkeley, 1968. Tchr. music Larkspur (Calif.)/Corte Madera Sch., 1961-62; libr. clk. Palo Alto (Calif.) Pub. Libr., 1962-67; cataloger Stanford (Calif.) U., 1968; children's libr. Santa Clara County Libr., Los Altos, Calif., 1975; cataloger Santa Clara County Libr., San Jose, Calif., 1976-78; instr. cataloging U. Calif., Berkeley, 1982, 84-85; with user svcs. staff Rsch. Librs. Group, Mt. View, Calif., 1978-80, systems analyst, 1980-89, mgr. online applications, 1989-92, sr. analyst, 1993—97, QA mgr., 1997—2000; ret., 2000. Contbr. articles to profl. jours. Chairperson curriculum com. Los Lomitas Sch., Menlo Park, Calif., 1975-77; bd. dirs. El Camino Youth Symphony, Los Altos, 1983-87, co-pres., 1985-87. Mem. ALA (chairperson cataloging and classification sect. 1991-92, various appts. 1982—), Nat. Info. Standards Orgn. (chairperson standards devel. com. 1990-92). Democrat. Avocations: music, gardening, needlework, theater. Home: 1225 Sherman Ave Menlo Park CA 94025-6012

BALES, GERTRUDE A. retired otolaryngologist; b. Greensboro, N.C., 1926; MD, U. Rochester, 1952. Diplomate Am. Bd. Otolaryngology. Intern Strong Meml. Hosp., Rochester, N.Y., 1952-53, resident, 1953-55; clin. assoc. prof. otolaryngology U. Rochester, 1968-96; chief of staff Canandaigua (N.Y.) VA Med. Ctr., 1994-96; ret., 1996. Fellow ACS; mem. Am. Acad. Otolaryngology/Head and Neck Surgery.

BALES, JOHN FOSTER, III, retired lawyer; b. Springfield, Mass., July 17, 1940; s. John Foster II and Jean (Torrence) Bales; m. Jane Lee Black, Sept. 11, 1965; children: Patricia, Elizabeth, Susan. BS in Engring., Princeton U., 1962; LLB, U. Va., 1965; LLM, Georgetown U., 1972. Bar: U.S. Supreme Ct. 1972. Staff atty. U.S. SEC, Washington, 1970-72; assoc. Morgan, Lewis & Bockius, Phila., 1972-76, ptnr., 1976—2001. Bd. dirs. Ind. Publs., Inc. Trustee U.S. com. refugees, 1998—2001; vice-chmn. bd. trustees Ind. Presbyn. Med. Ctr., Phila., 1988—95, Acad. Natural Scis., Phila., 1995—; trustee Presbyn. Found., Phila., 1995—96, Immigration Refugee Svcs. Am., 1998—2001. Mem.: ABA, Colo. Bar Assn., Phila. Bar Assn., Pa. Bar Assn., Va. Bar Assn. Republican.

BALES, ROBERT FREED, social psychologist, educator; b. Ellington, Mo., Mar. 9, 1916; s. Columbus Lee and Ada Lois (Sloan) B.; m. Dorothy Louise Johnson, Sept. 14, 1941. BA, U. Oreg., 1938, MS, 1941; MA, Harvard U., 1943, PhD, 1945. Research assoc. sect. on alcohol studies Yale U., 1944-45; instr. sociology Harvard U., Cambridge, Mass., 1945-47, asst. prof. sociology, research assoc. Lab. Social Relations, 1947-51, lectr. sociology, research assoc., 1951-55, assoc. prof., 1955-57, prof. social relations, 1957-86, prof. emeritus, 1986—, dir. Lab. Social Rels., 1960-67, chmn. social psychology program, dept. psychology and social rels., 1970-82; cons. psychology Harvard U. Health Svcs., 1970-82. Vis. lectr. sociology and social psychology U. Mich., summer 1949, Columbia U., summer 1950; lectr. Salzberg Austria Seminar of Am. Studies, summer 1952, 56; Mem. bd. sci. counsellors NIMH, 1957-60 Author: Interaction Process Analysis: A Method for the Study of Small Groups, 1950, The Fixation Factor in Alcohol Addiction, 1980, (with Talcott Parsons, Edward A. Shils) Working Papers in the Theory of Action, 1953, (with Talcott Parsons, et al) Family, Socialization, and Interaction Process, 1955, (with Stephen P. Cohen and Stephen A. Williamson) SYMLOG, A System for the Multiple Level Observation of Groups, 1979, SYMLOG Case Study Kit and Instructions for a Group Self Study, 1980; contbr. to Group Dynamics, Research and Theory, 1953, The SYMLOG Practitioner, 1988, Social Interaction Systems, Theory and measurement, 1999, several other compilations; editor: (with A. Paul Hare and Edgar F. Borgatta) Small Groups, Studies in Social Interaction, 1955; author various instruments and booklets, sr. rsch., cons. SYMLOG Cons. Group, 1983—. Trustee Ella L. Cabot Trust. Mem.: Boston Psychoanalytic Soc. (affiliate), Soc. Exptl. Social Psychology, Am. Psychol. Soc., Am. Acad. Arts and Scis., Eastern Sociol. Soc. (pres. 1962—63), Am. Sociol. Assn., APA (Outstanding Contbn. to Leadership and Orgnl. Excellence award Calif. chpt. divsn. of I/O psychology 1999, Disting. Contbn. to Psychology as a Profession award Calif. chpt. 2001). Home and Office: 17990 Bernardo Trails Pl San Diego CA 92128-1505

BALES, ROYAL EUGENE, philosophy educator; b. Pratt, Kans., Sept. 23, 1934; s. Harold Thomas and Gladys (German) B.; m. Flossie Kathleen O'Reilly, Apr. 16, 1960; children— David Scott, Elizabeth Laurel B.Music Edn. cum laude, U. Wichita, 1956, MA, 1960; PhD, Stanford U., 1968. Tchr. music Kans. Pub. Schs., 1956-57, 59-60; instr. philosophy Menlo Coll., Atherton, Calif., 1962-69, prof., 1970-2000, prof. emeritus, 2000—, chmn. social scis. and humanities, 1971-74, dean liberal arts, 1974-79, provost, 1979-87, standing mem. president's adv. council, 1971-87. Vis. fellow Harris-Manchester Coll.,

Oxford U., 1994, 98; Wong vis. prof. Guangdong U. of Law and Bus., Guangzhou, China, 1999. Contbr. articles to profl. jours. Pres. El Camino Youth Symphony Assn., 1985-87; bd. of govs. Manchester Coll., Oxford, 1994—. Scholar and fellow U. Wichita, 1952-60, Stanford U., 1966-67; prin. investigator NSF, Menlo Coll./Stanford, 1971-72; research grantee Stanford-Warsaw Exchange, Poland, 1969-70. Mem. Am. Philos. Assn., Soc. for Bus. Ethics, Save San Francisco Bay Assn., Phi Mu Alpha Sinfonia. Democrat. Avocations: classical music, designing and constructing furniture. Home: 1255 Sherman Ave Menlo Park CA 94025-6012 Office: Menlo Coll Florence Moore Bldg 1000 El Camino Real Atherton CA 94027-4300 E-mail: rbales@mindspring.com., ebales@menlo.edu.

BALES, SUSAN FORD, social service spokesperson; b. Washington, July 6, 1957; d. Gerald R. (38th Pres. U.S.) and Elizabeth Ann (Bloomer) Ford; m. Charles F. Vance, Feb. 10, 1979 (div. Dec. 1988); children: Tyne Mary, Heather Elizabeth; m. Vaden Frederick Bales, July 25, 1989. Student, Mount Vernon Coll., 1975-77. Spokesperson Nat. Breast Cancer Awareness, N.Y.C., 1985—99. Pub. spkr. Author: Double Exposure, 2002, Sharp Focus, 2003. Bd. dirs. Gerald R. Ford Libr. and Mus., Grand Rapids, Mich., 1981, Betty Ford Ctr., Rancho Mirage, Calif., 1990, Am. Cancer Soc. (Tulsa) chpt., 1990, Carl Albert State Coll., 1992, Bosque Sch., Albuquerque. Recipient John W. Sherrick Humanitarian award Peralta Cancer Rsch. Inst., 1987, Nat. Betty Ford award Susan G. Komen Found., 1991, Jonquils award Duke Comprehensive Cancer Ctr., 1992, Leadership award Congl. Families Action for Cancer Awareness, 1995. Republican.

BALES, VIRGINIA SHANKLE, health administrator; BA in Chemistry, Emory U., Atlanta, 1971, MPH, 1977. Dep. dir. Nat. Ctr. Chronic Disease Prevention and Health Promotion, 1988—98; dep. dir. program mgmt. CDC, 1998—. Office: CDC DHHS Mailstop D14 1600 Clifton Rd NE Atlanta GA 30329-4018

BALGEMAN, RICHARD VERNON, radiology administrator, alcoholism counselor; b. Berwyn, Ill., Dec. 25, 1929; s. Vernon Ernest and Regina Marie (Fitzgerald) B.; m. Wauneta Frances Laird, Nov. 15, 1952; children: Marcia, Kathleen, Barbara, Daniel. Radiology technician, Cook County Grad. Sch. of Med., 1951; BA in Health Svc., Governor State U., 1976, MA in Sci., 1978. Cert. technologist; ordained Deacon Roman Cath. Ch., 1997. Radiology adminstr. Manteno (Ill.) Mental Health Ctr., 1951-84; adminstrv. asst. bus. office Shapiro Devel. Ctr., Kankakee, Ill., 1984-88; with St. James Hosp., Chicago Heights, Ill., 1990-99. Inventor DuPont Cronex Tech. Aid, 1965. Trustee Village of Manteno, 1969-72, chmn. planning commn., 1985-93; pres. Village View TV Channel 4. With USNG, 1948-56. Gov.'s award Ill. Dept. Mental Health, Manteno, 1971; named Citizen of Yr. Manteno Hist. Soc., 1996. Mem. Am. Legion, Rotary. Roman Catholic. Avocations: camping, making miniature furniture, writing short stories. Home: 555 Park St Manteno IL 60950-1045

BALICK, HELEN SHAFFER, retired judge; b. Bloomsburg, Pa. d. Walter W. and Clarissa K. (Bennett) Shaffer; m. Bernard Balick, June 29, 1967. JD, Dickinson Sch. Law, 1966, LLD, 1997. Bar: Pa. 1967, Del. 1969. Probate adminstr. Girard Trust Bank, Phila., 1966-68; pvt. practice law Wilmington, Del., 1969-74; staff atty. Legal Aid Soc. Del., Wilmington, 1969-71; master Family Ct. Del., New Castle County, 1971-74; bankruptcy judge, U.S. magistrate Dist. Del., Wilmington, 1974-80, bankruptcy judge, 1974-94, chief judge, 1994-98. Guest lectr. Dickinson Sch. Law, 1981-87; lectr. Dickinson Forum, 1982. Pres. bd. trustees Cmty. Legal Aid Soc., Inc., 1972—74; trustee Dickinson Sch. Law, 1985—2000; mem. Citizens Adv. Com., Wilmington, 1973—74, Wilmington Bd. Edn., 1974; bd. dirs. Kutz Home, 1999—2001, Jewish Hist. Soc., 1999—; active U. Del. Libr. Assocs., 1998—, sec., 2000—, v.p., 2001—02; bd. govs. The Dickinson Sch. Law, Pa. State U., 2000—. Recipient Women's Leadership award Del. State Bar Assn., 1997; named to Hall of Fame of Del. Women, 1994. Mem.: AAUW, Dickinson Sch. Law Gen. Alumni Assn. (exec. bd. 1977—80, 1987—2000, v.p. 1981—84, pres. 1984—87, Outstanding Alumni award 1991, Career Achievement award 1998), Turnaround Mgmt. Assn. (bd. dirs. 1995—97), Wilmington Women in Bus. (bd. dirs. 1980—83), Del. Alliance Profl. Women (Trailblazer award 1984), Del. Bar Assn., Am. Bankruptcy Inst., Am. Coll. Bankruptcy, Am. Judges Assn., Nat. Conf. Bankruptcy Judges (bd. govs. 1986), Fed. Bar Assn. Home: 2319 W 17th St Wilmington DE 19806-1330

BALICK, KENNETH D. international business executive; b. Albany, N.Y., Nov. 27, 1960; s. Sidney M. and Carole (Kaufmann) B. BS in Indsl. and Labor Rels., Cornell U., 1983; MPA, Harvard U., 1986. Legis. aide to mem. Japan Parliament, Tokyo, 1983-84; dir. Asian programs Carnegie Coun. on Ethics and Internat. Affairs, N.Y.C., 1986-90; pres. Trans-Pacific Consulting Group, N.Y.C., 1990-94; asst. to CEO Nomura Securities Internat., Inc., N.Y.C., 1994-97; dir. internat. bus. devel. Capital Co. of Am., N.Y.C., 1998-99; founder, pres. RockBridge Global Advisors, 1999—. Pub. spkr. in field. Henry Luce scholar. Mem. Coun. on Fgn. Rels.

BALIGAR, VIRUPAX C. research soil scientist; b. Dharwar, Karnatak, India, June 1, 1942; BS with honors, Karnatak U., Dharwar, 1965, MS with distinction, 1967; MS, Utah State U., 1971; PhD, Miss. State U., 1975. Rsch. soil scientist Purdue U., West Lafayette, Ind., 1979; rsch. advisor Inst. Interamericano Ciencias Agricolas/Embrapa World Bank, Sete Lagoas, Brazil, 1979-81; rsch. agriculturist Allied Corp., Morristown, N.J., 1981-83; vis. prof. USDA/W.Va. U., Beckley, 1983-84; rsch. soil scientist, supervisory scientist USDA Agrl. Rsch. Svc., Beckley, 1984-2001; supervisory rsch. scientist USDA/Md., Beltsville, 2001—. Author: Growth and Mineral Nutrition of Field Crops, 1991, 2d edit., 1997; editor: Crops as Enhancers of Nutrient Use, 1990, Plant-Soil Interaction at Low pH, 1991, Adaptation of Plants to Soil Stresses, 1994; author more than 210 rsch. publs. Fellow Am. Soc. Agronomy, Soc. Soil Sci. Am.; mem. Internat. Union Soil Sci. Office: USDA Agrl Rsch Svc-ACSL BARC-West Bldg 001 Rm 342 Beltsville MD 20705-2350

BALILES, GERALD L. lawyer, former governor; b. Stuart, Va., July 8, 1940; BA, Wesleyan U., 1963; JD, U. Va., 1967. Bar: Va. 1967, U.S. Ct. Appeals (4th cir.), U.S. Supreme Ct. 1971. Ptnr. Bell, Lacy & Baliles, 1975-81; atty. gen. Commonwealth of Va., 1982-85, gov., 1986-90; with Hunton & Williams, 1990—. Mem. Va. Ho. of Dels., 1976-82, mem. appropriations com., 1978-82, com. corp. ins. and banking, 1976-82, com. conservation and natural resources, 1979-82; chmn. Joint House-Senate Ins. Study Com., 1977-79; Legal Drafting Sub-Com., State Water Study Commn., 1977-81; vice chmn. Joint House-Senate Com. on Nuclear Power Generation Facilities, 1977-79; chmn. Nat. Commn. Ensure Strong Competitive Airline Industry, 1993. Chmn. PBS; chmn. so. regional edn. bd. Commn. Ednl. Quality. Mem. Richmond Bar Assn., Va. Bar Assn. (exec. com. 1979), ABA (environ. quality com., natural resources law sect. 1973—, environ. control com., corp., banking and bus. law sect. 1974—), Va. State Bar (chmn. environ. quality com. 1975-77). Office: Hunton & Williams Riverfront Plz E Tower PO Box 1535 Richmond VA 23218-1535 Fax: 804-788-8218. E-mail: gbaliles@hunton.com.

BALINT, DAVID LEE, engineering company executive; b. Cleve., June 27, 1946; s. Robert Stephen and Edna Mae (Alward) S. BBA, Cleve. State U., 1969; grad., U.S. Naval War Coll., 1982; MBA, Temple U., 1986. Cert. purchasing mgr., profl. contracts mgr. Commd. ensign USN, 1970, advanced through grades to lt. comdr., retired, 1990; dep. dir. contract adminstrn. Teledyne Brown Engrıng., Huntsville, Ala., 1990-96, mgr. compliance programs, 1996-2000; mgr. export compliance The Boeing Co., Huntsville, Ala., 2000—. Adj. faculty Temple U., Phila., 1986-90, Southeastern Inst. Tech., Huntsville, 1991-94, U. Ala., Huntsville, 1994-96. Del. mem. People-to-People Contract Mgmt.; del. People's Republic China, 1986, 1989; vol. Family Svcs. Ctr., 1999—2000, Family Svcs. Ctr. Found., 2003—; North Ala. Internat. Trade Assn. Ala., 1999—; bd. dirs. Vol. Ctr. Huntsville-Madison County, 1995—97; bd. trustees Employees Cmty. Fun, 2001; bd. govs. Sigma Phi Epsilon Ednl. Found., 2001. Fellow Nat. Contract Mgmt. Assn. (nat. v.p. N.E. region 1989-90, nat. v.p. membership 1990-91, nat. functional dir. 1991-98, 2001, Nat. Edn. award 1994, Disting. Svc. award 1995), Soc. Logistics Engrs., Am. Assn. Adult and Continuing Edn. Home: 107 Huntington Ridge Rd Madison AL 35757-8501 Office: The Boeing Co 499 Boeing Blvd Huntsville AL 35824

BALIS, ANDREA F. historian, writer; b. Phila., Apr. 23, 1948; d. M. Earl and Bernice Balis; m. George V. Harris, Oct. 31, 1982; children: Jesse Andrew, Sophia Louise. BA, U. Pa., Phila., 1969; MFA, NYU, 1971; MA, CUNY, 1992, PhD, 1999. Artistic dir. Cutting Edge Theatre, N.Y.C., 1976—82; assoc. prof. history Hunter Coll., N.Y.C., 1990—97; adj. assoc. prof. thematic studies program John Jay Coll., N.Y.C., 1997—. Bd. mem. NARAL-New York State, N.Y.C., 1986—2002, Skysaver Prodns., N.Y.C., 1988—. Author: What Are You Using, 1984, P.J., 1986. Office: John Jay Coll Thematic Studies Program 899 Tenth Ave New York NY 10019

BALIS, JENNIFER LYNN, academic administrator, computer technology educator; b. Hamlin, W.Va., Nov. 23, 1946; 1 child, Theodore Berndt. AA, Del Mar Coll., 1987; BA, U. Tex., 1989; BS, So. Ill. U., 1992. Peer counselor U. Tex., Edinburg, 1989-90; tchr. Mission (Tex.) Ind. Sch. Dist., 1990; instr. San Diego Job Corps, 1992-95; instr. computer tech. Kaskaskia Coll., Centralia, Ill., 1997—2002. Coord. Kaskaskia Coll. Vandalia Ctr., Vandalia, 1999-2001. Chmn., sec. Mulberry Grove Zoning Bd. Appeals, 1999—2002; vol. advocate S.A.F.E., 2003—; asst. leader Living with Arthritis Support Group. With USNR, 1984—. Mem. Psi Chi (pres. 1989-90). Republican. Roman Catholic. Avocations: natural healing, folk medicine, mineral collector, archery.

BALIS, MOSES EARL, biochemist, educator; b. Phila., June 19, 1921; s. Harry and Frances (Spector) B.; m. Bernice M. Lamborg, Dec. 30, 1945; children— Frances Andrea, Ellen Joyce. BA, Temple U., 1943; MS, U. Pa., 1947, PhD, 1949. With Sloan-Kettering Inst., 1949-87, head nucleoprotein metabolism sect., 1957—, asso. mem., 1960-65, mem., 1965-87, chief div. cell metabolism, 1970-87; chair inst. senate, 1981-83; cons. Sloan-Kettering Inst., 1987-91; asso. prof. Med. Coll. Cornell U., 1954-66, prof. biochemistry, 1966-87, chmn. biochemistry unit, 1969-74; owner M.E. Balis, Inc., Fla. Vis. lectr. Adelphi U., 1963-64; cons. chemistry dept. Manhattan Coll., 1981-86; mem. study sects. Am. Cancer Soc., NIH.; mem. planning com. Nat. Cancer Plan; mem. rev. com. Nat. Large Bowel Cancer Program, 1977-81; pres. Med. Research Investment Fund, 1984-89. Mem. editorial bd. Cancer Rsch., 1969-73; assoc. editor, 1974-82. Served to lt. (j.g.) USNR, 1944-46. Recipient Research Career award USPHS, 1963 Mem. Am. Chem. Soc. (past sect. chmn.), AAAS, Am. Cancer Soc., Am. Soc. Biol Chemistry and Molecular Biology, Harvey Soc., Am. Assn. Cancer Rsch., Sigma Xi. Achievements include research, numerous publs. on metabolism of purines in normal and malignant tissues; determined biochem. action of anti-cancer drugs, biochemical nature of genetic defects. Home and Office: 11587 Pathway Ln Boynton Beach FL 33437-4932 E-mail: mebalis@att.net.

BALISH, RUTH REITZ, retired community health nurse; b. Palmerton, Pa., Oct. 1, 1919; d. Chas. B. and Minnie E. Reitz; m. George F. Balish, Nov. 5, 1949; children: Deidre B. Talarico, Vicki B. DelMonte, Lori S. Hedges. Student, Moravian Coll., 1937-38; diploma in nursing, Grandview Hosp. Sch. Nursing, 1942; BSN, Temple U., 1944; cert., New England Hosp. Women, 1943; diploma in med. tech., Sacred Heart Hosp. Sch., Allentown, Pa., 1945. Chief med. technician Morris County Chest Clinic, Morris Place, N.J.; pub. health nurse City of Summit, N.J., 1968-73; chief rsch. histologist Merck Co., Rahway, N.J.; pvt. duty nurse Clearwater, Fla., 1987-91, Lakeland, Fla., 1991-99; ret., 2000. Vol. nurse ARC Disaster Shelter, Boca Raton, Waynesville, N.C., Pinellas County, Fla., Lakeland Fla., 1978-82; co-owner, med. technologist North Summit Med. Lab., Summit, 1951-64. Vol. nurse Lakeland Regional Ctr., Morton Plant Hosp., Clearwater; adv. bd. J. Haley Vets. Hosp., Tampa, 1991-95, Bay Pines Vets. Hosp., St. Petersburg, Fla., VA Vol. Svc. Mem. DAR (officer 1961—, bd. dirs. to 1998, area chmn. commemorative WWII 50th anniversary Lakeland chpt. 1992-95, Excellence in Lakeland Cmty. Svc. award 1995), Am. Soc. Clin. Pathologists, Am. Chem. Soc., Daus. Am. Colonists, Order Ea. Star. Home: 4667 Yacht Ave Lakeland FL 33805-0501

BALK, ALFRED WILLIAM, journalist; b. Oskaloosa, Iowa, July 24, 1930; s. Leslie William and Clara Irene (Buell) B.; m. Phyllis Lorraine Munter, June 7, 1952; children: Laraine M., Diane M. Student, Augustana Coll., Rock Island, Ill., 1948-49; BS, Northwestern U., 1952, MS, 1953. Reporter Rock Island Argus, 1946-50; newswriter-producer WBBM (CBS), Chgo., 1952-53; reporter Chgo. Sun-Times, 1956; mag. writer, pub. relations J. Walter Thompson Co., Chgo., 1957-58; freelance writer nat. mags., including spl. writer Saturday Evening Post, 1958-66; feature editor Saturday Rev., 1966-68, editor at large, 1968-69; vis. scholar Russell Sage Found., 1968-69; lectr. journalism, editor Columbia Journalism Rev., 1969-73; editor World Press Rev., 1974, editor-pub., 1975-84, editorial dir., 1985-86, editorial cons., contbg. editor, 1986-94; mng. editor IEEE Spectrum, N.Y.C., 1989-91; assoc. prof. Syracuse U., 1991-94; freelance writer, cons., 1994—. Cons., rapporteur 20th Century Fund Task Force on Nat. News Coun., 1971-72, Ford Found., Markle Found.; faculty Bread Loaf Writers Conf., Middlebury, Vt., 1971; exec. sec. NY Gov.'s Com. on Employment Minority Groups in News Media, 1968-69; adv. com. World Press Inst., 1984-96. Author: The Free List: Property Without Taxes, 1970, A Free and Responsive Press, 1973, The Myth of American Eclipse: The New Global Age, 1990, Movie Palace Masterpiece: Saving Syracuse's Loew's State/Landmark Theatre, 1998; co-editor: Our Troubled Press, 1971. Bd. dir. Am. Jour. Nursing Co., 1990—93, Landmark Theatre Found., 1996—99. Mem. Am. Soc. Mag. Editors (exec. coun. 1977-83), Soc. Mag. Writers (pres. 1967), Soc. Profl. Journalists, Overseas Press Club (gov. 1978-79), Century Assn. Home: 13225 Michigan Ave Huntley IL 60142-7480

BALK, ROBERT A. medical educator; BA, U. Mo., Kansas City, 1976, MD, 1978. Resident internal medicine U. Mo., Kansas City, 1978—81; fellow pulmonary and critical care medicine U. Ark., Little Rock, 1981—83, instr. medicine, 1981—83, asst. prof. medicine, 1983—85; staff physician Little Rock VA Med. Ctr., 1983—85; asst. prof. medicine Rush-Presbyn.-St. Luke's Med. Ctr., Chgo., 1985—88, assoc. prof., 1988—95, prof. medicine, 1995—, asst. dir. sect. pulmonary medicine, 1985—90, med. dir. respiratory care svcs., 1985-93, med. dir. noninvasive respiratory care unit, 1985—87, co-dir. med. intensive care unit, 1986—88, dir. med. intensive care unit, 1988-95, assoc. dir. sect. pulmonary & crit. care medicine, 1993—97, assoc. dir. sect. critical care medicine, 1995—2002, dir. pulmonary & critical care medicine fellowship tng. program, 1994—, dir. pulmonary and critical care medicine, 2002—; J. Bailey Carter prof. med. ctr. Rush Med. Coll., Chgo., 2002. Contbr. articles to profl. jours. Recipient Dedicated Svc. & Superior Individual Effort in Patient Care Alice Sachs Meml. award, 1991, Alfred Soffer Rsch. award, Am. Coll. Chest Physicians, 1995, Take Wing award, U. Mo.-Kansas City Sch. Medicine, 1998. Office: Rush-Presbyn St Luke's Med Ctr 1653 W Congress Pkwy Chicago IL 60612-3833 E-mail: rbalk@rush.edu.

BALKA, SIGMUND RONELL, lawyer; b. Phila., Aug. 1, 1935; s. I. Edwin and Jane (Chernicoff) B.; m. Elinor Bernstein, May 29, 1966. AB, Williams Coll., 1956; JD, Harvard U., 1959. Bar: Pa. and D.C. 1961, N.Y. 1969, U.S. Supreme Ct. 1966. Sr. atty. Lilco, Mineola, N.Y., 1969-70; v.p., gen. counsel Brown Boveri Corp., North Brunswick, N.J., 1970-75; asst. gen. counsel Power Authority State N.Y., N.Y.C., 1975-80; gen. counsel Krasdale Foods, Inc., N.Y.C., 1980—. Pres. Graphic Arts Coun. N.Y., 1980—. Chmn. Hunts Point Environ. Protection Coun., N.Y.C., 1980—, Soc. for a Better Bronx, 1985—; chair fellows, mem. vis. com. Williams Coll. Mus. of Art, 1996—99; exec. com. bd. trustees Queens Mus. of Art, 2001—; chmn. law com. N.Y.C. Cmty. Bd. 6, Queens, 1980—88, chmn. econ. devel. com., 1988—99; chmn. Bronx Borough Pres.'s Adv. Com. on Resource Recovery, 1988—90; bd. dirs. Bronx Arts Coun., 1981—, Greater N.Y. Met. Food Coun., 1986—, Jewish Repertory Theatre, 1987—, chmn., 2001—. Fellow Am. Bar Found.; mem. ABA (co-chmn. pro bono project corp. law dept. 1986-88, chmn. 1988-90, com. of corp. gen. counsel 1974—, planning chmn. 1994-96, membership chmn. 1996-98, pro bono chair 2000—), Am. Corp. Counsel Assn. (bd. dirs. Met. N.Y. chpt. 1987—, bd. dirs. Found. 1992-99), Assn. Bar City N.Y. Office: Krasdale Foods Inc 400 Food Center Dr Bronx NY 10474-7098

BALKCOM, CAROL ANN, insurance agent; b. Newport, R.I., June 20, 1952; d. Robert Terrence and Barbara Ruth (Hilton) Hannaway; m. Richard Roger Balkcom, Oct., 1981; children: Richard Robert, Geoffrey Adam. BA, R.I. Coll., 1974, MA in Teaching, 1981; Cert. Life Underwriter, Am. Coll., 1984, ChFC, 1986. CLU, ChFC. Tchr. Lincoln (R.I.) Jr. High Sch., 1974-78; sales agt. Met. Life Ins. Co., Pawtucket, R.I., 1978-80; mgr., agt. Phoenix Mut. Life Ins. Co., Providence, 1980-94; instr. R.I. Lic. Sch., Providence, 1986-93; dist. mgr. New Eng. Fin., New Port Richey, 1994-99; brokerage mgr. Kaloust Brokerage, Tampa, Fla., 1999—. Mem. industry com., membership com. Com. 100; mem. Jr. Svc. League, treas. 1999—. Mem. R.I. Life Underwriters (bd. dirs. 1981-84, 90—, 1st v.p. 1983-84), Soc. of Fin. Svc. Profls. (bd. dirs., edn. chmn. Tampa chpt. 1999—, treas. 2000—). Avocations: cooking, entertaining.

BALKE, FRANK H. language educator, director; arrived in U.S., 1954; s. Bruno and Annemarie Balke; m. Nancy Gardner; children: Anacka, Koert. BS chemistry, Univ. Okla., Norman, Okla., 1961, MA German, 1964; PhD, Univ. Oreg., Eugene, Oreg., 1980. Instr. State Coll. Iowa, Cedar Falls, Iowa, 1964—69; asst. prof. Univ. No. Iowa, Cedar Falls, Iowa, 1969—72, Oreg. Coll. of Edn., Monmouth, Oreg., 1972—80; assoc. prof. Western Oreg. State Coll., Monmouth, Oreg., 1980—86; full prof. Western Oreg. Univ., Monmouth, Oreg., 1987—. Dir. Oreg. Summer Study Bd., Monmouth, Oreg., 1975—, Internat. Studies, Monmouth, Oreg., 1987—2000, Internat. Study Abroad, Monmouth, Oreg., 2000—. Author: A Summer Study Abroad Effect of Study Abroad on Students of German, 1980. Soccer ofcl. NISOA, OISA, SSRA, Salem, Oreg., 1985—. Recipient Tchr. of the Yr., Conf. of Oreg. Language Tchr., 1979, Hon. Citizen, C. of C., Austria, 1984. Mem.: Am. Assn. Tchrs. of German. Achievements include Initiated and directed internat. study abroad at Oreg. Coll. of Edn., now Western Oreg. Univ; development of and initiated cert. for German tchg. major at OCE and the internat. studies academic program of Western Oreg. Avocations: skiing, tennis, theater, reading, stamps. Office: Western Oreg Univ Office of Study Abroad Monmouth OR 97361

BALKE, VICTOR H. bishop; b. Meppen, Ill., Sept. 29, 1931; s. Bernard H. and Elizabeth A. (Knese) B.. BA in Philosophy, St. Mary of Lake Sem., Mundelein, Ill., 1954, STB in Theology, 1956, MA in Religion, 1057, STL in Theology, 1958; MA in English, St. Louis U., 1964, PhD, 1973. Priest Roman Cath. Ch., 1958. Asst. pastor, Springfield, Ill., 1958—62; chaplain St. Joseph Home Aged, Springfield, 1962—63; procurator, instr. Diocesan Sem., Springfield, 1963—70, rector, instr., 1970—76; ordained, installed 6th bishop Crookston, Minn., 1976—. Mem.: Lions, KC. Office: Chancery Office PO Box 610 Crookston MN 56716-0610*

BALKIN, DAVID BRUCE, management consultant, educator; b. Chgo., Apr. 16, 1948; s. Daniel Philip and Doris (Siegel) Balkin. BA, UCLA, 1970; MS, U. Minn. Mpls, 1979; PhD, U. Minn., 1981. Asst. prof. Northeastern U., Boston, 1981—85; asst. prof. La. State U., Baton Rouge, 1985—88, U. Colo., Boulder, 1988—90, assoc. prof., 1990—95, prof., 1995—. Mem. adv. bd. WorldatWork, Scottsdale, Ariz., 2000—02. Author: (book) Compensation, Organizational Strategy and Firm Performance, 1992, (Textbook) Managing Human Resources, 2001, Management, 2002; assoc. editor Human Resources Mgmt. Rev., 1997—2003; contbr. articles to profl. jours. Mem.: Mgmt. Acad. (Best article of Yr. 1992, Best Empirical Paper 2001). Avocations: tennis, skiing, jogging. Office: U Colo Coll Bus Adminstrn PO Box 419 Boulder CO 80309-0419

BALKO, GEORGE ANTHONY, III, lawyer, educator; b. Bklyn., June 22, 1955; s. George Anthony Jr. and Settimia (Palumbo) B. AB, Yale U., 1977; JD, U. Calif., San Francisco, 1986. Bar: Mass. 1986, U.S. Dist. Ct. Mass. 1987, U.S. Dist. Ct. Conn. 1999, U.S. Ct. Appeals (1st cir.) 1987, D.C 1990. Assoc. Swartz & Swartz, Boston, 1986-87, Bowditch & Dewey, LLP, Worcester, Mass., 1987-95, ptnr., 1996—. Adj. prof. Anna Maria Coll., Paxton, Mass., 1988-2000, mem. paralegal studies adv. bd., 1988-95. Author: Risk Management for Nursing Homes: A Primer In Long-Term Care Adminstration Handbook, 1993, Ambulatory Care and the Law: Lien Claims Where None Exist As of Right, 1995; legal columnist Jour. of Workers Compensation, 1996-99. Mem. Rice Sch. PTA, Holden, Mass., 1989-93; bd. health Town of Holden, 1995-99, chmn. 1996-99; moderator, 1999—; pres., bd. dirs. Elm Park Ctr. for Early Childhood Edn., 1994-96, mem. 1993-97. Recipient Am. Jurisprudence award for Ins. Law Lawyers Coop. Pub. Co. and Bancroft Whitney Co., 1985. Roman Catholic. Avocations: history, travel, tennis. Home: 4 Chestnut Hill Rd Holden MA 01520-1603 Office: Bowditch and Dewey LLP PO Box 15156 311 Main St Worcester MA 01615-0156 E-mail: gbalko@bowditch.com.

BALL, ALAN, screenwriter; b. Atlanta, 1957; Student in theater, Fla. State U. Founding mem., writer, actor, dir. Alarm Dog Rep. Screenwriter, co-prodr. (feature film) American Beauty, 1999 (Oscar for best screenplay 1999, Golden Globe for best screenplay motion picture 2000, Satellite award for best original screenplay 2000; best screenplay BFCA award, DGA award, ALFA award, SEFCA award and WGA Screen award 2000); screenwriter, creator, exec. prodr. (tv series) Grace Under Fire, 1993; co-exec. prodr. (tv series) Cybill, 1995; exec. prodr., creator (tv series) Oh Grow Up, 1999; screenwriter, dir., exec. prod. (tv series) Six Feet Under, 2001- (Emmy for outstanding director for a drama series 2002). Office: c/o Andrew Cannava United Talent Agy 9560 Wilshire Blvd Fl 5 Beverly Hills CA 90212-2401

BALL, ARDELLA PATRICIA, library media educator; b. Nashville, Dec. 15, 1932; d. Otis Hugh and Mary Ellen (Staples) Boatright; m. Wesley James Ball, June 15, 1931; children: Wesley James, Roderic Lynn, Weselyn Lynette, Patrick Wayne. AB, Fisk U., Nashville, 1953; MSLS, Atlanta U., 1956; ScD, Nova U., 1991. Tchr., libr. Fayetteville (Tenn.) H.S., 1954-57; children's libr. N.Y. Pub. Libr., summer 1957; cataloger Ala. A&M U., Huntsville, 1957-59; sr. cataloger St. Louis U., 1960-65; cataloger G.E.L. Regional Libr., Savannah, Ga., 1965-68, Armstrong Atlantic State U., Savannah, 1968-74, instrnl. devel. libr., 1974-77, libr. media educator, 1977—. Author course manuals for core media courses. Mem. Ga. Libr. Assn., Ga. Media Assn. Democrat. Mem. Ch. of Christ. Home: 67 Amanda Dr Savannah GA 31406 Office: Armstrong Atlantic State U 11935 Abercorn St Savannah GA 31419-1909

BALL, ARMAND BAER, former association executive, consultant; b. Dubach, La., Sept. 30, 1930; s. Armand Baer and Lovera (Sanderson) B.; m. Beverly Jane Hodges, Sept. 15, 1957; children— Kathryn Lynn, Robin Armand. BA, La. Coll., 1951; MRE, Southwestern Bapt. Theol. Sem., 1953; MS, George Williams Coll., 1960. Royal Ambassador dir. Fla. Bapt. Conv., Jacksonville, 1953-57; program dir. Woodlawn Boys' Club, Chgo., 1957-58; camp/youth dir. YMCA, Nashville, 1958-62; exec. dir. YMCA Camps Widjiwagan/duNord, St. Paul YMCA, 1962-74; exec. v.p. Am. Camping Assn., Martinsville, Ind., 1974-88; cons., 1988—; assoc. Campaign Assocs., Phila., 1989—. Author: (with Beverly H. Ball) Basic Camp Management, 2000; editor: A Cost Study of Resident Camps, 1985; Internat. Camping Fellowship newsletter, 1987-97; co-editor: Business and Finance, Site and Facilities; Trendlines newsletter. Cons. Ctr. for Disease Control, St. Petersburg (Russia) Children's Camps, Malaysian Tourist Bd., Pan-Am. Inst. of Phys. Edn. (Venezuela), Heritage Conservation and Recreation Svc., Project Reach, Boy Scouts Am., United Ch. of Christ, YMCA, Episcopal Ch.; mem. Internat. Camping Fellowship; bd. dirs. Sanibel-Captiva Conservation Found., Cmty. Housing Resources, Inc.; chair Sanibel Parks and Recreation Com. Recipient Disting. Svc. award Am. Camping Assn., 1989, Druszba award, 2002; named Citizen of the Yr., Sanibel, Fla., 1999, Disting. Alumni of Yr., Aurora U., 2003. Mem. Am. Soc. Assn. Execs. (cert. assoc. exec. life), World Future Soc., Audubon Soc., Canadian Camping Assn., Kiwanis (Hixon award). Home and Office: 1351 Middle Gulf Dr Apt 2A Sanibel FL 33957-4631 E-mail: alphaball@worldnet.att.net.

BALL, BETTY JEWEL, retired social worker, consultant; b. Sherman, Tex., Aug. 9, 1933; d. Emmett Jesse and Ethel Viola (Chesnut) B. BS, Okla. Bapt. U., 1954; M.Religious Edn., Carver Sch., 1958; MSW, Smith Coll., 1964. Cert. and lic. clin. social workers, Ill. Psychiat. social worker Inst. for Juvenile Rsch., Chgo., 1964-66; dir. child devel. ctr. Infant Welfare Soc. Chgo., 1966-71; dir. day hosp. for children Madden Mental Health Ctr., Chgo., 1971-78; child and adolescent coord. Ill. Dept. Mental Health, Chgo., 1978-83; pvt. practice social work cons. Hoffman Estates, Ill., 1983-93. Home and Office: 1225 Via Rafael San Marcos CA 92069-7102

BALL, CARROLL RAYBOURNE, anatomist, medical educator, researcher; b. Leakesville, Miss., Oct. 11, 1925; s. Marvin Hugh and Elizabeth (Hillman) B.; m. Jannie Vee Brooks, Sept. 5, 1947 (dec. 1954); children: Hugh Brooks, Peter Stephen; m. Sally Ann Montgomery, Mar. 22, 1963 (div. 1976); 1 child, Lou Ellen. BA, U. Miss., 1947, MS, 1948, PhD, 1963. Grad. asst. in zoology U. Miss., Oxford, 1946-48; instr. Duke U., 1948-51; instr. anatomy Med. Sch. W.Va. U., 1951-57; asst. prof. biology U. So. Miss., 1957-60; asst. prof. U. Miss. Med. Ctr., Jackson, 1963-66, assoc. prof., 1966-71, prof., 1971-99. Contbr. numerous articles to profl. jours. Pres. Jackson Civil War Round Table,

1983-84; chmn. Hist. Coker House Restoration Project, 1984-99; v.p. Magnolia chpt. Nat. Assn. Watch and Clock Collectors, 1980-82; bd. dirs. Miss. Hist. Soc., 1976-79, 85-88, 93-96. Lt. comdr. USNR, 1944-71, PTO. NIH predoctoral trainee, 1960-63; Miss. Heart Assn. grantee, 1963-66 Mem. Am. Assn. Anatomists, Soc. Exptl. Biology and Medicine, Am. Assn. Pathology, So. Assn. Anatomy, Miss. Acad. Sci., Hattiesburg Jr. C. of C. (sec. 1959-60), Order of First Families of Miss. (Gov. Gen. 2001-2003), Sigma Xi, Alpha Epsilon Delta, Theta Nu Sigma, Beta Beta Beta (pres. 1947-48), Omicron Delta Kappa, Pi Kappa Alpha (sec. 1943-44) Methodist.

BALL, DONALD L. retired English language educator; b. Balt., Oct. 25, 1922; s. Ambrose Markley and Daisy Gertrude (Anderson) B.; stepmother Thelma (Bonneville) B.; m. Barbara Jean Stevens, May 3, 1950; children: Helen Ball Williams, Ann S., Allison Ball Miller, Markley Ball Rizzi. BA, U. Richmond, 1948; MA, U. Del., 1951; PhD, U. N.C., 1965. Asst. mgr. resort hotels in Md. and Fla., 1948-53; instr. English Va. Mil. Inst., Lexington, 1953-57; part-time instr. U. N.C., Chapel Hill, 1957-60; faculty Coll. William and Mary, Williamsburg, Va., 1960-89, prof., 1976-89; vis. prof. English U.S. Mil. Acad., West Point, N.Y., 1984-85. Author: Samuel Richardson's Theory of Fiction, 1971, Fighting Amphibs The LCS(L) in World War II, 1997; contbr. articles to profl. publs. Served to lt. (j.g.) USNR, 1943-46, PTO. Research grantee Coll. William and Mary, 1978. Mem. MLA. Episcopalian. Avocations: genealogy, history, music. Home: 1 Cole Ln Williamsburg VA 23185-3313

BALL, DONALD MAURY, agronomist, consultant; b. Owensboro, Ky., Aug. 5, 1945; s. William Alonzo and Mary Ruth (Waltrip) B.; Vonda Lee Hatcher, June 3, 1967; children: Kelly Wayne, Allison Lee. BS, Western Ky. U., 1968; MS, Auburn U., 1973, PhD, 1976. Cert. profl. agronomist. Extension agronomist Auburn (Ala.) U., 1976-88, extension agronomist/prof., 1988-97, alumni prof., 1997—. Mem. nat. adv. com. Alfalfa Coun., Davis, Calif., 1983-2003; tech. advisor Oreg. Tall Fescue Commn., Salem, 1990—; tech. liaison Oreg. Clover Commn., Salem, 1994—; del. Internat. Grassland Congress, Nice, France, 1989; spkr. in field. Author: Southern Forages, 1991, Practical Forage Concepts, 1999; contbr. over 500 articles to profl. and applied jours. and trade mags. Elder First Presbyn. Ch., Auburn, 1982-85. With U.S. Army, 1968-71. Recipient Superior Svc. award USDA, Washington, 1986, Extension Excellence award Auburn Univ. Alumni Assn., 1988, Alumnus of Yr. award Western Ky. Univ. Dept. Agrl., Bowling Green, 1990, Hall of Disting. Alumni, 2000. Fellow Am. Soc. Agronomy (Crops and Soils award 1984, ext. Agronomy Edn. award 1993), Crop Sci. Soc. Am.; mem. Am. Forage and Grassland Coun. (pres. 1990-91, Merit award 1984, Medallion award 1993), So. Pasture and Forage Crop Improvement Conf. (chair 1987-88). Democrat. Office: Auburn Univ Dept Agronomy & Soils Auburn AL 36849

BALL, EDWARD DAVID, hematologist, oncologist; b. Syracuse, N.Y., Mar. 15, 1950; s. Edward and Della Lucille (Koehler) B.; m. Elizabeth Kate Rath, June 20, 1970 (div. 1975); 1 child, David; m. Susan Elaine Blonder, Jan. 15, 1977; children: Brian, Lindsey. BS in Biochemistry, U. Md., 1972; MD, Case Western Res. U., 1976. Resident Hartford Hosp., 1976-79; fellow in hematology and oncology Univ. Hosps. Cleve., 1979-81, Dartmouth-Hitchcock Med. Ctr., 1982-83; asst. prof. Dartmouth Coll., Hanover, N.H., 1982-86, assoc. prof., 1986-91; prof. U. Pitts., 1991-98; prof. medicine, chief divsn. blood and marrow transplant U. Calif., San Diego, 1998—. Co-founder Medarex, Inc., Princeton, N.J., 1987; dir. bone marrow transplant program Pitts. Cancer Inst., 1993-98, co-dir. leukemia/lymphoma program, 1991-98; mem. staff Montefiore U. Hosp., Pitts., 1991-98, Presbyn. U. Hosp., Pitts., 1991-98; assoc. mem. Hitchcock Clinic, Hanover, N.H., 1983-91; mem. clin. staff Mary Hitchcock Meml. Hosp., Hanover, 1983-91; mem. sr. staff Norris Cotton Cancer Ctr., Hanover, 1983-91. Contbr. articles to profl. jours. Bd. dirs. Leukemia Soc. Am., Pitts., 1991-98. Scholar Leukemia Soc. Am., 1986-91, Stolhman award; Tiffany Blake fellow Hitchcock Found., 1982-83. Mem. AAAS, ACP, Am. Soc. Hematology, Am. Soc. Clin. Oncology, Am. Assn. Immunologists, Am. Assn. Cancer Rsch., Am. Fedn. for Clin. Rsch., Am. Soc. for Blood and Marrow Transplantation (bd. dirs. 2001—), Am. Soc. for Clin. Investigation, Internat. Soc. for Exptl. Hematology (councilor 2003—, Internat. Soc. for Hematotherapy and Graft Engring., Inc., Assn. Subsplty. Profs., Assn. Hematology/Oncology Program Dirs. (pres. 1998-2000), Phi Beta Kappa, Phi Kappa Phi. Avocations: running, skiing, hiking, biking, surfing. Office: U Calif San Diego 9500 Gilman Dr La Jolla CA 92093-0961 E-mail: tball@ucsd.edu.

BALL, GORDON VICTOR, adult education educator, writer, editor, photographer; b. Paterson, N.J., Dec. 30, 1944; s. Gordon Victor and Daisy Belle Ball; m. Kathleen Louise Zobel, Aug. 11, 1980; 1 child, Daisy Barbara. BA, Davidson Coll., 1966; MA, U. N.C., 1976, PhD, 1980. Asst. prof. Old Dominion U., Norfolk, Va., 1981—85; fulbright specialist lectr. Am. Lit. Sophia, Rikkyo, Waseda Univs., Tokyo, 1983—84; asst. to assoc. prof. Tougaloo Coll., Tougaloo, Miss., 1985—89; Am. culture specialist Adam Mickiewicz U., Poznani, Poland, 1986, am. culture specialist, 1988; asst., assoc. and full prof. Va. Mil. Inst., Lexington, 1989—. Sec. Com. on Poetry, Inc., N.Y.C., 1969—; mem. nat. adv. bd. ALSOS, Va., 2000—. Author: (book) '66 Frames: A Memoir, 1999; editor (with Allen Ginsberg): three books, including Allen Verbatim: Lectures on Poetry, Politics, Consciousness, 1974 (Pulitzer nominee, 1974), films, photographs in numerous books and jours., films in galleries and instns., —. Recipient numerous ind. filmaking awards, 1977—90, Fulbright Specialist Lectureship, Coun. Internat. Exch. of Scholars, 1983—84. Mem.: Modern Lang. Assn. Avocations: photography, film making. Home: 339 Sugar Creek Rd Lexington VA 24450 Office: Va Mil Inst Lexington VA 24450 E-mail: ballgv@vmi.edu.

BALL, HAYWOOD MORELAND, lawyer; b. Jacksonville, Fla., June 29, 1939; s. John Willis and Margaret Ann (Moreland) Ball; m. Anne Towers, June 16, 1962; children: William Tucker, Sarah Anne Sheffield, David Winchester. BA, Washington and Lee U., 1961; JD, U. Fla., 1964. Bar: Fla. 1964, U.S. Dist. Ct. (mid. dist.) Fla. 1964, U.S. Ct. Appeals (11th cir.) 1964. Ptnr. Ulmer, Murchison, Ashby and Ball, Jacksonville, 1964-83, Donahoo, Ball & McMenamy P.A., Jacksonville, 1983—. Bd. dirs. Habitat for Humanity, Jacksonville Beaches, 1999—2003, pres., 2000—02. Mem.: Fla. Bar Assn. (bd. govs. young lawyers sect. 1970—74). Republican. Episcopalian. Avocation: golf. Office: Donahoo Ball & McMenamy P A Ste 2925 50 N Laura St Jacksonville FL 32202-3677 Home: 317 E Church St Jacksonville FL 32202 E-mail: hball@donahooball.com.

BALL, HOWARD GUY, education specialist educator; b. Lancaster, Ohio, Aug. 4, 1930; s. Howard Emitt and Edith Mildred (Clark) B.; married; children: Brian, Maryla. BS, Ohio State U., 1952, MS, 1969, PhD, 1972. Edn. specialist Ohio Dept. Edn., Columbus, 1964-71; assoc. prof. N.C. State U., 1971-74; mem. faculty Ala. A&M U., Normal, 1974—; prof. emeritus Ala. A&M U. (Sch. Library Media); chmn. bd. Communicon, Inc., Huntsville, Ala. Chmn. Media Svcs., Inc.; pres. Higby Inc.; dir. So. Inst. for Black Studies, 1995-96. Mem. editorial bd. Library Scene, 1979-80, Media and Methods: Early Years, 1984-85; contbr. articles to profl. jours.; authored, directed Training of Librarians in CATV, 1975. Mem. Ala. Council Human Relations, 1978—, Ala. Democratic Council, 1978— ; sec. Orgn. Inner City Govts., 1977— . Recipient NAACP Community award, 1976, Raleigh C. of C. educator's award, 1973 Mem. ALA, Assn. Educators Communication and Tech., Assn. Ednl. Research (regional v.p. 1985-86), Phi Beta Kappa, Phi Delta Kappa, Kappa Alpha Psi. Clubs: Masons. Presbyterian.

BALL, JACQUELINE SNYDER, librarian, educator; b. Winston-Salem, N.C., May 4, 1932; d. Henry Edward and Lucy Jane (Lambeth) Snyder; m. James Bryan Ball, Aug. 7, 1960; children: Michaela Anne, Jason Alan. BS in Edn., Appalachian State U., 1955; MS in Libr. and Info. Sci., U. Tenn., 1979; postgrad., Middle Tenn. State U., 1989. Cert. tchr., Tenn. Libr. media specialist Forsyth County Schs., Winston-Salem, 1955-57, Oak Ridge (Tenn.) Schs., 1957-68, 79-94; edn. reporter Freeman Comm., Oak Ridge, 1994—97. Adj. instr. Grad. Sch. Libr. and Information Sci. U. Tenn., 1991-1997. Host talk show Oak Ridge Today, 1987-89; book reviewer of young adult lit. The Oak Ridger, 1988-89, drama critic, 1992—; TV commentator ednl. news, Oak Ridge, 1992-1997. Mem. Am. Assn. Univ. Women, Nat. Edn. Assn. (life), Alpha Psi Omega, Beta Phi Mu. Episcopalian. Avocations: singer, actress. Home: 110 Berwick Dr Oak Ridge TN 37830-7831

BALL, JAMES CHARLES, biochemist, researcher, herpetologist; b. Denver, Jan. 30, 1953; s. George Monroe and Orel Louise Ball; m. Jill Elaine Shumaker; children: Andrea Marie, James Brennan, Steffen Michael, Nathaniel David. BS in Chemistry, Calif. State Poly. U., 1976; PhD in Chemistry, U. N.Mex., 1980. Postdoctoral rsch. fellow Mich. State U./Chem. Carcinogenesis Lab., East Lansing, 1980—82; rsch. scientist Ford Motor Co., Dearborn, Mich., 1982—. Adj. prof. biology Ctrl. Mich. U., Mount Pleasant; gen. conf. chmn. Toxic Air Pollutants from Mobile Sources, 1991. Contbr. articles to profl. jours. Mem.: Am. Cancer Soc., Environ. Mutagen Soc., Am. Chem. Soc., Chgo. Herpetol. Soc., Herpetologist's League, Am. Soc. Ichthyologists and Herpetologists, Soc. for Study of Amphibians and Reptiles. Avocations: herp hunting, photography. Office: Ford Motor Co Sci Rsch Lab MD 3083 Dearborn MI 48121-2053 Personal E-mail: jball@ford.com.

BALL, JAMES HERINGTON, retired lawyer; b. Kansas City, Mo., Sept. 20, 1942; s. James T. Jr. and Betty Sue (Herington) B.; m. Wendy Anne Wolfe, Dec. 28, 1964; children: James H. Jr., Steven Scott. AB, U. Mo., 1964; JD cum laude, St. Louis U., 1973. Bar: Mo. 1973. Asst. gen. counsel Anheuser-Busch, Inc., St. Louis, 1973-76; v.p., gen. counsel, sec. Stouffer Corp., Solon, Ohio, 1976-83; sr. v.p., gen. counsel Nestle Enterprises, Inc., Solon, 1983-91; gen. counsel, sr. v.p. Nestle USA, Inc., Glendale, Calif., 1991-99. Editor-in-chief St. Louis U. Law Jour., 1972-73. Bd. dirs. Alliance for Children's Rights, L.A., 1992-99, Am. Swiss Found., N.Y.C., 1996-99. Lt. comdr. USN, 1964-70, Vietnam. Mem. Mo. Bar Assn.

BALL, JAMES WILLIAM, financial executive; b. Tacoma, June 23, 1942; s. Montgomery McKinley and Ann Marie Ball; m. Patricia Miller, July 29, 1977; children: Katherine Kendall, Molly Elizabeth. Student, St. Martin's Coll., Lacy, Wash., 1960-61, San Jose City Coll., 1966-68; BA, San Jose State U., 1970, MA, 1971; postgrad., U. Calif., Irvine, 1971-72. Store mgr. Food Villa Inc., San Jose, Calif., 1972-76; asst. mgr. Ralph's Inc., San Jose, 1976-78; pres., owner Ball Liquors Inc., San Jose, 1978-88; pres. Fast Cash Inc., San Jose, 1984—. Mem. Fin. Svc. Ctrs. Am. Inc. (dir. 1994—, sec. 1998), Calif. Fin. Svc. Providers (v.p. 1988-97, pres. 1997). Office: Fast Cash Inc 2270 Quimby Rd San Jose CA 95122-1355

BALL, JENNIFER LEIGH, writer, editor; b. South Charleston, W.Va., Aug. 6, 1961; d. Robert Lee Ball and Lois Jean (Sovine) White. BA, Marshall U., Huntington, W.Va., 1983; MA, U. Colo., Colorado Springs, 1997. Copy writer Klausner Cooperage, Louisville, 1986; staff writer Ky. Power Co., Ashland, 1987-91; print buyer Focus on the Family, Colorado Springs, 1992-94; publs. mgr. Compassion Internat., Colorado Springs, 1994-96; editor Internat. Bible Soc., Colorado Springs, 1996-2000; comm. dir. Global Action, Colorado Springs, 2000—03. Editor: Discerning the Times, 1999, Light Inside, 1998; co-produced video/acad. rsch., Ethnic Minority Diversity at University of Colorado: Perceptions and Communication Processes, 1997. Avocations: equine sports, volleyball, camping, hiking. Home: 17620 Spur Ranch Rd N Peyton CO 80831-7653 E-mail: denmark86@earthlink.com.

BALL, JOHN FLEMING, advertising and film production executive; b. Evanston, Ill., Apr. 26, 1930; s. Edward Hyde and Kathleen (Fleming) B.; m. Anne Idabelle Firestone, Nov. 9, 1957; children— John Fleming, Jr., David Firestone, Sheila Ball Burkert. BA, Princeton, 1952. Assoc. producer, progam exec. CBS, N.Y.C., 1955-59; with J. Walter Thompson Co., N.Y.C., 1959—, v.p., 1965—, dir. programs, 1965-67, dir. broadcasting, 1967—83, pres., dir. Survival Anglia Ltd. div., 1972—; pres. Trident Anglia Inc., 1976—83; chmn. John F. Ball Prodns., John F. Ball Co., 1984—. Trustee Found. Am. Dance; chmn. instructional TV, Archidiocese of N.Y.; bd. dirs. Hist. Soc. Town of Greenwich, Conn. With USN, 1952-54. Mem. Knights of Holy Sepulchre of Jerusalem Knights of Sovereign Mil. Order of Malta, Knights of Order of St. Gregory the Gt., Cap and Gown Club of Princeton U. (N.Y.C.), Links Club, Round Hill Club (Greenwich), Nassau Club (Princeton), Am. Club (London), Princeton Triangle Club (chmn. emeritus grad. bd.). Home: Deer Park Greenwich CT 06830 also: Northport Point Northport MI 49670 Office: 4 Woodside Rd Greenwich CT 06830-3819 E-mail: jfbp@aol.com.

BALL, JOHN PAUL, publishing company executive; b. N.Y.C., Dec. 15, 1946; s. William Emil and Else (Schmid) B.; m. Jayne Barbara Irwin, Jan. 30, 1970 (div. 1991); m. Eileen M. Mitchell, Oct. 25, 1997. Student, N.Y. Sch. Printing, 1964. Prodn. assoc. Macmillan Co., N.Y.C., 1964-65; asst. to pres. Frederick Fell, Inc., N.Y.C., 1965-69; v.p. William Morrow & Co., Inc., N.Y.C., 1969-86; sr. v.p. mfg. and paper purchasing Macmillan Pub. Co., N.Y.C., 1986-94; pub. and graphic arts cons., chmn. bd. Electronic Pub. Svcs. Inc., N.Y.C., 1994—; exec. v.p., sec. Hungry Minds, Inc., N.Y.C., Calif., 1996—2001; cons. in pub. N.Y.C., 2001—. Recipient Comet Press award graphic arts, 1964, Columbia Scholastic Press Assn. Best Editorial Writing award, 1965. Office: Electronic Pub Svcs Inc 15 E 32d St 2d Fl New York NY 10016

BALL, JOHN ROBERT, healthcare executive; b. Opelika, Ala., July 16, 1944; s. John Cooper Jr. and Ellen Beverly (Williams) B.; m. Cornelia Anne Phillips, Aug. 13, 1966 (div. 1983); children: Kristen Anne, John Robert; m. Pamela Preston Reynolds, Jan. 9, 1988. AB, Emory U., 1966; JD, Duke U., 1971, MD, 1972. Rsch. assoc. Duke U. Sch. Medicine, Durham, NC, 1971—72, resident in medicine, 1972-74; asst. to dir. office asst. sec. for health USPHS, Rockville, Md., 1974-76; chief med. audit br. bur. quality assurance HEW, Rockville, 1976-77; sr. policy analyst Office Sci. and Tech. Policy Exec. Office of Pres., Washington, 1978-81; assoc. exec. v.p. ACP, Phila., 1981-86, exec. v.p., 1986-94, also master; sr. scholar Assn. Acad. Health Ctrs., Washington, 1994-95; exec. v.p., acting pres., CEO Pa. Hosp., Phila., 1995-96, pres., CEO, 1996-99; sr. v.p. The Lewin Group, Falls Church, Va., 2000; exec. v.p. Am. Soc. Clin. Pathology, Chgo., 2002—. Robert Wood Johnson clin. scholar George Washington U., Washington, 1977-79; bd. mgrs. Pa. Hosp., 1988-97; bd. dirs. Milbank Meml. Fund. Assoc. editor Jour. Am. Geriatrics Soc., 1984-86; mem. editorial bd. Internat. Jour. Tech. Assessment in Health Care, 1986-89, European Jour. Internal Medicine, 1988-94, Duke U. Law Jour., 1969-71; contbr. articles to profl. jours. Sr. surgeon USPHS, 1974-77. John Gordon Stipe scholar, Nat. Merit scholar, Emory U., 1962. Mem. Inst. Medicine of NAS, N.C. Bar Assn., Am. Clin. and Climatol. Assn., Soc. Med. Adminstrs. Democrat. E-mail: johnrball@hotmail.com.

BALL, KAREN MICHELE, music educator, musician, composer; b. Salem, Ohio, Dec. 21, 1952; d. Clifford David Aiken and Helen Rita Kovacik; m. Stephen Wayne Ball, Dec. 29, 1973; children: Rachel, Elizabeth, Judah. MusB, Temple U., 1976; MusM, No. Ill. U., 1992; D of Music Arts, U. Ill., 1992. Instr. piano pvt. practice, Columbus, Ohio, 1980—88, Wheaton, Ill., 1989—99, Wheaton Coll. Sch. Arts, 1989—99; assoc. prof. music Olivet Nazarene U., Bourbonnais, 2001—. Guest lectr. Wheaton Coll., 1998—2001; arranger various piano arrangements of hymns, 1976—. Rec. pianist (radio broadcast) Transworld Radio, Swaziland, South Africa, 1991; composer: (choral composition) The Three Psalms, 1988, various sacred solo songs. Ch. pianist Trinity Ch. Nazarene, Naperville, Ill., 1998—2001, Coll. Ch. Nazarene, Bourbonnais, 2001—. Recipient 1st pl. Music Downbeat award, 1992. Mem.: Nat. Coll. Musicians (judge piano guild 2001—), Ill. State Music Assn., Phi Kappa Lambda, Phi Kappa Phi. Republican. Avocations: reading, travel, research. Home: 1180 Lafite St Bourbonnais IL 60914 Office: Olivet Nazarene Coll 1 Univ Ave Bourbonnais IL 60914 E-mail: kball@olivet.edu.

BALL, KAY ATKINSON, health services consultant; b. Columbus, Ohio, Mar. 13, 1949; d. Donald Thomas and Betty Jean (Parton) Atkinson; m. David Allen Ball, May 6, 1967 (div. 1984); children: Christopher D., Trevor A.; m. Daniel Charles Flynn, May 4, 1991. ADN, Columbus Tech. Inst., 1975; B in Nursing, Otterbein Coll., Westerville, Ohio, 1983; M in Health Care Adminstrn., Cen. Mich. U., 1987. Cert. operating rm. nurse. Asst. dir. surgery and recovery rm. Drs. Hosp. North, Columbus, Ohio, 1975-85; laser program dir. Grant Med. Ctr., Columbus, Ohio, 1985-90, Mt. Carmel Health, Columbus, Ohio, 1990-93, United Med. Network, Dublin, Ohio, 1993-96; v.p. K&D Med. Inc., Lewis Center, Ohio. Cons. and lectr. in field. Author: Lasers: The Perioperative Challenge, 1990, 95 (Book of Yr. award Am. Jour. Nursing 1991), Endoscopic Surgery, 1997; author, editor: Nursing Clinics of North American Laser Technology, 1990; editor-in-chief jours. Mimimally Invasive Surgical Nursing, 1991-95, Today's Surg. Nurse, 1995-99; contbr. articles to profl. jours. Laser tech., surg. issues, healthcare reform presenter Kiwanis, Rotary, Cen. Ohio, 1986—. Recipient Alumnae of Yr. award Otterbein Coll., 1997, Columbus State C.C., 1998. Mem. ANA, Am. Soc. Laser Medicine (nursing chair 1990-92, bd. dirs. 1993-95, Nursing Excellence award 1998), Laser Inst. Am., Assn. Perioperative Nurses (bd. dirs. 1988-93, pres. 1992-93, award for excellence 2003), Assn. Perioperative RNs Found. (trustee 1992-01, sec. 1999-00, pres. 2000-2001), Am. Assn. Nurse Anesthetists (coun. pub. interest 1993-00, U.S. pharmacopei surg. drugs devices expert panel 1995-00), Assn. Practitioners Infection Control Epidemiology, Am. Soc. Post Anesthesia Nurses, Ohio Nurses Assn. (health policy coun. 1996—, chair 2000—, Legis. Excellence award 2003), Mid Ohio Nurses Assn. (bd. dirs. 1998-2000), Ohio Nursing Summit (chair 1995-97), Soc. Gastroent. Nurses and Assocs., Am. Acad. Nursing, Torch and Key Club, Sigma Theta Tau. Methodist. Avocations: scuba diving, ballroom dancing, skiing, traveling. Home: 6743 S Old State Rd Lewis Center OH 43035-9227 Office: K&D Med Inc 6743 S Old State Rd Lewis Center OH 43035-9227 E-mail: kayball@aol.com.

BALL, KENNETH LEON, manufacturing company executive, organizational development consultant; b. New York City, Aug. 11, 1932; s. Oscar and Elvira (Klein) B.; m. Patricia Ann (Whitley); children: David B. and Dana K. BA, Antioch Coll., Yellow Springs, Ohio, 1954; PhD, Washington Univ., St. Louis, 1958. Lic. psychologist, Mo. Gen. mgr. Pacific Coast div. Orchard Corp. Am., St. Louis, 1960-62, indsl. rels. dir., 1963-64, v.p. indsl. rels., 1965-66, v.p., dir., 1967-72, exec. v.p., dir., 1972-75, pres., dir., 1976-88; pres. Orchard Decorative Products, div. Borden, Inc., St. Louis, 1988-92, Ken Ball Mgmt. Resources, St. Louis, 1993—. Adj. prof. Washington Univ., 1978—79. Contbg. author: Humanizing Organizational Behavior, 1976; Making Organizatios Humane and Productive, 1981; contbg. articles to publ. Trust Antioch U., 1980-85, 89-2000; dir. Met. Employment and Rehab. Svc., St. Louis, 1975-2001, chair, 1985-86; dir. St. Louis chpt. Young Audiences, 1990; Narcotic Svc. Coun., 1976; MERS/Goodwill, 2001—. Human Rels. Rsch. Found. fellow, 1955-58. Mem.: APA, Soc. Psychologists in Mgmt. (dir. 1989—, pres. 1992—93). Home: 14312 Quiet Meadow Ct E Chesterfield MO 63017 Office: Ken Ball Mgmt Resources 165 N Meramec Ave Ste 400 Clayton MO 63105-3772 Mailing: PO Box 6607 Chesterfield MO 63005 E-mail: kenlball@aol.com.

BALL, LAURENCE ANDREW, microbiologist, educator, researcher; b. York, Yorkshire, Eng., July 9, 1944; came to U.S., 1969; s. Laurence Elinger and Christine Mary Ball; m. Anne Marguerite Gordon-Walker, July 20, 1968 (div. 1983); children: Jennifer Susan Truitt, Katherine Sarah; m. Gail Williams Wertz, May. 25, 1987. BA, Oxford (Eng.) U., 1966, MA, DPhil, Oxford (Eng.) U., 1969. Rsch. fellow U. Wis., Madison, 1969-71; mem. sci. staff Nat. Inst. Med. Rsch. Mill Hill, London, 1972-74; asst. prof. in residence U. Conn., Storrs, 1974-79; assoc. prof. U. Wis., Madison, 1979-82, prof. biochemistry, 1982-87; prof. microbiology U. Ala., Birmingham, 1987—. Pres. Internat. Com. for Taxonomy of Viruses, 2002—. Editor: The Insect Viruses, 1998; contbr. more than 100 articles to profl. jours. Grantee Nat. Inst. for Allergy and Infectious Diseases, 1974—. Fellow: Am. Acad. Microbiology; mem.: European Acad. Scis., Am. Soc. for Microbiology, Am. Soc. for Virology (coun. 1997—2000). Avocations: reading, music, skiing, sailing. Office: U Ala at Birmingham BBRB 373/17 845 19th St Birmingham AL 35294-2170

BALL, LAWRENCE, retired physical scientist; b. Albion, N.Y., Aug. 10, 1933; s. Harold Witheral and Gladys (Gibbs) B.; m. Caroline Moran, June 21, 1957; children: Daniel Lawrence, Logan Edward, Stacey Laura Ball Lucero, Ryan Laird (dec.). Diploma, Williston Acad., 1952; BSME, Antioch Coll., 1957; MSc in Elec. Engring., Ohio State U., 1962. Engring. aid Wright Air Devel. Ctr., Dayton, Ohio, 1957-60; engr. Deco Electronics Inc., Boulder, Colo., 1962-66; sr. engr. Westinghouse Rsch. Labs., Boulder, 1966-73, Westinghouse Ocean Rsch. Lab., Annapolis, Md., 1973-74; program mgr. div. geothermal energy U.S. Dept. Energy, Washington, 1974-79, lab. dir. Grand Junction, Colo., 1979-93; ret., 1993; resident inspector Armstrong Cons., Inc., Grand Junction, Colo., 2000—. Pres. Liberty Cons. Co., Grand Junction, 1984—; emergency coord. dist. 3 Amateur Radio Emergency Svcs., 1995-97. Co-inventor coal mine communications; contbr. articles to profl. jours. Mem. various vol. fire depts., 1954—79, Boulder Res. Police, 1968—74; sr. patroller Nat. Ski Patrol Sys., Md., Colo., 1973—92; mem. Grand Junction Safety Coun., 1992—98; active Amateur Radio Emergency Svcs., 1995—, dist. emergency coord., 1997—99; bd. dirs. Colo. Head Injury Found., chpt. pres., 1989—91. Named Profl. Govt. Employee of Yr., Western Colo. Fed. Exec. Assn., 1991. Mem. Toastmasters Internat. (area gov. 1991-92, divsn. gov. 1992-93, Toastmaster of Yr. Western Colo. 1990, DTM & ATM-S 1994), West Slope Wheelman (charter bd. dirs. 1992-93), Western Colo. Amateur Radio Club, Inc. (pres. 1994-96, bd. dirs. 1996-98), Black Ridge Comms. Site Users Assn. (charter bd. dirs. 1995—, sec. 1997-2001, sec., treas. 1999-2001). Avocations: fishing, scuba diving (divecon), woodworking, amateur radio (extra class), Bible archaeology.

BALL, LOUIS ALVIN, insurance company executive; b. Oct. 25, 1921; s. George Rhodom and Frances Mariam (Beals) B.; m. Norma Jane Laudenberger, Jan. 17, 1947. BA in Bus. Adminstrn., Kans. State U., 1947. Asst. purchasing agt. Kansas City (Mo.) br. Ford Motor Co., 1942-46; with Farm Bur. Mut. Ins. Co., Inc., Manhattan, Kans., 1947—, claims underwriting mgr., 1956-61, sys. and procedures mgr., 1961—, asst. sec., 1977-81, corp. sec., 1981-90; ret., 1990. Mem. Nat. Ind. Insurers, Conf. Casualty Cos., Assn. Sys. Mgmt. (Internat. Merit award 1971, Internat. Achievement award 1978, Kansas City chpt. Merit award 1970, Kansas City chpt. Diamond Merit award 1977, chmn. ann. conf. 1982), Manhattan Country Club. Home: 1101 Pioneer Ln Manhattan KS 66502-4624

BALL, MARGIE BARBER, elementary school educator; b. San Antonio, Tex., June 28, 1943; d. Truman Joseph and Margaret Evelyn (Norman) Barber; m. Flamen Ball Jr., Aug. 20, 1966; children: Michael David, Matthew Joseph, Marissa Anne. BS, U. Houston, 1963; MS, Stephen F. Austin State U., 1985. Texas Tchr. Cert. Spanish tchr. Spring Branch Ind. Sch. Dist., Houston, 1964-66, tchr., 1966-68; dir. mother's day out Holy Spirit Episcopal, Tex., 1977-78; tchr. Nacogdoches (Tex.) Ind. Sch. Dist., 1979-82; kindergarten tchr. Christ Episc. Sch., 1982-87; early childhood tchr. Hudson Ind. Sch. Dist., Lufkin, Tex., 1987-94; tchr. pre-kindergarten/bilingual Lufkin Ind. Sch. Dist., 1994-95, tchr. pre-kindergarten/multi-age, 1995-96; tchr. kindergarten Hudson ISD, Lufkin, 1996-97; supr. student tchrs., adj. faculty Stephen F. Austin State U., Nacogdoches, 1997—2003. Mem. Tex. State Tchr. Assn., East Tex. Assn. Educators Young Children, Nacogdoches, Med. Wives Auxillary, Kiwanis, Phi Delta Kappa. Republican. Presbyterian. Avocations: gardening, reading, travel, volunteering, family.

BALL, MARKHAM (ROBERT BALL), lawyer, arbitrator, educator; b. Wilmington, Del., Mar. 24, 1934; s. Robert William and Helen (Slepicka) B.; m. Harriet Laura Janney, July 6, 1957; children: Laurence Markham, Richard Janney, Martha Harriet, Julia Helen. BA magna cum laude, Amherst Coll., 1956; BA with honors, Oxford (Eng.) U., 1958, MA, 1973; LLB, Harvard U., 1960. Bar: D.C. 1961, U.S. Supreme Ct. 1968. Law clk. U.S. Supreme Ct., Washington, 1960-61; assoc. Covington and Burling, Washington, 1961 64; asst. gen. counsel U.S. Office Econ. Opportunity, Washington, 1964-66; staff dir. U.S. Peace Corps, Washington, 1966-67; from assoc. to ptnr. Leva, Hawes, Symington, Martin and Oppenheimer, Washington, 1967-77; gen. counsel U.S. Agy. for Internat. Devel., Washington, 1977-79, mem. adv. com. on vol. fgn. aid, 1981-88; ptnr. Wald, Harkrader and Ross, Washington, 1980-85, Morgan, Lewis and Bockius, Washington, 1986-98, Holland and Knight, Washington, 1998—2002. Sr. fellow, dir. internat. arbitration program Internat. Law Inst., Washington, 2002—; lectr. Law Sch. U. Va., 1991—2001; adj. prof. Law Sch. Georgetown U., 2002—. Mem. adv. bd. Brasenose Coll. Charitable Found., Oxford, 1988—. Fellow Am. Bar Found.; Rhodes scholar Phi Beta Kappa, 1956-58. Mem. ABA, Internat. Bar Assn., Am. Arbitration Assn. (mem. internat. arbitration adv. panel 2002—), Alexandria Literary Soc. (sec. 1981—). Home: 7223 Stafford Rd Alexandria VA 22307-1806 Office: Internat Law Inst 1615 New Hampshire Ave Washington DC 20009 E-mail: mball@ili.org.

BALL, MILLICENT JOAN (PENNY BALL), science educator, consultant; b. Buffalo, Sept. 15, 1939; m. Neil Baggett, Aug. 9, 1965 (div. Nov. 1991). BS, Antioch Coll., 1961; PhD, U. Md., 1969. Rsch. assoc. Inst. Hochenergiephysik, Heidelberg, Germany, 1969-71; sr. programmer Imperial Coll., London, 1971-73; asst. prof. Purdue U., West Lafayette, Ind., 1973-77; systems analyst Calculon Corp., Germantown, Md., 1978-80; computer analyst Brookhaven Nat. Lab., Upton, N.Y., 1980-90; data mgmt. group leader Super Collider Lab.,

Dallas, 1990-94; pres.;project dir. MJB Cons., DeSoto, Tex., 1994-97; pres. MJB Plus, Inc., DeSoto, Tex., 1998—. Recipient SBIR award Dept. Energy, 1994. Mem. AAUW, Assn. Computing Machinery, Assn. for Women in Sci. Avocations: square dancing, travel. Home and Office: 1415 Country Ridge Dr Desoto TX 75115-7423 E-mail: penny@mjb-plus.com.

BALL, REX MARTIN, urban designer, architect; b. Oklahoma City, June 14, 1934; s. Ralph Martin and Sarah Mae (Kellner) B. BArch, Okla. State U., 1956; MArch, MIT, 1958. Lic. arch. Nat. Coun. Arch. Registration Bd.; cert. planner Am. Inst. Cert. Planners. With HTB Inc. (archtl., engring., interior planning firm), Oklahoma City, 1958-94; chmn. emeritus HTB Inc., 1958-94; founder, pres. Planning Assocs. Inc., 1960—; founder, pres., chmn., CEO Mid Continent Design Group, 1968—. Presdl. appt. to U.S. Commn. of Fine Arts, 1994-97. Exhibitor U.S./USSR exhibit "The Socially Responsible Environment, 1980-90; contbr. articles to profl. jours. Past chair Tulsa Preservation Com., 1997—; facilitator Internat. Coalition Art Deco Socs., 2003; bd. dirs. Price Tower Mus., 1998—; past treas. Philbrook Mus.'s Pacers. Recipient Bus. in the Arts award, 1988, 5 Who Care Corp. Humanitarian award, Gannett Found., 1988, Curt Schwartz Bus. in the Arts award, 1989, Phoenix award/Downtown Now, 1992, Cityscape award City of Oklahoma City, 1992, Disting. Alumni award Okla. State U., 1995. Fellow: AIA (emeritus, mem. nat. com. on design, past pres. ea. Okla. chpt.); mem.: Soc. Am. Mil. Engrs. (former sustaining mem.), MIT Alumni Assn. (past Okla. pres.), Nat. Trust Hist. Preservation, Am. Planning Assn., Oklahoma City C. of C. (bd. dirs. 1980—90, former v.p.), Okla. State U. Alumni Assn. (life; past bd. dirs., pres. Tulsa and Okla. counties), Tulsa C. of C. (past bd. dirs.), Tulsa Art Deco Soc., Tulsa Hist. Soc. (bd. dirs. 2000—, chair 6th World Congress on Art Deco 2001), Air Force Assn. (past pres. Gerrity chpt.), Nat. Bldg. Mus., Okla. Heritage Assn., Blue Key Club, Urban League Greater Oklahoma City (former bd. dirs.), Sigma Nu, Alpha Rho Chi. Home: 2926 E 39th St Tulsa OK 74105-3704 Fax: 918-748-9688. E-mail: ballrexm@aol.com.

BALL, ROBERT M(YERS), social security, welfare and health policy specialist, writer, lecturer; b. N.Y.C., Mar. 28, 1914; s. Archey Decatur and Laura Elizabeth (Crump) Ball; m. Doris Jacqueline McCord, June 30, 1936; children: Robert Jonathan, Jacqueline Ball Smith. AB, Wesleyan U., 1935, MA, 1936, degree (hon.), U. Md., Wesleyan U., Yale U. With Bur. Old Age and Survivors Ins., Social Security Bd., 1939-46, asst. dir., 1949-52, acting dir., 1953, dep. dir., 1953-62, commr. social security, 1962-73; sr. scholar Inst. Medicine, Nat. Acad. Scis., 1973-80; writer, lectr., cons., 1980—. Asst. dir. com. edn. and social security Am. Coun. Edn., 1946—49; staff dir. adv. coun. Social Security, 1948—49, chmn., 1965, mem., 79, 91, 96; staff dir. pension study Nat. Planning Assn., 1950—52; mem. Nat. Commn. Social Security Reform, 1982—83, White Ho. Conf. Social Security, 1998. Author: (book) Pensions in the United States, 1952, Social Security Today and Tomorrow, 1978, Insuring the Essentials, Bob Ball on Social Security, Century Foundation, 2000, Social Security Plus, 2003; author: (with Thomas N. Bethell) Because We're All in This Together, 1989, Bridging the Centuries, The Case for Traditional Social Security, 1997, Straight Talk about Social Security, 1998; contbr. articles to profl. jours. Named to Health Care Hall of Fame, 1999; recipient Disting. Svc. award, Nat. Civil Svc. League, 1958, Rockefeller Pub. Svc. award, 1961, Arthur J. Atlmeyer award, 1968, Clarence A. Kulp award, Am. Soc. Risk and Ins., 1980, Presdl. award, Am. Soc. Aging, 1988, Elizur Wright award, 1990, Arthur S. Fleming award, 1989, Andrus award, AARP, 1990, Cruikshank award, Nat. Coun. Sr. Citizens, 1990, Nat. award, UN Internat. Yr. Older Persons, 1999, Maxwell A. Pollack award for productive living, 2000. Mem.: Nat. Acad. Social Ins. (founding chmn. bd.), Gerontol. Soc. Am. (award 1996), Nat. Coun. Aging (Ollie Randall award 1983), Nat. Acad. Pub. Adminstrn., Inst. Medicine (Lienhard award 1991), Phi Beta Kappa, Delta Kappa Epsilon. Home and Office: 10450 Lottsford Rd #5112 Mitchellville MD 20721-3302

BALL, TRAVIS, JR., educational consultant, editor; b. Newport, Tenn., July 13, 1942; s. Travis and Ruth Annette (Duyck) Ball. BA, Carson Newman Coll., 1964; MA, Purdue U., 1966. Instr., then asst. prof. English Ill. Wesleyan U., Bloomington, 1966—69; vis. prof. English Millikin U., 1969; asst. headmaster, chmn. English Brewster Acad., Wolfeboro, NH, 1969—72; dir. admissions, asst. to headmaster Park Tudor Sch., Indpls., 1972—88; cons. Selwyn Sch., Denton, Tex., 1988—89; pres. Travis Ball & Assocs., 1980—88; dir. comm. Verdey Valley Sch., Sedona, Ariz., 1988—91; editor Projects in Enrollment Mgmt., 1992—2000. Mem. commn. on curriculum and grad. requirements Ind. Dept. Pub. Instrn., 1974—76; mem. adv. coun. Ednl. Records Bur.; reviewer Nat. Stds. Project in Sci., Civics and Govt., 1994—95; ednl. cons., 1992—. Editor: Tchrs. Svc. Com. Newsletter for English Tchrs., 1977—82; dept. editor: English Jour., 1976—82, editor/pub.: Contact: Newsletter for Admissions Mgmt., 1980—88, contbg. editor: The Developing Leader, 2003—. Mem.: ASCD, Phi Delta Kappa, Pi Kappa Delta, Nat. Assn. Ind. Schs. (workshop faculty 1986, 1997), Coun. Advancement and Support Edn. (adv. com. on ind. schs.), Nat. Coun. Tchrs. English, Ind. Schs. Assn. Ctrl. States, Ind. Non-Pub. Edn. Assn. (treas., dir., vice chmn.), Sigma Tau Delta. Baptist. Office: 1739 Log Church Rd Newport TN 37821-5535 E-mail: ballt@juno.com.

BALL, WILLIAM KENNETH, lawyer; b. DeQueen, Ark., Jan. 15, 1927; s. William P. and Lucille (Jeter) B.; m. Ella Hubbard Scaife, Dec. 28, 1950; children— Lucy Jane, William Ramsay, Charles Scaife. JD, U. Ark., 1953. Bar: Ark 1953, U.S. Supreme Ct., 1971. Law clk. to assoc. justice Ark. Supreme Ct., 1953-54; practice in Monticello, 1954-99; ptnr. Ball, Barton & Hoffman, 1958-99; city atty. Monticello, 1961-93; of counsel Ball, Barton & Hoffman, 1999—. Spl. justice Supreme Ct. Ark., 1975. Served with AUS, 1945-47, 50-52. Mem. Fellow Ark. Bar Found.; mem. Ark. Bar Assn., S.E. Ark. Bar Assn. (pres. 1957-58), Rotary (pres. 1962-63), Kappa Sigma, Delta Theta Phi. Presbyterian. Home: 104 Westminster Dr Monticello AR 71655-4814 Office: Ball Barton & Hoffman 106 W Oakland Ave Monticello AR 71655-4114

BALL, WILLIAM LEE (ATLEY FALL), sportswriter; b. Dover, N.J., May 18, 1946; s. Frederick J. and Mary Elizabeth (Decker) B.; m. Gail Williams, Mar. 9, 1979. Grad., N.Y. Acad. Theatrical Arts, 1964; AS, La Salle Ext. U., 1978. Mem. staff West Coast Lit. Assocs., Aptos, Calif., 1993-95, Aardvark Lit. Agy., Amherst, N.Y., 1997-98; free lance writer Linden, N.J., 1998—. Contbr. over 65 articles to mags., including Ea. Outdoors, The Fisherman. Mem. Internat. Platform Assn., Authors Guild. Republican. Baptist. Avocations: fishing, photography. Home: 542 Springfield Rd Linden NJ 07036-5131

BALLAINE, JERROLD CURTIS, artist; b. Seattle, Feb. 16, 1934; s. Jerrold Felch and Elizabeth (Maxson) B.; m. JoAnn Heinbaugh, Dec. 3, 1960 (div. June 1972); children: Theresa, Peter; m. Nancy Carroll, May 24, 1980; children: Danielle, Emily. Student, U. Wash., 1952-55, Art Ctr. Sch., L.A., 1956-58; BFA, San Francisco Art Inst., 1958, MFA, 1961. One-person shows include Zabriskie Gallery, N.Y.C., 1960, Scott Gallery, Seattle, 1964-65, Richmond (Calif.) Art Ctr., 1966, San Francisco Mus. Art, 1970, Gallery Reese-Palley, San Francisco, 1971, Stephen Wirtz Gallery, San Francisco, 1977, San Jose Mus. Art, 1981, Joseph Chownig Gallery, San Francisco, 1986, Erickson and Elins Gallery, San Francisco, 1988, Malton Gallery, Cin., 1990, Ebert Gallery, San Francisco, 1991-93, Al-Adwani Gallery, Kuwait, 1995, Trosa, Sweden, 1998, Gallery "C" Internat., Paris, 1998, 2000, Athens Gallery, Greece, 1998; exhibited in group shows at San Francisco Mus. Art, 1960, Calif. Palace of Legion of Honor, 1962, Berkeley Gallery, San Francisco, 1966, Univ. Art Mus., U. Calif., Berkeley, 1967, Portland Art Mus., Seattle, 1968, Deane Coll., Crete, Nebr., 1969, Jewish Mus., N.Y.C., 1970, Seattle Art Mus., 1970, De Young Mus., San Francisco, 1997, others; represented in pub. collections San Francisco Mus. Modern Art, Seattle Art Mus., Whitney Mus. Am. Art, N.Y.C., Denver Art Mus., Joslyn Art Mus., Omaha, Login (Utah) Mus., Crocker Art Mus, Sacramento, Calif., San Jose (Calif.) Mus. Art, also pvt. collections; subject of 2 documentaries Sta. KQED, 1971. With U.S. Army, 1956-58. Recipient Award San Francisco Mus., 1960, 4th Internat. award Japanese Govt., 1967; fellowship U. Calif. Berkeley, 1969, rsch. fellowship, 1980.

BALLANCE, FRANK W., JR., congressman; b. Windsor, N.C., Feb. 15, 1942; s. Frank Winston Sr. and Alice (Eason) B.; m. Bernadine Smallwood, 1969; children: Garey Malcolm, Angela Denise, Valerie Michelle. BS, N.C. Cen. U., 1963, JD, 1965. Libr. prof. S.C. State Coll. Sch. Law, Orangeburg, 1965-66; atty. Clayton and Ballance, Warrenton, S.C., 1966-79; pvt. practice law Warrenton, 1979-84; atty. Ballance and Reaves, Warrenton, 1985-89, Frank W. Ballance, Jr. & Assocs., P.A., Warrenton, 1990—; senator State of N.C., 1988—2002; mem. U.S. Ho. of Reps. from 1st N.C. dist., 2003—. Mem. Warren County Polit. Action coun., Warrenton, 1988; rep. N.C. Ho. of Reps., Raleigh, 1982-84, 84-86; chmn. 2d Congl. Dist. Black Caucus. Chmn. Alcoholic Beverage Control; trustee Elizabeth City State U., N.C. Cen. U.; bd. deacons, mem. Greenwood Bapt. Ch., Warrenton. With USNG, 1968, with res., 1968-71. Mem. N.C. State Bar, N.C. Assn. Trial Lawyers, N.C. Assn. Black Lawyers. Office: 413 Cannon House Office Bldg Washington DC 20515-3301*

BALLANFANT, RICHARD BURTON, lawyer; b. Houston, Aug. 15, 1947; s. Richard Edward and Selma Autrey (Lewis) B.; children: Andrea Lavon, Benjamin Burton, Amy Lamer. BA, U. Tex., 1969, JD, 1972. Bar: Tex. 1972, U.S. Ct. Appeals (5th cir.) 1976, U.S. Ct. Appeals (11th cir.) 1981, U.S. Ct. Appeals (8th cir.) 1988, U.S. Dist. Ct. (so. dist.) Tex. 1974. Atty. FCC, Washington, 1973-74; asst. U.S. atty. Dept. Justice, Houston, 1974-78; sr. asst. city atty. City of Houston, 1978-80; atty. Shell Oil Co., Houston, 1980—. Mem. Citizens Adv. Bd. Met. Transit Auth., Houston, 1979-83; del. Rep. State Conv., 1978, 80, 82, 88, 90, 92, 96, del. to Rep. Nat. Conv., 1992; chmn. Personnel Bd., West University Place, Tex., 1975-85, city councilman, 1999-2001, mayor, 2003—; mem. Battleship Tex. Adv. Bd., 1989. Capt. USAR, 1972-82. Named Outstanding Asst. U.S. Atty. Dept. Justice, 1976, 77. Mem. Houston Bar Assn., Fed. Bar Assn. (pres. 1979-80), ABA, Houston C. of C. (govt. rels. com.). Episcopalian. Home: 3123 Amherst St Houston TX 77005-3009

BALLANTINE, JOHN TILDEN, lawyer; b. Louisville, Feb. 26, 1931; s. Thomas Austin and Anna Marie (Pfeiffer) B.; m. Mary January Strode, May 15, 1954 (div. 1964); children: John T. Jr., William Clayton, Douglas C.; m. Beverley Jo Hackley, Dec. 8, 1967; 1 child, Susan Marie. BA with high distinction, U. Ky., 1952; JD, Harvard U., 1957. Bar: Ky. 1957, U.S. Ct. Appeals (6th cir.) 1958, U.S. Supreme Ct. 1982. Law clk. to presiding judge U.S. Dist Ct. (we. dist.) Ky., 1957-58; assoc. then ptnr. Ogden Newell & Welch PLLC, Louisville, 1958—. Mem. civil rules com. Ky. Supreme Ct., 1988—2002. Bd. dirs. Family and Children Agy., Louisville, 1965-75, pres., 1971-74; bd. dirs. Our Lady of Peace Hosp., Louisville, 1968-73, 88—, chmn., 1968-69, 91-93; bd. dirs. Met. United Way, Louisville, 1975-81; mem. Hist. Landmarks and Preservation Dists. Commn., Louisville, 1976-88; bd. dirs. Ky. Derby Festival, Louisville, 1975-81, v.p., 1975. 1st lt. USAF, 1952-54. Recipient Outstanding Young Man in Field of Law award Louisville Jaycees, 1966. Fellow Am. Coll. Trial Lawyers; mem. ABA, Ky. Bar Assn. (bd. govs. 1996-2002, ho. of dels. 1985-91, chmn. 1989-90, clients' security fund 1993-96, Ky. evidence rules rev. commn. 1995-2002, Outstanding Lawyer award 2003), Louisville Bar Assn. (bd. dirs. 1969-71, 88, 89, 92, 93, 96-2002, pres. 1970, profl. responsibility com. 1988-93, past chmn. physician-atty. com.), U.S. 6th Cir. Ct. Appeals Jud. Conf. (life), Fed. Def. and Corp. Counsel, Ky. Def. Counsel (pres. 1981-82), Louis D. Brandeis Am. Inn of Ct., Ky. Character and Fitness Com., Pendennis Club, The Law Club, Phi Beta Kappa. Office: Ogden Newell & Welch PLLC 1700 Citizens Plaza 500 W Jefferson St Ste 1700 Louisville KY 40202-2874 Business E-Mail: jballantine@ogdenlaw.com.

BALLANTINE, MORLEY COWLES (MRS. ARTHUR ATWOOD BALLANTINE), newspaper editor; b. Des Moines, May 21, 1925; d. John and Elizabeth (Bates) Cowles; m. Arthur Atwood Ballantine, July 26, 1947 (dec. 1975); children— Richard, Elizabeth Ballantine Leavitt, William, Helen Ballantine Healy. AB, Ft. Lewis Coll., 1975; LHD (hon.), Simpson Coll., Indianola, Iowa, 1980, U. Denver, 2002. Pub. Durango (Colo.) Herald, 1952-83, editor, pub., 1975-83, editor, chmn. bd., 1983—; dir. 1st Nat. Bank, Durango, 1976—2002, Des Moines Register & Tribune, 1977-85, Cowles Media Co., 1982-86. Mem. Colo. Land Use Commn., 1975-81, Supreme Ct. Nominating Commn., 1984-90; mem. Colo. Forum, 1985—; trustee Choate/Rosemary Hall, Wallingford, Conn., 1973-81, Simpson Coll., Indianola, Iowa, 1981-2002, U. Denver, 1984-2002, Fountain Valley Sch., Colorado Springs, 1976-89, trustee emerita, 1993—; mem. exec. com. Ft. Lewis Coll. Found., 1991—. Recipient 1st place for editl. writing Nat. Fedn. Press Women, 1955, Outstanding Alumna award Rosemary Hall, Greenwich, Conn., 1969, Outstanding Journalism award U. Colo. Sch. Journalism, 1967, Disting. Svc. award Ft. Lewis Coll., Durango, 1970, Athena award Female Cmty. Leader, 1997; named to Colo. Cmty. Journalism Hall of Fame, 1987, Colo. Bus. Hall of Fame, 2002; named Citizen of Yr., Durango Area Chamber Resort Assn., 1990, Colo. Philanthropist of Yr. Colo. Assn. Found./Assn. Fundraising Profls., 2000, Bonfils-Stanton Found. award, 2002. Mem. Nat. Soc. Colonial Dames, Colo. Press Assn. (bd. dirs. 1978-79), Colo. AP Assn. (chmn. 1966-67), Federated Women's Club Durango, Mill Reef Club (Antigua, W.I.) (bd. govs. 1985-91). Episcopalian. Address: care Durango Herald PO Drawer A Durango CO 81302

BALLANTYNE, CHRISTIE MITCHELL, medical educator; b. Houston, Sept. 13, 1955; m. Yasmine Attie, June 21, 1980; children: Maria Leyla, Christina, Katina. BA magna cum laude, U. Tex., 1977; postgrad., NYU, Madrid, Spain, 1977; MD cum laude, Baylor Coll. Medicine, 1982. Diplomate Am. Bd. Internal Medicine, Am. Bd. Internal Medicine subspecialty Cardiovascular Disease; cert. ACLS instr. Resident in internal medicine U. Tex. Southwestern Med. Sch., Dallas, 1982-85; fellowship in cardiology Baylor Coll. Medicine, Houston, 1985-87, instr. sect. atherosclerosis and cardiology dept. medicine, 1988-89, asst. prof. atherosclerosis & cardiology dept. medicine, 1989-95, assoc. prof. dept. medicine, 1996-2000, assoc. chief and clin. dir. sect. atherosclerosis, 1997, dir. lipid and atherosclerosis lab., 1999—, prof. dept. medicine, 2000—; dir., Ctr. for Cardiovasc. Disease Prevention Meth. DeBakey Heart Ctr., 2000—. Attending Ben Taub Gen. Hosp. Cardiac Catherterization Lab., Houston, 1988—, Lipid Metabolism and Atherosclerosis Clinic, The Meth. Hosp., Houston, 1988—, Ben Taub Coronary Care Unit, Houston, 1989—; faculty mem. Am. Heart Assn./Squibb Tng. Ctr. for Clin. Mgmt. of Lipid Disorders, Baylor Coll. Medicine, 1990; co-investigator Lipoprotein and Coronary Atherosclerosis Study, 1990; sci. grant rev. com. Am. Heart Assn. Tex. Affiliate, 1991-96; pharmacy and therapeutics com. The Meth. Hosp., 1992-95. Editor: lipidsonline.org; editor: (assoc.) Circulation, Jour. Cardiovasc. Risk; contbr. chapters to books, articles to profl. jours. Recipient Mosby scholarship award, Grant-in-Aid awards Am. Heart Assn. Tex. Affiliate, 1989, 91, Sanofi-Winthrop Grant-in-Aid award, 1994, Established Investigator award, 1996, Clin. Investigator award Nat. Heart Lung and Blood Inst., NIH, 1990, Caroline Wiess Law award in Molecular Medicine, 1992; named fellow Am. Heart Assn./Bugher Found. Ctr. for Molecular Biology in the Cardiovascular Sys., 1987-89. Fellow ACP, Am. Coll. Cardiology (sec. Tex. chpt. 1997-98, gov. 2001), Coun. on Clin. Cardiology Am. Heart Assn., Coun. on Arteriosclerosis; mem. Am. Fedn. Clin. Rsch. (sch. rep. for Baylor 1992), Am. Soc. Clin. Investigation, Tex. Med. Assn., Harris County Med. Soc., Houston Cardiology Soc. (pres. 1996), Am. Heart Assn. (pres. Houston chpt. 1999), Phi Kappa Phi, Phi Beta Kappa, Alpha Omega Alpha. Office: Baylor Coll Medicine Sect Atherosclerosis 6565 Fannin St # A601 Houston TX 77030-2704 E-mail: cmb@bcm.tmc.edu.

BALLANTYNE, JOSEPH M. science educator, program administrator, researcher; b. Ariz. s. Alando and Annie Ballantyne; m. Martha Ballantyne; children: Joseph, Elizabeth, Catherine, Mary Joy, Annie, Richard, Merrill, Leonora. BS, BSEE, U. Utah, 1959; SM, MIT, 1960, PhD, 1964. Assoc. prof. Cornell U., Ithaca, N.Y., 1968-75, prof., 1975—, dir. elec. engring., 1980-84, v.p. rsch. adv. studies, 1984-89, dir. SRC ctr. of excellence in microscience and tech., 1992-98, L.B. Knight dir. nanofabrication facility, 1998-99, dir. Ctr. for Biochem. Optoelectronic Microsys., 2000—02. Bd. dirs. N.Y. Photonics Devel. Corp., Rome., vis. assoc. prof. Stanford U., Calif., 1970-71, vis. scientist IBM Watson Rsch. Ctr., Yorktown Heights, N.Y., 1978-79, vis. prof. U. Calif., Santa Barbara, 1990, Tech. U. Aachen, Germany, 1990, U. Calif., San Diego, 1997; mem. sci. adv. bd. Dimes, Delft U., The Netherlands, 1999-2001, Binoptics, Inc., 2000—; founding dir. Nat. Nanofabrication Facility, Ithaca, 1977-78; cons. in field. Contbr. articles to profl. jours. Bishop LDS Ch., Ithaca, 1972-77; v.p. bd. dirs. Tompkins County Area Devel. Corp., Ithaca, 1984-89, trustee Associated Univs. Inc., Washington, 1984-89, pres. Cornell Rsch. Found., Ithaca, 1984-89; high tech. adv. com. N.Y. State Urban Devel. Corp., N.Y.C., 1984-87; bd dirs. Coun. on Rsch. & Tech., Washington, 1987-89, Univ. Industry Partnership for Econ. Growth Waverly, N.Y., 1987-89; chmn. univ. adv. com. Semic Rsch. Corp., 1994-96. Recipient George Emery Fellows medal Phi Kappa Phi, 1959; Whitney fellow MIT, 1959-60, Schlumberger fellow MIT, 1961-62, sr. fellow NSF, 1970. Fellow IEEE. Achievements include patents for optoelectric devices. Office: Cornell U 313 Phillips Hall Ithaca NY 14853-5401

BALLANTYNE, MAREE ANNE CANINE, artist; b. Sydney, NSW, Australia, Oct. 22, 1945; came to U.S., 1946; d. Charles Venice and Yvonne Mavis (McSpeerin) Canine; m. Kent McFarlane Ballantyne, Apr. 22, 1967; children: Christopher Kent, Joel Sokson. AA, Del Mar Coll., 1966; BA in English, U. Tex., 1971; postgrad., U. South Ala., 1974, U. Houston, 1981, Sonoma State U., 1982, 84, 85. Exhibited paintings in Mass., Tex., Ala.; creator logo for Gulf Coast Area Childbirth Edn. Assn., 1972, logo for Calif. Health Resources, 1985; contbr. articles to profl. jours. Charter mem. Gulf Coast Area Childbirth Edn. Assn., Mobile, Ala., 1971-76; mem. Mus. Guild, Corpus Christi, 1978-80, Art Mus., Mobile, 1972-76, Nat. Trust for Hist. Preservation, 1977-80. Recipient Cert. Appreciation, USCG, 1993, Letter of Appreciation USCG, 1993. Mem. Nat. Mus. Women in Arts (charter). Avocations: reading about poet and artist william blake, women artists and literature, raising tropical plants, creating hand-painted greeting cards. Home: 1920 SW 56th Ave Plantation FL 33317-5938

BALLARD, BRUCE W. philosophy educator, religious studies educator; s. William Albert Ballard and Carolyn Louise Stevens; m. Barbara Marie Ballard, Nov. 27, 1989. BA, U. Tex., 1978, MA, 1982, PhD, 1986. Instr. U. Tex., Austin, 1986—87; asst. prof. U. S.C., Aiken; adj. instr. S.W. Tex. State U., San Marcos, 1989—90; prof. Stephens Coll., Columbia, Mo., 1990—. Author: The Role of Mood in Heidegger's Ontology, 1991, Understanding MacIntyre, 2000. Humanitarian Aid organizer Quest for Peace, Austin, 1989. Office: Stephens Coll 1200 E Broadway Columbia MO 65215 Business E-Mail: bballard@stephens.edu.

BALLARD, CARRIE, artist; b. Crockett, Tex., Oct. 22, 1930; d. Rufus Lee and Lillie Lee Turner; m. Travis Ballard, July 4, 1952; children: David Girard Ballard, Melanie Ballard Fahey. AB, Baylor U., 1951; MEd, U. Houston, 1967; student, Houston Mus. Fine Arts. Cert. tchr., Tex. Elem. tchr. Ector Co. Sch., Odessa, Tex., 1951-52, Waco Schs., Tex., 1952-53; tchr. Pasadena (Tex.) Sch. Dist., 1954-68, Deer Park (Tex.) Sch., 1969-84. One-woman shows include Archway Gallery, Houston, 1990, U. Houston O'Kane Gallery, 1990, 94, Spicewood Gallery, Austin, Tex., 1991, 93, 94, 95, 96, Lampros Gallery, Woodlands, Tex., 1993, Buchanan Gallery, Galveston, Tex., 1998, Tex. Trails Gallery, San Antonio, 1998; represented in numerous pvt. and corp. collections. Recipient Hon. Mention, Pasadena Art League, 1988, 2d Pl. award, 1989, 1st Pl. award Deer Park Juried Art Show, 1987, Hon. Mention, Houston Civic Arts Assn., 1992, 97, 2d. Pl. award Houston Civic Arts Assn., 1997, Tex. Star award KLRU-TV, Austin, 1992, Tex. Treasure award Sta. KLRU-TV, 1993. Mem. Oil Painters Am., Allied Artists Am., Houston Civic Arts Assn., Soc. Outdoor Painters, Alla Prima Internat., Houston Art League. Avocations: gardening, travelling, reading. Home: 14 Lilac Ridge Pl Conroe TX 77384-4649

BALLARD, CHARLES ALAN, investment banker; b. St. Louis; s. Fred William and Fern Ann (Markham) B. BBA, So. Meth. U., 1963. V.p. fin. Systems Capital Corp., Phila., 1967-69; exec. v.p., dir. Vanderbilt Corp., Phila., 1969-71; assoc. Dillon, Read & Co. Inc., N.Y.C., 1971-72, v.p., 1972-78, sr. v.p., 1979-80, mng. dir., 1980-90, sr. advisor, dir., 1990-99; chmn., dir. Ballard Properties Inc., Phila., 1982—; pres., dir. Ballard Marine, Inc., 1986—; sr. advisor UBS Warburg, N.Y.C., 1999—. Mem. council Nat. Municipal League, N.Y.C., 1981-85; mem. adv. bd. Nat. Entrepreneurship Found., Bloomington, Ind., 1983—, The Energy Bur., N.Y.C., 1981— . Recipient Merit award U. Wis.-La Crosse, 1975; recipient Achievement award Lions Club, Houston, 1963 Mem. N.Y. Stock Exchange (assoc.), Securities Industry Assn. (vice chmn. 1980-81, exec. com., bd. dirs. 1984-85), Investment Banking Com. (steering com. 1981—, vice chmn. 1981, 83, 86, 87, chmn. 1985). Clubs: Union League (Phila.); The Links (N.Y.C.); Merion Golf (Ardmore, Pa.); India House; Lighthouse Point (Fla.) Yacht and Racquet. Office: 299 Park Ave New York NY 10171-0002

BALLARD, CLYDE, state legislator; b. Batesville, Ark., June 8, 1936; s. Jeffery C. and Monnie F. Ballard; m. Ruth L. Guthrie, Feb. 6, 1955; children: Jeff, Shawn, Scott. Store mgr., gen. mgr. Peter Rabbit Stores, Wenatchee, Wash., 1955-66; owner Ballard Svcs., Wenatchee, 1967-87; caucus chmn., minority leader Wash. Ho. of Reps., Olympia, 1985-94, spkr. house, 1995-98, co-speaker house, 1999—2001, Republican leader, 2002. Republican. Free Methodist. Home: 1790 N Baker St East Wenatchee WA 98802-4157 Office: PO Box 40600 Olympia WA 98504-0600

BALLARD, ELIZABETH ANN, lawyer; b. Ada, Okla., Apr. 18, 1969; d. James R. and H. Arlene Treas. BS in Journalism, Okla. State U., 1991; JD, U. Okla., 1993. Bar: Okla. 1994, U.S. Dist. Ct. (ea., we. and no. dists.) Okla. 1994, U.S. Ct. Appeals (10th cir.). Assoc. Shelton Law Firm, Oklahoma City, Okla., 1994-96, Wilburn, Masterson & Smiling, Tulsa, 1997-99, Barkley, Titus, Hillis & Reynolds, Tulsa, 1999—. Pres. Tulsa Christian Legal Soc., 1998-99. Baptist. Office: Barkley Titus Hillis & Reynolds 401 S Boston Ave Ste 2700 Tulsa OK 74103-4063

BALLARD, GLEN, composer; b. Natchez, Miss., 1953; Grad. with honors, U. Miss., 1975. Recs. include Glen Ballard, co-writer, prodr. for Jagged Little Pill (Grammy award for Best Rock Album, 1996, Grammy award for Album of Yr., 1996), Hold On, Release Me, Shadows and Light; composer: You Oughta Know (Grammy award for Best Rock Song, 1996), The Places You Find Love, One Step, What's On Your Mind, Why is this Girl Giving Me Fever, Dance Electric, Try Your Love Again, All I Need, You Look So Good in Love (Country Song of Yr., 1986), Man in the Mirror, Nightline, State of Attraction, Keep the Faith, I Wonder Why, others; composer for various artists including Al Jarreau, Earth, Wind & Fire, Sheena Easton, Celine Dion, Philip Bailey, K.T. Oslin, Jack Wagner, Michael Jackson, Wilson Phillips, Curtis Stigers, others. Office: Chasen & Co 8899 Beverly Blvd Ste 405 Los Angeles CA 90048-2431

BALLARD, JACK STOKES, engineering educator; b. Gravette, Ark., July 23, 1928; s. Freeman Stokes and Chloe Katherine (Clarry) B.; m. Arleda Anne Greenwood, Feb. 21, 1954; children: Kenneth Stokes, Donald Steven, Cheryl Anne. BS in Edn., U. Ark., 1950; MA, U. So. Calif., 1953; PhD, UCLA, 1974. Cert. secondary tchr., Calif. Commd. 2nd lt. USAF, 1954, advanced through grades to lt. col., 1974, ret., 1980; tchr. Coalinga & Whittier (Calif.) High Schs., 1951-54; tng. and pers. officer USAF, Travis AFB, Calif., 1954—56, Elmendorf AFB, Alaska, 1956—59; asso. prof. air sci. Occidental Coll., L.A., 1959-64; asst. prof. history USAF Acad., Colorado Springs, Colo., 1964-69; sr. tng advisor Korean Air Force Tng. Wing, Taejon, Republic of Korea, 1969-70; air force historian Office of Air Force History, Washington, 1970-74; chief plans and requirement divsn. Lowry Tech. Tng. Ctr., Denver, 1974-80; chief strategic sys. tng. Martin Marietta Corp., Denver, 1980-92. Instr. history, U. Md., Alaska, 1958-59, U. Md., Taejon, Korea, 1969-70; adj. instr. history U. Colo., Colorado Springs, 1977-83, U. Colo., Denver, 1983-87. Author: Development and Employment of Fixed Wing Gunships, 1982, Shock of Peace, 1983; contbg. author USAF in S.E. Asia, 1977; contbr. articles to profl. jours. Pres. Occidental Coll. Faculty Club, 1962-63; chmn. Adv. Coun. Sch. Improvement, Littleton, Colo., 1984-89; sec. Large Sch. Dist. Accountability Coun., Denver, 1988-89; elected sch. bd. dirs. Littleton Pub. Schs., 1991; pres. Littleton Sch. Bd., 1995-99; recognized as Colo. All-State Sch. Bd. mem., 1996; bd. dirs. Friends of Fort Logan, 2000-03; mem. Arapahoe County Comprehensive Plan Adv. Com., 2000-01. Mem. Orgn. Am. Historians, Western History Assn., Air Force Hist. Found., Colo. Hist. Soc., Air Force Assn. (sec. Mile High chpt. 1988), Lions (pres. Littleton 1996-97). Republican. Methodist. Avocations: sports, tennis, racquetball, skiing. Home: 7820 S Franklin Way Centennial CO 80122-3116

BALLARD, JAMES OTIS, III, medical educator, physician; b. Nitro, W.Va., June 23, 1943; s. James O. and Madora Ann (Rodes) B.; m. Gretchen Noel Lang, Sept. 11, 1971; children: Elizabeth Noel, Sarah Marie. BA, W.Va. U., 1965; MD, U. Md., 1969. Diplomate Am. Bd. Internal Medicine, Am. Bd. Hematology. Resident in internal medicine Georgetown U., Washington, 1969-73, fellow in hematology, 1972-73; sr. resident in medicine Univ. Hosps. Vt., Burlington, 1971-72; rsch. fellow in hematology Pa. State U., Hershey, 1975-78, asst. prof. medicine, 1978-85, assoc. prof. medicine, 1985-91, Lawrence F. & Jane W. Kienle chair for humane medicine, 1990—, prof. medicine, 1991—. Dir. 3d yr. clerkship M.S. Hershey Med. Ctr., 1984-86, assoc. dir. Hemophilia Ctr., 1980—, co-dir. Spl. Hematology Lab., 1980—, attending physician, 1978—, chmn. com. for undergrad. med. edn., 1996-99; acting chair dept. humanities Pa. State U. Coll. of Medicine, 1999-02, prof.

medicine and pathology, 1999—, prof. humanities, 2002--. Author: (with others) Medical Consultation, 1998; co-editor: Time to Go, 1995; contbr. articles to profl. jours. Bd. dirs. Regional ARC, Harrisburg, Pa., 1981-94. Maj. U.S. Army, 1973-75. Fellow ACP; mem. Am. Soc. Hematology, Internat. Soc. for Haemostasis and Thrombosis, Alpha Omega Alpha. Presbyterian. Avocation: keyboard musical instruments. Office: Pa State U Coll Medicine 500 University Dr Hershey PA 17033-2360

BALLARD, JEFFREY LAWRENCE, surgeon, educator; b. L.A., Calif., May 26, 1960; s. James Larry and Ellen Ballard; m. Tami Lynn Haroldson, May 20, 1983; children: Lauren Nicole, Katelyn Paige. BS in Biology, Stanford U., 1982; MD, Vanderbilt U., 1986. Diplomate in vascular surgery Am. Bd. of Surgery, 2001, in general surgery Am. Bd. of Surgery, 2000. Surg. internship U. of Ariz., 1986—87; urgent care physician Cigna Southwest, Tucson, 1987—88; surg. residency Maricopa Med. Ctr., Phoenix, 1988—92; vascular residency Loma Linda U. Med. Ctr., Calif., 1992—93; prof. of surgery Sch. of Medicine Loma Linda (Calif.) U., 1993—. Mem.: ACS (bd. of governors 2002—), Am. Assn. for Vascular Surgery (chmn., young surgeons com. 2001—), Pacific Coast Surg. Assn., Western Vascular Soc. (sec., treas. 2002—), Peripheral Vascular Surgery Soc. (pres. 2002—03), Soc. for Vascular Surgery. Republican. Office: Loma Linda University Medical Center 11175 Campus Street CP 21123 Loma Linda CA 92354 Office Fax: 909-558-0337. E-mail: jballard@ahs.llumc.edu.

BALLARD, JOHN STUART, retired educator, former mayor, former lawyer; b. Akron, Ohio, Sept. 30, 1922; s. Irby S. and Sarah (McCormick) B.; m. Ruth Frances Holden, Oct. 22, 1949; children: Susan, Karen, John H., Mark, Ward; m. 2d, Patricia D. Whittenberger, Oct. 20, 1990. AB, U. Akron, 1943; LL.B., U. Mich., 1948. Bar: Mich. 1948, Ohio 1949. Spl. agt. FBI, 1949-52; atty. pvt. practice, Akron, Ohio, 1952—56, 1964—65; pros. atty. Summit County, 1957-64; mayor City of Akron, 1966-80; ret., 1995. Adj. assoc. prof. dept. pub. adminstrn. and urban studies U. Akron, 1980—95. Candidate for U.S. senator from Ohio, 1962. Served with inf. AUS, 1943-46. Recipient Distinguished Service award Akron Jr. C. of C., 1957 Episcopalian. Home: 171 Granger Rd Unit 144 Medina OH 44256-7312 *It is true that in giving we receive.*

BALLARD, JUDY THOMAS, real estate broker; b. Amory, Miss., Oct. 27, 1950; d. Ralph and Mary Frances (Falkner) Thomas; m. David C. Ballard, Dec. 4, 1982. BS, U. Ala., 1973. Realtor Re/Max Greater Atlanta, 1984—. Mem. Cobb County Jr. League, Cobb County Med. Aux. Named one of Top 25 Re/Max Agts. in Ga., 1990, 92. Mem. Residential Coun. (cert.), Ga. Realtors Inst. (grad. realtor), Real Estate Appraisal Inst. (cert.), Million Dollar Club (life). Home: 595 Keeler Woods Dr NW Marietta GA 30064-2043 Office: Re/Max Greater Atlanta Communities 135 Johnson Ferry Rd Marietta GA 30068

BALLARD, LOUIS WAYNE, composer; b. Miami, Okla., July 8, 1931; s. Charles Guthrie and Leona Mae (Quapaw) B.; m. Ruth Sands, Dec. 6, 1965; children by previous marriage: Louis Anthony, Anne Marie, Charles Christopher. B.Mus. and Music Edn., U. Tulsa, 1954; M.Mus., 1962; D.Mus. (hon.), Coll. Santa Fe, 1973; D.Mus. (hon.), William Jewell Coll., 2001. Dir. vocal and instrumental music Nelagoney (Okla.) Public Sch., 1954-56; dir. vocal music Webster High Sch., Tulsa, 1956-58; pvt. music tchr., 1959-62; music dir. Inst. Am. Indian Arts, Santa Fe, 1962-65, dir. performing arts, 1965-69; nat. dir. music edn. curriculum and rev. Bur. Indian Affairs, Washington, 1969-79. Lectr., clinician, 1960—; pres. First Am. Indian Films, Inc., 1969—; disting. vis. prof. music Wm Jewell Coll., Liberty, Mo., 2000—. Composer, Santa Fe, 1979—; guest composer West German Music Festival, Saarbrü, 1986, Musik im 20 Jahrhundert, Ariz. State U., 1992, U. Ill. at Champagne, 1992, Ea. Music Festival, Greensboro, N.C., 1994, 95, 96; gala concert Carnegie Hall, 1992; full concert in Beethoven Chamber Music Hall, Bonn (first Am. composer), 1989; (ballet) Koshare, 1964, The Four Moons, 1967, Maid of the Mist and the Thunderbeings, 1991; (orchl. music) Fantasy Aborigine, Nos. I, II, III, IV, V; (chamber music) Rhapsody for Four Bassoons, Incident at Wounded Knee, Desert Trilogy, Ritmo Indio, Katcina Dances for cello-piano suite; (choral cantatas) The Gods Will Hear, Portrait of Will Rogers, Thus Spake Abraham; (oratorio) Dialogue Differentia text in Latin, Lakota-Sioux, English, Live On, Heart of My Nation (choral cantate with native Am. dialect), Manitoo, Gitche Manitoo (Am. Indian Doxology); (band works) Nighthawk Keetowa; (percussion) Cecega Ayuwipi, Music for the Earth and the Sky; (guitar) Quetzalcoatl's Coattails, 1992, The Lonely Sentinel, 1993, The Fire Moon (string quartet), A City of Silver, A City of Fire, A City of Light (piano concert pieces), numerous others.; commd. writer Lila Wallace Reader's Digest Arts Ptnrs./Meet the Composer, 1991; commd. writer (opera) Ministry Lower Saxony (Germany), 1993-94; author: The American Indian Sings, Book 1, 1970, Book 2, 1991, American Indian Chants for the Classroom, Oklahoma Indian Chants for the Classroom, also articles. Recipient 1st Marion Nevins MacDowell award chamber music, 1969, Nat. Indian Achievement award, 1972, Catlin Peace Pipe award Nat. Indian Lore Assn., 1976, ASCAP award, 1966-88, Lifetime Music Achievement award First Americans in Arts, 1997; F.B. Parriott grad. fellow, 1969; grantee Ford Found., 1970; grantee Nat. Endowment Arts, 1967, 69, 76, 79; commd. by Martha B. Rockefeller Found., 1969, Am. Composers Orch., 1982, commd. by Ministry Lower Saxony for Opera in Norden Gymnasium, West Germany, 1994. Mem. ASCAP, Music Educators Nat. Conf. (chmn. minority concerns com. for N.Mex. 1976), Am. Symphony Orch. League, Internat. Soc. for Polyaesthetic Music Edn. and Performance (lectr.), Phi Beta Kappa (alumni mem. Beta chpt. Okla. 1999). Lodges: Masons, Scottish Rite (32d degree). Office: PO Box 2072 Santa Fe NM 87504-2072

BALLARD, MARION SCATTERGOOD, software development professional; b. Montclair, N.J., Dec. 19, 1939; d. Alfred G. and Helen F. (Galey) Scattergood; m. Frederic L. Ballard Jr., Dec. 20, 1974; children: William, Robert; 1 stepchild, Anne A. Ballard. BA, Smith Coll., 1961; MA, U. Pa., 1963; MBA, American Univ., 1990. Lectr. Temple U., Phila.; mathematician UNIVAC, Blue Bell, Pa.; v.p. FINPAC Corp., Narberth, Pa.; pres. DataPlus, Inc, Washington. Former chmn. bd. Sandy Spring Friends Sch., Washington Area Women's Found.; former sec. bd. Sidwell Friends Sch.; bd. dirs. Levine Sch. Music. Mem. Nat. Assn. Women Bus. Owners, Phi Beta Kappa, Sigma Xi. E-mail: marionballard@comcast.net

BALLARD, MARY MELINDA, financial communications and investment banking firm executive, consumer advocate; b. Sikeston, Mo., Apr. 21, 1958; d. Claude M. and Mary (Birnbach) B.; m. Emil Pena, Jan. 1, 1989 (div. July 1990); m. Ronald C. Allison, Oct. 1994; 1 child, Reese Colton Allison. BA, Monmouth U., 1976; MBA, NYU, 1980; postgrad., Columbia U. V.p. corp. comm. United Brands Co., N.Y.C., 1976-79; v.p. mktg. Oscar de la Renta Ltd., 1979-81; pres., CEO Ficom Internat., Inc., N.Y.C., 1981—89; exec. v.p. Ruder Finn Inc., N.Y.C., 1989—; dir., CEO MBP Interests Inc., 1989—; ptnr. Kamero Ptnrs., 1994—; officer, dir. Tex. Interlock Corp., 1995-96; exec. v.p., CFO Millenium Tech. Transfer, Inc., 1996—; officer dir. Capital Bank, 1997—. Bd. dirs. Reese Colton Enterprises, Inc., Millenium Tech. Transfer, Inc., Nat. Coun. Real Estate Investment Fiduciaries; pres. Policyholders Am., 2002—; adv. bd. me. Tex. Tech U., 2002—; cons., ins. adv. Contbr. articles to profl. jours. Trustee Ballard Family Found., Children's Aid Soc.; exec. mem. Tex. Dem. Roundtable, 1994—. Recipient CLIO Ann. Report award Fin. World, 1984, 86. Mem. Internat. Assn. Bus. Communicators (Golden Quill 1984), Pub. Investor Relsa. Inst. Methodist. Avocations: collecting art, thoroughbred race horses, ranching. Home and Office: PO Box 746 Dripping Springs TX 78620-0746

BALLARD, MILDRED LOUISE, retired adult nurse practitioner; b. Clearfork, Okla., Sept. 14, 1930; d. Clarence Edward and Fannie Elsie VanBeber; m. Carl Adrian Brown, Jan. 24, 1948 (div. Oct. 1978); children: Stephen P. Brown, Linda June Brown-Larson; m. Jerry Denton Ballard, Nov. 5, 1978 (dec. Nov. 1996). ASN, C.C. of Denver, 1978; BSN, U. North Colo., 1983. Cert. adult nurse practitioner. Lic. practical nurse Greeley (Colo.) Med. Group, 1972-78, staff nurse, 1978-85, adult nurse practitioner, 1985-86, Kaiser Permanente, East Hartford, conn., 1985-96, ret., 1996. Pioneer nursing practitioner receiving hosp. privileges No. Colo. Med. Ctr., 1985-86; citizen amb. to exchange med. info. People to People Program, Europe and China, 1988-90. Contbr. short story to book. Mem. adv. bd. RVNA, Greeley, 1985—86; chmn. Arthritis Found., Greeley, 1983—86; vol. organizer United Way, Greeley, 1984—86; preceptor for nursing practitioner students U. Conn., East Hartford, 1988—96; mem. com. Greeley C. of C., 1985; vol. West Springfield Meals on Wheels Program, Mass.; participant Ms. Senior Ma, 2001. Named Mother of Yr. for foster care of 56 children Radio Sta. KFKA, 1968. Democrat. Avocations: quilting, stained glass, writing, exercise, ballroom dance. Home: 165 Jeffrey Ln West Springfield MA 01089-4482

BALLARD, RONALD MICHAEL, lawyer, political consultant; b. Covina, Calif., Apr. 17, 1958; s. Gonzy Steven and Eleanor (Guarino) B.; m. Jamie S. Kemmerer, Aug. 17, 1980; children: Nathaniel, Kaitlyn, Nolan, Devin, Casadei, Cameron, Aliza, Damian. BA, Claremont McKenna Coll., 1980; JD, UCLA, 1983. Bar: Calif. 1983, U.S. Dist. Ct. (cen. dist.) Calif. 1984. Assoc. Reid and Hellyer, San Bernardino, Calif., 1984-85; pvt. practice law Irvine, Calif., 1985-95, Lake Forest, CA, 95—; owner Centrilink.net, 1999—, RapidWeb Presence.com, 1999—, Form Of Title.com., 1999—. Mem., v.p. Charter Oak Unified Sch. Dist. Bd. Edn., Covina, 1977-81; mem., sec. 62d A.D. Rep. Cen. Com., Covina, 1978-81; lector, commentator St. Elizabeth Ann Seton Ch., Irvine, 1987-92; nat. sec. Caths. Respect Life, Westminster, Calif., 1990. Mem. State Bar Calif. (bus. law, estate, probate and trusts sect.), South Orange County C. of C. Office: 22996 El Toro Rd Lake Forest CA 92630-4961

BALLARD, TERRY LEE, librarian, educator; b. Phoenix, Aug. 24, 1946; s. Sam Hugh and Florence May (Anderson) B.; m. Donna Gael Weiss, Jan. 23, 1972;1 child, Robert Daniel. BA, Ariz. State U., 1968, MEd, 1980; MLS, U. Ariz., 1989. Libr. asst. Phoenix Pub. Libr., 1969-90; systems librarian Adelphi U., Garden City, N.Y., 1990-95; libr. automation coord. NYU Law Sch., N.Y.C., 1995-97; automation librarian Quinnipiac U., Hamden, Conn., 1997—. Vis. prof. Palmer Libr. Sch., Brookville, N.Y., 1995—; adj. libr. St. Johns U., Jamaica, N.Y., 1992-95; adj. prof. So. Conn. State U., New Haven, 2000-01. Author: Innopac: A Reference Guide, 1995; co-author: Dictionary of American Biography, 1971-75, supplements, 1971-75, 76-80, Whole Library Handbook-2, 1994, Cybrarian's Manual, 1997, Scribners Encyclopedia of American Lives, 1998, 2000; columnist Info. Today, 1996-2001; contbr. articles to profl. jours. Recipient Productivity award City of Phoenix, 1983-88, Outstanding Article award Computers in Librs. mag. Mem. ALA, Nassau County Libr. Assn. (acad. & spl. librs. divsn., pres. 1995, v.p. 1994-95, bd. dirs.). Democrat. Avocations: astronomy, collecting first editions of Mark Twain. Office: Quinnipiac Univ Libr Mt Carmel Ave Hamden CT 06518 E-mail: terry.ballard@quinnipiac.edu.

BALLAS, ZUHAIR KHAMIS, physician; b. Beirut, Oct. 14, 1950; s. Khamis Mahmoud and Ellen (Kallenbach) B. BS, Am. U. Beirut, 1970, MD, 1974. Diplomate Am. Bd. Internal Medicine, Allergy/Clin. Immunology Bd., Diagnostic Lab. Immunology Bd. Resident Rutgers Med. Sch., N.J., 1974-75, Thomas Jefferson U., Phila., 1975-76; fellow in allergy Johns Hopkins U., Balt., 1976-78; assoc., sr. fellow Fred Hutchinson Cancer Rsch., U. Wash., 1978-80; asst. prof. U. Iowa Coll. Medicine, Iowa City, 1980-86, assoc. prof., 1986-93, prof., 1993—, dir. divsn. allergy, 1997—; staff physician allergy divsn. VA Med. Ctr., Iowa City, 1980—. Bd. dirs. Am. Bd. Allergy & Immunology. Mem. editl. bd. Jour. Allergy & Clinical Immunology, 2002—; contbr. articles to profl. jours. Recipient Rsch. Assoc. Career award, VA, 1981-84, Clin. Investigator Career award, 1984-87; grantee VA, 1980-81, 81—, NIH, 1982-85, 89-95, 96—, Am. Heart Assn., 1984-87. Fellow ACP, Am. Acad. Allergy, Am. Coll. Allergy; mem. N.Y. Acad. Sci., Am. Assn. Immunology, Am. Fedn. Clin. Rsch., Ctrl. Soc. Clin. Rsch., Am. Soc. Clin. Investigation. E-mail: ballasz@uiowa.edu.

BALLBACH, PHILIP THORNTON, political consultant, investor; b. Lansing, Mich., May 22, 1939; s. Nathan Anthony and Thelma Frances (Bowes) B. BA, Mich. State U., 1960; student, U. Mich., 1960-61; MA, Mich. State U., 1967. Social worker State of Mich., Corunna, 1961-64; legis. aide State Rep. H. James Starr, Lansing, Mich., 1964-67; exec. asst. State Atty. Gen.'s Dept., Lansing, Mich., 1967-81; county commr. Ingham County, Mason, Mich., 1980-93. Pub., Lansing This Weekend, 1963-64, The Gooseneck Tidings, 1977. Coord. Greater Lansing Assn. for Cmty. Edn., 1961-66; mem. Lansing Bd. Election Canvassers, 1965-69; dir. Cmty. Mental Health Bd., Lansing, 1977-99; treas. Zolton Ferency for Gov. Com., 1977-83; county liaison Eastside Neighborhood Orgn., Lansing, 1980-93; commr. Tri-County Regional Planning Com., Lansing, 1981-84; chairperson Ingham County Emergency Planning Com., Mason, Mich., 1988-93; campaign dir. Citizens for Pub. Recycling, Lansing, 1990; treas. People Achieving Legis. Power, 1992-95; campaign coord. Citizens for a Better Lansing, 1993-2003; bd. dirs. Peace Edn. Ctr., 1999-2003. Recipient Achievement award Nat. Assn. Counties, 1986, Dem. Party Ferency Activist Achievement award, 1998. Mem. Mich. Assn. Community Mental Health Bds. Democrat. Avocations: writing poetry, history studies, skiing, softball. Home: 312 Leslie St Lansing MI 48912-2723

BALLDIN, ULF INGEMAR, medical researcher; b. Malmö, Sweden, Apr. 5, 1939; arrived in U.S., 1992, naturalized, 2002; s. Anton and Ebba T. (Engholm) B.; m. Susanne Ploman, June 29, 1974; children: Carl H., B. Christian, Fredrik J. BA, U. Lund, Sweden, 1959, MD, 1967, PhD, 1973; D (hon.), State Scientific Rsch. Inst., Moscow, 1995. Lic. physician, Sweden. Instr. physiology U. Lund, Sweden, 1964-67, rsch. physician, 1968-73; resident U. Hosp., Lund, Sweden, 1974; acting assoc. prof. U. Lund, 1975; rsch. flight surgeon Nat. Defense Rsch., Linköping, Sweden, 1976; sr. rsch. med. officer Nat. Defense Rsch. Establishment, Stockholm, 1977-86; rsch. dir. Nat. Def. Rsch. Establishment, Stockholm, 1987-99, dir. Inst. Aviation Medicine Sweden, 1987-92; sr. scientist in aerospace medicine Wyle Labs., Inc., Brooks AFB, Tex., 2000—. Adj. prof., head dept. aerospace medicine Karolinska Inst. Med. Sch., Stockholm, 1982-91; liaison scientist Brooks AFB, USAF, San Antonio, 1992-98; clin. asst. prof. U. Tex. Med. Br., Galveston, 1997—. Co-author: (chpt.) Textbook of Military Medicine, 2002; contbr. articles to profl. jours. Sr. Rsch. Flight Surgeon Swedish Air Force, 1976-99. Fellow Aerospace Med. Assn. (v.p., coun. mem.); mem. Royal Swedish Acad. War Scis., Internat. Acad. Aviation and Space Medicine (dir. 1993-97, 2d v.p. 1997-99, 1st v.p. 1999-2001, pres. 2001-2003). Achievements include improving inert gas elimination for decreasing risk of decompression sickness in divers and during extravehicular space activity, improved G-tolerance in fighter pilots with balanced pressure breathing during G and extended coverage anti-G suit. Home: 14227 Parkhurst St San Antonio TX 78232-4733 Office: Wyle Labs USAF Rsch Lab 2485 Gillingham Dr Brooks City Base TX 78235-5105 E-mail: uballdin@swbell.net.

BALLENGER, CASS THOMAS (THOMAS BALLENGER), congressman; b. Hickory, N.C., Dec. 6, 1926; s. Richard E. and Dorothy (Collins) B.; m. Donna Davis, June 14, 1952; children: Cindy Ballenger Brinkley, Melissa Ballenger Jordan, Dorothy Davis Weaver. Student, U. N.C., 1944-45; BA, Amherst Coll., 1948. Pres. Plastic Packaging, Hickory, 1957-86, chmn. bd., 1986—; pres. Hickory Paper Box Co., 1961-80; mem. 100th-108th Congresses from 10th N.C. dist., 1987—. Mem. edn. and workforce com., internat. rels. com. County commr. Catawba County, N.C., 1966-74, chmn. commn., 1970-74; mem. N.C. Ho. of Reps., Raleigh, 1974-76, N.C. Senate, Raleigh, 1976-86. Mem. Hickory C. of C. Lodges: Rotary (pres. Hickory club). Republican. Episcopalian. Avocations: golf, swimming. Office: 2182 Rayburn House Office B Washington DC 20515-3310*

BALLESTEROS, PAULA MITCHELL, nurse; b. Jonesport, Me., Oct. 18, 1950; d. Paul Frederick and Janice Madeline (Beal) Mitchell; m. Ernesto Gascon Ballesteros, Apr. 4, 1981; children: Christopher, Jonathan. BS in Profl. Arts, St. Joseph's Coll., 1984; BSN, Husson/Ea. Me. Med. Ctr. Baccalaureate Sch. Nursing, 1994. Cert. Nursing Administrn. Patient care mgr. Ea. Me. Med. Ctr., Bangor, 1974—, bd. trustees, 1993-95. Chairperson adv. bd. Ea. Maine Tech. Coll., Bangor, Me., 1993-94; pres. Me. Coun. Nurse Mgrs., 1991-93, Ea. Me. Med. Ctr. auxiliary, Bangor, Me., 1993-95. Contbr. articles to profl. jours. Mem. St. Joseph Hosp. Auxiliary. Mem. Am. Orgn. Nurse Execs., Penobscot Med. Soc. Auxiliary, Me. Assn. Hosp. Auxiliaries (pres. 1994—). Democrat. Protestant. Avocations: skiing, tennis, reading. Home: 78 Packard Dr Bangor ME 04401-2531 Office: Ea Maine Med Ctr 489 State St Bangor ME 04401-6616 E-mail: pballesteros@emh.org.

BALLESTEROS, SEVERIANO, professional golfer; b. Pedrena, Spain, Apr. 9, 1957; s. Baldomero and Carmen (Sota) B.; m. Carmen Botin O'Shea; children: Javier, Miguel, Carmen. Chmn. Fairway, S.A., Madrid, 1981; main victories include Under 25 Nat. Championship, Vizcaya Open, 1974, Under 25 Nat. Championship, 1975, Profl. Championship Catalonia, Profl. Championship Tenerife, Dutch Open, Lancome Trophy, Donald Swaelens Meml., World Cup, 1976, French Open, Braun Internat., UniRoyal Internat., Swiss Open, Japanese Open, Dunlop-Phoenix (Japan), Otago Charity (New Zealand), World Cup, 1977, Kenia Open, Under 25 Nat. Open Championship, Greensboro Open, Martini Internat., German Open, Scandinavian Open, Swiss Open, 1978, Lada English Golf Classic, Brit. Open, El Prat Open (Spain), 1979, Masters, 1980, 83, Madrid Open, Martini Internat., Dutch Open, 1980, Scandinavian Open, Spanish Open, Suntory World Match Play, Australian PGA Championship, Dunlop-Phoenix, 1981, San Remo Masters, Madrid Open, French Open, Suntory World Match Play, 1982, M.H.T. Westchester Classic, Irish Open, Lancome Trophy, Sun City Challenge, Sun Alliance Championship, 1983, Brit. Open, 1984, 88, Suntory WMP, Sun City Challenge, 1984, USF&G Classic, World Match Play Championship, Irish Open, French Open, Sanyo Open, Spanish Open, Ryder Cup (mem. winning team), 1985, Dunhill Brit. Masters, Carrolls Irish Open, Johnnie Walker Montecarlo Open, Peugeot French Open, KLM Dutch Open, Lancome Trophy, 1986, Suze Open, APG Larios, Ryder Cup winning team, 1987, A.P.G. Larios, Mallorca Open de Baleares, Westchester Classic Scandinavian Enterprise Open, German Open, Lancome Trophee British Open, Visa Taiheiyo Club Masters, 1988, Epson Gran Prix, Cepsa Madrid Open, Swiss Open/Ebel European Masters, Ryder Cup (tied), 1989, Open Baleares, 1990, Volvo PGA Championship, Dunhill Brit. Masters, Chunichi Crowns, Toyota World Match Play, 1991, Turespaña Open de Baleares, Dubai Desert Classic, 1992, Benson and Hedges Internat. Open Mercedes (German) Masters, 1994, Tornoi Perrier, Peugeot Spanish Open, Five Tours Andersen Consulting, Ryder Cup, Campeonato Espana Profesionales, 1995, Ryder Cup, 1997, Seve Ballesteros Trophy, 2000. Capt. European Ryder Cup Team, 1997. Recipient Prince of Asturias award, 1989, Olympic Order, 1998. Roman Catholic. Office: Fairway SA Pasaje de Pena 2-4 39008 Santander Spain also: PGA 100 Ave of the Champions Palm Beach Gardens FL 33410 Address: Dep Tecnico S Ballesteros Pasaje de Pena 2 39008 Santander Spain

BALLEW, CAROL, epidemiologist, researcher; BA, U. Oreg.; Diploma in Human Biology, Oxford (Eng.) U., 1974; MA, Pa. State U., 1976, PhD, 1984. Vis. asst. prof. medicine U. Ga., Athens, 1985—86; NHLBI postdoctoral fellow Northwestern U. Med. Sch., Chgo., 1986—89; asst. dir. cmty. health rsch. Ill. Cancer Coun., Chgo., 1989—91; biostatistician Ctr. Clin. Rsch., Chgo., 1991—93; epidemiologist Ctrs. Disease Control, Atlanta, 1993—2001; dir., Alaska Native Epidemiology Ctr. Alaska Native Health Bd., Anchorage, 2001—. Instr. U. Alaska MPH program, Anchorage, 2002—; editl. bd. Nutrition Today, 2001—; numerous working groups and coms., 1994—. Author (with R. Wells): Selected Results from the Behavioral Risk Factor Surveillance System for Alaska Natives, 1995-2000, 2002; co-author (with L. White and H. Aronson): Navajo Health and Nutrition Survey: Patient Education Chartbook, 1997; contbr. chapters to books, articles to profl. jours. and conf. procs.; ad hoc reviewer numerous profl. jours., including Am. Anthropologist, Am. Jour. Clin. Nutrition, Archives Internal Medicine, Internat. Jour. Epidemiology, Oxford U. Press, Soc. Epidemiologic Rsch., others. Recipient numerous rsch. grants, Ctrs. Disease Control, 1991—. Mem.: APHA, Coun. State and Territorial Epidemiologists, Alaska Pub. Health Assn. Office: Alaska Native Health Bd 3700 Woodland Dr Ste 500 Anchorage AK 99517 E-mail: cloallew@anhlo.org.

BALLEW, KATHY I. controller; b. Sterling, Colo., Mar. 31, 1958; d. Arthur LeRoy Nelson and Dixie Irene Mann; m. Mark Ballew, Dec. 12, 1975 (div. Sept. 23, 1999); children: Mark Douglas, Amanda Jo. Diploma, Burns (Oreg.) Union H.S. Revenue audit Red Lion Casino, Elko, Nev., 1988, accounts payable, 1988, accounts receivable, 1988—89, office mgr., 1990—95, contr. Winnemucca Properties, 1995—99, contr. McClaskey Properties, 1999—. Avocations: fishing, camping, crafts, grandchildren. Home: 1910 Ruby View Dr Elko NV 89801

BALLHAUS, WILLIAM FRANCIS, JR., aerospace industry executive, research scientist; b. L.A., Jan. 28, 1945; s. William Francis Sr. and Edna A. Ballhaus; m. Jane Kerber; children from previous marriage: William Louis, Michael Frederick; stepchildren: Benjamin Joel, Jennifer Angela. BSME with honors, U. Calif., Berkeley, 1967, MS in Mech. Engring., 1968, PhD in Engring., 1971. Rsch. scientist U.S. Army Aviation R & D, Ames Rsch. Ctr., Moffett Field, Calif., 1971-79; chief applied computation aeronautics br. NASA-Ames Rsch. Ctr., Moffett Field, 1979-80, dir. astronautics, 1980-84, dir., 1984-89; acting assoc. adminstr. NASA Hdqrs., Washington, 1988-89; v.p. rsch. tech. Martin Marietta Astronautics Group, Denver, 1989-90, v.p., dir. Centaur program, 1990; pres. Civil Space and Communications, Denver, 1990-93, Aero & Naval Sys., 1993-94; v.p. sci. & engring. Lockheed Martin Corp., Bethesda, Md., 1995—. Co-chmn. Air Force Scientific adv. bd., 1996—. Contbr. articles on computational fluid dynamics to profl. jours. Mem. sci. and acad. adv. bd. U. Calif., 1987-92; mem. engring. adv. bd. U. Calif., Berkeley and Davis, U. Md., MIT Aero and Astro Dept.; chmn. govt. and edn. dir. United Way of Santa Clara County, Calif., 1987; mem. Air Force Sci. Adv. Bd., 1994—. Capt USAR. Decorated Presdl. Rank of Disting. Exec., 1985; recipient H. Julian Allen award NASA-Ames Rsch. Ctr., 1977, Arthur S. Flemming award Jaycees, Washington, 1980, Disting. Profl. Engring. Sci. and Tech. award NSPE, 1986, Disting. Exec. Svc. award Sr. Execs. Assn., 1989, Disting. Svc. medal NASA, 1989, Disting. Engring. Alumnus award U. Calif., Berkeley, 1989. Fellow AIAA (pres. 1988-89, Lawrence Sperry award 1980), Royal Aero. Soc.; mem. NAE, Internat. Acad. Astronautics, Tau Beta Pi (named Eminent Engr. Berkeley chpt.). Roman Catholic. Home: 981 Via Rincon Pls Vrds Est CA 90274-1627 Office: The Aerospace Corporation PO Box 92957 Los Angeles CA 90009-2957

BALLHAUS, WILLIAM LOUIS, engineering executive; s. William Francis Ballhaus and Susan Elizabeth Berghoff; m. Darrin Jennifer Mollett, Sept. 12, 1998. BS, UC Davis, 1989; MS, Stanford U., 1990, PhD, 1994; MBA, UCLA, 1998. Program dir. and sys. engring. mgr. Hughes Space and Comm., El Segundo, Calif., 1994—98; dir. Boeing Satellite Systems, Integrated Satellite Factory Ops., 1999—2000; gen. mgr. Boeing Electron Dynamic Devices, Inc., Torrance, Calif., 2000—01, Boeing Satellite Systems, Sys. Products Group, 2001—02; sr. v.p. Boeing Satellite Systems, Sys. Engring., 2002—. Mem. of the dean's coun. Loyola Marymount U., Coll. of Sci. and Engring., Westchester, Calif., 2002—. Mem.: AIAA. Achievements include patents for interconnective transponder systems and methods.

BALLIET, ARTHUR GERALD, molecular biologist, researcher; b. Nanticoke, Pa., Sept. 23, 1958; s. Arthur Stanley and Helen Mary Balliet. BS in Biology and Chemistry cum laude, King's Coll., 1980; MA in Biochem. Sci., Princeton U., 1982, PhD in Molecular Biology, 1991. Cert. profl. edn. Am. Chem. Soc. Sr. fellow U. Wash., Seattle, 1990-92; postdoctoral fellow U. Pa., Phila., 1993; postdoctoral rschr. Temple U., Phila., 1993-97, asst. scientist, 1997—. Mentor Minority Access to Rsch. Ctr. Program, Temple U., Phila., 1997- . Contbr. articles to profl. jours. Mem. AAAS. Avocations: reading, photography, bicycle riding, book collecting. Office: Temple U Sch Medicine Fels Inst Cancer Rsch and Mol Biology 3307 N Broad St AHP 331 Philadelphia PA 19140 E-mail: aballiet@unix.temple.edu.

BALLIETT, JOHN WILLIAM, entrepreneur, real estate executive; b. Rochester, N.Y., Sept. 10, 1947; s. Charles Garrison and Burnetta Elizabeth (Purtell) B.; m. Betsy Jane Van Patten, Jan. 25, 1969; 1 child, Noelle Elizabeth. BS in Physics, Grove City Coll., 1969; postgrad., U. Rochester, 1969 71. Devel. engr. Eastman Kodak Co., 1969-70; scientist Tropel Inc., 1970, mgr. applied optics, 1971-72, mktg. mgr., 1972-73; exec. v.p., dir. Quality Measurement Sys., Inc., Penfield, N.Y., 1973-77; pres. QMS Internat., Inc., Penfield, 1974-77, Balliett Assocs., Sarasota, Fla., 1978—, Shore Lane Devel. Corp. subs. (merger Sandbar Devel. Corp.), 1981—, 1990—. Pres., pub. Suncoast TV Facts, Inc., Sarasota, 1979-81; pres. Charter One, Inc., Sarasota, 1981—, Palma Sola Enterprises, Inc., 1990—; chmn., CEO Charter One Hotels & Resorts, Inc., 1989—; pres. Alacho Inc., 1992—; pres. Servus Hotel Group, Inc., N.Y.C., 1997—; spkr. at nat. and internat. timesharing confs. Contbr. articles on timesharing to profl. publs.; patentee optical sys. Founding dir. Internat. Found. for Timesharing. Mem. Fla. Bar (citizen mem. grievance com.), U.S. C. of C., Sarasota County C. of C., Am. Land Devel. Assn., Nat. Timeshare Coun., Fla. Hotel-Motel Assn. Home: 1404 Westbrook Dr Sarasota FL 34231-3549 Office: 2032 Hillview St Sarasota FL 34239-2334

BALLIETT, WHITNEY, writer, critic; b. N.Y.C., Apr. 17, 1926; s. Fargo and Dorothy (Lyon) B.; m. Elizabeth Hurley King, 1951; children: Julia, Elizabeth, Will; m. Nancy Kraemer, 1965; children: Whitney, Jamie. BA, Cornell U., 1951. Mem. editl. staff New Yorker mag., N.Y.C., 1951—, successively collator, proofreader, reporter, 1951-57, staff writer, 1957—; columnist on jazz; book,

movie, theater and art reviewer, reporter. Author: The Sound of Surprise, 1959, Dinosaurs in the Morning, 1962, Such Sweet Thunder, 1966, Super-Drummer: A Profile of Buddy Rich, 1968, Ecstasy at the Onion, 1971, Alec Wilder and His Friends, 1974, New York Notes, 1976, Improvising, 1977, Night Creature, 1981, Jelly Roll, Jabbo, and Fats, 1983, American Musicians: Fifty-Six Portraits in Jazz, 1986, American Singers: Twenty-Seven Portraits in Song, 1988, Barney, Bradley and Max: Sixteen Portraits in Jazz, 1989, Goodbyes and Other Messages: A Journal of Jazz, 1981-90, 91, American Musicians II: Seventy Two Portraits in Jazz, 1996, Collected Works: A Journal of Jazz, 1954-2001, 2002; contbr. to N.Y. Rev. Books, 1998—. Recipient Acad. award in lit. Am. Acad. Arts and Letters, 1996. Mem. Century Assn.

BALLIF-SPANVILL, BONNIE, psychologist, educator; BS with honors, Brigham Young U., 1962, PhD with distinction, 1966. Asst. rschr. R&D Ctr. U. Hawaii, Honolulu, 1966—68; with Fordham U. Grad. Sch. at Lincoln Ctr., N.Y.C., 1968—93, dir. Ctr. for Applied Motivation Rsch., 1975—84, coord. ednl. psychology and rsch. programs, 1979—83, 1985—87, chair divsn. psychology and edn. svcs., 1987—90; prof. psychology Brigham Young U., Provo, Utah, 1994—, dir. Women's Rsch. Inst., 1994—, mem. various univ. coms., 1994—. Cons. U.S. Govt., 1965—72, The Delphi Rsch. Group, N.Y.C., 1976—89; presenter in field. Contbr. articles to profl. jours. Recipient Bene Merenti award, 1988. Fellow: Am. Psychol. Soc.; mem.: AAUW, Consortium on Peace, Rsch., Edn. and Devel., Nat. Women's Studies Assn., Assn. for Women in Devel., Internat. Peace Rsch. Assn., Phi Kappa Phi. Office: Brigham Young Univ 337SWKT Provo UT 84602

BALLINGER, JAMES K. art museum executive; b. Kansas City, Mo., July 7, 1949; s. Robert Eugene and Yvonne (Davidson) B.; m. Nina Lundgaard, Aug. 21, 1971; children— Erin, Cameron BA, U. Kans., 1972, MA, 1974. Gallery coordinator Tucson Art Ctr., 1973; registrar U. Kans., Lawrence, 1973-74; curator collections Phoenix Art Mus., 1974-81, asst. dir., 1981, dir., 1982—. Author: (exhbn. catalogues) Beyond the Endless River, 1980, Visitors to Arizona 1846 to 1980, 1981, Peter Hurd, 1983, The Popular West, 1982, Thomas Moran, 1986, Frederick Remington, 1989. Bd. dirs. Balboa Art Conservation Ctr. Fellow Am. Assn. Mus. Dirs. (bd. dirs.), Western Assn. Art Museums; mem. Central Ariz. Mus. Assn. (v.p. 1983). Avocations: hiking; basketball; traveling. Office: Phoenix Art Mus 1625 N Central Ave Phoenix AZ 85004-1685

BALLINGER, RICHARD L. orchestra director; b. San Diego, Calif., Jan. 17, 1977; s. William Richard Ballinger and Kathleen Marie Beth Leavitt; m. Nicole Deanna Fabrizio-Ballinger, Feb. 17, 2001. MusB Fla. So. Coll., 2000. Violist Imperial Symphony Orch., Lakeland, Fla., 1993—98, Fla. So. Symphony, Lakeland, 1995—2000; string coach Treasure Coast Youth Orch., Ft. Pierce, Fla., 2000—; pvt. instr. Stuart (Fla.) Sch. of Music, 2000—; dir. founder Ocean Youth Orch., Stuart, 2010—; dor Jensen Beach Elem. Orch., Stuart, 2002—; violist Indian River (Fla.) Pops Orch., 2002—. V.p. programs Treasure Coast Music Tchr., Struart, 2003—; dir. Treasure Coast Music Tchr. Assn., Stuart, pres., 2002—03; founder Ocean Youth Orch.; co-founder Ocean String Quartet. Master: Fla. Fed. of Music Clubs, Music Rchrs. Nat. Assn. (assoc.); mem.: Fla. State Music Tchrs. Assn. (assoc.). Avocations: wine connoisseur, surfing, hockey, dancing, sailing. Home: 1021 SE 10th Street Stuart FL 34996 Office: 1608 S Kanner Highway Stuart FL 34996

BALLINGER, SANDRA LYNN, secondary education educator; b. Seattle, Nov. 25, 1942; d. Roy and Bette Ruth Marie Harker; m. Richard Long Ballinger, Jr., Mar. 20, 1968; 1 child, Pamela Lynn. BA in English, U. Wash., 1965; MA in Edn., City U., Seattle, 1993. English instr. Edmonds Sch. Dist., Lynnwood, Wash., 1965—. Instr. coll. in H.S. English, Lynnwood H.S. and Edmonds C.C., 1986—. Mem. NEA. Democrat. Avocations: reading, beach-combing, gardening. Home: 12016 NE 145th Kirkland WA 98034

BALLINGER, WALTER FRANCIS, surgeon, educator; b. Phila., May 16, 1925; s. Robert I. and Frances (Taylor) B.; children: Walter Francis, Christopher Bardin, David Gordon; m. Mary Randolph Gordon Dickson, Oct. 4, 1980. Student, Cornell U., 1942-44; MD, U. Pa., 1948. Intern 1st Surg. Div., Bellevue Hosp., N.Y.C., 1948-49, asst. resident surgery, 1949-50, chief resident surgery, 1955-56; asst. resident surgery Columbia-Presbyn. Med. Center, 1953-55; from instr. to assoc. prof. Jefferson Med. Coll., Phila., 1956-63; assoc. prof. surgery Johns Hopkins Sch. Medicine, 1964-67; Bixby prof., head dept. surgery Washington U. Sch. Medicine, St. Louis, 1967-78, prof. surgery, 1978-92, prof. emeritus surgery, 1992—. Med. dir. health adminstrn. program Wash. U. Sch. Medicine, 1993—99. Editor: Research Methods in Surgery, 1964, The Management of Trauma, 1968, 4th edit., 1985, (with T. Drapanas) Practice of Surgery: Current Review, 1972, 2d edit., 1974; editor-in-chief (with G. Zuidema) Surgery, 1971-97, (with J. Hepner) Best Practices and Benchmarking in Healthcare; mem. edit. bd. Brit. Jour. Surgery, 1989-94. Served to capt. U.S. Army, 1950-52. Markle scholar med. sci., 1961-66 Mem. Am. Surg. Assn., Soc. Clin. Surgery, Soc. Univ. Surgeons, A.C.S., James IV Assn., Halsted Soc. Home: 1203 Log Cabin Ln Saint Louis MO 63124-1528

BALLINGTON, DON AVELL, medical educator; b. Batesburg, S.C., Oct. 20, 1946; s. James Ralph and Theo Madgeilee Ballington; m. Linda Barnett, Nov. 20, 1982; children: Kristin, Mark. BS, Clemson U., 1968, MS, 1969. Animal nutritionist Spartan Grain & Mill, Spartanburg, SC, 1970—71; microscopist S.C. Dept. Agr., Columbia, SC, 1971—72; instr. health sci. Midlands Tech. Coll., Columbia, 1972—79, dir. pharmacy tech. program, 1979—. Cons. in field; founder Pharmacy Technician Educator's Coun., Charleston, SC, 1991. Author: Pharmacology for Technicians, 1999, Pharmacy Math for Technicians, 1999, Pharmacy Practice for Technicians, 1999. Mem.: S.C. Pharmacy Assn., S.C. Soc. Health Sys. Pharmacists (Pub. award 1991), Am. Soc. Health-Sys. Pharmacists, Am. Assn. Pharmacy Technicians (Founder's award 1987). Avocations: gardening, woodworking, RC model planes. Home: 210 Horace Ct Lexington SC 29073 Office: Midlands Tech Dept Health Sci PO Box 2408 Columbia SC 29202-2408

BALLMAN, B. GEORGE, lawyer; b. N.Y.C., Feb. 7, 1931; s. Bernard and Claire (Kahn) B.; m. Frances Hurst; children: Deborah, Lynda, B. George, Kimberly. AA, BS, Am. U., 1955, JD, 1957; LLM in Taxation, Georgetown U., 1980. Bar: Md. 1957, D.C. 1958, U.S. Supreme Ct. 1963. Former mng. prin. Conroy, Ballman & Dameron, Rockville, Md., 1981-97; of counsel Keegan & Sotelo PC, 2002—. Bd. dirs., treas. Bethesda-Chevy Chase Rescue Squad, 1948-50; co-founder, chancellor The Counsellors, 1963-64. Contbr. article to profl. jours. Mem. ABA, ATLA, Montgomery County Bar Assn. (treas. exec. com. 1960, chmn. law day com., 1962, pub. relations com. 1963, continuing legal edn. com. 1964, 65, 68, mem. grievance com. real estate sect. 1969-97), D.C. Bar, Montgomery County Bar Assn., Congl. Country Club. Republican. Episcopalian. Office: Keegan and Sotelo, PC 8120 Woodmont Ave Bethesda MD 20814

BALLMAN, PATRICIA KLING, lawyer; b. Cin., May 1, 1946; d. John Joseph and Margaret Elizabeth (Stacy) Kling; children: Andrew J., Cara E. BS with honors, St. Louis U., 1967; JD with honors, Marquette U., 1977. Bar: Wisc. 1977, U.S. Dist. Ct. (ea. and we. dist Wisc.) 1980, U.S. Ct. Appeals (7th Cir.) 1983, U.S. Ct. Appeals (8th Cir.) 1986, U.S. Supreme Ct., 1986; Systems analyst Gen. Electric Co., Cin., 1967-70; lectr. computer scis. Marquette U., Milw., 1971; ptnr. Quarles & Brady, Milw., 1977—. Mem. fin. divsn., chair pers. subcom. United Way, Shorewood Bd. of Rev. Mem. ABA, Am. Acad. Matrimonial Lawyers, Wis. Bar Assn. (marital property com., specialization com., nominating com., ins. for mems. com., pres. 2002-03), Milw. Bar Assn. (chair courts com., past pres., dir., legis. com., chair ct. of appeal bench/bar com.). Office: Quarles & Brady 411 E Wisconsin Ave #2040 Milwaukee WI 53202-4461*

BALLMER, STEVE, software company executive; Degree in applied math. and econs., Harvard U.; postgrad., Stanford U. Asst. product mgr. Procter and Gamble; v.p. mktg., v.p. corp. staffs, sr. v.p. sys. software Microsoft Corp., Redmond, Wash., 1980—, exec. v.p. sales and support, dir., CEO, 2000—. Bd. overseers Harvard U.; adv. coun. Stanford Bus. Sch. Avocations: exercise, jogging, playing basketball. Office: Microsoft Corp 1 Microsoft Way Redmond WA 98052-8300*

BALLON, CHARLES, lawyer; b. N.Y.C., Sept. 10, 1910; s. Herman and Anna (Platt) B.; m. Harriet Milk, Aug. 19, 1954; children— Howard, Hilary, Carla. B.A., Columbia U., 1930, LL.B., 1932. Bar: N.Y. 1933, U.S. Dist. Ct. (so. dist.) N.Y. 1935, U.S. Ct. Appeals (2d cir.) 1935, D.C. 1976, U.S. Dist. Ct. D.C. 1976, U.S. Ct. Appeals D.C. Ptnr., Hartman, Sheridan, Tekulsky & Pecora, N.Y.C., 1937-41; ptnr. Phillips, Nizer, Benjamin, Krim & Ballon, N.Y.C., 1946— . Bd. visitors Columbia U. Law Sch., 1975— ; chmn. bd. dirs. Benjamin N. Cardozo Sch. Law, Yeshiva U., N.Y.C., 1981-86, hon. chair, 1986—, trustee Yeshiva U., 1980— ; assoc. chmn. Fedn. Philanthropies of N.Y., 1979-86; v.p. United Jewish Appeal of N.Y., 1980-86, hon. chmn. . Served to lt. col. U.S. Army, 1942-46. Decorated Legion of Merit; recipient Proskauer medal Fedn. Jewish Philanthropies, 1973; Learned Hand award Am. Jewish Com., 1976; Israel Peace medal, Israel State Bonds, 1983; Disting. Service award Cardozo Sch. Law, 1979. Mem. Assn. Bar City of N.Y., N.Y. State Bar Assn. Home: 800 5th Ave New York NY 10021-7216 Office: Phillips Nizer Benjamin Krim & Ballon 40 W 57th St New York NY 10019-4001

BALLORA, MARK EDWARD, music educator; b. San Francisco, May 19, 1962; s. Paul Edward Ballora and Judith Schmidt; m. Jui-Chih Agatha Wang. BA in Theatre Arts, UCLA, 1984; MM in Music Tech., NYU, 1995, MA in Music Composition, 1996; Ph.D, McGill U., Montreal, Can., 2000. Computer graphics operator Lehman Brothers Am. Express, N.Y.C., 1985—92; grad. asst. NYU, N.Y.C., 1992—95; music specialist Bklyn. Music Sch., Bklyn., 1993—95; instr. McGill U., Montreal, 1998—2000; asst. prof. Pa. State U., University Park, 2000—. Author: (textbook) Essentials of Music Technology, 2002; composer: In and Around Your House, 1987, 9 Songs, 1988, Heart Rhythms: Healthy, 2002, (animated film series) Paradise Workshop, 1991; contbr. articles to profl. jours. Named Regents scholar, UCLA, 1980—84, Max Stern fellow in Music, McGill U., 1995—98; grantee, Pa. State U., 2001—02. Office: Pa State Sch Music 233 Music Bldg I University Park PA 16802-1901 Office Fax: 814-865-6785. Business E-Mail: ballora@psu.edu.

BALLOT, ALISSA E. lawyer; b. N.Y.C., Nov. 25, 1955; d. I. Martin and Barbara E. (Bendet) B. BA, Williams Coll., 1977; JD, Harvard U., 1980. Bar: N.Y. 1981, U.S. Dist. Ct. (so. and ea. dists.) N.Y. 1981. Assoc. Kramer, Levin et al, N.Y.C., 1980-83; counsel Lincoln Savs. Bank, N.Y.C., 1983-85; assoc. gen. counsel Am. Savs. Bank, White Plains, N.Y., 1985-86, dep. gen. counsel, 1987-92, gen. counsel North Side Savs. Bank, Floral Park, N.Y., 1992-96; sr. v.p. legal affairs, sec. Republic Security Bank, West Palm Beach, Fla., 1997-2001; sr. v.p. & gen. counsel BankAtlantic, Ft. Lauderdale, Fla., 2001—. Vice chmn. Williams Coll. Alumni Fund. Mem. ABA, Assn. of Corp. Counsel Am., Am. Soc. Corp. Secs. Jewish. Home: 80 Monterey Pointe Dr Palm Beach Gardens FL 33418-5809 Office: BankAtlantic 1750 E Sunrise Blvd Fort Lauderdale FL 33304 E-mail: alissa.ballot@wachovia.com.

BALLOU, JANICE DONELON, research director; b. New Brunswick, N.J., May 13, 1944; s. Peter and Kathryn (Koval) Donelon; m. Donald Thomas Ballou, Nov. 12, 1966 (div. 1984); children: Peter, David. BA, Douglas Coll., 1966; MA, Rutgers U., 1977. Tchr. Sayreville (N.J.) Jr. High Sch., 1966-71; dir. field ops. Eagleton Inst., Rutgers U., New Brunswick, N.J., 1977-80, assoc. dir., 1980-82, dir., 1989—; v.p. divsn. head Louis Harris & Assocs., N.Y.C., 1982-86; v.p. group head Response Analysis, Princeton, N.J., 1986-89; v.p. Mathematica Policy Rsch., Inc., Princeton, NJ, 2001—. Bd. dirs. Inst. Rsch. on Aging and Health Fin., Princeton, N.J., Essex C.C. Found. Co-founder Parents Drug and Alcohol Coun., Highland Park, N.J., 1991; bd. dirs. Rutgers Substance Abuse Task Force, New Brunswick, 1990-93, The Citizen's Com. on Biomed. Ethics, Summit, N.J., 1993-98; chair Pathways to Participation Civic Edn. Program com., New Brunswick, 1992; grad. bd. Leadership N.J., 1991-99; pres. Bd. Leadership N.J. Grad. Orgn., 1995; mayor Highland Park Econ. Devel. Com., 1999. Leadership N.J. fellow Partnership for N.J., 1990, Ford Found. fellow, 1990; named Alumnae of Yr. by Highland Park High Sch., 1992. Mem. Am. Assn. Pub. Opinion Rsch. (pubs. chair 1988-90, sec.-treas. 1991-93, standards chair 1999-2001, councillor-at-large 2002--), Nat. Network State Polls (mem. exec. coun. 1989—), Nat. Coun. Pub. Polls (mem. exec. coun. 1993—), N.J. Internat. Forum Women (sec.), Douglass Coll. Associate Alumnae Douglass Soc. Avocations: raising christmas trees, travelling, hiking, outdoor activities, reading. Office: Mathematica Policy Rsch PO Box 2393 Princeton NJ 08543-2392

BALLOU, KENNETH WALTER, retired business executive, university dean; s. Thomas Walter and Anne M. (Blanck) A.; m. Ann Dysart; children— Stephen K., Jeffrey S., Laura A., Ellen S. AB, Tufts U., 1953, Ed.M., 1954; postgrad., Rutgers U., 1955-56, UCLA, 1978, Wharton Sch., U. Pa., 1979, NYU, 1980. Tchr. pub. schs., Verona, N.J., 1954-56; asst. dir. admissions Northeastern U., Boston, 1954-59, dir. admissions, 1959-65, dean univ. relations, 1965-69, dean Univ. Coll., 1969-74, dean adult edn., 1974-78; pres. Wellesley Motor Coach Co., Mass., 1978-88; v.p., gen. mgr. Waters Bus. Systems, Inc., Framingham, Mass., 1978-88. Cons. U.S. Office of Edn., various colls.; corporator Framingham Savs. Bank, 1980-85; mem. Spl. Legis. Commn. on Sch. Transp. Safety; sr. lectr. in mngt. Northeastern U., 1979-90. Author monographs in field of adult edn. and sch. transp. Chmn. Framingham Sch. Com., 1962-68; corporator Framingham Union Hosp., 1969-79; corporator Northeastern U., 1986-2002, mem. nat. coun., bd. overseers, 1989-98, mem. long range planning com., life mem. President's Club; bd. dirs. Mass. Osteo Hosp., 1970-72; life mem. Danforth Mus. Art, Framingham Hist. Assn.; mem. Sudbury Valley Trustees, Cahoon Mus.; past mem. bd. assessors 1st Parish, Framingham; endowed Childrens Gallery of Danforth Mus. and established the Dean Kenneth W. Ballou Family Scholarship, Northeastern U. Mem. AAUP, Assn. Higher Edn., Am. Mgmt. Assn., Adult Edn. Assn., Am. Assn. Continuing Edn., Coun. Advancement of Edn., Am. Pers. and Guidance Asn., Mass. Sch. Transp. Assn. (pres. 1988—), Nat. Sch. Transp. Assn. (Golden Merit award 1988), Nat. Pupil Transp. Assn., Mass. Sch. Bus. Ofcls. Assn., Mass. Audubon Soc., Ariz. Hist. Soc., Zeta Psi, Heritage Mus., Hyannis Yacht Club. Home: 19 Roosevelt Rd Cotuit MA 02635

BALLOU, RONALD HERMAN, management educator; b. Columbus, Ohio, Aug. 20, 1937; s. Ralph Hunt Ballou and Selma Ann (Held) Weintritt; m. Carolyn Young, Dec. 21, 1960; children: Kevin Ronald, Brian Michael. BME, Ohio State U., 1960, MBA, 1963, PhD, 1965. Bus. adminstr. Westinghouse Electric Co., Columbus, 1960-63; asst. prof. quantitative methods Northwestern U., Evanston, Ill., 1965-68; prof. ops. and logists mgmt. Case-Western Res. U., Cleve., 1968—. Vis. assoc. prof. mktg. and transp. Mich. State U., East Lansing, 1972-73; editl. rev. bd. Jour. Bus. Logistics, 1983—, Internat. Jour. Phys. Distbn. and Logistics Mgmt., 1984—; cons. in field. Author: Business Logistics/Supply Chain Managment, 5th edit., 2004, Basic Business Logistics, 2d edit., 1987; contbr. numerous articles to profl. jours. Mem. Informs, Coun. Logistics Mgmt. Republican. Avocations: fishing, boating, musical performance. Office: Weatherhead Sch Mgmt Case Western Res U Cleveland OH 44106 Home: 5565 Hummingbird Cir Solon OH 44139

BALLOUN, JAMES S. service company executive; B in Indsl. Engring., Iowa State U.; MBA, Harvard U. Sr. governing leader, ptnr. election and review coms. McKinsey & Co.; chmn., CEO, pres. Nat. Svc. Industries, Inc., Atlanta, 1996—. Bd. dirs. Wachovia Corp., Georgia-Pacific Corp., Wachovia Bank, N.A., Radiant Sys. Inc. Bd. dirs. Westminster Schs.; past chmn. trustees Woodruff Arts Ctr. Mem. Atlanta C. of C., Commerce Club. Office: Nat Svc Industries 1420 Peachtree St NE Atlanta GA 30309

BALLSUN, KATHRYN ANN, lawyer; b. Calif., May 8, 1946; d. Zan and Doris (Pratt) B. BA, U. So. Calif., 1969, MA, 1971; JD, Loyola U., L.A., 1976. Bar: Calif. 1976, U.S. Dist. Ct. (cen. dist.) Calif. 1977. Ptnr. Sherer, Bradford, Lyster & Ballsun, L.A. Vis. prof. UCLA Law Sch., Loyola U. Law Sch., L.A.; adj. prof. U. So. Calif. Law Sch.; mem. planning com. U. So. Calif. Progate and Trust Conf., 1985-87; lectr. various schs. Author: (with others) Estate Planning for the General Practitioner; editor: How to Live and Die with California Probate; contbr. articles to profl. jours. Mem. graphic arts coun. L.A. County Mus. Art, Children's Coun., Westwood Meth. Ch.; co-chmn. for Class of 1976 Greater Loyola Law Sch. Devel. Program, 1983; advisor Am. Cancer Soc. Program; radio vol. sta. KUSC; bd. dirs. Planned Protective Svcs. Inc.; bd. dirs. L.A. Philharm. Orch., com. profl. women, treas. 1985-86. Fellow Am. Coll. Probate Counsel; mem. ABA (real property, probate and trust law, taxation sects., pre-death planning com.), State Bar Calif. (resolutions com., exec. com., co-vice chair estate planning techniques, post death, pre-death com., trust and probate, bus. law, taxation sects., law revision study team 1983-85), L.A. County Bar Assn. (trustee, exec. com., trust and probate, taxation sects.), Beverly Hills Bar Assn. (treas. 1985-86, bd. govs. 1982-84, 84-86, probate and trust com., taxation com., sr. vice chair resolutions com., del. State Bar Conv. 1981-85, v.p. 1987-89, pres.-elect, pres. 1989—, panelist), Nat. Acad. Elder Law Attys., Inc., Calif. Women Lawyers, L.A. Women Lawyers, Women in Business (sec., polit. action com.), Beverly Hills Estate Planning Com., Estate Counselor's Forum (past pres., v.p., bd. dirs.), Los Angeles County Mus. Art, L.A. C. of C., ACLU (L.A. chpt.), UCLA Ctr. for Study of Women, ACLU (L.A. chpt.), Kappa Alpha Theta. Office: Ballsun & Assocs 6fh Fl 2029 Century Park E Los Angeles CA 90067

BALLWEG, DAVID BRENT, music educator, conductor; b. Bartlesville, Okla., Oct. 6, 1956; s. Gus and Thersa Ballweg; m. Susan Kay Van Scyoc, June 4, 1977. MusB, Okla. Bapt. U., 1978; MusM, Southwestern Bapt. Theol. Sem., 1981; D in Musical Arts, U. Mo., Kansas City, 1987. Dir. choral activities Williams Bapt. Coll., Walnut Ridge, Ark., 1982—85; asst. prof. music Northwestern Okla. State U., Alva, 1987—88; asst. prof. music Grand Canyon U., Phoenix, 1988—89; dir. of choral activities U. Ark., Fort Smith, 1989—94; dir. choral activities Collin County C.C., Plano, Tex., 1994—2000; prof. music So. Nazarene U., Bethany, Okla., 2000—. Founder and condr. NE Ark. Chorale, Walnut Ridge, 1983—85; asst. condr. Kans. City (Mo.) Symphony Chorus, 1986—87; artistic dir., condr. Plano Civic Chorus, 1994—2000; condr. S.W. Condrs. Symposium, Phoenix, 1997; dir. orchestral instruments First Bapt. Ch., Richardson, Tex., 1998—2000. Recipient Gold award, Bison Glee Club, Okla. Bapt. U., 1978, First prize, Scarritt Grad. Sch. Nat. Choral Conducting Competition, 1986; John F. Skinner Meml. scholar, 1974, 1977, Conducting Performance scholar, Southwestern Bapt. Theol. Sem., 1981. Mem.: Okla. Music Educators Assn., Music Educators Nat. Conf., Okla. Choral Dirs. Assn. (newsletter editor 2003—), Internat. Fedn. Choral Music (condr. masterclass 1996), Am. Choral Dirs. Assn. (life; nat. r&s chair 1996—2000). Avocations: golf, scuba diving. Office: So Nazarene Univ 6729 NW 39th Expressway Bethany OK 73008 Office Fax: 405-717-6268. Personal E-mail: bballweg@juno.com. E-mail: bballweg@snu.edu.

BALLWEG, JANET C. artist, art educator; b. Madison, Wis., Apr. 16, 1961; d. Marvin J. and Norma J. Ballweg. BS, U. Wis., 1983; MFA, U. Ill., 1985. Adj. faculty Ind. State U., Terre Haute, Ind., 1988-90; asst. prof. art Bowling Green (Ohio) State U., 1990-94, assoc. prof. art, 1994—2001, prof., 2001—. Recipient Best of Show award Toledo Fedn. of Art, Toledo Mus., 1993; Individual Artists fellow Ind. Arts Coun., 1987. Mem.: So. Graphics Coun., Mid-Am. Print Coun. (v.p. 2000—02), Foundations in Art: Theory and Edn. (pres. 1994—95), Phi Kappa Phi (hon.). Avocations: home remodeling, gardening, weight training, walking. Office: Bowling Green State U Sch Of Art Bowling Green OH 43403-0001 Fax: (419) 372-2544. E-mail: jballwe@bgnet.bgsu.edu.

BALMAN, STEVEN K. lawyer; b. Wichita, Kans., Nov. 2, 1956; s. Nan Poston Balman, Gail Eugene Balman; m. Kelly Sue Knopp, June 1, 1991 (div. 2002); 1 child, Elizabeth Grace. AB, Harvard U., 1978; JD, U. Tex., 1981. Bar: Okla. 1981. Assoc. Conner & Winters, Tulsa, Okla., 1981—88; ptnr. Bond & Balman, Tulsa, 1988—96; sr. ptnr. Baker & Hoster, Tulsa, Okla., 1996—97; dir. Inhofe, Jorgenson & Balman, Tulsa, 1997—99, Sneed Lang, P.C., Tulsa, 1999—. Adj. prof. law U. Tulsa, Okla., 1991—; judge temporary divsn. panel LXL Okla. Ct. of Civil Appeals, Tulsa, 1992—93; adj. settlement judge U.S. Dist. Ct., No. Dist. Okla., Tulsa, 1998—. Editor-in-chief Am. Jour. Criminal Law, 1981; contbr. articles. Okla. membership chair U.S. Supreme Ct. Hist. Soc., Washington, 1992—93; mem. judicial conf. U.S. Ct. of Appeals, 10th cir., 1989—. Mem.: Tulsa County Bar Assn. (bd. dirs. 1997—), Am. Inns of Ct. Hudson Hall Wheaton Chpt. (sec. 1995—96), Am. Law Inst. (emeritus), Federalist Soc. (pres. Tulsa lawyers chpt. 2000—). Methodist. Office: Sneed Lang PC 2 W 2nd St Ste 2300 Tulsa OK 74103 Office Fax: 918-582-0410. Business E-Mail: sbalman@sneedlang.com.

BALMER, RANDALL, American religion historian; b. Chgo., Oct. 22, 1954; s. Clarence Russel Balmer and Nancy Ruth Froberg; m. Catharine Randall, Jan. 23, 1998; m. Kathryn Joyce Burkey, May 29, 1976 (div. Dec. 9, 1997); children: Christian Froberg, Andrew McKay. BA, Trinity Coll., 1976, M.A., 1980; PhD, AM, Princeton (N.J.) U., 1985; MDiv, Union Theol. Sem., 2001. Asst. prof. of religion Columbia U., N.Y.C., 1985—90, prof. of am. religion Barnard Coll., 1991—. Adj. prof. Union Theol. Sem., N.Y.C., 1995. Author: Growing Pains: Learning to Love My Father's Faith, 2001 (Book of the Yr. award, 2002), Religion in Twentieth Century America, 2001 (Named to Best Trade Books in the Social Studies, 2002), (3-part documentary) Mine Eyes Have Seen the Glory, 1992 (Emmy Award nomination, 1993), A Perfect Babel of Confusion: Dutch Religion and English Culture in the Middle Colonies, 1989 (Disting. Book award Soc. of Colonial Wars, 1991); editor: Christianity Today, 1999—. Mem. Dem. Town Com., Ridgefield, Conn., 2002, Parks and Recreation Commn., Ridgefield. Named to Hall of Fame, Hoover HS, Des Moines, IA, 1995. Mem.: Am. Acad. of Religion, Am. Soc. of Ch. History (mem. of coun. 2001, Sidney E. Meade prize 1983), Acad. of TV Arts & Scis. Democrat. Avocations: bicycling, travel. Home: 42 Beechwood Lane Ridgefield CT 06877-5803 Office: Barnard College Columbia University 3009 Broadway New York NY 10027-6598 Office Fax: 212-854-7491. Personal E-mail: rb281@columbia.edu. E-mail: rb281@columbia.edu.

BALMER, THOMAS ANCIL, state supreme court justice; b. Longview, Wash., Jan. 31, 1952; s. Donald Gordon and Elisabeth Clare (Hill) B.; m. Mary Louise McClintock, Aug. 25, 1984; children: Rebecca Louise, Paul McClintock. AB, Oberlin Coll., 1974; JD, U. Chgo., 1977. Bar: Mass. 1977, D.C. 1981, U.S. Dist. Ct. Mass. 1977, Oreg. 1982, U.S. Dist. Ct. Oreg. 1982, U.S. Ct. Appeals (9th cir.) 1982, U.S. Ct. Appeals (D.C. cir.) 1983, U.S. Supreme Ct. 1987. Assoc. Choate, Hall & Stewart, Boston, 1977-79, Wald, Harkrader & Ross, Washington, 1980-82; trial atty. antitrust div. U.S. Dept. Justice, Washington, 1979-80; assoc. Lindsay, Hart, Neil & Weigler, Portland, Oreg., 1982-84, ptnr., 1985-90, Ater Wynne LLP, Portland, Oreg., 1990—93, 1997—2001; dep. atty. gen. State of Oregon, Salem, 1993-97; justice Oreg. Supreme Court, Salem, 2001—. Adj. prof. of law Northwestern Sch. Law Lewis and Clark Coll., 1983-84, 90-92. Contbr. articles to law jours. Active mission and outreach com. United Ch. of Christ, Portland, 1984-87, Met. Svc. Dist. Budget Com., Portland, 1988-90; bd. dirs. Multnomah County Legal Aid Svc., Inc., 1989-93, chair 1992-93; bd. dirs. Chamber Music Northwest, 1997—, Classroom Law Project, 2000—. Mem. ABA, Oreg. Bar Assn. (chmn. antitrust sect. 1986-87, mem. fed. practice and procedure com. 1999-2001). Home: 2521 NE 24th Ave Portland OR 97212-4831 Office: Oreg Supreme Ct Supreme Ct Bldg 1163 State St Salem OR 97310

BALMUTH, BERNARD ALLEN, retired film editor; b. Youngstown, Ohio, May 19, 1918; s. Joseph and Sadie (Stein) B.; m. Rosa June Bergman, Mar. 2, 1952; children: Mary Susan, Sharon Nancy. BA in English, UCLA, 1942. Postal clk. U.S. Postal Svc., L.A., 1946-55; asst. and apprentice film editor, film editor L.A., 1955-90; ret., 1990. Instr. film editing dept. of the arts UCLA Extension, 1979-99 (cert. of appreciation); film editing cons. Am. Film Inst., L.A., 1982-92; peer group exec. com. TV Acad. Motion Picture Editors, 1988—. Author: The Language of the Cutting Room, 1979, Introduction to Film Editing, 1989. Initiator petition STOP Save TV Original Programming and Stop Excessive Reruns, 1971-75. Sgt. U.S. Army, 1942-45. Recipient Honor Cert. for Contribution Acad. TV Arts and Scis., 1974, Emmy nomination Best Editing, 1982, Mimes award for acting Youngstown Coll., 1937. Mem. Am. Cinema Editors (life, bd. dirs. 1982-85, 97-99, sec. 1985-87, v.p. 1987-91, chmn. spl. awards com. 1988-99, hon. historian 1993—), Hollywood Entertainment Labor Coun. (rep. for Editors Guild 1972-2002), Stage Soc. (bd. dirs., sec. 1949-54), TV Acad. Motion Picture Editors (mem. exec. com. peer group 1988—). Democrat. Jewish. Avocations: cinema, theatre, dancing, cinema books, tennis. Address: care Rosallen Publs PO Box 927 North Hollywood CA 91603-0927

BALMUTH, MICHAEL A. retail executive; With Bamberger's, Karen Austin Petites, Bon Marche, Seattle; joined Ross Stores, 1989, various positions including sr. v.p., gen. merchandise mgr., exec. v.p. merchandising, 1993-96, CEO, vice chmn., 1996—. Office: 8333 Central Ave Newark CA 94560

BALOG, IBOLYA, accountant; b. Subotica, Yugoslavia, July 11, 1953; came to U.S., 1969; d. Balint and Adela (Dohocki) B. BA, Lehigh U., 1975; MBA, Temple U., 1980. CPA. Adminstrv. asst. Chain Bike Corp., Allentown, Pa.,

1975-77; contr. Bicycle Corp. Am., Allentown, 1982-87; acct. Cohen & Rogozinski, CPA's, Allentown, 1987-92; mgr. Parente, Randolph LLC, CPA's, Allentown, 1992—. Bd. dirs. YWCA, Allentown, 1986-95, treas., 1993, pres., 1994, trustee, 1995—. Mem. AAUW (treas. 1984-85, Outstanding Woman 1985), AICPAs, Pa. Inst. CPAs (pres. Lehigh Valley chpt. 1998-99), Inst. Mgmt. Accts. (v.p. Lehigh Valley chpt. 1997-99, chpt. pres. 1999-2000), Am. Women's Soc. CPAs (pres. Lehigh Valley affiliate 1993-94), Allentown Rotary Club. Democrat. Home: 1522 1/2 W Chew St Allentown PA 18102-3645 Office: Parente Randolph LLC 1427 W Chew St Allentown PA 18102-3658

BALOG, RITA JEAN, retired librarian; b. Ashtabula, Ohio, Sept. 24, 1930; d. Frederick Carroll and Marguerite Ethel (White) Grady; m. Richard Francis Balog, Oct. 16, 1949 (dec. Feb. 1988); children: Rebecca Kay, Richard Francis Jr., Ronald Frank, Robert Henry; m. Charles R. Haapala, Oct. 24, 1999. AA, Kent State U., 1977, BA in Gen. Studies, 1978, MLS, 1980. Clk., typist Harbor Pub. Libr., Ashtabula, 1973-75, children's libr., 1975-80; libr., dir. Harbor-Topky Meml. Libr., Ashtabula, 1980-97; ret., 1997. Vol. libr. Thomas Jefferson Elem. Sch., Harbor Spl. Sch., Ashtabula, 1972-75. Sec., mem. Ashtabula Archtl. Restoration and Rev. Bd., 1975-95; vol. leader Lake River coun. Girl Scouts U.S., Niles, 1958-73, mem. nominating com., 1989-91, bd. dirs., 1991-95, child camp dir.; trustee Coun. Ashtabula County Librs., chair, 1994-96. Mem. ALA, AAUW, Ohio Libr. Assn., N.E. Ohio Libr. Assn. (regional adv. bd. 1984-86), Coun. Ashtabula County Librs. (pres. 1985-86), Ashtabula Area Mus. and Hist. Soc. (trustee 1992-98), Zonta (pres. 1987-89). Democrat. Avocations: collecting rocks, wild flowers, swimming, needlecraft.

BALON, RICHARD, psychiatrist, educator; b. Olomouc, Czechoslovakia, Oct. 11, 1951; s. Ota and Marie (Sindylek) B.; m. Helena Rachel Zador, July 24, 1976. MD, U. Karlova, Prague, Czechoslovakia, 1976. Diplomate Am. Bd. Psychiatry and Neurology; bd. cert. in psychiatry in Czechoslovakia, cert. clin. psychopharmacology Am. Soc. Clin. Psychopharmacology, 1998. Resident in psychiatry and clin. rsch. Psychiat. Rsch. Inst., Prague, 1978-81; resident in psychiatry Lafayette Clinic, Detroit, 1983-87; asst. prof. Wayne State U., Detroit, 1987-90, assoc. prof., 1990-96, prof., 1996—, assoc. dir. residency tng. in psychiatry, 2002—. Dir. jr. med. students program in psychiatry Wayne State U., Detroit, 1989-92, dir. med. student edn. psychiatry, 1993-97; staff psychiatrist Lafayette Clinic, Detroit, 1987-92, pres. med. staff, 1990-92; co-chair Mich. Tech. Adv. Rsch. com., 1991-99. Contbr. chpts to books and articles to profl. jours.; author, editor 4 books; co-author 1 book. Travel fellow Am. Coll. Neuropsychopharmacology, 1987. Fellow: Am. Coll. Psychiatrists, Am. Psychiat. Assn. (1st Nancy C.A. Roeske award 1991, George Tarjan award 1998); mem.: AMA, Mich. Psychiat. Soc. (pres. 2000—01), Assn. Dirs. Med. Student Edn. in Psychiatry, Collegium Internat. Neuro-Psychopharmacologicum, Soc. Biol. Psychiatry, Am. Assn. Suicidology, Internat. Soc. Psychoneuroendocrinology. Avocations: movies, books, politics, geography. Office: Univ Psychiat Ctr 2751 E Jefferson Ave Ste 200 Detroit MI 48207-4100 E-mail: rbalon@wayne.edu.

BALOUN, JOHN CHARLES, wholesale grocery company executive, retired; b. Chgo., May 1, 1934; s. John Nicholas and Anne (Giera) B.; m. Lynette Anne Jehs, July 27, 1963 (dec. Apr. 1998); children: John Christopher, Michael Warren. BSC, DePaul U., 1956. CPA, Ill. Audit staff Arthur Andersen & Co., Chgo., 1956-63; contr., asst. sec. Super Food Svcs., Inc., Chgo., 1963-67, treas., 1967-68, Dog'N Suds, Inc., Champaign, Ill., 1968-69; dir. planning and control distbn. divsn. Champion Internat., Inc., Chgo., 1969-74; treas. IGA, Inc., Chgo., 1974-77, v.p., 1977-80; v.p. fin. IGA Inc., Chgo., 1986-93, contr., 1993-96; ret. IGA, Inc., 1996; v.p. fin. Allied Van Lines, Inc., Broadview, Ill., 1980-83; contr., dir. corp. devel. Altair Corp., Northbrook, Ill., 1984-86. Pres. bd. dirs. No. Ill. Food Bank, St. Charles, Ill., 1990-91, bd. dirs., 1988-93, 96-2002. 2d lt. AUS, 1957. Republican. Home: 610 Western Ave Glen Ellyn IL 60137-4058 E-mail: jbaloun919@aol.com.

BALOW, IRVING HENRY, retired education educator; b. Wabasha, Minn., Jan. 19, 1927; s. Laurence Christian and Katherine (Yost) B.; m. Joyce Elizabeth Binner, June 8, 1950 (dec. 1980); children: Mary, Thomas, Michael, Robert, Ann.; m. Alta Sitton, June 27, 1981. BS, U. Minn., 1951, MA, 1957, PhD, 1959. Elementary sch. tchr., Theilmam, Minn., 1951-53; tchr. elem. sch. Wabasha, 1953-54, 56-57; instr. U. Minn., 1957-59; mem. faculty U. Calif., Riverside, 1959—, prof. edn., 1968—, chmn. dept., 1963-70, assoc. dean, 1970-71, acting dean, 1971-72, dean, 1972-87, acting dean Grad. Sch. Mgmt., 1990-92; retired, 1992. Reading cons., 1959—. Contbr. articles to profl. jours. Served with USAAF, 1945-47. Home: 29410 Winding Brook Dr Menifee CA 92584 E-mail: ibalow@earthlink.net.

BALOWS, ALBERT, microbiologist, educator; b. Denver, Jan. 3, 1921; s. Lazerus and Anna (Kleiner) B.; m. Patricia Ann Barker, Oct. 7, 1956; children: Eve Ellen, Daniel Scott. BA in Biology (Lowell scholar), Colo. Coll., 1942; MS in Microbiology, Syracuse U., 1948; PhD (Haggin fellow), U. Ky., 1952. Diplomate: Am. Bd. Med. Microbiology. Microbiologist St. Joseph Hosp., Lexington (Ky.) Clinic, 1952-69; dir. bacteriology div. Ctrs. Disease Control, USPHS, Atlanta, 1969-81; asst. dir. lab. sci. Ctrs. Disease Control, USPHS (Ctr. Infectious Diseases), 1981-88; dir. emeritus Ctr. Disease Control, USPHS (Ctr. Infectious Diseases), 1988. Asst. prof. medicine U. ky. Med. Ctr., Lexington, 1960-63, assoc. prof. medicine and cell biology, 1963-69; prof. lab. medicine Emory U. Sch. Medicine, 1970-98, prof. lab. medicine emeritus, 1998; prof. biology Ga. State U., Atlanta, 1970—; lectr. Am. Soc. Microbiology Found., 1974-76; cons. clin. microbiology VA Hosp., Good Samaritan Hosp., Lexington, 1965-69; Med. Svc. Corps Dept. Army, 1973-79; chair expert panel WHO Internat. Collaborating Ctr. for Rsch. Syphilis Serology and Immunology, 1974-82; bd. dirs. WHO Internat. Collaborating Ctr. for Rsch. and Ref. in Antibiotic Susceptibility Testing, 1975-82, WHO Internat. Collaborating Ctr. for Rsch. and Ref. in Diagnostic Methods and Materials, 1985-88; mem. expert panels bacterial diseases, biol. standardization, lab. sci. WHO, Geneva, 1977-88. Founding editor-in-chief Jour. Clin. Microbiology, 1974-79, Current Microbiology, 1982—; editor Applied Microbiology, 1965-74, Ann. Rev. Microbiology, 1979—, C.C. Thomas med. microbiology series, 1964-90; author, editor over 75 books on microbiology and infectious disease; mem. editorial bds. 6 sci. jours.; editor: The Prokaryotes, 1981, sr. editor: The Prokaryotes, 2d edit., 1991; gen. editor: Topley & Wilson's Microbiology & Microbial Infections, 9th edit., 1998 (winner Advanced Edited Book category Med. Soc. London 1998); contbr. articles to profl. jours. Bd. dirs. Lexington chpt. NCCJ, 1960—64. With U.S. Army, 1943—46, with M.C. U.S. Army, 1943—46, ETO. Named Lab World Microbiologist of Yr., 1980; recipient Becton-Dickinson award in clin. microbiology, 1981, Silver medallion for outstanding contbns. to clin. microbiology Italian Soc. Microbiology, 1983, Louis T. Benezet Disting. Alumni award Colorado Coll., 1988, Abbott Labs. award for devel. of rapid lab. diagnostic techs., 1990, Disting. Profl. Recognition award, Am. bd. Med. Microbiology, 1997, bioMerieux Sonnenwirth award for exemplary leadership in clin. microbiology, 1999. Fellow Am. Acad. Microbiology (bd. govs. 1973-77, 89-95, chmn. 1975-76), N.Y. Acad. Scis., AAAS, Am. Pub. Health Assn., Infectious Disease Soc. Am., Am. Acad. Lab. Physicians and Scientists; mem. Am. Soc. Microbiology (pres.-elect 1979-80, pres. 1980-81, council, also mem. council policy com. 1974-82, P.R. Edwards award for outstanding service furthering high profl. ideals and standards in microbiology from S.E. br. 1987, elected hon. mem. 1988), Am. Soc. Clin. Pathology, Soc. Gen. Microbiology, AAUP, Med. Mycol. Soc. Am., Soc. Applied Bacteriology, Am. Veneral Disease Assn., South Ctrl. Assn. Clin. Microbiology (hon.), Assn. State & Territorial Pub. Health Lab. Dirs. (hon.), Sci. Writers Guild, Sigma Xi, Blue Key, Omicron Delta Kappa, Tau Kappa Alpha, Zeta Beta Tau, B'nai B'rith. Home and Office: 105 Bay Colt Rd Alpharetta GA 30004-3531 E-mail: abalows@aol.com. *Self esteem, good will and understanding are achieved by effective communication. Regrettably we fail because we do not listen. I have patterned my life after an ancient Chinese proverb: "First you must learn to listen well; then you will know that you have talked too much."*

BALSAM, MARION JOYCE, retired naval officer, pediatrician; b. N.Y.C., Oct. 9, 1940; d. Emanuel and Dorothy Balsam; children: Ross Garret, Joclyn Page, Clifford Scott, Marissa Hale. BA, Cornell U., 1962; MD, NYU, 1966. Diplomate Am. Bd. Pediatrics. Chief Crippled Children's Svcs. Guam Dept. Pub. Health, 1971—74; joined M.C., USN, 1975, advanced through grades to Rear Adm., 1998; staff pediatrician Naval Hosp., Camp Pendleton, Oceanside, Calif., 1975—81; head inpatient pediats. Nat. Naval Med. Ctr., Bethesda, Md., 1981—85, dept. chair, 1985—89, dep. comdr., 1991—93; med. dir., chief of staff Naval Hosp., San Diego, 1989—91, comdr. Pensacola, Fla., 1993—95; fleet med. officer Naval Forces Europe, London, 1995—98; comdr. Naval Med. Ctr., Portsmouth, Va., 1998—2000; lead agt. Tricare, Mid-Atlantic Region, 1998—2000; dir. rsch. partnerships Nat. Children's Study, NICHD/NIH, 2000—. Fellow: Am. Acad. Pediatrics (mem. task force on terrorism and children, former mem. com. on pediat workforce, chmn. subcom. on women in pediats.). Avocations: photography, music, piano. Home: 5601 Beam Ct Bethesda MD 20817 E-mail: marionbalsam@aol.com.

BALSAM, RICHARD FREDRIC, cardiologist; b. Port Chester, N.Y., Mar. 8, 1938; s. Paul and Bertha (Jacobs) B.; m. Mary Kennedy, Feb. 18, 1989; children: Loren, Daniel. BS, Union Coll., Schenectady, N.Y., 1959; MD, Albany Med. Coll., 1964. Internal medicine intern Albany Med. Ctr. Hosp., 1964-65, internal medicine resident, 1965-67; cardiac fellow VA, Albany, 1967-69; internist/cardiologist Pankin & Balsam, MD, P.C., Albany, 1969-95, Cmty. Care Physicians, Albany, 1995—. Cons. Searle Pharms., Albany, 1992-95; mem. pharmacy adv. com. St. Peter's Hosp., Albany, 1969—; pres., founder Renaissance Mus. Arts, Inc., 1986—. Mem. bd. dirs. Albany Symphony Orch., 1977-83; pres. Empire State Youth Orch. Bd., Albany, 1983-87. Capt. USAR, 1965-72. Mem. Am. Coll. Cardiology, Am. Coll. Sports Medicine, Am. Heart Assn., Am. Soc. Internal Medicine, Cardiac Soc. of Upstate N.Y. (pres.). Jewish. Avocations: tennis, golf, swimming, chess, U.S. history. Office: Cmty Care Physicians Inc 1365 Washington Ave Ste 100 Albany NY 12206-1037

BALSAMELLO, MELISSA (MARLEY), educator; b. Red Bank, N.J., Aug. 5, 1975; d. Lucille (Perillo) M. BA in Psychology Douglass Coll., Rutgers U., 1997, EdM in Spl. Edn., 1998, postgrad., 1998—2001. Cert. early childhood edn., elem. edn., spl. edn., supr., psychology, dance/vocat. arts. Religious edn. tchr. St. Leo and Great, Lincroft, N.J., 1991-93; respite care provider, counselor ARC of Somerset, Manville, N.J., 1995; group leader, tchr. Happy Campers Ecology Camp, New Brunswick, 1996; tchg. asst., subsitute tchr. Douglass Child Study Ctr., New Brunswick, 1996-98; tchg. asst., field worker Douglass Devel. Disability Ctr., New Brunswick, 1995-96; store mgr. Pyramid Books, Highland Park, N.J., 1997-98; tchr., camp group leader Douglass Girl's Camp, New Brunswick, 1997-98; adminstrv. asst. to pres. United Bolt & Besel, 1998; tchr. 1st grade Franklin Park Sch., Somerset, NJ, 1998—2002, dance ensemble advisor, choreographer, 2000—02; 1st grade tchr. Woodrow Wilson Sch., Westfield, NJ, 2002—. Mem. selection com. Douglass Alumni Soc., 1995-97; program facilitator Coll. Orientation and Recruitment Svcs., 1995-96; house chairwoman Coll. Residence Life, 1995-98; mentor Douglass Coll. Emerging Leaders Program, 1995-98; divsn. leader, specialist Daisy Recreation, East Brunswick, 1997-99; counselor Friday Night Live, East Brunswick, 1999-2000; divsn. leader/specialist Daisy Recreation Ctr., East Brunswick, 1997-98; honors rev., tutor 2-8th, Edison, N.J., 1999—. Pres. Am. Assn. Mental Retardation, Rutgers chpt., 1995-96; vol., asst. coach N.J. Spl. Olympics, 1996-97. Recipient Presdl. Cmty. Svc. award, Ocean Twp., Washington, 1992, scholarship North Monmouth AAUW, 1996-97. Mem. ASCD, N.J. Edn. Assn., Am. Ednl. Rsch. Assn., Franklin Twp. Edn. Assn., Am. Assn. Mental Retardation (pres. chpt. 1995-97), N.J. Assn. Edn. Young Children, Rutgers U. Student Edn. Assn., Chi Sigma (pres. 1995). Avocations: crocheting, dance, drama, writing, art. Home: 24 Briar Cir Green Brook NJ 08812

BALSAMO, SALVATORE ANTHONY, technical and temporary employment companies executive; b. Boston, May 30, 1933; s. Anthony and Rosalia (Giambanco) B.; m. Yvonne Mollomo, Nov. 23, 1952; children: Anthony Joseph, Linda Marie Balsamo Wirta, Vicki Christine. Grad. high sch., Boston, 1951. Restranteur, 1955-61; asst. br. mgr. John Hancock, Boston, 1961-66; v.p. TAD Temporaries, Inc., Cambridge, Mass., 1966-69; chmn. bd., chief exec. officer, treas. Tech. Aid Corp. (now TAC Worldwide Cos.), Newton, Mass., 1969-99, chmn. bd., 1999—, also bd. dirs. Bd. dirs. Tech/Aid, TAC/Temps Inc., EDP/Temps and Contract Services, MicroTemps Systems and Programming, TAC/Medical Services Inc., Systems Mgmt. and Devel. Inc., Computer Enterprise Inc., Agy. for Personnel, TAC/Profl. Recruiters. Mem. fundraising com. Cath. Charitable Bur. Boston; founder, trustee Balsamo Meml. Charitable Found. Served to sgt. U.S. Army, 1953-55. Recipient award USAFR, 1977, Entrepreneurship Key to City of Cin., Mayor Charlie Luken, 1986. Mem. Nat. Assn. Temporary Services (1st v.p. 1987, 2d v.p. 1986-87, treas. 1985-86, exec. com. 1985—, bd. dirs. 1984—, govt. relations com.), Nat. Tech. Services Assn. (pres. New Eng. chpt. 1978-80, pres. 1983-84, exec. com., bd. dirs.), Mass. Assn. Temporary Services (v.p. tech. services 1982—, pres. 1979-81), New Eng. Design and Drafting Assn., Nat. Assn. Corp. Treas. Clubs: 100 of Mass. Avocation: tennis. Office: TAC Worldwide Cos PO Box 9100 Dedham MA 02027-9100*

BALSER, ROBERT EDWARD, animation film producer, director; b. Rochester, N.Y., Mar. 25, 1927; s. Syrel Jesse and Goldie (Weisenberg) B.; m. Cima Diane Feinberg, June 25, 1950; 1 child, Trevel Morley. BA, UCLA, 1950. Dir. animation TVC, London, 1967-68, WorldWide Prodn., Barcelona, Spain, 1969-70, Halas and Batcheler, London, 1971-72; owner, dir. Pegbar Prodns., Barcelona, 1972-93; dir. TV series Cromosoma, Barcelona, 1994-95; retired cons. Barcelona, 1995; animation cons., 1996, 1996-99. Pres. "CARTOON" (media program), 1988—; v.p. ASIFA Internat., 1979-94, pres. Spain, 1980-93; lectr. in field. Co-dir. The Yellow Submarine, 1967-68; supv. dir. The Jackson 5, 1971; producer numerous ednl. and TV series. V.p. Benjamin Franklin Found., Barcelona, 1986—, Am. Soc. Barcelona, 1986-90; pres. Benjamin Franklin Sch. Bd., Barcelona, 1986-95. With USN, 1945-46. Recipient EMMY award NATAS, 1980; 1st prize publicity Venice and Annecy Festivals, Italy and France, 1964, Acad. Motion Picture Arts Scis. Democrat. Jewish. Avocations: film, collecting stamps and coins.

BALSIGER, DAVID WAYNE, television-video director, researcher, producer, writer; b. Monroe, Wis., Dec. 14, 1945; s. Leon C. and Dorothy May (Meythaler) B.; m. Sylvia Roybal, 2003; children from previous marriages: Jennifer Anne, Lisa Atalie, Lori Faith. Student, Pepperdine U., Malibu, Calif., 1964-66, Cypress Jr. Coll., 1966, Chapman Coll. World Campus Afloat, Orange, Calif., 1967-68, Internat. Coll., Copenhagen, 1968; BA, Nat. U., San Diego, 1977; LHD (hon.), Lincoln Meml. U., Harrogate, Tenn., 1978. Chief photographer, feature writer Anaheim (Calif.) Bull., 1968-69; pub., editor Money Doctor, consumer mag., Anaheim, 1969-70; media dir. World Evangelism, San Diego, 1970-72; dir. mktg. Logos Internat. Christian Book Pubs., Plainfield, N.J., 1972-73; pres., dir. Master Media, advt. agy., Costa Mesa, Calif., 1973-75; pres. Balsiger Lit. Svc., Costa Mesa, 1973-78; v.p. communications Donald S. Smith Assocs., Anaheim, Calif., 1975-78; dir. creative devel. Sunn Classic Pictures, L.A., Salt Lake City, 1976-78; owner Writeway Lit. Assocs., Costa Mesa, 1978-92, Balsiger Enterprises, Costa Mesa, 1978-92, Bibl. News Svc., 1980-90; v.p. Donald S. Smith Assocs., Anaheim, 1982-86; owner BNS Publs., 1986-92; v.p. Am. Portrait Films Internat., Anaheim, 1990-91; chief rschr., field prodr., dir. Sun Internat. Pictures, Salt Lake City, 1992-94; exec. producer, dir. audio-video-media divsn. Group Pub., Loveland, Colo., 1994-98; sr. v.p., prodr., rights supr. Grizzly Adams Prodns., Loveland, Colo., 1998—. Vis. prof. Nat. U., San Diego, 1977-80 Author: (amazing stories books) The Satan Seller, 1972, The Back Side of Satan, 1973, Noah's Ark: I Touched It, 1974, One More Time, 1974, It's Good to Know, 1975, In Search of Noah's Ark, 1976, The Lincoln Conspiracy, 1977, Beyond Defeat, 1978, On The Other Side, 1978, 8 Mini Guide Books (travel series), 1975, (amazing coincidence books) Presidential Biblical Scorecard, 1980, 1984, 1988, Protection Scorecard, North Africa, 1987, 1988, 1989, Candidates Biblical Scorecard, 1986, Scoreboard Alert, 1989, (Amazing Books) Face in the Mirror, 1993, Ancent Secrets of the Bible, 1994, The Incredible Discovery of Noah's Ark, 1995, The Incredible Power of Prayer, 1996 (Dove Family Approved Seal, Film Adv. Bd. Excellence award, 1997, Freedom's Found. George Washington medal, 3 Telly awards, Worldfest Charleston award); dir.(field producer, writer, researcher): (TV films) Operation Thanks, 1965, The Life and Times of Grizzly Adams, 1976—77, In Search of Noah's Ark, 1976, The Lincoln Conspiracy, 1977, The Bermuda Triangle, 1977, Ancient Secrets of the Bible, 1992 (9 awards including Worldfest Charleston award, 1995), Ancient Secrets of the Bible II, 1993, Mysteries of the Ancient World, 1994, Ancient Secrets of the Bible Collectors Series, 1995 (6 awards including 2 communicator awards of excellence); prodr.(6 TV shows and videos): Angels Sent on Assignment, 1996; dir.(field producer, writer, researcher): (TV films) The Incredible Power of Prayer, 4 vols., 1997; exec. prodr.: (video) Chadder's Stowaway Adventure, 1996 (Film Adv. Bd, Excellence award, 1996), (videos) Sing and Play Music Video, 1996, Sing and Play Music Jamboree, 1997, Chadder's Wild Frontier Advemture, 1997, Encounter with the Unexplained (series 39 vols.) (21 awards including 3 Telly awards and 1 Omni Intermedia award); prodr.: (TV series, spls.) Secrets of the Bible Code Revealed, 1998, The Bible Code: Future and Beyond, 1999 (5 awards including 1 videographer award of excellence), Millenium Fears: Fact or Fiction?, 1999, Miracle and Wonder of Prayer (series), 2000 (7 awards including 2 communicator awards of distinction); chief rschr. : (TV series, and videos) many others.; author: numerous law enforcement publs. Press agt. John G. Schmitz congl. campaign, 1972, Gordon Bishop supr. campaign, Orange County, 1970; press agt. asst. Ronald Reagan for Gov., statewide, 1966; statewide campaign mgr. James E. Johnson for U.S. Senate, 1974; campaign mgr. Dave Gubler Congl. campaign, 1974; candidate Costa Mesa City Coun., 1980; Rep. candidate for Congress from 38th Dist. Calif., 1978; mem. Calif. Rep. Assembly, 1975-78, 81-84, Rep. Assocs. Orange County, 1977-79; mem. World Affairs Coun. Orange County and San Diego, 1969-70; assoc.mem. Calif. Rep. Cen. Com., 1969-70; bd. dirs. Chapman Coll. World Campus Afloat, 1967, Chrisma Ministries, Orange, Calif., 1969-73; founder Ban the Soviets Coalition, 1983-84; exec. com. Anatole Fellowship, 1983-87; founder, pres. Nat. Citizens Action Network, 1984-95; bd. dirs. Internat. Ch. Relief Fund, 1987-92. Recipient Vietnam appreciation citation Am. Soldiers in Vietnam, 1966, George Washington Honor medal Freedoms Found., 1978, 79, Religion in Media Angel trophy, 1981, 85, 87, 88, 89, 92, 93, 94, 95, 5 Telly awards for Ancient Secrets series, 1996; named Writer of Month Calif. Writer, 1967; grand winner Mercury award for Pub. Affairs, 1987, Gold Mercury award for Pub. Affairs Mag., 1987, Silver Mercury award for affairs video script, 1988, Nat. Faith and Freedom award Religious Heritage of Am., 1994; named to Lit. Hall of Fame, 1977; hon. tourism amb. Rep. of South Africa, 1991. Mem. Nat. Univ. Pres. Assocs., Coun. on Nat. Policy, Internat. Christian Visual Media Assn. (bd. mem.), Nat. Religious Broadcasters, Internat. Bible Reading Assn. (adv. bd.), Acad. TV Arts and Scis., Am. Film Mkt. Assn., Internat. Press Assn. (adv. bd.), Fellowship European Broadcasters. Address: PO Box 1987 Loveland CO 80539-1987 E-mail: dwbalsiger@ultrasys.net. *I believe successful people have a God given purpose strong enough to make them form the habit of doing things they don't like to do in order to accomplish their purpose. Every single qualification for success is acquired through habit. People form habits and habits form futures.*

BALSILLIE, JIM, information technology executive; Grad., U. Toronto, Harvard U. Chartered acct., Ont. Chmn., co-CEO Rsch. in Motion Ltd., Waterloo, Canada, bd. dirs. Clearnet. Office: Rsch in Motion Ltd 295 Phillip St Waterloo ON N2L 3W8 Canada

BALSLEY, PHILIP ELWOOD, entertainer; b. Augusta County, Va., Aug. 8, 1939; s. Henry Elwood and Marjorie Walden (Fielding) B.; m. Wilma Lee Kincaid, July 21, 1962; children— Gregory, Mark, Leah. Grad. high sch. With group Statler Bros., 1961—. Treas. Statler Bros. Prodns., 1973—. Bd. dirs. Happy Birthday U.S.A. Recipient numerous Grammy awards, Country Music Assn. awards. Presbyterian. Office: PO Box 2703 Staunton VA 24402-2703

BALSTER, ROBERT LOUIS, psychopharmacologist; b. St. Cloud, Minn., Oct. 12, 1944; s. Louis and Marion Mae (Vandergon) B.; m. Sandra Kay Herwig, June 25, 1966; 1 child, Sarah Elizabeth Balster. BS, U. Minn., 1966; PhD, U. Houston, 1970. Postdoctoral fellow in psychiatry and pharmacology U. Chgo., 1970-72; rsch. assoc. in psychiatry Duke U., Durham, N.C., 1972-73; asst. prof. pharmacology Med. Coll. Va., Richmond, 1973-78, assoc. prof., 1978-84, prof. pharmacology, 1984—2003, Luther A Butler prof. pharmacology, 2003—; dir. Inst. for Drug and Alcohol Studies, 1993—. Chmn. Drug Abuse Adv. Com., FDA, Rockville, Md., 1983-84; mem. Robert Wood Johnson Rsch. Network on Etiology of Tobacco Dependence, 1997—; mem. adv. bd. Partnership for Drug Free Am. Editor-in-chief Drug Alcohol Dependence, 1998—; contbr. more than 270 articles to profl. jours. Mem. med/sci. adv. bd. Partnership for a Drug Free Am. Recipient NIH Merit award, 1993—, Univ. award Excellence, 1999, Coll. on Problems of Drug Dependence Mentoring award, 2000. Fellow Coll. on Problems of Drug Dependence (charter fellow, pres. 1995-96), Am. Coll. Neuropsychopharmacology, Am. Psychol. Assn. (pres. psychopharmacology divsn. 1989-90, chair bd. sci. affairs 1995-96); mem. European Behavioral Pharmacology Soc. (coun. mem. 1986-94). Achievements include development of laboratory methods for studying the behavioral effects of drugs of abuse and procedures for drug abuse potential evaluation. Office: Va Commonwealth U PO Box 980310 Richmond VA 23298-0310 Fax: 804-827-0304. E-mail: balster@hsc.vcu.edu.

BALTA, ANDREW STEPHEN, oral and maxillofacial surgeon; b. Duquesne, Pa., Jan. 19, 1938; s. Andrew Victor and Eva Margaret (Kupra) B.; m. Joann Diremigio, Dec. 30, 1961; children: Andrew Brian, Stephen Adam. BS, U. Pitts., 1963, DMD, 1968. Diplomate Am. Bd. Oral and Maxillofacial Surgery. Asst. instr. histology U. Pitts. Sch. Dental Medicine, 1966-67; oral and maxillofacial surgeon Henry Ford Hosp., Detroit, 1971-72; asst. instr. anesthesia U. Pitts. Sch. Dental Medicine, 1972-73; dist. commr. Pa. Blue Shield, Camp Hill, 1973-91; founder, CEO Ctr. for Facial & Jaw Surgery, Washington, Pa., 1993—. Chief dept. oral and facial surgery Canonsburgh (Pa.) Hosp., 1975-94, Washington Hosp., 1992—. Chief dental forensic examiner Washington County Coroner, 1983-91; mem. exec. com. Washington County Rep. Party, 1987; pres. bd. health City of Washington, 1981-84; pres. CVO United Way of S.W. Pa., 1987-90, United Way of Washington County, 1985-87; pres.- and gov.-appointed mem. Selective Svc. Sys. Pa., 1987; pres. Washington unit Am. Cancer Soc., 1980-81; mem. Washington County Hosp. Authority, 1996—. Named Man of Yr. Jaycees, Washington, 1990, recipient Disting. Svc. award, 1990; recipient Disting. Svc. award United Way of S.W. Pa., 1977; fellow Internat. Coll. Dentists, 1981, fellow Pierre Fauchard Acad., 1983, Owens fellow Pitts. Dental Rsch. Club, 1966-68, fellow NIH, 1967-69. Fellow Am. Soc. Oral and Maxillofacial Surgeons (Scholars award, Masters award 1993-94), Am. Coll. Oral Surgeons, Am. Acad. Cosmetic Surgery; mem. NRA, ADA, Pa. Dental Assn. (Presdl. citations 1983-90), Pa. Soc. Oral and Maxillofacial Surgeons, Western Pa. Soc. Oral and Maxillofacial Surgeons, Dental Soc. Western Pa. (Presdl. citationss 1983-90), Rotary. Roman Catholic. Avocations: fly fishing, hunting, community activism, billiards. Home: 51 Fitzwilliams Rd Washington PA 15301-6331 E-mail: andrewbalta@mdnet.net.

BALTAKE, JOE, film critic; b. Camden, N.J., Sept. 16; s. Joseph John and Rose Clara (Bearint) B.; m. Susan Shapiro Hale. BA, Rutgers U., 1967. Film critic Gannett Newspapers (suburban), 1969, Phila. Daily News, 1970-85; movie editor Inside Phila., 1986—; film critic The Sacramento Bee, 1987—; syndicated movie critic Scripps Howard News Svc., 1999—. Leader criticism workshop Phila. Writer's Conf., 1977-79; film critic. Contbg. author: Encyclopedia of American Lives, Vol. 6, 2003; contbg. editor: Screen World, 1973-87; author: The Films of Jack Lemmon, 1977, updated, 1986; contbr. articles to Films in Rev., 1969-2000, broadcast criticism for Prism Cable TV, 1985; cons. Jack Lemmon: American Film Institute Life Achievement Award, 1987, Jack Lemmon: A Life in the Movies, 1990. Recipient Motion Picture Preview Group award for criticism, 1986, citation Phila. Mag., 1985, First Pl. commentary award Soc. of Profl. Journalists, 1995. Office: Sacramento Bee 2100 Q St Sacramento CA 95816 6899 *Life's philosophy: "Living well is the best revenge.".*

BALTARO, RICHARD J. pathologist, medical educator; came to the U.S., 1964; s. Dimitri and Maria Silvana (Vici) B.; m. Laura E. Neece, 1972; children: Elizabeth B., John C. BA, Earlham Coll., 1972; PhD summa cum laude, U. Rome, Italy, 1977; MD magna cum laude, Cath. U., Rome, 1983. Bd. cert. anatomic and clin. pathology Am. Bd. Pathology, cert. immunopathology Am. Bd. Pathology. Pathology resident Brown U., Providence, 1983-87; clin. pathology fellow George Washington U. Hosp., Washington, 1987-88; asst. in pathology George Washington Med. Sch., Washington, 1987-88; sr. staff fellow NIH Clin. Ctr. Immunology, Bethesda, Md., 1988-90; jr. active staff NIH Clin. Ctr., Bethesda, 1988-90; asst. prof. Marshall U. Sch. Medicine, Huntington, W.Va., 1990-93, dir. pathology residency program, 1991-93; staff pathologist lab. svc. VA Med. Ctr., Huntington, 1990-93; pathologist Med. Arts Lab., Oklahoma City, 1993-98; assoc. clin. prof. Med. Ctr. U. Rochester, 1999—2001; assoc. prof. Creighton U., Omaha, 2001—. Stockholder Med. Arts Lab., 1994-98; ptnr. Med. Arts Pathologists, 1995-98; adj. assoc. prof. U. Okla. Health Sci., Oklahoma City, 1993-99; spkr. in field. Contbr. articles to profl. jours. Recipient NIH grant, 1991. Fellow Coll. Am. Pathologists (lab. insp. 1985—), Am. Soc. Clin. Pathologists, Internat. Acad. Pathology, Acad. Clin. Lab. Physicians and Scientists, Am. Coll. Internat. Physicians, Assn. Clin.

Scientists; mem. AMA, AAAS, Am. Soc. Microbiology, Am. Assn. for Clin. chemistry, Assn. Med. Lab. Immunologists. Avocations: gardening, reading, dancing, child raising. Office: Creighton Univ Med Ct Path Dept 601 N 30th St Omaha NE 68131

BALTAS, GEORGE, finance educator; b. Athens, Greece, Sept. 15, 1968; s. Alexander and Helen Baltas. BSc in Econs., Athens U. Econs. and Bus., 1990, MBA, 1995; PhD in Bus. Studies, U. Warwick, Eng., 1998. Lectr. in mktg. Warwick Bus. Sch., Coventry, England, 1997—99; assoc. prof. mktg. Athens U. Econs. and Bus., 1999—. Contbr. articles to profl. jours. Mem. exec. com. Aetopoulio Cultural Ctr., Halandri, Greece, 2001—01. Cpl. Greek Army, 1992—93. Scholar, Nat. Scholarship Found., 1995—98. Mem.: Greek Mktg. Acad., European Mktg. Acad., Warwick Bus. Sch. Alumni. Office: Athens Univ Econs and Bus 76 Patission 10434 Athens Greece E-mail: gb@aueb.gr.

BALTAY, CHARLES, physicist, educator; b. Budapest, Hungary, Apr. 15, 1937; s. John A. and Ilona T. Baltay; m. Virginia Rohan Baltay, Oct. 7, 1961; children: Peter, Michael, Thomas, Matthew, Annemarie. BS, Union Coll., 1958; MS, Yale U., 1959, PhD, 1963. Lectr. Yale U., New Haven, 1963—64; instr. Columbia U., N.Y.C., 1964—65, asst. prof., 1965—68, assoc. prof., 1968—72, prof., 1972—88; Higgins Prof. of Physics, prof. astronomy Yale U., New Haven, 1988—. Dir. Nevis Labs. Columbia U., 1978—86; chmn. dept. physics Yale U., 1995—2001. Editor: 2 books; contbr. over 300 articles to profl. jours. Fellow: Am. Phys. Soc.; mem.: Sigma Xi. Home: 86 Lower Rd Guilford CT 06437 Office: Yale Univ Dept Physics New Haven CT 06520

BALTAYAN, ARA M. engineering executive; b. Istanbul, Turkey, Sept. 6, 1920; s. Karabet and Nuvart (Allahverdi) B.; m. Margarit Melkon, Sept. 9, 1943 (div. 1951); 1 child, Berc Hagen; m. Mary Arakelian; children: Charles Michael, Arthur Mark, Rosemary. BSEE, Robert Coll., Istanbul, 1944, BSME, 1945; cert. traffice engr., Yale U., 1952, M in Engring., 1960. Lic. profl. engr. Import, export officer H.K. Liman Co., Istanbul, 1944-47; devel. engr. Automatic Signal div. LFE Corp., Norwalk, Conn., 1952-62, mgr. R&D, 1962-67, M in Engring., 1967-70, systems mgr., 1970-71, asst. mktg. v.p., 1971-73; sr. signal assoc. Wilbur Smith & Assocs., New Haven, Conn., 1973-75; owner, prin. AMB Engring Svcs., New Haven, 1975-88; pres. AMB Engring., Inc., New Haven, 1988—. Patentee in field. Chmn. Com. on Edn. of CAC, New Haven, 1963; pres. Internat. Ctr., New Haven, 1987; sr. warden Christ Episcopal Ch., New Haven, 1986—; vol. Habitat for Humanity, New Haven, 1988—. 2d lt. Turkish Army, 1947-48. Fellow ITE; mem. IEEE, NSPE, CSPE, PEPP, N.Y. Acad. Scis., Rotary Internat. (pres. New Haven chpt. 1979, Paul Harris fellow 1983, Outstanding Svc. award 1988, Rotarian of Yr. award 1992-93), Yale Club of New Haven. Republican. Avocations: photography, computing, sailing, golfing. Office: AMB Engring Inc Amb Amity Sta PO Drawer New Haven CT 06525 E-mail: ambeng@snet.net.

BALTAZZI, EVAN SERGE, engineering research consulting company executive; b. Izmir, Turkey, Apr. 11, 1921; came to U.S., 1959, naturalized, 1964; s. Phocion George and Agnes Zoe (Varda) B.; m. Nellie Despina (Biorlaro), July 17, 1945; children— Agnes, James, Maria D.Phys. Scis., Sorbonne U., Paris, 1949; D.Phil. in Chemistry, Oxford (Eng.) U., 1954. Rsch. dir., prof. rsch. French Nat. Rsch. Ctr., Paris, 1947-59; group leader organic chemistry rsch. Nat. Aluminate Corp., Chgo., 1959-61; mgr. organic chemistry sect. IIT Rsch. Inst., Chgo., 1961-63; dir. rsch. lab. Addressograph-Multigraph Corp., Chgo. and Cleve., 1963-77; pres. Evanel Assocs., Sagamore Hills, Ohio, 1977—. Mem. com. on U.S. currency NRC, 1985-86. Author: Basic American Self-Protection, 1972, Kickboxing, 1976, Stickfighting, 1977, Self-Protection at Close Quarters, 1981, Self-Protection Complete: The A.S.P. System, 1992, Dog Gone West: A Western for Dog Lovers, 1994, Plato and Socrates Trial, 1995; patentee in field; originator Am. Self-Protection System. Mem. judo com. U.S. Olympic Com., 1967-74 Recipient Citizen of Yr. award Citizenship Coun. Met. Chgo., 1964; Outstanding Achievement award in sci. Immigrants Service League, 1965, citation, 1965; Outstanding Program award YMCA, 1967; recognition award Gordon Rsch. Confs., 1976; Ohio Spl. Olympics Gold medal volunteering award, 1999; named Outstanding Scientist of XXth Century Internat. Biog. Ctr., 2000; NRC Can. fellow, 1955, Brit. Coun. fellow, 1952-54 Fellow Am. Inst. Chemists (vice chmn. Chgo. chpt. 1970), Am. Chem. Soc. (sr.), Royal Chem. Soc. U.K., Soc. Photog. Scientists and Engrs. (pres., bd. dirs. Cleve. chpt. 1975-82), Am. Self-Protection Assn. (pres. 1965—), N.Y. Acad. Scis. Avocations: fencing, judo, aikido, Am. self-protection originator. E-mail: ebaltazzi@aol.com.

BALTENSPERGER, DAVID DWIGHT, education educator, researcher; b. Kimball, Nebr., Dec. 28, 1953; s. Dwight Doane and Josephine A. (DeCamp) B.; m. Jeanne R. Larson, May 29, 1976; children: Stacey R., Robert D., Katie S. BS, Nebr. Wesleyan U., 1976; MS, U. Nebr., 1978; PhD, N.Mex. State U. 1980. Asst. prof. U. Fla., Gainesville, 1981-86, assoc. prof., 1986-89, U. Nebr., Scottsbluff, 1989-95, prof. agrl. scis., 1995—. Adj. assoc. prof. Colo. State U., Ft. Collins, 1988-89; adj. prof. U. Wyo., 2003; cons. Am. Seed Trade Assn., Washington, 1986. Adv. Talbot Couns. Adv. Bd., Gainesville, 1986-88; chmn. Terwilliger Sch. Adv. Coun., Gainesville, 1988-89, Gering Booster Club, 2000-02. Recipient Rsch. award, Gamma Sigma Delta, 1998. Fellow Am. Soc. Agronomy (fin. com. 1989—), Crop Sci. Soc. Am.; mem. Soil and Crop Sci. Soc. Fla. (sec., treas. 1988-89), So. Breeders Work Group (sec., pres., past pres. 1987-89), Am. Forage and Grassland Coun. (Japan Travel award 1985), Agronomy Soils (adv. Gainesville chpt. 1985-88). Republican. Methodist. Home: 2670 Applewood Rd Gering NE 69341-1506 Office: Panhandle Rsch & Extension 4502 Avenue I Scottsbluff NE 69361-4907

BALTER, FRANCES SUNSTEIN, civic worker; b. Pitts. d. Elias and Gertrude Susntein; m. James Stone Balter, May 15, 1948; children: Katherine (Mrs. Ross Anthony) (dec.), Julia Frances, Constance Cantor, Daniel Elias. Student, Sarah Lawrence Coll., 1939-41, New Sch. Social Rsch., 1941-43; cert. Inst. Arts Adminstrn., Harvard U., 1973. Adminstrv. asst., assoc. prodr. Ednl. TV Sta. WQED-TV, Pitts., 1963-67; prodr., mng. dir. Freedom Readers, 1964-67; co-founder, incorporator, sec. bd. dirs. Pitts. Coun. Arts, 1967-70; cultural cons. Mayor's Office Dir. Office Cultural Affairs, Pitts., 1968. Initiator Three Rivers Arts Festival 1960; co-dir. Ohio and Miss. River Valley Art Festival, 1961-62; mem. Pa. Coun. Arts, 1972-78; co-founder Pioneer Crafts Coun., Mill Run, Pa., 1972; exec. dir. Poetry on the Buses, 1974—. Bd. dirs. Coun. for Arts MIT, 1985-93, Palm Beach Festival, 1987-89. Named Woman of Yr. Art Post-Gazette, 1969. Mem. Assn. Couns. on Arts, Nat. Soc. Arts and Letters (Pitts. chpt.).

BALTER, LESLIE MARVIN, business communications educator; b. N.Y.C., Feb. 27, 1920; s. Harry and Rose Balter; m. Frances Hughes; 1 child by previous marriage, Kenneth Robert (dec. 1979); 1 child by previous marriage, Sheila Beth. BSEE, Columbia U., 1941; postgrad., Rutgers U.; MA, NYU, 1969. Civilian radio engr. Signal Corps Devel. Lab., Ft. Monmouth, N.J., 1941-45, in ETO, 1942; chief engr. Masters Crystal Co., quartz crystal prodn., 1945-46; founder, dir. Jersey City Tech. Inst., 1947—; founder br. operation as Paterson (N.J.) Inst., 1956—; founder Sch. Bus. Machines tchg. IBM machines Plaza Sch., Paramus, N.J., 1958—; cons. test engr. Consumers Rsch., Washington, N.J. Contbr. articles to Electronic Design Mag., Bus. Edn. World, Tech. Edn. News. Mem. N.J. Vocat. Edn. Master Plan Com. Comm.; chmn. Jersey City CD Coun., 1950-53; pres. Ferncroft Park Coop. Mem. IEEE (life, participant Legacies 1994), N.J. Assn. Pvt. Career Schs. (pres. 1971), N.J. Bus. Edn. Assn., Columbia Club N.Y., Delta Pi Epsilon. Home: 41 Ferncroft Park Ramsey NJ 07446-2575 Office: Plaza Sch Bergen Mall Paramus NJ 07652 E-mail: lbalter@optonline.net.

BALTER, MURRAY, interior designer; b. Paterson, NJ, Oct. 1, 1923; s. Harry and Bertha (Krieger) Balter; m. Beverly Braverman, Apr. 7, 1945; children: Jeffrey, Kevin, Heidi. Student, NYU, 1946—48, Newark Fine and Indsl. Arts, 1948—50. Owner, operator Murray Balter A.S.I.D. Interiors, N.Y.C. and Fairlawn, NJ, 1948—. Chmn. Fair Lawn Beautification Com., 1982; mem. Fair Lawn Hist. Sites Preservation Corp., Inc., 1984—, Garretson Farm & Forge Restoration com.; trustee Cadmus House Preservation; active Fair Lawn Jewish Ctr. Served to 1st lt. AUS, 1943—45. Recipient citation, U.S. Dept. of Interior, 1998. Mem.: Boca West Landscape Com., Boca West Renovation Interior Design Com., Nat. Soc. Interior Designers (nat. bd. dirs. 1976—77), Assn. Lighting Arts, Am. Soc. Interior Designers (profl. mem., pres. NJ chpt. 1965—67, nat. v.p. 1976—77, bd. dirs. NJ 1983—84, NJ Gold Key award 1971), Fair Lawn Rotary (v.p. 1977—79). Home: 7363 Woodmont Ct Boca Raton FL 33434-3210

BALTHASER, JAMES HARVEY, lawyer; b. Columbus, Ohio, Oct. 7, 1954; s. James R. and Kathryn F. (Herman) B.; m. Dianne A. Davis, June 21, 1975; 1 child, Kathryn Dee. BA, Ohio State U., 1975, JD, 1978. Bar: Ohio 1978, U.S. Tax Ct. 1984. Supr. Touche Ross & Co., Columbus, 1978-82; mem. Schwartz, Warren & Ramirez, Columbus, 1982-96; ptnr. Thompson Hine, LLP, Columbus, 1996—. Mem.: Am. Inst. CPA's, Columbus Bar Assn. Home: 9417 Avemore Ct Dublin OH 43017-9672 Office: Thompson Hine LLP 10 W Broad St Ste 700 Columbus OH 43215-3435 E-mail: jim.balthaser@thompsonhine.com.

BALTIMORE, DAVID, academic administrator, microbiologist, educator; b. NYC, Mar. 7, 1938; s. Richard I. and Gertrude (Lipschitz) B.; m. Alice S. Huang, Oct. 5, 1968; 1 dau., Teak. BA with high honors in Chemistry, Swarthmore Coll., 1960; postgrad., MIT, 1960—61; PhD, Rockefeller U., 1964. Postdoctoral rschr. MIT, Cambridge, Mass., 1964—65; research assoc. Salk Inst. Biol. Studies, La Jolla, Calif., 1965—68; from assoc. prof. microbiology to dir. MIT, Cambridge, Mass., 1968—82, dir. Whitehead Inst. Biomed. Rsch., 1982—90; pres. Rockefeller U., N.Y.C., 1990—91, prof., 1990—94; pres. Calif. Inst. Tech., Pasadena, 1997—. Bd. govs. Weizmann Inst. Sci., Israel; co-chmn. Commn. on a Nat. Strategy of Aids; ad hoc program adv. com. on complex genome, AIDS rsch. adv. coun. NIH, chair vaccine adv. com., 1997—2002. Mem. editorial bd. Jour. Molecular Biology, 1971-73, Jour. Virology, 1969-90, Sci., 1986-98, New Eng. Jour. Medicine, 1989-94. Bd. govs. Weizmann Inst. Sci., Israel; bd. dirs. Life Sci. Rsch. Found. Recipient Gustav Stern award, 1970, Warren Triennial prize Mass. Gen. Hosp., 1971, Eli Lilly and Co. award, 1971, Nat. Acad. Scis. US Steel award, 1974, Gairdner Found. award, 1974, Nobel prize, 1975, Nat. medal of sci., 1999, Warren Alpert Found. prize, 2000, Sci. Achievement award AMA, 2002. Fellow AAAS, Am. Med. Writers Assn. (hon.), Am. Acad. Microbiology; mem. NAS, Am. Acad. Arts and Scis., Inst. Medicine, Am. Philos. Soc., Pontifical Acad. Scis., Royal Soc. (Eng., fgn.), French Acad. Scis. (fgn. assoc.). Office: Calif Inst Tech 1200 E California Blvd 204 Parsons Gate Pasadena CA 91125-0001

BALTIMORE, RUTH BETTY, social worker; b. Wilkes-Barre, Pa., Feb. 27, 1926; d. Samuel Jr. and Theresa (Bergsmann) Bloch; m. Martin Joseph Baltimore, Feb. 6, 1949; children: Francie, Sandy. BA in Psychology, Skidmore Coll., 1948; postgrad., U. Scranton, 1965, 70. Social worker Wyoming Valley West Sch. Dist., Kingston, Pa., 1966-89; ret. Cons. in field. Co-author: (booklet) Guide for Teachers on Reporting Child Abuse, 1970. Bd. dirs. Youth Svcs. Commn., Wilkes-Barre, 1986-87, Victims Resource Ctr., Wilkes-Barre, 1990—; bd. dirs. Luz County Adv. Bd. Children and Youth, Wilkes-Barre, 1988—, vice-chair, 1991, chair, 1992-96. Recipient Connie Coun. Svc. award Nat. Coun. Jewish Women, Wilkes-Barre, 1959. Mem. Valley Tennis and Swim Club (pres.-elect 1994, pres. 1995-96). Avocations: tennis, golf, reading. Home: 630 Newberry Estate Dallas PA 18612

BALTUCH, GORDON HIRSH, neurosurgeon; b. Montreal, Que., Can., Apr. 24, 1960; arrived in U.S., 1978; s. Siegmar Udo Baltuch and Carol Leila Wevrick; m. Vivian Ariane Barbara Wasmuht-Perroud, Mar. 28, 1997; 1 child, Orphee Sarah. BA, Harvard U., 1981; MSc, Stanford U., 1982; MD, McGill U., Montreal, 1986, PhD, 1995. Diplomate Am. Bd. Neurol. Surgery. Neurosurgery fellow CHUV, Lausanne, Switzerland; neurosurgeon Montreal Gen. Hosp., 1995—96; asst. prof. neurosurgery U. Pa, Phila., 1996—. Assoc. dir. PA-DRECC, Vets. Hosp., Phila., 2001—. Named Top Dr., Phila. Mag., 2002; grantee, NIH, 1998—, VA, 2001—. Fellow: FACS (Fellow Am. Coll. Surgeons), FRCSC (Fellow Royal Coll. Surgeons Canada); mem.: Am. Assn. Neurol. Surgeons. Office: Hosp U Pa 5 Silverstein 3400 Spruce St Philadelphia PA 19104 Home: 201 518th st #2516 Philadelphia PA 19103 Office Fax: 215-349-5534. Business E-Mail: baltuch@mail.med.upenn.edu.

BALTZ, DOUGLAS MATTHEW, artist; b. Cape Girardeau, Mo., Dec. 10, 1963; s. John Merton and Fern Helen (Light) B. BA in Art, S.E. Mo. State U., 1987. Owner Darkwater Studios, Cape Girardeau, 1998—, Gallery 127, Jackson, Mo. Mem. Art Addiction Internat. Artist Assn., Internat. Figurative Artist Soc. Office: Darkwater Studios 1303 Perry Ave Cape Girardeau MO 63701 E-mail: darkwaterstudios@hotmail.com., gallery127@hotmail.com.

BALTZ, PATRICIA ANN (PANN BALTZ), elementary education educator; b. Dallas, June 20, 1949; d. Richard Parks and Ruth Eileen (Hartschuh) Langford; m. William Monroe Baltz, Sept. 6, 1969; 1 childm Kenneth Chandler. Student, U. Redlands, 1967-68; BA in English Lit. cum laude, UCLA, 1971. Cert. tchr. K-8, Calif. Tchr. 4th grade Arcadia (Calif.) Unified Sch. Dist., 1972-74, 92—, substitute tchr., 1983-85, tchr. 3dr grade, 1985-87, tchr. 6th grade, 1987-90, tchr. 4th and 5th grade multiage, 1990—. Sci. mentor tchr. Arcadia Unified Sch. Dist., 1991-94; mentor Tech. Ctr. Silicon Valley, San Jose, Calif., 1991. Tchr. rep. PTA, Arcadia, 1980-93; mem. choir, children's sermon team, elder Arcadia Presbyn. Ch., 1980-93; chaperone, vol. Pasadena (Calif.) Youth Symphony Orch., 1988-90; vol. Am. Heart Assn., 1990-92. Recipient Outstanding Gen. Elem. Tchr. award, Outstanding Tchr. of the Yr. award Disney's Am. Tchr. Awards, 1993, Calif. Tchr. of Yr. award Calif. State Dept. Edn., 1993, Georgie award Girl Scouts of Am., 1993, The Self Esteem Task Force award L.A. County Task Force to Promote Self-Esteem & Personal & Social Responsibility, 1993, Profl. Achievement award UCLA Alumni Assn.; apptd. to Nat. Edn. Rsch. Policies & Priorities Bd., U.S. Sec. Edn. Richard Riley; Pann Baltz Mission Possible Scholar named in her honor. Mem. NEA, Nat. Sci. Tchrs. Assn., Calif. Tchr. Assn., Arcadia Tchrs. Assn. Avocations: reading, singing, calligraphy, book-making, computers. Home: 1215 S 3rd Ave Arcadia CA 91006-4205 Office: Arcadia Unified Sch Dist Camino Grove Elem Sch 700 Camino Grove Ave Arcadia CA 91006-4438

BALTZ, RICHARD ARTHUR, chemical engineer; b. Aug. 1, 1959; s. Arthur A. and Arlou M. Baltz. BSChemE, U. Mo., Rolla, 1981. Process design engr. Solutia Inc., 1981—83, process engr., 1983—89, process engring. specialist, 1989—2001, sr. process control specialist, 2001—. Mem. AIChE. Roman Catholic. Office: Solutia Inc 500 Monsanto Ave Sauget IL 62206-1198

BALTZ, RICHARD JAY, health care company executive; b. Kingston, N.Y., June 6, 1952; s. Harold H. and Virginia K. (Luedtke) B.; m. Mary Melissa White, May 26, 1974; 1 child, Christopher Jay. BS, St. Lawrence U., 1974; MA, George Washington U., 1978. Lic. nursing home adminstr. Adminstr. Hudson Valley Sr. Residence, Kingston, N.Y., 1974-76; adminstr. resident/asst. Buffalo VA Med. Ctr., 1977-80, asst. chief Med. Adminstrv. Svc., 1980-83; chief Med. Adminstrv. Svc. Syracuse (N.Y.) VA Med. Ctr., 1984-86; assoc. dir. trainee Albany (N.Y.) VA Med. Ctr., 1987; assoc. med. ctr. dir. Togus (Maine) VA Med. Ctr., 1988-90, VA Med. Ctr., Jackson, Miss., 1990-97, dir., 2000—, Fayetteville, NC, 1997—2000. Adj. prof. dept. health care adminstrn. U. Ala., Birmingham, 1990-94. Bd. dirs. Kennebec, Maine unit Am. Cancer Soc., 1988-90, pres., 1989, 90, Maine divsn., 1988-90. Fellow Am. Coll. Healthcare Execs. Address: 527 Northwind Dr Brandon MS 39047 Home: 527 Northwind Dr Brandon MS 39047-8688

BALTZLEY, PATRICIA CREEL, secondary mathematics educator; b. Ft. Benning, Ga., Dec. 14, 1952; d. Buckner Miller and Mary Madeleine (O'Neill) Creel; m. Kevin Gerard Robinson, Nov. 15, 1975 (div. Dec. 21, 1981); children: Kevin G. Jr., Timothy Eugene; m. Jeffrey Lynn Baltzley, July 23, 1988 (dec. Dec. 1996). Student, St. Joseph's Coll., 1971-72; BA in Math., Coll. Notre Dame, 1975; MS in Math., Shippensburg State U., 1986. Cert. advanced profl., Md.; cert. in adminstn. and supervision. Acct. trainee Md. Nat. Bank, Balt., 1975-76; math. tchr. Notre Dame Preparatory Sch., Towson, Md., 1976-78, Carroll County Bd. Edn., Westminster, Md., 1978-91; math. program developer Ctr. for Social Orgn. of Schs. Johns Hopkins U., Balt., 1991—95; K-12 math. specialist Baltimore County Pub. Schs., 1995—98, 6-12 math. supr., 1998—. Adj. prof. Coll. Notre Dame, Balt., 1992--, Johns Hopkins U., 1995-97, Western Md. Coll., 1997--, Loyola Coll., 2000--; cons. Ctr. for Social Orgn., Johns Hopkins U., Learning Inst.; ind. cons. in field. Pres. Seton Ctr., Emmitsburg, Md., 1982-86; vol. Seton Shrine Ctr., Emmitsburg, 1986—. Recipient Presdl. Award for Excellence in Teaching Math. NSF, 1989; named Md. Math. Educator of Yr., 1977. Mem. ASCD, NEA, Md. Coun. Tchrs. Math. (pres. 1991-93), Nat. Coun. Tchrs. Math., Coun. Presdl. Awardees in Math., Md. Coun. Suprs. Math. (pres., 2000—), Coun. Adminstrs. and Suprs. in Edn. Democrat. Roman Catholic. Avocations: reading, basketball, walking. Home: 830 Glendale Rd York PA 17403-4130 Office: Baltiore County Pub Schs 6901 Charles St Towson MD 21204

BALZEKAS, STANLEY, JR., museum director; b. Chgo., Oct. 8, 1924; s. Stanley and Emily B.; widowed; children— Stanley, III, Robert, Carole Rene. BS, DePaul U., Chgo., 1950, MA, 1951. Pres. Balzekas Mus. Lithuanian Culture, Chgo., 1966—, Balzekas Motor Sales, Chgo., 1952—; hon. consul Consulate of the Republic of Lithuania, Palm Beach, Fla. Hon. consul for Republic of Lithuania, Palm Beach, Fla. Trustee Lincoln Acad., Cath. Charities, Am.-Lithuanian Coun.; chmn. Sister Cities/Chgo.-Vilnius Friendship Com., Trade & Cultural Ctr.; mem. adv. bd. Chgo. Cultural Affairs; hon. consul Rep. of Lithuania, Palm Beach, Fla. Served with AUS, 1942-45, ETO. Decorated Bronze Star; decorated 3d degree order Grand Duke Gediminas, Pres. Lithuania; recipient Wigilia medal Polish Geneal. Soc. Am., medal DAR, Disting. Alumni award DePaul U., 1991. Mem. Am. Assn. Mus., Ethnic Cultural Preservation Coun. (pres. 1977—), Press Club (Chgo.), Literary Club (Chgo.), City Club (Chgo., ethnic chmn.), Exec. Club (Chgo.), Am. Legion Office: 4030 S Archer Ave Chicago IL 60632-1140

BALZER, ROBERT LAWRENCE, journalist; b. DesMoines, June 25, 1912; s. Albert Taylor and Selma Olivia (Peterson) Balzer; m. Emily Abel, Dec. 6, 1936 (div. Aug. 1945). BA in English cum laude, Stanford U., 1935. Buddhist monk 1956. Owner Balzer's on Larchment, L.A., 1935—59; wine columnist L.A. Times, 1964—96. Chmn. food and wine Taste of Am. Presdl. Inaugural Washington, Reagan, 1981, 85, Taste of Am. Presdl. Inaugural Reagan, 1989. Author: Beyond Conflict, 1962, Los Angeles Time Book of California Wine, 1984; wine/restaurant editor: Travel Holiday Mag., 1974—92; actor(priest): (films, with Gloria Swanson and dir. Curtis Harrington) Killer Bees, 1974, (minister); (films, with dir. John Shclesinger) Day of the Locust, 1975; anchor (radio K-MZT 105.1fm) RLB The Word on Wine, L.A., 1994—2003. Tchr. wines of Calif. Long Beach (Calif.) Parks and Recreation, 1970—2003. With USAF, 1942—43. Decorated Royal Order of Sahametrei King Norodom Sihanouk, Cambodia; recipient Cordon Bleu award, Wine and Food Soc., L.A., 1939, Golden Bacchus award, Italian Trade Commn., 1972. Home: 10551 Hillsboro Rd Santa Ana CA 92705

BALZHISER, RICHARD EARL, research and development company executive; b. Wheaton, Ill., May 27, 1932; s. Frank E. and Esther K. (Merrill Werner) B.; m. Christine Karnuth, 1951; children: Gary, Robert, Patricia, Michele. BS in Chem. Engring., U. Mich., 1955, MS in Nuclear Engring., 1956, PhD in Chem. Engring., 1961. Mem. faculty U. Mich., Ann Arbor, 1961-67; White House fellow, spl. asst. to sec. Dept. Def., Washington, 1967-68; chmn. dept. chem. engring. U. Mich., 1970-71; assoc. dir. energy, environ. and natural resources White House Office of Sci. and Tech., Washington, 1971-73; dir. fossil fuel and advanced systems Electric Power Rsch. Inst., Palo Alto, Calif., 1973-79, sr. v.p. R&D, 1979-87, exec. v.p. R&D, 1987-88, pres., chief exec. officer, 1988-96, pres. emeritus, 1996—. Bd. dirs. Reliant Energy, Electro Source, Aerospace Corp.; mem. adv. bd. Nat. Renewable Energy Lab.; mem. pres. com. on sci. and tech. energy studies I and II, Pres.'s Com. on Sci. and Tech. Energy Studies, 1997-99. Co-author: Chemical Engineering Thermodynamics, 1972, Engineering Thermodynamics, 1977. Mem. Ann Arbor City Coun., 1965-67, mayor pro tem, 1967. Mem. Nat. Acad. Engring. Lutheran. Office: Electric Power Rsch Inst 3412 Hillview Ave Palo Alto CA 94304-1344 Fax: 650-855-2090. E-mail: rbalzhis@epri.com.

BAM, FOSTER, lawyer; b. Bridgeport, Conn., Jan. 11, 1927; s. Frederick and Alma (Foster) B.; m. Sallie A. Baldwin; children: Sylvia Carol, Sheila Catherine, Eric Foster. Grad., Loomis Sch., 1944; AB, Yale U., 1950, LLB, 1953. Bar: N.Y. 1954, Conn. 1968. Mem. faculty acctg. Yale, 1952-53; with Spence & Hotchkiss, N.Y.C., 1954-55; asst. U.S. dist. atty. So. Dist. N.Y., 1955-58; ptnr. Kramer, Levin, Naftalis & Frankel (formerly Feldman, Kramer, Bam, Nessen), N.Y.C., 1958-67, Cummings & Lockwood, 1968—. Bd. dirs. The Evergreen Funds. Trustee Phoenix Sci. Ctr.; chmn. Am. Mus. Fly Fishing, Calif. Acad. Sci.; trustee Bermuda Biol. Sta. for Rsch. Recipient Johnny Foyle Meml. award, 1969. Mem. ABA, Conn. Bar Assn., Greenwich Bar Assn., Exptl. Aircraft Assn., Phi Beta Kappa. Home: 51 Londonderry Dr Greenwich CT 06830-3508 Office: Cummings & Lockwood 2 Greenwich Plz Ste 3 Greenwich CT 06830-6353

BAMBAKIDIS, PETER, neurologist, educator; b. Akron, Ohio, Nov. 2, 1948; s. Nicholas and Zopigi (Dragoumanou) B.; m. Anna Savaris, Aug. 18, 1974; children: Athe, John A., Theodore. Student, U. Akron, 1966-67; BMus, Cleve. Inst. Mus., 1971, MMus, 1973; postgrad., U. Pitts., 1974-75, Ohio State U., 1978-80; MD, Case Western Res. U., 1984. Diplomate Am. Bd. Psychiatry and Neurology, Am. Bd. Clin. Neurophysiology. Resident in neurology Mayo Grad. Sch. Medicine, Rochester, Minn., 1984-88, fellow EEG, 1988-89; pvt. practice Cleve., 1989-92; asst. prof. neurology Case Western Res. U., Cleve., 1992—; neurologist Fairview Med. Group, 1994—2000, Cleve. Clinic Found., 2000—02, Premier Physicians, 2003—. Violinist Akron Symphony Orch., 1966-67, Richmond (Va.) Sinfonia, Richmond Symphony Orch., 1973-74, West Australian Symphony Orch., Perth, 1976-78, Columbus (Ohio) Symphony Orch., 1978-80; freelance musician, 1967-73; tchg. asst. Cleve. Inst. Music, 1971-73; tchg. fellow dept. music U. Pitts., 1974-75; follow-up asst. regional pediat. intensive care transport sys. Rainbow Babies and Children's Hosp., Cleve., 1981-82; hosp. affiliations Fairview Hosp., Cleve., St. John & Westshore Hosp., Westlake, Ohio, Luth. Med. Ctr., Cleve., S.W. Gen. Hosp., Middleburgh Hts., Ohio, Lakewood Hosp., Lakewood, Ohio. Tuesday Musical Club scholar, 1968, Ranney Found. scholar, 1968, Hellenic U. Club scholar, 1983. Mem. Am. Acad. Neurology, Am. Clin. Neurophysiology Soc., Phi Kappa Lambda. Avocations: weight lifting, near/middle eastern music and mysticism, writings of early church fathers. Office: 18099 Lorain Ave Ste 145 Cleveland OH 44111-5610

BAMBERG, LOUIS MARK, wealth management specialist; b. Miami, Fla., Dec. 1, 1948; s. Harold Sidney and Estelle Grace (Nagorski) B.; children: Heather Rae, Elijah Louis; m. Andrea Bamberg. AA, Miami Dade Jr. Coll., Perrine, Fla., 1968; B Bus., Ga. State U., 1970; JD, John Marshall U., Atlanta, 1977. CLU, ChFC; Bar: Ga. 1977. Salesman, buyer, mgr. Levitz, Inc., 1970-78; atty. SBA, Atlanta, 1976-78; salesman Equitable Life Assurance, Miami, 1978-85; estate planning specialist Merrill Lynch Life, Ft. Lauderdale, Fla., 1985-1999; wealth mgmt. specialist, 1999—. Bd. dirs. United Hearing & Deaf Svcs., Ft. Lauderdale, 1990. Mem. ABA, Advanced Assn. Life Underwriters, Estate Planning Coun., Top of Table, Internat. Forum (bd. dirs.), Million Dollar Round Table. Avocations: jogging, softball, bike riding, basketball. Home: 310 N Gordon Rd Fort Lauderdale FL 33301-3775 Office: Merrill Lynch 2611 E Oakland Park Blvd Fort Lauderdale FL 33306

BAMBERGER, GERALD FRANCIS, plastics marketing consultant; b. Hannover, Germany, Sept. 20, 1920; came to U.S., 1938, naturalized, 1943; m. Ursula Friede, Mar. 27, 1946; children— Gale, Richard, Annette, Peter. Comml. diploma, Ecole Supérieure de Commerce, Neuchatel, Switzerland, 1938. Pres. A. Bamberger Corp., Bklyn., 1938-54, Interplastics Corp., N.Y.C., 1955-62; prodn. mgr. plastics div. Cities Service Corp., Hicksville, N.Y., 1963-67; pres. Bamberger Polymers, Inc., New Hyde Park, N.Y., 1967-85; plastics mktg. cons., 1985—. Served with M.I. AUS, 1943-46. Decorated Bronze Star. Mem. Soc. Plastics Industry, Soc. Plastics Engrs., Plastics Pioneers Assn.

BAMBERGER, JOSEPH ALEXANDER, mechanical engineer, educator; b. Hamburg, Germany, Nov. 21, 1927; came to U.S., 1940; s. Seligman and Else (Buxbaum) B.; m. Dorothy Frank, Dec. 24, 1950; children: David, Michael. BME, CUNY, 1949; MME, NYU, 1954. R & D engr. Kramer Trenton Co., Trenton, N.J., 1949-59; mech. engr., scientific staff Brookhaven Nat. Lab., Upton, N.Y., 1959-82; prof. mech. tech. Suffolk Community Coll., Selden, N.Y., 1982-95; mem. staff R&D objects conservation Met. Mus. Art, N.Y.C., 1996—. Cons. Typhoon Air Conditioning, Div. Hupp Corp., Bklyn., 1952-59. Contbr. articles to ASHRAE Jour., Advances in Cryogenic Engring., Cryogenics, ASME Transactions, Jour. Vacuum Sci. and Tech., Nuclear Instruments and Methods, Studies in Conservation. Dir. Temple Beth El, Patchogue, N.Y., 1962-84; chmn. Cryogenic Safety Com., Brookhaven Lab., 1980-82. Mem. N.Y. Acad. Sci., AAAS, ASHRAE. Achievements include patent for Electrically Insulating

Feedthrough for Cryogenic Applications; research in low temperature cooling systems for superconducting magnets, cryogenic pumping systems, liquid hydrogen bubble chamber design and operation.

BAMBERGER, MICHAEL ALBERT, lawyer; b. Berlin, Feb. 29, 1936; s. Fritz and Kate (Schwabe) B.; m. Phylis Skloot, Dec. 19, 1965; children—Kenneth A., Richard A. AB magna cum laude, Harvard U., 1957, LLB magna cum laude, 1960. Bar: N.Y. 1960, D.C. 1982. Assoc. Proskauer Rose Goetz & Mendelsohn, N.Y.C., 1960-69, Finley, Kumble, Wagner, Heine, Underberg, Manley, Myerson & Casey, N.Y.C., 1970, ptnr., 1971-87, Sonnenschein Nath & Rosenthal, N.Y.C., 1987—. Adj. prof. Benjamin Cardozo Sch. Law, Yeshiva U., 2001—; mem. faculty various legal seminars and insts.; mem. joint editl. bd. on uninc. orgn. acts. ABA/Nat. Conf. Commrs. on Uniform State Laws, 1994—, chair, 2003—; chmn. bd. Transcontinental Music Publs., New Jewish Music Press. Author: Reckless Legislation: How Lawmakers Ignore the Constitution, 2000; co-editor: State Limited Partnership Laws, 7 vols. and supplements, 1987—, State Limited Liability Company and Partnership Laws, 5 vols. and supplements, 1993-2003; editor Harvard Law Rev., 1958-60; contbr. articles to profl. jours. Vice chair bd. overseers Hebrew Union Coll.-Jewish Inst. Religion, N.Y.C.,; v.p., bd. dirs. Leo Baeck Inst., Selfhelp Cmty. Svcs.; bd. dirs. Ctr. Jewish History. Mem. ABA (com. on ltd. partnerships 1980—, chair com. on tech. and intellectual property 1992-95, chair, ad hoc com. on security interests in intellectual property 1990-98), First Amendment Lawyers Assn., N.Y. State Bar Assn. (exec. com. comml. and fed. litigation sect. 1989-93), Assn. Bar City N.Y. (com. on fed. legislation 1979-82, com. on civil rights 1982 86, chmn. 1983-86), N.Y. County Lawyers Assn. (securities com. 1980-82). Jewish. Home: 172 E 93d St New York NY 10128-3711 Office: Sonnenschein Nath & Rosenthal 1221 Ave of Americas New York NY 10020-1001

BAMBERGER-HERRMANN, JULIA KATHRYN, social worker; b. Phila., Dec. 23, 1960; d. William Thomas and Julia Kathryn (O'Brien) B; m. Robert F. Herrmann Jr., Nov.22, 1997. BA in Social Work, Holy Family U., Phila., 1983. Cert. social worker. Recreational therapy asst., phys. therapy asst. Ashton Hall Nursing Home, Phila., 1979—83; hairdresser asst. St. John Neumann Nursing Home, Phila., 1982—83; recreational therapy asst. Evang. Manor, Phila., 1983; social worker Consortium/Southwest Sr. Citizens Ctr., Phila., 1983—90; resource specialist Phila. Corp. for Aging, 1990—92, case mgr. Family Caregiver Support program, 1992—. Vol. Dear Neighbor program Am. Heart Assn.; mem. Pro-Life Coalition of Southeastern Pa., 1996—; majority inspector Election Bd., 1992—; solicitor Cath. Charities Appeal, 1979—82; mem. Gloria Dei Ch. Women's Ministries; soprano singer guitar Mass group Maternity Blessed Virgin Mary Roman Cath. Ch., Phila., 1977—; vol. Perpetual Adoration Soc. Our Lady of Fatima Roman Cath. Ch., 1988—97; mem., chair Alzheimer's Disease and Related Disorders Assn., Phila., 1983—, mem. Memory Walk com., 2001—; V.I.P. blood donor ARC, 1978—; vol. Ashton Hall Nursing Home, Phila., 1983—89. Named one of Outstanding Young Women Am., 1985; recipient cert. of appreciation, Alzheimer's Disease and Related Disorders Assn., 1985, 1991, 1995, 2002, ARC, 2002, 2003, Outstanding Young Women Am., 1986, 1988. Mem. Social Svc. Workers Assn. Nursing Homes, Archbishop Ryan H.S. for Girls ALumnae Assn. (corr. sec. 1985-95), Holy Family U. Alumni Assn. (rec. sec. 1985-90, cert. of appreciation 1984, 90, bd. dirs., class rep. 1983—, Disting. Alumni Svc. award 1992), Assn. Ch. Musician Phila., Classic Thunderbird Club (bd. dirs. 1994-95), Epsilon Nu, Cath. Adult Club, Phi Chi. Democrat. Avocations: tennis, bowling, singing, dining out, movies. Home: 9207 Rising Sun Ave Philadelphia PA 19115-3724 Office: Phila Corp for Aging 642 N Broad St Philadelphia PA 19130-3424 E-mail: jherrman@pcaphl.org.

BAMBRICK, JAMES JOSEPH, labor economist, labor relations executive; b. N.Y.C., Apr. 26, 1917; s. James Joseph and Mae (Murphy) B.; m. Margaret Mary Donlan, June 26, 1948; children: Patricia Bambrick Benek (dec.), Thomas G., Mary Alice Bambrick Schneider, Kathleen Bambrick Guzaukas, James Joseph Jr. BS, NYU, 1940, MBA, 1942; BS, U.S. Mcht. Marine Acad., 1946. Exec. dir. Labor Bur., N.Y.C., 1940-42; personnel dir. Allegheny Airlines, Wilmington, Del., 1942-44; mgr. labor relations research The Conf. Bd., N.Y.C., 1947-58; corp. labor economist Standard Oil Co., Cleve., 1958-81; exec. dir. Labor Econ. Inst., Cleveland Heights, Ohio, 1981—. Mem. bus. adv. council U.S. Bur. Labor Stats., Washington, 1971—, chmn. wages and indsl. relations com., 1980-85; instr. NYU, 1946-53, John Carroll U., University Heights, Ohio, 1968-71; lectr. Cleve. State U., 1963-68. Author: Preparing for Collective Bargaining, 1959, Handbook of Modern Personnel Administration, 1972; contbr. chpts. to The Foreman/Supervisor's Handbook, 1984; contbr. articles to profl. jours. Chmn. Ohio Rep. Fin. Com., Cuyahoga County, Cleve., 1963—; pres. Cath. Interracial Council, Cleve., 1965-68, bd. dirs. 1969—; v.p. Navy League of U.S., Cleve., 1984—. Served to lt. USNR, 1944-46. Named Hibernian Man of the Yr. Ancient Order of Hibernians, 1974. Fellow Soc. for Advancement of Mgmt. (pres. 1955-58); mem. Am. Econ. Assn., Indsl. Relations Research Assn., U.S. Mcht. Marine Acad. Alumni Assn. (pres., bd. dirs. N.E. Ohio, 1965-70). Clubs: City (Cleve.) (trustee 1972-75, v.p. Forum Found. 1981-88). Lodges: K.C. Republican. Avocations: fencing, sailing, golf.

BAMFORD, CAROL MARIE, marketing executive; b. Des Moines, May 18, 1948; d. Harry C. and Ellen T. (Andersen) Jensen; m. Bruce S. Nesbit, June 8, 1968 (div. Jan. 1978); m. Paul J. Bamford, June 9, 1979 (div. Dec. 1984); m. John V. Florian, Apr. 6, 1991. BA, Drake U., 1969, MA, 1972. Lic. tchr., Iowa. Tchr. English Des Moines Pub. Schs., 1969-79; mgr. product and promotional publs. Comshare, Inc., Ann Arbor, Mich., 1979-83; mgr. advt. and sales promotion Bell & Howell Learning subs. Bell and Howell Co., Ann Arbor, 1983-88, mktg. mgr., 1988-92, v.p. mktg., 1992-95, Briggs Corp., West Des Moines, 1995-2000, Briggs Tech., West Des Moines, 1997-2000; COO Enterprise Corp. Internat., Des Moines, 2000—03; v.p. mktg. Grand View Coll., 2003—. Bd. dirs. Ann Arbor Symphony, Mich., 1993—95. Recipient awards Soc. for Tech. Communication, 1980-86, Award of Excellence, Internat. TV Assn., 1988, Crystal Addy award Am. Advt. Fedn., 1988, Silver Cindy award Internat. Assn. Audio Visual Comms., 1999. Mem. Info. Industry Assn. (Mktg. Achievement award 1986-91, vice-chmn. mktg. com. 1991, chmn. mktg. com. 1992), Phi Beta Kappa. advisory coun. Business Sch. Grand view Coll., 2000-; Adj. instr. DesMoines area C.C., 2001-,. Democrat. Lutheran. Office: Grand View Coll 1200 Grandview Ave Des Moines IA 50316 E-mail: cbamford@guc.edu.

BAMFORD, JOSEPH CHARLES, JR., gynecologist, obstetrician, educator, medical missionary, writer; b. Paterson, NJ, Oct. 23, 1930; s. Joseph Charles and Luise (Whitehead) Bamford; m. Susan Jane Hall, Apr. 13, 1951; children: Joseph Charles III, Elizabeth Ann. BS, Rutgers U., 1952; MD, NY Med. Coll., 1956. Diplomate Am. Bd. Ob-Gyn. Intern U. Vt., 1956—57; resident in ob-gyn NY Med. Coll., N.Y.C., 1957—60, asst. clin. instr. dept. ob-gyn, 1960—64, clin. instr., 1964—65, asst. prof., 1965—70, assoc. prof., 1970—72, asst. dean, 1966—68, assoc. dean, 1968—72, acting v.p. hosp. affairs, 1971—72; sect. chief psychosomatic ob-gyn Met. Hosp. Ctr., N.Y.C., 1963—72, chief svc., 1971—72; practice medicien specializing in ob-gyn Paterson, NJ, 1962—66, St. Johnsbury, Vt., 1972—76; asst. obstetrician and gynecologist Flower and Fifth Ave. hosps., N.Y.C., 1960—66, asst. attending, 1966—70, attending, 1970—72; asst. vis. obstetrician and gynecologist Met. Hosp. Ctr., N.Y.C., 1960—66, assoc., 1968—70, vis., 1970—72; vis. ob-gyn Indian Health Svc. Hosp., Ft. Defiance, Ariz., 1981; clin. asst. ob-gyn Paterson Gen. Hosp., 1962—64, assoc. attending, 1964—66, attending, 1966—67; cons., 1967; attending obstetrician and gynecologist Northeastern Vt. Regional Hosp., St. Johnsburg, 1972—76, cons., 1976—85. Vis. obstetrician and gynecologist St. Jude Missions Hosp., St. Lucia, 1986; med. officer Tumutumu Mission Hosp., Kenya, 1987—88; cons. Beatrice D. Weeks Meml. Hosp., Lancaster, NH, 1972—80; vol. program steering com. for retired physicians Vt. Med. Soc., 1996—2001; chmn. subcom. for fact finding Mayor's Com. for Hosp. Facilities Planning, Paterson, 1964—66. Contbr. articles to profl. jours. Chmn. med. adv. com. Passaic County (NJ) Com. for Planned Parenthood, 1965—67; mem. NJ Com. on Med. Edn., 1965—66; trustee Greater Paterson Gen. Hosp., 1966—2000, So. Vt. Art Ctr., 1997—2002; pres. Lyndon State Coll. Found., 1980—84. Lt. comdr. USNR, 1960—62. Fellow: ACOG (mem. com. on course coord. 1977—79); mem.: Caledonia County Med. Soc. (v.p. 1974—75), Vt. Med. Soc. (mem. jud. com. 1975—77), Ob-Gyn. Soc. NY Med. Coll. (mem. exec. com. 1963—66), No. New England Acad. Medicine. Home: Box 724 Myrickview Vlg Dorset VT 05251

BAN, STEPHEN DENNIS, gas industry executive; b. Hammond, Ind., Dec. 16, 1940; s. Stephen and Mary Veronica (Holecsko) Ban; m. Margie Cahill, Aug. 17, 1963; children: Stephen, Mary Beth, Brian. BSME, Rose Hulman Inst. Tech., 1962; MS in Engring. Sci., Case Inst. Tech., 1964, PhD in Engring., 1967. Chief divsn. fluid and chem. processes Battelle Columbus (Ohio) Labs., 1970-72, chief divsn. emission sys., 1972-76, corp. coord. engring. scis. program, 1972-76; v.p. R & D Bituminous Materials, Inc., Terre Haute, Ind., 1976-81, Gas Rsch. Inst., Chgo., 1981-83, sr. v.p. R & D ops., 1983-86, exec. v.p., COO, 1986-87, pres., CEO, 1987—2000; dir. office tech. transfer Argonne Nat. Lab., 2002—. Mem. indsl. adv. bd. U. Ill., Chgo., 1983—93; mem. Coun. Energy Engring. Rsch., Washington, 1983—87; mem. energy rsch. adv. bd. U.S. Dept. Energy, Washington, 1987—90, mem. adv. com. renewable energy and energy efficiency joint ventures, 1992—95; bd. dirs. Energen Corp., Birmingham, Ala., 1991—; mem. Natural Gas Coun., 1993—97; bd. dirs. UGI Corp. Fellow, NDEA, 1962—65, NSF, 1965—67. Mem.: U.S. Energy Assn., Sigma Xi, Tau Beta Pi. Office: 9700 S Cass Ave Argonne IL 60439-4832

BANACH, ART JOHN, graphic artist; b. Chgo., May 22, 1931; s. Vincent and Anna (Zajac) B. Grad. Art. Inst. of Chgo., 1955; pupil painting studies Mrs. Melin, Chgo.; m. Loretta A. Nolan, Oct. 15, 1966; children: Heather Anne, Lynnea Joan. Owner, dir. Art J. Banach Studios, 1949—, cartoon syndicate for newspapers, house organs and advt. functions, 1954—, owner and operater advt. agy., 1954-56, feature news and picture syndicate, distbn. U.S. and fgn. countries. Dir. Speculators S Fund. Recipient award 1st Easter Seal contest Ill. Assn. Crippled, Inc., 1949. Chgo. Pub. Sch. Art Soc. Scholar. Mem. Artist's Guild Chgo., Am Mgmt. Assn., Chgo. Assn. of Commerce and Industry, Chgo. Federated Advt. Club, Am. Mktg. Assn., Internat. Platform Assn., Chgo. Advt. Club, Chgo. Soc. Communicating Arts, Am. Ctr. For Design, Chgo. Calligraphy Collective, Columbia Yacht Club, Advt. Execs. Club, Art Dirs. Club (Chgo.). Home: 1076 Leahy Cir East Des Plaines IL 60016-6050

BANAI, MOSHE, management educator; b. Tel Aviv, July 22, 1948; came to U.S., 1985; s. Asher and Nili (Breznitz) B.; m. Rachel Eliasaf, Aug. 15, 1971; children: Noit, Moran. BA in Behavioral Sci., Ben Gurion U., Ber Sheva, Israel, 1972; MSc in Orgnl. Behavior, Tel Aviv, 1977; PhD in Mgmt., London U., 1985. Youth counsellor Hadassim (Israel) Sch., 1970-80; rsch. mgr. Israel Inst. Rsch., Tel Aviv, 1974-80; mgmt. cons. Bank Leumi UK (Pub. Ltd. Co.), London, 1980-84, human resource dir., 1984-85; prof. Baruch Coll. CUNY, N.Y.C., 1985—. Vis. prof. U. Shanghai Sci. and Tech., Shanghai; vis. prof. dept. sci. and tech. Kazan State U., Russia, Tisom U., Tel Aviv, Sydney U., Interamericana U., PR; cons. to maj. orgns. internationally. Contbr. chpts. to: Comparative Management, 1988, Management and National Culture: A Global Perspective, 1993, Advancement in Organizational Behavior, 1997, Chinese Economic Transition and International Marketing Strategy, 2003; contbr. 60 articles to profl. jours. With Israeli Def. Force, 1966-69. Mem. Acad. Mgmt., Acad. Internat. Bus. Office: Zicklin Sch Bus One Bernard Baruch Way New York NY 10010-5518

BANAS, C(HRISTINE) LESLIE, lawyer; b. Swindon, Wiltshire, Eng., Oct. 29, 1951; arrived in U.S., 1957; d. Stanley M. and Helena Ann (Boryn) Banas; m. Dale J. Buras, May 1, 1976; children: Eric Buras, Andrea Buras. BA magna cum laude, U. Detroit, 1973; JD cum laude, Wayne State U., 1975. Bar: Mich. 1976, U.S. Supreme Ct. 1980. Atty. Hyman & Rice, Southfield, Mich., 1976-77, Hyman, Gurwin, Nachman, Friedman & Winkelman, Southfield, 1977-82, ptnr., 1982-87, Honigman Miller Schwartz and Cohn LLP, Detroit, 1987—. Contbr. articles to profl. jours. Chmn. bd. Women's Leadership Forum, bd. chair. Mem.: ABA, Fed. Bar Assn., State Bar Mich. (bd. dirs. real property sect. coun., coun. treas.), Detroit Athletic Club, Women's Econ. Club (past pres.). Roman Catholic. Avocations: gardening, photography, skiing. Office: Honigman Miller Schwartz and Cohn LLP 32270 Telegraph Rd Ste 225 Bingham Farms MI 48025-2457 E-mail: lbanas@honigman.com.

BANAS, EMIL MIKE, physicist, educator; b. East Chicago, Ind., Dec. 5, 1921; s. John J. and Rose M. (Valcicak) B; m. Margaret Fagyas Welton, Oct. 9, 1948; children: Mary K., Barbara A. French. BA, Benedictine U., 1943; postgrad. (U.S. Rubber fellow), U. Notre Dame, 1954, PhD, 1955. Recipient medal of St. Benedict, Benedictine U., 1999. Mem. Pres. Assocs. of Benedictine U., VFW (life), Sigma Pi Sigma. Home: 1426 SE Fancy Free Dr Pullman WA 99163-5522

BANAS, JOHN STANLEY, obstetrician, gynecologist; b. Chgo., May 27, 1955; s. Edward Thomas and Stephanie Victoria (Gatz) B.; m. Kerry Jeanine Keenan, June 7, 1981; children: Melissa, Kevin, Daniel, Amanda. BS in Biology cum laude, Loyola U., Chgo., 1977; MD, Loyola U., Maywood, Ill., 1981. Diplomate Am. Bd. Ob-Gyn. Resident in ob/gyn. SUNY, Buffalo, 1981-85; pvt. practice Ft. Wayne, Ind., 1985-88, Racine, Wis., 1988-90, Rock Island, Ill., 1990—. Fellow ACOG; mem. AMA, Ill. Med. Soc., Rock Island Med. Soc. Roman Catholic. Avocations: swimming, running, bicycling, gardening, reading. Home: 2130 Nathan Ct Bettendorf IA 52722-2100 Office: Trinity Med Ctr 2570 24th St Ste 122 Rock Island IL 61201-5394

BANAS, RICHARD FREDERICK, geographer; b. Hartford, Conn., June 8, 1948; s. Frank John and Sophie Wanda Banas. AB, Assumption Coll., 1971; MS, Cen. Conn. State U., 1987. Market rsch. analyst Advo-System, Inc., Hartford, 1971-72, Managed Mktg., Bolton, Conn., 1973; data technician Toner and Assocs., Inc., Seattle, 1974; rsch. asst. Urban Data Ctr. U. Wash., Seattle, 1974-75, City of Seattle, 1975; fin. clk. State of Conn., Hartford, 1977-81, rsch. analyst, 1981-82, accounts examiner, 1982-87; spl. air express package car operator United Parcel Svc., Hartford, Conn., 1988-90; salesperson Coldwell Banker, Coventry, R.I., 1991, Century 21, Newington, Conn., 1992; realtor JWL/Adamian, Hartford, Conn., 1993-94; driver tractor-trailer Direct Transit, Inc., North Sioux City, S.D., 1995-97; dedicated Sears driver Swift Transp., Inc., Syracuse, NY, 1998—2002, dedicated Staples driver Dayville, Conn., 2003—. Avocations: reading, concerts, hiking. Home: 8 Evans Ave East Hartford CT 06118-2610

BANASIAK, MAYME KAY HAMPTON, mathematician, educator; d. Arthur (Pete) and Mayme Yates Hampton; m. Edwin J. Banasiak, Jr., May 31, 1970 (dec. Dec. 3, 1990); children: Edwin J. (Jay) Banasiak, III, Mark H. Student, U. of N.C., Greensboro, 1968—70; BS in Math. Edn., N.C. State U., 1972; MA in Edn., Tusculum Coll., Greenville, Tenn., 2001. Cert. tchr. N.C., Tenn. Math. tchr. Raleigh City Schs., NC, 1971—72, Hamilton County Dept. of Edn., Chattanooga, 1973—74, 1981—82; supr./chief supr., devel. math. lab. U. of Tenn., Chattanooga, 1985—2000, interim dir. of devel. math., 2000—02, dir. of devel. math., 2002—. Math. tutor, 1973—2002; adj. faculty Chattanooga State Tech. C.C., 1995—2000; bd. of regents Oxford Grad. Sch., Dayton, Tenn., 2000—. Mem. LaSertoma, Chattanooga, 1980—88; elder Northminster Presbyn. Ch., Chattanooga, 1991—2002, educator, 1982—2002; bd. of dirs. U. Tenn.-Chattanooga Presbyn. Campus Ministry, 1986—92; pro bono math. tutoring; vol. Chattanooga Rm. In the Inn (homeless women and children). Mem.: Nat. Assn. of Tchrs. of Math., Math. Assn. of Am. Presbyterian. Office: University of Tenn at Chattanooga Dept 6956 Math 615 McCallie Ave Chattanooga TN 37403 E-mail: mayme-banasiak@utc.edu.

BANASIK, ROBERT CASMER, nursing home administrator, educator; b. Detroit, Dec. 8, 1942; s. Casmer John and Lucille Nathalie Banasik; m. Jacqueline Mae Miller, Aug. 28, 1965 (div. 1985); children: Robert John, Marcus Alan, Jason Andrew; m. Barbara Jean Willows, Oct. 12, 1985. BSME, Wayne State U., 1965; MS in Indsl. Engring., Tex. Tech Coll., 1967; MBA, Ohio State U., 1973, PhD, 1974. Registered profl. engr., Ohio; lic. nursing home adminstr., Ohio. Mgmt. systems engr. Riverside Meth. Hosp., Columbus, Ohio, 1970, 71; owner, mgmt. systems cons. Banasik Assocs., Columbus, 1972—; dir. mgmt. systems engring. Grant Hosp., Columbus, 1973-78; owner, mgr. RMJ Investment Enterprises, Columbus, 1975-85; pres. Omnilife Systems, Inc., Columbus, 1979—, RMJ Mgmt., Inc., 1983-85, Bryant Health Ctr., Inc., Ironton, Ohio, 1983—, Equity Mgmt., 1985—; owner Omnivend, 1985—. Adminstr. Patterson Health Ctr., Columbus, 1980-99, Parkview Health Ctr., Inc., Volga, S.D., 1986—, Hamilton (Ohio) Health Ctr., Inc., 1986-97, Shelby Manor Health Ctr., Inc., Shelbyville, Ky., 1986—; corp. sec. Clintonville Family Practice, Columbus, 1987—, Samaritan Care Ctr., Inc., Medina, Ohio, 1988—, Sanctuary at Whispering Meadows, Dayton, Ohio, 1997—, The Sanctuary at Tuttle Crossing, Columbus, 1997—, Patterson Resdl. Care, 1999—; asst. prof. Capital U. Grad. Sch. Adminstrn., Columbus, 1973-79, assoc. prof., 1979-97, prof., 1997—, Squire chmn. in small bus. and entrepreneurship, 1997—; pres. Banasik & Strayer Architects and Engrs., Columbus, 1988-93; dir. Asset Data Systems, Columbus; adj. prof. Union Inst., Cin., 1992—. Editor: Topics in Hospital Material Management, 1978-84; contbr. articles to profl. jours.; participant expert witness testimony forensic statis. methods. Pres. bd. dirs. United Cerebral Palsy Franklin County, 1979-80; mem. founding bd. Support Resources, Inc., 1978-85; bd. dirs. Transp. Resources, Inc., 1979-80, Dennison Health Systems, 1988-93, bd. dirs., 1988-97; bd. advisors Seicon, 1999—; pres. indsl. adv. bd. Tex. Tech U., 1987-88, mem. deans coun. Sch. Engring., 1995—; pres. Ohio Acad. Nursing Homes, Columbus, 1986-89, bd. dirs., 1986—; mem. adv. indsl. bd. dept. mech. engring. Wayne State U., 1994; mem. adv. bd. Sch. Nursing Capital U., 1995—. Named Disting. Engr. Tex. Tech U., 2000. Mem. Am. Hosp. Assn., NSPE (dir. Franklin County chpt. 1976-77), Ohio Soc. Profl. Engrs., Am. Inst. Decision Scis., Am. Coll. Health Care Adminstrs., Airplane Owner & Pilots Assn. (lic. pilot), Tex. Tech Acad. Engrs., Sigma Xi, Beta Gamma Sigma, Alpha Pi Mu, Phi Kappa Phi, Alpha Kappa Psi. Lutheran. Office: PO Box 8309 Columbus OH 43201-0309

BANCEL, MARILYN, fund raising management consultant; b. Glen Ridge, N.J., June 15, 1947; d. Paul and Joan Marie (Spangler) B.; m. Rik Myslewski, Nov. 20, 1983; children: Carolyn, Roxanne. BA in English with distinction, Ind. U., 1969. Cert. fund raising exec. Ptnr. The Sultan's Shirt Tail, Gemlik, Turkey, 1969-72; prodn. mgr. High Country Co., San Francisco, 1973-74; exec. dir. East Bay Performance, Inc., 1976—79; pub. Bay Arts Rev., Berkeley, Calif., 1976-79; dir. devel. Oakland (Calif.) Symphony Orch., 1979-81; assoc. dir. devel. Exploratorium, San Francisco, 1981-86, dir. devel., 1986-91; prin. Fund Devel. Counsel, San Francisco, 1991-93; v.p. The Oram Group, Inc., San Francisco, 1993—. Co-chmn. capital campaign com. Synergy Sch., San Francisco, 1995-2000; adj. prof. U. San Francisco, 1993—. Author: Preparing Your Capital Campaign, 2000. Mem. adv. bd. Mus. City of San Francisco, 1995—, San Francisco Bot. Gardens, 1998-99. Fellow U. Strasberg, France, 1968. Mem. Assn. Fundraising Profls. (bd. Golden Gate chpt. 1996-98, chmn. National Philanthropy Day, 2000, Outstanding Fundraising Exec. award 2002), Am. Assn. Fund Raising Counsel, Devel. Execs. Roundtable, Phi Beta Kappa. Democrat. Avocation: gardening. Office: The Oram Group Inc 275 Madison Ave New York NY 10016

BANCILA, MIHAELA, humanities educator; d. Florica Ileana Mira and Mihai Bancila; m. Timothy Dwight Pittman, Mar. 25, 2000; 1 child, Elena Joan Pittman. BA, U. of Bucharest, 1984—88; MA, U. of Pitts., 1994—96; PhD, U. of Va., 1996—2002. Asst. prof. U. of Bucharest, Romania, 1990—94; fellowship recipient U. of Pitts., 1994—96, U. of Va., 1996—2000. German Academic Exch. Svc., Germany, 1992—93, Academic Enhancement Program, U. of Va., 1999—2000. Mem.: Soc. of Romanian Germanists, MLA.

BANCROFT, ALEXANDER CLERIHEW, lawyer; b. N.Y.C., Feb. 6, 1938; s. Harding F. and Jane (Northrop) B.; m. Margaret A. Armstrong, Mar. 14, 1964; 1 dau., Elizabeth. AB, Harvard U., 1960, LL.B., 1963. Mem. Shearman & Sterling, N.Y.C., 1964—, ptnr., 1973—. Home: 15 E 91st St New York NY 10128-0648 Office: 599 Lexington Ave New York NY 10022-6030

BANCROFT, ANN E. polar explorer; b. 1955; d. Dick and Debbie Bancroft Former tchr., coach, wilderness instr., St. Paul, Minn. Mem. Steger Internat. Polar Expedition, 1986 (first woman to reach the North Pole by dogsled); leader Am. Women's Antarctic Expedition, 1993 (first women's team to reach the South Pole on skis); mem. The Bancroft Arnesen Expdn. (first all women's crossing of Antarctica), 2000. Subject (corp. video) Vision of Teams, 1998, (documentary) Poles Apart, 1999; featured in Remarkable Women of the 20th Century, 1998. Founder Ann Bancroft Found. Named Ms. Mag. Woman of Yr., 1987; inductee Girls and Women in Sport Hall of Fame, 1992, Nat. Women's Hall of Fame, 1995; recipient Women First award YWCA, 1993; first woman in world to travel across the ice to North and South poles. Office: yourexpedition 119 N 4th St Ste 406 Minneapolis MN 55401-1790 Fax: 612-333-1325. E-mail: susan@yourexpedition.com.

BANCROFT, ANNE (MRS. MEL BROOKS), actor, director, screenwriter; b. Bronx, NY, Sept. 17, 1931; d. Michael and Mildred (DiNapoli) Italiano; m. Mel Brooks, 1964; 1 son. Broadway stage appearances include Two for the Seesaw, 1957 (Tony award 1957), The Miracle Worker, 1959-60 (Tony award 1960), Devils, 1977, Golda, 1977-78, Duet for One, 1981; stage appearances include Mystery of the Rose Bouquet, 1989; motion pictures include Treasure of the Golden Condor, 1952, Don't Bother to Knock, 1952, Tonight We Sing, 1953, The Kid from Left Field, 1953, Demetrius and the Gladiators, 1954, Gorilla at Large, 1954, The Raid, 1954, A Life in the Balance, 1954, The Brass Ring, 1954, Naked Street, 1955, New York Confidential, 1955, The Last Frontier, 1955, Girl in the Black Stockings, 1957, Restless Breed, 1957, The Pumpkin Eater, 1964, Seven Women, 1966, Slender Thread, 1966, The Graduate, 1967 (Golden Globe for best actress, 1968), Young Winston, 1972, The Prisoner of 2nd Avenue, 1975, The Hindenburg, 1975, Lipstick, 1976, Silent Movie, 1976, The Turning Point, 1977, Fatso, 1979, The Elephant Man, 1980, To Be or Not to Be, 1983, Garbo Talks, 1984, Agnes of God, 1985, 'Night, Mother, 1986, 84 Charing Cross Road (Brit. Acad. award 1987), Torch Song Trilogy, 1988, Bert Rigby You're a Fool, 1989, Honeymoon in Vegas, 1992, Love Potion #9, 1992, Point of No Return, 1993, Mr. Jones, 1993, Malice, 1993, How to Make an American Quilt, 1995, Home for the Holidays, 1995, Dracula, Dead and Loving It, 1995, GI Jane, 1997, Critical Care, 1997, Great Expectations, 1998, Antz, 1998, Mark Twain's America in 3D, 1998, Up at the Villa, 1999, Deep in My Heart, 1999, Keeping the Faith, 2000, Heartbreakers, 2001; TV appearances include Kraft Music Hall, Jesus of Nazareth, 1977, Marco Polo, 1982, Broadway Bound, 1992, Mrs. Cage, PBS, 1992, Oldest Living Confederate Widow Tells All, 1994, The Homecoming, 1996, Sunchasers, 1997,AFI's 100 years ... 100 Movies, 1998, Deep in My Heart, 1999 (Emmy for best supporting actress, 1999), A Salute to Dustin Hoffman, 1999, Haven, 2001; dir., writer, star: (TV spl.) Annie-The Woman in the Life of Men, 1970 (Emmy award 1970). Recipient Acad. award for performance in The Miracle Worker, 1962, Best Actress award Cannes Internat. Film Festival for performance in Pumpkin Eater, 1964, inducted into Theater Hall of Fame, 1992, Lifetime Achievement in Comedy award Am. Comedy Awards, 1996. Address: c/o The Culver Studios 9336 Washington Blvd Culver City CA 90232-2628 Office: ICM 8942 Wilshire Blvd Beverly Hills CA 90211

BANCROFT, GEORGE MICHAEL, chemical physicist, educator; b. Saskatoon, Sask., Can., Apr. 3, 1942; s. Fred and Florence Jean B.; m. Joan Marion MacFarlane, Sept. 16, 1967; children: David Kenneth, Catherine Jean. B.Sc., U. Man., 1963; M.Sc., 1964; PhD, Cambridge (Eng.) U., 1967, MA, 1970, Sc.D. (E.W. Staecie fellow), 1979. Univ. demonstrator Cambridge U.; then teaching fellow Christ Coll.; mem. faculty U. Western Ont., London, now prof. dept. chemistry; 1 dir. rsch. Can. Light Source. Author: Mössbauer Spectroscopy, 1973; also articles in photoelectron spectroscopy, synchrotron radiation studies; revs. Mössbauer Spectroscopy. Recipient Harrison Meml. prize, 1972, Meldola medal, 1972, Rutherford Meml. medal, 1980, Alcan award, 1990, Herzberg award, 1991, Can. Inst. of Chemistry Palladium medal, 1996, Morley medal Am. Chem. Soc., 1998; Guggenheim fellow, 1982-83; named Officer of the Order of Can., 2003. Fellow Royal Soc. Can.; mem. Royal Soc. Chemistry, Can. Chem. Soc., Can. Geol. Soc., Can. Physics Soc. Mem. United Ch. Can. Clubs: Curling, Tennis (London). Office: U Western Ont Chem Dept London ON Canada N6A 5B7 E-mail: gmbancro@uwo.ca.

BANCROFT, JAMES ROGERS, consulting engineer; b. Cin., Jan. 4, 1952; s. William George and Patricia M. (Rogers) B.; m. Amy Jane McCully, Sept. 10, 1977; children: Adam James, Morgan Patrick, William Lawrence. BSCE, Purdue U., 1975; MBA, U. S.C., 1984. Registered profl. engr., Conn., Mass., NH, Ohio, SC, RI. Civil engr., resident engr. Bucher Willis and Ratliff, Kansas City, Mo., 1975-79; transp. engr. Wilbur Smith and Assocs., Columbia, S.C., 1979-82, transport planner Republic of Singapore, 1981; program mgr., indsl. engr. Naval Facilities Engring. Command, Charleston, S.C., 1982-86; br. mgr. SEA Consultants, Inc., Glastonbury, Conn., 1986-88; br. office mgr. Weston and Sampson Engrs., Inc., Glastonbury, Conn., 1988—95; mng. prin. Lenard Engring. Inc., Storrs, Conn., 1995—. Cub master Glastonbury (Conn.) area Boy Scouts Am., 1988—96, scoutmaster, 2002—. Mem.: ASCE, Am. Pub. Works Assn., Am. Water Works Assn., Inst. Transp. Engrs., Soc. Mktg. Profl. Svcs.

(pres. so. New Eng. chpt. 1991—92, treas. 1993—). Congregationalist. Home: 244 Buttonball Ln Glastonbury CT 06033-3224 Office: Lenard Engring 1066 Storrs Rd PO Box 580 Storrs CT 06268-0580

BANCROFT, MARGARET ARMSTRONG, lawyer; b. Mpls., May 9, 1938; d. Wallace David and Mary Elizabeth (Garland) Armstrong; m. Alexander Clerihew Bancroft, Mar. 14, 1964; 1 child, Elizabeth Armstrong. BA magna cum laude, Radcliffe Coll.-Harvard U., 1960; JD cum laude, NYU, 1969. Bar: N.Y. 1971. Reporter Mpls. Star and Tribune, 1960-61, UPI, N.Y., N.J., 1961-66; ptnr. Law Firm of Dechert LLP. Adj. prof. law NYU Sch. Law. Bd. dirs., mem. exec. com. Vis. Nurse Svc. N.Y.; pres. Vis. Nurse Svc. N.Y. Home Care, Inc. Mem. ABA (bus. law sect.), N.Y. State Bar Assn. (securities regulation com.), Assn Bar City N.Y. (com. on investment mngmt. regulation), Am. Law Inst. Office: Law Firm of Dechert LLP 30 Rockefeller Plz Fl 22 New York NY 10112-2200

BANCROFT, PEGGY, editor; b. Oakland, Pa., Nov. 30, 1919; d. Paul Meade and Claire Mildred (Culver) Thomas; m. Fred Ford Bancroft, June 28, 1941; children: Richard Lockyer, Joan Claire. BA, East Stroudsburg U., 1977. Editor This Week in the Poconos Mag., Pocono Pines, Pa., 1957-96, Greene Hills of Home, Greentown, 1984—2002. Author: Ringing Axes & Rocking Chairs, 1974, Falling Feathers, 1992, Of Rabbits, Rain & R I Reds, 1993, Tales From Pawdaddy Farm, 1994, A Cabin in the Clearing, 1997, Distant Days, 2002, More Distant Days, 2002, others. Mem. LaAnna U M Ch., Cresco, Pa., Newfoundland Libr., Newfoundland Theatre League. Mem. Greene Twp. Historical Soc., Del. Heritage Assn., Pike County Historical Soc., Hist. Soc. So. Wayne. Republican. Avocations: hiking, researching, genealogy, gardening. Home: Rt 191 PO Box 25 South Sterling PA 18460 Office: Rt 191 South Sterling PA 18460-0025

BANCROFT, WEBB ERNEST, lawyer; b. Webster, S.D., May 2, 1957; BA, U. Nebr., 1979, JD, 1983. Lawyer Assoc. Students U. Nebr., Lincoln, Nebr., 1984-86, Bancroft Law Office, Lincoln, 1984-89; dep. pub. defender Lancaster County Pub. Defender, Lincoln, 1989—. Office: Lancaster County Pub Defender 555 S 10th St Lincoln NE 68508-2810

BAND, JORDAN CLIFFORD, lawyer; b. Cleve., Aug. 15, 1923; s. Samuel Melville and Helen Rita (Krause) B.; m. Alice Jeanne Glickson, Apr. 27, 1946; children: Terril R., Stefanie Band Allweiss, Claudia Band McCord. Student, U. Ala., 1943-44; BBA, Case Western Res. U., 1947, LLB, 1948. Bar: Ohio 1948, U.S. Dist. Ct. (no. dist.) Ohio 1948. Assoc. Ulmer & Berne, Cleve., 1948-56, ptnr., 1956-94, ret., 1994—. Bd. dirs. numerous cos. Chmn. Greater Cleve. Conf. on Religion and Race, 1964-66, Greater Cleve. Project, 1978-81; nat. chmn. Nat. Jewish Community Rels. Adv. Coun., N.Y.C., 1967-70; presiding officer Cleve. Community Rels. Bd., 1970-90; nat. vice chmn. Am. Jewish Com., 1976-79; legal counsel Jewish Community Fedn. Cleve., 1984-87, also trustee, officer numerous civic and non-profit orgns. Recipient Kane Leadership award Jewish Community Fedn., 1961, Bronze medal, 1978, Cert. of Appreciation, City of Cleve., 1970-88, Cert. of Recognition, Ohio Senate, 1987. Mem. ABA, Ohio Bar Assn., Cuyahoga County Bar Assn., Cleve. Bar Assn., Order of Coif. Democrat. Avocations: community relations, civic activities, tennis. Office: 18483 Parkland Dr Shaker Heights OH 44122-3450

BANDAR, PRINCE BIN SULTAN BIN ABD AL-AZIZ AL SAUD, Saudi Arabian ambassador to U.S.; b. Taif, Saudi Arabia, Mar. 2, 1949; s. Prince Sultan ibn Abdulaziz al-Saud; m. Princess Haifa bint Faisal ibn Abdulazia al-Saud; children— Lulua, Rema, Khalid, Faisal. B.A., Brit. Royal Air Force Acad., Cranwell, Eng., 1969; Grad., Advanced Fighter and Instr. Pilot Program, USAF, 1979; M.A., Johns Hopkins U., 1980. Fighter pilot Royal Saudi Air Force, Dhahran Air Base, Khamis Mushayt Air Base, Taif Air Base, 1969-82, comdr. 7th Royal Saudi Air Force Squadron, 1976-79, comdr. Peace Hawk Project, Dhahran, 1976-79; in charge spl. AWACS Saudi Arabian Liaison Mission to U.S., 1981; mem. Saudi Arabia Mil. Mission to U.S., def. and mil. attache, 1982-83; mem. Saudi Del. to UN Gen. Assembly, 1983; Saudi Arabian ambassador to U.S., 1983—. Served to col. Royal Saudi Air Force. Decorated Flying Hawk medal; King Abdulaziz Sash, for work in attaining Lebanese ceasefire, King Fahd, 1983. Muslim. Home: Fgn Ministry Saudi Arabia Riyadh Saudi Arabia Office: Royal Embassy of Saudi Arabia 601 New Hampshire Ave NW Washington DC 20037-2405

BANDARCHI-CHAMKHALEH, BIZHAN, pathologist; b. Tehran, Mar. 8, 1965; s. Nasser Bandarchi-C. and Batool Fassihi-Langroudi. Med. Diploma, Shaheed Beheshti U. (formerly Nat. U. Iran), Tehran, 1990. Cert. Ednl. Commn. for Fgn. Med. Grads. Pathology resident Shaheed Modarres Hosp., Tehran, 1990-91, U. Fla. Health Sci. Ctr., Jacksonville, 1997-2000, Mass. Gen. Hosp./Harvard Med. Sch., Boston, 2000—02; fellow in dermatopathology U. Fla./Gainesville, 2002—03; physician-in-charge Mil. Base Clinic, Tehran, 1992-94, Ministry of Health, Qeshm, Iran, 1994-95; gen. practitioner Tehran, 1993-97; rsch. asst. Iran Pezeshk Clinic, Tehran, 1993-96; fellow in dermatopathology U. Fla. Coll. Medicine, Gainesville, 2002—03. Poster presenter in field. Translator: Clinical Neurology, 1993 (1st prize Med. Students Authorship Competition/Iran 1996); editor: (Farsi translation) Physiology of Special Senses, 1985, others; contbr. articles and abstracts to med. jours. including Breast Jour., Modern Pathology. Higher supr. in polio eradicating program, Ministry of Health in cooperation with WHO, Hormozgan, Iran, 1995. 1st lt. Iranian mil., 1992-94. Mem. AMA, U.S. and Can. Acad. Pathology, Internat. Soc. Dermatopathology, Med. Ethics Coun. of Iran, Am. Soc. Clin. Pathologists, Coll. Am. Pathologists, Am. Soc. Dermatopathology, Am. Soc. Cytopathology, Papanicolaou Soc. of Cytopathology. Home: 1105 Ft Clarke Blvd Apt 814 Gainesville FL 32606 Office: U Fla Diagnostic Referral Labs 4800 SW 35th Dr Gainesville FL 32608 E-mail: bizhanb@yahoo.com.

BANDEEN, ROBERT ANGUS, management consultant; b. Rodney, Ont., Can., Oct. 29, 1930; s. John Robert and Jessie Marie (Thomson) Bandeen; m. Mona Helen Blair, May 31, 1958; children: Ian Blair, Mark Everett, Robert Derek, Adam Drummond. BA, U. Western Ont., 1952; PhD, Duke U., 1959; LLD (hon.), U. Western Ont., 1975, Dalhousie U., 1978, Queens U., 1982; DCL (hon.), Bishop's U., 1978. Asst. economist Can. Nat. Rys., Montreal, 1955-56, research statistician, 1956-58, staff officer planning, 1958-60, chief costs and stats., 1960, chief devel. planning, 1960-66, dir. corp. planning, 1966-68, v.p. corp. planning and fin., 1968-71, v.p. Great Lakes region, 1971-72, exec. v.p. fin. and adminstrn., 1972-74, pres., CEO, 1974-82; chmn., pres., CEO Crown Life Ins. Co., 1982-84, chmn., CEO, 1984-85; chmn., pres., CEO Cluny Corp., Toronto, 1986—. Former chancellor Bishop's U.; gov. participation Can. Olympic Trust; bd. dirs. Clarke Inc., Nat. Challenge Sys., Inc. Gov. participation Can. Olympic Trust; senator Shakespearean Festival Found.; mem. Isle Maligne Soc. Duke U. Decorated knight Order St. John, officer Order of Can.; recipient Salzberg medal, Syracuse U., 1982. Mem.: York, Cambridge Club (Toronto), Mount Royal Club (Montreal), Delta Upsilon. Home and Office: Cluny Corp 305-1166 Bay St Toronto ON Canada M5S 2X8

BANDEEN, WILLIAM REID, retired meteorologist; b. Escanaba, Mich., Oct. 11, 1926; s. Orren I. and Jean (Guthrie) B.; m. Joan Sleeper, Dec. 17, 1960; children: Kevin Orren, Karen Jean, Keith Morse. BS, U.S. Mil. Acad., 1948; MS, NYU, 1955. Commd. 2d lt. U.S. Army, 1948, advanced through grades to capt., 1959, ret., 1959; with NASA, Goddard Space Flight Ctr., Greenbelt, Md., 1959-89, assoc. dir. space and earth scis. for ops., 1986-89, ret., 1989. Contbr. articles to profl. jours. Fellow AAAS, Am. Geophys. Union, Am. Meteorol. Soc.

BANDEL, DAVID BRIAN, accountant; b. Chgo., Aug. 18, 1951; s. Frank John and Lorraine Mary (Buzinski) B. BA in Psychology, So. Ill. U., 1974, BS in Acctg., 1977. CPA, Ill. Staff acct. Porte Brown LLC, Elk Grove Village, Ill., 1977-83, mgr., 1984-86, ptnr., 1987—; dir. Harris Bank, Elk Grove, Ill., 1996—. Treas. United Way, Elk Grove Village, 1990-96; bd. dirs. Greater O'Hare Assn., Elk Grove Village, 1994—, amb., 1979-86, treas., 1998—. Recipient Paul Harris fellow. Mem. AICPA, Ill. CPA Soc. (dir. pub. rels. O'Hare chpt. 1990), Rotary (pres. 1988-89). Roman Catholic. Avocations: sports, investing, community fundraising. Home: 72 Otis Rd Barrington IL 60010-5128 Office: Porte Brown LLC 845 Oakton St Elk Grove Village IL 60007-1904 E-mail: dbb@portebrown.com.

BANDEMER, NORMAN JOHN, healthcare consulting executive; b. Detroit, Sept. 13, 1949; s. Marvin Gustave and Helen Theresa (Jashinski) B.; m. Elaine Ellen Massie, Sept. 4, 1971; children: Norman John II, Marisa Nikol. BBA, Eastern Mich. U., 1971; MBA, Mich. State U., 1977. Field auditor Blue Cross and Blue Shield of Mich., Detroit, 1971-72; supr. State of Mich. Medicaid Program, Lansing, 1972-77; asst. dir. Mich. Hosp. Assn. Svc. Corp., Lansing, 1977-83; v.p. of operation Bronson/Beaumont Mgmt. Svcs., Kalamazoo, Mich., 1983-86; exec. dir. The Travelers Health Network, Grand Rapids, 1986-88; regional dir. Coopers & Lybrand, Detroit, 1988-90; mng. ptnr. ADA Consulting Group-Healthcare Consulting, Grand Rapids, 1990—. Guest speaker Health Care Benefits, Direct Contracting, 1992. Author: Health Care Costs in Michigan, 1991, Medicaid Program in Mich., 1992. Hon. coach Mich. State U. Athletic Booster Club, East Lansing, 1987. Mem. Lansing City Club, Healthcare Fin. Mgmt. Assn., Mich. Assn. CPAs Healthcare Com., Mich. State U. Alumni Club. Roman Catholic. Avocations: golf, travel, watching sporting events. Office: ADA Consulting Group 7705 Tobemory Ct SE Ste 100 Ada MI 49301-9362

BANDER, EDWARD JULIUS, law librarian emeritus, lawyer; b. Boston, Aug. 10, 1923; s. Abraham and Ida (Lendman) B. BA, Boston U., 1949, LLB, 1951; MLS, Simmons Coll., 1955. Bar: Mass. 1951. Asst. reference libr. Harvard U., Cambridge, Mass., 1954-55; libr. U.S. Ct. Appeals (1st cir.), Boston, 1955-60; asst. libr., asst. prof. NYU, N.Y.C., 1960-70, assoc. prof., curator, assoc. libr., 1970-78; prof., libr. Suffolk U. Law Sch., Boston, 1978-90, libr., prof. emeritus, 1991—. Author: Mr. Dooley and the Choice of Law, 1963, Mr. Dooley and Mr. Dunne, 1981, Justice Holmes Ex Cathedra, 1966, 91, Searching the Law, 1986, Shakespeare on Lawyers and the Law, 1998. Served with USN, 1942-46. Recipient Dean Frederick A. McDermott award, Suffolk U. Student Bar Ass, 1980. Mem. Assn. Am. Law Schs., New Eng. Law Libr. Democrat. Jewish. Office: 50 Church St Concord MA 01742-3050 E-mail: ebander@acad.suffolk.edu.

BANDER, MYRON, physics educator, university dean; b. Belzyce, Poland, Dec. 11, 1937; came to U.S., 1949, naturalized, 1955; s. Elias and Regina (Zielonka) B.; m. Carol Heimberg, Aug. 20, 1967. BA, Columbia U., 1958, MA, 1959, PhD, 1962. Postdoctoral fellow CERN, 1962-63; research assoc. Stanford Linear Accelerator Center, 1963-66; mem. faculty U. Calif., Irvine, 1966—, prof. physics, 1974—, dean phys. scis., 1980-86; chair dept. physics, 1992-95. Sloan Found. fellow, 1967-69 Fellow Am. Phys. Soc. Office: U Calif Irvine CA 92697-0001 E-mail: mbander@uci.edu.

BANDERAS, ANTONIO, actor; b. Malaga, Spain, Aug. 10, 1960; m. Ana Leza, 1988 (div. 1996); m. Melanie Griffith, 1996; 1 child. Films include: Labyrinth of Passion, 1982, Pestanas postizas, 1982, Y del sefuro...Ilbranos señor!, 1983,El Senor Galindez, 1983, El Caso Almeria, 1983, The Stilts, 1984, La corte de Faraon, 1985, Requiem por un campesino espanol, 1985, The Puzzle, 1986, 27 Hours, 1986, Matador, 1986, Delirios de amor, 1986, The Way They Were, 1987, Law of Desire, 1987, The Pleasure of Killing, 1988, El Acto, 1987, Baton Rouge, 1988, Women on the Verge of a Nervous Breakdown, 1988, Going South Shopping, 1988, Si que dicen que cai, 1989, The White Dove, 1989, Tie Me Up! Tie Me Down!, 1990, Against the Wind, 1990, New Land, 1991, Woman in the Rain, 1991, Madonna: Truth or Dare, 1991, Borges Tales, Part I, 1991, The Mambo Kings, 1992, Shoot!, 1993, Outrage, 1993, Philadelphia, 1993, The House of the Spirits, 1993, Il Giovane Mussolini, 1993, Of Love and Shadows, 1994, Interview With the Vampire, 1994, Never Talk to Strangers, 1995, Miami Rhapsody, 1995, Four Rooms, 1995, Desperado, 1995, Assassins, 1995, Two Much, 1996, Evita, 1996, The Mask of Zorro, 1997, Crazy in Alabama, 1998, The 13th Warrior, 1999, The White River Kid, 1999, Play It to the Bone, 1999, Dancing in the Dark, 2000, The Body, 2000, Spy Kids, 2001, Original Sin, 2001, Femme Fatale, 2002, Spy Kids: Island of Lost Dreams, 2002, Frida, 2002, Ballistics: Ecks vs. Sever, 2002, Spy Kids 3-D: Game Over, 2003, Imagining Argentina, 2003, And Starring Pancho Villa as Himself, 2003 (TV), Once Upon a Time in Mexico, 2003; dir. Crazy in Alabama, 1999, Malaga Burning, 2000; prodr. White River Kid, 1999, Forever Lulu, 2000. TV movies: La Otra historia de Rosendo Juarez, 1990 Office: c/o Emanuel Nunez Creative Artists Agy 9830 Wilshire Blvd Beverly Hills CA 90212-1804 also: Agents Assocs/Guy Bonnet 201 Rue du fauborg Saint Honore Paris 75008 France*

BANDERET, LOUIS EUGENE, psychologist; b. Des Moines, Aug. 9, 1943; s. Emil Raymond and Mable Elsie (Debele) B.; children: Paul Michael, Tanya Lynn, Suzanne Marie; m. Marilyn A. Heilbrunn, July 1996. BA, Concordia Coll., Moorhead, Minn., 1965; MS, Wash. State U., 1968, PhD, 1970. Rsch. animal psychologist U.S. Army Rsch. Inst. of Environ. Medicine, Natick, Mass., 1970-73, rsch. psychologist/simulation, 1974-80, rsch. psychologist/cognitive, 1981-84, rsch. psychologist/assessment, 1985—. Lectr. psychology Northeastern U., Boston, 1970—. Bell Atlantic Learning Ctr., Marlboro, Mass., 1985, 86, 97, 98, Quinsigamond C. C., Worcester, Mass., 1986-88, 93—, others; acad. reviewer McGraw Hill, West, Harper Collins, 1988—; prin. investigator Stress Study, 2000-02. Co-editor, co-author Spl. Issue Mil. Psychology Jour., 1997; co-author: (book chpt.) Handbook Military Psychology, 1991, (test bank) Understanding Psychology, 1990; co-author: (2 book chpts.) Textbook of Military Medicine, 2002; organizer symposium in field, 1986, 91, Workshop Organizer, 2003; chmn. psychology textbook com. Northeastern U., 1987, 95; reviewer sci. jours., 1997—. Fraternal communicator Luth. Brotherhood, Mpls., 1981-93; lay minister Christ King Luth., Holliston, Mass., 1980-92; com. chmn. troop 432, Boy Scouts Am., Milford, Mass., 1978-83; scientist judge Mass. State Sci. Fair, 1988-96, 98-99, Internat. Sci. Fair, 1997; originator funded idea Sml. Bus. Innovative Rsch. Program, Washington, 1993-96, 2002—; mem. Gov.'s Rsch. Evaluation Panel, 1998, 2000. Recipient 30-Yr. Tchg. award Northeastern Univ. Coll., 2001; rsch. grantee Def. Women's Health, 1996. Mem. Sigma Xi. Avocations: classical music, coffee, computers, books, mentoring exceptional people. Home: 10 Harvard Dr Milford MA 01757-1277 Office: USARIEM MCMR-EMP 42 Kansas St Natick MA 01760-5007 E-mail: banderetlm@sprynet.com.

BANDES, SUSAN ANNE, lawyer; b. N.Y.C., May 19, 1951; d. Seymour and Lucille Janet (Coleman) B.; m. Christopher McElroy, May 23, 1976 (div. 1979). B.A., SUNY-Buffalo, 1973; J.D., U. Mich., 1976. Bar: Ill. 1976, U.S. Dist. Ct. (no. dist.) Ill. 1976, U.S. Ct Appeals (7th cir.) 1978. Staff atty. Office Ill. Appellate Defender, Chgo., 1977-81; staff counsel ACLU, Chgo., 1981-84; asst. prof. DePaul Coll. Law, Chgo., 1984— ; mem. exec. com. Chgo. Law Enforcement Study Group, Chgo, 1981— . Mem. Chgo. Bar Assn., Chgo. Council Lawyers, Phi Beta Kappa. Democrat. Jewish. Office: De Paul Coll Law 25 E Jackson Blvd Chicago IL 60604-2289

BANDES, SUSAN JANE, museum director, educator; b. N.Y.C., Oct. 18, 1951; d. Ralph and Bessie (Gordon) B. BA, NYU, 1971; MA, Bryn Mawr Coll., 1973, PhD, 1978; postgrad., Mus. Mgmt. Inst., Berkeley, Calif., 1990. Asst. prof. Sweet Briar (Va.) Coll., 1978-83; project dir. Am. Assn. Mus., Washington, 1983-84; program officer J. Paul Getty Trust Grant Program, L.A., 1984-86; prof., dir. Kresge Art Mus. Mich. State U., East Lansing, 1986—. Author, editor: Caring for Collections, 1984, Affordable Dreams: The Goetsch-Winckler House and Frank Lloyd Wright, 1991; author: Abraham Rattner, The Tampa Museum of Art Collection, 1997; editor: The Prints of John S. de Martelly, 1903-1979. Recipient award Am. Philos. Soc., 1981, publ. award AIA, 1990; Samuel H. Kress fellow, 1972-73, 75-76, Whiting fellow, 1976-77; Fulbright-Hayes grant, 1974-75. Mem. Nat. Inst. for Conservation (treas. 1986-90), Mich. Alliance for Conservation (treas. 1994-95, sec. 1996-97, treas. 1997-98, pres. 1998-2000), Mich. Mus. Assn. (bd. dirs. 1987-92), Mich. Coun. for Humanities (coun. 1988-92), Midwest Art History Soc. (bd. dirs. 1997-2000). Avocation: collecting oriental rugs. Office: Mich State U Kresge Art Mus East Lansing MI 48824

BANDI, NAGESH, research scientist; b. Visakhapatnam, Andhra, India, Oct. 15, 1974; s. Narasayya Lakshmi and Sri Lakshmi Bandi; m. Kavitha Koushik Bandi. B.Pharmacy, Andhra U., 1995, M.Pharmacy, 1998; postgrad., U. Nebr., Omaha, 1998—. Rsch. fellow Andhra U., 1996—98; grad. rsch. asst. U. Nebr., Omaha, 1998—99, grad. tchg. asst., 1999—2000, grad. fellow, 2000—. Mem. bd. studies Andhra U., 1996—; co-moderator grad. symposium Edn. Beyond Grad. Studies to Become Successful Indsl. Scientists, 2002. Contbr. Grantee Grad. fellow, U. Nebr. Med. Ctr., 2001. Mem.: Am. Assn. Pharm. Scientists. Avocations: cooking, travel, sports, music, driving. Home: 411 S 41st St Apt 2 Omaha NE 68131 Office: Univ of Nebraska Med Ctr 986025 Nebraska Med Ctr Omaha NE 68198

BANDIX, GEORGE C. dean, chemist, educator; b. Braddock, Pa., Apr. 1, 1958; s. George J. and Eleanore K. Bandik. BS in Biochemistry, Pa. State U., 1980; PhD in Chemistry, U. Pitts., 1992. Dir. organic labs U. Pitts., 1986—, undergrad. coord. chemistry, 1998—2001, dir. undergrad. studies in chemistry, 2001—, asst. dean Coll. Arts and Scis., 1996—. Author: Organic Lab Manuals. Organist, choir dir. Holy Cross Parish, East Pittsburgh, 1984—. Recipient Chancellor's Tchg. award, U. Pitts., 1993, Tchg. Excellence award, Carnegie Sci. Ctr., Pitts., 1998, Bellet Tchg. award, Arts and Scis., U. Pitts., 2001. Mem.: Am. Chem. Soc. Avocations: gardening, music. Home: 336 Raymond St Pittsburgh PA 15218 Office: Univ of Pittsburgh 234 Chevron Science Ctr Pittsburgh PA

BANDLER, DONALD K. diplomat; BA in Polit. Sci., Kenyon Coll.; MA, St. John's Coll.; JD, George Washington U. Various fgn. svc. assignments, 1978—; dir. Israel and Arab-Israeli Affairs U.S. Dept. of State, 1994-95; dep. chief of mission, charge d'affaires Am. Embassy, Paris, 1995-97; spl. asst. to pres. and sr. dir. European Affairs Nat. Security Coun., 1997-99; amb. to Cyprus, 1999—; sr. v.p. Monsanto Co., Washington. Participant Sr. Seminar for fgn. affairs profls., 1993-94. Decorated French Legion of Honor, 1998; recipient Superior Honor awards State Dept. Home: 5624 Greentree Rd Bethesda MD 20817 Office: Monsanto Co 600 13th St NW Ste 660 Washington DC 20005

BANDLER, JOHN WILLIAM, electrical engineering educator, consultant; b. Jerusalem, Nov. 9, 1941; m. Beth; children: Lydia, Zoe. B.Sc., Imperial Coll. Sci. and Tech., London, 1963, PhD, 1967; D.Sc., U. London, 1976. With Mullard Research Labs., Eng., 1966-67; postdoctoral fellow, sessional lectr. U. Man., Can., 1967-69; asst. prof. McMaster U., Hamilton, Ont., Can., 1969-71, assoc. prof., 1971-74, prof. elec. engring., 1974-2000, prof. emeritus, 2000—, chmn. dept., 1978-79, dean faculty, 1979-81, coordinator group on simulation, optimization and control, 1973-83, dir. research in simulation optimization systems research lab., 1983—. Pres. Optimization Systems Assocs., Inc., 1983-97, Bandler Corp., Inc., 1997—. Author more than 350 tech. papers. Recipient Automated Measurements Career award Automatic Radio Frequency Techniques Group, 1994. Fellow IEEE, Inst. Elec. Engrs. U.K., Royal Soc. Can., Engring. Inst. of Can., Can. Acad. of Engring.; mem. Electromagnetics Acad., Assn. Profl. Engrs. Province of Ont. Office: McMaster U Dept Elec & Comp Engring Hamilton ON Canada L8S 4L7 *Proceeding in a direction not sanctioned by my peers has always proved tough, but the results achieved have almost always been worth the effort.*

BANDO, PATRICIA ALICE, university administrator; b. Detroit, Apr. 4, 1953; d. Hiro Walter and Fumi Patricia (Takemoto) B. BS in Dietetics, Mich. State U., 1975; MA in Food Svc. Adminstrn., NYU, 1985. Registered dietitian. Dietetic intern The N.Y. Hosp., N.Y.C., 1975-76, clin. dietitian, sr. dietitian/adminstrv., 1981-86; food and beverage mgr. Trump Palace Hotel, Atlantic City, N.J., 1986; gen. mgr., dining dept. Cornell U., Ithaca, N.Y., 1986-89, asst. dir., dining dept., 1989-92, dir., dining dept., 1992-95, Boston Coll., Chestnut Hill, Mass., 1995—. Fundraiser One to One Mentoring, Boston, 1998. Mem. ADA, Mass. Dietetic Assn., Nat. Assn. of Coll. and Univ. Food svcs. (conf. edn. chair 1996-97), N.Y. So. Tier Dietetic Assn. (treas. 1992-95), Soc. of Foodsvc. Mgmt., Nat. Restaurant Assn., New Seabury Country Club, Omicron Nu. Episcopalian. Avocations: golf, oil painting, watercolor, gourmet cooking. Home: 14 Holly Way Framingham MA 01701-4857 Office: Boston Coll Dining Svcs 66 Commonwealth Ave Chestnut Hill MA 02467-3843

BANDOPADHYAYA, AMITAVA (AMIT BANDO), economist, consultant, educator; b. Mombasa, Kenya, Oct. 2, 1957; (parents Indian citizens); came to U.S., 1979; s. Parry Mohan and Neelima (Chatterjee) B.; m. Carolyn A. Berry, Aug. 15, 1988; 1 child, Nikhil Alexander. BA with honors, St. Stephen's Coll., 1977; MA, Delhi Sch. Econs., 1979; PhD, U. Minn., 1987. Rschr. Indo-Can. Inst., Delhi, 1977-80; tchg. asst. U. Minn., Mpls., 1980-85; asst. prof. N.Mex. State U., Las Cruces, 1985-88; sr. economist environ. assessment and info. systems div. U. Chgo./Argonne (Ill.) Nat. Lab., 1988-92; adj. prof. Lewis U., Romeoville, Ill., 1990-92; v.p. RCF, Inc., Chgo., 1990-92; mgr. internat. environ. div. RCG/Hagler, Bailly, Inc., Arlington, Va., 1992-97; pres. Project Svcs. Group, Bethesda, Md., 1997—99; dir. energy-environ. svcs. Asia region Chemonics, 1999—2002; mng. dir. Deneb Cons., LLC, 2002—. Cons. nat. and internat. energy/environ. issues including climate change, clean prodn., market-based and regulatory incentives infrastructure development and project financing U.S. Govt., fgn. govts. and multilateral banks, including World Bank, ABD; cons. energy/environ./market analysis and forecasting U.S., Asia, Australia, Europe, Africa, Latin Am.; bd. dirs. Ctr. Econometric Modeling and Forecasting. Contbr. articles to numerous jours.; editor: Business Forecaster, 1987-90, Nat. Social Sci. Jour., 1988—. Sloan Found. fellow, 1984-85, Frost Found. fellow, 1986-88. Mem. AAAS, Am. Econ. Assn., Internat. Assn. for Energy Econs, Internat. Assn. Impact Assessment.

BANDOW, DOUGLAS LEIGHTON, editor, columnist, policy consultant; b. Washington, Apr. 15, 1957; s. Donald E. and Donna J. (Losh) B. AA, Okaloosa-Walton Jr. Coll., Niceville, Fla., 1974; BS in Econs., Fla. State U., 1976; JD, Stanford U., 1979. Bar: Calif. 1979 D.C. 1984. Sr. policy analyst Reagan for Pres. Com., Los Angeles, 1979 80, Arlington, Va., 1980, Office of Pres. Elect, Washington, 1980-81; spl. asst. to the Pres. for policy devel. White House, Washington, 1981-82; editor Inquiry Mag., Washington, 1982-84; sr. fellow Cato Inst., Washington, 1984 ; nat. syndicated columnist Copley News Svc., San Diego, 1983—. Author: Unquestioned Allegiance, 1986, Beyond Good Intentions: A Biblical View of Politics, 1988, Human Resources and Defense Manpower, 1989, The Politics of Plunder: Misgovernment in Washington, 1990, The Politics of Envy: Statism as Theology, 1994, Tripwire: Korea and U.S. Foreign Policy in a Changed World, 1996; editor: U.S. Aid to the Developing World, 1985, Protecting the Environment, 1986; co-editor: The U.S.-South Korean Alliance, 1992, Perpetuating Poverty, 1994; contbr. articles to periodicals. Recipient Freedom Leadership award Freedoms Found., Valley Forge, Pa., 1977; recipient cert. for polit. and journalistic activities Freedoms Found., Valley Forge, Pa., 1979; named Man of Yr. N.Y. State Coll. Reps., 1982; recipient Nat. Young Am. award Boy Scouts Am., 1977. Mem. Calif. Bar Assn., ABA, D.C. Bar Assn., Washington Ind. Writers. Office: Cato Inst 1000 Massachusetts Ave NW Washington DC 20001-5400

BANDSTRA, TED E. federal judge; b. Chgo., Jan. 27, 1948; m. Emmalee S. Shanks; one child. BA in Political Science, Calvin Coll., Grand Rapids, Mich., 1969; MA in Psychology, Ctrl. Mich. Univ., Mt. Pleasant, 1978; JD, Univ. of Miami Law Sch., 1981. Police officer Grand Rapids Police Dept., Grand Rapids, Mich., 1969-72; teacher Westminster Christian Sch., Miami, Fla., 1972-76; assoc. atty. Katten, Muchin et al., Chgo., 1981-83; prosecutor U.S. Attorney's Ofc., Miami, Fla., 1983-86; assoc. atty. Fowler, White, et al., Miami, Fla., 1986-89; magistrate judge U.S. Dist. Ct. (so. dist.) Fla., Miami, 1989—. Office: 105 US Courthouse 300 NE 1st Ave Miami FL 33132-2126

BANDT, PAUL DOUGLAS, physician, neurologist; b. Milbank, S.D., June 22, 1938; s. Lester Herman and Edna Louella (Sogn) B.; m. Mary King, Aug. 26, 1962 (div. Feb. 1974); children: Douglas, Peggy; m. Inara Irene Von Rostas, Apr. 1, 1974; 1 child, Jennifer. BS in Edn. with distinction, U. Minn., 1960, BS in Medicine, D in Medicine, U. Minn., 1966. Diplomate Am. Bd. Diagnostic Radiology, Am. Bd. Nuclear Medicine. Intern U.S. Pub. Health Svc., San Francisco, 1966-68, physician Las Vegas, 1968-69; resident Stanford U., Palo Alto, Calif., 1969-72; pres., physician Desert Radiologists, Las Vegas, 1972—. Vice chief med. staff Desert Springs Hosp., Las Vegas, chmn. dept. radiology; past chief of staff U. Med. Ctr. So. Nev., Las Vegas. Contbr. articles on diagnostic radiology to profl. jours. With USPHS, 1966-69. Recipient Nev. Physician Yr. award, 1998. Mem. Am. Coll. Radiology, Am. Coll. Nuclear Medicine, Clark Med. Soc., Nev. State Med. Soc. Avocations: skiing, scuba diving, photography. Office: Desert Radiologists 2020 Palomino Ln Las Vegas NV 89106-4812

BANDURA, ALBERT, psychologist, educator; b. Mundare, Alta., Can., Dec. 4, 1925; came to U.S., 1949, naturalized, 1956; m. Virginia Varns; 2 children. BA, U. B.C., 1949, D.Sc. (hon.), 1979; MA in Psychology, U. Iowa, 1951, PhD in Psychology, 1952. Prof. psychology Stanford U., 1953—, David Starr Jordan prof. social sci. in psychology, 1973—. Author: (with R.H. Walters) Adolescent Aggression, 1959, (with R.H. Walters) Social Learning and Personality Development, 1963, Principles of Behavior Modification, 1969, Aggression, 1973, Social Learning Theory, 1977, Social Foundations of Thought and Action: A Social Cognitive Theory, 1986; editor: Psychological Modeling: Conflicting Theories, 1971, Self-Efficacy in Changing Societies, 1995, Self-Efficacy: The Exercise of Control, 1997. Recipient Disting. Lifetime Contbn. award, Soc. for Advancement of Behavior Therapy, 2001; fellow, Guggenheim Found., 1972. Fellow: Ctr. Advanced Study in Behavioral Sci., Am. Acad. Arts and Scis.; mem.: APA (pres. 1974, Disting. Scientist award divsn. 12 1972, Disting. Sci. Contbn. award 1980), Can. Psychol. Assn. (hon. pres. 1999), Soc. Child Devel., Internat. Soc. Rsch. on Aggression (Disting. Contbn. award 1980), Western Psychol. Assn. (pres. 1980, Lifetime Achievement award 2003), Calif. Psychol. Assn. (Disting. Scientist award 1973, Lifetime Disting. Contbr. award 1998, Healthcare award for disting. contbns. to health promotion), Inst. Medicine NAS, Am. Psychol. Soc. (William James award 1989, James Cattell award 2003). Office: Stanford U Dept Psychology Stanford CA 94305-2130 E-mail: Bandura@psych.Stanford.edu.

BANDURSKI, BRUCE LORD, retired ecological and environmental scientist; b. Waterbury, Conn., June 28, 1940; s. Stanley Alexander Bandurski and Virginia Ann (VanRensselaer) Bandurski Hinckley. BS with honors, Mich. State U., 1962; postgrad., George Washington U., 1964-65, U.S. Dept. Agr. Grad. Sch., 1965-66. Pk. ranger Yellowstone Nat. Pk. Nat. Pk .Svc., Wyo., 1962-63; sci. reference analyst USPHS, Washington, 1963-65; intelligence ops. specialist U.S. Army, Washington, 1965-66; analyst planner U.S. Dept. Interior, Washington, 1966-74, coord., br. chief, Nat. Environ. Policy Act officer, 1974-83; on detail as ecologist, ecomgmt. advisor Internat. Joint Commn. U.S. and Can., Washington, 1983-85, sr. ecomgmt. advisor, ecologist, 1985-2000. Mem. faculty U.S. Dept. Agr. Grad. Sch., 1968-96, subcom. Fed. Interagy. Com. on Edn., 1967-74, Internat. Joint Commn. Task Force on Indicators Implementation, 1997-2000; watch dir., dep. and acting mission dir. U.S. Man-in-Sea program, St. John, V.I., 1970; chmn. Conservation Roundtable of Washington, 1970-71; chmn. com. on definitions, spl. com. on environ. protection U.S. nat. com. World Energy Conf., Washington, 1981-85; initiator, dir. Binat Workshop on Transboundary Monitoring, 1984; mem. exec. com. Great Lakes Sci. Adv. Bd., 1986-92; liaison Coun. Great Lakes Rsch. Mgrs.; mem. steering com. Great Lakes-St. Lawrence Ecosys. Model Framework; participant in ECE Seminar on Ecosys. Approaches to Water Mgmt. UN; mem. Steering Group on Marine Environ. Monitoring, Commn. on Engring. and Tech. Studies, NRC, 1986-87; mem. Lake Superior Biodiversity Project Adv. Com. Nat. Wildlife Fedn.; initiator multi year project Ecological Com. Great Lakes Sci. Adv. Bd., 1990-94; mem. Internat. Joint Commn. Task Force on Indicators for Evaluation, 1994-96; mem. Lake Erie Task Force, 1994-97; dir. Binat. Workshop on Indicators of Ecosystem Integrity/Diversity, 1998; guest lectr. No. Va. Cmty. Coll., U. Wis., Bucknell U., Am. U., U. Pitts., Am. Law Inst.-ABA. Complementarities between holism and reductionism as they pertain to governance of human/environ. rels.; Writer planning and recreation impact mgmt. series, 1967-73; originator of no action alt. in U.S. fed. govt.'s NEPA process, 1973; author U.S. Bur. Land Mgmt. Environ. Mgmt. Procedures, 1976-84 (Achievement award 1978, 79, 84), Ecology and Economics: Partners for Productivity, 1973; co-author The Ecosys. Approach: Theory and Ecosys. Integrity, 1990-94, More Recreation: Implications for the Tropical Ecosystem, 1969, Toward a Transboundary Monitoring Network, 1986. Mem. AAAS, Ecol. Soc. Am. (charter mem. Met. Washington chpt.), Internat. Assn. for Ecology, Am. Soc. Naturalists, The Wildlife Soc., Am. Soc. Mammalogists, Fed. Profl. Assn., Washington Soc. Engrs., Outdoor Ethics Guild, Nature Conservancy, Maine Coast Heritage Trust, Island Inst., Earthwatch, Assn. Ecosystem Rsch. Ctrs., Internat. Soc. for Ecosystem Health (charter mem.), Am. Mus. Women in the Arts (charter), Friesian Horse Assn. N.Am., Friesian Horse Soc., Alpha Zeta, Beta Beta Beta. Achievements include originator of no action alternative in U.S. Federal Government NEPA process; development of first college level course on NEPA process and instruction of same, 1971-96; inst. in 1974 of committed follow-up monitoring in decision documents when enviro. assessment findings of "no significant impact" of any actions to be taken are dependent upon mitigation measures; in what was then the USA's most extensive land/water mgmt. agency (Bureau of Land Mgmt.); took photograph which became the theme photo of USA's Nat. Trail Sys. Home: 355 Grover Criswell Rd Cynthiana KY 41031

BANDY, JACK D. lawyer; b. Galesburg, Ill., June 19, 1932; s. Homer O. and Gladys L. (Van Winkle) B.; m. Betty McMillan, Feb. 18, 1956; children: Jean A. Bandy Abramson, D. Michael, Jeffery K. BA, Knox Coll., 1954; LLB, U. La Verne, 1967. Bar: Calif. 1972, U.S. Supreme Ct. 2000. Safety engr. Indsl. Indemnity Co., L.A., 1960-65, sr. safety engr., 1965-69, resident safety engr., 1969-72; trial atty. Employers Ins. of Wausau, L.A., 1972-79; mng. atty. Wausau Ins. Cos., L.A., 1979-92; arbitrator, mediator L.A. Superior Mcpl. Ct., 1992—. Contbr. articles to profl. jours. Youth leader YMCA, Mission Hills, Calif., 1965-72. Served with U.S. Army, 1954-56. Mem. Calif. State Bar, Am. Soc. Safety Engrs. (cert. safety profl.). E-mail: bandy_jack@msn.com.

BANDYOPADHYAY, AMITABHA, engineering educator; b. Calbutta, West Bengal, India, Dec. 25, 1954; arrived in U.S., 1980; s. Ashoke Kumar and Kalpana Bandyopadhyay; m. Aditi Chattopadhyay, June 19, 1988; 1 child, Anika Banerjee. BE, U. Calcutta, 1976; MS, Pa. State U., 1987, PhD, 1991. Registered profl. engr., N.J., N.Y. Structural engr. M.N. Dastur & Co., Calcutta, 1976—80; lead engr. United Engrs. and Constructors, Phila., 1980—84; instr. Pa. State U., University Park, 1984—90; prof., dept. chair SUNY, Farmingdale, 1990—. Cons., Holbrook, NY, 1984—. Contbr. Named Engring. Educator Yr., NSPE, 2001. Mem.: ASEE (chmn. Mid Atlantic sect. 2003), ASCE, Chi Epsilon. Office: SUNY Farmingdale Lupton Hall RT 110 Farmingdale NY 11735

BANDYOPADHYAY, ARINDAM, endocrinologist; b. Calcutta, West Bengal, India, Sept. 5, 1959; s. Sadhan and Nirupama Bandyopadhyay; m. Sampa Bandyopadhyay, Dec. 25, 1963; children: Srijoni Rhea, Sharoni Neha. MB, BChir, MD, Calcutta U., 1982. Diplomate Am. Bd. Internal Medicine, 1995, Am. Bd. Endocrinology Diabetes and Metabolism, 1997. Ho. physician Med. Coll. Hosps., Calcutta, 1982—84, clin. asst., 1985—87; pvt. cons. physician Calcutta, 1988—91; fellow spl. immunology dept. medicine U. Miami/Jackson Meml. Hosp., 1991—92, resident dept. medicine; fellow endocrinology SUNY, Buffalo, 1995—97, asst. prof. clin. medicine, 2001—; cons. physician Kothari Med. Ctr., Calcutta, 1998—2001. Attending physician Diabetes Ctr. Millard Fillmore Hosp., Kaleida Health, Buffalo. Mem.: ACP, Am. Assn. Clin. Endocrinologist, Endocrine Soc., Am. Diabetes Assn. Achievements include research in Anti-Inflammatory Action Of Growth Hormone. Office: Diabetes Endocrinology Ctr Millard Fillmore Hospital 3 Gates Circle Buffalo NY 14209

BANDYOPADHYAY, RAM SHYAMAL, molecular biologist, researcher; b. West Bengal, India, Feb. 6, 1952; arrived in U.S., 1983; s. Ram Sekhar and Geeta Bandyopadhyay; m. Sabita Bandyopadhyay, Feb. 26, 1982. PhD, U. Calcutta, West Bengal, 1982. Fellow U. Fla., Gainesville, 1983—87; rsch. assoc. Tufts U., Boston, 1987—92, Boston U., Boston, 1992—2001; pvt. practice, 2001—03; fellow Shriver Ctr. U. Mass. Med., 2003; rsch. asst. Mass. Gen. Hosp., Boston, 2003—. Author: Cell Biochemistry and Biophysics, 1999. Avocations: painting, music, sports.

BANE, BERNARD MAURICE, publishing company executive; b. Nov. 23, 1924; s. Julius and Rhoda (Trop) B.. Student, Northeastern U., 1946—48. Various sales and merchandising positions, 1949—55; with BMB Pub. Co., Boston, 1965—, pub., 1965—. Author, pub.: The Bane in Kennedy's Existence, 1967, Is President John F. Kennedy Alive... and Well?, 1973, Is President John F. Kennedy Alive... and Well?, 16th edit., 1997, On the Impact of Morality in Our Times, 1985, Vatican "One": The Fault Line of Vatican II, 1986; prodr., host : The Fringe Voice, 1989—99. Chmn. Local Miss Am. Pageant, 1961. Mem.: Am. Soc. Notaries, Nat. Notary Assn. Home: 854 Massachusetts Ave Cambridge MA 02139-3024

BANE, JAMES WALLACE, music educator; b. Youngstown, Ohio, May 22, 1943; s. William Wallace and Evelyn June Bane; m. Glenice Gail DeWald, Feb. 16, 1974; children: Shannon Marie, Jamie Suzanne. M. Music, Cleve. Inst. of Music, Cleveland, OH, 1970; BA Music, Ohio State Univ., Columbus, OH, 1965; D. Music (hon.), Nat. Conservatory, Mexico City, Mexico, 1978. Cert. provisional Tchg. OH, 1966, permanent tchg. OH, 1978. Educator Ctrl. Jr. H.S., Cleveland, Ohio, 1966—70, Cuyahoga Heights H.S., Cuyahoga Heights, 1970—74, Cleve. Heights H.S., Cleveland Heights, 1974—2001, Hiram Coll., Hiram, 2001—. Assoc. dir. All-American Youth Honor Band, Miami, Fla., 1972—75; guest dir. Cleve. Youth Wind Symphony, Cleveland, Ohio; guest lectr. Cleve. State Univ., Cleveland, Ohio. Composer: (musical compositions) wrote 6 compositions for Jazz Ensemble. Bands com. Ohio Music Edn. Assn., Cleveland, Ohio, 2002—; adv. bd. Cleve. Music Sch. Settlement, Cleveland, Ohio, 1998—2002. Recipient Key to the City of U. Heights, OH, City of Cleve. Heights, 2001, Spl. Tribute Award, Tri-C Jazz Festival, 2001, Proclamation Award, City of Cleve. Heights, OH, 2001, Outstanding Jazz Educator of the Yr., 1996, Outstanding Tchr. Award, 1994. Mem.: Chautaugua Lit. and Sci. Cir., Internat. Assn. of Jazz Educators, Music Educators Nat. Conf. Avocation: boating. Office: Hiram College PO Box 67 Hiram OH 44234 E-mail: banejw@hiram.edu.

BANERJEE, AJOY KUMAR, engineer, constructor, executive; b. Dacca, Bangladesh, Apr. 23, 1945; came to U.S., 1966; s. Kalidas and Anjali (Mukherjee) B.; m. Marjorie Burren Friedman; children: Shonali Misha, Monisha Jenni. B Tech. in Civil Engring. with honors, Indian Inst. Tech., Kharagpur, 1966; M of Engring., U. Detroit, 1967; PhD in Structural Engring., Cornell U., 1973. Registered profl. engr., N.Y., Mass., Va., Mo., Ariz., Nev. V.p. Stone & Webster Internat., Boston, 1973-99, Pinnacle West Energy, 1999—. Mem. Presdl. Del. to India and China. Contbr. articles to Nuclear Safety Jour., Nuclear Engring. and Design Jour., Jour. Structural Div. ASCE, Am. Nuclear Soc. Proceedings, ASME Proceedings. Fellow ASCE, ASME; mem. IEEE (com. on probabilistic risk assessment 1981-82), Am. Nuclear Soc. Achievements include development of programs and methodologies for nuclear power plant life extension and increasing power rating; building, operating and acquiring several thousand MWs of power plants of various fuel types. Office: Pinnacle West Energy 400 N 5th St Phoenix AZ 85004 E-mail: ajoy.banerjee@pwenergy.com.

BANERJEE, KALYANI, science educator, researcher; b. Kolkatta, W. Bengal, India, Jan. 18, 1938; d. Mukti Pada and Nirupama Chatterji; m. Santosh Kumar, Aug. 6, 1970; 1 child, Kaberi. BS, Calcutta U., India, 1957, MS, 1959; PhD, U. Pitts, 1967. Cert. H.S. tchr. Northeastern Ill. U., 1994, H.S. math and sci. State of Ill. H.S. tchr., Calcutta, India, 1959—63; rsch. assoc. Bose Inst., Calcutta, India, 1969—70; substitute tchr. Evanston H.S., Ill., 1994—; adj. faculty Oakton CC, Des Plaines, Ill., 1988—, City Coll. of Chgo., 1992—. Mem.: NEA-IEA, Iota Sigma Pi.

BANERJEE, KAUSTAV, electrical and computer engineering educator; arrived in U.S., 1991; s. Gokul Chandra and Arati Banerjee; m. Sheetal Gavankar, Dec. 22, 1994. PhD, U. Calif., Berkeley, 1999. Rsch. asst. Elec. Engring. Computer Sci. Dept. U. Calif., Berkeley, 1993—99; vis. rschr. Tex. Instruments, Dallas, 1997—98; rsch. assoc. Ctr. for Integrated Systems, Stanford (Calif.) U., 1999—2002; vis. rsch. fellow Swiss Fed. Inst. of Tech., Lausanne, Switzerland, 2001; vis. faculty Microprocessor Rsch. Labs, Intel Corp., Hillsboro, Oreg., 2002; asst. prof. dept. elec. and computer engring. U. Calif., Santa Barbara, 2002—. Tech. cons. Magma Design Automation Inc., Cupertino, Calif., 2000—01; tech. cons. Fujitsu Labs of Am., Sunnyvale, 2002. Author: (paper (38th design automation conf.) Analysis of On-Chip Inductance Effects using a Novel Performance Optimization Methodology for Distributed RLC Interconnects, 2001 (Best Paper Award ACM/IEEE Design Automation Conf., 2001); contbr. articles (more than 75) to profl. jours. Mem.: IEEE.

BANERJEE, PRASHANT, industrial engineering educator; b. Calcutta, West Bengal, India, Apr. 15, 1962; came to U.S., 1986; s. Prabhat K. and Bani Banerjee; m. Madhumita Banerjee, Dec. 11, 1987; children: Jay, Ann. BSME, Indian Inst. Tech., Kanpur, India, 1984; MS in Indsl. Engring., Purdue U., 1987, PhD, 1990. Indsl. engr. Tata Steel Co., Jamshedpur, India, 1984-85; asst. prof. U. Ill., Chgo., 1990-96, assoc. prof., 1996—. Cons. Caterpillar Inc., Peoria, Ill., 1992, Motorola Inc., 1994-97, Monsanto, Inc., 1996—. Author: Automation and Control of Manufacturing Systems, 1991, Object-oriented Technology in Manufacturing, 1992; contbr. articles to profl. jours. NSF rsch. grantee, 1992, 95, Nat. Inst. Standards and Tech. rsch. grantee, 1995. Mem. ASME, Inst. Indsl. Engrs., Inst. Mgmt. Scis., Soc. Mfg. Engrs. Avocations: sports, current events, religious discussions. Home: 708 Kirstin Ct Westmont IL 60559 Office: Univ Ill Engring Dept Chicago IL 60607-7022

BANERJEE, SAMARENDRANATH, orthopedic surgeon; b. Calcutta, India, July 12, 1932; s. Haridhone and Nihar Bala (Mukherjee) B.; m. Hima Ganguly, Mar. 1977; 1 child, Rabindranath M.B. BS, R.G. Kar Med. Coll., Calcutta, 1957; postgrad., U. Edinburgh, 1965-66. Intern R.G. Kar Med. Coll., Calcutta, 1956-58; resident in surgery Bklyn. Jewish Hosp. Med. Ctr., 1958-60, Brookdale Med. Ctr., Bklyn., 1960-61, Jersey City Med. Ctr., 1961-63; orthopaedic registrar Royal Postgrad. Med. Sch., Hammersmith Hosp., London, 1966-67, Heatherwood Orthopaedic Hosp., Ascot, Eng., 1967-68; research fellow Hosp. for Sick Children, U. Toronto, Ont., Can., 1968-69; practice medicine specializing in orthopedics Sault Ste. Marie, Ont.; past pres. med. staff, chmn. exec. com. Gen. Hosp., Sault Ste. Marie, Ont., chief dept. surgery, mem. adv. com., 1980-88, chief div. orthopaedic surgery, 1980—. Cons. orthopaedic surgeon Gen. Hosp. Plummer Meml. Hosp., Crippled Children Ctr., Ministry Nat. Health and Welfare, Dept. Vets. Adminstrn; civilian orthopaedic surgeon to 44th Div. Armed Forces Base Hosp., Kaduna, Nigeria, 1969. Trustee, Gen. Hosp., Sault Ste. Marie, 1975-76 Miss Betsy Burton Meml. fellow N.Y. U. Med. Ctr., 1963-64 Fellow ACS, Royal Coll. Surgeons Can., Royal Coll. Surgeons Edinburgh; mem. Am. Fracture Assn. (regional v.p. Can. chpt., bd. govs. 1991—), Can. Orthopaedic Assn., Can. Med. Assn., Ont. Orthopaedic Assn., N.Y. Acad. Sci. Home: 50 Alworth Pl Sault Sainte Marie ON Canada P6B 5W5 Office: 50 Alworth Pl Sault Sainte Marie ON Canada P6B 5W5

BANERJEE, SANJAY KUMAR, electrical engineer, director; b. Khartoum, Sudan, Feb. 24, 1958; came to U.S., 1979; s. Sunil Chandra and Anima (Mukherjee) B.; m. Jaba Chatterjee, June 18, 1983; children: Anupam, Anurag. B in Tech. with honors, Indian Inst. Tech., Kharagpur, 1979; MS, U. Ill., 1981, PhD, 1983. Rsch. asst. U. Ill., Urbana, 1979-83; mem. tech. staff Tex. Instruments, Dallas, 1983-87; asst. prof. elec. engring. U. Tex., Austin, 1987—90, assoc. prof., 1990—93, prof., 1993—, Cullen trust endowed prof. engring., 1997—2001, Cockrell chair prof., 1999—; dir. Microelectronics Rsch. Ctr., 1999—. Contbr. articles to profl. jours.; patentee in field. Recipient Inst. medal Indian Inst. Tech., 1979, Swapan Shaha prize, 1979. Recipient NSF Presdl. Young Investigator award, 1988, Halliburton award Engring. Found., 1991, Callinan award Electrochem. Soc., 2003; fellow Tex. Atomic Energy Centennial, 1993-97. Fellow IEEE (Millennium medal 2000, ECS Callinan award 2003); mem. Phi Kappa Phi. Hindu. Avocations: reading, exercising. Home: 1742 Canonero Dr Austin TX 78746-2111 Office: U Tex Dept Elec & Computer Engring MER 1 606B/R9900 Austin TX 78712 E-mail: banerjee@ece.utexas.edn.

BANERJEE, SUJIT, environmental scientist, educator; b. Calcutta, India, Jan. 5, 1950; s. Debidas and Sujata Banerjee; m. Anu Sengupta; children: Joya, Ronjon. BSc, Indian Inst. Tech., Kharagpur, 1969; PhD, Concordia U., Montreal, 1974. Sr. scientist Syracuse (N.Y.) Rsch. Corp., 1977—83; prof., sr. fellow Inst. Paper Sci. and Tech., Atlanta, 1989—; group leader Brookhaven Nat. Lab., Upton, NY. Author 2 books; contbr. more than 100 articles to profl. jours. Grantee 41 rsch. grants, 1977—. Mem.: ACS, TAPPI. Achievements include patents in field. Office: Inst Paper Sci and Tech 500 10th St NW Atlanta GA 30318 Office Fax: 404-894-4778. Business E-Mail: s.banerjee@ipst.edu.

BANERJEE, (BIMAL BANERJEE), artist, educator; b. Calcutta, India, Sept. 4, 1939; naturalized, 1978; s. Dashurathee and Madhabilata B. BA with hons., Indian Coll. Art, Calcutta, 1960; student, Coll. Art, New Delhi, 1965-67, Atelier 17, Paris, 1967-69, Ecole des Beaux-Arts, 1967-70, Pratt Inst., N.Y.C., 1969-72, NYU, 1976; EdM, Columbia U., 1981, EdD, 1988. Lectr. NAD, N.Y.C., 1969, Bloomfield (N.J.) Coll., 1980-81, Parsons Sch. Design/New Sch., N.Y.C, 1979, faculty, 1983-88; art therapist St. John's Episc. Hosp., Queens, N.Y., 1981-83; tchr., art cons. N.Y.C. Pub. Schs., 1984-2001; art tchr. Cath. High Sch., N.Y.C., 1987; lectr. Columbia U. Tchrs. Coll., N.Y.C., 1988-2001. Guest lectr. Tchrs. Coll., Columbia U., 1984. Multi-media performance artist shows include Parsons Sch. Design/New Sch., 1986, Columbia U., 1978, 79, 84, Hofstra U., 1979, Just Above Midtown Gallery, N.Y.C., 1977, 78, Bertha Urdang Gallery, N.Y.C., 1976, Fremar Gallery, L.I., N.Y., 1974, Galerie du Haut Pave, Paris, 1968-69, Mcpl. Galeria, Levanto, Italy, 1968, Kumar Gallery, New Delhi, 1970, Arts & Prints Gallery, Calcutta, 1963, 64, Art Heritage Gallery, New Delhi, 1990, Chitrakoot Gallery, Calcutta, 1990, Bertha Urdang Gallery, N.Y.C., 1991, Chemould Gallery, Calcutta, 1993, Cite Internationale des Arts, Paris, 1994, 99, numerous others; internat. biennials in Paris, Tokyo, Rejika, Miami, Hawaii, Bradford, Eng., Biella, Ibiza, Triennale-India, Berlin Triennale, Joan Miro Drawing prize, Barcelona, Ljubljana, others; exhibited in 38 one-man shows, U.S., Europe and India; introduced new media Fumage and Carbontransfer; represented in permanent collections Mus. Modern Art, Paris, Mus. Modern Art, Barcelona, Spain, Mus. Fine Arts, Boston, Mus. Art, Iowa City, Mus. Modern Art de la Ville de Paris, Mus. Internat. of Electrography Art, Cuenca, Spain, Ctr. National d'Art Contemporain, Paris, Ministry Cultural Affairs, France, Neil Saek Gallery, Johannesburg, South Africa, Nat. Gallery Modern Art, New Delhi, Nat. Acad. Art, New Delhi, Essex Libr., London, The Pallas Gallery, London, Bibliothèque Nat., Paris, Honolulu Acad. Art, Rockefeller Bros. Found., N.Y.C., N.Y. Pub. Libr. Art Collection, N.Y.C., Bklyn. Mus., others; represented in pub. collections Mus. Modern Art, Paris, Mus. Modern Art, Barcelona, Mus. Fine Arts, Boston, Mus. Art, Iowa City, Mus. Modern Art de la Ville de Paris, Mus. Internat. Electrography Art, Cuenca, Spain, Centre National d'Art Contemporain, Paris, Min. Cultural Affairs, France, Neil Sack Gallery, Johannesburg, Nat. Gallery Modern Art, New Delhi, Nat. Acad. Art, New Delhi, Essex Libr., London, Pallas Gallery, London, Bibliotechque Nationale, Paris, Honolulu Acad. Art, Rockefeller Bros. Fund, N.Y.C., N.Y. Pub. Libr., N.Y.C., Radford U. Mus., Va., Bklyn. Mus. Inst. Arts and Scis., Radford U. Mus., Bklyn. Mus., others; contbr. articles, poetry, short stories, children's lit. to profl. jours. Founder Bill Clinton Presdl. Found., Little Rock. Recipient awards Hawaii Biennial, 1971, 73, 79, Arthur Kaplan award, 1978, award Painters and Sculptors Soc., 1972, Culturelle Internat. award, Paris, 1968, Nat. award Nat. Art Acad., India, 1967, 70, State Acad. award Bengal State, and Punjab State, 1967, Statue of Victory world cultural prize Nat. Ctr. Study and Rsch., Salsomiggiore, Italy, 1984, also others; grantee Govt. of India, 1965-67, Govt. of France, 1967-70, Adolph and Esther Gottlieb Found., 1989; India Govt. nat. scholar, French Govt. scholar. Mem. Mus. Modern Art, Found. for Community of Artists of N.Y.C., Coll. Art Assn. of Am., Print Club Philadelphia, World Print Council, Smithsonian Instn., Ancient Art—Paris. Home: Loft 2C 106 Ridge St New York NY 10002-2554 Office: Bertha Urdang Gallery 23 E 74th St New York NY 10021-2617 Home Fax: 212-228-8247.

BANERJI, RANAN BIHARI, mathematics and computer science educator; b. Calcutta, India, May 5, 1928; came to U.S., 1961, naturalized, 1969; s. Bijan Bihari and Setabja (Chatterji) B.; m. Purnima Purkayastha, July 8, 1954; children: Anindita Banerji Spielberg, Sunandita Banerji Ogawa. BS, Patna U., 1947; MS, Calcutta U., 1949, DPhil, 1956. Rsch. scholar Calcutta U., 1950-53, lectr., 1956; vis. asst. prof. Pa. State U., 1953-55; maintenance engr. Indian Statis. Inst., 1956-58; faculty Case Western Res. U., 1958-74, prof. computer sci., 1968-74, Temple U., Phila., 1974-82; prof. math. and computer sci. St. Joseph's U., Phila., 1983-92, prof. emeritus, 1993—. Vis. prof. U. Paris, U. Vienna, U. Calcutta, Czech Tech. U.; asst. prof. engring. U. N.B., Can., 1959-61; cons. in field. Author: Theory of Problem Solving, 1969, Artificial Intelligence, 1980; (with M. Mesarovic) Non-numerical Problem Solving, 1969; (with A. Elithorn) Artificial and Human Intelligence, 1986, Formal Techniques in Artificial Intelligence, 1989;assoc. editor Elsevier Sci. Pubs., Amsterdam; reviewer computing, mathematics reviews; contbr. articles to profl. jours. Gold medalist univs. Patna and Calcutta. Fellow Am. Assn. Artificial Intelligence; mem. ACLU, Common Cause, Sci. within Consciousnes, Computer Profls. for Social Responsibility. Hindu Quaker. Home: 7 Macarthur Blvd Apt N409 Westmont NJ 08108-3648 Office: St Joseph's U Dept Math and Computer Sci 5600 City Ave Philadelphia PA 19131-1308 E-mail: rbanerji@sju.edu. *It is my belief that the only successful actions by men and women are those done in selfless service to God. The rest, however laudable, are risky at best.*

BANET, CHARLES HENRY, academic administrator, clergyman; b. Ft. Wayne, Ind., Dec. 8, 1922; s. Henry Alexander and Cecilia Marie (Henry) B. Student, St. Charles Sem., 1949; BA, St. Joseph's Coll., 1950, LLD (hon.), 1991; AMLS, U. Mich., 1951; LittD (hon.), Calumet Coll. of St. Joseph, 1970; LLD (hon.), St. Joseph's Coll., 1991. Joined Soc. of Precious Blood, 1943; ordained priest Roman Cath. Ch., 1949. Librarian St. Joseph's Coll., Rensselaer, Ind., 1952-65, exec. v.p., 1964-65, pres., 1965-93, pres. emeritus, 1993—, also bd. dirs.; parochial vicar Holy Rosary Ch., Galveston, Tex., 1994—. Vice provincial Soc. Precious Blood, 1965-69. Assoc. editor: Philosophy Today, 1957-88; author: Our Lady of Precious Blood in Art, 1961. Bd. dirs. Ind. Colls. Ind. Found., sec.-treas., 1973, pres. 1980-82, exec. com.; bd. dirs. Ind. Colls. Ind., pres. 1975-76, 77-78; pres. Ind. Conf. Higher Edn., 1978-79; dist. chair Boy Scouts of Am., 1981; Ind. Bicentennial Commr., 1973-79. Recipient Sparks-Jones award, 1977; named Sagamore of the Wabash, 1979, 85, 93, Ky. Col., 1985. Mem. Ind. Acad., Blue Key, Phi Beta Kappa, Beta Phi Mu, Alpha Lambda Delta. Home: Holy Rosary Church 1420 31st St Galveston TX 77550-4321

BANEVER, THOMAS CLARK, surgeon, educator; b. Bridgeport, Conn., Dec. 21, 1945; s. Marshall and Elizabeth (Clark) B.; m. Jennifer Burke, June 29, 1969; children: Gregory, Andrew, Seth, Sarah Kate, Abigail, Matthew, Emily, Rebecca, Nadia Marie, Nicholas. BA in Chemistry, Yale U., 1968; MD, Tufts U., 1972. Diplomate Am. Bd. Surgery. Intern. New Haven Hosp, 1972-73; resident in surgery U. Conn., Farmington, 1974-75, Hartford (Conn.) Hosp., 1976-78; pvt. practice, Hartford, 1978—; asst. clin. prof. surgery primary dept. U. Conn. Med. Sch., Farmington, 1990—, asst. clin. prof. dept. emergency medicine and trauma, 1999—. Bd. dirs. Cmty. Health Svcs., Hartford, 1980-97. Finalist Am. Assoc. Med. Schs. Humanism & Medicine award, Am. Assoc. Med. Coll., 2001. Fellow ACS; mem. AMA, Conn. State Med. Soc., Hartford County Med. Assn. (Cmty. Svc. award 1992), Soc. Critical Care Medicine, Ea. Assn. Surg. Trauma, Physicians for Social Responsibility, Soc. Lapoendoscopic Surgery. Home: 31 Main St Farmington CT 06032-2229 Office: 100 Retreat Ave Ste 808 Hartford CT 06106-2569 Fax: 860-249-9180. E-mail: tbanever@pol.net.

BANEY, RICHARD NEIL, physician, internist; b. Phila., Apr. 13, 1937; s. Robert Emmet and Mary Elizabeth (Hedges) B.; m. Carolyn Vern Kurey, Feb. 17, 1962; children: Richard N. Jr., Michael D., Marisa V., Brian E. BS, Georgetown U., 1958; MD, U. Pitts., 1963. Diplomate Am. Bd. Internal Medicine, Am. Bd. Rheumatology. Intern VA & Parkland Hosp., Dallas, 1963-64; resident U. Pitts., 1967-70; internist Jess Parrish Hosp., Titusville, Fla., 1971-76, chief med. staff, 1974-76; internist Melbourne (Fla.) Internal Med. Assocs., Holmes Regional Med Ctr., 1976-95; sr. v.p. med. affairs Holmes Regional Med. Ctr., Melbourne, Fla., 1995-96; CEO Health First Physicians, 1995-98; ret., 1998; med. officer M.S. Endeavor, 1999—. Trustee Holmes Regional Med. Ctr., Melbourne, 1984-95; founding dir., chmn. bd. dirs. Reliance Bank Fla., Melbourne, 1985-95; founding dir., chmn. bd. Bank Brevard, 1996—. Trustee Fla. Inst. Tech., Melbourne, 1985—, mem. exec. com., 1987—, vice chmn. bd. trustees, 1991—2002; pres. Canaveral chpt. Am. Heart Assn., Rockledge, Fla., 1973—74; chmn. bd. trustees Sea Pines Rehab. Hosp., Melbourne, 1992—94. Fellow ACP; mem. Am. Coll. Rheumatology, Am. Coll. Physicians Execs., Brevard County Med. Soc. (pres. 1977-78), Navy League U.S., Eau Gallie Yacht Club (commodore 1985-86), Coast Club (bd. dirs. 1985-91, chmn. bd. 1989-91). Republican. Avocations: jogging, bicycling, travel, collecting antique maps, golf. E-mail: RNBaney@aol.com.

BANG, JENS, communications company executive; Dir. mktg. The Timberland Co., 1980-82; former sr. level mgr. various companies, including Reebok Internat., The Rockport Co.; pres., COO Cone Comms., Inc., Boston, 1999—. Office: Cone Inc 90 Canal St Boston MA 02114-2018

BANG, KI MOON, epidemiologist, educator; b. Korea, Oct. 2, 1940; came to U.S., 1972; m. Hanok Kim Bang, May 30, 1969; children: Sam, David. MPH in Epidemiology, Seoul Nat. U., 1966; MS in Biostats., U. Minn., 1974; PhD in Epidemiology, U. Tex. Med. Br., Galveston, 1981. Chief rsch. and stats. divsn.

Nat. Inst. Tuberculosis, Seoul, 1966-72; prof. Howard U., Washington, 1985-88; chief surveillance Nat. Inst. for Occup. Safety and Health, Ctrs. Disease Ctl. and Prevention, Morgantown, W.Va., 1993—. Adj. prof. W.Va. U. Sch. Medicine, Morgantown, 1993—. Author, editor: Occupational Epidemiology, 1997; contbr. chpts. to textbooks, papers and articles to profl. jours. Mem. Coun. Korea Peaceful Unification in N.Y., 1999. Fellow Am. Coll. Epidemiology; mem. APHA, Soc. for Epidemiologic Rsch. Presbyterian. Home: 1007 Brettwald Dr Morgantown WV 26508-9413 Office: Nat Inst Occupl Safety and Health CDC 1095 Willowdale Rd Morgantown WV 26505-2845 E-mail: kmb2@cdc.gov.

BANG, MARY JO, poet; b. Oct. 22, 1946; BA in Sociology, Northwestern U., Evanston, Ill., 1971, MA, 1975; BA in Photography, Westminster U., London, 1989; MFA, Columbia U., 1998. Asst. prof. English Washington U., St. Louis, 1999—2003, assoc. prof. English, 2003—. Poetry co-editor Boston Rev., 1995—; author (books of poetry) Apology for Want, 1997, Louise in Love, 2001, The Downstream Extremity of the Isle of Swans, 2001; contbr. poetry to lit. publs. Recipient Bakeless prize Bread Loaf Writers' Conf., 1996, New Writers award Gt. Lakes Colls. Assn., 1998, Hodder fellowship, Princeton U., 1999, Alice Fay di Castagnola award Poetry Soc. Am., 2000, Puschart Prize, 2002. Office: Washington U Dept English Box 1122 One Brookings Dr Saint Louis MO 63130

BANGASSER, RONALD PAUL, physician; b. Freeport, Ill., Jan. 25, 1950; s. Paul Francis and Florence (Ihm) B.; m. Susan Marie Andretta, June 19, 1971; children: Debra, Sandi. BA, Northwestern U., Chgo., 1971; MD, Chgo. Med. Sch., 1975. Physician Valley Family Med., Yucaipa, Calif., 1978-93, Beaver Med. Group, Redlands, 1993—. Med. dir. San Bernardino Found. for Med. Care, 1984-89, Redlands Med. Group, Redlands, Calif., 1986-92, Calif. Found. for Med. Care, San Francisco, 1991-94, Beaver Med., Redlands, 1997-2001; legis. com. CMA, 1991-95, 2000—, LOPAC, San Bernardino, 1992—, legis. affairs commn. Calif. Acad. Family Practice, 1994—; bd. dirs. CAL PAC. Bd. dirs. Blue Shield of Calif., 1998—. Mem. AMA (Calif. del. chair 1995-99), Calif. Med. Assn. (bd. dirs. 1995—, vice spkr. 1999-2001, exec. com. 1999—, spkr. 2001-03, pres.-elect 2002-03, pres. 2003—). Republican. Roman Catholic. Avocations: scuba diving, skiing, swimming, hiking. Home: 12724 Valley View Ln Redlands CA 92373-7632 Office: Beaver Med Group 242 Cajon St Redlands CA 92373-5202 E-mail: rbangass@epiclp.com.

BANGS, CATE (CATHRYN MARGARET BANGS), film production designer, interior designer; b. Tacoma, Mar. 16, 1951; d. Henry Horan and Belva Virginia (Grandstaff) B.; m. Steve Gobin, Nov. 1, 1986 (div. 2002). Student, Hammersmith Coll Art and Bldg., London, 1971; BA cum laude, Pitzer Coll., 1973; MFA, NYU, 1978. Owner Flying Pencil Design, L.A., 1981—. Prodn. designer: Lucky Day, 1990; (TV series) My So Called Life, 1994, Fudge-A-Mania, 1994; set designer: (TV series) Picket Fences, 1995-96, (film) Home Alone 3, 1997, Midnight in the Garden of Good and Evil, 1997; art dir.: (film) Volcano, 1997, (TV) The Notorious, 1997, Nothing Sacred, 1997-98 (Emmy and SMPTAD nomination 1998), Charmed, 1998-99, Level 9, 2000, The Huntress, 2000-2001, (film) The Fighting Temptations, 2002. 1st v.p. Friends of the Highland-Camrose Bungalow Village, 1985—97; bd. dirs. Ctr. Film and TV Design, 2002—, Hollywood Heights Assn., 1985—87, Cahuenga Pass Property Owners Assn., 1990. Recipient Dramalogue Critics award, 1983. Mem. Art Dirs. Guild (cert.; exec. bd. 1997-99, 2000—), Set Designers and Model Makers (cert., exec. bd. 1980—, v.p. 1989-91, pres. 1991-99), United Scenic Artists. Democrat. Buddhist. Home: 7754 Denivelle Rd Tujunga CA 91042-1115

BANGS, F(RANK) KENDRICK, former business educator; b. Lostant, Ill., May 17, 1914; s. Mark Howard and Mary Hay (Henning) B.; m. Elizabeth Jane Paisley, May 19, 1944; children— John Kendrick, James Paisley. B.E., Ill. State Normal U., 1936; M.P.S., U. Colo., 1946; Ed.D., Ind. U., 1952. Tchr. bus. Rosiclare (Ill.) High Sch., 1936-37, Carmi (Ill.) High Sch., 1937-42; asst. prof. bus. adminstrn. U. Colo., Boulder, 1946-58, assoc. prof., 1958-64, prof., 1964-81, chmn. gen. bus. div., 1964-79; vis. prof. Coll. Bus., Ill. State U., Normal, 1979-80, 84, U. Tex-Austin, 1982, Southwestern La U., Lafayette, 1983, 85, 86, 87, U. Colo., 1987-88. Cons. adminstrv. mgmt., small bus. Chmn. fin. stability bd. Colo. Pvt. Schs. Assn., 1977— Contbr.: articles to Jour. Bus. Edn. Served with inf. U.S. Army, 1942-46. Decorated Bronze Star; recipient Robert L. Stearns award U. Colo. Alumni, 1976; John Robert Gregg award Gregg div. McGraw-Hill Pub. Co., 1978 Mem. Mountain-Plains Bus. Edn. Assn. (pres. 1958-59, Leadership award 1967-68), Nat. Bus. Edn. Assn. (co-editor yearbook 1975, nat. pres. 1967-68), Adminstrv. Mgmt. Soc. (pres. Denver chpt. 1963-64, Diamond Merit award 1967), Colo. Bus. Edn. Assn. (pres. 1956-57), Beta Gamma Sigma, Delta Pi Epsilon (nat. pres. 1968-69, pres. Research Found. 1979—) Clubs: Rotary (Boulder). Presbyterian. Home: 4840 Thunderbird Dr Apt 188 Boulder CO 80303-3829

BANGS, WILL JOHNSTON, lawyer; b. N.Y.C., Oct. 7, 1923; s. Lawrence Cutler and Alma Elizabeth (Johnston) B.; m. Judith Esther Lindhal, July 27, 1957; children: Marjorie Elizabeth, Martha Ellen Alice. BA, Middlebury Coll., 1948; LLB, U. Mich., 1953. Bar: Mass. 1953, U.S. Dist. Ct. (Mass. dist.) 1955, U.S. Supreme Ct. 1973. Staff atty. Liberty-Mut. Ins. Co., Boston, 1953-56; sr. ptnr. Choate, Hall & Stewart, Boston, 1956—. Mem. fin. com., Concord, Mass., 1968-70; mem. Carlisle (Mass.) Conservation Commn., 1972-78, Carlisle Town Rep. Com., 1982-89. With U.S. Army, 1943-46. Fellow Am. Coll. Trial Lawyers; mem. ABA, Boston Bar Assn., Somerset Club, Concord Country Club. Home: 119 Bingham Rd Carlisle MA 01741-1537 Office: Exchange Pl 53 State St Boston MA 02109-2804

BANGSUND, EDWARD LEE, former aerospace company executive, consultant; b. Two Harbors, Minn, July 16, 1935; s. Ilo Henry and Hildur Margaret (Holter) B.; m. Caryl Ann Billingsley, Oct. 10, 1956; children: Julie Ann, Trina Lee, John Kirk, Edward Eric. BME, U. Wash., 1959. With Boeing Co., Cape Kennedy, Fla., 1956-71, engr. Apollo program, 1967-69, Houston, 1969-71; mgr. space vehicle design Space Systems div. Boeing Aerospace, Seattle, 1971-76, mgr. Inertial Upper Stage Futures, 1976-85, mgr. space transp., 1985-87, dir. strategic planning, 1987-90, dir. space mktg., 1990-95; pres., CEO BCA Enterprises, 1995—. Cons. engring. Orbital Techs. Corp., 1995—. Contbr. articles to profl. publs.; patentee in field. Pres. Springbrook Parents Adv. Com., 1972-75; chmn. Citizens Budget Rev. Com., 1973-75, 76-78, Citizens Facility Planning Com., 1977-78, Citizens for Kent (Wash.) Schs. Levy, 1974, 76; bd. dirs. Kent Youth Ctr., 1980-83; pres. Kent Sch. Bd., 1978-84. Named to Apollo-Saturn Roll of Honor, NASA, 1969; recipient Golden Acorn award Wash. Congress PTA, 1977, Vol. of Yr. award Kent Sch. Dist., 1977-78. Fellow AIAA (assoc., mem. space systems tech. com. 1985-87, dep. dir. region VI 1986-89, chmn. space transp. tech. com. 1987-90, pub. policy com. 1989-94); mem. Internat. Acad. Astronautics, Internat. Astronautical Fedn. (chmn. space transp. exec. com. 1991-94), Nat. Space Found., Aerospace Industries Assn. (mem. space com. 1987-94, chmn. 1990-94), Space Bus. Roundtable (pres. Seattle chpt., bd. dir. 1988-95), Boeing Mgmt. Assn. (vice chmn. 1990-91, chmn. 1993-94), pres.- Palm Valley Country Club 2003-, inducted WShS Hall of Fame, 2003 Republican. Lutheran. Home and Office: 13611 SE 251st St Kent WA 98042-6631

BANIAK, SHEILA MARY, accountant, educator; b. Chgo., Feb. 26, 1953; d. DeLoy N. and Ann (Pasko) Slade; m. Mark A. Baniak, Oct. 7, 1972 (div. Feb. 1994); 1 child, Heather Ann. Assocs. in Acctg., Oakton Community Coll., 1986; student, Roosevelt U., 1986—; MBA, North Park Coll., Chgo., 1995; Cert. in Human Resources, North Park U., Chgo., 2001. Cert. enrolled agt. IRS; accredited tax adviser Accreditation Coun. Accountancy and Taxation. Owner, mgr. Baniak and Assocs., Chgo., 1984—; acct. Otto & Snyder, Park Ridge, 1984-87; spl. projects coordinator, supplemental instr. Oakton Community Coll., Des Plaines, Ill., 1986—, acctg. computer instr., 1987—; acctg. and credit mgr. Fragomen, Delrey, Bernsen & Loewy P.C., 1996—, fin. and human resources mgr., 1999—. Adm. mem. acctg. Oakton C.C., Des Plaines, 1986—, cons., mem. Edn. Found., 1986—; instr. Ray Coll. Design, 1987—, dir. evening sch., 1994, fin. aid officer, Chgo. and Woodfield, 1994; mem. rsch. bd. advisors Am. Biog. Inst., Inc., 1988; tchr. fin. mgmt., retail math., bus. math., bus. computers, strategic retail mgmt. and econs.; part-time coll. instr. commerce dept. Northwestern Bus. Coll., 1995—; asst. to interim fin. dir. Art Inst. Ill., 1995-96. Author: A Small Business Collection Cycle Primer for Accountants, 1985, The Mathematics of Business, 1989. Ill. CPA Soc. scholar, 1984, Roosevelt U. scholar, 1986, Nat. Assn. Accts. scholar, 1985. Mem. Nat. Assn. Accts. (dir. community responsibility suburban Chgo. chpt. 1986—, speaker 1988, dir. profl. devel. seminars 1988, dir. communications 1989—), Nat. Assn. Tax Practitioners, Nat. Assn. Enrolled Agts., Ill. Soc. Enrolled Agts. (pres.; pres. N.W. Chgo. chpt. 1992, chmn. edn. 1990—). Home: 5718 W Cullom Ave Chicago IL 60634-1718

BANICH, FRANCIS EDWARD, surgeon; b. Chgo., Aug. 30, 1932; BS, Loyola U., 1953, MD, 1957. Diplomate Am. Bd. Surgery. Intern Cook County Hosp., Chgo., 1957-58, resident in surgery, 1958-63; attending surgeon Elmhurst (Ill.) Meml. Hosp., Good Samaritan Hosp., Downers Grove, Ill., 1970; clin. assoc. prof. surgery Stritch Sch. Medicine-Loyola Med. Ctr., 1985—. Mem. Am. Coll. Surgeons, Soc. Surgery Alimentary Tract. Office: 340 W Butterfield Rd Ste 1D Elmhurst IL 60126-5047 E-mail: FEBI@aol.com.

BANICK, CHERYL R. librarian; b. St. Johnsbury, Vt., Oct. 21, 1956; d. Joseph T. and Adeline Shelley Banick. AS in Computer Sci., C.C. of R.I., Warwick, 1984; BS in Bus. Adminstrn., U. R.I., 1986, M in Libr. Info. Studies, 1993. Med. libr. VA Med. Ctr., Providence, 1989—. Mem. adv. com. U. R.I. Grad. Sch. Libr. and Info. Studies, 2002—; severe weather spotter Nat. Weather Svc., 2002—. Author (written for Mrs. Tipper Gore): Resources in Mental HeaLth (White House Conf. on Mental Illness), 1999; contbr. (chpt.): Scientific and Clinical Literature for theDecade of the Brain, 1993, contbr. articles to profl. jours., contbr. essay: What the OCLC Interlibrary Loan Service Means to Me, 1999, contbr. bibliography resources listing Core Pub. Health Jours. Project, 2003, book reviewer. Recipient Gold Std. Search award, Nat. Libr. of Medicine, 1998. Mem.: Spl. Librs. Assn. (R.I. chpt. chair pub. rels. 1996—99, chair networking com. R.I. chpt. 1999—2001, pres. 2001—02, co-chair networking com., webmaster R.I. chpt. 2002—, pres. R.I. chpt. 2001—02). Avocations: christian chorale singing, writing, photography. Home: 27 Cedar Pond Dr Apt 9 Warwick RI 02886-0854

BANIK, SAMBHU NATH, psychologist; b. Joypara, India, Nov. 7, 1935; s. Padma L. and Kadambini B.; m. Promila Roy, Nov. 16, 1968; children: Sharmila, Kakali. BSc, Calcutta U., 1956, MSc, 1958; PhD, Bristol U., 1964. Staff psychologist Des Moines Child Guidance Ctr., 1965; sr. psychologist, dir. internship tng. Univ. Hosp., Saskatoon, Sask., Can., 1965-69, dir. psychol. svcs., 1969-71; asst. chief mental health svcs. Glenn Dale Hosp. and D.C. Village, 1971-81; chief South Cmty. Mental Health Ctr., Washington, 1981-84, chief child and youth svcs., 1984-88; clin. adminstr. NE/SE Family Ctr., Washington, 1988—. Pres. Family Diagnostic and Therapeutic Ctr., Washington, 1993—; exec. dir. Pres.'s Com. on Mental Retardation HHS, Washington, 1990-93, cons. psychologist, 1993—; pres. Banik and Assocs. Family Diagnostic and Therapeutic Ctr., 1993—; v.p. devel., chmn. Third World Found., 1993—; asst. prof. U. Sask., 1965-71; vis. prof. Bowie State Coll. (Md.), 1972-81, prof. psychology, 1993—; vis. prof. Thakur Hariprasad Inst., India, 1994. Contbr. articles to profj. jours. Mem. nat. adv. coun. drug abuse, 1987-90; mem. adv. bd. ARC, Washington, 1987-90; founder, pres. Prabashi, Inc., 1974-78, Assn. Indians in Am., 1980-84; pres. E.S.-Asia Found., 1995—; v.p. India Cultural Coordinating Com., 1979-80, Indian Am. Forum for Polit. Edn., 2000; sec. gen. Asian Pacific Am. Cultural Heritage Coun., 1981-82; treas. Asian Pacific Am. Heritage Coun., 1982-84; mem. spl. com. 3d Conv. Asian Indians in N.Am., 1984, chmn. Indian Am. Forum Polit. Edn., Md., 1986-88, 94—; chmn. Third World Found., 1993—; adv. bd. Ednl. India Found., Inc., 1993—, Commonwealth Assn. for the Mentally Handicapped and Developmental Dis., 1992—, Md. com. on diversity, 2000; chmn. Internat. Cooperation and Coordinating Com. 11th World Congress on Mental Retardation, 1993-94; bd. trustees Woodley House, Washington; pub. mem. Svc., Personel, Rev. Bd., Washington, 1996; commr. Commn. People with Disabilities, Montgomery County. Recipient Dept. Humanitarian Svcs. award D.C., 1986; Cmty. Svc. award U.S. Asia Found., 1995, Disting. Profl. Svcs. award Ariz. Brain Injury Assn., 1999, Mother Teresa Internat. Millennium award, 2002. Mem. APA, Am. Group Psychotherapy Assn., D.C. Psychol. Assn., Intenrat. Acad. Forensic Psychology, Nat. Health Svcs. Providers in Psychology. Home: 8606 Bradmoor Dr Bethesda MD 20817-3633 E-mail: sbanik@erols.com.

BANIKAZEMI, MOHAMMAD, computer scientist, researcher; MS in Elec. Engring., Ohio State U., 1994—96, PhD in Computer Sci., 1996—2000. Grad. rsch., tchg. assoc. Ohio State U., 1994—2000; rsch. staff mem. IBM Thomas J. Watson Rsch. Ctr., Hawthorne, NY, 2000—. Author pub., presented several rsch. papers in profl. jours. Grantee Presdl. Fellowship, Ohio State U., 2000. Mem.: Assn. for Computing Machinery (ACM), IEEE, Phi Kappa Phi Honor Soc., Upsilon Pi Epsilon Computer Sciences Honor Soc. Achievements include patents pending for Compressed IO with MXT. Office: IBM Thomas J Watson Research Center 19 Skyline Dr Hawthorne NY 10532

BANINO, CHRISTOPHER C. information technology administrator; b. N.Y.C., Aug. 28, 1969; s. Charles G. and Amelia M. Banino; m. Mary Louise Garde. BA, Fordham U., 1993. Asst. supr. Value Line, Inc., N.Y.C., 1993-94, corp. analyst, 1994-97, corp. database adminstr., 1997-98, dir. database adminstrn., 1998-99; dir. info. tech. N.Y. Stock Exch., N.Y.C., 1999—. Mem. Ardsley Country Club, Ardsley Curling Club. Republican. Roman Catholic. Avocations: golf, skiing. Home: PO Box 119 Ardsley On Hudson NY 10503-0119 Office: NY Stock Exch 11 Wall St Fl 17 New York NY 10005-1974

BANIS, ROBERT JOSEPH, pharmaceutical company executive, educator, publisher; b. N.Y.C., Oct. 26, 1943; s. Vincent Nicholas and Roberta Irma (Shwedo) B.; m. Lois Elaine Polson, Jan. 25, 1970 (dec. Sept. 30, 2002); children: Andrea Berit, Lauren Nicole. BS in Sci. Edn., Cornell U., 1967; MS in Animal Nutrition, Purdue U., 1969; PhD in Biochemistry, N.C. State U., 1973; MBA in Mktg. and Fin. with honors, U. Chgo., 1982. Cert. mgmt. acct. NIH postdoctoral fellow Harvard U., Cambridge, Mass., 1973-75; sr. rsch. scientist Armour Pharm. Co., Kankakee, Ill., 1975-79, tech. mgr. biochems. and parenterals, 1979-81, mgr. biochem. and pharm. devel., 1981-83; rsch. group leader health care div. Monsanto Co., St. Louis, 1983-85, mgr. rsch. ops. and fin. planning, 1985-86, mgr. rsch. ops. and fin. planning, Searle R&D Div., 1986-88, dir. ops. and fin., 1988-94; pres. 21st Century Stewardship Inc., St. Louis, 1994-2000; prin. Banis & Assocs., St. Louis, from 1994; mem. adj. faculty Vincennes U., St. Louis, 1994, Webster U., St. Louis, 1995; instr. St. Louis C.C., St. Louis, from 1994. Adj. asst. bus. prof. U. Mo., St. Louis, 1987-92, adj. assoc. prof., full-time lectr., 1992—; founder Sci. & Humanities Press, St. Louis, 1995, prin., pub., CEO, 1995—. Contbg. author: COMPUTE!'s Second Book of VIC, 1983, The Science of Meat and Meat Products, 3d edit., 1987; editor: Copyright Issues for Teachers and Authors, 1997, Sexually Transmitted Diseases, A Practical Guide, 1997, 2d edit., 2003, Inaugural Addresses--Presidents of the U.S. from George Washington to 2004, 1998, Copyright Issues for Librarians, Tchrs. and Authors, 1998; : 2d edit., 2001. Co-chmn. Searle-St. Louis divsn. United Way campaign, 1988-89, chmn., 1989-90, allocations panel vol. Greater St. Louis area, 1991-95, loaned exec. fundraisers, 1993, torchlight spkr., 1993-94; vol. St. John's Mercy Med. Ctr., 1992-98; pres., chmn. bd. Burns Recovered Support Group, Inc., 1993-96; mgmt. cons. United Way Mgmt. Assistance Ctr., 1994—; regional coord. The Phoenix Soc., 1993; gen. chmn. World Burn Congress VII, 1995. Recipient Vol. of Yr. award Trinity Luth. Ch., 1991, United Way Star Communicator award, 1993, 94. Mem. AAAS, Am. Chem. Soc., Inst. Mgmt. Accts. (St. Louis chpt. dir. civic activities, assoc. dir. CMA rev. course 1993-95), Inst. for Ops. Rsch. and Mgmt. Scis. (sec. Gateway chpt. 1993-94, v.p./pres.-elect 1994-95, pres. 1995-96), Am. Burn Assn., St. Louis Pub. Assn. (v.p. 1999), Phi Lambda Upsilon, Beta Gamma Sigma. Home: Manchester, Mo. Deceased.

BANISTER, JUDITH, demographer, educator; b. Washington, Sept. 10, 1943; d. William Price and Helen Barbara (Myers) B.; m. Kim Woodard, Dec. 17, 1966; children: Adrian Banard, Dawn Banard. BA in History, Swarthmore Coll., 1965; PhD in Demography, Stanford U., 1978. Postdoctoral rsch. fellow East-West Population Inst., Honolulu, 1978-80; statistician/demographer U.S. Bur. of Census, Washington, 1980-82; chief China br. Ctr. for Internat. Rsch., 1982-92, chief, 1992-94; chief Internat. Programs Ctr., 1994—97; part-time prof. George Washington U., Washington, 1981-92; prof. demography divsn. social sci. Hong Kong U. Sci. and Tech., 1997—2001. Sr. cons. Beijing Javelin Investment Consulting Co., 2001—; hon. prof. Social Sci. Rsch. Ctr., Hong Kong U., 2002—. Author: China's Changing Population, 1987, Vietnam Population Dynamics and Prospects, 1993; co-author: The Population of North Korea, 1992, Human Dimensions of Asian Security, 1996; contbr. articles to profl. jours. Mem.: Am. C. of C. Beijing, Assn. Asian Studies, Internat. Union for Sci. Study of Population, Population Assn. Am. Office: Beijing Javelin Investment Cons Co Guan Cheng Yuan (Citichamp Place) Building 16 Ste 21-A Madian, Haidian District Beijing 100088 China Fax: (8610) 6235 5459. E-mail: banister@163bj.com.

BANJOKO, ALIMI AJIMON, financial planner; b. Mona, St. Andrew, Jamaica, Nov. 11, 1954; arrived in U.S., 1980; s. Alton Alex and Martha Naomi (Needham) Harvey; m. Garnett Marlene St. Clair, Jan. 19, 1980; children: Che Lafianu, Pryha Krist-Loyé, Mikal Alaiye. BA honors, U. W.I., 1978; MA, Bklyn. Coll., 1992; LLB honor, U. Wolverhampton, 1999. Cert. CFP, registered investment advisor. Adminstrv. officer Ministry of Fgn. Affairs, Kingston, Jamaica, 1979; account exec., registered rep. John Hancock Cos., Boston, 1981-83; pres. PFS Group Inc., Bklyn., 1983—. Author: The Theory of Organic Capital Formation, 1996; co-prodr.(video): The Way to Wealth, 1999. Chmn. Capital Investment Plan First Ch. of God, Far Rockaway, 1986—90, trustee, 1985—87; mem. Allen AME, Jamaica, NY, 1990—; co-founder Lignum Vitae Soc., 1992—. Mem.: Inst. Cert. Fin. Planners, N.Y. CAP. Avocations: swimming, walking, flying, internat. politics. Office: The Organic Capital Group Inc 5306 Church Ave Brooklyn NY 11203-3609 E-mail: abanjoko@organiccapital.com., abanjoko@aol.com.

BANK, BARBARA J. sociology educator; b. Chgo., Dec. 13, 1939; d. Julius Charles and Anna Catherine (Damm) Bank; m. Bruce Jesse Biddle, June 19, 1976. BS in Edn., Ill. State U., Normal, 1961; MA, U. Iowa, 1968, PhD in Sociology, 1974. Tchr. Rich Twp. H.S., Park Forest, Ill., 1961-63; from instr. to prof. U. Mo., Columbia, 1969—, dir. grad. studies dept. sociology, 1978-82, chair dept. sociology, 1981-84. Vis. fellow Australian Nat. U., Canberra, 1984-85, 88, 93. Author: Contradictions in Women's Education, 2003; co-editor: Gender, Equity, and Schooling: Policy and Practice, 1997; assoc. editor Social Psychology of Edn., 1994-2000; contbr. articles to profl. jours.; presenter in field. Recipient Purple Chalk Tchg. award Coll. Arts and Scis., U. Mo., 1998; Fulbright sr. scholar, 1985; William T. Kemper fellow Excellence in Teaching, 2000. Mem. profl. orgns. Avocations: travel, reading. Home: 924 Yale Columbia MO 65203-1874 Office: U Mo Dept Sociology Columbia MO 65211-0001 E-mail: bankb@missouri.edu.

BANKER, GILBERT STEPHEN, industrial and physical pharmacy educator, administrator; b. Tuxedo Park, N.Y., Sept. 12, 1931; s. Gilbert Miller and Mary Edna (Gladstone) B.; m. Gwenivere May Hughes, Mar. 31, 1956; children: Stephen, Susan, David, William. BS in Pharmacy, Union Coll., Albany, N.Y., 1953; MS, Purdue U., 1955, PhD, 1957; DSc (hon.), Purdue Univ., 2003. Research found. fellow Purdue U., West Lafayette, Ind., 1955-57, asst. prof. pharmacy, 1957-61, assoc. prof., 1961-64, prof., 1964-67, head indsl. and phys. pharmacy dept., from 1967; dean, prof. pharmacy U. Minn., Mpls., 1985-92; dean emeritus, disting. prof. drug delivery U. Iowa, Iowa City, 1992. In coop. tng. program Upjohn Co., Kalamazoo, 1958. Editor: Modern Pharmaceutics, 1970, 90, Pharmaceuticals and Pharmacy Practice, 1980, Pharmaceutical Dosage Forms: Dispense Systems, 1988, 2d edit., 1994; contbr. articles to profl. jours.; patentee in field. Recipient Outstanding Alumnus of Yr. award Albany Coll. Pharmacy-Union U., 1977, Disting. Alumni award Sch. Pharmacy and Pharmacal Scis. Purdue U., 1989. Fellow Acad. Pharm. Scis. (v.p. 1971-72), Am. Pharm. Assn. (Indsl. Pharmacy award 1971, ho. dels. 1977-80), Am. Assn. Advancement of Scis., Am. Assn. Pharm. Scis. (chair 1993-94); mem. Sigma Xi (pres. Purdue chpt. 1971-72), Rho Chi. Office: Univ of Iowa Coll of Pharmacy Iowa City IA 52242 E-mail: gilgwenb@aol.com., gilbert-banker@uiowa.edu.

BANKERS, JAMES, military officer; BS in Psychology, ND State U., 1968; postgrad., Air Command and Staff Coll., 1982, Air War Coll. Commd. USAF, 1968, advanced through grades to maj. gen., 2001; student undergrad. pilot tng. Sheppard AFB, Tex., 1968—69; squadron pilot 604th Spl. Ops. Squadron, Bien Hoa Air Base, Vietnam, 1969—70; tng. officer 603d Spl. Ops. Squadron, Hurlburt Field, Fla., 1970—71; instr. pilot 426th Spl. Ops. Squadron, England AFB, La., 1971—72, 917th Spl. Ops. Squadron, Barksdale AFB, La., 1972—77; wing tactics officer 434th Tactical Fighter Wing, Grissom AFB, Ind., 1977—80; wing safety officer, squadron ops. officer, dir. 459th Tactical Airlift Wing, Andrews AFB, Md., 1980—84; wing dep. comdr. for ops. 459th Mil. Airlift Wing, Andrews AFB, Md., 1984—87; comdr. 910th Tactical Airlift Group, Youngstown Air Res. Base, Ohio, 1987—92, 315th Airlift Wing, Charleston AFB, SC, 1992—97, 439th Airlift Wing, Westover Air Res. Base, Mass., 1997—99; asst. vice comdr. Hdqrs. AF Res. Command, Robins AFB, Ga., 1999—2000; comdr. 22d AF AF Res. Command, Dobbins Air Res. Base, Ga., 2000—. Decorated Legion of Merit, DFC, Air medal with 9 oak leaf clusters. Office: AF Res Command 401 Atlantic Ave SE Marietta GA

BANKOFF, JOSEPH R. lawyer; b. Newark, Dec. 22, 1945; BS, Purdue U., 1967; JD, U. Ill., 1971. Bar: Ill. 1971, Ga. 1972. Law clk. to Hon. Walter P. Gewin U.S. Ct. Appeals (5th cir.), 1971-72; ptnr. King & Spalding, Atlanta. Asst. editor U. Ill. Law Forum, 1969-70. Mem. ABA, Ill. State Bar Assn., State Bar Ga., Atlanta Bar Assn., Nat. Inst. Trial Advocacy (trustee 1995—), Am. Law Inst., Order of Coif, Omicron Delta Kappa. Office: King & Spalding 191 Peachtree St NE Ste 4900 Atlanta GA 30303-1740

BANKS, ALLAN RICHARD, artist, art historian, researcher; b. Dearborn, Mich., Feb. 15, 1948; s. Henry Selman and Lillian Margaret (Radovic) B.; children: Christine Marie, Aaron Richard; m. Holly Hope Tumblin, Jan. 1997. Ind. pvt. study, Soc. Arts and Crafts, Detroit, 1966-69; student, Atelier Lack, Inc., Mpls., 1970-73, R.H. Ives Gammell Studio, Williamstown, Mass., 1976. Artist, with studio in Newburg, N.Y., 1979-81, Huron, Ohio, 1981-87; portrait artist, with studio in Spring Hill, Fla., 1987-93; dir. Atelier of Plein Air, Safety Harbor, Fla., 1993—. Lectr./demonstrator Portraits South, Inc., Raleigh, N.C., 1993, Atelier LeSueur, Mpls., 1995. Exhibited in group shows Sotheby's, N.Y.C., 1997, Guild of Boston Artists, 1996, 20th Century Exhbn., Amarillo Tex.-Springville, Utah, 1982, Butler Inst. Am. Art, Vixseboxse Art Galleries, Cleve., Salmagundi Club, Amarillo (Tex.) Art Ctr., Maryhill Mus. Art, Goldendale, Wash., Historic East-West Russia Exhibit, 1996, others; represented in collections at Wadsworth Athenaeum, Newark Art Mus., Montclair (N.J.) Mus., Hamilton Fish Meml. Libr., Nat. Portrait Gallery/Smithsonian. Trustee Mus. Natural History, Safety Harbor, 1995—; mem. bd. advisors Art Renewal Ctr., N.Y.C.; mem. Downtown Bus. Assn., Inc., Safety Harbor, 1994—. Elizabeth T. Greenshields Found. fellow, Montreal, 1972, 73; John and Anna Stacey Found. grantee, N.Mex., 1979, Ohio Arts Coun. grantee. Mem. Am. Soc. Portrait Artists (vice chmn. 2000-01), Am. Soc. Classical Realism (pres. 1997—), Met. Mus. Art, Appleton Mus. Art (Ocala, Fla.), Salmagundi Club, New Am. Acad. Ard. Lutheran. Avocations: travel, museums. Home: PO Box 233 Safety Harbor FL 34695-0233

BANKS, BETTIE SHEPPARD, psychologist; b. Birmingham, Ala., June 8, 1933; d. Francis Wilkerson and Bettie (Woodson) Sheppard; m. Frazer Banks, Jr., Mar. 22, 1952; children: Bettie Banks Daley, Lee Frazer Banks III. BA, Ga. State U., 1966, MA, 1968, PhD, 1970. Clin. assoc. lab. for Psychol. Svcs. Ga. State U., 1968-70; intern Ga. State U. Counseling Ctr., 1969-70, Ga. Mental Mental Health Inst., Atlanta, 1970-71, psychologist, 1971-72, chief psychologist, 1973; pvt. practice Atlanta, 1972—. Adj. assoc. prof. clin. psychology Ga. State U.; clin. asst. prof. dept. psychiatry and behavioral scis. Med. Sch. Emory U., 1974-79, 94—; mem. peer rev. panel Ga. Med. Care Found., 1980-86, chmn., 1986-88. Diplomate in clin. psychology Am. Bd. Profl. Psychology; Nat. Register Health Svc. Psychology Providers, 1977-97, Nat. Register Cert. Group Psychotherapists, 1994-2001. Cons. editor Voices, The Art and Science of Psychotherapy, 1978-84. Mem. Ga. Collaborative to Improve End-of-Life Care, 1997-2001, mem. steering com., 1999-2001. Fellow Ga. Psychol. Assn. (life), (chmn. divsn. E 1980, program chair ann. meeting 1991, pub. info. com. 1995-97, treas. divsn. F 1993-95, chair publicity divsn. F 1995-97); mem. APA (life), Am. Group Psychotherapy Assn. (clin. mem., co-chair local host com. 1995 Ann. Inst. and Conf.), Atlanta Group Psychotherapy Soc. (life) (bd. exec. com. 1982-83, 91-92, treas. 1995-99, fin. com. 1999-2001, faculty ann. group psychotherapy conf. 1995, 96, 97, instr. cert. course 1997), Jr. League. Episcopalian. Office: 18A Lenox Pointe NE Atlanta GA 30324-3168

BANKS, CHARLES AUGUSTUS, III, manufacturing executive; b. 1940; BA in Internat. Rels., Brown U., 1962. With Cameron Brown Co., 1965-67, Ferguson Enterprises Inc., Newport News, Va., 1967—, pres., COO, 1989-93, pres., CEO, 1993—. With USN, 1962—64. Office: Ferguson Enterprises Inc 12500 Jefferson Ave Newport News VA 23602-4314

BANKS, CHERRY ANN MCGEE, education educator; b. Benton Harbor, Mich., Oct. 11, 1945; d. Kelly and Geneva (Smith) McGee; m. James A. Banks, Feb. 15, 1969; children: Angela Marie, Patricia Ann. BS, Mich. State U., 1968; MA, Seattle U., 1977, EdD, 1991. Tchr. Benton Harbor Pub. Sch., 1968; staff assoc. Citizens Edn. Ctr. N.W., Seattle, 1984-85; edn. specialist Seattle Pub. Schs., Seattle, 1985-87; pres. Edn. Material and Svcs. Ctr., Edmonds, Wash., 1987—; asst. prof. edn. U. Wash., Bothell, 1992-96, assoc. prof. edn., 1996-2000, prof. edn., 2001—. Cons. Jackson (Miss.) Pub. Schs., 1988, Seattle Pub. Schs., 1988-90, Little Rock Pub. Schs., 1989, Scott Foreman Pub. Co., Glenview, Ill., 1992—; vis. asst. prof. Seattle U., 1991-92. Co-author: March Toward Freedom, 1978, Teaching Strategies for the Social Studies, 1999; co-editor: Multicultural Education: Issues and Perspectives, 1989, rev. edits., 1993, 97; assoc. editor Handbook of Rsch. on Multicultural Edn.; contbr. chpts. to books. Mem. Jack and Jill Am., Seattle, 1978-94, First AME Headstart Bd., Seattle, 1981-83; trustee Shoreline C.C., Seattle, 1983-95; bd. dirs. King County Campfire, Seattle, 1985-88. Recipient Outstanding Commitment and Leadership of C.C. award Western Region Nat. Coun. on Black Am. Affairs, 1989. Mem. ASCD, Nat. Coun. for Social Studies Programs Com. (vice chairperson Carter G. Woodson Book award com. 1991-92, chair person 1992-93, mem. nominating com.), Am. Rsch. Assn., The Links, Inc. (pres. Greater Seattle chpt.), Phi Delta Kappa (founding, Seattle U. chpt.), Alpha Kappa Alpha. Avocations: tennis, swimming, reading, traveling. Office: U Wash Edn Program 22011 26th Ave SE Bothell WA 98021-4900

BANKS, CHRISTOPHER PAUL, political science educator, lawyer; b. Wantagh, N.Y., Sept. 27, 1958; married. BA, U. Conn., 1980; JD, U. Dayton, 1984; PhD, U. Va. Bar: Conn. 1984, U.S. Dist. Ct. Conn. 1985. Assoc. Law Office of Jeffrey Reinen, Brookfield, Conn., 1985-86, Brown and Brown, Darien, Conn., 1986-87, Copp, Berall and Hempstead, Essex, Conn., 1987-88; ptnr. Banks & Banks, P.C., Ridgefield, Conn., 1988-90; assoc. prof. polit. sci. U. Akron, Ohio, 1995—. Pre-law advisor U. Akron. Author: Judicial Politics in the D.C. Circuit Court, 1999, (with John C. Green) Superintending Democracy: The Courts and the Political Process, 2001; contbr. articles to profl. jours., chpts. to books.; collections editor Law, Politics and Soc. series, U. Akron Press. Hearing officer Conn. Commn. on Human Rights and Opportunities, Hartford, 1988-91; Dem. candidate for state rep., Redding/Wilton, Conn., 1988. Mem. Am. Polit. Sci. Assn., Raven Soc., Omicron Delta Kappa. Office: U Akron 210 Olin Hall Akron OH 44325-1904

BANKS, DAVID RUSSELL, former health care executive; b. Arcadia, Wis., Feb. 15, 1937; s. J. R. and Cleone Banks; married; children: Melissa, Michael. BA, U. Ark., 1959. Vice pres. Dabbs, Sullivan, Trulock, Ark., 1963—74; chmn., chief exec. officer Leisure Lodges, Ft. Smith, Ark., 1974—77; registered rep. Stephens Inc., Little Rock, 1974—79; pres., CEO Beverly Enterprises, Ft. Smith, Ark., 1989—2001, chmn. bd., dir., 1990—2001. Dir. Nat. Coun. Health Ctrs., Pulaski Bank, Little Rock. With U.S. Army.

BANKS, DEIRDRE MARGARET, retired church organization administrator; b. Melbourne, Australia, May 9, 1934; came to U.S., 1975; d. Haldane Stuart and Vera Avice (Fisher) B. MA, Simpson Coll., 1980. Missionary nurse Leprosy Mission, Kathmandu, Nepal, 1960-69; dean of women Melbourne Bible Inst., 1970-75; asst. to dir. Bible Study Fellowship, Oakland, Calif., 1975-79; dir. adult ministries First Covenant Ch., Oakland, 1980-87, assoc. pastor for adults, St. Paul, 1987-89; exec. dir. Covenant Women Ministries, Chgo., 1989-99. Spkr. at women's retreats in U.S. and Australia. Chairperson ch. edn. bd. Pacific S.W. Conf. Evang. Ch., 1985-87, Gilead Group, Oakland, 1985-87; bd. dirs., chairperson Gilead Group Housing for Abused and Homeless Women and Children; bd. chmn. Barnabas Project for Abused and Homeless Women and Children, 1990-93; mem. bd. world mission Evang. Covenant Ch., 1986-89; bd. Covenant Enabling Residences Inc. for Developmentally Disabled Adults, pres., 1996-98; pastor Mission Covenant Ch., Orange, Mass., 2000--. Mem. Evangel. Covenant Ch.

BANKS, ERIC KENDALL, lawyer; b. St. Louis, Aug. 21, 1955; s. Willie James Banks Jr. and Grace (Kendall) Palmer; children: Brittany Renee, Bryson Kendall. BSBA, U. Mo., St. Louis, 1977; JD, U. Mo., Columbia, 1980. Bar: Mo. 1980, Ill. 1988, U.S. Dist. Ct. (we. dist.) Mo. 1980, U.S. Dist. Ct. (ea. dist.) Mo. 1984, U.S. Ct. Appeals (8th cir.) 1984, U.S. Ct. Appeals (D.C. cir.) 1998, U.S. Tax Ct. 1988, U.S. Supreme Ct. 1996. Asst. gen. counsel Mo. Pub. Svc. Commn., Jefferson City, 1980-84; asst. atty. Office Circuit Atty., St. Louis, 1984-87; pvt. practice, St. Louis, 1987-91, Clayton, Mo., 1991-92; corp. counsel Siegel-Robert, St. Louis, 1992-97; city counselor City of St. Louis, 1997-99; ptnr. Thompson, Coburn, 1999—, Thompson Coburn, St. Louis, 1999—. Adj. prof. civil law St. Louis U. Law Sch., 1987—92, Washington U. Sch., 1991; sec. bd. dirs. Black Leadership Tng. Program, St. Louis, 1975—77. Sec. bd. dirs. Wesley House Assn.; bd. trustees U. Law Sch. Found.; bd. dirs. DeSailes Cmty. Housing Corp., Am. Red Cross Bi-State chpt. St. Louis Met. Leadership Program fellow, 1975-77, named 100 Leaders for the New Millenium, St. Louis Bus. Jour., 2000; Cochran Cmty. Svc. award, Young Lawyers Sect. Mo. Bar Assn., 2002. Mem. ABA (labor and employment com.), Bar Assn. Met. St. Louis, Mo. Bar Assn., Mound City Bar Assn., Bar Assn. Met. St. Louis. Clubs: Toastmasters Internat. (adminstrv. v.p. 1983, William Tellman award 1982). Lutheran. Avocations: Karate, reading, photography, public speaking, community work. Home: 2755 Russell Blvd Saint Louis MO 63104-2137 Office: Thompson Coburn One US Bank Plz Saint Louis MO 63101 Fax: (314) 552-7256. E-mail: ebanks@thompsoncoburn.com.

BANKS, ERNEST (ERNIE BANKS), retired professional baseball player; b. Dallas, Jan. 31, 1931; s. Eddie B. Student, Northwestern U. Baseball player Kansas City Monarchs (Negro Am. League), 1950-51, 53, Chgo. Cubs, 1953-71, mgr. group sales, to 1982, 1st base coach, to 1989; spokesperson New World Van Lines, 1984—; now ret. Formerly co-owner, v.p. Bob Nelson-Ernie Banks Ford, Inc., Chgo.; with Associated Films Promotions, L.A., 1982-84. Author: (with Jim Enright) Mr. Cub. Past mem. bd. Chgo. Transit Authority; active Boy Scouts Am., YMCA. Served with AUS, 1951-53, Europe. Named most valuable player Nat. League, 1958, 59; recipient awards from Fans, 1969, awards from Press Club, 1969, awards from Jr. C. of C., 1971; inducted into Tex. Sports Hall Fame, 1971, Baseball Hall of Fame, 1977; mem. Nat. League All-Star Team, 1957-70; hold major league record for most career grand slam home runs. Office: Ernie Banks Internat Inc 520 Washington Blvd Ste 284 Marina Del Rey CA 90292-5442

BANKS, HELEN AUGUSTA, singer, actress; b. Petersburg, Va., Sept. 8, 1922; d. Robert Augustus and Helen (Fisher) B. Student, Victoria Sch. of Music, N.Y.C., 1940-43. Singer and actress. Mem. pub. safety com. Cmty. Bd. No. 9, 1983—. Recipient Svc. award The Bd. Christian Edn., St. John Bapt. Ch., N.Y.C., 1989. Mem. Am. Guild Variety Artists, Am. Assn. Ret. Persons, Sickle Cell Found., U.S. Ski Team Found., Internat. Skiing History Assn. Democrat. Baptist. Avocations: skiing, in line skating, tennis. Home: 408 W 150th St Apt 6 New York NY 10031-2828

BANKS, HENRY H. academic dean, physician; b. Boston, Mar. 9, 1921; s. Isaac and Bessie B.; m. Judith Epstein, June 1945; children: Nancy (Mrs. Curt Civin), Betsy (Mrs. David Epstein), Steven. AB cum laude, Harvard U., 1942; MD, Tufts U., 1945. Diplomate Am. Bd. Orthopedic Surgery (pres. 1978-79, exec. dir. 1979-86). Surg. intern Beth Israel Hosp., Boston, 1945-46, asst. resident in surgery, 1947-49; asst. resident orthopedic lab. and pathology Children's Hosp., Boston, 1949-50, asst. resident orthopedic surgery, 1950-51, Mass. Gen. Hosp., Boston, 1951-52; chief resident orthopedic surgery Peter Bent Brigham Hosp., Boston, 1952, Children's Hosp. Med. Center, Boston, 1952-53; practice medicine, specializing in orthopedic surgery Boston, 1953—; prof. Tufts U. Sch. Medicine, 1970-90, prof. emeritus, 1990—, chmn. dept. orthopedic surgery, 1970-84, assoc. dean, 1972-82, sr. assoc. dean med. affairs, 1982, acting med. dean, then med. dean, 1983-90, dean emeritus, 1990—; dir. orthopedic surgery Boston City Hosp., 1970-74; orthopedic surgeon-in-chief New Eng. Med. Center Hosps., 1970-84. Orthopedic surgeon children's Hosp. Med. Ctr., 1953-70, Peter Bent Brigham Hosp., 1953-70, chief orthopedic surgery, 1968-70. Author: A Century of Excellence: The History of Tufts University School of Medicine, 1893-1993, 1993, Orthopaedic Surgery at Tufts University School of Medicine, 1893-1998, 1998; editor: The Pediatric Clinics of North America-Musculoskeletal Disorder I, 1967; guest editor: Clinical Orthopedics and Related Research, 1968, Orthopedic Clinics of North America, 1976, 78; contbr. articles to profl. jours. With M.C. AUS, 1945-47. Mem. AMA, ACS, Am. Orthopedic Assn. (v.p. 1986-87), Am. Acad. Orthopedic Surgeons, Am. Acad. Cerebral Palsy (pres.), Eastern Orthopedic Assn., Mass. Med. Soc., Internat. Soc. Orthopedic Surgery and Traumatology, Boston Orthopedic Club (pres.), Pediatric Orthopedic Soc., Am. Bd. Orthopedic Surgery (sec., pres. 1973-79, exec. dir. 1979-86), Univ. Club (Boston). Home: 54 Commonwealth Ave Boston MA 02116-3043 Office: 136 Harrison Ave Boston MA 02111-1817

BANKS, HOLLY HOPE, artist; b. Columbus, Ohio, Apr. 16, 1957; d. Harold Russell and Ramona Faye (Corder) Tumblin; m. Allan R. Banks, Jan. 7, 1997. BA, U. Toledo, 1981; student, Atelier Plein-Air Studios, 1994. Artist, 1981—; instr. gifted children program Toledo Mus. Art, 1980-81; copyist Nat. Gallery Art, Washington, 1982-86; asst. instr. Atelier Plein-Air Studios, Safety Harbor, Fla., 1994-96. Masterpieces, 1997, Exhibited in group shows at Union Russian Artists, Moscow, 1996, Kolomna, 1996, Top 10 Emerging Artist Exhbn., 1999, The Butler Inst. Am. Art Mus. Exhbn., 2000—01, Audubon Artists Exhbn. (award), Catherine Lorillard Wolfe Art Club Exhbn., 2000—03; featured emerging artist Am. Artist Mag., 1998, featured artist, 2001; author: poems; contbr. The Best of Portrait Painting, 1998. Recipient Renee and Stephen McNeely award for best representational oil, 1998, Daler-Rowney award Salmagundi Club, 1999. Mem. Am. Soc. Classical Realism, Art Renewal Ctr., Audubon Artists, Portrait Soc. Am. Avocations: gourmet cooking, gardening. Office: PO Box 233 Safety Harbor FL 34695-0233

BANKS, JAMES ALBERT, educational research director, educator; b. Marianna, Ark., Sept. 24, 1941; s. Matthew and Lula (Holt) Banks; m. Cherry Ann McGee, Feb. 15, 1969; children: Angela Marie, Patricia Ann. AA, Chgo. City Coll., 1963; BE, Chgo. State U., 1964; MA (NDEA fellow 1966-69), Mich. State U., 1967, PhD, 1969; LHD (hon.), Bank St. Coll. Edn., 1993, U. Alaska, Fairbanks, 2000, U. Wis., Parkside, 2001, DePaul U., 2003. Tchr. elementary sch. Joliet, Ill., 1965, Francis W. Parker Sch., Chgo., 1965-66; asst. prof. edn. U. Wash., Seattle, 1969-71, assoc. prof., 1971-73, prof., 1973—, Russell F. Stark univ. prof., 2001—, chmn. curriculum and instrn., 1982-87; dir. Ctr. for Multicultural Edn., Seattle, 1991—. Vis. prof. edn. U. Mich., 1975, Monash U., Australia, 1985, U. Warwick, Eng., 1988, U. Minn., 1991; vis. lectr. U. Southampton, Eng., 1989, Harry F. and Alva K. Ganders disting. lectr. Syracuse U., 1989; disting. scholar lectr. Kent State U., 1978, U. Ariz., 1979, Ind. U., 1983; vis. scholar Brit. Acad., 1983; Sachs lectr. Tchrs. Coll. Columbia U., 1996; Tyler eminent scholar chair Fla. State U., 1998; Carl and Alice Daeufer lectr. U. Hawaii, Manoa, 1999; com. examiners Ednl. Testing Svc., 1974-77; nat. adv. coun. on ethnic heritage studies, U.S. Office Edn., 1975-78; com. on fed. role in ednl. rsch. NAS, 1991-92, mem. com. on developing a rsch. agenda on edn. of ltd. proficient and bilingual students, 1995-97; mem. bd. on children, youth and families NRC and Inst. of Medicine/NAS. Author: Teaching Strategies for Ethnic Studies, 1975, 7th edit., 2003, Teaching Strategies for the Social Studies, 1973, 5th edit., 1999, Teaching the Black Experience, 1970, Multiethnic Education: Practices and Promises, 1977, An Introduction to Multicultural Education, 1994, 2d edit., 1999, Educating Citizens in A Multicultural Soc., 1997, (with Cherry Ann Banks) March Toward Freedom: A History of Black Americans, 1970, 2d edit., 1974, rev. 2nd edit., 1978, Multiethnic Education: Theory and Practice, 1981, 3rd edit., 1994, 4th edit., (new title) Cultural Diversity and Education: Foundations, Curriculum, and Teaching, 2001, (with others) Curriculum Guidlines for Multicultural Education, 1976, rev. edit., 1992, We Americans: Our History and People, 2 vols., 1982; contbg. author Internat. Ency. of Edn., 1985, Handbook of Research on Teacher Education, 1990, Handbook of Research on Social Studies Teaching and Learning, 1991, Encyclopedia of Ednl. Rsch., 1992, Handbook of Research on the Education of Young Children, 1993, Review of Research in Education, vol. 19, 1993; editor: Black Self Concept, 1972, Teaching Ethnic Studies: Concepts and Strategies, 1973, (with William W. Joyce) Teaching Social Studies to Culturally Different Children, 1971, Teaching the Language Arts to Culturally Different Children, 1971, Education in the 80's: Multiethnic Education, 1981, (with James Lynch) Multicultural Education in Western Societies, 1986, (with C. Banks) Multicultural Education: Issues and Perspectives, 1989, 3d edit., 1997, 4th edit., 2001, Handbook of Research on Multicultural Education, 1995, Multicultural Education, Transformative Knowledge, and Action, 1996; editorial bd. Jour. of Tch. Edn., 1985-89, Coun. Interracial Books for Children Bull., 1982-92, Urban Edn., 1991-96, Tchrs. Coll. Record, 1998—, Multicultural Perspectives, 2000—; contbr. articles to profl. jours. Recipient Disting. Career Rsch. award, Nat. Coun. for the Social Studies, 2001, Outstanding Young Man award Wash. State Jaycees, 1975, Outstanding Service in Edn. award Seattle U. Black Student Union, 1985, Pres.'s award TESOL, 1998; Spencer fellow Nat. Acad. Edn., 1973-76; Kellogg fellow, 1980-83; Rockefeller Found. fellow, 1980. Mem. ASCD (bd dirs. 1976-79, Disting. lectr. 1986, Disting. scholar, lectr. 1994, 97), Nat. Acad. Edn., Nat. Coun. Social Studies (bd. dirs. 1973-74, 80-85, pres. 1982, Disting. Career Rsch. in Social Studies award 2001), Internat. Assn. Intercultural Edn. (editl. bd.), Social Sci. Edn. Consortium (bd. dirs. 1976-79), Am. Ednl. Rsch. Assn. (com. on role and status of minorities in edn. rsch. 1992-94, publs. com. 1995-96, pres.-elect 1996-97, pres. 1997-98, exec. bd. 1998-99, Disting. scholar/rschr. on minority edn. 1986, Rsch. Review award 1994, Disting. Career Contbn. award 1996), Phi Delta Kappa, Phi Kappa Phi, Golden Key Nat. Honor Soc., Kappa Delta Pi. Office: U Wash 110 Miller Hall PO Box 353600 Seattle WA 98195-3600 *One of the greatest strengths of our nation is its tremendous ethnic, racial, and cultural diversity. A major goal of my career is to increase understanding and communication across different ethnic, cultural and racial groups and to make it possible for each ethnic, cultural and racial group to make its greatest contribution to the nation. My belief that educational institutions can play a major role in improving race relations in our nation has greatly influenced my life and career.*

BANKS, LINDA T. legal assistant, massage therapist; b. Montgomery, Ala., Apr. 23, 1948; d. Robert Tillman and Margaret (Jackson) Tanner; m. R.O. Banks, Dec. 21, 1971 (div. Apr. 1978); 1 child, Charles R. BA, Brenau Coll., Gainesville, Ga., 1970; cert., Acad. Somatic Healing Arts, Atlanta, 1998. Cert. massage therapist. Legal asst. Powell, Goldstein et al, Atlanta, 1978-81, Martin & Young, Atlanta, 1981-84; adminstrv. asst. Yokogawa Corp., Peachtree City, Ga., 1984-86; legal asst. Sanders, Mottola & Haugen, Newnan, Ga., 1986-89; flight attendant ValuJet, Atlanta, 1996-98; self-employed massage therapist, Atlanta and Newnan, 1998—; legal asst. Sutherland Asbill & Brennan, Atlanta, 1989—2002, Alston & Bird LLP, 2002—. Bd. dirs. Manget-Brannon Alliance for Arts, Newnan, 1984; mem., patron Newnan Cmty. Theatre Co., 1981—. Mem. Internat. Massage Assn., Mu Phi Epsilon. Democrat. Episcopal/Methodist. Avocations: playing keyboards in local band, acting in local theatre, tennis, volunteer work for senior citizens. Home: 27 Chestnut Dr Newnan GA 30263-2201 Office: Alston & Bird LLP 1201 W Peachtree St Atlanta GA 30309

BANKS, LISA JEAN, government official; b. Dec. 19, 1956; d. Bruce H. and Jean P. (Como) Banks. BSBA, Northeastern U., Boston, 1979. Coop. trainee IRS, Boston, 1975-79, revenue officer Reno, 1979-81; spl. agt. Houston, 1981-84, Anchorage, 1984-90; spl. agt. Office Inspector Gen. procurement fraud task force DVA, Boston, 1990-92; spl. agt. Office Inspector Gen. NASA, Kennedy Space Center, Fla., 1992-2000, 2000—; spl. agt. Computer Crimes Div. NASA-OIG, Kennedy Space Center, Fla., 2000. Fed. womens program mgr., 1980—81. Pres. Make-A-Wish Found. of Cen. Fla., 1994-96, 99-2000, v.p. wish granting, 1996-99. Mem. Nat. Assn. Treasury Agts., Fed. Law Enforcement Officers Assn. Roman Catholic. Office: NASA Office of Inspector Gen PO Box 21066 Kennedy Space Center FL 32815-0066 E-mail: s.a.banks@worldnet.att.net.

BANKS, MONICA, sculptor; b. N.Y.C., Mar. 29, 1959; d. Stanley and Rela (Heuberg) B.; m. Philip A. Schultz, Jan. 28, 1995; children: Elias Banks Schultz, August Rawley Schultz. AB, Vassar Coll., 1981; student, Domus Acad., Milan, 1985. Graphic designer Milton Glaser Inc., N.Y.C., 1982-87, Monica Banks Inc., N.Y.C., 1987-95. One-woman shows include U. Mass., Amherst, Lizan Tops Gallery, East Hampton, N.Y., exhibitions include resin and fabric sculpture, Barneys N.Y., 1989, prin. works include steel rod horse sculpture, Binghamton (N.Y.) Visitor Ctr., 1996, Faces: Times Square, 1996, Louisa and Rusty, steel horse and dog sculpture, Hunts Pt. Recreation Ctr., Bronx, N.Y., 2001. Recipient Excellence in Design award, Art Commn. City N.Y., 1996. Mem.: Internat. Sculpture Ctr. Home: 88 Osborne Ln East Hampton NY 11937-2207

BANKS, PATRICIA ANNE, music educator, minister; d. Jethro Nichols and Rena Blanche Johnsey Banks. BS in Edn., U. of North Tex., 1966; MusM, S.W. Bapt. Theol. Sem., 1976; student, Southwestern Bapt. Theol. Sem., 1976—81, The Anglican Sch. of Theology, 2000—. Ordination to the diaconate Episcopal Diocese of Ft. Worth, 2002; cert. in piano and theory Music Teachers' Nat. Assn., 1996. Tchg. fellow and adj. prof. of music Southwestern Bapt. Theol. Sem., Fort Worth, Tex., 1973—81; pvt. tchr. of piano, music theory, music history Banks Piano Studio, Fort Worth, Tex., 1975—92; founder and dir. of precollege music dept. Howard Payne U. Sch. of Music, Brownwood, Tex., 1991—2000; assoc. prof. of music Howard Payne U. Sch. of Music and Fine Arts, 1991—; founder and dir. of music computer lab/music tech. dept. Howard Payne U. Sch. of Music, 1992—. Workshop clinician Van Cliburn Piano Inst., Fort Worth, 1994. Vestry mem. St. John's Episcopal Ch., Brownwood, Tex., 1998—2000. Mem.: Music Tchrs. Assns. (adjucator, workshop clinician), Nat. Guild Piano Tchrs. (adjucator 1997—), Heart of Tex. Music Tchrs.' Assn. (pres., student affiliate chmn., Tchr. of Yr. award), Tex. Music Tchrs.' Assn. (v.p. for student affairs, dir., tech. chmn., Tchr. of Yr. award 1996), Tex. Fedn. of Music Clubs (dist. junion festival chmn.), Ft. Worth Music Tchrs. Assn. (pres., student affiliate chmn., Tchr. of Yr. award), Am. Coll. of Musicians (faculty mem. 1976), Kappa Kappa Psi (hon.), Tau Beta Sigma (hon.). Episc. Avocations: reading, travel. Office: Howard Payne University School of Music and Fine Arts Brownwood TX 76801 Office Fax: 915-649-8945. E-mail: pbanks@hputx.edu.

BANKS, PETER MORGAN, physics educator, investor, business consultant; b. San Diego, May 21, 1937; s. George Willard and Mary Margaret (Morgan) B.; m. Mary E. Stewart, Dec. 28, 2002; children by previous marriage: Kevin, Michael, Steven, David. MS in E.E, Stanford U., 1960; PhD in Physics, Pa. State U., 1965. Postdoctoral fellow Institut d'Aeronomie Spatiale de Belgique, Brussels, 1965-66; prof. applied physics U. Calif., San Diego, 1966-76; prof. physics Utah State U., 1976-81, head dept. physics, 1976-81; vis. assoc. prof. Stanford U., 1972-73, prof. elec. engring., 1981-90, dir. space, telecommunications and radiosci. lab., 1982-90, dir. ctr. for aeronautics and space info. systems, 1983-90; prof. atmospheres, oceans, and space sci. U. Mich., 1990-95, adj. prof., 1996-2000; dean Coll. Engring., U. Mich., 1990-95; pres. Earth Data Corp., 1985-86; pres., CEO Environ. Rsch. Inst. Mich., 1995-97, ERIM Internat., Inc., 1997-99; ptnr. XR Ventures, LLC, 2000—; CEO, Akonni Biosystems, Inc. Vis. scientist Max Planck Inst. for Aeronomie, Germany, 1975; pres. La Jolla Scis., Inc., 1973—77, Upper Atmosphere Rsch. Corp., 1978—82; chmn. NASA adv. com. on sci. uses of space sta., 1985—87; prin. investigator space shuttle experiments, 1982, 85, 91; mem. Jason Group, 1983—97; bd. dirs. Tecumseh Products Corp., X-Rite Corp., Handylab, Inc., Chaos Telecomms., Inc., Triformix, Inc.; chmn. bd. trustees Consortium Internat. Earth Sci. Info. Networks, 1991—94; co-chmn. NRC Commn. on Phys. Scis., Math. and Applications, 1998—2000. Author: (with G. Kockarts) Aeronomy, 1973, (with J.R. Doupnik) Introduction to Computer Science, 1976; assoc. editor: Jour. Geophys. Research, 1974-77; assoc. editor: Planetary and Space Sci, 1977-83, regional editor, 1983-86; contbr. numerous articles in field to profl. jours. Mem. space sci. adv. council NASA, 1976-80. Served with U.S. Navy, 1960-63. Recipient Appleton prize Royal Soc. London, 1978, Space Sci. award AIAA, 1981, NASA Disting. Service medal, 1986; Alumni fellow Pa. State U., 1982 Fellow Am. Geophys. Union; mem. Internat. Union Radio Sci., Nat. Acad. Engrng., Cosmos Club. Episcopalian. Home: 9975 Joslin Lake Rd Gregory MI 48137 E-mail: pbanks@sonic.net.

BANKS, RELA, sculptor; b. Yaroslav, Poland, Oct. 8, 1933; came to U.S., 1947; d. Jacob and Frieda (Weintraub) Heuberg; m. Stanley Frederic Banks, Aug. 9, 1953; children: Andrew Howard, J. Monica, Gary Mitchell. Student, Mus. Modern Art, 1957, Art Students League, N.Y.C. and Woodstock, N.Y., 1958-61, Summit (N.J.) Art Ctr., 1966-75. Chmn. nat. juried exhibit Summit Art Ctr., 1976, mem. adminstrv. com., 1977-79, chmn. standing com. spl. events, trustee; mem. exec. com. Phoenix Gallery, N.Y.C., 1983; chmn. membership com. Stone Sculpture Soc. N.Y., 1980-82. One-woman shows include Robins Art Gallery, South Orange, N.J., 1973, Montclair (N.J.) Coll., 1974, Caldwell (N.J.) Coll., 1974, 83, Summit Art Ctr., 1976, Newark Acad., Livingston, N.J., 1976, Douglas Coll., New Brunswick, N.J., 1978, First Women's Bank, N.Y.C., 1979, Phoenix Gallery, 1979, 81, 83, Morris Mus. Arts and Scis., Morristown, N.J., 1983, Ann Leonard Gallery, Woodstock, 1983, NECCA Mus., Bklyn., Conn., 1985, Schiller-Wapner Galleries, N.Y.C., 1985, 87, Ann Norton Sculpture Galleries, West Palm Beach, Fla., 1987, David Gary Ltd, Millburn, N.J., 1988; exhibited in group shows at Phoenix Gallery, 1979, 83, Morris Mus. Art, 1979, 83, Invitational Woodstock Artists Assn., 1980, 84, Eilaine Benson Gallery, Bridgehampton, N.Y., 1980, Searles Art Ctr., Great Barrington, Mass., 1980, Nabisco Art Gallery, 1981, Summit Art Ctr., 1981, First Womens Bank, 1981, Fairleigh Dickinson U., Madison, N.J., 1983, NYU Grad. Sch. Bus., 1983, AT&T Gallery, Basking Ridge, N.J., 1984, Shering Plough Gallery, N.J., 1984, New Orleans Mus. Art, 1986, Gallery Contemporary Art at U. Colorado Springs, Colo., 1986, Schiller-Wapner Galleries, 1986, Lever House, N.Y.C., 1986, Aldrich Mus. Contemporary Art, Ridgefield, Conn., 1986, Okla. Art Ctr., Oklahoma City, 1987, "After Henry Moore", Emily Lowe Mus., Hofstra U., Hempstead, N.Y., 1988, group exhibition, Poland; represented in permanent collections New Orleans Mus. Art, Everson Mus., Syracuse, N.Y., Morris Mus. Sci. and Art, Okla. Art Ctr., Vassar Coll. Gallery, Poughkeepsie, N.Y., Millburn (N.J.) Pub. Library, Minn. Mus. Art, Mpls., Woodstock Hist. Soc., Fordham U., Lincoln Ctr., N.Y.C., Aldrich Mus. Contemporary Art, Warsaw Mus., Poland, various pvt. and corp. collections. Mem. Woodstock Artists Assn. Office: Rela Banks Studio 272 Yerry Hill Rd Woodstock NY 12498

BANKS, ROBERT J. bishop; b. Winthrop, Mass., Feb. 26, 1928; s. Robert Joseph and Rita Katherine (Sullivan) B. AB, St. John's Sem., Brighton, Mass., 1949; STL, Gregorian U., Rome, 1953; JCD, Lateran U., Rome, 1957. Ordained priest Roman Cath. Ch., 1952, ordained titular bishop of Taraqua, 1985. Prof. canon law St. John Sem., Brighton, Mass., 1959-71, acad. dean, 1967-71; rector St. John's Sem., 1971-81; vicar gen. Boston Archdiocese, 1984; aux. bishop Boston, 1985-90; bishop Diocese of Green Bay, Wis., 1990—. Roman Catholic. Office: Diocese of Green Bay PO Box 23825 Green Bay WI 54305-3825

BANKS, ROBERT LEE, publisher, author, jazz guitarist, composer, arranger; b. Buckingham County, Va., July 11, 1952; Student, Bronx C.C., 1970-71, L.I. U., 1994-96; broker's cert., Real Estate Tng. Ctr. Greater N.Y., Inc.; salesperson cert., Forest Hills Adult Edn. Sys. N.Y.C. Bd .Edn. Lic. real estate broker, N.Y. Broker/pres. Premier Nat. Realty, Inc., So. Ozone Pk., NY; tchr. music Beacon Sch. program Jr. H.S. 8, Jamaica, 1993—; pres. Total Package Pub., Ltd., So. Ozone Pk., 1997—. Former tchr. Henry Street Settlement Music Sch., 1976-87. Author: (autobiography) Against All Odds, 1993-97, The Art of Expressions are in the Progressions, vols. 1 & 2, Chord Melodies for the Innovative Guitarist, vols. 1, 2, 3, 4, Anthology of Scales, vols. 1, 2, 3, 4, 5, 6, The Pyramid Concet, vol. 1, The Virtuoso Pianist, vol. 1; guitarist, performed with Bobbie Humphrey, Gattertail Jackson, Stanley Turrentine, Delores Carr, Sherells, Charlie Rouse Quartet, bands of Dizzy Gillespie, Frank Foster and Ray Abams; TV appearances include Positively Black, Like It Is, CBS cable show; performed at Avery Fischer Hall, Lincoln Ctr., N.Y.C., Felt Forum, Manhattan Ctr., Mikell's, Munk's After Dark, Ariz.'s Tempi, Baker's Keyboard Lounge, Chgo., Just Jazz, Phila., Astrodome Stadium, Houston, Blues Alley, Washington, WRVR concert series with Bobbie Humphrey; performer jazz festivals of Kool and Newport, coll. concerts featuring Banks Brothers and Robert Banks Sextet; discography includes Sophisticated Funk (with Brother Jack McDuff) and Breezin', Funk Power, Moving World, Fight For What Is Right, and Approaching Storm (with Creative Funk). Pres. Creative Artists, Ltd., So. Ozone Pk., 2000—03. Recipient various honors and awards including Music Activity award L.I. U.; scholar United Fedn. Tchrs.; Trickle-up grantee Bus. Outreach Ctr. Mem. N.Y. State Assn. Realtors, Inc. (cert.). Office: Total Package Pub Ltd PO Box 200009 South Ozone Park NY 11420 Fax: 718-323-7828.

BANKS, RUSSELL, financial planner, consultant; b. N.Y.C., Aug. 2, 1919; s. Thomas and Fay (Cowen) B.; m. Janice Reed, June 19, 1949; 1 son, Gordon L. BBA, CCNY, 1936-40; JD, N.Y. Law Sch., 1960. Bar: N.Y. 1961. Sr. acct. Selverne, Davis Co., N.Y.C., 1940-45; pvt. practice N.Y.C., 1945-61; exec. v.p. Met. Telecomm. Corp., Plainview, N.Y., 1961-62; pres., former CEO Grow Group, Inc. (formerly Grow Chem. Corp.), N.Y.C., 1962-95, also dir., 1962-95; pres. Russell Banks & Co. Ltd., 1995—. Cons. Imperial Chem. Industries, PLC., 1995-96; adj. prof. bus. adminstrn. Baruch Coll., 1996-98. Editor: Managing the Small Company. Recipient award of achievement Sch. of Bus. Alumni Soc. of CCNY, 1977; Winthrop-Sears medal Chem. Industry Assn.,

1980 Mem. Nat. Paint and Coatings Assn. (past pres.), Am. Mgmt. Assn. (gen. mgmt. planning coun. 1966-95, former trustee, exec. com.), Met. Club, Sky Club. Home: 14 E 75th St New York NY 10021-2657

BANKS, THERESA ANN, retired elementary education educator; b. Camden, N.J., Apr. 5, 1946; d. Frederick Douglas and Betty Mae (Norman) Clarke; m. James Donald Banks, Feb. 14, 1987; 1 child, Elizabeth Pearl Banks. BS, Cheyney U., 1968. Third grade tchr. Loudenslager Elem. Sch., Paulsboro, N.J., 1968-81, tchr. basic skills, 1981-86, Billingsport Elem. Sch., Paulsboro, 1986-98; ret., 1998. Tchr. art activities Enrichment Prog., Paulsboro, 1988-98. Chmn. youth program ARC for Paulsboro Sch. System, 1970-80, Sunshine Club/Billingsport Sch., 1990-98, Billingsport Sch. Store, 1992-95; active Aluminum Tab Program, Camden, 1991-98. Mem. NEA, N.J. Edn. Assn., Paulsboro Edn. Assn., Nat. Coun. Tchrs. Math., N.J. Ret. Edn. Assn. Baptist. Avocations: reading, cooking, sewing, art, horses. Home: 253 Deptford Ave Woodbury NJ 08096-3508

BANKS, VIRGINIA ANNE (GINGER BANKS), association administrator; b. Dallas, Mar. 19, 1949; d. James Houston and Mary Virginia (Bussey) B. B of Journalism, U. Tex., 1971. Traveling cons. Alpha Omicron Pi Fraternity, Indpls., 1971-73, adminstrv. asst. Nashville, 1973-74; pub. info. officer Tex. Dept. of Community Affairs, Austin, 1974-76; asst. dir. of comm. State Bar of Tex., Austin, 1976-78, assoc. editor Tex. Bar Jour., 1977-79, mng. editor Tex. Bar Jour, 1979-91, comm. dir., 1991-99, dir. pub. svcs. divsn., 1992-99, dir. info. tech. divsn., 1999-2000, dir. mem. svcs. divsn., 2000-01. Internat. rush chmn. Alpha Omicron Pi, Nashville, 1976-77, internat. v.p. ops., 1977-81, internat. pres., 1981-85, v.p. found., 1985-90, mem. fraternity devel. com., 1985-89, pres. Pi Kappa Corp., 1991-95, mem. Austin Alumnae chpt., 1973—, alumnae adv. com. network specialist, 1996-98, del. nat. panhellenic Conf., 1987-93, chmn. Perry award com., 1992-98, mem. rituals, traditions and jewelry com., 1998—, chair rituals, traditions and jewelry com., 1998—; com. to devel. relationship statement, Nat. Panhellenic Conf., 1983, del., 1987-93, area advisor coll. Panhellenics com., 1985-88, chmn. liaison com., 1987-88, mem. Project Future collegiate concerns com., 1987-89, field cons. seminar com., 1987, chmn., 1988, resolutions com., 1988, chmn. pub. rels. com., 1991-93, mem. ednl. devel. com., 1991-93. Editor Alpha Omicron Pi Centennial History Book, 1995-97; contbr. articles to mags. Bd. dirs. Lone Star Girl Scout Coun., Austin, 1973-75, Nat. Interfraternity Found., 1986-89, M.L. Roller scholarship com., 1988-89, nominations com., 1988-89; mem. Humane Soc. Austin, 1981—; chmn. mag. adv. com. Ex-Students Assn., U. Tex., Austin, 1989-95; active Tarrytown United Meth. Ch. Recipient presdl. citation State Bar of Tex., 1981, 90, 94, presdl. citation Alpha Omicron Pi, 1988, 97. Mem. Am. Soc. Assn. Execs., Assn. Fraternity Advisors, Internat. Assn. Bus. Communicators, Nat. Assn. Bar Execs. (mem. pub. svcs. activities com. 1995-98, vice-chair pub. svc. activities com. 1996-97, chair pub. svcs. activities com. 1997-98, chair awards com. 1995-96, pub. rels. and comms. sect. 1991—, mem. sect.'s comms. audit com. 1994-95, chair sect.'s comms. audit com. 1995-98, mem. sect.'s coun., 1997-2000, sect.'s program com. 1995-98, co-chair sect.'s program com. 1996-98, sect.'s sec. 1998-2000, chair leadership award com. 2002, recipient, Wally Richter Leadership award, 2001), Women in Comms., PEO Sisterhood (chpt. R recording sec. 2002--), Alpha Omicron Pi (Austin alumnae chpt., Rose award 1991, Adele K. Hinton award 1997). Avocations: gardening, sailing, cooking. Home: 3108 W Terrace Dr Austin TX 78757-4332

BANKSON, MARJORY, religious association administrator; b. Y; m. Peter Bankson. BA in Govt. and Econs., Radcliffe Coll., 1961; M in Am. History, U. Alaska, 1961; postgrad., Va. Episcopal Sem., 1985; LLD, Va. Theol. Sem., 1999. H.S. history and English tchr.; counselor Dartmouth Coll., 1969-70; profl. potter, 1970-80; pres. Faith at Work, Falls Church, Va., 1985-2001. Author: Briaded Streams: Esther and a Woman's Way of Growing, Seasons of Friendship: Naomi and Ruth as a Pattern, This Is My Body...Clay, Creativity and Change, (videos) The Potter and Clay, With Tongues of Fire (Five Women from the Book of Acts), The Call to the Soul, 1999. Mem. Ch. of the Saviour. Office: 106-B East Broad St Falls Church VA 22046-4501 E-mail: faithatwork@aol.com.

BANKSTON, ARCHIE MOORE, lawyer; b. Memphis, Oct. 12, 1937; s. Archie M. and Elsie Bernice (Shaw) B.; m. Emma Ann Dejan, Apr. 16, 1966; children— Louis, Alice. BA, Fisk U., 1959; LLB, Washington U., St. Louis, 1962, MBA, 1964. Bar: Mo. 1963, N.Y. 1966. Asst. divsn. counsel Gen. Foods Corp., White Plains, N.Y., 1964-67, product mgr. Maxwell House divsn., 1967-69; asst. sec. and corp. counsel PepsiCo, Inc., Purchase, N.Y., 1969-72; divsn. counsel Xerox Corp., Stamford, Conn., 1973; sec. and asst. gen. counsel Consol. Edison Co. of N.Y. Inc., N.Y.C., 1974-89, sec., assoc. gen. counsel, 1989—2002. Sec. Consolidated Edison, Inc., N.Y.C., 1998—2002; exec.-in-residence Coll. New Rochelle, NY, 2002—. Mem. 100 Black Men, Inc., N.Y.C.; former trustee Beth Israel Med. Ctr.; trustee Hoff-Barthelson Music Sch., Scarsdale, NY; past mem. Westchester County African Am. Adv. Bd.; former trustee Coll. New Rochelle; former bd. dirs. Urban League of Westchester County, Associated Black Charities, Mental Health Assn. Westchester County. Recipient Black Achievers in Industry award, Harlem br. YMCA, 1971, Merit award, Black Exec. Exch. Program Nat. Urban League, 1974, Disting. Svc. Commendation awards, Mental Health Assn., 1987, 1992, Jerome H. Holland Power of Humanity Corp. award, Am. Red Cross, 2001. Mem.: ABA, Am. Soc. Corp. Secs. (mem. audit, edn. and securities industry com., chmn. budget com. and membership com., chmn. 50th anniversary nat. conf. com., bd. dirs., Disting. Svc. award 2000), N.Y. State Bar Assn., Westchester Clubmen (pres.), Alpha Phi Alpha, Sigma Pi Phi, Pi Delta Phi. Office: Consol Edison Co NY Inc 4 Irving Pl New York NY 10003-3502 also: The College of New Rochelle 29 Castle Place New Rochelle NY 10805 E-mail: bankstona@coned.com.

BANKSTON, WILLIAM MARCUS, lawyer; b. San Angelo, Tex., Feb. 16, 1946; s. Wyatt Lester and Mary Alice (Powell) B.; m. Janna Coe Herridge, Aug. 15, 1965 (div.); children: Darla Kae, Kendra Lynne; m. Judith Ann Railsback, Nov. 20, 1981 (div.); m. Frances J. Talbott. BA, BS, Tex. Tech U., 1968; JD, U. Tex., 1971. Bar: Alaska 1971, Tex. 1971, U.S. Tax Ct. 1983, U.S. Ct. Claims 1984, U.S. Supreme Ct. 1986. Assoc. Croft & Bailey, Anchorage, 1971-73; ptnr. Croft, Bailey, Gueschow & Bankston, Anchorage, 1973-74; instr. Anchorage C.C., 1972-74; ptnr. Greene & Bankston, Anchorage, 1974-76, Bankston, Gronning, O'Hara Sedor, Mills, Givens & Heaphy, Anchorage, 1976—. Mem. ABA, Alaska Bar Assn., State Bar Tex. Methodist. Office: Bankston Gronning O'Hara Sedor Mills Givens Heaphy PC 550 W 7th Ave Ste 1800 Anchorage AK 99501-3569

BANNARD, WALTER DARBY, artist, art critic; b. New Haven, Sept. 23, 1934; s. Homes and Janet (Darby) B. BA, Princeton U., 1956. Chmn. dept. art and art history U. Miami, Fla., 1989-97. Lectr. in field, 1969—; vis. prof. Princeton (N.J.) U., 1974, also other univs.; mem. grad. faculty Sch. Visual Arts, N.Y.C., 1984-89; curator Hans Hoffman Hirshorn Mus., 1976; mem. internat. exhbn. com., 1976-78; co-chmn. internat. panel for visual arts Nat. Endowment for Arts, 1979-81. Contbr. articles and revs. on modern painting to profl. jours.; contbg. editor: Artforum, 1973-74; 75 one-man shows internat. galleries and mus. include retrospective Balt. Mus. Art, 1973, retrospective U. Tampa, 1997, retrospective Lowe Mus., 1999; numerous internat. group shows; represented in permanent collections at Mus. Modern Art, N.Y.C., Whitney Mus. Am. Art, Met. Mus. Art, N.Y.C., Guggenheim Mus., N.Y.C., others; juror numerous competitions, 1969—; sole juror Australian Bi-Centenary Art Competition, 1988. Recipient Nat. Found. Arts award, 1968-69; Francis J. Greenburger Found. award, 1986; John Simon Guggenheim Meml. Found. fellow, 1968; Richard A. Florsheim Art Fund grantee, 1991. Office: 1540 Levante Ave Miami FL 33124 E-mail: wbannard@aol.com.

BANNATYNE, MARK WILLIAM MCKENZIE, technical graphics educator; b. West Chester, Pa., May 22, 1952; s. Isobel Steel B.; m. Tatiana Yurievna Shcherbakova, Sept. 2, 1990; children: Yuri Markovich, Kirill Markovich, Anna Ylizaveta. AAS, B.C. Inst. Tech., Burnaby, Can., 1982; BS, Utah State U., 1988, MS, 1991; PhD, Purdue U., 1994. Staff tchr. indsl. tech. and edn. dept. Utah State U., Logan, 1986-89, lectr. indsl. tech. and edn. dept., 1990, grad. prof. indsl. tech. and edn. dept., 1990-92; grad. instr. Purdue U., West Lafayette, Ind., 1992-94; asst. prof. dept. instnl. and curricular studies Coll. Edn. U. Nev., Las Vegas, 1995-97, assoc. dept. head, 2002—03; assoc. prof. tech. graphics dept. Purdue U., West Lafayette, 1997—. Instr. Bridgerland Applied Tech. Ctr., Logan, 1988-92; mem. Engring. State Com., Logan, 1990-92, Gov.'s Coun. on Fgn. Exch., Salt Lake City, 1991-92; presenter Far West Popular Am. Culture Conf., 1996, 97, Rocky Mountain States Conf., Moscow, 1992, Tech. Edn. Assn., Kansas City, Mo., 1994, Jistec '96, Jerusalem, 1996, Far West Popular and Am. Culture Conf., 1996, 97, ASEE Conf., Seattle, 1998, IV'98 Conf. IV'2000, London, 1998, IV' 99 Conf., London, 1999, Siggraph, L.A., 1999; dir. Focus 1996, Moscow, 1996; presenter Winter Sch. Computer Graphics '99 Conf., Plzen, Czech Republic, 1999, 2000. Author: (book review) Tech. Tchr., 1989, ERIC Document, 1996, Popular Culture Rev., 1997; editl. bd. Jour. Tech. Studies; contbr. articles to profl. jours. Leader Boy Scouts of Am., Logan, 1984-86. Fulbright scholar Tula (Russia) State U., 1999-01, 2002. Mem. Internat. Tech. Edn. Assn. (conf. chair fgn. and internat. programs 1991), Am. Soc. Engring. Edn. (vice chmn. internat. divsn.), Assn. for Computing Machinery-Spl. Interest Group for Graphics, Am. Vocat. Assn. (presenter conf. 1991), Internat. Visualisation Soc. (com. mem.), Phi Kappa Phi, Epsilon Pi Tau. Mem. Lds Ch. Avocations: ice hockey, opera, art, foreign travel, history. Office: Purdue U Dept Computer Graphics Tech 1419 Knoy Hall Rm 363 West Lafayette IN 47907-1419 Fax: (765) 494-9267. E-mail: mwbannatyne@tech.purdue.edu.

BANNEN, JOHN THOMAS, lawyer; b. LaCrosse, Wis., Oct. 29, 1951; s. James J. and Ruth J. (Frisch) Bannen; m. Carol A. Swanson, Aug. 16, 1975; children: Ryan M., Kelly A., Erin C. BA summa cum laude, Coll. St. Thomas, 1973; JD, Marquette U., 1976; LLM in Taxation, DePaul U., 1989; BA in Spanish, U. Wis., 2003. Bar: Wis. 1976, U.S. Dist. Ct. (ea. and we. dists.) Wis. 1976, U.S. Tax Ct. 1979, U.S. Claims Ct. 1983, U.S. Supreme Ct. 1984. Shareholder Charne, Clancy & Taitelman, S.C., Milw., 1976-91; ptnr. Quarles & Brady, Milw., 1991—. Bd. dirs. Guardianship Svcs. Indigents, Milw., 1983—87; mem. adv. bd. Sch. Sisters Notre Dame, 1993—98, pres., 1995—98; mem. coun. Christ the King Parish, Wauwatosa, Wis., 1989—93, trustee, 1996—98. Fellow: Am. Coll. Trust and Estate Counsel (state law coord. Wis. 1990—95, chmn. com. employee benefits 2001—); mem.: ABA, Wis. Bar Assn. (bd. dirs. probate sect.), Assn. Advanced Life Underwriters (assoc.). Avocations: reading, gardening, Spanish language, cooking. Office: Quarles and Brady LLP Ste 2040 411 E Wisconsin Ave Milwaukee WI 53202-4497 E-mail: jtb@quarles.com.

BANNER, LOIS WENDLAND, education educator, writer; b. Inglewood, Calif., July 20, 1939; d. Harry John Wendland and Melba Madeleine Parkes; m. John Laslett, Mar. 1, 1994; children: Olivia Parkes, Gideon Byrne. BA, UCLA, 1956—60; MA, Columbia U., 1970—72, PhD, 1965—70. Instr. Douglass Coll., Rutgers U., New Brunswick, NJ, 1967—71, asst. prof., 1971—77; lectr. Princeton U., NJ, 1977—78; nat. endowment for the humanities prof. U. of Scranton, Pa., 1979—80; vis. sr. lectr. U. of Md., Balt. County, 1980—81; vis. assoc. prof. (history and am. studies) George Wash. U., Washington, 1981—83; prof. U. of So. Calif., Los Angeles, 1983—; William Robertson coe prof. Stanford U., Palo Alto, Calif., 1983; Jane Watson Irwin prof. Hamilton Coll., Clinton, NY, 1983; adj. prof. Josai U., Japan, 1993—98. Program chair Berkshire Conf. of Women Historians, Cambridge, Mass., 1973—74; dir. Princeton Project on Women in the Coll. Curriculum, Princeton, NJ, 1976—77; pres. Conf. Group in Women's History, Am. Studies Assn., Los Angeles, 1979—81; dir. Nat. Endowment for the Humanities Summer Seminar for Coll. Teachers, George Wash. U., Men, Women, and Popular Culture, Washington, 1984; v.p. Am. Studies Assn., Los Angeles, 1984—86, pres., 1986—88; v.p. and pres. Am. Hist. Assn., Pacific Coast Br., Los Angeles, 1991—93; dir. Nat. Endowment for the Humanities Summer Seminar for Coll. Teachers, USC, Women and Men in US History, Los Angeles, 1992. Author: (book) Intertwined Lives: Margaret Mead, Ruth Benedict, and Their Circle, Elizabeth Cady Stanton: A Radical for Woman's Rights, Women in Modern America: A Brief History; editor: Clio's Consciousness Raised: New Perspectives on the History of Women; author: Finding Fran: History and Memory in the Lives of Two Women (best book, women's issues, Ind. publishers book awards, 1999), In Full Flower: Aging Women, Power, and Sexuality: A History, American Beauty; editor: (collection of essays) Reading Benedict/Reading Mead: Feminism, Race, and Imperial Visions. Commr. City of Santa Monica, Commn. on the Status of Women, Calif., 1985—86. Recipient Associates Award for Creativity in Rsch. and scholarship, USC, 1988, Innovative Rsch. award, 1988—89, Innovative Tchg. award, 1985—86; Curriculum Enrichment grant, James Irvine Found., 1993, Humanities fellow, Rockefeller Found., 1978—79, Fellow, Radcliffe Inst., 1974—75. D-Liberal. Avocations: research, travel. Home: 2111 Oak St Santa Monica CA 90405-5009 Office: Dept History USC 3520 Trousdale Pkwy SOS 153 Los Angeles CA 90089 Personal E-mail: lbanner@usc.edu. E-mail: history@usc.edu.

BANNICK, JANICE CAROL, automotive dealerships executive; b. Clinton, Iowa, Oct. 12, 1938; d. Claus John and Irma Jeanne (Switzer) Greve; m. Robert T. Gallagher, May 21, 1958 (div. Apr. 1967); children: Angela Jeanne, Carol Ellen; m. Mearl G. Bannick, June 24, 1967 (dec. Aug. 1991). Student, Old Dominion Coll., Norfolk, Va., 1956-58, U. Wis., Milw., 1980-83, U. Tex., Arlington, 1983-86, Bradley U., 1992-94. Contr. Kimberly Chrysler-Plymouth, Inc., Davenport, Iowa, 1974-79; cons. Davenport and Milw., 1979-80; contr. Stark Oldsmobile, Inc., Menomonee Falls, Wis., 1980-83; bus. mgr., field rep. Motors Holding divsn. Gen. Motors Corp., Detroit, 1986-89; contr., CFO S&K Chevrolet Pontiac and Oldsmobile, Peoria, Ill., 1989-96; automotive cons. Peoria and Springfield, Ill., 1996-97; contr., dealer acctg. Gen. Acceptance Corp., Bloomington, Ind., 1997-98; CFO Anthony Pontiac, Gurnee, Ill., 1998-2000, Lou Bachrodt Automall & Bachrodt Pontiac, Rockford, Ill., 2000-01; team sales rep. Internat. Teamworks Inc., Vacaville, Calif., 2001—; contr. Magouirk Chevrolet-Olds, Inc., Dodge City, Kans., 2001—02; cons. MSXI, Ford Motor Co. Dealer Devel., Detroit, 2003—. Bd. dirs., treas. St. Marks Luth. Ch., Chillicothe, Ill., 1994-96, Peoria Art Gild, 1995-96. Republican. Avocations: watercolor painting, reading, running, walking, antique refinishing, gourmet cooking, golf. Home: 6318 N Ripley St Davenport IA 52806-2126 E-mail: bannick777@aol.com.

BANNING, KEVIN CHARLES, finance educator, department chairman; b. Lafayette, Ind., Mar. 19; s. Charles Russell and Joan Banning; m. Allison Beth Banning, Sept. 30, 1989; children: Robert Charles, Sarah Beth. BS, Ind. U., 1986; PhD, U. Fla., 1996. Fin. mgr. Gen. Mills, Mpls., 1986—89; CFO Comml. Office Products & Supply, South Bend, Ind., 1989—92; asst. prof. Auburn U., Montgomery, Ala., 1997—2002, assoc. prof., 2001—. Mgmt. dept. head Auburn U., 2001—. Exec. bd. mem. Montgomery Area Non-Traditional Equestrians, 1998—2003. Mem.: Acad. Mgmt. Office: Auburn U PO Box 244023 Montgomery AL 36124 E-mail: kcbanning@yahoo.com.

BANNISTER, CANDIDA CLEVE, data processing executive; b. Lincoln, Nebr., Mar. 3, 1957; d. Robert L. and Miwako Cleve; m. Jerome Bannister II. BA, UCLA, 1980. Info. sys. mgr. UCLA, 1980-97; sr. sys. analyst Franklin (Tenn.) Am. Life, 1997-99; info. sys. mgr. Micro Diagnostics Inc., Nashville, 1999-2000; sys. analyst CNA Life Ins., Nashville, 2000—02; data analyst Am. Healthways, Inc., 2003—. Mem. NAFE, Augustan Soc. (bd. dirs. 1994—, v.p. elec. info. sys. 1999—). E-mail: ccbannister@comcast.net.

BANNISTER, DAN WESLEY, historian, retired; b. Erie, Pa., May 13, 1921; s. Earl Ford Bannister and Hortense Elizabeth Ashley; m. Audrey Marie Shell, May 20, 1944; children: Dan W. III, Shelley Ashley, James Earl. BS, Ind. U., 1942; JD cum laude, Albany Law Sch., 1946; LLD, Lincoln Coll., 1998. Pvt. practice law, Rochester, N.Y., 1947-50; contr. Vaisey Bristol Shoe Co., Rochester, 1949-50; fin. contr. dir. Allstate Ins. Co., Skokie, 1951-61; v.p. Security Ins. Group, Springfield, Ill., 1962-75; pres. Horace Mann Ins. Group, Springfield, 1974-80; sr. v.p. Comml. Credit Co., Balt., 1974-80; pres. Gulf Ins. Group, Dallas, 1981-85. Pres. Abraham Lincoln Assn., Springfield, 1946-47, dir., 1991—, exec. com., 1994—. Mem. Chartered Property and Casualty Underwriters, Casualty Actuarial Soc., Actuarial Assn. Am. Episcopalian. Home: 1309 S Douglas Ave unit H Springfield IL 62704 Office: Abraham Lincoln Assn 1 Old State Capitol Plz Springfield IL 62701-1512

BANNISTER, GEOFFREY, university president, geographer; b. Manchester, Eng., Sept. 19, 1945; came to U.S., 1973; s. Leslie and Doris (Shankland) B.; m. Margaret Janet Sheridan, Jan. 28, 1968; children: Katherine, Janet. BA, U. Otago, New Zealand, 1967, MA with honors, 1969; PhD, U. Toronto, Can., 1974. Asst. prof. Boston U., 1973-77, acting chmn. geography, 1977-78, dean liberal arts, grad. sch., 1978-87; exec. v.p. Butler U., Indpls., 1987-89, pres., 1989—. Cons. Urban Affairs Ministry of State, Can., 1973; legal cons. U.S. Dept. of State 1982-84; bd. dirs. Somerset Group, Ind. Nat. Bank. Co-author atlas Spatial Dynamics of Postwar County Economic Change, 1977; contbr. articles to profl. jours. Chmn. bd. trustees Cambridge (Mass.) Montessori Sch., 1979-80; mem. corp. Sea Edn. Assn., Woods Hole, Mass., 1979-87; bd. dirs. United Way of Cen. Ind., 1990—, chmn. 1992 Premeire Campaign, edn. chmn.; bd. dirs. Greater Indpls. Progress Com., 1988—; pres. Midwest Collegiate Cons; chmn. World Rowing Championship, 1994. Fellow U. Toronto, 1970-71, Can. Council, 1972. Mem. Nat. Labor/Higher Edn. Coun., Nat. Assn. Scholars, Indpls. Bus. Jour. Blue Ribbon Panel, Indpls. Commn. on African-Am. Males, C. of C., Econ. Club, English Speaking Union U.S. (Indpls. br.), Coun. Urban Coll. of Arts, Letter and Scis., Kiwanis, Phi Beta Kappa. Avocations: bicycling, golf, skiing.

BANNISTER, ROBERT CORWIN, JR., historian, educator, retired historian; b. Bklyn., June 4, 1935; s. Robert C. and Ruth (Allen) B.; m. Joan Turner, June 8, 1958; children: Robert Stanley, Emily E., Paul Andrew, James Peter. BA, Yale U., 1955, Oxford U., Eng., 1957, MA, 1961; PhD, Yale U., 1961. Instr. history Yale U., New Haven, 1960-62; asst. to full prof. Swarthmore Coll., Pa., 1962-98, ret., 1998. Bicentennial prof. U. Helsinki, 1977-78; Fulbright prof. U. Rome, 1985, U. Leiden, Netherlands, 1992; mem. advanced placement program Ednl. Testing Service, Princeton, N.J., 1963-79; vis. prof. U. Queensland, Australia, 1988. Author: Ray Stannard Baker, 1966, Social Darwinism: Science and Myth, 1978, Sociology and Scientism, 1987, Jessie Bernard: The Making of a Feminist, 1991; editor: American Values in Transition, 1972, On Liberty, Society and Politics: The Essential Essays of William Graham Sumner, 1992. Mem. Am. Studies Assn., Orgn. Am. Historians Democrat. Office: Swarthmore College Ave Swarthmore PA 19081-1390 E-mail: rbannis1@swarthmore.edu.

BANNON, ANTHONY LEO, museum director; b. Hanover, N.H., Dec. 6, 1942; s. Robert E. and Frances Ann (Cacioppo) B.; children: Nicholas, Brendan. BS, St. Bonaventure, 1964; MA, SUNY, Buffalo, 1974, PhD, 1996. Tchr. sci. and English Father Baker High Sch., Lackawanna, N.Y., 1964-66; critic Buffalo News, 1966-85; dir. Burchfield-Penney Art Ctr., asst. v.p. cultural affairs SUNY Coll. at Buffalo, 1985-96; dir. George Eastman House Internat. Mus. Photography and Film, Rochester, NY, 1996—. Chmn. visual arts program panel N.Y. State Coun. on Arts, N.Y.C., 1986—88; co-chmn. arts programming com. World Univ. Games, Buffalo, 1991—93, co-chmn. adv. coun. [illegible] NY, 1999—2002; vice chmn. Empire State Craft Alliance, Saratoga Springs, NY, 1988—93; chmn. adv. bd. Quick Fine Arts Ctr. St. Bonaventure U., 1996—2002. Author: The Photo-Pictorialists of Buffalo, 1981, The Taking of Niagara, 1983, Arcadia Revisited, 1989, (monographs) Painterly Photographs: Contemporary Handworked Images, 1980, Grace Woodworth: Photographer Outside the Common Lines, 1984, ArtPark, 1989; organized major exhibits for Albright-Knox Gallery, Buscaglia-Castellani Art Gallery, Niagara U., N.Y., Burchfield-Penney Art Ctr. and Rockwell Hall Performing Arts Ctr., SUNY Coll., Buffalo, David Anderson Gallery, others. Mem. vestry Ch. Good Shepherd, Buffalo, 1986—89; bd. dirs. Greater Rochester Visitors Assn., 1996—97, Rochester Arts and Cultural Coun., 1998—2003; trustee N.Y. State Alliance of Arts Orgns., 1998—2002, bd. sec., 1999—2001; bd. dirs. Rochester Sch. for the Deaf, 1998—, N.Y. State Coun. on Humanities, 1999—; mem. adv. coun. to the sec. Smithsonian Instn., 2001—; mem. adv. coun. Chautauqua Art Ctr., 1998—; bd. dirs. Santa Fe Ctr. Photography, 2002—. Recipient Excellence in Writing about Deafness award Gallaudet Coll., 1985, Merit award Am. Photog. Hist. Soc., 1982; Profl. Study Leave grantee N.Y. State/United Univ. Professions, 1993, Outstanding Arts Adminstr. award The Buffalo Partnership, 1995, Arts award, St. Bonaventure U., 2002. Mem. Am. Assn. Mus., Mus. Assn. N.Y. State (counselor 1994-2003), Gallery Assn. N.Y. State (trustee 1997-2000), Buffalo State Coll. Found. (trustee 1985-91), Soc. Photog. Edn., Am. Assn. Mus. Dirs. Office: George Eastman House 900 East Ave Rochester NY 14607-2298 E-mail: tbannon@frontiernet.net, tbannon@geh.org.

BANNON, GEORGE, retired economics educator, department chairman; b. Phila., May 25, 1925; s. Joseph Aloysius and Violet May (McCartney) B.; m. Rosemary Ann Chirico, Aug. 19, 1950; children: Patricia Ann, Christina Ann, Terence George. Student, U. Ga., 1944, N.C. State U., 1944; AB, Muhlenberg Coll., 1947; MBA, Lehigh U., 1967. Contr. Overseas Underwriters Ltd., Nassau, Bahamas, 1957-61; internal auditor Bethlehem (Pa.) Steel Corp., 1961-68, sr. systems and procedure analyst, 1968-72, adminstrv. asst., 1972-81; vis. assoc. prof. Moravian Coll., Bethlehem, 1981-85; asst. prof. Muhlenberg Coll., Allentown, Pa., 1985-88, chmn. dept. econs., 1988-96; ret., 1996. Official Ea. Collegiate Football Officials Assn., Princeton, N.J., 1955-65; Pa. Interscholastic Football Officials Assn., Harrisburg, Pa., 1952-71. Organizer Allentown Area Luth. Parish, Luth. Ch. in Am., 1964-67; bd. dirs. Allentown Area Luth. Parish, 1984-87. Recipient Outstanding Official award Pa. Interscholastic Football Officials Assn., 1971. Mem. Nat. Assn. Accts. (rsch. com. 1979-84, mktg. com. 1985-86, bd. dirs. 1987-93, v.p. 1995-96, mem. nat. exec. com. 1995-96), Am. Mgmt. Assn., Fin. Exec. Inst., Allentown C. of C., Am. Assn. Collegiate Schs. Bus., West Allentown Kiwanis Club (pres. 1986-87). Avocations: photography, coin collecting, gardening. Home: 9 W Sycamore Pl Lewisburg PA 17837-9229

BANNON, NANCY, performing arts educator; Grad., Juilliard Sch. Cert. yoga tchr. Instr. dance SUNY, Purchase, 2002—; dancer Doug Varone and Dancers, 1993—2000, Tere O'Connor Dance, 2000—02. Instr. dance Rutgers U. Recipient Bessie award, 2002. Office: SUNY Performing Arts Ctr MPO Box 140 Purchase NY 10577

BANOFF, SHELDON IRWIN, lawyer; b. Chgo., July 10, 1949; BSBA in Acctg., U. Ill., 1971; JD, U. Chgo., 1974. Bar: Ill. 1974, U.S. Tax Ct. 1974. Ptnr. Katten Muchin Zavis Rosenman, Chgo., 1974—. Chmn. tax conf. planning com. U. Chgo. Law Sch., 1993-94. Co-editor Jour. of Taxation, 1984—, contbr. articles to profl. jours. Mem. ABA, Chgo. Bar Assn. (fed. taxation com., mem. exec. coun. 1980—, chmn. large law firm com., 1999-2000), Am. Coll. Tax Counsel. Office: Katten Muchin Zavis Rosenman 525 W Monroe St Ste 1600 Chicago IL 60661-3693 E-mail: sheldon.banoff@kmzr.com.

BANOME, LYDIA M. elementary school educator; b. N.Y.C., NY, May 11; d. Salvatore and Ester Banome; children: Anna Marie, Lydia Antonio. BS in Early Childhood Edn., 1974. Joined Sisters of St. Joseph; cert. early childhood edn. Am. Montessori Soc. Profl. dancer; tchr. Montessori method. Cons. learning difficulties Pinellas County Literacy, Dunedin, Fla. Home: 835 Oxford Ct Dunedin FL 34698

BANOVETZ, JAMES M. public administration educator, consultant; Prof., dir. divsn. pub. adminstrn. No. Ill. U., DeKalb, 1979-97, prof., dir. emeritus divsn. pub. adminstrn., 1998—, sr. rsch. assoc. Ctr. for Govtl. Studies, editor Policy Profiles, 1998—. Albert Levin prof. urban studies and pub. svc. Cleve. State U., 1991—93. Editor: Managing Local Government Finance, 1996. Fellow Nat. Acad. Pub. Adminstrn.; mem. Ill. City Mgmt. Assn. (Lifetime Achievement award 1997), Internat. City/County Mgmt. Assn. (hon.). Address: 7 Miller Ct Dekalb IL 60115-2311

BANSAK, STEPHEN A., JR., investment banker, financial consultant; b. Bridgeport, Conn., Sept. 19, 1939; s. Stephen A. and Genevieve Bansak; m. Susan Jean Dizon, July 20, 1984; children: Cynthia A., Thomas S., Stephen A. III, Kirk C. BS, Yale U., 1961; MBA, U. Pa., 1968. With Kidder, Peabody & Co., Inc., N.Y.C., 1968-89, v.p., 1971-75, co-mgr. dept. corpl fin., 1975-84; vice chmn. Kidder, Peabody Internat., N.Y.C., 1984—. Bd. dirs. Kidder Peabody P.R., KP Realty Advisers; sr. cons. Concord Internat. Ptnrs., 1990—, Bentley Assocs., 1990-92; vice chmn. Myers, Craig, Vallone, Francois, Inc., 1992-93; sr. advisor Universal Tech. inst., 1995-97, Motay Electronics, Inc., 1993-97, Buenavenjura Filamor Echuas (Manila), 1991-94; vis. lectr. Wharton Grad. Sch., U. Pa., 1989; past bd. dirs. Filbrin, Inc., Lighthouse Ptnrs.; bd. dirs. Troy Bioscis., Inc.; bd. dirs., vice chmn. Computerized Med. Sys., Inc.; mem. adv. bd. Global Health Care Ptnrs. (DLJ Mcht. Banking 1998-2001); past adv. com. Manschot Opportunity Fund. Past trustee, v.p. Rumson (N.J.) Country Day Sch. Lt. USN, 1962-66, Vietnam. Mem. Philippine-Am. C. of C. (bd. dirs.), U.S.-Asia inst. (past bd. dirs.), India House (past pres. Broad St. Club), Yale Club N.Y.C., Troon Golf and Country Club, Securities Industry Assn. (chmn. corp. fin. com., rule 415 com.), Am. Stock Exch. (ofcl. 1988-91).

BANSAL, ARVIND KUMAR, computer scientist, educator; arrived in U.S., 1984; m. Rekha Gupta. Ph. D. (Computer Sci.), Case Western Res. U., Cleveland, Ohio, USA, 1984—88; M. Tech (Computer Sci.), Indian Inst. of Tech., Kanpur, UP, India, 1981—83, B. Tech (Elec. Engring.), 1974—79. Asst. exec. engr. Indian Tel. Industries, Allahabad, India, 1979—81; sys. analyst Tata Engring. and Locomotive Co., Pune, India, 1983—84; grad. rsch. asst. Case Western Res. U., Cleve., 1984—88; asst. prof. Kent (Ohio) State U., 1988—93; summer rsch. faculty Argonne (Ill.) Nat. Lab., 1994—94; vising scientist European Molecular Biology Lab., Heidelberg, Germany, 1995—95; rsch. fellow U. of Melbourne, Melbourne, Australia, 1996—96; assoc. prof. Kent (Ohio) State U., 1993—. Contbr. articles to profl. jours. Mem.: AAAS, IEEE (Appreciation award 2001), Internat. Soc. of Computational Biology, Assn. of Computing Machinery, N.Y. Acad. of Sci. Office: Kent State U Kent OH Office Fax: 330-672-7824. Personal E-mail: arvind@adelphia.net. E-mail: arvind@cs.kent.edu.

BANSE, KARL, retired oceanography educator; b. Koenigsberg Pr., East Prussia, Germany, Feb. 20, 1929; came to U.S., 1960, naturalized; s. Karl and Wally B. PhD in Oceanography, U. Kiel, Germany, 1955, Dr. honoris causa, 1995. Postdoctoral fellow in marine sci. U. Kiel, 1955-57; Govt. India scholar Ctrl. Marine Fish Rsch. Sta., India, 1958—60; asst. prof. oceanography U. Wash., Seattle, 1960-63, assoc. prof. oceanography, 1963-66, prof. oceanography, 1966-95, retired, 1995. Recipient Lifetime Achievement award ASLO, 1998. Fellow Marine Biology Assn. India. Office: U Wash Sch Oceanography Box 357940 Seattle WA 98195-7940

BANSIL, ARUN, research scientist; s. P. C. and L. Bansil; m. Rama Bansil; children: Nisha, Amit, Rajat. PhD, Harvard U., Cambridge, Massachusetts, 1969—73; MA, SUNY at Stonybrook, Long Island, New York, 1967—69; B.Sc. (Honors), U. of Delhi, Delhi, India, 1964—67. Prof. of physics Northeastern U., Boston, Mass., 1987—, assoc. prof. of physics, 1981—87, asst. prof. of physics, 1976—81, founding dir., advanced sci. computation ctr., 1999—; editor, jour. of physics and chemistry of solids Elsevier Sci., Oxford, United Kingdom, 1994—; founding dir., elmo lab. Northeastern U., Boston, Mass., 1998—; exec. officer Physics Dept., Northeastern U., Boston, Mass., 1998—2000; hon. prof. (docent) Tampere U. of Tech., Tampere, Finland, 1989—; sci. cons. Netherlands Energy Rsch. Found. (ECN), Petten, Netherlands, 1987—; resident assoc. Argonne Nat. Lab., Argonne, Ill., 1991—; mem., commn. on charge, spin and momentum densities Internat. Union of Crystallography, 1993—2002. Author (authored or co-authored 145 publications) and 7 conference proceedings as of 2002. Recipient Robert D. Klein U. Lectr., Northeastern U., 2002, Listed in Am. Men and Women of Sci., 1991-, Mem., Phi-Beta-Delta Internat. Honor Soc., 1995-, Mem., Internat. Adv. Bd., Jour. of Advanced Materials (Algeria), 1996-, Mem., Editl. Adv. Bd., Materials Sci. Found., Trans Tech Publications, Switzerland, 1997-; fellow TOKTEN Fellow, UN Devel. Program (UNDP), 1993,1994; grantee Many grants from nat. and internat. funding agencies, 1976-. Mem.: Am. Phys. Soc. (life).

BANTA, DON ARTHUR, retired lawyer; b. Chgo., Mar. 10, 1926; s. George A. and Grace Regina (Donnelly) B.; m. Mickey Edwards, Mar. 31, 1951; children: Stephanie, Meredith, John, Hillary. BS, Northwestern U., 1948, LLB, 1950. Bar: Ill. 1950, U.S. Ct. Appeals (7th cir.) 1951, U.S. Dist. Ct. (no. dist.) Ill. 1953, U.S. Ct. Appeals (6th cir.) 1963, U.S. Supreme Ct. 1967, U.S. Ct. Appeals (3d cir.) 1972, U.S. Ct. Appeals (11th cir.) 1982. Assoc. Vogel & Bunge, Chgo., 1950-51; atty. Montgomery Ward & Co., Chgo., 1951-53; assoc. Pruitt & Grealis, Chgo., 1953-55; ptnr. Naphin Banta & Cox and predecessor firms, Chgo., 1956-90, Banta Hennessy & Graefe, Chgo., 1990-99, Michael Best & Friedrich, Chgo., 1999—2001; ret., 2001. Cons. Chgo. Vol. Legal Svcs. Found., 1983—, arbitrator and mediator, 2002-. Author: (with others) Labor Arbitration-A Practical Guide for Advocates. 1990, Supplement to How Arbitration Works 1985-89, 1991, How Arbitration Works, 5th edit., 1997, Discipline and Discharge in Arbitration, 1998. Bd. edn. Deerfield (Ill.) Sch. Dist., 1964-70, pres., 1968-69. With U.S. Army, 1944-46, ETO. Fellow Coll. Labor and Employment Lawyers; mem. ABA (labor sect. com. on alternative dispute resolution in labor and employment law), Ill. State Bar Assn., Chgo. Bar Assn., Phi Delta Phi, Delta Tau Delta, Union League Club. Roman Catholic. Home: 1000 Lake Shore Plz 36B Chicago IL 60611-1308 E-mail: outerdrive@msn.com.

BANTEL, LINDA MAE, former museum curator, consultant; b. King City, Calif., May 30, 1943; d. Clifford Burnett and Helen Vernelle (Mallicotte) Bantel; m. David Hollenberg, June 15, 1980; 1 child, Matthew Bantel Hollenberg. MA, NYU, 1973. Rsch. cons. N.Y. Hist. Soc., N.Y.C., 1975—76; guest co-curator Art Mus. of South Tex., Corpus Christi, 1977—79; rsch. assoc. Met. Mus. Art, N.Y.C., 1978—80; curator, dir. Mus. Pa. Acad. Fine Arts, Phila., 1980—95. Co-author (with James Thomas Flexner): The Face of Liberty: Founders of the U.S., 1975; author (with Marcus Burke): Spain and New Spain: Mexican Colonial Arts in Their European Context, 1979; author: The Alice M. Kaplan Collection, 1980, William Rush, American Sculptor, 1982; contbr. American Paintings in the Metropolitan Museum of Art Vol. II: A Catalogue of Works by Artists Born Between 1816-1845, 1985, Raphaelle Peale Still Lifes, 1988, contbr. (with others) Searching Out the Best, 1988, contbr. to Antiques mag., 1989; editor (with Jacolyn A. Mott): American Sculpture in the Museum of American Art of the Pennsylvia Academy of the Fine Arts, 1997. Mem.: Am. Assn. Mus., Coll. Art Assn. Home: 703 W Phil Ellena St Philadelphia PA 19119-3513 E-mail: lindabantel@aol.com.

BANTON, STEPHEN CHANDLER, lawyer; b. St. Louis; s. William Conwell and Ruth (Chandler) B. AB, Bowdoin Coll., 1969; JD, Washington U., St. Louis, 1973, MBA, 1974. Bar: Mo. 1973, U.S. Dist. Ct. (ea. and we. dists.) Mo. 1973. Asst. pros. atty. St. Louis County, 1973-75; sole practice Clayton, Mo., 1975-83; ptnr. Quinn, Ground & Banton, Manchester, Mo., 1983—. Pres. Coll. for Living, 1997-98. Exploring chmn. St. Louis coun. Midland Dist. Scouts, 1975-77; pres. Am. Youth Hostels Ozarks area, 1976-80; trustee St. Louis Art Mus., 1985-94; mem. Rockwood Sch. Bd., 1997—. Served with USMC. Recipient Leadership award Lafayette Community Assn., 1983, Service award The Meramec Palisades Community Assn., 1985, Service award Profl. Remodeling Assn., 1985, Service award St. Louis Symphony Orch., 1985. Mem. ABA, Mo. Bar Assn., St. Louis County Bar Assn., Bar Assn. Met. St. Louis, Assn. Trial Lawyers Am., St. Louis County League of C. of C. (pres. 1978), West Port C. of C. (bd. dirs. 1978-81, Service award 1983), Rotary (pres. Ballwin club 1997-98), Toastmasters (adminstrv. v.p.), Lions (pres. 1977), Kiwanis (pres. West County club 2001-02), Gideons (pres. Frontenac 1999-2002). Republican. Office: Quinn Ground & Banton 14611 Manchester Rd Ballwin MO 63011-3700 Home: 929 Saint Paul Rd Ballwin MO 63021-6061

BANTRY, BRYAN, entrepreneur, producer, director; b. Jacksonville, Fla., Oct. 12, 1956; Owner, operator dog-walking svc., 1969-73; photographer's agt. Patrick Demarchelier, 1973—; owner Bryan Bantry Hair-Makeup Agy., N.Y.C., 1973—, Bryan Bantry Celebrity Model Mgmt., N.Y.C., 1992—; chmn., chief exec. officer Royal Atlantic Airways, N.Y.C., 1987—. Co-prodr. (Broadway plays) You Can't Take it With You, 1983, Aren't We All, 1985, (off-Broadway plays) Greater Tuna, 1982, Hey Ma...Kaye Ballard, 1984; creator TV pilot Man's Best Friend, 1983; prodr. (feature documentary) The Cream Will Rise: The Sophie B. Hawkins Story, 1998; theatre prodr. (Broadway musical) Street Corner Symphony, 1997-98; prodr., co-dir. feature short film Eventual Wife, 2000. Chmn. Batoto Yetu inner-city youth program, N.Y.C., 1992-2002; bd. dirs. The Trevor Project, L.A. Mem. League of Am. Theatres and Prodrs. E-mail: bb@waggingtail.com.

BANUELOS, BETTY LOU, rehabilitation nurse; b. Vandergrift, Pa., Nov. 28, 1930; d. Archibald and Bella Irene (George) McKinney; m. Raul, Nov. 1, 1986; children: Patrice, Michael. Diploma, U. Pitts., 1951; cert., Loma Linda U., 1960. RN, Calif.; cert. chem. dependency nurse, addictions treatment specialist; ordained to ministry Ch. of God. Cons. occupl. health svc. Bd. Registered Nurses, 1984—. Lectr., cons. in field. Recipient Scholarship U. Pitts. Mem. Dirs. of Nursing, Calif. Assn. Nurses in Substance Abuse. Home and Office: 15 Oak Spring Ln Laguna Hills CA 92656-2980 E-mail: BettyB8@hotmail.com.

BANUK, RON EDWARD (RON BANUK), mechanical engineer; b. Brockton, Mass., Oct. 22, 1944; s. Joseph John and Leocadia Marilyn (Gusciora) B.; m. Patricia Audrey Ryan, July 4, 1969; children: Kim, Lance. BSME, Northea. U., 1967; MSME, San Diego State U., 1971. Design and stress engr. in advanced systems Ryan Aero. Co., San Diego, 1967-76; sr. tech. specialist Northrop Corp., Pico Rivera, Calif., 1976-94, program mgr., 1987-89, structures tech. area mgr., 1991, prin. investigator in advanced structure and foam devel., 1986-93; prin. engr. structures Advt. Tech. Transit Bus, 1993-99. Tech. lead for Navy's Composite Destroyer Deck, 737-700 Wedgetail Cert. Contbr. articles to profl. jours., including SAMPE, DOE, ASME, WVU. Mem. Soc. Adv. Material and Process Engring. Avocation: writing on religion. Home: 311 Sarahrose Ct Severna Park MD 21146-1913 Office: Northrop Grumman-ES MS 368 Linthicum MD 21090

BANWART, WAYNE LEE, agronomy, environmental science educator; b. West Bend, Iowa, Jan. 9, 1948; s. Albert R. and Betty R. (Zaugg) B.; m. Charlen Ann Schrock, Mar. 22, 1970; children: Krista, Kara, Neil. MS, Iowa State U., 1972, PhD, 1975. Asst. prof. U. Ill., Urbana, 1975-79, assoc. prof., 1979-84, prof., 1984-89, prof., assoc. head dept. agronomy, 1989-94, asst. dean, 1994—. Vis. scientist Constrn. Engring. Lab., Champaign, 1985-86; chmn. Nat. Atmospheric Deposition Program, 1986. Co-author: (textbook) Soils and Their Environment, 1992. Mem. patient satisfaction com. HMO, Champaign, 1987-93; pres. citizen's adv. com. Mahomet-Seymour Schs., 1981. Nat. Coll. Tchrs. of Agr. fellow, 1987. Fellow Am. Soc. Agronomy (George D. Scarseth award 1973). Soil Sci. Soc. Am.; mem. Internat. Soil Sci. Soc., Gamma Sigma Delta (pres.). Achievements include discovery that agricultural crops subject to acid rain will suffer little or no yield reduction or physiological damage; discovery that plant uptake and translocation of TNT is very limited while RDX is readily taken up and concentrated in plant tissues; that organic amendments offer promise for bioremediation of soils contaminated with these explosives. Home: 3201 Sandhill Ln Champaign IL 61822 Office: U Ill 1301 W Gregory Dr Urbana IL 61801-9015 E-mail: wanwart@uiuc.edu.

BANYA, SANTONINO KU'CAYA, science educator; b. Gulu, Uganda, July 10, 1957; arrived in U.S., 1989; s. Zakeo Kal Ocaya and Aburijina Ocaya Lapura. Diploma in sci. edn., Kenya Sci. Tchrs/ Coll., 1982; BA in Judaic Studies, U. Judaism, 1993; MEd in Phys. Sci., Ea. Ill. U., 1998; postgrad., So. Miss. U., 1999—. Cert. educator Commonwealth of Mass., 1997, Ministry of Higher Edn., Kenya. Tchr. Eng. Amboni HS, Kiganju, Kenya, 1977—78; tchr. Eng. and biology Lirhanda Girl's HS, Kakamega, Kenya, 1978; tchr. chemistry and biology Kangaru HS, Embu, Kenya; tchr. biology and Eng. Kaumoni HS, Makueni, Kenya, 1981—82; tchr. physics and chemistry Nguviu Boy's HS, Embu, Kenya, 1982—89; tchr. world culture S.E. Halifax (N.C.) HS, 1993—94; tchr. physics and chemistry N. Chgo. (Ill.) Cmty. HS, 1994—95; sci. dept. chair St. Martin Poress Acad., Chgo., 1995—97; tchr. chemistry De La Salle Inst., Chgo., 1997—99; instr. sci. Miss Porter's Sch., Farmington, Conn., 1999—. Author: Sketches of the Soul, 1997, The Best Poems & Poets of 2002, 2002. Mem.: AAAS, N.Y. Acad. Sci., Am. Chem. Soc. Avocations: music, dancing, reading, cooking, travel. Home: 60 Garden St Farmington CT 06032 Office: Miss Porter's Sch 60 Main St Farmington CT 06032 E-mail: kallidobo@aol.com.

BANZHAF, JOHN F., III, legal association administrator, lawyer; b. N.Y.C., July 2, 1940; s. John F., Jr. and Olga Banzhaf; m. Ursula Maag, 1971. BS in Elec. Engring, M.I.T., 1962; JD magna cum laude, Columbia U., 1965. Civilian research asst. Signal Corps Engring. Labs., 1957; research engr., cons. Lear Siegler Corp., 1959-62; editor Columbia Law Rev., 1964-65; research fellow Nat. Municipal League, 1965; law clk. to U.S. Dist. Judge Spottswood W. Robinson III, 1965-66; assoc. firm Watson, Leavenworth, Kelton & Taggart, N.Y.C., 1967; founder, exec. dir. Action on Smoking and Health, Washington, 1968—, Nat. Inst. Legal Activism, 1980—; prof. law and legal activism Nat. Law Center, George Washington U., 1968—; exec. dir. Action on Safety and Health, 1971-80, Open America, 1975-80; founder Nat. Center for Law and the Deaf, 1975—. Bd. dirs. Consumers Union, 1971 Recipient 17th ann. Sat. Rev. award distinguished TV programming in pub. interest, 1969; Advt. Age award, 1967, 68; those who made advt. news, 1967, 68; Benjamin Franklin Lit. and Med. Soc. award, 1981 Mem. Sigma Xi, Eta Kappa Nu, Tau Beta Pi. Home: 2810 N Quebec St Arlington VA 22207-5215 Office: Nat Center for Law and the Deaf 2013 H St NW Washington DC 20006-4207 *Despite the increasing complexity of society, and the seemingly overwhelming power of large institutions both public and private, one determined individual can still have a significant and beneficial impact on society. (I was responsible, as an individual, for over 200 million dollars worth of free radio and television time for anti-smoking commercials which led to the ban on cigarette commercials.).*

BAO, JOSEPH YUE-SE, orthopedist, microsurgeon, educator; b. Shanghai, Feb. 20, 1937; s. George Zheng-En and Margaret Zhi-De (Wang) B.; m. Delia Way, Mar. 30, 1963; children: Alice, Angela. MD, Shanghai First Med. Coll., 1958. Intern affiliated hosps. Shanghai First. Med. Coll.; resident Shanghai Sixth People's Hosp., orthopaedist, 1958-78, orthopaedist-in-charge, 1978-79, vice chief orthopaedist, 1979-84; rsch. assoc. orthop. hosp. U. So. Calif., L.A., 1985-90, 94—, vis. clin. assoc. prof. dept. orthopedics, 1986-89; coord. microvascular svcs. Orthopaedic Hosp., L.A., 1989-91; clin. assoc. prof. dept. orthopedics U. So. Calif., L.A., 1989—, clin. assoc. prof. plastic surgery, 1997—; attending physician Los Angeles County and U. So. Calif. Med. Ctr., L.A., 1986, 90—, Orthopaedic Hosp., L.A., 1998—, Coast Plaza Doctors Hosp., Norwalk, Calif., 1999—. Cons. Rancho Los Amigos Med. Ctr., Downey, Calif., 1986. Contbr. articles to profl. jours., chpts. to books. Mem. Internat. Microsurg. Soc., Am. Soc. for Reconstructive Microsurgery, Am. Soc. for Peripheral Nerve, Orthop. Rsch. Soc., Societe Internationale de Chirurgie Orthopedique et de Traumatologie, Calif. Med. Assn., Calif. Orthopedic Assn., L.A. Med. Assn. Home: 17436 Terry Lyn Ln Cerritos CA 90703-8522 Office: 13132 Studebaker Rd Ste 7 A Norwalk CA 90650

BAO, KATHERINE SUNG, pediatric cardiologist; b. Soochou, Kiangsu, China, Sept. 7, 1920; came to U.S., 1953; d. Yung H. Bao and Ming King; m. William S. Ting, May 2, 1948; children: Gordon K., Albert C. MD, Nat. Ctrl. Univ. Med. Coll., Nanking, China, 1944. Diplomate Am. Bd. Pediatrics. Intern Mercer Hosp., Trenton, N.J., 1953; resident Children's Meml. Hosp. Northwestern U., Chgo., 1954-57; fellow in pediatric cardiology Children's Hosp. L.A., Calif., 1957-59, attending cardiologist, 1960—; chief pediatric cardiology City of Hope Med. Ctr., Duarte, Calif., 1965-68; chief heart bd. L.A. Unified Sch. Dist. and PTA Specialty Health Clinics, L.A., 1968—; attending pediatrician, cardiologist Hollywood Presbyn. Med. Ctr., L.A., 1970—, UCLA, L.A., 1973—. Vis. pediatric cardiologist to univs. in Taipei Nat. Sci. Coun., Republic of China, 1983; pres.'s appointee Pres.'s Com. on Nat. Medal of Sci., 1983-85; adv. com. on health and med. care svcs. Dept. Health Svcs., Calif., 1988-90; pres. Chinese Physicians Soc. of So. Calif., 1969; speaker in field. Active Rep. Eagle, Rep. Presdl. Task Force, Rep. Presdl. Round Table. Rsch. Fellow Cardiologist, NIH, 1960-63; recipient Physician of Yr., Hon. Svc. award Calif. Congress of PTA, Inc., 1984, U.S. Rep. Senatorial Medal of Freedom, 1994; named Internat. Scientist of Yr., IBC, Cambridge, Eng., 2001, Woman of the Yr., ABI, 2002. Fellow Am. Acad. Pediatrics; mem. AMA, AAAS, World Med. Assn., Calif. Med. Assn., L.A. County Med. Assn., Am. Heart Assn., Internat. Cir. of L.A. World Affairs Coun., N.Y. Acad. Scis., Hollywood Acad. Medicine (pres. 1995), Scripps Clinic La Jolla (coun.). Office: PO Box 10456 Beverly Hills CA 90213-3456

BAO, LICHUN, application developer, educator; m. Chunhua Pan. Ph.D. U. Calif., Santa Cruz, 2002. Rsch. engr. Cenus Techs., Inc., Scotts Valley, Calif., 2000—02, Meru Networks, Inc., 2002—03; asst. prof. U. Calif., Irvine, 2003—. Mem.: IEEE/ACM (Computer Society 1997—2002).

BAO, SHUMING, economist, researcher; s. Sifu Bao; m. Xiaohong Xu; children: Zhe Charlie, Dylan Herbert. PhD, Clemson U., 1996. Rsch. scientist MathSoft, Inc, Seattle, 1996—97; sr. rsch. assoc. China Data Ctr., U. Mich., Ann Arbor, Mich., 1997—. Sr. rsch. coord. for China initiatives Internat. Inst., U. of Mich., Ann Arbor, Mich., 1997—. Mem.: Regional Sci. Assn. Internat. (assoc.), Chinese Economist Soc. (assoc.; v.p. 2002—03), Assn. for Chinese Profls. in Geog. Info. Sci. (life; pres. 1999—2000), Gamma Sigma Delta, Alpha Epsilon Lambda. Achievements include development of S-PLUS for ArcView GIS, a software for spatial analysis. Office: U Mich Ste 3630 1080 S University Ave Ann Arbor MI 48109-1106 Office Fax: 734-764-5540. E-mail: sbao@umich.edu.

BAO, XUE-MING, librarian, educator; b. Shanghai, People's Republic of China, June 8, 1957; came to U.S., 1985; s. Si-Wen Bao and Xi-Kun Cao; m. Yi-Ping Tao, July 23, 1984; 1 child, David. MEd, U. Victoria, Can., 1983; MLS, No. Ill. U., 1991, EdD, 1989. Cert. profl. libr. Head cmty. learning ctr. Paterson (N.J.) Free Pub. Libr., 1991-94; asst. libr. dir. Belleville (N.J.) Pub. Libr. and Info. Ctr., 1994-97; libr., assoc. prof. Seton Hall U., South Orange, NJ, 1997—. Computer sys. libr. info. ctr. Belleville Pub. Libr., 1997—. Contbr. articles to profl. jours. Grantee numerous fed. and state govts., and pvt. founds., 1991-2000. Mem. ALA, Libr. and Info. Tech. Assn., N.J. Libr. Assn. (mem. coll. and univ. sect.). Avocations: reading, traveling, movies. Office: Univ Libr Seton Hall U 400 South Orange Ave South Orange NJ 07079-2671 E-mail: baoxuemi@shu.edu.

BAPTIST, ALLWYN J. healthcare consultant; b. India, July 10, 1943; came to U.S., 1971; s. Peter L.G. and Trescilla (Lobo) B.; m. Anita Lobo, Sept. 8, 1973; children: Alan, Andrew, Annabel, Arthur. BCS, U. Calcutta, India, 1962; cert. mgmt., U. Chgo., 1978. CPA, Ill; chartered acct., India. Divisional acct. Rallis India Ltd., Bombay, 1967-71; mgr. Chgo. Blue Cross, 1972-79; sr. mgr. Price Waterhouse, Chgo., 1979-84; v.p., dir. Truman Esmond and Assocs., Barrington, Ill., 1984-86; ptnr. Laventhol and Horwath, Chgo., 1986-90, BDO Seidman, Chgo., 1991-2000; pres. Baptist Cons. Inc., 2000—. Mem. adv. bd. St. Mary of Nazareth Hosp., 1989—, mem. gov. bd., 1992-94, 96-98, lifetime trustee. Contbr. articles to profl. jours. Mem. fin. com. St. James Ch., Arlington Heights, Ill., 1987; mem. AICPA Health Care Com., 1991-94. Mem. Healthcare Fin. Mgmt. Assn. (dir., sec. 1983-85, pres. 1988-89, recipient William J. Follmer award 1984, Reeves award 1989, Muncie Gold award 1992, founders medal of honor 1998), India Cath. Assn. Am. (treas. 1980, 87, pres. 1988). Avocations: travel, reading, tennis, golf. Office: Bapt Cons Inc 126 E Wing St Arlington Heights IL 60004

BAPTIST, ERROL CHRISTOPHER, pediatrician, educator; b. Colombo, Sri Lanka, Feb. 24, 1945; came to U.S., 1974; s. Egerton Cuthbert and Hyacinth Margaret (Colombo) B.; m. Christine Rosemary Francke, Aug. 7, 1976; children: Lauren Marianne, Erik Christopher. MB, BS, U. Ceylon, 1969. Diplomate Am. Bd. Pediat. Intern Colombo Gen. Hosp. and Children's Hosp., 1969-70; resident house officer Dist. Hosp., Gampola, Sri Lankda, 1970-71, Base Hosp., Kegalle, Sri Lankda, 1971-74; family practitioner Marawila, Sri Lankda, 1974; resident in pediat. Coll. Medicine and Dentistry N.J., Newark, 1975-77; pvt. practice, Rockford, Ill., 1977—. Asst. prof. pediat. U. Ill. Coll. Medicine, Rockford, 1977-94, assoc. prof., 1994-2000, clin. prof. pediats., 2000—; chmn. dept. pediat. St. Anthony Med. Ctr., Rockford, 1986—. Fellow Am. Acad. Pediat.; mem. So. Med. Assn. Roman Catholic. Home: 5112 Parliament Pl Rockford IL 61107-5066 Office: Mulford Village Office Park 461 N Mulford Rd Rockford IL 61107-5190

BAPTISTE, THOMAS L. career officer; BSBA in Fin., Calif. State U., 1973; student navigator tng., Mather AFB, Calif., 1973-74; student, MacDill AFB, Fla., 1974-75, 81-82, Williams AFB, Ariz., 1977-78, Squadron Officer Sch., 1977; student F-4 qualification tng., George AFB, Calif., 1978-79; student, Air Command and Staff Coll., 1986; MPA, Golden Gate U., 1987; student, Air War Coll., 1990, Johns Hopkins U., 1997. Commd. 2d lt. USAF, 1973, advanced through grades to brig. gen., 1997; weapons sys. officer and instr. 44th Tactical Fighter Squadron, Kadena Air Base, Japan, 1975-77; aircraft comdr., standardization and evaluation officer 334th Tactical Fighter Squadron, Seymour Johnson AFB, N.C., 1979-81; stationed at MacDill AFB, Fla., 1982-84, 85-89; F-16 instr. pilot and chief, standardization/evaluation div. 8th Tactical Fighter Wing, Kunsan Air Base, S. Korea, 1984-85; asst. dir. nuc. ops. Hdqs. Def. Nuc. Agy., Alexandria, Va., 1990-92; comdr. 52d Ops. Group, Spangdahlem Air Base, Germany, 1992-94; chief weapons tech. control div. Joint Staff, Pentagon, Washington, 1994-96, asst. dep. dir. internat. negotiations, 1994-96, directorate strategic plans and policy, 1994-96; dep. comdr. Can. N. Am. Aerospace Def. Command Region, Winnipeg, Manitoba, 1996-98; comdr. Cheyenne Mountain Ops. Ctr., Cheyenne Mountain Air Sta., Colorado Springs, Colo., 1998-99; asst. chief of staff ops. HQ Allied Air Forces Southern Europe, Naples, Italy, 2000—. Decorated Air medal. Office: USAF/CC Air South Allied Air Forces Apo AE 09014-6001

BAQUET, CHARLES R., III, former federal agency administrator, international studies educator; b. New Orleans, Dec. 24, 1941; BA, U. Xavier, 1963; MPA, Syracuse U., 1975. With Fgn. Svc., 1968, consular officer, 1969-71; gen. svcs. officer bldg. mgmt. Dept. of State, 1971, adminstrv. officer Bur. Adminstrn., 1971-75, spl. asst. to Asst. Sec. of Adminstrn., 1978-79; gen. svcs. officer U.S. Consulate Gen., Hong Kong, 1975-76; councillor adminstrv. affairs U.S. Embassy, Beirut, 1976-78; dep. Office of Ops., 1979-83; dir. regional mgmt. ctr. U.S. Embassy, Paris, 1983-87; sr. seminar Fgn. Svc. Inst., 1987-88; with U.S. Consul Gen., Cape Town, South Africa, 1988-91; U.S. amb. to Djibouti, 1991-93; dep. dir. Peace Corps, Washington, 1994—2002; dir. Ctr. for Internat. Studies, Xavier U., La., 2002—. Vol. Peace Corps, Somali Republic, 1965-67.

BARA, JEAN MARC, finance and communications executive, artist; b. Roubaix, France, Aug. 22, 1946; came to U.S., 1970; s. Henri and Marie Antoinette (Dousseau) B.; m. Marian Yu, May 8, 1973; 1 child, Patrick Luc. B in Engring., Fed. U. Rio Grande do Sul, Brazil, 1969; MBA, Columbia U., 1972. With Chase Manhattan Bank, 1972-88; assigned Chase's Brazilian affiliate Banco Lar Brasileiro, 1978-80, mng. dir., head corp./retail mktg., planning, product mgr., 1980; v.p., head Brazil/Argentina/Paraguay liaison office Chase Manhattan Bank, N.Y.C., 1980-82, v.p. corp. banking team, Latin Am. coord. mining and metals, 1983, v.p. nat. positioning group, 1984; corp. fin. exec. Chase Investment Bank, 1985-88; with Young & Rubicam, N.Y.C., 1988—, v.p., corp. treas., 1988-89, sr. v.p., corp. treas., 1989-91; exec. dir., CFO Landor Assocs., N.Y.C., 1992-94; CFO Burson Marsteller, 1997-98; pres. Ams.-Ea. Region, chief learning officer Landor Assocs., 1998—; pres. Americas, 2000—; generative artist, 2001—. Mem. Beta Gamma Sigma. Home: PO Box 4446 Greenwich CT 06831-0408 Office: PO Box 4446 Greenwich CT 06831-0408

BARAB, MARVIN, financial consultant; b. Wilmington, Del., July 16, 1927; s. Jacob and Minnie (Press) B.; m. Gertrude Klein, June 13, 1951; children: Jordan, Neal, Caryn. BS with distinction, Ind. U., 1947, MBA, 1951. Dir. mktg. Edward Weiss & Co., Chgo., 1951-56; dir. bus. rsch. Parker Pen Co., Janesville, Wis., 1956-59; dir. mktg. rsch. packaging and graphics Mattel Inc., Hawthorne, Calif., 1959-65; pres. Barcam Pub. Co., Rolling Hills Estates, Calif., 1959-70, Rajo Publs., Rolling Hills Estates, 1967-70, So. Calif. Coll. Med. & Dental Careers, Anaheim, 1970-81, Barbrook, Inc., Rolling Hills Estates, 1981—96. Cons. Marvin Barab & Assocs., Rolling Hills Estates, Calif., 1981—. Editor: Rand McNally Camping Guide, 1967-70; contbr. articles to various publs., 1982-87. Treas. Harbor Free Clinic, 1990-92; bd. dirs. So. Bay Contemporary Art Mus., 1993-94, sec., 1994, peer couns., South Bay Health Dist., 2003-. Mem. Nat. Assn. Trade and Tech. Schs. (hon. life, sec. 1977-79, pres. 1979-81, bd. dirs.), Calif. Assn. Paramed. Schs. (pres. 1973-77). Avocations: travel, music, art. Office: 904 Silver Spur Rd # 110 Palos Verdes Peninsula CA 90274-3800 E-mail: marvbarab@hotmail.com.

BARABASH, CLAIRE, lawyer, special education administrator, psychologist; b. N.Y.C., Oct. 22, 1940; d. Maurice Isaac and Sarah (Libowsky) B. BA, Bklyn. Coll., 1960; MS, CUNY, 1962; PhD, NYU, 1979; JD, Bklyn. Law Sch., 1994. Bar: N.J. 1994, N.Y. 1995, Ala. 2000; Diplomate Am. Coll. Forensic Examiners; lic. psychologist, sch. psychologist; cert. sch. dist. adminstr. Psychology intern Bklyn. Coll. Edn. Clinic, 1962-63; sch. psychologist Yonkers (N.Y.) Bd. Edn., 1963-65, N.Y.C. Bd. Edn., 1965-78, regional coord., 1978-82, dept. asst. supt., 1982-95, asst. supt. for clin. svcs., 1991-92; pvt. practice Marguretville, NY, 1996—; forensic cons., 1999—. Adj. assoc. prof. NYU, 1979-80, L.I. U., Bklyn., 1988-93. Named Outstanding Spl. Educator of Yr. Orthodox Jewish Tchrs., 1990, Brian E. Tomlinson award for disting. contbns. in psychology, 1991. Mem. APA, ABA, N.Y. State Bar Assn., N.Y.C. Assn. Sch. Psychologists (pres. 1979-80), Adminstrv. Women in Edn. (Woman of Yr. 1989, chair mentoring com. 1989-90), Acad. for Pub. Edn. Home: 101 Clark St Brooklyn NY 11201-2746

BARABINO, WILLIAM ALBERT, science and technology researcher, inventor; b. Bay Shore, N.Y., Feb. 11, 1932; s. John Joseph and Anna Marie (Gates) B.; children: Susan Beth, Diane Marie, William John. Student, Fordham U., 1951; AS, SUNY, Farmingdale, 1952; student, St. Louis U., 1957; diploma,

Alexander Hamilton Inst., N.Y.C., 1963. Dist. mgr. Piper Aircraft Corp., Ctrl. Am., Mex., 1960-62; application engr. Lab. for Electronics, Boston, 1962-63; mktg. mgr. spl. equipment divsn. Itek Corp., Waltham, Mass., 1963-65; bus. cons. North Reading, Mass., 1965-68; dir. Andover (Mass.) Inst. Bus., 1968-70; sci. and tech. rschr. North Reading, 1970—; founder, mng. gen. ptnr. Mass Light Internat. Group, Agoura Hills, Calif., 1992—; founder, CEO In-Case Products, Inc., Agoura Hills, Calif., 1990. Cons. CTS Corp., Proctor and Gamble, Scovill Corp., Am. Enviro Products, Inc., Plessey Co., Ltd., GM, Goodyear Aerospace, Ford Motor Co. Patentee tire pressure alarm and warning systems (6), brake wear warning system, fluid level and condition detection systems, personal, feminine and infant hygiene products (7), treatment for causes of scalp diseases, based on theory then electron-microscopy capture of mitochrondia with dual set of double-walled membranes, liquid dispensing swab applicator, others; contbr. articles to profl. jours. Mem. 2000 Rep. Presdl. Task Force. Capt., rated pilot/rated navigator USAF, 1952-59. Mem. VFW, Am. Legion. Republican.

BARACK, PETER JOSEPH, lawyer, educator; b. Cleve., Nov. 3, 1943; s. Louis Barry and Florence (Schenberg) B.; m. Elise Hoffman, June 6, 1971; children: Sarah, Jonathan, David. AB summa cum laude, Princeton U., 1965; BPhil, Oxford (Eng.) U., 1967; JD magna cum laude, Harvard U., 1970. Bar: Ill. 1970, U.S. Ct. Appeals (7th cir.) 1976, U.S. Supreme Ct. 1978. Asst. prof. bus. adminstrn. Harvard U. Grad. Sch. Bus. Adminstrn., Cambridge, Mass., 1970-72; asst. prof. law Northwestern U. Sch. Law, Chgo., 1972-74, dir. JD-MM joint degree program, 1972-80, assoc. prof., 1974-79, adj. prof. corp. law, Edward Avery Harriman lectr., 1979—; ptnr. Levy and Erens, Chgo., 1969-74; founding, sr. ptnr. Barack, Ferrazzano, Kirschbaum Perlman & Nagelberg LLC, Chgo., 1984—. Adj. prof. fin. Kellogg Grad. Sch. Mgmt. Northwestern U., 1998—; of counsel Mayer, Brown & Platt, Chgo., 1977-79; pres. Chgo. Mgmt. Group, Inc., 1972—; bd. dirs. Christian Dior Perfumes, Inc., Duty Free Stores, Inc., Hillels of Ill.; lectr. in field. Contbr. articles to profl. jours. Pres. Highland Park (Ill.) Libr., 1982-84. Recipient Lt. John A. Larkin, Jr. Meml. prize, 1965; Marshall scholar, 1965; Nuffield scholar, 1966. Mem. ABA, Ill. State Bar Assn., Chgo. Bar Assn., Chgo. Coun. Lawyers, Assn. Marshall Scholars. Home: 1379 Sheridan Rd Highland Park IL 60035-3406 Office: 333 W Wacker Dr Ste 2700 Chicago IL 60606-1227 E-mail: peter.barack@bfkpn.com.

BARAD, JILL ELIKANN, family products company executive; b. N.Y.C., May 23, 1951; d. Lawrence Stanley and Corinne Elikann; m. Thomas Kenneth Barad, Jan. 28, 1979; children: Alexander David, Justin Harris. BA English and Psychology, Queens Coll., 1973. Asst. prod. mgr. mktg. Coty Cosmetics, N.Y.C., 1976-77, prod. mgr. mktg., 1977; account exec. Wells Rich Greene Advt. Agy., L.A., 1978-79; product mgr. mktg. Mattel Toys, Inc., L.A., 1981-82, dir. mktg., 1982-83, v.p. mktg., 1983-85, sr. v.p. mktg., 1985-86, sr. v.p. product devel., 1986, exec. v.p. product design and devel., exec. v.p. mktg. and worldwide product devel., 1988-89; pres. girls and activity toys div. Mattel Toys, Inc. (name now Mattel, Inc.), L.A., 1989-90; pres. Mattel USA, 1990-92; pres., COO Mattel, Inc., 1992-97, pres., CEO, 1997, chmn., CEO, 1997-2000. Bd. dirs. Pixar Animation Studios, Leap Wireless Internat.; bd. fellows Claremont U. Ctr. and Grad. Sch. Trustee emeritus Queens Coll. Found.; chair exec. adv. bd. Children Affected by AIDS Found.; bd. advs. Girls Inc., White House Project, The For All Kids Found., Inc.; vice chmn., bd. govs. Town Hall of Los Angeles. Exec. bd. Med. Scis. UCLA,

BARAGWANATH, ALBERT KINGSMILL, curator, writer; b. Lima, Peru, July 20, 1917; s. John Gordon and Leila Radcliff (Morris) B.; m. Eileen Mary Flanagan, Sept. 1, 1943; children— Joan Baragwanath Shaw, Janice, John Blackburn, Patricia. Grad., Hill Sch., Pottstown, Pa., 1936; BA, Princeton, 1940; MA in Am. History, Columbia, 1952. With traffic and sales dept. Eastern Air Lines, N.Y.C., 1946-50; librarian Mus. City N.Y., 1952-58, curator prints and portraits, 1959—, sr. curator, 1963-79, sr. curator emeritus, 1980—. Mem. N.Y.C. Mayor's Task Force on Municipal Archives, 1966; mem. adv. com. Mus. Am. Folk Art, 1969— Author: More Than a Mirror to the Past: The First Fifty Years of the Museum of the City of New York, 1973, 50 Currier & Ives Favorites, 1978, 100 Currier & Ives Favorites, 1978; New York Life at the Turn of the Century in Photographs, 1985; contbr.: New York City Guide, 1964, Currier and Ives, Chronicles of America, 1968. Served from pvt. to capt. AUS, 1941-46, ETO; Served from pvt. to capt. AUS, PTO. Decorated Combat Inf. badge. Mem. Am. Hist. Print Collectors Soc. (dir.) Home: 20 Summit Ave Larchmont NY 10538-2930 Office: 1220 5th Ave New York NY 10029-5221

BARAMKI, THEODORE ATALLAH, gynecologist, reproductive endocrinologist; b. Jerusalem, May 6, 1931; s. Atallah T. and Cecile (Madbak) B.; m. Ingrid Ringe, Dec. 27, 1969. MD, Cairo U. Sch. Medicine, 1957. Diplomate in ob-gyn. and in reproductive endocrinology Am. Bd. Ob-Gyn. Intern Johns Hopkins Hosp., Balt., 1960-61, resident in ob-gyn., 1961-64; fellow in reproductive endocrinology Johns Hopkins U., Balt., 1964-66; head divsn. reproductive endocrinology Greater Balt. Med. Ctr., 1978-2001, dir. prenatal diagnostic ctr., 1981—2000. Assoc. prof. ob-gyn. Johns Hopkins Med. Sch., 1980—. Co-author: Medical Cytogenetics, 1967. Recipient 1st Class Independence medal, Jordan, 1974. Fellow Am. Coll. Ob-gyn.; mem. Md. Ob-gyn. Soc. (pres. 1976-77, cert.). Republican. Office: Johns Hopkins Hosp Phipps 247 600 N Wolfe St Baltimore MD 21287

BARAMOVA, IRINA ANTONOVA, investment banker; b. Geneva, May 5, 1972; d. Anton Donchev and Eugenia Nedialkova B.. BA in Applied Econs., BA in Bus. Adminstrn., Am. U. in Bulgaria, Bulgaria, 1995; MBA, Duke U., Durham, NC, 1999. Series 7 NASD, 1999, Series 63 NASD, 1999. Client svc. dir. Leo Burnett & Co., Sofia, Bulgaria, 1995—97; tchg. asst. Duke U., Durham, NC, 1998—99; sr. assoc. Merrill Lynch & Co., N.Y.C., 1999—2003; convertible securities analyst trainer Merrill Lynch & Co., N.Y.C., 2000—02, co-head recrutiting team to Duke U., 2001—02; assoc. v.p. HSH Nordbank, N.Y.C., 2003—. Founder Marco Polo Global Hedge Fund, Sofia, Bulgaria, 2003—. Translator: confidential documents for the UNDP. Fuqua fellowship, Duke U., 1997, 1998, Ann. Scholarship, Am. U. in Bulgaria, 1991 - 1995. Mem.: PADI (licentiate), BalkanTourist (assoc.; ski instr. 1988—95). Greek Orthodox. Avocations: skiing, jogging, fitness, tennis, rollerblading.

BARAN, CHRISTINE, systems analyst; b. Rochester, N.Y., Apr. 21, 1958; d. Wolodymyr and Olha (Zyrak) B. AS, Rochester Inst. Tech., 1978, BS, 1980. Computer programmer Infodata Sys., Rochester, N.Y., 1980-83; sys. analyst Acumenics, Bethesda, Md., 1983-85; staff cons. Martin Marietta, Greenbelt, Md., 1985-88; sys. analyst, computer specialist Smithsonian Inst., Washington, 1988—. Cons. USAID, Washington, 1983-90 Recipient Discovering Undeveloped Engrng. Scientific Talent, Eastman Kodak Co., 1975—80. Mem. NAFE, LWV. Republican. Mem. Ukrainian Catholic. Home: 8607 Chase Glen Cir Fairfax Station VA 22039-3308 Office: Smithsonian Instn Comptr Office 955 Lenfant Plz SW Washington DC 20024-2119

BARAN, DAVID A, cardiologist; s. Henri and Lisa Baran; m. Carol T Gorski; 1 child, Matthew. MD, U. of South Fla. Coll. of Medicine, Tampa, 1992. Bd. Cert. in Cardiovascular Dis. Am. Bd. of Internal Medicine, 1999. Asst. prof. of medicine Mt. Sinai Med. Ctr., New York, NY, 1999—. Fellow: Am. Coll. Cardiology; mem.: Internat. Soc. of Heart and Lung Transplantation. Achievements include research in Risk factors for renal failure in cardiac transplant patients. Avocations: computers, travel. Office: Mt Sinai Hosp 1 Gustave L Levy Pl New York NY 10029

BARAN, JAN WITOLD, lawyer, educator; b. Ingolstadt, Germany, May 14, 1948; came to U.S., 1951; s. Jerzy Leopold and Leonce Sidonie (Vanden Bussche) B.; m. Kathryn Kavanagh, June 16, 1979; children: Brendan Jerzy, Maria Leonce, Elise Jett, Anna Margaret. BA, Ohio Wesleyan U., 1970; JD, Vanderbilt U., 1973. Bar: Tenn. 1973, D.C. 1976, U.S. Dist. Ct. D.C. 1980, U.S. Ct. Appeals D.C. 1980, U.S. Ct. Appeals (10th cir.) 1994, U.S. Supreme Ct. 1980, U.S. Ct. Appeals (5th cir) 2001. Legal counsel Nat. Rep. Congl. Com., Washington, 1975-77; exec. asst. Fed. Election Commn., Washington, 1977-79; assoc. Baker & Hostetler, Washington, 1979-81, ptnr., 1981-85, Wiley, Rein & Fielding, Washington, 1985—. Gen. counsel, George Bush for Pres., Inc., 1987-88; gen. counsel, Bush-Quayle, Inc., 1988; lectr., co-chair Practicing Law Inst., Corp. Polit. Activities, Washington, 1978—. Author: The Election Law Primer for Corporations, 1984, 88, 92, 2000, 2002. Chmn. nat. adv. bd. Jour. of Law and Politics, 1983—; gen. counsel Am. bicentennial Presdl. Inaugural Inc., 1989, Rep. Nat. Com., 1989-92; mem. Pres. Commn. Fed. Ethics Law Reform; amb., head U.S. del. World Adminstrv. Radio Conf. WARC, Malaga, Spain, 1992; gen. counsel, dir. Bus.-Industry Polit. Action Com., 1996—. Patrick Wilson scholar, 1970-73. Mem. ABA (chmn. com. election law 1981-2000), D.C. Bar Assn., FBA (chmn. polit. campaign and election law com. 1981-83). Roman Catholic. Home: 1608 Walleston Ct Alexandria VA 22302-3928 Office: Wiley Rein & Fielding LLP 1776 K St NW Ste 900 Washington DC 20006-2332

BARAN, PAUL, computer executive; b. Poland, Apr. 29, 1926; came to U.S., 1928; m. Evelyn Murphy, 1955; 1 child, David. BSEE, Drexel U., 1949; MS in Engrng., UCLA, 1959; DSc in Engrng. (hon.), Drexel U., 1997; PhD in Policy Analysis (hon.), RAND Grad. Sch., 2000. With Eckert-Mauchley Computer Co., 1949, Rosen Engrng. Products Co., 1950-54; systems group Hughes Aircraft Co., 1955-59; with RAND Corp., 1959-64; co-founder Inst. for Future, 1968; founder CableData Assocs., 1972; co-founder Equatorial Comm., 1978-80; founder Packet Techs., 1980, Telebit, 1980, Metricom, Inc., 1985; founder, chmn. bd. Com21, Inc., Milpitas, Calif., 1992—. Trustee IEEE History Ctr., 2000—, Charles Babbage Found., 2000—; bd. dirs. Marconi Internat. Fellowship Found. Named Entrepreneur of Yr. Tech., Silicon Valley Bus. Jour., 1999; recipient Edwin H. Armstrong award, IEEE Comm. Soc., 1987, 1st Ann. award, ACM Spl. Interest Group in Comm., 1989, Fellowship award, Marconi Internat., 1991, Centennial 100 medal, Drexel U., 1992, Pioneer award, Electronic Frontier Found., 1993, Computers and Comm. Found. award, 1996, award, NAE, 1996. Fellow AAAS, IEEE (life, Alexander Graham Bell medal 1990, Centennial medal 2000, Internet award 2000), Franklin Inst. (2001 Bower award and prize achievement in sci. 2001). Achievements include design of first doorway gun detector; inventor packet switching. Home: 83 James Ave Atherton CA 94027-2009 E-mail: paul@baran.com.

BARANDES, ROBERT, lawyer; b. Bklyn., May 15, 1947; s. Max and Helen (Berger) B.; m. Joan Noveck, May 28, 1970 (div. Jan. 1981); m. Kathleen Lindsey, Aug. 22, 1982 (div. Jan. 1986). Student, U. Coll., London, 1967-68; BA magna cum laude, Union Coll., Schenectady, N.Y., 1969; JD, Harvard U., 1972. Bar: N.Y. 1973, U.S. Dist. Ct. (so. and ea. dists.) N.Y. 1976. From assoc. to ptnr. Barandes, Rabbino & Arnold, N.Y.C., 1972-81; ptnr. Roper, Barandes & Fertel, LLP, N.Y.C., 1981-99; of counsel Beckman, Millman & Sanders LLP, N.Y.C., 2000; ptnr. Beckman, Lieberman & Barandes, LLP, N.Y.C., 2001—02. Prodr. (on Broadway) The News, 1986, Broadway revival of Damn Yankees, 1994-96, (on Broadway) Epic Proportions, 1999, Broadway revival of Bells Are Ringing, 2001. Assoc. producer: (Broadway Play) On The Waterfront, 1995, Lyricist Musical Etched in Stone, 1984; writer, lyricist, musical Star Crossed Lovers, 1984; bookwriter, lyricist musical Almost Eden, 1990. Mem. ABA, League Am. Theatres and Producers, Phi Beta Kappa. Jewish. Avocations: writing, skiing, golf, tennis. Office: Beckman Lieberman & Barandes LLP 116 John St Rm 1313 New York NY 10038-3303

BARANNYK, LYUDMYLA LEONIDIVNA, mathematician, educator, researcher; b. Poltava, Ukraine, Apr. 17, 1972; d. Leonid Feodosiyovych and Mariya Yuriivna Barannyk; m. Paata Tsiklauri. Dipl. in Math., Math. Physics, Tchg. in Math.(hon.), Kharkiv State U., Ukraine, 1994; PhD in Physics and Math. Sci., Nat. Acad. Sci. Ukraine, Kyiv, 1997; postgrad., N.J. Inst. Tech., 1998—. Tchr. computer sci. Secondary Sch. #8470, Poltava, Ukraine, 1994; asst. prof. applied rsch. Inst. Math., Nat. Acad. Sci. Ukraine, Kyiv, 1997—98. Contbr. articles; tech. editor math. sect.: Dopovidi Natsional'noi Akademii Nauk Ukrainy, 1996—98. Recipient Student Achievement award, Grad. Student Assn., N.J. Inst. Tech., 2000—02; scholar Honor stipend, Kharkiv State U., 1990—94; Tchg. Asst. fellow, N.J. Inst. Tech., 1998—2003. Mem.: Am. Phys. Soc., Soc. Indsl. and Applied Math., Math. Sciences Group, NJIT, Math. Sciences Group, NJIT, Who's Who Among Students in Am. Universities & Colleges. Home: 35 Marsac Pl Newark NJ 07106 Office: NJ Inst Tech University Heights Newark NJ 07102 Home Fax: 973-375-7022; Office Fax: 973-596-6467. Personal E-mail: barannyklyu@hotmail.com. E-mail: llb1313@njit.edu.

BARANOVA, ELENA, basketball player; b. Russia, Jan. 28, 1972; arrived in U.S., 1997; Ctr., Israel, 1992—94, CKSK, Russia, 1994—97, WNBA - Utah Starzz, Salt Lake City, 1997—99, Cleve. Rockers, 1999—. Recipient Gold medal, European Championship, Soviet Nat. Team, 1991, Barcelona Olympics, 1992, Bronze medal, European Championship, 1995. Avocations: shopping, housekeeping, electric piano. Office: Cleveland Rockers Gund Arena 1 Center Ct Cleveland OH 44115-4001

BARANOVICH, DIANA LEA, music educator; b. New Orleans, Nov. 1, 1961; d. Walter Horace and Margaret (Rothman) B.; m. Robert Charles Shoup, June 12, 1982; children: Nadia Lea, Raymond Christopher., Tammy Tran MusB, Loyola U., 1983, MEd, 1986; Dalcroze cert., Carnegie-Mellon U., 1993; postgrad., U. Houston, 1990-93. Cert. tchr. music, dance, drama, English, h.s. counselor, Tex. Tchr. music St. Tammany Schs., Slidell, La., 1983-84, Lynn Oaks Sch., Braithwaite, La., 1984-86; choir dir. Fort Bend Pub. Sch., Houston, 1990-93; tchr., cons. music and dance New Orleans, 1996—. Prof. music edn. Normal U. Beijing, China, 1995-97; cons., trainer tchrs. music and dance Kinderland Learning Ctr., Singapore, 1996—; vol. tchr. dance, movement and Chinese studies Alice Harte Elem. Sch., New Orleans, 1996-99; pvt. tchr. piano and movement, 1996—; tchr. tap dancing and choreography New Orleans Dance Acad., 1997-99; fine arts coord. Malaysian Ministry Edn., Kuala Lumpur, 2002—. Contbr. articles to profl. jours. Sponsor St. Joseph's Indian Sch., Childreach, Food for the Poor. Mem. Music Tchrs. Nat. Assn., Music for People, Dalcroze Soc. Am. (patron). Avocations: theater, ethnic dancing, creative writing, composing children's music, piano. Home: 2531 Binz St Houston TX 77004-7565

BARANSKI, JOAN SULLIVAN, publisher; b. Andover, Mass., Apr. 6, 1933; d. Joseph Charles and Ruth G. (McCormack) Sullivan; m. Kenneth E. Baranski, Apr. 20, 1970. BS, U. Mass., Lowell, 1955. Tchr. Andover Public Schs., 1955-61; assoc. editor sci. and reading sch. dept. Holt, Rinehart and Winston, N.Y.C., 1961-65; promotion coord. sch. dept. Harcourt Brace Jovanovich, N.Y.C., 1965-74, mgr. div. verifiability and testing, 1974-75; editor-in-chief Teacher mag., Macmillan Co., Stamford, Conn., 1975-81; editor-in-chief sch. dept. Harper & Row Pubs., N.Y.C., 1981-84; v.p., editor-in-chief Globe Book Co., Simon and Schuster Edn. Group, 1984-88; pub. Joint Coun. Econ. Edn., N.Y.C., 1989-92; pub. Econs. Am., Nat. Coun. on Econ. Edn., N.Y.C., 1992-98; writer, editor, 1999—. Home and Office: 250 E 87th St New York NY 10128-3116

BARANY, JAMES WALTER, industrial engineering educator; b. South Bend, Ind., Aug. 24, 1930; s. Emery Peter and Rose Anne Barany; m. Judith Ann Flanigan, Aug. 6, 1960 (div. 1982); 1 child, Cynthia Getty. BSME, Notre Dame U., 1953; MS in Indsl. Engrng., Purdue U., 1958, PhD, 1961. Prodn. worker Studebaker Corp., 1949-52; prodn. liaison engr. Bendix Aviation Corp., 1955-56; mem. faculty Sch. Indsl. Engrng. Purdue U., West Lafayette, Ind., 1958—, now prof., assoc. head indsl. engrng. Sch. Indsl. Engrng. Cons. Taiwan Productivity Ctr., Western Electric, Gleason Gear Works, Am. Oil Co., Timken Co. Served with U.S. Army, 1954-55 Recipient Best Counselor award Purdue U., 1978, Best Engrng. Tchr. award, 1983, 89, Outstanding Indsl. Engrng. Tchr. award, 1983, 87, 89, Outstanding Tchr. award Purdue U., 1989, Marion Scott Faculty Exemplary Character award Purdue U., 1993, 2000, Work Measurement award, Inst. Indsl. Engring., 2000, Young Engr. award, 2001; named to Purdue Book of Great Tchrs., 1999; NSF and Easter Seal Found. rsch. grantee, 1961, 63, 64, 65; Purdue Tchg. Acad. founding fellow, 1997, Indiana Gov.'s Sagamore of the Wabash award, 1998; named Purdue Book Great Tchrs., 1999. Mem. Inst. Indsl. Engrng. (life, Fellows award 1982, Disting. Educator award 1989, Disting. Svc. award 1992, Cert. of Svc. Appreciation 1994, Work Measurement award 2000, Young Engr. Mentoring award 2001), Soc. Mfg. Engr., Am. Soc. Engrng. Edn., Methods Time Measurement Rsch. Assn., Human Factors and Ergonomics Soc., Order of Engr., Sigma Xi, Alpha Pi Mu, Tau Beta Pi (Eminent Engr. award 1982). Home: 101 Andrew Pl Apt 201 West Lafayette IN 47906-3928 Office: Purdue U iE GRIS 315 N Grant St West Lafayette IN 47907-2023 E-mail: jwb@ecn.purdue.edu.

BARASCH, CLARENCE SYLVAN, lawyer; b. N.Y.C., May 20, 1912; s. Morris and Bertha Lydia (Herschdorfer) B.; m. Naomi Bosniak, July 1, 1957; children: Lionel, Jonathan. AB, Columbia U., 1933, JD, 1935. Bar: N.Y. 1936, U.S. Dist. Ct. (so., ea. and no. dists.) N.Y. 1936, U.S. Ct. Appeals (2d cir.) 1936. Pvt. practice, N.Y.C., 1935—. Lectr. law of real estate brokerage at various real estate bds.; faculty of N.Y. Real Estate Bd. on courses for lic. renewals required by the Dept. of State of N.Y.; chmn. Columbia U. Law Sch. Class of 1935 Ann. Fund 1965—, Columbia Coll. Class of 1933 Ann. Fund, 1977-79; decade chmn. Columbia Coll. Ann. Fund; pres. Jewish Campus Life Fund, Inc. of Columbia U., 1970-87. Author: (with Elliot L. Biskind) The Law of Real Estate Brokers, 1969; also cumulative supplements, 1971-83; contbr. articles to profl. jours. Capt. Signal Corps AUS, 1942-46. Recipient cert. of appreciation Columbia U., 1981, medal for conspicuous svc. Columbia U., 1984. Mem. ABA, N.Y. State Bar Assn. (real property com.), N.Y. County Lawyers Assn. (com. on real estate brokerage matters), Real Estate Bd. N.Y. (mem. legis and law cms., 1970—, mem. arbitration panel 1989—, rev. ann. Diary and Manual and author of summary of real estate brokerage law and related legal matters 1991—), Am. Arbitration Assn. (arbitration panel 1986—), Men's Club (bd. dirs. 1972-80), Columbia U. Law Sch. Alumni Assn. (bd. dirs. 1985-89). Jewish (mem. adv. bd. to chaplain Columbia 1950-70). Home: 1016 5th Ave New York NY 10028-0132 Office: 425 Park Ave New York NY 10022-3506

BARASCH, MAL LIVINGSTON, lawyer; b. NYC, May 14, 1929; s. Joseph and Ernestine (Livingston) Barasch; m. Ann Beckley, May 19, 1962; children: Amy Pitacairn, Jody Taylor. BS in Econs. with distinction, U. Pa., 1951; LL.B., Yale U., 1954. Bar: NY 1957, US Dist Ct (so dist) NY 1960, US Tax Ct 1960. Assoc. Mudge Rose Guthrie Alexander & Ferdon, N.Y.C., 1957-62; assoc. Rosenman & Colin, N.Y.C., 1962-67; ptnr. Rosenman & Colin, LLC, 1968-2000; counsel Katten Muchin Zavis Rosenman and predecessor, 2000—. Mem exec comt, 2d vpres library NY Law Inst, 1979—2000. Treas, bd dirs Lenox Hill Neighborhood House; dist leader, mem exec comt NY County Dem Comt, 1961—65; bd dirs Visions, Servs for the Blind and Visually Impaired. With U.S. Army, 1954—56. Fellow: Am Col Trust and Estate Counsel, NY Bar Found; mem.: ABA, Int Acad Estate and Trust Law (acamedician, exec com.), Asn Bar City NY (chmn. com. trusts, estates and surrogates cts. 2000—03), NY State Bar Asn, Univ Club (New York, NY), Beta Gamma Sigma. Home: 1225 Park Ave New York NY 10128-1132 E-mail: mal.barasch@kmzr.com.

BARASCH, SHIRLEY RUTH, musician, educator; b. Pitts., Jan. 13, 1933; d. Irving Arthur and Elizabeth Schiffman; m. Ronald Henry Barasch, Aug. 15, 1954; children: Larry E., Karen B., Miriam S. BA, U. Pitts., 1954, MusM in Vocal Performance, B of Music Edn., 1969, postgrad., 1973, PhD, 1976. Cert. tchr., secondary edn., elem. and early childhood, music edn., Dalcroze Eurythmics, vocal pedagogy. Tchr. English, speech and drama J.T. Hutchinson Jr. High Sch., Lubbock, Tex., 1954-56; tchr. drama and music Ursuline Acad. and Hebrew Inst., Pitts., 1958-79; voice tchr. Ctrs. for Musically Talented, Bd. of Edn., Pitts., 1968-79; tchr. music and speech Point Pk. Acad., Point Pk. Coll., Pitts., 1969-72; asst. prof. edn. Point Pk. Coll., Pitts., 1969-74, assoc. prof., dir. student teaching, 1974-80, prof. edn. and music, fine arts dir., 1981-86, dir. music, 1981—, chair dept. fine, applied and performing arts, 1993=98; cons. music. Contbr. master classes, writer text chpt. for Generations Together; presenter workshops/master classes in mus. theatre/acting, 1999, 2000. Lyricist, author, composer (children's musicals) Button for Yarmulke, 1986, Emperor's Nightingale, 1986, Alice in Wonderland, 1987, Robin Hood, 1988, Wind in the Willows, 1989, Legend of Sleepy Hollow, 1991, Canterville Ghost, 1992, Rapunzel, 1993; composer (original script/new prodn.) Alice in Wonderland, 1996, (original scripts) Starmaker's Gala, 1995, 96; composer numerous songs and choral pieces; original sketch 45th Anniversary Playhouse, Jr. Celebration; contbg. author tng. manual; contbr. poems, articles on ednl. theory and teaching music to publs.; creater dance-drama: Pied Piper-A Rappin Romp for Rats (with original lyrics and music), 1997—; composer, lyricist: (book, musical drama) Mary Shelley and Her Frankenstein, (one-act plays) The Red Wagon, I Was My Grandmother's Shabbos Goy for Professional Purposes, 2002; contbr. poetry to Crossing Limits. Bd. dirs. Pitts. Boys and Girls Choir, 1986-90, Pitts. Concert. Soc., 1988-2002. Recipient award Warner TV Best Ednl. Children's Music Demo on Cable, 1984. Mem.: ASCAP (Spl. awards 1997—2003), Theater Alliance, Children's Theatre Assn., Tuesday Mus., Early Childhood Assn., Music Edn. Nat. Assn., Nat. Assn. Tchrs. of Singing (bd. dirs. 1989—91), Mu Phi Upsilon. Office: Point Park Coll 201 Wood St Pittsburgh PA 15222-1984

BARASH, PAUL GEORGE, anesthesiologist, educator; b. Bklyn., Feb. 22, 1942; s. Abraham Malcolm and Rose (Shenker) B.; m. Norma Ellen Bernard, Aug. 19, 1967; children: David, Daniel, Jed BA, CCNY, 1963; MD, U. Ky., 1967; MA (hon.), Yale U., 1982. Diplomate Am. Bd. Anesthesiology. Intern SUNY Kings County Hosp., Bklyn., 1967-68; resident Yale-New Haven Hosp., 1970-72, chief resident, 1972-73; asst. prof. anesthesiology Yale U., New Haven, 1973-78, assoc. prof., 1978-82, prof., 1982—, assoc. dean clin. affairs, 1991-94. Chmn. dept. anesthesiology, Yale U., New Haven, 1983-94. Assoc. editor: Advances in Anesthesia, 1984; assoc. editor Jour. Clin. Monitoring, 1984 Surgeon USPHS, 1968-70 Fellow Am. Coll. Anesthesiology, Am. Coll. Chest Physicians; mem. Soc. Cardiovasc. Anesthesiologists (pres. 1984-86), Conn. Soc. Anesthesiologists (pres. 1982-83), Internat. Anesthesia Rsch. Soc., Am. Soc. Anesthesiologists (editor-in-chief Anesthesia Refresher Courses 1985-96). Home: 867 Robert Treat Ext Orange CT 06477-1649 Office: Yale U Sch Medicine 333 Cedar St New Haven CT 06510-3289

BARASH, SUSAN SHAPIRO, writer, humanities educator; b. N.Y.C. d. Herbert Lester and Selma (Meyerson) Shapiro; m. Richard J. Ripps (div.); 3 children; m. Gary A. Barash, Nov. 8, 1997. BA, Sarah Lawrence Coll.; M in English and Creative Writing, NYU, 1987. Prof. critical thinking, gender studies Marymount Manhattan Coll., N.Y.C., 1997—. Mem. adv. bd. Collegiate Press, San Diego; vice chairperson mentoring com. Kennedy Sch. Govt. Harvard U. Author: (book) A Passion for More: Wives Reveal the Affairs that Make or Break Their Marriages, Sisters: Devoted or Divided, The Men Out There: A Woman's Little Black Book, Second Wives: The Pitfalls and Rewards of Marrying Widowers and Divorced Men, Mothers In Law and Daughters In Law: Love, Hate, Rivalry, and Reconciliation, Reclaiming Ourselves: How Women Dispel a Legacy of Bad Choices, Inventing Savannah, Women of Divorce: Mothers, Daughters, Stepmothers - The New Triangle; syndicated radio talk show host; author: The New Wife: The Evolving Role of the American Wife, Tripping the Prom Queen: The Myth of Female Solidarity. Avocations: films, swimming, travel. Office: Marymount Manhattan Coll 221 E 71st St New York NY 10021

BARATTA, EDMOND JOHN, radiochemist, radiation safety officer; b. Somerville, Mass., June 22, 1928; s. Rose Catherine and Joseph Baratta; m. Rose Marie Doucette, July 25, 1953; 1 child, Susan Blaufuss. BSCheme, Northeastern U., 1949—53. With Shell Oil Co., Houston, 1953—56, USN Fuel Depot, Newport, RI, 1957—59, AEC (Nat. Lead Co.), Winchester, Mass., 1959—61, Pub. Health Svc., Winchester, 1961—70, EPA, Winchester, 1970—72; nat. expert, radioactivity U.S. FDA, Winchester, 1984—87, internat. expert, radioactivity, 1988—. Radiation safety officer U.S. FDA, 1986—. Author: (book) Manual of Food Quality Control 16 Radionuclides in Foods, 1994. Storekeeper, disbursing USN, 1946—48, Norfolk, Va. Recipient Exceptional Achievement award, U.S. HHS, 1963, 1982, 2000. Fellow: AOAC Internat. (gen. referee, radioactivity 1978—). Avocation: travel. Home: 5 Fairlane Terrace Winchester MA 01890-3207 Office: US Food and Drug Administration 109 Holton St Winchester MA 01890-1152 Office Fax: 781-729-3593. Personal E-mail: edmbarma@aol.com. Business E-Mail: ebaratta@ora.fda.gov.

BARATTA-LORTON, ROBERT, educator; b. Fresno, Calif., June 19, 1939; s. Paul Vernon and Jean (Steinbeck) Lorton; BA in Econs. with honors, Stanford U., 1961; MA in Edn., U. Calif., Berkeley, 1968; widower. Classroom tchr., tchr. educationally handicapped, Calif., 1966-73; instr. Miller Math. State Specialized Tchr. Improvement Program, also Center Improvement Math. Edn., San Diego, 1971-74; co-founder, 1975, since chmn. bd. dirs., dir. Center Innovation in Edn., Saratoga, Calif.; pres., bd. govs. Center Grad. Coll., Saratoga, 1980—. Lt. USNR, 1963-66; Vietnam. Mem. Internat. Reading Assn., Nat. Council Tchrs. Math., Assn. Supervision and Curriculum Devel., Nat. Assn. Edn. Young Children, Council Exceptional Children, Calif. Math. Council. Author: Mathematics. . .A Way of Thinking, 1977; Baratta-Lorton Reading Program, 1985; creator Power Blocks, 1993. Office: 14599 Big Basin Way Saratoga CA 95070-6069

BARATTO, STEFAN, mathematics educator; b. Bklyn., N.Y., Nov. 28, 1966; s. Robert and Marilyn Baratto; m. Margaret Hughes. B of Gen. Studies, U. of Mich., 1988; MS in Math., U. of Oreg., 1996. Chair, faculty in math and sci.

York County Tech. Coll., Wells, Maine, 1998—2000; faculty in math. Clackamas C.C., Oregon City, Oreg., 2000—. Chair mfg. ops. tech. York County Tech. Coll., Wells, 1999—2000; vis. instr. of math. S.E. Mo. State U., Cape Girardeau, 1997—98; instr., tchg. fellow U. of Oreg., Eugene, 1993—97, statistician, 1996—97; mid. sch. tchr. math and sci. Jr. H.S. 142 Ind. Sch. 88K, Bklyn., 1989—91. Mem.: Am. Math. Assn. 2-Yr. Colls. Office: Clackamas C C 19600 S Molalla Ave Oregon City OR 97045 Office Fax: 503-650-6658. E-mail: sbaratto@clackamas.edu.

BARAZZONE, ESTHER LYNN, academic administrator, educator; b. Charleston, W.Va., Mar. 7, 1946; d. Vincent and Alma Gladys (Wilson) B.; m. Jay Reise, Aug. 25, 1977 (div. 2003); children: Matthew, Nicholas. BA, New Coll., 1967; MA, Columbia U., 1969, PhD, 1982; cert. bus. adminstrn., U. Pa., 1981; D (hon.), Doshisha Women's Coll., 1999, Seoul Women's U., 2000. Mem. faculty Hamilton and Kirkland Coll., Clinton, NY, 1974-81; assoc. dir. corp. and found. rels. U. Pa., Phila., 1982-83; assoc. provost, dir. corp. and found. rels. Swarthmore (Pa.) Coll., 1983-87; v.p., acad. affairs, dean Phila. Coll. Textiles, 1987-92; pres. Chatham Coll., Pitts., 1992—. Bd. dirs. Dollar Bank. Author: (with others) To Beijing and Beyond, 1998; contbr. author: Succes Stories' Presidential Essays, 2000. Bd. dirs. Benedum Found., 2003, Coun. Internat. Exchange of Scholars, NCAA Divsn. III Coun. Presidents, The Carnegie, Pitts., 1993, Hist. Soc. Western Pa., 1993, World Affairs Coun., Pitts., 1994, Allegheny Conf., 1998, Duquesne Club, 2001; mem. adv. bd. Pitts. Symphony Orch., 1993. Grantee Am. Coun. Edn.-Nat. Identification Program Forum, 1992, YWCA, 1996; fellow Columbia U., 1968-72; Fulbright scholar Fulbright Internat. Scholar Exch., 1967-68; named Woman of Yr. Edn., Vectors of Pitts., 1999, Disting. Daughter of Pa., 2001; recipient Susan B. Anthony award, 1999, Pres.' medal Fatima Jinnah Women's U., Pakistan, 2001. Mem. Internat. Women's Forum (founding mem.), Coun. Ind. Colls. (bd. dirs., exec. com.), Duquesne Club, Longue Vue Club, Pitts. Golf Club. Office: Chatham Coll Woodland Rd Pittsburgh PA 15232 E-mail: barazzone@chatham.edu.

BARBA, HARRY, author, educator, publisher; b. Bristol, Conn., June 17, 1922; s. Michael Hovanessian and Sultone (Mnatsignanian) B.; m. Roberta Ashburn Riley, 1955 (div. 1963); 1 child, Gregory Robert; m. Marian Andrea Homelson, Oct. 29, 1965. AB, Bates Coll., 1944; MA, Harvard U., 1951; MFA, U. Iowa, 1960, PhD with honors, 1963; postgrad., NYU, 1955-56, Boston U., 1950-51, NYU, 1955-56, CCNY, 1956-57, Columbia U., 1957-58, U. Middlebury, 1945. Stringer, feature writer Bristol (Conn.) Press, 1944-45; file clk. supr. new departure GM Corp., 1944-45; instr. English and writing Wilkes Coll., 1947, U. Conn., Hartford, 1947-49; tchr. English Seward Park H.S., N.Y.C., 1955-59; instr. U. Iowa, 1959-63; asst. prof. Skidmore Coll., 1963-68; prof. English, dir. writing Marshall U., Huntington, W.Va., 1968-70, title I writing arts dir., 1969-70; comml. and pub. svcs. radio-TV interviewee, reader, lectr., 1961—; prof. English, dir. writing Marshall U., Huntington, W.Va., 1968-70; Title I Writing Arts dir. W.Va., 1969-70. Vis. prof., Fulbright grantee, vis. Am. specialist Damascus U., 1963-64; disting. vis. lectr. contemporary lit., cons. SUNY, Albany, 1977-78; reader, lectr. USIS Libr., Damascus, Syria, 1963-64; innovator, dir., devel. writers confs. for creative growth in several nat., regional and urban contexts, 1964—; dir. The Workshop Under the Sky, 1968—; pres., pub., exec. dir. Harian Creative Books, Ballston Spa, N.Y., 1967—; cons. Bantam Books, Random House, 1967, 69-70, Nat. Found. for Arts, Nat. Found. for Humanities, U.S. Dept. Edn., N.Y. State Coun. Arts, N.Y. State Edn. Dept., Poets & Writers, Inc., Harvard U., others; pres. several instns. (acad. and civic), 1963—, founding pres. and socially functional writer; founder, dir. Skidmore's Writers and Educator's Conf., 1967, The Workshop Under the Sky, 1970—. Author: For the Grape Season, 1960, 3 By Harry Barba, 1967, 3 X 3, 1969, The Case for Socially Functional Education, Art and Culture, 1970—74, One of A Kind (The Many Faces and Voices of America), 1976, The Day the World Went Sane, 1979; author: (compiled and co-edited with Marian Barba) (series) What's Cooking in Congress? A Congressional Smorgasbord of Recipes, 1979, 1983; author: Gospel According to Everyman, 1981, Round Trip to Byzantium, 1985 (Pulitzer prize nominee, 1985), When the Deep Purple Falls, a Story (PEN Syndicated Fiction award, 1985); author: (co-published with Princeton U. Press) Mona Lisa Smiles, 1993; reviewer: plays Three Plays by William Saroyan; author: The Nightingale Sings. Founder, dir. Skidmore Coll. Writers and Educators Conf., 1967, Adirondack-Metroland Writers and Educators Conf., 1967—. Recipient cert. of merit Dictionary Internat. Biography Ctr., 1974, Internat. Man of Yr. award Cambridge (Eng.) Internat. Biographical Ctr., 1995-96, Internat. Biog. Inst.; grad. fellow U. Iowa, 1961-62, Yaddo residence fellow, 1950, Macdowell Colony residence fellow, 1970, World's Hall of Fame in Lit., 1997—, Guggenheim fellow, 1989-90; Skidmore rsch. grantee, 1965-68, N.Y. State coun. Arts grantee, 1971, U. Benedeum grantee, 1969; established Harian Creative awards for fiction, poetry, essays, mus. compositions, photography and graphic arts, 1973. Mem. MLA, Coll. English Assn., Authors Guild, Writers Union PEN, Com. Small Press Editors and Pubs., Harvard Grad. Soc. Advanced Study and Rsch., Harvard Alumni Assn., Harvard Club Ea. N.Y. (dir. 1975-79). Achievements include writing and educating for the mainstreaming of Am.'s multiple ethnic, religious, and racial groups, and for increasing the authority of the UN for the benefit of world's peoples. Home and Office: 47 Hyde Blvd Ballston Spa NY 12020-1607

BARBA, JULIUS WILLIAM, lawyer; b. Arlington, N.J., May 22, 1923; s. John and Rose (Lettiere) B.; m. Susan Vartanian, Oct. 24, 1970; children: Susan Elizabeth, Christina Barba. BA, Princeton U., 1947; LLB, U. Pa., 1950. Bar: N.J. 1950, N.Y. 1981, U.S. Supreme Ct. 1959, U.S. Ct. Appeals (D.C. cir.) 1960, U.S. Dist. Ct. D.C. 1969, U.S. Ct. Appeals (2d cir.) 1973. Assoc. Young, Shanley, Foehl, Congleton & Fisher, Newark, 1950-54; asst. spl. counsel to Pres. Eisenhower, Washington, 1954-57; ptnr. Shanley & Fisher, P.C., Morristown, 1957—; bd. dirs. Selective Ins. Group, Inc., Branchville, N.J., 1983. Bd. trustees Peck Sch., Morristown, N.J., 1982, Kent Place Sch., Summit, N.J.; mem. membership corp. Morristown Meml. Hosp., 1979, trustee, 1984; chmn. N.J. State Fin. Com., 1974-76; bd. dirs. Atlantic Health Systems, Inc. Served to lt. (j.g.) USNR, 1943-46, PTO. Mem. ABA, N.J. State Bar Assn., D.C. Bar Assn., Morris County Bar Assn., Essex County Bar Assn. Republican. Roman Catholic. Clubs: Met. (Washington); Baltusrol Golf (Springfield, N.J.), Morris County Golf (Convent, N.J.); Shinnecock Hills Golf (Southampton, N.Y.). Home: Long Hill Rd New Vernon NJ 07976 Office: Shanley & Fisher PC 131 Madison Ave Morristown NJ 07960-6086

BARBA, ROBERTA ASHBURN, retired social worker, writer; b. Morgantown, W.Va., June 23, 1931; d. Robert Russell and Mary Belle (Rogers) Ashburn; m. Harry C. Barba, Jan. 28, 1956 (div. June 1963); 1 child, Gregory Robert; m. Robert Franklin Church, May 10, 1972. BSSW, W.Va. U., 1953; postgrad., U. Conn., Hartford, 1953-54; MSSW, NYU, 1957. Diplomate in Am. Bd. Examiners; lic. N.Y., W.Va. Pvt. practice, W.Va., 1968—; evaluator P.A.C.E., Star City, W.Va., 1973-74; social worker Family Svc. Assn., Morgantown, W.Va., 1974-75, 85-87; human resources asst., social worker Sundale Rest Home, Morgantown, 1977-79; cons., residential svcs. specialist Coordinating Coun. for Ind. Living, Morgantown, 1983-88; provider W.Va. Dept. Welfare, Human Svcs., Morgantown, 1980-87, social worker maternity svcs. Monongalia County Health Dept., Morgantown, 1985-87; social worker Hospice of Preston County, Kingwood, W.Va., 1988-89; shelter worker, field work instr. Bartlett House W.Va. Sch. Social Work, Morgantown, 1986-90; case mgr. Region VI Area Agy. on Aging, Fairmont, W.Va., 1990-92; case mgr. geriatric program W.Va. U., Morgantown, 1992-95; ret., 1995. Author: (with others) Working with Terminally Ill, 1990, (short fiction) Kids Know, 1992, Walk West on Bleecker Street, 1999; freedom writer Amnesty Internat., 1987—. Grantee George Davis Bivens Found., 1953-54. Mem. NASW (charter mem., cert. diplomate), ACLU, NOW, Acad. Cert. Social Workers, W.Va. Human Resources Assn., Phi Beta Kappa. Avocations: gardening, reading, dogs, cats, travel. Home: 429 Fairmont Rd Morgantown WV 26501-4244

BARBAGELATA, ROBERT DOMINIC, lawyer; b. San Francisco, Jan. 9, 1925; s. Dominic Joseph and Jane Zeffra (Frugoli) B.; m. Doris V. Chatfield, June 8, 1956; children: Patricia Victoria, Robert Norman, Michael Alan. BS, U. San Francisco, 1947, JD, 1950. Bar: Calif. bar 1950, U.S. Supreme Ct. bar 1964. Pvt. practice, San Francisco, 1950—; judge pro-tem San Francisco County Superior Ct., 1992-95. Lectr. U. San Francisco Law Sch., Pacific Med. Center. Contbr. to legal jours. Served with USNR, 1943-46. Mem. Calif. State Bar, Calif. Trial Lawyers Assn. (lectr., v.p.), Am. Bd. Trial Advocates (nat. pres. 1981-82, Trial Lawyer of Yr. 1986-87), Assn. Trial Lawyers Am., San Francisco Trial Lawyers Assn. (Lifetime Achievement award 2003), Am. Coll. Trial Lawyers, Internat. Soc. Barristers, San Francisco Lawyers Club. Roman Catholic. Home: 819 Holly Rd Belmont CA 94002-2214 Office: 109 Geary St San Francisco CA 94108-5632

BARBAKOW, JEFFREY C. former healthcare industry executive; b. Apr. 1944; BS, San Jose U.; MBA, U. So. Calif. With Merrill Lynch Capital Mkts. and several additional affiliates, 1972—88; chmn., CEO, pres. MGM/UA Communications Inc., 1988—91; with Donaldson, Lufkin & Jenrette Securities Corp., 1991; dir. Tenet Healthcare, Santa Barbara, Calif., 1990—2003, chmn. bd., CEO, 1993—2003.*

BARBAN, ARNOLD MELVIN, advertising educator; b. San Antonio, Sept. 17, 1932; s. Sam and Ida Dollie (Wolfson) B.; m. Barbara Marie Fox, June 2, 1955; children: Polly Gwen, Pamela Florence. BBA, U. Tex., 1955, MBA, 1959, PhD, 1964. Asst. to v.p. Joske's of Tex., San Antonio, 1955-56; asst. prof. U. Houston, 1959-64; from asst. prof. to prof. in communications U. Ill., Urbana, 1964-83; prof. U. Tex., Austin, 1983-87; prof. advt. U. Ala., Tuscaloosa, 1987-2000, chmn. advt. and pub. rels. dept., 1992-97, prof. emeritus, 2000—. Rsch. prof. communications dept. U. Ill., 1972-83, head advt. dept., 1978-83; cons. Gulf Oil Corp., Houston, 1962, 64, Farm Rsch. Inst., Urbana, 1965-83, Dept. Def., Ft. Sheridan, Ill., 1984; cons. editor Grid Pub. Co., Columbus, Ohio, 1974-84. Author: Readings in Advertising and Promotion Strategy, 1968, Essentials of Media Planning, 1987, 3d edit., 1993, Advertising Media Sourcebook, 4th edit., 1997, Advertising: Its Role in Modern Marketing, 8th edit., 1994, Advertising Media: Strategy and Tactics, 1992, Advertising Campaign Strategy, 1996; editor U. Houston Bus. Rev., 1962-64; cons. editor Jour. Advt., 1979-81; mem. editl. rev. bd. Jour. Current Issues and Rsch. in Advt., 1980-2001, Jour. Advt., 1983-88, 91-94; contbr. articles to profl. jours. Cons. Democratic congl. campaign, Champaign, Ill., 1972. Sgt. U.S. Army, 1956-58. Recipient Outstanding Svc. award Houston Advt. Club, 1964, disting. svc. award Dicionary Internat. Biography, Cambridge, England; fellow U. Tex., Austin, 1960, 1962, Am. Acad. Advt., 1986. Fellow Am. Acad. Advt. (pres. 1981-82, Sandy award 1997). Jewish. Avocations: gardening, reading, listening to classical music. Home: 136 N Stallion Estates Dr Spring Branch TX 78070 E-mail: barban@gvtc.com.

BARBANEL, SIDNEY WILLIAM, engineering consulting firm executive; b. N.Y.C., July 2, 1921; s. Morris A. and Sadie (Rosenbloom) B.; m. Hilda Helen Hirsch, Oct. 10, 1942 (dec. Nov. 1999); children: Marsha Barbanel Elser, Stephanie Barbanel Simon, Geraldine Barbanel Kapchan, Samara Barbanel Rosenberg, Karen Sue Barbanel Estis. Registered profl. engr., Md., Pa., Mass., Conn., D.C., N.J., N.Y., Ariz., Del., Va., Ga., Fla., Okla., Tenn., Mich., Ill., Wyo., Ohio, Nev. Owner, exec. Sidney W. Barbanel, Long Island City, N.Y. and Paris; cons. engr. internat. practice, specializing in office bldgs., shopping centers, housing complexes, comml., indsl. facilities, energy systems. Trustee Hebrew Acad. Nassau County, 1962, pres., 1974—76. Home: 99 Crows Nest Ct Manhasset NY 11030-4023 Office: 29-15 Queens Plaza N Long Island City NY 11101-2931

BARBANTI, PAOLO, management consultant; b. Milan, Mar. 22, 1956; s. Emilio and Carla (Ravini) B. MS in Biology, U. Milan, 1980, PhD in Toxicology, 1984; MBA, SDA Bocconi, Milan, 1990. Cert. biologist. Rschr. Nat. Cancer Inst., Milan, 1981-84, Recordati SpA, Milan, 1985; rschr. Sch. Medicine U. Brescia, Italy, 1986-88; mgr. nat. biotech. program Nat. Rsch. Coun., Milan, 1988-90; mgmt. cons. Thinktank srl, Milan, 1991-96, Pivot/Cross Border, Milan, 1997—. Vis. scientist NIH, Bethesda, 1988; mgmt. cons. Value Ptnrs., Milan, 1995; lectr. Scuola Normale Superiore Studi S. Anna, Pisa, Italy, 1993—, SDA Bocconi, Milan, 1995—, Sch. Pharmacy, U. Milan, 1996—, Advanced Biotech. Ctr., Genoa, Italy, 1994-95; bd. dirs. nat. biotech program CNR, 1998—; prof. U. Bologna (Italy) Sch. Biotech., 2000—. Contbr. chapters to books, articles to profl. jours. Fellow Nat. Cancer Inst., 1982, Associazione Italiana Ricerca Cancro, 1983; recipient fellowship Fondazione Marco Senepa, 1989. Fellow Italian Fedn. Immunol. Socs., Gruppo di Cooperazione Immunologia, MBA Alumni SDA Bocconi (bd. dirs. 1991—); mem. Ordine Nazionale Biologi, Italian Assn. Pharm. Mktg., Soc. Pharm. Scis. Roman Catholic. Avocations: skiing, trekking, motorcycling, reading. Home: Via Placido Riccardi 19 20132 Milan Italy E-mail: barbanti@eurotecnes.it.

BARBARA, PAUL FRANK, chemistry educator; b. Jamaica, N.Y., Apr. 23, 1953; s. Dominic and Virginia (Bambara) B. BA, Hofstra U., 1974; PhD, Brown U., 1978. Postdoctoral assoc. Bell Labs., Murray Hill, N.J., 1978-80; asst. prof. Univ. Minn., Mpls., 1980-86, assoc. prof., 1986-90, prof., 1990-95, 3M-Alumni Distg. prof. chemistry, 1995—, R. J.V. Johnson-Welch Regents chair chemistry, 1998—; dir. Ctr. Nano & Molecular Sci. and Tech., 2000—. Assoc. editor Accounts of Chem. Rsch., 1995—. Recipient Presdl. Young Investigator award NSF, 1984-89; Alfred P. Sloan fellow Sloan Found., 1983-85. Fellow Am. Phys. Soc.; mem. AAAS, Am. Chem. Soc., Optical Soc. Am. Office: U Tex Dept Chemistry and Biochem Austin TX 78712

BARBARESE, J. T. poet, educator; s. Joseph Anthony and Antionette Danibale Barbarese; m. Karen Irma Henly, June 7, 1980; children: Julianna Claire, Niccolo John. PhD, Temple U., 1994, MA, 1981, BA, 1976. Author: (book) Under the Blue Moon, 1985; author: (Poetry) New Science, 1989; author: Children of Herakles, 1999. Recipient Poetry fellowship, Pa. Arts Coun., 1990, 1994. Office: Rutgers U Dept English 311 N 5th St Camden NJ 08102 Personal E-mail: barbares@camden.rutgers.edu. E-mail: barbares@camden.rutgers.edu.

BARBAROSH, MILTON HARVEY, merchant banking executive; b. Montreal, Que., Can., Apr. 22, 1955; came to U.S., 1986; m. Ricki Tucker, June 1, 1980; children: Marli, Lori, Liana. BCom with honours in Acctg., Concordia U., Montreal, 1976; Can. Chartered Acct., McGill U., Montreal, 1977; MBA, York U., Toronto, Ont., Can., 1980. CPA. Sr. staff acct. Thorne, Ernst & Whinney/KPMG Peat Marwick, Montreal, 1976-79; mgr. merger and acquisitions Clarkson Gordon/Ernst Young, Toronto, 1980-84, Royal Bank of Can., Toronto, 1984-86; pres. JW Charles Group, Inc., Boca Raton, Fla., 1987-88, JW Charles Capital Corp., Boca Raton, 1986-89. Pres. Stenton Leigh Group, Inc., Boca Raton, 1989—. Author: (with others) The Acquistion Decision; editor M&A in Canada for Harris-Bentley Ltd. Fellow Can. Inst. Chartered Bankers; mem. Nat. Assn. Cert. Valuation Analysts, Inst. Bus. Apprasers, Can. Inst. Chartered Bus. Valuators, Am. Soc. Appraisers (sr.), Inst. Chartered Accts. Ont., Quebec Order Chartered Accts., McGill U. Alumni, Concordia U. Alumni, York U. Alumni (chpt. exec.), Boca Raton Golf and Country Club. Office: Ste 305W 1900 Corporate Blvd Boca Raton FL 33431-8502

BARBATO, JOSEPH ALLEN, writer; b. N.Y.C., Feb. 23, 1944; s. Joseph Michael and Florence (Kelly) B.; m. Augusta Ann DeLait, Oct. 23, 1965; children: Louise, Joseph. BA, NYU, 1964, MA, 1969. Newswriter NYU, N.Y.C., 1964-68, dir. alumni comms., 1969-74, sr. devel. writer, 1974-78; staff writer Shell Oil Co., N.Y.C., 1968-69; ind. writer N.Y.C., 1978-90; editl. dir. The Nature Conservancy, Arlington, Va., 1990-98; pres. Barbato Assocs., Alexandria, Va., 1999—. Mem. editl. bd. Small Press mag., N.Y.C., 1984-86; communications cons. univs., hosps., etc., 1978-90; v.p. Washington Ind. Writers. Co-author: You Are What You Drink, 1989, Writing for a Good Cause, 2000; editor: What We Really Know About Mind-Body Health, 1991; co-editor: Heart of the Land, 1995, Patchwork of Dreams, 1996, Off the Beaten Path: Stories of Place; contbg. author: The Book of the Month, 1986; columnist edn., health, lit. numerous mags. and newspapers including Smithsonian, N.Y. Times, Village Voice, Christian Sci. Monitor, others. Mem.: Soc. Profl. Journalists, Nat. Book Critics Cir., Authors Guild. Office: Barbato Assocs 5420 Gary Pl Alexandria VA 22311-1505 E-mail: jabarbato@aol.com.

BARBE, BETTY CATHERINE, retired financial analyst; b. Chgo., Dec. 24, 1930; d. Norbert Lambert and Helen Weishaar; m. Edward William, Aug. 8, 1953; children: Leonard Walter, Roger Andrew. Student, U. Toledo, 1970, 85. Acct. Gorr Printing, Allstate Ins., Muntz TV, Chgo., 1947-53; hostess Welcome Wagon Internat., Maumee, Ohio, 1965-70; v.p. sec., cost acctg. Craftmaster, Toledo, 1970-72; sec., estimator Grinnell Fire Protection, Toledo, 1972-73; exec. sec., payroll Crow, Inc. Aviation, 1973-77; asst. city clk., payroll City of Perrysburg, 1977-83, tax adminstr., 1983-98; ret., 1998. Sec., vice chair Ohio Women's Policy and Rsch. Commn.; mem. adv. coun. Ohio Bicentennial Commn.; reading coach Evening St. Sch., Park Elem. Sch., Bluffsview Elem. Sch., 2001; active Big Sisters of Toledo, 1979, YWCA; vol. New Albany LPGA Golf Classic, Jamie Farr LPGA Golf Classic, Worthington Rep. Women's Club, 1999. Ptnrs. for Citizenship and Character. Paul Harris fellow Dublin-Worthington Rotary, Rookie Rotarian of Yr., 1999-00; honoree Maumee Valley coun. Girl Scouts U.S., 1990; named Woman of Yr., Bus. and Profl. Women Black Swamp Region II. Mem. Internat. Inst., Nat. Notary Assn., Nat. Fedn. Bds. and Profl. Women, Key to the Sea Bus. and Profl. Womens Orgn. (pres. 1982-84), Maumee Bus. and Profl. Women (pres. 1995-97), Maumee Valley Toastmasters (pres. 1989—, area gov.), Toledo Opera Soc. Assn., Two Toledos (sec., 1st v.p.), Christ Child Soc., Maumee C. of C. (sec.), Samagama Club, Zonta II (treas.), Maumee Valley Historical Soc., Rotary (sec. Dublin-Worthington chpt.). Republican. Roman Catholic. Avocations: football, reading, sewing, crafts, travel. Home: 55 Highland Ter Worthington OH 43085-2627 E-mail: kellyfoz@aol.com.

BARBE, DAVID FRANKLIN, electrical engineer, educator; b. Webster Springs, W.Va., May 26, 1939; s. Damon and Mary K. (Cooper) Barbe; m. Irene Theresa Barbe; children: John David, Jane Suzanne. BSEE with high honors, W.Va. U., 1962, MSEE, 1964; PhD in Elec. Engring., Johns Hopkins U., 1969. Instr. elec. engring. W.Va. U., Morgantown, 1962-65; fellow engr. Westinghouse Advanced Tech. Lab, Balt., 1965-71; head functional devices sect. Electronics divsn. Naval Rsch. Lab., Washington, 1971-74, head microelectronics br., 1974-79, asst. electronics and phys. scis., 1979-83; dir. Submarine and ASW Programs Submarine and ASW Sys., Office Sec. of Navy, 1983-85; prof. elec. and computer engring. U. Md., College Park, 1985—, assoc. dir. Md. Tech. Enterprise Inst., 1985-87, exec. dir. Md. Tech. Enterprise Inst., 1987—, interim dir., assoc. dean engring., 1999-2000; co-dir. Hinman CEO's Program, 1999—. Mem. adv. group electron devices Dept. Def., 1971—79, 1987—90; mem. steering com. Internat. Conf. Charge-Coupled Devices, Edinburgh, 1974, Edinburgh, 76, San Diego, 75; lectr. 1st Internat. NATO Course Charge-Coupled Devices U. Louvain-La Neuve, Belgium, 1975; mem. program com. Internat. Solid State Circuits Conf., 1993—; pres. Elec. Engring. Acad. W.Va. U., 1995—97; co-dir. Hinman Campus Entrepreneurship Opportunities Program, 2000—. Contbr. articles on electronics and tech. entrepreneurship to profl. jours. Recipient Dept. Def. award, 1979, Very High Speed Integrated Circuits Pioneer award, 1987, Disting. Alumni award, Elec. and Engring. Acad., W.Va. U., 1990. Fellow: IEEE (assoc. editor Electron Devices Newsletter 1975—79, adminstrv. com. Electron Devices Soc. 1977—83, nat. lectr. 1987—88, awards bd. 1990—94); mem.: Soc. Photographic and Instrumentation Engrs., Am. Soc. Engring. Edn. (Outstanding Entrepreneurship Educator award 2003), Eta Kappa Nu (charter mem.), Tau Beta Pi. Home: 6532 Burgundy Ln Clarksville MD 21029-2600 Office: U Md Md Tech Enterprise Inst Potomac Bldg College Park MD 20742-0001

BARBE, WALTER BURKE, education educator; b. Miami, Fla., Oct. 30, 1926; s. Victor Elza and Edith (Burris) B.; m. Marilyn E. Wood, Feb. 7, 1967; 1 child, Frederick Walter. BS, Northwestern U., 1949, MA, 1950, PhD, 1953. Tchr. Dade County Bd. Pub. Instrn., 1947; asst. Psycho-Ednl. Clinic Northwestern U., 1949-50; instr. psychology, dir. reading clinic Baylor U., 1950; asst. prof. elementary edn. Kent State U., 1952-53, prof., head spl. edn. dept., 1960-64; adj. prof. U. Pitts., 1964-72, Ohio State U., 1972-89; pub. Modern Learning Press, 1997—. Editor Highlights for Children, 1964—, bd. dir.; prof. edn., bd. dir. Jr. League Reading Center, U. Chattanooga, 1953-59; bd. dir. Zaner-Bloser; bd. dirs. internat. council Improvement of Reading Inst. Author: Reading Clinic Directory, 1955, (with Ralph Roberts) Teenage Tales, 1957, (with Dorothy Hinman) We Build Our Words, 1957, Educators Guide to Personalized Reading, 1961, Helping Children Read Better, 1970; sr. author: (with Paul Witty) Creative Growth with Handwriting Series, 1975, Personalized Reading Instruction: New Techniques that Increase Reading Skill and Comprehension, 1975, (with Jerry Abbott) Barbe Reading Skills Check Lists, 1975, (with Swassing and Milone) Teaching through Modality Strengths: Concepts and Practices, 1979; sr. editor: (with Joseph Renzulli) Psychology and Education of the Gifted: Readings, 3d edit, 1980, Basic Skills in Kindergarten, 1980, Resource Book for Kindergarten Teachers, 1980, (with Kurt Reed) The Glass Industry in Wayne County, PA, 1802 to Present, 2003; editor: Teaching of Reading: Selections, 1965, (with Edward Frierson) Educating Children with Learning Disabilities, 1967, Compass Points in Literature, Searchlights in Literature, 1969, Helping Children with Special Needs Series, 1974; author: (with Francis, Braun) Spelling: Basic Skills for Effective Communication, 1982, (with Lucas, Wasylyk) Basic Skills for Effective Communication, 1984, (with others) Handwriting: Basic Skills and Application Series, 1984, Growing Up Learning, 1985, (with Francis, Gentry, San Jose) Spelling Connections: Words Into Language, 1988, (with others) Reading and Study Skills Mastery, 1996, (with others) Vocabulary, Word Analysis and Comprehension, 1996, Some Folks Like Cats and Other Poems, 2002, I Asked a Tiger to Tea and Other Poems, 2002. Chair exec. com. bd. dirs. Dorflinger-Suydam Wildlife Sanctuary, 1992—. With AUS, 1944-46. Fellow Am. Psychol. Assn.; mem. Nat. Assn. Gifted Children (pres. 1958), Touchstone Applied Sci. Assn. (bd. dirs. 1997—), Internat. Reading Assn. (Disting. Svc. award 1992). Democrat. Presbyterian. Address: 214 9th St Honesdale PA 18431-1911 E-mail: drbarbe@ezaccess.net.

BARBEE, GEORGE E.L. financial services and business executive; b. Washington, Jan. 26, 1943; s. H. Randolph and Grace Lunt (Davenport) B.; m. Molly Morse Johnson, May 21, 1977; children: Gregory, John, Scott, Jefferson. AB, Brown U., 1965; MBA, U. Va., 1967. Fin. analyst W. R. Grace & Co., N.Y.C., 1968; product mgr. Wilkinson Sword Inc., Mountainside, N.J., 1968-70; mgr. new products Noxell divsn. Procter & Gamble, Balt., 1970-74; sr. mktg. exec. Gillette Corp., Boston, 1974-79; co-founder, exec. dir. Consumer Fin. Inst., Newton, Mass., 1979-86; ptnr., exec. dir. personal fin. svcs. Price Waterhouse, Waltham, Mass., 1986-91, ptnr., exec. dir. client svcs. nat. office N.Y.C., 1991-92; ptnr. Worldwide Client Svc. PriceWaterhouseCoopers LLP, 1992—2002; ptnr. emeritus PriceWaterhouseCoopers LLP, 2002—. Dir. Victory Van Internat., Washington; TV commentator fin. and bus. news NBC, CNN, PBS, ABC, CBS, 1981—; Batten faculty fellow Darden Grad. Bus. Sch., U. Va., 2000—. Contbr. articles to profl. jours. Republican. E-mail: barbeeg@comcast.net.

BARBEE, STEVEN GEORGE, engineer; b. Hastings, Nebr., Feb. 2, 1953; s. James Max and Betty Lavonne (Gustafson) B.; m. Deborah Kay Hultman, June 7, 1975; children: Paul Steven, David Lyle. BA in Physics and Math. summa cum laude, Doane Coll., 1974; MS in Plasma Physics, Columbia U., 1976. Sr. engr. mgt. data mining methods Semiconductro R&D Ctr., microelectronics divsn. IBM Corp., East Fishkill, NY, 1978—. Auditor Engring. Rsch. Ctr. for Nat. Sci. Found., 1990-91; troop scoutmaster Boy Scouts Am., 1992-2000; active Nat. Jamboree Staff, 1993, 97; instr. NRA, 1992-2000, sr. warden St. James Episcopal Ch., 1993-95, deacon Warren Congrl. Ch., 2002—. Mem. IEEE, IEEE Computer Soc., Am. Vacuum Soc., N.Y. Acad. Scis., Nat. Eagle Scout Assn., Project Mgmt. Inst., Amateur Radio Relay League (vol. examiner). Republican.

BARBEHENN, ELIZABETH, research analyst; d. Sanford and Lillian Rosenthal; m. Kyle Barbehenn, Sept. 8, 1956; children: Raymond, Katharine, Michael. PhD, Wash. U., St. Louis, 1974. Biochemist NIH, Bethesda, 1974—85; pharmacologist FDA, Rockville, 1985—98; rsch. analyst pharmaceuticals Pub. Citizen, Washington, 1998—. Achievements include research in Mammalian embryo biochemistry. Avocations: gardening, swimming. Office: Public Citizen 1600 20th St NW Washington DC 20009 Office Fax: 202-588-7796. E-mail: ebarbehe@citizen.org.

BARBEOSCH, WILLIAM PETER, bank executive, lawyer; b. N.Y.C., Nov. 25, 1954; s. Peter Joseph and Marie Delores (Slesiona) B.; m. Marta B. Varela, Sept. 6, 1986. AB magna cum laude, Brown U., 1976; JD, Columbia U., 1979; MBA, Yale U., 1989. Bar: N.Y. 1980, U.S. Tax Ct. 1985. Atty. Casey, Lane and Mittendorf (and successor firms), N.Y.C., 1979—86, Milbank, Tweed, Hadley and McCloy, N.Y.C., 1986—87; mgmt. assoc. Swiss Bank Corp., N.Y.C., 1989—90; v.p. J.P. Morgan Chase & Co. (and predecessor firms), N.Y.C., 1990—99; mng. dir. Chase Manhattan Bank & Trust Co. (Bahamas) Ltd., 1999—2002, Citigroup Trust, N.Y.C., 2002—. Bd. advisor The Chase Jour., 1997—2002. Mem. profl. adv. com. Mus. of Arts and Design, N.Y.C., 2002—. Mem. N.Y. State Bar Assn., Assn. of the Bar of City of N.Y., Brown U. Club N.Y., Stone House Club, Yale Club (N.Y.C.), Phi Kappa Psi (sec. R.I. Alpha

chpt. 1974-75). Republican. Roman Catholic. Avocations: swimming, history, politics. Home: 545 W 111th St Apt 7E New York NY 10025-1965 Office: Citigroup Trust 153 E 53d St 23d Fl New York NY 10022 E-mail: williampbarbeosch@citigroup.com.

BARBER, AARON, golfer; b. Willmar, Minn., Nov. 15; married. Student, U. Minn. Profl. golfer Can. Tour, 1996—. Named winner, TELUS Edmonton Open, 2001, Barefood Classic, 2001. Office: Canadian Tour 212 King St W Ste 203 Toronto ON Canada M5H 1K5

BARBER, BEN BERNARD ANDREW, journalist; b. Warwick, Eng., May 2, 1944; came to U.S., 1948; s. Stephen S. and Miriam (Idler) B.; m. Risa Richman (div. Apr. 1982); children: Karen Cloud, Forest; m. Nognoy Pinsanoa, Apr. 23, 1983 (div. Feb. 2000); children: Stephanie, Natalie. Cert. in French lang. and civilization, Sorbonne U., Paris, 1964; BA, Trinity Coll., Hartford, Conn., 1964; cert. in Asian studies, Gannett fellow, U. Hawaii, 1987; MJ, Boston U., 1979. Reporter Middlesex News, Framingham, Mass., 1979; free-lance reporter Miami (Fla.) Herald, Boston Globe, Balt. Sun, Toledo Blade, San Francisco Examiner, London Observer, Newsweek, Network News Svc., San Diego Union, Omni mag., MacLean's mag., L'Actualite, Atlantic mag.; Miami corr. USA Today, 1983-86; internat. desk editor United Press Internat., 1989-90; policy analyst Refugee Policy Group, 1991-92; correspondent Sunday Age, Melbourne, Australia; state dept. corr. The Washington Times, 1994—2003; sr. writer/editor U.S. AID, 2003—. Trainer journalism workshops U.S. Info. Agy., Africa; adj. prof. Sch. Fgn. Svc., Georgetown U., 1999. Contbr. articles to profl. jours. Jewish. Avocation: international travel. Office: US AID 1300 Pennsylvania Ave NW Washington DC 20523

BARBER, BENJAMIN R. director, educator; Cert., London Sch. Econ. & Polit. Sci, 1959; BA with honors, Grinnell Coll., 1960; MA, Harvard U., 1963, PhD, 1967; PhD (hon.), Grinnell Coll. With Ecole des hautes etudes en sci. sociol., Paris, 1990-91, Princeton U., 1991; prof. polit. sci. Rutgers U. Walt Whitman Ctr. for Culture and Politics of Democracy, New Brunswick, 1969—2001; prof. Gershon and Carrol Kekst Civil Soc. U. Md., 2001; chmn., chief strategic vision officer Bodies Electric, 2001—. Cons. White House Millennial Com., Corp. for Nat. Svc., U.S. Info. Agency, NEH, UNESCO, European parliament, Swedish parliamentary commn., Mission 2000 (French commn.), various polit. and civic leaders including Pres. Bill Clinton, V.p. Al Gore, Senator Bill Bradley, Germany Pres. Roman Herzog. Author: Marriage Voices, 1981, Strong Democracy, 1984, Jihad vs. McWorld, 1995 (recent internat. best seller), The Struggle for Democracy, 1988, A Place for Us, 1998, The Truth of Power: Intellectual Affairs in the Clinton White House, 2001; founding editor, editor-in-chief Political Theory; contbrs. articles to Harper's Mag., N.Y. Times, The Atlantic, The Nation, Le Nouvel Observateur, Die Zeit, and numerous others in U.S. and Europe; co-scriptwriter The Struggle for Democracy, Greek Fire (U.K.), The American Promise, and other ednl. documentaries; (theater) Kaspar. Named Guggenheim, Fulbright and Social Sci. fellow, Grinnell Coll.; recipient Berlin prize, Am. Acad. of Berlin, 2001, Palmes Academiques (Chevalier), French Govt. Office: Democracy Collaborative 400 W 59th St New York NY 10019 also: Am Acad Berlin Am Sandwerder 17-19 14109 Berlin Germany E-mail: bbarber@sorosny.org.

BARBER, CHARLES EDWARD, newspaper executive, journalist; b. Miami, Fla., Oct. 30, 1939; s. James Plemon and Margaret Katherine (Grimes) B. m. Judith Margaret Tuck, May 28, 1960; children: Janet Lynn Wood, Christopher Edward AA, Santa Fe Community Coll., 1971. Prodn. mgr. dept. student publs. U. Fla., Gainesville, 1966-68, ops. mgr., 1968-70, asst. dir., 1970-72, dir. div. publs., 1974; prodn. mgr. State Univ. System Press, Gainesville, 1975-76; pres., gen. mgr. Campus Communications, Inc., Gainesville, 1976—. Pres. The Herald Pub. Co., Inc., 1990—, Tuck Barber & Assocs., 1995—; pub. The High Springs Herald, 1990—; dir. Campus Press; cons. in field. Co-author: (with Judy Barber) screenplay This Small Island, 1989; adv. editor Fla. Quar., 1973-74; contbr. articles to profl. jours. Mem. citizens adv. coun. Stephen Foster Elem. Sch., Gainesville, 1976-77, Santa Fe H.S., 1991, Spring Hill Mid. Sch., 1992; mem. Friends of Five, 1975-77, Friends of Libr., 1975-77; mem. Fla. Newspaper Oral History Project, 1996—; chmn. book com. Fla. State Prison, 1973-85, 89-94; bd. dirs. Gainesville H.S. Band Boosters, 1978-79, 83-84, treas., 1984; key communicator Alachua County Sch. Bd., 1980-91, judge countywide spelling bee, 1997—; spl. registered dep. sheriff Alachua County Sheriff's Dept., 1979-92, Monroe County Sheriff's Dept.; mem. gifted students boosters Howard Bishop Mid. Sch., 1980-82; dir. Howard Bishop Band Boosters, 1980-82; mem. pres.'s coun. U. Fla., 1978—; mem. Leadership Gainesville, 1979, Leadership Fla., 1997—; mentor Coll. Leadership Fla., U. Fla. English Lang. Inst.; mem. steering com. Fla. Alliance for Better Campaigns, chair regional coalition, 1998; mem. Fla. Correct Ct. Com. for 2000 Census, 1998-2000; pack com. chmn. Cub Scouts Am., 1977-78; dir. The Prevention Partnership, 1992-94, Hippodrome State Theatre, 1992-95, bd. advisors. With USCGR, 1957-65. Recipient Nat. 1st pl. for Editl. Writing Hearst Found., 1965, Svc. award Santa Fe C.C., 1982, Cert. of Appreciation Big Bros. and Big Sisters of Gainesville, 1984, Vols. for Internat. Student Affairs, 1986, 88, 89, 90, Fla. Track Club, 1988, U. Fla. Divsn. Housing, 1990, 91, Addy award Gainesville Advt. Fedn., 1986, 87, Recognition for Cold War Svc. U.S. Sec. Def.; named to Ind. Fla. Alligator Hall of Fame, 1996. Mem.: Soc. Profl. Journalists (treas. No. Fla. chpt. 1972—75, 1986—91, pres.'s club 1994—95, Helen Thomas award for lifetime achievement in journalism 2003), First Amendment Found (trustee), So. Univ. Newspapers (bd. dir. 1980—89), Soc. of News Design, New Media Fedn., Newspaper Assn. Am., Nat. Newspaper Assn. (H.M. for weekly newspaper promotion 1996), Col. Media Advisers, Internat. Newspapers Mktg. Assn., Internat. Newspapers Fin. Execs., Gainesville Advt. Fedn. (bd. dir. 1979—80, Addy award 1986), U. Fla. Coll. Journalism and Comm. (journalism adv. coun.), Foresight Inst., Fla. Bus. Leadership Network, Fla. Press Found (bd. trustees 2001—, 1st pl. award for newspaper promotion 1992, award for weekly newspaper advt. 1993, 1st pl.. award for editl. writing 1994, 1st pl. award for weekly newspaper advt. 1994, Best of Show award weekly newspaper advt. 1994, 1st pl. award weekly newspaper promotion 1995, 1st pl. award for weekly newspaper cmty. svc. 1995, 3rd. pl. award weekly newspaper advt. 1996, 3rd pl. weekly newspaper promotion 1997, award of appreciation,US Census 2000), Fla. Press Assn. (bd. dir. 1992—2001, chmn. continuing edn. com. 1992—2001, v.p. 1997, pres. 1998, chmn. bd. dirs. 1999—2000, Award of Appreciation 1999, Award of Appreciation for 10 years Svc. on Bd. Dirs. 2001, 1st pl. award for Creative Use of Newspaper 2001), Fla. Newspaper Advt. and Mktg. Execs. (chmn. edn. com. 1984—87), Fla. Scholastic Press Assn. (newspaper judge 1981—85, Gold Medallion for svc. 2003), Coll. Newspaper Bus. and Advt. Mgrs. (bd. dir. 1980—81), Am. Advt. Fedn., Am. Collegiate Network (adv. com. 1989—91), Leadership Gainesville Alumni Assn., Substance Abuse Prevention Partnership (coun. 1992—95), Alligator Alumni Assn. (bd. dir. 1980—, named Mr. Alligator 1986), Gainesville Area C. of C., Alachua C. of C., High Springs C. of C., U. Fla. Nat. Alumni Assn., Alachua County Am. Red Cross (bd. dir.), Red Herring Club, Nat. Press Club, Rotary Internat. (sustaining, sec. 1993—94, Paul Harris fellow), Alpha Phi Gamma. Office: Campus Comm Inc PO Box 14257 Gainesville FL 32604-2257

BARBER, CLARENCE LYLE, economics educator; b. Wolseley, Sask, Can., May 5, 1917; s. Richard Edward and Lulu Pearl (Lyons) B.; m. Barbara Anne Patchet, May 10, 1947; children— Paul Edward, Richard Stephen, David Stuart, Alan Gordon. BA, U. Sask., 1939; MA, Clark U., 1941; postgrad., U. Minn., 1941-43, PhD, 1952; LLD (hon.), U. Guelph, 1988. With Stats. Can., 1945-48; mem. faculty McMaster U., 1948-49, U. Man., Winnipeg, Can., 1949-85, prof. econs., 1956-85, disting. prof., 1982-85, emeritus, 1985—, head dept., 1963-72; vis. prof. Queen's U., 1954-55, McGill U., 1964-65. Commr. Royal Commn. on Farm Machinery, 1966-71; spl. adviser on nat. income Phillipines Govt., 1959-60; commr. for study welfare policy in Man., 1972; mem. Nat. Commn. on Inflation, 1979, Royal Commn. Econ. Union and Devel. Prospects for Can., 1982-85; received Order of Manitoba, 2002. Author: Inventories and the Bus. Cycle, 1958, The Theory of Fiscal Policy as Applied to a Province, 1966, (with others) Inflation and Unemployment: The Canadian Experience, 1980, Controlling Inflation: Learning from Experience in Canada, Europe and Japan, 1982, False Promises: The Failure of Conservative Econ., 1993. Served with RCAF, 1943-45. Named Officer in Order of Can., 1987; Can. Coun. Profl. Leave fellow, 1970-71 Fellow Royal Soc. Can.; mem. Canadian Assn. U. Tchr. (pres. 1958-59), Canadian Econ. Assn. (pres. 1971-72), Am. Econ. Assn., Royal Econ. Soc., Social Sci. Rsch. Coun. Can. (mem. exec. 1972-73), U. Victoria Faculty Club.

BARBER, EARL EUGENE, consulting firm executive; b. Dayton, Ohio, Dec. 8, 1939; s. Earl Garnet and Mary Helen (Brown) B.; m. Sandra Kay Reese, Mar. 11, 1960; children: Steven, Amy, Dana. BS, Ball State U., 1963; MDiv., Asbury Theol. Sem., Wilmore, Ky., 1977. Tchr. Muncie (Ind.) Community Schs, 1963-65; exec. mem. Gen. Motors, Muncie, 1965-73; pres. Barber Electric, Wilmore, 1973-77; sr. pastor Calvary Temple, Plainview, Tex., 1977-79; exec. Borg Warner Corp., Muncie, 1979-84; chief ops. officer Barber Cons. Resources, Muncie, 1984—. Author: Statistical Process Control for the Worker, 1985, Statistical Process Control: The Basic Tools, 1986, Team Leader Training, 1989, Problem Solving, 1992, 96, Understanding SPC for Short Production Runs, 1990, Total Quality Management, 1991, Team Building, 1992, Problem Solving, 1994, Time Management, 1995. Mem Mayor's Task Force, Muncie 1980. Mem. Am. Soc. Quality Control (Ptnrs. award for quality 1989, sustaining mem.), Delaware County Ministerial Assn., Epsilon Pi Tau. Republican. Methodist. Avocations: writing, music, boating. Office: Barber Cons Resources Inc 4501 N Wheeling Ave #2-209 Muncie IN 47304-6028

BARBER, EDWARD BRUCE, medical products executive; b. Chgo., Mar. 11, 1937; s. Edward Vanrennsaler and Alice (Reinertsen) B.; m. Louise Joy Griebler, May 23, 1964. BS, Lake Forst (Ill.) Coll., 1957; MBA, U. Chgo., 1958. Market rsch. cons. Container Corp. of Am., Chgo., 1959-61; pres. Christiansen & Barber Assoc. Ltd., Chgo., 1961—. Chmn., CEO Odyssey Travel Ltd., Chgo., 1974—; founder, chmn. M.E. Team, Inc., South Plainfield, N.J., 1980—, also bd. dirs.; pres. Colts Necks Farms, Inc. 1990—; cons. Lab. Supply Co., Louisville, 1990—, Graham-Field Surg., Inc., Hauppage, N.Y., 1990—; ptnr. Wynne Med./Statco Med., 1996—, Sci. Supply Co., Schiller Park, Ill., 1990—; bd. dirs. Golden Eagle Travel, Huntington Beach, Calif. Mem.: AAONMS, Health Industries Distbr. Assn., Internat. Assn. Travel Agys., Masons. Republican. Lutheran. Avocations: travel, coin collector. Office: Christiansen Barber Assocs Ltd Ste 310 6800 W Raven St Chicago IL 60631-2528 E-mail: pandabruce@aol.com.

BARBER, ELAINE T. See FUDA, SIRI NARAYAN K.K.

BARBER, GERARD RENO, pharmacist, writer; b. Bklyn., Oct. 27, 1960; s. Earl William and Adeline Margaret Barber; m. Marie McCormick, Apr. 12, 1991. BS in Pharmacy, L.I. U., 1983; MPH in Health Edn., NYU, 1992. Intern Clayton & Edwards Chemists, N.Y.C., 1982-83; sr. clin. pharmacist infectious disease Brookdale (N.Y.) Hosp. Med. Ctr., 1985-89; fellow in infectious disease Meml. Sloan-Kettering Cancer Ctr., N.Y.C., 1989-90, epidemiologist, 1990-95; clin. specialist in respiratory medicine Lakeland (Fla.) Regional Med. Ctr., 1995—. Reviewer Am. Soc. Health Sys. Pharmacists, Bethesda, Md., 1993—; cons. Health Edn. Awareness Assocs., Valrico, Fla., 1996—; intern Nat. Cancer Inst.-Cancer Info. Svc., N.Y.C., 1990; adj. asst. prof. Schwartz Coll. Pharmacy, Bklyn., 1993—; clin. asst. prof. U. Fla. Coll. Pharmacy, Gainesville, 1999—. Contbr. articles to profl. jours. including New Eng. Jour. Medicine, Am. Jour. Health-Sys. Pharmacy, Cancer Care, Archives Surgery, Am. Jour. Medicine. Mem. Assn. Practitioners in Infection Control and Epidemiology (cert., New Investigator award 1993), Am. Soc. Health-Sys. Pharmacists, APHA. Avocations: freelance writing, health-related issues. Office: Lakeland Regional Med Ctr Lakeland Hills Blvd Lakeland FL 33804 E-mail: gbarberrx@aol.com.

BARBER, JAMES ALDEN, navy officer, educator; b. Poplar Bluff, Mo., May 6, 1934; s. James Alden and Ellamay (Morris) B.; m. Beverly June Kingsbury, June 12, 1955; children: Judith Lynn Barber Joyce, Steven Alden, Susan Barber Blackwell. BA in Econs., U. So. Calif., 1955; MA in Econs., Vanderbilt U., 1960; MA in Internat. Rels., Stanford U., 1964, PhD in Polit. Sci., 1965. Commd. ensign USN, 1955, advanced through grades to capt., 1975; comdg. officer USS Hissem, 7th Fleet, Vietnam, 1966-68; Stephen B. Luce Prof. of Naval Strategy U.S. Naval War Coll., Newport, R.I., 1968-71; comdg. officer USS Schofield, 7th Fleet, Vietnam, 1971-72; exec. asst. to under sec. of Navy Washington, 1975-76; comdg. officer USS Horne, 7th Fleet, 1977-79; dep. dir. Politico-Mil. Affairs, Navy Dept., Washington, 1979-82; dep. dir., sr. fellow Strategic Concepts Devel. Ctr., Washington, 1982-84; CEO, pub. U.S. Naval Inst., Annapolis, Md., 1984-99; sr. lectr. sys. mgmt. U.S. Naval Postgrad. Sch., Annapolis, 1998—. Author: Social Mobility and Voting Behaviour; co-author: Military and American Society; contbr. articles to encys. and profl. jours. Decorated Bronze Star with combat V, Legion of Merit, also others; recipient Alfred Thayer Mahan award, U.S. Navy League, 1971, Meritorious Pub. Svc. award USCG, 1999, Dist. Pub. Svc. award Dept. Navy, 2000. Mem. Coun. on Fgn. Rels., U.S. Naval Inst., Interuniv. Seminar on Armed Forces and Soc., Naval Inst. Found., U.S. Naval Acad. Found., U.S. Naval Sailing Assn., N.Y. Yacht Club. Democrat. Presbyterian. Avocations: gardening, book collecting, sailing.

BARBER, JANICE ANN, lawyer; b. Buffalo, May 30, 1947; d. Warren Richard and Betty A. (Stabler) B. BA with high distinction, U. Ky., 1969; JD cum laude, SUNY, Buffalo, 1977. Bar: N.Y. 1978, U.S. Dist. Ct. (we. dist.) N.Y. 1978, U.S. Supreme Ct., 1994. Reporter The Times-Union, Rochester, N.Y., 1969-74; assoc. Smith, Murphy & Schoepperle, Buffalo, 1977-84, ptnr., 1985-95, Brown & Tarantino, LLP, 1995—. Warden Episcopal Ch. of the Good Shepherd, 2001—; bd. dirs. Parkside Cmty. Assn., 1996—, Pro-Zoo, Buffalo Zoo, 2000-2001, Preservation Coalition Buffalo, 2003—. Mem. N.Y. State Bar Assn., Erie County Bar Assn., AAUW, Audubon Soc., Roycrofters (life), Buffalo Olmsted Conservancy, Preservation Coalition of Buffalo and Erie Co. (trustee 2003—), 20th Century Club, Phi Beta Kappa. Democrat. Episcopalian. Home: 139 Woodward Ave Buffalo NY 14214-2311 E-mail: JanBfflo@cs.com.

BARBER, JERRY RANDEL, medical device company executive; b. Killarney, W.Va., Sept. 23, 1940; s. Edward Clay and Nora (Mullins) B.; m. Carrolyn Rae Acree, June 9, 1964; 1 child, Alyssa Rae. BSChemE, W.Va. U., 1962; MSChemE, Ohio State U., 1964, PhD, 1968. Rsch. engr. Union Carbide Corp., South Charleston, W.Va., 1968-73, group leader rsch., 1973-77, assoc. dir. rsch., 1977-81, dir. rsch. Tarrytown, N.Y., 1981-89, dir. new bus. and tech. devel. Danbury, Conn., 1989-93; gen. mgr. Medisyn Techs., Corp., Las Vegas, Nev., 1993-94; mng. dir. Medisyn Techs. Ltd., Arklow, Ireland, 1994-97; exec. v.p. techs. McGhan Med. Corp., Santa Barbara, Calif., 1997-98; v.p. R & D Mentor Corp., Irving, Tex., 1998-2000, Santa Barbara, Calif., 2000—. Mem. AIChE, Am. Acad. Sci., Sigma Xi. Democrat. Methodist. Home: 2785 Poli St Ventura CA 93003-1556 Office: Mentor Corp 301 Mentor Dr Santa Barbara CA 93111-2360

BARBER, JOHN JOSEPH, minister, writer; b. N.Y.C., Aug. 2, 1955; s. John Frederick and Anna Mary Barber; m. Bonnie Cheryl Howard, June 30, 1990; children: Paul Joseph, Haley Genevieve. BFA, Fla. Atlantic U., 1979; M in Religion, Westminster Theol. Sem., 1981; MDiv, Yale U., 1984; postgrad., Whitefield Theol. Sem., 2002—. Dive Master Pa. Diving Instr., 1980, Personal Trainer Nat. Fedn. Profl. Trainers, 1996. Dir. New Eng. Evangelistic Ministries, New Haven, Conn., 1984—88; evangelist Presbyn. Evangelistic Fellowship, Decatur, Ga., 1985—92; ch. planter Potomac Presbytery, 1990—97; dir. Am. Revival Ministries, Fairfax, Va., 1993—; radio prodr. Campus Crusade for Christ, Orlando, 1997—2000, writer/theol. editor, 2000. Author: (book) Earth Restored, America Restored, The Book God Wrote, Christ For The Third Millenium, Written By The Hand Of God; contbr. articles. Commentator Am. In Focus, Fairfax, Va., 1993—97; radio prodr. Campus Crusade for Christ, Orlando, Fla., writer, theol. editor, 2000. Recipient numerous music related awards. R-Consevative. Achievements include research in developed the ethical model for the relationship of Christianty with culture. Avocations: scuba diving, surfing, weightlifting.

BARBER, LARRY EUGENE, financial planner; b. Sabetha, Kans., Aug. 4, 1931; s. Paul W. and Nellie C. (Nicholas) B.; m. Norma J. Schroeder, Sept. 9, 1951; children: Mark E., Gary P., Jay D., Craig A., Kirk N. BSBA, U. Nebr., Omaha, 1952; M in Fin. Svcs., Am. Coll., 1981. CLU; accredited tax preparer. Ins. agt. Conn. Gen., Omaha, 1970-77; tax and fin. planning, cons. Colo. Agy. State Mut. Life (now Allmerica Fin. Svcs.), Denver, 1977—; v.p. Bus. and Personal Fin. Planning Ltd., Denver, 1985—; pres. Barco Enterprises, Inc., 1996—. Lt. col. USAFR, 1951-52. Mem. Nat. Assn. Life Underwriting, Am. Soc. CLUs, Optimists. Home: 1030 S Garrison St Lakewood CO 80226-4129

BARBER, LLOYD INGRAM, retired university president; b. Regina, Sask., Can., Mar. 8, 1932; s. Lewis Muir and Hildred (Ingram) B.; m. Muriel Pauline MacBean, May 12, 1956; children: Muir, Brian, Kathleen, David, Susan, Patricia. BA, U. Sask., 1953, BComm, 1954; MBA, U. Calif., Berkeley, 1955; PhD, U. Wash., 1964; LLD (hon.), U. Alta., 1983, Concordia U., 1984; postgrad., U. Regina, 1993. Hon. chartered acct. Instr. commerce U. Sask., 1955-57, asst. prof., 1957-64, assoc. prof., 1964-65, prof., 1965-68, 74-76, dean commerce, 1965-68, v.p., 1968-74; pres. U. Regina, Sask., prof. adminstrn., 1976-90. Indian claims commr. Govt. of Can., 1969-76, hon. lt. col.; spl. inquirer for Elder Indian Testimony, 1977-81; bd. dirs. Bank of N.S., 1976-03, The Molson Cos., Teck-Cominco, N.W. Co. Ltd., 1990-02, Can. West Global Comm. Corp., Greystone Capital Mgmt. Inc.; cons. to bus. and govt.; hon. prof. Shandong U. Trustee Inst. Rsch. on Public Policy, 1972-79; bd. dirs. Indian Equity Found., 1978-79, Can. Scholarship Trust Fund, Regina United Way, 1977-79; past bd. dirs. Wascana Centre Authority; bd. dirs. Nat. Mus. Nature, Inst. Saskatchewan Enterprise, Can. Polar Commn.; bd. dirs., past trustee Can. Scheneley Football Awards; adv. com. to Rector on pub. affairs award Concordia U., 1983; past mem. Northwest Territories Legis. Coun., 1967-70, Natural Sci. and Engring. Rsch. Coun. Officer Aboriginal Order of Can.; recipient Vanier medal, 1978; named hon. Sask. Indian Chief Little Eagle. Mem. Am. Inst. Pub. Adminstrn., Nat. Stats. Coun., Assn. Univs. and Colls. Can. (past pres.), Am. Econ. Assn., Can. Econ. Assn., Order of Can. (companion), Sask. Order of Merit, Assn. Commonwealth Univs. (coun.), Assinobia Club, Regina Beach Yacht Club, Masons. Mem. United Ch. Office: PO Box 510 Regina SK Canada S0G 4C0 E-mail: barberl@uregina.ca.

BARBER, MARSHA, company executive; b. Peoria, Ill., Dec. 7, 1946; d. Jack R. and Dorothy M. Hursey; m. Thomas L. Barber, June 15, 1968; 1 child, Brett A. BS, So. Ill. U., Carbondale, 1968; postgrad., So. Ill. U., Edwardsville. Pres. Plus 1 Exec. Suites, Columbus. Instr. elem. edn., Alton, Ill.; regional coun. rep. Ill. Edn. Assn.; mem. So. Ill. U. Edn. Adv. Coun.; mem. Columbus Bd. Realtors; mem. Real Estate Buyers Agt. Coun. Mem. Women's Bus. Bd., Columbus, Ohio. Mem. NEA, Columbus Area C. of C. (small bus. adv. coun., exec. com., chair N.W. Area Bus. Coun.), Sports Car Club Am., Nat. Assn. Realtors, Ohio Assn. Realtors, Nat. Assn. Women Bus. Owners, Nat. Assn. Watch and Clock Collectors, Exec. Suite Assn., Dublin C. of C., So. Ill. U. Alumni Assn.

BARBER, NICHOLAS CARL, tax specialist, consultant, real estate executive; b. Schenectady, N.Y. s. Joseph F. and Philomena (Savignano) B.; m. Laura A. Sherak, Mar. 20, 1987; children: Courtney, Robyn. AAS, SUNY, Cobleskill, 1966; student, Rochester Inst. Tech., 1967-68; BS in Mgmt., Empire State Coll., 1998. Cert. county dir., N.Y. Claims rep. Hartford Ins. Group, Albany, N.Y., 1968-76; owner, prin. N.C. Barber Agy., Schenectady, 1978—. Account exec. Jardine Ins. Brokers, Schenectady, 1981-82; v.p. Complete Coverage Ins., Schenectady, 1982-84; county dir. Real Property Tax Agy., Schenectady, 1991—; trustee Schenectady County C.C., 1999—. Mem. Schenectady County Legislature, 1980-91, majority leader, 1982-84, 90-91; bd. mem. City-County Youth Bd., Schenectady, 1980-91, Schenectady Boys Club, 1980-82, Aeroscis. Mus., Schenectady, 1982-85; bd. dirs. County Econ. Devel. Corp., Schenectady, 1986-91. Sgt. USNG, 1967-73. Mem. Sons of Italy in Am. (trustee 1980-82), Masons, Elks. Republican. Avocations: public speaking, acting. Home: 905 Nott St Schenectady NY 12308-2318 E-mail: ncbarber@juno.com.

BARBER, PATRICIA LOUISE, clinical specialist; b. St. Paul, Jan. 11, 1953; d. James Bernard and Margaret Mary (Neagle) B. BSN, U. Minn., 1975; cert. nurse practitioner, U. Ill., 1978. RN, Colo., Ill., Minn. Staff nurse U. Minn., Mpls., 1974-75; transplant coord. U. Ill., Chgo., 1978-90; nurse practitioner emergency rm. Denver Presbyn., 1990-93; nurse practitioner in-patient svc. cardiovascular Denver Presbyn. St. Luke's Med. Ctr., 1993-95, nurse practitioner nephrology, 1995-96, nurse practitioner in-patient svc., 1996-99; mem. clin. faculty Health Edn. Ctr. C.C. Denver, 1999—; nurse practitioner cardiovasc. Cardiovasc. Assocs., Denver, 2003—. Cons. in field, Chgo., 1983—. Editor: Resource Manual for Transplant Coordinators, 1982. Co-chmn. S/A Patient Svcs. Com., 1983-90. Mem. N.Am. Transplant Coords. Orgn. (co-chmn. 1979-90, Honors 1983), Am. Diabetes Assn. (speakers bur. 1982—), Nat. Kidney Found. (bd. dirs. 1983-90). Avocations: fundraiser, volunteer, profl. image, pet therapy. Office: C C Denver Health Edn Ctr 1070 Yosemite Cir Denver CO 80230-6921

BARBER, PHILLIP ROBERT, III, communications executive; b. Ashland, Ky., Nov. 24, 1959; s. Phillip Robert Jr. and Rahe Darlynn (Church) B; m. Tammi Ruth Davis, Mar. 17, 1969; children: Ashley Brooke, Phillip Robert IV, William Christian, Joshua David. BA, U. Ky., 1982. Freelance illustrator David E. Carter Corp. Communications, Ashland, 1978-79; cartographer U.S. Census Bur., Ashland, 1980; photography instr. Lyndhurst Found., Whitesburg, Ky., 1981; darkroom technician Stone Photography, Lexington, Ky., 1982; art dir. The Photography Gallery, Nashville, 1982-83, Carden and Cherry Advt. Agy., Nashville, 1985-86; from creative dir. to pres. Barber Comm., Nashville, 1983-96, pres. Ashland, 1996—, Exodus Records, Nashville, 1987-91; producer Koinonia Radio Show, Nashville, 1987-90; pres. The Idea Factory, 1990—96, Net Ltd., Ashland, 1998-99, Cliksilver.com., Ltd., 1999—2001, Mossy Bottom LLC, 2001—. V.p. Mission Unto the Chronically Hip, Nashville, 1987-90, One Road Ministries, 1987-90; dir. Christmas in Apr. Nashville, 1995-96, Love Helps, 1995-96; mktg. com. Paramount Arts Ctr., Ashland; adv. bd. Salvation Army. Lyndhurst Found. grant, 1981; named one of Outstanding Young Men of Am., 1987. Mem. Nashville Advt. Fedn., Gospel Music Assn., Am. Film Inst., Optimists Club. Republican. Office: 515 Wheatley Rd Ashland KY 41101-2343

BARBER, PHYLLIS NELSON, writer, educator; b. Henderson, Nev., May 11, 1943; d. Herman Evans and Thora Jane (Mickelson) N.; m. David Henry Barber, May 29, 1964 (div. Jan. 1997); children: Geoffrey Stevenson, Christopher Jon, Jeremy Scott, Bradley Nelson Barber; m. William Traeger, Sept. 30, 2000 (div. June 2002). BA, San Jose State U., 1968; MFA, Vt. MFA in Writing Program, 1984. Pres. bd. dirs. Writers at Work, Park City, Utah, 1985-87; co-dir., 1988-89; mem. faculty MFA in Writing program Vt. Coll., Montpelier, 1991—; fellowship panelist, mem. profl. devel. com. NEA, Washington, 1992; vis. writer U. Mo., Columbia, 1994; cmty. sch. tchr. Rochester, Minn., 1998, Park City, 2000. Mem. literary arts panel Utah State, Salt Lake City, 1985-89; exec. co-chair Utah Women's Art Project, Salt Lake City, 1989-90; founder Summit County Artists Series, Frisco, Colo., 1990-92; judge writing competitions. Author: Smiley Snake's Adventure, 1980, The School of Love, 1990, Legs: The Story of a Giraffe, 1991, And the Desert Shall Blossom, 1991 (1st prize Utah Fine Arts Lit. Competition Utah Fine Arts Coun. novel category, 1988, chosen by Utah Endowment for the Humanities to be discussed by The Book Group Libr. Series), paperback, 1993, How I Got Cultured: A Nevada Memoir, 1992 (Assoc. Writing Program award series prize in creative nonfiction, 1993, excerpts published in Literary Las Vegas: The Best Writing About America's Most Fabulous City, 1995, NBC Today Show, 1997), paperback, 1994, Parting the Veil: Stories from a Mormon Imagination, 1999, short stories, published in numerous lit. mags. including Kenyon Rev., N.Am. Rev., Fiction Internat., The Chariton Rev., others. Bd. dirs. Utah Symphony, Salt Lake City, 1972-75; dir. pub. rels. Utah Symphony Guild, Salt Lake City, 1970-71. Recipient Pro-Journalism award 1st Sigma Delta Chi, 1982, 1st prize D.K. and Brookie Brown Short Story Contest Sunstone Found., 1997. Mem. AAUW, Assn. Mormon Letters, Assoc. Writing Programs. Mem. Lds Ch. Avocations: piano, hiking, biking, tinsmithing.

BARBER, RICHARD WILLIAM, publishing executive; b. Dunmow, Essex, Eng., Oct. 30, 1941; s. Geoffrey Osborn and Daphne (Drew) B.; m. Helen Rosemary Tolson, May 7, 1970; children: Humphrey Thomas, Elaine Mary. BA, Cambridge (Eng.) U., 1963, PhD, 1982. Editor G. Bell & Sons, London, 1968-72; mng. dir. Boydell & Brewer, Woodbridge, Eng., 1972—. Chmn. Boydell & Brewer Inc., Rochester, N.Y., 1987—. Author: The Knight and Chivalry, 1970, rev. edit., 1996 (Somerset Maugham prize 1970), Edward Prince of Wales & Aquitaine, 1976, King Arthur, 1984, Penguin Guide to Medieval Europe, 1984, 20 other books. Fellow Royal Soc. Lit., Soc. Antiquaries, Royal Hist. Soc.

BARBER, ROBERT CUSHMAN, lawyer; b. Columbus, Ga., Aug. 30, 1950; s. Robert Kennard and Kathleen (Cushman) B.; m. Bonnie A. Neilan, Apr. 30, 1983; children: Nicholas, Benjamin, Alexander. AB, Harvard U., 1972, M in City Planning, 1977; JD, Boston U., 1977. Bar: Mass. 1978, N.Y. 1978, U.S. Dist. Ct. Mass. 1981, U.S. Dist. Ct. (ea. and so. dist.) N.Y. 1981. Asst. dist. atty.

N.Y. County, N.Y.C., 1977-81; assoc. Looney & Grossman, Boston, 1981-84, ptnr., 1985—, mng. ptnr., 2000—. Trial advisor Harvard Law Sch., 1985—. Bd. dirs. Fayerweather Edn. Found., 1995—; trustee Social Law Libr., 1998—. Mem. ABA, Boston Bar Assn. Office: Looney & Grossman LLP 101 Arch St Ste 900 Boston MA 02110-1117 E-mail: rbarber@lgllp.com.

BARBER, RUSSELL BROOKS BUTLER, television producer; b. Nov. 11, 1934; s. Russell Brooks and Verga Merrill (Lesher) Butler. BA, U. Puget Sound, 1957; AM, Stanford U., 1959; PhD, Northwestern U., 1963. Exec. prodr. Sta. WCBS-TV, N.Y.C., 1964-71; religion editor Sta. WNBC-TV, N.Y.C., 1973-90, media lectr., 1993—. Adj. prof. pub. comm. Nova Southeastern U., Ft. Lauderdale, Fla., 2002—. Author: Among First Patriots, 1976. Advisor Templeton Found., London, 1976—; dir. Coun. Chs. N.Y.C., 1979—; mem. comms. com. Am. Cancer Soc. N.Y., N.Y.C., 1978—, N.Y.C. Mission Soc., 1979—, Laymen's Nat. Bible Com., N.Y.C., 1983—, Conn. Diocese Episcopal Ch., Hartford, 1984—, media cons., prodr., host Diocese Armenian Ch. of Am., 1992—; established Barber Scholars, U. Puget Sound, Tacoma, 1978—, Nat. Lecture Tours on Media; bd. dirs. Inst. for Religion & Pub. Policy, Washington, D.C., 1998—. Recipient Faith and Freedom award Religious Heritage Am., St. Louis, 1982, Emmy awards NATAS, N.Y.C., 1984, 85, 88, U. Thant Peace award UN Peace Meditation, 1986, Gabriel award Nat. Cath. Assn. for Broadcasters and Communicators, 1987, Trisccort award Roman Cath. Ch., 1988, Nat. Cmty. Svc. award, U. Puget Sound, 2003; named Knight Comdr. Order St. John of Jerusalem, N.Y.C., 1985. Mem. NATAS, World Assn. Christian Comms. Home: Oasis Tower 434 180 Isle of Venice Dr Fort Lauderdale FL 33301 Office: Enlightenment Enterprises Inc 419 E 57th St Ste 8F New York NY 10022-3060 E-mail: rbbb2@aol.com.

BARBER, THEODORE FRANCIS, aircraft mechanics professional; b. Port Jervis, N.Y., Jan. 29, 1931; s. Theodore and Frances Mary (Wozniak) B.; m. Beverly Ann Horton, Mar. 15, 1961 (div. Dec. 1965); 1 child, Theodore Francis Barber, Jr. Student, Arlington Sch. Flight & Engring., Tillamook, Oreg., 1951-52; grad., Jet Engine Specialist Sch., Chanute, Ill., 1952. Lic. comml. eel fisherman, Pa., 1964. Quiller Tex Ray Fabrics, Port Jervis, NY, 1945; laborer Erie RR, Port Jervis, NY, 1947-49; fireman, night watchman Tex Ray Fabrics, 1949; carpenter Erie R.R., Port Jervis, N.Y., 1950, mail handler Jersey City, 1950-51; locomotive fireman Erie RR, Port Jervis, N.Y., 1951-59, locomotive engr., 1959-66; miniature golf course owner/operator Matamoras, Pa., 1963-65; lipstick moulder Kohmar Lab., Port Jervis, N.Y., 1965; interior installer Douglas Aircraft Co., Long Beach, Calif., 1966-67; car salesman Brookhurst Dodge, Garden Grove, Calif., 1967; field and svc. aircraft mechanic Douglas and McDonnell Douglas Aircraft Co., Long Beach, 1967-93; structure assembly mechanic Northrop Corp., Anaheim, Calif., 1969-70, exptl. flight test mechanic McDonnell Douglas Aircraft Co., Long Beach, 1971, 77; systems mechanic Airco Cryogenics, Costa Mesa, Calif., 1977; co-owner C&B Sabot Fiberglass Boat Mfrs., 1976; mech. test technician Space Shuttle Arrowhead Products, Los Alamitos, Calif., 1976-77; B-1 bomber tool maker North Am. Rockwell, El Segundo, Calif., 1977. Realtor Real Estate Store, Fullerton, Calif., 1976-79; metal fitter toolmaker F-18, Northrop, Hawthorn, Calif., 1978-79; toolmaker satellite and Space Shuttle divsn. North Am. Rockwell, Seal Beach, Calif., 1984; walnut orchard grower C & B Orchard, Fresno, Calif., 1982-83. With USAF, 1951-55. Mem. VFW, Gold Wing Rd. Riders Assn., Jacksonville Real Estate Investors Assn., Am. Legion, Moose, Eagles. Republican. Roman Catholic. Avocations: motorcycling, classic auto restoration, gourmet cooking.

BARBER, WILLIAM JOSEPH, educator, economist; b. Abilene, Kans., Jan. 13, 1925; s. Ward Seymour Henry and Esther (Roop) B.; m. Sheila Mary Marr, Apr. 16, 1955; children: Thomas, John, Charles. AB, Harvard U., 1949; BA, Oxford (Eng.) U., 1951, MA, 1955, DPhil, 1957; MA (hon.), Wesleyan U., Middletown, Conn., 1965. Asst. prof. Kans. State U., 1951-52; lectr. Balliol Coll., Oxford U., 1956; mem. faculty Wesleyan U., Middletown, Conn., 1957—, prof. econs., 1965—, Andrews prof. econs., 1972-93, acting pres., 1988; vis. prof. econs. Yale U., 1982-84. Am. sec. Rhodes Scholarship Trust, 1970-80; bd. electors Eastman professorship Oxford U., 1970-81 Author: The Economy of British Central Africa, 1961, A History of Economic Thought, 1967, British Economic Thought and India 1600-1858, 1975, From New Era to New Deal, 1985, Designs within Disorder: Franklin D. Roosevelt, the Economists, and the Shaping of American Economic Policy, 1933-1945, 1996; contbr. to Asian Drama: An Inquiry into the Poverty of Nations, 1968, Exhortation and Controls, 1975, Energy Policy in Perspective, 1980, Economists in Government, 1982; co-author, editor: Breaking the Academic Mold: Economists and American Higher Learning in the Nineteenth Century, 1988; editor: Perspectives on the History of Economic Thought, Vols. V-VI, 1991; gen. editor, The Works of Irving Fisher (14 vols.), 1997. Served with AUS, 1943-46, ETO. Decorated Order Brit. Empire; Rhodes scholar, 1949-51; Ford Found. Fgn. Area fellow Africa, 1955-56 Mem. Am. Econ. Assn., Royal Econ. Soc., Am. Assn. Rhodes Scholars, History of Econs. Soc. (pres. 1989-90, Disting. Fellow 2002), Phi Beta Kappa. Home: 306 Pine St Middletown CT 06457-3119

BARBER, X. THEODORE, archivist; b. Boston, Nov. 29, 1957; s. Theodore X. and Catherine (Spinos) B. BA, Harvard U., 1980; MA, NYU, 1983, PhD, 1993. Instr. NYU, N.Y.C., 1984-87, Rutgers U., New Brunswick, N.J., 1987-88; rschr. Nat. Portrait Gallery, Washington, 1993; archivist Parsons Sch. Design, New Sch. U., N.Y.C., 1994—. Contbr. articles to profl. publs. Mem. Am. Studies Assn., Orgn. Am. Historians, Soc. Am. Archivists, Phi Beta Kappa. Home: 40 Waterside Plz Apt 21H New York NY 10010-2632 Office: Parsons Sch Design New Sch U 2 W 13th St Fl 2 New York NY 10011-7902 E-mail: barberx@newschool.edu.

BARBERA, ANTHONY THOMAS, accountant, educator; b. Bklyn., Oct. 5, 1955; s. Thomas Anthony and Rachelle Regina (Crocitto) Barbera. BS summa cum laude, St. John's U., N.Y., 1977; MBA, 1987. CPA N.Y. Staff acct. Price Waterhouse, N.Y.C., 1977-80, sr. acct., 1980-83, audit mgr., 1983-84; grad. asst. St. John's U., Jamaica, NY, 1985-87, asst. prof., 1987-96; vis. asst. prof. SUNY, Old Westbury, 1996—, dir. internships, placement and adminstrn., 1998—. Mem. com. fin. acctg. Savs. Banks Assn. N.Y. State, N.Y.C., 1983—84. Contbr. articles to profl. jours. Recipient William R. Donaldson award, Cath. Accts. Guild, Diocese of Bklyn., 1977; N.Y. State Regents scholar, 1973—77, Robert E. Gillece fellow, CUNY Grad. Sch., 1989—93, AICPA doctoral fellow, 1989—92. Mem.: AICPA, Decision Scis. Inst., Securities Industry Assn., Am. Acctg. Assn., N.Y. State Soc. CPAs (prof. conduct com., mem. recruitment com. CPA careers, mem. cooperation com. with ednl. instns.), KC, Omicron Delta Epsilon, Beta Gamma Sigma, Beta Alpha Psi. Republican. Roman Catholic. Home: 32 Northcote Rd Westbury NY 11590-1504 Office: SUNY-Old Westbury Sch Bus Old Westbury NY 11568

BARBERA, JOSEPH, motion picture and television producer, cartoonist; b. N.Y.C., Mar. 24, 1911; s. Vincente and Frances Barbera; m. Sheila Holden; children: (by former marriage) Lynne Meredith, Jayne Earl, Neal Francis. Grad., Am. Inst. Banking. Banking clk. Irving Trust Co., N.Y.C., 1930-32; storyboard writer, sketch artist Van Beuren Studio, N.Y.C., 1932-34; animator Terrytoons, New Rochelle, 1934-37; head animation dept. MGM, 1955-57; co-founder with William Hanna Hanna-Barbera Prodns., 1957—. Dir. with Hanna of short animated films including Puss Gets the Boot, 1940 (Academy award nomination best animated short subject 1940), The Nightmare Before Christmas, 1941 (Academy award best animated short subject 1941), Yankee Doodle Mouse, 1943 (Academy award best animated short subject 1943), Mouse Trouble, 1944 (Academy award best animated short subject 1944), Quiet, Please!, 1945 (Academy award best animated short subject 1945), The Cat Concerto, 1946 (Academy award best animated short subject 1946), Dr. Jekyll and Mr. Mouse, 1947 (Academy award nomination best animated short subject 1947), The Little Orphan, 1948 (Academy award best animated short subject 1948), Hatch Up Your Troubles, 1949 (Academy award nomination best animated short subject 1949), Jerry's Cousin, 1950 (Academy award nomination best animated short subject 1950), The Two Mouseketeers, 1951 (Academy award best animated short subject 1951), Johann Mouse, 1952 (Academy award best animated short subject 1952), Touche, Pussy Cat, 1954 (Academy award nomination best animated short subject 1954), Good Will to Men, 1955 (Academy award nomination best animated short subject 1955), One Droopy Knight, 1957 (Academy award nomination best animated short subject 1957); animated programming series with Hanna include The Ruff and Reddy Show, 1957-60, The Huckleberry Hound Show, 1958-62 (Emmy award 1960), Yogi Bear, 1958-62, The Quick Draw McGraw Show, 1959-62, The Flintstones, 1960-66 (Golden Globe award 1965), Top Cat, 1961-62, Lippy the Lion, 1962, Touche Turtle, 1962, Wally Gator, 1962, The Jetsons, 1962-67, 69-76, 79-81, 82-83, 85, The Adventures of Jonny Quest, 1964-65, 67-72, 79, 80-81, The Magilla Gorilla Show, 1964-67, The Peter Potamus Show, 1964-67, Tom and Jerry, 1965-72, 75-78, 80-82, The Atom Ant/Secret Squirrel Show, 1965-68, Sinbad, Jr., the Sailor, 1966, The Abbott and Costello Cartoon Show, 1966, Laurel and Hardy, 1966 67, Space Kiddettes, 1966 67, Space Ghost, 1966-68, Frankenstein, Jr. and the Impossibles, 1966-68, Sampson and Goliath, 1967-68, Birdman and the Galaxy Trio, 1967-68, The Herculoids, 1967-69, Moby Dick and the Mighty Mightor, 1967-69, Shazzan!, 1967-69, The Fantastic Four, 1967-70, The Wacky Races, 1968-70, The Adventures of Gulliver, 1969-70, The Perils of Penelope Pitstop, 1969-71, The Cattanooga Cats, 1969-71, Dastardly and Muttley in Their Flying Machines, 1969-71, Scooby-Doo, Where Are You?, 1969-74, Where's Huddles?, 1970-71, The Harlem Globetrotters, 1970-73, Josie and the Pussycats, 1970-76, Pebbles and Bamm Bamm, 1971-72, Help! It's the Hair Bear Bunch, 1971-72, The Funky Phantom, 1971-72, Wait Til Your Father Gets Home, 1972, Sealab 2020, 1972-73, The Roman Holidays, 1972-73, The Amazing Chan and the Chan Clan, 1972-74, The Flintstones Comedy Hour, 1972-74, Josie and the Pussycats in Outer Space, 1972-74, Speed Buggy, 1971-74, Butch Cassidy and the Sundance Kids, 1973-74, Peter Puck, 1973-74, Inch High, Private Eye, 1973-74, Yogi's Gang, 1973-75, Jeannie, 1973-75, Goober and the Ghost Chasers, 1973-75, The Addams Family, 1973-75, Super Friends, 1973-83, Wheelie and the Chopper Bunch, 1974-75, The Partridge Family: 2200 A.D., 1974-75, Hong Kong Phooey, 1974-76, These Are the Days, 1974-76, Devlin, 1974-76, Valley of the Dinosaurs, 1974-76, The Scooby-Doo/Dynomutt Hour, 1976-77, Mumbly, 1976-77, Jabberjaw, 1976-78, The Skatebirds, 1977-78, The Tom and Jerry/Great Grape Ape Show, 1977-78, Scooby's All-Star Laff-a-Lympics, 1977-78, Fred Flintstone and Friends, 1977-78, Captain Caveman and the Teen Angels, 1980, The Scooby-Doo and Scrappy-Doo Show, 1980-82, The Drak Pack, 1980-82, Fonz and the Happy Days Gang, 1980-82, The Richie Rich Show, 1980-82, The Kwicky Koala Show, 1981-82, Trollkins, 1981-82, Laverne and Shirley in the Army, 1981-82, The Smurfs, 1981-90 (Emmy award 1982, 83), Laverne and Shirley with the Fonz, 1982-83, Scooby, Scrappy, and Yabba Doo, 1982-83, Snorks, 1984-86, The Funtastic World of Hanna-Barbera, 1986-87,87-88, Pound Puppies, 1986-87, The Flintstone Kids, 1986-87, Wildfire, 1986-87, Foofur, 1986-87, Popeye and Son, 1987-88, The Completely Mental Misadventures of Ed Grimley, 1988-89; animated spls. include Alice in Wonderland, 1966, Jack and the Beanstalk, 1967 (Emmy award 1967), Last of the Curlews, 1972 (Emmy award 1973), My Smurfy Valentine, 1982, Smurfily-Ever-After, 1985, The Flintstones' 25th Anniversary Celebration, 1986, The Jetsons Meet the Flintstones, 1987, Hanna-Barbera's 50th: A Yabba Dabba Doo Celebration, 1989, I Yabba Dabba Doo!, 1993; live action spls. include The Runaways, 1974 (Emmy award 1974); live action TV movies include Hardcase, 1972, Shootout in a One-dog Town, 1974, The Gathering, 1977 (Christopher award 1978, Emmy award 1978), The Gathering Part II, 1979, Stone Fox, 1987; animated feature films include Hey There, It's Yogi Bear, 1964, A Man Called Flintstone, 1966, Charlotte's Web, 1973 (Annie award 1977), Heidi's Song, 1982, Once Upon a Forest, 1993; live action feature films C.H.O.M.P.S., 1979, The Flintstones, 1994; co-creator Huckleberry Hound, Yogi Bear, Flintstones, Jetsons, Top Cat, Jonny Quest, Scooby-Doo; author: (with Alan Axelrod) My Life in Toons, 1994. Recipient TV Acad. Gov.'s award, 1988, Hall of Fame award Acad. Arts and Scis., 1993, Movie Guide award Tom & Jerry the Movie, 1993, The Flintstones, 1994. *I have a simple goal; make people laugh.*

BARBERI, MATTHEW, physical education and health educator; b. New Haven, Nov. 12, 1916; m. Maryhannah Slingerland, Sept. 22, 1941; children: Robert, Richard, Susan, Marnie, Tom. BS, Arnold Coll., 1938; MS, NYU, 1949; postgrad., Yale U., 1953. Recreation dir. Children's Ctr., Hamden, Conn., 1938-40; tchr. phys. edn. New Haven Pub. Schs., 1940-41, tchr. health and phys. edn., 1945-46; asst. supr. phys. edn. dept. Hamden (Conn.) Pub. Schs., 1947-54, dir. health and phys. edn., 1955-81; adj. prof. So. Conn. State U., New Haven, 1956-98. Mem. Conn. Gov.'s Fitness Com., Hartford, 1968-75. Contbr. articles to profl. jours. Instr. water safety and first aid ARC, New Haven, 1945-81. Lt. USNR, 1941-45, PTO. Recipient cert. of achievement ARC, 1960; named Adminstr. of Yr. City Dirs. Coun. of AAHPERD. Mem. Conn. Assn. Health, Phys. Edn. and Recreation (pres. 1958-59, Profl. Honor award), Hamden Edn. Assn. (pres. 1952-53). Roman Catholic. Avocations: farming, fishing. Home: 42 Thornton St Hamden CT 06517-1320

BARBEY, ADÉLAÏDE, publisher; b. Vallorcine, France, Aug. 21, 1948; 1 child, Alice Gissinger-Barbey. Attachée de direction Inst. Etudes Politiques, Paris, 1971-74; chargée de mission French Ministry Culture, Paris, 1974-79; exec. editor Hatier, Paris, 1979-82; pub. Hachette Littérature Générale, Paris, 1982-95, mng. dir. TF1 Édits., 1996; cons. World Book, NYC, 2002—.

BARBEZAT, EUGENE LAVAR, computer systems engineer, retired air force officer; b. St. Johns, Ariz., Sept. 28, 1936; s. Fred Eugene Barbezat and Madge (Gibbons) Kindall; m. Karen Elizabeth Leichner, Dec. 22, 1970; children: Michele Lynn, Sean Michael. BS in Sociology, Brigham Young U., 1963; MA in Internat. Rels., U. So. Calif., 1980. Probation officer Ada County Probate Ct., Boise, Idaho, 1963-65; state probation officer 9th Dist. Ct., Ogden, Utah, 1965-66; commd. 2d lt. U.S. Air Force, 1966, advanced through grades to lt. col., 1981; chief Intelligence Report Ctr., 497th Reconaissance Tech. Group, Wiesbaden, Fed. Republic Germany, 1968-73; staff officer Def. Intelligence Agy., Washington, 1973-77, 84-85, Hdqrs. U.S. European Command, Vaihaingen, Fed. Republic Germany, 1977-80; chief Indications and Warning Ctr., Hdqrs. Mil. Airlift Command, Scott AFB, Ill., 1980-84; ret., 1985; staff integration and test software engr. Martin Marietta, Denver, 1985-92; documentation specialist Computer Data Systems Inc., Lakewood, Colo., 1992—98. Staff mem. com. on imagery and exploitation Dept. Def., 1975-77, mem. indications and warning study group, 1980-84. Commr., scoutmaster Boy Scouts Am., Denver, 1986-92, commr., Ft. Collins, 1994-98; mem. Operation Santa Claus, Denver, 1987-92; pres. Homeowners Assn., 1994-95. Mem.: DAV (life), Order of Arrow, Am. Legion, Denver Zool. Found., Denver Mus. Natural History, Air Force Assn., Assn. Former Intelligence Officers, Mil. Officer Assn. of Am. (life). Republican. Mem. Lds Ch. Avocations: camping, skiing, fishing, reading, music. Home: 2144 Andrews St Fort Collins CO 80528 Office: TEK Sys 6300 S Syracuse Way Englewood CO 80111-2215

BARBIER, EDWARD B. economist, educator; b. Washington, D.C., July 22, 1957; s. Clarence E. and Marietta N. Barbier; m. Joanne C. Burgess, July 3, 1993; children: James children: Lara, Rebecca. BA in Econ. & Polit. Sci., Yale U., 1979; MSc in Econ., London Sch. Econ. & Polit. Sci., 1980; PhD in Econ., U. of London, 1986. Reader U. York, York, England, 1993—2000; John S. Bugas prof. econ. U. Wyo., Laramie, 2000—; dir. London Environ. Econ. Ctr., 1990—93. Author: (book) Blueprint for a Sustainable Economy, 2000, The Economics of Environment and Development: Selected Essays, 1998. Office: Univ Wyo PO Box 3985 Laramie WY 82071-3985

BARBIERI, CHRISTOPHER GEORGE, professional society administrator; b. Bklyn., Jan. 9, 1941; s. Nicholas Joseph and Marie Anne (Bacigalupo) B.; m. Joanne Lee Barnett, Jan. 30, 1965 (div. 1980); children— Matthew, Deborah, Lisa; m. Laurel E. Praet, July 6, 1985 BS, Cornell U., 1962; MS, U. Vt., 1964. Adminstrv. asst., asst. new products mgr., new products mgr., retail sales mgr. H.P. Hood & Sons, Boston, 1964-69; pres. Vt. C. of C., Montpelier, 1969—2003, internat. trade v.p. Shanghai, 2003—. Dir. Vt. World Trade Office, 2001—. Past mem. adv. bd. Congl. Travel and Tourism Caucus; bd. dirs. Union 32 H.S., 1977-80; del. White House Conf. on Better Librs., 1979; mem. Vt. Travel and Recreation Coun., 1988-91; chmn. Vt. Metric Coordinating Coun., past chair Vt. Employer Support for Guard and Res. Com.; past bd. dirs. New Eng. Trade Adjustment Assistance Ctr.; past chmn. New Eng.-USA Found., 1990-92; adv. coun. U. Vt.; former mem. Washington County Rep. Com.; past bd. dirs. Vt. Employers Health Alliance; trustee Ea. States Expdn.; active Vt. State Rep. Exec. Com. With Air N.G., 1964-70. Mem. Vt. Assn. Execs. (pres. 1972), Vt. Assn. Chamber Execs. (pres. 1971), Small Bus. Adv. Coun. (past chmn.), Vt. Auto Enthusiasts (dirs.), Coun. State C. of C. (chair 1996-98). Lodges: Kiwanis (pres. Burlington 1972-73). Roman Catholic. Office: PO Box 37 Montpelier VT 05601-0037

BARBIERI-LIGHTNER, PATRICIA, state representative; b. Kansas City, Mo., Dec. 15, 1957; m. David L. Lightner; 1 child. BA in Personal Adminstrn. and Art History, U. Kans., 1981; JD, Western State U., 1984. Enforcement atty. FAA, 1989—92; mem. Kans. Ho. of Reps., 1999—. Mem.: Kans. City Met. Bar Assn., Wycliff Homes Assn. (sec., treas.). Republican. Roman Catholic. Office: 175-W State Capitol 300 SW 10th Ave Topeka KS 66612*

BARBINI, RICHARD JOHN, chemical engineer, marketing manager; b. Bronx, N.Y., Feb. 4, 1946; s. Alesandro J. and Theresa (Caggiano) B. BSChE, Rensselear Polytech. Inst., 1969. Registered profl. engr., N.J. Chemical engr. Grumman Aerospace, Bethpage, N.Y., 1969-73; process engr. Charles Ross & Son, Co., Hauppauge, N.Y., 1973-76; sales rep. Day Mixing, Cin., 1976-78; sales engr. Chemineer, Dayton, Ohio, 1978; sr. engr. Arco Indsl. Gases, Murray Hill, N.J., 1979-82, 84-87; sales engring mgr. Draiswerke, Inc., Allendale, N.J., 1982-83; products mgr. Arde Barinco, Inc., Norwood, N.J., 1987—. Speaker Engring. Found., N.H., 1974, Interphex, N.Y.C., 1993, Soc. Cosmetic Chemists, Chgo., 1994. Mem. rsch. com. Mt. Olive (N.J.) Residents Against Transfer Sta., 1987; catechist St. Elizabeth Ann Seton Ch., Flanders, N.J., 1989-97; chmn. alumni scholarship com. Rensselear Polytech. Inst., No. N.J., 1990-95. Mem. NSPE (mem. Discover E com. 1990-97), Italian Club of Mt. Olive, (pres., treas., sec. 1987-95; Outstanding Svc. award 1989), Phi Kappa Theta. Republican. Roman Catholic. Achievements include U.S. Patents on: Motionless Mixer, Controlling Temperature of a Cryogenically Refrigerated Product, CO2 Snow Horns; invention and commercialization of powder induction mixer. Office: Arde Barinco Inc 500 Walnut St Norwood NJ 07648-1389 Home: 146 Mount Grove Rd Califon NJ 07830-4214 E-mail: abmixer@optonline.net.

BARBOI, ALEXANDRU CEZAR, neuroscientist, researcher; b. Bucharest, Apr. 10, 1966; arrived in U.S., 1990; s. Alexandru and Constanta B.; m. Cristina Barboi; children: Mihnea, Christopher MD, Faculty Medicine, 1990. Diplomate Am. Bd. Internal Medicine, Am. Bd. Psychiatry and Neurology, Am. Bd. Clin. Neurophysiology. With customer svc. dept. Chgo. Clin. Lab., 1990-93; intern, resident in internal medicine West Suburban Hosp., Oak Park, Ill., 1993-96; resident in neurology Rush Presbyn., Chgo., 1996-99; fellow in neurophysiology St. Luke's Med. Ctr., Chgo., 1999—2000; asst. prof. neurology Med. Coll. Wis. Mem. Am. Acad. Neurology. Avocations: physics, philosophy. Office: Med Coll Wis 9200 W Wisconsin Ave Milwaukee WI 53226

BARBOR, JOHN HOWARD, lawyer; b. Pitts., Mar. 4, 1952; s. Thomas Sharp and Irene (Park) B.; m. Gretchen Suzanne Kunst, Mar. 20, 1982; children: Peter Howard, Katherine Suzanne. AB, Dartmouth Coll., 1974; JD, Boston Coll., 1977. Bar: Pa. 1977. Ptnr. Barbor and Barbor, Indiana, Pa., 1978-89, Barbor & Cicola, Indiana, 1989-93, Barbor, Vaporis & Sottile, P.C., Indiana, 1993—2002, Barbor Sottile & Darr, P.C., Indiana, 2003—. Bd. dirs., solicitor Indiana County YMCA, 1985-94; solicitor Indiana County Red Cross, 1979—; bd. dirs. Indiana Arts Coun., 1986-89; bd. dirs. Indiana County Zoning Appeals Bd., 1995—, chmn., 1998—. Mem. ABA, Pa. Bar Assn., Pa. Bar Inst. (bd. govs. 1995-97), Ind. County Bar Assn. (exec. bd. 1988, 95), Ind. Country Club, Phi Beta Kappa. Republican. Lutheran. Home: 217 Forest Ridge Rd Indiana PA 15701-7443 Office: Barbor Sottile & Darr PC 917 Philadelphia St Indiana PA 15701-3911

BARBOSA, RUBENS ANTONIO, Brazilian ambassador; b. Sao Paulo, June 13, 1938; s. Jose Orlando and Lice (Farina) B.; m. Maria Ignez Correa da Costa, June 13, 1969; children: Joao Bernardo, Mariana. BA in Law, U. Sao Paulo; BA in Diplomacy, Brazil's Fgn. Svc. Acad.; MA in Latin Am. Politics, London Sch. Econs./Polit. Sci. 3rd sec. Brazil's Ministry of Fgn. Rels., Brasilia, Brazil and London, 1962-66; 2d sec. Brazilian Embassy, London, 1966-73, counselor, 1976-79, min., 1979-84; chief of staff to min. of fgn. rels., 1985-86; undersec. gen. for multilateral and spl. polit. affairs Ministry of Fgn. Rels., 1986-87; sec. for internat. affairs Brazilian Fin. Ministry, 1987-88; Brazilian amb. Latin Am. Integration Assn., 1988-91, pres. com. of reps., 1991-92; undersec. gen. for trade, regional integration/econ. affairs Ministry of Fgn. Rels., 1991-93, v.p. permanent com. on fgn. trade, 1992-93; Brazilian amb. to the Ct. of St. James London, 1994-99; Brazilian amb. to the U.S., 1999—. Brazilian govt. coord. Mercosul Issues, 1991-93; exec. sec. com. on trade with East European Countries, 1976-83. Author: American Latina em Perspectiva: a Integraçao Regional da Retórica à Realidad, 1991, Panorama visto de Londres, 1998, The Mercosur Codes, The British Institute of International and Comparative Law, 2000, O Brasil dos Brasilianistas, Um Guia dos Estudos sobre o Brasil nos Estados Unidos (1945-2000), 2002; contbr. articles to profl. jours. and newspapers. Mem. Assn. of Coffee Producing Countries (pres. 1994-99). Avocations: tennis, classical music. Office: Brazilian Embassy 3006 Massachusetts Ave NW Washington DC 20008-3699

BARBOUR, ALTON BRADFORD, human communication studies educator; b. San Diego, Oct. 13, 1933; s. Ancel Baxter and Mary Jane (Fay) B.; m. Betty Sue Burch, Aug. 19, 1961 (div. 1991); children: Elizabeth, Christopher, Damon, Meagan; m. Jacqueline Moorhead, Feb. 29, 1996. BA, U. No. Colo., 1956; MA, U. Denver, 1961, PhD, 1968; postdoctoral, Moreno Inst., 1976. Diplomate Am. Bd. Psychotherapy. Lectr. Colo. Sch. Mines, Golden, 1964-65; instr. U. Denver, 1965-68, asst. prof. human comm. studies, 1968-71, assoc. prof., 1971-77, prof., 1977—, chairperson dept. human comm. studies, 1980—98. Vis. lectr. Swiss Inst. for Group Psychotherapy, Switzerland, 1992, Remin U., China, 1999, Chinese U. of Hong Kong. Co-author: Interpersonal Communication: Teaching Resources, 1972, Louder Than Words: Nonverbal Communication, 1974, Assessing Functional Communication, 1978; editor: Free Speech Yearbook, 1974-76; contbg. editor Internat. Jour. Action Methods, Psychodrama, Skill Tng., and Role Playing, Psychodrama Network News; contbr. articles to profl. jours. With USN, 1956-58. Recipient Intellectual Freedom award Nat. Coun. Tchrs. English, 1997, William McBride Writing award Colo. Lang. Arts Soc., 1998. Fellow Am. Soc. for Group Psychotherapy and Psychodrama (Disting. Profl. Svc. award 1998, Outstanding Scholar award 2002), Am. Bd. of Med. Psychotherapists, Internat. Acad. of Behavioral Medicine, Counseling and Psychotherapy; mem. Am. Bd. Examiners in Group Psychotherapy (sec. 1983-93, chair 1997-98). Avocation: trapeze catcher and flier. Home: 1195 S Vine St Denver CO 80210-1830 Office: Univ Denver Human Comm Studies Denver CO 80208-0001

BARBOUR, CATHERINE JEAN, actress, director, mime, set designer; b. Dover, Del., Nov. 8, 1932; d. Peter Joseph Callovini and Lydia Clara Shane; m. Alan Gregory Barbour, June 18, 1960. Cert., Am. Acad. Dramatic Arts, 1960; BA magna cum laude, Marymount Manhattan Coll., 1987; MFA, NYU, 1991. Tchr., dir. Am. Acad. Dramatic Arts, N.Y.C., 1963-71; performer, tchr., dir. The Am. Mime Theatre, N.Y.C., 1965—. Adminstrv. asst. Internat. Mimes and Pantomimists, N.Y.C., 1973-74. Set piece design for Music Box; performances with The Am. Mime Theatre include Dreams, Evolution, Sludge, Six, Couplings, Abstraction, Peepshow, Unitaur, Pageant; appeared in Captain Celluloid vs. The Film Pirates (film), 1968; appeared on The Today Show, 1975, TV Tokyo-Asayan, 1999; watercolor exhbn. Nat. Arts Club, N.Y.C., 2001. Recipient Jehlinger award Am. Acad. Dramatic Arts, N.Y.C., 1960. Mem. Am. Watercolor Soc. (assoc.), Rehoboth Art League, Inc., Art Students League N.Y., 1100 Watercolor Soc., Sons of the Desert, Nat. Movement Theater Assn. Avocations: art, sculpture, writing, set designing. Office: The American Mime Theatre 61 4th Ave New York NY 10003-5204 E-mail: AmMime@aol.com., Mimestar@aol.com.

BARBOUR, CLAUDE MARIE, minister, educator; b. Brussels, Oct. 2, 1935; came to U.S., 1969; Diploma d'État d'Infirmières, École d'Infirmières, Paris, 1956; diploma d'Études Religieuses, Faculté Libre de Théolog, Paris, 1958; MST, N.Y. Theol. Sem., 1970; DST, Garrett Evang. Theol. Sem., 1973. Ordained to ministry Presbyn. Ch., 1974. Youth counselor Young Women's Christian Assn., Geneva, 1959-61, Edinburgh, 1965-67; missionary Paris Evang. Missionary Soc., So. Africa, 1962-64; deaconess Ch. of Scotland, Edinburgh, 1967-69; from asst. to assoc. pastor First United Presbyn. Ch., Gary, Ind., 1974-80; from asst. to assoc. prof. Cath. Theol. Union, Chgo., 1976-86, prof., 1986—, McCormick Theol. Sem., Chgo., 1990-96. Founder, dir. Shalom Ministries and Community, Chgo., 1975—; parish assoc. First Presbyn. Ch., Evanston, Ill., 1983—. World Coun. Chs. scholar, Geneva, 1969, United Presbyn. Ch. Commn. on Ecumenical Mission and Rels., N.Y., 1972; recipient Laskey award United Meth. Ch. Womens Div. the Bd. Global Ministries, N.Y., 1972, Civic award Ind. Women's Coun., 1976, Challenge of Peace award Chgo. Ctr. for Peace Studies, 1991, Martin P. Wolf O.F.M. award Justice, Peace and Integrity of Creation Coun. of the English-Speaking Conf. of the Order of Friars Minor, 1996. Mem. AAUW, Internat. Assn. for Mission Studies, Nat. Assn. Presbyn. Clergywomen, Am. Soc. Missiology, Assn. Prof. Mission, Midwest

Fellowship Prof. Mission, Assn. Presbyn. in Cross-Cultural Mission. Home: 1649 E 50th St Apt 21A Chicago IL 60615-6110 Office: Catholic Theological Union 5401 S Cornell Ave Chicago IL 60615-5664

BARBOUR, MICHAEL G(EORGE), botany educator, ecological consultant; b. Jackson, Mich., Feb. 24, 1942; s. George Jerome and Mae (Dater) B.; m. Norma Jean Yourist, Sept. 30, 1963 (div. 1981); m. Valerie Ann Whitworth, Jan. 25, 1987; children: Julie Ann, Alan Benjamin, Steven Allan Whitworth. BS in Botany, Mich. State U., 1963; PhD in Botany, Duke U., 1967. Asst. prof. botany U. Calif., Davis, 1967-71, assoc. prof., 1971-76, prof., 1976—, chmn., 1982-85; prof. environ. horticulture U.. Calif., Davis, 1993—; ptnr. Ecolabs Cons., Davis, 1969—. Vis. prof. botany dept. Hebrew U., Jerusalem, 1979-81; vis. prof. marine scis. dept. La. State U., Baton Rouge, 1984; vis. prof. plant biology dept. Complutense U., Madrid, 1999. Co-author: Coastal Ecology, Bodega Head, 1973, Botany, 6th edit., 1982, Terrestrial Vegetation of California, 1977, 2d edit., 1988, Terrestrial Plant Ecology, 1980, 3d edit., 1998, North American Terrestrial Vegetation, 1988, 2d edit., 2000, California's Changing Landscapes, 1993, Plant Biology, 1998. Fulbright Found. fellow Adelaide, Australia 1964; Guggenheim Found. fellow, 1978; NSF rsch. grantee, 1968-78, MAB/NSF rsch. grantee, 1989-92, USDA rsch. grantee, 1992—. Mem. Ecol. Soc. Am., Brit. Ecol. Soc., Sigma Xi Democrat. Jewish. Office: U Calif Environ Horticulture Dept Davis CA 95616

BARBOUR, WILLIAM RINEHART, JR., retired book publisher; b. N.Y.C., Mar. 2, 1922; s. William Rinehart and Mary (McKelvey) B.; m. Mary Munsell, Nov. 17, 1951; children: Bruce R., Elizabeth M., Alan W. Student, Mich. State Coll., 1941-42. With Fleming H. Revell Co., 1944-83, pres., 1968-80, chmn., 1980-83. Co-author: (with wife) Trading Places, 1991, Home Exchange Vacationing, 1996, What Kids Say About Life, Love, and God, 2001. Served with USAAF, 1942-44. Named Pub. of Year Religious Heritage Am., 1974 Home: Shell Point Village 6810 Turban Ct Fort Myers FL 33908-1669

BARBOZA, ANTHONY, photographer, artist; b. New Bedford, Mass., May 10, 1944; s. Anthony Canto and Lillian (Barros) B.; m. Laura Carrington, June 15, 1985; children: Danica Chizu-Alita, Alexio Kyoshi-Tuari, Lien Orianna; children by previous marriage: Leticia, Laryssa. Grad. high sch., New Bedford. Lectr. Internat. Ctr. Photography, 1975, 83, Mass. State Coun. of Arts, 1982, Columbia Coll. Photography, Chgo., 1983, Oberlin (Ohio) Coll., 1984, Ohio U., Athens, 1986, Mus. Sch. Fine Arts, Boston, 1989, Lowell (Mass.) U., 1989, Rochester (N.Y.) Inst. Tech., 1991; asst. curator, photo exhibitor Bklyn. Mus. Art, 2001. Freelance photographer for advt. campaigns including Clairol, Hanes, Coca-Cola, Pepsi-Cola, United Negro Coll. Fund., Burger King, Soft Sheen Products, Kodak, McDonalds, Anheiser Busch, AT&T, Coors, Universal Pictures, Spike Lee Prodns., numerous others; panelist, judge Mass. State Coun. of Arts, 1978, Nat. Endowment Arts, 1981; lectr. R.I. Sch. of Design, 2001. Solo exhbns. include Pensacola (Fla.) Art Mus., 1966, Jacksonville (Fla.) Art Mus., 1969, Light Impressions Gallery, Rochester, N.Y., 1973, Friends Gallery of N.Y., 1974, Studio Mus. Harlem, N.Y.C., 1982; group shows include Addison Gallery Am. Arts, Andover, Mass., 1971, Mus. Modern Art, N.Y.C., 1978, Photokina, Germany, 1982, 84, City of Munich, 1985, Washington Project for Arts, 1989, Bklyn. Mus., 2001; in permanent collections Mus. Modern Art, N.Y.C., Newark Art Mus., U. Ghana, U. Mex., others; contbr. to books A Day in the Life of Hollywood, 1992, Color of Fashion, 1992, Songs of My People, 1992, The African Americans, 1993, A Day in the Life of Israel, 1994, A Day in the Life of Africa, 2002. Grantee N.Y. State Coun. of Arts, 1974, 76, Nat. Endowment Arts, 1980, N.Y. State Coun. of Arts, 2002. Avocations: painting, writing, gardening, design, literature. Home: 915 Gloucester Ct Westbury NY 11590-5301 Studio: 13 Laight St Apt 17 New York NY 10013-2119

BARBOZA, SANDRA LIVINGSTON, language educator; BA, Columbia College, SC, 1984; MAT, Univ. SC, 1989. Instr. Univ. SC, 1984—89, Midlands Tech. Coll., Columbia, SC, 1988—89; prof. Coll. Charleston, 1989—90, The Citadel, 1991—94; instr. Trident Tech. Coll, Charleston, SC, 1994—. Mem.: SC Tech. Educators Assoc. (assoc.), SC Fgn. lang. Tchr. Assoc. (assoc.), SC Internat. Edn. Consortium (assoc.). Avocations: yoga, Kung Fu. Office: Trident Tech Coll 7000 Rivers Ave Charleston SC 29423-8067

BARCA, GEORGE GINO, winery executive, financial investor; b. Sacramento, Jan. 28, 1937; s. Joseph and Annie (Muschetto) B.; m. Maria Sclafani, Nov. 19, 1960; children: Anna, Joseph, Gina and Nina (twins). AA, Grant Jr. Coll.; student, LaSalle U., 1963. With United Vintners, U.S.A., St. Helena, Napa Valley, Calif., 1960—. Chmn., pres. Barca Internat., USA, Barca Internat. USA, Calif. Grape Growers, USA, Calif. Vintage Wines, USA, Am. Vintners, USA, Barca Wineries and Vineyards USA, Barca Investment Co. USA. Named Best Prodr. of Sales, United Vintners, U.S.A. Mem. KC. Roman Catholic. Achievements include development of wine trademarks and brands.

BARCA, JAMES JOSEPH, fire department administrative services executive; b. New London, Conn., Feb. 20, 1944; s. Mariano and Angeline (Curzio) B.; m. Elizabeth Drake Garrison, Mar. 28, 1969 (div. Jan. 1983); m. Janet Louise Shields, Jan. 14, 1984. BSE in Indsl. Engring., U. Cen. Fla., 1972. Launch tech. IBM Corp., Cape Canaveral, Fla., 1968-69; indsl. engr. Honeywell, Inc., St. Petersburg, Fla., 1972-75, Tampa, Fla., 1975; mgr. mgmt. div., budget & mgmt. dept. City of St. Petersburg, 1975-81; mgr. fire adminstrv. svcs. St. Petersburg Fire and Rescue Dept., 1981-2000, ret., 2000. Exec. mem. Pinellas County (Fla.) Disaster Adv. Com., 1981-2000; mem. ARC Disaster Com., St. Petersburg, 1985-94, adv. coun., Pinellas, 1994-2000. Author: Disaster Planning for Adult Congregate Living Facilities, 1985, St. Petersburg Disaster Operations Plan, 1986-2000. Guest speaker representing St. Petersburg Emergency Mgmt. program at various civic assn. mtgs., 1981-2000. With USN, 1962-66. Recipient NASA Apollo Achievement award for Apollo 11 Moon landing participation. Republican. Roman Catholic. Avocations: computers, photography, home video. E-mail: jbarca2@tampabay.rr.com.

BARCA, KATHLEEN, marketing executive; b. Burbank, Calif., July 26, 1946; d. Frank Allan and Blanch Irene (Griffith) Barnes; m. Gerald Albino Barca, Dec. 8, 1967 (dec. May 1993); children: Patrick Gerald, Stacia Kathleen. Student, Pierce Coll., 1964; B in Bus., Hancock Coll., 1984. Teller Security Pacific Bank, Pasadena, Calif., 1968-69, Bank Am., Santa Maria, Calif., 1972-74; operator Gen. Telephone Co., Santa Maria, Calif., 1974-83, supr. operator, 1983-84; account exec. Radio Sta. KRQK/KLLB, Lompoc, Calif., 1984-85; owner Advt. Unltd., Orcutt, Calif., 1986-88; regional mgr. A.L. Williams Mktg. Co., Los Alamos, Calif., 1988-89; supr. Matol Botanical Internat., 1989-91; account exec. Santa Maria Times, 1989-95; owner a-garagesale.com, 2000—03. Author numerous local TV and radio commercials, print advt. Activist Citizens Against Dumps in Residential Environments, Polit. Action Com., Orcutt and Santa Maria; chmn. Community Action Com., Santa Maria, Workshop EPA, Calif. Div., Dept. Health Svcs. State of Calif.; vice coord. Toughlove, Santa Maria, 1988-89; parent coord., mem. steering com. ASAP and Friends, 1988-89; mem. Sloco Access, 1997-99; mem. Friends San Luis Obispo Bot. Gardens, 1997-99; v.p. Seneca Hosp. Aux., 1998-2000; active Fire Svcs., 1998-2000. Mem. NAFE, Womens Network-Santa Maria, Ctrl. Coast Ad (recipient numerous awards), Santa Maria C. of C. (amb. representing Santa Maria Times 1990-94, asst. chief amb. 1993-94), Chester Piecemakers Quilt Club, Lake Almaner Womens Club. Democrat. Avocations: raising exotic birds, writing childrens books.

BARCAN, STEPHEN EMANUEL, lawyer; b. Buffalo, N.Y., July 10, 1942; s. Abe and Goldie (Irom) Barcan; m. Bettye Ann Grossman, June 13, 1965; children: Sara Ellen, Daniel Jonathan, Adam Michael. AB, Columbia Coll., 1963; JD cum laude, Rutgers U., 1966. Bar: N.J. 1966, U.S. Dist. Ct. N.J. 1966, U.S. Ct. Appeals (3d cir.) 1971. Law sec. to presiding judge Appellate divsn. N.J. Superior Ct., 1966—67; assoc. Wilentz, Goldman & Spitzer, P.A., Woodbridge, NJ, 1967—74, ptnr., 1974—, adminstrv. shareholder, 1999—. Pres. Westfield Symphony Orch., 1999—2001, Temple Emanu-El, Westfield, NJ, 1984—86. Mem.: Middlesex County Bar Assn., N.J. Bar Assn. (chmn. land use sect. 1997—98). Democrat. Jewish. Office: Wilentz Goldman & Spitzer PO Box 10 90 Woodbridge Ctr Dr Ste 900 Woodbridge NJ 07095-1142

BARCEL, ELLEN NORA, secondary school educator, free-lance writer, editor; b. N.Y.C., Jan. 25, 1945; d. Oliver Vincent and Anna (Goss) B. BA, SUNY, Stony Brook, 1967, MA, 1969. Cert. elem. and secondary tchr., N.Y. Tchr. Patchogue (N.Y.)-Medford Sch. Dist., 1967-96. Dir., cataloguer Southold Indian Mus., 1985—, editor 1986—. Contbr. articles to profl. jours. Grantee N.Y. State Coun. on Arts, Mus. Aid Program 1987, 88, 89, 90. Mem. Am. Philatelic Soc., Am. Tropical Assn., Am. Soc. for Philatelic Pages and Panels (bd. dirs., sec. 1992-95), L.I. Coun. for Social Studies (grant 1991), Soc. for Am. Archaeology, Ea. States Archaeol. Fedn., N.Y. State Archaeol. Assn. (L.I. chpt., trustee 1986-89, v.p. 1989-2001, pres. 2001—), Archaeol. Soc. Ohio, Suffolk County Archaeol. Assn., Delta Kappa Gamma (v.p. Beta Psi chpt. of Pi state 1997-98, chpt. pres. 1998-2000). Avocations: genealogy, photography, philately. Home and Office: PO Box 39 East Setauket NY 11733-0039 E-mail: ebarcel@aol.com.

BARCELLA, ERNEST LAWRENCE, JR., lawyer; b. Washington, May 23, 1945; s. Ernest Lawrence and Louise Marion (Berniere) B.; m. Mary Elizabeth Lashley, June 1, 1970; 1 child, Laura Louise. AB, Dartmouth U., 1967; JD, Vanderbilt U., 1970. Bar: D.C. 1971, U.S. Dist. Ct. D.C. 1971, U.S. Ct. Appeals (D.C. cir.) 1971, U.S. Supreme Ct. 1976. Asst. U.S. atty., Washington, 1970-86; ptnr. Katten, Muchin, Zavis & Dombroff, Washington, 1991-94, Paul, Hastings, Janofsky & Walker, Washington, 1994—. Recipient John Marshall award, U.S. Dept. Justice, 1983. Fellow Am. Coll. Trial Lawyers; mem. ABA (white collar crimes com. criminal justice sect., complex crimes com. litigation sect.), Assn. Trial Lawyers Am., Fed. Bar Assn. (younger lawyer award 1979). Roman Catholic. Office: Paul Hastings Janofsky and Walker 10th Fl 1299 Pennsylvania Ave NW Washington DC 20004-2400

BARCELO, JOHN JAMES, III, law educator; b. New Orleans, Sept. 23, 1940; s. John James Jr. and Elfrida Margaret (Bisso) B.; m. Lucy L. Wood, July 14, 1974; children— Lisa, Amy, Steven. BA, Tulane U., 1962, JD, 1966; SJD, Harvard U., 1977. Bar: La. 1967, D.C. 1974, U.S. Supreme Ct. 1974, N.Y. 1975. Fulbright scholar U. Bonn, Fed. Republic Germany, 1966-67; prof. law Cornell U. Law Sch., Ithaca, N.Y., 1969—, A. Robert Noll. prof. of law, 1984-96, William Nelson Cromwell prof. internat. and comprative law, 1996—, dir internat. legal studies, 1972-88, 90—. Cons. Import Trade Adminstrn., Dept. Commerce Author: (with others) Law: Its Nature, Functions and Limits, 3rd edit., 1986, International Commercial Arbitration, 1999, 2d edit., 2003; co-editor: Lawyers' Practice and Ideals: A Comparative View, 1999, A Global Law of Jurisdiction and Judgments: Lessons from the Hague, 2002; contbr. articles to profl. jours. Mem. Am. Assn. for Comparative Study of Law (bd. dirs.), Am. Soc. Internat. Law, Am. Soc. Comparative Law, Maritime Law Assn. U.S. Office: Cornell U Law Sch Myron Taylor Hall Ithaca NY 14853

BARCENAS, CAMILO GUSTAVO, physician; b. Managua, Nicaragua, Sept. 18, 1944; came to U.S., 1969; s. Camilo and Margarita (Levy) B.; M.D., U. Nicaragua, 1968; m. Aurora Cardenas, Dec. 22, 1969; children: Margarita, Marcela, Camilo. Diplomate Am. Bd. Internal Medicine. Intern, Managua (Nicaragua) Gen. Hosp., 1967-68, Mt. Sinai Hosp., U. Conn., 1969; resident internal medicine Baylor Coll. Medicine, Houston, 1970-72; chief resident St. Luke's Episcopal Hosp., Houston, 1971; chief resident VA Hosp., Houston, 1972; fellow nephrology U. Tex. Health Sci. Ctr., Dallas, 1972-74; practice medicine specializing in nephrology, Dallas, 1974-76, Houston, 1976— ; chief home dialysis unit VA Hosp., Dallas, 1974-75, chief hemodialysis unit, 1975; chief nephrology sect. St. Luke's Episcopal Hosp., Houston, 1976— ; chief nephrology Tex. Heart Inst., dir. renal transplant svc.; asst. prof. medicine U. Tex. Health Sci. Ctr., Dallas, 1974-75; clin. asst. prof. medicine Baylor Coll. Medicine, Houston, 1976-79, clin. asso. prof., 1979-85, clin. prof., 1985— . Gen. sec. Juventud Social Christiana, 1968. Fellow A.C.P.; mem. Internat. Soc. Nephrology, Houston Soc. Internal Medicine, Am. Soc. Nephrology, Harris County Med. Soc., Tex. Med. Assn., Colegio Medico Nicaraguense. Roman Catholic. Contbr. articles on nephrology to med. jours. Office: 6624 Fannin St Ste 2510 Houston TX 77030-2337 also: 9197 Winkler Dr Ste D Houston TX 77017-5970

BARCEY, HAROLD EDWARD DEAN (HAL BARCEY), real estate counselor; b. Flint, Mich., Sept. 11, 1949; s. Glen Edward and Joyce Paulene (Dean) B.; children: Allen, David, Richard, Jackson, Joseph, Chris, Andrew. BA, U. Fla., 1971, postgrad., 1971-76. Cert. residential mktg. specialist, cert. residential brokerage mgr., cert. residential appraiser, accredited buyer rep., cert. buyer rep. Activist, lectr., fundraiser various environ. orgns. and projects, Fla., Ga., 1970-75; advt. mgr., salesman Towne & Suburban Realty, Salem, Ohio, 1977-87; broker-mgr. Seasons Real Estate Counselors, Salem, 1987—. Artist "Man in Balance with Nature" symbol, 1969. Campaign worker McCarty for Pres., Youngstown, 1967; bd. dirs. adult edn. program Alachua County, Fla., 1969; bd. dirs. Balance Fund Found., Balt., 1970-73, Good Earthkeeping, Inc., Gainesville, Fla., 1971-73; del. Conf. on Population Explosion and the Devel. Profl., Airlie, Va., 1969; solicitor LifeBanc of Ohio, Salem, 1989—; campaign worker Morris Udall for Pres., Gainesville, 1975. Named for Outstanding Citizen Contbn., Village of Canfield, Ohio, 1967. Mem. Nat. Assn. Realtors, Am. Assn. Cert. Appraiser, Realtors Nat. Mktg. Inst., Alpha Gamma Sigma. Independent. Roman Catholic. Avocations: travel, writing, music. Home and Office: 1288 W Perry St Salem OH 44460-3550

BARCH, DAVIS R. neuroscientist, application developer; b. Pitts., Sept. 14, 1956; s. Dwight Richard Barch and Margaret Halleran. BS, George Washington U., 1977; MS, U. Pitts., 1981, U. Calif., Santa Barbara, 1989; PhD, U. Calif., Berkeley, 2001. Rsch. asst. divsn. hematology and oncology U. of Pitts.; rsch. asst. Repligen Corp., Cambridge, Mass., 1984—85; software engr. Unisys, Camarillo, Calif., 1989—92, Neuron Data Corp., Palo Alto, Calif., 1993—95; programmer, analyst dept. physics U. Calif., Berkeley, 2002—. Neighborhood rep. Highlands Cmty. Assn., San Mateo, Calif., 2002—03. Mem.: AAAS. Achievements include research in Elucidation of the role of distributed activity patterns in the processing of sensory information.

BARCHAS, ERIC G. veterinarian; b. Idaho, July 1971; s. Rudy D. and Jean L. Barchas. BA, Rice U., 1993; DVM, U. Calif., Davis, 2000. Lic. vet., Calif. Lectr. U. Calif., Berkeley, 1994-96; vet. Bayshore Animal Hosp., San Mateo, Calif., 2000, Balboa Pet Hosp., San Francisco, 2000—. Regents scholar U. Calif.-Davis, 1996-2000, Max Roy scholar Rice U., 1989-93. Mem. Am. Animal Hosp. Assn., Am. Vet. Med. Assn. (student del. 1999-2000), Phi Beta Kappa, Phi Zeta, Phi Lambda Upsilon. Avocations: travel, outdoor recreation. Office: Balboa Pet Hosp 3329 Balboa St San Francisco CA 94121

BARCHAS, JACK DAVID, psychiatrist, educator; b. L.A., Calif., Nov. 2, 1935; s. Samuel Isaac and Cecile Margaret (Pasarow) B.; m. Patricia Ruth Corbitt, Feb. 9, 1957; 1 son, Isaac Doherty. BA, Pomona Coll., 1956; MD, Yale U., 1961. Lic. physician N.Y., Pa., Va., Calif. Intern Pritzker Sch. Medicine, U. Chgo., 1961—62; postdoctoral fellow in biochemistry and pharmacology NIH, 1962—64; resident in psychiatry Stanford Med. Sch., 1964—67, instr., 1966—67, asst. prof., 1967—71, assoc. prof., 1971-76, Nancy Friend Pritzker prof. psychiatry and behavioral scis., 1976—89; prof. psychiatry UCLA Sch. Medicine, L.A., 1990—93, dean for neurosci. and rsch. devel., 1990—93; Barklie McKee Henry prof., chmn. dept. psychiatry, psychiatrist-in-chief Weill Cornell Med. Ctr. and N.Y.-Presbyn. Hosp., N.Y.C., 1993—. Dir. Nancy Pritzker Lab. of Behavioral Neurochemistry, 1976— Editor; author: Serotonin and Behavior, 1973, Neuroregulators and Psychiatric Disorders, 1977, Psychopharmacology from Theory to Practice, 1977, Catecholamines - Basic and Clinical Frontiers, 1979, Isoquinolines and Beta-Carbolines, 1981, Research on Mental Illness and Addictive Disorders: Progress and Prospects, 1984, Neuropeptides in Neurology and Psychiatry, 1986, In Situ Hybridization in Neurobiology, 1987, Perspectives in Psychopharmacology, 1988, Biological Rhythms and Mental Illness, 1988; contbr. articles to profl. jours. Served with USPHS, 1962-64. Lt. comdr. USPHS, 1962—64. Recipient Psychopharmacology award Am. Psychol. Assn., 1970, Research Scientist award NIMH, 1980— Fellow Am. Psychiat. Assn., Am. Coll. Neuropsychopharmacology; mem. Soc. Neurosci., Am. Coll. Neuropsychopharmacology (Daniel Efron award 1978), Am. Soc. Pharmacology and Exptl. Therapeutics, Am. Physiol. Soc., Am. Soc. Neurochemistry, Am. Chem. Soc., Am. Psychosomatic Soc., Psychiat. Research Soc., Soc. Biol. Psychiatry (A.E. Bennett award 1968), Am. Psychopathol. Assn., Inst. Medicine Nat. Acad. Scis. (chmn. bd. Mental Health and Behavioral Medicine). Achievements include patents in field; investigation of neuroregulators in terms of identification of previously unrecognized substances; study of formation and inactivation of neuroregulators and determination of their role in brain, behavior, and mental disorders; research in studies of neurobiology and psychobiology of depressive illnesses. Avocations: photography, classical music, Scottish-Irish culture in America. Office: Cornell U Weill Med Coll Dept Psychiatry 1300 York Ave Box 171 New York NY 10021

BARCHET, STEPHEN, physician, former naval officer; b. Annapolis, Md., Oct. 25, 1932; s. Stephen George and Louise (Lankford) B.; m. Marguerite Joan Racek, Aug. 9, 1965. Student, Brown U., 1949-52; MD, U. Md., 1956. Diplomate Am. Bd. Ob-Gyn.; cert. physician exec. Commd. ensign M.C. U.S. Navy, 1955, advanced through grades to rear adm., 1978; intern Naval Hosp., Chelsea, Mass., 1956-57, resident in ob-gyn, 1958-61, resident in gen. surgery, 1957-58; fellow Harvard Med. Sch., 1959-60; obstetrician-gynecologist Naval Hosp., Naples, Italy, 1961-63, Portsmouth, N.H., 1963-64, Beaufort, S.C., 1964-66, Bremerton, Wash., 1967-70, chief ob-gyn Boston, 1970-73; asst. head, tng. br. Bur. Medicine and Surgery, Washington, 1973, head, 1973-75; dep. spl. asst. to surgeon gen. Navy, 1975; assoc. dean Sch. Medicine, Uniformed Services U. Health Scis., Bethesda, Md., 1976-77, exec. sec. bd. regents, 1976-77; spl. asst. to surgeon gen. for med. dept. edn. and tng. Bur. Medicine and Surgery, Navy Dept., Washington, 1977-79, insp. gen., 1979-80; comdg. officer Naval Health Scis. and Edn. and Tng. Command, Nat. Naval Med. Center, Bethesda, 1977-79; asst. chief planning, resources BUMED, 1980-82; dep. surg. gen., dep. dir. naval medicine Dept. Navy, 1982-83; ret., 1983; with Pacific Med. Ctr., Seattle, 1985-91; cons. Mil. Health Care, Seattle, 1987—; prin. MSA Programs, Seattle, 1995—; mng. ptnr. Benefit Payment $olutions, 1998—. Clin. asst. prof. Boston U. Sch. Medicine, 1971—; alt. regent Nat. Libr. Medicine, Bethesda, 1977-79; adj. prof. health care scis. George Washington U. Sch. Medicine and Health Scis., Washington, 1978—; ex officio mem. grad. med. edn. nat. adv. com. HEW, 1978-79; chmn. med.-dental com. Intersvc. Tng. Rev. Orgn., Washington, 1977-79; chmn. Washington Med. Savs. Accounts Project, 1994; coord. Health Plan for Life, 2003— Contbr. articles to med. jours. Sec. The Rainier Club, 1992-93; bd. dirs. North Seattle C.C. Found., 1992-95. Decorated Bronze star, others. Fellow Am. Coll. Obstetricians and Gynecologists, Am. Coll. Physician Execs.; mem. AMA, Assn. Mil. Surgeons U.S., Soc. Med. Cons. Armed Forces, Wash. State Med. Assn., King County Med. Assn., N.W. Mil. Health Benefit Assn. (exec. dir. 1991-94). Home and Office: 18601 SE 64th Way Issaquah WA 98027-8616 *Lasting achievements depend not only upon knowledge well applied but also upon doing what ought to be done.*

BARCHI, ROBERT LAWRENCE, clinical neurologist, neuroscientist, educator; b. Phila., Nov. 23, 1946; s. Henry John and Elizabeth (Pesci) B.; children: Jonathan Robert, Jennifer Elizabeth. BS, Georgetown U., 1968, MS, 1969; PhD, U. Pa., 1972, MD, 1973. Diplomate Am. Bd. Neurology and Psychiatry, Am. Bd. Med. Examiners. Resident in neurology U. Pa. Hosp., 1973-75; asst. prof. biochemistry U. Pa. Med. Sch., Phila., 1974-75, asst. prof. neurology and biochemistry, 1975-78, assoc. prof., 1978-81, prof., 1981—, David Mahoney prof. neurol. scis., 1985—, chmn. neurosci. grad. program, 1983-89, dir. Mahoney Inst. Neurol. Scis., 1983-96, vice-dean rsch. sch. medicine, 1989-91, chmn. dept. neurosci., 1992-95, chmn. depts. neurology and neurosci., 1995-99; provost and chief acad. officer U. Pa., 1999—. Mem. med. adv. bd. Muscular Dystrophy Assn., 1982—94, Soc. To Prevent Blindness, 1999—2001, Cephalon Inc., 1992—, chmn., 1996—; mem. sci. adv. bd. Phila. Ventures Inc., 1992—95, TransMolecular, Inc., 1996—; bd. dirs. Internat. House, Inc.; bd. mgrs. The Wistar Inst., 2000—; bd. dirs., vice chair Pa. BioAdvance, Inc., 2002—; bd. dirs. The Lauder Inst., 1999—, Benjamin Franklin Partnership, 2002—, Covance, Inc., 2003—. Author: (with Rosenberg, Prusiner, DiMauro) Molecular and Genetic Basis of Neurological Disease, 3 edits.; mem. editorial bd. Muscle and Nerve Jour., 1981-82, 95—, Jour. Neurochemistry, 1981-90, Jour. Neurosci., 1988-91, Ion Channels, 1988—, Current Opinion Neurology and Neurosurgery, 1992—, The Neuroscientist, 1993—, Neurobiology of Disease, 1994—; contbr. chpts. to textbooks, numerous articles to profl. jours. Recipient Lindback award U. Pa., 1979, Javits award NIH, 1985, Sci. Achievement award Am. Heart Assn., 1997, Disting. Grad. award U. Pa. Med. Sch., 2000. Fellow AAAS, Am. Acad. Neurology, Am. Neurol. Assn. (bd. councillors 1992-94); mem. Inst. Medicine of the NAS, Biophys. Soc., Soc. for Neurosci. (pub. lectr. 1985), Am. Soc. Clin. Investigation, Assn. Am. Physicians, Phila. Coll. Physicians, Phi Beta Kappa, Alpha Omega Alpha. Avocation: antiquarian horology. Office: U Pa Office of Provost 122 College Hall Philadelphia PA 19104 E-mail: barchi@mail.med.upenn.edu.

BARCIA, JAMES A. state senator, former congressman; b. Bay City, Mich., Feb. 25, 1952; Grad., Saginaw Valley State U., 1974. Staff asst. to U.S. Senator Philip Hart, 1971; cmty. svc. coord. Mich. Cmty. Blood Ctr., Bay City, 1974-75; mem. Ho. of Reps. from 101st Mich. Dist., 1977-82, mem. edn. com., 1977-82, chmn. pub. works com., 1979-82, majority whip, 1979-82; mem. Mich. Senate, 1983-92, U.S. Congress from 5th Mich. dist., 1993—2002; mem. sci. and transp. and infrastructure coms.; senator, State of Mich., 31st Dist., 2003—. Mem. UAW Local 688, 1970-71, Saginaw Valley Univ. Bd. Control, 1973-74. Recipient disting. svc. award Saginaw Valley State U. Alumni Assn., 1977, Golden Eagle award Am. Fedn. Police; named Fed. Legislator of Yr., Mich. Credit Union League, Legislator of Yr., Satari Club Internat.; elected to Bay City Ctrl. Hall of Fame, 1981. Mem. NRA, Bay Area C. of C., Mich. Assn. Osteopathic Physicians and Surgeons (hon. lay mem.), Bay City Jaycees (Disting. Svc. award 1982), United Conservation clubs, Elks, Bay City Lions. Democrat. Home: 3190 Hidden Rd Bay City MI 48706-1203 Office: PO Box 30036 Lansing MI 48909-7536 also: 301 E Genessee Ste 502 Saginaw MI 48607*

BARCLAY, H(UGH) DOUGLAS, lawyer, former state senator; b. N.Y.C., July 5, 1932; s. Hugh and Dorothy Barclay; m. Sara Seiter, Aug. 15, 1959; children: Kathryn D., David H., Dorothy G., Susan M., William A. BA, Yale U., 1955; JD, Syracuse U., 1961; LLD (hon.), St. Lawrence U., 1980; ScD (hon.), Clarkson Univ., 1981; LLD (hon.), SUNY, 1990, Syracuse U., 1997. Bar: N.Y. 1962. Ptnr. Hiscock & Barclay and predecessors, Syracuse, N.Y., 1961—. Sec., gen. counsel KeyCorp and subs., Albany, N.Y., 1971-89; mem. N.Y. State Senate, 1965-84, chmn. Judiciary com., chmn. Select Task Force on Ct. Reorgn., chmn. senate codes com.; dir., chmn. bd. Syracuse Supply Co; chmn. bd. Eagle Media, Inc. Mem. N.Y. State Econ. Power Allocation Bd., N.Y. Racing Assn., bd. trustees; pres. Met. Devel. Assn.; trustee, former chmn. Syracuse U., chair chancellor search com.; vice chmn. N.Y. State George Bush for Pres., 1988; chmn. N.Y. State Bush-Quayle campaign, 1992; mem. policy coun. Gov. Pataki's Transition Team; bd. visitors Syracuse U. Coll. Law; mem. Onondaga C.C. Found.; bd. dirs. Overseas Pvt. Investment Corp., 1990-93; mem. panel of conciliators, Internat. Ctr. of Settlement of Investment Disputes, 2002. Lt. arty. U.S. Army, 1955-57, Korea. Mem. ABA, N.Y. State Bar Assn. Office: Hiscock & Barclay PO Box 4878 221 S Warren St Syracuse NY 13202-1633

BARCLAY, MARTHA JANE, science educator, research scientist; b. Warren County, Ill., July 5, 1948; d. George Leonard and Edna Virginia Ault; children: Brad children: Austin. BS, U. Ill., 1970; MS, Ind. U., 1972; PhD, U. Tenn., 1979. Registered dietitian. Asst. prof. U. Iowa, Iowa City, 1979—86; prof. Western Ill. U., Macomb, Ill., 1986—2002. Rschr. Coun. Food and Agrl. Rsch., Champaign/Urbana, 1997—2002. Treas. McDonough County Teen Ct. Bd., Macomb, 2000—02. Named Hospitality Educator of Yr., Illinois Hotel and Lodging Assn., 2001-2002. Mem.: Ill. Assn. Family and Consumer Scis., Am. Assn. Family and Consumer Scis., Ill. Dietetic Assn., Am. Dietetic Assn., Midwest CHRIE (pres. 1990—91), Internat. CHRIE. Office: Western Ill U 1 University Cir Macomb IL 61455 Office Fax: 309-298-2688. Business E-Mail: MJ-Barclay@wiu.edu.

BARCLAY, PETER ROY, minister, counselor; b. Mass., 1963; s. David and Florence Barclay. BS summa cum laude, Boston U., 1991, MA, 1994; MDiv honors, Gordon-Conwell Sem., 2002, ThM, 2003. Lic. min. United Ch. Christ, 2002. Rschr., social analyst Mass. Family Inst., Newton, 1995—97; sales rep. Colo. Prime, Weymouth, Mass., 1997—99; assoc. chaplain Boston Seafarers Mission, Chelsea, Mass., 2000—. Tchr., asst. prof. Gordon-Conwell Sem., Boston, 2000—; assoc. min. Elm St. Bapt. Ch., Everett, Mass., 2001—02; pastor Scotland Congl. Ch., Bridgewater, Mass., 2002—; cons. Boston City Mission Soc., 2002—; com. mem. Restorative Justice Task Force United Ch. Christ, Framingham, Mass., 2002—. Mem. Hanover Hist. Soc., 2000—, Bridgewater Coun. Churches, 2002—. Mem.: Assn. Profl. Chaplains, Evang. Theol. Soc., N.Am. Meritime Ministry Assn., Am. Correctional Assn., Am.

Acad. Religion, Soc. Study Social Problems, Am. Sociol. Assn., Am. Acad. Mins. Avocations: hiking, travel. Home: 107 Park Ave Bridgewater MA 02324-2610 Office: Seafarers Friend Mission 25 Williams St Chelsea MA 02150

BARCLAY, ROBERT, JR., chemist; b. Mt. Vernon, N.Y., Apr. 1, 1928; s. Robert and Emma Josephina (Neher) B. AB, Cornell U., 1948; PhD, U. Md., 1957. Chemist Barrett Div. Allied Chem. Corp., Edgewater, N.J., 1948-51, Am. Cyanamid Co, Linden, N.J., 1951-52; project scientist Union Carbide Corp., Bound Brook, N.J., 1956-69; sr. rsch. scientist Chem. Div. Morton Thiokol, Trenton, N.J., 1969-79; sect. head Hydrocarbon Rsch. Inc., Lawrenceville, N.J., 1979-86; cons. Amoco Performance Products Inc., Bound Brook, 1986-90. Contbr. chpt. to book Condensation Monomers, 1972. Mem. Am. Chem. Soc. (sec. Trenton sect. 1979-81, alt. councillor 1983-84). Roman Catholic. Achievements include 13 patents for synthesis of high performance condensation polymers and ultraviolet cured urethane acrylate polymers, and others. Home: 6 Berrywood Dr Hamilton NJ 08619-1906

BARCLAY, STEVEN CALDER, lawyer; b. Phoenix, Ariz., Jan. 17, 1956; s. Leslie Calder and Ruth (Lindke) B.; m. Janice Marie Reno, Sept. 25, 1982; 1 child, Jordan Nicole. BA magna cum laude, Oral Roberts U., 1977; JD cum laude, Notre Dame U., 1980. Bar: Ariz. 1980, U.S. Dist. Ct. Ariz. 1980, U.S. Ct. Appeals (9th cir.) 1980. Assoc. Snell & Wilmer, Phoenix, 1980-83; corp. counsel S.W. divsn. CIGNA Healthplans, Inc., Phoenix, 1983-85; ptnr. Barclay & Reece, Phoenix, 1985-87; pvt. practice Phoenix, 1987-90; shareholder, pres. Barclay & Goering, PC, Phoenix, 1990-00, Steven C. Barclay, PC and Advocates West, Inc., 2001—. Mem. editl. bd. Today's Health Care Mag., 1994-96. Mem. March of Dimes (Az. chap., dir.), Project Citizen (adv. coun.); dir., counsel Ariz. Sports Coun./Grand Canyon State Games. Mem.: Pub. Affairs Profls. Ariz. (dir., pres. 1998—99), Am. Health Lawyers Assn., Ariz. Assn. Health Care Lawyers, State Bar Ariz. Republican. Avocations: camping, hiking, jogging, scuba diving, travel. Office: Law Offices of Steven C Barclay PC PO Box 93746 Phoenix AZ 85070-3746 E-mail: scbarclay@cox.net.

BARCLAY, WARREN M. human resources specialist, researcher; b. New Bedford, Mass., Feb. 27, 1952; s. Emil Barclay, Alice (Stamler) Barclay. BA, U. Bridgeport, 1974; MPA Maxwell Sch., Syracuse U., 1975. Cert. Pub. Mgr. State of N.J., 1999. Bur. chief divsn. EEO and Affirmative action N.J. Dept. Pers., Trenton, 1977—93, chief rsch. projects Office Planning and Rsch., 1993—. Chair State Data Ctr. Adv. Com. N.J. Dept. Labor, Trenton, 1992—96; chair Employee Action Com. N.J. Dept. Pers., Trenton, 1991—98; adj. instr. Mercer County C.C., Trenton, 1983. Author (profl. monthly newspaper): PA TIMES, 1991; author: (jour.) Pub. Adminstrn. Rev., 1979; editor (employee monthly newsletter): N.J. Dept. Pers., 1986—90. Pres. Condo Assn. Soc. Hill at Hamilton, Hamilton, NJ, 1987—88; mem. Mercer County Exploring com. Boy Scouts Am., Trenton, NJ, 1984—93; pres. Greater Princeton Jaycees, Princeton, NJ, 1982—83; rec. sec. religious institution, Trenton, NJ, 1992—96, youth advisor, 1980—82. Named Outstanding Young Man Am., 1985. Mem.: Am. Soc. Pub. Adminstrn. (Nat. Coun. 1997—98, Pres. N.J. chpt. 1998—99, chair nat. steering group 2001—02, Joseph E. McLean Chpt. Svc./Devel. award 1995), Acad. Polit. Sci., Assn.Govt. Accts., Commonwealth Assn. Pub. Adminstrn. and Mgmt., Soc. Human Resource Mgmt., Internat. Pers. Mgmt. Assn., Am. Acad. Cert. Pub. Mgrs., Am. Soc. Notaries (life). Avocation: travel, photography, antiques, history, flea markets. Office: New Jersey Dept Personnel PO Box 319 Trenton NJ 08625 Office Fax: 609-984-3800. Business E-Mail: warren.barclay@dop.state.nj.us.

BAR-COHEN, AVRAM, mechanical engineering educator; b. Bklyn., Jan. 19, 1946; s. Simon and Dorothy (Halperin) Markowitz; m. Annette Pavony, Sept. 11, 1966; children: Barak, Raanan, Talia Dvora. SB, SM, MIT, 1968, PhD, 1971. Sr. engr. Raytheon Co., Bedford, Mass., 1968-73; lectr. dept. mech. engring. Ben Gurion U., Beer Sheva, Israel, 1973-75, sr. lectr., 1975-77, 79-81; assoc. prof. Ben Gurion U. of the Negev, Beer Sheva, Israel, 1981-84, prof., 1988; vis. assoc. prof. U. Minn., 1984-85, adj. prof., 1985-87, 89, assoc. prof., 1989-91, prof. dept. mech. engring., 1992—, dir. Thermodynamics and Heat Transfer divsn., 1992-98, James J. Renier vis. chair Tech. Leadership, 1996-99, exec. dir. Ctr. Devel. Tech. Leadership, 1998—2002, H.W. Sweatt chair in technol. leadership, 2000—02; chair dept. of mech. engring. U. Md., 2002—. Vis. assoc. prof. MIT, Cambridge, 1977-78; adj. prof. Naval Postgrad. Sch., Monterey, Calif., 1982; exec. cons. Control Data Corp., Mpls., 1985-89. Author: (with A.D. Kraus) Thermal Analysis and Control of Electronic Equipment, 1983, Design and Analysis of Heat Sinks, 1995; editor: (with A.D. Kraus) Advances in Thermal Modeling of Electronic Components and Systems, vol. I, 1988, vol. II, 1990, vol. III, 1992, vol. IV, 1998; contbr. articles to profl. jours. Recipient Edwin F. Church medal Am. Soc. of Mechanical Engineers, 1994. Fellow ASME (v.p. rsch. 1998—, recipient Heat Transfer meml. award 1999, Worcester Reed Warner medal 2000), IEEE (editor-in-chief Transaction on Components and Packaging Technologies 1995—), N.Y. Acad. Scis., Sigma Xi, Pi Tau Sigma, Tau Beta Pi.

BARCUN, GAIL E. forensic economics executive; b. Newark, Sept. 20, 1945; d. Milton and Miriam (Jenett) Rosen; m. Leon Weinglass, June 11, 1967 (div. Nov. 1995); children: Ronny, Jodi; m. Seymour David Barcun, June 2, 1985; children: Louis Isaac, Tania Jo. BA in Edn., Coll. N.J., 1967; MA in Edn., Kean Coll., 1974. Cert. nursery sch. 2d grade tchr. Washington Sch., Union, N.J., 1967-69; music/dance/party specialist 20 Nursery, K & Day Care Ctr., N.J., 1977-89; exec. v.p., adminstr. Fin. Freedom, Inc., Edison, NJ, 1985—. Pres. Rutgers U. Parents Assn., Piscataway, N.J., 1988-91. Mem. NAFE, AAUW, N.J. Activity Profls. Assn. (assoc.), Jewish Women Internat. Jewish. Avocations: travel, music, volunteer work, theatre. Home: 39 Merker Dr Edison NJ 08837-2733

BARCUN, SEYMOUR, economics educator; b. N.Y.C., June 4, 1932; s. Oscar and Tanya (Fein) B.; m. Esther Schachter (div. 1981); children: Louis, Tania; m. Gail Ellen Rosen, June 2, 1985. BA, CUNY, 1956; MBA, NYU, 1969, MS, 1973, PhD, 1977. Mgr. mktg. sci. Mathematica, Princeton Junction, N.J., 1968-70; assoc. prof. econs. Rider Coll., Lawrenceville, N.J., 1970-73; asst. prof. econs. Montclair State Coll., Upper Montclair, N.J., 1971-72; supr. ops. rsch. AT&T, various locations, 1973-75; dir. forecasting svcs. Am. Paper Inst., N.Y.C., 1975-77, prof. L.I. U., N.Y.C., 1977-83, Rutgers U., New Brunswick, N.J., 1980-84; pres., econ. analyst, forensic economist ECO-STAT, Edison, N.J., 1977—; prof., dept. chmn. St. Francis Coll., N.Y.C., 1983—. Cons. mktg. sci., 1977—; tchr. St. John's U., Queens and S.I., 1990—. Producer pub. svc. radio messages on economy, 1977-79. With U.S. Army, 1957. Mem. AAAS, Nat. Assn. Bus. Economists, Nat. Bus. Edn. Assn., Decision Scis. Inst., N.Y. Acad. Scis., Sigma Xi, Alpha Kappa Psi, Delta Sigma Pi. Jewish. Home: 39 Merker Dr Edison NJ 08837-2733

BARCUS, ROBERT GENE, retired educational association administrator; b. Oct. 22, 1937; s. Harold Eugene and Marjorie Irene (Dilling) B.; m. Mary Evelyn Shull, Aug. 9, 1959; children: Jennifer Sue, Debra Lynn. BPE, Purdue U., 1959; MA, Ball State U., 1963; postgrad., Ind. U., summer 1966; supts. lic., Butler U., 1967. Tchr., coach Wabash (Ind.) Jr. H.S., 1959-63; tchr. Wabash H.S., 1963-64; tchr., coach North Cen. H.S., Indpls., 1964-65; salary cons. Ind. State Tchrs. Assn., Indpls., 1965-67, asst. dir. rsch., 1967-68, dir. spl. svcs., 1968-70, exec. asst., 1971-72, adminstrv. asst., 1972-73, asst. exec. dir. spl. svcs. and tchr. rights, 1973-82, asst. exec. dir. adminstrn., pers. and governance, 1982-85, asst. exec. dir. labor rels. and adminstrn., 1985-93, assoc. exec. dir. labor rels. and adminstrn., 1993—2002, ret., 2003. Clk. Ch. of the Brethren, 1966-74, chmn., 1979-83, 87, 92-96, 97-98, 98-99, fin. sec., 2000; mem. Ind State Libr. and Hist. Bd., 2000. Alumni scholar Purdue U., 1959. Mem. NEA, Wabash City Tchr. Assn. (past pres.), Washington Twp. Tchr. Assn. (past pres.), Indpls. Press Club. Home: 2230 Brewster Rd Indianapolis IN 46260-1521 Office: 150 W Market St Indianapolis IN 46204-2806 E-mail: rbarcus@ista-in.org.

BARCZYNSKI, JOHN LESLIE, periodontist; b. Bethlehem, pa., July 19, 1956; s. John Peter and Theresa Marie (Mariano) B.; m. Lisa Kay Christner, May 29, 1982; children: John Edward, Heather Lynn and Kristen Marie (triplets). BS in Chemistry summa cum laude, Lehigh U., 1978; DMD, U. Pitts, 1982, MDS, 1987. Periodontist Sto-Rox Health Corp., McKees Rocks, Pa., 1982, 84-87, 1987—, dental dir., 1988—, clin. dir., 1990—; gen. dentist USPHS, Phila., 1982-84; periodontist Highland Dr. Med. Ctr., Pitts., 1986—; periodontal instr. U. Pitts. Dental Sch., 1989—. Dental cons. Pa. Forum Clin. Svcs. Com., Wormleysburg, 1991—, Alma Ilery Med. Ctr., Pitts., 1998-2000; cons., bd. dirs. Cmty. Integrated Network of Pa., Wormleysburg, 1996—. Capt. USPHS, 1982-84, Res., 1984—. Recipient Fellowship award AGD, 1987, Healthcare State Recognition award Pa. Forum Primary Health Care, 1991, Dr. Nealon Pub. Health award, 1998. Mem. ADA, Am. Acad. Periodontology, Internat. Assn. Dental Rsch., Clin. Regional Adv. Network, Pa. Dental Assn., Dental Soc. Western Pa., Northeastern Soc. Periodontists, Pa. Soc. Periodontologists, Pitts. Acad. Periodontology (pres. 1995-96, exec. com. 1993-97), Am. Assn. Dental Rsch., Am. Dental Soc. Anesthesiology, Acad. Gen. Dentistry (affiliate), USPHS Commissioned Officer's Assn., Nat. Network Oral Health Access, Am. Legion, Elks, Am. Philatelic Soc., Tau Beta Pi, Omicron Kappa Upsilon, Psi Omega, Delta Sigma Phi. Avocations: reading, piano, collecting. Office: Sto-Rox Health Corp 710 Thompson Ave Mc Kees Rocks PA 15136-3808

BARD, ALLEN JOSEPH, chemist, educator; b. Dec. 18, 1933; m. Fran; children: Eddie, Sara. BSc in Chemistry summa cum laude, CCNY, 1955; MA in Chemistry, Harvard U., 1956, PhD in Chemistry, 1958; PhD (hon.), U. Paris-VII, 1986. Instr. chemistry The U. Tex., Austin, 1958-60, asst. prof., 1960-62, assoc. prof., 1962-67, prof., 1967—, Jack S. Josey Professorship Energy Studies, 1980-82, Norman Hackerman Prof. Chemistry, 1982-85, Hackerman-Welch Regents Chair Chemistry, 1985—. US nat. com. Internat. Union Pure and Applied Chemistry-Nat. Rsch. Coun., 1983-93, chair, 1988-89, bd. energy and environ. sys., 1983-86, 93-96, bd. chem. scis. tech., 1982-87, co-chair, 1985-87, nat. materials adv. bd. com. on electrochem. aspects of energy conservation and prodn., 1985, com. on chem. scis. and ad hoc panel on DOE rsch., 1980-84, NAS, NRC liaison com. on high temp. sci. and tech., 1984; pres. Internat. Union Pure and Applied Chemistry, 1991-93; adv. bd. Dept. Energy and Energy Rsch., panel on Cold Fusion, 1989; chem. adv. com. NSF, 1981-84; external adv. com. Beckman Inst., 1989-97; bd. govs. Weizmann Inst., 1995—, sci. & acad. adv. com., 1995-98; lectr. in field. Author: Chemical Equilibrium, 1966, Integrated Chemical Systems, 1994; co-author: Electrochemical Methods, 1980; editor Electroanalytical Chemistry, 21 vols., 1966—, Encyclopedia of the Electrochemistry of the Elements, 16 vols., 1973—, (with others) Standard Potentials in Aqueous Solution; mem. editl. bd. Jour. Am. Chem. Soc., editor-in-chief, 1982-2001; mem. editl. bd. Electrochimica Acta, divsn. editor, 1978-80; mem. editl. bd. Dictionary Modern Sci. and Tech., 1989—, Ency. Sci. Instrumentation, 1990—, Ency. Phys. Sci. and Tech., 1984—, Ency. Sci. and Tech., 1992-1997, Analytical Letters, 1967—, Analytical Scis., 1985-99, Catalysis Letters, 1988-94, Chem. Instrumentation, 1967-77, Chem. Physics Letters, 1992—, Critical Revs. in Analytical Chemistry, 1985-91, Jour. Photoacoustics, 1982-84, New Jour. Chemistry, 1978-93, Jour. Supercritical Fluids, 1988-95, Organic Thin Films and Surfaces, 1991—, Heterogeneous Chemistry Revs., 1993—, Accounts of Chem. Rsch., 1993—, Russian Chem. Bull., 1995—; contbr. over 700 articles to profl. jours. Recipient Outstanding Achievement in Fields of Analytical Chemistry award Eastern Analytical Symposium, 1990, Townsend Harris medal City Coll. N.Y., 1989, Edward Mack award Ohio State U., 1989, Math. and Phys. Scis. award N.Y. Acad. Scis., 1986, Bruno Breyer Meml. award Royal Australian Chem. Inst., 1984, Scientific Achievement award City Coll. N.Y., 1983, Sherman Mills Fairchild scholar Calif. Inst. Tech., 1977, Ward Medal in Chemistry, 1955, Luigi Galvani medal Societa Chimica Italiana, 1992, Sigillum Magnum di Bologna, 1996, Pitts. Analytical Chemistry award, 2001. Fellow Electrochem. Soc. (Olin-Palladium medal 1987, Henry Linford award 1986, Carl Wagner Meml. award 1981); mem. AAAS (coun. del. 1992-95, chair-elect chemistry sect. 1996), Am. Chem. Soc. (G.M. Kosolapoff award 1992, Oesper award Cin. sect. 1989, Analytical Chemistry award 1988, Willard Gibbs award Chgo. sect. 1987, Fisher award in Analytical Chemistry 1984, Harrison Howe award Rochester sect. 1980, Priestley medal, 2002), NAS (chmn. chemistry sect. 1996-99, award in chem. scis. 1998), Am. Acad. Arts and Scis. (award 1990), Internat. Soc. Electrochemists (Linus Pauling award 1998), Am. Philos. Soc. (award 2000), Assn. Harvard Chemists (Priestley medal 2002), Sigma Xi. Achievements include research involving application of electrochemical methods to study of chemical problems and include investigations in electroanalytical chemistry, electron spin resonance, electro-organic chemistry, high resolution electrochemistry, electrogenerated chemiluminescence and photoelectrochemistry. Office: U Tex Austin 1 Univ Station A5300 Dept Chemistry Austin TX 78712-0165 E-mail: ajbard@mail.utexas.edu.

BARD, JUDY KAY, librarian; b. Topeka, Kans., May 10, 1943; d. Wilbur Dean and Kathryn Lucille (Bauer) White; m. Nelson Parker Bard Jr., June 20, 1965; children: Daniel Oliver, Nathaniel Arthur. BA in English cum laude, Hiram (Ohio) Coll., 1965; MA, U. Va., 1968; MLS in Libr. Sci., Ind. U., 1984. Prof. ESL Internat. Lang. Inst., Elkins, W.Va., 1974-84; prof. English Davis & Elkins Coll., Elkins, 1975-85; sch. libr. Harman (W.Va.) Sch., 1985-86; libr. Lancaster (Pa.) County Libr., 1988-92; libr. Lebanon (Pa.) Campus Harrisburg Area C.C., 1992—, sec. faculty coun., 1997-98, mem. exec. com. faculty coun., 1997-99. Mem. exec. com. Middle States Re-Accreditation Self-Study, 1996, mem. strategic planning com., 1998, 2003, mem. joint budget adv. com., 1999-2002, affirmative action com. 2000—, mid. states mid-term report com. 2000-02, coll. master plan com., 2002—; charter mem. Lebanon County Mediation Svcs., 1999-2002, sec. 1999-2000; chairperson One World Festival, 2003. Compiler, editor Historic Beverly booklet, 1970. Charter mem., sec., Randolph County Creative Arts Coun., Elkins, 1969-86, Beverly (W.Va.) Cmty. Action, 1969-86; delivery person Randolph County Meals on Wheels, Elkins, 1970-85; deacon Elizabethtown Ch. of Brethren, 1986—; mem. nominating com. N.E. Atlantic Ch. of Brethren, 2000—. Recipient award for Excellence in Cmty. Coll. Tchg., Nat. Inst. Staff and Orgnl. Devel., 2002. Mem.: Assn. Coll. Librs. Ctrl. Pa. (sec. 2000—02), Pa. Libr. Assn. (past relocation round table chair, co--chair ann. conf. bookstore 1998, past regional sec., chairperson South Ctrl chpt. ann. conf. registration 2000, chairperson scholarship com. 2001). Avocations: kayaking, biking, needlework, modern dance. Office: Pushnik Family Libr 735 Cumberland St Lebanon PA 17042-5235 E-mail: jkbard@hacc.edu.

BARD, MARJORIE, social welfare administrator; b. Balt. d. Harry B. and Eleanore M. Friedgood. BA, UCLA, 1956, MA, 1958, MA, 1982—83, PhD, 1988. Tchr. L.A. Sch. Dist., 1957—60; instr. Coll. Balt. County, 1971—78, UCLA, 1983—84; mgmt. crisis cons. L.A., 1985—; folklorist, oral historian, dir., pres. Women Organized Against Homelessness, 1985—. Workshop leader Gov.'s Conf. on Crime Victims, 1985; domestic violence victim adv., L.A., 1985—95; advisor W. L.A. Vets. Hosp., 1990—95; cons. in field; presenter in field. Author: Shadow Women: Homeless Women's Survival Stories, 1990, Organizational and Community Responses to Domestic Abuse and Homelessness, 1994; contbr. articles to publs., web pages. Recipient Giraffe award, The Giraffe Found., 1995, Helping Vets. Step Out of Homelessness award, W. L.A. Vets. Hosp., 1994. Mem.: Authors Guild, Women in Film, Internat. Documentary Assn. Avocations: goldsmithing, sculpting, welding, carousel preservation, beachcombing. E-mail: islandr@goeaston.net.

BARD, TERRY ROSS, rabbi, psychologist, educator; b. Chgo., Jan. 17, 1944; s. Bernard David and Lillian (Terry) B.; m. Kay Elsa Bard, Aug. 6, 1966 (dec. 1974); children: Michael Aaron, Amy Shira; m. Linda Faye Bard, Dec. 18, 1975; 1 child, Rachel Joy. AB with distinction, Brown U., 1966; BHL, Hebrew Union Coll., 1968; MAHL, Hebrew Union Coll., Cin., 1971; postgrad., Harvard U., 1975; DD, Hebrew Union Coll., 1996. Ordained rabbi, 1971; bd. cert. chaplain Assn. Profl. Chaplains, 1998; cert. chaplain Assn. Mental Health Chaplains, 1978, Nat. Assn. Jewish Chaplains, 94. Asst./assoc. rabbi Temple Shalom, Newton, Mass., 1971-76; rabbi Congregation Shalom, Chelmsford, Mass., 1976-98, rabbi emeritus, 1998—; dir. dept. pastoral care and edn. Beth Israel Deaconess Med. Ctr., Boston, 1984—, coord. med. ethics program, 1985-98, dir. Ctr. Excellence in Spiritual Care, Edn., Tng. and Rsch., 1998—, dir. Rsch. Subject's Safety Program, Gen. Clin. Rsch. Ctr., 2001—. Dir. dept. pastoral care and edn. Mass. Mental Health Ctr., Boston, 1976-96; dir., psychotherapist Rabbinic Counseling Ctr., Newton, Mass., 1976—, dir. ctr. of Excellence in spiritual Care, Edn., Tng. and Rsch., Beth Israel Deaconess Med. ctr., 1999—, Rsch. Subject Safety Program, Beth Israel, 2001—; bd. dirs. Jewish Cmty. Coun., Boston, 1976-84; v.p. Interfaith Counseling Svcs., Inc., Newton, 1988-93; lectr., cons. in field. Author: Medical Ethics in Practice, 1990; editor, Cura Animarum, 1987-94; editl. adv. com. Jour. Health Care, 1987—, Jour. Pastoral Care, 1984—, chmn. bd. mgrs., 1991-97; abstract and book rev. editor Jour. of Assn. Mental Health Clergy, 1980-87; contbr. articles to profl. jours. Adv. bd. Health Decisions USA, The Boston Experience, 1990—96, Mass. Health Decision, 1990—98, New Eng. Organ Bank, 1990—; mem. devel. com. Beth Israel Hosp., 1986—95, resuscitation com., pharmacy com., 1993—, pub. affairs com., 1985—96, com. clin. investigations, 1985—, originator ethics adv. group, coord. clin. ethics program, 1984—, human subjects com. Harvard Pilgrim Health Plan, 1991—97; others; inst. rev. bd. Harvard Med. Sch., 1975—90, 1999—, faculty divsn. med. ethics, 1993—; faculty clin. investigation tng. program BIDMC Harvard Med. Sch., MIT, 1987—; mem. Cath. Jewish com. Archdiocese of Boston, 1973—. Recipient Nat. Conf. Christians and Jews, spl. recognition, 1971, Farband Labor Zionist award for excellence in field of religious studies, 1966, Founder's award Hebrew Union Coll.-Jewish Inst. Religion, 1996. Mem. Am. Psychiat. Assn. (ex-officio mem. com. on religion and psychiatry), Assn. Mental Health Clergy (pres. 1982-84, Anton T. Boisen award 1994), Mass. Bd. Rabbis (pres. 1980-82), Ctrl. Conf. Am. Rabbis, Chelmsford Clergy Assn., Assn. Clin. Pastoral Edn., Nat. Assn. Jewish Chaplains. Office: Beth Israel Deaconess Med Ctr 330 Brookline Ave Boston MA 02215-5400 Business E-Mail: tbard@bidmc.harvard.edu.

BARDACH, JOAN LUCILE, clinical psychologist; b. Albany, N.Y., Oct. 3, 1919; d. Monroe Lederer and Lucile May (Lowenberg) B. BA, Cornell U., 1940; AM in Psychology, NYU, 1951; PhD in Clin. Psychology, 1957; cert. in psychoanalysis and psychotherapy, NYU, 1970. Supr. clin. psychologist NYU Rusk Inst. Rehab. Medicine, 1959-61; asst. chief and acting chief psychologist Rusk Inst. Rehab. Medicine, 1962-65, dir. psychol. services, 1965-82; research psychologist, mem. faculty N.Y. Med. Coll., 1961-62, clin. prof. rehab. medicine (psychology), 1976—; supr. postdoctoral program psychoanalysis and psychotherapy NYU, 1978—; pvt. practice clin. psychology and psychoanalysis N.Y.C., 1957—. Non-govtl. orgn. rep. to UN Internat. Ctr. Sociol., Penal and Penitentiary Rsch. and Studies, Messina, Italy, 1985—; prin. investigator NIMH, 1976-81; mem. adv. bd. Coalition Sexuality and Disability, Planned Parenthood, 1983-89; cons. in field. Contbr. articles to profl. jours., chpt. to books. Recipient 3 awards for ednl. film, Choices: In Sexuality With Physical Disability, Internat. Film Festivals, Pioneer award for Sexual Attitude Reassessment Workshops The Coalition on Sexuality and Disability, 1989; NIMH fellow Inst. Sex Rsch., U. Ind., 1976. Fellow Am. Orthopsychiat. Assn.; mem. APA, Am. Congress Rehab. Medicine, Sex Info. and Edn. Council U.S., Nat. Register Health Service Providers in Psychology, Eastern Psychol. Assn., N.Y. State Psychol. Assn. Home and Office: 50 E 10th St New York NY 10003-6223

BARDACK, PAUL ROITMAN, lawyer, consultant; b. N.Y.C., Nov. 13, 1953; s. Lawrence Stanley and Charlotte (Sebold) B.; m. Esther Roitman, May 27, 1979; children: David, Avi, Daniella. BA, Yale U., 1975; JD, Am. U., 1978. Bar: D.C. 1980. Atty. U.S. Dept. HUD, Washington, 1978-79; gen. counsel to U.S. congressman Robert Garcia, Washington, 1979-81; atty. Barrett Smith Schapiro Simon & Armstrong, N.Y.C., 1981-83; mgr. econ. devel. dept. City of Cleve., 1983-84; chief exec. officer, gen. counsel Econ. Devel. Resources, Inc., Phila. and Washington, 1984-86; sr. policy advisor Gov. Thomas Kean, Trenton, N.J., 1986-89; dep. asst. sec. for econ. devel. HUD, Washington, 1989-93; v.p. Nat. Mentoring Partnership, Washington, 1993-99; cons. Booz Allen Hamilton, McLean, Va., 1999—. Mem. ABA, D.C. Bar Assn., U.S. Distance Learning Assn. Jewish. Home: 105 Dunloggin Dr Rockville MD 20850-5615 Office: Booz Allen Hamilton 8251 Greensboro Dr Mc Lean VA 22102-3812

BARDACKE, PAUL GREGORY, lawyer, former attorney general; b. Oakland, Calif., Dec. 16, 1944; s. Theodore Joseph and Frances (Woodward) B.; children: Julie, Brynn, Francheska, Chloe. BA cum laude, U. Calif.-Santa Barbara, 1966; JD, U. Calif.-Berkeley, 1969. Bar: Calif. 1969, N.Mex. 1970. Lawyer Legal Aid Soc., Albuquerque, 1969; assoc. firm Sutin, Thayer & Browne, Albuquerque, 1970-82; atty. gen. State of N.Mex., Santa Fe, 1982-86; ptnr. Sutin, Thayer & Browne, 1987-90, Eaves, Bardacke, Baugh, Kierst & Kiernan, P.A., 1991—2003, Eaves, Bardacke, Baugh, Kierst & Larson, 2003—. Adj. prof. N.Mex. Law Sch., Albuquerque, 1973— ; mem. faculty Nat. Inst. Trial Lawyers Advocacy, 1978— Bd. dirs. All Faiths Receiving Home, Albuquerque; bd. dirs. Friends of Art, 1974, Artspace Mag., 1979-80, Legal Aid Soc., 1970-74; bd. trustees Albuquerque Cmty. Found., 2001-. Reginald Heber Smith fellow, 1969 Fellow Am. Coll. Trial Lawyers; mem. ABA, Calif. Bar Assn., N.Mex. Bar Assn., Am. Bd. Trial Advocates (pres. N.Mex. chpt. 1992-93). Democrat. Office: Eaves Bardacke Baugh Kierst & Larson PO Box 35670 Albuquerque NM 87176-5670

BARDAGLIO, PETER WINTHROP, humanities educator; b. Hartford, Conn., Apr. 25, 1953; s. George William and Mary Frances (White) B.; m. Wrexie Anne Lainson, Dec. 21, 1983; children: Sarah Jennings Agan, Jesse Barrett Agan, Anne Winthrop. BA, Brown U., 1975; MA, Stanford U., 1978, PhD, 1987. Vis. lectr. U. Md., College Park, 1981-83; instr. Goucher Coll., Balt., 1983-87, asst. prof., 1987-93, assoc. prof., 1993-95, Elizabeth Conolly Todd disting. assoc. prof., 1995-99, prof., 1999—2002, Elizabeth Connolly Todd disting. prof., 1999-2000, chair History Dept., 1996-98, interim v.p., acad. dean, 2000—02; provost, v.p. acad. affairs, prof. history Ithaca (NY) Coll., 2002—. Spkr. Md. Humanities Coun. Spkrs. Bur., 1996-99. Author: Reconstructing the Household: Families, Sex, and the Law in the Nineteenth Century South, 1995 (Orgn. Am. Historians James A. Rawley prize 1996); contbr. articles to profl. jours. Elder Catonsville (Md.) Presbyn. Ch., 1992-02; mem. Lyman Award Com., 2002-03, Jameson Fellowship Com., 2002-03. Jesse Ball duPont fellow Nat. Humanities Ctr., 1999-2000. Mem. Am. Hist. Assn. (Littleton-Griswold Rsch. grant 1989), Orgn. Am. Historians, So. Hist. Assn. (membership com. 1991-92, local arrangements com. 2002), Am. Soc. for Legal History, So. Assn. for Women Historians (Taylor prize com. 2000). Home: 9748 Arden Rd Trumansburg NY 14886 Office: Ithaca Coll Ithaca NY 14850-7001

BARDANA, EMIL JOHN, JR., allergist, immunologist, internist; b. N.Y.C., May 21, 1935; BS in Biology/Philosophy, Georgetown U., 1957; MD, McGill U., 1961. Diplomate Am. Bd. Allergy and Immunology, Am. Bd. Internal Medicine. Intern Calif. Med. Ctr., 1961-62; resident in medicine U. Oreg., Portland, 1965-68; fellow in allergy and immunology Nat. Jewish Hosp. Rsch. Ctr., Denver, 1969-71; divsn. allergy and clin. immunology Oreg. Health Scis. U., Portland, 1985—, prof. medicine, 1984—. Editor-in-chief Allergy Watch. Fellow: ACP, Am. Coll. Allergy, Asthma and Immunology, Am. Acad. Allergy, Asthma and Immunology (pres. 2000—01), Am. Coll. Chest Physicians; mem.: AMA, Am. Soc. Internal Medicine. Home: 12389 Clara Ln Lake Oswego OR 97035-1166 Office: Oregon Health Sci Univ OP34 3181 SW Sam Jackson Park Rd Portland OR 97239-3011

BARDEEN, WILLIAM ALLAN, research physicist; b. Washington, Pa., Sept. 15, 1941; s. John and F. Jane (Maxwell) B.; m. Marjorie Ann Gaylord; children: Charles Gaylord, Karen Gail. AB in Physics, Cornell U., 1962; PhD in Physics, U. Minn., 1968, DSc (hon.), 2002. Rsch. assoc. SUNY, Stony Brook, 1966-68; mem. Inst. for Advanced Study, Princeton, N.J., 1968-69; asst. prof. Stanford (Calif.) U., 1969-72, assoc. prof., 1972-75; scientist Fermilab, Batavia, Ill., 1975-93, head theoretical physics, 1987-93, scientist, 1994—; head theoretical physics SSC Lab., Dallas, 1993-94. Vis. scientist CERN, Geneva, Switzerland, 1971-72, Max Planck Inst. for Physics, Munich, 1977, 86. Author: Bardeen-Bardeen Genealogy, 1993; editor: Symp. on Anomalies, Geometry, Topology, 1985; mem. editl. bd. Phys. Rev., 1981-84, 92-94, Jour. Math. Physics, 1986 90, European Physics Jour. C, 1997-2000; contbr. numerous articles to profl. jours. Trustee Aspen Ctr. for Physics, 1987-91. Fellowship Alfred P. Sloan Found., 1971-74, John Simon Guggenheim Found., 1985-86; recipient sr. scientist award Alexander von Humboldt Found., 1977 Fellow Am. Phys. Soc. (exec. com. divsn. of particles and fields 1988-90, J. J. Sajurai prize for theoretical particle physics 1996); mem. Am. Acad. Arts and Scis., NAS. Avocations: genealogy, basketball. Office: Fermilab MS 106 PO Box 500 Batavia IL 60510-0500

BARDELAS, JOSE ANTONIO, allergist; b. Havana, Cuba, Feb. 3, 1948; came to U.S., 1961; s. Jose A. and Georgina (Leyva) B.; m. Sallie Young, July 3, 1971; children: Joseph, Mary. BA in Human Biology, Johns Hopkins U., 1970, MD, 1973. Intern, then resident in pediats. Johns Hopkins Hosp., Balt., 1973-75; fellow in allergy and immunology Nat. Jewish Ctr., Denver, 1975-77; pvt. practice Greensboro, N.C., 1977—. Asst. clin. prof. pediats. U. N.C., Chapel Hill, 1979—. Fellow Am. Acad. Allergy and Immunology; mem. AMA, N.C. Soc. Allergy and Immunology (pres. 1982), N.C. Med. Soc. (mem. exec. coun. 1990, 91), High Point Med. Soc. (pres. 1989). Roman Catholic. Avocations: golf, reading. Home: 400 Edgedale Dr High Point NC 27262-2908 Office: 100 Westwood Ave High Point NC 27262-4320

BARDELLI, FREDERICK KETCHELL, artist, art educator; b. Apr. 22, 1940; s. Guido Firpo Bardelli and Mary Widitz-Bardelli. Student, U. Mont., 1958—59, student, 1970, student, 1991, U. Oreg., 1960—61; BA in Fine Arts, Whitworth Coll., 1964; postgrad., Loyola Marymount U., 2001. Edn. credential secondary art Idaho Dept. Edn. Art tchr. Wallace (Idaho) H.S., 1967—2001. Exhibitions include Nat. Art Edn. Assn. Conf., N.Y.C., 2001. Activist Sierra Club, Kalispell, Mont., 1992, Defenders of Wildlife, Silverton, Idaho, 1997, Nat. Resources Def. Coun., Spokane, Wash., 2000. Mem.: Nat. Art Edn. Assn. Roman Catholic. Avocations: hiking, studying Renaissance drawings, boxing history, photography, writing. Mailing: PO Box 124 Osburn ID 83849-0124

BARDEN, GEORGE V. county official, watershed specialist; b. Penn Yan, NY, Jan. 20, 1948; s. Gerald and Helen Lou Barden (div.); children: Peter, Thomas. Assoc., Agrl. & Tech. Coll., Canton, N.Y., 1968. Cert. profl. soil erosion and sediment control specialist. Gen. farm laborer Ej-Lo Farms, Penn Yan, 1963-66; gen. constrn. laborer Penn Yan Builders, 1967-68; designer, design draftsman MRB Group, Rochester, N.Y., 1969-78, Sear Brown Assocs., Rochester, 1979-83; owner, operator Barden Tech. Svcs., Penn Yan, 1984-90; watershed inspector Canandaigua Lake, Ontario County Soil & Water Conservation Dist., Canandaigua, N.Y., 1991—. Canandaigua Lake Watershed Commn. rep. Watershed Task Force, Canandaigua, 1991—. Euphonium player, pres. Finger Lakes Concert Band, 1984-87. Recipient map competition award N.Y. State Assn. Profl. Land Surveyors, 1980, spl. project award N.Y. State Conservation Dist. Employees Assn., 1994, Merit award N.Y. State Conservation Dist. Employees Assn., 1996, recognition award Canandaigua Lake Watershed Task Force, 1998. Mem.: Finger Lakes Water Works Assn., N.Y. State Bldg. Ofcls. Assn., Am. Water Works Assn., Finger Lakes Bldg. Ofcls. Assn., Am. Design Drafting Assn., Am. Inst. Design and Drafting. Avocations: music, woodworking, furniture refinishing, vegetable gardening. Office: Ontario County Soil & Water Conservation Dist 480 N Main St Canandaigua NY 14424-1049 E-mail: ontswcd6@rochester.rr.com.

BARDEN, JANICE KINDLER, personnel company executive; b. Cleve. d. Norman Allen and Bessie G. (Black) Kindler; m. Hal Barden, Nov. 12, 1944 (dec. Jan. 1985) 1 child, Sheryl Andrea Barden Coholan BBA, Miami U., Oxford, Ohio, 1947; M in Indsl. Psychology, Kent State U., 1948. Asst. dir. admissions Fairleigh Dickinson U., Teaneck, N.J., 1950-53; gen. mgr. Pilots Employment Assocs., Teterboro, N.J., 1953-71; founder, pres. Aviation Pers. Internat., New Orleans, 1971—. Commr. jury U.S. Dist. Ct. (ea. dist.) La., New Orleans, 1965—; lectr. in field. Chmn. History of Aviation Collection U. Tex., Dallas, 1980—; served on Pres. Com. Rehab. Vietnam POW Pilots; mem. FAA's Blue Ribbon Panel. Recipient Disting. Alumnus award Kent State U., 1986, Cuyahoga Falls H.S., 1988, Doswell award Nat. Bus. Aircraft Assn., 1994. Mem. AAUW, Nat. Bus. Aircraft Assn. (chmn. conf. 1975, 85, 87, 90, 94, 2000, 2001, Am. Spirit award 2000), Flight Safety Found. (chmn. corp. seminar), Profl. Aircraft Maint. Assn., Bus. and Profl. Women's Club, Kent State Alumni Assn. (bd. dirs. 1976-82), Women in Aviation, Order of Rainbow (grand coord. 1973-84), Psi Chi. Republican. Episcopalian. Office: Aviation Pers Internat PO Box 6846 New Orleans LA 70174-6846 E-mail: jkbarden@apiaviation.com.

BARDEN, ROBERT CHRISTOPHER, lawyer, psychologist, educator, legislative analyst, speaker, writer; b. Richmond, Va., June 7, 1954; s. Elliott Hatcher and Jane Elizabeth Cole (Ferris) B.; m. Robin Jones, Nov. 14, 1987. BA summa cum laude, U. Minn., 1976, PhD in Clin. Psychology, 1982; postgrad., U. Calif., Berkeley, 1977; JD cum laude, Harvard U., 1992. Lic. cons. psychologist, Minn., Tex.; diplomate Am. Bd. Forensic Examiners. Project asst. NSF, 1978-79; intern in psychology VA Med. Ctr., Stanford Med. Ctr., Palo Alto, Calif., 1979-80; dir. psychology Internat. Craniofacial Surg. Inst., Dallas, 1980-87; corp., civil litigation, family and health law atty. Lindquist and Vennum, Mpls., 1992-96; psychologist, lawyer, expert witness, pub. policy analyst R.C. Barden & Assocs., 1996—. Asst. prof. psychology So. Meth. U., Dallas, 1980—84; asst. prof., coord. child clin. psychology U. Utah, Salt Lake City, 1984—87, rsch. faculty dept. surgery, 1987—93; vis. faculty, asst. prof. psychology Gustavus Adolphus Coll., St. Peter, Minn., 1988; pres. Optimal Performance Sys., Inc., Cambridge, 1989—; mem. Minn. Bd. Psychology, 1993—97; adj. prof. law U. Minn. Law Sch., 1995—97; cons. and spkr. in field. Consulting editor Devel. Psychology, 1989; editor Harvard Jour. Law and Pub. Policy, 1990-91; contbr. to profl. publs. Project dir. ch. cmty. svc. projects, Mpls. and Cambridge, 1988—; mem. Minn. Bd. Psychology, 1993-97, Higher Edn. Coordinating Bd., 1993-94; rep. Minn. Sixth Congl. Dist. Recipient Young Scholar award Found. for Child Devel., Faculty Scholar award W.T. Grant Found., 1987-89; NSF fellow, 1978, NIMH fellow, 1976, 77. Mem. ABA, Am. Psychol. Soc., Soc. for Rsch. in Child Devel., Internat. Soc. Clin. Hypnosis, Harvard Law Sch. Soc. Law and Medicine, Lowell House Commons Rm. Harvard U., Nat.Assn. for Consumer Protection in Mental Health Practices (pres. 1995—), Sigma Xi, Phi Beta Kappa. Avocations: church and service work, tennis, martial arts, mountain climbing, music. Office: RC Barden and Assocs 1093 Duffer Ln North Salt Lake UT 84054-3313 E-mail: rcbarden@aol.com.

BARDENWERPER, WILLIAM BURR, lawyer; b. Jan. 12, 1952; s. H. William and Dorothy (Weix) Bardenwerper; m. Gail Smith, Apr. 11, 1959. BA, U. Va., 1974; JD, U. Louisville, 1977. Bar: Ky. 1978, Wis. 1985, U.S. Dist. Ct. (we. dist.) Ky. 1978. Counsel, dir. intergovtl. affairs Jefferson County, Louisville, 1978—84; ptnr. Bardenwerper Law Firm, Louisville, 1987—. Author (editor): Kentucky Methods of Practice (4 vols.), 1989, 2d edit., 1998; editor (in-chief): Louisville Lawyer mag., 1977—81. Vice chmn. Louisville C. of C., 1993—96; mayor City of Hurstbourne, Ky., 1994—2002; bd. dir. Homebuilders Assn. of Louisville, 1993—96, 2002—. Named Assoc. of Yr., Home Builders Assn. of Louisville, 1995, 2002; recipient Disting. Svc. award, U. Louisville Sch. Law, 1977. Mem.: ABA, Louisville Bar Assn. (chmn. real estate and zoning sect. 1988), Ky. Bar Assn., Wis. Bar Assn., Rotary (pres. Hurstbourne 1994—95). Roman Catholic. Home: 8620 Blackpool Dr Louisville KY 40222-5667 Office: Bardenwerper Law Firm PLLC 8311 Shelbyville Rd Louisville KY 40222-5544

BARDGETT, JOHN E. lawyer; b. St. Louis, Apr. 28, 1927; s. Alfred L. and Catherine C. (Heverin) Bardgett; m. Mary Jean Branch, Aug. 1, 1953; children: John E., Suzanne, Bruce, Beth. LLB, St. Louis U., 1951. Bar: Mo. 1951, Ill. 1963, US Dist. Ct. (ea. dist.)/ Mo. 1954, US Supreme Ct. 1957. Sole practice, St. Louis, 1955—68; city atty. Normandy, Mo.; judge St. Louis County Cir., 1968—70; justice Supreme Ct. Mo., Jefferson City, Mo., 1970—82; chief justice, 1982—84; ptnr. Guilfoil, Petzall, Shoemake, St. Louis, 1984—. Office: Cen States SE and SW Areas Health Welfare and Pension Funds 8550 W Bryn Mawr Ave Chicago IL 60631-3203

BARDIN, CLYDE WAYNE, biomedical researcher; b. McCamey, Tex., Sept. 18, 1934; s. James A. and Nora Irene (Barnett) B.; m. Bonnie Lambdin, June 24, 1958 (div.); m. Dorothy Kreiger, Aug. 11, 1978 (dec. Apr. 1985); m. Beatrice MacDonald, June 12, 1987; children: Charlotte E., Stephanie F. BA in Biology, Rice U., 1957; MS with honors, MD with honors, Baylor U., 1962; Docteur (hon.), U. de Caen, France, 1990, U. Pierre et Marie Curie, Paris, 1997, U. Helsinki, Finland, 2000. Cert., licensed MD, Tex., Pa., N.Y. Resident in medicine N.Y. Hosp., N.Y.C., 1962-64; clin. assoc. NIH, Bethesda, Md., 1964-67, sr. investigator, 1967-70; assoc. prof. Milton S. Hershey Med. Ctr., Pa. State U., Hershey, 1970-72, prof. medicine, 1972-78; v.p. The Population Coun., N.Y.C., 1978-95; pres. Bardin LLC, N.Y.C., 1996—; pres., CEO Thyreos Corp., Newark, 1997—2003. Adj. prof. Rockefeller U., N.Y.C., 1978—, Cornell Med. Ctr., N.Y.C., 1985—; cons. WHO, 1972-73; chmn. bd. sci. counselors Nat. Inst. Child Health and Human Devel., Bethesda, 1982-83; chmn. endocrine study sect. NIH, Bethesda, 1977-79; mem. nat. prostate cancer task force Nat. Cancer Inst., 1973-78; endocrinologist Nat. Inst. Child Health and Human Devel., NIH, 1996-97. Editor 18 books on medicine and endocrinology; mem. editl. bd. 16 sci. jours.; contbr. over 500 articles to profl. jours. Advisor internat. divsn. Ford Found., N.Y.C., 1975-79; bd. dirs. Harris and Harris Group, Inc., 1994—, Internat. Assn. Axel Munthe Awards, 1982-92; chmn. bd. dirs. The Hormone Found., 1997-98. Decorated Order of Comdr. of Lion (Finland), 1983; recipient Transatlantic medal Brit. Endocrine Socs., 1988; named fellow Josiah Macy Jr. Found., 1976-77, Disting. Alumnus Rice U., 1994, Disting. Alumnus N.Y. Hosp.-Cornell Med. Ctr., 1992. Mem. Am. Assn. Physicians, Am. Soc. Clin. Investigation, Am. Soc. Andrology (coun., v.p., pres. 1984-89, Serono award 1984, Disting. Andrologist award 1992), Endocrine Soc. (coun. 1976-79, pres. 1993-94, Sidney H. Ingbar Disting. Svc. award 1996), Internat. Soc. Andrology (exec. coun. 1981-85), Internat. Com. Contraception Rsch. (chmn. 1978-95), Inst. Medicine. Democrat. Achievements include direction of a team of scientists that developed seven contraceptives as well as treatments for menopause and cancer. E-mail: cwbardin@aol.com.

BARDIN, DAVID J. lawyer; b. N.Y.C., June 2, 1933; s. Shlomo and Ruth (Jonas) Bardin; m. Livia Goldeen, Mar. 12, 1961; children: Jacob, Matthew, Joseph, Sarah. AB, Columbia U., 1954, JD, 1956. Bar: N.Y. 1956, D.C. 1966, Israel 1970. Atty., dep. gen. counsel FPC, Washington, 1958-69; asst. to atty. gen. Israel, Jerusalem, 1970-72; counsel Israel Environ. Protection Svc., Jerusalem, 1973; commr. N.J. Dept. Environ. Protection, Trenton, 1974-77; dep. adminstr. FEA, Washington, 1977; adminstr. Econ. Regulatory Adminstrn., Dept. Energy, Washington, 1977-80; of counsel, mem. Arent Fox Kintner Plotkin & Kahn PLLC, Washington, 1980-2001, ret., 2001. Lectr. law Bar-Ilan U., Tel Aviv U., U. Va. Ext. Co-author: AGA Select Gas Use Handbook: Natural Gas for Environmental Control, 1985; contbr. ; author: Psychological Coercion and Human Rights, 1994. Mem. Mayor's Coun. on Environment, 1999—2001, D.C. Zoning Adv. Panel, 2003—; bd. mgrs. Adas Israel Congregation, 1998—99; trustee The Found. Jewish Studies, 1991—99; moot ct. panel Nat. Assn. Atty. Gens., 1993—; trustee Liberty State Pk. Devel. Corp., 1990—2000, Pinelands Preservation Alliance, 1991—99, Mental Health Liaison Group, 1993—; adv. neighborhood commr. of D.C., 1999—; mem. Mayor's Com. on Adoption Law, 2000—01; bd. dirs. D.C. Water and Sewer Authority, 2000—; mem. D.C. Bldg. Code Adv. Com., 2002—. Served with U.S. Army, 1956—58. Mem.: ABA, Found. for Energy Law Jour. (bd. dirs. 1987—90), Fed. Energy Bar Assn. (bd. dirs. 1985—87), Fed. Bar Assn. Democrat. Jewish. Office: Arent Fox Kintner Plotkin & Kahn 1050 Connecticut Ave NW Ste 400 Washington DC 20036-5339 E-mail: BardinD@arentfox.com. *Combine careful thought with timely action: rely on oneself, work with others, and procrastinate only if there's a very strong reason. Finally, apply this test: How will I explain my acts and omissions to a grandchild?.*

BARDO, JOHN WILLIAM, university administrator; b. Cin., Oct. 28, 1948; s. John Thomas and Grace Roberta (Day) B.; m. Deborah Joan Davis, Aug. 8, 1975; 1 child, Christopher. Student, U. Southampton, Eng., 1968-69; BA in Econs., U. Cin., 1970; MA in Sociology, Ohio U., 1971; PhD in Sociology, Ohio State U., 1973. Asst. prof. Wichita (Kans.) State U., 1973-79, assoc. prof., 1979-83, chmn. dept. sociology, 1978-83; prof. Southwest Tex. State U., San Marcos, 1983-86, dean Sch. Liberal Arts, 1983-86; prof. U. N. Fla., Jacksonville, 1986-90, provost, v.p., 1986-89; prof. dept. sociology and anthropology Bridgewater (Mass.) State Coll., 1990-95, v.p. acad. affairs, 1990-95, provost, 1993-95; chancellor Western Carolina U., Cullowhee, N.C., 1995—. Vis. lectr. Monash U., Clayton, Australia, 1977; vis. prof. Univ. Coll. Wales, Swansea, 1981; cons. various orgns. and govt. agys. Co-author: Urban Sociology: An Integrated Approach, 1982; editor: Defining the Mission of AASCU Institutions, 1990; contbr. articles to profl. jours. and books chpts. Co-chair N.C./Estern Band of Cherokee Indians Econ. Devel. Task Force, 1996—; bd. dirs. N.C. Arboretum, 1995—; trustee N.C. Ctr. for the Advancement of Teaching, 1995—. Recipient Humanities award Kans. Com. for Humanities, 1978; named one of Outstanding Young Men in Am., Jaycees, 1979. Mem. Am. Sociol. Assn., Assn. for Consumer Rsch., Mid-South Sociol. Assn., Am. Assn. Higher Edn., Am. Assn. State Colls. and Univs. (coll. rep. resource ctr.), Soc. Applied Multivariate Rsch. (pres.-elect 1993—), Alpha Kappa Delta, Phi Kappa Phi. Greek Orthodox. Avocations: photography, golf. Home: 10 Chancellor Dr Cullowhee NC 28723-6874 Office: W Carolina Univ Chancellor Cullowhee NC 28723

BARDOLIWALLA, DINSHAW FRAMROZE, chemical executive; b. Bombay, Jan. 19, 1945; came to U.S., 1968; s. Framroze Shapurji and Shirin (Langrana) B.; m. Hutoxi Edulji Madon, July 19, 1971; children: Nenshad, Shanaz. BS in Chemistry, U. Bombay, India, 1965; BS in Textile Chemistry, 1968; MS in Plastics, U. Mass., Lowell, 1971, PhD in Polymer Sci., 1974; MBA, Rutgers U., 1986. Rsch. chemist Am. Cyanamid Co., Stamford, Conn., 1974-80, sr. rsch. chemist, 1980-82; mgr. polymer chemistry Diamond Shamrock Corp., Morristown, NJ, 1982-85, mgr. devel., 1985-87; tech. dir. Oakite Products, Inc., Berkeley Heights, NJ, 1987, dir. rsch. and tech. svcs., 1988, v.p. rsch. and tech., 1988-93, corp. v.p. tech. and quality mgmt., 1993—95; tech. dir. John C. Dolph Co., Monmouth Junction, NJ, 1996—2002; chief tech. officer Zinsser Co., Inc., Somerset, NJ, 2002—. Patentee (8) in field. Sec., Zoroastrian Assn. Greater N.Y., New Rochelle, 1982-84, v.p., 1984-86, 99-2002, sec., 1997-99. Polaroid Corp. fellow, 1971-74. Mem. Am. Chem. Soc. Republican. Avocations: tennis, music, swimming. Office: Zinsser Co Inc 173 Belmont Dr Somerset NJ 08550 Home: 12 Maidenflower Ln West Windsor NJ 08550-2431

BARDOLPH, RICHARD, historian, educator; b. Chgo., Feb. 18, 1915; s. Mark and Anna (Veldman) B.; m. Dorothy Corlett, July 28, 1945; children: Virginia Ann (Mrs. George Haskett), Mark III, Richard. BA, U. Ill., 1940, MA, 1941, PhD, 1944; Litt.D., Concordia Coll., 1968; LL.D., Concordia Theol. Sem., 1983. Mem. faculty dept. history U. N.C. at Greensboro, 1944-80, head dept., 1960-80, Jefferson Standard prof., 1970-80; Fulbright lectr. Denmark, 1953-54. Mem. regional selection com. Woodrow Wilson Nat. Fellowship Found.; mem. commn. theology and ch. relations Luth. Ch.-Mo. Synod. Author: Agricultural Literature and Illinois Farmer, 1948, Negro Vanguard, 1959 (Mayflower award 1960), Civil Rights Record, 1849-1970, 1970; Mem. bd. editors: Jour. So. History; Contbr. articles to profl. jours. and encys. Active ACLU, NAACP. Recipient Max O. Gardner award for Outstanding Contbns. to Welfare of Human Race U. N.C., 1979; Ford Found. fellow HArvard U., 1952-53, Guggenheim fellow, 1956-57, sr. fellow NEH, 1971-72. Mem. ACLU, NAACP, Am. Hist. Assn., Orgn. Am. Historians, So. Hist. Assn., Phi Beta Kappa. Home: 207 Tate St Greensboro NC 27403-1838 E-mail: rbardolph@aol.com.

BARDOS, THOMAS JOSEPH, chemist, educator; b. Budapest, Hungary, July 20, 1915; came to U.S., 1946, naturalized, 1952; s. Arthur and Vilma (Brachfeld) B.; m. Mary Jane Choate, Mar. 24, 1951 (wid. Mar. 1995); m. Maria Csonka (Dec. 20, 2002). Diploma in chem. engring., Royal Hungarian Tech. U., Budapest, 1938; PhD in Chemistry, U. Notre Dame, 1949. Chem. engr. Vacuum Oil Co., Budapest, 1938-46; rsch. assoc. U. Tex., Austin, 1948-51; sect. head Armour & Co., Chgo., 1951-60; prof. med. chemistry and biochem. pharmacology SUNY, Buffalo, 1960-94, prof. emeritus, 1994—. Contbr. articles sci. jours. Recipient Ebert prize Acad. Pharm. Scis., 1971 Fellow AAAS, N.Y. Acad. Scis.; mem. Am. Chem. Soc. (Schoellkopf medal Western N.Y. sect. 1974), Royal Chem. Soc. (London), Hungarian Acad. Scis. (hon.), Am. Soc. Biol. Chemists, Am. Assn. Cancer Rsch., Am. Pharm. Assn., Cosmos Club (Washington), Sigma Xi, Rho Chi. Achievements include isolation and first synthesis of folinic acid (leukovorin); design and synthesis of antifolates, nucleoside analogs, dual antagonists (phosphoraziridines) and antitemplates (modified DNA, RNA and oligonucleotides) as anticancer and antiviral agents. Home: 705 Renaissance Dr Apt 202 Buffalo NY 14221-8030 E-mail: tbardos@aol.com.

BARDSLEY, KAY, historian, archivist, dance professional; b. Port Said, Egypt, Apr. 17, 1921; came to U.S., 1928; d. Chris and Helen (Jones) Lanitis; m. James Calvert Bardsley, May 30, 1947 (wid. Sept. 1978); children: Wendy Jane, Amy Kim; m. Donald Marshall Kuhn, Feb. 25, 1990. Student, Duncan Dance Tng./Carnegie Hall, Steinway Hall Studios, N.Y.C., 1931—35; BA in Journalism cum laude, Hunter Coll., 1942. Dance debut Maria-Theresa Duncan Heliconiades, N.Y.C., 1934; prin. dancer Maria-Theresa Heliconiades, N.Y.C., 1935-42; Duncan tchr. Maria-Theresa Sch., N.Y.C., 1937-46; tchr. Creative Dance for Children, N.Y.C., 1960-66, Isadora Duncan-Maria-Theresa Heritage Group, N.Y.C., 1977-81; fashion editor Woman's Day, N.Y.C., 1943-46; TV Script WPIX Gloria Swanson Hour, 1948-49; writer TV Guide, 1949; writer/prodr. culture news and fashion ABC Network/Don Ameche-Langford Show, 1949-50. Syndicated film series prodr., Your Beauty Clin., 1950-60; prodr. video documentation of Duncan Repertory, 1976-80. Writer, lectr. in field: ; prodr.: (documentaries) The Last Isadorable, 1988, re-issued, 1997; contbr. to profl. dance jours. and pubs. including Dance Scope, 1977, Ballet Rev., 1991, 1994, staging of ReAnimations of Duncan Masterworks, A Four-year Project, presented at Dance ReConstructed Conf., Rutgers U., 1992; author: numerous conf. presentations and earliest documentation of Isadora Duncan's 1st sch.; resident dancer scholar U. Oreg., Eugene, 1997—98, staging of Duncan solos for Colo. Ballet Dancelab, 1999, Duncan's masterwork to seventh Symphony of Beethoven, 2000; owner, curator Legacy of Isadora Duncan: The Kay Bardsley Collection. Trustee Coun. for the Arts in Westchester, N.Y., 1973-76; bd. dirs. Bicentennial Com., Chappaqua, N.Y., 1973-76; co-chmn. Community Day, 1973, 75. Grantee NEA, N.Y.C., 1980; pioneer NYU/Master Tchr. Dance Tng. Inst., 1987; recipient 1997-98 Creativity award in Dance U. Oreg. Mem.: Isadora Duncan Internat. Inst. (dir., founder 1978—), Dance Critics Assn. (bd. dirs. 1997—2000), World Dance Alliance, Am. Dance Guild, Soc. Dance History Scholars. Office: Isadora Duncan Internat Inst 6305 S Geneva Cir Englewood CO 80111-5437 E-mail: kaybardsley@earthlink.net.

BARDWICK, JUDITH MARCIA, management consultant; b. N.Y.C., Jan. 16, 1933; d. Abraham and Ethel (Krinsky) Hardis; m. John Bardwick, III, Dec. 18, 1954 (div.); children: Jennifer, Peter, Deborah; m. Allen Armstrong, Feb. 10, 1984. BS, Purdue U., 1954; MS, Cornell U., 1955; PhD, U. Mich., 1964. Lectr. U. Mich., Ann Arbor, 1964-67, asst. prof. psychology, 1967-71, assoc. prof., 1971-75, prof., 1975-83, assoc. dean, 1977-83; clin. prof. psychiatry U. Calif., San Diego, 1984—; pres. In Transition, Inc. (name changed to Judith M. Bardwick, PhD, Inc., 1991), La Jolla, Calif., 1983—. Mem. population rsch. study group NIH, 1971—75. Co-author: (book) Feminine Personality and Conflict, 1970; author: Psychology of Women, 1971, In Transition, 1979, The Plateauing Trap, 1986, Danger in the Comfort Zone, 1991, In Praise of Good Business, 1998, Seeking the Calm in the Storm, 2002; mem. editl. bd. Women's Studies, 1973—, Psychology Women Quar., 1975—; contbr. articles to profl. jours. Mem. social sci. adv. com. Planned Parenthood Am., 1973. Fellow: APA; mem.: Am. Psychosomatic Soc., N.Y. Acad. Scis., Midwest Psychol. Assn., Phi Beta Kappa. Home and Office: 1389 Caminito Halago La Jolla CA 92037-7165 E-mail: jmbwick@san.rr.com. *I am particularly grateful to the principle of academic freedom which has allowed me to pursue intellectual questions that I considered important. No other institution would have supported my pursuit of the answers to questions that seemed significant for theoretical or applied reasons before those issues were obviously important to society.*

BARDWIL, JOSEPH ANTHONY, investments consultant; b. Bklyn., Oct. 29, 1928; s. Najeb B. and Malvina (Galaini) B.; m. Valerie Pavilonis, Feb. 11, 1961; children: Anita, James, David, Joanna. BS in Econs, U. Pa., 1950; MBA, NYU, 1956. Reporter, mgr. Dun & Bradstreet, Inc., N.Y.C., 1950-57; gen. investment mgr. Prudential Ins. Co., 1957-69; v.p. Hartz Mountain Corp., Harrison, N.J., 1960-88; prin. Bardwil Assocs., Cranford, N.J., 1989—. Mem. N.Y. Soc. Security Analysts. Republican. Roman Catholic. Home and Office: 321 North Ave E Unit 128 Cranford NJ 07016-2451

BARDYGUINE, PATRICIA WILDE, ballerina, ballet theatre executive; b. Ottawa, Ont., Can., July 16, 1928; came to U.S., 1943; d. John Herbert and Eileen Lucy (Simpson) White; m. George Bardyguine, Dec. 14, 1953; children: Anya, Youri. Student, Profl. Children's Sch., N.Y.C. Dancer Am. Concert Ballet, N.Y.C., 1943-44, Marquis De Queras Ballet Internat., N.Y.C., 1944-45, Ballet Russe De Monte Carlo, tours nationwide, 1945-49; guest artist Roland Petit Ballet De Paris, 1949; prin. ballerina Met. Ballet, touring throughout Europe, 1950, N.Y.C. Ballet, 1950-65; dir. Harkness House, N.Y.C., 1965-67; ballet mistress Am. Ballet Theater, N.Y.C., 1969-82; ret. artistic dir. Pitts. Ballet Theatre, 1997—, advisor, tchr., 1997—. Dir. Am. Ballet Theater Sch., 1979-82; dance panelist Nat. Endowment for Arts, N.Y. State Coun. for the Arts; judge Lausanne Internat. Competition; guest tchr., coach N.Y.C. Ballet, Joffrey Ballet, Dance Theater of Harlem, The Royal Ballet of Stockholm, Internat. Summer Seminar, Cologne, Germany, Heinz Bosl Found., Munich, St. Moritz, Japan, Australia, Republic of Korea. Soloist six European tours, also tour of Orient; numerous TV appearances; commd. by N.Y. Philharm. to choreograph ballets Festival, 1964, At the Ball, 1965, Viennese Evening, 1966, Petite Suite, 1967. Adminstr. scholar fund Sch. A. Ballet Group; mem. Nat. Bd. Regional Ballet; Fulbright panelist. Recipient YWCA award for Leadership in Arts and Letters, 1990, Cultural award for Extraordinary Contbns. to Cultural Life in Region, Pitts. Ctr. for Arts, 1997, Cultural award for outstanding contbns. to cultural climate of the region Pitts. Ctr. for Arts, 1997; named Pitts. Woman of Yr. in Arts and Music, 1994. Mem. Am. Guild Mus. Artists, AFTRA, Dance/USA (bd. dirs.). Office: Pitts Ballet Theatre 2900 Liberty Ave Pittsburgh PA 15201-1511

BARE, BRUCE, retired life insurance company executive; b. Pierson, Iowa, May 26, 1914; s. Edward E. and Myrtle Viola (Sloan) B.; m. Adaline Light, June 14, 1936; children: Bruce Jr., Barbara Bare Spaulding, John. BA, Grinnell (Iowa) Coll., 1935; LL.D. (hon.), Westmont Coll., Santa Barbara, Calif., 1971. C.L.U. With New Eng. Mut. Life Ins. Co., 1935—, gen. agt., 1946-80, field v.p., 1979-82. Trustee Westmont Coll., 1947—, chmn., 1965; past pres. Fuller Evangelistic Found., Pasadena, Calif.; chmn. bd. trustees African Enterprise Internat., 1979-84. Recipient Farrell award Los Angeles C. of C., 1968; named to Hall of Fame Gen. Agts. and Mgrs. Assn., 1977 Mem. Am. Soc. C.L.U.'s (pres. 1964, trustee 1974), Life Underwriters Assn. (past pres. Los Angeles chpt.), Los Angeles Life Ins. Mgrs. Assn. (past pres.) Presbyterian. E-mail: bbaresr@aol.com. *The important thing is to establish goals a step at a time as you go through life. College diploma, proper job with opportunity, careful discharge of all responsibilities assumed, proper marriage and complete commitment to the Christian way of life. A periodic check on goal and accomplishments should provide incentive for greater goals. Success will be a result of never turning aside from Christian principles in all aspects of life.*

BARE, STEVEN WAYNE, consulting services company executive; b. Ames, Iowa, Aug. 27, 1958; s. Donald Wayne Bare and Helen Louise Towne, Leon Victor Towne (Stepfather); m. Marilyn Kay Allen, Dec. 10, 1957; children: Sara, Matthew. BS, Ball State U., 1980. CPA. Acct. Trinidad Roofing Co., Anderson, Ind., 1981—82; CPA Whitinger & Co., Muncie, Ind., 1982—86, Clifton, Gunderson & Co., various, 1986—94; pres. Savannah Software Co., Yorktown, Ind., 1994, Whitinger Consulting, LLC, Muncie, 2001—. Contbr. articles to profl. jours. Treas. Del. County Rep. Fin. Com., Muncie, 1985—86; local govt. com. Del. County C. of C., Muncie, 1984—86. Mem.: AICPA (mem. info. tech. exec. com. 1992—93, info. tech. practices subcom. 1993—96), Constrn. Fin. Mgmt. Assn., Info. Security and Control Assn., Ind. CPA Soc. Methodist. Avocation: sailing.

BAREFOOT, ALDOS CORTEZ, JR., forester, educator; b. Angier, NC, Feb. 25, 1927; s. Aldos Cortez Barefoot, Sr. and Eva Kathleen (Benson) Barefoot; m. Naomi Gertrude Pugh; children: Aldos, James, Rebecca. BS, NC State Coll., 1950, Master of Wood Tech., 1951; D Forestry, Duke U., 1958. Registered forester N.C., 1981. Lab. asst. (zoology) NC State Coll., Raleigh, NC, 1948—49; supr. quality control Henry County Plywood Corp., Ridgeway, Va., 1951; grad. asst. dept. stats. N.C. State Coll., Raleigh, 1952—54; statistician Forest Products Lab., U.S. Dept. Agr., 1953; technologist and supt., wood products lab. N.C. State Coll., Raleigh, 1954—55, asst. prof. to assoc. prof. Sch. Forestry, 1955—68; advisor (utilization), forest products rsch. inst. Internat. Cooperation Agy., US State Dept., Chittagong, Bangladesh, 1959—61; prof. wood and paper sci. N.C. State U., Raleigh, 1968—86; leader, wood products sect. Coop. Ext. Svc., NC State U., Raleigh, 1972—75; head divsn. interdisciplinary studies N.C. State U., Raleigh, 1975—82; chief of party, reforestation and watershed mgmt. project, U. of Ga., SECID, Chapel Hill, NC, Colombo, Sri Lanka, 1982—84; prof. emeritus of wood and paper sci. and multidisciplinary studies N.C. State U., Raleigh, 1986—. Cons.; tree-rings, statis. quality control, and wood identification, Raleigh, NC, 1955—; dendrochronologist Winchester Rsch. Unit, Winchester and Oxford, England, 1964—; dir., vis. scientist program, soc. of wood sci. and tech. NSF, Raleigh, 1968—74; chmn. pres.'s adv. com. U. N.C., Chapel Hill, 1970—71. Chmn. tchr.'s and state employee's benefits study commn. Gen. Assembly N.C., Raleigh, 1969—71, mem. commn. on pre-paid health benefits, 1979—81; mem. health adv. com. to the state treas. and bd. of trustees of the tchr. and state employee's retirement sys. The State Treas. Office, State of NC, Raleigh, 1971—81. Served in USN, 1945—46. Recipient 'Second-Mile' award, N.C. Assn. of Educators, 1971, outstanding contbn. award, State Employees Assn., 1972; grantee Fulbright-Hayes Rsch. Scholarship, United States-UK Ednl. Commn., 1973—74, The Furniture R & D Inst., NSF, 1973—78. Fellow: The Inst. of Wood Sci.; mem.: TAPPI (chmn. ann. biology conf. 1966), N.C. Govtl. Ret. Employees' Assn., N.C. State U. Club, Tree-Ring Soc., Forest Products Soc., Kiwanis (trustee). Democrat. Baptist. Avocation: hunting, hiking, travel, bridge, dancing. Home: 3401 Hampton Road Raleigh NC 27607-3131 Office: Divsn Multidisciplinary Studies NC State Un Raleigh NC 27695-7107 Home Fax: 919-834-9495; Office Fax: 919-515-1828.

BAREIS, DONNA LYNN, biochemist, pharmacologist; b. Abington, Pa., May 1, 1954; d. Walter Charles and Doris (Cameron) B.; m. Paul Joseph Amico, Jan. 24, 1981. BS in Biochemistry, Pa. State U., 1975; PhD in Pharmacology, Duke U., 1979. Staff fellow NIH, Bethesda, Md., 1979-81; pharmacologist U.S. Army Med. Rsch. Inst. Chem. Def., Aberdeen Proving Ground, Md., 1981-82; program mgr. U.S. Army C.E., Washington, 1982-83; sr. scientist Sci. Applications Internat. Corp., Joppa, Md., 1983-87, div. mgr., 1987-89, asst. v.p. Frederick, Md., 1989-94, v.p., 1994-97, corp. v.p., dep. mgr. biomed. scis., 1997—2002, sr. v.p., 2002—. Bd. dirs. Tech. Coun. Md., 1998—. Contbr. articles to sci. jours. Lighting designer Rockville (Md.) Musical Theater, 1980—; pres. Swan Point Condominium Assn., Columbia, Md., 1982-84. Mem.: AAAS, Soc. for Risk Analysis, Am. Chemical Soc., Cattail Creek Country Club (bd. dirs. 1995—96), Potomac Region Porsche Club of Am. (tech. chmn. 1998—2001, instr. 1999—), Porsche Club Racing (nat. scrutineer 2000—, chief nat. scrutineer 2001—), Sigma Xi. Home: 8805 Blue Sea Columbia MD 21046-1412

BARENBOIM, DANIEL, conductor, pianist; b. Buenos Aires, Nov. 15, 1942; s. Enrique and Aida (Schuster) Barenboim; m. Jaqueline DuPre, June 15, 1967 (dec.); m. Elena Bashkirova, Nov. 28, 1988; 2 children. Student, Mozarteum, Salzburg, Austria, Accademia Chigiana, Siena, Italy; grad., Santa Cecilia Acad., Rome, 1956. Music dir. Chgo. Symphony Orch., 1991—; gen. music dir. Deutsche Staatsoper Berlin, 1992—. Debut with Israel Philharm. Orch., 1953, Royal Philharm. Orch., 1953, debut as pianist Carnegie Hall, N.Y.C., 1957, Berlin Philharm. Orch., 1963, N.Y. Philharm. Orch., 1964, 1st U.S. solo recital, N.Y.C., 1958, as pianist performed in N.Am., South Am., Europe, Soviet Union, Australia, New Zealand, Near East, condr., 1962—, conducted English Chamber Orch., London Symphony Orch., Israel Philharm. Orch., N.Y. Philharm. Orch., Phila. Symphony, Boston Symphony, Chgo. Symphony Orch., others, musical dir. Orch. de Paris, 1975—89, Staatsoper Berlin, 1992—, artistic advisor Israel Festival, 1971—74, over 100 recs. as pianist and condr., debut as pianist at age 7, Buenos Aires. Named to Legion of Honor, France, 1987; recipient Beethoven medal, 1958, Harriet Cohen Paderewski Centenary prize, 1963. Office: 29 rue de la Coulouvreniere 1204 Geneva Switzerland also: Chgo Symphony Orch c/o Synneve Carlino 220 S Michigan Ave Chicago IL 60604-2596 Office: Unter den Linden 7 D-10117 Berlin Germany*

BARENTYNE-TRULUCK, ROSS, musicologist, educator, voice educator; b. Denton, Tex., Nov. 30, 1939; s. Henry F. Ross and Josie Lee Barentine; life ptnr. Cordell M. Truluck, Aug. 20, 1995; children: Ellan Ross Willis, Ross, Ross. MusM, Mich. State U., East Lansing, MI, 1965—67; MusB, U of North Tex., Denton, TX, 1958—62. Adj. faculty U of Miami Sch. of Music, Coral Gables, Fla., 2000—; accompanist/vocal coach self-employed, New York, NY, 1974—2000; musical dir. La Gran Scena Opera Co., New York, NY, 1984—97. Scholar Grad. Asst. Scholarship, Mich. State U, 1967-1967, Full Undergraduate Scholarship, U of North Tex., 1958-1962. Mem.: Phi Mu Alpha Sinfonia (life). Democrat-Npl. Episcopalian. Avocations: gourmet, international, cinema. Office: University of Miami 5501 San Amaro Drive Coral Gables FL 33146 Personal E-mail: r.barentyne@miami.edu. E-mail: r.barentyne@miami.edu.

BARFIELD, KENNY DALE, religious school administrator; b. Florence, Ala., Nov. 17, 1947; s. Henry Perry and Bernice Elizabeth (Olive) B.; m. Nancy Ann Cordray, Aug.7, 1970; children: Amber Elizabeth, Lora Allyn. BA in Speech Communication, David Lipscomb Coll., 1969; MA in Speech Communication, U. Ala., Tuscaloosa, 1972; EdS in Ednl. Adminstrn., U. North Ala., 1986; EdD in Ednl. Adminstrn., U. Ala., Tuscaloosa, 1989. Dir. debate, instr. Mars Hill Bible Sch., Florence, 1969—, acad. dean, 1986-2000, prin., 1990-95, v.p., 1999-2000, pres., 2001—; minister Highland Park Ch. of Christ, Muscle Shoals, Ala., 1970-74, Jackson Heights Ch. of Christ, Florence, 1974-78, Sherrod Ave Ch. of Christ, Florence, 1978—. Instr. speech communication Internat. Bible Coll., 1972-75, U. North Ala., Florence, 1981-83. Author: 50 Golden Years: The N.F.L. Nationals, 1980, Why The Bible Is Number One, 1988, The Prophet Motive, 1995; editor Pacesetter; contbr. articles to profl. jours. Recipient Outstanding Young Religious Leader award Ala. Jaycees, 1976, Ala. Speech Tchr. of Yr. award 1977, Outstanding Speech and Debate Coach award Comml. Appeal, 1977, Key Coach award Barkley Forum for High Schs., Emory U., 1981, High Sch. Debate Coach of Yr. award Bishop's Guild, Samford U., 1983, Disting. Svc. award Nat. Forensic League, 1981, 86, Gregg Phifer svc. award Fla. State U., 1997; named Four Diamond Coach Nat. Forensic League, 1999, H.S. Debate Coach of Yr. Carson Newman U., 1992, 2000; Faulkner fellow U. Miss., 1987. Mem. Am. Forensic Assn. (ednl. practices com. 1984-86, high sch. affairs com. 1988-90, pub. rels. com. 1990-93, v.p. high sch. affairs 1998-00), Ala. Forensic Educators Assn. (pres. 1976-77, 82-83, 85-86), Nat. Assn. Secondary Sch. Prins., So. Assn. Colls. and Schs. (cen. rev. com. 1991-95), Deep South Nat. Forensic League (chmn. 1977-79, 81-85), Nat. Debate Coaches Assn. Office: Mars Hill Bible Sch 698 Cox Creek Pky Florence AL 35630-6624

BARFIELD, ROBERT ELLIOTT, music educator; b. St. Petersburg, Fla., Feb. 18, 1965; s. Edith Katherine Dinwiddie. BA in Edn., U. of North Fla., 1990—92. Cert. tchr. Fla. State Bd. Edn., 2002. Band dir. S.E. H.S., Bradenton, 1992—93, Wolfson H.S., Jacksonville, 1993—99, Tarpon Springs H.S., 1999—. Visual caption head Carolina Crown Drum and Bugle Corps, Ft. Mill, SC, 1995—96, Boston Crusaders Drum and Bugle Corps, Boston, 2000—. Mem.: Music Educators Nat. Conv., Fla. Bandmasters Assn., Fla. Music Educators Assn. Avocations: travel, sports, arts/entertainment. Home: 90-Highland Ave S #318 Tarpon Springs FL 34689 Office: Tarpon Springs High School 1411-Gulf Rd Tarpon Springs FL 34689 Office Fax: 727-943-4907. Personal E-mail: reb1224999@aol.com.

BARFIELD, ROBERT F. retired mechanical engineer, educator, dean; b. Thomaston, Ga., Feb. 8, 1933; s. Jason Malcome and Nettie Lee Barfield; m. Marion Janelle Neill, June 25, 1953 (div. Jan. 1980); children: Kimberly Faith, Robert Frederick Jr.; m. Sara de Saussure Davis, Nov. 27, 1981 (div. Jan. 1984); m. Leonette Walker, May 1990 (div. June 1994). B.M.E., Ga. Inst. Tech., 1956, MSM.E., 1958, PhD, 1965. Diplomate: registered profl. engr. Preliminary design engr. AiResearch Corp., Los Angeles, 1957-59; asst. prof. mech. engring. Ga. Inst. Tech., Atlanta, 1959-65; corp. mech. engr. Thomaston Mills Corp., Ga., 1965-67; prof. mech. engring. U. Ala., Tuscaloosa, 1967-94, prof. emeritus, 1994, dean of engring., 1982-94, dean emeritus, 1994. Dir., sr. adv. Shiraz Tech. Int., Iran, 1975-77; gen. bd. Assn. Internt. practical Tng., 1980-85; dir. Capstone Engring. Soc., 1982-94; head mech. engring. program, dir. Oil Testing Ctr., U. Petroleum and Minerals, Dhahran, Saudi Arabia, 1971-73; advisor King Saud U., Riyhad, Saudi Arabia, 1982-89, U. Jordan, 1984, Yarmouk U., Jordan, 1986, Birzeit U., Israel, 1985, Kabul U., Afghanistan, 1963; mem. Accreditation Bd. for Engring. and Tech., visitor in Mech. engring., 1982-94; mem. Ala. Commn. High Tech. Bd. dirs. Salvation Army Ala., 1996—, Turning Point, Inc., 1995—. Recipient Disting. Service award Inperial Orgn. for Social Services, Tehran, Iran, 1977, U. Ala. Faculty Senate, 1980, Engr. of Yr. award Ala. Soc. Profl. Engrs., 1987, Liberty Bell award Ala. Law Assn., 1987; inductee Engring. Hall of Fame, 1998. Fellow ASME; mem. Am. Soc. Engring. Edn., Nat. Soc. Profl. Engrs., Ala. Acad. Sci., Tuscaloosa C. of C., Sigma Xi, Tau Beta Pi, Pi Tau Sigma, Phi Kappa Phi, Upsilon Pi Epsilon, Tau Alpha Pi. Presbyterian. Home: 703 Shallow Creek Rd Tuscaloosa AL 35406-2085 Office: Univ Ala PO Box 870200 Tuscaloosa AL 35487-0200

BARFIELD, STEWART BAYNE, counseling therapist; b. Macon, Ga., May 19, 1957; s. Lee Bayne and Corinne Powers (Cole) B. BA in Psychology, Furman U., 1980; MAEd in Counseling, Washington U., St. Louis, 1982, MSW in Family Therapy, 1984. Residence counselor Marshall I. Pickens Hosp., Greenville, S.C., 1978-81; counselor Reproductive Health Services, St. Louis, 1981-82, Luth. Family and Children's Services, St. Louis, 1983-84; hospice counselor Charter Hosp., St. Louis, 1983-85; family therapist Cen. Bapt. Family Services, St. Louis, 1984-86; med. social worker Am. Nursing Resources, St. Louis, 1985-87; substance abuse counselor Magdala Found., St. Louis, 1986-88; social worker Carpenter Healthcare Systems, St. Charles, Mo., 1988-89; adult outpatient therapist Piasa Health Care, Alton, Ill., 1990-95; family therapist extern Provident Counseling, St. Louis, 1995-99. Instr. Mo. Valley Coll., St. Charles, 1987; seasonal employee Meadowbrook Country Club, Ballwin, Mo., 2000. Vol. phone counselor Life Crisis Svcs., St. Louis, 1984-87; active Wellness Assn., St. Louis, 1991-92. Named one of Outstanding Young Men of Am., 1984, 85. Methodist. Avocations: running, cycling, weight training, reading, theatre, golf.

BARFIELD, THOMAS JEFFERSON, III, anthropology educator, consultant; b. Atlanta, Apr. 21, 1950; s. Thomas J. Jr. and Susan A. B. BA, U. Pa., 1972; MA, Harvard U., 1974, PhD, 1978. Assoc. prof. Harvard U., Cambridge, prof. anthropology, 1986-89; prof., chmn. anthropology Boston U., 1989—. Adv. com. Inner Asia, U. Cambridge. Editl. bd. Anthropological Theory, 1997—; author: The Central Asian Arabs of Afghanistan, 1981, The Perilous Frontier: Nomadic Empires and China, 1989, The Nomadic Alternative, 1993, Afghanistan: An Atlas of Indigenous Domestic Architecture, 1991; editor: The Dictionary of Anthropology, 1997. Recipient Outstanding Acad. Book in Art and Architecture ALA, 1992; Sr. fulbright scholar U.S. Dept. of State, 1997. Fellow Am. Anthropol. Assn. Home: 51 Chilton St #2 Cambridge MA 02138 Office: Boston U Anthropology Dept 232 Bay State Rd Boston MA 02215 E-mail: barfield@bu.edu.

BARFIELD, W. LEON, federal judge; b. Moultrie, Ga., Sept. 8, 1947; m. Lennie Shore. AA, Abraham Baldwin Agrl. Coll., 1971; BS (magna cum laude), Univ. of Ga. Law Sch., 1973, JD, 1976. Law clk. Hon. Elie L. Holton Ga. Superior Ct., Waycross, 1976-77; asst. dist. atty. City of Augusta, Ga., 1979-81; asst. U.S. atty. So. Dist. Ga., 1981-93; magistrate judge U.S. Dist. Ct. (so. dist.) Ga., Augusta, 1993—. Served with U.S. Army, 1967-69. Office: 500 Ford St E Augusta GA 30901-2358

BARGELLINI, PIER LUIGI, electrical engineer; b. Florence, Italy, Feb. 7, 1914; came to U.S., 1948, naturalized, 1956; s. Angelo and Giovanna (Cecchi) B.; m. Anna Cioni, Sept. 8, 1941; children: Clara, Angela, Leonard M. Grad., U. Florence, 1933; DEng, Poly. Inst., Turin, 1937; MSEE, Cornell U., 1949. Engr. Italo Radio Co., Rome, 1937-41; head spl. tests lab. Fivre Co., Florence, 1941-44; researcher microwave physics Inst. Italian Nat. Research Council, 1945-50; mem. faculty U. Pa., Phila., 1950-68; sr. scientist COMSAT Labs., Clarksburg, Md., 1968-83, cons., 1984—. Mem. adv. engring. faculty Montgomery County C.C., 1970-75, trustee nominating com., 1975-82; adj. prof. elec. engring. U. Pa., 1987-89. Editor: Communications Satellite Systems and Communications Satellite Technology, 1974; contbr. articles to profl. jours.; lectr. internat. univs. Recipient City of Columbus (Ohio) award Inst. Internat. Communications, 1975, Columbus Gold medal City of Genoa, Italy, 1987; Inst. Internat. Edn. fellow, 1948. Fellow IEEE (life), AIAA (assoc.); mem. Internat. Acad. Astronautics. Democrat. Home: PO Box 517 South Wellfleet MA 02663-0517 E-mail: pbarge@c4.net.

BARGER, DON P. conservation association administrator; b. Charleston, W.Va., Aug. 28, 1950; s. Warren Doyle and Alta Smith Barger; m. Maureen Cunningham, Jan. 9, 1978 (div. 1989); 1 child, Erin Eileen; m. Linda Jean Creswell, May 29, 1995; 1 child, Jillian Sage. BArch, U. Tenn., 1973. Svc. rep. Social Security Adminstrn., Maryville, Tenn., 1976-82; cmty. organizer Save Our Cumberland Mountains, Lake City, Tenn., 1982-90; policy analyst Environ. Policy Inst., Washington, 1990-92; S.E. regional dir. Nat. Pks. Conservation Assn., Washington, 1992—2000; sr. dir. S.E. region, 2000—. Cumberland Island Nat. Seashore adv. com. Nat. Park Svc., Washington, 1999-2000. Active Recreation Commn., City of Norris, Tenn., 1997-99, Mcpl. Watershed Bd., 1999—02. Recipient First Annual Searching for Success award Renew Am., Washington, 1990, Congl. Record citation Sen. Max Cleland, 2000; named Air Conservationist of Yr., Tenn. Conservation League, 2001. Mem. Assn. Nat. Pk. Rangers, Tenn. Citizens for Wilderness Planning (bd. dirs. 1996-98), So. Appalachian Mountains Initiative (pub. interest rep., ops. com. 1995—02), George Wright Soc. Avocations: archery, badminton, canoeing, hiking, music. Office: Nat Pks Conservation Assn 706 Walnut St Ste 200 Knoxville TN 37902 E-mail: dbarger@npca.org.

BARGER, JAMES EDWIN, physicist; b. Manhattan, Kans., Dec. 28, 1934; s. Edgar Lee and Carolyn Marie (Grantham) B.; m. Mary Elizabeth Rupp, Aug. 24, 1957; children: Elaine Marie Fleckenstein, Carolyn Ruth Hanson, James Rupp, Corinne Elizabeth Noordzij. BS, U. Mich., 1957; MS, U. Conn., 1960; PhD, Harvard U., 1964. Teaching asst. Harvard U., Cambridge, 1961-64; v.p. BBN Techs. (formerly Bolt Beranek & Newman, Inc.), Cambridge, Mass., 1965-75, chief scientist, 1975—. Trustee Winchester Savs. Bank. Mem. Methods and Procedures Com., Town of Winchester, 1967-71; trustee Winchester Hosp., 1972—; corp. mem. Mt. Vernon House, 1979—. Served with USNR, 1957-63. NSF fellowship, 1960-64 Fellow AAAS, Acoustical Soc. Am.; mem. Marine Tech. Soc., Indsl. Noise Control Engring., Winchester Country Club, Cosmos Club, Tau Beta Pi, Pi Tau Sigma. Congregationalist (deacon). Home: 3 Lakeview Rd Winchester MA 01890-3801 Office: BBN Techs 70 Fawcett St Cambridge MA 02138-1110

BARGER, LINDA KALE, choral director; b. Charlotte, N.C., Apr. 14, 1948; d. Jack and Alma Kale; children: William Jackson, Chastity Lynn Barger Page. MusB, U. N.C., Greensboro, 1972; postgrad., U. N.C., 1988; postgrad., Belmont Abbey U., 1994—95; degree computer applications with windows, Gaston Coll., 1999; degree music comp. and theory, N.C. Sch. Sci. and Math, 2001. Band dir. Highland Jr. High, Gastonia, NC, 1974—76; music specialist Ashley Jr. H.S., Gastonia, NC, 1976—81, Highland Jr. H.S., Gastonia, NC, 1978—81; dir. choral William C. Friday Jr. H.S., Dallas, 1981—91; Cherryville HS choral dir. Gaston County Schs., Cherryville, 1991—2002. Choir dir. First Presbyn. Ch., Cherryville, NC, 1977—79; chmn. All-County Choral Festival, Gaston County, NC, 1981—82; interim music dir. First Bapt. Ch., Cherryville, NC, 1981; choral dir. William C. Friday Jr. H.S., Dallas, 1981—91; mem. bd. dirs. Lincoln Arts Guild Cmty. Concerts, Lincolnton, NC, 1981; interim choir dir. Dallas Bapt. Ch., Dallas, 1984, New Hope Bapt. Ch., Gastonia, NC, 1985—87; choir dir. First United Meth. Ch., Cherryville, NC, 1987—95; chs cheerleading coach of the award-winning chs cheerleaders Cherryville H.S., Cherryville, NC, 1992—97; state bd. dirs. N.C. Music Educators Assn., NC, 1994—2002; pres. Dist. 2 NC Music Educators, Gaston, Lincoln, Cleve., Polk, Rutherford, McDowell Counties, NC, 1994—2002; theater arts tchr. Cherryville H.S., Cherryville, NC, 1999—2002; mem. barbara bair scholarship com. NC Music Educators Assn., NC, 2000—02; Gaston County music textbook adoption com. Gaston County Schs., Gastonia, NC. Musician (accompanist): (first all-county choral festival) Gaston County Choral Festival, 1977; dir.(choral director): (musical) All-County Junior High Choral Festival, 1978, (state choral contests) William C. Friday chorus, Various performances, 1986. Mem. team Relay for Life Cancer Orgn., Cherryville, NC, 2001—02. Mem.: NEA, Assn. of Classroom Tchrs., Gaston County Theater Arts Tchrs. Assn., Gaston County Choral Dirs. Assn., Am. Choral Dirs. Assn., N.C. Assn. Educators, Cherryville Music Club (past pres. 1981—83). Office: Cherryville HS 313 Ridge Ave Cherryville NC 28021 Home Fax: 704-435-4989. Business E-Mail: bargerl@gaston.gcs.k12.nc.us.

BARGER, LOUISE BALDWIN, religious organization administrator; b. Mexia, Tex., Nov. 7, 1938; d. Curtis Arthur and Vada Irene (Barker) Baldwin; m. Billy Joe Barger, June 15, 1957; children: Kenneth Gene, Keith Dean, Kimberly Ann Barger Moeller. BS, Tex. Woman's U., 1961; MS in Nursing, St. Louis U., 1974, PhD in Higher Edn., 1981; MRE, So. Bapt. Theol. Sem., 1982. Ordained to ministry Am. Bapt. Chs. in U.S.A., 1986. Faculty Mo. Bapt. Hosp. Sch. Nursing, 1973, St. Louis U., 1974-80; min. Christian edn., mem. pastoral staff 3d Bapt. Ch., St. Louis, 1980-86; dir. leader devel. Am. Bapt. Chs. Pa. and Del., Valley Forge, Pa., 1986-93, interim dir. evangelism and social concern, 1989-91; exec. min. Am. Bapt. Chs. of the Rocky Mountains, 1993—. Mem. Christian edn. com., Area V, Gt. Rivers region, Am. Bapt. Chs. Mo., and Am. Bapt. Chs. U.S.A., 1981-86; Handicapped Ministry, Home Mission Bd. So. Bapt. Conv., 1983; mem. Mins. Coun., Am. Bapt. Conv., U.S.A., Am. Bapt. Chs., U.S.A. Author: Growing through the Sunday School: A Sourcebook for Sunday School Growth, 1988; co-author: New and Renewed Churches: A Time of Prayer and Preparation for Invitation to New Life, 1991, New and Renewed Churches; A Time of Invitation to New Life, 1992; contbr. Bapt. Leader. Mem. Handicapped Ministry Home Mission Bd., So. Bapt. Conv., 1983. Recipient Richard Hoiland citation Am. Bapt. Chs. U.S.A.; grantee Fund of Renewal Am. Bapt. Chs. U.S.A., 1980, Hazle Fund, 1984. Mem. Religious Edn. Assn., Assn. Profs. and Rschrs. in Religious Edn. Office: Am Bapt Ch Rocky Mts Ste 365 3900 S Wadsworth Blvd Lakewood CO 80235-2220 E-mail: abcrm@office.org. *As Christians we are called first to BE the persons we were intended to become. All of our DOING is to be an expression of our BEING.*

BARGER, RICHARD WILSON, hotel executive; b. Cleve., Aug. 16, 1934; s. Harold Wilson and Blanche (Smith) B.; m. Barbara K. Schroeder, July 20, 1963; children— Scott Wilson, Christopher Armon. BS, Cornell U., Ithaca, N.Y., 1956. Resident mgr. Sheraton Cleve. Hotel, 1964-67; gen. mgr. Sheraton Biltmore Hotel, Providence, 1967-68, Sheraton Peabody Hotel, Memphis, 1968-69, Sheraton Boston Hotel, 1969-72; v.p., regional mgr. Sheraton Corp., Boston, 1972-79; chmn. Barger Hotel Corp., Boston, 1979—, Conf. Planning Assoc., 1987—. Cons., lectr. hotel adminstrs. Mem. coun. Cornell U., Ithaca, N.Y. Mem. Boston C. of C., Boston Conv. Bur. (dir.), Cornell U. Alumni Fund, Sigma Chi. Republican. Episcopalian. Home: 63 Neptune St Beverly MA 01915-4746 Office: Barger Hotel Corp 63 Neptune St # A Beverly MA 01915-4746 E-mail: bargerhotel@attbi.com.

BARGER, VERNON DUANE, physicist, educator; b. Curllsville, Pa., June 5, 1938; s. Joseph F. and Olive (McCall) Barger; m. Annetta McLeod, 1967; children: Victor A., Amy J., Andrew V. BS, Pa. State U., 1960, PhD, 1963. Rsch. assoc. U. Wis., Madison, 1963-65, from asst. prof. to assoc. prof., 1965-68, prof. physics, 1968—, J.H. Van Vleck prof., 1983—, dir. Inst. Elem. Particle Physics Rsch., 1984—, Hilldale prof., 1987-91, Vilas prof., 1991—. Vis. prof. U. Hawaii, 1970, 79, 82, U. Durham, 1983, 84; vis. scientist CERN, 1972, Rutherford Lab., 1972, SLAC, 1975, Kavli Inst. for Theoretical Physics, U. Calif., Santa Barbara, 2003. Co-author: (book) Phenomenological Theories of High Energy Scattering, Classical Mechanics, Classical Electricity and Magnetism, Collider Physics. Recipient Alumni Fellow award, Pa. State U., 1974; Guggenheim fellow, 1972, Fermilab Frontier fellow, 1999. Fellow: Am. Phys. Soc. Methodist. Achievements include research in in elementary particle theory and phenomenology; classification of hadrons as Regge recurrences; analyses of neutrino scattering and oscillations; research in weak boson, Higgs boson and heavy quark production; electroweak models; supersymmetry and grand unification; future collider physics, cosmology. Office: U Wis Dept Physics 1150 University Ave Madison WI 53706-1302

BARGER, WILLIAM JAMES, management consultant, educator; b. Los Angeles, Nov. 1, 1944; s. James Ray and Aylene M. (Skinner) B.; m. Jane A. Cox, Jan. 30, 1988. BA, U. So. Calif., 1966; MA, Harvard U., 1970, PhD, 1972. Asst. prof econs. U. So. Calif., Los Angeles, 1971-76; v.p. Bank Am., Los Angeles, 1976-81; sr. v.p. Gibraltar Savs. Co., Beverly Hills, Calif., 1981-84, exec. v.p., 1984-88; pres. High Point Acad., Pasadena, Calif., 1995—2001; dir. Maxson Young Assocs., San Francisco, 1995—. Mem. Phi Beta Kappa.

BARGETTO, PAUL C. theater director; b. San Jose, Calif., June 26, 1969; s. Lawrence John and Patricia Margaret Bargetto. BA in Drama, San Francisco State U., 1994; MFA in Directing, Columbia U., 2003. Artistic dir. East River Ensemble, Bklyn., 1996—. Dir.: (plays) Hecuba, 2002, Striptease, 2002, A Midsummer Nights Dream, 2003. Named a semifinalist, Ring Award Competition, Graz Austria; Dept. Rsch. Assoc. fellow, Columbia U.

BARGFREDE, JAMES ALLEN, lawyer; b. Seguin, Tex., Sept. 10, 1928; s. Herman Fred and Elsie (Vorpahl) B.; m. Virginia Felts, Nov. 27, 1970; 1 child, Charles Allen. BS, Tex. A&M U., 1950; postgrad., Ohio State U., 1952-53; JD, St. Mary's U., 1957. Bar: Tex. 1957, U.S. Patent and Trademark Office 1961; registered profl. engr., Tex. Engr. Signal Corps, San Antonio, 1950-52; elec. engr. San Antonio Pub. Svc. Bd., 1953-58; patent counsel Hubbard & Co., Chgo., 1958-59; pvt. practice law Butler, Binion, Rice, Cook & Knapp, 1960-68, 1968-74, 75—; patent and legal counsel Hydrotech Internat., Inc., 1977-81; ptnr. Bargfrede & Thompson, 1974-75. Subcom. chmn. dist. com. on admissions Supreme Ct. Tex., 1988—. Served with USAF, 1952-53. Mem. Houston Bar Assn. (chmn. automated equipment com. 1971-75), State Bar Tex., Assn. Former Students Tex. A&M U., Houston Livestock Show and Rodeo (life), Briarcroft Civic Club (pres. 1979-82), Houston A&M Club (treas. 1990, sec. 1991, v.p., 1992, pres. 1993), Delta Theta Phi. Home: 5649 Piping Rock Ln Houston TX 77056-4028 Office: 5649 Piping Rock Ln Houston TX 77056-4028

BARGMANN, CORNELIA, anatomist, educator, biochemist, educator, biophysicist, educator; B, U. Ga.; PhD, MIT. Postdoctoral rschr. MIT; prof. anatomy, vice chair dept. anatomy U. Calif., Berkeley, prof. biochemistry, prof. biophysics. Recipient Lucille P. Markey award, Takasago prize, W. Alden Spencer award, Charles Judson Herrick award, 2000; Searle scholar. Mem.: NAS, AAAS. Office: 4000 Jones Bridge Rd Chevy Chase MD 20815-6789*

BARGMANN, ROLF ERWIN, computer scientist, educator; b. Glückstadt, Schleswig, Germany, May 13, 1921; arrived in U.S., 1955, naturalized, 1962; s. Erwin Bargmann and Martha (née)Bargmann; m. Ilse Heckenbach, May 24, 1920; children: Dorie children: Monika Brown, Evelyn, Cornelia. PhD in Stats., U. N.C., Chapel Hill, 1958. Ct. interpreter Nuremberg Trials, Office of Chief of Counsel for War Crimes, Nürnberg, Germany, 1947—48; fellow, Rockefeller Found. Psychometrics Lab., U. Chgo., 1951—52; rsch. asst., head stats. dept. Inst. for Internat. Edn. Rsch., Frankfurt, Germany, 1952—55; rsch. asst. Psychometric Lab, U. N.C., Chapel Hill, 1955—57; prof. stats. Va. Poly. Inst., Blacksburg, 1957—61; rsch. staff mem., mgr. info. scis. IBM Thomas J. Watson Rsch. Ctr., Yorktown Heights, NY, 1961—65; prof. of stats. and computer sci. U. Ga., Athens, 1965—, prof. stats. and computer sci., emeritus dept. stats., 1990—. Vis. lectr. Institut nat. d'études démographiques; U. of Paris, 1965; exch. prof. U. Erlangen/Nürnberg, Bavaria, Germany, 1978; vis. prof. U. Dortmund, Rhineland Westphalia, Germany, 1980; rsch. fellow US Dept. of Agr., Washington, 1990. Assoc. editor: Psychometrica, 1957—74, Jour. Statistical Computation, 1970—74. Pres. U. Ga. chpt. AAUP, Athens, 1975—77. Fellow: AAAS, Am. Statis. Assn.; mem.: Am. Assn. for Computing Machines, Internat. Statis. Inst., Sigma Xi. Lutheran. Avocations: music (piano, accordion), travel. Home: 170 Colonial Dr Athens GA 30606 Office: Univ Ga Dept Stats Athens GA 30602-1952 Office Fax: 706-542-3391. E-mail: reb2@stat.uga.edu.

BARGMEYER, BRAD D. communications exectuve, advocate; b. Tacoma, Wash., Nov. 1970; s. Larry Bargmeyer and Deanna Johnson. BA in Polit. Sci., U. Redlands, 1993; cert. econ. devel., U. Calif., Riverside, 1994; MBA, Claremont U., 1999, MA in Am. Politics, 2000; Cert. in Internat. Human Rights, Simon Greenleaf Inst., 1999. Regional rsch. coord. TCI Media Svcs., Ontario, Calif., 1993-97; mktg. coord. Charter Comm., Alhambra, Calif., 1997—2000, bus. mgr., 2001—. Pres. Ctr. for Human Rights and Mgmt., Rancho Cucamonga, Calif., 1997 2000. Mem. dist. bd. dirs. Cal-Nev-Ha Circle K Internat., 1990-91; mem. steering com. Inland Empire (Calif.) Prayer Breakfast, 1994-96. Mem. Christian Mgmt. Assn. Home: PO Box 3271 Rancho Cucamonga CA 91729-3271 Office: Charter Comm 7337 Central Riverside CA 92504-

BARHAM, CHARLES DEWEY, JR., electric utility executive, lawyer; b. Goldsboro, N.C., July 7, 1930; s. Charles Dewey and Helen Wilkinson (Douglass) Barham Hughes; m. Margaret Wright Crow, June 17, 1960; children: Margaret Douglass, Charles Dewey III. BS, Wake Forest U., 1952, JD, 1954. Bar: N.C. 1954. Asst. atty. gen. N.C. Dept. Justice, Raleigh, 1958-66; assoc. gen. counsel Carolina Power & Light Co., Raleigh, N.C., 1966-73; ptnr. Douglass & Barham, Raleigh, 1974-80; v.p., sr. counsel Carolina Power & Light Co., Raleigh, 1981-82, sr. v.p., gen. counsel, 1982-87, sr. v.p., 1982-90, exec. v.p, 1990-95; bd. of dir., 1990—95; ptnr. Douglass & Barham, 1995—. Chmn. bd., pres. Nuclear Mut., Ltd., Hamilton, Bermuda, 1981-86, bd. dirs. 1973-95; bd. dirs. Nuclear Elec. Ins. Ltd., 1987-95 Hamilton; gen. counsel World Nuclear Fuel Mkt., Atlanta, 1974-80; gen. counsel Meredith Coll., Raleigh, 1977-80, trustee, 1984-87, 90-93, 95—2001; mem. regional bd. dirs. Wachovia Bank of N.C., 1990-95. Pres. Raleigh YMCA, 1982-92; bd. vis. Sch. Law Wake Forest U., 1998—. Capt. USNR, 1955-77. Mem.: ABA, N.C. Bar Assn., Glen Forest Club (pres. 1977), Raleigh Civitan Club (dir. 1974—77, 1999—).

BARHAM, MACK ELWIN, lawyer, educator; b. Bastrop, La., June 18, 1924; s. Henry Alfred and Lockie Izorie (Harper) B.; m. Ann LeVois, June 3, 1946; children: Bret L., Megan. JD, La. State U., 1946; postgrad., U. Colo., 1964-65. Judge City Ct., Bastrop, 1948-61, 4th Jud. Dist. Ct., Parishes of Ouachita and Morehouse, 1961-67, 2d Circuit Ct. of Appeal, 1967-68; assoc. justice La. Supreme Ct., 1968-75; prof. Sch. Law, Tulane, 1975-78; counsel Lemle, Kelleher, Kohlmeyer & Matthews, 1975-78; pres. Barham & Churchill, 1979-88; founder Barham & Arceneaux, New Orleans, 1988—. Mem. faculty Am. Acad. Jud. Edn., U. Ala., 1968-73. Chmn. Ouachita Valley council Boy Scouts Am. Recipient award Freedoms Found. at, Valley Forge, 1969; Outstanding Service award ACLU, 1976; Creative Intelligence award Found. Sci., 1976 Mem. La. Juvenile Judges Assn. (past pres.), La. Law Inst. (council),

Internat. Acad. Estate and Trust Law, Scribes, Kiwanis, Blue Key, Order of Coif, Omicron Delta Kappa, Lambda Chi Alpha, Phi Delta Phi, Phi Alpha Delta. Home: 5837 Bellaire Dr New Orleans LA 70124-1103

BARIE, PHILIP STEVEN, surgeon, educator; b. Buffalo, Aug. 18, 1953; s. Kenneth George and Eleanor Lucille (Davis) B.; m. Elaine Catherine Dash, May 31, 1981; children: Catherine, Steven, Alexandra. AB cum laude, MD, Boston U., 1977. Diplomate and surg. critical care cert. Am. Bd. Surgery. Jr. resident in surgery N.Y. Hosp.-Cornell Med. Ctr., N.Y.C., 1977-79; fellow in surgery and physiology Albany (N.Y.) Med. Coll., 1979-81; sr. resident in surgery N.Y. Hosp.-Cornell Med. Ctr., 1981-83, adminstrv. chief resident surgery, 1983-84; asst. prof. surgery Weill Med. Coll. Cornell U., NYC, 1984—89, prof. pub. health Weill Med. Coll., 2003—, assoc. prof. Weill Med. Coll., 1989-2001, prof. Weill Med. Coll., 2001—, chief divsn. trauma and critical care dept. surgery Weill Med. Coll., 1998—; attending surgeon, dir. surg ICU, N.Y. Presbyn. Hosp., N.Y.C., 1984—. Cons. in surgery Cath. Med. Presbyn. Ctr., N.Y.C., 1985—; chmn. inst. rev. bd. Med. Coll. Cornell U., N.Y.C., 1988-92; cons. specialist, med. control bd. Health Ins. Plan Greater N.Y., 1990-98; cons. in critical care therapeutics U.S. Pharmacopeial Conv., 1991—; med. adv. bd. N.Y. Blood Ctr., 1999—. Editor-in-chief Surg. Infections; mem. editl. bd.: Surg. Infections: Index and Revs., 1993-99, Shock, 1996-2000, Contemporary Surgery, 1996-2002, Air Med. Jour., 1997— Jour. of Surg. Outcomes, 1997-2000, Jour. of Trauma, 1998—, Critical Care Medicine, 1998—, New Horizons, 1998-2000, Pediat. Critical Care Medicine, 2000-01, New Surgery, 2000-02; co-editor: Surg. Intensive Care, 1993 (Best New Book in Med Scis. Assn. Am. Pubs. 1994); contbr. articles to profl. jours. Fellow: ACS, Am. Surg. Assn., Am. Coll. Critical Care Medicine; mem.: Surg. Infection Soc. (coun. mem. 1995—98, found. trustee, treas. 1998—, treas. 1998—2003, pres.-elect 2003), Critical Care Medicine Edn. and Rsch. Found. (trustee 2000—02), Ea. Assn. for Surgery of Trauma (bd. dirs. 1996—99, pres.-elect 2003), Shock Soc., Assn. for Acad. Surgery, Soc. Civil War Surgeons, N.Y. Acad. Scis., N.Y. State Soc. Surgeons (bd. dirs. 1992—95, sec. 1995—97, pres.-elect 1997—99, pres. 1999—2001, bd. dirs. 2001—02), Soc. Univ. Surgeons, Am. Physiol. Soc., Internat. Surg. Soc., Am. Assn. for Surgery of Trauma (Peter C. Canizaro award 1992), Am. Thoracic Soc., Soc. Critical Care Medicine (sec.-treas. surg. sect. 1995—96, chair-elect surg. sect. 1996—97, chair surg. sect. 1997—98, mem. coun. 1997—), N.Y. Surg. Soc. (coun mem.-at-large 1995—2000), N.Y. Acad. Medicine (sec. surg. sect. 1991—92), Halsted Soc. (sec.-treas. 2002—), Am. Med. Writers Assn. Office: NY Presbyn Hosp-Weill Cornell Med Ctr Dept Surgery 525 E 68th St New York NY 10021-4885

BARIFF, MARTIN LOUIS, information systems educator, consultant; b. Chgo., Jan. 26, 1944; s. George and Mae (Goldberg) B. BS in Acctg., U. Ill., 1966, MA in Acctg., 1967, PhD in Acctg., 1973. CPA, Chgo. Asst. prof. acctg. and decision scis. Wharton Sch., Phila., 1973-78; vis. asst. prof. acctg. U. Chgo., 1978-79; assoc. prof. acctg. and mgmt. info. decision systems Case Western Res. U., Cleve., 1979-83; assoc. prof. info. mgmt., dir. Ctr. for Rsch. on Impacts of Info. Systems Ill. Inst. Tech., Chgo., 1983—, acad. dir. MS e-commerce program Ctr. for Rsch. on Impacts of Info. Systems, 2000—. Exec. v.p. EDP Auditors Found., 1979-80; program chmn. Internat. Conf. Info. Systems, Phila., 1980; co-founder Info. Integrity Coalition, 2001-; cons. in field. Contbr. articles to profl. jours. Bd. dirs. Community Accts. Inc. of Phila., 1974-75; co-founder Info. Integrity Coalition, 2001—. Mem. AICPA, IEEE (computer soc.) INFORMS, Ill. CPA Soc., Am. Acctg. Assn. (chmn. acctg., behavior and orgns. sect. 1987-88), Assn. Computing Machinery (sec. spl. interest group on security, auditing and control 1981-85), Soc. Info. Mgmt. (treas. Chgo. chpt. 1988-90, 95-96), Internat. Engring. Consortium (bd. dirs. ednl. overseers 1991-96), Internat. Internal Auditors (rsch. chair Chgo. chpt., 2001-03). Jewish. Avocations: running, flying, photography. Office: Ill Inst Tech 565 W Adams St Ste 450 Chicago IL 60661-3613 E-mail: bariff@stuart.iit.edu.

BARIK, SUDHAKAR, microbiologist, research scientist; b. Sainkula, Orissa, India, Aug. 14, 1949; came to U.S., 1980; s. Ananda Chandra and Sakhamani (Behera) B.; m. Dharashri Behera, Mar. 4, 1979; children: Santwana, Sambit. BSc, Utkal U., Orissa, 1972, MSc, 1974, PhD, 1979. Postdoctoral fellow U. Okla., 1980-82; rsch. assoc. U. Ill., Urbana, 1982-84, U. Ark., Fayetteville, 1984-87; asst. prin. scientist Atlantic Rsch. Corp., Alexandria, Va., 1987-88; prin. scientist, group leader ARCTECH, Inc., Chantilly, Va., 1988-92; sr. devel. microbiologist Lederle Labs. Am. Cyanamid Co., Pearl River, N.Y., 1992-94; group leader process devel. Wyeth-Lederle Vaccines and Pediat. Am. Home Products, Inc., Pearl River, N.Y., 1994-98; mgr. vaccines devel. Wyeth-Lederle Vaccines, Am. Home Products, Inc., Pearl River, N.Y., 1998-99, assoc. dir. clin. supplies mfg. and distbn., 2000-01; dir. clin. supplies mfg. and distbn. Wyeth, Inc., Pearl River, 2001—. Contbr. articles to profl. jours., chpts. to books. Fund raiser PTA, Annandale, Va., 1987-92; sci. fair judge for high schs., Annandale and Alexandria, 1987-92. Mem. Am. Soc. Microbiology, Soc. Indsl. Microbiology. Avocations: reading, outdoor activities, community service, travel, collecting stamps. Home: 8 Ambrey Ln Thiells NY 10984-1608 Office: Lederle Labs 401 N Middletown Rd Pearl River NY 10965-1299 E-mail: bariks@wyeth.com.

BARIL, MAURICE, career officer; b. Saint-Albert de Warwick, Qué., Can., Sept. 22, 1943; m. Huguette Desjardins; children: François, Hélène. Student, U. Ottawa, 1961-64; cert., Officer Tng. Corps, 1964, École Supérieure de Guerre, Paris, 1977. Commd. 2nd lt. Royal 22nd Regiment, 1963, advanced through ranks to gen., 1997; with 1st Commando Airborne Rgt., Valcartier and Edmonton, Can., 1968-71; comdr. tng. co. Recruit Sch.; ops. officer, adjutant 3d Bn., Valcartier, Can., and Cyprus; comdr. 2d Bn., La Citadelle, Québec, 1980; comdt. Inf. Sch. Comd. Forces Command and Staff Coll., 1984; dep. commdt. Can. Forces Command and Staff Coll., 1985; dir. land ops., tng., and resources, dir. inf. Nat. Def. Hdqs., Ottawa, Can., 1986, dir. gen. land doctrine ops., 1989; mil. advisor UN Dept. Peacekeeping Ops., 1992; comdr. Land Force Que. Area, Montréal, 1995, Land Force Command, 1995-97; chief of def. Govt. of Canada, 1997—2001. Avocations: ultralight flying, fishing, hunting, markmanship, golfing.

BARILICH, THOMAS ANTHONY, loss control specialist; b. South Bend, Ind., Sept. 24, 1955; s. John Joseph and Agnes B. (Sostritz) Barilich. AS in Bus., Ind. U., 1977, BA, 1977, M in Safety, 1979; AS in Risk Mgmt., Ins. Sch. of Chgo., 1985, AS in Mgmt., 1996. Engring. rep. Aetna Life & Casualty, Chgo., 1980-85; sr. loss control rep. Hartford Ins., Chgo., 1985-87; loss control specialist Continental Ins., Chgo., 1987-93; regional tech. constrn. mgr. AIG Cos., Chgo., 1993—. Instr. first aid Aetna Life & Casualty, 1983—84, instr. def. driving, 1984—85. Contbr. articles to Skismoke newsletter. Club instr. Chgo. Met. Ski Coun., 1990—91. Mem.: Constrn. Safety Assn. Am., Am. Soc. Safety Engrs., Sundowner Ski Club (chmn. racing bd. dirs. 1991—, Male Racer of the Yr. 1991). Roman Catholic. Avocations: sports officiating, basketball, volleyball, softball, philately. Home: 2121 Tahoe Pkwy Algonquin IL 60102-4282

BARILLA, FRANK (ROCKY BARILLA), lawyer, consultant, educator; b. Los Angeles, Jan. 26, 1948; s. Bruno Frank and Lucera (Campos) B. Student Glendale Coll., 1966-68; B.A., U. So. Calif., 1970, J.D., 1975; M.B.A., Stanford U., 1972. Bar: Calif. 1975, Oreg. 1976, U.S. Dist. Ct. (no. dist.) Calif. 1976, U.S. Dist. Ct. Oreg. 1976, U.S. Ct. Appeals (9th cir.) 1977. Adj. asst. prof. immigration law Sch. Law, U. Oreg., Eugene, 1976-88; adj. asst. prof. Willamette U., Salem, Oreg., 1979, 83, 86; instr. bus. law Linfield Coll., McMinnville, Oreg., 1983; adminstr. labor and edn. com. Oreg. Legislature, Salem, 1979, 81, 83, legal counsel joint judiciary com., 1984-86, legislator, state rep. Oreg. Legis. Assembly, 1986-89; cons. Interface Cons., Portland, Oreg., 1981-84; hearings officer Oreg. Employment Div., Salem, 1982-83; adj. instr. Lewis and Clark Law Sch., Portland, Oreg., 1977, 80; cons. in field; vice chmn. Housing and Urban Devel. Com., mem. various other coms. Oreg. State Legislature; bd. dirs. La Alianza Legal de Oregon, 1983-88. Author tng. manual Enabling Legislation for Multicultural Education, 1981. Mem. Salem Pub. Schs. Affirmative Action, 1976-78; chmn. Salem Chpt. Hispanic Polit. Action Com., 1983-84; bd. dirs. Oreg. Soccer Assn., Salem, 1978, United Way, Portland, 1980. Recipient Civil Liberties award Oreg. chpt. ACLU, 1984. Calif. State fellow/scholar, 1968-72; fellow Merrill Trust, 1970-72, Council Grad. Mgmt. Edn., 1970-72, Kellogg Found., 1981-82. Mem. Oreg. State Bar (com. on affirmative action 1978-80, com. on fgn. and internat. law 1980-83, com. legal aid 1983-86), Calif. State Bar, Marion County Bar Assn. Home: 2429 Hastings Dr Belmont CA 94002-3319 Office: 1118 10th St Ste 200 Sacramento CA 95814-3504

BARILLEAUX, RYAN J. politcal science educator; b. Lafayette, La., June 15, 1957; s. Ira C. and Joanna (Beyt) B.; m. Marilyn Wasick, May 23, 1981; children: Gerard, Madeleine, Christine, Paul, Thomas, Michael. BA summa cum laude, U. Southwestern La., 1979; MA, U. Tex., 1980, DPhil, 1983. Asst. prof. polit. sci. U. Tex., El Paso, 1983-87; assoc. prof. Miami U., Oxford, Ohio, 1987-95, prof., 1995—, chmn. dept. polit. sci., 2001—. Steering com. mem. Presidency Rsch. Group, Washington, 1993-95. Author: The President and Foreign Affairs, 1985, The Post-Modern Presidency, 1988, The President as World Leader, 1991, Leadership and the Bush Presidency, 1993, American Government in Action, 1995, Presidential Frontiers, 1998, Power and Prudence: The Presidency of George H.W. Bush, 2003; editor-in-chief Cath. Social Sci. Rev., 1999—; contbr. articles to profl. jours. Intern/aide Sen. J. Bennett Johnston, Washington, 1977-78. Salvatori fellow Heritage Found., Washington, 1994-95. Mem. Am. Polit. Sci. Assn. (com. chmn. 1994), Soc. Cath. Soc. Scientists, Ctr. Study Presidency. Roman Catholic. Avocations: reading, camping, scouting. Office: Miami U Dept Polit Sci Oxford OH 45056 E-mail: barillrj@muohio.edu.

BARISH, CHARLES FRANKLIN, internist, gastroenterologist, researcher; b. Franklin, N.J., Jan. 5, 1955; s. Philip and Laura (Freedman) Barish; m. Debrah Lee Kaufman, Aug. 13, 1977; children: Philip, Stefanie, Jacob. BS in Chemistry with honors, U. Fla., 1976, MD, 1980. Diplomate in internal medicine and gastroenterology Am. Bd. Internal Medicine. Resident, fellow Wake Forest U. Sch. Medicine, Winston-Salem, N.C., 1980-85; physician Wake Internal Medicine Cons., Raleigh, N.C., 1985—; pres., founder Wake Rsch. Assocs., Raleigh, 1985—; clin. asst., prof. medicine U. N.C. Sch. Medicine, Chapel Hill, 1985—. Co-founder Peak Rsch., 1998; chmn. nutritional care com. Rex Hosp., Raleigh, 1987—97. Co-author: Gastroesophageal Reflux Disease, 1985; contbr. numerous sci. articles to med. jours. Pres. Jewish Cmty. Ctr., Raleigh, 1995—97; v.p. Raleigh-Cary Jewish Fedn., 1993—97, bd. dirs., 1990—. Fellow: ACP, Am. Coll. Gastroenterology; mem.: AMA, Crohn's and Colitis Found. (bd. dirs.), Wake County Med. Soc., N.C. Med. Soc., Am. Liver Found., Am. Soc. Gastrointestinal Endoscopy, Am. Coll. Physician Execs., Am. Gastroenterol. Assn., B'nai Brith, Alpha Epsilon Delta, Phi Kappa Phi, Alpha Omega Alpha. Avocation: golf, skiing, gardening. Office: Wake Internal Medicine Cons 3100 Blue Ridge Rd Ste 300 Raleigh NC 27612-8035 E-mail: CFBGastro@aol.com.

BARISH, LAWRENCE STEPHEN, nonpartisan legislative staff administrator; b. Bklyn., Nov. 30, 1945; s. Louis C. and Anna (Sanders) B.; m. Sharon Lee Shapiro, July 2, 1967; 1 child, Lauren. BS in Polit. sci., U. Wis.-Madison, Wis., 1967; MA in Govt., U. Ariz., 1970. Legis. analyst Legis. Reference Bur., Madison, Wis., 1971-87, dir. of reference and info. svcs., 1987—. Chmn. rsch., comm. staff sec. Nat. Conf. State Legislatures, Denver, 1995-97; redistricting cons. Wis. Legis. and Local Govt. units, 1980—. Editor State Almanac, 1987—; contbr. articles to profl. jours. Home: 1429 W Skyline Dr Madison WI 53705-1134 Office: Wis Legis Reference Bur 100 N Hamilton St Madison WI 53703-4118 E-mail: larry.barish@legis.state.wi.us.

BARIST, JEFFREY, lawyer; b. Jersey City, Dec. 29, 1941; s. Irving and Lillian (Finkelstein) B.; m. Joan Elaine Travers, Feb. 19, 1967; children: Jessica, Alexis. AB, Rutgers U., 1963; JD, Harvard U., 1966. Bar: N.Y. 1967, U.S. Ct. Appeals (2d cir.) 1968, U.S. Dist. Ct. (so. dist.) N.Y. 1969, U.S. Supreme Ct. 1975. Law sec. U.S. Dist. Judge Irving Ben Cooper, N.Y.C., 1966-67; ptnr., chmn. nat. litigation group Milbank, Tweed, Hadley & McCloy, N.Y.C., 1996—. Author: Commercial Arbitration Law and Clauses, 1994; contbr. articles to profl. jours. Bd. dirs. Lawyers Com. for Civil Rights Under Law; trustee Rutgers U. Fellow Am. Coll. Trial Lawyers, Am. Bar Found.; mem. Am. Law Inst. Office: Milbank Tweed Hadley McCloy 47th Fl 1 Chase Manhattan Plz Fl 47 New York NY 10005-1413 E-mail: jbarist@milbank.com.

BARITZ, LOREN, history educator; b. Chgo., Dec. 26, 1928; s. Joseph Harry and Helen (Garland) B.; m. Phyllis L. Handelsman, Dec. 26, 1948; children: Tony, Joseph. BA, Roosevelt U., 1953; MA, U. Wis., 1954, PhD, 1956. Asst. prof. history Wesleyan U., Middletown, Conn., 1956-62; assoc. prof. Roosevelt U., Chgo., 1962-63; prof. U. Rochester, 1963-69, chmn. dept. history, 1964-67; leading prof. SUNY, Albany, 1969-71; exec. v.p. Empire State Coll., exec. dir. univ. commn. on purposes and priorities, 1975-76; from exec. v.p. to provost SUNY, 1971-79; dir. N.Y. Inst. Humanities; prof. history NYU, 1979-80; provost, vice chancellor for acad. affairs U. Mass., Amherst, 1980-83, prof. history, 1980-91, prof. emeritus, 1991—. Vis. lectr. U. Wis.-Madison, 1959-60; cultural cons. to UNESCO, Paris, 1968-71; mgmt. cons. Balykchy Inst. of Bus. and Law, Kyrgyzstan, 1997, 99, Slovak U. of Tech., Bratislava, Slovak Republic, 1997, Comenius U., Bratislava, 1998. Author: City on a Hill, 1964, Servants of Power, 1960, Sources of the American Mind, 2 vols., 1966, The Culture of the Twenties, 1970, The American Left, 1971, Backfire, 1985, 98, The Good Life, 1989. Co-chmn. policy coun. rsch. and svc. Assembly Univ. Goals, Am. Acad. Arts and Scis., 1969-70; del. Dem. Nat. Conv., 1968; bd. govs. chmn. com. on acad. affairs Haifa U., 1975-92; mem. exec. bd. Nat. Com. for Labor, Israel, 1984-94; mgmt. cons. Am. Stock Exchange, 1994-95, 97. Rsch. Tng. fellow Social Sci. Rsch. Coun., 1955-56, grantee, 1960; grantee Am. Council Learned Socs., 1963. Home: 12 Glennana Way Sheffield MA 01257 E-mail: lbaritz@earthlink.net.

BARK, MARTHA W. state legislator; BA in Econs., DePauw U. Mayor City of Medford, N.J., 1981-895; mem. N.J. Assembly, 1995-97, N.J. Senate, Dist. 8, Trenton, 1998—. Mem. econ. growth com. N.J. State Senate, chair agr. and tourism com., cmty. and urban affairs com. Mem. Medford Sch. Bd., 1973-78; mem. Medford Twp. Com., 1980-87; mem. Burlington County Freeholder, 1984—. Republican. Office: NJ State Senate Dist Office 3000 Midlantic Dr Ste 103 Mount Laurel NJ 08054-1513 Address: NJ State Senate PO Box 098 Trenton NJ 08624-0098 E-mail: SenBark@njleg.state.nj.us.*

BARKAN, JOEL DAVID, political science educator, consultant; b. Toledo, Apr. 28, 1941; s. Manuel and Toby (Wolfe) B.; m. Sandra Lynn Hackman, Sept. 9, 1962; children: Bronwyn Michelle, Joshua Manuel. AB, Cornell U., 1963; MA, UCLA, 1965, PhD, 1970. Asst. prof. polit. sci. U. Calif., Irvine, 1969-72; asst. prof. polit. sci. U. Iowa, Iowa City, 1972-76, assoc. prof., 1976-81, prof., 1981—, chmn. dept. polit. sci., 1985-87, dir. ctr. internat. and comparative studies, 1981-83. Vis. rsch. fellow Makerere U., Uganda, 1966—67, U. Dar es Salaam, Tanzania, 1973—74, Fondation Nat. des Scis. Politiques, Paris, 1978—79, U. Nairobi, Kenya, 1979, 80, Ctr. Study of Developing Socs., New Delhi, 1984, Cornell U., 1990, U.S. Inst. Peace, 1997—98, Nat. Endowment for Democracy, 2000, Woodrow Wilson Internat. Ctr., 2001—02; regional governance advisor for Ea. and So. Africa USAID, 1992—94; sr. cons. on governance World Bank, 2000—. Co-author, editor: Politics and Public Policy in Kenya and Tanzania, 1979, rev. edit., 1984, Beyond Capitalism Versus Socialism in Kenya and Tanzania, 1994; co-author: The Legislative Connection, 1984; author: An African Dilemma, 1975; contbr. articles to profl. jours. Pres. Iowa City Fgn. Rels. Coun., 1989—90. Fellow, Social Sci. Rsch. Coun., 1966—68, Fulbright fellow, 1978—79, Indo-Am. fellow, 1984, Randolph fellow, 1997—98, Woodrow Wilson fellow, 2001—02; grantee, Rockefeller Found., 1973—74, US-AID, 1978—81, Ford Found., 1992—99. Mem. Am. Polit. Sci. Assn., African Studies Assn. (bd. dirs. 1990-93), Coun. Fgn. Rels. Office: U Iowa Dept Polit Sci Iowa City IA 52242 E-mail: joel-barkan@uiowa.edu.

BARKAN, JOHN MARTIN, JR., architect; b. Warren, Ohio, Mar. 16, 1945; s. John Martin and Esther (Wagoner) B.; m. Darlene Rose Kast, Oct. 14, 1972; children: Leilani, John III. BArch, Kent State U., 1969. Registered architect, Ohio. Draftsman Mallalieu, Ross & Roberts, Massillon, Ohio, 1968-72, architect, 1972-76; architect capt. Lawrence, Dykes & Goodenberger, Canton, Ohio, 1977-80; project architect Wilson Archtl. Group, North Canton, Ohio, 1982-86; pvt. practice Canton, Ohio, 1986-89; ptnr. Goodenberger, Dansizen & Barkan Architects, Canton, Ohio, 1989-95; v.p. L.D. Design Group, Canton, 1995—. Prin. works include Massillon City Hall, McKinley Centre, Ergun residence, Aultman North Med. Ctr., Akron Canton Regional Airport Expansion. Local coord. for Russian med. clinic. adminstr. Ctr. for Citizen Initiatives, 2000, 2003. Mem.: AIA (sec. Akron chpt. 1985), Rotary (Paul Harris fellow 2000). Republican. Roman Catholic. Avocations: golf, art, literature. Home: 3809 Tuscarawas St W Apt 11 Canton OH 44708-5539

BARKAN, STEVEN EDWARD, sociology educator; b. Phila., Dec. 11, 1951; s. Morry and Sylvia B. PhD, SUNY, Stony Brook, 1980. Asst. prof. to prof. dept. sociology U. Maine, Orono, 1979—. Office: Dept Sociology/Univ Maine 5728 Fernald Hall Orono ME 04469-5728

BARKEMEIJER DE WIT, JEANNE SANDRA, graphic artist, illustrator, writer, multimedia consultant; b. Santa Ana, Calif., July 6, 1955; d. Hendrik Pieter and Nelly Maria Barkemeijer de Wit; m. Johnne J. Johnson, Sept. 6, 1996. Student, Am. Coll. Paramed. Arts Scis., Santa Ana, 1977-78, Computer Learning Ctr., Anaheim, Calif., 1985-86, Regional Occupational Program, Buena Park, Calif., 1986, Cen. Counties Regional Occupational Program, Santa Ana, 1986-87, 90-94, Rancho Santiago Coll., 1990-94. Cert. respiratory therapy tech. Freelancer, Santa Ana, 1972—; respiratory therapist Good Samaritan Hosp., Anaheim, 1978-79, Tustin (Calif.) Community Hosp., 1979-81, United Western Med. Ctrs., Santa Ana, Anaheim, 1981-86; office mgr., asst. dir. internat. sales, dir. spl. accounts D-Link Systems, Inc., Irvine, Calif., 1986-90; graphic artist, illustrator, contbg. writer West 17th mag., Santa Ana, 1990-94, also editor-in-chief, 1991. Graphic artist Santa Ana Unified Schs., 1974. Exhibited in group shows including Torrana Art League, 1970-72, Buzza Gibson Gallery, 1970, various galleries in Japan, Amsterdam, and N.Y., 1970, Very Spl. Arts Gallery, 1999-2000; illustrator: Sexual Positions for Chronic Lung and Cardiac Patients, 1984; author, designer numerous storyboard diskettes, 1988—; illustrations exhibited, The Very Special Arts Gallery, 1999-2000; webmaster for numerous sites. Vol. lab. technician Health Fair Expo 1992; vol. therapist Cancer Assn. Great Am. Smoke-Out, Costa Mesa, 1979-86, Lung Assn. Scamp Camp for Asthmatic Children, Santa Ana, 1986; vol. artist Heart Assn., L.A., 1986; vocalist, guitarist Easter Seal Telethon Orange County, 1978. Recipient Cert. Thanks Heart Assn., 1985, Cert. Appreciation Health Fair Expo Nat. Health Laboratories, 1992, Columbia medal Front Page Graphics, 1990, Peacemaker award, 1991, 2d Pl. for layout and design, 2nd Pl., 1993, 1st, 2d and 4th pl., 3d Hon. Mention award JACC State Competition for mag. illustration, 1992. Democrat. Avocations: piano, guitar, singing, theater arts, cosmetology. Home: 1551 W Chateau Ave Anaheim CA 92802-1315 Fax: 714-772-2036.

BARKEN, BERNARD ALLEN, lawyer; b. St. Louis, July 20, 1924; s. Gottlieb and Hattie E. (Rubin) B.; m. Jocelyn Moss Kopman, Sept. 1, 1948; children: Thomas L., Dale Susan. JD, Washington U., 1947. Bar: Mo. 1947, U.S. Dist. Ct. (ea. dist.) Mo. 1947, U.S. Ct. Appeals (8th cir.) 1954, U.S. Tax Ct. 1966, U.S. Ct. Appeals 2nd cir.) 1985, U.S. Supreme Ct. 1984. Sole practice, St. Louis, 1947-80; ptnr. Shifrin & Treiman, St. Louis, 1980-88; pres. Bernard A. Barken, St. Louis, 1988-91; ptnr. Barken & Bakewell L.L.P., St. Louis, 1991—. With USAAF, 1943-44. Mem. ABA, Bar Assn. Met. St. Louis (v.p. 1958, chmn. young lawyers 1953). Jewish. Avocations: piano, tennis, gardening. Home: 30 Vouga Ln Saint Louis MO 63131-2628 Office: Barken & Bakewell LLP 500 N Broadway Ste 2000 Saint Louis MO 63102-2130 Fax: 314-444-7892. E-mail: babarken@hotmail.com.

BARKER, ALAN FREUND, internist; b. St. Louis, Aug. 27, 1944; s. Irven M. and Gladys (Freund) B.; m. Julieann Brixner; children: Sara, David. BA, Carleton Coll., 1966; MD, U. Mo., 1970. Internship internal medicine U. Wash. Affiliated Hosps., Seattle, 1970-71, residency internal medicine, 1971-73; chief med. resident internal medicine U. Wash. Affiliated Hosps., USPH Hosp., Seattle, 1973-74; fellow pulmonary medicine U. Calif., San Diego, 1974-76; asst. prof. medicine Oreg. Health Scis. U., Portland, 1976-82, assoc. prof. medicine Divsn. Pulmonary & Critical Care, 1982-95; prof., 1995—. Med. dir., cons Respiratory Therapy Program, Mt. Hood C.C., 1978—, chair adv. com., 1992—; cons. Multnomah County Tuberculosis Clinic, 1981—. Contbr. articles to profl. jours. and chpts. to books. Mem. Gov.'s Commn. for Pub. Health Policy, 1984-85; bd. dirs. Univ. Med. Assocs., 1980-85, pres., 1983-85; mem. Med. Bd. Univ. Hosp., 1984-87, exec. coun., 1984-85. Grantee NIH, 1989-94, Genentech, 1993-94, Miles, 1993-94. Fellow Am. Coll. Chest Physicians; mem. Am. Thoracic Soc., Oreg. Thoracic Soc. (pres. 1982-83). Avocations: tennis, squash, gardening. Office: Oreg Health Scis U Pulmonary/Critical Care Portland OR 97239

BARKER, BARBARA, registered nurse, medical researcher; b. Vancouver, Canada, Jan. 11, 1934; arrived in U.S., 1955, naturalized, 1979; d. William James and Mary Anne Graham; m. Richard Lloyd Barker, Nov. 21, 1960. RN, Vancouver Gen. Hosp., Vancouver, Canada, 1952—55; BA, MA, PhD hist., U of Wash., Seattle, WA, 1979—89. Psychiat. nurse UCLA Med. Ctr., Los Angeles, Calif., 1956—59; oper. room nurse Mt. Sinai Hosp., Los Angeles, Calif., 1960; claims exam. OR Physicians Svc., Portland, Oreg., 1963—65; biomedical rschr. Physio-Control Co., Redmond, Wash., 1988—91; freelance rschr. self-employed, Seattle, 1991—. Adv. art com. U of Wash., Seattle, 1987—89. Author: (article) hist. article/Sonoma County Hist. Soc., 1981; poet (poetry) Spindrift, 2000 (Metro Bus. poet, 2000); author: (plays) Raven Chronicals Bricolage, 2000, (non-fiction) Fireworks, 2002—. Named one of Phi Beta Kappa, U of Wash., Magna Cum Laude, 1981; scholar scholarship, Vancouver Gen. Hosp. Sch. of Nursing /Can., 1952, U of Wash./ US, 1988. Mem.: Friends of Bancroft Library (assoc.), Nordic Heritage Museum (assoc.), Friends of Frye Museum (assoc.), Wash. Poets Assoc. (assoc.; treas. 1995). Avocations: jazz, gardening, art. Home: 110 West 13th Street Port Angeles WA 98362

BARKER, BARBARA ANN, ophthalmologist; b. Paterson, N.J., Nov. 10, 1943; d. Earle Louis and Dorothy Louise (Williamson) Barker; m. Joel Ira Papernik, July 28, 1972; children: Deborah Papernik, Ilana Papernik. BA magna cum laude, Conn. Coll., 1965; BS, Yale U., 1967; MA, Rutgers Med. Sch., 1974; MD, Mt. Sinai Sch. Medicine, 1976. Diplomate Am. Bd. Ophthalmology Intern Beth Israel Med. Ctr., 1977; resident Mt. Sinai Sch. Medicine/Beth Israel Med. Ctr., 1980, fellow in glaucoma, 1980-81, fellow cornea, refractive surgery, 1981-82; pvt. practice medicine specializing in ophthalmology, N.Y.C., 1983—. Rsch. technician The Rockefeller U., N.Y.C., 1965—66; tchr. Riverdale Country Sch., N.Y.C., 1967—68; rsch. asst. Sloan Kettering Inst., N.Y.C., 1969—72; asst. clin. prof. Mt. Sinai Sch. Medicine, N.Y.C., 1982—; mem. staff N.Y. Eye and Ear Hosp., Beth Israel/St. Luke's/Roosevelt Hosp. Recipient Resident Best Paper award, Beth Israel Med. Ctr., 1989, Honor award, Am. Acad. Ophthalmology, 1955; grantee Beth Israel Rsch. grant, 1983, NSF, 1966. Fellow: ACS, N.Y. Acad. Medicine; mem.: AMA, N.Y. County Med. Assn., Women's Med. Soc. NYC, Am. Med. Women's Assn., Phi Beta Kappa. Home and Office: 11 E 86th St New York NY 10028-0501 E-mail: bbarkermd@aol.com.

BARKER, CELESTE ARLETTE, computer scientist; b. Redding, Calif., Apr. 19, 1947; d. Edwin Walter Squires and Rachel (Kinkead) Layton; m. Julius Jeep Chernak, Sept. 13, 1970, (div. 1980); children: Sean Matthew, Bret Allen; m. Jackson Lynn Barker, Oct. 8, 1988. BA in Art, San Francisco State U., 1970; AA in Engring. Tech., Coll. Marin, 1980; MBA in Mgmt., Golden Gate U., 1988. Cert. netware engr. Art tchr. San Rafael (Calif.) Schs., 1971-75; owner, photographer Julius Chernak Photography, Novato, Calif., 1970-76; draftsman Donald Foster Drafting, San Rafael, 1975-76; surveyor Parks Dept. State Calif., Inverness, 1976; electric draftsman Pacific Gas & Electric, San Rafael, 1976-78, electric engring. estimator, 1978-79, mktg. rep. Santa Rosa, 1980-85, valuation analyst San Francisco, 1985-86, budget analyst, 1986-88, budget system project mgr., 1988-89, fin. asset mgr. Vallejo, Calif., 1989-90; ops. mgr. San Francisco Mus. Modern Art, 1990-91; cons. CB Cons., Atlanta, 1991-93; computer local area network mgr. Ga. Inst. Tech., Atlanta, 1993-94; systems integrator Bank South, Atlanta, 1994-95; mgmt. info. sys. mgr. Dinwiddie Constr., San Francisco, 1995-96; process/project mgr. Sybase, Inc., Emeryville, Calif., 1996-98; Wintel delivery mgr. Fair-Isaac Cos., San Rafael, Calif., 1998—2000; dir. support Kabira Techs., San Rafael, Calif., 2000—01; dir. tech. support PC Guardian, San Rafael, Calif., 2002—. Dir. Mariner Green Townhomes Assn., treas. 1987-88. Mem. Sierra Club. Avocations: photography, painting, backpacking. Home: 29 Woodside Way San Rafael CA 94901-1439

BARKER, CLAYTON ROBERT, III, lawyer; b. Statesville, N.C., Aug. 27, 1957; s. Clayton Robert Jr. and Alta Jo Barker; m. Sandra Ann Mills, June 30, 1990. AB with distinction, Stanford U., 1979; postgrad., Tufts. U., 1982; JD, U.

Va., 1983. Bar: N.Y. 1984, Ga. 1995. Assoc. Shearman & Sterling, N.Y.C., 1983-85, Skadden, Arps, Slate, Meagher & Flom, N.Y.C., 1985-91; counsel The Coca-Cola Co., Atlanta, 1991-2000; ptnr. Smith Helms Mulliss & Moore, LLP, Atlanta, 2000—01, Powell, Goldstein, Frazer & Murphy LLP, Atlanta, 2001—. Contbr. articles to profl. jours. Mem. Am. Coun. on Germany. Mem. Internat. Bar Assn., Am. Soc. Internat. Law, Nat. Assn. Corp. Dirs., N.Y. State Bar Assn. (internat. law and practice sect., fgn. investment in U.S. bus. com.), Am. Coun. on Germany (young leader 1992), Assn. for Corp. Growth (pres. Atlanta chpt. 1999-2000), Federalist Soc., Omicron Delta Kappa. Republican. Presbyterian. Office: Powell Goldstein Frazer & Murphy LLP Ste 1600 191 Peachtree St Atlanta GA 30303 E-mail: rbarker@pgfm.com.

BARKER, CLYDE FREDERICK, surgeon, educator; b. Salt Lake City, Aug. 16, 1932; s. Frederick George and Jennetta Elizabeth (Stephens) B.; m. Dorothy Joan Bieler, Aug. 11, 1956; children: Frederick George II, John Randolph, William Stephens, Elizabeth Dell. BA, Cornell U., 1954, MD, 1958. Diplomate Am. Bd. Surgery. Intern Hosp. U. Pa., Phila., 1958-59, resident in surgery, 1959-64, fellow in vascular surgery, 1964-65; fellow in med. genetics U. Pa. Sch. Medicine, Phila., 1965-66, assoc. in surgery, 1964-68, assoc. in med. genetics, 1966-72; attending surgeon Hosp. U. Pa., Phila., 1966—; chief div. transplantation U. Pa. Sch. Medicine, Phila., 1966—2001, asst. prof. surgery, 1968-69, assoc. prof. surgery, 1969-73, prof. surgery, 1973—, J. William White prof. surg. research, 1978-82, chief div. vascular surgery, 1982—2001, Guthrie prof. surgery, 1982—, John Rhea Barton prof. surgery, 1983—2001, chmn. dept. surgery, 1983—2001; chief surgery Hosp. U. Pa., Phila., 1983—2001. Dir. Harrison Dept. Surgery Rsch. U. Pa., Phila., 1983-2001; mem. immunobiology study sect. NIH; chmn. clin. practices U. Pa., 1987-89; v.p. United Network for Organ Sharing, 2001-02, pres., 2002--. Mem. editl. bd. Jour. Transplantation, 1977-2001, Clin. Transplantation, 1988—, Jour. Surg. Rsch., 1979-85, Jour. Diabetes, 1981-86, Archives of Surgery, 1987-96, Transplantation Procs., 1990-2001, Surgery, 1991-95, Cell Transplantation, 1991—, Postgrad. Gen. Surgery, 1991-95, Jour. ACS, 1994—, Annals of Surgery, 1995—; contbr. articles to profl. jours. and textbooks. Markle Found. Scholar, 1968-74; NIH grantee, 1974—; recipient Merit award NIH, 1987-95. Fellow AOA, NAS (Inst. Medicine), ACS (com. Forum on Fundamental Surg. Problems 1983-88, vice chmn. 1987-88, bd. govs. 1994-2001, pres. Phila. chpt. 1991-92), Coll. Physicians Phila., Royal Coll. Surgeons Eng. (hon.), Royal Coll. Surgeons Ireland (hon.); mem. AMA, Royal Coll. Surgeons of Ireland (hon.), Assn. Acad. Surgery, Am. Diabetes Assn., Am. Soc. Artificial Internal Organs, Am. Fedn. Clin. Rsch., Juvenile Diabetes Found., Soc. Univ. Surgeons, Am. Surg. Assn. (recorder 1991-96, pres. 1996-97), Soc. Clin. Surgery (chmn. membership 1984-85), Halsted Soc. (chmn. membership 1984-85, v.p. 1985-86, pres. 1986-87), Surg. Biology Club II, Soc. Vascular Surgery, Internat. Cardiovascular Soc., Internat. Surg. Group (treas. 1988-94, pres. 1994-95), Internat. Soc. Surgery (v.p. U.S. chpt. 1995-97, pres. 1997-99), Transplantation Soc. (councilman 1978-84, 94—), Am. Soc. Transplant Surgeons (chmn. membership 1980-81, treas. 1988-91, pres. 1992-93), Unitd Network for Organ Sharing (v.p. 2001-02), (pres.2002-03), Am. Acad. Arts and Scis., Assn. Am. Physicians, Phila. Acad. Surgery (program chmn. 1984-86, v.p. 1986-88, pres. 1988-89), Greater Delaware Valley Soc. Transplant Surgeons (pres. 1978-80), Am. Philos. Soc. (coun. 2003—). Home: 3 Coopertown Rd Haverford PA 19041-1012 Office: Hosp Univ Pa Dept Surgery 3400 Spruce St Philadelphia PA 19104-4206

BARKER, DAVID MATTHEW, music educator; b. Charlton Heights, W.Va., Apr. 13, 1965; s. George Peter and Jeanette Ann (Engelking) Barker; m. April Rockstead, Aug. 5, 1995. MusB, U. Wis., 1988. Cert. tchr. Wis. Dept. Pub. Instrn. Music tchr. Milw. Pub. Schs., 1988—90; band dir. Clinton (Iowa) Pub. Schs., 1990—91; music tchr. Madison (Wis.) Sch. Dist., 1991—92; band dir. Lourdes Acad., Oshkosh, Wis., 1992—95, Arlington Heights (Ill.) Sch. Dist., 1995—96, Notre Dame Acad., Green Bay, Wis., 1995—98, 2001—03, Edgewood H.S., Madison, 1999—2001, Fall River (Wis.) Pub. Schs., 2003—. Pres. Milw. Music Dirs. Assn., 1989—90; music dir. Regimental Vol. Band Wis., Dousman, Wis., 1994—. First E-flat cornet First Brigade Band, Watertown, Wis., 1988—95. Mem.: Wis. Music Educators Assn., Music Educators Nat. Conv. Avocations: Civil War history, music. Office: Fall River Pub Schs PO Box 118 Fall River WI 53932

BARKER, DONALD DEWAYN, psychotherapist; b. Fairmont, W.Va., July 10, 1945; s. Wayne Everson and Ruth Brown Barker. BA, W.Va. U., 1967; postgrad., U. Utah, 1967-69, 73; MA, Columbia Pacific U., 1985, PhD, 1987; MBA, Calif. Pacific U., 1989. Lic. profl. counselor; cert. clin. addictions counselor; diplomate in psychotherapy Clin. assoc. Bette Ann Weinstein, ASCW, Chevy Chase, Md., 1975-77; adminstrv. dir., therapist Turn About Counseling Ctr., Seaford, Del., 1976-78; program dir. Western Dist. Guidance Ctr., Parkersburg, W.Va., 1978-87; counselor, therapist So. Highlands CMHC, Princeton, W.Va., 1987—. Human rels. cons. Don Barker & Assocs., 1974—. Contbr. articles to profl. jours. Del. W.Va. Dem. Party Conv., Charleston, 1996; cons. Charlotte Pritt for Gov., Charleston, 1992, 96. With USN, 1969-72. Mem. Assn. for Humanistic Psychology, W.Va. Counseling Assn., Am. Psychotherapy Assn. Avocations: dog, practicing alternative medicine, meeting people with alternative life styles. Home: PO Box 5333 Princeton WV 24740-5333

BARKER, EDWIN BOGUE, musician; b. Tucson, Apr. 14, 1954; s. Francis Hustis and Mary Jeanne (Austin) B.; m. Pamela Paikin, 1980; children: Rachel Leigh, Ilana Michelle. Studies with Henry Portnoi, Peter Mercurio, Angelo LaMariana, Richard Stephan, David Perleman, 1965-76; MusB with honors, New Eng. Conservatory Music, 1976. Prin. bass Lake George Opera Orch., N.Y., 1971-72; substitute mem. N.Y. Philharm., 1976; prin. bass Lake George Opera Orch., N.Y., 1971-72; mem. Chgo. Symphony Orch., 1976-77; prin. bass Boston Symphony, 1977—; mem. Boston Symphony Chamber Players, 1977—; instr. double bass New Eng. Conservatory Music, 1977-90, 98—, Boston Conservatory Music, 1980-83; instr. double bass and chamber music Berkshire Music Ctr. (Tanglewood), 1978—; tchg. assoc. double bass Boston U., 1983—. Bass and string clinics Am. String Tchrs. Assn. and U. Mich., Ann Arbor, 1982, 83; instr. double bass Teton Orchestral Tng. Seminar, Wyo., 1984-86; mem. player's com. Boston Symphony Orch., 1989-93; prin. bass and faculty mem. Georg Solti Orchestral Tng. Project, Carnegie Hall, 1994—; prin. bass UN Orchestra Musicians of the World, Geneva, 1995—; master classes U. Ga., 1997, Juilliard Sch., 1999. Solo appearances with Boston Symphony Orch., Tanglewood, New England Conservatory Symphony Orch., Bergen (Norway) Music Festival, others; concerto performance with Boston Symphony, Madrid, 1993; other performances include: Concerto for Double Bass and Chamber Orch. by Gunther Schuller, Boston premiere with Pro Arte Chamber Orch., 1987, Concerto for Double Bass and Chamber Orch. by James Yannatos, premiere performance, 1986, Concerto for Double Bass and Orchestra by Edward Tubin, with Boston Symphony Orch., Boston premiere, 1994, Juilliard Quartet, Libr. of Congress, 1992, Muir Quartet, 1998, 99, premiere performance James Yannatos' Variations for Solo Contrabass, 1998, premier performance with Lydian String Quartet of Serenade in D by Harold Shapiro, for String Quartet and Double bass, 1999, World Premiere of Concertino for Double Bass and Chamber Orch. with Pro Arte Chamber Orch., 2000; soloist with Boston Symphony Orch., 2001; recs. include Three Sonatas for Double Bass, 1998, Variations for Solo Contrabass, 2000. Mem. Players com. Boston Symphony, 1988-92. Recipient Benjamin H. Delson award Berkshire Music Ctr., 1975; named one of Outstanding Young Men of Am., 1986, Most Outstanding Alumni New Eng. Conservatory of Music, 1993. Mem. Am. Fedn. Musicians., Internat. Soc. Bassists (dir. 1983) Office: CAMI Foster Division 165 W 57th St New York NY 10019-2201

BARKER, HAROLD GRANT, surgeon, educator; b. Salt Lake City, June 10, 1917; s. Frederick George and Elizabeth Jennetta (Stephens) B.; m. Kathleen Butler, July 29, 1949; children: Janet Stephens, Douglas Reid. AB, U. Utah, 1939, postgrad., 1939-41; MD, U. Pa., 1943. Diplomate Am. Bd. Surgery. Intern. Hosp. U. Pa., 1943-44, asst. resident in surgery, 1947-51, sr. resident in surgery, 1951-52, asst. attending surgeon, 1952-53; also asst. instr., research fellow U. Pa., 1946-51, instr., research fellow, 1951-52, assoc. in surgery, 1952-53; asst. prof. surgery Columbia U., 1953-57, assoc. prof., 1957-68, prof., 1968-82, prof. emeritus, 1982—. Asst. attending surgeon Presbyn. Hosp., 1953-57, assoc. attending surgeon, 1957-69, attending surgeon, 1969-89, cons. surgeon, 1989—, dir. med. affairs, 1974-82; pvt. practice, Phila., 1952-53, N.Y.C., 1953-88. Contbr. articles med. jours. Served from 1st lt. to capt., M.C. AUS, 1944-46, ETO. Fellow ACS; mem. Soc. U. Surgeons, N.Y. Surg. Soc., Am. Physiol. Soc., Soc. Exptl. Biology and Medicine, AMA, Halsted Soc., N.Y. State (chmn. surg. sect. 1961-62), N.Y. County med. socs., Am. Surg. Assn., N.Y. Gastroent. Assn., Société Internationale de Chirurgie, Soc. Surgery Alimentary Tract, Allen O. Whipple Surg. Soc., Am. Assn. History Medicine, Collegium Internationale Chirurgiae Digestivae, Century Assn., Manursing Island Club, Am. Yacht Club. Home: 1 Forest Ave Rye NY 10580-4209

BARKER, HAROLD KENNETH, former university dean; b. Louisville, Apr. 14, 1922; s. J.M. and Fannie Mae (Elliott) B.; m. Elizabeth Johns, Mar. 11, 1948 (dec.); children: Leslie Ann, Glenn Lewis.; m. Beverly Williams, Feb. 28, 1984. AB, U. Louisville, 1948, MA, 1949; PhD, U. Mich., 1959. Instr. Gunfire Prep. Sch., Hanau, Germany, 1946; sch. psychologist, vis. tchr. Bay City (Mich.) Pub. Schs., 1949-52; also instr. Bay City Jr. Coll.; sch. psychologist Ypsilanti (Mich.) Pub. Schs., 1952-53; instr. Eastern Mich. U., 1954-58; asst. dir. Bur. Appointments and Occupational Info., U. Mich., 1954-59; assoc. exec. sec. Am. Assn. Colls. Tchr. Edn., Washington, 1959-66, dir., 1972—; dean Coll. Edn., U. Akron, 1966-85, asst. to pres., 1985-87, dean emeritus, 1987. Bd. dirs. World U., San Juan, P.R., 1966—, Joint Council Econ. Edn., 1979 Editor: AACTE Handbook of International Education Programs, 1963; contbr. articles to profl. jours. and periodicals. Chmn. bd. dirs. Edwin Shaw Hosp., 1989; trustee U. Akron Found., 1994—. Recipient award outstanding profl. svc. Am. Assn. Colls. Tchr. Edn., 1966; named Hon. Alumni U. Akron, 1992. Mem. Phi Delta Kappa (internat. commn. 1962-69) Home: 1811 Brookwood Dr Akron OH 44313-5061 Office: Dept Devel Martin Univ Ctr U Akron Akron OH 44325-2603

BARKER, HILDA JEAN, retired library director; b. New Hill, N.C., Aug. 12, 1938; d. John Hollie and Vila Belle (Melton) Barker; children: Rheth Alexander Fish, Hollie Ann Fish. BS, East Carolina U., 1960; MS in Edn., N.C. Agrl. and Tech. U., 1979; MLS, U. N.C., Greensboro, 1990. Cert. librarian, N.C. Bus. tchr. Contentnea H.S., Kinston, N.C., 1960-61; math. tchr. Great Bridge (Va.) Jr. H.S., 1961-62; spl. edn. tchr. Craddock Jr. H.S., Portsmouth, Va., 1962-63; sec. Dan River Mills, Danville, Va., 1963-64; bus. tchr. Bartlett Yancey H.S., Yanceyville, N.C., 1964-67, Rockingham C.C., Wentworth, N.C., 1967-72; dir. vols. Annie Penn Meml. Hosp., Reidsville, N.C., 1973-78; librarian Caswell County Schs., Yanceyville, 1978-87; bibliographer Elem. Sch. Libr. Collection, Greensboro, 1987-89; reference librarian Franklin County Libr., Louisburg, N.C., 1991, libr. dir., 1991-2001. Contbr. video revs. to Libr. Jour. Treas. Franklin County Partnership for Children, Louisburg, 1994—2001; ch. vol., 2001—. Avocations: sewing, crafts. E-mail: hildajeanbarker@aol.com.

BARKER, JAMES REX, water transportation executive, director; b. Cleve., Aug. 3, 1935; s. William Wardel and Elizabeth Ranghild (Wandler) B.; m. Kaye Elizabeth Schumacher, Aug. 3, 1957; children: James Arthur, Karen Elizabeth, Mark William. BA, Columbia U., 1957; MBA with distinction, Harvard U., 1963; DSc (hon.), Maine Maritime Acad., 1978. Planning exec. Pickands Mather & Co., Cleve., 1963-67; v.p. Harbridge House, Boston, 1967-69; founder, exec. v.p. Temple, Barker & Sloane, Wellesley, Mass., 1970-71; chmn. bd. Moore McCormack Resources, Inc., Stamford, Conn., 1971-87, chief exec. officer, 1971-87; vice chmn., founder, co-owner Mormac Marine Group Inc., Stamford, Conn., 1987—; chmn., prin. Interlake Steamship Co., Stamford, 1987—. Vice chmn., prin. owner Moran Towing Co.; bd. dirs. Brink's Co., Verizon. Lt. (j.g.) USCG, 1975-61. Mem. Am. Bur. Shipping (bd. mgrs.) Clubs: Wee Burn Country, Noroton Yacht, N.Y. Yacht, Rolling Rock, Union, Links. Episcopalian. Home: 180 Long Neck Point Rd Darien CT 06820-5816 Office: Mormac Marine Group Inc Ste 300 1 Landmark Sq Stamford CT 06901-2501

BARKER, KEITH RENE, investment banker; b. Elkhart, Ind., July 28, 1928; s. Clifford C. and Edith (Hausmna) B.; children by previous marriage: Bruce C., Lynn K.; m. Elizabeth S. Arrington, Nov. 24, 1965; 1 child, Jennifer Scott. AB, Wabash Coll., 1950; MBA, Ind. U., 1952. Sales rep. Fulton, Reid & Co., Inc., Ft. Wayne, Ind., 1951-55, office, 1955-59, asst. v.p. then v.p., 1960, dir., 1961, asst. sales mgr., 1963, sales mgr., 1964, dir. Ind. ops.; sr. v.p. Fulton, Reid & Co., 1966-75; pres., CEO Fulton, Reid & Staples, Inc., 1975-77; ptnr. William C. Roney & Co., 1977-79; exec. com. Cascade Industries, Inc.; assoc. A.G. Edwards & Sons, Inc., 1984-89, v.p. investments, 1989—. Dir. Fulton, Reid & Staples, Inc., Craft House Corp., Nobility Homes, Inc. Pres. Historic Ft. Wayne, Inc.; cons. to Mus. Historic Ft. Wayne; nominee, trustee Ohio Hist. Soc.; mem. Smithsonian Assocs.; mem. fin. com. E. Tenn. Hist. Soc., dir., treas. collections com.; v.p. Ft. Wayne Hist. Soc.; bd. dirs. Ft. Wayne YMCA, 1963-64. Recipient Achievement cert. Inst. Investment Banking, U. Pa., 1959. Mem. Alliance Française, VFW (past comdr.), Co. Mil. Historians, Cleve. Grays, Am. Soc. Arms Collectors, 1st Cleve. Cavalry Assn., Nat. Assn. Securities Dealers (bus. conduct com.), Beaver Creek Hunt Club, Cleve. Athletic Club, Rockwell Springs Club, Hill and Dale Club, Masons, Phi Beta Kappa. Episcopalian. Home: 16300 Mansion Cir Apts 1001 and 1005 Independence MO 64055 Office: AG Edwards & Sons Inc 8848 Cedar Springs Ln Knoxville TN 37923-5408

BARKER, LARRY LEE, communications educator, educator; b. Wilmington, Ohio, Nov. 22, 1941; s. Milford and Ruth Maxine (Garringer) B.; children: Theodore Allen., Robert Milford. BA, Ohio U., 1962, MA, 1963, Ph. D, 1965. Asst. prof. So. Ill. U., Carbondale, 1965-66, Purdue U., West Lafayette, Ind., 1966-69; assoc. prof. Fla. State U., Tallahassee, 1969-71, prof., 1971-75; prof. emeritus Auburn (Ala.) U., 1995—. Pres. Spectra Inc., New Orleans, 1979—. Author: (with R. Kibler) Conceptual Frontiers in Speech Communication, 1969, Behavioral Objectives and Instruction, 1970, Listening Behavior, 1971, Speech Communication Behavior, 1971, Communication Vibrations, 1974, Speech—Interpersonal Communication, 1974, (with R. Edward) Intrapersonal Communication, 1980, (with R. Kibler) Objectives for Instruction and Evaluation, 1981, Communication, 1982, Communication in the Classroom, 1982, (with others) Effective Listening, 1982, (with L. Malandro) Nonverbal Communication, 1983, (with K. Wahlers) Groups in Process, 1983, (with others) Intrapersonal Communication Processes, 1987, (with K. Watson) Interpersonal and Relational Communications, 1989, Listen Up, 2000, Fishing Florida's Top Ten Bass Lakes: Vol. I, 2003; contbr. articles to profl. jours. Recipient outstanding award in discussion Tau Kappa Alpha, 1962, outstanding tchr. award Central States Speech Assn., 1969. Mem. APA, ASTD, Speech Comm. Assn. (Robert J. Kibler Meml. award 1986), Internat. Comm. Assn. (v.p. 1972-74), Internat. Listening Assn. (chmn. rsch. com. 1979-82, pres. 1986-87). Home: 30617 US Hwy 19 N Ste 630 Palm Harbor FL 34684 E-mail: lbarker933@cs.com.

BARKER, LLYLE JAMES, JR., management consultant, journalism educator; b. Columbus, Ohio, July 28, 1932; s. Llyle James and Mabel Lucile (Johnson) B.; m. Maxine Ruth Metcalf, Jan. 15, 1956; children: Llyle J., Daryl Alan. BS, Ohio State U., 1954, postgrad., U. Wis., 1961; MS in Mass. Comm., Shippensburg State Coll., 1975. Commd. officer U.S. Army, advanced through grades to maj. gen.; served in Korea, Vietnam, Thailand and Germany; pub. affairs officer Hawaii, 1957-59, NORAD, 1961-63, Dept. Army, 1966-69, 7th Army, 1969-71, Joint Casualty Resolution Ctr., 1974, European Command, 1975-77, U.S. Army Europe, 1979-80; dep. chief info. Dept. Army, 1980-81, chief pub. affairs, 1981-84; prof. Sch. Journalism Ohio State U., Columbus, 1984-98. Cons. mgmt. comm.; assoc. Gannett Ctr. Media Studies (now Freedom Forum Media Studies Ctr.), Columbia U. Contbr. articles to profl. jours. Decorated D.S.M., Legion of Merit, others. Mem. World Future Soc., Pub. Rels. Soc. Am., Assn. Edn. Journalism and Mass Comm. Home: 6844 Chateau Chase Dr Columbus OH 43235-3942 Office: Ohio State U Sch Journalism 242 W 18th Ave Columbus OH 43210-1107 E-mail: llylej@aol.com.

BARKER, MICHAEL, social scientist; b. N.Y.C., Nov. 22, 1949; s. Norman Mayford and Rosalie Estelle Barker; m. Sabrina Michelle Miller-Barker; children: Malcolm, Michael. BA, SUNY, Albany, 1979. Dir. food svcs. Richard Femster Meml. Bldg., N.Y.C., 1987—88, HIV/AIDS unit coord., 1988—94, supr. treatment, 1994—96, dir. treatment, 1996—97, supr. counselors, 1997—99, dir. data info., 1999—2000; free-lance writer, founder, pres. Michael Barker Enterprises, N.Y.C., 2000—. Author: A Peek With Mauk, 1975, The King Still Reigns Amidst The Pains, 1996, From Slauby to Food Stamps, 2000. Named Gaylor S. White scholar, East Larley/Union Settlement, 1977. Mem.: Prince Hall Masons (poet laureate 1997—). Avocations: poetry, public speaking. Home: 225 E 106th St #12B New York NY 10029 Office: Richard Feimster Meml Bldg 2015 Madison Ave New York NY

BARKER, NANCY LEPARD, university official; b. Owosso, Mich., Jan. 22, 1936; d. Cecil L. and Mary Elizabeth (Stuart) Lepard; m. J. Daniel Cline, Jun 6, 1960 (div. 1971); m. R. William Barker, Nov. 18, 1972; children: Mary Georgia Harker, Mark L. Cline, Richard E., Daniel P., Melissa B. Van Arsdel, John C. Cline MD, Helen Grace Garrett, Wiley D., James G. BSc, U. Mich., Ann Arbor, 1957; DHum, Northwood U., 2001. Spl. edn. instr. Univ. Hosp. U. Mich., Ann Arbor, 1958-61; v.p. Med. Educator, Chgo., 1967-69; asst. to chmn., dir. careers for women Northwood U., Midland, Mich., 1970-77, asst. prof., chmn. dept. fashion mktg. and merchandising, 1972-77, dir. arts programs and external affairs, 1972-77, v.p. univ. rels., 1978-2001, office of the pres., 2001—. Cons. and lectr. in field. Co-author: (children's books) Wendy Well Series, 1970-72; contbr. chpts. to books, articles to profl. jours. Advisor Mich. Child Study Assn., 1972—; chmn. Matrix: Midland Festival, 1978; bd. dirs. Nat. Coun. of Women, 1971—, pres., 1983-85, chmn. centennial com., 1988; mem. exec. bd. Mich. ACE Network for Women Leaders in Higher Edn., 2001—; bd. dirs. ArtServe, Mich., Family and Children's Svcs., Internat. Coun. Women, Paris. Nominee, (3) Mich. Women's Hall of Fame; named 1st ann. Disting. Educator of Yr., Am. Coun. on Edn., 2001; named one of Outstanding Young Women in U.S. and Mich., 1974; recipient Hon. award, Ukrainian Nat. Women's League, 1983, Disting. Woman award, Northwood U., 1970, Outstanding Young Woman award, Jr. C. of C., 1974. Mem. Internat. Coun. Women (bd. dirs. Paris 1991—), The Fashion Group, Internat. Furnishings and Design Assn. (pres. Mich. chpt. 1974-77), Mich. Women's Studies Assn. (founding mem.), Arts Midland Coun. (pres. 2 terms, 25th Anniversary award), Internat. Women's Forum, Mich. Women's Forum, Contemporary Rev. Club, Midland County Lawyers' Wives, Zonta, Phi Beta Kappa, Phi Kappa Phi, Alpha Lambda Delta, Phi Lambda Theta, Phi Gamma Nu, Delta Delta Delta. Home: 209 Revere St Midland MI 48640-4255 Office: Northwood U Office of the Pres Midland MI 48640-2398 E-mail: barkermid@aol.com., barker@northwood.edu.

BARKER, OREL O'BRIEN, retired activity and social service director; b. Wis., June 6, 1918; d. Otto Fahrenkrug and Margaret (Berg) Machenske; m. Wilbert Ervin O'Brien, Sept. 20, 1935 (dec. Aug. 1965); children: Marilyn, Maureen, Marleen, Merridith, Wilbert Jr., Margaret. Lic. activity dir., activity dir. coord., social svc. coord., Ind. U., 1975. Occupl. therapy asst. Westview Nursing Home, Racine, Wis., 1971-73; occupl. therapist asst. Pine Manor Nursing Home, Clintonville, Wis., 1973-75; activity dir. Rynard Ent., Indpls., 1975-85; ret., 1985. Author, poet: Echo' of the Heart, 1990, Sunshine and Shadows, 1995; contbr. poetry to various publs. Active St. Stephen's Luth. Ch. Named Activity Dir. of the Yr., Ind. Health Care, 1985. Mem. Wis. Fellowship Poets, Westview Retirement Club. Home: 1628 N Auburn St Indianapolis IN 46224-5709

BARKER, PETER EUGENE, biologist, researcher; b. Ithaca, NY, May 30, 1951; s. Eugene Gilbert Hammond and Mary Lesyk Barker; m. Soni Jo Anderson, Oct. 2, 1983; 1 child, Lydia Rachel. AB in Biol. Scis., Cornell U., Ithaca, NY, 1973; MS in Biol. Scis., U. Tex., Houston, 1978, PhD in Biomed. Scis., 1981. Postdoctoral fellow in biology Yale U., 1980—85; asst. med. educator U. Ala., Birmingham, 1985—91; guest rschr. German Cancer Rsch. Ctr., Heidelberg, Germany, 1991—93; staff scientist Cold Spring Harbor Lab., Cold Spring Harbor, NY, 1993—96; project leader NIST, Gaithersburg, Md., 1997—. Office: NIST-NCI Biomarker Validation Lab; Biote 100 Bureau Drive Gaithersburg MD 20899-8311 Office Fax: 301-975-8967. E-mail: peter.barker@nist.gov.

BARKER, REX J. music educator; b. Omaha, Nebr., Oct. 13, 1959; s. James R. and Noreen M. Barker; m. Mary J. Barker, Aug. 13, 1982; children: Joshua, Erin. MME, U. of Nebr., Omaha, 1991—99; BA, U. of Nebr., Kearney, 1977—81. Professional Nebr., 1982. Dir. of bands NW H.S., Grand Island, Nebr., 1982—89; dir. of bands & dept. chair Millard South H.S., Omaha, Nebr., 1989. Pres. Nebr. State Bandmasters Assn., Nebr., 1999—2001. Mem.: Music Educators Assn., Nebr. State Bandmasters Assn. (pres. 1999—2001). Achievements include 50 Directors Who Make Difference Band & Orchestra Magazine. Home: 4204 S 148th St Omaha NE 68137 Office: Millard South High School 14905 Q St Omaha NE 68137 Office Fax: 402-895-8472. E-mail: rbarker@mpsomaha.org.

BARKER, RICHARD ALEXANDER, organizational psychologist; b. San Diego, Aug. 11, 1947; s. Alexander Markewich and Donna Lee Barker; m. Barbara Yvonne Schutt, Aug. 1, 1987; children: Jaime Lynn, Cory Richard AB in Psychology, San Diego State U., 1974, MS in Indsl. and Organizational Psychology, 1976, EdD, U. San Diego, 1990. Statis. analyst U.S. Navy Pers. R & D Center, San Diego, 1974-75; pers. and testing analyst City of San Diego, San Diego, 1976, cons. various orgns., 1976-78; employment mgr. Computer Scis. Corp., San Diego, 1978; indsl. psychologist Gen. Dynamics Corp., San Diego, 1978-91; instr. music San Diego City Coll., 1976-91; lectr. psychology, mgmt. sci., stats., orgnl. behavior U. Redlands, 1978-91; asst. prof. bus., chair mgmt. dept. Marist Coll., Poughkeepsie, N.Y., 1991-98; assoc. prof. bus. Clarke Coll., Dubuque, Iowa, 1998-2000, Upper Iowa Univ., Fayette, Iowa, 2000—. Author: On the Nature of Leadership, Horse's Hoofs, At Story Time - The Story of Charles COleman Parker and Upper Iowa University; mem. editl. bd. Jour. Leadership Studies, 1994—; contbr. articles to profl. jours. Bd. dirs. San Diego Youth Svcs., Inc., chmn. pers. com., 1978-81. Served with USNR, 1968-69 Mem. APA, Computer Automated Systems Assn./Soc. Mfg. Engrs., Nat. Mgmt. Assn., Am. Fedn. Musicians, Psi Chi. Office: Upper Iowa Univ 605 Washington St Fayette IA 52142

BARKER, ROBERT JEFFERY, financial executive; b. Glendale, Calif., Feb. 22, 1946; s. Albert and Margaret E. (Windle) B.; m. Ildiko Barker, Jan. 1, 1989; 1 child, Alexander A. BSEE, UCLA, 1968, MBA, 1970. Cert. mgmt. acctg. Cost analyst Lockheed, Sunnyvale, Calif., 1976-78; from cost acctg. supr. to fin. systems mgr. Monolithic Memories Inc., Sunnyvale, 1976-84; dir. fin. Waferscale Integration, Inc., Fremont, Calif., 1984-88, v.p. fin., CFO, 1988-94; CFO Micrel, San Jose, Calif., 1994, v.p. corp. bus. devel., 1999—. Bd. dirs., treas. Am. Electronics Assn. Credit Union, Santa Clara, Calif., 1988—, bd. chmn., 1991; dir. Monolithic Memories Integration Fed. Credit Union, Sunnyvale, 1977-84, pres. 1983-84. Dir. Vets. Task Force, Palo Alto, Calif., 1980-87, pres. 1987. Capt. USAF, 1970-74. Mem. Nat. Assn. Accts., Fin. Execs. Inst., Toastmasters (pres. 1986-87). Republican. Presbyn. Avocations: beach doubles volleyball, jogging, sports. Home: 1 Winchester Dr Atherton CA 94027-4040

BARKER, ROBERT OSBORNE (BOB BARKER), educator, mediator; b. Cleve., June 13, 1932; m. Sharon Ann (div.); children: Debra, Stephen, Dawn, Michael, Colleen. Student, Henry Ford C.C., 1950; BA in Comm. Arts and Sci., Mich. State U., 1954; LLB, LaSalle U., 1969; postgrad., U. Wis., 1989, U. Fla., 1996, postgrad., 2000—03. Lic. cmty. assn. mgr. 1993—, real estate agent; registered lobbyist Nat. Assn. Mfrs. 1972-87; cert. ct./pvt. mediator Alternative Dispute Resolution, 1995—. With pub. rels. dept. Ford Motor Co., Dearborn, Mich., 1953; mgr. Kaiser Aluminum Co., Chgo., 1956-58; advt. mgr. Bastian Blessing Co., Chgo., 1958-59; mgr., regional mgr. Sun Oil Co., Ohio and Detroit, 1959-71; mgr. Goodyear Tire & Rubber Co., Detroit, 1971-72; mgr., v.p. Nat. Assn. Mfrs., Washington, Boston and Detroit, 1972-87, pres., CEO Barker Cons. Inc., 1987-96; mgr., v.p. seminars and materials dept. Am. Supplier Inst. (div. of FoMoCo), 1987-90; nat. mdse./mktg. mgr. Costa del Mar Sunglasses, Ormond Beach, Fla., 1990-91; resort mgr. Oceanside 99 Condo, Ormond Beach, Fla., 1992-93, Outrigger Beach Club, Ormond Beach, Fla., 1994-95. Adj. prof. pub. rels., advt., retailing, sales fundamentals, global and internat. mktg., quality svc. mgmt. Daytona Beach C.C., 1994—; owner Dolphin Beach Club Condo, 1981-2001, bd. dirs., 1991-99. Twp. trustee, Findlay, Ohio, 1962; lay min. Episcopal ch., 1960-85, vestry, 1981-2001; mem. exec. bd. dirs. Volusia County Rep., 1991-2000; bd. dirs. Am. Cancer Soc., 1991—; bd. dirs. Dearborn Civic Theatre, 1980-84, Volusia Presdl. forum, 1991-99, Dearborn City Beautiful commr. emeritus, 1970-90; commr. Ormond Beach Quality of Life, Beautification and Planning bds., 1990-99; mem. adv. coun. bd. Habitat Humanity, 1995-99; res. police officer, Dearborn, 1968-88; pres. Dearborn High and Lindbergh Elem. PTA; bd. dirs. Bldg. Assn. Mgrs., 1991-95, Cmty. assoc. Inst., 1993-97, Volusia County Pers. Bd., 1991-93; mem. adv. coun. bd. Coun. of Aging, 1991-2000; mem. Fla. Police Benevolent Assn., Fla. Sheriffs Assn.; bd. dirs. Daytona and Ormond Beach Rep. Club, 1991-99, heritage mem. Ormond Meml. Art Mus., 1991-2001; amb. Daytona Internat. Airport, 1996-2002; team selection scout Fla. Citrus Sports for New Year's Bowl football game, Orlando, Fla., 1997—; mem. elder voice focus group

Genesis Elder Care, 2001; asst. publicity dir. bd. dirs. Ormond Sr. Games, 1994-96. Served with USNR, 1949-58, AFROTC, 1951-54. Recipient Vol. of Yr. award Am. Cancer Soc., 1998. Mem. Advt. Fedn., Assn. Execs., Am. Heart Assn. (bd. dirs. Volusia/Flagler 2002-), Fla. Pub. Rels. Soc. (Volusia chpt., former v.p. bd. dirs. 1996-98), Am. Legion (life), Mich. State U. Alumni (life, past. pres. 4 alumni clubs), Mich. State Varsity Alumni Club (life), U. Fla. Alumni Assn. (bd. dir. 1997- Gator Club Volusia County, v.p. edn. 1999-2002), Ormond Beach C. of C. (former amb., chmn. pub. rels. Beautification, JazzMatazz, social com. 1990-2002), Nat. Assn. Sr. Friends of Volusia/Flagler Counties (pres. 2000—), Ormond Shrine Club (pres. 1994-95), Elks, Exch. Club, Rotary (pres. 1987-88), Masons, Moose-Legion, Shriners (dir. pub. rels. 1984, provost unit, Fez on Wheels and Vets. unit), Delta Tau Delta. Home: Unit 613 229 S Ridgewood Ave Daytona Beach FL 32114-4334 E-mail: bobbarker13_99@yahoo.com., robert_barker42@falconmail.dbcc.edu.

BARKER, ROBERT WILLIAM, television personality; b. Darrington, Wash., Dec. 12, 1923; s. Byron John and Matilda Kent (Tarleton) B.; m. Dorothy Jo Gideon, Jan. 12, 1945 (dec. Oct. 1981). BA in Econs. summa cum laude, Drury Coll., 1947. Master of ceremonies: Truth or Consequences, Hollywood, Calif., 1957-75, Price is Right, 1972—, Miss Universe Beauty Pageant, 1966-87, Miss U.S.A. Beauty Pageant, 1966-87, Pillsbury Bake-Off, 1969-85, Bob Barker Fun and Games Show, 1978—; host: Rose Parade, CBS, 1969-88; appeared in (feature film) Happy Gilmore, 1996. Served to lt. (j.g.) USNR, 1943-45. Recipient Emmy award for Best Audience Participation Host, 1981-82, 83-84, 86-87, 87-88, 89-90, 90-91, 91-92, 93-94, 94-95, 95-96, 99-00, 00-01. Mem. AGVA, AFTRA, Screen Actors Guild. Office: The Price is Right care CBS TV 7800 Beverly Blvd Los Angeles CA 90036-2112

BARKER, SARAH EVANS, judge; b. Mishawaka, Ind., June 10, 1943; d. James McCall and Sarah (Yarbrough) Evans; m. Kenneth R. Barker, Nov. 25, 1972. BS, Ind. U., 1965, LLD (hon.), 1999; JD, Am. U., 1969; LLD (hon.), U. Indpls., 1984; D in Pub. Svc. (hon.), Butler U., 1987; LLD (hon.), Marian Coll., 1991; LHD, U. Evansville, 1993; LLD (hon.), Wabash Coll., 1999, Hanover Coll., 2001; D of Civil Law (hon.), 2003. Bar: Ind. 1969, U.S. Dist. Ct. (so. dist.) Ind., 1969, U.S. Ct. Appeals (7th cir.) 1973, U.S. Supreme Ct., 1978. Legal asst. to senator U.S. Senate, 1969-71; spl. counsel to minority, govt. ops. com. permanent investigations subcom., 1971-72; dir. rsch. scheduling and advance Senator Percy Re-election Campaign, 1972; asst. U.S. atty. So. Dist. Ind., 1972-76, 1st asst. U.S. atty., 1976-77, U.S. atty., 1981-84; judge U.S. Dist. Ct. (so. dist.) Ind., 1984-94, chief judge, 1994—2000. Assoc., then ptnr. Bose, McKinney & Evans, Indpls., 1977-81; mem. long range planning com. Jud. Conf. U.S., 1991-96, exec. com., 1989-91, standing com. fed. rules of practice and procedure, 1987-91, dist. judge rep., 1988-91; mem. jud. coun. 7th cir. Ct. Appeals, 1988-2000, jud. fellows commn. U.S. Supreme Ct., 1993-98; jud. adv. com., sentencing commn., 1995-97, bd. advisors, Ind. U., Purdue U., Indpls., 1989—; mem. pres.'s cabinet Ind. U., 1995—; bd. visitors Ind. U. Sch. of Law, Bloomington, 1984—; bd. dirs. Clarian Health Ptnrs., 1996—, Christian Theol. Sem., 1999-2001; bd. dirs. Einstein Inst. for Sci., Health and the Cts., 2001— Recipient Peck award Wabash Coll., 1989, Touchstone award Girls Club of Greater Indpls., 1989, Leach Centennial 1st Woman award Valparaiso Law Sch., 1993, Most Influential Women award Indpls. Bus. Jour., 1996, Paul Buchanan award of excellence Indpls. Bar Found., 1998, Thomas J. Hennessy award Ind. U., 1995, Disting. Citizen fellow Ind. U., 1999-2001; named Ind. Woman of Yr., Women in Comm., 1986, Ind. Univ. Disting. Alumni, 1996, Disting. Citizen fellow Ind. U., 1999-2001, Singing Hoosiers Disting. Alumni award Ind. U., 2000, Man for All Seasons award St. Thomas More Soc., 2000. Mem. ABA, Ind. Bar Assn., Indpls. Bar Assn. (Antoinette Dakin Leach award 1993), Fed. Judges Assn. (exec. com., bd. dirs. 2001—), Com. on Budget (judicial conf. 2001-), Einstein Inst. Sci., Health and Cts. (bd. dirs. 2001-), U.S. Judicial Conf. (spl. redaction rev. panel 2000-), Christian Theol. Sem. (bd. trustees 1999-), Lawyers Club, Kiwanis. Republican. Methodist. Office: US Dist Ct 210 US Courthouse 46 E Ohio St Indianapolis IN 46204-1903

BARKER, SYLVIA MARGARET, nurse; b. Glens Falls, N.Y., Sept. 11, 1914; d. Victor Howell and Julia Helen (Lansing) B. Student, Green Mountain Coll., 1933; diploma, Mt. Sinai Hosp. Sch. Nursing, 1936; BS, Columbia U., 1947, MA, 1951. RN, N.Y. Staff nurse Mt. Sinai Hosp., N.Y.C., 1936-37, gynecology head nurse, 1937-40, nursing arts asst. instr., 1940-41, nursing of children instr., 1941-45, nursing arts instr.-in-charge, 1945-48; instr. in charge nursing arts Michael Reese Hosp., Chgo., 1948-50; nursing of children supr. Mt. Sinai Hosp., N.Y.C., 1951-66, asst. dir. insvc. edn., 1966-72, assoc. dir. nursing, 1972-77, acting dir. nursing, assoc. dir. nursing, 1972, assoc. dir. nursing affairs, 1977-86, cons. nursing adminstrn., 1986-94. Hon. clin. assoc. faculty CUNY, 1984-87, 89-91; presenter SUNY, Downstate, 1982, N.Y. State Nurses Assn., 1982, Mt. Sinai Hosp., N.Y.C., 1983, 91, 92, United Hosp. Fund and Office of Profl. Discipline, N.Y.C., 1983, Cornell Med. Ctr., 1984, CCNY, 1984-91, Charleston W.Va. Eye, Ear, Nose and Throat Clinic, 1986, Hunter-Bellevue Sch. Nursing, 1987-91. Co-author: The Sinai Nurse; author: SMB-A Memoir, 2001; contbr. Bd. dirs. Nurses House, 1991—95, 2001—, sec., 1995—97, pres., 1997—2001. Recipient Alumni Achievement award Nursing Edn. Alumni Assn. Tchrs. Coll., 1994, Leadership in Profl. and Allied Orgns. Achievement award, 1999; writings and papers in Archives of Found. N.Y. State Nurses Assn., 1993; Guggenheim scholar Mt. Sinai Hosp. Sch. Nursing, 1936. Mem.: ANA (Coun. Nursing Adminstrn. Membership award 1998, Disting. Membership award 1998), N.Y. Counties RNs Assn. (bd. dirs. 1983—85, chair bylaws com. dist. 13 1983—91, exec. dir. 1993—94, search com., Recognition 50 Yr. Membership award 1989, Jane Delano Disting. Svc. award 1982), N.Y. State Nurses Assn. (bylaws com. 1982—85, nominating com. 1995, Nursing Svc. Adminstrn. award 1984, Recognition 50 Yr. Membership award 1986, Hon. Recognition award 1992), So. N.Y. League for Nursing, Nat. League for Nursing, Alumni Assn. of Mt. Sinai Hosp. Sch. Nursing (bd. dirs. 1981—84, pres. 1987—91, treas. 1991—95, sec. 1995—2002, bd. dirs. 2002—), Sigma Theta Tau. Avocations: ballet, philharmonic orchestra, reading, writing, collecting owls. Home and Office: 788 Columbus Ave Apt 6K New York NY 10025-5942

BARKER, THOMAS CARL, retired health care administration educator, executive; b. Cedar Rapids, Iowa, May 25, 1931; s. Carl Edward and Bertha Olive (Simons) B.; m. Mary Irene Beorkrem, Sept. 1, 1952 (dec. 1995); children: Cheryl Lynn, Thomas Carl Jr. (dec.), Laura Ann, David Edward; m. Patricia Blount Moore, May 2, 1998. Student, Loras Coll., 1949-50, Coe Coll., 1950-51; BS, U. Iowa, 1954, MA, 1960, PhD, 1963. Acct. Wilson & Co., Cedar Rapids, Iowa, 1951-54; contract adminstr. Collins Radio Co., Cedar Rapids, 1956-57; with customer rels. The Cryovac Co., Cedar Rapids, 1957-58; bus. officer Mercy Hosp., Iowa City, Iowa, 1958-59; rsch. asst. U. Iowa, 1959-60, tchg. asst., 1961-63, asst. prof., 1963-64; adminstrv. assoc. U. Iowa Hosp., 1960-62; rsch. assoc. UAW Internat. Union, Detroit, 1964-67; dir. Mich. Health and Social Security Rsch. Inst., Detroit, 1964-67; adj. assoc. prof. health econs. Wayne State U., Detroit, 1966-67; Arthur Graham Glasgow prof., dir. Sch. Hosp. Adminstrn. Med. Coll. Va., Richmond, 1967-71; prof., dean and CEO Sch. Allied Health Professions Va. Commonwealth U., Richmond, 1969-96, dean emeritus, prof. emeritus, 1996—. Mem. com. on allied health edn. and accreditation AMA, chmn. com., 1988-91; served as mem. or cons. to various pub. health svcs., including NIH, Health Resources Adminstrn., VA, HEW agys.; mem. dean's com. VA Med. Ctr., Richmond, 1974-96; mem. Ctrl. Va. Health Sys. Agy., 1976-88, pres., 1979-80; mem. Va. Health Coord. Coun., 1986-88. Contbr. articles to profl. jours. With USN, 1949-56; capt. Res., ret. Named Hon. Alumni, Med. Coll. Va. Fellow APHA, Am. Soc. Allied Health Professions (pres. 1975-76); mem. Am. Health Planning Assn., Assn. Univ. Programs in Health Adminstrn., Soc. Sons. Revolution in State of Va., Va. Assn. Allied Health Professions, Va. Hosp. Assn., Rotary (pres. Richmond club 1991-92), Phi Kappa Phi. Roman Catholic. Home: 2251 Winterfield Rd Midlothian VA 23113-4145 Office: The Grant House PO Box 980203 Richmond VA 23298-0203 Fax: 804-828-1894. E-mail: tcbarker@hsc.vcu.edu.

BARKER, VERLYN LLOYD, retired minister, educator; b. Auburn, Nebr., July 25, 1931; s. Jack Lloyd and Olive Clara (Bollman) B. AB, Doane Coll., 1952, DD, 1977; BD, Yale U., 1956, STM, 1960; postgrad., U. Chgo., 1960-61; PhD, St. Louis U., 1970. Ordained to ministry United Ch. of Christ, 1956. Instr. history, chaplain Doane Coll., Crete, Nebr., 1954-55; pastor U. Nebr., 1956-59; sec. ministry higher edn. United Ch. Bd. Homeland Ministries, N.Y.C., 1961-96, ret. Cleve., 1996. Author: Premises about Education, 1981, Creationism, the Church and Public Education, 1981, Health and Human Values: A Ministry of Theological Inquiry and Moral Discourse, 1987; editor: The Church and the Public School, 1980, Science, Technology and the Christian Faith, 1990; contbg. author: Campus Ministry, 1964, Religious Colleges in America: A Selected Bibliography, 1988, The New Faith-Science Debate, 1989; mem. editorial adv. com. Jour. Current Social Issues; contbr. articles to various publs. Pres. United Ministries in Higher Edn., N.Y.C., 1971-77. Mem.: ACLU, AAAS, Nat. Assn. for Sci., Tech. and Society, Soc. Health and Human Values, Am. Acad. Polit. and Social Sci., Acad. Polit. Sci., Am. Studies Assn., Am. Assn. Higher Edn., Doane Coll Alumni Assn. (pres. 1957—58), Yale Club N.Y.C.

BARKER, VIRGINIA LEE, nursing educator; Diploma, Ind. U. Sch. Nursing, 1952, BS, 1955, MS, 1961, EdD, 1969. Dean sch. nursing, prof. Alfred (N.Y.) U., 1969-78; prof., dean nursing U. Louisville, 1978-81; dean Mary Black Sch. Nursing, prof. U. S.C., Spartanburg, 1981-90; dean profl. studies, prof. nursing SUNY, Plattsburg, 1990-98; dir. virtual reality devel. Plattsburgh State U., New York, prof. nursing, 1998—. Cons. N.Y. Regents Coll. Nursing Program, 1972—91; project dir. federally funded telenursing project rural upstate N.Y., 1993—98; dir. project to develop virtual reality simulations edn. physicians, nurses, allied health pers., 1995—. Contbr. articles to profl. jours., papers nat. and internat. confs. Mem. ARC. Grantee Disting. Practitioners, N.Y. State Nurses Assn. Mem.: AAUW, ANA, Internat. Coun. of Nurses, S.C. Deans and Dirs. Nursing Fedn. (chair), Am. Assn. Higher Edn., S.C. League Nursing, Nat. League Nurses (com. mem.), N.Y. Nurses Assn. (pres.), Ind. U. Sch. Nursing Alumni Assn. (pres.), Kappa Delta Pi, Phi Kappa Phi, Sigma Theta Tau. E-mail: virginia.barker@plattsburgh.edu.

BARKER, WALTER LEE, thoracic surgeon; b. Chgo., Sept. 9, 1928; s. Samuel Robert, M.D., and Esther (Meyerovitz) B.; m. Betty Ruth Wood, Apr. 4, 1967 AB cum laude, Harvard U., 1949, MD, 1953. Diplomate Am. Bd. Surgery, Am. Bd. Thoracic Surgery. Intern, resident in gen. and thoracic surgery Cook County Hosp. and Presbyn. St. Luke's Med. Ctr. and affiliated hosps., Chgo., 1953-62; practice medicine specializing in thoracic surgery Chgo., 1962-95; clin. prof. surgery U. Ill.; prof. emeritus, 1998; head sect. thoracic surgery Cook County Hosp., 1972-93, cons. sect., 1993-98; chmn. dept. surgery St. Joseph Hosp., Chgo., 1982-97. Researcher on tuberculosis, pleural infections, lung cancer Author: The Post Operative Chest, 1977; editl. bd. Chest, 1984-89; cons. to editor, 1989—; contbr. articles to profl. jours. Served with M.C., USNR, 1955-57 Fellow Am. Coll. Chest Physicians (credentials com. 1984-89), ACS, mem. Am. Assn. Thoracic Surgery, AMA (rep. to HD of dels. 1988-94), Boylston Med. Soc., Chgo. Med. Soc., Ill. Med. Soc., Chest Club, Chgo. Surg. Soc. (v.p. 1990-91, chmn. membership com. 1991-92), Ill. Surg. Soc., Central Surg. Soc., Inst. Medicine, Soc. Thoracic Surgeons (founding mem., cons. editor Ann. Thoracic Surgery), Sigma Xi Home: 2912 N Commonwealth Ave Apt 11C Chicago IL 60657-6215 Fax: 773-525-0561. E-mail: b.b.barker@worldnet.att.net.

BARKER, WALTER WILLIAM, JR., artist, waiter; b. Coblenz, Germany, Aug. 8, 1921; s. Walter William and Selma Rosalie (Zinke) B.; children: Emily Croy, Michael Brendan. B.F.A., Washington U., 1948; M.F.A., Ind. U., 1950. Mem. faculty Sch. Art, Washington U., St. Louis, 1950-63, Bklyn. Mus. Sch., 1963-66; mem. faculty dept. art U. N.C., Greensboro, 1966—, prof., 1984-92, prof. emeritus, 1992, lectr. on art, 1992-99. Chmn. Venice Com., N.C., 1969-75. One-man shows include Otto Gerson Gallery, N.Y.C., 1959, Albert Landry Gallery, N.Y.C., 1963, Betty Parsons Gallery, N.Y.C., 1966, 69, Webster Coll., St. Louis, 1991, Weatherspoon Gallery U. N.C., Greensboro, 1994; represented in permanent collections U. Tex., Austin, Mus. Modern Art, N.Y.C., City Art Mus. of St. Louis, Washington U., St. Louis, L.A. County Mus., Phila. Mus. Fine Art, Boston Mus. Fine Art, Corcoran Gallery Art, Ark. Art Ctr., Little Rock, U. Minn., Mpls., U. Mass., Amherst, Hirschorn Mus., Washington, Libr. of Congress, Washington, St. Louis U., U. Mo., Columbia, Swan Hill Art Mus., Victoria, Australia; columnist on art St. Louis Post Dispatch, 1962-78. Served with AUS, 1942-45. Recipient Disting. Alumni citation Washington U., St. Louis, 1972 Episcopalian. Home: 1606 Walker Ave Greensboro NC 27403-2319 also: 39 Dogfish Head Rd West Southport ME 04576 Office: PO Box 207 West Southport ME 04576-0207 *As an artist I have found that search for self can only be undertaken successfully if there is deep respect for the visual world.*

BARKER, WILEY FRANKLIN, surgeon, educator; b. Santa Fe, Oct. 16, 1919; s. Charles Burton and Bertha (Steed) B.; m. Nancy Ann Kerber, June 8, 1943; children: Robert Lawrence, Jonathan Steed, Christina Lee. BS, Harvard, 1941, MD, 1944. Intern, then resident Peter Bent Brigham Hosp., Boston, 1944-46; Arthur Tracy Cabot fellow Harvard Med. Sch., 1948-49; asst. chief surg. service, then chief surg. sect. Wadsworth VA Hosp., Los Angeles, 1951-54, attending physician, 1951—; mem. faculty U. Calif. at Los Angeles Med. Sch., 1954—, prof. surgery, 1964-86, prof. emeritus, 1986—, chief div. gen. surgery, 1955-77; cons. Sepulveda VA Hosp., 1966-78, chief of staff, 1978-83. Mem. com. trauma NRC, 1964-68; mem. bd. advisors UCLA Med. Ctr., 1982—. Author: Surgical Treatment of Peripheral Vascular Disease, 1962, Peripheral Arterial Disease, 1966, 2d edit., 1976, Clio Chirugica: The Arteries, vols. I and II, 1992,, also papers, chpts. in books. Served as lt. (j.g.) M.C. USNR, 1946-47. Harvard Nat. scholar, 1937-44 Fellow ACS (2d v.p. 1986-87); mem. AMA, Am. Surg. Assn., Am. Bd. Surgery (diplomate, bd. dirs. 1964-70), Soc. Clin. Surgery (pres. 1972-74), Soc. Univ. Surgeons, Soc. Vascular Surgery (pres. 1972-73), Internat. Cardiovascular Soc. (v.p. N.Am. chpt. 1964-65, pres. 1979-80), So. Surg. Assn., Pacific Coast Surg. Assn. (pres. 1982-83), Pan Pacific Surg. Assn. (pres. 1986-88), Calif., Los Angeles County med. assns., Phi Beta Kappa, Sigma Xi, Alpha Omega Alpha. Republican. Episcopalian. Address: 29129 Paiute Dr Agoura CA 91301-2938 Office: Univ Calif Sch Medicine Dept Surgery Los Angeles CA 90024

BARKER, WILLIAM DANIEL, hospital administrator; b. New Orleans, July 21, 1926; s. William Daniel and Ada (Will) B.; m. Nancy Pool, Sept. 23, 1949; children: Nancy Louise, Julia Ann, William Daniel III, Marion DeVilbiss. B in Bus. Adminstrn., Emory U., 1949; M in Hosp. Adminstrn., Ga. State U., 1966. Bus. office mgr. Emory U. Hosp., Atlanta, 1949-50; asst. adminstr. Griffin (Ga.) Spalding County Hosp., 1950-51; adminstr. Winder-Barrow (Ga.) Hosp., 1951-52; hosp. field rep. Ga. Dept. Pub. Health, Atlanta, 1952-54, hosp. cons., 1954-55; asst. adminstr. Tri-County Hosp., Ft. Oglethorpe, Ga., 1955-60; asst. dir. Crawford Long Hosp. Emory U., Atlanta, 1960-73, adminstr., 1973-84, dir. hosps., 1984-90, exec. dir. hosp., 1987-90; ret., 1991; prof. Emory U., Atlanta, 1988-93. Bd. dirs. Ga. Fed. Bank, Atlanta, Blue Cross Blue Shield Ga., Inc.; provider affairs com. Blue Cross Blue Shield Assn., United Network for Organ Sharing, bd. dirs., 1991—; bd. govs. SunHealth, Charlotte, N.C., chmn., 1988-89; bd. commrs. Joint Commn. on Accreditation of Healthcare Orgns., 1981-86; v.p. Greater Atlanta Coalition on Health Care, 1983-84; mem. Gov.'s Coun. Malpractice Ins., 1975-83, Medicaid Adv. Com. Ga. Dept. Human Resources, 1973-77, Health Facilities Planning Com. Met. Atlanta Coun. for Health, 1971-74, Atlanta Regional Commn. Emergency Med. Task Force 1969-73, Gov.'s Commn. on Nursing, 1970-71, adv. commn. Internat. Implant Registry, 1989—, vice-chmn., 1991, chmn., 1992; pres. Health Careers of Ga., Inc., 1969-70, Ga. Coun. Paramed. Edn., 1968. Contbr. articles to profl. jours. With U.S. Army, 1944-46. Recipient R.C. Williams award Ga. State U., 1966, Disting. Alumni award, Ga. State U., 1979, Disting. Svc. award. Ga. Med. Assn. Atlanta, 1980; Disting. Guest Lectr. Ga. State U., 1978. Fellow Am. Coll. Healthcare Execs. (regent 1972-75); mem. Am. Hosp. Assn. (chmn. 1979, Speaker of Ho. 1980, Disting. Svc. award 1987), Ga. Hosp. Assn. (pres. 1966-79, Gold Honor award of Excellence 1980), Ansley Golf Club. Baptist. Home: 50 S Prado NE Atlanta GA 30309-3309 E-mail: dbarker@emory.edu.

BARKER, WILLIAM M. state supreme court justice; b. Chattanooga, Sept. 13, 1941; married; 3 children. BS, U. Chatanooga, 1964; JD, U. Cin., 1967. Bar: Tenn. 1967. Pvt. practice, 1967-83; cir. ct. judge, 1983-95; justice Ct. of Appeals, 1995-98, Tenn. Supreme Ct., 1998—. Adj. prof. U. Tenn., Chatanooga, 1984—. Chmn. bd. deacons 1st Presbyn. Ch. Chattanooga, 1995-97. With USAMC, 1967-69. Fellow Tenn. Bar Found., Chattanooga Bar Found.; mem. Am. Legion, Alpha Soc., U. Tenn. Chattanooga Alumni Coun., Chattanooga Rotary Club. Office: Tenn Supreme Ct 540 Mccallie Ave Ste 410 Chattanooga TN 37402-2096*

BARKER, WILLIAM THOMAS, lawyer; b. Feb. 28, 1947; s. V. Wayne and Cordelia (Whitten) B.; m. June K. Robinson, Jan. 30, 1981. BS, MS, Mich. State U., 1969; JD, U. Calif., Berkeley, 1974. Bar: Calif. 1975, Ill. 1976. Assoc. programmer-analyst Control Data Corp., Sunnyvale, Calif., 1969-71; law clk. Pa. Supreme Ct., Erie, 1974-75; assoc. Sonnenschein Carlin Nath & Rosenthal, Chgo., 1975-82, ptnr., 1982—. Moderator Ill. Ins. Law Forum, Counsel Connect, 1994-98; co-moderator Nat. Ins. Law gen. forum, 1996-98; moderator Ins. Law Forum, Lexis One, 2001. Bd. editors: Def. Counsel Jour., 1987—; editor Bad Faith Law Report, 1999-2001, contbg. editor 1990-99; mem. editl. bd. Ins. Litigation Reporter, 1987—. editl. dir. and sr. contbg. editor, 2001—; editor Covered Events, 1995-96, editor emeritus, 1996—; ins. law publs. bd. Def. Rsch. Inst., 1992-97; contbr. articles to profl. jours. Fellow Am. Bar Found. (life); mem. ABA (chair-elect com. on appellate advocacy, tort and ins. practice sect. 1994-95, chair 1995-96, chair gen. comm. bd. 1996-97), Internat. Assn. Def. Counsel (Yancey Meml. award for best article 1995, chair spl. com. on Amicus Curie 1996-97, chair ad hoc com. on interstate practice 2000-03), Chgo. Coun. Lawyers (sec. 1987-88, bd. govs. 1989-91, chair com. profl. responsibility 1990-95), Chgo. Bar Assn. (chmn. com. constl. law 1984-85), Def. Rsch. Inst., Assn. Profl. Responsibility Lawyers (chair com. on internat. trade in legal svcs. 2002—), Am. Law Inst., Ill. Assn. Def. Trial Coun. Home: 132 E Delaware Pl Apt 5806 Chicago IL 60611-4951 Office: Sonnenschein Nath Et Al 8000 Sears Tower 233 S Wacker Dr Ste 8000 Chicago IL 60606-6491 E-mail: wtb@sonnenschein.com.

BARKER-BENFIELD, GRAHAM JOHN, historian; b. London, May 28, 1941; came to U.S., 1963; s. E. James and Eleanor (Sinfield) Barker-B.; 1 child, Chloe. BA with honours, Cambridge U., Eng., 1963; PhD with distinction, UCLA, 1968; MA (hon.), Cambridge U., 1968. Vis. asst. prof. Am. U., Washington, 1969-72, Lewis & Clark Coll., Portland, Oreg., 1972-74; asst. prof. SUNY, Albany, 1974-79, assoc. prof., 1979-93, prof., 1993—. Author: The Horrors of the Half-Known Life: Male Attitudes Towards Women and Sexuality in Nineteenth-Century America, 2000, The Culture of Sensibility: Sex and Society in Eighteenth-Century Britain, 1992; co-editor: Portraits of American Women: From European Settlement to the Present, 1998, Sensibility in An Oxford Companion to the Romantic Age: British Culture 1776-1832, 1999, The Origins of Anglo-American Sensibility in Charity, Philanthropy and Civility in American History, 2003. Office: Dept of History Suny At Albany Albany NY 12222-0001

BARKER-NUNN, JEANNE BEVERLY, English educator; b. Mpls., Nov. 24, 1946; d. Paul Barker and Beverly Jeanne (Nunn) Johnson; m. Lee Gordon Hesselroth, Nov. 26, 1982; children: Tyler Hesselroth, Andrew Hesselroth. BS in English, U. Minn., 1968, MA in English, E. Carolina U., 1977, PhD in Am. Studies, U. Minn., 1985. Instr. U. Minn., Mpls., 1977-85, E. Carolina U., Greenville, N.C., 1974-76; asst. prof. Mich. State U., East Lansing, 1985-91; mng. editor Signs: Jour. of Women in Culture and Soc., Mpls., 1991-95; dir. J.B. Barker-Nunn & Assocs., St. Paul, Minn., 1996—. Adj. prof. dept. English, U. Minn., Mpls., 1995—; cons. editor various bus. and univs., 1992—. Editor: (book) History and Theory, 1996; contbr. articles to profl. jours. Adv. bd. dirs. Linwood A+ Sch., St. Paul, 1995-97, Groveland Park Elem. Sch., St. Paul, 1994-95; ministry mem. spiritual devel. Unity Unitarian Universalist Ch., St. Paul, 1997—. Rsch. grantee Mich. State U., 1987, 89, 90; recipient Presdl. Svc. award U. Minn., 1985, Dissertation fellowship U. Minn., 1983-84. Mem. Am. Studies Assn., Nat. Coun. Tchrs. of English, MLA. Avocation: attending arts performances and events. Home and Office: JB Barker-Nunn & Assocs 1833 Berkeley Ave Saint Paul MN 55105-1659 E-mail: jbbn@barker-nunn.com.

BARKETT, ROSEMARY, circuit judge; b. Ciudad Victoria, Tamaulipas, Mex., Aug. 29, 1939; arrived in U.S., 1946, naturalized, 1958; BS summa cum laude, Spring Hill Coll., 1967; JD, U. Fla., 1970; LLD (hon.), Stetson U., St. Petersburg, Fla., 1987; LHD (hon.), Fla. Internat. U., Miami, 1987; LLD (hon.), John Marshall Law Sch., Chgo., 1990; LHD (hon.), U. So. Fla., Tampa, 1990; DCL (hon.), Spring Hill Coll., Mobile, Ala., 1990; LLD (hon.), Rollins Coll., Orlando, Fla., 1992, Nova U., Ft. Lauderdale, Fla., 1992. Bar: Fla., U.S. Dist. Ct. (so. dist.) Fla., U.S. Ct. Appeals (5th cir.), U.S. Supreme Ct. Pvt. practice, West Palm Beach, Fla., 1971—79; judge 15th Jud. Cir. Ct., Palm Beach County, Fla., 1979—82, administrative judge civil divsn., 1982—83, chief judge, 1983—84; appellate judge 4th Dist. Ct. Appeal, West Palm Beach, Fla., 1984—85; justice Supreme Ct. Fla., Tallahassee, 1985—92, chief justice, 1992—94; cir. judge U.S. Ct. Appeals (11th cir.), Miami, 1994—. Bd. dirs. Lawyers for Children, U.S. Assn. Constl. Law; faculty U. Nev., Reno, Nat. Jud. Coll., Fla. Jud. Coll., Appellate Judges Seminar, Inst. Jud. Adminstrn., NYU; lectr. in field; vis. com. Miami U. Law Sch.; bd. visitors St. Thomas U. Mem. editl. bd.: The Florida Judges Manual. Named Women of Distinction, Crohn's & Colitis Found., 1997; named to Fla. Women's Hall of Fame, 1986, Miami Centennial Hall of Fame, 1996; recipient Woman of Achievement award, Palm Beach County Commn. on Status of Women, 1985, Hannah G. Solomon award, Nat. Coun. Jewish Women, 1991, Lifetime Achievement award, Latin Bus. Profl. Women, 1992, Breaking the Glass Ceiling award, Fla. Fedn. Bus. Profl. Women's Clubs, Inc., 1993, Disting. Jurist award, Miss. State U., 1995, Margaret Brent Women Lawyers of Achievement award, ABA Commn. Women in Profession, 1996, Harriette Glasner Freedom award, ACLU, 1999. Mem.: ABA (Minority Justice Honoree 1992), Dade Marine Inst., Fed. Judges Assn., Am. Law Inst., Assn. Trial Lawyers Am. (Achievement award 1986), Acad. Fla. Trial Lawyers (Achievement award 1988, Rosemary Barkett award named in her honor 1992), Palm Beach Marine Inst., Nat. Assn. Women Judges (Honoree of Year 1999), Fla. Assn. Women Lawyers (Judge Mattie Belle Davis award 1991, Rosemary Barkett Outstanding Achievement award named in her honor 1999), Am. Acad. Matrimonial Lawyers (award 1984), Palm Beach County Bar Assn., Fla. Bar Assn. Office: US Ct of Appeals (11th cir) Fla 99 NE 4th St Rm 1223 Miami FL 33132-2140

BARKEY, BRENDA, technical writer, publications manager; b. Hawthorne, Calif., Dec. 22, 1959; d. Greta E. B.; 1 child, Tiffany. BSCE, Comm., U. Washington, 1983. Cert. aerobics instr. and personal trainer Am. Coun. on Exercise. Tech. writer, editor Care Computer Sys., Bellevue, Wash., 1983-87, tech. writing supr., 1987-88; tech. writer Municipality of Met. Seattle, 1988-91; project mgr. West Point Treatment Plant Ops. Documentation, King County, Seattle, 1991-96; pvt. practice Edmonds, Wash., 1997—. Presenter in field. Co-author: A Team Approach to Training and Documentation in a Changing Organization, 1993, Putting Operations and Maintenance Manuals to Work for You, 1991; author: West Point Treatment Plant Operations and Maintenance Manual. Bd. dirs., sec. Edmonds (Wash.) Greenery Assn., 1996-2000. Recipient Merit awards Soc. Tech. Comm., Seattle, 1989, 91, 2000.. Avocations: swimming, bicycling, running, aerobics. E-mail: bbarkey@earthlink.net.

BARKHUIZEN, ANDRE, academic rheumatologist; b. Johannesburg, Mar. 15, 1961; s. Johan Nicholas and Helena Charlotta Barkhuizen; m. Cecelia Linda Barker, Apr. 25, 1992; children: Helene Jean, Daniel Nicholas. MBBCh, U. Witwatersrand, Johannesburg, South Africa, 1984; MMED, U. Cape Town, 1994. Specialist Physician South African Med. and Dental Coun., 1992, Specialist Rheumatologist South African Med. and Dental Coll., 1994. Intern Johannesburg (South Africa) Hosp., 1985; med. officer South African Med. Svcs., Voortrekkerhoogte, 1985—87; registrar Groote Schuur Hosp., Cape Town, South Africa, 1988—92, sr. registrar, 1992—94; fellow Oreg. Health & Sci. U., Portland, 1994—97, asst. prof. medicine, 1997—; staff physician, rheumatologist Portland VA Med. Ctr., 1998—. Bd. mem., rsch. and edn. com. chair Oreg. Rheumatology Alliance, Portland, 2002—. Editor: (section of jour.) Current Pain and Headache Reports. Chmn. rsch. and edn. com. Oreg. Rheumatology Alliance, Portland, 2002—03. Lt. Med. Svcs., 1986—87, Voortrekkerhoogte, South Africa. Recipient Housestaff Tchg. award, 2002; fellow, Coll. of Med. of South Africa, 1992, Am. Coll. Rheumatology, 1997; grantee Fellowship Tng. Grant, Am. Coll. Rheumatology, Rsch. and Edn. Fund, 2000—. Fellow: South African Coll. of Medicine, Am. Coll. of Rheumatology; mem.: NW Rheumatism Soc., Arthritis Found. of Am., Lupus Found. of Am. Dutch Reformed Church. Avocations: marathon and ultra-marathon running, travel. Office: Oregon Health & Sci U 3181 SW Sam Jackson Pk Rd OP-09 Portland OR 97239 Office Fax: 503-494-1022. E-mail: barkhuiz@ohsu.edu.

BARKIN, MARVIN E. lawyer; b. Winter Haven, Fla., Nov. 9, 1933; s. Isadore and Jean (Epstein) B.; m. Gertrude Parnes, Sept. 20, 1959; children: Thomas I., Michael A., Pamela L. AB, Emory U., 1955; LLB cum laude, Harvard U., 1958. Bar: Fla. 1958, U.S. Dist. Ct. (mid. and so. dists.) Fla., U.S. Ct. Appeals (5th and 11th cirs.), U.S. Supreme Ct. Research aide Dist. Ct. Appeal Fla., Third Dist., Miami, 1958-60; assoc., then ptnr. Fowler, White, Collins, Gillen, Humkey & Trenam, Tampa, 1960-69; ptnr. Trenam, Kemker, Scharf, Barkin, Frye, O'Neill & Mullis, Tampa, 1970—; mem. Fla. Bd. Bar Examiners, 1979-84, chmn., 1982-83. Chmn. corp., banking and bus. law sect. Fla. Bar, 1974-75, chmn.

appellate ct. rules subcom., 1972-73 Mem. Am. Law Inst., Am. Bar Found., Nat. Conf. Bar Examiners (bd. mgrs. 1985-95, chmn. 1993-94, 11th cir. ct. appeal com. on lawyer qualifications and conduct, chair 2001—), Fla. Bar, Omicron Delta Kappa. Democrat. Jewish. Home: 1605 Culbreath Isles Dr Tampa FL 33629-4824 Office: Trenam Kemker Scharf Barkin Frye O'Neill & Mullis 101 E Kennedy Blvd Tampa FL 33602-5179

BARKIN, ROBERT ALLAN, graphic designer, newspaper executive, consultant; b. Toronto, Ont., Can., Sept. 2, 1939; came to U.S., 1940, naturalized, 1950; s. Jacob and Mildred Barkin; m. Susan Davis, Jan. 23, 1987; children: Craig, Robin, Richard, Jamie. BA, George Washington U., 1960. From artist to advt. and sales promotion dir. Giant Food Inc., Washington, 1960-69; freelance artist, designer Washington, 1969-72; v.p. Lawrence Dobrow & Assos., Washington, 1972-73, Taft Communications Corp., Washington and N.Y.C., 1973-74. Cons. MacHarmans Assos., Auckland, N.Z., 1975; Freelance cons., Washington, 1976-77; art dir. Washington Post mag., 1977-78; asst. mng. editor Washington Post, 1978-85; cons. Barkin & Davis Inc., 1986—; tchr. life drawing and anatomy Georgetown U., 1973-76; inst. D.C. St. Acad., 1970 Exhbns. in, Washington, Phila. and Auckland; rep. pvt. and pub. collections. Recipient Silver Lions award Venice, Italy, 1975, also awards N.Y.C. Art Dirs. Club, Print Mag., Soc. Newspaper Design, Communications Art Assn., Ad Club Washington, Am. Inst. Graphic Arts, Printing Industry Am., Beckett Paper Co. Mem. Art Dirs. Club Washington (Gold medal 1979), Soc. Publ. Designers, Soc. Newspaper Designers. Home and Office: 1107 Notley Rd Silver Spring MD 20904-6243 E-mail: Barkinr@washpost.com., robert.barkin@verizon.net.

BARKIN, ROBERT LYN, pharmacologist, pharmacist; b. Chgo., July 10, 1940; s. Saul R. and Annette L. (Rosen) B.; m. Diana Sue Geifman, Sept. 5, 1965; children: Stacy, Stephanie. BS in Pharmacy, St. Louis Coll. of Pharmacy, 1963; MBA in Healthcare Mgmt., DePaul U., 1978; D Pharmacy, Purdue U., 1985. Diplomate Am. Acad. Pain Mgmt., Am. Bd. Forensic Examiners, Am. Bd. Forensic Medicine, Am. Bd. Psychol. Specialities in Psychopharmacology, cert. in gerentology, Ill.; registered nursing home adminstr., Ill. Dir. pharmacy St. Francis X. Cabrini Hosp., Chgo., 1971-76; asst. dir. pharmacy Rush-Presbyn. St. Luke's Med. Ctr., Chgo., 1976-90; assoc. prof., anesthesiology, family medicine, pharmacology Rush Med. Coll., Chgo., 1995—, cons. dept. psychiatry, 1985—; cons. in pharmacotherapy Rush Pain Ctr. of Rush-Presbyn. St. Lukes Med. Ctr. and Pain Ctr. of North Shore Hosp., Skokie, Ill., 1990—. Expert witness in pharmacologic, pharmaco-kinetic, pharmacodynamics and drug interaction for numerous law firms, 1976—; cons. Lake County Substance Abuse Planning Commn., Waukegan, Ill., 1975—80, Dangerous Drugs Commn., Chgo., 1976—79, Ill. Dept. Alcohol and Substance Abuse, Chgo., 1979—85, City of Chgo. Corp., 1990—; cons. to chief surgeon Chgo. Police Dept., 1990—, med. review officer, 2002—. Author: (texts) Pharmacology in Nursing, 15th edit., 1983, Pharmacology in Nursing, 16th edit., 1986; author: (editor) Pocket Guide to Most Commonly Prescribed Drugs, 1993; editor (reviewer): AMA Drug Evaluations, 1992; editor: (jours.) Am. Jour. Therapeutics, 1994, Am. Jour. Hospice and Palliative Care, Jour. Terminal Oncology, Pharmacotherapy, Jour. Clin. Psychiatry Primary Care Companion, Critical Care Medicine, Am. Family Physician, The Pain Clinic, Drugs; contbr. more than 120 articles to profl. jours. L. Lohman scholar, 1984. Fellow Am. Assn. Integrative Medicine (diplomate), Am. Coll. Clin. Pharmacology; mem. Am. Soc. Clin. Psychopharmacology, Am. Pain Soc., Am. Coll. Healthcare Adminstrn., Pain Soc. of Philippines, Am. Acad. Pain Mgmt. (diplomate), Assn. of Acad. Physiatrists, Sigma Xi, Delta Mu Delta. Achievements include research in areas of neuro-psychopharmacology, pharmacology, pharmacodynamics, pharmacokinetics, pharmacotherapy, geriatrics and pain related issues; extensive national and international presentations. Avocation: antique pocket watches, antique medical and pharmacy objects, antique firearms, travel, sports car collection. Home: 1211 Blackthorn Ln Deerfield IL 60015-3103 Office: Rush Presbyn St Lukes Med Ctr Dept Anesthesiology Rush Pain Ctr Chicago IL 60015

BARKLEY, BRIAN EVAN, lawyer, political consultant; b. Teaneck, NJ, Jan. 30, 1945; s. Henry E. and Alice M. (Schultz) Barkley; m. Pamela A. Martin, May 5, 1979; children: Leigh Elizabeth, Christine Elizabeth, Brett Evan. BA, U. Md., 1967; JD with honors, George Washington U., 1970. Bar: Md. 1970, D.C. 1976, U.S. Dist. Ct. Md. 1973. Assoc. Everngam & Goldstein, Silver Spring, Md., 1970—72; pvt. practice Silver Spring, 1972—80, Rockville, Md., 1980—86; spl. asst. Rep. Michael Barnes, Washington, 1981—84; sr. ptnr. Barkley and Kennedy, Chartered, 1987—. Vice chmn. Nat. Capital chpt. Nat. Multiple Sclerosis Com., Washington, 1980—86, Nat. Multiple Sclerosis Soc., Washington, 1998—2001, chmn. chpt. svcs. com., 1985—2001; chmn. Montgomery County Multiple Sclerosis Com., Rockville, Md., 1980; major gifts chmn. Shady Grove Hosp., 1980; chmn. Nat. Capital chpt. Nat. Multiple Sclerosis Com., 2001—; campaign mgr. Barnes for Congress, Rockville, 1980, campaign chmn., 1982—84; campaign mgr. Montgomery County for Mondale, 1984; del. Dem. Nat. Conv., 1984; vice chmn. Montgomery County for Dukakis, 1988. Recipient Humanitarian award, Nat. Multiple Sclerosis Soc., 1989. Mem.: Montgomery County Bar Assn., Md. Bar Assn., Rockville C. of C. (pres. 1996—97), Bethesda Country Club, Masons. Democrat. Home: 12405 Copenhaver Ter Potomac MD 20854-3028 Office: 51 Monroe St Ste 1407 Rockville MD 20850-2408

BARKLEY, BRONSON LEE, minister; b. Austin, Tex., July 30, 1949; s. Junius Paul and Ellie Montgomery (Neal) B.; m. Darlene Lynette Hickman, July 21, 1972; children: John Paul, Jared Patrick. BA, Lamar U., 1971, MA, 1974. Ordained to ministry Assemblies of God, 1977. Assoc. pastor 1st Assembly of God, Tyler, Tex., 1972-74; pastor Faith Assembly of God, Alvin, Tex., 1974-76, Golden Acres Assembly of God, Pasadena, Tex., 1979-82, Chapel in the Forest Assembly of God, Kingwood, Tex., 1983-99; revivalist Assemblies of God, Port Arthur, Tex., 1976-78, 83; pastor Congregation Shalom, Porter, Tex., 1999—. Founding pres. WZZJ Radio, Pascagoula, Miss., 1991—98; bd. dir. KSBJ Radio, Humble, Tex.; co-founder Assn. Jewish and Christian Believers, Inc., 2000—. Author play: The Lady and the Middle Cross, 1989; composer, publisher various songs. Bd. dirs. Birthright of Humble (Tex.), 1990-92, Leadership Tng. Internat., Inc., Ocala, Fla., 1991—; precinct chmn. Rep. Party of Harris County, 1988-90; state del. Tex. Rep. Party Conv. Mem. Kingwood Area Clergy Assn., Christian Coalition, Phi Eta Sigma. Office: Shalom Hebraic Christian Congregation 806 Russel Palmer Rd 7 Kingwood TX 77339 E-mail: PastorBarkley@aol.com. *I owe everything that I am to the personally-transforming power I have experienced in Jesus Christ. Remember Jesus loves you—and so do I!.*

BARKLEY, CHARLES WADE, sports broadcaster, retired professional basketball player; b. Leeds, Ala., Feb. 20, 1963; Student, Auburn U., 1981—84. With Phila. 76ers, 1984—92, Phoenix Suns, 1992—96, Houston Rockets, 1996—2000, ret., 2000; co-host Inside the NBA, TNT, 2001—; host Listen Up, TNT, 2002—. Mem. U.S. Olympic team, 1992, 96. Author (with Roy S. Johnson): Outrageous! The Fine Life and Flagrant Good Times of Basketball's Irresistible Force, 1992; actor: (films) Forget Paris, 1995. Named to All-Rookie team, 1985, NBA All-Star team, 1988—93; recipient Schick Pivotal Player award, 1986—88, IBM award, 1986—88, NBA All-Star Game Most Valuable Player award, 1991, NBA Most Valuable Player award, 1993. Achievements include holding single game records for most offensive rebounds in one quarter-11, 1987; holding single game record for most offensive rebounds in one half-13, 1987.

BARKLEY, HENRY BROCK, JR., research and development engineering executive; b. Raleigh, N.C., Apr. 5, 1927; s. Henry Brock and Thelma Maurine (Dutt) B.; m. Edith Sumner Stowe, June 24, 1950; children: Margaret Susan, Henry Brock III, Jane Stowe. Student, U. N.C., 1944-45; BS, U.S. Naval Acad., 1949; BSEE, U.S. Naval Postgrad. Sch., 1954, MSEE, 1955. Commd. ensign USN, 1949, advanced through grades to lt. comdr., 1960; ret., 1961; supr. space power sect. Bendix, Ann Arbor, Mich., 1962-63; chief reactor divsn. Lewis Rsch. Ctr. NASA, Sandusky, Ohio, 1963-73; asst. gen. mgr., dir. power reactors EG&G Idaho, Inc., Idaho Falls, 1973-81; mgr. internat. bus. Babcock & Wilcox Co., Lynchburg, Va., 1981-83, mgr. 205 plant project svcs., 1983-87, mgr. space power and propulsion, 1987-89, dir. space and def. sys., 1989-92; cons., 1992—. Dir. Devel. Workshop, Inc., Idaho Falls., 1977-81; IEEE disting. lectr. in S.Am. and C.Am., 1984. Bd. dirs. Sandusky Concert Assn., 1965-73; chmn. Huron (Ohio) Sch. Levy Campaigns, 1970. Lt. comdr. USN, 1960. Mem. IEEE, Am. Nuc. Soc., Am. Guild Organists. Presbyterian. Home: 501 VES Rd Apt WG25 Lynchburg VA 24503-4638 E-mail: brock.barkley.jr@worldnet.att.net.

BARKLEY, MARLENE A. NYHUIS, nursing educator; b. Waupun, Wis., Aug. 31, 1934; d. Fred and Esther Elsie (Leu) Nyhuis; m. Peter Don Barkley, Sept. 1, 1956; children: Peter Scott, John Fredric. Dipl. nursing, Milw. County Hosp., 1955; cert. nurse practitioner, U. Miami, Fla., 1976; AA, Miami Dade C.C., Fla., 1983; BSN cum laude, U. Miami, 1985; MSN, Barry U., 1996. RN, Fla.; cert. advanced RN, ANCC. Nurse Waupun (Wis.) Meml. Hosp., 1956-57; nurse coord. Courtland Med. Ctr., Milw., 1958-61, Planned Parenthood, Bloomington, Ind., 1971-74; nurse practitioner Miami VA Med. Ctr., 1976-83, program dir., 1983-98, cons. on home care, 1997—; adj. prof. Barry U., Miami Shores, Fla., 1997; cons. on home care Miami VA Med. Ctr., 1997; clin. adj. faculty ARNP program Barry U., Naples, Fla., 1997—; asst. dir. nursing Nursing Network of Naples, 2001—. Mem.: ANA, U. Miami Alumni Assn., Fla. Nurses Assn., Advanced Practice Coun., Am. Acad. Nurse Practitioners, Honor Soc. Fla. Gulf Coast U. Sch. Nursing, Sigma Theta Tau. Presbyterian. Avocations: rollerblading, bicycling. Home: 321 31st St NW Naples FL 34120-1705

BARKLEY, MONIKA JOHANNA, general contracting professional; b. Lexington, Ky., Feb. 22, 1961; d. Ellis Leon McCollum and Doris Leni (vonderLippe) Hutson; m. Samuel Custer Barkley II, Feb. 14, 1986. Constrn. sec. Price, Inc.-Neal, Inc., Lexington, 1982-84; quality control adminstr. Jacobs Builders, Inc., Jacksonville, N.C., 1984-90; pres. Unicorn Constrn., Goldsboro, N.C., 1984—; quality control adminstr. Flynn Co., Inc., Dubuque, Iowa, 1988-89; sec. to pres. Wooten Oil Co., Goldsboro, N.C., 1990-91; contract adminstr. Colejon Corp., Cleve., 1991-95; office mgr.-adminstr. JC&B Constrn. Co., Goldsboro, N.C., 1995-97; pres. Phoenix Constrn. Assocs., Inc., Goldsboro, 1995—. Rep. dist. chair, Lexington, 1979; county coord. Dole for Pres., Hayes for Gov., Jones for Congress, 1996, 98; alt. del. to Rep. Nat. Conv., 1996; sec. exec. com. Wayne County Rep. Com., 1997-99, media dir., Winders for Sheriff, 1998; mem. Wayne County Elections Task Force, 2001; Wayne County coord. Elizabeth Dole for U.S. Senate, 2002. Recipient Contractor Safety award U.S. Army Corp Engrs., Seymour Johnson AFB, N.C., 1988, Contractor of Yr. award, 1988. Fellow VFW Aux. (Outstanding Svc. award 1985), Order of Ea. Star; mem. Vets. United for Strong Am. (nat. sec. 1985-89), Pearl Harbor Commemorative Assn. (nat. sec. 1989—, Wayne County Rep. Women's Club (v.p. 1995, 99), Wayne County C. of C. (amb. 1999), Wayne County Citizens For Better Tax Control (sec. 1995), Wayne County Rep. Women's Club (v.p. 1999), Wayne County C. of C. (amb. 2000, mem. mil. affairs com. 2000, Ambassador of Yr. 2001, N.C. ea. region exec. com. 2000—, mem. mil. affairs ad hoc com.). Baptist. Avocations: political campaigns, travel. Home and Office: PO Box 10627 Goldsboro NC 27532-0627 E-mail: monyb@aol.com.

BARKLEY, PAUL HALEY, JR., architect; b. Washington, Sept. 24, 1937; Paul Haley Sr. and Mary Barrett (Brewer) B.; m. Jeanette Frances Nickerson, Dec. 20, 1975. Student, Ecole D'Art Americaines, Fontainebleau, France, 1959; BArch, U. Va., 1960. Registered architect, Va., Md., D.C. Archtl. designer Strang & Childers Architects, Annandale, Va., 1960-61; project designer Alan J. Lockman Architect, Washington, 1962-63; design assoc. D.G. Chase & Assocs., Alexandria, Va., 1964; pres. Barkley Pierce Assocs., Falls Church, Va., 1965-94; sole practice Paul H. Barkley, FAIA, Architect, Falls Church, Va., 1994—. Bd. dirs. Hist. Falls Church; lectr. archtl. divsn. continuing edn., 1966-91; mng. ptnr. Village Ctr. Assocs., Falls Church, 1983-99. Prin. works includes Falls Ch. Community Ctr., 1967, Vega Precision Labs., 1972, 1st Va. Bank, Arlington, 1979, Sullyfield Commerce Ctr., 1986, Rigg's Nat. Bank, McLean, Va., 1988; contbr. articles to profl. jours. Chmn. Falls Church Bus. Devel. Commn., 1987—93; mem. exec. com. Citizens for a Better City, Falls Church, 1987—92; mem. Falls Church Econ. Devel. Authority, 2002, Falls Church Pvt. Pub. Partnership, 1991—98, bd. dirs., 1991—98, pres., 1993—94. With USAF, 1960—63. Recipient excellence in design award Falls Church Village Preservation and Improvement Soc., 1979, Indsl. Devel. Vol. of Yr. award So. Indsl. Devel. Coun., 1982, Bus. Person of Yr. award City of Falls Church, 1988; Margaret Thompson Biddle fellow U. Va., 1959. Fellow AIA (bd. dirs. 1986-89, pres. Va. Soc. 1984, regional rep. Coll. of Fellows 1993-95, chair, Coll. Fellows Reg. Rep., 2002-03, numerous other offices, Disting. Svc. award 1983, Outstanding Svc. award No. Va. chpt. 1982, award of recognition of outstanding achievement 1988, Noland award 1991); mem. Falls Church C. of C. (bd. dirs. 1973-75, 99—, pres. 1976, 3d v.p. 1977-79, vice chmn. 2003), Va. Found. for Arch. (pres. 1988-89, trustee 1993-99). Avocations: photography, travel, collecting art. Home and Office: 311 Chestnut St Falls Church VA 22046-2404 E-mail: pbarkley@cox.net.

BARKLEY, RICHARD CLARK, ambassador; b. Chgo., Dec. 23, 1932; s. Harold Clark and Chrystal Leone (Boddiger) B.; m. Nina Margretha Schultz, Feb. 27, 1954; children: Katharina Lynn, Crystal Nina. BA, Mich. State U., 1954; MA, Wayne State U., 1958; postgrad., U. Frieburg, Germany, 1961. Joined Fgn. Svc., Dept. State, Washington, 1962; 2d sec. Am. Embassy, Helsinki, Finland, 1963-65; vice consul Am. Consulate, Santiago, Dominican Republic, 1965-67; 1st sec. U.S. Mission, Berlin, 1972-74; dep. chief mission Am. Embassy, Oslo, 1979-82, polit. counselor Bonn, Fed. Republic Germany, 1982-85, dep. chief mission Pretoria, Republic of South Africa, 1985-88; amb. to German Dem. Republic Berlin, 1988-90; amb. to Turkey Ankara, 1991-94. Bd. dirs. Inst. for Turkish Studies; chmn. Palace Arts Found. Inc., 1998—. Capt. U.S. Army, 1955-57. Recipient Disting. Alumni award Wayne State U., 1991, Disting. Honor award Dept. State, 1991. Mem. Am. Fgn. Svc. Assn., Alpha Tau Omega. E-mail: rcbnmb@aol.com.

BARKLEY, ROY REID, historian, educator, editor, writer; b. Brownwood, Tex., Nov. 2, 1941; s. Joseph Calvin Barkley and Nita Myrl Ussery; m. Flordeliza Oville. BA, Abilene Christian Coll., 1963; MA, U. of Tex., 1965, PhD, 1974. Cert. Secondary tchg. 1964. Instr. English Lamar U., Beaumont, Tex., 1965—68; asst. prof. Bowling Green State U., Firelands Campus, Huron, Ohio, 1974—75; asst. editor then assoc. editor Mid. English Dictionary U. of Mich., Ann Arbor, Mich., 1975—84; sr. editor Tex. State Hist. Assn., Austin, 1984—2003. Contbr. hist. dictionary; author: The Catholic Alcoholic, 1990, Catholic Ministry to the Addicted, 1992, The Mysteries of the Rosary: Mirror of Scripture and Gateway to Prayer, 2001, Journey of Faith: Catholic Marriage Preparation, 2002; editor: (ency.) New Handbook of Texas, 7 vols., 1996 (Tex. Reference Source award Tex. Libr. Assn., 1997), Portable Handbook of Texas, 2000, Handbook of Texas Music, 2003; contbr. articles to profl. jours. Deacon Cath. Diocese of Austin, Austin, TEX., 1991—2002; pres., bd. of directors Natural Family Planning for Ctrl. Tex., Austin, TEX., 1995—98; sch. bd. mem. St. Mary's Cathedral Sch., Austin, TEX., 1989—94; editl. bd. mem. Cath. SW (jour.), Austin, TEX. Mem.: West Tex. Hist. Assn., Mariological Soc. of Am., Soc. of Cath. Social Scientists, Tex. Cath. Hist. Soc. (pres. 1996—98, Carlos E. Castañeda award 2000), Fellowship of Cath. Scholars. Conservative. Avocations: music, hunting, travel, politics. Home: 711 Pigeon Forge Rd Pflugerville TX 78660 Office: Texas State Historical Association SRH 2.316 Capitol Station Austin TX 78712 Fax: 512-990-7068., 512-471-1551. Personal E-mail: rbarkley@mail.utexas.edu. Business E-Mail: rbarkley@mail.utexas.edu.

BARKLEY, TERRELL WAYNE, school librarian, museum curator; b. Tokyo, July 22, 1950; arrived in U.S., 1950; s. Hillard Rhoda and Violet Beatrice (Taylor) Barkley. BS, U. N. Ala., 1973; MA, The Citadel, 1974; MLS, U. Ala., 1987; cert. in mus. studies (grad.), Harvard U., 1990. Cert. tchr. Ala., 1975, Va., 1978. Social studies tchr. Randolph Sch., Huntsville, Ala., 1975—78; chmn. Social Studies Dept. Augusta Mil. Acad., Ft. Defiance, Va., 1978—83; social studies tchr. Huntsville (Ala.) City Schs., 1984—86; asst. archivist Birmingham (Ala.) Pub. Libr., 1988—89; spl. collections libr. Ala. A&M U., Huntsville, 1990—92; archivist and mus. curator Bridgewater (Va.) Coll., 1993—. Editl. asst.: The Brethren Encyclopedia, 1996—97, rsch. asst.:, 2001—; author: One Who Served Brethren Elder Charles Nesselrodt, 1996; contbr. articles to profl. jours.; musician: Ala. Music Hall Fame (drums), 1999. Mem. com. Valley Brethren Mennonite Cultural Ctr., Harrisonburg, Va., 1998—2001, Shenandoah Valley Battlefields Found., New Market, Va., 2000—02; chmn. Shenandoah Dist. Hist. Com. Ch. of the Brethren, 1996—99; mem. exec. bd. Shenandoah Valley Civil War Roundtable, 1993—98. Advanced army grad. ROTC, 1973. Mem.: ALA, Am. Assn. Mus., Soc. Am. Archivists, Rockingham Area Hist. Assn., Nat. Soc. Scabbard and Blade, Phi Alpha Theta. Avocations: music, history, travel. Office: Box 147 Bridgewater College Bridgewater VA 22812 Home: 117-B S Main St Bridgewater VA 22812 E-mail: tbarkley@bridgewater.edu.

BARKLEY, THIERRY VINCENT, lawyer; b. Paris, Mar. 21, 1955; s. Jacques and Michéline Marie (Rossi) B.; came to U.S., 1967, naturalized, 1974; m. Mary Ellen Gamble, June 18, 1983; children: Richard A., Robert V., Marriah E., Christopher R. BA in Polit. Sci., UCLA, 1976; JD, Calif. Western Sch. Law, San Diego, 1979. Bar: Nev. 1980, U.S. Dist. Ct. Nev. 1982, U.S. Supreme Ct. 1986. Intern, Calif. Ct. Appeals 4th Circuit, San Diego, 1978-79; law clk. Nev. Dist. Ct., 7th Jud. Dist., Ely, 1979-81; assoc. firm C.E. Horton, Ely, 1982-83; asst. city atty. Ely, 1982-83; assoc. firm Barker, Gillock & Perry, Reno, 1983-87, Perry & Spann, 1987-89, ptnr., 1990—. Editor Internat. Law Jour., 1979. Mem. Internat. Moot Ct. Team, 1978; recipient Dean's award Calif. Western Sch. Law, 1979. Mem. Rep. Presdl. Task Force, 1990. Mem. Nev. Bar Assn., Washoe Bar Assn., U.S. Jaycees (past pres. White Pine, Nev.). Republican. Roman Catholic. Lodge: Elks (past treas. Ely club). Office: Perry & Spann 6130 Plumas St Reno NV 89509-6041

BARKMAN, JON ALBERT, lawyer; b. Somerset, Pa., Oct. 8, 1947; s. Blair Albert and Billie (Dietz) B.; m. Annette E. Shaulis, Dec. 1, 1983. BA, Washington and Jefferson U., 1969; JD, Duquesne U., 1975. Bar: Pa. 1975, U.S. Dist. Ct. (we. dist.) Pa. 1975, U.S. Supreme Ct. 1984, U.S. Ct. Appeals (3rd cir.) 1989. Mem. claims dept. Liberty Mut. Ins. Co., Pitts., 1969-71; dist. justice Commonwealth of Pa., Somerset, 1973-93; pvt. practice Somerset, 1975—; pres. Barkman Realty, Inc., Somerset County Settlement and Abstract Co. Inc. Advisor Com. Against Sexual Assault, Somerset, Pa., 1984; Pa. del. Nat. Spl. Ct. Judges Conv., Honolulu, 1989, Atlanta, 1991; mem. Somerset County Com. for prison overcrowding, 2002-03. Paul Harris fellow, 1989. Mem. ABA, Pa. Trial Lawyers Assn., Somerset County Bar Assn. (pres. 1990—), Allegheny County Bar Assn., Elks, Rotary, Sons of the Am. Legion. Republican. Methodist. Home: 388 High St Somerset PA 15501-1301 Office: Somerset County Com Jailho County 116 N Center Ave Somerset PA 15501-2027

BARKMEIER, WAYNE W. academic administrator; b. Friend, Nebr., Mar. 29, 1944; m. Carolyn A. Johnsen; children: Kimberly, Jennifer, Wayne Jr. Postgrad., U. Nebr., Lincoln, 1962—65; DDS, U. Nebr. Med. Ctr. Coll. Dentistry, 1965—69; MS, U. Tex. Health Sci. Ctr., Houston, 1973—75. Asst. prof., oral surgery Creighton U., 1978—79; pvt. practice Omaha, 1978—82; asst. prof., operative dentistry Creighton U., 1979—82; rsch. dentist L.D. Caulk Divsn., Dentsply Internat., Milford, Del., 1982—85, intramural rsch. mgr., 1985; asst. dean rsch. and assoc. prof. operative dentistry, Sch. Dentistry Creighton U., 1985—87, dir., Ctr. Oral Health Rsch., 1986—95, assoc. dean rsch., Sch. Dentistry, 1991—94, prof., operative dentistry, Sch. Dentistry, 1991—2000, prof. gen. dentistry, Sch. Dentistry, 2000—, dean, Sch. Dentistry, 1994—. Cons. on dental materials Nat. Bd. Test Constrn. Com. for Joint Commn. on Nat. Dental Exams.; past mem. Am. Dental Assn. Coun. on Dental Rsch. Contbr. ; mem. editl. and adv. bds. Operative Dentistry, Jour. Esthetic Dentistry, Military Medicine, Dental Advisor, article rev. cons. Jour. Am. Dental Assn., Am. Jour. Dentistry, Dental Materials, Jour. Dentistry, Quintessence Internat., Jour. Dental Edn. Active duty USAF, 1969—78, brig. gen. USAFR, 1991—94. Office: 2500 Calif Plza Omaha NE 68178

BARKOFF, RUPERT MITCHELL, lawyer; b. New Orleans, May 7, 1948; s. Samuel and Martha B.; m. Susan Joyce Levitt, May 31, 1970; children: Stuart, Jeffrey, Lisa. BA in Econs. with high distinction, U. Mich., 1970, JD magna cum laude, 1973. Bar: Ga. 1973. Assoc. Kilpatrick Stockton LLP, Atlanta, 1973-80, ptnr., 1980—. Contbr. articles to profl. jours. Mem. ABA (bus. law sect., antitrust sect., forum on franchising, panelist ann. forums 1980-92, chmn. 1989-92, assoc. editor Franchise Law Jour. 1981-86), Ga. Bar Assn. (corp. and banking sect.), Atlanta Bar Assn., Phi Beta Kappa. Democrat. Jewish. Home: 5215 Vernon Springs Trl NW Atlanta GA 30327-4511 Office: Kilpatrick Stockton LLP 1100 Peachtree St NE Ste 2800 Atlanta GA 30309-4530 E-mail: rbarkoff@kilpatrickstockton.com.

BARKOVICH, ANTHONY JAMES, pediatric neuroradiologist, educator, researcher; b. Ft. Lee, Va., July 29, 1952; s. Anthony and Mildred Margaret (Donner) B.; m. Karen Kaye Jernstedt, May 24, 1986; children: Matthew, Krister, Emil. BS in Chemistry, U. Calif., Davis, 1974; MS in Chemistry, U. Calif., Berkeley, 1977; MD, George Washington U., 1980. Diplomate Am. Bd. Radiology. Intern, then resident in radiology Letterman Army Med. Ctr., 1980-84; fellow in neuroradiology Walter Reed Army Med. Ctr., 1984-86; maj. U.S. Army, 1980-89; neuroradiologist Letterman Army Med. Ctr., San Francisco, 1986-89; prof. radiology, pediatrics, neurology and neurosurgery U. Calif., San Francisco, 1989—. Author: Pediatric Neuroimaging, 1995, 3d edit., 2000; editor: Magnetic Resonance Neuroimaging, 1994, Teaching Atlas of Neuroradiology, 2000. Sec. gen. World Fedn. Neuroradiol. Societies, 2002—; chmn. bd. trustees Neuroradiology Rsch. and Edn. Found., 2001—. Grantee NIH, 1993, 1996, 2002. Mem. AAAS, Am. Soc. Neuroradiology (sec. 1994-96, v.p. 1996-97, pres.-elect 1997-98, pres. 1998-99), Am. Soc. Pediatric Neuroradiology (pres. 1992-94), Soc. Pediatric Radiology, Soc. Neurosci., World Fedn. Neurol. Socs. (sec. gen. 2002—), Neuroradiology Edn. and Rsch. Found. (chmn. bd. 2001—). Avocations: history, basketball. Office: UCSF-Dept Neuroradiology 505 Parnassus Ave San Francisco CA 94143-0628 E-mail: jimb@radiology.ucsf.edu.

BARKSDALE, BARRY W. career officer; BS in History, USAF Acad., 1972; student pilot tng., Columbus AFB, Miss., 1972-73, Davis-Monthan AFB, Ariz., 1973, 81, 86; student, Squadron Officer Sch., 1981, USMC Command and Staff Coll., 1984, Air Command and Staff Coll., 1985, Air War Coll., 1988; MA in Mgmt., U. Phoenix, 1989, Army War Coll., 1991; student Phase II, Joint Profl. Mil. Edn., 1992. Commd. 2d lt. USAF, 1972, advanced through grades to brig. gen., 1997; aircraft comdr. 75th Tactical Fighter Squadron, England AFB, La., 1973-76; forward air controller tng. Patrick AFB, Fla., 1976-77; wing scheduler 51st Composite Wing, Osan Air Base, S. Korea, 1977-78; chief weapons and tactics then asst. ops. officer 549th Tactical Air Support Tng. Squadron, Patrick AFB, 1978 81; flight comdr. 355th Tactical Fighter Squadron, Myrtle Beach AFB, S.C., 1981-83; action officer then exec. officer to dep. chief plans Hdqs. Tactical Air Command, Langley AFB, Va., 1983-86; various positions Davis-Monthan AFB, 1986-90, 95-97; chief detection and monitoring br., counternarcotics ops. Joint Staff, Pentagon, Washington, 1991-93; comdr. 554th Support Group, Nellis AFB, Nev., 1993-94, 57th Ops. Group, Nellis AFB, Nev., 1994-95, 37th Tng. Wing, Lackland AFB, Tex., 1997-99; vice comdr. 12th Air Force U.S. So. Com., Davis-Monthan AFB, Ariz., 1999—. Decorated Legion of Merit. Office: 12 AF Davis Monthan AFB AZ 85707

BARKSDALE, CLARENCE CAULFIELD, banker; b. St. Louis, June 4, 1932; s. Clarence M. and Elizabeth (Caulfield) B.; m. Emily Catlin Keyes, Apr. 4, 1959; children: John Keyes, Emily Shepley. AB, Brown U., 1954; postgrad., Washington U. Law Sch., St. Louis, 1957-58, Stonier Grad. Sch. Banking, Rutgers U., 1964, Columbia U. Grad. Sch. Bus., 1968; LLD (hon.), Maryville Coll., St. Louis, 1976, Westminster Coll., Fulton, Mo., 1982, St. Louis U., 1989. From asst. cashier to chmn. bd., CEO Centerre Bank NA (formerly 1st Nat. Bank), St. Louis, 1960—76, chmn. bd., chief exec. officer, 1976-88; vice chmn. Bank of Am. (formerly Boatmen's Bancshares, Inc.), St. Louis, 1988-89; vice chmn. bd. dirs. Washington U., St. Louis, 1989—. Bd. dirs. SBC Comms., Inc., Thomas Lawrence & Assocs., Inc. Bd. dirs. Mo. Bot. Gardens, Alzheimers Assn., Grand Ctr. Inc., Wash. U. Mus. Contemporary Art, St. Louis Boy Scouts, and Girls, Inc. With M.I., U.S. Army, 1954-57. Mem. St. Louis Club, St. Louis Country Club, Noonday Club, Bogey Club of St. Louis, Harbor Point Golf Club, Little Harbor Club), Wequetosing Golf Club (Harbor Springs, Mich.), Ocean Club, Gulfstream Golf Club, Gulf Stream Bath & Tennis Club (Delray Beach, Fla.), Alpha Delta Phi. Office: Washington U 7425 Forsyth Blvd Saint Louis MO 63105-2161 E-mail: clarence_barksdale@aismail.wustl.edu.

BARKSDALE, JACQUELINE YVONNE, elementary school educator; b. Memphis, Feb. 24, 1954; d. Jesse M. (Stepfather) and Lucille (Townsend) Beasley; married; 1 child, Jaslin L. EdB, Ind. U., 1975, EdM in Counseling, 1979, EdM in Reading, 1981; EdD in Counseling, Lael U., 1985. Elem. tchr. Ft. Wayne (Ind.) Cmty. Schs., 1976—81, tchr., 1985—88, 1992—; elem. sch. counselor Dept. Edn., St. Croix, 1981—84; prin. Nazarine Christian Sch., Christiansted, St. Croix, 1981—84; tchr., sch. counselor Memphis Acad. Word

of Faith, 1989—90; sch. counselor Memphis Pub. Schs., 1990—92. Contbr. poem to (anthology) Before They are Gone; camera operator, editor: pub. access TV programs. Mem. adv. bd. Voices of Unity Cmty. Choir, Ft. Wayne, 2002—; tchr., tutor After Sch. Tutoring Project, Ft. Wayne, 2000—; dir. Sunday sch. New Zion Tabernacle, Ft. Wayne, 2000—. Mem.: Ind. Reading Assn., Ind. State Tchrs. Assn. Avocations: writing and producing school and church plays, reading, travel, attending conferences. Office: Ft Wayne Cmty Schs Dr LeVan R Scott Acad 950 Fairfax Ave Fort Wayne IN 46806 E-mail: jacquelinebarksdale@fwcs.k12.in.us.

BARKSDALE, MARY ALICE, education educator; b. Roanoke, Va., Feb. 12, 1954; d. Byrd H. and Mary Anne (St. Clair) Barksdale. BA in Elem. Edn., Clemson U., 1976, MEd in Reading Edn., 1979; EdD in Curriculum and Instrn., Va. Tech., 1988. Tchr. Greenville (S.C.) Schs., 1976-81, Bedford (Va.) County Schs., 1981-83; grad. asst. Va. Tech., Blacksburg, 1983-88; prof. W.Va. U., Morgantown, 1988-94, U. South Fla., Tampa, 1994—2001, Va. Tech., Blacksburg, 2001—. Presenter in field. Co-editor Jour. Computing in Childhood Edn., 1995-97; contbr. articles to profl. jours.; reviewer publs. in field. Fulbright scholar 1995. Mem. Internat. Reading Assn. (Albert J. Harris award 1995), Nat. Reading Conf., Coll. Reading Assn., Ea. Ednl. Rsch. Assn., Fulbright Assn., Phi Delta Kappa. Office: 217 War Meml Hall Va Tech Blacksburg VA 24061 E-mail: mbarksda@vt.edu.

BARKSDALE, RHESA HAWKINS, federal judge; b. Jackson, Miss., Aug. 8, 1944; s. John Woodson Jr. and Mary Bryan (Saunders) Barksdale. BS, U.S. Mil. Acad., 1966; JD, U. Miss., 1972. Law clk. to Hon. Byron R. White U.S. Supreme Ct., 1972—73; assoc., then ptnr. Butler, Snow, O'Mara, Stevens & Cannada, Jackson, 1973—90; judge U.S. Ct. Appeals (5th cir.), Jackson, 1990—. Instr. U. Miss. Sch. Law, Jackson, 1975—76, Miss. Coll. Sch. Law, Jackson, 1976. Chmn. Miss. Vietnam Vets. Leadership Program, Jackson, 1982—85; del. Rep. Nat. Conv., New Orleans, 1988; elector election of Pres. of U.S., Jackson, 1988. Capt. U.S. Army, 1966—70, Vietnam. Decorated Silver Star, Bronze Star for Valor, Purple Heart, Cross of Gallantry with silver star (Republic of Vietnam). Mem.: Phi Delta Phi (Nat. Grad. of Yr. 1972). Episcopalian. Office: US Ct Appeals 5th Cir James O Eastland Courthouse 245 E Capitol St Ste 200 Jackson MS 39201-2414*

BARKSDALE, RICHARD DILLON, civil engineer, educator; b. Orlando, Fla., May 2, 1938; s. William Spruil and Lucile Dillon B.; m. Bonnie Alice McClung, Nov. 16, 1962; children— Cheryl Lynn, Richelle Denise. A.S., So. Tech. Inst., Marietta, Ga., 1958; B.C.E., Ga. Inst. Tech., 1962, MS, 1963; PhD, Purdue U., 1966. Registered profl. engr., Fla., Ga., S.C., N.C., Ala., Tenn., La. Asst. prof. civil enging. Ga. Inst. Tech., 1965-69, asso. prof., 1969-75, prof., 1975-95, prof. emeritus, 1995—. V.p. Soil Systems, Inc., Marietta, 1972-79, Soil Systems of the Carolina, 1976-79; spl. lectr. So. Tech. Inst., 1958-60; mem. com. longterm pavement performance Strategic Hwy. Rsch. Program. Contbr. articles in field to profl. jours. Co-pres. Briarcliff High Sch. Booster Club, 1983-84, Briarcliff High Sch. PTA, 1985-86 Recipient Ga. Engring. Soc. award, 1961; co-recipient Croda prize Instn. Highway Engrs., 1989; NSF grantee, 1966-67; rsch. fellow Brit. Sci. and Engring. Rsch. Coun., 1988. Mem. ASCE (Norman medal 1978, pres. Ga. sect. 1975-76, chmn. nat. com. structural design of roadways), Nat. Stone Assn. (prof. of yr. 1996), Appalachee Sportsman Club (pres. 1974-95), Phi Kappa Phi (pres. Ga. Tech. chpt. 1979). Republican. Baptist. Office: Ga Tech Institute Sch Civil Engring Atlanta GA 30332-0001 E-mail: rbarksda@mindspring.com.

BARLAND, PETER, rheumatologist, medical educator; b. N.Y.C., June 5, 1936; s. Samuel and Marion (Angrist) B.; m. Tina Saleh, Apr. 15, 1951; children: Susan, Julie. BA, NYU, 1955; MD, Yeshiva U., 1959. Intern Strong Meml. Hosp., Rochester, N.Y., 1959-60; resident in internal medicine Bronx (N.Y.) Mcpl. Hosp. Ctr., Bronx, N.Y., 1960-63; prof. medicine and pathology Albert Einstein Coll. Medicine, Bronx, 1965—2002; attending physician Montefiore Med. Ctr., Bronx, 1969—, dir. rheumatology divsn., 1992—2002, dir. immunodiagnostic lab., 1970—; mem. Mid-Westchester Med. Assocs., White Plains, NY, 2002—. Fellow Am. Coll. Rheumatology; mem. N.Y. Rheumatism Assn. (pres., sec.-treas. 1975). Office: 33 Davis Ave White Plains NY 10605 E-mail: pbarland@montefiore.org.

BARLAS, JULIE SANDALL, computer scientist, former librarian; b. Eugene, Oreg., Sept. 15, 1944; d. Wendell Mervin Sandall and Edna Marie (Shrock) Kehl; m. Arthur Barlas, Aug. 10, 1974 BA, U. Oreg., Eugene, 1965; M.L.S., U. Pitts., 1967; MS, Harvard U., 1985. Cataloguer Grad Sch. Edn., Harvard U., Cambridge, Mass., 1967-70, cataloguer, asst. librarian Gordon McKay Library, 1970-71, librarian, 1971-86; mem. tech. staff MITRE Corp., Bedford, Mass., 1986-91, Racal-Redac, Inc., Westford, Mass., 1991-93; software engr. Viewlogic Sys., Inc., Marlboro, Mass., 1993—98, IBM, Westford, Mass., 1998—. Mem. IEEE. Democrat. Home: 360 Littleton Rd Unit B18 Chelmsford MA 01824-3370

BAR-LEV, ZEV, linguist, educator; b. Bklyn., N.Y., Mar. 27, 1943; s. Daniel and Florence Lefkowitz; m. Shoshana Wirth, June 20, 1965; children: Rebecca, Naomi, Joshua. AB, Columbia Coll., 1963; MA, Cornell U., 1965; PhD, Ind. U., 1969. Asst. prof. Syracuse (N.Y.) U., 1969—73; lectr. linguistics Ben-Gurion U. in Negev, Beer-Sheva, Israel, 1972—78; prof. linguistics San Diego State U., 1979—. Author: (book) Computer Talk for the Liberal Arts, 1987, Hebrew Free Speech, 2000, Shush and Say Six, 2001, Aleph-Bet Puzzle, 2002. Jewish. Achievements include invention of sheltered initiation language learning; discovery of Hebrew Key-Letters. Office: Dept Linguistics and Oriental Langs San Diego State Univ San Diego CA 92182 E-mail: zev.bar-lev@sdsu.edu.

BARLIN, L. PAUL, dance director; b. Bklyn., Ny, Oct. 31, 1916; s. Hyman and Anna Braun Barlin; m. Anne Goodman, Sept. 0, 1948; children: Douglass, Michael children: Leanne Mennin, Jo Anne Pieracci. BFA in Dance, Evergreen State Coll., 1982. Turbine blade prodn. specialist Westinghouse Mfg., Lester, Pa., 1941—45; dance dir. Dance Ctr., Paul Barlin Dance Theater, L.A., 1950—73, Paul Barlin Dance Theater, Mercer Island, Wash., 1973—97. Spkr. in field. Choreographer (books, dance concerts) Learning Through Movement, Dance-A-Stories, Dance-A-Folk-Song, 1963—73; author: From Andrew, With Love, 2001, A Dancer on the Edge, Only in A White World, The Yellow Line, All My Fathers. Club pres. Strivers, Mercer Island, Wash., 2000—03. Mem.: Strivers (pres. 2000—02). Avocations: organic gardening, natural medical cures. Home: 5702 80th Ave SE Mercer Island WA 98040 Office: Strivers 8236 SE 24th St Mercer Island WA 98040 Personal E-mail: paulbarlin@msn.com.

BARLINE, JOHN, lawyer; b. Tacoma, Dec. 29, 1946; s. John Dean Barline and Jane (Greiwe) Moosey; m. Sally Harris, Oct. 21, 1984. B.A., Netherland Sch. Internat. Bus., Breukelen, 1968; B.A., U. Puget Sound, 1969; J.D., Willamette U., 1972; LL.M. in Taxation, NYU, 1973. Bar: Wash. 1972, U.S. Dist. Ct. (we. dist.) Wash. 1974. Ptnr., Dolack, Hansler, et al, Tacoma, 1973-85, ptnr. Williams, Kastner & Gibbs, Tacoma, 1985—. Bd. dirs., treas. Bldg. a Scholastic Heritage, Tacoma, 1980-85; bd. dirs., chmn. Bellarmine Prep. Sch., 1981— ; chmn. bd. dirs. Tacoma Community Coll. Found.; trustee U. Puget Sound, 1988—. Named among Leaders of Tomorrow, Time Mag., 1983. Mem. Wash. State Bar Assn. (com. mem., spl. dist. counsel, mem. gift and estate tax com.), Pierce County Bar Assn., ABA, U. Puget Sound Alumni Assn. (chmn. 1984—, bd. dirs. 1984). Republican. Roman Catholic. Clubs: Tacoma, Tacoma Yacht (bd. dirs. 1978-80), Tacoma Country and Golf. Lodge: Elks. Office: Williams Kastner & Gibbs 1000 Financial Ctr 1145 Bro Tacoma WA 98402

BARLOW, ANNE LOUISE, pediatrician, medical research administrator; b. Skipton-in-Craven, Eng., Jan. 28, 1925; came to U.S., 1951, naturalized, 1954; m. Howard Cadwell, May 19, 1951; children: Barbara Anne, John James Stewart; m. Alastair Ramsay, Dec. 19, 1969. MB BS, London (Royal Free Hosp.) Sch. Medicine for Women, U. London, 1948; diploma in child health, Royal Colls. Eng., 1950; MPH with honors, Yale U., 1952. House physician North Lonsdale Hosp., Barrow-in-Furness, Lancashire, Eng., 1948-49; house surgeon Royal Infirmary (Glasgow), Scotland, 1949; resident to profl. unit of child health Royal Hosp. for Sick Children, Glasgow, 1949-50; jr. hosp. med. officer Knightswood Infectious Diseases Hosp., Glasgow, 1950; Rotary Found. Internat. fellow U. Toronto Med. Sch., Ont., Can., 1950-51; research asst. Yale U. Sch. Pub. Health, New Haven, 1952-53; clinic physician in cancer prevention Arlington, Va., part-time 1953-54; resident, staff physician William H. Maybury Tb Sanatorium, Northville, Mich., 1954-56; research dir. Detroit Feeding Study with the Detroit City Health Dept., 1954-56; research asst., instr. sch. health U. Pitts. Grad. Sch. Pub. Health, 1957-62; pvt. practice medicine specializing in pediatrics Pitts., 1959-62; mem. courtesy staff St. Margaret Hosp., Pitts., 1959-62; research assoc. Tice Lab for Tb research, Cook County Hosp., Chgo., Ill., 1962; med. writer product info. Abbott Labs., North Chicago, Ill., 1963-66, med. specialist antibiotic medicine, 1966-68; mgr. clin. devel. pharm. products div. Abbott Lab., North Chicago, Ill., 1968-71, asst. med. dir., 1971-72, mgr. parenteral nutrition hosp. products div., 1972-73, med. dir., 1973-80, v.p. med. affairs hosp. products div., 1980-84; pres. Albamed, Inc., 1985—; asst. clin. prof. Med.Coll. Pa., 1988. Cons. maternal, child and sch. health, dir. well baby clinic Lake County (Ill.) Health Dept., 1963-76; pres. Tb Sanatorium Bd. Lake County Health Dept., Ill., 1976-79; dir., pres. Lake County Bd. Health, 1979-82; health officer Village of North Barrington, Ill., 1964-67; physician-adviser Head Start Lake County Community Action Project, 1970-84; chmn. profl. adv. com. Lake County Health Dept., 1972-84; preceptor Pediatric Nurse Assoc. Program; chmn. bd. Sutton Place Behavioral Health Inc., 2000—. Contbr. articles on maternal and infant care, pediatrics and nutrition; patentee high calorie solution of low molecular weight glucose polymer mixtures useful for intravenouse adminstrn. Bd. dirs. Heart Assn. of Lake County, 1979-84, chmn. nutrition com. 1980-82, v.p. 1982-83, pres., 1983-84; mem. sch. bd. Grant Twp. Cmty. H.S. (Ill. Dist. 124), 1973-79; sec. to governing bd. Spl. Edn. Dist. of Lake County, 1977-79; assoc. Nat. Coll. Edn., Evanston, Ill., 1976-84; chmn. Am. Women's Hosp. Svc., 1986-95; vol. Guardian ad Litem, 1989—. Recipient Charlotte Danstrom award for excellence Women in Mgmt., 1984, award of merit for outstanding contns. to pub. health Ill. Pub. Health Assn., 1975; recipient award of merit for outstanding community service to Lake County Community Action Project, 1976, award for outstanding and dedicated service as pres Lake County TB Sanatorium Bd., 1979, TWIN award YWCA, 1983. Mem. AAAS, NOW, LWV, AMA (chair sr. physician gov. com. 1996—), Am. Med. Women's Assn. (councilor for orgn. and mgmt. 1977-79, treas. 1980, 1st v.p. 1981, pres. 1983, chair found. 1992-95, Elizabeth Blackwell medal 1992), Fla. Med. Assn. (vice chair Internat. Med. Grad. sect. 1998—), Med. Women's Internat. Assn. (v.p. N. Am. 1993-95), Pan-Am. Med. Women's Alliance (pres. 2000), Nassau County Med. Soc. (pres. 2002-03). Home and Office: 20 S 19th St Fernandina Beach FL 32034-2767 E-mail: czarduska@aol.com

BARLOW, AUGUST RALPH, JR., minister; s. August Ralph and Kathryn Viola (Adams) B.; m. Elizabeth Evone Anderson, Aug. 27, 1960; children: Paul Martin, Andrew Ralph, Ann Kathryn. BA, Haverford Coll., 1956; BD, Yale U., 1959, STM, 1964. Ordained to ministry Meth. Ch., 1959. Pastor Fox Chapel Meth. Ch., Pitts., 1959-60, Butler St. Meth. Ch., Pitts., 1961-62, Lawrenceville Cmty. Ch., Pitts., 1962-63; intern Cleve. Inner City Protestant Parish, 1960-61; from tchg. min. to pastor Beneficent Congl. Ch., Providence, 1964-97, pastor emeritus, 1997—. Bd. govs. Beneficent House, 1970-97, Beneficent Commons Housing, Providence, sr. min., devel. team, 1991-95; bd. dirs. Pastoral Counseling Ctr., Greater Providence, v.p., 1984-86, pres., 1995-97; pres. Steere House, Providence, 1983-86, past bd. dirs.; bd. dirs. Home Health Svcs. of R.I., 1986-93, chmn. ch. in soc. com., 1985-86; mem. R.I. Conf., United Ch. of Christ, 1964—, mem. com. on ministry, 1981-83, past bd. dirs.; mem. urban divsn. R.I. Coun. Chs., 1979-82. Editor-in-chief: jour. Expanding Horizons, 1996—; contbr. articles to profl. jours., newspapers and mags.; Religious Broadcasting Sta. WEAN, 1964—87. Adv. coun. Providence Pub. Libr., 1968-71; bd. dirs. Mouthpiece Coffee House, Providence, 1969-75, pres., 1974-75; bd. dirs. Citizens United Renewal Enterprises, 1972-77; alumni class agt. for scholarship funds Haverford Coll. and Yale U. Div. Sch., 1979-95; corp. mem. R.I. Hosp. Corp., 1980-95. Rsch. fellow Yale U. Div. Sch., 1979; recipient Alumnal Bd. award Yale U. Div. Sch., 1997. Mem. Providence Intown Chs. Assn., Mins. Assn. R.I. Conf. United Ch. of Christ, Dodeka Symposium, Rotary (trustee Rotary Charities Found. 1977-82, Paul Harris fellow), Beneficent Order of Spike, Phi Beta Kappa. Democrat. Home and Office: 103 Angell Rd Lincoln RI 02865-4710 E-mail: bararbor@earthlink.net.

BARLOW, CARROLEE, physician, scientist, educator; b. Page, Ariz., Sept. 24, 1963; d. Eslie and Carrol (Burham) B.; m. Kleanthis Gabriel Xanthopoulos, June 10, 1989. BA, U. Utah, 1985, MD, 1989; PhD, The Karolinska Inst., Stockholm, 1995. Diplomate Am. Bd. Endocrinology, Am. Bd. Internal Medicine. Study rsch. fellow Sch. Medicine U. Utah, Salt Lake City, 1986-89, The Rockefeller U., N.Y.C., 1988; resident N.Y. Hosp.-Cornell Med. Ctr.-U. Utah Med. Ctr., N.Y.C. and Salt Lake City, 1989-91; clin. assoc. NIH, Bethesda, Md., 1995-98; asst. prof. The Salk Inst., San Diego, 1998—. Presenter in field. Contbr. numerous articles to profl. jours. Recipient Caine scholarship U. Utah, 1988-89, Olga A. Logan scholarship, 1986-89, scholarship Nat. Panhellenic Assn., 1984-85, U. Utah Women's Club, 1982-83. Mem. Am. Women's Med. Assn. (Outstanding Women in Medicine award 1989), Alpha Omega Alpha, Phi Beta Kappa. Avocations: skiing, rollerblading, gardening. Office: The Salk Inst Genetics Lab 10010 N Torrey Pines Rd La Jolla CA 92037-1099

BARLOW, CATHERINE MAURICE, curator; b. St. Louis, Sept. 17, 1944; BA, Eckerd Coll., 1994; MA, U. Ark., 2002. Various to exec. asst. YMCA of Greater St. Louis, St. Louis, 1995—98; intern Washington County Hist. Soc., Fayetteville, Ark., 2001—02, Prairie Grove State Park, Prairie Grove, Ark., 2002—03; comptroller The Village, Inc., 2002—. Mem.: Lambda Pi Eta. Avocation: hist. rsch., writing, photography, travel. Home: PO Box 4522 Fayetteville AR 72702

BARLOW, F(RANK) JOHN, mechanical contracting company executive; b. Milw., July 12, 1914; s. Ernest A. and Alice E. (Norton) B.; m. Dorothy M. Marx, Oct. 13, 1935; children: Joyce D., Bonnie M., Joan C., Grace M., Jacqueline S., Wendy J., Terri L., Alice M. BS in Mech. Enging., U. Wis., 1937; DSc (hon.), 1994. Engr. Buffalo Forge Co., 1937-40, sales engr., 1940-42; plant engr. A.O. Smith Corp., Milw., 1942-44; chief mech. engr. Western Condensing Co., Appleton, Wis., 1944-46, profl. mgr., 1946-53; owner Azco, Inc., Appleton, Wis., 1953—98; pres. Sanco, Ltd., Appleton, 1959—98, Baldwin Barlow Corp., Appleton, 1965-83, The Downey Co., Milw. Pres. Ave. Dept. Inc., Appleton, Inc.; treas. Winagamie Corp., 1965-88; bd. dirs. Beta Color Inc., First Nat. Bank Appleton; dir., mem. exec. com. Air Wis., 1965-92; chmn. bd. dirs. Transpace Carriers, 1986-88. County chmn. March of Dimes, 1957—, state co-chmn., 1958; industry chmn. com. fund dir., 1968-69; bd. dirs. Nat. Cert. Pipe Welding Bur., Cmty. Found., 1986—, Beth Color Inc., 1991—, Bergstrom-Mahler Mus., 1993-95 (also pres. 1995); trustee Azco Employees Profit Sharing Trust, Wis. Acad. Scis., Arts & Letters, 1988—; pres. Appleton Devel. Coun., 1983-86; mem. adv. bd. Mich. Tech. U. Seaman Mus., 1995. Recipient Industry award Wis. Soc. Profl. Engrs., 1967, Cert. Commendation Gov. Tommy Thompson, 1998, Disting. Svc. award Curtis J. Tompkins, 2000, Carnegie Mineralogical award Carnegie Mus. Natural History, 2001. Mem. CAP, ASCE, Mech. Contractors Assn. Am. (nat. dir., pres. 1974-75, disting. service award 1982), Mech. Contractors Assn. Wis. (pres.), Wis. Soc. Profl. Engrs. (chpt. pres. 1968—), Am. Soc. Heating, Refrigerations and Airconditioning Engrs., Appleton C. of C., Flying Engrs., Nat. Soc. Profl. Engrs. Clubs: Butte Des Morts Golf (dir., pres. 1961, 62). Lodges: Masons, Shriners, Rotary, Elks (past exalted ruler). Home: 2703 Fox Run Appleton WI 54914-8727 Address: PO Box 177 Appleton WI 54912-0177

BARLOW, JEAN, art educator, painter; b. L.A., Dec. 13, 1940; d. Sydney R. and Rose (Ballen) Barlow; m. Gordon M. Nunes, Sept. 21, 1973 (dec. Dec. 1991). BA cum laude, UCLA, 1963, MA, 1965, MFA, 1968. Tchg. assoc. UCLA, 1964-68; instr. Univ. Adult Sch., L.A., 1966-70; lectr. Calif. State U., Long beach, 1967-69; instr. Beverly Hills (Calif.) Adult Edn., 1969, East L.A. Jr. Coll., 1969-70; lectr. UCLA, 1986, instr. ext. divsn., 1969-96; instr. Santa Monica (Calif.) City Coll., 1969—. Mentor program mem. Santa Monica City Coll., 1989-90; pvt. art tchr., L.A., 1970-96; cons. in field. One woman shows include Jenet Gallery, L.A., 1965, Santa Monica City Coll., 1974; new works on view at home, invitation only, 2001—03; exhibited in group shows at So. Calif., 1965, Orlando Gallery, L.A., 1967, 68, Santa Monica City Coll., 1974, 78, 80, 87, 88, 91, 94, 95, Living Room Gallery, 1997, Bergemot Station T2, 1999, Brentwood Park Group Art Exhibit; invitational pastel drawing Scripps Coll., So. Calif., 1965. Avocations: drawing and painting, photography, home landscape and decoration, creative cooking, writing.

BARLOW, JESSE LOUIS, computer scientist, educator; b. Lawrence, Kans., July 8, 1955; s. Richard Lewis and Elizabeth Marie (McCaffrey) B.; m. Ramsey Stade, Jan. 10, 1981; children: Hilary, Zachary. B.A. in Computer Sci. and Math., U. Kans., 1977; M.S. in Computer Sci., Northwestern U., 1979, M.S. in Stats., 1980, Ph.D., 1981. Asst. prof. computer sci. Pa. State U., University Park, 1981-87, assoc. prof. computer sci., 1987-92, prof. computer sci., 1992—. Vis. prof. U. Manchester, Eng., 1996, Courant Inst. Math. Sci., 1988, CUNY Grad. Ctr., 2002; vis. Inst. of Maths. and It's Applications, Inst. Math. Scis. Contbr. articles to profl. jours. NSF grantee, 1982-84, 84-86, 87, 90-2002, AFOSR grantee, 1988-90; recipient 2d prize L. Prize Meeting, London, 1986. Mem. Soc. Indsl. and Applied Math., IEEE Computer Soc., Assn. for Computing Machinery, Phi Beta Kappa. Office: Pa State U Computer Sci & Engring Dept University Park PA 16802 E-mail: barlow@cse.psu.edu.

BARLOW, JIM B. retired columnist; b. Port Arthur, Tex., Aug. 19, 1936; s. Joseph B. and Goldie (Johnson) B.; m. Karleen Ann Smith, Aug. 24, 1968 (div. Jan. 1974); 1 child, Samantha Lynn; m. Susan Ann Bischoff, June 20, 1975. BA, U. North Tex., Denton, 1972. Newsman KPAC-TV, Port Arthur, Tex., 1959-61; news dir. KPNG-Radio, Port Neches, Tex., 1962-63; reporter Beaumont (Tex.) Enterprise, 1963-64, Denton Record-Chronicle, 1964-66; asst. city mgr. City of Denton, 1967; staff writer U. North Tex., Denton, 1968; newsman AP, Dallas-Houston, 1968-75; dir. info. svcs. Houston Ind. Sch. Dist., 1975-77; reporter Houston Chronicle, 1977-87, columnist, 1987—2002; ret., 2002. Co-author: Big Town, Big Money, 1974. With U.S. Army, 1956-59. Avocations: reading, cooking, exercise. Home: # 112 2929 Buffalo Speedway Houston TX 77098

BARLOW, JOHN SUTTON, neurophysiologist, electroencephalographer, lexicographer; b. Raleigh, N.C., June 10, 1925; s. David Henry and Anne Mary (Sutton) B.; m. Sibylle E. Jahrreiss, Aug. 5, 1950; children: Thomas Walter, Robert Sutton, Lisa Katharine. BS, U. N.C., 1944, MS, 1948; MD, Harvard U., 1953. Diplomate Am. Bd. Cert. EEG. Clin. and rsch. fellow, asst. resident in neurology Mass. Gen. Hosp., Boston, 1953-57; clin. and rsch. fellow Harvard Med. Sch., Boston, 1953-57; rsch. assoc. in elec. engring. MIT, Cambridge, 1954-64, rsch. affiliate Rsch. Lab. of Electronics, 1964-99; asst. neurology Mass. Gen. Hosp., Boston, 1957-61, neurophysiologist neurology svc., 1961—; rsch. assoc. neurology Harvard Med. Sch., Boston, 1961-69, prin. rsch. assoc., 1969-78, sr. rsch. assoc. neurology, neurophysiology, 1979—. Mem. neurology study sect. NIH, Bethesda, Md., 1966-70; mem. rev. panel on neurol. devices FDA, Washington, 1974-76; cons. dept. neurology VA Med. Ctr., Boston, 1979-89, part-time staff, 1989-98; cons. dept. neurology New Eng. Med. Ctr., Boston, 1979-89. Author: The Electroencephalogram: Its Patterns and Origins, 1993, A Chinese-Russian-English Dictionary, 1995, A Pocket Chinese-Russian-English Dictionary, 2000, The Cerebellum and Adaptive Control, 2002; editor: (with Karenina Kollmar-Paulenz) Otto Ottonovich Rosenberg and his Contribution to Buddhology in Russia, 1998; cons. editor EEG Clin. Neurophysiology, 1970-86; translator/editor books from the Russian, Czech and Chinese; contbr. articles and revs. to profl. jours. Served from ensign to lt. (j.g.) USN, 1944-46. Recipient Rsch. Career Devel. award NIH, 1962-71, Sr. Scientist award Alexander von Humboldt Found., Göttingen, Germany, 1979, Sr. Scientist Exch. award NAS, U.S.A./USSR Acad. Scis., Moscow, 1982, 83, 88; rsch. grantee NIH, 1962-88; Fogarty Internat. fellow, 1979. Mem. Internat. Brain Rsch. Orgn., Am. EEG Soc. (pres. 1975-76), Am. Neurol. Assn., Am. Acad. Neurology, Soc. Neurosci., Am. Geophys. Union, Ea. Assn. EEG (pres. 1971-72), Assn. Asian Studies, European Assn. Chinese Studies, Dictionary Soc. North Am. Avocations: music, rail travel, foreign languages, international relations.

BARLOW, MARA LISE, public relations executive; b. Newark, July 20, 1963; d. David M. Litman and Ann (Zinnes) Newman; m. Jeffrey P. Barlow, May 5, 1991. BA in Comm., Rutgers U., 1986. News reporter The Times, Scotch Plains, N.J., 1984; advt. salesperson The Police News of N.J., Scotch Plains, 1983-85; asst. to dir. pub. relations, pubs. and spl. projects Seton Hall U., South Orange, N.J., 1987-88; pub. relations writer Bozell/Poppe Tyson, Morris Plains, N.J., 1988-90, pub. relations account exec., 1991-92; pub. info. asst. Dept. Commerce State of N.J., Trenton, 1990-91; pub. affairs dir. N.J. Organ and Tissue Sharing Network, Springfield, N.J., 1992—. Mem. NAFE, Pub. Relations Soc. Am., Internat. Assn. Bus. Communicators. Avocations: reading, bicycling, tennis, crafts, volunteer work. Office: The Sharing Network 841 Mountain Ave Springfield NJ 07081-3437 E-mail: mbarlow@sharenj.org.

BARLOW, NADINE GAIL, planetary geoscientist; b. La Jolla, Calif., Nov. 9, 1958; d. Nathan Dale and Marcella Isabel (Menken) B. BS, U. Ariz., 1980, PhD, 1987. Instr., planetarium lectr. Palomar Coll., San Marcos, Calif., 1982; grad. rsch. asst. U. Ariz., Tucson, 1982-87; postdoctoral fellow Lunar and Planetary Inst., Houston, 1987-89; NRC assoc. NASA/Johnson Space Ctr., Houston, 1989-91, vis. scientist, 1991-92, support scientist exploration programs office, 1992; vis. scientist Lunar and Planetary Inst., Houston, 1992-95; assoc. prof. U. Houston, Clear Lake, 1991-95; pres. Minerva Rsch. Enterprises, 1995-99; asst. prof. astronomy, dir. Robinson Obs. U. Ctrl. Fla., Orlando, 1996—2002; asst. prof. dept. physics and astronomy No. Ariz. U., Flagstaff, 2002—. Co-dir. intern program Lunar and Planetary Inst., 1988-89. Editor (slide set) A Guide to Martian Impact Craters, 1988; assoc. editor Encyclopedia of Earth Sciences, 1996; contbr. articles to profl. jours. Named among Outstanding Women and Ethnic Minorities Engaged in Sci. and Enging., Lawrence Livermore Nat. Lab., 1991, Alumna of Yr., Palomar Coll., 2003. Mem. AAUW (pres. Clear Lake chpt. 1991-93, program v.p. 1993-95, v.p. interbr. coun. 1990-91, chmn. Tex. task force on women and girls in sci. and math. 1991-92, dir. state pub. policy 1991-94, Tex. Woman of Yr. 1992, mem. pub. policy com. 1994-95, chmn. steering com. Tex. edln. equity 1994-95), Am. Astron. Soc. (pres. officer divsn. planetary scis. 1993-99, status of women in astronomy com. 1987-90, 1995-98, exec. com. divsn. for planetary scis. 1999-02), Meteoritical Soc., Am. Geophys. Union, Geol. Soc. Am. (planetary geology divsn. nominating com. 1996-97). Achievements include research and compilation of primary data source on 42,283 impact craters on Mars; identification of possible source craters for Martian meteorites. Office: No Arizono Univ Dept Physics and Astronomy NAU Box 6010 Flagstaff AZ 86011-6010

BARLOW, WALTER GREENWOOD, public opinion analyst, management consultant; b. Liverpool, Eng., Sept. 10, 1917; came to U.S., 1920, naturalized, 1928; s. Walter and Sarah Ellen (Greenwood); m. Hanna Hansen, 1951 (dec. 1974); children: Eric, Francine, Deborah, Alison; m. Joan K. Frahm, June 21, 1980 (div. 1989). BA, Cornell U., 1939. Reporter Washington Daily News, 1940; mem. editorial staff Time mag., 1941; with Opinion Rsch. Corp., 1946-65, pres., 1960-65, Howard Chase Assocs., Inc., N.Y.C., 1965-68; founder Rsch. Strategies Corp., N.Y.C., 1965, pres., 1966—. Bd. dirs. A.D. Publs. (formerly Presbyn. Life Mag.), 1968-72, pres., 1970-72; pres. Crawford House, Inc., 1988-90. Mem. N.J. Bd. Pub. Welfare, 1966-80, vice chmn., 1973-80; mem. adv. coun. Electric Power Rsch. Inst., 1977-81; trustee Cornell U., 1968-75, univ. coun., 1968—; bd. dirs. support agy. United Presbyn. Ch. in U.S.A., 1973-80; bd. dirs. Renewal Found., 1990—, pres., 1995; bd. dirs. Family Svc. Assn. Am., 1958-69, v.p., 1964-67, pres., 1967-69; commr. Middle States Assn. Colls. and Schs., 1982-88. Maj. AUS, 1941-46, ETO. Decorated Bronze Star. Mem. Am. Assn. Pub. Opinion Rsch., Phi Beta Kappa, Phi Kappa Phi. Clubs: Cornell of N.Y., Nassau (Princeton, N.J.). Presbyterian. Office: 217 Wall St Princeton NJ 08540-1512

BARLOW, WILLIAM KYLE, lawyer, state legislator; b. Smithfield, Va., Mar. 13, 1936; s. Gordon E. and Gladys (Holleman) B.; 1 child, Todd R.; m. Taylor Rowell; 1 child, Amy Elizabeth Barlow Britt. MS in Agrl. Econs. with honors, Va. Poly. Inst., 1958; LLB, U. Va., 1965. Assoc. Law Office of A. E. S. Stephens, Va., 1965-72; ptnr. Delk and Barlow, Smithfield, Va., 1972-87, Barlow, Councill & Riddick, Smithfield, Va., 1987-92; pres. Barlow & Riddick, Smithfield, Va., 1992—2002, Barlow, Riddick & Farmer, 2002—; mem. Va. Ho. of Dels., 1991—2001, mem. fin., agr., sci. & tech., general law, mem. cts. of justice, gen. laws, militia, police, pub. safety, 2001—. Past mem. PTA; past chmn. Isle of Wight County Dem. Com., past chmn. bd. selection commn., mem. C. of C.; past trustee Walter Cecil Rawls Regional Libr., Courtland Va.; mem. Smithfield Bapt. Ch., past chmn. bd. deacons, trustee, ch. moderator; former Little League baseball coach; former mem. and chmn. bd. trustees Walter Cecil Rawls Regional Libr.; mem. bd. dirs. Obici Hosp., Suffolk, Va.;

legal advisor Isle of Wright County Rescue Squad. With USAF, 1958-62. Mem. Va. Tech. Alumni Assn. (past pres., bd. dirs.; mem. Peanut Alumni chpt.), Isle-Wight County-Smithfield C. of C., Rotary (past pres.), Ruritan Club, Phi Alpha Delta.

BARLOW, WILLIAM PUSEY, JR., accountant; b. Oakland, Calif., Feb. 11, 1934; s. William P. and Muriel (Block) B. Student, Calif. Inst. Tech., 1952-54; AB in Econs., U. Calif., Berkeley, 1956. CPA, Calif. Acct. Barlow, Davis & Wood, San Francisco, 1960-72, ptnr., 1964-72, J.K. Lasser & Co., 1972-77, Touche Ross & Co., San Francisco, 1977-78; self employed acct., 1978-89; ptnr. Barlow & Hughan, 1990—. Co-author: Collectible Books: Some New Paths, 1979, The Grolier Club, 1884-1984, 1984; editor: Book Catalogues: Their Varieties and Uses, 2d edit., 1986, Officially Sealed Notes, 1996—; contbr. articles to profl. jours. Fellow Gleeson Libr. Assocs., 1969, pres., 1971-74; mem. coun. Friends Bancroft Libr., 1971-98, chmn., 1974-79; bd. dirs. Oakland Ballet, 1982-99, pres., 1986-89, chmn., 1995-98. Recipient Sir Thomas More medal Gleeson Libr. Assocs., 1989; named to Water Ski Hall of Fame, 1993. Mem. Am. Water Ski Assn. (bd. dirs., regional chmn. 1959-63, pres. 1963-66, chmn. bd. 1966-69, 77-79, hon. v.p. 1969—), Machine Cancel Soc. (pres., 2003—), Internat. Water Ski Fedn. (exec. bd. 1961-71, 75-78), Bibliog. Soc. Am. (coun. 1986-92, pres. 1992-96), Grolier Club (N.Y.C.), Roxburghe Club (San Francisco), Book Club of Calif. (bd. dirs. 1963-76, pres. 1968-69, treas. 1971-83). Home: 1474 Hampel St Oakland CA 94602-1346 Office: 1182 Market St Ste 400 San Francisco CA 94102-4922 E-mail: wpbjr@barlowandhughan.com.

BARLOWE, RALEIGH, economist, educator; b. Lincoln, Idaho, Nov. 10, 1914; s. George Edward and Charlotte (Campbell) B.; m. Jeanette Topp, Oct. 4, 1941; 1 child, Raleigh R.B. BS, Utah State Agrl. Coll., 1936; postgrad., USDA Grad. Sch., 1938-40; MA, Am. U., 1939; PhD, U. Wis., 1946. Instr. Am. U., 1937-38; asst. Libr. of Congress, 1937-40; land economist Southwestern Land Tenure Research Project, Fayetteville, Ark., 1942-43; agrl. economist U.S. Dept. Agr., Milw., 1943-47; economist FAO, Washington, 1947; from lectr. to prof. agrl. econs. Mich. State U., 1948-59, prof., 1959-81, disting. prof., 1981, adj. prof., 1982—84, chmn. dept. resource devel., 1959-71, 80, dir. William Vogt Ctr. Population-Environment Balance, 1986; vis. prof. U. Calif., Riverside, 1982; economist Robert R. Nathan Assn., Bogotá, Colombia, 1959, Cons. U. P.R., 1958, Govt. Colombia, 1959, U. Nigeria, 1967, Pub. Land Law Rev. Commn., 1969, Korea, 1971-72; cons. Agr. Devel. Council, 1972, Orgn. for European Cooperation and Devel., 1973, Govt. Thailand, 1976-77; mem. U.S. del. to Indo-U.S. Pugwash Conf. on Sci. and Tech., 1974; Mem. Gov.'s Water Com., 1955-56; staff Mich. Tax Study, 1957-58; chmn. tech. com. Lansing Water Adv. Com., 1961-63; staff Mich. Constl. Conv. Prep. Commn., 1961; treas. Mich. Natural Resources Council, 1961-63, chmn., 1963-65; mem. Gov.'s Task Force on Water Rights, Use and Pollution Control, 1964-66 Author: Land Resource Economics, 1958, rev. 1972, 78, 86, (with V. Webster Johnson) Land Problems and Policies, 1954, Fain Would I Climb: Sir Walter Raleigh Tells His Life Story, 1996, The Blackening of Richard III, 1999, The Kingmaker, 2003; contbr. articles to profl. jours. Fellow Soil Conservation Soc. Am. (pres. Mich. chpt. 1980-81); Mem. Am. Agrl. Econs. Assn., Am. Econ. Assn., Econ. History Assn., Agrl. History Soc. Home: 907 Southlawn Ave East Lansing MI 48823-3038

BARLOWE BODMAN, AMY, violinist, composer; b. Copiague, N.Y., Jan. 20, 1952; d. Sy and Dorothea (Kay) Barlowe; m. Alan Kingsley Bodman, Dec. 27, 1988; children: Alanna, Ariel Rose. BMus, Juilliard Sch. Music, N.Y.C., 1975, MMus, 1976. Violinist Oregon Trio, Salem, 1976-86; assoc. prof. violin Willamette U., Salem, 1976-86; tchr. Bowdoin (Maine) Music Festival, 1983, Estherwood Music Festival, Oneonta, N.Y., 1984, Juilliard Pre-Coll., N.Y.C., 1986-88; faculty Sch. for Strings, N.Y.C., 1986-88; violinist Duo AB2, Akron, Ohio, 1988—; assoc. concertmaster Arkon Symphony Orch., 1988—2000; artist/faculty Meadowmount Sch. Music, Westport, N.Y., 1988—. Violinist, recitalist numerous chamber ensembles, U.S., Can., Mex., 1976—. Author: Guide for Enjoyable Listening, 1983, Happy Listening Guide, 1992, Come Listen With Me, 1993; composer: Reflections from the Edge of the Millennium, 1999, Hebraique Eiegie, 2000, Requiem, 2002; violinist recording on Medici label, 1990, Azica label, 1999; numerous violin appearances various radio stas., N.Y., Oreg., Ohio, Calif., Wash., 1976—. Recipient Atkinson award Willamette U., 1983, Helena Rubinstein Found. award, 1975; Willamette U. Northwest Area grantee, 1983; Bach Aria Group fellow. Mem. Am. Fedn. Musicians, Am. String Tchrs. Assn., Music Educators Nat. Conf., Music Tchrs. Nat. Assn. Avocation: photography. Home: 338 Castle Blvd Akron OH 44313-6504

BARMANN, BERNARD CHARLES, SR., lawyer; b. Maryville, Mo., Aug. 5, 1932; s. Charles Anselm and Veronica Rose (Fisher) B.; m. Beatrice Margaret Murphy, Sept. 27, 1965; children: Bernard Charles Jr., Brigit. PhD, Stanford U., 1966; JD, U. San Diego, 1974; MPA, Calif. State U., Bakersfield. Bar: Calif. 1974, U.S. Dist. Ct. (so. dist.) Calif. 1974, U.S. Dist. Ct. (ea. dist.) Calif. 1978, U.S. Ct. Appeals (9th cir.) 1984, U.S. Supreme Ct. Asst. prof. Ohio State U., Columbus, 1966-69, U. Toronto, Ont., Can., 1969-71; dep. county counsel Kern County, Bakersfield, Calif., 1974-85, county counsel, 1985—. Adj. prof. Calif. State U., Bakersfield, 1986—. Editor: The Bottom Line, 1991-93, contbr. articles to profl. jours. Mem. exec. bd. So. Sierra coun. Boy Scouts Am., Bakersfield, 1986—; bd. dirs. Kern County Acad. Decathlon, Bakersfield, 1988—. Danforth Found. fellow, 1963-65; grantee Fulbright Found., 1963-65. Mem. Calif. Bar Assn. (law practice mgmt. sect. exec. com., jud. nominees evaluation commn. 1997-2000), County Counsel Assn. Calif. (bd. dirs. 1990—, chair 1993-94), Kern County Bar Assn. (pres. 2001), Rotary. Avocations: golf, skiing, travel, photography. Office: Kern County Office of County Counsel 1115 Truxtun Ave Bakersfield CA 93301-4639 E-mail: bbarmann@co.kern.ca.us.

BARMANN, LAWRENCE FRANCIS, history educator, retired; b. Maryville, Mo., June 9, 1932; s. Francis Lawrence and Clary Weber (LaMar) B. BA, St. Louis U., 1956, Ph.L., 1957, S.T.L., 1964; MA, Fordham U., 1960; postgrad., Princeton, 1965-66; PhD, Cambridge U., Eng., 1970. Tchr. history St. Louis U. High Sch., 1957-59; asst. prof. history St. Louis U., 1970-73, assoc. prof., 1973-78, prof., 1978—, asst. dir. Am. Studies Program, 1981-83, prof. Am. studies, 1981-01; dir. Am. Studies Program, 1983-88; prof. theol. studies St. Louis U., 1996-01, ret., 2001, prof. emeritus, 2002—. Author: Newman at St. Mary's, 1962, Baron Friedrich von Hügel and the Modernist Crisis in England, 1972, The Letters of Baron Friedrich von Hügel and Professor Norman Kemp Smith, 1982; editor Sanctity and Secularity, 1999; contbr. articles profl. jours. Recipient award Mellon Faculty Devel. Fund, 1987, 92, 94, Emerson Electric Outstanding Tchr. award, 1999; rsch. grantee Am. Philos. Soc. PHila., 1971, Beaumont Fund, 1977, 82; Danforth assoc., 1978—. Mem. Am. Acad. Religion, Cambridge Soc. (founding 1977), Am. Cath. Hist. Assn., Phi Beta Kappa. Home: The Lindell Ter 12-A 4501 Lindell Blvd Saint Louis MO 63108-2038 Office: 221 N Grand Blvd Saint Louis MO 63103-2006 E-mail: barmann@slu.edu. *I have found for myself that the meaning of life is the joy of continuous discovery in unending intellectual, emotional and spiritual growth, and the satisfaction which comes from sharing my vision and concerns with the young people who will lead the next generation.*

BARMASH, ISADORE, writer, journalist; b. Phila., Nov. 16, 1921; s. Samuel and Sarah (Griff) Barmash; m. Sarah Jasnoff, July 22, 1945; children: Elaine, Stanley, Marilyn, Pamela. Diploma in Journalism, Charles Morris Price Sch., Phila., 1941. Bur. news reporter Fairchild Pubs., Phila., 1947—50, bur. chief, 1950—51, ctrl. copy chief N.Y.C., 1952—58, mng. editor, 1958—59, editor-in-chief, 1960—62; fin. feature writer N.Y. Herald Tribune, N.Y.C., 1962—64; bus. writer, editor N.Y. Times, N.Y.C., 1965—91; freelance writer, 1991. Columnist Nihon Keizai Shimbun (Japan), Tokyo, 1988—91, Money Talks (Online), N.Y.C., 1995—99; feature writer Reuters Am., N.Y.C., 1996—2000; lectr. in field. Contbr. ; author: (book) The Self-Made Man, 1969, (mergers trend) Welcome to Our Conglomerate - You're Fired!, 1971, (bus. novel) Net-Net, 1972, (book) The World is Full of It, 1974, (documentary) For the Good of the Company, 1976, The Chief Executives, 1978, More Than They Bargained For, 1981, (biography) Always Live Better Than Your Clients, 1983, (documentary) Macy's for Sale, 1989, (book) The Not-So Tender Offer, 1995; co-author: Healing Our Health-Care System, 1990, Everybody Wins, 1986; editor: (anthology) Great Business Disasters, 1972. With U.S. Army, 1942—45. Avocations: music appreciation, painting, reading. Home: 85-33 215th St Hollis Hills New York NY 11427

BARMETTLER, JOSEPH JOHN, lawyer; b. Omaha, Sept. 10, 1933; s. William Thomas and Dorothy Lucy (Flynn) B.; m. Jeanne Waller, June 21, 1958; children: Joseph Jr., Gregory, Richard, Katie, Peggy Carbullido, Timothy, Michael. BSC, Creighton U., 1956, JD, 1959. Bar: Nebr. 1959, US Dist. Ct. Nebr. 1959, US Ct. Appeals (8th cir.) 1963, US Ct. Claims 1963. Assoc. Fitzgerald, Hamer, Brown & Leahy, Omaha, 1959-64; prin. Fitzgerald, Schorr, Barmettler & Brennan, P.C., L.L.O., Omaha, 1964—, CEO, 1988—. Gen. counsel Met. C.C., Omaha, 1974—, Village of Boys Town, Nebr., 1991—, City of La Vista, Nebr., 1963—. Mem. pres.'s coun. Creighton U., Omaha, 1990—; trustee La Vista Cmty. Found. Fellow Nebr. Bar Found.; mem. Nebr. Bar Assn. (chmn. ways, means and planning com. 1993-94, ho. of dels. 1985—, chmn. budget and adminstrn. com. 1993-94), Omaha Bar Assn., Omaha Downtown Rotary (dir. 1986-89, Paul Harris fellow). Avocations: golf, photography. Office: Fitzgerald Schorr Barmettler & Brennan PC Ste 400 13320 California St Omaha NE 68154

BARNA, DOUGLAS PETER, collection agency executive; b. Passaic, N.J., Nov. 28, 1945; s. Peter Richard and Marie (Saltamachia) B.; m. Nancy M. Viverito, Oct. 1971 (div. Oct. 1974); m. Norma Rae Hudson Fitzsimmons, July 3, 1983; stepchildren: Sherry, Michael, Gail, Laura, Kelly, Kenneth. BS in Bus. Mgmt., Fairleigh Dickinson U., 1968. Product control and accounts receivable specialist IBM Corp., Franklin Lakes, N.J., 1964-72; credit mgr. Star Graphic Sys., Clifton, N.J., 1972-74; corp. credit mgr. The Harvey Group, Woodbury, N.Y., 1975; sales exec. Contract Equity Corp., Melville, N.Y., 1976, Media Coords. Ltd., Levittown, N.Y., 1976-78; v.p. sales Valer Enterprises Inc., Patchogue, N.Y., 1978-84; pres. Douglas Equity Enterprises Ltd. divsn. Nat. Recovery Svcs., Patchogue, 1985—; owner Douglas Enterprises, Patchogue, 1985—; pres. Bulldog Devel. Inc., Patchogue, 1988-94. Mem. Comml. Law League Am., Greater Patchogue C. of C. (dir. 1987-96, treas. 1994-96), Kiwanis (bd. dirs. 1994-97, Kiwanian of Yr. 1996), Phi Gamma Pi (pres. 1967-68). Avocations: swimming, traveling, reading, gourmet foods. Home: PO Box 800 Medford NY 11763-0800 Office: Nat Recovery Svcs PO Box 469 Patchogue NY 11772-0469 E-mail: NRSDEEL@cs.com.

BARNA, RICHARD ALLEN, lighting company executive, broadcasting executive; b. N.Y.C., Oct. 7, 1948; s. Raymond Alexander and Miriam (Friedman) B.; m. Eileen Maisel; children: Ross, Hayley. BA, Brown U., 1970; OPM degree, Harvard U., 1985. Program dir. WHCN Concert Network, Inc., Hartford, Conn., 1970-71; pres. ProMedia, Inc., Northvale, N.J., 1971-96; v.p. RAB Electric Mfg., Inc., Bronx, N.Y., 1976-78, pres., CEO Northvale, N.J., 1978—; COO ZyDoc.com, Happauge, NY, 1997—2001. Cons. Harvard Bus. Sch. Cmty. Ptnrs., N.Y.C., 1998—; Internet cons. N.Y. Pub. Libr., 1998-2001; bd. dirs. The Exec. Alliance, N.Y. Vice pres. Banksville Fire Dept., Bedford, N.Y., 1987-94; trustee, treas. North Castle Pub. Libr., Armonk, 1991-96. With U.S. Army, 1971-77. Avocations: sailing, skiing. Office: RAB Electric Mfg 170 Ludlow Ave Northvale NJ 07647-2306

BARNARD, ALLEN DONALD, lawyer; b. Williston, N.D., Feb. 22, 1944; s. Donald J. and Ruth E. (Franklin) B.; m. Andra Lynn Lebsock, Nov. 24, 1962; children: Alana, Aaron. BA in Social Scis., U. N.D., 1965; JD, U. Notre Dame, 1968. Bar: Minn. 1968, U.S. Dist. Ct. Minn. 1968, U.S. Ct. Appeals (8th cir.) 1971, U.S. Supreme Ct. 1973. Assoc. Best & Flanagan, Mpls., 1968-72, ptnr., 1972—, mng. ptnr., 1991-93. City atty. City of Golden Valley, Minn., 1988—, housing and redevel. authority atty., 1978— Mem. ABA, Hennepin County Bar Assn., Minn. State Bar Assn., Madeline Island Yacht Club (bd. dirs. 1991-97, 2003—). Avocations: sailing, skiing. Office: Best & Flanagan 225 S Sixth St #4000 Minneapolis MN 55402-4331 E-mail: abarnard@bestlaw.com.

BARNARD, ANNA MARION, county official; b. Magnolia, Ark., Oct. 30, 1953; d. Harvey Wesley and Virginia Sue (Herring) Callicott; m. Robert Richard Edington, Aug. 5, 1972 (dec. Oct. 1974); m. Rickie Lynn Barnard, May 15, 1976; children: Melanie Lynn, Hilary Anne, Matthew Ryan. Student, So. State Coll., 1975-76. Cert. treas., Ark. Teller, ins. clk. Peoples Bank, Waldo, Ark., 1971-74; teller collections, sec. to pres. First Nat. Bank, Magnolia, Ark., 1976-80; acct., bookkeeper Hamlin & Nolte Water Wells, Taylor, Ark., 1987-95; adminstrv. asst. Columbia County, Magnolia, Ark., 1995-96, county treas., 1997—. Mem. Leadership Magnolia, 1998—; bd. dirs., treas. Bussey/Sharman Fire Dist., Taylor, Ark., 1996—; mem. South Ark. Women's Network, Magnolia, 1997-98, Magnolia Econ. Devel. Corp., 1999—; bd. dirs. Columbia County United Way, 2002—. Mem. Ark. County Treas. Assn. Baptist. Avocations: church pianist, singing, reading, cooking, cross-stiching. Office: Columbia County Treas 101 S Court Sq Magnolia AR 71753-3511 E-mail: ccto@magnolia-net.com.

BARNARD, ANNETTE WILLIAMSON, elementary school principal; b. Phoenix, Nov. 29, 1948; d. Water Albert and Geraldine Williamson; m. Richard W. Heinrich, Sept. 1969 (div.); 1 child, Jennifer Anne; m. Charles Jay Barnard, June 6, 1981. AA, Mesa C.C., 1979; BA in Spl. Edn., Elem. Edn., Ariz. State U., 1981, postgrad., 1989; M in Edn. Leadership, 1996, No. Ariz. U., 1996. Cert. tchr., prin., Ariz. Tchr. spl. edn. Tempe (Ariz.) Sch. Dist., 1981-83, tchr. Indian community, 1983-84; tchr. elem. sch. Kyrene Sch. Dist., Tempe, 1984-97; sch. dist. mentor coord., 1994-96; tchr. Chandler (Ariz.) Sch. Dist., 1986-89; v.p. Pendergast Elem. Sch., Phoenix, 1997-98; prin. Arredondo Elem. Sch., Tempe Sch. Dist., 1999—. Chair profl. stds. and cert. com. Ariz. Bd. Edn., Phoenix, 1990-94; chair facilitator Kyrene Legis. Action Community, 1991-94; mentor Kyrene Sch. dist., 1990—; commencement spkr. Ariz. State U., 1981; design. team. mem. Quality Cert. Employee Appraisal System; speaker in field. Contbg. author: Environmental Education Compendium for Energy Resources, 1991, System of Personnel Development, 1989; contbr. articles to profl. jours. Bd. dirs. Ariz. State Rep. Caucus, Phoenix, 1990-93, precinct committee-woman, Tempe, 1990-92. Recipient Profl. Leadership award Kiwanis Club Am., Tempe, 1984; nominee to talent bank Coun. on Women's Edn. Programs U.S. Dept. Edn., 1982; named Tchr. of Yr., local newspaper, 1993. Mem. ASCD, Kyrene Edn. Assn. (chair legis. com. 1990-94), Kappa Delta Pi, Phi Kappa Phi, Phi Theta Kappa, Pi Lambda Theta. Achievements include being featured in PBS Cornerstones video, 1994. Home: 3080 S Greythorne Way Chandler AZ 85248-2149

BARNARD, CHARLES NELSON, editorial consultant, author; b. Arlington, Mass., Oct. 5, 1924; s. Charles Nelson and Mae E. (Johnson) B.; m. Diana Lee Pattison, Aug. 6, 1949 (div. Aug. 1970); children: Jennifer Lee, Rebecca, Charles Nelson, Patrick; m. Karen Louise Zakrison, Apr. 18, 1971 (div. Jan. 1987). B.J., U. Mo., 1949. Editor Dell Pub. Co., N.Y.C., 1949; assoc. editor True mag., Fawcett Pubs., N.Y.C., 1949-54, mng. editor, 1954-63; sr. editor Sat. Evening Post, N.Y.C., 1964-65; exec. editor True Mag., 1965-67, editor, 1968-70; travel editor Modern Maturity, publ. of Am. Assn. Ret. Persons, 1982-2000; editorial cons., freelance writer, 1971—; mgn. editor Travel Classics.com. Author: The Winter People, 1973, 20,000 Alarms, 1974, I Drank the Water Everywhere, 1975, The Money Pit, 1976, It Was a Wonderful Summer for Running Away, 1977; editor: A Treasury of True, 1957, Official Automobile Handbook, 1959, Anthology of True, 1962; contbr. to: Ency. Brit., Readers Digest, Smithsonian mag., Nat. Geographic, Travel and Leisure, Nat. Wildlife. Served from pvt. to sgt. AUS, 1944-46; war corr. Mem. Alpha Tau Omega, Sigma Delta Chi, Kappa Tau Alpha. Home: 225 Valley Rd Cos Cob CT 06807-2213

BARNARD, DONALD ROY, medical and veterinary entomologist; b. Santa Ana, Calif., June 7, 1946; s. Alan Whittaker and Ethel Mae (Kennedy) B.; m. Priscilla Margaret Grier, Aug. 12, 1967; children: Jennifer Erin, David Michael. BS in Zoology, Calif. State U., 1969, MA in Biology, 1972; PhD in Entomology, U. Calif., Riverside, 1977. Postdoctoral fellow Colo. State U., Ft. Collins, 1977-79; rsch. entomologist agrl. rsch. svc. USDA, Poteau, Okla., 1979-85, supervisory rsch. entomologist, 1985-88, rsch. leader agrl. rsch. svc., 1988—. Adj. prof. entomology Okla. State U., 1988—, U. Fla., 1991—; tech. reviewer NIH, 1989-96, NSF, 1995-96, Ctrs. for Disease Control and Prevention, 1990. Ill. Soybean Program Operating Bd., 1995-96; mem. USDA, NRI Competitive Grants Program, 1994—, Dept. Def., Def. Logistics Agy., 1995-96; cons., tech. reviewer WHO/FAO, 1980—, USAID, Somali Dem. Republic, 1981—, Dept. of Def., AFPMB, 1985—, Republic South Africa, 1988—, State of Fla., DOACS, DAI, DOH, 1992—, Unilever Rsch., 1999—, Consumers Union, 2000—, USDA, APHIS, 1996—, EPA, 2000—; external reviewer U. Orange Free State, Republic South Africa, 1995-96, Tripura U., India, 1999—, Kongunadu Coll., India, 2001—, Ministry of Health, Brazil, 1988—; active Fla. Coordinating Coun. for Mosquito Control.; rsch. adv. com. Fla. Mosquito Control Assn. Contbr. chpts. to books, articles to profl. jours.; editor Jour. of Med. Entomology, 2000—; mem. editl. bd. Bull. of the Soc. Vector Ecologists. Mem. Am. Mosquito Control Assn., Internat. Orgn. Biol. Control, Entomol. Soc. Am., Entomol. Soc. Can., Ecol. Soc. Am., Internat. Soc. Travel Medicine, Am. Soc. Tropical Medicine and Hygiene. E-mail: dbarnard@gainesville.usda.ufl.edu.

BARNARD, GEOFFREY W. magistrate judge; b. Batavia, N.Y., Apr. 4, 1945; Diploma, Univ. of Madrid, Spain, 1965; BA, Alleghany Coll., 1966; JD, Cornell Univ. Sch. of Law, Ithaca, 1969. Magistrate judge for V.I., U.S. Magistrate Ct., Charlotte Amalie, St. Thomas, 1986—. Office: US Magistrate Ct 345 US Courthouse 5500 Veterans Dr Charlotte Amalie VI 00802-6424*

BARNARD, GEORGE SMITH, lawyer, former federal agency official; b. Opelika, Ala. s. George Smith and Caroline Elizabeth (Dowdell) B.; m. Muriel Elaine Outlaw, July 26, 1945; children: Elizabeth Elaine Barnard Crutcher, Charles Dowling, Beverly Laura Barnard Parker, Andrew Carey. BA, U. Ala., 1948, LLB, 1950. Bar: Fla. 1978, Ala. 1950, U.S. Tax Ct. 1950, U.S. Dist. Ct. Ala. 1950, U.S. Dist. Ct. Fla. 1978, U.S. Dist. Ct. (so. dist. trial bar) Fla. 1995, U.S. Supreme Ct. 1965, U.S. Ct. Claims 1979, U.S. Ct. Appeals (Fed. cir.) 1984, U.S. Ct. Appeals (11th cir.) 1985. Pvt. practice, Opelika, 1950-51; with IRS, 1951-78; attache, revenue service rep. Sao Paulo Brazil, S.Am. and Lesser Antilles, 1965-71, Mexico City, Bermuda Is., Bahamas, Panama, Major Antilles, C.Am., 1971-77; ptnr. Barnard, P.A., Miami, Fla., 1978-87, of counsel, 1987-91. Lectr. taxation U. Ala., 1958-60. Pres. Rocky Ridge Vol. Fire Dept., 1956-58, Rocky Ridge Civic Club, 1959, Ala. chpt. Nat. Assn. Internal Revenue Employees, 1962; commr. Rocky Ridge Civic Water Works, 1960-62; bd. dirs. S.E.Pompano Homeowners Assn., 1996-99. With USAAF, 1942-46. Recipient Albert Gallatin award U.S. Treasury Dept., 1978; named Hon. Citizen of Tex., 1979, Hon. Admiral in Tex. Navy, 1979. Mem. Fgn. Svc. Retirees Assn. of Fla. (advisor/dir. for S.E. Fla. 1987-98, dir. emeritus 1998—, original incumbent historian 1998—), Kappa Sigma. Republican. Home: 671 SW 6th St Apt 602 Pompano Beach FL 33060-7735 Office: Charles D Barnard PA 3940 N Andrews Ave Fort Lauderdale FL 33309-5240 E-mail: memebarn@attbi.com.

BARNARD, IAN, writer, educator; b. Johannesburg, Gauteng, S. Africa, Jan. 3, 1960; came to U.S., 1984; s. Wessel and Iona B. BA with honors, U. Witwatersrand, Johannesburg, S. Africa, 1984; MA, San Diego State U., 1986; PhD, U. Calif., San Diego, 1992. Vis. asst. prof. Ohio State U., Columbus, 1996-97; lectr. San Diego State U., 1997-99, Calif. State U., Chico, 1999-2000, U. So. Calif., L.A., 2001—03; asst. prof. Calif. State U., Northridge, 2003—. Office: Dept English Calif State U Northridge CA 91330-8242

BARNARD, JOHN PHILLIP, technology educator; b. Watertown, NY, Jan. 30, 1950; s. Lewis Addison and Emma (Halsey) B.; m. Che du Puich, Aug. 26, 1977. BS, USNY Regents Coll., Albany, 1989; MEd, Ariz. State U., 1990, PhD, 2000. Cert. CC instr. Photographer Ariz. State U., Tempe, 1971-81, media specialist, 1981-90, instrnl. specialist, 1990-91, acad. profl., 1991—2002; asst. prof. instl. tech. Gordon Coll., Barnesville, Ga., 2002—. Contbr. articles to profl. jours. Mem. Am. Ednl. Rsch. Assn., Assn. for Ednl. Comm. and Tech., Ariz. Ednl. Media Assn. (pres. 1994-95), Phi Kappa Phi. Democrat. Office: Gordon Coll Barnesville GA 30204

BARNARD, KURT, retail trend/consumer spending forecaster, publisher; b. Hamburg, Germany, Apr. 16, 1927; s. León and Senta (Künstlinger) Barnard-Jeserski; m. Wendy Holly Love, Dec. 9, 1979; 1 child, Lance Jonathan. Student, NYU, 1948, N.Y. State U., 1953; grad., New Sch. for Social Research, 1957. N.Y. corr. European and Japanese bus. publs., 1957-60; dir. Latin Am., Far Eastern pub. relations Anglo-Affiliated Corp., N.Y.C., 1955-60; mktg. dir. Am. Research Merchandising Inst., Chgo., 1960-67; founding exec. dir. Internat. Mass Retail Assn., N.Y.C., 1967-69; exec. v.p. Internat. Mass Retailing Assn., N.Y.C., 1969-74, pres., 1974-76; exec. dir. Fedn. Apparel Mfrs., N.Y.C., 1976-86; launched Barnard's Retail Cons. Group and Barnard's Retail Mktg. Report, 1984. Launched Barnard's Retail Cons. Group and Barnard's Retail Mktg. Report, 1984 (now Barnard's Retail Trend Report); cons. on wage-price freeze to dir. U.S. Office Emergency Preparedness, 1971-72; condr. retailing seminars in Europe, U.S.; frequent forecaster and commentator on retailing and consumer spending issues on TV, Radio, including McNeil-Lehrer Newshour, CBS Evening News, NBC's Today Show, ABC's Good Morning Am. show, CNN, CNNfn, CNBC, Wall Street Journal Radio, Nat. Pub. Radio; organizer Nat. Loss Prevention Coun., 1972, Store Thieves and Their Impact, A Study, 1973; named mem. U.S. Govt. Industry Sector Adv. Com., 1978; mem. U.S. Govt. Exporters Adv. Com., 1979; chmn. bd. N.Y. Internat. Fashion Fair, 1980; leader nat. campaign against fair trade laws. Author: Cargo of Death, 1966, An Untapped Source of Store Profits, 1974, Picture of a Tragedy, 1974, How Chains Succeed With Non-Foods, 1974, Can Supermarkets Capture Non-Food Sales?, 1974, In Retailing: Future Shock is Now, 1975, Guidelines to Effective Marketing Strategies for Self-Service Retailers, 1975; co-author: Mass Merchandisers Guide to Sales and Expense Reporting, 1969, Marketing: Key to Retail Prosperity, 1985; contbr. articles to mags. and profl. jours. Recipient Disting. Service award U.S.O., 1965, Am. Soc. Assn. Execs. award, 1965; commd. Ky. col., 1975; DuPont Co. grantee, 1971-75 Mem. Nat. Assn. Bus. Economists, Mus. Modern Art. Office: 17 Kenneth Rd Montclair NJ 07043-2541

BARNARD, ROBERT N. lawyer; b. Madison, Wis., Dec. 15, 1947; s. Robert Julian and Dorothy Jane (Nichol) B.; m. Katherine Elaine Chott, Mar. 1, 1980; children: Suzanna Katherine, Sarah Elizabeth. AB, Harvard U., 1969; JD, Stanford U., 1975. Bar: Ill. 1975, U.S. Dist. Ct. (no. dist.) Ill. 1975, N.Y. 2003. Assoc. Mayer, Brown & Platt, Chgo., 1975-81, ptnr. London, Eng., 1982-88, Chgo., 1988—2001, New York, NY, 2001—. Trustee U. Notre Dame, London, 1986-88. Lt. U.S. Army, 1969-72. Office: Mayer Brown Rowe & Maw LLP 1675 Broadway New York NY 10019-5820

BARNARD, ROLLIN DWIGHT, retired financial executive; b. Denver, Apr. 14, 1922; s. George Cooper and Emma (Riggs) B.; m. Patricia Reynolds Bierkamp, Sept. 15, 1943; children: Michael Dana, Rebecca Susan (Mrs. Paul C. Wulfestieg), Laurie Beth (Mrs. Kenneth J. Kostelecky). BA, Pomona Coll., 1943. Clk. Morey Merc. Co., Denver, 1937-40; ptnr. George C. Barnard & Co., Denver, 1946-47; v.p. Foster & Barnard, Inc., 1947-53; instr. Denver U., 1949-53; dir. real estate U.S. P.O. Dept., Washington, 1953-55, dep. asst. postmaster gen., bur. facilities, 1955-59, asst. postmaster gen., 1959-61; pres., dir. Midland Fed. Savs. & Loan Assn., Denver, 1962-84; vice-chmn. Bank Western Fed. Savs. Bank, 1984-87; vice-chmn., pres. Western Capital Investment Corp., 1985-87. Mayor City of Greenwood Village, Colo., 1989-93, chmn. Planning and Zoning Commn., 1969-73, mem. coun., 1975-77; pres. Denver Area coun. Boy Scouts Am., 1970-71, mem. exec. bd., 1962-73; mem. adv. bd. Denver Area coun. Boy Scouts Am., 1973—; bd. dirs. Downtown Denver Improvement Assn., pres., 1965; bd. dirs. Bethesda Found., Inc., 1973-82, Children's Hosp., 1979-84, treas., 1983-84; bd. dirs. Children's Health Corp., Inc., 1982-93; trustee Mile High United Fund, 1969-72, Denver Symphony Assn., 1973-74; bd. dirs. Colo. Coun. Econ. Edn., 1971-80, chmn. 1971-76; trustee, v.p., treas. Morris Animal Found., 1969-81, pres., chmn. 1974-78, trustee emeritus, 1981—; trustee Denver Zool. Found., 1994—, exec. vice-chmn., 1996-2000, vice-chmn., 2000-01; mem. acquisitions com. Friends Found. Denver Pub. Libr., 1994-2003; dir. Wings over the Rockies Air & Space Mus. Found., 1998-2002; treas. Roundup Riders of the Rockies Heritage and Trails Found., Inc., 1988-97, pres., 1997—. Named one of Ten Outstanding Young Men in Am., U.S. Jaycees, 1955, 57; recipient Disting. Svc. award Postmaster Gen. U.S., 1960; Silver Beaver award Boy Scouts Am., 1969; named Outstanding Citizen of Yr., Sertoma, 1982, Colo. Citizen of Yr., Colo. Assn. Realtors, 1982, Citizen of West, Nat. Western Stockshow, 1994. Mem. Greater Denver C. of C. (pres. 1966-67), U.S. League Savs. Instns. (bd. dirs. 1972-77, vice-chmn. 1979-80, chmn. 1980-81, mem. nat. legis. com., exec. com. 1974-77), Savs. League Colo. (exec. com. 1969-73, pres. 1971-72), Colo. Assn. Commerce and Industry (dir. 1971-76), Fellowship Christian Athletes (Denver area dir. 1963-76), Western Stock Show Assn. (dir. 1971—, exec. com. 1982-94, 1st v.p. 1985-94, trustee Western Stock Show scholarship trust 2002—,), Mountain and Plains Appaloosa Horse Club (pres. 1970-71),

Roundup Riders of the Rockies (bd. dirs. 1979-2000, dir. emeritus 2000—, treas. 1980-87, v.p. 1987-89, pres.-elect 1989-91, pres. 1991-93). Republican. Presbyterian. Home: Surrey Ridge Estates 9902 N Heather Dr Castle Rock CO 80108-9133

BARNARD, WILLIAM MARION, psychiatrist; b. Mt. Pleasant, Tex., Dec. 17, 1949; s. Marion Jaggers and Med (Cody) B. BA, Yale U., 1972; MD, Baylor Coll. Medicine., 1976. Diplomate Am. Bd. Psychiatry and Neurology. Resident NYU/Bellevue Med. Ctr., 1976-79; liaison, consultation fellow L.I. Jewish/Hillside Med. Ctr., 1979-80; chief, liaison, consultation psychiatrist Queens (N.Y.) Med. Ctr., 1980-83; liaison, consultation psychiatrist Mt. Sinai Med. Ctr., N.Y.C., 1983-84; clin. asst. prof. NYU Med. Sch., N.Y.C., 1984-87; emergency psychiatrist VA Med. Ctr., N.Y.C., 1984-87; pvt. practice Pasadena, Calif., 1987—2000. Chief psychiat. svc. Las Encinas Hosp., Pasadena, 1989, chief staff, 1990, med. dir. gen. adult. psychiat. svc., 1990-92, asst. med. dir., 1992; med. dir. BHC Alhambra Hosp., Rosemead, Calif., 1992-2000; dir. inpatient psychiatry Contra Costa Regional Med. Ctr., Martinez, Calif., 2001—. Chmn. mental health com. All Saints AIDS Svc. Ctr., Pasadena, 1990-94, bd. dirs., 1991-94; bd. dirs. Pasadena Symphony, 1989-97, v.p., 1996-97; bd. dirs. Whiffenpoof Alumni, New Haven, 1991—, haberdasher, 1995—. Wilson scholar Yale U., 1970-72. Mem. NYU-Bellevue Psychiat. Assn., Am. Soc. Addiction Medicine, Acad. of Psychosomatic Soc., Am. Psychiat. Assn., East Bay Psychiat. Assn., Univ. Club NYC, St. Francis Yacht Club, Venerable Order of St. John (knight). Republican. Episcopalian. Office: 2500 Alhambra Ave 4E Martinez CA 94553 E-mail: wmbarnard@aya.yale.edu.

BARNAT, RHONDA KATZ, public relations executive, writer; b. Champaign, Ill., Apr. 24, 1952; d. Harold William and Lee (Pankler) Katz; children: Dara Katz, Jeremy Allan. BA, U. Rochester, 1973; MUP, U. Mich., 1976. Rsch. analyst Washtenaw County Planning, Ann Arbor, Mich., 1973-76; community relations editor U. Mich. Hosp., Ann Arbor, 1976-79; freelance writer Ann Arbor, 1979-89; instr. Washtenaw Community Coll., Ann Arbor, 1984-89; cmty. affairs and mktg. mgr. River Bank Am., New Rochelle, NY, 1989-92; asst. v.p. The Bank of N.Y., 1992-96; mng. dir. The Abernathy MacGregor Group, N.Y.C., 1996—. Adj. prof. Marymount Manhattan Coll., N.Y.C., 1997—. Author feature and fiction articles. Mem. Murry Bergtraum High Sch. for Bus. Careers Bus. Adv. Coun., N.Y.C., Marymount Manhattan Community Adv. Bd.; v.p. Chapel Hill Condominium Assn., Ann Arbor, 1980; mem. adv. bd. N.Y.C. First Book. Recipient Appreciation award Iona Coll., 1991. Mem. Women in Communications (co-chair Ann Arbor 1980-81), Oratorio Soc. N.Y. Home: 150 Theodore Fremd Ave Apt A2 Rye NY 10580-2839 Office: The Abernathy MacGregor Group 501 Madison Ave New York NY 10022-5602

BARNEA, URI N. music director, conductor, composer, violinist; b. Petah-Tikvah, Israel, May 29, 1943; came to U.S., 1971; s. Shimon and Miriam Burstein; m. Lizbeth A. Lund, Dec. 15, 1977; 2 children. Tchg. cert., Oranim Music Inst., Israel, 1966; postgrad., Hebrew U., Israel, 1969-71; MusB, Rubin Acad. Music, Israel, 1971; MA, U. Minn., 1974, PhD, 1977; D (hon.), Rocky Mountain Coll., 1999. Music dir. Jewish Cmty. Ctr., Mpls., 1971-73; condr. Youval Chamber Orch., Mpls., 1971-73; asst. condr. U. Minn. Orchs., Mpls., 1972-77; music dir., condr. Unitarian Soc., Mpls., 1973-78, Kenwood Chamber Orch., Mpls., 1974-78, Knox-Galesburg Symphony, 1978-83, Billings (Mont.) Symphony Soc., 1984—, Mont. Ballet Co., 1998—; asst. prof. Knox Coll., Galesburg, Ill., 1978-83; violinist, violist Yellowstone Chamber players, Billings, 1984—; violist Tri-City Symphony, Quad-Cities, Ill., Iowa, 1983-84; condr. Cedar Arts Forum String Camp, Cedar Falls, Iowa, 1981, 82. Guest condr., Ark., Calif., Colo., Fla., Ill., Iowa, Maine, Mich., Minn., Mont., Pa., SD, Va., Wis. European conducting debut, London, Neuchatel and Fribourg, Switzerland, 1986; Can. conducting debut No. Music Festival, North Bay, Ont., 1989; Violin Concerto, 1990; Russian conducting debut Symphony Orch., Kuzbass, Kemerovo, 1993; recordings include: W. Piston's Flute and Clarinet Concertos, Mario Lombardo's Oboe Concerto, two compact discs of Am. music; composer numerous compositions including String Quartet (1st prize Aspen Composition Competition 1976), Sonata for Flute and Piano, 1975 (Diploma of Distinction 26th Viotti Internat. Competition, Italy 1975), Ruth, a ballet, 1974 (1st prize Oberhoffer Composition Contest 1976). Music adv. panel Ill. Arts Coun., 1980-83; v.p. Cmty. Concert Assn., Galesburg, 1980-83; bd. dirs. Knox Coll. Credit Union, Galesburg, 1982-83, Radio Sta. KEMC, Billings, 1984—, Fox Theater Corp., Billings, 1984-86. Recipient Friend of the Arts title Sigma Alpha Iota, 1982, Mont. Gov. Arts award, 2003; Ill. Arts Coun. grantee, 1979; Hebrew U. Jerusalem scholar, 1972-74, Hebrew U. and Rubin Acad. Mus. scholar, 1969, 70; Individual Artist fellow Mont. Arts Coun., 1986. Mem. NEA (music adv. panel 1990-95), ASCAP, Am. Composers Forum, Condrs. Gukld, Am. String Tchrs. Assn. Office: Billings Symphony Soc 201 N Broadway Ste 350 Billings MT 59101-1936

BARNEBEY, KENNETH ALAN, food company executive; b. Fremont, Nebr., Apr. 16, 1931; s. Hoyt F. and Mae S. (Mott) B.; m. Faith Price, May 10, 1969; children: Robert, Mark, Holiday, Cindy, Kendra, Valerie, Bonnie, Laurel, Susan. Student, U. Md., 1950, U. Tampa, 1951; BA in Transp., U. Wash., Seattle, 1953; grad. advanced mgmt. program, Harvard U., 1977. With Tropicana Products, Inc., Bradenton, Fla., 1955-80, gen. sales mgr., then v.p. mktg. and sales, 1957-77, exec. v.p., 1977, pres., chief adminstrv. officer, 1977-79, chmn. bd., chief exec. officer, 1979-81, also dir.; corp. v.p. Beatrice Foods, Inc., 1979-81; pres., dir., dep. chmn. Am. Agronomics Corp., Tampa, Fla., 1981-86; bus. acquisition cons. Bradenton, Fla., 1981—. Bd. dirs. Dependable Ins. Group Inc. Am., Exmart, Cmty. Bank Holding Co.; mem. sch. mktg. program Fla. Citrus Dept., 1973—; dir. First Union Bank. Bd. dirs., pres. Am. Acad. Achievement; bd. dirs. Manatee Jr. Coll., Asolo State Theatre, Blowing Rock (N.C.) Hosp., Blowing Rock Stage Co. Theater; mem. Fla. Coun. of 100; adv. coun. Fla. State U.; exec. svc. corp. pres. Manasota Basin Bd. Served with U.S. Army, 1953-55. Mem. Am. Mgmt. Assn. (lectr.), NAM (mktg. adv. com., dir.), Fla. Canners Assn. (mktg. adv. com.), Manatee County C. of C. (dir., chmn. econ. devel. com.) Clubs: Manatee County Exchange (past pres.), Bradenton Country, Blowing Rock Country (past pres.), State of Fla. Govs. Coun. of 100. Home and Office: PO Box 2490 Blowing Rock NC 28605-2490 also: 2302 63d St W Bradenton FL 34209

BARNER, BRUCE MONROE, former state agency administrator, not-for-profit company chairman; b. Delaware, Ohio, Jan. 16, 1951; s. Charles Ray and Annabel (Monroe) B. BA in Philosophy with honors, Muskingum Coll., 1973; postgrad., Cleve. State U., 1975-77. Adminstrv. researcher Dept. Pub. Safety State of Ohio, Columbus, 1980—98; bd. chmn. ALIVE Ministries, Inc., Columbus, Ohio, 1999—. Fatal crash analyst Nat. Hwy. Traffic Safety Adminstrn., Washington, 1982-83, 85, Nat. Accident Sampling System, 1983; researcher study on motorcycle/moped crash trends, 1985, study on driving edn. in Ohio, 1987, study on semi-truck crash trends, 1986, 87, 88, study on child safety seat usage in Ohio, 1989, study on driver errors in serious heavy truck crashes in Ohio, 1989, studies on shoulder belt usage by roadway functional class in Ohio, 1991, 92, 93, 94, study on fatal crash involvement of repeat DWI offenders in Ohio, 1991-93. Contbr. articles to profl. jours. Co-founder Ohio Safety Belt Coalition, 1983-84; adminstrv. rschr. gov.'s motor carrier adv. com. State of Ohio, 1986-90, adminstrv. rschr. Ohio hwy. safety elderly driver task force, 1990, DWI task force, 1992, 93; advisor Safety Mgmt. Sys., 1994, 95. Mem. Assn. Advancement Automotive Medicine, Planetary Soc., World Future Soc., Nat. Space Soc., Search for Extra-Terrestrial Intelligence Inst., Saved by the Belt Club. Avocations: distance running, internet web-page design, extemporaneous music, chess. Home: PO Box 510 Galloway OH 43119-0510

BARNES, A. JAMES, academic dean; b. Napoleon, Ohio, Aug. 30, 1942; s. Albert James and Mary Elizabeth (Morey) Barnes; m. Sarah Jane Hughes, June 19, 1976; children: Morey Elizabeth, Laura LeHardy, Catherine Farrell. BA with high honors, Mich. State U., 1964; JD cum laude, Harvard U., 1967. Asst. prof. bus. adminstrn. Ind. U., 1967—69; trial atty. Dept. Justice, 1969—70, asst. to dep. atty. gen., 1973; asst. to adminstr. EPA, 1970—73; campaign mgr. for Gov. Milliken of Mich., 1974; ptnr. Beveridge, Fairbanks & Diamond, Washington, 1975—81; gen. counsel Dept. Agr., 1981—83; adj. prof. Georgetown U. Sch. Bus. Adminstrn., Washington, 1978—80; gen. counsel EPA, 1983—85, dep. adminstr., 1985—88; dean Sch. Pub. Environ. Adminstrn., prof. pub. and environ. affairs Ind. U., 1988—2000, prof. pub. and environ. affairs, 1988—, adj. prof. law, 2001—. Spl. counsel Beveridge, Fairbanks & Diamond, Washington, 1988—97; cons., mediator, expert witness Nat. Acad. Pub. Adminstrn., 1988—; adj. prof. law Ind. U., 2001—. Co-author: Essentials of Business Law, 1994, Law of Commercial Transactions and Business Associations, 1995, Bus. Law and the Regulatory Environment, 2000, Law for Bus., 2002, Business Law: The Ethical, Global and E-Commerce Environment, 2004, Bus. Law: The Ethical, E-Commerce and Internat. Environ., 12th edit., 2004. Del. Ind. Rep. Conv., 1968, Mich. Rep. Conv., 1974. Named Sagamore of Wabash, 2000; recipient Outstanding Tchg. award, Ind. U., 1969. Fellow: Nat. Acad. Pub. Adminstrn.; mem.: Sagamore of Wabash, Vineyard Haven Yacht Club (Mass.), Edgartown (Mass.) Yacht Club, Met. Club (Washington). Office: Ind U SPEA 418 Bloomington IN 47405 E-mail: barnesaj@indiana.edu.

BARNES, ANDREW EARL, newspaper executive; b. Torrington, Conn., May 15, 1939; s. Joseph and Elizabeth (Brown) B.; m. Marion Otis, Aug. 26, 1960; children: Christopher Joseph, Benjamin Brooks, Elizabeth Cheney. BA, Harvard U., 1961. Reporter, bur. chief Providence Jour., 1961-63; from reporter to edn. editor Washington Post, 1965-73; met. editor, asst. mng. editor St. Petersburg Times, Fla., 1973-75, mng. editor, 1975-84; editor, pres. St. Petersburg (Fla.) Times, 1984-99, chief exec. officer, 1988—. Chmn. bd. dirs. Congl. Quar., Times Pub. Co., Poynter Inst.; mem. Pulitzer prize bd. Mem. Fla. Coun. of 100. With USAR, 1963-65. Alicia Patterson fellow, 1969-70 Mem. Newspaper Assn. Am. (chair 2000-01), Am. Soc. Newspaper Editors, Fla. Soc. Newspaper Editors (pres. 1980-81), Internat. Press Inst. Home: 15724 Puckett Rd Dade City FL 33525-7066 Office: Saint Petersburg Times 490 1st Ave S PO Box 1121 Saint Petersburg FL 33731-1121

BARNES, ANTHONY CLARKE, music educator; b. Mobile, Ala., July 3, 1970; s. Douglas Earl (Stepfather) and Elizabeth Betty Holwadel, Conrad Ray Barnes; m. Jennifer Lynn Stewart, Dec. 19, 1998. MusB, U. So. Miss., 2000. Class A liscense State Dept. of Edn. for Miss., 2000. Choir dir. Christ United Meth. Ch., Long Beach, Miss., 1989—92; dir. of musical activities Richton United Meth. Ch., Richton, Miss., 1992—99, Chickasaw United Meth. Ch., Chickasaw, Ala., 2001—; tchr. music West Elem. - Moss Point (Miss.) Sch. Dist., 2000—. Cons. Moss Point H.S. Band, 1999—, dir., 1999—. Chmn. Chickasaw Concerts in the Pk. Mem.: Am. Choral Directors Assn. (ACDA) (life), Music Educators Nat. Conf. (MENC) (life), Phi Mu Alpha Sinfonia (life; treas. 1994—98, Most Outstanding Active Mem. 1997, Outstanding Active Mem. 1998). Home: 6521 Hertiage Trace Ct Mobile AL 36695 Office: West Elementary - Moss Point School Dist 3524 Prentiss Ave Moss Point MS 39563 Office Fax: 228-474-3307. Personal E-mail: abarnesmusic@aol.com. E-mail: abarnesmusic@aol.com.

BARNES, ARTHUR ROOSEVELT, advertising executive; b. Bklyn., May 14, 1971; s. Calvin Coolidge Nettles and Marion Palteen Barnes; children: Arthur Mendez, Amanda Mendez. Mng. editor African Profiles mag., N.Y.C., 1999—2001; advt. and circulation mgr. The Am. Jewish Congress, N.Y.C., 2000—. Cons. in advt., NY, 2001. Democrat. Seventh-Day Adventist. Avocations: writing, travel, swimming, reading. Home: 142-23 253rd St Rosedale NY 11422 Office: The American Jewish Congress 15 East 84th St New York NY 10028 Office Fax: 212-249-3672. E-mail: arbarnes30@hotmail.com.

BARNES, BETTY JEAN, educational administrator; b. Aug. 11, 1948; BS, Miss. State U., Starkville, 1971, MEd, 1978; postgrad., U. Miss., Oxford, 1987. Tchr. Burnsville (Miss.) Sch., 1972-84; dir. exceptional children Tishomingo County Schs., Iuka, Miss., 1984—. Vol. Am. Cancer Soc., 8 yrs., Tishomingo Manor Nursing Home, 9 yrs. Mem.: Miss. Profl. Educators, Coun. Adminstrs. in Spl. Edn., Miss. Spl. Edn. Coop, Delta Kappa Gamma. Office: Tishomingo County Schs 1620 Paul Edmondson Dr Iuka MS 38852-1212

BARNES, CARLA LEDDY, social worker, developmental psychologist; b. Zanesville, Ohio, Dec. 9, 1938; d. William Fredrick and Mary (Kopchak) Leddy; m. Patrick Dwyer Barnes, July 8, 1967; children: Michael Leddy, Jennifer Dwyer. BA, Hanover Coll., 1960; MSW, Ind. U., 1962; PhD, Mich. State U., 1986. Lic. clin. social worker, Mich.; diplomate social worker. Psychiat. social worker LaRue D. Carter Meml. Hosp., Indpls., 1962-66; social worker supr. Lafayette Clinic, Detroit, 1966-69, St. Lawrence Community Mental Health Clinic, Lansing, Mich., 1969-71; prof. social work Mich. State U., East Lansing, 1971-79, 86-96, asst. prof. Coll. Nursing; clin. social worker East Lansing Ctr. for the Family, 1986-97; pvt. practice Psychol. and Behavioral Cons., Lansing, 1997—. Contbr. articles to profl. jours. Mem.: NASW, Acad. Cert. Social Workers. Roman Catholic. Office: 2535 E Mount Hope Ave Lansing MI 48910-1913

BARNES, CARLYLE FULLER, manufacturing executive; b. Bristol, Conn., Feb. 16, 1924; s. Fuller Forbes and Myrtle (Ives) B.; m. Elizabeth Anne May, Oct. 1, 1949; children: Lynne Elizabeth, Janis Lee, Joan Wells, Fuller Forbes. AB, Wesleyan U., 1948. Staff asst. Wallace Barnes Co. div. Barnes Group Inc., 1948-50, gen. mgr., 1951-53, dir., 1951-92, pres., 1953-64, chmn. bd., 1964-77, chmn. exec. com., 1977-94, ret., 1994. Bd. dirs. Bushnell Meml. Hall. Home: Peacedale St Bristol CT 06010

BARNES, CHARLES ANDREW, physicist, educator; b. Toronto, Ont., Can., Dec. 12, 1921; came to U.S., 1953, naturalized, 1961; m. Phyllis Malcolm, Sept., 1950. BA, McMaster U., 1943; MA, U. Toronto, 1944; PhD, Cambridge U., 1950. Physicist Joint Brit.-Canadian Atomic Energy Project, 1944-46; instr. physics U. B.C., 1950-53, 55-56; mem. faculty Calif. Inst. Tech., 1953-55, 56—, prof. physics, 1962-92; prof. emeritus physics, 1992—. Guest prof. Niels Bohr Inst., Copenhagen, 1973-74. Editor, contbr. to profl. books and jours. Recipient medal Inst. d'Astrophysique de Paris, 1986, Alexander von Humboldt U.S. Sr. Scientist award, Fed. Republic of Germany, 1986; NSF sr. fellow Denmark, 1962-63. Fellow AAAS, Am. Phys. Soc. Office: Calif Inst Tech 1201 E California Blvd Pasadena CA 91125-0001

BARNES, CLOYD RAY, sculptor, retired engineer; b. Hartford, Ark., July 18, 1934; s. Cloyd Hiram and Esta Elizabeth (McCafferty) B.; m. Wanda Jean Carlton, Oct. 17, 1954; children: Mark E., Stephanie Barnes Veasman. BS in Physics, Tulsa U., 1968. Mem. tech. staff N.Am. Rockwell, Tulsa, 1964-68; sr. aerosystems engr. Gen. Dynamics, Alamogordo, N.Mex., 1968-72; mgr. project engring. Dynalectron Corp., Alamogordo, 1972-77, mgr. ops. dept. Alamagordo, 1977-80, tech. dir. radar backscatter divsn., 1980-84, tech. dir., site mgr., 1984-86; mgr. radio frequency test ops. Martin Marietta Denver Aerospace, 1986-89, dept. staff engr., 1989-91. Represented by Nedra Matteuccis Gallery, Santa Fe; interim instr. Denver Art Students League, 1994. Exhibited in group shows at Southeastern Wildlife Expo, Charleston, S.C., Nat. Acad. Design, N.Y.C., Audubon Show, N.Y.C., Am. Artists Profl. League, N.Y.C., (Helen G. Oehler award), 1991, Nat. Wildlife Show, Kansas City, 1993 (Best of Show), Cantigny Park, Chgo., BCCFA Show, Clifton, Tex. (Best of Show award), Western Regional Show, Cheyenne, Wyo., N.Am. Sculpture Exhibit, Golden, Colo., Rough Rider Art Show, Williston, N.D., 1993 (Grand Prize 1993), Ho. Reps. Office Bldg.-Rotunda, Washington, 1994, Am. Artists Profl. League, 1994 (Leila G. Sawyer award), Visual Individualists United, Bklyn., 1995 (Grumbacher Gold Medallion award), Pacific Rim Wildlife Art Exhbn., Seattle; commd. works include life-size bronze portrait figure of C.L. Tutt, Colo. Coll., Colorado Springs, 1992, monumental bronze running buffalo Buffalo Run Golf Course, Adams County, Colo., 1996; monumental 9 feet high gold miner and pack burro installed in Colorado Springs, Colo., 1999, Life-Size Arabian Horse with Two Children, Golden, 2001. Fellow Am. Artists Profl. League; mem. Allied Artists Am. (assoc.), Knickerbocker Artists (assoc.). Avocations: hunting, hiking, travel, reading. Home: 7425 S Milwaukee Way Centennial CO 80122-1951

BARNES, CRAIG MARTIN, minister; b. Oak Park, Ill., May 5, 1949; s. Raymond Herbert and Barbara Anne (Barlow) B.; m. Joyce Marie Brainard, Jan. 31, 1971; children: Annette Marie, Walter Martin. BS in Music Edn., U. Ill., 1971; BA in Acctg. and Fin., U. So. Fla., 1976. CPA, Tenn., tax acct., Tenn. Contr. Fore Line Safe Co., Tampa, Fla., 1973-75, Fore Line Bldgs., Largo, Fla., 1973-75; EDP audit mgr. Comptr. of Treasury State of Tenn., Nashville, 1976-88; pvt. practice Cottontown, Tenn., 1986-97; owner CMB Capital Mgmt., Cottontown, 1991—98. Chaplain, dir. Cave Springs, 1997—. Mem., singer Nashville Symphony Chorus, 1982-86, coach Comptroller Sox Softball Team, Nashville, 1984-86; commr. State Softball Leagues, 1985-86. Ernst and Whinney scholar, 1976. Mem.: Tenn. Ctrl. Ry. Mus., Nashville N-Trak R.R. Club. Adventist. Avocations: softball, baseball, model railroading, music. Home and Office: 350 Cave Springs Rd Pegram TN 37143-2215

BARNES, DONALD MICHAEL, lawyer; b. Hazleton, Pa., June 15, 1943; s. Donald A. and Margaret (Resuta) B.; m. Mary Catherine Gibbons, June 3, 1967; children: Donald M., Stephanie A., Susan E. BS in Indsl. Engring., Pa. State U., 1965; JD cum laude, George Washington U., 1970. Bar: D.C. 1970, U.S. Dist. Ct. D.C. 1970, U.S. Ct. Appeals (D.C. cir.) 1970, U.S. Supreme Ct. 1975, U.S. Ct. Appeals (5th cir.) 1980, U.S. Ct. Appeals (4th cir.) 1980, U.S. Ct. Appeals (8th cir.) 1981, U.S. Ct. Appeals (6th cir.) 1993, U.S. Ct. Appeals (10th cir.) 2003. Assoc. Arent, Fox, Kintner, Plotkin & Kahn, Washington, 1970-78, ptnr., 1978-97; mng. shareholder Jenkens & Gilchrist, Washington, 1997-2000; ptnr. Seyfarth Shaw, Washington, 2000—02, Porter Wright Morris & Arthur, LLP, Washington, 2002—. Notes editor George Washington Law Rev., 1969-70 Mem.: ABA (criminal justice, antitrust, litigation and adminstrv. law sects.), DC Bar Assn., Order of Coif, Phi Delta Phi. Office: Porter Wright Morris & Arthur LLP Ste 500 1919 Pennsylvania Ave NW Washington DC 20006-3434

BARNES, EDWARD LARRABEE, architect; b. Chgo., Apr. 22, 1915; s. Cecil and Margaret Helen (Ayer) B.; m. Mary Elizabeth Coss, Mar. 4, 1944; 1 child, John Cecil. BS cum laude, Harvard U., 1938, M.Arch. (Sheldon Travelling fellow), 1942; D. Fine Arts (hon.), R.I. Sch. Design, 1983; L.H.D. (hon.), Amherst Coll., 1984. Architect, N.Y.C., 1949—; practice includes prefabricated house, pvt. houses, camps, acad. bldgs. & master plans, office bldgs. and corp. headquarters, museums, bot. gardens; archtl. design critic, lectr. Pratt Inst., Bklyn., 1954-59; design critic, lectr. Yale U., New Haven, Conn., 1957-64; Eliot Noyes critic Harvard U., 1979; Thomas Jefferson prof. architecture U. Va., 1980. Mem. Westchester Council of Arts, 1967-71, Urban Design Council of N.Y.C., 1972-76; trustee Am. Acad., Rome, 1963-78, 1st v.p., 1973, 1st vice chmn., 1975; vis. com. MIT, 1965-68, Harvard Grad. Sch. Design. 1978-88; assoc. Nat. Acad. Design, 1969, academician, 1974—; bd. dirs. Municipal Art Soc., 1960, treas., 1961; trustee Mus. Modern Art, N.Y.C., 1975-93, life trustee, 1993—; mem. adv. council Trust for Pub. Land, 1984-90; mem. Westchester County Planning Bd., 1976-88. Work exhibited Mus. Modern Art., N.Y.C., Sarah Scaife Gallery, Pitts., Whitney Mus., N.Y.C., Nat. Bldg. Mus., Washington; work pub. in archtl. mags. Recipient award for distinction in arts Yale, 1959, Arnold Brunner prize Nat. Inst. Arts and Letters, 1959, Silver medal Archtl. League N.Y., 1960, Harleston Parker medal Boston Soc. Architects, 1972, Bard award for Excellence in Archtl. and Urban Design, 1978, 85, Louis Sullivan award, 1979, Honor award Conn. Soc. Architects, 1980, award of Honor for Art and Culture Mayor of N.Y.C., 1982, Honor award N.Mex. Soc. Architects, 1983, Excellence in Design award N.Y. State Assn. Architects, 1984, Thomas Jefferson medal U. Va., 1981, Harvard U. 350th Anniversary medal, 1986, Alumni Lifetime Achievement award Harvard U. Grad. Sch. Design, 1993, Am. Craft Coun. award of distinction for Haystack Sch., 1998. Fellow AIA (Medal of Honor N.Y. chpt. 1971, collaborative achievement in architecture 1972, Honor award 1972, 77, 86, Firm award 1980, 25 Yr. award 1994, Pres. award N.Y. chpt.), Am. Acad. Arts and Scis.; mem. Am. Acad. and Inst. Arts and Letters, Century Assn. Home: 975 Memorial Dr Cambridge MA 02138-5753

BARNES, FRANK STEPHENSON, electrical engineer, educator; b. Pasadena, Calif., July 31, 1932; s. Donald Porter and Thedia (Schellenberg) B.; m. Gay Dirstine, Dec. 17, 1955; children: Stephen, Amy. BS, Princeton U., 1954; MS, Stanford U., 1955, PhD, 1958. Fulbright prof. Coll. Engring., Baghdad, Iraq, 1957-58; rsch. assoc. Colo. Rsch. Corp., Broomfield, 1958-59; assoc. prof. U. Colo., Boulder, 1959-65, prof. dept. elec. engring., 1965—, chmn. dept., 1964-81, faculty rsch. lectr., 1965, acting dean Coll. Engring. and Applied Sci., 1980-81, disting. prof., 1997—, dir. interdisciplinary telecom. program, 1971-75, 88-89, 1996-99. Disting. lectr. IEEE Elec. Device Soc., 1994-01. Regional editor Electronics Letters of Brit. Instn. Elec.Engrs., 1970-75; exec. editor Ann. Rev. Telecom. Bd. dirs. Accreditation Bd. Engring. and Tech., 1980-82. Recipient cert. of merit Internat. Comm. Assn., 1989, Meritorious Svc. award IEEE Edn. Soc., 1993, Leon Montgomery award Internat. Comm. Assn., 1994, Univ. Colo. Centennial Celebration Engring. Recognition award, 1994; fellow Internat. Engring. Consortium, 1995. Fellow AAAS, IEEE (editor Student Jour. 1967-70, mem. G-Ed Adcom 1970-77, v.p. publ. activities 1974-75, pres. device soc. 1974-75, ednl. activities bd. 1976-82, editor IEEE Transactions on Edn. 1988-94, mem. press bd. 1989-90, ednl. activities bd., cert. of merit, Centennial medal, Millennium medal 2000); mem. NAE, Am. Soc. Elec. Engring. (Elec. and Computer Engring. Disting. Educator award 2002), Soc. Lasers in Medicine, Engrs. Coun. Profl. Devel. (dir. 1976-82, chmn. com. on advanced level accreditation 1976-78), Bioelectromagnetics Soc. (bd. dirs. 1982-84, 96-98, pres. 2000-01), Engring. Info. (bd. dirs. 1984-90). Home: 225 Continental View Dr Boulder CO 80303-4516 *There are always more interesting problems to solve than time to solve them. The trick is to find important problems which can be solved with an effort which is small compared to the value of the results and where one can have a good time learning new ideas at the same time.*

BARNES, GALEN R. insurance company executive; b. Vevay, Ind. m. June Ann Ladd; two children. Degree in maths., Ind. U. Actuarial officer Nationwide Mut. Ins. Co., Columbus, Ohio, 1975-81, vice pres. actuary, 1981—83; pres., COO Colonial Ins. Co., Calif., 1983-87; v.p. personal and comml. ins. svcs. Nationwide Ins. Co., Columbus, Ohio, 1987-89, sr. v.p. nationwide personal and comml. ins. svcs., 1989-93; pres., COO Wausau Ins. Co., Columbus, 1993-96; pres. Nationwide Ins. Enterprise, 1996-99; pres., COO Nationwide Ins., 1999—. Bd. dirs. Ohio Dominican Coll., Franklin County United Way, Arthur C. James Cancer Hosp. Fellow Casualty Actuarial Soc., Am. Acad. Actuaries, Nat. Urban League Bd. Office: Nationwide Mut Ins Co 1 Nationwide Plz Columbus OH 43215-2220

BARNES, HARPER HENDERSON, movie critic, editor, writer; b. Greensboro, N.C., July 2, 1937; s. Bennett Harper and Cora Emmaline Barnes; m. Janice Stauffacher, May 10, 1961 (div. 1985); m. Roseann Marie Weiss, May 31, 1986. Critic, reporter St. Louis Post-Dispatch, 1965-70, editor, critic, 1973-97; editor The Phoenix, Boston, 1970-72, St. Louis mag., 1997-99. Instr. Washington U., St. Louis, 1990, 94. Author: Blue Monday, 1991, Standing on a Volcano, 2001. With U.S. Army, 1959-62. Avocations: bicycling, fishing. Office: St Louis Mag 6358 Delmar Blvd Saint Louis MO 63130-4719 E-mail: hbarnesl@mindspring.com.

BARNES, HARREY MCGWINN, III, internist, oncologist; b. May 31, 1951; MD, U. Ala., 1976. Diplomate Am. Bd. Internal Medicine, Am. Bd. Med. Oncology. Intern U. Ala. Hosps., Birmingham, 1976-77, resident in internal medicine, 1977-79, fellow in hematologic oncology; pvt. practice, Montgomery, Ala., 1981—. Mem. Ala. Soc. Clin. Oncology (past pres.), Alpha Omega Alpha. Office: 4145 Carmichael Rd Montgomery AL 36106-2803

BARNES, HARRY FRANCIS, federal judge; b. Memphis, May 14, 1932; m. Mary Milburn Mann, four children. Student, Vanderbilt U., 1950-52; BS, U.S. Naval Academy, 1956; LLB, U. Ark., 1964. With Pryor & Barnes, Camden, Ark., 1964-66, Barnes & Roberts, Camden, 1966-68, Gaughan, Laney, Barnes & Roberts, Camden, 1968-78, Gaughan, Laney & Barnes, Camden, 1978-82; mcpl. judge Camden and Ouachita Counties, 1975-82; circuit judge 13th jud. dist. State of Ark., 1982-93; judge U.S. Dist. Ct. (we. dist.) Ark., 1993—. Mem. Ark. Jud. Discipline and Disability Comm. With USMC, 1956-86, col. res. ret. Named Outstanding Trial Judge in Ark., Ark. Trial Lawyers Assn., 1986, 2000. Mem. ABA, Ark. Bar Assn., Ark. Jud. Coun. (bd. dirs.). Office: US Dist Ct We Dist PO Box 1735 El Dorado AR 71731-1735

BARNES, HARRY G., JR., human rights activist, conflict resolution specialist, retired ambassador; b. St. Paul, June 5, 1926; s. Harry George and Bertha Pauline (Blaul) B.; m. Elizabeth Ann Sibley; children: Pauline, Adrienne, Douglas, Sibley. BA summa cum laude, Amherst Coll., 1949, LLD (hon.), 1984; MA in History, Columbia U., 1968; PhD in Engring. (hon.), Stevens Inst., 1985; LLD (hon.), Monterey Inst. Internat. Studies, 1989. With fgn. service U.S. Dept. State, 1951-88; vice-consul Bombay, India, 1951-53; vice consul, 2d sec. Prague, Czechoslovakia, 1953-55, Moscow, 1957-59; polit. officer Office of Soviet affairs, Dept. State, Washington, 1959-62; dep. chief mission Kathmandu, Nepal, 1963-67; dep. chief of mission Bucharest, Romania, 1968-71; chief jr. officer program Dept. State, Washington, 1971-72, dep. exec. sec., 1972-74; amb. to Romania Bucharest, 1974-77; dir. gen. fgn. service, dir. pers. Dept. State, Washington, 1977-81; amb. to India, New Delhi, 1981-85, Chile, Santiago, 1985-88; ret.; exec. dir. Critical Langs. and Area Studies Consortium, 1989-94; dir. conflict resolution and human rights programs The Carter Ctr., Atlanta, 1994-99, chmn. rights com., 1997-99; sr. advisor Asia Soc., 1999—.

Cyrus Vance vis. prof. internat. rels. Mt. Holyoke Coll., spring 1990; Sol Linowitz vis. prof. internat. rels. Hamilton Coll., fall 1990; James and Joan Warburg vis. prof. internat. rels. Simmons Coll., fall 1991-spring 1993; sr. fellow World Wild Life Fund-Conservation Found., 1989-91; interim dir. Human Rights Program Career Ctr., 1993-94, dir. human rights and conflict resolution programs, 1995-99; chmn. bd. dirs. Romanian-Am. Enterprise Fund, 1996—. With U.S.Army, 1944-46. Decorated Grand Cross, Order of Bernardo O'Higgins (Chile), 1990; recipient Pres.' Meritorious Svc. award, 1983, 88, Pres.' Disting. Svc. award, 1987. Fellow AAAS (mem. adv. com. internat. program). Presbyterian. Avocation: trekking. Home: PO Box 73 Peacham VT 05862-0073 Fax: (802) 592-3046. E-mail: hgbarnes@attglobal.net.

BARNES, HOWARD G. communications executive, film and video producer; b. N.Y.C., Dec. 27, 1913; m. Joan Lesavoy, Jan. 9, 1949 (div. Nov. 1957); foster children: Marshall Alan (dec.), Denis Joy; m. Mary Ellena Mock, Dec. 7, 1958 (div.); children: Christie Ann, Paul Louis Lloyd; m. Partricia Lee Sills, August 4, 1965 (div.); children: Paxton Louise, Gillian Leigh. AB, U. Mich., 1935. Announcer radio sta. WIP, Phila., 1935, KYW, Phila., WHN, N.Y.C., 1936; producer WOR Mut., 1936-38; exec. producer MCA, 1938; producer, writer, exec. CBS, N.Y.C., 1938-46; v.p. in charge network programs CBS Radio, 1955-60; dir. programs CBS-TV, Hollywood, 1960-63; producing independently, 1946-48; v.p. in charge radio and TV Dorland, Inc., N.Y.C., 1948-51; pres. Gen. Entertainment Corp., 1949-60; TV exec. Ashley Famous Agy., Inc., 1963-66; dir. film prodn. Westinghouse Broadcasting Co., N.Y.C., 1966-67, exec. v.p. Group W Films, 1967-73, also dir. parent co., ind. producer, 1973-89, gen. mgr., dir. advt. The Walking Ctr., Beverly Hills, Calif., 1989-91. Pres. Ragazza Inc., Washington, Conn., 1980-81; bd. govs. Dramalites, Washington, Conn., 1979-89; dir. Trio Films, Ltd., London, 1973-79; ptnr. The Barnes/Sabinson Partnership, 1976-84; exec. dir. Entertainment Hall of Fame Found., 1974-77; cons. film and video Conn. State Dept. Edn., 1985-89; lectr. Sch. Comm., San Diego State U., 1996-97. Lt. USNR, 1942-45. Home: 1930 W San Marcos Blvd Spc 358 San Marcos CA 92069-3930

BARNES, HUBERT LLOYD, geochemistry educator; b. Chelsea, Mass., July 20, 1928; s. George Lloyd and Mary Ellen (MacPherson) B.; m. Mary Talbot Westergaard; children: Roy Malcolm, Catherine Patricia. BS, MIT, 1950; PhD, Columbia U., 1958. Resident geologist Peru Mining Co., Hanover, N.Mex., 1950-52; lectr. geology Columbia U., N.Y.C., 1952-54; postdoctoral fellow Geophys. Lab. Carnegie Inst., Washington, 1956-60; prof. Pa. State U., University Park, 1960-96, dir. ore deposits rsch. sect., 1969-96, emeritus, 1997. Vis. prof. Mineralogy-Petrology Inst., Heidelberg, 1974, Academia Sinica, 1983, U. Sydney, 1987, U. Witwatersrand, 1990; Crosby lectr. MIT, Cambridge, 1983, mem. geophysics rsch. bd. NRC, 1976-80; mem. U.S. Nat. Com. on Geology, 1983-86; cons. numerous corps.; dir. NATO Advanced Study Inst., Salamanca, 1987; gen. chmn. 1st Goldschmidt Conf., Balt., 1988, co-chmn. PA. State U., 1995; chmn., sec. Internat. Symposium on Hydrothermal Reactions, Pa. State U., 1985; guest prof. Nanjing U., People's Republic of China, 1996; Air-India disting. lectr. Indian Inst. Tech., Bombay, 1996; hon. prof., disting. vis. fellow U. Wales, 1996-2001; pres. Applied Rsch. & Exploration, 1994—. Author: Uranium Prospecting, 1956. Editor: Geochemistry of Hydrothermal Ore Deposits, 1967, 79, 97; co-editor: Hydrothermal Experimental Techniques, 1987; consulting editor Internat. Geol. Rev., 1999—. Vice-pres. Pa. chpt. Humboldt Found., 1996-99. N.L. Britton scholar, 1955-56; Guggenheim fellow, 1966-67, Japan Soc. Promotion Sci. fellow, 1997; lecturer, World Famous Scientists Forum, Nanjing, 2002; recipient Sr. Humboldt prize Humboldt Found. Germany, 1988; named Disting. Prof. Geochemistry Pa. State U., 1990, Disting. Svc. award, Geochemical Soc., 2003; Can. Inst. Mining and Metallurgy lectr., 1969, C.F. Davidson lectr., St. Andrews, Scotland, 1971. Fellow Mineral Soc. Am., Geol. Soc. Am., Geochem. Soc. (councillor 1970-73, v.p. 1983, pres. 1984-85, Disting. Svc. award 2003); mem. Soc. Econ. Geologists (councilor 1981-84, Thayer Lindsley lectr. 1980-81), Am. Geologic Inst. (governing bd. 1981-83), Penrose Gold Medal, Soc. Econ. Geol. 2002, disting. svc. award Geochem. soc. 2003, U.S. Nat. Geochemistry Com. (chmn. 1976-78). Home: 213 E Mitchell Ave State College PA 16803-3655 Office: Pa State U Dept Geoscis 235 Deike Bldg University Park PA 16802-2711 E-mail: barnes@geosc.psu.edu.

BARNES, JACQUELINE C. LINSCOTT, education consultant, retired educator; b. Franklin, N.C., Feb. 26, 1941; d. Clyde W. and Katherine (Ray) Clark; m. Leonard Lee Linscott, Aug. 16, 1964; 1 child, Laura Leigh Linscott Bledsoe; m. Graham B. Barnes, Sept. 2, 2001. BS in Edn., U. N.C., 1964; M in Elem. Edn., Adminstrn. Supr., Stetson U., 1980. Edn. Cert., Fla. Tchr. Riverview Elem. Sch., Titusville, Fla., 1964-66, Jackson Middle Sch., Titusville, Fla., 1966-67, Coquina Elem. Sch., Titusville, Fla., 1967-86, Challenger 7 Elem. Sch., Cocoa, Fla., 1986-89, PRIME specialist, 1989-91, YRE coord., 1991-96, Cons. on yr.-round edn. Dept. Edn., Tallahassee, 1990—. Author: Blue Bell Paper Weights and Other Bells, 1990, rev. edit., 1992, addendum, 1995, rev. edit., 2003. Grantee PAC-MAN Reading Program Brevard Pub. Schs., Melbourne, Fla., 1982, Caring Adults Reading with Elem. Students, Brevard Pub. Schs., 1990. Mem. ASCD, Nat. Assn. Yr.-Round Edn. (presenter confs. 1993—), Fla. Assn. Yr.-Round Edn. (presenter conf. 1991—, pres.), Alpha Delta Kappa. Avocations: antiques, reading, crafts. Home: 3557 Nicklaus Dr Titusville FL 32780-5356 E-mail: bluebellwt@aol.com.

BARNES, JAMES JOHN, history educator; b. St. Paul, Nov. 16, 1931; s. Harry George and Bertha (Blaul) B.; m. Patience Rogers Plummer, July 9, 1955; children— Jennifer Chase, Geoffrey Prescott BA, Amherst Coll., 1954, New Coll., Oxford, 1956, MA, 1961; PhD, Harvard U., 1960; DHL, Coll. of Wooster, 1976, Amherst Coll., 1999. Instr. history Amherst Coll., 1959-62; asst. prof. history Wabash Coll., Crawfordsville, Ind., 1962-67, assoc. prof. history, 1967-76, prof. history, 1976—, chmn. dept. history, Hadley prof., 1979-97. Author: Free Trade in Books: A Study of the London Book Trade since 1800, 1964, Authors, Publishers and Politicians: The Quest for an Anglo-American Copyright Agreement 1815-54, 1974, (with Patience P. Barnes) Hitler's Mein Kampf in Britain and America 1930-39, 1980, (with Patience P. Barnes) James Vincent Murphy: Translator and Interpreter of Fascist Europe, 1880-1946, 1987, (with Patience P. Barnes) Private and Confidential Letters from British Ministers in Washington to the Foreign Secretaries in London, 1849-67, 1993, (with Patience P. Barnes) Nazi Refugee turned Gestapo Spy: The Life of Hans Wesemann, 1895-1971, 2001, (with Patience P. Barnes) The American Civil War through British Eyes: Dispatches from British Diplomats, Vol. 1: Nov. 1860-Apr. 1862, 2003; contbr. articles to profl. jours. Mem. Rhodes Scholar Selection Com. for Ind., 1965-89, Crawfordsville Community Action Coun., 1966-69, Crawfordsville Community Day Care Com., 1966-67; mem. vestry St. John's Episcopal Ch., 1966-69; mem. Ind. Adv. Com. State Rehab. Svcs. for Blind, 1979-81; trustee Ind. Hist. Soc., 1982—. Recipient Disting. Alumni award St. Paul Acad. and Summit Sch., 1989; Rhodes scholar, 1954-56, Fulbright scholar, 1978; Woodrow Wilson fellow, 1956-57, Kent fellow, 1958, Great Lakes Colls. Assn. Teaching fellow, 1958, Great Lakes Colls. Assn. Teaching fellow, 1975; rsch. grantee Amherst Coll., 1960-61, Social Sci. Rsch. Coun., 1962, 70, Wabash Coll., 1962—, Am. Coun. Learned Socs., 1964-65, 80, Am. Philos. Soc., 1964, 68, 76, 91; named Hon. Alumnus, Wabash Coll., 1994. Mem. Am. Hist. Assn., Ouiatenon Literary Soc., Conf. Brit. Studies, Rsch. Soc. Victorian Periodicals, Am. Rhodes Scholars, Soc. Historians Am. Fgn. Rels., Ind. Hist. Soc., Montgomery County Hist. Soc., Midwest Victorian Studies Assn. (pres. 1989-91), Ind. Assn. Historians, N.E. Victorian Studies Assn., Soc. for History of Authorship, Reading and Pub., Am. Coun. of Blind, United Oxford and Cambridge Club of London, Phi Beta Kappa. Home: 7 Locust Hl Crawfordsville IN 47933-3347 Office: Wabash Coll History Dept Crawfordsville IN 47933 E-mail: barnesj@wabash.edu.

BARNES, JAMES MILTON, physics and astronomy educator; b. Ypsilanti, Mich., July 5, 1923; s. J. Milton and Elsie (Fischer) B.; m. Marjorie Ruth Petersen, Dec. 17, 1949. BS, Eastern Mich. U., 1948; MS, Mich. State U., 1950, PhD, 1955. Asst. prof. Eastern Mich. U., Ypsilanti, 1955-58, asso. prof., 1958-61, prof., 1961-88, prof. emeritus, 1988—, head dept. physics and astronomy, 1961-74. Served with AUS, 1942-46. Mem. A.A.A.S. (life), Nat. Sci. Tchrs. Assn. (life), Am. Assn. Physics Tchrs., Sigma Xi, Sigma Pi Sigma, Pi Mu Epsilon. Clubs: Ann Arbor (Mich.) Country. Home: 4872 N Whitman Cir Ann Arbor MI 48103-9774 Office: Eastern Mich U Physics Dept Ypsilanti MI 48197

BARNES, JHANE ELIZABETH, fashion design company executive, designer; b. Balt., Mar. 4, 1954; d. Richard Amos and Muriel Florence (Chase) B.; m. Howard Ralph Feinberg, Dec. 12, 1981 (div.); m. 2d, Katsuhiko Kawasaki, Feb. 12, 1988. A.S., Fashion Inst. Tech., 1975. Pres., designer Jhane Barnes for ME, N.Y.C., 1976-78; pres., designer, owner Jhane Barnes Inc., N.Y.C., 1978—; owner Jhane Barnes Textiles, LLC, 1998—. Recipient Coty award Menswear Am. Fashion Critics, 1980, 1984, Contract Textile award Am. Soc. Interior Designers, 1983, 84, Product Design awards Inst. Bus. Designers and Contract Mag., 1983-86, 94, Outstanding Am. Menswear Designer award Woolmark, 1990, Dalmore, 1990, Good Design award 1997, 98, 99, Best of Neo Con award. I.D. 40, 1996, 97, 98, 99, 2000; named Most Promising Designer Cutty Sark, 1980, Outstanding Designer, 1982, Outstanding Menswear Designer, Coun. of Fashion Designers Am., 1982, Design Resources Coun., 1989, 94, Designer of Yr., Neckwear Assn. Am., 1997. Office: Jhane Barnes Inc 119 W 40th St Fl 20 New York NY 10018-2500 Fax: 212-575-2506.

BARNES, JO ANNE, investment advisor; b. Berwyn, Ill., Feb. 1, 1947; d. Robert Marshall and Margaret Hickman Barnes; children: Katherine Dorothy Schock, Alice Margaret Schock. BA in English, U. Minn., 1969; MAT in English, Northwestern U., 1972. Cert. fin. planner. Tchr., adviser New Trier H.S., Winnetka, Ill., 1972-75; editl. proofreader Arthur Andersen & Co., St. Charles, Ill., 1980-82; registered rep., v.p. investments Howe Barnes Investments, Chgo., 1983-91; exec. v.p., dir. mktg. Podesta & Co., Chgo., 1992; pres., chief investment officer Barnes Alliance, Inc., Chgo., 1993-96; portfolio mgr. Vestor Capital Corp., Chgo., 1997; sr. investment mgr. Vanguard Group, Valley Forge, Pa., 1997—. Host, prodr., writer (TV show) On Your Side, 1985-86; co-author, editor Investor's Workshop, 1994-96. Chmn. Planning Commn., Hampshire, Ill., 1978-80; dir. Builders Skills, Niles, Ill., 1988-90; pres., trustee Salem United Meth. Ch., Barrington, Ill., 1991-93; dir., treas. Women's Opportunity Fund, Oakbrook, Ill., 1995-98. Mem.: Nature Conservancy, Audubon Soc. Avocations: poetry, hiking, biking, writing. Home: 2025 Greens Way Cir Collegeville PA 19426

BARNES, JOHN ALLEN, writer; b. Angola, Ind., Feb. 28, 1957; s. John Donald and Beverly Anne Hoopes B.; m. Kathleen Reese Albe, Jan. 3, 1981 (div. Aug. 1990); m. Kara Mia Dalkey, Aug. 6, 1993 (div. May 2001). AB, Washington U., St. Louis, 1978, AM, 1981; MFA, MA, U. Mont., 1988; PhD, U. Pitts., 1995. Sys. analyst Mid. South Svcs., New Orleans, 1982-84; from asst. to assoc. prof. Western State Coll., Gunnison, Colo., 1994-2001; sr. cons. in semiotics Criteria LLC, 2002—. Cons. in field. Contbr. articles to profl. jours.; author: The Man Who Pulled Down the Sky, 1987, Sin of Origin, 1988, Orbital Resonance, 1991, Wartide, 1992, Battle Cry, 1992, Union Fires, 1992, A Million Open Doors, 1992, Mother of Storms, 1994, Kaleidoscope Century, 1995, One for the Morning Glory, 1996; author: (with Buzz Aldrin) Encounter with Tiber, 1996; author: Patton's Spaceship, 1997, Washington's Dirigible, 1997, Caesar's Bicycle, 1997, Earth Made of Glass, 1998, Apostrophes and Apocalypses, 1998, Finity, 1999, Candle, 2000; author: (with Buzz Aldrin) The Return, 2000; author: The Merchants of Souls, 2001, The Sky So Big and Black, 2002, The Duke of Uranium, 2002, A Princess of the Aerie, 2003, In the Hall of the Martian King, 2003. Bertha Morton fellow, 1985-86, Mellon fellow, 1991-92, 93-94; Erasmus scholar, 1986-87, Marshall scholar, 1993. Mem. Sci. Fiction Writers Am., Am. Soc. for Theatre Rsch. Avocations: Judo, cooking, theater, astronomy. E-mail: johnbarnes@sprintmail.com.

BARNES, JOHN GILBERT PRESSLIE, computer language designer; b. London, Aug. 19, 1937; s. Gilbert Arthur and Edith Helen (Presslie) B.; m. Barbara Winifred Juffkins, Sept. 8, 1962; children: Janet Elizabeth, Helen Jane. BA in Math., Cambridge U., 1961, MA, 1964. Mathematician Imperial Chem. Industries, Reading, Eng., 1961-68, sect. mgr., 1969-75, cons. Slough, Eng., 1975-78; vis. fellow U. Edinburgh (Scotland), 1968-69; dir. lang. research S P L Internat., Abingdon, Eng., 1978-84; tech. dir. Systems Designers, Camberley, Eng., 1984-85; mng. dir. Alsys Ltd., Henley, Eng., 1985-91; owner John Barnes Informatics, 1985—. Cons. Dept. Industry, London, 1976-78; indsl. fellow Wolfson Coll., Oxford, Eng., 1979-81; vis. prof. Imperial Coll., London, 1982-84; mem. bd. ADA, Washington, 1986-87, pres. ADA-Europe, 1991-2001. Author: RTL/2 Design and Philosophy, 1976, Programming in ADA, 1982, 3d edit., 1996, High Integrity ADA, 1997, ADA 95 Rationale, 1995; editor: ADA in Use, 1985, High Integrity Software, 2003; contbr. articles to software to profl. publs. Fellow Brit. Computer Soc. (chartered engr.). Home: 11 Albert Rd Caversham Reading RG4 7AN England

BARNES, JUDITH ANN, real estate executive; b. Milw., Mar. 10, 1949; d. Einar and Eleanor Svea (Russell) B.; divorced; children: Krista Svea, Erik Leif. BA, Gustavus Adolphus Coll., 1970; grad., Wis. Sch. Real Estate, Milw., 1979; postgrad., Carroll Coll., 1980, U. Wis., 1978-80, 92. Tchr. Oak Grove Mid. Sch., Bloomington, Minn., 1970-71, Mukwonago (Wis.) H.S., 1971-72; sales mgr. Lincoln Park Homes, West Allis, Wis., 1972-73, v.p., 1973-74, pres., 1974-97, Palm Coast, Fla., 1997-2000; assoc. Coldwell Banker Comml. (Nicholson-Williams), 2000—01; with Hammock Dunes Real Estate Co., 2001—. Chmn. Mfrd. Housing Subdivision S.E. Wisc., Madison, 1978-80; sec. Southeastern Wis. Housing, Milw., 1981-82, treas., 1982-84. Bd. dirs. Waukesha YMCA, 1985-87, v.p. 1987-89; bd. dirs. YMCA Heritage Found., 1994-97; bd. dirs. Waukesha County United Way, 1984-87; coun. pres. Stetson U., 1996-2000; mem. alumni bd. Gustavus Adulphus Coll., St. Peter, Minn., 1974-80; trustee The Cooper Inst., Naples, Fla., 1987-93, mem. adv. bd., 1993—. Recipient Dedicated Svc. award Wis. Mfrd. Housing, 1975-84, 88, Vol. of Yr. award Univ. Lake Sch., 1995. Mem. Wis. Mfrd. Housing Assn. (bd. dirs. 1975-80), Ind. Bus. Assn. Wis. (trustee U. Lake 1991-96), Merrill Hills Country Club (chair golf 1991), Milw. Women's Dist. Golf Assn. (bd. dirs. 1993, v.p. 1994, pres. 1995-96), Vasa Lodge, Hammock Dunes Country Club (adv. bd.). Republican. Lutheran. Avocations: golf, photography. Home: 3 Anastasia Ct Palm Coast FL 32137-2273 E-mail: jbhd@bellsouth.net .

BARNES, KAREN KAY, lawyer; b. June 22, 1950; d. Walter William and Vashti (Greenlee) Sessler; m. James Alan Barnes, Feb. 12, 1972; children: Timothy Matthew, Christopher Michael. BA, Valparaiso U., 1971; JD, DePaul U., 1978, LLM in Taxation, 1980. Bar: Ill. 1978, U.S. Dist. Ct. (no. dist.) Ill. 1978. Ptnr. McDermott, Will & Emory, Chgo., 1978-88; prin. William M. Mercer, Inc. and predecessor firm, Chgo., 1989-93; staff dir. legal dept. McDonald's Corp., Oak Brook, Ill., 1993-95, home office dir. legal dept., 1995-97, regulatory practice group leader and mng. counsel, 1998—. Instr. John Marshall Grad. Sch. Law, Chgo., 1986-87; mem. adv. bd. John Marshall Sch. Law, 1996—; bd. dirs. Flutes Unlimited; mem. adv. bd. dirs. Plan Sponsor Mag., 2000—. Contbr. case note to DePaul Law Rev., 1976, note and comment editor DePaul Law Rev., 1976-77, editor Taxation For Lawyers, 1986-88. Mem. Am. Coll. Employee Benefit Attys., Chgo. Bar Assn. (chair employee benefits com. 1991-92, co-chair symphony orchestra 1999—), Midwest Pension Conf. (name chged to Midwest Benefits Coun.), WEB (pres. Chgo. chpt. 1986-88, v.p. nat. bd. 1988, pres. 1989-90), Profit Sharing Coun. Am. (legal and legis. com. 1994—, bd. dirs. 1997—, 2d vice chair 1997-98, 1st vice chair 1998-2000, chair 2000—). Lutheran. Home: 586 Crescent Blvd # 402 Glen Ellyn IL 60137 Office: McDonald's Corp 2915 Jorie Blvd Oak Brook IL 60523 E-mail: karen.barnes@mcd.com.

BARNES, KATHLEEN CAROLE, medical educator; b. Akron, Ohio, Oct. 27, 1960; d. Robert and Carole Barnes; m. Edward M. Horowitz, Sept. 4, 1994; children: Nora, Sofia, Clara. Student, James Madison U., 1979—82; BSN, Va. Commonwealth U., 1984; PhD, U. Fla., 1992. RN Md. State Bd. Nursing, 92. Charge nurse Med. Coll. Va. Va. Commonwealth U., Richmond, Va., 1984—86; RN Shands Tchg. Hosp., Gainesville, Fla., 1986—92; rsch. asst. U. Fla., Gainesville, 1987—92; from postdoctoral fellow to assoc. prof. Johns Hopkins U., Balt., 1993—2002, assoc. prof., 2002—. Mem. med. task force on women's academic careers Johns Hopkins U., 1996—; cons. Glaxo-Wellcome Pharm., 1999—; spkr. in field. Contbr. articles to profl. jours.; mem. editl. bd.: Current Opinion in Allergy & Clin. Immunology, reviewer: Genomics, Human Genetics, Am. Jour. of Respiratory & Critical Care Medicine, Jour. Allergy and Clin. Immunology, Clin. and Exptl. Allergy, Allergy, European Jour. Human Genetics. Fellow, Women's Bus. Assn. Danville, 1982; grantee Vining Davis grant, 1988, S.C. Johnson, 1988, Dow-Elanco, 1991, U. Fla., 1992, Boehringer Rsch. grant, 1994, Caribbean Med. Rsch. Coun., 1994, Glaxo Rsch. Travel grant, 1994, Asthma and Allergy Found. Am., 1997, 1999. Mem.: AAAS, Soc. Applied Anthropology, Am. Anthrop. Assn., Am. Acad. Allergy, Asthma and Immunology (mem. various coms. 1996—, grant 1994, 1995), Phi Kappa Phi. Office: Johns Hopkins Univ 5501 Hopkins Bayview Circle Room 3B 65A Baltimore MD 21224

BARNES, KAY, mayor; BS in Secondary Edn., U. Kans.; MS in Secondary Edn. and Pub. Adminstrn., U. Mo., Kansas City. Staff mem. Westport area Cross-Lines Coop. Coun.; pres. Kay Waldo, Inc., human resources devel. co., Kansas City, Mo.; mayor City of Kansas City, Mo., 1999—. Condr. over 400 pub. seminars Nat. Seminars, Inc.; cons., keynote spkr. 14 reginal confs. through U.S., Am. Bus. Women's Assn.; former co-host, prodr. cable TV show Let's Talk; former instr. U. Mo., Kansas City, U. Kans., Ctrl. Mich. U. Author: About Time! A Woman's Guide to Time Management. Co-founder Ctrl. Exch.; vol. Cross-Lines Coop. Coun.; a founder women's resource svc. U. Mo., Kansas City; developer multicultural women's speaking panels through western U.S.; mem. Jackson County (Mo.) Legislature, from 1974; mem. Kansas City City Coun., from 1979; chmn. Tax Increment Financing Commn., 1993-97; pres. bd. dirs. Women's Employment Network; mem. or dir. numerous other orgns., including Women's Found. Greater Kansas City, Greater Kansas City Sports Commn.; mem. chancellor's adv. bd. of Women's Ctr., U. Mo., Kansas City. Named One of 7 Outstanding Women in Kansas City, 1977. Mem. Greater Kansas City C. of C. (com.). Office: Mayor's Office City Hall 29th Fl 414 E 12th St Ste 2902 Kansas City MO 64106-2778*

BARNES, KEITH LEE, electronics executive; b. San Francisco, Sept. 14, 1951; s. Arch Lee and Charlotte Mae (Sanborn) B.; m. Sharon Ann Tosaw, June 9, 1986; children: Allecia, Alexandra, Wyatt. BS, Calif. State U., San Jose, 1976. Mgr. engring. and mktg. Gould, Inc., Rolling Meadow, Ill., 1976-79; v.p., gen. mgr. Kontron Electronics, Mountain View, Calif., 1979-85; v.p. Valley Data Scis., Mountain View, 1985-86; pres., CEO Integrated Measurement Sys., Beaverton, Oreg., 1986-2000, chmn., CEO, 2000—. Bd. dirs. Data Io Corp., LWG, Inc., Clarity Visual Systems, Inc. Patentee in field. Bd. dirs. Am. Electronics Assn., 1992-93, chmn. Oreg. bd., 1993; trustee Oreg. Grad. Inst. for Sci. and Industry, 1996—; vice chair Oreg. Growth Account, 1998; regent U. Portland, 2000. Mem. IEEE, PGC. Republican. Roman Catholic. Office: Integrated Measurement Systems 9525 SW Gemini Dr Beaverton OR 97008-7149

BARNES, MAGGIE LUE SHIFFLETT (MRS. LAWRENCE BARNES), nurse; b. Redmond, Tex., Mar. 29, 1931; d. Howard Eldridge and Sadie Adilene (Dunlap) Shifflett; m. T.C. Fagan, Jan. 1950 (Dec. Feb. 1952); 1 child, Lawayne; m. Lawrence Barnes, Sept. 2, 1960. Student, Cogdell Sch. Nursing, 1959-60, Western Tex. Coll., 1972-76; postgrad., Meth. Hosp. Sch. Nursing, Lubbock, Tex., 1975; BSN, West Tex. State U., 1977; cert. legal nurse cons., Kaplan Coll., 2001. RN Tex., cert. gerontol. nurse. Floor nurse D.M. Cogdell Meml. Hosp., Snyder, Tex., 1960-64, medication nurse, 1964-76, asst. evening supr., 1976-78, charge nurse, after 1978, evening nursing supr., 1980; nursing supr. for 5 counties West Ctrl. Home Health Agy., Snyder, 1980-83; emergency rm. evening supr. Mitchell County Hosp., 1983-89; dir. nurses Snyder Oak Care Ctr., 1989-91, Mountain View Lodge, Big Spring, Tex., 1991-92, Med. Arts Hosp. Home Health, Big Spring, 1992-93, Metplex Home Health Svcs., Snyder, 1993-94, ret., 1994; weekend RN Snyder Oaks Care Ctr. Part time nurse 1994—, CNA Sch. instr.; leader Bible study, 1997—; vol. Helping Children Read Sch., Bible study at nursing homes; regional coord. home health svcs. Beverly Enterprises, 1983; legal nurse cons. Grad. Kaplan Coll., Boca Raton, Fla., 2001. Den mother Cub Scouts, Boy Scouts Am., Holliday, Tex., 1960-61; mem. PTA, Snyder, 1960-69; adviser Sr. Citizens Assn.; mem Tri-Region Health Sys. Agy., 1979—; mem. adv. bd. Scurry County Diabetes Assn., 1982—; mem. vol. reading program; ch. sec.-treas. Apostolic Faith Ch., 1956-58 Mem.: DAR, Emergency Dept. Nursing Assn., Vocat. Nurses Assn. Tex. (bd. dirs. 1963—65, divsn. pres. 1967—69), Rock and Roll Quilting Club (coord.). Avocation: bible study with nursing home residents. Home: 8239 County Road 473 Hermleigh TX 79526-3303

BARNES, MARGARET ANDERSON, business consultant; b. Johnston County, N.C. m. Benjamin Barnes, Dec. 26, 1959. BS, N.C. Ctrl. U., 1958; MA, U. Md., 1975; PhD, Columbia Pacific U., 1986. Lic. ins. agt., Md.; ordained Christian min. and elder in World Evangelism, 1992. Math. tchr. Tarboro (N.C.) Sch. Sys., 1959-61; math. statistician Bur. of Census, Suitland, Md., 1962-67, 69-70, Govt. of D.C., 1967-68; cons. NIH, Bethesda, Md., 1970-72; chief of data stds. Nat. Insts. of Health, Bethesda, Md., 1972-73; with exec. clearance office HEW, Rockville, Md., 1973-77; founder, pres. MABarnes Cons. Assoc., Lanham, Md., 1978-95. Commr. State of Md. Accident Fund, Balt., 1979-89; mem. adv. bd. Universal Bank, Lanham, 1980-83, Interstate Gen. Corp., St. Charles, Md., 1981-83; founder Christian Ministries, 1983—, Christ Centered Ministries Esprit, 1995—, Mleecole Pub., 1997—; profiled for First Record: "Women of Achievement in Prince George's County History", 1994. Chairwoman Glenwood Park Civic Assn., Lanham, 1967-80. Democrat. Avocations: piano, sewing, reading, prose writing, artistic designing. Home: PO Box 586 Lanham Seabrook MD 20703-0586 Office: Christ Centered Ministries Esprit PO Box 802 Lanham Seabrook MD 20703-0802

BARNES, MARK JAMES, lawyer; b. Oak Park, Ill., Jan. 10, 1957; s. James W. and Lorraine (Brady) B.; m. Ellice Halpern, 1988; children: Julia Elizabeth, Katherine Claire, John Halpern. BS in Polit. Sci. summa cum laude, Ariz. State U., 1978; JD, UCLA, 1981. Staff atty. Senator Ted Stevens U.S. Senate, Washington, 1981-83, chief counsel Senator Ted Stevens, 1983-84; assoc. Davis, Wright & Jones, Anchorage, 1984-86; dep. gen. counsel U.S. Office of Personnel Mgmt., Washington, 1986-87; assoc. dir. adminstrn. U.S. Office Personnel Mgmt., Washington, 1988-89; counsel to sec. for drug abuse policy HHS, Washington, 1989-93; pvt. practice Washington, 1993—. Alaska ambassador organizing com. Anchorage Olympics, 1986; mem. exec. com., World Forum on Future of Sport Shooting Activities, 1998—. Mem. ABA, Alaska Bar Assn., Ariz. Bar Assn., D.C. Bar Assn., Phi Beta Kappa. Republican. Roman Catholic. Avocations: travel, movies, stamps. Office: 1350 Eye St NW Ste 1255 Washington DC 20005-3390 E-mail: markb17@aol.com.

BARNES, MARYLOU RIDDLEBERGER, retired academic administrator, educator; b. Bridgewater, Va., Feb. 27, 1930; d. Hensel Dorsey Riddleberger and Ruby Elizabeth Heltzel; children: Tenley Elizabeth, Rachel Patricia. BS, Madison Coll., 1952; MS, Med. Coll. Va., 1957; MA, James Madison U., 1968; EdD, W. Va. U., 1975; DSc (hon.), U. Indpls., 1993. From staff phys. therapist to dir. clin. edn. Woodrow Wilson Rehab. Ctr., Fishersville, Va., 1958-64, dir clin. edn., 1964-67; chief phys. therapy Rockingham Meml. Hosp., Harrisonburg, Va., 1958-59; prof., dir., chair dept. phys. therapy W. Va. U., Morgantown, W. Va., 1968-79; from prof., chair dept. phys. therapy to prof. emeritus Ga. State U., Atlanta, 1979-95, ret., 1995, prof. emeritus, 1995—. Adv. bd. Perry Inst., Strafford, Pa., 1993-95; co-chair program com. Joint Am.-Can. Phys. Therapy Annual Conf. Author: Patient at Home, 1972, Neurophysiological Basis of Physical Therapy Care, vol. I, 1973, vol. II, 1977, Physical Therapy, 1989, Motor Control and Motor Learning in Rehabilitation, 1993; contbr. articles to profl. jours. Vol. Centennial Olympic Games, Atlanta, 1996, Goodwill Industries Book Ctr., Atlanta, 1999. Mem. Am. Phys. Therapy Assn. (nat. survey pool for accreditation of schs. 1974-95, pres. neurology sect. 1985-87, task force on profl. devel. 1994, chair continuing edn. bd. 1994-95, Mary McMillan Lectr. award 1992, Catherine Worthingham fellow 1994, leadership in edn. award 1995, svc. to neurology sect. award 1998, Lucy Blair Svc. award 1988). Presbyterian. Avocations: amateur archaeologist, travel, reading, tree climbers of am. Home: 133 Santolina Park Peachtree City GA 30269-3245 E-mail: mloubarnes@mindspring.com.

BARNES, MELVER RAYMOND, retired chemist; b. nr. Salisbury, N.C., Nov. 15, 1917; s. Oscar Lester and Sarah Albertine (Rowe) B. AB in Chemistry, U. N.C., 1947; D of Physics (hon.), World U., 1983; DSc in Chemistry (hon.), Assoc. Univs., 1987, PhD in Chemistry (hon.), 1990, Albert Einstein Internat. Acad. Found. and Associated Univs., 1990. Chemist Pitts. Testing Labs., Greensboro, N.C., 1948-49, N.C. State Hwy. and Pub. Works Commn., Raleigh, 1949-51, Edgewood (Md.) Arsenal, 1951-61, Dugway (Utah) Proving Ground, 1961-70. Recipient Albert Einstein Bronze medal, 1988, Alfred Nobel Medal award Albert Einstein Internat. Acad. Found., 1991, Albert Einstein Acad. Found. Cross of Merit, 1992. Mem. AAAS, Am. Statis. Assn., Am. Chem. Soc., Am. Phys. Soc. Home and Office: 1486 Swicegood Rd Linwood NC 27299-9386

BARNES, MYRTLE SUE SNYDER, editor; b. Farmville, Va., July 14, 1933; d. George McClure and Alma White (Hillsman) Snyder; m. Shelton W. Barnes, Dec. 23, 1954 (dec. Aug. 1979); children: Donna Barnes Boulter, David Brian. BJ, Northwestern U., 1955. Reporter Times-Herald, Newport News, Va., 1956-60, 67-72, city editor, 1972-75, asst. mng. editor, 1975-82; mng. editor Daily Press & Times Herald, Newport News, 1982-87; adminstrv. editor Daily Press, Newport News, Va., 1987-95, reader editor, 1995-96, ret., 1996. Mem. jury for Pulitzer prize Columbia U., 1977, 78; mem. Accreditation Coun. on Edn. in Journalism and Mass Comm., 1986-91. Past pres., now treas. Newport News Libr. Friends. Named to Va. Comm. Hall of Fame, 1993; recipient Founding Dir.'s award Va. Coalition on Open Govt., 2000. Mem. AP Mng. Editors (chmn. com. 1986-88, bd. dirs. 1988-91, Meritorious Svc. award 1993), Va. AP Newspapers (chmn. 1987), Nat. Fedn. Press Women (bd. dirs. 1972-74, numerous awards for writing and editing), Va. Press Women (pres. 1970-72, Press Woman of Yr. 1973, numerous awards for writing and editing), Soc. Profl. Journalists (pres. Tidewater chpt. 1978, George Mason award Richmond chpt. 1986), Nat. Congress Parents and Tchrs. (life). Avocations: reading, traveling, theater, handwork. Home: 19 Rose Briar Pl Hampton VA 23666-6818 E-mail: msbarnes@widomaker.com.

BARNES, NATASHA LYNN, lawyer; b. Woodward, Okla., Aug. 24, 1971; d. Lex V. and Bonnie A. Barnes. BS, Okla. State U., 1993; JD with honors, U. Okla., 1996. Bar: Tex. 1996. Assoc. Thornton, Summers, Biechlin, Dunham and Brown, Austin, Tex., 1996-2000, Thompson, Coe, Cousins and Irons, L.L.P., Austin, 2000—. Mem. Austin Young Lawyer's Assn., Travis County Bar Assn. Office: Thompson Coe Cousins Irons 1500 Austin Ctr 701 Brazos Austin TX 78701 Fax: 512-708-8777.

BARNES, PAUL EDWIN, concert pianist, music educator; b. Lima, Ohio, Oct. 29, 1961; s. Harry S and Joan Marie Barnes; m. Ann Chang, Aug. 10, 1985; children: Sarah Young, Hannah Michel, Peter Chang. MusB, Ind. U., 1985, MusM, 1987, MusD, 1991. Cert. music tchr. Music Teachers Nat. Assn., 1998. Asst. prof. of piano DePauw U., Greencastle, Ind., 1991—94; assoc. prof. of piano U. of Nebr. Lincoln Sch. of Music, Lincoln, 1995—; piano faculty Boesendorfer Internat. Piano Acad., Austria, 1999—. Musician: (recording) American Piano Concertos, Vol. One; musician: (piano soloist) (lecture-recital in Jerusalem) Liszt and the Cross: Music as Sacrament in the B Minor Sonata, (lecture recital in Thessaloniki, Greece) Liszt and the Cross: Music as Sacrament in the B minor Sonata; author (pianist): (lecture-recital in Washington, D.C.) Liszt and the Church: Dogma and Devotion, (lecture recital at 2000 MTNA, Mpls.) New Music for a New Millenium; musician: (Internat. Computer Music Festival) Keyed Up by Jeff Hass; author (chanter): (lecture-recital at Internation Religion) From Antioch and Constantinople to Kearney and Lincoln: Arab and Greek Liturgical Adaptation to the Great Plains; musician (transcriber): (piano transcriptions of Philip Glass) Orphee Suite for Piano; editor: (piano transcriptions from Philip Glass) Trilogy Sonata; musician: (world premier performance, piano concert) Ancient Keys by Victoria Bond; musician: (transcriber) (world premier performance, piano solo) Orphee Suite for Piano by Philip Glass; author (pianist): (lecture-recital) Liszt and the Cross: Music as Sacrament in the B Minor Sonata; musician (piano soloist): (performance with Slovak Radio Orch.) Gershwin Variations, Bond Ancient Keys, (solo recital at Liszt Acad., Budapest) piano works of Liszt, Glass, (solo recital at Moscow Conservatory) works by Liszt, Barber, Tower. Mem. Nat. Forum of Greek Orthodox Ch. Musicians, Bloomington, Ind., 2002—03; head chanter Annunciation Greek Orthodox Ch., Lincoln, 1997—2003. Grantee Lied Ctr. for Performing Arts grantee, 2003—, Nebr. Lewis and Clark Bicentennial Commn. grantee, 2003—, UNL Rsch. Coun. grantee, 2003—, Hixson-Lied Coll. Fine and Performing Arts grantee, 2003—, U. Nebr. Found. grantee, 2002—03, UNL Rsch. Coun. grantee, 1999—2000. Mem.: Am. Liszt Soc. (chair of chpt. devel. 2002—03, nat. bd. dirs. 2001—), Music Tchrs. Nat. Assn. Greek Orthodox. Avocation: tennis. Home: 2300 S 75th St Lincoln NE 68506 Office: University of Nebraska-Lincoln 241 Westbrook Music Bldg Lincoln NE 68588-0100 Home Fax: 402-488-9555; Office Fax: 402-472-8962. Personal E-mail: pbarnes@unl.edu. E-mail: pbarnes@unl.edu.

BARNES, PAUL MCCLUNG, lawyer; b. Phila., June 27, 1914; s. Andrew Wallace and Luella Hope (Andrew) B.; m. Elizabeth McClenahan, Dec. 28, 1940 (dec.); children: Andrew M., Margaret L. Lenart, James D., John R. (dec.). BA, Monmouth (Ill.) Coll., 1936; JD, U. Chgo., 1939. Bar: Colo. bar 1939. Assoc. Bannister & Bannister, Denver, 1939-40, Foley & Lardner, Milw., 1940-47, ptnr., 1948-88, of counsel, 1988—. Dir. Wis. Public Service Corp., 1974-77, Kickhaefer Mfg. Co., 1965-85, Attys. Liability Assurance Soc., Ltd., 1979-87; sec. Sta-Rite Industries, Inc., 1965-73 Mem. adv. bd. Milw. Protestant Home, 1975-87. Served with USNR, 1942-45. Mem. ABA, Wis. Bar Assn., Order of Coif. Office: Foley & Lardner 777 E Wisconsin Ave Ste 3800 Milwaukee WI 53202-5367 E-mail: pbarnes@webtv.net.

BARNES, PETER, retired lawyer; b. Cambridge, Mass., Apr. 13, 1940; s. Tracy Barnes and Janet (White) Lawrence; m. Jan Adair; children from previous marriage: K. Tracy, John E. BA magna cum laude, Yale U., 1962; LLB cum laude, Harvard U., 1965. Bar: DC 1966, Md. 1984. Assoc. Leva, Hawes, Symington, Martin & Oppenheimer, Washington, 1965-71, ptnr., 1972-83, Venable, Baetjer & Howard, Balt., 1983-86; mem., shareholder Swidler & Berlin, Chtd., Washington, 1987-98; mem. Swidler Berlin Shereff Friedman, LLP, Washington, 1998-99, counsel, 1999—2001; ret., 2002. Bd. dirs. Walker & Dunlop, Inc., Washington. Mem.: Elkridge Club, Met. Club. Home: 4 Deep Run Ct Cockeysville MD 21030-1600 E-mail: PtrBrs@aol.com.

BARNES, PETER J., JR., assemblyman; b. East Providence, R.I., Sept. 12, 1928; BA in Polit. Sci., Providence Coll.; BA in pub. adminstrn., Kean Coll. Assemblyman N.J. Gen. Assembly, 1996—; majority whip, 2002—. Spl. agt. FBI, 1954—81; Edison dir. pub. safety, 1991—93. Pvt. Mil. Police U.S. Army, 1946—48. Democrat. Office: 1967 Rt 27 Ste 20 Edison NJ 08817 E-mail: AsmBarnes@njleg.org.*

BARNES, RICHARD DALE, college basketball coach; b. Hickory, North Carolina, July 17, 1954; m. Candace, July 31, 1976; children: Nicholas, Caroline. Degree in Health Physical Edn., Lenoir-Rhyne Coll., 1977. Head coach North State Acad., 1977-78; asst. coach Davidson, 1978-80, George Mason, 1980-85, Ala., 1985-86, Ohio State, 1986-87; head coach George Mason, 1987-88; head basketball coach Providence Coll., 1988-94, Clemson U., 1994-98, U. Tex., Austin, 1998—. Office: U Tex Intercoll Athletics-Men Campus Mail Code E2400 Austin TX 78712

BARNES, RICHARD GEORGE, physicist, educator; b. Milw., Dec. 19, 1922; s. George Richard and Irma (Ott) B.; m. Mildred A. Jachens, Sept. 9, 1950; children: Jeffrey R., David G., Christina E., Douglas A. BA, U. Wis., 1948; MA, Dartmouth Coll., 1949; PhD, Harvard U., 1952. Teaching fellow Harvard, 1950-52; asst. prof. U. Del., 1952-55, asso. prof., 1955-56, Iowa State U., 1956-60, prof., 1960-88, chmn. dept. physics, 1971-75, prof. emeritus, 1988—; sr. physicist Ames Lab., U.S. Dept. Energy, 1960-88; assoc. Ames lab. US Dept. Energy, 1988—; chief physics divsn. Ames lab. AEC, 1971-75. Vis. rsch. prof. Calif. Inst. Tech., 1962-63; guest profl. Tech. U. Darmstadt, Germany, 1975-76; vis. prof. Cornell U., 1982-83; program dir. solid state physics NSF, 1988-89, condensed matter physics NSF, 1995; chmn. Metal Hydrides Gordon Rsch. Conf., 1987. Served with USAAF, 1942-43; C.E. AUS, 1944-46 (Manhattan Project). Recipient U.S. Sr. Scientist award Alexander von Humboldt Found., 1975-76 Fellow Am. Phys. Soc. Home: 3238 Aspen Rd Ames IA 50014 Office: Iowa State U Physics Dept Ames IA 50011-0001

BARNES, ROBERT VINCENT, retired elementary and secondary school art educator; b. Flint, Mich., May 27, 1948; s. Albert J. and Mary Elizabeth (Morey) B.; m. Sandra E. Mathews-Barnes, Dec. 20, 1986; 1 child, Kathryn R. BA, Adrian Coll., 1970; postgrad., U. Mich., 1973-75, Ctrl. Mich. U., 1976-80, Getty Ctr. Edn. Arts, Cin. Art Mus., Cranbrook Acad. Art, Marygrove Coll., Cranbrook Acad. Art, 1995—; MA, Marygrove Coll., 1997. Cert. tchr. art grades kindergarten through 12, Mich. Tchr. art Flushing (Mich.) Cmty. Schs., 1971—2002; instr. Flint Inst. Arts, 1975-76; tchr. genealogy adult edn. program Mott C.C., Flushing, Fenton and Grand Blanc, Mich., 1976-84; pvt. art tchr., 2002—. Tchr. pvt. art lessons. Author: Flushing Area Families, 1981, Fenton Area Families, 1984; editor Flint Geneal. Quar., 1981. Past pres. Flint Geneal. Soc., Fenton Hist. Soc.; bd. dirs., past pres. Flushing Area Hist. Soc.; pres. Fenton Mus. Bd., 1984-86; chmn. Fenton 150th Com., 1984; co-chmn. Fenton Civic Com. for New Mus., 1985-86; com. mem. Genesee County Sesquicentennial, Flint, 1986; mentor for jr. h.s. youth Logas program Fenton United Meth. Ch., mem. edn. commn., 2000—. Recipient 1st prize Flushing Art Fair, Flushing Jr. Women's League, 1975, 78, Orren Hart award Flushing Area Hist. Soc., 1983. Mem. NEA, Mich. Edn. Assn., Nat. Art Edn. Assn., Mich. Art Edn. Assn., Ohio Geneal. Soc., Ohio Hist. Soc. Methodist. Avocations: pottery, painting, family history research.

BARNES, ROBERT F, agronomist; b. Estherville, Iowa, Feb. 6, 1933; s. Chester Arthur and Pearl Adella (Stoelting) B.; m. Bettye Jeanne Burrell, June 25, 1955; children: Bradley R., Rebecca L. Reinalda, Roberta K. Nixon, Brian L. AA, Estherville Jr. Coll., 1953; BS, Iowa State U., 1957; MS, Rutgers U., 1959; PhD, Purdue U., 1963. Rsch. agronomist USDA-Agrl. Rsch. Svc., West Lafayette, Ind., 1959-70, lab. dir. University Park, Pa., 1970-75, staff scientist nat. program staff Beltsville, Md., 1975-79, assoc. dep. adminstr. So. region New Orleans, 1979-84, dep. adminstr. So. region, 1984-86; exec. v.p. Am. Soc. Agronomy, Madison, Wis., 1986-99; exec. dir. Agronomic Sci. Found., exec. dir. emeritus, 1999—; also fellow Am. Soc. of Agronomy, Madison, Wis. Asst. prof. Purdue U., West Lafayette, 1963-66; assoc. prof., 1966-70; adj. prof. Pa. State U., University Park, 1966-70; adj. prof. agronomy U. Wis., Madison, 1986-99; pres. Internat. Grassland Congress, Lexington, Ky., 1981; cons. Agronomic Sci. Found., Am. Soc. Agronomy. Editor: Forages, 1995; contbr. articles to profl. jours. With U.S. Army, 1953-55, Germany. Recipient H.S. Stubbs Meml. Lecture award Tropical Grassland Soc., Brisbane, Australia, 1984, Henry A. Wallace award Iowa State U., 1991. Fellow AAAS, Crop Sci. Soc. Am. (pres. 1984-85); mem. Am. Forage and Grassland Coun. (medallion 1981, Disting. Grasslander award 2001), Grazing Lands Forum (pres. 1986-87), Forage and Grassland Found. (pres. 1993-97). Avocations: walking, reading. Office: Am Soc of Agronomy 677 S Segoe Rd Madison WI 53711-1048 E-mail: rbarnes@agronomy.org.

BARNES, ROBERT VERTREESE, JR., masonry contractor executive; b. Dallas, Oct. 7, 1946; s. Robert Vertreese and Doris Corinne (Haffen) B.; m. Deborah Dee Brown, May 31, 1968; children: Robert V. III, John David, Leslie Shannon. BS in Indsl. Tech., Tex. A&M U., 1976. Registered bldg. contractor, Ariz.; registered and cert. bldg. contractor, Fla. Salesman Sears, Roebuck and Co., Dallas, 1965-66, dept. mgr., 1967-69; estimator Dee Brown Masonry, Inc., Dallas, 1970-75, contract adminstr., 1976-77; v.p. Cardinal Masonry Co., Houston, 1978-79, Dee Brown Masonry, Inc., Houston, 1980-85, exec. v.p., 1985-89, Dee Brown, Inc., Houston, 1985-89, pres., COO, 1990-99; chmn., pres., CEO, 2000—. V.p., sec./treas., dir. Shiloh Investment Co., 1974-99, chmn., pres. 2000—, Stone Erectors, Inc., 1989-93; exec. v.p. Dee Brown Masonry/Hatch, Inc., 1989-90, chmn. 2000—; pres., CEO, dir. Masonry Tech., Inc., 1993-95, chmn., pres., CEO, 1996-2002; dir. Stone Anchor, Inc., 1993-2003; ptnr. Pacific Water Jet LLC, 1996-2003, Skinner Marble and Granite LLC, 1997-99, Kepco & DBI, LLC, 2000, Salesmanship Club Dallas, 1997—; trustee, chmn. bricklayers health and welfare Bricklayer's Pension Fund, 1983-85; pres. Youngblood Masonry Inc., 2000—; trustee Episcopal Founds. of Dallas, 2000—; mem. archtl. and constrn. com. Dallas Arboretum, 2000—, chmn. archtl. and constrn. com., 2003—, exec. com., 2003—; bd. dirs. Innovative Masonry, Inc. Pres. Katy Youth Soccer Assn., 1980-81; mgr. Solar "74" Soccer Club, 1986-88, Diggers Soccer Club, 1989-92; dir. Whiterock Ch.'s Athletic Assn., 1972-77; bishop warden St. Cuthbert's Episcopal Ch., 1985-86; bd. dirs. St. John's Episc. Sch., 1987-93, v.p., 1988-89, sch. fin. com., health, safety and ins. com., bldg. facility com., chmn. bldg. and grounds com., 1988-90, co-chmn. devel. com., vestry mem., fin. com., athletic dir., 1999-2001; exec. com. Constrn. Rsch. Ctr., U. Tex., Arlington, 1992-94, vice chmn., 1994, chmn. elect, 1995, chmn., 1995-96; trustee Episcopal Found. Diocese Dallas, 2000—, Gaston Episcopal Hosp. Found., 2000—, John Charles Brown Parish Scholar Fund, 1996—; exec. adv. bd. mem. Cir. Ten coun. Boy Scouts Am., 2000—, chmn. camping facilities, 2002. Mem. ASTM (C12, C15, C18 coms. 1990—), Mason Contractors Assn. Am. (contract rsch. com. 1982-83, chmn. labor com., codes and stds. com., state chmn. 2003, liaison com., regional v.p.), Tex. Masonry Coun. (bd. dirs.) Marble Inst. Am., Constrn. Specification Inst., Associated Gen. Contractors Dallas (subcontractor rels. com. 1988-89, AGC mktg. com. 1990-93, co-chmn. gencontractor/subcontractor rels. com. 1993-94, bd. dirs. 1995-98, transition com. AGC/ABC 1995-96, nat. assn. bd. dirs. assoc. mem. AGC 1995-98), Masonry Alliance Codes and Stds. (treas. 1996-2000), Constrn. Edn. Found. (trustee 1996-98), Baylor Inst. Rehab. (trustee 1997-2003, vice chmn. 1998-2000, chmn. 2001-2003), Assn. Masonry Contractors Tex. (pres. 1983, sec./treas. 1981-82, v.p. 1990-91), So. Bldg. Congress, Nat. Bldg. Environment and Thermal Envelope Counsel, Assn. Masonry Contractors Houston (pres. 1982-84, v.p. 1981), Am. Subcontractor Assn. (v.p. 1982-83, bd. dirs. Houston 1982-85, also mem. nat. coms., dir. north Tex. chpt. 1995-97), United Masonry Contractors Dallas (dir. constrn. edn. found. 1996-98, mem. program com. 1996-98, bd. dirs. 2003—), Dallas Exec. Assn., Houston C. of C., N.W. Houston C. of C., Dallas C. of C., East Dallas Younglife (bd. dirs. 1990—), Tex. A&M U. Blue and Gold Alumni Assn., Tex. A&M U.-Commerce Mayo Found., Tex. A&M U. Commerce Amb., John Brown U. Parents Cabinet (founder, pres. 1989-93), Dallas Pioneer Assn., Pine Forest Country Club (Houston), Dallas Athletic Club, Baylor Health Club, Tom Landry Ctr., Dallas Country Club, Delta Sigma Pi. Republican. Home: 6531 Meadow Road Dallas TX 75230

BARNES, ROSEMARY LOIS, minister; b. Grand Rapids, Mich., Sept. 17, 1946; d. Floyd Herman and Cora Agnes (Beukema) Herms; m. Louis Herbert Adams, Feb. 22, 1969 (div. Oct. 1976); 1 child, Louis Herbert Jr.; m. Robert Jearold Barnes, Oct. 8, 1976. BA, Calvin Coll., 1968; postgrad., Wagner Leadership Inst., 1999—. Ordained to ministry Home Ministry Fellowship, 1980; cert. social worker. Group worker Kent County Juvenile Ct., Grand Rapids, Mich., 1966-68; tchr. Sheldon Elem. Sch., Grand Rapids, 1968-69; social worker Kent Dept. Social Services, Grand Rapids, 1969-75, 75-84; tchr., mission worker Emmanuel House, San Diego, 1975; co-pastor, founder River of Life Ministries, Grand Rapids, 1980—; instr. Gt. Lakes Inst. Bible Studies, Grand Rapids, 1988. Tchr., founder River of Life Sch. Christian Leadership, Grand Rapids, 1981—; v.p. Aglow, Grand Rapids, 1982-83; sec., treas. Western Mich. Full Gospel Ministers Fellowship, Grand Rapids, 1984-85; mem. bd. chaplains Dunes Correctional Facility, Saugatuck, Mich., 1986-91; coord. 1988 Washington for Jesus March, One Nation Under God, Inc.; co-pastor Gun Lake River of Life, 1988; prof. Great Lakes Inst., 1988; county coord. Grand Rapids Full Gospel Ministers Fellowship, 1990-92; co-pastor Defiance, Ohio River of Life, 1992-93; founder St. Joseph Sch. Christian Leadership. Participant TV show Ask the Pastor, 1993—; dir., producer TV show River Reflections, 1994—; Mich. women's coord. Let The Redeemed of the Lord Say So, 1994; sponsor Grand Rapids cable TV Jewish Jewels, 1995—. Bd. dirs. Alcohol Incentive Ladder, Grand Rapids, 1979; overseer River City Outreach Ch., 1994—. Mem. Women in Leadership. Republican. Mem. Ind. Charismatic Ch. Avocation: playing the trumpet. Address: PO Box 140735 Grand Rapids MI 49514-0735 E-mail: RBarnesROL@aol.com. *My passion to see the Lord's church grow into Him, mature and spotless, is the force that motivates me to teach the Word of God. I believe that when His Bride is fully mature He will come to her and together they will rule and reign forever.*

BARNES, ROY EUGENE, former governor, lawyer; b. Atlanta, Mar. 11, 1948; m. Marie Dobbs Barnes; children: Harlan, Allison, Alyssa. AB, U. Ga., 1969, JD cum laude, 1972. Bar: U.S. Ct. Appeals 1972, Ga. 1972, U.S. Dist. Ct. 1973, U.S. Ct. Appeals (5th cir.) 1973, U.S. Supreme Ct. 1979, U.S. Ct. Appeals (11th cir.) 1983. Ptnr. Barnes & Browning, Marietta, Ga., 1975—; mem. Ga. Senate, 1974-90, chmn. com. on spl. judiciary, 1978-80, chmn. com. on judiciary, 1980-82, chmn. com. on constl. revision, 1981, adminstrn. floor leader, 1983-89; mem. Ga. Ho. of Reps., 1993-99; gov. State of Ga., 1998—2003; pvt. practice, 2003—. Vol. Atlanta Legal Aid Soc., 2003. Recipient John F. Kennedy Profile in Courage award, 2003. Mem. Am. Judicature Soc., Assn. Trial Lawyers Am., ABA, State Bar Ga., Ga. Trial Lawyers Assn., Inc., Cobb County Bar Assn. Democrat.*

BARNES, SALLY ANDERSON, human resources consultant, organization effectiveness and employee involvement facilitator; b. Sioux City, Iowa, Feb. 9, 1955; d. William David and Betty Ruth (Smith) Anderson; m. Barney B. Barnes, Oct. 22, 1986. BS in Journalism, U. Houston, 1979. Asst. tng. specialist U. Tex., Austin, 1975-77; client coord. Bus. Internat. Corp., NY, Houston, 1978-79; employment counselor John L. Cloud Placement Svc., Houston, 1979; sr. employment recruiter Tex. Commerce Bank, Houston, 1979-81; dir., pers. officer Post Oak Bank, Houston, 1981-82; pers. rep. Austin divsn. Lockheed Corp., 1982-90, TQM/employee involvement facilitator, 1991-94, mgr. Career Transition Ctr., 1994-95; pres., CEO The Right People, Inc., 1995—. Exec. dir. Lockheed's Bucks of the Month Club, 1983-84; dir. Lockheed Employee Recreation Assn., 1982-84; bd. dirs. Lockheed Lone Stars Assn. Mem. Nat. Employee Recreation Assn., Nat. Mgmt. Assn. Republican. Methodist. Avocations: sailing, cooking, reading. Home: 3611 Black Mesa Holw Austin TX 78739-7534

BARNES, SAMUEL HENRY, political scientist, educator; b. Miss, Jan. 20, 1931; s. Eugene Ludlow and Christine (Thompson) B.; m. Annabelle Bivona, Nov. 30, 1954; children: Christopher F.E., Michael Andrew, Catherine Ann. BA, Tulane U., 1952, MA, 1954; PhD, Duke U., 1957; postgrad. (Fulbright scholar), Institut des Hautes Etudes Politiques, Paris, 1956-57. Instr. polit. sci. U. Mich., Ann Arbor, 1957-60, asst. prof. polit. sci., 1960-64, assoc. prof., 1964-68, prof., 1968-91, James Orin Murfin prof. polit. sci., 1982-85, acting chmn. dept. polit. sci., 1968-69, chmn. dept., 1977-82, research assoc. Survey Research Ctr., 1969-70, program dir. Ctr. for Polit. Studies, 1970-91; prof. Comparative European Politics, dir. Ctr.for German and European Studies Georgetown U., Washington, 1991—2003; emeritus prof. and dir. Graf Goltz, 2003. Fulbright lectr. U. Florence, Italy, 1962-63, U. Rome, 1967-68; Ctr. Advanced Study in Behavioral Scis. fellow Stanford U., 1982-83, Hoover Instn. fellow Stanford U., 1989. Author: Party Democracy: Politics in an Italian Socialist Federation, 1967, Representation in Italy: Institutionalized Traditions and Electoral Choice, 1977, (with Max Kaase and others) Political Action: Mass Participation in Five Western Democracies, 1979, Politics and Culture, 1989, (with others) Continuities in Political Action, 1990 (with others) Cultural Dynamics of Democratization in Spain, 1998; contbr. articles to profl. publ., book chpt. Trustee Duke U., 1989-2001. Served with USN, 1949-50. Mem. Am. Polit. Sci. Assn. (sec. 1972-74), Conf. Group for Italian Polit. Studies (v.p. 1975-77, pres. 1977-79), Cosmos Club (Washington).

BARNES, SANDRA HENLEY, publishing company executive; b. Seymour, Ind., Jan. 15, 1943; d. Ray C. and Barbara Henley; m. Ronald D. Barnes, Sept. 3, 1961; children: Laura, Barrett and Garrett (twins). Student, Ind. State U., 1962-63. Asst. sales mgr. Marquis Who's Who, Indpls., 1973-79, sales, svc. mgr., 1979-82, mktg. ops. mgr., 1982-84, mktg. mgr. Chgo., 1984-86, dir. mktg. Wilmette, Ill., 1986-87; v.p. mktg. Macmillan Directory Div., Wilmette, 1987-88; group v.p. product mgmt. Marquis Who's Who, Wilmette, 1988-89, pres., 1989-92; v.p. Reed Reference Pub., New Providence, N.J., 1992-96; v.p., fulfillment Reed Elsevier-New Providence, 1996-97, LEXIS-NEXIS, Dayton, Ohio, 1997-98, Lexis Law Pub., Charlottesville, Va., 1997-98, Congrl. Info. Svc., Bethesda, Md., 1997-98; sr. v.p. Ednl. Comms., Inc., Lake Forest, Ill., 1998—2001; gen. mgr. Marquis Who's Who, New Providence, NJ, 2002—. Republican. Avocation: reading. Office: 121 Chanlon Road New Providence NJ 07974

BARNES, SHIRLEY ELIZABETH, foreign service officer; b. St. Augustine, Fla. d. James Albert and Evelyn (Findley) B. Student, Boston U., 1959-60; BBA, CUNY, 1959; MBA, Columbia U., 1970; student, Nat. Def. U., 1990. Adminstrv. assoc. Ford Found. Ecole Nat. de Droit et d'Adminstrn., Kinshasa, Zaire, 1962-65; program asst. African Am. Inst., N.Y.C., 1965-66; adminstrv. asst. U.S. Info. Svc. English Lang. Sch., Kinshasa, 1966-68; account exec. J. Walter Thompson Advt., N.Y.C., 1970-73; v.p., account supr. John F. Small Advt., N.Y.C., 1973-76, Uniworld Advt., N.Y.C., 1976-79; Norman, Craig & Kummel, 1979-80; owner, pres. Barnes Findley Internat., N.Y.C., 1980-83; sr. fgn. svc. officer U.S. Dept. State, Washington and abroad, 1983—2001, U.S. amb. to Madagascar, 1998-2001; U.S. consul gen. Strasbourg, France. Cons. Richard K. Manoff Advt., U.S. Agy. for Internat. Devel., Kinshasa, Port-au-Prince, Haiti, 1981-83. Mem. nat. adv. bd. Hampshire Coll., Amherst, Mass., 1972-74; bd. dirs. Cinque Gallery, N.Y.C., 1974—. Mem. Delta Sigma Theta. Avocations: art of african diaspora, african and african-american history, jazz, opera. Office: Ste 1531 3001 Veazey Terr NW Washington DC 20008 E-mail: theta320@msn.com.

BARNES, STEVEN W. diagnostic equipment company executive; BS, Syracuse U., 1982. Various exec. level positions Executone Bus. Solutions; dir. Miltex Instruments; pres., COO, dir. Holson Burnes Group Inc.; exec. v.p. Bain Capital, 1996; COO Dade Behring, Deerfield, Ill., 1996—97, CEO, 1997—2000; mng. dir Bain Capital, Boston, 2000—. Office: Bain Capital 111 Huntington Ave Boston MA 02199*

BARNES, STUART ROBERT, physician assistant; b. Wilkes-Barre, Pa., July 11, 1952; s. Stanley Fenton and Arlene Violet Barnes; m. Dawn Marie Barnes, Oct. 24, 1992; children: Patricia Ann, Rebecca Paige. Paramedic cert., St. Petersburg Jr. Coll., 1974; physician asst. cert., King's Coll., 1983. Cert. physician asst. King's Coll., ACLS; firefighter Fla. State Fire Coll., 1973, smoke diver Fla. State Fire Coll., 1973. Firefighter/EMT New Port Richey Fire Dept., 1972-74; EMT/paramedic Pasco County Emergency Svcs., Newport Richey, Fla., 1974-76; paramedic Manatee County Emergency Svcs., Bradenton, Fla., 1976-80; physician asst. Ariz. State Dept. of Corrections, Florence, 1984-87, Caroline Health Svcs., Denton, Md., 1988-90, Genessis Physician Svcs., Salisbury, Md., 1990—2002, Breton Med. Group/Shah Assocs., California, Md., 2003—. Contbr. articles to profl. jours. Pres. Chestnut Hill Civic Assn., Delmar, Md., 1996, Leonard's Mill Pond Assn., Delmar, 1999. Fellow Am. Acad. Physician Assts., Md. Acad. Physician Assts., Assn. Family Practice Physician Assts.; mem. N.Am. Fishing Club (life), Masons. Avocations: music, fishing, woodworking, collecting old medical books. Office: Breton Med Group/Shah Assoc San Souci Plz 22576 MacArthur Blvd California MD 20619 E-mail: STUnDAWN@cs.com.

BARNES, THOMAS G. law educator; b. 1930; AB, Harvard U., 1952; DPhil, Oxford U., 1955. From asst. prof. to assoc. prof. Lycoming Coll., Williamsport, Pa., 1956-60; from lectr. to prof. history U. Calif., Berkeley, 1960—, humanities rsch. prof., 1971-72, prof. history and law, 1974—, co-chmn. Canadian studies program, 1982—. Dir. legal history project Am. Bar Found., 1965-86; com. mem. on ct. records 9th Cir. Ct. Author: Somerset 1625-1640: A County's Government During the Personal Rule, 1961, List and Index to Star Chamber Procs., James I, 3 vols., 1975, Lawes and Libertyes of Massachusetts, 1975, Hastings College of Law: The First Century, 1978; mem. editl. bd. Gryphon Legal Classics Libr.; editor Pub. Record Office. Huntington Libr. fellow, 1960, Am. Coun. Learned Socs. fellow, 1962-63, John Simon Guggenheim Found. fellow, 1970-71. Fellow Royal Hist. Soc.; mem. Selden Soc. (councillor, state corr.), Assn. Canadian Studies (pres. 2001-). Office: U Calif Sch Law 454 Boalt Hl Berkeley CA 94720-7200

BARNES, THOMAS JOHN, lawyer; b. Grand Rapids, Mich., Apr. 1, 1943; s. James and Adeline (Molenda) B.; m. Lynn Marie Owens, Aug. 19, 1967; children: Nicolle, Cynthia. BA in Acctg., Mich. State U., 1965, BA in Polit. Sci., 1966; JD, Wayne State U., 1972. Bar: Mich. 1972, U.S. Dsit. Ct. (ea. and we. dists.) Mich. 1972, U.S. Ct. Appeals (6th cir.) 1974, U.S. Dist. Ct. (no. dist.) Ind. 1994, U.S. Ct. Appeals (7th cir.) 1995. Ptnr. Varnum, Riddering, Schmidt & Howlett, Grand Rapids, 1972—. Arbitrator Mich. Employment Rels. Commn.; spkr. in field. Editor-in-chief Wayne Law Rev.; contbr. articles to profl. jours. Fellow Coll. Labor and Employment Lawyers; mem. ABA (nat. labor rels. bd. practice and procedures com.), Am. Employment Law Coun., Mich. Bar Assn. (labor coun., sec., treas. 1987-88, chmn. 1989-90), Grand Rapids Bar Assn. (chair labor sect.) Roman Catholic. Avocations: reading, horse racing, sports. Office: 333 Bridge St NW Grand Rapids MI 49504-5356

BARNES, THOMAS JOSEPH, writer; b. St. Paul, June 18, 1930; s. Ralph Weikert and Helen (O'Connor) B.; m. Mai Tang; children: An, Kim, Kevin; children by previous marriage: Christopher, Ross, Karen, Shannon. BA, U. Minn., 1950, MA, 1951. With fgn. service, 1957-80; vice consul, 1958-60; prin. officer Am. consulate, Hue, Viet Nam, 1960-61; polit. officer Bangkok, 1962-64, Vientiane, Laos, 1964-67; province sr. adviser Binh Long, Vietnam, 1967-68; country officer for Laos State Dept., 1968-70; prin. officer Am. Consulate, Udorn, Thailand, 1970-71; assoc. dir. AID, Nhatrang, Vietnam, 1971-72; consul gen. Tangier, Morocco, 1972-73, Can Tho, Vietnam, 1973; polit. counselor Bangkok, 1973-75; sr. staff mem. for East Asia Nat. Security Council, 1975-76; student Sr. Seminar in Fgn. Policy, State Dept., 1976-77; regional refugee coordinator Bangkok, 1977-78; diplomat-in-residence U. Hawaii, 1978-79; dir. Interagy. Working Group on Kampuchea, Dept. State,

Washington, 1979-80; with UN High Commn. for Refugees, Somalia, 1980-81, chief S.W. Asia sect., 1982-86, head supplies and food aid service, 1986-87, head orgn. and mgmt., 1987-90; coord. for ops. and program devel. Internat. Cath. Migration Commn., Geneva, 1991—95. Author: (novel) Tay Son: Rebellion in 18th Century Vietnam, 2000, Coping with Lust and the Colonel: Wartime Korea From Sokchang-ni, 2000, (memoir) Anecdotes of a Vagabond: The Foreign Service, The UN, and a Volag, 2000, (photographic art book) Southeast Asian Portraits, 2002. Capt. AUS, 1951-56. Decorated UN Svc medal, Korean Svc. medal, Bronze Star with 2 oak leaf clusters, Nat. Def. Svc. medal; recipient Award for Valor, Meritorious Honor award State Dept., Superior Honor awards State Dept, AID. Home: 15005 Solera Drive Austin TX 78717-4449

BARNES, VERNON ANTHONY, research scientist; b. Calgary, Alta., Can., June 24, 1950; Naturalized US citizen, 1996. s. John A. and Jeanne L. Barnes; m. Helene T. Martin, Sept. 18, 1996. BS, U. Calgary, Alta., Can., 1973; MSci, Maharishi European Rsch. U., Seelisberg, Switzerland, 1981; MS, Maharishi Internat. U., 1993, PhD, 1996. Lectr. stress reduction Maharishi European Rsch. U., Seelisberg, Switzerland, 1974—86; asst. prof. Maharishi Internat. U., Fairfield, Iowa, 1996-97; postdoc. rsch. fellow Med. Coll. Ga., Augusta, 1997-98, asst. rsch. scientist, 1999—. Reviewer Annals of Behavioral Medicine, 1999, Am. Jour. Hypertension, 1999, Pediats., 1999, Clin. Physiol, 2000, Psychsom Med, 2000, Jour. Complementary and Alternative Medicine, Ann. Behavioral Medicine, Am. Jour. Hypertension, Biological Psychology, Internat. Jour. Psychophysiology, 2001-03, Health Psychology, 2003; contbr. articles to med. jours. Scientist Devel. grantee AHA, 1999-2002. Mem. Am. Psychosomatic Soc. (Scholars award 1999), Soc. Behavioral Medicine, Internat. Soc. Hypertension in Blacks. Avocations: photography, audio, home theater. Office: Med Coll Ga Ga Prevention Inst Bldg HS 1640 Augusta GA 30912

BARNES, VIRGIL EVERETT, II, physics educator; b. Galveston, Tex., Nov. 2, 1935; s. Virgil Everett and Mildred Louise (Adlof) B.; m. Barbara Ann Green, 1957 (dec. 1964); 1 son, Virgil Everett III; m. Linda Dwight Taylor, 1970; children— Christopher Richard Dwight, Charles Jeffrey, Daniel Woodbridge. AB magna cum laude with highest honors, Harvard U., 1957; PhD, Cambridge (Eng.) U., 1962. Rsch. assoc. Brookhaven Nat. Lab., Upton, N.Y., 1962-64, asst. physicist, 1964-66, assoc. physicist, 1966-69; mem. faculty Purdue U., 1969—, prof. physics, 1979—; asst. dean Purdue U. (Sch. Sci.), 1974-78. Cons. in field. Author papers on exptl. high energy particle physics. NSF predoctoral fellow Gonville and Caius Coll., Cambridge U., 1959-62; Marshall scholar Cambridge U., 1957-59; recipient Perkin Elmer prize Harvard U., 1956. Mem. AAAS, AAUP, Am. Phys. Soc., N.Y. Acad. Scis., Phi Beta Kappa, Sigma Xi. Home: 801 N Salisbury St West Lafayette IN 47906-2715 Office: Purdue U Dept Physics West Lafayette IN 47907

BARNES, WALLACE, manufacturing executive; b. Bristol, Conn., Mar. 22, 1926; s. Harry Clarke and Lillian (Houbertz) B.; m. Audrey Kent, June 14, 1947; children: Thomas Oliver, Jarre Ann Betts; m. Mrs. Frederick B. Hollister, Jr.; 1 adopted son, Frederick Hollister; m. Joan C. Fierri, Mar. 3, 1973; m. Barbara Hackman Franklin, Nov. 29, 1986. BA, Williams Coll., 1949; LLB, Yale U., 1952; grad., Advanced Mgmt. Program, Harvard, 1973; LLD (hon.), U. Hartford, 1988; LLD (hon.), Briarwood Coll., 2002. Bar: Conn. 1952. Pres. Nutmeg Air Trans. Inc., 1949-55; asst. to treas. Northeast Airlines Inc., Boston, 1951; assoc. firm Beach, Calder & Barnes (and predecessor), Bristol, 1952-55, partner, 1956-62; exec. v.p. Assoc. Spring Corp. (name changed to Barnes Group Inc.), 1960-64, pres., 1964-77, chmn., chief exec. officer, 1977-91, chmn. bd., 1991-95, ret., 1995; chmn. bd. Rohr Inc., Chula Vista, Calif., 1995-98; chmn. Coun. Employment and Tng. Commn. State of Conn., 1997—; sr. ptnr. Sky Bight Ptnrs. Dir. Aetna Life and Casualty Co., 1971-96, Barnes Group Inc., 1954-96, DeMaria ElectroOptics Systems Inc., 1996—, Loctite Corp., 1990-96, Rogers Corp., 1983-98, Rohr Inc., 1988-98; chmn. bd. Tradewind Turbines Corp., 1994—; ptnr. Green Acres Farm, 1986—. Pres. Bristol Cmty. Chest, 1956; bd. dirs., mem. exec. com. Bristol Boys Club, pres., 1965-68; bd. regents U. Hartford, 1961-94, lifetime regent, 1995, chmn., 1988-93; trustee Bristol Girls' Club Assn.; bd. dirs. New Eng. Legal Found., 1986-90, New Eng. Coun., 1980-83, Jr. Achievement North Ctrl. Conn., 1980-90; nominee for Congress, 1st Congl. Dist. Conn., 1954; Rep. town chmn. Bristol, 1953-55; mem. Conn. Senate from 5th Dist., 1958-62, 8th Dist., 1966-70, minority leader, 1969; Gov.'s Clean Water Task Force, 1966-67; bd. dirs. Cmty. Coun. of Capital Region, 1975-77, Hartford Symphony Soc., 1971-78, Coun. on Employment and Fair Taxation, 1978-80, Bus. Coalition on Health, 1983-88, Conn. Pub. Expenditure Coun., 1979-85; trustee Am. Clock and Watch Mus., Environ. Learning Ctrs. Conn. Inc., The Family Ctr.; bd. trustees New Eng. Air Mus.; corporator Inst. of Living, Hartford, Bristol Hosp., St. Francis Hosp., Hartford Hosp.; co-chair Conn. Children's Med. Cap. Campaign, chmn. CBIA, 1982-93; bd. dirs. Conn. Econ. Devel. Corp. Served as aviation cadet USAAF, 1944-45. Recipient Disting. Svc. award Bristol Jaycees, Keystone award Boys Clubs Am., 1967, Humanitarian award Tunxis C.C., 1982, Human Rels. award Nat. Conf. Christians and Jews, 1985, Hon. Alumnus award U. Hartford, 1985, Salute to Wallace Barnes Bristol C. of C., 1991, Hall of Fame award Jr. Achievement North Ctrl. Conn., 1996, Exec. Philanthropist of Yr. Nat. Soc. Fund Raising Exec., 1996; Bartels fellow U. New Haven, 1992. Mem. ABA, Conn. Bar Assn., Am. Judicature Soc., Am. Arbitration Assn., Bristol Hist. Soc., Newcomen Soc., Conn. Bus. and Industry Assn. (past chmn., dir.), Metro Hartford C. of C. (bd. dirs., exec. com. 1991—), Am. Legion, Elks, Econ. Club N.Y.C., Yale Club, Williams Club, Farmington Country Club, Chippanee Golf Club. Home and Office: Sky Bight 1875 Perkins St Bristol CT 06010-8910

BARNES, WALLACE RAY, retired lawyer; b. Easton, Pa., Nov. 7, 1928; s. Charles Hicks and Erma (Saylor) B.; m. Helen Honey Bartley, July 2, 1958; children: Charles Calvin, Elizabeth McKee, Douglas Wittmer. AB, Duke U., 1950; LLB, Harvard U., 1957. Bar: Pa. 1958, Ohio 1973. Atty. Allegheny Ludlum Steel, Pitts., 1957-62, Columbia Gas, Md., N.Y., Pa., 1962-73, sec., gen. counsel, 1973-78, sr. counsel, 1978-81, assoc. gen. counsel, 1981-88, dep. gen. counsel, 1988-96, ret., 1996. Corp. dir. Columbia Gas Ohio, 1973-78, N.Y., 1973-78 Bd. dirs. Pitts. Better Bus. Bur., 1972—74. With USN, 1947—54. Mem. FBA (pres. chpt. 1961), ABA, Ohio Bar Assn., Phi Beta Kappa, Fox Chapel Racquet Club, Racquet Club of Columbus, Sawmill Athletic Club, Wickertree Tennis Club. Home: 2438 Sandover Rd Columbus OH 43220-2845 E-mail: wallacerbarnes@hotmail.com.

BARNES, WESLEY EDWARD, energy and environmental executive; b. Chgo., Sept. 11, 1937; s. Donald Edson and Helen Mary (Popovich) B.; m. Constance Arlene Simpson, Nov. 9, 1957; children: Dawn Ellen, Wesley Edward II. Grad., Indsl. Coll. of Armed Forces, 1973; BS, Cen. Mich. U., 1976, MBA, 1981. Chief warrant officer USN, 1955-68; sr. mktg. rep. UNIVAC, Washington, 1968-70; regional mgr. Weismantel Assocs. Inc., Washington, 1970-71; dir. computer ops. U.S. SBA, Washington, 1971-75; asst. dir. legis. affairs U.S. ERDA, Washington, 1975-77; dir. bus. rels. U.S. Dept. Energy, 1977-80, dir. major projects, 1980-83; chief exec. officer Western Rsch. Inst., Laramie, Wyo., 1983-90; pres., chief exec. officer Mktg. Bus. Assocs., Ltd., Washington, 1990-94; project mgr. Dept. of Energy, Yucca Mountain Project, 1995-97; energy and environ. cons. Dagsboro, Del., 1997—. Bd. dirs. Econ. Devel. Corp., Laramie, 1986-90. Mem. Rep. Nat. Com. Mem. Am. Mgmt. Assn. (pres.'s assn.), Cripple Creek Country Club, K. of C. (lector 1981-82). Roman Catholic. E-mail: barnes188@mchsi.com.

BARNES, WILLIAM DAVID, non-profit charities consultant, publisher; b. Gary, Ind., July 14, 1938; s. Frank J. and Marie M. (Jasorka) B.; m. Suzanne Frost Barnes, June 10, 1961 (div. June 1977); children: Adam Frost, Eric Earl. BA in Edn., Ariz. State U., 1960; Cert., Northwestern U., Chgo., 1965. Asst. editor The Arizonian Newspaper, Scottsdale, 1960-61; asst. v.p. First Security Bank, Mesa, Ariz., 1962-65; dir. mktg., v.p. Great Western Bank, Phoenix, 1966-67; dir. alumni fund Ariz. State U., Tempe, 1967-71; pres., sr. editor Barnes Assocs., Inc., Phoenix, Sacramento and Modesto, Calif., 1971—. Author: How to Build Your Development Program, 1973, More on How to Build Your Development Program, 1974, Fund Raiser's Planning and Budgeting Guide, 1976. V.p. United Way, Mesa, 1962; Ariz. bus. chmn. Com. to Re-elect Pres., 1972; cons. to 68 local, state and nat. polit. campaigns, 1960-84 (62 victories); chair pub. rels. com. Ariz. Bankers Assn., 1968. Recipient Nat. 1st pl. award in mktg. Chrysler Corp. Young and Rubicam, 1974, Silver Triange award Am. Advt. Assn., 1977, Exec. Leaders Inst. award Lilly Endowment/Assn. Fundraising Profls., 1990, Man of Yr. award for vol. work Rainbow Acres Ranches for Developmentally Challenged, 1982. Mem. Assn. Fundraising Profls. (cert., nat. bd. dirs. 1975-78, One of 25 Authors Worldwide Contributing Most to Profession 1985, Outstanding Fund Raising Exec. No. Calif. 1987). Roman Catholic. Avocations: tennis, gardening. Office: Barnes Assocs Inc 909 15th St Ste 9 Modesto CA 95354-1130 E-mail: barnesnfr@sbcglobal.net.

BARNES, WILLIAM DOUGLAS, advertising executive; b. Washington, Sept. 1, 1953; s. Berry Carter and Virginia Mae (Keeler) Barnes; m. Jeannette Avendano, July 3, 1990; 1 child, Chadsworth. BBA, U. Miami, Fla., 1980, MBA, 1984. Staff acct. Arthur Andersen & Co., Miami, 1980-81; sr. acct. Storer Comm., Miami, 1981-84; pres., personnel cons. Profl. Resources, Miami, 1984-86; acct. exec. Miami Herald, 1986-90; pres. Barnes & Assoc. Advt., Ft. Lauderdale, 1990-97; acct. exec. Sun-Sentinel, 1991—97; CEO Strategic Resource Group, Inc., Ft. Lauderdale, 1997—; dir. bus. devel. Am. Home Guides, 1999—. Mem. Beta Alpha Psi (chmn. alumni com. 1980). Republican. Home and Office: 1146 Hidden Valley Way Weston FL 33327 E-mail: srginc@prodigy.net.

BARNES-BROWN, PETER NEWTON, lawyer; b. Rutland, Vt., Aug. 22, 1948; s. Rufus Enoch and Julia Pottwin (Morgan) Brown; m. Susan Linda Barnes, Aug. 11, 1974; children: Diana Morgan, David Alexander, Julia Elizabeth. AB, Brown U., 1970; JD, U. Pa., 1976. Bar: Ga. 1978, N.Y. 1979, Mass. 1985. Law clk. Assoc. Justice Alfred H. Joslin R.I. Supreme Ct., Providence, 1977-78; assoc. Olwine, Connelly, Chase, O'Donnell & Weyher, N.Y.C., 1978-84, Goodwin, Procter & Hoar, Boston, 1984-86; internat. counsel Cullinet Software, Inc., Westwood, Mass., 1986-89; co-founder, prin. Van Wert & Zimmer, P.C., Lexington, Mass., 1989-93; co-founder Morse, Barnes-Brown & Pendleton PC, Waltham, Mass., 1993—. Co-founding dir., clk. New Eng.-Latin Am. Bus. Coun., Inc., Boston, 1992-2000. Contbr. articles to profl. jours. Mem.: ABA, Boston Bar Assn., State Bar Ga., NY State Bar Assn., Mass. Bar Assn. Office: Morse Barnes-Brown & Pendleton PC Reservoir Place 1601 Trapelo Rd Waltham MA 02451-7333

BARNES-KEMPTON, ISABEL JANET, microbiology educator, college dean; b. Union City, N.J., Sept. 22, 1936; d. Carl Robert and Isabel Sarah (Cappelletti) B.; m. John D. Bowman, June 15, 1978 (dec. Nov. 1986); m. Arnold J. Kempton, Feb. 5, 2000. BS, Pa. State U., 1958; MS, Cornell U., 1960; PhD, Hahnemann Med. Coll., 1969; postgrad., Inst. Ednl. Mgmt. Harvard U., 1991. Asst. prof. microbiology Hershey Med. Ctr., Pa. State U., 1968-73; asst. prof., then assoc. prof. Sangamon State U., Springfield, Ill., 1973-76; assoc. prof. med. tech. U. Wis., Madison, 1976-85; interim dean Sch. Allied Health Professions, 1981-84; prof. med. tech. Ferris State U., Big Rapids, Mich., 1985-2000; dean Coll. Allied Health Scis., 1985-2000, acting v.p. Acad. Affairs, 1992-93. Bd. dirs. Mecosta County Gen. Hosp., 1988-99, sec. 1991-94, pres., 1996-97, v.p. 1997-99, Alliance for Health, 1993-2002, Mich. Hemophilia Found., 1989-95, 97—, sec. 1991-94; active Mecosta Health Svcs., 1998-2002, Mecosta County Cmty. Found., 1999—; coord. St. Andrews Manna Food Pantry, 2002—; mem. Tamarack Dist. Libr. Bd., 2003—; pres. bd. Tamarack Dist. Libr., 2003—. Fellow Assn. of Schs. of Allied Health Professions (bd. dirs. 1989-91); mem. Coll. Health Deans (pres. 1988-90), Mich. Bd. Podiatric Medicine and Surgery.

BARNESS, LEWIS ABRAHAM, physician; b. Atlantic City, N.J., July 31, 1921; s. Joseph and Mary (Silverstein) B.; m. Elaine Berger, June 14, 1953 (dec. Jan. 1985); children: Carol, Laura, Joseph; m. Enid May Fischer Gilbert, July 5, 1987; stepchildren: Mary, Elizabeth, Jennifer, Rebecca. AB, Harvard U., 1941, MD, 1944; MA (hon.), U. Pa., 1971; DS U. Wis. (hon.), 2002. Intern Phila. Gen. Hosp., 1944-45; resident Boston Children's Hosp., 1947-50; asst. chief, then chief dept. pediatrics Phila. Gen. Hosp., 1951-72; vis. physician U. Pa. Hosp., 1952-57, acting chief, then chief, 1957-72. Mem. faculty U. Pa. Sch. Medicine, 1951-72, prof. pediat., 1964-72; chmn. dept. U. So. Fla. Med. Sch., Tampa, 1972-88, prof. pediat., 1988—, Disting. Univ. prof., 2000—; vis. prof. Univ. Wis., 1987-92, prof. emeritus, 1993—. Author: Pediatric Physical Diagnosis Yearbook, edits. 1-6, 1957—; editor: Advances in Pediatrics, 1976—, Pediatric Nutrition Handbook, 3d edit., 1991; asst. editor Pediatric Gastroenterology and Nutrition, 1981-91; editl. bd. Cons., 1960-84, Pediatrics, 1978-83, Core Jour. Pediatrics, 1980-96, Contemporary Pediatrics, 1984—, Jour. Clin. Medicine and Nutrition, 1985-95, Nutrition Rev., 1985-87. Served to capt. AUS, 1945-46. Recipient Lindback Teaching award U. Pa., 1963; Borden award nutrition, 1972; Noer Disting. Prof. award, 1980, Joseph B. Goldberger award in clin. nutrition, 1984, Joseph St. Geme Leadership award 7 pediatric socs., 1991, U. So. Fla. Svc. award, 1997, President's Award, U. So. Fla., 2000, Distinguished Prof. award, 2000; inductee Phila. Pediat. Soc. Hall of Fame, 1996. Fellow Am. Inst. Nutrition; mem. AAAS, Am. Pediatric Soc. (recorder-editor 1964-75, pres. 1985-86, John Howland award 1993), Soc. Pediatric Rsch., Am. Acad. Pediatrics (chmn. com. on nutrition 1974-81, Abraham Jacobi award 1991, Med. Edn. Lifetime Achievement award 1995), Sigma Xi, Alpha Omega Alpha. Home: 3301 Bayshore Blvd Unit 403 Tampa FL 33629-8841 Office: U South Fla Dept Pediat 17 Davis Blvd Tampa FL 33606 E-mail: lbarness@hsc.usf.edu. *Most people, when given the opportunity, try to be unselfish and prefer to do good. The human brain is a fantastic instrument, which when exercised, can solve most problems.*

BAR-NESS, YEHESKEL, electrical engineer, educator; b. Baghdad, Iraq, Apr. 28, 1932; arrived in Israel, 1950; came to U.S., 1978; m. Varda Bar-Ness, Aug. 21, 1952; children: Yael, Yaron, Yegal. BEE, Technion U., Haifa, Israel, 1958, MEE, 1963; PhD, Brown U., 1969. Chief engr. Elscint Inc., Haifa, 1971-75; assoc. prof. Tel-Aviv U., 1973-78; vis. prof. Brown U., 1978-79, U. Pa., Phila., 1979-81; prof. elec. engring. Drexel U., Phila., 1981-83; tech. staff mem. AT&T Bell Lab., Holmdel, N.J., 1983-85; disting. prof. elec. and computer engring. N.J. Inst. Tech., Newark, 1985—, dir. ctr. communication and signal processing rsch., 1985—, found. chair comm. and signal processing, 2000—. Vis. prof. elec. engring. Tech. U. Delft, The Netherlands, 1993-94, Stanford U., 2000-01. Recipient Kaplan Price award Gov. of Israel, 1974. Fellow IEEE; mem. Communication Soc. of IEEE (sec. communications systems engring. com. 1985-87, vice chmn., 1987-89, chmn. 1990-91, editor IEEE transaction on comm., founder and editor-in-chief IEEE Comm. Letters). Home: 2 Etna Ct Marlboro NJ 07746-1307 Office: NJ Inst of Tech 323 King Blvd Newark NJ 07102-1824

BARNET, RICHARD JACKSON, author, educator; b. Boston, May 7, 1929; s. Carl J. and Margaret L. (Block) B.; m. Ann Birnbaum, Apr. 10, 1953; children: Juliana, Beth, Michael. AB summa cum laude, Harvard U., 1951, LLB cum laude, 1954. Bar: Mass. bar 1954. Rsch. fellow Am. Law Inst., 1957-58; assoc. Choate, Hall & Stewart, Boston; fellow Russian Rsch. Ctr. Harvard U., 1959-60; spl. asst. Dept. State, 1961; dep. dir. Office of Polit. Rsch. U.S. ACDA, 1961-62; fellow Ctr. for Internat. Studies Princeton U., 1963; co-dir. Inst. for Policy Studies, Washington, 1963-77, 90—, sr. fellow, 1977—. Vis. prof. Yale U., 1970, Nat. U. Mexico, 1973, U. Paris, 1982; vis. com. Harvard U. Author: Who Wants Disarmament, 1960, (with Marcus Raskin) After Twenty Years, 1965, (with Richard Falk) Security in Disarmament, 1965, Intervention and Revolution, 1968, The Economy of Death, 1969, (with Marcus Raskin) An American Manifesto, 1970, Roots of War, 1972, (with Ronald Muller) Global Reach, 1974, The Giants, 1977, The Lean Years, 1980, Real Security, 1981, The Alliance, 1983, The Rockets' Red Glare, 1990, (with John Cavanagh) Global Dreams, 1994, (with Ann Barnet) The Youngest Minds, 1998; contbg. editor: Sojourners mag., 1979-2000. 1st lt. JAGC U.S. Army, 1955-57. Recipient Sidney Hillman prize Amalgamated Clothing Workers Am., 1975, U. Mo. Sch. Journalism award, 1981. Mem. World Peacemakers, Coun. on Fgn. Rels. Home: 1716 Portal Dr NW Washington DC 20012-1116 E-mail: arbarnet@gwu.edu.

BARNET, ROBERT JOSEPH, cardiologist, ethicist; b. Port Huron, Mich., Apr. 27, 1929; s. John A. and Ruth Elizabeth (Wittliff) B.; m. Helen Kresoja, Dec. 8, 1969; children: Benedict, Maria, Antonia, Peter, Elizabeth, Rebecca, Christina, Jacqueline, Ann. Student, Port Huron Jr. Coll., summers 1947, 49; MD, Loyola U., Chgo., 1951; BS in Chemistry magna cum laude, U. Notre Dame, 1954; MA in History, U. of Nev., 1986; MA in Philosophy, U. Notre Dame, 1988. Diplomate Am. Bd. Internal Medicine, Nat. Bd. Med. Examiners. Intern Boston City Hosp., 1954—55; rotating intern Mercy Hosp., Chgo., 1955; asst. resident in medicine Boston City Hosp., 1958-59; clin. and research fellow in cardiology Children's Med. Center and House of the Good Samaritan, Boston, 1959-60; cons. fellow in rheumatic fever pediatric service Boston City Hosp., 1959-60; research fellow in pediatrics Harvard U., Boston, 1959-60; clin. fellow in cardiology Mass. Meml. Hosps., Boston, 1960-61; physician-in-charge St. Francis Mission Hosp., Solwezi, No. Rhodesia, 1961-62; dir. clinics, assoc. in medicine Stritch Sch. Medicine, Loyola U., Chgo., 1962-65; physician-in-charge Cardiac Clinic, Loyola U., Chgo., Fantus Outpatient dept. Cook County Hosp., Chgo., 1962-65, Hypertension Clinic, Fantus Outpatient dept. Cook County Hosp., 1962-65; assoc. attending physician dept. medicine Cook County Hosp., 1962-63, attending physician, 1963-65; practice medicine specializing in cardiology Reno, 1965-87; med. staff Washoe Med. Center, 1965—, St. Mary's Hosp., 1965—; assoc. clin. prof. cardiology U. Nev.; also assoc. dir. Lab. Environ. Patho-Physiology, Desert Research Inst., U. Nev., Reno, 1965-68; dir. Cardiac Care unit Washoe Med. Center, 1965-83, exec. com., 1967-71, 73-77, vice chief dept. medicine, 1969, chief, 1970-71, 78, chief dept. emergency services, 1973-77. Vis physician Solwezi Boma Rural Hosp., 1961-62; cons. in cardiology disability determination unit State of Nev., 1966-87, Crippled Children's Svc., 1966-76, Reno VA Hosp., 1967-80; asst. clin. prof. med. edn. U. Utah, 1968-71; cons. Churchill Pub. Hosp., Fallon, Nev., 1969-87, Pershing Gen. Hosp., Lovelock, Nev., 1969-87; clin. assoc. U. Nev., Reno, 1971-72, assoc. clin. prof. medicine, 1973-77, prof., 1978—; vis. scholar U. Notre Dame, 1989-90, 96-97; prof. med. ethics St. Louis U., 1993-95; med. reviewer, cons. Nev. State Bd. Med. Examiners, 1994—; affiliated scholar Ctr. Clin. Bioethics, Georgetown U., 2000—; lectr. in electrocardiography and cardiology Loyola U., Chgo., 1962-65. Contbr. articles to med. jours. Served with U.S. Army, 1955-58. Recipient Clin. Faculty Honor award Loyola U., 1963-64. Fellow A.C.P. (bd. govs. 1980-85), Am. Coll. Cardiology (bd. govs. 1974-77), Am. Coll. Chest Physicians; mem. Nev., Washoe County med. socs., Am. Fedn. Clin. Research, Nev. Heart Assn. (bd. dirs., exec. com., pres. 1974-75) Home: 166 Greenridge Dr Reno NV 89509-3927 E-mail: phbobmd@aol.com. *I have tried to dedicate my life to the service of all and the betterment of the community while striving for professional excellence without compromise of my moral and religious principles.*

BARNET, WILL, artist, educator; b. Beverly, Mass., May 25, 1911; s. Noah and Sarah (Toahnich) B.; m. Mary Sinclair, Feb., 1935 (div.); children: Peter George, Richard Sinclair, Todd Williams; m. Elena Ona Ciurlys, Mar. 4, 1953; 1 dau., Ona Willa. Student, Boston Mus. Fine Arts Sch., 1927-30, Art Students League, N.Y.C., 1930-33; DFA (hon.), Mass. Coll. Art, 1989. Instr. painting Art Students League, NYC, 1946—; faculty Cooper Union, NYC, 1945—, prof., 1965—; instr., critic Pa. Acad., Phila., 1967—; faculty Famous Artists Painting Course, Westport, Conn., 1954—, Mont. State Coll., summer 1951, Summer Artists Workshop, Regina Coll., U. Sask., Canada, 1957; instr. advanced painting U. Minn. at Duluth, summer 1959, Wash. State U., Spokane, summer 1963, Pa. State U., summer 1965, Des Moines Art Center, summer 1965. Distinguished vis. prof. Pa. State U., 1965-66; vis. critic Yale, 1952-53; vis. prof. Cornell U., 1968-69; condr. grand art tour of, Europe, April, 1959, Ford Found. artist in residence program, 1964 Contbr. to: Art Students League Mag; one-man shows, Hudson D. Walker Gallery, 1938, Galerie St. Etienne, 1943, Berthe Schaefer Gallery, Arthur Harlow & Co., Inc., all NYC, 1946, U.S. Nat. Mus., Washington, 1946, Bertha Schaefer Gallery, NYC, 1947, 48, Krasner Gallery, NYC, Gallery Trastevere, Rome, 1960, Terry Dintenfass Gallery, NYC, 1982, Kennedy Galleries, NYC, 1984, 86, 88, retrospective, Inst. Contemporary Art, Boston, 1961, Mary Harriman Gallery, Boston, 1963, 64, Va. Mus., Richmond, 1964, Waddell Gallery, NYC, 1965, 66, 68, 70, Des Moines Art Center, 1965, Pa. Acad. Phila., 1969, Fairweather Hardin Gallery, Chgo., 1971, David and David, Phila., 1972, print retrospective, Asso. Am. Artists, NYC, 1972-79, Hirschl & Adler Galleries, Inc., 1973, 76, 81, Essex Inst., Salem, Mass., 1980, painting retrospective, Neuberger Mus., Purchase, N.Y., 1979, 94, Ringling Mus., Sarasota, Fla., 1980, Wichita Art Mus., Wichita, Kans., 1983, traveling mus. retrospective, Currier Gallery Art, Manchester, N.H., 1984, Huntsville Mus. Art, Ala., 1984, Minn. Mus. Art, St. Paul, 1984-5, Art Gallery of Hamilton, Ont., Can., 1985, Farnsworth Libr. and Art Mus., Maine, 1985, Meek-Harmon Gallery, Naples, Fla., 1990, Terry Dintenfass Gallery, 1991, 94, Butler Inst., Youngstown, Ohio, 1992, Philharm. Ctr. Arts, Naples, Fla., 1994, Ogonquit Mus. Am. Art, Maine, 1994, Worcester Art Mus, Mass., 1995, Nat. Mus. Am. Art, Washington, 1995, Terry Dintenfars Gallery, 1996; drawing retrospective Ark. Art Ctr., Little Rock, 1991—; The Farnsworth Art Mus., Maine, 2002; exhibited, Art USA, 1959, Glenn Horowitz Bookseller, inc., East Hampton, NY, 1997, Nat. Acad. Mus., NYC, 1997, Maine Coast Artists, 1998, Tabor De Nagy Gallery, NYC, 1998, Retrospectives Montclair Art Mus., NJ, 2000, Boca Raton Mus. Art, Fla., 2000, Portland Mus. Art, Maine, 2000, Retrospective Ark. Art Ctr., 2001, Alexandre Gallery, NY, 2002; represented in permanent collections, Minn. Inst. Arts, Met., NYC, Fogg Art Mus., Library of Congress, Art Gallery, U. ND, U. Art Gallery, Berkeley, Calif., Cin. Art Mus., Duncan Phillip Meml. Mus., Washington, Phila. Art Mus., Honolulu Acad., Mus. Modern Art, Bklyn. Mus., Mont. State Coll., Whitney Mus. Am. Art, Mus. Fine Arts, Boston, Guggenheim Mus., NYC, Farnsworth Mus. Maine, Butler Inst., Ohio, Ashmolean Mus., Oxford, Eng., Brit. Mus., London; exhibited in museums throughout, US, including, Art Inst. Chgo., Los Angeles Mus., Portland Mus., John Herron Inst., Carnegie Inst., Virginia Mus. Fine Arts, Columbia (SC) Mus. Art (1st Biennial); pub. Will Barnet 27 Master Prints, 1982; illustrator The World in a Frame; subject of Robert Doty work: Publisher Abrams, 1984. Recipient Bronze medal, 3d prize Corcoran Biennial, 1961, Benjamin Altman 1st prize NAD, 1977, Medal of Honor, Nat. Arts Club, 1990, The Winthrop Rockefeller Meml. award, 1992, The Butler Medal for Life Achievement in Am. Art award Butler Inst. of Am. Art, 1992, Arts & Tourism Coun. Killy Carlisle Hart award, 1999; named to Gallery of Honors, Art World Mag., 1990. Fellow Royal Soc. Arts; mem. Art Students League (life), NAD (life), Am. Abstract Artists, Soc. Am. Graphic Artists, Inc., Fedn. Modern Painters and Sculptors, Century Assn. Liberal, Am. Acad. and Inst. Arts and Letters, NY Acad. of Art, Dr. of Fine Arts, 2002, and the Lyme Acad. Coll. of Fine Arts, 2003. Unitarian Universalist. Home: 15 Gramercy Park S New York NY 10003-1705

BARNETT, ALLEN, pharmacologist, consultant; b. Newark, N.J., May 5, 1937; s. Samuel Boroviak and Lillian (Bloomberg) Barnett; m. MaryLou Victoria Selva, June 6, 1965; children: Carole A. Barnett Collard, David Allen. BS Pharmacy, Rutgers Univ., Newark, N.J., 1959; PhD Pharmacology, SUNY, Buffalo, 1965. Registered pharmaist N.J., N.Y. Sr. scientist Roche, Nutley, NJ, 1965—66; sr. scientist, drug discovery Schering-Plough, Bloomfield, NJ, 1966, dir., 1966, sr. dir., 1966, v.p., 1966—98; pres. AB Cons., Pine Brook, NJ, 1999—. Mem. sci. adv. bd. Singapore Biotechnology, Singapore, 2000—; cons. Schering-Plough, Kenilworth, NJ, 1999—; rsch. prof. of pharmacology SUNY, Buffalo, 2001—. Contbr. articles to over 135 profl. jour. Pvt. reserves U.S. Army, 1959—62. Mem.: AAAS, CINP, ASPET. Achievements include discovery of Loratadine (Claritin) as leading non-sedating anthistamine; Doral (Quazepam) marketed sedative-hypnotic. Contributed to discovery of Clarenex and Zetia, two newly marketed drugs. Avocations: tennis, golf, reading.

BARNETT, AMY DUBOIS, editor-in-chief; B, Brown U.; MFA, Columbia U. Mng. editor Fashion Almanac Mag., 1996—98; editor-in-chief Edition Inside NY, 1999; mng. editor Fashion Planet Website; columnist, features editor Total NY Website; editor Essence Mag., 1999—2000; editor-in-chief Honey Mag., 2000—03; editor Teen People, 2003—. Office: Teen People/Time Inc 1271 Ave of the Americas New York NY 10020-1393

BARNETT, ARTHUR LYN, land use and environmental planner; b. Glendale, Calif., Dec. 1, 1959; AA, Lake Tahoe C.C., 1981; BS, Humboldt State U., 1984. Cert. mem. Am. Inst. Cert. Planners. Chief project rev. divsn. Tahoe Regional Planning Agy., Zephyr Cove, Nev., 1998—. Chair parish coun. St. Theresa Parish, South Lake Tahoe, 1991-95, new ch. design & capital com., 1996-2000; pres. bd. dirs., St. Joseph Cmty. Land Trust, Lake Tahoe, Calif. and Nev., 2002—. Mem. Am. Planning Assn. Office: Tahoe Regional Planning Agy PO Box 1038 Zephyr Cove NV 89448

BARNETT, BENJAMIN LEWIS, JR., retired physician, educator; b. Woodruff, S.C., July 22, 1926; s. Benjamin Lewis and Mattie Bernice (Skinner) B.; m. Annalyne Louise Hall, Oct. 25, 1958; children: Benjamin Lewis III, Jane Kristen. BS, Furman U., 1946, LLD, 1978; MD, Med. U. S.C., 1949. Diplomate Am. Bd. Family Practice. Intern Protestant Episcopal Hosp., Phila., 1949-50; pvt. practice Woodruff, 1950-70; assoc. prof. family practice Med. U. S.C., Charleston, 1970-74, prof. family practice, 1974-77, asst. dir. family practice residency program, 1970-75, chief undergrad. curriculum, 1970-77, vice-chmn. dept. family practice, 1973-77, asst. dean for student affairs, 1975-77; clin. staff

Med. U. Hosp., Charleston County Hosp., 1970-77; Walter M. Seward prof. U. Va. Med. Sch., 1977-2000, chmn. dept. family medicine, 1977-96, faculty senate, 1988-92, prof. emeritus, 2000—; family medicine physician-in-chief U. Va. Med. Center Hosp., 1977-96. Admissions com. U. Va. Med. Sch., 1997-99; Stoneburner lectr. Med. Coll. Va., 1975; Daniel Drake lectr. U. Cin., 1976; Robert P. Walton lectr. Med. U. S.C., 1978; Goodlark prof. U. Tenn., 1979; Roy J. Gerard lectr. Mich. State U., 1992; vis. scholar U. Mich. Med. Sch., 1984; vis. lectr. Med. Coll. of Ga., 1982; vis. prof. Case Western Res. Sch. Medicine, 1984, U. Vt., 1988, U. N.Mex., 1991, U. S.C. Sch. Medicine, 1999; spkr. baccalaureate address U. Va., 1986, 2000; Mack Lipkin vis. prof. U. Oreg., 1987, U. Utah, 1989; Donald J. Welter Meml. lectr. Med. Coll. Wis., 1989; Frederick Lytel Meml. lectr., Abington, Pa., 1989; Bradford Strock lectr. Harrisburg (Pa.) Gen. Hosp., 1989; 7th Leland Blanchard Meml. lectr. Soc. Tchrs. Family Medicine ann. meeting, Nashville, 1985; health officer, Town of Woodruff, 1950-54; keynote speaker Assn. Depts. Family Medicine, Clearwater, Fla., 1991; commencement speaker U. Va. Med. Sch., 1992, 97; Grand Prof. Rounds St. Margaret's Hosp., Pitts., 1993; Julian Keith lectr. Bowman Gray Sch. Medicine, 1993; keynote speaker leadership conf. Fla. Med. Assn., Ponta Vedra, 1994, AHEC conf. S.C. Family Practice, Myrtle Beach, 1994; B. Leslie Huffman lectr. Med. Coll. of Ohio, Toledo, 1994; lectr. Atlanta Med. Ctr., 2000—; grad. speaker McLennan County Med. Edn. and Rsch. Found., Waco, Tex., 1995; Inaugural Buck Crockett lectr., Roanoke, Va., 2000; founder's prof. U. Okla. Health Scis. Ctr., Tulsa, 2000; Harlan Thomas Meml. lectr.; Hiram B. Curry Meml. lectr. MUSC, 1990, 2001; lectr. and cons. in field. Author: Between the Lines (Reflections of a Physician), 1989, Pebbles in the Water, 2003; editor: S.C. Family Physician, 1973—74; contbr. Mem. Spartanburg County Bd. Edn., 1968-70, sec. 1969-70; trustee Bethea Bapt. Home for Aged, Darlington, S.C., 1972-73; mem. bd. trustees Furman U., 1994-99; dir. Marietta-Lost Mtn. Kiwanis, 2003—; mentor character curriculum Kennesaw Mountain HS, 2002—. Named Citizen of Year Woodmen of World, 1968; recipient Golden Apple award for clin. teaching Student AMA, 1973; Thomas W. Johnson award Am. Acad. Family Physicians, 1976, Disting. Alumnus award Med. U. S.C., 1993; endowed Barnett Professorship in Family Medicine established U. Va. Bd. Visitors, 1997; Thomas Jefferson award U. Va., 1997. Mem. AMA (mem. residency rev. com. for family practice 1974-79), Am. Bd. Family Practice (exam. bd. 1975-81, dir. 1976-81, exec. com. 1979-81, pres. 1980-81), Va. Med. Soc., Albemarle County Med. Soc., Soc. Tchrs. Family Medicine (v.p. 1974, sec.-treas. 1975, dir. 1981-85, Cert. of Excellence 1983, F. Marian Bishop award 1996), Am. Acad. Family Physicians, S.C. Acad. Family Physicians (v.p. 1973, pres. 1975-76), Spartanburg County Med. Soc. (v.p. 1968), Am. Philatelic Soc., Coun. Acad. Socs., Furman U. Alumni Assn. (dir. 1972-77), U. Va. Raven Soc., Kiwanis, Alpha Omega Alpha (faculty councilor, vis. prof. U. S.C. Sch. Medicine 1999), Alpha Kappa Kappa (pres. 1948), Kappa Alpha (v.p. 1944) Baptist (deacon, chmn. bd.). Home: 4734 Talleybrook Dr NW Kennesaw GA 30152-5484

BARNETT, BERNARD, accountant; b. N.Y.C., Oct. 14, 1920; s. Abraham L. and Rose (Albert) B.; m. Helen Salla, July 9, 1953; children: Susan Barnett Christiensen, Douglas (dec.). BBA magna cum laude, CCNY, 1941. CPA, N.Y., Mich., La., N.C., Va. Ptnr. Apfel & Englander, CPAs, N.Y.C., 1941-69, Seidman & Seidman, CPAs, N.Y.C., 1970, sr. ptnr., nat. dir. tax practice, 1971-86; sr. cons. BDO Seidman, LLP, N.Y.C., 1987—; pres. Found. Acctg. Edn., 1977-78; exec. dir. Fiduciary Income Tax Inst., 1986—. Adv. commn. to commr. IRC; mem. N.Y. State Bd. Pub. Accountancy; mem. faculty, mem. adv. com. Inst. Estate Planning, U. Miami (Fla.) Law Sch., 1972—; mem. adv. bd. Tax Mgmt. Inc.; mem. faculty Am. Law Inst/ABA Estate Planning Course, 1978-91, Nat. Trust Sch. of Am. Bankers Assn.; cons. CBS News Ann. Income Tax Program, 1977-90; pres. N.Y.C. Estate Planning Coun., 1967-68. Co-author: Estate Planning and the CPA, 1958, Attorneys Handbook of Accounting, 2d edit., 1979, 3d edit., 1991, Analysis of the Tax Reform Act of 1969, 1970; mem. editorial bd. Trusts and Estates, 1979—, Tax Adviser, 1970-94, emeritus, 1994—, Taxation for Accts., 1973-98, Practical Tax Strategies, 1999—. Pvt. to capt. AUS, 1942—46, maj. USAF, 1951—52. Mem. AICPA (gov. coun. 1971-80, chmn. task force on estate and gift tax reform 1979-83, chmn. joint disciplinary trial bd. 1982-84, chmn. task force on income taxation of trusts and estates 1983-87, v.p. 1985-86, bd. dirs. 1985-86, chmn. joint trial bd. divsn. 1984-93, mem. nat. rev. bd. 1984-88, trustee benevolent fund 1983-86, AICPA Disting. Svc. award for CPA in tax practice 1984, chmn. liaison AICPA tax divsn. with ABA tax sect., mem. faculty ann. adv. estate planning conf.), N.Y. State Soc. CPAs (pres. 1976-77), Nat. Conf. Lawyers and CPAs (co-chmn. 1978-81), Accts. Club Am. (pres. 1977-80), Royal Berkshire Golf Club (res., Ascot, Eng.). Office: BDO Seidman LLP 330 Madison Ave New York NY 10017-5001

BARNETT, CHARLES DAWSON, lawyer; b. Louisville, Jan. 27, 1951; s. Bernard Harry and Marian (Spiesberger) B.; m. Maureen Liel Stewart, Nov. 17, 1980; children: Rachel Langfeld, Jacob Bernard, Hannah Marian. BS in Commerce, U. Louisville, 1973; JD, U. Fla., 1976. Bar: Fla. 1977, Ky. 1977, D.C. 1977, U.S. Dist. Ct. (so. dist.) Fla. 1981. Assoc. Barnett & Alagia, Louisville, 1977-81, ptnr., Palm Beach, Fla., 1981-88, Nat. Fin. Realty Trust, Louisville, 1986-88; pvt. practice, West Palm Beach, Fla., 1988—. Bd. dirs. Ralph E. Mills Found., Frankfort, Ky., 1980— , Active Louisville-Jefferson County Republican Exec. Com., 1978-80. Served with USCG, 1969-74. Jewish. Home: 8412 Native Dancer Rd E Palm Beach Gardens FL 33418-7728 Office: 400 S Australian Ave Ste 700 West Palm Beach FL 33401-5044

BARNETT, CRAWFORD FANNIN, JR., internist, educator, cardiologist, travel medicine specialist; b. Atlanta, May 11, 1938; s. Crawford Fannin and Penelope Hollinshead (Brown) B.; m. Elizabeth McCarthy Hale, June 6, 1964; children: Crawford Fannin III, Robert Hale. Student, Taft Sch., 1953-56, U. Minn., 1957; AB magna cum laude, Yale U., 1960; postgrad. (Davison scholar), Oxford (Eng.) U., 1963; MD (Trent scholar), Duke U., 1964. Intern internal medicine Duke U. Med. Ctr., Durham, N.C., 1964-65, resident, 1965; resident internal medicine Wilmington (Del.) Med. Ctr., 1965-66; dir. Tenn. Heart Disease Control Program, Nashville, 1966-68; pvt. practice medicine in internal/travel medicine Atlanta, 1968—. Dir. Travel Immunization Ctr., Atlanta; mem. staff Crawford Long, Northside, Grady Meml., West Paces, Piedmont, North Fulton hosps. (all Atlanta); mem. tchg. staff Vanderbilt Med. Ctr., Nashville, 1966-68, Crawford Long Meml. Hosp., 1969—; clin. instr. internal medicine, dept. medicine Emory U. Med. Sch., Atlanta, 1969—. Contbr. articles to profl. publs. Bd. govs. Doctors Meml. Hosp., 1971-80; bd. dirs. Atlanta Speech Sch., 1976-80, 92—, Historic Oakland Cemetery, 1976-86, So. Turf Nurseries, 1977-92, Tech Industries, 1978-92; bd. dirs. Am. Chestnut Found., 1990, bd. trustees Mary Brown Found. of Atlanta, 1998—, Woodward Found., 2001—. Surgeon USPHS, 1966-68. Fellow Am. Geog. Soc., Royal Soc. of Tropical Medicine and Hygiene, Royal Geog. Soc., Royal Soc. Medicine, Explorers Club (life, N.Y.C.); mem. Am. Soc. Tropical Medicine and Hygiene, Am. Fedn. Clin. Rsch., Coun. Clin. Cardiology, AMA, Ga. Med. Assn., Atlanta Med. Assn., Am. Heart Assn., Ga. Heart Assn., Am. Soc. Internal Medicine, Am. Assn. History, Medicine, Ga. Hist. Soc., Atlanta Hist. Soc. (bd. govs. 1976-84), Ga. Trust for Hist. Preservation, Nat. Trust Hist. Preservation, Internat. Hippocratic Found. Soc. (Greece), Faculty of History of Medicine and Pharmacy Worshipful Soc. Apothecaries of London, Atlanta Com. on Fgn. Rels. (chmn. exec. com. 1972-88), So. Coun. Internat. and Pub. Affairs, Newcomen Soc., Atlanta Clin. Soc., Wilderness Med. Soc., Internat. Soc. Travel Medicine (founding), Travelers Century Club, Circumnavigators Club, South Am. Explorers Club, Victorian Soc. Am. (bd. advisers Atlanta chpt. 1971-86), Mensa, Gridiron, Piedmont Driving Club, Yale Club (dir. 1970-74), Nine O'Clocks Club, Pan Am. Doctors Club, Phi Beta Kappa. Episcopalian. Home: 2739 Ramsgate Ct NW Atlanta GA 30305-2817 Office: Ste 302 3193 Howell Mill Rd NW Atlanta GA 30327-2100

BARNETT, DAVID HUGHES, software engineer, computer systems architect; b. Rockville Centre, N.Y., Oct. 9, 1947; s. Paul Wilson Jr. and Patricia (Hughes) B.; m. Rosemary Friday, July 9, 1979 (div. 1983); m. Demery Culum, Apr. 10, 1996. BA, Drew U., 1970. Cert. software quality engineer, cert. quality engr. Program analyst So. Nev. Drug Abuse Coun., Las Vegas, 1974-75; project supr. Treatment Alternatives to Street Crime, Las Vegas, 1975-78; sr. project assoc. Helix Group, Berkeley, Calif., 1978-81; cons. Pacific Inst. for Rsch. and Evaluation, Berkeley, 1979-80; rsch. tech. Sonoma State U., Rohnert Park, Calif., 1981-82; system mgr. Database Minicomputers, San Francisco, 1982-84; cons. sys. programmer Wells Fargo Bank, San Francisco, 1984-89; messaging arch. Kaiser Permanente, Walnut Creek, Calif., 1989-96; info. tech. arch. IBM, San Ramone, Calif., 1996, Digital Equipment Corp., Walnut Creek, 1996-98; security sys. arch. Kaiser Permanente, Walnut Creek, 1998—2002; prin. architect Applera Corp., 2002—. Contbr. articles to profl. jours. Mem. IEEE, Am. Soc. for Quality Control, Assn. for Computing Machinery. Office: 850 Lincoln Centre Dr M/S 401-3 Foster City CA 94404 E-mail: dave.barnett@computer.org.

BARNETT, DAVID PHILIP, horticulturist; b. Jacksonville, N.C., Nov. 18, 1956; s. Frederick D. and Janet (Holdridge) B.; m. Eileen Nickerson, Aug. 19, 1978; children: Jake, Marie. BS, U. Conn., 1978; MS, U. Calif., Davis, 1983, PhD, 1987. Collections crew leader The Morton Arboretum, Lisle, Ill., 1978-81; asst. dir. Planting Fields Arboretum, Oyster Bay, N.Y., 1986-93; dir. horticulture Mt. Auburn Cemetery, Cambridge, Mass., 1993-99, dir. ops. and horticulture, 1999—. Asst. scoutmaster Boy Scouts Am., Boxborough, Mass., 1996—. Mem. Am. Assn. Botanical Gardens & Arboreta (bd. dirs. 1995-98, chmn. N.Am. plant collections consortium 1998-2002), Worcester County Horticultural Soc. (chmn. Cary award plant selection com. 1995-2001), Internat. Dendrology Soc., Internat. Soc. Arboriculture, N.Y. Hortus Club (v.p. 1990-93), Horticultural Club Boston (chair program com. 1996-00). Avocations: running marathons, hockey, camping, hiking, gardening. Office: Mt Auburn Cemetery 580 Mount Auburn St Cambridge MA 02138-5529

BARNETT, DONALD BLAKE, corporate financial executive; b. Corsicana, Tex., Oct. 2, 1957; s. Donald Wayne and Patricia (Anderson) B.; m. Karen Bryant Tripp; 1 child, Hamilton Chase. BA, Yale U., 1980. Account exec. E.F. Hutton, Houston, 1980-82, Rotan Mosle, Houston, 1982-83, Merrill Lynch, Houston, 1983-84; collections supr. Security Nat. Bank, Nacogdoches, Tex., 1984-85; owner Barnett Investments, Nacogdoches, Tex., 1985-94; pres., CEO, dir. of trading, underwriting Taylor, Pruitt & Sylvester, Houston, 1994; chmn., CEO Blake, Barnett & Co., Inc., Houston, 1996—. Chmn. Pinnacle Advantage Capital, Houston, 1994—, Banita Creek Farms, Nacogdoches, Tex., 1992—; chmn. Money Mgrs. Co., 2000—, The Train Store, Inc., 2001—. Recipient scholarships Yale Alumni Assn. of N.Y., 1976-80, Yale Alumni Assn. of Houston, 1978-80, Philiips Exeter TAD Jones, 1977-80. Mem. NASD, Yale Alumni Assn., Yale Alumni, Houston Soc. Club, Houston Polo Club, Houston Ctr. Club. Presbyterian. Avocations: golf, reading and researching, coaching boy's basketball, pub. speaking. Home: 2245 Shakespeare St Houston TX 77030-1112 Office: 2245 Shakespeare St Houston TX 77030-1112 E-mail: bbarnett@moneymanagers.com.

BARNETT, EDWARD WILLIAM, lawyer; b. New Orleans, Jan. 2, 1933; s. Phillip Nelson and Katherine (Wilkinson) B.; m. Margaret Mauk, Apr. 3, 1933; children: Margaret Barnett Stern, Edward William. BA, Rice U., 1955; LL.B., U. Tex.-Austin, 1958. Bar: Tex. 1958. Mem. Baker Botts LLP, Houston, 1958—, mng. ptnr., 1984-98, sr. counsel, 1998—. Bd. dirs., chmn. Cen. Houston, Inc., 1989-91. Trustee Rice U., Houston, 1991—, chmn. bd. trustees, 1996—; trustee Baylor Coll. Medicine, St. Luke's Episcopal Health System, Tex. Heart Inst.; life trustee U. Tex. Law Sch. Found.; bd. dirs., former chmn. Greater Houston Partnership, 1992; bd. dirs. Ctr. for Houston's Future, Reliant Resources, Inc.; chmn. bd. dirs. Houston Zoo, 2002-. Fellow Am. Coll. Trial Lawyers; mem. ABA (chmn. sect. antitrust law 1981-82), State Bar Tex., Houston Bar Assn., Coronado Club (pres. 1989), Houston Country Club, Old Baldy Club, Riverhill Country Club. Office: Baker Botts LLP 3000 One Shell Plaza Houston TX 77002

BARNETT, ELIZABETH HALE, organizational consultant; b. Nashville, Mar. 17, 1940; d. Robert Baker and Dorothy (McCarthy) Hale; m. Crawford F. Barnett Jr., June 6, 1964; children: Crawford F. III, Robert H. BA, Vanderbilt U., 1962. Receptionist, sec. U.S. Atty. Gen. Robert F. Kennedy, Washington, 1962-64; free-lance cons. Atlanta, 1973-76; pres. E.H. Barnett & Assocs. orgnl. cons., trainers, Atlanta, 1976-86; trustee The Ga. Conservancy, Atlanta, 1978-92, chmn. bd. trustees, 1986-88, chmn. adv. bd., 1994-98; legis. asst. to Senator Michael J. Egan Ga. State Senate, Atlanta, 1990-93. Bd. dirs. Jr. League Atlanta, 1973-75, High Mus. Art, Atlanta, 1977—; bd. dirs. United Way Met. Atlanta, 1981-84, ARCS Found., Atlanta chpt., found. mem.; bd. dirs. Student Aid Found., 2002—; active White House Fellows Southeastern Region Selection Panel, 1995-96; chmn., pres. bd. dirs. Vol. Coms. Art Mus. U.S. and Can., 1976-79; chmn. bd. dirs. Met. Atlanta chpt. ARC, 1978-80, hon. bd. dirs., 1980—; cmty. adv. com. NW Ga. Coun. Girl Scouts Am., 1979-83; coun. mem. USO Ga., 1981-1993; bd. sponsors Atlanta Women's Network; apptd. to Ga. Clean and Beautiful Citizens Adv. Com., 1990, Ga. Solid Waste Mgmt. Commn., 1990; appt. sec. to Gov.'s Environ. Edn. Coun., 1992—; sci. coun. Ga. Coalition for Sci. Tech. and Math. Edn., 1993-, Student Aid Found., Atlanta, 2002-(bd. dirs.). Named One of 10 Outstanding Young Women of Am., 1977, Outstanding Young Woman of Ga., 1977; honored by Ga. State Legis., Atlanta, 1978. Mem. LWV. Episcopalian. Avocations: gardening, travel, hiking, snorkeling, politics.

BARNETT, GARY, lawyer; b. Chgo., Dec. 20, 1955; s. Lawrence Barnett and Deena Mae Goldberg; children: Matthew, James. BS, U. Tulsa, 1978, JD, 1981; LLM, NYU, 1986. Bar: Okla. 1981, N.Y. 1986, Calif. 1989. Legal intern Gordon & Gordon, Claremore, Okla., 1980-81; assoc. Sublett, McCormick, Andrew & Keefer, Tulsa, 1981-82; prin. Barnett & Assocs., Claremore and Tulsa, 1982-85; assoc. Cadwalader, Wickersham & Taft, N.Y.C., 1986-92, ptnr., 1993-95, O'Melveny & Myers LLP, N.Y.C., 1995-99, Shearman & Sterling, N.Y.C., 1999—. Chmn. confs. on new devel. in securitization Practising Law Inst., N.Y.C., 1995—. Contbr. articles to profl. jours. Achievements include patents in field. Office: Shearman & Sterling 599 Lexington Ave 16th Fl New York NY 10022-6030 E-mail: gbarnett@shearman.com.

BARNETT, GENE HENRY, neurosurgeon; b. Phila., Feb. 2, 1955; s. Edgar Tryon and Anne Shirley (Wenner) B.; m. Kathleen Marie Seng, May 9, 1984 (div. Sept. 1989); 1 child, Alexander; m. Cathy Ann Sila, Dec. 9, 1990; children: Austin, Addison. BA summa cum laude, Case Western Res. U., 1976, MD, 1980. Intern Cleve. Clinic Found., 1980-81, neurosurgery resident, 1981-86, staff neurosurgery, 1987—, co-dir. residency program, 1992-95, vice chmn. dept. neurosurgery, 1993—2002, program dir. dept. neurosurgery, 1995—, dir. Brain Tumor Ctr., 1995—2001, chmn. Brain Tumor Inst., 2001—, dir. Gamma Knife Ctr., 1997—. Hon. registrar U. Edinburgh, Scotland, 1985; fellow Harvard Med. Sch., Mass. Gen. Hosp., 1986-87; cons. in field. Editor: Image Guided Neurosurgery: Clinical Applications of Surgical Navigation Systems, 1998; contbr. over 120 articles to profl. jours., 27 chpts. to books. Grantee Epilesy Found. Am., 1979, NINDS, 1995; clin. and rsch. fellow Harvard Med. Sch., Mass. Gen. Hosp., Boston, 1986-87. Office: Cleve Clinic Found 9500 Euclid Ave Cleveland OH 44195-0001

BARNETT, GUY OCTO, physician, educator; b. Chula Vista, Calif., Sept. 18, 1930; married; 3 children. BA, Vanderbilt U., 1952; MD, Harvard U., 1956. Resident Peter Bent Brigham Hosp., 1956—61; clin. assoc. Nat. Heart Inst., 1958—60; investigator Am. Heart Assn., 1961—67; physician, prof. medicine, dir. computer sci. lab Mass. Gen. Hosp., 1979—; prof. medicine Harvard U., 1980—. Lectr. elec. engring. MIT, 1972—. Fellow: Inst. Medicine-NAS; mem.: ACP, IEEE, Am. Med. Informatics Assn. (bd. dirs. 1984—), Biomed. Engring. Soc., Assn. Computing Machinery. Office: Mass Gen Hosp Lab Computer Sci 50 Staniford St Boston MA 02114-2517

BARNETT, JAMES A. state legislator; m. Yvonne Barnett. Mem. Kans. State Senate, 2001—, vice chair pub. health and welfare com., mem. fed. and state affairs com., mem. fin. instns. and ins. com., mem. health care reform legis. oversight com. Home: 1400 Lincoln Emporia KS 66801 Office: Ste 202 1301 W 12th Emporia KS 55801 Fax: 316-342-6520. E-mail: jbarnett@cadvantage.com., barnett@senate.state.ks.us.*

BARNETT, JAMES MONROE, lawyer; b. Hulah, Okla., Dec. 24, 1933; s. Irvin M. and Ida Ruth (Loy) B.; m. Vicki L. Smith, Dec. 30, 1985. BBA, Washburn U., 1955, JD, 1959. Bar: Kans. 1959. Mem. firm Ross & Wells, Kansas City, Kans., 1959-63, Ross, Wells & Barnett, Kansas City, Kans., 1963-73; pres. Barnett & Ross, Chartered, Kansas City, Kans., 1973—. Bd. govs. Washburn Law Sch., 1974—, pres. 1982-83. Served with U.S. Army, 1956-58. Mem. ABA, Am. Judicature Soc., Wyandotte County Bar Assn., Kans. Bar Assn., Kans. Trial Lawyers Assn., Assn. Trial Lawyers Am. Republican. Methodist. Home: 14236 Benson St Overland Park KS 66221-2176 also: Gen Sq Bldg 9800 Metcalf Ave Overland Park KS 66212-2216

BARNETT, JOEY VICTOR, pharmacologist, educator, researcher; b. Evansville, Ind., June 18, 1958; s. Victor Alan and Judy Kay (Kohlmeyer) B. BS in Biology, U. So. Ind., 1980; PhD in Pharmacology, Vanderbilt U., 1986. Rsch. intern Argonne (Ill.) Nat. Lab., U.S. Dept. Energy, 1981; rsch. fellow Brigham & Women's Hosp., Harvard Med. Sch., Boston, 1986-89, instr. medicine, 1989-92; asst. prof. medicine and pharmacology Vanderbilt U., Nashville, 1992-99, assoc. prof. medicine and pharmacology, 1999—, dir. grad. studies in pharmacology, 2001—. Rsch. investigator Tenn. affiliate Am. Heart Assn., 1993-95, established investigator Am. Heart Assn., 1996—; mem. devel. mechanisms panel NSF, 1995-98. Co-author: Heart Failure: Basic Science and Clinical Aspects, 1993; contbr. articles and abstracts to profl. jours. Founding bd. dirs. Dismas House in Ctrl. Mass., Worcester, 1987-90; co-chair cardiovasc. devel. panel Nat. Am. Heart Assn., 1997-98, chair, 1999-2000. Mass. affiliate Am. Heart Assn. fellow, 1986-88; recipient Nat. Rsch. Svc. award Nat. Heart Lung and Blood Inst./NIH, Boston, 1988-90, Disting. Alumni award U. So. Ind., 1991. AAAS, N.Y. Acad. Scis., Ind. Acad. Sci., Basic Rsch. Coun. Am. Heart Assn., Sigma Zeta, Sigma Xi. Roman Catholic. Achievements include research on the molecular mechanisms that regulate development of the cardiovascular system. Office: 383 Prb 2220 Pierce Ave Nashville TN 37232-0021 E-mail: joey.barnett@vanderbilt.edu.

BARNETT, JONATHAN, architect, urban planner, educator; b. Boston, Jan. 6, 1937; s. David and Josephine Barnett; m. Nory Miller, Mar. 19, 1983. BA magna cum laude, Yale U., 1958, MArch, 1963; MA Mellon fellow, U. Cambridge, Eng., 1960. Designer Haines, Lundberg & Waehler, Archts., N.Y.C., 1963, 64; assoc. editor Archtl. Record, N.Y.C., 1964-67; cons. New City Exhbn. Mus. Modern Art, 1966, 67; prin. urban designer N.Y.C. Planning Dept., 1967-68, dir. urban design group, 1969-71; prof., dir. grad. program in urban design CCNY, 1971-98; prof. city and regional planning, dir. urban design program U. Pa., Phila., 1998—. Planning cons., 1971—; mem. vis. com. Sch. Architecture Yale U., 1974—80, William Henry Bishop prof., 1983; mem. vis. com. Harvard U. Grad. Sch. Design, 1976—81, UCLA, 1990, MIT Planning Dept., 1999; vis. prof. U. Wis., Milw., 1981; Kea disting. vis. prof. U. Md., 1988, 89; Sam Gibbons eminent scholar U. S. Fla., 1991—94; cons. AIA, South St. Seaport Mus., Nat. Pk. Svc., Louisville, Kansas City, Cleve., Charleston, SC, Norfolk, Va., Omaha, Pitts., Salt Lake City, Sioux City, Iowa, Wildwood, Mo., N.Y.C., Miami, Fla., Brookfield, Wis., Dallas, others; lectr. in field. Editor: (book) Perspecta 9, 1968; co-author: New Zoning, 1970, Collaborations: Artists and Architects, 1981, The Practice of Local Government Planning, 1988, 3d edit., 2000, Cities in Our Future, 1997, Charter of the New Urbanism, 1999; author: Urban Design as Public Policy, 1974; author: (with John C. Portman, Jr.) The Architect as Developer, 1976; author: Introduction to Urban Design, 1982, The Elusive City, 1986, The Fractured Metropolis, 1995, Planning for the New Century, 2000, Redesigning Cities, 2003; editl. cons. Archtl. Record, 1968—90, mem. adv. bd. Jour. Urban Design, 1996—; contbr. articles to profl. jours. Mem. adv. bd. Environment and Behavior, 1968—78; bd. dirs. DC Preservation League, 1996—2000; mem. Com. 100 Fed. City, 1997—2002. Fellow: AIA, Am. Inst. Cert. Planners; mem.: Congress New Urbanism (bd. dirs. 1995—), N.Y. Landmark Conservancy (bd. dirs. 1972—97), Berzelius Soc., Inst. Urban Design (bd. dirs. 1989—99), Mcpl. Art Soc. (bd. dirs. 1970—78, 1981—86), Archtl. League N.Y. (v.p. 1968—70, dir. 1975—98, pres. 1977—81), Century Assn., Elizabethan Club Yale, Yale Club. Unitarian Universalist. Home: 225 S Bonsall St Philadelphia PA 19103 Office: Dept of City and Regional Planning Univ Pa Philadelphia PA 19104

BARNETT, JOYCE LYNDEL, freelance/self-employed writer; b. Louisville, Ky., Apr. 21, 1956; d. Otis and June LaVern Cleveland; m. Lloyd Barnett; children: Luciene, Lloyd Jr. Travel agent diploma, Walters Coll., Louisville, Ky., 1989; BSBA, Barrington U., Birmingham, Ala., 2001. Mental health nurse Vis. Nurses Assn.; sales and mktg. staff Time Life Books, Washington. Motivational spkr. For the Spirit, Inc., Louisville; lectr. on autism Jewish Hosp., Louisville; speaker Vis. Nurses Assn. Author: (Book) Understanding the Autistic Person, 1994, For the Spirit, 1998, While on My Journey, 2000, (Poem) Strange Fruit, 1993. Avocation: story telling. Home: 5403 Red Leaf Rd Louisville KY 40218 E-mail: bchaplainL@aol.com.

BARNETT, JUDY JANNETTE, healthcare technology company executive, consultant; b. Irumagawa, Japan, July 22, 1958; came to U.S., 1961; d. Earl Vestal Barnett and Earlene Geneva Woosley; m. David Hatherill Brown, Aug. 27, 1993. BJ, U. Tex., 1981. News reporter, anchor Sta. KAVU-TV, Victoria, Tex., 1984-85; sr. account exec. Dublin-McCarter, San Antonio, 1985-88; account supr. Atkins & Assocs., San Antonio, 1988-90; pub. rels. mgr. Fidelity Investments, Miami, Fla., 1990-93; comm. dir. Metro-Dade County, Miami, 1993-94; v.p. Zynyx Mktg. Comm., Miami, 1994-96; dir. mktg. comm. North Broward Hosp. Dist., Fort Lauderdale, Fla., 1997—2001; dir. pub. rels. Eclipsys Corp., 2001—. Named Excellence in Commn., Am. Heart Assn., 1999, 2000; recipient 51 mktg./PR awards including Clarion award, Women in Comm., 1996, Comprehensive Comm. award, Fla. Soc. Healthcare Pub. Rels. and Mktg., 1998—2000. Mem.: Pub. Rels. Soc. Am. (bd. dirs. Miami chpt. 1994—97, sec. 1996). Office: 1750 Clint Moore Rd Boca Raton FL 33487 E-mail: judybarnett@eclipsys.com.

BARNETT, MARGARET EDWINA, nephrologist, researcher, business consultant, entrepreneur, clinical hypertension specialist; b. Ft. Benning, Ga., July 28, 1949; d. Eddie Lee and Margaret Thomas Barnett. BS magna cum laude with distinction in Zoology, Ohio State U., 1969; MD, Johns Hopkins U., 1973; PhD in Cellular and Molecular Biology, Case Western Res. U., 1984; postgrad., Purdue U., 1992; postgrad. in med. acupuncture, UCLA, 1996, MBA, 1999. Med. technologist blood bank Johns Hopkins Hosp., Balt., 1971-73; intern Greater Balt. Med. Ctr., Towson, Md., 1973-74; med. resident Cleve. Clinic Edni. Found., 1974-75, Univ. Hosps. Cleve., 1975-76, nephrology fellow, 1976-78, med. tchg. fellow, 1978-84; nephrology rounding physician Cmty. Dialysis Ctr., Cleve., Mentor, Ohio, 1978-83; rsch. assoc. Case Western Res. U., Cleve., 1978-79, 83-84; physician emergency medicine Huron Regional Urgent Care Ctrs., Inc., Cleve., 1983-84; preceptor renal correlation conf. Case Western Res. Sch. Medicine, 1980-81, lectr. anatomy and histology, 1979-83; asst. prof. medicine/nephrology Milton S. Hershey Med. Ctr., Pa. State U., Hershey, 1984-87, acting chief renal and electrolyte divsn., 1985, dir. peritoneal, 1986-87, assoc. dir. hypertension, 1986-87. Pvt. practice medicine specializing in nephrology and hypertension Arnett Clinic, Lafayette, Ind., 1987—93; dir. outpatient dialysis St. Elizabeth Hosp. Med. Ctr., Lafayette; clin. asst. prof. medicine Ind. U. Sch. Medicine, 1989—94; pharmacology clin. preceptor Purdue U., West Lafayette, 1988—93; spl. guest lectr. hypertension Drugs Cos. Ill., Ind., S.D., Ky., Ohio, Pa., 1988—94, Drugs Cos. Calif., 1995—; assoc. dean rsch. and grad. studies Sch. Allied Health Scis. Ind. U., 1993—94, vis. prof. medicine dept. health info adminstrn. Allied Health Scis., 1994; medicine dept. phys. therapy Nat. Inst. Fitness & Sport, 1993—94; dir. dialysis svcs. King/Drew Med. Ctr., L.A., 1994—99; asst. prof. medicine Charles R. Drew U., 1994—2002, assoc. dir. nephrology fellowship program, 1995—99, adj. assoc. prof. medicine, 2003—; pres., CEO Barnett Rsch. & Comm. Med. Corp., 2000—; faculty mem. Nat. Bur. Info. on Coronary Heart Disease Risk, 1991—94, mem. cardiorenal subcom., 1995—97; rep. rsch. and grad. studies alumni adv. coun. Ohio State U., 1990—93; regional adj. faculty mem. Vascul Biology Working Group U. Fla., 2001—; part-time attending physician Brotman Med. Ctr., Culver City, Calif., 2000—. Del. in nephrology and hypertension amb. program People to People Internat. to Russia, Belarus and Lithuania, 1994, Chinese Med. Assn. 80th Anniversary, Beijing, 1995, Johannesburg and Capetown, South Africa, 1996; rep. So. Calif. regional quality coun. GAMBRO Healthcare, Inc., Lakewood, Colo., 1998—99; mem. internat. adv. bd. Shire Pharm. Devel. Recipient Nat. Rsch. Svc. award, NIH, 1979—82, Pres.'s Scholarship award, 1967—69; grantee, Am. Heart Assn. Ohio divsn., 1980—81, Ohio Kidney Found., 1977—78; scholar, GM, Leo Yassinoff, Alpha Epsilon Delta, Beanie Drake, Am. Heart Assn., 1977. Fellow: ACP; mem.: AMA (physician rsch. evaluation panel 1981—83, Physician Recognition award 1984—87), John Hopkins Med. and Surg. Soc., Am. Acad. Med. Acupuncture (assoc.), Nat. Kidney Found., Am. Soc. Hypertension (specialist in clin. hypertension 1999—), Assn. Black Cardiologists, Inc., Internat. Soc. Nephrology, Am. Film Inst., World Tae Kwon Do Fedn., Seoul, Korea, Mensa, Alpha Kappa Alpha, Alpha Epsilon Delta (scholar), Phi Beta Kappa. Democrat.

BARNETT, MARILYN, advertising agency executive; b. Detroit; d. Henry and Kate (Boesky) Schiff; children: Rhona, Ken. BA, Wayne State U. Founder, part-owner, pres. Mars Advt. Co., Southfield, Mich. Bd. dirs. Mich. Strategic

Fund; apptd. to Mich. bi-lateral trade team with Germany. Named Outstanding Retail Woman of Yr., Outstanding Retail Mktg. Exec., bd. dirs. Oakland U., Entrepreneur of Yr., Oakland Exec. of Yr.; named to Mich.'s Top 25 Women Bus. Owner's List. Mem. AFTRA (dir.), SAG, Exec. Women Am., Am. Women in Radio & TV (Top Agy. Mgmt. award, Outstanding Woman of Yr.), Internat. Women Forum, Com. of 200, Women's Econ. Club (Ad Woman of Yr.), Adcraft. Office: MARS Advt 23999 Northwestern Hwy Southfield MI 48075 2528 also: MARS Advt Co 6671 W Sunset Blvd Ste 1591 Los Angeles CA 90028-7170

BARNETT, MARK A. psychology educator; b. Chgo., Sept. 7, 1949; s. Robert and Mona Barnett; children: Megan, Neil. PhD, Northwestern U., 1975. Prof. dept. psychology Kans. State U., Manhattan, 1975—. Contbr. numerous articles on psychology to profl. jours. Mem. APA, Soc. for Rsch. in Child Devel., Soc. for Rsch. in Human Devel. Office: Kans State U Dept Psychology 1100 Mid-Campus Dr Manhattan KS 66506

BARNETT, MARK WILLIAM, former state attorney general; b. Sioux Falls, S.D., Sept. 6, 1954; s. Thomas C. and Dorothy Ann (Lievrance) Barnett; m. Deborah Ann Barnett, July 14, 1979. BS in Govt., U. S.D., 1976; JD, 1978. Bar: S.D. Pvt. practice, Sioux Falls, 1978—80; asst. atty. gen. State of S.D., Pierre, 1980—83, spl. prosecutor, 1984—90; ptnr. Schmidt, Schroyer, Colwill and Barnett, Pierre, 1984—90; atty. gen. State of S.D., Pierre, 1991—2003. Mem. S.D. Bar Commn., 1986—92, S.D. Law Enforcement Tng. Commn., 1987, S.D. Corrections Commn., 1987. Bd. dirs. D.A.R.E. Mem.: State's Atty. Assn. (bd. dirs. 1987—90), Am. Judicature Soc. (nat. bd. dirs. 1984—88), S.D. Bar Assn. (pres. young lawyers' sect. 1985). Republican. Avocations: golf, weight lifting, snowmobiling.*

BARNETT, MARY LORENE, real estate manager; b. Saline County, Mo., Nov. 29, 1927; d. Grover Cleveland Renno and Emma Zue Rennison; m. Eugene Earl Boone, Aug. 24, 1946 (div. Aug. 1961); 1 child, Priscilla Sue Boone; m. Charles Owen Barnett, Nov. 11, 1961; 1 child, Robert E. BA in Psychology magna cum laude, Washburn U., 1979. Asst. contr. 1st State Savs., Sedalia, Mo., 1960-61; bookkeeper New Empire Ins., Sedalia, 1961-63; office mgr. Klassic Mfg., Sedalia, 1963-66; real estate mgr. Topeka, Kans., 1970—. Author: Charles Renno Family Record, 1996, Charles Renno Family, 1997. Bd. dirs. Shawnee County Coun. on Aging, Topeka. Recipient cert. of appreciation Bd. of County Commrs., Topeka, 1995. Mem. DAR, AAUW, LWV, Topeka Women's Club (1st v.p.), Fa. Star, Phi Kappa Phi, Psi Chi. Republican. Avocations: genealogy, poetry. Home: 3819 SW Lincolnshire Rd Topeka KS 66610-1360

BARNETT, PATRICK SHAWN, music educator; b. Woodstock, Ill., Oct. 13, 1965; s. Arlis Wade and Clara Marie Barnett; m. Lisa Maureen Kiener-Barnett; 1 child, Sophie. B of Music Edn., No. Ill. U., 1987; M of Music Edn., DePaul U., 1993. Cert. tchg. Mid. sch. music tchr. Round Lake (Ill.) Area Schools, 1988—89, Villa Park (Ill.) Sch. Dist. 45, 1989—90; organist St. Johns Luth. Ch., Woodstock, 1980—83, Messiah Luth. Ch., Chgo., 1983—84; music dir. 1st Presbyn. Ch., Woodstock, 1985—87, St. Lukes Luth. Ch., Glen Ellyn, Ill., 1987—88, Luth. Ch. of St. Phillip, Glenview, Ill., 1988—91; organist Redeemer Luth. Ch., Highland Park, Ill., 1993—94; assoc. music dir. Holy Cross Cath. Ch., Deerfield, Ill., 1994—98; min. of music St. Michaels Luth. Ch., LaGrange Park, Ill., 1998—99; assoc. music dir. Divine Savior Parish, Downers Grove, Ill., 1999—2000, Gloria Dei Luth. Ch., Downers Grove, Ill., 2001—; choral dir. Maine Twp. H.S. East, Park Ridge, Ill., 1990—. Dir. of choir Ill. Ambs. Music, Littleton, 1998—2000. Mem. Boy Scouts Am. Mem.: NEA, Ill. Music Educators Assn. (chair dist. 7 chorus 1999—2002), Am. Guild of Organists, Am. Choral Dirs. Assn. (chair youth and student activitites 1991—95, dir. youth and student activities 1991—95). Liberal. Avocation: home rehabbing. Office: Maine Twp H S E 2601 W Dempster St Park Ridge IL 60068 Office Fax: 847-692-8499. Business E-Mail: Pbarnett@maine207east.k12.il.us.

BARNETT, PEGGY G. music educator; b. Dallas, Sept. 15, 1935; d. Garnald Morris and Thelma Christean (Turner) Gregory; m. John Curtis Jones, Aug. 24, 1957 (div. June 1980); children: Lewis Gregory, Michael Wayne, Scott Carlton, Cynthia Luanne; m. Edward Ralph Burnett, Aug. 31, 2002. BS in Home Econs., Baylor U., 1956; MS in Housing and Interior Design, Okla. State U., 1957; student, Rykyu Classical Acad., Okinawa, Japan, 1964-68, Hampton (Va.) Inst., 1968-70. Nat. cert. tchr. music; cert. profl. master. Pvt. practice piano tchr., 1964—2002; founder, dir., piano thcr., music theory tchr. Music Arts Conservatory, Albuquerque, 1984—2002; ret., 2002. Mem. piano faculty Summer Piano Camp at Mary Hardin-Baylor U., Belton, Tex., summers 1980, 86. Performed two-piano and duet music, 1980-85; performed with ptnr. in master classes for well-known duettists. Choir dir., pianist and organist various chs., Okinawa, 1964-68, Hampton, Va., 1969-72, Las Vegas, Nev., 1972-74; talent judge Miss Teen Pageant, Albuquerque, 1993-96. Mem. Profl. Music Tchrs. N.Mex. (state membership chair 1982-83, adjudicator 1975—Tchr. of Yr. 1998), Music Tchrs. Nat. Assn., Nat. Guild Piano Tchrs., Tex. Music Tchrs. Assn., Abilene Music Tchrs. Assn. Avocations: downhill skiing, hiking, gardening.

BARNETT, PHILIP, science librarian, educator; b. N.Y.C., May 26, 1946; s. Paul and Beatrice (Blume) G.; m. Sarah Ellen Friend; children: David, Reena. BS in Chemistry, Bklyn. Coll., 1967; MS in Libr. Svc., Columbia U., 1981; PhD in Biochemistry, Rutgers U., 1973. USPHS postdoctoral fellow NYU, Tuxedo, 1972-74; postdoctoral staff assoc. Columbia U., N.Y.C., 1974-81; indexer H. W. Wilson Co., Bronx, N.Y., 1981-82; info. scientist Ayerst Labs., N.Y.C., 1982-87; corp. libr. Becton Dickinson Inc., Franklin Lakes, N.J., 1987-88; sr. info. scientist Warner-Lambert Co., Morris Plains, N.J., 1988-90; assoc. prof. CUNY, 1990—. Author: (with others) Methods Enzymol., 1982; contbr. articles to sci. jours. Mem. AAAS, Am. Chem. Soc. Democrat. Jewish. Office: CUNY Convent Ave # 138 New York NY 10031-9127

BARNETT, R(ALPH) MICHAEL, theoretical physicist, educational agency administrator; b. Gulfport, Miss., Jan. 25, 1944; s. Herbert Chester and Lisa Margaret (Kielley) B.; children: Leilani Pinho, Julia Alexandra, Russell Alan. BS, Antioch Coll., 1966; PhD, U. Chgo., 1971. Postdoctoral fellow U. Calif., Irvine, 1972-74; rsch. fellow Harvard U., Cambridge, Mass., 1974-76; rsch. assoc. Stanford (Calif.) Linear Accelerator Ctr., 1976-83; vis. physicist Inst. Theoretical Physics U. Calif., Santa Barbara, 1983-84; staff scientist Lawrence Berkeley Nat. Lab., 1984-89, sr. scientist and head particle data group, 1990—; co-dir. QuarkNet Ednl. Project, 1999—. V.p. Contemporary Physics Edn. Project, 1987-98, pub. info. coor. Am. Phys. Soc. Dvsn. of Particles and Fields, 1994-97; edn. coord. ATLAS experiment at CERN, Geneva; prodr. film: The Atlas Experiment, 2000. Author: Teachers' Resource Book on Fundamental Particles and Interactions, 1988, Review of Particle Physics, 1990, 6th edit., 2002, Particle Physics—One Hundred Years of Discoveries, 1996, Guide to Experimental Particle Physics Literature, 1993, 2d edit., 1996, The Charm of Strange Quarks, Mysteries and Revolutions of Particle Physics, 2000, (chart) Fundamental Particles and Interactions, 1987, 4th edit., 1999, World-Wide Web feature, The Particle Adventure, 1995, rev. edit. 2000, (CD ROM) The Quark Adventure, 2000. Fellow Am. Phys. Soc. (pub. info. coord. divsn. particles and fields 1994-97, taskforce on informing the public, chair-elect Calif. sect.), Am. Assn. Physics Tchrs. (v.p., sect. North Calif.). Achievements include research on the Standard Model and its extensions, including studies of nature and validity of quantum chromodynamics; analyses of neutral current couplings; calculations of the production of heavy quarks; predictions of properties and decays of supersymmetric particles and higgs bosons. Office: Lawrence Berkeley Nat Lab MS-50-308 1 Cyclotron Rd Berkeley CA 94720-0001

BARNETT, RANDY EVAN, law educator; b. Chgo., Feb. 5, 1952; s. Ronald Evan and Florice Jane (Abrahams) B.; m. Beth E. Black, Dec. 2, 1979; 2 children. B.A., Northwestern U., 1974; J.D., Harvard U., 1977. Bar: Ill. 1977, U.S. Dist. Ct. (no. dist.) Ill. 1977. Asst. State's Atty. Cook County, Chgo., 1977-81; research fellow U. Chgo. Law Sch., 1981-82; asst. prof. law Ill. Inst. Tech. Chgo.-Kent Coll. of Law, 1982-86, assoc. prof. law, 1986—; adj. scholarCato Inst.; adv. com. Speaker Ill. Ho. of Reps.; dir. law and philosophy program and Leonard P. Cassidy fellowship program Inst. for Humane Studies, George Mason U., Fairfax, Va., 1982— . Editor: Assessing the Criminal, 1977. Contbr. articles to profl. jours. Mem. Mid Am. Legal Found. (chmn. bd. legal advisors), Wash. Legal Found. (bd. advisors), Heartland Inst. (bd. advisors).

BARNETT, RICHARD CHAMBERS, historian, educator; b. Davenport, Fla., Apr. 27, 1932; s. Jones Richard and Helen June (Chambers) B.; m. Betty May Tribble, Oct. 18, 1957; children— Amelia Carlton, Colin Warwick BA, Wake Forest Coll., 1953; M.Ed., U. N.C., 1954, PhD, 1963. Instr., acting chmn. dept. social sci. Gardner-Webb Coll., 1956-58; instr. history Wake Forest U., Winston-Salem, N.C., 1961-62, asst. prof., 1962-67, assoc. prof., 1967-76, prof., chmn. dept. history, 1968-75, 83-87, acting dean Grad. Sch., 1979; retired. Contbg. author history and polit. sci. vols., also articles and book revs. Pres Winston-Salem-Forsyth PTA, 1969-71; bd. mgrs. N.C. PTA, 1971-73, exec. com., 1972-73, life mem.; adv. com. N.C. Bd. Edn., 1973-76. Served with CIC, AUS, 1954-56 Southeastern Inst. Medieval and Renaissance Studies fellow, summer 1974 Mem. Am. Hist. Assn. (pres. elect N.C. conf. 1991-92, pres. 1992-93), AAUP, Carolinas Symposium Brit. Studies (pres. 1979-80), So. Conf. Brit. Studies (pres. 1990-92), N.Am. Conf. Brit. Studies (coun. 1990-92), Danforth Assocs. Home: 2130 Royall Dr Winston Salem NC 27106-5234

BARNETT, RICHARD EARL, lawyer, film distributing company executive; b. Lake Charles, La., Aug. 1, 1927; s. George and Freida (Goldsmith) B.; student Princeton, 1944-45; B.A., Amherst Coll., 1950; LL.B., Columbia U., 1953; m. Harriet Schottland, July 21, 1950; children: Pamela Jane, James Richardson, Thomas Schuyler. Bar: N.Y. 1953. Atty., N.Y.C., 1953-56; atty. with gen. counsel's office N.Y. Ctrl. R.R., 1956-58; v.p., dir. Modern Film Corp., N.Y.C., 1958-71, sec., 1961-71, pres., 1971-87, ret., 1987; chmn. Movies En Route, Inc., N.Y.C.; dir. Walport (Overseas) Ltd., London. Served to warrant officer U.S. Mcht. Marine, 1945-47. Mem. Am., N.Y.C. bar assns., Theta Xi, Phi Delta Phi. Home: 225 Clinton Ave Dobbs Ferry NY 10522-3003

BARNETT, ROBERT BRUCE, lawyer, educator; b. Waukegan, Ill., Aug. 26, 1946; s. Bernard and Betty Jane (Simon) Barnett; m. Rita Lynn Braver, Apr. 10, 1972; 1 child, Meredith Jane. BA, U. Wis., 1968; JD, U. Chgo., 1971. Bar: D.C. 1971. Law clk. to Hon. John Minor Wisdom U.S. Ct. Appeals (5th cir.), 1971-72; law clk. to assoc. justice Byron R. White U.S. Supreme Ct., Washington, 1972-73; legis. asst. Sen. Walter F. Mondale, Washington, 1973-75; assoc. Williams & Connolly, Washington, 1975-78, ptnr., 1979—. Adj. prof. Georgetown Law Sch., 1973—80. Trustee John F. Kennedy Ctr. for Performing Arts, 1994—; mem. bd. visitors Sanford Inst. of Pub. Policy, Duke U., 1998—2001, U. Chgo. Law Sch., 2001—. Office: Williams & Connolly LLP 725 12th St NW Washington DC 20005-5901

BARNETT, SAMUEL TREUTLEN, international company executive; m. Rena H. Earnhardt, Sept. 22, 2001; children: Elizabeth L., Katharine T., Emily R., Alexander W. BA, Wesleyan U., 1969; MEd, Temple U., 1973, EdD, 1975. Tchr. The Haverford Sch., 1969-74; leadership devel. specialist Phila. Sch. Dist., 1974-75; freelance cons., 1971-76; tng. cons. U.S. Office Personnel Mgmt., Pa., 1976-79; founder, chief cons. Barnett Internat. a subsidiary PAREXEL Internat., Media, Pa., 1979-99; lead ptnr. N.Am. pharm. sector mgmt. consulting svcs. Pricewaterhouse Coopers, Phila., 1999—2002; lead ptnr. Am. Life Sci. Pharm. Practice IBM Bus. Consultancy Svcs., Phila., 2002—. Spkr. in field. Contbr. articles to profl. jours. Mem. ASTD, Drug Info. Assn. Office: IBM Bus Cons Svc 30 S 17th St Philadelphia PA 19103-7044 E-mail: sam.barnett@us.ibm.com.

BARNETT, STEVEN R. director, music educator; b. Humboldt, TN, Sept. 11, 1957; s. John Grady and Carolyn Bowles Barnett; children: John, Chris. MusB, Univ. of Miss., Univ., MS, 1979; MusM ed., Miss. Coll., Clinton, MS, 1992. Asst. band dir. Pear HS, Pearl, Miss., 1979—81; band dir. Newton HS, Newton, Miss., 1981—83, Oxford HS, Oxford, Miss., 1983—85, Forest HS, Forest, Miss., 1985—88, Madison-Ridgeland HS, Madison, Miss., 1988—91, Copiah-Lincoln Cmty. Coll., Wesson, Miss., 1991—99; asst. bd. dir. Univ. of Miss., Oxford, Miss., 1999—. Arranger: songs Jalen Publ., 1999—. Sec. Oxford Athletic Booster Club, Oxford, Miss., 2002—03; pres. Oxford Band Boosters, Oxford, Miss., 2001—02, v.p., 2000—01. Recipient HEADWAE - Outward Tchr. Award, Copiah- Lincoln Cmty. Coll., 1999. Mem.: Phi Beta Mu Internat. (internat. editor 2002). Home: 121 Lakeway Dr Oxford MS 38655 Office: 178 Township Rd 1252 Proctorville OH 45669

BARNETT, STUART ADRIAN, English language educator; b. Ft. Sill, Okla., Dec. 15, 1960; s. Frederic Eugene and Regina (Prestel) B.; m. Patricia Mary Festa, July 16, 1988; children: Nicholas Fenton, Katherine Egan. BA, Columbia U., 1983; MA in German, U. Va., 1985; MA in Comparative Lit., SUNY, Buffalo, 1988; PhD in Comparative Lit., SUNY, 1990. Asst. prof. English Cen. Conn. State U., New Britain, 1992-96, assoc. prof., 1996—2001, prof., 2001—. Vis. asst. prof. Hampshire Coll., Amherst, Mass., 1990-91, U. Rochester, N.Y., 1991-92. Editor collection: Hegel After Derrida, 1998; translator: Friedrich Schlegel: On the Study of Greek Poetry, 2000; contbr. articles to profl. jours. Mem. MLA, Am. Soc. for 18th Century Studies. Home: 65 Avonwood Rd C10 Avon CT 06001 Office: Ctrl Conn State Univ Willard Hall Dept English New Britain CT 06050

BARNETT, SUZANNE WILSON, historian, educator; b. Columbus, Ohio, June 1, 1940; d. George Leedom and Dorothy May (Macklin) Wilson; m. Redmond James Barnett, June 7, 1969. BA, Muskingum Coll., New Concord, Ohio, 1961; AM, Harvard U., 1963, PhD, 1973. Lectr. Suffolk U., Boston, 1970-72, Boston U., 1971-72; instr. Wellesley (Mass.) Coll., 1972-73; from asst. prof. to assoc. prof. U. Puget Sound, Tacoma, 1973—85, prof., 1985—, Robert G. Albertson prof., 1998—2003. Asst. prof. U. Va., Charlottesville, 1973. Author, co-editor: book Christianity in China: Early Protestant Missionary Writings, 1985; co-editor: Asia in the Undergraduate Curriculum: A Case for Asia in Liberal Arts Education, 2000; contbr. articles to profl. jours. Bd. dirs. Chinese Reconciliation Project Found., Tacoma, 1994—. Named Wash. Prof. of the Yr., Carnegie Found. Advancement Tchg., 2002; Fulbright-Hays Grd. fellow, U.S. Office Edn., 1967—68, Lang. and Rsch. fellow, Inter-Univ. Program and Academia Sinica, 1986—87, Postdoctoral fellow, History Christianity China Project, 1990. Mem.: Soc. History Edn. (mem. nat. adv. coun. 1996—), ASIANetwork (bd. dirs. 1996—2000, chair 1998—99), Assn. Asian Studies (bd. dirs. China and Inner Asia Coun. 1979—82, mem. program com. 1998—2000, chair 1999—2000), Am. Hist. Assn. (mem. coun. tchg. divsn. 1992—95). Democrat. Avocations: jogging, dining, opera. Home: 3401 N 29th St Tacoma WA 98407-6250 Office: U Puget Sound Dept History 1500 N Warner #1033 Tacoma WA 98416-1033 E-mail: sbarnett@ups.edu.

BARNETT, VIVIAN ENDICOTT, curator; b. Putnam, Conn., July 8, 1944; d. George and Vivian (Wood) Endicott; m. Peter Herbert Barnett, July 1, 1967; children: Sarah, Alexander. AB magna cum laude, Vassar Coll., 1965; MA, NYU, 1971; postgrad., CUNY, 1979-81. Research asst. Solomon R. Guggenheim Mus., N.Y.C., 1973-77, curatorial assoc., 1978-79, assoc. curator, 1980-81, rsch. curator, 1981-82, curator, 1982-91; dir. Roethel Benjamin Archive at Guggenheim Mus., N.Y.C., 1991—. Author: (book) The Guggenheim Museum: Justin K. Thannhauser Collection, 1978, The Guggenheim Museum Collection 1900-1980, Kandinsky at the Guggenheim, 1983, 100 Works by Modern Masters from the Guggenheim Museum, 1984, Kandinsky and Sweden, 1989, Kandinsky in Major Collections in the West, 1989, Kandinsky Watercolours: Catalogue Raisonné, vol I 1900-1921, 1992, Kandinsky Watercolours: Catalogue Raisonné, vol II 1922-1944, 1994, Kleine Freuden, 1992, Das bunte Leben: Kandinsky in Lenbachhaus, 1995, The Blue Four: Feininger, Jawlensky, Kandinsky, Klee in the New World, 1997; contbr. book, ; author: Exiles and Emigre's, 1997, Mies in America, 2001, Die Bruche in Dresden, 2001; contbr. Fellow John Simon Guggenheim, 1990. Mem.: Col Art Asn Am, Int Coun Museums, Am Asn Museums, Soc Kandinsky (secy 1992—). Office: Solomon R Guggenheim Mus 1071 5th Ave New York NY 10128-0112

BARNETT, WILLIAM ARNOLD, economics educator; b. Boston, Oct. 30, 1941; s. Marcus Jack and Elizabeth Leah (Forman) B.; m. Melinda Gentry, Sept. 1, 1991. BS, MIT, 1963; MBA, U. Calif., Berkeley, 1965; MS, Carnegie Mellon U., 1972, PhD, 1974. System devel. engr., Apollo Project, Rocketdyne div. Rockwell Internat. Corp., Canoga Park, Calif., 1963-67; research econometrician Bd. Govs., Fed. Reserve System, Washington, 1973-81; Stuart Centennial prof. econs. U. Tex., Austin, 1981-90; prof. econs. Washington U., St. Louis, 1990—; Oswald Disting. prof. macroeconomics U. of Kans., 2002—. Vis. prof. econs. U. Aix-Marseille, Aix-en-Provence, France, 1979, Duke U., Durham, N.C., 1987-88; organizer ann. symposia in econ. theory and econometrics; assoc. dir. Ctr. for Econ. Rsch., U. Tex., Austin, 1981-90. Author: Consumer Demand and Labor Supply, 1981; editor three spl. edits. Jour. of Econometrics, 1979, 80, 85, Cambrige U. Press Monograph series, 1985—, Cambridge U. Press Jour. Macroeconomic Dynamics, 1997—; assoc. editor Jour. of Bus. and Econ. Stats., 1982-97; contbr. approx. 75 articles to profl. jours. Contract selection panel mem. NIH, Washington, 1983; cons. World Bank, Washington, 1985. R.K. Mellon Found. fellow, 1971-73; rsch. grantee NSF, Washington, 1977-89, Hogg Found., Houston, 1983. Fellow ICC Inst. (sr., editor 1983—), Am. Statis. Assn. (assoc. editor 1982—, fellow 1989—, program chair 1992—), Jour. Econometrics (charter fellow 1989—); mem. Inst. Math. Stats., Econometric Soc. (contbr. to jour.), Am. Econ. Assn., MIT Club (St. Louis). Home: 1904 Inverness Dr Lawrence KS 66047-1832 Office: U Kans Dept Econs Lawrence KS 66045

BARNETT, WILLIAM MICHAEL, lawyer; b. New Orleans, June 15, 1925; s. Herman Lyon Barnett and Irma Samson; m. Audrey Steinert, Mar. 17, 1954 (dec. June 30, 1995); children: Robert Alan, James Michael; m. Doris Berthelot, May 4, 2002. BA, Yale U., 1950; LLB, Tulane U., 1953. Assoc. Guste, Barnett & Redmann, New Orleans, 1953-57; ptnr. Guste, Barnett & Little, New Orleans, 1957-70; mng. ptnr. Guste, Barnett & Colomb, New Orleans, 1970-75, Guste, Barnett & Shushan, New Orleans, 1975—2002. Asst. editor Tulane Law Rev., 1952-53. Pres. Madonna Manor, Jefferson Parish, La., 1964-65, Upper Audubon Assn., New Orleans, 1986-88; trustee Boy Scouts of Am., New Orleans, 1970-75, Pharm. Mus., New Orleans, 1985-93; dir. La. Civil Svc. League, New Orleans, 1985-2002, La. Landmark Soc., New Orleans, 1963-65, Continental Savs. & Loan Assn., New Orleans, 1971-82, 1st v.p. Cultural Attractions Fund, New Orleans, 1966-68; pres. New Orleans Jr. C. of C., 1960-61; chmn. New Orleans Civil Svc. Commn., City of New Orleans, 1963-75. Sgt. inf. U.S. Army, 1943-46, ETO. Decorated Bronze Star, Combat Inf. badge; recipient M.M. Lemann award City of New Orleans, 1982. Mem.: Soc. Escargot Orleanais (master chancellor 1990—92), Exeter Acad. Alumni Assn. of La. (pres. 1968—75), Yale Alumni Assn. La. (pres. 1968—70), Nat. Assn. Yale Alumni (dir. 1973—75), La. Bar Assn. (mem. ho. of dels. 1961—64), Order of the Coif, Chevaliers du Tastevin (commandeur), Omicron Delta Kappa. Republican. Unitarian Universalist. Home: 7227 Benjamin St New Orleans LA 70118-3505 Office: Guste Barnett & Shushan 25th Fl 639 Loyola Ave New Orleans LA 70113-3125 E-mail: billbarney@webtv.net.

BARNETTE, CURTIS HANDLEY, steel company executive, lawyer; b. St. Albans, W.Va., Jan. 9, 1935; s. Curtis Franklin and Garnett Drucella (Robinson) Barnette; m. Loris Joan Harner, Dec. 28, 1957; children: Curtis Kevin, James David. AB with High Honors, W.Va. U., 1956; postgrad. (Fulbright scholar), U. Manchester, 1956—57; JD, Yale U., 1962; grad. advanced mgmt. program, Harvard U., 1974—75; LLD (hon.), W.Va. U., 1995, DeSales U., 1996, U. Charleston, 1998, Lehigh U., 1999, Moravian Coll., 2002. Cert. Conn., 1962, Pa., 1968, D.C., 1988, W.Va., 1990. Atty. Wiggin & Dana, New Haven, 1962—67, Bethlehem (Pa.) Steel Corp., 1967—92, sec., 1976—92, gen. counsel, 1977—92, sr. v.p., 1985—92, chmn., CEO, 1992—2000, also bd. dirs. 1986—2000; of counsel Skadden, Arps, Slate, Meagher & Flom, LLP, 2000—. Lectr. U. Md., 1958—59; law tutor Yale U., 1962—67; chmn. bd. dirs. Am. Iron and Steel Inst., 1997, dir., 1992—2000; bd. dirs. Met Life Ins. Co., Lehigh Valley Partnership; chmn. Internat. Iron and Steel Inst., 1994—95, dir., 1992—2000; comenius prof., exec. in residence Moravian Coll., 2000—. Trustee Leigh U., 1993—; Pa. Soc., 1993—; mem. Adminstrv. Conf. U.S., 1988—89; chmn. bd. govs. W.Va. U., 2002—; dir. W.Va. U. Found., 1982—, chair, 1987—88; mem. adv. com. Trade Policy and Negotiations, 1989—2002, Coal Commn., 1990, Pa. 21st Century Environ. Com., 1997—98. With Counterintelligence Corps U.S. Army, 1957—59, maj. USAR, 1959—67. Mem.: Nat. Mus. Indsl. History (chmn.), Pa. Pk. Found., Pa. Bus. Roundtable (dir. 1986—2000, chmn. 1994—95), Bus. Roundtable (policy com. 1992—2000), Bus. Coun., Pa. Chamber Bus. and Industry (dir. 1985—93), Am. Law Inst., Am. Soc. Corp. Secs. (chmn. 1986), Assn. Gen. Coun. (pres. 1988—90), W.Va. Bar Assn., D.C. Bar Assn., Northampton County Bar Assn., Conn. Bar Assn., Pa. Bar Assn., Fed. Bar Assn., ABA, Met. Club Washington, Blooming Grove Hunting and Fishing Club, Bethlehem Club, Lobolly, Links, Saucon Valley Country Club, Yale Club of N.Y.C., Univ. Club of Washington, Phi Delta Phi, Phi Alpha Theta, Beta Theta Pi, Phi Beta Kappa. Home: 1112 Prospect Ave Bethlehem PA 18018-4914 Office: 1170 8th Ave Bethlehem PA 18016-7699 also: 1440 New York Ave NW Washington DC 20005-2111 E-mail: barnette@bethsteel.com., hbarnett@skadden.com.

BARNEY, AUSTIN DUNHAM, II, estate planner; b. Hartford, Conn., Apr. 27, 1945; s. Philip Cushman and Elizabeth Cole (Freeman) B.; m. Susan C. Rumney, Aug. 26, 1976 (div. Mar. 1998); children: Austin C. D. III, Amanda Brandegee. BA in Polit. Sci., Yale U., 1967; MPA, Syracuse U., 1969. Lic. real estate broker, Conn., N.Y., Mass.; lic. life/health ins., securities, Conn.; cert. ins. cons., risk profl. Mgmt. asst. U. Hartford, Conn., 1967-68; jr./sr. planner Hartford Police Dept., 1969-70; sr. planner Commn. on City Plan City of Hartford, 1970; sr. adminstrv. analyst fin. dept. City of Hartford Budget and Rsch. Divsn., 1970-71, prin. adminstrv. analyst fin. dept., 1971-72; dir. land use policy planning State of Conn., Dept. Environ. Protection, 1972-73; exec. dir. Environ. Ctrs. Inc., 1973-75; pvt. practice cons., 1975-76; dir. natural resources mgmt. and community design Westledge Ctr. for Edn., 1976-78; sr. cons. corp. citizenship Cigna Corp. (Conn. Gen. Ins. Corp.), 1979-82; dir. contbns. and civic affairs Cigna Corp., Conn. Gen. Ins. Corp., 1982-84; pres., founder Farmvest, Inc., 1984—; prin. Bus. Planning Assocs., 1991-96; pres. Life Legacy Advisors, LLC, Avon, Conn., 1996—. Dir. Spiritus Wines, Inc., Aid to Artesans; ptnr. Folly Farm Assocs., 1983-90; pres. Folly Farm, Inc., 1983-90. Zoning commr. Town of Simsbury, Conn., 1976—, sec., 1993—; del. People's Republic China, Yale-China Assn., fall 1979, 80; corporator Hartford Pub. Libr., 1981—; corporator The Ctr. Families and Children, 1996—; bd. dirs., exec. com. Riverfront Recapture, Inc., 1981-90; bd. trustees Hartford Art Sch., 1969-2003, pres. 1984-86, 96-2003, hon. trustee, 2003—; bd. dirs. Conn. Trust for Hist. Preservation, 1982-85, The Nature Conservancy, treas. 1986-89, vice-chmn., 1989-2000, Oak Leaf award, 1995; bd. dirs. U. Conn. Found., 1988-92, Ensign-Bickford Found., 1987-93, v.p., 1989-93; bd. dirs. Ea. States Expo.; chmn. Conn. trustees 1993-96; elector Wadsworth Atheneum, 1983—; bd. dirs., chmn. fin. com. Conn. Earth Day 20, Inc., 1990; regent U. Hartford, 1980-86, 90-2003. Recipient Oak Leaf award Nature Conservancy, 1995, Pubs. Svc. award State of Conn., 2001, Gold medal for outstanding leadership excellence Hartford Art Sch., 2003. Mem. Nat. Assn. Life Underwriters, Am. Assn. Life Underwriters, Conn. Assn. Life Underwriters, Hartford Assn. Life Underwriters, Conn. Life Leaders. E-mail: acdb2@att.net.

BARNEY, CAROL ROSS, architect; b. Chgo., Apr. 12, 1949; d. Chester Albert and Dorothy Valeria (Dusiewicz) Ross; m. Alan Fredrick Barney, Mar. 22, 1970; children: Ross Fredrick, Adam Shafer, John Ross. BArch, U. Ill., 1971. Registered architect, Ill. Assoc. architect Holabird & Root, Chgo., 1972-79; prin. architect Orput Assoc., Inc., Wilmette, Ill., 1979-81; prin. architect, pres. Ross Barney & Jankowski, Inc., Chgo., 1981—, also bd. dirs. Studio prof. Ill. Inst. Tech., Chgo., 1993-94; asst. prof. U. Ill., Chgo., 1976-78. Prin. works include Cesar Chavez Elem. Sch., Chgo., Glendale Heights (Ill.) Post Office, Little Village Acad. Pub. Sch., Fed. Campus, Oklahoma City. Plan commr. Village of Wilmette, 1986 88, mem. Econ. Devel. Commn., 1988-90, chmn. Appearance Rev. Commn., 1990-2000; trustee Children's Home and Aid Soc. Ill., Chgo., 1986—; mem. adv. bd. Small Bus. Ctr. for Women, Chgo., 1985—. Recipient Fed. Design Achievement award, 1992, Firm award AIA Chgo., 1995; Francis J. Plym travelling fellow, 1983. Fellow AIA (bd. dirs. Chgo. chpt. 1978-80, v.p. 1981-82, Disting. Svc. award Chgo. chpt. 1978, Ill. Coun. 1978, Honor award 1991, 94, 99, 2002); mem. Nat. Coun. Archtl. Registration Bds. (cert.), Chgo. Women in Architecture (founding pres. 1978-79), Chgo. Network, Cliff Dwellers Club (bd. dirs. 1995). Home: 601 Linden Ave Wilmette IL 60091-2819 Office: Ross Barney & Jankowski Inc 10 Hubbard St Chicago IL 60610 E-mail: crossbarney@rbjarchitects.com.

BARNEY, CHARLES RICHARD, retired transportation executive; b. Battle Creek, Mich., June 7, 1935; s. Charles Ross and Helena Ruth (Croose) Barney; m. Grace Leone Nightingale, Aug. 16, 1958; children: Richard Nolan, Patricia Lynn. BA, Mich. State U., 1957; MBA, Wayne State U., 1961. Fin. analyst Ford Motor Co., Dearborn, Mich., 1958—65; gen. mgr. RentCo divsn. Fruehauf Corp., Detroit, 1965—72; pres. Evans Trailer Leasing, Des Plaines, Ill., 1973—77; v.p., gen. mgr. U.S. Rlwy. Equipment Co., Des Plaines, 1972—77; pres. Evans Railcar divsn. Evans Trans. Co., 1978—84; pres. W.H. Miner divsn. Miner Enterprises, Geneva, Ill., 1985—2000; ret., 2000. Mem. exec. com.

Rlwy. Progress Inst., 1984—2000, chmn., 1990—. Served to 1st lt. inf. U.S. Army, 1958. Mem.: Ry. Supply Assn. (bd. dirs. 1977—80), Wildcat Run Country Club (bd. dirs. 2003—). Congregationalist. Home: 20411 Wildcat Run Dr Estero FL 33928-2014

BARNEY, CHRISTINE J. artist; b. Bath, NY, Sept. 9, 1952; d. Willis H. and Elsa P. (Heney) Barney. BA, Goddard Coll., 1975; MA, NYU, 1988. Proprietor, designer, craftsperson Laurel Mountain Glass, Bosswell, Pa., 1975-83; tchg./tech. asst. Alfred (N.Y.) U., 1983-85; freelance designer Seguso Arte Vetro, Murano, Venice, Italy, 1985-87. Artist-in-residence Golden Glass Studio and Sch., Cin., 1991—92; guest artist Artpark, Lewiston, NY, 1992, Lewiston, 94; vis. artist Ohio State U., 1992, Tyler Sch. Art, Phila., 1993; lectr. in field. One-woman shows include Kavesh Gallery, Sun Valley, Kethun, Idaho, 1991, Christy/Taylor Gallery, Boca Raton, Fla., 1990—92, Vespermann Gallery, Atlanta, 1994, Portia Gallery, Chgo., 1997, 1997, Glass Gallery, Bethesda, Md., 2000, Art Elements Gallery, Milw., 2001, exhibited in group shows at Traver-Sutton Gallery, Seattle, 1982, So. Alleghenies Mus. Art, Loretto, Pa., 1983, Querini Stampaglia Gallery, Venice, 1984, U. di Architettura de Venezia, 1985, 80 Washington Sq. East Galleries, N.Y.C., 1988, Spaso Ho., Am. Embassy, Moscow, 1988—89, Grohe Gallery, Boston, 1989, 1995, Newark Mus., 1989, Sotheby's, N.Y.C., 1990, N.J. Ctr. Visual Arts, 1990, Morris Mus., Morristown, N.J., 1991, 1997, Mus. Am. Glass, Millville, N.J., 1993, Gallery at Wheaton Village, Millville, 1994, S. Shore Art Ctr., Cohasset, Mass., 1996, Holsten Gallery, Stockbridge, Mass., 1999—2001, Morgan Glass Gallery, Pitts., 2001, Yates County Arts Ctr., NY, 2002, Oxford Gallery, Rochester, 2002, Eleven Eleven Sculpture Space, Washington, 2003, Represented in permanent collections Corning Mus. Glass, Mus. Am. Glass, Millville, Tropicana Products, Inc., Bradenton, Fla., Centeon Pharm., King of Prussia, Pa.; contbr. articles to profl. jours. Creator Arts in Achievement awards Middlesex County Cultural and Heritage Commn., 1990—94; creator Artpark award, 1993. Recipient Carnegie Inst. prize, 1981; Creative Glass Ctr. Am. fellow, 1988, 1996, N.J. State Coun. Arts fellow, 1989—90. Avocation: dancing. Home: 432 Monmouth St Jersey City NJ 07302-2326

BARNEY, DONNA NADYNE, writer; d. Sadie Barney. MS in Agronomy, Iowa State U., 2003. Mem. adv. bd. Jocelyn Project, Chgo., 2001—; cons. Houghton-Mifflin, Itasca, Ill., 2000—02. Author: The Carver's Gift. Bacterial Rsch. grantee, NIH, 1995, Ecol. Devel. grantee, Ill. Natural Resource, 1999, Ill. Dept. Natural Resources, 1998—2000. Achievements include invention of electronic voting machine and software. Avocations: gardening, reading, biking, camping, watching sports.

BARNEY, JOHN CHARLES, lawyer; b. Nov. 18, 1939; s. Harold Lamont and Sara Eleanor (Johnston) B.; m. Joyce Marie Ebbinge; children: John C., Karen E., William L. BA, Wesleyan U., 1961; LLB, Columbia U., 1964. Bar: N.Y. 1964, U.S. Dist. Ct. (so. and ea. dists.) N.Y. 1966, U.S. Dist. Ct. (no. and we. dists) N.Y. 1977, U.S. Ct. Appeals (2d cir.) 1973, U.S. Supreme Ct. 1979. Assoc. Donovan, Leisure, Newton and Irvine, N.Y.C., 1964-66; staff atty. N.Y. State Law Revision Commn., Ithaca, 1966-68; ptnr. Barney, Grossman, Dubow & Marcus, Ithaca, 1968—. Asst. dist. atty. Tompkins County, N.Y., 1968-70; mem. N.Y. State Com. on Profl. Standards, 3d Jud. Dept., 1984-90, chmn. 1989-90. Chmn. Bd. Zoning Appeals, Lansing, N.Y., 1975-92; mem. Bd. Edn., Lansing, 1981-96, v.p., 1983-89, pres., 1989-96; bd. edn. Tompkins-Seneca-Tioga Bd. Coop. Ednl. Svcs., 1997, v.p., 2000—; bd. dirs. Challenge Industries (sheltered workshop), Ithaca, 1970-80. Mem. Tompkins County Bar Assn. (pres. 1983-84), N.Y. State Bar Assn. Republican. Unitarian Universalist. Home: 12 Stormy View Rd Ithaca NY 14850-9774 Office: Barney Grossman Dubow & Marcus 119 E Seneca St Ithaca NY 14850-4352

BARNEY, KLINE PORTER, JR., engineering company executive, consultant; b. Dec. 16, 1934; s. Kline Porter and Doris (Nielsen) B.; m. Cheryl Kathleen Taylor, June 14, 1957; children: Peter, Suzanne, Cathleen, Patrick, Andrew. BS, U. Utah, 1957; MPA, San Diego State U., 1971. Registered profl. engr., 7 states. Asst. engr. Fallbrook (Calif.) Pub. Utility Dist., 1960-63; pres. Engring. Sci., Inc., Arcadia, Calif., 1963-85, Parsons Mcpl. Svcs., Inc., Pasadena, Calif., 1985-89; sr. v.p. Parsons Engring. Sci., Inc., Pasadena, 1989-97; cons., 1997—; owner Kline Barney Engrs., 1999—. Presenter on field of privatization, 1983—; environ. cons. Contbr. articles to profl. jours. Mem. exec. bd. San Gabriel coun. Boy Scouts Am., 1981-96. Capt. USMC, 1957-60. Mem. ASCE, Am. Acad. Environ. Engrs. (diplomate), Am. Waterworks Assn., Water Environ. Fedn., Tau Beta Pi, Chi Epsilon, Phi Eta Sigma. Republican. Mem. Lds Ch. Avocations: hiking, astronomy. Home: 800 Juniperpoint Dr Salt Lake City UT 84103-3331 E-mail: kline.barney@usa.net.

BARNEY, THOMAS MCNAMEE, lawyer; b. Indpls., Mar. 14, 1938; s. John R. and Helen (Adams) B.; m. Marjorie Joan Eckhert, Sept. 9, 1961; children: Lynn M., Thomas M. Jr., Katherine J. BA, Cornell U., 1960; JD, Ind. U., 1966; LLM in Taxation, NYU, 1967. Bar: Ind. 1966, N.Y. 1967, Fla. 1977. Assoc. Barney & Hughes, Indpls., 1966-67, Dewey, Ballantine, Bushby, Palmer & Wood, N.Y.C., 1967-69, Phillips, Lytle, Hitchcock, Blaine & Huber, Buffalo, 1969-74, ptnr., 1975—99, of counsel, 2000—. Lectr. in taxation SUNY, Buffalo, 1969-82, mem. adv. bd. grad. tax. cert. program, 1981-2000. Author: Major Changes in Estate Tax, 1981. Sec. Upstate N.Y. Synod. Evang. Luth. Ch. Am., Syracuse, 1987-96; bd. dirs. Luth. Theol. Sem., Phila., 1988-91, Niagara Luth. Home Found., 1988—. Lt. (j.g.) USN, 1960-63. Mem. Erie County Bar Assn. (chmn. tax com. 1981-84), Fla. Bar Assn., Ind. Bar Assn., Am. Coll. Trust and Estate Counsel. Office: Phillips Lytle Hitchcock Blaine & Huber 3400 Marine Midland Ctr Buffalo NY 14203-2887

BARNHARDT, ZEB ELONZO, JR., lawyer; b. Winston-Salem, N.C., Dec. 28, 1941; s. Zeb Elonzo and Katie Sue (Taylor) B.; m. Pam Hall; children: Daniel Black, Kathleen Martin. AB, Duke U., 1964; JD, Vanderbilt U., 1969. Bar: N.C. 1969; cert. mediator, N.C.. Assoc. Womble Carlyle Sandridge & Rice, PLLC, Winston-Salem, 1969-75, mem., 1975-97, of counsel, 1997-98; owner, mgr., cons. Barnhardt & Assocs., Inc., Leland, NC, 1998—; pvt. practice law, Leland, 1998—. Bd. dirs. BarCARES of N.C., Inc., 1999—. Alumni admissions adv. com. Duke U., 1970-72; bd. dirs. Industries for Blind, Winston-Salem, 1973-85, vice chmn., 1983-84, chmn., 1985; bd. dirs. Goodwill Industries, Winston-Salem, 1973-80,bd. dirs.; BarCARES of N.C., Inc., 1999—; bd. dirs. The Little Theatre, Winston-Salem, 1979-85, asst. treas., 1980, treas., 1981-82, v.p., 1983-84, pres., 1984-85; adv. bd. Salvation Army, Winston-Salem, 1973-85, chmn., 1979-80; bd. dirs. Leadership Winston-Salem, 1984-92, v.p. adminstrn., 1988-89, pres. 1989-90; com. mem. Winston-Salem Found., 1975-84, vice chmn., 1978-80, chmn., 1983-84; trustee High Point U., 1984-96; chmn. Second Journey Inc., 2002—. With USN, 1964—66. Recipient Disting. Service award as Young Man of Yr. Winston-Salem Jaycees, 1974; Disting. Alumni award Duke U., 1979 Mem. ABA (fed. regulation securities laws com., law firms com., com. on law and acctg., bus. law sect.), ABA Comm. on Lawyer Assistance Programs (2002-), N.C. Bar Assn. (chmn. securities regulation com. 1985-87, vice chmn. bus. law sect. 1987-89, chmn. bus. law sect. 1989-91, bd. govs. 1991-94, chmn. membership recruitment and retention com. 1997-2000, chair lawyer effectiveness and quality of life com. 2001—), Winston-Salem Jaycees (life, pres. 1973-74), N.C. Jaycees (regional dir. 1974-75, legal counsel 1975-77), Greater Winston-Salem C. of C. (bd. dirs. 1973-74), Rotary. Democrat. Methodist. Office: Barnhardt & Assocs Inc 1158 Willow Pond Ln Leland NC 28451 E-mail: zbarnhardt@ec.rr.com.

BARNHART, CHARLES ELMER, animal sciences educator; b. Windsor, Ill., Jan. 25, 1923; s. Elmer and Irma (Smysor) B.; m. Norma McCarty, Dec. 28, 1946 (dec. Dec. 25, 1970); children: John D., Charles E., Norman R.; m. Jean M. Hutton, Jan. 12, 1973; stepchildren: Mark, David, Bonnie, Beth Hutton. BS in Agr., Purdue U., 1945; MS, Ia. State U., 1948, PhD, 1954. Mem. faculty U. Ky., Lexington, from 1948, assoc. prof. animal sci., 1955-57, prof., 1957-88, prof. emeritus, 1988—, dean, dir. exptl. sta. and coop. extension service, 1969-88, dean emeritus, 1988—. Pres. So. Assn. Agrl. Scientist, 1982-83 Patentee in field. Bd. dirs. Ky. Bd. Agr., 1966-88, Ky. State Fair and Expn. Ctr., 1969-88, Ky. Tobacco Rsch. Bd., Farm Credit Svcs. Mid Am., 1988-93, Ky. Farm Bur., 1969-76; mem. Gov.'s Coun. on Agrl., 1971-80. Named Man of Yr. in Ky. Agr. Progressive Farmer, 1962, Man of Yr. for Ky. Agr. Ky. Agrl. Communicators, 1979; elected to Saddle and Sirloin Portrait Gallery, 1987. Mem. Am. Soc. Animal Sci., Ky. Hist. Soc., Farmhouse Fraternity, Masons (32 deg.), Shriners, Epsilon Sigma Phi, Gamma Sigma Delta., Omicron Delta Kappa, Sigma Xi. Methodist. Home: 1017 Turkey Foot Rd Lexington KY 40502-2712 Address: 5013 Southern Pine Cir Venice FL 34293-4245

BARNHART, GENE, lawyer; b. Pineville, W.Va., Dec. 22, 1928; s. Forrest H. and Margaret (Harshman) B.; m. Shirley L. Dunn, Jan. 28, 1952; children: Sheryl Lynne (Mrs. John Dickey), Deborah Lee (Mrs. Kim Orians), Taffie Elise (Mrs. Tony Knight), Pamela Carole (Mrs. Michael Dean), Margaret Melanie (Mrs. Thomas Atkinson). Student, W.Va. U., 1946-48, Coll. Steubenville, 1949-50; JD, U. Cin., 1953. Bar: Ohio 1953. Counsel, clothing br. Armed Svcs. Procurement Agy., Washington and Phila., 1953-55; assoc. Black, McCuskey, Souers & Arbaugh, L.P.A., Canton, Ohio, 1955-60, ptnr., 1961-84, pres., 1984-86, vice chmn., 1986-88, chmn., 1988-98, of counsel, 1999—. Lectr. Ohio Legal Center Inst., Ohio Bar Assn., Am. Inst. Banking. Mem. Jackson Local Bd. Edn., 1966-74, pres., 1970; mem. Jackson Twp. Bd. Zoning Appeals, 1963-94, chmn., 1978-94; vice chmn. Jackson Zoning Ordinance Revision Com.; past pres. Coun. of Chs. of Ctrl. Stark County, Family Counseling Svcs. of Ctrl. Stark County; mem. Stark County Bd. Health, 1985-93; com. chmn. Congressional Action Com., Greater Canton Chamber; past pres., trustee Canton Preservation Soc.; deacon Grace Bible Ch. With USNR, 1948-49. Recipient Disting. Svc. award Jackson Twp. Jaycees, 1981, Cmty. award Jackson-Belden C. of C., 1982. Mem. Ohio State Bar Assn. (comml. law com., com. legal specialization), Stark County (grievance, disputed fee, meml., voluntary pro bono coms.), Order of Coif, Phi Alpha Delta. Home and Office: 2805 Coventry Ln NW Canton OH 44708-1321

BARNHART, JO ANNE B. federal agency administrator; b. Memphis, Aug. 26, 1950; d. Nelson Alexander and Betty Jane (Fitzpatrick) Bryant; m. David Lee Ross, Feb. 14, 1976 (div. June 1983); m. David Ray Barnhart, May 24, 1986. Student, U. Tenn., 1968—70; BA, U. Del., 1975. Space and time buyer DeMartin-Marona & Assocs., Wilmington, Del., 1970—73; adminstrv. asst. Mental Health Assn., Wilmington, 1973—75; dir. SERVE nutrition program Wilmington Sr. Ctr., 1975—77; legis. asst. to Sen. William V. Roth, Jr., Washington, 1977—81; dep. assoc. commr. Office Family Assistance, HHS, Washington, 1981—83, assoc. commr., 1983—86; rep. staff dir. U.S. Senate Govt. Affairs Com., 1987—90; asst. sec. family support HHS, Washington, 1990—91, asst. sec. for children and families, 1991—92; staff U.S. Sen. William V. Roth, 1993—; comnr. Social Security Admin., Baltimore, Md., 2001—. Mem. adv. bd. on welfare indicators U.S. Dept. HHS, 1996—. Campaign mgr. U. S. Sen. William V. Roth, 1988, 1994; polit. dir. Nat. Rep. Senatorial Com., 1995—97, polit. and pub. policy cons., 1997—2001; mem. Social Security adv. bd., 1997—2001; commr. Social Security, 2001—. Republican. Methodist. Office: Social Security Admin Office of Commr Altmeyer Bldg 6401 Security Blvd Baltimore MD 21235-6401 Office Fax: 410-966-1463.

BARNHART, MARY C. health facility administrator; b. Milw., Wis., Mar. 7, 1951; d. Zenon and Olga Soblewski; m. Clayton F. Barnhart, Feb. 22, 1997; children: Clayton D., Lucille. BA, U. of Wis. - Milw., 1983—2002. Certified IRB Mgr. Nat. Assn. of IRB Managers, 2001, Certified IRB Profl. Pub. Responsibility in Medicine, 2002. Sec. Milw. County Children's Ct., 1986—96; mgr., irb programs Oakwood Healthcare Sys., Dearborn, Mich., 1996—. Contbr. newsletter articles; editor: (jour.) Oakwood Healthcare Rsch. Quar., (newsletter) Ch. Newsletter, author short stories, poetry. Exec. bd. mem. Allen Pk. Bapt. Ch., Mich., 1996—2001; assoc. program dir. Nat. Assn. of IRB Manager's, Atlanta, 2001—03. Baptist. Avocations: reading, poetry, music, travel, graphic design. Home: 5137 Jackson Rd Trenton MI 48183 Office: Oakwood Healthcare Sys 18101 Oakwood Blvd Dearborn MI 48123 Office Fax: 313-436-2783. Personal E-mail: barnharm@wideopenwest.com. E-mail: barnharm@oakwood.org.

BARNHILL, CHARLES JOSEPH, JR., lawyer; b. Indpls., May 22, 1943; s. Charles J. and Phyllis (Landis) Barnhill; m. Elizabeth Louise Hayek, Aug. 14, 1971; children: Eric Charles, Colin Landis. BS in Econs., U. Pa., 1965; JD, U. Mich., 1968. Bar: Ill. 1968, U.S. Dist. Ct. (no. dist.) Ill. 1968, U.S. Ct. Appeals (7th cir.) 1969, U.S. Supreme Ct. 1972. Assoc. Kirkland & Ellis, Chgo., 1968; Reginald Heber Smith fellow Chgo. Legal Aid, 1968-69; assoc. Katz & Friedman, Chgo., 1969-72; ptnr. Davis, Miner, Barnhill & Galland, P.C. (now Miner, Barnhill & Galland), Madison, Wis., 1972—. Spl. master Fed. Dist. Ct. (no. dist.) Ill. Asst. editor: Mich. Law Rev., 1968. Chmn. Wis. Ctr. Tobacco Rsch. and Intervention, 1996; bd. dirs. Combined Health Appeal, Legal Assistance Found., Chgo., 1972—74, Old Town Triangle Assn., Chgo., 1972—75. Fellow: Am. Coll. Trial Lawers; mem.: Order of Coif, Barristers Soc., Chgo. Coun. Lawyers (bd. dirs. 1974—76), ABA (chmn. employment litig. litig. section 1975—78). Office: Miner Barnhill & Galland 44 E Mifflin St Ste 803 Madison WI 53703-2800

BARNHILL, DAVID STAN, lawyer; b. Washington, N.C., May 10, 1949; s. Arthur David and Ida Bea (Cox) B.; m. Katherine C. Felger, July 26, 1975; children: Hannah Katherine, Mary Rachel. BS, Va. Poly. Inst., 1971, MS, 1973; doctoral studies, U. Va., 1976-79; JD magna cum laude, Washington and Lee U., 1983. Bar: Va. 1983, U.S. Ct. Appeals (4th cir.) 1983, U.S. Supreme Ct. 1990, Federal Ct. Claims 1994. Asst. prof. social sci. Va. Intermont Coll., Bristol, Va., 1973-76; soc. sci. researcher U. Va., Charlottesville, Va., 1979-80; assoc. Woods, Rogers & Hazlegrove, Roanoke, Va., 1983-88, ptnr., 1989—. Contbr. articles to profl. jours.; lead articles editor Washington & Lee Law Rev., 1982-83. Bd. dirs. Total Action Against Poverty, Roanoke, 1987-90, DePaul Children's Svcs., Roanoke, 1985-95, Legal Aid Roanoke Valley, 1990-92. Sgt. USNG, 1972-78. Named to Legal Elite Litigation, Va. Bus. Mag., 2000, Legal Elite Constrn. Law, 2002. Mem.: ABA (forum on constrn. industry, civil litigation sect.), Va. Assoc. Gen. Contractors (legal affairs and contract documents coms. 1992—), Roanoke Bar Assn. (bd. dirs. 1992—94), Va. Bar Assn. (civil litigation coun. 1994—99, constrn. law coun.), Va. State Bar (chmn. 6th dist. ethics com. 1990—91, bd. govs. constrn. law sect. 1991—99, state bar coun. 1995—2001, state bar disciplinary bd. 1995—2001, vice chair bench-bar and media rels. com. 1996—2000), Va. Tech. Alumni Assn., Order of the Coif. Democrat. Baptist. Avocations: middle distance running, writing. Home: 5145 Falcon Ridge Rd Roanoke VA 24014-5720 Office: Woods Rogers & Hazlegrove 10 S Jefferson St Ste 1400 Roanoke VA 24011-1319 E-mail: barnhill@woodsrogers.com.

BARNHILL, GREGORY HURD, investment banker; b. Balt., Feb. 20, 1953; s. Robert Bell and Margaret Katherine (Hurd) B. Student, Inst. d'Etudes Européennes, 1974, Banque Nat. de Paris, 1974; BA in Econs., Brown U., 1975; postgrad., Inst. Fin., N.Y.C., 1975. Lic. N.Y. Stock Exch./NASD series 7, 9, 10, 63. Internat. investment banking mng. dir. Deutsche Bank Securities Inc., Investment Bankers, Balt., 1975—2003; ptnr. Brown Adv. Securities, LLC, Balt., 2003—, also bd. dirs. Bd. dirs. Agora Press, BTAB-Cook Overseas Ltd., BTAB-Stark Ltd. Partnership/AB-Stark Overseas Ltd., Captel-Nat. Cap. Telesvcs., L.L.C., View Tech., NASA/Goddard Space Flight Ctr. Balt. Incubator, Innovative Med. Svc.; chmn. bd. Ocean Race Chesapeake. Mem. adv. bd. Inst. d'Etudes Européenes; affiliate Balt. Mus. Art, Walters Art Gallery; chmn. fundraising com. Balt. Arts Festival, 1980-84; bd. dirs. Palm Beach Maritime Mus., 1990—, Balt. Heritage Inc., 1981-83, Md. Ballet, 1982-83, Nat. Taxpayers Union Found., 1984—, The Netherlands-Am. Amity Trust, Inc., 1993—, Balt. Columbus 500, 1987—; bd. dirs. Md. Art Place, 1982-90, pres. 1982-86, pres. bd. trustees, 1985-86; co-chmn. Businesspeople for Mayor Schaefer's Re-election, 1982-83; mem. fin. com. Congresswoman Helen Delich Bentley; mem. Balt. Operation Sail (chmn. fin. com., bd. dirs. 1987—, pres. 1988-93), hon. mem. Christopher Columbus Quincentennary Commn., 1989—; mem. Nat. Rep. Fin. Com., 1991—; vice chmn. bd. dirs. Greater Balt. Med. Ctr., 1992—; trustee Md. Internat. Ctr. Md., 1993—; mem. bd. govs. Faberge Arts Found., 1992—; mem. 2000 com. Walters Art Gallery, 1978—; nat. vice-chmn. The Pres.'s Dinner, 1989—; mem. mayor's adv. com. internat. affairs, 1988—; mem. gov's bus. com. for Md.-St. Petersburg, 1993—; trustee St. Paul's Sch., 2000—, Alexander Brown Charitable Found., 2002—; chmn. Found. for Govt. House, 2003—. Mem. Bond Club Md., Balt. Hist. Soc. (trustee), Md. Hist. Soc. (trustee 1992—, co-chmn. MHS 150 1993—), Md. Soc. Preservation of Antiquities (dir. 1981-83), Mcpl. Arts Soc. (trustee 1985—, dir. 1981), Md. Acad. Scis. (bd. dirs), Brown U. Club of Md. (pres. 1976-81), McDonogh Sch. Alumni Assn. (dir. 1976—), Nature Conservancy (bd. dirs. 1987—), SAR, Soc. Colonial Wars, Maryland Club (bd. govs., treas. exec. com, bd. dirs. 1995), Volvo Ocean Race Chesapeake (formerly Whitbread Ocean Race Chesapeake) (pres. 1998—), Newport Reading Room Club, Greenspring Valley Hunt Club, N.Y. Yacht Club, Ocean Reef Club, Rehoboth Country Club, Henlopen Acres Beach Club, Sigma Chi. Republican. Home: 10801 Stevenson Rd Stevenson MD 21153-0679 Office: Brown Adv Securities LLC 901 S Bond St 4th Fl Baltimore MD 21231

BARNHILL, HENRY GRADY, JR., lawyer; b. Buena Vista, Ga., Aug. 24, 1930; s. Henry Grady and Imogene (Hogg) B.; m. Sarah Carolyn Haire, Oct. 29, 1953; children: Grady Michael, Stephen Drew, Kevin Scott, Carol Kelly. JD, Wake Forest U., Winston-Salem, N.C., 1958. Bar: N.C. 1958, U.S. Dist. Ct. (ea., mid. and we. dists.) N.C. 1958, U.S. Ct. Appeals (4th cir.) 1961, U.S. Supreme Ct. 1983, U.S. Ct. Appeals (fed. cir.) 1985. Assoc. Womble Carlyle Sandridge & Rice, Winston-Salem, 1958-61, ptnr., 1961—. Bd. visitors Sch. of Law Wake Forest U. Lt. USAF, 1951-55. Fellow Am. Coll. Trial Lawyers (state chmn. 1986-88); mem. Am. Bd. Trial Advs., N.C. Assn. Def. Attys., N.C. Bar Assn. (litigation sect.), 4th Cir. Jud. Conf., Forsyth County Bar (pres. 1979-80), Inns of Ct. (Chief Justice Joseph Branch). Democrat. Presbyterian. Avocation: tennis. Home: 3121 Robinhood Rd Winston Salem NC 27106-5610 Office: Womble Carlyle Sandridge & Rice PLLC PO Drawer 84 One W 4th St Winston Salem NC 27102 E-mail: gbarnhill@wcsr.com.

BARNHILL, HOWARD EUGENE, insurance company executive; b. Nankin, Ohio, Oct. 2, 1923; s. William Wallace and Juliaette (Garver) B.; m. Evelyn Lucille Poorman, Aug. 24, 1944; children: Eric Stephen, Phillip William. BA, Ashland (Ohio) Coll., 1946; grad., Advanced Mgmt. Program, Harvard U., 1967. C.L.U. With Mut. Ins. Co. N.Y., 1946-72, sr. v.p., 1969-72; pres., chief exec. officer N.Am. Life & Casualty Co., Mpls., 1972-79, chmn. bd., pres., chief exec. officer, 1979-85, chmn. bd., chief exec. officer, 1985-88, ret., 1989; owner Barnhill & Assocs., Cons., 1989—. Former bd.. dirs. Nat. City Bank, Mpls., Preferred Life Ins. Co. of N.Y. Former bd. dirs. North Am. Life & Casualty Allianz of Am. Served to lt. USNR, 1943-46, 50-52. Mem. Life Ins. Mktg. Research Assn. (past chmn.), Greater Mpls. Area C. of C. (past chmn.), Comty. Ch. Club, Lafayette Club. Home: 18775 11th Ave N Minneapolis MN 55447-2508

BARNHILL, JAMES ORRIS, theater educator; b. Sumner, Miss., May 23, 1922; s. James Arthur and Louise (Sullivan) B. BA, Yale U., 1947, MFA, 1954; MA, NYU, 1949; MA (hon.), Brown U. Instr. in English Brown U., Providence, 1954-56, from asst. prof. to assoc. prof., 1956-70, prof., 1970-78, prof. in theater arts, 1978-86, prof. emeritus, 1986—. Vis. prof. English R.I. Sch. Design, Providence, 1987-88, 93-94, Tougaloo (Miss.) Coll., 1989; actor Trinity Square Repertory Theatre, Providence, 1971-73. Lt. (j.g.) USNR, 1943-46, PTO. Fulbright prof. English M.S. U. Baroda, India, 1984-85, St. Xavier Coll., Ahmedabad, India, 1988-89, Am. Lit. Univ. Punjab, Pakistan, 1994-96. Mem. Univ. Club, Players Club. Baptist. Avocations: hobbies, calligraphy, sculpture. Home: 81 Transit St Providence RI 02906-1022 Office: Brown U Dept Theatre Arts PO Box 1897 Providence RI 02912-1897

BARNHOLDT, TERRY JOSEPH, chemical, industrial, and general engineer; b. Wiota, Iowa, Sept. 22, 1921; s. Claus Edward and Leona (Consaul) B.; m. Martha Francis Cannon, 1946 (dec. 1975); children: Martha Jane, Terry (Ted) Joseph Jr. BChE, Clarkson Coll. Tech., 1943; postgrad. degree in chem. engring. and adminstrn. engring., Cornell U., 1947; MBA (hon.), U. N.C., Charlotte, 1967; JD, Atlanta Law Sch., 1981. Project, process engr. Std. Oil Co., Richmond, Calif., 1947-49; Perth Amboy, N.J., 1949-51; br. mgr. The Clorox Co., Charlotte, N.C., 1949-51; pres., gen. mgr. Allied Prodrs. Supply Co., Charlotte, 1959-66; mgr. mfg. and engring. BASF Wyandotte, Charlotte, 1966-68; sales mgr. Detrex Chem. Industries, Charlotte, 1969-70; chem. mfg. sales rep. Valchem Chem. United Mchts., Charlotte, 1970-74; sales, mfg. rep. Star Chemicals Co., Macon, Ga., 1976-78; mgr. shipping Pepsi-Cola Beverage Corp., Atlanta, 1979; project engr. Metro Atlanta Rapid Transit Authority, 1981-84; comml. real estate specialist Gen. Svc. Adminstrn., Atlanta, 1984-85; gen., indsl. engr. Def. Logistics Agy., Manassas, Alexandria and Ft. Belvoir, Va., 1986—. 1st lt. U.S. Army, 1943-46. Mem. NSPE, AIChE, ATLA, Am. Chem. Soc., Assn. Energy Engrs., Def. Acquisition Corps, Alpha Chi Sigma. Republican. Presbyterian. Avocations: running, handball, free weights, golf. Home: 12301 Strong Ct Fairfax VA 22033-2846 Office: Def Logistics Agy DLSC-BIS 8725 John J Kingman Rd Ste 2533 Fort Belvoir VA 22060-6217

BARNHOLT, BRANDON K. gas station/convenience store executive; COO, exec. v.p. mktg. Clark USA Inc. (now Clark Retail Group Inc.); CEO, pres. Clark Retail Group, Inc., Glen Ellyn, Ill., 1999—. Office: Clark Retail Group Inc 3003 Butterfield Rd Oak Brook IL 60523*

BARNHOLT, EDWARD W. computer company executive; b. N.Y.C., 1943; BEE, MEE, Stanford U. R&D engr., mktg. engr., product mgr. Hewlett-Packard, Palo Alto, Calif., 1966—73, product mktg. mgr. Stanford Pk. divsn., 1973—76, mktg. mgr. Santa Clara divsn., 1979—80, gen. mgr. divsn. microwave and commns. group, 1980—84, gen. mgr. electronic instruments group, 1984—88, v.p., 1988—90, gen. mgr. test and measurement orgn., 1990—93, sr. v.p., 1993—96, exec. v.p., 1996—99; pres., CEO Agilent, Palo Alto, Calif., 1999—, chmn., 2002—. Dir. KLA-Tencor Corp. Mem.: N.Y. Stock Exch. (listed co. adv. com.). Address: Agilent Technologies 3000 Hanover St Palo Alto CA 94304-1112*

BARNICK, HELEN, retired judicial clerk; b. Max, ND, Mar. 24, 1925; d. John K. and Stacy (Kankovsky) B. BS in Music cum laude, Minot State Coll., 1954; postgrad., Am. Conservatory of Music, Chgo., 1975-76. With Epton, Bohling & Druth, Chgo., 1968-69; sec. Wildman, Harrold, Allen & Dixon, Chgo., 1969-75; part-time assignments for temporary agy. Chgo., 1975-77; sec. Friedman & Koven, Chgo., 1977-78; with Lawrence, Lawrence, Kamin & Saunders, Chgo., 1978-81; sec. Hinshaw, Culbertson et al., Chgo., 1982; sec. to magistrate judge U.S. Dist. Ct. (we. dist.) Wis., Madison, 1985-91; dep. clk., case adminstr. U.S. Bankruptcy Ct. (we. dist.) Wis., Madison, 1992-94; ret., 1994. Chancel choir 1st Bapt. Ch., Mpls., Fourth Presbyn. Ch., Chgo., Covenant Presbyn. Ch., Madison; choir, dir. sr. high choir Moody Ch., Chgo.; dir. chancel choir 1st Bapt. Ch., Minot, ND; bd. dirs., sec.-treas. Peppertree at Tamarack Owners Assn., Inc., Wisconsin Dells, Wis.; mem. Festival Choir, Madison. Mem. Christian Bus. and Profl. Women (chmn.), Bus. and Profl. Women Assn., Participatory Learning and Tchg. Orgn., Madison Symphony Orch. League, Madison Civics Club, Sigma Sigma Sigma. Home: 7364 Old Sauk Rd Madison WI 53717-1213

BARNICLE, STEPHAN PATRICK, secondary school educator; b. Worcester, Mass., Jan. 23, 1948; s. John Francis and Catherine Mabel (Kilgore) B.; m. Mary Anne Petrovick, Aug. 23, 1969; children: Michael Edward, Patricia Ann, Daniel John, Kevin Patrick. MusB cum laude, U. Hartford, 1970, M of Music Edn., 1974, postgrad., 1987, 88. Tchr. music Farmington (Conn.) High Sch., 1970-74, Simsbury (Conn.) High Sch., 1974—. Singer-bass soloist Concora Conn. Choral, New Britain, 1974—; exec. dir. Simsbury Music and Arts Ctr., 1988-94; music dir., prin. condr. Visit Can. Internat. Polychoral Festivals, Montreal and Quebec City, 1994—; project chmn. HS music panel Preparing Tomorrow's Tchrs. to Use Tech., 2002—. Author: Teaching Examples: Ideas for Music Education, 1994, Music at the Middle Level, 1994, Teacher's Guide to Classical Music For Dummies, 1997; pub. choral compositions & arrangements; contbr. articles to profl. jours.; author of poetry. Goodwill amb. Simsbury-Wittmund (Germany) Sister Town Com., 1990, 98, 99; music dir. Sacred Heart Ch., Bloomfield, Conn., 1990—; mem. Simsbury Bd. Assessment Appeals, 1999—, Simsbury Dem. Town Com., 2000—, Simsbury Hist. Dist. Commn., 2000—. Recipient Excellence in H.S. Tchg. award U. Conn., 1995, Disney Channel and McDonald's Am. Tchrs. Awards honoree, 1996; named Winning Composer, Am. Choral Dirs. Assn. Choral Composition Contest, 1995; Travel grantee Ptnrs. of Ams., Washington, 1984. Mem. Music Edn. Technologists Assn. (past pres., co-founder, grantee 1995), Conn. Music Educators Assn. (chair music tech. com. 1993-95, chair music composition com. 2000, Music Tchr. of Yr. 1994-95), Music Educators Nat. Conf. (tchg. music adv. com. 2000-02), Assn. Ednl. Comms. and Tech. (H.S. music chmn. project 2002—). Democrat. Roman Catholic. Avocations: sports, family, travel, swimming, flying. Home: 91 E Weatogue St Simsbury CT 06070-2503 Office: Simsbury High Sch 34 Farms Village Rd Simsbury CT 06070-2399 E-mail: stephanB2@attbi.com.

BARNIDGE, JASON, biomedical researcher; b. Loring AFB, Maine, June 30, 1975; s. Leroy Barnidge, Jr. and Cassandra Louise Barnidge. BS in Biomedical Engring., La. Tech U., 1993—98; MS in Bioengineering, Pa. State U., 1998—2000; MBA, Fla. State U., 2000—01. Internship Rapid City Regional Hosp., SD, 1996—96, SW Rsch. Inst., San Antonio, 1997—97; rsch. asst. Pa. State U., 1998—2000; sci. and tech. analyst III, project mgr. Geo-Centers, Inc., Wash., DC, 2001—. Author: (jour. pub.) Requirement of arteriovenular pairing for increased capillary filtration during acute inflammation., Role of arteriovenular pairing in FMLP-induced capillary filtration. Mem.: Biomedical Engring. Soc., Congress of Grad. Students (grad. sch. rep. 2000—01), Fla. State U. Student Senate (grad. sch. rep. 2000—01), Fla. State U. Bus. Rev. (assoc.; founding mem., assoc. editor, fin. officer 2000—01), Kappa Sigma Frat. (life). Avocations: travel, tennis, running.

BARNIDGE, LEROY, JR., military officer; BSME, La. Tech. U., 1971; grad., Squadron Officer Sch., 1976; M in Logistics Mgmt., Air Force Inst. Tech., 1978; grad., Air Command and Staff Coll., 1983, Indsl. Coll. of Armed Forces, 1989; program for sr. ofcls. in nat. security, Harvard U., 1990; seminar on fgn. polit. & internat. rels., MIT, 1991. Commd. 2d lt. USAF, 1971, advanced through grades to brigadier gen., 1997; maintenance supr. 55th Orgnl. Maintenance Squadron Offutt AFB, Nebr., 1978-80, reconnaissance sys. officer Hdqs. Strategic Air Command, Offutt AFB, 1980-82; dir. acads. B-1B Combat Crew Tng. Squadron Dyess AFB, Tex., 1985-86; comdr. 338th Combat Crew Tng. Squadron, dep. comdr. 96th Combat Support Group, Dyess AFB, 1986-88; chief force design divsn. Joint Chiefs of Staff J-8, Washington, 1989-91; asst. dep. comdr. for maintenance 28th Bomb Wing, Ellsworth AFB, S.D., 1991-92; comdr. 28th Logistics Group Ellsworth AFB, 1992-93, comdr. 319th Ops. group, dep. comdr. for ops. 319th Bomb Group, Grand Forks AFB, N.D., 1993-94; comdr. Coll. Aerospace Doctrine, Rsch. and Edn. Air U., Maxwell AFB, Ala., 1994-95; comdr. 28th Bomb Wing, Ellsworth AFB, 1995-97; vice comdr. San Antonio Air Logistics Ctr., Kelly AFB, Tex., 1997-98; comdr. 509th Bomb Wing, Whiteman AFB, Mo., 1998-2000; dep. comdr. U.S. Ctrl. Command Air Forces; vice comdr. 9th Air Force, Air Combat Command. Decorated Def. Superior Svc. medal, Legion of Merit, D.F.C., Meritorious Svc. medal with 4 oak leaf clusters.

BARNOFF, ROBERT MARK, civil engineering educator; b. Punxsutawney, Pa., Aug. 28, 1926; s. Joseph A. and Ruth A. (Morris) B.; m. Norma Gugliemi; children: Joni, Janice, Mark, Joseph. BS, Pa. State U., 1951, MS, 1956; PhD, Carnegie Inst. Tech., 1966. Steel detailer Am. Bridge Co., 1951-52; constrn. engr. John Mohr & Sons, 1952-53; bridge designer Gannett Fleming Corddry & Capenter, 1953-55; from instr. to prof. civil engring. Pa. State U., University Park, 1955-79, prof., chmn. dept. civil engring., 1979-85. Vis. prof. Bucknell U. Contbr. articles to profl. jours. With USNR, 1944-46. Sci. Faculty fellow NSF, 1965-66. Mem. ASTM, ASCE, Am. Concrete Inst., Sigma Xi, Tau Beta Pi, Chi Epsilon. Achievements include patents on concrete testing device and bridge deck systems. Home and Office: 606 Nimitz Ave State College PA 16801-6415 E-mail: rmb1@psu.edu.

BARNOW, BURT S. economist; b. Chgo., Sept. 3, 1947; s. Samuel and Ann Y. Barnow; B.S., M.I.T., 1969; M.S. (Ford Found. fellow), U. Wis., Madison, 1972, Ph.D., 1973. Asst. prof. econs. U. Pitts., 1973-75; with Dept. Labor, 1975-84, dir. Office Research and Devel., Employment and Tng. Adminstrn., 1980-82, dir. Office Research and Evaluation, 1982-84; project mgr. ICF, Inc., 1984-87; v.p. Levin/ICF, Washington, 1988-92; prin. rsch. scientist Inst. Policy Studies Johns Hopkins U., Balt., 1992—, assoc. dir. for rsch., 2000—; referee NSF. Mem. Am. Econ. Assn., Indsl. Rels. Rsch. Assn. Author articles, reports in field. Home: 6232 30th St NW Washington DC 20015-1514 Office: Johns Hopkins U Inst Policy Studies Wyman Bldg Baltimore MD 21218 E-mail: barnow@jhu.edu.

BARNUM, BARBARA STEVENS, writer, retired nursing educator; b. Johnstown, Pa., Sept. 2, 1937; d. William C. and Freda Inzes (Claycomb) Burkett; m. H. James Barnum (dec.); children: Lauren, Elizabeth, Catherine, Anne (dec.), Shauna, Sallee, David. AA in Nursing, St. Petersburg Jr. Coll., 1958; BPh, Northwestern U., 1967; MA, DePaul U., 1971; PhD, U. Chgo., 1976. RN, Ill., N.Y. Dir. nursing svcs. Augustana Hosp. and Health Care Ctr., Chgo., 1970-71; dir. staff edn. U. Chgo. Hosps. and Clinics, 1971-73; prof. U. Ill., Chgo., 1973-79; dir. div. health svcs., sci. and edn. Columbia U. Tchrs. Coll., N.Y.C., 1979-87; editor Nursing & Health Care Nat. League for Nursing, N.Y.C., 1989-91; editor div. nursing Columbia-Presbyn. Med. Ctr., Columbia U., N.Y.C., 1991-95; prof. Sch. Nursing Columbia U., N.Y.C., 1995-98; ret., 1998. Chmn. bd. Barnum & Souza, N.Y.C., 1989-92; civilian cons. to surgeon gen. USAF, 1980-87. Author: Nursing Theory, Analysis, Application and Evaluation, 4th edit., 1994, Writing for Publication: A Primer for Nurses, 1995; author: (with K. Kerfoot) The Nurse as Executive, 4th edit., 1995; author: Spirituality and Nursing: From Traditional to New Age, 1996, Spirituality and Nursing: From Traditional to New Age, 2002, Teaching Nursing in the Era of Managed Care, 1999, The New Healers: Minds and Hands in Complementary Medicine, 2002, (fiction) The Haunting of Lisa Tilden, 1999; editor: Nursing Leadership Forum, 1994—98. Mem. governing bd. Nurses House, 1979-86, Nat. Health Coun., 1981-90, others. Fellow Am. Acad. Nursing (governing bd. 1982-84); mem. Sigma Theta Tau (Founders' award 1979). Home: 80 Park Ave Apt 15G New York NY 10016-2547

BARNUM, JOHN WALLACE, lawyer; b. N.Y.C., Aug. 25, 1928; s. William Wallace Atterbury and Frances (Long) Barnum; m. Nancy Russell Grinnell, Sept. 13, 1958; children: Alexander Stone, Sarah Kip, Cameron Long. BA, Yale U., 1949; LLB, Inst. Derecho Internat. Comparativo, Havana, Cuba, 1957. Bar: Conn. 1957, N.Y. 1958, D.C. 1977; on Brussels fgn. lawyer list, 1995. Adminstrn. asst. Cerro de Pasco Copper Corp., Lima, Peru, 1946; jr. asst. purser Grace Lines, 1946; analyst 1st Banking Corp., Tangier, Morocco, 1950; reg. rep. Bache & Co., London and Paris, 1951-52; assoc. Cravath, Swaine & Moore, N.Y.C., 1957-62, ptnr., 1963-71; gen. counsel U.S. Dept. Transp., Washington, 1971-73, undersec., 1973-74, dep. sec., 1974-77; resident fellow Am. Enterprise Inst. for Pub. Policy Rsch., Washington, 1977-78, vis. fellow, 1978-86; ptnr. White & Case, Washington, 1978-94, McGuireWoods, LLP, Brussels, 1995—; pres. McGuireWoods Internat. LLC, Brussels, 1999—; mng. ptnr. McGuire-Woods Kazahhstan LLP, Almaty, 1999—. U.S. del. Inter-Am. Comml. Arbitration Commn., 1969—71; del. NATO Com. for Challenges to Modern Soc., 1973—76; adv. mem. Coun. on Wage and Price Stability, 1974—77; mem. Coun. Adminstrv. Conf. U.S., 1973—77. Bd. editors Regulation: AEI Jour. on Govt. and Soc., 1977-86. Chmn. bd. Internat. Play Group, 1962-77; bd. dirs., mem. exec. com. N.Y C. Ctr. Music and Drama, 1969-75; trustee Washington Drama Soc. (Arena Stage), 1983-93; bd. overseers Corcoran Gallery of Art, Washington, 1994-2000; pres. U.S. Fedn. Friends Mus., 2002-. Mem.: Am. Arbitration Assn. (exec. com. 1968—72, bd. dirs. 1968—98), Nat. Def. Transp. Assn. (chmn.mil. airlift com. 1983—94, bd. dirs. 1988—94), Am. Bar Found., D.C. Bar Assn., N.Y. State Bar Assn. (exec. com., chmn. antitrust law sect. 1979—80), Internat. Bar Assn., N.Y. Yacht Club, Amateur Ski Club, Chevy Chase Club, Met. Club, Watersportvereniging Noord-Beveland, Cercle Royal Gaulois Artistique et Litteraire, Am. Club of Brussels (gov., exec. com.). Home: 182 Ave Franklin Roosevelt 1050 Brussels Belgium also: 2029 Connecticut Ave NW Washington DC 20008-6141 Office: McGuireWoods LLP 250 Ave Louise, Bte 64 1050 Brussels Belgium E-mail: jbarnum@mcguirewoods.com.

BARNUM, MEL BLOYCE, company executive; b. Peoria, Ill., Aug. 9, 1949; s. Bloyce William Barnum and Joan Patricia (Meece) Keen; m. Janet L. McCall, June 8, 1968 (div. Oct. 1980); 1 child, Brenda; m. Nan Martin, Jan. 1, 1982 (div. Dec. 1996); 1 child, Samantha; m. Ann M. Martz, 1997; children: Joseph, Morgan. Student, So. Ill. U., Edwardsville, 1967-70. Microsoft cert. systems engr.; MSF cert. instr. Computer operator ITT Blackburn, Overland, Mo., 1969-70, programmer, analyst, 1970-74, sr. programmer, analyst, 1974-76, systems and programming mgr., 1976-78, data processing mgr., 1978-80; project mgr. Central Hardware, Bridgeton, Mo., 1980-82; sr. systems analyst Maritz Inc., Fenton, Mo., 1982-84, mgr. PC svcs., 1984-87, office automation mgr., 1987-95; cons. Technology Source, Inc., 1995-97; Enterprise Messaging cons. Hewlett-Packard, 1997—. Pres. New Leaf Software, Belleville, Ill., 1982-83; treas. N.M. Barnum & Assocs. Ltd., Belleville, 1986-90; owner Bottomline Cons., Belleville, 1985—; instr. SIU Carbondale, 1991—, Jefferson Coll., 1994-96. Mem. bus. adv. coun. Goodwill Industries, 1980-88. Mem. St. Louis Lotus Notes Users Group (pres. 1993-94). Avocations: woodworking, model trains, motorcycling, electronics. Home: 72 Hillsborough Dr Collinsville IL 62234-1547 Office: Hewlett Packard Collinsville IL 62234 E-mail: cycleguy@bikerider.com.

BARNUM, WILLIAM DOUGLAS, retired communications company executive; b. Denton, Tex., July 28, 1946; s. Billie Douglas and Leticia Christina Barnum; m. Mary Ann Mook, Aug. 10, 1968. BSBA in Econs. with distinction, Georgetown U., 1967; MBA, Fairleigh Dickinson U., 1985. Acct. RCA Corp., Cherry Hill, N.J., 1967-68, Andros Island, Bahamas, 1968-70, budget and cost analyst Cherry Hill, 1970, adminstr. tel. sys., 1970-73; mgr. project adminstrn. white sands radar project RCA Svc. Co., Holloman AFB, N.Mex., 1973-74; coord. profit ctr. acctg. RCA Global Comms., N.Y.C., 1974-76, adminstr. globcom. sys., 1976-77, mgr. spl. project and accts. payable, 1978-79; mgr. fin. RCA Globcom Sys., Inc., N.Y.C., N.J., 1979-81; mgr. gateway ops. RCA Global Comms., Edison, N.J., 1982, dir. field support svcs., 1982-88; sr. mgr. network svcs. MCI Internat., Piscataway, N.J., 1988-90, sr. mgr. sys. support and adminstrn., 1990-92, sr. mgr. messaging and marine ops., 1992-93, sr. staff internat. alliances, 1994; owner, sr. cons. Lake Road Assocs. Consulting, Far Hills, N.J., 1994-99; ret., 1999. Author: Kroodley Made Knife Catalog, 1977. Mem. Am. Security Coun., 1981—92, Far Hills (N.J.) Bd. Health, 1993—99, vice-chmn., 1994—95, chmn., 1996—99; adviser Jr. Achievement, Cherry Hill, NJ, 1968—69, Cherry Hill Jaycees, 1973—74; mem. spl. commn. Far Hills Police Dept., 1993, 1998; sustaining mem. Rep. Nat. Com., 1984—2003; bd. dirs. United Cerebral Palsy Somerset/Morris County, 1989. Mem.: NRA (life), Woodcreek Country Club, Knifemakers Guild (hon.), Mensa, Am. Knife Throwers Alliance (hon.), Wildewood Country Club, Delta Mu Delta, Delta Phi Epsilon. Presbyterian. Home: PO Box 23329 Columbia SC 29224

BARNUM, WILLIAM MILO, architect; b. June 17, 1927; s. Phelps and Catharine (Davis) B.; m. Katharine Miller, Aug. 10, 1971; children: Anne Lyttleton, Catharine Hollerith, William Milo, Nathaniel Phelps, Caleb Townsend; 1 stepchild, Elizabeth Pierce. BA, Yale U., 1950; MArch, U. Pa., 1952. Archtl. asst. job capt. Eggers & Higgins, 1952-54; job capt. W. Stuart Thompson & Phelps Barnum, archs., 1954-58, jr. ptnr., 1958-60; sr. ptnr. Phelps Barnum & Son, N.Y.C., 1960-68; pres. William Milo Barnum Assocs., Inc., N.Y.C., 1968—. Cons. to judges com.; interior designer new U.S. Courthouse Ho., 500 Pearl St., N.Y.C., Scudder Stevens & Clark 5 Fls. Prin. works include Westminster Sch. Chapel, 1961, Westminster Sch. Acad. Ctr., 1964, Howmet Office Bldg., Greenwich, Mfrs. Hanover Bank, Bklyn., Pickwick Pla., Greenwich, R.T. Vanderbilt Corp. Hdqs., Norwalk, Conn., Union Trust Sq., Greenwich, Gen. Host. Corp. Hdqs., Stamford, Conn., Gateway Ctr., Greenwich, The Boatyard Condominium, City Island, N.Y., Gorham Island Office Bldg., Westport, Conn., N.Y. Offices Scudder Stevens and Clark, Mason Place Mixed Use Hist. Restoration, Greenwich, Shawmut Bank offices and Br. Landmark Sq. Bldg., Stamford, Shawmut br., New Canaan, St. Andrews by the Sea Episcopal Ch. Renovation and Reconstruction, Little Compton, R.I. Chmn. Archtl. Rev. Bd., Greenwich, Conn.; mem. selectmen's com. H.S. Property, Greenwich, 1964-68; bd. dirs. Cmty. Chest, Greenwich, 1964-68; mem. alumni coun. Phillips Acad., Andover, Mass., 1965-68; v.p. bd. trustees Putnam Indian Field Sch., vice-chmn.; bd. dirs. Episcopal Ch. at Yale; bd. dirs. Episcopal Ch. Bldg. Fund. With USNR, 1945-46, PTO. Mem. AIA (N.Y. chpt. office practices com.), Concrete Industry Bd. (bd. dir.), Met. Builders Assn. (liaison com.), Andover Alumni Assn. N.Y.C. (pres. 1964-65), Hist. Soc. Greenwich (v.p.), Soc. Colonial Wars, Yale Club (coun. 1958-79, pres. 1970-72) (N.Y.C.), Acoaxet Club, Providence Art Club, St. Andrews-By-The-Sea (sr. warden), Spindle Rock Club. Office: 32 Custom House St Providence RI 02903-2614 E-mail: WMBarnum@hotmail.com.

BARNWELL, FRANKLIN HERSHEL, zoology educator; b. Chattanooga, Oct. 4, 1937; s. Columbus Hershel and Esther Bernice (Ireland) B.; m. Adrienne Kay Knox, June 13, 1959; 1 child, Elizabeth Brooks. BA, Northwestern U., 1959, PhD, 1965. Instr. biol. sci. Northwestern U., Evanston, Ill., 1964, research assoc., 1965-67; asst. prof. U. Chgo., 1967-70; from asst. prof. to prof. zoology, ecology and behavioral biology U. Minn., Mpls., 1970—, head dept. ecology, evolution and behavior, 1986-93. Mem. adv. panel NASA, 1963-67, NSF, Washington, 1980; faculty Orgn. for Tropical Studies, San Jose, Costa Rica, 1966-85, bd. dirs.; Nat. Confs. on Underground Rsch., bd. dirs., treas., 1990-96; investigator rsch. R/V Alpha Helix, various locations, 1979, vis. scientist. Contbr. articles on zoology to profl. jours. NSF fellow, 1965; named Minn. Coll. Sci. Tchr. of Yr., Minn. Acad. Sci. and Minn. Sci. Tchrs. Assn., 1997, dist. tchg. prof. of ecolgoy, U. Minn., 1997. Fellow Linnean Soc. London, AAAS; mem. Soc. Intergrative and Comparative Biology, Internat. Soc. for Chronobiology, Assocs. Orgn. for Tropical Studies, Crustacean Soc. (founding and sustaining mem., bd. dirs., sec. 1991-98), Phi Beta Kappa, Sigma Xi. Office: U Minn Dept Ecology Evol & Behav 1987 Upper Buford Cir Saint Paul MN 55108-1051 E-mail: fhb@umn.edu.

BARNWELL, MADGE OWEN, volunteer; b. Milltown, Ala., Oct. 8, 1920; d. Edgar Eugene and Cenus Rosa (Denney) O.; m. George Price Barnwell, Dec. 31, 1953. Student, Samford U., Birmingham, Ala., 1938-40. Clk. War Dept., South Atlantic Divsn. C.E., World War II, adminstrv. asst., 1940-53. Contbr. articles to profl. jours. Dir. Painted Rock Arts Soc., Valley, Ala.; vol. hosp. aux. hon. life George Lanier Meml. Hosp., Valley; chmn. bicentennial com., cmty. appearance chmn. Mcpl. Planning Bd., West Point, Ga. Mem. Riverside Country Club (bd. dirs., house chmn.), Charter Garden Club (pres.), Highland Country Club (LaGrange, Ga.), Big Eddy Club (Columbus, Ga.), Garden Club Ga. (hon. life), Nat. Trust Historic Preservation, Tallapoosee Hist. Soc., Mid. Ga. Hist. Soc., Chattahoochee Hist. Soc., Troup County Hist. Soc. and Archives, Muscogee Geneal. Soc., Geneal. Soc. East Ala., DAR, Colonial Dames XVIIC, Daus. Am. Colonists, Nat. Soc. Magna Charta Dames, Colonial Order of Crown, Sovereign Colonial Soc. Ams. of Royal Descent, Soc. Descendants of Knights of Most Noble Order of Garter, Plantagenet Soc. Republican. Baptist. Avocations: gardening, flower arranging, bridge, family genealogy, history. Home: PO Box 407 124 Hillcrest Rd West Point GA 31833-5208

BAROFF, GEORGE STANLEY, psychologist, educator; b. Bronx, N.Y., Nov. 27, 1924; s. Irving and Ida (Herman) B.; m. Rose Kislin, June 15, 1952 (dec. May 1992); children: Marina Binet, Roy James. BS in Zoology, George Washington U., 1948, MA in Clin. Psychology, 1950; PhD in Clin. Psychology, NYU, 1955. Research psychologist dept. med. genetics N.Y. State Psychiat. Inst., 1952-60; chief clin. psychologist Vineland (N.J.) Tng. Sch., 1960-63; asso. prof. psychology U. N.C., Chapel Hill, 1963-67, prof., 1967-2000, prof. emeritus, 2000—, dir. devel. disabilities tng. inst., 1964-2000. Forensic psychologist with criminal defendants who may be mentally retarded, 1987—. Author: Mental Retardation: Nature, Cause and Management, 1974, 3d edit., 1999, Developmental Disabilities: Psychosocial Aspects, 1991; contbr. articles to profl. jours. Served with U.S. Army, 1943-45. Mem. APA, Assn., Am. Assn. Mental Retardation. Jewish. Home: 417 Granville Rd Chapel Hill NC 27514-2723 E-mail: gbaroff@earthlink.net.

BAROLINI, HELEN, writer, translator, educator; b. Syracuse, N.Y., Nov. 18, 1925; m. Antonio Barolini, Nov. 8, 1950 (dec.); children: Teodolinda, Susanna, Nicoletta. AB magna cum laude, Syracuse U., 1947; MLS, Columbia U., 1959. Lectr. Pace U., Pleasantville, N.Y., 1990—. Lectr. Padua, Italy and Westchester C.C., Valhalla, N.Y., 1988; writer-in-residence Quarry Farm, Elmira Coll., 1989; resident scholar Rockefeller Found.'s Bellagio Study Ctr., Lake Como, Italy, 1991; vis. artist Am. Acad. Rome, 2001. Creative works include Umbertina, 1979, 1999, The Dream Book, 1985, 2000, Love in the Middle Ages, 1986, Festa, 1988, 2002, Aldus and His Dream Book, 1991, Chiaroscuro, 1999, More Italian Hours, and Other Stories, 2001, stories in Literary Olympian II, Love Stories by New Women, An Inn Near Kyoto, and numerous jours.; cited in The Best American Essays, 1991, 93, 98, 99, 2000; scholar-cons., advisor to film Tarantella. Recipient MELUS 2000 Lifetime Achievement award, Soc. for Study of Multi-Ethnic Lit. of U.S., 2000, Susan Koppelman award, Am. Culture Asn., 1987, Am. Book award, 1986, Marina-Velca Journalism prize, Italy, 1970, Sons of Italy Lit. Award, 2003; fellow, MacDowell Colony, 1974; grantee, Nat. Enwodment for Arts, 1976. Mem. PEN Am. Ctr., Authors Guild, Hudson Valley River Writers Assn., Phi Beta Kappa. Home and Office: 86 Maple Ave Hastings On Hudson NY 10706 E-mail: helenbarolini@juno.com.

BAROLINI, NICOLETTA E. artist; b. Tarrytown, N.Y., Jan. 13, 1962; d. Antonio and Helen Barolini; children: Darla, Antonia. BA in Sculpture, Sarah Lawrence Coll., Bronxville, N.Y.; postgrad. studies in graphics, Sch. Visual Arts, N.Y.C. Assoc. art dir. Raven Press, N.Y.C., 1987—91; art dir., graphic designer, illustrator Barolini Computer Graphics, Hastings, NY, 1992—97, Education People, Inc, Katonah, NY, 1997—. Pres., owner Go Leap Figurines, 1999 ; freelance artist, Hastings, NY, 1992—. Logo, Village of Hastings, 1999, painting, Cow Parade, 2000, illustration, Side by Side, 2001, Village of Hastings, 2002. Fax: 914-478-7119. E-mail: NBaraloni@aol.com.

BAROLINI, TEODOLINDA, literary critic; b. Syracuse, N.Y., Dec. 19, 1951; d. Antonio and Helen (Mollica) B.; m. Douglas Gardner Caverly, June 21, 1980 (dec. Nov. 1993); 1 child: William Douglas; m. James J. Valentini, Feb. 10, 2001. BA, Sarah Lawrence Coll., 1972; MA, Columbia U., 1973, PhD, 1978. Asst. prof. Italian U. Calif., Berkeley, 1978-83; assoc. prof. Italian NYU, 1983-89; prof., 1989-92; prof. Italian, chmn. dept. Italian Columbia U., N.Y.C., 1992—, Lorenzo Da Ponte prof. Italian, 1999—. Author: Dante's Poets, 1984 (Howard R. Marraro prize MLA 1986, John Nicholas Brown prize Medieval Acad. Am. 1988, transl. into Italian as Il miglior fabbro 1993), The Undivine Comedy, 1992, transl. into Italian as La Commedia Senza Dio, 2003; contbr. articles to profl. jours. AAUW fellow, 1977, ACLS fellow, 1981, NEH fellow, 1986, Guggenheim fellow, 1998. Fellow Medieval Acad. Am., Am. Acad. Arts and Scis., Am. Philos. Soc.; mem. MLA, Dante Soc. Am. (v.p. 1983-86, 91-94, 95-97, pres. 1997-2003), Renaissance Soc. Am. Office: Columbia U Dept Italian 510 Hamilton Hall New York NY 10027

BARON, ALMA FAY S. management educator; b. Pitts., July 26, 1923; d. Max J. and Emma C. (Aronson) Spann; m. Lee A. Baron, Dec. 23, 1944; children—Ellen J., Michael A., Jill S. BA, U. Pitts., 1943; PhD, U. Wis-Madison, 1974. Advt. mgr. Kaufmann's, Pitts., 1943; head copywriter Levy Bros., Houston, 1945; fashion coordinator Baron's, Madison, Wis., 1946-54; host TV Talent, Sta. WMTV, Madison, Wis., 1953-54, Sta. WQED, Pitts., 1954-58, Sta. KORN, Mitchell, S.D., 1958-66, Sta. KELO, Sioux Falls, S.D., 1959-66; co-owner Lee Baron's Women's Store, Madison, 1966-71; instr. U. Wis. Mgmt. Inst., Madison, 1974-77, assoc. prof. mgmt., 1978-81, prof. mgmt., 1981-88, prof. emeritus, 1988—. Mem. internat. bd. Inst. Cert. Profl. Secs., 1977-81; vis. faculty La. State U., Baton Rouge, Pa. State U.. Univ. Park, U. Okla., Norman, Purdue U., W. Lafayette; lectr. in Scandanavia, U.K., India; started Sr. Class TV progam in Madison, Wis., 1996, now statewide. Author: Assertiveness in the Business Environment, 1979, Nonverbal Communication, 1981, Women in Management: Strategies for Success, 1995; host, prodr.: (TV show) Mature; contbr. articles to profl. jours. Pres. Madison Civic Music Assn., 1971-73; v.p. YWCA, Madison, 1973-76; pres. Madison Civics Club, 1985-86; chmn. bd. advisers St. Mary's Hosp., 1986—; bd. ethics com. Inst. on Aging, St. Mary's Health Ctr.; chmn. blue ribbon millennium com. U. Wis. Ret. Assn.; pres. U. Wis. Faculty-Staff Assn., 1999-2000. Recipient Woman of Achievement award This is Madison, 1977, Outstanding Women award Select mag., 1976, Madisonian award Wis. State Jour., 1975, Sales and Mktg. award Sales Mktg. Execs., 1977, Meritorious Ind. Study Course award Nat. Univ. Extension Assn., 1980, Disting. Service award U. Wis. Extension, 1982, Outstanding Prof. award U. Wis.-Madison, 1985, Robert A. Jerred award U. Wis. Sch. Bus., 1988, Women of Distinction award YWCA, 1993, U. Wis. Disting. Alumni award, 1995, Jean Harris Rotary Dist. award, 1998. Mem. AAUW, Am. Bus. Comm. Assn., Am. Soc. Tng. and Devel. (mem. sr. faculty symposium 1980), Wis. Internat. Women's Forum (initiator 1987—), Gen. Semantics Assn., Wis. Acad. Arts and Scis., Assn. Platform Speakers, Nat. Telemedia Coun. (Journalist award 1996), U. Wis.-Madison Ret. Faculty Assn. (1st pres.), B'nai B'rith, Blackhawk Country Club, Zeta Phi Eta. Home: 8301 Old Sauk Rd Apt 12 Middleton WI 53562-4391 E-mail: afbaron@facstaff.wisc.edu.

BARON, BARRY CAMP, otolaryngologist; b. San Francisco, Apr. 15, 1945; s. Shirley Harold and Gene Doris (Camp) B.; 1 child, Julia Elizabeth. MD, U. Calif., San Francisco, 1975. Diplomate Am. Bd. Otolaryngology. Intern N.C. Meml. Hosp., Chapel Hill, 1975-76; resident in otolaryngology U. Calif., 1976-77, 78-80; resident in gen. surgery San Joaquin Gen. Hosp., Stockton, Calif., 1977-78; chmn. dept. otolaryngology Calif. Pacific Med. Ctr., San Francisco, 1992—; pvt. practice San Francisco. Assoc. clin. prof. U. Calif., San Francisco. Mem. AMA, Am. Acad. Otolaryntology, Pacific Coast Oto-Ophthal. Soc. Office: 2100 Webster St Ste 329 San Francisco CA 94115-2378

BARON, BARTON LEONARD, engineer; b. N.Y.C., Mar. 8, 1943; s. Harry Abraham and Sophie Duber B.; m. Leslie Stone, Feb. 6, 1966 (div. Dec. 1995); children: Brett, Amy. BS in Indsl. Engring., Pratt Inst., 1967. V.p. corp. ops. Diversified Ind., St. Louis, 1979-80; dir. mfg. engring. Smith Internat., Inc., Houston, 1981-86; dir. corp. engring. Van Dresser, Detroit, 1986-92; dir. quality corp. Harley Davidson, Milw., 1993-96; cons. Process Devel. Corp., Livonia, Mich., 1996-99, 99—; v.p. lean bus. Fairchild Fasterners, Torrance, Calif., 1999. Rep. candidate for U.S. Ho. of Reps. 12th Congl. Dist., Mich., 2000. Contbr. articles to jours. Mem. Troy Cmty. Coalition, Troy, 1999. Mem. Automotive Industry Action Group (vice chmn. 1997-99).

BARON, CHARLES HILLEL, lawyer, educator; b. Phila., Aug. 18, 1936; s. Samuel A. and Rose (Bailinky) B.; m. Irma Elaine Frankel, June 15, 1958 (dec. 1985); children: Jessica Susan, Ira Benjamin, David Hume; m. Dianne M. Quartarone, Sept. 9, 1988; 1 child, Samuel Guy. AB in Philosophy with honors, U. Pa., 1958, PhD in Philosophy, 1972; LLB, Harvard U., 1961. Bar: Pa. bar 1967, U.S. Supreme Ct. bar 1970, Mass. bar 1972. Asst. prof. law U. Pa., 1965-66; assoc. firm Blank Rome Klaus & Comisky, Phila., 1966-68; chief law reform, consumer's adv. Community Legal Svcs., Inc., Phila., 1968-70; assoc. prof. law Boston Coll., 1970-74, prof., 1974—, assoc. dean, 1972-74. Exec. dir. Resource Ctr. Consumers Legal Svcs., 1975-77. Author: (with M. Saks) The Use, Nonuse, and Misuse of Applied Social Research, 1980, Droit Constitutionnel et Bioéthique: L'Expérience Americaine, 1997; contbr. articles to profl. jours. Chmn. Cheltenham Twp. (Pa.) Dem. Party, 1966-68; mem. Mass. Health Facilities Appeals Bd., 1974-75; chmn. Mass. Gov.'s Adv. Com. on Prepaid Legal Svcs., 1978-86; bd. dirs. CEPA Found., Death With Dignity Nat. Ctr., Washington, 2001—; mem. bd. overseers Mass. Supreme Jud. Ct. Hist. Soc., 1999—. Recipient various community awards; U. Pa. fellow, 1961 63 Mem. ABA, Am. Assn. Law Schs., Soc. Am. Law Tchrs., Am. Soc. Law and Medicine (bd. editors Am. Jour. Law and Medicine 1978—, bd. dirs.), Civil Liberties Union Mass. (bd. dirs., pres. 1989-91, trustee Mass. Civil Liberties Found.), ACLU. Jewish. Home: 60 Grove Hill Ave Newton MA 02460-2335 Office: Boston Coll Law Sch 885 Centre St Newton MA 02459-1148 E-mail: baron@bc.edu.

BARON, FRANK, language educator; b. Budapest, Hungary, Jan. 13, 1936; arrived in U.S., 1947; s. Leo Baron and Gertrude Herold; m. Betty Baron; children: Christopher, Maya. BA, U. Ill., 1958; MA, Ind. U., 1960; PhD, U. Calif. Berkeley, 1966. Instr. U. Notre Dame, Notre Dame, Ind., 1960—61; asst. prof., assoc. prof. U. Kans., Lawrence, 1970—80, prof., 1980—. Editor (with E. Dick and W.R. Maurer): Rilke: Alchemy of Alienation, 1979; editor: Rilke and the Visual Arts, 1982; editor: (with R. Auernheimer) Johannes Trithemius: Humanismus und Magie im vorreformatorischen, 1991, Das Faustbuch von 1587. Entstehung und Wirkung, 1991; editor: German Poetry in War and Peace. A Dual-Language Anthology, 1995; editor: (with H. Arntzen and D. Cateforis) Albert Bloch: Artistic and Literary Perspectives, 1997; editor: (with Gert Sautermeister) Thomas Mann's Der Tod in Venedig, Wurklichkeit, Dichtung Mythos, 2003; editor: (with Richard Auernheimer) War der Faustus in Kreuznach? Realität und Fiktion im Faust-Bild des Abtes Johannes Trithemius, 2003; editor: (with Gert Sauermeister) Goethe im Exit, 2003. Fellow NEH, 1974, NSF, 1980, Fulbright Found., 1985, German Acad. Exch., 1986, 1987, 1992, NEH, 1995. Mem.: GSA, AATG. Home: 1108 Sunset Dr Lawrence KS 66044 Office: Dept Germanic Lang and Lit Univ Kansas Lawrence KS 66045

BARON, FREDERICK DAVID, lawyer; b. New Haven, Dec. 2, 1947; s. Charles Bates and Betty (Leventhal) B.; m. Kathryn Green Lazarus, Apr. 4, 1982; children: Andrew K. Lazarus, Peter D. Lazarus, Charles B. BA, Amherst Coll., 1969; JD, Stanford U., 1974. Bar: Calif. 1974, D.C. 1975, U.S. Supreme Ct. 1978, U.S. Dist. Ct. D.C. 1979, U.S. Ct. Appeals (D.C. cir.) 1979, U.S. Dist. Ct. (no. dist.) Calif. 1982, U.S. Ct. Appeals (9th cir.) 1982. Counsel select com. on intelligence U.S. Senate, Washington, 1975-76; spl. asst. to U.S. atty. gen. Washington, 1977-79; asst. U.S. atty. for D.C., 1980-82; atty. Clark, Baron & Korda, San Jose, Calif., 1982-83; ptnr. Cooley, Godward, Palo Alto, Calif.,

1983—; assoc. dep. atty. gen., dir. Exec. Office for Nat. Security U.S. Dept. of Justice, 1995-96. Lectr. U.S. Info. Svc., 1979-80; pres. bd. trustees Keys Sch., Palo Alto, 1983-87; bd. dirs. Retail Resources, Inc., 1987-88; mem. bd. vis. Stanford Law Sch., 2003-. Co-author, editor U.S. Senate Select Com. on Intelligence Reports, 1975-76; also articles. Issues dir. election com. U.S. Senator Alan Cranston, 1974, Gov. Edmund G. Brown Jr., 1976; mem. transition team Pres. Carter, 1976-77, Pres. Clinton, 1992; del. Calif. Dem. Conv., 1989-90. Mem. ABA, Calif. Bar Assn., D.C. Bar Assn., Santa Clara County Bar Assn., Univ. Club. Office: Cooley Godward LLP 5 Palo Alto Sq Palo Alto CA 94306-2122

BARON, JEFFREY, retired pharmacologist; b. Bklyn., July 10, 1942; s. Harry Leo and Terry (Goldstein) Baron; m. Judith Carol Rothberg, June 27, 1965; children: Stephanie Ann, Leslie Beth, Melissa Leigh. BS in Pharmacy, U. Conn., 1965; PhD in Pharmacology, U. Mich., 1969. Rsch. fellow in biochemistry U. Tex. Southwestern Med. Sch., Dallas, 1969-71, rsch. asst. prof. biochemistry and pharmacology, 1971-72; from asst. prof. pharmacology to prof. emeritus U. Iowa, Iowa City, 1972—2002, prof. emeritus, 2002—. Mem. chem. pathology study sect. NIH, Bethesda, Md., 1983—87, mem. environ. health scis. rev. com., Nat. Inst. Environ. Health Scis., Research Triangle Park, NC, 1990—94. Contbr. chapters to books, articles to profl. jours. Recipient Rsch. Career Devel. award, NIH, 1975—80. Mem.: Internat. Soc. Study Xenobiotics, Soc. Toxicology, Am. Assn. Cancer Rsch., Am. Soc. Biochem. and Molecular Biology, Am. Soc. Pharmacology and Exptl. Therapeutics. Achievements include discovery of of the role of heme synthesis in regulating the induction of cytochrome P450 in liver; participation in the discovery of oxygenated cytochrome P450; research in immunohistochemical localization of cytochromes P450 and other xenobiotic-metabolizing enzymes in liver and extrahepatic tissues. E-mail: jeffrey-baron@uiowa.edu.

BARON, JUDSON RICHARD, aerospace educator; b. N.Y.C., July 28, 1924; s. Louis and Leah (Berzin) B.; m. Selma Francine Wasserman, Sept. 4, 1949; children— Jason Roberts, Jeffrey Scott. B.Aero. Engring., NYU, 1947; SM, MIT, 1948, ScD, 1956. Registered profl. engr., Mass. Stress analyst Chance Vought Aircraft Co., 1947; mem. research staff MIT, 1948-54, research asst., 1954-56, mem. faculty, 1957—, prof. aeros. and astronautics, 1957-89, prof. emeritus, sr. lectr., 1989-2000; cons. in field, 1957—. Mem. Air Force Sci. Adv. Bd., 1987-91. With AUS, 1943-46. Decorated Bronze Star; recipient Exceptional Civilian Svc. award. Dept. Air Force, 1991. Fellow AIAA (assoc. editor jour. 1989-96), Sigma Xi, Tau Beta Pi, Gamma Alpha Rho. Home: 7 Gould Rd Lexington MA 02420-1003 Office: 77 Massachusetts Ave Cambridge MA 02139-4307 E-mail: jrbaron@mit.edu.

BARON, LEE ANN, chemist, educator; d. Albert Leonard and Marion Jean Fisher; m. Keith Wayne Baron, Aug. 12, 1978; children: Kendra Elizabeth, Caitlin Constance. BA in Chemistry, Wittenberg U., 1977; MS in Chemistry, U. Mich., 1979, PhD in Chemistry, 1984, postgrad., 1986—88. Tchg. asst. organic and gen. chemistry Wittenberg U., 1975—76, tchg. asst. gen. chemistry, 1977, U. Mich., 1977, tchg. asst. organic chemistry, 1978, 1979, 1981, tchg. asst. organic chemistry Interflex Program, 1978—80, tchg. asst. honors organic chemistry, 1980, 1981, rsch. asst., 1979—84, lectr. organic chemistry, 1984—86, post-doctoral fellow, 1986—88; asst. prof. chemistry Adrian (Mich.) Coll., 1988—89, Hillsdale (Mich.) Coll., 1989—93, assoc. prof. chemistry, 1993—2003, prof. chemistry, 2003—, chair dept. chemistry, 2000. Contbr. articles to profl. jours. Mem.: Ctrl. Assn. of the Health Professions, Nat. Assn. Advisors for the Health Professions, Midwest Assn. Chemistry Tchrs. at Liberal Arts Colls., Am. Chem. Soc., Phi Lambda Upsilon, Sigma Zeta. Achievements include research in effects of alcohol on membrane fats and water-soluble metabolites in developing chick embryos using 13C NMR; diffusion and adsorption of dichlortiazyl dyes by chitin; development of laboraties used during the Hillsdale College Summer Science Camp and a K-12 science curriculum. Avocations: reading, gardening, volleyball. Office: Hillsdale Coll 33 E College Hillsdale MI 49242

BARON, MARTIN, editor; BA, MBA, Lehigh U., 1976. Reporter, bus. writer Miami Herald, 1976—79; reporter, bus. editor, asst. mng. editor L.A. Times, 1979—93, editor Orange County Edit., 1993—96; editor, assoc. mng. editor N.Y. Times, 1996—99; exec. editor Miami Herald, 1999—2001; editor Boston Globe, 2001—. Named Editor of Yr., Editor & Pub. Mag., 2001; recipient Pulitzer prize, 2001. Mem.: Phi Beta Kappa. Office: Boston Globe PO Box 2378 135 Morrissey Blvd Dorchester MA 02107

BARON, MELVIN FARRELL, pharmacy educator; b. L.A., July 29, 1932; s. Leo Ben and Sadie (Bauchman) B.; m. Lorraine Ross, Dec. 20, 1953; children: Lynn Baron Friedman, Ross David. PharmD, U. So. Calif., 1957, MPA, 1973. Lic. pharmacist, Calif. Pres. Shield Health Care Ctrs., Van Nuys, Calif., 1957-83; dir. externship program U. So. Calif., L.A., 1991—; v.p. Shield Health Care Ctrs., Inc. (C.R. Bard, Inc. subsidiary), 1983-86; pres. Merit Coll., 1988-92, PharmaCom., L.A., 1990—; assoc. prof. clin. pharmacy U. So. Calif., L.A., 1991—, asst. dean pharm. care programs, 1995—97, dir. PharmD/MBA program, asst. dean programmatic advancement, 1998—; prin. New Horizon Pharmacy Cons. Adj. asst. prof. U. without Walls, Shaw U., Raleigh, NC, 1973; project dir. Haynes Found. Drug Rsch. Ctr., U. So. Calif., L.A., 1973; assoc. dir. Calif. Alcoholism Found., 1973—75; adj. asst. prof. clin. pharmacy Sch. Pharmacy, U. So. Calif., 1981—91; cons. Topanga Terr. Convalescent Hosp., 1970—80, Calif. Labor Mgmt. Plan of alcoholism programs and coords., 1974, Office of Alcoholism, State of Calif., Nat. In-Home Health Svc., 1975, Continuity of Life Team, 1975, Triad Med., Longs Drug Stores, HealthTek, others; vis. prof. Tokyo Coll. Pharmacy, 1994, Sandoz Pharm. Co., 1995, Clin Oscar Romero, 2000; lectr. Meijo U., Nagoya U., Japan, 1994; presenter Nat. Pharmacy Dir. Conf., 1995; cons., mem. sci. adv. bd. Leiner Health Products, 1998—; cons. Prime Care Pharmacy, 1998—, Jackson Meml. Hosp., 1998, New Horizon Pharmacy, Avalon Hosp., Queenscare Family Clinics; cons., mem. adv. bd. Medpin, 2001; chair nominating com. CPHA, 1998; co-developer Trends in Healthcare Svcs.; presenter in field. Adv. bd. Pharmacist Newsletter, 1980—. Chmn. Friends of Operation Bootstrap, 1967-77; svc. chmn. tng. coord. Am. Cancer Soc., San Fernando Valley, Calif., 1980; mem. adv. bd. L.A. VNA, 1982; bd. dirs. pres. QSAD, 1987-88; pres. bd. Everywoman's Village, 1988-89; bd. dirs. Life Svcs., 1988-94; pres. bd. counselors, U. So. Calif., 1988-92, co-chmn. good neighborhood campaign Sch. Pharmacy, 1998; mem. Calif. Bd. Pharmacy Com. on Student/Preceptor Manual, 1991-92. Named Disting. Alumnus of Yr., U. So. Calif., Sch. of Pharmacy Alumni Assn., 1983, U. So. Calif. Torchbearer, 1990-91, Hon. Tchr. of Yr. U. So. Calif. Sch. Pharmacy, 1997. Fellow Am. Coll. Apothecaries; mem. Am. Pharm. Assn., Am. Soc. Health Sys. Pharmacists, Calif. Pharmacist Assn. (chair edn. com.), Am. Soc. Pub. Adminstrn., Am. Assn. Colls. of Pharmacy (spkr. ann. meeting 2000), Phi Kappa Phi, Phi Lambda Sigma (hon., faculty advisor), Rho Chi. Home: 1245 Wellesley Ave Apt 201 Los Angeles CA 90025-1170 Office: 1985 Zonal Ave Los Angeles CA 90089-0105 E-mail: mbaron@usc.edu.

BARON, PATRICIA BURRELL, university director; b. Glen Ridge, N.J., Dec. 16, 1949; d. Leo Duncan and Mollie Amelia (Scard) B.; m. William Robert Baron, June 17, 1972. BA, Allegheny Coll., 1972; MA in Librarianship, U. Denver, 1973; MEd in Ednl. Adminstrn., U. Maine, 1980; EdD in Ednl. Adminstrn., No. Ariz. U., 1987. Reference libr. U. Maine, Orono, 1975, asst. to grad. dean, 1976-80, asst. to acad. v.p., 1980-82; asst. to grad. dean No. Ariz. U., Flagstaff, 1982-87, asst. grad. dean, 1987-93, assoc. grad. dean, dir. grad. admissions, 1993—. Contbr. articles to profl. jours., 1998-. Active commn. on status of women Ariz. Bd. of Regents, Phoenix, 1989-91. Named Woman of Distinction, Soroptimist Internat., 1993. Mem. Am. Assn. U. Women, Nat. Assn. Women in Edn., Nat. Assn. Grad. Admissions (exe. bd. 1998-), Univ. Career Women (founder, chair 1991-92), Phi Kappa Phi. Avocations: needlework, gardening. Office: No Ariz U PO Box 4125 Flagstaff AZ 86011-4125

BARON, RICHARD L. health services administrator; b. Springfield, Mass., Mar. 11, 1949; s. Gilbert Whitney and Carolyn Cahan B.; m. Shirley Reynolds, June 5, 1971; children: Timothy, Christine. BA, Yale Coll., 1972; MD, Washington U. Sch. Medicine, 1976. Diplomate Am. Bd. Radiology. Instr. dept. radiology Washington U. Sch. Medicine, St. Louis, 1980-81; asst. prof. dept. radiology U. Pa. Sch. Medicine, Phila., 1981-82; staff Radiol. Assocs., Everett, Wash., 1982-86; assoc. prof. dept. radiology U. Wash. Sch. Medicine, 1986-90; prof. dept. radiology U. Pitts. Sch. Medicine, 1990-92, chair dept. radiology, 1992-99; pres., CEO U. Pitts. Physicians, 1997—2002; prof., chmn. dept. radiology U. Chgo., 2002—. Bd. dirs. U. Pitts. Med. Ctr. Health Sys., 1997-2002. Assoc. editor Radiology, 1991-96; editl. bd. Jour. Computer Assisted Tomography, 1994-98; contbr. articles to profl. jours., chpts. to books. Fellow Am. Coll. Radiology; mem. Soc. Gastrointestinal Radiologists (traveling fellow 1995, Roscoe E. Miller award 1990, meml. award 1988), Soc. Computed Body Tomography & Magnetic Resonance (pres. 1998-99, Hounsfield award 1989, 97), Radiol. Soc. N.Am., Am. Roentgen Ray Soc. Home: 111 E Chestnut St # 50K Chicago IL 60611 Office: U Chgo Dept Radiology 5841 S Maryland Ave MC 2026 Chicago IL 60637 E-mail: rbaron@uchicago.edu.

BARON, ROBERT, folklorist; b. N.Y.C., Jan. 27, 1951; s. Charles and Helen Esther (Suss) B.; m. Lise May Korson, Jan. 2, 1982; 1 child, Violet. BA, U. Chgo., 1972; MA, U. Pa., 1976, PhD, 1994. Sr. rsch. specialist Bklyn. Mus., 1977-79; folk arts coord. N.Y. State Coun. on Arts, N.Y.C., 1980-84, mus. program assoc., 1984-85, dir. folk arts program, 1985-2000, 01—; dir. museum program, 1996-2000. Folklore adminstr. NEH, 2000-01; presenter in field; cons. Artpark, 1979, Bklyn. Rediscovery, 1978-79; adj. lectr. Am. Studies dept. Rutgers U., Newark, 1979-80; bd. dirs. Mid Atlantic Arts Found., 1995-96, also chair, mem. traditional arts com., 1996-99, mem. performing arts com., 1995-96. Co-editor: Public Folklore, 1992; contbr. articles to profl. publs. Pres. U. Chgo. Folklore Soc., 1970-71; mem. N.J. Folklife adv. coun. N.J. Hist. Commn., 1979-80; field rschr., presenter Festival Am. Folklife, Smithsonian Instn., 1974; mem. multi-disciplinary panel N.J. State Coun. on Arts, 1984, mem. presenting orgns. panel, 1994; mem. folk arts orgn. panel, 2001; mem. traditional arts adv. com. New Eng. Found. for Arts, 1990-93; mem. nat. adv. com. Fund for Folk Culture, 1991-95, bd. dirs. 2000—, chair program com., 2002—; coord. ethnic folklife festival Caribbean traditions Internat. House of Phila., 1978; mem. panel N.J. Folk Arts Apprenticeships, 1995, 2003, Folk Arts Orgn., 1997, 99, 2003; mem. orgn. granting panel Conn. Commn. on Arts, 1995. U. Pa. teaching fellow, 1976-77; Wenner-Gren Found. grantee, 1976. Mem. Am. Folklore Soc. (state of profession com. 1992-94, nominating com. 1996-98, exec. bd. 2000, membership com. 2000, chair ann. meeting program com. 2002, Benjamin A. Botkin prize 2002), Nat. Coun. for Traditional Arts (bd. dirs. 1992-2001), Mid. Atlantic Folklife Assn. (v.p. 1991-93, pres. 1993-95, bd. dirs. 1995-2000, 2002—). Jewish. Home: 211 8th Ave Brooklyn NY 11215-2658 E-mail: rbtbaron@aol.com.

BARON, ROBERT CHARLES, publishing executive; b. L.A., Jan. 26, 1934; s. Leo Francis and Marietta (Schulze) B.; m. Faye Helen Rogers, Jan. 28, 1961 (div. 1984); m. Charlotte Rose Persinger, Nov. 29, 1986; stepchildren: Brett, Kristen. BS in Physics, St. Joseph's Coll., 1956. Registered profl. engr., Mass. Engr. RCA, Camden, N.J., 1955-57, Computer Control Co., Framingham, Mass., 1959-61, program mgr. Mariner II and IV space computers, 1961-65, engring. mgr., 1965-69; worldwide systems mgr. Honeywell Minicomputer, Framingham, 1970-71; founder, pres., CEO Prime Computer, Framingham, 1971-75; pvt. practice Boston, 1976-83; founder and pres. Fulcrum Pub., Golden, Colo., 1984—. Bd. dirs. Prime Computer, Framingham, Mass., Alling-Lander, Cheshire, Conn., Oxion, Hugoton, Kans., Fulcrum Pub., Golden Colo. Author: Digital Logic and Computer Operations, 1966, Micropower Electronics, 1970, America in the Twentieth Century, 1995, Footsteps on the Sands of Time, 1999, What Was It Like Orville: The Early Space Program, 2002; editor: The Garden and Farm Books of Thomas Jefferson, 1987, Soul of America: Documenting Our Past, 1492-1974, 1989, Colorado Rockies: The Inaugural Season, 1993, Thomas Hornsby Ferril and the American West, 1996. Trustee Lincoln Filene Ctr., Tufts U., Medford, Mass., 1982-84; vice chmn. bd. dirs. Mass. Audubon Soc., Lincoln, 1980-85; bd. dirs. Rocky Mountain Women's Inst., Denver, 1987-90; bd. dirs. Denver Pub. Libr. Friends Found., 1989-96, pres., 1994-96. Mem. Am. Antiquarian Soc. (bd. dirs., chmn. 1993—), Internat. Wilderness Leadership Found. (bd. dirs. 1990—, chmn. 1994-2000), Thoreau Soc., Mass. Hist. Soc., Western History Assn., Hakluyt Soc., Grolier Club, Explorer's Club. Avocations: writing, reading, sports, gardening, collecting clocks. Office: Fulcrum Pub Ste 300 16100 Table Mountain Pkwy Golden CO 80403-1672 E-mail: bob@fulcrum_books.com.

BARON, SAMUEL HASKELL, historian; b. N.Y.C., May 24, 1921; s. James and Dinah (Bader) B.; m. Virginia Wilson, Dec. 22, 1949; children— Sheila, Carla, Laura. BS, Cornell U., 1942; MA, Columbia U., 1948; PhD, 1952. Instr. history U. Tenn., 1948-53; vis. lectr. Northwestern U., 1953-54, U. Mo., 1954-55, U. Nebr., 1955-56; from asst. prof. to prof. Grinnell (Iowa) Coll., 1956-66; prof. U. Calif.-San Diego, 1966-72; Alumni Disting. prof. history U. N.C., Chapel Hill, 1972-91, prof. emeritus, 1991—; chmn. Conf. Slavic and Ea. European History, 1976. Author: Plekhanov: The Father of Russian Marxism, 1963, The Travels of Olearius in Seventeenth Century Russia, 1967, Muscovite Russia: Collected Essays, 1980, Explorations in Muscovite History, 1991, Plekhanov in Russian History and Soviet Historiography, 1994, Bloody Saturday in the Soviet Union: Novocherkassk, 1962, 2001; co-editor: Windows on The Russian Past: Essays on Soviet Historiography since Stalin, 1977, Introspection in Biography: The Biographer's Quest for Self-Awareness, 1985, Religion and Culture in Early Modern Russia and Ukraine, 1997, Adventures in Russian Historical Research, 2003. Served from pvt. to capt. AUS, 1942-46. Ford Found. fellow, 1958-59, Guggenheim Found. fellow, 1970-71, Nat. Endowment Humanities fellow, 1976; chair named in his honor U. N.C., 1994. Mem. AAUP (council 1962-65), Am. Hist. Assn., Am. Assn. Advancement Slavic Studies, Early Slavic Studies Assn. (pres. 1991). Home: 2 Carolina Meadows Chapel Hill NC 27517 Office: U NC Dept History Chapel Hill NC 27599-0001 E-mail: shbaron@email.unc.edu.

BARON, SHELDON, research and development company executive; b. Bklyn., May 13, 1934; s. Harry and Edna (Schleifer) B.; m. Doris Earl Rudd, Aug. 11, 1961; 1 son, David. BS, Bklyn. Coll., 1955; MA, Coll. William and Mary, 1961; PhD, Harvard U., 1966. Simulation engr. USAF-NACA, Hampton, Va., 1955-57; aerospace technologist NASA, Hampton, 1958-65, Cambridge, Mass., 1965-67; mgr., researcher Bolt Beranek & Newman, Cambridge, 1967-71, mgr., prin. scientist, 1971-79, v.p., 1979-94, sr. v.p., 1994-98; ind. cons. Lexington, Mass., 1999—. Mem. sci. adv. bd. U.S. Army Missile Command, Huntsville, Ala., 1975-77; mem. working group on simulation, 1982-84; chmn. working group on human performance modelling Nat. Acad. Scis.-NRC, 1983-87; bd. vistors BBN Techs., 1998-2000; bd. councillors U. S.C. Integrated Media Systems Ctr., 1998—; cons. U.S. Army Sci. Bd., 2000—. Assoc. editor: Jour. Cybernetics and Info. Scis., Washington, 1976-81. Served to 1st lt. USAF, 1955-57. Fellow IEEE; mem. Control Systems Soc. (sec., treas. 1982-84), AIAA, Harvard Soc. Engrs. and Scientists (pres. 1976-78) Home: 7 Birch Hill Ln Lexington MA 02421-7445 E-mail: baron@bbn.com.

BARON, SHERI, advertising agency executive; b. Bklyn., Sept. 3, 1955; d. Irwin Murray Glaser and Rosalind (Mendelson) Krasik; m. Peter T. Colonel, Sept. 20, 1981 (dec.); m. Alan R. Baron, Dec. 14, 1996. BA in Psychology, SUNY, Courtland, 1977. Account exec. Ted Bates Co., N.Y.C., 1978-80, SSC&B Advt. (name now Lowe), N.Y.C., 1980-82, v.p. acct. supr., 1983-84, sr. v.p. mgmt. supr., 1984-88, exec. v.p., 1988-94, bd. dirs., 1990-94; pres. Gotham Inc., 1994—. Named to Am. Advt. Fedn. Hall of Achievement, 1993, 40 Under 40 List, Crain's N.Y. bus., 1994. Mem. Advt. Women N.Y., Cosmetic Exec. Women, Fashion Group Internat. Home: 11 W 20th St New York NY 10011-3704 Office: Gotham Inc 100 5th Ave Fl 16 New York NY 10011-6996 Business E-Mail: sherib@gothaminc.com.

BARON, THEODORE, public relations executive; b. Harbin, Manchuria, China, Aug. 20, 1928; came to U.S., 1946; s. Solomon and Bella (Gelesny) B.; m. Irene Cunnington, Oct. 23, 1958; children: Susan Elaine, Michael. BA, U. Calif., Berkeley, 1950; LLB, NYU, 1957. Bar: N.Y. 1958. Newspaper reporter The Record, Coalinga, Calif., 1950-51; writer, editor Associated Press, San Francisco, 1951-52; writer, acct. exec. N.Y.C. Pub. Rels. firms, N.Y.C., 1952-58; pres. Ted Baron Inc., N.Y.C., 1958-98; ret., 1998. Contbr. articles to profl. jours. and consumer mags. Fellow Pub. Rels. Soc. Am. (pres. N.Y. 1990-91); mem. Far Eastern Soc., Salty Flyrodders N.Y., Princeton Club. Home and Office: 2300 Lindenmere Dr Merrick NY 11566-4312 E-mail: tedbaron@aol.com.

BARONDES, SAMUEL HERBERT, psychiatrist, educator; b. Bklyn., Dec. 21, 1933; s. Solomon and Yetta (Kaplow) B.; m. Ellen Slater, Sept. 1, 1963 (dec. Nov. 22, 1971); children: Elizabeth Francesca, Jessica Gabrielle; m. Louann Brizendine, Sept. 14, 2002. AB, Columbia U., 1954, MD, 1958. Intern, then asst. resident in medicine Peter Bent Brigham Hosp., Boston, 1958-60; sr. asst. surgeon USPHS, NIH, Bethesda, Md., 1960-63; resident in psychiatry McLean and Mass. Gen. hosps., Boston, 1963-66; asst. prof., then assoc. prof. psychiatry and molecular biology Albert Einstein Coll. Medicine., Bronx, N.Y., 1966-69; prof. psychiatry U. Calif., San Diego, 1969-86, prof., chmn. dept. psychiatry, dir. Langley Porter Psychiat. Inst. San Francisco, 1986-94, dir. Ctr. Neurobiology and Psychiatry, 1994—, Jeanne and Sanford Robertson Prof. Neurobiol. and Psychiatry, 1996—. Pres. McKnight Endowment Fund for Neurosci., 1989-98, bd. dirs., 1987—; mem. sci. adv. com. Rsch. Am.; mem. governing coun. Internat. Brain Rsch. Orgn., 1994-2000; mem. bd. sci. counselors NIMH, 1997-2002, chair, 2000-02; mem. internat. adv. coun. to develop the biomed. scis. industry in Singapore, 2001-. Author: Molecules and Mental Illness, 1993, Mood Genes, 1998, Better Than Prozac, 2003; mem. editl. bds. profl. jours.; contbr. numerous articles to profl. publs. Recipient Rsch. Career Devel. award USPHS, 1967, Elliott Royer award, 1989, P.H. Stillmark medal Estonia, 1989; Fogarty Internat. scholar NIH, 1979; J. Robert Oppenheimer lectr., 2000. Fellow AAAS, Am. Psychiat. Assn., Am. Coll. Neuropsychopharmacology; mem. Inst. Medicine Nat. Acad. Sci. Office: U Calif-San Francisco Langley Porter Psychiat Ins 401 Parnassus Ave San Francisco CA 94143-0984 E-mail: barondes@cgl.ucsf.edu.

BARONDESS, JEREMIAH ABRAHAM, physician; b. N.Y.C., June 6, 1924; s. Benjamin and Dora (Greenberg) B.; m. Sue Kaufman, Nov. 22, 1953 (dec. 1977); 1 child, James Joseph; m. Linda Hiddemen, Dec. 10, 1982. MD, Johns Hopkins U., 1949; DSc (hon.), Albany Med. Coll., Union U., 1978; LittD (hon.), N.Y. Inst. Tech., 1992; DMedSci (hon.), Med. Coll. Pa., 1993; DSc (hon.), N.Y. Med. Coll., 1998. Diplomate Am. Bd. Internal Medicine (bd. govs., council gen. internal medicine 1975-81). Intern, then asst. resident in medicine Osler Med. Svc. Johns Hopkins Hosp., 1949-51; asst. medicine Johns Hopkins U. Med. Sch., 1950-51; mem. virology sect., research div. Children's Hosp., Phila., also; rsch. fellow virology U. Pa. Med. Sch., 1951-53; asst. resident, then chief resident in medicine N.Y. Hosp.-Cornell U. Med. Center, 1953-55; mem. faculty Cornell U. Med. Coll., 1953—, clin. prof. medicine, 1971-78, prof. clin. medicine, 1978-87, Irene F. and I. Roy Psaty Disting. Prof. Clin. Medicine, 1987-89, William T. Foley Disting. Prof. in Clin. Medicine, 1989-90, adj. prof. clin. medicine, 1990, prof. emeritus, 1993—; mem. staff N.Y. Hosp., 1953—, attending physician, 1971—; chief pvt. med. svc., 1971-92; hon. staff mem. N.Y. Hosp., 1992—; assoc. chmn. dept. medicine, 1983-90; asst. vis. physician Bellevue Hosp., 1960-67; assoc. medicine Meml. Hosp. Cancer and Allied Diseases, 1972-90; Alpha Omega Alpha vis. prof. U. P.R. Med. Sch., 1972; Meyerowitz meml. lectr. U. Rochester Sch. Medicine, 1980. Disting. lectr. U. N.C., 1982; vis. prof. medicine U. Ill. Med. Sch., 1974, U. Va. Med. Sch., 1976, Mayo Clinic and Med. Sch., 1978, U. Iowa Sch. Medicine, 1979, U. Tex. Med. Ctr., 1986, 90, U. Pa., 1986, U. Va., 1989, N.Y. Med. Coll., 1990, SUNY Health Sci. Ctr., Bklyn., 1992; mem. nat. resources com. Johns Hopkins U., 1965—, trustee, 1977-94, trustee emeritus, 1994—, chmn. vis. com. Sch. Medicine, 1978-92. Author: (with A.M. Harvey and J. Bordley) Differential Diagnosis, (with J. McGovern and C. Roland) The Persisting Osler, 1985, (with A.H. Samiy and R.G. Douglas) Textbook of Diagnostic Medicine, 1987, (with C. Roland) The Persisting Osler II, 1994, (with C. Roland) The Persisting Osler III, 2002; editor: Diagnostic Approaches to Presenting Syndromes, 1971; co-editor Differential Diagnosis, 1994; mem. editl. bd. Forum on Medicine, Pharos, Internat. Jour. Technol. Assessment in Health Care, Jour. Royal Soc. Med.; contbr. articles to profl. jours. Bd. dirs. Am. Fedn. Aging Rsch., 1996—. Served with AUS, 1943-46; Served with USPHS, 1951-53. Recipient Wiggers award Albany Med. Coll. Union U., 1978, Alfred Stengel award ACP, 1983; named Hon. Alumnus Cornell U. Med. Coll., 1974. Fellow AAAS, Am. Acad. Arts and Scis., Royal Coll. Physicians London, ACP (chmn. bd. govs. 1973-75, bd. regents 1975—, pres. 1978-79, pres. emeritus 1988), Federated Coun. Internal Medicine, Royal Soc. Medicine, Royal Soc. Health. Royal Coll. Physicians Ireland (hon.); mem. Am. Clin. and Climatol. Assn. (coun. 1975-78, pres. 1994), Am. Osler Soc. (pres. 1983-84), Am. Fedn. Clin. Rsch., APHA, Assn. Am. Physicians, Harvey Soc., N.Y. Heart Assn., Inst. Medicine NAS (coun. 1979-81, co-chair coun. on health care tech., chair com. on managed care and chronic disease 1996, chair com. on musculoskeletal disorders and the workplace 1999-2001), N.Y. Acad. Scis., N.Y. Acad. Medicine (pres. 1990—), Internat. Soc. Internal Medicine, Phi Beta Kappa, Alpha Omega Alpha (dir. 1978-79, pres. 1987-89), Century Club (N.Y.C.), Cosmos Club (Washington). Jewish. Home: 544 E 86th St New York NY 10028-7536 Office: NY Acad Medicine 1216 5th Ave New York NY 10029-5202 E-mail: jbaronde@nyam.org.

BARONE, ANGELA MARIA, artist, researcher; b. Concesio, Brescia, Italy, June 29, 1957; came to U.S., 1983; d. Giuseppe and Adelmina (D'Ercole) B. Laurea cum laude in geol. scis., U. Bologna, Italy, 1981; PhD in Marine Geology, Columbia U., 1989. Cert. in profl. photography, N.Y. Inst. Photography, N.Y.C., 1992; cert. in the fine art of painting and drawing North Light Art Sch., Cin., 1993. Collaborative asst. Marine Geology Inst., Bologna, 1981-83, Inst. Geology and Paleontology, Florence, Italy, 1982-83, Sta. de Geodynamique, Villefranche, France, 1982; grad. rsch. asst. Lamont-Doherty Geol. Obs., Palisades, N.Y., 1983-89, postdoctoral rsch. asst., 1989; postgrad. rschr. Scripps Instn. of Oceanography, La Jolla, Calif., 1990-92; artist San Diego, 1993—. Contbr. articles to profl. jours. Mem. Am. Geophys. Union (co-pres. meeting session 1990), Nat. Mus. Women in Arts (assoc.). Home: 7540 Charmant Dr Apt 1222 San Diego CA 92122-5044

BARONE, JAMES L. state legislator; b. Chgo., May 20, 1941; m. Donita Barone. BSBA, Pitts. State U., 1962. With Bell Sys.-S.W. Bell Telephone, 1962-91; mem. Kans. Senate from 13th dist., Topeka, 1996—; ranking minority mem. commerce com.; mem. fin. instns. and ins. com.; ranking minority mem. utilities com.; mem. joint com. on econ. devel.; mem. joint com. on pensions, investments and benefits com. Named to Order Ky. Cols. Mem. Pittsburg State Alumni Assn. (bd. dirs.), Pittsburg C. of C., Eagles, Rotary, KC. Democrat. Office: 300 SW 10th Ave Rm 504-n Topeka KS 66612-1504*

BARONE, JOHN ANTHONY, academic administrator emeritus; b. Dunkirk, NY, Aug. 30, 1924; s. John A. and Josephine (Audino) B.; m. Rose Marie Pace, Aug. 23, 1947. BA, U. Buffalo, 1944; MS, Purdue U., 1948, PhD, 1950; ScD (hon.), Fairfield U., 1992. Research fellow Purdue U., 1948-50; instr. Fairfield U., Conn., 1950-51, asst. prof., 1951-56, assoc. prof., 1956-62, prof. chemistry, 1962-92, dir. rsch. and grants, 1963-66, v.p. planning, 1966-70, provost, 1970-92, emeritus, 1992—. Mem. rev. and evaluation com. Conn. Regional Med. Program, 1970-76; dir. NSF In-Service Inst., 1961-69; mem. steering com. comprehensive health planning United Community Svc.; bd. dir., mem. Corp. Conn. Blue Cross, 1973-77; bd. dir., mem. exec. com. Blue Cross-Blue Shield Conn., 1977-94 ; project mgr. HUD New Rural Soc. contract, 1972-76; mem. adv. com. on fed. matters Conn. Commn. for Higher Edn., 1974-77; pres. UN Assn. Conn., 1970-72; mem. Conn. Health and Edn. Facilities Authority, 1987-2001, vice-chmn., 1988-2001; mem. adv. com. Conn. Dept. Health Svc., 1987-93. Contbr. articles profl. jour. Trustee Conn. Coun. for Sci. Edn., Hall-Brooke Found., St. Vincent's Coll., Ctr. for Fin. Studies, vice chmn., 1977-94; bd. dir. Jesuit Rsch. Coun. Am., chmn., 1968-70; bd. dir. Higher Edn. Ctr. for Urban Studies, Health Systems Agy. S.W. Conn., 1977-84; mem. Conn. Statewide Health Coordinating Coun., 1979-87, chmn., 1984-87. Served with AUS, 1944-46. Barone Campus Ctr. at Fairfield U., Barone Resource Ctr. at St. Vincent's Coll. named in his honor, 1992; cancer rsch. grantee NIH, dir. NSF undergrad. rsch. program, 1961-67. Fellow AAAS; mem. Am. Chem. Soc. (chmn. western Conn. sect. 1966), AAUP (1st pres. Fairfield U. chpt.), Newcomen Soc., Phi Beta Kappa, Sigma Xi, Phi Lambda Upsilon. Clubs: Algonquin. Democrat. Roman Catholic.

BARONE, ROSE MARIE PACE, writer, retired educator, entertainer; b. Buffalo, Apr. 26, 1920; d. Dominic and Jennie (Zagara) Pace; m. John Barone, Aug. 23, 1947 BA, U. Buffalo, 1943; MS, U. So. Cal., 1950; cert. advanced study, Fairfield (Conn.) U., 1963. Tchr. Angola (N.Y.) High Sch., 1943-46, Puente (Calif.) High Sch., 1946-47, Jefferson High Sch., Lafayette, Ind., 1947-50; dir. Warren Inst., Bridgeport, Conn., 1951-53; instr. U. Bridgeport, 1953-54; tchr. bus. subjects Bassick H.S., Bridgeport, 1954-74, Harding H.S., Bridgeport, 1974-80; instr. Fairfield U., Conn., 1969; freelance writer, 1980—. Chair State Poetry Festival, 1987. Founder Pet Rescue; chmn. comty. affairs com. Area Coun. Cath. Women, 1988-90, sec., 1990-91, chmn. family affairs com., 1991, v.p., 1992-93; chmn. comty. affairs Ch. Women United, 1992—, state area chmn., 1995-97, sec., 2003, state UN chair, 1997—. Pace-Barone Minority yearly scholar Fairfield U., Auerbach Found. scholar, 1956; recipient Playwriting prize Conn. Federated Women's Clubs, 1955, 1st prize for poetry,

1985, Short Story award Federated Women Conn., 1987, 88, 90, Citizen award Bridgeport Dental Assn., 1982, State/Town Hero award, 1986, Anniversary medal and marble statuette Fairfield U., Cmty. Care Successful Aging award, 1992, Salute to Women award YWCA, 1993, Woman of Substance award, 1994, State Commission Arts award, 2000, RSVP award, 2001. Mem. NEA, AAUW (treas. 1957-58, named gift grant 1989, cultural and poetry chair 1992—, rec. sec. 1992-93, internat. rels. 1993-94, v.p. program 1995-97, contest chair 1995—, Conf. of Women award 1997, Fairfield Citizen, Vol. Extraordinaire, 2001), Am. Assn. Ret. People (v.p. 1987-88, pres. 1988-89, 94-95, instr. 55 Alive, cmty. affairs chair 1990—), Owl (sec. 1987-89, pres. 1989-90), Nat. League Am. PEN Women (Bridgeport historian 1966-84, state historian 1983—, treas. br. 1985-88, state pres. 1986-88, state lit. chair 1988-95, br. membership chair 1990, Nat. Historian award 1976, 88), Fairfield Area Poets (founder, pres. 1990—, editor 5 vols. Conn. poets), UN Assn. USA (pres. Bridgeport 1964-66, 68-70, v.p. 1988—, chmn. area UN Days 1960—, pres. Conn. 1971—, state chmn. UNICEF to 1984, area UNICEF Ctr. 1984—, state historian 1984—), Conn. Bus. Tchrs., Bridgeport Edn. Assn. (sec. 1966-68), VFW (aux. 1989—), Am. Legion (aux. contest chair 1989—, historian 1993-95, Aux. Nat. Cmty. Svc. award 1993), Fairfield Arts Coun., Fairfield Philatelic Soc. (sec. 1971-78, founder advisor Philatelic Jrs. 1972-80), Fairfield U. Women's Club (founder, pres. 1950, 74—, v.p. 1973-74), Southport Women's Club (garden dept. sec. 1981-85, chmn. 1985-87), John & Rose Marie Barone Resource Ctr. St. Vincent's Coll., Pi Omega Pi. Home: 1283 Round Hill Rd Fairfield CT 06430-7329

BARONI, BARRY JOSEPH, law educator, mediator, arbitrator; b. New Orleans, Dec. 21, 1939; s. Frank and Frances (Coniglio) B.; m. Eve Mary Davis, June 8, 1971. B.B.A., Loyola U., New Orleans, 1961, M.B.A., 1965, J.D., 1967; LL.M. in Labor Law, Tulane U., 1974. Bar: La. 1967, D.C. 1972, U.S. Dist. Ct. (ea. dist.) La. 1967, U.S. Ct. Appeals (5th cir.) 1967, U.S. Supreme Ct. 1971, U.S. Dist. Ct. D.C. 1971, U.S. Ct. Claims, U.S. Tax Ct., U.S. Ct. Mil. Appeals, U.S. Ct. Customs and Patent Appeals. Mem. faculty Coll. Bus., U. New Orleans, 1967—, prof. labor law and arbitration, 1967— ; mgmt. cons. and tng. specialist in indsl. relations, 1970— ; trial atty. enforcement div. SEC, Washington, summers 1971-75; prof. law U. Innsbruck, Austria, summers, 1979, 80, 82, 85, 87, 95, U. N.C., Chapel Hill, summer 1983; vis. prof. Coll. Bus., dep. gen. counsel NLRB, Washington, summer 1984; mem. arbitrator list Fed. Mediation and Conciliation Service, 1979—, Am. Arbitration Assn., 1975, Nat. Acad. of Arbitrators, 1987—. Editor Loyola U. Law Rev., 1965-66. Contbr. numerous articles to bus. and legal jours. Served to lt. comdr. JAGC, USNR, 1975-95. Mem. D.C. Bar Assn., La. Bar Assn., Am. Bus. Law Assn., So. Bus. Law Assn., Am. Arbitration Assn., Soc. for Profls. in Dispute Resolution. Office: U New Orleans Lakefront Coll Of Business New Orleans LA 70148-0001

BAROODY, ALBERT JOSEPH, JR., pastoral counselor; b. Columbia, S.C., Sept. 8, 1952; s. Albert Joseph and Hazel (Haskin) B.; m. Nancy Dell Weatherford, Jan. 3, 1976; children: Joseph McKinley, Blakely Adelle. BS in Sociology, U. S.C., 1974; MDiv, S.E. Bapt. Theol. Sem., Wake Forest, N.C., 1978, D of Ministry, 1984. Ordained to ministry Bapt. Ch., 1977; lic. profl. counselor, S.C., 1992; cert. pastoral counselor. Chaplain intern and resident Palmetto Bapt. Med. Ctr., Columbia, S.C., 1977-79; dir. pastoral svcs. Easley (S.C.) Bapt. Med. Ctr., 1979-80, McLeod Regional Med. Ctr., Florence, 1980-91; pastoral counselor McLeod Counseling Svcs., Florence, 1991-94, Cmty. Care and Counseling, Florence, 1994-2000, Baroody Pastoral Counseling, St. John's Episcopal Ch., Florence, 2000—; interim pastorate Florence Bapt. Fellowship, 2003—. Chaplain Lions Club, Florence, 1980-83; interim pastor Florence Bapt. Fellowship, 2003—; pastoral cons. Tuomey Hosp., Sumter, S.C., 1983, Conway (S.C.) Hosp., 1985-86, 92-94, Williamsburg County Hosp., Kingstree, S.C., 1986-88. Author (with others): Ministry to Youth in Crisis; contbr. articles to profl. jours. Continuing edn. state rep. Coll. Chaplains, 1983-92; mem. adv. bd. Salvation Army, Florence, 2000—, vice chmn. adv. bd., 2002, 03; mem. adv. bd., Hospice, Florence, 1988-94, chmn., 1993-94; chmn. Devel. Com. of S.E. Region Assn. for Clin. Pastoral Edn., 1986-90; liason coun. S.C. Organ Procurement Assn., 1988-91; mem. Pee Dee Coalition Against Domestic and Sexual Assault cmty. svcs. adv. coun., 1996-2001. Fellow Am. Assn. Pastoral Counselors (cert., S.E. region fin. com. 1996-99, profl. concerns com. 2000); mem. Assn. Profl. Chaplains (cert. chaplain). Avocations: traveling, reading, walking, movies. Office: Baroody Pastoral Counseling St John's Episcopal Ch 252 S Dargan St Florence SC 29506-2534 E-mail: Joebaroody@aol.com.

BAROODY, ARTHUR JAMES, mathematician, educator; b. Auburn, N.Y., Aug. 15, 1947; s. Arthur and Martha (Keeley) B.; m. Sharon Coslick, Mar. 29, 1970; children: Alison, Alexis, Arianne. BS, Cornell U., 1969, PhD, 1979. Asst. prof. Keuka Coll., Keuka Park, N.Y., 1977-80; rsch. assoc. U. Rochester, N.Y., 1980-86; prof. early childhood and elem. math. edn. U. Ill., Champaign, 1986—. Co-author of TEMA and SCREEN tests. Author: Children's Mathematical Thinking, 1987, Problem Solving, Reasoning and Communicating, 1993, Fostering Children's Mathematical Power, 1998. 1st lt. U.S. Army, 1969-72. Grantee NIH, 1983—86, NSF, 1985—88, 2001—. Mem. Am. Edni. Rsch. Assn., Internat. Group for Psychology of Math. Edn., Soc. Rsch. Child Devel. Office: Coll Edn Univ Ill 1310 S 6th St Champaign IL 61820-6925

BAROODY, JUDITH RAINE, federal official, educator; b. Richmond, Va., Nov. 28, 1953; d. Alfred Fred and Elizabeth Irwin Baroody; m. Richard Dale Krueger, June 14, 1986. BA, William and Mary, 1975; MA, U. Va., 1985; PhD, Am. U., 1993; MS, Nat. War Coll., 2000. Reporter Sta. WVEC-TV, Norfolk, Va., 1977-83; fgn. svc. officer Dept. State, Washington, 1984—; pub. affairs officer U.S. Consulate, Casablanca, Morocco, 1992—95, Am. Embassy, Nicosia, Cyprus, 1996—99; dir. pub. affairs and pub. diplomacy Bur. Near Ea. Affairs, 2000—02; dir. strategic planning and external affairs Bur. Democracy, Human Rights and Labor Dept. State, Washington, 2002—. Instr. Am. U., Washington. Author: Media Access and the Military: the Case of the Gulf War, 1998; chmn. editl. bd. Fgn. Svc. Jour., 2003 Bd. dirs. State Dept. Fed. Credit Union, Alexandria, Va., 1999-2000. Named Outstanding Individual Report Va. AP Broadcasters, 1982; recipient Marks Found. award USIA, 1999, Col. Higgins award NWC, 2000; fellow MIT Seminar XXI, 2003. Mem. Exec. Women Govt., Washington Classical Guitar Soc., Phi Kappa Phi. Episcopalian. Avocations: classical guitar, snorkeling, photography, travel. Home: 6601 Forsythia St Springfield VA 22150 Office: Dept State DRL Rm 7802 2201 C St NW Washington DC 20520 E-mail: jrbaroody@aol.com.

BAROODY, MICHAEL ELIAS, trade association executive; b. Washington, Sept. 14, 1946; s. William J. and Nabeeha (Ashooh) B.; m. Mary Cecilia Patton, Dec. 16, 1967; children— Michael Elias, Timothy, Catherine, Matthew, Peter, Meghan BA in Polit. Sci., U. Notre Dame, 1968. Legis. asst. Senator Roman Hruska, Washington, 1970-71; speech writer, exec. asst. Senator Bob Dole, Washington, 1972-75; congl. liaison FEA, Washington, 1975-77; dir. pub. affairs Republican Nat. Com., Washington, 1977-81; exec. asst. to U.S. trade rep. William Brock, Washington, 1981; dep. asst. to Pres., dir. pub. affairs The White House, Washington, 1981-85; asst. sec. for policy Dept. Labor, Washington, 1985-89; sr. v.p. for policy and comms. Nat. Assn. Mfrs., 1990-93; pres. nat. policy forum A Rep. Ctr. for Exch. of Ideas, 1993-94; v.p. pub. affairs Nat. Assn. Mfrs., Washington, 1994-96, sr. v.p. pub. affairs, 1997-99, sr. v.p. policy comm. and pub. affairs, 1999-2001, exec. v.p., 2001—. Editor-in-chief: Commonsense: A Republican Jour. Thought and Opinion, 1978-80, 94, Rep. Platform, 1980. Chmn. bd. Nat. Ctr. for Neighborhood Enterprise, 1997—2002. Lt. (j.g.) USN, 1968-70 Greek Catholic Home: 4628 Newcomb Pl Alexandria VA 22304-1505

BAROTT, PAT ROBERT, broadcast technician; b. St. Paul, Minn., Oct. 26, 1953; s. Robert Wilfred Barott and Erma Janet Hagaan. Grad. HS, Forest Lake HS, Forest Lake, Minn., 1972. Contbr. Emergency comacetions; mem. Amature Radio Emergency Svc. Mem.: AAAS (assoc.), Minn. Assn. Radio Operators, N.Y. Acad. Scis., Twin Cities Receptor Club, Anacka County Radio Club. Avocations: ham radio, astro physics. Home: 13702 Jordell St Circle Pines MN 55014-2049

BAROUCH, DAN HUNG, physician, scientist; b. Gottingen, Germany, Feb. 4, 1973; s. Eytan and Winifred Wendy B.; m. Fina Canas, May 15, 1999. BA summa cum laude, Harvard U., 1993; PhD, Oxford (U.K.) U., 1995; MD summa cum laude, Harvard U., 1999. Rschr. HIV immunology and vaccines Oxford U., 1993-95; rschr. Beth Israel Deaconess Med. Ctr., Boston, 1995—; clin. fellow in medicine Harvard Med. Sch., Boston, 1999—2002; resident physician in internal medicine, fellow in infectious diseases Mass. Gen. Hosp., Brigham and Women's Hosp., Boston, 1999—; instr. in med. Harvard Med. Sch., 2002—. Investigator HIV Vaccine Trials Network, Boston, 2000—. Contbr. articles to profl. jours. British Marshall scholarship Marshall Commn., 1993-95, Barry M. Goldwater scholarship U.S. Govt., 1991-93, USA Today Coll. scholar, 1993. Mem. AMA, ACP, AAAS, Mass. Med. Soc. Avocations: calligraphy, violin, skiing, travel. Home: ONE LONGFELLOW PL APT 3222 BOSTON MA 02114 Office: Mass Gen Hosp 55 Fruit St Boston MA 02114 E-mail: dbarouch@bidmc.harvard.edu.

BAROUDY, BAHIGE MOURAD, biochemist, researcher; b. Beirut, July 1, 1950; came to U.S., 1973, naturalized, 1988; s. Mourad Bahige and Ludmila Adelheid (Obermuller-Haddad) BSc, Am. U. of Beirut, 1972; PhD, Georgetown U., 1978. Teaching asst. Wesleyan U., Middletown, Conn., 1973-74; rsch. asst. Georgetown U., Washington, 1974-78, fellow, 1982, rsch. assoc. prof., 1985-89; dir. molecular virology div. James N. Gamble Inst. Med. Rsch., Cin., 1989-95; assoc. dir. antiviral therapy Schering-Plough Rsch. Ins., Kenilworth, N.J., 1996-2000, dir., 2000—01, group dir., 2001—02, group dir. antiviral and antimicrobial therapy, 2002—. Vis. fellow scientist NIH, Bethesda, Md., 1979-81, vis. assoc. scientist, 1982-85. Contbr. articles to profl. jours., chpts. to books. Mem. Am. Assn. for Study of Liver Diseases, Am. Chem. Soc., Am. Soc. Biochemistry and Molecular Biology, Am. Soc. for Microbiology, Am. Soc. for Virology, N.Y. Acad. Scis., NIH Alumni Assn., Sigma Xi. Lutheran. Avocations: fencing, viola. Office: Antiviral Therapy Schering Plough Rsch Inst K-15 4-4650 2015 Galloping Hill Rd Kenilworth NJ 07033-1310 E-mail: bahige@comcast.net.

BARQAWI, ALBAHA Z. urologist, researcher; b. Khubar, Saudi Arabia, Nov. 8, 1966; s. Zuhair K. Barqawi and Nadera A. Al-Hanbali; m. Dina A. Abu-Hilal, Dec. 9, 1995; children: Natasha A., Zuhair A., Sandra Jean. Bachelor of Medicine, Med. Acad., Sofia, Bulgaria, 1990. Resident in surgery Royal Coll. Surgeons, Dublin, 1993—98; registrar in gen. surgery/urology Portlaoise Gen. Hosp., Laois, Ireland, 1998—99; hon. fellow Leicester Gen. Hosp., 1999—2000; specialist registrar Worthing Gen. Hosp., West Sussex, 1999—2000; rsch. fellow dept. oncology and urology U. Colo., Denver, 2000—. Prin. investigator U. Colo. Health Sci. Ctr., Denver. Contbr. articles to profl. jours. Fellow: Royal Coll. Surgeons, Royal Acad. Medicine in Ireland (life). Avocation: travel. Office: University of Colorado Health Science Ce 4200 E 9th Ave C-319 Denver CO 80262 Home Fax: 801-516-3021; Office Fax: 303-864-5570. Personal E-mail: albahadina@yahoo.com. E-mail: al.barqawi@uchsc.edu.

BARQUERO, PEDRO BENJAMIN, mathematician, researcher; b. Barcelona, Apr. 18, 1973; s. Benjamin Barquero and Maria Carmen Salavert. BSc, U. Bath, Eng., 1996; MA, UCLA, 1998, PhD, 2000. Lectr. Calif. State U., Carson, 2001—02; prof. N.Y. Inst. Tech., N.Y.C., 2003—; assoc. prof. Santa Monica Coll., Calif., 2000—03. Textbook reviewer Brooks/Cole Pub., 2003—. Contbr. Fellow Chancellor's fellow, Dept. Math., UCLA; scholar UCLA scholar, 1996. Mem.: Math. Assn. Am., Am. Math. Soc. Office: Mathematics NYIT-Manhattan Campus 1855 Broadway New York NY 10023

BARR, CHARLES JOSEPH GORE, lawyer; b. Saginaw, Mich., Sept. 17, 1940; s. Joseph Gore and Maja T. (Strand) B.; m. Carolyn Conn, Aug. 26, 1961; children: Maja Irene, Shannon Conn, Meaghan Won. BA, U. Mich., 1962, LLB, 1965. Bar: Mich. 1965, U.S. Dist. Ct. (ea. dist.) Mich. 1965, U.S. Ct. Appeals (6th cir.) 1968. Assoc. Clark Klein Winter, Detroit, 1965-67, Goodman, Eden, Millender & Bedrosian, Detroit, 1967-73; ptnr. Moore, Barr & Kerwin, Detroit, 1974-78, Barr & Walker, Detroit, 1978-83, Barr & Arsenault, Detroit, 1984-90, Barr & Assocs., Detroit, 1990—. Mem. State Bar of Mich. (chmn. negligence sect. 1985-86), Assn. Trial Lawyers Am. (gov. 1982-85), Mich. Trial Lawyers Assn. (sec. 1986-87, pres. 1988-89), Nat. Lawyers Guild (pres. Detroit chpt. 1983-84, exec. bd.). Home: 19430 Cumberland Way Detroit MI 48203-1458 Office: 2201 Cadillac Tower Detroit MI 48226 Fax: 313-965-2043. E-mail: cjgbarr@aol.com.

BARR, CYRILLA PATRICIA, music educator; b. Carroll, Iowa, Feb. 9, 1929; d. Ernest Melvin and Elizabeth Marie (Schumacher) B. B in Music Edn., Viterbo Coll., 1956; MusM, U. Wis., 1957; PhD, Cath. U. of Am., 1965. Assoc. prof. Viterbo Coll., La Crosse, Wis., 1957-61, 65-74; prof. Cath. U. of Am., Washington, 1976-99, prof. emeritus, 1999—. Cons. Opera Am., Washington, 1991. Author: (book) Monophonic Lauda, 1988, (monograph) The Coolidge Legacy, 1997, (biography) Elizabeth Sprague Coolidge: American patron of Music; co-author, co-editor: (book) Cultivating Music in America, 1997. Fulbright scholar U.S. Cultural Exch., 1963-64; I. Tatti fellow Harvard U., 1974-75; grantee-in-aid (3) Am. Coun. Learned Socs., 1978, 79, 88. Mem. Am. Musicol. Soc., Sonneck Soc. Roman Catholic. Avocations: reading, traveling, cooking. Office: Cath U Of Am Washington DC 20064-0001

BARR, DAVID JOHN, civil, geological engineering educator; b. Evansville, Ind., Mar. 5, 1939; s. Ralph Emerson and Selma Louise (Sander) B.; m. Kay Arlene Porter, Jan. 23, 1965; 1 child, John Matthew. C.E., U. Cin., 1962; MSCE, Purdue U., 1964, PhD, 1968. Registered profl. engr., Ohio. Asst. prof. civil engring. U. Cin., 1968-72; prof. geol. engring. U. Mo., Rolla, 1972—, chmn. dept. geol. and petroleum engring., 1987-92, dir. Mo. Mining and Mineral Resources Rsch. Inst., 1980-87, asst. to vice chancellor for acad. computing, 1986-87. Cons. in field. Author: (with others) Remote Sensing for Resource Managemnt, 1983; contbr. Ency. Applied Geology, 1984. Bd. dirs., fireman Rolla Rural Fire Protection Assn., 1975-88. Recipient New Tech. award NASA, 1973-74; NASA rsch. fellow Manned Spacecraft Ctr., Houston, 1969, 70. Mem. NSPE, ASCE (chmn. aerospace div. 1977), Mo. Soc. Profl. Engrs. (Rolla chpt. pres. 1992-93), Am. Soc. Photogrammetry (pres. Rolla region 1975), Soc. Mining Engrs., Assn. Engring. Geologists, Am. Soc. for Engring. Edn., Nat. Assn. Mineral Inst. Dirs. (nat. chmn. 1987-88). Avocations: hunting, fishing. Office: U Mo-Rolla Dept Geol and Petroleum Engring 129 McNutt Rolla MO 65401-0249

BARR, DAVID JOHN, retired art educator; b. Detroit, Oct. 10, 1939; s. John A. and Phyllis E. (Prince) B.; m. Elizabeth Margaret Dwaihy, June 19, 1982; children: Heather, Gillian. BFA, Wayne State U., 1962, MFA, 1965. Prof. art Macomb C.C., Warren, Mich., 1965—2002, ret., 2002. Founder, artistic dir. Mich. Legacy Art Park, Thompsonville, Mich., 1995—. One-man shows include Hanamura Gallery, Detroit, 1965, Kazimir Gallery, Chgo., 1968-69, 71-72, Evanston (Ill.) Art Ctr., 1969, Donald Morris Gallery, Detroit, 1973, Art Rsch. Ctr., Kansas City, Mo., 1974, Marianne Friedland Gallery, Toronto, Ont., Can., 1975, Richard Gray Gallery, Chgo., 1975, 86, U. Pitts., 1975, Donald Morris Gallery, Birmingham, Mich., 1976, 79, 81, 84, 87, 89, 92, San Jose Mus. Art, 1978, Kent (Ohio) State U., 1979, Meadowbrook Art Gallery, Oakland U., Rochester, Minn., 1982, Mot Coll., Flint, Mich., 1985, Momentum Gallery, Mpls., 1986, Swords into Plowshares Gallery, Detroit, 1990, Dennos Mus., Traverse City, Mich., 2000, Krasl. Mus., St. Joseph, Mich., 2002, Midland (Mich.) Art Ctr., 2002, Washtenaw Coll., Ann Arbor, Mich., 1993; exhibited in group shows at Flint Inst. Art, 1990, Pontiac (Mich.) Art Ctr., 1992; commns. include Fairlane Town Ctr., Dearborn, Mich., 1976, Macomb C.C., 1976, Meadowbrook Festival Ground, Oakland U., 1981, Lakeview Sq., Battle Creek, Mich., 1983, Mich. Hist. Mus., Lansing, 1988, Hoffman Corp., Appleton, Wis., 1989, Bishop Internat. Airport, Flint, 1994, Detroit Zoo Wildlife Interpretive Ctr. Butterfly-Hummingbird Garden, 1995, Chrysler World Hdqrs., Auburn Hills, Mich., 1996, Revolution II, Brussels, Belgium, 1998, Dennos Mus., Traverse City, 1999-2000, Mich. Legacy Art Pk., 2002, Thompsonville, Mich., 2002, Pfizer, Ann Arbor, Mich., 2002, Pisa Town Hall, Pisa, Italy, 2002, Hart Plaza, Detroit, 2003, others; represented in permanent collections Dennos Mus. Ctr., Northwestern Mich. Coll., Traverse City, Detroit Inst. Arts, Flint Inst. Arts, Ft. Lauderdale Mus., Oakland U., Portland (Oreg.) Art Recipient Mich. Arts award Arts Found. Mich., 1977, Disting. Alumni award Wayne State U., 1983, Gov. of Mich.'s artist award Concerned Citizens for Arts in Mich., 1988, Humanity in the Arts award Wayne State U., 1988. Mem. AIA (hon.). Home: 22600 Napier Rd Novi MI 48374-3202

BARR, DONALD ROY, statistics and operations research educator, statistician; b. Durango, Colo., Dec. 10, 1938; s. Russell Wesely and Elizabeth Joanette B.; m. Loudean Suttle, June 14, 1958; children: Mark Edward, Bryan Michael. BA, Whittier Coll., 1960; MS, Colo. State U., 1962, PhD, 1965. Instr. Colo. State U., 1964-65; asst. prof. math. U. Wis.-Oshkosh, 1965-66; prof. stats. and ops. rsch. Naval Postgrad. Sch., Monterey, Calif., 1966-87; v.p. Evaluation Tech. Inc., 1987-88, pres., 1988-89; v.p. VRC Corp., Monterey, 1988-89; prof. math. Naval Postgrad. Sch., Monterey, CA, 1990-93; prof. systems engring. U.S. Mil. Acad., West Point, N.Y., 1993-99; ret., 1999—. Liaison scientist London br. Office Naval Rsch., 1982-83; vis. prof. systems engring., U.S. Mil. Acad., West Point, N.Y., 1992-93. Author: College and University Mathematics, 1968, Finite Statistics, 1968, Probability, 1971, Analytic Geometry: A Vector Approach, 1971, Probability: Modeling Uncertainty, 1981, Statistics by Calculator, 1983; contbr. articles to profl. jours. Recipient Rist prize for best paper in mil. ops. rsch. Mil. Ops. Rsch. Soc., 1996, Payne award for ops. rsch. U.S. Army, 1997. Mem. Am. Stat. Assn., Ops. Research Soc. Am., Internat. Test and Evaluation Assn., Sigma Xi. Home: PO Box 2071 Paradise CA 95967-2071 E-mail: dbarrz@aol.com.

BARR, HARVEY STEPHEN, lawyer; b. N.Y.C., June 4, 1941; s. Lillian (Meslin) B.; m. Willyce Selman, Dec. 18, 1962: children: Shari Lynn, Amy Sue, Pamela Jan, Matthew Scott. LLB, N.Y. Law Sch., 1964. Bar: N.Y. 1964, U.S. Ct. Appeals 1966, U.S. Dist. Ct. 1968, U.S. Supreme Ct. 1969. Village atty. Village of Spring Valley, N.Y., 1965-67, Village of Sloatsburg, N.Y., 1969-82, Village of Suffern, N.Y., 1975-77; asst. county atty. Rockland County, N.Y., 1970-74; ptnr. Barr & Faerber, Spring Valley, N.Y., 1979-90, Barr & Rosenbaum, 1990-2001, Barr & Haas LLP, 2002—. Mem. editl. bd. N.Y. Law Forum, 1961-64. Active Rockland County Republican Com., 1964-82; chmn. Town of Ramapo Rep. Com. Mem. Rockland County Bar Assn., Bar Assn. State of NY. Jewish. Office: Barr & Haas LLP 664 Chestnut Ridge Rd Spring Valley NY 10977-1901 Business E-Mail: hbarr@barrandhaas.com.

BARR, IRWIN ROBERT, retired aeronautical engineer; b. Newburgh, N.Y., May 16, 1920; s. Abraham Herman and Esther (Reibel) B.; m. Florence Lenore Skliar, Oct. 19, 1941 (dec. Feb. 1957); children: Mary Barr Megee, Betty Barr Mackey, Joan Barr Blanco, Alan Howard; m. Dorothy Friendly Weeks, Sept. 20, 1958. Cert. aero. engring., Inst. Aeros., 1940. Registered profl. engr., Md. Design group engr. Glenn L. Martin Co., Balt., 1940-50; chief ordnance engr., then pres. and chief exec. officer AAI Corp., Hunt Valley, Md., 1950-89, chmn. bd. emeritus, 1989—. Patentee rocket stblzn. and control sys., aircraft, weapons, wheels, suspensions, bearings, solar energy collectors, med. catheter, heart pump, aluminum-powered batteries. Served with USAAF, 1944-46. Named to Ordnance Hall of Fame, Aberdeen Proving Ground, Md., 1985 Home: 13801 York Rd Apt S207 Cockeysville Hunt Valley MD 21030-1826

BARR, JAMES, III, telecommunications company executive; b. Oak Park, Ill., Mar. 2, 1940; s. James Jr. and Florence Marie (Erichsen) B.; m. Joan Benning, Aug. 12, 1961; children: James IV, Brett Christopher, Heather Kathryn, Stephanie Alexandra. BS in Engring., Iowa State U., 1962; MBA, U. Chgo., 1967. Engr. Ill. Bell Tel. Co., Chgo., 1962-66, staff mgr. for regulatory affairs, 1966-69; dist. mgr. for planning AT&T, N.Y.C., 1969-72, dir. regulatory affairs, 1975-80, dir. product mgmt. Basking Ridge, N.J., 1980-85, sales v.p. N.Y.C., 1985-90; gen. mktg. mgr. Bell Can., Ottawa, Ont., 1972-75; pres., CEO, TDS TELECOM, Madison, Wis., 1990—. Exec. vp., bd. dirs. NY Bd. Trade, 1985—90; bd. dirs. Tel. and Data Sys., Chgo., Ctr. for Telecom. Mgmt., L.A., TDS Telecom, Madison, Wis. Mem. dean's adv. coun. Bus. Sch. U. Wis., 1997— Republican. Roman Catholic. Office: TDS TELECOM 301 S Westfield Rd Madison WI 53717-1799

BARR, JAMES HOUSTON, III, lawyer; b. Louisville, Nov. 2, 1941; s. James Houston Jr. and Elizabeth Hamilton (Pope) Barr; m. Sarah Jane Todd, Apr. 16, 1970 (div.); 1 child, Lynn Jamison; m. Cindy Ann Jeffries, May 31, 1997; children: Worden Pope Washington, Augustine Washington Jeffries. Student, U. Va., 1960-63, U. Tenn., 1963-64; BSL, JD, U. Louisville, 1966. Bar: Ky. 1966, U.S. Ct. Appeals (6th cir.) 1969, U.S. Supreme Ct. 1971, U.S. Ct. Mil. Appeals 1978. Law clk. Ky. Ct. Appeals, Frankfort, 1966-67; asst. atty. gen. Ky. Frankfort, 1967-71, 79-82; asst. U.S. atty. U.S. Dept. Justice, Louisville, 1971-79, 83—; 1st asst. U.S. Atty., 1978-79; asst. dist. counsel U.S. Army C.E., Louisville, 1982-83. Lt. comdr. USNR, 1967-81, lt. col. USAR, 1981-91. Mem. FBA (pres. Louisville chpt. 1975-76, Younger Fed. Lawyer award 1975), Ky. Bar Assn., Louisville Bar Assn., Soc. Colonial Wars, SAR, Washington Family Soc., Pendennis Club, Louisville Boat Club, Filson Club, Delta Upsilon. Republican. Episcopalian. Home: 100 Westwind Rd Louisville KY 40207-1520 Office: US Atty 510 W Broadway Ste 1000 Louisville KY 40202-2281

BARR, JAMES NORMAN, federal judge; b. Kewanee, Ill, Oct. 21, 1940; s. James Cecil and Dorothy Evelyn (Dorsey) B.; m. Trilla Anne Reeves, Oct. 31, 1964 (div. 1979); 1 child, James N. Jr.; m. Phyllis L. DeMent, May 30, 1986; children: Renae, Michele. BS, Ill. Wesleyan U., 1962; JD, Ill. Inst. Tech., 1971. Bar: Ill. 1972, Calif. 1977. Assoc. Pretzel, Stouffer, Nolan & Rooney, Chgo., 1974-76; claims counsel Safeco Title Ins. Co., L.A., 1977-78; assoc. Kamph & Jackman, Santa Ana, Calif., 1978-80; lawyer pvt. practice Law Offices of James N. Barr, Santa Ana, 1980-86; judge U.S Bankruptcy Ct. Ctrl. Dist. Calif., Santa Anna, 1987—. Adj. prof. Chapman U. Sch. Law, 1996—. Lt. USN, 1962-67, Vietnam. Mem. Fed. Bar Assn. (Orange County chpt. bd. dirs. 1996-2000), Orange County Bar Assn. (cmty. outreach com.), Nat. Conf. Bankruptcy Judges, Orange County Bankruptcy Forum (bd. dirs. 1989—), Peter M. Elliott Inn Ct. (founder, first pres. 1990-91), Warren J. Ferguson Am. Inn of Ct. (founder). Office: US Bankruptcy Ct 411 W 4th St Santa Ana CA 92701-4500

BARR, JOHN BALDWIN, chemist, research scientist; b. Niagara Falls, N.Y., Nov. 8, 1932; s. Lorne Haworth and Myra (Baldwin) B.; m. Patricia Jane Kromer, Sept. 18, 1954; children: Mark Kromer, John Robert, Kathryn Jean, Karen Patricia. BA, U. Buffalo, 1954; MS, U. Mich., 1956; PhD, Pa. State U., 1961. Rsch. chemist Corning Glass Works (N.Y.), 1961-62; sr. rsch. chemist Union Carbide Corp., Parma, Ohio, 1962-71, rsch. scientist, 1971-82, sr. rsch. scientist, 1982-86, Amoco Performance Products, Parma, 1986-90, Alpharetta, Ga., 1990-91, assoc. rsch. scientist, 1991-95; cons. Rsch. Opportunities, Inc., Torrance, Calif., 1996—2001; cons. for carbon fiber industry, 2002—. Contbr. articles to profl. jours.; patentee in field. Shell Oil Co. fellow, 1959. Mem. Am. Chem. Soc., Am. Carbon Soc., N.Am. Thermal Analysis Soc., Sigma Xi, Phi Lambda Upsilon. Republican. Episcopalian.

BARR, JOHN MICHAEL, investor, management consultant; b. Columbus, Ohio, May 13, 1957; s. William Harvey and Mary Louise (Chesser) B.; m. Mary Elizabeth Mudd, Sept. 4, 1982. BA in History and Polit. Sci., Ohio Dominican Coll., 1979; MA in Polit. Sci., Ohio State U., 1980. Tchr. pub. schs., 1981-88; secondary edn. educator Whitehall City Schs., 1981-83, South Western City Schs., 1983-88; profl. investor, speaker, cons. Westerville, Ohio, 1988—; pres. Decisive Response, Westerville, 2000—. Active Rep. Nat. 500 Club, Washington, 1991, Franklin County Reps., Columbus, 1990, Rep. Nat. Campaign Coun., 1988—, Ohio Rep. Party, 1993—; mem. Rep. Presdl. Task Force. Mem. ASTD, Am. Assn. Individual Investors (life), NRA (life, chmn. second ammend. task force 1993—), Am. Bd. Hypnotherapy, Japan Aikido Assn. (life), Am. Soc. Cybernetics, Internat. Listening Assn., Shingitai Jujitsu Assn., Nat. Guild of Hypnotists. Methodist. Avocations: shooting, Aikido, travel, poetry. Office: PO Box 506 Westerville OH 43086-0506

BARR, JOHN MONTE, lawyer; b. Mt. Clemens, Mich., Jan. 1, 1935; s. Merle James and Wilhelmina Marie (Monte) B.; student Mexico City Coll., 1955; BA, Mich. State U., 1956; JD, U. Mich., 1959; m. Marlene Joy Bielenberg, Dec. 17, 1954; children: John Monte, Karl Alexander, Elizabeth Marie. Admitted to Mich. bar, 1959, since practiced in Ypsilanti; mem. Ellis B. Freatman, Jr., 1959-61; ptnr., chief trial atty. Freatman, Barr, Anhut & Moir and predecessor firm, 1961-63; pres. Barr, Anhut, Assoc. PC, 1963-01; pres. Barr, Anhut, Gilbreath, 2001—; city atty. City of Ypsilanti, 1981—, City of Belleville, 2000—. Lectr. bus. law Eastern Mich. U., 1968-70. Pres., Ypsilanti Family Service, 1967; mem. Ypsilanti Public Housing Com., 1980-84; sr. adviser Explorer law post Portage Trail council Boy Scouts Am., 1969-71, commr. Potawatomi dist., 1973-74, commr. Washtenong dist., 1974-75, dist. committeeman, 1984, wolverine coun. v.p., 1992, v.p. Great Saulk Trail coun., 1995—; bd. dirs. Mich. Mcpl. League Legal Def. Fund., pres. 1989-90, sec. High/Scope Ednl. Rsch. Found., 2003-, past pres. Washtenaw 100 Club, 1980—. Served with AUS, 1959-60. Recipient Silver Beaver award Boy Scouts Am., 1992, Mich. Mcpl. League award of Merit Mcpl. League Legal Def., 1992. Mem. State Bar Mich. (grievance bd. hearing panel 1969-97, state rep. assembly 1977-82, bd. commrs. 1993—), Am., Ypsilanti, Washtenaw County (pres.

1975-76, Profl. and Civility award 1998) Bar Assns., Washtenaw County Trial Lawyers Assns., Mich. Mcpl. Attys. Assn. (pres. 1989-90, MAMA dist. mcpl. atty. award, 1993), U.S. (instr. piloting, seamanship, sail), Ann Arbor (comdr. 1972-73) power squadrons. Lutheran. Club: Washtenaw Country. Contbr. articles to boating mags. Home: 1200 Whittier Rd Ypsilanti MI 48197-2152 Office: 105 Pearl St Ypsilanti MI 48197-2611

BARR, JOHN ROBERT, retired lawyer; b. Gary, Ind., Apr. 10, 1936; s. John Andrew and Louise (Stentz) B.; m. Patricia A. Ferris, July 30, 1988; children: Mary Louise, John Mills, Jennifer Susan. BA, Grinnell Coll., 1957; LL.B. cum laude, Harvard U., 1960. Bar: Ill. 1960. Assoc. Sidley Austin Brown & Wood, Chgo., 1960—69, ptnr., 1970—99, sr. counsel, 2000—02; ret., 2002. Mem. Ill. Ho. of Reps., 1981-83, Commn. on Presdl. Scholars, Washington, 1975-77; mem. Ill. Electric Utility Property Assessment Task Force, 1998-99. Chmn. Ill. Bd. Regents, 1971-77; mem. Ill. Bd. Higher Edn., 1971-77, 87—; chmn. Ill. Student Assistance Commn., 1985—; chmn. Rep. Ctrl. Com. of Cook County, Chgo., 1978-85; mem. Rep. state ctrl. com. 9th Congl. Dist. Ill., 1986-93; trustee Grinnell Coll., 1996—, Evanston Hist. Soc., 2001—; bd. dirs. Steppenwolf Theatre Co., Chgo., 1992—. Mem. ABA (chmn. task force on utility deregulation of state and local tax coms.), Ill. State Bar Assn. (chmn. state tax sect. coun. 1986-87), Chgo. Bar Assn. (chmn. com. on state and mcpl. taxation 1974-75), Taxpayers' Fedn. Ill. (treas. 1990-92, vice chmn. 1992-95, chmn. 1995-97), The Civic Fedn. (bd. dirs. 1993-97), Selden Soc., Nat. Assn. State Bar Tax Sects. (sec.-treas. 1989-90, vice chmn. 1990-91, chmn. 1991-92), Emil Verban Soc., Lawyer's Club Chgo., Chgo. Club, Phi Beta Kappa. Episcopalian. Home: 1144 Asbury Ave Evanston IL 60202-1137 Office: Sidley Austin Brown & Wood Bank One Plz 10 S Dearborn Chicago IL 60603 E-mail: jrbarr@sidley.com.

BARR, KENNETH L. former mayor; b. Fort Worth, TX, 1942; s. Willard B.; married; 1 daughter. BBA, postgrad., Tex. Christian U. With The Barr Printers, now pres., CEO; mem. Ft. Worth Transp. Authority, chair, 1992-93; mem. City Coun. for the Near South Side Coun. Dist., 1993—96; mayor City of Ft. Worth, 1996—2003. Mem., elder Univ. Christian Ch.; bd. dirs. Dallas-Ft. Worth Internat. Airport, Casa Manana Theater, The Gladney Fund; chair Work Force Devel. Bd., Strategy 2000 Bd.; former bd. dirs. Lena Pope Home Bd., Child Study Ctr. Bd. Recipient Rotary Found. Paul Harris fellow. Mem. Printing Industry Assn.-Tex. CEO Roundtable (organizing mem., bd. rep.).*

BARR, KEVIN CURTIS, poet, computer graphics designer; b. Cin., Sept. 26, 1963; s. Fred Curtis Sutton and Betty Jane B. Pvt. security officer Burns Security Co., Cin., 1994—. Author: (poetry books) My Love Is, 1997, Once Sprinkled By A Saintly Tear, 1997, Oh Chaka Fame Tonite, 1998, The Red Eagle Soars from Heaven, 1998, The Hunting Grounds of Social Knowledge. Recipient Cert. of achievement Talent Search Am., Nashville, 1994, Cert. of merit Nashville Newsletter, 1996. Avocations: creating comic book characters, dancing, beginning novelist.

BARR, LESLIE GLEN, family practice physician; b. Ft. Benning, Ga., Aug. 1, 1965; d. Glen Woodard Smith and Barbara Jean Mills; children: Shannon Leslie, Chelsea Patricia. BA, SUNY, Buffalo, 1993, MD, 1998; MBA, Niagara U., N.Y., 2000. Diplomate Nat. Bd. Family Practice, Minn. Bd. Med. Practice. Resident U. Buffalo, 1998—2001; family physician Mayo Health Sys., Waseca, Minn., 2001—; clin. instr. dept. family practice and cmty. health U. Minn. Med. Sch. Contbr. chpt. Sexism and Stereotypes in Modern Society, 1999. Mem.: AMA, Minn. Acad. Family Practice (del.), Am. Bd. Family Practice, Minn. Med. Assn., Rotary Internat. (bd. dirs. for internat. svcs.), Phi Beta Kappa. Roman Catholic. Avocation: teaching church school. Home: 2101 4th St NE Waseca MN 56093

BARR, LOIS I. personnel administrator; b. Olympia, Wash., Feb. 8, 1949; d. Jacob Hatfield Barr and Irene Tourangeau; m. Steven Gottlieb Huber, May 1, 1966 (div. July 1976); children: Heidi Irene Pettenger, Hyrum H. Huber. BA, Pacific Western U., 1980, MBA, 1981, Stanford U., 1981. Newspaper statistics reporter Fairfield (Calif.) Daily Republic, 1972-73; pers. adminstr. Intel Corp., Livermore, Calif., 1978-81; massage therapist 4 Doctors, Aurora, Colo., 1984-85; jewelery buyer CVJ, Minden, Nev., 1992; vol. coord. Sierra Recovery, Gardnerville, Nev., 1993-95; grant writer URS Ch., Carson City, Nev., 1999—; vol. tchr. AARP Guardianship, Carson City, 1999—. Author: Caregiving and Guardianship for Seniors in Nevada, 2001; author numerous poems. Vol., v.p. Nev. Network Against Domestic Violence, Reno; bd. dirs. Sunflower Ministry. Named Poet of Yr., Nat. Libr. Congress, Washington, 1989. Mem. Humane Soc. Democrat. Avocations: writing poetry, movie critic. Home and Office: PO Box 691 5LT Ca South Lake Tahoe CA 96156

BARR, MARLENE JOY, volunteer; b. Grosse Pointe Farms, Mich., Feb. 25, 1935; d. Max John and Viola Christina (Funke) Bielenberg; m. John Monte Barr, Dec. 17, 1954; children: John Monte Jr., Karl Alexander, Elizabeth Marie Letter. Student, Mex. City Coll., 1955; BA, Mich. State U., 1956; MA, Ea. Mich. U., 1959. Cert. elem. edn. Tchr. A.G. Erickson Sch., Ypsilanti, Mich., 1956-66; chair 5th grade tchrs., sec. curriculum coun. Ypsilanti Pub. Schs., 1961-66; receptionist Barr, Anhut, and Assoc., P.C., Ann Arbor, Mich., 1989-95; vol. Thrift Shop Assn. Ypsilanti, 1969—; block coord. Ypsilanti Recycling, 1990—. Mem. Fletcher Sch. Adv. Coun., 1980—81; v.p. Thrift Shop Assn., Ypsilanti, 1979—81, pres., 1981—83, 2002, scheduling chmn., 1993—96, chmn. nominating com., 1998, 1999; asst. leader Girl Scouts U.S., 1978—81; sec. troop 290 Boy Scouts Am., 1989—95, treas., 2000—; rm. mother Fletcher Elem. Sch., Ypsilanti, 1982—83; mem. chancel choir Emmanuel Luth. Ch., 1980—96, 1998—, youth coord., 1983—89, sec. youth standing com., 1983—89, ch. coun., 1986—90, sec. endowment com., 1995—96, chmn. ch. nominating com., 1999—2000; bd. dirs. Ypsilanti Cmty. Choir, 1984—; mem. High/Scope Ednl. Rsch. Fedn. Endowment Bd., 1993—96. Mem.: AAUW (life; chmn. gourmet arts study group 1968—), Ann Arbor Power Squadron of U.S. Power Squadron, Geneal. Soc. Wash. County, Law Wives of Washtenaw County (editor 1970—72), P.E.O. (chaplain 1991—93, chpt. pres. 1997—99, program com. chair 2000—01, treas. 2001—), Depot Town Assn., Ypsilanti Hist. Soc. (life), Marquette County Hist. Soc. (life), Friends of the Ypsilanti Dist. Libr., Ann Arbor Bike Touring Soc. (co-chair One Hell of a Ride 1995), Chandler Birthday Club (treas. 1990), Ladies Lit. Club (corr. sec. 1976—78, sec. bd. trustees 1982—86, v.p. 1986—90, pres. 1990—92, treas. bd. trustees 1992—97), Ann Arbor Women's City Club (life; chmn. ways and means com. 1995—97, chmn. Home Tour 1996, 1997, asst. membership chmn. 1998—99, nominating com. 2000—02, chmn. Home Tour 2001, 2001, mem. com. 2001—02, chmn. 2001—02), Alpha Delta Kappa (pres. Beta Zeta chpt. 1965—68, pres. Area X Pres. Coun. Mich. chpt. 1966—68, historian 1986—88, chmn. ways and means com. 1994—96, co-historian 2002—, 2002—). Lutheran. Avocations: skiing (7th in 50-59 age group Mich. divsn. NASTAR 1993), biking, hiking, boating, guiding youth ski trips.

BARR, MARTIN, health care and higher education administrator; b. Phila., Nov. 11, 1925; s. Louis and Bella (Moskowitz) B.; m. Nancy Lipschutz, July 15, 1951; children: Lawrence Allen, Richard Andrew, Debra Ann, Steven Bruce. B.Sc. in Pharmacy, Temple U., 1946; M.Sc. in Pharmacy, Phila. Coll. Pharmacy and Scis., 1947; PhD, Ohio State U., 1950. Grad. asst., then instr. Ohio State U. Coll. Pharmacy, 1947-50; from asst. prof. pharmacy to prof. phys. pharmacy and pharm. research Phila. Coll. Pharmacy and Sci., 1950-61; prof. pharmaceutics Wayne State U. Coll. Pharmacy, 1961-87, prof. emeritus, 1987—, chmn. dept., 1961-63, dean, 1963-72, v.p. spl. assignments, 1972-76, v.p., sec. to bd. govs., 1976-78, sec. to bd. govs., acting v.p. for health affairs, 1978-80, v.p., dep. provost, 1980-82, dean Coll. Pharmacy and Allied Health Professions, 1982-87; exec. v.p. corp. bus. and med. devel. Mich. Health Care Corp., Detroit, 1987-90, v.p. bd., profl. rels., 1990-92, v.p. continuous quality improvement, 1992-95. Cons. HEW, 1964-69 Contbg. author: Pharmacy, Compounding and Dispensing, 2d edit, 1956, Remington's Practice of Pharmacy, 11th edit, 1956, 12th edit., 1965; Profl. editor: Mid-Atlantic Apothecary, 1953-64, Apothecary, 1953-64, Central Pharm. Jour, 1961-64. Chmn. Mayor's Com. for Narcotics Rehab., Detroit, 1971-73; pres. Oakland County unit Mich. Heart Assn., 1970-72; chmn. Vis. Nurse Assn. S.E. Mich., 1999-2002, vice chmn., 2002—. Recipient Disting. Service award, Disitng. Alumnus award Alumni Assn. Coll. Pharmacy, Temple U., 1957, Disting. Alumnus award Temple U., 1964, Alpha Zeta Omega award, 1979, Meritorious Service award Wayne State U. Pharm. Alumni Assn., Ann. Alumus award Phila. Coll. Pharmacy and Sci., 1983, John H. Webster award Met. Detroit Pharmacist Assn., 1985, Disting. alumnus award Pharmacy Alumni Assn., 1987, Jack L. Beal Postbaccalaureate award Ohio State U. Coll. Pharmacy Alumni Assn., 1989, Disting. Svc. award Wayne State U. Pharmacy Alumni Assn., 1993, Advocate award Detroit Occupl. Therapy Assn., 1995. Fellow Am. Coll. Apothecaries, Acad. Pharm. Scis.; mem. Am. Pharm. Assn. (pres. Phila. 1954-55, chmn. sci. sect. 1959-60, Ebert medal 1956), Am. Soc. Hosp. Pharmacists, Mich. State Pharm. Assn. (pharmacist of yr. 1971), Am. Assn. Colls. Pharmacy (chmn. sect. tchrs. pharmacy 1959-60, chmn. conf. tchrs. pharmacy 1961-62), Sigma Xi, Rho Chi. Home: 7430 Tall Timbers West Bloomfield MI 48322-1082 E-mail: mbarr@nshore.net.

BARR, M.E. See BIGELOW, MARGARET ELIZABETH BARR

BARR, MICHAEL BLANTON, lawyer; b. Freeport, N.Y., July 24, 1948; s. Harry Kyle and Rosemary (Blanton) B.; m. Nancy Nickeson, Aug. 11, 1979; children: Nicholas Upton, Jessica Nickeson, Alice Primrose. BS, Georgetown U., 1970; JD, George Washington U., 1973. Bar: D.C. 1973, U.S. Dist. Ct. D.C. 1973, U.S. Ct. Appeals (3d cir.) 1979, U.S. Ct. Appeals (4th cir.) 1976, U.S. Ct. Appeals (6th cir.) 1981, U.S. Supreme Ct. 1980. Assoc. LeBoeuf, Lamb, Lieby & McRae, Washington, 1973-76, Hunton & Williams, Washington, 1976-80, ptnr., 1980—, mng. ptnr. Washington office, 1985-2000, exec. com., 1985-94, 2000—. Contbr. articles to profl. jours. Bd. trustees Georgetown Day Sch., 1999—; bd. dirs. Am. Sch. of Tangier, Morocco, 1989—. Mem. ABA, Internat. Bar Assn., D.C. Bar Assn., City Tavern Club (Washington), Union League (N.Y.). Home: 8004 Glendale Rd Chevy Chase MD 20815-5903 Office: Hunton & Williams 1900 K St NW Washington DC 20006-1110

BARR, MICHAEL CHARLES, financial journalist; b. White Plains, N.Y., Nov. 2, 1947; s. Charles Yerger and Joan Tames (Biggar) B.; m. Helen June Rumsey, Mar. 17, 1973. Student, Washington and Lee U.; BA summa cum laude, Rutgers Coll., 1969; JD, Columbia U., 1972, MBA, 1980. Bar: N.J. 1976, N.Y. 1978, U.S. Supreme Ct. 1976. Assoc. McCarter & English, Newark, 1976-77, Conboy, Hewitt, O'Brien & Boardman, N.Y.C., 1977-78; investment banker Kidder, Peabody & Co., Inc., N.Y.C., 1980-82; v.p. Mfrs. Hanover Trust Co., N.Y.C., 1982-90, A-L Assocs., N.Y.C., 1990-92; corp. sec., dir. H. Rivkin & Co., Inc., N.Y.C., 1992-93; securities analyst Standard & Poor's Corp., N.Y.C., 1993-98; Russian securities specialist H. Rivkin & Co., Inc., N.Y.C., 1998-99; emerging markets specialist HP Capital Mkts. Group, N.Y.C., 1999-2000; fin. cons. AXA Advisors, Inc., N.Y.C., 2000; corp. bond corr. Dow Jones and Co., N.Y.C., 2001—. Guest commentator on Russia, CNN, 1998-2000. Mem. adv. bd. Washington and Lee Alumni Coll., 1996-98; mem. 30th Reunion planning com. Columbia Law Sch. Class of 1972, 2002. Lt. USN, 1972-76. Recipient Loyal Son award Rutgers Alumni Assn., 1976. Mem. U.S. Polo Assn., Phi Beta Kappa.

BARR, RICHARD STUART, computer science and management science educator; b. Austin, Tex., Sept. 3, 1943; s. Howard Raymond and Margaret (Pressler) B.; m. Mary Shipp Sanders, Mar. 10, 1990; 1 child, Johnathan Austin. BSEE, U. Tex., 1966, MBA, 1972, PhD, 1978. Assoc. dir. Coll. of Bus. Computer Ctr. U. Tex., Austin, 1968-72; exec. v.p. Analysis, Rsch. & Computation, Inc., Austin, 1975-76; asst. prof. mgmt. info. scis. So. Meth. U., Dallas, 1976-80, assoc. prof., 1980-84, assoc. prof. ops. rsch. and engring. mgmt., 1984-89, assoc. prof. computer sci. and engring., 1989-2001, dir. parallel processing lab., 1989-97, dir. telecomm. mgmt. rsch. lab., 1997—, assoc. prof., chair dept. engring. mgmt., info. and sys., 2001—; co-founder, pres. Teloptica, Inc., Dallas, 1996-99. Cons. Dept. Treas., Dept. Agr., Dept. Health and Human Svcs.; vis. fellow Dept. Treas., 1977-78; vis. scholar, Princeton (N.J.) U., 1984, U. Colo., Boulder, 1992. Mem. editl. bd. Jour. of Heuristics; area editor Jour. on Computing; contbr. articles to profl. jours. Recipient Rsch. Excellence award So. Meth. U. Sch. Bus., 1980, Outstanding Grad. Instr. award, 1983; named Outstanding Instr., Nat. Tech. U., 1991-99, 2001-02; grantee NSF, 1993-2002. Mem. Inst. for Ops. Rsch. and Mgmt. Scis., INFORMS, Computing Soc. (chmn. 1997-98). Home: 6812 Velasco Ave Dallas TX 75214-3763 Office: So Meth U Sch Engring Dallas TX 75275-0123 E-mail: barr@engr.smu.edu.

BARR, ROBERT LAURENCE, JR., congressman, lawyer; b. Iowa City, Iowa, Nov. 5, 1948; s. Robert Laurence and Beatrice Emily (Radenhausen) B.; children: Adrian Robert, Derek Ryan; m. Jerilyn Dobbin, Dec. 31, 1986. BA in Internat. Rels., U. So. Calif., 1970; JD, Georgetown U., 1977; MA, George Wash. Univ., 1972. Bar: Ga. 1977, Fla. 1979. Analyst, atty., chief legis. staff CIA, Washington, 1970-78; assoc. Law Offices of Edwin Marger, Atlanta, 1979-81; pvt. practice Marietta, Ga., 1981-85, 91-94; ptnr. Brock & Barr, Marietta, 1985-86; U.S. atty. for No. Ga., 1986-90; mem. U.S. Congress from 7th Ga. dist., Washington, 1995—. Mem. banking and fin. svcs., govt. reform and oversight, and judiciary coms., chmn. subcom. on Comml. and Adminstrv. Law, 2001-02; gen. counsel Cobb County Rep. Com., 1981-83, 1st vice-chmn., 1983-85, chmn., 1985-86; pres. Southeastern Legal Found., Atlanta, 1990-91; bd. dirs. Met. Atlanta Coun. Alcohol and Drugs, 1989-91. Mem. editl. staff Am. Criminal Law Rev., 1974-77. Mem. Ga. Bar Assn., Fla. Bar Assn., Kiwanis, Phi Alpha Delta, Delta Phi Epsilon, Tau Kappa Epsilon. Republican. Wesleyan. Office: US Ho of Reps 1207 Longworth Bldg Washington DC 20515-4611 Home: 328 William Falls Dr Canton GA 30114-6866

BARR, RONALD JEFFREY, dermatologist, pathologist; b. Mpls., Jan. 5, 1945; s. Maxwell Michael and Ethel Deana (Ring) B.; m. Ulla Elisabet Edstam; children: Anna, Jessica, Sara. BA, Johns Hopkins U., 1967, MD, 1970. Diplomate Am. Bd. Pathology, Am. Bd. Dermatology. Intern U. Calif., San Diego, 1970-71, resident in pathology, 1971-75, resident in dermatology Irvine, 1975-78, fellow in dermatopathology, 1975-78, asst. prof. dermatology, 1977-83, assoc. prof. dermatology and pathology, 1983-86, prof. dermatology and pathology, 1987—, dir. Dermatopathology Lab., 1979—, prof., chmn. dept. dermatology Davis, 1986-87. Bd. dirs. Am. Bd. Dermatology, 1989—, pres., 1997. Contbr. more than 10 chpts. to books. more than 100 articles to profl. jours. Lt. USN, 1971-73. Fellow Am. Soc. Dermatopathology (pres. 1988-89); mem. Internat. Soc. Dermatopathology, Internat. Com. for Dermatopathology (sec.-treas. 1987-91, pres. 1992-93). Office: U Calif Irvine Med Ctr Dermatopathology Lab 101 The City Dr S Orange CA 92868-3201

BARR, ROSEANNE See ROSEANNE

BARR, SANFORD LEE, dentist; b. Chgo., Jan. 18, 1952; s. Mike and Bernice (Kaplan) B.; m. Randy Joyce Briskman, Dec. 24, 1973; children: Shelby Paige, Blake Jared, Taylor Ashley. BS, U. Ill., 1972; DDS, Northwestern U., 1976. Resident gen. practice VA Hosp., Chgo., 1976-77; gen. practice dentistry Chgo., 1977—. Attending dentist Rush Med. Coll., Chgo., 1977—; asst. prof. Presbyn.-St. Luke's Hosp., Chgo., 1977—, Northwestern U. Sch. Dentistry, Chgo., 1977-83; cons. VA Hosp., Chgo., 1978—. Mem. adv. bd. Homehealth of Ill. Chgo., 1984—. Fellow Acad. Gen. Dentistry, Acad. Facial Aesthetics; mem. ADA, Acad. Hosp. Dentistry, Chgo. Dental Soc., Alpha Omega (treas. 1984, pres. elect 1988), Tau Delta Phi. Lodges: B'nai B'rith (v.p. Chgo. chpt. 1984—). Jewish. Avocations: computers, photography, golf, baseball. Home: 632 Dauphine Ct Northbrook IL 60062-2256 Office: 25 E Washington St Chicago IL 60602-1708

BARR, SOLOMON EFREM, allergist, educator; b. Washington, Mar. 24, 1929; s. Barney and Jennie Florence (Brickman) B.; m. Rita Zeasla Cohan, June 20, 1954; children: Linda, Steven, Carol, Sharon. BA, George Washington U., 1951, MD, 1954. Diplomate Am. Bd. Internal Medicine, Am. Bd. Allergy and Immunology. Intern Phila. Gen. Hosp., 1954-55; resident D.C. Gen. Hosp., 1957-58, George Washington U., 1959-60; practice medicine specializing in allergies Silver Spring, Md., 1978—. Mem. staff Holy Cross Hosp., George Washington U. Contbr. articles to med. pubs., most recent in insect sting allergy. Served as capt. M.C., U.S. Army, 1955-57. Emma K. Carr scholar, 1948-49, Maria M. Carter scholar; recipient Freshman award in chemistry Alpha Chi Sigma, 1948, award in chemistry Sigma Kappa, 1948, John Ordronaux award in medicine George Washington U., 1954. Fellow Am. Acad. Allergy, ACP, Am. Coll. Allergists, Am. Assn. Cert. Allergists; mem. Washington Allergy Soc., Montgomery County, Md. State med. socs., AMA (Physician's Recognition award 1974-77, 77-80), Smith-Reed-Russell, William Beaumont, Jacobi Med. soc. Washington, Phi Beta Kappa, Alpha Omega Alpha. Club: Phi Delta Epsilon Grad. of Washington (pres. 1971-72). Home: 5713 Magic Mountain Dr Rockville MD 20852-3233 Office: 121 Congressional Ln Rockville MD 20852-1542 E-mail: sobarr@erols.com.

BARR, WALLACE R. electronics executive; m. Roberta Barr; children: Karyn, Michael. BS in Bus. Adminstrn., Calif. State Poly. U., 1968. Casino auditor Arthur Anderson & Co., Las Vegas; fin. dept. MGM Grand Hotel, Las Vegas; casino controller, then casino adminstr. Caesars, Atlantic City, 1979—81; corp. controller, treas. then sr. v.p. Bally's Park Place, Atlantic City, 1981; exec. v.p. Hilton Gaming Corp., Park Place Entertainment, 1998—2001, co-COO, 2001, COO, 2001—02, pres., CEO, 2002—. Named Exec. of Yr., Casino Jour., 1995, Businessman of Yr., Greater Atlantic City C. of C., 1999. Mem.: Casino Assn. NJ (chmn., pres. 1996—2001). Office: 3930 Howard Hughes Pkwy Las Vegas NV 89109-0943*

BARR, WALLY, social worker, researcher; b. Hull, Yorkshire, England, Dec. 5, 1951; s. Wally Barr and Ena Deane; m. Margaret Mary Richards, Jul. 3, 1976; children: Dyfan, Iestyn, Bethan. BSc with hons. in Sociology, Univ. London, 1975; MA, Univ. Manchester, Eng., 1983, PhD, 1996. Registered mental nurse; cert. social worker. Psychiatric nurse Birmingham (Eng.) Health Authority, 1976-80; social worker Turning Point, Chester, Eng., 1980-81; generic social worker Clwyd Social Svcs. Dept., Rhyl, Wales, 1983-89, mental health social worker, 1989-97; rsch. assoc. Univ. Liverpool, Eng., 1997-99, rsch. fellow, 1999—. Editor: (with L. Cotterill) Targeting in Mental Health Services: a multidisciplinary challenge, 2000; contbr. articles to profl. jours. Avocations: buddhist meditation, archaeology. Office: HaCCRU Univ Liverpool Brownlow Hill L69 3GB Liverpool England Office Fax: 0151 7945434. E-mail: wallybarr@yahoo.co.uk., walb@liv.ac.uk.

BARR, WARREN PAUL, optometrist; b. Hawthorne, Calif., Dec. 9, 1955; s. Paul C. and Betty Patricia Barr; m. Peggy Duncan, Sept. 3, 1993. BS, So. Calif. Coll. Optometry, Fullerton, 1978, OD, 1980. Cert. in therapeutics Calif. State Bd. Optometry. Pvt. practice optometry, Hermosa Beach, Calif., 1980—. Pres. Optometric Care Coun. So. Calif., 1986-87. Contbr. articles to profl. jours. Recipient Lens Design award Gordon Optics, 1980. Mem. Am. Optometric Assn., Calif. Optometric Assn. (chair Congress 1996-2001, Calif. Young Optometrist of Yr. 1986), South Bay Optometric Soc. (pres. 1985-86), Hermosa Beach C. of C. (pres. 1994-95, Hermosa Beach Man of Yr. 1990). Libertarian. Avocations: motocross racing, skiing, water skiing. Office: 1200 Artesia Blvd Ste 1 Hermosa Beach CA 90254-2755

BARR, WILLIAM PELHAM, lawyer, former attorney general of United States; b. NYC, May 23, 1950; s. Donald and Mary (Ahern) B.; m. Christine Moynihan, June 23, 1973; 3 children. AB, Columbia U., 1971, MA, 1973; JD, George Washington U., 1977. Bar: Va. 1977, D.C. 1978. Staff officer CIA, Washington, 1973-77; law clk. to presiding judge Cir. Ct., Washington, 1977-78; assoc. Shaw, Pittman, Potts & Trowbridge, Washington, 1978-82, 83-84, ptnr., 1985-89, 93-94; dep. asst. dir. domestic policy staff The White House, Washington, 1982-83; asst. atty. gen. Office Legal Counsel, U.S. Dept. Justice, Washington, 1989-90, dep. atty. gen., 1990-91, atty. gen., 1991-93; exec. v.p., gen. counsel GTE Corp., Washington; exec v.p., gen. counsel Verizon Communications, New York; vice chmn., bd. of dir. The Coll. of William & Mary. Mem. ABA, Va. State Bar Assn., D.C. Bar Assn., KC. Republican. Roman Catholic. Office: Verizon Communications Legal Dept 38th Fl 1095 Avenue of the Americas New York NY 10036*

BARR, WILLIAM ROBERT, industrial engineer, consultant; b. Detroit, Oct. 25, 1947; s. Robert Webb and Marion (Squire) B.; m. Diane Gayle Buddemeier, June 25, 1988 (dec.). BSIE, U. Mich., 1970, MSIE, 1974; MBA, Western Mich. U., 1977. Registered profl. engr., Mich. Indsl. engr. Pharmacia Corp., Kalamazoo, 1974-82; program mgr. Kellogg Co., Battle Creek, Mich., 1982-91; pres. William Barr Assoc. Inc., Augusta, 1991—. Instr. Western Mich. U., Kalamazoo, 1980-92. Contbr. articles to profl. jours. Active ordinance com. Ross Twp., Mich., 1987, chmn. road improvement com., 1989, active zoning bd., 1995-99. With U.S. Army, 1972-73. Mem. Inst. Indsl. Engrs. (chpt. officer 1995—), Indsl. and Ops. Engring. Acad. U. Mich., Alpha Pi Mu, Tau Beta Pi. Achievements include the development of computer model for the analysis of capacity in production facilities. Office: William Barr Assoc Inc PO Box 507 Augusta MI 49012-0507

BARRACANO, HENRY RALPH, retired oil company executive, consultant; b. Bklyn., Apr. 8, 1926; s. Ralph Henry and Josephine (Chianese) B.; m. Dorothy Sue Bartlow, Aug. 19, 1945; children: Ralph Robert, Susan Jo Barracano Ratterree, Linda Joyce Barracano Swartz. BSEE, Pa. State U., 1948. Registered profl. engr., Okla. Distbn. engr. Pub. Svc. Co. Okla., Tulsa, 1948-51; elec. engr. W.R. Holway & Assocs., Tulsa, 1951-56; from staff engr. to asst. to sr. v.p. engring. and constrn. Arabian Am. Oil Co., 1956-83; ind. cons., 1983-89; sr. project mgr. Hudson Engring. and Project Mgmt. Corp., 1990-91; ind. cons., 1992—. Mem. grievance com. State Bar Tex., 1994-99; arbitrator NASD, 1994—. Precinct chair Dem. Party, Harris County, Tex., 1984-98; precinct judge Harris County, 1984-90; bd. dirs. The Pinemont Apts., 2002-2003. 1st Lt. Signal Corps U.S. Army, 1943-59. Named Outstanding Engring. Alumnus, Pa. State U., 1993, Alumni Fellow award, 1997, Pa. State Pioneer, 1998. Mem. IEEE (life sr. mem., various offices held), Petroleum Club Houston (resident mem.), Northgate Country Club. Avocation: travel. Home and Office: 7723 Allegro Dr Houston TX 77040-2508 E-mail: barracano@ieee.org.

BARRACK, WILLIAM SAMPLE, JR., petroleum company executive; b. July 26, 1929; s. William Sample and Edna Mae (Henderson) B.; m. Irene Ball, Sept. 12, 1953; children: William, Elizabeth. BS, U. Pitts., 1950; postgrad., Dartmouth Coll. With Texaco, Inc., N.Y., 1953—, mktg. mgr. Northeast, 1953-62, dist. mgr., 1962-65, asst. mgr. distbn. and devel. N.Y., 1965-66, asst. mgr. mktg. research and project devel., 1966-67, asst. div. mgr. Norfolk, Va., 1967-68, area dir. Brussels, Belgium, 1968-70; v.p. Texaco Europe Ltd., N.Y., 1970; asst. to chmn. bd. Texaco, Inc., N.Y.C., 1971, v.p. internat. Europe, 1971-76, v.p. producing Eastern hemisphere, 1976-77, v.p. personnel and corp. services, 1977-80; chmn., chief exec. officer Texaco Ltd., London, Eng., 1980-83; sr. v.p. Texaco Inc., White Plains, N.Y., 1983-92, ret., 1992. Bd. dirs. Standard Comml. Corp., Wilson, N.C., Consol. Natural Gas Co., Pitts., Dominion Resources Inc., Richmond, Va.; mem. Naval War Coll. Found., Newport, R.I.; bd. vis. U. Pitts. Sch. Engring.; dir. Arabian Am. Oil Co., 1977-78; sr. dir. Caltex Petroleum Corp., 1983-92. Trustee Manhattanville Coll.; bd. dirs. Texaco Found. Inc., Mary Rose Soc., Disting. Alumni U. Pitts., Internat. Exec. Svc. Corps. Comdr. USNR, 1951-53. Mem. Fgn. Policy Assn. N.Y. (gov.). Clubs: N.Y. Yacht; Ida Lewis Yacht; North Sea Yacht (Belgium); Woodway Country, Ox Ridge Hunt; Clambake (Newport, R.I.); Australian (Sydney), 25 Yr. Club of The Petroleum Industry; The Pa. Soc., Naval War Coll. Found.

BARRACLOUGH, CHARLES ARTHUR, retired endocrinologist, educator; b. Vineland, N.J., July 13, 1926; s. Charles A. and Martha (Romain) B.; m. Eleanor Pauline Kolakowski, June 28, 1952; children: Janet, Patricia. BS, St. Joseph's Coll., 1947; MS, Rutgers U., 1952, PHD, 1953. Asst. prof. UCLA, 1959-61; spl. rsch. fellow Cambridge (Eng.) U., 1961-62; assoc. prof. U. Md., Balt., 1962-65, prof. physiology, 1965-93, dir. Ctr. Studies Reproduction, 1985-93, dir. emeritus, prof. emeritus, 1993—. Reproduction biology study sec. NIH, Bethesda, 1967-69, 70-74. Contbr. over 125 articles to profl. jours., 25 chpts. to books. Recipient Rsch. award Soc. Study Reproduction, 1984, Carl Hartman award 1990. Fellow AAAS; mem. Endocrine Soc. (editorial bd. 1965-72), Soc. Neurosci., Soc. Exptl. Biology and Medicine (editorial bd. 1974-87), Am. Physiol. Soc. (editorial bd. 1979-83). Research on regulation by the brain of reproduction in females.

BARRAGĀN, CELIA SILGUERO, junior high school educator; b. Corcoran, Calif., Feb. 4, 1955; d. Frutoso Silguero and Olinda Gonzalez S.; m. Mario Barragān Jr., Nov. 12, 1977; children: Maricela Aimē, Mario Armando. BS, S.W. Tex. State U., 1976, MA, 1977. 3d grade tchr. Crockett Elem. Sch., San Marcos, Tex., 1977—78, Bowie Elem. Sch., San Marcos, 1978—84; 5th grade tchr. Travis Elem. Sch., San Marcos, 1984—94, Hernandez Intermediate Sch., San Marcos, 1994—99; asst. prin., bilingual coord. Bonham Elem. Sch., San Marcos, 1985—86, title I reading tchr., trainer, cons., 1995—99; coord., tchr. AVID Miller Jr. H.S., San Marcos, Tex., 1999—2000; ESL/Dyslexia tchr. Miller Jr. High, 2000—01; ESL/dyslexia tchr. Goodnight Jr. H.S., 2001—. Winter High ability program tchr. S.W. Tex. State U.; project math trainer, migrant tchr., Princeville, Ill.; cons., nat. trainer Lang. Cir. Project Read, Minn. Recipient Latino award for cmty. recognition S.W. Tex. State U. Mem. Internat. Reading Assn., Tex. Reading Assn., Tex. State Tchrs. Assn., Tex. Assn.

Bilingual Edn., Tex. Classroom Tchrs. Assn., San Marcos (Tex.) Assn. Bilingual Edn. (v.p. 1990-91, 94—, pres. 1995—, Bilingual Tchr. of Yr. 1991, Travis Elem. Tchr. of Yr. 1993, Hernandez Intermediate Tchr. of Yr. 1995, Secondary Tchr. of Yr. 1995), Orton Dyslexia Soc., Nat. Coun. Tchrs. Math., Tex. Assn. Bilingual Educators, Ill. Migrant Edn. Assn., Tex. Assn. Gifted and Talented, N.J. Writing Project, Assn. Comprehensive Edn. in Tex. Roman Catholic. Home: 1763 Loma Verde Dr New Braunfels TX 78130-1297 Office: Goodnight Jr H S 1805 Peter Garza Dr San Marcos TX 78666-5062 E-mail: celia.barragan@san-marcos.isd.tenet.edu.

BARRAN, THOMAS PAUL, language educator; b. Warren, Ohio, July 8, 1946; s. Paul Thomas and Sophia Catherine Barran; m. Barbara Caplan, June 5, 1983. AB, Columbia Coll., 1968; PhD, Columbia U., 1984. Preceptor Columbia U., N.Y.C., 1978—79; prof. Russian Bklyn. Coll., N.Y.C., 1986—. Vis. prof. Hunter Coll., N.Y.C., 1991; bd. dirs. Classic Rug Collection, Inc., N.Y.C.; cons. in field; expert witness in field; lectr. in field. Author: Russia Reads Rousseau 1762-1825, 2002; contbr. articles to profl. jours. Bd. dirs. ROSAS Neighborhood Assn., Bklyn., 1998—2002. Fellow, U.S. State Dept., 1972—74, Internat. Rsch. & Exchanges Bd., 1976—77. Mem.: N.Y. Pub. Libr., Slavic Lang. Profl. Assn., Modern Lang. Assn. Am., Bigelow Soc. Avocations: deep sea fishing, archaeology. Home: 417 16th Street Brooklyn NY 11215 Office: Brooklyn College CUNY Bedford Ave at Ave H Brooklyn NY 11210

BARRATT, CYNTHIA LOUISE, pharmaceutical company executive; b. El Paso, Tex., Feb. 13, 1953; d. John Edward and Louise Joy (Lacy) B.; m. Nat G. Adkins, Jr., Oct. 5, 1980. BJ, U. Tex., 1975. Buyer Joske's of Tex., San Antonio, 1975-80, Craigs of Tex., Houston, 1981-83; v.p. sales ops. Akorn, Inc., Abita Springs, La., 1980-86; CEO, chmn. bd. dirs. NGLC Corp., Richmond, Tex., 1983—; pres., CEO, bd. dirs. CynaCon/Ocusoft, Richmond, 1986—. Mem. NAFE, Rosenberg/Richmond C. of C., DAR, Ft. Bend County Mus. Assn. Avocations: golf, snorkeling, skiing. Office: OcuSoft Inc PO Box 429 Richmond TX 77406-0429 E-mail: cbarratt@ocusoft.com.

BARRATT, DONNA LEE, elementary school educator; b. Westwood, N.J., Nov. 23, 1965; d. Robert Roy B. and Arlene Rose (Solar) Landwehr. BA in English Edn. cum laude, Trenton St. Coll., 1988; MA in Edn., Georgian Ct. Coll., 1998, supervisory cert., 1999, instrnl. tech. cert., 2000. Cert. tchr. English, N.J., Pa., elem. tchr., N.J. Tchr. English St. Mary H.S., South Amboy, N.J., 1989-92; mid. sch. lang. arts tchr. Joyce Kilmer Sch., Milltown, N.J., 1992-94; lang. arts tchr. Manalapan-Englishtown (N.J.) Mid. Sch., 1994—. Presenter inservice writing workshop Manalapan-Englishtown Bd. Edn., Manalapan, N.J., 1997; presenter interdisciplinary instr. N.J. ASCD state conf., East Windsor, N.J., 1999, N.J. Ednl. Assn. Good Ideas Forum, 2000, N.J. Sch. Bd. Assn., 2000. Recipient Outstanding Ednl. Program award N.J. ASCD, 1998. Mem. Nat. Coun. Tchrs. English, Kappa Delta Pi Edn. Honor Soc.. Roman Catholic. Avocations: reading, music, bike riding, hiking. Office: Manalapan Englishtown Middle Sch 155 Millhurst Rd Manalapan NJ 07726-4002

BARRATT, ERIC GEORGE, accountant; b. Stokenchurch, England, Apr. 15, 1938; s. Frank Ronald and Winifred Mary (Hayward) B. Chartered acct. Ptnr. Tansley Witt & Co., London, 1966-79, Arthur Andersen & Co., London, 1979-82; sr. ptnr. MacIntyre & Co., London, 1982-2000. Dir. Automotive Products P.L.C., Leamington, 1977-86, Montague Boston Investment Trust P.L.C., London, 1982-85, Milton Keynes Devel. Corp., 1980-85; chmn. MacIntyre Strater Internat. Ltd., 1990-2000. Chmn. Stokenchurch Parish Council, 1975-86; vice-chmn. buckinghamshire County Council, Aylesbury, 1981-85; dir. Commn. for New Towns, 1986-90; treas. Oriel Coll., Oxford, 1986-2000, St. Augustine's Found., Canterbury; bd. trustees Alzheimer's Rsch. Trust. Fellow Inst. Chartered Accts. Clubs: City of London. Conservative. Anglican. Home: Stockfield Stokenchurch HP14 3SX England

BARRATT, ERNEST STOELTING, psychologist, educator; b. North Charleroi, Pa., Mar. 31, 1925; s. Robert Duff and Marie Agnes (Stoelting) B.; m. Karen Marie Creel, Dec. 18, 1968; 1 son, Christopher Robert; 1 dau. by previous marriage, Robin Rhein. BA, Tex. Christian U., 1947, MA, 1949; PhD, U. Tex., 1952. Asst. prof. U. Del., Newark, 1951-57; prof. Tex. Christian U., Fort Worth, 1957-62; prof., chief psychophysiology lab. and psychology sect. U. Tex. Med. Br., Galveston, 1962—, Marie B. Gale Centennial prof. psychiatry, 1998—. Contbr. articles to profl. jours. Trustee Galveston Ind. Sch. Dist., 1971-89. Served with USN, 1943-46. Spl. fellow UCLA Brain Research Inst., 1961-62 Fellow APA, Am. EEG Soc., Soc. for Personality Assessment, Am. Psychol. Soc., Internat. Orgn. Psychophysiology; mem. Soc. for Neurosci., Soc. Psychophysiol. Rsch., Soc. Biol. Psychiatry, Internat. Soc. for Study Individual Differences (pres. 1989-91). Roman Catholic. Home: 2641 Gerol Dr Galveston TX 77551-1529 Office: U Tex Med Br Dept Psychiatry & Behavioral Sci Galveston TX 77555-0189 E-mail: ebarratt@utmb.edu.

BARRÉ, LLOYD MILTON, retired religion educator, researcher, writer; b. Regina, Sask., Can., Jan. 7, 1952; s. Vern Victor and Alexandra Eva Barré; 1 child, Linda. BA, San Jose State U., 1979; C of Christian Studies, Regent Coll., 1980; MA, Vanderbilt U., 1983, PhD, 1986. Rschr., tchg. asst. U. B.C., Can., 1979; tchg. asst. Vanderbilt U., 1982, instr. bibl. Hebrew, 1983-84; asst. prof. So. Meth. U., 1984-85. Author: The Rhetoric of Political Persuasion: The Narrative Artistry and Political Intentions of 2 Kings 9-11, 1988, El and Yahweh: The Early History and Formative Traditions of Ancient Israel, 1998, A Brilliant Deceit and Other Essays, 2001; Tradition and History in Early Israel, 2001; contbr. articles to profl. jours. Recipient Beach Carré fellowship, 1982-83.

BARRECA, CHRISTOPHER ANTHONY, lawyer; b. Pittsfield, Mass., Sept. 15, 1928; s. Christopher Joseph and Jennie (Cannici) B.; m. Alice Hazlehurst, Sept. 5, 1953. AA, Boston U., 1950, JD, 1953; LLM, Northwestern U., 1968. Bar: Mass. 1954, Ky. 1969, U.S. Dist. Ct. Ky. 1970, U.S. Dist. Ct. Mass. 1995, U.S. Ct. Appeals (6th cir.) 1970, Conn. 1988. With Gen. Electric Co., Fairfield, Conn., 1953-93, labor arbitration and litigation counsel, 1971-80, sr. labor and employment law counsel, 1980-93; ptnr., office chair Paul, Hastings, Janolsky & Walker LLP, Stamford, Conn., 1993-99, sr. counsel, 1999—. Mem. arbitration services adv. com. Fed Mediation and Conciliation Service, 1973—; adj. prof. U. Louisville, 1970-71, U. Bridgeport (Conn.) Sch. of Law, 1986-90; selectman Weston, 1997-00. Co-author, editor: Labor Arbitrator Development, 1983, A Practical Guide for Advocates, 1990; contbr. articles to profl. jours. Chmn. Weston (Conn.) Bd. Edn., 1977-82; trustee, vice chair exec. com., chmn. com. legal affairs, sec. bd., 2001, sec. bd. Boston U., 1977—. Served with AUS, 1946-47. Mem. ABA (chmn. labor and employment law sect. com. labor arbitration advocacy, elected to governing council of labor and employment law sect. 1986—, chair 1996-97, elected to governing coun. dispute resolution sect. 2001—), Boston U. Sch. Law Alumni Assn. (Silver Shingle award 1982), Aspetuck Valley Country Club (Weston, pres. 1995-96). Home: 6 Aspetuck Hill Ln Weston CT 06883-2601 Office: Paul Hastings Janolsky & Walker LLP 1055 Washington Blvd Stamford CT 06901-2216 E-mail: christopherbarreca@paulhastings.com.

BARREDO, RITA M. auditor; b. Torrington, Conn., June 24, 1953; d. Avelino and Josephine (DiNoia) B. BA, U. Conn., 1975; BS, Post Coll., 1981; MS in Acctg., U. Hartford, 1984, MBA, 1990. CPA, Conn.; cert. info. sys. auditor, cert. internal auditor; cert. mgmt. acct.; cert. govt. auditing profl.; diplomate Am. Bd. Forensic Accts., Am. Bd. Forensic Examiners. Timekeeper Timex Corp., Waterbury, Conn., 1976-85; auditor Def. Contract Audit Agy., Lowell, Mass., 1985—. Mem. AICPA, Am. Coll. Forensic Examiners, Am. Womens Soc. CPAs, Conn. Soc. CPA (continuing profl. edn. com. 1989-95, 97— social and recreation com. 1996-97), Inst. Mgmt. Accts. (sec. Waterbury chpt. 1994—), Inst. Internal Auditors, Info. Sys. Audit and Control Assn. Home: 130 Dawes Ave Torrington CT 06790-3627 Office: Def Contract Audit Agy 400 Main St East Hartford CT 06108-0968 E-mail: rbarredo01@snet.net.

BARRELL, DAWN HOLMAN, marketing specialist; b. Chattanooga, Dec. 7, 1940; d. Eldridge Martin Sr. and Althea Lois (Smead) B.; m. John MacMillin Barrell, Oct. 7, 1972 (dec. Sept. 1996). Student, U. Ga., 1958-62. Sec. Dr. Wm. Benton U. Ga., 1960-62; sec. supt. Delta Air Lines, 1963-93; terr. mgr. Panasonic, Atlanta, 1995-96, Delta Staff Svcs., Atlanta Airport, 1997-98, mgr. placement, 1998—; dir., treas. Barrell Investments Inc., Atlanta, 1986-96. Author numerous poems. Del. Conty and State Rep. Conv., 1984-86; mem. adminstrv. bd. First United Meth. Ch., Peachtree City, Ga., 1998. Named Lt. Col. aide-de-camp Gov. State Ga., 1979, Dame of Grand Cross of Order St. Stanislaus, Dame Merit Order of St. John Jerusalem, Holder of Cross of Holy Land, Dame of Justice Sovereign Order of Oak. Mem. DAR. Avocations: stamp collecting, waterskiing, antiques. Home: 101 Parkway Dr Peachtree City GA 30269 E-mail: deltadawn12@juno.com.

BARREN, BRUCE WILLARD, merchant banker; b. Olean, N.Y., Jan. 28, 1942; s. James Lee and Marion Frances (Willard) B.; children: James Lee, Christina Roseanne. Student, The Hun Sch. of Princeton, 1959; BS, Babson Coll., 1962; MS, Bucknell U., 1963; grad. cert., Harvard U., 1967, Cambridge U., England, 1968. Exec. v.p. Am. Extract Co., 1960—62; sr. cons. Price Waterhouse, N.Y., 1963-67; v.p. Walston & Co., Inc., N.Y., 1967-70; sr. v.p. Delafield Childs, Inc., N.Y., 1970-71; chmn. The EMCO/Hanover Group Ltd., L.A., 1971—; sr. v.p. Goodway, Inc., 1972-73; pres. Park West Med. Group, Inc., 1980-81; CEO First Pacific Bank, 1984-85; exec. editor The Mgmt. Gazette, 1988-98; chmn., mem. exec. adv. com. Vitafort Internat. Corp., L.A., 1996-97. Vice-chmn. Four Winds Enterprises Inc., San Diego 1985-87, F.W. Myers & Co., Rouses Point, N.Y., 1990-91; vice chmn., CEO Hydro-Mill Co., Chatsworth, Calif., 1996-98; bd. dirs. various U.S. and internat. cos., 1978-95; author, instr. CPA, CPE courses, Tex., Calif. and N.Y.; mem. editl. adv. bd. Prentice-Hall, 2001-02; U.S. rep. Transatlantic Bio-scis. Fund, London, 1988-91; instr. loan documentation and valuation procedures Sanwa Bank, 1995-96; CEO, dir. Potomac Worldwide, 1998-2000; chmn. Tech. Asset Mgmt. Ltd., Eng., 2000-01, lectr. exec. MBA program UCLA, 1988-98, U. S.C. Grad. Sch., Pepperdine Exec. MBA Program. Whittier Sch. Law, Chapman U. Sch. Law; spkr. in field. Contbr. over 100 articles to profl. jours. including CFO, Contr. Alert, KPMG Banking Insider. Recipient Disting. Svc. awards Calif. State Senate and State Assembly, Office of the Gov., Office of State Treas., Counties of L.A. and Orange, Calif., San Diego, City of L.A., Congl. Tribute, U.S. Senate, 1986-2002, U.S. Ho. of Reps., 1988, 89, Mayor L.A., 1987, 90-91, Office of U.S. Pres. and V.p., 1999, 2001-2002; named to Athletic Hall of Fame, HUN/Princeton, 1999. Mem. Am. Mgmt. Assn. (author, instr. 1991-92. v.p. 2002), Society Register of So. Calif., Mil. and Hospitaller Order St. Lazarus of Jerusalem (comdr.), K.M. (chevalier), Ordo Supremus Militaris Templi Hierosolymitani. Roman Catholic. Avocation: writing. Home: London England Office: 11740-11 West Sunset Los Angeles CA 90049

BARRERA, ELVIRA PUIG, counselor, therapist, educator; b. Alice, Tex., Dec. 11, 1943; d. Carlos Rogers and Delia Rebecca (Puig) B.; 1 child, Dennis Lee Jr. BA, Incarnate Word Coll., 1971; M of Counseling and Guidance, St. Mary's U., San Antonio, 1978; specialist degree in marriage and family therapy, St. Mary's U., 1989. Lic. profl. counselor; lic. marriage & family therapist; lic. chem. dependency counselor. Tchr. Edgewood Ind. Sch. Dist., San Antonio, 1965-74, Dallas Ind. Sch. Dist., 1971-72, Northside Ind. Sch. Dist., San Antonio, 1974; ednl. cons. Region 20-Edn. Service Ctr., San Antonio, 1974-79; career edn. coordinator San Antonio Ind. Sch. Dist., 1979-84, counselor, 1984-91; family coord. C.A.T.C.H. Project, U. Tex. Health Sci. Ctr., Houston and Austin, 1991-94; counselor Austin Ind. Sch. Dist., 1994-97, dist. transition counselor, 1997-98; vice prin. San Antonio Ind. Sch. Dist., 1998—. Cons. SBA, 1981, U.S. Office Edn., Washington, 1981-82, Tex. Edn. Agy., Austin, 1979-80; cons., writer San Antonio Ind. Sch. Dist. and Tex. Edn. Agy., 1985; cons. to various edn. pubs. Chairperson career awareness exploring div. Boy Scouts Am., 1982-87. Named Disting. Alumna, Incarnate Word Coll., 1983; recipient Spurgeon award Boy Scouts Am., 1985, Merit award, 1986, Growth award, 1986, Internat. Profl. and Bus. Women's Hall of Fame, 1995. Mem. Am. Assn. Marriage and Family Therapy, San Antonio Hash House Harriers (treas. 1990-91), San Antonio Assn. Women Adminstrs. Counselors, Incarnate Word Coll. Alumni Assn. (mem. adv. bd. 1990—), St. Mary's U. Alumni Assn. (v.p. Austin alumni chpt. 2003—), The Harp and Shamrock Soc. of Tex., Delta Kappa Gamma (2d v.p. 1982-84, 1st v.p. 1986-88), Chi Sigma Iota. Roman Catholic. Avocation: running. Home: 907 Aurora Cir Austin TX 78757-3415 Office: San Antonio Ind Sch Dist 515 Willow San Antonio TX 78202-1255

BARRERE, CLEM ADOLPH, business brokerage company executive; b. Bradford, Pa., Jan. 5, 1939; s. Clem A. and Ruth Eleanore (Brauner) B.; m. Jamie Elizabeth Newton, Aug. 30, 1969; 1 child, John Coleman Barrere. B Engring., Yale U., 1960; PhD in Chem. Engring., Rice U., 1965; postgrad., Emory U., 1975. Registered profl. engr., Tex., Okla.; bd. cert. broker; cert. bus. intermediary. Group leader rsch. dept. Conoco, Inc., Ponca City, Okla., 1965-69, dir. gas engring. Houston, 1969-72, dir. gas ops., 1972-77, mgr. loss control, 1977-81; mgr. Dupont-Transp. Svc., Houston, 1981-87, Dupont-Safety and Environ., Houston, 1987-89; pres. Barrere & Co. Ventures, Houston, 1989—. Dir. Barrere & Co. Realtors, Houston, 1978—. Contbr. articles to profl. jours.; 7 patents in field. Mem. Mus. Fine Arts, Houston, Zool. Soc., Houston, Mus. Natural Sci., Houston, 1970-96. Recipient Citations for Svc., Am. Petroleum Inst., 1988, Gas Processors Assn., 1989; NSF rsch. grantee, 1963-65. Fellow Internat. Bus. Brokers Assn. (dir. 1998-2003, Pres. award, 2002); mem. Tex. Bus. Brokers Assn., Houston Gas Processors Assn. (pres. 1981-82), Tex. Rolls-Royce Assn. (dir. 1987-96, Spl. award 1991), Houston Gun Collectors (pres. 1964), Houston Area Realtors, Petroleum Club, Lakeside Country Club, Phi Lambda Upsilon. Republican. Methodist. Avocations: car restorations, travel, sailing, genealogy. Office: Barrere & Co Ventures 5652 Doliver Dr Houston TX 77056-2322 E-mail: clembarrer@earthlink.net.

BARRERE, JAMIE NEWTON, real estate executive; b. Russellville, Ark., June 7, 1946; d. James Edward Jr. and Martha (Spillers) Newton; m. Clement Adolph Barrere Jr., Aug. 30, 1969; 1 child, John Coleman. BA in Math., U. Ark., 1968; graduate, Realtor Inst., 1984. Cert. real estate brokerage mgr.; grad. Realtor Inst.; accredited relocation coord. Asst. programmer, analyst Conoco, Ponca City, Okla., 1968-69; programmer, analyst Bonner & Moore Assocs., Houston, 1969-70; tchr. math. Lamar Consol. H.S., Rosenberg, Tex., 1970-72; assoc. broker Betty James, Realtors, Houston, 1972-78; pres. Barrere & Co., Realtors, Houston, 1978-96, Barrere Relocation Svcs. affiliate Heritage Tex. Properties, Houston, 1996—. Mem. adv. bd. Western Bank-Westheimer, Houston, 1986; mem. Employee Relocation Coun. Mem. Harris County Heritage Soc., Houston, 1970—, Houston Jr. Forum, 1980—, Am. Heart Assn. Guild, Houston Zool. Soc.; guild mem. Mus. Fine Arts, Houston, 1978—, Covenant House; trustee St. Luke's United Meth. Ch.; bd. dirs., children's dept. vol. bd. dirs. Moores Sch. Music Soc. U. Houston, 1992—; life mem. Tex. Real Estate Polit. Action Com.; former cub scout leader Boy Scouts Am. Mem. Nat. Assn. Realtors (mem. Equal Opportunity Com. 1985), Tex. Assn. Realtors (bd. dirs. 1989-98, mem. Multiple Listing Svc. com. 1985-90), Houston Assn. Realtors (bd. dirs. 1986-89, 93-95, v.p. 1993, mem. and chmn. various coms.), Houston C. of C. (amb. 1986), DAR, U. Ark. Alumnae Assn. (life, v.p. Houston chpt. 1985-88), RELO Internat. Relocation Network, Lakeside Country Club, Petroleum Club, Tanglewood Garden Club (bd. dirs. 1973-86, 93-95), Delta Delta Delta (past pres. Houston alumnae), Tri Delta Art Show for Charity (past pres.). Avocations: swimming, travel, music, geneology, historical preservation. Office: Barrere & Co 4295 San Felipe St Ste 300 Houston TX 77027-2915

BARRETO, BERNARDO, artist; b. Lima, Peru, Sept. 30, 1959; s. Juan Barreto and Sara Valverde. Student, Cath. U. Sch. Fine Arts, Lima, Peru, 1977—80. Cert. electronic technology Ctr. For The Media Arts, N.Y.C., 1992. Art supr. Fine Arts Decorating, N.Y.C., 1984—88; art studio mgr. R.B.S. Fabrics, N.Y.C., 1990—92; fine art studio artist Novo Arts, N.Y.C., 1999—2001. Art cons. Randa Corp., N.Y.C., 1992—2000; press corr. The Illus. Wild One Mag., N.Y.C., 1994—. Mem.: Graphic Artists Guild N.Y. (assoc.; bd. mem. 1993—96).

BARRETO, ERNEST, science educator, researcher; b. New York, June 12, 1968; s. Ernesto and Ana Lucia B.; m. Terri Kathrine McClain, Dec. 28, 1996. BA, U. Chgo., 1990; MS, U. Md., 1995, PhD, 1996. Lectr. U. Md., College Park, 1996-97, faculty rsch. asst., 1997, rsch. assoc., 1997-98; rsch. asst. prof. George Mason U., Fairfax, Va., 1998—2001, asst. prof., 2001—. Contbg. author: Dynamics and Chaos in Manufacturing Processes, 1997, Control and Chaos, 1997; Synchronization:theory and application, 2003 contbr. articles to profl. jours. Recipient 3d place award Internat. Grand Champion Whitsler, 2002, 2003; Nat. Phys. Sci. Consortium fellow, 1990-96, Nat. Scholastic Art scholar, 1986. Mem. Am. Phys. Soc., Soc. Indsl. and Applied Math., Sigma Xi. Avocation: music performance and composition. Office: The Krasnow Inst MS2A1 George Mason U Fairfax VA 22030 E-mail: ebarreto@gmu.edu.

BARRETO, HECTOR, federal agency administrator; Grad., Rockhurst U. Pres. Barreto Ins. an dFin. Svcs., L.A.; adminstr. Small Bus. Adminstrn., Washington, 2001—. Vice chmn. bd. U.S. Hispanic C. of C. Office: Small Bus Adminstrn 409 3d St SW Washington DC 20416

BARRETT, ANDREA FULLER, writer; b. Boston, Nov. 16, 1954; d. Norman Fuller Jr. and Anne Tucker (Jensen) B.; m. Barry M. Goldstein, 1979. BS, Union Coll., 1974, LLD (hon.), 1996. Author: (stories) Ship Fever, 1996 (Nat. Bk. award 1996), Servants of the Map, 2002, (novels) Secret Harmonies, 1989, The Middle Kingdom, 1991, Lucid Stars, 1988, The Forms of Water, 1993, The Voyage of the Narwhal, 1998; contbr. to Prize Stories: The O. Henry Awards, 2000, 01, Best American Short Stories, 1995, 2001. Recipient fellowship Nat. Endowment for Arts, 1992, Guggenheim Found., 1997, MacArthur Found., 2001.

BARRETT, ARCHIE DON, retired federal official, educator; b. Paris, Tex., Aug. 13, 1935; s. Archie Lafayette and Mabel Clara (Dickinson) B.; m. Miriam Meda Rowell, Aug. 31, 1958; children: Julie Ann, Cynthia Dawn, Archie Don Jr. BS, U.S. Mil. Acad., 1957; MPA, Harvard U., 1962, PhD in Polit. Economy and Govt., 1971. Commd. 2d lt. USAF, 1957, advanced through grades to col., 1979, ret., 1981; instr. to asst. prof. USAF Acad., Colo., 1965-67, assoc. prof., 1969-71; fighter pilot 13th Tactical Fighter Squadron, Thailand, 1968-69; instr. NATO-Weapons Sys. Sch., Oberammergau, Germany, 1971—73; plans officer 86th Tactical Fighter Wing, Ramstein, Germany, 1973-75; air staff USAF Hdqrs. Pentagon, Washington, 1975-79; rsch. assoc. Nat. Def. U., Ft. McNair, Washington, 1979-81; legis. staff House Armed Svcs. Com., Washington, 1981-94; prin. dep. asst. sec. Army, Manpower and Res. Affairs, Washington, 1994-97. Vis. disting prof. nat. security affairs Naval Postgrad. Sch., Monterey, Calif.; cons., 1998-2002 Author: Reappraising Defense Organization, 1983; contbr. chpts. in books and articles to profl. jours. Mem. Assn. of U.S. Army, Ret. Officers Assn., Order of Daedalians, Air Force Assn., Phi Kappa Phi. Democrat. Methodist. Home: 18002 Austin Blvd Lago Vista TX 78645 E-mail: adbarret@nps.navy.mil.

BARRETT, BEATRICE HELENE, psychologist; b. Cin., Dec. 8, 1928; d. Oscar Slack and Helen (Kaiper) B.; m. Harold Sheffield Van Buren, Oct. 6, 1966 (div. Oct. 1985). BA, U. Ariz., 1950; MA, U. Ky., 1952; PhD, Purdue U., 1957. Grad. tchg. asst. in psychology U. Ky., Lexington, 1950-52; psychology asst. Longview State Hosp., Cin., 1951, staff psychologist, 1952; staff psychologist Children's Outpatient and Cons. Svcs. Ind. U. Med. Ctr., Indpls., 1954-57, chief psychologist, 1957-59; instr. psychology Ind. U. Med. Sch., Indpls., 1956-60; rsch. assoc. dept. psychiatry Ind. U. Med. Ctr., Indpls., 1959-60; pvt. practice clin. psychology Indpls., 1957-60; research fellow in psychology Sch. of Medicine Harvard U., Boston, 1960-62; lectr. in spl. edn. Grad. Sch. Edn., Boston U., 1962-63; dir. psychol. rsch. Walter E. Fernald State Sch., Belmont, Mass., 1962-69, dir. behavior prosthesis lab., 1963-92; chief psychologist, 1969-92; assoc. psychologist Eunice Kennedy Shriver Ctr. for Mental Retardation, Inc., Waltham, Mass., 1982-98. Instr. Mass. Psychol. Ctr., 1972; lectr. in spl. edn. Lesley Coll. Grad. Sch., 1974-76; adj. assoc. prof. Northeastern U., 1983-92; psychology cons. Carter Meml. Hosp., Indpls., 1959-60; mem. exec. com. Boston Behavior Therapy Interest Group, 1973-74; mem. human studies com. Eunice Kennedy Shriver Ctr., 1980-98. Cons. editor, mem. adv. bds. various profl. jours.; contbr. numerous articles to profl. jours. Mem. Ind. Gov.'s Youth Coun., 1959-61; mem. spl. adv. com. on mental retardation Ind. Dept. Pub. Instrn., 1959-61; mem. task force Mass. Mental Retardation Planning Project, 1965-66; mem. adv. bd. Cambridge Ctr. for Behavioral Studies, 1981-87, 93-2000, trustee, 1987-93, 94-2000, sr. fellow, 2001—, chair devel. com., 1987-89, mem. subcom. on planned giving, 1992-95, chmn. nominating com., 1992-93, mem., 1993-98, exec. com., 1993, 94-99, mem. subcom. on acad. and sci. programs, 1992-97, mem. editl. bd., 1998-99; treas. B.F. Skinner Found., 1996-2003, bd. dirs., 1997—; mem. com. on dance edn. Spl. Commn. on Performing Arts, 1976-77; mem. art acquisition com. DeCordova Mus., 1978-80, mem. contemporary arts coun., 1985-87; trustee Boston Repertory Ballet, 1977-79, Boston Ballet Co., 1970-76, sec. bd., 1974-75, exec. com., 1974-76. Grantee Nat. Assn. for Retarded Citizens, 1963, NIHM, 1963-76; recipient Lifetime Contbn. to frequency based rsch. and ednl. tech., Standard Celeration Soc. award, 1997. Fellow APA, Mass. Psychol. Assn. (Ezra Saul Psychol. Svc. award 1979), Behavior Therapy and Rsch. Soc. (charter clin.); mem. Assn. for Mentally Ill Children (human rights com. 1979-81), Eunice Kenndey Shriver Ctr. (mem. human studies comm. 1980-98), Am. Acad. on Mental Retardation (v.p. 1969-74, at-large exec. com. 1975-77), Am. Psychol. Assn., Am. Psychol. Soc., Ea. Psychol. Assn., Assn. Behavior Analysis (jour. adv. bd. 1983-87, chair task force on right to effective edn. 1986-91, presdl. adv. group on edn. and pub. policy 1994-95), Stage Harbor Yacht Club (Chatham, Mass., race com. 1984-86), Sigma Xi, Phi Kappa Phi. Home and Office: RFD 5 Box 236A Winter St Lincoln MA 01773

BARRETT, BERNARD MORRIS, JR., plastic and reconstructive surgeon; b. Pensacola, Fla., May 3, 1944; s. Bernard Morris and Blanche (Lischkoff) B.; children: Beverly Frances, Julie Blaine, Audrey Blake, Bernard Joseph. BS, Tulane U., 1965; MD, U. Miami, 1969. Diplomate Am. Bd. Plastic Surgery. Surg. intern Meth. Hosp. and Ben Taub Hosp., Houston, 1969-70; resident in gen. surgery Baylor Coll. Medicine, Houston, 1970-71, UCLA, 1971-73; resident in plastic surgery U. Miami (Fla.) Affilated Hosps., 1973-75, chief resident in plastic surgery, 1975; fellow in plastic surgery Clinica Ivo Pitanguy, Rio de Janeiro, 1973; instr. surgery Baylor Coll. Medicine, 1970-71, clin. instr. plastic surgery, 1977-80, clin. asst. prof., 1980-90, clin. assoc. prof., 1991-97, clin. prof. surgery, 1997—; instr. surg. emergeicies L.A. County Paramedics, 1972-73; plastic surgery coord. for jr. med. students Sch. Medicine U. Miami, 1975; practice medicine specializing in plastic and reconstructive surgery Houston, 1976—. Pres., chmn. bd. dirs. Plastic and Reconstructive Surgeons, P.A., 1978—; chmn. Tex. Inst. Plastic Surgery, Houston; assoc. chief plastic surgery St. Luke's Episcopal Hosp., Houston, 1991—; attending physician Jr. League Clinic, Tex. Children's Hosp., Houston, 1977—; active staff St. Luke's Hosp., Houston, Meth. Hosp., Houston; clin. assoc. in plastic surgery U. Tex. Med. Sch., Houston, 1976—; instr. surg. emergencies Harris County C.C.; dir. Am. Physicians Ins. Exch., Austin, 1976—, vice chmn., bd. dirs., 1995—; past chief of staff, chief plastic surgery Travis Centre Hosp., Houston, 1985—; dir. Physicians for Peace, Norfolk, Va., 1991—; cons. physician Houston Oilers, 1978-97; attending physician Ontario Motor Speedway, Calif., 1972-73. Author: Patient Care in Plastic Surgery, 1982, 2d edit., 1996, Manuel de Ciudados en Cirugia Plastica, 1985, Atencion al Paciente de Cirugia Plastica, 1998; contbr. articles to med. publs., presentations to profl. confs.; inventor Barrett sterling surgigrip. Bd. dirs. Plastic Surgery Ednl. Found., Chgo.; mem. Fed. Coun. on Aging, Washington, 1991-93, Pres.'s Coun. U. Miami, 1997—; adv. bd. Johnson & Johnson, New Brunswick, N.J. Lt. comdr. M.C., USNR, 1969-74. Surg. exch. scholar to Royal Coll. Surgeons, London, 1968; hon. dep. sheriff Harris County, Tex. (Houston). Fellow ACS; mem. Am. Assn. Plastic Surgery, Am. Soc. Plastic Surgeons, Royal Soc. Medicine, Michael E. DeBakey Internat. Cardiovascular Surg. Soc., Am. Soc. for Aesthetic Plastic Surgery, Denton A. Cooley Cardiovascular Surg. Soc., Tex. Med. Assn., Tex. Soc. Plastic Surgery, Harris County Med. Soc., Houston Soc. Plastic Surgery, D. Ralph Millard Plastic Surg. Soc. (pres. 1993-94, v.p. 1977-79, sec., treas. 1975 77, historian 1980—), U. Miami Sch. Medicine Nat. Alumni Assn. (bd. dirs. 1975-77, pres. coun. 1997—), Houston City Club, Houstonian Club, Royal Biscayne Racquet Club, Commodore Club, Coral Beach and Tennis Club, Sweetwater Country Club, Alpha Kappa Kappa (pres. 1968-69). Office: 6624 Fannin St Ste 2200 Houston TX 77030-2334 E-mail: txips@swbell.net.

BARRETT, BRUCE RICHARD, physics educator; b. Kansas City, Kans., Aug. 19, 1939; s. Buford Russell and Miriam Aileen (Adams) B.; m. Gail Louise Geiger, Sept. 3, 1961 (div. Aug. 1969); m. Joan Frances Livermore, May 21, 1979. BS, U. Kans., 1961; postgrad., Swiss Poly., Zurich, 1961-62; MS, Stanford U., 1964, PhD, 1967. Research fellow Weizmann Inst. Sci., Rehovot, Israel, 1967-68; postdoctoral research fellow, research assoc. U. Pitts., 1968-70; asst. prof. physics U. Ariz., Tucson, 1970-72, assoc. prof., 1972-76, prof., 1976—, assoc. chmn. dept., 1977-83, mem. faculty senate, 1979-83, 88-90, 91-97, program dir. theoretical physics NSF, 1985-87, mem. tech. transfer com., 1996-97, 98-99, mem. grad. coun., 1998-2000. Chmn. adv. com. Internat. Scholars, Tucson, 1985-96; chmn. rsch. policy com. U. Ariz. Faculty Senate, 1993-94, 95-96; affiliate prof. U. Wash.-Seattle, 2000—. Woodrow Wilson fellow, 1961-62; NSF fellow, 1962-66; Weizmann Inst. fellow, 1967-68; Andrew Mellon fellow, 1968-69; Alfred P. Sloan Found. research fellow,

1972-74; Alexander von Humboldt fellow, 1976-77; Japan Soc. for Promotion of Sci. rsch. fellow, 1998; NSF grantee, 1971-85, 87—; Netherlands F.O.M. research fellow Groningen, 1980; recipient sr. U.S. scientist award (Humboldt prize) Alexander von Humboldt Found., 1983-85. Fellow Am. Phys. Soc. (publs. com. divsn. nuclear physics 1983-86, program com. 1993-94, 2002—, chmn. steering com. for Nuclear Physics Summer Sch. 1996-98, mem. exec. com. four corners sect. 1998—, chair 2003, vice chmn. forum on internat. physics 2000, chair 2002, chmn. com. internat. sci. affairs 2003), Phi Beta Kappa (pres. Alpha Ariz. chpt. 1992, 2000-02), Sigma Xi, Sigma Pi Sigma, Omicron Delta Kappa, Beta Theta Pi, Phi Beta Kappa (senate 2000—, fellow). Office: U Ariz Dept Physics PO Box 210081 Tucson AZ 85721-0081 E-mail: bbarrett@physics.arizona.edu.

BARRETT, CAROLE A. American Indian studies educator; b. Quantico, Va., May 19, 1947; d. Gilbert A. and Lucille H. Barrett; children: Matthew A., Christopher J. BA with honors, Seton Hill Coll., 1969; MA, St. Louis U., 1971. Instr. English St. Louis U., 1969-71, Sinte Gleska U., Rosebud, S.D., 1972-75, U. S.D., Vermillion, 1972-73; tchr. lang. arts St. Francis (S.D.) Indian Sch., 1972-77; coll. coord. Indians into Medicine U. N.D., Grand Forks, 1977-81; placement officer United Tribes Tech. Coll., Bismarck, N.D., 1981-82; assoc. prof. Am. Indian studies U. Mary, Bismarck, N.D., 1982—. Program evaluator Collaboration for Advancement of Coll. Tchg. and Learning, Mpls., 1998—; panel mem. NEH, Washington, 2000; bd. dirs. tribal mgmt. program United Tribes Tech. Coll., Bismarck, 2000—. Cons. editor: (ency.) Racial and Ethnic Relations in America, 1999; contbr.: (encyc.) Ready Reference: American Indians, 1994; contbr. articles to profl. jours. Chairperson N.D. Adv. Com. on Civil Rights, Rocky Mountain Region, 1993—; mem. diversity com. Girl Scouts Am., Bismarck, 1999—; sec. Indian Parent Bd., Bismarck, 1994-99. Recipient Rsch. Grant award Mont. Hist. Soc., 1986, 87, 88; Larry Remele fellow N.D. Humanities Coun., 1989, 95, 98. Mem. MLA, Nat. Indian Edn. Assn., Am. Studies Assn. Home: 402 Ashwood Ave Bismarck ND 58504 Office: U of Mary 7500 University Dr Bismarck ND 58504-9652

BARRETT, CRAIG R. computer company executive; b. 1939; Assoc. prof. Stanford U., 1965-74; with Intel Corp., Chandler, Ariz., 1974—, v.p. components tech. and mfg. group, sr. v.p., gen. mgr. components tech. and mfg. group, exec. v.p., mgr. components tech., now pres., CEO. Mem. NAE, 1994—. Office: 2200 Mission College Blvd Santa Clara CA 95054-1537

BARRETT, DAVID EUGENE, judge; b. Hiawassee, Ga., June 25, 1955; s. Homer and Laura Arispah (Wilson) B.; m. Donna L. Barrett; children: Laura Elizabeth, Thomas Jeffrey. BA summa cum laude, U. Ga., 1977, JD cum laude, 1980. Assoc. Erwin, Epting, et al, Athens, Ga., 1980-84, Blasingame, Burch, et al, Athens, 1984; pvt. practice Hiawassee, 1984-92; judge Recorders Ct., 1986-92, Superior Ct., Enotah Cir., 1992—. Counsel Towns County Humane Soc., Hiawassee, 1985-92; counselor Alzheimer Support, Hiawassee, 1985. Mem. ABA, Ga. Bar Assn., Mountain Bar Assn. (sec. 1987-88, v.p. 1988-89, pres. 1989-90), Western Bar Assn. (sec. 1983-84), Trial Lawyers Assn. Am., Towns County C. of C. (bd. dirs. 1986-87, 90-92, pres. 1988), Demosthenian Lit. Soc. (bd. dirs., sec. bd. trustees 1978-89, chmn. bd. 1986-89), Athens Jaycees (v.p. 1983-84). Home: 924 Mining Gap Ln Young Harris GA 30582-2324 Office: Superior Ct Enotah Cir 59 S Main St Ste K Cleveland GA 30528-1376

BARRETT, DAVID M. urologist; b. Detroit, Mar. 25, 1942; MD, Wayne State U., 1968. Diplmate Am. Bd. Urology. Intern Detroit Gen. Hosp., 1968-69; resident in gen. surgery Mayo Clinic, Rochester, Minn., 1969-70, resident in urology, 1972-75, staff, dept. urology, 1975-99, chair, dept. urology, 1991—; faculty Mayo Med. Sch., Rochester, Minn., 1986-99; chair, dept. urology, 1991-99; pres. Am. Bd. Urology, Charlottesville, Va.; CEO Lahey Clinic, 1999—. Bd. govs. Mayo Clinic, 1988-96, trustee, 1991-97; pres. Am. Bd. Urology, 1999. Mem. ACS. Office: Lahey Clinic 41 Mall Rd Burlington MA 01805-0002

BARRETT, DAVID OLAN, lawyer; b. Indianapolis, May 25, 1970; m. Jacqueline R. Barrett. BA in Polit. Sci. and Journalism, Ind. U., 1992, JD cum laude, 1995. Bar: Ind. 1995, U.S. Dist. Ct. (no. and so. dists) Ind., 1995, U.S. Ct. Appeals (7th cir.), 1998, U.S. Supreme Ct., 1999. Assoc. Ice Miller, Indpls., 1995-99; corp. counsel Emmis Comm. Corp., Indpls., 1999—. Mem. bd. editors Ind. Law Jour.; contbr. numerous articles to lay publs. and profl. jours; presenter on topics relating to corp. and comm. law. Mem. Indpls. New Leaders Project, 1997-98; past pres., hon. v.p. No. Am. Fedn. Temple Youth (NFTY); bd. mem. Union of Am. Hebrew Conregations, 1988-89; alumni bd. dirs. Ind. U. Sch. Journalism, 2001-. Mem. ABA, Ind. State Bar Assn., Indpls. Bar Assn., Order of Barristers. Home: 10823 Diamond Dr Carmel IN 46032-9309 Office: Emmis Comm Corp One Emmis Plaza 40 Monument Cir Ste 700 Indianapolis IN 46204-3017 E-mail: dbarrett@emmis.com.

BARRETT, EDWARD MITCHELL, lawyer; b. NYC, July 18, 1920; s. Edward F. and Elizabeth (Schoder) Barrett; m. Rita F. Ferris, June 8, 1946; children: Edward M., James F. BS engring., Princeton U., 1942; LLB, Bklyn. Law Sch., 1949. Bar: NY 1949. Asst. engr. planning dept. L.I. Lighting Co., 1945—48; atty., legal dept., 1950—53; gen. atty., 1953—66; sec., gen. atty., 1966—70; gen. counsel, 1970—85; counselor firm Hunton & Williams, NYC, 1984, Richmond, Va., 1984—. Capt. USAAF, 1942—45. Mem.: Nassau County Bar Assn., NY State Bar Assn., ABA (pub. utility sect.). Office: Hunton & Williams 100 Park Ave New York NY 10017-5516

BARRETT, ELIZABETH ANN MANHART, nursing educator, psychotherapist, consultant; b. Hume, Ill., July 11, 1934; d. Francis J. and Grace C. (Manhart) Fridy; children: Joseph B., Jeffrey F., Paula G. Brown, Pamela M. Temple, Scott D. BSN summa cum laude, U. Evansville, 1970, MA, 1973, MSN, 1976; grad., Gestalt Assocs. Psychotherapy, 1982; PhD in Nursing, NYU, 1983; grad., Am. Inst. for Mental Imagery, 1995. From instr. to asst. prof. nursing U. Evansville, Ind., 1970-76; staff nurse Welborn Bapt. Hosp., Evansville, 1975-76, Bellevue Psychiat. Hosp., N.Y.C., 1976-79; clin. tchr. CUNY, 1977-82; asst. prof. Adelphi U., 1979-80; group practice Nurse Healers, 1979-82; pvt. practice psychotherapy, 1980—. Nurse rschr. Mt. Sinai Med. Ctr., N.Y.C., 1982-86, asst. dir. nursing, 1983-86; assoc. prof. Hunter Coll., N.Y.C., 1986-89, prof., 1994-2001, prof. emerita, 2001—, dir. grad. studies, 1989-92, coord. Ctr. for Nursing Rsch., 1993-2001; cons. Internat. Soc. Univ. Nurses; co-chair adv. com. Martha E. Rogers Ctr. for Study of Nursing Svc., 1994-96; sec., treas. Am. Inst. for Mental Imagery, 2002—; com. mem. Regional Health Planning Coun., Evansville, 1974-77. Mem. editl. bd. Alt. Therapies in Health and Medicine, 1995—. Recipient Disting. Nursing Alumnus award NYU, 1994, Disting. Nurse Rschr. award Found. N.Y. State Nurses Assn., 1995. Fellow Am. Acad. Nursing; mem. ANA (cert. psychiat.-mental health), NOW, Nat. League Nursing, Ea. Nursing Rsch. Assn. (charter), Ea. Nursing Rsch. Soc., Soc. Rogerian Scholars (co-founder, 1st pres. 1988-90), Phi Kappa Phi, Sigma Theta Tau (Upsilon chpt. pres. 1986-88), Alpha Tau Delta, Sigma Xi. Home: 415 E 85th St Apt 9E New York NY 10028-6358 Office: 16 E 96th St Ste 1 A New York NY 10128

BARRETT, EUGENE JOSEPH, researcher, medical educator, physician; b. Jersey City, N.J., May 22, 1946; s. Joseph Francis and Margaret (Harney) B.; m. Paul Marie Quiricani, Jan. 31, 1976; children: Nora, Matthew. BS in Physics, St. Peters Coll., Jersey City, N.J., 1968; MD, PhD in Biophysics, U. Rochester, 1975. Intern in medicine Strong Meml. Hosp., Rochester, N.Y., 1975-76, asst. resident in medicine, 1976-77; fellow in endocrinology and metabolism Yale U. Sch. Medicine, New Haven, Conn., 1977-80, asst. prof. medicine, 1980-85, assoc. prof. medicine, 1985-91, chief diabetes unit, 1988-91; prof. internal medicine and pediats. U. Va. Sch. Medicine, Charlottesville, 1991—; dir. U. Va. Diabetes Ctr., 1991—. Dir. diabetes unit Yale U. Sch. Medicine, 1987-91; dir. diabetes ctr. U. Va., 1991—. Contbr. over 70 articles to profl. jours. Recipient Rsch. Career award NIH, 1981-85. Mem. NIH (mem. metabolism study sect. 1993-96), Am. Diabetes Assn. (bd. dirs. Va. affiliate 1993-96, pres.-elect 2002, mem. nat. profl. practice com., rsch. award 1996), Am. Heart Assn. (Established Investigator 1987-92, mem. Conn. affiliate grant rev. panel 1985-90, mem. grant rev. panel New Eng. region 1986-91, chair 1991), Am. Fedn. Clin. Rsch., Am. Soc. Clin. Investigation. Roman Catholic. Avocations: sailing, tennis. Office: U Va Sch Medicine Diabetes Rsch Ctr PO Box 801410 Charlottesville VA 22908

BARRETT, EVELYN CAROL, retired secondary education educator; b. Ocean Springs, Miss., Feb. 6, 1928; d. Charles Edward and Irene Effie (Hopkins) Engbarth; m. Arthur James Barrett, June 10, 1951; children: George Stanley, Ruth Anne, James Sidney, Carolyn Jean. Diploma with honors, Jr. Coll. (now Miss. Coast Coll.), Perkinston, Miss., 1945; BS in Commerce with high honors, Miss. So. Coll. (now U. So. Miss.), 1947; MBA in Acctg., La. State U., 1950; also numerous continuing edn. courses, 1950-82. Bookkeeper-sec. Non-Commn. Officers Club, Kessler AFB, Miss., summer 1947; asst., secretarial practice office and divsn. rsch.; instr. in typing Coll. Commerce, La. State U., 1947-50; instr. Miss. So. Coll., summer 1950; clk.-stenographer dept. physics U. Ill., Urbana, 1951-52; instr. in shorthand Ill. Comml. Coll., 1951-52; tchr. Milford (N.H.) H.S., 1957-58; tchr. bus. edn. Merrimack (N.H.) H.S., 1958-90, head dept. bus. edn., 1971-81; ret., 1990. Grad. asst. La. State U., 1947-50; instr. auditing Rivier Coll., 1982; registered rep. R. Danais Investment Co., Manchester, N.H.; account exec. John, Edward & Co., Lebanon, N.H.; ind. beauty cons. Mary Kay Cosmetics, Merrimack; tutor in shorthand, acctg.; cons. acctg. sys. Organizer, 1st pres. Merrimack Group Hillsborough County Ext. Svc., 1957-58; active Girl Scouts U.S.A., including Cadette leader, 1959-63, sr. troop leader Switwater coun., 1970-72, adult vol. trainer, 1964-66, troop program cons., 1963-64. Mem. AAUW, NEA, N.H. Edn. Assn., N.H. Bus. Educators Assn. (v.p. 1964-65, pres. 1965-67, rep. to N.H. Vocat. Assn. 1986-87, sec. 1967-68, treas. 1973-75, historian 1986-87), N.H. Supervisory Union 27 (sec.-treas. 1961-62), Merrimack Tchrs. Assn. (sec. 1984-85, Disting. Educator award 1980, Excellence in Edn. award 1985), New Eng. Bus. Educators Assn., Assn. Career Tech. Edn., N.H. Assn. Computer Edn. Statewide, Ea. Bus. Edn. Assn., Nat. Bus. Edn. Assn., Manchester User's Group of Apple Computers (treas. 2000), Delta Zeta, Phi Theta Kappa, Pi Omega Pi, Delta Pi Epsilon, Alpha Delta Kappa (chpt. award of appreciation 1980, historian N.E. region 1981-83, sec. N.E. region 1995-97, v.p. N.H. Alpha chpt. 1978-79, pres. N.H. Alpha chpt. 1979-82, N.H. state sgt.-at-arms 1982-84, N.H. state treas. 1984-88, N.H. state membership chmn. 1988-92, N.H. state chaplain 1992-94, N.H. state pres. elect 1994-96, N.H. state pres. 1996-98, N.H. state immediate past pres. 1998-2000), Audubon Soc. N.H., Delta Sigma Epsilon (chpt. corr. sec.), Gen. Electric Women's Club, Reeds Ferry Women's Club, Manchester Coll. Women's Club, Our Lady of Mercy Ladies Guild (v.p. 1999, pres. 2000), Merrimack Sr. Citizen Club, Manchester Area Ret. Educators Assn., Nashua Area Ret. Educators Assn., N.H. Ret. Educators Assn. Roman Catholic.

BARRETT, FRANK JOSEPH, lawyer, former insurance company executive; b. Greeley, Nebr., Mar. 2, 1932; s. Patrick J. and Irene L. (Printy) B.; m. Ruth Ann Nealon, Aug. 20, 1956; children: Patrick, Mary, Anne, Karen, Thomas. BS in Law, U. Nebr., 1957; LLB, Nebr. Coll. Law, 1959. Bar: Nebr. 1959, U.S. Supreme Ct. 1976. Asst. gen. counsel, asst. sec. Nebr. Nat. Life Co., 1957-61; dir. ins. State of Nebr., Lincoln, 1961-67; exec. v.p., sec., gen. counsel Ctrl. Nat. Ins. Group of Omaha, 1967-75; exec. v.p., chief counsel Mut. of Omaha (and Affiliates), 1975-81; pres., CEO Ctrl. Nat. Ins. Co. of Omaha, 1981-89, Ins. Rsch. Svc. Co., Omaha, 1989—; of counsel Lamson, Dugan & Murray, Omaha, 1990—. Bd. dir. Am. Family Life Assurance Co., West Coast Life Ins. Co. State organizational chmn. 3 Nebr. gubernatorial campaigns. Served in U.S. Army, 1953-55, Korea. Recipient service citation Am. Nat. Red Cross, 1964, 65 Mem. Nebr. Bar Assn., Omaha Bar Assn., Am. Arbitration Assn., Fedn. Ins. Counsels, Consumer Credit Ins. Assn. (past pres. and dir.), Nat. Assn. Ind. Insurers (gov., past chmn.), Nat. Assn. Ins. Commrs. (past pres.), Am. Legion, Irish-Am. Cultural Soc., KC, ARIAS-U.S. (cert.). Democrat. Roman Catholic. Home: 516 S 119th St Omaha NE 68154-3115 Fax: 402-333-2341. E-mail: fbarrett@ldmlaw.com.

BARRETT, GEORGE EDWARD, lawyer; b. Nashville, Oct. 19, 1927; s. George E. and Annie (Conroy) B.; m. Eloise McBride Barrett, Sept. 14, 1957 (div. 1988); children: Anne-Louise Barrett Thompson, Mary Eloise Barrett Brewer, Kathryn Conroy Barrett Cain. BS, Spring Hill Coll., 1952; diploma, Oxford U., Eng., 1953; JD, Vanderbilt U., Nashville, 1957. Bar: Tenn., U.S. Ct. Appeals (6th cir.), U.S. Supreme Ct. Atty. Barrett, Johnston & Parsley, Nashville. Office: Barrett Johnston & Parsley 217 2nd Ave N Nashville TN 37201-1601 E-mail: gbarrett@barrettjohnston.com.

BARRETT, HERBERT, artists management executive; b. N.Y.C., May 31, 1910; s. John and Mollie (Pike) B.; m. Betty Palash, May 29, 1937; children: Nancy, Katherine. BA, Cornell U., 1930. Pub. rels. counsel Cadillac Car Co., N.Y.C., 1934—, GM, N.Y.C., 1935—; mgr., pres. Herbert Barrett Mgmt. (artists mgmt. assn.), N.Y.C., 1940—; mgr. inaugural Great Performers series Avery Fisher Hall, Lincoln Center for Performing Arts, N.Y.C., 1965. Mem. adv. com. Town Hall, N.Y.C., 1970—; mem. recommendation bd. Avery Fisher Artist Program, Lincoln Center Performing Arts; mem. nat. adv. bd. Van Cliburn Internat. Quadrennial Piano Competition. Recipient Patrick Hayes award for outstanding svc. to Internat. Soc. for the Performing Arts Found., 1997. Mem. Little Orch. Soc. (treas. 1970—, mgr. 1967—), Internat. Assn. Festival and Concert Mgrs. (exec. bd. 1969—), Phi Beta Kappa. Home: 15 W 72nd St New York NY 10023-3402 Office: Fl 20 266 W 37th St New York NY 10018-6648

BARRETT, IZADORE, retired fisheries research administrator; b. Vancouver, B.C., Can., Oct. 4, 1926; came to U.S., 1956; s. Samuel Barrett and Rose (Hyatt) Gordon; m. Fulvia Mercedes Quesada, July 5, 1958; children: Marcus, Byron, Norman, Dora. BA, U. B.C., 1947, MA, 1949; postgrad., U. Toronto, 1949-52; PhD, U. Wash., 1980. Chief hatchery biologist B.C. Game Commn., Vancouver, 1952-56; scientist Inter-Am. Tropical Tuna Commn., La Jolla, 1956-67; chief biologist UNDP Fisheries Devel. Project, Santiago, Chile, 1967-69; fisheries advisor FAO, Santiago, 1969-70; dep. dir. S.W. Fisheries Ctr., La Jolla, 1970-77, dir., 1977-88; sci. and research dir. S.W. region, Nat. Marine Fisheries Svc., 1988-92; ret., 1992. Rsch. assoc. Scripps Inst. Oceanography, La Jolla, 1977-98; mem. sci. and statis. com. Pacific Fisheries Mgmt. Coun., Portland, Oreg., 1977-90; chmn. sci. and statis. com. Western Pacific Fisheries Mgmt. Coun., Honolulu, 1976-79. Contbr. articles to profl. jours. Bd. govs. San Diego Oceans Found., 1985-95; chmn. Mayor's San Diego/La Jolla Underwater Park Com., 1978-92; mem. adv. coun. Inst. Marine Resources U. Calif., La Jolla, 1979-85; bd. govs. San Diego Sci. Fair, 1984-92. Fellow Am. Inst. Fisheries Rsch. Biologists (v.p. 1973-76), U. Calif. San Diego Retirement Assn. (v.p. 2003-). E-mail: ibarrett@ucsd.edu.

BARRETT, J. CARL, cancer researcher, molecular biologist; b. Portsmouth, Va., Dec. 28, 1946; s. Jacob Weaver and Dixie Wike (Ring) B.; m. Roberta Mick, June 8, 1968; children: James, Paul, Lia. BS in Chemistry, Coll. of William and Mary, 1969; PhD in Biophysical Chemistry, Johns Hopkins U., 1974. Postdoctoral fellow divsn. biophysics Johns Hopkins U., Balt., 1974-77; sr. staff fellow lab. pulmonary function and toxicology Nat. Inst. Environ. Health Scis., Rsch. Triangle Park, N.C., 1977-82, group leader environ. carcinogenesis group, 1977-87, rsch. chemist, 1982-87, chief lab. molecular carcinogenesis, 1987-2000, dir. program environ. carcinogenesis div. intramural rsch., 1992-96, sci. dir., 1995-2000; dir. divsn. basic scis. Nat. Cancer Inst., Bethesda, Md., 2000—. Adj. prof. dept. pathology U. N.C., 1978—, dept. epidemiology, 1992—; adj. mem. genetics curriculum U. N.C., 1979—, toxicology curriculum, 1985—; adj. sr. fellow Ctr. Study of Aging and Human Devel. Duke U. Med. Ctr., 1993—; mem. study sections NIH, Nat. Cancer Inst., Nat. Cancer Inst. Can.; ad hoc reviewer; vis. prof. Sun Yat-Sen U., People's Rep. China, 1987, Inst. Zoology Academia Sinica, Taiwan, 1992, NYU, 1992; keynote speaker, organizer, chair numerous symposia, conferences, workshops; invited speaker more than 125 symposia, conferences, univs. worl dwide, 1986—; mem. Task Force Health Effects of Synthetic Fuels Dept. Energy, 1980; mem. workshop Internat. Program Chem. Safety, 1982; mem. working group WHO, 1983, Internat. Agy. Rsch. Cancer, France, 1985, 86, peer rev. com. sci. coun., 1988; mem. adv. panel Calif. Biotech., Inc., 1990, Greenwall Found., 1989; mem. various adv. bds., coms. Nat. Coun. Radiation Protection & Measurements, Am. Health Found., Nat. Cancer Inst., U.S. EPA, Health Effects Inst.-Asbestos Rsch. Com., Chem. Industry Inst. Toxicology, also external expert, ad hoc mem.; cons. Abbott Labs., 1989-91, Chem. Industry Inst. Toxicology, 1991-92; chmn. sci. coun. Internat. Agy. for Rsch. on Cancer, 1998. Author: Mechanisms of Environmental Carcinogenesis: Volume I-Role of Genetic and Epigenetic Changes, 1987, Vol. II-Multistep Models of Carcinogenesis, 1987; co-author: Carcinogenesis-A Comprehensive Survey: Volume 9, Mammalian Cell Transformation: Mechanisms of Carcinogenesis and Assays for Carcinogens, 1985, Comparative Molecular Carcinogenesis: Volume 376-Progress in Clinical and Biological Research, 1992; editor-in-chief Molecular Carcinogenesis, 1992—, mem. editl. bd., 1988—; assoc. editor Cancer Rsch., 1984—, Mutagenesis, 1985-88, Toxicology in Vitro, 1986-90; mem. editl. bds. profl. jours., 1988—; contbr. over 405 articles to profl. jours. Recipient merit awards NIH, 1989, 94, 97, Dir.'s award, 1995, 96, Ramazzini award Collegium Ramazzini, Italy, 1995, Secretary's award for Disting. Svc., Dept. Health and Human Svcs., 1996; NSF grantee, 1966; Dow Chem. Co. fellow, 1968. Mem. AAAS, Am. Chem. Soc., Am. Assn. Cancer Rsch. (program com., Rhodes award com., chair spl. membership com., bd. dirs. 1998—), Internat. Soc. Diffrentiation (bd. dirs. 1998—). Office: Nat Cancer Inst Dir of Ctr for Cancer Rsch 31 Center Dr Bldg 31 Rm 3A11 Bethesda MD 20892-2440 E-mail: barrett@mail.nih.gov.

BARRETT, JALMA See BOERSMA, JUNE

BARRETT, JAMES EDWARD, JR., management consultant; b. Lowell, Mass., Dec. 9, 1929; s. James E. and Margaret A. (Holland) B.; m. Dorothy G. Walle; children: James Edward III, Dorothy Anne, William H., M. Stephen. BA, Harvard U., 1951; postgrad., Air Command and Staff Coll., 1953. Asst. prof. Harvard U., 1955-58; staff mgr. Raytheon Co., 1958-62; staff Kepner-Tregoe, Inc., Princeton, N.J., 1963-68; pres. Cresheim Co., Inc., Phila., 1968—. Chmn. Cresheim, Ltd. (U.K.), 1979-95, Cresheim do Brasil, Sao Paulo, 1980-99. bd. dirs. Swansea Press, Inc. 1986-95. Author: Managing Your Distributors; columnist Family Bus. mag., 1994—; contbr. numerous articles to profl. jours. Pres. Wyndmoor (Pa.) Cmty. Assn., 1977-79; dir. Alzheimer's Assn. Southeastern Pa., 1995-2001, v.p., 1996-99. Capt. USAF, 1951-55. Mem. Harvard Club (N.Y.C., Phila.), Adcesno Inst. (chmn. 1999). Home: 8315 Flourtown Ave Wyndmoor PA 19038-7924 Office: Cresheim Management Cons PO Box 27785 Philadelphia PA 19118-0785 E-mail: jebcmc99@att.net.

BARRETT, JAMES EMMETT, retired judge; b. Lusk, Wyo., Apr. 8, 1922; s. Frank A. and Alice C. (Donoghue) Barrett; m. Carmel Ann Martinez, Oct. 8, 1949; children: Ann Catherine Barrett Sandahl, Richard James, John Donoghue. Student, U. Wyo., 1940—42, LLB, 1949; student, St. Catherine's Coll., Oxford, Eng., 1945, Cath. U. Am., 1946. Bar: Wyo. 1949. Mem. firm Barrett and Barrett, Lusk, 1949—67; atty. Niobrara Sch. Dist., 1950—64; county and pros. atty. Niobrara County, Wyo., 1951—62; atty. Town of Lusk, 1952—54; atty. gen. State of Wyo., 1967—71; judge U.S. Circuit Ct. Appeals (10th cir.), 1971—2003, now sr. judge. Active Boy Scouts Am.; trustee St. Joseph's Children's Home, Torrington, Wyo., 1971—85; sec.-treas. Niobrara County Rep. Ctrl. Com. Cpl. U.S. Army, 1942—45, ETO. Recipient Disting. Alumni award, U. Wyo., 1973, Coll. Law U. Wyo., 2002. Mem.: VFW, Am. Legion, Order of Coif (hon. mem. Wyo. Coll. Law/U. Wyo. chpt.).

BARRETT, JAMES GRESHAM, congressman; b. Oconee, S.C., Feb. 14, 1961; m. Natalie Barrett; 3 children. BS in Bus. Adminstrn., The Citadel, 1983. Operator Barrett's Furniture, 1987; mem. S.C. Ho. Reps., 1996—2002, U.S. Ho. Reps. from 3rd S.C. dist., 2003—; mem. budget and fin. svcs. com. U.S. Ho. Reps. SME chair Oconee Boy Scouts, 1995, chmn.; mem. S.C. GOP steering com. Pres. George W. Bush Candidacy, 2000. Capt. U.S. Army, 1983—87. Mem.: Oconee County C. of C. (pres.), Westminster Rotary Club (pres.). Republican. Baptist. Office: 1523 Longworth HOB Washington DC 20515*

BARRETT, JAMES THOMAS, immunologist, educator; b. Centerville, Iowa, May 20, 1927; s. Alfred Wesley and Mary Marjorie (Taylor) B.; m. Barbro Anna-Lill Nilsson, July 31, 1967; children— Sara, Robert, Annika, Nina BA, State U. Iowa, 1950, MS, 1951, PhD, 1953. Asst. prof. bacteriology and parasitology U. Ark. Sch. Medicine, Little Rock, 1953-57; asst. prof. microbiology U. Mo. Sch. Medicine, Columbia, 1957-59, assoc. prof., 1959-67, prof., 1967-94, St. George's (Grenada, W.I.) U. Sch. Medicine, 1994—2002; prof. emeritus U. Mo. Sch. Medicine, 1994—, ret., 2003. Exchange prof. U.S. and Romanian Acads. Sci., 1971; vis. scientist Spanish Ministry Edn. and Sci., 1986, Sch. Vet. Medicine, 2000 Author: Textbook of Immunology, 5th edit., 1988, Basic Immunology and Its Medical Application 2d edit., 1980, Medical Immunology, 1991, Microbiology and Immunology Casebook, 1995, Microbiology and Immunology Concepts, 1998; editor: Contemporary Classics in the Life Scienes, 1986, Contemporary Classics in Clinical Medicine, 1986, Contemporary Classics in Plant, Animal and Environmental Sciences, 1986. Served with USN, 1944-45 NIH Fogarty sr. fellow, 1977-78; Fulbright scholar, 1984 Mem. Am. Assn. Immunology, Am. Soc. Microbiology. Home: 901 Westport Dr Columbia MO 65203-0741 E-mail: niann@aol.com.

BARRETT, JANE, lawyer; AB magna cum laude, Vassar Coll., 1969; MA in Chinese Studies, U. Mich., 1973; JD, NYU, 1976. Bar: N.Y. 1977, Mass. 1985. Staff atty. Legal Svcs. Corp., Bklyn., 1977-79; law asst. N.Y. County Supreme Ct., N.Y.C., 1979-81; asst. atty. gen. N.Y. State, N.Y.C., 1981-84; asst. corp. counsel N.Y.C., 1984-87; sole practitioner N.Y.C., 1988-95; ptnr. Spodek & Barrett LLP, N.Y.C., 1995—. Bd. dirs. Bklyn. Legal Svcs. Corp. A. Contbg. author: Everywoman's Legal Guide, 1983; editor newsletter N.Y. County Lawyers Assn., 1977. Mem. N.Y. State Bar Assn., Assn. Bar City N.Y., N.Y. State Trial Lawyers, Nat. Assn. Ins. Women, Princeton Club. Office: Spodek & Barrett LLP 61 Broadway Rm 1050 New York NY 10006-2701

BARRETT, JANE HAYES, lawyer; b. Dayton, Ohio, Dec. 13, 1947; d. Walter J. and Jane H. Barrett BA, Calif. State U.-Long Beach, 1969; JD, U. So. Calif., 1972. Bar: Calif. 1972, U.S. Dist. Ct. (cen. dist.) Calif. 1972, U.S. Ct. Appeals (9th cir.) 1982, U.S. Supreme Ct. Assoc. Lawler, Felix & Hall, L.A., 1972—84; ptnr. Arter & Hadden, L.A., 1984—94; mng. ptnr. Preston, Gates & Ellis, L.A., 1994—2002; ptnr. Piper Rudnick, L.A., 2002—. Lectr. bus. law Calif. State U., 1973-75. Mem. adv. bd. Harriet Buhai Legal Aid Ctr., 1991-96, mem. bd. pub. counsel, 1996-98; pres. Pilgrim Parents Orgn. 1990-91; chmn. fin. Our Mother Good Counsel Sch.; bd. regents Loyola, H.S., 2000—. Named Outstanding Grad. Calif. State U., Long Beach, 1988, Outstanding Alumnae Polit. Sci., 1993. Fellow Am. Bar Found.; mem. ABA (bd. govs. 1980-84, chmn. young lawyers divsn. 1980-81, com. on delivery of legal svcs. 1985-89, exec. coun. legal edn. and admissions sects. 1985-89, fin. sec. torts and ins. practice 1982-83, adv. mem. fed. judiciary com. 9th circuit rep. 2000—, v.p. 1997—, Am. Bar Endowment 1999, bd. dirs. 1990—, sec. 1993-95, v.p. 1998-99, pres., 1999-2000, bd. fellows young lawyers divsn. 1992—, del 9th cir. jud. conf., atty. del. U.S. Dist. Ct. ctrl. dist. Calif. Atty. Conf. 2002—), 9th Cir. Atty. Conf. (del. 2003), Calif. State Bar (com. adminstrn. of justice, editl. bd. Calif. Lawyers 1981-84), Legion Lex (bd. dirs. 1990-93), Los Feliz Homeowners Assn. (bd. dirs.). Democrat. Office: Piper Rudnick 1999 Ave of the Stars Los Angeles CA 90067 E-mail: jane.barrett@piperrudnick.com.

BARRETT, JANET TIDD, academic administrator; b. Crystal City, Mo., Nov. 29, 1939; d. Lewis Samuel and Mamie Lou (Hulvey) Tidd; m. David Clark Barrett, June 3, 1961; children: Barbara, Pam. Diploma in nursing, St. Lukes Hosp. Sch. Nursing, 1960; BSN with honors, Washington U., St. Louis, 1964, MSN, 1979; PhD, St. Louis U., 1987. Assoc. prof. Maryville Coll., St. Louis, 1979-89; acad. dean Barnes Coll., St. Louis, 1989-91; dir. BSN program Deaconess Coll. Nursing, St. Louis, 1991-2000, acad. dean, 2000—02; nursing cons., 2002—. Contbn. author to Beare and Meyers: Principles of Medical-Surgical Nursing. St. Lukes Hosp. scholar; recipient Sister Agnita Claire Day Rsch. award St. Louis U. Mem.: Mo. League Nursing, Nat. League Nursing, St. Luke's Alumni Assn., Phi Delta Kappa, Pi Lambda Theta, Sigma Theta Tau. E-mail: jtbarrett02@earthlink.net.

BARRETT, JESSICA (DONNA ANN NIPERT), psychotherapist; b. Paterson, N.J., July 25, 1952; d. Donald Alfred and Gloria Emma (Lustica) Nipert; m. John David Barrett, Sept. 9, 1977 (div. June 1982); 1 child, Ashley Elizabeth. BA, UCLA, 1975; MA, Azusa Pacific U., 1981. Lic. marriage, family, child therapist; cert. hypnosis prof. With employee relations Engrs. and Architects Exec. Assn., L.A., 1975-79; practicing psychotherapy Toluca Lake and Burbank, Calif., 1983—; instr., supr. Phillips Grad. Inst., Encino, Calif., 1986-2000; psychotherapist Pasadena (Calif.) Outpatient Eating Disorders Program, 1987-88. Cons. Texaco Employee Assistance Program, Studio City, 1985—86, NBC Employee Assistance Program, Burbank, 1986—87, Burbank, 1993—; spl. therapist United Behavioral Health, Managed Health Networks, Cigna Behavioral Health, 1989—, Value Options Provider, 1986—, Health Mgmt. Resource Svcs., 1985—99; assessment and referral liaison Nat. Resource Cons., San Diego, 1983—93, Employee Support Sys. Corp., Orange, Calif., 1985—,

Health and Human Resource Ctr., 1984—92, Blue Cross Preferred Provider and EAP Network, 1995—, U.S. Behavioral Health, 1998—. Mem. Employee Assistance Profls. Assn. (bd. dirs. 1983-86), Am. Assn. Marriage and Family Therapists (clin. 1983—), Phillips Grad. Inst. Alumni Assn. (sec.-treas. 1987-88, v.p. programs 1988-89), Eye Movement Desensitization Reprocessing Internat. Assn. (charter). Avocations: theater, improvisational comedy, piano, literature, travel. E-mail: ncrrgbl1@aol.com.

BARRETT, JOHN J(AMES), JR., lawyer; b. Phila., May 19, 1948; s. John J. and Carmela (DiJohn) B.; m. Rosemary A. Campagna, Aug. 23, 1969; children: Jeffrey, Kristin, Jacqueline. BA, Temple U., 1970, JD, 1973. Bar: Pa. 1973, N.J. 1987, U.S. Dist. Ct. (ea. dist.) Pa. 1973, U.S. Ct. Appeals (3rd cir.) 1975, U.S. Dist. Ct. (mid. dist.) Pa. 1986, U.S. Supreme Ct. 1986, U.S. Dist. Ct. N.J. 1987. Assoc. Saul, Ewing, Remick & Saul, Phila., 1973-80; ptnr. Saul Ewing LLP, 1980—. Mem. Nat. Assn. R.R. Trial Counsel, Phila. Assn. Def. Counsel. Office: Saul Ewing LLP 3800 Centre Sq W 1500 Market St Philadelphia PA 19102

BARRETT, JUDITH ANN, salon owner; b. N.Y.C., Dec. 15, 1940; d. William Patrick and Eleanor Margaret (McClaurey) B. Grad., Aquinas H.S., 1958. Sec. Avon Products, N.Y.C., 1960-73; owner The Girl's Beauty Shop, Port Richey, Fla., 1974—2002. CEO, founder Enraged People Against Rape, Pasco, Fla., 1990-93. With USNR, 1969-72. Recipient Outstanding Contbrn. and Dedication to Fla Residents, U.S. Congress M. Bilirakis, Washington, 1992, Cmty. Svc. Pres. award Cmty. Svc. Coun. of W. Pasco, 1992, Humanitarian award Pasco County Sheriffs Dept., 1991-92, J.C. Penney Golden Rule award, 1996, Cmty. Hero award Pasco County, 1997. Mem.: Waves Nat., 2d Amendment Rep. Club, West Pasco Rep. Club, Am. Legion. Republican. Roman Catholic. Avocations: tennis, writing, poetry.

BARRETT, KAREN MOORE, lawyer; b. Pitts., Jan. 16, 1950; d. James Newton and Grace Naomi (Gigax) Moore; m. Jay Elliott Barrett, June 24, 1972; children: Catherine Grace, Elizabeth Alice. AB, Bryn Mawr Coll., 1972; JD, Harvard U., 1977. Bar: Pa. 1977, U.S. Dist. Ct. (we. dist.) Pa. 1977. Assoc. Buchanan Ingersoll Profl. Corp., Pitts., 1977-84, ptnr., 1984-89; counsel CBS Corp. (formerly Westinghouse Electric Corp.), Pitts., 1989-90, sr. counsel, 1990-93, asst. gen. counsel, 1993-2000; sr. counsel The PNC Fin. Svcs. Group, Inc., Pitts., 2000—. Bd. dirs. Planned Parenthood of Western Pa., Inc., 1983-95, v.p., 1988-92; trustee Southminster Presbyn. Ch., 1995-98. Mem. ABA, Pa. Bar Assn., Allegheny County Bar Assn., Bryn Mawr of Western Pa. (Pitts., v.p. 1984-87, pres. 1987-91). Democrat. Office: PNC Fin Svcs Group Inc 249 5th Ave Pittsburgh PA 15222-2707

BARRETT, KATHERINE, writer, multimedia producer; b. N.Y.C., May 24, 1954; d. Herbert and Betty (Palash) B.; m. Richard H. Greene, Feb. 21, 1982; children: Benjamin, Sandra. BS in Journalism, Northwestern U., 1976. Reporter Comml. Appeal, Memphis, 1976-78; assoc. editor, sr. writer, sr. editor Ladies' Home Jour., N.Y.C., 1980-84, contbg. editor, 1984-98; free-lance writer, columnist numerous publs., 1984—; prodr. Walt Disney Family Edn. Found., San Francisco, 1996—; spl. project editor Governing mag., Washington, 1997—. Spkr. on state and city mgmt., 1992—; mem. adv. bd. Govtl. Acctg. Stds. Bd., Norwalk, Conn., 1996—, Urban Inst., Washington, 1996-99; curator Walt Disney Family Mus. web site. Author: The Man Behind the Magic, 1991, Frankly, My Dear, 1996, Powering Up, 2000, Inside the Dream, 2001; co-prodr.: (plays, CD-ROM) Walt Disney: An Intimate History, 1998; co-prodr., writer (TV documentary) Walt: The Man Behind the Myth, 2001; contbr. articles to Redbook, Reader's Digets, Glamour, Ladies Home Jour., others. Recipient award for excellence N.Y. Soc. CPA's, 1991, Children's Choice award Internat. Reading Assn., 1992, Washington Monthly Journalism award, 1999. Folio Editorial Excellence award, 2002.

BARRETT, LAURENCE IRWIN, public relations executive, writer; b. N.Y.C., Sept. 6, 1935; s. Harold and Ruth (Gaier) B.; m. Paulette Singer, Mar. 9, 1957 (div. 1983); children: Paul M., David A., Adam S.; m. Martha Priddy Patterson, July 24, 1988. BA, NYU, 1956; MS in Journalism, Columbia U., 1957. Polit. reporter and columnist N.Y. Herald Tribune, N.Y.C., 1958-62, Washington correspondent, 1962-65; assoc. editor Time Inc., N.Y.C., 1965-69, sr. editor, 1970-75, N.Y. regional bur. chief, 1975-78, sr. White House correspondent, 1978-85, nat. polit. correspondent, 1986 92, contbr., 1993 97; Washington dep. bur. chief, 1989-91; v.p. Powell Tate, Washington, 1998—2002, sr. v.p., 2003—. Panelist various TV and radio talk shows; asst. prof. sch. comm. Am. U., 1995-97. Co-author: The Winning of the White House, 1988, 89; author: Gambling with History: Reagan in the White House, 1983, The Mayor of New York, 1965; contbr. articles to mags., newspapers, profl. jours. With U.S. Army, 1957. Mem. Nat. Press Club, Soc. of the Silurians. Jewish. Office: Powell Tate 700 13th St NW Ste 1000 Washington DC 20005-6618 E-mail: labarrett@webershandwick.com.

BARRETT, LINDA L. real estate consultant; b. Hudson, Mich., Aug. 16, 1948; d. David John and Georgia Elizabeth (Spengler) B.; m. Carl Gugino; 1 dau., Toni. Student, U. Mich., 1970-73. Cert. residential brokerage mgr. Sales mgr. Collins Real Estate, Hudson, Mich., 1973-79; owner, broker Homeland Real Estate, Lake Leann, Mich., 1979-82; mgr. broker Mid-Mich. Real Estate, Jackson, Mich., 1982-85; exec. v.p. Michael Saunders & Co., Sarasota, Fla., 1986-95, cons., 1995—. Mem. adv. bd. Sotheby's Internat. Mem. Econ. Devel. Coun., Com. of 100. Mem. AAUW, NAFE, Internat. Real Estate Fedn., Nat. Mktg. Inst., Nat. Assn. Realtors, Fla. Assn. Realtors, Sarasota C. of C., Global Travel Internat. Network, 2000 Notable Am. Women, Econ. Devel. Coun., CRB, Holistic Options, Profl.'s Network Investment Orgn., Field Club, The Oaks, Longboat Key Club. Avocations: gardening, golfing, yoga, travel, writing.

BARRETT, LISA MARIE, acupuncture physician, herbologist, hypnotherapist; b. Hudson, Mich., Feb. 26, 1954; d. David John and Georgia Elizabeth (Spengler) B. Grad., Lansing Bus. U., Mich., 1972, Sch. Natural Healing Arts, Sarasota, Fla., 1997. Diplomate acupuncture, Chinese herbology, Nat. Certification Commn. for Acupuncture & Oriental Medicine; cert. herbologist, Nambudripad's allergy elimination technique practitioner. Pvt. practice acupuncture, Sarasota, Fla., 1997—. Mem. MENSA, Am. Assn. Oriental Medicine, Fla. State Oriental Med. Assn. Avocations: feng shui, qigong, reading, horseback riding, walking. E-mail: drlisa@lotushealthcenter.com.

BARRETT, LORETTA ANNE, literary agent; b. Mt. Vernon, N.J., July 1, 1941; d. Edward Vincent and Irene (Wynne) B. Student, Rosemont (Pa.) Coll.; BA with honors, U. Pa., Phila., 1962, MS in Edn., 1965. Editor Doubleday & Co., N.Y.C., 1965, editl. dir. spl. projects, 1967-72, exec. editor Anchor Press, 1972—83, editor, v.p., 1983—90; pres. Loretta Barrett Books, Inc., N.Y.C., 1990—. Mem. trustee coun. of Penn Women U. Pa.; bd. dirs. Reading Is Fundamental, Nathaniel Wharton Found., Grandparenting Found., Lake Placid, NY. Mem.: Assn. Author Reps., Women's Media Group NY. Office: 101 5th Ave Fl 11 New York NY 10003-1008

BARRETT, LOUIS C. mathematician, educator; b. Murray, Utah, Jan. 23, 1924; s. John Taylor Barrett, Louise Caroline Matilda Dahl; m. Betty Jene Grist, June 13, 1947; children: Louis LeeGrande, Linda Jene Stokes, Lori Lynn Prause, Louise Ann Kingston. BS, U. Utah, 1948, MS, 1951, PhD, 1956. Instr. math. U. Utah, Salt Lake City, 1953—56; assoc. prof. math. Ariz. State U., Tempe, 1956—57; prof. and head dept. math. S.D. Sch. Mines and Tech., Rapid City, 1957—65; prof., chmn. dept. math. Clarkson Coll. Tech., Potsdam, NY, 1965—67; prof., head dept. math. Mont. State U., Bozeman, 1967—89, prof. emeritus, 1989—; math. cons. Inline Diagnostics, Ogden, Utah, 1999—2000. Math. rschr. Holloman Air Devel. Ctr., N.Mex., 1955—56; math. cons. Naval Weapons Ctr., China Lake, Calif., 1957—72; army and navy rschr. U. Utah, 1950—53. Co-author: Advanced Engineering Mathematics, 5th edit., 1982, 6th edit., 1995; contbr. 1st lt. U.S. Army, 1943—46, ETO. Ch. Of Jesus Christ Of Latter Day Saints. Avocations: gardening, sports, travel. Mailing: 1721 S Willson Ave Bozeman MT 59715

BARRETT, MARTIN JAY, financial executive; b. N.Y.C., Mar. 12, 1949; s. Nat and Pearl Barrett; m. Bette Sue Levy, Sept. 9, 1984. BS in Acctg., Lehmann Coll., CUNY, 1976. V.p. fin., CFO N.Y. Jr. Tennis League Inc., Sports and Arts in Schs. Found. Inc., Long Island City, 1999—2003; assoc. exec. dir. for ops. Hetrick-Martin Inst., N.Y.C., 1998-99; CFO Ackerman Inst. for Family Therapy, N.Y.C., 1992-98; COO NY Jr. League, 2003—. Pres. 40 Plus of N.Y., N.Y.C., 1992, 99; chief auditor N.Y.C. Carpenters Benefit Funds, N.Y.C., 1972-92; mgr. pension and med. benefits Nat. Health and Welfare Assn., N.Y.C., 1967-72. Editor: (newsletter) The Good News Is ... The Bad News Is ..., 1993-98. Chmn. cmty. planning bd. #6, Manhattan, 1998-2000, pks. and landmarks com. Cmty. Bd. 6, N.Y.C., 1991—, chmn. budget priority com., 2002—, chmn. pub. safety com., 1992-94, vice chmn. planning bd., 1996-98, chmn. budget and legis. affairs, 1996-98; mem. Sutton Area Com., 1993—; pres. Phipps Plz. West Tenant's Assn., N.Y.C., 1989-92, treas., 1985-89; v.p., trustee Belleview South Pk. Assn., N.Y.C., 1991-2000; chmn. pub. safety Ams. for Dem. Action, N.Y.C., 1995-96; campaign treas. various local and state elected ofcls. and judges, N.Y.C., 1978-94; mem. Nat. Trust Hist. Preservation Soc., 1990—, Wildlife Conservation Soc., 1992—; commr. of deeds N.Y.C., 1984—; pres. Stuyvescent Cove Pk. Assn., 1998—; bd. trustees 14th St. Bus. Improvement Dist.; bd. dirs. Grand Ctrl. Neighborhood Social Svcs. Corp., 2000—; mem. Manhattan Borough Bd.; bd. dirs. 440 E. Owers Coop. Recipient Congression Record for Civic and Comty. Svc. award, 2001, Proclamatia award N.Y.C. Coun., 2001, citation N.Y. State Assembly, 2001, resolution N.Y. State Senate, 2001, citation Manhattan Borough Pres., 2001. Mem. Am. Mgmt. Assn., Inst. Mgmt. Accts., Knights of Pythias (Hubert H. Humphrey chancellor comdr. 1995-97, fin. sec. 1997-2000). Avocations: literature, performing arts, fine arts, travel, civil affairs. Office: NY Jr Tennis League Inc 2416 Queens Plz S Long Island City NY 11101-4620

BARRETT, MICHAEL BAKER, historian, educator; b. Honolulu, Oct. 12, 1946; s. John P. and Bernice (Baker) B.; m. Sara Harriet McKerley, Sept. 20, 1969; 1 child, Michael M. AB, The Citadel, 1968; MA, U. Mass., 1969, PhD, 1977. Lectr. history U. Mass., Amherst, 1973-74, 75-76; instr. history The Citadel, Charleston, S.C., 1976-78, asst. prof., 1978-82, assoc. prof., 1982—, dean of grad. studies, 1985—. Contbr. articles to profl. jours. Brig. gen. U.S. Army, 1969—2001. Recipient Legion of Merit, U.S. Army, others; Fulbright fellow, 1974-75, Citadel Devel. Found. fellow, 1977, 82, NDEA fellow, 1977. Mem. Am. Hist. Assn., Am. Mil. Inst., Conf. Group Cen. European History, So. History Assn., S.C. History Assn., Soc. Mil. History, Hibernian Soc., U.S. Army Armor Assn., Transp. Corps. Res. Officers Assn., Phi Alpha Theta, Phi Kappa Phi, Delta Phi Alpha. Roman Catholic. Office: The Citadel Grad Studies Office Of The Dean Charleston SC 29409-0001 Mailing: 1170 Chersonese Rd Mount Pleasant SC 29464-9506

BARRETT, MICHAEL HENRY, civil engineer; b. Dove Creek, Colo., June 20, 1932; s. Frank Ace and Carrie Ethel (Snyder) B.; m. Barbara Jane Kreutz, Aug. 7, 1954; children: Robert, Mary, Bonnie, William. BS in Civil Engring, U. Colo., 1955, postgrad., 1955-64; MBA, U. Denver, 1979. Registered profl. engr., Colo., Calif., Fla., Wis., N.C., Minn., N.Mex., Utah. Design engr., then partner Ketchum & Konkel, Denver, 1955-69; pres. Ketchum, Konkel, Barrett, Nickel, Austin, Denver, 1969-79, chmn. bd., 1979-85, pres., chmn., 1986-88; prin., cons. Martin/Martin, 1988—; cons. MMFX Steel Co., 2000—. Dir. Testing Cons., Inc., Martin Assoc. Group; mem. faculty U. Colo., 1963-64, U. Denver, 1968-69; lectr. Civil Def., 1962-68. Patentee in field. Exec. bd. Denver Area council Boy Scouts Am., 1970—, pres., 1974-75, area v.p., 1976-82, area pres., 1982; mem. Westminster (Colo.) Planning Commn., 1971-72; chmn. bd. dirs. Denver Boys, Inc. Served with USNR, 1951-54, USAR, 1955-63. Recipient Lincoln Arc Welding award, 1966, 68, award Am. Inst. Steel Constrn., 1969, Disting. Engring. Alumnus award U. Colo., 1984, Honor award Colo. Engring. Coun., 1984, Silver Beaver award Boy Scouts Am., 1977, Silver Antelope award, 1983. Fellow ASCE (life); mem. Nat. Soc. Profl. Engrs., Am. Concrete Inst., Soc. Exptl. Stress Analysis, Profl. Engrs. Colo. (pres. 1970), Am. Cons. Engrs. Coun. (1st place award 1973, pres. Colo. chpt. 1982, Orley Phillips award 1992, com. of fellows 1993, peer reviewer 1984—, George Washington Leadership award 1998), Structural Engrs. Assn. Colo., Am. Arbitration Assn., Harvard Bus. Sch. Club, Denver C. of C., Rotary (dir. 1976-78). Office: Martin & Martin Inc 4251 Kipling St Wheat Ridge CO 80033-2896 E-mail: mbarrett@martinmartin.com.

BARRETT, MICHAEL JOHN, anesthesiologist; b. Milw., Feb. 27, 1954; s. Walter Joseph and Valerie Clara (Wisniewski) Baclawski; m. Joan Marie Rowley, May 28, 1983; children: Michael J. Jr., Jessica Marie, Monica Jane. BS in Math. with honors, U. Wis., 1974; MD, Med. Coll. Wis., 1981; MBA, U. Toledo, 1998. Diplomate Am. Bd. Anesthesiology, Nat. Bd. Medicine and Surgery, Nat. Bd. Med. Examiners, Am. Acad. Pain Mgmt., Am. Bd. Anesthesiology Pain Mgmt. Intern Med. Coll. Wis. Affiliated Hosps., Milw., 1981, resident in anesthesiology, 1982—84; dir. anesthesiology Putnam Cmty. Hosp., Palatka, Fla., 1984—92, dir. Putnam Pain Ctr., 1985—92; clin. asst. prof. anesthesiology Ohio U. Coll. Osteo. Medicine; chief dept. anesthesia Putnam Cmty. Hosp., Palatka, 1984—92. Pres. Putnam Anesthesia Assocs., Palatka, 1985-92; staff anesthesiologist St. Vincent Med. Ctr., Toledo, 1992—, dir. Pain Mgmt. Ctr., 1994—; ptnr. Assn. Anesth. of Toledo, 1993—, fiduciary pension plan, 1999—, vice chmn. dept. Anesthesia SVMMC, v.p. AAT. Bd. dirs. Round Lake Park Homeowners Assn., Palatka, 1986-88. Walter Zeit fellow; recipient St. Vincents Physician Excellence award, 1996. Mem. AMA, Internat. Anesthesia Rsch. Soc., Am. Soc. Anesthesiologists, Am. Soc. Regional Anesthesiologists, Ohio Med. Assn., Acad. Medicine of Toledo and Lucas County, Am. Neuromodulation Soc., Ohio Soc. Anesthesiologists, Putnam County Med. Soc. (pres. 1989-91), Phi Beta Kappa, Phi Kappa Phi. Republican. Roman Catholic. Avocations: boating, private pilot, swimming. Home: 8646 Plum Hollow Pt Holland OH 43528-8487 Office: Assoc Anesthesiologists Ste 305 2409 Cherry St Toledo OH 43608-2600

BARRETT, MICHAEL JOSEPH, priest; b. N.Y.C., Oct. 6, 1952; s. Patrick Joseph and Margaret Mary (Rogan) B. BA, Columbia Coll., 1974; STD, Pontifical U. Holy Cross, Rome, 1987. Ordained priest by Pope John Paul II, Rome, 1985. Sales rep. Gulf Oil Chems. Co., N.Y.C., 1974-76; acct. exec. Merrill Lynch & Co., N.Y.C., 1976-78; dir. devel. The Heights Found., Inc., N.Y.C., 1978-83; asst. prof. Roman Coll. of Holy Cross, Rome, 1985-88; del. vicar for Tex. Opus Dei Prelature, Houston, 1988-99; dir. Holy Cross Chapel and Cath. Info. Ctr., 1999—; chaplain St. Thomas More Soc. Legal Ethics, 2001—. Retreat master Featherock Conf. Ctr., Schulenburg, Tex., 1988-99; chaplain Southgate Cultural Ctr., Houston, 1988-99; co-host (radio talk show) Faith Matters, 1997-98. Alumnus advisor Columbia U. Secondary Schs. Com., N.Y.C., 1981-83. Roman Catholic. Avocations: tennis, jogging, classical music, reading. Home: 5505 Chaucer Dr Houston TX 77005-2631 Office: Holy Cross Chapel 905 Main St Houston TX 77002-6408 E-mail: info@holycrosschapel.org.

BARRETT, NANCY SMITH, university administrator; b. Balt., Sept. 12, 1942; d. James Brady and Katherine (Pollard) Smith; children: Clark, Christopher. BA, Goucher Coll., 1963; MA, Harvard U., 1965, PhD, PhD, Harvard U., 1968. Dep. asst. dir. Congl. Budget Office, Washington, 1975-76; sr. staff Council of Econ. Advisors, Washington, 1977; prin. research assoc. The Urban Inst., Washington, 1977-79; dep. asst. sec. U.S. Dept. Labor, Washington, 1979-81; instr. Am. U., Washington, 1966-67, asst. prof. econs., 1967-70, assoc. prof., 1970-74, prof., 1974-89; dean Coll. of Bus. Adminstrn. Fairleigh Dickinson U., Teaneck, N.J., 1989-91; provost, v.p. acad. affairs Western Mich. U., Kalamazoo, 1991-96, U. Ala., Tuscaloosa, 1996—2003, Wayne State U., Detroit, 2003—. Author: Theory of Macroeconomic Policy, 1972, 2d rev. edit., 1975, Theory of Microeconomic Policy, 1974, (with G. Gerardi and T. Hart) Prices and Wages in U.S., 1974; contbr. articles on econs. to profl. jours. Woodrow Wilson fellow, 1963-64; Fulbright scholar, 1973. Mem. Am. Econs. Assn., Phi Beta Kappa. Office: Wayne State Univ 4092 Faculty Adminstrn Bldg Detroit MI 48202 Home: 2033 Shorepointe Grosse Pointe Woods MI 48236 E-mail: nancy.barrett@wayne.edu.

BARRETT, PAUL J. pharmacist; b. Pryor, Okla., July 14, 1962; s. Joe C. and Lenna M. (McMillen) B.; m. Susan G. Cartier, Feb. 14, 1989; 1 child, Drew Phillip. BS in Pharmacy, Purdue U., 1985, PharmD, 1986; MPA, U. Maine, 1992. Registered pharmacist, Ind., Maine; bd. cert. pharmacotherapy specialist. Staff pharmacist Ind. U. Hosp., Indpls., 1985-86, R.I. Hosp., Providence, 1986-87; clin. pharmacist Aroostook Med. Ctr., Presque Isle, Maine, 1987—. Cons. pharmacist Aroostook Residential Ctr., Presque Isle, 1991-2001, So. Acres Boarding Home, Westfield, Maine, 1998-2000. Bd. dirs. Maine Sch. Adminstrn. Dist. #1, Presque Isle, 1993-96; cubmaster Katahdin Area Boy Scouts Am., 2002—; treas. Pine St. Sch. PTO, 2002—. Fellow Am. Soc. Cons. Pharmacists; mem. Am. Coll. Clin. Pharmacists, Am. Soc. Health Sys. Pharmacists, Maine Soc. Health Sys. Pharmacists (dir. 1992-96, pres. 1996-98, treas. 2000—). Republican. Congregationalist. Home: 132 Canterbury St Presque Isle ME 04769-3021 Office: Aroostook Med Ctr 140 Academy St Presque Isle ME 04769-3171

BARRETT, PAULETTE SINGER, public relations executive; b. Paris, Dec. 20, 1937; came to U.S., 1947; d. Andrew M. and Agatha (Kinsbrunner) Singer; m. Laurence I. Barrett, Mar. 9, 1957 (div. 1983); children: Paul Meyer, David Allen, Adam Singer. BA, NYU, 1957; MS in Journalism, Columbia U., 1958. News dir. Yardney Electric Corp., N.Y.C., 1958-61; freelance writer newspapers and pub. relations orgns., N.Y.C. and Washington, 1961-73; assoc. dir. pub. info. Columbia U., N.Y.C., 1973-77; from account exec. to v.p., then sr. v.p. Edelman Pub. Rels. Worldwide, N.Y.C., 1977-80, sr. v.p. and gen. mgr., 1980, exec. v.p., gen. mgr., 1986-88, exec. v.p., dir. corp. affairs div., 1988-89; exec. v.p. Rowland Co., N.Y.C., 1980-82; exec. dir. communications UJA-Fedn./N.Y., N.Y.C., 1982-86; sr. v.p., mng. dir. Hill and Knowlton, Chgo., 1989-90; pres. Barrett Comm., Chgo. and N.Y.C., 1990—. Established The Barrett Workshops, tng. svcs., 1999—; comm. counsel The Barrett Group, 2002—. Pres. Found. of Women Execs. in Pub. Rels., 2003—. E-mail: paulettebarrett@earthlink.net.

BARRETT, PHILLIP HESTON, lawyer, director; b. Detroit, May 7, 1943; s. Richard Hamilton and Jeanne Marcille (Webb) Barrett; m. Nancy Rose Samson, June 17, 1966 (div. Aug. 1979); children: Jeffrey Adam, Douglas Austin; m. Karen Lee Hock, Jan. 10, 1981 (div. Sept. 1999); 1 child, Andrew Hamilton. BS, Ohio State U., 1965, JD, 1968. Bar: Ohio 1968, US Dist. Ct. (so. dist.) Ohio 1971, US Ct. Appeals 1982. Assoc Porter, Wright, Morris & Arthur LLP, Columbus, Ohio, 1970—74, ptnr., 1975—. Trustee United Way of Franklin County, Inc., 1985—96, chmn., 1992—95; trustee Columbus Speech & Hearing Ctr., 1972—82, chmn., 1978—80; trustee Met. Human Svcs. Commn., 1986—91, chmn., 1987—89; trustee Children's Hosp. Found., 1993—98, Children's Rsch. Inst., 1998—. Capt. Signal Corps U.S. Army, 1968—70, Vietnam, Capt. JAG Corps Ohio Nat. Guard, 1971—73. Mem.: ABA, Columbus Bar Assn., Columbus Bar Found., Ohio Bar Assn., Capital Club (Columbus), New Albany Country Club, Ohio State U. Pres.'s Club. Avocations: squash, skiing, golf, photography. Office: Porter Wright Morris & Arthur LLP 41 S High St Ste 3100 Columbus OH 43215-6194

BARRETT, REGINALD HAUGHTON, biology educator, wildlife management educator; b. San Francisco, June 11, 1942; s. Paul Hutchison and Mary Lambert (Hodgkin) B.; m. Katharine Lawrence Ditmars, July 15, 1967; children: Wade Lawrence, Heather Elizabeth. BS in Game Mgmt., Humboldt State U., 1965; MS in Wildlife Mgmt., U. Mich., 1966; PhD in Zoology, U. Calif., Berkeley, 1971. Rsch. biologist U. Calif., Berkeley, 1970—71, acting asst. prof., 1971—72; rsch. scientist divsn. wildlife rsch. Commonwealth Scientific and Indsl. Rsch. Orgn., Darwin, Australia, 1972—75; from asst. prof. to prof. U. Calif., Berkeley, 1975—, George and Wilhelmina Goertz disting. prof. wildlife mgmt., 2002—. Author: (with others) Report on the Use of Fire in National Parks and Reserves, 1977, Research and Management of Wild Hog Populations, Proceedings of a Symposium, 1977, Sitka Deer Symposium, 1979, Symposium on Ecology and Management of Barbary Sheep, 1980, Handbook of Census Methods for Birds and Mammals, 1981, Wildlife 2000: Modeling Habitat Relationships of Terrestrial Vertebrates, 1986, Translocation of Wild Animals, 1988, Wildlife 2001: Populations, 1992; contbr. articles, abstracts, reports to profl. jours. Recipient Outstanding Profl. Achievement award Humboldt State U. Alumni Assn., 1986, Bruce R. Dodd award, 1965, Howard M. Wight award, 1966; Undergrad. scholar Nat. Wildlife Fedn., 1964, NSF grad. fellow, 1965-70; Union found. Wildlife Rsch. grantee, 1968-70. Mem. The Wildlife Soc. (pres. Bay Area chpt. 1978-79, pres. western sect. 1997-98, cert. wildlife biologist, R.F. Dasmann Profl. of Yr. award western sect. 1989), Am. Soc. Mammalogists (life), Soc. for Range Mgmt. (life), Ecol. Soc. Am. (cert. sr. ecologist), Soc. Am. Foresters, Australian Mammal Soc., Am. Inst. Biol. Scis., AAAS, Calif. Acad. Scis., Internat. Union for the Conservation of Nature (life), Calif. Bot. Soc., Orgn. Wildlife Planners, Sigma Xi, Xi Sigma Pi. Episcopalian. Avocations: hunting, fishing, photography, camping, backpacking. Office: U Calif 151 Hilgard Hall Berkeley CA 94720-3110

BARRETT, RICHARD DAVID, university director, consultant, bank executive; b. Cin., Sept. 27, 1931; s. Oscar Slack and Helen Rust (Kaiper) B.; m. Pamela P. Soldwedel, Feb. 25, 1971; children: David, Kimball, Randall. Grad., Choate Sch.; BA, Yale U., 1953; postgrad., George Washington U., NYU. Prodn. control Reynolds Metals Co., 1954-56; v.p. ops. Nat. Bank Washington, 1956-66; officer Irving Trust Co., N.Y.C., 1966-70; v.p. mktg. First Am. Bank, N.A., Washington, 1970-74, sr. v.p., 1974—, head internat. div., head retail ops. and mktg. group, v.p. internat. and pvt. banking group, exec. v.p. mktg. and community rels.; dir. planned giving Georgetown U., Washington; pres. Barrett Planned Giving, Inc., Washington. Past mem. Bankers Assn. Fgn. Trade, Greater Washington Area Bd. Trade Internat. Com. Author: (with Molly E. Ware) Planned Giving Essentials: A Step-by-Step Guide to Success, 2d edit., 2002. Past trustee Meridian House Internat.; past bd. dirs., treas. Hospice Care of D.C., Watergate South Inc.; past trustee Washington Hosp. Ctr.; past chmn., past mem. bd. dirs. Nat. Capitol Area Health Care Coalition, Hospice Care of D.C. Lt. (j.g.) USNR, 1953-54. Mem. Assn. Fundraising Profls., Nat. Com. on Planned Giving, Yale Club, Met. Club, Chevy Chase Club (Md.). Home: 700 New Hampshire Ave NW # 906 Washington DC 20037-2406 E-mail: richard@barretplannedgiving.com.

BARRETT, ROBERT JAMES, III, investment banker; b. Bangor, Maine, July 23, 1944; s. Robert James and Catherine Pauline (Rogan) B.; m. Susan Hopkins Vander Poel, July 26, 1975 (div.); children: Robert James IV, Graham Halsted; m. Catherine Moore Tankoos, Apr. 22, 1995. BA cum laude, Georgetown U., 1966; JD, Columbia U., 1969; MBA with honors, Harvard U., 1971. Bar: N.Y., 1969, Maine 1970. Assoc. Morgan Stanley, N.Y.C., 1971-76; sr. v.p. E.F. Hutton & Co. Inc., N.Y.C., 1976-83; dir. Prudential-Bache Securities, N.Y.C., 1983-90; ptnr. Barrett & Whitman., N.Y.C., 1991-92; sr. fin. cons. Merrill Lynch, 1992-95; pres. R.J. Barrett, Inc., 1998—. Dir. Gen. George Mitchell Inst.; founder Bar Harbor Preservation Trust; trustee Husson Coll., Bangor, 1989—96, U. Maine, R.J. Barratt, Beatrix J. Farrand Fund, Landscape Hort. Mem.: Beach Club (Palm Beach, Fla.), Bear Lakes Club (West Palm Beach, Fla.), Everglades Club (Palm Beach, Fla.), Northeast Harbor Club(Bar Harbor, Maine), Union Club (N.Y.C.). Republican. Roman Catholic. Avocations: tennis, squash, hunting, fishing, golf. Home: Nobe House 608 Island Dr Palm Beach FL 33480

BARRETT, ROBERT MATTHEW, law educator, lawyer; b. Bronx, N.Y., Mar. 18, 1948; s. Harry and Rosalind B. AB summa cum laude, Georgetown U., 1976, MS in Fgn. Service, JD, 1980. Bar: Calif. 1981. Assoc. Latham & Watkins, L.A., 1980-82, Morgan, Lewis & Bockius, L.A., 1982-84, Skadden, Arps, Slate, Meagher & Flom, L.A., 1984-86, Shea & Gould, L.A., 1986-87, Donovan, Leisure, Newton & Irvine, L.A., 1988-90; ptnr. Barrett & Zipser, L.A., Calif., 1991-93; prof. law U West L.A. Law Sch., Woodland Hills, Calif., 1993— Civilian vol. L.A. Sheriff's Dept., 1997-99. Mem. State Bar Calif. (standing com. on profl. responsibility and conduct 1995-99, chair 1997-98, spl. advisor 1998-99), L.A. Bar Assn. (bd. advisors vols. in parole com. 1981—). Address: 21300 Oxnard St Woodland Hills CA 91367-5058 Fax: 818-883-8142. E-mail: robertbarrett@charter.net.

BARRETT, ROBERT TODD, surgeon, retired; b. Cranford, N.J., Apr. 6, 1933; MD, Wayne State U., 1968. Diplomate Am. Bd. Surgery. Intern Detroit Gen. Hosp., 1968-69; resident in surgery David Grant USAF Med. Ctr., Travis AFB, Calif., 1969-73; staff surgeon USAF TAC, SAC and ATC Hosps., 1973-83; mem. staff American River Hosp., Mercy San Juan Hosps., Carmichael, Calif., 1984-95; ret., 1995. Fellow Am. Coll. Surgeons; mem. Am. Bd. Surgery.

BARRETT, ROGER WATSON, lawyer; b. Chgo., June 26, 1915; s. Oliver R. and Pauline S. B.; m. Nancy N. Braun, June 20, 1940; children— Victoria Barrett Bell, Holly, Oliver. AB, Princeton U., 1937; JD, Northwestern U., 1940. Bar: Ill. 1940. Mem. firm Poppenhusen, Johnson, Thompson & Raymond, Chgo., 1940-43; 45-50; charge documentary evidence Nuremberg Trial, 1944-45; regional counsel Econ. Stablzn. Agy., Chgo., 1951-52; ptnr. Mayer, Brown & Platt, Chgo., 1952-91, of counsel, 1991—. Life trustee Mus. Contemporary Art, Chgo. With AUS, 1943-45. Mem. ABA, Ill. Bar Assn., Chgo. Bar Assn.,

Am. Coll. Trial Lawyers, Indian Hill Club (Winnetka), Old Elm Club, Commonwealth Club (Chgo.), Caxton Club (Chgo.). Home: 84 Indian Hill Rd Winnetka IL 60093-3934 Office: Mayer Brown Rowe & Maw 190 S La Salle St Chicago IL 60603-3410

BARRETT, ROLIN FARRAR, JR., mechanical engineer, consultant; b. Raleigh, N.C., May 18, 1962; s. Rolin Farrar and Dixie Hobbs Barrett; m. Petra Arabaszova Barrett, Feb. 27, 2001. BSEE, N.C. State U., 1986, BS in Mech. Engring., 1991; MS in Mech. Engring., La. Tech. U., 1996. Registered profl. engr., N.C. Engr. Barrett Engring., Raleigh, 1986—. Rschr. N.C. State U., Raleigh, 2001—. V.p. bd. dirs. Ruston (La.) Symphony, 1992—94; mem., fundraiser Krewe of Janus, Monroe, La., 1994—97. Named Duke, Krewe of Janus, Monroe, 1997. Mem.: Triangle Soc., Cardinal Club, Sir Walter Gun Club (bd. dirs. 1997—). Achievements include patents for guided bullet; patents pending for electronic aid for visually impaired; gun sight; firearm bolt assembly. Office: Barrett Engring Ste 280 3141 John Humphries Wynd Raleigh NC 27612

BARRETT, STEPHEN, psychiatrist, educator, consultant; b. N.Y.C., Sept. 6, 1933; s. Joseph and Rebecca Barrett; m. Judith Barrett; children: Daniel, Deborah, Benjamin. AB, Columbia U., 1954, MD, 1957. Intern Highland Park (Mich.) Gen. Hosp., 1957-58; resident in psychiatry Temple U. Hosp., Phila., 1958-61; chief psychiat. svc. Scott AFB Hosp., Ill., 1961-63; pvt. practice psychiatry, 1963-93; instr. health edn. Pa. State U., 1987-89. Psychiatrist San Francisco Child Psychiatry Clinic, 1963—66, Ctr. Spl. Problems, 1966—67, Allentown Hosp. Psychiat. Clinic, 1968—90, Muhlenberg Med. Ctr. Psychiat. Clinic, 1971—86; cons. San Francisco Dept. Welfare, 1964—65, 1964—65, San Francisco Adult Probation Dept., 1966—67, Pa. Bd. Probation and Parole, 1967—69, Lehigh Valley Mental Health Assn., 1967—69. Co-author: The Health Robbers-How to Protect Your Money and Your Life, 1976, The Health Robbers-How to Protect Your Money and Your Life, 2d edit., 1980, Consumer Health-A Guide to Intelligent Decisions, 1980, 7th edit., 2001, The Tooth Robbers-A Pro-Flouridation Handbook, 1980, Vitamins and "Health" Foods: The Great American Hustle, 1981, Shopping for Helath Care, 1982, Health Schemes, Scams and Frauds, 1990, Your Guide to Good Nutrition, 1991, Reader's Guide to "Alternative" Health Methods, 1993, The Health Robbers-A Close Look at Quackery in America, 1993, The Vitamin Pushers: How the Health Food Industry is Selling America a Bill of Goods, 1994, Chemical Sensitivity: The Truth About Environmental Illness, 1998; editor: Consumer Health Digest, 2001—. Trustee Lehigh Valley Opportunity Ctr., 1970—72; mem. com. on health fraud Pa. Health Coun., 1972—74; mem. com. on quackery Pa. Med. Soc., 1972—79; mem. bd. advisors Calif. Coun. Against Health Fraud, Inc., 1977—84; mem. bd. sci. advisors Am. Coun. on Sci. & Health, 1978—; cons. on unproven health practices Pa. Med. Soc. Coun. on Edn. & Sci., 1979—84; sci. cons. Com. for Sci. Investigation of Claims of Paranormal, 1980—; chmn. bd. dir. Quackwatch, Inc., 1970—; v.p. Nat. Coun. Against Health Fraud, 2000—. Recipient Dr. Francis J. Trembley Outstanding Citizen award, Lehigh Valley Dental soc., 1975, FDA Commr.'s Spl. Citation award, 1984, Hon. Lifetime Meml. award, Lehigh Valley Dietetic Assn., 1986, Hon. Meml. award, Am. Dietetic Assn., Disting. Svc. to Health Edn. award, Am. Assn. Health Edn., 2001; fellow, Com. Sci. Investigation of Claims of the Paranormal, 1992. Mem.: Am. Assn. Health Edn. (Disting. Svc. award 2001). Address: PO Box 1747 Allentown PA 18105-1747 E-mail: sbinfo@quackwatch.org.

BARRETT, THOMAS J. military officer; BS in Biology, LeMoyne Coll.; JD (with hons.), George Washington U.; grad., Army War Coll., Carlisle, Pa., 1989. Commd. US Coast Guard, 1969, advanced through grades to vice commandant, 2002—. Decorated 5 Legion of Merit, Meritorious Svc. medal, 2 Coast Guard Commendation medal, Coast Guard Achievement medal. Office: Coast Guard Hdqrs 2100 Second St SW Washington DC 20593*

BARRETT, THOMAS JOSEPH, sales executive, computer systems consultant; b. Montclair, N.J., June 18, 1955; s. Joseph Thomas and Marion Helen (Staples) B.; m. Wendy Irene Stout, Mar. 15, 1980; children: John, Christopher. Student, Syracuse U., 1973-74; BS in Agronomy and Plant Genetics, U. Ariz., 1979. Asst. supt. Skyline Country Club, Tucson, 1979-81, USN, China Lake, Calif., 1981-83; supt. Palos Verdes Golf Club; Palos Verdes Estates, Calif., 1983-87; dist. mgr. Rain Bird Sales, Glendora, Calif., 1987-92, regional sales mgr., 1992-97, mtkg. mgr., 1997-99, bus. mgr., 2000—02; mktg. mgr. MacAllister Machinery, Indpls., 2003—. V.p., dir. Tucson Women's Hockey Club, 1978-81. Author software Estimator, 1992. Mem. Am. Mktg. Assn. Home: 104 Ash Cir Noblesville IN 46060-9101 Office: MacAllister Machinery 7515 E 38th St Indianapolis IN 46219

BARRETT, THOMAS M. congressman; b. Milwaukee, Wis., Dec. 8, 1953; m. Kristine Barrett; children: Thomas John, Anne Elizabeth. BA in Economics, U. Wis., 1976, JD with honors, 1980. Atty. Smith & O'Neill, Milw., 1982-84; mem. Wis. State Assembly, 1984-89, Wis. State Senate from 5th Dist., 1989-92, U.S. Congress from 5th Wis. dist., Washington, 1993—2002; mem. energy and commerce com. Bd. dirs. Sojourner Truth House, Shalom High Sch., Transcenter Home for Youth. Recipient Circle of Friends award Milw. Advocates for Retarded Citizens, 1989, Health Leadership award State Med. Soc., Govt. Leadership award Rehab. for Wis.; named to Clean Sixteen list for environ. voting record by Wis. Environ. Decade, 1987, 89, 90. Mem. Wis. Bar Assn., Phi Beta Kappa. Democrat.*

BARRETT, TINA, professional golfer; b. Balt., Md., June 5, 1966; d. Barbara Smith; m. Dan Friedman, Nov. 27, 1993. BA cum laude, Longwood Coll., 1988. Winner Eastern Amateur, 1987, Md. State Amateur, 1988; golfer Ladies Pro Golf Assn., 1988—. Avocations: Balt. Orioles and Pheonix Suns fan. Office: c/o LPGA 100 International Golf Dr Ste B Daytona Beach FL 32124-1082

BARRETT, WILLIAM E. former congressman; b. Lexington, Nebr., Feb. 9, 1929; s. Harold O. and Helen Stuckey B.; m. Elsie L. Carlson, 1952; children: William C., Elizabeth A., David H., Jane M. AB, Hastings (Nebr.) Coll., 1951; grad., Nebr. Realtors Inst. Cert. real estate broker, Nebr. Admissions counselor Hastings Coll., 1952-54, asst. dir. admissions, 1954-56; ptnr. Barrett Agy., Lexington, 1956-59; pres. Barrett-Housel & Assocs., Inc., 1970-90; former pres. Dawson County Young Rep.; del. Rep. Co. Conv., from 1958; mem. Nebr. Rep. State Exec. Com., 1964-66; chmn., formerly mem. Rep. Nat. Com., state coord. Mobilization of Rep. Enterprise Programs, 1965-66; del. Rep. Nat. Conv., 1968; mem. Nebr. Legislature, 1979-90, speaker, 1987-90; mem. 102nd-106th Congresses from 3rd Nebr. Dist., 1991-2001. Work in campaigns for various rep. candidate, 1960; officer Barrett-Housel & Assocs., Inc., 1969—; dir. Farmers State Bank; chmn. Agr. subcom. on Gen. Farm Commodities, mem. forestry, resource conservation & rsch. coms.; mem. oversight & investigations, worker protections, agr., edn. and workplace coms.; mem. Econ. & Edn. Opportunity Com. Trustee, co-founder Nebr. Real Estate Polit. Edn. Com.; elder First Presbyn. Ch., Lexington; moderator Presbytery of Platte, 1972-73, chmn. gen. coun., 1973, mem. staff nominating com. Synod of Lakes and Prairies, from 1973. With USN, 1951-52. Named Legislator of Yr. Nat. Rep. Legislators Assn., 1990. Mem. Nebr. Assn. Ins. Agts., Nat. Assn. Ins. Agts., Dawson Co. Bd. Realtors, Nebr. Assn. Realtors, Nat. Assn. Realtors, Nebr. Jaycees (named one of three outstanding young men of Nebr. 1962), Rotary (Lexington). Republican.*

BARRETT, WILLIAM GARY, advertising and marketing executive; b. N.Y.C., Oct. 24, 1943; s. Herbert Mark and Toni Eileen (Craig) B.; m. Christina Louise Sjogren, Sept. 11, 1977 (div. 1980); m. Donna Lou Barnes, May 11, 1984; 1 child, Daniel Martin. BA, U. Buffalo, 1964. Sr. media planner Grey Advt., N.Y.C., 1966-69; v.p., supr. network rels. Batten, Barton, Durstine & Osborn Advt., N.Y.C., 1969-71; v.p., media dir. Martin Landey, Arlow, N.Y.C., 1971-74; v.p. media and mktg. Shaller-Rubin Assocs., N.Y.C., 1974-77; sr. v.p., dir. media and mktg. svcs. Young & Rubicam and Dentsu, Young & Rubicam, N.Y.C., 1977-86; exec. v.p., dir. communications svcs. Earle Palmer Brown, Washington, 1986-88; exec. v.p., dir. client svcs. S.F.M./Havas Media, MPG, LLC, Real Time Direct, N.Y.C., 1988-2000; founding ptnr., specialist in mktg./comm. Barrett Consulting LLC, 2000—. Bd. dirs. PriceCompare.com, Story Inc., Easy Planet. Lt. U.S. Army, 1964-65. Avocations: skiing, golf, photography, scuba diving, wine collecting. Home: 297 Miller Rd Hudson NY 12534 Office: PO Box 249 Claverack NY 12513-0249 E-mail: 105132.157@compuserve.com.

BARRETT, WILLIAM JOEL, investment banker; b. Darien, Conn., Aug. 26, 1939; s. William J. and Virginia Barrett; m. Sara Schrock, Sept. 1, 1962; children: William, Brian, Christopher, Peter. BA, DePauw U., Greencastle, Ind., 1961; MBA, NYU, 1963. Investment analyst Met. Life Ins. Co., 1961-66; v.p. Gregory & Sons, investment bankers, 1966-69, G.A. Saxton, investment bankers, 1969-74; sr. v.p. Janney Montgomery Scott, Inc., N.Y.C., 1974—. Bd. dirs. Supreme Industries, Inc., TGC Industries, Inc.; chmn. bd. Rumson-Fair Haven, Bach & Trust Co. Bd. trustees De Pauw U., Diocesan Investment Trust N.J. Mem. Univ. Club, India House Club, Bond of N.Y. Club, Shrewsbury Sailing and Yacht Club, Sea Bright Lawn Tennis Club, Seabright Beach Club, Rumson Country Club. Republican. Episcopalian. Office: Janney Montgomery Scott Inc 26 Broadway Fl 9M New York NY 10004-1776

BARRETT, WILLIAM MARTIN, environmental engineer, chemical engineer, researcher; s. William Martin and Barbara Lee Barrett; m. Anna Speros Georgiou, Mar. 11, 1991; children: Sara Evanthia, William Martin Barrett, III. BS in Chem. Engring., U. of Fla., 1987; MS in Engring., U. of Ctrl. Fla., 1989; PhD, U. of South Fla., 1998. Registered profl. engr., Fla., 1992. Project engr. IT Corp., Tampa, Fla., 1989—91, Westinghouse Remediation Svcs., Tampa, 1991—93; assoc. Bruder Stephens, Tampa, 1993—99; project mgr. HSA Engrs. and Scientists, Tampa, 1999—2001; environ. engr. U.S. EPA, Cin., 2001—. Fellow, U.S. EPA, 2001. Mem.: AAAS, AIChE. Office: US Environmental Protection Agency 26 W Martin Luther King Drive MS-445 Cincinnati OH 45268

BARRETT-CONNOR, ELIZABETH LOUISE, epidemiologist, educator; b. Evanston, Ill., Apr. 8, 1935; m. James D. Connor; 3 children. BA, Mt. Holyoke Coll., 1956, DSc (hon.), 1985; MD, Cornell U., 1960; PhD (hon.), U. Utrecht, The Netherlands, 1996, U. Bergen, Norway, 1996, U. Helsinki, Finland, 2000. Diplomate Am. Bd. Internal Medicine, Nat. Bd. Med. Examiners. Instr. medicine U. Miami, Fla., 1965-68, asst. prof. medicine, 1968-70; asst. prof. community and family medicine U. Calif., San Diego, 1970-74, assoc. prof. community and family medicine, 1974-81, prof. community and family medicine, 1981—, acting chair dept. community and family medicine, 1981-82, chmn. dept. family and preventative medicine, 1982-97. Mem. hosp. infection control com. VA Med. Ctr., San Diego, 1971-81; Kelly West Meml. lectr. Am. Diabetes Assn., Indpls. 1987; vis. prof.Royal Soc. Medicine, London, 1989; John Rankin lectr. U. Wis., 1989; Don McLeod Meml. lectr., Halifax, N.S., Can., 1990; Elizabeth Blackwell lectr., Rochester, Minn., 1991; Lila Wallace vis. prof. N.Y. Hosp.-Cornell Med. Ctr., N.Y.C., 1992; Donald P. Shiley vis. lectr. Scripps Clinic and Rsch. Found., La Jolla, Calif., 1993; Leonard M. Schuman lectr. U. Mich., 1993; disting. vis. U. Western Australia, 1997; disting. lectr. geriatrics Duke U. Med. Ctr., Durham, N.C., 1998; Heath Clark lectr-.,London, 1989, Pickering lectr., Cambridge, England, 2000. Contbr. articles to profl. jours. Recipient Frederick Murgatroyd prize, 1965, Kaiser award for excellence in tchg., 1982, Dr. of Yr. award San Diego Health Care Assn., 1987, merit award Nat. Inst. Aging, 1987, Making a Difference for Women's Health award Soroptimists, La Jolla, 9195, clin. svc. award Soc. for Advancement Women's Health Rsch., 1997; NIH grantee, 1970—. Fellow ACP (James D. Bruce Meml. award 1994, Masters award 2001), Am. Heart Assn. (chmn. budget com. coun. on epidemiology 1987-88, chmn. coun. on epidemiology 1988-89m Ancel Keys lectr. 1995, Elizabeth Barrett-Connor rsch. award 1995, Merit award 1998), Royal Soc. Health, Am. Coll. Preventive Medicine (Katharine Boucot Sturgis lectr. 1986, Am. Coll. Nutrition, Royal Soc. Medicine; mem. APHA (chmn. epidemiology sect. 1989-90, Wade Hampton Frost lectr. 1993), Assn. Tchrs. Preventive Medicine (bd. dirs. 1987-92, Outstanding Educator award 1992), Inst. Medicine, Soc. Epidemiol. Rsch. (pres. 1983, John Cassell Meml. lectr. 1997), Phi Beta Kappa. Office: U Calif San Diego Family and Preventive Medicine 9500 Gilman Dr # Mc0607 La Jolla CA 92093-0607

BARRETTE, JEAN, physicist, researcher; b. Montreal, May 1, 1946; s. Bertrand and Marguerite Ducharme B. BSc, U. Montréal, 1967, MSc, 1968, PhD, 1974. Postdoctoral fellow Max-Planck Inst., Heidelberg, Germany, 1974-76; physicist Brookhaven Nat. Lab., Upton, N.Y., 1976-82; engring. physicist Commissariat a l'energie Atomique, Saclay, France, 1982-87; prof. McGill U., Montréal, 1987—, chair dept. physics, 1997—2002; dir Foster Radiation Lab., Montréal, 1988-97. Mem.: Can. Assn. of Physicists, Am. Physical Soc. Achievements include research in nucleus-nucleus reactions and heavy-ion physics with particular interest in the study of reaction mechanism at intermediate and relativistic bombarding energies. Office: McGill U Dept Physics 3600 University St Montreal QC Canada H3A 2T8 E-mail: barrette@physics.mcgill.ca.

BARRETTE, LINDA JONES, dean; b. Johnson City, Tenn., Mar. 30, 1946; d. Horace Easterly Jones and Una Mae Scott; m. Pierre Philip Barrette, Aug. 20, 1977. BS, East Tenn. State U., 1967; MSLS, Cath. U. Am., 1977; PhD, So. Ill. U., 1992. Cert. distance learning adminstr. profl., VTEL ESA installation, operation and svc. Libr. Park Rd. Elem. Sch., Charlotte, N.C., 1967-69; hed libr. Williamsburg Jr. High, Arlington, Va., 1969-77; libr. Harrisonburg (Va.) Jr. High, 1977-78; dean for learning resources John A. Logan Coll., Carterville, Ill., 1981—2002; pres. Learning, Tech. and Librs., Inc., Carbondale, Ill., 1982-91; sec.-treas. IPDN, Inc., St. Louis, 2000—02. Trainer-cons. So. Ill. Collegiate Common Market, Herrin, Ill., 1998-2000, mem. tech. adv. bd., 1998—; mem. adv. bd. Ill. State Libr., Springfield, 1998-2000, Ill. Digital Acad. Libr., Champaign, 1999—. Author: (software program) CARDPREP: Microcomputer Catalog Card, Label, Proofsheet and List Writer, 1985. Del. Ill. Regional White Ho. Conf. on Libr. and Info. Svcs., Carterville, 1990; bd. trustees Grace United Meth. Ch., 2002—. Recipient Outstanding Regional Leadership award Chair Acad., 1999, Excellence award John A. Logan Coll. Ctr. for Excellence in Tchg., Learning and Leadership, 2000. Fellow Postdoctoral Acad. Higher Edn.; mem. A Consortium of Midwest Colls. and Univs. (pres. 1999-2000), Am. Libr. Assn., So. Ill. Learning Resource Consortium (sec. 2000-01), Ill. Coun. C.C. Adminstrs. (sec. 1993-94, bd. dirs. 1993-96, pres. 1994-95), Ill. Libr. Assn., Rotary (pres. Carbondale-Breakfast chpt. 1992-93, award of merit 1996, Paul Harris fellow 1988, 99), Carbondale C. of C. (bd. dirs. 2001, chair online com. 1998), Phi Kappa Phi, Phi Kappa Delta. Methodist. Avocations: golf, swimming, crafts. Home: 662 Lake Shore Dr Murphysboro IL 62966-5222 E-mail: ljb@onemain.com.

BARRICKLO, JACK NELSON, small business owner; b. Houston, Tex., Apr. 30, 1945; s. Charles Burton and Bernice Helen Barricklo; m. Ingrid Maria Kremer, July 28, 1972; children: Donald Burton, Thomas Nelson. Grad. H.S., Houston, Tex., 1964. Pers. specialist USAF, 1964—73; adjudicator VA Regional Office, Houston, 1973—75; owner, Windswept Pool Svc. Co., Houston, 1981—. Author: Pythogaras, This Cross Is For You, 2001. Staff sgt. USAF, 1964—73. Named Tex. Admiral, Gov. of Tex., 1989. Mem.: Tex. Lodge of Rsch., VFW (life), Masons (Past Master S.P. Waltrip Lodge #1328). Achievements include patents for Cube of Pythagoras, Cross of Pythagoras, 2002. Home and Office: 8631 McDade Houston TX 77080

BARRICKMAN, LES L. psychiatrist; b. Centerville, Iowa, Nov. 2, 1953; s. Bob and Margie (Gorden) B. BA, William Penn Coll., 1976; DO, Kirksville Coll. Osteopathic, 1982. Diplomate in adult psychiatry and in child and adolescent psychiatry Am. Bd. Psychiatry and Neurology. Intern Des Moines Gen. Hosp., 1982-83; resident adult psychiatry U. Iowa Coll. Medicine, Iowa City, 1983-86, resident child/adolescent psychiatry, 1986-88, assoc. faculty, 1989-90, instr., 1990-93, asst. prof., 1991-93; clin. asst. prof. U. N.Mex., Iowa City, 1995; dir. child/adolescent edn. tng. program U. Iowa, 1991-93; assoc. prof. U. Hawaii, Honolulu, 1996-98; clin. assoc. prof. dept. psychiatry Coll. Medicine, 1999—; pvt. practice, 1998—. Mem. AMA, Am. Psychiat. Assn., Am. Acad. Child/Adolescent Psychiatry.

BARRICKS, MICHAEL ELI, retinal surgeon; b. Chgo., Feb. 22, 1940; s. Arthur Goetz and Ruth (Zuckerman) B.; m. Zondra Dell Natman, Jan. 18, 1992; 1 child, Charleigh Ruth. BA, Harvard Coll., 1961; MD, U. Chgo., 1965; PhD, Stanford U., 1973. Diplomate Nat. Bd. Med. Examiners; lic. physician, Calif. Intern then resident in surgery Stanford (Calif.) U., 1965-67, postdoctoral fellow, 1967-72; resident, fellow in ophthalmology Bascom Palmer Eye Inst., Miami, Fla., 1972-76; fellow in retinal surgery U. Calif., San Francisco, 1976-77; asst. prof., dir. retina svc. U. Tex., San Antonio, 1977-78; retinal surgeon, dir. retina svc. Permanente Med. Group., Oakland, Calif., 1979—. Asst. clin. prof. U. Calif., San Francisco, 1980-92, assoc. clin. prof., 1993-2001, clin. prof., 2001--. Contbr. articles to profl. jours. Recipient Gold award Am. Acad. Pediatrics, Outstanding Physician award Kaiser Hosp., 1982, Cert. of Appreciation for Outstanding Teaching, U. Calif, San Francisco; ; Nat. scholar Fisher Body Craftsmans Guild; USPHS fellow Stanford U., 1967-70, Atholl McBean fellow Stanford Rsch. Inst., 1970-71. Fellow Am. Acad. Ophthalmology; mem. Permanente Ophthalmologic Soc. (pres. 1981), Vitreous Soc., Harvard Varsity Club, Crimson Key Soc. E-mail: michael.barricks@worldnet.att.net.

BARRIE, JOHN PAUL, lawyer, educator; b. Burbank, Calif., Oct. 7, 1947; s. John and Virginia (Feagans) B.; children: Sean, Tyler. AB in Pol. Sci., UCLA, 1969; JD, U. Calif., San Francisco, 1972; LLM in Tax, NYU, 1973. Bar: Calif. 1972, D.C. 1975, Mo. 1977, N.Y., 2001. Atty. advisor to judge U.S. Tax Ct., Washington, 1973-75; atty. office of gen. counsel Renegotiation Bd., Washington, 1975-77; assoc. Lewis & Rice, St. Louis, 1977-82, ptnr., 1982-86, Gallop, Johnson & Neuman, St. Louis, 1986-93, Bryan Cave L.L.P., St. Louis, 1993-98, Washington and NYC, 1998—. Adj. prof. Washington U. Sch. Law, St. Louis, 1979-99, Georgetown Law Ctr., 1999—; past mem. IRS Dist. Dirs.'s Liaison Group, Practitioners Coun., IRS Kansas City Svc. Ctr. Liaison Group, Mo. Dept. Rev. Adv. Group, past chmn. Editor Mo. Bar Ct. and CLE Bull.; editl. advisor Jour. Multistate Taxation; contbr. articles on tax to profl. jours. Commr., Commn. Bot. Garden Subdist., St. Louis, 1989-99. Recipient Dir.'s award IRS, 1993. Fellow Am. Coll. Tax Counsel, Exec. Inst. for Advanced Study Washington U., St. Louis Tax Lawyers Group (past chmn.), St. Louis Corp. Tax Group (chmn.), St. Louis Internat. Tax Group; mem. ABA (tax sect., chmn. com. on govtl. submissions, past chmn. com. on affiliated corps.), Am. Tax Policy Inst. (life, sponsor), Mo. Bar Assn. (tax. sect., past chmn. tax com., Pres.'s award 1983), Calif. Bar Assn. (tax sect.), DC Bar Assn. (tax sec., steering com. 2001—), NY Bar Assn. (tax sect.), Bar Assn. Met. St. Louis (tax sect.), Nat. Assn. State Bar Tax Sects. (N.Y. bar tax sect. chmn. 1983-84), Noonday Club, City Club (Washington). Episcopalian. Home: 420 7th St NW Apt 1010 Washington DC 20004-2215 Office: Bryan Cave LLP 700 13th NW Ste 700 Washington DC 20005 also: 1290 Ave of the Americans 35th Flr New York NY 10104

BARRIER, JOHN WAYNE, engineer, management consultant; b. Savannah, Tenn., June 17, 1949; s. John H. and Evelyn (Williams) B.; m. Janet Putnam, Aug. 27, 1969; children: Jennifer, Jamar, Joseph, Jeremy. BS in Chem. Engring., U. Tenn., 1972, MS in Adminstrn., 1975. Chem. engr. Monsanto Co., Decatur, Ala., 1972-76, TVA, Muscle Shoals, Ala., 1976-82, process devel. leader, 1982-85, project mgr., 1985-86, program mgr., 1986-2000; instr. Heritage U., Florence, Ala., 1992—. Instr. mgmt. Faulkner U., Florence, Ala., 1980-2000; bd. dirs. Met. Energy Systems, Inc. Contbr. articles to profl. jours. Named one of Outstanding Young Men in Am., 1979; recipient Tech. Achievement award U.S. Dept. Energy, 1985. Mem. Nat. Mgmt. Assn. Avocations: travel, sports, hiking. Home: 3000 County Road 10 Florence AL 35633-2942

BARRIGER, JOHN WALKER, IV, transportation executive; b. St. Louis, Aug. 3, 1927; s. John Walker and Elizabeth Chambers (Thatcher) B.; m. Evelyn Dobson, Dec. 29, 1955; children: John Walker V., Catherine B. Dunsby. BS, MIT, 1949; CT, Yale U., 1950; D Artsa nd Letters (hon.), U. Mo., St. Louis, 2003. With Santa Fe Railway, 1970—83, 1950—68, GTE Sylvania Info. Sys., 1968-70, Santa Fe Pacific Corp., 1983-85, CM&W Ry., 1986-90; v.p. Derson Group Ltd., 1990—. Trustee John W. Barriger Ill. Nat. R.R. Libr., St. Louis, Hegeler-Carus Found., LaSalle, Ill.; bd. dirs. St. Louis Merc. Libr. Served with USN, 1946. Recipient Bronze Beaver award MIT, 1975. Mem. Newcomen Soc., Econ. Club. Chgo., Exec. Club Chgo., MIT Club Chgo., Kenilworth Club, Union League Chgo., Sheridan Shores Yacht Club, Delta Kappa Epsilon. Republican. Roman Catholic. Homes: 155 Melrose Ave Kenilworth IL 60043-1248 Office: 332 S Michigan Ave Ste 700 Chicago IL 60604-4303

BARRINGER, JOAN MARIE, counselor, educator, artist, writer; b. Washington, Sept. 30, 1955; d. John Thomas and Maria Regina Barringer. BA in Latin Am. Studies, George Mason U., 1981; grad. in Creating and Selling Short Stories, Inst. Childrens Lit., 1995; MA in Edn. and Counseling, George Mason U., 1999. Translator and receptionist Brazilian Emb., Washington, 1975—83; dir. day care Army-Navy Country Club, Arlington, Va., 1983—87; visitors svcs. Nat. Gallery Art, Washington, 1991—94; workshop asst. Women's Ctr., Vienna, Va., 1996—2000; career counselor Dept. Rehab. Svcs., Alexandria, Va., 1998—99. Author: (book of poems) Metronome, 1979; designer CD cover, singer Gift of Life with Michael Patterson; Fairfax (Va.) Jour., 1992, Montgomery (Va.) Jour., 1992, exhibitions include Graffiti Gallery, 2002, Greenbelt Cmty. Ctr., 2003, Govt. Ctr., 2003. Election officer U.S. Govt., Va., 2001; mem. Unity Ch. Mem.: Assn. Rsch. and Enlightenment (wayshower 2001—), Women's Caucus for Art (active newsletter 1999—), Sigma Pi Alpha. Avocations: genealogy, travel, ice skating, yoga, photography. Home: 11107 Hampton Rd Fairfax Station VA 22039

BARRINGER, PAUL BRANDON, II, lumber company executive; b. Sumter, S.C., Aug. 22, 1930; s. Victor Clay and Gertrude (Hampton) B.; m. Merrill Underwood, May 27, 1957; children: Merrill U., Victor Clay, Ann Hampton. BS, U. Va., 1952; postgrad., George Washington U., 1954. With Human Relations Lab., Washington, 1954; with Coastal Lumber Co., Weldon, N.C., 1954—, chmn. bd., 1967—. Bd. dirs. BB&T Corp., Sea Pines Co., Inc.; mem. Pres.'s Task Force on Internat. Pvt. Enterprise, Industry Policy Adv. Com. for trade policy matters; mem. U. Va. Exec. Com. Capital Fund Campaign, 1994-2000. Mem. coll. bd. trustees U. Va., 1995-96. With USAF, 1952-54. Mem.: NAM (bd. dirs.), Chief Execs. Orgn. (dir.), Farmington Country Coub, Sea Pines Country Club, Chockoyotte Country Club, Lamda Chi, Sigma Delta Psi, Zeta Psi. Episcopalian. Home: 14 S Calibogue Cay Rd Hilton Head Island SC 29928-2912 Office: Coastal Lumber Co PO Box 829 Weldon NC 27890-0829

BARRINGER, PHILIP E. retired government official; b. Haverford, Pa., Oct. 2, 1916; s. D. Moreau and Margaret (Bennett) B.; m. Sophia F. Hazard, Aug. 10, 1946 (dec. Apr. 1979); children: Thomas H., C. Frances, Paul M.; m. Bettyanne Rusen, Oct. 15, 1988. Student, Heidelberg (Germany) Coll., 1934; AB cum laude in European History, Princeton U., 1938; LL.B., U. Pa., 1948; grad., Nat. War Coll., 1952. Bar: Pa. 1949. U.S. sec. Legal Directorate, Allied Control Council for Germany, 1945-46; with Office Sec. Def., 1949-64; dep. dir. European region Office Asst. Sec. for internat. security affairs, 1956-64; attaché, politico-mil. affairs Am. embassy, London, Eng., 1964-66; dep. dir. Near East and South Asia region Office Asst. Sec. Def. for internat. security affairs, Washington, 1966-67; dir. fgn. mil. rights Dept. Def., 1967-99; ret., 1999. Mem. numerous U.S. dels.; dir. emeritus Barringer Crater Co., Flagstaff, Ariz. Pres. Alexandria (Va.) Civic Orch., 1950-52; co-founder, mem. Cleveland Park Chamber Music Group, 1955—; trustee All Souls Unitarian Ch., Washington, 1964, 67-70, chmn., 1969-70; del. to Unitarian-Universalist Gen. Assemblies, 1968-80, Internat. Assn. for Religious Freedom meetings, 1975, 84, 87. Mem. Pa. N.G., 1937-40; served to lt. col. AUS, 1941-46, ETO. Decorated Army Commendation medal; recipient Meritorious Civilian Svc. medal Sec. Def., 1975, 81, Disting. Civilian Svc. award, 1989, 99; Meritorious Exec. award Sr. Exec. Svc., 1990. Mem. Am. Soc. Internat. Law, Internat. Inst. Strategic Studies (London), Am. Hiking Soc. (bd. dirs. 1988-94), Cosmos Club, Princeton Club, Cleveland Park Club, Potomac Appalachian Trail Club (pres. 1990-91), Appalachian Trail Conf. (bd. mgrs. 1991-97). Home: 4609 38th St NW Washington DC 20016-1803 E-mail: pbarringer@aol.com.

BARRINGER, WILLIAM CHARLES, retired chemist; b. Cleve., Feb. 28, 1934; s. Donald Frederick and Elsa (Smith) Barringer; m. Vera Evelyn Dodge, July 8, 1955; children: Laura Elizabeth, Donna Lee, Mary Jane, Judy Lynn. BS in Chemistry Honors, Denison U., 1956; MS in Chemistry, NYU, 1964, PhD of Chemistry, 1968. Devel. chemist, group leader Lederle Labs., Pearl River, NY, 1957—95; sr. rsch. scientist Wyeth-Ayerest Rsch., Pearl River, 1995—2000; ret., 2000. Adj. prof. King's Coll., Briarcliff Manor, NY, 1969—71. Contbr. Mem.: N.Y. Acad. Scis., Am. Chem. Soc. Achievements include patents in field. Avocations: gardening, sports, travel, photography. Home: 155 Pearce Pkwy Pearl River NY 10965*

BARRINGTON, JUDITH M. writer, educator; b. Brighton, Eng., July 7, 1944; came to U.S., 1976; d. Reginald Jack and Violet Elizabeth (Lambert) B.; life ptnr., R.E. Gundle. BA, Marylhurst Coll., 1978; MA, Goddard Coll., 1980. Interpreter Perelada Castle, Gerona, Spain, 1964-66; pub. rels. exec. Eric White

& Ptnrs., London, 1966-68; mktg. dir. Utilair Ltd., London, 1968-73; dir. Flight of the Mind, Portland, Oreg., 1983—2000; pres. Soapstone: A Writing Retreat for Women, 1997—. Author: (poetry) Trying to Be An Honest Woman, 1985, History and Geography, 1989, Writing the Memoir: From Truth to Art, 1997, Lifesaving: A Memoir, 2000; editor lit. anthology: An Intimate Wilderness, 1991. Recipient award Dulwich Festival Poetry Competition, 1996, Stuart Holbrook award Lit. Arts Inc., 1997, Lambda Lit. Found. award for nonfiction; fellow in creative nonfiction Oreg. Arts Commn., 1997, Lit. Arts Inc., 1997. Mem. Pen Am., Poetry Soc. Am., Poetry Soc. U.K., Nat. Writers Union. Avocation: music.

BARRIOS, SOLEDAD, dancer; b. Madrid; m. Martin Santangelo; children: Gabriela Santangelo, Stella Santangelo. Dancer Noche Flamenca, N.Y.C. Recipient Bessie award, 2001. Office: Noche Flamenca 168 W 86th St New York NY 10024

BARRIO TERRAZAS, FRANCISCO, government official of Mexico; b. Chihuahua, Mex., Nov. 25, 1950; B in Pub. Acctg., Autonomous U. Chihuahua, Mex.; MBA with hon. mention, Autonomous U. Chihuahua. Cert. pub. acct. Mgmt. positions various cos. including Mercados Amigo, S.A., Consultores en Planeación del Norte, S.C.; founder Adminstrn. Profl. de Negocios, S.A. de C.V., Bate, S.A. de C.V.; served as pres. Bus. Ctr., Ciudad Juarez; joined Nat. Action Party (PAN), 1983, mem. Nat. Coun., 1986—, mem. Nat. Exec. Com., 1999—; mayor Ciudad Juarez; cand. gov. State of Chihuahua, 1986, constl. gov., 1992—98; mem. State Coun. Chihuahua; sec. of comptroller, gen. and adminstrn. devel. Govt. of Mex., 2000—. Office: Ave Insurgentes Sur 1735 Col Guadalupe Inn 10o Piso 01020 Mexico City Mexico*

BARRISH, CAROL LAMPERT, psychologist; b. N.Y.C., Oct. 6, 1945; d. J. William and Sally (Bobrick) Lampert; m. Michael Louis Barrish, June 30, 1974; children: Jordan Seth, Jessica Lynne. BA, Queens Coll., 1967; MA, Columbia U., 1972; PhD, NYU, 1993. Licensed psychologist; cert. learning disabilities cons.; lic., cert. spl. edn. tchr.; cert. reading specialist; cert. tchr. Tchr., team leader elem. sch. Englewood (N.J.) Bd. Edn., 1969-72, reading cons., 1973-74; curriculum coord. Adams Town House, N.Y.C., 1974-75; ednl., learning disabilities cons. N.Y.C., 1974—; reading/learning disabilities specialist, 1975—; clin. psychology intern Risk Inst., NYU Hosp., N.Y.C., 1990-91; psychologist com. for spl. edn. N.Y.C. Bd. Edn., 1992—; spkr. for tchr. trainer groups, project coord. dist. 4, lecturer, 1998—. Pvt. clin. practice for cognitive psychology, sch., N.Y.C. Author: (with others) Assessment of Social Skills Problems with Learning Disabled Adolescents, 1993. Mem. APA, N.Y. State Psychol. Assn., Orton Dyslexia Soc., Children and Adults with Attention Deficit Disorder, Nat. Assn. Sch. Psychologists, Kappa Delta Pi. Avocations: tennis, skiing. Office: 305 E 86th St Apt 4G West New York NY 10028-4702

BARRITT, CHRISTY, freelance/self-employed writer; b. Chesapeake, Va., Sept. 9, 1976; d. Charles Nichols and Louise (Sprull) Mohorn; m. Scott M. Barritt, June 24, 2000. BA in Comm., Cin. Bible Coll., 1998. Asst. editor Std. Pub., Cin., 1998—2000; freelance writer Chesapeake, 2000—; mng. editor WillWrite4food.com, 2002—03. Author: (novels) The Waiting, 2003. Mem.: Am. Christian Romance Writers. E-mail: christybarritt@cox.net.

BARRITT, EVELYN RUTH BERRYMAN, nurse, educator, university dean; b. Detroit, Sept. 4, 1929; d. George C. and Ruby (Mathews) Berryman; m. Ward LeRoy Barritt, Oct. 28, 1951; 1 dau., Kelli Jo. AA, Graceland Coll., 1949; diploma, Independence (Mo.) Sanitarium and Hosp. Sch. Nursing, 1952; BSN., Ohio State U., 1956, MA, 1962, PhD, 1971. Asst. instr. nursing Atlantic City Hosp., 1952-53; staff nurse Shore Meml. Hosp., Somers Point, N.J., 1953-54, Ohio State U. Hosp., Columbus, 1954-55; instr. White Cross Hosp., Columbus, 1955-57; asso. dir. nursing service Riverside Meth. Hosp., Columbus, 1957-64; asst. exec. dir. Ohio Nurses Assn., Columbus, 1964-65; dean Capital U. Sch. Nursing, Columbus, 1965-72, Coll. Nursing, U. Iowa, Iowa City, 1972-79, prof. nursing, 1972-80; prof. Sch. Nursing U. Miami, Fla., 1980—, dean, 1980-85. Bd. dirs. Health Coun. South Fla., 1988—, pres., 1990-92; bd. dirs. So. Fla. Perinatal Network, Inc., 1980-89, pres., 1984-86; mem. Fla. Bd. Ind. and Pvt. Colls. and Univs., 1980; co-chmn. Dade County Indigent Care Task Force, 1991-93. Author: Florence Nightingale: Her Wit and Wisdom, 1975; author, editor: Thoughts on CareGiving, 1998; contbr. articles to profl. jours. Mem. Am. Nurses Assn., Ohio Nurses Assn. (pres. dist. 1966-68), Iowa Nurses Assn., Fla. Nurses Assn., Graceland Univ. Alumni Assn., Am. Assn. Higher Edn., Am. Assn. Colls. Nursing (pres. 1976-78), Independence Hosp. Sch. Nursing Alumnae Assn. Home: 416 Park Blvd N Venice FL 34285-1332

BARR-KUMAR, RAJ, architect; b. Colombo, Ceylon, Feb. 5, 1946; arrived in U.S., 1974; s. Alexander Barr-Kumarakulasinghe and Francesca ThangaRanee (Winslow) Barr-Kumar; m. Athina Kambouri, 1975 (dec. Feb. 1977); m. Bernadette Dipica Wikramanayake, 1994. BS, U. Ceylon, Colombo, 1971; grad. diploma in architecture, U. London, 1974; MArch, U. Kans., 1975; postgrad., Harvard U., 1978; D of Arch., U. Hawaii, 2002. Lic. architect Washington, N.Y., Va., Md., Fla., Kans.; cert. Nat. Coun. Archtl. Registration Bds. Designer Panditaratna & Adithiya RIBA, Ceylon, 1967-71, Jon Prescott RIBA, Hong Kong, 1971-72, NE Met. Regional Hosp. Bd./Watkins Gray Internat., London, 1972-73, Llewellyn-Davies Assocs., London, 1973-74, Patty Berkebile Nelson Assocs./Seligson Assocs., Kansas City, Mo., 1975-78; sr. designer Barret Daffin & Carlan, Tallahassee, 1979-80; mgr. computer aided design Wolfberg, Alvarez, Taracido Assocs., Rosslyn, Va., 1982-83; pres. Barr-Kumar Architects Engrs., Washington, 1981—; asst. prof. U. Kans., Lawrence, 1975—79; assoc. prof. Fla. A&M U., Tallahassee, 1979—85, dir., assoc. prof. Arch. Ctr. Washington, 1981—84; assoc. prof. Howard U., Washington, 1986—94. Vis. prof. Washington Alexandria Ctr. Va. Polytech. Inst., 1984—86, 1998, Cath. U. Am., 2003; Emens disting. vis. prof. Ball State U., 1999; spkr., panelist Smithsonian Inst., Washington, 1982—, Nat. Bldg. Mus., Washington, 1985—, Corcoran Art Gallery, 1998—, Lambda Alpha Internat., 1994—; mem. adv. coun. on arch. No. Va. C.C.'s, 1983—; apptd. mem. FIDER Nat. Interior Design Accrediting Bd., 1986—92; chair Anne Arundel County Devel. Design Awards, Md., 1985—90; examiner Nat. Coun. Archtl. Registration Bd., 1990; lectr. in field. Author: Green Architecture - Strategies for Sustainable Development, 2003. Chair archtl. group Luther Pl. Shelter for Homeless, Washington, 1990—; co-chair DC-HOME Housing Assistance Team, Washington, 1990—; pres. Sri Lanka Assn., Washington, 1991-93; mem. bldg. and preservation coms. Washington nat. Cathedral, 1995—. Recipient County Exec. Appreciation cert. Anne Arundel County, Md., 1990. Fellow AIA (bd. dirs. Washington chpt. 1984-97, pres. 1990, host chpt. chair nat. conv. 1988-91, nat. bd. dirs. 1991-97, nat. v.p. 1994, nat. pres. 1997, Outstanding Svc. award Washington chpt. 1990, Walter Wagner fellow 1992, Richard Upjohn fellow 1994, Nat. citation for exceptional svc. 1997), Bahamian Inst. Architects, Japan Inst. Architects (hon.), Philippine Inst. Architects (hon.), United Architects of Philippines (hon.), Sri Lanka Inst. Architects (hon.), Royal Archtl. Inst. Can. (hon.), Mex. Soc. Architects (hon.), Pan Am. Fedn. Architects (hon.); mem. Royal Inst. Brit. Architects. Office: Barr-Kumar Architects Engrs PC 1825 I St NW Ste 400 Washington DC 20006-5415

BARRON, ALMEN L. microbiologist, department chairman; b. Toronto, Ont., Can., Jan. 19, 1926; came to U.S., 1954, naturalized, 1963; s. Max and Bena (Sussman) B.; m. Shirley Brovender, Sept. 14, 1949; 1 child, Joshua Charles. BSA, Ont. Agrl. Coll., U. Toronto, 1948, MSA, 1949; PhD, Queen's U., Kingston, Ont., 1953. Mem. faculty SUNY, Buffalo, 1954-74, prof. microbiology, 1968-74; dir. Erie County (N.Y.) Virology Lab., 1968-74; prof. microbiology, chmn. dept. microbiology and immunology U. Ark. Med. Sci., Little Rock, 1974-91, prof. emeritus, 1991—. Cons. Little Rock VA Med. Ctr., 1974-91; vis. prof. Hadassah Med. Sch., Hebrew U., Jerusalem, 1972, Kaohsiung Med. Coll., (Taiwan), 1982 Co-editor: Microbiology: Basic Principles and Clinical Applications, 1983; editor: Microbiology of Chlamydia, 1988. Recipient Commonwealth Fund travel award, 1964, Golden Apple award Student AMA, 1975, 77, Disting. Faculty award Ark. Caduceus Club, 1990; Fulbright rsch. scholar Israel, 1964. Mem. Am. Acad. Microbiology (emeritus 1991—), Am. Soc. Microbiology (pres. South Central br. 1980), Infectious Diseases Soc. Am. (emeritus 1991—), Am. Assn. Immunologists. Achievements include research on Chlamydia organisms.

BARRON, BRUCE ALBRECHT, physician, educator, medical researcher; b. N.Y.C., Nov. 3, 1934; s. Alexander and Beatrice (Albrecht) B.; m. Mary Cahill, Dec. 19, 1975; 1 child, Amy. BA, Allegheny Coll., 1955; MPH, Yale U., 1960, PhD, 1965; MD, NYU, 1971. Diplomate Am. Bd. Ob-Gyn., Nat. Bd. Med. Examiners. Fellow in public health Sch. Medicine Yale U., New Haven, Conn., 1959-60, fellow in biometry Grad. Sch., 1960-65; intern dept. of medicine NYU-Bellevue Med. Ctr., N.Y.C., 1971-72, sr. resident dept. ob-gyn., 1972-73, chief resident, clin. instr. ob-gyn., 1973-74; rsch. assoc. Rockefeller U., N.Y.C., 1965-67, asst. prof., 1967-74; assoc. prof. dept. ob-gyn. Coll. Physicians and Surgeons Columbia U., N.Y.C., 1974-95, 98—; prof., vice chmn. dept. ob-gyn NYU Sch. Medicine, N.Y.C., 1995-97; assoc. attending physician Columbia-Presbyn. Med. Ctr., N.Y.C., 1974-95; sr. attending physician NYU Hosp., N.Y.C., 1995-97; attending physician Columbia-Presbyn. Med. Ctr., 1998—. Advisor biomed. divsn. The Poplation Council, NYC, 1966-74, divsn. of reproductive biology The Ford Found., 1969-74, The Hettinger Found., 1988—; vis. lectr. Albert Einstein Coll. Med., Bronx, N.Y.; mem. spl. study sect. epidemiology Fogerty Ctr. divsn. grants and contracts NIH, Bethesda, Md.; adj. prof. The Rockefeller U., 1992-95; pres. Columbia-Presbyn. Health Services, Inc.; cons. Empire Blue Cross Blue Shield, 1993-96, sr. med. dir., 1996—. Author: Outsmarting Managed Care, 1999, chmn. editl. com., Physician's Reference Guide: Obstetrics and Gynecology, 1993—; contbr. articles to profl. jours. With U.S. Army, 1957-59. Mem. N.Y. Acad. Medicine (vice chmn. divsn. computer scis

BARRON, CHARLES ELLIOTT, retired electronics executive; b. Midland, Tex., Feb. 17, 1928; s. Thomas Paul and Hollie Belle (Pickerill) B.; m. Sarah Alice Crawford, July 18, 1950; children: Thomas, Sarah, Robert. BSEE, Vanderbilt U., 1949; BD, Southwestern Bapt. Theol. Sem., 1958. Geophysicist Shell Oil Co., various locations, 1949-54, Tex. Pacific Coal and Oil Co., Ft. Worth, 1954-59; engring. mgr. then gen. mgr. Gen. Electric Co., Utica, Syracuse and Binghamton, N.Y., 1959-87; pres. ops. Eaton Corp., Melville, N.Y., 1987-88; pres., chief exec. officer AIL Systems, Inc. (sub. of Eaton Corp.), Deer Park, N.Y., 1989-91, also bd. dirs., 1989-93. Bd. dirs. Roberson Ctr., Binghamton, N.Y., 1981-84, United Way L.I., 1991; chmn. major firms drive Broome County (N.Y.) United Way, 1981-83, bd. dirs.; mem. engring. adv. bd. Syracuse U., 1986-91; mem. engring. sch. council SUNY, Binghamton, 1982-83 Mem. Nat. Security Indsl. Assn. (Comcac com. 1986-88, trustee 1989-91), L.I. Assn. (bd. dirs. 1988-91), Security Affairs Support Assn. (bd. dirs. 1989-91). Republican. Baptist.

BARRON, HAROLD SHELDON, lawyer; b. Detroit, July 4, 1936; s. George Leslie and Rose (Weinstein) B.; m. Roberta Yellin, Nov. 17, 1963; children: Lawrence Ira, Jean Louise. AB, U. Mich., 1958, JD, 1961. Bar: N.Y. 1963, Mich. 1961, Ill. 1983, Pa. 1992. Pvt. practice, N.Y.C., 1962-68; practice in Southfield, Mich., 1968-83, Chgo., 1983-93, 1991—2002; atty. Hughes Hubbard & Reed, 1962-68; corp. counsel Bendix Corp., 1968-69, sec., assoc. gen. counsel, 1969-72, sec., gen. counsel, 1972-83, v.p., 1974-83; ptnr. Arnstein, Gluck, Lehr, Barron & Milligan, Chgo., 1983-86, Seyfarth, Shaw, Fairweather & Geraldson, Chgo., 1986-91; v.p., gen. counsel Unisys Corp., Blue Bell, Pa., 1991-92, sr. v.p., gen. counsel, 1992-94, sr. v.p., gen. counsel, sec., 1994-99, sr. v.p., gen. counsel, 1999-2001, vice chmn., 2001—02; counsel McDermott, Will & Emery, 2002—. Mem. nat. adv. coun. and faculty Practising Law Inst., N.Y.C.; bd. dirs. Royal Maccabees Life Ins. Co., Southfield, 1983-94; chmn. bd. F.A. Tucker Group, Inc., 1991-95. Editor The Business Lawyer. Com. visitors U. Mich. Law Sch.; trustee Children's Hosp. Mich., Detroit, 1976-84; mem. Census Adv. Com. on Privacy and Confidentiality, 1975-76; mem. governing bd., adv. coun. Purdue U. Info. Privacy Rsch. Ctr.; bd. dirs. Citizens Rsch. Coun. of Mich., 1982-83, Greater Phila. Econ. Devel. Coalition. Served with AUS, 1961-62. Mem. ABA (coun. bus. law sect., bus. law sect.(chmn. 2002-03, standing com. on fed. judiciary, editor The Bus. Lawyer, Latin Am. legal initiatives coun., chmn. com. of corp. gen. counsel, sect. bus. law coun., com. corp. law and taxation, internat. bus. law com., com. devels. in investment svcs., com. long-range issues affecting bus. law practice, com. on corp. laws, commn. on asbestos litigation), Am. Arbitration Assn., Am. Soc. Corp. Secs. (securities law com.), CPR Inst. for Dispute Resolution (exec. com., nat. panel disting. neutrals), Mich. Bar Assn., Assn. Bar City NY (com. corp. law depts.), Carlton Club, Chgo. Club, Bryn Mawr Country Club (Chgo.), The Reserve (Indian Wells, Calif.). Office: McDermott Will & Emery 227 W Monroe Chicago IL 60606-5096

BARRON, HOWARD ROBERT, lawyer; b. Chgo., Feb. 17, 1930; s. Irwin P. and Ada (Astrahan) B.; m. Marjorie Shapira, Aug. 12, 1953; children: Ellen Barron Feldman, Laurie A. PhB, U. Chgo., 1948; BA, Stanford U., 1950; LLB, Yale U., 1953. Bar: Ill. 1953. Assoc. Jenner & Block, Chgo., 1957-63, ptnr., 1964-97; assoc. Schiff Hardin & Waite, Chgo., 1953, of counsel, 1997—. Contbr. articles to profl. jours. and books. Mem., then pres. Lake County Sch. Dist. 107 (now Dist. 112) Bd. Edn., Highland Park, 1964-71; pres. Lake County Sch. Bd. Assn., 1970-71; mem. Lake County High Sch. Dist. 113 Bd. Edn., Highland Park, 1973-77; mem. Highland Park Zoning Bd. Appeals, 1984-89. Lt. (j.g.) USNR, 1953-57. Mem.: ABA (com. corp. counsel litigation sect. 1983—2002, co-chmn. subcom. labor and employment law), Yale Club (N.Y.C.), Met. Club, Internat. Bar Assn., Yale Law Sch. Assn. of Ill. (pres. 1962), Yale Law Sch. Assn. (v.p. 1978—81), Chgo. Bar Assn., Fed. Bar Assn., Ill. State Bar Assn. (chmn. antitrust sect. 1968—69, sr. counselor 2003), Standard Club. Democrat. Home: 1366 Sheridan Rd Highland Park IL 60035-3407 Office: Schiff Hardin & Waite 6600 Sears Tower Chicago IL 60606 E-mail: hbarron@schiffhardin.com.

BARRON, ILONA ELEANOR, reading educator, consultant; b. Mass, Mich., Sept. 19, 1929; m. George Barron; 1 child, Fred. Cert. in elem. teaching No. Mich. U., 1951; BS in Elementary Edn., Cen. Mich. U., Mt. Pleasant, 1961; MA in Edn., U. Mich., Ann Arbor, 1966; postgrad. Mich. State U., East Lansing. Reading specialist. Tchr. elem. schs., 1952-67; Title I dir. Saginaw (Mich.) Twp. Community Schs., 1967-68, reading cons., 1971—; elem. intern cons. Mich. State U., 1968-71; elem. reading cons. Saginaw Twp. Pub. Schs., 1972—. Mem. NEA, Mich., Saginaw Twp. Edn. Assns., Saginaw Area Reading Coun. Specialist in reading, methods of teaching developmental reading skills and enrichment. Home (Winter): 35702 Clubber Ct Zephyrhills FL 33541 Home: 25366 W State Hwy M 64 Ontonagon MI 49953

BARRON, JEROME AURE, law educator; b. Tewksbury, Mass., Sept. 25, 1933; s. Henry and Sadie (Shafmaster) B.; m. Myra Hymovich, June 18, 1961; children— Jonathan Nathaniel, David Jeremiah, Jennifer Leah AB magna cum laude, Tufts Coll., 1955; JD, Yale U., 1958; LL.M., George Washington U., 1960. Bar: Mass. 1959, D.C. 1960. Law clk. to chief judge U.S. Ct. Claims, Washington, 1960-61; assoc. firm Cross, Murphy & Smith, Washington, 1961-62; asst. prof. law U. N.D., Grand Forks, 1962-64; vis. assoc. prof. U. N.Mex., Albuquerque, 1964-65; dean Syracuse U. Coll. Law, 1972-73; assoc. prof. George Washington U., from 1965, prof., 1973—, dean, 1979-88, Lyle T. Alverson prof. law, 1987-2000, Harold H. Greene prof. law, 2000—. Author: (with Donald Gillmor and Todd Simon) Mass Communication Law, Cases and Comment, 6th edit., 1998, First Amendment in a Nutshell, 2d edit. 2000, Constitutional Law: Principles and Policy, 6th edit., 2002, (with C. Thomas Dienes, Wayne McCormack and Martin Redish) Constitutional Law In A Nutshell, 5th edit., 2002; contbr. articles, chpts. to profl. publs. Served with U.S. Army, 1959-60 Mem. ABA, D.C. Bar, Cosmos Club, Phi Beta Kappa. Office: George Washington U 2000 H St NW Washington DC 20006-4234

BARRON, JONATHAN, language educator; b. Washington, May 20, 1962; s. Jerome and Myra Bertha Barron; m. Ellen Mary Weinauer, June 8, 1991; children: Liana, Raphael. BA, Tufts U., 1984; MA, Ind. U., 1987, PhD, 1990. Postdoctoral fellow Marquette U., Milw., 1990—92; asst. prof. St. Olaf Coll., Northfield, Minn., 1992—94, U. N.C., Charlotte, 1994—95, U. So. Miss., Hattiesburg, 1995—99, assoc. prof., 1999—. Dir. Robert Frost Soc., Hattiesburg, 2000—; editor-in-chief Robert Frost Review, Hattiesburg, 2000—. Co-editor: Roads Not Taken: Rereading Robert Frost, 2000, Jewish American Poetry, 2000; contbr. articles to profl. jours. Mem.: MLA. Democrat. Home: 114 Lesley Ln Hattiesburg MS 39402 Office: Univ So Miss Dept English Box 5037 Hattiesburg MS 39406

BARRON, LINDSEY HAND, real estate broker; b. Greenville, S.C., Dec. 16, 1923; s. Zeddie Pleasant and Opal Carolyn (Hand) B.; m. Genet Louise Heery, May 22, 1948; children: Thomas W., Frank H. BBA, Emory U., 1944; grad., Northweston USN Midshipman Sch., 1944. Owner, pres. Coweta Developers, Inc., Newnan, 1962-79, with, 1979—; salesman Proctor & Gamble, Atlanta, 1947-48; owner, pres. Lindsey's, Inc., Newnan, Ga., 1948-79, chmn., 1979—. Bd. dirs. Newnan Hosp., 1969-79, Residential Care for Elderly of Coweta County, Newnan, 1996—, Wesley Woods Found., Atlanta, 1995—; pres. Newnan-Coweta United Way, 1979. Lt. USN, 1944-47, PTO. Named Coweta County Citizen of Yr., Optimist Club, Newnan, 1965. Mem. Newnan-Coweta Realtors Assn. (pres. 1968), Newnan Mchts. Assn. (pres. 1955), Newnan-Coweta C. of C. (pres. 1967, 75, Citizen of Yr. award 1996), Kiwanis (pres. Newnan 1948, George F. Hixson award 1995, Man of Half Century award 1975). Baptist. Avocations: reading, travel, spectator sports. Office: Lindsey's Inc 14 Jackson St Newnan GA 30263-1929

BARRON, LOWELL RAY, state legislator; b. Jackson County, Ala., Apr. 22, 1942; m. Susan Holloway; children: Shala, Lowell Ray, Lauren, Collier. BS in Pharmacy, Auburn U., 1965. Mem. Fyffe City Coun., 1968-69; mayor Fyffe City, 1969-82; mem. Ala. State Senate, Montgomery, 1983—, pres. pro tem., 2000—. Businessman Sand Mountain Drugs, Fyffe Constrn. Co., Fyffe Glass Co., Bank of Fyffe, Barron Land Co., Rainsville Fin.; chairperson Fin. and Taxation Gen. Fund Com., Animal Agr. subcom. Agr. and Forestry Com.; mem. Tourism and Mktg. Com. Trustee Auburn U., 1993—. Democrat. Baptist. Avocations: golf, tennis, fishing. Home and Office: PO Box 65 Fyffe AL 35971-0065 Office: Ala State House 11 S Union St Rm 726 Montgomery AL 36130 2103*

BARRON, MARLENE, education educator; b. Balt., May 14, 1939; d. Alexander and Lillian Ray (Sklar) Bass; m. Joseph Lackey Barron (div.); children: Leslie Rachel, Charles Jeffrey, Joshua Simon. BA in Psychology, Barnard Coll., 1965; Montessori Tchr. Edn., Fairleigh Dickinson U., 1966-67; MS in Edn., Wagner Coll., Staten Island, N.Y., 1966 68; postgrad., Richmond Coll., Staten Island, 1968-70; PhD in Curriculum and Instrn., NYU, 1995. Cert. tchr., N.Y.; cert. tchr. and cons. Am. Montessori Soc. Founding head of sch. S.I. Montessori Sch., 1965-79; head of sch. West Side Montessori Sch., N.Y.C., 1979—, co-dir. tchr. edn. program, 1992—; prof. NYU, N.Y.C., 1982—. Cons.; workshop facilitator; presenter in field. Author: Sensorial Ideas, 1984, I Learn to Read and Write the Way I Learn to Talk, 1991, Ready, Set, Count, 1995, Ready Set, Read and Write, 1995, Ready, Set, Cooperate, 1996, Ready, Set, Explore, 1996, others; contbr. numerous articles to profl. jours. Bd. dirs. Early Childhood Resource and Info. Ctr., 1986—91, NY Pub. Libr., 1986—96. Mem.: ASCD, Nat. Coun. Tchrs. Math., Nat. Coun. Tchrs. English, Nat. Assn. for Edn. of Young Children, Nat. Assn. for Early Childhood Tchrs., Internat. Reading Assn., Assn. for Childhood Edn. Internat., Internat. Assn. for Montessori Edn. (sec.-treas. 1997—2000), Ind. Sch. Admissions Assn. Greater N.Y. (bd. dirs. 1989—, treas. 1994—), Am. Montessori Soc. (bd. dirs. 1984—87, treas., pres. 1987—89). Office: West Side Montessori Sch 309 W 92d St New York NY 10025-7213

BARRON, MYRA HYMOVICH, lawyer; b. July 5, 1938; d. Leo and Lillian Estelle (Berman) Hymovich; m. Jerome Aure Barron, June 18, 1961; children: Jonathan Nathaniel, David Jeremiah, Jennifer Leah. AB cum laude, Smith Coll., 1959; student, L'Institut des Hautes Etudes, Geneva, 1957—58; MA, Johns Hopkins U., 1961; JD, Georgetown U., 1970. Bar: Va. 70, DC 72, NY. Instr. econs. U. ND, Grand Forks, 1962—64; econ. rsch. asst. U. N.Mex., Albuquerque, 1964—65; legal aid staff atty. Fairfax County, Va., 1971—72, asst. county atty., 1974—81; assoc. Melvin & Melvin, Syracuse, NY, 1973; counsel Fairfax County Redevel. and Housing Authority, Fairfax, Va., 1981—88; ptnr. Sprenger & Lang (formerly Weissbrodt, Swiss & Mc Grew, 1989—98, Weinberg & Jacobs, Rockville, Md., 1998—2000, of counsel, 2001—. Dep. gen. counsel Housing and Devel. Law Inst., 1988—94, of counsel, 1994—2000. Editor: Jour. Affordable Housing and Cmty. Devel. Law, ABA, 1993—99; contbr. articles to housing jours.; mem.: Georgetown Law Jour., 1967—68. Recipient Samuel Bowles award, Smith Coll., 1959. Mem.: LWV (local chmn. nat. events 1962—64), ABA (mem. governing com. 1994—99, co-chmn. profit practice group 2000—03, mem. forum on affordable housing and cmty. devel. law). Home: 3231 Ellicott St NW Washington DC 20008-2061 Office: Weinberg & Jacobs LLP 11300 Rockville Pike Ste 1200 Rockville MD 20852

BARRON, PEGGY PENNISI, management consultant; b. Chgo., Jan. 27, 1958; d. Louis Legendre and Jane Harriet (Peters) Pennisi; m. Stan Barron, May 3, 1986; children: Brian Alexander, Christine Deanna. BS with honors, U. Ill., Chgo., 1979. Data processing mgr. Oasis Aviation, Inc., L.A., 1980-87; pres. Millennium Enterprises, L.A., Calif., 1987—. Author: Broken Bloodlines, 1997, The Big Daddy, 1999. Mem. NAFE, Phi Beta Kappa, Phi Kappa Phi. Avocations: scuba diving, sky diving, cooking and travel.

BARRON, ROS, artist; b. Boston, July 4, 1933; d. Louis and Ida (Titel) Myers; m. Harris Barron, Apr. 19, 1953; children: Matt Lewis, Nina Rebecca. B.F.A., Mass. Coll. Art, 1954. Fellow Bunting Inst., Harvard U., 1966-68; co-dir. Zone Visual Theater Co., 1970; assoc. prof. art U. Mass.-Harbor Campus, Boston, 1974—. Vis. artist U. Colo., Boulder, 1983; presenter Arts at the Bunting, 1997. Producer numerous video performance tapes.; one-woman shows include North Hall Gallery, Mass. Coll. Art, Boston, 1988, Watson Gallery, Wheaton Coll., Norton, Mass., 1989, Harbor Gallery U. Mass., Boston, 1990, Mobius, Boston, 1993, Brick Bottom Gallery, Boston, 1996; exhbns. include Whitney Mus. Am. Art, 1967-68, Helen Shlien Gallery, Boston, 1979, 82, Mus. Modern Art, N.Y.C., 1980, 84, Le Nouveau Musee, Lyon, France, 1979, Montevideo Gallery, Amsterdam, Holland, 1979, World Wide Video Festival, Kijkhuis, Holland, 1984, Hirschhorn Mus., Washington, 1984, North Hall Gallery; travelling group exhbns. include Project Rembrandt Biennial, 1991-92, Women's Caucus for Art, 1992; represented in permanent collections Mus. Fine Arts, Boston, Harvard U., Smith Coll. Collection, Worcester Art Mus., Addison Gallery Am. Art., Inst. Contemporary Art, Boston, Samuel P. Harn Mus. Art, U. Fla., Gainesville, Mus. of Modern Art, N.Y.C., Mus. Modern Art, N.Y.C.; performance Art: (with Harris Barron) Mr. & Mrs. Zone: Art Life Art, Mobius Theatre, Boston, 1987, Performance Art: (with Harris Barron) Mr. & Mrs. Zone Again, Mobius Theatre, Boston, 1997, Eartheart and other video works, Mobius Theatre, Boston, 1999, Eagle Air, The Life and Work of Harris Barron, 2001. Bd. dirs. Boston Performance Artists. Recipient Design award HUD, 1968; N.Y. Found. for Arts grantee, 1972; Guggenheim Found. grantee, 1972; Nat. Endowment Arts grantee, 1975; Rockefeller Found. grantee, 1978-80; Mass. Council Arts grantee, 1981-82, 83 Address: 30 Webster Pl Brookline MA 02445-7937 *I am a visual artist. As a painter and video artist, my work involves how I see and transform reality. My life force feels the ontological mystery, an intense state of wonder, and the endlessness of seeing. Strategies of surrealism and the transformational process provide emotional, intellectual, and metaphysical coherence to my work.*

BARRON, STEPHANIE, curator; AB, Columbia U., 1972; student, Harvard Inst. Arts Adminstrn., 1973; MA, Columbia U., 1974; postgrad., CUNY, 1975-76. Intern, curatorial asst. Solomon R. Guggenheim Mus., 1971-72; Nat. Endowment Arts intern in edn. Toledo Mus. Art, 1973-74; exhbn. coord. Jewish Mus., N.Y.C., 1975-76; assoc. curator modern art L.A. County Mus. Art, 1976-80, curator Twentieth Century art, 1980-94, coord. curatorial affairs, 1993-96, sr. curator Twentieth Century art, 1995—, v.p. edn. and pub. programs, 1996—. Lectr., panelist in field. Contbr. articles to profl. jours. Mem. art adv. panel IRS, 1996—; advisor U.S. Holocaust Mus., 1996—; mem. bd. trustees Scripps Coll., 1996—; mem. steering com. Villa Aurora, 1994—. Recipient George L. Wittenborn award ARLIS, 1991, award for best Am. exhbn. of yr. Assn. Internat. Critics Art, 1991, 97, Theo Wormland Kunstpreis, 1992, George L. Wittenborn award, 1992, Alfred H. Barr Jr. award Coll. Art Assn., 1992, E.L. Kirchner prize, Switzerland, 1997, award for best exhbn. catalogue Assn. Internat. Art Critics Art, First Pl. award Am. Assn. Art Mus., 1998, Hon. Mention, ARLIS, 1998; named Woman of Yr., Bus. and Profl. Women of UJA, Jewish Fedn., 1991, Friends of Tel Hashomer, 1991; named to Order of Merit, Fed. Republic of Germany, 1984; fellow Nat. Endowment of Arts, 1986-87; John J. McCloy fellow in art, 1981. Fellow Am. Acad. Arts and Scis.; mem. Art Table. Office: LA County Mus Art 5905 Wilshire Blvd Los Angeles CA 90036-4597

BARRON, SUSAN, clinical psychologist; b. Chgo., May 13, 1940; d. Earl and Trixie (Chernoff) B.; m. Eugene Pratt, Jan. 18, 1975 (div. 1983). BBA, CCNY, 1960, MA, 1963; PhD, CUNY, 1973. Lic. psychologist, diplomate Am. Bd. Psychol. Specialties, bd. cert. fellow Am. Coll. Advanced Practice Psychologists, cert. alcohol and related substance abuse APA Coll. Profl. Psychology. Intern psychologist Bellevue Psychiat. Hosp., N.Y.C., 1964-65, psychologist, 1966-67; tchg. fellow CUNY, 1965-66; staff psychologist Lighthouse, N.Y.

Assn. for the Blind, N.Y.C., 1968-71, sr. clin. psychologist, 1971-74; dir. psychol. counseling svcs. Peninsula Ctr. for the Blind, Palo Alto, Calif., 1974-75; cons. psychologist N.Y. State Commn. for Blind and Visually Handicapped, N.Y.C., 1975-78, 86—; dir. psychol. svcs. Thoms Rehab. Hosp., Asheville, N.C., 1978-79; state coord. psychol. svcs. N.Y. State Office Vocat. Rehab., Albany, 1979-85; founder, dir. Family Support Program ICU N.Y. Infirmary-Beekman Downtown Hosp., N.Y.C., 1982-84; cons. clin. psychologist N.Y. Hosp. Cornell U. Med. Ctr., 1987—; pvt. practice, 1987—; behavioral scientist diabetes control/complications trial NIH Cornell U. Med. Ctr., N.Y.C., 1987—; cons. clin. psychologist Joslin Ctr. for Diabetes St. Luke's-Roosevelt Hosp. Ctr./Columbia U. Phys. and Surg., N.Y.C., 1994-95. Cons. clin. psychologist Joslin Ctr. Diabetes, St. Lukes-Roosevelt Hosp. Ctr., U. Hosp. of Columbia U. Coll. of Physicians and Surgeons, N.Y.C., 1994-95, Health Psychology Assocs., Calif., 1997—, N.Y.C., 1997—; mem. Nat. Human Svcs. Adv. Bd.-Retinitis Pigmentosa Found., Balt., 1975-82; cons. Del. State Commn. for Blind, 1975-78, Am. Found. Blind, 1974-82, Calif. Dept. Rehab., 1974-82, Hawaii State Svcs. Blind, 1974-82, Ariz. State Svcs. Blind, 1974-82, Nev. State Svcs. Blind, 1974-82; spkr. Nat. Multiple Disabilities Conf., 1982, NAS, 1981; mem. adv. bd. doctoral psychology internship program Rusk Inst. of Rehab. Medicine, NYU Med. Ctr., 1979-84; behavioral scientist Diabetes Control and Complications Trial NIH-Cornell U. Med. Ctr., 1987—; mem. mended hearts NYU Med. Ctr., Cardiac Prevention and Rehab. Ctr. Contbr. articles to profl. jours. Recipient Leadership award Alumni Assn. CCNY, 1960, 62, Rsch. award Retinal Dystrophy Soc., Australia, 1975, Charles H. Best medal for disting. svc. Am. Diabetes Assn., 1994. Fellow Am. Coll. Advanced Practice Psychologists (bd. cert.), Am. Orthopsychiat. Assn. (life); mem. APA, AAAS, Am. Coll. Forensic Examiners, Calif. State Psychol. Assn., N.Y. Acad. Scis., Mended Hearts. Office: 347 5th Ave Rm 603 New York NY 10016-5010

BARRON, THOMAS WILLIS, real estate broker; b. Newnan, Ga., Apr. 9, 1949; s. Lindsey Hand and Genet Louise (Heery) B.; m. Margaret Rose MacLennan, Aug. 17, 1973; children: Catharine Lindsey, Thomas Willis Jr., John Taliaferro Gaines. BA, Emory U., 1971; JD, Mercer U., 1974. Assoc. Sanders, Mottola, Haugen, Wood, Goodson and Odom, Newnan, 1974-77; real estate broker Lindsey's, Inc., Newnan, 1977—, Coweta Developers, Inc., Newnan, 1977—. Dir., mem. local adv. bd. BB&T (formerly First Citizens Bank); dir. Ga. Multi-List, Inc., Atlanta. Dir., sec.-treas. Newnan Hosp., 1992—, chmn. bd. 1997-2002, vice-chmn., immediate past chmn.; trustee Mercer U., Macon, Ga., 1990-95, 96-97, 2002—, Coweta Cmty. Found., 1999; past pres. Newnan-Coweta United Way, 1982—, Newnan Coweta chpt. ARC, 1980—; chmn. deacons Bapt. Ch., 1988-89, 95-96. Mem. Newnan-Coweta Bd. Realtors (past pres. 1984—, Realtor of Yr. 1991, Million Dollar Club 1989—, Phoenix award 1999), Newnan Country Club (past dir.), Newnan Kiwanis Club (past pres.), Sigma Chi (life, past consul), Newnan-Coweta C. of C. (chmn. bd. 1994). Baptist. Avocations: sports, history, historical autographs. Office: Lindseys Inc Realtors 14 Jackson St Newnan GA 30263-1929

BARROW, CHARLES HERBERT, investment banker; b. Evanston, Ill., July 23, 1930; m. Patricia Wandelt, Dec. 27, 1952; children: Paula, Carla, Barbara. AB, Princeton U., 1952; MBA, U. Chgo., 1956. With No. Trust Co., Chgo., 1952-86, v.p., 1962-68, sr. v.p., 1968-74, exec. v.p., 1974-78, sr. exec. v.p., 1978-81, pres., 1981-86, also dir.; with Blunt Ellis & Loewi, Inc. Kemper Securities, Inc., Chgo., 1987-91, sr. dir., 1987-91; mng. dir. Everen Securities, Inc. (formerly Kemper Securities, Inc.), 1991-99; sr. advisor Howe Barnes Investments, 1999—. Sr. advisor Sumitomo Trust and Banking Co., 1989-93; life mem. adv. coun. J.L. Kellogg Grad. Sch. of Mgmt., Northwestern U. Bd. dirs. Planned Parenthood Assn., Chgo., 1965-81, pres., 1972-73; bd. dirs. Rehab. Inst. Chgo., 1974—, chmn., 1982-83; trustee McCormick Theol. Sem., Chgo., 1984-95, treas., 1988-92, chmn., 1992-95, nat. trustee, 1995-96, trustee, 1996—. Mem. Chgo. Club, Comml. Club, Univ. Club, Commonwealth Club, Econ. Club, Bankers Club (pres. 1979-80), Bond Club, Glen View Club (Ill.), Michigan Shores Club (Wilmette, Ill.), Ocean Reef Club (Key Largo, Fla.), Pentwater (Mich.) Yacht Club. Presbyterian.

BARROW, CLYDE WAYNE, political scientist, educator; b. Alice, Tex., Feb. 15, 1956; s. Floyd Smith and Wanda Ruth (Conner) B. BA in Polit. Sci., Tex. A&I U., 1977; MA in Polit. Sci., UCLA, 1979, PhD in Polit. Sci., 1984. Teaching fellow UCLA, 1978-82, dir. instrnl. devel., 1982-84; vis. asst. prof. U. Tex., San Antonio, 1984-85, Tex. A&M U., College Station, 1985-87; from asst. prof. to prof. polit. sci. U. Mass. at Dartmouth, North Dartmouth, 1987-96, prof., 1996—, acting chmn. dept., 1992-93, 95, sr. rsch. assoc. Ctr. for Policy Analysis, 1993-94, dir. Ctr. for Policy Analysis, 1994—. Mem. adv. bd. Arnold Dubin Labor Edn. Ctr., North Dartmouth, 1988—; policy cons. Office of Mayor, City of Fall River, Mass., 1993—, New Bedford CEO Club, 1994—99, Fall River Sch. Dept., 1995—, Sandwich Sch. Dept., 1996—, Fall River Housing Authority, 1997—, New Bedford Housing Authority, 1999—; exec. staff analyst Gov.'s Commn. on Commonwealth Port Devel., Mass., 1994, Gov.'s Regional Econ. Devel. Strategies Project, 1996, 2000—01; regional analyst Mass. Benchmark Project, 1997—; pub. mem. Cranberry Mktg. Com., 2003—. Author: Universities and the Capitalist State, 1990, Critical Theories of the State, 1993, More Than a Historian: The Political and Economic Thought of Charles A. Beard, 2000, Economic Impacts of the Textile and Apparel Industries in Massachusetts, 2000, Portuguese-Americans and Contemporary Civic Culture in Massachusetts, 2002; co-author: Globalisation Trade Liberalisation and Higher Education in North America, 2003; mem. bd. editors Acad. Labor, 2003-, Sociol. Inquiry, 1992-95, Jour. Politics, 1993-97, Acad. Labor, 2003-; mng. editor New England Jour. Pub. Policy, 1994-97; also articles. Recipient Fontera Meml. award Arnold Dubin Labor Edn. Ctr., 1991, Disting. Svc. award Mass. Fedn. Tchrs., 2001. Mem. Am. Polit. Sci. Assn., Western Polit. Sci. Assn., Caucus for a New Polit. Sci., Policy Studies Orgn., U. Mass. Faculty Fedn. (treas. 1991-96, 2002-03, pres. 1998-2000). Office: U Mass Ctr Policy Analysis 285 Old Westport Rd North Dartmouth MA 02747-2356

BARROW, FREDERICA HARRISON, education educator, social worker; b. Monroe, N.C., Apr. 10, 1939; d. Frederick Perry Crowell and Hattie Berthenia Alexander; m. Lionel Ceon, Jr. Barrow, Sept. 5, 1992; m. Claude McKinely Harrison, July 2, 1960 (dec. June 1980); children: Emily Harrison Smith, Brenda M. Feliciano, Rhonda Patricia Liquori, Aurea Adams, Kirsten Erin, Lia Barrow Ward, Laura Elaine Harrison. BA (cum laude), N.C. Coll., 1960; M in Social Work, Atlanta U., 1962; M in Adminstr. Sci., Johns Hopkins U., Balt., 1980; PhD, Howard U., Washington, DC, 2001. LCSW Md., 2004, lic. Independent Social Worker D.C., 2003. Rsch. adminstrn., social policy The Social Security Adminstrn., Balt., 1995—2002; asst. prof. U. of South Fla., Tampa, 2002—. Clincal social worker U. of N.C. Child Psychiatry, Chapel Hill, 1962—66; dir. sch. social work program Durham Edn. Improvement Program, NC, 1966—70; clin. social worker Duke U., Divsn. of Child Psychiatry, Durham, NC, 1970—73, Linwood Children's Ctr., Ellicott City, Md., 1974—75; coord. child and adolescent svcs. Md. Dept. of Health & Hygiene, Balt., 1976—85; dir. social work dept. The Sheppard & Enoch Pratt Hosp., Balt., 1982—85; employee assistance br. chief Social Security Adminstrn., Balt., 1985—91. Author: (dissertation) The Social Welfare Career and Contributions of Forrester Blanchard Washington, A Life Course Analysis, (book chpt.) How can ethnic, cultural issues be integrated into EAP supervisory/management and union training and into Employee Assistance program delivery. In An Emerging Paradigm, EAPs and the New American Workorce; co-author: Work and Wellbeing. The Occupational Social Work Advantage. Mem. bd. dirs. Long Reach Village Bd., Columbia, Md., 1977—80; mem. Howard County Coordination Coun. for Criminal Justice, Ellicott City, Md., 1979—80, Handel Choir, Howard County Social Svcs. Bd., Ellicott City, Md., 1982—84, USO of Ctrl. Md., Balt., 1984—85, Girl Scouts of Ctrl. Md., Balt., 1984—86. Fellow NIMH, Atlanta U., 1960—62; grantee Svc. Learning Grant, The U. of South Fla., 2002. Mem.: Sch. Social Work Assn. of Am., Coun. on Social Work Edn., NASW, N.C. Ctrl. U. Alumni Assn. (life), Delta Sigma Theta, Inc. (life). Democrat. Episcopalian. Avocations: African Am. family devel. and history, art collecting, gardening, choral singing. Home: 17842 Arbor Greene Dr Tampa FL 33647 Office: U of South Fla 4202 E Fowler Ave MGY 132 Tampa FL 33620-6600 Office Fax: 813-974-4675. Personal E-mail: fhbarrow@aol.com. E-mail: fbarrow@chuma1.cas.usf.edu.

BARROW, JOHN J. lawyer; b. Athens, Ga., Oct. 31, 1955; s. James and Phyllis (Jenkins) B.; m. Victoria Pentlarge, Dec. 19, 1953. AB, U. Ga., 1976; JD, Harvard U., 1979. Bar: Ga., U.S. Dist. Ct. (no. and mid. dists.) Ga., U.S. Ct. Appeals (11th cir.), U.S. Ct. Appeals (5th cir.). Clk. to Hon. Tom Clark U.S. Ct. Appeals, Tampa, Fla., 1979-81; assoc. Winburn & Assocs., Athens, Ga., 1981-83; ptnr. Winburn, Lewis Barrow & Stolz, PC, Athens, Ga., 1983—. Mem. rev. panel State Bar Disciplinary Bd., 1997-99; mem. Ga. Com. on Continuing Lawyer Competency, 1984-87. Commr. Athens-Clarke County Commn., Athens, 1991—. Mem. Ga. Trial Lawyers Assn., Assn. Trial Lawyers Am. Democrat. Baptist. Avocations: govt., tennis, backpacking, spectator sports. Home: 255 Milledge Hts Athens GA 30606-4927

BARROW, LIONEL CEON, JR., communications and marketing consultant; b. N.Y.C., Dec. 17, 1926; s. Lionel Ceon and Wilhelmina Barrow; m. Frederica Harrison; children: Lea, Kirsten Erin; stepchildren: Brenda Marie, Aurea Nellie, Rhonda Patricia, Emily Harrison Smith, Laura Harrison. BA in English, Morehouse Coll., 1948; MA in Journalism, U. Wis., 1958, PhD in Mass Communications, 1960. Reporter Richmond Afro-Am., Va., 1953-54; teaching and research asst. U. Wis., Madison, 1954-60; asst. prof. dept. communication Mich. State U., Lansing, 1960-61; research project dir. Bur. Advt., N.Y.C., 1961-63; research project supr. Kenyon & Eckhardt Advt. Agy., N.Y.C., 1963-64; research group head Foote Cone & Belding, N.Y.C., 1964-68, assoc. research dir., v.p., 1968-71; chmn. dept. Afro-Am. studies U. Wis., Milw., 1971-72, 74-75, prof. mass comms. and Afro-Am. studies, 1971-75; dean Sch. Communications Howard U., Washington, 1975-85, prof. communications, 1975-86; pres. The Barrow Info. Group, Columbia, Md., 1986—. Vis. prof. Stanford U., 1971, Ohio State U., 1986; pres. Journalism Coun. Inc., 1971-79; sec. elected advs. Md. Conf. on Small Bus., 1987-89. Contbr. articles to profl. jours. Active Higher Edn. Group Washington, 1985-92. Served with AUS, 1945-47, 50-53. Recipient media citation Journalism Edn. Assn., 1974; recipient radio pioneer award Medgar Evers Coll., 1979 Mem. Assn. for Edn. in Journalism and Mass Communications (founder, first head minorities and comm. divsn.), Nat. Assn. Black Journalists, Soc. Profl. Journalists, Capitol Press Club, NAACP (life), 24th Infantry Regimental Combat Team Assn. (life, Combat Infantry badge).

BARROW, ROBERT EARL, retired agricultural organization administrator; b. Swansea, Mass., Jan. 30, 1930; s. Charles H. and Etta (Campbell) B.; m. Dolores A. Pannoni, Jan. 30, 1954; children: Kyle A. Kawa, Susan E. Gregory. Grad. high sch., Swansea, 1948. Sr. v.p. 1st Fed. Savs. & Loan Assn., Providence, 1949-77; mgr. Old Red Bank, Fall River, Mass., 1978-79; mgr. bookkeeping Uncle Matty's Tropical Gardens, Warwick, R.I., 1980-87; sec. Nat. Grange, Washington, 1983-85, lectr., program dir., 1985-87, pres., 1987-95; sec. Mass. State Grange, 1997—2001. Master Swansea Grange #148, 1959-60, Bay State Pomona #33, 1965-66, Mass. State, 1981-85. Mem. Bretton Woods Com., 1988—, Agrl. Policy Adv. Com., 1988-94, transp. alternatives group Transp. 2020, 1988, 4-H Coun., 1988—, Bd. Hwy. Users Fedn., 1988—, Nat. Farm Coalition, 1988—, Coalition for Fiscal Restraint, 1988—. With U.S. Army, 1951-53. Avocations: profl. singer, gardening, bell collecting.

BARROW, SALLY SETTLE, media specialist, librarian; b. Moore Haven, Fla. m. John Guy Barrow, III, June 15, 1969 (div. Jan. 19, 2001); children: Mollie Susan Barrow-Huggins, John Daniel. BA, Fla. State U., Tallahassee, FL, 1974; MSLS, Fla. State U., Tallahassee, FL, 1987. Cert. in Mental Retardation Fla. State U., 1974. Tchr. Duval County Sch. Bd., Duval County, Fla., 1970—72, media specialist, 1970—72; educator Jefferson County Sch. Bd., Jefferson County, Fla., 1974—88; media specialist Duval County Sch. Bd., Long Br. Elem., Jacksonville, Fla., 1988—93, Duval County Sch. Bd., Ctrl. Riverside Elem., Jacksonville, Fla., 1993—. Tchr. rep. Demse Title III. Contbr. co-author for curriculum guide. County coord. Fla. Spl. Olympics, Fla., 1982—86, Fla. Big Bend Spl. Arts Festival, Fla., 1983—88; educator First Nazarene Ch., Monticello, Fla., 1984—88, libr., 1984—88, First Presbyn. Ch., Fernandina Beach, Fla., 1993—99; vacation bible sch. tchr. and coord. First United Meth. Ch., Monticello, Fla., 1970—89; tchr. Nassau Nazarene Ch., Yulee, Fla., 1984—88, coord. social teas Yulle, Fla., 1993—99. Recipient Outstanding Young Women Award, Outstanding Young Women Award, 1982, Selected Participant, Teachers' Seminar Fla. Humanities Coun., 1996. Mem.: Duval County Media Educators In Action, Fla. Humanities Coun., Duval County Reading Coun., Alpha Delta Kappa, Beta Phi Mu Libr. Sci. Honor Frat. D-Liberal. Presbyterian. Avocation: studying Florida history. Home: 123 West Hirth Road #1031 Fernandina Beach FL 32034 Office: Central Riverside Elementary School 2555 Gilmore Street Jacksonville FL 32204 Personal E-mail: barrows2@net-magic.net.

BARROW, THOMAS DAVIES, oil and mining company executive; b. San Antonio, Dec. 27, 1924; s. Leonidas Theodore and Laura Editha (Thomson) B.; m. Janice Meredith Hood, Sept. 16, 1950; children: Theodore Hood, Kenneth Thomson, Barbara Loyd, Elizabeth Ann BS, U. Tex., 1945, MA, 1948; PhD, Stanford U., 1953; grad. advanced mgmt. program, Harvard U., 1963. With Humble Oil & Refining Co., 1951-72, regional exploration mgr., 1962-64, sr. v.p., 1966—70, pres., 1970-72, also bd. dirs.; exec. v.p. Esso Exploration, Inc., 1964-65; sr. v.p. Exxon Corp., N.Y.C., 1972-78; chmn., CEO Kennecott Corp., Stamford, Conn., 1978-81; vice chmn. Standard Oil Co., Ohio, 1981-85; investment cons. Houston, 1985-89; chmn. GX Tech., Houston, 1990—; pres. Thomson-Barrow, 1989—; sr. chmn., bd. dir. GeoQuest Internat. Holdings, Inc., Houston, 1990-97; pres. Tecolotita, Inc., 1991—, T-BAR-X, Houston, 1995—. Chmn. bd. dirs. GPS Tech. Corp., Houston, 1986-98, Tobin Internat., 1998—; mem. commn. on natural resources NRC, 1973-78, commn. on phys. sci., math. and natural resources, 1984-87, bd. on earth scis., 1982-84; trustee Woods Hole Oceanographic Instn., 20th Century Fund-Task Force on U.S. Energy Policy; chmn. bd. dirs. Petroleum Info./Dwights, 1994-97. Pres. Houston Grand Opera, 1985-87, chmn., 1987-91; trustee Am. Mus. Natural History, 1972-82, Stanford U., 1980-90, Tex. Med. Ctr., 1983—, Geol. Soc. Am. Found., 1982-87; trustee Baylor Coll. Medicine, 1984—, vice chmn bd. trustees, 1991-99. Served to ensign USNR, 1943-46. Recipient Disting. Achievement award Offshore Tech. Conf., 1973, Disting. Engring. Grad. award U. Tex., 1970, Disting. Alumnus, 1982, Disting. Geology Grad., 1985, Disting. Natural Sci. Grad., 1990; named Chief Exec. of Yr. in Mining Industry, Fin. World, 1979 Fellow N.Y. Acad. Scis.; mem. Nat. Acad. Engring., Am. Mining Congress (bd. dirs. 1979-85, vice chmn. 1983-85), Am. Assn. Petroleum Geologists, Geol. Soc. Am., Internat. Copper Research Assn. (bd. dirs. 1979-85), Nat. Ocean Industry Assn. (bd. dirs. 1982-85), AAAS, Am. Soc. Oceanography (pres. 1970-71), Am. Geophys. Union, Am. Petroleum Inst., Am. Geog. Soc., Houston Country Club, The Hills Club, Petroleum Club, River Oaks Country Club, Houston Club, Sigma Xi, Tau Beta Pi, Sigma Gamma Epsilon, Phi Eta Sigma, Alpha Tau Omega Episcopalian. Office: 5847 San Felipe St Ste 3830 Houston TX 77057-3008

BARROW, THOMAS FRANCIS, artist, educator; b. Kansas City, Mo., Sept. 24, 1938; s. Luther Hopkins and Cleo Naomi (Francis) Barrow; m. Laurie Anderson, Nov. 30, 1974; children: Melissa, Timothy, Andrew. B.F.A., Kansas City Art Inst., 1963; MS, Ill. Inst. Tech., 1965. With George Eastman House, Rochester, N.Y., 1966-72, asst. dir., 1971-72; assoc. dir. Art Mus., U. N. Mex., Albuquerque, 1973-76; assoc. prof. U. N.Mex., 1976-81, prof., 1981—2001, Presdl. prof., 1985-90. Author: The Art of Photography, 1971; sr. editor: Reading into Photography, 1982; contbr. to Brit. Ency. Am. Art, 1973, A Hundred Years of Photographic History: Essays in Honor of Beaumont Newhall, 1975, Experimental Vision, 1994; forward The Valiant Knights of Daguerre, 1978; contbr. articles to profl. jours.; one-man shows include Light Gallery, N.Y.C., 1974-76, 79, 82, Amarillo Art Ctr., 1990, Andrew Smith Gallery, Santa Fe, 1992, Laurence Miller Gallery, N.Y.C., 1996, U. N.Mex. Art Mus., 1997, Richard Levy Gallery, Albuquerque, 2000; exhibited in group shows including Pace Gallery, N.Y.C., 1973, Hudson River Mus., Yonkers, N.Y., 1973, Internat. Mus. Photography, Rochester, 1975, Seattle Art Mus., 1976, Mus. Fine Arts, Houston, 1977, Retrospective exhbn. L.A. County Mus. Art, 1987—; represented in permanent collections Nat. Gallery Can., Mus. Modern Art, Getty Ctr. for Arts and Humanities. Nat. Endowment for Arts fellow, 1971, 78.

BARROWS, FRANK CLEMENCE, editor; b. Lewes, Del., Nov. 2, 1946; m. Mary S. Newsom, Nov. 16, 1985; 1 child, Margaret S. BA, St. Andrews Coll., 1968. Reporter, columnist Charlotte (N.C.) Observer, 1969-72, 76-81, asst. sports editor, 1981-82, asst. met. editor, 1982-83, exec. sports editor, 1983-84, 86, dep. features editor, 1985, dep. met. editor, 1986-87, asst. mng. editor, 1987-88, dep. mng. editor, 1988-92, mng. editor, 1992—. Contbr. articles to mags. Recipient Ethel Fortner Writer and Cmty. award, 2000, Reporting award, NC Press Assn., 1972—80. Mem.: Investigative Reporters and Editors, Soc. News Design, Am. Soc. Newspaper Editors. Home: 1810 Shoreham Dr Charlotte NC 28211-2134 Office: Charlotte Observer 600 S Tryon St Charlotte NC 28202-1842 E-mail: fbarrows@charlotteobserver.com.

BARROWS, JOSEPH HOWARD, state representative; b. Fort Ord, Calif., Apr. 16, 1950; m. Jean Barrows; children: Parry, Hayden. BA, DePauw U., 1973; JD, U. Ky., 1977. Atty., 1977—; staff analyst Legis. Rsch. Commn., 1977—78; mem. Ky. Ho. of Reps., 1980—, majority whip, 1997—98. Vice chair legis. adv. coun. So. Regional Edn. Bd., 1985—; bd. dirs. Appalachian Ednl. Lab., United Way, Woodford County, Ky. Democrat. Office: Capitol Annex Rm 432 A Frankfort KY 40601*

BARROWS, MICHAEL JOHN, endodontist, educator; b. Chgo., Jan. 26, 1949; s. Glendon Leroy and Mabel Rose (Thorn) B.; m. Susan Kay Straub, June 20, 1970; children: Aimee Susan, Laura Michelle. DDS, U. Ill., 1973, MS, 1981. Pvt. practice, Oak Lawn, Ill., 1977-93; asst. prof. U. Ill., Chgo., 1986—, instr., 1977-81, endodontic clinic dir., 1999—. Part-time supr. dentist Prairie State Coll., 1994-97. Editor (ch. newsletter) The Voice, 1994—; co-author videotapes in field. Chmn. pastoral adv. com. St. Paul Community Ch., Homewood, Ill., 1985-88, v.p. coun., 1995-97; nation chief Indian Guide program YMCA, Harvey, Ill., 1984-87. Capt. U.S. Army, 1973-75. Mem. Am. Dental Assn., Am. Assn. Endodontists, Ill. State Dental Soc., Chgo. Dental Soc., Edgar D. Coolidge Endodontic Study Club, Phi Eta Sigma, Omicron Kappa Upsilon. Republican. Avocations: photography, video, stereo, electronics. Home: 21162 Raintree Ct Frankfort IL 60423-8819 Office: Dept Endodontics 801 S Paulina St Chicago IL 60612

BARRS, JAMES THOMAS, linguistics educator; b. Danville, Ga., Sept. 2, 1904; s. Andrew Robert and Dollie Lee (Brown) B.; m. Vida Fitz Randolph, Sept. 2, 1931; children: Dorothy Caroline, Ann Radcliffe, Andrew Fitzrandolph. AB summa cum laude, U. Ga., 1927; AM, Harvard U., 1932, PhD, 1936; student, Mercer U., 1928. Registrar, tchr. English South Ga. Coll., Douglas, 1937-42, dean, 1940-42; asst. prof. English Washington Coll., Chestertown, Md., 1943-45; from asst. prof. to prof. English Northea. U., Boston, 1945-71, prof. emeritus, 1971—. Lectr. Sta. WAYX, Waycross, Ga., 1940-42, Sta. WBZ-WBZA, Boston and Springfield, Mass., 1959-60, Stas. WEEI, WCRB, WILD, Boston, and Concert Network, 1960s, Sta. WGBH-TV, Boston, 1958-59. Contbr. to scholarly publs. Recipient Cert. of Distinction Assn. Coll. Honor Socs., 2000. Mem. MLA (life), N.E. MLA (chmn. linguistics sect. 1972-73), Nat. Coun. Tchrs. of English (bd. dirs. 1969-70, chmn. semantics sect. 1972, mem. com. on pub. and profl. rels. 1967-70, mem. com. on semantics in sch. programs 1960-71), N.Y. Acad. Scis., Coll. English Assn. (bd. dirs. 1962-65), Conf. on Coll. Composition and Comm., New England Assn. Tchrs. of English (adv. mem. exec. bd. 1960-70, chmn. sch. and coll. liaison com. 1962-65, chmn. nominating com. 1966-69), Phi Beta Kappa (sec. Newton com. 1972-97, pres. Northea. U. assocs. 1965-68), Phi Kappa Phi (copy editor nat. forum, copy editor extraordinaire award 2000). Home and Office: PO Box 215 Onset MA 02558

BARRY, ALLAN RONALD, ship pilot, corporate executive; b. Chgo., Jan. 28, 1945; s. Robert Edward and Stella Yvonne (Pellonari) B.; m. Ellen Conerly, May 1, 1971; 1 child, Elizabeth Anne. BS, U.S. Mcht. Marine Acad., 1967. Unltd. masters lic., Houston Ship Channel pilot's lic. USCG; commd. branch pilot Galveston Bar and Houston Ship Channel, State of Tex. Ship's officer Lykes Bros. S.S. Co., Inc., New Orleans, 1967-74; ship's pilot Houston Pilots, 1975—; pres., chief exec. officer Allan Barry, Inc., Houston, 1979—. Commd. to office of br. pilot, Galveston Bar and the Houston Ship Channel by State of Tex. Lt. USNR, 1967-82. Mem. U.S. Mcht. Marine Acad. Alumni Assn. (leadership contbr. 1978—), Nat. Audubon Soc., Houston Audubon Soc., Nat. Maritime Hist. Soc., Coun. Am. Master Mariners, Am. Pilots Assn., Am. Mcht. Marine Vets., Propeller Club (bd. govs. Port of Houston 1986-88), Nature Conservancy, Nat. Wildlife Fed. Republican. Office: Houston Pilots 8150 South Loop E Ste 118 Houston TX 77017-1796

BARRY, DAVE, columnist, author; b. Armonk, N.Y., July 3, 1947; m. Michelle Kaufman, 1996; children: Robert, Sophie. Grad., Haverford Coll., 1969. Reporter, editor Daily Local News, West Chester, Pa., 1971-75; with AP, instr. bus. writing Phila., 1975-83; columnist The Miami (Fla.) Herald, 1983—. Author: Taming of the Screw: Several Million Homeowner's Problems Sidestepped, 1983, Babies and Other Hazards of Sex, 1984, Bad Habits: A One Hundred Percent Fact Free Book, 1985, Stay Fit and Healthy Until You're Dead, 1985, Dave Barry's Guide to Marriage and/or Sex, 1987, Claw Your Way to the Top, 1987, Dave Barry's Greatest Hits, 1988, Dave Barry Slept Here, 1989, Dave Barry Turns 40, 1990, Dave Barry Talks Back, 1991, Dave Barry's Only Travel Guide You'll Ever Need, 1991, Dave Barry Does Japan, 1992, Dave Barry Is Not Making This Up, 1994, Dave Barry's Complete Guide to Guys, 1995, Dave Barry in Cyberspace, 1996, Dave Barry is from Mars and Venus, 1997, Dave Barry Turns 50, 1998, Dave Barry Is Not Taking This Sitting Down, 2000, Dave Barry Hits Below the Beltway, 2001, (novel) Big Trouble, 1999, (novel) Tricky Business, 2002, Boogers Are My Beat, 2003. Recipient Disting. Writing award, Soc. Newspaper Editors, 1987, Pulitzer prize for commentary, 1988. Office: Miami Herald 1 Herald Plz Miami FL 33132-1693

BARRY, DAVID EARL, lawyer; b. N.Y.C., Nov. 25, 1945; s. David J. Barry and Beatrice A. Richtmyer; m. Teresa M. Anderson, July 26, 1969; children: Andrea, David R., Kristin. BA, Coll. Holy Cross, Worcester, Mass., 1966; JD, Harvard U., 1969. Bar: N.Y. 1969, Conn. 1978. Ptnr. Kelley Drye & Warren, LLP, N.Y.C., 1969—. Mem. ABA, Univ. Club, Apawamis Club. Roman Catholic. Home: 2 Puritan Rd Rye NY 10580-1931 Office: Kelley Daye & Warren LLP 101 Park Ave New York NY 10178-0002

BARRY, DESMOND THOMAS, JR., lawyer; b. N.Y.C., Mar. 26, 1945; s. Desmond Thomas and Kathryn (O'Connor) B.; m. Patricia Mellicker, Aug. 28, 1971; children: Kathryn, Desmond Todd. AB, Princeton U., 1967; JD, Fordham U., 1973. Bar: N.Y. 1974, U.S. Dist. Ct. (so. and ea. dist.) N.Y. 1974, U.S. Ct. Appeals (2d cir.) 1974, U.S. Ct. Appeals (9th cir.) 1980, U.S. Ct. Appeals (5th cir.) 1983, U.S. Ct. Appeals (3d cir.) 1984, U.S. Supreme Ct. 1985. Assoc. Condon & Forsyth, N.Y.C., 1973-79, ptnr., 1979—. Trustee Canterbury Sch., New Milford, Conn., 1970-80. Capt. USMC, 1967-70, Vietnam. Decorated Navy Commendation medal with combat V, Combat Action medal, 1969, Vietnamese Cross of Gallantry, 1969. Mem.: ABA (chmn. aviation and space law com. 1996—97), Internat. Assn. Def. Counsel (exec. com.), Assn. Bar City NY, NY State Bar Assn., Queenwood Golf Club (London), Hawk's Nest Golf Club (Vero Beach, Fla.), Winged Foot Golf Club (bd. govs. 1999—2001), Univ. Club N.Y.C. Republican. Roman Catholic. Home: 40 Charter Oak Ln New Canaan CT 06840-6705 Office: Condon & Forsyth LLP 685 3rd Ave Fl 14 New York NY 10017-4024

BARRY, EDWARD WILLIAM, retired publisher; b. Stamford, Conn., Nov. 24, 1937; s. Edward and Elizabeth (Cosgrove) B.; m. Barbara Helen Walker, Sept. 14, 1963; children— Wendy Elizabeth, Neil Edward. BA with honors, U. Conn., 1960; LittD (hon.), U. Oxford, 2000. Pres. The Free Press, N.Y.C., 1972-82, Oxford U. Press Inc., N.Y.C., 1982-2000—; sr. v.p. Macmillan Pub. Co., N.Y.C., 1973-82; ret., 2000. Exec. coun. mem. Profl. and Scholarly Pubs., 1993; adv. bd. Pace U. Grad. Program in Pub., 1990—; bd. dirs. Rsch. Lib. Group, iuniverse.com, knovel.com, Ctrl. European Univ. Press, Univ. Alliance; mem. mgmt. coun. Flora N.Am., 2000—; trustee Columbia U. Press, 2000—; adj. prof. Pace U., 2000—. Mem. Assn. Am. Pubs. (bd. dirs. 1995-99), Am. Assn. Higher Edn. (bd. dirs. 1995-96), Phi Alpha Theta. Home: 266 Old Poverty Rd Southbury CT 06488-1769 E-mail: edwardbarry7@cs.com.

BARRY, FRANCIS JULIAN, JR., lawyer; b. New Orleans, Oct. 7, 1949; s. Francis Julian and Bertha Anna (Lion) B.; m. Janice Leigh Gonzales, May 8, 1976; children: Francis III, Marianna. BA, Tulane U., 1970, JD, 1973. Bar: La. 1973, U.S. Dist. Ct. (ea. dist.) La. 1973, U.S. Ct. Appeals (5th cir.) 1973, U.S. Dist. Ct. (we. dist.) La. 1978, U.S. Ct. Appeals (11th cir.) 1982, U.S. Supreme Ct. 1991. Assoc. Deutsch, Kerrigan & Stiles, New Orleans, 1973-78, ptnr., 1978—. Editor Admiralty Law Inst. Symposium Tulane U., New Orleans, 1973. Adv. editor Tulane Maritime Law Jour. (formerly The Maritime Lawyer), 1975—. Served to capt. USAR. Mem. Fed. Bar Assn., La. Bar Assn., New Orleans Bar Assn., Maritime Law Assn. U.S. (proctor, carriage of goods com. 1982-87, 2000—, transp. hazardous substances com. 1987—), Admiralty Law

Inst. New Orleans (mem. planning com. 1998—, mem. program com. 2000—), U.S. Naval Inst., Southeastern Admiralty Law Inst., La. Assn. Def. Counsel, Def. Rsch. Inst., Assn. Average Adjusters London, Am. Legion, Navy League U.S., Army-Navy Club (Washington), La. Landmarks Soc., Bienville Club, Univ. Club (N.Y.C.), Plimsoll Club, Mariners Club, The Round Table Club. Republican. Roman Catholic. Home: 4301 Dumaine St New Orleans LA 70119-3617 Office: Deutsch Kerrigan & Stiles 755 Magazine St New Orleans LA 70130-3672 E-mail: fbarry@dksno.com.

BARRY, HERBERT, III, psychologist, educator; b. N.Y.C., June 2, 1930; s. Herbert and Lucy Manning (Brown) Barry. BA, Harvard U., 1952; MS, Yale U., 1953, PhD, 1957. USPHS-NIMH rsch. fellow Yale U., 1957-59, asst. prof. psychology, 1960-61, U. Conn., Storrs, 1961-63; rsch. assoc. prof. pharmacology Sch. Pharmacy U. Pitts., 1963-70, prof., 1970-87, prof. pharm. scis., 1995—2001, prof. emeritus, 2001—, prof. pharmacology and physiology Sch. Dental Medicine, 1987-94. Mem. alcohol rsch. rev. com. Nat. Inst. Alcohol Abuse and Alcoholism, 1972—76; mem. sociobehavioral subcom. AIDS rsch. rev. com. Nat. Inst. Drug Abuse, 1988—89. Author (with H. Wallgren): (book) Actions of Alcohol, 1970; author: (with A. Schlegel) Adolescence: An Anthropological Inquiry, 1991; field editor: book Psychopharmacology, 1974—91; contbr. articles to profl. jours. Bd. dirs. Schalkenbach Found., 1997—, Ctr. Study Econs., 1988—; mem. Allegheny County Dem. Com., 1984—. Recipient Rsch. Scientist Devel. award, NIMH, 1967—77. Fellow: APA (coun. reps. 1975—76, pres. divsn. psychopharmacology 1980—81), AAAS; mem.: Am. Coll. Neuropsychopharmacology, Psychonomic Soc., Am. Name Soc. (mem. exec. com. 2000—), Sigma Xi, Phi Beta Kappa. Unitarian Universalist. Home: 552 N Neville St Apt 83 Pittsburgh PA 15213-2830 Office: U Pitts 526 Salk Hall Pittsburgh PA 15261-1905 Business E-Mail: barryh@pitt.edu. *I believe that the contrasting behaviors of persistence and innovation both contribute to effective learning and creativity. Awareness of the need for both contrasting behaviors may help people to avoid the failures caused by overemphasis of either one.*

BARRY, JAMES P(OTVIN), writer, editor; b. Alton, Ill., Oct. 23, 1918; s. Paul Augustine and Elder (Potvin) B.; m. Anne Elizabeth Jackson, Apr. 16, 1966 BA cum laude, Ohio State U., 1940. Commd. 2d. lt. Arty. U.S. Army, 1940, advanced through grades to col., served ETO, 1944-46; adviser to Turkish Army, 1951-53; detailed Army Gen. Staff, Washington, 1953-56; ret., 1966; adminstr. Capital U., Columbus, Ohio, 1967-71; freelance writer, editor Columbus, 1971-77; dir. Ohioana Library Assn., 1977-88; editor Ohioana Quar., 1977-88; sr. editor Inland Seas, 1984—; photographer, documentary and book illustrator, 1968—. Author: Georgian Bay: The Sixth Great Lake, 1968, 3rd edit., 1995, The Battle of Lake Erie, 1970, Bloody Kansas, 1972, The Noble Experiment, 1972, The Fate of the Lakes, 1972, The Louisiana Purchase, 1973, Henry Ford and Mass Production, 1973, Ships of the Great Lakes, 1973 (Dolphin Book Club selection), Ships of the Great Lakes, rev. edit., 1996, The Berlin Olympics, 1975, The Great Lakes: A First Book, 1976, Wrecks and Rescues of the Great Lakes, 1981 (Dolphin Book Club selection), Georgian Bay: An Illustrated History, 1992, Old Forts of the Great Lakes, 1994, Hackercraft, 2002, American Powerboats, 2003; contbr. articles to mags. and jours.; over 300 photographs accepted for permanent collection Inst. Gt. Lakes Rsch. Recipient award Am. Soc. State and Local History, 1974, Nonfiction History award Soc. Midland Authors, 1982; named Gt. Lakes Historian of Yr., Marine Hist. Soc. Detroit, 1995. Mem. Internat. Assn. Gt. Lakes Rsch., Assn. Gt. Lakes Maritime History, Can. Nautical Rsch. Soc., Gt. Lakes Hist. Soc., Marine Hist. Soc., Ohio Hist. Soc., World Ship Soc., Antique and Classic Boat Soc., Royal Can. Yacht Club, Columbus Country Club, Capital Club, Phi Beta Kappa. Home: 353 Fairway Blvd Columbus OH 43213-2507

BARRY, JOAN, clinical researcher; b. N.Y.C., Sept. 17, 1953; BA in Polit. Sci., UCLA, 1978. Rsch. assoc. cardiovasc. divsn. UCLA Med. Ctr., 1980-83; rsch. assoc. cardiovascular div. Brigham and Women's Hosp., Boston, 1983-96, assoc. scientist Ischemia Lab., 1987-96; co-dir. Brigham Ischemia Group, Boston, 1989-96; rsch. assoc. Harvard Med. Sch., 1987-93, prin. assoc. in medicine, 1993-97. Cons. Boston U. Sch. Medicine, 1983. Contbr. articles to profl. jours. Mem. Am. Heart Assn. (mem. pub. edn. forum com. 1982-83, cons. com. to enhance cardiac patient family support groups). Home: 55 Hallwood Rd Chestnut Hill MA 02467-2720

BARRY, JOHN J. labor union leader; Internat. pres. Internat. Brotherhood Elec. Workers, Washington. Office: Internat Brotherhood Elec Workers 1125 15th St NW Washington DC 20005-2707

BARRY, JOHN L. military officer; BS in Internat. Affairs & Polit. Sci., USAF Acad., 1973; grad., Squadron Officer Sch., 1977; M in Pub. Adminstrn., U. Okla., 1980; grad., Armed Forces Staff Coll., 1984, Harvard U., 1994. Commd. 2d lt. USAF, 1973, advanced through grades to brigadier gen., 1997; air staff tng. officer Office of Inspector Gen. Hdqs. USAF, Washington, 1979-80; aide to comdr. 12th Air Force, Bergstrom AFB, Tex., 1983-84; action officer for fighter programs Dep. Chief Staff for Pers. Resources, Hdqs. USAF, Bergstrom AFB, 1985; White House fellow, exec. officer, liaison to NASA adminstr. NASA, Washington, 1985-86; chief of safety 8th Tactical Fighter Wing, Kunsan Air Base, South Korea, 1987-88; ops. officer 421st Tactical Fighter Squadron, Hill AFB, Utah, 1988-89; comdr. 34th Tactical Fighter Squadron, Hill AFB, 1989-90; mil. asst. to sec. of def. The Pentagon, Washington, 1990-92; comdr. 56th Ops. Group, MacDill AFB, Fla., 1992-93, 39th Wing and 7440th Composite Wing, Incirlik Air Base, Turkey, 1994-96; dir. plans and programs Hdqs. U.S. Air Forces in Europe, Ramstein Air Base, Germany, 1996-98; comdr. 56th Fighter Wing, Luke AFB, Ariz., 1998-2000; dir. strategic planning Dep. Chief of Staff Plans and Programs, HQ USAF, Washington, 2000—. Decorated Def. Superior Svc. medal, Legion of Merit, Meritorious Svc. medal with 3 oak leaf clusters; Nat. Security fellow Harvard U., 1994. Office: USAF Pentagon 1030 Air Force Pentagon Washington DC 20330-1030

BARRY, JOHN MAYNARD, urologist; b. Winona, Minn., Mar. 14, 1940; MD, U. Minn., 1965. Intern SUNY, Syracuse, 1965-66; resident U. Oreg. Med. Sch., Portland, 1969-73; prof., chmn. urology Oreg. Health Sci. U., Portland, 1980—, dir. renal transplantation, 1976—, chmn. abdominal organ transplantation, 2000—02. Office: Oreg Health SciU Divsn Urology 3181 SW Sam Jackson Park Rd Portland OR 97201-3011

BARRY, JOYCE ALICE, dietitian; b. Chgo., Apr. 27, 1932; d. Walter Stephen and Ethel Myrtle (Paetow) B. Student, Iowa State Coll., 1950-52, Loyola U., 1952-58; BS, Mundelein Coll., 1955; postgrad., Simmons Coll., 1963-64, U. Ga., 1979, Calif. We. U., 1980. Registered dietitian. Prodn. supr. Marshall Field & Co., Chgo., 1955-59; dir. food svcs. Women's Ednl. and Indsl. Union, Boston, 1959-62, Wellesley Pub. Schs., Mass., 1962-70; regional dietitian Canteen Corp., Chgo., 1970-83; gen. mgr. bus. devel. Plantation-Sysco, Orlando, Fla., 1983-87; dir. product devel., corp. quality assurance, procurement Marriott Internat. Hdqrs., Washington, 1987-95; owner food svc. cons. svc., 1995—. Cons. Stokes Food Services, Newton, Mass., 1960-70; vis. lectr. Affiliate Produce for Better Health Found. Mem.: AAUW, Sch. Nutrition Svcs., Cons. Dietitians in Healthcare Facilities, Am. Dietetics Assn. (career adv. cons.), Food and Culinary Profls., Dietitians in Bus. and Comm., Washington Opera Guild, Met. Opera Guild. Republican. Roman Catholic. Home and Office: 1009 Pearce Dr Apt 102 Clearwater FL 33764-1107

BARRY, LANCE LEONARD, judge; b. Boston, Dec. 18, 1965; s. Leonard and Theodora Ann Pawlak. BEE, Cath. U. Am., 1988; MS, Johns Hopkins U., 1991; JD, George Mason U., 1995. Bar: Va. 1995, U.S. Ct. Appeals (fed. cir.) 1995, bar: D.C. 1998. Engring. analyst RCI Internat., Vienna, Va., 1987; engring. aide MPR Assocs., Washington, 1987; engring. technician BBN Labs., Arlington, Va., 1988; cons. Booz, Allen & Hamilton, Bethesda, Md., 1988-90, sr. cons., 1990—91; patent examiner U.S. Patent and Trademark Office, Arlington, Va., 1991-95, primary examiner, 1996-99, adminstrv. patent judge, 1999—. Spkr. Va. State Bar, Richmond, 1998—; instr. U.S. Patent and Trademark Office, Arlington, 1996-97, curriculum com., 1999—; law lectr. U.S. Patent and Trademark Office, Arlington, 1997-99, EEO counselor, 1999. Pub. adv. com. mem. Lawyers Coop. Pub., Raleigh, N.C., 1995; contbr. articles to profl. jours. Head tutor St. Francis Xavier Sch., Washington, 1997-2001; cmty. svc. v.p. St. Mary's Ch., Alexandria, Va., 2001; vol. Greater D.C. Cares, Washington, 1999—; social officer Holy Trinity Ch., Washington, 1997-98; tutor kids and chemistry program Am. Chem. Soc., 2002—; lector Our Lady of Lourdes Ch., 2002—; vol. Alexandria Christmas in April, 2000—, house capt., 2003. Mem. IEEE (manuscript referee Potentials mag. 1989—), Am. Intellectual Property Law Assn., Patent and Trademark Office Soc. (rep. 1996-98), Mensa, Phi Theta Kappa, Tau Beta Pi. Avocations: volunteering, Italian, birdwatching, travel, skiing. Office: US Patent and Trademark Office 10-A12 1225 Jefferson Davis Hwy Arlington VA 22202

BARRY, MARILYN WHITE, retired special education educator, dean; b. Weymouth, Mass., Sept. 12, 1936; d. Harland Russell and Alice Louise (Dwyer) White; m. Dennis Edward Barry, July 11, 1959; children: Dennis Edward, Christopher Gerard. BS in Edn., Bridgewater State Coll., 1958; EdM in Spl. Edn., Boston U., 1969, EdD in Spl. Edn., 1974. Tchr. Weymouth (Mass.) pub. schs., 1958-60; spl. edn. instr. Boston U., 1972-74; ast. prof. in spl. edn. Bridgewater (Mass.) State Coll., 1974-79, assoc. prof., 1979-83, prof., 1983-87, chmn. spl. edn. dept., 1979-87, coord. dept. grad. programs, 1979-87, adminstr. bilingual spl. edn., 1983-86, dean Grad. Sch., 1987-98; ret., 1998. Co-author human svc. workers curriculum materials. Recipient 3 Disting. Svc. awards Bridgewater State Coll., 1980, 82, 85; Bilingual Spl. Edn. grantee, 1980, 83; Boston U. fellow, 1967-74 Mem. CEC (Mass. chpt. founder, past pres., learning disabilities chpt.), Mass. Assn. Children with Learning Disabilities (past v.p.), Phi Delta Kappa, Pi Lambda Theta. Democrat. Roman Catholic. Home: 138 Bedford St Lakeville MA 02347-1351

BARRY, MARYANNE TRUMP, federal judge; b. N.Y.C., Apr. 5, 1937; d. Fred C. and Mary Trump; m. John J. Barry, Dec. 26, 1982; 1 child, David W. Desmond. BA, Mt. Holyoke Coll., 1958; MA, Columbia U., 1962; JD, Hofstra U., 1974, LLD (hon.), Seton Hall U.; LLD (hon.), Caldwell Coll.; LLD (hon.), Kean Coll. Bar: N.J. 1974, N.Y. 1975, U.S. Ct. Appeals (3d cir.), U.S. Supreme Ct. Asst. U.S. Atty., 1974-75; dep. chief appeals div., 1976-77; chief appeals div., 1977-82; exec. asst. U.S. Atty., 1981-82; 1st asst., 1981-83; judge U.S. Dist. Ct., N.J., 1983-99, U.S. Ct. Appeals (3d cir.), Newark, 1999—. Chmn. Com. on Criminal Law Jud. Conf. of U.S., 1994-96. Fellow Am. Bar Found.; mem. ABA, N.J. Bar Assn., Am. Judicature Soc. (bd. dirs.), Assn. Fed. Bar State of N.Y. (pres. 1982-83). Office: US Ct Appeals PO & Courthouse Bldg Rm 333 PO Box 999 Newark NJ 07101-0999*

BARRY, MILDRED CASTILLE, artist; b. Sunset, La., Feb. 23, 1924; d. Joseph Hippomene and Beatrice Victoria (Tinney) Castille; m. Francis Xavier Barry, Aug. 16, 1947; children: Christopher, Kevin, Maureen, Robin, Shane, Kim. BA in Edn., Sam Houston U., 1958. Cert. tchr., Tex. Tchr. Sacred Heart Elem., Conroe, Tex., 1959-67, Conroe Sam Houston Elem., 1967-68, Houston Ind. Sch. Dist. Elem., 1968-69. Tchr., stuent of Ernest Gaines, author-in-residence U. So. La., Lafayette, 1985-87, instr. memoir writing classes, 1995-96. Exhibited in group shows Opelonsas, La., 1973 (1st pl.). With WAC, 1944-45. Mem. Writers Guild. Roman Catholic. Avocations: reading, writing, painting, sewing, traveling. Home: 309 Beverly Dr Lafayette LA 70503-3109

BARRY, MIRANDA ROBBINS, educator, internet and television producer, writer; b. NYC, Jan. 18, 1951; d. Philip Semple and Patricia Allen (White) B. AB, Stanford U., 1972; postgrad., Columbia Law Sch., N.Y.C., 1978-79, Bank St. Coll. Edn., 2003—. Prodn. rsch. coord. The Best of Families/CTW, N.Y.C., 1975-77; freelance story analyst CBS Inc., N.Y.C., 1976-81; asst. mgr. spl. programs devel. Sta. WNET 13, N.Y.C., 1977-78; exec. coord. Nat. TV Theatre, N.Y.C., 1981-82; story editor Am. Playhouse, N.Y.C., 1982-83, dir. program devel., 1983-87, exec. story cons., 1987; dir. internat. prodn. McNeil/Allyn Films, London, 1987-88; sr. prodr. (TV series) Ghostwriter CTW, 1990, supervising prodr., 1991-94; tchg. fellow N.Y.C. Bd. Edn., 2002—; dir. Mirror Repertory Co., Arts in Edn., 2003—. Instr TV writing New Sch. Social Rsch., N.Y.C., 1982-83; instr. screen writing Womens Interart Ctr., N.Y.C., 1981-83; adj. assoc. prof. Columbia U. Sch. Film, 1986-87, prof., 1988, 94-96; writer One Life to Live, ABC-TV, N.Y.C., 1994-95; co-dir., organizer TV Theater Workshop Sta. KTCA, Mpls., 1983; creator TV series Mom and Dad/Embassy-NBC, 1983; v.p., lic. support Zing Sys. LP, Denver, 1995; cons. feature film Children's TV Workshop, 1996—; exec. in charge of devel. JP Kids, 1996-97, v.p. creative affairs, 1997-99, sr. v.p. creative affairs, 2000-03. Author: Time for Kids Readers, 2003; (play) Friends and Relations, 1981, (TV adaptation) A World to Care For, (TV series) MedSchool, 1980, (TV miniseries) Sara and Gerald, 1988, Who is Mouse Max?, 1993; co-author: Quincy Script Blood Ties, 1980, Basil, 1990; (screenplay) Pinkerton's Angel, 1989; scriptwriting resource person Sundance Inst., 1984-86; story editor Eugene O'Neill Nat. Playwright's Conf., 1984—; co-exec. prodr. (TV series) Green Wilma, 1997; exec. prodr. Yahooligans, 1999—; project dir. Going Global, KQED and World Affairs Coun., 1999-2000; dir. Romeo and Juliet, Mirror Repertory Co., 2003. Rape victim counselor St. Luke's Hosp., N.Y.C., 1979-81; mem. alumnae bull. com. Miss Porter's Sch., 1979-84, vol. Children's Aid Soc. McKnight grantee Playwright's Ctr., Mpls., 1983. Mem. Writers Guild Am-East, Dramatists Guild, N.Y. Women in Film (sec., bd. dirs. 1984-85, 90-91). E-mail: mrbarry237@aol.com.

BARRY, NADA DAVIES, retail business owner; b. London, Dec. 2, 1930; d. Ernest Albert J. and Natalie Emma (Rossin) Davies; m. Jacob J. Ebeling-Koning, Aug. 1952 (div. 1962); m. Robert I Barry, 1963 (div. 1976); children: Natasha E.-K. Sigmund, Derek B. Ebeling-Koning, Gwen E.-K. Waddington, Trebor C. Barry. Student, Mills Coll., 1948-50; BA, Barnard Coll., 1952. Owner The Wharf Shop, Sag Harbor, N.Y., 1968—. Founder Sag Harbor Youth Com. Bd. dirs. The Hampton Day Sch., Bridgehampton, N.Y., 1966-74, Youth Advocacy Resource Devel., 1997-01; active Noyac Civic Coun., LWV of The Hamptons; founder Sag Harbor Youth Com. Mem. AAUW, Sag Harbor C. of C. (bd. dirs.), Nat. Trust Historic Preservation, Nature Conservancy, Sanibel-Captiva Conservation Found., So. Poverty Law Ctr., Sag Harbor Hist. Soc., Sag Harbor Whaling Museum, Bailey-Matthews Shell Mu., Mills Coll. Club (N.Y. chpt.), Williams Coll. Club. Avocations: gardening, photography, traveling, shelling, theatre. Office: The Wharf Shop PO Box 922 Sag Harbor NY 11963-0025

BARRY, NANCY MARIE, bank executive; b. Kansas City, Kans., Aug. 2, 1949; d. John Joseph and Lorna Marie Barry. BA in Econs., Stanford U., 1971; MBA, Harvard U., 1975. Divsn. chief pub. sector mgmt. World Bank, Washington, 1986-87, divsn. chief indsl. devel., 1987-90; pres. Women's World Banking, N.Y.C., 1990—. Founding mem. World Bank Consultative Group to Assist the Poorest-Policy Advisory Group, Washington; adv. com. Harvard Social Enterprise, Mass. Mem. Harvard Club. Office: Women's World Banking 8 W 40th St Fl 9 New York NY 10018-3993 Fax: (212) 768-8519. E-mail: nmbarry@swwb.org.

BARRY, RICHARD A. public relations executive; b. Chgo., Ill., Nov. 11, 1934; BS in Polit. Sci., Loyola U., 1956; cert. in publ. and graphics, U. Chgo., 1958. Asst. editor No. Ind. Pub. Svc. Co., Hammond, 1956-58; dir. pub. rels. Loyola U., Chgo., 1958-66; dir. devel. and pub. rels. St. Xavier Coll., Chgo., 1966-68; sr. v.p. Daniel J. Edelman, Inc., Chgo., 1968-70; exec. v.p. PCI, Chgo., 1970-72; pres. Pub. Comms., Inc., Chgo., 1972—. Office: Public Communications Inc 35 E Wacker Dr Chicago IL 60601-2109

BARRY, RICHARD FRANCIS, retired life insurance company executive; b. N.Y.C., Aug. 28, 1917; s. Thomas Francis and Gertrude Mary (Spillane) B.; m. Irene Patricia Schulties, July 24, 1948. BBA, St. John's U., Bklyn., 1948; JD, Fordham U., 1953. Bar: N.Y. 1954. With Met. Life Ins. Co., N.Y.C., 1937-82, v.p., office of pres., then v.p. human resources, 1979-80, sr. v.p. human resources, 1980-81, sr. v.p. office of chmn., 1981-82, ret. 1982. Mem. faculty St. John's U., 1955-60 Bd. dirs. Urban Acad. for Mgmt., Inc., 1979-82, Met. Life Found., 1981-82; sec. Nat. Assn. Drug Abuse Problems, N.Y.C., 1979-82; mem. Coop. Edn. Commn. N.Y.C., 1979-82. Served with AUS, 1943-45. Mem. Adminstrv. Mgmt. Soc. (pres. N.Y.C. chpt. 1972-73), Life Office Mgmt. Assn., Bar Assn. State N.Y., N.Y. C. of C. and Industry. Republican. Roman Catholic. Home: 237 Berry Hill Rd Syosset NY 11791-2105

BARRY, RICHARD FRANCIS, III, publishing executive; b. Norfolk, Va., Jan. 18, 1943; s. Richard F. and Mary Margaret (Perry) B.; m. Carolyn Ann Kennett, Aug. 7, 1965; children: Carolyn Michelle, Christopher David. BA, LaSalle Coll., 1964; JD, U. Va., 1967. Bar: Va. 1967. Assoc. Kaufman, Oberndorfer & Spainhour (now Kaufman and Canoles), Norfolk, 1967-71, ptnr., 1972-73; corp. sec. Landmark Comm., Inc., Norfolk, 1973-74; pres. Roanoke Times & World-News, Va., 1974-76, The Virginian-Pilot and The Ledger-Star, Norfolk, 1976-78, pub., 1983-90; pres., COO, dir. Landmark Comm., Inc., Norfolk, 1978—, CEO, 1984-91, vice chmn., 1991—. Bd. dirs. The Weather Channel, Greensboro News and Record, Inc., Times World Corp., Trader Pub. Co., Capital Gazette Comm. Inc., AutoTrader.com LLC. Trustee or past trustee Norfolk Acad., Chrysler Mus., U. Va. Colgate Darden Bus. Sch. Found., Cath. H.S. Found., Old Dominion Univ. Ednl. Found., Suffolk Ctr. for Cultural Arts; bd. dirs., past pres., campaign chmn. United Way of South Hampton Rds.; bd. visitors, past rector Old Dominion U., co-chmn. capital campaign. Office: Landmark Comm Inc 150 W Brambleton Ave Norfolk VA 23510-2018

BARRY, ROBERT MICHAEL, education educator; b. N.Y.C., N.Y., Sept. 11, 1927; s. Michael Joseph Barry and Barbara June Earley; m. Dorothy A. Barry, May 22, 1985; children: Timothy J., Rosemary F. Nole, Regina M., Thomas A., Gregory M. AB, Iona Coll., 1946—50; AM, Fordham U, 1950—53, PhD, 1953—63; post studies, U. Chgo., 1969—70. Asst. dean, registrar Iona Coll., New Rochelle, NY, 1950—53; asst. prof. Rider Coll., Trenton, NJ, 1953—56; assoc. prof. Coll. of Scholastica, Duluth, Minn., 1956—63; prof., assoc. prof. Loyola U, Chgo., 1963—99, emeritus prof. of Philosophy, 2000—. Cons. Carnegie Found. and Acad. for Edn. Devel., Princeton, NJ, 1981; cons. Career Devel. Maricopa Cmty. Coll., Phoenix, 1982; cons. U of Mich., Ann Arbor, 1984, Lilly Endowment, Inc., Indpls., 1988; faculty devel. State of Pa., 1988; cons. retirement programs numberous Colleges and Universities. Author: Jour. of the History of Ideas, Am. Bebedictine Review, Internat. Philos. Quar., Inquiry, 1965, Am. Philos. and the Future, On Coll. Tchg., Chronicle of Higher Edn., Nat. Cath. Reporter; editor (author): The Medieval: New Dimensions, Listening: Am. Culture; contbr. articles papers. Bd. mem. Family Svc. Soc. of Am., Duluth, Minn., 1959—62. USNR, 1945—46. Grantee Post Doc Fellow, Soc. for Values in Higher Edn., 1969—70, Fund for the Improvement of Post-secondary Edn., Office of Edn. Dept. of Health, Edn., and Welfre, 1976—77, Career Devel. Program, Dpt. of Health, Edn., and Welfare, 1978—81, Nat. Dissemination Conf., Faculty Devel. and Retirement Program. Mem.: Gold Key, Blue Key. Home: PMB 271 2859 Central St Evanston IL 60201 Office: 112 Vista Del Mar Dr Santa Barbara CA 93109-1050

BARRY, STEVE, sculptor, educator; b. Jersey City, June 22, 1956; s. Thomas Daniel and Lorraine (Lowery) B. BFA, Sch. Visual Arts, N.Y.C., 1980; MFA, Hunter Coll., N.Y.C., 1984. Adj. lectr. Hunter Coll., 1984-89; assoc. prof. U. N.Mex., Albuquerque, 1989—. Kohler Arts and Industry Residency, 1996; bd. dirs. Albuquerque Ctr. Contemporary Arts. Exhbns. include Bklyn. Army Terminal, N.Y.C., 1983, City Gallery, N.Y.C., 1986, 90, Storefront for Art and Architecture, 1988, Artists Space, N.Y.C., 1989, Santa Barbara Art Mus., 1990, Kohler Arts Ctr., Sheboygan, Wis., 1991, Hirshhorn Mus., Washington, 1990, Fla. State U., 1992, Contemporary Art Mus., Houston, 1992, CAFE Gallery, Albuquerque, 1993, Charolette Jackson, Santa Fe, 1993, Ctr. for Contemporary Arts, Santa Fe, 1994, U. Wyo. Art Mus., 1995, Site Santa Fe, 1996, Sheldon Art Mus., Lincoln, Nebr., 1997, U. N.Mex. Art Mus., Albuquerque, 1997, Cedar Rapids (Iowa) Mus. of Art, 1998, Albuquerque Contemporary Art Ctr., 2000, Plan B, Santa Fe, 2000. Grantee Clocktower Nat. Studio, 1985, NEA, 1986, 88, 90, N.Y. State Coun. for the Arts, 1987, N.Y. Found. for the Arts, 1988, Rsch. grantee Coll. Fine Arts N.Mex., 2002; recipient AVA award, 1990. Home: PO Box 1046 Corrales NM 87048-1046 Office: U NMex Dept Art & Art History Albuquerque NM 87131-0001

BARRY, TERENCE PATRICK, endocrinologist, aquaculturist; b. Washington, Sept. 20, 1954; s. Harry Joseph and Carol (Esser) B.; m. Amy Lynn Reyes, Jan. 11, 1986; children Thomas Patrick, Timothy Patrick, Caroline Catherine. BS, U. Wis., 1977, PhD, 1994; MS, U. Hawaii, 1989. Rsch. assoc. U.S. AID, Philippines, 1986-88; rschr. U. Wis. Aqua. Program, Madison, 1990—. Chmn. N. Ctrl. Regional Aquaculture Ctr., USDA, 1996— Contbr. articles to profl. jours. including Jour. Exptl. Zoology, Aquaculture, Gen. and Comparative Endocrinology, Fish Physiology and Biochemistry; assoc. editor Progressive Fish Culturist, Bethesda, Md., 1996—. Rsch. fellow Fulbright Program, U. Tokyo, 1988. Mem. Am. Fisheries Soc. (exec. com physiology sect. 1996—), Asian Fisheries Soc., Am. Soc. of Integrative and Comparative Biology. Democrat. Roman Catholic. Achievements include contributions to understanding the regulation of: (1) the physiological stress response in cultured fish species; (2) interactions between stress and reproductive physiology in fish. Office: U Wis Aquaculture Program 123 Babcock Hall Madison WI 55706

BARRY, THOMAS CORCORAN, investment counselor; b. Cleve., Feb. 9, 1944; s. Willard Corcoran and Harriet (Mullin) Barry; m. Patricia Ryan, Feb. 14, 1976; children: Hannah McGrath(dec.), Ryan Nichols(dec.), Oliver Mullin, Lillian Nicholson, Michael Corcoran. BA in Latin Am. Studies, Yale U., 1966; MBA, Harvard U., 1969. Chartered Fin. Analyst. Market research analyst Corning Glass Works, Brazil and Japan, 1966-67; investment analyst T. Rowe Price Assos., Inc., Balt., 1969-70; partner Cole, Thompson and Barry, Inc., Cleve., 1971-73; pres. Rowe Price New Horizons Fund, Balt., 1973-81, Saratoga Assocs., 1981-83; pres., CEO Rockefeller and Co. Inc., 1983-93; pres. Zephyr Mgmt., L.P., 1994—. Dir. numerous cos. Trustee William T. Grant Found., 1989—, Univ. Sch., Cleve., 1998—; mem. Yale Pres.'s Coun. on Internat. Activities; mem. dean's coun. Harvard U.-Kennedy Sch. Govt. Office: 320 Park Ave New York NY 10022-6815

BARRY, WAYNE STEPHEN, physician, educator; b. Oak Ridge, Tenn. s. Lewis Arthur and Ruth Florence (Benjamin) B.; m. Patricia Marie Lysaght, June 29, 1974 (div.); children: Shannon Sinnott, Cara Nevin; m. Diana Lynn Harmon, Aug. 10, 1986; children: Marya Frances Eileen, Caryn Alexa Charlotte. Diplomate Am. Bd. Internal Medicine, Am. Bd. Emergency Medicine. Intern Cleve. Met. Gen. Hosp., 1973—74; resident Balt. City Hosps., 1974—76; med. dir. Md. Penitentiary, Balt., 1978—83, Balt. City Jail, 1980—83; med. dir. emergency dept. Harbor Hosp. Med. Ctr., Balt., 1984—87, Health Ctrl., Orlando, Fla., 1987—94; regional med. dir. mil. svcs. Emergency Med. Svcs. Assocs./InPhyNet, Ft. Lauderdale, Fla., 1994—97; regional med. dir. DOC Emergency Med. Svcs. Assocs. Correctional Care, Jessup, Md., 1997—99; staff emergency dept. physician Fla. Hosp. Fish Meml., Orange City, 2000—, asst. med. dir. emergency dept. Instr., asst. prof. medicine Johns Hopkins U., Balt., 1978-84; asst. clin. prof. medicine U. Md., Balt., 1984-87; asst. med. dir. emergency dept. Nat. Naval Med. Ctr., Bethesda, 1984-97, med. dir. emergency dept Naval Hosp. Patuxent River, Md., 1994, Naval Hosp. Cherry Point, N.C., 1995; asst. prof. medicine Uniformed Svcs. U. Health Scis., Bethesda, Md., 1997—. Contbr. articles to profl. jours. Fellow Am. Coll. Emergency Physicians. Democrat. Jewish. Avocations: golfing, gardening, nascar racing. Home and Office: 397 Caddie Dr Debary FL 32713-4514

BARRY, WILLIAM ANTHONY, priest, writer; b. Worcester, Mass., Nov. 22, 1930; s. William and Catherine (McKenna) B. AB, Boston Coll., 1956, STL, 1963; MA, Fordham U., 1960; PhD, U. Mich., 1968. Joined S.J., Roman Cath. Ch., 1950, ordained priest, 1962. Tchr. high sch. Fairfield (Conn.) Prep., 1956-58; lectr. U. Mich., Ann Arbor, 1968-69; from asst. to assoc. prof. Weston Jesuit Sch. of Theology, Cambridge, Mass., 1969-78; rector Jesuit community Boston Coll., Chestnut Hill, Mass., 1988-91; vice provincial S.J. of New Eng., Boston, 1978-84, asst. novice dir., 1985-88, provincial, 1991-97; co-dir. S.J. Tertianship, 1997—. Dir. staff Ctr. for Religious Devel., Cambridge, 1971-78; trustee Boston Coll., Chestnut Hill, 1988-91, adj. assoc. prof., 1989-91. Co-author: Communication, Conflict, Marriage, 1974, The Practice of Spiritual Direction, 1982, Contemplatives in Action, 2002; author: God and You, 1987, Seek My Face, 1989, Now Choose Life, 1990, Paying Attention to God, 1990, Finding God in All Things, 1991, Spiritual Direction and the Encounter with God, 1992, God's Passionate Desire and Our Response, 1993, Allowing the Creator to Deal with the Creature, 1994, What Do I Want in Prayer?, 1994, Who Do You Say I Am?, 1996, Our Way of Proceeding, 1997, With an Everlasting Love, 1999, Letting God Come Close, 2001; editor-in-chief (quar. jour.) Human Development, 2003—. Mem. Phi Beta Kappa, Phi Kappa Phi. Democrat. Roman Catholic. Avocations: reading, writing. Home and Office: Campion Ctr 319 Concord Rd Weston MA 02493-1310 E-mail: frbarry@bc.edu.

BARRYMORE, DREW, actress; b. L.A., Feb. 22, 1975; d. John Jr. and Jaid Barrymore. Appearances include (films) Altered States, 1980, E.T.: The Extra-Terrestrial, 1982, Irreconcilable Differences, 1984, Firestarter, 1984, Cat's Eye, 1985, Poison Ivy, 1992, Bad Girls, 1994, Boys on the Side, 1995, Batman Forever, 1995, Mad Love, 1995, Wishful Thinking, 1996, Scream, 1996, Like a Lady, 1996, Everyone Says I Love You, 1996, All She Wanted,

1997, Best Men, 1997, Never Been Kissed, 1998 (also prodr.), Home Fries, 1998, The Wedding Singer, 1998, Ever After: A Cinderella Story, 1998, Never Been Kissed (also exec. prodr.), 1999, Olive, the Other Reindeer, 1999 (voice & exec. prodr.), Titan A.E., 2000 (voice), Charlie's Angels, 2000 (also prodr.), Donnie Darko (also exec. prodr.), 2001, Riding in Cars With Boys, 2001, Confessions of a Dangerous Mind, 2002, Charlie's Angels: Full Throttle (also prodr.), 2003, Duplex, 2003 (also prodr.); (TV episodes) Amazing Stories, 1985, Con Sawyer and Hucklemary Finn, 1985, 2000 Malibu Road, 1992; (host) Hansel and Gretel, 1986; (TV movies) Suddenly Love, 1978, Bogie, 1980, The Screaming Woman, 1986, Babes in Toyland, 1986, Conspiracy of Love, 1987, Beyond Control: The Amy Fisher Story, 1993; (TV spls.) Screen Actors Guild 50th Anniversary, 1984, Night of 100 Stars II, 1985, Happy Birthday, Hollywood, 1987, Disney's 30th Anniversary, 1987.

BARSALONA, FRANK SAMUEL, theatrical agent; b. S.I., N.Y., Mar. 31, 1938; s. Peter and Mary (Rotunno) B.; m. June Harris, Sept. 1, 1966; 1 dau., Nicole. BA, Wagner Coll., S.I., 1958; postgrad., Herbert Berghof Sch., N.Y.C., 1959-60. Agt. Gen. Artists Corp., N.Y.C., 1960-64; founder, since pres. Premier Talent Agy. (merged with William Morris Agy.), N.Y.C., 1964—2002; co-founder, pres. Phila. Fury, 1977-80. Lectr., moderator music industry; founding ptnr. Precision Media Corp., 1984-97. Bd. govs., trustee Rock & Roll Hall of Fame Mus., Cleve. Named to Performance Mag. Hall of Fame, 1988; recipient numerous awards (cover subject spl. issue), Billboard Publs., 1984, Silver Clef award, Nordoff Robbins, 2002. Mem. Mus. Am. Folk Art. (internat. adv. bd.). Office: William Morris Agy 1325 Ave of Ams New York NY 10019

BARSAMIAN, J(OHN) ALBERT, lawyer, judge, educator, criminologist, arbitrator; b. Troy, N.Y., May 1, 1934; s. John and Virginia Barsamian; m. Alice Missirilan, Apr. 21, 1963; children: Bonnie, Tamara. BS in Psychology with honors, Union Coll., 1956; JD, 1968; LLB, Albany Law Sch., 1959; postgrad., SUNY, Albany, 1964, Nat. Jud. Coll., 1997. Bar: N.Y. 1961, U.S. Dist. Ct. (no. dist.) N.Y. 1961, U.S. Supreme Ct. 1967; fire tng. cert. N.Y. State Exec. Dept. Pvt. practice, 1961—; dir. criminal sci., chmn. dept. Russell Sage Coll., 1970-88, assoc. prof. criminal sci., 1977-82, prof., 1982-87, prof. emeritus, 1987—. Lectr. office local govt. divsn. criminal justice svcs. State N.Y., 1964—72, N.Y. State Police Acad., 1970; judge adminstrv. law N.Y. State Pub. Employment Rels. Bd., 1996—2001, supervising judge, asst. dir. pub. employment practice and representation, 2001—; faculty pub. affairs and policy pub. svc. tng. program Nelson A. Rockefeller Coll., 1986—91, Sch. Labor Rels. Ext. divsn. Cornell U., 1986; gaming cons. Gov's Office Indian Rels., NY, 1991—92; spl. counsel Office of Police Chief, Cohoes, NY, 1986—92, to city mgr., Troy, NY, 1993; counsel Watervliet Police Assn., 1967—74, Cohoes Police Assn., 1967—74, Colonie Police Assn., 1977—80, Troy Police Command Officers Assn., 1981—85, North Greenbush Police Assn., 1985—90, Office of the Police Chief, Syracuse, NY, 1985—90, Fire Dept. Union, Albany, NY, 1986, Shenectady Fire Fighters Union, 1992—95; gen. counsel Internat. Narcotic Enforcement Officers Assn., 1982—84, Troy Uniformed Firefighters Assn., 1977—97; spl. investigator Rensselaer County Dist. Atty., 1959—61; mem. law guardian panel N.Y. State Family Ct., 1967—77; mem. mediation panel N.Y. State Pub. Employment Rels. Bd., 1968—73; supervising judge, asst. dir. Pub. Employment Practices and Representation, 2001—; lectr. Inst. Legal Studies Albany (N.Y.) Law Sch., 2003. Founder, chmn. dept. police sci. Hudson Valley C.C., 1961-69; mem. adv. bd. History Ctr. Skidmore Coll., 1993—; bd. dirs. Rensselaer County ARC, 1966-70; mem. alumni coun. Union Coll., 1981-86; mem. parish coun. St. Peter Armenian Ch., Watervliet, N.Y., 1979-83, chmn., 1981-83, vice chmn., 1984; evaluator office of non-collegiate programs N.Y. State Dept. Edn., 1985—; hon. dep. sheriff St. Mary Parish (La.); mem. Rensselaer County Criminal Justice Coordinating Coun., 1976-78. Decorated chevalier, knight comdr. Sovereign Order of Cyprus; recipient Lawyers Coop. Pub. Co. prize in criminal law, 1957, Police Sci. Students award, Hudson Valley C.C., 1968, meritorious svc. to law enforcement award, Law Enforcement Officers Soc., 1969, Archbishop's cert. merit, Armenian Ch. Am., 1973, Gabrielli Meml. award, Albany Law Sch., 2003; scholar Tarzian, Union Coll., 1952—56, Porter, Albany Law Sch., 1954—56, Saxton, 1956—59. Mem.: Internat. Coll. Master Advocates, N.Y. State Assn. Adminstrv. Law Judges (bd. dirs. 1999, 2001), Am. Coll. Barristers, N.Y. State Trial Lawyers Assn., Union Coll. Alumni Assn. (Silver medal 1956), Am. Assn. Criminology, Acad. Criminal Justice Scis., Am. Arbitration Assn. (svc. award 1983), Nat. Assn. Adminstrv. Law Judges, N.Y. Bar Assn. (chmn. com. on police 1970—72, trial lawyers sect. com. contg. legal edn. 1977—97, subcom. on adminstrv. law judges 2000), ABA (com. on police selection and tng. 1967—69), ATLA, N.Y. Vet. Police Assn. (life; counsel), Rose Croix (most wise master Delta chpt. 1986), Masonic Vet. Assn. Troy (life), Les Amis d'Escoffier Soc., Lambda Epsilon Chi, Alpha Phi Sigma, Phi Delta Theta. Home and Office: 5 Sage Hill Ln Albany NY 12204-1315

BARSAN, ROBERT BLAKE, dentist; b. Akron, Ohio, Apr. 7, 1948; s. Emil O. and Letitia (Dobrin) B.; m. Cheryl Lee Adams, Dec. 16, 1972; children: Erin Lee, Kathleen Letitia. BS, U. Cin., 1970; DDS, Ohio State U., 1974. Resident U. Chgo., 1976; gen. practice dentistry Cuyahoga Falls, Ohio, 1976—. Contbr. editor Modern Dental mag., 1984-89. Bd. dirs. Akron Civic Theatre, 1996—. Fellow Acad. Gen. Dentistry (bd. dirs. Ohio chpt.); mem. ADA (chmn. CPR 1984-90), Am. Endodontic Soc., Akron Gnathological Soc. (pres. 1986), Am. Acad. Cosmetic Dentistry, Fedn. Dentaire Internat., Canton Akron Cleve. Orthodontic Study Club (pres. 1994-98). Home: 3084 Silver Lake Blvd Silver Lake OH 44224-3033 Office: 330 Stow Ave Cuyahoga Falls OH 44221-2516

BARSANO, CHARLES PAUL, medical educator, dean; BS in Biology, Loyola U., Chgo., 1969; PhD in Pathology, U. Chgo., 1974, MD, 1975. Diplomate Am. Bd. Internal Medicine. Resident internal medicine Barnes Hosp./Washington U., St. Louis, 1975-77; fellow endocrinology U. Chgo. Sch. Medicine, 1977-79, rsch. assoc. endocrinology, 1979-80; asst. prof. medicine Northwestern U. and Lakeside VA Med. Ctr., 1980-85, U. Health Scis./Chgo. Med. Sch. and North Chgo. VA Med. Ctr., 1985-87, assoc. prof., 1987-92, prof. medicine, 1992-98, assoc. prof. pharmacology and molecular biology, 1992-94, prof. pharmacology and molecular biology, 1994-98, acting dean Med. Sch., 1998—99, assoc. dean for clin. affairs, vice-chmn. dept. medicine, 1999—2001, interim dean, 2001—; staff physician med. svc./endocrinology sect. North Chgo. VA Med. Ctr. Mem. editl. bd. Thyroid, 1990-95; mem. adv. bd. Toxic Substance Mechanisms, 1993-99. Recipient Bausch and Lomb Nat. Sci. award, 1965, Individual Nat. Rsch. Svc. award, 1979-80. Mem. Internat. Coun. for Control of Iodine Deficiency Disorders, Assn. Am. Med. Colls. (group on ednl. affairs sect. on resident edn.), Am. Assn. Clin. Endocrinologists, Am. Thyroid Assn. (fiscal com. 1982-85, pub. health com. 1986-88, membership com. 1990-93, chmn. membership com. 1993, local organizing com. 1994, bylaws com. 1995—), Endocrine Soc., Chgo. Endocrine Club (pres. 1984-85), Sigma Xi, Alpha Omega Alpha. Office: Office Clin Affairs Finch Univ Health Scis Chgo Med Sch North Chicago IL 60064 Fax: 847-578-3320. E-mail: barsanoc@finchcms.edu.

BARSHIS, VICTORIA R. GARNIER, social worker; b. Oakland, Calif., Dec. 31, 1956; children: Bradley, Christopher. BA summa cum laude, Bridgewater (Va.) Coll., 1980; MSW, Washington U., 1982. Cert. divorce mediator, acad. of cert. social worker; bd. cert. diplomate social work; qualified clinc. social worker; lic. clin. social worker. Therapist Kids in the Middle, 1980-81, 85-86; social worker Luth. Family and Children's Svcs., 1981-88, Hyland Child and Adolescent Ctr., 1988-89; dir. Adoption Assocs., 1989-92; therapist Cancer Family Care, 1992-94; social worker Multiple Sclerosis Soc., 1992-96; psychiat. social worker Barnes Hosp., 1993-96; pvt. practice Stonebridge Counseling, 1993-96; patient svcs. mgr. Leukemia and Lymphoma Soc., 1996—; pvt. practice Affiliated Psychotherapists and the Attention Deficit Ctr., 1996—; owner Creative Memories, 1996—. Contbr. articles to profl. jours. Mem. St. Louis Cmty. Adoption Coun., 1985-93, St. Louis Foster Care Coalition, 1989-93, Teen Pregnancy Network, 1990-93, Youth Svcs. Network, 1990-93, Am. Adoption Congress, 1989-93, N.Am. Coun. on Adoptable Children, 1984-93, St. Louis Task Force on Substance Impacted Children, 1990-93; adminstrv. vol. Girl Scouts, St. Louis, 1985—; pres. Cancer Aygs. Network, 1999-. Recipient Gold Laurel award, 1994. Mem. NASW (women's issues com. 1982—), Acad. of Family Mediators, Assn. Oncology Social Workers, Soc. Social Work Leaders in Health Care.

BARSKY, CONSTANCE KAY, education educator; b. Newark, Nov. 3, 1944; d. Bernard Benjamin Barsky and Evelyn Josephine Hach; m. Steven George Katz. BS, Denison U., Granville, Ohio, 1966; PhD, Washington U., St. Louis, 1975. Rsch. assoc. geology U. Mo., Columbia, 1971—77; advanced scientist Owens-Corning Fiberglas, Gransville, 1977—78, lab. supr., 1978—86; adminstrv. mgr. chemistry Ohio State U., Columbus, 1987—92, dir. Discovery, 1992—96; dir. Learning by Redesign, Ohio State U., Columbus, 1996—. Mem. nat. adv. coun. NSF/Nat. Ctr. of Excellence for Advanced Mfg. Edn, Dayton, 1995—98; sec. Denison U. Rsch. Found., Granville, 1984—; trustee Denison U., 1995—2001; fellow, sr. vis. rsch. scholar Dibner Inst., Cambridge, Mass., 2002. Contbr. Chair com. Granville Profl. and Bus. Assn., 1998—2001; advisor Alpha Chi Omega, Granville, 1985—. Mem.: Internat. History, Philosophy and Sci. Tchg. Group, Am. Assn. Physics Tchrs., Sigma Xi. Avocations: travel, needlecrafts. Office: Learning by Redesign Ohio State Univ 174 W 18th Ave Columbus OH 43210

BARSKY, IRENE J. graphics designer; b. Kiev, Ukraine, USSR, May 25, 1978; d. Edward Grinyov and Lana Barsky; m. Richard S. Schwalb, Mar. 19, 1997. BFA, B in Graphic Design, RISD, 2001. Graphic designer Roplab, 1999—2000, Sequel Comm., Providence, 2000, Hasbro, Providence, 2001; graphic designer, cons. Tupperware, Orlando, Fla., 2001—03; media design specialist Your Net Connection, Schaumburg, Ill., 2003—. Tchr. Buffalo Grove (Ill.) Pk. Dist., 1999; instr. RISD, Providence, 2000—01. Co-author, illustrator: book, CD ROM Que and His Missing Dot, 2000, book Once in Numberland..., 2001. Scholar, RISD, 1997—2001. Avocations: painting, graphic design, writing. Personal E-mail: barskyi@aol.com.

BARSNESS, RICHARD WEBSTER, management educator, administrator; b. Elbow Lake, Minn., Apr. 26, 1935; s. Russel E. and Joanna (Warga) B.; m. Dorothea L. Gother, Aug. 22, 1964; children: Karen Louise, Erik Richard. BS, U. Minn., 1957, MA, 1958, MAP.A., 1960, PhD, 1963. Budget analyst U.S. Bur. Budget, Washington, 1960-61; instr., asst. prof. Northwestern U., Evanston, Ill., 1962-69, assoc. prof., 1969-78, assoc. dean, 1972-78; dean, prof. Lehigh U., Bethlehem, Pa., 1978-92, prof., 1978—, Iacocca prof. bus., 1992-93, exec. dir. Iacocca Inst., 1992-95, Univ. disting. svc. prof., 1995—; pres. Lexington Group, Inc., 1997—. Exec. sec. Lexington Group in Transport History, 1969-89; pres. Bus. History Conf., 1981-82; lectr. Transp. Ctr., Evanston, Ill., 1964-84; editl. cons. Various pubs. Contbr.: articles to profl. jours.; editor: Lexington Newsletter. Mem. Gov.'s Adv. Coun. State of Ill., 1969—72; gen. chmn. United Way Lehigh U., 1981; v.p., bd. dirs. Episcopal Ho., Allentown, Pa., 1999—, pres., 2003. Recipient R.R. and E.C. Hillman award Lehigh U., 1991. Mem.: Acad. Internat. Bus., Internat. Assn. for Bus. and Soc., Bus. History Conf. (trustee 1978—81, pres. 1981—82), Transp. Rsch. Forum, Acad. Mgmt., Phi Beta Kappa, Beta Gamma Sigma. Republican. Episcopalian. Home: 769 Apollo Dr Bethlehem PA 18017-2556 Office: Lehigh U Coll Bus 621 Taylor St Bethlehem PA 18015-3117 E-mail: rwb0@lehigh.edu.

BARSON, ROSS J. music educator, assistant principal; s. Vaughn P. and Gertrude M. Pat Barson; m. Peggy B. Bowen, June 3, 1982; children: Sarah, Crystal, Steven. MusB, Boise State U., 1985; MEd in Adminstrn., U. Idaho, 2000. Cert. Idaho Secondary Educator 1985, Idaho Sch. Adminstr. 2000. Dir. bands/choirs Shelley Sch. Dist., Shelley, Idaho, 1985—86; dir. bands Sugar-Salem Sch. Dist., Sugar City, Idaho, 1986—91; dir. bands Minidoka County Sch. Dist., Rupert, Idaho, 1991—; asst. prin. Paul (Idaho) Elem. Sch., 2002—. Dir.(All-State Jr. High Band): Idaho Music Educators Assn. All-State Conf./Insvc., 2000 (I.M.E.A. Cert., 2000). Mem.: Idaho Music Educators Assn. (pres. Dist. VI 1990—91, pres.-elect Dist. IV 2002), Music Educators Nat. Conf. Mem. Lds Ch. Avocations: fishing, hiking, camping, travel.

BARSOUM, MICHEL W. materials engineer, educator; b. Cairo, Jan. 1, 1955; s. Wadie and Nathalie Barsoum; m. Patricia Lyons; children: Katherin Melchiore, Michael. BSc, American Univ, Cairo, Egypt, 1977; MSc, U. Mo., 1980; PhD, MIT, 1985. Disting. prof. Drexel U., Phila., 1985—. Author: Fundamentals of Ceramics, 1997 (, , .), over 100 refereed publs. Recipient Humboldt/Max Planck award sr. US scientists, Humboldt Found., Germany. Mem.: Am. Ceramic Soc. Achievements include patents in field. Office: Drexel U 32 and Chesnut Philadelphia PA 19104 Home Fax: 215 895 6760; Office Fax: 215 895 6760. Personal E-mail: barsoumw@drexel.edu. Business E-Mail: barsoumw@drexel.edu.

BARSUGLI, JESSE BENJAMIN, lab administrator; b. Pasadena, Calif., Mar. 29, 1972; s. Norman L. and Adelfa F. Barsugli. BS in biology, BS in psychology, Liberty U., 1999. Lab. / tchg. asst. Liberty U. - Chemistry Dept., Lynchburg, Va., 1993—94; med. nursing technician Centra Health - Lynchburg Gen. Hosp., Lynchburg, Va., 1996—98; prodn. lab. technician ARC Blood Services, Los Angeles, Calif., 2001—02, lab. supr. Irvine, Calif., 2002—. Spiritual life dir. Liberty U. Student Affairs Dept., Lynchburg, Va., 1993—96; vol. / pre-med rotation Riverside Regional Med. Ctr., Riverside, Calif., 1991. Recipient Outstanding Young Men of Am., OYA, 1996, Outstanding Student Citizen, LA Times/ LA Dodgers Orgn., 1988, Outstanding Achievement in Promoting Profession of Lab. Medicine, Am. Soc. Clin. Pathology, 2003. Mem.: Nat. Forensic League (life; spkr./debator 1989—90, Degree of Merit 1990). Conservative. Bapt. Avocations: travel, hiking, camping, sports, photography. Home: 1120 Euclid Ave San Gabriel CA 91776-3011 Office: American Red Cross Blood Services 1130 S Vermont Ave Los Angeles CA 90006 Personal E-mail: phoenixlight@hotmail.com. E-mail: barsuglij@usa.redcross.org.

BARSUK, SIDNEY ALAN, management consultant, educator; b. Batavia, N.Y., June 22, 1941; s. Max and Nellie (Greenberg) B.; m. Maxene Frances Soloway, Aug. 19, 1967; children: Peter Scott, Jeffrey Howard. BS, Rochester Inst. Tech., 1969, MBA, 1971. Cert. fundraising exec. Acting devel. dir. Rochester Inst. Tech., 1969-72, spl. asst. to v.p., 1971-72; dir. devel. Upper Iowa Coll., Fayette, 1972-73; regional devel. officer Northwood Inst., Midland, Mich., 1973-75; asst. v.p. devel. Jackson Park Hosp., Chgo., 1975-80, v.p. resource devel., 1980-90; v.p. devel. St. Francis Hosp. and Health Ctr., Blue Island, Ill., 1990-92; v.p. Brakeley, John Paul Jones, Inc., Stamford, Conn., 1992-94; bus., mktg. & mgmt. instr. Rosevelt U., Nat. Louis U., Chgo., 1994—. Dir. devel. Five Hosp. Program, Chgo., 1995-97; pres. Barsuk Group, 1997—; ptnr. Ednl. Facilities Planners, 1997—. Author: Hector Bear's Homecoming, 2000. Chmn. Citizens Referendum Com., Homewood, Ill., 1980; mem. Homewood Sch. Dist. 153 Bd., 1980-93, chmn. property and fin. com., 1982—; chmn. South Shore Revitalization Ctr., Chgo., 1980; vice chmn. Rosenblum Boys Club, Chgo., 1980-84, chmn., 1984-88; mem. Homewood Cultural Arts Com., 1986-89; bd. dirs. South Shore YMCA, 1984-90. Named Outstanding Young Person, Chgo.-Southend Jaycees, 1977. Mem. Nat. Soc. Fund Raising Execs. (dir., exec. com. 1977-82), Nat. Assn. Hosp. Devel. (legis. chmn. 1983—), South Shore C. of C. (pres. 1978-79), Cosmopolitan C. of C. (vice chmn. 1986-90). Republican.

BART, POLLY TURNER, real estate developer; b. Peterborough, N.H., Feb. 28, 1944; 1 child, Greta Rose Bart. BAcl, Radcliffe Coll., 1965; PhD in City Planning, U. Calif., Berkeley, 1979. Contbr. President's Nat. Urban Policy Report to Congress, Washington, 1980; asst. prof. U. Md., College Park, 1981-84; real estate salesperson Coldwell Banker Comml. Real Estate Services, Balt., 1984-87; pres. Investment Properties Brokerage, Inc., Balt., 1988-98. Faculty Johns Hopkins U., Berman Real Estate Inst., 1993—. Fellow Danforth Found., 1975-79, Ford Found., 1981. Mem. Comml. Real Estate Women (co-founder). Home and Office: 4033 Osborne Rd Reisterstown MD 21136

BART, ROGER, actor; b. Norfolk, Conn., Sept. 29, 1962; Actor with Broadway/first nat. tour credits including: You're a Good Man, Charlie Brown (Tony award, Drama Desk award), The Producers, Triumph of Love, London's West End, U.S. Tour, German prodns. of: The Who's Tommy, King David, How to Succeed in Business, The Secret Garden, Big River; actor: (off-Broadway) Henry IV, Parts I and II, Up Against It, role of Whizzer in Falsettos; singing voice title role of Walt Disney's animated feature Hercules, other canine credits include singing voice of Scamp in Disney's Lady and the Tramp Part II, acting role in The George Carlin Show, Fox TV; actor: (George St. prodn.) Ancestral Voices, 2002; (TV series) Alice and Bram, 2002, Law & Order: Special Victims Unit, 1999. Office: c/o SAG 1515 Broadway Fl 44 New York NY 10036-8901

BART, TEDDY, journalist; b. Johnstown, Pa., Feb. 7, 1936; s. Herbert and Blanche Kaminsky; m. Jana L. Bart, Nov. 2, 1959; children: Jody, Kevin. Host WSM Radio and TV, Nashville, 1970—81; news anchor WKRN TV, Nashville, 1981—83, WSMV TV, Nashville, 1983—86; host Teddy Bart's Round Table, Nashville, 1986—. Author: Insde Music City USA, 1972, The Mensh, 1979. Pvt. U.S. Army, 1958—59. Named one of 100 Most Influential, Nashville Bus. Jour., 1999, 2000, 2001. Jewish. Avocation: writing. Home: PO Box 150263 Nashville TN 37215

BARTA, DANIEL STEPHEN, music educator, composer; b. Cleve., Mar. 20, 1953; s. Donald William and Rosemary Jane Barta; m. Peggy Jane Marcouiller, Sept. 14, 1990; children: Jessica, Jonathan. Ch. Music Diploma, Moody Bible Inst., Chgo., 1975; MusB, Temple U., Phila., 1984; MusM, Temple U., 1988, DMA, 2003. Adj. faculty Temple U., Phila., 1986—93, Phila. Bibl. U., Langhorne, Pa., 1991—94, asst. prof., 1994—. Composer: Suite for Piano, 2001, Duo for Flute and Cello, 2001, Tranquillo (String Quartet), 2003; author: Lead Me in Your Truth, I'm the Good Shepherd. Mem.: Phila. Christian Fellowship0, Pi Kappa Lambda. Avocations: travel, carpentry. Home: 3015 Lincoln Ave Glenside PA 19038 Office: Philadelphia Biblical Univ 200 Manor Ave Langhorne PA 19047

BARTA, JAMES OMER, priest, psychology educator, church administrator; b. Fairfax, Iowa, Oct. 22, 1931; s. Omer J. and Bertha (Brecht) B. BA, Loras Coll., 1952; Sacrae Theologiae Licentiatus, Gregorian U., Rome, 1956; PhD, Fordham U., 1962. Ordained priest Roman Cath. Ch., 1955. Prof. psychology Loras Coll., Dubuque, Iowa, 1957-94, v.p. acad. affairs, 1977-87, pres., 1987-94; archbishop's vicar Cedar Rapids (Iowa) region, 1994-99; vicar Gen. Archdiocese of Dubuque, 1999—. Roman Catholic. Office: Archdiocesan Chancery 1229 Mount Loretta Ave Dubuque IA 52003-7826

BARTALINI, C. RICHARD, judge; b. Kincaid, Ill., Sept. 25, 1931; s. Chester Richard and Florinda (Galli) B.; m. Anne M. Evanoff, June 4, 1955; children: Robert Charles, Denise Anne, David Chester. BA, U. Calif., Berkeley, 1954; JD, U. Calif, San Francisco, 1957. Bar: Calif. 1957. Practice law, Oakland, 1957-66, Alameda, 1966-77; dep. dist. atty. Alameda County, 1957-59; chief def. counsel Transit Casualty Co., 1959-60; chief trial atty. Alameda/Contra Costa Transit Co., 1960-61; asso. Nichols, Williams, Morgan & Digardi, 1961-66; partner Davis, Craig & Bartalini, 1966-77, judge Superior Ct. Calif., 1977-93, ret. 1993. Atty., counselor Supreme Ct. U.S.; del. Calif. Bar Conf., 1963-68; cons. U.S. Dept. Justice, U.S. Dept. Edn.; faculty Nat. Inst. for Trial Advocacy, Ctr. for Trial and Appellate Advocacy, Hastings Coll. Law, Calif. Ctr. for Jud. Edn. and Rsch. Chmn. Alameda Youth Activities Com., 1958-63, Nat. Coun. on Mental Health and Retardation, 1965-69; mem. President's Coun. on Youth Opportunity, 1965-70; pres. Alameda Bd. Edn.; pres., v.p., bd. dirs. Alameda Boys Club; mem. exec. com. Nat. Found. March of Dimes; chmn. No. Calif. Area coun., mem. Nat. Commn. for Constl. Revision and mem. nat. area coun. com. Boys Clubs Am.; chmn. bd. dirs. Moreau High Sch., Hayward, Calif., Alameda Hosp. Found.; mem. adv. bd. Partners Program, The Close-Up Found.; mem. civil svc. bd. City of Alameda, 1992-96, mem. housing authority, 1996—; mem. Alameda County Grand Jury, 1997-98, chair Measure A oversight com., superintendents edn. adv. com. Recipient Service award Nat. Congress Parents and Tchrs., 1972, Disting. Svc. award Alameda Unified Sch. Dist., 1972, Man and Boy award Boys Clubs Am., 1975; Bronze Keystone award Boys Club Am., 1979, Bronze Keystone and Svc. Bar awards Boys and Girls Clubs of Am., 1989; named Young Man of Yr. City of Alameda, 1965, Outstanding Civic Leader of Am., 1967. Mem. ATLA, ABA, Calif. Bar Assn., Alameda County Bar Assn. (dir.), Criminal Cts. Bar Assn., Com. for Advancement and Support of Edn., Nat. Assn. Ind. Schs., Alameda Collaborative for Children, Youth and Their Families, Alameda County Lawyers Club (past pres.), Calif. C. of C. (past dir.), Alameda Jaycees (past pres.), U.S. Jaycees (past legal counsel), Elks, Eagles, Kiwanis, Alameda Rod and Gun Club, Commonwealth Club, Chabot Gun Club, Phi Alpha Delta. Home: 1224 Bay St Alameda CA 94501-3914

BARTCHY, S(TUART) SCOTT, history educator, researcher; b. Canton, Ohio, Nov. 9, 1936; s. Jacques Robert Bartchy and Dorothy Elizabeth Engle; m. Diane Walker, June 13, 1956 (div. Jan. 1988); children: Beth, Christopher; m. Nancy L. Breuer, Nov. 19, 1988. BA cum laude, Milligan Coll., 1958; MDiv, Harvard U., 1963, PhD, 1971. Dir. Inst. zur Erforschung des Urchristentums, Tuebingen, Germany, 1971-74, 77-79; Gast prof. Eberhard-Karls Universitaet, Tuebingen, various 1977-87; prof. Bibl. studies Emmanuel Sch. Religion, Johnson City, Tenn., 1974-77; resident New Testament scholar Westwood Christian Found., L.A., 1979-87; assoc. prof. history dept. UCLA, 1988-96, prof. Christian origins and history of religion, 1996—, dir. Ctr. for the Study of Religion, 1997—, chair Chancellor's com. on religion, ethics and values, 1992—96. Cons. Arts and Entertainment Network, 1996-97; vis. prof. Fuller Theol. Sem., Pasadena, Calif., 1981, 85, 96, 2001, external examiner grad. programs, 1998; lectr. in field. Author: First Century Slavery and Corinthians, 1973, 85, 03; assoc. editor Religion, 1996—; contbr. chpts. to books and articles to profl. jours. Recipient Hebrew Scholar's award Indpls. Hebrew Congregation, 1960, Thomas Evans award U. Religious Conf., L.A., 1999. Fellow The Context Group; mem. Am. Acad. Religion (pres. western region 1998-99), Soc. Bibl. Lit. (nat. com. chair 1997—), Cath. Bibl. Assn., Inst. for Bibl. Rsch., Studiorum Novi Testamentum Socs. Avocations: jazz piano improvising, competitive running. Office: UCLA Dept History Box 951473 Los Angeles CA 90095-1473 E-mail: bartchy@history.ucla.edu.

BARTEAU, MARK ALAN, chemical engineering and chemistry educator; b. St. Louis, Sept. 8, 1956; s. Dallas Frank and Charlotte Jean (Shelker) B.; m. Diane Viola Jorgensen, June 25, 1983; children: Katherine Pearl, Alexander Bradford. BSChemE, Washington U., 1976; MSChemE, Stanford U., 1977, PhD, 1981. Postdoctoral fellow Tech. U. Munich, 1981-82; asst. prof. U. Del., Newark, 1982-87, assoc. prof., 1987-90, prof. chem. engring. and chemistry, 1990-94, Robert L. Pigford prof., 1994—, dir. Ctr. for Catalytic Sci. and Tech., 1996-2000, chmn. dept. chem. engring., 2000—. NSF Postdoctoral fellow, 1981; recipient Presdl. Young Investigator award NSF, 1985, Ipatieff prize Am. Chem. Soc., 1995, Internat. Catalysis award Internat. Assn. Catalysis Socs., 1998, Alpha Chi Sigma award, 2001.. Mem. AAAS, AIChE (Allan P. Colburn award 1991, assoc. editor jour.), Am. Chem. Soc. (Ipatieff prize 1994, Victor K. LaMer award 1982), Catalysis Soc. (Paul H. Emmett award 1993), Materials Rsch. Soc., Am. Vacuum Soc. Democrat. Office: Univ of Del Dept Chem Engring Newark DE 19716 E-mail: barteau@che.udel.edu.

BARTEE, NEALE, music educator, musician, conductor; b. Springfield, Mo., Feb. 23, 1947; s. Josephus Christian and Thelma Ruby Bartee; m. Debra Elaine Austin. BS in Edn., U. Ill., 1969, MEd, 1970, PhD, 1977. Tchr. instrumental music pub. schs., Norman, Okla., 1972—73; prof. music Ark. State U., Jonesboro, 1973—. Condr. Delta Symphony Orch., Jonesboro, 1975—; trombonist ch. music programs, Ark., Mo., Tenn., 1973—. Condr. Internat. Trombone Festivals. Condr. Clinician fellow, Coll. Band Dirs. Nat. Assn., Austin, Tex., 1989, Bapt. Nat. Music Conf., Glorietta, N.Mex., 1992, Friend of the Arts fellow, Sigma Alpha Iota, Epsilon Gamma chpt., 1999. Mem.: Music Edn. Nat. Conf. (assoc.; state pres. 1997—98). Baptist. Home: 3713 Burdyshaw Jonesboro AR 72401 Office Fax: 870-972-3932. Personal E-mail: nebartee@cox-internet.com.

BARTEE, ROY MCKINLEY, II, anesthesiologist; b. Denver, Feb. 21, 1946; s. Roy Arianog and Evelyn Grace (Peck) B.; m. Katharine Dianne Hayden, July 15, 1967; children: Roy M. III, Dianne Carolyn. BS, U. Denver, 1968; MD, U. Colo., 1971. Diploamte Am. Bd. Anesthesiology. Intern, resident U.S. Naval Regional Med. Ctr., Oakland, Calif., 1971-75, asst. chmn. dept. anesthesiology, 1975-78; chmn. dept. anesthesiology Swedish Med. Ctr. Porter Hosp., Englewood, Colo., 1982-84; practice medicine specializing in anesthesiology, Denver, 1978—. Cons. Swedish Med. Ctr., Englewood, 1980—. Contbr. articles to profl. jours. Trustee Arapahoe Med. Soc., Englewood, 1979-88, Arapahoe Med. Found., Englewood, 1980-88; cons. staff Denver Area coun. Boy Scouts Am., 1984. Lt. comdr. USNR, 1970-78. Fellow Am. Coll. Anesthesiologists; mem. Am. Soc. Anesthesiologists, Colo. Med. Soc. (del. 1981—, bd. dirs. 1985-88), Internat. Anesthesia Rsch. Soc. Office: South Denver Anesthesiologists PC 333 W Hampden Ave Ste 600 Englewood CO 80110-2336

BARTEE, THOMAS CRESON, computer scientist, educator; b. Moberly, Mo., Dec. 18, 1926; s. Thomas Monroe and Verna Miller (Tippett) B.; m. Mildred Higdon, Sept. 5, 1953; 1 child, Thomas Quentin. BA, Westminster

Coll., 1949. Mem. staff computer research M.I.T.-Lincoln Lab., Lexington, Mass., 1955-63; Gordon MacKay lectr. in computer engring. Harvard U., Cambridge, Mass., 1963-69, dir. electronic design center, 1969-72, Gordon MacKay prof. computer engring., 1970—. Cons. Nat. Acad. Scis., IDA, IBM, Honeywell, Raytheon; IEEE disting. computer sci. lectr., 1972-74 Author: (with G. Birkhoff) Modern Applied Algebra, 1971, Introduction to Computer Science, 1972, Digital Computer Fundamentals, 7th edit., 1989, Basic Computer Programming, 1981, 2d edit., 1985, Data Communications, Networks and Systems, 1985, 2d edit., 1992, Digital Communications, 1986, Expert Systems in AI, 1987, ISDN, SNA AND DECNET, 1989; editor: IEEE-IRE Computer Jour., 1963-66. Recipient Disting. contbn. in computer sci. award Westminster Coll., 1980 Mem. IEEE (chmn. N.E. computer group 1973-74), Am. Math. Soc. Office: Aiken Computation Lab Harvard Univ Cambridge MA 02138 Home: 2534 S Walter Reed Dr Apt A Arlington VA 22206-1287

BARTEK, GORDON LUKE, radiologist; b. Valparaiso, Nebr., Dec. 27, 1925; s. Luke Victor and Sylvia (Buner) B.; m. Ruth Evelyn Rowley, Sept. 10, 1949; children: John, David, James. BSc, U. Nebr., 1948, MD, 1949. Diplomate Am. Bd. Radiology. Intern Bishop Clarksen Hosp., Omaha, 1949-50; resident in medicine Henry Ford Hosp., Detroit, 1952-53, resident in radiology, 1953-56; staff radiologist Ferguson Hosp., Grand Rapids, Mich., 1956-76, Holland City Hosp., Mich., 1956-76, Logan Hosp., Utah, 1976-78, St. Lawrence Hosp., Lansing, Mich., 1978-97, Spectrum Health, Grand Rapids, 1997—. Asst. clin. prof. dept. radiology Mich. State Univ. Coll. Medicine, 1977-93, asst. prof. radiology, 1993-97; organizer Care Choices HMO, Lansing, 1983, bd. dirs., 1983-93. Served to lt. USN, 1949-52. Fellow: Am. Coll. Radiology (councilor 1972 76, emeritus); mem.: Mich. Radiology Practice Assn. (bd. dirs. 1984—97, chmn. western Mich. sect. 1970—71), Cascade Hills Country Club, Terravita Country Club. Republican. Roman Catholic. Avocations: flying, photography, skiing, snorkeling. Home and Office: 1350 Briarcliff Dr SE Grand Rapids MI 49546-9679

BARTEL, BARBARA M. educator; arrived in U.S., 1986; d. Edmund and Irena Slota. Masters Degree, Coll. Edn., Katowice, Poland, 1965, Jagiellonian U., Krakow, Poland, 1985; Doctorate Degree, Ednl. Credential Evaluators, Inc., 1993. Lectr. MX Coll., Chgo., 1987—88; prof. Wright Coll., Chgo., 1988—; cashier Bank, Chgo., 1988—90; tchg. asst. Chgo. Pub. Sch., 1990—91, tchr., 1991—2001. Editor: Ancient History, 1991, The World Past to Present, 1992. Bd. dirs. Educators in Polonia, Chgo., 1987. Mem.: Polish Women's Alliance Am., Am. Tchr. Assn. Avocations: travel, tennis. Office: Wright Coll 4300 N Narragansett Ave Chicago IL 60634

BARTELL, ANGELA GINA BALDI, judge; b. Milw., Jan. 25, 1946; d. John Batiste and Marie Alma (Rank) Baldi; m. Jeffrey Bruce Bartell, Aug. 31, 1968; children: Jessica Marie, Carey Laurel, Chad Gerald, Dana Joyce, Nicholas John. BA, U. Wis., 1969, JD, 1971. Bar: Wis. 1972, U.S. Dist. Ct. (we. dist.) Wis. 1972. Intern Wis. Dept. Justice, Madison, 1970; law clk. to Hon. James E. Doyle U.S. Dist. Ct. (we. dist.) Wis., Madison, 1971-72; assoc., then ptnr. LaFollette Sinykin Law Firm, Madison, 1973-78; county judge Dane County Ct., Madison, 1978-79; chief judge Wis. Fifth Jud. Dist., 1982-88; cir. judge Dane County Cir. Ct., Madison, 1979—. Mem. Professionalism Commn., Madison, 1990-93; mem. Legal Edn. Commn., 1994-95; mem. adv. bd. Scan Child Abuse Prevention Project, Madison, 1988-90; assoc. dean Wis. Jud. Coll., 2000—. Jud. editor Wisconsin Judician Benchbooks, 3 vols., 1980-92 (Supreme Ct. award 1992), Wisconsin Jury Handbook, 1983; contbr.: State Bar Civil Forms Manual, 1992-99, Wisconsin Jury Instructions-Criminal, 1992-2002. Pres. Young Lawyers divsn. Wis. State Bar, Madision, 1974; bd. dirs. Dane County United Way, 1995-2001, chair bd., 2000-01; chair United Way Allocation Com.; planner, presenter Leadership Madison Forum, 1994. Fellow Am. Bar Found.; mem. Am. Law Inst., Nat. Assn. Women Judges, Rotary Club of Madison (pres.-elect 2002-2003, pres. 2003—), Phi Beta Kappa. Office: Dane County Cir Ct 210 Martin Luther King Jr Blvd Madison WI 53709-0002

BARTELL, ERNEST, economist, educator, priest; b. Chgo., Jan. 22, 1932; PhB, U. Notre Dame, 1953; AM, U. Chgo., 1954; MA, Coll. Holy Cross, 1961; PhD, Princeton U., 1966; LLD (hon.), China Acad., Taipei, Taiwan, 1975, St. Joseph's Coll., 1983, King's Coll., 1984, Stonehill Coll., 1992. Ordained priest Roman Cath. Ch., 1961. Instr. econs. Princeton (N.J.) U., 1965-66; asst. prof. econs. U. Notre Dame, Ind., 1966-68, assoc. prof., 1968-71, chmn. dept. econs., 1968-71, dir. Ctr. Study of Man in Contemporary Soc., 1969-71, prof. econs., 1981—2003, prof. emeritus, 2003—; exec. dir. Helen Kellogg Inst. Internat. Studies, Ind., 1981—97, fellow, 1997—; pres. Stonehill Coll., North Easton, Mass., 1971-77; dir. Fund for Improvement Post Secondary Edn. U.S. Dept. Health, Edn. and Welfare, Washington, 1977-79; dir. Project 80 Assn. Cath. Colls. and Univs., Washington, 1979-80; overseas mission coord. Priests of Holy Cross, Ind. Province, 1980-84, assoc. dir. Holy Cross Mission Ctr., 1984-95; asst. to pastor St. Anthony Ch., Ft. Lauderdale, Fla., 1993—2003. Active Inst. East-West Securities Studies Working Group on Sources in Instability, 1989-90, Internat. Ctr. Devel. Policy Commn. on U.S.-Soviet Rels., 1988-89, Overseas Devel. Coun., 1988-2000, The Bretton Woods Com., 1992-2002; mem. policy planning commn. Nat. Inst. Ind. Colls. and Univs., 1982-85; bd. dirs. Ctr. for Health Promotion, Internat. Life Scis. Inst.; hon. trustee Stonehill Coll., 2002—. Author; Costs and Benefits of Catholic Elementary and Secondary schools, 1969; co-editor: Business and Democracy in Latin America, 1995, The Child in Latin America, 2000; contbr. articles to profl. jours. Bd. regents U. Portland, Oreg., 1984—; bd. dirs. Missionary Vehicle Assn. Am., 1981-88, Big Bros. and Big Sisters Am., 1978-80, Brockton Community Housing Corp., 1974-77, The Brighter Day, 1974-77, Brockton Hosp., 1973-77, King's Coll., Wilkes-Barre, Pa., 1969-82; bd. trustees Emmanuel Coll., 1977-78, U. Notre Dame, 1974-2002, bd. fellows, 1974-2002; bd. trustees Regis Coll., 2002--; adv. bd. Brockton Art Ctr., 1974-77; exec. com. Opera New Eng., 1977. Recipient Fenwick Alumni Recognition award, 1974; named to Fenwick Hall of Fame, 1990; faculty fellow Kellogg Inst., 1997—. Fellow Soc. Values in Higher Edn.; mem. Am. Econ. Assn., Am. Assn. Higher Edn., Nat. Cath. Ednl. Assn. (chmn. govtl. rels. com. 1976-77, vice chmn. exec. com. 1976-77, chmn. mgmt. and planning com. 1974-76), Assn. Soc. Econs., Latin Am. Studies Assn., Young Pres. Orgn. (sec. 1974-77), Delta Mu Delta (hon.). Home: 227 Corby Hall Notre Dame IN 46556-5680 Office: U Notre Dame Kellogg Inst 211 Hesburgh Ctr Notre Dame IN 46556-5677 E-mail: ebartell@nd.edu.

BARTELL, JEFFREY BRUCE, lawyer; b. Madison, Wis., Jan. 29, 1943; s. Gerald Aaron and Joyce Meta (Jaeger) B.; m. Angela Gina Baldi, Aug. 31, 1968; children: Jessica, Carey, Chad, Nicholas, Dana. BS in Econs., U. Wis., 1965, JD cum laude, 1968. Bar: Wis. 1968, U.S. Dist. Ct. (we. dist.) 1968, U.S. Dist. Ct. (ea. dist.) 1969, U.S. Ct. Appeals (7th cir.) 1970, U.S. Supreme Ct. 1971. Asst. atty. gen. State of Wis., Madison, 1968-71; counsel Wis. Citizens Study Com. on Jud. Orgn., Madison, 1971-72; commr. securities State of Wis., Madison, 1972-79; pres. N.Am. Securities Administrators Assn., 1978-79; ptnr. Michael, Best & Friedrich, Madison, 1979-83; mng. ptnr. Quarles & Brady, Madison, 1983—99, ptnr., 2000—. Lectr. on securities regulation U. Wis. Law Sch., Madison, 1982, 86, 92; mem. adv. com. on tender offers SEC, 1983. Pres. Madison Repertory Theatre, 1978—80; trustee Wis. Meml. Union, Madison, 1984—; chair Madison Civic Ctr. Endowment Fund, 1988—91, Wis. Found. for Arts, 1990—; officer, bd. dirs. Forward Wis., Inc., 1984—; bd. dirs. Madison Civic Ctr. Found., 1985—95, Friends of WHA-TV, 1996—2000, Ten Chimneys Found., 1997—2003, Overture Devel. Corp., 1998—, Friends of Monona Ter., 1999—2002, Meriter Health Svcs., Inc., 2000—, Meriter Hosp., Inc., 2000—, Wis. Med. Soc. Found., 2001—. Capt. JACG USAR, ret. Mem. ABA (gavel awards com. 1992—), State Bar Wis. (dir. bus. law sect. 1983-91, chmn. sect. 1990-91, mem. bus. corp. law com. 1989-96), Dane County Bar, Wis. Law Alumni Assn. (pres. 1989-91), Rotary (bd. dirs. Madison 1987-88). Avocations: skiing, biking, music, golfing. Office: Quarles & Brady US Bank Plaza PO Box 2113 Madison WI 53701-2113 E-mail: jbb@quarles.com.

BARTELL, LAWRENCE SIMS, chemist, educator; b. Ann Arbor, Mich., Feb. 23, 1923; s. Floyd Earl and Lawrence (Sims) B.; m. Joy Hilda Keer, Aug. 16, 1952; 1 son, Michael Keer. BS, U. Mich., 1944, MS, 1947, PhD, 1951. Research asst. Manhattan project U. Chgo., 1944-45; mem. faculty Iowa State U., 1953-65, prof. chemistry, 1959-65, U. Mich., 1965—, Philip J. Elving prof. chemistry, 1987-94, prof. emeritus, 1994—. Vis. prof. Moscow (USSR) State U., 1972, U. Paris XI, Orsay, France, 1973, U. Tex., 1978, 86; cons. Gillette Co., Chgo., 1956-62, Mobil Oil Corp., Paulsboro, N.J., 1960-84; mem. commn. on electron diffraction Internat. Union Crystallography, 1966-75 Assoc. editor: Jour. Chem. Physics, 1963-66; mem. editorial bd.: Jour. Computational Chemistry, 1979-90, Chem. Physics Letters, 1981-84. Served with USNR, 1945. Recipient Disting. Faculty Achievement award U. Mich., 1981, Disting. Faculty award Mich. Assn. Governing Bds., 1982, Creativity award NSF, 1982. Mem. Am. Chem. Soc. (petroleum research fund adv. bd. 1970-73), Am. Phys. Soc. (chmn. div. chem. physics 1977-78), Am. Crystallographic Assn., AAAS, Phi Beta Kappa, Sigma Xi, Phi Kappa Phi, Phi Lambda Upsilon, Alpha Chi Sigma. Home: 381 Riverview Dr Ann Arbor MI 48104-1847 E-mail: lbart@umich.edu.

BARTELS, BETTY JANE, nurse; b. Cin., Mar. 7, 1925; d. William Charles and Irene Agnes (McLean) Roth; m. Donald Arthur Bartels Sr., 1946; children: Donald A. Jr., Virginia, Frederick, Bernadette. Nursing diploma RN, Good Samaritan Hosp., 1946; postgrad., Barry Coll., 1966—70. Mem. U.S. Nurse Cadet Corps, 1943—46; nursing staff Hines Vets. Hosp., Chgo., 1945—46; RN Sun Ray Health Resort, Miami, Fla., 1949-51; vol. libr. St. James Cath. Sch., Miami, 1966-70; RN North Shore Med. Ctr., Miami, 1970-72; charge RN Villa Maria Rehab. Ctr., Miami, 1972-76; pvt. duty RN Miami, 1976-80; staff RN North Shore Med. Ctr., Miami, 1979-91. Author: Amotrophic Lateral Sclerosis: Helping the Patient with Lou Gehrigs Disease, 1979, RN Mag., 1979. Vol. Bon Secours Hosp./Villa Maria Nursing Ctr., 1990—. Mem. Third Order of St. Dominic (pres., moderator 1974-80, 92-2000, 02). Democrat. Roman Catholic. Avocations: do-it-yourself projects, fishing.

BARTELS, BRUCE MICHAEL, health care executive; b. Chgo., Oct. 13, 1946; s. John Phillip Frederick and Margaret Florine (Michael) B.; children: Sarah, Jennifer, Rebecca. BA, U. Wis., 1969, MBA, U. Chgo., 1975. Adminstrv. asst. U. Chgo. Hosp., 1975-77; asst. adminstr. Meth. Hosp., Indpls., 1977-81; exec. v.p. Med. Ctr. Hosp. Vt., Burlington, 1981-88; pres. York (Pa.) Hosp. and Found., 1988-95, York Health Sys., 1995-99, WellSpan Health, York, 1999—. Contbr. articles to profl. jours. Bd. dirs. YMCA, York, 1989-98, chmn., 1994-96; bd. dirs. ARC, 1990-96, United Way, 1991-96, WITF, Inc., Ctrl. Pa. Pub. Broadcasting, 1994-2002, chmn., 1999-2001; bd. dirs. Pa. Trauma Systems Found., Mechanicsburg, 1990-, chmn., 1997-99; bd. dirs. Novation, Inc., 2003-. With U.S. Army, Korea. Fellow Am. Coll. Healthcare Execs. (membership com. 1990-93); mem. Am. Hosp. Assn., Hosp. Assn. Pa. (bd. dirs., chmn.), York C. of C., U. Chgo. Health Adminstrn. Alumni Assn. (exec. com. 1991-95), Rotary. Avocations: reading, running, travel. Office: WellSpan Health 45 Monument Dr Ste 200 York PA 17403-3676 E-mail: bbartels@wellspan.org.

BARTELS, RANDY A. science educator, researcher; b. Seoul, Republic of Korea, Nov. 19, 1974; arrived in U.S., 1975; s. Linda and Winston Rice(Stepfather); m. Malini Ramakumar, Dec. 28, 1974; 1 child, Maya. MS, U. of Mich., 1999, PhD in Elec. Engring., 2002. Rsch. asst. Microelectronics Rsch. Ctr., Ames, Iowa, 1994, Ctr. for Lasers and Photonics Rsch., Stillwater, Okla., 1994—97, Lawrence Livermore Nat. Lab., Livermore, Calif., 1996—97, Ctr. for Ultrafast Optical Sci., Ann Arbor, 1997—99, Joint Inst. Lab. Astrophysics, Boulder, 1999—2001, postdoctoral fellow, 2002; prof. Colo. State U., Fort Collins, 2003—. Contbr. scientific papers to profl. jours. Named Del. Mem. for the 51st meeting of Nobel Laureates in Lindau, Germany, U.S. Dept. of Energy, 2001; recipient LEOS Grad. Student fellowship, IEEE Laser and Electroptics Soc., 2000, Nat. Def. Sci. and Engring. Grad. fellowship, U.S. Dept. of Def., 1997—2001, GAANN Grad. fellowship, U.S. Dept. of Edn., 1997, William L. Everitt award, Internat. Engring. Consortium, 1997, Summer Inst. in Applied Physics award, Fannie and John Hertz Found., 1996. Mem.: IEEE, Laser and Electroptic Soc. (v.p. Rocky Mountain sect.), Am. Phys. Soc., Optical Soc. of Am. (New Focus Student award 2001). Achievements include invention of Attosecond control of electronic wavefunctions; Self Compression of Ultrafast Optical Pulses using Molecular Rotational Wavepackets; research in Coherent Control of Atomic and Molecular Systems; invention of Pinhole Diffraction Spectrometer; Nonlinear freqeuency conversion with aligned molecular quasi-crystals. Office: Colo State U 104 Engineering Fort Collins CO 80523-1373 Office Fax: 970-491-2294. E-mail: bartels@engr.colostate.edu.

BARTELS, ROBERT EDWIN, aerospace engineer; b. Des Moines, May 24, 1955; s. Everett M. and Iola J. (Van Wyck) B. BS, Iowa State U., 1977; MDiv cum laude, N.W. Baptist Sem., Tacoma, Wash., 1983; MS, Iowa State U., 1992, PhD, 1994. Sr. engr. Boeing Comml. Airplane Co., Seattle, 1984—87; teaching asst. Iowa State U., Ames, 1987—92, grad. rsch. fellow NASA, 1992—94; NRC rsch. assoc. NASA Langley Rsch. Ctr., Hampton, Va., 1994—97, aerospace engr., 1997—2003, sr. rsch. engr., 1997—. Adj. prof. Tidewater C.C., 1998. Bd. dirs., treas. Second Wind Contemporary Dance Co., 1996-98. Recipient Grad. Student Tchg. Excellence award Iowa State U., 1991. Mem. AIAA (sr.), Phi Kappa Phi. Home: 6310 Sentry Way S Suffolk VA 23435 Office: Nasa Langley Rsch Ctr Hampton VA 23681-0001

BARTELSTONE, RONA SUE, gerontologist; b. Bklyn, Jan. 10, 1951; d. Herbert and Hazel (Mittman) Canarick; m. Alan Joel Markowitz. BS in Social Welfare, SUNY, Buffalo, 1972; MSW, Ind. U., 1974. Lic. clin. social worker Fla., diplomate in social work, cert. care mgr., advanced social work case mgr. Social worker YM-YWHA of Greater Ny, NY, 1974-75; dist. supr. NYC Housing Authority, Bklyn., 1975-77; field instr. Barry U. Sch. Social Work, 1980-81; project dir. United Family & Children's Svc., 1977-81; faculty Miami Dade Cmty. Coll., 1981-82; adult educator Sch. Bd. Dade County, 1981-82; med. social worker Mederi Home Health Agy., 1979-82; mem. adj. faculty Nova U., 1986-88; pvt. practice Rona Bartelstone Assocs., Inc., Ft. Lauderdale, Fla., 1981—; team leader curriculum devel., cert. in geriatric care mgmt. U. Fla., 2002. Adj. faculty Fla. Internat. U. S.E. Ctr. on Aging, 1996; team leader curriculum devel., cert. in geriatric care mgmt. U. Fla., 2002; conf. co-chair, Vancouver, BC, Canada, 01; co-chair Internat. Care Mgmt. Conf., 2003; adv. bd. Caregivers Marketplace, 2003; coalition ptnr. And They Shalt Honor Care Mgmt. Conf., 2003; cons. and trainer in field. Contbr. articles to various mags., chapters to books. Mem. funding panel Area Agy. on Aging, Miami, 1985—89; active Friends of the Family Counseling Svcs., Miami, 1983—88; adv. bd., chair internship subcom. Lynn U., 1993—97; exec. bd. Fla. Geriatric Care Mgrs., 1993—2000, pres.-elect, 1998—2000; chair tng. com., exec. v.p. Alzheimer's Assn., Miami, 1994—97, bd. dirs., 1999, v.p., 1999—2002; co-chair Nat. Acad. Cert. Care Mgrs., 1994—97, v.p., 1997—; trustee Fla. Coun. on Aging, 1996—2002; bd. dirs. Jewish Vocat. Svcs., Miami, 1985—92. Recipient Dade County Citizen of the Yr. award, 1982, NASW Social Worker of the Yr. award, 1982-83, Trail Blazer award, 1984, Up & Comers award in health care Price Waterhouse and So. Fla. Bus. Jour., 1990. Mem.: NICLC (del. coun. 1999—), NASW (treas. 1987—89), Internat. Care Mgmt. Conference (co-chair 2003), Univ. of Fla., Dept. of Continuing Ed., Develop. for Geriatric Care Mgmt. Cert. program (team leader 2002—03), Fla. Coun. on Aging (bd. trustees 1996—2002), Fla. Geriatric Care Mgr. Assn. (exec. bd. 1993—2000, pres.-elect 1998—2000, Broward County Care Mgmt. Licensing com. 2001—), Nat. Acad. Cert. Care Mgr. (co-chmn. 1994—97, v.p. 1997—2001), Assn. Profl. Geriatric Care Mgr. (pres. 1988—94, chmn. credential com. 1993—), Nat. Coun. on Aging, Am. Soc. on Aging (bd. of dir. 2003—06), Gerontology Soc. Am., Caregivers Mkt. Pl., (advisory bd. 2003—04), And Thou Shjalt Honor, Town Hall Meetings, Car Mgmt. and Fla. Coalition (co-chair, ptnr. 2003—04). Democrat. Jewish. Home: 5342 SW 33rd Way Fort Lauderdale FL 33312-5574 Office: 2699 Stirling Rd Ste C304 Fort Lauderdale FL 33312-6592 E-mail: rbartelstone@rbacaremanagement.com.

BARTER, JAMES DUNCAN, physicist; b. Portland, Oreg., Aug. 14, 1946; m. Beverly Jean Thomas. BS, Portland State U., 1968; MS, U. Wis., 1974, PhD, 1976. Physicist Northrop Grumman Space Tech., Redondo Beach, Calif., 1977—. With U.S. Army, 1969-71, Vietnam. Mem. Am. Phys. Soc. Office: NGST R1/1008 1 Space Park Blvd Redondo Beach CA 90278-1071

BARTH, DAVID KECK, distribution industry consultant; b. Springfield, Ill., Dec. 7, 1943; s. David Klenk and Edna Margaret (Keck) B.; m. Dian Oldemeyer, Nov. 21, 1970; children— David, Michael, John. BA cum laude, Knox Coll., Galesburg, Ill., 1965; MBA, U. Calif., Berkeley, 1971. With data processing div. IBM Corp., Chgo., 1966; with No. Trust Co., Chgo., 1971-72; mgr. treasury ops., then treas. fin. services group Borg-Warner Corp., Chgo., 1972-79; treas. W.W. Grainger, Inc., Skokie, Ill., 1979-83, v.p., 1984-90; pres. Barth Smith Co., 1991—2001. Mem. faculty Lake Forest (Ill.) Grad. Sch. Mgmt., 1994—; bd. dirs. Indsl. Distbn. Group Inc., Atlanta, Gen. Roofing Svcs., Inc., Ft. Lauderdale, Fla. Served to lt. USNR, 1966-69. Mem. Econ. Club Chgo., Univ. Club of Chgo., Beta Gamma Sigma, Phi Delta Theta. Lutheran.

BARTH, DAVID VICTOR, computer systems designer, consultant; b. Tulsa, Sept. 23, 1942; s. Vincent David and Norma (Bell) B. BS summa cum laude, Met. State Coll., Denver, 1977; MS, U. No. Colo., 1982; PhD, Kennedy-Western U., Boise, Idaho, 1995. Programming mgr. Am. Nat. Bank, Denver, 1967-72; cons. Colo. Farm Bur. Ins. Corp., Denver, 1972; systems analyst Mid-Continent Computer Services, Denver, 1972-73; programming mgr. Bayly Corp., Denver, 1973-75, project leader Cube Labs. Inc., Denver, 1976-84; sys. analyst Affiliated Banks Svc. Co., Denver, 1985-87, tech. supr., 1987-89; software engr. Computer Data Sys., Inc., Aurora, Colo., 1990-91, 94-98; sr. computer sys. designer Martin Marietta Corp., Golden, Colo., 1991-92; owner, operator Computer Shop, Lakewood, Colo., 1992-93; sr. software engr. Perot Sys., Englewood, Colo., 1998-99, Anderson Consulting, Denver, Colo., 1999-2000, Computer Scis. Corp., Denver, 2000—, Perot Systems, Englewood, Colo., 1998-99, Andersen Consulting, Denver, Colo., 1999-2000. Freelance flight instr., 1977—; part-time tchr. Met. State Coll., 1982-83; real estate broker Van Schaack & Co., Denver, 1985; cons. Ross Co., Denver, 1993-95. Vol. Am. Red Cross, 1987—; Served with USN, 1961-66. Mem. Soc. for Info. Mgmt. (editor newsletter 1983), Exptl. Aircraft Assn. (editor newsletter chpt. 660, 1989-91), Aircraft Owners and Pilots Assn., Flying Circus Skating Club, Air West Flying Club (editor newsletter 1997-99). Republican. Avocations: ice skating, flying, creative writing. Home: 509 S Cody St Lakewood CO 80226-3047 Office: Computer Scis Corp Fed Sector Def Group 5445 DTC Pky Ste 1250 Englewood CO 80111 E-mail: dvbarth@aol.com.

BARTH, DIANA, actress, playwright, journalist, editor; b. LA, Calif., May 31, 1929; d. Harry and Sarah (Pressman) Newman; m. Leslie Klein, Nov. 21, 1951 (div. Oct. 1974); 1 child, Randall. BA in Social Scis. summa cum laude, Fordham U., 1979. Profl. actress, NYC, 1950—; co-founder, sec. Equity Libr. Theatre West, 1959-62; theatre adminstr. Bklyn. Acad. Music, 1970-72, NY State Coun. on the Arts, 1972-75; assoc. editor Simon & Schuster, NYC, 1968-70; pvt. practice Knopf, Doubleday, McGraw-Hill, and others, NYC, 1970—; assoc. dir., pub. rels. Internat. Ctr. for Women Playwrights, NYC, 1995—. Critic, feature writer Playbill, Irish Voice, New Millennium, Back Stage, Show Business, Western European Stages, N.Y.C. Playwright: Tides, Legacy, Bound Together, Struggles of Stefania, Always, Do the Rules, Girl!; prodr.: (plays) UCG, The Lion Theatre, U. Athens, New Fed. Theater, Alice's Fourth Fl., 42d St. Workshop, 1988—, Pen & Brush Club, 1990—. Playwrights fellow Ctr. for Creative Arts and Scis., Hambidge, Ga., 1992; recipient Sussman/Stevenson/Davis 2d prize prose award, 1994, 3rd prize prose award, 1995, 3rd prize playwriting award, 1999, finalist Samuel French Short Play Competition, 1999, 2d prize Sussman/Stevenson/Davis Playwriting award, 2000. Mem. Actors Equity Assn., AFTRA, SAG, Am. Theatre Critics Assn., Drama Desk, Outer Critics Cir., Pen & Brush Club, Workshop Theater Co., Am. Renaissance Theatre Co. Home and Office: 535 W 51st St Apt 3A New York NY 10019-5071 E-mail: diabarth@juno.com.

BARTH, ELMER ERNEST, wire and cable company executive; b. Phila., May 15, 1922; s. Paul Adolph and Anna (Miller) B.; m. Ruth Bradstreet Stone, Sept. 18, 1943 (dec. Aug. 1990); 1 dau., Rebecca Barth Gallucci; m. Barbara E. Burbridge, Jan. 25, 1992. Ed., Bentley Sch. Accounting, 1947-51; BBA, Northeastern U., 1956. Asst. treas. Hayward Hosiery Co., Ipswich, Mass., 1945-56; v.p. ops. Rockbestos Co.; Mem. Marmon Group, New Haven, 1956-86; sec., treas., dir. Applied Data, Inc., North Haven, 1961-97. Trustee Ipswich Savs. Bank, 1947-56 Bd. govs., vice chmn. fin. com. Children's Center, Hamden, Conn., 1965-68. Served with USNR, 1942-45. Recipient Charles D. Scott Disting. Career award New Eng. Wire & Cable Club. Mem.: Branford Yacht (commodore 1976), Ipswich Outboard, Inc. (sec., bd. dirs. Commodore 1988-89). Home: 1 Riverside Dr Ipswich MA 01938-2427 E-mail: elmerbarth@vfw-online.com., EEBarth22@aol.com.

BARTH, FRANCES, artist; b. N.Y.C., July 31, 1946; d. Frank and Helen Barth. BFA, Hunter Coll., 1968, MA, 1970. Instr. Princeton U., 1975-79, Sarah Lawrence Coll., Bronxville, N.Y., 1979-85; prof. Yale U., 1986—. One-woman shows include, N.Y.C., 1974—, Jan Cicero Gallery, Chgo., 1981, 1985, U. Mass. Amherst, 1994, E.M. Donahue Gallery, N.Y.C., 1994, 1997, 2000, Millersville Coll., Pa., 1995, Marcia Wood Gallery, Atlanta, 1998, 2001, 2002, Moravian Coll., Pa., 1999, Donahue Sosinski, N.Y.C., 2000, exhibited in group shows at Moore Coll. Art, 1970, Whitney Mus. Am. Art, N.Y.C., 1972—73, Houston Mus. Contemporary Art, 1972, Corcoran Gallery Art, Washington, Bard Coll., Annandale-on-Hudson, N.Y.C., 1973, Trenton State Coll., 1974, Princeton U. Art Mus., 1975, High Mus. Art, Atlanta, 1976, Bennington Coll., 1976, San Francisco Art Inst., 1978, U. Pa., 1978, MIT, 1978, Jan Cicero, CHI, 1995, Moravia Coll., Pa., 1999, William Patterson Coll., Wayne, N.J., 1979, NYU, 1979, Va. Commonwealth U., Richmond, 1980, Sarah Lawrence Coll., 1981, Mus. Modern Art, 1981, Cleve. Mus. Art, 1983, Indpls. Mus., 1984, 1985, Princeton U., 1985, Hunter Coll., 1986, Yale U., 1987, Bennington Coll., 1991, Am. Acad. Arts and Letters, 1988, Met. Mus. Art, 1990, Andre Emmerich Gallery, 1991, La Viglie, Nimes, France, 1995, Charles Cowles Gallery, N.Y.C., 1996, Amer. Acad. of Arts and Letters, 1999, Tucson Mus. Art, 2003, Represented in permanent collections New 20th Century Wing, Met. Mus. Art, N.Y.C., Mus. Modern Art, Akron Art Inst., Albright-Knox Gallery, Am. Can Co., Greenwich, Conn., Amerada Hess Corp., N.Y.C., Chase Manhattan Bank, Cornell U., IBM Corp., N.Y.C., Mobil Oil Corp., Prudential Inst. Co., N.J., Whitney Mus. Am. Art, Lehman Bros., N.Y.C. and Chgo., Isham, Lincoln & Beale, Chgo., Security Pacific Nat. Bank, L.A., Swiss Bank Corp., N.Y.C., Cameron Iron Works, Houston, Mus. Modern Art, N.Y.C., Paul Haim Found., Paris, Humana, Inc., Louisville, Coudert Bros., N.Y.C., Dallas Mus. Art, Tucson (Ariz.) Art Mus. Grantee Creative Artists Pub. Svc., 1973, NEA, 1974, 82, N.J. State Coun. on Arts, 1987, Adolph and Esther Gottlieb Ind. Support, 1993; John Guggenheim fellow, 1977; recipient Joan Mitchell Found. award, 1995.

BARTH, J. EDWARD, lawyer, shareholder; b. Oklahoma City, Oct. 24, 1937; s. Richard L. and Vera S. Barth; m. Gene Bloomston, Apr. 15, 1972; children: Lance Rothstein, Rodney Rothstein, Lee P. Barth. BA, Yale U., 1959; JD, U. Mich., 1962. Bar: Okla. 1963, U.S. Dist. Ct. (we. dist.) Okla., U.S. Ct. Appeals (10th cir.) 1964. Law clk., Chief Judge A.P. Murrah U.S. Ct. Appeals 10th Cir., Oklahoma City, 1963-64; ptnr. Bohanon & Barth, Oklahoma City, 1964-79; shareholder, dir. Andrews Davis Legg Bixler Milsten & Price, Oklahoma City, 1979—. Chmn. com. on admissions and grievances, U.S. Dist. Ct. (we. dist.) Okla., 1987—; judge Okla. Temporary Ct. Appeals, Oklahoma City, 1991-92. Chmn. Met. Area Projects Oversight Bd., Oklahoma City, 1994—; pres., trustee Oklahoma City Cmty. Found., 1989-98; chmn., dir. ARC, Oklahoma County, 1979—. Mem. ABA, Okla. Bar Assn. (Lawyer of Month 1994), Oklahoma County Bar Assn. (dir. 1975-77). Home: 6020 Riviera Dr Oklahoma City OK 73112-7356 Office: Andrews Davis Legg Bixler Milsten & Price 500 W Main St Ste 500 Oklahoma City OK 73102-2275

BARTH, JOHN ROBERT, English educator, priest; b. Buffalo, Feb. 23, 1931; s. Philip C. and Mary K. (Eustace) B. AB, Bellarmine Coll., 1954, PhL, 1955; MA, Fordham U., 1956; STB, Woodstock Coll., 1961, STL, 1962; PhD, Harvard U., 1967. Joined Society of Jesus, Roman Catholic Ch., 1948; tchr. English, French, Latin (Canisius High Sch.), Buffalo, 1955-58; asst. prof. English Canisius Coll., Buffalo, 1967-70, Harvard U., Cambridge, Mass., 1970-74; assoc. prof. English U. Mo.-Columbia, 1974-77, prof., 1977-79, Catherine Paine Middlebush prof. English, 1979-82, prof. English, chmn. dept., 1980-83, prof. English, 1983-85; Thomas I. Gasson prof. English Boston Coll., 1985-86; prof. English U. Mo.-Columbia, 1986-88; dean Coll. Arts and Scis. Boston Coll, 1988-99; James P. McIntyre prof. English Boston Coll., 1999—. Author: Coleridge and Christian Doctrine, 1969, 2d edit., 1987, The Symbolic Imagination: Coleridge and the Romantic Tradition, 1977, 2d edit., 2000 (Book of Yr. award, Conf. on Christianity and Lit. 1977), Coleridge and the Power of Love, 1988 (U. Mo. Curators Publ. award 1989), Romanticism and Transcendence: Wordsworth, Coleridge, and the Religious Imagination, 2003; editor: Religious Perspectives in Faulkner's Fiction, 1972, The Fountain Light: Studies in Romanticism and Religion, 2002; co-editor: Marginalia in Collected Works of Samuel Taylor Coleridge, 1984—, Coleridge, Keats and the Imagination: Romanticism and Adam's Dream, 1990; mem. bd. advisors Wordsworth Circle, Phila., 1976—; mem. editl. bd. cons. Thought, 1980-93, mem. adv. bd. Studies in Romanticism, 1981—, European Romantic Rev., 1990—, Renascence, 1993—; mem. editl. adv. bd. Christianity and Literature, 1989—; mem. editl. planning bd. Religion and the Arts, 1996—. Trustee St. Louis U., 1974-79, St. Peter's Coll., 1985-91, Coll. of the Holy Cross, 1989-93, Canisius Coll., 1992-98. Recipient Howard Mumford Jones prize Harvard U., 1967; Dexter

fellow, 1967; NEH summer grantee, 1969; Am. Council Learned Socs. grantee, 1970; Harvard U. research grantee, 1973. Mem. AAUP, Conf. on Christianity and Lit. (dir. 1980-83), MLA (del. assembly 1979-83, exec. com. romantic divsn. 1975-79, exec. com. religious approaches 1983-87), N.Am. Soc. Study Romanticism, Wordsworth-Coleridge Assn. (v.p. 1978, pres. 1979), Keats-Shelley Assn., Friends of Coleridge. Address: St Mary's Hall Boston College Chestnut Hill MA 02467 Office: Boston Coll Dept English 24 Quincy Rd Chestnut Hill MA 02467-3937 E-mail: robert.barth@bc.edu.

BARTH, KAREN ANN, lawyer; b. Dubuque, Iowa, Dec. 8, 1966; d. Henry Victor and Janet Marie Barth. BA, Colo. State U., 1989; JD, U. Calif., Davis, 1995. Bar: Calif. 1995, U.S. Dist. Ct. (cen. dist.) Calif. 1995, U.S. Dist. Ct. (so. dist.) Calif. 1999, U.S. Ct. Appeals (9th cir.) 1999. Law clk. Colo. Atty. Gen.'s Office, Denver, 1993; law clk. to Justice Davis, Calif. 3d Dist. Appellate Ct., Sacramento, 1994; legal intern Calif. Atty. Gen.'s Office, Sacramento, 1994, Sacramento Dist. Atty.'s Office, Sacramento, 1995; shareholder Baum, Hedlund, Aristei, Guilford & Schiavo and predecessor firms, L.A., 1995—. Mem. ABA, State Bar of Calif., Nat. Assn. Women Lawyers, L.A. Women Lawyers Assn., George McBurney Complex Litigation Inn of Ct. Avocations: rock climbing, diving, skiing, basketball, volleyball. Office: Baum Hedlund et al 12100 Wilshire Blvd Ste 950 Los Angeles CA 90025-7107 E-mail: kbarth@baumhedlundlaw.com.

BARTH, KARL LUTHER, retired seminary president; b. Milw., Nov. 7, 1924; s. G. Christian and Louise A. (Schneemann) B.; m. Jean L. Kelly, June 8, 1947; children: Linda, Karl, Laurel, Kurt, Lisa. BA, Concordia Sem., 1945, M.Div., 1947; D.D. (hon.), Concordia Theol. Sem., 1975. Ordained to minstry, Lutheran Ch., 1947. Asst. pastor First English Lutheran Ch., New Orleans, 1947-50; pastor Trinity Evan. Lutheran Ch., Centralia, Ill., 1950-52, St. Paul's Lutheran Ch., West Allis, Wis., 1956-70; pres. So. Wis. Dist. Luth. Ch. Mo. Synod, Milw., 1970-82, bd. for mission svcs., 1982-90, bd. dirs., 1992—; pres. Concordia Sem., St. Louis, 1982-90. Exec. dir. 150th Anniversary Luth. Ch. Mo. Synod. Contbr. articles to profl. jours. Vice pres. So. Wis. dist. Lutheran Ch., Mo. Synod, 1966-70; chmn. Com. on Theology and Ch. Relations, St. Louis, 1974-82; denominational rep. Div. Theol. Studies Lutheran Council U.S.A., N.Y.C., 1975-81; mem. adv. bd. Wis. Citizens Concerned for Life, 1976-82. Mem. Badger Assn. of the Blind (adv. coun. 2000—). Republican. Home: Apt 208 8220 Harwood Ave Milwaukee WI 53213

BARTH, MARK HAROLD, lawyer; b. Lincoln, Ill., June 22, 1951; s. rev. Harold Julius and Maxine Virginia Barth; m. Jannette Morgan Berg, June 29, 1974; children: Katherine, Erica. BA, The Johns Hopkins U., 1973; JD, Georgetown U., 1977. Bar: N.Y. 1978. Assoc. Curtis, Mallet-Prevost, Colt & Mosle, N.Y.C., 1977-86, ptnr., 1986—, mng. ptnr. London office, 1988-92. Mem. ABA, Internat. Bar Assn., Assn. Bar City N.Y. Office: Curtis Mallet-Prevost Colt & Mosle 101 Park Ave New York NY 10178-0061

BARTH, MICHAEL CARL, economist; b. Newark, Apr. 3, 1941; s. Abe and Frances (Keller) B.; m. Marilyn Levy, Dec. 11, 1966; children: Christopher Jay, Karen Rebecca Simon. BA, Harpur Coll., Binghamton, N.Y., 1962; MA, U. Ill., Champaign, 1963; PhD, CUNY, 1971. Rsch. assoc. CCNY Rsch. Found., N.Y.C., 1965-67; lectr. econs. CCNY, 1966-68; economist Pres.'s Commn. on Income Maintenance, Washington, 1968-69, Office Econ. Opportunity, Washington, 1969-73; dir. income sec. policy/analysis U.S. Dept. HEW, Washington, 1973-75; vis. assoc. prof. econs. U. Wis., Madison, 1975-76; dep. asst. sec. U.S. Dept. HHS, Washington, 1976-80; prin. ICF Inc., Washington, 1980-87, sr. v.p., 1987—; pres. ICF Info. Tech. Inc., Washington, 1992-95; exec. v.p. ICF Cons., Fairfax, Va., 1995—. Bd. dirs. ICF Info. Tech., Inc, ICF Resources. Author: (with G. Carcagno and J. Palmer) Toward an Effective Income Support System: Problems, Prospects and Choices, 1974; editor: Greenhouse Effect and Sea Level Rise, 1984 contbr. articles to profl. jours. Recipient Sec.'s Spl. citation HEW, 1975, Sec.'s Outstanding Achievement award, 1977 Mem. Am. Econ. Assn., Am. Evaluation Assn. Home: 3818 Military Rd NW Washington DC 20015-2704 Office: ICF Cons 9300 Lee Hwy Fairfax VA 22031-1207 E-mail: mbarth@icfconsulting.com.

BARTH, RICHARD, pharmaceutical executive; b. N.Y.C., May 23, 1931; s. Alexander Haddon and Georgine (Grant) B.; m. Mary Elizabeth McAnaney, June 13, 1959; children: Leanore, Jennifer, Richard, Michele, Alexander. AB cum laude, Wesleyan U., 1952; LLB, Columbia U., 1955; postgrad., NYU, 1959-62. Bar: N.Y. 1958, N.J. 1966. Assoc. firm Burke & Burke, 1957-65; gen. counsel, sec., mem. mgmt. com. Ciba, 1965-70; dir. Radio Shack Corp., 1964-65; v.p., gen. counsel, mem. mng. com., dir. Ciba-Geigy Corp., Ardsley, N.Y., 1971-86; chmn., pres., chief exec. officer, dir. CIBA-GEIGY Corp., Ardsley, N.Y., 1986-96; dir. Novartis Corp., 1997-2000. Bd. dirs. Bowater, Inc. Contbr. articles to profl. jours. Mem. Pres. Clinton's Coun. Sustainable Devel.; trustee Wesleyan U., Middletown, Conn., 1987—90, N.Y. Med. Coll., 1990—2002, chmn. bd. dirs., 1994—99; mem. substandard housing bd., Summit, NJ, 1968—70. Mem. ABA, N.Y. Bar Assn., N.J. Bar Assn., Phi Delta Phi, Psi Upsilon. Home and Office: 470 W End Ave # 15A New York NY 10024-4933

BARTH, ROBERT HENRY, nephrologist, educator; b. Newark, Oct. 31, 1944; s. Robert Henry and Wilma Elizabeth (Van Ness) B.; m. Elettra Nerbosi, May 10, 1976. BA in Chemistry, Cornell U., 1967; MD cum laude, U. Bologna, Italy, 1976. Diplomate Am. Bd. Internal Medicine, Am. Bd. Nephrology. Chemist Sandoz, Inc., Hanover, Basel, N.J., Switzerland, 1967-68, 70, Internat. Flavors and Fragrances, Union Beach, N.J., 1968-69; resident Berkshire Med. Ctr., Pittsfield, Mass., 1976-80; fellow, rsch. assoc. Rogosin Kidney Ctr. N.Y. Hosp.-Cornell U. Med. Ctr., 1980-83; assoc. dir. Baumritter Kidney Ctr. Albert Einstein Coll. Medicine, Bronx, N.Y., 1983-86; physician, chief nephrology, chief dialysis VA Med. Ctr., Bklyn., 1986—. Instr., asst. prof. Albert Einstein Coll. Medicine, Bronx, 1983-86, attending physician, 1983-86; asst. prof., assoc. prof. SUNY Health Sci. Ctr., Bklyn., 1986—; attending physician Bronx Mcpl. Hosp. Ctr., 1983-86. Contbr. chpts. in books and articles to profl. jours.; software program developer. Pres. Bklyn. VA Med. Ctr. Med. Soc., 1996—. Mem. Am. Soc. for Artificial Internal Organs (bd. trustees 1996-2000, program chmn. 1998, ann. meeting), Am. Soc. Nephrology (abstract reviewer 1993 ann. meeting session chmn.), Internat. Soc. Peritoneal Dialysis, Internat. Soc. Nephrology, Nat. Kidney Found. (exec. bd., coun. on Dialysis 1990-94), N.Y. Soc. Nephrology, Physicians for Nat. Health Program, Adirondack Mountain Club. Avocations: hiking, skiing, photography, jazz. Home: 392 11th St Brooklyn NY 11215 Office: VA Med Ctr 800 Poly Pl Brooklyn NY 11209-7104 E-mail: ebarth@ix.netcom.com., robert.barth@med.va.gov.

BARTH, ROLF FREDERICK, pathologist, educator; b. N.Y.C., Apr. 4, 1937; s. Rolf L. and Josephine Barth; m. Christine Ferguson, Oct. 30, 1965; children: Suzanna, Alison, Rolf, Christofer. AB, Cornell U., 1959; MD, Columbia U., 1964. Diplomate Am. Bd. Pathology. Surg. intern Columbia-Presbyn. Med. Ctr., N.Y.C., 1964-65; postdoctoral fellow Karolinska Inst., Stockholm, 1965-66; rsch. assoc. Nat. Inst. Allergy and Infectious Diseases, NIH, Bethesda, Md., 1966-68; resident pathology br. Nat. Cancer Inst., 1966-68, Nat. Inst. Health, 1968-70; Prof. dept. pathology and oncology U. Kans. Med. Ctr., Kansas City, 1970-77; clin. prof. dept. pathology Med. Coll. Wis. and U. Wis., Madison, 1977-79; prof. dept. pathology Ohio State U., Columbus, 1979—. Contbr. articles to profl. jours. Sr. asst. surgeon USPHS, 1966-70, inactive Res., 1970—. Grantee Dept. Energy, NIH. Mem. Am. Assn. Exptl. Pathology, Am. Assn. Immunologists, Am. Assn. Cancer Rsch., Internat. Soc. for Neutron Capture Therapy, Sigma Xi, Phi Kappa Phi. Office: Ohio State U Dept Pathology 165 Hamilton Hall 1645 Neil Ave Columbus OH 43210-1218

BARTHEL, WILLIAM FREDERICK, JR., engineer, electronics company executive; b. Washington, July 14, 1940; s. William Frederick and Eva (Buday) B.; m. Barbara Joan Adams, Nov. 18, 1961; 1 son, William Frederick III. BS, McNeese State U., 1972. Shop mgr. Electronic Unlimited, Lake Charles, La., 1968; quality control engr. Rockwell Internat., Cedar Rapids, Iowa, 1974-79, mgr. quality assurance, 1979, sr. engring. scientist, process control devel., 1980-81; engring. mgr. process reliability Digital Equipment Corp., Andover, Mass., 1981-87, engring. mgr. performance assurance, 1987-91; dir. quality Gables Engring., Inc., Coral Gables, Fla., 1991-93, v.p. ops., 1993—. Served with USAF, 1958-62. Mem. Am. Chem. Soc., Am. Inst. Chemists. Republican. Home: 745 SE 25th Ln Homestead FL 33033-5234 Office: Gables Engring Inc 247 Greco Ave Miami FL 33146-1808

BARTHELD, ROBERT LYLE, dentist; b. McAlester, Okla., Jan. 4, 1933; s. Floyd Thomas Bartheld and Nedra Larae Ackors; m. Patricia Elizabeth McCann, June 10, 1956; children: Thomas, William, Joseph, Elizabeth. BS, Okla. U., 1955; DDS, U. Mo., Kansas City, 1958. Registered dentist. Pres. Okla. State Dental Assn., McAlester, 1962, pres., bd. trustees Oklahoma City, 1964-95; ho. of dels. ADA, Chgo., 1969-95, v.p., 1996. Dir. The Bank NA, McAlester, 1973—. Pres. Navy League, McAlester, 1968; mem. Red Cross of St. Constantine. Capt. U.S. Army, 1958-60, 61-62. Fellow Internat. Coll. Dentists (regent, v.p., pres. elect, 2003), Am. Coll. Dentists; mem. Jester and Shrine (33d degree Scottish Rite, pres. Scottish Rite Edn. Found.), Lions Club (bd. dirs. 1969-75, pres.), McAlester C. of C. (bd. dirs. 1968). Anglican. Avocation: golf. Office: Ste 101 301 N 2d Mcalester OK 74501 Fax: (918) 423-1548.

BARTHELMAS, NED KELTON, investment and commercial real estate developer; b. Circleville, Ohio, Oct. 22, 1927; s. Arthur and Mary Bernice (Riffel) B.; m. Marjorie Jane Livezey, May 23, 1953; children: Brooke Ann, Richard Thomas. BS in Bus. Adminstrn., Ohio State U., 1950. Stockbroker Ohio Co., Columbus, 1953-58; pres. First Columbus Securities Corp., 1958—; pres., dir. Ohio Fin. Corp., Columbus, 1960—; pres. Thwirs, Inc., Columbus, 1996—. Trustee, chmn. Am. Guardian Fin., Republic Fin.; bd. dirs. Nat. Foods, Midwest Capital Corp., Capital Equity Corp., Midwest Nat. Corp., 1st Columbus Realty Corp., Dublin Nat. Corp. (all Columbus). Served with Adj. Gen.'s Dept., AUS, 1944-47. Recipient Merit award, State of Ohio, 2001. Mem. Nat. Assn. Securities Dealers (past vice chmn. dist. bd. govs.), Investment Bankers Assn. (exec. com. 1973), Investment Dealers Ohio (sec., treas. 1956-72, pres. 1973), Nat. Stock Traders Assn., Young Pres.'s Orgn. (pres. 1971), World Bus. Coun., Columbus Pres.'s Assn., Nat. Investment Bankers (pres. 1973), Internat. Real Estate Inst., Columbus Jr. C. of C. (pres. 1956), Ohio C. of C. (trustee 1957-58), World's Pres.'s Assn. (Exec. Hall of Fame award 1993), Columbus Area C. of C. (dir. 1956, named an Outstanding Young Man of Columbus 1962), Newcomen Soc., Coun. for Ethics in Econs., Coun. of Orgn. of Am. States, Winston Churchill's Wisdom Hall of Fame, Internat. Soc. Financiers, Oxford Club, Nat. Assn. Appraisers Execs. Club, Pres.' Club (Ohio State U.), Internat. Platform Assn., Stock and Bond Club (past pres.), named top 25 corp. Dirs. (1984-90), Columbus Club, Scioto Country Club, Crystal Downs Country Club, Ohio State U. Faculty Club, Kiwanis (legion of honor 1992), Am. Legion, Columbus Admirals Club, Alpha Kappa Psi, Phi Delta Theta (Golden Legion award). Office: 1241 Dublin Rd Columbus OH 43215-7000

BARTHOLD, WALTER, lawyer; b. Toronto, Ont., Can., June 8, 1924; came to U.S., 1924; s. Walter and Josephine (Salmon) B.; m. Denise Buffington, May 2, 1957 (div. 1996); children: Charles F., David F., Nancy L.; m. Dorothy True LaValle, Sept. 7, 1996. BS, Northwestern U., 1948; LLB, Yale U., 1951. Bar: N.Y. 1952, U.S. Supreme Ct. 1963, U.S. Ct. Appeals (2d cir.) 1955. Assoc. Arthur, Dry & Kalish, N.Y.C., 1952-60, ptnr., 1961-78, Barthold & McGuire, N.Y.C., 1978-81, Kissam, Halpin & Genovese, N.Y.C., 1981-82, Barthold & Eikenberry, N.Y.C., 1983-84; pvt. practice N.Y.C., 1984-88; counsel Leaf Sternklar & Drogin, N.Y.C., 1988-89, Ferber, Greilsheimer, Chan & Essner, 1989-92. Author: Attorney's Guide to Effective Discovery Techniques, 1965. With U.S. Army, 1943-46, ETO. Fellow Am. Coll. Trial Lawyers, Am. Bar Found., N.Y. Bar Found.; mem. ABA, Assn. Bar City N.Y., N.Y. State Bar Assn., Yale Club. Democrat. Episcopalian. Avocations: music, biking, stamp collecting. Home: 323 Stevens Ave Ridgewood NJ 07450-5203 Office: 489 5th Ave New York NY 10017-6105

BARTHOLOMAUS, BRETT WILLIAM, small business owner; b. Milw., Jan. 19, 1944; s. Weber and Beatrice (Elmergreen) B.; m. Joan Anne Cavosi, Feb. 19, 1977; children: Laura, Thomas, Eric. Student, Milw. tech. Coll. Lic. pvt. security Wis. Motorcycle sales rep. Vic Panetti & Sons, Milw., 1963-75; maint. supr. U. Wis., Milw., 1977; owner North Trail Inn Supper Club, Tigerton, Wis., 1978-82; security supr. Sentinal Detective agy., Wausau, Wis., 1988—. Author: (poetry book) Moments Beautiful, Moments Bright, 1993, (novel) Reflection of Evil, 1998; poetry pub. various pubs.; numerous poetry readings. Vol. numerous charitable orgns. Recipient Golden Poets award World of Poetry, 1988, 89, 90, 92.. Democrat. Roman Catholic. Avocations: motorcycling, backpacking, weight lifting, family. Address: Wildwood Apts 100 Wall St Apt 1 Bowler WI 54416

BARTHOLOMAY, WILLIAM C. insurance brokerage company executive, professional baseball team executive; b. Evanston, Ill., Aug. 11, 1928; s. Henry C. and Virginia (Graves) B.; m. Sara Taylor, 1950, (div. 1964); children: Virginia, William T., Jamie, Elizabeth, Sara; m. Gail Dillingham, May 1968 (div. Apr. 1980). Student, Oberlin Coll., 1946-49, Northwestern U., 1949-50; BA, Lake Forest Coll., 1955. Ptnr. Bartholomay & Clarkson, Chgo., 1951-63; v.p. Alexander & Alexander, Chgo., 1963-65; pres. Olson & Bartholomay, Chgo. and Atlanta, 1965-69; sr. v.p. Frank B. Hall & Co. Inc., N.Y.C. and Chgo., 1969-72, exec. v.p., 1972-73, pres., 1973-74, vice chmn., 1974-90; chmn. bd. dir. Atlanta Braves, 1966—; pvt. practice cons. Chgo., 1990-91; pres. Near North Nat. Group, 1991—; vice chmn., chmn. exec. com. Turner Broadcasting Sys., Inc., Atlanta, 2001—. Bd. dirs. WMS Industries Inc., Chgo., Midway Games, Inc., Exec. Coun. Maj. League Baseball, Maj. League Baseball Players Pension Plan; dir. Internat. Steel, 2002—. Commr. Chgo. Park Dist., 1980-2002, Chgo. Pub. Bldg. Commn., 1989—; bd. dirs. Chgo. Maternity Ctr., Lincoln Park Zool. Soc.; trustee Adler Planetarium, Mus. Sci. and Industry, Roosevelt U., Chgo., Ill. Inst. of Tech.; former trustee Lake Forest (Ill.) Coll., Ogelthorpe Coll., Atlanta, Marymount Manhattan Coll., N.Y. With USNR, 1951-54. Mem. Chief Execs. Orgn., World Pres.'s Orgn., Chgo. Pres.'s Orgn., Nat. Assn. CLU, Chgo. Assn. CLU, Chgo. Club, Racquet Club, Saddle and Cycle Club, Econ. Club, Onwentsia Club, Shoreacres Club (Lake Forest), Brook Club, Links Club, Racquet & Tennis Club, Doubles Club (N.Y.C.), Piedmont Driving Club, Atlanta Country Club, Peachtree Golf Club, Commerce Club. Episcopalian. Home: 180 E Pearson St Chicago IL 60611-2130 Office: Near North Nat Group 875 N Michigan Ave Ste 2000 Chicago IL 60611-1954 also: Atlanta Braves PO Box 4064 Atlanta GA 30302-4064 E-mail: wbarthol@nnng.com.

BARTHOLOMEW, ARTHUR PECK, JR., accountant; b. Rochester, N.Y., Nov. 20, 1918; s. Arthur Peck and Abbie West (Dawson) B.; m. Mary Elizabeth Meyer, Oct. 4, 1941(wid. Oct. 1992); children: Susan B. Hall, Arthur Peck III, James M., Virginia B. Keyser. AB, U. Mich., 1939, MBA, 1940. With Ernst & Whinney (name now Ernst & Young), 1940-79, successively jr. accountant, partner charge Eastern dist., Detroit office, 1940-64; nat. office, Cleve. Ernst & Whinney, 1964-65, N.Y. office, 1965-79, also mem. mng. com. Instr. accounting U. Mich., 1940, George Washington U., 1945-46 Mem. Mich. Gov.'s Task Force for Expenditure Mgmt., 1963-64; mem. 2d Regional Plan Commn. N.Y.; bd. dirs. Detroit League for Handicapped, 1952-64; bd. dirs., dir., treas. Bethesda Hosp. Found.; treas. Grosse Pointe War Meml. Assn., 1961; life trustee Greater N.Y. council Boy Scouts Am. Served from pvt. to capt. AUS, 1942-46. Mem. AICPA, Inst. Mgmt. Accts. (pres. Detroit 1963-64, nat. pres. 1974-75), The Conf. Bd., Mich. Soc. CPAs, N.Y. Soc. CPAs, Detroit Country Club, Gulf Stream Golf Club, Wall St. Club (pres. 1976-78), Ocean Club Fla. (pres. 1993-94), Phi Beta Kappa, Phi Kappa Phi, Beta Gamma Sigma, Phi Eta Sigma, Beta Alpha Psi, Phi Kappa Sigma. Republican. Presbyterian. Home: 6665 N Ocean Blvd Boynton Beach FL 33435-3312

BARTHOLOMEW, DEBRA LEE, publishing executive; b. Cobleskill, NY, Sept. 11, 1958; d. Donald Walter Mochrie, Sr. and Jean Marie (Hamm) Mochrie; m. Richard Ray Bartholomew, July 8, 2001; 1 child, Robert Wayne Kucienski, Jr. Author: Hope: Discovering the Power of 'No' (Merit from the Writer's Digest, 2001). Organizer fundraiser poster contest For the children, boost the moral of the soldiers, Richmondville, NY, 1991. Home: 297 Main St Richmondville NY 12149-0150 Home Fax: 518-294-8860. Personal E-mail: debilee@capital.net.

BARTHOLOMEW, DENNIS, sculptor, fine arts company executive; b. Youngstown, Ohio, Dec. 1, 1947; s. Rocco and Mary Magdalene Bartholomew; m. Lynette Womer, Feb. 19, 2000. BSBA, Youngstown State U., 1970. 1st class FCC lic. Radio Engring. Inst., Fredericksburg, Va., 1971. Engr., Denver, 1971—84; prodr., dir., 1971—80; dir. devel. Easter Seal Soc., Youngstown, Ohio, 1984—89; creative dir. The Media Team, L.A., 1989—94; pres., owner Bartholomew Fine Art and Design, Vero Beach, Fla., 1994—. Author: How to Market Your Art, 1998, Guide for Automobile Importation, 1982. Recipient award of excellence, Colo. Broadcasters Assn., 1982, Armory Art Ctr., Palm Beach, Fla., 1996, Hoyt Mus. Art, New Castle, Pa., 1998. Fellow: Artworks (bd. dirs. 1985—90), Escondido Sculptors Guild (bd. dirs. 1990—94, dir. Art in Pub. Places 1990—94), South East Sculpture Assn. (v.p., bd. dirs. 1994—99, dir. Art in Pub. Places program 1994—2000). Avocations: sports cars, travel, movies, reading, bicycling.

BARTHOLOMEW, GILBERT ALFRED, retired physicist; b. Nelson, C., Can., Apr. 8, 1922; s. Alfred and Anna (Lenzman) B.; m. Rosalie May Dinzey, Apr. 19, 1952 (dec. Dec. 10, 1990); m. Anna Lubicz-Luba, July 24, 1992. BA, U. B.C., 1943; PhD, McGill U., 1948. With Atomic Energy of Can., Ltd., 1948-83, head neutron physics br., 1962-71, dir. physics div., 1971-83. Contbr. articles to profl. jours. Fellow AAAS, Royal Soc. Can., Am. Phys. Soc.; mem. Can. Assn. Physicists, Can. Nuclear Soc., Assn. for Baha'i Studies, Sigma Xi. Home: PO Box 150 Lions Bay BC Canada V0N 2E0 E-mail: gilanna@direct.ca.

BARTHOLOMEW, JOHN NILES, retired church administrator; b. Rochester, N.Y., Dec. 30, 1934; s. Donald Hague and Adair (Wellington) B.; m. Mary Townsend, June 18, 1955; children: David Malcolm, Jean Elizabeth Bartholomew Parker. BA, Cornell U., 1955; BD, Princeton Theol. Sem., 1958, ThD, 1971. Sunday sch. missionary Presbyn. Bd. Nat. Missions, Tok, Alaska, 1958-61; pastor First Presbyn. Ch., Sayre, Pa., 1962-66; instr. Princeton (N.J.) Theol. Sem., 1968-69; asst. to assoc. prof. sociology, dean The Lindenwood Colls., St. Charles, Mo., 1969-82; mem. office of rev. & evaluation Presbyn. Ch. (U.S.), Atlanta, 1982-87; synod exec., stated clk. Presbyn. Ch. (U.S.A.), Jacksonville, Fla., 1988-99; ret. Hon. assoc. rector Trinity Episcopal Ch., St. Charles, 1972-80; vis. asst. min. Ch. of Scotland, Glasgow, 1980; stated clk. Presbytery of Elijah Parish Lovejoy, St. Louis, 1980-82; cons. Evang. Presbyn. Ch., Ghana, 1988; vis. lectr. Peki Sem., Ghana, 2001. Author: (with others) Administration in the Church, 1969; contbr. articles and revs. to profl. jours. Mem. City Coun., St. Charles, 1971-75. Fellow Soc. Sci. Study of Religion; mem. Am. Sociol. Assn., Religious Rsch. Assn. Presbyterian. Avocations: sailing, woodturning and working. Home: 930 River Rd Orange Park FL 32073-4130

BARTHOLOMEW, LLOYD GIBSON, physician; b. Whitehall, N.Y., Sept. 15, 1921; s. Emerson F. and Minnie (Swinton) B.; m. Elisabeth Thrall, Dec. 27, 1943; children: Suzanne, Lynne, Lloyd Gibson, Deborah, Douglass Thrall. AA, Green Mountain Jr. Coll., 1939; BA, Union Coll., Schenectady, 1941; MD, U. Vt., 1944; MS in Internal Medicine (fellow), U. Minn., 1952; LHD (hon.), Green Mountain Coll., 1984. Diplomate Am. Bd. Internal Medicine, subsplty. bd. gastroenterology. Intern Mary Hitchcock Meml. Hosp., Hanover, N.H., 1944-45, resident, 1945-46, 48-49; asst. internal medicine Dartmouth, 1948-49; 1st asst. div. internal medicine Mayo Clinic, Rochester, Minn., 1949-52, asst. to staff div. internal medicine, 1952-53; practice medicine, specializing in gastroenterology Rochester, 1952—; instr. internal medicine Mayo Found., U. Minn., 1952-58, asst. prof., 1958-63, assoc. prof. internal medicine, 1963-67, prof. medicine, 1967—, Mayo Med. Sch., 1973—. Attending physician St. Mary's, Meth. hosps., Rochester, 1952; mem. adv. bd. to surgeons gen. of armed forces and asst. sec. def., 1978-86; mem. policy bd. Bush Found., 1978-87. Contbr. articles profl. publs. Trustee Green Mountain Coll. Poultney, Vt., 1991—, chmn. bd. trustees, 1997—. Capt. M.C. AUS, 1946-47; col. M.C., 1960-86, ret. Recipient Woodbury prize in medicine, 1944, Carbee prize in obstetrics, 1994, disting. svc. award U. Vt. Coll. Medicine, 1977, Henry J. Plummer disting. clinician award Mayo Found. Internal Medicine, 1992, disting. svc. award Green Mtn. Coll. Alumni Assn., 1995. Mem. AMA (sec. gastroenterology sect. 1962-68, vice chmn. gastroenterlogy sect. 1968-69, chmn. 1969-70, mem. council sci. assembly 1969, chmn. program planning com. 1971-75, chmn. council sci. assembly 1974-76, chmn. council continuing physician edn. 1976-77), Minn. Med. Assn. (del. ho. dels. 1964—, chmn. scholarship and loan com. 1967—, alt. del. to AMA 1974-77, 85—, del. to AMA 1978-83, Pres.'s award 1983, Disting. Service award 1987), So. Minn. Med. Assn. (pres. 1963-64), Zumbro Valley Med. Soc. (sec.-treas. 1969-70, v.p. 1970-71, pres. 1971-72), Soc. Med. Cons. to Armed Forces (mem. governing council 1980-86, pres. 1984, del. to AMA 1984-92), Am. Gastroent. Assn. (com. on procedures 1970-72, presdl. commn. on future of assn. 1973-74, com. on constn. and by-laws 1980-85), Minn. Soc. Internal Medicine, Sigma Xi. also: 1201 6th St SW Rochester MN 55902-1918 Office: Mayo Med Sch 200 1st St SW Rochester MN 55902 Home: 1201 6th St SW Rochester MN 55902-1918

BARTHOLOMEW, REGINALD, diplomat; b. Portland, Maine, Feb. 17, 1936; m. Rose-Anne Dognin; children: Sylvie, Christian, Damien, Jonathan. BA, Dartmouth Coll., 1958; MA, U. Chgo., 1960. Instr. U. Chgo., 1961-64; instr. Wesleyan U., Conn., 1964-68; dep. dir. Policy Planning Staff Dept. State, 1974-77, dep. dir. Bur. Politico-Mil. Affairs, 1977, dir. Bur. Politico-Mil. Affairs, 1979-81; with NSC, 1977-79; spl. Cyprus coordinator Dept. State, 1981-82, spl. negotiator for U.S.-Greek def. and econ. cooperation negotiations, 1982-83, U.S. amb. to Lebanon, 1983-86; with NSC, 1977-79; U.S. amb. to Spain, 1986-89; with Sec. State Internat. Security Affairs, 1989-92; U.S. perm. rep. to NATO, 1992-93; U.S. amb. to Italy, 1993-97; vice-chmn., mng. dir. Merrill Lynch Europe Holdings Ltd, London, 1997—. Chmn. Merrill Lynch, Italy. Mem. Council on Fgn. Relations (internat. inst. for strategic studies) Office: Merrill Lynch Largo Fontanella Borghese 00186 Rome Italy

BARTKIW, ROMAN, artist; b. Montreal, Que., Can., Mar. 8, 1935; s. Ivan and Annastasia Bartkiw; 4 children. Assoc., Ont. Coll. Art, 1960; student, Sheridan Sch. Design, Mississauga, 1969, Alfred U., 1970, 74-75. Owner, operator pottery studio, Toronto, Markdale, Ont., Can., 1961-71, glass blowing studio, Combermere, Ont., 1975-77, pottery studio, N.S., Can., 1981. Pottery tchr. pvt. studio, Toronto, 1961-62, No. Coll. Inst., Toronto, 1962; head ceramics Ont. Coll. Art, 1968-69; instr. ceramics and glass blowing Georgian Coll. Applied arts, 1971-74; founder arts and crafts program Chesterfield Inlet, N.W.T., Can., 1978; instr. various summer and night courses; resident master craftsman potter St. Clair Coll., Chatham, Ont.; demonstrator, panel mem. Internat. Glass Symposium, Denmark, 1976; presenter pottery workshop Cambrian Coll., 1977; craft cons. Upper Clements Park, 1988; head master craftsman, glass blower and presser Upper Clements Park, N.S., 1989, 90. One-man ceramic exhibits include Can. Guild Crafts Gallery, Toronto, 1964, Can. Guild Potters, 1967, Wells Gallery, Ottawa, 1985, Dresden Gallery, Halifax, 1985; one-man glass exhibits include Wells Gallery, Ottawa, 1976, Thomas Gallery, Winnipeg, 1976, Alice Peck Gallery, Hamilton, 1976; group exhibits Umea and Gothenburg Mus., Sweden, Denmark and Finland, 1974-76, Masters Exhbn., Toronto, 1976; represented in permanent collections Royal Ont. Mus., Umea and Gothenburg Mus., Mus. Decorative Arts, Copenhagen, N.S. Dept. Culture and Recreation, Cultural Ctr. Japan, Massey Coll., Industry Min. Coll., Seagram Coll. Recipient Design award in ceramics Can. Guild Crafts, 1965, Carling Festival Arts award, Toronto, 1969, Can. Coun. award, 1969, Marriott award for hand blown glass, 1977; J.S. McClean scholar Ont. Coll. Art, 1960, Can. Scandinavian Found. traveling scholar, 1974; travel grantee Can. Scandinavian Found., 1974, Can. Guild Crafts, 1975; grantee Can. Coun., 1973, Ont. Arts Coun., 1979, Dept. Culture grantee N.S. Province Govt., Internat. Art Glass Mus., Ebeltoft, Denmark, 1986. Mem. Royal Can. Acad. Arts, Visual Arts Ont., N.S. Designer's Craftsman, Can. Crafts Coun., Ont. Crafts Coun., Can. Ceramic Soc., Ont. Potters Assn., Ont. Arts Coun. Address: PO Box 2313 Wolfville NS Canada B4P 2N5

BARTKUS, RICHARD ANTHONY, magazine publisher; b. Chgo., Mar. 14, 1931; s. Anthony J. and Mary (Petraitis) B.; m. Betty Ann Luetke, Jan. 2, 1954; children: Susan Kimberly, David Richard. Student, U. Ill., 1949-55. Circulation trainee Chgo. Tribune, 1955-58; asst. advt. mgr. Kilner Pub. Co., Chgo., 1958-59; advt. mgr. Cox Publs., Arcadia, Calif., 1959-60, Bond Pub. Co., 1960, western advt. mgr., advt. dir., 1969-75; pub. Road & Track mag., Newport Beach, Calif., 1975-91; v.p. CBS Publs., 1977-91. With USMC, 1951-53. Mem. Univ. Athletic Club. Home: 18681 Via Torino Irvine CA 92612-3438

BARTKUS, ROBERT EDWARD, lawyer; b. Kearny, N.J., Sept. 30, 1946; s. Edward Charles and Dorothy Agnes (Konschott) B.; m. Mary Bartkus. BA with honors, Swarthmore Coll, 1968; JD, Stanford U., 1976. Bar: Calif. 1976, N.J. 1977, N.Y. 1977, U.S. Supreme Ct. (3d, 2d cirs.), U.S. Dist. Ct. N.J., U.S. Dist. Ct. (so. and ea. dist.) N.Y. Spl. counsel Schulte, Roth & Zabel, N.Y.C., 1985-88; ptnr. Dillon, Bitar, & Luther, LLC. Tchg. asst. Stanford U. Law Sch., 1976; mem. Dist. X Ethics Com., 1992-97, chair, 2002-03; lectr. N.J. Inst. for Continuing Edn., 1988—; master John J. Gibbons Intellectual Property Inn of

Ct. Articles co-editor Stanford Law Rev., 1974-76; author Innovation Competition 28 Stanford Law Rev. 1976; author, editor: New Jersey Federal Civil Practice, 1992, N.J. Federal Civil Procedure, 1999; mem. editl. bd. N.J. Law Jour. (Alfred C. Clapp award 1995). Atty. Community Law Office, 1976-79, Legal Aid Soc., 1979-87; mem. alumni coun. Swarthmore Coll., 1977-78. Lt. USNR, 1968-73. Mem. ABA (ethics com. Dist. X), Nat. Assn. Securities Dealers (arbitrator), N.J. Bar Assn. (chair fed. practice com.), Assn. Fed. Bar of State of N.J., Am. Arbitration Assn. (arbitrator), Delta Upsilon. Home: 6 Terrill Dr Califon NJ 07830-3443 Office: Dillon Bitar & Luther LLC 53 Maple Ave Morristown NJ 07963-0398 E-mail: rbartkus@dbl-law.com.

BARTLE, HARVEY, III, federal judge; b. Bryn Mawr, Pa., June 6, 1941; s. Harvey Jr. and Dorothy L. (Baker) B.; m. Nathalie Akin Vanderpool, June 12, 1993; 3 children, 2 stepchildren. AB in History, Princeton U., 1962; LLB, U. Pa., 1965. Bar: Pa. 1965, U.S. Dist. Ct. (ea. dist.) Pa. 1965, U.S. Ct. Appeals (3d cir.) 1969, U.S. Supreme Ct. 1978. Law clk. to Hon. John Morgan Davis U.S. Dist. Ct. (ea. dist.) Pa., 1965-67; assoc. Dechert, Price & Rhoads, 1967-73, ptnr., 1973-79, 81-91; Pa. Ins. Commr., 1979-80; Pa. Atty. Gen., 1980-81; judge U.S. Dist. Ct. (ea. dist.) Pa., 1991—. Editor Law Review U. Pa. Capt. U.S. Army Res. Mem. ABA, Phila. Bar Assn., Am. Law Inst. Episcopalian. Office: US Dist Ct 601 Market St Philadelphia PA 19106-1713

BARTLE, JOHN R. social sciences educator; b. Urbana, Ill., Nov. 23, 1958; s. Robert Gardner and Doris Sponenberg Bartle; m. Lori Lynn Elliott, June 1, 1963; children: Alexander Elliott, Sarah Emily Gray. BA, Swarthmore Coll., 1979; MPA, U. Tex., 1983; PhD, Ohio State U., 1990. Rsch. asst. Am. Enterprise Inst., Washington, 1979—81; rsch. analyst Minn. Tax Study Commn., St. Paul, 1983—85, Minn. Taxpayers Assn., St. Paul, 1985—87; asst. prof. SUNY, Binghamton, 1990—94, U. Nebr., Omaha, 1994—99, assoc. prof., 1999—. Editor: (book) Evolving Theories of Public Budgeting, 2001; co-editor: Benchmark Ohio, 1989, Benchmark Ohio, 1991, 1991; contbr. articles to profl. jours. Bd. mem., treas. Mcpl. Dock Bd., Omaha, 1995—; pres. Great Plains Rugby Union, Omaha, 1999—2001. Master: Gt. Plains Rugby Referees Soc. (chair 1995—98, 2001—); mem.: ASPA (mem. fin. com.), Pi Alpha Alpha. Avocation: rugby. Office: Univ Nebr Omaha 6001 Dodge St Omaha NE 68182-0276

BARTLE, RICHARD ALLAN, computer games designer; b. Ripon, Eng., Jan. 10, 1960; s. Frederick Allan Bartle and Edith Anne Toase; m. Gail Christine Martin, Apr. 13, 1985; children: Jennifer Gail, Madeleine Anne. BSc in Computer Sci. 1st class honors, Essex (Eng.) U., Colchester, 1981, PhD in Artificial Intelligence, 1988. Lectr. dept. computer sci. Essex U., 1984-89; mng. dir. Multi-User Entertainments Ltd., Colchester, 1989—, also bd. dirs. Cons. to various cos. including Brit. Telecom, Mercury Comms., London, 1985—. Author: Artificial Intelligence and Computer Games, 1985, Designing Virtual Worlds, 2003, (computer game) MUD 2, 1985—; co-author: (computer game) MUD, 1978. Mem. Soc. for Study Artificial Intelligence and Simulation of Behavior. Achievements include co-invention of class of multi-player computers MUDs—multi-user dungeons used as text-based virtual realities and played in shared virtual worlds. E-mail: richard@mud.co.uk.

BARTLE, ROBERT GARDNER, retired mathematics educator; b. Kansas City, Mo., Nov. 20, 1927; s. Glenn Gardner and Wanda (Mittank) B.; m. Doris Marie Sponenberg, Oct. 6, 1951; children— James, John; m. Carolyn June Bloemker, Apr. 1, 1982 BA with highest honors, Swarthmore Coll., 1947; S.M., U. Chgo., 1948, PhD, 1951. Postdoctoral fellow Yale U., New Haven, 1951-52, instr., 1952-55; from asst. prof. to prof. math. U. Ill., Urbana, 1955-90, prof. emeritus, 1990—; prof. math Ea. Mich. U., Ypsilanti, 1990-97. Exec. editor Math. Revs., 1976-78, 1986-90; mem. editorial bds. various math. jours.; contbr. articles to profl. jours. and books. Mem. Am. Math. Soc., Math. Assn. Am., London Math. Soc. Home: 3340 Alpine St Ann Arbor MI 48108-1704

BARTLEMAN, JAMES K. lieutenant governor; b. Orillia, Ont., Dec. 24, 1939; m. Marie-Jeanne Rosillon, 1975; children: Anne-Pascale, Laurent, Alain. BA in History with honors, U. Western Ont., 1963, LLD (hon.). Lt. gov., Ont., 2002—; amb. to Cuba, 1981—83; amb. to Israel, 1986—90; high commr. to Cyprus, 1986—90; amb. to North Atlantic Coun. NATO, 1990—94; high commr. to Australia, 1999—2000; Can.'s amb. to European Union, 2000—02. Author: (memoir) Out of Muskoka, 2002. Named Knight of Justice in Order of St. John, hon. chief, Toronto Police Svc.; named to Order of Ont.; recipient Golden Jubilee Medal in Commemoration of Queen Elizabeth II, Nat. Aboriginal Achievement award, 1999, Anishinabek Lifetime Achievement award. Office: Lt Gov of Ont Queen's Park Toronto ON Canada M7A 1A1*

BARTLESON, AMY AILEEN, psychotherapist; b. Park Ridge, Ill., Sept. 28, 1968; d. Warner H. and Mary Lou B. MA, St. Mary's U., Mpls., 1993; postgrad., Walden U. Psychotherapist St. Joseph's Home for Children, Mpls., 1994-96, Luth. Social Svcs., Washburn, Wis., 1996, Behavioral Health Svcs., Ashland, Wis., 1996-99; rsch. coord. Ind. U., Bloomington, 1999—; assessment counselor BHC Meadows Hosp., Bloomington, 2000—. Mem. Soc. Of Friends. Avocations: hiking, reading, volunteer activities. Home: 506 Ballantine Rd Bloomington IN 47401-5018

BARTLETT, ALEX, lawyer; b. Warrensburg, Mo., Aug. 7, 1937; s. George Vest and May (Woolery) B.; m. Sue Gloyd, June 5, 1961 (div. June 1978); children: Ashley R., Nathan G.; m. Eleanor M. Veltrop, Oct. 27, 1978. BA, Cen. Mo. State U., 1959; LLB, U. Mo., 1961. Bar: Mo. 1962, U.S. Ct. Mil. Appeals 1963, U.S. Supreme Ct. 1965, U.S. Dist. Ct. (we. dist.) Mo. 1966, U.S. Ct. Appeals (8th cir.) 1968. From assoc. to ptnr. Hendren & Andrae, Jefferson City, Mo., 1965-79; mem. Bartlett, Venters, Pletz & Toppins, P.C., Jefferson City, 1980-87; pvt. practice Jefferson City, 1987-90; mem. Husch & Eppenberger, LLC, Jefferson City, 1990—. With Transit Casualty Co. Receivership, 1986-90, commr. claims, 1986-87, spl. claims counsel, 1987-89, dir. legal affairs dept., 1989-90; lectr. law U. Mo., Columbia, 1965-66. Contbr. editor Mo. Law Rev., 1960-61. Served to capt. JAGC, U.S. Army, 1962-65. Mem. ABA, FBA, Mo. Bar Assn. (chmn. young lawyers sect. 1972-73, ct. modernization com. 1972-74, jud. reform com. 1974-76, chmn. cts. and jud. com. 1978-79, legis. com. 1981-84, President's award 1976, Smithson award 1976), Cole County Bar Assn., Am. Coll. Trial Lawyers (chmn. Mo. 1994-96), Order of Coif. Democrat. Office: Husch and Eppenberger PO Box 1251 235 E High St Jefferson City MO 65102-3236

BARTLETT, ALLEN LYMAN, JR., retired bishop; b. Birmingham, Ala., Sept. 22, 1929; s. Allen Lyman and Edith Buell (West) B.; m. Jerriette L. Kohlmeier, Dec. 28, 1957; children: Christopher, Stephen, Catherine. BA, U. of South, 1951, D.D. (hon.), 1988; M.Div., Va. Theol. Sem., 1958, D.Min., 1980, D.D. (hon.), 1986. Ordained to ministry Episcopal Ch. 1958, ordained priest 1959. Vicar St. James' Ch., Alexander City, Ala., 1958-61, St. Barnabas Ch., Roanoke, Ala., 1958-61; rector Zion Ch., Charles Town, W.Va., 1961-70; dean Christ Ch. Cathedral, Louisville, 1970-85; ordained bishop, 1986; bishop coadjutor Diocese of Pa., Phila., 1986-87, bishop, 1987-98; assisting bishop Diocese of Washington, 2001—04. Dep. Episcopal Gen. Convention, 1964-67, 73-85; mem. exec. coun. Episcopal Ch., 1979-85. Lt. (j.g.) USN, 1952-55. Mem.: Union League, Phi Beta Kappa. Democrat. Episcopalian. Avocations: tennis, hiking. Home: 316 S 10th St Philadelphia PA 19107-6149

BARTLETT, ARTHUR EUGENE, food service executive; b. Glens Falls, N.Y., Nov. 26, 1933; s. Raymond Ernest and Thelma (Williams) Bartlett; m. Collette R. Bartlett, Jan. 9, 1955 (dec.); 1 child, Stacy Lynn. Sales mgr. Forest E. Olson, Inc., 1960-64; co-founder, v.p. Four Star Realty, Inc., Santa Ana, Calif., 1964-71, v.p., sec., 1964-71; founder, pres. Comps, Inc., Tustin, Calif., 1971-81; co-founder, chmn. of bd., pres., CEO Century 21 Real Estate Corp., Tustin, 1980—; pres. Larwin Sq. LLC Shopping Ctr, Tustin, 1979—2002. Chmn. bd. dirs. United Western Med. Ctrs., 1981—87. Mem.: Internat. Franchise Assn. (v.p., bd. dirs. 1975—80, Hall of Fame 1987), Masons.

BARTLETT, BRUCE REEVES, economist, columnist; b. Ann Arbor, Mich., Oct. 11, 1951; s. Frank and Marjorie (Stern) B.d BA, Rutgers U., 1973; MA, Georgetown U., 1976. Spl. asst. to Congressman Jack F. Kemp, Washington, 1977-78; chief legis. asst. to U.S. Senator Roger Jepsen, Washington, 1979-80; dep. dir. Joint Econ. Com., U.S. Congress, Washington, 1981-83, exec. dir., 1983-84; v.p. Polyconomics, Inc., Morristown, N.J., 1984-85; sr. fellow Heritage Found., Washington, 1985-87; sr. policy analyst The White House, Washington, 1987-88; dep. asst. sec. for econ. policy Dept. Treasury, 1988-93; sr. fellow CATO Inst., Washington, 1993, Alexis de Tocqueville Instn., 1993-94, Nat. Ctr. for Policy Analysis, 1995—. Author: Coverup: The Politics of Pearl Harbor, 1941-46, 1978, Reaganomics: Supply Side Economics in Action, 1981; co-editor: The Supply Side Solution, 1983; syndicated columnist Creators Syndicate, L.A., 1997—; contbr. articles to Washington Post, N.Y. Times, Wall Street Jour., numerous others. Served with USAF, 1973. Mem. Am. Econ. Assn. Republican. Home: 439 Seneca Rd Great Falls VA 22066-1113 Office: Nat Ctr for Policy Analysis 655 15th St NW Ste 375 Washington DC 20005-5707 E-mail: bartlettb@cox.net.

BARTLETT, CHARLES LEFFINGWELL, foundation executive, former newspaperman; b. Chgo., Aug. 14, 1921; s. Valentine C. and Marie (Frost) B.; m. Josephine Martha Buck, Dec. 16, 1950; children: Peter B., Michael V., Robert S., Helen B. Student, St. Mark's Sch., Southboro, Mass., 1934-39; AB, Yale U., 1943. Reporter Chattanooga Times, 1946-62, Washington corr., 1948-63; editor News Focus Service, 1958-63; columnist Field Syndicate, 1962-80, Chgo. Sun-Times, 1963-75, Chgo. Daily News, 1975-78, Field Syndicate, 1978-81; pres. Jefferson Found., 1982—; editor Coleman/Bartlett's Washington Focus, 1988 . Author: (with Edward Weintal) Facing the Brink, 1957. Served as lt. USNR, 1943-46. Recipient Pulitizer prize for nat. reporting, 1955 Mem.: Gridiron, Federal City. Roman Catholic. Home: 4615 W St NW Washington DC 20007-1515 Office: Washington Focus 2208 46th St NW Washington DC 20007-1031

BARTLETT, CLIFFORD ADAMS, JR., lawyer; b. N.Y.C., Mar. 17, 1937; s. Clifford Adams and Frances (Burke) B.; m. Eileen Marie McCarthy; children: Elizabeth, Kathleen, Clifford III, Christopher, Karen, Charles, Eileen, Kevin, Jamison. BA, St. Francis Coll., N.Y.C., 1959; JD, St. John's U., N.Y., 1962. Bar: N.Y. 1963, U.S. Dist. Ct. (so. dist.) N.Y. 1964, U.S. Supreme Ct. 1966. Ptnr. Bartlett, McDonough, Bastone & Monaghan, Mineola, N.Y., 1992—. Mem. faculty Nassau Acad. Law, Mineola, N.Y. & N.Y.C., 1984—. Mem. ABA, N.Y. State Bar Assn., Nassau County Bar Assn., Nassau-Suffolk Trial Lawyers Assn., Suffolk County Bar Assn. Avocations: golf, skiing, swimming. Office: 300 Old Country Rd Mineola NY 11501-4198 also: 230 Park Ave New York NY 10169 also: 81 Main St White Plains NY 10601-1711

BARTLETT, CODY BLAKE, lawyer, educator; b. Syracuse, N.Y, Apr. 21, 1939; s. Stanley Jay and Izora Elizabeth (Blake) B.; m. Claudine Germaine Bouthillette, Dec. 27, 1968; 1 child, Cody Blake. AAS, Auburn C.C., 1960; BA with high honors, Mich. State U., 1963; JD, Harvard U., 1966. Bar: Mich. 1967, N.Y. 1967, Colo. 1993, U.S. Dist. Ct. (ca. dist.) Mich. 1967, U.S. Dist. Ct. (no. dist.) N.Y. 1967, U.S. Supreme Ct. 1984, U.S. Dist. Ct. (we. dist.) N.Y. 1985, U.S. Ct. Appeals (2d cir.) 2002, U.S. Tax Ct. 1999, U.S. Ct. Fed. Claims 1999. Law clk. Onondaga County Dist. Atty.'s Office, Syracuse, 1965; assoc. Touche, Ross, Bailey & Smart, Detroit, 1966; law clk. Onondaga County Family Ct., Syracuse, 1967; assoc. Melvin & Melvin, Syracuse, 1967; budget and accounts officer Appellate Divsn., 4th Dept., Rochester, N.Y., 1967-69, dep. dir. adminstrn., 1969-72, dir. adminstrn., 1972-80; chief atty. State Commn. on Jud. Conduct, 1980-84; ptnr. Newman, Kehoe, Wunder and Bartlett, Lyons, N.Y., 1984-91, Kehoe, Bartlett & Kehoe, Wolcott, N.Y., 1992-94, Bartlett Law Offices, Wolcott, 1994—. Spl. adminstr. N.Y. State Dangerous Drug Program, Western N.Y., 1973-75; adj. prof. polit. sci. dept. SUNY, Brockport, 1983-85, Grad. Sch. Pub. Adminstrn., 1985-90; adj. prof. Syracuse U. Coll. Law, 1980-84, Coll. Criminal Justice, Rochester Inst. Tech., 1979-80; grad. asst. polit. sci. dept. Mich. State U., 1962-63; lectr. jud. ethics and discipline Office Ct. Adminstrn., 1990. Author: Staying Fit Past Fifty, 1992; contbr. articles on legal issues and sports and fitness to publs.; drafter numerous legis. bills that became law. Mem. adv. com. Regional Criminal Justice Edn. and Tng. Ctr., Monroe C.C., Rochester, 1974-80; divsn. leader YMCA, Midtown Rochester membership drive, 1976; mem. East Bloomfield Planning Bd., 1984-87, chmn., 1985-87; trustee Village of East Bloomfield, 1985-87; mem. Sodus Point (N.Y.) Zoning Bd. Appeals, 1986-87; mem. adv. bd. Sodus Bay Hist. Soc., 1992; justice Sodus Point Village, 1994-95; mem. adv. bd. Wolcott C. of C., 1993; mem. Circuit of Reebok Profls. and Specialists, 1992-94. Recipient Disting. Alumni award Assn. Bds. Trustees SUNY, 1980, nat., regional and state powerlifting and bench press champion, 1982, 83, 96-2002; N.Y. State and Am. nat. and world bench press record holder, 1996-2002. Mem. N.Y. State Bar Assn. (spl. com. on jud. conduct 1984-90, profl. sports com. 1988-90), Wayne County Bar Assn., Onondaga County Bar Assn. (chmn. Syracuse City Ct. com. 1968-72), Nat. Strength and Conditioning Assn. (cert. strength and conditioning specialist, bd. dirs., lectr. 1989-96), Phi Kappa Phi, Pi Sigma Alpha. Home: 7094 Overlook Dr Sodus Point NY 14555-9620 Office: 12032 E Main St Wolcott NY 14590-1022 E-mail: bartlaw@dreamscape.com.

BARTLETT, DAVID, management consultant; b. Bethlehem, Pa., Mar. 23, 1946; s. Bertram Francis and Sally Caroline (Lewis) Bartlett; m. Joan Carol Benevelli, Dec. 27, 1975. BA, Trinity Coll., Hartford, Conn., 1969. News dir. WRC Radio, Washington, 1979-81; mng. editor Metromedia TV news, Washington, 1981-83; dir. news and English broadcasts Voice of Am., Washington, 1984-85; program dir. NBC Radio Networks, N.Y.C., 1986-88, v.p., 1988-89; pres. Radio-TV News Dirs. Assn., Washington, 1989-97; dir. global news svcs. Worldspace Corp., Washington, 1998-2000; v.p. Rowan & Blewitt Inc., Washington, 2000—.

BARTLETT, DAVID CARSON, state legislator; b. New London, Conn., Feb. 2, 1944; s. Neil Riley and Susan Marion (Carson) B.; m. Barbara Hunting, July 14, 1973 (div. 1974); m. Janice Anne Wezelman, Feb. 11, 1979; children: Daniel Wezelman, Elizabeth Anne. Student, Wesleyan U., Middletown, Conn., 1962-64; BA, U. Ariz., 1966, MA, 1970; JD, Georgetown U., 1976. Teaching asst. U. Ariz., Tucson, 1967-69; program analyst U.S. Dept. Labor, Washington, 1970-76; assoc. Snell & Wilmer, Tucson, 1976-77; pvt. practice Tucson, 1976-79; assoc. Davis, Eppstein & Hall, Tucson, 1979-85; mem. Ariz. Ho. of Reps., Tucson, 1983-88, Ariz. State Senate, 1989-92; chief counsel for civil rights Ariz. Atty. Gen.'s Office, Tucson, 1993-99, spl. couns., 1999—2002. Democrat. Home: 3236 E Via Palos Verdes Tucson AZ 85716-5854

BARTLETT, DAVID FARNHAM, physics educator; b. N.Y.C., Dec. 13, 1938; s. Frederic Pearson and Margaret Mary (Boulton) B.; m. Roxana Ellen Stoessel, Nov. 19, 1960; children: Andrew, Susannah, Christopher, Jennifer AB, Harvard U., 1959; AM, Columbia U., 1961, PhD, 1965. Instr. Princeton U., N.J., 1964-67, asst. prof., 1967-71; assoc. prof. physics U. Colo., Boulder, 1971-82, prof., 1982—. Editor: The Metric Debate, General Relativity and Gravitation, 1989; contbr. articles to profl. jours. Fellow Am. Phys. Soc.; mem. Am. Assn. Physics Tchrs., Am. Geophys. Union. Democrat. Home: 954 Lincoln Pl Boulder CO 80302-7234 Office: U Colo Dept Physics PO Box 390 Boulder CO 80309-0390

BARTLETT, DEDE THOMPSON, communications consultant; m. James Wesley Bartlett; children: Katherine Morgan, John Eriksen. BA, Vassar Coll.; MA, NYU. V.p., corp. sec. Philip Morris Cos. Inc., 1991-94, v.p. corp. affairs programs, 1995—2002; comms. cons., 2002—. Chmn. adv. coun. Nat. Domestic Violence Hotline; bd. dirs. Domestic Voilence Crisis Ctr., Women's Forum of N.Y., Corp. Alliance to Edn Ptnr. Violence, Women's Forum of N.Y. Recipient honors, YWCA, N.Y.C., Nat. Ctr. for Victims of Crime, Plays for Living, Nat. Coun. Jewish Women, Ctr. for Elimination of Violence in the Family. Mem.: Vassar Club (Fairfield County, Conn.). Home: 643 Oenoke Ridge New Canaan CT 06840

BARTLETT, DESMOND WILLIAM, engineering company executive; b. Southampton, Eng., Feb. 11, 1931; came to U.S., 1971; s. Walter Hayward and Gladys (Akerman) B.; m. Joan Margaret Mitchell, July 19, 1952; children: Jennie Claire. Grad. Marine Engring., U. Coll., Southampton, 1951; diploma, Shippingport Nuclear Sch., Pitts., 1961; exec. devel. diploma, Cornell U., 1978. Registered profl. engr., Europe; chartered engr. U.K.; lic. chief engr., U.K. Ministry of Transport, nuclear power plant operator, U.K. Ministry of Def. Engr. officer Cunard Steamship Co., Liverpool, Eng., 1952-57; engr. Vickers Armstrong Ltd., Southampton, 1957-59; project mgr. Rolls Royce & Assocs., Derby, Eng., 1959-65; chief engr. Cammell Laird Shipbuilders & Engrs., Birkenhead, Eng., 1965-71; cons. Gibbs & Hill, Inc., N.Y.C., 1971-72; project dir. Westinghouse Electric Co., Pitts., 1972-79; pres. Dravo Engrs. Inc., Pitts., 1979-85, C.F. Braun, Inc., Alhambra, Calif., 1986-89; v.p. bus. devel. Raytheon Engrs. and Constructors, Inc., Phila., 1991-95; v.p. Corp. Ventures Flour Daniel, Irvine, Calif., 1995-98, Bartlett Consulting Ltd., Sewickley, Pa., 1998—. Bd. dirs. Dravotec spa, Milan, Italy, F.C. de Weger Bv, Rotterdam, Dravo-Still, Inc., Pitts., Worley Santa Fe Ltd., London, Santa Fe Braun (UK) Ltd, London, Biomechanics Corp. Am. Melville, N.Y., Badger Catlytic Ltd., New Malden, England, Catalytic Svcs., Caracas, Venequela, Cosa United C.A., Caracas, United Yemen, Sana Yemen. Decorated officer Order Brit. Empire (Eng.). Fellow Inst. Marine Engrs.; mem. ASME, Am. Nuclear Soc., Am. Mgmt. Assn., Project Mgmt. Inst., Am. Petroleum Inst., Coun. on Fgn. Rels. (L.A. com. on fgn. relations). Clubs: Duqesne. E-mail: bartlettobe@aol.com.

BARTLETT, DIANE SUE, clinical mental health counselor, family therapist; b. Laconia, N.H., Dec. 6, 1947; d. Fred Elmer and Dorothy Pearl (Wakefield) Davis; m. Josiah Henry Bartlett, Aug. 23, 1980; 1 child by previous marriage, Fred Louis Hacker; 1 stepchild, Juliet. AA, Plymouth State Coll., 1982, MEd, 1988; B Gen. Studies summa cum laude, U. N.H., 1984. Lic. clin. mental health counselor. Mental health counselor, Ossipee, N.H., 1995—; police comm. specialist Divsn. Motor Vehicles, Concord, N.H., 1970-76, br. office mgr., 1976-83, coord. motor vehicle registrations, 1983-84; tax collector City of Dover, N.H., 1984; intern Lakes Region Mental Health Divsn., Laconia, N.H., 1985; counselor Latchkey Pastoral Counseling, Laconia, 1984-87; family therapist Children's Best Interest, Laconia, 1988—. Mental health counselor Carroll County Mental Health Svcs., Wolfeboro, N.H., 1988-95; participant N.H. Ann. Conf. on Status and Role of Women, Concord, 1985-87; mem. Carroll County Domestic Violence Coun., 1997—. Mem. Moultonboro (N.H.) Sch. Feasibility Study Commn., 1978; mem. adminstrv. bd. dirs., chmn. pastor-parish rels. com. United Meth. Ch., Moultonboro, 1983-94, N.H. ann. conf., 1986-88; mem. Friends of Families in Carroll County, 1995—. Grantee N.H. Charitable Found., 1985. Mem. ACA, Am. Mental Health Counselors Assn., Internat. Soc. for Study Dissociation. Avocations: skiing, swimming, reading, writing. Home: PO Box 14 Moultonborough NH 03254-0014 Office: Mountainside Bus Ctr 127 Route 28 Ossipee NH 03864-7300

BARTLETT, ELIZABETH SUSAN, audio-visual specialist; b. Bloomington, Ind., Sept. 11, 1927; d. Cecil Vernon and Nell (Helfrich) Bartlett; m. Frederick E. Sherman, July 8, 1955 (div. 1978). Student, Ind. U., 1946-48. Traffic-continuity dir. WTTS-Radio, Bloomington, Ind., 1947-48; program dir. WTTV-TV, Indpls., 1949-59; creative dir. Venus Advt. Agy., Indpls., 1960-68; prodn. mgr. Nat. TV News, Detroit, 1968-71; owner, producer Susan Sherman Prodns., Greenwich, Conn., 1971-73; audiovisual officer NSF, Washington, 1973-2001; lectr. in field. Cons. NSF, 2001—. Concept writer/prodr. film: The Observatories, 1981; prodr.: Science: Woman's Work, 1982, Keyhole of Eternity, 1975, What About Tomorrow?, 1978, The American Island, 1970, The New Engineers, 1986, Discover Science, 1988, A Brain, Books and a Curiosity, 1992, Radio Astronomy: Observing the Invisible Universe, 1999, Breaking the Code: The Arabidopsis Genome, 2000, others. Recipient Silver award Internat. Film and TV Festival of N.Y., 1970, 74, 2001, Gold medal Nat. Ednl. Film Festival, 1982, 89, Chris Bronze plaque Columbus Film Festival, 1982, Bronze award Internat. Film & TV Festival of N.Y., 1982, Gold award 1976, Gold Camera award U.S. Indsl. Film Festival, 1982, Silver Cindy award, Info. Film Producers Assn., 1982, award for creative excellence U.S. Indsl. Film Festival, 1975, Techfilm Festival award, 1979, 80, 88, Gold award Houston Internat. Film Festival, 1987, Art Direction Mag. Creativity award, 1988, Videographer award of Distinction, 2001, Silver award, 2001, Aurora Festival Gold award, 2001; named Outstanding Woman for Contbn. in Arts, Federally Employed Women, 1984. Mem. Am. Women in Radio and TV (chpt. pres. 1953-56, 69-70), Washington Film and Video Coun. (pres. 1978-79), Coun. on Internat. Non-Theatrical Events (adv. bd., Golden Eagle award 1970, 74, 76-79, 82, 87, 99). Home: 809 S Columbus St Alexandria VA 22314-4206

BARTLETT, EUGENE FRED, retired surgeon; b. Spokane, Wash., 1933; MD, Washington U., 1958. Diplomate Am. Bd. Surgery. Intern U. Va. Hosp., 1958-59; resident in surgery U.S. Naval Hosp., Phila., 1961-65, mem. staff Oak Harbor, Wash., to 1997. Fellow ACS.

BARTLETT, JAMES LOWELL, III, investment company executive; b. Boston, May 26, 1945; s. James Lowell and Shirley Victoria (Wyatt) B.; m. Shannon Mara McMillion, May 4, 1979; children: James Lowell IV, Zachary Morgan, Matthew Wyatt. BS, U. Calif., Berkeley, 1967, MBA, 1968. Loan officer nat. div. Bank of Am., Los Angeles, 1968; fin. mgr. Psychology Today mag., Del Mar, Calif., 1969; pres. Forum Communications Corp.; pub. Cuisine, Politics Today, Volleyball mags., N.Y.C., 1970-82; pres. Bartlett & Co., Santa Barbara, Calif., 1982—. Commr. Internat. Volleyball Assn., 1977-80 Mem. Lds Ch. Office: 5662 Calle Real Santa Barbara CA 93117-2317

BARTLETT, JAMES WILSON, III, lawyer; b. Pasadena, Calif., Mar. 21, 1946; s. James Wilson Jr. and Helen (Archbold) B.; m. Jane Edmunds Graves; children: Matthew Archbold, Polly Graves. BA, Washington & Lee U., 1968; JD, Vanderbilt U., 1975. Bar: Md. 1975, U.S. Dist. Ct. Md. 1975, U.S. Dist. Ct. (no. dist.) Ohio, 1992, U.S. Ct. Claims 1984, U.S. Ct. Appeals (4th cir.) 1976, U.S. Ct. Appeals (6th cir.) 1992, U.S. Supreme Ct. 1995. Assoc. Semmes, Bowen & Semmes, Balt., 1975-85; pvt. practice Balt., 1985-86; ptnr. Kroll & Tract, Balt., 1986-87, Wilson, Elser, Moskowitz, Edelman & Dicker, Balt., 1987-98, mng. ptnr., 1998-2001; ptnr. Semmes, Bowen & Semmes, Balt., 2001—. Permanent mem. jud. conf. 4th Cir. Assoc. editor: Am. Maritime Cases, 1997—; contbr. articles to profl. jours. Chmn. law firm campaign United Fund, Balt., 1979; bd. dirs. Roland Park Civic League, 1987-90, Balt. (Md.) Maritime Exchange, 2001—. 1st lt. U.S. Army, 1969-71. Mem.: ABA (vice chmn. 1985—88, chmn. admiralty and maritime law tort and ins. practice sect. 1990—91, vice chmn. 1992—95, chmn. admiralty and maritime litig. com. litig. sect. 1997—99, vice chmn. 1999—), Assn. Average Adjusters U.S., Assn. Average Adjusters (Eng.), Md. Def. Counsel Inc., Def. Rsch. Inst., Maritime Law Assn. U.S. (proctor, bd. dirs. 1998—2001, chair practice and proc. com. 2000—), Balt. City Bar Assn., Md. Bar Assn., St. Andrews Soc., Am. Boat and Yacht Coun., Propeller Club U.S. (gov. Balt. chpt. 1984—87, 1997—2003, v.p. 1987—88, exec. v.p. 1988—89, pres. 1989—90, nat. regional v.p. 1991—92, nat. 3d v.p. 1995—96), Md. Club. Republican. Presbyterian. Home: 307 Edgevale Rd Baltimore MD 21210-1913 Office: Semmes Bowen & Semmes 250 W Pratt St Baltimore MD 21201 E-mail: jbartlett@mail.semmes.com.

BARTLETT, JANET SANFORD (JANET WALZ), school nurse; b. Bryn Mawr, Pa., Aug. 13, 1930; d. Edward Joseph Walz and Anna Downing (Little) Walz Tomlin; m. Joseph Richard Bartlett, May 6, 1952 (div. April 1972); children: Cheryl, Elaine, Karen, Lee, Patrick, Michael. Diploma nursing, Meml. Mission Sch. Nursing, 1953; EMT-I cert., El Paso C.C., 1983. RN, N.C., Tex. Office nurse William F. Hillier, M.D., Asheville, N.C., 1953-55; school nurse Ysleta Ind. Sch. Dist., El Paso, 1973-93. Author: (manual) Sch. Nurse Manual, 1979, Volunteer's Handbook, 1979, (cookbook) Bartlett Heritage Cookbook; editor: (newsletter) Nurses Notes Newsletter, 1983-88; co-creator, copyright, D.K. Buster, 1989. Mem. El Paso Health Issues Forum, 1985—88; co-chair El Paso Oral Health Commn., 1987—; life mem. PTA; pres. El Paso coun., bd. dirs. Campfire Girls, Inc., 1971—74, leader Blue Birds, Camp Fire guardian; active Boy Scouts Am., Girl Scouts Am.; com. chair El Paso chpt. Am. Cancer Soc.; co-chair Ysleta Sch. Dist. Employee Wellness, 1989—90, compiler manual; sec. Unite El Paso Birth Packet Com., 1993—96, chmn., 1996—; founder, chmn. Health Connection, 1996—; apptd. oral health svcs. adv. com. Tex. Bd. Health, 1995—, vice chmn., 1999—2001; mentor Sageland Elem. Sch., 1994—97; mem. vestry St. Alban's Anglo Cath. Ch., 1996—99, sr. warden, 1997—99. Recipient Outstanding Staff Support award Ysleta Vol. Svcs., 1988-89, Stand Up for El Paso award KDBC TV, 1991, REACH award YWCA/El Paso Healthcare System, 1992, Pub. Health Partnership award El Paso City-County Health and Environ. Dist., 1998, Older El Pasoans Hall of Fame award Mayor's Adv. Bd. on Aging, 1999, Access award ADA, 2003; named Woman of Yr. El Paso Parks and Recreation, 1995; named to Ysleta Ret. Sch. Employees Assn. Hall of Fame, 2000, El Paso Women's Hall of Fame, El Paso Women's Comm., 2002. Mem. Nat. Assn. Sch. Nurses, Tex. Assn. Sch. Nurses (Pres.'s award 1990, Tex. Sch. Nurse of Yr. 1991), Tex. Assn. Sch. Nurses Region 19 (v.p. 1982, 83, Sch. Nurse of Yr. 1990), Ysleta Sch. Nurses Assn. (pres. 1988, Sch. Nurse of Yr. 1987, World Healer award 1995), Assistance League of El Paso (yearbook chmn. 1994, 95, Sch. Bell. com. 1994—). Avocations: swimming, knitting, cooking, children, traveling. Home: 10249 Bayo Ave El Paso TX 79925-4347

BARTLETT, JOHN GILL, infectious disease physician; b. Syracuse, N.Y., Feb. 12, 1937; s. Kenneth Gill and Bernice (Kleinhaus) B.; m. Jean Scott; children: Valerie, Joshua, Scott. BS, Dartmouth Coll., 1959; MD, Upstate Med. Ctr. Internship Peter Bent Brigham Hosp., Boston, 1963-65; assoc. prof. U. Ala., Birmingham, 1967-68; residency UCLA-Wadsworth Hosp., L.A., 1968-70; asst. prof. medicine UCLA, Balt., 1970-75; assoc. prof. Tufts U. Sch. Medicine, Boston, 1975-80; prof., 1980, Johns Hopkins U. Sch. Medicine, Balt., 1980—, chief of staff. Contbr. articles to profl. jours. and chpts. to books; author 10 books in field of infectious diseases. Mem. Assn. Am. Physicians, Am. Soc. Microbiology, A Thoracic Soc., Infectious Diseases Soc. Am., Am. Fedn. Clin. Rsch., AAAS, ACP, Interurban Club, Peripatetic Club, Assn. Subsplty. Profs., Assn. Profs. Medicine. Avocation: painting. Home: Apt 705 1101 Saint Paul St Baltimore MD 21202-2626

BARTLETT, JOHN LAURENCE, lawyer; b. L.A., June 9, 1942; s. Oswald and Sarah Elisabeth (Caldwell) B.; m. Jane Helen Dormann, June 22, 1963; children: Jennifer Lynn, George Andrew. AB, UCLA, 1963; LLB, Stanford Law Sch., 1967. Bar: D.C. 1967, U.S. Dist. Ct. D.C. 1968, U.S. Ct. Appeals (D.C. cir.) 1969, U.S. Ct. Appeals (4th cir.) 1976, U.S. Supreme Ct. 1976, U.S. Ct. Appeals (2d cir.) 1977. Assoc. Kirkland & Ellis, Washington, 1967-72, ptnr., 1972-83, Wiley, Rein & Fielding, Washington, 1983—. Bd. dirs. Arinc Inc., Aeronautical Radio, Inc., Cmty. Residences Found., chmn. 1995—. Bd. dirs. Found. for Ministry of the Laity, Inc. Mem. ABA, Fed. Comm. Bar Assn. Home: 2757 N Nelson St Arlington VA 22207-5033 Office: Wiley Rein & Fielding 1776 K St NW Washington DC 20006-2304 E-mail: jbartlett@wrf.com.

BARTLETT, JOHN WESLEY, consulting firm executive; b. Camden, N.J., Oct. 18, 1935; s. William W. and Naomi Verna (Snook) B.; m. Helen Barbara Boulas, Mar. 2, 1968 (dec. Feb. 1986); children: Larah, Tanya; m. Joan R. Field, June 21, 2000. BSChemE, U. Rochester, 1957; MChemE, Rensselaer Poly. Inst., 1959, PhD, 1962. Staff engr. Knolls Atomic Power Lab., Schenectady, N.Y., 1957-62; asst. prof. U. Rochester, N.Y., 1962-68; Fulbright prof. nuclear engring. Istanbul (Turkey) Tech. U., 1968-69; program mgr. Pacific N.W. Labs., Richland, Va., 1969-78; presdl. exch. exec. Nat. Bur. Standards, Washington, 1973-74; dir. energy and environment Analytic Scis. Corp., Reading, Mass., 1978-89; cons. to sec. U.S. Dept. Energy, Washington, 1989-90, dir. Office Civilian Radioactive Waste Mgmt., 1990—, pres. The Bartlett Co., Vienna, Va., 1993-96, SC&A, McLean, Va., 1996—. Contbr. articles to profl. jours. Mem. Sch. Bd., Richland, 1970-73; mem., mayor pro tem City Coun., Richland, 1974-78; vice chair Conservation Commn., Lynnfield, Mass., 1979-89. Rsch. grantee NSF, 1963-64, NIH, 1965-68, recipient Robert E. Wilson award, AIChE, 1993. Mem. AAAS, Am. Nuclear Soc. (exec. com. 1976-80, 86-90), Rotary (bd. dirs. Richland club 1976-78), Sigma Xi. Republican. Avocations: model shipwright, piano. Home: 1300 Crystal Dr #403 Arlington VA 22202 Office: SC&A Inc 1355 Beverly Rd Mc Lean VA 22101-3623 E-mail: jbvienna@aol.com.

BARTLETT, JOSEPH WARREN, lawyer; b. Boston, June 14, 1933; s. Charles W. and Barbara (Hastings) B.; m. May Parish, Apr. 28, 1956 (div.); children: Charles, Susan, Henry; m. Barbara Bemis, Sept. 20, 1980. AB, Harvard U., 1955; LLB, Stanford U., 1960. Bar: Mass. 1962, D.C. 1969, N.Y. 1981. Law clk. Chief Justice Warren, U.S. Supreme Ct., 1960-61; pvt. practice Boston, 1961-66; ptnr. Gaston & Snow, Boston, 1966-80, Gaston & Snow (formerly Gaston Snow Beekman & Bogue), N.Y.C., 1980-90, of counsel, 1990-91; ptnr. Mayer, Brown & Platt, 1991-96, Morrison & Foerster, N.Y.C., 1996—2002; of counsel Fish & Richardson P.C., N.Y.C. Counsel Mass. Commn. Adminstrn., 1964-65; gen. counsel, under sec. Dept. Commerce, Washington, 1967-69; prin. adviser on universal social security coverage Sec. of HEW, Washington, 1978-79; acting prof. Stanford U., 1978; trustee, mem. fin. com. Montefiore Med. Ctr.; mem. Council on Fgn. Relations; adj. prof. NYU Law Sch. Served to 1st lt. U.S. Army, 1956-57. Fellow Am. Bar Found.; mem. Am. Law Inst., Am. Bar Assn., Boston Bar Assn. (pres. 1977-78) Democrat. Episcopalian. Home: 200 E 71st St Apt 16C New York NY 10021-5147 Office: Fish and Richardson PC 45 Rockefeller Plaza Ste 2800 New York NY 10111 Office Fax: 212-258-2291. E-mail: joseph.bartlett@fr.com.

BARTLETT, KATHARINE TIFFANY, law educator; b. New Haven, Feb. 16, 1947; d. Edgar Parmelee and Elizabeth (Clark) B.; m. Christopher H. Schroeder, Aug. 13, 1975; children: Emily, Ted, Elizabeth. BA, Wheaton Coll., 1968; MA, Harvard U., 1969; JD, U. Calif., Berkeley, 1975. Bar: Calif. 1975, N.C. 1980, U.S. Dist. Ct. (no. dist.) Calif. 1975, U.S. Dist. Ct. (mid. dist.) N.C. Law clk. to presiding justice Calif. Supreme Ct., San Francisco, 1975-76; atty. Legal Aid Soc. of Alameda County, Oakland, Calif., 1976-79; A. Kenneth Pye prof. of law Duke U., Durham, NC, 1979—; dean, 2000—. Vis. prof. UCLA, 1985-86, Boston U., 1990. Grad. prize fellow Harvard U., 1968-69, fellow Nat. Humanities Ctr., 1992-93. Mem. Am. Law Inst., Soc. Am. Law Tchrs., N.C. Women Attys., Am. Law Inst. (reporter for principles of family dissolution), Phi Beta Kappa. Democrat. Office: Duke Univ Law Sch Sci Dr and Towerview Rd Box 90362 Durham NC 27708-0362

BARTLETT, LEONARD LEE, retired communications educator, retired advertising agency executive; b. Mountain Home, Idaho, May 31, 1930; s. Harold Roberts and Alma Martina (Nixon) B.; m. Sue Ann Kipfer, Nov. 5, 1966; children: Jennifer, Deborah; children by previous marriage: Linda Lee, Cynthia, Nancy, Pamela, William Charles. BA, Brigham Young U., Provo, Utah, 1957, MA, 1989. Advt. mgr. Steiner Co., Chgo., 1957-59; sr. v.p. Marsteller Inc., Chgo., 1959-67; vice chmn. Cole & Weber, Inc., Seattle, 1966-84; chmn. Cole & Weber Calif., San Francisco, 1984-86, Los Angeles, 1986-87; assoc. prof. communications Brigham Young U., Provo, 1989 2000; ret., 2000. Acting chmn. dept. comms. Brigham Young U., Provo, 1995—96, chmn. dept. comm., 1996—97, asst. to pres. univ. comms., 1997—2000. Mem. Am. Assn. Advt. Agys. (chmn. Western region 1980, nat. bd. 1980-81). Republican. Mem. Ch. Jesus Christ of Latter-day Saints. Home: 1211 East 2080 North Provo UT 84604-2123 E-mail: leeber30@comcast.net.

BARTLETT, LINDA GAIL, lawyer; b. Bklyn., Apr. 6, 1943; d. Manny Max and Lottie (Sandler) Katz; m. Randall David Bartlett, Feb. 10, 1979; children: Gregory, Jeremy. AB, Bklyn. Coll., 1964; JD cum laude, U. Miami, 1977. Bar: U.S. Dist. Ct. (so., ea. and no. dists.) N.Y. 1979, U.S. Dist. Ct. N.Mex. 1979, U.S. Ct. Appeals (2d, 5th and 10th cirs.) 1979, U.S. Supreme Ct. 1980. Vol. U.S. Peace Corps, 1964-66; clin. intern U.S. NLRB, Coral Gables, Fla., 1976; assoc. Klecan & Roach, P.A., Albuquerque, 1977-78, Benjamin Wyle, N.Y.C., 1978-81; arbitrator Civil Ct. State of N.Y., 1981-90; pvt. practice law, 1990-94; ptnr. Bartlett, Bartlett & Ziegler, P.C., 1994—; mediator N.Y. County comml. divsn. N.Y. State Supreme Ct., 1996—. Adminstrv. law judge N.Y C. Dept. Environ. Protection, 1983-85; dep. gen. cunsel Dirs. Guild Am., Inc., N.Y.C., 1981-90, asst. exec. sec., 1985-90; adj. prof. law CUNY, 1986-87, 93—, vis prof. law, 1987-88; adj. prof. law Cornell U., 1989, N.Y. State Sch. Indsl. and Labor Rels., Ithaca. Bd. dirs. Lake Peekskill Civic Assn., 1972-73; planning and zoning chmn. LWV, 1972-73. Mem. ABA, Assn. Bar City N.Y. (labor rels. com., com. on labor arbitration), N.Y. State Bar Assn. (dist. del. employment and labor law sect. 1984-89, chair St. John's Law Sch., Ann. Employment Law Litigation Inst. 1996—, exec. com.). Avocations: sailing, skiing. Office: 10 E 40th St Fl 46 New York NY 10016-0301

BARTLETT, LYNN CONANT, English literature educator; b. Bethlehem, Pa., Dec. 14, 1921; s. Fay Conant and Marie Agnes (McGuiness) B.; m. Margaret Emma Johnson, June 29, 1946; 1 dau., Anne Elston. BA, Lehigh U., 1943; A.M., Harvard, 1947, PhD, 1957; B. Litt., Oxford U., Eng., 1952. Instr. English Lehigh U., 1946; teaching fellow Harvard, 1948-50; instr. Vassar Coll., 1952-57; asst. prof., 1957-62; asso. prof., 1962-70; prof., 1970-92; prof. emeritus, 1992—; asst. dean coll., 1958-61; sec. coll., 1966-76. Editor: (with W.R. Sherwood) The English Novel, Background Readings, 1967. Served with AUS, 1943-46. Decorated Bronze Star. Mem. Phi Beta Kappa, Sigma Phi Epsilon. Clubs: Harvard (N.Y.C.), Circumnavigators Club. Home: 170 College Ave Poughkeepsie NY 12603-2806 E-mail: Lcbartlett6@cs.com.

BARTLETT, MICHAEL JOHN, lawyer; b. Paterson, N.J., June 8, 1943; s. Ernest John and Alice Edith (Schrell) B.; children: Tara Christine, Jessica Simons, Darren Michael. BA cum laude, Amherst Coll., 1965; JD, U. Va., 1969. Bar: Va. 1969, D.C. 1971, U.S. Supreme Ct. 1976. Atty. Office Gen. Counsel, NLRB, Washington, 1969-71; atty. law offices Joseph C. Wells, Washington, 1971-74; assoc. Vedder, Price, Kaufman, Kammholz & Day, Washington, 1974-76, ptnr., 1976-80; ptnr. (Michael J. Bartlett, P.C.) Ogletree, Deakins, Nash, Smoak & Stewart, Washington, 1980-86; staff v.p. employee rels. Ea. Airlines, Inc., 1986-87; shareholder Verner, Liipfert, Bernhard, Mc Pherson and Hand, Chartered, 1987-94; pvt. practice, 1994-98; dir. labor law policy U.S. C. of C., 1998—2002; mem. NLRB, Washington, 2002—. Contbr. articles to profl. jours. Mem. exec. bd. Arlington (Va.) YMCA, 1982-86, treas., 1984-86. Andrew D. Lawrie scholar, Amherst Coll., 1964-65; Am. Jurisprudence award in labor law Lawyer Coop. Pub. Co., 1969. Mem. ABA (sect. on labor law), Va. State Bar, D.C. Bar. Home: 4650 Washington Blvd Apt 926 Arlington VA 22201-5776 Office: 1099 14th St NW Washington DC 20570-2000

BARTLETT, NEIL, chemist, emeritus educator; b. Newcastle-upon-Tyne, Eng., Sept. 15, 1932; s. Norman and Ann Willins (Vock) B.; m. Christina Isabel Cross, Dec. 26, 1957; children: Jeremy John, Jane Ann, Christopher, Robin. B.Sc., Kings Coll., U. Durham, Eng., 1954; PhD in Inorganic Chemistry, Kings Coll., U. Durham, 1957; D.Sc. (hon.), U. Waterloo, Can., 1968, Colby Coll., 1972, U. Newcastle-upon-Tyne, 1981, McMaster U., Can., 1992; D.Univ. (hon.), U. Bordeaux, France, 1976, U. Ljubljana, Slovenia, 1989, U. Nantes, France, 1990; LLD, Simon Fraser U., Can., 1993; Dr. rer. nat. (hon.), Freie U., Berlin, 1998. Lectr. chemistry U. B.C., Vancouver, Canada, 1958—63, prof., 1963—66; prof. chemistry Princeton U., NJ, 1966—69, U. Calif., Berkeley, 1969—99; guest sr. scientist chem. sci. divsn. LBNL, Berkeley, 1999—. Mem. adv. bd. on inorganic reactions and methods Verlag Chemie, 1978—; mem. adv. panel Nat. Measurement Lab., Nat. Bur. Stds., 1974-80; E.W.R. Steacie Meml. fellow NRC, Can., 1964-66; Miller vis. prof. U. Calif., Berkeley, 1967-68; 20th G.N. Lewis Meml. lectr., 1973; William Lloyd Evans Meml. lectr. Ohio State U., 1966; A.D. Little lectr. Northeastern U., 1969; Phi Beta Upsilon lectr. U. Nebr., 1975; Henry Werner lectr. U. Kans., 1977; Jeremy Musher Meml. lectr., Israel, 1980, Randolph T. Major Meml. lectr. U. Conn., 1985, J.C. Karcher lectr. U. Okla., 1988; Brotherton vis. prof. U. Leeds, Eng., 1981; Erskine vis. lectr. U. Canterbury, New Zealand, 1983; Wilsmore fellow Melbourne U., Australia, 1983; vis. fellow All Souls Coll., Oxford U., 1984; Miller prof. U. Calif.-Berkeley, 1986-87; George H. Cady lectr. U. Wash., Seattle, 1994; Leermakers lectr. Wesleyan U., 1995; Davis Meml. lectr. U. New Orleans, 1997, Pierre Duhem seminaires, U. Bordeaux, 1998. Bd. editors Inorganic Chemistry, 1967-79, Jour. Fluorine Chemistry, 1971-80, Synthetic Metals, Revue Chimie Minerale; mem. adv. bd. McGraw-Hill Ency. Sci. and Tech. Recipient Rsch. Corp. prize; E.W.R. Steacie prize, 1965; Elliott Cresson medal Franklin Inst., 1968; Kirkwood medal Yale U. and Am. Chem. Soc. (New Haven sect.), 1969; Dannie-Heinemann prize The Gottingen acad. 1971; Robert A. Welch award in chemistry, 1976; Alexander von Humboldt Found. award, 1977; medal Jozef Stefan Inst., Slovenia, 1980; Moissan medal, 1986; Prix Moissan, Paris, 1988; fellow Alfred P. Sloan Found., 1964-66; Bonner Chemiepries, Bonn, 1991; Berkeley citation, 1993. Fellow Royal Soc. (Davy medal, 2002), Royal Soc. Chemistry (U.K., hon.), Am. Acad. Arts and Scis., Chem. Inst. Can. (1st Noranda lectr. 1963), Royal Soc. Can.; mem. NAS (fgn. assoc.), Leopoldina Acad. (Halle, Salle), Akademie der Wissenschaften in Gottingen, Associé Etranger, Academia Europaea, Académie des Sciences, Institut de France, Am. Chem. Soc. (chmn. divs. fluorine chemistry 1972, inorganic chemistry 1977, award in inorganic chemistry 1970, W.H. Nichols award N.Y. sect. 1983, Pauling medal of Pacific N.W. sects. 1989, Disting. Svc. award 1989, award for Creative Work in Fluorine Chemistry 1992), Phi Lambda Upsilon (hon.) Home: 6 Oak Dr Orinda CA 94563-3912 Office: Bldg 70A c/o Rm 3307 LBNL Berkeley CA 94720 Office Fax: 510-486-6033. E-mail: nbartlett@lbl.gov.

BARTLETT, NORMA THYRA, retired administrative assistant; b. Raymond, S.D., June 7, 1922; d. Wilhelm Emil and Olga Sophie (Mailand) Claussen; m. Fred Otis Metcalf, Mar. 29, 1941 (dec. Apr. 1963); children: Linda E. Lepak, Barry Otis (dec. Feb. 2000); m. Francis Grindal Bartlett, Dec. 27, 1963. BA, U. Wash., 1969; Diploma, Inst. of Children's Lit., 1997. Cert. profl. sec. Office mgr. Fed. Old Line Ins. Co., Everett, Wash., 1949-55; supr. office svc. Scott Paper Co., Everett, Wash., 1958-63; tchr. bus. edn. Canyon Park Jr. H.S., Seattle, 1969, Bellevue (Wash.) C.C., 1969; exec. asst. Peoples Bank, Starkville, Miss., 1970-76; prin. Satellite Steno Svc., Starkville, Miss., 1976-77; office mgr. Donald Wiley & Assocs., Sydney, Australia, 1977-80. Bd. dirs. United Cmty. Fund Snohomish County, Everett, Wash., 1961-62; pres. Scott Paper Co. Fellowship Fund, Everett, 1961. Hon. life mem. United Luth. Ch. Women, Everett, Wash., 1958—; organizer, charter pres. Starkville Bus. and Profl. Women, 1972-74; pres. Welcome Wagon Club, Ocean Springs, Miss., 1982-83; tutor Jackson County Literacy, Ocean Springs, 1985-88; organizer Discourse, Ocean Springs, 1985-86. Norma T. Bartlett scholarship named in her honor Starkville Area Bus. and Profl. Women, 1978. Mem.: AAUW (Gig Harbor br. media rep. 1997—99), Intertel, Mensa (local sec. 1989—91, editor newsletter 1987—89), U. Wash. Alumni Assn. Democrat. Lutheran. Avocations: needlework, reading, writing, travel. Home: 1305 N Highlands Pkwy Apt C1 Tacoma WA 98406-2171 E-mail: fgbart@comcast.com.

BARTLETT, PAUL DANA, JR., agribusiness executive; b. Kansas City, Mo., Sept. 16, 1919; s. Paul D. and Alice May (Hiestand) B.; m. Joan Jenkins, May 14, 1949; children— J. Alison Bartlett Jager, Marilyn Bartlett Hebenstreit, Paul Dana III, Frederick Jenkins. BA, Yale U., 1941. Chmn. Bartlett and Co., Kansas City, Mo., 1961-77; pres., chmn. bd. Bartlett and Co. (formerly Bartlett Agri Enterprises, Inc.), Kansas City, 1977—, chmn., dir. Bd. dir. United Mo. Bank, United Mo. Bancshares. Lt. USN, 1942-46 Office: Bartlett and Company 4800 Main St Ste 600 Kansas City MO 64112-2509

BARTLETT, RICHARD ADAMS, American historian, educator; b. Boulder, Colo., Nov. 23, 1920; s. John Thomas and Margaret Emily (Abbott) B.; m. Marie Regina Cosgrove, Dec. 26, 1945; children: Richard, Margaret, Thomas, Mary. BA, U. Colo., 1942; MA, U. Chgo., 1947; PhD, U. Colo., 1953. Instr. Tex. A&M U., College Station, 1945-51; asst. prof. Fla. State U., Tallahassee, 1955-63, assoc. prof., 1963-67, prof., 1968-89, prof. emeritus, 1989—. Author: Great Surveys of the American West, 1962, 66, paperback, 1980, 86, 89, 93 (Spur award Western Writers Am. 1962, Desert Mag. award 1962), The Wilderness and the Indians: Challenges in the New World, 1970, Nature's Yellowstone, 1974, paperback, 1989, The New Country: A Social History of the American Frontier, 1776-1890, 1974, paperback, 1976, 86, Freedom's Trail, 1979, 2d edit., 1981, Yellowstone: A Wilderness Besieged, 1985, paperback, 1989, From Cody to the World: The First Seventy-Five Years of the Buffalo Bill Memorial Association, 1992, Troubled Waters: Champion International and the Pigeon River Controversy, 1995, Yellowstone Holiday, 1998; editor: The Gilded Age: America, 1865-1900, 1969, Rolling Rivers: An Encyclopedia of America's Rivers, 1984; contbr. articles and book revs. to profl. jours. Huntington Libr. fellow, 1967, Woodrow Wilson fellow Smithsonian Inst., 1979-80; recipient fellowship Am. Philos. Soc., 1967, Rsch. grant Fla. State U., grant Am. Philos. Soc. Mem. Western History Assn. (governing coun. 1976-79, edtl. bd. The Am. West 1980-82), Fla. Coll. Tchrs. History (pres. 1974-75), Phi Alpha Theta. Episcopalian. Home: 2205 Mendoza Ave Tallahassee FL 32304-1319 E-mail: rbartlet@mailer.fsu.edu.

BARTLETT, RICHARD CHALKLEY, business executive, writer, conservationist; b. L.A., May 23, 1935; s. Theodore Lester Bartlett and Maud (Colley) Newsom; m. Joanne Krieger; children: Lisa, Christopher. BS in Communications, U. Fla., 1956. With advt. sales dept. The Miami (Fla.) Herald, 1958; internat. sales and mgmt. exec. for home parties div. Tupperware Inc., Orlando, 1959-65; v.p. advt. and sales promotion Vanda Beauty Counselor div. Dart Industries, Orlando, Fla., 1965-71; exec. v.p. mktg. Dynasty Industries Inc., Dallas, 1971-73; dir. mktg. svcs. Mary Kay Inc., Dallas, 1973-76, v.p. mktg., 1976-85, exec. v.p. mktg., 1986-87, pres., COO, 1987-93, vice-chmn., 1993—. Bd. dirs. Vital Voices Global Partnership; chmn. U.S. Direct Selling Assn., Washington, 1991-93, U.S. Direct Selling Edn. Found., Washington, 1993-94, bd. dirs.;; vice chmn. edn. World Fedn. Direct Selling, 1997-99; adv. bd. U. Fla. Ctr. for Retailing Edn. and Rsch., Gainesville; adv. coun., bd. dirs. mem. adv. coun. U. Tex. Press; mem. adv. com. Coll. Agrl. Sci. and Natural Resources, Tex. Tech. U.; vice chmn. bd. dirs. Nat. Environ. Edn. and Tng. Found.; bd. dirs. com. Nat. Inst. for the Environment, Nat. Coun. Sci. and Environ.; mem. nat. environ. edn. adv. bd. coun. US EPA. Author: The Direct Option, 1994, Saving the Best of Texas: A Partnership Approach to Conservation, 1995; co-author: The Sportsman's Guide to Texas, 1988. Chmn. Tex. Environ. Edn. Partnership Fund Bd.; bd. dirs. Better Bus. Bur. Met. Dallas, The Aldo Leopold Found., Nature Conservancy N.Mex.; hon. trustee The Nature Conservancy of Tex.; chmn. edn. and outreach adv. com. Tex. Parks and Wildlife Dept. With U.S. Army, 1957. Named Outstanding Marketer of Yr., Southwestern Mktg. Assn., 1991, Chief of Exec. of Yr., Internat. TV Assn., 1992; named to U.S. Direct Selling Assn. Hall of Fame, 1994, U.S. Direct Selling Edn. Found. Circle of Honor, 1995, Pi Kappa Phi Nat. Hall of Fame, 1996; recipient Oak Leaf award Nature Conservancy, 1997. Mem. Acad. Mktg. Sci. (Disting. Marketer of Yr. 1995), Dallas Com. on Fgn. Rels. Avocations: conservation work, performing arts. Office: Mary Kay PO Box 799045 Dallas TX 75379-7045

BARTLETT, RICHARD JAMES, lawyer; b. Glens Falls, N.Y., Feb. 15, 1926; s. George Willard and Kathryn M. (McCarthy) Bartlett; m. Claire E. Kennedy, Aug. 18, 1951; children: Michael, Amy. BS, Georgetown U., 1945; LLB, Harvard U., 1949; LLD (hon.), Union Coll., 1974; ScD (hon.), Albany Med. Coll., 1986. Bar: N.Y. 1949. Pvt. practice, Glens Falls, 1949-73; with Clark Bartlett & Caffry, 1962-73; justice N.Y. State Supreme Ct., 1973-79; chief adminstr. cts. N.Y. State, 1974-79; dean Albany (N.Y.) Law Sch., Union U., 1979-86; mem. Bartlett, Pontiff, Stewart, & Rhodes P.C., Glens Falls, 1986—. Mem. N.Y. Bd. Law Examiners, 1986—2001, chair, 1998—2001; chmn. N.Y. Jud. Commn. Justice for Children, 1988—90; trustee Nat. Conf. Bd. Examiners, 1987—97, pres., 1996; dir. Nat. Conf. Bar Founds., 2001—; del. N.Y. Constl. Conv., 1967. Trustee Hyde Collection, Glens Falls, 1967—98. Capt. USAF, 1951—53. Fellow: Am. Bar Found.; mem.: ABA (ho. dels. 1997—2001), N.Y. State Bar Assn. (ho. dels. 2002—), N.Y. Bar Found. (bd. dirs. 1989—, pres. 2000—03), Am. Law Inst. (life), Warren County Bar, Assn. Bar City of N.Y. Republican. Roman Catholic. Office: 1 Washington St PO Box 2168 Glens Falls NY 12801-2168

BARTLETT, ROBERT WILLIAM, lawyer; b. Chgo., Nov. 11, 1941; s. Robert C. and Rita E. Bartlett; m. Mary Lou Holtzman, Mar. 8, 1988; 1 child, Brooke Ann. AB, Stanford U., 1963; LLB, U. Va., 1966. Bar: Ill. 1966. Assoc. counsel U.S. League Savs. Instns., Chgo., 1970-77, assoc. gen. counsel, editor legal bull., 1977-81, sr. v.p., 1981-91; exec. editor bus. and fin. group Commerce Clearing House, Riverwoods, Ill., 1991-2000. Mem. ABA (mem. com. on savs. instns. 1973--). Roman Catholic. Avocation: running. Home: 8 Anglican Ln Lincolnshire IL 60069-3316 E-mail: bartlettrw@earthlink.net.

BARTLETT, ROGER DANFORTH, engineering executive; b. Brentwood, Mo., Dec. 10, 1940; s. Robert Danforth and Margaret Elizabeth (Gruber) B.; m. Cynthia A. Adkins, July 1, 1978; children: Rex Danforth, Ryan Andrew, Megan Leigh. BSEE, Bradley U., 1971. Engr. Revomat, Parkville, Mo., 1971-72; divsn. engr. Am. Multi-Cinema, Inc., Kansas City, Mo., 1972-75, project mgr., 1975-78, assoc. dir. corp. engring., 1978-82, dir. corp. engring., 1982-85; dir. constrn. Commonwealth Theatres, Inc., 1985-87, dir. purchasing/tech. svcs., 1987-88; dir. midwest constr. United Artist Theatre Cir., 1988-89; pres. Bartlett & Assocs., Inc., Shawnee Mission, Kans., 1989—. Mem. IEEE, SMPTE, Constrn. Specifications Inst. Home and Office: 8701 W 72nd St Shawnee Mission KS 66204-1132 E-mail: rogerbart@aol.com.

BARTLETT, ROSCOE G. congressman; b. Ky., June 3, 1926; married; 10 children. BA, Columbia Union, 1947; MS, U. Md., 1948, PhD, 1952. Asst. prof. Loma Linda Med. Sch., 1952-54, Howard Med Sch., 1954-56; rschr. NIH, 1956-59; engr. Naval Aerospace Med. Inst., 1959-62, 62-67; dir. Space Life Scis. Divsn. Johns Hopkins U., 1968-74; dir. rsch. devel. IBM, 1975-87; owner Roscoe Bartlett & Assocs.; mem. U.S. Congress from 6th Md. Dist., 1993—, mem. armed svcs. com., sci. com., vice chmn. small bus. com. Republican. Office: US Ho of Reps 2412 Rayburn House Ofc Bldg Washington DC 20515-0001*

BARTLETT, THOMAS ALVA, educational administrator; b. Salem, Oreg., Aug. 20, 1930; s. Cleave Wines and Alma (Hanson) B.; m. Mary Louise Bixby, Mar. 20, 1954; children: Thomas Glenn, Richard A., Paul H. Student, Willamette U., 1947-49, DCL (hon.), 1986; AB, Stanford U., 1951, PhD, 1959; MA (Rhodes scholar), Oxford U., 1953; L.H.D. (hon.), Colgate U., 1977, Mich. State U., 1978, Union Coll., 1979; D.C.L. (hon.), Pusan Nat. U., Korea, 1985, U. Ala., 1983. Mem. U.S. Permanent Mission to UN, 1956-63; advisor Gen. Assembly Dels., 1956-63; pres. Am. U., Cairo, 1963-69, Colgate U., Hamilton, N.Y., 1969-77, Assn. Am. Univs., Washington, 1977-82; chancellor U. Ala. System, 1982-89, Oreg. State System of Higher Edn. Office, Eugene, 1989-94, SUNY, 1994-96; ret., 1996. Mem. UAR-U.S. Ednl. Exch. Commn., 1966-69; mem. Task Force on Financing Higher Edn. in N.Y. State (Keppel Commn.), 1972-73; chmn. Commn. Ind. Colls. and Univs. N.Y., 1974-76; bd. dirs. Nat. Assn. Ind. Colls. and Univs., 1975-76; trustee Univs. Field Staff Internat., 1985-87; mem. NASA Comml. Space Adv. Com., 1988-90. Mem. nat. bd. examining Chaplains Episcopal Ch., 1978-91; trustee Gen. Theol. Sem., 1977-82, Am. U. in Cairo, 1978— (vice chair 1998-2002), U.S.-Japan Found., 1988— (chm. 1996-2001), bd. mem. Internat. Assn. of Univs., 1995-2000. Mem. Coun. Fgn. Rels., Phi Beta Kappa, Century Assn. Home: 1209 SW 6th Ave Apt 904 Portland OR 97204

BARTLETT, THOMAS FOSTER, international management consultant; b. Oklahoma City, Nov. 28, 1918; s. Martin Johnson and Clara Nell (Mattingly) B. BS, Harvard U., 1943, MBA, 1948; cert., Sorbonne, Paris, 1987, Oxford (Eng.) U., 1988, Cambridge (Eng.) U., England, 1989, U. Salamanca, 1993, U. Genoa, 1994; grad., US Command and Gen. Staff Coll, Ft. Leavenworth, Kans., 1945. Asst. to pres. Am. Express Co., N.Y.C., 1948-50; export promotion specialist Dept. of State, Paris; mem. U.S. Mission to NATO Dept. Def., London and Paris; econ. cons. Am. Embassy, Rome, 1950-55; exec. asst. to pres. for internat. devel. Kaiser Industries, Oakland, Calif., 1955-56; mktg. specialist Bigelow-Sanford Inc., N.Y.C., 1957-59; pres. Internat. Mgmt. Cons. Thomas F. Bartlett & Assocs., N.Y.C., 1959—. Cons. for UN, U.S. and fgn. govts., corps., other orgns. Capt. U.S. Army, 1943-46, maj. USAF Res. Mem. Am. Soc. Profl. Cons., Am. Mgmt. Assn., Am. Mktg. Assn., Harvard Club. Avocations: travel, photography, lecturing. Office: Thomas F Bartlett & Assoc 330 E 52nd St New York NY 10022-6718

BARTLETTE, DONALD LLOYD, social worker, counselor, educator; b. Walhalla, N.D., Dec. 17, 1939; s. Abraham Bruno and Lily Alice (Houle) B.; m. Julie Gay Poer, Feb. 1, 1969; children: Lisa Maaca, Joanna Leigh, Andrea Gay, Marisa Anne,m Laura Bethany, Sara Elizabeth, Seth VanAdams, Vanessa Joy. PhB, U. N.D., 1962; MA, N.D. State U., 1966; PhD, CPU, 1981. Camp worker, program dir. Camp Grassick, N.D., 1957-62; unit supr., counselor Cambridge State Sch. and Hosp., 1963-64; group worker Children's Village, Fargo, N.D., 1964-65; supr. Meth. Children's Village, Detroit, 1966-68; program dir. Mich. Children's Inst., Ann Arbor, 1968-70; exec. program dir. Madison County (Ind.) Assn. for Retarded, 1970-71; dir. program and social work svcs. Outreach Cmty. Ctr., Mpls., 1972-73; exec. dir. Minn. Epilepsy League, St. Paul, 1974-75; pvt. cons. in retardation, 1972-75; coord. spl. svcs., adviser Human Rights Commn. City of Bloomington, Minn., 1975-78; assoc. pastor, dir. social svcs. Am. Indian Evang. Ch., Mpls., 1978-79; dir. social svcs. Stark County (Ohio) Bd. Mental Retardation, 1979-80; field work instr. Sch. Social Work U. Minn., Augsburg Coll., Mpls., 1972-73; off-campus tchr. in retardation and social work Anderson Coll., 1970-71; adj. faculty Univ. Without Walls, U. Minn., 1972-73. Author presentation: Macaroni at Midnight; film participant Believing for the Best in You, 1985; film subject When Nobody Loves You, 1988; focus of play Macaroni at Midnight, Erie, Pa., 1986. Pres. Nat. Minority Affairs Coalition, 1977-78, sec., 1976-77; mem. Met. Developmental Disabilities Task Force, 1975; chmn. Pub. Info. Coalition Project on Developmental Disabilities Task Force, 1974-75; vol. mem. Pres.'s Minn. Gov.'s coms. on employment handicapped; task force minority affairs Pres.'s Com. Mental Retardation; bd. dirs. N.W. Hennepin Human Svcs. Coun., 1975-76; bd. dirs., chmn. poverty com. Anoka County Assn. for Retarded, 1974-79; bd. dirs. Family and Children's Svcs. of Greater Mpls., Stark County Mental Health Bd., Citizen Advocacy Program of Stark County; cons. People First of Stark County; adv. Indian Children Coun. for Exceptional Children; patron and com. mem. Lake Ctr. Christian sch., Hartville, Ohio; trustee Cuyahoga Valley Christian Acad., 1985-86; patron Heritage Christian Sch., 1986-94, Good Shepherd Christian Sch., 1994-2000; bd. dirs. Pretty Shield Found., 1999—; spkr. Fellowship of Christian Athletes; adv. cons. Christian Berets, Keystone Acad. and Navajo Missions; spkr. Assn. Christian Schs. Internat.; founder travel ministry, 1974—; cons. Children's Harbor, Ala.; nat. bd. dirs. Teen Ranch, Mich.; mem. Nat. Assn. Native Am. Children of Alcoholics; lectr. Nat. Edn. Svcs., Insts. Drug Addictions and Alcoholism; guest lectr. Jennings Inst. Outstanding Educators in Ohio; spkr. Promise Keepers; lectr. series spkr. Staley Found.; prayer breakfast spkr. Ashtabula County Concerts of Prayer, Ohio; spkr.

Concerned Women of Am., Old Time Gospel Hour, Bill Gaither Family Fest, Gaither Gathering. Recipient Hon. Grad. award Chemawa Indian Sch., Hon. Citizen award W.Va., Ark.; Don Bartlette Day proclaimed by City of Cin. and N.D. Fellow Acad. Ednl. Disciplines. Mem. Am. Acad. Mental Retardation, Nat. Assn. Christian Social Workers, Nat. Assn. Retarded Citizens (bd. dirs., chmn. com. on poverty and mental retardation 1973-74), Internat. Platform Assn., Assn. Am. Indian Social Workers, Soc. for Protection Unborn through Nutrition (life mem.), Focus on Family, Civitan Club (hon.), Internat. Inst. for Christian Sch. Tchrs., Christian Home Educators Ohio, Christian Coun. on Disabilities, The 700 Club, Phi Delta Kappa, Kappa Delta Pi. Home: 2602 Ocelot St NE Canton OH 44721-2144

BARTLETTI, DON, photographer, editor; b. Phila., Pa., Dec. 29, 1947; m. Diana Bartletti; children: Adrienne, Jay. AA in Art, Palomar Coll., 1968. Photographer Vista (Calif.) Press, 1972—75, San Diego Union;/Tribune, 1977—83; freelance photographer, 1975—77; photographer Oceanside (Calif.) Blade Tribune, 1976—77; photographer San Diego edit. L.A. Times, 1983—92, photographer Orange County edit., 1992—. 1st lt. inf. U.S. Army, 1968—71, Vietnam. Recipient award, World Press Photo, Pictures of the Yr., Inter-Am. Press Assn., Ruben Salazar award, Nat. Assn. Hispanic Journalists, award, Nat. Press Photographers Assn., AP, UPI, L.A. Pres Club, San Diego Press Club, Orange County Press Club, Copley Newspapers, L.A. Times Editl. Awards, Pulitzer prize for feature photography, 2003, George Polk award, award, Scripps-Howard Found. Office: The Times Orange County 1375 Sunflower Ave Costa Mesa CA 92626-1697 E-mail: don.bartletti@latimes.com.

BARTLETT-POWERS, JOHN DAVID, social worker, elementary education educator; b. Chgo., Aug. 1, 1952; s. Fred William and Marianne (Braun) P.; m. Jane Ellen Andres, May 29, 1976 (div. Aug. 1986); children: Zachary, Renah; m. Debera Ann Bartlett, June 10, 2001; 1 stepson, David Ross. AB, U. Ill., 1974; MS in Social Work, U. Wis., 1976; cert. in elem. edn., Metro. State Coll. Denver, 2001. Vol. VISTA, Boulder, Colo., 1974-75; social worker No. Wis. Ctr. Developmentally Disabled, Chippewa Falls, Wis., 1978-81, Wheat Ridge (Colo.) Regional Ctr., 1981-87, 89-90; program dir. case mgmt. North Metro Cmty. Svcs., Thornton, Colo., 1988-89; social worker Ptnrs. Home Health, Lakewood, Colo., 1992-97, Centura Sr. Care, Denver, 1992-98; case mgr. St. Joseph Hosp., Denver, 1998-99; student tchr. Gov.'s Ranch Elem. Sch., Littleton, Colo., 2001; substitute tchr. Jefferson County R-1 Schs., Golden, Colo., 2001; tchr. Dutch Creek Elem. Sch., Littleton, Colo., 2001—02, Century Mid. Sch., Thornton, Colo., 2002—, S. Elem., Castle Rock, Colo., 2003—. Mem. profl. adv. com. Ptnrs. Home Health, Lakewood, Colo., 1995-97; hospice friend Hospice of Peace, Denver, 1996-97, mem. profl. adv. com., 1996-98; field instr. U. Denver, 1997-98. Mentor kid connection Jewish Family Svcs., Denver, 1998-99; vol. lit. program Denver Pub. Schs., 1999. Mem.: NASW, Colo. Coun. Tchrs. of Math., Assn. Childhood Edn., Kappa Delta Pi. Jewish. Avocations: stamp collecting, photography, bicycling. E-mail: djbartlettpowers@cs.com.

BARTLEY, BURNETT GRAHAM, JR., oil company and manufacturing executive; b. Pitts., Nov. 10, 1924; s. Burnett Graham and Helen (McKee) McKenney B.; m. Mary Lou Gilbert, Aug. 7, 1947; children: Burnett III, Davison Wittmer, Richard McKenney, Parker Bowen, Heather Swinston, Tiffany Gilbert; m. Wendy K. Keyes, May 12, 2001; 1 child, Timothy Lee Vogler. BA, Yale U., 1949; grad. advanced mgmt. program, Harvard U., 1967. Rep. sales Koppers Co. Inc., Pitts., 1949-52, dist. mgr. sales, 1952-56, v.p. sales, 1956-58, v.p., gen. mgr. forest products, 1958-69, dep. chmn. bd., 1969-79, exec. v.p., 1979-88; chmn., chief exec. officer chems. and coatings Kop-coat, Inc., Pitts., 1988-90; chmn., chief exec. officer Anegada Group, Inc., Pitts., 1990—. Chmn., CEO Ameritex Chem. and Coatings Co., Irving, Tex.; chmn. Bridgewater Steel Corp., N.J., Trans-Ocean Trading Corp., Ltd.; chmn. bd. Edgewater Marine Corp., Morgantown, W.Va. Dir. World Affairs Coun., Pitts., 1987; Trustee Rehab. Ctr. Pitts., 1989, Children's Hosp., Pitts., 1989, Mich. Inst. Tech., 1989; chmn. bd. trustees Point Park Coll., Pitts., 1989; bd. dirs. Penn. Economy League, 1989; pres. Health Rsch. and Svcs. Found., Pitts., 1989. Lt. inf. U.S. Army, 1943-45, ETO. Mem. Am. Wood Preservers Inst. (pres. 1970), Am. Wood Preserver's Assn. (pres. 1975), So. Pressure Treaters Assn. (pres. 1974), Harvard-Yale-Princeton Club, Duquesne Club, Fox Chapel Golf Club, Annapolis Yacht Club, Buffalo Launch Club, Rolling Rock Club, Laurel Valley Golf Club, Pitts. Athletic Club, St. John (V.I.) Yacht Club, St. Thomas (V.I.) Yacht Club, Chautauqua Lake Yacht Club (Lakewood, N.Y.). Republican. Presbyterian. Avocations: hydroplanes, flying, sailing, fishing, motorcycling. Office: Anegada Group Inc 2335 Koppers Bldg Pittsburgh PA 15219 also: Fairwinds Estate PO Box 248 Mayville NY 14757-0248 also: Villa # 4113 Virgin Grand, Great Cruz Bay Cruz Bay VI 00830

BARTLEY, MURRAY HILL, retired dental educator; b. Jamestown, N.Y., June 15, 1933; s. Merle Campbell and Doris Ann (Keller) B.; m. Anita Estelle Glatfelter, July 29, 1956; children: Todd L., Brian C., Kathleen A. Student, Lewis & Clark Coll., 1951-54; DMD, U. Oreg., 1958; PhD, U. Utah, 1968. Cert. in oral pathology. Teaching fellow U. Oreg. Dental Sch., Portland, 1961-64; assoc. dir. rsch. D.N. Sharp Hosp., San Diego, 1964-65; post-doctoral fellow dept. anatomy Sch. Medicine U. Utah, Salt Lake City, 1965-68; acting assoc. prof. oral biology and pathology UCLA, 1968-69; assoc. prof. oral pathology Dental Sch. U. Oreg., Portland, 1969-77; prof. oral pathology Sch. Dentistry Oreg. Health Sciences U., Portland, 1977—95, prof. emeritus, 1995—, chmn. dept. oral pathology, 1972—76, 1980—95. Cons. Wadsworth VA Hosp., 1968-69, Barnes VA Hosp., Vancouver, Wash., Portland Med. Ctr., 1968—, Coun. on Hosp. Dental Svcs., ADA, Chgo., 1970, Oreg. State Dental Assn. Biohazards Com., Portland, 1976-82, chmn. dental care counsel, 1992—, Oreg. Dept. Health AIDS Task Force, Portland, 1981-91, Project Hope-Stomatology Faculties, Peoples Republic of China, 1984, Mich. AMC. Contbr. sci. articles to profl. jours. Mem. com. ORE div., profl. edn. Am. Cancer Soc., Portland, 1974—; bd. dirs. Oreg. regional med. program O.C.C.P., Portland, 1973-81. Col. USAR, 1958-92. USPHS Tchr.'s Tng. grantee NIH, Portland, 1961-64; Post-Doctoral Teaching fellow NIH, 1965-68; recipient Presdl. citation Oreg. Dental Assn., 1979, 89; decorated U.S. Army Meritorious Svc. medal, 1981. Mem. AAAS, ADA, Am. Acad. Oral Pathology, Soc. Mil. Surgeons, Sigma Xi, Omicron Kappa Upsilon (chpt. pres. 1988-89), Delta Sigma Delta. Avocations: watercolor, wood working, sculpture. Home: 6020 SW Arrow Wood Ln Portland OR 97223-7700 Office: OHSU Sch Dentistry Dept Oral Pathology 611 SW Campus Dr Portland OR 97201-3001

BARTLEY, ROBERT LEROY, newspaper editor; b. Marshall, Minn., Oct. 12, 1937; s. Theodore French and Iva Mae (Radach) B.; m. Edith Jean Lillie, Dec. 29, 1960; children: Edith Elizabeth, Susan Lillie, Katherine French. BS, Iowa State U., 1959; MS, U. Wis., 1962; LLD (hon.), Macalester Coll., 1982, Babson Coll., 1987; HHD (hon.), Adelphi U., 1992. Reporter Grinnell (Iowa) Herald-Register, 1959-60; staff reporter Wall Street Jour., Chgo., 1962-63, Phila., 1963-64, editorial writer N.Y.C., 1964-70, Washington, 1970-71, editor editorial page N.Y.C., 1972-78, editor, 1979—, v.p., 1983—, Dow Jones. With ASian Wall Street Jour., Wall Street Jour. Europe, WSJ.com, OpinionJOurnal-.com, others. Author: The Seven Fat Years: And How to Do It Again, 1992. Trustee emeritus Mayo Found. Served to 2d lt. USAR, 1960. Recipient Overseas Press Club citation, 1977, Gerald Loeb award, 1979, Pulitzer prize for editorial writing, 1980 Mem. Am. Soc. Newspaper Editors, Soc. Profl. Journalists, Nat. Conf. Editl. Writers, Am. Polit. Sci. Assn., Coun. on Fgn. Rels., Heights Casino Club. Office: The Wall Street Jour 200 Liberty St New York NY 10281-1003

BARTLEY, WILLIAM CALL, science administrator; b. Mason, Mich., Dec. 4, 1932; s. Hugh Jerome and Daisy Ione (Call) B.; m. W. Dee Gray, July 14, 1956; children: Carol Sue Gourlas, Gregory William Bartley, Christopher Gray Bartley. BS in Electircal Engring., Mich. State U., 1955, MS in Electircal Engring., 1959. Registered Profl. Engr., Tex.; commercial pilot/instr., FAA. Rsch. scientist/dir. space-sci. lab. U. Tex., Richardson, 1963-67; exec. sec. Fed. Coord. Coun. Sci., Engring. and Tech. The White House, Washington, 1967—74; sr. staff dir. Nat. Acad. Sci., Washington, 1974-78; asst. dir. Office Energy Rsch. U.S. Dept. Energy, Washington, 1978-82; min.-counselor for health and sci. Geneva, 1982-88; spl. asst. to FDA commr., 1988-89; sr. advisor to U.S. Trade Rep. The White House, Washington, 1989-91; sr. adv. to asst. sec. oceans, environ., sci. U.S. State Dept., Washington, 1991-95; chmn./CEO Bartley Tech., Inc., Bandera, Tex., 1995—; founder, co-owner TreeLife Tech., Boerne, Tex., 1998—2000. Co-investigator NASA, U. Tex., Richardson, Tex., 1965-67, study dir./exec. dir. Nat. Acad. Sci., Washington, 1969-74. Contbg. author: International Orbital Debrie, 1994; patentee in field. Mem. panel on trends in aviation Davos World Econ. Forum, Switzerland, 1987, vice-chair, Bandera County Federated Libr. Bd., 1999-2001; pres. bd. trustees Bandera Libr., 2000-01; chair Bandera Frontier Times Mus. Expansion Com., 2003-; rectory renovation project leader Vestry of St. Christopher's Ch., 2002—; delagate coun. Diocese of West Tex., 2003—, mem., task Force on Mission and Ministry, Diocese of West Tex., 2003-. Recipient Certificate of Appreciation, U.S. State Dept., Geneva, Switzerland, 1984, 86, Washington, 95. Mem. NY Acad. Sci., Am. Geophysical Union, Am. Men an Women Sci., Free Trade Alliance. Episcopalian. Avocations: tennis, skiing, travel, historical restoration, aviation. Home: PO Box 2246 2628 English Crossing Rd Bandera TX 78003-2246 Office: Bartley Tech Inc PO Box 821 Bandera TX 78003-0821 E-mail: bill@bartleytech.com.

BARTLING, PHYLLIS MCGINNESS, oil company executive; b. Chillicothe, Ohio, Jan. 3, 1927; d. Francis A. McGinness and Gladys A. (Henkelman) Bane; m. Theodore Charles Bartling; children: Pamela, Theodore, Eric C. Student, Ohio State U., 1944-47. Bookkeeper, Bartling & Assocs., Bartling Oil Co., Houston 1974-80; sec.-treas., dir. both cos., 1980—. Co-chmn. ticket sales Tulsa Opera, 1956-61; bd. dirs. Tex. Speech and Hearing Ctr., Houston, 1967 70. Republican. Episcopalian. Avocations: gardening, bicycling, cooking, golf. Home and Office: 11 Inwood Oaks Dr Houston TX 77024-6803

BARTLOW, GENE STEVEN, association executive, retired air force officer; b. Alva, Okla., Dec. 19, 1939; s. C. Merle and Mildred Violet (Stevens) B.; m. Carolyn F. Strickland, Dec. 31, 1960 (div. Apr. 4, 1962); 1 child, Karie Jean Bartlow Parsons; m. Karin C. Jacobsen, Jan. 13, 1967; children: Christina K., Erik K. BA in Ednl. Comm., N.W. Okla. State U., 1962; disting. grad., Indsl. Coll. Armed Forces, Washington, 1972; MPA, Ball State U., 1978; grad., Air War Coll., Maxwell AFB, Ala., 1984; MS in Computers and Info. Mgmt., Webster U., St. Louis, 1995. Life cert. assn. exec., Am. Soc. Assn. Execs. Tchr. speech, debate coach Liberal (Kans.) Pub. H.S., 1962-63; commd. 2d lt. USAF, 1964, advanced through grades to full col.; chief logistics plans divsn. 68th tactical air support group Tactical Air Command, Shaw AFB, S.C., 1971-73; chief logistics plans inspection br. Hdqs. Tactical Air Command, Langley AFB, Va., 1973-76; chief NATO logistics plans br. Hdqs. USAF in Europe, Ramstein Air Base, Germany, 1976-80; dep. comdr. for resource mgmt. 474th tactical fighter wing Tactical Air Command, Nellis AFB, Nev., 1980-83; chief congl. activities divsn. Office Asst. Sec. Air Force (Acquisition), Washington, 1984-87; dean adminstrn., prof. sys. acquisition mgmt. Indsl. Coll. Armed Forces, Nat. Def. U., 1987 90; ret., 1990; asst. exec. dir., CFO, Assoc. Cath. Charities, Archdiocese of Washington, 1990-91; dep. exec. dir. Internat. Assn. for Dental Rsch.-Am. Assn. for Dental Rsch., Washington, 1991-94; pres., CEO, Am. Wood Preservers Inst., Fairfax, Va., 1995-97; exec. v.p., COO, Painting and Decorating Contractors Am., 1998-2000; exec. dir., COO Assn. Old Crows, Alexandria, Va., 2002—. Adj. prof. mgmt. Nat.-Louis U., McLean, Va., 1989-97, U. Md. U. Coll., 1998-99; lectr. congl. liaison activities exec. mgmt. course Def. Sys. Mgmt. Coll., Ft. Belvoir, 1986-92. Contbr. articles to profl. jours. Decorated Legion of Merit, others. Mem.: Greater Washington Soc. Assn. Execs., Air Force Assn., Mil. Officers Assn. Republican. Congregationalist. Avocations: Am. Civil War history, photography, music, politics. Home: 6501 Tiburon Ct Springfield VA 22152-2824 E-mail: eagle85@verizon.net.

BARTNICKI, KAREN JO, social services administrator; b. Beverly, Mass., May 2, 1958; d. Edward W. and Ruth B. Bartnicki. BA in Sociology, Regis Coll., 1980; MA in Psychology, Calif. State U., Sacramento, 1997. Cert. Coun. on Social Work Edn., Meeting Planners Internat. Activities dir. Redwood Villa Retirement Residence, Mountain View, Calif., 1989-90; dir. social svcs., admissions and mktg. Southpark Cmty. Hosp., Sacramento, 1990-91, Gold Country Health Ctr., Placerville, Calif., 1991-92; social worker, social work cons. Vital Care Am., Gardena, Calif., 1993-94, Mediplex, Lowell, Mass., 1994-95; adminstr. John Bertram House Assisted Living, Salem, Mass., 1995-96; event cons. Interface Found., Newton, Mass., 1997; mgr. social svcs. Vencor Hosp., Boston-North Shore, Peabody, Mass., 1998-99; exec. dir. Valley Terrace, Terrace Cmtys., Hartford, Vt., 1999-2000; dir. social svcs. Danvers (Mass.) Nursing and Rehab. Ctr., 2000—02. Mem. adv. bd. City of Santa Clara-Silicon Valley 1986 Conv., Santa Clara, Calif., 1986; exec. dir. Meetings Plus, Fremont, Calif., 1986-89; program cons., event planner Computer Faire Inc./The Interface Group, Needham, Mass., 1984-86; program mgr., conf. dir. CW Comms., Inc., Framingham, Mass., 1981-84; mem. adv. bd. West Coast Computer Faire, San Francisco, 1987, 88. Author: (book) An Exploration of Life Experiences, Personality Traits and Sleep Habits in Relation to Dream Recall and Dream Content, 1997; prodr., author: (videotape) Microcomputer Application Spotlight: Desktop Publishing, 1987. Mem. Inst. Noetic Scis., Assn. Rsch. and Enlightenment, Am. Soc. Psychical Rschrs., Assn. for Study of Dreams, Psi Chi, Pi Gamma Mu. Avocations: sleep and dream research, philosophy and religion, poetry, creative writing, outdoor recreation. Address: PO Box 156 Amesbury MA 01913 E-mail: KJ.Bartnicki@verizon.net.

BARTNICKI-GARCIA, SALOMON, microbiologist, educator; b. Mexico City, May 18, 1935; came to U.S., 1957; s. Israel Bartnicki and Refugio Garcia; m. Ildiko Nagy, Aug. 10, 1975; children— Linda Laura, David Daniel. Bacteriological Chemist, Inst. Politecnico Nacional, Mexico City, 1957; PhD, Rutgers U., 1961. Rsch. assoc. microbiology Rutgers U., 1961-62; mem. faculty U. Calif., Riverside, 1962—, prof. plant pathology and microbiology, 1971-94, prof. emeritus, 1994, rsch. prof., 1994-2000, chmn. dept. plant pathology, 1989-92, dir. grad. program in microbiology, 1997-2000; sci. rschr. Ctr. Scientific Investigation and Higher Studies Ensenada, Ensenada, Mexico, 2000—. Vis. prof. Organic Chemistry Inst., U. Stockholm, 1969-70; selected faculty rsch. lectr. U. Calif., Riverside, 1989. Author research and rev. papers. Grantee NIH, 1963-96, NSF, 1971-96. Fellow AAAS, Am. Phytopathol. Soc. (Ruth Allen award 1983); mem. Am. Soc. Microbiology, Mycol. Soc. Am. (Disting. Mycologist award 1994), Brit. Soc. Gen. Microbiology, Brit. Mycol. Soc. (hon.), Am. Soc. Biol. Chemists. Home: 3787 Elliott St San Diego CA 92106-1235 Office: U Calif Dept Plant Pathology Riverside CA 92521-0001 also: CICESE Ensenada Mexico E-mail: bart@citrus.ucr.edu.

BARTNIKAS, RAYMOND, electrical engineer, educator; b. Kaunas, Lithuania, Jan. 25, 1936; s. Andrius and Eugenia (Kanisauskas) B.; m. Margaret McLachlan, Aug. 19, 1967; children: Andrea Marie, Thomas Benedict. BASc, U. Toronto, 1958; M in Engring., McGill U., Montreal, 1962, PhD, 1964; D in Engring. (hon.), U. Waterloo, 2002. Rsch. engr. No. Electric Co. (now Nortel), Lachine, Canada, 1958—63; mem. sci. staff phys. scis. divsn. No. Electric R&D Labs. (now Nortel Techs.), Ottawa, Canada, 1963—68; research scientist, sci. dir. materials sci. research div., Disting. Sr. Scientist Hydro-Quebec Inst. Rsch., Varennes, Que., 1968-98; rschr. emeritus Hydro-Quebec Inst. Research, 1998—. Adj. prof., lectr. theory of dielectrics McGill U., 1968—; adj. prof. Fleming Found., visitor dept. elec. and computer engring. U. Waterloo, Ont., 1969—; adj. prof. dept. engring. physics Ecole Poly. U. Montreal, 1982—; vis. prof. U. Rome, 1994—; cons. Cepel Inst. Rsch., Rio de Janeiro, 1973-84; mem. Task Force on Long Term Performance of Insulating Materials Nat. Acad. Scis., 1976-77; mem. elec. engring. com. Nat. Scis. and Engring. Rsch. Coun. Can., 1987-90; mem. Commn. de la recherche universitaire Conseil des Universites, Que., 1989-93. Author, editor: ASTM book series on Engring. Dielectrics, 1979, Elements of Cable Engineering, 1980, Power Cable Engineering, 1987, Power and Communication Cables, 1999; contbr. articles on dielectric and discharge loss mechanisms in elec. insulating systems to profl. jours. Decorated officer Order of Can.; recipient Golden Jubilee medal Can. Fellow IEEE (mem. energy com. 1978—, mem. insulated condrs. com. 1966—, mem. awards and recognition com. 1984-88, mem. electric machinery materials com. 1993—, IEEE Thomas Dakin Disting. Sci. Achievement award 1980, Centennial medal 1984, Whitehead Meml. award 1987, Morris Leeds award 1989, MacNaughton Gold medal 1993, 3d Millennium medal 2000), ASTM (chmn. elec. insulation com. 1979-85, mem. editl. bd. Jour. Testing and Evaluation 1985—, award of merit 1985, Charles Dudley medal, appreciation award, Arnold Scott award), Can. Acad. of Engring., Inst. Elec. Engrs. Japan (Disting. hon. lectr. symposium on elec. insulating materials 1983), Inst. Physics (U.K.), Royal Soc. Can. Acad. Scis. (Thomas W. Eadie medal 1994); mem. Dielectrics and Elec. Insulation Soc. of IEEE (pres. 1976-78, mem. editl. bd. Elec. Insulation Mag. 1984-91), Internat. Electrotech. Commn. (mem. com. insulation materials, chmn. subcommittee on tests 1993—), Order Engrs. Que., Can. Stds. Assn. (Merit award 1986, John Jenkins award 1989), Can. Elec. Assn., Can. Stds. Coun. (J.P. Carrière award 1992), French-Can. Assn. for Advancement of Scis. (Urgel Archambault award 1993), U. Toronto Engring. Alumni Assn. (engring. medal 1993). Roman Catholic. Office: Hydro-Québec Inst Rsch 1800 Boul Lionel-Boulet CP 1000 Varennes QC Canada J3X 1S1

BARTNOFF, JUDITH, judge; b. Boston, Apr. 14, 1949; d. Shepard and Irene F. (Tennenbaum) B.; m. Eugene F. Sofer, Sept. 10, 1978; 1 child, Nelson Bartnoff Sofer. BA magna cum laude, Radcliffe Coll., 1971; JD (Harlan Fiske Stone scholar), Columbia U., 1974; LLM, Georgetown U., 1975. Bar: D.C. 1975, U.S. Dist. Ct. D.C. 1975, U.S. Ct. Appeals (D.C. cir.) 1980, U.S. Ct. Appeals (fed. cir.) 1985, U.S. Ct. Appeals (11th cir.) 1988, U.S. Ct. Appeals (3d cir.) 1989, U.S. Claims Ct. 1991. Fellow Inst. Pub. Interest Representation, Georgetown Law Ctr., Washington, 1974-75; staff atty. Coun. Pub. Interest Law, Washington, 1975-77; spl. asst. to asst. atty. gen. criminal divsn. Dept. Justice, Washington, 1977-78, assoc. dep. atty. gen., 1978-80; spl. asst. U.S. atty. Office of U.S. Atty., Washington, 1980-81, asst. U.S. atty., 1982-85; assoc. firm Patton, Boggs & Blow, 1985-87, ptnr., 1988-94, assoc. ind. counsel, 1993-94; assoc. judge Superior Ct. of D.C., Washington, 1994—. Mediator U.S. Dist. Ct. D.C., 1991-94; mem. com. on pro se litig. U.S Dist. Ct., 1991-94. Mem. D.C. Bar Task Force on Children at Risk, 1997—98, D.C. Child Support Guidelines Commn., 2003—. Fellow Am. Bar Found.; mem. Nat. Assn. Women Judges, D.C. Bar, Women's Bar Assn. Office: 500 Indiana Ave NW Washington DC 20001-2131 E-mail: bartnofj@dcsc.gov.

BARTO, BRADLEY EDWARD, small business owner, educator; b. N.Y.C., N.Y., Nov. 25, 1956; s. Kenneth William and Edna Ruth (Dalton) B.; m. Cheryl Annette Pray, Nov. 28, 1987; 1 child, David Bradley. B in Engring., N.Y. Maritime Coll., 1982; M in Gen. Adminstrn., U. Md., 1989; postgrad., U. Sarasota. Sr. engr. Advanced Tech., Inc., McLean, Va., 1982-85, Arinc Rsch., Inc., Annapolis, Md., 1985-87; pres., owner B Square Computing, Inc., Riva, Md., 1987—; pres. BCD Enterprises, Riva, Md., 1995—. Prof. U. Md., College Park, 1990—, portfolio reviewer Prior Learning program, 1995—. Inventor Chocks, 1995. Republican. Lutheran. Avocations: golf, writing children's books, gofl, baseball, tennis, writing children's books. Home: 905 Malvern Hill Dr Davidsonville MD 21035-1242 Office: B Square Computing PO Box 606 Riva MD 21140-0606 Personal E-mail: bbarto@mindspring.com.

BARTO, DEBORAH ANN, physician; b. West Chester, Pa., July 27, 1948; d. Charles Guy and Jeannette Victoria (Golder) B. BA, Oberlin Coll., 1970; MD, Hahnemann U., 1974; grad., NWSH, 2003. Cert. Reiki master. Intern, resident Kaiser Permanente Hosp., San Francisco, 1974-77; dir. med. oncology Evergreen Hosp., Kirkland, Wash., 1980-85, head oncology quality assurance, 1992-94; med. dir. Cmty. Home Health Care Hospice, Seattle, 1981-84. Mem. hosp. ethics com. Evergreen Hosp., 1995-98, mem. integrative care com., 1996-2001. Mem. Evergreen Women's Physicians, Reiki III. Democrat. Buddhist. Avocation: horseback riding. Office: Evergreen Profl Plz 12911 120th Ave NE Ste E60 Kirkland WA 98034-3047

BARTO, REBECCA LYNN, business analyst; b. Tokyo, Aug. 9, 1962; came to U.S., 1968; d. Jackie Don Baize and Hisako (Ogawa) Ishimoto; children: Tanya Lynn, Andrew James. Student, U. Pitts., 1982-87, U. Tex., 1980-82. Coordinator data mgmt. and outreach, liaison to Ctr. Continuing Edn. Health Scis. U. Pitts., 1983-87; cons. TRW-Fla. Ops. Def. Systems Group, Cape Canaveral Air Force Sta., 1987-90, bus. analyst, 1987-90; self-employed bus. analyst Pt. Saint John, Fla., 1990-97; nurse emergency dept. and case mgr., 1997—. Democrat. Roman Catholic. E-mail: hlfbreed@earthlink.net.

BARTO, SUSAN CAROL, writer; b. Bklyn., June 21, 1941; d. William O. and Eda (Birra) Forcellon; m. Harry W. Barto, Mar. 11, 1960; 1 child, William M. Cert., Katherine Gibbs, 1960; student, Union Coll., 1979-82. Sec. dean of students Montclair (N.J.) State Coll., 1960; sec. Presbyn. Synod of N.J., East Orange, N.J., 1961-62; exec. sec. Union County Rep. Com., Westfield, N.J., 1971-79; legis. aide State Senator James Vreeland-Morris County, N.J., 1977-79. Author of short stories. County com. woman Union County Rep. Com., Westfield, 1970-82; active New Providence (N.J.) Libr. Bd., 1979-86. Recipient plaque of appreciation New Providence (N.J.) Libr. Bd., 1986. Mem. Friends of the Hunterdon Mus. of Art (pres. 1996-99). Presbyterian. Home and Office: 1 Fisher Ct Lebanon NJ 08833-2107

BARTOES, RICHARD ALAN, agricultural products executive; b. Norwich, Conn., July 29, 1928; s. Francis Florian and Katherine Brown Bartoes; m. Nancy Pettice Smith, June 22, 1952; children: Daniel Ryland, Nancy Elizabeth, Karen Francis, Marilyn Pettice, Richard Smith. BS in Geology, Trinity Coll., Hartford, Conn., 1951. Plant expediter Charles C. Hart Seed Co., Wethersfield, Colo., 1951—91, sales mgr., 1960—91, prodn. mgr.; purchasing dir. Helen's Greenhouses, Aquebogue, NY, 1980—; owner, v.p. Blue Ridge Garden Ctr. INc., Charlottesville, Va., 1992—99. Cons. Town of Rocky Hill, Conn., 1960—62; spkr. in field. Scoutmaster Boy Scouts Am. Recipient Silver Beaver, Boy Scouts Am., 1989. Mem.: Lions Club (pres. Rocky Hill chpt. 1988). Episcopalian. Avocations: collecting ships and lighthouses, gardening, running, swimming. Home: 1050 Earlysville Forest Dr Earlysville VA 22936-9550

BARTOK, MICHELLE, cosmetic company executive; b. Youngstown, Ohio, Feb. 18, 1961; d. Albert James and Judith Ann (Phillips) Bartok; m. John Anthony Garruto, Apr. 2, 1988 (div. 1997); children: Catherine Michelle, Gabrielle Bartok; m. Lee Edward Dupuis, Nov. 27, 1999 (div. 2000). BS in Physiol. Psychology, U. Calif., Santa Barbara, 1984. EMT, Calif. Asst. to phys. therapist Santa Barbara Phys. Therapy, 1983-84, Escondido (Calif.) Phys. Therapy, 1984-85; regional sales rep. Ft. Dodge Labs., San Francisco, 1985-87; owner North Coast Therapeutics, Oceanside, Calif., 1986—92; CEO Innovative Bioscis. Corp., Carlsbad, Calif., 1992—; owner Beaches Cafe Inc., Encinitas, Calif., 1999-2000. Tchr. mktg. and entrepreneurism Fashion Inst. Design and Merchandising, San Diego, L.A., 2003—. Named Entrepreneur of Yr., Beauty Industry West, 2003. Mem. Soc. Cosmetic Chemists, Beauty Industry West (pub. rels. dir. 1991-92, chair symposium 1996, named Entrepreneur of Yr., 2003), Internat. Spa and Fitness Assn. (sponsor Ironman competition 1989). Avocations: outrigger canoes, yoga. Home: 178 Grandview St Encinitas CA 92024 1009 E-mail: michelle@innovativebodyscience.com.

BARTOK, WILLIAM, environmental technologies consultant; b. Budapest, Hungary, May 1, 1930; s. Imre and Irma (Singer) B.; m. Susan V. Roth; Aug. 11, 1957; children: Michael F., Sylvia D., Richard E. BEng in Chem. Engring., McGill U., 1954, PhD in Phys. Chemistry, 1957. Research chemist Exxon Research & Engring. Co., Linden, N.J., 1957-61, sr. research chemist, 1961-66, research assoc., 1966-73, sr. research assoc., 1973-80, sci. advisor Clinton and Linden, N.J., 1980-86; sr. v.p. Energy and Environ. Research Corp., Irvine, Calif., 1986-91; sr. v.p. tech. Rsch.-Cottrell Cos., Somerville, N.J., 1991-92; cons., 1993—. Editor: Combustion of Synthetic Fuels, 1983; co-editor: Fossil Fuel Combustion, 1991; contbr. articles to profl. jours., chpts. to books. Mem. Combustion Inst. (bd. dirs. 1980-92), Am. Chem. Soc. (award in chemistry of comtemporary tech. problems 1987). Avocations: music, reading, tennis, swimming, photography. Home and Office: 956 Wyandotte Trl Westfield NJ 07090 3733 E-mail: wbartok@ix.netcom.com.

BARTOK-BARATTA, EDWARD, poet, artist; b. Jersey City, Apr. 5, 1959; s. Emanuel Baratta and Doris Elsaesser. BA in Lit./Philosophy, N.J. State U., 1982; MFA in Poetry/Fiction, U. Mass., 1986. Counselor St. Francis House, Boston, 1985—94; poet, author, artist, 1995—. Author: Fox Has His Day: Tales and Poems from the Far Far North, 1998; contbr. to literary jours. and anthologies. Recipient Paumanok Poetry award, SUNY, Farmingdale, 2001; grantee, Ludwig Vogelstein Found., N.Y., 1999; Artist grantee, Mass. Cultural Coun., Northampton, 1999. Mem.: Fridays Are for Prisoners (founder), Murder Victims Families for Reconciliation, Hampshire County Citizens Against the Death Penalty (founder). Home: PO Box 358 Northampton MA 01061

BARTOL, ERNEST THOMAS, lawyer; b. Mineola, N.Y., Feb. 2, 1946; s. Frank Henry and Mary Ann (Kretlein) Bartol; m. Christine Ann Pillis; children: Jacqueline Marie, Aimee Elizabeth, Suzanne Melissa. BS in Acctg., Fordham U., 1967; JD, Villanova U., 1970. Bar: N.Y. 1971, U.S. Dist. Ct. (ea. and so. dists.) N.Y. 1973, U.S. Ct. Appeals (2d cir.) 1975, U.S. Supreme Ct. 1974. Staff acct. Pustorino, Puglisi, Behan & Co., N.Y.C., 1965-70; tax specialist Arthur Young & Co., Phila., 1970; acct. Arthur Andersen & Co., N.Y.C., 1970-71;

assoc. Gehrig, Ritter, Coffey et al, Hempstead, N.Y., 1971-78; founder, mng. ptnr., sr. ptnr. Murphy, Bartol & O'Brien, LLP, Mineola, 1978—. Mem. exec. com. United Cerebral Palsy Assn. Nassau County, 1978—, chmn. forget-me-not-ball, 1987—92; pres., founder cmty. adv. coun. Syosset Cmty. Hosp., 1987—92; bd. dirs. LI Children's Mus., 1996—99; exec. leader Oyster Bay Rep. Com., 1978—2003; vice chmn. Nassau County Rep. Com., 2003—; sec., mem. parish coun. and spl. sch. com. St. Edward Roman Cath. Ch., Syosset, NY, 1978—80; trustee N.Y. Inst. Tech., 1997—99; bd. dirs. LI Coalition Fair Broadcasting, Inc., 2001. Named Man of the Yr., United Cerebral Palsy Assn. Nassau County, 1993, Heart Coun. L.I., Inc., 2001. Mem.: ABA, Cath. Lawyers Guild Diocese Rockville Centre, N.Y. State Trial Lawyers Assn., Fed. Bar Coun. N.Y., Nassau Lawyers Assn. LI (bd. dirs. 1977—, chmn. 1992—93, rec. sec. 1993—94, corr. sec. 1994—95, 1st v.p. 1995—97, pres. 1997—98), Criminal Cts. Bar Assn., Nassau County Bar Assn. (estates and trusts law com. 1975—, mem. profl. ethics com. 1980—86, 1989—93), N.Y. State Bar Assn. (trusts and estates law com. 1983—, lectr. estate topics), Chaminade HS Alumni Assn. (class rep. 1971, class dir. 1971—72, 1st v.p. 1972—74, pres. 1974—76), Rotary (sec.-treas. Syosset Club 1980—90), Alpha Kappa Psi. Roman Catholic. Avocations: racquetball, tennis, fishing, softball, stamp collecting. Office: Murphy Bartol & O'Brien LLP 22 Jericho Tpke Ste 103 Mineola NY 11501-2976 E-mail: etbartol@aol.com.

BARTOLACCI, PAULETTE MARIE, middle school educator, aerobics instructor; b. Phillipsburg, Pa., Aug. 19, 1969; d. Anthony Thomas and Pauline Virginia (Leh) B. BS in Elem. Edn., St. Joseph U., Phila., 1991; MS in Bilingual, Bicultural Studies, Lehigh U., 1997. 6th grade tchr. Our Lady of Prepetual Help, Bethlehem, Pa., 1992-93; 1-4th grade lang. arts tchr. for ESOL children Allentown (Pa.) Sch. Dist., 1993-97, interim asst. to dir. instrl. support svcs., 1998, 6th grade lang. arts tchr., 1997—, insvc. steering com. mem. Fellow Pa. State Nat. Writing Project, Fogelsville, Pa., 1993—, outreach mem., 1995—; cheerleading coach S. Mountain Middle Sch., Allentown, 1998-99, mem. leadership team for stds.-based edn., support tchr. for student tchrs., peer mentor for peer edn., also mem. sch. coun. Grantee Nat. Writing Project, Pa. State U., 1995-99. Mem. ASCD, Pa. Edn. Assn., Allentown Edn. Assn., Nat. Coun. Tchrs. of English, Aerobics and Fitness Assn. Am. (cert., instr. summer 1998) Republican. Roman Catholic. Avocations: aerobics, singing, jazz dancing, guitar. Home: 4139 Waterford Dr Center Valley PA 18034-8690

BARTOLINI, BRUCE ANTHONY, real estate executive; b. Framingham, Mass., Mar. 4, 1950; s. Benjamen A. and Eleanor H. (Connery) B.; m. Elaine A. Dowd, Dec. 30, 1990; 1 child, Bethany Nicole. Student, Northeastern U., Boston, 1967-69, postgrad., 1986-88; BA in Biology, Framingham State Coll., 1971; postgrad., Keene State Coll., 1972. Cert. in hematology. Sci. instr. Orford (N.H.) Acad., 1971-73; biology, chemistry instr. J.P. Keefe Tech. Sch., Framingham, 1973—; pres. Bartolini Motor Sales, Inc., Medway, Mass., 1979—. Trustee Milford Realty Devel., 1979—, Blackstone Realty Trust, 1980, Bartolini Realty Trust, High Rock Realty Trust, Lake Williams Realty Trust, Worcester Realty Trust; securities investor A.G. Edwards & Sons; mem. Adesa Auto Auctions, 1979—. Contbr. articles to profl. jours. With USAR, 1984—, Op. Desert Storm. Decorated Army Achievement medal, Nat. Def. medal. Mem. NEA, Am. Soc. Clin. Pathologists, Keefe Tech. Tchrs. Assn., Mass. Tchrs. Assn. Clubs: Southboro Rod and Gun (Mass.), Framingham Militia, Chatham Yacht Club. Republican. Roman Catholic. Avocations: skeet and trap shooting, skiing, sailing.

BARTOLINI, JAMES DANIEL, lawyer; b. New Haven, Apr. 13, 1946; s. Dante J. and Mariella (Cestaro) B.; m. Roni Goldstein, Dec. 22, 1975; 1 child, Jessica Marie. B.A., Trinity Coll., Hartford, Conn., 1968; M.A., Hartford Sem., 1970, M.Div., 1972; J.D., U. Conn., 1975. Bar: Conn. 1975, U.S. Ct. Appeals (2d cir.) 1975. Ptnr. RisCassi and Davis, Hartford, Conn., 1975— . Editor-in-chief Conn. Bar Jour., 1997—. Recipient Book award Harvard U., 1964. Mem. Am. Coll. Trial Lawyers, Nat. Bd. Trial Advocates (cert. Civil trial Specialist), Conn. Bar Assn. (bd. dirs. civil law sect. 1984—), Conn. Trial Lawyers Assn. (dir. 1982—, pres. 1988-89), Hartford County Med. Soc. (co-chmn. legal com. 1982—). Roman Catholic. Home: 47 Wood Pond Rd Glastonbury CT 06033-3703 Office: PO Box 6550 Hartford CT 06106

BARTOLINI, LEONARDO, economist; b. Florence, Italy, May 15, 1958; arrived in U.S., 1984; s. Alberto and Carla Bartolini; m. Jin M. Choi, Sept. 3, 1994; 1 child, Lorenzo. Laurea in Econs., U. Florence, 1983; MA in Econs., Rutgers U., 1986; PhD in Econs., Princeton U., 1991. Economist IMF, Washington, 1990—98, Fed. Res. Bank N.Y., N.Y.C., 1995—98, v.p., 2000—02, sr. v.p., 2002—. Adj. assoc. prof. Econs. Columbia U., N.Y.C., 2003—. Contbr. articles to profl. jours. With inf. Italian Army, 1980—81. Mem.: European Econ. Assn. Avocations: music, bicycling, gourmet food. Home: 27 8th Ave Brooklyn NY 11217 Office: Fed Res Bank NY 33 Liberty St New York NY 11217

BARTOLINI, ROBERT ALFRED, electrical engineer, researcher; b. Waterbury, Conn., Apr. 4, 1942; s. Alfred N. and Maria D. (Cartoceti) B.; M. Janice M. Daly, June 13, 1964; children: Jill C., Ellen G., Robin M. BSEE, Villanova U., 1964; MSEE, Case Western Res. U., 1966; PhD, U. Pa., 1972. Rsch. scientist RCA Labs., Princeton, N.J., 1966-79, leader optical sys., 1979-83, head optoelectronic rsch., 1983-87; head laser diode rsch. David Sarnoff Rsch. Ctr., Princeton, 1987-89, dir. integrated cir., 1989-96, sr. dir. inegrated cir. lab., 1996-97; v.p. integrated cir. lab. Sarnoff Corp., Princeton, 1997—2001, v.p. internat. ops., 2001—02, sr. v.p. comm. ops., 2002—. Chmn. elect. engring. dept. LaSalle U., 1982-90. Contbr. 35 articles to jours. in field; presenter 65 profl. presentations. Chmn. Sewer Oper. Com., West Windsor, N.J., 1974-82, chmn. assessment bd., West Windsor, N.J., 1984; vice chmn. Stony Brook Regional Sewerage Authority, Princeton, N.J., 1980-96, chmn., 1997—. Recipient 3 labs. achievement awards RCA Labs., 1970, 76, 80, Outstanding Paper award Soc. Internat. Display, 1979, Engring. Alumni award Villanova U., 1986, Sarnoff award RCA Corp., 1986, Career Engring. award Villanova U., 2002. Fellow IEEE (Centennial medal 1984), Optical Soc. Am. (chmn. laser conf. 1987-91); mem. Sigma Xi (nat. lectr. 1983-84), Tau Beta Pi, Eta Kappa Nu. Achievements include 22 U.S. patents and research in embossable holographic development, optical data storage media development, optical data storage system development, surface emitting diode laser development. Office: Sarnoff Corp 201 Washington Rd Princeton NJ 08540-6449 E-mail: rbartolini@sarnoff.com.

BARTOLO, DONNA MARIE, health association executive, retired nurse; b. Springfield, Ill., Mar. 21, 1941; d. Elmer Ralph Bartolomucci and Zoe (Rose) Cavatorta. Diploma in nursing, St. John's Sch. Nursing, Springfield, Ill., 1962; BS, Milliken U., 1976; MA, Sangamon State U., 1978. Pediatric nurse Springfield Clin., 1962—64, physician's asst., 1972—74; gynecol. nurse Watson Clin., Lakeland, Fla., 1964—66; cons. state sch. nurses Office of Edn. State of Ill., Springfield, 1974—78; assoc. dir. operating rm. svcs. Cedars-Sinai Med. Ctr., L.A., 1978—82, co-dir. div. nursing, 1981—82; surg. nurse Emory U. Hosp., Atlanta, 1966—70, asst. dir. nursing, surg. svcs., 1982—94; v.p. Clinical Oper., Heart Care Plus, Inc., 1999—2001; dir. surg. svcs., dir. nursing Emory U. Hosp., Atlanta, 1994—97, dir. nursing for surg. scis., 1998—2000; nurse surveyor Joint Commn. of Accreditation of Health Care Orgns., 2000—01; v.p. clin. ops. TeleHealth Home Monitoring Co., Atlanta, 2001—; v.p. nursing St. Mary's Hosp., Athens, Ga., 2001—02, nurse adminstr. cons. Cenetalin, Ill., 2002—. Adj. prof. Nell Hodgson Woodruff Sch. Nursing Emory U. Mem. editorial bd. Perioperative Nursing Quarterly; contbr. articles to nursing jours. Mem. Org. Nurse Execs., Ga. Assn. Nurse Exec. (pres. elect, pres. 1992), Assn. Operating Rm. Nurses, Sigma Theta Tau (sec. 1990—). Home: 1424 So Douglas Springfield IL 62704

BARTON, ALAN JOEL, lawyer; b. N.Y.C., NY, Sept. 2, 1938; s. Sidney and Claire (Greenfield) B.; m. Ann Rena Beral, Jan. 29, 1961; children: Donna Frieda Olsen, Brian Joseph. AB, U. Calif., Berkeley, 1960, JD, 1963. Assoc. Nossaman, Krueger & Mash, L.A., 1963—70, prin., 1970—80, Paul, Hastings, Janofsky & Walker, LLP, LA, 1980—2002, sr. counsel L.A., 2002—. Lectr. UCLA Sch. Law, 2001—; lectr. corp. and securities law U. Calif. Continuing Edn. Bar, 1980—; lectr. venture capital and securities law Practicing Law Inst., 1986—. Assoc. editor U. Calif. Law Rev., 1963. Dir. Ctr. for Study of Young People in Groups, L.A., 1988—, Planned Parenthood, L.A., 1999—; trustee Dubnoff Ctr. for Ednl. Therapy, North Hollywood, Calif., 1976-80. Mem. ABA (com. on fed. regulation of securities), Calif. Bar Assn. (com. on corps.), Order of Coif, The Calif. Club. Republican. Jewish. Avocations: movies, Torah study, contemporary art, tennis, travel. Office: Paul Hastings Janofsky & Walker LLP 515 S Flower St Fl 25 Los Angeles CA 90071-2300

BARTON, ALICE, physician, educator; b. West Long Branch, N.J., Sept. 29, 1953; d. David Knox and Ruth B. Barton; children: Lara, Seth, Peter. BA, Harvard U., 1975; MD, N.Y. Med. Coll., 1992. Diplomate Am. Bd. Internal Medicine. Tchr. art history Westover Sch., Middlebury, Conn., 1975-78; gen. surgery intern N.Y. Med. Coll., N.Y.C., 1992-93, resident in neurol. surgery, 1993-95; resident in internal medicine Stamford (Conn.) Hosp., 1995-97; attending physician ER Horton Hosp., Middletown, N.Y., 1997-98; attending physician HIV Ctr. St. Luke's-Roosevelt Hosp., N.Y.C., 1998-99; attending physician, asst. prof. medicine Ctr. Spl. Studies Cornell U. Med. Sch., N.Y.C., 1999—. Contbr. essays, articles to profl. jours. Recipient Janet M. Glasgow Meml. Achievement award, Am. Med. Women's Assn., Samuel Spiegel, MD Meml. award, N.Y. Med. Coll., 1992. Mem.: Phi Beta Kappa, Alpha Omega Alpha. Office: Cornell Chelsea Ctr Spl Studies 119 W 24th St New York NY 10011-1913

BARTON, ALLEN HOISINGTON, sociologist, educator; b. Greenwich, Conn., Oct. 7, 1924; s. Horace Allen and Elizabeth (Hoisington) B.; m. Judith Schneider, Mar. 11, 1949; children: Stephen, Hugh, Matthew, Julia. AB, Harvard U., 1947; PhD, Columbia U., 1957. Dir. Bur. Applied Social Rsch. Columbia U., N.Y.C., 1962-77, instr. sociology, 1953-54; rsch. assoc. Bur. Applied Social Rsch., Columbia U., N.Y.C., 1957-62; asst. prof. to prof. Columbia U., N.Y.C., 1957-90, chmn. sociology dept., 1989-90; ret., 1998. Lectr. sociology U. Oslo, Norway, 1948-49; adj. prof. sociology U. Fla., 1993-98; vis. scholar Sch. Journalism and Comm. U. N.C., 2001—. Author: Studying the Effects of College Education, 1959, Organizational Measurement, 1961, Communities in Disaster, 1969, Background Attitudes and Activities of American Elites, 1985; co-author: Opinion-Making Elites in Yugoslavia, 1973, Decentralizing City Government, 1977; co-editor: Making Bureaucracies Work, 1980. Del. Conn. Dem. Conv., 1968; mem. Dem. Town Com., Greenwich, 1971-90. With U.S. Army, 1943-46. Recipient Worcester prize for best pub. opinion article, 1996, E.L. Quarantelli award for contbns. to social sci. theory of disasters, 2002; Social Sci. Rsch. Coun. grantee, 1949-50, Carnegie Corp. grantee, 1968-71, Ford Found. grantee, 1970-74, grantee NIMH, NSF, 1972-75. Mem. AAAS, Am. Sociol. Assn., Am. Assn. Pub. Opinion Rsch., Internat. Sociol. Assn., Soc. For Study Social Problems. Avocations: travel, hiking, snorkeling, photography. Home: 118 Wolf's Trail Chapel Hill NC 27516-9060

BARTON, ANN ELIZABETH, retired financial executive; b. Long Lake, Mich., Sept. 8, 1923; d. John and Inez Mabel (Morse) Seaton; m. H. Kenneth Barton, Apr. 3, 1948; children: Michael, John, Nancy. Student Mt. San Antonio Coll., 1969-71, Adrian Coll., 1943, Citrus Coll., 1967, Golden Gate U., 1976, Coll. Fin. Planning, 1980-82. CFP. Tax cons., real estate broker, Claremont, Calif., 1967-72, Newport Beach, Calif., 1972-74; v.p., officer Putney, Barton, Assocs., Inc., Walnut Creek, Calif., 1975-94, ret., 1997; bd. dir. Fin. Svc. Corp. Cert. fin. planner. Mem. Internat. Assn. Fin. Planners (registered investment advisor), Calif. Soc. Enrolled Agts., Nat. Assn. Enrolled Agts., Inst. CFP.

BARTON, BABETTE B. lawyer, educator; b. Los Angeles, Apr. 30, 1930; d. Milton Vernon and Ruth (Schreiber) Barancik; children: Jeffrey B. Barton, David R. Barton, Baird R. Barton. BS, U. Calif., Berkeley, 1951, LLB, 1954. Bar: Calif., U.S. Dist. Ct., U.S. Ct. Appeals 1955. Law clk. to Hon. Phil S. Gibson Calif. Supreme Ct., San Francisco, 1954-55; lectr., acting prof. U. Calif. Sch. Law, Berkeley, 1961-72, prof., 1972-99, prof. emeritus, 1999—; Adrian A. Kragen chair U. Calif., Berkeley. Cons. Calif. Inter Agy. Task Force on Electronic Funds Transfers, 1978-79, Dept. Treasury, 1963; adv. com. Calif. Bd. Legal Specialization, 1980-83. Contbr. chpts. to books in field. Adv. com. Alameda County Dir. Welfare, 1970-73; bd. dirs. Family Service Berkeley, 1967-74, Univ. Students' Coop. Assn., 1966-74. Recipient Citation award Boalt Hall Alumni Assn., 1997. Fellow Am. Law Inst., Am. Bar Found.; mem. ABA (taxation sect. chmn. tchg. tax. com. 1994-96, real property probate and trust sect. coun. 1977-79), Calif. State Bar (chmn. taxation sect. 1976-77, Joanne M. Garvey award taxation sect. 1997), Western Regional Bar Assn. (chmn. 1978-79), Am. Coll. Tax Counsel, San Francisco Tax Club, San Francisco Estate Planning Coun., Berkeley Tennis Club (bd. dirs. 1988-90, pres. 1990-91). Home: 16 Saint James Dr Piedmont CA 94611-3533 Office: U Calif Berkeley Sch Law 691 Simon Boalt Hl Berkeley CA 94720-0001

BARTON, BERNARD ALAN, JR., lawyer; b. Glens Falls, N.Y., Aug. 13, 1948; s. Bernard A. Sr. and Geraldine (Bushey) B.; children: Lindsey, Kylie. BA, U. Fla., 1969, JD, 1975, LLM, 1976. Bd. cert. tax lawyer. Ptnr. Holland & Knight, Tampa, Fla., 1976—. Editor, contbg. author Florida Taxation, State Taxation Series, 1994. Mem. ABA, Nat. Assn. Bond Attys., Fla. Bar Assn. (exec. coun. tax sect., chmn. various coms. 1980-99). Republican. Episcopalian. Office: Holland & Knight 400 N Ashley Dr PO Box 1288 Tampa FL 33601-1288

BARTON, DAWN KANANI, elementary school educator; b. Landstuhl, Germany, Mar. 6, 1971; came to U.S., 1971; d. Brian Leigh and Georgina Allyne (Plucker) Clevenger; m. Charles Raymond Barton II, Sept, 5, 1992; children: Faith C., Mary E., Hannah M. BS in Elem. Edn. cum laude, Towson U., 1994; MS in Sch. Adminstrn., Western Md. Coll., 1998. Camp leader Dept. Pks. and Recreation, City of Balt., 1990-93; substitute tchr. Baltimore County Pub. Schs., Owings Mills, Md., 1992, long-term substitute, 1994; substitute tchr. Harford County Pub. Schs., Jarrettsville, Md., 1993; tchr. 3rd grade Anne Arundel County Pub. Sch., Glen Burnie, Md., 1994-95, tchr. 5th grade, 1995 98, Sandymount Elem., 1999—. Chmn. reading/writing com., 2001—; team leader pub. sch. Glen Burnie, 1995-97, chairperson ednl. mgmt. team, prin. designee, 1996-97; table leader Staff Devel. Ctr., Arnold, Md., 1996; instr. Md. Summer Ctr. Gifted & Talented, 1998; office mgr. Electronics Boutique, 1998-99. Camp leader Baltimore County Renaissance Program, 1997; active PTA, liaison, 1995-96; tchr. Sunday sch. Baltimore County Bapt. Ch., Reisterstown, Md., 1994-98; youth leader Balt. County Bapt., 1999—; child care dir. YMCA, 1998. Lions Club scholar, Reisterstown, 1989. Avocations: reading, writing, computers. Home: 9416 Fitzharding Lane Owings Mills MD 21117 E-mail: cbarton2@mindspring.com.

BARTON, ELLEN LOUISE, lawyer, educator, consultant; b. Harrisburg, Pennsylvania, Jan. 17, 1946; d. George Michael and Irene Catherine (Gregor), Schmeltzer; m. Norman W. Barton, Nov. 28, 1987; children: William Michael, Ian Christopher, Michael Alexander. AB Psychology, Rosemont Coll., 1972; JD, Ohio U, Cin., Ohio, 1978. Dist. Fellow Am. Soc. Healthcare Risk Mgmt. Bar: Ohio 1978, U.S. Dist. Ct. (so. dist.), Ohio, 1979; Pa., 1985, U.S. Ct. Appeals (3d cir.), 1985,; Maryland 1989; CPCU. Occupl. analyst Commonwealth of Pa., Harrisburg, Pa., 1972-74; ins. adjuster Lloyd Deist, Inc., Cin., 1977-78; asst. editor FC and S Bulls, Nat. Underwriter Co., Cin., 1978-81; assoc. dir. risk mgmt. Ohio U., Cin., 1981-84, dir. risk mgmt., 1984-85, Pa. State U., 1985-87; ptnr. Fischer, Klimon, Salman, and Harpster, Cin., 1984-85, Klimon, Salman, Greve, and Harpster, Phila., 1985-89, Barton and Salman, Balt., 1990-91; pres. Neumann Ins. Co., 1987-97; corp. dir. risk mgmt. Franciscan Health Sys., Aston, Pa., 1987-97, sr. v.p., legal svc. gen. counsel, 1993-97; dir., chairperson Alternative Ins. Mgmt. Svc., Inc., 1989-97; dir., chmn. Preferred Physicians Ins. Co., 1988-97; dir., chairperson Consol. Cath. Casualty Risk Retention Group, Inc., 1987-97; CEO, gen. counsel New Am. Health, LLC., Glen Burnie, Md., 1997-98; health care practice leader Aon Risk Svc., Inc., Balt., 1998; v.p. risk mgmt. MedStar Health, Columbia, Md., 1999-2000, cons., 2000—. Cons. Don Malecki & Assocs., Fort Thomas, Ky., 1983-85; asst. atty. gen. State of Ohio, Columbus, 1983-85; asst. prof. family medicine U.Cin., 1984-85; legal advisor Children's Internat. Summer Villages, Cin., 1984-85. Editor: Insuring the Lease Exposure, Part II, 1981; contbr. articles to profl. jour. Mem. Our Lady of Rosary Sch. bd., Greenhills, Ohio, 1974-81; v.p. Covered Bridge Civic Assn., Cin., 1979-81, area rep., 1979-82; pres. Nat. Underwrite Co. Fed. Credit Union, Cin., 1980-81. Pa. Higher Edn. Assistance Agy. Scholar, Rosemont Coll., Phila., 1971-72. Mem.: ABA, Am. Inst. for Property and Liability Underwriters (chartered property and casualty underwriter 1981), Am. Soc. Healthcare Risk Mgmt. (pres. 1990—91, pres 2002—03, Disting. Svc. Award 1993, Ellen Barton Cert. in Healthcare Risk Mgmt. 2001), Nat. Health Lawyers Assn., Am. Soc. Law and Medicine, Soc. CPCUs, Md. Bar Assn., Pa. Bar Assn., Ohio Bar Assn. Republican. Roman Catholic. E-mail: ellenbarton@earthlink.com.

BARTON, FREDRICK PRESTON, English language educator, administrator; b. Alexandria, La; life ptnr.: Joyce Markrid Dombourian. BA, Valparaiso U., 1970; MA, UCLA, 1973, CPhil, 1975; MFA, U. Iowa, 1979. Tchr., coach Luth. HS, St. Louis, 1970-72; carnival barker Ted Towne Entertainment, LA, 1973-75; tchg. asst. UCLA, 1975-76; asst. editor Instns. Mag., Chgo., 1978; tchg. fellow U. Iowa, Iowa City, 1978—79; English prof. U. New Orleans, 1979—, dean Liberal Arts Coll., 2000—. Film critic Gambit Weekly, New Orleans, 1980—. Author: (novels) A House Divided, 1999 (William Faulkner award 2000), The El Cholo Feeling Passes, 1985, Counting Pandemonium, 1986, With Extreme Prejudice, 1993, (play) Ash Wednesday, 1998, (screenplay) Early Warning, 2001, (film column) Balcony Seats, 1984 (Alex Waller Meml. award 1984); actor: (film) Early Warning, 2001. Bd. dir. Tennessee Williams/New Orleans Literary Festival, 1986--; mem. Valparaiso U. Christ Coll. Nat. Coun. Recipient Lit. prize La. Divsn. Arts, 1989. Mem. PEN (treas. Gulf South 1993-94), Authors Guild, Press Club New Orleans (bd. dir. 1993-95, Criticism prize 1984, 86-90, 92, 94, 97, 2000, 2002). Baptist. Avocations: tennis, squash, golf. Home: 63 Versailles Blvd New Orleans LA 70125 Office: U New Orleans Lakefront New Orleans LA 70148 Fax: 504-280-6468. E-mail: fbarton@uno.edu.

BARTON, GERALD LEE, farming company executive; b. Modesto, Calif., Feb. 24, 1934; s. Robert Paul and Alice Lee (Hall) B.; m. Janet Murray, June 24, 1955; children: Donald Lee, Gary Michael, Brent Richard. BA with distinction, Stanford U., 1955. Owner, pres. Barton Ranch, Escalon, Calif., 1961—; v.p. R.P. Barton Mfg. Co., Escalon, 1963-86; chmn. bd. Diamond Walnut Growers Inc., 1976-81, chmn. emeritus, 1981—, pres., 1986-90. Chmn. Growers Harvesting Com., Modesto, 1976-77, Diamond-Sunsweet Co., Stockton, Calif., 1978-80, Sun Diamond Growers, Inc., 1980-81; bd. dirs. Calif. Fin. Holding Co., Stockton, Stockton Savs. Bank, Union Safe Deposit Bank; vice-chmn. Fed. Land Bank, Modesto, Calif., 1976-81; pomology rsch. adv. bd. U. Calif., Davis, 1968-74, Walnut Mktg. Bd., San Francisco, 1971-73, 77-2000; mem. Calif. Walnut Commn., 1987-99; agribus. adv. bd. U. Santa Clara, 1979-89; dir. Ross Hort. Found.; ext. adv. bd. San Joaquin County U. Calif. Chmn. bd. edn. Escalon Unified Sch. Dist., 1963—75; vice chmn. San Joaquin County Sch. Bds. Assn., 1965; trustee Yosemite Assn., 1999—; dir. Union Safe Deposit Bank, 2000—; elder Trinity United Presbyn. Ch., Modesto, 2002—; bd. dirs. St. Joseph's Healthcare Corp., 1991—95; bd. dirs. v.p. Stanislaus River Flood Control Assn., 1965—. With U.S. Army, 1956—58. Decorated Order of the Golden Walnut; named Outstanding Young Farmer in San Joaquin County C. of C., 1965, Farmer of Yr. Escalon C. of C.; recipient U. Calif. Friend of Extension award, 1992; named to San Joaquin County Agrl. Hall of Fame, 1993; recipient Disting. Svc. award Calif. Walnut Commn., 1998; named Co-op Farmer of Yr. Agrl. Coun. Calif., 2001. Mem. Stanford U. Alumni Assn., Delta Chi. Republican. Presbyterian. Office: 22398 Mcbride Rd Escalon CA 95320-9637

BARTON, GLEN A. manufacturing company executive; b. Alton, Mo. BS in Civil Engring., U. Mo., Columbia, 1961; grad. Exec. Program, Stanford U., 1977. With Caterpillar Inc., Peoria, Ill., 1961—, mgr. merchandising divsn. gen. offices, 1983-84, mgr. products control, 1984-86, v.p., 1987-89, exec. v.p., 1989-90, group pres., 1990-98, vice chmn., CEO, 1998—99, chmn., CEO, 1999—. Mem. adv. bd. Bank One, Peoria, Bradley U., Peoria, INCO Ltd. Mem. Nat. Mining Assn. (bd. dirs., chmn. mfrs. divsn. bd. govs.), Mineral Info. Inst.

BARTON, GREGORY MARK, Olympic athlete, kayak racer; b. Jackson, Mich., Dec. 2, 1959; BS in Mech. Engring., U. Mich., 1983. Olympic kayak racer, 1000 meter singles, L.A., 1984; Olympic kayak racer, 1000 meter singles and doubles Seoul, Korea, 1988; Olympic kayak racer, 1000 meter singles Barcelona, Spain, 1992. Recipient Bronze medal 1000 meter kayak singles Olympics, L.A., 1984, Gold medal 1000 meter kayak singles Olympics, Seoul, 1988, Gold medal 1000 meter kayak doubles Olympics, Seoul, 1988, Bronze medal 1000 meter kayak singles Olympics, Barcelona, 1992. Office: c/o US Olympic Com 1750 E Boulder St Colorado Springs CO 80909-5724

BARTON, HUGH PERRY, bank executive; b. Modesto, Calif., Apr. 6, 1932; s. Robert Paul and Alice B.; m. Sheila Grieve, Dec. 29, 1954; children: Elizabeth, James. BS, U. Calif., Berkeley, 1954. Pres., CEO R.P. Barton & Co., Escalon, Calif., 1955-91; chair bd. Modesto (Calif.) Banking Co., 1977-94, Barton McLean & Waters, San Francisco, 1992-97; dir. Bank of Los Altos (Calif.), 1994—, Heritage Commerce Corp.; chmn. bd. dirs. Pvt. Bank of Peninsula, Palo Alto, Calif., 2003—. Dir. Heritage Commerce Corp., San Jose, 2000—. Mem. Carmel Valley Ranch Golf Club, Pebble Beach Tennis Club, Old Capitol Club. Republican. Episcopalian. Home: 9906 Club Place Ln Carmel CA 93923-8507 Office: PO Box 222097 Carmel CA 93922-2097

BARTON, JAMES CARY, lawyer; b. Raymondville, Tex., Sept. 1, 1940; s. Dewey Albert and Dorothy Marie (Keene) B.; m. Isabel Pattee Critz, Sept. 12, 1964 (div. June 1975); children: Hamilton Keene, James Albert, John Franklin; m. Carolyn Ann Cox, Dec. 20, 1975; stepchildren: Holly Ann Adams, Laura Lee Adams, Jennifer Lynn Adams. BA, Baylor U., 1962; LLB, Harvard U., 1965. Bar: Tex. 1965, U.S. Dist. Ct. (so. dist.) Tex. 1972, U.S. Tax Ct. 1977. Trial atty. FPC, Washington, 1965-67; atty.-advisor U.S. Tax Ct., Washington, 1967-68; assoc. to ptnr. Kleberg, Mobley, Lockett & Weil, Corpus Christi, Tex., 1969-75, Brown, Maroney, Rose, Baker & Barber, Austin, Tex., 1975-82; ptnr. to of counsel Johnson & Swanson, Austin, 1982-88; dir. Smith, Barshop, Stoffer & Millsap, Inc., San Antonio, 1988-91; prin. J. Cary Barton, P.C., San Antonio, 1991-93; prin Barton & Schneider, L.L.P., San Antonio, 1993—2003, Barton, Schneider, & Russell, L.L.P., 2003—. Speaker in field. Sgt. USAF, 1968-69. Mem. ABA, State Bar Tex. (mem. coun. of real estate probate and trust law sect. 1982-85, mem. real estate forms com. 1986—), Am. Coll. Real Estate Lawyers, Tex. Bd. Legal Specialization (cert. in comml. real estate law), Tex. Coll. Real Estate Attys. Democrat. Episcopalian. Office: Barton Schneider & Russell LLP 700 N Saint Marys St Ste 1825 San Antonio TX 78205-3596

BARTON, JAMES MILLER, lawyer, international business consultant; b. Scarsdale, N.Y., Apr. 13, 1942; s. Ralph Miller and Eleanor (LaRose) B.; m. Nancy Claudia Bishop, Aug. 7, 1965; children: James Miller Jr., Timothy Ralph, Allison Megen. BA, Yale U., 1964; LLB, U. Va., 1967. Bar: Conn. 1967, U.S. Tax Ct. 1971, U.S. Supreme Ct. 1971. Assoc. Cummings & Lockwood, Stamford, Conn., 1967-75, ptnr., 1975-96, mem. exec. and fin. coms., 1980-95; ptnr. Levett Rockwood, Westport, Conn., 1996-99. Legal cons. fgn. investment; active Ministry Privatization Czech Republic, Prague, 1992-93; v.p. Avian Farms, Inc., Waterville, Maine, 1996-99; sr. cons. internat. affairs Preferred Health Systems, LCC, Bethesda, Md., 1995-98; dir. corp. afairs Advanced Cell Tech., Inc., Worcester, Mass., 1996-99; CEO, Cyagra, LLC, Westport, Conn., 1999—, Hematech, LLC, Worcester, 1999—. Contbr. articles to profl. jours. Trustee Greenwich Acad., 1988-96, chmn., 1993-96; bd. dirs. Greenwich Choral Soc., 1970's, Stamford Symphony, 1994—. Mem. Stanwich Club (Greenwich), Yale Club (N.Y.); Yale Club (Greenwich) (bd. dirs. 1970s). Avocations: opera, theater, reading, tennis. Office: 33 Riverside Ave Westport CT 06880-4223

BARTON, JANICE SWEENY, chemistry educator; b. Trenton, N.J., Mar. 22, 1939; d. Laurence U. and Lillian Mae (Fletcher) S.; m. Keith M. Barton, Dec. 20, 1967. BS, Butler U., 1962; PhD, Fla. State U., 1970. Postdoctoral fellow Johns Hopkins U., Balt., 1970-72; asst. prof. chemistry East Tex. State U., Commerce, 1972-78, Tex. Woman's U., Denton, 1978-81; assoc. prof. Washburn U., Topeka, 1982-88, prof., 1988—, chair chemistry dept., 1992—. Mem. undergrad. faculty enhancement panel NSF, Washington, 1990; mem. NSF instr. lab. improvement panel, 1992, 96, 99; mem. NSF-AIRE site visit team, 2000; WUKBRIN (NIH grant) coord., 2001—. Contbr. articles to profl. jours. Active Household Hazardous Waste Collection, Topeka, 1991, Solid Waste Task Force, Shawnee County, Kans., 1990; mem. vol. com. YWCA, Topeka, 1984-87; bd. dir. Helping Hand Humane Soc., 2002—; grant coord. Kans. Biomedical Rsch Infrastructure Network, 2002—. Rsch. grantee Petroleum Rsch. Fund, Topeka, 1984-86, NIH, Topeka, 1985-88; instrument grantee NSF, Topeka, 1986, 95. Mem. Am. Chem. Soc. (sec. Dallas-Ft. Worth sect. 1981-82), Kans. Acad. Sci. (pres.-elect 1991, pres. 1992, treas. 1995—), Biophys. Soc., Sigma Xi (pres. TWU club 1980-81), Iota Sigma Pi (mem.-at-large coord. 1987-93). Home: 3401 SW Oak Pky Topeka KS 66614-3218 Office: Washburn U Dept Chemistry Topeka KS 66621 E-mail: janice.barton@washburn.edu.

BARTON, JEAN MARIE, psychologist, educator; b. Pitts., Mar. 24, 1945; d. Joseph Paul and Jean Marie (Anderson) Adamchic; m. Robert L. Barton, Jr., Aug. 14, 1965; children: Robert Joseph, Katherine Anne. BS summa cum laude, U. Pitts., 1965; MEd, Boston U., 1969; CAGS, Cath. U. Am., 1985, PhD in Ednl. Psychology, 1988. Cert. sch. psychologist, Md., nationally cert. sch. psychologist. Tchr./curriculum Wellesley (Mass.) pub. schs., 1965-69; lectr. U. R.I./R.I. Coll., Providence, 1969-72; curriculum specialist/tchr. St. Jane DeChantal Sch., Bethesda, Md., 1977-83, computer prog. dir., 1982-84; psychology assoc. Long Assocs., Bethesda, 1988—; psychol. cons. gifted unit Montgomery County Pub. Schs., Rockville, Md., 1985-99; sch. psychologist various schs. Archdiocese of Washington (Md.), 1987—; adj. mem. faculty Cath. U. Am., Washington, 1989—. Mem. evaluation team Cath. Schs. Studies, 1987-92; dir. Profl. Devel. Inst., Cath. U. Am., 1985-86; mem. adv. com., chairperson identification com. Jacob Javits Grant, Montgomery County Pub. Schs., 1989-92, project coord. Jacob Javitz grant, 1992-95, supt. adv. com. on Edn. of Gifted, 1992-96, on Spl. Edn.; assoc. dir. Ctr. for Advancement Cath. Edn. at Cath. U. Am., 1998—; mem. adv. com. on gifted edn. Md. State Dept. Edn., 1999-2000. Contbr. articles to profl. jours. U. Pitts. scholar, 1962-65. Mem. APA, ASCD, NASP, Am. Ednl. Rsch. Assn., Md. Sch. Psychologists Assn., Nat. Assn. for Gifted Children, Pi Lambda Theta. Home: 5008 Benton Ave Bethesda MD 20814-2804 Office: Cath U of America O'Boyle Hall Washington DC 20064-0001 E-mail: docjeanbarton@cs.com. *Meaningful achievement consist of recognizing one's unique talents, working hard to develop them to the fullest, and then striving to seize opportunities to use them so that in some small way humanity is better for one's having lived.*

BARTON, JOE LINUS, congressman; b. Waco, Tex., Sept. 15, 1949; s. Larry Linus and Bess Wynell (Buice) Barton; children: Bradley Linus, Allison Renee, Kirsten Elizabeth. BS in Indsl. Engring., Tex. A&M U., 1972; MS in Indsl. Adminstrn., Purdue U., 1973. Asst. to v.p. Ennis (Tex.) Bus. Forms, 1973-81; White House fellow, aide to energy sec. James B. Edwards Washington, 1981-82; cost control cons. ARCO, Dallas, 1982-84; mem. U.S. Congress from 6th Tex. dist., 1985—; mem. energy and commerce com.; mem. sci. com.; chmn. energy and air quality subcom. of commerce com.; mem. Rep. steering com. Mem. Assn. Former Students Tex. A&M U. (councilman at large 1985—) Republican. Methodist.*

BARTON, JOHN HAYS, law educator; b. Chgo., Oct. 27, 1936; s. Jay and Agnes (Heisler) B.; m. Julianne Marie Gunnis, June 13, 1959; children: John II, Robert, Anne, Thomas, David. BS, Marquette U., 1958; JD, Stanford U., 1968. Bar: D.C. 1969. Engr. Sylvania Electronic Def. Labs., Mountain View, Calif., 1961-68; assoc. Wilmer, Cutler and Pickering, Washington, 1968-69; George E. Osborne prof. Stanford (Calif.) U. Law Sch., 1969—. Vis. prof. U. Mich. Law Sch., fall 1981, Harvard Law Sch., 1988. Author: Politics of Peace, 1981; co-author: Law in Radically Different Cultures, 1983 (Am. Soc. Internat. Lawe award 1984), International Trade and Investment, 1986; co-editor Words over War, 2000. Former chair Nat. Genetic Resources Adv. Coun.; former mem. NAFTA Dispute Settlement Panel; mem. NRC Com. Intellectual Property Rights in Knowledge Based Econ., 2000-03; chair comm. intellectual property rights UK Dept. Internat. Devel., 2001-02; vice chmn. Ctr. for Mgmt. Intellectual Property in Health Rsch. and Devel. Lt. (j.g.) USN, 1958-61. Rockefeller Found. fellow, 1976-77. Fellow AAAS, Chartered Inst. Arbitrators; mem. Am. Soc. Internat. Law. Home: 1340 Harwalt Dr Los Altos CA 94024-5815 Office: Stanford U Sch Law Stanford CA 94305

BARTON, JOHN JOSEPH, obstetrician, gynecologist, educator, researcher; b. Rockford, Ill., Mar. 19, 1933; s. L. David and Helen M. (Fox) B.; m. Lois Maltby, 1959 (div. 1965); children: Mary Katherine, Karen Ann. BA in History, U. Ill., 1957; BS in Medicine, U. Ill., Chgo., 1959, MD, 1961; student Law, Loyola U., Chgo., 1966-69. Diplomate Am. Bd. Ob.-Gyn.; cert. Advanced Cardiac Life Support. Rotating intern Cook County Hosp., Chgo., 1961-62, resident in ob.-gyn., 1962-65; fellow gynecologic pathology Northwestern U., Chgo., 1963, clin. asst. ob.-gyn., 1963-64, clin. instr. ob.-gyn., 1964-65, assoc. in ob.-gyn., 1965-71; prof. ob.-gyn. Cook County Grad. Sch. of Medicine, Chgo., 1965—; dir. ob.-gyn. rsch. and edn. Cook County Hosp., Chgo., 1965-69; chmn. ob.-gyn. Ill. Masonic Med. Ctr., Chgo., 1970—2001; assoc. prof. ob.-gyn. U. Ill. Coll. Medicine, Chgo., 1971-83, prof., 1983-93, lectr. in ob.-gyn., 1993—; prof. ob.-gyn. Rush Med. Coll., Chgo., 1993—; chmn. emeritus ob-gyn Ill. Masonic Med. Ctr., 2002—. Clin. clerkship subcom. U. Ill. Coll. Medicine, 1974-90, acad. senate 1977-91, 85-87, perinatal steering com., 1977-92, admissions com. 1985-91, screening subcom. 1988-89; ad hoc com. on rules for governance, Rush Med. Coll., Chgo., 1993—, curriculum com. 1993, com. on student evaluation and promotions, 1994—, core ckerkship subcom. of curriculum com. 1995—; editl. bd. Jour. Obstetrics and Gynecology, Am. Jour. Obstetrics and Gynecology, Internat. Jour. Obstetrics and Gynecology Contbr. numerous articles to profl. jours., chpts. to books. including Laparoscopy in Gynecologic Practice, 1972, Guidelines for Perinatal Care, 1983, Antepartum HIV Screenings: A Comparison of Methodologies, 1990. Vol. cons. Ob.-Gyn. Claremore (Okla.) Indian Hosp., 1979-80, 86, Fort Defiance (Ariz.) Indian Hosp., 1981, Red Crescent Soc., Heliopolis, Cairo, Egypt, 1987; vol. surgeon Internat. Red Cross and Red Crescent Soc. Vols., West Beirut, Lebanon, 1982; mem. Ill. Gov.'s AIDS adv. coun.; advisor, expert witness Atty. Gen. State of Ill. on Standards of Practice in Ob.-Gyn.; mem. com. formation of outcome-oriented surveillance systems for Ill. Dept. of Pub. Health, adv. com. to Health Planning Com. for Chgo., perinatal adv. com. Ill. Dept. Health, steering com. Mayor Washington's Infant Mortality Reduction Initiative and others. Sgt. USMC, 1950-55, Korea. Fellow Am. Coll. Obstetricians and Gynecologists (adv. coun. 1977-81, adv. coun. dist. VI 1977-81, chmn. Ill. sect. 1977-78, com. on profl. liability 1989-92, Jr. Fellow Rsch. prize award 1991), Ctrl. Assn. Obstetricians nd Gynecologists (ctrl. travel club, sci. awards com. 1985-89. chmn. 1987-89, Ann. prize award 1988), Chgo. Gynecol. Soc. (exec. com. 1994—, pres. 1995-96), Am. Coll. Surgeons, Soc. Contemporary Medicine and Surgery, Am. Soc. Clin. Hypnosis, Chgo. Inst. Medicine, Royal Soc. Medicine (London); mem. Ill. Assn. Maternal and Child Health, Assn. Profs. Gynecology and Obstetrics, Am. Pub. Health Assn., Phi Kappa Phi, Nu Sigma Nu. Avocations: rancher quarter horses, exotic animals, hounds, harleys. Home: Bar T Ranch 20516 Bunker Hill Rd Marengo IL 60152-8003 Office: Ill Masonic Med Ctr 836 W Wellington Ave Chicago IL 60657-9224

BARTON, JONATHAN MILLER, clergyman; b. Elizabeth, N.J., June 26, 1952; s. Douglas William and Deborah (Gray) B.; m. Elizabeth Dora Rinehart, May 19, 1985 (div. June 1990); 1 child, Katherine Nicole; m. Elizabeth Wood Stark, July 17, 1994; stepchildren: Liza, Archer Blair. Student, Union Coll., 1970-72; BA in Psychology, Kean Coll., 1974; MDiv, Drew U, 1978. Ordained to ministry Presbyn. Ch., 1981. Asst. chaplain Drew U., Madison, N.J., 1976-78, resident dir., 1977-81; hunger action enabler Elizabeth, Newark, Newton presbyteries United Presbyn. Ch. U.S.A., 1978-82; cons. World Hunger Edn. Svc., Washington, 1983; assoc. regional dir. Ch. World Svc., Rocky Hill, N.J., 1983-85, regional dir. Richmond, Va., 1985-2000; gen. min. Va. Coun. Churches, Richmond, 2000—. Mem. Nat. IMPACT Briefings, Washington, 1978-84; mem. coord. com. N.J. State Food Conf., 1979; spl. asst. to coord. U.S. Nat. Com. for World Food Day, 1981-83; mem. 4th World Food Issues Conf., Cornell U., 1982; testifier Senate Subcom. on edn., ARts and Humanities, 1982; mem. NGO Com. for UN Internat. Conf. on Population Consultation, 1984, UN/NGO Com. on Food and Rural Devel. Food Forum, 1985, UN/NGO Consultation on African Crisis, 1985; mem. Summer Inst. in Devel. Edn., Tao, N.Mex., 1986; mem. prep. com. for visit Dir.-Gen. UN/FAO on FAO's 50th anniversary commemoration, Washington, 1993; attended US AID Conf. Global Edn., Williamsburg, Va., 1989; mem. Gov.'s Conf. Infant Mortality, Richmond, Va., 1986. Regional editor Va. Steps, Ch. World Svc., 1985-2000; contbr. articles to various publs. in field. Co-chair grant com. Va. Hands Across Am., 1986; co-founder, chair Madison, N.J. chpt. Amnesty Internat., 1976-80; chair program adv. com. Ch. World Svc., 1987-89; chair Divsn. Mission and Svc., Presbytery of James, 1992-93; bd. dirs. Va. Interfaith Ctr. Pub. Policy, 1987-93; bd. dirs. Direct Ministries, Va. Coun. Chs., 1986-94, mem. Va. refugee adv. coun., 1992— ; co-founder, convener Va. Congress on Hunger, 1987-93; founding mem. bd. dirs. Va. Hunger Found., 1992-95. Recipient C.J. Helen svc. award Miquin Lodge #68, 1967, Virgil honor Order of the Arrow, 1968, Lighthouse award Foodbank S.E. Va., 1993. Mem. Internat. Platform Assn. Office: Va Coun Churches 1214 W Graham Rd Ste 3 Richmond VA 23220-1409 E-mail: barton@vcc-net.org.

BARTON, JUDITH MARIE, lawyer, lobbyist; b. Grosse Pointe, Mich., Feb. 19, 1953; d. Joseph J. and Shirley (Fisher) B.; m. A. Scott MacGuidwin, Sept. 19, 1980; children: Stephen Fisher, Richard Joseph, Elizabeth Ashley, James Scott, Scott Thomas. BA, U. Mich., 1975; JD, Thomas M. Cooley Sch. Law, 1979. Bar: Mich. 1981, U.S. Dist. Ct. (we. and ea. dists.) Mich. 1982. Mgr. bus. and circulation Football News/Basketball Weekly, Grosse Pointe, 1975-77; legis. asst. Mich. Ho. of Reps., Lansing, 1977-80, legal specialist, 1980-81; staff dir. Mich. State Senate, Lansing, 1981-83; pvt. practice Lansing, 1983-93; majority gen. coun. Mich. House of Reps., 1993—, chief policy and legal counsel, 1994—. Lobbyist Mich. Rental Housing Assn., 1989-93. Bd. dirs. Common Cause, Lansing, 1983-89, state chairperson, Mich., 1987-89; bd. dirs. Landlords of Mid-Mich., Lansing, 1985-89. Mem. ABA, Mich. Bar Assn., Ingham County Bar Assn., Women's Law Assn., Pub. Action Com., Capitol Area Women's Network (bd. dirs. 1983-84), Civitan Internat., Pi Beta Phi. Republican. Roman Catholic. Home: 4317 Manitou Dr Okemos MI 48864-2715 Home (Winter): 5117 Sea Bell Rd Sanibel FL 33957

BARTON, KEITH CASEY, college educator; b. Louisville, Ky., Feb. 9, 1961; s. Earl Harlan Barton, Thelma Jesse Casey; m. Shaunna Lynn Scott; 1 child, Hannah. BA, U.Ky., 1982; MA, U.Calif., L.A., 1985; EdD, U.Ky., 1994. Cert. K-8 Multiple Subject Credential Calif., 1985, 5-8 Social Studies Credential Ky., 1994. Elem. tchr. L.A. Unified Sch. Dist., L.A., 1985—86; tchr. Antioch Unified Sch. Dist., Antioch, Calif., 1986—90; prof. No. Ky. U., Highland Heights, Ohio, 1991—97; assoc. prof. U. Cin., Cincinnati, Ohio, 1998—. Home: 220 Boone Ave Winchester KY 40391 Office: University of Cincinnati Division of Teacher Education Cincinnati OH 45221-0002 Office Fax: 513-556-1001. Personal E-mail: keith.barton@uc.edu. Business E-Mail: keith.barton@uc.edu.

BARTON, LAURA ANN, aerospace experimental psychologist, consultant, researcher; d. Nayland B. Barton and Margaret A. Summers Barton; children: Joshua A., Jacob B. BA, MA, Calif. State U.; PhD, U. Denver. Aerospace Experimental Psychologist Naval Aerospace Med. Inst.; Victim's Services Cert. Calif. State U., Cockpit Resource Management Program Manager Naval Aviation Schools Command, Fla., Operational Risk Management Transp. Safety Inst. Aerospace physiol. tng. specialist USAF, Edwards Air Force Base, Calif., 1980—86; aviation maintenance officer/oic Army N.G., Fresno, Calif.; head, msc aerospace med. tng. Naval Operational Med. Inst., Naval Air Station Pensacola, Fla.; head, force aviation human factors US Naval Air Forces, Naval Station Norfolk, Va. Cons. Nat. Transp. Safety Bd., Washington; field naval aviator evaluation bd. Naval Air Forces Atlantic Fleet, Naval Station Norfolk, Va. Lcdr USN. Decorated USAF Commendation Medal USAF, USN Commendation Medal USN, USN Achievement Medal, USAF Marksmanship Medal USAF; recipient Medallion Excellence, Fresno City Coll.; grantee Rsch. Award, Office Naval Rsch.; scholar Golden Key Nat. Honor Soc., Calif. State U. Chpt. Mem.: APA, Aerospace Med. Assn., Am. Psychol. Soc., Golden Key (Scholarship), Phi Kappa Phi. Achievements include research in Coping and Adjustment in Pervasive Low Situations. Office: Naval Air Forces Atlantic Fleet 1279 Franklin St Naval Base VA 23511 Office Fax: 757-445-4271. E-mail: bartonla@cnal.navy.mil.

BARTON, LESLIE L. physician; b. N.Y.C., Feb. 22, 1943; d. Raymond and Beatrice Liebesman; m. William Holmes; 1 child, Todd Barton. BA cum laude, Hunter Coll., 1963; MD, U. Chgo., 1966. Diplomate Am. Bd. Pediat. Combined pediat.-medicine intern Cook County Hosp., Chgo., 1966-67; resident Boston Children's Hosp. Med. Ctr., 1967-69; fellow in rsch. virology Nat. Children's Hosp. Med. Ctr., Washington, 1969-70; instr. pediat. Washington U. Sch. Medicine, St. Louis, 1971-73, asst. prof. pediat., 1973-76, St. Louis U. Sch. Medicine, 1977-81, assoc. prof. pediat., 1981-88, prof. pediat., 1988-90; prof. pediat., dir. pediat. housestaff U. Ariz. Sch. Medicine, Tucson, 1990—. Pediat. cons. Montgomery County Health Dept., Rockville, Md., 1970-71; cons. Malcolm Bliss Mental Health Ctr., St. Louis, 1977-85; asst. dir. pediat. St. Louis County Hosp., 1971-73, dir. pediat., 1974-76; dir. pediat. St. Louis City Hosp., 1977-85; mem. ambulatory divsn. Cardinal Glennon Children's Hosp., St. Louis, 1985, joint appt. infectious disease and ambulatory divsn., 1986, interim dir. divsn. infectious diseases, 1989-90; med. staff U. Med. Ctr., Tucson, 1990, Tucson Med. Ctr., 1990. Reviewer numerous pediat. and infectious disease jours., 1978—; contbr. articles to profl. jours. N.Y. Pub. Health Rsch. fellow, 1963. Fellow: Infectious Diseases Soc. Am., Am. Acad. Pediat. (editl. bd.); mem.: Assn. Pediat. Program Dirs., Pediat. Infectious Diseases Soc., Phi Beta Kappa. Avocations: gardening, music, reading. E-mail: llb@peds.arizona.edu.

BARTON, LEWIS, consultant; b. N.Y.C., Mar. 9, 1940; s. Louis and Mary (Mosca) Bologna; m. Barbara Joan Hummell, Sept. 6, 1964; children: Glenn Scott, Gregory Jon. Student, Adelphi U., 1957-59. Sales rep. Olivetti Corp., N.Y.C., 1962-64, W. Ralston Co., Chgo., 1964-65, Milprint Co., N.Y.C., 1965-66; pres., founder Sigma Quality Foods, Farmingdale, N.Y., 1966-88, Sigma Star Food Corp., N.Y.C., 1993-98; pres. The Barton Group, Inc., N.Y.C., 1998—. Lectr. various confs. Patentee several package design constructions and methods. With USAF, 1961-62. Named to Pres. Coun. for Ednl. Distinction, Adelphi U. Mem. Nat. Single Svc. Food Assn. (charter, chmn. 1977-79, Svc. award 1982), Assn. Dressings and Sauces, Dwight D. Eisenhower Soc. (founder), Columbus Citizen's Found., Internat. Orgn. Packaging Profls., NY Athletic Club. Home: 45 Sutton Pl S New York NY 10022-2444 E-mail: lb@consultbarton.com.

BARTON, PAUL B. artist, sculptor; b. Worcester, Mass., Oct. 2, 1946; s. Walter E. and Elsa Barton; m. Lorraine Barton-Haas, July 1, 1967; 1 child, Hannah C. BFA, Boston U., 1980. Journeyman carpenter Brotherhood Carpenters & Joiners, 1972—80; artist, 1980—. Prin. works include pub. sculpture Beulah Cmty. Ctr., 1997. Recipient Silver medal Boston U. Alumni, 1980. Mem. Internat. Sculpture Ctr., Nat. Sculpture Soc., Colorado Springs Art Guild, Pueblo Art Guild. Mem. Soc. Of Friends. Avocations: fly fishing, fly tying, fly rod building. Home and Office: PO Box 176 Beulah CO 81023-0176

BARTON, PAUL J. lawyer; b. Price, Utah, Sept. 24, 1946; s. John O. and Mae L. Barton; m. Elaine L. York, Oct. 12, 1974 (div. Sept. 1997); children: Susan, John, James. BA in Econs., Brigham Young U., 1970, JD, U. Utah, 1973, LLM in Taxation, Washington U., 1974. Pvt. practice, Salt Lake City, 1973—; real estate broker Utah and Mo., 1979—; investment advisor, 1988—. Contbr. articles to profl. jours. With U.S. Army, 1969. Scholar Hinckley Inst., 1971, John A. Widtsoe Meml. scholar, 1972-73. Mem. Internat. Assn. Fin. Planners, Estate Planning Coun., Utah State Bar Assn. (probate and tax sect. 1974-2003, unauthorized practice law sect. 1994-99, advt. com. 1994-99). Mem. Ch. Jesus Christ Latter Day Sts. Avocations: basketball, hunting. Office: 345 E 400 S Ste 201 Salt Lake City UT 84111-2971

BARTON, RICHARD N. computer company executive; BS in Indsl. Engring., Stanford U., 1989. Strategy cons. Alliance Consulting Group, 1989-91; with Microsoft Corp., Redmond, Wash., 1991-94; gen. mgr. traveler bus. unit Microsoft Corp. (Expedia), Redmond, Wash., 1994—. Office: Microsoft Corp One Microsoft Way Redmond WA 98052-6399

BARTON, ROBERT H., III, automotive executive; CEO Meridian Automotive Sys., Dearborn, Mich. Office: Meridian Automotive Systems 550 Town Center Dr Dearborn MI 48126 Office Fax: (313) 336-4184.

BARTON, ROBERT LEROY, JR., judge, educator; b. Ballston Spa, N.Y., June 19, 1943; s. Robert L. Sr. and Bertha (Di Pasquale) B.; m. Jean M. Adamchic, Aug. 14, 1965; children: Robert Joseph, Katherine Anne. BA, U. Pitts., 1965; JD, Boston Coll., 1969. Bar: Mass. 1969, R.I. 1970, D.C. 1972, U.S. Ct. Appeals (1st cir.) 1970, U.S. Ct. Appeals (D.C. cir.) 1973, U.S. Dist. Ct. R.I., 1971, U.S. Dist. Ct. D.C. 1973, U.S. Dist. Ct. Md. 1973. Law clk. U.S. Dist. Ct. R.I., Providence, 1969-70; staff atty. R.I. Legal Svcs., Providence, 1970-71; spl. asst. to solicitor U.S. Dept. Labor, Washington, 1971-72; assoc. Sherman, Dunn, Cohen & Leifer, Washington, 1972-75; trial atty. FTC, Washington, 1975-88; judge Pa. Office of Hearing & Appeals, Pitts., 1988-90, Office of Hearings, Washington, 1990-95, Office of Adminstr. Law Judges, Washington, 1995—. Trial instr. Nat. Inst. Trial Advocacy, Washington, 1982-86, U.S. Dept. Justice, Washington, 1986-96. Chair com. Cath. League for Religious Rights, Milw., 1983-84. Master Am. Inn of Ct.; mem. Fed. Bar Assn. (co-chair adminstrv. jud. com.), Fed. Adminstrn. Law Judges Assn. (exec. com.), Nat. Lawyers Assn. Roman Catholic. Avocations: travel tennis, swimming. Office: Office Adminstrv Law Judges 5107 Leesburg Pike Ste 1905 Falls Church VA 22041-3249 E-mail: robert.barton@usdoj.gov.

BARTON, SARAH MURIEL, lawyer; b. London, Mar. 23, 1958; d. Russell William Andrew Charles and Katherine Grizel (Maitland-Makgill-Crichton) B.; children: Daniel Russell Bernard, Caroline Sarah Katherine. BA, U. Toronto, Ont., Can., 1978; JD, Union U., Albany, 1981; LLM in Admiralty, Tulane U., 1982. Bar: N.Y. 1982, La. 1983, U.S. Dist. Ct. (ea. dist.) La. 1983, N.J. 1985, U.S. Dist. Ct. (we. dist.) La. 1985, U.S. Dist. Ct. (so. dist.) N.Y., U.S. Ct. Appeals (5th cir.) 1986. Assoc. Law Offices Frederick Gisevius, New Orleans, 1982-83, James Hanemann and Assocs., New Orleans, 1983-85; assoc. counsel Am. Bur. Shipping, N.Y.C. and London, 1985-96; gen. counsel ABS Group of Cos., Inc., Houston, 1997—, v.p., 1998—. Spkr. Maritime Cyprus Legal Forum, 1993, Nat. Inst. and Royal Inst. Naval Archs., London, 1994. Mem. Am. Corp. Counsel Assn., Maritime Law Assn. (proctor). Home: 1511 Potomac Dr Houston TX 77057-1925 Office: ABS Group of Cos Inc 16855 Northchase Dr Houston TX 77060-6006

BARTON, STANLEY FAULKNER, management consultant; b. Halesowen, Worcestershire, Eng., Dec. 30, 1927; came to U.S., 1957, naturalized, 1963; s. Lazarus and Alice (Faulkner) B.; m. Marion Brittain, Dec. 20, 1952; children: Carolyn Francesca, Andrea Elizabeth. B.Sc. (hons.), U. Birmingham, Eng., 1949; PhD, U. Birmingham, 1952. Group leader Naval Rsch. Establishment, Halifax, N.S., Can., 1953-56; project coord. Def. Rsch. Chem. Labs., Ottawa, Ont., Can., 1956-57; devel. engr. Procter & Gamble, Cin., 1957-58, R & D group leader, 1958-59, R & D sect. head, 1959-69; tech. dir. food products-natural resources ITT, N.Y.C., 1969-76; sr. v.p. tech. and quality ITT Rayonier, Inc., Stamford, Conn., 1976-90; v.p., dir. Spectrum Internat. Assocs., Inc., Tucson, 1990-92. Pres. Catalina Cons., 1990—. Mem. Am. Theater Organ Soc. Home and Office: Catalina Cons 4051 N Circulo Manzanillo Tucson AZ 85750-1879 E-mail: stanb@prodigy.net.

BARTON, STANLEY L. ophthalmologist, consultant; b. Columbia Station, Ohio, May 30, 1920; 1 child, Randal L. BA, Bowling Green State U., 1943; MD, Wayne State U., 1946. Cert. Am. Bd. Ophthalmology. Capt. U.S. Army, 1946—49, Korea. Mem.: AMA (life), Wayne County Med. Soc., Mich. State Med. Soc. Home: 17400 Ft St Riverview MI 48192-6646 Office: Troy Med Clinic 1663 Stephenson Hwy Troy MI 48083

BARTON, THOMAS DONALD, lawyer, educator; b. July 1, 1949; s. Donald Walter and Dorothy Louise (Farlin) B.; m. Sharon Lee Foster, July 26, 1980. BA, Tulane U., 1971; JD, Cornell U., 1974; PhD, Cambridge (Eng.) U., 1982. Bar: N.Y. 1974, Calif. 1990. Assoc. Harris, Beach & Wilcox, Rochester, N.Y., 1974-76; asst. prof. W.Va. U. Coll. Law, Morgantown, 1978-80; assoc. prof., assoc. dean acad. affairs, 1982-84; prof., 1984-87; posten prof. law, 1987-89; prof. Calif. Western Sch. Law, 1990—; dir. Brown Program in Preventive Law, 2000—. Mem. panel arbitrators, Am. Arbitration Assn.; mem. Morgantown Bd. Zoning Appeals, 1983-86; bd. dirs. W.Va. Tax Inst., 1978-80; cons. W.Va. State Elections Commn., 1979. NEH fellow, 1979. Contbr. articles to profl. jours. Recipient Gustavus Hill Robinson award, 1974; W.D.P. Carey Exhbn. prize, 1972. Mem. Phi Beta Kappa, Phi Sigma Delta, Delta Alpha Pi. Office: Calif Western Sch Law 225 Cedar St San Diego CA 92101-3046

BARTON, THOMAS HEISLER, management consultant; b. Chgo., Apr. 12, 1924; s. Jay and Agnes Heisler Barton; m. Jo Jeanne Millon, Apr. 5, 1952; children: Avril Barton Moore, Brooke Millon. BS, Northwestern U., 1945, BSEE, 1946; postgrad., Navy Russian Lang. Sch., Boulder, Colo., 1945—46; MBA, Harvard U., 1948. Asst. to pres. Automatic Electric Co., Chgo., 1948—49; dist. sales mgr. Beckman Instruments, Inc., Fullerton, Calif., 1949—52; govt. mktg. staff BG Corp., N.Y.C., 1952—53; asst. to pres. Nickel Cadmium Battery Co., N.Y.C., 1953—55; v.p. Barrington & Co., Inc., N.Y.C., 1955—65, Am. Express Co., N.Y.C., 1965—71; fin. cons. A.T. Kearney, Inc., N.Y.C., 1971—73; pres. Thomas H. Barton & Co., Inc., N.Y.C., 1973—. Author: Japanese Technology for the Graphic Arts, 1986; contbr. articles to profl. jours. Trustee St. Vincents Hosp., N.Y.C., 1973—2000. Lt. j.g. USNR, 1942—46. Mem.: AAAS, IEEE, Union Club City N.Y., Tau Beta Pi. Roman Catholic. Avocations: travel, languages. Home: 1192 Park Ave New York NY 10128 Office: Thomas H Barton & Co Inc Ste 1700 521 Fifth Ave New York NY 10175

BARTON, THOMAS JACKSON, chemistry educator; b. Dallas, Nov. 5, 1940; s. Ralph and Florence (Whitfield) Barton; m. Elizabeth Burton, Oct. 1, 1966; children: Ralph, Brett. BS, Lamar U., 1962; PhD (hon.), U. Fla., 1967. NIH fellow Ohio State U., 1967; mem. faculty Iowa State U., Ames, 1967—, prof. chemistry, 1978—, disting. prof., 1984—, program dir. Ames Lab., 1986—88, dir. Ames Lab, 1988—, dir. Inst. for Phys. Rsch. and Tech., 1998—. NAS exch. scientist, Former Soviet Union, 1975; assoc. prof. U. Montpellier, France; mem. coun. on materials scis. Dept. Energy, 1992—97. Contbr. rsch. papers to profl. publs. Recipient Fredric Stanley Kipping award in organosilicon chemistry, 1982, Gov.'s medal for sci. tchg., 1983, Excellence in Tchg. faculty achievement award, Burlington No. Found., 1988, Outstanding Sci. Accomplishment in Materials Chem. award, Dept. Energy, Materials Sci. Divsn., 1989. Fellow: Japan Soc. Promotion of Sci.; mem.: Am. Chem. Soc. (Midwest award 1995). Methodist. Home: 815 Onyx Cir Ames IA 50010-8429 Office: Iowa State Univ Dept Chemistry Ames IA 50011-0001

BARTOO, EUGENE CHESTER, academic administrator, educator; b. Wellsboro, Pa., Jan. 31, 1940; s. Eldred Llewellyn and Viola May (Mudge) Bartoo; m. Ruth Grace Walker, June 27, 1961 (div. May 1986); children: Steven, James, Thomas, Jennifer. BS, Pa. State U., 1961; MEd, SUNY, Buffalo, 1967, EdD, 1972. Tchr. Onondaga Ctrl. Sch., Syracuse, NY, 1961-63, Hamburg (N.Y.) Sr. HS, 1963-65; tchr., dept. head Newfane (N.Y.) Ctrl.. Sch., 1965-69; asst. supt. Griffith Inst., Springville, NY, 1970-71; asst. prof. Case Western Res. U., Cleve., 1971-78; assoc. prof. U. Tenn., Chattanooga, 1978-84, prof., 1984—. Cons. State Edn. Dept. Ohio, Columbus, 1974—77, Lillian Ratnor Montessori Sch., Cleve., 1975—78, State Edn. Dept. Tenn., Nashville, 1983—86. Co-author: (book) Curriculum: An Introduction to the Field, 1978. Bd. dirs., past pres. ACLU Tenn., 1985—90. Named Best Supporting Actor, Chattanooga Little Theatre, 1992, Mildred Routt Disting. Tchg. Prof., 2000. Mem.: Soc. Advancement Am. Philosophy, Am. Ednl. Rsch. Assn. Avocation: amateur acting. Office: U Tenn 615 Mccallie Ave Chattanooga TN 37403-2504 E-mail: ebartoo@cecasun.utc.edu.

BARTOS, JERRY GARLAND, corporate executive, mechanical engineer; b. Dallas, Feb. 5, 1933; s. Vladimir Thomas and Ella Marie (Rezek) B; m. Marlene Louise Buehrer, Sept. 25, 1954 (div. 1978); children: Marla Jeanette, Sara Jane, Julie Ann; m. Candye Laverna Gould, Feb. 24, 1979; 1 child, Mary Meghan. BSME, So. Meth. U., 1954. Registered profl. engr., Tex., Mont. Sales engr. Trane Co., Dallas, 1957-61, asst. v.p. LaCrosse, Wis., 1961-62; chief engr. Linskie Co., Dallas, 1962-64; pres. Bartos, Inc., Dallas, 1964—. Hon. Consul Czech Republic for North Tex., 1996—. Contbr. articles to profl. jours. Mem. Dallas City Coun., 1987—; chmn. Clean Dallas, Inc., 1974, Greater Dallas Planning Coun., 1986, pres., 1984-86; bd. dirs. Dallas Ind. Sch. Dist., 1979-81; pres. North Dallas C. of C., 1975-76; hon. consul Czech Republic for North Tex., 1995—. Recipient Speakers-Authors award Am. Air Filter Co., 1972, Svc. award Luth. Ch., 1975, Life Mem. award State PTA, 1976, Rotarian award, 1993, Pro Deo Schola award Luth. Ch., 2001; Paul Harris fellow, 1993. Mem. Am. Soc. HVAC Engrs. (life, chair com. Dallas chpt. 1957—, Alco Nat. Svc. award), Tex. Soc. Profl. Engrs., U.S. C. of C. (founder, regional chair small bus. orgn. 1978-79), Dallas C. of C. (vice chmn. 1976-77), North Dallas C. of C. (pres. 1975-76, chmn. 1976), Small Businessmen Assn. (Small Businessman of Yr. award 1974). Republican. Office: Bartos Inc Dallas TX 75209

BARTOSHUK, LINDA J. otolaryngologist, educator; BA in Psychology, Carleton Coll., 1960; MS in Psychology, Brown U., 1963, PhD in Psychology, 1965; DSc (hon.), Carleton Coll., 2001. Pre-doctoral fellow PHS, 1960—64, NSF, 1960—64; lectr. Brown U., 1966—68; affiliate asst. prof. Clark U., 1966—69; rsch. psychologist Natick Labs, 1966—70; asst. John B. Pierce Found., 1970—73, assoc., 1974—85, fellow, 1985—89; asst. prof. dept. epidemiology and pub. health Yale U., 1971—76, assoc. prof. depts. epidemiology and pub. health and psychology, 1976—85, prof. depts. epidemiology and

pub. health and psychology, 1985—88, prof. sect. otolaryngology dept. surgery and prof. dept. psychology, 1989—. Chair Gordon Conf. on Chem. Senses, 1978; mem. various coms. NIH, NRC. Editor: Chem. Senses, 1982—84; cons. editor: Perception and Psychophysics, 1972—86, Sensory Processes, 1976—79; contbr. articles to profl. jours. Recipient Pepper Neuroscience Investigator award, 1984—92, Manheimer award, Monell Chem. Senses Inst., 1990, Kreshover award, Nat. Inst. Dental Rsch., 1990, Disting. Contbn. award, New Eng. Psychol. Assn., 2000. Fellow: AAAS; mem.: APA (mem. at large exec. com. div. 6 1984—87, mem. NSF working group for com. on rsch. support 1985—87, program chair div. 6 1987, pres. div. 6 1988—89, pres. elect div. 1 2001, fellow div. 6 comparative and physiol. psychology, Neal Miller Lectr. 2000), NAS, Am. Assn. Dental Schs. (mem. women's affairs adv. com.), Soc. Exptl. Psychologists, Soc. for Study of Ingestive Behavior (bd. govs. 1987—89, 2000—03), Psychonomic Soc. (mem. publ. com. 1987—92), Ea. Psychol. Assn. (mem. program com. 1983—86, bd. govs. 1987—90, pres. 1990—91), Assn. Chemoreception Scis. (exec. chair 1980—81, Award for Outstanding Achievement in chem. senses 1998), Am. Psychol. Soc. (bd. dirs. 2001—03), Phi Beta Kappa, Sigma Xi. Office: Dept Surgery Yale U Sch Medicine PO Box 208041 New Haven CT 06520-8041*

BARTOSIC, FLORIAN, law educator, lawyer, arbitrator; b. Danville, Pa., Sept. 15, 1926; s. Florian W. and Elsie (Woodring) B.; m. Eileen M. Payne, 1952 (div. 1969); children: Florian, Ellen, Thomas, Stephen; m. Alberta C. Chew, 1990. BA, Pontifical Coll., 1948; B.C.L., Coll. William and Mary, 1956; LL.M., Yale U., 1957. Bar: Va. 1956, U.S. Supreme Ct. 1959. Asst. instr. Yale U., 1956-57; assoc. prof. law Coll. William and Mary, 1957, Villanova U., 1957-59; atty. NLRB, Washington, 1956, 57, 59; counsel Internat. Brotherhood of Teamsters, Washington, 1959-71; prof. law Wayne State U., 1971-80, U. Calif., Davis, 1980-92; recalled to tchg., 1994-99; prof. emeritus law U. Calif., Davis, 1993—, dean law, 1980-90. Adj. prof. George Washington U., 1966-71, Cath. U. Am., 1960-71; mem. panel arbitrators Fed. Mediation and Conciliation Service, 1972— ; hearing officer Mich. Employment Relations Commn., 1972-80, Mich. Civil Rights Commn., 1974-80; bd. dirs. Mich. Legal Services Corp., 1973-80, Inst. Labor and Indsl. Relations, U. Mich., Wayne State U., 1976-80; mem. steering com. Inst. on Global Conflict and Cooperation, 1982-83; mem. adv. bd. Assn. for Union Democracy Inc., 1980—, adv. coms. Calif. Jud. Council, 1984-85, 87; vis. scholar Harvard Law Sch., 1987, Stanford Law Sch., 1987; sr. rsch. scholar ILO, 1990-91; acad. visitor Oxford U., London Sch. Econs., 1991; mem. exec. bd. Pub. Interest Clearinghouse, 1988-90. Co-author: Labor Relations Law in the Private Sector, 1977, 2d edit., 1986; contbr. articles to law jours. Mem. ABA (sec. labor rels. law sect. 1974-75), Fed. Bar Assn., Am. Law Inst. (acad. mem. labor law adv. com. on continuing profl. edn.), Soc. Profls. in Dispute Resolution (regional v.p. 1979-80), Indsl. Rels. Rsch. Assn., Internat. Soc. Labor Law and Social Legis., Internat. Indsl. Rels. Assn., Lawyers Guild, ACLU (dir. Detroit chpt. 1976-77), Order of Coif (hon.), Scribes. Home: 235 Ipanema Pl Davis CA 95616-0253 Office: U Calif Sch Law Mrak Hall Dr Davis CA 95616 E-mail: fbartosic@ucdavis.edu.

BARTOW, DIANE GRACE, marketing and sales executive; b. Maspeth, N.Y., Apr. 20, 1948; d. Alfred Otto and Charlotte Florence (Bronnenkant) Bruggeman; m. Eugene A. Bartow, aug. 29, 1992; children: Jason, Trudi. AAS, Queensborough C.C., 1967; BS, Nova Southeastern U., 1979. Jr. acct. Exxon, N.Y.C., 1967-69; acct. BRM Assocs., N.Y.C., 1969, Texaco, N.Y.C., 1969-74; supr. Eutectic, Flushing, N.Y., 1974-76; regional industry dir. Am. Express, N.Y.C., 1976-83; v.p. Eastern Exclusives, Boston, 1983-85; pres. The Mktg. Dept., 1985-86; sr. v.p., gen. mgr. Rogers Merchandising Inc., 1986-92; exec. v.p., COO Bartow Ins. Agy., Inc., 1992—. Seminars Marketing to Win. Author tng. manual, travel newsletter, 1982, Ins. Update, 1992. Trustee, v.p. Murray Hill Neighborhood Assn., 1982, pres., 1997, 98, 99, 00, 01, 02, 03, 04; trustee 7 E 35th Corp., 1983; chmn. judging Promotion and Advt. awards, 1990, awards chair, 2001-02. Mem. Nat. Assn. Advt. and Promotional Allowances (judging chair 1996-00), Am. Soc. Travel Agts. (tour rels. com. 1983), Am. Hotel and Motel Mgmt. Assn., Am. Film Assn., Am. Mgmt. Assn., Life Underwriters, Sigma Mu Omega (pres. Bayside (N.Y.) 1966-67). Home: 7 E 35th St New York NY 10016-3810

BARTRAM, RALPH HERBERT, physicist; b. N.Y.C., Aug. 16, 1929; s. Herbert L. and Grace L. Bartram; m. Ellen Anderson Devlin, Oct. 9, 1953; children: Ellen Ruth, Robert Arthur. Student, Northwestern U., 1948-49; BA cum laude, NYU, 1953, MS, 1956, PhD, 1960. Engr. Sylvania Electric Products Inc., Kew Gardens, NY, 1953-56; advanced rsch. physicist GTE Labs., Inc., Bayside, NY, 1956-61, cons., 1961-85; mem. faculty U. Conn., Storrs, 1961—, prof. physics, 1971-92, dept. head, 1986-92, prof. emeritus, 1992—. Rsch. assoc. Atomic Energy Rsch. Establishment, Harwell, England, 1967—68; vis. prof. U. Oxford, England, 1978; sr. vis. fellow U. Strathclyde, Scotland, 1993; cons. U.S. Army, 1966—71, Am. Optical Co., 1966—78, Brookhaven Nat. Lab., 1971—85, Timex Corp., 1981—82, Polaroid Corp., 1987—88, Boston U., 1993—99, ALEM Assocs., 1996—, Photonics Materials Ltd., 2002—. Author (with J. M. Spaeth and J. R. Niklas): (book) Structural Analysis of Point Defects in Solids, 1992; author: (with B. Henderson) Crystal-Field Engineering of Solid-State Laser Materials, 2000; contbr. articles to profl. jours. With USN, 1946—48. Grantee, U.S. AEC, 1963—69, U.S. Army Rsch. Office, 1971—78, 1982—92, NSF, 1974—77, 1983—91, NATO, 1985—90. Fellow: Am. Phys. Soc.; mem.: AAUP, Conn. Acad. Sci. Engring., Optical Soc. Am., Phi Beta Kappa, Phi Eta Sigma, Sigma Pi Sigma, Phi Kappa Phi, Sigma Xi. Achievements include patents in field. Home: 67 Independence Dr Mansfield Center CT 06250-1541 Office: U Conn Dept Physics Storrs Mansfield CT 06269-3046 E-mail: RHBartram2@aol.com.

BARTREM, DUANE HARVEY, retired military officer, designer, building consultant; b. Lansing, Mich., June 4, 1928; s. Harvey Theodore and Ruby Leola (Thomas) B.; m. Frances Lillie Bushee, Sept. 12, 1948 (dec. Jan.19, 2000); children: Lawrence Duane, Jeffrey Earl. BA in Bus. Adminstrn., Columbia Coll., Mo., 1976. Enlisted U.S. Army N.G., Lansing, 1948, commd. 2d lt., 1951, advanced through grades to col., 1951-76, comdr. battery, 1956-60; facilities engr. Mich. Nat. Guard, Lansing, 1960-69, chief engr., 1969-76, comdr. 119 FA Bn., 1971-75, comdr. 46th Brigade, 1975-76, comptr., 1976-83, ret., 1983; prin. residential design office Lansing, 1955-60, Grand Ledge, Mich., 1967—. Leader local and regional levels Boy Scouts of Am.; chmn. congregation Bretton Woods Covenant Ch., Mich., 1986—89, v.p. congregation, 1995—. With USNR, 1946—48. Decorated Army Commendation with 3 clusters, Meritorious Svc. medal with 2 clusters, Legion of Merit. Mem. Mil. Officers Assn., Mil. Order Fgn. Wars (sr. vice comdr. gen., 2003—), Assn. of the U.S. Army (mem. resolutions com. 1973, 74, chair resolutions com. 1975, area v.p. 1976—, mem. adv. bd. 1978—, chair by-laws com. 1978—, past state pres., past region pres. 1988-92, coun. of trustees 1992-96, Pres.'s medal 1998), Grand Lodge Rotary (pres. 1989-90, Paul Harris award 1992), Boy Scouts Am. (pres. 1973-79, exec. bd. 1970—; disting. Eagle Scout 1989, Silver Beaver award 1969, Silver Antelope 1983, God and Svc. award 1992, James E. West fellow, 1910 Soc., Ernest Thompson Seton Mem. 1999). Avocation: golf.

BARTSCHAT, KLAUS RICHARD WILHELM, physics educator; b. Steinfurt, Westfalen, Germany, June 17, 1956; s. Richard Ewald and Helmine Angela Käthe (Busch) Bartschat; m. Teresa Elisabeth Zweerman, Aug. 13, 1988; children: Nicholas, Erika. Diploma in physics, U. Münster, Germany, 1981; PhD, U. Münster, 1984, Habilitation, 1989. Rsch. scientist U. Münster, 1984-88; asst. prof. physics Drake U., Des Moines, 1988-91, assoc. prof. physics, 1991-94, prof. physics, 1994-2000, Ellis and Nelle Levitt Disting. prof. physics, 2000—. Author: Computational Atomic Physics, 1996, Polarization, Alignment, and Orientation in Atomic Collisions, 2000; contbr. over 200 articles to profl. jours. Grantee NSF, 1991—, NATO, 1990, 93, 2000, Rsch. Corp., 1989. Fellow Am. Phys. Soc.; mem. Deutsche Physikalische Gesellschaft, Theoretical Atomic, Molecular and Optical Cmty. (chair 1998-2000), Internat. Conf. Photonic, Electronic, and Atomic Collisions (sec. 2001—). Baptist. Avocations: family, exercise, travel. Home: 4301 101st St Urbandale IA 50322 Office: Drake U Dept Physics and Astronomy Des Moines IA 50311 Fax: 515-271-1943. E-mail: klaus.bartschat@drake.edu.

BARTTER, BRIT JEFFREY, investment banker; b. Berea, Ohio, Dec. 27, 1949; s. Lynn Martin Bartter and Scharlie Ellen (Watson) Handlan; m. Marilyn McCullough, Aug. 25, 1973; children: Bryndl Lynn and Blake McCullough (twins). AB in Econs., Duke U., 1972; MS in Fin., Cornell U., 1976, PhD in Fin., 1977. Asst. prof. computer sci. Grad. Sch. Bus. Cornell U., Ithaca, N.Y., 1976; asst. prof. fin. Grad. Sch. Mgmt. Kellogg Grad. Sch. Mgmt., Northwestern U., Evanston, Ill., 1977-79; assoc., then v.p. Merrill Lynch Capital Markets, Chgo., 1979-83; v.p. The First Boston Corp., Chgo., 1983-87, dir., 1988-89, mng. dir., 1989-94, Merrill, Lynch Investment Banking, Chgo., 1995—. Bd. dirs. Coun. for Young Profls., Chgo., 1985-87. Contbr. articles to Jour. of Fin., Fin. Mgmt. Bd. dirs. Cornell Coun. Chgo., 1987-88, Duke Campaign Chgo., 1987-88; mem. governing bd. Chgo. Symphony Orch. Mem. Econ. Club Chgo., Northwestern U. Assocs., Glen View Golf Club, Chgo. Club. Home: 221 Apple Tree Rd Winnetka IL 60093-3703 Office: Merrill Lynch Investment Bkng 5500 Sears Tower Chicago IL 60606

BARTUNEK, JAMES SCOTT, psychiatrist; b. Flint, Mich., Oct. 20, 1962; s. Steven James and Frances Annabelle (Peters) B.; m. Carol Lynn Tobis, Feb. 26, 1994; 1 child, Rebecca. BS, U. Mich., Flint, 1985; MD, Wayne State U., 1989. Resident in psychiatry Sinai Hosp. Detroit, 1989-92; pvt. practice Psychiatry, Rochester, Minn., 1992—. Mem. Am. Psychiat. Assn., Founder's Soc. Detroit Inst. Arts, U. Mich. Club, Wayne State U. Med. Alumni Club. Avocations: reading, sports, travel, shakespearean theater. Home: 3541 Hidden Forest Ct Orion MI 48359-1477 Office: 1460 Walton Blvd Ste 215 Rochester Hills MI 48309-1779

BARTUNEK, JEAN MARIE, management consultant, educator; b. Cleve., Oct. 25, 1944; d. Robert Richard Bartunek and Clare Elizabeth Lonsway. PhD, U. Ill., Chgo., 1976. Vis. asst. prof. orgnl. behavior U. Ill., Urbana, 1976—77; asst. prof., assoc. prof., prof. orgn. studies Boston Coll., Chestnut Hill, Mass., 1977—. Author: (book) Organizational and educational change: The life and role of a change agent group, 2003, Insider-Outsider team research, 1996; editor: Hidden conflict in organizations: Uncovering behind the scenes disputes, 1992; author: Creating alternative realities at work: The quality of worklife experiment at FoodCom, 1990; mem. editl. bd.: Adminstrv. Sci. Quar., 1997—, Jour. Applied Behavioral Sci., 1986—, Jour. Orgnl. Behavior, 1999—, Qualitative Orgnl. Rsch., 2001—; co-editor: Jour. Mgmt. Inquiry, 1994—97. Recipient Best Manuscript award, Mass. Soc. CPAs, 1980; grantee, Marion and Jasper Whiting Found., 1997—99, Soc. for Orgnl. Learning, 1998—99. Fellow: Acad. Mgmt. (exec. com., chmn. orgn. and devel. change divsn. 1986—91, exec. com. women in mgmt. divsn. 1993—96, editl. bd. Acad. Mgmt. jour. 1997—2001, officer 1998—2003, pres. 2001—02, coord. external rels. 2002—03, Best Practice-Related Paper orgn. devel. and change divsn. 1996); mem.: Ea. Acad. Mgmt. (bd. dirs. 1993—96), Soc. for Orgnl. Learning, Am. Ednl. Rsch. Assn. Roman Catholic. Office: Boston Coll 140 Commonwealth Ave Chestnut Hill MA 02467-3808

BARTUNEK, KENNETH STEVEN, financial consultant; b. Flint, Mich., May 11, 1965; s. Steven James and Frances Annabelle (Peters) B. Student, U.S. Naval Acad., 1983; BS in Math., U. Mich., Flint, 1987; PhD in Bus. Adminstrn., La. State U., 1991; MS in Fin. Math., U. Chgo., 1998. Chemistry rsch. asst. U. Mich., Flint, 1984; intern Mich. Bell Telephone, Detroit, 1987; instr. fin. La. State U., Baton Rouge, 1991; asst. prof. fin. Fla. Atlantic U., Boca Raton, 1991-97, assoc. prof. fin., 1997-2000. Mem. Met. Mus. Art La. State U. Alumni Fedn. fellow, 1987-91. Roman Catholic. Office: Ste 2300 333 Clay St Houston TX 77002

BARTUNEK, ROBERT R(ICHARD), JR., lawyer; b. Cleve., July 2, 1946; s. Robert Richard and Clare Elizabeth (Lonsway) B.; 1 child, Kathryn Elizabeth. BS, Bucknell U., 1968; MBA, Ohio State U., 1974, JD, 1975; LLM, U. Mo., Kansas City, 1986. Bar: Mo. 1975, Kans. 1997, U.S. Dist. Ct. (we. dist.) Mo. 1975, U.S. Tax Ct. 1981, U.S. Dist. Ct. Kans. 1997. Ptnr. Beckett, Lolli & Bartunek, Kansas City, 1975-96, Swanson Midgley, LLC, Kansas City, 1997—2003, Siegfreid, Bingham, Levy, Selzer & Gee, Kansas City, 2003—. Mem. Men's Sr. Baseball League. Decorated Bronze Star. Mem. ABA, Lawyers Assn. Greater Kansas City, Kansas City Met. Bar Assn. (former chmn. tax law com.). Roman Catholic. Office: Seigfried Bingham Levy Selzer & Gee 2800 Commerce Tower 911 Main St Kansas City MO 64105 Home: 10314 Howe Ln Leawood KS 66206-2517 E-mail: rbartunek@sblsg.com.

BARTUS, RAYMOND THOMAS, neuroscientist, pharmaceutical executive, writer; b. Chgo., May 19, 1947; s. Frank A. and Katherine (Bogus) B.; m. Cheryl Marie Gyure, Feb. 11, 1967; children: Raymond T., Kristin Marie. BA, California State U. Pa., 1968; MS, N.C. State U., 1970, PhD, 1972. NRC postdoctoral fellow, research assoc. Naval Med. Rsch. Lab., Groton, Conn., 1972; scientist Parke-Davis Rsch. Labs., Ann Arbor, Mich., 1973-75, sr. scientist, 1975-78, Lederle Labs., Am. Cyanamid Co., Pearl River, N.Y., 1978-79, group leader neuroscience, dir. geriatric discovery program, 1979-88; sr. v.p. R & D, chief sci. officer Cortex Pharms. Inc., Irvine, Calif., 1988-91, interim pres., 1990, exec. v.p., chief oper. officer, 1991-92, chief sci. officer, 1988-92; sr. v.p. neurobiology Alkermes Inc., Cambridge, Mass., 1992-96, sr. v.p. preclin. R&D, 1996—2001; sr. v.p. Worldwide Life Sci. R&D, 2001—02; v.p., rsch. and devel. Ceregene Inc., San Diego, 2002—. Bd. dir. Net Met; prof. N.Y.U. Med. Ctr., 1979—; adj. prof. Tulane U., 1978—87, U. Calif., Irvine, Calif., 1988—92, Tufts U., 1992—; v.p. R&D Ceregene, Inc., San Diego, 2002—. Editor-in-chief, founder, Neurobiology of Aging, 1980-89; contbr. articles on neurosci. to profl. jours. Fellow Am. Coll. Neuropsychopharm.; mem. Alzheimers Assn. (sci. med. bd. 1986-92), Soc. Neurosci., N.Y. Acad. Sci., Brain Tumor Soc., Am. Assn. Pharm. Sci., Am. Soc. Pharmacology and Exptl. Biology. Office: Ceregene Inc 9381 Judicial Dr #130 San Diego CA 92121 E-mail: rtbartus@ceregene.com.

BARTZ, DAVID JOHN, lawyer; b. Appleton, Wis., Feb. 15, 1955; s. Frederick Carl and Dorothy Lucille (Weckwerth) B. BA, U. Wis., 1976; MA in Pub. Affairs, U. Minn., 1979; JD, Ariz. State U., 1985. Bar: Ariz. 1985, U.S. Dist. Ct. Ariz. 1985, U.S. Ct. Appeals (9th cir.) 1985, Wis. 1989, U.S. Dist. Ct. (we. dist.) Wis. 1996, U.S. Dist. Ct. (ea. dist.) Wis. 1997. Policy analyst Minn. Dept. Transp., St. Paul, 1978-79; office dir. Wis. Senate, Madison, 1979-82, 86; pvt. practice, Phoenix, 1985-86; adminstr. Wis. Dept. Justice, Madison, 1987-91; pvt. practice, Madison, 1991—. Mem. ASPA (sec. Wis. Capital chpt. 1981-82), Ariz. Bar Assn., Wis. Bar Assn., Dane County Bar Assn.

BARTZATT, RONALD LEE, research biochemist, consultant; b. Lincoln, Nebr., Dec. 18, 1953; s. Frank Wright and Lorretta (Warta) B.; m. Patricia Ann Dockham, July 30, 1979 (div. Oct. 1983). BS, U. Nebr., 1978, MS, 1980, PhD, 1982. Cert. med. lab. technician. Research biochemist U. Nebr., Lincoln, 1983-84, Eppley Cancer Ctr., Omaha, 1984-85, Theodor Gildore Ctr., San Diego, 1985, U. Calif., San Diego, 1985-88; rsch. biochemist Eppley Cancer Ctr., 1988—. Cons. IRCS Med. Sci., Lancaster, England, 1985—. Author: Proceedings of ACS Symposia on Computer Data Analysis and Optimization; contbr. articles to profl. jours. Deacon Luth. Ch., San Diego. Served with U.S. Army, 1973-76. Towle Scholar U. Nebr., 1973; NIH fellow, 1984; grantee Nebr. Water Co., 1981. Mem. Am. Soc. Clin. Pathologists, Am. Chem. Soc., AAAS, Planetary Soc., Phi Lambda Upsilon. Republican. Avocations: kayaking, ice skating, skiing, music.

BARUCH, EDUARD, management consultant; b. Bklyn., Dec. 19, 1907; s. Emile and Grace (Willis) B.; m. Dorothy Hurd, Sept. 8, 1934 (dec. Aug. 1994); 1 child, Hurd; m. Malyn Crusius, Feb. 9, 1996. Mech. engr., Rhenania Coll., Switzerland, 1924-26; AB, Columbia U., 1930; postgrad., Law Sch., 1933. Trust adminstr. spl. loan div. Irving Trust Co., N.Y.C., 1933-39; sales exec. Bankers Life Co., Des Moines, 1939-42; v.p. charge sales James H. Rhodes & Co., 1942-47; nat. sales mgr. vending div. Pepsi Cola Co., 1947-49; v.p. Heli-Coil Corp., Danbury, Conn., 1949-55, exec. v.p., 1955-56, pres., 1956-70; indsl. commr. State Conn., 1973-75; corp. cons., 1970—. Exec. com., mem. bd. Barden Corp. (acquired by F.A.G. Schinefert Germany), Danbury, Conn.; bd. dirs. Savs. Bank, Danbury. Comdr. Conn. State Police Aux., 1967-70. Recipient Cecil J. Previdi Meml. award for civic accomplishment, leadership and entrepreneurial spirit State of Conn. Gen. Assembly and City of Danbury, 2000. Mem. Soc. Automotive Engrs., Rotary (past pres., Paul Harris fellow), Masons, Shriners, Jesters, KT (Bridgeport, Conn.), Princeton U. Club, Wings Club (N.Y.C.), Ridgewood Country Club (Danbury), Coral Ridge Yacht Club (gov.), Tower Club, Lago Mar Beach and Tennis Club, Navy League (Ft. Lauderdale), Danbury Hosp. Pres. Coun., Psi Upsilon, Phi Delta Phi. Presbyterian. Home and Office: 936 Intracoastal Dr Fort Lauderdale FL 33304-3640 *I learned from yesterday, it is past. Today is my gift to use - it is a present.Both will prepare me for tomorrow, the future.*

BARUCH, HURD, lawyer; b. N.Y.C., Nov. 29, 1937; s. Eduard and Dorothy (Hurd) B.; m. Mary Ellen Kinney, July 8, 1964; children: Edward, Michael, Amy. BA, Hamilton Coll., 1957; LLB, Yale U., 1960; MBA, Columbia U., 1961. Bar: Conn. 1960, N.Y. 1966, D.C. 1971, Pa. 1972, Ill. 1988, U.S. Supreme Ct. 1964. Ptnr. Winston & Strawn, Chgo. Spl. counsel divsn. trading and markets, SEC, 1969-72. Author: Wall Street Security Risk, 1971. Capt. USAFR, 1961-64. Mem. Ill. State Bar Assn., KM, Order of Coif, Phi Beta Kappa, Beta Gamma Sigma. Office: Winston & Strawn 35 W Wacker Dr Ste 4200 Chicago IL 60601-1695

BARUCH, JORDAN JAY, management consultant, consultant; b. N.Y.C., Aug. 21, 1923; s. Solomon L. and Minnie (Kessner) B.; m. Rhoda Wasserman, June 3, 1944; children: Roberta, Marjory, Lawrence. BS, MS, Mass. Inst. Tech., 1948, Sc.D., 1950. V.p., dir. Bolt, Beranek & Newman, Inc., Cambridge, Mass., 1949-66, dir., 1949-77, Boston Broadcasters, 1963-77, 81-83, Inst. for Mental Health Initiatives, Washington, 1982—, treas., 1982-98; dir. Gould Corp., 1985-88, Baupost Group, Cambridge, Mass., 1984-98; asst. prof. elec. engring. MIT, Cambridge, 1950-53, lectr., 1954-70; lectr. bus. adminstrn. grad. sch. bus. adminstrn. Harvard U., Boston, 1970-74; prof. Amos Tuck Sch. Bus. Adminstrn., Thayer Sch. Engring., Dartmouth Coll., Hanover, N.H., 1974-77; asst. sec. sci. and tech. Dept. Commerce, Washington, 1977-81; pres. Jordan Baruch Assocs., Washington, 1981—. Mem. bd. sci. and tech. for internat. devel. Nat. Rsch. Coun.; advisor to U.S./Israel Hightech Commn.; advisor Nat. Ctr. Indsl. Sci. & Tech., Dalian, China; founder, U.S. advisor U.S./Israel Bianational Indsl. R&D Found., 1978—; regent Nat. Libr. Medicine, Washington, 1998-2001. Contbr. articles to books and profl. jours.; patentee loudspeakers, acoustical treatments, automotive mufflers. Bd. dirs. Inst. Mental Health Initiatives, Washington. Served with AUS, 1942-46. Named Outstanding Young Elec. Engr. Eta Kappa Nu, 1956 Fellow Acoustical Soc. Am., IEEE, AAAS, Nat. Acad. Engring. (Augustine sr. scholar 2001—), Am. Acad. Arts and Scis. Patentee loudspeakers, acoustical treatments, automotive mufflers. Home and Office: 5630 Wisconsin Ave Apt 905 Chevy Chase MD 20815-4456 E-mail: jbaruch@erols.com.

BARUCH, RALPH M. communications executive; came to U.S., 1940, naturalized, 1944; s. Bernard and Alice B.; m. Jean Ursell de Mountford, June 9, 1963; children by previous marriage: Eve, Renee, Alice, Michele. Student Sorbonne, U. Paris. Account exec. SESAC, 1947-50, Dumont TV, 1950-54; Eastern Sales mgr. Enterprises, N.Y.C., 1954-59, v.p. internat. sales, 1959-67, v.p., gen. mgr., 1967-70; group pres. CBS, 1970-71; pres., chief exec. officer Viacom Internat. Inc., N.Y.C., 1971-78, chmn. bd., mem. office of chief exec., 1979-87; sr. fellow Gannett Ctr. for Media Studies Columbia U., 1988. Cons. Adv. Commn. on Com., USIA, 1979-86. Bd. dirs., vice chmn. exec. com. Internat. Rescue Com., N.Y.C., 1975-88; mem. Pres.'s Coun. for Internat. Youth Exch., 1982; trustee Mus. of TV and Radio, Carnegie Hall, Lenox Hill Hosp., 1980-94, Thirteen-WNET, Carnegie Hall; adv. Mayor's Coun. on Cultural Affairs, N.Y.C., 1994. Fellow Internat. Council TV Acad. Arts and Scis. (pres. 1973-76, 85-87, dir. 1976—); mem. Internat. Radio and TV Soc. (pres., past pres. Found.), Nat. Acad. Cable Programming (chmn. emeritus), Nat. Assn. Broadcasters (task force on pub. broadcasting, chmn. program producers and distbrs. com.), Cable TV Edn. Found. (chmn.). Office: Viacom Inc 1633 Broadway New York NY 10019-6708

BARUSCH, AMANDA SMITH, social welfare educator, researcher; b. Long Beach, Calif, Sept. 8, 1955; d. Gilbert T. and Helen (Dauphine) Smith; m. Lawrence Roos Barusch, Aug. 7, 1983; children: Ariana Grace, Nathaniel Morris. BA, Reed Coll., Portland, Oreg., 1977; M in Social Welfare, U. Calif., Berkeley, 1981, D in Social Welfare, 1985. Planner Govt. of Guam, Agana, 1980-82, supr. Title XX, 1983-84; teaching asst. U. Calif., Berkeley, 1982-83; asst. prof. U. Guam, Mangilao, 1984-85; asst. prof. grad. sch. social work U. Utah, Salt Lake City, 1985-90, assoc. prof. grad. sch. social work, 1990-94, prof. grad. sch. social work, 1994—. Chmn. rev. bd. Salt Lake City Alcohol/Drug Abuse Svc., 1985—; tng. cons. Sr. Companion Program, Salt Lake City, 1985—; mem. Gov. Task Force, Agana, 1984, Gov. Commn., Agana, 1984-85. Author: Elder Care: Family Training and Support, 1991, Caring for the Frail Elderly: Family Support, Public Services and Case Management, 1992, Older Women in Poverty: Pvt. Lives and Pub. Policies, 1994, Found. of Social Policy: Social Justice, Pub. Programs, and the Social Work Profession, 2002, with Robert Atchley Social Forces and Aging, 2003; contbr. articles on social work and psychology to profl. jour. Recipient Nat. Leadership award in gerontology Assn. for Gerontology Edn and Social Work, 2002; Regent's fellow U. Calif., Berkeley, 1982, 83. Mem. Guam Assn. Social Workers (pres. 1984-85), Nat. Assn. Social Workers, Nat. Council on Aging, Am. Soc. on Aging, Gerontol. Soc. Am. Democrat. Office: U Utah Social Work Bldg 395S1500E 1 University Of Utah Salt Lake City UT 84112-1107 E-mail: abarusch@socwk.utah.edu.

BARUSCH, LAWRENCE ROOS, lawyer; b. Oakland, Calif., Aug. 23, 1949; s. Maurice Radston and Phyllis (Rose) B.; m. Susan Amanda Smith, Aug. 7, 1983; children: Nathaniel M., Ariana G. BA summa cum laude, Harvard U., 1971, JD cum laude, 1975. Bar: Calif. 1975. Assoc. Cotton, Seligman & Ray, San Francisco, 1975-77; gen. counsel Jones & Guerrero Co., Inc., Agana, Guam, 1977-82; ptnr. Klemm, Blair & Barusch, PC, Agana, Guam, 1982-85; assoc. Davis, Graham & Stubbs, Salt Lake City, 1986-87; counsel Parsons, Behl & Latimer, Salt Lake City, 1987-89, shareholder, 1989—; counsel Guam Tax Code Commn., 1990-94. Adj. prof. U. Utah Coll. Law, 1998-99, 2000—, vis. assoc. prof., 1999-2000; mem. com. U.S. activities of foreigners and tax treaties, tax sect. ABA, 1994—. Contbr. articles to profl. jours. including Guam Bar Jour., Utah Bar Jour., Offshore Investment and Tax Notes. Chmn. Dem. Party, Davis County, Utah, 1997-99; mem. bd. dirs. The Road Home, 2002—. Sheldon fellow Harvard U., 1971. Mem. Guam Bar Assn. (pres. 1982-84), No. Marianas Bar Assn., Utah Bar Assn. (chmn. tax sect. 1994-95), Calif. Bar Assn., Utah Tax Review Commn., Phi Beta Kappa. Office: Parsons Behle & Latimer 201 S Main St Ste 1800 Salt Lake City UT 84111-2218 E-mail: lbarusch@pblutah.com.

BARWICK-SNELL, KATHERINE LANE, family human relations and women's studies educator, home economics consultant; b. Jackson, Miss., Feb. 9, 1955; d. Jim Drane and Doris Eloise (Langford) Barwick; m. Daniel Clair Snell, June 28, 1986; children: James David, Abigail Katherine. BS, Miss. State U., 1977; MS, U. Okla., 1981; EdD, Okla. State U., 1995. Cert. home economist, Okla. Adminstrv. asst. Women's Resource Ctr., Norman, Okla., 1977-78; mgr. Norman Shelter, Inc., 1978-80; tchr. Washington (Okla.) High Sch., 1980-81; instr. home econs. U. Okla., Norman, 1981-83, instr. sociology and human rels., 1990-95, 1997—, asst. prof. human rels., faculty fellow Coll. Liberal Study, 1995—97. Caterer, tchr. pvt. cooking class, Norman, 1982—. Pres. bd. dirs. Women's Resource Ctr., 1983-85; mem., chmn. Human Rights Commn., Norman, 1983-86. Grantee Okla. Arts Coun., 1988. Mem. Am. Home Econs. Assn., Internat. Home Econs. Fedn., Okla. Home Econs. Assn., Adult Edn. Assn., Phi Kappa Phi. Democrat. Avocations: sewing, gardening, cooking. Home: 504 Miller Ave Norman OK 73069-5930 Office: U Okla Dept Human Rels Norman OK 73019-0001

BARWIG, REGIS NORBERT JAMES, priest; b. Chgo., Jan. 16, 1932; s. Ladislas-Joseph and Josepha Agnes (Neugebauer) B. AB, St. Procopius Coll., 1954; postgrad., Georgetown U., 1957, Pontifical Lateran U., Rome, 1959-61. Ordained priest Roman Cath. Ch., 1959. Sec. to abbot of Lisle, 1955-61; sec. gen. Christian Unity Apostolate, 1961-64; founding prior Claremont Priory, Cedarburg, Wis., 1964-67; prior Community of Our Lady, Oshkosh, Wis., 1968—. Co-chmn. 1st Festival Faith, Milw., 1966; chmn. Ecumenical Conf. Spiritual and Liturgical Renewal Religious Life, 1969—; mem. Green Bay Diocese Ecumenical Commn., 1970-73; theol. cons. Consortium Perfectae Caritatis, 1974—; preacher, U.S. and Europe; U.S. liaison for beatification of Pope Pius IX, 1975—; assoc. Wanda Landowska Music Ctr., Lakeville, Conn., 1969; bd. dirs. Inter-Cath. Press Agy., N.Y., 1967-72. Author: Changing Habits, 1971, Waiting for Rain, 1975, Reflections on Spiritual Life for Order of Malta, 1982; translator: His Will Alone, 1971, Wanda Landowska Diaries, 1971, Pius XI-A Close-up, 1975, Pius IX-More than a Prophet, 1977, Writings of Blessed Maximilian Maria Kolbe, 1977, Evaluations of the Possibility of Constructing a Christian Ethic on the Assumptions of the Philosophy of Max Scheler, 1982; editor: Conferences of Mother Mary of Jesus, 1968; contbr. articles to religious publs. Decorated Bruderschaft, Collegio Teutonico, Vatican City, Knight Comdr., Order Isabel la Catolica, Spain, Grand Cross of Merit, Sovereign Mil.

Order of Malta, Magistral Chaplain, Conventual Grand Cross Chaplain of Honor, Prelatial Councillor, Chief of Chaplains, Polish Assn., Sovereign Mil. Order of Malta, knight comdr. Ecclesiastical Grace, Gold Benemerenti medal Sacred Mil. Constantinian Order of St. George-Bourbon Two Sicilies, Chaplain Am. Del., knight Order of Francis I, Bourbon-Two Sicilies, Knight Comdr. Equestrian Order Holy Sepulcher of Jerusalem, Grand Priory of Poland, Gold Cross Merit Primate of Poland, hon. Canon. Royal Coll. Chpt., Wilanow-Warsaw, Archbishop Weber HS Madonna award, Skowyrow Found. award Pastoral Inst. Cath. U. Lublin, Spl. Fgn. award Warsaw Soc. Civitas Christiana, Person of Yr. award St. John Cantius Soc. Chgo., Gold Cross Merit Polish Cath. Mission Eng. and Wales, Meml. medal Cardinal Stefan Wyszynski, Merit medal Arch. Warsaw. Mem. Selden Soc., Queen Mary Coll., Polish-Am. Assn. Wis. (chaplain 1979—), Polish Arts Club. Home and Office: 2804 Oakwood Ln Oshkosh WI 54904-8406 *From my Roman Catholic faith and my Polish heritage I imbibed early a sense of the importance of Divine Providence in one's life. In this context, then, regret and disappointment are both futile and destructive emotions. Everything can be redeemed. Radical eternalism makes one look Above and Beyond.*

BARZ, PATRICIA, lawyer; b. Mattoon, Ill., Oct. 18, 1953; d. William E. Barz and Rosemary A. (Easton) Scott; m. Herbert P. Wiedemann, Feb. 12, 1983; children: Sarah Barz Wiedemann, Andrew Barz Wiedemann. BA, Yale U., 1974; JD, U. Va., 1978. Bar: Va. 1979, Conn. 1982, Ohio 1985. Assoc. Hunton & Williams, Richmond, Va., 1978-81, Davis, Graham & Stubbs, Denver, 1981-82; counsel legal dept. Aetna Life and Casualty Co., Hartford, Conn., 1982-84; assoc. Jones, Day, Reavis & Pogue, Cleve., 1984-92; dir. law Cleve. Metroparks, 1992—. Trustee St. Anthony Trust Assn., New Haven, 1983-86; class agt. Yale Alumni Fund, New Haven, 1985-89. Mem. ABA, Ohio State Bar Assn., Cleve. Bar Assn., Conn. Bar Assn., Va. Bar Assn., Yale Alumni Assn. (v.p. Cleve. chpt. 1986-88, trustee 1988-95, 98—, pres. 1995-98). Methodist. Avocations: figure skating, raquetball, theater, reading, travel. Home: 18040 S Woodland Rd Shaker Heights OH 44120-1773 E-mail: pabarz@aol.com., pb@clevelandmetroparks.com.

BARZA, HAROLD A. lawyer; b. Montreal, Que., Can., July 28, 1952; came to U.S., 1969; s. Solomon A. and Evelyn (Elkin) B. BA, Boston U., 1973; JD, Columbia U., 1976. Bar: N.Y. 1977, Calif. 1978, U.S. Dist. Ct. (ctrl. dist.) Calif. 1978. Law clk. to Hon. Milton Pollack U.S. Dist. Ct. (so. dist.) N.Y., 1976-77; assoc. Munger, Tolles & Rickershauser, L.A., 1978-81; ptnr. Gelles, Singer & Johnson, L.A., 1982-83, Gelles, Lawrence & Barza, L.A., 1983-87, Loeb & Loeb, L.A., 1987-99, Quinn, Emanuel, Urquehart, Oliver and Hedges, L.A., 1999—. Adj. prof. mass comm. law Southwestern U. Sch. Law, L.A., 1979-82; judge pro tem., L.A. Mcpl. Ct., 1985—. Mem. bd. editors Columbia Law Rev., 1975-76. Mem. steering com. Jewish Nat. Fund, L.A., 1983. James Kent scholar, 1974-76, Harlan Fiske Stone scholar, 1973-74. Mem. ABA (mem. com. on antitrust litigation), Los Angeles County Bar Assn. (trial lawyers, litigation and intellectual property sects.). Office: Quinn Emanuel Urquhart Oliver and Hedges 865 S Figueroa St Los Angeles CA 90017-2543 E-mail: hab@qeuo.com.

BARZELATTO, JOSE S. social welfare organization executive; b. Santiago, Chile, Apr. 6, 1926; arrived in U.S., 1989; s. Jose Q. Barzelatto and Veronica G. Sanchez; m. Juanita Ramirez Barzelatto, Jan. 8, 1950 (dec. Nov. 21, 1999); children: Veronica, Ana Maria, Jovan, Marcos, Cristina, Virginia. MD, U. Chile, 1949. Lic. physician Fla. Mem. faculty U. Chile, Santiago, 1950—68; postgrad. trainee Mass. Gen. Hosp., Boston, 1951—53, rsch. fellow, 1959—60; spl. advisor OAS, Washington, 1968—75; med. officer, dir. WHO, Geneva, 1975—89; dir. reproductive health The Ford Found., N.Y.C., 1989—97; v.p. Ctr. for Health & Social Policy, N.Y.C. and San Francisco, 1997—. Founder, exec. sec. Chile's Nat. Coun. Sci. and Tech., Santiago, 1967—68; mem. coun. Pugwash Conf. Sci. and World Affairs, 1971—82; mem. ethics com. Internat. Fedn. Ob-Gyn., London, 1997—; pres. directive coun. Civil Soc. Forum of the Ams., Rio de Janeiro, 2000—. Co-editor: Ethics and Human Values in Family Planning, 1989; contbr. articles to profl. jours., chapters to books. Mem.: Latin Am. Assn. Rsch. in Human Reprodn. (hon.). Avocations: family, politics. Home: 5800 Nicholson Ln Apt 1201 Rockville MD 20852 Office: Ctr Health & Social Policy 847 25th St San Francisco CA 94121 Fax: 301-468-4999.

BARZILAI, HAREL, education educator; s. Dina Meyerhof Lewis and Uzi Barzilai. BA, Dartmouth Coll., 1985—88; MS, U. of Chgo., 1988—90; PhD, Cornell U., 1991—97. Temp. asst. prof. U. of Minn., 1997—98; asst. prof. Lynchburg Coll., Va., 1998—2000, Salisbury U., Md., 2000—. Recipient Academic citations (9), Dartmouth Coll., 1985—88, Project NEXT fellow , Math. Assn. of Am., 1998—99; fellow, Cornell Dean of A&S, 1996; McCormick fellowship, U. of Chgo., 1988, Lemuel G. Hodgkins 1900 Meml. scholarship, Dartmouth Coll., 1986—87, Rufus Choate scholar, 1986—88, NSF grantee, 2001, grantee, Md. Higher Edn. Comm., 2002. Mem.: ASCD, Mathematicians and Edn. Reform (MER), MAA Spl. Interest Group on Rsch. in Undergraduate Math Edn. (biographies database, lit., and nominating committees), Math. Assn. of Am. Green Party. Avocations: hiking, music, nature, biking. Office: Salisbury University 1101 Camden Ave Salisbury MD 21801 Office Fax: 410-548-5559. E-mail: hxbarzilai@salisbury.edu.

BARZUN, JACQUES, author, literary consultant; b. Créteil, France, Nov. 30, 1907; came to U.S., 1920, naturalized, 1933; s. Henri Martin and Anna-Rose B.; m. Mariana Lowell, Aug. 1936 (dec. 1979); children: James Lowell, Roger Martin, Isabel; m. Marguerite Davenport, June 1980. Ed., Lycée Janson de Sailly, Paris; AB, Columbia U., 1927, MA, 1928, PhD, 1932. From lectr. history to assoc. prof. Columbia U., N.Y.C., 1927-45, prof., 1945, dean grad. faculties, 1955-58, dean faculties and provost, 1958-67, prof. emeritus, spl. adviser on arts, 1967-75; lit. adviser Scribner's, N.Y.C., 1975-93. Author: The French Race, 1932, Teacher in America, 1945, Berlioz and the Romantic Century, 1950, 3d edit., 1969, Pleasures of Music, 1951, 2d edit., 1977, God's Country and Mine, 1954, Music in American Life, 1956, Darwin, Marx, Wagner, 1941, The Energies of Art, 1956, Of Human Freedom, 2d edit, 1964, Race: A Study in Superstition, 1937, The Modern Researcher, 1957, 5th edit., 1993, The House of Intellect, 2d edit, 1975, Classic, Romantic and Modern, 1961, Science: The Glorious Entertainment, 1964, The American University, 1968, 2d edit., 1995, A Catalogue of Crime, 1971, 2d edit., 1986, On Writing, Editing and Publishing, 1971, The Use and Abuse of Art, 1974, Clio and the Doctors, 1974, Simple and Direct, 1975, 2d edit., 1993, Critical Questions, 1982, A Stroll With William James, 1983, A Word or Two Before You Go, 1986, The Culture We Deserve, 1989, Begin Here: On Teaching and Learning, 1990, An Essay on French Verse, 1991, From Dawn to Decadence: 1500 Years of Western Cultural Life, 2000, A Jacques Barzun Reader, 2001, What Is a School?, 2002; mem. editl. bd. The American Scholar, 1946-76, Ency. Brit, 1979—; editor: Selected Letters of Lord Byron, 1953, Nouvelles Lettres de Berlioz, 1954, The Selected Writings of John Jay Chapman, 1957, Follett's Modern American Usage, 1966. Trustee NY Soc. Libr., 1968-97; adv. coun. U. Buckingham. Decorated Legion of Honor; Extraordinary fellow Churchill Coll., U. Cambridge (Eng.), Presdl. medal of Freedom Fellow Royal Soc. Arts, Royal Soc. Lit.; mem. Soc. Am. Historians, Mass. Hist. Soc. (corr.), AAAL (pres. 1972-75, 77-78), Am. Philos. Soc., Am. Acad. for Liberal Edn. (hon. pres.), Acad. Delphinale (Grenoble), Century Assn., Phi Beta Kappa.

BASA, ENIKÖ MOLNAR, librarian; b. Huszt, Hungary, Sept. 7, 1939; came to the U.S., 1950; d. Julius Valentine and Terézia (Fejér) Molnár; m. Péter Basa, Nov. 19, 1966. BA, Trinity Coll., 1962; MA, U. N.C., 1965, PhD, 1972. Instr. U. Md., College Park, 1965-69; asst. prof. Dunbarton Coll., Washington, 1970-72; lectr. Am. U., Washington, 1972-75, Hood Coll., Frederick, Md., 1975-76; editor, serials cataloger Libr. of Congress, Washington, 1977—. Mem. symposium Libr. Congress, 1996. Author: Sandor Petöfi, 1980; editor: Twayne World Authors, 1974—, Hungarian Literature, 1993; translator: (play) Screenplay from Örkény, 1983; assoc. editor The Comparatist, 1976-82, editorial bd., 1992—; jour. rev. editor: Hungarian Studies Newsletter, 1975-82; guest editor: Rev. Nat. Lits., 1992; contbr. chpts. to books and articles and book revs. to profl. jours. Recipient Gold medal Pres. of Republic of Hungary, 1997; Kluge Staff fellow Libr. of Congress, 2002-03. Mem. MLA (Hungarian sect. chair 1980, 90), So. Comparative Lit. Assn. (founding v.p. 1977-79, 89—, sec.-treas. 1985-89, pres. 1992-94), Am. Hungarian Educators Assn. (pres. 1974-80, 88-92, exec. dir. 1980—), Internat. Assn. Hungarian Studies, Libr. Congress Profl. Assn. (v.p. 1991, pres. 1996). Avocations: reading, travel, needlework. Home: 4515 Willard Ave Apt 2210 Chevy Chase MD 20815-3685 Office: Serial Record Libr Congress Washington DC 20540-4160 E-mail: ebas@loc.gov.

BASAÑEZ, MIGUEL EBERGENYI, opinion pollster, political science educator; b. Tuxpan, Ver, Mex., Oct. 24, 1947; came to U.S., 1995; s. Miguel Sorcini and Magdalena Ebergenyi Basáñez; m. Tatiana Beltran, Feb. 7, 1970; children: Tatiana, Alejandro, Pamela, Nicolas. BA in Law, UNAM, Mexico City, 1969; MA in Adminstrn., U. Warwick, Coventry, Eng., 1974; PhD in Polit. Sci., London Sch. Econs., 1991. Prof. U Nat. Autonoma Mex., U. Autonoma Estado Mex., Inst. Tech., Mexico City and Toluca, 1975-95; atty. gen. State of Mex., Toluca, 1985-86; chief of staff Ministry of Energy, Mexico City, 1986-88; pres. Mori-Mexico, Mexico City, 1988—2002; vis. prof. U. Mich., Ann Arbor, 1995-96; sr. v.p. MORI-Internat., Princeton, NJ, 1996—98; CEO MORI-USA, Princeton, 1998-2000; CEO, Global Quality Rsch. Corp., Princeton, 2000—. Pub. Este Pais mag., Mexico City, 1990-95; bd. dirs. Serfin Bank, Mexico City, 1986-88, Mexican-Am. Binat. Found., Mexico City/Washington D.C., 2002. Co-author: Human Values and Beliefs, 1998, North American Trajectories, 1996; author: El Pulso de Los Sexenios, 1990, La Lucha por La Hegemonia, 1981. Pres. Acude-Alianza Democratica, Mexico City, 1992-93. LSE Alumnai in Mex., Mexico City, 1980-83; del. PRI, Mex., 1970-72. Recipient Nat. prize Nat. Pub. Adminstrn. Inst., 1982. Mem. World Assn. for Pub. Opinion Rsch. (pres. 1999-2000, Nelson award 1993), Am. Polit. Sci. Assn., Am. Assn. for Pub. Opinion Rsch., Latin Am. Studies Assn. Avocations: photography, water skiing, computers, films. Office: Global Quality Rsch Corp 116 Village Blvd Ste 200 Princeton NJ 08540-5740

BASAR, TAMER, electrical engineering educator; b. Istanbul, Turkey, Jan. 19, 1946; came to U.S., 1969; s. Munir and Seniye (Pirilsu) B.; m. Tangul Unerdem, Dec. 27, 1975; children: Gozen, Elif. BS in Elec. Engring., Robert Coll., Istanbul, 1969; MS, Yale U., 1970, M.Phil., 1971, PhD, 1972. Research fellow Harvard U., Cambridge, Mass., 1972-73; sr. researcher scientist Marmara Research Inst., Gebze, Kocaeli, Turkey, 1973-80; adj. assoc. prof. Bogazici U., Istanbul, 1974-80; assoc. prof. elec. engring. U. Ill., Urbana, 1980-83, prof., 1983—, disting. prof., 1998—. Co-author: Dynamic Noncooperative Game Theory, 1982, 3d edit., 1999, H-infinity Optimal Control and Related Minimax Design Problems, 1991, 2d edit., 1995; editor: Dynamic Games and Applications in Econs., 1986, Control Theory: Twenty-Five Seminal Papers (1932-1981), 2001; co-editor: Differential Games and Applications, 1989, Advances in Dynamic Games and Applications, 1994; contbr. articles to profl. jours.; editor 2 jours. in control theory; assoc. editor 1 jour. in games and 1 in control. Recipient Young Scientist award in Applied Math., Turkish Nat. Rsch. Coun., 1976, Sedat Simavi Found. award, 1979, Medal of Sci., Turkey, 1993. Fellow IEEE (v.p. Control Sys. Soc. 1997-98, pres.-elect 1999, pres. 2000, Disting. Mem. award 1993, Best Paper award 1995); mem. Soc. for Indsl. Applied Math., Internat. Soc. Dynamic Games (pres. 1990-94), Game Theory Soc., Am. Math. Soc., Nat. Acad. of Engring., European Acad. Scis. Home: 2810 Valley Brook Dr Champaign IL 61822-7621 Office: U Ill 1308 W Main St Urbana IL 61801-2307 E-mail: tbasar@control.csl.uiuc.edu.

BASART, JOHN PHILIP, electrical engineering and remote sensing researcher; b. Des Moines, Feb. 26, 1938; s. Philip Edwin and Hildreth Pauline (Belden) B.; m. Luann Kay Stow, Mar. 2, 1960; children— Jill Eileen Urban, Ann Marie BS, Iowa State U., 1962, MS, 1963, PhD in Elec. Engring., 1967. Rsch. assoc. Nat. Radio Astronomy Obs., Charlottesville, Va., 1967-69; system scientist Very Large Array, Socorro, N.Mex., 1979-81; asst. prof. elec. engring. Iowa State U., Ames, 1969-73, assoc. prof., 1973-80, prof., 1980-2000, prof. emeritus, 2000—. Rschr. in radio astronomy, image processing, wave propagation, remote sensing; campus coord. Iowa Space Grant Consortium. Contbr. articles to profl. jours. Served with USAF, 1955-59 Recipient student award IRE, 1962 Mem. IEEE (sr. mem.), AIAA, Am. Geophys. Union, Am. Astron. Soc., Royal Astron. Soc., Internat. Astron. Union, Internat. Soc. for Optical Engring., Sigma Xi, Eta Kappa Nu, Tau Beta Pi, Phi Kappa Phi. Office: Iowa State U 2271 Howe Hl Rm 2348 Ames IA 50011-0001 E-mail: jpbasart@iastate.edu.

BASAVAPPA, RAVI, biophysical scientist, educator; b. Bangalore, India, Feb. 7, 1961; arrived in U.S., 1968; BS, Duke U., 1980; MS, Clemson U., 1983; PhD, U. Chgo., 1991. Postdoctoral fellow Harvard Med. Sch., Boston, 1991—95; asst. prof. dept. biochemistry and biophysics U. Rochester (N.Y.) Med. Ctr., 1995—2002, assoc. prof., 2002—. Rsch. scholar Leukemia and Lymphoma Soc. Am. Contbr. articles to sci. jours. Postdoctoral fellow NIH, 1992-95, rsch. grantee, 1998—. Mem. Am. Crystallograpers Assn. Achievements include research in biochemistry and biophysics. Office: U Rochester Med Ctr Dept Biochem and Biophys 601 Elmwood Ave Dept And Rochester NY 14642-0001 E-mail: ravi_basavappa@urmc.rochester.edu.

BASCH, RICHARD VENNARD, photographer, producer, writer, director; b. Inpls., Jan. 22, 1945; s. Richard and Helen Louise (Vennard) B.; m. Meredith Baker, Feb. 12, 1966; 1 child, Nicholas; m. Vicki Sylvester, Aug. 15, 1977. Cert., U. Fine Arts, Perugia, Italy, 1965, London Film Sch., 1966; BA, Antioch Coll., 1968; DFA, London Inst. for Applied Rsch., 1995. Dir. filmmaker tng. Am. Film Inst., Washington, 1968-69; instr. film history R.I. Sch. Design, Providence, 1970-73; cons. in theatre Antioch Coll., Yellow Springs, Ohio, 1976-77; prin., photographer Richard Basch Studio, Washington, 1979—. Dir. film programs Brown U., 1972-73; cons. Smithsonian Instn., Washington, 1979—. Author: Faces of Fairmont Heights, 1970; producer (films) The Burning Issue, 1984, News from the Future, 1996. Mem. Am. Soc. Mag. Photographers. Episcopalian. Office: Richard Basch Studio 2627 Connecticut Ave NW Washington DC 20008-1545 E-mail: richardbasch@mindspring.com.

BASCOM, C. PERRY, retired foundation administrator; b. Boston, July 30, 1936; s. William Richardson and Jean Ames (Hall) B.; m. Sally Cissel Greenwood, July 18, 1995; children: Elisabeth Brooke, Heather Ames, Sarah Duff Greenwood, Amy Greenwood Dunaway. BA, Yale U., 1958; LLB, Harvard U., 1961. Assoc. Bryan Cave, St. Louis, 1962-72, ptnr., 1972-95; adminstr. Gateway Found., St. Louis, 1995—2001, ret., 2001. Judge St. Louis Night Housing Ct., 1970-72; lectr. on various topics, including Truth in Lending, Real Estate Settlement Procedures Act, techniques in comml. bank lending, devels. in Mo. banking law, electronic funds transfers. Sr. warden Trinity Ch., St. Louis, 1974-78. Served with USAR, 1961-68. Mem. Mo. Bar Assn. Home: 4650 Pershing Pl Saint Louis MO 63108-1908

BASCOM, LIONEL CYRIL, writer, educator; b. Danbury, Conn., Apr. 25, 1947; s. Lionel Roper and Lucy Bascom; m. Virginia Bascom, Jan. 15, 1986; children: Rachel, Lauren, Molli. Cert., Western Conn. State U., 1989. Reporter Danbury (Conn.) News Times, 1970, New Haven (Conn.) Register, 1970; reporter, editor United Press Internat., N.Y.C., Chgo., 1971-77; freelance editor, 1977-80; metro editor The Advocate, Stamford, Conn., 1980-83; reporter Time Inc., N.Y.C., 1983-86; prof. dept. English Western Conn. State U., Danbury, 1987—. Author: Full Circle, 1990, Rubouts, 1991, Bail Out, 1993, By The Light, 1995; editor: A Rennaissance in Harlem, 1999, The Last Leaf, 2000, The Harlem Renaissance, 2003. Juror, editor Pulitzer Prize Jury Columbia U., 1984, 85. With USN, 1966-70. Office: Dept English Western Conn State U 181 White St Danbury CT 06810 E-mail: lcbascom@netscape.net.

BASCOM, RUTH F. retired mayor; b. Ames, Iowa, Feb. 4, 1926; d. Frederick Charles and Doris Hays Fenton; m. John U. Bascom, June 14, 1950; children: Lucinda, Rebecca, Ellen, Thomas, Paul, Mary. BS, Kans. State U., Manhattan, 1946; MA, Cornell U., 1949. Tchr. Dickinson County Cmty. H.S., Kans., 1946-48, Nat. Coll. Edn., Chgo., 1949-51. Co-chair Cascadia High Speed Rail, 1995-98. Chair City and State Bicycle Com., 1971-83; mem., chair Met. Park Bd., Eugene, 1972-82; past bd. pres. Youth Symphony, 1962-68; city councilor City of Eugene, Oreg., 1984-92, coun. v.p., pres., 1988-90, mayor, 1993-97; v.p., pres. LWV, Eugene, 1967-69; chair, Oreg. Passenger Rail Com., 2000—; state bd. 1000 Friends of Oreg., 1999—. Recipient Gold Leaf award Internat. Soc. Arboriculture, 1993; dedicated Ruth Bascom Riverbank Trail Sys., 2003. Democrat. Congregationalist. Avocations: music, tree farm, bicycling. Home: 2114 University St Eugene OR 97403-1542 Fax: 541-484-2646. E-mail: jbascomr@pacinfo.com.

BASCONI, PAMELA BRAY, lawyer; b. Louisville, Sept. 10, 1951; d. Walter Andrew and Roberta Lee (Schrodt) Wimberg; children: Zachary Andrew, Michael D. BBA, U. Ky., 1973, JD, 1976. Bar: Ky. 1976, U.S. Dist. Ct. (ea. dist.) Ky. 1977, U.S. Ct. Appeals (6th cir.) 1988. Atty. Fowler Measle & Bell, Lexington, Ky., 1976-84, Gallion Baker & Bray, Lexington, Ky., 1984—2002; pvt. practice Pamela Bray Basconi PLLC, Lexington, Ky., 2002—. Instr., land transfer, U. Ky. Coll. Law, Lexington, 1991-92; dir. Fayette County Bar Assn., Lexington, 1995-98. Pres., dir. Providence Montessori Sch., Lexington, 1991-95; bd. dirs. Family Care Ctr., Lexington, 1991-95; Leadership Lexington C. of C., 1990-91. Mem. Ky. Bar Assn. (chair partnership com. 1986), Lexington Jour. Club, Bluegrass Estate Planning Coun. (dir. 1978-81). Avocations: biking, skiing. Office: Pamela Bray Basconi PLLC 881 Corporate Dr Ste 204 Lexington KY 40503

BASE, GRAEME ROWLAND, illustrator, author; b. Amersham, Eng., Apr. 6, 1958, s. Geoffrey Donald and Elizabeth Enid (Philips) B.; m. Robyn Anne Paterson, Aug. 1, 1981; children: James Geoffrey, Katherine Gabrielle, William Alexander. Art diploma, Swinburne Inst. Tech., 1978. Author (illustrator): (novels) My Grandma Lived in Gooliguich, 1983, Animalia, 1983 (Australian Children's Book award Children's Book Coun. Australia, 1987, Kids Own Australia Literature award, 1988), The Eleventh Hour: A Curious Mystery, 1988 (Australian Children's Book Coun. Australia, 1989, Book Design award Australian Book Pub. Assn., 1988, Young Australian Best Book award, 1989, Kids Own Australia Literature award, 1989), The Sign of the Seahorse, 1992, The Disovery of Dragons, 1996, The Worst Band in the Universe, 1999, The Water Hole, 2001; illustrator (novels) Adventures with My Best Worst Friend, 1982, The Island Bike Business, 1982, Jabberwocky From "Through the Looking Glass", 1985. Office: Penguin Australia PO Box 701 Hawthorn VIC 3122 Australia

BASEFSKY, STUART MARK, law librarian, library and information scientist, journalist; b. Denver, Oct. 31, 1949; s. Stanley S. and Ilene U. (Sunshine) Basefsky; m. Claire M. Germain, Aug. 16, 1976; 1 child, Nicolas. Student, U. Erlangen, Fed. Republic of Germany, 1969-70; BA, U. Colo., 1971; MA in Tchg., Duke U., 1975; MSLS, U. N.C., 1979. Info. specialist N.C. Sci. & Tech. Rsch. Ctr., Research Triangle Park, NC, 1980; documents libr. N.C. State U., Raleigh, 1980-83, Duke U., Durham, NC, 1983-93; reference libr. Sch. Indsl. & Labor Rels., Cornell U., Ithaca, NY, 1993—, editor, dir. IWS news bur., 2002—. Adj. instr. sch. info. and libr. sci. U. N.C., Chapel Hill, 1990—92; mem. adv. bd. Washington Alert Svc. Congl. Quar. Inc., 1990—; pres. Ithaca Pub. Edn. Initiative, 1996—2003; mem. adv. bd. HR Advisor West Group, 1998—. Contbr. articles to profl. jours. Recipient Key Vol. award, Durham County, 1978, Indsl. and Labor Rels. Recognition award, 1999, H. W. Wilson Co. award, Spl. Librs. Assn., 2002. Mem.: ALA, Can. Assn. Journalists, Internat. Platform Assn., Am. Assn. Law Librs. (founder, chmn. citation reform com. 1980—83), Patent Documentation Soc., N.C. Libr. Assn. (mem. exec. bd. 1984—85, lobbyist 1987). Democrat. Avocation: swimming. Home: 10 Wedgewood Dr Ithaca NY 14850-1063 Office: Cornell U Sch Indsl & Labor Rels Catherwood Lib Ives Hall Ithaca NY 14853-3901 E-mail: smb6@cornell.edu.

BASENER, RICHARD FRANCIS JOSEPH, mathematician, application developer; b. Pitts., Pa., Feb. 9, 1947; s. Eric William and Anna Irene Basener; m. Carol Tambasco, Aug. 26, 1967 (div. Dec. 2002); children: Mary Ann Gallaher, William, John. BS in Math., Manhattan Coll., 1967; PhD in Math., Brown U., 1972. J. Willard Gibbs instr. Yale U., New Haven, 1972—74; asst. prof. Lehigh U., Bethlehem, Pa., 1974—78; adv. software engr. IBM Corp., Poughkeepsie, NY, 1978—. Vis. asst. prof. Ecole Polytechnique, Paris, 1975. Contbr. articles to profl. jours., procs., and symposia. Recipient rsch. grant, NSF, 1975; fellow, Woodrow Wilson Found., 1967—68, NSF, 1968—71. Mem.: Am. Math. Soc. Avocations: bridge, Bible study. Office: IBM Corp South Rd Poughkeepsie NY 12603 Personal E-mail: basener@alumni.brown.edu. E-mail: basener@us.ibm.com.

BASFORD, JAMES ORLANDO, container manufacturing company executive; b. Akron, Ohio, Apr. 17, 1931; s. Napoleon Orlando and Hazel Martha (Fersner) B.; m. Mary Eleanor Hagmeyer, Mar. 16, 1957; children: Jeffrey James, Gregory Robert, Lisa Jean Cullity. Student, Kent State U., 1949-51, 55-58. Asst. sales mgr. San Hygene Mfg. Co., Akron, 1958-60; gen. sales mgr. Adjusta Post Mfg., Akron, 1960-64; area sales mgr. Gaylord Container, Columbus, Ohio, 1964-74; v.p. Buckeye Container Co., Wooster, Ohio, 1974-78, pres., 1978-95, chmn. bd. dirs., 1994-96. Bd. dirs. Wayne County Nat. Bank, Wooster; chmn. bd. dirs. Pahaque Wilderness, Inc., San Diego; pres. Jelige LLC, Wooster, Ohio. Bd. dirs. Boys Village, Smithville, Ohio, 1985— (pres., 1998—); chmn. Wayne County Econ. Devel. Commn., 1995. With USAF, 1951-54, Korea. Recipient John B. Gerlach Recognition award Ohio State U., 2000. Mem. Wooster C. of C. (bd. dirs. 1977-80, named to Hall of Fame 1998). Clubs: Wooster Country (pres. 1981-83). Lodges: Rotary (bd. dirs. Wooster club 1978-81). Republican. Lutheran. Avocations: golf, tennis, skiing. Home: 1097 Greens View Dr Wooster OH 44691-2659 E-mail: basfordbox@aol.com.

BASFORD, ROBERT EUGENE, retired biochemistry educator, researcher; b. Montpelier, N.D., Aug. 21, 1923; s. Eugene M. and Bertha (Cudworth) B.; m. Carol Kaufman Phebus, Dec. 23, 1965; 1 child, Lee A. Phebus BS, U. Wash., 1951, PhD, 1954. Postdoctoral fellow U. Wis.-Madison, 1954-58; asst. prof. U. Pitts., 1958-63, assoc. prof., 1963-70, prof., 1970-93, prof. emeritus, 1993—. Cons. Mine Safety Appliance Co., Pitts., 1966-69; mem. neurol. scis. study sect. NIH, Washington, 1977-80. Home (Winter): 4160 E Aquarius Dr Tucson AZ 85718-5221 E-mail: rbust87388@aol.com.

BASH, PHILIP EDWIN, publishing executive; b. Huntington, Ind., Aug. 13, 1921; s. Philip Purviance and Nell (Johnson) B.; m. Flora Wiley Oberg, Mar. 11, 1944; children: Barbara, Kingsley, Roger, Amy. BA, DePauw U., 1943. Account exec. Leo Burnett Co., Inc., Chgo., 1947-54; account supr., v.p., sr. v.p. mktg. services Clinton E. Frank Inc., Chgo., 1954-64, pres., 1964-72, Barrington (Ill.) Press, Inc., 1972-86, also bd. dirs. Bd. dirs. Fla. Family Inst. Co. Chmn. bd. trustees Shimer Coll., 1989—; trustee Garrett Theol. Sem., 1976—, chmn. bd., 1989-95. Served to lt. (j.g.) USNR, 1943-46, PTO. Mem. Am. Assn. Advt. Agys. (bd. govs. Chgo. council), Am. Mktg. Assn., Sigma Chi. Methodist (trustee). Clubs: University (Chgo.), Economics (Chgo.); Barrington Hills Country. Office: 200 James St Barrington IL 60010-3328

BASHA, EDWARD N., JR., grocery chain owner; CEO, chmn. Bashas Inc, Chandler, AZ. Recipient Disting. Svc. award Nat. Art Edn. Assn., 1992. Office: Bashas Inc 22402 S Basha Rd Chandler AZ 85248*

BASHAM, KAY, music teacher; b. Webster City, Iowa, Aug. 15, 1955; d. Estelle Floyd and Lois Bethel (Johnson) Voss; m. Robert Lynn Basham, July 2, 1977; children: Diane, Sharon. B of Music Edn., Wartburg Coll., Waverly, Iowa, 1977. Cert. and NCTM. Pvt. tchr. piano, Bettendorf, Iowa, 1977-98; pvt. tchr. piano and voice Thibodaux, La., 1998—. Author articles. Mem.: PEO, Nat. Music Tchrs. Assn., Bayou Jr. Woman's Club (v.p.). Methodist. Avocations: computers, playing piano for organizations, reading. Home: 100 Allendale Dr Thibodaux LA 70301-8030

BASHAM, LLOYD MOMAN, manufacturing service company executive; b. Paris, Tex., June 30, 1947; s. Ralph Allen and Faye (Frith) B.; m. donna Jean Walker, aug. 27, 1965; children: Jason, Adam. BBA, Tex. A&M U., Commerce, 1968; MBA, 1970; MA in Internat. Corp. Mgmt., U. Tex., Dallas, 1979. Div. cost mgr. Tex. Instruments, Inc., Dallas, 1973-75; corp. fin. analyst, 1975-76; div. contr., 1977-78; subs. copr. contr. Ciba Geigy, Richardson, Tex., 1979-80; also bd. dirs.; v.p. fin. Cable & Wireless N.Am., Dallas, 1981-85; v.p. ops., 1985-87; exec. v.p., 1987-88; cont. gen. sys. sector field svc. ops. Motorola, Inc., 1988-92; v.p. N.Am. svc. ops., 1992-93; v.p. worldwide svc. ops., 1993-94; v.p. customer svc. multimedia comms. sys. Nortel, Richardson, 1994-95; v.p. bus. devel. engerprise and wireless networks Nortel Networks, 1995-96; corp. v.p. ATM svc. U.S. Brinks Co., Irving, Tex., 1996—2001; pres. LMB LLC, 2001—03; corp. contr. King Supply Co., Inc., 2003—. Online faculty mem. U. Phoenix; adj. instr. Tex. A&M U., Commerce, Tex. State adv. to U.S. Adv. Bd. Fgn. Policy Nat. Security and Internal Affairs, Rep. Presdl. Task Force; bd. dirs., mem. adv. bd. Coll. Bus. and Tech. Tex. A&M U., Commerce. With USAF, 1970-73. Mem. Nat. Assn. Wholesalers Distbrs. Fin. Execs. Inst., Nat. Assn. Corp. Treas., Nat. Assn. Corp. Dirs., Nat. Assn. Purchasing Mgmt., Am. Mgmt.

Assn., Assn. MBA Execs., Nat. Assn. Accts., Assn. Svcs. Mgmt. Internat., Rotary Internat. Republican. Avocation: cattle rancher. Home: 330 Marriott Ln Garland TX 75040-3651 Office: LMB LLC Mgmt Cons PO Box 450912 Garland TX 75045 E-mail: lmbasham@evl.net.

BASHAM, W. RALPH, federal agency administrator; m. Judith A. O'Bryan; three children. BA in Bus. Adminstrn., Southeastern U. Various positions to deputy asst. dir. for trng. U.S. Secret Svc., Washington, 1993-94; spl. agent in charge Office of Investigations Washington, Louisville, 1970-74, 76-79, 86-87, 90-92; spl. agt. of Protective support Divsn. U.S. Secret Svc., Washington, 1974-76; spl. agt., asst. spl. agt. in charge Vice Presdl. Protective Svc. Washington, 1979-83; dep. chief Fin. Mgmt. Divsn. U.S. Secret Svc., Washington, 1983-85; spl. agt. in charge of Vice Presdl. Protective Svc. U.S. Svc., Washington, Cleve., 87-89, 92-93; spl. agt. in charge of Dignitary Protective Divsn. U.S. Secret Svc., Washington, 1989-90, asst. dir. for Adminstrn., 1994-98; insp. Office of Inspections Washington, 1985-86; dir. Fed. Law Enforcement Tng. Ctr. U.S. Dept. Treasury, 1998—2001; chief of staff Transp. Security Adminstrn., Washington, 2002—03; dir. US Secret Svc., Washington, 2003—. Mem. Sr. Exec. Svc. Office: US Secret Svc Comm Ctr PO Box 6500 Springfield VA 22150*

BASHIR, KHURRAM, neurologist; b. Lahore, Pakistan, Apr. 13, 1967; came to U.S., 1992; s. Mohammad Bashir Chaudhry and Fakhar (Mir) B.; m. Rabiya Zaman; children: Ahad, Zoya. BSc, Punjab U., 1988; MBBS, King Edward Med. Coll., Lahore, 1990; MPH, U. Ala., Birmingham, 2001. Resident house officer Mayo Hosp., Pakistan, 1991; resident So. Ill. U. Sch. Medicine, Springfield, 1992-97; clin. instr., fellow U. Ala., Birmingham, 1997-99, asst. prof. dept. neurology, 2000—, dir., Birmingham Multiple Sclerosis Clinic, 2000—. Mem. ACP-Am. Soc. Internal Medicine, Am. Acad. Neurology, Alpha Omega Alpha. Avocations: reading, sports. Office: U Ala Birmingham 1205 JT 625 South 19th St Birmingham AL 35233-7340 E-mail: kbashir@uab.edu.

BASHIRI, IRAJ, Central Asian studies educator; b. Behabahan, Iran, July 31, 1940; came to US, 1966; s. Muhammad and Robab Bashiri; m. Carol L. Sayers, Apr. 18, 1968; children: Mariam, Manuchehr, Mehrdad. BA cum laude, Pahlavi U. Shiraz, Iran, 1963; MA, U. Mich., 1968, PhD, 1972, Tajikstan State U., 1996. Coord., tchr. Peace Corps, Brattleboro, Vt., 1967—68; asst. prof. Iranian studies U. Minn., Mpls., 1972—77, coord. Middle East studies program, 1975—77, assoc. prof. Iranian studies, 1977—87, acting chair South Asian studies, 1990—91, assoc. chair Russian and Eastern European studies, 1987—90, acting chair Russian and Eastern European studies, 1990—91, assoc. prof. Ctrl. Asian studies, 1987—96, prof. Ctrl. Asian studies, 1996—; assoc. prof. Iranian studies U. Tex., Austin, 1982, chair Slavic and Ctrl. Asia langs. and lit., 1997—98; hon. internat. academician Acad. Sci. of Tajikistan, 1996—. Rev. bd. Internat. Rsch. and Exch. Bd. for Tajikistan, Princeton, NJ, 1991—; editor bilingual series Mazda Pub., Encino, Calif., 1985-90; selection com. MacArthur Found., Mpl., 1990-91, internat. seminar, 1990; prof. internat. rels. Kyrgyz State Nat. U., 1998-99. Author: Fiction of Sadeq Hedayat, 1984, The Black Tulip (English, Persian), 1985, Firdowski's Shahname: 1000 Yrs. After, 1994, Kamal Khujandi: Epoch and its Importance in the History of Ctrl. Asian Civilization, 1996, The Samanids and the Revival of the Civilization of Iranian Peoples, 1998, 2002, The Nowruz Scrolls, 2001; editor: The Pearl Canon, 1986, Tajikistan in the 20th Century, 2002, Beginnings to AD 2000: A Comprehensive Chronology of Ctrl. Asia, Afghanistan and Iran, 2001, The Nowruz Scrolls (English, Russian, Tajiki, Persian), 2002, Prominent Figures of the 20th Century, 2003, History of a Nat. Catastrophe, 1996; contbr. articles to profl. jours. Internat. Edn. Travel grant U. Minn., 1990-92; IREX resident scholar, Tajikistan, 1993-94. Fellow Middle East Studies Assn.; mem. Am. Inst. Iranian Studies (trustee 1975-79), Assn. for Cen. Asian Studies, Assn. Advancement Cen. Asian Rsch. (chair devel. com. 1990—), Am. Assn. Tchr. of Slavic and Eastern European Lang. Avocations: writing realist fiction, painting, fishing, travel. Home: 518 8th St SE Minneapolis MN 55414-1208

BASHKIN, LLOYD SCOTT, marketing and management consultant; b. Bridgeport, Conn., July 11, 1951; s. Jules Bernard and Luella (Kobre) B.; children: Marisa Elizabeth, Carly Michelle. BS in Fin., Syracuse U., 1973, MBA in Mktg. and Acctg., 1974; postgrad., Columbia U., 1975-78. Corp. staff mktg. cons. RCA, N.Y.C., 1974-77, mgr. entertainment, indsl. mktg. and nat. sales Cherry Hill, N.J., 1977-79; v.p. mktg. and sales CCA Electronics Corp. div. Singer Co., Cherry Hill, 1979-80; pres. Lloyd Scott & Co., Cherry Hill, 1980—, Sydex, Cherry Hill, 1987-88. Adj. instr. Temple U. Grad. Sch., Phila., 1980-82; adj. prof. Drexel U. Grad. Sch., Phila., 1982—; speaker in field. Trustee, chmn. mktg. com. Food Bank South Jersey, 1985—; mem. Camden County Pvt. Industry Coun., 1989-90; mem. cabinet World Affairs Coun., 1989, Community Leaders Recognition Com., 1991—. Recipient Commendation award Gov. of N.J., 1981, SBA, 1983, Nat. Distbn. and Logistics Honorary award Delta Nu Alpha, 1973, Nat. Broadcasting Honorary award Alpha Epsilon Rho, 1979. Mem. Am. Mktg. Assn., C. of C. of So. N.J. (chmn. small bus. action com. 1982-85, strategic planning and mktg. com. 1985—, bd. dirs. 1984—, chmn. programming com. 1989-92), Greater Cherry Hill C. of C. (chmn. small bus. coun. 1982-83), Rotary (bd. dirs. Garden State club 1980-81). Avocations: skiing, photography, guitar. Office: Lloyd Scott & Co Commerce Ctr Ste 192 1820 Chapel Ave W Cherry Hill NJ 08002 E-mail: lbashkin@lloydscott.com.

BASHKOW, JACK SIMON, musician; b. Bklyn., Dec. 7, 1954; s. David and Sylvia Bashkow; m. Lorraine Shemesh, Sept. 12, 1993. Student, Queens Coll., 1972—74, Columbia U., 1991—93. Mem. orch. West Side Story traveling road co., 1978—79, Richard III with Kevin Kline, N.Y.C., 1984, Big River Broadway co., N.Y.C., 1985, Grease Broad co., N.Y.C., 1997—98, Footloose Broad co., N.Y.C., 1999, Fosse Broadway co., N.Y.C., 2000, Annie Get Your Gun Broadway co. with Reba McEntire, N.Y.C., 2001, Hairspray -Broadway co., N.Y.C., 2002—03, Laughing Room Only - Broadway co., 2003—. Music prodr. Moo Music Prodns. Recording credits include albums with: Jane Olivor, 1982, Keith Richards, 1992, Lionel Hampton, 1999, performed with: Aretha Franklin, The Temptations, The Four Tops, Cyndi Lauper, Natalie Cole, Manhattan Transfer, Michael Bolton, Darlene Love, Peter Allen, others, musician for numerous TV commls.:. Nominee Helen Hayes award for Outstanding Musical Direction. Home and Office: 22 W 30th St # 4-5 New York NY 10001-4423 E-mail: JBashkow@aol.com.

BASHKOW, THEODORE ROBERT, electrical engineering consultant, former educator; b. St. Louis, Nov. 16, 1921; s. Maurice Louis and Caroline (Davidson) B.; m. Delphina Brownlee, Sept. 12, 1960; 1 stepdau., Lynn Michele. BS, Washington U., St. Louis, 1943; MS, Stanford U., 1947, PhD, 1950. Mem. tech. staff David Sarnoff Research Labs., RCA, 1950-52, Bell Telephone Labs., 1952-58; mem. faculty Columbia U., 1958-91, prof. elec. engring., 1967-79, prof. computer sci., 1979-91, chmn. dept. elec. engring., 1968-71, mgr. Sch. Engring. Computing Center, 1961-64. Cons. to industry, 1959—; dir. MSI Inc., Woodside, N.Y., 1961— ; chmn. tech. program 1968 Spring Joint Computer Conf.; chmn. sci. sect. Internat. Fedn. Info. Processing Congress, 1965 Author articles, chpts. in books. Served to 1st lt. USAAF, 1943-45. Mem. Assn. Computing Machinery, IEEE, Profl. Group Circuit Theory and Electronic Computers. Home: 92 Jay St Katonah NY 10536-3729

BASHORE, GEORGE WILLIS, retired bishop; b. Lancaster, Pa., Jan. 21, 1934; m. Carolyn Ruth Baumgartner, Sept. 20, 1957; children: Wanda Bashore Allison, John, Barbara Bashore Heagy. BA, Princeton U., 1955; MDiv, United Theol. Sem., Dayton, Ohio, 1958, D.Ministry, 1976; DD, Albright Coll., 1974. Ordained elder Evang. United Brethren Ch., 1958. Pastor Cen. Pk. Ch., Reading, Pa., 1959—73; supt. Lebanon-Reading Dist., Ea. Pa. Conf., 1973—79; sr. pastor 1st United Meth. Ch., Lancaster, Pa., 1979—80; elected bishop United Meth. Ch., Boston, 1980—88, bishop, Pitts., 1988—2000; ret., 2000. United Methodist. Home: 2409 Broadlawn Dr Pittsburgh PA 15241-2407

BASHORE, IRENE SARAS, art association administrator; b. San Jose, Calif. d. John and Eva (Lionudakis) Saras; m. Vincent Bashore (div.); 1 child, Juliet Ann. BA, Pepperdine U., 1950; MA in Theatre Arts, Calif. State U., Fullerton, 1977. Founder, exec. dir. Inst. for Dramatic Rsch., Fullerton, Calif., 1967—.

BASHOUR, FOUAD ANIS, cardiology educator; b. Tripoli, Lebanon, Jan. 3, 1924; s. Anis E. and Mariana (Yazigi) B.; m. Val Imm, Sept. 28, 1978. BA, Am. U. of Beirut, Lebanon, 1944, MD, 1949; PhD, U. Minn., 1957. Intern Am. U. of Beirut Hosp., Beirut, 1949-50; med. officer UNRWA, 1950-51; resident in internal medicine U. Minn. Hosps., 1951-54; rsch. fellow U. Minn. Med. Schs., 1954-55; instr. in medicine U. Minn., 1955-57; rsch. assoc. Am. U. Med. Sch., Beirut, 1957, asst. prof. medicine cardiopulmonary lab. sect., 1957-59; instr. internal medicine U. Tex. Southwestern Med. Ctr., Dallas, 1959-60, assoc. prof. internal medicine, 1963-71, dir. Cardiovascular Inst., 1967-78, prof. medicine, 1971-85, prof. medicine and physiology, 1985-95; mem. staff Parkland Meml. Hosp., Dallas; prof. emeritus of physiology and internal medicine, 1995-99; mem. staff Zale-Lipshy Univ. Hosp., Dallas, Ashbel Smith prof. medicine and physiology, 1999—. Founder, pres. Cardiology Fund, Inc., 1972-93; program dir. consultation agreement lectrs. Univ. Kuwait, U. Tex., 1977-85; mem. chancellor adv. coun. U. Tex., 1982—; mem. bd trustees of coms. on promotions and med. sch. Am. U. Beirut, 1996—; cons. in field. Mem. editorial bd. Chest, 1963-69, Lebanese Med. Jour., 1957-59, cited in the Warren Commn. Pub., 1963; contbr. more than 200 articles to profl. publs. Elder Christ Luth. Ch., Dallas. Recipient Americanism award DAR, 1970; named Knight Order of Holy Cross Jerusalem; Fouad Bashour ann. lectr. disting. physiologist in their honor, 1974—, Fouad A. and Val Imm Bashour distinguished chair in physiology in his honor, 1990, eminent scholar, Tex., 1985, Wisdom Hall of Fame, eminent Wisdom fellow, 1998. Fellow Am. Coll. Chest Physicians (emeritus), Am. Physiol. Soc. (circulation group), Am. Heart Assn. (coun. on basic sci., coun. on circulation); mem. Am. Fedn. Clin. Rsch. (emeritus), Ctrl. Soc. Clin. Rsch. (emeritus), So. Soc. Clin. Investigation (emeritus), Tex. Med. Assn., Dallas County Med. Assn., Am. Soc. Internal Medicine, Tex. Med. Found., Order of Cedars of Lebanon (officer 1971), cons. Tex. Bd. of Med. Examiners. Office: U Tex Southwestern Med Ctr 5323 Harry Hines Blvd Dallas TX 75390-9040 Fax: 214-648-9376.

BASHSHUR, RASHID L. health facility administrator, educator; arrived in U.S., 1956; s. Lutfallah M. and Yamna D. Bashshur; m. Naziha S. Sima'an, Sept. 15, 1957; children: Ramona R., Noura R. PhD, U. of Mich., 1962. Prof. of health mgmt. and policy U. of Mich., Ann Arbor, 1977—; dir. of telemedicine U. of Mich. Health Sys., Ann Arbor, Mich., 1998—. Staff assoc. Inst. of Medicine, NAS, Washington, 1970—72. Editor in chief: Telemedicine Jour. and eHealth. Pres. Am. Telemedicine Assn., Washington, 2000—02. Grantee Effects of Telemedicine on Cost, Quality and Access, Health Care Financing Adminstrn., 1996—98. Mem.: APHA. Achievements include first original evaluation of telemedicine in the U.S. Avocations: watercolor painting, swimming. Office: U of Mich Health Sys 1500 E Medical Center Dr Ann Arbor MI 48109-0825

BASHWINER, STEVEN LACELLE, lawyer; b. Cin., Aug. 3, 1941; s. Carl Thomas and Ruth Marie (Burlis) B.; m. Arden J. Lang, Apr. 24, 1966 (div. 1978); children: Heather, David; m. Donna Lee Gerber, Sept. 13, 1981; children: Margaret, Matthew. AB, Holy Cross Coll., 1963; JD, U. Chgo., 1966. Bar: Ill. 1966, U.S. Dist. Ct. (no. dist.) Ill. 1967, U.S. Ct. Appeals (7th cir.) 1968, U.S. Supreme Ct. 1970, U.S. Dist. Ct. (ea. dist.) Wis. 1988, U.S. Ct. Appeals (4th cir.) 1990. Assoc. Kirkland & Ellis, Chgo., 1966-72, ptnr., 1972-76, Friedman & Koven, Chgo., 1976-86, Katten Muchin Zavis Rosenhan, Chgo., 1986—. Served to sgt. USAFR, 1966-72. Mem. ABA, 7th Cir. Bar Assn., Chgo. Bar Assn., Chgo. Inn of Ct., Lawyers Club Chgo. Home: 834 Green Bay Rd Highland Park IL 60035-4630 Office: Katten Muchin Zavis Rosenhan 525 W Monroe St Ste 1600 Chicago IL 60661-3693

BASICHIS, GORDON ALLEN, writer, scriptwriter, marketing professional, media consultant; b. Phila., Aug. 23, 1947; s. Martin and Ruth (Gordon) B.; m. Marcia Hammond; 1 child, Casey James. BS, Temple U., 1969. Reporter Phila. Bull., 1969; writer, reporter Santa Fe News, 1971-72; with advt., pub. rels. Jay Bernstein Pub. Rels., L.A., 1978-80; screenwriter Metro Goldwyn Mayer Feature Films, Culver City, Calif., 1982-83; exec. dir. media and mktg. Laclede, Inc., 2002—. Exec. v.p. Antigua Rd. Prodns., 1996; sr. v.p. market and ops. Nextworld Entertainment Zone; pres. Big Venus Entertainment, 2003. Author: Constant Travelers, 1978, Beautiful Bad Girl: The Vicki Morgan Story, 1985; prodr., dir.: Jerry: One Man's Triumph, 1980; screenwriter: Breach of Trust, 1994; exec. prodr.: Land of Dreams, 2001. Mem. ASCAP, Writers Guild Am. West, Am. Film Inst., Nat. Sports Mktg. Assn., Simon Wiesenthal Inst., Statue of Liberty/Ellis Island Found. Office: PO Box 1511 Beverly Hills CA 90213-1511 E-mail: gordonbasichis@usa.net.

BASIL, DOUGLAS CONSTANTINE, writer, educator; b. Vancouver, C., Can., May 30, 1923; s. William and Christina (Findlay) B.; m. Evelyn Margaret Pitcairn, 1950; 1 dau., Wendy Patricia. B.Commerce, U. B.C., 1949; BA, 1949; PhD, Northwestern U., 1954; postgrad., London Sch. Econs., 1950. Instr. Marquette U., 1951-54; asst. prof. Northwestern U., 1954-57; asso. prof. U. Minn., 1957-61; prof. mgmt. U. So. Calif., 1961-88, prof. emeritus, 1988—. Cons. mgmt. devel.; lectr., Brussels, Caracas, Bogota, Paris, London, others. Author: Executive Development, 1964, (Paul Cone, John Fleming) Effective Decision Making Through Simulation, 1972, Organacao E Controls Da Pequena Empresa, 1968, La Direccion de la Pequena Empresa, 1969, Managerial Skills for Executive Action, 1970, Leadership Skills for Executive Action, 1971, Women in Management: Performance, Prejudice, Promotion, 1972, Autorite Personnelle et Efficacite des Cadres, 1972, Conduccion y Liderazgo, 1973, Developing Tomorrow's Managers, 1973, Management of Change, 1974, others.; Contbr. (Paul Cone, John Fleming) articles to profl. jours. Served to capt. Canadian Army, 1943-46. Home: 2201 Warmouth St San Pedro CA 90732-4532 Office: U So Calif Grad Sch Bus Adminstrn Los Angeles CA 90007

BASILE, LEON EDMUND, writer, editor; b. Woburn, Mass., Dec. 12, 1955; s. Mario Joseph and Charlene (Chesteen) B. BA, U. Mass., Boston, 1977; MA, U. Ga., 1979. Editor: The Civil War Diary of Amos E. Stearns, A Prisoner at Andersonville, 1981; contbr. articles to hist. publs. Recipient Jefferson Davis gold medal UDC, 1976. Mem.: New England Historic Genealogical Soc. Republican. Roman Catholic. Avocation: reading. Home: 9 Colonial Rd Woburn MA 01801-2814

BASILE, PAUL LOUIS, JR., lawyer; b. Oakland, Calif., Dec. 27, 1945; s. Paul Louis and Roma Florence (Paris) B.; m. Linda Lou Paige, June 20, 1970; m. 2d Diane Chierichetti, Sept. 2, 1977. BA, Occidental Coll., 1968; postgrad., U. Wash., 1969; JD, UCLA, 1971. Bar: Calif. 1972, U.S. Dist. Ct. (cen. dist.) Calif. 1972, U.S. Dist. Ct. (no. dist.) Calif. 1985, U.S. Ct. Appeals (9th cir.) 1972, U.S. Tax Ct. 1977, U.S. Ct. Claims. 1978, U.S. Customs Ct. 1979, U.S. Ct. Customs and Patent Appeals 1979, U.S. Ct. Internat. Trade 1981, U.S. Supreme Ct. 1977; cert. specialist in taxation law Bd. of Legal Specialization, State Bar of Calif. Assoc. Parker, Milliken, Kohlmeier, Clark & O'Hara, L.A., 1971-72; corp. counsel TFI Cos., Inc., Irvine, Calif., 1972-73; pvt. practice L.A., 1973-80, 90-96, 98-99; mem. Basile & Siener, L.A., 1980-86, Clark & Trevithick, L.A., 1986-90; ptnr. Wolf, Rifkin & Shapiro, L.A., 1990, of counsel, 1990-92; ptnr. Basile & Lane, LLP, L.A., 1996-97; of counsel Shaffer, Gold & Rubaum, L.L.P., L.A., 1996—; sr. ptnr. Basile & Assocs., L.A. and Pasadena, Calif., 1999—; pres., CEO, dir. 765 Inc., Cliffside Park, NJ, 1997—. Gen. counsel J.W. Brown, Inc., L.A., 1980—, asst. sec., 1984—92; sec., gen. counsel Souriau, Inc., Valencia, Calif., 1981—90; v.p., sec., dir., gen. counsel Pvt. Fin. Assocs., L.A., 1983—94; gen. counsel Quest Relocation Group, Toluca Lake, Calif., 1994—97, v.p. real estate, 1996—; pres., CEO, dir. 765, Inc., Cliffside Park, NJ, 1997—. Trustee, sec. Nat. Repertory Theatre Found., 1975-94, mem. exec. com., 1976-94, chmn. bd. dirs., 1991-94; mem. fin. com., bd. dirs. Calif. Music Theatre, 1988-92; bd. dirs. March of Dimes Birth Defects Found., Los Angeles County, 1982-87, mem. exec. com., 1983-86, sec., 1985-86; dist. fin. chmn. L.A. Area coun. Boy Scouts Am., 1982-83; trustee Occidental Coll., L.A., 1989-94; active L.A. Olympic Organizing Com., Ketchum Downtown YMCA, Vols. Am. L.A., others. Mem. ABA (taxation sect., corp. tax com., vice chmn. closely held bus. com. 1992-94, chair, 1994-96, chmn. subcom. on continuing legal edn. 1990-94, chmn. subcom. on estate planning 1992, sec. 1996-97, small firm lawyers com., bus. law sect., real property sect., probate and trust law sect., spl. problems of bus. owners com., estate planning and drafting, pre-death planning issues com.), State Bar Calif. (bus. law sect., nonprofit and unincorporated orgns. com. 1989-92, taxation sect., estate planning, trust and probate sect., taxation law adv. commn. 1994-97, vice chmn. 1995-96, chair 1996-97, mem. bd. legal specialization 1996-97), L.A. County Bar Assn. (taxation sect., com. on closely-held and pass-through entities, bus. and corps. law sect., sole practitioner section exec. com. 1995-99), Beverly Hills Bar Assn. (probate, trust and estate planning sect., taxation sect., vice chmn. Estate and Gift Tax Com., 1998—, law practice mgmt. sect.), Can. Calif. C. of C. (dir. 1980-89, 2d v.p. 1983-84, 1st v.p. 1984-85, pres. 1985-87), L.A.-Vancouver Sister City Assn. (dir., exec. com. 1987-92, treas. 1987-89, pres. 1989-92), French-Am. C. of C. (councilor 1979-84, v.p. 1980, 82-84), L.A. Area C. of C. (dir. 1980-81), Occidental Coll. Alumni Assn. (pres. 1979-80, v.p. 1978-79, alumni bd. govs. 1977-81, chmn. ann. fund campaign 1990-91), Grand People (bd. dirs. 1985-92, chmn. bd. 1986-92), Rotary Club of L.A. (dir. 1994-96, sergeant-at-arms 1986-87, chmn. gateway com. 1993-94, chmn. world cmty. svc. com. 1991-93, chmn. vols. Am. of L.A. com. 1988-90, chmn. golf com. 1986-87, vice-chmn. pres. com. 1985-86), Rotary Internat. (chmn. club extension com. 1995-96, cmty. svc. dir. 1993-95, chmn. gift of life com. 1992-93), Small Bus. Coun. of Am., Inc. (legal adv. bd. 1989—), The Group, Inc. (dir. 2003—), Attys. for Family Held Enterprises. Democrat. Baptist. Home: 3937 Beverly Glen Blvd Sherman Oaks CA 91423-4404 Office: Basile and Assocs 12011 San Vicente Blvd Ste 600 Los Angeles CA 90049-4948 also: 180 S Lake Ave Ste 540 Pasadena CA 91101-2666

BASILE, RICHARD EMANUEL, retired management consultant, educator; b. Buffalo, Dec. 24, 1921; s. Giustino Gregory and Minnie (Bailey) B.; m. Mariette Ruth Borocco, Oct. 12, 1946 (dec. Feb. 1994). BA, Washington and Lee U., 1943; postgrad., U. Mo., 1947-48, Columbia U., 1965; L.H.D., Combs Coll., Phila., 1969. Geologist U.S. Geol. Survey, 1946-49; mgr. hotel industry, 1948-51; head hotel mgmt. dept. Paul Smith's Coll., 1951-57, adminstrv. dean, 1961-66; mgr. Am. Mgmt. Assn. Acad., 1957-61; dir. devel. Aramark, Phila., 1966-67, v.p. purchasing, 1966-68, v.p., 1968-70; prof. U. Nev., Las Vegas, Nev., 1970-88; pres. Univ. Assoc., Inc., Las Vegas, Nev., 1971-92; adv. bd. Paul Smith's Coll., NY, 1994. Instr. geology U. Mo. Rolla Sch. Mines, 1948-49; cons. Indsl. Rels. Counselors, Area Redevel. Act, US Govt., XIX and XXI Olympiads, 1968, 76; com. chmn. XI Internat. Congress on Nutrition, Rio de Janeiro, 1978; US Dept. Commerce tech. rep. Cyprus Internat. Trade Show, Nicosia, 1982; mem. Nev. Employee-Mgmt. Rels. Bd., 1981— ; bd. dir. Marriott's Camelback Inn and Resort, Scottsdale, Ariz., 1987-91; cons. to hospitality industry. Cons. editor: Restaurant Hospitality Mag. Contbr. articles to profl. jour. Sec. treas. Paradise Valley Phys. Therapy Clinic, Las Vegas, Nev., 1987—89; arbitrator Teamsters local 995, Nev. Resort Assn., Nat. Assn. Security Dealers Regulations, 1997—. With USNR, 1943—46. Paul Harris fellow, 1980—; eminent fellow Wisdom Hall of Fame, 1998; Winston Churchill medal of wisdom and eminent Churchill fellow, 1999. Mem. Utility Shareholders Assn. Nev. (bd. dir. 1994-99, v.p. 1997-99), Am. Arbitration Assn. (panel arbitrators 1961—), Pa. Acad. Fine Arts, Masons, K.T., Rotary (pres. 1962-63), Washington and Lee Univ. Doremus Soc., Sigma Phi Epsilon, Alpha Kappa Psi. Home: 1800 S 14th St Las Vegas NV 89104-3124 Office: 4505 S Maryland Pky Las Vegas NV 89154-9900 *Success? Is it not in the eye of the beholder? A strong hero worship from childhood days of those selected educators, religious and business leaders who were honest, unselfish, and who enjoyed pure living—not solely materialistic gain. A family who exemplified the work ethic, and a wife who was almost psychic in her ability to keep me from wearing an oversized hat.*

BASILICO, FREDERICK CALVIN, cardiologist; b. Providence, Oct. 23, 1948; s. Panfilo and Mary Basilico; m. Judith A. Waligunda, Dec. 8, 1973; children: Justin, Matthew. BS, Fairfield U., 1970; MD, Cornell U., 1974. Intern Cornell-N.Y. Hosp., resident, Dartmouth-Affiliated Hosps.; trustee New Eng. Baptist Hosp., Boston, 1990—, chief cardiology, 1993—, chmn. medicine, 1998—. Bd. dirs. New Eng. Baptist Health Svcs. Fellow Am. Coll. Cardiology; mem. AMA, Am. Heart Assn. Avocations: sailing, skiing, golf. Office: One Brookline Pl Ste 305 Brookline MA 02445 E-mail: fbasilic@caregroup.harvard.edu.

BASILIOUS, NAGI MOUSSA, artist, painter; b. Cairo, Dec. 12, 1949; BA in Painting, Helwan U. Graphic designer Egyptian TV, 1973-75, graphic designer, scene painter, 1977-83, painter, designer, 1983—. Exhibited in one-man shows and in group shows. Recipient award Ministry of Culture, 1979, award Fine Arts Assn., 1976. Mem. Nat. Assn. Fine Arts, Cairo Atelier. Avocations: photography, electronics, reading. Office: 26 July St # 28 Flat # 24 Cairo Egypt

BASINGER, KAREN LYNN, renal dietitian; b. Mechanicsville, Md., July 4, 1955; d. Leonard Marcus and Mary Jane (Harding) Brookbank; m. Joseph Andrew Basinger, Nov. 17, 1984; 1 child, James Marcus. BS, U. Md., 1977; MS, Hood Coll., 1987. Lic. nutritionist. Libr. technician Bowie (Md.) State Coll., 1973-79; instr. St. Mary's County Adult Edn., Leonardtown, Md., 1979-80; home economist Zamoiski Co., Balt., 1977-83; nutritionist/WIC coord. South County Health Plan, Prince Frederick, Md., 1979-80; nutritionist Walter Reed Army Med. Ctr., Washington, 1980-82; renal dietitian Mid Atlantic/BMA, Camp Springs, Md., 1982-87, Kidney Care Ctr., Landover, Md., 1987-99; instr. dietary intern program Andrews AFB, 1988-91; renal dietitian Silver Spring (Md.) Artificial Kindey Ctr., 1998—; outpatient dietitian Holy Cross Hosp., Silver Spring, 1999-2000; renal dietitian DaVita-Wheaton, Md., 1999—. Cons. Leisure World, 2002-; lectr. in field. Profl. adv. bd. Nat. Kidney Found./NCA, 1989-94; chair coun. on renal nutrition Nat. Kidney Found., 1993-94, program chair, 1990-92. Recipient Spl. Recognition Nat. Kidney Found./NCA, 1990, 92, Recognized Renal Dietitian/NCA, 1991, 94. Mem.: Washington Met. Coun. on Renal Nutrition (chair 1986—94, nutrition symposium chair 1989, chair 1986—94, 2001—02), Am. Dietetic Assn. (legis. chair renal practice group 2003—), Md. Home Econs. Assn. (bylaws chair 1982—94), Am. Home Econs. Assn., Am. Nutritionists Assn., U. Md. Aumni Assn. Democrat. Lutheran. Avocation: cross-stitch.

BASINGER, RICHARD LEE, lawyer; b. Canton, Ohio, Nov. 24, 1941; s. Eldon R. and Alice M. (Bartholomew) B.; m. Rita Evelyn Gover, May 14, 1965; children: David A., Darron M. BA in Edn., Ariz. State U., 1963; postgrad. Macalester Coll., 1968-69; JD, U. Ariz., 1973. Bar: Ariz. 1973, U.S. Dist. Ct. Ariz. 1973, U.S. Tax Ct. 1977, U.S. Ct. Appeals (6th cir.) 1975, U.S. Ct. Appeals (9th cir.) 1976, U.S. Supreme Ct. 1977; cert. arbitrator. Assoc. law offices, Phoenix, 1973-74; pvt. practice, Scottsdale, Ariz. 1974-75; pres. Basinger & Assocs., P.C., Scottsdale, 1975—, also bd. dirs. Contbr. articles to profl. jours. Bd. dirs. Masters Trail Ventures, Scottsdale, 1984-85, Here's Life, Ariz., Scottsdale, 1976—; precinct committeeman Republican Party, Phoenix, 1983—; bd. dir. Ariz. Coll. of the Bible, 1992-93. NSF grantee, 1968-69. Mem. ABA, Ariz. Bar Assn., Maricopa County Bar Assn., Ariz. State Horseman's Assn. (bd. dirs. 1984-86, 1st v.p. 1986), Scottsdale Bar Assn., Western Saddle Club (bd. dirs. 1983-86, pres. 1985-86), Scottsdale Saddle Club, Saguaro Saddle Club. Baptist. Office: Mohave County Atty Dep County Atty Civil Divsn PO Box 7000 Kingman AZ 86402-7000

BASINGER, WILLIAM DANIEL, computer programmer; b. Washington, Feb. 14, 1952; s. James Samuel and Eleanor (Freeburger) B.; m. Martha Kecskes, July 1, 1978 (div. 1983); m. Mary Teresa Richardson, June 11, 1988. BA in Linguistics, U. Md., 1974; MS in Linguistics, Georgetown U., 1977; MS in Computer Sci., Johns Hopkins U., 1989. Programmer Evaluation Techs., Arlington, Va., 1977-78; programmer, analyst, cons. Vitro Corp., Silver Spring, Md., 1978-84, 87-88; programmer, analyst Tracor Applied Scis., Rockville, Md., 1984-88, PRC, Inc., McLean, Va., 1988-89; sr. programmer, analyst Systems & Computer Tech. group George Washington U., Washington, 1989-95; sr. programmer, statistician PRC, Inc., Reston, 1996-97; sr. systems analyst, Yr. 2000 Assessment Project M-Cubed Info. Systems, Rockville, Md., 1997-2000; sr. computer specialist, statistician VGS, Fairfax, Va., 2000—01; statistician U.S. Dept. Transp., 2001—02; sr. computer specialist Ajilon Cons., Rockville, 2002—. Cons. applications software dept. geology George Washington U., Washington, 1990-91, 93—. Contbr. articles to profl. jours. Contbr., sponsor Statue of Liberty/Ellis Island Found., N.Y.C., 1985—. Md. State Sen. scholar U. Md., 1970-74. Mem. Assn. Computing Machinery, Am. Geophys. Union, Am. Statis. Assn., N.Y. Acad. Scis. Republican. Roman Catholic. Home: Apt 203 11342 Cherry Hill Rd Beltsville MD 20705-3735 Office: Ajilon Cons 11400 Rockville Pike Ste 210 Rockville MD 20852 E-mail: wdbasinger@hotmail.com.

BASINSKI, ANTHONY JOSEPH, lawyer; b. Pitts., Apr. 11, 1947; s. Anthony F. and Emily C. (Klocko) B.; m. Elisabeth Fawcett, Oct. 4, 1980; children: Ann Elisabeth, Robert Anthony. BA, U. Pitts., 1969, JD, 1974. Bar: Pa. 1974, U.S. Dist. Ct. (we. dist.) Pa. 1974, U.S. Ct. Appeals (3d cir.) 1981, U.S. Ct. Appeals (4th cir.) 1992, U.S. Ct. Appeals (fed. cir.) 1995. Law clk. to presiding justice Pa. Supreme Ct., Pitts., 1974-76; ptnr. Reed, Smith, Shaw and McClay, Pitts., 1976—. Served with U.S. Army, 1969-71, Vietnam. Mem. Allegheny County

Bar Assn., Am. Arbitration Assn. (arbitrator 1983—). Democratic. Roman Catholic. Home: 1749 Taper Dr Pittsburgh PA 15241-2623 Office: Reed Smith Shaw & McClay 435 6th Ave Ste 2 Pittsburgh PA 15219-1886 E-mail: abasinski@reedsmith.com.

BASISZTA, MARTIN WINSTON, lawyer; b. Antioch, Calif., Jan. 10, 1943; m. Catherine Dawn Czarnecki, Mar. 3, 1978; children— Kelly Jane, Meghan Aileen. B.A. summa cum laude, U. Calif.-Davis, 1968; J.D., U. Calif.-Berkeley, 1972. Bar: Calif. 1973. Assoc., McNamara, Lewis & Craddick, Walnut Creek, Calif., 1973-75, Maloney, Chase, Fisher & Hurst, San Francisco, 1975-76; ptnr. Van Voorhis & Skaggs, Walnut Creek, 1976-78; sole practice law, Walnut Creek, 1978-83; ptnr. Basiszta & Daniels, Hayward, Calif., 1983— . Assoc. editor Calif. Law Rev., 1971-72. Contbr. articles to legal jours. Served with submarine service U.S. Navy, 1960-63. Recipient deptl. citation German studies U. Calif.-Davis, 1968; regents scholar U. Calif., 1966-68; German Govt. grad. grantee, German Govt. Grad. Exchange Program, 1969; John Woodward Ayer fellow in law, 1971-72; Alexander Von Humboldt grad. fellow in law, 1982; hon. Woodrow Wilson fellow, 1968. Mem. Bar Assn. San Francisco, Contra Costa County Bar Assn., Mt. Diablo Bar Assn., Santa Clara Bar Assn., San Mateo Bar Assn., Calif. Trial Lawyers Assn., Contra Costa/Alameda Trial Lawyers Assn., Assn. Def. Counsel, Def. Research Inst., Lawyers Club San Francisco, Barristers Club San Francisco, Phi Beta Kappa, Alpha Gamma Sigma, Phi Kappa Phi.

BASKA, JAMES LOUIS, wholesale grocery company executive; b. Kansas City, Kans., Apr. 3, 1927; s. John James and Stella Marie (Wilson) B.; m. Juanita Louise Carlson, Oct. 14, 1950; children: Steven James, Scott David. BSBA, U. Kans., 1949; JD, U. Mo., 1960. Bar: Kans. 1960. Pres., chief exec. officer Baska Laundry Co., Kansas City, 1951-62; ptnr. Rice & Baska, Kansas City, 1962-76; corporate sec., gen. counsel Assoc. Wholesale Grocers Inc., Kansas City, 1976-77, v.p., sec., gen. counsel, 1977-79, exec. v.p., chief fin. officer, sec., gen. counsel, 1979-84, pres., chief exec. officer, 1984-92; pres. emeritus, 1992. Mem. SDC com. Wakefern Food Corp., 1998—; bd. dirs. Raley's, Riverwood Homes, Inc. Served as staff sgt. U.S. Army, 1944-46. Mem. Nat. Grocers Assn. (bd. dirs. 1980-89, chmn. 1987-88), Food Mktg. Inst. (bd. dirs. 1988-93). Republican. Roman Catholic. Avocations: hunting, golf. Office: Assoc Wholesale Grocers Inc PO Box 2932 5000 Kansas Ave Kansas City KS 66106-1135 *There is always room at the top and my objectives whatever they may be and no matter how big or wild, are always attainable. The only questions are— am I ready to make the move and willing to pay the price?.*

BASKE, C. ALAN, manufacturing company executive; b. Detroit, Apr. 19, 1927; s. Clarence A. and Alice Loraine (Severance) B.; m. Shirley Ann Duckworth, Feb. 24, 1945; children: Nance, Roger, Douglas, Brian. Radio officer, USCG Hoffmann Island, Bklyn., 1944. Radio officer U.S. Maritime Svc., Atlantic, Pacific, Caribbean, 1944-45; owner/mgr. Alan's Auto Svc., Dearborn, Mich., 1946; svc. parts mgr. Detherage-McDonald Auto Sales, Dearborn, Mich., 1946-48; field sales agt. Sun Electric Corp., Detroit/Jackson, 1948, asst. dir. Chgo., 1948-53; mfg. rep. Valley Bearing, Chgo., 1953-74, owner/pres., 1974-86; cons. Libertyville, Ill., 1986—. Advisor Boy Scouts Am. troop 80, Libertyville, 1954-65; vestryman St. Lawrence Ch., Libertyville, 1958-66; bd. dirs. Libertyville/Fremont High Sch. Dist., 1962-64; chmn. Condell Hosp., 1968-72, 84-86, bd. dirs., 1963-72, 77-86; trustee Lake Forest (Ill.) Acad., 1969-75; pres. Waukegan (Ill.) Symphony Chorus, 1984-88; founding mem. Coll. Lake County Found., pres., 1975-82. Mem. Libertyville Country Side Assn. (bd. dir./officer), Island Goat Sailing Soc. (commodore), Waukegan Power Squadron (life), Waukegan Yacht Club (dir., past commodore), Libertyville Boat Club (founder dir.), U.S. Sailing Assn. (judge 1998—), Waukegan Yacht Club Jr. Found. (founder, pres. 1997—). Republican. Episcopalian. Avocations: sailing, flying, skiing, traveling. Home and Office: 15252 W Oak Spring Rd Libertyville IL 60048-1620 E-mail: casab@att.net.

BASKERVILL, CHARLES THORNTON, lawyer; b. South Boston, Va., May 26, 1953; s. William Nelson and Julia Alice (Moore) B.; m. Pamela Temple Shell, July 17, 1976; children: Ann Cabell, Susannah Thornton. BA, Hampden-Sydney Coll., 1975; JD, U. Richmond, 1978. Bar: Va. 1978, U.S. Dist. Ct. (ea. dist.) Va. 1978. Assoc. White, Hamilton, Wyche & Shell, P.C., Petersburg, Va., 1978-96; asst. commonwealth's atty Petersburg, Va., 1985—; assoc. Shell, Johnson, Andrews, Baskervill & Baskervill, P.C., Petersburg, Va., 1996-2001, Shell, Johnson, Andrews & Baskervill, P.C., Petersburg, Va., 2001—. Commr. of accts. City of Petersburg, Va., 1996—. Former dir. Petersburg Crime Prevention Found.; bd. trustees Mary Baldwin Coll., 2003—. Named to Athletic Hall of Fame, Hampden-Sydney Coll., 1988. Mem. Prince George County Bar Assn. (sec.-treas. 1990-91, pres. 1991-92), Petersburg Bar Assn. (pres. 2001-02). Methodist. Avocations: golf, tennis. Office: Shell Johnson Andrews Baskervill PC 43 Rives Rd Petersburg VA 23805-9255

BASKERVILLE, CHARLES ALEXANDER, geologist, educator; b. Jamaica, N.Y., Aug. 19, 1928; s. Charles H. and Annie M. (Allen) Baskerville; children: Mark Dana, Shawn Allison, Charles Morris, Thomas Marshall. BS, CCNY, 1953; MS, NYU, 1958, PhD, 1965. Cert. profl. geologist Maine. Asst. civil engr. N.Y. State Dept. Transp., Babylon, 1953-66; prof. engring. geology CUNY, N.Y.C., 1966-79, dean sch. of gen. studies, 1970-79, prof. emeritus, 1979—; project rsch. geologist U.S. Geol. Survey, 1979-90; prof. geology Ctrl. Conn. State U., New Britain, 1990—, dept. chmn., 1992-94. Commonwealth vis. prof. George Mason U., Fairfax, Va., 1987-89; mem. U.S. Nat. Com. on Tunnelling Tech., NRC, chmn. subcom. on edn. and tng.; mem. Am. del Internat. Tunnelling Assn. to Internat. Colloquim of Tunnelling and Underground Works, Beijing, People's Republic of China, 1984; geol. cons. N.Y.C. Dept. Environ. Protection Water Tunnel #3; guest lectr. various colls., 1964—; geol. program evaluator for colls. seeking continued mid. states accreditation. Author numerous sci. papers. Mem. com. for minority participation in the geoscis. U.S. Dept. Interior, 1972-75; panelist Grad. Fellowship Program NRC; chmn. Minority Grad. Fellowship Program, 1979-80; mem. com. of visitors for edn. and human resources program divsn. earth scis. NSF, 1991; mem. N.Y. State Low Level Radioactive Waste Com. NAS, 1994-96. Recipient Founders Day award N.Y. U., 1966, 125th Anniversary medal The City Coll., 1973, award for excellence in engring. geology Nat. Consortium Black Profl. Devel., 1978, Recognition award Nat. Assn. Black Geologists and Geophysicists, 1998. Fellow Geol. Soc. Am. (sr., com. on minorities in geoscis., chmn. com. on coms. 1989), N.Y. Acad. Scis., Geol. Soc. Washington, Am. Inst. Profl. Geologists, Assn. Engring. Geologists (rep. to nat. bd. dirs. 1973-74, chmn. N.Y.-Phila. sect. 1973-74), Internat. Assn. Engring. Geology, Yellowstone-Bighorn Rsch. Assn., Sigma Xi. Office: Ctrl Conn State Univ 1615 Stanley St New Britain CT 06050-4010 E-mail: baskerville@ccsu.edu.

BASKES, MICHAEL I. materials engineer; b. Chgo., Ill., June 13, 1943; s. Charles George Baskes, Fae Baskes; m. Carole Elaine Dixon, Mar. 17, 1968; children: Michelle, David. BSc, Calif. Inst. Tech., Pasadena, 1965, PhD, 1969. Tech. staff mem. Los Alamos National Lab., Los Alamos, N.Mex., 1999—; mgr., tech. staff Sandia Nat. Labs., Livermore, Calif., 1969—99. Mem. nat. materials adv. bd. Nat. Rsch. Coun., Washington, 1996—98. Contbr. articles to profl. jours.; editor-in-chief: Modelling and Simulation in Materials Sci. and Engring., 1990-. Fellow: Inst. Physics; mem.: MRS, TMS, ASM Internat., Sigma Xi. Office: Los Alamos Nat Lab MST-8; MS G755 Los Alamos NM 87545 Office Fax: 5056678021. Business E-Mail: baskes@lanl.gov.

BASKIN, C. R. retired civil engineer, physical scientist; b. Houston, Mar. 6, 1926; s. Charles Todd and Bessie Emma (Heilig) B.; m. Peggy June Holden, Dec. 31, 1952; children: Richard Karl, Sheila Frances. BSCE, La. State U., 1953. Design engr. City-Parish Dept. Pub. Works, Baton Rouge, 1953-57; city engr. City of Plaquemine, La., 1957-58; sect. head, asst. chief engr. Tex. Bd. Water Engrs., Austin, 1958-62; asst. chief engr. Tex. Water Commn., Austin, 1962-65; asst. chief engr., chief engr. Tex. Water Devel. Bd., Austin, 1965-77; dir. data and engring. svcs. divsn. Tex. Dept. Water Resources, Austin, 1977-83; spl. asst. Office of Asst. Dir. Info. Sys./U.S. Geol. Survey, Reston, Va., 1983-92; ret., 1992. Chmn. Tex. Mapping Adv. Com., 1968-83; chmn. water oriented data programs sect. Tex. Interagy. Council on Natural Resources and the Environment, 1968-72, Tex. Natural Resources Info. System Task Force, 1972-83; mem. Non-Fed. Adv. Com. on Water Data for Public Use, 1970-83; chmn. Water Data Coordination Task Force, Interstate Conf. on Water Problems, 1975-83. Contbr. articles to profl. jours. With U.S. Army, 1944-47, POW; commd. Adm. Tex. Navy, 1961. Recipient John Wesley Powell award U.S. Geol. Survey, 1972, Combat Inf. badge. Mem.: Am. Ex-POWs, Sigma Tau Sigma (pres. 1950), Phi Eta Sigma, Chi Epsilon, Tau Beta Pi (chpt. pres. 1950), Phi Kappa Phi. Adventist (elder). Avocations: photography, walking. Home: 304 N Woodlake Dr Columbia SC 29229-8932

BASKIN, DAVID STUART, neurosurgeon, educator; b. N.Y.C., Feb. 11, 1952; s. Norman and Selma (Schorr) B. BA with high honors, Swarthmore Coll., 1974; MD, Mt. Sinai Sch. Medicine, CUNY, 1978. Diplomate Am. Bd. Neurol. Surgery. Intern in surgery U. Calif., San Francisco, 1978-79, resident in neurosurgery, 1979-84; asst. prof. Baylor Coll. Medicine, Houston, 1984-89, assoc. prof., 1989-94, assoc. prof. anesthesiology, 1993-94; chief neurosurgery VA Hosp., Houston, 1984-92, attending neurosurgeon, 1992—; prof. neurosurgery Baylor Coll. Medicine, Houston, 1994—, prof. anesthesiology, 1994—. Attending physician Meth. Hosp., Ben Taub Hosp., Tex. Children's Hosp., St. Luke's Episc. Hosp., Inst. for Rehab. and Rsch., Houston, 1984—, Tex. Orthopedic Hosp., 1994—. Contbr. numerous articles to profl. jours. Mem. Alzheimer's Exec. Coun. Recipient Acad. award Am. Acad. Neurol. Surgeons, 1983, Wakeman award for rsch. in neurosci., 1990, Disting. Alumni awadr Mt. Sinai Sch. Medicine, 1990. Fellow ACS, Stroke Coun. of Am. Heart Assn.; mem. AMA, AAAS, Congress Neurol. Surgeons, Joint Sect. on Spinal Disorders of Congress Neurol. Surgeons/Am. Assn. Neurol. Surgeons, Pituitary Found. Am., Soc. Univ. Neurosurgeons, Soc. Neurol. Surgeons, Rocky Mountain Neurol. Soc., So. Med. Assn., Houston Neurol. Soc., Pituitary Soc. Houston, Tex. Med. Assn., Harris County Med. Soc., Phi Beta Kappa, Sigma Xi, Alpha Omega Alpha. Avocations: scuba diving, hunting, fishing, skiing. Office: Baylor Coll Medicine 6560 Fannin St Ste 944 Houston TX 77030-2706

BASKIN, FRANK ELLIS, social worker, educator; b. Phila., June 3, 1943; BS in Social Welfare, Temple U., 1965; MSW, U. Mich., 1967. Cert. Acad. Cert. Social Worker; bd. cert. diplomate; lic. ind. clin. social worker. Social worker VA Hosp., Phila., 1967-74, Phila. Geriatric Ctr., 1974-77; dir. social svc. Lowell (Mass.) Gen. Hosp., 1979-80; counselor Lowell Indsl. Ctr., 1981-83; pvt. practice Phila. and Lowell, 1977—. Instr. Salem (Mass.) State Coll. Grad. Sch. Social Work, 1990—; instr. dramatics Ea. Coop. Recreation Sch., 1991—, staff coord., 1995—; coord. project to develop practice stads. for nursing home social workers in Mass., 1993. Author: (with others) Play & Playfulness, 1990, Your Nursing Home Social Worker, 2000; author (with others) law which amends Mass. Legislation on nursing home abuse, (articles on nursing home social policy issues) Ask Frank. Recipient Greatest Contbn. to Social Work Practice award NASW Mass. chpt., 1989. Achievements include development of long range plan for elder home care agency; coor. devel. of Web site on elder mental health, 2003. Home and Office: 18 E Meadow Ln Lowell MA 01854-1557

BASKIN, OTIS WAYNE, business educator; b. Houston, Oct. 26, 1945; s. Samuel and Ollie Estell (Key) B.; m. Maryan Kay Patrick, Dec. 26, 1970. BA, Okla. Christian Coll., 1968; MA, U. Houston, 1970; PhD, U. Tex., 1975. Asst. prof. Tex. Luth. Coll., Seguin, 1970-75; prof. U. Houston, 1975-87; prof., acad. dir. Ariz. State U., Phoenix, 1987-91; prof., dean Memphis State U., 1991-92, prof., dir. family bus., 1992-95; dean George L. Graziadio Sch. Bus. and Mgmt. Pepperdine U., Malibu, Calif., 1995-2001, prof. mgmt., 1995—. Vis. faculty U. Md., London, 1979, Oxford U., 1994; ons. Ministry Trade, Sophia, Bulgaria, 1990, Utara U., Malaysia, 1992; spl. advisor to the pres. AACSB Internat. Author: Guidelines for Research in Business Communication, 1977, (With Craig Aronoff) Interpersonal Communication in Organizations, 1980, Getting Your Message Across, 1981, Public Relations: The Profession and the practice, 1983, (with Grover Starling) Issues in Business and Society: Capitalism and Public Purpose, 1985; contbr. articles to profl. jours. Bd. dirs. Jr. Achievement Memphis, 1991-92, Econ. Club Memphis, 1991-94, Margurite Piazza Gala for St. Jude's Hosp., Memphis, 1992-95, Durham Found., Memphis, 1992-95, World Affairs Coun. Ventura County, 2001, L.A. Econ. Devel. Corp., 2000-02. Recipient Advancing Pub. Rels. Through Rsch. award Tex. Pub. Rels. Soc., Houston, 1983. Mem. Acad. Mgmt. (divsn. chair 1985), Rotary, Sigma Iota Epsilon (bd. dirs. 1986—), Beta Gamma Sigma. Mem. Ch. of Christ. Avocations: reading, travel. Office: George L Graziadio Sch Bus & Mgmt Pepperdine Univ Malibu CA 90263 E-mail: Otis.Baskin@pepperdine.edu.

BASKIN, RONALD JOSEPH, cell biologist, physiologist, biophysicist educator, dean; b. Joliet, Ill., Nov. 25, 1935; s. Mack Robert and Evelyn Josephine (Rudzinski) B.; m. Lydia Olga Lendl, Mar. 29, 1957; children— Ronald James, Thomas William. AB, UCLA, 1957; MA, 1959, PhD, 1960. Asst. prof. biology Rensselaer Poly. Inst., Troy, N.Y., 1961-64; asst. prof. zoology U. Calif., Davis, 1964-67, assoc. prof., 1967-71, prof., 1971—, chmn. dept. zoology, 1971-78, assoc. dean coll. letters and sci., 1986-90. Mem. editorial bd. U. Calif. Press. Contbr. articles to sci. pubs. Nat. Heart Inst. predoctoral fellow, 1957-60 Mem. Biophys. Soc., Soc. Cell Biology, Am. Physiol. Soc., N.Y. Acad. Scis., Sigma Xi. Office: Molecular & Cellular Biology Sect U Calif Davis CA 95616

BASKIN, SCOTT DAVID, lawyer; b. N.Y.C., Oct. 24, 1953; s. George and Anne (Strauss) B.; m. Sherry Nahmias, Mar. 13, 1982; children: Jonathan, Felicia. BA, Stanford U., 1975; JD, Yale U., 1978. Bar: Calif. 1978, U.S. Dist. Ct. (cen., ea., so. and no. dists.) Calif. 1979, U.S. Appeals (2d and 9th cirs.) 1979. Law clk. Hon. Herbert Choy, 9th Cir. Ct., Honolulu, 1978-79; ptnr. Irell & Manella, Newport Beach, Calif., 1979—. Lectr. Calif. Continuing Edn. of the Bar, 1985—. Contbr. articles to profl. publs. Office: Irell & Manella 840 Newport Center Dr Ste 400 Newport Beach CA 92660-6323 E-mail: sbaskin@irell.com.

BASKIN, WILLIAM GRESHAM, counselor, music educator, vocalist; b. Cameron, Tex., July 14, 1933; s. James Dollar and Ruth (McKinney) B.; m. Margaret Lee Williams, Mar. 26, 1959; 1 child, Susan Elizabeth. Student, U. Tex., 1951-54; B of Music Edn., S.W. Tex. State U., 1955; postgrad., Ea. Wash. U., 1956; MEd, S.W. Tex. State U., 1961. Cert. life elem. and secondary tchr., profl. music tchrs., provisional vis. techr., profl. counselor, profl. prin., Tex.; lic. profl. counselor, Tex.; nat. cert. counselor; nat. cert. career counselor; nat. cert. sch. counselor. Choral dir. San Marcos (Tex.) Bapt. Acad., 1957-58, Carrizo Springs (Tex.) Ind. Sch. Dist., 1958-62, Victoria (Tex.) High Sch., 1962-68; counselor Brazosport Ind. Sch. Dist., Freeport, Tex., 1968—. Music dir. 1st Bapt. Ch., Carrizo Springs, 1958 62, Bapt. Temple, Victoria, 1962 64; interim music dir. 1st Bapt. ch., Victoria, 1965, Freeport, 1972-73, 87-88, 89, Lake Jackson, Tex., 1978-79, Temple Bapt. Ch., Clute, Tex., 1990; mem. Music Educators Nat. conf., 1958-68; del. Am. Mental Health Counselors Assn. and Citizen Amb. Program People to People Internat. to Chinese Assn. Mental Health and Chinese Assn. for Sci. and Tech. of People's Republic of China in Beijing, Shanghai and Kunming, 1994; del. from Am. Sch. Counselor's Assn. and Citizen Amb. Program of People to People Internat. to 1st U.S./Russia Joint Conf. on Edn., Moscow, 1994. Mem. Victoria Fine Arts Assn. (pres. 1964-66), 1963-68; mem. Brazosport Fine Arts Coun., Lake Jackson, 1970-73, Brazoria County Hist. Mus., Angleton, Tex., 1990—; del. Tex. Gov.'s Conf. on Arts, Austin, 1966-68; del. Dem. Precinct Conv., Lake Jackson, 1976, 77, 93, Brazoria County Dem. Conv., Angleton, 1977, Tex. Dem. Conv., San Antonio, 1977; deacon 1st Bapt. Ch., Lake Jackson, 1989, also youth worker. Scholar PTA, Victoria, 1966. Mem. Music Educator's Nat. Conf., NEA (del. 1977-79), Am. Sch. Counselors Assn., Nat. Career Devel. Assn., Assn. for Specialists in Group Work, Assn. for Measurement and Evaluation in Counseling and Devel., Tex. Assn. for Measurement and Evaluation in Counseling and Devel., Tex. Career Guidance Assn., Tex. Sch. Counselors Assn., Tex. Assn. for Counseling and Devel. (senator 1979-82, legis. com. 1984-87), Tex. Music Educators Assn. (state bd. dirs. 1964-68, dist. choral chmn. 1964-68), Tex. State Schrs. Assn., Brazosport Edn. Assn. (pres. 1977-78), Brazoria County Assn. Counseling and Devel. (legis. chmn. 1984—), Rotary (Brazosport club, Paul Harris fellow 1988). Avocations: gardening, flying. Home: 111 Oyster Bend Ln Lake Jackson TX 77566-3105 Office: PO Box Z Freeport TX 77542-1926

BASKIR, GEOFFREY SCOTT, airport planner; b. Rochester, N.Y., June 10, 1956; s. Emanuel and Helene (Reiser) B.; m. Regina, June 9, 1984; 1 child, Emma Jane. BS, MIT, 1978; MS, Stanford U., 1979. Analyst Peat Marwick Mitchell & Co., San Mateo, Calif., 1979-80; project planner Dallas-Ft. Worth Internat. Airport, 1981-88; staff planner Turner, Collie & Braden, Inc., Dallas, 1988-90; supr. airport planner Parsons, Brinckerhoff, Quade & Douglas, Inc., Herndon, Va., 1990—. Mem. ASCE (pres. nat. capital sect. 2003—), Am. Planning Assn., N.Am. SIMMOD Users Group. Jewish. Avocations: cartooning, soccer, distance running, internet radio broadcasting. Office: Parsons Mgmt Cons Inc Ste 200 45045 Aviation Dr Sterling VA 20166

BASKIR, LAWRENCE M. chief judge; b. N.Y.C., Jan. 10, 1938; s. Philip and Florence B.; m. Marna S. Tucker, May 13, 1973; children: Cecily Elizabeth, Micah Tucker. AB magna cum laude, Princeton U., 1959; LL.B., Harvard U., 1962. Bar: N.Y. 1963, D.C. 1964, U.S. Supreme Ct. 1968. Assoc. Weaver and Glassie, 1963-65; counsel Ho. of Reps. Judiciary Com., 1965-66; chief counsel Constl. Rights Subcom., U.S. Senate, 1968-74; dir. Presidential Clemency, Bd., 1974-75; faculty fellow U. Notre Dame, 1975-77; dep. asst. sec. Dept. Treasury, Washington, 1977-79; legis. dir. Sen. Bill Bradley, 1979-80; sole practice Washington, 1981-93; prin. dep. gen. counsel U.S. Army, 1994-98; judge U.S. Ct. Federal Claims, Wash., D.C., 1998-2000, chief judge, 2000—. Adj. prof. Georgetown Law Center, Cath. U. Law Sch.; cons. U.S. Senate Intelligence Com., ABA Contbr. articles to profl. jours.; author: Reconciliation After Vietnam, 1977, Chance and Circumstance: The Draft, the War and the Vietnam Generation, 1978. Grantee, Ford Found., 1975—77. Office: 717 Madison Pl NW Washington DC 20439-0002

BASKIYAR, SANJEEV, engineering educator;, U.S.1986; m. Smita Baskiyar, 1995; 1 child, Swati. BSc in Physics, St. Xavier's Coll., Ranchi, 1981; B in Electronics and Comm., Indian Inst. Sci., Bangalore, India, 1984; MSEE, U. Minn., 1988, PhD, 1993. Asst. computer engr. Tata Engring. & Locomotive Co., Jamshedpur, India, 1984—86; sr. software engr. O'Systems/Unisys Corp., Mpls., 1993—96; asst. prof. We. Mich. U., Kalamazoo, 1996—99, Auburn U., Ala., 1999—. Contbr. articles. Mem.: IEEE. Avocations: tennis, music, bicycling. Home: 1309 Gatewood Dr #2018 Auburn AL 36830 Office: Auburn Univ Dept Computer Sci & Software Engring Auburn AL 36849 Office Fax: 334-844-6329. E-mail: baskiyar@eng.auburn.edu.

BASKOUS, ATHAN A. retired civil engineer; b. Schenectady, N.Y., June 12, 1921; s. Alexander and Beatrice B.; m. Dena Julia Xanthos, Feb. 7, 1945 (dec. Dec. 1968), children: Alexander, Patricia; m. Bertha Esther Caranikas, Aug. 26, 1973. B in Civil Engring., Cornell U., 1943; MPH, U. Mich., 1955. Profl. engr. N.Y., profl. land surveyor, N.Y. Engr. Havens & Emerson, Cleve., 1946-49, N.Y. State Dept. Health, Albany, 1949-55, regional engr., 1955-71; regional dir. N.Y. State Dept. Environ. Conservation, Albany, 1971-78, regional engr. Schenectady, 1978-83; cons., 1983—95. Mem. Sr. Concert Orch., Schenectady; bd. dirs. St. George Greek Orthodox Ch., Schenectady; merit badge counselor Boy Scouts Am., Schenectady, 1950-55. 1st Lt. U.S. Army, 1943-46. Mem. APHA, Adirondack Water Works Assn., Classical Mandolin Soc. Am., Adirondack Fiddlers, Chi Epsilon. Avocations: violin restoration, violinist, mandolinist, tennis, travel. Home: 825 Jamaica Rd Schenectady NY 12309-6411

BASLER, THOMAS G. librarian, administrator, educator; b. Cleve., Mar. 8, 1940; s. Gordon Fred and Bertha Elizabeth (Gerspacher) B.; m. Samille Jones, Nov. 25, 1986; children from previous marriage: William T., Elizabeth E., Charles G. BEd, U. Miami, Coral Gables, Fla., 1962; MS, Fla. State U., 1964; PhD, Laurence U., Santa Barbara, Calif., 1977. Intern Emory U., Atlanta, 1965; asst. prof., librarian Insts. Marine Scis., Miami, Fla., 1966-68; librarian Am. Mus. Natural History, N.Y.C., 1968-70, N.Y. Acad. Medicine, N.Y.C., 1970-72; prof., dir. library Med. Coll. Ga., Augusta, 1972-91; dir. libr. and learning resources ctrs. Med. U. S.C., Charleston, 1991—, dir. environ. hazards assessment program info. sys., 1994—, chair dept. of libr. sci. and informatics. Cons. Abbott Pharm. Co., North Chicago, Ill., 1973-83; chmn. Regents Acad. Com. on Libraries, Univ. System Ga., 1984-85; mem. adv. council SE Atlantic Regional Med. Library, 1984— Author: Health Science Librarianship, 1977, Medical School Library Directorship, 1977, also articles Mem. Consortium So. Biomed. Libraries, Inc. (sec.-treas. 1983—) Home: 1205 Manor Ln Mount Pleasant SC 29464-5188 Office: Med U SC 171 Ashley Ave Charleston SC 29425-0001

BASMAJIAN, JOHN VAROUJAN, medical scientist, educator, physician; b. Constantinople, Turkey, June 21, 1921; came to Can., 1923, naturalized, 1927; s. Mihran and Mary (Evelian) B.; m. Dora Belle Lucas, Oct. 4, 1947; children: Haig, Nancy, Sally. MD with honors, U. Toronto, 1945; LLD (hon.), Queen's U., 1999; DSc (hon.), McMaster U., 2001. Intern Toronto Gen. Hosp., 1945; surg. resident Sunnybrook Hosp. and Hosp. for Sick Children, Toronto, 1946-48; from lectr. to prof. U. Toronto, 1949-57; prof. anatomy, chmn. dept. anatomy Queen's U., Kingston, Ont., 1957-69; prof., dir. regional rehab. rsch. and tng. ctr. Emory U., Atlanta, 1969-77; prof. medicine McMaster U., Hamilton, Ont., Can., 1977-86, prof. emeritus, 1986—; dir. rehab. ctr. Chedoke-McMaster Hosps., Hamilton, 1977-86. Exec. sec. Banting Rsch. Found., Toronto, 1954-57; chmn. rsch. com. Fitness Coun. Can., Ottawa, Ont., 1965-69; spl. cons. med. rsch. Ga. Inst. Tech., Atlanta, 1984-90; dir. rsch. and tng. grants Ea. Seal Rsch. Inst., Toronto, 1990 95; bd. dirs. Can. Physiotherapy Found., Toronto, 1984-89; lectureships in Europe, Asia, South Am., Australia, Japan, others. Author 11 med. sci. and clin. books in multiple edits. and transls., 1953—; editor 9 med. clin. books in multiple edits., and transls., 1977—; series editor: Rehabilitation Medicine Library, 24 vols., 1977—; editl. bd. Am. Jour. Phys. Medicine, 1968-90, Am. Jour. Anatomy, 1971-74, Electromyography and Clin. Neurophysiology, 1966-85, Electro-diagnostic-therapy, Physiotherapy Can., 1979-84, Jour. Motor Behavior, 1980—, Med Post; assoc. editor Anat. Record, 1970-73, 77—, BMA Audiotape Series, 1970-77; contbr. articles to profl. jours.; prodr. several motion pictures; inventor sci. and med. devices and techniques. Mem. and chmn. Bd. Edn., Kingston, Ont., 1960-68; founding chmn. bd. govs. St. Lawrence Coll. Applied Arts and Tech., Ont., 1964-69. Served to capt. M.C., Can. Army, 1943-46 Decorated officer Order of Ont., officer Order of Can.; recipient awards including Starr Gold medal U. Toronto, 1957, Kabakjian award Armenian Youth Fedn., 1967; NRC (Can.) vis. scientist Soviet Acad. Scis., 1963, Henry Gray Laureate, 1991,. Fellow Am. Acad. Angiology, Royal Coll. Physicians (Can.), Royal Coll. Physicians and Surgeons (Glasgow, hon.), Royal Coll. Physicians (Edinburgh, hon.), Physicians Coll. Rehabilitative Medicine (Australia, hon., Edinburgh, hon.); mem. Am. Assn. Anatomists (pres. 1985-86, Henry Gray Laureate award 1991), Can. Assn. Anatomists (founding, sec. 1965-69, J.C.B. Grant award 1985), Am. Congress Rehab. Medicine (Gold Key award 1977, Coulter lectr. 1988), Biofeedback Soc. Am. (founding, pres. 1978-79), Internat. Soc. Electromyographic Kinesiology (founding, pres. 1955-60), Order St. John of Jerusalem (hon. life mem.), Am. Orthopedic Foot Soc. (hon. life), Australian Biofeedback Soc. (hon. life), Venezuelan Biofeedback Soc. (hon. life), Mex. Soc. Anatomy (hon. life), Columbian Assn. Phys. Medicine (hon. life), Physiotherapy Assn. North Greece (hon. pres. 1995—). Avocations: travel, music, gardening, writing. Office: McMaster U Med Sch Box 2000 Hamilton ON Canada L8N 3Z5

BASMAJIAN, THOMAS STEPHEN, actor, performing arts association administrator; s. John and Frances Basmajian. BS Advanced Comm. Tech.,Interactive Multimedia, Design, Wilmington Coll., Wilmington, Del., 2001—02; AAS, The Art Inst. of Phila., Phila., PA, 1991—93. Pres. & ceo Zephyr Media, Inc., Mt. Holly, NJ, 1998—; sr. faculty mem. The Art Inst. of Phila., Phila., 1994—2003. Prodr.(writer, performer): (musical) My Dear. Recipient Valedictorian, The Art Inst. of Philladelphia, 1993, The Ruth VanYoungman Award, The Art Inst. of Phila., 1993, Outstanding Achievement Award, 1993, Gold Bond Award, Wilmington Coll., 2002; scholar Presdl. Scholarship, The Art Inst. of Phila., 1993. Mem.: AAUP (assoc.). Achievements include patents pending for A new system for public global electronic communications and commerce; A new human computer interface; New computer and mobile device designs. Office: Zephyr Media Incorporated PO Box 4076 Mount Holly NJ 08060

BASNAKIAN, ALEXEI G. biochemist, researcher; b. Rostov-na-Donu, Russia, Oct. 19, 1953; s. Georgiy A. and Irina A. Basnakian; m. Marina V. Philimonova, May 4, 1958; children:Serguei A., Ekaterina A. Grigoriants, Diana A. MD, Sechenov Moscow Med. Acad., 1976; PhD, Russian Acad. Med. Scis., Moscow, 1981. Med. diplomate Russia. Sr. scientist Russian Acad. Med. Scis., Moscow, 1981—92; vis. scientist Nat. Ctr. Toxicological Rsch., Jefferson, Ark., 1992—96; asst. prof. U. Ark. Med Scis., Little Rock, 1996—. Cons. Coun. Healthcare Advisors, N.Y.C. Contbr. articles to profl. jours. Mem.: FASEB (assoc.), Am. Soc. Nephrology (assoc.). Achievements include patents for method of DNA isolation. Office: U Ark Med Scis 4301 W Markham St Box #501 Little Rock AR 72205 Office Fax: 501-257-4822. Business E-Mail: basnakianalexeig@uams.edu.

BASNETT, MARGARET G. reading and language arts educator, consultant; b. Avoca, Iowa, Oct. 7, 1946; d. Fay and Mary Gertrude (Grote) Osborn; m. Richard John Socwell, Mar. 11, 1971 (div. May 1979); 1 child, Benjamin Adam;

m. William C. Basnett, Dec. 19, 1999. BS, Ohio State U., Columbus, 1968; MS, U. Wis., 1979. Cert. reading specialist, libr. media specialist, Spanish and French tchr., Ariz. Tchr. French Mason (Ohio) Pub. Schs., 1969-70; tchr. Spanish and French St. Matthias Cath. Girls H.S., L.A., 1970-71; tchr. French Whitewater (Wis.) Pub. Schs., 1971-72, tchr. Spanish, 1972-78; reading specialist Chilton (Wis.) Pub. Schs., 1978-79, Tolleson (Ariz.) Elem. Schs., 1979-80; tchr. reading and Spanish Deer Valley Unified Schs., Phoenix, 1980-88; tchr. reading Rio Salado C.C., Phoenix, 1987-91, tchr. lang. arts, 1989-93, tchr. social studies, 1993-96, libr. media specialist, 1996-2000. State forensics judge Whitewater Pub. Schs., 1974—; test designer Deer Valley Reading Curriculum Com., Phoenix, 1986-87, participant lang. arts pilot program Deer Valley Unified Sch. Dist., 1989; designer integrated social studies curriculum, Hillcrest Mid. Sch., Deer Valley Unified Pub. Schs., Phoenix, 1994-96; ret. Deer Valley Unified Sch. Dist., 2000. Recipient grant Deer Valley Edn. Found., Inc., 1992. Mem.: Ariz. Quilters Guild (chair Calico Cut-Ups chpt. 2003, cmty. svcs. coord. Calico Cut-Ups chpt. 2002). Democrat. Avocations: reading, quilting, machine embroidery, cross-stitch, travel.

BASNIGHT, MARC, state senator, small business owner, construction executive; b. May 13, 1947; m. Sandy Tillett; children: Vicki, Caroline. Grad. high sch.; degree (hon.), Chowan Coll., 1998; JD (hon.), U. N.C., 1999. Senator State of N.C., 1985—; pres. pro tempore N.C. Senate, Raleigh, NC, 1993—; part owner Basnight's Lone Cedar Cafe, 2002—; pres., ptnr., part owner Basnight Constrn. Co., 1992—. Recipient Pres.'s Pub. Svc. award Nature Conservancy, 1989. Mem. Masons, Lions (Manteo chpt.). Methodist. Office: Legislative Bldg Room 2007 Raleigh NC 27601-2808*

BASON, GEORGE R., JR., lawyer; b. N.Y.C., 1954; AB magna cum laude, Harvard U., 1975, JDcum laude, 1978. Bar: N.Y. 1979, U.S. Dist. Ct. (so. and ea. dists.) N.Y. 1979; cert. Avocat à la Cour de Paris 1992. Assoc. Davis Polk & Wardwell, N.Y.C., 1978-85, ptnr., 1986—. Mem. ABA, Bar Assn. City N.Y., Phi Beta Kappa. Office: Davis Polk & Wardwell 450 Lexington Ave New York NY 10017-3982

BASQUIN, MARY SMYTH (KIT BASQUIN), museum administrator; b. NYC, July 3, 1941; d. Joseph Percy and Virginia Sandford (Gibbs) Smyth; m. Maurice Hanson Basquin, Feb. 4, 1967 (div. Feb. 1984); children: Susan, Peter Lee, William. BA, Goucher Coll., Balt., 1963; MA, Ind. U., 1970. Asst. dir. pub. rels. Indpls. Mus. Art, 1971-72; dir. Washignton Gallery, Frankfort, Ind., 1972-79, Indpls., 1977-79, Kit Basquin Gallery, Milw., 1981-83; curator edn. Haggerty Mus. Marquette U., Milw., 1988-95; dir. outreach Milw. Wis. Humanities Coun., 1995-98; curator Marvin Lowe Retrospective, Ind. U. Art Mus., 1998; mktg. William Doyle Galleries, NYC, 1999, exhbn. mgr., 2000; rsch. assoc. Bklyn. Mus. Art, 2000; asst. print study rm. Met. Mus. Art, NYC, 2000—. Instr. art history Concordia U., Mequon, Wis., 1991, instr. Marquette U., Gaza, 1996; pres. contemporary art soc. Milw. Art Mus., 1986-87, prints and drawings subcom., 1991-99, pres. Print Forum, 1996-97; mem. program com. Midwest Mus. conf., Milw., 1992. Wis. editor: New Art Examiner, 1980—81; mem. St. Barts Singers, 1999—; contbr. articles to profl. jours. Trustee Ten Chimneys Found., Genesee Depot, Wis., 1997-99; mem. adv. bd. Ten Chimneys Found., 2000-01. Mem. Univ. Club NY, Univ. Club Milw. Episcopalian. Avocations: singing, fashion, theater, swimming. Home: 1675 York Ave Apt 19A New York NY 10128-6756

BASS, AARON, school system administrator; b. Phila., May 26, 1950; m. Jade King, July 3, 1999; children: Naja Killebrew, Clyde Killebrew, Aaron III, Jared, Sharita. BA in Psychology, Lincoln (Pa.) U., 1972; MA in Social Psychology, Temple U., Phila., 1974; AA in Data Processing, Phila. Cmty. Coll., 1982; MDiv, Luth. Theol. Seminary, Phila., 1998. Learning specialist Urban Career Edn. Ctr., Phila., 1974; rsch. asst. Sch. Dist. Phila., 1974-94, rsch. assoc., 1994-96, rsch. asst., 1996-2000, pupil data analyst, 2000—. Author numerous studies and evaluations. Tchr. Germantown Cmty. Photography Workshop, Phila., 1972-74; elder Eagles Nest Christian Fellowship, Phila., 1999-2001, eler Mt. Airy Ch. of God in Christ, 2001—. Temple U. scholar, 1972; recipient award Most Unique Reporting Technique for Career Edn. Accumulative Report, Am. Ednl. Rsch. Assn., 1980. Mem.: Phi Delta Kappa, Omega Psi Phi. Avocations: running, biking, swimming, reading, travel. Home: 6025 Morton St Philadelphia PA 19144 Office: Sch Dist Phila 2120 Winter St Rm 414 Philadelphia PA 19103 E-mail: abass@voicenet.com., abass@phila.k12.pa.us.

BASS, BETTY ZOE PASSMORE (MRS. ERIC BASS), artist; b. Burlington, Wis., Mar. 26, 1926; d. Dempster Stewart and Bettina (Rakow) Passmore; student U. Ariz., 1943, U. Miami, 1944-47; B.A., UCLA, 1955; M.A., Stanford U., 1963; m. Eric Bass, Oct. 10, 1948. Designer, partner haute couture firm Eric Bass, Beverly Hills, Calif., 1949-53; fine art painting, Lakeside and Los Angeles, Calif., 1953— ; exhibited UCLA Art Gallery, 1955, Art Center, LaJolla, Calif., 1957, So. Calif. Exposition, 1961; Oriental art research travel to Japan, Thailand, India, 1959-60. Chmn. opening night dinners San Diego Opera Guild, also chmn. LaJolla Assos.; mem. Asian arts com. Fine Arts Soc.; v.p. San Diego com. Los Angeles Philharmonic; v.p. Women's Assn. Salk Inst.; chmn. benefit ball San Diego Symphony, 1971; chmn. dinners Civic Light Opera. Bd. dirs. U. Calif. at San Diego Hosps. Aux.; bd. dirs. women's com. San Diego Symphony Assn. Named a San Diego Woman of Elegance, 1972; Makua life patroness, 1972; chmn. Social Service League benefit for Darlington House, 1976; chmn. benefit fashion show for U. San Diego, 1979; chmn. Women of Dedication Benefit, Door of Hope, 1985. Mem. Soc. Mayflower Descs., DAR, Social Service League, La Jolla Civic Orch. Assn., Old Globe Theater 400, Klee Wyk Soc. Mus. Man, La Jolla Mus. Contemporary Art, World Affairs Council, Country Friends, Starlight Women's Assn. (v.p.), U. San Diego Aux. (v.p.), Delta Gamma. Club: Stanford (San Diego). Home: PO Box 14407 Palm Desert CA 92255-4407

BASS, CHARLES F. congressman; b. Jan. 8, 1952; s. Perkins and Katharine J. Bass; m. Lisa L.; children: Lucy, Jonathan. AB, Dartmouth Coll., 1974. Field worker Congressman William S. Cohen, 1974; legis. asst. Congressman David F. Emery, 1975-76, chief of staff, 1976-79; v.p. High Std., Inc., Dublin, N.H., 1980-94; chmn. Columbia Archtl. Products, Beltsville, Md., 1980-94; mem. U.S. Congress from 2nd N.H. dist., 1995—; mem. ho. budget com., energy and commerce com.,mem. working groups on nat. security and govt. reform; vice chmn. subcom. on civil svc., subcom. on govt. mgmt., info. and tech. Trustee N.H. Higher Edn. Assistance Found., Monandnock Conservancy, N.H. Humanities Coun. Mem. Monadnock Rotary (pres. 1992-93), Amoskeag Vets., Masons. Republican. Office: US Ho of Reps 2421 Rayburn HOB Washington DC 20515-2902 also: 142 N Main St Concord NH 03301-4917 also: 170 Main St Nashua NH 03060-2731 also: 78 Main St Littleton NH 03561-4012*

BASS, EVELYN ELIZABETH, educator; b. Magnolia, Ark., Sept. 28, 1948; d. Marvin and Catherine (Grissom) Scott; m. Burlin Lee Hughes, July 17, 1971 (div. Aug. 1984); children: Tionna Latrice, Lee Otis Williams Jr.; m. John W. Bass Sr., July 23, 2000. BA, Ark. Bapt. Coll., 1971; MS in Edn., Ouachita Bapt. Coll., Arkadelphia, Ark., 1988; postgrad., U. Little Rock, 2000—02. Tchr. Pulaski County Spl. Sch. Dist., Little Rock, 1971-97; exec. dir. Lenea's Children's Cottage, Little Rock, 1997—; advisor Choice Care Inc., Little Rock, 1998—; owner, pres. Evelyn's Tutoring Svc., Little Rock, 1998—; presch. tchr. Graceland Kids' Educare Ctr., 2000—. Child devel. assoc. instr., advisor Grace Holiness Christian Acad., 1999—, also head instr.; cons. in field. Author, composer: (poetry and songs) The Printed Word, 1993; (CDs) The Printed Word, 2003, Never Say Never, 2003; author: The Printed Word/Woman of God, 1995. Traffic judge Willard Proctor, Jr. Campaign, 1996, cir. ct. judge, 2000. Democrat. Apostolic. Avocations: singing, songwriting, writing fiction. Home: 2918 Dorset Dr Little Rock AR 72204 Office: c/o Pastor LD Jenkins Scott Adminstr 7601 Scott Hamilton Dr Little Rock AR 72209-3167

BASS, GEORGE FLETCHER, retired archaeology educator; b. Columbia, S.C., Dec. 9, 1932; s. Robert Duncan and Virginia (Wauchope) B.; m. Ann Singletary, Mar. 19, 1960; children: Gordon Wauchope, Alan Joseph. MA, Johns Hopkins U., 1955; PhD, U. Pa., 1964; PhD (hon.), Bogazici U., Istanbul, Turkey, 1987, U. Liverpool, 1998. Asst. prof. U. Pa., Phila., 1964-68, assoc. prof., 1968-73; prof. archaeology Tex. A&M U., College Station, 1976-80, disting. prof., 1980-2000, George T. and Gladys H. Abell prof. nautical archaeology, 1986-2000, Yamini Family prof., 1994-2000, prof. emeritus, 2001—. Dir. excavations of ancient shipwrecks off Turkish coast, 1960—; pres. Inst. Nautical Archaeology, 1972-82, 96-98. Author: Archaeology Under Water, 1966, Cape Gelidonya, 1967, History of Seafaring, 1972, Archaeology Beneath the Sea, 1975, Yassi Ada I, 1982, Ships and Shipwrecks of the Americas, 1988; adv. editor Am. Jour. Archaeology, 1987-99, Archaeology, 1987—, Internat. Jour. Nautical Archaeology, 1987—, Nat. Geog. Rsch., 1987-94. Lt. U.S. Army, 1957-59, Korea. Recipient Centennial award Nat. Geog. Soc., 1988, La Gorce Gold medal, 1979, Lowell Thomas award Explorers Club, 1986, Nat. Medal of Sci., 2002 (presented by Pres. George W. Bush); named one of Outstanding Young Men of Yr., Jaycees, 1967. Mem. Inst. Nautical Archaeology (pres. 1973-82), Archaeol. Inst. Am. (Gold medal for disting. archaeol. achievement 1986), Soc. for Hist. Archaeology (J.C. Harrington medal 1999), Nat. Maritime Hist. Soc., Mothers Against Drunk Driving. Presbyterian. Avocation: classical music. Home: 1600 Dominik Dr College Station TX 77840-3623 Office: Tex A&M U Nautical Archaeology College Station TX 77843-0001 E-mail: gfbass@neo.tamu.edu.

BASS, JAMES ORIN, lawyer; b. Sumner County, Tenn., July 12, 1910; s. Francis Marion and Sadie (Dunn) B.; m. Susanne Warner, June 9, 1937; children: James Orin, Edwin Warner, Francis Marion II, Susan Richardson. BA, U. of South, 1931; LL.B., Harvard, 1934. Bar: Tenn. 1934. Ptnr. Bass, Berry & Sims, Nashville, 1937—. Mem. Tenn. Ho. of Reps. from Davidson County, 1936-38, Tenn. Senate, 1940-42. Served to lt. col. AUS, 1942-45, ETO. Mem. ABA, Tenn. Bar Assn., Nashville Bar Assn. (pres. 1951), Am. Coll. Trial Lawyers. Presbyterian. Home: 4412 Georgian Pl Nashville TN 37215-4528 Office: Bass Berry & Sims PLC 315 Deaderick St Ste 2700 Nashville TN 37238-3001 E-mail: jbasssr@bassberry.com.

BASS, LYNDA D. retired medical/surgical nurse, retired nursing educator; b. Suffolk, Va. d. H.M. and Katie Lea Bass. BSN, N.C. Agrl. and Tech. State U., Greensboro, 1968; MS in Nursing, Cath. U. Am., 1974; Gen. Surgery Clin. Specialist, George Washington U. Hosp., Washington. Cert. BCLS instr., CPR instr.-trainer. Med. surg. nurse Walter Reed Army Hosp., Washington; clin. instr. Suburban Hosp., Bethesda, Md.; edn./tng. quality assurance coord. Howard U. Hosp., Washington; clin. educator Providence Hosp., Washington; edn. specialist Vets. Affairs Md. Healthcare Sys., Balt.; ret., 2003. Coord. clin. staff Devel. Mount Vernon Hosp., Alexandria, Va. Capt. USAR, 1967—71, Vietnam. Mem. Nat. Nursing Staff Devel. Assn., Vietnam Vets. Am., Chi Eta Phi.

BASS, MARY LEE, education educator, administrator; b. Phila., Jan. 1, 1947; d. Leon Jr. and Mary Katherine (Magarian) Attarian; m. Harris Merrill Bass, July 1, 1973; 1 child, Mandy Michelle. BS, Millersville U. Pa., 1969; MS in Edn., Monmouth U., 1992; EdD., Rutgers U. Cert. tchr., N.J., Pa.; cert. reading specialist, N.J. Pers. clk. Jefferson Med. Ctr., Phila., 1965-67; elem. tchr. Lancaster (Pa.) City Schs., 1969-71; transition elem. tchr. Springfield (Pa.) Sch. Dist., 1971-77; lang. arts tchr. Benchmark Sch., Media, Pa., 1987-90; reading lab. instr. Brookdale C.C., Lincroft, N.J., 1990-92; adj. instr., dir. Reading Ctr. Monmouth U., West Long Branch, N.J., 1992—. Mem. steering com. N.J. Consortium for Placement Testing, 1994—. Contbr. articles to profl. jours. Exec. bd. dirs. Adult Edn., Marple Newtown, Pa., 1987; vol. program coord. Neighborhood Model Cities, Lancaster, 1971; vol. tchr.'s asst. Headstart, Lancaster, 1969. Mem. Internat. Reading Assn., N.J. Reading Assn., Coll. Reading Assn., Phi Delta Kappa, Alpha Upsilon Alpha, Kappa Delta Pi. Avocations: reading, writing, concerts, piano, crossword puzzles. Office: Monmouth U Coll Skills Ctr Cedar Ave West Long Branch NJ 07764 E-mail: mbass@monmouth.edu.

BASS, NORMAN HERBERT, physician, scientist, university and hospital administrator, health care executive; b. N.Y.C., July 10, 1936; s. Julius and Celia (Annex) B.; m. Kathleen Bass; children: Joel Martin, Rebecca Pier, Robert Farrell. BS (Ford Found. scholar 1953, N.Y. State Regents scholar 1954), Swarthmore (Pa.) Coll., 1958; MD, Yale U., 1962. Diplomate: Am. Bd. Psychiatry and Neurology. Intern Med. U. Wash. Hosp., Seattle, 1962-63; resident in neurology U. Va. Hosp., Charlottesville, 1963-65; clin. fellow in neurology Mass. Gen. Hosp., Boston, 1965-67; NIH fellow Harvard U. Med. Sch., 1965-67; from asst. prof. to prof. neurology U. Va. Med. Sch., Charlottesville, 1967-79, dir. Clinic Neurosci. Rsch. Ctr., 1973-79; prof. neurology, chmn. dept. Albert B. Chandler Med. Center, U. Ky., Lexington, 1979-85; neurologist in chief Univ. Hosp., 1979-85; dir. lab. neurochemistry Sanders-Brown Ky. Rsch. Ctr. Aging, 1979-85; dean Sch. Medicine, prof. dept. Neurology Med. Coll. Ga., 1985-86; prof. neurology, rehab. medicine, chief div. rehab. medicine U. Md. Sch. Medicine, Balt., 1986-89; prof. neurology, rehab. medicine U. Pitts., 1989-92; sr. v.p., chief med. officer Harmarville Rehab. Ctr. Inc., Pitts., 1989-92; prof. pediatrics and neurology Sch. Medicine, Boston U., 1992—; sr. v.p. med. affairs Franciscan Childrens Hosp. and Rehab Ctr., 1992-94; pvt. practice Cape and Islands, 1994—. Cons. neurology VA Med. Ctr., Lexington, Augusta, Balt., Pitts., Boston; chmn. nat. rsch. program merit rev. bd. in neurobiology VA, 1978-81; mem. bd. sci. advisers Delta Regional Primate Ctr., Tulane U., 1978-81, chmn., 1979-81; chmn. profl. adv. bd. Epilepsy Assn. VA Ky., 1978-82; chmn. study sect. Nat. Inst. Disability and Rehab. Rsch., 1986-89; program surveyor Comm. on Accreditation of Rehab. Facilities, 1987-92; mem. panel co-chari Task Force Med. Rehab. Rsch. Office Sci. Policy, NIH, 1990; vis. prof. pharmacology U. Goteborg, Sweden, 1972-73. Assoc. editor Neurochem. Rsch. Jour., Jour. Neurol. Rehab.; mem. editorial bd. Stroke jour.; contbr. numerous articles to med. jours. Served to maj. M.C. USAR, 1963-69. Recipient Rsch. Career Devel. award NIH, 1971-75, Nat. Inst. Neurologic Disease rsch. fellow in neurochemistry, 1965-67; Markle scholar in acad. medicine, 1969-74 Fellow Am. Acad. Neurology (S. Weir Mitchell rsch. award 1967, chmn. sect. on geriatrics 1986, sect. on neurol. rehab. 1987), AAAS, Stroke Coun. of Am. Heart Assn., Am. Acad. Cerebral Palsy and Devel. Medicine; mem. Am. Assn. U. Profs. Neurology (v.p. 1980-81), Am. Assn. Anatomists, Am. Soc. Neurochemistry, Am. Soc. Neuro. Rehab., Soc. Neurosci., Internat. Soc. Neurochemistry, Child Neurology Soc., Am. Neurol. Assn., Assn. Rsch. Nervous and Mental Disease, Nat. Head Injury Found., Inc., AMA, Am. Congress Rehab. Medicine, Nat. Assn. Rehab. Facilities Inc., Nat. Multiple Sclerosis Soc., Nat. Head Injury Found., Alpha Omega Alpha. Office: PO Box 1050 West Falmouth MA 02574

BASS, PAUL, pharmacology educator; b. Winnipeg, Man., Can., Aug. 12, 1928; came to U.S., 1958; s. Benjamin and Sarah B.; m. Ruth Zipursky, May 31, 1953; children: Stuart, Susan. BS in Pharmacy, U. B.C., 1953, MA in Pharmacology, 1955; PhD in Pharmacology, McGill U., 1957, fellow in Biochemistry, 1957-58; fellow in Physiology, Mayo Found., 1958-60. Research asst. Ayerst, McKenna & Harrison, Can., 1956; assoc. lab. dir. Parke, Davis & Co., 1960-70; prof. pharmacology Sch. Pharmacy and Sch. Medicine, U. Wis., Madison, 1970-2000, prof. emeritus, 2001—. Mem. editorial bd.: Am. Jour. Physiology, 1976-79, 81-92, Jour. Pharmacology and Exptl. Therapeutics, 1980-99 ; contbr. chpts. to books, articles to profl. jours. Mem. Am. Soc. Pharmacology and Exptl. Therapeutics, Am. Gastroent. Assn. Home: 777 Highland Ave Madison WI 53705-2222 E-mail: pbass@wisc.edu.

BASS, ROBERT OLIN, retired manufacturing executive; b. Denver, July 22, 1917; s. Olin R. and Cora (Durham) B.; m. Isabelle Cantrell, Mar. 22, 1941; 1 dau., Susan. BS in Bus. Adminstrn., U. Denver, 1941. Pres. Eberhardt-Denver Co., 1956; exec. v.p., asst. gen. mgr. Morse Chain Co., Ithaca, N.Y., 1956-58, pres., 1958-66; group v.p. indsl. Borg-Warner Corp., 1966-68, exec. v.p., 1968-75, pres., 1975-79, vice chmn., 1979-82, chief oper. officer, 1975-80, dir., 1973-83; ret. Chmn. metals and machinery sect. Chgo. Met. Crusade of Mercy, 1968; mem. bus. adv. council Coll. Bus. Adminstrn., U. Denver, 1976-89; trustee Field Mus. Natural History, Chgo. Mem. Am. Mgmt. Assn. (v.p., chmn. gen. mgmt. planning council 1976-79, trustee 1979-82) Home: Chicago, Ill. Died Apr. 25, 2002.

BASS, RONALD, screenwriter; Screenplays include Code Name: Emerald, 1985, Black Widow, 1987, Gardens of Stone, 1987, (with Barry Morrow) Rainman, 1988 (Academy award best original screenplay 1988), Sleeping with the Enemy, 1991, (with Amy Tan) The Joy Luck Club, 1993; screenwriter, exec. prodr.: (with Al Franken) When a Man Loves a Woman, 1994, Dangerous Minds, 1995, (with Terry McMillan) Waiting to Exhale, 1995, My Best Friend's Wedding, 1997, What Dreams May Come, 1998, Stepmom, 1998, How Stella Got Her Groove Back, 1998, Entrapment, 1999, Snow Falling on Cedars, 1999, Passion of Mind, 1999. Office: Creative Artists Agency care Beth Swofford 9830 Wilshire Blvd Beverly Hills CA 90212-1825

BASS, SCOTT ARTHUR, community psychologist, gerontologist, educator; b. Detroit, Oct. 25, 1949; s. Seymour Everett and Marcia Louise B.; m. Elyse Ellen Jacob, June 1979; children: Stephen Jacob, Brian Jacob, Coleman Jacob. BA, U. Mich., 1971, MA, 1973, PhD, 1976. Assoc. prof. U. Mass., Boston, 1979-90, prof. coll. pub. and cmty. svc., 1990-96; dean grad. sch., vice provost rsch. U. Md., Balt. County, 1996—2002, dean grad. sch., vice provost rsch. and planning, 2002—, disting. prof. sociology and pub. policy, 1996—. Pres., co-dir. Ctr. Rsch. Inc., Newton, Mass., 1976-84; assoc. rsch. scientist Am. Insts. for Rsch., Washington, 1975; dir. gerontology program U. Mass., Boston, 1983-88, head gerontology ctr., 1984-96. Editor: Older and Active: How Americans Over 55 Are Contributing to Society, 1995; co-editor: Challenges of the Third Age: Meaning & Purpose in Later Life, 2002, Public Policy and the Old Age Revolution in Japan, 1996, International Perspectives on State and Family Support for the Elderly, 1993, Achieving a Productive Aging Society, 1990, Diversity in Aging: Challenges Facing Planners & Policymakers in the 1990s, Retirement Reconsidered: Economic and Social Roles for Older People, 1988; co-author: School Vandalism, 1980. Recipient Clark Tibbits award Assn. for Gerontology in Higher Edn., 1997; Fulbright rsch. scholar, Japan, 1994-95. Fellow Gerontological Soc. Am. Office: UMBC Grad Sch 1000 Hilltop Cir Baltimore MD 21250

BASS, STEVEN CRAIG, computer science educator; b. Indpls., July 29, 1943; s. Leland Ellsworth and Isabelle Frances (Ross) B.; m. Sara Ann Hiday, Sept. 4, 1965 (div. Apr. 1988); children: Leland Kai, Marshall Lynn; m. Kevyn Anne Salsburg, Jan. 2, 1989. BSEE, Purdue U., 1966, MSEE, 1968, PhD in Elec. Engring., 1971. Prof. elec. engring. Purdue U., Lafayette, Ind., 1971-88; prof. elec. and computer engring. George Mason U., Fairfax, Va., 1988-91; prin. engr. Mitre Corp., McLean, Va., 1988-91; prof. computer sci. and engring., chmn. dept. U. Notre Dame, Notre Dame, Ind., 1991-2000. Cons. Magnovox Co., Ft. Wayne, Ind., 1971-73, Admiral Corp., Chgo., 1973-76, Kimball Internat., Jasper, Ind., 1978-84, Tektronix Corp., Wilsonville, Oreg., 1987-88. Contbr. over 25 articles to profl. jours., delievered over 35 papers at sci. confs. Rescue officer Stockwell (Ind.) Vol. Fire Dept., 1985-88. Recipient numerous grants from NSF, USAF, IBM, Mitre Corp., others. Fellow IEEE (v.p. circuits and sys. soc. 1981, 91-93, mem. audio engring. soc.); mem. Tau Beta Pi. Roman Catholic. Achievements include 3 U.S. and 6 fgn. patents in the field of digital signal processing. Office: U Notre Dame Dept Computer Sci & Engring 384 Fitzpatrick Hl Engrng Notre Dame IN 46556-5637 E-mail: bass@cse.nd.edu

BASS, SUZANNE, social worker; b. Pittston, Pa., Aug. 9, 1949; d. Edward Spower and Lala Hamlin; m. John C. Bass, Sept. 9, 1971; children: Allison, Jayne. MSW, Marywood U., 1973, MPA, 1990. Diplomate Am. Bd. Clin. Social Work. Dir. social work, discharge planning dept. Cmty. Med. Ctr., Scranton, Pa., 1971—. Pvt. practice clin. social work, Clarks Summit, Pa. Fellow, HEW, 1972. Mem.: NASW (N..E. divsn. Scranton chpt. Social Worker of Yr. 1996), Sigma Phi Sigma. Home: RD 6 Box 6372 Moscow PA 18444 Office: Bass Counseling 311 Davis St Clarks Summit PA 18411 Fax: 570-586-3840. E-mail: jcb50262@aol.com.

BASSECHES, ROBERT TREINIS, lawyer; b. N.Y.C., Jan. 24, 1934; s. Jacob Thomas and Paula (Treinis) B.; m. Harriet Itkin, July 6, 1958; children: K.B., Joshua, Jessica. BA, Amherst Coll., 1955; LLB, Yale U., 1958. Bar: D.C. 1962, U.S. Ct. Appeals (D.C. cir.) 1962, U.S. Ct. Appeals (2d cir.) 1978, U.S. Ct. Appeals (4th cir.) 1998. Law clk. to judge David L. Bazelon U.S. Ct. Appeals (D.C. cir.), Washington, 1958-59; law clk. to justice Hugo L. Black U.S. Supreme Ct., Washington, 1959; assoc. Shea & Gardner, Washington, 1959-63, ptnr., 1963—, adminstrv. ptnr., 1980-86, chmn., exec. com., 1988-93. Trustee Green Acres Sch., Rockville, Md., 1971-76, pres., chmn. bd. trustees, 1973-75; pres. Chevy Chase (Md.) Village Citizens Assn., 1976. Mem. Maritime Adminstrv. Bar Assn. (pres. 1969-71, sec. 1967-69), Phi Beta Kappa. Office: Shea & Gardner Ste 800 1800 Massachusetts Ave NW Washington DC 20036-1872

BASSEN, NED HENRY, lawyer; b. N.Y.C., June 8, 1948; s. Harold Russell and Annette (Frankfeldt) B.; m. Susan Millington Campbell, July 2, 1999; children: Amanda Lee, Susannah Spence. BS, Cornell U., 1970, JD, 1973. Bar: N.Y. 1974, U.S. Dist. Ct. (so. and ea. dists.) N.Y. 1974, U.S. Dist. Ct. (ea. dist.) Mich. 1990, U.S. Dist. Ct. (we. dist.) N.Y. 1999, U.S. Ct. Appeals (11th cir.) 1984, U.S. Ct. Appeals (2d cir.) 2001. Assoc. Baer Marks & Upham, N.Y.C., 1975-80, Kelley Drye & Warren, N.Y.C., 1973-75, 80-83, ptnr., 1983-92; ptnr., labor group head Mudge Rose Guthrie Alexander & Ferdon, N.Y.C., 1993-95; ptnr., chair labor and employment group Hughes Hubbard & Reed LLP, N.Y.C., 1995—. Note and comment editor Cornell Law Rev., 1972-73. Mem. ABA (labor and employment law sect.), U.S. Coun. for Internat. Bus., Indsl. Rels. Com., Indsl. Rels. Rsch. Assn., N.Y. State Bar Assn. (labor law sect., com. on equal employment opportunity law), N.Y. State Mgmt. Attys. Conf. Office: Hughes Hubbard & Reed LLP 1 Battery Park Plz Fl 12 New York NY 10004-1482

BASSETT, ALTON HERMAN, health care company executive; b. Hartford, Conn., Nov. 27, 1930; s. Arthur and Martha B.; m. Joan Tolley, Jan. 7, 1956; children: Linda, Barbara. BA, Middlebury (Vt.) Coll., 1953. Plant chemist Am. Viscose Corp., Front Royal, Va., 1955-58; rsch. dir. Chicopee Inc., div. Johnson & Johnson, Milltown and Dayton, N.J., 1958-88, cons., 1988-94; ret., 1994. Patentee in field. Lt. USMC, 1953-55. Republican. Avocations: sailing, photography, radio control, sports cars. Home: 73 Harriet Dr Princeton NJ 08540-3934 Office: Products & Materials Rsch Johnson & Johnson Worldwide Dayton NJ 08810-0940

BASSETT, ANGELA, actress; b. N.Y.C., Aug. 16, 1958; Appeared in (plays) Colored People's Time, 1982, The Mystery Plays, 1984-85, The Painful Adventures of Pericles, Prince of Tyre, 1986-87, Joe Turner's Come and Gone, 1986 87, (Broadway) Ma Rainey's Black Bottom, (Broadway) Joe Turner's Come and Gone, 1988, King Henry IV Part I, 1987; (TV movies) Line of Fire: The Morris Dees Story, 1991, The Jacksons: An American Dream, 1992, A Century of Women, 1994); (films) F/X, 1986, Kindergarten Cop, 1990, Boyz N the Hood, 1991, City of Hope, 1991, Innocent Blood, 1992, Malcolm X, 1992, Passion Fish, 1992, What's Love Got to Do with It, 1993 (Acad. award nominee for best actress 1993, Golden Globe award best actress in a musical or comedy 1994), Strange Days, 1995, Panther, 1995, Waiting to Exhale, 1995, A Vampire in Brooklyn, 1995, Contact, 1997, How Stella Got Her Groove Back, 1998, Wings Against the Wind, 1999, Cosm, 1999, 50 Violins, 1999, Music of the Heart, 1999, Supernova, 2000. Office: care Doug Chapin Mgmt # 430 9465 Wilshire Blvd Beverly Hills CA 90212 also: Creative Artists Agy Wilshire Blvd Beverly Hills CA 90212-2613

BASSETT, CAROL ANN, journalism educator, writer; b. Langley AFB, Va., Mar. 2, 1953; d. William Brainard and Genevieve (Rivaldo) B. BA summa cum laude in Humanities, Ariz. State U., 1977; MA in Journalism, U. Ariz., 1982. Ptnr. Desert West News, Tucson, 1985-90; freelance writer Tucson, 1980-95; freelance writer for mags. Missoula, Mont., 1995-98; mem. faculty Sch. Journalism U. Mont., Missoula, 1996-98; mem. faculty Sch. Journalism and Comm. U. Oreg., Eugene, 1998—. Author: A Gathering of Stones: Journeys to the Edges of a Changing World, 2002, Essays in American Nature Writing, 2000, American Nature Writing, 2001; editor Tucson Weekly, 1989-90; contbr. numerous articles to nat. and internat. mags. including N.Y. Times. Recipient 2d Place Gen. Reporting award Ariz. Press Club, 1987, Gold medal for best environ. documentary Houston Internat. Film Festival, 1990, 1st Place Gen. Reporting award Ariz. Press Club, 1992, Silver Medal for Energy Issues documentary, Houston Internat. Film Festival, 1992; co-recipient Alfred I. duPont Columbia award, 1984-85, First Place award Investigative Reporting, 1986, 1st Place Polit. Reporting, 1989, First Amendment Journalism award, 1986; grantee Fund for Investigative Journalism, 1985, 87, Corp. for Pub. Broadcasting, 1988, Oxfam Am., 1991. Address: Sch Journalism Univ Oreg Eugene OR 97403

BASSETT, CHARLES WALKER, English language educator; b. Aberdeen, S.D., July 7, 1932; s. Wilfred Walker and Angela (Jewett) B.; m. Carol Hoffer, Sept. 15, 1956 (dec. Feb. 5, 1995); children— David, Elizabeth. BA, U. S.D., 1954, MA, 1956; PhD, U. Kans., 1964; LHD (hon.), U. S.D., 2000. Asst. instr. English U. S.D., 1954-56, U. Kans., 1958-64; instr. U. Pa., Phila., 1964-66, asst. prof., 1966-69; asst. prof. English Colby Coll., Waterville, Maine, 1969-74, assoc. prof., 1974-80, prof., 1980-83, Charles A. Dana prof. Am. studies and

English, 1983-93, Lee Family prof. Am. studies and English, 1993-99, dir. Am. studies, 1971-87, 89-96, chmn. dept. English, 1987-89, Lee family prof. Am. Studies & English emeritus, 1999—. Book rev. editor Am. Quar., 1983-91; assoc. editor: Ency. of Polit. Parties and Elections in the U.S., 1991; contbr. articles to profl. jours. Recipient Charles Bassett/Sr. Class Tchg. award, 1993, Charles Bassett award for dedicated svc. Colby Alumni Assn., 1997; S.L. Whitcomb fellow, 1961-62, U. Kans. fellow, 1962-63; U. Pa. Faculty Rsch. grantee, 1966-68; Humanities and Mellon grantee, 1973-96. Mem. MLA (New Eng. rep. del. assembly), Am. Studies Assn. (Mary C. Turpie award 1994). Democrat. Roman Catholic. Home: 9 Martin Ave Waterville ME 04901-4625 Office: Colby Coll Dept English Waterville ME 04901

BASSETT, CHUCK, English educator; b. Langdale, Ala., July 30, 1953; s. Earl and Evelyn Bassett; m. Beverly Cobb. MA in English, U. West Fla., 1979. Instr. English, head dept. Munson H.S., Milton, Fla., 1976-83, Ctrl. H.S., Milton, 1983— Sports editor Milton Press-Gazette, 1979-81; sports adj. writer Pensacola (Fla.) News Jour., 1981-85, N.W. Fla. Daily News, Ft. Walton Beach, 1987—; author: Once in a Lifetime, 2001. Missionary Trinidad, 1991, Jamaica, 1993, Russia, 1994, 99, Ukraine, 1996, Romania, 1996, 2000, Paris, 2002. Named Tchr. of the Yr., Ctrl. H.S., 1987, 94, 2001. Mem. Assn. of Am. Educators, Santa Rosa Profl. Educators. Republican. Avocations: golf, writing, collecting old-time radio shows. Home: 6548 Cedar St Milton FL 32570 Office: Central High School 6180 Central School Rd Milton FL 32570 E-mail: bassette@mail.santarosa.k12.fl.us.

BASSETT, CLYDE M. music educator; s. Ralph L. and Rebecca L. Bassett; m. Esther A. Anania, July 9, 1979; 1 child, Anthony R. BM, So. Ill. U., 1972—76; MA, Western Ill. U., 1990—92, Post Baccalaureate Cert. in Distance Edn., 2000—02. Cert. Tchg. Cert. Ill., 1981. Orch. dir. Pub. Schools, Charleston, SC, 1976—81, Mt. Vernon Twp. H.S., Ill., 1981—89, Quincy Pub. Schools, Ill., 1989—; music dir. Quincy Symphony Orch. Mem.: Ill. Music Educators Assn. (dist. rep. 1991—2002). Avocation: jazz musician. Personal E-mail: cbassett@adams.net.

BASSETT, DEBRA LYN, lawyer, educator; b. Pleasanton, Calif., Oct. 28, 1956; d. James Arthur and Shirley Ann (Russell) Bassett. BA, U. Vt., 1977; MS, San Diego State U., 1982; JD, U. Calif., Davis, 1987. Bar: Calif. 1987, DC 1990, U.S. Dist. Ct. (no. and ea. dists.) Calif. 1988, U.S. Ct. Appeals (9th cir.) 1988, U.S. Supreme Ct. 1991. Guidance counselor Addison Cen. Supr. Union, Middlebury, Vt., 1982-83, Milton (Vt.) Elem. Sch., 1983-84; assoc. Morrison & Foerster, San Francisco, 1986; jud. clk. U.S. Ct. Appeals (9th cir.), Phoenix, 1987-88; assoc. Morrison & Foerster, San Francisco and Walnut Creek, Calif., 1988-92; sr. atty. Calif. Ct. Appeal (3d appellate dist.), Sacramento, 1992-99; assoc. prof. Mich. State U., East Lansing, 2002—. Tutor civil procedure, rsch. asst. U. Calif., Davis, 1985—87, instr., 1995—2002, lectr., 1997—2002; adj. prof. McGeorge Sch. Law, 1998—99, dir. legal process, 1999—2000, vis. prof., 2000—01. Editor: U. Calif. Law Rev., 1985—86; sr. articles editor:, 1986—87. Mem. Steiner Chorale, 2002—. Mem.: ABA (vice chmn. ethics com. young lawyers divsn. 1989—91, exec. com. labor and employment law com. 1989—90), AAUW, APA (assoc.), Scribes. Democrat. Avocations: music, tennis, travel, hiking. Home: 915 Snyder Rd East Lansing MI 48823 Office: Mich State U DCL Coll Law 417 Law Coll Bldg East Lansing MI 48824 E-mail: debbie.bassett@law.msu.edu.

BASSETT, ELIZABETH EWING (LIBBY BASSETT), writer, editor; b. Cleve., July 22, 1937; d. Ben and Eileen Grace (Ewing) B.; m. Robert Richter, Feb. 20, 1994. AA, Bradford Jr. Coll., Mass., 1957. Girl Friday Time-Life, animated film cos., others, 1957-63; asst. producer, stage mgr. N.Y. State Pavilion at N.Y. World's Fair, 1963-64; writer, reporter, editor AP, N.Y.C., 1965-72; free-lance corr. AP, Newsweek, Voice of America, UNICEF, ABC Radio, Africa, 1972-74; resident corr. ABC News, Cairo, 1974-77; dir. publs. and comm. World Environment Ctr., N.Y.C., 1978-85; cons. writer, editor, editorial designer Women's Environ. and Devel. Orgn., 1989—98, UN orgns. and others, 1985—; co-organizer Project on Religion and Human Rights, 1994-95. Guest lectr. Am. U. Cairo, Rutgers U., Columbia U., L.I. U., Hunter Coll., CUNY; press officer Global Survival Conf., Oxford, Eng., 1988; press coord. Global Forum on Environ. and Devel., Moscow, 1990, Parliamentary Earth Summit, Rio de Janeiro, 1992; info. officer Internat. Green Cross/Global Forum, Kyoto, Japan, 1993; comm. coord. World Women's Congress for Healthy Planet, Miami, 1991; press. coord. WEDO Web, NGO Forum on Women, China, 1995. Author: The Growth of Environment in the World Bank, World Environment Center, 1982, UNEP N.Am. News, 1986-91, Shared Vision, 1988-92, The Global Forum Decade, 1995, Earth and Faith: A Book of Reflection for Action, 2000, also others; assoc. editor, designer: The Bella Abzug Reader, 2003. Mem. Soc. Profl. Journalists, Soc. Environ. Journalists, Internat. Sci. Writers Assn.

BASSETT, JOHN E. academic administrator, English educator; b. Washington, May 12, 1942; s. J. Earl and Frances E. (Walker) B.; m. Kay E. Hobart, Sept. 5, 1964; children: Laura, Gregory. BA in History, Ohio Wesleyan U., 1963, MA in English, 1966; PhD in English, U. Rochester, 1970. Instr. U. Rochester, N.Y., 1969-70; asst. prof. Wayne State U., Detroit, 1970-75, assoc. prof., 1975-84; prof., head dept. English No. Carolina State U., Raleigh, 1984-93; dean Coll. Arts and Scis., prof. English Case Western Res. U., Cleve., 1993-2000; pres. Clark U., Worcester, 2000—. Author: William Faulkner: An Annotated Checklist of Criticism, 1972, Faulkner: The Critical Heritage, 1975, Faulkner: A Checklist of Recent Criticism, 1983, Vision and Revisions: Essays on Faulkner, 1989, Faulkner in the Nineties: A Bibliography of Criticism, 1991, A Heart of Ideality in My Realism and Other Essays on Howells and Twain, 1991, Harlem in Review: Critical Reactions to Black American Writers 1917-1939, 1992, Defining Southern Literature, 1997, Thomas Wolfe: An Annotated Bibliography of Criticism, 1996; contbr. articles to profl. jours. Mem. MLA, Mark Twain Soc., Thomas Wolfe Soc., Soc. for Study of So. Lit., Assn. Depts. of English (pres. 1990-91), Phi Beta Kappa, Phi Kappa Phi, Phi Alpha Theta. Office: Clark U 950 Main St Worcester MA 01610-1477 E-mail: jbassett@clarku.edu.

BASSETT, JOHN WALDEN, JR., lawyer; b. Roswell, N.Mex., Mar. 21, 1938; s. John Walden Sr. and Evelyn (Thompson) B.; m. Patricia Lubben, May 22, 1965 (dec. Apr. 1995); children: John Walden III, Loren Patricia; m. Nolana Knight, May 2, 1998. AB in Econs., Stanford U., 1960; LLB with honors, U. Tex., 1964. Bar: Tex. 1964, N.Mex. 1964. Assoc. Atwood & Malone, Roswell, 1964-66; White House fellow, spl. asst. to U.S. Atty. Gen., Washington, 1966-67; ptnr. Atwood, Malone, Mann & Turner and predecessors, Roswell, 1967-95, Bassett & Copple, LLP, Roswell, 1995—. Bd. dirs. Belo Corp., Dallas, AMMA Found., Washington. Assoc. editor U. Tex. Law Rev., 1962. Mem. N.Mex. State Bd. Edn., 1987-91; pres., chmn. bd. United Way of Chaves County, N.Mex., 1973; bd. dirs. Ednl. Achievement Found., Roswell, 1992—, N.Mex. Bus. Roundtable for Ednl. Excellence, Albuquerque. 1st lt. U.S. Army, 1961-68. Mem. ABA, Tex. Bar Assn., N.Mex. Bar Assn., Chaves County Bar Assn., Order of Coif, Rotary (pres. 1976), N.Mex. Amigos, Phi Delta Phi. Republican. Episcopalian. Home: 5060 Bright Sky Rd Roswell NM 88201-8800 Office: Bassett & Copple 400 N Pennsylvania Ave Ste 250 Roswell NM 88201-4788 E-mail: anabassett@aol.com.

BASSETT, LAWRENCE C, management consultant; b. N.Y.C., Dec. 11, 1931; s. David Isaac and Genia Esther Bassett; m. Charlotte Corinne Margolis, Jan. 24, 1960; children: Wendy Jill, Craig Henrid, Heidi Jill, Evan Henrid. BA, NYU, 1953, MBA, 1958. Pers. mgr. Republic Carloading & Distbg. Co., N.Y.C., 1956-61; dir. pers. Clay Adams Inc., N.Y.C., 1961-63; asst. dir. pers. Montefiore Hosp. and Med. Ctr., N.Y.C., 1963-65; dir. pers. Hosp. for Joint Diseases and Med. Ctr., N.Y.C., 1965-67; sr. cons. Orgn. Resources Counselors Inc., N.Y.C., 1967-76; pres. Applied Leadership Tech. Inc., Bloomfield, N.J., 1976-86, The Bassett Cons. Group Inc., Thornwood, N.Y., 1986—. Adj. prof. NYU, 1978—, N.Y. Med. Coll., 1992, Fairleigh Dickenson U., Teaneck, N.J., 1964-86; instr. Helene Fuld Sch. for RN's, N.Y.C., 1966-67. Author: Achieving Excellence, 1986; producer & presenter audio & video tape tng. albums; contbr. articles to profl. jours. Pres., v.p. Mt. Pleasant Bd. Edn., Thornwood, N.Y., 1973-76, 81-87; docent Am. Mus. Natural History. With U.S. Army, 1953-55. Mem. Soc. Profl. Mgmt. Cons. (bd. dirs., v.p.), Inst. Mgmt. Cons. (cert. mgmt. cons.), Am. Soc. for Tng. and Devel., Am. Hosp. Assn., Am. Arbitration Assn., Nat. Speakers Assn., Masons. Avocations: clock making, baking, beekeeping, skiing, orchid growing. Home and Office: The Bassett Cons Group Inc 1 Ilana Ln Thornwood NY 10594-2001 E-mail: larrybass@cttgroup.com.

BASSETT, LESLIE RAYMOND, composer, educator; b. Hanford, Calif., Jan. 22, 1923; s. Archibald Leslie and Vera (Starr) B.; m. Anita Elizabeth Denniston, Aug. 21, 1949; children— Wendy Lynn (Mrs. Lee Bratton), Noel Leslie, Ralph (dec.). BA in Music, Fresno State Coll., 1947; M.Music in Composition, U. Mich., 1949, A.Mus.D., 1956; student, Ecole Normale de Musique, Paris, France, 1950-51. Tchr. music pub. schs., Fresno, 1951-52; mem. faculty U. Mich., 1952—, prof. music, 1965—, Albert A. Stanley disting univ. prof., 1977—, chmn. composition dept., 1970, Henry Russel lectr., 1984, emeritus, 1992. Guest composer Berkshire Music Center, Tanglewood, Mass., 1973 Served with AUS, 1942- 46. Fulbright fellow, 1950-51; recipient Rome prize Am. Acad. in Rome, 1961-63; grantee Soc. Pub. Am. Music, 1960, Nat. Inst. Arts and Letters, 1964, Nat. Council Arts, 1966; Guggenheim fellow, 1973-74, 80-81; recipient Pulitzer prize in music for Variations for Orch., 1966; citation U. Mich. regents, 1966; Walter Naumburg Found. rec. award for Sextet, 1974; Disting. Alumnus award Calif. State U., Fresno, 1978; Disting. Artist award Mich. Council Arts, 1981; Citation of Merit, U. Mich. Sch. Music Alumni, 1980 Mem. Am. Composers Alliance, Mich. Soc. Fellows, Am. Acad. of Arts and Letters, Pi Kappa Lambda, Phi Kappa Phi, Phi Mu Alpha. Methodist.

BASSETT, PETER Q. lawyer; b. Buenos Aires; s. John Jewett and Helen (Gibbs) B.; m. Wendy O. Bassett, Sept. 2, 1972; children: Elisabeth E., Laura G. AB, Princeton U., 1971; JD, George Washington U., 1975. Assoc. Alston, Miller & Gaines, Atlanta, 1975-81; ptnr. Alston & Bird LLP, Atlanta, 1981—. Mem. Ga. Bar Assn., Atlanta Bar Assn. Avocation: motorcycles. Office: Alston & Bird LLP 1201 W Peachtree St NW Ste 4200 Atlanta GA 30309-3449

BASSETT, TINA, communications executive; b. Detroit; m. Leland Kinsey Bassett; children: Joshua, Robert. Student, U. Mich., 1974, 76-78, 81, Wayne State U., 1979-80. Advt. dir. Greenfield's Restaurant, Mich. and Ohio, 1972-73; dir. advt. and pub. rels. Kresco, Inc., Detroit, 1973-74; pub's. rep. The Detroiter mag., 1974-75; pub. rels. dir. Detroit Bicentennial Commn., 1975-77; prin. Leland K. Bassett & Assocs., Detroit, 1976-86; intermediate job devel. specialist Detroit Coun. of the Arts, 1977; project dir. Detroit image campaign dept. pub. info. City of Detroit, 1975, spl. events dir., 1978, dep. dir. dept. pub. info., 1978-83, dir. dept. pub. info., 1983-86; pres., prin. Bassett & Bassett, Inc., Detroit, 1986—. Publicity chmn. Under the Stars IV, V, VI, VII, VIII, IX and X, Benefit Balls, Detroit Inst. of Arts Founders Soc., 1983-88, Detroit Inst. of Arts Founders Centennial Ball, 1985, publicity chmn. Mich. Opera Theater, Opera Ball, 1987; program lectr. Wayne County Close-Up Program, 1984; mem. ctrl. planning com. Am. Assn. Mus.; mem. Founders Soc., Detroit Inst. Arts, 1988—; mem., publicity chair Grand Prix Ball, 1989; co-chair, prodr. Mus. Hall Ctr. for Performing Arts; bd. dirs. arts coun. Detroit Inst. Arts, 1996, bd. dirs. cinema arts coun., 1996—; bd. dirs. Weizman Inst. Sci., 1996-97. Named Outstanding Woman in Agy. Top Mgmt., Detroit chpt. Am. Women in Radio and TV, 1989, one of Most Powerful Women in Mich., CORP Mag., 2002. Mem. AIA (hon., pub. dir. 1990-91, Richard Upjohn fellowship 1991), Detroit Hist. Soc., Internat. Women's Forum, Music Hall Assn., Pub. Rels. Soc. Am. (Advt. Woman of Yr. 1989), Woman's Advt. Club Detroit, Cinematic Arts Coun., DIA (bd. dirs. 1996-99). Home: 30751 Cedar Creek Dr Farmington Hills MI 48336-4989 Address: Bassett & Bassett 1502 Randolph St Ste 200 Detroit MI 48226-2295

BASSETT, WILLIAM AKERS, geologist, educator, retired; b. Bklyn., Aug. 3, 1931; s. Preston Rogers and Jeanne Reed (Mordorf) B.; m. Jane Ann Kermes, Sept. 8, 1962; children: Kari Nicalo, Jeffrey Kermes, Penelope North. BA, Amherst Coll., 1954; MA, Columbia U., 1956, PhD, 1959. Research assoc. Brookhaven Nat. Lab., 1960-61; Asst. prof. U. Rochester, NY, 1961-65, asso. prof., 1965-69, prof. geology, 1969-77, Cornell U., Ithaca, NY, 1978—99, ret., 1999. Vis. prof. Brigham Young U., 1967-68; Crosby vis. prof. MIT, 1974 Research, publs. on the devel. of techniques for investigation of properties of minerals at pressures and temperatures within the earth's interior Recipient Bridgman award Internat. Assn. for Rsch. at High Pressure and Temperature, 1997; NSF grantee; Guggenheim fellow, 1985. Fellow Geol. Soc. Am., Mineral. Soc. Am. (Roebling medal 1994, Bridgman award 1997), Am. Geophys. Union, AAAS; mem. Sigma Xi (pres. Rochester chpt. 1977-78). Home: 765 Bostwick Rd Ithaca NY 14850-9310 E-mail: bassett@geology.cornell.edu.

BASSETT, WOODSON WILLIAM, JR., lawyer; b. Okmulgee, Okla., Nov. 7, 1926; s. Woodson William and Bee Irene (Knerr) B.; m. Marynm Shaw, Dec. 16, 1950; children: Woodson William III, Beverly M., Tod Corbett. JD, U. Ark., 1949. Bar: Ark. 1949. Employed in New Orleans and Monroe, La., 1949-51; claims examiner Employers Group Ins. Cos., 1949-51; mgr. Light Adjustment Co., 1951-56; v.p. legal dept. Preferred Ins. Cos., 1957-62; sr. partner Bassett Law Firm, 1962—. Spl. chief justice Ark. Supreme Ct., 1991—; mem. Ark. Bd. Law Examiners Mem. editorial staff: Ark. Law Review, 9. Pres. Sherman Lollar Boys Baseball League, 1962; v.p. Babe Ruth Baseball Assn., 1968; chmn. bd. dirs. Fayetteville Public Library, 1975-79. Served with AUS, 1950-51. Fellow Am. Coll. Trial Lawyers; mem. ABA, Ark. Bar Assn., Washington County Bar Assn. (pres. 1973-74), Am. Bd. Trial Advs., Delta Theta Phi, Kappa Sigma. Home: 2210 E Manor Dr Fayetteville AR 72701-2640 Office: Bassett Law Firm 221 N College Ave Fayetteville AR 72701-4238

BASSFORD, LYNN FOSTER, physicist, engineer; b. Webster, Mass., Jan. 23, 1969; d. George E. and Carolyn M. F. BS in Physics, U. Lowell, Lowell, 1991. NASA cert. for Hubble Space Telescope's Flight Ops. sci. instruments, data mgmt., instrumentation and comms., elec. power, shift supr., and thermal control subsystems. Satellite flight contr. Lockheed Martin Tech. Ops. Co., GSFC, NASA, Greenbelt, Md., 1991-95; Hubble Space Telescope satellite shift supervisor flight ops Lockheed Martin Tech. Ops., NASA, Goddard Space Flight Ctr., Greenbelt, Md., 1995-99, HST sci. instrument systems engr., 1999-2000, sci. instruments sys. engr. group leader, 2000—. Mem. Nat. Soc. Physics Students.

BASSI, SUZANNE HOWARD, volunteer; b. Santa Ana, Calif., Feb. 26, 1945; d. David Gould and Marian (Matthews) H.; Roger Joseph Bassi, Aug. 25, 1973; children: Carrie, Steven, Gregory. BA, Rosary Coll., River Forest, Ill., 1966; MA in Teaching, U. Ill., Champaign, 1973. Tchr. Resurrection H.S., Chgo., 1966-67, Proviso Twp. H.S., Hillside, Ill., 1967-76; home day care operator Palatine, Ill., 1980-84; mem. bd. Palatine Elem. Sch. Dist. # 15, 1987-95. Rep. candidate for state rep. dist. 54, Ill., 1996, 98, state rep., 54th Dist., 1998—; vice chmn. Ed-Red, Park Ridge, Ill., 1993, chmn., 1994-96; legis. chmn. Ill . Assn. of Sch. Bds., North Cook divsn., Lombard, Ill., 1994-96; staff mem. Gar y Skoien for Congress, Palatine, 1994. Named Those Who Excel, Ill. State Bd. Edn., 1992. Mem. LWV (bd. dirs., legis. chair), Palatine Rep. Women's Orgn. Republican. Roman Catholic. Home: 2509 Honeysuckle Ln Rolling Meadows IL 60008*

BASSIN, GILBERT SHELDON, manufacturing executive, engineer; b. N.Y., N.Y., June 7, 1932; m. Doreen Bassin; children: Pamela, Elisabeth, William. BME, NYU, New York, NY, 1953. Cert. Professional Engineer, NY, 1957. Engr. Cornel Dubilier Electric Co, Cambridge, Mass., 1953—56; chief engr. Litton Industries-Components Div, Mt Vernon, NY, 1956—61; pres., owner Bassin Tech. Sls. Co, Mamaroneck, NY, 1961—, Logicomp Electronics Inc, Mamaroneck, NY, 1967—, Pres:Air:Trol Corp, Mamaroneck, NY, 1977—. Mem. bd. of trustees Neuberger Mus. of Art, Purchase, NY, 1994—. Recipient Pi Tau Sigma, Hon. Engring. Frat., 1952. Mem.: ASME. Achievements include patents for Fluid Actuated Control-1988,Control Housing-1993, Bellows Switch Actuator-1999, Bellow Actuator-2000. Avocations: boating, art collecting. Office Fax: 914-698-9456. E-mail: presair@aol.com., dorbert@aol.com.

BASSIN, JULES, foreign service officer; b. N.Y.C., Apr. 16, 1914; s. Abe and Bessie (Brooks) B.; m. Beatrice M. Kellner, Dec. 25, 1938; children: Arthur Jay, Nelson Jay. BS, CCNY, 1936; JD, N.Y.U., 1938; student, Criminal Investigation Sch., U.S. Army, 1943, Security Intelligence Sch., 1944, Mil. Govt. Sch., U. Va., 1944, Far East Civil Affairs, Harvard, 1945; grad., Armed Forces Staff Coll., 1960. Bar: N.Y. bar 1939. Dir. law div. Gen. Hdqrs., Supreme Comdr. Allied Powers, Tokyo, Japan, 1945-51; legal attache Am. embassy, Tokyo, 1951-56; also spl. asst. to ambassador for politico-mil. affairs; spl. asst. to ambassador for mut. security affairs Am. Embassy, Karachi, 1956-59; State Dept. faculty adviser Armed Forces Staff Coll., Norfolk, Va., 1960-62; chief titles and rank br. Dept. State, 1962-63, chief functional assignments br., 1963-65, dir. functional personnel program, 1965-67, spl. asst. to dep. undersec. state for adminstrn., 1967-69, exec. sec. Bd. Fgn. Service, 1967-69; dep. rep. of U.S. to European office UN and other internat. orgns.; also dep. chief U.S. mission with personal rank of minister, Geneva, Switzerland, 1969 74; cons. on refugee and migration affairs Dept. State, 1974—; cons. USIA, 1975-76. Served from 2d lt. to maj., Judge Adv. Gen. Corps. AUS, 1942-46; col. Res. Mem. Am. Fgn. Service Assn. Clubs: American Internat. (Geneva) (exec. com.). Home: 2891 Audubon Ter NW Washington DC 20008-2309

BASSINGTHWAIGHTE, JAMES BUCKLIN, physiologist, educator, medical researcher; b. Toronto, Sept. 10, 1929; s. Ewart MacQuarrie and Velma Emeline B.; m. Joan Elizabeth Graham, June 18, 1955; children: Elizabeth Anne, Mary, Alan, Sarah, Rebecca. BA, U. Toronto, 1951, MD, 1955; postgrad., Med. Sch. London, 1957-58; PhD, Mayo Grad. Sch. Medicine U. Minn., 1964. Intern Toronto Gen. Hosp., 1955-56; physician Internat. Nickel Co., Sudbury and Matheson, Ont., 1956-57; house physician Hammersmith Hosp., London; postgrad. Med. Sch. London, 1957-58; teaching asst. physiology U. Minn., Mpls., 1961-62; fellow Mayo Grad. Sch. Medicine, Rochester, Minn., 1958-64, instr., 1964-67, asst. prof., 1967-69, assoc. prof., 1969-72; vis. prof. Pharmacology Inst., U. Bern, Switzerland, 1970-71; asso. prof. bioengring. U. Minn., 1972-75; prof. physiology Mayo Grad. Sch. Medicine, 1973-75, prof. medicine, 1975; prof. bioengring., radiology and biomath U. Wash., Seattle, 1975—; dir. Ctr. for Bioengring., 1975-80; vis. prof. medicine and physiology McGill U., 1979-81, affiliate prof. physiology Limburg U., Maastricht, The Netherlands, 1990—. Mem. study sect. NIH, 1970-74, 80-83; chmn. Biotech. Resources Adv. Com., 1977-79, chmn. 1st Gordon Rsch. Conf. on Water and Solute Transport in Microvasculature, 1976; chmn. workshop on metabolic imaging Nat. Heart, Lung and Blood Inst., 1985; bd. dirs. Nat. Space Biomed. Rsch. Inst., NASA, 2002; Lewellen-Thomas lectr., U. Toronto, 1991; Coulter lectr. U. N.C., 1995; Oxford lectr. Internat. Soc. Magnetic Resonance Medicine, 1996. Author: (with L.S. Liebovitch and B.J. West) Fractal Physiology, 1994; contbr. over 200 articles to profl. publs. Recipient NIH Rsch. Career Devel. award, 1964-74, Louis and Artur Lucian award McGill U., 1979, Witzig award Cardiovasc. Sys. Dyamics Soc., 1982, Faculty Achievement award for outstanding rsch. U. Wash. Coll. Engring., 1993; Edmund Hustinx chair Maastricht U., 1999. Mem. AAAS, Am. Heart Assn. (coun. on circulation 1976—), Biophys. Soc. (assoc. editor Biophys. Jour. 1980-83), Biomed. Engring. Soc. (dir. 1971-74, pres. 1977-78, Alza award 1986, editor-in-chief Annals of Biomedical Engring. 1993—, Disting. Svc. award 1999), Microcirculatory Soc. (mem. coun. 1975-78, 80-83, pres. 1990-91, Landis award 1995), Nat. Acad. Engring., Am. Physiol. Soc. (mem. circulation group, editorial bd. 1972-76, 79-83, mem. edn. com.), Internat. Union Physiol. Scis. (U.S.A. nat. com. 1978-86, U.S. del. to assembly 1980, 83, 86, chmn. 1983-86, chmn. Commn. on Bioengring. and Clin. Physiology 1986-97, chmn. satellite to 30th Congress on Endothelial Transport 1986, co-chmn. satellite on microvascular networks 1989, chmn. satellite on Physiome Project 1997). Achievements include research in cardiovascular physiology and bioengineering, biomathematics and computer simulation with emphasis on ion and substrate exchange in heart, fractals in physiology, integrative biology and originator of the Physiome Project. Home: 3150 E Laurelhurst Dr NE Seattle WA 98105-5333 Office: U Wash Dept Bioengring PO Box 35-7962 Seattle WA 98195-7962 E-mail: jbb@bioeng.washington.edu.

BASSIS, AILEEN, artist; b. N.Y.C., Dec. 23, 1949; d. Bouris and Frances Bassis; m. Andrew Kapochunas, May 28, 1975; children: Rachel Rose Kapochunas, Simon Vincent Kapochunas. BA, SUNY, Binghamton, 1971; MA, Hunter Coll., 1976. One-woman shows include Ohio U., Athens, 1994, Gallery 402, N.Y.C., 2000, The Ceres Project Room, 2002, exhibited in group shows at City Without Walls Gallery, Newark, 1994, 2000, 2003, Morehead (Ky.) State U., 2001, Hunterdon Mus. Art, Clinton, N.J., 2000. Photography fellow, N.J. State Coun. on the Arts, 1999. Home: 884 Bellis Pky Oradell NJ 07649 Personal E-mail: aileenbassis@hotmail.com.

BASSIS, MICHAEL STEVEN, academic administrator; b. N.Y.C., Sept. 8, 1944; s. Lewis and Barbara (Fay) B.; m. Mary Suzanne Wilson, Dec. 27, 1977; children: Anne Elizabeth, Christina, Jessica, Nicholas. BA with honors, Brown U., 1967; MA, U. Chgo., 1968, PhD, 1974. Asst. dir. acad. potential project Brown U., 1966-67; rsch. assoc. Ctr. for the Study of the Acts of Man U. Pa., 1968; instr., asst. prof.-assoc. prof. dept. sociology and anthropology U. R.I., 1971-81, acting asst. dean Coll. Arts and Scis., 1977-78; assoc. Harvard U. Grad. Sch. Edn., 1980-81; assoc. dean faculty U. Wis., Parkside, 1981-85, assoc. prof. sociology, 1981-86, interim asst. chancellor ednl. svcs., 1985-86; v.p. acad. affairs Ea. Conn. State U., 1986-89; exec. v.p., univ. provost Antioch U., Yellow Springs, Ohio, 1989-93; pres. Olivet (Mich.) Coll., 1993-98; dean, warden New Coll., U. South Fla., Sarasota, 1998—2001; president Westminster Coll. of Salt Lake City, 2002—. Presenter in field. Author (with W.R. Rosengren) The Social Organization of Nautical Education: The U.S., Great Britain and Spain, 1976, (with R.J. Gelles and A. Levine) Sociology: An Introduction, 4th edit., 1991, Social Problems, 1982; editor Teaching Sociology, 1982-85; contbr. articles to profl. jours. NIMH grantee, 1967-71, Exxon Edn. Found. grantee, N.Y.C., 1975, Fund for Improvement of Post-Secondary Edn. grantee, Washington, 1978. Mem. Am. Sociol. Assn. (undergrad. edn. sect., membership com. 1979-81, coun. 1980, 82, 86-89, teaching resources group 1984-86, publs. com. 1985, chair 1987-88), Am. Assn. Higher Edn., Nat. Soc. Experiential Edn. Home: 4055 East Adonis Circle Salt Lake City UT 84124 Office: Office of the President Westminster College 1840 South 1300 East Salt Lake City UT 84105 E-mail: mbassis@westminstercollege.edu.

BASSITT, JANET LOUISE, lawyer; b. Macomb, Ill., Oct. 8, 1941; d. James Russell Hoover and Louise Loretta (Lawrence) Hoover Reed; children: Teri Beth, William Jefferson, Margaret Louise. BA in Psychology with honors, U. Ill., Chgo., 1976; JD, John Marshall Law Sch., 1980. Bar: Ill. 1981, U.S. Dist. Ct. (no. dist.) Ill. 1982, U.S. Ct. Appeals (7th cir.) 1982, U.S. Tax Ct. 1983, U.S. Supreme Ct. 1985. Sole practice, Roselle, Ill., 1982—. Instr. Harper Coll., Palatine, Ill., 1983-88, Coll. Fin. Planning, Denver, 1985-88. Author: Attorney Conduct, 1985, Trust Yourself, 1990; contbr. articles to profl. jours. Vol. lawyer Constl. Rights Found., Chgo., 1982—; chmn. March of Dimes, Wenatchee, Wash., 1971-72; bd. dirs. United Way Schaumburg-Hoffman Estates, 1986-89; leader Wenatchee area Boy Scouts Am., 1971-72, Camp Fire Girls. Mem. ABA, Ill. Bar Assn. Address: PO Box 72277 Roselle IL 60172-0277

BASSLER, BONNIE, molecular biologist; BS, U. Calif., Davis, 1984; PhD, Johns Hopkins U., 1990. Rsch. scientist Agouron Inst., La Jolla, Calif., 1993—94; faculty dept. molecular biology Princeton U., 1994—96, faculty environ. inst., 1996—. Contbr. articles to profl. jours. Fellow Rsch. fellow, Agouron Inst., 1990—93, MacArthur Found. fellow, 2002. Achievements include research in quorum sensing. Office: Princeton U 329 Lewis Thomas Lab Princeton NJ 08544*

BASSLER, ROBERT COVEY, artist, educator; b. N.Y.C., Nov. 9, 1935; s. Robert Stein and Joan (Covey) B.; m. Linda Marie Allen, June 14, 1964. BA, Bard Coll., 1957; MFA, U. So. Calif., 1960. Instr. sculpture Occidental Coll., 1960-64; prof. sculpture Calif. State U., Northridge, 1964-97, prof. emeritus, 1998—. Artist in residence Calif. Inst. Tech., 1970-71; art film tour Arts Coun. Gt. Britain. Solo exhbns. include Comara Gallery, L.A., 1961, 63, Occidental Coll., L.A., 1961, 70, Calif. State U. Bakersfield, 1964, L.A. Mcpl. Art Gallery, Barnsdall Park, 1965, 81, Calif. State U., Northridge, 1965, Santa Barbara (Calif.) Mus. Art, 1968, Molly Barnes Gallery, L.A., 1969, Baxter Art Gallery, Calif. Inst. Tech., 1971, Galerie La Demeure, Paris, 1972, Amerika-Haus, West Berlin, 1972, Wenger Gallery, L.A., 1988, Security Pacific Pla., L.A., 1989-90, Calif. State U., Northridge, 1997, Orlando Gallery, Sherman Oaks, Calif., 1997; exhibited in group shows at Jewish Mus., N.Y.C., Milw. Art Ctr., San Francisco Mus. of Art, Los Angeles County Mus. of Art, Pasadena Mus. of Art, Long Beach (Calif.) Mus. of Art, LaJolla (Calif.) Mus. of Art, San Francisco Mus. of Art, Newport Harbor Art Mus., Oakland Mus. of Art, Esther Bear Gallery, Santa Barbara, Houston Mus. of Art, Ackland Meml. Art Ctr., Chapel Hill, N.C., Mus. Fine Arts, St. Petersburg, Fla., Jacksonville (Fla.) Art Mus., Musée d'Art Moderne, Paris, Galerie La Demeure, Paris, Redfern Gallery, London, U.S. Embassy, London, Wenger Gallery, L.A., Calif. Inst. Tech., Amerika Haus, Berlin, Century City, Calif., Fine Arts Gallery, San Diego, Art Park, L.A., Design Ctr., L.A., Washington Sq., Washington, Fine Arts Bldg., L.A., Valerie

Miller Gallery, Palm Desert, Calif., Tom Bradley Terminal, L.A. Internat. Airport, Finegood Art Gallery, West Hills, Calif., Pacific Design Ctr., L.A., L.A. Contemporary Exhibitions; represented in permanent collections including Atlantic Richfield Corp., Container Corp. Am., Quinn & Assocs., L.A., Security Pacific Nat. Bank, Carter Hawley Hale Stores Inc., Home Savs. & Loan, The Ahmanson Collection, Chgo. Convention Ctr., Arts Coun. of Gt. Britain, U. So. Calif., Bard Coll., N.Y., Kirk O' The Valley, Reseda, Calif., Calif. State U., Northridge. With AUS, 1959-62. Recipient Pres.'s Creativity award Calif. State U., Northridge, 1978, Meritorious Performance award, 1989, 96. Achievements include developing technique for casting clear polyester resin. Address: 8329 Melvin Ave Northridge CA 91324-4132 E-mail: robert.c.bassler@csun.edu. *My current work explores visual phenomena created by light and structural juxtapositions and their resulting effects upon one's concept of reality. Most recently painted interpretations of NASA photographs of our planet's atmospheric patterns have been incorporated as provocative elements of beauty, fragility, order and chaos.*

BASSNETT, PETER JAMES, retired librarian; b. Sutton Coldfield, Warwickshire, Eng., Nov. 16, 1933; emigrated to Can., 1966; s. Lionel and Phyllis (Mair) B.; m. Ann Gorham, Dec. 12, 1959; children: Madeline Jane, Sarah Catherine. A.Library Assn., N. Western Poly. Sch. Librarianship, London, 1963. Chartered librarian, U.K. Library asst. City of Westminster, London, 1958-61; tech. librarian Cement & Concrete Assn., London, 1963-64; librarian-in-charge London Borough of Haringey, 1964-66; adminstrv. asst. to dir. Calgary Pub. Library Bd., Alta., 1966-72; dir. systems and mgmt. North York Pub. Library Bd., Ont., 1972-75; CEO librs. Scarborough Pub. Library Bd., Ont., 1975-95; ret., 1995; exec. coordinator Ont. Pub. Libraries Programme Rev., Toronto, 1980-82. Contbr. articles to profl. jours. Chmn. adv. com. on library arts programme So. Alta. Inst. Tech., 1969-72. Fellow Libr. Assn. (U.K.); mem. Alta. Libr. Assn. (pres. 1969-70), Powys Soc. Home: 29 Highbridge Pl Scarborough ON Canada M1V 4R7

BASSO, KEITH HAMILTON, cultural anthropologist, linguist, educator; b. Asheville, N.C., Mar. 15, 1940; s. Joseph Hamilton and Etolia (Simmons) B.; div. BA, Harvard U., 1962; MA, Stanford U., 1965, PhD, 1967. Asst. prof. anthropology U. Ariz.-Tucson, 1967-71, assoc. prof., 1972-76, prof., 1977-81; prof. anthropology Yale U., 1982-88, U. N.Mex., Albuquerque, 1988—. Fellow Inst. Advanced Study, Princeton, N.J., 1975-76; Weatherhead fellow Sch. Am. Research, Santa Fe, N.M., 1977-78; cons. cultural and historical topics White Mountain and San Carlos Apache Tribes, Alfonso Ortiz Ctr. for Intercultural Studies, 2000—, Native Nations Inst., 2000—; mem. steering com. Nat. Coalition for Am. Indian Religious Freedom; bd. trustees Nat. Mus. of the Am. Indian, 1991-96. Author: Wisdom Sits in Places: Landscape and Language Among the Western Apache, 1996 (Western States Book award 1996, Victor Turner prize for ethnographic writing 1997, J.I. Staley award 2001), Western Apache Language and Culture: Essays in Linguistic Anthropology, 1991, Portraits of the White Man, 1979, The Cibecue Apache, 1970; editor: Senses of Place, 1996, Meaning in Anthropology, 1976, Western Apache Witchcraft, 1969. Mem. AAAS, Assn. Am. Indian Affairs (bd. dirs. 1978-86), Am. Anthropol. Assn., Am. Ethnol. Soc. (pres. 1983-84), Linguistic Soc. Am. Democrat. Home: 12 Pool St NW Albuquerque NM 87120-1809

BASSOPPO-MOYO, SHEILA, elementary school educator; b. St. Louis, Mo., Mar. 1, 1955; d. Elmer and Rumell Perry; m. Temba Charles Bassoppo-Moyo, Oct. 31, 1981; 1 child, Tinima. BA in English lit., Barnard Coll., 1978; MS, Florida State U., 1993; EdD, U. of Memphis, 1999. Dir. Consumer Coun., Harare, Zimbabwe, 1984—87; overseas edn. adv. U.S. Embassy, Harare, Zimbabwe, 1987—90; edn. and tng. specialist Fla. Dept. of Labor, 1991—94; coord., learning resource ctr. U. of Memphis, 1996, tchg./grad. asst., 1994—95, 1997—99; asst. prof. Troy State U., Japan and South Korea, 1999—2002; online edn. adj. faculty U. of Md., Troy State U., 2002—; lang. arts tchr. St. Louis Pub. Sch., 2002—; tchr., gifted, mid. sch. level McKinley Classical Jr. Acad., 2003—; tchr., undergraduate courses over the Internet Univ. of Md., 2003—; owner bus. Tea, 2003—. Vol. St. Louis Pub. Libr., 2002. Mem.: Assn. for the Study of Higher Edn., Am. Edn. Rsch. Assn. Democrat. Home: 2100 Portis Ave, Apt 1 S Saint Louis MO 63110 Office: McKinley Classical Jr Acad 2156 Russell Blvd Saint Louis MO 63110 Personal E-mail: bassoppomoyo@hotmail.com.

BASSUK, ELLEN LINDA, psychiatrist; b. N.Y.C., Feb. 8, 1945; d. Irving and Molly (Pakarow) B.; children: Daniel, Sarah. BA, Brandeis U., 1964; MD, Tufts U., 1968; Dr.P.S. (hon.), Northeastern U., 1993. Diplomate Am. Bd. Psychiatry. Intern Mt. Auburn Hosp., Cambridge, Mass., 1968-69; resident psychiatry Univ. Hosp., Boston, 1969-70, Boston State Hosp., Boston, 1970-71, Beth Israel Hosp., Boston, 1971-73, dir. psychiat. emergency svcs., 1974-82; fellow Bunting Inst., Cambridge, Mass., 1982-84; assoc. prof. psychiatry Harvard Med. Sch., Boston, 1983—. Founder, pres. Nat. Ctr. on Family Homelessness, Newton, Mass., 1988—; mem. Com. on Health Care of Homeless Persons Inst. of Medicine, Washington, 1986-88. Editor: The Practitioners Guide to Psychoactive Drugs, 1977, 83, 91, 97; editor-in-chief Am. Jour. Orthopsychiatry, 1994-98; contbr. numerous articles to profl. jours. Fellow Am. Psychiat. Assn.; mem. Mass. Psychiat. Soc. Home: 20 Randolph Rd Chestnut Hill MA 02467-2338 Office: Nat Ctr on Family Homelessness 181 Wells Ave Newton MA 02459-3332 E-mail: ellen.bassuk@familyhomelessness.org.

BAST, JAMES LOUIS, retired trade association executive; b. Balt., Apr. 19, 1936; s. Louis and Evelyn Frances (Alling) B.; m. Mary Margaret Griffin, June 13, 1959; children: Andrew Griffin, James Mark, Cynthia Elizabeth. BA, Columbia U., 1958, BSM.E., 1959; MBA, NYU, 1968. With Pitney Bowes Inc., Stamford, Conn., 1963-72, 73-90, chief fin. officer, 1976-82, v.p. fin., contr., 1976-77, sr. v.p. fin. and adminstrn., 1977-82; pres. Pitney Bowes Bus. Systems, Stamford, Conn., 1987-90; pres., chief exec. officer Dictaphone Corp. subs. Pitney Bowes Inc., Rye, N.Y., 1982-87; CEO A. B. Dick Co., Chgo., 1990-92; CEO, pres. Presstek, Inc., Hudson, N.H., 1993; pres., CEO, Coun. Better Bus. Burs., Inc., Arlington, Va., 1994-99. Cons., contr. Bunker Ramo Corp., Trumbull, Conn., 1972-73. Served to lt. USN, 1959-63. Home: 128 Monument Rd Orleans MA 02653-3514 E-mail: jimbast@aol.com.

BAST, ROBERT CLINTON, JR., medical researcher, medical educator; b. Washington, Dec. 8, 1943; s. Robert Clinton and Ann Christine (Borland) B.; m. Blanche Amy Simpson, Oct. 21, 1972; 1 child, Elizabeth Simpson Bast. BA cum laude, Wesleyan U., Middletown, Conn., 1965; MD magna cum laude, Harvard U., 1971. Diplomate Am. Bd. Internal Medicine, Am. Bd. Med. Oncology, Am. Bd. Hematology. Predoctoral fellow dept. pathology Mass. Gen. Hosp., Boston, 1967-69; intern Johns Hopkins Hosp., Balt., 1971-72; rsch. assoc. biology br. Nat. Cancer Inst., NIH, Bethesda, Md., 1972-75; asst. resident Peter Bent Brigham Hosp., Boston, 1975-76; fellow med. oncology Sidney Farber Cancer Inst., Boston, 1976-77; asst. prof. medicine Harvard U. Med. Sch., Boston, 1977-83, assoc. prof., 1983-84; prof. Duke U. Med. Ctr., Durham, N.C., 1984-92, Wellcome clin. prof. medicine in honor of R. Wayne Rundles, 1992-94, co-dir. div. hematology-oncology, 1984-94; dir. clin. research programs Duke U. Comprehensive Cancer Ctr., Durham, 1984-87; dir., 1987-94; Harry Carothers Wiess chair cancer rsch. U. Tex. M.D. Anderson Cancer Ctr., 1994—, head divsn. med., 1994-2000, v.p. translational rsch., 2000—; dir. divsn. med. oncology dept. medicine U. Tex. Health Sci. Ctr., Houston, 1994-2000. Hosp. appointments include asst. in medicine Peter Bent Brigham Hosp., 1976-77; jr. assoc. in medicine Brigham and Women's Hosp., 1977-82; cons. oncologist Boston Hosp. Women, 1978-80; physician Duke U. Med. Ctr., 1984-94; internist M.D. Anderson Cancer Ctr., 1994—; mem. biol. response modifiers decision network com. Nat. Cancer Inst., 1984-87, exptl. immunology study sect., 1983-84, 90-92; mem. grant rev. com. Leukemia Soc. Am., 1985-87, adv. com. oncologic drugs FDA, 1985-89, chmn. 1988-89; bd. dirs. Cancer and Leukemia Group B., 1986-88, Am. Council Transplantation, 1985-87; mem. grant rev. com. Am. Cancer Soc., 1987; numerous other coms.; Edward G. Waters Meml. lectr., 1987; John Ohtani Meml. lectr., 1991; D. Nelson Henderson lectr., 1991; Stolte Meml. lectr., 1992; Arnold O. Beckman Disting. Lectureship, 1993; Robert C. Knapp lectr., 1996; Alan Dembo Meml. Keynote lectr., 1997, George Willbanks lectr., 2000. Contbr. numerous articles on tumor immunology, immunodiagnosis and immunotherapy of cancer and cellular immunology to profl. jours. Served as surgeon USPHS, 1972-75. Named Disting. Spkr., Chas Family Comprehensive Cancer Ctr., 2002; recipient Dominus award, 1984, Robert C. Knapp award, 1990, Recognition Outstanding Leadership and Advocacy award, Nat. Coalition for Cancer Rsch., 1995, Smith Kline Beecham Clin. Labs. award, Clin. Ligand Soc., 1996, award of Achievement, Ptnrs. in Courage, ACS, 1998, Abbott award, Internat. Soc. Oncodevelopmental Biology and Markers, 2001; grantee, Nat. Cancer Inst., NIH, HHS, 1978—; scholar, Leukemia Soc. Am., 1978—83. Fellow: AAAS, ACP; mem.: Am. Clin. and Climatological Assn., Am. Soc. Hematology, Soc. Biol. Therapy (bd. dirs. 1984—86), Internat. Soc. Immunopharmacology, Am. Soc. Clin. Investigation, Am. Fedn. Clin. Rsch., Am. Soc. Clin. Oncology, Assn. Am. Physicians, Am. Assn. Immunologists, Am. Assn. Cancer Rsch., Am. Soc. Microbiology, The Reticuloendothelial Soc., Internat. Gynecol. Cancer Soc. (coun. 1997—), Soc. Gynecol. Oncology (assoc.). Achievements include development of monoclonal antibodies to react with human ovarian cancer, leading to CA125 blood test; techniques for selective elimination of tumor cells from human bone marrow; identification of molecular changes associated with malignant transformation of ovarian epithelium. Office: U Tex MD Anderson Cancer Ctr 1515 Holcombe Blvd # 355 Houston TX 77030-4009

BASTA, CARLO R. information systems specialist, consultant; b. Syracuse, N.Y., Feb. 14, 1959; s. Dominick A. Basta and Maria A. Dragano; m. Joanne Bergman, June 20, 1980. Student, Syracuse U., SUNY, Syracuse, Am. Inst. Computer Sci., Birmingham, Ala. Cert. Novell specialist, 1997; notary pub. Vol. Syracuse Police Dept., 1975-77, police dispatcher/systems specialist, 1980-88; police dispatcher Manlius (N.Y.) Police Dept., 1977-80; sys. adminstr. State of Fla., Tallahassee, 1994-96; mgr. info. systems Monroe County Sheriff's Office, Rochester, N.Y., 1997-98, Onondaga County Health Dept., Syracuse, 1997—. Supr. comm. divsn. Syracuse Police Dept.; adminstrv. mgr. engring. dept. Syracuse City Hall, 1988-94 Bd. dirs. Underground Facilities Protection Orgn., Syracuse, 1994; mem. design com. Criminal History Arrest-Incident Reporting Sys., Syracuse, 1985-87. Recipient award State of Fla, 1995, Gov.'s Office, 1996, commendations Syracuse Police, 1987. Mem. Associated Pub. Safety Comm. Ofcls. Office: Onondaga County Sheriff's OFfice 407 S State St Syracuse NY 13202

BASTA, PAUL M. lawyer; b. Cairo, Mar. 23, 1966; BA with honors, U. Mich., 1988; JD, George Washington U., 1992. Bar: R.I. 1992, N.Y. 1993, Mass. 1993. Ptnr. Weil, Gotshal & Manges LLP, N.Y.C., 1996—. Contbr. articles to profl. jours. Named one of 40 Young Rising Stars in N.Y., Crain's N.Y. Bus., 2003, Outstanding Young Bankruptcy Lawyers, Crossroads, 2002, 2003, Beard Group, 2002, 2003. Mem.: Order of Coif. Office: Weil Gotshal and Manges LLP 767 Fifth Ave New York NY 10153 Office Fax: 212-310-8007. E-mail: paul.basta@weil.com.*

BASTIAANSE, GERARD C. lawyer; b. Holyoke, Mass., Oct. 21, 1935; s. Gerard C. and Margaret (Lally) B.; m. Paula E. Paliska, June 1, 1963; children: Elizabeth, Gerard. BSBA, Boston U., 1960; JD, U. Va., 1964. Bar: Mass. 1964, Calif. 1970. Assoc. Nutter, McClennen & Fish, Boston, 1964-65; counsel Campbell Soup Co., Camden, N.J., 1965-67; gen. counsel A&W Internat. (United Fruit Co.), Santa Monica, Calif., 1968-70; ptnr. Kindel & Anderson, Los Angeles, 1970—. Mem. ABA, Calif. Bar Assn., Mass. Bar Assn., Japan Am. Soc., Asia Soc., World Trade Ctr. Assn. Clubs: California (Los Angeles); Big Canyon Country (Newport Beach, Calif.). Home: 2 San Sebastian Newport Beach CA 92660-6828 Office: Kindel & Anderson 2030 Main St Ste 1300 Irvine CA 92614-7220

BASTIAN, DONALD NOEL, retired bishop; b. Estevan, Sask., Can., Dec. 25, 1925; s. Josiah and Esther Jane (Millington) B.; m. Kathleen Grace Swallow, Dec. 20, 1947; children: Carolyn Dawn, Donald Gregory, Robert Wilfrid, John David. BA, Greenville Coll., 1953, DST (hon.), 1974; BD, Asbury Theol. Sem., 1956, DD (hon.), 1991, Seattle Pacific U., 1965; DHL (hon.), Roberts Wesleyan Coll., 1990. Ordained to ministry Free Meth. Ch. N.Am., 1954; pastor chs. Lexington, Ky., 1953-56, New Westminster, B.C., Can., 1956-61; pastor College Free Meth. Ch., Greenville, Ill., 1961-74; bishop Free Meth. Ch. N.Am., Toronto, Ont., Can., 1974-90, mem. bd. adminstrn., 1964-90, exec. editor Light and Life mag., 1974-84, chmn. editorial adv. com. Light and Life mag., 1980-86; bishop Free Meth. Ch. in Can., 1990-93. Author: The Mature Church Member, 1960, Along the Way, 1974, Belonging, 1974; editor: The Joy of Christian Fathering: Five First Person Accounts, 1979, Counterfeit: The Lie of Living Together Unmarried, 1988. Recipient Disting. Svc. award Asbury Theol. Sem., 1974; Presdl. award Greenville Coll., 1972; Donald N. and Kathleen G. Bastian chair Wesley studies established at Tyndale Sem., Toronto, 2000. Mem. Can. Holiness Fedn. (pres. 1977, 78), Christian Holiness Assn. (v.p. 1977-78), Evang. Fellowship of Can. (pres. 1989-91). Mem. Free Methodist Ch. Home: 63 Adirondack Cres Brampton ON Canada L6R 1E5 E-mail: dnbasti@aol.com. *I live by the conviction that, however durable it may seem, evil is by nature unstable. Righteousness, by contrast, gives stability to life in the long pull.*

BASTIAN, GARY WARREN, judge; b. St. Paul, Nov. 07; s. Warren John and Virginia (Brower) Bastian; children: Alexander, Christopher. BS, Wis. State U., 1970; JD, William Mitchell Co., 1974. Bar: Minn. 1975. Rschr. Minn. Taxpayers Assn., 1970-73; dir. IR rsch. staff Minn. Senate, 1974-85; project dir. labor mgmt. com. Minn. Sch., 1985-87; pvt. practice, 1987-91; asst. commr. Dept. Labor and Industry, 1991, dep. commr., 1991-95, commr., 1995-97; judge 2d Jud. Dist. Ramsey County, 1997—. Mem. Maplewood City council, Minn., 1980-90. mayor 1990-97; bd. dirs. East Communities Family Ctr., 1986-90, Minn. League of Cities, 1988-92, Nat. Assn. Govt. Labor Officials, 1995-97, sec.-treas., 1996-97, Ramsey-Washington Counties Suburban Cable Commn., 1991-97, State Fund Mut. Ins. Co., 1995-97, Minn. Safety Coun., 1996-97; chmn. Minn. Workers' Compensation Adv. Coun., 1995-97. Mem. Criminal Def. Svcs. Bd., 1998—; bd. dirs. U. Wis.-River Falls Found., 1997—; mem. Ramsey County Violence Coord. Coun., 1999—. Recipient award of merit Local 320, Pub. and Law Enforcement Teamsters Mpls., 1979. Mem. Assn. Met. Municipalities (bd. dirs. 1981-89, pres. 1987-88), Suburban C. of C. (bd. dirs. 1979-84), Polar Wrestling Club. Roman Catholic. Office: Ramsey County Courthouse 15 W Kellogg Blvd Saint Paul MN 55102

BASTIDAS, HUGO XAVIER, painter; b. Quito, Ecuador, Aug. 18, 1956; came to U.S., 1960; s. Hugo Enrique and Leonor (Jaramillo) B.; m. Susan Kay Bengston, Nov. 22, 1989. BA, Rutgers U., 1979; Cert. in Sculpture, Bklyn. Mus. Sch. of Art, N.Y.C., 1979-80; MFA, Hunter Coll./CUNY, N.Y.C., 1987. Bd. dirs. Aljira: A Ctr. for Contemporary Art, chair artist adv.; artist-in-residence Ctr. Innovative Printmaking, Rutgers U., N.J., 2000, Artomi Internat., 2001. One-man shows include Nohra Haime Gallery, N.Y.C., 1994, 1995, 1996, 1997, 1998, 2000, Aljira: A Ctr. for Contemporary Art, 1996, ETS Gallery, Princeton, N.J., 1989, N.J. City U., 1998, Rutgers U., 1999, Art Gallery Art Guild Rahway (N.J.), 1999, QCC Art Gallery CUNY, 2000, others, exhibited in group shows at Nohra Haime Gallery, 1994—97, Ben Shahn Galleries William Paterson Coll. N.J., Wayne, 1996, Muscarelle Mus. Art, Williamsburg, Va., 1996, Art Chgo./Nohra Haime Gallery, Chgo., 1996, Jersey City Mus., 1996, Kentler Internat. Drawing Space, N.Y.C., 1994, Matsuzakaya Art Gallery, Osaka, Japan, 1995, John Woodward Gallery, 1998, 1999, Cuenca (Ecuador) Biannual, 1998, 2000, 2001, 2002, Sharjah Biennial, United Arab Emirates, 2001, others. Co-chair hist. preservation Weehawken Environ. Com., N.J., 1997. Recipient Robert Smithson Meml. scholarship, 1979-80, Schwartz and Hofflich CPA award Silvermine Artists' Guild, 1986, Fulbright fellowship, 1990, awards Colombian Ecuadorian Assn. of Am., 1995; grantee Pollock-Krasner Found., 1992. Mem. Ecuadorian House of Culture (bd. dirs. 1994-96). Home: 445 E 86th St Apt 10E New York NY 10028-6439

BASTIEN, JANE SMISOR, music educator; b. Hutchinson, Kans., Jan. 15, 1936; d. Herbert D. and Gladys I. (Haston) Smisor; m. James W. Bastien; children: Lisa Bastien Hanss, Lori Bastien Vickers. AA, Stephens Coll., 1955; BA, Barnard Coll., 1957; MA, Columbia U., 1958. Asst. prof. Tulane U., New Orleans, 1958-75; pvt. piano tchr., La Jolla, Calif., 1975—. Author/composer: Bastien Piano Books/Ednl. Piano Books for Children and Adults. Recipient Alumnae award Stephens Coll., 1960. Mem. Nat. Assn. Music Tchrs. (Lifetime Achievement award 1999), Music Tchrs. Assn. of Calif. (State Tchg. award 1996). Republican. Presbyterian. Avocations: gardening, collecting antiques. Home: 2431 Vallecitos Ct La Jolla CA 92037-3146 E-mail: jsbastien@aol.com.

BASTOKY, BRUCE MICHAEL, human resources executive; b. Cleve., June 15, 1953; Student, Cuyahoga Community Coll., 1971-73, U. Akron, 1984-85. Personnel/tng. adminstr. The May Co., Cleve., 1974-77; cons. Roth Young, Cleve., 1978-80; dir. human resources The Lawson Co., Cuyahoga Falls, Ohio, 1980-86, Cardinal Industries, Columbus, Ohio, 1986-89; pres. January Mgmt. Group, Columbus, 1989—. Mem. strategic planning bd. Profl. Secs. Internat., 1989. Author: (Book) Supervisor's Guide, 1985, Sixty Minute Mastery, 1987, Property Management First Aid Kit, 1988, The January Report, 1989, The Human Resources Executive Guide to Mergers and Acquisitions, 1989, Executive Development: At the Crossroads, 1990, The Board of Directors: A Peek Behind the Boardroom Doors, 1990, Human Resources and the Quest for Corporate Quality, 1992, Selecting the Chief Executive Officer, 1993; prodr.: (films, and videos) The Visitor, 1984, Dell Heros, 1985. Mem. Youth Motivation Task Force, Akron, Ohio, 1983-86; officer Pvt. Industry Council, Akron, 1983-86. Recipient Silver Quill for Scriptwriting award Internat. Assn. Bus. Communicators, 1985, Best Film/Video Series award Nat. Assn. Convenience Stores, 1985, Exec. of Yr. award Profl. Secs. Internat., 1987. Mem. Soc. for Human Resources Mgmt. (bd. dirs. 1985-86), Am. Soc. Tng. and Devel., Internat. Assn. of Corp. and Profl. Recruiters. Address: 22 E Gay St #801 Columbus OH 43215

BASTOW, RICHARD FREDERICK, civil engineer, educator, surveyor; b. Waterville, Maine, Apr. 20, 1934; s. Frank W. and Susan (Strong) B.; m. Nancy Dodge, Sept. 13, 1958; children: Susan Weimer, Bonnie Jean Kuykendall. BS in Civil Engring., U. Maine, Orono, 1961; MS, U. So. Maine, Gorham, 1975. Site planner, engr. Harriman Assocs., Architects and Engrs., Auburn, Maine, 1957-65, Taylor Engring., C.E., Auburn, 1966-68; chmn. archtl. and civil engring. tech. Ctrl. Maine Tech. Coll., Auburn, 1968—. Pres. Maine Planning & Engring. Assocs., Auburn, 1969—; mem., chmn. Maine Bd. Land Surveyors, 1978-87. Contbr. articles to profl. jours. Fellow ASCE; mem. Maine Soc. Land Surveyors (charter; bd.dirs., sec., pres., Appreciation award 1987), Am. Congress Surveying and Mapping (chmn. New Eng. sect. 1992). Home: 10 Weaver St Auburn ME 04210-4627 Office: Ctrl Maine Tech Coll 1250 Turner St Auburn ME 04210-6436 E-mail: RFBastow@cmtc.net.

BASTRENTA, BRIGITTE ELISABETH, school administrator; b. Moutiers, Savoie, France, Jan. 7, 1952; came to U.S., 1979; d. Marcel Rinaldo and Jeanne Eulalie (Chaville) B.; m. Rudolph Andrew Walter, Dec. 27, 1979; children: Laurie Nicole Walter, Julian Thomas Walter. BA, U. Paul Valéry, Montpellier, France, 1973, MA, 1974. Tchr. French Marin Acad., San Rafael, Calif., 1980-83, Arrowsmith Acad., Berkeley, Calif., 1989-96, dir. admission and devel., 1996—. Tchr. French Diablo Valley Coll., Pleasant Hill, Calif., 1990-95; mem. WASC Accreditation Commn., 1998—. Editor (newsletter) Arrowsmith in Action, 1999—. Co-pres. East Bay French-Am. Sch. PTA, Berkeley, 1991-93; mem. Natural Resources Def. Coun. Mem. Amnesty Internat., Doctors Without Borders, So. Poverty Law Ctr. Democrat. Avocations: swimming, skiing, hiking, travel, cooking. Home: 333 Scottsdale Rd Pleasant Hill CA 94523 Office: Arrowsmith Acad 2300 Bancroft Way Berkeley CA 94704

BASTRON, JAMES ARTHUR, retired neurologist; b. Ottumwa, Iowa; s. Alexander E. and Grayce Margaret Bastron; m. Louise Frances Lomas; children: Malcolm Dewitt, Mary Jo, James Arthur. BA, U. Iowa, 1941, MD, 1944; MS in Neurology, U. Minn., 1954. Rotating intern Wesley Meml. Hosp., Chgo., 1944-45; resident pathology Columbia U. Coll. Physicians and Surgeons, N.Y.C., 1947-48; fellw in surgery, internal medicine and neurology Mayo Found., Rochester, Minn., 1948-53; cons. in neurology and electromyography Mayo Clinic, Rochester, 1954-91, Jacksonville, Fla., 1954-91, head neurology dept., 1989-90, emeritus staff, 1990—. Hosp. dir. Fed. Med. Ctr., Rochester, 1985-87. Elder First Presbyn. Ch., Rochester. Capt. U.S. Army, 1945-47, USAF, 1954. Mem. Alpha Omega Alpha. Avocations: golf, gardening, fishing. Home: 2220 Hillside Ln SW Rochester MN 55902-1147 Office: Mayo Clinic 200 1st St SW Rochester MN 55905-0002

BASU, ASIT PRAKAS, statistician; b. India, Mar. 17, 1937; arrived in U.S., 1962, naturalized, 1979; m. Sandra Bergquist; children: Amit K., Shumit K. BS with honors, Calcutta U., 1956, MS, 1958; PhD, U. Minn., 1966. Asst. prof. stats. U. Wis., Madison, 1966-68; mem. research staff IBM Research Center, Yorktown Heights, N.Y., 1968-70; asst. prof. indsl. engring. and mgmt. sci. Northwestern U., Evanston, Ill., 1970-71; asso. prof. math. U. Pitts., 1971-74; prof. stats. U. Mo., Columbia, 1974—, chmn. dept., 1976-83. Co-author: Statistical Methods for the Reliability of Repairable Systems, 2000; co-editor: Reliability and Quality Control, 1986, Advances in Reliability, 1993, The Exponential Distribution: Theory, Methods and Application, 1995, Frontiers in Reliability, 1997; contbr. articles to profl. jours. Fellow AAAS, Royal Statis. Soc., Am. Statis. Assn., Inst. Math. Stats.; mem. Calcutta Statis. Assn., Internat. Statis. Inst., Am. Soc. Quality Control, Biometric Soc. Office: Univ Mo Dept Stats Columbia MO 65211-0001

BASU, PARANTAP, economist, educator; s. Sunil and Indu Basu; m. Barsha S. Sinha, July 4, 1987. PhD, U. of Calif., Santa Barbara, 1985. Assoc. prof. Fordham U., Bronx, NY, 1988—. Avocation: Indian classical music. Office: Dept of Economics Fordham University Bronx NY 10458 Personal E-mail: basu@fordham.edu. E-mail: basu@fordham.edu.

BASU, PRODYOT KUMAR, civil engineer, educator; b. Lucknow, India, Nov. 15, 1939; came to U.S., 1974; s. Krishna Kamal and Usha Rani (Ghosh) B.; m. Liliya Bhattacharya, Jan. 26, 1966; 1 child, Devraj. MS, Calcutta (India) U., 1963; ScD, Washington U., St. Louis, 1977. Registered profl. engr., Tenn. Lectr., then asst. prof. civil engring. Calcutta U., 1964-74; instr., sr. rsch. engr. Washington U., 1975-79, asst. prof., then assoc. prof. civil engring., 1980-84; assoc. prof., now prof. civil engring. Vanderbilt U., Nashville, 1984—. Cons. Ala. A&M U., Huntsville, 1990—. Contbr. articles to tech. publs. Fellow: ASCE; mem.: AIAA, ASME, Internat. Assn. Computational Mechanics. Achievements include development of p- and hp- version of finite boundary element and wavelet methods; research in high performance concrete jointless bridges, fire resistance of buildings, active control of structures and multiscale modeling. Office: Vanderbilt U PO Box 15 Nashville TN 37202-0015

BASU, SUDESHNA, mathematician, educator, researcher; b. Kolkata, West Bengal, India, July 1, 1966; d. Biplap Kumar and Bandana Basu; m. Subrata Kundu, Sept. 23, 1996. BS, Calcutta U., 1984—88, MS, 1988—91; PhD, Indian Statis. Inst., 1992—98. Lectr. Howard U., Washington, 1998—. Mem.: Banach Bulletin Bd., Am. Math. Soc. Avocation: singing. Home: 17628 Sequoia Drive # 203 Gaithersburg MD 20877 Office: Department of Mathematics Howard University Washington DC 20059 Personal E-mail: sbasu@howard.edu.

BASYE, CHARLES BENJAMIN, engineering educator; b. Fayette, Mo., June 10, 1927; s. Charley Bradley and Dorothy Elizabeth (Crews) B.; m. Joanne Brown, Dec. 12, 1954; children: George Levon, Stuart Randall, Charles Roger, Scott Kennedy. BS, U. Mo., 1953; MS, Iowa State U., 1960, PhD i Engring., 1965. Registered profl. engr., Mo. Engr. Westinghouse, Kansas City, Mo., 1953-58; prof. Iowa State U., Ames, 1958-65, U. Mo., Rolla, 1965-67, 69-92, prof. emeritus, 1992—; sr. staff engr. Emerson Electric, St. Louis, 1967-69. Cons. in field, Mo., 1970—. Mem. St. Charles (Mo.) Sch. Bd., 1973-79. Capt. USNR, 1945-87. Me. Mid. Mo. Ret. Officers Assn., Pachyderm Club (pres. 2000), Kiwanis, Tau Beta Pi, Pi Tau Sigma, Pi Mu Epsilon, Sigma Xi. Mem. Reform Party. Avocations: farming, travel. Home: 15001 W Hwy 40 Rocheport MO 65279

BATA, RUDOLPH ANDREW, JR., lawyer; b. Akron, Ohio, Jan. 9, 1947; s. Rudolph Andrew and Margaret Eleanor (Ellis) Bata; m. Genevieve Ruth Brannan, Aug. 25, 1968 (div. May 1985); 1 child, Seth Andrew; m. Linda Lee Waldo, Apr. 7, 1985; 1 child, Sarah Ariel. BS, So. Coll., Collegedale, Tenn., 1969; JD, Emory U., 1972. Bar: D.C. 1973, N.C. 1978, U.S. Dist. Ct. N.C. 1991, U.S. Ct. Appeals (4th cir.) 1991, cert.: Adminstrv. Office of Cts. (arbitrator, mediator). Assoc. ICC, Washington, 1972-73; in house counsel B.F. Saul Real Estate Investment Trust, Chevy Chase, Md., 1973-74; staff atty. Martha, Cafferky, Powers & Jordan, Washington, 1974-75; asst. corp. counsel Hardee's Food Systems, Inc., Rocky Mount, N.C., 1975-78; ptnr. Bata & Blomeley, Murphy, N.C., 1978-87, 88-90, Bata & Sumpter, Murphy, 1987-88; sole practice, 1990—. Bd. dirs. Cherokee County United Fund, Murphy, 1981-83. Mem. ABA, N.C. Bar Assn., D.C. Bar Assn., 30th Jud. Dist. Bar Assn., So. Soc. of Adventist Attys. (pres. 1984-85), Cherokee County C. of C. (bd. dirs. 1980-82). Avocations: golf, tennis, hiking. Office: 225 Valley River Ave Ste A Murphy NC 28906-3000 E-mail: batalaw@dnet.net.

BATABYAL, AMITRAJEET AMARNATH, economics educator; b. Chittaranjan, India, Sept. 6, 1965; came to US 1983; s. Amar Nath and Sutapa (Bhattasali) B.; m. Swapna Bhattacharya, Mar. 8, 1995; 1 child, Sanjaña S. BS with honors and distinction, Cornell U., 1987; MS, U. Minn., 1990; PhD, U. Calif., Berkeley, 1994. Asst. prof. econ. UT State U., Logan, 1995-98; assoc. prof. Utah State U., Logan, 1998—2000; Arthur J. Gosnell prof. econ. Rochester Inst. Tech., Rochester, NY, 2000—. Vis. asst. prof. econ. Coll. William and Mary, Williamsburg, Va., 1994-95; legal asst. Spiegel & McDiarmid, Washington, 1987-88; Smith lectr. Brigham Young U., 1997. Contbr. articles to profl. jour. Rsch. grantee USDA, Berkeley, 1992-94; Dorab Tata scholar, India, 1983. Mem. Am. Econ. Assn., Assn. Environ. and Resource Economists, Am. Agrl. Econ. Assn., Internat. Soc. for Ecol. Econ. Achievements include rsch. in field. Home: 35 Crandon Way Rochester NY 14618-4427 E-mail: aabgsh@rit.edu.

BATALDEN, PAUL BENNETT, pediatrician, health care educator; b. Mpls., Dec. 4, 1941; s. Abner Bennett and Martha (Bjornstad) B.; m. LaVonne Marie Olson; children: Maren, Sonja. BA, Augsburg Coll., 1963; MD, BS, U. Minn., 1967. Diplomate Am. Bd. Pediatrics. Clin. assoc. Nat. Cancer Inst., Bethesda, Md., 1969; med. dir. Job Corps, Washington, 1970-72; dir. Community Health Svcs., Rockville, Md., 1972-73; dir., Bur. Community Health Svc., Rockville, 1973-75; pediatrician Park Nicollet Med. Ctr., Mpls., 1975-86, quality assurance dir., 1976-84, chief oper. officer, 1984-86; v.p. med. care, head quality resource group Hosp. Corp. of Am., Nashville, 1986-94; Breech chmn. Dept. Health Care Quality Improvement Edn. and Rsch. Henry Ford Health Sci. Ctr., 1990—2000; prof., dir. Ctr. Healthcare Improvement Leadership Devel. Dartmouth Med. Sch. Founding chmn., bd. dirs. Inst. for Healthcare Improvement. Author: Quality Assurance in Ambulatory Care, 1980, Clinical Improvement Action Guide, 1998; contbr. articles on quality in healthcare and aspects of pediatric practice to profl. jours. Regent Augsburg Coll., Mpls., 1978-90. Recipient Guild of Honor, 1963, Pub. Svc. award Nat. Med. Assn., 1974, Disting. Alumnus award Augsburg Coll., 1984, Award of Honor, Am. Hosp. Assn., 1997, Codman award, 1998, Nemours Found. award for improving quality, 2002. Mem. Inst. of Medicine of NAS, Am. Acad. Pediatrics, Minn. Med. Assn., Tenn. Med. Assn., N.H. Med. Assn., Alpha Omega Alpha

BATAVIA, MITCHELL, physical therapist, educator; b. Bklyn., Nov. 8, 1959; s. Gabriel and Renée (Hyman) Batavia; m. Evgenia Yakovleva, Aug. 12, 2001; 1 child, Michael Andrew. BS, U. of Del., 1978—81; MA, Teachers Coll., Columbia U., 1986; PhD, N.Y. U, 1994—97. Lic. Physical Therapist N.Y. State, 1981. Staff phys. therapist Inst. for Rehab. Medicine, NY U. Med. Ctr., 1981—84; home care phys. therapist Vis. Nurse Svc. of NY, 1984—86; pediatric phys. therapist NY Foundling Hosp., 1986—91; phys. therapy cons. Terence Cardinal Cooke Health Care Ctr., N.Y.C., 1989—97; adj. lectr. Hunter Coll. Phys. Therapy Program, N.Y.C., 1992—93, 1996; asst. prof. of phys. therapy NYU, 1998—. Manuscript reviewer Neurology Sect., Am. Phys. Therapy Assn., Alexandria, Va., 2000—; manuscript reviewer for book submissions Butterworth-Heinemann, Boston, 1999—2001. Author: (book) The Wheelchair Evaluation: A Practical Guide, Clinical Research for Health Professionals: A User Friendly Guide; contbr. articles to profl. jours. Vol., food distbr. Coalition for the Homeless, N.Y.C, 2002. Recipient NY U. Arch award, NY U., 1997; DeWitt Wallace Reader's Digest fellow, Inst. for Rehab. Medicine; NY U. Med. Ctr., 1978, Trainee for Phys. Therapy Clin. Rsch. in Doctoral Studies, Nat. Inst. for Disabilities Rsch. in Rehab., NY U., 1993—97, Robert Salant Post Doctoral fellow, Dept. of Phys. Therapy, NY U., The Inst. for Rehab., NY U. Med. Ctr., 1997—98, Rsch. Challenge fund, NY U., Sch. of Edn., 2000. Mem.: Neurology Sect. of the Am. Phys. Therapy Assn., Am. Phys. Therapy Assn. Achievements include constructed a functional rotation test to measure a person's rotation ability; construction of a mechanical stretch reflex model for teaching; construction of a tissue compliance meter for research. Avocation: music. Office: New York U 380 Second Ave 4th floor New York NY 10010 Office Fax: 212-995-4190. E-mail: mitchell.batavia@nyu.edu.

BATBIE, JOHN J., JR., military officer; BBA, Ariz. State U., 1973; postgrad., Air Command and Staff Coll., 1976, Indsl. Coll. Armed Forces, 1977; MBA, La. Tech. U., 1990. Commd. 2d lt. USAF, 1967, advanced through grades to maj. gen., 1997; tng. officer I Corps, Camp Red Cloud, Republic of Korea, 1967—68; platoon leader 3d Armored Cavalry Regiment, Ft. Lewis, Wash., 1968; cobra weapons platoon leader, ops. officer 101st Airborne Divsn., Quang Tri, Vietnam, 1970—71, staff officer Ft. Campbell, Ky., 1971—72; helicopter instr. pilot 302d Air Rescue and Recovery Squadron, AF Res., Luke AFB, Ariz., 1972—79; pilot, group tng. officer, instr. pilot, exec. officer 917th Tactical Fighter Group, Barksdale AFB, La., 1979—83; staff officer Hdqrs. U.S. Air Forces in Europe, Ramstein AB, Germany, 1973—76; asst. dir. ops. 452d Air Refueling Wing, March AFB, Calif., 1987—88; comdr. 916th Air Refueling Group, Seymour Johnson AFB, NC, 1988—91, 434th Air Refueling Wing, Grissom AFB, Ind., 1991—94; dir. plans and programs AF Res. Command, Robins AF Base, Ga., 1994—98; comdr. 22d AF, Dobbina Air Res. Base, Ga., 1998—2000; dir. mobilizationand res. component affairs U.S. European Command, Stuttgart, Germany, 2000—01; vice comdr. AF Res. Command, Robins AFB, Ga., 2001—. Decorated Bronze Star, Air medal with 20 oak leaf clusters, DSM, DFC, Legion of Merit. Office: Robins AFB Robins AFB GA 31098-5009

BATCHA, GEORGE, retired mechanical and nuclear engineer; b. Marblehead, Ohio, Oct. 24, 1928; s. John and Anna (Groholy) B.; m. Erika Voelker, Jan. 1, 1982; 1 child, Susan Kolodziejczyk. BA, Bowling Green State U., 1951; MS in Engring. Sci., U. Toledo, 1968; R&D test and evaluation program cert., U.S. Army Logistics Mgmt. Coll. and Assn. for Sys. Mgmt.; certs., numerous U.S. Army Tng. Schs. R&D test and evaluation program cert, U.S. Army Logistics Mgmt. Coll. and Assn. for Systems Mgmt.; certs. numerous U.S. Army tng. schs.; registered profl. engr., Ohio, Mich.; cert. nat. engring. examiners. With Standard Products Co., Port Clinton, Ohio, 1951, A.O. Smith Co. Landing Gear Divsn., Toledo, 1951; army rep. Glenn L. Martin Co., Balt., 1952-54, Cleve. Pneumatic Tool Co., 1954-55, Hardware Stamping divsn. Ford Motor Co., Sandusky, Ohio, 1955-59; mech. design and test engr. Missile and Def. Engring. divsns. Chrysler Corp., Detroit, 1959-62; mech. and nuclear engr. NASA, Lewis Rsch. Ctr., Plum Brook Sta., Sandusky, 1962-74; mech. and system mgmt. engr. Armament Rsch. & Devel. Command, U.S. Army, Dover, N.J., 1974-81, Rock Island, Ill., 1974-81; mech. engr. Tank Automotive and Armaments Command, Warren, Mich., 1981—2002; ret., 2002. Author numerous tech. reports. With U.S. Army, 1952-54. Recipient Apollo Achievement award, NASA, 1969, accomplishments awards, 1981, 82, Cost Reduction awards, 1971-74, Dept. Army Achievement award Tank Automotive and Armaments Command, 1985, Superior Performance award Spl. Act award, 1990-2002; Bowling Green State U. scholar, 1948. Mem. NSPE, Order of Engr., Nat. Coun. engring. Examiners (cert.), Am. Acad. Environ. Engrs. (diplomate, radiation protection), Soc. Logistics Engrs. (cert. prof. logistician), U.S. Army Logistics Mgmt. Coll. and Assn. for Systems Mgmt. (cert. in R&D), Am. Legion. Byzantine Catholic. Achievements include serving as team leader of Logistics Engring. Team; research in technical assessment and guidance of developmental programs of all elements of integrated logistics support in tank-automotive weapon system and equipment; subspecialties include:mechanical engineering and nuclear engineering. Home: 12851 E Outer Dr Detroit MI 48224-2730

BATCHELDER, ALICE M. federal judge; b. Aug. 15, 1944; m. William G. Batchelder III; children: William G. IV, Elisabeth. BA, Ohio Wesleyan U., 1964; JD, Akron U., 1971; LLM, U. Va., 1988. Tchr. Plain Local Sch. Dist., Franklin County, Ohio, 1965-66, Jones Jr. High Sch., 1966-67, Buckeye High Sch., Medina County, 1967-68; assoc. Williams & Batchelder, Medina, Ohio, 1971-83; judge U.S. Bankruptcy Ct., Ohio, 1983-85, U.S. Dist. Ct. (no. dist.) Ohio, Cleve., 1985-91, U.S. Ct. of Appeals (6th cir.), Cleveland, 1991—. Mem. ABA, Fed. Judge's Assn., Fed. Bar Assn., Medina County Bar Assn. Office: US Ct of Appeals (6th cir) 143 W Liberty St Medina OH 44256-2215

BATCHELDER, ANNE STUART, retired publisher, political party official; b. Lake Forest, Ill., Jan. 11, 1920; d. Robert Douglas and Harriet (McClure) Stuart; m. Clifton Brooks Batchelder, May 26, 1945; children: Edward, Anne Stuart, Mary Clifton, Lucia Brooks Student Lake Forest Coll., 1941-43. Clubmobile driver ARC, Eng., Belgium, France, Holland and Germany, 1943-45; pub., editor Douglas County Gazette, 1970-75, 79-90. Bd. dirs. Firstier Bank Omaha; dir., treas. U.S. Checkbook Com. Mem. Rep. Ctrl. Com. Nebr., 1955-62, 70-83, vice chmn. Ctrl. Com., 1959-64, chmn., 1975-79, mem. fin. com., 1957-64; chmn. women's sect. Douglas County Rep. Fin. Com., 1995, vice chmn. com., 1958-60; v.p. Omaha Woman's Rep. Club, 1957-58, pres., 1959-60; alt. del. Nat. Conv., 1956, 72, del., 1980, 84, 88; mem. Rep. Nat. Com. for Nebr., 1964-70; asst. chmn. Douglas County Rep. Ctrl. Com., 1971-74; 1st v.p. Nebr. Fedn. Rep. Women, 1971-72, pres., 1972-74; chmn. Nebr. Rep. Com., 1975-79; vice-chmn. Bldg. Fedn. Rep. Women, 1998—; mem. Nebr. State Bldg. Commn., 1979-83; Rep. candidate for lt. gov., 1974. Sr. v.p. Nebr. Founders Day, 1958; trustee Hastings Coll., 1977—; bd. dirs. YWCA, 1983-89, Omaha Libr. Found., 1991-2000, Libr. Found., 2000—; past trustee Brownell Hall, Vis. Nurse Assn.; past pres. Nebr. chpt. Freedoms Found. at Valley Forge; chmn. fin. George Bush for Pres., Nebr., 1987-88; apptd. Kennedy Ctr. Performing Arts, 1989, 94, Pres.' Adv. Com. on the Arts, 1990-92, Nat. Com. for the Performing Arts, 1992—; mem. Nebr. Rep. State Fin. Com., 1990, Nat. Fin. Com. Bush-Quayle, 1992; active Omaha Meth. Hosp. Found., Brownell-Talbot Sch. Found.; mem. Uta Halee Home for Girls, 1980—. Elected to Nebr. Rep. Hall of Fame, 1984; named Citizen of the Yr. Midlands Coun. Boy Scouts Am., 1997; recipient Silver Beaver, Boy Scouts Am., Spirit award Uta Halee Home for Girls, 1999. Mem. Mayflower Soc., Colonial Dames, P.E.O., Nat. League Pen Women Omaha Country, Omaha, Halee Spirit of Youth. Presbyterian. Home: 6875 State St Omaha NE 68152-1633

BATCHELDER, SAMUEL LAWRENCE, JR., retired corporate lawyer; b. Boston, Apr. 3, 1932; s. Samuel L. and May W. (Read) B.; m. Jane B. Borden, 1955 (div. 1965); children: John H., Benjamin A.; m. Marion C. Thomas, 1967; children: Timothy C., Lily L. AB, Harvard U., 1954, LLB, 1960. Bar: Mass., 1960, U.S. Dist. Mass. 1961. Assoc. Goodwin, Procter LLP, Boston, 1960-67, ptnr., 1968-97, of counsel, 1997—. Active ARC, bd. dirs. local orgns., Boston, 1966-2003, chmn. Mass. Bay unit, 1979-83, mem. various nat. coms., 1981-98, chmn. resolutions com., 1998, NE Blood Svcs., 1981-92; mem. grad. coun. Milton Acad., 1986-91, chmn., 1989-91, trustee, 1989-92; trustee Mass. Continuing Legal Edn., 1995—; dir. Exec. Svc. Corps. N.E., 1998—, vice chair, 2001-03, chair, 2003—. Served to 1st lt. U.S. Army, 1954-57. Mem. ABA, Mass. Bar Assn., Boston Bar Assn. (chmn. corp. law com. 1985-88, mem. gov. coun. 1988-91, legal edn. com. 1995-2000), Brookline Cmty. Fund (trustee 1998—). Clubs: The Country Club (Brookline, Mass.). Democrat. Avocations: tennis, skiing, gardening, music, art. Office: 66 Laurel Rd Chestnut Hill MA 02467-2211 also: Goodwin Procter LLP Exchange Pl Boston MA 02109-2803

BATCHELLER, JOE ANN, entrepreneur; b. Jacksonville, Fla., Dec. 11, 1932; d. Osmer St. Clair and Lorena (Jones) Deming; m.David Springsteen Batcheller, Aug. 8, 1957; children: Elizabeth Batcheller Whalen, Osmer Deming, John Alden. AA, Stephens Coll., Columbia, Mo., 1952; BA, U. N.C., 1955. Sec. Seminole Oil Co., Miami, Fla., 1957-61, pres., bd. dirs., 1961-65; pres., chmn. Blue Water Mobile Home Sales, Inc., Tavernier, Fla., 1967-76; dir. Miami Heart Inst., Miami Beach, 1973—, v.p., 1975—, exec. v.p., 1986-89, pres., chief exec. officer, 1989-93. Sec., bd. dirs. Bluegrass Plant Foods, Inc., Cynthiana, Ky., 1958-72; chmn. Superior Plant Foods, Inc., Lakeland, Fla., 1958-60; v.p., bd. dirs. Pensacola Petroleum Co., Inc., Miami, 1961-65, Top Power Stas., Miami, 1961-65, Atico Savs. Bank, Miami, 1987-88, Pan Am. Bank, Miami, 1984-87; bd. dirs. Intercontinental Bank; vice chmn. Miami Heart Rsch. Inst., Inc., 1993—. Bd. dirs. Am. Heart Assn., Miami, 1989-91; mem. adv. bd. Convent of Sacred Heart, Miami, 1973-77; mem. parents adv. bd. Furman U., Greenville, S.C., 1979-83. Mem. Surf Club on Miami Beach (pres. bd. govs. 1993-97, vice chmn. 1997-99), Surf Club Debutante Com. (chmn. 1976-82, 86, 87), Bay Point Property Owners Assn. (pres. 1991-96), Young Patronesses of Opera, English Speaking Union, DAR. Episcopalian. Avocations: reading, boating, Beaux Arts. Home: 4595 Sabal Palm Rd Miami FL 33137-3363

BATCHELOR, BARRINGTON DE VERE, civil engineer, educator; b. Lucea, Jamaica, W.I., July 2, 1928; s. Reginald Augustus and Vera Louise (O'Connor) B.; m. Alison Yvonnie Johnston, Sept. 14, 1960; children: Roger, Nicola, Wayne. B.Sc. with honors (Elias Issa scholar), U. Edinburgh, 1956; PhD (Commonwealth scholar), U. London, 1963; student, Nat. Def. Coll. Can., 1982-83. Registered profl. engr., Ont. Asst. engr. Sir William Halcrow & Partners, London, 1956-58; exec. engr. Ministry Edn., Jamaica, 1958-63, sr. exec. engr., 1963-64; ptnr. Franks & Batchelor, cons. engrs., Kingston, Jamaica, 1964-66; asst. prof. civil engring. Queen's U., Kingston, Ont., Can., 1966-68, assoc. prof., 1968-72, prof., 1972-93, prof. emeritus, 1993—. Bd. govs. Kingston Gen. Hosp. Fellow Engring. Inst. Can., Can. Soc. Civil Engrs.; mem. ASCE, Am. Concret Inst., Instn. Engrs. Jamaica, Instn. Engrs. Ont. Home: 150 Collingwood St Kingston ON Canada K7L 3X5 Office: Queen's U Dept Civil Engring Kingston ON Canada K7L 3N6

BATCHELOR, JAMES KENT, lawyer; b. Long Beach, Calif., Oct. 4, 1934; s. Jack Morrell and Edith Marie (Ottinger) B.; m. Jeanette Lou Dyer, Mar. 27, 1959; children: John, Suzanne; m. Susan Mary Leonard, Dec. 4, 1976. AA, Sacramento City Coll., 1954; BA, Calif. State U., Long Beach, 1956; JD, U. Calif., 1959. Bar: Calif. 1960, U.S. Dist. Ct. (cen. dist.) Calif. 1960, U.S. Supreme Ct. 1968; cert. family law specialist Calif. Bd. Legal Specialization, 1980. Dep. dist. atty., Orange County, Calif., 1960-62; assoc. Miller, Nisson, Kogler & Wenke, Santa Ana, Calif., 1962-64; ptnr. Batchelor, Cohen & Oster, Santa Ana, Calif., 1964-67, Kurilich, Ballard, Batchelor, Fullerton, Calif., 1967-72; pres. James K. Batchelor, Inc. Tchr. paralegal sect. Santa Ana City Coll.; judge pro-tem Superior Ct., 1974—; lectr. family law Calif. Continuing Edn. of Bar, 1973—. Contbr. articles to profl. jours. Named one of Best Lawyers in Am., 1989—. Fellow Am. Acad. Matrimonial Lawyers (pres. So. Calif. chpt. 1989-90); mem. ABA, Calif. State Bar (plaque chmn. family law sect. 1975-76, advisor 1976-78), Orange County Barristers (founder, pres., plaque 1963), Calif. State Barristers (plaque 1964, v.p.), Orange County Bar Assn. (plaque sec. 1977, pres. family law sect. 1968-71). Republican. Methodist. Office: 765 The City Dr S Ste 270 Orange CA 92868-6908

BATCHELOR, ROBERT PAUL, corporate communications specialist, writer; b. Wellsville, N.Y., Aug. 29, 1968; s. Linda Ellen and Jon Bowen(Stepfather); m. Katherine Elizabeth Roda, Nov. 15, 1997. BA, U. of Pitts., 1991; MA, Kent (Ohio) State U., 1993. Sr. writer UpStart Comm., Emeryville, Calif., 2000—01; v.p. corp. comm. Bank of Am., San Francisco, 2001—. Author: The 1900s, 2002. Home: 1100 Clayton Court Novato CA 94945 Personal E-mail: bob@bobbatchelor.com.

BATCHELOR, RUBY STEPHENS, retired nurse; b. Rocky Mount, N.C., Sept. 27, 1931; d. Paul Madison and Ruby Legin (Coggins) Stephens; m. Sherwood H. Batchelor, Nov. 1, 1952; children: Paula S. Liggon, G. Brooks. Diploma, Wilson Sch. Nursing, 1953; student, Atlantic Christian Coll. (now Barton Coll.). Cert. med.-surg. nurse. Assessment nurse Wilson (N.C.) Med. Ctr. (formerly Wilson Meml. Hosp.), head nurse pediat., primary care nurse ob.-gyn. unit, primary care nurse med.-surg. unit, primary care nurse psychiat. unit, 1991—93, ret., 1993. Organizer Al-A-Non, Wilson, N.C., 1973. Deacon Westview Christian Ch., 1995, 96, 97. chmn. membership com., 1996, moderator bd., 1997, v.p. Sunday Sch. class, 2002-2003; trustee Westview Christian Ch., 1998-99, mem. 60+ Singers, 1999—, sec. bd., 2000; vol. Wilson Pregnancy Ctr.; past dist. pres. Wilson, N.C. Nurses Assn.; pres. Wilson Active Artist, 2001-2003, sec., 1999-2001; co-chmn., Lowe Gallery Arts Coun., 2003-2004. Mem.: ANA, Arts Coun. Lowe Gallery (asst. 2003—), Wilson Active Artist Assn. (sec. 1999, 2000, pres. 2001—03). Avocation: oil, watercolor and acrylic painting. Home: 1300 Dogwood Ln NW Wilson NC 27896-1420

BATCHO, RONALD FRANK, automotive company executive; b. Hackensack, N.J., Mar. 31, 1947; s. Edward Stephen and Anna (Korley) B.; m. Michele Jean (Kosmider) McAndrew, Dec. 23, 1984; children: Ronald Frank, Rebecca Louise; stepchildren: William A Reardon, Alexandra Reardon. AAS, Fashion Inst. Tech., 1967. Indsl. engr. Can. Garment Ltd., Winnipeg, Man., 1967-68; asst. product mgr. Ea. Isles, Inc., N.Y.C., 1968-73; product mgr. Windjammer Fashions, N.Y.C., 1973-77; pres. Crewco, Inc., Cornelius, N.C., 1977-83, United Sportswear, Inc., Locust, N.C., 1983-87; v.p. United Screen Printers, Locust, 1983-97; automotive after-market agt. Dealer Devel. Svcs., Charlotte, N.C., 1997—. Mem. Cornelius bd. Piedmont Bank and Trust Co., Davidson, N.C., 1980-87. First lt. Maywood (N.J.) First Aid Squad, 1975-77; CPR instr. Am. Heart Assn., Englewood, N.J., 1975-77. Mem. Am. Mgmt. Assn., Ctrl. Piedmont Employers Assn. Democrat. Roman Catholic. Office: Dealer Devel Svcs 206 Woodlawn Rd Ste 229A Charlotte NC 28217 Fax: 704-523-9311. E-mail: rbatcho@earthlink.net.

BATCHVAROVA, MADLEN TODOROVA, music educator, conductor; d. Todor Bachvarov and Stefka Bachvarova. MusB, Acad. for Music and Dance Art, Bulgaria, 1991; MusM in Choral Conducting, Ga. state U., 1997; Mus D, U. of Ala., 2000. Condr. Plovdiv Choral Soc., Bulgaria, 1992—94; piano accompanist Secondary Music Sch., Plovdiv, Bulgaria, 1992—94; grad. tchg. asst. U. of Ala., Tuscaloosa, 1997—2000; asst. prof. music Columbus State U., Ga., 2000—01; asst. prof. music, dir. choral programs Hanover Coll., Ind., 2001—. Mem. internat. jury Internat. Choral Festival, Preveza, Greece, 2002. Singer: (CD recording) John Adams (GRAMMY for Best Choral Performance, 1997); singer: (chorus) (music performance at carnegie hall) Brahms, Requiem. Mem.: Am. Choral Dirs. Assn., NARAS, Pi Kappa Lambda. Office: Hanover Coll POBox 890 Hanover IN 47243 Office Fax: 812-866-2164. E-mail: batchvarova@hanover.edu.

BATDORF, LYNN ROBERT, horticulturist; b. Lebanon, Pa., Aug. 4, 1954; s. Robert LeVoy Smith Jr. and Rudella Louise (Brandt) Batdorf; m. Holly A. Hamilton, Oct. 24, 1998; children: Jessica Zischka, Theodore Robert. AA in Horticulture, Inst. of Applied Agrl., 1974; BSBA, U. Coll., 1984; BS in Ornamental Horticulture, U. Md., 1994. Cert. profl. horticulturist. Agrl. rsch. technician U.S. Nat. Arboretum, Washington, 1977-80, horticulturist, 1980—, Horticultural cons. TJ Horticultural Svcs., Washington, 1989—; instr. water garden mgmt. course Montgomery Coll., Germantown, Md., 1996—. Author: Boxwood Handbook: A Practical Guide to Knowing and Growing Boxwood, 1995, revised 1997, Caring for Box, 2003; contbr. National Arboretum Book of Outstanding Garden Plants, 1989, Time-Life Gardener's Guide, Perennials, 1988, The Washington Star Garden Book, 1988. Recipient Cert. of Merit U.S. Dept. Agrl., 1980, 89, 91, (2) 93, 96. Mem. Am. Boxwood Soc. (hon. life, bd. dirs.,) Internat. Registration Authority for Cultivated Boxwoods, Am. Hemerocallis Soc., Internat. Water Lily Soc., Internat. Soc. for Horticultural Sci., Am. Assn. of Botanic Gardens and Arboreta, Royal Horticulture Soc., European Boxwood and Topiary Soc. (hon. life), Office: US Nat Arboretum 3501 New York Ave NE Washington DC 20002-1958

BATDORF, SAMUEL B(URBRIDGE), physicist; b. Jung Hsien, China, Mar. 31, 1914; s. Charles William and Nellie (Burbridge) B.; m. Carol Catherine Schweiss, July 19, 1940 (dec.); children: Samuel Charles, Laura Ann. AB, U. Calif., Berkeley, 1934, AM, 1936, PhD, 1938. From instr. to assoc. prof. physics U. Nev., 1938-43; aero. rsch. scientist Langley Lab., NACA, 1943-51, chmn. advanced study com., 1946-51, mem. NACA subcom. on aircraft structural metals, 1946-51; from adv. physicist in rsch. lab. to dir. devel. Westinghouse Elec. Corp., Pitts., 1951-56; from asst. dir. rsch. to tech. dir. weapons sys. Lockheed Missile & Space Co., Palo Alto, Calif., 1956-58; mgr. comm. satellites Inst. Def. Analysis, Washington, 1958-59; from mgr. product planning to dir. rsch. in physics, electronics and bionics Aeronutronic, Newport Beach, Calif., 1959-62; from dir. office of rsch. to prin. staff scientist Aerospace Corp., El Segundo, Calif., 1962-77. Aeromechanics adv. com. Air Force Office Sci. RSch., 1965-71, tech. assessment panel Engrs. Joint Coun., 1968-71; cons. NSF, 1967-71; Sigma Xi lectr. communication satellites; Disting. prof. Tsing Hua U., Republic of China, 1969; adj. prof. engring. and applied sci. UCLA, 1973-86; vis. scholar Va. Poly. Inst. and State U., 1984. Contbr. articles to profl. jours. Pres. Engrs. Club Va. Peninsula, 1948. Fellow AIAA (edn., structures and materials coms.), ASME (hon., edn. materials and space structures coms., chmn. applied mechanics divsn. exec. com. materials and space structures com. 1960), Am. Phys. Soc., Am. Acad. Mechanics (pres. 1982-83); mem. Aerospace Club, Academians Leisure World Club (pres. 2002-03), Phi Beta Kappa, Phi Kappa Phi. Republican. Presbyterian. Home: 1106 Tower 1 24055 Paseo Del Lago Laguna Woods CA 92653-2678 E-mail: sbbatdorf@aol.com.

BATE, BRIAN R. psychologist; b. Cleve., July 4, 1940; s. Paul A. and Claire N. B.; children: Jennifer Bate Tyler, Julia L. Bate-Poxon. BA in English, Western Res. U., 1963, MS in Psychology, 1965; PhD in Psychology, Case Western Res. U., 1972. Instr. Cuyahoga C.C. Western Campus, Parma, Ohio, 1969, from asst. prof. to prof. of psychology, 1970—; pvt. practice, Cleve., 1972-96. Contbr. articles to profl. jours. Nat. Merit Scholar Princeton U., 1958-61, Western Res. U., 1962-63; USPHS fellow, 1963-67. Mem. APA, Am. Fedn. Musicians, Edelweiss Ski Club, Cleve. Buddhist Temple. Achievements include development and teaching of the first underclass-level behavior modification course in United States, 1970-77. Home: 8498 Vera Dr Cleveland OH 44147-2204 Office: Cuyahoga Cmty Coll Western Campus Parma OH 44130-5199

BATE, JENNIFER LUCY, musician; b. London, Nov. 11, 1944; d. Horace Alfred and Dorothy Marjorie B. BA with honors, Bristol U., 1966. Shaw libr. London Sch. Econs., London U., 1966-69. Organizer tchg. programs. Collaboration with Olivier Messiaen, 1975-92; designer portable organ with Mander Organs, 1984; designer prototype computer organ, 1987; compositions: Toccata on a Theme of Martin Shaw, Introduction and Variations on an Old French Carol, Four Reflections, Homage to 1685, Lament, An English Canon, Variations on a Gregorian Theme; recordings include concertos and solo works of all periods. Recipient Grand Prix du Disque, Messiaen, Music Retailers' Assn. award for 18th century series From Stanley to Wesley; named Young Musician, 1972, Personnalité de l'Année, France, 1989, One of Women of Yr., U.K., 1990-97; named hon. Italian citizen for svcs. to music, 1996. Fellow: Royal Coll. of Organists (F.J. Read prize), Royal Soc. Arts; mem.: Royal Acad. of Music (licentiate), Royal Coll. of Music (assoc.). Avocations: cooking, theatre, philately, gardening. Address: 35 Collingwood Ave Muswell Hill London N10 3EH England Fax: 44 0 20 8444 3695. E-mail: jenniferbate@classical-artists.com.

BATEMAN, CHRISTOPHER (KIP BATEMAN), state legislator; b. Somerville, N.J., Oct. 9, 1957; m. Susan Bateman; children: Christopher, Joseph, Stephanie, Kate. BA in Polit. Sci. and History, Ithaca Coll., 1980; JD, Seton Hall Law Sch., Newark, 1984. Bar: N.J. Assoc. Wharton, Stewart & Davis, Somerville, N.J., 1984-85; with Office of the Gov., Trenton, N.J., 1985-86; dir intergovtl. affairs N.J. Dept. Environ. Protection, Trenton, 1986-87; asst. gen. counsel Colfax Cos., Skillman, N.J., 1987-88; ptnr. Bateman & Bateman, 1988-94, DiFrancesco, Kynzman, Coley, Yospin, Bernstein & Bateman, 1994—; mem. N.J. Gen. Assembly, 1994—, asst. majority whip, 1994-95. Office: 36 E Main St Somerville NJ 08876-2308*

BATEMAN, CONNIE RAE (HANSON), entrepreneur, finance educator; b. Grand Forks, ND, Apr. 12, 1962; d. Henry Arnold and Hazel Ann Hanson; m. Micheal George Bateman, Apr. 15, 1995; 1 child, Kristopher Lee Dallmann. B in psychology and sociology, U. of ND, 1985—89, MBA, 1989—90; D of bus. adminstrn., So. Ill. U., 1992—98. Instr. of mktg. U. of ND, 1990—92, instr. of mgmt., 1991; lectr. -spl. appointment So. Ill. U., 1992—95; prof. of mktg. U. of ND, 1995—. Cons. U. of ND, 1995—; bus. owner Bateman Devel., Grand Forks, ND, 1995—. Contbr. articles to profl. jours. (Best Paper Award by Allied Acadmies, 2002). Flood relief Bateman Devel., 1997—97; ministry support - musical Living Word Ch., 2002. Mem.: MBA Steering Com. (assoc.). Conservative-R. Christian. Achievements include research in quantitatively and significantly validated theories supporting situational ethics in the consumer reasoning process. Avocations: travel, singing, religion. Office: University of North Dakota PO Box 8366 Grand Forks ND 58202-8366 Office Fax: 1-701-777-2225. E-mail: connie_bateman@und.nodak.edu.

BATEMAN, ERIC, literature educator; b. Huntington Park, Calif., Oct. 18, 1965; s. Linden B. and Deann Willes Bateman; m. Michele Dee McDonald, Aug. 12, 1988; children: Foster M., Charlie J., Andy W. BA in English, Brigham Young U., 1990; MA in English, Idaho State U., 1992. English prof. Great Basin Coll., Winnemucca, Nev., 1994—. Faculty senate chair Great Basin Coll., Elko, Nev., 1999—2000; freelance writer, photgrapher Humboldt Sun, Winnemucca, 2000—01; English instr. Ricks Coll., Rexburg, Idaho; adj. English instr. Idaho State U., Pocatello, writing tutor. Contbr. essays to books. Recipient Regent's Tchg. award for C.C., U. and C.C. Sys. Nev. Bd. Regents, 2002. Mem.: Coll. Composition and Comm., Nat. Coun. Tchrs. English, Two Year Coll. English Assn. (west region rep. to nat. assn. 2002—, west regional exec. com. 1996—2001). Democrat. Mem. Lds Ch. Avocations: photography, backpacking, travel, woodcarving. Office: Great Basin Coll Winnemucca Campus 5490 Kluncy Canyon Rd Winnemucca NV 89445

BATEMAN, HEIDI S. lawyer; b. Spokane, Wash., June 17, 1965; d. John Alan and Carole L. Havens; children: Ryan, Matthew; m. David Alan Bateman. BA with honors, Gonzaga U., 1987; JD, U. Wash., 1990. Bar: Wash. 1990, U.S. Dist. Ct. (we. dist.) Wash. 1994. Assoc. Bogle & Gates, PLLC, Seattle, 1990-96, sr. litigation atty., 1997-98; founding ptnr. Miller Bateman, LLP, Seattle, 1999—. Active Guardian Ad Litem Program, Seattle, 1990—; fund raiser U. Wash. Alumni Orgn., Seattle, 1990—. Mem. ABA (comml. and corp. litigation coms. 1998—), Wash. State Bar Assn. (legis. coms. 1995-96), King County Bar Assn. (jud. screening com. 1996-97). Office: Miller Bateman LLP 1426 Alaskan Way Ste 301 Seattle WA 98101-2045 E-mail: hbateman@millerbateman.com.

BATEMAN, JOHN JAY, classics educator; b. Elmira, N.Y., Feb. 17, 1931; s. Joseph Earl and Etha M. (Edwards) B.; m. Patricia Ann Hageman, July 5, 1952; children: Kristine M., Kathleen A., John Eric. BA, U. Toronto, 1953; MA, Cornell U., 1954, PhD, 1958. Lectr. Univ. Coll., U. Toronto, 1956-57; lectr., then asst. prof. U. Ottawa, 1957-60; mem. faculty U. Ill., Urbana, 1960—, prof. classics and speech, 1968-93; prof. emeritus, 1993—; head dept. classics U. Ill., 1966-73, chmn., 1988-92, acting dir. Sch. Humanities, 1973-74. Author, editor books and articles. Dem. precinct committeeman, 1964-68; sec. Champaign Dem. Central Com., 1965-66. Mem. Am. Philol. Assn. (sec.-treas. 1968-73), Soc. Bibl. Lit., Renaissance Soc. Am. Home: 5508 41st Ave E Bradenton FL 34208-6835 E-mail: jjbateman@aol.com.

BATEMAN, MERRILL JOSEPH, church administrator; b. Lehi, Utah, June 19, 1936; s. Joseph Fredric and Belva (Smith) Bateman; m. Marilyn Scholes, Mar. 23, 1959; children: Michael, Mark, Michele, Melisa, Merilee, Matthew, McKay. BA, U. Utah, 1960; PhD, MIT, 1965. Exec. Mars, Inc., 1971—75; dean Sch. Mgmt. Brigham Young U., Provo, Utah, 1975—79, pres., 1996—2003; mgmt. cons., 1979—92; mem. 2d Quorum of 70 LDS Ch., Salt Lake City, 1992—94, presiding bishop, 1994—95, mem. 1st Quorum of 70, 1996—; pres. Quorum of 70 Ch. of Jesus Christ of Latter Day Saints, Salt Lake City, 2003—. Pres. Deseret Mgmt. Corp., Salt Lake City, 1993—95. 1st lt. USAF, 1964—67. Fellow, Danforth, 1960—64, Woodrow Wilson, 1960—61. Mem.: Phi Beta Kappa, Phi Kappa Phi. Office: Quorum of Seventy 47 E South Temple St Salt Lake City UT 84150

BATEMAN, MILDRED MITCHELL, retired psychiatrist; b. Cordele, Ga., Mar. 22, 1922; married; 2 children. BS, J.C. Smith U., 1941; MD, Woman's Med. Coll. Pa., 1946. Staff physician Larkin (W.Va.) State Hosp., 1947-48, clin. dir., 1951-52, 55-58, supt., 1958-60; supr. dir. profl. svcs. W.Va. Dept. Mental Health, 1960-62; dir. State Capital, 1962-77; prof., chmn. psychiat. Sch. Medicine Marshall U., Huntington, W.Va., 1977-82, prof. psychiatry, 1982-2000; staff psychiatrist Mildred Mitchell Bateman Med. Ctr., 1986—96; clin. dir. Sch. Medicine, Huntington, W.Va., 1996—; prof. part-time Marshall U., Huntington, W.Va., 2000—. Mem. com. mental illness and mental retardation Commn. Aging, W.Va. Commn. Mental Retardation, Govt. W.Va. Commn. Status of Women & Coop. Health Statis. Adv. Com., Nat. Ctr. Health Statis.; trustee Menninger Found. Mem. AMA, Inst. Medicine-NAS, Am. Psychiat. Assn. (v.p. 1973, Warren Williams Disting. award 1991). Home: 1016 1st Ave Charleston WV 25302-1422 E-mail: bateman8@marshall.edu.

BATEMAN, PAUL WILLIAM, government official, business executive; b. Whittier, Calif., Feb. 28, 1957; s. John William and Glenus Bernice (Redman) B.; m. Marguerite Cameron; children: Ellen Ryan, Nancy Cameron, Greer Aidan. BA, Whittier Coll., 1979. Asst. to former pres. Office of Richard Nixon, N.Y.C. and San Clemente, Calif., 1979-81; dep. dir. adminstrv. ops. div. The White House, Washington, 1981-82; exec. asst. to asst. sec. for econ. devel. U.S. Dept. Commerce, Washington, 1982-84, dep. asst. sec. for econ. devel., 1984-85; dep. treas. of U.S. Dept. Treasury, 1985-88; sr. v.p. New Eng. Council, Inc., Boston, 1988-89; dep. asst. to Pres. The White House, 1989-93; dir. pub. affairs Gold Inst., Washington, 1994-95, exec. v.p., 1995-99, pres., 2000—; v.p. Klein & Saks, Inc., 1995-96, pres., 1996—2002, KSG, LLC, 2003—. V.p. George Washington Boyhood Home Found., 1994-96; exec. dir. Silver Inst., 1996—. Trustee Whittier Coll., 2000—; mem. Adv. Coun. on Hist. Preservation, 1989-93; bd. dirs. Internat. Cyanide Mgmt. Inst., 2002—. Republican. Episcopalian. Home: 490 Fort Williams Pky Alexandria VA 22304-1810 Office: 1112 16th St NW Ste 240 Washington DC 20036-4818

BATEMAN, ROBERT MCLELLAN, artist; b. Toronto, Ont., Can., May 24, 1930; s. Joseph Wilbur and Ann (McLellan) Bateman; m. Suzanne Bowerman, June 1961; children: Alan, Sarah, John; m. Birgit Freybe, Aug. 1975; children: Christopher, Rob. BA in Geography with honors, U. Toronto, 1954; postgrad., Ont. Coll. Edn., 1955; DSc (hon.), Carleton U., Ottawa, 1982; LLD (hon.), Brock U., St. Catherine, Ont., 1982; D Letters for Fine Arts (hon.), McMaster U., Hamilton, Ont., Can., 1983; LLD (hon.), U. Guelph, Ont., 1984; LittD (hon.), Lakehead U., Thunder Bay, Ont., 1986; LLD (hon.), Laurentian U., Sudbury, Ont., 1987; DFA (hon.), Colby Coll., 1989, Northeastern U., 1991; DSc (hon.), McGill U., Montreal, 1995. Tchr. Nelson H.S., Burlington, Ont., 1958-63, 65-69; tchr. geography Nigeria, 1963-65; tchr. art Lord Elgin H.S., Burlington, Ont., 1970-76. One-man shows include Tryon Gallery, London, 1975, 79, Beckett Gallery, Hamilton, Ont., Can., 1978, 87, Smithsonian Instn., 1987, Nat. Mus. Natural Sci., Ottawa, 1981-82, Everard Read Gallery, Johannesburg, South Africa, 2000, Beckett Fine Art Gallery, Toronto, 2002, Retrospective Tour, USA, 2002-03, also touring U.S. and Can., Can. Embassy, Tokyo, 1992; represented in permanent collections Govt. Ont. Art Collection, Toronto Bd. Trade, Hamilton Art Gallery, Leigh Yawkey Woodson Art Mus., Wausau, Wis., H.R.H. The Prince of Wales, H.R.H. Prince Phillip, The Late Princess of Monaco, Am. Artists Collection, Gilcrease Mus., Tulsa, Art Gallery of Greater Victoria; commd. World Wildlife Fund, 1971, Endangered Species Silver Bowl, 1971, Endangered Species Postage Stamp Series, 1976-81, "Northern Reflections - Loon Family", 1981, Govt. Can. wedding gift to Prince of Wales, 1981, Can. Post Office, Royal Can. Mint-Platinum Polar Bear series, 1990, Nat. Capital commn. Canadiana Fund; subject of the Art of Robert Bateman, 1981, A Day in the Life of Robert Bateman, 1985, The World of Robert Bateman, 1985, Robert Bateman An Artist in Nature, 1990, Natural Worlds: Robert Bateman, 1996, The Life and Times of Robert Bateman, 1997, Safari, 1998, Thinking Like a Mountain, 2000, Birds, 2002. Bd. dirs. Elsa Wild Animal Appeal, Toronto, 1975—, Ecotrust, Jane Goodall Inst. Can.; hon. chmn. Harmony Found., Ottawa; hon. dir. Kenya Wildlife Fund, Long Point Bird Obs., Ont., Sierra Legal Def. Fund. Decorated Queen Elizabeth Silver Jubilee medal Govt. of Can., 1977, Officer of Order of Can., 1984; recipient award of excellence Soc. Animal Artists, 1979, 80, 86, 90, Gov. Gen. award for conservation, Quebec City, Can., 1987, Lescarbot award Can. Govt., 1992, Rachel Carson award, 1996, Golden Plate award Am. Acad. Achievement, 1998; named Artist of Yr., Am. Artist Collection, 1980, Master Artist, Leigh Yawkey Woodson Mus., Wausau, Wis., 1982, Environ. Hero, Nat. Aububon Soc., 1998, others. Mem. Order B.C., Brit. Soc. for Wildlife Artists, Jane Goodall Inst. (bd. dirs.), N.Am. Native Plant Soc. (hon. dir.), Audubon Soc. (hon. life), Royal Can. Acad. Arts, Can. Nat. Wildlife Fedn. (hon. life), Fedn. Ont. Naturalists (hon. life), Sierra Club (hon. life), Kenya Wildlife Fund (hon. dir.), Sierra Legal Def. Fund (hon. dir.). E-mail: boshkung@saltspring.com.

BATEMAN, SHARON LOUISE, public relations executive; b. St. Louis, Oct. 18, 1949; d. Frank Hamilton and Charlotte Elizabeth (Hogan) B. Student, Drury Coll., 1967-69; BJ, U. Mo., 1971. Asst. dir. pub. relations Cardinal Glennon Hosp. for Children, St. Louis, 1971-76; staff asst. pub. relations Ozark Air Lines, St. Louis, 1976-80; mgr. corp. relations Kellwood Co., St. Louis, 1980-83; mgr. corp. communications May Dept. Stores Co., St. Louis, 1983-86, dir. corp. communications, 1986-94; mgr. comm. Arthur Andersen, St. Louis, 1995-96; mgr. editl. and adminstrv. svcs. The Falk Design Group, St. Louis, 1996—2000; v.p. corp. comms. May Dept. Stores Co., St. Louis, 2000—. Bd. dirs. St. Michael's Houses, 1996-97, Gateway Greening, 1999-2001. Recipient Best Regional Airline Employee Publ. award Editor's Assn. Am. Transp. Assn., 1978. Mem.: Pub. Rels. Soc. Am. (sec.St. Louis chpt. 1983, bd. dirs. 1988—90, v.p. 1991), Internat. Assn. Bus. Comms. (pres. St. Louis chpt. 1977). Office: May Dept Stores Co 611 Olive St Saint Louis MO 63101-1721

BATEMAN, THOMAS ROBERT, lawyer; b. Winchester, Mass., Dec. 9, 1944; s. Richard Holt and Phyllis (Brown) B.; m. Katherine Elizabeth Elliott, Sept. 9, 1972; children: Kyra Elizabeth, Richard Holt, Robert Elliott. BA, Harvard U., 1967; JD, NYU, 1971. Bar: N.Y. 1972, U.S. Dist. Ct. (so. dist.) N.Y. 1973, U.S. Ct. Appeals (2d cir.) 1974, Mass. 1978, U.S. Dist. Ct. Mass. 1978, U.S. Ct. Appeals (1st cir.) 1978. Assoc. Winthrop, Stimson, Putnam & Roberts, N.Y.C., 1971-77, Skadden, Arps, Slate, Meagher & Flom, Boston, 1977-79, ptnr., 1980—. Class agent Phillips Exeter Acad., N.H., 1969—; class steering com. Harvard U., Cambridge, Mass. 1985—. Mem.: ABA, Assn. of Bar of City of N.Y., N.Y. State Bar Assn., Somerset Club, Harvard Club (Boston). Episcopalian. Home: 33 Bullard Rd Weston MA 02493-2203

BATES, ALAN (ARTHUR BATES), actor; b. Derbyshire, Eng., Feb. 17, 1934; s. Harold Arthur and Florence Mary (Wheatcroft) B.; m. Victoria Ward, May 1970 (dec. June 1992); 2 sons (twins, 1 dec.). Student, Royal Acad. Dramatic Art, London. Appeared in stage prodns. including Hamlet, London, Butley, London and N.Y.C. (Antoinette Perry award for Best Actor 1973, Drama League N.Y. award), Poor Richard, N.Y.C., Merry Wives of Windsor and Richard III, Stratford, Ont., Taming of the Shrew, Stratford-on-Avon, Eng., 1973, Life Class, 1974, Otherwise Engaged, 1975 (variety club awards), The Seagull, 1976, Stage Struck, 1979-80, A Patriot for Me, London and L.A., 1983, One for the Road, Victoria Station, 1984, The Dance of Death, 1985, Yonadab, Nat. Theatre, 1986, (with Patrick Garland) Down Cemetery Road, 1986, Melon, 1987, Ivanov, Much Ado About Nothing, 1989, Stages, Nat. Theatre, 1992-93, The Showman, London, 1993, Antony & Cleopatra, Stratford-on-Avon, 1999; films include The Fixer (Oscar award nomination), Women in Love, The Three Sisters, A Day in the Death of Joe Egg, The Go-Between, Second Best, Impossible Object, In Celebration, Royal Flash, An Unmarried Woman, The Shout, The Rose, Nijinsky, Quartet, The Return of the Soldier, 1982, The Wicked Lady, 1983, Duet for One, 1986, A Prayer for the Dying, 1987, We Think the World of You, 1988, Force Majeur, 1988, Mr. Frost, 1989, Dr. M., 1989, Hamlet, 1990, Shuttlecock, 1991, Losing Track, 1991, Silent Tongue, 1992, St. Patrick, 1999; TV shows include The Collection, 1977, The Mayor of Casterbridge, 1978, Very Like a Whale, The Trespasser, 1981, A Voyage Round My Father, 1982, An Englishman Abroad, 1985 (Brit. Acad. Film & TV Arts award, Ace award Nat. Cable TV Acad.), Separate Tables, 1983 (Ace award Nat. Cable TV Acad.), Dr. Fischer of Geneva, 1984, One for the Road, 1985, Pack of Lies, 1987, The Dog It Was That Died, 1988, 102 Boulevard Haussmann, 1990, Secret Friends, 1991, Unnatural Pursuits, 1992, Hard Times, 1994, Oliver's Travels, 1994, Nicholas' Gift, 1997, Love in a Cold Climate, 2000, The Unexpected Man, N.Y., 2000, Salem Witch Trials, U.S., 2001, Bertie and Elizabeth, U.K., 2001, Dorian Gray Theatre Royal, Windsor, Yvonne Arnaud Theatre, Guildford, U.K., 2001, The Prince and the Pauper, 2001; (film) The Grotesque, 1995, The Cherry Orchard, 1998, St. Patrick, 1999, Gosford Park, U.K., 2001, Sum of All Fears, U.S., 2001, Mothman Prophecies, Evelyn, Ireland, 2002, (TV) Arabian Nights, In the Beginning, The Prince & the Pauper, (U.S. TV film narration) The Arabian Nights, 1999, (British TV series narration) The Spying Game, 1999, (theater) The Master Builder, London, 1995, Ont., 1996, Simply Disconnected, 1996, Fortune's Fool, 1996, Life Support, 1997, Fortune's Fool, Music Box Theatre, N.Y.C., 2002; (radio) Art, Murder in Paris, Man and Boy, 1998. Served with RAF. Recipient Clarence Derwent award, Evening Std. award, 1972. Office: Chatto & Linnit Ltd 123A Kings Rd London SW3 4PL England

BATES, BARBARA J. NEUNER, retired municipal official; b. Mt. Vernon, N.Y., Apr. 8, 1927; d. John Joseph William and Elsie May (Flint) Neuner; m. Herman Martin Bates, Jr., Mar. 25, 1950; children: Roberta Jean Bates Jamin, Herman Martin III, Jon Neuner. BA, Barnard Coll., 1947. Confidential clk. to supr. Town of Ossining, N.Y., 1960-63, receiver of taxes, 1971-90; ret.; pres. BNB Assocs., Briarcliff Manor, N.Y., 1963-83, Upper Nyack Realty Co., Inc., Briarcliff Manor, 1966-71. V.p. Ossining (N.Y.) Young Rep. Club, 1958; pres. Young Womens Rep. Club Westchester County (N.Y.), 1959-61; regional committeewoman N.Y. State Assn. Young Rep. Clubs, 1960-62; mem. Westchester County Rep. Com., 1963-95; mem. Ossining Women's Rep. Club, 1960-92, pres., 1984-85; mem. Westchester County Women's Rep. Club, 1957-92. Mem. DAR, Jr. League Westchester-on-Hudson, Receivers Taxes Assn. Westchester County (legis. liaison, v.p., pres. 1984-85), Hackley Sch. Mothers Assn. (pres. 1968), R.I. Hist. Soc., Ossining Hist. Soc., Westchester County Hist. Soc., Landmark Preservation Soc. of S.E., Ossining Woman's Club. Home: 23 Bloomer Rd Brewster NY 10509-1026 also: 663 Reynolds Rd Chepachet RI 02814-1629

BATES, BENJAMIN JOHNSON, telecommunications educator, researcher; b. Chilicothee, Ohio, Jan. 25, 1954; s. Philip Knight and Myrna (Mademann) B. BA in Math. and Econ., Pomona Coll., Claremont, Calif., 1976; MS in Statistics, U. Wis., Madison, 1978; MA in Comms., U. Wis. Stevens Point, 1981; PhD in Comms., U. Mich., Ann Arbor, 1986. Instr. Rutgers U., 1985-86; lectr. U. Calif., Santa Barbara, 1986-88; vis. asst. prof. Mich. State U., 1988-89; vis. lectr. The Chinese U. of Hong Kong, 1992-93; asst. prof., dir. Inst. Comm. Rsch. Tex. Tech. U., 1989-94; prof. U. Tenn. Knoxville, 1994—. Contbr. articles to profl. jours. Mem.: Nat. Comm. Assn., Internat. Comm. Assn., Broadcast Edn. Assn., Assn. Internet Rschrs., Am. Assn. Pub. Opinion Rsch., Assn. for Edn. in Journalism and Comms. Office: Sch Journalism Electronic Media U Tenn 333 Communication Bldg Knoxville TN 37996-0333 E-mail: bjbates@utk.edu.

BATES, BEVERLY BAILEY, lawyer; b. Atlanta, Jan. 23, 1938; d. Fred Eugene and Justine Elizabeth (Marques) B. AB, Mercer U., 1959, LLB, 1961. Bar: Ga. 1961, U.S. Ct. Mil. Appeals 1963, U.S. Supreme Ct. 1965, D.C. 1966, U.S. Dist. Ct. (no. dist.) Ga. 1966, U.S. Ct. Appeals (5th cir.) 1967, U.S. Ct. Appeals (11th cir.) 1981, U.S. Ct. Appeals (fed. cir.) 1982, U.S. Dist. Ct. (so. dist.) Ga. 1982, U.S. Dist. Ct. (mid. dist.) Ga. 1985. Asst. U.S. atty. No. dist. Ga. U.S. Dept. Justice, Atlanta, 1966-74; ptnr. Bates & Baum, Atlanta, 1974—. Spl. master Ga. Commn. on Equal Employment, 1986-95. Contbr. articles to profl. jours. Rep. Buckhead Neighborhood Planning Unit, Atlanta, 1982-85; v.p., bd. dirs. Pine Hills Civic Club, Atlanta, 1982-85. Served to capt. U.S. Army, 1961-66. Mem. ABA, Fed. Bar Assn. (pres. 1972-73, named Younger Fed. Lawyer of Yr. Atlanta chpt. 1972), Atlanta C. of C. (pres. downtown coun. 1982-83, bd. dirs. 1982-83), Mercer U. Law Sch. Alumni Soc. (pres. 1971-72), Mercer U. Alumni Soc. (pres. Atlanta chpt. 1974-75), Atlanta Lawyers Club, Resurgens Atlanta (pres. 1981-82). Office: Bates & Baum 3151 Maple Dr NE Atlanta GA 30305-2503

BATES, CHARLES BENJAMIN, elementary school administrator; b. Balt., Aug. 24, 1934; s. Charles Benjamin and Mary Elizabeth (Holden) B.; m. Martha Pearl Copenhaver, Apr. 9, 1960; children: Benjamin Madison, Lelia Ann, William Andrew. BS, Towson State Tchrs. Coll., 1961; MEd, Loyola Coll., Balt., 1968; PhD, Columbia Pacific U., 1982. Cert. tchr., Md. Tchr. Balt. County Pub. Schs., 1958-68, vice prin., 1968-77, prin., 1977-78, elem. adminstr., 1979-86; cons. edn. and history Joppa, Md., 1986—. Adj. prof. Columbia Pacific, Balt., 1982-87; curriculum cons. Balt. County Pub. Schs., Towson, 1986; cons. history Am. History Workshop, N.Y.C., 1990. Editor: Edward Fenner (book); editor Bates Chronicles, 1981-93; contbr. articles to profl. jours. Trustee Balt. Streetcar Mus., 1988—96, dir. sch. tours, 1998—; historian; pres. The Bates Assn., 1993—96, 1998—, mem. exec. bd., 1996—98, PTA, 1961—86. Sgt. U.S. Army, 1957—63. Recipient Svc. to Cmty. award VFW, 1986, Katharine Lee Bates award, 1998. Mem. Orton Soc. (bd. dirs. 1974-77), Assn. Elem. Sch. Adminstrs. (exec. bd. 1974-77), Rwy. Hist. Soc. (exec. bd. 1986-88), New Eng. Hist. and Geneal. Soc., Nat. Hist. Soc., Md. Geneal. Soc., Md. Hist. Soc., NRHS (historian). Republican. Avocations: streetcars and trains, flags, civil war, genealogy. Home: 202 Frazier Ct Joppa MD 21085-4434

BATES, CHARLES CARPENTER, oceanographer; b. Rockton, Ill., Nov. 4, 1918; s. Carl and Vera B.; m. Pauline Barta; children: Nancy, Priscilla, Sally. Grad. (Rector scholar 1936-39), DePauw U., 1939; MA, U. Calif. at Los Angeles, 1944; PhD in Geol. Oceanography, Tex. A. and M. Coll., 1953; student, Cath. U., 1947-48, Johns Hopkins, 1951, George Washington U., 1954. Geophys. trainee Carter Oil Co., 1939-41; spl. asst. to pres. Am. Meteorol. Soc., 1945-46; mem. survey phys. and geol. environment Marshall Is. relative to pending Bikini atomic bomb tests, 1946; with div. oceanography U.S. Navy Hydrographic Office, 1946- 57, dept. dir. div., 1953-57; environmental surveillance coordinator Office Devel. Coordinator, Office Naval Research, 1957-60; chief underground nuclear test detection br. Advanced Research Projects Agy., Office Sec. Def., 1960-64; sci. and tech. dir. U.S. Naval Oceanographic Office, 1964-68; sci. adviser to comdt., also chief scientist Office Research and Devel., USCG, 1968-79. V.p. Spectrum Internat. Assocs., 1986-88; mem. bd. experts Civil Service Examiners, 1954-60; mem. adv. com. postdoctoral awards for Fulbright grants NRC, 1957-60; vis. geoscientist Am. Geol. Inst., 1959-60; mem. meteorology panel, space sci. bd. Nat. Acad. Sci., 1959-61; mem. Mcht. Marine Council, 1968-71, Nat. Transp. Research Bd., 1968-71; mem. sea grant adv. council La. State U. System, 1968-79; co-chmn. U.S.-Japan panel marine facilities U.S.-Japan Natural Resource Program, 1969-71. Author: Geophysics in Affairs of Man, 1982, 2nd edit., 2001, America's Weather Warriors, 1814-1985, 1986; numerous articles, reports in field. Served to capt. USAAF, 1941-45, lt. col. USAFR, 1941-65. Decorated Bronze Star; recipient U.S. Navy Meritorious Civilian award, 1962, U.S. Navy Superior Civilian Service award, 1969, U.S. Dept. Transp. Silver medal, 1973, gold medal, 1979. Mem. Am. Geophys. Union (chmn. com. interaction sea and atmosphere 1950, mem. council 1964-67), Soc. Exploration Geophysicists (council 1963-67, v.p. 1965-66, hon. mem. 1981), Am. Meteorol. Soc. (chmn. com. indsl. bus. and agrl. meteorology 1946-48), Am. Assn. Petroleum Geologists (President's award 1954), Am. Mgmt. Assn. (research and devel. council 1970-79), Sigma Xi. Home and Office: 501 S La Posada Cir Apt 388 Green Valley AZ 85614

BATES, CHARLES TURNER, lawyer, educator; b. Tarrytown, N.Y., Jan. 3, 1932; s. Harry Cole and Helen Morris (Turner) B. AB, Hamilton Coll., 1953; LL.B., Yale U., 1958. Bar: N.Y. 1958. Atty. firm Townley & Updike, N.Y.C., 1958-69; atty. CBS Inc., N.Y.C., 1969-71, asst. sec., 1971-74, sec., asso. gen. counsel, 1974-88; instr. in history Hackley Sch., Tarrytown, NY, 1988—99; ret., 1999. Trustee Hackley Sch., Tarrytown, N.Y., 1972-76, 81-88, hon. trustee, 1999—; trustee Hamilton Coll., 1975-79. With Ordnance Corps, U.S. Army, 1953-55. Mem. Phi Beta Kappa, Sigma Phi. Republican. Episcopalian.

BATES, CHARLES WALTER, lawyer, human resources executive, politician; b. Detroit, June 28, 1953; s. E. Frederick and Virginia Marion (Nunneley) B. BA in Psychology and Econs. cum laude, Mich. State U., 1975, M in Labor and Indsl. Rels., 1977; postgrad., DePaul U., 1979-80; JD, William Mitchell Coll. Law, 1984. Bar: Wash. 1990, U.S. Dist. Ct. (we. dist.) Wash. 1992, U.S. Ct. Appeals (9th cir.) 2002; cert. sr. profl. in human resources. Job analyst Gen. Mills, Inc., Mpls., 1977-78, plant pers. asst. II Chgo., 1978-80, plant asst. pers. mgr., 1980-81, pers. mgr. consumer foods mktg. Mpls., 1981-82, pers. mgr. consumer foods mktg. divsns. and Saluto Pizza, 1982-84; human resources mgr. Western divsn. Godfather's Pizza, Inc., Costa Mesa, Calif., 1984-85, human resources mgr. western U.S. and Can. Bellevue, Wash., 1985-91; dir. human resources Royal Seafoods, Inc., Seattle, 1991-92, dir. human resources and employee rels. counsel, 1992-94, dir. human resources and counsel, 1994-95; sr. internal auditor PACCAR, Inc, Bellevue, Wash., 1995-97; dir. field human resources PACCAR Automotive, Inc., Renton, 1997, dir. human resources, 1997—2000, TransAlta Corp.-Centralia Ops., 2000—02; dir. adminstrn., corp. sec. TransAlta USA Inc., 2002—. Instr. employee labor rels. Lake Washington Tech. Coll., 1992-94; bd. dirs., TransAlta USA Inc., 2000-01, TransAlta Investments LLC, 2000-01, Olympia Symphony Orch., 2001-02. Candidate for lt. gov. of Minn., 1982; mem. Sammamish Cmty. Coun., Bellevue, 1990-93; mem. Bellevue Civil Svc. Commn., 1997-2000, vice chmn., 1999, chmn., 2000; commr. Scott Lake Drainage Commn., 2002-; asst. scoutmaster Boy Scouts Am., 1971—. Recipient Scouter's Tng. award Boy Scouts Am., 1979, Vantage Recruiting award Recruitment Today mag., 1989, Vigil Honor award Order of the Arrow, Boy Scouts Am., 1990, Dist. Award of Merit, Boy Scouts Am., 1991. Mem. ABA, Wash. State Bar Assn., Am. Soc. Corp. Secs., Soc. Human Resource Mgmt., Nat. Eagle Scout Assn. Office: TransAlta USA Inc 913 Big Hanaford Rd Centralia WA 98531-9101 E-mail: charlie_bates@hotmail.com.

BATES, DWIGHT LEE, retired mechanical engineer; b. Miles City, Mont., Aug. 19, 1943; s. Edmond Russell and Verna Elizabeth (Johnson) B.; m. Diane Marie Seppi, Aug. 19, 1967. BSME, U. Wyo., 1966; MBA in Mktg., Seattle U., 1971. Registered profl. engr., Wash. Rsch. engr. comml. airplane div. Boeing Co., Seattle, 1966-70; product devel. engr. internat. mktg. div. Warn Industries, Seattle, 1972-73, 1972-73; prin. engr. Heath Tecna, Kent, Wash., 1973-74; mech. design engr. Puget sound naval shipyard U.S. Dept. Def., Bremerton, Wash., 1974-78; supervisory indsl. engr. Supship Seattle, 1978-85; sr. specialist engr. comml. airplane div. Boeing Co., Seattle, 1985-99, ret., 1999. Cons. in field. Contbr. publs. in field. Pres. Melrose E. Condo Assn., Seattle, 1978-81; bus. adv. coun. Resource Ctr. for Handicapped. With USCG Aux. Recipient 2 letters of appreciation and 2 letters of commendation U.S. Dept. Def., award Am. Mktg. Assn., 1973; honored as grad. with successful career U. Wyo. Coll. Engring., 1993. Mem. Resource Ctr. for Handicapped Bus. Adv. Coun. (7 letters of commendation, Mus. Flight award, Seattle Block Capt. award), AIAA (pres. Laramie, Wyo. chpt. 1966), NSPE, Wash. State Profl. Engrs. Soc., Wash. State Power Squadron, Am. Inst. Indsl. Engrs., Seattle U. MBA Assn.. Republican. Lutheran. Avocations: skiing, hiking, climbing, photography, computers. Home: 1509 Brick Rd Ellensburg WA 98926-9564

BATES, EDWARD BRILL, retired insurance company executive; b. Lexington, Mo., May 14, 1919; s. Worth and Faye Marvin (Brill) B.; m. Mary Louise Van Sickle (dec. Mar. 1999); m. Elizabeth Curtis, 2002; children: Lynn Bates Russell, Stephen Worth. BABA, U. Chgo., 1940; LLD (hon.), Trinity Coll., Hartford, Conn., 1974; LHD (hon.), U. Hartford, 1976. Agt., gen. agt. Conn. Mut. Life Ins. Co., 1946—59, v.p., 1960—62, exec. v.p., 1962-67, pres., 1967-77, chmn., 1977-84, chmn. exec. com., 1985-87. Mem. Country Club Fla., Ocean Club. Home: 6861 N Ocean Blvd Ocean Ridge FL 33435 Home (Summer): PO Box 528 Manchester VT 05254

BATES, GEORGE WILLIAM, obstetrician, gynecologist, educator, medical products executive; b. Durham, N.C., Feb. 15, 1940; s. George W. and Lillian M. (Streete) B.; m. Susanne Rayburn, Oct. 18, 1969; children: Jonathan Rayburn, Jeffrey William, Robert Wiser. BS, U. N.C., 1962, MD, 1965; SM, MIT, 1984. Diplomate Am. Bd. Ob-Gyn. (examiner 1984-93). Intern U. Ala., Birmingham, 1965-66; resident ob-gyn U. N.C., Chapel Hill, 1966-70; prof., chmn. ob-gyn U. Tenn., Knoxville, 1972-76; fellow reproductive endocrinology U. Tex., Dallas, 1976-78; prof., dir. reproductive endocrinology U. Miss. Med. Ctr., Jackson, 1978-86; prof. ob.-gyn. Coll. Medicine, Med. U. S.C., Charleston, 1986-90, dean, 1986-89; v.p. med. edn. Greenville (S.C.) Hosp. System, 1990-96; exec. v.p., chief med. officer Prin.Care, Inc., Brentwood, Tenn., 1996-98; v.p. devel. Vanderbilt U. Med. Ctr., Nashville, 1998—. CEO digiChart, Inc. Co-author: Obstetrics and Gynecology for Medical Students, 1992, 95; editor: Manual of Clinical Problems in Obstetrics and Gynecology, 1982, 86, 90; contbr. numerous articles to profl. publs. Commr. coun. Boy Scouts Am., 1989-90, v.p. adminstrn., 1992, pres., 1993-94, bd. dirs. Mid. Tenn. Coun., 2002--; elder Mt. Pleasant Presbyn. Ch., Westminster Presbyn. Ch.; mem. pres.'s adv. coun. Mars Hill Coll., Presbyn. Coll., Nat. Devel. Coun., U. N.C. Maj. USAF, 1970-72. Morehead scholar, 1958; NIH rsch. trainee, 1976-78; Sloan fellow, 1983; recipient Eagle Scout award, 1955, Henry Fordham award, 1966, Golden Apple award, 1987, Silver Beaver award, 1989, Hon. Alumnus award Med. U. S.C., 1990, Disting. Eagle Scout award, 1991; named Prof. of Yr., U. Miss., 1980, Top 100 Healthcare Exec., 2002. Mem. ACOG (chmn. fin. com. 1990-94, health care commn. 1994-97, Jr. Fellow Profl. of Y. award dist. IV 1991), AMA, AAAS, Assn. Profs. Ob-Gyn. Found. (bd. dirs. 1993), Am. Gyn.-Ob. Soc., Nat. Bd. Med. Examiners, Gynecol. Investigation, Am. Fertility Soc. (bd. dirs. 1991-94, treas. 1994-96), Soc. Gynecol. Surgeons, Accreditation Coun. Grad. Med. Edn., So. Atlantic Assn. Obstetricians and Gynecologists, Ctrl. Assn. Obstetricians and Gynecologists, Endocrine Soc., Rotary, Alpha Omega Alpha. Office: digiChart Inc 102 Woodmont Blvd Ste 500 Nashville TN 37205-5254

BATES, GERALD EARL, bishop emeritus; b. Caldwell, Ohio, Sept. 12, 1933; s. Earl and Lillian Inez (Merritt) B.; m. Marlene Rachel Parsons, Aug. 21, 1954; children: David Earl, William Randall, Elizabeth Ann. AA, Spring Arbor Coll., 1953; AB, Greenville Coll., 1955; MDiv, Asbury Theol. Sem., 1958; ThM, Western Theol. Sem., 1964; PhD, Mich. State U., 1975; DD (hon.), Roberts Wesleyan Coll., 1986, Greenville Coll., 1998. Missionary with Gen. Missionary Bd. Free Meth. Ch. of N.Am., Winona Lake, Ind., 1957-85, area adminstrv. asst. for Cen. Africa, 1973-85, bishop, 1985-99, bishop emeritus, 1999—. Adj. prof. Union Inst., Cin., West Africa Theol. Sem., Nigeria. Author: Soul Afire, 1981, 2d edit., 1993; chmn. bd. editors: Book of Discipline, 1985. Trustee Spring Arbor U., Mich.; bd. dirs. King Trust N.A.; bd. dirs. India Missionary Tng. Bd., J. Wesley Bible Coll., Budapest, Hungary, Ctr. for Study of Wesley and Soc.; pres. Free Meth. World Fellowship, 1989-95; pres. U.S. bd. Hope Africa U., Kenya. Recipient Alumnus of Yr. award Spring Arbor Coll., 1974, Goodwill Amb. award Noble County C. of C., 1988, Alumnus of Yr. award Asbury Theol. Sem., 1991. Mem. Am. Soc. Missiology, Phi Kappa Phi. Republican. Mem. Free Methodist Ch. Avocations: reading, travel, photography. Home: 6715 Oak Lake Dr Indianapolis IN 46214-2038 E-mail: nijewe@cs.com.

BATES, HAMPTON ROBERT, JR., pathologist; b. Roanoke, Va., Feb. 1, 1933; s. Hampton Robert and Mary Mildred (Crowder) B.; m. Carole Harrison Young, Apr. 12, 1958; children: Hampton Robert III, Catherine Louise Franck. BS in Chemistry, Roanoke Coll., 1953; MD, Med. Coll. Va., 1957. Diplomate Am. Bd. Pathology, Am. Bd. Nuc. Medicine, Nat. Bd. Med. Examiners; cert. radiation safety officer. Intern Med. Coll. Va. Hosp., Richmond, 1957-58, resident in pathology, 1958 62, faculty, 1962-63; practice medicine specializing in pathology and nuc. medicine Richmond, 1963-95; ind. rschr., 1995—. Pathologist Johnston-Willis Med. Ctr., Chippenham Med. Ctr.; v.p. Clin. Lab. Consultants, Inc., Richmond, 1972-95; forensic pathologist Richmond Met. Area, 1959-95. Contbr. articles on descriptive, exptl. and forensic pathology to med. jours. Fellow Coll. Am. Pathologists (life); mem. AMA, AAAS, Med. Soc. Va., Richmond Acad. Medicine, Rokitansky Soc., Diogenes Club. Episcopalian. Avocations: dancing, card magic. Home: 122 W Square Dr Richmond VA 23233-6162

BATES, HAROLD MARTIN, lawyer; b. Wise County, Va., Mar. 11, 1928; s. William Jennings and Reba (Williams) B.; m. Audrey Rose Doll, Nov. 1, 1952 (div. Mar. 1978); children: Linda, Carl; m. Judith Lee Farmer, June 23, 1978 (div. Feb. 2002). BA in Econs., Coll. William and Mary, 1952; LLB, Washington and Lee U., 1961. Bar: Va. 1961, Ky. 1961. Spl. agt. FBI, Newark and N.Y.C., 1952-56; tech. sales rep. Hercules Powder Co., Wilmington, Del., 1956-58; investigator U.S. Def. Dept., Lexington, Va., 1959-62, Louisville, 1959-62; practice law Louisville, 1961-62; sec.-treas., dir., house counsel Life Ins. Co. of Ky., Louisville, 1962-66, practice law Roanoke, Va., 1966—; sec., dir. James River Limestone Co., Buchanan, Va., 1970-96; sec. Eastern Ins. Co., Roanoke, 1984-87. Pres., Skil, Inc., orgn. for rehab. Vietnam vets., Salem, Va., 1972-75; freshman football coach Washington and Lee U., 1958-60. With airborne U.S. Army, 1946—47. Mem. Va. Bar Assn., Roanoke Bar Assn., William and Mary Alumni Assn. (bd. dirs. 1972-76), Soc. Former Spl. Agts. of FBI (chmn. Blue Ridge chpt. 1971-72). Republican. Home: 241 Knoll Rd Roanoke VA 24019 Office: 320 Elm Ave Roanoke VA 24016 E-mail: hbates6802@aol.com.

BATES, JAMES EARL, academic administrator; b. Ligonier, Pa., Aug. 10, 1923; s. Earl Barrington and Margaret (Kinsey) B.; m. Lauralou Courtney, Apr. 15, 1950; children: Susan Bates Jaren, Sara Bates Hudson, James Barrington, Willa Bates Leitten. DSc, Temple U., 1946; DPM, Pa. Coll. Podiatric Medicine, 1970, LHD (hon.), 1996; EdD (hon.), Franklin Pierce Coll., 1972; DSc (hon.), Calif. Coll. Podiatric Med., 1995; LLD, Barry U., 1995; LHD (hon.), Pa. Coll. Podiatric Medicine, 1996. Practice podiatric medicine, Phila., 1946-71; assoc. prof. roentgenology Temple U., Phila., 1948-60; prof., pres. Pa. Coll. Podiatric Medicine, Phila., 1962-95, chancellor, 1995-96, chancellor, CEO, 1997-98; cons. to dean Sch. Podiatric Medicine Temple U., 1998—; chancellor Temple Sch. Podiatric Medicine. Cons. BHRD Region IX, HEW, San Francisco, 1973-74, Region V, Chgo., 1974-75; del. Nat. Commn. on Certifying Health Manpower; mem. health adv. com. HEW, 1972-73; adv. panel for podiatry Inst. Medicine, Nat. Acad. Scis., 1972-74; adv. council for comprehensive health planning Pa. Dept. Health, 1972-75, health manpower task force edn. com., 1976; task force on health manpower distbn. Nat. Health Council, 1973, com. on manpower, 1976-83; mem. Nat. Adv. Council on Health Professions Edn., 1983-87; cons. team So. Regional Ednl. Bd. Feasibility Study for So. Podiatry Sch., 1975-76; mem. Statewide Profl. Standards Rev. Council, 1976-82, Greater Phila. Com. for Med.-Pharm. Scis. Contbr. articles to profl. jours. Trustee First United Meth. Ch. of Germantown, 1965-72, past chmn. fin. com.; v.p. bd. Germantown Businessmen's Assn., Disting. Service award, 1964; chmn. 277th and 278th Ann. Germantown Week, 1958-59; dep. service dir. Phila. CD Council, 1966-73; mem. Health Adv. Commn., Phila., 1976; past pres., bd. mgrs. Germantown YMCA; v.p. Phila. Boosters Assn.; trustee Univ. City Sci. Center, Phila. Served with M.C. AUS, WWII. Recipient citation Pa. Coll. Podiatric Medicine, 1970, citation Gov. Pa., 1973, Lifetime Achievement award Podiatric Mgmt. Mag., 1993. Fellow Internat. Acad. Preventive Medicine (dir. 1973-78), Brit. Soc. Podiatric Medicine (hon.), Royal Soc. Health (Eng.), Am. Coll. Foot Roentgenologists (pres. 1958-59), Coll. Physicians Phila.; mem. Am. Podiatry Assn. (Merit award 1962, gen. chmn. Region Three Ann. Conv. 1975—), Pa. Podiatry Assn. (pres. 1959-60, Man of Yr. award 1961, Spl. citation 1973), Greater Phila. Podiatry Soc. (pres. 1955-56), Fedn. Assns. Schs. of Health Professions (pres. 1975-76), Am. Assn. Colls. Podiatric Medicine (pres. 1969-72), Pi Epsilon Delta, Pi Delta. Clubs: Greate Bay Country, Union League, Pyramid Club. Republican. Office: Pa Coll Podiatric Medicine 810 N Race St Philadelphia PA 19107-2496

BATES, JOHN CECIL, JR., lawyer; b. Buffalo, May 27, 1936; s. John C. and Geraldine K. Bates; m. Ellen Clare Eyler, June 28, 1964; children: Andrew, Jeremy, Eliot, Emily. AB magna cum laude, Harvard U., 1958; JD, U. Mich., 1961; LLM, NYU, 1962. Bar: N.Y. 1962, D.C. 1977. Assoc. Milbank, Tweed, Hadley & McCloy, N.Y.C., 1963-72; spl. asst. tax policy Treasury Dept., Washington, 1973-76; ptnr. Squire, Sanders & Dempsey, Washington, 1977-84, Reid & Priest, Washington, 1984-91, Foley & Lardner, Washington, 1992-94; tax policy advisor Dept. Treas. Tech. Assistance Program (Ctrl. and Eastern Europe), 1995-98; cons. to fgn. govts. on taxation, 1998; cons. to fgn. govts. on decentralization, 2000—. Tax and fin. cons. state and local govts., also others, 1977—; adj. prof. Fordham U. Grad. Sch. Bus. Administrn., 1992. Co-author: Federal Law of Public Finance, 1988; contbr. numerous articles on tax, energy and fin. to profl. jours. Fellow: Internat. Law Inst. (sr.); mem.: ABA (chmn. com. tax sect. 1981—83), D.C. Bar Assn., Harvard Club. Avocations: historic preservation, environmental protection, music. Home: PO Box 293 Tenants Harbor ME 04860-0293

BATES, JOSEPH HENRY, physician, educator; b. Little Rock, Sept. 19, 1933; s. Henry Ermer and Susan Elizabeth (Wallis) B.; m. Patsy McGinnis, Aug. 6, 1955; children— Patricia, Susan Elizabeth, Joseph Henry, III, Elisabeth Lee. BS, MD, U. Ark., 1957, MS, 1963. Diplomate in internal medicine and pulmonary diseases Am. Bd. Internal Medicine, also mem. exam. bd. Med. intern U. Ark. Med. Center, 1957-58, resident in internal medicine, 1958-61, fellow in infections diseases, 1961-63; clin. investigator Little Rock VA Med. Ctr., 1963-66; mem. faculty U. Ark. Med. Ctr., Little Rock, 1967—, prof. medicine, 1973—, vice chmn. dept., 1978 98; assoc. dean U. Ark. Coll. Pub. Health, 2001—, Coll. Pub. Health, U. Akr. for Med. Sci., 2002—. Chief med. service Little Rock VA Hosp., 1970-98, dep. state health officer, Ark. Dept. Health, 1998—. Author research papers in field, chpts. in books. Chmn. Ark. chpt. NCCJ, 1980; chmn. biracial commn. Little Rock public schs., 1977-79; bd. dirs. Am. Lung Assn., 1972-90. Served as officer M.C. AUS, 1956-65. Grantee USPHS, 1961-63; Grantee NIH, VA, also pvt. founds. and corps., 1963— Mem. ACP (gov.), Am. Coll. Chest Physicians (gov.), Am. Fedn. Clin. Rsch., Am. Thoracic Soc. (pres. 1988-89), Infectious Disease Soc., So. Soc. Clin. Rsch., Am. Lung Assn. (pres. 1994-95), Aassn. Am. Physicians, Assn. Profs. Medicine. Presbyterian. Home: 5 Glenridge Rd Little Rock AR 72227-2208 Office: 4815 W Markham St Little Rock AR 72205-3866 E-mail: jbates@healthyarkansas.com.

BATES, KATHY, actress; b. Memphis, June 28, 1948; BFA, So. Meth. U., 1969. Film appearances include Taking Off, 1971, Straight Time, Come Back to the Five and Dime, Jimmy Dean, Jimmy Dean, Summer Heat, Arthur 2: On the Rocks, Signs of Life, High Stakes, Men Don't Leave, Dick Tracy, White Palace, Misery, 1990 (Acad. award for Best Actress 1990, Golden Globe award), At Play in the Fields of the Lord, 1991, Fried Green Tomatoes, 1991 (Golden Globe nomination, BAFTA nomination), The Road to Mecca, 1992, Prelude to a Kiss, 1992, Used People, 1992, A Home of Our Own, 1993, North, 1994, Curse of the Starving Class, 1994, Dolores Claiborne, 1994, Angus, 1995, Diabolique, 1996, The War at Home, 1996, Primary Colors, 1998, Swept from the Sea, 1998, Titanic, 1998, The Waterboy, 1998, Baby Steps, 1999, Dash and Lilly, 1999, My Life as a Dog, 1999, Bruno, 2000, Rat Race, 2001, American Outlaws, 2001, About Schmidt, 2002, Love Liza, 2002; stage appearances include Vanities, 1976, Semmelweiss, Crimes of the Heart, The Art of Dining, Goodbye Fidel, 1980, Chocolate Cake and Final Placement, 1981, 5th of July, 'night, Mother, 1983 (Tony nomination, Outer Critics Circle award), Two Masters: The Rain of Terror, 1985, Curse of the Starving Class, Frankie and Johnny in the Clair de Lune (OBIE award 1988), The Road to Mecca; TV appearances include (series) The Late Shift (Golden Globe award, Am. Comedy award, SAG award), The Love Boat, St. Elsewhere, Cagney & Lacey, L.A. Law, China Beach, Homicide, N.Y.P.D. Blue, (pilot) Fargo, (miniseries) Murder Ordained, The Stand, 1994, (movies of the week) Johnny Bull, No Place Like Home, Roe vs. Wade, Hostages, The West Side Waltz, 1995, The Late Shift, 1996 (Golden Globe, 1997), Annie, 1999, My Sister's Keeper, 2002, Six Feet Under, 2003; dir. Talking With, PBS Great Performances, (NBC) Office: Susan Smith & Assocs 121 N San Vicente Blvd Beverly Hills CA 90211-2303*

BATES, LURA WHEELER, retired trade association executive; b. Inboden, Ark., Aug. 28, 1932; d. Carl Clifton and Hester Ray (Pace) Wheeler; m. Allen Carl Bates, Sept. 12, 1954; 1 child, Carla Allene. BSBA, U. Ark., 1954. Cert. constrn. assoc. Sec.-bookkeeper, then office mgr. Assoc. Gen. Contractors Miss., Inc., Jackson, 1958-77, dir. adminstrv. svcs., 1977-98, asst. exec. dir., 1980-98; owner Ditty Bay Supply Co., 1987-98; ret., 1998. Adminstr. Miss. Constrn. Found., 1977-98; sec. AIA-Assoc. Gen. Contractors Liaisonship Coms., 1977-98; sec. Carpenters Joint Apprenticeship Coms., Jackson and Vicksburg, 1977-98. Editor NAWIC Image, 1968-69, Procedures Manual, 1965-66, Public Relations Handbook, 1967-68, Profl. Edn. Guide, 1972-73, Guidelines & Procedures Handbook, 1987-88; author digests in field. Sec. Marshall Elem. Sch. PTA, Jackson, 1962-64, v.p., 1965; sec.-treas. Inter-Club Coun. Jackson, 1963-64; tchr. adult Sunday sch. dept. Hillcrest Bapt. Ch., JAckson, 1975-82; dir. Bapt. Women WMU, 1987—, sec., 1992—; tchr. adult Sunday sch. dept. 1st Bapt. Ch., Crystal Springs, Miss., 1989-98; mem. exec. com. Jackson Christian Bus. and Profl. Women's Coun., 1976-80, sec., 1978-79, pres., 1979-80. Named Outstanding Woman in Constrn. Miss., 1962-63, Fellow Internat. Platform Assn.; mem. AAUW, NAFE, Nat. Assn. Women in Constrn. (life, chpt. pres. 1963-64, 76-77, 92-93, 2003—, nat. v.p. 1965-66, 77-78, nat. dir. Region 5 1967-68, nat. sec. 1970-71, 71-72, pres. 1980-81, coord. cert. constrn. assoc. program 1973-78, 83-84, guardian-contr. Edn. Found. 1981-82, chmn. nat. bylaws com 1974-75, 82-83, 85-86, 95-96, nat. parliamentarian 1983-92, Named Outstanding Mem., 1964, 74-84, 85-86, 95-96, Miss Hospitality 2002-03), Nat. Assn. Parliamentarians, U. Ark. Alumni Assn. (life, pres. ctrl. Miss. chpt. 1992-95), Delta Delta Delta (50 Yr. Golden Cir. 2002) Home: 1007 Lee Ave Crystal Springs MS 39059-2546

BATES, MARCIA JEANNE, information scientist educator; b. Terre Haute, Ind., July 30, 1942; d. Robert Joseph and Martha Jane B. BA, Pomona Coll., 1963; MLS, U. Calif., Berkeley, 1967; PhD, U. Calif., 1972. Peace corps vol., Saraburi, Thailand, 1963-64, Nongkhai, Thailand, 1964-65; jr. specialist Inst. Libr. Rsch., U. Calif., Berkeley, 1968; acting instr. U. Calif., Berkeley, 1969-70; asst. prof. U. Md., College Park, 1972-76, U. Wash., Seattle, 1976-80, assoc. prof., 1980-81, U. Calif., Los Angeles, 1981-91, prof., 1991—, prof. and dept. chmn. libr. and info. sci. Cons. U.S. Libr. Congress, Washington, 1986, 91, 2002-03, Getty Art Hist. Info. Program, Santa Monica, Calif., 1988-91, Info. Access Co., Foster City, Calif., 1992-95; mem. editl. bd. Jour. of Asis &T, 1989—, Libr. Quar., 1993-2001. Co-author: For Information Specialists, 1992; contbr. articles to profl. jours. Recipient Distinguished Lectureship award N.J. Am. Soc. for Info. Sci., New Brunswick, 1991. Fellow AAAS (sect. T electorate nominating com. 1980-84, chmn. 1983-84, sect. T com. mem.-at-large, 2001-04), mem. ALA (Frederick G. Kilgour award, 2001), Am. Soc. Info. Sci. and Tech. (bd. dirs. 1973-74, Best Jour. Article Yr. award, 1980, 99, Rsch. award 1998), Assn. Records Mgrs. Adminstrs., Calif. Libr. Assn. (mem. task force on future of Libr. profession, 1993-95), Phi Beta Kappa. Achievements include design of information systems and interfaces for search and subject access in information retrieval systems. Office: Grad Sch Edn & Info Studies UCLA 405 Hilgard Ave Los Angeles CA 90095-1520

BATES, MICHAEL, professional football player, former Olympic athlete, track and field; b. Dec. 19, 1969; Olympic track and field participant, Barcelona, Spain, 1992; kick off/returns football player Seattle Seahawks, 1993-95; running back, football player Carolina Panthers, 1996—. Recipient Track & Field Bronze medal in the 200 meter, Olympics, Barcelona, 1992; named All-Pro Sports Illustrated, Coll. and Pro Football Newsweekly, Football News, Pro-Football Weekly/Pro Football Writers Assn., Sporting News, USA Today, 1996; named All-Pro Sports Illustrated, Pro Football Weekly, Sporting News, Football Digest, 1997; named All-NFC Pro-Football Weekly, Football News, 1997; named All-NFC as Spl. Teamer Pro-Football Weekly, 1998, 99; became 1st player to lead kick-off return, 1996-97; mem. Pro Bowl, 1997, 98. Office: c/o Carolina Panthers 800 S Mint St Ste 2 Charlotte NC 28202-1502

BATES, MICHAEL LAWRENCE, curator; b. Louisville, Ky., Oct. 14, 1941; s. Hugh Louis and Emily Stiles (Willyard) B.; m. Katalin Uzdi, 1996; 1 child, Andrew. AB, U. Chgo., 1963, PhD, 1975. Curator of Islamic coins Am. Numismatic Soc., N.Y.C., 1970—; numismatist Fustat Excavations, Cairo, Egypt, 1978-80; sec. Am. Inst. for Yemeni Studies, Chgo., 1978-81; mem. council Internat. Numismatic Commn., 1979-91, v.p., 1986-91; cons. curator Kuwait Nat. Mus., 1981-85. Author: Islamic Coins, 1982; co-author: Greek, Roman and Islamic Coins from Sardis, 1981; editor Internat. Numismatic Newsletter, 1986-90. Fellowship Nat. Endowment for the Arts, 1976, Am. Rsch. Ctr. in Egypt, 1981-82, Samir Shamma Vis. Islamic Numismatic fellow St. Cross Coll. Oxford U., 1994, Near East Ctr. fellow UCLA, 1996; Gen. Motors Nat. scholar, 1959-63. Fellow Am. Oriental Soc., Middle East Studies Assn., Middle East Medievalists (v.p. 1990-92). Office: Am Numismatic Soc Broadway at 155th St New York NY 10032-7598 E-mail: bates@amnumsoc.org.

BATES, PATRICIA C. state official; m. John Bates; children: Jason, J'Amy. BA in Psychology, Occidental Coll.; postgrad., Calif. State U., Long Beach. Bus. owner, 1973—; councilwoman; social caseworker; mayor, 1989; state assembly mem. Dist. 73 Calif. State Assembly, 1998—. Mem. budget com.; mem. health com.; mem. judiciary com.; mem. transp. com.; vice-chair appropriations com.; mem. Orange County Charter Commn., 1995; chair Rep. Women's Caucus. Laguna Niguel Rep. Women Federated; mem. Orange County Mentoring Program Task Force, 1997, Gang Suppression Task Force; Jr. League Orange County; mem. Saddleback C.C. Found. Bd.; mem. South Coast Med. Ctr. Found., Taxpayers for Responsible Planning Adv. Bd. Mem.: Conservative Women's Leadership Assn., C. of C. (pres.), Laguna Niguel Rotary Club. Republican. Mailing: Rm 6031 PO Box 942849 Sacramento CA 94249 Office: Ste 120 30012 Ivy Glenn Dr Laguna Niguel CA 92677

BATES, PATTI JEAN, protection services official; b. Cin., Apr. 19, 1959; d. Harold Lee and Emily (Cox) Blinkhorn; m. Michael Bates, Apr. 12, 1986. BS in Forestry Recreation, U. Wis., Stevens Point, 1982; MA in Pub. Adminstrn., No. Ky. U., 1997. Cert. pub. safety communicator Assn. Pub. Safety Comm. Officials, Fla. Groundskeeper Cinti Tech. Coll., Cin., 1984-86; comm. specialist Union Twp., Cin., 1986-99; dir. adminstrn. Kenton County (Ky.) Detention Ctr., 1999—. Named Outstanding Student Alumni Assn., No. Ky. U., 1997. Mem.: Alumni Assn. No. Ky. U. Avocations: environ. issues, hiking, softball, phys. fitness. Office: Kenton County Jail Court St Covington KY 41011

BATES, WALTER ALAN, former lawyer; b. Wadsworth, Ohio, Oct. 27, 1925; s. Edwin Clinton and Gertrude (Connor) B.; m. Aloise Grasselli O'Brien, Feb. 9, 1957; children: Charles, Aloise, Walter Alan Jr., Thomas, David BS cum laude, Harvard U., 1945, LLB, 1950. Bar: Ohio 1950, U.S. Dist. Ct. (no. dist.) Ohio 1954, U.S. Ct. Appeals (6th cir.) 1965, U.S. Ct. Appeals (7th cir.) 1966, U.S. Dist. Ct. Conn. 1976, U.S. Ct. Appeals (2nd cir.) 1977, U.S. Dist. Ct. Minn. 1978, U.S. Ct. Appeals (8th cir.) 1980, U.S. Ct. Appeals (5th cir.) 1984, U.S. Dist. Ct. (no. dist.) Tex. 1988, U.S. Supreme Ct. 1989. Assoc. McKeehan, Merrick, Arter & Stewart, Cleve., 1950-60; ptnr. Arter & Hadden, Cleve., 1960-94; ret., 1994. Chmn. bd. trustees Cleve. Inst. Music, 1980-85, hon. trustee, 1985—; assoc. v.p., chmn. new programs com. United Way Svcs., Cleve., 1982-85, trustee, 1985-88; mem. Cleve. panel Ctr. for Pub. Resources; trustee Apollo's Fire, 1998—. Lt. USN, 1945-46, 51-53. Mem. ABA (antitrust sect.), Ohio State Bar Assn. (chmn. bd. govs. antitrust sect. 1987-91), Cleve. Bar Assn. (joint com. on bar admissions 1990-97, cert. grievance com. 1992-95). Clubs: Kirtland Country (sec., bd. dirs. 1981-86), Mentor Harbor Yachting (emeritus, bd. dirs. 1980-89, commodore 1988), Tavern, Harvard (Cleve. pres. 1968-69). Republican. Roman Catholic. Avocations: sailing, traveling. Home: 18235 Shaker Blvd Cleveland OH 44120-1754 E-mail: sailor74@prodigy.net.

BATES, WILLIAM, III, lawyer; b. Phila., May 1, 1949; s. William and Elizabeth (Martin) B. BA, Yale U., 1971; JD, Stanford U., 1974. Bar: Calif. 1974, U.S. Dist. Ct. (no. dist.) Calif. 1976, U.S. Dist. Ct. (ea. dist.) Calif. 1978, U.S. Dist. Ct. (ctrl. dist.) Calif. 1984, U.S. Ct. Appeals (9th cir.) 1986, U.S. Dist. Ct. (so. dist.) Calif. 1987, U.S. Supreme Ct. Law clk. to chief judge U.S. Dist. Ct. Conn., Hartford, 1974—75; assoc. McCutchen, Doyle, Brown & Enersen, San Francisco, 1975—81; ptnr. Bingham, McCutchen (formerly McCutchen, Doyle, Brown & Enersen), 1981—. Bd. visitors Stanford Law Sch., 2003—. Mem. ABA (mem. bus. bankruptcy com.), State Bar Calif. (chair rules of ct. com. 1979-80, mem. uniform comml. code com. 1985-88, mem. debtor/creditor rels. com. 1989-92), San Francisco Bar Assn. (chair comml. law and bankruptcy sect. 1991-92). Democrat. Episcopalian. Avocations: wine tasting, bicycling, travel. Office: Bingham McCutchen 1900 University Ave East Palo Alto CA 94303-2223 E-mail: bill.bates@bingham.com.

BATES, WILLIAM HUBERT, lawyer; b. Lexington, Mo., Apr. 14, 1926; s. George Hubert and E. Norma (Comer) B.; m. Joy LoRue Godbehere, Oct. 20, 1956; children: William Brand, Joy Ann. BA, U. Mo., 1949; JD, U. Mich., 1952. Bar: Mo. 1952. With Lathrop & Gage L.C., Kansas City, Mo., 1952—, chmn., 1988-95. Mem., pres. bd. curators U. Mo. Multi-Campus U., 1983-89. Sgt. U.S. Army, 1943-46, ETO. Recipient Brotherhood award NCCJ, 1984; Disting. Alumni award U. Mo., 1989, Geyer award for pub. svc., 1991. Fellow Am. Bar Found. (state chmn. 1990-97); mem. ABA (ho. of dels. 1990-93), Mo. Bar Assn. (bd. dirs. 1982-91, v.p., pres. 1988-91), Kansas City Bar Assn. (pres. Found. 1985-87), Lawyers Assn. Kansas City (Charles Evans Whittaker award 1990), Mo. C. of C. (chmn., bd. dirs. 1983-85), Greater Kansas City C. of C. (bd. dirs., chmn. 1975-92), Van Guard Club, Mercury Club, Beta Theta Pi (Man of Yr. award Kansas City 1985, Oxford Cup 1996). Democrat. Methodist. Avocations: golf, swimming, music. Home: 310 W 49th St Apt 1002 Kansas City MO 64112-3400 Office: Lathrop & Gage L C 2345 Grand Blvd Ste 2600 Kansas City MO 64108-2617

BATEY, SHARYN REBECCA, clinical research scientist; b. Nashville, Apr. 19, 1946; d. Robert Thomas and Sue (Alred) B. BS in Pharmacy, U. Tenn., 1969, D of Pharmacy, 1975; MS in Pub. Health, U. S.C., 1984. Hosp. pharmacist Vanderbilt Hosp., Nashville, 1969—71, VA Hosp., Beckley, W.Va., 1971—72, Gainesville, Fla., 1972—73, Battle Creek, Mich., 1973—74; hosp. pharmacy resident VA Hosp., Memphis, 1974—76; psychopharmacy resident Menninger Found., Topeka, 1976—77; clin. pharmacist William S. Hall Psychiat. Inst., Columbia, SC, 1977—82; asst. prof. U. S.C. Coll. Pharmacy, Columbia, 1977—83, asst. prof. Sch. Medicine, 1981—83, assoc. prof. Coll. Pharmacy and Sch. Medicine, 1983—89, prof., 1989; chief clin. pharmacy svcs. and ednl. programs William S. Hall Psychiat. Inst., Columbia, 1982—89; clin. rsch. scientist Burroughs Wellcome Co., Research Triangle Park, NC, 1989—95; clin. program head Glaxo Wellcome, Inc., Research Triangle Park, 1995—97, sr. clin. rsch. program head, 1997 2001; dir., clin. devel. Elan Pharmaceuticals, San Diego, 2001—02, sr. dir. clin. devel., 2003—. Clin. drug rsch./drug devel. fellow U. N.C. and Burroughs Wellcome, Research Triangle Park, 1983-84; pharmacist cons. NIMH, Bethesda Md., 1983-84, Health Care Fin. Adminstrn., Balt., 1983-84. Author audio visual programs Psychotropic Medication Edn. Program for Adults, Adolescents and Children, 1978, 84, 88, 89; contbr. articles on psychopharmacology to profl. jours. Recipient Significant Achievement award Am. Psychiat. Assn., 1980, Sci. Exhibit award Am. Psychiat. Assn., 1981. Mem. Am. Coll. Clin. Pharmacy, Am. Soc. Hosp. Pharmacists (chmn. edn. and tng. working group of psychopharmacy spl. interest group 1983-85, chmn. elect 1985-86, chmn. 1986-87, past chmn. 1987-88, project leader psychopharmacy specialty recognition petition 1986-89, psychopharmacy fellow selection com. 1986-88, chmn. psychopharmacy spl. practice group 1989), S.C. Dementia Registry (pres. user policy coun. 1989). Avocations: travel, reading. Home: 2645 28th St San Diego CA 92104 Office: Elan Pharms San Diego CA 92121 E-mail: sharyn.batey@elan.com.

BATH, RONALD J. military officer; BS in Bus. and Agr., U. Nev., Reno, 1968, MBA, 1971; JD, U. Pacific, 1975; postgrad., Air Command and Staff Coll., 1982, Air War Coll., 1993. Commd. 2d lt. USAF, 1969; advanced through grades to maj. gen., 2002; reconnaissance pilot 192d Tactical Reconnaissance Squadron, Reno, 1970—84, RF-4C pilot and flight comdr., 1984—90; flight safety officer 35th Tactical Fighter Wing, Sheikh Isa AB, Bahrain, 1990—91; chief of safety 152d Tactical Reconnaissance Group, Reno, 1991—92, chief of plans, 1993; nat. security fellow John F. Kennedy Sch. Govt. Harvard U., Cambridge, Mass., 1993—94; mem. profl. staff Commn. on Roles and Missions of Armed Forces, Washington, 1994—95; Air Nat. Guard advisor Army Divsn. Redesign Study, Washington, 1995—96; Air Nat. Guard asst . to dir. AF Quadrennial Def. Rev., Washington, 1996—97; divsn. chief Nat. Def. Rev. Directorate of Air Force Strategic Planning and Programming, Washington, 1997—99; dep. dir. AF Quadrennial Def. Rev., Washington, 1999—2001; dir. AF Quadrennial Def. Rev. and Def. Integration Hdqrs. USAF, Washington, 2001—02, spl. asst. to dep. chief of staff for plans and programs, 2001—02, dir. AF stragetic planning Dep. Chief of Staff for Plans and Programs, 2002—. Nat. security fellow John F. Kennedy Sch. Govt. Harvard U., Cambridge, Mass., 1994. Decorated DFC, Air medal with 3 oak leaf clusters. Office: USAF The Pentagon Washington DC 20330-1690

BATHAEE, SOUSSAN, engineering technician; b. Tehran, Iran, Jan. 23, 1953; arrived in U.S., 1983; d. Mohammad Bathaee and Farokhlagha Hassanpour. BSCE, Calif. State U., Fullerton, 2003. Overseas supr. Atomic Energy Orgn., Tehran, Iran, 1972—80; overseas drafts person London, 1980—83; drafts person Earl Walls Assocs., San Diego, 1984—85; job capt. Rsch. Facilities Design, San Diego, 1985—90; engrng. svc. technician County of San Bernardino, Calif., 1991—2002, ret., 2002; freelance engr. LDIC, San Jose, Calif., 2002—. Moslem. Home: 42045 Kaffirboom Ct Temecula CA 92591

BATHER, PAUL, state representative; b. June 30, 1947; MBA, U.Louisville; MSW, CUNY; degree in Liberal Arts, Fairfield U. Pres., CEO Bather Group; mem. Ky. Ho. of Reps., 2000—. Recipient Lena Coleman award, G.K. Offult/C. Eubank Tucker award, NAACP Freedom award, Stand UP award, NAACP Cmty Svc. award. Democrat. Office: Capitol Annex Rm 432 A Frankfort KY 40601 Address: 4706 Varble Ave Louisville KY 40211*

BATIUK, THOMAS MARTIN, cartoonist; b. Akron, Ohio, Mar. 14, 1947; s. Martin and Verna (Greskovics) B.; m. Catherine L. Wesemeyer, June 26, 1971; 1 child, Brian. B.F.A., cert. edn., Kent (Ohio) State U., 1969. Tchr. art Eastern Heights Jr. High Sch., 1969-72; syndicated cartoonist, 1972—. Cartoonist: comic strip Funky Winkerbean, 1972—, John Darling, 1979—, Crankshaft, 1987—; collections include Funky Winkerbean, 1973, Funky Winkerbean, Play It Again Funky, 1975, Funky Winkerbean, Closed Out, 1977, Yearbook, 1979, You Know You've Got Trouble When Your Mascot is a Scpaegoat, 1984, Football Fields are for Band Practice, 1986, Sunday Concert, 1987, Henry C. Dinkle-Live at Carnegie Hall, 1988, A Pizza Pilgrim's Progress, 1990, Funky Winkerbean: Gone with the Woodwinds, 1992, Would the Ushers Please Lock the Doors, 1994, Crankshaft: I've Still Got It, 1995; co-author: And One Slice With Anchovies!, 1993, Crankshaft, 1992; forward: A PArent's Guide to Band and ORchestra, 1991, Attack of the Band Moms, 1996. Recipient 46th Annual Ohio Gov.'s award-Journalism, 1995. Mem. Nat. Cartoonists Soc., Newspaper Features Coun. Office: care Universal Press Syndicate 4520 Main St Ste 700 Kansas City MO 64111-1816

BATLA, RAYMOND JOHN, JR., lawyer; b. Cameron, Tex., Sept. 1, 1947; s. Raymond John and Della Alvina (Jezek) B.; m. Susan Marie Clark, Oct. 1, 1983; children: Sara, Charles, Michael, Traci. BS with highest honors, U. Tex., 1970, JD with honors, 1973. Bar: Tex. 1973, D.C. 1973, U.S. Dist. Ct. (so. dist.) Tex. 1982, U.S. Ct. Appeals (D.C. cir.) 1974, U.S. Ct. Appeals (5th cir.) 1982, U.S. Ct. Appeals (10th cir.) 1978, U.S. Supreme Ct. 1977; registered Fgn. Lawyer, Law Soc. of Eng. and Wales, 2000. Structural engr. Tex. Hwy. Dept., Austin, 1970; assoc. Hogan & Hatson, Washington, 1973-82, gen. ptrn., 1983—. Mem. Am. Endowment for Democracy Internat. Observer Del. to Czechoslovakia, 1990; sec. Coun. on Alt. Fuels, 1987-97. Author: Petroleum Regulation Handbook, 1980, Natural Gas Yearbook, 1991; columnist, mem. editorial bd. Natural Gas mag., 1984-91, Energy Law Jour., 1991-93; contbr. articles to profl. jours. Mem. ABA (mem. spl. com. for energy fin., vice chmn. energy com. 1981), Fed. Energy Bar Assn. (chmn. internat. energy transactions com. 1993-94), Fed. Bar Assn., D.C. Bar Assn., State Bar Tex., City Club of Wash., London Capital Club, Order of Coif, Chi Epsilon, Tau Beta Pi. Home: 12406 Shari Hunt Grv Clifton VA 20124-2056 also: 5 Half Moon St London W1Y 7RA England Office: Hogan & Hartson 555 13th St NW Ste 800W Washington DC 20004-1109 also: Hogan & Hartson One Angel Ct London EC2R 7HJ England E-mail: rjbatla@hhlaw.com.

BATLIN, ROBERT ALFRED, retired newspaper editor; b. San Francisco, Aug. 24, 1930; S. Philip Alfred and Lavenia Mary (Barnes) B.; m. Diane Elise Giblin, July 4, 1956; children— Lisa, Philippa. BA, Stanford U., 1952, MA, 1954. Reporter San Bruno Herald, 1952-53; copy editor, then dept. editor San Francisco News, 1956-59; dept. editor San Francisco News-Call Bull., 1959-65; feature editor San Francisco Examiner, 1965-74, arts editor, 1974-85, asst. style editor, 1985-2001; copy editor San Francisco Chronicle mag., 2001—02, ret., 2002. Served with AUS, 1954-56. Mem. Soc. of Profl. Journalists. Home: 91 Fairway Dr Daly City CA 94015-1215

BATLIVALA, ROBERT BOMI D. oil company executive, economics educator; b. Bombay, Feb. 17, 1940; came to U.S., 1962, naturalized, 1968; s. Dean Shaw and Rose (Engineer) B.; m. Carole Gretchen Feustel, May 9, 1964; children: Amy, Dina. BS in Geology, Chemistry, St. Xavier Coll., Bombay, Ind., 1960; MBA in Bus., Econs., Loyola U., Chgo., 1970; PHD in Bus., Econs., Ill. Inst. Tech., 1971; postgrad., U. Chgo., 1972-73. Rsch. chemist Reynolds Metals Co., McCook, Ill., 1962-64; from sales engr. to staff dir. econs. Amoco Corp., Chgo., 1964-1988, dir. antitrust econs., 1988-93, dir. regulatory econs., 1993-99. Adj. prof. bus. and econs. Rosary Coll., Dominican U., River Forest, Ill., 1976—, Graduate Sch. Bus., 1980-99; bd. dirs. Vesta Ins. Group, Inc., Ill. Ins. Exch. (INEX), Parsee Internat. Ltd. Contbr. articles to profl. jours. Bd. dirs. Ctr. for Conflict Resolution, 1991-96. Stuart Tuition scholar Ill. Inst. Tech., 1970-71; recipient Recognition award Rosary Coll. Grad. Sch. Bus. Alumni Assn., River Forest, 1986. Mem. ABA (assoc.), Nat. Assn. Mfrs. (corp. fin., mgmt. & competition com., regulation, transp. com. 1980-99), Am. Econ. Assn., Assn. of Energy Economists, Loyola U. Grad. Bus. Alumni Assn. (pres., sr. v.p. 1971-73, Disting. Alumni award 1975), Oak Park Country Club. Avocations: ancient history, reading, writing, travel, languages. Home: 1106 Keystone Ave River Forest IL 60305-1326

BATMASIAN, MARTA TERSAKIAN, investment company owner; b. Istanbul, Turkey, Oct. 4, 1949; came to U.S., 1970. Garo and Anjel Tersakian; m. James H. Batmasian, Aug. 10, 1974; children: Jimmy, Armen. Student, Robert Coll., Istanbul, 1966-69, Leiden (The Netherlands) U., 1969-70; BA, Emerson Coll., 1972; MA, Brandeis U., 1975, postgrad., 1972-76; MBA, Barry U., 1987. Supt. Sahag Mesrob Sch., Watertown, Mass., 1974-75; lectr., prof. U. Mass., Boston, 1975-83, owner, pres. Mar-Mel Travel, Ins. and Real Estate, Cambridge, Mass., 1979-83; co-owner Investments, Ltd., Boca Raton, Fla., 1983—. Co-owner Investments Ltd., Cambridge, Mass., 1983—. Mem. Elem. Sch. Bd. of Watertown, 1979-81, Boca Raton Hist. Soc., South Fla. Symphony, Boca Raton Mus. Art, St. David's Armenian Ch.; bd. dirs. Boca Delray Sci. Mus., 1986-88; rec. sec. Fla. Symphonic Pops-Pro-Pops, 1986-87; v.p. Friends of Children's Mus. Boca Raton, 1987-89; Rep. nominee for Mass. Senate, 1982; bd. dirs. YMCA of Boca Raton, 1988-92; founder, v.p. Children's Sci. Explorium, Boca Raton, pres., chmn. bd., 1989—; active Men's Rep. Club of Baca Raton, Cystic Fibrosis Assn., St. Andrew's Sch. PTA; bd. trustees Am. Assembly, 1986—, Caldwell State Theater, 1990—, Children's Mus. of Boca Raton, 1986-90; founder, pres. Caldwell Theater Guild, 1991—; active Humanitarian Soc., 1989—; founder, bd. dirs. Boca Raton Literary Soc., 1991—. Mem. Nat. Assn. Armenian Studies and Rsch., Boca Raton C. of C., Jr. League of Baca Raton, AGBU Pres.'s Club, Allegro Soc. Club, Pro Pops (founder), Poinciana Women's Rep. Club (legis. chair 1985-87), YMCA Y's Women's Club (v.p. 1987—), Daus. of Vartan Lodge (treas. 1983—). Armenian Apostolic. Avocations: jogging, music, theater, stamp collecting. Office: Investments Ltd 215 N Federal Hwy Ste 1 Boca Raton FL 33432-3992

BATOR, FRANCIS MICHEL, economist, educator; b. Budapest, Hungary, Aug. 10, 1925; came to U.S., 1939, naturalized, 1944; s. Victor and Franciska Elisabeth (Sichermann) B.; m. Micheline Charlotte Martin, June 30, 1949; children: Nina, Christopher Francis. Grad., Groton Sch., 1943; BS, MIT, 1949, PhD, 1956; MA (hon.), Harvard U., 1967. Exec. asst. to dir. Center Internat. Studies, MIT, 1951-54; sr. research staff Center Internat. Studies, Mass. Inst. Tech., 1954-63, asst. prof. econs., 1957-60, assoc. prof., 1960-63; sr. econ. adviser AID, Dept. State, 1963-64; sr. staff NSC, 1964-65; dep. asst. to Pres. for nat. security affairs White House, 1965-67; prof. polit. economy John F. Kennedy Sch. Govt. Harvard U., 1967-87, Ford Found. prof. internat. polit. economy John F. Kennedy Sch. Govt., 1987-92; Lucius N. Littauer prof. polit. economy John F. Kennedy Sch. Govt., Harvard U., 1992-96, emeritus Lucius N. Littauer prof. polit. economy, 1996—. Cons. Rand Corp., Inst. Def. Analysis, Office Sec. Treasury, 1961-63, under sec. state for econ. affairs, 1961; U.S. mem. consultative group on econ. projections UN, 1962, on internat. monetary arrangements, 1969; spl. cons. sec. treasury, 1967-69; mem. Pres.'s Adv. Com. Internat. Monetary Arrangements, 1967-69; vis. fellow Collegium Budapest Inst. Advanced Study, 1993. Author: The Question of Government Spending, 1960; co-author: Energy, the Next Twenty Years, 1979; contbr. Agenda for the Nation, 1968, Employment and Growth, 1987, The Theory of Market Failure, 1998, also articles. Mem. fgn. affairs task force Dem. Adv. Coun. Elected Ofcls., 1974-76; mem. nat. adv. bd. Ctr. Nat. Policy, 1981-90; mem. adv. bd. Scudder New Europe Fund, 1990-92, McKinsey and Co. Global Inst., 1991-95; bd. dirs. Hungarian-Am. Enterprise Fund, 1994—, Exxel/Atmos Inc., 1994—. 1st lt. inf. AUS, 1944-46. Recipient Disting. Service award Treasury Dept., 1968; Guggenheim fellow, 1959; named to US Army Officer Candidate Sch. Hall of Fame. Fellow Am. Acad. Arts and Scis.; mem. Coun. Fgn. Rels., Am. Econ. Assn., Royal Econ. Soc., Century Assn. (N.Y.C.), Harvard Club of N.Y.C. Home: 17 Farrar St Cambridge MA 02138-2007 Office: Harvard U 79 Jfk St Cambridge MA 02138-5801

BATORY, RONALD LOUIS, rail transportation executive; b. Detroit, Jan. 25, 1950; s. Louis Frank and Bonita Faye (Hall) B.; m. Barbara Ellen Berger, Apr. 19, 1975; 1 child, Erin Faye. BA, Adrian Coll., 1971; MA, Eastern Mich. U., 1975. With Detroit, Toledo & Ironton R.R., 1971-81; adminstrn. asst. to v.p. ops. Dearborn, Mich., 1972-75; asst. engr. track Flat Rock, Mich., 1975-76; mgr. indsl. engr. Dearborn, 1976-77; dir. material procurement and planning, 1977-81; with Grand Trunk Western R.R., 1981-87; transp. supr. Pontiac, Mich., 1981-82; trainmaster Toledo, 1982-84; terminal mgr. Chgo., 1984-86; dist. mgr. ops, 1986-87; dir. transp. planning Detroit, 1987; v.p., gen. mgr. Chgo. Mo. & Western Rlwy., Springfield, Ill., 1987-89; asst. gen. mgr. ea. region So. Pacific Transp., Lisle, Ill., 1989-92, gen. mgr. Midwest region, 1992-94; pres. The Belt Railway Co. of Chgo., 1994-98; sr. v.p., COO Conrail, Mt. Laurel, NJ, 1998—, COO, 1998—. Bd. dirs. Kansas City Terminal Rlwy., Terminal Railroad Assn. St. Louis. Author: Purchasing Perspective, 1979, Econs. of Planning, 1980. Mem. The R.R. Tie Assn., Am. Ry. Engr. Assn., Ry. Ops. Officers, Inc., Am. Short Line R.R. Assn. (bd. dirs.), Am. Assn. R.R. Supts. (bd. dirs.), Fairlane Club, Laurel Creek Country Club, Union League Club of Chgo. Republican. Methodist. Avocations: photography, historical transportation readings. Home: 13 Leeds Rd Moorestown NJ 08057-1887 Office: Consol Rail Corp 1000 Howard Blvd Mount Laurel NJ 08054-2371

BATRA, INDER P. physics educator, researcher; b. Punjab, Punjab, India, June 25, 1942; s. Sawan Mal and Santi Devi Batra; m. Uma Leekha, Sept. 16, 1949; children: Puja, Mala. PhD, Simon Fraser U., Burnaby, B.C., Can., 1969; MS, BS with honors, Delhi U., India, 1964. Rsch. scientist, and mgr. IBM Corp., San Jose, Calif., 1969—98; head dept. of physics U. of Ill., Chgo., 1998—. Fellow, Am. Phys. Soc., 1974—. Office: U Ill-Chgo MC 273 845 W Taylor St Chicago IL 60607 Office Fax: 312-996-9016. E-mail: ipbatra@uic.edu.

BATRA, ROMESH CHANDER, engineering mechanics educator, researcher; b. Dherowal, Punjab, India, Aug. 16, 1947; came to U.S., 1969; s. Amir Chand and Dewki Bai (Dhamija) B.; m. Manju Dhamija, June 26, 1972; children: Monica, Meenakshi. BSME, Panjabi U., Patiala, India, 1968; MASc, U. Waterloo, Ont., Can., 1969; PhD, Johns Hopkins U., 1972. Postdoctoral rsch. assoc. Johns Hopkins U., Balt., 1972-73; rsch. assoc. McMaster U., Hamilton, Ont., 1973-74; asst. prof. U. Ala., Tuscaloosa, 1976-77; asst. prof. engring. mechanics U. Mo., Rolla, 1974-76, assoc. prof., 1977-81, prof., 1981-94; Clifton C. Garvin prof. Va. Polytech. Inst. & State U., Blacksburg, 1994—. Mem. NRC Panel on Armaments, 1996—99, NRC Panel on Survivability and Lethality, 2001—; S.W. Mechanics Series lectr., 2000; Michael L. Sadowski mechanics lectr. Rensselaer Poly. Inst., 2000. Editor: Contemporary Research in Engineering Science, Springer Verlag, 1995; co-editor: Contemporary Research in the Mechanics and Mathematics of Materials, Internat. Ctr. for Numerical Methods in Engring., 1996, Constitutive Laws, Experiments and Numerical Implementation, Internat. Ctr. for Numerical Methods in Engring., 1995, Material Instabilities, Theory and Applications, 1994, Impact, Waves and Fracture, 1994, Contemporary Research in Mechanics, 2002; mem. editl. bd. Internat. Jour. Plasticity, 1989-2003, Internat. Jour. Engring. Design and Analysis, 1992—, Continuum Mechanics and Thermodynamics, 1993—, Computational Mechanics, 1994—, Jour. Engring. Materials and Tech., 1996-2001, Polish Jour. Theoretical and Applied Mechanics, 2000—, Computer Modeling in Engring. and Sci., 2003—; editor: Mathematics and Mechanics of Solids, 1995—; reviewer for various jours. in field; contbr. articles to profl. jours. Grantee NSF, 1980-83, 87—, Army Rsch. Office, 1985—, Office of Naval Rsch., 1994—; recipient Alexander von Humboldt award for sr. scientists, 1992, Jai Krishna award Indian Geotech. Soc., 1994, Eric Reissner medal Internat. Congress in Computational Engrg. Sci., 2000; inducted into Hopkins Soc. Scholars, 1993. Fellow ASME (chair elasticity com. 1995-2000, co-editor symposium procs. 1991, 94-95, co-editor meeting procs. 1999, awards nominating com. 1997—), Am. Acad. Mechanics (awards nominating com. 2002—, sec. 2003—), Am. Soc. Engring. Edn. (Centennial award 1993), Soc. Engring. Sci. (bd. dirs. 1991-96, editor meeting procs. 1982, v.p. 1995, pres. 1996); mem. Midwestern Mechanics Conf. (editor procs. 1991, bd. dirs. 1989-93), Soc. Natural Philosophy (treas. 1987-89, editor meeting procs. 1981), Mechs. and Materials Conf. (organizer, cochair 1999), U.S. Nat. Congress Theoret. and Applied Mechs. (organizer, co-chmn. 2002). Office: Va Polytech Inst & State U Dept Engring Sci & Mechanics 220 Norris Hall Blacksburg VA 24061-0219 E-mail: rbatra@vt.edu.

BATROUNEY, CLIVE M. corporate financial executive; Vice chmn. Australian Stock Exch., Melbourne. Office: Australian Stock Exch 530 Collins St Melbourne VIC 3000 Australia

BATSAKIS, JOHN GEORGE, pathology educator; b. Petoskey, Mich., Aug. 14, 1929; s. George John and Stella (Vlahkis) B.; m. Mary Janet Savage, Dec. 28, 1957; children: Laura, Sharon, George. Student, Va. Mil. Inst., 1947, Albion Coll., Mich., 1948-50; MD, U. Mich., 1954. Diplomate Am. Bd. Pathology. Intern George Washington Univ. Hosp., Washington, 1954-55; resident in pathology U. Mich. Hosp., Ann Arbor, 1955-59; prof. pathology U. Mich., Ann Arbor, 1969-79; chmn. dept. pathology M.D. Anderson Hosp. U. Tex., Houston, 1981-96, chm. and prof. emeritus dept pathology, 1996—. Ruth Legett Jones prof. U. Tex., Austin, 1982-96; adj. prof. oral pathology U. Tex. Dental Br., Houston; cons. Armed Forces Inst. Pathology, 1972—, VA Hosp., Ann Arbor, 1968-79; Hayes Martin lectr. Am. Soc. for Head and Neck Surgery, 1994; Gunnar Holmgren lectr. Swedish Nat. Ear, Nose, Throat Meeting, 1994; William Christopherson lectr. U. Louisville Dept. of Pathology, 1995; external examiner U. Hong Kong Dental Sch., 1995—; Francis A. Sooy lectr. dept. otolaryngology, head and neck surgery U. Calif., San Francisco, 1997; 2d Matthews lectr. dept. pathology Emory U., 1997; spkr. in field. Author: Tumors of the Head and Neck, 2d edit., 1979; co-editor: Oral Cancer, 2003; editor: Clin. Lab. Ann., 1981—86; co-editor: Advances in Anatomic Pathology, 1994—98; contbr. articles. Bd. trustees, v.p. Mike Hogg Found., Houston, 1991—; trustee George C. Marshall Found., Lexington, Va., 1995-00, emeritus trustee, 2000—. Capt. U.S. Army, 1959-61. Recipient William H. Rorer award Am. Coll. Gastroenterology, 1972, Disting. Alumnus award Albion Coll., 1987, Reviewer of the Decade award AMA Archives Orolaryngology Head Neck Surgery, 1990, Presdl. award Am. Soc. Head and Neck Surgery, 1991, Harlan Spjut award Houston Soc. Clin. Pathologists, 1992, Honor award Am. Laryngologic Assn., 1995; Spl. Honored Guest of Am. Soc. for Head and Neck Surgery, 1993. Fellow ACP, Am. Soc. Clin. Pathologists, Coll. Am. Pathologists (Disting. Svc. award 2002), Am. Acad. Otolaryngology (assoc., honor award 1994), Royal Soc. Medicine. Republican. Episcopalian. Home: 1701 Hermann Dr Unit 3304 Houston TX 77004-7373 Office: 1452 W Bear Lake Rd NE Kalkaska MI 49646-9051

BATSHAW, MARILYN SEIDNER, education administrator; b. East Orange, N.J., Aug. 19, 1946; d. Gerald and Sylvia (Weinstein) Seidner; 1 child, Andrew Curt. BA, Newark State Coll., Union, N.J., 1968; MA, Kean Coll., Union, 1972, prin. cert., 1984. Cert. hearing aid dispenser, audiologist, elem. and deaf and hearing impaired tchr., supr., prin., N.J. Tchr. of deaf N.J. Dept. Edn., Trenton, 1972-74, audiologist, 1974-82, cons. in spl. edn., 1982-86; prin., dir. edn. Lakeview Sch., Cerebral Palsy Assn. Middlesex County, Edison, NJ, 1986-94; prin. ARC Essex Sch., Livingston, NJ, 1994-96; billing and eligibility case mgr. Prudential Health Care Group, Cranbury, NJ, 1997-99; dir. ESC Sch. West Amwell Campus Hunterdon County Ednl. Scvs. Commn., Lambertville, NJ, 1999; supr. Bright Beginnings Learning Ctr. Middlesex County Ednl. Svcs. Commn., Piscataway, NJ, 1999—2001; supr. special edn. North Arlington Bd. Edn., NJ, 2001—. Officer Parents for Deaf Awareness. Mem. ASCD, N.J. ASCD, Ednl. Audiology Assn., Am. Speech-Lang. and Hearing Assn. (cert. clin. competence in audiology), N.J. Speech-Lang. and Hearing Assn., A.G. Bell Assn., Am. Auditory Soc., Am. Acad. Audiology, N.J. Acad. Audiology, Coun. Exceptional Children, N.J. Coun. Exceptional Children, Nat. Assn. Edn. Young Children. Home: 166 Westgate Dr Edison NJ 08820-1158 Office: North Arlington HS Child Study Team 222 Ridge Rd North Arlington NJ 07031 E-mail: mbatshaw@optonline.net.

BATSON, DAVID WARREN, lawyer; b. Wichita Falls, Tex., Jan. 4, 1956; s. Warren M. Batson and Jacqueline (Latham) B. BBA, Midwestern State U., 1976; JD, U. Tex., 1979. Bar: Tex. 1980, U.S. Dist. Ct. (no. dist.) Tex. 1981, U.S. Tax Ct. 1981, U.S. Ct. Appeals (5th cir.) 1983, U.S. Ct. Appeals (D.C. cir.) 1983, U.S. Ct. Claims 1984, U.S. Supreme Ct. 1984. Atty. Arthur Andersen & Co., Ft. Worth, 1980-81; tax atty. The Western Co. of N.Am., Ft. Worth, 1981-85; sr. tax atty. Alcon Labs., Inc., Ft. Worth, 1985; gen. counsel Data Tailor, Inc., Ft. Worth, 1985-87; sr. tax atty. Arco, 1988-90; atty. pvt. practice, Wichita Falls, Tex., 1990—99; pvt. practice Stephenville, Tex., 1999—. Lectr. U. of Tex., Arlington, 1984-85; of counsel Means & Means, Corsicana, Tex., 1985-86. Contbr. articles to profl. jours. Speaker A Wish With Wings, Arlington, Tex., 1984-85, Habitat for Humanity (bd. dirs. 1999-). Fellow Tex. Bar Found.; mem. ATLA, Tex. Bar Assn., Christian Legal Soc., Tex. Trial Lawyers Assn., Phi Delta Phi. Avocations: negotiations, camping, self improvement. Address: PO Box 585 Stephenville TX 76401-0585

BATSON, DAWN KIRSTEN, music educator, cultural consultant; b. Port-of-Spain, Trinidad and Tobago, Oct. 7, 1959; d. Henry Arthur Batson and Esther Stephanita Kafiluddi-Batson. BSc in Music Edn., Hofstra U., 1981; Diploma in Radio and TV Prodn., Announcer Tng. Studios, N.Y.C., 1982; MusM in Music Industry, U. Miami, Coral Gables, Fla., 1993, PhD, 1995. Announcer, prodr. Trinidad and Tobago Radio and TV, Port-of-Spain, 1982—; music tchr. Trinity Coll., Maraval, Trinidad and Tobago, 1983—91; conf. coordination staff U. Miami Office of Confs., Coral Gables, 1992—93; dir. steelband ensemble U. Miami, Coral Gables, 1991—96; asst. prof. music, dir. steelband Fla. Meml. Coll., Miami, 1996—; chmn., bd. dirs. Trinidad and Tobago Nat. Steel Orch., Port-of-Spain, 2000—03. Musical dir. Pamberi Steel Orch., San Juan, Trinidad and Tobago, 1986—98, Woodtrin Steel Orch., Maraval, Trinidad and Tobago, 1983—90; cultural cons. Consulate Gen. Trinidad and Tobago et. al., 1998—2002. Composer: works for steel orch. Fulbright-Hayes fellow, North Africa, 2000, Inter-Am. Found. fellow, 1994. Mem.: Fla. Steelband Assn. (pub. rels. officer 2001—). Avocations: drums, dancing, hiking, reading. Home: 8611 NW 29th St Sunrise FL 33322 Office: Fla Meml Coll 15800 NW 42d Ave Miami FL 33054

BATSON, RAYMOND MILNER, retired cartographer; b. Lincoln, Nebr., July 8, 1931; s. Avery A. and Margaret Elizabeth (Milner) B.; m. Rhoda May Meier, Aug. 31, 1955; children: Beverly Ann Batson Platten, Frederick Avery, Thomas Raymond. Student, U. Colo., 1953-57, BA, 1962. Field engr., photogrammetrist U.S. Geol. Survey, Denver, 1957-63, rsch. cartographer Flagstaff, Ariz., 1963-94, chief planetary cartography, 1963-92; ret., 1994. Mem. planetary cartography working group NASA, Washington, 1978-94, mem. planetary geol. and geophys. working group, 1982-92, expert mem. U.S./USSR joint working group for planetary data exch., 1988-92. Author, editor: Planetary Mapping, 1990, NASA Atlas of the Solar System, 1997, The Compact NASA Atlas of the Solor System, 2001. Staff sgt. USAF, 1951-52. Fellow Am. Soc. for Photogrammetry; mem. Am. Soc. Photogrammetry (chmn. extraterrestrial sci. com. 1981-88), Astron. Soc. of the Pacific (hon.), Internat. Soc. PHotogrammetry (chmn. working group 3 com. IV 1982-85), Internat. Astron. Union (working group for planetary system nomenclature com. 16, 1991-94).

BATSON, RICHARD NEAL, lawyer; b. Nashville, May 1, 1941; s. John H. and Mildred (Neal) B.; m. Jean Elizabeth Flanagan; children: John Hayes, Richard Davis. BA cum laude, Vanderbilt U., 1963, JD, 1966. Bar: Ga. 1967. Law clk. to Judge Griffin B. Bell U.S. Ct. Appeals (5th cir.), Atlanta, 1966-67; assoc. Alston & Bird (formerly Alston, Miller & Gaines), Atlanta, 1967-71, ptnr., 1971—. Spkr. Nat. Conf. Bankruptcy Judges, 1982, 86, 87, 88, 94, 96, Bank Lending Inst., 1986-87, also other instns. and assns.; adj. prof. Emory U. Sch. Law, 1994-95; co-lectr. Ga. State U., fall 1984; mem. bankruptcy rules com. Jud. Conf. U.S., 1993-99. Co-author: Problem Loan Strategies, 1985, rev. 1998; contbg. author Bankruptcy Litigation Manual, 1990—; contbg. editor Norton Bankruptcy Law and Practice, 1990—. Sgt. USAF, 1967-73. Fellow Am. Coll. Trial Lawyers, Am. Coll. Bankruptcy (bd. dirs., pres. 1997-2001, chmn. bd. dirs. 2001-03); mem. Atlanta Bar Assn. (pres. 1979-80), Am. Law Inst., Southeastern Bankruptcy Law Inst. (bd. dirs., pres. 1986-87), Nat. Bankruptcy Conf. Avocations: hiking, outdoor activities. Office: Alston & Bird One Atlantic Ctr 1201 W Peachtree St Atlanta GA 30309-3400 Home: PO Box 5201 Snowmass Village CO 81615

BATT, ALYSE SCHWARTZ, technical officer; b. Bronx, NY, Aug. 8, 1960; d. Irwin Aaron and Beryl (Leff) Schwartz; m. David Charles Batt, Feb. 14, 1993; children: Shannon Paige, Megan Brooke. AAS in Data Processing, SUNY, Farmingdale, 1980; BBA in Bus. Computers, Hofstra U., 1987; MS in Mgmt. Engring., L.I. U., 1995. Programmer trainee State Ins. Fund, N.Y.C., 1980; programmer analyst cons. Bradford Nat. Corp., N.Y.C., 1981-83; programmer E.F. Hutton, N.Y.C., 1983; programmer analyst Chase Manhattan Bank, N.Y.C., 1983-87; sr. systems analyst Met. Life Ins. Co., N.Y.C., 1987-89; sr. programmer analyst Orion Pictures Corp., N.Y.C., 1989-91, JPMorgan Chase, N.Y.C., 1991—. Mem.: Ladies Aux. Massapequa Fire Dept. (pres., v.p., treas.), Greater L.I. Road Runners Club, N.Y. Road Runners Club, Massapequa Road Runners Club, Commack Skating Club, Bayshore Skating Club. Republican. Jewish. Avocations: roller skating, running. Home: 153 Massachusetts Ave Massapequa NY 11758-4111

BATT, H. WILLIAM, political scientist; b. Springfield, Mass., May 30, 1940; s. Henry W. and Nellie K. Batt. BA, U. Mass., 1962; MA, No. Ill. U., 1967; PhD, SUNY, Albany, 1974. Vol. Peace Corps, Thailand, 1962-65; instr. grad. sch. pub. affairs Russell Sage, Siena Colls., Albany, 1972-73; asst. prof. SUNY, Binghamton, 1976-78; dir. Ctrl. Rsch. Group, Ithaca, N.Y., 1978-80; v.p. Interwolf, Inc., Ithaca, 1979-80; asst. rsch. dir. legis. commn. N.Y. State Senate, Albany, 1982-83; staff polit. scientist, legis. com. N.Y. State Assembly, Albany, 1983-92; exec. dir. Cen. Rsch. Group, Albany, N.Y., 1994—; dir. Ctr. for Study of Econs., Phila., 1997—. Cons. in field, Ithaca, 1974-76, Albany, 1980—. Contbr. articles to profl. jours. Pres. Returned Peace Corps Vols., N.Y., 1986-91; dir. Robert Schalkenbach Found., N.Y.C., 2002—. Mem. Am. Soc. for Pub. Adminstrn., Hemlock Soc. (pres. N.Y. chpt. 1987-97, nat. bd. dirs. 1989-94, treas. 1993-94). Democrat. Unitarian Universalist. Avocation: social and political action groups. Home and Office: 680 N Pearl St Albany NY 12204

BATT, NICK, property and investment executive; b. Defiance, Ohio, May 6, 1952; s. Dan and Zenith (Dreher) B. BS, Purdue U., 1972; JD, U. Toledo, 1976. Asst. prosecutor Lucas County, Toledo, 1976-80, civil divsn. chief, 1980-83; village atty. Village of Holland, Ohio, 1980-91; law dir. City of Oregon, Ohio, 1984-91; spl. counsel State of Ohio, 1983-93; pres. Property & Mgmt. Connection, Inc., Toledo, 1993—2002, All Rental Property Mgmt. Co., 2002—. Mem. Maumee Valley Girl Scout Coun., Toledo, 1977-80; bd. mem. Bd. Cmty. Rels., Toledo, 1975-76; mem. Lucas County Dem. Exec. Com., 1981-83. Named One of Toledo's Outstanding Young Men, Toledo Jaycees, 1979. Mem. KC, Elks. Democrat. Roman Catholic. Office: All Rental Property Mgmt Co 1732 Arlington Ave Toledo OH 43609-3050 E-mail: NICKBATT@TOAST.NET.

BATT, RONALD ELMER, gynecologist, scientist, historian; b. Buffalo, Sept. 24, 1933; s. Elmer Lawrence and Mary Catherine (Roll) B.; m. Carol Mary Schaab, Dec. 28, 1957; children: Paula, Douglas, Thomas, Neil, Jennifer, John; m. 2d, Kathleen Over Cansdale, May 19, 1982; stepchildren: William, James, Suzanne, Timothy, John, Mark. BS in Biology, Niagara U., 1954; MD, U. Buffalo, 1958; MA in History, SUNY, Buffalo, 2002. Intern Millard Fillmore Hosp., Buffalo, 1958-59; resident in ob-gyn SUNY, Buffalo, 1959-60, 62-66; rsch. fellow Harvard U. Med. Sch., 1963-64; asst. in surgery Peter Bent Brigham Hosp., Boston, 1963-64; fellow in gynecologic surgery Mayo Clinic, 1965; practice gynecology specializing in endometriosis and reproductive surgery Buffalo, 1966-98; researcher, 1966—. Prof. clin. gynecology, clin. prof. social and preventive medicine SUNY Buffalo. Co-author: Another Era: A Pictorial History of the School of Medicine and Biomedical Sciences, State University of New York at Buffalo 1846-1996; contbr. chpts. to books, articles to profl. jours. With M.C., USN, 1960-62. Recipient Lifetime Career Achievement award Med. Alumni Assn. Sch. Medicine and Biomed. Scis. SUNY, 1998. Fellow Royal Coll. Surgeons Can., Am. Coll. Obstetricians and Gynecologists, ACS; mem. Am. Soc. Reproductive Medicine, Soc. Reproductive Surgeons, Am. Assn. History Medicine, Internat. Soc. History Medicine, Am. Assn. Gynecol.Laparoscopists. Office: 5648 Broadway Lancaster NY 14086-2317

BATTAGLIA, ANTHONY SYLVESTER, lawyer; b. Binghamton, N.Y., Aug. 21, 1927; s. Sylvester Anthony and Helen B.; m. Catherine Jean, Oct. 1, 1972; children: Christina, Marc Anthony; children by previous marriage— Anthony, Sandra, Brian, Brenda Lee. AA, U. Fla., 1948, BA, 1949, LL.B., 1953, JD, 1967. Bar: Fla. 1953, U.S. Dist. Ct. (mid. and so. dists.) Fla., U.S. Ct. Appeals (5th, 11th cirs.), U.S. Tax Ct., U.S. Ct. Appeals (D.C. cir.), U.S. Ct. Mil. Appeals; cert. ct. approved abritrator U.S. Dist. Ct., U.S. Supreme Ct. 1966. Asst. to U.S. dist. atty., So. Dist. Fla., 1953-56; ptnr. Parker, Parker & Battaglia, St. Petersburg, Fla., 1953-56, Parker, Battaglia & Ross, St. Petersburg, 1965-73, Parker, Battaglia, Parker, Ross & Ross, St. Petersburg, 1973-75, Battaglia, Parker, Ross, Parker & Stolba, St. Petersburg, 1975-76, Battaglia, Ross & Stolba, 1976-77, Battaglia, Ross, Stolba & Forlizzo, 1977-78, Battaglia, Ross & Forlizzo, 1978-80, Battaglia, Ross, Hastings, Dicus & Andrews, 1980-93, Battaglia, Ross, Dicus & Wein PA, 1993-2001. Mem. Fla. Pub. Svc. Commn., 1971; chmn. bd. Metrocare, Inc., 1975-78; mem. grievance com. U.S. Dist. Ct., 1985-88; pres. Asst. U.S. Attys. Assn. for Mid. Dist. Fla., 1994; guest lectr. Stetson U., 1994; bd. dirs. Intervest Bank, 1st Bankers Tampa Bay, N.A., St. Petersburg, Nat. Bank Fla., St. Petersburg, Operation PAR, Inc.; chmn. adv. bd. 1st Union Nat. Bank, South Pinellas, Fla. Republican nat. committeeman, Fla., 1956-64, bd. dirs., Tampa div.; bd. dirs. San Carlo Opera Fla., 1972-74, pres., chmn. bd. dirs., Pinellas County div., 1974-76; bd. dirs. St. Petersburg Opera Co., 1976-77; chmn. bd. Pinellas County Arthritis Found., 1985; founding sponsor Civil Justice Found.; trustee Ctr. Against Spouse Abuse, 1999. Elected to U. Fla. Hall of Fame, 1951 Master Ferguson-White Am. Inn of Ct.; fellow Am. Coll. Mortgage Attys.; mem. ABA, ATLA (sustaining), Fla. Bar Assn. (bd. govs. 1993-99), St. Petersburg Bar Assn. (pres. 1990), Fed. Bar Assn. (v.p. Mid. Fla. dist.), U.S. Attys. Assn. for Mid. Dist. Fla. (pres. 2001), Internat. Bar Assn., Hillsborough County Bar Assn., Acad. Fla. Trial Lawyers (judge student competition 1985), Am. Judicature Soc. (Supreme Ct. Hist. Soc. 1985-89), Nat. Assn. Criminal Def. Lawyers, Acad. Criminal Justice Scis., Fla. Criminal Def. Trial Lawyers, Criminal Def. Lawyers Hillsborough County, Pinellas County Trial Lawyers Assn. Roscoe Pound Am., Trial Lawyers Found. (judicial nominating com.), U. Fla. Nat. Alumni Assn., St. Petersburg C. of C. (gov.), Pinellas Inns Ct. (master bench), Herbert G. Goldberg Criminal Law Am. Inn Ct., Fla. Bar Bd. of Govs. Clubs: Treasure Island Tennis and Yacht (bd. dirs.), Suncoast Tiger Bay, St. Petersburg Yacht, Nat. Italian Am. Found., Italian-Am. Unico Internat. Lodges: K.C. Roman Catholic. Office: 980 Tyrone Blvd N Saint Petersburg FL 33710-6333

BATTAGLIA, BASIL RICHARD, company executive, former political party official; b. Wilmington, Del., Oct. 28, 1935; s. Bruno and Carmella (Cannatelli) B.; m. Sandra Battaglia; children: Lisa Maria, Michael Basil. AB, LaSalle Coll., 1959; LLB, Mt. Vernon Sch. Law, 1963. Owner title search firm, chmn. Chmn. Rep. Eighth Councilman Dist., Wilmington; mem. Mayor's Citizens Adv. Com. Urban Renewal; v.p. Del. Fedn. Young Reps.; bd. dirs. Active Young Reps. Wilmington; mem. Rep. City Edn. Com.; chmn. Rep. Fund Raising Dinners; registrar in chancery New Castle County; chmn. Wilmington Rep. City Exec. Com.; fin. chmn. Del. State Rep. Party, 1993-2001; co-chmn. Presdl. Pers. Advt. Com.; mem. fin. com. George Bush for Pres. Campaign, 1988; chmn. Rep. Nat. Com. Northeastern Chmn. Com.; adminstr. Del. Mem Turnpike; mem. bd. Del.

Visitors and Conv. Bur.; bd. dirs. Nat. Constn. Ctr. Named Outstanding Young Rep., Wilmington, 1969. Mem. Nat. Assn. County Officers. Roman Catholic. Office: 1419 Riverview Ave Wilmington DE 19806

BATTAGLIA, BRIAN PETER, lawyer; b. St. Petersburg, Fla., Oct. 10, 1960; s. Anthony S. and Virginia A. (Knopick) B.; m. Nancy L. Pateras, Sept. 27, 1986; children: Jason Michael, Matthew Brian. BS in Criminology, Fla. State U., 1982; JD, Drake U., 1985; LLM in Health Law, Loyola U., Chgo., 1996. Bar: Fla. 1986, U.S. Dist. Ct. (mid. dist.) Fla. 1987, U.S. Ct. Appeals (11th cir.) 1992, U.S. Supreme Ct. 1993. Cert. mediator cir. and county ct., Fla., 1995—. Assoc. Battaglia, Ross, Dicus and Wein, P.A., Tampa, St. Petersburg, 1986-90, shareholder litigation dept., 1990—. Adj. prof. Stetson U. Coll. of Law, 1997-2001, 2003—; mem. 6th cir. unlicensed practice of law com. Fla. Supreme Ct., 1993-95. Contbr. articles to law jours. Bd. dirs. Pinellas Opportunity Coun., 1988-92, pres., 1990-92; bd. dirs. Head Start, 1989-91, Bay Area Legal Svcs., 1994-97; v.p. Comty. Law Program, 1990-92, pres., 1992-95. Recipient pro bono cert. of appreciation Cmty. Law Program, 1993. Mem. ABA (com. on condemnation, zoning and land use litigation 1991-95), Fla. Bar (vice chmn. eminent domain com. 1994-95, health law sect. 1996-2003, clients' security fund com., 2002-03, Pres.'s Pro Bono Svc. award 6th jud. cir. 1994), St. Petersburg Bar Assn. (exec. com. 1993-95, 1999-2000, sec. 2000-01, Pro Bono award 1990, chair law day com. 1999), Delta Theta Phi, Alpha Phi Sigma. Office: Battaglia Ross Dicus and Wein PA 980 Tyrone Blvd N Saint Petersburg FL 33710-6382 E-mail: bbatt@brdwlaw.com.

BATTAGLIA, FRANCINE, mechanical engineering educator, researcher; b. Buffalo, N.Y., Nov. 28, 1968; d. Charles Robert Battaglia and Paula Beatrice Radice. BSME, SUNY, Buffalo, 1991, MS in Aerospace Engring., 1992; PhD in Mech. Engring., Pa. State U., 1997. Grad. rsch. asst. SUNY, 1991-92, Pa. State U., University Park, 1992-93, grad. tchg. fellow, 1994, grad. rsch. asst., 1995-96, lectr., 1997; NRC postdoctoral fellow Nat. Inst. Stds. and Tech., Gaithersburg, Md., 1997-99; prof. mech. engring. Iowa State U., Ames, 1999—. Contbr. articles to profl. jours., including AIAA Jour., Physics of Fluids, others. Paul H. Schweitzer Meml. grad. fellow Pa. State U., 1992-93, nat. need fellow Dept. Energy and Pa. State U., 1995-96, postdoctoral fellow NRC, 1997-99. Mem. AIAA (life), Am. Phys. Soc., Am. Soc. Engring. Edn., ASME, The Combustion Inst. Fax: (515) 294-3261. E-mail: francine@iastate.edu.

BATTAGLIA, FREDERICK CAMILLO, physician; b. Weehawken, N.J., Feb. 15, 1932; m. Jane B. Donohue; children: Susan Kate, Thomas Frederick. BA, Cornell U., 1953; MD, Yale U., 1957; DSc (hon.), U. Ind. Diplomate Am. Bd. Pediat. Intern in pediat. Johns Hopkins Hosp., 1957—58, USPHS postdoctoral fellow biochemistry Cambridge (Eng.) U., 1958—59; Josiah Macy Found. fellow in physiology Yale U. Med. Sch., 1959—60; asst. resident, fellow in pediat. Johns Hopkins Hosp., 1960—61, resident, fellow, 1961—62; USPHS surgeon lab. perinatal physiology NIH, San Juan, PR, 1962—64; asst. prof. Johns Hopkins Med. Sch., 1963—65; mem. faculty U. Colo. Med. Sch., Denver, 1965—, prof. pediat., prof. ob-gyn., 1969—, dir. divsn. perinatal medicine, 1970—74, chmn. dept. pediat., 1974—89. Attending pediatrician Children's, Denver Gen., Fitzsimons Gen. Hosps. Editor (assoc.): Pediatrics; med. progress contbg. editor Jour. Pediat., 1966—74, editl. bd. European Jour. Ob-Gybn., 1971—, assoc. Jour Perinatal, med. editor Biol. Neonate, 1979—, contbr. numerous articles to med. jours., —. Mem.: Inst. Medicine NAS, Soc. Exptl. Biology and Medicine, Internat. Congress Perinatal Medicine (pres. 1996), Am. Pediatric Soc. (pres. 1996), Soc. Gynecol. Investigation (coun. 1969—72), We. Soc. Pediatric Rsch. (pres. 1987—), Perinatal Rsch. Soc. (pres. 1974—75), Soc. Pediatric Rsch. (pres. 1976—77), Am. Gynecologic and Obstetric Soc., Am. Acad. Pediat. (E. Mead Johns award 1969), Assn. Am. Physicians, Sigma Xi, Phi Beta Kappa. Home: 2975 E Cedar Ave Denver CO 80209-3211 Office: Fitzsimons Bldg 260 13243 E 23d Ave Aurora CO 80010

BATTAGLIA, LYNNE ANN, judge; b. Buffalo, 1946; BA Intl Relations, Amer. Univ., 1967, MA, 1968; JD, Univ. of Maryland, 1974. U.S. atty., Md., 1993-2001; chief of staff Office of U.S. Sen. Barbara A. Mikulski, 1991—93; judge Md. Ct. Appeals, 2001—. Office: Md Ct Appeals Robert C Murphy Bldg 361 Rowe Blvd Annapolis MD 21401*

BATTAGLIA, PHILIP MAHER, lawyer; b. Pasadena, Calif., Jan. 18, 1935; s. Philip N. and Helen Margaret (Maher) B.; m. Lorraine Marie Moore, Dec. 29, 1962; children: Karen, Steven, Kristen, Scott. B.S.L., U. So. Calif., 1956, LL.B., 1958. Bar: Calif. 1959, U.S. Dist. Ct. (cen. dist.) Calif. 1959, U.S. Supreme Ct. 1967. Assoc., then sr. ptnr. Flint & MacKay, Los Angeles, 1960—; with Donovan Leisure Newton, L.A., 1986-94; with Sidley & Austin, L.A. 1994—. adminstrv. asst. to Gov. Ronald Reagan, 1966-67; dir. First Colony Life Ins. Co. (Va.), others. Past pres. Santa Barbara (Calif.) Theatrefest. Served to 1st lt. USAF. Mem. Los Angeles County Bar Assn., U. So. Calif. Law Alumni Assn. (pres.), Trojan Barristers (pres.), Calif. Jr. Chamber (named Outstanding Young Man of Yr. 1967-68), Los Angeles Jr. Chamber, Phi Alpha Delta. Republican. Roman Catholic. Clubs: Chancery, Lincoln (Los Angeles). Office: PO Box 209 Los Olivos CA 93441-0209

BATTAT, EMILE A. management executive; b. Mar. 17, 1938; s. Abe N. and Marguerite (Elias) B.; m. Vivian L. Masri, Apr. 12, 1964; children: Lisa, David. BS, MIT, 1959, MS, 1960; MBA, Harvard U., 1962. Mktg. analyst Standard Oil Co., N.Y.C. and N.J., 1962-65; mgr. corp. diversification Kaiser Aluminum, Oakland, Calif., 1965-69; v.p., dir. Kaiser Internat., Oakland, 1969-78; pres., CEO, dir. Minemet Inc., Stamford, Conn., 1978-94; pres. Piedmont Enterprises Inc., Riverside, Conn., 1994-98; chmn., CEO Atrion Corp., 1998—; pres. Quest Med., Inc., 1998—. Chmn. Halkey Roberts Corp., 1998—. Treas. Harbor Point Assn., 1987-97; tax collector Harbor Point Tax Dist., 1987-97. Mem. Sigma Xi, Pi Tau Sigma, Tau Beta Pi. Office: Atrion Corp One Allentown Pkwy Allen TX 75002

BATTEN, ALAN HENRY, astronomer; b. Tankerton, Kent, Eng., Jan. 21, 1933; emigrated to Can., 1959, naturalized, 1975; s. George Cuthbert and Gladys (Greenwood) B.; m. Lois Eleanor Dewis, July 30, 1960; children: Michael Henry John, Margaret Eleanor. BSc with 1st class honors, U. St. Andrews, Scotland, 1955, DSc, 1974; PhD, U. Manchester, Eng., 1958. Rsch. asst. in astronomy, jr. tutor St. Anselm Residence Hall, U. Manchester, 1958-59; postdoctoral fellow Dominion Astrophys. Obs., Victoria, B.C., Can., 1959-61, mem. staff, 1961-91, assoc. rsch. officer, 1970-76, sr. rsch. officer, 1976-91, guest scientist, 1991—. Part-time lectr. astronomy U. Victoria, 1961-64; guest investigator Vatican Obs., 1970, Inst. de Astronomia y Fisica del Espacio, Buenos Aires, 1972; lectr. history U. Victoria, 2002-03. Author: Binary and Multiple Systems of Stars, 1973, Resolute and Undertaking Characters: The Lives of Wilhelm and Otto Struve, 1988; editor: Extended Atmospheres and Circumstellar Matter in Spectroscoscopic Binary Systems, 1973, Algols, 1989, Astronomy for Developing Countries, 2001; sr. author: Eighth Catalogue of the Orbital Elements of Spectroscopic Binary Systems, 1989; co-editor: The Determination of Radial Velocities and Their Applications, 1967; translator: L'Observation des Etoiles Doubles Visuelles par P. Couteau, 1981; contbr. articles to profl. jours. Pres. Willows Elem. Sch. PTA, Victoria, 1971-73; mem. Anglican Ch. Can. Diocesan Synod, B.C., 1966-68, 74; mem. adv. coun. Ctr. Advanced Studies in Religion and Soc., U. Victoria, 1993-2002, chmn., 1997-2000. Erskine Vis. fellow U. Canterbury, New Zealand, 1995; recipient Queen's Silver Jubilee medal Can., 1977. Fellow Royal Soc. Can. (convenor interdisciplinary sect. 1980-81, mem. coun. 1980-81), Royal Astron. Soc., Explorers Club; mem. Internat. Astron. Union (v.p. 1985-91, pres. commn. 30 1976-79, pres. commn. 42 1982-85, chmn. nat. orgn. com. XVII Gen. Assembly 1975-79), Royal Astron. Soc. Can. (pres. 1976-78, hon. pres. 1993-98, editor jour. 1981-88), Astron. Soc. Pacific (v.p. 1965-68), Can. Astron. Soc. (pres. 1972-74), Am. Astron. Socs., Ancient Soc. Coll. Youths. Home: 2987 Westdowne Rd Victoria BC Canada V8R 5G1 Office: Dominion Astrophys Obs 5071 W Saanich Rd Victoria BC Canada V9E 2E7

BATTENBERG, J. T., III, automotive company executive; BS in Indsl. Engring., Kettering U.; MBA Columbia U.; grad. advanced mgmt. program, Harvard U. With GM, 1986, mng. dir. GM Continental divsn., gen. mgr. overseas truck ops., v.p. Buick-Oldsmobile-Cadillac group, 1986, v.p., group exec. Buick-Oldsmobile-Cadillac, v.p., group exec. automotive components group, 1992, sr. v.p., pres. group, 1992-95, exec. v.p., 1995; pres., CEO, chmn. bd. Delphi Automotive Systems (formerly ACG Worldwide), Troy, Mich., 1995—. Mem. GM's Pres. Coun.; nat. adv. bd. Chase Manhattan Corp. Bd. trustees Kettering U.; bd. overseers Columbia U. Bus. Sch.; exec. bd. Detroit area Coun. of Boy Scouts Am.; exec. bd. Oakland County Automation Alley; bd. dirs. For Inspiration and Recognition of Sci. and Tech.; mem. Coun. on Competitiveness; adv. bd. Covisint; mem. Bus. Roundtable and Bus. Coun. Named Internat. Bus. Coun. World Trader of the Yr. Detroit Regional Chamber, 1998. Mem. Soc. of Automotive Engrs., Soc. of Body Engrs., Engring. Soc. of Detroit, Exec. Leadership Coun., Automobile Nat. Heritage Area, Econ. Club of Detroit. Office: Delphi Automotive Systems Corp 5725 Delphi Dr Troy MI 48098-2815

BATTERBURY, SIMON PEREGRINE JOHN, geographer, educator; s. Paul T.S. Batterbury and Sheila M. Watson; m. Judith Clare Longbottom, June 29, 2002. BA in Geography with honors, Reading U., 1982—85; MA in Geography, Clark U., Worcester, Mass., 1987—90, PhD in Geography, 1990—97. Lectr. Brunel U., London, 1993—99, LSE, London, 1999—2001; asst prof. Dept of Geography and Regional Devel., Tucson, 2001—. Contbr. articles to profl. jours. Fellow: Royal Geog. Soc. Office: Dept of Geography and Regional Devt Univ Arizona Tucson AZ 85721

BATTERDEN, JAMES EDWARD, retired business executive; b. Balt., Dec. 25, 1925; s. James Edward and Mary Elizabeth (Noonan) B.; m. Berenice Brown, Apr. 22, 1950; children: James, Julia, Mark, Mary, Stephen, Margaret, John, Brigid. Student, U. Md., 1946-47, U. Balt., 1947-48, Balt. Inst., 1948-50. Auditor State of Md., Balt., 1947-52; salesman Uniroyal Corp., Balt., 1952-61, Comml. Envelope Co., Balt., 1961-63, Oscar T. Smith Co., Balt., 1963-97, v.p., 1971-97, ret., 1997, also bd. dirs. With USN, 1944-46. Named to Hall of Fame Mt. St. Joseph H.S., Balt., 1987. Mem. VFW, Mt. St. Joseph Alumni Assn., KC. Democrat. Roman Catholic. Avocations: theatre, travel, cards, ping pong, swimming.

BATTERMAN, BORIS WILLIAM, physicist, educator, academic director; b. N.Y.C., Aug. 25, 1930; children: Robert W., William E., Thomas A. Student, Cooper Union Coll., 1949-50, Technische Hochschule, Stuttgart, Germany; SB, MIT, 1952, PhD, 1956. Mem. tech. staff Bell Tel. Labs., Murray Hill, N.J., 1956-65; assoc. prof. Cornell U., Ithaca, N.Y., 1965-67, prof. applied and engring. physics, 1967—, dir. Sch. Applied and Engring. Physics, 1974-78, dir. Synchrotron Radiation Lab. (CHESS), 1978-97, Walter S. Carpenter Jr. prof. engring., 1985—2001, Walter S. Carpenter Jr. prof. emeritus, 2002—. Mem. U.S.A. Nat. Com. Crystallography, NAS, 1969-72. Assoc. editor Jour. Crystal Growth, 1964-74. Fulbright scholar, 1953-54; Guggenheim fellow, 1971, Fulbright Hayes fellow, 1971, Alexander von Humboldt fellow, 1983. Fellow AAAS, Am. Phys. Soc. Office: 150 Lombard St #603 San Francisco CA 94111 E-mail: bwb1@cornell.edu.

BATTERMAN, STEVEN CHARLES, engineering mechanics and bioengineering educator, forensic engineering and biomechanics consultant; b. Bklyn., Aug. 15, 1937; s. Jacob and Anna (Abramowitz) B.; m. Judith Wilpon, Mar. 29, 1959; children: Scott David, Risa Karen, Daniel Adam. BCE, Cooper Union, 1959; ScM (NSF fellow), Brown U., 1961, PhD, 1964; MA (hon.), U. Pa., 1971. Mem. faculty U. Pa., 1964-97, prof. mech. engring. and applied mechanics, 1974-79; assoc. prof. orthopaedic surgery rsch. U. Pa. (Sch. Medicine), 1972-74, prof. orthopaedic surgery research, 1974-97; prof. biomechanics in vet. medicine U. Pa Sch. Vet Medicine, 1975-84, prof. bioengring., 1974-97; emeritus prof. Sch. Engring. and Applied Sci., Sch. Medicine U. Pa., 1997—; pres. Cons. Assocs., Inc., Cherry Hill, N.J.; mng. ptnr. Batterman Engring., LLC, Cherry Hill. Forensic enring. and biomechanics cons. to govt., industry, ins. cos., attys. Contbr. numerous articles to profl. jours.; patentee apparatus for acoustically determining periodontal health. Recipient S.R. Warren Disting. Teaching award U. Pa., 1982. Mem. ASCE, ASME, Am. Acad. Mechanics, Am. Soc. Engring. Edn., Biomed. Engring. Soc., Soc. Exptl. Mech., Soc. Automotive Engrs., Am. Soc. Safety Engrs., Am. Acad. Forensic Scis. (Founder's award 1992, pres.-elect 1993-94, pres. 1994-95, Disting. Fellow 2001), Assn. for Advancement Automotive Medicine, Sigma Xi, Tau Beta Pi, Chi Epsilon. Jewish. Home: 109 Charlann Cir Cherry Hill NJ 08003-2906 E-mail: batterma@upenn.edu., batterman@aol.com.

BATTERSBY, HAROLD RONALD, retired anthropologist, archaeologist, linguist; b. Guildford, Surrey, Eng., Nov. 16, 1922; came to U.S., 1960, naturalized, 1972; s. Eric and Lillian (Darnell) B.; m. Betty Yertchenig O'Hannesian, Apr. 22, 1944. BA in Modern Near Eastern Studies, U. Toronto, Can., 1960; PhD in Altaic Studies-Anthropology Linguistics, Ind. U., 1969. Corr. Surrey Times, London-Guildford, 1947-55; adv. dir. Turkish Post, Istanbul, 1949-53; instr. English Istanbul Med. Faculty, 1948-49, Amerikan Lisan ve San'at Dersanesi, Istanbul, 1948-54, Pangalti Ermeni Orta Okulu, Istanbul, 1949-56; coordinator athletic events USO, Istanbul, 1948-54; asst. Royal Ont. Mus., Toronto, 1957-59; asst. mgr. City of Toronto, 1957-59; research asst. in med. anthropology U. Pitts., 1960-62; asst. Ind. U., Bloomington, 1962-69; assoc. prof. anthropology SUNY-Geneseo, 1970-98, dir. linguistics program, 1978-98, adj. prof., 1999-2001; ret. Author: Anatolian Archaeology: A Comprehensive Bibliograph, 2 vols., 1976; sect. editor: Altaic and Uralic Studies, Ultimate Reality and Meaning, 1982—; contbr. articles to profl. jours., translations, proofreading and editing of Biblical ethnographic and linguistic texts into Altaic langs. and from Altaic langs. into English. Served with RAF Vol. Res., 1939-46. NDEA fellow; Ind. U. grantee; Geneseo Found. grantee, 1973, 77, 78— Fellow Royal Anthrop. Inst. Gt. Brit. and Ireland, Am. Anthrop. Assn., Royal Asiatic soc.; mem. Am. Oriental Soc., Royal Ctrl. Asian Soc., Royal Soc. Asian Affairs, Hakluyt Soc., Internat. Soc. Oriental Rsch., Middle East Inst., Chgo. Anthrop. Soc., Inst. Ency. of Human Ideas on Ultimate Reality and Meaning, Brit. Inst. Archaeology at Ankara, Am. Oriental Soc., Am. Soc. Study People of Ea. Europe and No. and Ctrl. Asia, Linguistic Soc. Am., Niagara Linguistic Soc., N.Y. State Coun. Linguistics, Soc. Armenian Studies, Zoryan Inst., Ind. U. Alumni Assn., The Smithsonian Assocs., The Wilson Ctr. Assocs., Lambda Alpha. Clubs: Ind. U. Linguistics. Republican. Episcopalian. Avocation: reservation birds, cats, ducks. Home: 7339 Groveland Station Rd Groveland NY 14462 Office: SUNY Anthropology Dept Sturges Office and Lab Geneseo NY 14454

BATTERSBY, JAMES LYONS, JR., English language educator; b. Pawtucket, RI, Aug. 24, 1936; s. James Lyons and Hazel Irene (Deuel) B.; m. Lisa J. Kiser, Aug. 6, 1990; 1 child, Julie Ann. BS magna cum laude, U. Vt., 1961; MA, Cornell U., 1962, PhD, 1965. Asst. prof. U. Calif., Berkeley, 1965-70; assoc. prof. English Ohio State U., Columbus, 1970-82, prof., 1982—. Cons. Ohio State U. Press, U. Ky. Press, U. Calif. Press, Prentice-Hall, McGraw Hill, Fairleigh Dickinson U. Press, U. Mich. Press, U. Ala. Press. Author: Typical Folly: Evaluating Student Performance in Higher Education, 1973, Rational Praise and Natural Lamentation: Johnson, Lycidas and Principles of Criticism, 1980, Elder Olson: An Annotated Bibliography, 1983, Paradigms Regained: Pluralism and the Practice of Criticism, 1991, Reason and the Nature of Texts, 1996, Unorthodox Views: Reflections on Reality, Truth, and Meaning in Current Social, Cultural, and Critical Discourse, 2002; contbg. author: Domestick Privacies: Samuel Johnson and the Art of Biography, 1987, Fresh Reflections on Samuel Johnson: Essays in Criticism, 1987, Criticism, History and Intertextuality, 1988, Beyond Poststructuralism: The Speculations of Theory and the Experience of Reading, 1996; contbr. articles to profl. jours. With U.S. Army, 1954—57. Woodrow Wilson fellow, 1961-62, 64-65, Samuel S. Fels fellow, 1964-65, U. Calif. Summer Faculty fellow, 1966, Humanities Research fellow, 1969; recipient Kidder Medal U. Vt., 1961. Mem. MLA, Am. Soc. 18th Century Studies, Midwest Soc. 18th Century Studies, Royal Oak Found., Phi Beta Kappa, Phi Kappa Phi, Kappa Delta Pi. Home: 472 Clinton Heights Ave Columbus OH 43202-1277 E-mail: batterjay@msn.com.

BATTESTIN, MARTIN CAREY, retired English language educator; b. N.Y.C., Mar. 25, 1930; s. Martin Augustus and Marion (Kirkland) B.; m. Ruthe Rootes, June 14, 1963; children: David (dec. 1999), Catherine. BA summa cum laude, Princeton U., 1952, PhD, 1958. English master Westminster Sch., Simsbury, Conn., 1952-53; instr. Wesleyan U., Middletown, Conn., 1956-58, asst. prof., 1958-61, U. Va., Charlottesville, 1961-63, assoc. prof., 1963-67, prof., 1967-75, William R. Kenan, Jr. prof. English, 1975-98, emeritus prof., 1998—, chmn. dept. English, 1983-86. Vis. prof. Rice U., Houston, 1967-68; assoc. Clare Hall, Cambridge (Eng.) U., 1972. Author: The Moral Basis of Fielding's Art, 1959, 1975, The Providence of Wit, 1974, 1989, Henry Fielding: A Life, 1989, 2d edit., 1993, New Essays by Henry Fielding, 1989, 1993, A Henry Fielding Companion, 2000; editor: Joseph Andrews (Henry Fielding), 1961, 1967, Shamela (Henry Fielding), 1961, Tom Jones (Henry Fielding), 1974, 2d edit., 1975, Amelia (Henry Fielding), 1983, Tom Jones: A Collection of Critical Essays, 1968, British Novelists, 1660-1800, 1985, Tobias Smollett, translator Cervantes' Don Quixote, 2003; co-editor: The Correspondence of Henry and Sarah Fielding, 1993. Am. Coun. Learned Socs. fellow, 1960-61, 72; Guggenheim fellow, 1964-65; Sr. fellow Coun. Humanities, Princeton U., 1971; Ctr. for Advanced Studies fellow U. Va., 1974-75; NEH Bicentennial Rsch. fellow, 1975-76. Mem. MLA (chmn. sec. VII 1967, adv. editor publs. 1982-86), South Atlantic Modern Lang. Assn., Internat. Assn. Univ. Profs. English (chmn. sect. V 1990-92), Assn. of Lit. Scholars and Critics, Nat. Assn. Scholars, The Johnsonians. Mem. Ch. of England. Home: 1832 Westview Rd Charlottesville VA 22903-1648 E-mail: mcb9g@virginia.edu.

BATTEY, JAMES F., JR., federal agency administrator; BS in Physics with honors, Calif. Inst. Tech.; MD, PhD, Stanford U. Mem. staff, then head molecular structure sect. lab. biol. chemistry Nat. Cancer Inst., NIH; chief molecular neurosci. sect. lab. neurochemistry Nat. Inst. Neurol. Disorders and Stroke; acting dir. divsn. intramural rsch. Nat. Inst. Deafness and Other Comm. Disorders, Bethesda, Md., 1995—, dir., 1998—. Adj. prof. George Washington U. Sch. Medicine. Author: (with Leonard Davis and Michael Kuehl) Basic Methods in Molecular Biology; contbr., co-contbr. over 120 rsch. articles to profl. jours. Recipient Commendation medal Pub. Health Svc., 1990, Outstanding Svc. medal, 1994; postdoctoral fellow Harvard Med. Sch. Office: Nat Inst Deafness & Comm Disorders 31 Center Dr Msc 2320 Bldg 31 Bethesda MD 20892 0001

BATTILEGA, JOHN A. research and development company executive; b. Portland, Oreg., Nov. 25, 1941; s. Ercole Anthony and Odelia Francis Battilega; m. Nancy Ann Scott, May 2, 1964; children: Catherine, Edward, Michael, David. BS, Gonzaga U., 1963; PhD, Oreg. State U., 1967. Rsch. asst. Tektronix, Beaverton, Oreg., 1961—62; Sandia Nat. Lab., Livermore, Calif., 1965; staff engr. Martin Marietta Corp., Denver, 1971—73; corp. v.p., gen. mgr., rsch. dir. Sci. Applications Internat. Corp., Englewood, Colo., 1973—99; pres. John Battilega Assocs., Littleton, Colo., 1999—. Adj. prof., sr. lectr. Grad. Sch. Internat. Studies U. Denver, 2000—; mem. U.S. Def. Sci. Bd., Washington, 1984—85; dir. Fgn. Sys. Rsch. Ctr., Sci. Applications Internat. Corp., Englewood, Colo., 1978—99; dir. strategic rsch. on def. policy and planning and internat. issues U.S. govt. nat. security orgns., Washington, 1973—; mem. modeling and simulation rev. com. U.S. Space Command, Colorado Springs, Colo., 1986; mem. U.S. strategic def. initiative Soviet red team Dept. Def., Washington, 1985—90; sr. cons. various U.S. govt. agys., Washington, 1973—; adj. prof. U.S. Def. Intelligence Coll., Washington; mem. several adv. panels U.S. govt., Washington, 1980—; seminar developer over 20 seminars on def. planning topics, Washington, 1973—; lectr. def. and intelligence colls., 1978—; mem. AirLand Battle Future Spl. Study Group U.S. Army, Ft. Leavenworth, Kans., 1988; mem. select com. on computer tech. Nat. Def. U., Washington, 1983. Author, editor: book The Military Applications of Modeling, 1984; contbr. Coach youth baseball, Lakewood and Littlewood, Colo., 1975—98; Pres. parish coun. St. Jude Cath. Ch., Lakewood, Colo., 1972—74. Maj. U.S. Army, 1963—71. Decorated Meritorious Svc. medal, Bronze star, Vietnamese Cross of Gallantry. Mem.: AIAA, IEEE, Denver Coun. Fgn. Rels., U.S. Mil. Ops. Rsch. Soc. (bd. dirs. 1983—85), Inst. for Ops. Rsch. and Mgmt. Sci., Internat. Inst. Strategic Studies. Roman Catholic. Avocations: travel, reading, fishing, baseball, bridge. Home: 7706 S Forest St Littleton CO 80122 E-mail: j.battilega@worldnet.att.net.

BATTIN, JAMES F., JR., state legislator, sales executive; b. Billings, Mont., July 28, 1962; s. James F. and Barbara (Choate) B.; m. Mary E Shook, June 15, 1985; 1 child, Christopher Paul. BS in Psychology, U. Oreg., 1985. With Sta. KMIR-TV, Palm Desert, Calif.; mem. Calif. Ho. of Reps., Sacramento, 1995-2000, Calif. Senate from 37th dist., Sacramento, 2001—. Mem. C. of C., Desert Ad Club. Republican. Presbyterian. Home: 78-650 Saguaro Rd La Quinta CA 92253-2464 Office: Sta KMIR-TV 72-920 Parkview Dr Palm Desert CA 92260-9357*

BATTIN, PATRICIA MEYER, librarian; b. Gettysburg, Pa., June 2, 1929; d. Emanuel Albert and Josephine (Lehman) Meyer; m. William Thomas Battin, June 16, 1951 (div. 1975); children— Laura, Joanna, Thomas BA, Swarthmore Coll., 1951; MS in LS, Syracuse U., 1967. Asst. libr. SUNY-Binghamton, 1967-69, asst. dir. for reader svcs., 1969-74; dir. libr. svcs. Columbia U., N.Y.C., 1974-78, v.p., univ. libr., 1978-87; interim pres. Research Libraries Group, Palo Alto, Calif., 1982, also dir., 1974-87; pres. Commn. on Preservation and Access, Washington, 1987-94. Trustee Coun. on Libr. Resources, Washington, 1984-94, EDUCOM, Princeton, N.J., 1982-88, Lehigh U., 1989-98, CAUSE, Boulder, Colo., 1993-96; mem. adv. com. on coun. on libr. and info. resources Frye Leadership Inst. Contbr. articles to profl. jours. Mem. ALA, Assn. Rsch. Librs. (trustee 1982-85), Cosmos Club, Phi Beta Kappa, Beta Phi Mu.

BATTIN, R. RAY (ROSABELL HARRIET RAY), audiologist, neuropsychologist; b. Rock Creek, Ohio; d. Harry Walter and Sophia (Boldt) Ray; m. Tom C. Battin, Aug. 27, 1949. AB, U. Denver, 1948; MS, U. Mich., 1950; PhD, U. Fla., 1959; postgrad., U. Miami (Fla.) Sch. Medicine, 1957, U. Iowa, 1958. Diplomate Am. Bd. Forensic Medicine, Am. Bd. Profl. Disability Cons., Am. Bd. Psychol. Specialties, Am. Bd. Forensic Examiners (cert. forensic examiner, cert. med. examiner), forensic neuropsychology, devel. psychology, psychol. assessment, lic. psychologist Tex. Instr. in speech pathology U. Denver, 1949-50; audiologist Ann Arbor (Mich.) Sch., 1950-51, Houston Speech and Hearing Ctr., 1954-56; clin. fellow divsn. Clin. Svcs. U. Fla., Gainesville, 1952-54; dir. speech pathology/psychology Hedgecroft Hosp. and Rehab. Ctr., Houston, 1956-59; audiologist Drs. Guilford, Wright and Draper, Houston, 1959-63; pvt. practice psychology, audiology, and neuropsychology Houston, 1959—. Clin. instr. dept. otolaryngology U. Tex. Sch. Medicine, Galveston, 1964-80; dir. of audiology vestibulography and speech pathology lab. Houston Ear, Nose and Throat Hosp. Clinic, 1963-73; adj. clin. instr. U. Houston, 1981-86; lectr. The First Word program Sta. KUHT-TV, 1959; v.p. Behavioral Perceptual Ctr., 1986-90; neuropsychol. cons. edn. divsn. Environ. Health Screening Lab., 1989-99, adv. bd., 1989-99; lectr. in field. Author: (with C. Olaf Haug) Speech and Language Delay, 1964, Vestibulography, 1974, Private Practice: Guidelines for Speech Pathology and Audiology, 1971; editor (with Donna R. Fox) Private Practice in Audiology and Speech and Language Pathology, 1978; contbg. author: Seminars in Speech, Language, Hearing (Northern), Auditory Disorders in School Children (Roeser and Downs), Current Therapy of Communications Disorder (Perkins); editor Jour. Acad. Pvt. Practice in Speech Pathology and Audiology, 1981-84; contbr. articles in field to profl. jours.; author: (with Irvin A. Kraft) The Dysynchronous Child (film), 1971, Symposium Brain Plasticity As it Relates to the Remediation of Attention, Auditory Processing, Language and Reading Disorders, 1999; The Battin Clinic Language Learning Screening Test for Preschool Children, 1985, The Battin Scale of Parent's Attitude Toward Family Experience and Need for Child Cochlear Implant Candidates. Bd. dirs. Juvenile Ct. Vols., 1980—83, Children's Resource and Info. Ctr., 1981—85, Dyslexic Adult Support Svcs., 1986—90, Musicfest, 1990—2002, Houston Repretory Theater, 1993—98; mem. adv. bd. Caring Choices, 1993—, H.S. for the Performing and Visual Arts Friends, 1998—. Recipient Gold award for Ednl. Exhibit, Am. Acad. Pediats., 1969, Lifetime Achievement award Houston Psychol. Assn., 1996, Leadership award Sci. Learning Corp., 2000. Fellow: World Acad. Inc., Am. Speech and Hearing Assn. (profl. svcs. bd. 1967—70, com. on pvt. practice 1971—74); mem.: APA, Am. Acad. Audiology, Tex. Biofeedback Soc., Internat. Assn. Logopedics and Phoniatrics, Acad. of Aphasia, Harris County Biofeedback Soc. (pres. 1984), Houston Psychol. Assn., Tex. Acad. Audiology, Tex. Psychol. Assn., Tex. Speech and Hearing Assn. (v.p. 1968), Am. Acad. Pvt. Practice in Speech Pathology and Audiology (pres. 1968—70), Am. Coll. Forensic Examiners, Internat. Assn. Applied Psychology. Home: 3837 Meadow Lake Ln Houston TX 77027-4029 Office: Battin Clinic Inc 4545 Post Oak Place Dr Ste 375 Houston TX 77027-3121 E-mail: rhrb@pdq.net.

BATTIN, RICHARD HORACE, astronautical engineer; b. Atlantic City, Mar. 3, 1925; s. Horace Leslie and Martha Esther (Scheu) B.; m. Margery Katheryn Milne, Aug. 25, 1947; children: Thomas, Pamela, Jeffrey. BS, MIT, 1945, PhD, 1951; DSc (hon.), Tex. A&M U., 1999. Instr. math. MIT, Cambridge, 1946-51, research mathematician Instrumentation Lab., 1951-56, adj. prof. aero. and astronautics, 1979-95, sr. lectr., 1995—. Sr. staff mem. Ops. Research Group, Arthur D. Little, Inc., Cambridge, 1956-58; tech. dir. Apollo Mission Devel.;

assoc. dir. Instrumentation Lab., 1958-73; assoc. head NASA program dept. Charles Stark Draper Lab., Inc., 1973-87, mem. aerospace safety adv. panel, 1980-86. Author: (with J.H. Laning, Jr.) Random Processes in Automatic Control, 1956, Astronautical Guidance, 1964, An Introduction to the Mathematics and Methods of Astrodynamics, 1987; Mem. editorial com.: Celestial Mechanics, 1968-74. Pres. Project Impact, 1981-90; Mem. Lexington (Mass.) Town Meeting, 1956—; mem. Lexington Appropriations Com., 1958-64. Lt. (j.g.) Supply Corps USNR, 1945-46. Recipient Superior Achievement award, Inst. of Navigation, 1980, 1st Tycho Brahe award, 2000, Tchg. award, dept. aeros. and astronautics MIT, 1981. Fellow: AIAA (hon.; assoc. editor jour. 1967—87, chmn. astrodynamics tech. com. 1978—80, dir. tech. 1979—82, Louis W. Hill Space Transp. award 1972, Mechanics and Control of Flight award 1978, Pendray Aerospace Lit. award 1987, von Karman Disting. Lectureship award in astronautics 1989, Summerfield Book award 2002, Aerospace Guidance, Nav. and Control award 2002), Am. Astronautical Soc. (Dirk Brouwer award 1996); mem.: Celestial Mechanics Inst., Internat. Acad. Astronautics, Nat. Acad. Engring., Hancock Men's Club (pres. 1974—76), Sigma Xi. Home: 15 Paul Revere Rd Lexington MA 02421-6632 Office: 9-470 MIT 77 Massachusetts Ave Cambridge MA 02139-4307 E-mail: battin@alum.mit.edu.

BATTINO, RUBIN, chemistry educator, retired; b. N.Y.C., June 22, 1931; s. Sadik and Anna (Decastro) B.; m. Charlotte Alice Ridinger, Jan. 30, 1960; children— David Rubin, Benjamin Sadik BA, CCNY, 1953; MA, Duke U., 1954, PhD, 1957; MS, Wright State U., 1978. Lic. profl. clin. counselor, Ohio. Research chemist Leeds & Northrup Co., Phila., 1956-57; asst. prof. Ill. Inst. Tech., Chgo., 1957-66; prof. Wright State U., Dayton, Ohio, 1966-95, ret., 1995, prof. emeritus, 1995—. Vis. prof. U. Vienna, Austria, Oxford U., Eng., Hebrew U. Jerusalem, Ben Gurion U., U. New Eng., Australia, U. Canterbury, N.Z., Okayama U. Sci., Japan, Rhodes U., U. Turku, Finland. Author: (with S.E. Wood) Thermodynamics-An Introduction, 1968; Oxygen and Ozone, 1981, Nitrogen and Air, 1982, (with S.E. Wood) The Thermodynamics of Chemical Systems, 1990, (with T.L. South) Ericksonian Approaches, A Comprehensive Manual, 1999, Guided Imagery and other Approaches to Healing, 2000, Coping: A Practical Guide for People Who Have Life-Challenging Diseases and Their Caregivers, 2001, Meaning: The Life of Viktor E. Frankl, 2002, Metaphoria: Metaphor and Guided Metaphor for Psychotherapy and Healing, 2002; mem. edtl. bd. Solubility Data Series, Jour. Chem. and Engring. Data; contbr. tech. papers to profl. jours. Fulbright fellow, 1979; recipient Outstanding Tchr. award Wright State U., 1979, 93, Outstanding Engr. award Engring. and Sci. Found., Dayton, 1985, Bd. Trustees award Wright State U., 1985. Mem. AAAS, Am. Chem. Soc., Internat. Union Pure and Applied Chemistry (commn.), Sigma Xi, Phi Lambda Upsilon Democrat. Jewish. Office: Wright State U Chemistry Dept Dayton OH 45435 E-mail: rubin.battino@wright.edu.

BATTIS, DAVID GREGORY, lawyer; b. Rahway, N.J., July 25, 1945; s. Robert A. and Ruth (Augustine) B.; m. Florence B. Daly, Sept. 9, 1967; children— Seth, Melissa, Anna. B.A., Swarthmore Coll., 1967; M.A., Stanford U., 1968; J.D., U. Pa., 1975. Bar: Pa. 1975, U.S. Dist. Ct. (ea. dist.) Pa. 1976, U.S. Ct. Appeals (3d cir.) 1981. Law clk. U.S. Ct. Appeals 3d circuit Phila., 1975-76; assoc. Schnader, Harrison, Segal & Lewis, Phila., 1976-83, ptnr., 1984— . Rec. clk. sch. com. Germantown Friends Sch., Phila., 1980— ; bd. mgrs. Springfield Retirement Residence-All Saints Rehab. Hosp., Phila., 1983-87; trustee Alfred Cope Book Trust, 1986—. Mem. ABA, Pa. Bar Assn., Phila. Bar Assn., Order of Coif. Mem. Soc. of Friends. Office: Schnader Harrison Segal 1600 Market St Ste 3600 Philadelphia PA 19103-7287

BATTIS, EMERY JOHN, actor; b. Arlington, Mass., May 30, 1915; s. Floyd Rumney and Myrtle Evelyn (Davis) Battis; m. Elaine Goodell (dec.); children: Christopher, Michael, Peter, Robert, Wendy; m. Elizabeth Neuman. BA, Harvard U., 1942; MA, Columbia U., 1948, PhD, 1959; hon. degree, Clark U., 2001. Assoc. prof. history Rutgers U., New Brunswick, N.J., 1948-68; actor Guthrie Theatre, Mpls., 1968-72, Long Wharf Theatre, New Haven, Conn., 1972-84, The Shakespeare Theatre, Washington, 1984—. Recipient Helen Hayes award for Disting. Lifetime Achievement in Theatre. Address: 324 S Carolina Ave SE Washington DC 20003

BATTISTA, JOHN ROBERT, psychiatrist; b. N.Y.C., Dec. 14, 1946; s. Joseph Victor and Mary Rose Battista; m. Justine Anne McCabe, Aug. 6, 1989; children: Jenny, Jessa, Jared. BA in Psychology, Princeton U., 1968; MD, MA in Psychology, Stanford U., 1972; postgrad., Calif. Inst. Asian Studies, 1973—75. Diplomate Am. Bd. Psychiatry and Neurology, Nat. Bd. Med. Examiners. Intern Mt. Zion Hosp. and Med. Ctr., San Francisco, 1972—73; resident gen. psychiatry U. Calif., San Francisco, 1973—76, chief resident, 1976—77, asst. prof. psychiatry Davis, 1976—83, dir. Adolescent Day Treatment Ctr., 1977—79, staff psychiatrist Faculty Psychotherapy Clinic, 1977—82, clin. dir. Psychiat. Outpatient Clinic, 1980—81, dir. residency tng. dept. psychiatry, 1981—82; psychiatrist pvt. practice Riverbend Assocs., New Milford, Conn., 1983—. Dir. edn. East Sacramento Cmty. Mental Health Ctr., 1977—79; Nat. Rsch. Svc. scholar, Davis, 1979—80; psychiat. cons. Adolescent Day Treatment Ctr., Sacramento, 1979—80; clin. dir. The Country Place, Litchfield, Conn., 1982—83; consulting bd. Am. Assn. for the Study of Mental Imagery, 1979—82; psychait. dir. Wellspring Found., Bethlehem, Conn., 1983—84, Danbury (Conn.) Psychiat. Day Hosp., 1983—84, Temenos Inst., Westport, Conn., 1983—85; dir. Waramaug Assocs., New Milford, Conn., 1983—88; psychiat. cons. Wykeham Rise Sch., Washington, 1983—89; pres. Litchfield County Psychotherapists Network, 1991—93; psychiat. cons. Marvelwood Sch., Cornwall, Conn., 1992—2000; coord. Conn. Coalition for Universal Health Care, 1997—; host Health Care in Mind WPKN, Bridgeport, Conn., 1999—2002; host Progressing Voices WPNK, Bridgeport, Conn., 2002—; commentator News and Views Charter Comm. TV Network, 1999—2002. Editor: Textbook of Transpersonal Psychiatry, 1996; contbr. articles to profl. jours. Bd. dirs. Grass Roots Coalition, New Milford, Conn., 2000—02, Housatonic Environ. Action League, 2001—; pres. Grass Roots Coalition New Milford, 2001—03; Conn. del. Green Party Nat. Nominating Conv., 2000; coordinating com. Green Party of the U.S., 2000—03. Recipient Bausch Lomb Sci. award, 1964, Warner Chilcott Sci. award, 1965, Laughlin prize, Nat. Psychiat. Endowment Fund, 1976, Physicians Recognition award, AMA, 1976, award, Nat. Rsch. Svc., 1979, Will Solimene award of excellence, Am. Med. Writers Assn., 1997. Mem.: AAAS, Physicians for Human Rights, Am. Assn. for the Anthropology Consciousness, Assn. for the Sci. Study Consciousness, Physicians for a Nat. Health Program (exec. steering com. 1994—), Internat. Soc. for the Study of Multiple Personality and Dissociation, Soc. for Gen. Sys. Rsch., Assn. for Transpersonal Psychology, Assn. for Humanistic Psychology. Home: 88 Cherniske Rd New Milford CT 06776

BATTISTA, ROBERT A. otolaryngologist, educator; b. Trenton, NJ, Sept. 10, 1960; BA in Chemistry, Franklin and Marshall Coll., Lancaster, Pa., 1982; MD, U. Medicine and Dentistry-N.J., 1986. Diplomate Am. Bd. Otolaryngology. Attending physician EAR Consultants of Mich., Royal Oak, 1992-94; asst. prof. otolaryngology Rush-Presbyn.-St. Luke's Med. Ctr., Chgo., 1994-97; clin. asst. prof. otolaryngology Northwestern U. Med. Sch., Chgo., 1997—. Dir. Cochlear Implant Team, Rush-Presbyn.-St. Luke's Med. Ctr., Chgo., 1994-97. Author: (book chpt.) Textbook of Otolaryngology, 1997; med. editor: eMedicine, 1999—; contbr. articles to profl. jours. Fellow ACS, Otolaryngology-Head and Surgery Found.; mem. Am. Neurotology Soc. (assoc.). Avocations: bicycling, swimming, running. Office: Chgo Otology Group Ste 102 950 N York Rd Hinsdale IL 60521-8608

BATTISTELLA, FELIX D. physician, educator; MD, U. of Calif. Cert. General Surgery Am. Bd. of Surgery. Assoc. prof. U. of Calif., Sacramento, 1998—2002. Office: Univ of Calif Davis 2315 Stockton Blvd Rm 4209 Sacramento CA 95817 Office Fax: 916-734-7821.

BATTISTELLI, JOSEPH JOHN, electronics executive; b. Bridgeport, Conn., Oct. 22, 1930; s. Joseph John and Maria (Brunetti) B.; m. Helen Josephine Thompson, Apr. 5, 1961; children: Jay Dominick, Randall Victor. BSEE, U. Conn., 1958; MSEE, U. Ariz., 1960. Registered profl. engr., Ariz., Ohio. V.p. Electro Tech. Analysis Corp., Tucson, 1960-68; rsch. engr. Ohio U., Athens, 1968-72; sr. engr. Hughes Aircraft Co., Culver City, Calif., 1972-74; dir. engring. Lockheed Aircraft Co., Ont., Calif., 1974-80; dir. Riyadh area Litton Industries, Beverly Hills, Calif., 1980-91; v.p. Orion Ltd., Reston, Va., 1991—. Cons. FAA, Washington, 1962-72, U.S. Army Electronics Command, Ft. Monmouth, N.J., 1962-74, Lockheed Aircraft Co., Ont., 1980—, Nat. Airlines, 1998—; adj. prof. elec. engring. Embry-Riddle U., 1997—; adj. prof. math. Yavapi C.C., 1997—. Contbr. articles to profl. jours. With U.S. Army, 1952-54. Mem. IEEE, Sigma Xi, Tau Beta Pi, Eta Kappa Nu, Phi Kappa Phi.

BATTISTI, PAUL ORESTE, retired county supervisor; b. Herkimer, N.Y., Mar. 16, 1922; s. Oreste and Ida (Fiore) B.; m. Constance Muth Drais, May 18, 1985; children— Paul J., Kate, Deborah, Thomas, Daniel, Melora, Stephen. Student, Cornell U., Ithaca, N.Y., 1947-48, U. Neb., 1951-52. With VA, 1946-75; dir. VA Hosp., Martinez, Calif., 1969-73; western region dir. San Francisco, 1973-75; adminstr. State Vets. Home Calif., 1976-86; supr. County of Napa, 1989-97. Chmn., CEO Medam., Inc.; dir. Med. Am. Corp.; health care cons. 1975-88; chmn. Bay Area Air Quality Mgmt. Dist.; mem. exec. bd. Assoc. Bay Area Govts.; chmn. Bay Area Regional Planning Com.; mem. exec. bd. Bay Area Econ. Forum; chmn. Napa River Flood Control Dist. Fellow Am. Coll. Hosp. Adminstrs.; mem. Hosp. Conf. No. Calif. (pres.), Nat. Assn. State Vets. Homes (pres.). Home: Silverado Country Club 117 Milliken Creek Dr Napa CA 94558-1240

BATTLE, EMERY ALFORD, JR., sales executive; b. McComb, Miss., May 23, 1947; s. Emery Alford and Torrey Wofford (Copenhaver) B.; m. Martha Lee Kuntz, July 1971 (div. Jan. 29, 1985); children: Emery Alford III, Meredith Lindsay. BS in Pharmacy, U. Miss., 1971. Staff pharmacist Wilson-Quick, Super-X Foxall Pharmacy, Nashville, 1971-74; sales rep. Eli-Lilly and Co., Nashville, 1974-79, Deknatel Suture Co., Nashville, 1979-81, U.S.C.I. Inc., Nashville, 1981-84; mfr. rep. Cardiac Systems, Inc., Nashville, 1984-85; sales rep. Cordis Corp., Nashville, 1985-87, mgr. sales Dallas, 1987-91, Nashville, 1991-98, regional dir. sales, 1998-2000, corp. account dir., 2001—02; corp. account exec. Johnson & Johnson Health Care Systems, 2002—. Mem. Dallas Symphony Assn., 1990. Recipient Pres.'s Club award U.S.C.I. Inc, 1981-83, Pres.'s award Eli-Lilly, 1975-77. Mem. Mayflower Soc., Pilgrim Soc. Episcopalian. Avocations: golf, reading, jazz music, fitness and exercise.

BATTLE, HILARY HOWARD, minister, educator; b. Cleve., July 1, 1936; s. Joseph Battle and Alice Lee Thomas-Battle; m. Kathleen Ann Harris-Battle, July 4, 1987; 1 child, Rubin. AB, Cuyahoga CC, 1972; BA, Cleve. State U., 1975; MDiv, Princeton (NJ) Theol. Sem., 1978; post grad., U.S. Army Chaplain Sch., 1987. Cert. U.S. Army Chaplain Sch., 1987, ordained Mt. Olive Miss. Bapt. Ch., Cleve., 1975. Chaplain (major) U.S. Army, 1955—96, ret.; pastor Mt. Olive Bapt. Ch., Highstown, NJ, 1977—78; substance abuse counselor Cleve. Treatment Ctr., 1978—80; Hosp. chaplain Ohio Dept. of Mental Health, Cleve., 1981—96, U.S. Army 256 Comat Support, Parma, Ohio, 1982—96. Substitute tchr. Cleve. Pub. Sch., 1974—81; chaplain V.A. Hosp., East Orange, 1977—78; adj. prof. Ashland Theol. Sem., Cleve., 1985—88. Author: (book) Thee of Come Things All, 2002. Founder, dir. instl. choir Cleve. Psychiat. Hosp., 1989—91; choir dir. several ch. choirs, 1955—85; 2 v.p. Ohio State Chaplain Assn., Cleve., 1994—96; chaplain Tuskegee Airmen (north coast chpt.), Beachwood, Ohio, 1996—. Mem.: Clin. Privileges Cleve. Psychiat. Inst. (cert.). Avocations: music, skating. Home: 3178 E 121st St Cleveland OH 44120 Office Fax: 216-283-1320. E-mail: kathleen@buckeyeweb.com.

BATTLE, JEAN ALLEN, writer, educator; b. Talladega, Ala., June 15, 1914; s. William Raines and Lemerle McLemore Allen Battle; m. Lucy Troxell, Aug. 25, 1940; 1 child, Helen Carol Battle Salmon. Student, Birmingham So. Coll., 1932-33; BS, Middle Tenn. State U., 1937; MA, U. Ala., 1941; Ed.D., U. Fla., 1952; postgrad., Oxford U., 1980. Dept. chmn., dean students Fla. So. Coll., 1940-55, dean coll., 1956-59; dean Coll. Edn. U. South Fla., Tampa, 1959-71, prof. higher edn., 1971. Guest lectr. Rewley House, Oxford U., 1981; editor, pub. Tenn. Valley News.; Mem. Fla. Tchrs. Edn. Adv. Council, Fla. Continuing Edn. Council; mem. courses study com. Fla. Bd. Edn.; mem. Tampa Bay Com. on Fgn. Affairs; adv. com. Hillsborough County Hosp.; bd. dirs. Fla. Univ. System Honduras Program, World Trade Council, Tampa, Poynter Found., St. Petersburg, Fla., Harold Benjamin Found., U. Md.; bd. dirs., v.p. Southeastern Edn. Lab., Atlanta. Author: Culture and Education for the Contemporary World, 1969, (with others) The New Idea in Education, 1974, Choices for an Intelligent and Humane School and Society, 1981, Education: The Fate of Humanity, 1982, rev., 1983; Contbr. papers to tech. lit. Served to capt. USAAF, 1942-46. Recipient Disting. Service awards Fla. So. Coll., 1952, Disting. Service awards Fla. Citizenship Clearing House, 1957; Outstanding Alumnus award Middle Tenn. State U. Mem. SAR, Fla. Hist. Soc., Nat. Edn. Assn., Fla. Edn. Assn. (co-chmn. tchr. recruitment com.), Tampa C. of C. (edn. com.), Acad. Polit. Sci., Oxford Soc. (sec. Fla. br. 1990—), Omicron Delta Kappa, Pi Gamma Mu, Kappa Delta Pi, Phi Delta Kappa, Sigma Alpha Epsilon. Clubs: Carrollwood Village Golf and Tennis. Methodist. Home: 11011 Carrollwood Dr Tampa FL 33618-3905

BATTLE, JOE DAVID, engineer; b. Montgomery, Ala., Apr. 11, 1958; s. Marvin Andrew and Mary Della (Reynolds) B.; m. Margaret Carol Gillum, Jan. 18, 1980; children: Chloe Christine, John Edward. BS in Civil Engring. Tech., U. Ala., 1981. Coop. engr. Harbert Internat., Birmingham, Ala., 1977-78, B,E&K Inc., Birmingham, 1979-80; estimator Campbell & Assocs., Tuscaloosa, Ala., 1980-81; project coord. Pitts.-Desmoines Corp., Birmingham, 1981-83; staff project engr. VA, Dublin, Ga., 1983-85, asst. chief engr. Indpls., 1985-88, chief engr., 1988—, acting COO, 1999-2000. Named Va. Fed. Engr. of Yr. Nat. Soc. Profl. Engrs. Mem. Fed. Exec. Assn., Am. Soc. Hosp. Engrs., Ind. Soc. Healthcare Engrs., Lions. Baptist. Avocations: golf, outdoor sports. Office: VA Med Ctr 1481 W 10th St Indianapolis IN 46202-2803

BATTLE, LEONARD CARROLL, lawyer; b. Toronto, Ont., Can., Oct. 25, 1929; s. Leonard Conlon and Beatrice Hester Battle; m. Marjory Estelle Holland, Dec. 28, 1953; children: David, Tracy, Thomas, Patricia, John, Mary. AB, U. Mich., 1950; JD, Ind. U., 1958. Bar: Mich. 1961, Ind. 1961, U.S. Ct. Mil. Appeals 1964, U.S. Supreme Ct. 1964. Claims adjuster State Farm Ins. Co., 1959-61; asst. pros. atty. Midland County, Mich., 1961-67; pvt. practice, Midland, Mich., 1967—. Lt. col. JAG, USAFR, 1950-84. Mem. ATLA, Mich. Bar Assn. (mil. law com.), Midland County Bar Assn. (pres.), Air Force Ret. Judge Advs. Assn. Home: 408 Harper Ln Midland MI 48640-7321 Office: 200 E Main St Midland MI 48640-6510 E-mail: afjag05ret@webtv.net.

BATTLE, LUCIUS DURHAM, retired educational institution administrator, former diplomat; b. Dawson, Ga., June 1, 1918; s. Warren Lazarus and Jewel Beatrice (Durham) B.; m. Betty Jane Davis, Oct. 1, 1949; children: Lynne, John, Laura, Thomas. AB, U. Fla., 1939, LL.B., 1946; LL.D.; L.H.D., Fla. State U. Mgr. student staff U. Fla. Library, 1940-42; assoc. adminstrv. analyst War Dept., 1942-43; fgn. affairs specialist Dept. State, Washington, 1946-49, spl. asst. to sec. of state, 1949-53, 61-62, also exec. sec., 1961-62; asst. sec. of state for edtl. and cultural affairs, 1962-64; 1st sec. Am. Embassy, Copenhagen, 1953-55; dep. exec. sec. NATO, Paris, 1955-56; ambassador to UAR, 1964-67; asst. sec. state for Nr. Eastern and South Asian affairs, 1967-68; v.p. corp. affairs Communications Satellite Corp., 1968-73, sr. v.p. corp. affairs, 1974-80; dir. COMSAT Gen. Corp., 1974-80; chmn. Fgn. Policy Inst., Sch. Advanced Internat. Studies, Johns Hopkins U., 1980-84; pres. Middle East Inst., Washington, 1973-74, 86-91, bd. dirs., 1973-81. Chmn. UNESCO Gen. Conf., Paris, 1962; pres. Found. for Mid. East Peace, 1994—. V.p. Colonial Williamsburg, Inc., Williamsburg Restoration, Inc., 1956-61; chpt. mem. Protestant Episcopal Cathedral Found., Washington; chmn. bd. St. Albans Sch., 1973-76; vice chmn. Meridian House Internat., 1976-77; trustee George C. Marshall Research Found., Am. U., Cairo, 1970-79; chmn. vis. com. Ctr. for Middle Eastern Studies, Harvard, 1973-76; bd. dirs. Fgn. Policy Assn., 1974-84, Sch. Advanced Internat. Studies, 1975—, World Council of Washington, 1980, Smithsonian Assocs., 1981-85; Am. Near East Refugee Aid, 1985—; mem. fine arts com. Dept. State, 1973-77; mem. Nat. Study Commn. on Records and Documents Fed. Ofcls., 1975-76; pres. Bacon House Found., 1975-85, v.p. DACOR Bacon House Found. adv. bd. Ctr. for Contemporary Arab Studies, Georgetown U., 1976-86; mem. founders council Inst. for Study of Diplomacy, 1978-87; chmn. nat. com. to honor 14th centennial of Islam, 1979-84; chmn. Am. Inst. Islamic Affairs, 1984-87; pres. Found. for Middle Eastpeace, 1994. Served to lt. USNR, 1943-46. Decorated Order of Republic 1st class Egypt; recipient Fgn. Service Cup, Diplomatic and Consular Officers Ret., 1984, Founders award Sch. Advanced Internat. Studies. Mem. Am. Fgn. Service Assn. (pres. 1962-63), Order of Coif, Phi Beta Kappa, Alpha Tau Omega, Phi Delta Phi. Clubs: Met. (Washington); Alibi. Home: 4856 Rockwood Pky NW Washington DC 20016-3249

BATTLE, TURNER CHARLES, III, art educator, educational association administrator; b. Oberlin, Ohio; s. Turner and Annie (McClellan) B.; m. Carmen Helena Gonzalez Castellanos; children: Anne E. McAndrew, Turner C. IV, Conchita Yvonne, Carmen Rosario. Student, Andrews U.; BA, Oakwood Coll.; postgrad., Wagner Inst. Sci., Cheyney State Coll., Temple U., Columbia U., NYU; MFA, Temple U.; HHD, Wiley Coll. Instr. art Oakwood Coll., Huntsville, Ala.; auditor, acct. Navy Regional Acct. Office; instr. art Phila.; dir. Sch. Art League Sch. Gifted Children, Phila.; asst. prof. art Elmira Coll., NY; assoc. prof. art Moore Coll. Art, Phila.; vis. assoc. prof. NYU, NY; tchg. fellow. Vis. assoc. prof., dir. program Westminster Choir Coll.; art cons., lectr. pvt. and pub. orgns.; edn. cons. cmty. planners group U.S. Office Edn.; cons. E. Africa, Mid. E. Exhibited in group shows ea. U.S., including Bucknell U., Phila. Art Alliance, Newport (R.I.) Art Assn., Phila. Mus. Art, Susquehanna U., Atlantic City Boardwalk Show, Greenwich Village, N.Y.C., numerous others; represented in pvt. collections throughout U.S., India, Eng., Africa, Japan. Exec. dir. Higher Edn. Coalition Southeastern Pa.; dir. Open Door Program, LaSalle U.; asst. exec. dir., sec. corp. United Negro Coll. Fund, N.Y.C., pres. ednl. devel. svc., 1994—. Mem. Am. Assn. Higher Edn., Tyler Sch. Temple U. Alumni Assn. (pres. 1965-66), Am. Mus. Natural History, Smithsonian Inst., Sierra Club, Phi Delta Kappa. Home: 1519 W Turner St Allentown PA 18102-3634 also: 175 Adams St Apt 7G Brooklyn NY 11201-1815 E-mail: turnercbattle3@cs.com.

BATTLE, VINCENT M. ambassador; b. Teaneck, N.J., Sept. 1940; MA, Columbia U., 1967, PhD, 1974. Consular officer U.S. Fgn. Svc., Manama, Bahrain, 1977—79; head of Immigrant Visa sect., Port-au-Prince, Haiti, 1985—88; polit. officer Muscat, Oman, 1983—85; consular officer Bur. of Near East Affairs, Damascus, Syria, 1980—83; various to dep. chief of mission U.S. Embassy, Cairo, 1996—99; U.S. amb. to Lebanon, 2001—. Office: DOS Amb 6070 Beirut Pl Washington DC 20521*

BATTLE, WILLA LEE GRANT, clergywoman, educational administrator; b. Webb, Miss., Sept. 30, 1924; d. James Carlton and Aslean (Young) Grant; m. Walter Leroy Battle, July 4, 1941. Diploma, Northwestern Coll., Mpls., 1956; B.A. cum laude, U. Minn., 1975, M.A., 1979; Ph.D. summa cum laude, Trinity Sem., 1982. Ordained to ministry, 1959. Founder, pastor Grace Temple Del. Ctr., Mpls., 1958— ; founder, pres., Willa Grant Battle Ctr., Mpls., 1980— ; founder House of Refuge Mission, Haiti, W.I., 1957— ; adminstr., dir. Kiddie Haven Pre-Sch., Mpls., 1982— . Mem. Interdenominational Ministerial Alliance (sec. 1986—), Mpls. Ministerial Assn., AAUW, AAUP, U. Minn. Alumni Assn. (life), NAACP, Nat. Council Negro Women, Christian Educators, Nat. Assn. Female Execs. Home: 220 E 42nd St Minneapolis MN 55409-1634 Office: Willa Grant Battle Ctr 1816 4th Ave S Minneapolis MN 55404-1844

BATTLE, WILLIAM ROBERT (BOB BATTLE), retired newspaper executive; b. Nolensville, Tenn., Dec. 25, 1927; s. William Robert and Cleo (Smith) B.; m. Elizabeth Ogilvie, Dec. 23, 1948; children: Valerie Elizabeth Kienzle, William Robert III. Student, George Peabody Coll., 1946-49. Exec. offcl. Nashville Banner, 1943-98, police beat, county polit. beat, 1943-53, city editor, 1953-64, movie columnist, 1955-72, mng. editor, 1964-71, exec. editor, 1971-75, asst. to editor, 1975-78, regional editor, 1978-80, sr. editor, 1980-84, v.p., bus. editor, 1984-89, v.p., sr. bus. editor, 1989-98; staff writer Country Style mag., Livin Country. Columnist Williamson A.M., Tennessean; mem. exec. bd. Tenn. Dept. Agr. Agrl. Mus., 2002—. Appeared as newspaperman in: film Teacher's Pet, 1957, also in Country Music on Broadway, 1963; contbr. World Book Ency., numerous articles to nat. publs. Supt. gates and admissions Tenn. State Fair, 1953-64; pub. rels. chmn. Davidson County Coun. for Retarded Children, 1961-66; mem. exec. bd. Mid. Tenn. coun. Boy Scouts Am.; mem. 4-H Club Found.; exec. bd. dirs., past sec. Nashville Boys Club, now life mem. bd. dirs. Recipient Big Story award NBC-TV, 1956; named Man of Yr., 4-H Club, 1974, Man of Yr., Future Farmers Am., 1975, Silver Beaver award Boy Scouts Am., 1997; Robert Battle scholarship established in his honor Belmont U. Sch. Bus., By Opryland, U.S.A., 1989. Mem. Nashville Area C. of C., Tenn. Press Assn., Nat. Screen Coun., Country Music Assn., Masons (33d deg., knights commdr. ct. of honor), Shriners (potentate 1976), Royal Order of Jesters (former dir.), Elks (former chmn. scholarship com.), Sigma Delta Chi (former chmn. scholarship com., former pres.). Methodist. Home: 8889 Horton Hwy College Grove TN 37046-9280

BATTLES, ROXY EDITH, novelist, consultant, educator; b. Spokane, Wash., Mar. 29, 1921; d. Rosco Jirah and Lucile Zilpha (Jacques) Baker; m. Willis Ralph Dawe Battles, May 2, 1941 (dec. 2000); children: Margaret Battles Holmes, Ralph, Lara. AA, Bakersfield (Calif.) Coll., 1940; BA, Calif. State U., Long Beach, 1959; MA, Pepperdine U., 1976. Cert. tchr. English, adult basic edn. and elem. edn., Calif. Free-lance writer 50 nat. and regional mags., 1940—; tchr. elem. Torrance (Calif.) Unified Schs., 1959-85; tchr. adult edn. Pepperdine U., Torrance, 1969-79, 88-89; free-lance children's author, 1966—; mystery novelist Pinnacle Publs., N.Y.C., 1980; with Tex. A&M U., 1988. Instr. Mary Mount Coll., Harbor Coll., 1995; author-in-residence Young Authors Festival, Am. Sch. Madrid, 1991; lectr. in field. Author: Over the Rickety Fence, 1967, The Terrible Trick or Treat, 1970, 501 Balloons Sail East, 1971, The Terrible Terrier, 1972, One to Teeter-Totter, 1973, 2d edit., 1975, Eddie Couldn't Find the Elephants, 1974, reprints, 1982, 84, 88, What Does the Rooster Say, Yoshio?, 1978, reprinted in Swedish, German, French, 1980, The Secret of Castle Drai, 1980, The Witch in Room 6, 1987, 3d edit., 1989 (nominee Garden State, Nene, and Hoosier awards), The Chemistry of Whispering Caves, 1988, rev. edit., 1997, Computer Encryptions in Whispering Caves, 1997; playwright: Roxy, 1995, The Lavender Castle, 1996, mus. version, 1997, Sacred Submarine, 2000, Embarking on Rebellion, 2001. Active So. Calif. Coun. on Lit. for Children and Young People, 1973-80, 87 . Recipient Commendation UN, 1979; Hoosier award nominee, 1990; Garden State award nominee, 1990, Nene award nominee, 1992, 93. Mem. S.W. Manuscripters (founder), Surfwriters. Home: 560 S Helberta Ave Redondo Beach CA 90277-4353 E-mail: groxy@aol.com. *However I rail at prejudice, some prejudgment is inevitable and, except in extremity, foreseeable. Whether caused by neglect or studied plan, negatives are noticed. When the fixable remains unfixed, I deserve to be judged for my part, however I blame my adjudicator.*

BATTS, MICHAEL STANLEY, German language educator; b. Mitcham, Eng., Aug. 2, 1929; s. Stanley George and Alixe Kathleen (Watson) B.; m. Misao Yoshida, Mar. 19, 1959; 1 dau., Anna. BA, U. London, 1952, BA with honors, 1953, LittD, 1973; PhD, U. Freiburg, Germany, 1957; M.L.S., U. Toronto, 1974. Mem. faculty U. Mainz, Germany, 1953-54, U. Basel, Switzerland, 1954-56, U. Wurzburg, Germany, 1956-58; instr. German U. Calif., Berkeley, 1958-60; mem. faculty dept. German U. B.C., Can., 1960-91, prof., 1967-91, head dept., 1968-80. Author: Die Form der Aventiuren im Nibelungenlied, 1961, Bruder Hansens Marienlieder, 1964, Studien zu Bruder Hansens Marienliedern, 1964, Das Hohe Mittelalter, 1969, Das Nibelungenlied-Synoptische Ausgabe, 1971, Gottfried von Strasburg, 1971, A Checklist of German Literature, 1945-75, 1977, The Bibliography of German Literature: An Historical and Critical Survey, 1978, A History of Histories of German Literature, 1835-1914, 1993, Germanic Studies at Canadian Universities From the Beginning to 1995, 1998; editor: Seminar, 1970-80. Served with Brit. Army, 1947-49. Alexander von Humboldt fellow, 1964-65, 83; Can. Council sr. fellow, 1964-65, 71-72; Killam fellow, 1981-82. Fellow Royal Soc. Can.; mem. Canadian Assn. Univ. Tchrs. German (pres. 1982-84), Modern Humanities Rsch. Assn., Alcuin Soc. (exec. v.p. 1972-79, pres. 1979-80), Internat. Assn. for Germanic Studies (pres. 1990-95). Office: U Brit Columbia German Dept Vancouver BC Canada V6T 1Z1 E-mail: msb@interchange.ubc.ca.

BATTS, WARREN LEIGHTON, retired diversified industry executive; b. Norfolk, Va., Sept. 4, 1932; s. John Leighton and Allie Belle (Johnson) B.; m. Eloise Pitts, Dec. 24, 1957; 1 dau., Terri Allison. BEE, Ga. Inst. Tech., 1961; MBA, Harvard U., 1963. With Kendall Co., Charlotte, N.C., 1963-64; exec. v.p. Fashion Devel. Co., Santa Paula, Calif., 1964-66; dir. mfg. Olga Co., Van Nuys, Calif., 1964-66; v.p. Douglas Williams Assocs., N.Y.C., 1966-67; co-founder Triangle Corp., Orangeburg, S.C., 1967, pres., chief exec. officer, 1967-71; v.p. Mead Corp., Dayton, Ohio, 1971-73, pres., 1973-80, chief exec. officer, 1978-80; pres., chief operating officer Dart Industries, Inc., L.A., 1980-81, Dart & Kraft, Inc., Northbrook, Ill., 1981-86; chmn., chief exec. officer Premark Internat. Inc., Deerfield, 1986-96, chmn., 1996-97; chmn., CEO Tupperware Corp., Orlando, Fla., 1996-97. Trustee Children's Meml. Hosp., Chgo., 1984—, Northwestern U., 1989.

BATTY, HUGH KENWORTHY, physician; b. Kansas City, Kans. s. James Jacob and Genevieve Adeline (Johnston) B.; m. Mercedes Aguirre, Mar. 17, 1979; 1 child, Henry Briton. BS in Zoology, U. Wash., 1970; PhD in Anatomy, U. Utah, 1974; MD, Ciudad Juárez, Mex., 1977. Intern, asst. resident St. Vincent's Med. Ctr., Bridgeport, Conn., 1977-78, resident, 1978-79, chief resident, 1979-80; pvt. practice Sheridan, Wyo., 1980—. Chmn. dept. medicine Meml. Hosp. Sheridan, 1989, 91, 95, 96, 97, 98, chmn. ICU, 1995. Contbr. articles to profl. jours. Del. Citizen Ambassador Program, India. Eleanor Roosevelt Cancer Rsch. Found. grantee, 1972. Mem. ACP, Wyo. Med. Soc., Sheridan County Med. Soc. Avocations: archeology, reading, hiking, wrestling, fishing. Office: 1260 W 5th St Sheridan WY 82801-2702

BATULE, ROBERT JOHN, priest, writer; b. Bklyn., May 23, 1958; s. Robert Philip and Ann Marie (Reilly) B. BA in Sociology, Cathedral Coll., 1980; MDiv, Immaculate Conception, 1985; MA in Sociology summa cum laude, Adelphi U., 1990; MA in Theology summa cum laude, St. Johns U., 1996. Ordained priest Roman Cath. Ch., 1985. Parish priest St. Boniface Roman Cath. Ch., Elmont, NY, 1985-90, St. Martha Roman Cath. Ch., Uniondale, NY, 1990-93, Corpus Christi Roman Cath. Ch., Mineola, NY, 1993—2002, adminstr., 2001—, 2001—02. Del. for Pastoral Intervention, 2002—, chmn., moderator Cath. Youth Orgn. Nassau and Suffolk, Hicksville, NY, 1997-2000; adj. faculty St. Vincent's Coll. divsn. humanities, dept. theology, St. John's U., 1996-99. Contbr. Cath. Ency., 1991, 98, Cath. Dictionary, 1993; columnist, The Catholic Answer, 1987-96, The Catholic Transcript, 1993-95, The Long Island Cath. Newspaper; contbr. numerous homilies, revs. and articles to profl. jour. 2d lt. USAF, 1981-82. Mem. Fellowship of Cath. Scholars, Soc. Cath. Social Scientists, Nat. Assn. of Scholars. Roman Catholic. Avocations: athletics, reading. Office: Diocese of Rockville Ctr 50 No Pk Ave Rockville Centre NY 11570

BATYGIN, YURI KONSTANTINOVICH, accelerator physicist; b. Moscow, Sept. 25, 1954; s. Konstantin Stepanovich and Valentina Fedorovna (Muhina) B.; m. Galina Zinov'evna Batunina, Oct. 6, 1979; children: Ekatherine, Konstantin. BS, Moscow Engring. Physics Inst., 1977, PhD, 1984; DSc in Physics and Math., Dubna Joint Inst. Nuc. Rsch., Russia, 1998. Rschr. Moscow Engring. Physics Inst., 1977-86, sr. rschr., 1987-94; contract rschr. Inst. Phys. and Chem. Rsch., Japan, 1994-99; sr. scientist high energy sys. divsn. Am. Sci. & Engring., Inc., Santa Clara, Calif., 2000; accelerator physicist-engring. Stanford Linear Accelerator Ctr., Stanford U., Calif., 2000—. Vis. scientist Eindhoven U. Tech., Netherlands, 1986—87, Instituto Nazionale di Fisica Nucleare, Frascati, Italy, 2002. Editor: American Institute of Physics Proceedings Series, vol. 480, 1999; contbr. articles to profl. jours.; inventor in field. Mem.: Am. Phys. Soc. Office: Stanford Linear Accelerator Ctr PO Box 20450 MS 66 Stanford CA 94309 Home: 572 Cadburry Ct San Jose CA 95123-1302 E-mail: batygin@slac.stanford.edu.

BATZEL, EDWARD LEE, surgeon; b. Scranton, Pa., Aug. 20, 1951; s. Edward Morris and Lillian (Cavalieri) B.; m. Marie Homentosky, Jan. 16, 1982; children: Zachary, Jacob, Nicholas, Kimber Lee, Callin. BA cum laude, U. Scranton, 1973; postgrad., U. Rome, 1973-76; MD, Mt. Sinai Sch. Medicine, 1978. Diplomate Am. Bd. Surgery, Am. Bd. Vascular Surgery. Intern in surgery Mt. Sinai Med. Ctr., N.Y.C., 1978-79, resident in surgery, 1987-92, chief resident, 1991-92; pvt. practice gen. medicine, Bklyn., 1979-87; fellow in vascular surgery Mt. Sinai Hosp., N.Y.C., 1992-93; pvt. practice gen., vascular and thoracic surgery, Scranton, 1993—. Co-med. dir. Vascular Diagnostic Ctr., Scranton. Contbr. articles to med. jours. Fellow ACS; mem. AMA, Am. Coll. Breast Surgeons, Am. Soc. Gen. Surgeons, Pa. Med. Soc., N.Y. Med. Soc., Lackawanna County Med. Soc., Scranton C. of C., Alpha Omega Alpha. Office: 790 Northern Blvd Olyphant PA 18447

BATZER, JOHN L. systems engineer; b. Elizabeth, N.J., Feb. 21, 1946; s. R. Kirk and Marjorie W. (Batzer) Batzer; m. Elizabeth Ashe Cranmer; children: John L. Batzer Jr., Jessica L. Batzer. BS in Engring. Physics, Lehigh U., 1973; MBA, NYU, 1975. Staff scientist ITT Industries, 1978—. Patentee in field. Pres. New Providence Music Boosters, 1991-96; mem. vestry St. Andrew's Ch., New Providence, N.J., 1994-97; bd. trustees, treas. St. Andrew's Nursery Sch., New Providence, 1996-97. With U.S. Army, 1969-72. Mem. IEEE. Episcopalian. E-mail: john.batzer@itt.com.

BATZLI, GEORGE OLIVER, ecology educator; b. Mpls., Sept. 23, 1936; s. Oscar H. and Bertha M. B.; m. Sandra Lou Scharf, Jan. 2, 1959; children—Jeffrey, Samuel. BS in Psychology, U. Minn., 1959; MA in Biology, San Francisco State U., 1965; PhD in Zoology (Ecology), U. Calif., Berkeley, 1969. Research assoc. U. Calif., Davis, 1969-71, lectr. biology Santa Cruz, 1971; asst. prof. zoology U. Ill., Urbana, 1971-76, assoc. prof. ecology, 1976-80, prof. ecology, 1980—, head dept. ecology, ethology and evolution, 1983-88, 95-97. Sr. scientist research in arctic environs., 1976-78, mem. ecology program adv. panel NSF, 1984-87, 2003; research scientist DSIR, N.Z., 1979; chmn. ecology program U. Ill., 1976-82. Contbr. articles on ecology to profl. jours.; spl. issue editor Arctic and Alpine Research, 1980, Oikos, 1983; mem. editorial bd. Ecology, Ecol. Monographs, 1981-84. Fellow NSF, 1962-63, NIH, 1967-69, 69-71, Zool. Inst. U. Oslo, Norway, 1982. Fellow AAAS; mem. Am. Inst. Biol. Scis., Am. Soc. Mammalogy (C. Hart Merriam award 2002), Ecol. Soc. Am., Brit. Ecol. Soc., Intecol, Am. Soc. Naturalists, Comp. Nutrition Soc. Office: U Ill Shelford Vivarium 606 E Healey St Champaign IL 61820-5502 E-mail: g-batzli@life.uiuc.edu.

BATZLI, TERRENCE RAYMOND, lawyer; b. Dec. 28, 1946; s. Marion Raymond and Kathryn Velma (Hudran) Batzli; m. Sharon Lee Heinatz, Aug. 2, 1969; children: Catherine Barrett, Jonathan Raymond. BS, U. Richmond, 1974, JD, 1975. Bar: Va. 1975, U.S. Dist. Ct. (ea. dist.) Va. 1975, U.S. Dist. Ct. (we. dist.) Va. 1983, U.S. Ct. Appeals (4th cir.) 1984. Ptnr. Mays & Valentine and predecessor firms, Richmond, 1982-93, Durrette, Irvin & Bradshaw, Richmond, Va., 1993-96; prin. Barnes & Batzli, PC, 1996—. Mediator McCammon Group; adj. prof. law Reynolds C.C., Richmond, 1980—82. Mem. adv. bd. Nat. Head Injury Found., 1988—, VA Head Injury Found., 1990—91. Capt. U.S. Army, 1966—70. Named Best Divorce Atty. in Richmond in a pub. opinion poll, Richmond Mag., 2000; named one of Top Three Family Law Lawyers in Richmond in a survey of lawyers, 1999, Top 5 Family Law Attorneys in Stat of Va., 2000, 2001, 2002. Fellow: Internat. Acad. Matrimonial Lawyers, Am. Acad. Matrimonial Lawyers; mem.: Hanover Assn. Bus. (pres. 1989, bd. dirs.), Va. State Bar (bd. govs. family law sect. 1996—, sec. 1997, vice-chair 1999, chair 2000—), Metro Richmond Family Law Bar Assn. (founding pres. 1994), Hanover County Bar Assn. (treas. 1997, sec. 1998, pres.-elect 1999, pres. 2000), Richmond Bar Assn. (chmn. family law sect. 1982—83, exec. com. 1982—83), Ruritan Club (pres., zone gov., dist. sec.), Rotary (bd.dirs. 1980—84). Republican. Methodist. Home: 11910 Aberdeen Landing Ter Midlothian VA 23113-1394 Office: Barnes & Batzli PC 4701 Cox Rd Ste 320 Glen Allen VA 23060-6804

BAUCCIO, LISA VALENTINE, obstetric nurse, high-risk perinatal nurse; b. Pitts., May 4, 1967; d. Raymond D. and Ruthann L. (Stevens) Valentine; m. Carmen J. Bauccio, May 12, 1990; children: Anthony M., Julia R. BSN, Carlow Coll., 1989. RN, Pitts. Asst. patient care Forbes Regional Health Ctr., Monroeville, Pa., 1987-89; clin. nurse II West Penn Hosp., Pitts., 1989—, instr. obstet. edn., 1991-94, mem. core com. critical care obstet. unit, 1992-97. Speaker perinatal outreach program West Pa. Hosp., Pitts., 1993—. Fellow Nightingale Soc.; mem. Sigma Theta Tau, Delta Epsilon Sigma, Phi Eta Sigma, Alpha Lambda Delta. Home: 174 Regal Court Monroeville PA 15146 Office: The Western Pa Hosp E5DR Labor and Delivery 4800 Friendship Ave Pittsburgh PA 15224-1793

BAUCH, THOMAS JAY, financial/investment advisor, lawyer, educator, former apparel company executive; b. Indpls., May 24, 1943; s. Thomas and Violet (Smith) B.; m. Ellen L. Burstein, Oct. 31, 1982; children: Chelsea Sara, Elizabeth Tree. BS with honors, U. Wis., 1964, JD with highest honors, 1966. Bar: Ill. 1966, Calif. 1978. Assoc. Lord, Bissell & Brook, Chgo., 1966-72; lawyer, asst. sec. Marcor-Montgomery Ward, Chgo., 1973-75; spl. asst. to solicitor Dept. Labor, Washington, 1975-77; dep. gen. counsel Levi Strauss & Co., San Francisco, 1977-81, sr. v.p., gen. counsel, 1981-96, of counsel, 1996-2000; pvt. practice, Tiburon, Calif., 1996-2000; mng. dir. Offit Hall Capital Mgmt. LLC, San Francisco, 2000—. Cons. prof. Stanford (Calif.) U. Law Sch., 1997—; ptnr. Ika Enterprises. Mem. U. Wis. Law Rev., 1964-66. Bd. dirs. Urban Sch., San Francisco, 1986-91, Gateway H.S., San Francisco, Charles Armstrong Sch., Belmont, Calif., 1998-2001, San Francisco Opera Assn., 1998-2001, Telluride Acad., 1996-2000, Corinthian Acad.; bd. visitors U. Wis. Law Sch., 1991-95. Mem. Am. Assn. Corp. Counsel (bd. dirs. 1984-87), Bay Area Gen. Counsel Assn. (chmn. 1994), Univ. Club, Villa Taverna Club, Corinthian Yacht Club, Order of Coif, San Francisco Yacht Club. Office: Offit Hall Capital Mgmt One Maritime Plz Ste 500 San Francisco CA 94111 E-mail: tbauch@offithall.com.

BAUCKHAM, JOHN HENRY, lawyer; b. Royal Oak, Mich., Mar. 16, 1923; s. Henry Charles and Mabel Lillian (Stratford) B.; m. Nancy Lee Bassett, Aug. 5, 1943 (div. 1972); children: Thomas, Laura Bauckham Callander, David, Robert; m. Dorothy Ann Kobussen, Jan. 29, 1973 (div. 1988); m. Rosalie Kirklin, Feb. 14, 1993. JD, U. Mich., 1949. Bar: Mich. 1949, U.S. Dist. Ct. (we. dist.) Mich. 1953, U.S. Ct. Appeals (6th cir.) 1971, U.S. Dist. Ct. (ea. dist.) Mich. 1977, U.S. Supreme Ct. 1978. Assoc. Adams Smith & Yenner, Kalamazoo, 1949-50; ptnr. Harry F. Smith, 1950-55, Bauckham & Enslen, Kalamazoo, 1957-60, Bauckham, Reed, Lang, Shaefer & Travis, Kalamazoo, 1960-79; with Bauckham, Sparks Rolfe, Lohrstorfer & Thall PC/predecessors, 1979—, pres., 1979—. Author: Duties and Responsibilities of Michigan Townships Officials, Boards, and Commissioners, 1976, rev., through 2003. With USAF, 1943-45. Mem. ABA, Mich. Bar Assn., Kalamazoo County Bar Assn. (pres. 1966-67, chmn. state grievance panel 1982—, mem. state character and fitness com. 1987—), Elks. Republican. Episcopalian. Avocations: golf, travel, sports. Home: 259 Ballantrae Ct Kalamazoo MI 49006-4349 Office: Bauckham Sparks et al 458 W South St Kalamazoo MI 49007-4621 E-mail: bauckham@bsrlt.com.

BAUCOM, SIDNEY GEORGE, lawyer; b. Salt Lake City, Oct. 21, 1930; s. Sidney and Nora (Palfreyman) B.; m. Mary B., Mar. 5, 1954; children: Sidney, George, John JD, U. Utah, 1953. Bar: Utah 1953. Pvt. practice, Salt Lake City, 1953-55; asst. city atty. Salt Lake City Corp., 1955-56; asst. atty. Utah Power and Light Co., Salt Lake City, 1956-60, asst. atty., asst. sec., 1960-62, atty., asst. sec., 1962-68, v.p., gen. counsel, 1968-75, sr. v.p., gen. counsel, 1975-79, exec. v.p., gen. counsel, 1979-89, dir., 1979-89; of counsel Jones, Waldo, Holbrook & McDonough, Salt Lake City, 1989—. Past chmn. Utah Coordinating Coun. Devel. Svcs., Utah Taxpayers Assn.; past pres. Utah State Fair Found.; past dir. Utah Power & Light Co., El Paso Electric Co., vice chmn. Mem. Alta Club, Lions, Phi Delta Phi Mem. Lds Ch. Home: 2248 Logan Ave Salt Lake City UT 84108-2715 Office: Jones Waldo Holbrook & McDonough 1500 Wells Fargo Bank Bldg 170 S Main St Salt Lake City UT 84101-1605 E-mail: sbaucom@janeswaldo.com.

BAUCUS, MAX S. senator; b. Helena, Mont., Dec. 11, 1941; s. John and Jean (Sheriff) B.; m. Wanda Minge, Apr. 23, 1983. BA, Stanford U., 1964, LLB, 1967. Bar: D.C. 1969, Mont. 1972. Staff atty. CAB, Washington, 1967-68; lawyer SEC, Washington, 1968-71, legal asst. to chmn., 1970-71; sole practice Missoula, Mont., 1971-74; mem. Mont. Ho. of Reps., 1973-74, 94th-95th congresses from 1st Dist. Mont., 1975-79, mem. com. appropriations; senator from Mont. U.S. Senate, 1979—, ranking minority mem., mem. environ. and pub. works com., mem. fin. subcom. on internat. trade, mem. health com., taxation and IRS oversight com., mem. agrl./nutrition and forestry coms., mem. intelligence/joint com. on taxation, mem. Senate Dem. steering and coordination com. Democrat. Office: US Senate 511 Hart Senate Bldg Washington DC 20510-0001 also: District Office 207 N Broadway Billings MT 59101*

BAUDOIN, LARRY ANTHONY, academic administrator; b. New Orleans, July 29, 1946; s. Louis Joseph Baudoin Sr. and Mildred Marie Bourgeois; m. Anna Marie Knobloch, May 29, 1968; children: Troy, Danica. BS, Nicholls State U., 1968; MBA, Nova Southeastern U., 1987. Acct. Union Carbide, Taft, La., 1968-70, Honeywell Aerospace, St. Petersburg, Fla., 1970-72, U. South Fla., Tampa, 1972-75, assoc. bus. mgr., 1975-84, dir., 1984-86, asst. v.p., 1986-93; dean fin. and adminstrn. Tulane U. Med. Sch., New Orleans, 1993—. Vol. Metro Ministries for the Homeless, Tampa, 1990-93, St. Feed for the Homeless, New Orleans, 1994-96; chmn. med. ctr. United Way, 1988-90; officer Homeowner's Assn., Tampa, 1981-92; sec.-treas., bd. dirs. New Villa Condo. Assn., 1995-01; bd. dirs., sec., Orlando Internat. Resort, 1996-2003. Recipient Svc. award Tulane Med. Students, 1994-95. Mem. Am. Mgmt. Assn., Assn. Am. Med. Coll. (prin. bus. officer, chmn. so. region 1992, 2002), Med. Group Mgmt. Assn., Inst. Mgmt. Accts. New Orleans (v.p. 1997, treas. 1998-2000, pres. 2001-03). Republican. Avocations: travel, photography, cooking. Home: 29 Briarfield Dr Marrero LA 70072-5067 Office: Tulane U Med Sch 1430 Tulane Ave New Orleans LA 70112-2699 E-mail: larry.baudoin@tulane.edu.

BAUE, ARTHUR EDWARD, surgeon, educator, administrator; b. St. Louis, Oct. 7, 1929; s. Arthur Christian and Viola (Wegener) B.; m. Rosemary Dysart, Nov. 24, 1956; children: Patricia Sage Baue Nizen, Arthur Christian II, William Dysart, 6 grandchildren. AB summa cum laude, Westminster Coll., 1950; MD cum laude, Harvard, 1954; M Honoris Privatum, Yale U., 1975; Doctoris Medicinae Gradum Honoris Causa, Ludwig Maxmillian U., Munich, Germany, 2000. Diplomate Am. Bd. Surgery (dir.), Am. Bd. Thoracic Surgery (dir.). Cpt. asst. chief of surgery USAF Hosp., Philippine Islands, 1955-57; from intern to chief resident surgery Mass. Gen. Hosp., Boston, 1954-61; asst. prof. surgery U. Mo. Sch. Medicine, 1962-64; sr. registrar in thoracic surgery Bristol, Eng., 1961-62; from asst. prof. to assoc. prof. surgery U. Pa. Sch. Medicine, Phila., 1964-67; Harry Edison prof. surgery Washington U. Sch. Medicine, St. Louis, 1967-75; surgeon-in-chief, dir. dept. surgery Jewish Hosp., St. Louis, 1967-75; chief of surgery Yale-New Haven Hosp., 1975-85; prof., chmn. dept. surgery Yale U., 1975-85, Donald Guthrie prof. surgery, 1977-85; assoc. dean for clin. affairs St. Louis U. Sch. Medicine, 1985-86; v.p. for the med. ctr. St. Louis U., 1986-90, prof. surgery, 1986-97, prof. emeritus, v.p. emeritus for the med. ctr., 1997. Dir. surg. edn. St. Mary's Health Ctr., 1990-97; cons. surgery Nat. Bd. Med. Examiners; cons. to chief of staff VAMC, St. Louis, 1994-97; chmn. NIH surgery B study sect., 1978-82; bd. dirs., med. dir. Healthcare Mgmt., Inc.; vis. prof. various colls.; hon. pres., Internat. Symposium Critical Care Medicine, Trieste, 2003. Chief editor Archives of Surgery, 1977-88, sr. cons. editor, 1989-93; editor: Parameters of Health Care, 1986-90; mem. editl. bd. JAMA, 1977-88, Circulatory Shock, Am. Jour. Physiology, 1975-87, Postgrad. Gen. Surgery, Jour. Shock, 1994—; sr. editor: Glenn's Thoracic and Cardiovascular Surgery; contbr. more than 650 articles to profl. jours. Life trustee Westminster Coll.; trustee Nat. Commn. for Quality Health Care, 1986-92, Health Care Leadership Coun.; bd. dirs. United Way. Capt. USAF, 1959-69. John and Mary R. Markle scholar acad. medicine, 1963; recipient Rsch. Career Devel. award USPHS, 1965-68, Scientist of Yr. award Sigma Xi, 1991. Mem. ACS, AMA (trustee jour., editl. bd. jour.), Assn. Am. Med. Colls. (coun. acad. socs.), Am. Assn. Thoracic Surgery, Am. Coll. Cardiology, Am. Coll. Chest Physicians, Assn. Acad. Surgery, New Eng. Surg. Soc., New Eng. Vascular Soc., Internat. Cardiovasc. Soc., Soc. Thoracic Surgeons, Soc. Univ. Surgeons, Soc. Vascular Surgery, Shock Soc. (scientific achievement award 2003), Internat. Fedn. Shock Socs. (pres. 1992-95), Internat. Vascular Soc. Surgery, Am. Assn. for Surgery of Trauma, Am. Assn. Artificial Internal Organs, Organ Failure Acad. (Trieste, Italy, hon. pres. 1983—), Surgical Biol. Club, Soc. U. Surgeons, Am. Physiol. Soc., Soc. Critical Care Medicine, Am. Surg. Assn., Ctrl. Surg. Assn., Halsted Soc. Societeé Internat. de Chirurgie, Soc. of Clin. Surgery, Surg. Infection Soc., James IV Assn. of Surgeons, Southern Thoracic Surg. Soc., Soc. for Surgery Alimentary Tract, St. Louis Surg. Soc. (hon.), Soc. Grad. Surgeons L.A. County-U. S.C. Med. Ctr. (hon.), Assn. VA Surgeons (hon.), Colombia Surg. Soc. (hon.), Chgo. Surg. Soc. (hon.), L.A. Surg. Soc. (hon.), Mpls. Surg. Soc. (hon.), Indonesian Shock Soc. (hon.), Organ Failure Soc. (hon. pres.), Alpha Omega Alpha. Home and Office: PO Box 396 Fishers Island NY 06390 Fax: 631-788-5591.

BAUER, ANTONIE GERTRUD, journalist; b. Munich, Dec. 12, 1961; d. Martin Simon and Gertrud (Wild) B. Diploma in Econs., Munich U., 1988, PhD in Econs., 1992. Journalist Sueddeutscher Rundfunk, Stuttgart, Germany, 1983-85, Bayerischer Rundfunk, Munich, 1985-86; editor-in-chief APF, Munich, 1986-91; asst. prof. Munich U., 1988-94; editor Forbes, Munich, 1994-95, Sueddeutsche Zeitung, Munich, 1995—2000, U.S. corr., 2001—. Author: Der Treibhauseffekt, 1993; co-author: Mikrooekonomie, 1994, Stichwort Spezial: Geld, 1996; contbr. articles to profl. jours.

BAUER, A(UGUST) ROBERT, JR., surgeon, medical educator; b. Dec. 23, 1928; s. A(ugust) Robert and Jessie Martha-Maynard (Monie) Bauer; m. Charmaine Louise Studer, June 28, 1957; children: Robert, John, William, Anne, Charles, James. BS, U. Mich., 1949, MS, 1950, MD, 1954; M in Med. Sci.-Surgery, Ohio State U., 1960. Diplomate Am. Bd. Surgery. Intern Walter Reed Army Med. Ctr., 1954—55; resident in surgery Univ. Hosp., Ohio State U., Columbus, also instr., 1957—61; pvt. practice medicine, specializing in surgery Mt. Pleasant, Mich., 1962—74; chief surgery Ctrl. Mich. Cmty. Hosp., Mt. Pleasant, 1964—65, vice chief of staff, 1967, chief of staff, 1968; clin. faculty Mich. State Med. Sch., East Lansing, 1974; mem. staff St. Mark's Hosp., Salt Lake City, 1974—91; pvt. practice surgery Salt Lake City, 1974—91. Clin. instr. surgery U. Utah, 1975—91; rschr. surg. immunology. Contbr. articles to profl. publs. Trustee Rowland Hall, St. Mark's Sch., Salt Lake City, 1978—84; mem. Utah Health Planning Coun., 1979—81. With M.C. U.S. Army, 1954—57. Fellow: ACS, Southwestern Surg. Congress; mem.: AAAS (affiliate), AMA, Pan Am. Med. Assn. (affiliate), Salt Lake Surg. Soc., Utah Soc. Certified Surgeons, Utah Med. Assn. (various coms.), Salt Lake County Med. Soc., Zollinger Club, Phi Rho Sigma, Sigma Phi Epsilon. Episcopalian. Office: PO Box 17533 Salt Lake City UT 84117-0533 Address: 1366 Murray Holladay Rd Salt Lake City UT 84117-5050

BAUER, BARBARA A. financial consultant; Student, Syracuse U., 1973-75, Wilma Boyd Airline Travel Sch., 1975. Script editor various networks, L.A., 1976-88; v.p. You, Inc., Palos Verdes Estates, Calif., 1980-83; cons. Pub. Broadcasting Systems, L.A., 1981-89; fin. cons., pres. Fin. Diversified Mgmt., Laguna Niguel, Calif., 1989—. Founder Bauer Living Fulfillment Found., 1992—. sr. health homecare and estate cons., 1993-; sr. health and rehab. cons. and svs., 1994-. Fashion model at charitable events. Mem. NAFE, Orange County Bus. Women, Entrepreneurs of Am., Delta Delta Delta. Office: Fin Diversified Mgmt 28241 Crown Valley Pkwy Suite F-600 Laguna Niguel CA 92677-4441

BAUER, BARBARA ANN, marketing consultant; b. Fairfield, Ohio, Dec. 4, 1944; d. Charles P. and Grace J. (Peteka) B.; m. Joseph J. Strojnowski. AA, So. Sem. Jr. Coll., Buena Vista, Va., 1964; BA, Am. U., 1966. Pub. relations, advt. specialist Sta. WOR-AM-FM-TV, N.Y.C., 1966-67; pub. relations mgr. Continental Corp., N.Y.C., 1967-68; dir. corp. communications Am. Internat. Group, N.Y.C., 1968-80; dir. mktg. mgmt. infos. CIGNA Corp., Phila., N.Y.C., 1980-83; asst. v.p. Citicorp Credit Services Inc., N.Y.C., 1983-87; v.p., dir. mktg. Skandia Am. Group, N.Y.C., 1987-88, v.p. corp. communications, 1988-89; pres. Bauer Mktg. and Communications, Goshen, N.Y., 1989—. Mem. Reinsurance Cons. Network. Lifetime mem. Girl Scouts U.S. Mem. Pub. Rels. Soc. Am. (accredited, counselors' acad.), Assn. Profl Ins. Women (chair pub. rels., advisor bd. dirs.), Wed Pub. Rels. Group. E-mail: barbarabauer@pioneeris.net.

BAUER, BERNARD OSWALD, geography educator; b. Salmon Arm, B.C., Can., Feb. 7, 1957; s. Joseph and Gerda (Frisch) B. BSc. with honors, U. Toronto (Can.), 1980, MSc., 1982; PhD, Johns Hopkins U., 1988. Instr. U. Toronto, 1985-86; asst. prof. U. So. Calif., L.A., 1987-93, assoc. prof., 1993—2000, prof., dept. chair, 2001—. Prin. GeoCan Cons., Toronto, 1985—; dir. geography and regional sci. program NSF, 1997-99; mem. com. on geography NRC/NAS, 2001—. Author: (reference bibliography) Council of Planning Librarians, 1981, (lab. manual) Laboratory Exercises in Physical Geography, 1990; contbr. articles to profl. jours. Recipient J. Warren Nystrom award Assn. Am. Geographers, 1989, Hydrolab award Internat. Assn. for Great Lakes Rsch., 1986, Presdl. Young Investigator award Nat. Sci. Found., 1991; Postgrad. scholar Nat. Scis. and Engring. Coun., Ottawa, Can., 1981-85. Mem. Assn. Am. Geographers (bd. dirs. coastal and marine geography specialty group 1990-92, vice chair 1992-93, chair 1993-95, geomorphology specialty group sec.-treas. 2000-01, chair, 2001-02, assoc. editor jour., 1996—), Am. Geophys. Union, Can. Assn. Geographers.

BAUER, BETSY (ELIZABETH BAUER), artist; b. Mt. Holly, N.J., Jan. 18, 1959; d. Richard Byram and Melvina Barnett (Miller) B. Student, MIT, 1979; BFA, Phila. Coll. Art, 1980; postgrad., Santa Fe Art Inst., 1995, Sch. Visual Arts, Parsons Sch. Design. One-woman shows include Hahn Ross Gallery, Santa Fe, 1996, 98, 2000, 02, NAS, Washington, 1997, Bridgewater/Lustberg Gallery, N.Y.C., 1998, 99; exhibited in group shows at Visual Arts Mus., N.Y.C., 1984, N.Y. Feminist Art Inst., N.Y.C., 1987, Hunter Mus., Chattanooga, 1996, Site Santa Fe, 1997, 98, 99, 2000, 01, 02, Bridgewater/Lustberg Gallery, N.Y.C., 1997, 98, Addison/Ripley Gallery, Washington, 1998, 2000, Nat. Mus. Women, 1999, N.Mex. Fine Arts Mus., 1999—, David Floria Gallery, Aspen, Colo., 1999, Jenkins Johnson Gallery, San Francisco, 1999, 2000, Evelyn Siegel Gallery, Ft. Worth, 2000; represented in permanent collections at Gen. Electric, N.Y., Hallmark Fine Art Collection, Kansas City, Mo., Rohm and Haas Corp., Phila. (award), U.S. State Dept.-Am. Embassies, Bolivia and Sarejevo, Nat. Acad. Scis., Washington, Sloane Kettering Meml. Cancer Ctr./Lawrence S. Rockefeller Pavilion, N.Y., U. Pa. Hosp., Phila.; Poster and notecards designed for SFO, 1996, 98, 99, 2000; animator for advt. Fox-TV, 1993; contbr. articles to profl. jours.; included in New Am. Paintings, 1998, Women Artists in the Land of Enchantment Catalogue, 1999, N.Mex. 2000 Catalogue, 1999-2000, Betsy Bauer: Memoria Catalogue, Bridgewater/Lustberg and Blumenfeld Gallery, 1999, Southwest Art, 2000, U.S. Embassy, Art in Embassies Catalogue, La Paz, Bolivia, 2000. Mem. Santa Fe Coun. for Arts. Home: 66 Two Trails Rd Santa Fe NM 87505-9357 Office: Hahn Ross Gallery 409 Canyon Rd Santa Fe NM 87501-2717 E-mail: betbauer@aol.com.

BAUER, BRUCE F. former aerospace engineer; b. Washington, Sept. 7, 1912; s. C. Max and Clara Z. Bauer; m. Myfanwy Rhys Bauer; children: Bruce Rhys, Byron Richard, Vicki Bauer Tucker, David R. Student, U. Colo., 1930-35; Aero. Engring. Degree, Curtiss-Wright Tech., 1937; Degree in Structural Engring., U. Calif., Long Beach, 1972. Design and devel. engr., flight test engr. XP-38 Lockheed Aircraft Co., Burbank, Calif., 1937-46; flight test engr. Lark Missile and B-36 and XF-92 Consolidated-Vultee, San Diego and Downey, Calif., 1947-48; design and devel. engr. for C-74 and C-124 Douglas Aircraft Co., 1948-50; design and devel. and flight test engr. on C-125, F-89, F-5 Air Conditioner Northrop Aircraft Co., 1950-64, design and devel. engr. Snark Missle and Polaris Navy Submarine Datico Surveillance Computer System, 1950-64; Apollo space, reliability and acceptance engr. N.Am. Space Div., 1964; Saturn S-IVB design, reliability and acceptance engr. Douglas Spare Div., 1964-68; DC-10 air-conditioning system design and devel. engr. Douglas Aircraft Co., 1968-72; contract specifications, reliability, and acceptance engr. for landing assault ships Litton Ships, Pasagoula, Miss., 1973; prin. engr. for final assembly and test facilities for Orbit Shuttle Rockwell Internat., 1973-79; cons. aerospace engr., 1978-84. Math. and drafting instr. Curtiss-Wright Tech., Glendale, Calif., 1936-37; prefabricated housing engr., sales mgr. So. Calif. Homes, Inc., 1947-48 With USAAF, 1942-46, CBI, lt. col. USAFR, ret. Mem. AIAA (life, 7 awards 1980-88), Soc. Aeornautical W. Engrs. (charter), Inst. for Advance of Engring., Air Force Assn. (life, 3 meritorious awards, 3 state awards, nat. meritorious award, nat. exceptional svc. award), Res. Officers Assn. (life), Ret. Res. Officers Assn. (life), Phi Kappa Tau. Home: 18882 Parkview Ter Santa Ana CA 92705-1232*

BAUER, BURNETT PATRICK, state legislator; b. LaPorte, Ind., May 25, 1944; s. Burnett Calix and Helen (Cryan) B.; m. Karen Bella, 1980; children: Bartholomew, Meagan, Maureen. BA, U. Notre Dame, 1966; postgrad., Miami U., 1966-68; MS, Ind. U. Ind. state rep. Dist. 7, 1970-91, Dist. 6, 1991—; asst. minority leader, 1977, 83; ranking minority leader Ind. Ho. Reps., 1984-89, chmn., ways and means, 1989, ranking minority mem., state budget com., 1989, ho. spkr., 2002—. Tchr. Muessel Jr. H.S., South Bend, Ind., 1968-74, Madison Jr. H.S., 1974-75, Dickinson Jr. H.S., 1976-78, Washington H.S.; asst. to supt. South Bend Cmty. Sch. Corp. Recipient Legis. award EPA Region V, 1976. Mem. K.C., Am. Fedn. Tchrs., Ind. State Tchrs. Assn. Home: 1307 Sunnymede Ave South Bend IN 46615-1017*

BAUER, EDWARD ALPHONSE, electrical contractor; b. Waite Park, Minn., Aug. 6, 1942; s. Michael Frank and Olive Ann (Lardy) B.; m. Carol Ann Lobb, July 8, 1967; children: Steven J., Gwen Marie, John Edward. Grad. jr. acct., Drews Bus. Coll., St. Cloud, 1961; elec. grad., Dunwoody Indsl. Sch., Mpls., 1967; AA, St. Cloud State Coll., 1969. Owner, pres. Bauer Inc., elec. contractors, Waite Park, 1969—. Sec., v.p. JAB, Inc., 1975-82. Chief Waite Park Fire Dept., 1980-91; scoutmaster Boy Scouts Am., 1979-84. With USNR, 1961-62, Res. ret. Decorated Naval Meritorious Svc. medal, Nat. Def. medal. Mem. U.S. C. of C., Minn. Elec. Assn., Waite Park C. of C., Am. Legion, Minn. Street Rod Assn., Studebakers Drivers, Avanti Drivers, Rock City Rods,

Pantowners, North Star DriversEagles, Moose, Lions, Boosters, Rifle Club. Republican. Roman Catholic. Home: 149 7th Ave N Waite Park MN 56387-1150 Office: Bauer Inc 250 6th Ave N Waite Park MN 56387-1147 E-mail: edbauer@cloudnet.com.

BAUER, ERNST GEORG, physicist, educator; b. Schoenberg, Germany, Feb. 27, 1928; MS, U. Munich, 1953, PhD in Physics, 1955. Rsch. asst. U. Munich, 1955-58; head crystal physics br. Michelson Lab., China Lake, Calif., 1958-69; prof. Tech. U. Clausthal, Germany, 1969-96. Disting. rsch. prof. Ariz. State U., Tempe, 1993—. Author: (book) Elektronenbeugung, 1958. Recipient Gaede prize, German Vacuum Soc., 1988, Niedersachsenpreis, 1994. Fellow: Am. Vacuum Soc. (Welch award 1992), Am. Phys. Soc.; mem.: German Electron Microscopy Soc., Materials Rsch. Soc., Goettingen Acad. Sci. Office: Ariz State Univ Dept Phys Astronomy Tempe AZ 85287-1504

BAUER, EUGENE ANDREW, dermatologist, educator; b. Mattoon, Ill., June 17, 1942; s. Eugene C. and Madge L. (Armer) B.; m. Gloria Anne Hehman, Feb. 19, 1966; childen: Marc A., Christine A., J. Michael, Amanda F. BS, Northwestern U., 1964, MD, 1967. Diplomate Am. Bd. Dermatology, Nat. Bd. Med. Examiners. Intern Barnes Hosp., St. Louis, 1967-68; resident, fellow div. dermatology Washington U. Med. Ctr., St. Louis, 1968-70; instr. Washington U., St. Louis, 1971-72, asst. prof. dermatology, 1974-78, assoc. prof., 1978-82, prof., 1982-88; prof., chmn. Stanford U. Sch. Medicine, 1988-95, dean, 1995-2001; program dir. Gen. Clin. Rsch. Ctr., 1990-93; v.p. med. affairs Stanford U., 1997-2000, v.p. Med. Ctr., 2000—01. Mem. adv. coun. Nat. Inst. Arthritis and Musculoskeletal and Skin Diseases, 1997—2000; bd. dirs. U. Calif. San Francisco-Stanford Health Care, Connetics Corp., Reconstructive Techs., Arbor Vita Corp., Medgenics. Contbr. numerous articles to profl. jours. Served to lt. comdr. USNR, 1972-74. Recipient Alumni Merit award Northwestern U., 1999. Fellow Am. Acad. Dermatology; mem. Am. Fedn. Clin. Rsch., Am Soc. Clin. Investigation, Am. Dermatol. Assn., Soc. Investigative Dermatology (bd. dirs. 1981-86, assoc. editor Jour. Investigative Dermatology 1982-87, pres.-elect 1994-95, pres. 1995-96), Ctrl. Soc. Clin. Rsch., Assn. Am. Physicians, Inst. of Medicine of NAS, Am. Clin. and Climatological Assn. Office: Stanford U Sch Medicine Office of the VP M121 Stanford CA 94305

BAUER, FRED L. judge, lawyer, accountant, arbitration; b. Bklyn., Sept. 8, 1951; s. Sidney and Beatrice (Roth) B. BS in Acctg. cum laude, NYU, 1973, JD cum laude, 1976, MBA in Tax, 1977, LLM in Tax, 1979. Bar: Ill., N.Y. Tax ptnr. Griggs Baldwin & Baldwin, N.Y.C., 1979-84; tax assoc. Ernst & Ernst, N.Y.C., 1976, Trubin Sillcocks Edelman & Knapp, N.Y.C., 1977; arbitration judge N.Y.C. Civil Ct., Queens, 1994—. Editor John Marshall Law Rev., 1976. Mem. N.Y.C. Assn. Arbitrators (arbitration judge), Queens Bar Assn.

BAUER, GEORGE A., III, lawyer; b. Queens, N.Y., Nov. 2, 1954; s. George A. Jr. and Mariella (Hoffman) B.; m. Marcy F. Greenberg, Aug. 6, 1978; children: Garrett J., Melissa I., Maren A.A. BBA magna cum laude, CUNY, 1976; JD, NYU, 1979. Bar: N.Y. 1980, U.S. Dist. Ct. (so. and ea. dists.) N.Y. 1980, U.S. Ct. Appeals (2d and 4th cirs.) 1988, U.S. Supreme Ct. 1988. Ptnr. Milberg Weiss Bershad Hynes & Lerach LLP, N.Y.C., 1979—. Mem. ATLA, ABA, N.Y. State Bar Assn., N.Y. County Lawyers Assn. Office: Milberg Weiss Bershad Hynes & Lerach LLP 1 Penn Plz New York NY 10119-0002

BAUER, HENRY HERMANN, chemistry and science educator; b. Vienna, Nov. 16, 1931; came to U.S., 1965, naturalized, 1969; s. Martin Josef and Anne (Rafael) B.; m. Barbara Bush, Aug. 25, 1986; children from previous marriage: Helen Suzanne, Judith Ann. B.Sc., U. Sydney, 1952, M.Sc., 1953, PhD, 1956. Rsch. assoc. U. Mich., 1956-58, vis. scientist, 1965-66; lectr., sr. lectr. U. Sydney, 1958-66; assoc. prof., prof. U. Ky., 1966-78; vis. prof. Southampton (Eng.) U., 1972-73; dean Coll. Arts and Scis. Va. Poly. Inst. and State U., Blacksburg, 1978-86, prof. chemistry and science studies Coll. Arts and Scis., 1986-99. Author: Alternating Current Polarography and Tensammetry, 1963, Electrodics, 1973, Instrumental Analysis, 1978, Beyond Velikovsky, 1984, Enigma of Loch Ness, 1986, (under pseudonym Josef Martin) To Rise Above Principle, 1988, Scientific Literacy and the Myth of the Scientific Method, 1992, Science or Pseudoscience, 2001, Fatal Attractions: The Troubles with Science, 2001; editor-in-chief Jour. Sci. Exploration, 2000—. Fulbright fellow, 1956-58; Japan Soc. fellow for promotion of sci., 1974 Mem. Soc. Sci. Exploration (founding mem.), Internat. Soc. Cryptozoology. Unitarian Universalist. E-mail: hhbauer@vt.edu.

BAUER, JAMES RICHARD, academic administrator; b. Salt Lake City; s. Richard Leuting and Lois (Saathoff) Bauer; m. Lonna Robinette Bauer, May 24, 1980; children: Hannah Marie, Lydia Sophia. BS in interpersonal comm., U. Idaho, 1982, EdM in counseling, 1988. V.p. adminstrn. Willamette Univ., Salem, Oreg., 2002—, dean of Res. & Aux. Svc., 1995—2002; dir. of Res. Life Univ. of Idaho, Moscow, Idaho, 1992—95, dir. of Housing, 1988—92, dir. of Student Activities, 1983—88. Bd. mem. Salem Chamber Orch., Salem, Oreg., Garten Svc. Corp., Salem, Oreg. Mem.: Nat. Assoc. Coll. & Univ. Bus. Officers, Nat. Assoc. Student Pers. Admin., Nat. Assoc. of Coll. Auxilliary Svc. Catholic. Office: Willamette Univ 900 State St Salem OR 97304

BAUER, JEAN MARIE, accountant; b. Morristown, N.J., Sept. 10, 1958; d. Earl F. and Patricia A. (O'Brien) W.; m. Ronald F. Bauer, Sr. AA in Acctg., County Coll. of Morris, 1978; BSBA, Coll. of St. Elizabeth, Convent Station, N.J., 1986. Sec. to payroll supr. Monroe Calculator, Morris Plains, N.J., 1979-80; clk. typist Stewart Title, Morris Plains, 1980-81; with BASF Corp., Mount Olive, N.J., 1981—, credit rep. chems. div. Parsippany, N.J., 1986-88, property acct. III Mount Olive, N.J., 1988—. Co-leader folk group Sacred Heart Ch. of Dover, N.J., 1981, adult leader youth group, 1982, eucharistic minister, 1993—, vol. religious edn. chr. St. Jude Ch., Budd Lake, N.J., 1993; spl. dep. registrar boro Mountain Lakes, N.J., 1976. Named one of Outstanding Young Women in Am., U.S. Jaycees, 1985. Mem. Cath. Daughters Am. (treas. Dover chpt. 1987-89, regent 1989-91). Republican. Avocations: needlepoint, cooking, travel, gardening. Home: HC 1 Box 1896 Tafton PA 18464-9718 Office: BASF Corp Property Acctg 3000 Continental Dr N Budd Lake NJ 07828-1234

BAUER, JEROME LEO, JR., chemical engineer; b. Pitts., Oct. 12, 1938; s. Jerome L. and Anna Mae (Tucker) B.; children from previous marriage: children: Lori, Trish, Jeff. BSChemE, U. Dayton, 1960; MSChemE, Pa. State U., 1963; postgrad., Ohio State U., 1969. Registered profl. engr., Ohio. Asst. prof. chem. engring. U. Dayton, Ohio, 1963-67; mgr. advanced composites dept. Ferro Corp., Cleve., 1967-72; engring. material and process specifications mgr. Lockheed Missiles & Space Co., Inc., Sunnyvale, Calif., 1972-74; gen. dynamics design specialist Convair Div., San Diego, 1974-76, project devel. engr., 1976-77; dir. research Furane div. M&T Chems. Inc., Glendale, Calif., 1980-82; mem. tech. staff Jet Propulsion Lab., Calif. Inst. Tech., Pasadena, Calif., 1977-80, 82-90; mem. tech. staff mfg. engring. The Aerospace Corp., El Segundo, Calif., 1990—, engring. specialist, 1997—. Editor: Materials Sciences for Future, 1986, Moving Foreward With 50 Years of Leadership in Advanced Materials, 1994, Materials and Processes Challenges, 1996, Evolving & Revolutionary Technologies for the New Millennium, 1999; contbr. articles to profl. jours. Jr. warden St. Luke Episcopal Ch., La Crescenta, Calif., 1980, sr. warden 1981. Fellow Internat. Electronics Packaging Soc. (pres. L.A. chpt. 1982), Soc. Advancement of Material Process Engring. (membership chmn. no. Calif. sect. 1973-74, vice chmn. San Diego sect. 1974-75, chmn. 1975-76, chmn. 1976, chmn. L.A. sect. 1977, 2003, internat. treas. 1978-82, internat. exec. v.p. 1989, internat. pres. 1990, gen. chmn. 31st internat. symposium exhbn., Las Vegas, Nev., 1986, dep. chmn. 1999, 2003, Long Beach, Calif., Meritorious Achievement award 1983, internat. v.p. 1987-89, internat. pres. 1989-90), Am. Inst. Chem. Engrs. (founder, chmn. Dayton sect. 1964-66, spl. projects chmn. Cleve. sect. 1968-69); mem. Phi Lambda Upsilon, Delta Sigma Epsilon. Republican. Avocations: carpentry, photography, camping. Home: PO Box 3298 El Segundo CA 90245-8398 Office: The Aerospace Corp 2350 E El Segundo Blvd El Segundo CA 90245-4691

BAUER, JUDY MARIE, minister; b. South Bend, Ind., Aug. 24, 1947; d. Ernest Camiel and Marjorie Ann (Williams) Derho; m. Gary Dwane Bauer, Apr. 28, 1966; children: Christine Ann, Steven Dwane. Ordained to ministry Christian Ch., 1979. Sec. adminstrv. asst. Bethel Christian Ctr., Riverside, Calif., 1975-79; founder, pres. Kingdom Advancement Ministry, San Diego, 1979—; co-pastor Bethel Christian Ctr., Rancho Bernardo, Calif., 1991—; coll. funding advisor, 2002—03. Trainer, mgr., cons. Tex., Ariz., Calif., Oreg., Wash., Alaska, Okla., Idaho, Rep. South Africa, Guam, Egypt, The Philippines, Australia, Can., Mozambique, Malawi, Mex., Zimbabwe, Poland, Guatemala, Israel, Scotland, Ireland, Japan, Eng., others, 1979—; pres. Witty Outerwear Distbrs. Internat., Inc., 1993—96; mktg. exec. Melalueca, 1999—2002; founder, co-pastor Bernardo Christian Ctr., San Diego, 1981—91; adult tchr. Bethel Christian Ctr., 1973—81, undershepherd minister, 1975—79, evangelism dir., 1978—81; chaplain La Mesa Fed. Penitentiary, Tijuana, Mexico, 1998—2001; bd. dirs. Strong Tower Rehab. Ministry, San Diego; pres., founder Bethel Christian Ctr., Ranco Bernardo, Calif., 1991—; condr. leadership tng. clinics, internat. spkr., lectr. in field. Author syllabus, booklet, tng. material packets. Pres. Bernardo Christian Ctr., San Diego, 1981-91. Mem. Internat. Conv. Faith Ministries, Inc. (area bd. dirs. 1983-88). Address: PO Box 501711 San Diego CA 92150-1711 also: Kingdom Advancement Min PO Box 501711 San Diego CA 92150-1711

BAUER, MARIA CASANOVA, computer engineer; b. Cienfuegos, Las Villas, Cuba, Jan. 1, 1954; came to U.S., 1979; d. Manuel José and Loida Eugenia (Ojeda) Casanova; m. Lawrence D. Bauer, Feb. 14, 1997; 1 child, Ingrid. BSEE cum laude, U. Miami, 1985; MS, U. Cen. Fla., 2000. Software engr. Martin Marietta Corp., Orlando, Fla., 1986-89; computer engr., mgr. software acquisition, Tng. Sys. divsn. Naval Air Warfare Ctr., Orlando, 1989-97; project dir. U.S. Army Simulation, Tng. and Instrumentation Command, Orlando, 1000—. Software arch. U.S. Army Simulation. Tng. and Instrumentation Command, Orlando, 1997-2000. Mem. IEEE, Golden Key, Sigma Xi, Tau Beta Pi, Eta Kappa Nu, Phi Kappa Phi. Achievements include co-development of weapons system for Desert Storm. Home: 3212 Lake George Cove Dr Orlando FL 32812-6844 E-mail: maria_bauer@stricom.army.mil.

BAUER, MARION DANE, writer; b. Oglesby, Ill., Nov. 20, 1938; d. Chester and Elsie (Hempstead) Dane; m. Ronald C. Bauer, June 25, 1959 (div. Dec. 1988); children: Peter Dane, Elisabeth Alison. AA, LaSalle-Peru-Oglesby Jr. Coll., 1958; student, U. Mo., 1958—59; BA in Lang. Arts, U. Okla., 1961, postgrad., 1961—62. Author: Shelter from the Wind, 1976 (Notable Children's Book ALA, 1976), Foster Child (Golden Kite Honor Book award Soc. Children's Book Writers, 1977), Tangled Butterfly, 1980, Rain of Fire, 1983 (Tchrs.' Choices award Nat. Coun. Tchrs. of English, 1984, Revs. Choice award ALA Booklist, 1983, Children's Book award Jane Addams Peace Assn., 1984), Like Mother, Like Daughter, 1985, On My Honor, 1986 (Newbery Honor Book, 1987, Notable Children's Book ALA, 1986, Best Books of 1986 Sch. Libr. Jour., Editors' Choice Booklist, 1986, Pub.'s Weekly Choice the Yrs.'s Best Books, 1986, Flicker Tale Children's Book award, N.D., 1989, Golden Archer award, Wis., 1989, William Allen White Children's Book award, Kans., 1989, BBY, IRA selection for Janusc Korczak Lit. Competition Poland, 1990), Touch the Moon, 1987, A Dream of Queens and Castles, 1990, (drama) God's Tears: A Woman's Journey, Face to Face, 1991 (Children's Book of Distinction, Hungry Mind Rev., 1992), What's Your Story? A Young Person's Guide to Writing Fiction, 1992 (Notable Children's Book ALA, 1992), Ghost Eye, 1992, A Taste of Smoke, 1993, A Question of Trust, 1994; editor: Am I Blue? Coming Out from the Silence, 1994, When I Go Camping With Grandma, 1995, A Writer's Story, From Life to Fiction, 1995, Alison's Wings, 1996, Our Stories, A Fiction Workshop for Young Authors, 1996, Alison's Puppy, 1997, If You Were Born a Kitten, 1997, Turtle Dreams, 1997, Alison's Fierce and Ugly Halloween, 1997, Bear's Hiccups, 1998, Christmas in the Forest, 1998, An Early Winter, 1999, Sleep, Little One, Sleep, 1999, Jason's Bears, 2000, Grandmother's Song, 2000, My Mother is Mine, 2001, If You Had a Nose Like an Elephant's Trunk, 2001, Frog's Best Friend, 2002, Love Song for a Baby, 2003, Runt, 2002, Land of the Buffalo Bones, 2003, Toes, Ears and Nose, 2003, Why Do Kittens Purr, 2003, Wind, 2003, Snow, 2003; contbr. short stories to mags. and books in field. Mem.: Soc. Children's Book Writer and Illustrators, Authors League Am., Authors Guild. Democrat. Home: 8861 Basswood Rd Eden Prairie MN 55344-7407 Office: Clarion 215 Park Ave S New York NY 10003-1603 E-mail: mdanebauer@aol.com. *Children are our future, of course, but they are also the touchstone for our present. To discover who we are and how we are doing we need only check our reflections in our children's eyes.*

BAUER, MARVIN AGATHER, lawyer; b. Milw., June 28, 1940; m. Gray Bauer; children: Laura, Andrew. BS, U. Wis., 1962; JD, U. Chgo., 1965. Bar: Calif. 1966. Dep. atty. gen. State of Calif., Los Angeles, 1965-69; ptnr. Archbald & Spray, Santa Barbara, Calif., 1969-82, Bauer, Harris Clinkenbeard & Ramsey, Santa Barbara, 1982—. Lectr. U. Calif., 1975—77; instr. Santa Barbara Coll. Law, 2001; bd. dir. Summerland Citizens Assn. Bd. dirs. Carpinteria Valley Assn., Calif., 1980-83, Carpinteria Boys Club, 1983-84. Mem. Am. Coll. Trial Lawyers, Am. Bd. Trial Advocates, Santa Barbara Bar Assn. (pres. 1978-79, bd. dirs. 1974-80), Calif. Med.-Legal Com. (pres. 2003—), Santa Barbara Med. Legal Com. Home: PO Box 1307 Summerland CA 93067-1307 Office: Bauer Harris Clinkenbeard & Ramsey 925 De La Vina St Santa Barbara CA 93101-3243

BAUER, MICHAEL, lawyer; b. Chgo., Nov. 8, 1952; s. Morris and Tema (Posalski) B.; B.A., Northwestern U., 1973, J.D., 1976. Bar: Ill. 1976, D.C. 1977. Assoc. firm Williams & Jensen, P.C., Washington, 1976-78; atty. Am. Hosp. Supply Corp., Evanston, Ill., 1978-81; asst. gen. counsel AM Internat., Inc., Chgo., 1981-83; group counsel Bell & Howell Co., Chgo., 1983—. Class gift chmn. Norhtwestern U. Ten-Yr. Reunion, Evanston, 1983. Mem. ABA, Ill. Bar Assn., D.C. Bar Assn., Chgo. Bar Assn., Northwestern U. Coll. Arts and Scis. Alumni Assn. (bd. dirs. 1984). Jewish. Club: John Evans (Evanston). Home: 1636 N Wells St Apt 2805 Chicago IL 60614-6022 Office: Bell & Howell Co 5215 Old Orchard Rd Skokie IL 60077-1035

BAUER, MICHAEL ANTHONY, computer scientist, educator; b. Dayton, Ohio, Feb. 18, 1948; married; 2 children. BSc, U. Dayton, 1970; MSc, U. Toronto, 1971, PhD in Computer Sci., 1978. Rschr. artificial intelligence Edinburgh U., 1974-75; prof. computer sci. U. Western Ont., 1975—, chmn. dept., 1991-96, assoc. v.p. IT, 1996—2001. Cons. Geac Computers Internat., 1984—88, IBM, 1991—94; advisor IBM Ctr. Advanced Studies, 1990—91, vis. scientist, 1991—2001. Mem.: Assn. Computing Machinery (bd. dirs. 1989—94), Can. Info. Processing Soc. (bd. dirs. 1984—88). Achievements include research in in distributed computing, especially distributed systems and applications management, distributed algorithms, correctness, languages for distributed computing, verfication; software engineering, including methodologies, testing, formal specifications, development environments. Office: University of Western Ontario Middlesex College Rm 355 London ON Canada N6A 5B7

BAUER, PETER, publishing executive; Degree, U. Colo. From advt. sales rep. to pres. People Mag., 1986—2002, pres., 2002—. Office: People/Time Inc 1271 Ave of Americas New York NY 10020-1393*

BAUER, R. ANDRE, lieutenant governor; b. Charleston, S.C., Mar. 20, 1969; s. William R. and Saundrea J. Bauer. BS, U. S.C., 1991. Rep. S.C. Ho. of Reps., 1997; senator S.C. State Senate, Columbia. Sec.-treas. freshman cuacus S.C. Ho. of Reps., 1997; mem. agr. and natural resources, fish, game and forestry, gen., med. affairs coms. S.C. State Senate. Mem. Union Meth. Ch. Mem. SAR, TKE. Republican. Office: State House 1st Fl PO Box 142 Columbia SC 29202

BAUER, RANDY MARK, management training firm executive; b. Sept. 2, 1946; s. Ralph I. and Gloria P. Bauer; m. Sue Deliva, July 4, 1975; children: Sherri, Kevin. BS summa cum laude, Ohio State U., 1968; MBA, Kent State U., 1971. Auditor Peat Marwick Mitchell & Co., Cleve., 1971-72; mgmt. devel. specialist GAO, Denver, 1972-80; adj. prof. mgmt. Columbia Coll., Denver, 1979—. Pres. Leadership Tng. Assos., Denver, 1979—; condr. exec. devel. workshops U. Colo., Denver, 1979—. Recipient Best in 1976 award GAO. Mem. Am. Soc. for Tng. and Devel., Beta Gamma Sigma. Address: 10022 Oak Tree Ct Lone Tree CO 80124-9714

BAUER, RAYMOND GALE, sales professional; b. Merchantville, N.J., June 19, 1934; s. Robert Irwin and Florence Winifred (Guyer) B.; m. Jayne Whitehead, Feb. 15, 1955; 1 child, Linda Joan. AA, Monmouth Coll., 1955; BBA, U. Miami, 1958. Divsn. mgr. R.J. Reynolds Tobacco Co., Winston-Salem, N.C., 1959-68; mgr. Mid-Atlantic U.S. Envelope Co., Springfield, Mass., 1968-74; divsn. sales mgr. Eastern Tablet Corp., Albany, N.Y., 1974-75; owner Ray Bauer Assocs., mfrs. reps., Haddonfield, N.J., 1975—. With USAFR, 1959-64; officer USAF Aux. Mem. Friends of Haddonfield Libr., Haddonfield Civic Assn., Smithsonian Assn., U. Miami Alumni Assn., Monmouth U. Alumni Assn., Nat. Philatelic Soc., Am. Security Coun., Air Force Assn., Am. Conservative Union, Am. Mgmt. Assn., Internat. Platform Assn., Sch. and Home Office Products Assn., Am. Legion, Rep. Club Haddonfield, U.S. Senatorial Club, Arrowhead Racquet Club, Iron Rock Swim and Country Club, Lambda Sigma Tau, Lambda Chi Alpha. Home and Office: 132 Maple Ave Haddonfield NJ 08033-1432 E-mail: RayGBauer@aol.com., raygbauer@hotmail.com.

BAUER, RICHARD CARLTON, nuclear engineer; b. Batavia, N.Y., July 15, 1944; s. Willard Ronald and Ethel Bauer; m. Madeline Joy Amreich, June 28, 1969; children: Jason Todd, Cheryl Robyn. BS in Chem. Engring., Clarkson Coll. Tech., 1966; M in Engring., Cornell U., 1968; PhD in Nuclear Sci., Engring., Carnegie-Mellon U., 1974. cert. in bus. mgmt. Am. Mgmt. Assn. Extension Inst., 1989; registered profl. engr., Pa.; cert. fallout shelter analyst, multiprotection designer. Technician Graham Mfg. Co., Batavia, summer 1965; engr. Linde divsn. Union Carbide Corp., Tonawanda, N.Y., summer 1966; hot cell operator asst. Cornell U., Ithaca, N.Y., 1967; engr. Bettis Atomic Power Lab divsn. Westinghouse Corp., West Mifflin, Pa., 1968-73, sr. engr., 1973-78, staff engr., 1978, mgr. AIW performance analysis, 1979-82, AIW/S5G performance analysis, 1982-86, mgr. centralized safety and plant analysis support, 1986-93, mgr. centralized thermal hydraulic devel. group, 1994—2002, mgr. centralized thermal hydraulic advanced analysis methods devel. group, 2002—. Employee tng. lectr. reactor safety, mem. and sec. lab. reactor ops. safety com. Contbr. articles to sci. jours. Chmn. Cornell Secondary Schs., Pitts., PEI Pitts. Clarkson Trustee scholar; Regents fellow, 1962, Bettis Doctoral Program fellow, AEC spl. fellow, 1967. Mem. Nat. Soc. Profl. Engrs., Pa. Soc. Profl. Engrs. (chmn. sustaining assocs. com., dir. chpt. 1981-83, 2d v.p. 1984, 1st v.p. 1985, chpt. pres. 1987, chpt. past pres. 1988, alt. state dir. 1989, state dir. 1990-94, Mathcounts com. 1984, chpt. award for meritorious svc. 1984, restructuring task force 1992-93, chpt. award dedicated svc. 2000), Cornell Soc. Engrs. (regional v.p. 1970-83), Am. Nuclear Soc., Am. Mgmt. Assn., N.Y. Acad. Scis., Am. Inst. Chem. Engrs., Soc. Am. Mil. Engrs., Tau Beta Pi, Sigma Xi, Omega Chi Epsilon, Triangle Fraternity.

BAUER, ROGER DUANE, chemistry educator, science consultant; b. Oxford, Nebr., Jan. 17, 1932; s. Albert Carl and Minnie (Lueking) B.; m. Jacquelyn True, Aug. 10, 1956; children— Lisa, Scott, Robert. BS, Beloit Coll., 1953; MS, Kans. State U., 1957, PhD, 1959. Asst. prof. chemistry Calif. State U., Long Beach, 1959-64, assoc. prof., 1964-69, prof., 1969-92; dean Calif. State U. (Sch. Natural Scis.), 1975-88. Served with U.S. Army, 1954-56. USPHS fellow, 1966; Am. Coun. on Edn. fellow, 1971 Mem. Am. Chem. Soc., Radiation Rsch. Soc., Sigma Xi, Phi Lambda Upsilon. Home: 6320 E Colorado St Long Beach CA 90803-2202 Office: Calif State U Coll Natural Sci Long Beach CA 90840-0001

BAUER, SAMUEL THOMAS, gynecologist, researcher, obstetrician; b. Hutchison, Kas., July 6, 1975; s. Thomas Anderson and Donna Moody Bauer; m. Leslie Elizabeth Williams, June 24, 2000. BMA in organ performance with high honors, BA in women's studies with distinction, U. Mich., Ann Arbor, Mich., 1999; MD, U. Kans., Kans. City, Kans., 2003. Grad. student instr. in biochemistry U. Mich., 1997—98, res. dir. U. housing, 1997—99, rsch. assoc., 1998—99; EKG instr. and tech.,cardiac catheterization lab. U. Kans., 2001—02; med. student note svc. rep. U. Kans. Med. Ctr., 1999—2001; rsch. assoc. dept. obstet. and gynecology U. Mich., 2003; rsch. asst. dept. preventive med. U. Kans. Med. Ctr., Kans., 2000—. Vol. trauma burn ICU U. Mich. Hosp., Ann Arbor, 1995, vol. emergency dept., 1996—99, vol. phys. med. hydrotherapy, 1996, vol. dept. ob-gyn., 1997—99; vol. mentors program Mott Children's Hosp., Ann Arbor, Mich., 1998—99. Author (with Z.J. Surprenant): Physicians for a Violence-Free Soc. Coord. Handbook: Creating a Student Chapt., 2002, co-author rsch. and program devel. grants; contbg. editor (assoc. editor): Physicians for a Violence-Free Soc. Abuse Assessment Course, 2002; contbr., to profl. jours.; presenter (to conf.). Vol. instr. HIV/AIDS and domestic violence Washtenaw County Dept. of Corrections Women's Divsn., Ann Arbor, 1998; vol. children's divsn. Safe House, Ypsilanti, Mich., 1998—99. Recipient Material Contest winner, Kans. Pub. Health Assn., 2000; grantee edn. and rsch. foundn. scholarship, AMA, 2002, Mahlon Delp acad. scholarship, 2001. Mem.: AMA, Am. Acad. of Family Physicians, Am. Med. Sch. Assn., Am. Coll. of Obstetricians and Gynecologists, Physicians for a Violence Free Soc. (bd. dir. 2000—, nat. med. sch. coord. 2000—, mem. family violence curr. task force 2001—02, pres. 2001—03, founder), Physicians for Soc. Responsibility, Obstet. and Gynecology Interest Group (co-pres. 2001—03, co-founder), Nat. Coalition Against Domestic Violence, Med. Students for Choice (co-pres. 1999—2002), Students for Women's Wellness (mem. exec. coun. 1999—2003, co-founder), Phi Kappa Phi. Home: Apt 103 1443 Natalie Lane Ann Arbor MI 48105 Business E-Mail: sbauert@umich.edu.

BAUER, SIMON HARVEY, chemistry educator; b. Kaunas, Lithuania, Oct. 12, 1911; came to U.S., 1921; BS, U. Chgo., 1931, PhD, 1935. Postdoctoral fellow Calif. Inst. Tech.; instr. fuel tech. Pa. State U.; mem. faculty Cornell U., Ithaca, N.Y., 1939—, prof. dept. chemistry, 1950—. Fgn. adj. prof. Inst. Molecular Sci., Okazaki, Japan; cons. Los Alamos Nat. Lab., Argonne Nat. Lab., Calspan, Arco-Harvey Tech. Ctr., 1945-85, Lockheed Calic. Co.; lectr., tour speaker Am. Chem. Soc., 1975, 76, 77, 80, 89; Sievers lectr. U.S.C., 1974; Emerson lectr. Emory U., 1989; vis. prof. N.D. State U., 1974, U. Calif., Irvine, 1978, Riverside, 1978. Mem. editorial bd. Combustion and Flame; contbr. over 365 articles to profl. jours. Recipient Alexander von Humboldt award, 1979; Guggenheim fellow, 1949, NAS Interacad. Exch. fellow USSR, 1966. Fellow AAAS, Am. Phys. Soc., Am. Inst. Chemists; mem. Am. Chem. Soc., Sigma Xi, Phi Beta Kappa. Achievements include research in molecular structure determinations by diffraction, EXAFS and spectroscopic techniques, measurement of physical and thermochemical properties of boranes, kinetics of fast reactions and spectral emissions at high temperatures. Studies of condensation from supersaturated vapors. Office: Cornell U Dept Chemistry Baker Lab Ithaca NY 14853-5123 E-mail: shb6@cornell.edu.

BAUER, STEVEN ALBERT, English educator, writer; b. Newark, Sept. 10, 1948; s. Albert Henry Bauer and Alice Marian Horrocks; m. Elizabeth Ann Arthur, June 19, 1982. BA in English, Trinity Coll., Hartford, Conn., 1970; MFA in English, U. Mass., 1975. Lectr. Colby Coll., Waterville, Maine, 1979-81, asst. prof., 1981-82, Miami U., Oxford, Ohio, 1982-86, assoc. prof., 1986-96, prof. English, 1996—. Mem. adv. bd. Co. of Animals Fund, Columbus, Ohio, 1988—. Author: Satyrday, 1982 (ALA Book award 1982), Daylight Savings, 1989 (Peregrine Smith Poetry prize), The Strange and Wonderful Tale of Robert McDoodle, 1999, A Cat Of A Different Color, 2000 (Parents' Choice award 2000). Fellow Fine Arts Work Ctr., 1978-79; Allan Collins fellow Bread Loaf Writers Conf., 1981, Master Artist fellow Ind. Arts Coun., 1988, Associated Student Govt. Outstanding Prof. award, 1991, 2001, Arts and Sci. Disting. Educator award, 1995, E Phillips Knox Tchg. award, 1997. Mem. Assoc. Writing Program (dir. member program 1986-2001), Poets and Writers. Democrat. Home: 14100 Harmony Rd Bath IN 47010-9701 Office: Miami U Dept English Oxford OH 45056 E-mail: bauersa@muohio.edu.

BAUER, STEVEN MICHAEL, cost containment engineer; b. Hemet, Calif., Nov. 8, 1949; s. Donald Richard and Jeanne Patricia (Lamont) B.; m. Myung-Hee Min, Sept. 10, 1983; children: Claudia Margaret, Monica Anne. BA in Physics, Calif. State U., San Bernardino, 1971, BS in Physics, 1984, cert. in acctg., 1980, cert. in computer programming, 1986; postgrad., U. Calif., 1974, Calif. State U., 1982-87; cert. in counseling skills, U. Calif. Ext., 1991, cert. in alcohol and other drug studies, 1992, cert. in micro computer applications, 1996, cert. in air quality mgmt., 2001. Registered engr. in tng., Calif., 1976. Asst. nuclear engr. So. Calif. Edison Co., Rosemead, 1973-76, assoc. nuclear engr., 1976-88, cost containment engr., 1988—. Cons. rsch. dept. Jerry L. Pettis Meml. Vets. Hosp., 1978-79, Calif. State U., San Bernardino, 1983-84; cons. planning San Bernardino County, 1975-76; cons. alumni rels. Calif. State U., San. Bernardino, 1989-90. Supporter St. Labre Indian Sch., 1984, Asian Relief Fund, 1985—, So. Poverty Law Ctr., Amnesty Internat., Freedom Writer, 1988; mem. Greenpeace, Wilderness Soc., Internat. Platform Assn.; supporter United Negro Coll. Fund, 1985, vol., 1988; vol. counselor San Bernardino Girls' Juvenile Hall, ARC, 1990—; fellow Casa Colina Hosp.; mem. Robert V. Fullerton Art Mus.; campaign vol. Congressman George E. Brown, 1986; block

capt. Neighborhood Watch Assn., sec., 1991-92, v.p., 1992-93, pres., 1994-96. Mem. Am. Nuclear Soc. (assoc.)., Calif. State U. San Bernardino Alumni Assn. (sec. bd. 1979-80, rep. food com. 1980-82), Nat. Assn. Accts., Astron. Soc. Pacific, Assn. Computing Machinery (assoc.), Ams. for Energy Independence (bd. dirs. 1990-93), KC (sec., recorder 1989, cmty. dir. Outstanding Svcs. award 1989), Toastmasters, UCLA Alumni (life), Calif. State U. Fullerton Computer Club, Sierra Club (sec. San Gorgonio chpt. 1992). Avocations: personal computers, reading, walking, gardening. Home and Office: 131 Monroe Ct San Bernardino CA 92408-4137 E-mail: stevenmbauer125@hotmail.com.

BAUER, STUART BARRY, urologist; b. Bklyn., Feb. 23, 1943; BA in Chemistry, Bklyn. Coll., 1964; MD, U. Rochester, 1968. Intern Harborview Hosp. U. Wash., Seattle, 1968-69; resident in surgery Tufts New Eng. Med. Ctr., Boston, 1971-72, resident in urology, 1972-75; assoc. in urology Children's Hosp., Boston, 1977-90, sr. assoc. urology, 1990—; asst. prof. surgery/urology Harvard Med. Sch., Boston, 1977-90, assoc. prof. surgery/urology, 1990-2000, prof. surgery, urology, 2000—. Contbr. 40 chpts. to books and articles to profl. jours. Scholar Jonas E. Salk scholar, City of N.Y., 1964. Mem. Am. Acad. Pediatrics (chmn. sect. on urology 1994-95, sec. 1991-93, exec. com. mem. 1984-87, Rsch. awards 1998), Am. Urol. Assn., Urodynamics Soc., Internat. Continence Soc., Internat. Children's Continence Soc. Avocations: skiing, sailing, hiking, bird watching, traveling. Office: Dept Urology Children's Hosp 300 Longwood Ave Boston MA 02115-5724 E-mail: stuart.bauer@tch.harvard.edu.

BAUER, SYDNEY MEADE, lawyer; b. Seguin, Tex., Sept. 18, 1957; s. Sydney Moore and Dorothy Meade (Bruns) B.; m. Ann Thompson, Dec. 18, 1982. BBA, U. Tex., 1979, JD, 1982. Bar: Tex. 1982; cert. Am. Bd. Comml. Real Estate Law. Shareholder Clark, Thomas & Winter, Austin, Tex., 1989—. Mem. BSA Friends of Scouting, chmn., 1997; election judge Precinct 237, 1994-97; cubmaster Pack 20, 1996-98; trustee Headliners Club, 2003—. Named one of The Best Lawyers in Am., 1995. Mem. ABA (real estate financing com. 1985—), Tex. Bar Assn. Travis County Bar Assn., San Antonio Bar Assn., State Bar Tex., Tex. Exes Alumni Assn.(chmn. scholarship com. for bus. majors, 1996—), Rotary Club Austin (v.p. 1997-98, 2003—), Austin Woods and Water Club (pres. 1993-94), Pi Kappa Alpha (pres. 1978-79), Phi Delta Phi. Republican. Episcopalian. Office: Clark Thomas & Winter PC 300 West 6th St Ste 1500 Austin TX 78701-3109 E-mail: SMB@CTW.com.

BAUER, THEODORE JAMES, physician; b. Iowa City, Nov. 18, 1909; s. Charles A. and Anna (Braun) B.; m. Helen Mattes, Sept. 1, 1938; children: Jane Helen Bauer Gray, Virginia Ann Bauer Biedron, Martha Jean Bauer. MD, U. Iowa, 1933, BS, 1934. Diplomate Am. Bd. Preventive Medicine and Pub. Health. Intern U.S. Marine Hosp., N.Y., 1933-34, resident in internal medicine, 1934-36; spl. tng. USPHS, 1936-37; regional cons. venereal disease control Dist. 5, San Francisco, 1938-41, veneral disease control officer Kansas City, 1941-42; chief nat. div. venereal disease Washington, 1948-53; med. officer in charge Communicable Disease Ctr., Altanta, 1953-56; asst. surgeon gen., dep. chief Bur. State Svcs., Washington, 1956-60; chief Bur. State Services, 1960-62; veneral disease control officer Chgo. Health Dept.; also med. officer charge Chgo. Intensive Treatment Ctr., 1942-48; med. dir. Becton, Dickinson and Co., 1962-67, sr. v.p. rsch. and med. affairs, 1967-75, dir., 1965-85, cons., 1975—; dir. Med. Rsch. Mgmt. Group Inc., 1985-89. Assoc. prof. bacteriology and immunology Emory U., 1954-58; mem. adv. com. Inst. Agrl. Medicine U. Iowa, 1954-72; spl. lectr. on venereal diseases Georgetown U. Sch. Medicine, Washington, Calif. U., Northwestern U.; mem. expert com. on venereal infections, trepinematoses WHO; bd. dirs. Nat. Council, 1972-76; mem. Surgeon Gen.'s Adv. Com. on Community Health Services, Adv. Council on the Chronic Sick of N.J., N.J. Health Care Adminstrn. Bd., 1975-86. Editor: Jour. Venereal Disease Info; mem. editorial bd.: Am. Jour. Syphilis, Gonorrhea and Other Venereal Diseases. Mem. gov's. adv. council Chronic Sick of N.J. Recipient Disting. Svc. award USPHS, 1962, Disting. Svc. medal Pub. Health Svc., Dept. Health, Edn., Welfare, 1962, Disting. Achievement award U. Iowa Alumni Assn., 1997. Fellow APHA (chmn. program area com. drugs), Am. Colls. Physicians; mem. AMA, Am. Veneral Disease Assn., Am. Soc. Hygiene Assn. (internat. adv. com.), Pharm. Mfrs. Assn. (med. sect.), Am. Venereal Disease Assn. (Disting. Achievement award 1934-35), Sci. Rsch. Soc. Am. (pres. Communicable Disease Ctr. Br. 1954), Am. Social Health Assn. (bd. dirs.), Nat. Adv. Cmty. Health Com., Bergen County Tuberculosis and Health Assn. (bd. dirs.), U.S.-Mex. Border Pub. Health Assn. (hon. life), Assn. Mil. Surgeons U.S., Bergen County Med. Soc., Med. Assn. N.J., Sigma Xi. Democrat. Roman Catholic. Avocations: golf, travel, investing. Home and Office: 451 Weymouth Dr Wyckoff NJ 07481-1216

BAUER, TRICIA, publishing executive, writer; m. Bill Bozzone; 1 child, Lia. Mng. editor Joshua Morris Pub., Inc., Wilton, Conn., 1988—89; fiction reader Redbook Mag., N.Y.C., NY, 1990—94; asst. editor The Millbrook Press, Inc., Brookfield, Conn., 1992—94, dir. spl. sales, 1995—98; dir. spl. mkts. The Rosen Pub. Group, N.Y.C., NY, 1998—. Author: Working Women and Other Stories, 1995, Boondocking, 1997 (selected by Barnes & Noble's Discover Great New Writers Program, 1997), Hollywood & Hardwood, 1999, Shelter-belt, 2000; contbr. fiction & poetry to profl. jours., columns in newspapers. Fellow, Fundación Valparaiso, Spain, 1998. Office: 29 E 21st St New York NY 10010

BAUER, WILLIAM JOSEPH, federal judge; b. Chgo., Sept. 15, 1926; s. William Francis and Lucille (Gleason) Bauer; m. Mary Nicol, Jan. 28, 1950; children: Patricia, Linda. AB, Elmhurst Coll., 1949, LLD, 1969; JD, DePaul U., 1952, LLD (hon.), 1993, John Marshall Law Sch., 1987, Roosevelt U., 1994. Bar: Ill. 1951. Ptnr. Erlenborn, Bauer & Hotte, Elmhurst, Ill., 1953—64; asst. state's atty. Du Page County, Ill., 1952—56; 1st asst. state's atty., 1956—58; state's atty., 1959—64; judge 18th Jud. Cir. Ct., 1964—70; U.S. dist. atty. No. Ill. Chgo., 1970—71; judge U.S. Dist. Ct. (no. dist.), Chgo., 1971—75, U.S. Ct. Appeals (7th cir.), 1975—86, chief judge, 1986—93, senior judge, 1994—. Instr. bus law. Elmhurst Coll., 1952—59; adj. prof. law DePaul U., 1978—91; former mem. Ill. Supreme Ct. Com. on Pattern Criminal Jury Instrns.; chmn. Fed. Criminal Jury Instrn. Com. 7th Cir. Trustee Elmhurst Coll., 1979—, DePaul U., 1984—, DuPage Meml. Hosp.; bd. advisors Mercy Hosp. With U.S. Army, 1945—47. Mem.: FBA (former bd. dirs.), ABA, Chgo. Bar Assn., DuPage County Bar Assn. (past pres.), Ill. Bar Assn., Legal Club (Chgo.), Law Club, Union League Club. Roman Catholic. Office: US Ct Appeals 219 S Dearborn St Ste 2754 Chicago IL 60604

BAUERLE, JAMES ERNEST, oral surgeon; b. Hamilton Pool, Tex., Sept. 24, 1923; s. Ernest and Nancy Ima Bauerle; m. Frances Irene Tankers, June 25, 1945 (div. Sept. 1979); children: Frances Diane, Nancy Lea, Janet Elizabeth; m. Charlotte Margaret Ehlers, May 27, 1983. BS in Pharmacy, U. Tex., 1943; DDS, St. Louis U., 1946; MS in Oral Surgery, U. Pitts., 1950; LLD, U. Tex., 1969. Regent U. Tex. System, Austin, 1973—79, chmn. bldg. & grounds, 1975—79; clin. prof. oral surgery U. Tex. Health Sci. Ctr., San Antonio, 1979—; Bauelre prof. U. Tex. Coll. Pharmacy, Austin, 1982. Capt. U.S. Army, 1950—52. Recipient Alumni Merit award, St. Louis U., 1973. Fellow: Am. Coll. Dental & Maxilofacial Surgeons, Internat. Coll. Dentists, Am. Coll. Dentists, Royal Soc. Health (life); mem.: San Antonio Assn. Oral and Maxillofacial Surgeons, Soc. Advancement Gen. Anesthesia in Dentustry (life), Tex. Dental Assn. (life), Fedn. Dentaire Internat. (life), Tex. Pharm. Assn. (hon.), Am. Assn. Oral and Maxillofacial Surgeons, Tex. State Bd. Dental Examiners, San Antonio Break-fast Club (pres. 1968—2003), Scottish Rite, Masons, Rho Chi, Delta Sigma Delta. Republican. Prsbyterian. Avocation: ranching. Home: 150 Oak Park San Antonio TX 78209 Office: Oral & Maxillofacial Surgery 1100 NW Look 410 Ste 500 San Antonio TX 78213

BAUERLY, RONALD JOHN, marketing educator; b. Monroe, Wis., Oct. 31, 1953; s. Jack Leroy and Josephine (Wiegel) B.; m. Robin Rochelle Kramer, Aug. 8, 1981; children: Shannon Marie, Thomas Joseph. BBA, U. Iowa, 1975, MBA, 1977; DBA, Southern Ill. U., Carbondale, 1989. Asst. mgr. K-Mart Corp., Racine, Wis., 1977-78; instr. Metropolitan Tech. Community Coll., Omaha, 1978, Loras Coll., Dubuque, Iowa, 1979-81, Northwest Mo. State U., Maryville, 1981-82; asst. prof. Brescia Coll., Owensboro, Ky., 1983-86; asst. prof. mktg. Western Ill. U., Macomb, 1987-91, assoc. prof., 1991-96, prof., 1996—. Editor Jour. of Contemporary Business Issues; contbr. articles to jours. Mem. Am. Acad. Advt., Am. Mktg. Assn., Assn. for Consumer Rsch., Acad. Mktg. Sci., Mktg. Mgmt. Assn., Phi Kappa Phi, Beta Gamma Sigma. Office: Western Ill U 424 Stipes Macomb IL 61455 E-mail: moviefan@macomb.com.

BAUERNFEIND, JAMES CHARLES, secondary education educator; b. N.Y.C., Aug. 23, 1948; s. James Charles and Genveive Anne (Fitzgerald) B.; m. Monica Lynne Hangey, Mar. 2, 1973; children: James III, Christina, Rebecca, Jessica. BE, S.W. Tex. State U., San Marcos, 1980; MA, Webster U., St. Louis, 1990. Cert. secondary tchr., Tenn. Tchr. Mt. Juliet H.S., Mt. Juliet, Tenn., 1994—. Maj. USAF, 1966-94. Mem. Kiwanis, Phi Delta Kappa. Republican. Roman Catholic. Avocations: reading, travel, computering. Home: 619 Noel Dr Mount Juliet TN 37122-2027 Office: Mt Juliet H S 3565 N Mount Juliet Rd Mount Juliet TN 37122-3047 E-mail: mrb1948@comcast.net.

BAUERSFELD, CARL FREDERICK, lawyer; b. Balt., June 9, 1916; s. Emil George and Irene Marie (Hulse) B.; m. Ann Yancey, Mar. 3, 1944 (div.); children: Elizabeth Bauersfeld Garnett, Carl F. Student, George Washington U., 1937-42; LLB, Am. U., 1937. Bar: D.C. 1937, U.S. Dist. Ct. D.C. 1937, U.S. Ct. Appeals (D.C. cir.) 1937, U.S. Supreme Ct. 1941, U.S. Ct. Claims 1946, U.S. Tax Ct. 1946, Md. 1957, U.S. Ct. Appeals (5th cir.) 1947, (9th cir.) 1956, (3d cir.) 1958, (8th cir.) 1960, (4th cir.) 1966, (2d cir.) 1970. Practiced in, Washington, 1937—; ptnr. Bauersfeld, Burton, Hendricks & Vanderhoof, L.L.C., 1956—. Lectr. on fed. taxation at various univs. Lt. comdr. USNR, 1942-46. Mem. ABA, Md. Bar Assn., Bar Assn. D.C., Congl. Country Club, Burning Tree Club, Sigma Nu Phi, Phi Sigma Kappa. Lutheran. Office: 7101 Wisconsin Ave Bethesda MD 20814-4805 E-mail: c.bauersfeld@bbhv.net.

BAUGH, BRADFORD HAMILTON, occupational and environmental health advisor; b. Seattle, Jan. 18, 1943; s. Sheppard McReynolds and Naomi Emma (Hugel) B.; m. Karyl Eileen Onstad, June 8, 1974; children: Taggart, Darin, Robyn, Patrick, Tracy. BS in Zoology, BS in Psychology, Wash. State U., 1972; MS in Biology, Ea. Wash. State U., 1976, BSN, 1983, MS in devel. psychology, 1992; PhD in Environ. Engring., Kennedy-Western U., 2002; student, U. Fla., 2002—. Cert. med. lab. tech., Community Health Nurse. Environ. chemist, research and devel. USCG, Groton, Conn., 1975-76, occupational health advisor Alameda, Calif., 1983—; adj. prof. Whitworth Coll., Spokane, Wash., 1973-82; counselor Morning Star Ranch, Spokane, 1982-83; instr. Chapman Coll., Alameda, 1983—; indsl. hygienist, fire chief VA, American Lake, Wash., 1986-87; child mental health specialist Tamarack Ctr., Spokane, Wash., 1987-92; occupational and environ. health cons., Nine Mile Falls, Wash., 1987—; indsl. hygienist Wash. State U., Pullman, 1990-93; environ. protection specialist no. cluster USDA Agr. Rsch. Svc., Pullman, 1993—. With USCGR, 1961-93. Mem. Am. Med. Techs., Nat. Environ. Health Assn. (registered environ. health specialist and sanitarian), Am. Conf. Govt. Indsl. Hygienists World Safety Orgn., Assn. Profl. Indsl. Hygeinists, Am. Indsl. Hygiene Assn. (Pacific N.W. sect.). Mem. Lds Ch. Home: PO Box 209 Nine Mile Falls WA 99026-0209 Office: USDA Agr Rsch Svc Pullman WA 99164-0001

BAUGH, CHARLES H. music educator, actor; b. Atlanta, Sept. 12, 1960; s. Charles H. Baugh Sr. and Jacqueline H. Baugh. AS in Comml. Music/Rec., Ga. State U., 1988, B of Music in Music Theory, 1983. Cert. tchr. Profl. Stds. Commn., Ga. Tchr. choral and gen. music Miller Grove Jr. H.S., Atlanta, 1992—93, Haynes Bridge Mid. Sch., Alpharetta, Ga., 1993—. Bd. dirs. Theatre Noble, Roswell, Ga.; curriculum writer mid. sch. choral and gen. music Fulton County Schs., Atlanta, 1998—2000; founder, artistic dir. Ensemble Concordia, 2002—. Contbg. author: Book Strategies for Teaching Music: General Music, Grades 6-8, 1994; singer: (solo concert) A Concert of American Song, Saint Martin-in-the-Fields, 1995, Poets, Priests, and Peasants: Songs from the British Isles and the United States, Saint Martin-in-the-Fields, 1996, (CD) Informal Buffet by Wine, Woman, and Song, 1995, Pretty Close to D by Wine, Woman, and Song, 1997, Around My Cabin Door by Wine, Woman, and Song, 1999, But We Digress by Wine, Woman, and Song, 2001, The Sacred Sounds of John Rutter by Michael O'Neal Singers, 1995, Allelujah: A Randal Thompson Tribute by Michael O'Neal Singers, 1997; actor: (plays) A Christmas Carol, 1995—97, 1996, Hamlet, 2000, A Midsummer Night's Dream, 2000, Paradise Lost, 2001; scenic designer : Ali Baba and the Magic Cave, 1998; Taming of the Shrew, 2001; singer: (Operas) Amahl and the Night Visitors, 2001; actor: (polit. comedy and music rev.) Georgia Cracker Crumble, 1999; condr.: choral composition The Wave by Mary McAuliff, 2000; actor: (Renaissance festival) Adventures of Robin Hood, 1995; singer: (vocal trio) Wine, Woman, and Song, 1995—; actor: Much Ado About Nothing, 2002; singer: (Opera Chorus) Die Fliegende Holländer, 2002. Scholar Outstanding scholar, Mortar Bd. Soc., Ga. State U., 1983, Coll. Arts and Scis., Ga. State U., 1983, Mortar Bd. Soc., Ga. State U., 1987. Mem.: NARAS (gov. Atlanta chpt. 2000—02), Ga. Music Educators Assn. (gen. music chair 1998—2003), Golden Key. Avocations: travel, exercise. Office: Haynes Bridge Mid Sch 10665 Haynes Bridge Rd Alpharetta GA 30022 Personal E-mail: chazbaugh@yahoo.com.

BAUGH, GARY TODD, lawyer; b. Sweetwater, Tex, Oct. 12, 1941; BA, Rice U, 1964; LLB, U. Tex., 1967—. Bar: Mont. 1967, Tex. 1967, Colo. 1967. Practice Billings, Mont., 1967—, sole practice, 1968; ptnr. Scott, & Baugh, Billings, 1969—71; assoc. Kurth Davidson & Calton, Billings, 1972—74; ptnr. Davidson, Veeder, Baugh, Broeder, Poppler & Michelotti, Billings, 1975; asst. atty. Yellowstone County (Mont.), 1970—72; US magistrate US Dist. Ct. Mont., 1972—82. Mem.: Colo. Bar Assn., Mont. Bar Assn., ABA, Housing Authority of Billings. Office: 805 First Bank Bldg Billings MT 59101

BAUGH, JEREMY RICHARD, music educator; b. Indianapolis, Ind., Sept. 6, 1977; s. Richard Allen Baugh and Kathryn Carmel Morrow, Robert Joseph Morrow, Jr. (Stepfather) and Gloria Baugh(Stepmother); m. Tamara Joy Irwin, June 16, 2001. B, Ind. State U., 1995—2000. Music specialist North Putnam Cmty. Sch. Corp., Bainbridge, Ind., 2000—02, Pittsboro Elem. Sch., Ind., 2002—. Musician: Terre Haute Symphony Orchestra. Creative & Performing Arts award, Ind. State U., 1995—99, Robert L. Hotchkins award, Robert L. Hotchkins Found., 1995—99, Robert Amos Outstanding Jr. award, Ind. State U., 1998. Mem.: Percussive Arts Soc., Music Educator's Nat. Conf., Omicron Delta Kappa (life), Delta Sigma Phi, Phi Mu Alpha Sinfonia (pres. 1998—99, Man of Sinfonia 1999). United Methodist.

BAUGH, JERRY PHELPS, lawyer; b. Evansville, Ind., July 20, 1933; s. Emmanuel Henry and Elva Lorene (Winkler) B.; m. Mary Frances Jones, July 16, 1960; children: David E., Matthew K., Carolyn G. Student, Exeter (Eng.) U., 1953-54; AB, DePauw U., 1955; JD, U. Mich., 1958. Bar: Ind. 1958, U.S. Dist. Ct. (so. dist.) Ind. 1958, U.S. Supreme Ct. 1971. Fgn. service officer U.S. Dept. State, Washington, 1958-66; ptnr. Baugh & Baugh, Evansville, Ind., 1966-74; asst. city atty. City of Evansville, 1967-70, city atty., 1970-71; ptnr. Lacey, Terrell, Annakin, Heldt & Baugh, Evansville, 1974—, Terrell, Baugh, Salmon & Born LLP, Evansville, 1998—. Asst. sec., dir. Cen. Ind., Evansville, 1982-91, sec., 1991-98. Mem. ABA, Ind. State Bar Assn., Evansville Estate Planning Coun. (pres. 1982-83), Evansville Bar Assn. (pres. 1983-84), Order of Coif. Democrat. Episcopalian. Home: 100 NW 1st St Unit 104 Evansville IN 47708-1223 Office: Terrell Baugh Salmon & Born 5011 Washington Ave Evansville IN 47715-4865 E-mail: jpmfb@earthlink.net.

BAUGH, L. DARRELL, financial executive; b. Prairie Grove, Ark., Oct. 7, 1930; s. Lacey D. and Mary Grace (Brown) Baugh; m. Wileeta Claire Gray, June 15, 1958 (dec. Sept. 2001); children: Adrienne Leigh Calvo, John Grayson. BBA, U. Ark., 1954; MBA, U. Colo., 1960; CLU, Am. Coll., 1967. CLU, Am. Coll. 1967; chartered fin. cons.; cert. estate planner. With Penn Mutual Life Ins. Co., 1961-71; gen. agt. Penn Mut. Life Ins. Co., Sacramento, 1968-71; pres. Nat. Estate Planning Inst., Boulder, Colo., 1974—. Faculty estate planning seminars Colo. State U.; dir. Nat. Assn. Estate Planner/Coun., 1992-95; cons. U. Colo. Center for Confs. Mgmt./Tech. Programs, 1975-80; sponsor ednl. programs for profl. estate planners and estate owners. Contbr. articles to profl. jours. Bd. dirs. Boulder Men's Christian Fellowship. With U.S. Army, 1954-56. Mem. Boulder C. of C., Soc. of Profl. Fin. Advisors, Boulder County Estate Planning Coun. (pres. 1972-73), Sacemento Estate Planning Coun., Soc. Fin. Svc. Profls., Nat. Registry Fin. Planners (interview com.), Nat. Assn. Estate Planners (planners accreditation com., mem. Denver study group), Student Venture (bd. dirs.), Flatirons Country. Office: PO Box 3582 Boulder CO 80307-3582

BAUGH, LISA SAUNDERS (LISA SAUNDERS BOFFA), research chemist; b. Houston, Aug. 27, 1969; d. James Robert Saunders Jr. and Diane Hussey Young; m. Alexander Bowman Boffa, June 7, 1991 (div. Oct. 2000); m. Simon David Peter Baugh, Sept. 15, 2001. BS in Chemistry with high honors, U. Tex., 1991; PhD in Chemistry, U. Calif., Berkeley, 1996. Vis. scholar polymer sci. and engring. dept. U. Mass., Amherst, 1994-96; sr. rsch. chemist Air Products and Chems., Allentown, Pa., 1996-97; sr. chemist ExxonMobil Rsch. and Engring., Annandale, N.J., 1997—. Lectr. in field. Editor: Transition Metal Catalysis in Macromolecular Design, 2000, Late Transition Metal Polymeriza-tion Catalysis, 2003; contbr. articles to profl. jours. Violinist/violist Ctrl. Jersey Symphony Orch.; prin. violist Hunterdon (N.J.) Symphony. Nat. Merit scholar U. Tex., 1987-91; fellow NSF, 1991-94; named Dean's Honored Grad., 1991. Mem.: AAAS, Am. Chem. Soc. (polymer sci. engring. divsn. mem.-at-large 2000—03, sec-gen./program chmn. catalysis and surface sci. secretariat 2001, assoc. women chemists com. 2002—03, editl. adv. bd. Chemistry mag. 2003—), Alpha Chi Sigma, Phi Beta Kappa. Achievements include patents in field. Office: ExxonMobil Rsch & Engring Route 22 East LC124 Annandale NJ 08801 Business E-Mail: Lisa.S.Baugh@ExxonMobil.com.

BAUGH, STEVEN MICHAEL, theology studies educator; b. McMinnville, OR, Apr. 1, 1954; s. Fred Allen and Patricia Ann Baugh; m. Kathleen Diane Schild, June 22, 1980; children: Stephanie Grace, Leah Hope, Isaac Christopher Michael. BA in Telecomms., U. Oreg., 1980, BA in Classics, 1982; MDiv, Westminster Theol. Seminary, Escondido, CA, 1985; PhD, U of CA, Irvine, CA, 1990. Tchg. fellow in Greek Westminster Theol. Sem. Calif., 1983—86, lectr. Hebrew, 1987—88, lectr. Greek, 1988—90, asst. prof. New Testament, 1991—94, assoc. prof., 1994 , chmn. dept. Bibl. Studies, 2002—. Author: (novels) A New Testament Greek Primer, 1995, A First John Reader, 1999, (articles) various theol. and journals. E5 USN, 1973—77, Mediterranean. Fellow Regent Fellowship, U of Calif., 1986—87. Fellow: Inst. for Bibl. Rsch.; mem.: Evang. Theol. Soc., Soc. of Bibl. Lit., Phi Beta Kappa (assoc.). Office: Westminster Theol Sem Calif 1725 Bear Valley Pky Escondido CA 92027

BAUGHER, PETER V. lawyer; b. Chgo., Oct. 2, 1948; s. William and Marilyn (Sill) Baugher; m. Robin Stickney, Nov. 25, 1978; children: Julia Allison, Britton William Herbert. AB, Princeton U., 1970; JD, Yale U., 1973. Bar: Ill. 1974, U.S. Dist. Ct. (no. dist.) Ill. 1974, U.S. Ct. Appeals (7th cir.) 1974, U.S. Supreme Ct. 1987. Law clk. to judge U.S. Ct. Appeals (7th cir.), Chgo., 1973-74; from assoc. to ptnr. Schiff Hardin & Waite, Chgo., 1974-85; ptnr. Adams, Fox, Adelstein & Rosen, Chgo., 1985-89, Schopf & Weiss, Chgo., 1989—. Trustee Sta. WTTW Channel 11, Chgo., 1976—81, Kendall Coll., Evanston, 1980—92, WBEZ, Chgo. Pub. Radio, 1992—98, Ill. Humanities Coun., 1997—. Mem. adv. com. Rep. Nat. Conv., Detroit, 1980; bd. dirs. Protestants for the Common Good, 2001—; mem. adv. com. Northwestern U. Sch. Law Ctr. Internat. Human Rights; pres. Lincoln Inn of Ct., 1994—96. Mem.: ABA, Chgo. Coun. Fgn. Rels., Am. Law Inst., Chgo. Bar Assn. (chair internat. and fgn. law com., chair fed civil procedure com.), Ripon Soc. (chmn. 1975—76), Am. Coun. Germany, Mich. Shores Club, Econ. Club Chgo., Univ. Club. Home: 1310 Sheridan Rd Wilmette IL 60091-1834 Office: Schopf & Weiss 312 W Randolph St Chicago IL 60606-1721 E-mail: baugher@sw.com.

BAUGHMAN, FRED HUBBARD, aeronautical engineer, former naval officer; b. Michigan City, Ind., Feb. 7, 1926; s. Palmer Hubbard and Mary Moore (Munson) B.; m. Marilyn Ann Weaver, June 20, 1947; children: Lynne Ann, Elizabeth Louise, Bruce Palmer, Laura Alice, Julia Ellen, Robert Alan. BS, U.S. Naval Acad., 1947; BS in Aero. Engring., U.S. Naval Postgrad. Sch., 1956; MS in Nuclear Engring., Iowa State Coll., 1957; MS in Aeros. and Astronautics, MIT, 1967. Commd. ensign U.S. Navy, 1947, designated naval aviator, 1950, advanced through grades to rear adm., 1973; service in Korean conflict, 1950-53; S-3A project mgr. (Naval Air Systems Command Hdqrs.), Washing-ton, 1968-73; force material officer staff (Naval Air Force, U.S. Pacific Fleet), San Diego, 1973-76; vice comdr. Naval Air Systems Command, 1976-79; comdr. Pacific Missile Test Center, 1979-82; ret., 1982. Engr. cons. Aerospace Def. Mgmt. Decorated Legion of Merit with two stars, Air medal with star. Asso. fellow AIAA; mem. Internat. Test and Evaluation Assn. (charter sr. mem.), U.S. Naval Inst. (life), Naval Acad. Alumni Assn. (life), Sigma Xi. Episcopalian. Home and Office: 1542 Crump Farm Rd New Bern NC 28562-3653 E-mail: fredradm@aol.com.

BAUGHMAN, J. ROSS, photographer, writer, educator; b. Dearborn, Mich., May 7, 1953; s. Charles T. and Patricia Jane (Hill) B.; m. Jonalyn Sue Schuon, May 9, 1987 (div. 1995); 1 child, Henry Marshall. BA cum laude; BA (J. Winton Lemen Photojournalism scholar), Kent State U., 1975. Staff photographer, writer Lorain (Ohio) Jour., 1975-77; contract photographer, writer AP in, Africa & Mid. East, 1977-78; co-founder Ind. Visions Internat., Inc., 1978; pres. Visions Photo Group, N.Y.C., 1978-97; dir. photography The Day Publ. Co., New London, Conn., 1997-98; dep. dir. photography The Washington Times, dir. photography, 2003—. Mem. faculty New Sch. for Social Research, N.Y.C., 1979-97, NYU, 1980-82; co-founder, program dir. Focus Photography Sympo-siums, N.Y.C., 1981-88; adj. prof. U. Mo. Grad. Program in Journalism, N.Y.C., 1984-86. Author: Graven Images: a thematic portfolio, 1976, Forbidden Images: a secret portfolio, 1977, Some Ancestors of the Baughman Family in America: Tracing Back Twelve Generations from Switzerland through Virginia, 1989, Harvest Time, 1994, Apart From the World, 1997, A Lake Beneath the Crescent Moon, 2000, The Chain Rejoined, 2003. Recipient Pulitzer prize in journalism for feature photography, 1978; finalist Pulitzer prize in journalism for news photography, 2003. Mem. Nat. Press Photographers Assn., Photogra-phers Gallery, Am. Soc. Mag. Photographers (sustaining 1984—), White House News Photographers' Assn. (edn. chair), Sigma Delta Chi. Office: The Wash-ington Times 3600 New York Ave NE Washington DC 20002-1996

BAUGHMAN, JAMES CARROLL, information and communication educa-tor; b. President Township, Pa., Nov. 13, 1941; s. Lewis Carroll and Viola Leah (Motter) B.; m. Carolyn England, Apr. 18, 1965; children: Sharon Elizabeth, Susan Carol. BS, Clarion U., 1963; MS, Drexel U., 1967; MA, Case We. Res. U., 1970, PhD, 1971. Tchr., media specialist Phillipsburg (N.J.) Pub. Schs., 1963-65, Weymouth (Mass.) Pub. Schs., 1965-66; supr. edn., demonstration ctr. coord. Mass. Dept. Edn., Boston, 1966-68; asst. prof., assoc. prof. Simmons Coll., Boston, 1971-87, prof., 1987—, dir. media program, 1980—. Prin. cons. tchrs. ctr. project Boston Pub. Schs., 1975-78. Author: Trustees, Trusteeship and the Public Good, 1987, Policy Making for Public Library Trustees, 1993; editor: Trustee Voice Jour., 1994—; contbr. articles to profl. jours. Trustee Medfield (Mass.) Pub. Libr. Bd., 1989-94, vice-chair, 1991, chair, 1992; mem. com. Walpole (Mass.) Sch., 1980-83. Grantee Whiting Found., 1978, Hollowell Rsch. Fund, 1987, 90. Mem. ALA (life, mem. chmn., 1998-99, com. on accreditation 1995-99 Avocation: gardening. Home: 101 Green St Medfield MA 02052-1924 Office: Simmons Coll 300 Fenway Boston MA 02115-5820

BAUGHMAN, KENNETH LEE, cardiologist, educator; b. Kansas City, Mo., Oct. 8, 1946; m. Cheryl Jean Cain, Aug. 10, 1968; children: Matthew Tyler, Christopher Rolle. AB in Chemistry, U. Mo., 1968, MD, 1972. Diplomate Am. Bd. Internal Medicine, Am. Bd. Cardiology. Intern dept. internal medicine The Johns Hopkins Hosp., Balt., 1972-73, jr. and sr. asst. resident dept. internal medicine, 1973-75, asst. chief Osler Med. Svc., 1975-77; clin. and rsch. fellow div. cardiology Mass. Gen. Hosp., Boston, 1977-79; asst. prof. medicine div. cardiology The Johns Hopkins Hosp., Balt., 1979-84, assoc. prof. medicine div. cardiology, 1984-94, prof. medicine div. cardiology, 1994—, asst. dean postoc-toral programs, 1985-91, acting dir. div. cardiology, 1991-92, dir. div. cardiol-ogy, 1992—2002; sr. physician Brigham and Women's Hosp., Boston, 2002—. Chmn. joint com. housestaff and postdoctoral program The Johns Hopkins U. Med. Hosp., Balt., 1985—91, mem. med. bd., 1985—91; lectr. in field. Contbr. articles to profl. jours. Mem.: Am. Clin. and Climatologic Assn., Internat. Soc. Heart Transplantation, Am. Fedn. Clin. Rsch., Am. Coll. Cardiology (nat. program com. 1992—93, gov.-elect Md. chpt. 1993, gov., pres. 1994—96), Am. Heart Assn. (fellow coun. clin. cardiology 1980—), Paul Dudley White Soc. Home: 21 Dembeigh Hill Cir Baltimore MD 21210-1020 Office: Brigham and Women's Hosp Divsn Cardiology Tower 3A 15 Boston MA 02115 Home: 83 Beethoven Ave Waban MA 02468

BAUGHMAN, PAULINE CLARA, librarian; b. Portland, Oreg., July 29, 1971; d. John Junior and Norma Winifred (Strohschein) Baughman. BA in English, Oreg. State U., 1993; MA in Libr. Sci., U. Ariz., 1994. Libr., asst. prof. U. Idaho, Moscow, 1995—97; reference libr., team leader sci. and bus. dept.

Multnomah County Libr., Portland, Oreg., 1998—. Reviewer for libr. jours., mags. for librs. Vol. gardener Hinson Meml. Bapt. Ch., Portland, 2002—, music and arts camp instr., 2002—02. Grantee, Multnomah County Libr., 2000, U. Ariz., 1996. Mem.: ALA (comm. adv. com. 2001—02, chmn. 2003—), Pub. Libr. Assn. Achievements include creator of the Knowmobile a mobile reference desk. Avocations: art, piano, cooking. Office: Multnomah County Libr 801 SW 10th Ave Portland OR 97205

BAUGHMAN, R(OBERT) PATRICK, lawyer; b. Zanesville, Ohio, Nov. 18, 1938; s. Robert G. and Kathryn E. B.; m. Joyce Hall, June 17, 1959; 1 dau., Patricia. BS, Ohio State U., 1960, JD, 1963. Bar: Ohio 1963. Assoc. firm Sindell & Sindell, Cleve., 1964-71, Jones, Day, Reavis & Pogue, Cleve., 1972-73; asst. atty. gen. State of Ohio, Columbus, 1971-72; pres., prin. firm Baughman & Assocs., Cleve., 1973—. Mem. ABA, Ohio Bar Assn., Cuyahoga County Bar Assn., Nat. Council Self-Insurers, Internat. Assn. Indsl. Accident Bds. and Commns., Internat. Platform Assn. Clubs: Columbia Hills Country. Episcopalian. Office: Baughman & Assocs 55 Public Sq Ste 2215 Cleveland OH 44113-1996

BAUGHMAN, ROBERT PHILLIP, physician; b. Warren, Ohio, Oct. 31, 1951; s. George May and Ellen (Van Huffel) B.; m. Elyse Ellen Lower, May 25, 1984. BS, Yale U., 1973; MD, Case Western Res. U., 1977. Intern, resident U. Cin., 1977-80, prof. Editor: Bronchoalveolar Lavage, 1990. Fellow ACP, Am. Coll. Chest Physicians; mem. Ctrl. Soc., Am. Thoracic Soc., European Respiratory Soc. Roman Catholic. Office: U Cin 1001 Holmes Eden Ave Cincinnati OH 45267-0565 E-mail: bob.baughman@uc.edu.

BAUGHMAN, WALTER DAVID, parochial school educator; b. Akron, Aug. 17, 1953; s. Howard Walter Baughman and Margaret Jean Paton Baughman. BA, Mt. Vernon Nazarene Coll., 1971—76. Tchr. Open Door Christian Sch., Elyria, 1989—92; bookkeeper Mill Manor Nursing Home, Vermilion, 1995—2000; tchr. Faith Meml. Christian Sch., Sandusky, 1996—2000, St. Mary Ctrl. Cath., Sandusky, 2000—. Ch. organist Grace United Meth. Ch., Vermilion, 1993—97, St. Matthew Luth. Ch., Vermilion, 1997—. Property and grounds com. Beulah Beach Corp., Vermilion, 1998—2000, archivist, 2000—02; asst. treas. The Christian and Missionary Alliance, Vermilion, 1993—06, treas. Sandusky, 1995—98. Avocations: teach private piano, tutor in math. Home: 126 Kentucky Ave, Beulah Beach Vermilion OH 44089 Personal E-mail: cen28378@centurytel.net.

BAUGHN, CYNTHIA J. human services administrator; b. Austin, Tex., Dec. 15, 1948; BA, Tarleton State U., 1970. Cert. secondary educator Tex. Edn. Agy. Exec. dir., founder The House That Kerry Built Inc., Abilene, Tex., 1993—; adminstr., founder Home Health Agy., Abilene, 1997—, adminstr., founder Medically Fragile Children's Daycare and Respite Program. Cons., Tex., 1995—; spkr. in field. Mem. children with spl. health care needs com., Austin, 1998—, Tex. State Respite Taskforce, Austin, 1996-2000; rep. Abilene Children's Taskforce, 1996-2000. Mem. Tex. Homecare Assn., Nat. Soc. Fundraising Execs., Nat. Assn. Edn. of Young Children, Abilene for the Children Conf. Republican. Roman Catholic. Avocations: music, reading, needlepoint, writing. also: 751 Hickory St Abilene TX 79601-5005

BAUGHN, MARY ALICE JACKSON, journalist; b. Grove Hill, Ala., Dec. 28, 1952; d. Riley G. and Mary Agnes Jackson; m. W. Ronald Baughn, Apr. 20, 1985; children: Tracy, Trent. BS, Miss. U. for Women, 1975. News editor Magee (Miss.) Courier, 1975-77; reporter Sun Herald, Biloxi, Miss., 1977-84, 92-99; exec. editor WLOX-TV, Biloxi, 1984-91; v.p. news Love Comms., Biloxi, 1991-92; contract stringer Time and People mags., N.Y.c., 2000—. Bd. dirs. Miss. Ctr. Freedom of Info., Jackson, 1999-. Mem.: Soc. Profl. Journalists (Miss. state sunshine chmn. 1997—). Roman Catholic. Avocation: writing. Home and Office: 9425 Seacliff Blvd Ocean Springs MS 39564 E-mail: ajaxbaughn@aol.com.

BAUGHN, WILLIAM HUBERT, former business educator and academic administrator; b. Marshall County, Ala., Aug. 27, 1918; s. J.W. and Beatrice (Jackson) B.; m. Mary Madiera Morris, Feb. 20, 1945; children: Charles Madiera, William Marsteller. BS, U. Ala., 1940; MA, U. Va, 1941, PhD, 1948. Instr. U. Va., 1942-43, asst. prof., 1946-48; assoc. prof., then prof. econs. and bus. adminstrn. La. State U., 1948-56; prof. U. Tex., 1956-62, chmn. fin. dept., 1958-60, assoc. dean Coll. Bus. Adminstrn., 1959-62; assoc. dir. Sch. Banking of South, 1952-66; dean Coll. Bus. and Pub. Adminstrn. U. Mo., 1962-64; dean Coll. Bus. and Adminstrn. U. Colo., 1964-84, pres., 1985, acting chancellor, 1986-87; pres. U. Colo. System, Boulder, 1990-91. Pres. Am. Assembly Collegiate Schs. Bus., 1973-74; chmn. Big Eight Athletic Conf., 1970-71, 78-79, 86-87; dir. Stonier Grad. Sch. of Banking, Rutgers U., 1966-86; mem. council Nat. Collegiate Athletic Assn., 1983-86. Author: (with E.W. Walker) Financial Planning and Policy, 1961; editor: (with C.E. Walker) The Bankers' Handbook, 1966, (with C.E. Walker and T.I. Storrs) 3d rev. edit., 1988, (with D. R. Mandich) The International Banking Handbook, 1983. Served to 1st lt. USAAF, World War II; lt. col. Res. Home: 555 Baseline Rd Boulder CO 80302-7421 Office: U Colo System Boulder CO 80309-0001

BAUHN, PER ROALD, sociology educator; b. Ljungby, Sweden, July 23, 1960; s. Per Gustaf and Karla Bauhn. BA, Lund (Sweden) U., 1985, PhD in Practical Philosophy, 1989. Lectr. practical philosophy Umea U., 1990-91; asst. prof. peace and conflict rsch. Lund U., 1992-97, assoc. prof., 1996—, lectr., 1998—, head of the sociology dept., 2000; mem. Assoc. Study of Law, Culture, and the Humanities, 2002. Lectr. practical philosophy Kalmar U., 2002—. Author: Ethical Aspects of Political Terrorism, 1989, Nationalism and Morality, 1995, Multiculturalism and Nationhood in Canada, 1995, The Value of Courage, 2003. Office: Lund U Dept Sociology Box 114 SE-22100 Lund Sweden E-mail: per.bauhn@soc.lu.se.

BAUKAL, CHARLES EDWARD, JR., mechanical engineer; b. Phila., Dec. 15, 1959; s. Charles Edward Sr. and Elaine Claire (Zimmerman) B.; m. Elizabeth Frances Hagerty, Mar. 3, 1990; children: Christine Elaine, Caitlyn Elizabeth, Courtney Elyse. BS in Mech. Engring., MS in Mech. Engring., Drexel U., 1982; PhD in Mech. Engring., U. Pa., 1996; MA in Bibl. Studies, Dallas Theol. Sem., 2001. Registerd profl. engr., Pa.; diplomate in environ. engring., qualified environ. profl. Tech. dir. Marsden, Inc., Pennsauken, N.J., 1982-85; devel. engr. Air Products and Chems., Inc., Allentown, Pa., 1985-88, sr. devel. engr., 1988-91, prin. devel. engr., 1991-96, sr. prin. devel. engr., 1996-98; dir. R&D test ctr. John Zink Co. LLC, Tulsa, 1998—. Instr. Burlington County Coll., Pemberton, N.J., 1984-90; teaching asst. U. Pa., Phila., 1992-96; adj. instr. Phila. Coll. Textiles and Sci., 1997-98; expert witness, 2001—. Author: (book) Heat Transfer in Industrial Combustion, 2000; editor: Oxygen-Enhanced Combustion, 1998, Computational Fluid Dynamics in Industrial Combustion, 2001, The John Zink Combustion Handbook, 2001; contbr. articles to profl. jours. Mem. ASME (mem. NOx com. 1993-96), Am. Soc. Safety Engrs., Air and Waste Mgmt. Assn., Combustion Inst., Phi Kappa Phi, Tau Beta Pi, Pi Tau Sigma. Republican. Achievements include 9 patents in field. Office: John Zink Co LLC 11920 E Apache St Tulsa OK 74116 Fax: 918-234-1827. E-mail: baukalc@kochind.com.

BAUKNIGHT, CLARENCE BROCK, consultant; b. Anderson, S.C., May 14, 1936; s. John Edward and Theodosia (Brock) B.; m. Harriet League, June 29, 1959; children: Harriet League, Clarence Brock. BS, Ga. Inst. Tech., 1958. Exec. v.p. Builder Marts Am., Inc., Greenville, SC, 1965-87, pres., chief exec. officer, 1970—88, chmn. bd. dirs., 1987—2003. Chmn. bd. dirs. Enterprise Computer Sys., Inc. Mem. policy adv. bd. Joint Ctr. Urban Studies Harvard U., 1982-87; trustee Bumcombe St. United Meth. Ch., 1985-90, chmn., 1989-90, Greenville Hosp. System, 1987-93, chmn., 1991-92; bd. dirs. Greenville Health Corp., 1994-97. Mem. Chief Exec. Orgn., Greenville Country Club, Cullasaja and Highlands, Masons, Shriners, Phi Delta Theta. Methodist. Home and Office: PO Box 2183 Greenville SC 29602-2183

BAUKOL, RONALD OLIVER, company executive; b. Chgo., Aug. 11, 1937; s. Oliver Peter and Clara Marie (Haugstad) B.; m. Gay Lynn Gollan, Aug. 29, 1959; children: David, Andrew, Kathlyn. BSChemE, Iowa State U., 1959; MSChemE, MIT, 1960. Engr., group leader Procter & Gamble, Cin., 1960-66; lab. supr. 3M Co., 1966-70; White House fellow Washington, 1970-71; dept. mgr. dental, new enterprises, diagnostic depts. Minn. Mining & Mfg. Co., St. Paul, 1972-82; v.p., gen. mgr. 3M/Riker Labs., 1982-86; mng. dir., CEO 3M U.K. PLC, 1986-89; mng. dir. 3M Ireland, 1988-89; group v.p. Pharms. and Dental Products Group, 3M Co., St. Paul, 1989-90, Med. Products Group, 1990-91; v.p. Asia Pacific, 1991-94, Asia Pacific Can. and L.Am., 1994-95, exec. v.p. internat. ops., 1996—2002; ret., 2002. Bd. dirs. The Toro Co.; mem. exec. bd. Internat. C.of C., 2001-. Chmn. bd. ARC St. Paul, 1979-81, dir. regional blood com., 1972-86; mem. alumni assn. bd. dirs. Iowa State U., 1974-76, gov. found., 1990—; trustee Minn. Med. Found., 1990-93, Children's Hosp., St. Paul, 1993-95; trustee U.S. Coun. Internat. Bus., 1994—, vice-chmn., 2000—; mem. adv. coun. U. St. Thomas Ctr. Health and Med. Affairs, Minn., 1990-97, internat. programs adv. coun. Carlson Sch. Mgmt., U. Minn., 1998—, Children's Hosps. and Clinics Fedn., Minn., 2003; bd. dirs. Children's Health Care, St. Paul, 1995-97. Named Outstanding Young Alumnus, Iowa State U., 1969. Mem. Brit. Inst. Mgmt. (companion 1988-89). Methodist. Avocation: tennis. Home: 70 Spruce St Saint Paul MN 55115-1947 Office: 30 Seventh St East Ste 3050 Saint Paul MN 55101

BAUL, MARY ANN, correctional counselor; b. Chgo, Nov. 28, 1958; d. Robert Louis and Shirley Mary Ann (Jones) B. BA in Sociology/Criminology, Spelman Coll., 1980; MA in Criminal Justice Adminstrn., Atlanta U., 1986. Cert. pers. cons., counselor, vol. probation counselor, victim impact facilitator, basic and advanced group counselor, substance abuse educator, sex offender counselor. Intern Gov.'s Intern Program, Atlanta, 1984-85; alcohol/drug counselor New Start Drug Program, Atlanta, 1985-86; legal asst. Hyatt Legal Svcs., Atlanta, 1986-90; pers. cons. Charlie Brown's Legal Resources, Atlanta, 1987-88; night counselor Salvation Army Youth Lodge, Atlanta, 1990-93; correctional counselor Ga. Dept. of Corrections, Savannah, 1993—2001, Pa. Dept. Corrections, Phila., 2002—. Vol. Ga. Dept. of Corrections, Atlanta, 1985—. Dem. pollster, Atlanta, 1993. Fellow NAFE (cert.), NAACP, Spelman Coll. Alumnae; mem. Nat. Coun. Negro Women, Nat. Register of Outstanding Coll. Grads., Sigma Gamma Rho. Democrat. Avocations: reading, volunteering, crocheting, walking, social services, art, crafts.

BAULDOFF, GERENE S. nursing researcher, educator; b. Butler, Pa., Nov. 11, 1958; d. Melvin J. and Frieda A. Bauldoff. BSN, LaRoche Coll., 1982; MSN, U. of Pitts., 1993, PhD in Nursing, 2001. RN Pa., Ohio. Cardiothoracic transplant coord. U. of Pitts. Med. Ctr., Pitts., 1993—2001; asst. prof. of nursing Ohio State U. Coll. of Nursing, Columbus, 2001—. Fellow: Am. Coll. of Chest Physicians; mem.: Sigma Theta Tau (chpt. pres. 1997—99). Avocations: reading, cooking, travel. Office: Ohio State U Coll Nursing 1585 Neil Ave Columbus OH 43210 Office Fax: 614-292-7976. E-mail: bauldoff.1@osu.edu.

BAULE, STEVEN MICHAEL, principal; b. Southfield, Mich., Sept. 2, 1966; s. Charles L. and Betty Ann (Lange) B.; m. Kathy Ann Schilling, June 13, 1992; children: Sydney Elizabeth, Samuel Michael. BA, Loras Coll., Dubuque, Iowa, 1988; MALS, U. Iowa, 1991; EdD, No. Ill. U., 1997; PhD, Loyola U., 2002. Cert. tchr. Ill., Iowa, adminstr. Ill. Tchr. Aquin Sch., Cascade, Iowa, 1989-90; libr. media specialist Haines Mid. Sch., St. Charles, Ill., 1991-94; coord. info. svcs. Glenbrook South H.S., Glenview, Ill., 1994-97; dir. info. tech. New Trier H.S. Dist., Winnetka, Ill., 1997-2001, asst. supt., 2001—03; prin. Zion (Ill.) Benton HS Dist., 2003—. Editl. cons. Linworth Pub., Worthington, Ohio, 1995—; affiliate prof. No. Ill. U., DeKalb, 1994—. Author: Technology Planning, 1997, Facilities Planning for School Libraries and Technology Centers, 1999, Technology Planning for Effective Teaching and Learning, 2001, Case Studies in Educational Technology Management, 2003; contbr. articles to profl. jours.; author: British Army Officers Who Served in the American Revolution 1775-1783, 2003. Firefighter, St. Charles Fire Dept., 1992-96. Recipient Iowa Gov.'s Cup for Outstanding ROTC Grad., Gov. of Iowa, 1987; named Sch. Libr. of Yr., North Suburban Libr. Sys., Wheeling, Ill., 1997. Mem. Am. Assn. Sch. Adminstrs., Ill. Sch. Libr. Media Assn. (bd. dirs. 1997-2000, Highsmith Innovation award 1996), Am. Assn. Sch. Librs. (awards com. 1999-2000, chair 2000-01, conf. planning com. 2000-2001), Ill. Assn. Ednl. and Comms. Tech., Ill. Libr. Assn. (mem. technology task force 1997). Home: 3918 Carousel Dr Northbrook IL 60062-7535 Office: Zion-Benton Twp HS 21st & Kenosha Rd Zion IL 60099 E-mail: baules@zbths.org.

BAULEKE, HOWARD PAUL, lawyer; b. Lawrence, Kans., Apr. 16, 1959; s. Maynard Paul and Virginia (Shirley) P. BA, U. Kans., 1981; JD, Georgetown U., 1984. Bar: Kans. 1985, D.C. 1985, U.S. Dist. Ct. Kans. 1985. Legis. asst. U.S. Rep. Jim Slattery, Washington, 1984-87, legis. dir., 1987, Washington staff dir., 1987-90, adminstrv. asst., 1991-95, U.S. Rep. Karen McCarthy, 1995; assoc. counsel U.S. House Dem. Policy Com., 1995-97; counsel U.S. House Commerce Com., 1997-99; chief of staff U.S. Rep. Dennis Moore, 1999—. Contbr. articles to profl. jours. Mem. D.C. Bar Assn., Phi Beta Kappa. Democrat. Unitarian Universalist. Home: 1840 California St NW # 10 Washington DC 20009-1822 E-mail: howard.bauleke@mail.house.gov.

BAUM, ALAN STUART, lawyer; b. Phila., Aug. 5, 1955; s. Seymour Zangwill and Harriet (Berlin) B.; m. Marjorie Fisher, May 28, 1978; children: Ryan Michael, Andrew Eric. BS in Mktg. and Real Estate with honors, Syracuse U., 1977; JD, Ohio No. U., 1980. Bar: Pa. 1980, N.J. 1981, U.S. Supreme Ct., 1995. Assoc. Zarwin & Baum, Phila., 1980-82, Grigsby, Gaca & Davies, Pitts., 1982-86, ptnr., 1987-93, Gaca, Matis, Baum & Rizza, Pitts., 1993—, mng. ptnr., 1993-98. Lectr. med. malpractice and nursing home litig. seminars; advisor Pa. Statewide Mock Trial Competition, 1991—; adj. settlement judge U.S. Dist. Ct. (we. dist.) Pa.; apptd. spl. master civil litig. Ct. Common Pleas, Allegheny County. Editor: Ohio No. U. Law Rev. Recipient Eagle Scout award Boy Scouts Am. Fellow Acad. Trial Lawyers Allegheny County; mem. Pa. Bar Assn., Allegheny County Bar Assn. (ct. rules com., civil litig. sect. counsel 1998—, officer 2002--). Avocation: tenor saxophone. Home: 149 Monticello Dr Monroeville PA 15146-4851 E-mail: abaum@gaca.com.

BAUM, ALISSA L. lawyer; b. Ft. Worth, Jan. 21, 1968; d. Kenneth Sidney and Sandra B. BA, U. Tex., 1990, JD, 1993. Bar: Tex. 1993, DC 1995. Legis. asst. Office of Congressman Martin Frost, Washington, 1993-96; assoc. McLeod, Watkinson & Miller, Washington, 1996—. Democrat. Jewish. Office: McLeod Watkinson & Miller One Massachusetts Ave NW Washington DC 20001

BAUM, AXEL HELMUTH, lawyer; b. Berlin, July 14, 1930; came to U.S., 1933; s. Stefan H. and Gertrud (Goette) B.; m. Elisabeth K. Nordwall, Dec. 11, 1982; children— Nicholas S., Andreas S. BA cum laude, Amherst Coll., 1952; LL.B., Yale U., 1957. Bar: Conn. 1957, N.Y. 1958, U.S. Supreme Ct. 1976; Conseil Juridique, France, 1971; Avocat à la Cour (Paris) 1972. Assoc. Hughes, Hubbard & Reed, N.Y.C., 1957-64; fgn. atty. Lovell, White & King, London, 1959-60; ptnr. Hughes, Hubbard & Reed, N.Y.C., 1964—, ptnr.-in-charge European office Paris, 1996—2002, counsel, 2002—. Lectr., spkr. various internat. forums and seminars, France, Germany, U.S., Mid. East, 1970—; arbitrator, U.S. mem. Internat. Ct. of Arbitration of ICC, Paris, 2000—; Ctr. Pub. Resources Panel of Disting. Internatl. Mediators. Mng. editor Yale Law Jour., 1957; contbr. articles to profl. jours. Bd. dirs. Am. Aid Soc., France, 1981, chmn. 1995—, Am. Ch. Com. France, 1991-96, World Monuments Fund France, 1989-; Bd. trustees, Amer. Libr. of Paris 1999-2002, Served to lt. USNR, 1952-54. Mem. ABA, Am. Arbitration Assn., U.S. Coun. Internat. Bus., ICC Commn. Internat. Arbitration, Union Internat. des Avocats, Assn. Bar N.Y.C., London Ct. Internat. Arbitration, German Inst. Arbitration, Swiss Arbitration Assn., French Comite Arbitrage, Internat. Arbitration Inst., Polo Club (Paris), Yacht Club France, Swedish Cruising Club, Yale Club of N.Y.C. Avocations: sailing; tennis; swimming. Home: 8 Rue des Dames Augustines 92200 Neuilly Seine France Office: Hughes Hubbard & Reed 47 Ave Georges Mandel 75116 Paris France E-mail: baum@hugheshubbard.com.

BAUM, BERNARD HELMUT, sociologist, educator; b. Giessen, Germany, Apr. 18, 1926; arrived in U.S., 1933, naturalized, 1934; s. Theodor and Beatrice (Klee) Baum; m. Barbara B. Eisendrath, June 13, 1953; children: David Michael, Jonathan Klee, Victoria, Lisa Baum Kritz. PhB, U. Chgo., 1948, MA, 1953, PhD, 1959. Qualifications rating examiner, bd. adviser U.S. CSC, Chgo., 1952-54; instr. human relations, psychology Chgo. Police Officers' Coll. Edn. Program, 1955-59; dir. orgnl. analysis CNA Ins., Chgo., 1960-66; assoc. prof. mgmt. and sociology U. Ill., Chgo., 1966-69, assoc. dean Coll. Bus. Adminstrn., 1967-68, prof. mgmt. and sociology, 1969—2002, prof. mgmt. and sociology emeritus, 2002—, prof. health policy and adminstrn. Sch. Pub. Health, 1973—2002, prof. emeritus, 2002—, dir. health policy and adminstrn. Sch. Pub. Health, 1977-92. Lectr. Roosevelt U., 1955—66, U. Chgo., 1961—68, Northwestern U., 1968—70, U. Colo., 1971—76; mem. spkr.'s bur. Adult Edn. Coun. Greater Chgo., 1963—76; team leader joint evaluation mission UN devel. program WHO primary health care and health mgmt. devel. projects in South Pacific, 1985; vis. scholar Chiang Mai U., Thailand, 1988. Author: (book) Decentralization of Authority in a Bureaucracy, 1961; author: (with others) Basics for Business, 1968; contbr. articles to profl. jours.; editor (with others): (book) Intervention: the Management Use of Organizational Research, 1975. Bd. dirs. Selfhelp Home for Aged, Chgo. With AUS, 1944—46, brig. gen. Ill. Army N.G., ret. Decorated Legion of Merit, Bronze Star; recipient Bus. Adminstrn. and Social Sci. Doctoral Dissertaion award, Ford Found., 1960. Mem.: APHA, AAAS, Acad. Mgmt., Am. Acad. Polit. and Social Sci., Am. Sociol. Assn., Sigma Xi. Office: U Ill Sch Pub Health M/C 923 Chicago IL 60680 Home: Apt 3B 2610 Central St Evanston IL 60201-1354 E-mail: bhbaum@uic.edu.

BAUM, BERNARD RENE, research scientist; b. Paris, Feb. 14, 1937; s. Kurt and Martha (Berl) B.; m. Danielle Habib, May 24, 1961; 1 child, Anat. BS, MS, Hebrew U., Jerusalem, 1963, PhD, 1966. Research scientist Agr. Can., Ottawa, Ont., 1966-74, sr. research scientist, 1974-80, prin. research scientist, 1980—, chief vascular plants sect. Biosystematics Research Inst., 1981—. Author: Oats: Wild and Cultivated, 1977, Monograph of Tamarix, 1978, World Registry of Avena Cultivars, 1972, World Registry of Barley Cultivars, 1985, World Registry of Triticale, (on Internet), 1994; assoc. editor Can. Jour. Botany, 1986—, Euphytica, 1987—, Plant System Evolution, 1992—2000, Genetic Resources and Plant Evolution, 1992—, Kurtziana, 1999—. Fellow Acad. Sci.-Royal Soc. Can.; mem. Can. Bot. Assn. (Lawson medal 1979), Bot. Soc. Am., Am. Soc. Plant Taxonomists, Internat. Assn. Plant Taxonomists, Classification Soc., Linnean Soc. London, Orgn. Plant Taxonomy of the Mediterranean Area Home: 15 Murray St Ste 408 Ottawa ON Canada K1N 9M5 Office: Ea Cereal & Oil Seed Rsch Ctr Agrl Food Can Rsch Br Cen Exptl Farm Ottawa ON Canada K1A 0C6 E-mail: baumbr@agr.gc.ca., baumbd@attcanada.ca.

BAUM, BRANDON, lawyer, law educator; AB, U. Calif., Berkeley, 1982; JD, Hastings Coll. Law, 1985. Ptnr. Cooley Godward LLP, Palo Alto, Calif., 1996—. Adj. prof. Hastings Coll. Law, San Francisco, 2003—. Pub. adv. Calif. Child Advocates, Martinez, 1985—90. Avocation: watch collecting. Office: Cooley Godward LLP 5 Palo Alto Square 3000 El Camino Real Palo Alto CA 94306-2155 E-mail: baumbd@cooley.com.

BAUM, CARL EDWARD, electromagnetic theorist; b. Binghamton, N.Y., Feb. 6, 1940; s. George Theodore and Evelyn Monica (Bliven) B. BS with honors, Calif. Inst. Tech., 1962, MS, 1963, PhD, 1969. Commd. 2d lt. USAF, 1962, advanced through grades to capt., 1967, resigned, 1971; project officer Air Force Rsch. Lab. (formerly Phillips Lab.), Kirtland AFB, N.Mex., 1963-71, sr. scientist for electromagnetics, 1971—; pres. SUMMA Found. U.S. del. to gen. assembly Internat. Union Radio Sci., Lima, Peru, 1975, Helsinki, Finland, 78, Washington, 81, Florence, Italy, 84, Tel Aviv, 87, Prague, Czech Republic, 90, Kyoto, 93, Lille, France, 96, Toronto, Canada, 99, Maastricht, Netherlands, 2002; mem. Commn. B U.S. Nat. Com., 1975—, Commn. E, 1982—, Commn. A, 1990—. Author: (with others) Transient Electromagnetic Fields, 1976, Electromagnetic Scattering, 1978, Acoustic, Electromagnetic and Elastic Wave Scattering, 1980, Fast Electrical and Optical Measurements, 1986, EMP Interaction: Principles, Techniques and Reference Data, 1986, Lightning Electromagnetics, 1990, Modern Radio Science, 1990, Recent Advances in Electromagnetic Theory, 1990, Scattering, 1992, Direct and Inverse Methods in Radar Polarimetry, 1992, (with A.P. Stone) Transient Lens Synthesis: Differential Geometry in Electromagnetic Theory, 1991; editor: (with H.N. Kritikos) Electromagnetic Symmetry, 1995, (with L. Carin and A.P. Stone) Ultra-Wideband, Short-Pulse Electromagnetics 3, 1997, Detection and Identification of Visually Obscured Targets, 1998, Scattering, 2002; contbr. articles to profl. jours. Recipient award Honeywell Corp., 1962, R&D award USAF, 1970, Harold Brown award Air Force Systems Command, 1990; Air Force Rsch. Lab. fellow, 1996; Electromagnetic pulse fellow. Fellow IEEE (Harry Diamond Meml. award, 1987, Richard R. Stoddart award, 1984); mem. Electromagnetics Soc. (pres. 1983-85), Electromagnetics Acad., Sigma Xi, Tau Beta Pi. Roman Catholic. Home: 5116 Eastern Ave SE Apt D Albuquerque NM 87108-5618 Office: AFRL/DEHP Bldg 909 3550 Aberdeen Ave SE Kirtland Afb NM 87117-5776

BAUM, CAROL GROSSMAN, physician; b. NYC, June 14, 1958; d. Jacob Joseph and Anita Pearl (Serbrinsky) Grossman; m. Michael Seth Baum, June 16, 1985; 1 child, Daniel Joseph. BS, CCNY, 1979; MD, NYU, 1983; MBA, Pace U., 2001. Diplomate Nat. Bd. Med. Examiners, Am. Bd. Internal Medicine, Am. Bd. Allergy & Immunology. Resident in internal medicine St. Luke's Hosp., NYC, 1983-86; fellow in allergy & clin. immunology Cornell U. Med. Coll., NYC, 1986-88; pvt. practice internal medicine, allergy-clin. immunology NYC, 1988-90; asst. attending allergy N.Y. Hosp., NYC, 1988—; dir. allergy clinic St. Luke's Hosp., NYC, 1989-90, William F. Ryan Cmty. Health Ctr., 1990; dir. dept. allergy and clin. immunology N.E. Permanente Med. Group, White Plains, NY, Stamford, Conn., 1990-98; med. dir. Hudson Valley Ind. Health, Tarrytown, NY, 1998-2001, Empire Blue Cross Blue Shield Sr. Plan, NYC, 2001; vis. attending Albert Einstein Coll. Medicine, 2002—03; pvt. practice allergy and clin. immunology Ridgefield and Danbury, Conn., 2003—. Clin. instr. medicine Cornell U. Med. Coll., N.Y.C.; lectr., presenter in field. Mem. editl. bd. Bronx Asthma Newsletter Project, 2002—03; contbr. articles to profl. jours. Fellow: ACP, Am. Acad. Allergy, Asthma and Immunology; mem.: AMA. Avocations: horseback riding, hebrew studies, sailing, playing piano.

BAUM, CHRISTOPHER FREDERICK, economics educator, consultant; b. Chgo., Aug. 13, 1951; s. Clare Frederick and Olga Jean (Sturm) B.; children: Erik M., Elisabeth A., Christopher J., Jonathan A. BA, Kalamazoo Coll., 1972; MA, Fla. Atlantic U., 1973; PhD, U. Mich., 1977. Asst. prof. econs. Boston Coll., Chestnut Hill, Mass., 1977-83, assoc. prof. econs., 1983—. Sec.-treas. Soc. Econ. Dynamics and Control, 1989-92; econ. cons., 1982—. Assoc. editor Computational Econs. Jour., 1990—, Stata Jour., 2001—; contbr. articles to profl. jours. Mem., vice chair, chair Sudbury (Mass.) Fin. Com., 1984-87. Mem. Am. Econ. Assn., Econometric Soc., Soc. for Computational Econs. Office: Econs Dept Boston Coll Chestnut Hill MA 02467

BAUM, GEOFFREY LEO, director; b. Long Beach, Calif., Oct. 22, 1963; s. Morton Alex and Sherry L. Baum; m. Lisa Kay Gallaway, Oct. 23, 1993. B.A., Claremont McKenna Coll., 1985; M.A., U. So. Calif., 1989. Sr. prodr. C-SPAN, Washington, 1989—93, exec. prodr., 1999—2001; asst. v.p. mktg. and pub. rels. Claremont (Calif.) McKenna Coll., 1994—99; dir. pub. affairs U. So. Calif., LA, 2001—. Trustee Pasadena City Coll., 2001; pres. Pasadena Cmty. Access Corp., 1999; mem. state ctrl. com. Calif. Rep. Party, Burbank; bd. dirs. West Pasadena Residents Assn., 1999, Armory Ctr. for Arts, Pasadena, 2001. Paul Miller Wash. Reporting fellow, Freedom Forum, 1993. Mem.: Acad. TV Arts and Scis. Office: U So Calif 3502 Watt Way Los Angeles CA 90089-0281 Personal E-mail: glbaum@msn.com. E-mail: gbaum@usc.edu.

BAUM, GORDON LEE, lawyer, non-profit organization administrator; b. St. Louis, Aug. 24, 1940; s. James Paul and Johnnie Thelma (Thompson) B.; m. Georgia Dee Thompson, Sept. 12, 1959 (div. 1977); children: Gordon Lee II, Mark Evans Sterling, Duane Russell Stuart; m. Linda Gaye Gulledge, Feb. 10, 1978; children: Laura Leigh, Renee Gabrielle. Grad., U. Mo., 1965; JD, St. Louis U., 1969. Bar: Mo. 1969, U.S. Dist. Ct. Mo. 1969. Sr. inspection clk. Chevrolet Divsn. GM Corp., St. Louis, 1961-65, work standards engr., 1965-69; field dir. mid-west Citizens Coun. Am., Jackson, Miss., 1969-84; pvt. practice civil law St. Louis, 1969—. Chief exec. officer, Coun. Conservative Citizens, St. Louis, 1985—, Conservative Citizens Found., St. Louis, 1985—; dir. St. Louis Met. Area Citizens Coun. Assoc. editor (newspaper) Citizens Informer, 1971—; talk show host WGNU Radio, St. Louis, 1995—. State Coord. Wallace Presdl. Campaign, Mo., 1972, 76; del. Dem. Party State Conv., 1976. Yeoman 2d class petty officer USN, 1958-61. Mem. Mo. Bar Assn., Phi Alpha Delta, MENSA, NRA, Sons of Confederate Vets., Hist. Soc. Berks County, Pa., Ger.-Am. Heritage Soc., Am. Legion. Lutheran. Avocations: politics, history, hunting, gardening, travel. Home: 2412 Park Ave Saint Charles MO 63301 Office: Coun of Conservative Citizens PO Box 221683 Saint Louis MO 63122-8683 E-mail: baum@bbs.galilei.com.

BAUM, HERBERT MERRILL, consumer products company executive; b. Chgo., Dec. 6, 1936; s. Jack William and Ruth Frances (Ginsburg) Baum; m. Diane Jean Kale, Nov. 1, 1975 (div. Sept. 1977); m. Karen Rochelle Oberman, Dec. 22, 1983. BSBA, Drake U., 1958. Account exec. Stern, Walters & Simmons, Chgo., 1962-66, Doyle, Dane & Bernbach, Chgo., 1966-69; v.p., account dir. Needham, Harper & Steers, Chgo., 1969-78; assoc. dir., dir. new products Campbell Soup Co., Camden, NJ, 1978, v.p. mktg., gen. mgr. soup div., 1978-84, exec. v.p. U.S. divsn., 1984-85; pres. Campbell USA, Camden, NJ, 1985-90, sr. v.p., 1986-89, exec. v.p., 1989-93; pres. Campbell N.Am., Camden, NJ, 1990-92, Campbell North & South Am., Camden, NJ, 1992-93; chmn., CEO Quaker State Corp., Irving, Tex., 1993-98; pres., COO Hasbro Inc., Providence, R.I., 1999-2000; chmn., CEO Dial Corp., Scottsdale, Ariz., 2000—. Bd. dir. Grocery Mfr. Am.; bd. dirs. Meredith Corp., Pepsi Ams. Inc., Dial Corp., Action Performance Cos. Inc., Am. West Airlines. With U.S. Army, 1958—59. Mem.: Am. Mktg. Assn. Home: 702 Ocean Dr Juno Beach FL 33408-1911 Office: Dial Corp 15501 N Dial Blvd Scottsdale AZ 85260 E mail: baum@dialcorp.com.

BAUM, HOWARD RICHARD, research scientist; b. NYC, Apr. 3, 1936; s. Samuel and Rachel (Papernick) B.; m. Alice Linda Prince, June 25, 1961; children: Allen, Sarah. B of Aero. Engring., Polytech U., 1957, MS in Applied Mech., 1959; PhD, Harvard U., 1964. Lectr. Harvard U., Cambridge, Mass., 1964-66, asst. prof., 1966-71; sr. scientist Aerodyne Rsch., Inc., Billerica, Mass., 1971-75; rsch. physicist Nat. Inst. Stds. & Tech., Gaithersburg, Md., 1975-83, NIST fellow, 1983—. Com. on microgravity rsch. NRC, 2001—. Mem. editl. bd. Combustion Theory and Modelling Inst. Physics, London, 1997—, Combustion and Flame, Combustion Inst., 2001—. Recipient Silver medal U.S. Dept. Commerce, Washington, 1981, Gold medal, 1985; Medal of Excellence, Internat. Assn. Fire Safety Sci., 1991, 99; Gulse Medal Soc. Fire Profl. Engrs., 1999, Japan Soc. Promotion Sci. fellow, Tokyo, 1994, Arthur Newell Talbot Lecture, U. of Ill., 2002. Fellow Inst. Physics; mem. NAE, Internat. Assn. Fire Safety Sci., Combustion Inst., Soc. Indsl. and Applied Math. Jewish. Office: Nat Inst Stds & Tech 100 Bur Dr Stop 8663 Gaithersburg MD 20899-8663

BAUM, JOHN, physician; b. N.Y.C., June 2, 1927; s. Louis Israel and Lilian (Treitman) B.; m. Erna Rose Bailis, Jan. 28, 1950; children: Nina, Jane, Carl, Antonia, Theodore. BA, NYU, 1949, MD, 1954. Intern Baltimore City Hosp., 1954-55; resident in medicine Lenox Hill Hosp., N.Y.C., 1955-56, VA Hosp., N.Y.C., 1956-57; NIH clin. trainee N.Y.U.-Bellevue Hosp., 1957-58; NIH research fellow Rheumatism Research Unit, Taplow, Eng., 1958-59; asst. prof. medicine U. Tex. Southwestern Med. Sch., 1962-68; dir. arthritis clinic Parkland Meml. Hosp., Dallas, 1959-68, dir. med. clinics, 1965-67; co-dir. pediatric arthritis clinic Scottish Rite Hosp., Dallas, 1960-68; mem. faculty U. Rochester (N.Y.) Med. Sch., 1968—, prof. medicine pediatrics and rehab., 1972-93, prof. medicine emeritus, 1993—, chmn. rsch. subjects rev. bd., 1987-96, prof. orthopedics (rehabilitation), 1991-93, prof. pediatrics, 1997—. Vis. prof. rheumatology, hon. sr. rsch. fellow U. Birmingham, Eng., 1988-89; vis. prof. U. Kiev Med. Sch., 1995; dir. arthritis and clin. immunology unit Monroe Cmty. Hosp., 1968-93; dir. pediatric arthritis clinic Strong Meml. Hosp., 1970—; mem. drug efficacy panel NRC-NAS, 1960-65; mem. rsch. rev. bd. immunology VA, 1970-76; adv. panel U.S. Pharmacopeia, 1975—; coord. therapeutics U.S.-USSR Program Rheumatology, 1974—; mem. test com. for rheumatology Am. Bd. Internal Medicine, 1971-76; locum pediat. rheumatologist Princess Margaret Hosp. for Children, Perth, Australia, 1999-2000. Mem. editl. bd. Clin. Rheumatology (Brussels), Jour. Rheumatology (Can.), Japanese Rheumatology, 1984-93; contbr. articles to profl. jours., chpts. to books. Served with AUS, 1944-46. Recipient award of merit Rochester Acad. Medicine, 1999, Sr. Role Model award, 2000, Earl Brewer award, Am. Juvenile Arthritis Orgn., 2002; Fulbright scholar, 1958; clin. scholar rheumatology Arthritis Found., 1964-69. Mem. Am. Coll. Rheumatology (master 1993, coun. pediat. rheumatology 1975-80, 85-00), Heberden Soc., Am. Fedn. Clin. Rsch., Am. Soc. Human Genetics, Am. Assn. Immunologists, Reticuloendothelial Soc., So. Soc. Clin. Investigation, Tex. Rheumatism Assn., Brit. Soc. Rheumatology, Midlands Rheumatology Soc. (Eng.), Polish Rheumatol. Soc. (hon.), La Found. Rheum Argentina (Dr. Oswaldo Garcia Morteo int. sci. com. 1997—), Great Lakes Interurban Club, Sigma Xi. Home: 1470 East Ave Rochester NY 14610-1619 Office: Strong Meml Hosp 601 Elmwood Ave Rochester NY 14642-0002 E-mail: john_baum@urmc.rochester.edu. *If what I have achieved is called success, it is not because it has been my goal. As a clinician, teacher and researcher, I realize that success comes mostly with the latter, but my greatest satisfaction, which must have been my "secret goal," has been with the personal contacts that come through taking care of people and sharing my knowledge with students. The lagniappe of a supportive wife and fascinating children makes achieving the goals more worthwhile.*

BAUM, JOSEPH HERMAN, retired biomedical educator; b. Chgo., Sept. 9, 1927; s. Herman and Esther (Rosenzweig) B.; m. Mireille Josephe Jomain, Mar. 23, 1970 (dec. 1978); stepchildren: Eric Morin, Arthur Morin; m. Susan Harding, Apr. 10, 1994; stepchildren: L. Stephanie Smith, Gordon MacDonald Promish. BS, Roosevelt U., 1953; PhD, Northwestern U., 1962. Instr. pathology Northwestern U., Chgo., 1962-63, asst. prof. pathology, 1963-68; assoc. prof. pathology Temple U., Phila., 1968-80, asst. dean grad. sch., 1972-78, prof. pathology, 1981-90, prof. emeritus, 1990—, asst. dean Sch. Medicine, 1986-89, acting dean Sch. Medicine, 1989-90, univ. exec. cabinet, 1989-90. Cons. in field. Committeeman Boy Scouts Am., Hatboro, Pa., 1974-78; bd. govs. St. Christopher's Hosp. for Children, Phila., 1989-90, Temple U. Hosp., 1989-90; chmn. South Ga. cmty. svc. bd. Ga. State Mental Health, Retardation, Substance Abuse Delivery System, 1994-96. With U.S. Army, 1944, col. inf. AUS, ret. Decorated Meritorious Svc. medal U.S. Army; recipient Lindback award for disting. tchg. C. & M. Lindback Found., 1981, Golden Apple award Student AMA, 1987. Mem. Am. Soc. Cell Biology, Am. Soc. Investigative Pathology, Multidiscipline Edn. in Health Scis. (founding mem.), Internat. Acad. Pathology. Avocations: military history, art history, baroque music, blues, poetry. Home: PO Box 5202 Quitman GA 31643-5202

BAUM, JULES LEONARD, ophthalmologist, educator; b. N.Y.C., Mar. 13, 1931; children from previous marriage: Jeffrey Stuart, Alison Rachel; m. Laura Klabin, 1990; stepchildren: Alexander Matthew, Samantha Merrill. AB, Dartmouth Coll., 1952; MD, Tufts U., 1956. NIH fellow in research in ophthalmology N.Y. U., 1958-59, researcher in ophthalmology, 1961-62; asst. prof. N.Y. U. (Med. Sch.), 1965-68; resident in ophthalmology Bellevue Hosp., N.Y.C., 1962-64; mem. faculty Tufts U. Med. Sch., 1968—, prof. ophthalmology, 1974-91; sr. surgeon New Eng. Med. Center Hosp., Boston, 1973-91; rsch. prof. Tufts U. Med. Sch., 1991—2002, prof. ophthalmology emeritus, 2002—. Assoc. editor Ophthalmic Lit., 1967-85; mem. editl. bd. Investigative Ophthalmology and Vision Sci., 1978-82, Survey of Ophthalmology, 1970-79, Am. Jour. Ophthalmology, 1985-91, Ophthalmic Surgery, 1985-95, Cornea Jour., 1989-98; contbr. articles to profl. jours. Served to capt. M.C. AUS, 1959-61. Recipient William Warner Hoppin award N.Y. Acad. Medicine; Alcon Rsch. Inst. award, 1991; NIH fellow, 1958-59, 64-65; Nat. Eye Inst. grantee. Fellow: Royal Coll. Ophthalmologists; mem.: Chaine des Rotisseur, Conferie des Chevaliers du Tastevin, Ocular Microbiology Immunology Group (pres. 1990—91, Thygeson lecture 2001), Mass. Ophthalmology Soc. (sec. 1974—76), Castroviejo Soc. (exec. sec., treas. 1979—87, v.p. 1987—89, pres. 1989—91, Castroviejo Corneal medalist 1997), Assn. Rsch. in Vision and Ophthalmology (trustee 1981—86, v.p. 1986), Am. Acad. Ophthalmology (bd. councillors 1981—83, honor award 1979, sr. honor award 1990), Internat. Wine and Food Soc., Phi Beta Kappa. Jewish. Office: 1244 Boylston St Chestnut Hill MA 02467-2116 E-mail: julebaum@massmed.org.

BAUM, KENNETH FRANCIS, medical educator, physician; b. Dyersville, Iowa, July 25, 1950; s. F. Gerald and Clarabelle (Loes) B.; m. Patti Jo Thureen, June 17, 1978; children: Alexander, Christina. BS, St. John's U., Collegeville, Minn., 1972; MS, U. N.D., 1975, MB, 1977; MD, U. Pa., 1979. Diplomate Nat. Bd. Med. Examiners, Am. Bd. Internal Medicine (infectious diseases). Intern U. Wis. Hosp., Madison, 1979-80, resident in internal medicine, 1980-82; fellow in infectious diseases U. Colo. Health Sci. Ctr., Denver, 1984-87, instr. divsn. infectious diseases, dept. medicine, 1987-89, asst. prof. divsn. infectious diseases, dept. medicine, 1989-97, dir. Sexually Transmitted Diseases Clinic, 1991-92, assoc. clin. prof., 1997—. Clin. investigator MRC Sickle Cell Unit, U. W.I., Kingston, Jamaica, 1982-83; staff Riverside Hosp., Wisconsin Rapids, Wis., 1984, Univ. Hosp., Denver, 1987—, Denver VA Med. Ctr., 1989—; med. dir. Antero Healthplans, 1995-97, Cmty. Health Plan of the Rockies, 1997-99, Colo. Access, 2000-01; sr. med. cons. Digital Med., 2002—; prin. investigator Ctr. for Disease Control Hantavirus Treatment Task Force, State of Colo.; dir. Colo. Clin. Guidelines Collaborative, 1997—. Contbr. articles to profl. jour. Nat. Found. for Infectious Diseases and Eli Lilly Corp. fellowship, 1986-87. Mem. ACP, Infectious Disease Soc. Am., Am. Coll. Physician Exec. Office: Univ of Colo HSC Divsn Infectious Diseases 4200 E 9th Ave # B168 Denver CO 80220-3706

BAUM, KERRY ROBERT, retired military officer, director; b. LaGrande, Oreg., May 25, 1939; s. Guy Hiatt Baum and Niola (Anderson) Jones; m. Lynda Sue Christian, Dec. 18, 1964; children: Kerry Jr., Tatia D., Christian H., Buffy Jo, Patrick H., Britta Sue, Natalie A. BA in History, Brigham Young U., 1967; MBA in Mktg., Murray State U., 1978; postgrad., Webster Coll., St. Louis, 1979-80; MA in Nat. Security & Strategic Studies, U.S. Naval War Coll., 1986. Cert. bus. continuity planner Disaster Recovery Inst. Internat. Commd. 2d lt. U.S. Army, 1957, advanced through grades to col., 1990; mgr. emergency preparedness Brigham Young U., 1993—. Joint staff rep. LIVE OAK, 1986—90; U.S. rep. Maj. NATO Comdrs. Alert Conf., 1987—90. Author, editor: book NATO Alert Procedures for Joint Staff, 1988, Focal Point Procedures Manual, 1989. Mem., past pres. Utah Campus Safety Assn.; apptd. mem. Utah Seismic Safety Commn., 2001; bishop Mormon Ch., Hopkinsville, Ky., 1974—78, councilor, bishopric Newport, RI, 1985—86; bishop Mormon Ch. BYU 185th Ward, 1996—99. Decorated Bronze Star, Army Commendation medal, Air Force Commendation medal, Def. Superior Svc. medal; named Mem. of the Yr., Utah Emergency Mgmt. Assn., 2000. Mem.: Internat. Assn. Emergency Mgrs. (cert. emergency mgr.), Assn. Contingency Planners (treas. Utah chpt.), Res. Officers Assn. Home: 10938 N 5870 W Highland UT 84003-9487 E-mail: kerry_baum@byu.edu.

BAUM, LAURA, educator; b. NYC, Jan. 3, 1948; d. Morton and Selma (Wallman) Berdy Roblin; children: Alexander Klabin, Samantha Klabin; Stepchildren: Jeffrey Baum, Alison Baum Hook; m. Jules Baum, June 16, 1990. BS with distinction, Boston U., 1969, EdM, 1974. Cert. spl. edn. adminstrn., moderate spl. needs children elem. edn., instr. perceptually handicapped, Mass. Tchr. spl. edn. elementary, middle and high schs. Wellesley (Mass.) Pub. Schs., 1969—; chmn. spl. svcs. dept. Wellesley Middle Sch., 1974-77; adminstr. spl. edn. Dover (Mass.) Pub. Schs., 2000—01, Upham Elem. Sch., Wellesley, 2001—02, Sprague Elem. Sch., Wellesley, 2002—. Instr., supr. Lesley Coll., Cambridge, Mass., 1980-84, supr. spl. edn. student tchrs., 1980-84, instr., 1988-89, mentor Curry Coll., Milton, Mass., 1988; pvt. practice assessment, evaluation and diagnosis, Wellesley, 1969—; participant internship program Simmons Coll., 1992-96; spkr. in field; assoc. tchr. in edn. Wellesley Coll., 1993-94. Bd. dirs. Wellseley Cmty. Children's Ctr., 1979—; mem. children/youth com. Mass. Dept. Mental Health and Mental Retardation, 1979-81; chmn. mental retardation com. 1981-82, co-chmn. cmty. edn. com. 1982-84, bd. dirs., 1981-84; corr. sec. Wellesley Players, 1997-99; adminstr. spl. needs Dover (Mass.) Pub. Schs., 2000. Mem. AAUW (1st v.p. Wellesley chpt. 1978-79), NEA, Mass. Tchr.'s Assn., Wellesley Tchr.'s Assn., Coun. Exceptional Children. Avocations: cooking, travel, computers, photography. Home: 81 Maugus Ave Wellesley MA 02481-7614 Office: Wellesley Pub Sch 40 Kingsbury St Wellesley MA 02481-4831

BAUM, M(ARY) CAROLYN, occupational therapist; b. Chgo., Mar. 26, 1943; d. Gibson Henry and Nelle (Curry) Manville; 1 child, Kirstin Carol. BS, U. Kans., 1966; MA, Webster Coll., 1979; PhD, Washington U., 1993. Occupl. therapist U. Kans. Med. Ctr., 1966-67; staff occupl. therapist Rsch. Med. Ctr., Kansas City, Mo., 1967, dir. occupl. therapy, 1967-73, dir. phys. medicine and rehab., 1973-76; dir. occupl. therapy, clin. svcs. Washington U. Sch. Medicine, St. Louis, 1976—88. Dir. program in occupl. therapy Rehab. Inst. St. Louis; assoc. prof. occupl. therapy and neurology, 1988—; vis. prof. NYU, U. Mo., 1985—87; mem. adv. com. Nat. Ctr. Med. Rehab. Rsch. NIH; allied health rep. AMA Health Policy Agenda for Am. People; mem. com. on assessing rehab. sci. and engring. Inst. Medicine; bd. dirs. Rehab. Inst. St. Louis. Author: Understanding the Prospective Payment System: A Business Perspective, 1986, Occupational Therapy: Overcoming Human Performance Deficits, 1991, Occupational Therapy: Enabling Function and Well Being, 1997, Measuring Occupational Performance: Supporting Best Practice in Occupational Therapy, 2001, Occupation-Based Practice: Fostering Performance and Participation, 2001; contbg. author: Occupational Therapy, 1978, 83; editor Jour. OTJR; Occupation, Participation and Health; contbr. articles to profl. jours. Coord. St. Louis Ind. Living Coun., 1980-81; mem. nominating com. Greater Kansas City Health Sys. Agy.; vice-chmn. Village Ch. Accessibility Task Force, 1974-76; bd. dirs. Rehab. Inst. St. Louis. Named Employee of Yr., Rsch. Hosp., 1974, Kans. Occupl. Therapist of Yr., 1975, Outstanding Alumni Sch. Allied Health U. Kans., 1999. Fellow Am. Occupl. Therapy Assn. (chmn. stds. and ethics commn. 1973-77, nat. v.p. 1978-82, pres. 1982-83, pres. elect, 2003—, Eleanor Clarke Slagel Lectureship award 1980, award of Merit 1984); mem. Occupl. Therapy Certification Bd. (pres. 1986-93, pres.-elect 2003—), Mo. Occupl. Therapy Assn. (Occupl. Therapy Clinician of Yr. 1985), Mo. Assn. Rehab. Facilities (bd. dirs.), St. Louis Med. Rehab. Soc. (pres. 1987). Office: Program Occupll Therapy Washington U Sch Medicine 4444 Forest Park Ave Saint Louis MO 63108-2212 E-mail: baumc@msnotes.wustl.edu.

BAUM, MICHAEL LIN, lawyer; b. Clinton, Okla., Apr. 10, 1952; s. William Eldon and Patricia (Schumacher) B.; m. Colleen Margaret Condon, Apr. 6, 1991; children: Elizabeth, Alexandra, Kevin. BA summa cum laude, UCLA, 1982, JD, 1985. Bar: Calif. 1985, D.C. 1993, U.S. Dist. Ct. (ctrl. dist.) Calif. 1986, U.S. Dist. Ct. (ea. and no. dists.) Calif. 1989, U.S. Dist. Ct. (we. dist.) Mich. 1991, U.S. Dist. Ct. (no. dist.) Ohio 1993, U.S. Dist. Ct. (no. dist.) N.Y. 1996, U.S. Ct. Appeals (9th cir.) 1990, U.S. Ct. Appeals (4th cir.) 1996, U.S. Ct. Appeals (7th cir.) 1997, U.S. Supreme Ct. 1991. Assoc. Kananack, Murgatroyd, Baum & Hedlund,and predecessors, L.A., 1985-87; ptnr., shareholder Baum, Hedlund, Aristei, Guilford & Schiavo, L.A., 1987—. Mem. discovery and trial teams MDL 817 United Airlines 1989 aircrash at Sioux City, Iowa, Chgo.; mem. plaintiffs' steering com. MDL 891 Northwest Airlines 1990 aircrash at Detroit Met. Airport, Ill. State Ct. procs. for USAir 427 crash near Aliquippa, Pa., 1994, MDL 1041 USAir 1994 crash at Charlotte, N.C.; trial team for consolidated hemophilia-AIDS cases, New Orleans, 1999. Recipient Safety award, Nat. Air Disaster Found., 2002. Mem. State Bar Calif., D.C. Bar, Bar Assn. D.C., Consumer Attys. Calif., Consumer Attys. L.A. Office: Baum Hedlund Aristei Guilford & Schiavo 12100 Wilshire Blvd Ste 950 Los Angeles CA 90025-7107 E-mail: mbaum@baumhedlundlaw.com.

BAUM, PETER ALAN, lawyer; b. Jamaica, N.Y., Sept. 22, 1947; s. Morris and Elsa (Sturtz) B.; m. Barbara Hartman, Nov. 29, 1969; children: Benjamin, Lisa, Alexander. BA, Colgate U., 1969; JD, Syracuse U., 1972. Bar: N.Y. 1973, U.S. Dist. Ct. (no. dist.) N.Y. 1974. House counsel William Porter Real Estate Co., Syracuse, N.Y., 1972-73; pvt. practice Syracuse, 1973-82; ptnr. DiStefano and Baum, Syracuse, 1983-85, Baum and Woodard, Syracuse, 1985-90; prin. Peter A. Baum Law Offices, Chittenango, N.Y., 1990-96; ptnr. Iaconis, Iaconis and Baum, Chittenango, 1997—. Lectr. Onondaga C.C., Syracuse, 1976-79. Chmn. bd. dirs. Syracuse Area Landmark Theater, 1982-83, bd. dirs. Syracuse Opera Co., 1979-85. Mem. N.Y. State Bar Assn. (ho. of dels. 1992-93), Madison County Bar Assn. (pres. 1993), Onondaga County Bar Assn. (continuing edn. chmn. 1977-78), Onondaga Title Assn. Office: Iaconis Iaconis & Baum 282 Genesee St Chittenango NY 13037-1705

BAUM, PHYLLIS GARDNER, travel management consultant; b. Ashtabula, Ohio, Dec. 13, 1930; d. Charles Edward Schneider and Stella Elizabeth (Schaefer) Gardner; m. Kenneth Walter Baum, Oct. 21, 1948 (div. July 1971); children: Deidre Adair, Cynthia Gail; m. Dennis Carl Marquardt, Sept. 22, 1979 (dec. 1991). Grad. high sch., Cleve. Am. Soc. Travel Agents. Travel cons. Fredo Travel Svc., Ashland, Ohio, 1960-66; sales mgr. Travelmart, Willoughby, Ohio, 1966-68, br. mgr. Mentor, Ohio, 1966-68, Diners Fugazy Travel, Sun City, Ariz., 1968-69; travel cons. Jarrett's Travel Svc., Phoenix, 1969-72; sr. cons. Loyal Travel, Phoenix, 1972-74; co-mgr. Phil Carr Travel, Sun City, 1974-77; tour ops. mgr. ASL Travel, Phoenix, 1978-79; owner, mgr. Travel Temporaries, Glendale, Ariz., 1979-2000; ret. Cons. and lectr. in field. Adv. bd. mem. Small Bus. Devel. Ctr., Phoenix, 1986-2000. Mem. Pacific Asia Travel Assn. Ariz. (bd. dirs. 1986—), Ariz. Women in Travel, NAFE, Altrusa. Republican. Avocations: music, travel, tatting, knitting, horseback riding. Home and Office: Travel Temps 10249 N 45th Ave Glendale AZ 85302-1901

BAUM, RICHARD THEODORE, engineering executive; b. N.Y.C., Oct. 3, 1919; m. Jean Knapp, June 15, 1946 (dec. Sept. 1, 1994); children: Kathryn, Judith. BA, Columbia U., 1940, BS, 1941, MS, 1948. Registered profl. engr., N.Y., D.C., and 20 other states, Nat. Bur. Engring. Registration. Engr. Electric Boat Co., Groton, Conn., 1941-43; with Jaros, Baum & Bolles, N.Y.C., 1946—, ptnr., 1958-86, ptnr. emeritus, cons. to firm, 1986—. Mem. adv. coun., faculty of engring. and applied sci. Columbia U., N.Y.C., 1972—. 1st lt. USAAF, 1943-46. Egleston medalist Columbia U., 1985 Fellow ASME, ASHRAE, AAAS, Am. Cons. Engrs. Coun.; mem. NAE (mech. engring. peer com. 1991-93), NSPE, N.Y. Acad. Scis., Nat. Soc. Energy Engrs., NRC (chmn. bldg. rsch. bd. 1987-91), Am. Arbitration Assn. (panel arbitrators 1973—), Coun. on Tall Bldgs. and Urban Habitat (vice chmn. N.Am. chpt.), Univ. Club N.Y.C. Office: Jaros Baum & Bolles 80 Pine St New York NY 10005-1702

BAUM, RICHARD A. radiologist; b. Phila., Aug. 27, 1960; s. Stanley and Jeanne Baum; m. Cathe Chiaramonte; children: Zachary, Michael, Sophia. MD, Med. Coll. Pa., 1987. Diplomate Am. Bd. Radiology, 1993, cert. added qualification in interventional radiology Am. Bd. Radiology, 1995. Attending interventional radiologist Phila. Vets. Adminstrn. Med. Ctr., 1993—2001, Presbyn. Med. Ctr., Phila., 1996—2001, chief divsn. interventional radiology Brigham and Women's Hosp., Boston, 2001—. Editor: (textbook) Endoleaks and Endotension. Mem.: Soc. Interventional Radiology, Am. Coll. Radiology, Radiol. Soc. N.Am. Office: Brigham and Womens Hosp 75 Francis St Boston MA 02115 Office Fax: 617-277-8331. E-mail: rbaum@partners.org

BAUM, ROBERT M. religious studies educator, researcher; s. Myron C. and Beatrice S. Baum. BA, Wesleyan U., 1974; MA, Yale U., 1976, PhD, 1986. Asst. prof. history Ohio State U., Columbus, 1987—94; asst. prof. African studies Wesleyan Coll., Macon, Ga., 1995—97; resident fellow DuBois Inst. Harvard U., Cambridge, Mass., 1997—98; asst. prof. religious studies Iowa State U., Ames, 1998—2000, assoc. prof. religious studies, 2000—. Mellon fellow in history Bryn Mawr (Pa.) Coll., 1991—92; vis. asst. prof. history Kenyon Coll., Gambier, Ohio, 1994—95; dir. Ohio Humanities Coun. Workshop, Columbus, Ohio, 1994, Columbus, 95; mem. spkrs. bur. Humanities Iowa, Iowa City, 2002—; bd. dirs. West Africa Rsch. Assn. Author: Shriners of the Slave Trade, 1999; contbr. articles to profl. jours. Bd. dirs. Iowa Civil Libertieis Union, DesMoines, 2002—. Mem.: Am. Hist. Assn., Am. Acad. Religion (Best First Book in the History of Religions 2000), African Studies Assn. Office: Iowa State Univ 402 Catt Hall Ames IA 50011

BAUM, ROGER S. writer; b. Los Angeles, Calif., Mar. 21, 1938; s. Joslyn S. and Elizabeth Baum; m. Charlene S. Baum. Author: (novels) Lion of Oz and The Badge of Courage, 1997, Dorothy of Oz, 1990, Green Star of Oz, 2001, (hardcover short stories) SillyOZbul Trilogy, 1991—93, (short stories) Rewolf of Oz, 1998, Toto in Candy Land of Oz, 2002, Wizard of Oz and The Magic Merry Go Round, 2003, (novella) Longears and Tailspins Adventure, 1962, (musical) Lion of Oz, 2001. Schools/hospitals. Po 3 U.S. Navy, 1958—61. Achievements include Animated Musical - Lion of Oz/ Sony Wonder; Legends of Oz / CD Rom. E-mail: totototoofoz@cs.com.

BAUM, STANLEY, radiologist, educator; b. N.Y.C., Dec. 26, 1929; s. Herman and Fannie (Harris) B.; m. Jeanne Masch, June 29, 1958; children: Richard Arthur, Laura Dianne, Carol Lisa. BA, NYU, 1951; MD, U. Utrecht, Holland, 1957. Intern Kings County Hosp., N.Y.C., 1957-58; resident in radiology Grad. Hosp., U. Pa., Phila., 1958-61; trainee Nat. Cancer Inst., Bethesda, Md., 1958-61; fellow cardiovascular radiology Stanford (Calif.) U., 1961-62; instr. radiology U. Pa., Phila., 1962-63, asst. prof., 1963-66, assoc. prof., 1966-70, prof., 1970—, Eugene P. Pendergrass prof. radiology, 1977-96, chmn. dept. radiology, 1975-96; chmn. med. bd. Hosp. of U. Pa., 1983-86; chief cardiovascular radiology Mass. Gen. Hosp., Boston, 1971-75; prof. radiology Harvard Med. Sch., Boston, 1971-75. Cons. Radiation Effects Research Found., Hiroshima, Japan, 1975-76; mem. cardiovasc. rev. bd. Am. Heart Assn., 1970-90. Editorial bd.: Investigative Radiology, 1970-80, New Eng. Jour. Medicine, 1975-76, Radiology, 1975-85, Gastrointestinal Radiology, 1975-79, Jour. Continuing Edn., 1978-80, Postgrad. Radiology, 1980-90; editor-in-chief: Acad. Radiology, 2000—. Fellow Am. Coll. Radiology, Am. Coll. Cardiology; mem. Inst. Medicine Nat. Acad. Sci., Soc. Cardiovascular Radiology (pres. 1974-76), Soc. Chmn. Acad. Radiology Depts. (pres. elect 1985-86, pres. 1986), Acad. Radiol. Rsch. (pres. 1997-2000). Home: 401 W Moreland Ave Philadelphia PA 19118-4207 Office: U Pa 3400 Spruce St Philadelphia PA 19104-4206

BAUM, STANLEY DAVID, lawyer; b. Bklyn., Feb. 22, 1954; s. Irwin and Muriel A. (Margolis) B.; m. Ilyne Rhona Fried, June 9, 1979; children: Andrew, Miranda. BS, U. Pa., 1976, JD, 1980; LLM, NYU, 1984. Bar: N.Y. 1981, U.S. Tax Ct. 1993. Lawyer Carter, Ledyard & Milburn, N.Y.C., 1988-98; of counsel Swidler, Berlin, Shereff, Friedman, LLP, N.Y.C., 1998—. Contbr. articles to profl. jours. Mem. N.Y. State Bar Assn. (com. on employee benefits tax sect.). E-mail: sdbaum@swidlaw.com.

BAUM, STANLEY M. lawyer; b. Bronx, N.Y., Mar. 6, 1944; s. Abraham S. and Mae (Weiner) B.; m. Louise Rae Iteld, Aug. 30, 1970; children: Rachel Jennifer, Lauren Amy. BS in Commerce, Rider Coll., 1966; JD summa cum laude, John Marshall Law Sch., 1969. Bar: Ga. 1970, U.S. Dist. Ct. (no. dist.) Ga. 1970, U.S. Ct. Appeals (5th cir.) 1970, U.S. Supreme Ct. 1973, U.S. Ct. Appeals (11th cir.) 1981, U.S. Tax Ct. 1983. Law clk. to U.S. atty. No. Dist. Ga., 1969; legal aide Ga. Gen. Assembly, 1970-71; asst. U.S. atty. No. Dist. Ga., 1971-74; ptnr. Bates & Baum, 1974—. Pres. Congregation Shearith Israel, 1976-78; chmn. Rep. Party of DeKalb County, 1983-85, 4th Dist. Rep. Party, 1985-89; pres. Resurgens, Atlanta, 1987-88, Electoral Coll., 1988; del. Rep. Nat. Conv., 1992; mem. DeKalb County Bd. Ethics, 1991—, chair, 1993-95, 2001; mem. Met. Atlanta Rapid Transit Authority Bd. Ethics, 1993—. Mem. ABA (criminal justice sect. white collar com.), Ga. Bar Assn., Atlanta Bar Assn. (chmn. criminal law sect. 1985-86, bd. dirs. 1986-87), Fed. Bar Assn. (pres. Atlanta chpt. 1976-77, nat. council 1974-77), DeKalb Bar Assn. (pres. 1989-90), Am. Judicature Soc., Nat. Dist. Attys. Assn. Clubs: Atlanta Lawyers. Lodge: Masons. Office: 3151 Maple Dr NE Atlanta GA 30305-2503

BAUM, STEPHEN L. utilities company executive; Grad., Harvard U.; JD, U. Va. Sr. v.p., gen. counsel N.Y. Power Authority, 1982-85; various positions with SDG&E, 1985-93, exec. v.p., 1993-96; pres., CEO Enova Corp., 1996-97, chmn., CEO, 1998; vice-chmn., pres., CEO Sempra Energy, San Diego, 1998—2000, chmn., pres., CEO, 2000—. Bd. dirs. Computer Sci. Corp., mem. audit com. Capt. USMC, 1966—69. Office: Sempra Energy 101 Ash St San Diego CA 92101-3017

BAUM, WILLIAM ALVIN, astronomer, educator; b. Toledo, Jan. 18, 1924; s. Earle Fayette and Mable (Teachout) B.; m. Ester Bru, June 27, 1961. BA summa cum laude, U. Rochester, 1943; PhD magna cum laude, Calif. Inst. Tech., 1950. Physicist U.S. Naval Research Lab., Washington, 1946 49; astronomer Mt. Wilson and Palomar observatories, Pasadena, Calif., 1950-65; dir. Planetary Research Center, Lowell Obs., Flagstaff, Ariz., 1965-90; with astronomy dept. U. Wash., Seattle, 1990—. Adj. prof. astronomy Ohio State U., 1969-91; adj. prof. physics No. Ariz. U., 1973-91; rsch. prof. astronomy U. Wash., Seattle, 1990-97, prof. emeritus, 1997—; cons. physics, astronomy, optics; cons. U.S. Army Research Office, Durham, N.C., 1967-74; vis. prof. Am. Astronomy Soc., 1961-98; adv. com. Nat. Acad. Sci., 19 58-67; mem. optical instrumentation panel adv. Air Force, 1967-76; coms. and panels NSF and NASA Office Space Scis., 1967-91; mem. NASA Viking Orbiter Imaging Team, 1970-79, Hubble Space Telescope Camera Team, 1977-96. *In 1946 Baum was a member of the team that made the very first successful astrophysical observation above the earth's atmosphere by installing an ultraviolet spectrograph in a German V2 rocket. Later, he designed and used a photoelectric "Photon counter" at Palomar Observatory to extend reliable photometry of stars and galaxies about 4 magnitudes fainter than previously possible. Over the years, Baum's publications have dealt with topics ranging from planetary science to cosmology. In the 1990s, he used the Hubble Space Telescope to investigate globular star clusters, the cosmetic distance scale, and of the universe.* Contbr. articles to tech. publs. Served to lt., jr. grade USNR, 1943-46. Guggenheim fellow, 1960-61; Asteroid 4174 named Billbaum, 1990. Mem. Am. Astron. Soc. (chmn. div. planetary scis. 1976-77), Royal Astron. Soc., Astron. Soc. Pacific, Internat. Astron. Union, Phi Beta Kappa, Sigma Xi, Theta Delta Chi. Achievements

include asteroid 4175 named "Billbaum" in his honor, 1990. Home: 2124 NE Park Rd Seattle WA 98105-2422 Office: U Wash Dept Astronomy Seattle WA 98195-0001 E-mail: baum@astro.washington.edu.

BAUM, WILLIAM WAKEFIELD CARDINAL, archbishop emeritus; b. Dallas, Nov. 21, 1926; s. Harold E. and Mary Leona (Hayes) Baum. Student, Kenrick Sem., St. Louis, 1947—51, U. St. Thomas Aquinas, Rome, 1956—58, STD, 1958; STL, Muhlenberg Coll., Allentown, Pa., 1957, DD, 1967; LLD, Georgetown U., St. John's U., Bklyn. Ordained priest Roman Cath. Ch., 1951. Assoc. pastor St. Aloysius Parish, Kansas City, Mo., 1951—56; adminstr. St. Cyril's Parish, Sugar Creek, Mo., 1960—61; assoc. pastor St. Therese's Parish, Kansas City, Mo., 1961—64, St. Peter's Parish, Kansas City, Mo., 1967—68; pastor St. James Parish, Kansas City, 1968—70; chancellor Diocese Kansas City-St. Joseph, 1967—70; bishop of Springfield-Cape Girardeau, Mo., 1970—73; archbishop of Washington, 1973—80; elevated to cardinal Roman Cath. Ch., 1976; prefect Sacred Congregation for Cath. Edn., Rome, 1980—90; grand penitentiary cardinal Apostolic Penitentiary, Rome, 1990—2001. From instr. to prof. Avila Coll., Kansas City, Mo., 1954—56, Kansas City, 1958—63; Hon. chaplain of The Pope, 1961, 68; 1st exec. dir. Bishops' Commn. Ecumenical and Inter-Religious Affairs, 1964—67, joint working group; reps. Cath. Ch. and World Coun. Chs., 1965—69, Cath. Ch. and Lutheran World Fedn., 1965—66; active Vatican's Congregations Cath. Edn., Doctrine of Faith and Secretariat for Non Christians, Bishop's Welfare Emergency Relief Com., Mixed Commn. Author: The Teaching of Cardinal Cajetan on the Sacrifice of the Mass, 1958, Considerations Toward the Theology on the Presbyterate, 1961. Trustee, chancellor Cath. U. Am.; chmn. bd. trustees Nat. Shrine Immaculate Conception. Mem.: Nat. Conf. Cath. Bishops (adminstrv. com.). Roman Catholic. Address: Via Rusticucci 13 Rusticucci 13 00193 Rome Italy*

BAUMAN, DALE ELTON, nutritional biochemistry educator; b. Detroit, Dec. 26, 1942; s. Elton Blaine and Waneta Mary (Taylor) B.; m. L. Marie Vinande, Aug. 28, 1965; children: Rebecca, Todd, Jeffrey. BS, Mich. State U., 1964, MS, 1968; PhD, U. Ill., 1969. Asst. prof., assoc. prof. U. Ill.-Urbana, 1969-78; vis. prof. Mich. State U., East Lansing, 1978; assoc. prof., then prof. Cornell U., Ithaca, N.Y., 1979—, Liberty Hyde Bailey prof., 1987. Chmn. NAS/NRC Bd. Agr., 1990-97. Contbr. articles to profl. jours. Leader and scoutmaster Boy Scouts Am., Mich., N.Y., 1970-83. Recipient N.Y. Farmers award, 1983, Alexander von Humboldt award, 1985, USDA Superior Svc. award, 1986, U. Ill. Alumni award, 1995, Cornell Alumni Faculty award, 2000, Disting. Scientist, U.S. Libr. of Congress, 2001, Outstanding Alumni award Mich. State U., 2003. Mem. NAS, Am. Dairy Sci. Assn. (Nat. Student award 1967, Nutrition Rsch. award 1982, Biotech. award 1987, Physiology Rsch. award 1994), Am. Soc. Animal Sci. (Young Scientist award 1977, Growth Biology award 1996, Fellow Rsch. award 1999), Am. Soc. Nutritional Sci. (pres-elect 2002, pres. 2003), Coun. Agr. Sci. Tech. (Black award 1995). Methodist. Home: 2 Eagleshead Rd Ithaca NY 14850-9659 Office: Cornell U 262 Morrison Hall Ithaca NY 14853-4801 E-mail: debb@cornell.edu.

BAUMAN, EARL WILLIAM, accountant, government official; b. Jan. 30, 1916; s. William A. and Gracia M. (Jones) Bauman; m. Margaret E. Blackman, Oct. 21, 1940 (dec. 1984); children: Carol Ann Bauman Ammerman(dec.), Earl William Jr.; m. Jessie C. Morgan, Dec. 23, 1990. BS with honors, U. Wyo., 1938; postgrad., Northwestern U., 1938—39. Acct. Haselmire, Cordle Co., Casper, Wyo., 1939—42; asst. dir. fin. VA, Chgo., 1946—49, chief acctg. group Washington, 1949—52; supr. sys. acctg. GAO, Washington, 1952—55, supervising auditor, 1955—58; dir. fin., asst. dir. Directorate Acctg. and Fin. Policy, Office Asst. Sec. Def., Washington, 1958—63; tech. asst. to comdr. AF Acctg. and Fin. Ctr., Denver, 1963—73; mem. investigations staff Ho. of Reps. Appropriations Com., 1953—54; prof. acctg. Benjamin Franklin U., 1960—63; mem. exec. coun. Army Finance, 1963—64; dir. Real Estate Investment Corp., 1962—64; sr. ptnr. EMB Enterprises, 1973—; chmn. Acctg. Careers Coun. Colo., 1969—71. Chmn. Aurora Citizens Adv. Budget Com., 1975—76; chmn. fin. and taxation com. Denver Met. Study, 1976—78. Served with AUS, 1942—46, col. Res., now ret. Mem.: AICPA, Nat. Assn. Ret. Fed. Employees (Aurora 1072 pres. 1986—87), Denver Am. Soc. Mil. Comptrollers (pres. 1968—69), Am. Soc. Mil. Comptrollers, Army Fin. Assn., Fed. Govt. Accts. Assn. (nat. v.p. 1972—73, pres. Denver 1973—74), Wyo. Assn. CPAs, Citizens Band Radio Assn. (pres. 1963), Columbine Sertoma Club (pres. 1975—76), Phi Kappa Phi, Beta Alpha Psi, Alpha Kappa Psi. Avocations: photography, tennis, collector cars. Home: 536 Newark Ct Aurora CO 80010-4728

BAUMAN, FRANK ANTHONY, lawyer; b. Portland, Oreg., June 10, 1921; s. Frank Anthony and Josephine Louise (Carolan) Bauman; m. Mildred Inez Packer, Sept. 9, 1950 (dec. June 1997); children: Barbara Ann, Todd Anthony, Patricia Jean; m. Jane Carter, Aug. 15, 1998 (div. July 29, 2003); m. Barbara Baumen Tyran. Student in Japanese, U.S. Naval Sch. U. Colo., 1943-44; AB, Stanford U., 1944; JD, Yale U., 1949; postgrad., U. London, 1951-52. Bar: Oreg. 1950, U.S. Dist. Ct. Oreg. 1950. Assoc. Wilbur Beckett Oppenheimer Mautz & Souther, Portland, 1950-51; pvt. practice Portland, 1952-55, 68-71, 1978-91; ptnr. Veatch Bauman Lovett, Portland, 1955-63, Keane Haessler Bauman & Harper, Portland, 1963-68; rep. UN, Australia, 1971-76, 1971—76, 1971-73. Property advisor Frank M. Packer Trust, Dallas, 1971—; adj. prof. internat. law Lewis and Clark Sch. Law, Portland, 1979—80; advisor Lillian Bauman Fund, Portland, 1985—; co-trustee Mildred P. Bauman Trust, Portland, 1997—. Past trustee, pres. World Affairs Coun., Oreg., 1954—; past chmn. Portland Com. Fgn. Rels., 1978—; bd. dirs., mem. exec. com. English Speaking Union U.S., N.Y.C., 1997—; bd. dirs., past pres. English Speaking Union, Portland, 1992—. Recipient World Peace award, Assembly of the Bahia's, 1985, MacNaughton Civil Liberties award, ACLU, 1998. Mem.: ABA, UN Assn. U.S., UN Assn. Oreg., Internat. Law Assn. (Am. br.), Am. Soc. Internat. Law (patron), Yale Club N.Y.C., Arlington Club, Univ. Club (past pres. scholarship found.), Masons (past master). Democrat. Christian Scientist. Office: Ladd Carriage Ho 1331 SW Broadway Portland OR 97201

BAUMAN, JERRY L. pharmacy researcher, educator; b. Rutland, Ill., Aug. 15, 1953; s. Ronald H. and Wilma J. Bauman; m. Judith M. Hicks, July 26, 1975; children: Gregory L., Tracy J., Kevin M. BS in Pharmacy, U. of Ill., Chgo., 1976. Lic. pharmacotherapy specialist with added qualifications in cardiology Bd. of Pharm. Specialties. Prof. dept. pharmacy practice and medicine, sect. cardiology U. of Ill., 1989—. Head dept. of pharmacy practice U. of Ill., Coll. of Pharmacy, Chgo., 1997—. Named Disting. Practitioner, Nat. Acad. of Practice, 1996. Fellow: Am. Coll. of Cardiology, Am. Coll. of Clin. Pharmacy (sec., mem. bd. of regents and pres. 1985—97, Russell Miller award for sustained rsch. 1994). Achievements include research in side effects of antiarrhythmic drugs and helped to define the clinical profile of drug-induced torsade de pointes; electrophysiology of cocaine with implications of mechanisms of arrhythmic death and treatments for cocaine-induced arrhythmias; development of clinical pharmacy (pharmacotherapy) as a specialized discipline within pharmacy; training program in cardiovascular drug research for clinical pharmacists; one of first clinical pharmacy practices in cardiology with emphasis in the treatment of arrhythmias. Office: U Ill 833 Wood St Chicago IL 60612 Office Fax: 312-996-0379. E-mail: jbauman@uic.edu.

BAUMAN, JOHN ANDREW, law educator; b. 1921; BSL, U. Minn., 1942, LLB, 1947; JSD, Columbia U., 1958. Bar: Wis. 1947, Minn. 1948. Assoc. prof. U. N. Mex., 1947—54; spl. fellow Columbia U., 1950—51; assoc. prof. Ind. U., 1954—59, prof., 1959—60, UCLA, 1960—91, prof. emeritus, 1991; exec. dir. Assn. Am. Law Schs., Washington, 1980—83. Author (with York): Cases and Materials on Remedies, 1967, 5th edit., 1991. Mem.: Order of Coif (sec.-treas. 1983—92). Office: UCLA Sch Law 405 Hilgard Ave Los Angeles CA 90095-9000

BAUMAN, JOHN DUANE, lawyer; b. Kaskaskia, Ill., Aug. 22, 1930; s. Louis Wells and Veronica Genevieve (Schmerbauch) B.; m. Avis Crysella Moore, Sept. 15, 1956; children: Mark Duane, Thomas Jon, Jeffery Paul. BA, S.E. Mo. U., 1952; JD, Washington U., St. Louis, 1957. Bar: Mo. 1957, Ill. 1957. Assoc. Baker, Kagy & Wagner, East Saint Louis, Ill., 1957-62; ptnr. Wagner, Bertrand, Bauman & Schmieder, Belleville, Ill., 1962-86, Hinshaw & Culbertson, Chgo. and Belleville, 1986—. Bd. dirs. Breeders Cup/Nat. Thoroughbred Racing Assn. Pres. Ill. Thoroughbred Breeders and Owners Found., 2001—03; gen. counsel Okaw Valley coun. Boy Scouts Am., 1980—90. With U.S. Army, 1952—54. Mem. ABA, Ill. Bar Assn., Internat. Assn. Ins. Counsel (state membership chmn.), Assn. of Def. Trial Counsel (pres. 1975-76), St. Clair County Bar Assn. (pres. 1972-73), Horsemen's Benevolent and Protective Assn. (v.p. 1989-98), Ill. Thoroughbred Breeders and Owners Found. (bd. dirs. 1999-2002, v.p. 1996-99, sec.-treas. 1999-2000, pres. 2000—), Bradenton Country Club, St. Clair Country Club (pres. 1972-74), Paducah Country Club, Elks, Mo. Athletic Club (emeritus 1998). Roman Catholic. Avocations: horse racing, golf. Office: Hinshaw & Culbertson PO Box 509 521 W Main St Belleville IL 62220-1533 E-mail: jb222555@aol.com.

BAUMAN, JOHN E., JR., chemistry educator; b. Kalamazoo, Jan. 18, 1933; s. John E. and Teresa A. (Wauchek) B.; m. Barbara Curry, June 6, 1964; children— John, Catherine, Amy BS, U. Mich., 1955, MS, 1960, PhD, 1962. Chemist Midwest Research Inst., Kansas City, Mo., 1955-58; research assoc. U. Mich., Ann Arbor, 1958-61; prof. chemistry U. Mo., Columbia, 1961-97, prof. emeritus, 1997—. Active Mo. Symphony Soc. Recipient Faculty Alumni award, 1969, Amoco Teaching award, 1975, Purple Chalk award, 1980, all U. Mo. Mem. Am. Chem. Soc. (nat. lectr.), Mo. Acad. Sci., U. Mo. Retirees Assn. (pres. 2000—), Kiwanis, Sigma Xi, Alpha Chi Sigma. Roman Catholic. Home: 3703 S Woods Edge Rd Columbia MO 65203-6607 Office: Univ Mo 125 Chemistry Building Columbia MO 65211-7600 E-mail: baumanj@missouri.edu.

BAUMAN, KAY A. physician; b. Nov. 25, 1942; MPH, Tulane U., 1967; MD, U. Mich., 1973. Prof. U. Hawaii Sch. Medicine, Honolulu, 1992—; med. dir. Dept. Pub. Safety, Honolulu, 2002—. Office: Rm 407 919 Ala Moana Blvd Honolulu HI 96814 E-mail: Kay_Bauman@exec.state.hi.us.

BAUMAN, LAURIE JULIA, sociologist, researcher; b. Rockville Center, N.Y., May 18, 1949; d. Maurice Joseph and Madelon Joan (Broz) Bauman; m. Richard Henry Pereira Mendes, Mar. 5, 1983. BA in Polit. Sci., CUNY, 1970; MA in Sociology, Columbia U., 1975, MPhil in Sociology, 1981, PhD in Sociology, 1984. Rsch. asst., field dir. Bur. Applied Social Rsch. Columbia U., N.Y.C., 1970-75, rsch. staff assoc. Ctr. for Social Scis., 1975-77, rsch. staff assoc. grad. sch. bus., 1977-85; rsch. assoc. Meml. Sloan Kettering Cancer Ctr., N.Y.C., 1982-86; asst. prof. Albert Einstein Coll. Medicine, Bronx, 1986-91, assoc. prof., 1991-95, prof. pediat., 1996—, co-dir. Preventive Intervention Rsch. Ctr., 1986—. Assoc. editor Jour. Devel. and Behavioral Pediat., 1992-96; contbr. articles to profl. jours. Recipient Lela Rowland Prevention award Nat. Mental Health Assn., 1992, Robert Wood Johnson Investigator award, 2000. Fellow N.Y. Acad. Medicine; mem. Am. Assn. Pub. Opinion Rsch. (bd. dirs. pubs. 1993-95), Am. Sociol. Assn. Avocations: needlepoint, bird watching. Office: Albert Einstein Coll of Med PIRC NR 7 South 21 1300 Morris Park Ave Bronx NY 10461-1926 E-mail: bauman@aecom.yu.edu.

BAUMAN, M. GARRETT, English educator; b. Paterson, N.J., Aug. 7, 1948; s. M. Garrett and Dorothy Otley Bauman; m. Carol Nobles, June 3, 1978; children: Cynthia J., Diana M., Amy E., Jeremy N. BA, Upsala Coll., 1969; MA, Binghamton U., 1971. Prof. English Monroe C.C., Rochester, N.Y., 1971—. Author: Ideas and Details, 1993, 1995, 1998, 2000, 2003; author, editor: The Shape of Ideas, 1995; contbr. articles to mags., newspapers, jours. Recipient Leavy award Freedom's Found., 1988, Creative Nonfiction award N.Y. Found. for Arts, 1995, Saltonstall Found., 1997, N.Y. State Coun. on the Arts, 1999, New Letters Nat. award, 2000. Avocations: nature studies, travel, tennis. Office: Monroe CC 1000 E Henrietta Rd Rochester NY 14623-5701 E-mail: garrettbauman@cs.com.

BAUMAN, MARGARET ESTELLE LANG, pediatric neurologist; b. New Haven, Aug. 6, 1938; d. Otto John and Margaret Pauline (Roney) Lang; m. Roger Alan Bauman, May 11, 1968; children: Karen Lang, Margaret Sprague, David Westcott. AB, Smith Coll., 1960; MD, Med. Coll. Pa., 1965. Diplomate Am. Bd. Pediat., Am. Bd. Psychiatry & Neurology. Intern U. Md. Hosp., Balt., 1965-66, resident in neurology, 1968-69; resident in pediat. Johns Hopkins U. Hosp., Balt., 1966-68; fellow in child neurology Mass. Gen. Hosp., Boston, 1969-71; instr. neurology Mass Gen. Hosp., Boston, 1971-81, asst. prof. neurology, 1981-96; assoc. prof. neurology Mass. Gen. Hosp., Boston, 1996—, asst. neurologist, 1977—, asst. pediatrician, 1986-99, assoc. pediatrician, 1999—, med. dir. Ladders at MGH-Riverside, 1997-2000, dir. Ladders at MGH-Spaulding, 2000—; staff pediatrician Eunice Kennedy Shriver Ctr. Hosp., Waltham, Mass., 1975-2000. Med. dir. pediat. Braintree (Mass.) Rehab. Hosp., 1995-96; pediat. neurologist, dir. Learning and Devel. Disabilities Evaluation and Rehab. Svc. Program (Ladders)/Youville Hosp., Cambridge, 1990-95; pediat. neurologist in charge of seizure clinic Paul A Dever State Sch., Taunton, Mass., 1977-79; instr. neurology Harvard Med. Sch., Boston, 1973-85, asst. prof. 1985-96, assoc. prof. neurology, 1996—; adj. prof. dept. psychology Northeastern U., Boston, 1980-93; adj. prof. Mass. Gen. Hosp. Inst. Allied Health Professions, 1991-95; sr. physician Walter E. Fernald State Sch., Waltham, Mass., 1971-88, dir. pediat. tng., 1973-75, pediat. neurologist in charge of seizure clinic, 1979-94; dir. EEG lab. Cambridge Hosp., 1973-85; staff physician Cmty. Evaluation and Rehab. Ctr., Waltham, 1971-200, staff neurologist, CASA Colina Ctrs. for Rehab., Inc., Pomona, Calif., 2001—; clin. prof. pediat., U. Calif., Irvine, Calif.; med. adv. bd. May Inst., Chatham, 1991—, Rsch. for Rett Found., Linwood, N.J., 1991—, spl. rev. com., Mobile, Ala., 1994—; profl. adv. bd. New Eng. Ctr. for Autism, Southborough, Mass., 1990—, Am. Inst. for Neuro-Integrative Devel., Fairfield, Conn., 1994—; utilization rev. com. Eunice Kennedy Shriver Ctr., Waltham, 1976-77, chair audit com., 1977-78, human studies com., 1983-97; cons. and reviewer in field; med. dir. LADDERS Mass. Gen. Hosp., Riverside, 1997-2000; dir., Ladders at Mass. Gen. Hosp./Spaulding, Wellesley. Co-author: The Neurobiology of Autism, 1994; mem. editl. bd. Behavior Specialist, 1990—, Neurology Chronicle, 1990—. Bd. adv. Found. for Educating Children with Autism, Inc., Mt. Kisco, N.Y., 1994—, Higashi Sch., Lexington, Mass., 1991—. NIH fellow, 1969-73, Clin. and Rsch. fellow Mass. Gen. Hosp., 1970-74; Emma Willard Sch. scholar, 1954-56, Quota Club scholar, 1961, Med. Coll. Pa. scholar, 1963-65; grantee June Rockwell Levy Found., 1986-87, Natalie Z. Haar Found., 1987-95, Combined Jewish Philanthropies, 1986-87, Nancy Lurie Marks Found., 1987-95, NIH, 1990-98, Internat. Rett Syndrme Assn., 1993-94, NIMH, 1996-98, Stallone Fund for Austism Rsch., 1996—, NINDS, 2000—; recipient Excellence award Boston Inst. for the Devel. Infants and Parents, 1993, Ctr. for Outreach and Svcs. for the Autism Cmty., Inc. award, 1994, Enid Peschel Meml. Lectureship award, 1994, Cert. Appreciation Nat. Assn. Sch. Psychologists, 1995. Fellow Am. Acad. Pediat., Am. Acad. Neurol. and Psychiatry; mem. Am. Epilepsy Soc., Am. Acad. Neurology, Am. Soc. Autism, Am. Acad. Cerebral Palsy and Devel. Medicine, Internat. Rett Syndrome Assn. (profl. adv. bd. 1989—), Mass. Med. Soc., Child Neurology Soc. (membership com. 1978-79, archives and history com. 1989-90, fin. com. 1991-94, ethics com. 1995—), Boston Soc. for Psychiatry and Neurology, Soc. for Auditory Integration Tng. (adv. bd. 1995—), Neurobiol. Disorders Soc., Inc. (sci. bd. 1994—), Autism Soc. of Conn. (award 1997). Avocations: skiing, figure skating, opera. Office: Ladders at MGH/Spaulding 65 Walnut St Wellesley MA 02481

BAUMAN, MARILYN ADRIENNE, artist, educator; b. Bronx, N.Y., Jan. 21, 1941; d. Arthur Lionel Moldoff and Mildred Isabel Heyman; m. Donald Lee Bauman, Sept. 16, 1964; children: Andrew, Alisa, Mark. BS, SUNY, Cortland, 1962; MA, Pa. State U., 1965. Tchr. P.S. 100, Bronx, 1962-63; reporter Davis (Calif.) Enterprise, 1965-67; instr. U. Calif., Davis, 1965-67; pvt. tchr. art, Wilmington, Del., 1979—; instr. U. Del., Newark, 1988-91; dir. Del. Inst. Arts Edn., Wilmington, 1991-99; tchr., editor Violette de Mazia Trust, 2000—, dir. edn., 2002—. Author: (book) Edward L. Loper, Sr., The Prophet of Color, 1999; contbr. articles to profl. jours. Avocations: jogging, reading, hiking. E-mail: baumanart@comcast.net.

BAUMAN, MARK KEITH, historian, educator; b. Bklyn., Apr. 12, 1946; s. David and Marcia (Schack) Bauman; m. Sandra G. Woolf, July 1, 1967; children: Joel, Peter. BA, Wilkes Coll., 1967, Lehigh U., 1968; MA, U. Chgo., 1972; PhD, Emory U., 1975. Asst. prof. Clayton Jr. Coll., Morrow, Ga., 1975—76; prof. History Atlanta Met. Coll., 1976—2002; editor So. Jewish History, Ellenwood, Ga., 1998—. Adj. instr. DeKalb Coll., Decatur, Ga., 1976—84; gen. and juvenile mediator, 2002—. Author: Warren A. Candler, Conservative Amidst Change, 1981, Harry H. Epstein and the Rabbinate as Conduit for Change, 1994; editor: Quiet Voices: Southern Rabbis and Black Civil Rights, 1997. Exhibit historian 250 Yrs. of Ga. Jewish History, 1983; chair humanities team, catalog co-author Creating Community: 150 Yrs. of Atlanta Jewish History, 1994—95. Sp5 U.S. Army, 1969—72, Vietnam. Decorated Bronze Star for Svc.; named Bangel lectr., Coll. William and Mary, 1999; fellow, Am. Jewish Archives, 1999—2000. Mem.: Ga. Assn. Historians (pres. 1996—97, editor 1991—94, Disting. Svc. award 2002), So. Jewish Hist. Soc., Immigration and Ethnic Hist. Soc. (nominating com. 1998—2000). Home and Office: 2517 Hartford Dr Ellenwood GA 30294

BAUMAN, RICHARD ARNOLD, coast guard officer; b. Fitchburg, Mass., Aug. 16, 1924; s. Frederick Adams and Dorothy Arnold (Farnham) B.; m. Dorothy Helen Schmalz, June 5, 1948; children: Elizabeth Kay, Richard Arnold, Jr., Robert Arthur, William Lawrence. BS in Marine Transp., Mass. Maritime Acad., 1976, DPA (hon.), 1982; student, Armed Forces Staff Coll., Norfolk, Va., 1966-67, Nat. War Coll., Washington, 1974-75. Officer U.S. Mcht. Marine, 1944-57; commd. lt. USCG, 1957, advanced through grades to rear admiral, 1980, comdr. divsn. 12 squad one, 1967—68; liaison officer to comdr. in chief U.S. Atlantic Fleet, Norfolk, 1968-71; comdg. officer USCG Cutter Ingham, 1971-73; chief info. systems div. Coast Guard Hdqrs., Washington, 1973-74, chief port safety and law enforcement, 1975-78; ops. officer 9th Coast Guard Dist., Cleve., 1978-80; chief Office Navigation, Coast Guard Hdqrs., Washington, 1980-83; comdr. 1st Coast Guard Dist., Boston, 1983-85. U.S. commr. Permanent Internat. Assn. Navigation Congresses, 1980-84 Decorated Legion of Merit, Bronze Star Medal with combat V, Meritorious Service medal (2), Coast Guard Commendation medals (3), Joint Service Commendation medal, Navy Commendation medal with combat V, Vietnamese Gallantry Cross with Gold Star. Mem. Retired Officers Assn., Boston Marine Soc., Masons.

BAUMAN, ROBERT ALAN, humanities educator, consultant; b. Wooster, Ohio, May 25, 1964; s. Robert Benjamin and Betty Lou Bauman; m. Stephanie Kris San Miguel, Sept. 1, 1990; children: Robert Benjamin, Rachel Marie. BA in History, Biona U., 1986; MA in History, U. Calif., Santa Barbara, 1989, PhD, 1998. From historian to cons. History Assoc., Inc., Rockville, Md., 1989—96; instr. Washinton State U., Richland, 1997—2001, asst. prof., 2001—. Cons. in field. Co-author: Guide to the Historian Records of LA County, 1991, Stearns Wharf, 1994, The Evolution of Los Angeles County Government, 2003. Active Tri-Cities Lewis & Clark Bicentennial Coun., Richland, 1999—. Fellow, U. Calif., 1996; Rsch. grant, Lydon Baines Johnson Rsch. Found., 1996. Mem.: Am. Hist. Assn., Orgn. Am. Historians, Nat. Coun. on Pub. History. Office: Washington State Univ 2710 University Dr Richland WA 99352

BAUMAN, ROBERT PATTEN, diversified company executive; b. Cleve., Mar. 27, 1931; s. John Nevin and Lucille (Patten) B.; m. Patricia H. Jones, June 15, 1961; children: John, Elizabeth. BA, Ohio Wesleyan U., 1953; MBA, Harvard U., 1955. Mktg. adminstrn. Maxwell House div. Gen. Foods, White Plains, N.Y., 1958-65, gen. mgr. Post div., 1967, corp. v.p., 1968, exec. v.p., 1968, pres., dir. internat. ops., 1973; dir. Avco Corp., Greenwich, Conn., 1980-85, chmn., CEO, 1981-85; vice chmn. Textron Inc., Providence, R.I., 1985-86; chmn. Beecham PLC, 1986-89; CEO SmithKline Beecham Plc., Brentford, Eng., 1989-94; chmn. Brit. Aerospace PLC, Farnborough, Eng., 1994-98, BTR plc, London, 1998-99. Bd. dirs. Morgan Stanley, Russell Reynolds, Panorama, Invensys plc., Boleo.net. Author: Plants as Pets, 1982; co-author: From Promise to Performance, 1997. Mem.: Pine Valley Golf, Wisley Golf (Surrey, Eng.), Blind Brook (Port Chester, N.Y.), Webhannet Golf (Kennebunk, Maine). E-mail: RPBauman@aol.com.

BAUMAN, SANDRA SPIEGEL, nurse practitioner, mental health counselor; b. N.Y.C., June 30, 1949; d. Siegmund and Ruth (Josias) S.; m. H. Lee Bauman, Nov. 3, 1978 (div.); 1 child, Brandon Spiegel; m. P. McGrath, 1991. Student, Boston U., 1967-70; BSN, Adelphi U., 1971, postgrad., 1973-74; MS in Cmty. Counseling, Barry Coll., 1981; postgrad., Fla. Atlantic U./Fla. Internat, 1982—, Gestalt Inst., Miami, 1982—; PhD, Kennedy-Western U., 2000. Staff nurse educator obstetrics Albert Einstein Hosp., N.Y.C., 1971-72, head nurse newborn nurseries, 1973-74; asst. instr. maternity nursing St. Johns Riverside Hosp., 1972-73; head nurse obstetrics and nurseries, high risk nursery Mt. Sinai Hosp., Miami Beach, Fla., 1974-78; clin. nursing supr., divsn. pediatrics Jackson Meml. Hosp., Miami, 1978, coord. divsn. clin. edn., 1978-81; quality assurance coord. Maternal-Child Hosp. Ctr., 1979-81, perinatal coord., 1980-81, also core nursing mem. child protection team, 1979-81, asst. adminstr. ob-gyn., 1981-82; adminstr. Meadowbrook Med. Ctr., Inc., Danta, Fla., 1982—; pvt. practice psychotherapy, 1983—; asst. adminstr. nursing Miami Gen. Hosp., 1985, assoc. adminstr. pvt. care svcs., 1985—; contract nursing supr. Griswold Spl. Care, Miami, 2001—. Asst. prof. Sch. Nursing, Fla. Internat. U., North Miami, 1982-84; coord. child bearing and child rearing courses, 1982-84; mem. Fla. Bd. Nursing, 1979-85, vice chmn. 1981-82, chmn. 1982-85; CPR instr., 1978; dir. nursing HCA Grant Ctr. Hosp., Miami, 1986-89, asst. adminstr. Dr.'s Hosp., 1990-91, pvt. practice 19991—; cons. State Fla., 1992-95; interim dir. nursing Charter Hosp., Miami, 1995-96; surveyor Fla. Correctional Med. Authority, 1996; cons. State of Fla. Children's and Family Svcs., 2000. Contbr. articles to RN mag., Fla. Nursing News, Fla. Nurses Assn. Newsletter and Nursing Mgmt. Mem. mental health disaster team ARC, 2001—, vol. disaster response team, 2000—. Mem. ANA (regional editor 1980—), Fla. Nurses Assn., Fla. Soc. Nurse Execs., Fla. Nursing Adminstn. Assn., Fla. Hosp. Assn., Fla. Nursing Adminstrn. Soc., Sigma Theta Tau, Victim Advocate Com., bd., 2001. Office: 7800 SW 57th Ave Ste 203 South Miami FL 33143-5523

BAUMAN, SUSAN JOAN MAYER, mayor, lawyer; b. N.Y.C., Mar. 2, 1945; d. Curt H. J. and Carola (Rosenau) Mayer; m. Ellis A. Bauman, Dec. 29, 1968. BS, U. Wis., 1965, JD, MS, 1981; MS, U. Chgo., 1966. Bar: Wis. 1981, U.S. Dist. Ct. (we. dist.) Wis. 1981, U.S. Ct. Appeals (7th cir.) 1983, U.S. Dist. Ct. (ea. dist.) Wis. 1985. Tchr. Madison (Wis.) Pub. Sch., 1970-78; research asst. U. Wis. Law Sch., Madison, 1981; ptnr. Thomas, Parsons, Schaefer & Bauman, Madison, 1981-84; sole practice Madison, 1984-85; ptnr. Bauman & Massing, Madison, 1985-87; pvt. practice, Madison, 1987-97; mayor City of Madison, 1997—. Alderman Madison Common Coun., 1985-97, coun. pres., 1989-90; commr. equal opportunities com. City of Madison, 1985-89; mem. Econ. Devel. Commn., 1986-87, chmn. human resources com., 1987-90, mem. affirmative action com., 1988-93; mem. Cmty. Action Commn., 1988-97, pres., 1991-96; mem. Pub. Health Commn., 1991-97, Monona Terr. Conv. and Cmty. Ctr. Bd., 1993-97; pres. South Madison Health and Family Ctr., Inc., 1993-97; bd. visitors U. Wis. Coll. Letters and Scis., Madison, 1997—; mem. exec. com. Wis. Alliance Cities, 1996—; mem. adv. bd. U.S. Conf. Mayors, 1999—. Mem. Wis. Bar Assn., Dane County Bar Assn., Wis. Indsl. Rels. Alumni Assn. (pres. 1985-86), Madison Civics Club. Democrat. Avocations: knitting, reading, backpacking, cross-country skiing. Home: 430 W Main St #309 Madison WI 53703 Office: Office of the Mayor 210 Martin Luther King Blvd Madison WI 53709-0001 E-mail: sjmbauman@aol.com.

BAUMAN, WILLIAM ALLEN, pediatrician, educator, health systems consultant; b. N.Y.C., Nov. 23, 1923; s. Louis and Stella (Kraus) B.; m. Joan Carlsen, June 28, 1952; children: William Carlsen, Phillip Allen, Pamela Joan. Student, Harvard U., 1942-43, 46; MD, Columbia U., 1947; postgrad. in biostats., Sch. Pub. Health, 1960-63. Intern L.I. divsn. Kings County Hosp., Bklyn., 1947-48; resident The Babies Hosp., N.Y.C., 1948-50, practice medicine specializing in pediatrics, 1953-75; chief pediatric clinic Vanderbilt Clinic, N.Y.C., 1954-65; dir. med. data processing Presbyn. Hosp., N.Y.C., 1966-74, assoc. attending pediatrician, 1973-93, emeritus staff, 1994—. V.p. med. adminstrv. svcs. Group Health Inc., N.Y.C., 1974-77; chmn. bd. govs. Hillcrest Gen. Hosp.-Group Health Inc., 1975-79, attending pediatrician, 1975-79; sr. v.p. Health Svcs. Group Health Inc., 1977-79; v.p. med. affairs Danbury Hosp., Conn., 1979-90; mem. faculty dept. pediatrics Columbia U., 1952-73, assoc. clin. prof. pediatrics, 1973—; mem. med. bd. Maternity Ctr. Assn., 1969-95; chmn. faculty-student adv. bd. P&S Club, Coll. Physicians and Surgeons, Columbia U., 1970-90; chmn. com. on data processing N.Y. County Health Rev. Orgn., 1976-79; mem. exec. com. Babies Hosp. Alumni Assn., 1998—. Contbr. articles to profl. jours. Mem. data protection rev. bd. N.Y. State Dept. Health, 1993—. With M.C. USAF, 1951-52. Fellow Am. Coll. Med. Informatics, N.Y. Acad. Medicine; mem. Am. Acad. Pediatrics, N.Y. County Med. Soc., AMA, Med. Soc. State N.Y. (chmn. com. info. tech. in medicine 1967-93), Assn. Ambulatory Pediatrics, Assn. Computing Machinery, Soc. Computer Medicine (bd. dirs.), Bioengring. Inst., Am. Soc. Info. Scis., N.Y. Acad. Scis., N.Y. State Assn. Professions, Am. Assn. Med. Systems and Infomatics (pres. 1983). Home and Office: 667 Heritage Hls Somers NY 10589-1927 E-mail: drg@aol.com.

BAUMAN, WINFIELD SCOTT, finance educator; b. Dayton, Ohio, Nov. 7, 1930; s. Carl Louis and Lillian Elizabeth (Limpert) B.; m. Shirlee Ann Madden, June 20, 1953; children: Dale, Kent, Kimberly, Van. BBA, U. Mich., 1953,

MBA, 1954; D Bus. Adminstrn., Ind. U., 1961. Securities rsch. analyst Wells Fargo Bank, San Francisco, 1956-57; stock broker UBS Paine Webber Group, Palo Alto, Calif., 1957-58; asst. prof. fin. Coll. Bus. Adminstrn. U. Toledo, 1961-63, assoc. prof. fin., 1963-66; prof. fin. U. Oreg., Eugene, 1966-72, head dept. fin., 1969-72; prof. bus. adminstrn. Darden Grad. Sch. Bus. Adminstrn. U. Va., Charlottesville, 1972-81; prof. fin. No. Ill. U., DeKalb, 1981—2001, prof. emeritus, 2001—, chair dept. fin., 1981-90. Hon. vis. prof. City U. Bus. Sch., London, 1995. Contbr. articles to profl. jours., chpt. to Handbook of Modern Finance, 1997. Pres. Western Fin. Assn., 1971-72; nat. bd. dirs. Inst. Quantitative Rsch. in Fn., 1973-82; trustee, v.p., treas. Bedford (Mich.) Pub. Sch. Bd. Edn., 1963-66; chmn. endowment fund investment com. U. Oreg., 1969-72. Capt. USAF, 1954-56. Mem. Inst. CFA (exec. dir. 1972-78, Investment Analysts Soc. Chgo. (bd. dirs. 1996-2000, Rsch. Found. grantee), Midwest Fin. Assn. (bd. dirs. 1984-87, 95-98), Fin. Mgmt. Assn., Beta Gamma Sigma. Methodist. Avocations: boating, travel, swimming. E-mail: wsbauman@umich.edu.

BAUMANN, ARTHUR NICHOLAS, chemist, consultant; b. Bogota, N.J., Dec. 15, 1922; s. Arthur Rudolph and Theresa Baumann; m. Elizabeth Theresa McNelis, Feb. 15, 1947; children: Suzanne, Mark Steven. BS in Chemistry, Fla. So. Coll., 1951; postgrad., Fla. State U., 1951—52. Analytical technician Internat. Minerals and Chem., Mulberry, Fla., 1949—50, rsch. chemist, 1952—65, chief chemist tech. svcs. Bartow, Fla., 1966—70, supr. devel. lab., 1971—80, mgr. devel. agrl. ops. divsn. Mulberry, 1980—86, mgr. devel. engring. New Wales chem. ops.; cons. in chemistry Mulberry, 1986—. Tech. adv. com. Fla. Inst. Phosphate Rsch., 1985 ; vol. exec. Internat. Exec. Svc. Corp., Stamford, Conn., 1987—2000; mem. liaison com. Fertilizer Inst.; prin. investigator chem. projects Fla. Inst. Phosphate Rsch. Contbr. Mem.: AIChE, Am. Chem. Soc. (chair Fla. sect., councilor fertilizer and soil chemistry divsn. of governing coun.). Roman Catholic. Achievements include patents for 20 U.S. patents in field. Avocations: dancing, travel, photography. Home: 4275 Creekwoods Ln Mulberry FL 33860

BAUMANN, CAROL EDLER, retired political science educator; b. Plymouth, Wis., Aug. 11, 1932; d. Clarence Henry and Beulah Hanetta (Weinhold) E.; m. Richard Joseph Baumann, Feb. 28, 1959; children: Dawn Carol, Wendy Katherine. BA in Internat. Rels., U. Wis., 1954; PhD in Internat. Rels., London Sch. Econs./Polit. Sci., 1957. Chmn. Internat. Rels. Major U. Wis., Milw., 1962-79; dep. asst. sec. Bur. of Intelligence and Rsch./Dept. of State, Washington, 1979-81; prof. U. Wis., Milw., 1972-95, dir. internat. studies and programs, 1982-88, prof. emeritus, 1995—; dir. Inst. of World Affairs, Milw., 1964-97, dir. emeritus, 1997—. Internat. edn. adv. coun. U. Wis. Milw., 2000—. Author: Program Planning About World Affairs, 1991, The Diplomatic Kidnappings, 1973; editor: Europe in NATO: Deterrence, Defense, and Arms Control, 1987, Western Europe: What Path to Integration?, 1967. Active Gov.'s Commn. on the UN, 1964-79, 82-89; Dem. candidate 9th Congl. Dist., 1968; mem. World Affairs Coun. of Milw., 1964-75; bd. dirs. Wis. World Trade Ctr., 1987-2001, Wis. Dist. Export Coun., 1987—, Ea. Shores Libr. Sys., 1999—, Inst. World Affairs, U. Wis., Milw., 2000—. Recipient pub. svc. achievement award Common Cause, Wis., 1991; Marshall scholar, 1954-57. Mem. Coun. on Fgn. Rels., Fgn. Policy Assn. (bd. dirs. 1990—, editl. adv. com. 1977-79, 82-88), Nat. Coun. World Affairs Orgns. (pres. 1977-79, bd. dirs. 1992-96), UN Assn. of USA (bd. dirs. 1977-79, 82-89), Soc. for Citizen Edn. in world Affairs (pres. 1977-79), Phi Kappa Phi, Phi Beta Kappa. Democrat. Lutheran. Avocations: walking, swimming, reading, travel, writing fiction. Home: W6248 Lake Ellen Dr Cascade WI 53011-1322 E-mail: cbaumann@excel.net.

BAUMANN, CAROL KAY, clinical nurse specialist; b. Summersville, Mo., Dec. 12, 1946; d. Vern Underwood and Jean E. (Lay) Hines; children: Joell Christine, Richard Douglas. Diploma, Barnes Hosp., St. Louis, 1967; BS in Nursing, St. Louis U., 1981, MS in Nursing Rsch., 1989. Cert. oper. rm. nurse; cert. RN 1st asst.; cert. clin. nurse specialist. Staff nurse Barnes Hosp., St. Louis, 1967-68, head nurse neurosurgery, 1969-71; staff nurse St. John's Mercy Hosp., St. Louis, 1980-81, neurosurgery specialty nurse, 1981-85; surgery edn. coord. Mo. Bapt. Med. Ctr., St. Louis, 1985-90; asst. head nurse neuro/ophthalmology oper. rm. Barnes Hosp., St. Louis, 1990-92; clin. nurse specialist St. Louis U. Med. Ctr., 1992—2001; staff nurse Barnes-Jewish Hosp., 2002—. Speaker in field. Contbr. articles to profl. jours. Mem. ANA, Assn. Oper. Rm. Nurses, Am. Assn. Neurosci. Nurses (Gateway City chpt. 1988—, charter sec.-treas. 1988-89, pres. 1989-91), Am. Assn. Neurol. Surgeons (assoc.), Mo. Assn. RN First Assts., Mo. Nurses Assn., Congr. Neurol. Surgeons, Sigma Theta Tau. Home: 14515 Coeur Dalene Ct Chesterfield MO 63017-2401

BAUMANN, CHRISTOPHER ANTHONY, chemist, educator; b. Portland, Oreg., Dec. 22, 1955; s. Albert W. and Dorothy F. (Nudo) B.; m. Lisa Ahrens, July 13, 1985. BS, Oreg. State U., 1978; PhD, U. Fla., 1982. Postdoctoral fellow Ind. U., Bloomington, 1982-84; asst. prof. U. Scranton, Pa., 1984-89, assoc. prof., 1989-98, prof., 1998—. Mem. Am. Phys. Soc., Am. Chem. Soc. (grantee 1985, 87), Sigma Xi, Acacia, Phi Lambda Upsilon (moderator 1987-90). Office: U Scranton Dept Chemistry Scranton PA 18510

BAUMANN, DANIEL E. retired newspaper executive; b. Milw., Apr. 10, 1937; s. Herbert F. and Agnes V. (Byrne) B.; m. Karen R. Weinkauf, Apr. 29, 1961; children: James W., Jennifer R., Colin D. BJ, U. Wis., 1958, MA in Polit. Sci., Cert. in Russian Area Studies, U. Wis., 1962. Reporter South Milwaukee (Wis.) Voice Jour., 1958-59, East St. Louis (Ill.) Jour., 1959-60; pub. relations rep. Credit Union Nat. Assn., Washington, 1962-64; reporter Paddock Publs., Inc., Arlington Heights, Ill., 1964-66, mng. editor, 1966-68, exec. editor, 1968-70, editor and pub. Paddock Circle newspapers, 1970-75, v.p., editor, 1975-83, sr. v.p., gen. mgr., editor, 1983-86, pres., editor, 1986-90, dir., 1986—, pres., chief operating officer, 1990—2002, chmn., pub., 2002—, ret., 2002. Recipient William Alan White award U. Kans., 1976. Avocation: travel. Office: Paddock Publs Daily Herald 155 E Algonquin Rd Arlington Heights IL 60005-4617

BAUMANN, EDWARD ROBERT, environmental engineering educator; b. Rochester, N.Y., May 12, 1921; s. John Carl and Lillie Minnie (Roth) B.; m. Mary A. Massey, June 15, 1946; children: Betsy Louise, Philip Robert. BSCE, U. Mich., 1944; BS in San. Engring, U. Ill., 1943, MS, 1947, PhD, 1954; NSF faculty fellow, U. Durham, Eng., 1959-60. Research assoc. U. Ill., 1947-53; assoc. prof. civil engring. Iowa State U., 1953-56, prof., 1956-91, Anson Marston Disting. prof. engring., 1972-91, emeritus Disting. prof., 1991—. Cons. Water Quality Office of EPA, Culligan Internat., Lakeside Engring. Co., Bolton & Menk, many cities and industries. Author: Sewerage and Sewage Treatment, 1958; mem. editorial bd.: Internat. Jour. Air and Water Pollution, London, 1960-67; asst. editor: San. Engr. Newsletter of ASCE, 1962-74; contbr. articles to profl. jours. V.p., treas. Water Found., Inc., 1978-83; mem. Iowa Bd. Health, 1975-76, Iowa State U. Rsch. Found., 1975-78, 83-91. With C.E., AUS, 1944-46. Recipient George B. Gascoigne medal Water Pollution Control Fedn., 1962, 80, Publs. award, 1963, Purification divsn. award Am. Water Works Assn., 1965, Anson Marston medal Iowa Engring. Soc., 1966, Disting. Svc. award, 1968, Gold medal Filtration Soc. Eng., 1970, Bedell award, 1977, Rsch. award, 1978, Philip F. Morgan award Water Pollution Control Fedn., 1986; named Water Works Man of Yr., 1972, Disting. Alumni award U. Ill. Alumni Assn., 1992. Fellow ASCE (life), Iowa Acad. Scis. (disting. sci. 1990), Am. Filtration Separations Soc. (F.M. Tiller award 1994); mem. NSPE (nat. bd. dirs.), AAUP, Am. Water Works Assn. (hon., life, internat. bd. dirs. 1978-80), Assn. Environ. Engring. Profs. (pres. 1967-70, 86-87, Nalco award, Founders award 1991), Am. Soc. Engring. Edn., Am. Inst. Chem. Engrs., Am. Acad. Environ. Engring. (diplomate), Filtration Soc. (Eng., bd. dirs., tech. editor, vice chmn. 1993, chmn. 1994, Fluid/Particle Separation Jour.), Rotary, Sigma Xi, Phi Kappa Phi (Centennial medal 1997), Chi Epsilon. Home: 1627 Crestwood Cir Ames IA 50010-5520 *It isn't enough to build a "big pie"; we must also protect its quality and learn how to cut it fairly.*

BAUMANN, GERHARD PAUL, endocrinologist, educator; b. Basel, Switzerland, Sept. 15, 1941; m. Mary Paula Casey, June 25, 1972; 1 child, Catherine. MD, U. Basel, 1967. Diplomate Am. Bd. Internal Medicine. Intern in medicine VA Hosp., Bklyn., 1968-69; fellow in endocrinology Peter Bent Brigham Hosp., Boston, 1969-71; resident in medicine U. Basel, U. Lausanne, Switzerland, 1971-74; vis. scientist NIH, Bethesda, Md., 1974-77; asst. prof. medicine Northwestern U., Chgo., 1977-82, assoc. prof., 1982-88, prof. medicine, 1988—, dir. endocrine tng. program, 1982—; chief endocrinology sect. VA Lakeside Med. Ctr., 1999—. Vis. prof. U. Göteborg, Sweden, 1989, U. Umea, Sweden, 1989, Mass. Gen. Hosp./Harvard Med. Sch., Boston, 1991; spkr. in field. Mem. editl. bd. Endocrinology, 1986-89, 2003—, Jour. Clin. Endocrinology and Metabolism, 1991-94; reviewer Am. Jour. Physiology, Jour. AMA, Archives Internal Medicine, European Jour. Clin. Investigation, Jour. Clin. Investigation, Jour. Molecular Endocrinology, New Eng. Jour. Medicine, Proc. Nat. Acad. Sci., Procs. Soc. Exptl. Biology and Medicine, Jour. Endocrinol. Investigation, Jour. Biochem. and Biophys. Methods, Trends in Endocrinology and Metabolism, Scis., New Eng. Jour. Medicine, others; contbr. articles to profl. jours. Grantee NIH, 1980-84, 87-93, Am. Diabetes Assn., 1987—, others. Mem. AAAS, Assn. Am. Physicians, Am. Soc. Clin. Investigation, Am. Fedn. Med. Rsch., Endocrine Soc., Cen. Soc. Clin. Rsch., Chgo. Endocrine Club (pres. 1981-82). Avocations: music, violin, piano, skiing. Office: Northwestern U Med Sch 303 E Chicago Ave Chicago IL 60611-3072 E-mail: gbaumann@northwestern.edu.

BAUMANN, JON PAUL, music educator, director; b. Bismarck, N.Dak., May 2, 1973; s. Martin Paul and Jane Elizabeth Baumann. BSc, U. of Mary, 1995; MA, So. Oreg. Univ., 2003. Band dir. Bismarck (N.Dak.) Cath. Schs., 1995—2001, Bismarck (N.Dak.) HS, 2001—. Prin. trombone Bismarck-Mandan (N.Dak.) Symphony Orch., 1991—. Mem.: Nat. Band Assn. (assoc. Allegro Band award). Office: Bisamrck High School 800 N 8th Street Bismarck ND 58501

BAUMANN, JULIAN HENRY, JR., lawyer; b. Ft. Leavenworth, Kans., Feb. 20, 1943; s. Julian Henry and Helene (Claiborne) B.; m. Karen Ann Hofmann, July 14, 1973; children: Andrew H., Allison C. BS, Clemson U., 1965; postgrad., U. Tenn., 1966; JD, U. S.C., 1968; LLM in Taxation, NYU, 1975. Bar: S.C. 1968, Del. 1976. Assoc. Richards, Layton & Finger, Wilmington, Del., 1975-80, dir., 1980—. Served to capt., JAGC, U.S. Army, 1969-74. Fellow Am. Coll. Tax Counsel; mem. ABA, S.C. Bar Assn., Del. State Bar (chmn., sec. taxation 1990-91), Wilmington Tax Group (chmn. 1988-89), The Com. of 100 (pres. 1994-96), Bd. of Mgrs., The Nemours Found., Wilmington Club. Democrat. Roman Catholic. Home: 8 Brendle Ln Wilmington DE 19807-1300 Office: Richards Layton & Finger One Rodney Sq 10th & King Sts Wilmington DE 19801

BAUMANN, KARL H. health and medical products executive; Vice chmn. bd. Siemens Corp., N.Y.C.; dep. dir. Siemens AG, N.Y.C. Office: Siemens Corp 153 E 53rd St New York NY 10022-4611

BAUMANN, LARRY R(OGER), lawyer; b. Chadron, Nebr., Feb. 19, 1946; s. Robert R. and Mary Nadine (Simpson) B.; children: Brenda Sue, Andrea Lynn; m. Marcia Lynn Bliefernich; children: Abigail Lynn, Jeffrey Scott. BA, Chadron State Coll., 1968; JD, U. Nebr., 1974. Bar: Nebr. 1974, U.S. Dist. Ct. Nebr. 1974, U.S. Ct. Appeals (8th cir.) 1989, U.S. Tax Ct. 1983. Ptnr. Fillman & Baumann, York, Nebr., 1974-80, Kelley, Scritsmier & Byrne PC, North Platte, Nebr., 1981—. Pres. York Jaycees, 1976; bd. dirs. C. of C., 1992-94, Nebraskaland Days, Inc., 1994-98. With U.S. Army, 1968-71, Vietnam. Mem. Nebr. Bar Assn., Lincoln County Bar Assn., Western Nebr. Bar Assn., Nebr. Coun. Sch. Attys. (pres. 1988-89). Democrat. Methodist. Office: 221 W 2nd St North Platte NE 69101-3905 E-mail: lbaum@nponline.net.

BAUMANN, MARTIN F. savings and loan association executive; BA in Acctg., Queens Coll.; MBA in Fin., Baruch Coll.; degree in Bus. Adminstrn., Columbia U. CPA. Banking leader PricewaterhouseCoopers; ptnr. World Fin. Svcs. Practice, dep. chmn.; exec. v.p. for fin. Freddie Mac, McLean, Va., 2003, exec. v.p., 2003—, CFO, 2003—. Office: Freddie Mac 8200 Jones Branch Drive Mc Lean VA 22102-3110*

BAUMANN, PAUL ARTHUR, radiation oncologist; b. West Allis, Wis., Sept. 30, 1932; s. Erwin Harry and Lydia Emma (Steinke) B.; m. Bethel Horter Smith, May 13, 1961; children: Bethel Ann, Annette, Ruth. BS in Med. Sci., U. Wis., 1954, MD, 1957. Intern U. Pitts., 1957, resident in pathology, 1960; resident in radiology U. Minn., 1963-66; fellow U. Tex. M.D. Anderson Hosp. & Tumor Inst., Houston, 1967-68; chief dept. radiation therapy Wesley Med. Ctr., Wichita, Kans., 1968—2000; practice medicine specializing in radiation oncology Wichita, 1968—. Pres. Kans. Div. Am. Cancer Soc., Topeka, 1979. Served to lt. comdr. USPHS, 1962-63. Fellow Am. Coll. Radiology; mem. AMA, Radiology Soc. N.Am., Am. Radium Soc., Am. Soc. Therapeutic Radiology and Oncology, Kans. Radiol. Soc. Republican. Presbyterian. Avocations: stamp collecting, swimming, carpentry, wind surfing. Home: 6042 E 13th St N Wichita KS 67208-2652 Office: 550 N Hillside Ave Wichita KS 67214 Fax: 316-962-2620. E-mail: TumorZapr@aol.com.

BAUMANN, RICHARD GORDON, lawyer; b. Chgo., Apr. 7, 1938; s. Martin M. and Harriet May (Granof) B.; m. Terrie Bemel, Dec. 18, 1971; children: Michelle, Alison. BS cum laude, U. Wis., 1960, JD, 1964. Bar: Wis. 1964, Calif. 1970, U.S. Supreme Ct. 1973. Congressional intern U.S. Senator Hubert H. Humphrey, 1959; assoc. firm Kohner, Mann & Kailas, Milw., 1964-69, Sulmeyer, Kupetz & Alberts, L.A., 1969-73; mem. firm Sulmeyer, Kupetz, Baumann & Rothman, L.A., 1973—. Judge pro tem L.A. Ct., 1980. Assoc. editor Comml. Law Jour., 1991—. Fellow Comml. Law Found. (bd. dirs.); mem. Nat. Inst. on Credit Mgmt. (bd. dirs.), Am. Bd. Cert. (bd. dirs.), Acad. Comml. and Bankruptcy Law Specialists (bd. dirs.), Comml. Law League (pres. 1990-91, bd. govs. 1986-92, chmn. Western Region Mem. Assn. 1982-83). Office: 300 S Grand Ave Fl 14 Los Angeles CA 90071-3109

BAUMANN, RICHARD WILLIAM, science educator, consultant; b. Castle Dale, Utah, 1940; s. William Baumann and Elsie Elizabeth Anderson; m. Myrna Rae Morrill, 1964; children: Karin, Jeffrey, Heidi, Rebecca, Susan, Peter. BA, U. Utah, 1965, MS, 1967, PhD, 1970; postgrad., U. Mont., 1968—69. Postdoctoral awardee Max-Planck Soc., Schlitz, Germany, 1971; asst. prof. S.W. Mo. State U., Springfield, 1972; asst. curator Smithsonian Instn., Washington, 1973—75; asst. prof. Brigham Young U., Provo, Utah, 1976—80, assoc. prof., 1981—87, prof., 1988—2002. Dir. Monte L. Bean Life Sci. Mus., Provo, 1980—83, curator of insects, 1985—2002; editor Gt. Basin Naturalist, Provo, 1993—99, Western North Am. Naturalist, Provo, 2000—02. Lt. U.S. Army, 1965—73. Mem.: N.Am. Benthological Soc. (assoc.), Am. Entomol. Soc. (assoc.), Entomol. Soc. Am. (assoc.). Mormon. Avocations: fishing, tennis. Home: 575 WIDB Brigham Young U Provo UT 84604 Personal E-mail: richard_baumann@byu.edu.

BAUMANN, ROBERT JAY, child neurology educator; b. Chgo., Oct. 22, 1940; s. Stephen S. and Evelyn (Hellerstein) B.; m. Judith Kravitz, Oct. 1964; children: Barbara, Stephen, Lauren. BS magna cum laude, Tufts U., 1961; MD, Western Res. U., 1964. Diplomate Am. Bd. Psychiatry and Neurology (examiner 1976—). Intern, resident in pediatrics and neurology U. Chgo. Hosps., 1965-69, fellow in child neurology, 1971-72; asst. prof. neurology U. Ky., Lexington, 1972-78, assoc. prof., 1987-92, prof., 1992—, assoc. prof. rehab., 1987—, assoc. prof. pediatrics, 1989-92, prof., 1992—, dir. regional neurology program, 1972—, dir. child neurology program, 1979—. Cons. U.S. Commn. for Control Epilepsy, Washington, 1976; reviewer, cons. Nat. Inst. Neurol. Disease and Stroke, Bethesda, Md., 1979-95; neuroepidemiology cons. Ky.-Ecuador Ptnrs. of Ams., Quito, 1987-91, Am. Acad. Pediatrics, 1991—, Instituto de Investigaciones, Facultad de Ciencias Medicas, U. Ctrl. Del Ecuador, Quito, 1991-93; cons. Min. of Health, Ecuador, 2000—, Shandong Med. Ctr., Jinan, China, 2001—; vis. lectr. Pan Am. Health Orgn., Quitos, Ecuador, 2000—. Chmn. United Jewish Appeal Campaign, Lexington, 1986-87; v.p. Cen. Ky. Jewish Fedn., Lexington, 1988-92. Capt. M.C., USAF, 1969-71. Mem. Child Neurology Soc., Am. Acad. Neurology, Am. Acad. Pediatrics (neuroepidemiologic cons. 1992—), Am. Coll. Epidemiology, Soc. for Epidemiologic Rsch., Profs. Child Neurology (bd. dirs. 1988-92). Office: U Ky Dept Neurology Ky Clinic 800 Rose St Dept L409 Lexington KY 40536-0284

BAUMANN, ROLAND M. historian, archivist, consultant; b. Sheboygan, Wis., Mar. 7, 1942; s. Roland A. and Frieda M. Baumann; m. Phyllis A. Langerak, Dec. 18, 1965; children: Karyn J., Philip M. BS in History, U. Wis., 1964; MA in History, No. Ill. U., 1966; PhD in History, Pa. State U., 1970. Cert. editing hist. documents NHPRC & U. SC., 1976, modern archives adminstrn. Nat. Archives, Libr. of Congress, Am. U., 1976, archivist Acad. Cert. Archivists, 1989, Acad. Cert. Archivists, 1996, Acad. Cert. Archivists, 2002. Instr. U.S. history Monmouth Coll., Ill., 1966—67; asst. prof. history Bowling Green State U., Ohio, 1970—73; archival/hist. cons. Pa. Hist. & Mus. Commn., Harrisburg, 1975—76, chief divsn. archives & manuscripts, 1977—86; archivist & adj. prof. of history Oberlin Coll., Oberlin, Ohio, 1987—. Exch. archivist IREX, US-USSR Commn. on Archival Cooperation, Moscow, 1989; faculty exch. Yunnan U., Kunming, China, 1996, Obirin U., Machida City, Tokyo, 1998. Author: (book) The 1858 Oberlin-Wellington Rescue: A Reappraisal; contbr. chapters to books; editor: (book) Guide to the Women's History Sources in the Oberlin College Archives (Finding Aids Prize, Mid-Atlantic Regional Archives Conf., 1991); author: A Manual of Archival Techniques (Arline Custer Award, Mid-Atlantic Regional Archives Conf., 1983); contbr. chapters to books, articles; mem. editl. bd.: Pa. History, 1977—88. Trustee emeritus Oberlin Hist. & Improvement Orgn., Ohio, 1987—2002; mem. City Records Commn., Oberlin, Ohio, 1988—2002; bd. dirs. Ohio State Hist. Records Adv. Bd., Columbus, Ohio, 1987—2002; bd. dirs., pres. Lorain County Hist. Soc., Elyria, Ohio, 1991—95. Grantee, Am. Philos. Soc., 1972, N.J. Hist. Commn., 1978, Dana Found. Grant, 1989—90, Nat. Hist. Pub. & Records Commn., 1991—92, Graham Found. for Advanced Studies in Fine Arts, 1994—95; NDEA fellow, Pa. State U., 1967—70, Andrew W. Mellon fellow, U. Mich., 1985. Fellow: Soc. Am. Archivists (chair coll. & u. archives sect. 1990—92, chair awards com. 1999—2001, Dist. Svc. award 1992); mem.: Pa. Hist. Assn. (life; chair Philip S. Kklein prize com. 1985—89, coun. 1978—89). D-Liberal. Lutheran. Avocations: book collecting, golf, travel. Home: 146 Pyle Rd Oberlin OH 44074 Office: Oberlin Coll Archives 148 W College St Oberlin OH 44074 Office Fax: 440-775-8016. E-mail: roland.m.baumann@oberlin.edu.

BAUMANN, SARA MARGARET CULBRETH, retired elementary school educator; b. Camilla, Ga., Oct. 20, 1949; d. Max Ronald and Sara Emily (Rivers) Culbreth; m. Curtis Darrah Baumann; children: Ford Pearce, Brad Pearce. BS in Edn., U. Ga., 1971; MEd, Ga. State U., Atlanta, 1974. Tchr. 5th and 6th grades Carver Elem. Sch., Columbus, Ga., 1971-78; tchr. 5th grade Gould Elem. Sch., Savannah, Ga., 1979; tchr. 7th grade Edwards Mid. Sch., Conyers, Ga., 1981-91; tchr. Salem H.S., Conyers, 1991-93, Meml. Mid. Sch., Conyers, 1993-2001, Woodstock (Ga.) Mid. Sch., 2001—03; ret., 2003. Tchr. of gifted, 1999-2003. Recreation, all-star, premier and classic coach Rockdale Youth Soccer Assn., Conyers, 1984-94, dir., 1990; youth, H.S. and coll. soccer referee. Named Rockdale County Tchr. of the Yr. 1991, Edwards Middle Sch. Tchr. of the Yr. 1990, Math./Sci. Outstanding Tchr. in Ga., 1990, Female Referee of Yr., Ga. State Soccer Assn., 1998. Mem.: Ga. Ret. Educators Assn. Methodist. Avocations: tennis, photography, soccer, bridge. Home: 906 Audrey Dr Woodstock GA 30188-4209 Personal E-mail: scbaumann@hotmail.com.

BAUMANN, THEODORE ROBERT, aerospace engineer, consultant, army officer; b. Bklyn., May 13, 1932; s. Emil Joseph and Sophie (Reiblein) B.; m. Patricia Louise Drake, Dec. 16, 1967; children: Veronica Ann, Robert Theodore, Joseph Edmund. B in Aerospace Engring., Poly. U., Bklyn., 1954; MS in Aerospace Engring., U. So. Calif., L.A., 1962; grad., US Army C&GS Coll., 1970, Indsl. Coll. of Armed Forces, 1970, US Army War Coll., 1979, Air War Coll., 1982. Structures engr. Glenn L. Martin Co., Balt., 1954-55; structural loads engr. N.Am. Rockwell, L.A., 1958-67; dynamics engr. TRW Systems Group, Redondo Beach, Calif., 1967-71, systems engr., 1971-75, project engr., 1975-84, sr. project engr., 1984-92. Cons. SAAB-Scania Aerospace Div., Linkoping, Sweden, 1981-82; asst. dir. Dir. Weapons Systems, U.S. Army, Washington, 1981-85, staff officer Missile & Air Def. System div., 1975-81. Contbr. articles to Machine Design, tech. publs., tech. symposia. Asst. scoutmaster Boy Scouts Am., Downey, Calif., 1985-93; instr. Venice Judo Boys Club, 1966-86. Served from 2d lt. U.S. Army to col. USAR, 1954-88. Decorated Legion of Merit. Mem. AIAA; mem. Soc. Am. Mil. Engrs (life), Am. Legion, Res. Officers Assn. (life), U.S. Judo Fedn., Nat. Rifle Assn, Knights of Columbus. Republican. Roman Catholic. Achievements include developing a new method for the analysis and classification of random data; contbr. to air force ballistic missile program; devel. procedure for design of prestressed joints and fittings. Office: Theodore R Baumann & Assoc 7732 Brunache St Downey CA 90242-2206

BAUMANN-SINACORE, PATRICIA LYNN, nursing administrator; b. Carbondale, Pa., Jan. 30, 1962; d. John Frederick and Catherine Anne Hunt; married: children: Donnell Patricia and Taryn Frances Thorne. BSN, Wilkes Coll., 1987. Staff nurse, pulmonary and float Mercy Hosp., Scranton, Pa., 1987-88; asst. mgr. CMC Found., Scranton, 1988-89; mgr. CMCI Community Med. Ctr. Found., Scranton, 1989-90; dir. profl. svcs. Above All Home Health and Hospice, Taylor, Pa., 1991-93; surveyor, cons. Primary Care and Home Health divsn., Pa. Dept. Health, 1993-95; asst. adminstr. Interim Healthcare Svcs., Inc., Hughestown, Pa., 1995; quality assurance/risk management specialist Pa. Dept. Pub. Welfare, Clark Summit, 1997-98; RN mgr. Mountain View Care Ctr., Scranton, 1998—. Instr. DEPMED Power Distbn. 348th Gen. Hosp., Ashley, Pa. Capt. USAR, Desert Shield/Desert Storm, Saudi Arabia, 1990-91. Mem. Rotary (charter, v.p. 1994-95). E-mail: trish.sinacore@cmchealthsys.org.

BAUMBERGER, CHARLES HENRY, lawyer; b. Port Huron, Mich., Sept. 13, 1941; s. Peter Julius and Evelyn Margaret (Jackson) B.; m. Martha Carolyn Mighallin, Aug. 8, 1969; children: Peter Scott, Charles Henry Jr. BA, Vanderbilt U., 1963; JD, U. Fla., 1966. Bar: Fla. 1966, U.S. Dist. Ct. (so. dist.) Fla. 1967; cert. civil trial lawyer. Atty. Stephens, Demos & Magill, Miami, Fla., 1967-68; ptnr. Hastings, Goldman & Baumberger, Miami, Fla., 1969-74; founding ptnr. Rossman & Baumberger P.A., Miami, Fla., 1974—. Lectr. various continuing legal edn. programs; guest on numerous radio, TV talk shows, 1987—. Contbr. articles to profl. jours. Mem. Gov.'s Task Force on Emergency Room and Trauma Care, 1987; So. Fla. Health Action Coalition, Inc., 1984; task force on trauma and trauma systems Dept. Transp., 1987—. Served to 1st lt. U.S. Army Res., 1966-72. Mem. ABA, ATLA (past chair of Profl. Negligence Sect.), Dade County Bar Assn. (bd. dirs. 1977-88, pres. 1989-90), Fla. Bar (exec. coun. trial lawyers sect. 1983-89, chmn. 1990-91), Acad. Fla. Trial Lawyers (bd. dirs. 1980-89), Dade County Trial Lawyers Assn. (founding mem. bd. dirs. 1981-84), Am. Bd. Trial Advocates (Miami chpt. past pres.), Fla. Lawyers Action Group, So. Fla. Trial Lawyers Assn., Trial Lawyers for Pub. Justice (founding mem. 1982—), Am. Coll. Trial Lawyers, Internat. Soc. Barristers, Coral Reef Yacht Club. Democrat. Methodist. Home: 5755 Suncrest Dr Miami FL 33156-5704 Office: Rossman Baumberger Reboso & Spier 44 W Flagler St Fl 23 Miami FL 33130-1808 E-mail: Baumberger@rbrlaw.com.

BAUMEL, HERBERT, violinist, conductor; b. N.Y.C., Sept. 30, 1919; s. Leon and Fannie (Beckerman) B; m. Rachael Bail, Oct. 17, 1949 (div. Nov. 1970); children: Susan, Samuel, Mary Elizabeth (dec.); m. Joan Patricia French, July 11, 1971. Student, Mannes Sch. of Music, 1932-34; diploma, Curtis Inst. of Music, 1937-42; postgrad., Santa Cecilia, Accademia Chigiana, Rome and Siena, 1954-56. Violinist, concertmaster, conductor with orchs., chamber groups, Broadway shows, jazz ensembles, ballets, operas worldwide, 1939—. Baumel-Booth-Smith Trio (1st integrated classical trio to tour deep south), 1968-71; Baumel-Booth Duo, 1968-96; violinist/storyteller, 1970—, co-dir., Baumel Assocs., Yonkers, N.Y., 1984—; judge Fulbright Nat. Screening Com., 1965-67; guest artist Sponsors' Concerts of Dallas Chamber Music Soc., 1991, Internat. Piano Archives U. Md., College Park, Beveridge Webster Celebration Concert, 1991; lectr. and violinist with Dr. Joan French Baumel, 1991—, Yonkers Pub. Libr., 1992, Greenburgh (N.Y.) Pub. Libr., 1992, Waverly Heights, Gladwyne, Pa., 1993, 94, 95, Alliance Francaise, Westchester, N.Y., 1993, 94, 95, 96, 1st Unitarian Soc. Westchester, 1994, Workmen's Circle Lodge, Sylvan Lake, N.Y., 1994, Thomas Paine/Huguenot/New Rochelle (N.Y.) Hist. Soc., 1995, 96, others; commentator All Things Considered, Nat. Pub. Radio, 1999—; contbr. (mag.) Opera News, 2000—. Violinist Phila. Orch. with Ormandy, Toscanini, Walter, Monteux, Mitropoulos, Szell; first to play Samuel Barber's Violin Concerto with Curtis Symphony (Reiner), 1939 and Phila. Orch. (Ormandy); concert artist with: Stokowski, Stravinsky, Copland, Bernstein, Benny Goodman; concertmaster Phila. Opera, N.Y.C. Opera, N.Y.C. Ballet, Joe Bushkin Jazz Ensembles, (original Broadway musicals) New Girl in Town, Fiorello!, She Loves Me, Fiddler on the Roof, A Little Night Music, Rex, Dancin', also three Presdl. galas with Marilyn Monroe, Bill Cosby, Woody Allen, Jack Benny, Johnny Carson, Rudolph Nureyev, Margot Fonteyn; recs. with Heifetz, Horowitz, Rubinstein, Leonard Warren, Frank Sinatra, Edith Piaf, Tallulah Bankhead, many others; writer script and music edml. audio-visual program The Art of Listening, 1972—; composer: Fiddlers Two, 1976, Caprice #48 1/2, 1978, Sentiment America, 1984, arranger selections from Fiddler on the Roof, 1971, 2001. Mem. adv. bd. Mark Brent Dolinsky Found., White Plains, N.Y., 1982—; played benefits for Westchester Assn. Retarded Citizens,

1982—, Coalition for the Homeless,Westchester County, N.Y., 1986—. Recipient Silver medal New York Music Week Assn., 1928, Gold medal New York Music Week Assn., 1929; 2-time Fulbright scholar to Rome, 1954-56; chosen for both Stokowski All-American Youth Orch. tours, S.Am., U.S., 1940, 41; chosen to organize, present and play concerts for U.S. Embassy and Cultural Offices throughout Italy with Anna Moffo, Ezio Flagello, Ivan Davis, Gimi Beni, and in honor of Queen Elisabeth of Belgium, 1954-56, Phila. Drama Guild Lectr. Series, 1978. Mem. Am. Fedn. Musicians, Curtis Inst. of Music Alumni Assn., Phila. Orch. Retirees and Friends. Democrat. Jewish. Avocations: tennis, gardening, reading, photography, chess. Home and Office: Baumel Assocs 86 Rosedale Rd Yonkers NY 10710-3033

BAUMEL, JOAN PATRICIA FRENCH, educator, writer, lecturer; b. Winona, Minn., Mar. 12, 1930; d. William Oswald and Gertrude Marie (Fitzgerald) French; m. Herbert Baumel, July 11, 1971. Student, l'Ecole du Louvre, France, 1950-51; student with high honors, Inst. Phonétique Sorbonne, Paris, 1950-51; BA magna cum laude, Douglass Coll., 1952; postgrad., U. Detroit, 1952-55, Case Western Reserve U., 1960, U. Akron, 1962, U. Notre Dame, 1963, Manhattanville Coll., 1971; MA in French, Rutgers U., 1965; PhD in Modern Langs., Fordham U., 1985. Tchr. French lang. and culture, elem. and coll. levels various schs. including Mother House of Religious of the Sacred Heart, Kenwood, Albany, N.Y., Ohio, Mich., 1955-66; tchr. French White Plains (N.Y.) Pub. High Sch., 1966-86; curricula creator Akron (Ohio) Pub. Schs., 1962-63; co-dir. Baumel Assocs., Yonkers, N.Y., 1984—, Concerts and Lectures with Herbert Baumel, 1991—, Words and Music Programs with Herbert Baumel, 1991—, Yonkers Pub. Libr., 1992, Waverly Heights, Gladwyne, Pa., 1993-95, Workmen's Circle Lodge, Sylvan Lake, N.Y., 1994, Thomas Paine/Huguenot Hist. Soc., New Rochelle, N.Y., 1995—. Lectr. French lang. and culture Yonkers (N.Y.) Pub. Libr., 1992, Greenburgh (N.Y.) Pub. Libr., 1992; lectr. anti-semitism CUNY Grad. Ctr., 1988—, B'nai B'rith Internat. Mus., Washington, 1st Unitarian Soc., Westchester, N.Y., Rockland (N.Y.) Ctr. for Holocaust Studies, Unitarian Ch. of All Souls, N.Y.C., Temple Beth Israel, Port Washington, N.Y., Holocaust Resource Ctr. and Archives, Queensborough C.C., CUNY, 1991, Women's Am. ORT, Midchester Jewish Ctr., Yonkers, 1992, 2000, Ctrl. Queens YM & YWCA, N.Y.C., 1992, 2000, Jewish Cmty. Ctr., Scarsdale, N.Y., 2001. Author: Paul Claudel and the Jews: A Study in Ambivalence, 1985; lectr. topics include French Anti Semitism: The Gallic Road to the Concentration Camp: Klaus Barbie and the Children of Izieu, Kristallnacht Remembered, numerous others. Mem. adv. bd. Mark Brent Dolinsky Meml. Found. Recipient Woodrow Wilson fellowship, 1958-59, Yearbook Dedication award White Plains (N.Y.) Pub. H.S., 1980. Mem. Am. Assn. Tchrs. French, White Plains Tchrs. Assn., N.Y. State Assn. Fgn. Lang. Tchrs., French Inst./Alliance Francaise, Alliance Francaise Westchester, Phi Beta Kappa. Avocations: tennis, gardening, music, reading. Home and Office: Baumel Assocs 86 Rosedale Rd Yonkers NY 10710-3033

BAUMER, BEVERLY BELLE, journalist; b. Hays, Kans., Sept. 23, 1926; d. Charles Arthur and Mayme Mae (Lord) B.; BS, William Allen White Sch. Journalism, U. Kans., 1948. Summer intern reporter Hutchinson (Kans.) News, 1946-47; continuity writer, women's program dir. Sta. KWBW, Hutchinson, 1948-49; dist. editor Salina (Kans.) Jours., 1950-57; commd. writer State of Kans. Centennial Year, 1961; contbg. author: Ford Times, Kansas City Star, Wichita (Kans.) Eagle, Oljibway Publs., Billboard, Modern Jeweler, Floor Covering Weekly, other bus. mags., 1962-69; owner and mgr. apts., Hutchinson, 1970— ; broadcaster Reading Radio Room, Sta. KHCC-FM, Hutchinson, 1982—, columnist The Hutchinson (Kans.) Record, 1983-86; info. officer, maj. Kans. Wing Hdqrs. CAP, 1969-72; participant People to People Citizen Ambassador program, People's Republic of China, summer 1988. Mem. Republican Presdl. Task Force. Recipient Human Interest Photo award Nat. Press Women, 1956, News Photo award AP, 1952. Mem. Fellows Menninger Found., Suffolk County Hist. Soc., Nat. Fedn. Press Women, Kans. Press Women (Comm. Contest award 1986), Am. Soc. Profl. and Exec. Women, Am. Film Inst., Nat. Soc. Magna Charta Dames, Nat. Soc. Daus. Founders and Patriots Am., Nat. Soc. Daus. Am. Colonists, Kans. Soc. Daus. Am. Colonists (organizing regent Dr. Thomas Lord chpt., state chmn. insignia com.), Nat. Soc. Sons and Daus. Pilgrims (elder Kans. br.), D.A.R., Ben Franklin Soc. (nat. adv. bd.), Daus. Colonial Wars, Order Descs. Colonial Physicians and Chirurgiens, Colonial Dames 17th Century (chaplain, charter mem. Henry Woodhouse chpt.), Plantagenet Soc., Internat. Platform Soc., U. Kans. Alumni Assn., Nat. Geneal. Soc. Author book of poems, 1941; editor: A Simple Bedside Book for People Who Are Kinda, Sorta Interested in Genealogy, 1983. Home and Office: 122 Downing Rd Hutchinson KS 67502-4453 *Kindness belongs in business, the professions and the trades. It is the most sincere form of good will and leaves no one uncomfortable.*

BAUMGARDNER, JAMES LEWIS, history educator; b. Bristol, Va., Jan. 26, 1938; s. John Richard and Roxie Katherine (Lewis) B.; children: Ellen Lorena, James Michael; m. Paula Louise Jones; stepchildren: Joseph Branscome, Sarah Elizabeth Brock. AA, Bluefield Jr. Coll., 1957; BA, Carson-Newman Coll., 1959; MA, U. Tenn., Knoxville, 1964, PhD, 1968. Ordained to ministry Baptist Ch., 1955. Asst. prof. history Carson-Newman Coll., Jefferson City, Tenn., 1964-67, assoc. prof., 1967-73, prof., 1973—, chmn. history-polit. sci,. dept., 1974-95. Contbr. articles to learned jours. Interim mem. Jefferson County (Tenn.) Bd. Sch. Commrs., 1978; mem. Anderson County (Tenn.) Bd. Edn., 1990-94; active interim, bivocation pastor. Served with U.S. Army, 1959-62. Named Bivocational Pastor of the Yr., Tenn. Bapt. Conv., 1997. Mem. Am. Hist. Assn., Acad. Polit. Sci., Orgn. Am. Historians, So. Hist. Assn., Bapt. History & Heritage Soc., Phi Alpha Theta. Office: Carson-Newman Coll PO Box 71929 Jefferson City TN 37760-7001

BAUMGARDNER, JOHN ELLWOOD, JR., lawyer; b. Balt., Jan. 6, 1951; s. John Ellwood and Nancy G. (Brandenburg) B.; m. Astrid Rehl, Sept. 7, 1974; children: Jeffrey Mark, Julia Alexis. Bar: N.Y. 1976. Assoc. Sullivan & Cromwell, N.Y.C., 1975-83, ptnr., 1983—. Supervisory dir. The Turkish Pvt. Equity Investment Co., 1991-93; trustee JPM Advisor Funds, 1996. Vice chair gen. dir.'s coun. N.Y.C. Opera. Mem.: ABA, Assn. Bar City NY (chair com. on investment mgmt. regulation), NY State Bar Assn., Nat. Dance Inst. (bd. dirs. 1988—89), Princeton Club. Office: Sullivan & Cromwell LLP 125 Broad St Fl 32 New York NY 10004-2498 E-mail: baumgardnerj@sullcrom.com.

BAUMGARDNER, MATTHEW CLAY, artist; b. Columbus, Ohio, Feb. 5, 1955; s. Alan Wirth and Mary Lou (Weidner) B.; m. Heather Evans; children: Zoe Klee, Eva Evans, Lila Joy, Sofi Clare. MFA, U. N.C., 1982. One-man shows include Presbyn. Coll., Clinton, S.C., 1980, Sumter (S.C.) Gallery, 1981, Wilkov/Goldfeder, N.Y.C., 1987, Wessel O'Connor Ltd., N.Y.C., 1988, 89, Howard Yezerski Gallery, Boston, 1992, Charles Cowles Gallery, N.Y.C., 1993, Gallery A, Chgo., 1995, Bentley Gallery, Scottsdale, Ariz., 1998, MD Modern, Houston, 1998, Jeffrey Coploff Fine Art, 2000, 2001, Bentley Gallery, Scottsdale, Ariz., 2000, Jeffrey Coploff Fin Art, 2001; group exhbns. include Spartenburg (S.C.) Arts Ctr., 1979, Columbia (S.C.) Mus., 1979, Clemson (S.C.) U., 1980, Greenville (S.C.) County Mus., 1980, Greater Birmingham (Ala.) Arts Alliance, 1981, Gibbes Mus., Charleston, S.C., 1981, Mint Mus., Charlotte, N.C., 1981, Ackland Mus., Chapel Hill, N.C., 1982, Huntington (W.Va.) Mus., 1982, Edward Thorp Gallery, N.Y.C., 1985 Hudson Ctr. Gallery, N.Y.C., 1985, Edward Thorp Gallery, N.Y.C., 1985, Mokotoff Gallery, N.Y.C., 1985, 86, Wilkov/Goldfeder, N.Y.C., 1987, Trenton (N.J.) City Mus., 1988, Wessel O'Connor Ltd., N.Y.C., 1989, Stephanie Theodore Gallery, N.Y.C., 1991, Art Dealers Assn. Am., N.Y.C., 1993, New Mus. Contemporary Art, N.Y.C., 1993, Trans Hudson Gallery, Jersey City, 1993, N.Y.C., 1997, Gallery A, Chgo., 1994, 95, 98, Gallerie Marie-Louise Wirth, Zurich, Switzerland, 1995, Bentley Gallery, Scottsdale, Ariz., 1997, MD Modern, Houston, 1998, Jeffrey Coploff Fine Art, N.Y.C., 1999, 2000, Bemis Ctr., Omaha City, Nebr., 1999, LewAllen Contemporary, Santa Fe, N. Mex., 2000. Recipient Purchase awards Mint Mus., Charlotte, N.C., 1981, Gibbes Mus., Charleston, S.C., 1981; Visual Artist fellow Nat. Endowment for the Arts, Washington, 1993. Episcopalian. Office: Baumgardner Studio 12 E 2nd St New York NY 10003-8906 E-mail: baumeye@hotmail.com.

BAUMGARDT, BILLY RAY, professional society administrator, agriculturist; b. Lafayette, Ind., Jan. 17, 1933; s. Raymond P. and Mildred L. (Cordray) Baumgardt; m. D. Elaine Blain, June 8, 1952; children: Pamela K. Baumgardt Farley, Teresa Jo Baumgardt Adolfsen, Donald Ray. BS in Agr., Purdue U., 1955, MS, 1956; PhD, Rutgers U., 1959. From asst. to assoc. prof. U. Wis., Madison, 1959-67; prof. animal nutrition Pa. State U., University Park, 1967-70, head dept. dairy and animal sci., 1970-79, assoc. dir. agrl. expt. sta., 1979-80; dir. agrl. research, assoc. dean Purdue U., West Lafayette, Ind., 1980-98; exec. v.p. Am. Registry Profl. Animal Scientists, Savoy, Ill., 1998—2003. Contbr. chapters to books, articles to profl. sci. jours. Recipient Wilkinson award, Pa. State U., 1979. Fellow: AAAS, Am. Dairy Sci. Assn. (pres. 1984—85, Nutrition Rsch. award 1966, award of Honor 1993, Disting. Svc. award 2003); mem.: Nat. Agrl. Biotech. Coun. (chair 1993—94), Am. Soc. Animal Sci., Am. Inst. Nutrition, Rotary, Sigma Xi. Home and Office: 2741 N Salisbury St West Lafayette IN 47906-1431

BAUMGART, MATTHEW, congressional aide; b. Seattle, Mar. 5, 1966; s. William Joseph Baumgart and Shirley Ann McBride. BA in Comms., Wash. State U., 1988. Legis. corr. to Sen. Joseph R. Biden, Jr., Washington, 1988-91; legis. asst. to Sen. Joseph R. Biden, Jr., 1991-99; sr. policy advisor to Sen. Barbara Boxer, 1999-2000; legis. dir. to Sen. Barbara Boxer, 2000—. Democrat. Home: 850 N Randolph St Apt 1831 Arlington VA 22203-4050 Office: US Senator Barbara Boxer US Senate Washington DC 20510-0001 E-mail: matthew_baumgart@boxer.senate.gov.

BAUMGARTEN, JONATHAN, flutist; s. Howard and Jeanne Baumgarten; m. Amy Wilkinson Frost, May 10, 1986. MusB, The New Sch. of Music, Phila., 1983; MusM, The Juilliard Sch., N.Y.C., 1985. Prin. flute Mexico City Philharm. Orch., Mexico City, 1986—87; freelance musician New Haven Symphony/Neighborhood Music Sch./U. of Bridgeport, New Haven, 1987—94; dir. El Camino Youth Symphony Flute Ensembles, Palo Alto, Calif., 1994—2000; lectr. Am. U., Washington, 2000—. Soloist Isleworth Festival, London, San Francisco Concerto Orch., New Am. Chamber Orch., Detroit, Wallingford Symphony Orch., Conn., Eastern Conn. Symphony, New London. Fellow W.W. Smith fellow, Nat. Endowment for the Arts, 1979—83. Mem.: Am. Fedn. of Musicians. Avocations: hiking, backpacking. Home: 5554 Kendrick Ln Burke VA 22015 Office: American University 4400 Massachusetts Avenue NW Washington DC Personal E-mail: jbaumgarten@yahoo.com.

BAUMGARTEN, PAUL ANTHONY, retired lawyer; b. N.Y.C., July 31, 1934; s. Louis S. and Margaret (Karol) B.; m. Susan T., Feb. 21, 1960; children Stephen, Michael, Lisa, Deborah BA, Swarthmore Coll., 1955; LLB, Harvard U., 1958. Bar: N.Y. Assoc. Otterbourg Steindler, Houston Rosen, N.Y.C., 1958-66; assoc. Halperin, Morris, Granett & Cowan, N.Y.C., 1960; with legal dept. Hill & Range Songs Inc., 1960-62, Warner Bros. Pictures Inc., 1962-64, Embassy Pictures Corp., 1964-70; ptnr. Krause, Hirsch & Gross, 1970-77, Rosenman & Colin, LLP, N.Y.C., 1977—2001, counsel, 2001—. Co-chmn. workshops on motion picture industry Practicing Law Inst.; trustee Copyright Soc. U.S., 1989-91. Co-author: Producing, Financing & Distributing Film (revised and expanded edition), 1992. Mem. Columbia Artists Mgmt. Inc. (dir.). Avocations: classical music, sailing, tennis. Home: 61 W Gate Blvd Plandome NY 11030-1452 Office: Katten Muchin Zavis Rosenman 575 Madison Ave New York NY 10022-2585 E-mail: paulbaumgarten@kmzr.com.

BAUMGARTEN, RONALD NEAL, lawyer; b. Chgo., May 13, 1942; s. Albert and Beatrice (Loseff) B.; m. Aloha Herman, Aug. 27, 1966; children: Brett, Reed, Jaclyn, Blake. BA, U. Ill., 1964, JD, 1966. Bar: Calif. 1970, U.S. Dist. Ct. (cen. dist.) Calif. 1970, U.S. Ct. Appeals (9th cir.) 1973, U.S. Supreme Ct. 1975. Gen. counsel, chief ops. officer Elgin Jewelry Distbrs. Inc., L.A., 1967-72, also bd. dirs.; assoc. Grobe, Rinestein, Freid & Katz P.L.C., Beverly Hills, Calif., 1972-75; ptnr. Jacobs & Baumgarten P.L.C., Beverly Hills, 1975-80, Baumgarten & Greene P.L.C., Santa Monica, Calif., 1980-88; pvt. practice law Santa Monica, 1988-89, L.A., 1989—; sr. v.p. Comml. Fin. Ctr., 1991-95, also bd. dirs.; pres. Occidental Svcs., Inc., 1992-95; pres., CEO, majority shareholder Holmby Investments, Inc., 1994—, Baumgarten Property Mgmt. Svcs., Inc., 1994—; v.p., sec. Sierra Crest Equities, LLC, 1997—, Corner Stone Real Estate Investment, Inc., 1997—; CEO Sierra Sr. Cmtys. LLC, 2001—. Chmn., bd. dirs., CEO, COO, J.D. Alexander & Assocs., Inc., L.A., 1980-92; asst. prof. law U. San Fernando Valley, Calif., 1974. Mem. L.A. World Affairs Coun., 1974—, L.A. Olympic Citizens Adv. Commn., 1982-84, Town Hall, 1983—; exec. v.p., gen. counsel, bd. dirs. Variety-The Children's Charity, 1974-2000, Variety Boy's and Girl's Club, L.A., pres., 1996-99, bd. dirs., 1981—; founder 1st Bus. Bank, L.A., 1981. Mem. ABA, Calif. Bar Assn., L.A. County Bar Assn., Beverly Hills Bar Assn., Phi Delta Phi. Office: 10590 Wilshire Blvd Ste 201 Los Angeles CA 90024 E-mail: rbpacpal@aol.com.

BAUMGARTEN, SIDNEY, lawyer, company executive; b. N.Y.C., July 30, 1933; s. Abraham and Doris (Kanarick) B.; children: Douglas, Frederick, Roger, Julia. AB, Brown U., 1954; JD, NYU, 1960. Bar: N.Y. 1961, U.S. Dist. Ct. (ea. and so. dists.) N.Y. 1961, U.S. Ct. Claims 1961, U.S. Ct. Appeals (2d cir.) 1961. Asst. mgmt., field underwriter Home Life Ins. Co., 1957-61; sole practice, 1961-67; asst. dist. atty. Queens County, N.Y., 1967-68; law sec. to presiding justice State of N.Y., Queens, 1968-73; asst. to Mayor City of N.Y., 1974-77; gen. counsel Phoenix House Found., 1978-80; sr. ptnr. Baumgarten, Swiedler & Waxman, N.Y.C., 1980-88; pvt. practice N.Y.C., 1989-94; pres., CEO Spectral Biosci. Corp., 1994—. Lectr. various seminars, assns. and ednl. instns; adj. prof. law N.Y. Inst. Tech.; vis. prof. Found. U. Cardiology, Brazil, 1996. Pres. N.Y.'s Finest Found., 1993; bd. dirs., chmn. N.Y. Therapeutic Communities, Inc.; trustee Lawrence County Day Sch. (pres. 1985-87). Served with U.S. Army, 1954—56, with Res., 1956—73, col. chief of staff Army Div., 2001—, N.Y. Guard. Decorated Companion Order of Merit SMOTJ, N.Y. State Conspicuous Svc. medal. Mem.: NAHC, VFW, NRA (life), East Side C. of C. (pres. 1983—86, chmn. 1987—), Am. Legion. Office: 350 Fifth Ave Ste 7310 New York NY 10118

BAUMGARTNER, ANTON EDWARD, automotive sales professional; b. N.Y.C., May 18, 1948; s. Hans and Carmen Maria (Figueroa) B.; m. Brenda Lee Lemmon, May 24, 1969 (div. 1990); 1 child, Anton Nicholaus; m. Virginia Thiele, 1992; 1 child, Bree Alexandra. BS, Woodbury U., 1970. Sales mgr. Maywood Bell Ford, Bell, Calif., 1966-69, O.R. Haan, Inc., Santa Ana, Calif., 1969-72; pres. Parkinson Volkswagen, Placentia, Calif., 1972-77; exec. v.p. United Moped, Fountain Valley, Calif., 1975-82; pres. Automobili Intermeccanica, Fountain Valley, 1975-82; gen. mgr. Bishop (Calif.) Volkswagen-Bishop Motors, 1982-85, Beach Imports-Irvine Imports, Newport Beach, Calif., 1985-88; chmn. bd. Stan and Ollie Ins. Co., Santa Ana, Calif., 1989—92; exec. v.p. Asterism, Inc., 1992-96; chmn. Marich Acceptance Inland Empire, 1996—98; gen. mgr. Saturn Retail Enterprises, Anaheim, Calif., 1999—. Mem. faculty, Automotive World Congress, Detroit, 1980. Contbr. articles to weekly serial publs. Mem. Coachbuilders Assn. N.Am. (sec. 1975-78). Office: Saturn Retail Enterprises Anaheim CA 92806 E-mail: tbaumgartner@cox.net.

BAUMGARTNER, BRUCE, airport terminal executive; Mgr. aviation Denver Internat. Airport. Office: Denver Internat Airport Airport Office Bldg 8500 Pena Blvd Denver CO 80249-6205

BAUMGARTNER, FREDERIC JOSEPH, history educator; b. Medford, Wis., Sept. 26, 1945; s. Michael and Theresa Mary (Stauner) B.; m. Lois Ann Hoffman, Jan 31, 1970; children: Eric Michael, Nathan Robert. BA, Mt. St. Paul Coll., 1967; MA, U. Wis., 1969, PhD, 1972. Asst. prof. history Ga. Coll., Milledgeville, 1972-76; assoc. prof. Va. Poly. Inst. and State U., 1976-85, prof., 1985—. Author: Radical Reactionaries, 1976, Change and Continuity, 1986, Henry II King of France, 1988 (Charles Smith prize 1989), From Spear to Flintlock, 1991, Louis XII, 1995, France in the Sixteenth Century, 1996, Longing for the End, 1999, Behind Locked Doors, 2003; contbr. articles to profl. jours. Mem. Am. Cath. Hist. Assn. Office: Va Poly Inst Blacksburg VA 24061-0117

BAUMGARTNER, JAMES EARL, mathematics educator; b. Wichita, Mar. 23, 1943; s. Earl Benjamin and Gertrude J. (Socolofsky) B.; m. Yolanda Yen-Hsu Loo, Jan. 29, 1966; children: Eric James, Jonathan David AB, U. Calif., Berkeley, 1964, PhD, 1970; AM (hon.), Dartmouth Coll., 1981. J. W. Young rsch. instr. Dartmouth Coll., Hanover, N.H., 1969-71, asst. prof. math., 1971-76, assoc. prof., 1976-80, prof., 1980-83, J.G. Kemeny prof. math., 1983—; dept. chmn., 1995-98. Vis. asst. prof. Calif. Inst. Tech. Pasadena 1971-72; cons. Coll. Bd., 1990—. Cons. editor Jour. Symbolic Logic, 1983-90; editor: Axiomatic Set Theory, 1984; contbr. articles to profl. jours., chpts. to books. Mem. Am. Math. Soc. (editor Transactions and Memoirs 1988-92, mng. editor 1992-94), Math. Assn. Am., Assn. Symbolic Logic (exec. coun. mem. 1993-95). Home: Lindy Ln Hanover NH 03755 Office: Dartmouth Coll Dept Math Hanover NH 03755

BAUMGARTNER, JOHN H. refining and petroleum products company executive; b. 1936; married. With Clark Oil & Refining Corp., Milw., 1956-82, retail sales rep., 1960-65, dist. mgr., 1965-72, regional mgr., 1972-74, v.p. retail mktg., asst. gen. sales mgr., 1974-75, sr. v.p. mktg., 1975-78, exec. v.p., 1978-82; pres. J.H. Baumgartner Enterprises, Brookfield, Wis., 1982—; v.p., owner Robert Kidd & Assocs. Inc., 1990—. Served with USMC, 1954-56.

BAUMGARTNER, MARY ANNE SGARLAT, academic administrator, entrepreneur; b. Boston, Apr. 5, 1958; d. Francis Abbott and Elizabeth Maria (Paragallo) Sgarlat; m. Michael von Arx Baumgartner, Nov. 18, 2000. Grad., Milton Acad.; student, Roedean Sch., Brighton, Eng.; BA, Bennington Coll., 1979. Adminstr. Harvard U., Cambridge, Mass., 1979-86; pub. rels. dir. Graham Gund Architects, Cambridge, 1986-89; mktg. and comms. mgr. Elkus/Manfredi Architects, Boston, 1989-90; comms. mgr. Turan Corp., Boston, 1990-92; mktg. dir. The Design Partnership of Cambridge, 1992-97; mng. dir. The Bounty Group, 1997—; mktg. mgr. Yolles Ptnrship. Ltd., 1998-99, Bishoff Solomon Comms., 1999-2000; adminstr. Kennedy Sch. Govt., Cambridge, 2000—. Mem.: LWV, Mus. Fine Arts, Harvard U. Art Museums, Focus Internat., Bennington Coll. Alumni Assn. (regional dir. 1993—97, exec. com. 1986—93). Avocations: politics, music, dancing, antiques, sailing. Office: Kennedy Sch Govt 79 JFK St Cambridge MA 02138

BAUMGARTNER, REUBEN ALBERT, retired school administrator; b. Pearl City, Ill., Dec. 30, 1912; s. Albert Centennial and Laura Anna (Hummermeir) B.; m. Arleigh Camille Mears, June 27, 1942 (dec. Aug. 1969); 1 child, Richard. BA, U. Ill., 1934, MA, 1935; postgrad., U. Iowa, 1938, 41, 55. Math. instr. Polo (Ill.) High Sch., 1935-38, N.D. State U., Fargo, 1938-40; dept. head, math. instr. Freeport (Ill.) High Sch., 1940-56; dir. adult edn. Freeport Pub. Schs., 1949-55; prin. Freeport High Sch., 1956-72; curriculum dir. Freeport Pub. Schs., 1972-77. Contbr. articles to profl. jours. State coord. 55 Alive/Mature Driving, Ill., 1985-88; pres. Stephenson County Sr. Ctr., Freeport, 1975-77; mem. Sec. of State Sr. Adv. Com., Ill., 1983-88. Lt. USN, 1942-46. Mem. Kiwanis (pres. 1954-55, lt. gov. 1975-76). Presbyterian. Avocations: reading, swimming, walking. Home: # 221 1234 S Park Blvd Freeport IL 61032-4602

BAUMGARTNER, ROBERT, consultant; b. Dallas, Aug. 20, 1934; s. Oren Floyd and Jessie Elizabeth (Seale) B.; m. Sabina Jumatayeva, Aug. 1, 1998; children: Janet, Cathy, Diane, Mitchell. BBA, So. Meth. U., 1956. V.p. Rep. Nat. Bank, Dallas, 1958-70, Bank of Southwest, Houston, 1970-71; v.p., treas. Marathon Mfg. Co., Inc., Houston, 1971-78; CEO Amistad Well Svc., Houston, 1978-79; treas. Anderson Clayton & Co., Inc., Houston, 1980-82; pres. Baumgartner Capital, Austin, Tex., 1982—. Mem. Assn. Corp. Growth, Fin. Execs. Inst., Beta Gamma Sigma. Republican. Methodist. Avocations: golf, travel. Home and Office: Tex Bus Svcs 12400 Wycliff Ln Austin TX 78727-5219 E-mail: bb@onr.com.

BAUMGARTNER, WILLIAM ANTHONY, cardiac surgeon; b. Covington, Ky., Apr. 18, 1947; s. Nicholas Raymond and Rosemary (Blank) Baumgartner; m. Betsy Reik; children: Bill Jr., Amy, Mark. BS, Xavier U., 1969; MD, U. Ky., 1973. Intern surgery Stanford (Calif.) U. Med. Ctr., 1973-74, asst. resident gen. surgery, 1974-75, asst. resident cardiothoracic surgery, 1975-76, asst. resident cardiovasc. surgery, 1976-77, chief resident cardiovasc. surgery, 1977-78, chief resident thoracic surgery, 1978, asst. resident gen. surgery, 1978-80, chief resident, 1980-81; cardiac surgeon-in-charge Johns Hopkins U. Sch. Medicine, Balt., 1993—. Vincent L. Gott prof. Editor: (book) Heart and Heart Lung Transplantation, 1990, 2001. Grantee, NIH, 1988, 1992, 1995, 2000. Mem.: ACS, Clin. Practice Assn. (pres., vice dean clin. practice 1999—), Soc. Univ. Surgeons, Am. Assn. Thoracic Surgery, Am. Soc. Transplant Surgeons, Internat. Soc. Heart and Lung Transplantation, Soc. Thoracic Surgeons (pres. 2002—03), Am. Surg. Assn. Office: Johns Hopkins Hosp 600 N Wolfe St # 618 Baltimore MD 21287-0005 E-mail: wbaumgar@csurg.jhmi.jhu.edu.

BAUMHART, RAYMOND CHARLES, Roman Catholic church administrator; b. Chgo., Dec. 22, 1923; s. Emil and Florence (Weidner) B. BS, Northwestern U., 1945; PhL, Loyola U., 1952, STL, 1958; MBA, Harvard U., 1953; DBA, Harvard, 1963; LLD (hon.), Ill. Coll., 1977; DHL (hon.), Scholl Coll. Podiatric Medicine, 1983, Rush U., Chgo., 1987, Northwestern U., 1993, Xavier U., Cin., 1994, Ill. Benedictine Coll., 1994. Joined Jesuit Order, 1946; ordained priest Roman Cath. Ch., 1957. Asst. prof. mgmt. Loyola U., Chgo., 1962-64, dean Sch. Bus. Adminstrn., 1964-66, exec. v.p., acting v.p. Med. Ctr., 1968-70, pres., 1970-93; cons. to Cardinal George, Cath. Archdiocese of Chgo., 2000—. Alfred Ring lectr. U. Fla., 1988; John and Mildred Wright lectr. Fairfield U., 1992; D. B. Reinhart lectr. Viterbo Coll., 2000; bd. dirs. Ceres Food Group, Inc. Author: An Honest Profit, 1968, (with Thomas Garrett) Cases in Business Ethics, 1968, (with Thomas McMahon) The Brewer-Wholesaler Relationship, 1969; corr. editor: America, 1965-70. Trustee St. Louis U., 1967-72, Boston Coll., 1968-71; bd. dirs. Coun. Better Bus. Burs., 1971-77, Cath. Health Alliance Met. Chgo., 1986-93; mem. U.S. Bishops and Pres.'s Com. on Higher Edn., 1980-84, Jobs for Met. Chgo., 1984-85, Chgo. Health Care Industry, 1990-94. Decorated cavalier Order of Merit, Italy, 1971, commendatore, 1994; recipient Rale medallion Boston Coll., 1976, Daniel Lord S.J. award Loyola Acad., Wilmette, Ill., 1992, Mary Potter Humanitarian award Little Company of Mary Hosp., Ill., 1993, Sword of Loyola Loyola U., Chgo., 1993, Theodore Hesburgh award Assn. Cath. Colls. and Univs., 1995; John W. Hill fellow Harvard U., 1961-62, Cambridge Ctr. for Social Studies Rsch. fellow, 1966-68. Mem. Comml. Club, Mid-Am. Club, Tavern Club. Roman Catholic. Home: 6525 N Sheridan Rd Chicago IL 60626-5344 E-mail: rbaumhart@archdiocese-chgo.org.

BAUMHEFNER, CLARENCE HERMAN, banker; b. Lester Prairie, Minn., Apr. 1, 1912; s. Walter P. and Clare A. (Jacobs) B.; m. Virginia Haight, May 11, 1941; children— Robert, Bonnie. Grad., Am. Inst. Banking, 1940; student, Grad. Sch. Banking, Rutgers U., 1951. With Bank of Am., 1940—, Bank of Am. (inspection dept.), 1940-43, insp., 1943-47, asst. chief insp., 1947-50, asst. to cashier, 1950-56, cashier and v.p., 1956-65, sr. v.p., cashier, 1965-66, exec. v.p., 1966-70, vice chmn. bd., 1970—2003. Mem.: Merchants Exchange (San Francisco), Bankers (San Francisco), Bohemian (San Francisco), Pacific Union (San Francisco). Home and Office: 555 California St Ste 1100 San Francisco CA 94104-1514

BAUMHEINRICH, THORSTEN FRANK, electrical engineer; b. Oberhausen, Germany, Jan. 13, 1969; s. Klaus Juergen and Margot Baumheinrich. MSEE in elec. engring., Ruhr U., Bochum, Germany, 1995, PhD in Elec. Engring., 2000. Rsch. asst. Ruhr U., 1995-99; sr. design engr. Tex. Instruments Inc., Dallas, 2000—02; prin. design engr. Inphi-Corp., Westlake Village, Calif., 2002—. Contbr. articles to profl. jours., confs. Mem. IEEE. Avocations: sports, reading, music, travel, family. Home: 7176 University Dr Moorpark CA 93021-3235 Office: Inphi Corp 2393 Townsgate Rd Ste 101 Westlake Village CA 91361 Office Fax: 805-446-5190. E-mail: tbaumheinrich@inphi-corp.com.

BAUMLER, ROBERT ALBERT, cardiologist; b. Buffalo, Aug. 26, 1927; s. Raymond John and Alma Gertrude (Gebhardt) B.; m. Jane Watts Hatch, Oct. 10, 1959; 1 child, Ann Elizabeth Baumler Harrington. MD, U. Buffalo, 1952; BA, Canisius Coll., 1982. Diplomate Am. Bd. Internal Medicine, Am. Bd. Cardiovascular Disease, Am. Bd. Geriatric Medicine. Rotating intern E.J. Meyer Meml. Hosp., Buffalo, 1952-53; resident in medicine Buffalo Gen. Hosp., 1953-55; resident in cardiology New Eng. Ctr. Hosp., Boston, 1955-56; physician Buffalo Gen. Hosp., 1956—; clin. asst. prof. medicine SUNY, Buffalo, 1960—. Fellow Am. Coll. Physicians, Am. Coll. Cardiology, Coun. Clin. Cardiology, Am. Heart Assn.; mem. Buffalo Med. Hist. Soc. Avocations: lit., history, philosophy. Home: 92 South Dr Buffalo NY 14226-4127 Office: 77 Broadway St Ste 110 Buffalo NY 14203-1642

BAUMRIN, BERNARD STEFAN HERBERT, lawyer, educator; b. N.Y.C., Jan. 7, 1934; s. David and Regina (Zuckerbrg) B.; m. Judith Anne Marti, Dec. 20, 1953; children: Seth, Jeanne, Rachel. Student, Marietta Coll., 1951-52, NYU, 1952-53; BA, Ohio State U., 1956; PhD, Johns Hopkins U., 1960;

postgrad., Washington U., St. Louis, 1965-67; JD, Columbia U., 1970. Dir. forensics Johns Hopkins U., Balt., 1957—59; vis. asst. prof. philosophy Butler U., 1960—61, Antioch Coll., 1961; asst. prof. philosophy U. Del., Newark, 1961—64, Washington U., 1964—67; assoc. prof. philosophy Hunter Coll., CUNY, 1967—68, assoc. prof. philosophy Grad. Sch. and Lehman Coll., 1968—72, prof., 1972—, treas. univ. faculty senate, 1978—81, 1990, exec. com., 1976—84, 1987—91, 1992—93, 1998—99, 2002—; ptnr. Baumrin, Galub & Volkomer, 1979—. Adj. prof. med. edn. Mt. Sinai Sch. of Medicine, 1988—; bd. dirs. CUNY Acad. for the Humanities and Scis. Author: Philosophy of Science, 2 vols., 1963, British Moralists, 1964, Hobbes's Leviathan, 1968, Moral Responsibility and the Professions, 1983; U.S. editor: Jour. Applied Philosophy, 1986—2001, mem. adv. bd.: Jour. Philosophy Psychiatry and Psychology, 1995—; cons. editor Metaphilosophy, 1968—; contbr. articles to profl. jours. AEC fellow, 1963, U. Del. fellow, 1962, Washington U. Forsyth fellow, 1964-67; CUNY grantee, 1968, 70, 89, 91, 93, N.Y. Council for Humanities grantee, 1976, NEH grantee, 1977-79, 91, Mellon Found. grantee, 1980-84, Am. Council Learned Socs. grantee, 1987. Mem. AAAS, AAUP, ACLU, N.Y. State Bar Assn. (chmn. ethics subcom., com. on legal edn. and admission to bar 1986—), Mind Assn., Am. Philos. Assn. (chmn. standing com. on philosophy and medicine 1988-92, chmn. standing com. on philosophy and law 1998-2001), Soc. for Philosophy and Pub. Affairs, Internat. Assn. Philosophy of Law and Social Philosophy, Conf. on Methods in Philosophy and the Scis. (chmn. 1988-90), Internat. Hobbes Assn. (exec. com. 1986—), Internat. Soc. Econs. and Philosophy (treas. 1994—). Office: CUNY Grad Sch 365 5th Ave New York NY 10016-4334 also: Lehman Coll Philosophy Dept Bronx NY 10468 E-mail: bhaumrin@tiac.net.

BAUMRIND, DIANA, research psychologist; b. N.Y.C., Aug. 23, 1927; AB, Hunter Coll., 1948; MA, U. Calif., Berkeley, 1951, PhD, 1955. Cert. and lic. psychologist, Calif. Project dir. psychology dept. U. Calif., Berkeley, 1955-58; project dir. Inst. of Human Devel., 1960—, also rsch. psychologist and prin. investigator family socialization and devel. competence project. Lectr. and cons. in field; referee for rsch. proposals Grant Found., NIH, 1970—, NSF, 1970—. Contbr. numerous articles to profl. jours. and books; author 2 monographs; mem. editorial bd. Devel. Psychology, 1986-90, Parenting: Science and Practice, 2000—. Recipient Rsch. Scientist award, NIMH; grantee NIMH, 1955-58, 60-66, Nat. Inst. Child Health and Human Devel., 1967-74, MacArthur Found., Grant Found., 1967—. Fellow Am. Psychol. Assn., Am. Psychol. Soc. (G. Stanley Hall award 1988), Soc. Research in Child Devel. Office: U Calif Inst of Human Devel 1217 Tolman Hall Berkeley CA 94720-1691

BAUMSTEIN, PASCHAL M. priest; b. Coffee County, Tenn., Sept. 16, 1950; s. Josef ben-Abram and Mae (Winton) Baumstein. AA, Aquinas Coll., Nashville, 1972; AB, Holy Apostles Coll., Cromwell, Conn., 1973; MDiv, St. Meinrad Coll., Ind., 1979; AM, Ind. U., 1979. Monk Benedictine Order, 1974, ordained priest Roman Cath. Ch., 1979. Faculty Belmont Abbey Coll., Belmont, NC, 1977—80; archivist-historian Belmont Abbey/Belmont Abbey Coll., 1979—96, archivist-historian emeritus, 1996—; editor CRESCAT, Belmont, 1977—87; book editor Cistercian Studies Quar., Gethsemani, Ky., 1997—98. Chaplain Abbey Players of Belmont Abbey Coll., 1977—; calligrapher Cath. Worker, 1999—; expert, cons. on work and life of Anselm of Canterbury and Robert Hugh Benson. Author: My Lord of Belmont, 1985, Blessing the Years to Come, 1997; contbr. over 100 revs. to profl. jours., numerous articles to profl. jours. Mem. Pax Christi, Cath. Peace Fellowship; mem. archivists exec. bd. Cath. Libr. Assn., 1982—96; bd. trustees Belmont Abbey Coll., 1986—94. Mem.: Am. Cath. Philos. Soc., Acad. Cert. Archivists (cert. archivist), Internat. Arthurian Soc. (life), Am. Cath. Hist. Assn. (life), Phi Sigma Tau (sec. 1979—84), Delta Epsilon Sigma, Alpha Phi Gamma. Home and Office: Belmont Abbey 100 Belmont-Mount Holly Rd Belmont NC 28012-1802

BAUNER, RUTH ELIZABETH, library administrator, reference librarian; b. Quincy, Ill. d. John Carl and M. Irene (Nutt) B. BS in Edn., Western Ill. U., 1950; MS, U. Ill., 1956; postgrad., So. Ill. U., 1974, PhD, 1978. Asst. res. libr. Western Ill. U., Macomb, 1950; tchr., libr. Sandwich (Ill.) Twp. High Sch., 1950-54; circulation dept. asst. U. Ill. Libr., Urbana, 1955; asst. edn. libr. So. Ill. U., Carbondale, 1956-63, acting edn. libr., 1963-64, edn. and psychology libr., 1965-93, assoc. prof. curriculum and instrn. dept., 1971-93; coord. freshman yr. experience program, vis. assoc. prof. Coll. of Liberal Arts, Carbondale, 1994-96. Dir. Grad. Residence Ctr. Librs., So. Ill. U., 1973-79; subject matter expert Learning Resources Svc. Interactive Video, Carbondale, 1990-91, also scriptwriter. Co-author: The Teacher's Library, 1966; contbr. articles to profl. jours. Pres. alumni constituency bd. Coll. Edn., Carbondale, 1988—89; mem. Carbondale Bd. Ethics, 1989—2001; tchr. I Can Read Program, 2001—03; mem. Carbondale Citizens Adv. Commn., 1999—2001; bd. dirs. So. Ill. U. chpt. UN, 1985—86, 1994—97, So. Ill. Learning in Retirement, So. Ill. U. Emeritus Assn., Jackson County AARP, 1997—99, 2001—. Recipient Luck Has Nothing To Do With It award Oryx Press, 1993. Mem.: AAUW (univ. rep. Carbondale br. 1988—89), ALA, Ill. Libr. Assn., Assn. Coll. and Rsch. Librs. (chmn. edn. and behavioral scis. sect. 1976—77, Most Active Mem. award 1968—93), AAUP (v.p. So. Ill. U. chpt. 1972—73), Delta Kappa Gamma (Inter-Varsity Christian Fellowship award for svc. 1956—2001), Phi Kappa Phi, Phi Delta Kappa (Women of Distinction award 1999). Office: 1206 W Freeman St Carbondale IL 62901-2351

BAUR, WERNER HEINZ, mineralogist, educator; b. Warsaw, Aug. 2, 1931; came to U.S., 1962; s. Heinrich Ernst and Melanie B.; m. Renate, June 22, 1962; children: Wolfgang, Brigitte. Dr. rer.nat, U. Gottingen, Germany, 1956, privatdozent, 1961. Sci. officer U. Göttingen, 1956-63; asst. to assoc. prof. U. Pitts., 1963-65; asso. prof. to prof. U. Ill.-Chgo., 1965-86, head dept. geol. scis., 1967-80, asso. dean Coll. Liberal Arts and Scis., 1978-80; prof. crystallography, chair dept. Johann Wolfgang Goethe U., Frankfurt am Main, Fed. Republic Germany, 1986-96; sr. scientist, dept. geophys. sci. U. Chgo., 1997—. Postdoctoral fellow U. Berne, Switzerland, 1957; vis. asso. chemist Brookhaven Nat. Lab., 1962-63; vis. prof. U. Karlsruhe, Germany, 1971-72 Assoc. editor Crystallography Revs.; editor, author multivol. treatise on Microporous and other Framework Materials with Zeolite Type Structures, 5 vols., 2000, 2002; contbr. articles to sci. jours. Fellow Mineral. Soc. Am.; mem. Am. Crystallographical Assn., Am. Geophys. Union. Achievements include research on crystal chemistry of minerals and inorganic compounds, electronic databases, crystal structure determination, zeolites, computer simulation of crystal structures, empirical theories of chem. bonding, predictive crystal chemistry. E-mail: whbaur@eudoramail.com.

BAURES, MARY MARGARET, clinical psychotherapist, author; b. St. Petersburg, Fla., Sept. 13, 1947; d. Robert A. and Ruth S. Baures; divorced. BS, U. Fla., 1969; MA, Boston U., 1976, EdM, 1984; Cert. Advanced Grad. Study in Human Devel., Harvard U., 1986; D in Clin. Psychology, Antioch New Eng., 1994; MS in Psychopharm. Instr. Emerson Coll., Boston, 1981-86; counselor Beverly (Mass.) Hosp., 1984-86; emergency svc. clinician Ctr. for Mental Health, Waltham, Mass., 1987-91; psychotherapist Mass. Sch. Profl. Psychology, Danvers, Mass., 1989—2002, Human Resource Inst., Brookline, Mass., 1993—. Mem. neuropsychology intern Northshore Children's Hosp., Salem, Mass., 1990-91; founder, dir. Boycott Anorexic Mktg., 1993—. Author: (novels) Undaunted Spirits-Portraits of Recovery from Trauma, 1994; co-prodr.: (documentaries) Strong at the Broken Places-Turning Trauma into Recovery, 1998, Letting Go of Bitterness and Hate Jour. of Humanistic Psychology, 1996; exhibitions include Animal Dreams watercolor show, Hooper Mansion, 2001. Office: Essex Green Dr Ste 65 Peabody MA 01960

BAURICHTER, JOHN DANIEL, osteopath; b. Columbia, Mo., Dec. 13, 1961; s. Cletus Edwin and Hazel Frances (Newcomer) B.; m. Kathleen Diane Ramsey, June 27, 1987; children: Katherine, Joshua. AB in Biology, U. Mo., 1984; DO, U. Health Scis., 1989. Diplomate Am. Coll. of Ostepathic Family Physicians. Resident Still Regional Med. Ctr., Jefferson City, Mo., 1989-92; physician Family Med. Ctr., Rogersville, Mo., 1992-98, East Sunshine Family Practice, Springfield, Mo., 1998—. Mem. Am. Osteopathic Assn., Mo. Assn. of Osteopathic Family Physicians, Am. Coll. of Osteopathic Family Physicians, Ozark Dist. Osteopathic Assn. (v.p. 1995-96, pres. 1997), Sigma Sigma Phi, Phi Sigma Alpha. Southern Baptist. Avocations: fly fishing, sports. Office: E Sunshine Family Practice 2730 E Sunshine St Springfield MO 65804-2047 E-mail: jbaurichter@mchsi.com.

BAUSCH, JAMES JOHN, foundation executive; b. New Brunswick, N.J., May 1, 1936; s. Charles John and Colette (Perdoni) B.; m. Janet Ellen Safer, May 22, 1970; children: Jennifer, David. Student, Fordham U., 1953-54; BS, St. Peter's Coll., 1955-58; postgrad., Emory U., 1958-61, Wharton Sch., U. Pa., 1977. Lectr. in social sci. Emory U., Ga. Inst. Tech., Atlanta, 1958-61; vol. U.S. Peace Corps, Bangladesh, 1961-63; chief U.S. Peace Corps South Asia div., Washington, 1965-69; dir. tng. Experiment in Internat. Living, Brattleboro, Vt., 1963-64; dir. edn. Coun. on Internat. Ednl. Exch., N.Y.C., 1964-65; program officer Ford Found., N.Y.C., 1969-71, 73-76, rep. Jakarta, Indonesia, 1971-73; v.p., sec. The Population Coun., N.Y.C., 1976-88; pres. Save the Children Fedn., Westport, Conn., 1988-92; vice chmn. A.T. Hudson & Co., Oradell, N.J., 1992-94; pres. J.J. Bausch Cons. Svcs., River Vale, N.J., 1992-94, Nat. Charities Info. Bur., N.Y.C., 1994-99; cons. in philanthropy, 1999—. Trustee, mem. exec. com., chmn. fin. com., chmn. investment com., co-chmn. N.Y. Assocs. World Learning, Inc., Brattleboro, Vt., 1980-88; trustee, sec.-treas. Internat. Child Health Found., Columbia, Md., 1985-87, chmn. bd. trustees, 1987-94; mem. fin. com. Population Coun. 1976-88; trustee Ctr. Pvt. Vol. Orgns./Univ. Collaboration, N.C., 1990-92, Ind. Sector, Washington, 1991-93. Chmn. UNICEF Action for Children, N.Y.C., 1985—89; mem. Bretton Woods Com., Washington, 1991—; chmn. bd. advisors U. South Fla. Sr. Acad., 2003—; trustee Selby Bot. Gardens, 2001—, sec. bd. trustees, 2002—03. Mem. N.Y. Acad. Scis., Population Assn. Am., Am. Pub. Health Assn., Nat. Coun. Internat. Health (mem. exec. com. 1991-92), Carnegie Coun. on Ethics and Internat. Affairs, Nat. Peace Corps Assn. Democrat. Home: 4865 Featherbed Ln Sarasota FL 34242-1558

BAUSCH, RICHARD CARL, writer, educator; b. Ft. Benning, Ga., Apr. 18, 1945; s. Robert Carl and Helen (Simmons) B.; m. Karen Miller, May 3, 1969; children: Wesley, Emily, Paul, Maggie, Amanda. BA, George Mason U., 1973; MFA, U. Iowa, 1975. Instr. No. Va. C.C., Annandale, Va., 1975-80; prof., Heritage chair of creative writing George Mason U., Fairfax, Va., 1980—. Vis. prof. U. Va., Charlottesville, 1985, 88, Wesleyan U., Middletown, Conn., 1986, 90, 92, 93; lectr., reader in field. Author: (stories) Spirits and Other Stories, 1987 (PEN/Faulkner award nomination 1988), The Fireman's Wife & Other Stories, 1990, Rare & Endangered Species, 1994, Modern Library Selected Stories, 1996, Someone to Watch Over Me, 1999; (novels) Real Presence, 1980, Take Me Back, 1981 (PEN/Faulkner award nomination 1982), The Last Good Time, 1984, Mr. Field's Daughter, 1989, Violence, 1992, Rebel Powers, 1993, Good Evening Mr. & Mrs. America and All the Ships At Sea, 1996, In the Night Season, 1998. Recipient Lila Wallace Reader's Best Writer's award Lila Wallace Fund, 1992, Acad. award in Lit. AAAL, 1993; grantee Nat. Endowment for the Arts, 1982; Guggenheim fellow John Simon Guggenheim Found., 1984. Fellow So. Writers; mem. PEN Am. Democrat. Roman Catholic. Avocations: songwriting, singing. Office: George Mason U Dept English 4400 University Dr Fairfax VA 22030-4444

BAUSCHINGER, SIGRID ELISABETH, German literature educator, researcher; b. Frankfurt am Main, Germany, Nov. 2, 1934; came to U.S., 1962; d. Klement Johann and Luise Elisabeth Bauschinger. DPhil, Goethe U., Frankfurt am Main, 1959. Editor Ullstein Verlag, Frankfurt am Main, 1960-62; instr. to asst. prof. German Oberlin (Ohio) Coll., 1962-68; asst. prof. German U. Mass., Amherst, 1968-70, assoc. prof. German, 1970-76, prof. German, 1976—2000; ret., 2000. Author: Else Lasker-Schüler, ihr Werk und ihre Zeit, 1980, The Trumpet of Reform, English translation, 1999; editor: Ich labe etwas zu sagen, Annette Kolb 1870-1967, 1993. Mem. Am. Assn. Tchrs. German (hon.). Avocations: theatre, hiking, skiing. Home: 7 Pease Pl Amherst MA 01002 E-mail: baushin@german.umass.edu.

BAUSE, DAVID FRANCIS, printing company professional; b. Boyertown, Pa., Feb. 16, 1936; s. Daniel Eagle Sr. and Frances Margaret (Dieter) B.; m. Janice Elaine Croyle, Aug. 19, 1961; children: Erin Elaine Bause Landry, Amy F. Bause Bartra. BA in Communications, Am. U., 1957. Radio announcer Sta. WRAW, Reading, Pa., 1959-61; mdse. mgr. Bause Super Drug Stores, Boyertown, Pa., 1961-64; area dir. Dale Carnegie Courses, Phila., 1964-68; owner, operator Copy Fast Printing, Pottstown, Pa., 1968—. Instr. color photography Albright Coll., Reading, 1988; seminar presenter Nat. Assn. Quick Printers, 1988; instr. Owen J. Roberts Evening Sch., Pottstown, 1991—, Boscov's Evening Sch., 1991—; entertainer The Great Am. Juggling and Fun Show; coord. June Jugglefest, Kutztown (Pa.) U., 1998; instr. juggling Boscov's Dept. Stores, Owen J. Roberts Schs., Internat. Juggling Workshop, Montreal, 2000; participant Adobe Photoshop Tng., 1999, Nat. Assn. Photoshop Profls., 1999, Kris Kremo Juggling Workshop at Internat. Jugglers Conv., Niagara Falls, N.Y., 1999, Digital Photo Workshop, Fla.; workshop leader, media dir. 55th Internat. Jugglers Festival, Reading, 2002; advanced Reiki tng., 1999. Author: Create Your Own Newsletter, 1985, Dave Bause's Laugh Book, 2000, Thought Lifters, 2002; editor Season, 1977— (Print award 1991); photographer Country Mag., Juggler's Mag.; contbr. articles and photographs to profl. jours.; exhibited photo display at Borders Books, Reading, Pa. Staff vol. Found. "I", Inc., 1989-94; bd. dirs. Fellowship Farm, Sanatoga, Pa., 1984, Grace Luth. Ch., Pottstown, Pa., 1970-74, Transfiguration Luth. Ch., Pottstown, 1986-89; media dir. Internat. 55th Juggling Festival, 2002. Scholar Am. U., 1956; recipient photog. awards Kodak, 1985, Individual Achievement award Freedoms Found., 1986. Mem. Internat. Jugglers Assn. (life), Phila. Jugglers Club, Reading Jugglers Club (co-founder, coord., Contbr.'s award 1992), Pottsgrove High Twelve Club (pres., sec. 1987-91), Pottstown Writer's Group (co-founder), Limelight Theater (Limelight award), Masons (25 Yr. award 1991), Omicron Delta Kappa. Republican. Lutheran. Avocations: photography, swimming, juggling, racquetball. Home: 2156 N Hill Camp Rd Pottstown PA 19465-7127 Office: Copy Fast Printing 246 King St Pottstown PA 19464-5542

BAUSE, GEORGE STEPHEN LONERAVEN, anesthesiologist; b. Chester, Pa., Nov. 22, 1955; BS in Biophysics, Ursinus Coll., 1977; MPH in Epidemiology, Johns Hopkins U., 1981, MD, 1981. Diplomate Am. Bd. Anesthesiology. Intern Johns Hopkins Hosp., Balt., 1981-82, resident in anesthesiology, 1982-84; fellow geriatric anesthesiology Johns Hopkins Hosp.-Nat. Inst. Aging, Balt., 1984-85; attending physician Yale-New Haven Hosp., 1985-92, dir. geriatric anesthesia, 1987-92; chief dept. anesthesia West Haven (Conn.) VA Med. Ctr., 1990-92; Whitacre dir. anesthesia edn. Meridia Health Sys., Ohio, 1992-96; asst. prof. Yale U., New Haven, 1985-91, assoc. prof., 1991-92; assoc. clin. prof. anesthesiology Case Western Res. U., Cleve., 1994—. Hon. curator USA's Wood Libr.-Mus. Anesthesiology, 1987—; assoc. curator USA's United Ch. of Christ, 2000—, George and Ramona Bause Collection, USA's Wood Libr. Mus., 2002. Pres. Yale Assn. Native Americans, 1988—90. Recipient Internat. William Halsted prize in Anesthesiology, 1993. Fellow: Coll. Physicians Phila., Internat. Coll. Surgeons, Acad. Anesthesiology, Royal Soc. Medicine; mem.: AMA, Soc. Cardiovasc. Anesthesiologists, Soc. Advancement Geriatric Anesthesiology, Internat. Anesthesia Rsch. Soc., Am. Soc. Regional Anesthesia, Am. Soc. Anesthesiologists, Am. Geriat. Soc. Office: 5247 Wilson Mills # 282 Cleveland OH 44143-3016

BAUSELL, R. BARKER, JR., research methodology educator; s. Rufus B. and Nellie (Bowman) B.; m. Carole R. Vinograd, Jan. 6, 1978; children: Jesse T., Rebecca B. BS in Edn., U. Del., 1968, PhD in Ednl. Rsch. and Evaluation, 1975. Rsch. methodologist Med. Coll. Pa., 1975-76; prof., coord. faculty rsch. U. Md., Balt., 1976-91, dir. office rsch. methodology, 1991-94, prof. rsch., 1994-98, dir. rsch. complementary medicine program, 1998—. Sr. scientist Demarna Found. for Med. Care, 1994-98; cons., part-time dir. prevention rsch. ctr. Rodale Press, Inc.; presenter numerous seminars and confs. Author: (with C.R. Bausell and N.B. Bausell) The Bausell Home Learning Guide: Teach Your Child to Read, 1980, (with C.R. Bausell and N.B. Bausell) The Bausell Home Learning Guide: Teach Your Child to Write, 1980, (with C.F. Waltz) Nursing Research: Design, Statistics and Computer Analysis, 1981, (with C.R. Bausell and N.B. Bausell) The Bausell Home Learning Guide: Teach Your Child Math, A Practical Guide to Conducting Empirical Research, 1986, An Instructor's Manual for a Practical Guide to Conducting Empirical Research, 1986, (with C. Inlander and M. Rooney) How to Evaluate and Select a Nursing Home, 1988, Advanced Research Methodology: An Annotated Guide to Sources, 1991, Conducting Meaningful Experiments, 1994, (with Yu-Fang Li) Power Analysis for Experimental Research, 2002; editor: Evaluation and the Health Professions; author numerous monographs; contbr. numerous articles to profl. jours. Recipient Outstanding Rsch. award Nat. Wellness Conf., 1986, 87, Gov.'s award Meritorious Svc., 1992, award for Disting. Assessment Project Md. Assessment Resource Ctr., 1993. Achievements include research on documented effects of class size on student learning, effects of teacher experience on student learning, and determinants of health seeking (preventative) behavior. Home: 1311 Doves Cove Rd Baltimore MD 21286-1426 Office: U Md Complementary Med Program 2200 Kernan Dr Baltimore MD 21207-6665

BAUSHER, VERNE C(HARLES), banker; b. Reading, Pa. s. La Verne H. and Helen M. (Dornes) B.; m. Sandra Stamm Bausher, May 22, 1965; children: Christopher S., Gretchen S., Samantha A., Andrew P. BS, Drexel U., 1961; MBA, Northwestern U., 1962. Asst. v.p. Cen. Nat. Bank of Cleve., 1962-69; v.p. Meridian Bank (formerly American Bank and Trust Co. of Pa.), Reading, 1969-83; exec. v.p. Penn Savs. Bank, Wyomissing, 1983-87; exec. v.p., chief lending officer Germantown Savs. Bank, Bala Cynwyd, Pa., 1987—. Trustee, v.p. Pub. Edn. Found. for Berks County, 1986—; bd. dirs. Wilson Sch. Dist., West Lawn, Pa., 1977—, pres., 1989-90; bd. dirs. Berks County Intermediate Unit, Reading, 1977—, YMCA of Reading, 1987-89. Republican. Lutheran. Avocations: reading, swimming, diving. Home: 4152 Hill Terrace Dr Sinking Spring PA 19608-9384 Office: Germantown Savs Bank One Belmont Ave Bala Cynwyd PA 19004

BAUTISTA, MICHAEL PHILLIP, school system administrator; b. Merced, Calif., June 15, 1952; s. Ynacio and Frances (Garcia) B.; m. Nancy Ruth End, Aug. 4, 2000; children: Michael P., Lisa M., Rachel, Sam. B Music Edn., Emporia State U., 1974, MA, 1975; PhD, Tex. Tech U., 1981; adminstrv. cert., Okla. State U., 1986. Cert. adminstr., Colo., Supt., secondary prin., Okla., bldg. adminstr., Kans. Instr. U. Nebr., Lincoln, 1977-79; asst. prof. U. Tulsa, 1979-82; dir., adminstr. Jenks Pub. Schs., Tulsa, 1983-92; coord., adminstr. Denver Sch. of the Arts, Denver Pub. Schs., 1991-97, adminstrv. dir., 1997-99, divsn. dir. Kenneth King Acad. and Performing Arts Ctr., 1999—. Part-time instr. Tex. Tech U., Lubbock, 1975-77, Tulsa Jr. Coll., 1982-83; theatrical cons. MPB Assocs., Tulsa, 1983-91; v.p. internat. Network for Performing and Visual Arts Schs. Author: Ten Years of Stage Design at the Met (1966-1976); theatrical designer for various stage prodns. Bd. dirs. Carson-Brierly Dance Libr., Denver, 1992-99, Friends of Chamber Music, Denver, 1992-99, Rocky Mountain Coll. of Art and Design, 1997—; mem. steering com. Harwelden Inst., Tulsa, 1983-91; inactive Boy Scouts Am.; mem. Mayor's subcom. Arts Edn.; mem. exec. bd. Colo. Arts Assn. for Edn.; cantor Holy Family Cath. Ch. Recipient Svc. award St. Bernhards Parish, 1990, Amoco award for set design Am. Coll. Theatre Festival, 1989, Documentary citation Kansas City, Mo. Star, 1970. Mem. ASCD, U.S. Inst. Theatre Tech. Roman Catholic. Avocations: hiking, photography, music, design, painting, videography. Home: 5980 Dunraven Ct Golden CO 80403 Office: Kenneth King Acad and Perf Arts Ctr Auraria Higher Edn Ctr BoxR PO Box 173361 Denver CO 80217-3361

BAUTZ, JEFFREY EMERSON, mechanical engineer, educator, researcher; b. Milw., Apr. 13, 1966; s. Thomas W. and Dona J. (Emerson) Bautz; m. Heather Sienkiewicz; 1 child, Madison;1 child, Kyle. BS in Math. and Engring. Mechanics, U. Wis., 1988, MS in Engring. Mechanics, 1989; postgrad., Stanford U., 1992—, Wayne State U., 1996—. Devel. engr. McDonnell Douglas Corp., St. Louis, 1989-90; rsch. engr. GE, Milw., 1990-91; engring. project mgr., cons. on finite element method GM & Body Structure Design, Detroit, 1991—; project mgr. internat. experience GM-Opel, Germany, 1997-99; project mgr. Ford Motor Co., Dearborn, Mich., 1999—, master black belt, 2003—. Instr. engring. mechanics U. Wis., Madison, 1988-89; pres. PEB Profls.; instr. indsl. tech. and math. Macomb C.C., Warren, Mich., 1992—; part-time engring. cons., facilitator Am. Speaks Orgn. Patentee in field. Mem. Rep. party, Macomb County, Mich. Recipient Master Mason Utica Lodge, Wayne State Univ., Hitchman Endowed Scholarship, 2002, Kean Meml. Scholarship, 2003. Mem. Am. Soc. Body Engrs., Engring. Soc. Detroit. Avocations: basketball, volleyball, golf, racquetball, six sigma black belt. Home: 48550 Brittany Parc Dr Macomb MI 48044-2119 Office: Mail Drop 69 21500 Oakwood Blvd Dearborn MI 48124-4080

BAUZA, CHRISTINE DIANE, special education educator; b. Santa Monica, Calif., Sept. 16, 1961; d. William Gene and Dorothy Louise (Evans) Lough; m. Joseph Henry Bauza, July 26, 1986; 1 child, Crystal Marie. AA in Liberal Arts, Crafton Hills Coll., Yucaipa, Calif., 1981; BA in Liberal Studies, Calif. State U., Northridge, 1983, MA in Deaf Edn., multiple subjects-spl. edn. credentials, Calif. State U., Northridge, 1986. Tchr. comm. handicapped edn. San Bernardino County Supt. Schs., Rialto, Calif., 1986-98, Rialto Unified Sch. Dist., 1998—. Tchr., cons. Cmty. Adv. Com., San Bernardino, Calif., 1990-91. Avocations: bowling, reading, crafts. Home: 1031 Cimarron Dr Redlands CA 92374-6335 Office: Bemis Elem Sch 774 E Etiwanda Ave Rialto CA 92376-4508

BAVASI, PETER JOSEPH, sports management executive; b. Bronxville, N.Y., Oct. 31, 1942; s. Emil Joseph and Evit E. (Rice) B.; m. Judith Marzonie, June 13, 1964; children: Patrick, Cristina BA in Philosophy, St. Mary's Coll., Moraga, Calif., 1964. Minor league gen. mgr. Los Angeles Dodgers, 1964-68; dir. minor league ops. San Diego Padres, 1968-73, v.p., gen. mgr., 1973-76; pres., chief exec. officer Toronto Blue Jays, Ont., Can., 1976-81; pres. Peter Bavasi Sports, Inc., Tampa, Fla., 1981-84; pres., chief operating officer Cleve. Indians, 1984-87; pres., chief exec. officer Telerate Sports and SportsTicker, Jersey City, 1987-94; pres. ESPN/SportsTicker, Jersey City, 1995-96; prin. Bavasi Sports Ptnrs., LLP, La Jolla, 2001—. Office: Bavasi Sports Ptnrs LLP 1001 Genter St Unit 3G La Jolla CA 92037-5531 E-mail: peter@bavasisports.com.

BAVER, ROY LANE, retired protection services official, consultant; b. Dayton, Ohio, Sept. 20, 1942; s. Paul Vincent and Winifred (Korn) B.; m. Sandra Jean Stephen, Oct. 7, 1967; children: Dawn Maria, Denise Michele, Diana Melissa. AAS, Sinclair C.C., Dayton, 1979; BA in Urban Affairs, Wright State U., Dayton, 1985. Cert. state fire safety inspector, class IV automatic sprinkler inspector, fire inspector level I, sr. fire inspector, paramedic, CPR/first aid instr. Mechanic Casey's Union Oil, Centerville, Ohio, 1967-70; sales rep. Hauer Music, Dayton, Ohio, 1970-73; dep. fire marshal Washington Twp. Fire Dept., Centerville, 1973-96; ret., 1996. Cons., RLB Consulting, Centerville, 1989—, R&S Enterprises, Centerville, 1997—; bd. dirs., treas. Americana Festival Inc.; mem. Ohio Bd. Bldg. Stds. Edn. Ad Hoc Com. Apptd. edn. ad hoc com. Ohio Bd. Bldg. Stds. With U.S. Army, 1964—66. Charter mem. Ohio Fire Off. Assn.; mem. Bldg. Ofcls. and Code Adminstrs. Internat., S.W. Ohio Fire Safety Coun. (bd. dirs., treas.), Ohio Bldg. Ofcls. Assn. (bd. dirs., Fire Ofcl. of Yr. 1993-94), Ohio Assn. Profl. Fire Fighters, Washington Twp. Fire Fighters Assn., Internat. Assn. Fire Fighters, Masons, Scottish Rite, Shriners, Order Ea. Star, Centerville HighTwelve Club, Internat. Shrine Clown Assn., Great Lakes Shrine Clown Unit Assn., Wright State Alumni Assn., City of Centerville Sister City Com. Assn. (assoc.), Phi Theta Kappa, Phi Alpha Alpha. Lutheran. Avocations: travel, collecting fire memorabilia, collecting stamps. Home: 145 Boyce Rd Centerville OH 45458-2475

BAVERO, RONALD JOSEPH, lawyer, legal educator; b. N.Y.C., Jan. 11, 1950; s. Joseph Carmine and Nancy (Martino) B.; m. Carolyn Angela Grippi, Aug. 20, 1972; children— Christen, Theresa, James, Joanna. B.A., Fordham U., 1971; J.D., St. John's U., N.Y.C., 1974. Bar: N.Y. 1975, U.S. Ct. Appeals (2d cir.) 1975, U.S. Dist. Ct. (ea. and so. dists.) N.Y. 1975, U.S. Supreme Ct., 1990. Law asst. appellate div. N.Y. State Supreme Ct., 1974-76; asst. dist. atty. Westchester County Dist. Atty.'s Office, White Plains, N.Y., 1976-82; prin. law sec. N.Y. State Family Ct., White Plains, 1982-85; ptnr. Fink & Weinberger, P.C., 1985-93, Hall Dickler Kent Friedman and Wood, 1993—; acting village justice Village of Elmsford, 1987-89; prof. law Pace U., Pleasantville, N.Y., 1982— . Editor Symposium on Law of Condominiums, 1974; assoc. editor St. John's Law Rev., 1974. Mem. N.Y. State Bar Assn., Westchester County Bar Assn., Columbian Lawyers Assn. Republican. Roman Catholic. Address: 11 Martine Ave White Plains NY 10606-1934

BAVICCHI, JOHN ALEXANDER, music educator; b. Apr. 25, 1922; s. Alexander and Sarah Elizabeth (Nolfi) B. Student, New Eng. Conservatory, 1948-52, Harvard U., 1952-55. Music instr. Rivers Country Day Sch., Weston, Mass., 1959-63; prof. composition Berklee Coll. Music, Boston, 1964—; condr. Arlington (Mass.) Philharm. Soc., 1968—2003. Composer band, percussion, choral, chamber and orchestral works. Served to lt. (j.g.) USN, 1942-46, also Res. Office: BKJ Publs PO Box 610377 Newton MA 02461-0377 E-mail: jbavicchi@berklee.edu.

BAVINGTON, BETTE ANNE, special needs educator; b. Malden, Mass., July 3, 1954; d. Edward Thomas and Laurel Anne Todd; m. Brian Anthony Bavington, Aug. 23, 1994; children: Ivy, Misty, Charles, Michael, Laurel, Rebecca, Regina. Tchrs. asst. Mentally Retarded Sch., Rockledge, Fla., 1972-73; ESL tchr. Cherrywood Elem. Sch., Berryessa, Calif., 1979-80; presch. tchr. Adlersgate Christian Sch., Seminole, Fla., 2000—; tchr. asst. for emotionally handicapped Bardmoor Elem. Sch., Seminole, Fla., 1999—, bus. asst., 1999—. Author: (poetry) Childhood Reality or Not Okay It's a Dream, 1997. PTA pres. Horace Cureton Elem. Sch., San Jose, Calif., 1982-83. Avocations: reading, writing, ceramics, wordsearch puzzles, painting.

BAVOTA, MICHAEL FRANCIS (MICHAEL RYAN), food products executive, freelance writer; b. Balt., Feb. 16, 1952; s. Roland Paul and Thelma (Baier) B.; m. Linda Sue DenBoer, Apr. 13, 2001; children: Ryan, Darrell, Noelani, Nicki, Jacob, Annice. Diploma, Inst. Children's Lit., 1980, Writers Digest Sch., 1983, 85. Seafood sales mgr. N.Y. region Grand Union, Elmwood Park, N.J., 1982-84; corp. seafood merchandiser Shoprite, Freehold, N.J., 1984-86; perishable dir. Carrefour U.S.A., Phila., 1986-88; sr. seafood cons. B.L.R. Assocs., Lakehurst, N.J., 1988-93; lead trainer U.S. Dept. Comml. Nat. Marine Fishery Svc./NOAA, 1993-96; corp. seafood merchandiser Kash N' Karry, Tampa, 1996-98, seafood dir. program sales and mktg., 1998—; pres. Michael Bavota, Inc. Author: Seafood Lover's Bible, 1999; bd. editl. advisors Seafood Bus. mag.; contbr. numerous stories and articles to profl. and pop. jours. and mags. Avocations: collecting coins, old and rare books. E-mail: bavota@msn.com.

BAWA, RAJ, education educator, educator, biodefense specialist, biotechnology company executive, patent agent; b. Chandigarh, Punjab, India, Dec. 1, 1963; came to U.S., 1979; s. Sukhdev Raj and Sudesh (Bhalla) B. *Dr. Bawa's doctoral research involved the purification and characterization of a novel potassium transport protein from mitochondria of various mammals. His masters research focused on the study of membrane transport of various anticancer drugs and polyamines in mammalian mitochondria.* BSc in Microbiology with honors, Panjab U., India, 1985; MS in Biology, Rensselaer Poly. Inst., 1987, PhD in Biology, 1990. Registered patent agent. Rsch. and tchg. asst. biology dept. Rensselaer Poly. Inst., Troy, NY, 1985-90; patent examiner Patent and Trademark Office, U.S. Dept. Commerce, Washington, 1990-96; instr. U.S. Patent Acad., Washington, 1995—2002; primary examiner, supervisory patent examiner (acting) U.S. Dept. Commerce, Washington, 1996—2002. Vis. asst. prof. Sch. Sci. Rensselaer Polytechnic Inst., Troy, NY, 1999—2002, adj. asst. prof., 2002—; judge Intel Internat. Sci. & Engring. Fair, 1997, 98; host Ultimate Invention Contest, Discovery Channel, 1999—2000; pres. Bawa Biotechnology Cons., LLC, Arlington, Va., 2002—; prin. con. Shimizu Patent Office, Ibaraki, Japan, 2002—; adv. Office Tech. Commercialization, Rensselaer Polytechnic Inst., Troy, 2003—; mem. adv. bd. Infocast Intellectual Property Landscape Series, 2003; spkr. in field. *Bawa Biotechnology Consulting, LLC is a biotechnology firm based in Arlington, Virginia and Schenectady, New York. The firm specializes in all aspects of biotechnology and chemical patent prosecution, including application drafting, patent searching, assignment searching, and validity opinions. In addition, Bawa Biotechnology Consulting, LLC has expertise in nanotechnology, HIV/AIDS, and biodefense-related issues. Currently, it represents both international and domestic clients. Dr. Bawa is a registered patent agent licensed to practice before the U.S. Patent and Trademark Office in Washington, DC.* Contbr. articles to profl. jours. and books. Recipient Talbot award U.S. Biophys. Soc., Bethesda, Md., 1988, Performance award U.S. Dept. Commerce, 1992, 93, 95, 98, 2000, Cert. Appreciation U.S. Dept. Commerce, 2001, EEO Svc. award, U.S. Patent Office, 1997, 98, Rensselear Alumni Assn. Dir.'s award, 2001. Mem.: Am. Soc. for Microbiology, Patent and Trademark Office Soc., Am. Physiol. Soc., Alpha Epsilon Delta (pres. N.Y. Theta chpt. 1989—90), Sigma Xi (life Travel award 1988, 1990). Achievements include research in isolation and biochemical characterization of a potassium transport protein from mammalian mitochondria, research on membrane transport of cationic anticancer drugs and polyamines in mammalian mitochondria, electron microscopy of animal sperm cells. Office: Bawa Biotechnology Consulting LLC 1801 Crystal Dr Ste 907 Arlington VA 22202 E-mail: doctorhockey@aol.com.

BAWDEN, NINA (MARY BAWDEN), author; b. Eng., 1925; Author: Who Calls the Tune (in U.S. as Eyes of Green), 1953, The Odd Flamingo, 1954, Change Here for Babylon, 1955, The Solitary Child, 1956, Devil by the Sea, 1957, Just Like a Lady (in U.S. as Glass Slippers Always Pinch), 1960, In Honour Bound, 1961, Tortoise by Candlelight, 1963, The Secret Passage (in U.S. as The House of Secrets), 1963, On the Run (in U.S. as Three on the Run), 1964, Under the Skin, 1964, A Little Love, A Little Learning, 1966, The White Horse Gang, 1966, The Witch's Daughter, 1966, A Handful of Thieves, 1967, A Woman of My Age, 1967, The Grain of Truth, 1968, The Runaway Summer, 1969, The Birds on the Trees, 1970, Squib, 1971, Anna Apparent, 1972, Carrie's War, George Beneath a Paper Moon, 1974, The Peppermint Pig, 1975, Afternoon of a Good Woman, 1976, Rebel on a Rock, 1978, Familiar Passions, 1979, Walking Naked, 1981, Kept in the Dark, 1982, The Ice House, 1983, The Finding, 1985, Circles of Deceit, 1987, Keeping Henry, 1988, The Outside Child, 1989, Family Money, 1991, Humbug, 1992, The Real Plato Jones, 1993, In My Own Time, 1994, A Nice Change, 1997, Off the Road, 1998, Ruffian on the Stair, 2001. Address: care Curtis Brown Ltd 10 Astor Pl New York NY 10003-6935 also: 22 Noel Rd London NI 8HA England also: 19 Kapodistriou Nauplion 21100 Greece E-mail: ninakrak@talk21.com.

BAXLEY, LUCY, lieutenant governor; Lt. gov. State of Ala., Montgomery, 1996. Office: Ste 725 11 S Union St Montgomery AL 36130

BAXT, WILLIAM GORDON, medical educator; b. Mar. 31, 1941; BA, Brown U., 1963; MD, Yale U., 1967. Diplomate Am. Bd. Internal Medicine, Am. Bd. Emergency Medicine. Intern Columbia-Presbyn. Hosp., N.Y.C., 1967-68, resident in internal medicine, 1970-71, fellow in hematology, 1971-73; from asst. prof. medicine to prof. clin. medicine & surgery U. Calif., San Diego, 1973-94; prof., chmn. dept. emergency medicine U. Pa. Med. Ctr., Phila., 1994—. Rsch. biologist U. Calif., La Jolla, 1976-77; med. dir. life flight aeromed. program U. Calif. Med. Ctr., San Diego, 1980-89, assoc. dir. divsn. emergency med. svcs., 1978-80, dir. dept. emergency medicine, 1980-94; chmn. dept. emergency medicine U. Pa. Med. Ctr., 1994—. Co-author: (with others) Cellular Modifiction and Genetic Transformation by Exogenous Nucleic Acids, 1973, The Leukemia Cell, 1979, Systems Approach to Emergency Medical Care, 1983, Trauma: The First Hour, 1985; mem. editl. bd. Emergency Care Quar., Annals of Emergency Medicine; contbr. articles to profl. jours. Surgeon USPHS, 1968-70. Leukemia Soc. Am. scholar, 1976; recipient Physicians Recognition award AMA, 1985, Best Oral Clin. Sci. Paper U. Assn. for Emergency Medicine, 1988, Best Oral Methodology Paper Soc. for Acad. Emergency Medicine, 1990. Mem. Nat. Acad. Scis., Soc. for Acad. Emergency Medicine, Phi Beta Kappa. Office: Hosp U Pa Dept Emergency Med Ground Ravdin 3400 Spruce St Philadelphia PA 19104-4206 E-mail: baxt@mail.med.upenn.edu.

BAXTER, BETTY CARPENTER, educational administrator; b. Sherman, Tex., Oct. 10, 1937; d. Granville e. and Elizabeth (Caston) Carpenter; m. Cash Baxter; children: Stephen Barrington, Catherine Elaine. AA in Music, Christian Coll., Columbia, Mo., 1957; MusB in Voice and Piano, So. Meth. U., Dallas, 1959; MA in Early Childhood Edn., Tchrs. Coll., Columbia, 1972, MEd, 1979, EdD, 1988. Tchr. Riverside Ch. Day Sch., N.Y.C., 1966-71; headmistress Episcopal Sch., N.Y.C., 1972-87, headmistress emeritus, 1987—. Founding head Presbyn. Sch., Houston, 1988-94; dir. Chadwick Village Sch., Palos Verdes Peninsula, Calif., 1995—; head of sch. St. Margaret's Episcopal Sch., Palm Desert, Calif., 2001-02. Author: The Relationship of Early Tested Intelligence on the WPPSI to Later Tested Aptitude on the SAT. Mem. ASCD, Nat. Assn. Episcopal Chs. (former gov. bd., editor Network publ.), Nat. Assn. Elem. Sch. Prins., Ind. Schs. Assn. Admissions Greater N.Y. (former exec. bd.), Nat. Assn. for Edn. of Young Children, L.A. Assn. Sch. Heads, Nat. Assn. Elem. Sch. Prins., Assn. Supervision and Curriculum Devel., Kappa Delta Pi, Delta Kappa Gamma. Republican. Presbyterian. Office: 72-828 Joshua Tree St Palm Desert CA 92260 E-mail: baxterbuty@jps.net.

BAXTER, CECIL WILLIAM, JR., retired college president; b. Stockton, Kans., Aug. 11, 1923; s. Cecil William and Marjorie LaVerne (Fitzpatrick) B.; m. Pat Ann Layman, June 6, 1951; children: Cecil William, Michael Kent, Patrick Alan. BA, Kans. Wesleyan U., 1950; MBA, U. Denver, 1954; PhD, U. Tex., 1967. Secondary edn. tchr., then secondary sch. prin., 1951-60; bus. mgr. Cottey Coll., Nevada, Mo., 1960-65; dean instrn. Kansas City Community Jr. Coll., Kans., 1967-68, Forest Park Community Coll., St. Louis, 1968-70; pres. North Seattle Community Coll., 1970-85, pres. emeritus, 1985—; exec. dir. Coun. on Naturopathic Med. Edn., 1989-92. Mem. faculty U. Wash., 1971; mem. Comm. on Colls. N.W. Assn. Schs. and Colls., 1981-85 Bd. dirs. Sr. Citizens Orgn., Seattle, 1972. Served with AUS, 1944-46. Ford Found. fellow U. Okla.; Kellogg Found. fellow U. Tex. Mem. Phi Delta Kappa Lodges: Rotary.

BAXTER, CINDI CHOATE, librarian; b. Nashville, Tenn., Mar. 21, 1958; d. Ralph Edsil and Patty Gail (Kennemur) Choate; m. Michael Wayne Baxter, June 20, 1976; 1 child, Barry Michael. Assoc. degree, Columbia State C.C., 1979; Bachelor's degree, U. North Ala., 1981. Social worker Dept. Human Svcs., Hohenwald, Tenn., 1981-82; libr. asst. Blue Grass Regional Libr., Columbia, Tenn., 1982; tchr. Lewis County Mid. Sch., Hohenwald, 1982-85; libr. Lewis County High Sch., Hohenwald, 1985—. Mem. Profl. Educators Tenn., Tenn. Assn. Sch. Librs., Am. Quilters Soc. Avocations: reading, quilting, quilt history, sports.

BAXTER, DECIMA CHRISTINE, hospital administrator, military officer; b. Temple, Tex., Aug. 13, 1963; d. Edward Lee Messer and Janice Faye Jaafari. BS in Bus. Adminstrn.and Mktg., N.E. Mo. State U., Kirksville, 1984; MBA in Bus. Adminstrn., Healthcare Adminstrn. Cert., Fla. State U., 1990; postgrad., Pa. State U., State College, 2000—. Cert. healthcare exec. Am. Coll. of Healthcare Execs. Dept. mgr. Jack's Discount Retail Store, Ft. Madison, Iowa, 1984—85; dept. head of patient adminstrn. Naval Hosp. Camp LeJeune, Jacksonville, NC, 1986—89; dept. head of patient adminstrn. and managed care Naval Hosp., Beaufort, SC, 1991—93; dir. for adminstrn. U.S. Naval Dental Ctr., 1993—96; med. adminstrv. officer USS Kitty Hawk, San Diego, 1996—98; hosp. adminstr., dept. head of patient adminstrn. U. S. Naval Hosp., Naples, Italy, 1998—2000. Total quality mgmt. instr. USN, San Diego, 1993—98. Founder, coord. State College Alateen Support Group, 2002; svc. planning and social work adv. com. mem. Ctr. Vols. in Medicine, State College, 2002; mentor Naples H.S. Mentorship Program, Naples, 1999; vol. instr. SAT-U exam. prep. course, 1995; vol. office mgr. and coach Spl. Olympics Hdqs., 1995; hotline vol. Christmas Hotline, 1994; vol. tchr. elem. sch. program Standing Tall, 1996; vol. Sunday sch. tchr. Calvary Bapt. Ch., State College, 2001—02. Comdr. USN, 1986—2002. Decorated Navy Commendation Medal (5) USN, Desert Storm medal; recipient Gov. of Guam's Cert. of Commendation for the Golden Salute to the 50th Anniversary Celebration of Liberation, Gov. of Guam, 1994. Mem.: Acad. for Health Svcs. Rsch. and Health Policy, Acad. of Mgmt., Am. Coll. of Healthcare Execs. (regent's adv. counsel 1999—2000). Baptist. Avocations: scuba diving, running, travel. Personal E-mail: dcb190@psu.edu.

BAXTER, DUBY YVONNE, government official; b. El Campo, Tex., July 21, 1953; d. Ray Eugene and Hazel Evelyn (Roades) Allenson; m. Loran Richard Baxter, April 7, 1979. Student, Alvin Jr. Coll., 1971, Tex. Tech U., 1972; cert. legal sec., Alaska Bus. Coll., 1974; student, Alaska Pacific U., 1981, Anchorage Community Coll., 1981-85, U. Santa Clara, 1982-83; BBA in Mgmt. cum laude, U. Alaska, Anchorage, 1985. Sr. office assoc., legal sec. Municipality of Anchorage, 1975-78; exec. sec. Security Nat. Bank, Anchorage, 1978-80, Alaska Renewable Resources Corp., Anchorage, 1980-82; pers. mgmt. specialist Dept. of Army, Ft. Richardson, Alaska, 1986-87; pers. mgmt. specialist, position classification specialist 10th Mtn. Div. (Light) Civilian Pers. Office, Ft. Drum, N.Y., 1987-89; pers. mgmt. specialist Civilian Pers. Office Alaska Dist. U.S. Army C.E., Anchorage, 1989-90; position classification specialist Civilian Pers. Office, 6th Inf. Divsn. (Light)-USA Garrison, Ft. Richardson, Alaska, 1990-91, 11th AF 3Wg, Civilian Personnel Office, Elmendorf AFB, Alaska, 1991-93, U.S. Army C.E., Anchorage, 1994-96, spl. project advisor, 1996-97; position classification specialist Pacific Region Civilian Pers. Ops. Ctr., Ft. Richardson, Alaska, 1997-98, 11th AF, 3Wg, Civilian Pers. Flight, 1998—2002; lead program support specialist U.S. Army Corps of Engrs. Europe Dist., 2002; human resource specialist U.S. Army Corps of Engrs., North Atlantic Divsn., 2002—. Avocations: travel, big game hunting, collecting alaskan and native artwork.

BAXTER, ELIZABETH PALM, music educator; b. Detroit, Oct. 25, 1955; d. Gerald Victor and Virginia Leech Palm; m. Timothy Edward Baxter, June 17, 1982; children: Ryan Timothy, Erin Elizabeth, Bridget Hannah. Diploma, Interlochen (Mich.) Arts Acad., 1973; MusB, Mich. State U., 1977; MusM, Northwestern U., 1979. Pvt. piano tchr., Farmington Hills, Mich., 1979—; piano accompanist Southfield (Mich.) Christian Sch., 1998—; pianist Grace Chapel Evang. Presbyn. Ch., Farmington Hills, 2001—. Musician: (multi-media presentation) Jerusalem (C. H. H. Parry). Mem.: Livonia Area Piano Tchrs. Forum, Camerata Music Club, Nat. Fedn. Music Clubs, Mich. Music Tchrs. Assn. (cert. pvt. piano tchr. 2003), Music Tchrs. Nat. Assn. Presbyterian. Avocations: reading, travel.

BAXTER, FRANK EDWARD, brokerage executive; b. Baxter, Calif., Nov. 20, 1936; s. Erwin Williard and Alice Mary (Byrne) B.; m. Kathrine Forest Stacey, June 9, 1962; children: Stacey, Matthew, Katherine. BA, U. Calif., Berkeley, 1961. V.p., dir. J.S. Strauss & Co., San Francisco, 1963-74; chmn. emeritus, dir. Jefferies & Co., L.A., 1974—. Served with USAF, 1955-58. Mem. Security Traders Assn. N.Y., Nat. Security Traders Assn., Equity Dealers Assn., London, Siwanoy Country Club, L.A. Country Club, Regency Club, Wilshire Country Club (L.A.). Office: Jefferies & Co Inc 11100 Santa Monica Blvd Los Angeles CA 90025-3384 E-mail: fbaxter@jefco.com.

BAXTER, GENE FRANCIS, chemical researcher, consultant; b. Sanish, Nd, July 25, 1922; s. Leslie Valentine and Frances (Ellertson) Baxter; m. Elizabeth Rose Turner, Feb. 14, 1970; children: Marsha Lynn, Michael James, Anthony Frederick. BS Chem., Univ. Wash., Seattle, WA, 1944. Rsch. chemist Adhesive Products Co., Seattle, Wash., 1944—46, Martin-Marietta Corp., Seattle, 1946—53; group leader Weyerhaeuser Co., Seattle, 1953—62, rsch. scientist, 1962—73, Georgia-Pacific Corp., Decatur, 1973—83, sr. scientist, 1983—85, cons., 1985—99. Recipient Disting. Scientist Award, Georgia-Pacific Resins Corp., 1986. Achievements include patents for 22 US patents granted between 1940-1990. Avocation: playing cards. Home: 195 Tiburon Drive Lithonia GA 30038

BAXTER, GENE KENNETH, mechanical engineer, company executive; b. Emmett, Idaho, Sept. 4, 1939; s. Glen Wilton Sr. and Mable Velhelmina (Casper) B.; m. Laraine Marie Mitchell, Jan. 20, 1968; children: Gretchen Lynn, Aaron Gregory. AA in Mech. Engring. (scholar), Boise Jr. Coll., 1959; BS in Mech. Engring., U. Idaho, 1961; MS in Aero. Engring. (NDEA fellow), Syracuse U., 1966, PhD in Mech. Engring., 1971. Registered profl. engr., N.Y., Ariz. Engr. Pratt & Whitney Aircraft Co., East Hartford, Conn., 1961; tchg. and rsch. asst. Syracuse (N.Y.) U., 1962-67; engr. Galson & Galson Cons. Engrs., Syracuse, 1968; sr. mech. engr., staff engr. electronic sys. divsn. GE Co., Syracuse, 1968-77, advanced project mgr. mech. design engring. mgr., space div. Daytona Beach, Fla., 1977-82; engring. dept. head Schlumberger Tech. Corp., Rosharon, Tex., 1982-83; mgr. engring., downhole svcs. divsn. Exploration Logging, Inc. divsn. Baker Internat. Corp., Sacramento, 1983-85; mgr. handling qualities sect. engring. and tng. simulation McDonnell Douglas Helicopter Co., Mesa, Ariz., 1985-87, mgr. projects mgmt., 1987-88, project mgr. Advanced Apache Simulation projects, 1988-91; pres. Exodyne Electric Motors, Inc., Tempe, Ariz., 1991-93, Baxter Engring., Mesa, 1993—. Dir. mech. projects creating visual simulation and tng. sys., nuc. power controls, shipboard digital control sys.; dir. equipment for measurement, analysis and control of wellhead, formation and drilling parameters for oil well svcs. industry; dir. hardware sys. and software models of flight, avionics, displays, controls and aircraft subsys. for helicopter simulation and tng. sys.; dir. for design and manufacture of submersible electric motors and accessories for indsl. turbine pumping applications; dir. mech. engring. cons. for forensic applications; tchr. refresher course N.Y. State Profl. Engrs., Syracuse, 1975-76; spkr. numerous profl. confs. Contbr. articles to profl. jours. Chmn. fin. and stewardship com. United Ch. of Christ, Liverpool, N.Y., 1974-77, chmn. bd. trustees, 1977; ruling elder Ormond Beach (Fla.) Presbyn. Ch., 1979-82, chmn. stewardship com., 1979-80, pres. corp., 1980-82, chmn. fin. com., 1981-82; pres. bd. dirs. Hope Women's Ctr., 1995-2000. Recipient Design award Machinery Mag., 1961, Raymond J. Briggs award Idaho Bd. Engring. Examiners, 1961. Mem. IEEE (sr., treas. Daytona sect. 1978-79, chmn. 1979-80, treas. Phoenix Area Cons. Network 1995-2000), ASME, SAE, ASHRAE, NSPE, NAFE, Nat. Assn. Profl. Accident Reconstruction Specialists, Southwestern Assn. Tech. Accident Investigators, Ariz. Soc. Profl. Engrs., Phi Kappa Phi, Tau Beta Pi. Home: 1243 N Norwalk Mesa AZ 85205-4038

BAXTER, HOWARD H. retired lawyer; b. Cleve., July 31, 1931; s. Harold H. and Bessie (Bovee) B.; m. Ona Mae Miller, June 25, 1955; children: Kevin, Douglas, John, Susan. BS, Iowa State Coll., 1953; JD, Case Western Res. U., 1956. Bar: Ohio 1956, D.C. 1982; U.S. Dist. Ct. (no. dist.) Ohio 1962, U.S. Ct. Appeals (3rd cir.) 1978, U.S. Supreme Ct. 1978, U.S. Ct. Appeals (fed. cir.) 1982. Assoc. McNeal & Schick, Cleve., 1956-60; group counsel Harris Corp., Cleve., 1960-76; sec., gen. counsel Molins USA Inc., Richmond, Va., 1976-79; v.p., gen. counsel The Langston Co., Inc., Cherry Hill, N.J., 1976-79, Cuyahoga County Hosp. System, Cleve., 1979-81; v.p., sec., gen. counsel Macey Machine Co., Inc., Cleve., 1981-88, exec. v.p., 1988-91; ptnr. Kasdan & Baxter Co., Cleve., 1992-2000; pvt. practice Cleve., 2000—. Chmn. zoning com. Lakewood (Ohio) Rep. Club, 1959-60; vestry, sr. warden St. Stephens Episcopal Ch., Beverly, N.J., 1977-79, Lakewood, 1981—, Ch. of the Ascension, Lakewood. Mem. NRA, Ohio State Bar Assn., Cleve. Bar Assn., Great Lakes Hist. Soc. (vice chmn. 1981-88, exec. v.p. 1968-76, trustee 1968—, chmn. exec. com. 1982-94), Ohio Gun Collectors Assn., Inc., Edgewater Yacht Club. Avocations: marine history, sailing, shooting sports, scale model railroading. Home and Office: 18107 Clifton Rd Lakewood OH 44107-1024

BAXTER, JAMES THOMAS, III, lawyer; b. Columbus, Miss., Nov. 23, 1947; s. James Thomas Jr. and Doris Gaynell (Gaither) B.; m. Sharon Kay Smith, Aug. 7, 1971; children: Katherine, Jennifer. BSBA, Auburn U., 1970; JD cum laude, Samford U., 1973. Bar: Ala. 1973, U.S. Dist. Ct. (no. dist.) Ala. 1973, U.S. Ct. Appeals (5th cir.) 1977, U.S. Ct. Appeals (11th cir. 1981), U.S. Dist. Ct. (mid. dist.) Ala. 1989, U.S. Dist. Ct. (ea. dist.) Tenn. 1989. Assoc. Cloud, Berry, Ables, Blanton & Tatum, P.C., Huntsville, Ala., 1973-75, ptnr., 1975-78, Berry, Ables, Tatum, Little & Baxter, P.C., Huntsville, 1978-93, Berry, Ables, Tatum, Baxter, Parker & Hall P.C., Huntsville, 1995—. Co-author: (handbooks) Foreclosure and Repossession, 1989, Basic Bankruptcy, 1989, Protection of Security Interests in Bankruptcy, 1988. Capt. USAFR, 1970—. Mem. ABA (litigation and family law practice mgmt. sect.), ATLA, Nat. Assn. Retail Collection Attys., Ala. State Bar Assn., Comml. Law League, Am. Arbitration Assn. Democrat. Methodist. Home: 1206 Kennamer Dr SE Huntsville AL 35801-1633 Office: Ables Baxter Parker & Hall PC PO Box 165 315 Franklin St SE Huntsville AL 35801-4208 E-mail: tbaxter@abphlaw.com.

BAXTER, JEFFREY Q. graphic artist, sculptor; b. Rockford, Ill., Sept. 25, 1959; Grad. high sch., Rockford. Painter, 1988—; sculptor, 1993—. Exhbns. include Gallery 10, Rockford, 1995-99, Art Guild of Rockford, 1995, 1997-2003, Arts Chatteau, Butte, Mont., 1996, 98, Joan Cawley Gallery, Scottsdale, Ariz., 1997, Charlene's Gallery 10 Ltd., Gills Rock, Wis., 1998-2001; commd. On The Water Front festival, Rockford, 1997, 98, Art of the Lawn, U. Ill. Coll. Medicine at Rockford U., 2001-2003; represented in permanent collections Bachrodt Motors Inc., Ill., numerous pvt. collections; featured in International Encyclopedia Dictionary of Modern and Contemporary Art, 2000-2001. Recipient 1st and 2d place sculpture awards Minn. Aquarium Soc. Nat. Art Show, Mpls., 1993, award of Excellence, Manhattan Arts Internat. Art Competition, N.Y.C., 1996, 97, 99. Mem. Rockford Area Arts Coun., Internat. Sculpture Ctr., Internat. Acad. Arts and Scis. (corr. acad.), Am. Ceramic Soc. (charter mem. potters coun.). Home: 5299 Village Ct Rockford IL 61108-6617 E-mail: fishart2@earthlink.net.

BAXTER, JOHN MICHAEL, editor; b. Upper Darby, Pa., Mar. 25, 1945; s. Allen and Judith Bryner (Bushey) B.; m. Carolyn Jane Johnson, Nov. 7, 1970 (div. May 1984); children: Jeffrey Michael, Wendy Beth. BA in English, Hobart Coll., 1967. Automotive editor Chilton Book Co., Radnor, Pa., 1971-79, mng. editor Specialist Mag., 1979-82, sr. assoc. editor Automotive Industries Mag., 1982-83; automotive book editor Chilton Automotive Books, Radnor, Pa., 1983-89, sr. assoc. editor Owner-Operator Mag., 1989-2001; sr. assoc. editor Comml. Carrier Jour., 2001—. Author: Chilton's Auto Troubleshooting Guide, 1973; editor: About Sexual Abuse, 1989, Gas Turbine Engine, 1974; author: Working Toward Homogeneous Diesel Combustion: A Fresh Look at the Work of Max Fiedler, 2001. Dir. Gundaker Found. Inc., Wayne, Pa., 1984-90, treas., 1985-86; trustee Marple Presbyn. Ch., Broomall, Pa., 1993-98; bd. dirs., treas. Huaguang Arts and Culture Ctr., 1998—. With U.S. Army, 1967-70, Vietnam. Mem. ASME, Soc. Automotive Engrs. (treas. Phila. sect. 1998—), Truck Writers N.Am. (tech. achievement award com.), Rotary (treas. Wayne chpt. 1990-98, sec. 1998, v.p. 1999, pres. 2000-01, v.p. 2001-02). Avocations: running, bicycling, rollerblading. Home: 3209 W Chester Pike Apt D-5 Newtown Square PA 19073-4260 Office: Randall Publ 643 Lancaster Ave Berwyn PA 19312 E-mail: jmbaxt@aol.com.

BAXTER, JUDITH LEE, academic administrator, mathematician; b. Marlinton, W.Va., Nov. 8, 1948; d. Ernest and Anne Baxter; m. Stephen D. Smith, June 14, 1980; children: Dallas Kevin Williams, Dawn Krystal Williams. MS in Applied Math., U. of Ill., Chgo., 1984. Dir. undergrad. studies U. of Ill., Chgo., 1987—98, dir. LAS Acad. Advising Ctr., 1998—. Contbr. articles to profl. jours. Mem.: Nat. Assn. of Advisors for the Health Professions, Am. Math. Soc. E-mail: baxter@uic.edu.

BAXTER, LARRY K. electrical engineer, consultant; b. Boston, Mar. 27, 1938; s. Gerald A. and Jean Slocombe Baxter; m. Carol Sue Marby, Aug. 1, 1981; children: A.J., Shenna, Kathy. At, Mass. Inst. Tech., Cambridge; BSEE, Rensselaer Poly., Troy, NY. V.p. engring. Shintron Co., Cambridge, Mass., 1962—70; engr. E. G. & G., Bedford, Mass., 1970—76; v.p. engring. Kronos, Inc., Chelmsford, Mass., 1976—80, Echolab, Inc., Chelmsford, Mass., 1980—98; cons. engr. Pictuetel, Inc., Andover, Maine, 1993—98; owner, cons. Capsense.com, Gloucester, Maine, 1998—. Bd. dirs. Echolab, Inc., Chelmsford, Mass., 1976—90, Kronos, Inc., Chelmsford, Mass., 1978—82, XRF, Inc., Somerville, Mass., 1999—2003; cons. on capacitive sensing. Author: (book) Capacitive Sensors, 1998, (novels) The Mayan Glyph, 2003. Achievements include 15 patents. Avocations: music, skiing, tennis. Home: 63 Norwood Hts Gloucester MA 01930 E-mail: larry@capsense.com.

BAXTER, MARVIN RAY, state supreme court justice; b. Fowler, Calif., Jan. 9, 1940; m. Jane Pippert, June 22, 1963; children: Laura, Brent. BA in Econs., Calif. State U., 1962; JD, U. Calif.-Hasting Coll. Law, 1966. Bar: Calif. 1966. Appointments sec. to Gov. George Deukmejian, 1983-88; dep. dist. atty. Fresno County, Calif., 1967-68; assoc. Andrews, Andrews, Thaxter & Jones, 1968-70, ptnr., 1971-82; apptd. sec. to Gov. George Deukmejian, 1983-88; assoc. justice Calif. Ct. Appeal (5th dist.), 1988-90; state supreme ct. assoc. justice Calif. Supreme Ct., 1991—. Mem. Jud. Coun. of Calif., chmn. policy coord. and liaison com., 1996—. Mem. Fresno County Bar Assn. (bd. dirs. 1977-82, pres. 1981), Calif. Young Lawyers Assn. (bd. gov. 1973-76, sec.-treas. 1974-75), Fresno County Young Lawyers Assn. (pres. 1973-74), Fresno County Legal Svcs., Inc. (bd. dirs. 1973-74), Fresno State U. Alumni Assn. (pres. 1970-71), Fresno State U. Alumni Trust Coun. (pres. 1970-75). Office: Calif Supreme Ct 350 Mcallister St San Francisco CA 94102-4712

BAXTER, MYRTLE MAE (BOBBI BAXTER), artist; b. Weableau, Mo., Nov. 10, 1928; d. Maxwell and Maude Bell Dorrel; m. Clarence Edgar Baxter, Dec. 31, 1945; children: Kenneth Wayne, Gary Dee, Joyce Evelyn. Profl. cert., Nevada (Mo.) Beauty Sch., 1970; degree in art, Am. Art Sch., 1987. Hair stylist Beauty Box, Butler, Nev., 1993-96; tchr. art to children Baxter Art Gallery, Butler, 1993-95. Exhibited in group shows Roscoe (Mo.) Mus. Soc., 1978-79 (1st place best of show award), Iola (Kans.) Guild, 1985-86, 1st award), Cottey Coll., Nevada, 1985-86, Royal Arts Coun., Versailles, Mo., 1985-86, (1st, 2d, 3d. awards, Best of Show), Table Rock (Mo.) Art Assn., 1996-97 (Best of Show award), Stover (Mo.) Art Assn., 1990-91, Warrensburg Coll. Art Gallery, 1995, Image Art Gallery, Carthage, Mo., 1997, Lamar (Mo.) Art League, 1996-97 (1st, 2d and 3d awards), Royals Arts Coun. Art Show, 1997 (Best of Show award), Harrisonville, Mo. Best of Show Fine Arts award, 1997; contbr. poetry On the Wing of Poetry. Leader, v.p. Summit 4-H Club, Butler, 1975-80; pres. Ladies Aid Club, Butler, 1985-86; in charge festival Roscoe (Mo.) Art Festival, 1996-97. Mem. Butler Art Club (pres. 1973-74), Tri-County Art Assn. (v.p., show chmn. 1980-81, bd. dirs. 1980, sec. 1980-81), Bates County Art League (mem. 1980-81, 89, show chmn. 1978-79), Harrisonville Art Assn. (v.p. 1995-96, program organizer), Mo. Coun. Arts (program organizer 1995),

Warrensburg Art Assn., Greater Kansas City Art Assn., Nat. Mus., Women in the Arts, Bates County Art League. Democrat. Methodist. Avocations: painting on location, hiking, bicycling, exercising, attending art meetings. Home: RR 5 Butler 52 E Box 65 Butler MO 64730-1852

BAXTER, NATHAN DWIGHT, dean; b. Coatesville, Pa., Nov. 16, 1948; s. Belgium Nathan and Augusta Ruth (Byrd) Baxter; m. Mary Ellen Walker, June 10, 1969; children: Timika Ann, Harrison David. MDiv with honors, Lancaster Theol. Sem., 1976, DMin, 1984; STD (hon.), Dickinson Coll., Carlisle, Pa., 1990; DD (hon.), St. Paul's Coll., Lawrenceville, Va., 2000; DST (hon.), Messiah Coll., Grantham, Pa., 2001; DHL (hon.), York Coll., Pa., 2002; DD (hon.), Colgate U., Hamilton, N.Y., 2003. Ordained Episcopal Ch., 1977. Curate St. John's Episcopal Ch., Carlisle, Pa., 1976—78; rector St. Cypman's Episcopal Ch., Hampton, Va., 1978—84; chaplain, prof. religious studies St. Paul's Coll., Lawrenceville, Va., 1984—86; dean, assoc. prof. church and ministry Lancaster Theol. Sem., Pa., 1986—90; adminstrv. dean, assoc. prof. pastoral theology Episcopal Div. Sch., Cambridge, Mass., 1990—91; dean Washington Nat. Cathedral, 1991—. Bd. dirs. Faith and Politics Inst., Washington, 1996; lectr., Medina Seminar Princeton U., NJ, 1997—2002; preacher Chautaugua Inst., NY, 1997—2002; bd. mem. U. Va. Ctr. on Religion & Democracy, 2002; bd. dirs. Riggs Nat. Bank, Washington, 2002. Author: Visions for the Millennium: Thoughts on Christian Living. E-5 U.S. Army, 1968—70. Decorated Vietnam Cross of Gallantry with Palm U.S. Army; fellow, Coll. of Preachers, 1990; Charles E. Merrill fellow, Harvard Div. Sch., 1998. Mem.: NAACP (life), Cosmo Club. Episcopalian. Avocations: black poetry, walking, jazz. Office: Washington Nat Cathedral Massachusetts and Wisconsin Aves NW Washington DC 20016-5098

BAXTER, NEVINS DENNIS, bank consultant; b. N.Y.C., June 29, 1941; s. Sol and Beatrice B.; m. Anne Susan Hatow, July 30, 1972; children: S.J., Keith. BA, Columbia Coll., 1961; MA, Princeton U., 1962, PhD in Econs., 1964. Asst. prof. fin. U. Pa., 1965-69; v.p. Mathematica, Princeton, N.J., 1969-71; pres. Baxter & Co., Washington, 1971-75, Golembe Assocs., Inc., Washington, 1975-89; chmn. BEI Golembe Cons., Washington, 1989-90; vice chmn. BEI Holdings Ltd., Washington, 1990-93; prin. Baxter & Co., Washington. Contbr. articles to numerous profl. jours. Office: Baxter & Co Ste 260 1667 K St NW Washington DC 20006

BAXTER, RALPH H., JR., lawyer; b. San Francisco, 1946; AB, Stanford U., 1968; MA, Cath. U. Am., 1970; JD, U. Va., 1974. Chmn. Orrick, Herrington & Sutcliffe LLP, San Francisco, 1990—. Mem. adv. bd. Nat. Employment Law Inst. Author: Sexual Harassment in the Workplace: A Guide to the Law, 1981, Sexual Harassment in the Workplace: A Guide to the Law, 2d rev. edit., 1989, 1994, Manager's Guide to Lawful Terminations, 1983, Manager's Guide to Lawful Terminations, rev. edit., 1991; mem. editl. bd.: Va. Law Rev., 1973—74, mem. editl. adv. bd.: Employee Rels. Law Jour. Mem.: ABA (mgmt. co-chair com. on employment rights and responsibilities 1987—90). Office: Orrick Herrington & Sutcliffe LLP Old Fed Res Bank Bldg 400 Sansome St San Francisco CA 94111-3143

BAXTER, ROBERT BANNING, insurance company executive; b. Rochester, N.Y., Aug. 26, 1946; s. Robert Clarkson and Flora Corinne (Banning) B.; m. Sandra Anne Weber, Apr. 21, 1973; children: Matthew Hamilton, Darcy Colson, Jeffrey Ford. BA, U. Rochester, 1968. Chartered property casualty underwriter; cert. ins. counselor. Personal lines account underwriter Allstate Ins. Co., Rochester, 1973-77; asst. personal lines underwriting mgr. Reliance Ins. Co., Pitts., 1977-78, personal lines underwriting mgr. Canandaigua, N.Y., 1978-79, regional personal lines underwriting mgr. Cin., 1979-81, mktg. mgr., 1981-84, Hartford Ins. Group, Cleve., 1984-85; regional mktg. mgr. Nat. Grange Mut. Ins. Co., Syracuse, N.Y., 1985-88; asst. br. mgr., mktg. mgr. Gen. Accident Ins., Syracuse, 1988-90, br. mgr., 1990-93; CEO, gen. mgr. Dryden Mut. Ins. Co., Dryden, N.Y., 1994—. Capt. USAF, 1968-73, Thailand, also West Germany. Decorated Air Force Commendation medal (2). Mem. Soc. Chartered Property Casualty Underwriters, Soc. Cert. Ins. Counselors, Ins. Mgrs. Coun., Syracuse (sec.-treas. 1992, v.p. 1993, pres. 1994-95), Ind. Ins. Agts. Assn. N.Y. (assoc.), Profl. Ins. Agts. N.Y. (assoc.), Honorable Order of Blue Goose Internat., N.Y. Ins. Alliance (bd. dirs.), DeWitt Hist. Soc. (bd. trustees 2003-). Republican. Unitarian Universalist. Avocation: numismatics. Home: 29 Forest Acres Dr Ithaca NY 14850-9782 Office: Dryden Mut Ins Co PO Box 635 12 Ellis Dr Dryden NY 13053 E-mail: bob@drydenmutual.com.

BAXTER, ROBERT HAMPTON, insurance executive; b. Glassport, Pa., Mar. 27, 1931; m. Barbara Miller, Aug. 4, 1956. Student, Carnegie Inst. Tech., 1949-50; AB, U.S.C., 1954, JD, 1958. Bar: S.C. bar 1959. Trust officer Citizens & So. Nat. Bank, Charleston, S.C., 1958-60, First Citizens Bank & Trust Co., Charlotte, N.C., 1960-68; with Aetna Life & Casualty Co., Atlanta, 1968-91; pres. The Resource Group, Atlanta, 1991—. Served to lt. (j.g.) USNR, 1954-57; comdr. USNR; ret. Mem. Bernardo Heights (Calif.) C.C., Phi Delta Phi. Presbyterian. Home: 12143 Caminito Corriente San Diego CA 92128-4569

BAXTER, STEPHEN BARTOW, retired history educator; b. Boston, Mar. 8, 1929; s. James Phinney 3d and Anne (Strang) B.; m. Ann Sweeney, Aug. 22, 1953; children: Clare, Persis Baxter Andrews, James, Nicholas, Stephen, Michael. AB in Econs. with honors, Harvard U., 1950; PhD, Cambridge U., 1955. Instr. history Dartmouth Coll., Hanover, N.H., 1954-57; asst. prof. U. N.C., Chapel Hill, 1958-62, assoc. prof., 1962-66, prof. history, 1966-91, Kenan prof. history, 1975-91. Vis. asst. prof. U. Mo., Columbia, 1957-58; dir. post-doctoral summer seminars Clark Meml. Libr. UCLA, 1973, 88, Clark libr. prof., 1977-78; dir. summer seminars NEH, Chapel Hill, 1974, post-doctoral seminar, 1978-79. Author: The Development of the Treasury, 1660-1702, 1957, William III and the Defense of European Liberty, 1650-1702, 1966; (with Paul R. Sellin) Anglo-Dutch Cross Currents in the Seventeenth and Eighteenth Centuries, 1976; (with others) Major Crises in Western Civilization, vol. 1, 1965, Eighteenth Century Studies Presented to Arthur M. Wilson, 1973, The Revolution of 1688 and the Birth of the English Political Nation, 1973, Biography in the Eighteenth Century, 1980, Changing Views on British History, 1984; editor: Basic Documents of English History, 1968, England's Rise to Greatness, 1660-1763, 1983; mem. editorial bd. Jour. Modern. History, 1971-77, Albion, 1982-92. Guggenheim fellow, 1959-60, 73-74; Charles Henry Fiske III scholar Trinity Coll., 1950-51.

BAXTER, WILLIAM, federal agency administrator; Grad., Duke U., U. Tenn. Commr. Tenn. Dept. Econ. and Cmty. Devel., 1997—2001; mem. Tenn. Valley Authority, Knoxville, 2001—. Office: Tenn Valley Authority 400 W Summit Hill Dr Knoxville TN 37902-1499

BAXTER-LOWE, LEE ANN, educator; b. Oshkosh, Wis., June 28, 1950; d. James Paul and Jane G. Matejowec; m. Kenneth N. Lowe, Nov. 12, 1983; children: Ashley, Lindsay. BS, U. Wis., 1972, PhD, 1976. Lab. investigator Blood Rsch. Inst., Milw., 1987-94; dir. DNA diagnostics Blood Ctr. Southeast Wis., Milw., 1987 94; dir. molecular genetics program Richland Meml. Hosp., Columbia, S.C., 1994-98; prof. U. Calif., San Francisco, 1998—. Cons., reviewer NIH, Bethesda, Md., 1990—. Contbr. articles to profl. jours.; inventor/patentee in field. Rsch. grantee NIH, 1988—. Mem. AAAS, Am. Soc. Immunologists, Am. Soc. Histocompatibility & Immunologenetics, Am. Soc. Hematology, Transplantation Soc. Office: U Calif Box 0508 San Francisco CA 94143-0508

BAXTER-SMITH, GREGORY JOHN, lawyer; b. Davenport, Iowa, Sept. 27, 1949; s. James Sanford Baxter and Doris Arlene (Olson) Smith; m. Carolyn Imes, June 10, 1975 (div. Oct. 1980); children: Bradley Imes, Brian McBride; m. Karen Ruth Thomas, Dec. 12, 1986. BA in English, Bucknell U., 1971; JD, U. Mo., 1974. Bar: Mo. 1974, U.S. Dist. Ct. (we. dist.) Mo. 1975, U.S. Tax Ct. 1975. Clk. Hon. Charles Shangler Mo. Ct. Appeals, Kansas City, 1974-75; assoc. Miller & Poole, Springfield, Mo., 1975-76; shareholder Poole & Smith, P.C., Springfield, 1976-78, Gregory J. Smith, P.C., Springfield, 1978-86, Poole, Smith & Wieland, P.C., Springfield, 1986-90, Smith & Fels, P.C., Springfield, 1990—. Mem. Springfield Met. Bar Assn., Greene County Estate Planning Coun., Mo. Bar Assn., Elks, Delta Upsilon. Republican. Lutheran. Avocation: golf. Home: 5027 S Glenhaven Ave Springfield MO 65804-7800 Office: Smith & Fels PC 528 W Battlefield St Ste 103 Springfield MO 65807-4122

BAY, JOANN REEDER, financial planner; b. Williamsport, Pa., Sept. 29, 1926; d. Rollin A. and Esther Ellen (Costello) Reeder; m. John William Bay Sr., Aug. 22, 1948; children: John William Jr., Neil Andrew. BA in English & Psychology, Bucknell U., 1948. Cert. Paralegal Inst. Paralegal Tng., Phila., 1973, Fin. Planner Coll. Fin. Planning, 1984. Analyst HAY Assoc., Phila., 1973—75, fin. planning cons., 1975—77; prin., owner J.R. Bay Assoc., Drexel Hill, Pa., 1978—. Chmn. investment com. Cmty. Y of Ea. Del. County, Upper Darby, Pa., 1992—97, Cmty. Y Found. Bd., Upper Darby, 1995—97. Adv. com. Upper Darby Sch. Bd., Upper Darby, 1970—72; exec. v.p. Upper Darby H.S. Mother's Group, Upper Darby, 1970—71; pres. Upper Darby H.S. Parent's Group, Upper Darby, 1971—72; pro bono work for financially needy women. Named 1 of 200 Best Fin. Adv. in U.S., Money Mag. Silver Anniversary Issue, 1987. Democrat. Presbyterian. Avocations: piano, reading, concerts, museums. Office: JR Bay Associates 5022 Sylvia Rd Drexel Hill PA 19026

BAY, MICHAEL BENJAMIN, film director; b. Los Angeles, Feb. 17, 1965; Dir. films Bad Boys, 1995, The Rock, 1996, Armageddon, 1998, Pearl Harbor, 2001, Bad Boys II, 2003; prodr. Armageddon, 1998, Pearl Harbor, 2001; actor: Armageddon, 1998, Mystery Men, 1999, Coyote Ugly, 2000, Zigs, 2000. Office: Creative Artists Agy care Adam Krentzman 9830 Wilshire Blvd Beverly Hills CA 90212-1825

BAY, YEW CHUAN, conglomerate company executive; b. Singapore, June 12, 1943; s. Khong Khai and Lian Huay (Tan) B.; m. Keng Wa Phoa, Mar. 18, 1967; children: Bay Chin Hao, Bay Chern Chieh. B of Elec. Engring., Melbourne U., 1965, MBA, 1970. Asst. tech. mgr. Jardine Waugh L, Malaysia, 1965-68; various positions Mobil Oil, N.Y.C., Singapore, Australia, and Malaysia, 1970-82; group gen. mgr., exec. dir. Amcol Holdings Ltd., Singapore, 1982-96; vice chmn. Store+Deliver+Logistics Pte Ltd., Singapore, 1997—. Lectr. Prahan Tech. Coll., 1970-71, Singapore Inst. of Mgmt., 1972-73. Chmn. Regulatory Affairs Singapore Chemical Industry Coun., Jurong Inst. ADv. Com., Singapore, 1989—. Fellow Inst. Dirs. (U.K.); mem. Inst. Elec. Engrs. (assoc.), Melbourne Bus. Sch. Alumni, Singapore Chpt. (chmn), Rotary (pres. Singapore West Club 1993-94, Best Rotarian 1991-92). Mgmt. Com. Rotary Family Svc. Ctr., Rotary Student Care Ctr. Avocations: golf, reading, social work. Home: 94 Westlake Ave Singapore 574279 Singapore

BAYACK, PATRICIA ELAINE, psychotherapist, social welfare administrator, social worker; b. Bklyn., Jan. 18, 1950; d. Augustine Joseph and Rose Marie (Azzarelli) Merola; m. Raymond Stanley Bayack, Nov. 29, 1969; children: Raymond S. Jr., Nicholas P. Cert. in spiritual devel., Archdiocese N.Y. Sch. of Spiri, 1987; BSW, Dominican Coll., 1990; MSW, NYU, 1991. Cert. social worker, N.Y. Social work intern Middletown (N.Y.) Psychiat. Ctr., 1989, Orange County Dept. Mental Health, Newburgh, N.Y., 1989-90, Monroe-Woodbury (N.Y.) Sch. Dist., 1990-91; dir., counselor Youth Adv. Programs, Inc., Liberty, N.Y., 1991-92, program dir. Newburgh, 1994-95, cons., supr. improving families, 1995—, early intervention svc. provider, 1996—; social work supr. Abbott House, Liberty, 1992-94. Adj. prof. Dutchess C.C., Poughkeepsie, N.Y., 1991-92; clin. cons. Vails Gate (N.Y.) High Tech. Magnet Sch., N.Y., 1991-93. Pres., v.p., elected lifetime mem. Balmville Sch. PTA, Newburgh, 1977—; umpire, coach, mgr. aux. mem. Town of Newburgh Little League, 1980-98; catechist Sacred Heart Ch., Newburgh, 1981-87; sec., treas. Helping Children, Newburgh, 1983-92; founding mem. Primary Concerns Found., exec. officer, 2000—. Recipient Bella Holzer Meml. award Dominican Coll., Orangeburg, 1990; acad. scholar Dominican Coll., 1988-90, NYU scholar, 1990-91. Mem. NASW (cert. sch. social work specialist)., Pi Gamma Mu (pres. 1988-89, v.p.1989-90, Social Work scholar, 1990-91), Alpha Chi. Avocations: golf, gardening, reading, traveling.

BAYAR, JULIA BERYL, interior designer; b. Washington, June 12, 1949; BA, Vassar Coll., 1971; MS, Boston U., 1972. Press aide Dem. Nat. Com., Washington, 1972-73, U.S. Ho. Reps., Washington, 1973-76, U.S. Senate, Washington, 1976-77; speechwriter U.S. Dept. Justice, Washington, 1977-79; cons. Jules Kroll Assocs., N.Y.C., 1980-81; interior designer, owner Interiors by Julia Bayar, Scarsdale, N.Y., 1984—. Home: 47 Lynwood Rd Scarsdale NY 10583-2701

BAYARD, MRS. ARNOLD A. See NESS, EVALINE

BAYARD, RICHARD H. political party official; Chmn. Del. Democratic Party, Newport. Office: Delaware Democratic Party 19 E Commons Blvd 2d Fl New Castle DE 19720*

BAYARD, SUSAN SHAPIRO, adult education educator, small business owner; b. Boston, Dec. 26, 1942; d. Morris Arnold and Hester Muriel (Blatt) Shapiro; m. Edward Quint Bayard, Jan. 4, 1969; children: Jeffrey David, Lucy Quint. BA, Syracuse U., 1964; MA, U. Calif., Berkeley, 1966; cert. in advanced grad. study, Boston U., 1984. Rsch. chemist Harvard Med. Sch., Boston, 1966; asst. scientist Polaroid Corp., Cambridge, Mass., 1966-67; instr. Boston U., 1968-70, Wheelock Coll., Boston, 1978-81; chmn. sci. dept. Tower Sch., Marblehead, Mass., 1981-85; dir., owner Bayard Learning Ctr., Marblehead, 1985—94; vis. lectr. Salem (Mass.) State Coll., 1994—2000, coord. Instrnl. Design Lab., 1995—2000, coord. PALMS presvc. program, 1998—2000; dir. Ctr. Tchg., Learning and Assessment N. Shore CC, Danvers, Mass., 2003—. Ednl. cons., workshop facilitator Swampscott (Mass.) Pub. Schs., Lynn (Mass.) Pub. Schs.; instr., cons. N.E. Consortium, North Andover, Mass., 1986—94. Mem. Curriculum Evaluation Com., Swampscott, 1978—80, Mass. Ednl. TV Program Selection Com., 1979—87, Supt. Screening Com., Swampscott, 1987, Town Meeting, Swampscott, 1988—, Sch. Improvement Coun., Swampscott, 1988—89. Named Outstanding Woman Grad. Student, Boston U. Women's Guild, 1977; grantee, NSF, Syracuse U., 1962, 1964. Mem.: Nat. Sci. Tchrs. Assn., Pi Lambda Theta. Jewish. Avocations: tennis, reading, computers, piano.

BAYDA, EDWARD DMYTRO, judge; b. Alvena, Sask, Can., Sept. 9, 1931; s. Dmytro Andrew and Mary (Bilinski) B. BA, U. Sask., 1951, LLB cum laude, 1953; LLD (hon.), 1989. Bar: Sask. 1954; created Queen's Counsel, 1966. Barrister, solicitor, Regina, Sask., 1953-72; sr. ptnr. Bayda, Halvorson, Scheibel & Thompson, 1966-72; justice Ct. Queen's Bench for Sask., Regina, 1972-74, Ct. Appeal for Sask., Regina, 1974-81; chief justice Sask., Regina, 1981—. Roman Catholic. Home: 3000 Albert St Regina SK Canada S4S 3N7 Office: Ct Appeal Sask Courthouse 2425 Victoria Ave Regina SK Canada S4P 3V7

BAYE, MICHAEL ROY, economics educator; b. Dallas, Apr. 6, 1958; s. Firmin Joseph and Exia Jaynet (Cawley) B.; m. M'Lissa Arlene, Aug. 6, 1977; children: Natalie, Mitchell. BS in Econs., Tex. A&M U., 1980; MS in Econs., Purdue U., 1981, PhD in Econs., 1983. From asst. prof. econs. to assoc. prof. Tex. A&M U., College Station, 1985—88; from assoc. prof. econs. to prof. econs. Pa. State U., University Park, 1991—97; Bert Elwert prof. bus. Ind. U., 1997—. Cons. in field. Author: Consumer Behavior, 1986, Managerial Economics and Business Strategy, 1994, 4th edit., 2003, Russian translation, 1999, Korean translation, 2002, Money, Banking, and Financial Markets: An Economic Approach, 1995, Indian edit., 1996; mem. editl bd. Jour. Pub. Policy and Mktg., Lecture Notes in Econs. and Math. Systems, Econs. of Governance, Advances in Applied Microeconomics, 1996-; contbr. articles to profl. jours. Recipient Alfred Chalk award, 1980, Tchg. Excellence award KBS, 1997-2000; David Ross fellow, 1982-83, NSF grantee 1984-85, Fulbright fellow 1985-86, Ctr. Economic Rsch. fellow, 1990-; vis scholar KBS, 1995-2002; named Outstanding Rschr. KBS, 1999-2000. Mem. Econometric Soc., Am. Econ. Assn., Royal Econ. Soc., European Econ. Assn. Office: Kelley Sch Bus Bloomington IN 47405

BAYER, RICHARD STEWART, lawyer; b. Laurel, Md., July 7, 1951; s. James Theodore and Patricia Ruth (Stewart) B.; m. Roberta Ann Cruise, July 9, 1977; children: Andrew Stewart, Henry Eliot, Hannah Caitlin AB, Middlebury Coll., 1973; JD, Colo. U., 1976. Bar: Colo. 1976, U.S. Dist. Ct. Colo. 1976, U.S. Ct. Appeals (10th cir.) 1976, U.S. Supreme Ct. 1987, Calif. 1989. Assoc. Brownstein Hyatt, Farber & Madden, Denver, 1976-81, ptnr., 1981-86, Kutak, Rock & Campbell, Denver, 1987-89; gen. counsel Hoskings Trust, San Diego, 1989—. Author: Colorado Appellate Advocacy, 1984; contbr. articles to legal jours. Mem. ABA (chmn. 10th cir. comml., banking, fin. transactions subcom., litigation sect. 1984-89), Denver Bar Assn., Denver Law Club (sec. 1982-83) Democrat. Home: 785 Bellevue Pl La Jolla CA 92037-8023 Office: Hoskings Trust 4817 Santa Monica Ave San Diego CA 92107-2850

BAYER, ROBERT EDWARD, retired defense department official, consultant; b. Cleve., Oct. 26, 1941; s. Charles and Pauline (Kamuf) B.; m. Mary Ellen Horrigan, Dec. 27, 1965 (div. 1981); m. Rozanne Deane Oliver, Jan. 29, 1983; children: Sylvia M., Laura A., Anne M., John C. BS in Social Sci. magna cum laude, John Carroll U., 1962; postgrad., Loyola U., 1962-63. Commd. 2nd lt. USAF, 1963, advanced through grades to lt. col., 1979, ret., 1983; mem. profl. staff Office of Sen. Sam Nunn U.S. Senate, Washington, 1983-86; mem. profl. staff Senate Com. on Armed Svcs., Washington, 1986-93; dep. asst. sec. of def. installations U.S. Dept. Def., Washington, 1993-97, ret., 1997. Mem. Creative Team Concepts LLC; cons. in field. Pastor, spiritual dir. The Seeker Ch., Washington, 1989-93; co-chair Bridge Builders Fund, 1998-2000; mem. Mt. Olivet United Meth. Ch., Arlington, Va., chmn. stewardship. Nat. Def. fellow Loyola U., 1962-63. Mem.: Nat. Assn. Installation Developers, Meth. Fedn. for Social Action, Nat. Alliance for the Mentally Ill, Parents, Families and Friends of Lesbians and Gays. Methodist. Avocations: bicycling, swimming, travel, teaching. E-mail: roliver52@comcast.net.

BAYER, THORA ILIN, professor; b. Philadelphia, PA, Oct. 15, 1966; d. Manfred Eric and Margret Helene Bayer. BA magna cum laude(hon.), Bryn Mawr Coll., 1990; MA, Emory U., 1994, PhD, 1998. Asst. prof. Xavier U of LA, New Orleans, 1998—. Tech. editor New Vico Studies, Atlanta, 1998—. Author: Cassirer's Metaphysics of Symbolic Forms, 2001. Fellow: Soc. of Philos. in Am.; mem.: Hegel Soc. of Am., Am. Philos. Assoc., Internat. Ernst Cassirer Soc., So. Soc. of Philos. and Psychol., Phila. H.S. for Girls Assoc. Home: 3443 Esplanade Ave Apt. #401 New Orleans LA 70119 Office: Xavier U of La 1 Drexel Drive Philosophy Dept New Orleans LA 70125

BAYER, WILLIAM, writer; b. Cleve., Feb. 20, 1939; s. Leo Bayer and Eleanor (Rosenfeld) Perry; m. Paula Wolfert, Aug. 10, 1983. BA, Harvard U., 1960. Fgn. svc. officer USIA, Washington and Saigon, Republic of Vietnam, 1963-68; freelance documentary filmmaker, 1968-72; freelance writer, 1972—. Author: In Search of a Hero, 1966, Stardust, 1974, Visions of Isabelle, 1976, Tangier, 1978, Punish Me With Kisses, 1980, Peregrine, 1981 (Edgar award 1982), Switch, 1984, Pattern Crimes, 1987, Blind Side, 1989, Wallflower, 1991, Mirror Maze, 1994, The Dream of the Broken Horses, 2002, (as David Hunt) The Magician's Tale, 1997 (Lambda Lit. award 1998), Trick of Light, 1998, (nonfiction) Breaking Through, Selling Out, Dropping Dead, 1971, The Great Movies, 1973; (teleplay) Internal Affairs, 1988, Murder X Seven, 1991. When Love Kills, 1993; contbr. articles to profl. jours. Mem. PEN, Writers Guild Am. West, Authors Guild, Internat. Assn. Crime Writers (pres. 1991-93), Mystery Writers of Am. Avocations: photography, book collecting. Office: 1592 Union St # 475 San Francisco CA 94123-4531 E-mail: crimenovelist@aol.com.

BAYERN, ARTHUR HERBERT, lawyer; b. Jan. 28, 1934; s. Henry V. and Rose (Strumer) Bayern; m. Janice O'Banion, June 10, 1961; children: William T., Robert M.(dec.). AB, Colgate U., 1954; JD, U. Tex., 1965. Bar: Tex. 1965, U.S. Dist. Ct. (we. dist.) Tex. 1966, U.S. Tax Ct. 1968, U.S. Ct. Appeals (5th cir.) 1970, U.S. Supreme Ct. 1978. Salesman IBM, Houston, 1959—62; ptnr. Remy, Bayern & Paterson, San Antonio, 1965—84, Bayern, Paterson & Aycock, San Antonio, 1984—98, Bayern & Aycock, San Antonio, 1998—. Pres. San Antonio Estate Planners Coun., 1972—73. Co-editor: (non-fiction) How to Live and Die with Texas Probate, 1983; editor (contbg.): Texas Probate System, 1974, Texas Guardianship System, 1983. Capt. USAF, 1954—57. Fellow: Am. Coll. Probate Counsel; mem.: ABA (chmn. com. on post-mortem estate and tax planning), San Antonio Bar Assn. (pres. 1980—81), State Bar Tex. (bd. dir. 1982—85, chmn. real estate, probate and trust law sect. 1981—82). Office: Bayern & Aycock 745 E Mulberry Ave Ste 300 San Antonio TX 78212-3167

BAYES, MARJORIE ANDRESS, psychologist; b. Chgo., Dec. 1, 1934; d. Allan Wallace and Mary (Nixon) Andress; m. Andrew H. Bayes, Aug. 25, 1957 (div. 1965); m. Kenneth Purcell, Jan. 17, 1987; children: Stephen Bayes, Christopher Bayes. BA, U. Fla., 1956; MA, U. Ky., 1959; PhD, U. Miami, 1970. Faculty mem. dept. psychiatry Yale Sch. Medicine, New Haven, 1970-80; pvt. practice psychotherapy and consultation Northampton, Mass., 1980-87, Denver, 1987—. Cons. staff group relations confs. Yale U. Sch. Medicine, 1970-80. Co-editor: Women and Mental Health, 1981; contbr. articles to profl. jours. Mem. Am. Psychol. Assn., Am. Assn. Univ. Profs., Phi Beta Kappa, Sigma Xi. Democrat. Mem. Unitarian Universalist Ch. Avocation: stained glass objects. Home: 3254 S Heather Gardens Way Aurora CO 80014-3666 Office: 8000 E Prentice Ave Ste B13 Englewood CO 80111-2726

BAYES, RONALD HOMER, English language educator, author; b. Freewater, Oreg., July 19, 1932; s. Floyd Edgar and Mildred Florence (Cochran) B. BS, East Oreg. State Coll., 1955, MS, 1956; postgrad., U. Pa., 1959-60; DDM, U. Delle Arti, Termi, Italy, 1982. Asst. prof. English Ea. Oreg. State Coll., LaGrande, 1955-56, assoc. prof. English, 1960-68; lectr. English U. Md., College Park, 1958-59, 66-67; disting. prof. creative writing St. Andrews Presbyn. Coll., Laurinburg, 1968—. Founder, exec. bd. St. Andrews Rev. & Press, Laurinburg, 1970-95; mem. N.C. State Arts Coun., Raleigh, 1987-89; master poet Atlantic Ctr. for Arts, New Smyrna Beach, Fla., 1988; cons. Nat. Coun. for Arts, Washington, 1969-71. Author: (poetry) Dust & Desire, 1961, Cages & Journeys, 1964, Child Outside My Window, 1965, History of the Turtle, 1970, The Casketmaker, 1972, Porpoise, 1974, Tokyo Annex, 1977, King of August, 1979, Fram, 1979, Beast in View, 1985, Guises, 1992, Greatest Hits 1969-2002, 2003; (fiction) Sister City, 1971. Chmn. Rep. Ctrl. Com., Union County, Oreg., 1967-68, Scotland County, N.C., 1980-81; bd. dirs. Scotland County Humane Soc., Laurinburg, 1993—. With U.S. Army, 1956-58. Named one of Outstanding Young Men of Am., 1960, master poet Atlantic Ctr. for the Arts, 1988, Disting. Prof. Creative Writing Chair named in his honor, 1999, Emeritus, 2002, Lifetime Achievement award in writing named in his honor, N.C. Writers' Network, 2001; recipient Outstanding Alumni award Ea. Oreg. State Coll., 1973, Roanoke-Chowan prize for poetry, 1973, N.C. Writers' Conf. award, 1987, N.C. award for Literature, 1989, cert. honor Poetry Coun. N.C., 1994, Honor for contr. to N.C. Writers, N.C. State Senate, 2002; fellow Woodrow Wilson Nat. fellow, 1959—60; grantee N.C. arts grantee, 1988. Mem. Danforth Found. (assoc.), Internat. House Japan, Japan Soc., N.C. Poetry Soc. (life), Oregon Poetry Assn. (life), Mason. Episcopalian. Avocations: gardening, reading, jogging, travel. Home: PO Box 206 Laurinburg NC 28353-0206

BAYH, EVAN, senator, former governor; b. Terre Haute, Ind., Dec. 26, 1955; s. Birch Evans Jr. and Marvella (Hern) B.; married. BS in Bus. Econs., Ind. U., 1978; JD, U. Va., 1981. Atty. Bingham, Summers, Welsh & Spilman; sec. of state State of Ind., Indpls., 1987-89, gov., 1989-96; ptnr. Baker & Daniel Assocs., Indpls., 1997-98; U.S. senator from Ind., 1999—. Chmn. State Recount Commn. & Corp. Law com.; mem. Nat. Edn. Goals Panel & Nat. Assessment Edn. Panel; chmn. Edn. Commn. States; vice chmn. Nat. Govs. Assn. Task Force Workforce Devel. Democrat. Office: US Senate 463 Russell Senate Office Bldg Washington DC 20510-0001 also: 10 W Market St Ste 1650 Indianapolis IN 46204-2934*

BAYLEN, JOSEPH OSCAR, retired history educator; b. Chgo., Feb. 12, 1920; s. Leo and Mary (Lakin) B.; m. Margaret Pringle, June 16, 1979; 1 son, James Leo; 1 stepdaughter, Julia. AA, Wright Jr. Coll., 1939; BE, No. Ill. U., 1941; MA, Emory U., 1947; PhD, U. N.Mex., 1949. Instr. history U. N.Mex., 1948-49; asst. prof. history N.Mex. Highlands U., Las Vegas, 1950-52, assoc. prof., 1952-54; prof. history, chmn. div. social sci. Delta State Tchrs. Coll., 1954-57; prof. history Miss. State U., 1957-61, U. Miss., 1961-66, chmn., 1963-66; chmn. dept. history Ga. State U., 1966-78, Regents' prof., 1969-83, emeritus Regents' prof. history, 1983—; lectr. in history Ctr. for Continuing Edn., U. Sussex, 1985-89. Vis. asst. prof. U. Md. Overseas Program, Europe, 1952-53; vis. assoc. prof. Agnes Scott Coll., 1953; vis. prof. summers Emory U., 1952, U. Ala., 1960, Georgetown U., 1964, 65, Tulane U., 1966, 68, U. York, 1979; Fulbright-Hays lectr., U.K., 1961-62, 72-73; mem. Miss. Hist. Commn., 1954-57, 63-66; vice chmn. So. Humanities Conf., 1964-65, chmn., 1965-66; mem. Nat. Fulbright Adv. Screening Com., 1962-64, chmn., 1964-65; cons. NEH, 1969-83, BBC-TV, 1988—; mem. Fed. Govt. Regional Archives Com., 1971-74; chmn. adv. com. on history Univ. System of Ga., 1970-72, 76-78, British Libr., Consultative Group on Newspapers, 1990-2000; lectr. U. Sussex, City Univ., London. Author: (monographs) Mme. Juliette Adam,

Gambetta, and the Idea of a Franco-Russian Alliance, 1960, Lord Kitchener and the Viceroyalty of India, 1980, 1965, Soldier-Surgeon: The Crimean War Letters of Dr. D.A. Reid, 1855-1856, 1968, W.T. Stead and the Russian Revolution of 1905, 1969; author: (with O.S. Pidhainy) East-European and Russian Studies in the American South, 1972; author: (with others) Dictionary of Labour Biography, 1977, British Literary Magazines, 1984; : Biographical Dictionary of Peace Leaders, 1985, Victorian Britain: An Encyclopaedia, 1988, Papers for the Millions: The New Journalism in Britain..., 1988, Biographical Dictionary of American Journalism, 1989, Ency. of the British Press, 1992, Dictionary of Literary Biography (British Publishing Houses 1881-1965), 1992; co-editor: Biographical Dictionary of Modern British Radicals, 1770-1914, 3 vols., 1979—88, The 1890's An Encyclopeadia of British Literature, Art and Culture, 1993, Twentieth Century Britain: An Encyclopeadia, 1995, Shaping the Collective Memory, Government and International Historians through Two World Wars, 1996, A Journalism Reader, 1997, American National Biography, 1999; mem. editl. bd.: Encyclopedia of 1848 Revolutions: So. Humanities Rev., mem. editl. adv. bd.: Ency. of the World Press; contbr. . Capt. AUS, 1941-45. Guggenheim fellow, 1958-59, rsch. fellow Inst. Advanced Studies, Princeton, 1966; summer fellowships and awards include So. Fellowship Found., 1955, Am. Philos. Soc., 1956, 65, Am. Coun. Learned Socs., 1961-62; English-Speaking Union, 1978; recipient Most Disting. Alumni award No. Ill. U., 1976, Disting. Prof. award Ga. State U., 1979, Disting. Prof. award Ga. State U. chpt. Omicron Delta Kappa, 1980, Hugh McCall award for disting. achievement in hist. studies, 1982 Fellow: Royal Hist. Soc.; mem.: N.Am. Conf. Brit. Studies (chmn. so. conf. 1977—79), So. Hist. Assn. (chmn. European history sect. 1972—73), Am. Hist. Assn. (exec. coun. 1972—75), European Movement, London Press Club (bd. dirs. 1995—2001), Travellers Club, Phi Kappa Tau, Kappa Delta Pi, Pi Gamma Mu, Phi Alpha Theta, Omicron Delta Kappa, Phi Kappa Phi. Home: The Hawthorns Apt 50 4 Carew Rd Eastbourne BN21 2BG England

BAYLES, JENNIFER LUCENE, museum program director, educator; b. Tokyo, May 26, 1953; d. Lewis Allen Bayles and Rosemary (Beuhler) Fraser; m. Robert Steinfeld, July 4, 1992; children: Noah Isaac Steinfeld, Ezra Milton Steinfeld. BA in Art History with honors, Ind. U., Bloomington, 1976; MA in Art History, U. Mich., 1984, cert. in mus. practice, 1984. Curatorial apprentice Indpls Mus Art 1976; mus apprentice Portland (Oreg.) Art Mus., 1976-78, asst. curator edn., 1978-81; asst. curator photographic collection dept. art history U. Mich., Ann Arbor, 1981-83, rsch. and editl. asst. Mus. Art, 1982-83; intern dept. mus. edn. Art Inst. Chgo., 1983-84; from asst. curator edn. adult programs to educator spl. projects Albright-Knox Art Gallery, Buffalo, 1984—2001, educator spl. projects, 2001—. Horace H. Rackman Grad. scholar, 1981—83, Acad. scholar, U. Mich., 1982. Mem.: Am. Assn. Mus. (regional rep. edn. com. 1979—81). Office: Albright-Knox Art Gallery 1285 Elmwood Ave Buffalo NY 14222-1096

BAYLESS, BETSEY, state official; b. Phoenix; BA in Latin Am. Studies and Spanish, U. Ariz., 1966; MPA, Ariz. State U., 1974; DHL (hon.), U. Ariz. V.p. pub. fin. Peacock, Hislop, Staley & Given, Inc., Phoenix; asst. dir. Ariz. Bd. Regents; acting dir. dept. revenue State of Ariz., dir. dept. adminstrn., sec. of state, 1997—2003; dir. Ariz. Dept. Adminstrn., 2003—. Bd. suprs. Maricopa County, 1989-97, chmn. bd., 1992, 94, vice chair, 1997; mem. Ariz. Bd. Investment, 2003—; bd. dirs. Child Help Ariz.; mem. Nat.bd. dirs. U. Ariz. Coll. of Bus. and Pub. Adminstrn.; adv. bd. Ariz. State U. West.. Bd. dirs. Xavier Coll. Preparatory Found., Ariz. Ctr. for the Book; commr. Gov.'s Commn. Violence Against Women; mem. Ariz. Town Hall, Charter 100, Valley Leadership Class VI, Ariz. Rep. Caucus, Ariz. Women's Forum. Named to Hall of Fame, Ariz. State U. Coll. Pub. Programs; recipient Disting. Citizen award U. Ariz. Alumni Assn., Woman of Yr. award Capitol chpt. Bus. and Profl. Women, Disting. Achievement award NEH Fellowship, Achievement award Nat. Assn. Counties, 1993, Citizen award Bur. Reclamation, 1993, Woman of Achievement award Xavier Coll. Preparatory, 1995. Mem. Phi Beta Kappa (Freeman medal 1966). Republican.*

BAYLESS, CAROLYN COTTON, nurse; b. Marietta, Ga., Aug. 16, 1948; d. John Lamar Cotton and Jeanne Walker Garriss; m. Luke Edward Bayless, Dec. 17., 1995. BSN, Brenau U., 1990; MBA, Mercer U., 1998. Cert. nurse adminstr. ANA, 1992; lic. nursing home adminstr., RN. Coord. chem. dependency unit N.E. Ga. Med. Ctr., Gainesville, 1984-90, unit dir., 1990-95; dir. NGHS LTC Svcs./Northeast Ga. Health System, Inc., Gainesville, 1995-2001; co-founder One Voice, Inc., Hiawassee, Ga., 2001—; RN Piedmont Hosp., Atlanta, 2001—02, clin. mgr. transplant unit and med./surg. unit, 2002—. Mem. Am. Coll. Healthcare Adminstrs. (Ga. chpt.), Complimentary Alternative Med. Assn., Ga. Nurses Assn., Sigma Theta Tau. Office: One Voice Inc 1435 Long Ridge Rd Hiawassee GA 30546 Home: 1435 Long Ridge Rd Hiawassee GA 30546

BAYLESS, DAVID J. engineer; s. Jerry R. and Shirley L. Bayless; m. Sally J. Howe, Aug. 14, 1993; children: Michael H., Laurel H. BSME, U. Mo., 1987; PhD, U. Ill., 1995. Registered profl. engr., Mo., 1998, Ohio, 1998. Assoc. prof. mech. engring. Ohio U., Athens, 1998—. Dir. Ohio Coal Rsch. Ctr., Athens, 1998—. Lt. USN, 1987—91. Achievements include patents for Membrane Electrostatic Precipitator. Office: Ohio U 248 Stocker Ctr Athens OH 45701-2979 Home Fax: 740-593-4902; Office Fax: 740-593-4902. Personal E-mail: bayless@ohio.edu. E-mail: bayless@ohio.edu.

BAYLESS, THEODORE M(ORRIS), gastroenterologist, educator, researcher; b. Atlantic City, Apr. 14, 1931; s. David N. and Fan (Halpern) B.; m. Janet M. Nides, June 22, 1954; children: Jeffrey, Andrew, Neal. BS, Bucknell U., 1953; MD, Chgo. Med. Sch., 1957. Intern Cornell div. Bellevue Hosp., also Meml. Cancer Ctr., N.Y.C., 1957-58, 58-60; fellow gastroenterology Johns Hopkins U., Balt., 1960-62, prof., 1981—; physician Johns Hopkins Hosp., Balt., 1964—; clin. dir. Meyerhoff Digestive Disease-Inflammatory Bowel Disease Ctr. Johns Hopkins U. Editor: Current Therapy-Gastroenterology, 1994, Advanced Therapy of Inflammatory Bowel Disease, 2001; co-author: NOD2 Gene in Crohn's Disease, 2001. Capt. USAR, 1962-64. Recipient Corson Nutrition medal Franklin Inst., Phila., 1987. Fellow ACP; mem. Am. Soc. Clin. Investigation, Am. Gastroenterology Assn. (dir. immunology, microbiology and inflammatory bowel disease 1991-96, Disting. Educator award 1987), Am. Coll. Phys. (Md. chpt. Clin. Investigation award, 1996, Janssen Disting. Clin. award, 1997), Alpha Omega Alpha. Jewish. Home: 2206 South Rd Baltimore MD 21209-4428 Office: Johns Hopkins Hosp 600 N Wolfe St Baltimore MD 21287-0005

BAYLIFF, EDGAR W. lawyer; b. Hazelwood, Ind., Feb. 23, 1927; s. Henry A. and Grace Eva (Bourn) B.; m. Betty L. Whitman, June 4, 1949; children: Bradford W., Dixie L. BA, Ind. U., 1951; JD, Ind. U., Indpls., 1954. Bar: Ind. 1954, U.S. Dist. Ct. (so. and no. dists.) Ind. 1954; diplomate Nat. Bd. Trial Advocacy. Ptnr. Bayliff, Harrigan, Cord & Maugans, Kokomo, Ind., 1955—. Contbr. articles to profl. jours. Recipient Disting. Alumni Svc. award Ind. U. Sch. Law, 1990. Mem. ABA, Assn. Trial Lawyers Am. (gov. 1969-72), Ind. Trial Lawyers Assn. (pres. 1965, life dir. coll. fellow, Hoosier Freedom award 1983, Trial Lawyer of Yr. 1993, Lifetime Achievement award 1995), Ind. Bar Assn. Home: 1901 Greytwig Dr Kokomo IN 46902-4516 Office: Bayliff Harrigan Cord & Maugans PO Box 2249 Kokomo IN 46904-2249 Fax: 765-459-3974.

BAYLINSON, CHRISTOPHER MICHAEL, lawyer; b. Atlantic City, Aug. 31, 1962; s. Roy S. and Florence B.; m. Marlena, July 18, 1992; children: Christopher Stone, Jackson Graham. BA, Rollins Coll., 1984; JD, Quinnipiac Sch. Law, 1988. Bar: N.J. 1988, U.S. Dist. Ct. N.J. 1988, U.S. Ct. Appeals (3d cir.) 2000; cert. civil. trial atty. Law clk. Atlantic County Civil Divsn., Atlantic City, 1988—99; ptnr. Cooper, Perskie, April, Niedelman, Wagenheim & Levenson, Atlantic City, 1999, Perskie Nehmad & Perillo, Egg Harbor Twp., NJ, 1999—. Master Haneman Inns Ct., Atlantic City, 1998. Bd. dirs. Atlantic City Art Ctr. Mem. NJ State Bar Assn. (trustee 2003—), Atlantic County Bar Assn. (trustee 1997-2002, treas. 2002—, sec. 2003, Outstanding Young Lawyer award 1998), Boardwalk Runners Club. Avocations: running, surfing. Office: PO Box 730 Somers Point NJ 08244-0730 E-mail: cmbaylinson@pnplaw.com.

BAYLIS, ROBERT MONTAGUE, investment banker; b. N.Y.C., Aug. 20, 1938; s. Chester, Jr. and Dorothy Montague (Smith) B.; m. Lois Margaret Wells, Apr. 6, 1963; children: Robert Wells, David Martin, John Chester. AB, Princeton U., 1960; MBA, Harvard U., 1962. CFA. Chartered fin. analyst CS First Boston, N.Y.C., 1963-96, vice chmn., 1992-96; chmn. CS First Boston Pacific, Hong Kong, 1993-94. Bd. dirs. Covance, Inc., Host Marriott Corp., N.Y. Life Ins. Co., Gildan Activewear, Ptnr. Re Inc. Served with M.C. U.S. Army, 1962-63. Mem. N.Y. Soc. Security Analysts, Nat. Assn. Bus. Economists, Weeburn Country Club, Univ. Club, Nassau Club, Cap and Gown Club, Ocean Reef Club. Home: 116 Delafield Island Rd Darien CT 06820-6017 Office: 105 Rowayton Ave Norwalk CT 06853

BAYLIS, THOMAS ARTHUR, political science educator; b. Providence, R.I., Feb. 28, 1937; s. Charles A. and Ruth Weage B.; m. Theresa M. Kelley, Nov. 23, 1986; children: Helen E. Ullrich, Aug. 28, 1969 (div. Oct. 1979); 1 child, Patrick. AB, Duke U., 1958; postgrad., Free U., Berlin, 1958-59; MA, U. Calif., Berkeley, 1961, PhD, 1968. Acting instr. in polit. sci. U. Calif., Berkeley, 1966-67; instr. polit. sci. Duke U., Durham, N.C., 1967-69; asst. prof. polit. sci. SUNY, Albany, 1969—74; assoc. prof. of polit. sci. U. Tex., San Antonio, 1974-90, prof. polit. sci., 1990-2000; sr. lectr. polit. sci. U. Wis., Madison, 2001—. Vis. assoc. prof. govt. U. Tex., Austin, 1990, 2000; vis. fellow Western Socs. Program Cornell U., Ithaca, N.Y., 1984-85; fellow Inst. for Sino-Soviet Studies George Washington U., 1987-88. Author: The Technical Intelligentsia and the East German Elite, 1974, Governing by Committee, 1989, The West and Eastern Europe, 1994; contbr. articles to profl. jours. Recipient Fulbright rsch. award U.S. Govt., 1980-81, Rsch. and Publ. award 20th Century Fund, 1986-93. Mem. German Dem. Republic Studies Assn. (pres. 1986-89), Southwestern Assn. of Slavic Studies (pres. 1996-97). Avocation: music. Home: 725 Oneida Pl Madison WI 53711 Office: Dept Polit Sci U Wis 110 North Hall 1050 Bascom Mall Madison WI 53706-1389 Fax: 608-265-2663. E-mail: tbaylis@polisci.wisc.edu.

BAYLIS, WILLIAM THOMAS, systems engineering specialist, writer; b. Bay Shore, N.Y., Oct. 21, 1952; s. William Wood and Viola Elaine (Burtis) B.; m. Milagros Marfisi, July 3, 1988; children: Christopher Thomas, Justin William Andrew. BSBA, U. Tenn., 1981; MBA in Mgmt., Dowling Coll., Oakdale, N.Y., 1984; PhD in Mgmt., Columbia Pacific U., San Raefel, Calif., 1986; postgrad., N.Y. Inst. Tech., 1987—. Asst. mgr. AIL div. Eaton Corp., Deer Park, N.Y., 1984-86, group leader, 1986-88; program mgr. Gen. Instrument Corp., Hicksville, N.Y., 1988-89, mgr. logistics engring., 1988-89, sr. logistics engr., logistics support analysis engring. lead McDonnell Douglas Space Systems Co., Kennedy Space Center, Fla., 1989-94; sys. engr. Avionics Rsch. Corp., Orlando, Fla., 1994—, systems engr., 1994—; engring. specialist, ILS, systems engr. Northrop Grumman, Melbourne, Fla., 1996—, lead assessor ISO 9001, 1996. Level II Integrated Database adminstr., security coord. for Space Sta. Freedom Program; pres. WTB Enterprises, Melbourne, Fla., 1990—; cons. in logistics and systems engring., systems devel. computer-based tng.; instr. space logistics tech. Brevard C.C. (adv. com. logistics systems tech. program), tchr. various logistics engring. courses; creator on-line college level courses; panel spkr. on space sta. group ops./logistics integration, Cocoa Beach, Fla., 1991, logistics support analysis spkr. Internat. Conf. and Tech. Exposition, Indpls., 1992; chmn. tech. adv. bd. SOLE Logistics Engring., 1992-94; chmn. tech. adv. bd. BCC's Multimedia Devel., 1994; spkr. in field. Author, editor: Starting a Retail Business, 1988, Trainer's Guide to Task Analysis, 1989, Logistics Engineer's Desk Reference, 1991, 2d edit., 92, LSA/LSAR Manual, 1992-94, Excel Manual, 1992-94, Word/Windows Manual, 1992-94; author: Training Requirements for Defense Contracts: A Practitioner's Desk Reference, 1989, Developing, Designing and Delivering Productive and Efficient Training, 1992, Mission Rehearsal and Synthetic Training, 2001, Life Cycle Costing in Defense and Aviation, 2001, Simulation Based Acquisition, 2001; editor Training Issues column in Soletter, 1994; developer software course Lotus 123, 1989. With USN, 1974-78. Recipient Chmn. award SOLE, 1992, Guest Speaker award, 1992, Paper award, 1997, Space Congress Achievement award, 1992, Speaker award Fla. Conf. and Workshop, 1994, Cert. of Appreciation Air Force Jour. of Logistics, 1995, Brevard C.C. Outstanding Adjunct of Yr. award, 1994-95; named Coord. of Yr. Total Quality, 1994-99, Total Quality Facilitator of Yr., 1995. Mem. AIAA, Am. Mgmt. Assn., Soc. Logistics Engrs. (Splty. award in logistics support analysis 1991, 92, 93, Splty. award Logistics & Supportability Engring. Edn. 1996, Sole Paper award Logistics Edn. 1996, Sole Paper award ISO 9000, 97, Guest Spkr. award 1997, 98, 99, ISO 9000), Internat. Orgn. for Standardization (trained lead assessor, instr. and course developer in ISO 9000), Internat. Soc. Philos. Enquiry, Assn. MBA Execs., Mensa, Intertel, Am. Legion, Phi Eta Sigma. Avocations: developing software, writing, photography, woodworking, reading. Home: 1988 Trevino Cir Melbourne FL 32935-4459 Office: Northop Grumman Corp Melbourne FL 32935 E-mail: baylibi@mail.northgrum.com., drwtb@aol.com.

BAYLISS, E. VIRGINIA, psychiatrist, educator; b. Richmond, Va. BA, Duke U., 1978; MD, U. Va., 1983. Diplomate Am. Bd. Psychiatry and Neurology. Resident in psychiatry U. Va., Charlottesville, 1983-87, clin. asst. prof. psychiat. medicine, 1987—; med. dir. Piedmont Psychiatric Profls., Charlottesville, 1990-2000. Fellow Am. Psychiat. Assn. (disting.); mem. Psychiat. Soc. Va. (bd. dirs. 1993-2000). Office: Piedmont Psychiatric Profls 175 S Pantops Dr Charlottesville VA 22911-8671 Fax: 434-296-1195.

BAYLISS, JOHN TEMPLE, retired science educator, retired energy executive; b. Richmond, Va., July 6, 1939; s. William Murray and Catherine Williams Bayliss; m. Mary Lynn Skinner, Aug. 14, 1971; children: William Temple, Ann Forbes, Albert Thompson. BA, Bowdoin Coll., 1957—61; PhD, U. of Va., 1961—67. Asst. prof. of physics Va. Commonwealth U., Richmond, Va., 1967—74; asst. dir., energy divsn. Va. Dept. of Mines Minerals and Energy, Richmond, 1975—79; dir., energy divsn. Va. Dept. of Mines, Minerals, and Energy, 1979—86; energy cons. Tech. Associates, Inc., Richmond, 1986—93, J. T. Bayliss Cons. Inc., Richmond, 1993—2001. Contbr. articles; editor: (book of newspaper columns) Out in the Noonday Sun. Mem.: James River Bridge Club, Fishing Bay Yacht Club. Home: 1114 Dover Rd Manakin Sabot VA 23103 Home Fax: 804-784-5213. Personal E-mail: jtempbay@aol.com.

BAYLOR, DENIS ARISTIDE, neurobiologist; b. Oskaloosa, Iowa, Jan. 30, 1940; s. Hugh Murray and Elisabeth Anne (Barbou) B.; m. Eileen Margaret Steele, Aug. 12, 1983; children: Denis Murray, Michael Randel; 1 stepchild, Michele Gonelli. BA in Chemistry magna cum laude, Knox Coll., 1961, DS (hon.), 1989; MD cum laude, Yale U., 1965. Post-doctoral fellow Yale Med. Sch., New Haven, 1965-68; staff assoc. NINDS, Bethesda, Md., 1968-70; USPHS spl. fellow Physiol. Lab. Cambridge U., England, 1970-72; assoc. prof. physiology U. Colo. Med. Sch., Denver, 1972-74, Stanford U., Calif., 1974-75, assoc. prof. neurobiology, 1975-78, prof. neurobiology, 1978—2001, chmn. dept. neurobiology, 1992-95; First Annual W.S. Stiles lecturer U. Coll., London, 1989; Jonathan Magnes lecturer Hebrew U., Jerusalem, 1990; Woolsey lectr. U. Wis., 1992; E. Hille lectr. U. Wash., 1995. Mem. NIH Visual Scis. Study Sect., 1984-88, chmn., 1986-88; vis. com. med. scis. Harvard U., 1987-93; chmn. Summer conf. on Vision FASEB, 1989; Wellcome vis. prof. U. Miami, 1995; mem. sci. adv. com. Alcon Rsch. Inst., 1994-99; mem. HHMI Sci. adv. bd. 1997—, Med. adv. bd. 1998-01; mem. sci. adv. bd. Found. Fighting Blindness, 1998—; trustee The Grass Found., 1995-99. Mem. editorial bd. Jour. Physiology, 1977-84, Neuron, 1988-93, Jour. Neurophysiology, 1989—, Visual Neurosci., 1990-93, Jour. Neurosci., 1991—; contbr. articles to profl. jours. Recipient Sinsheimer Found. award, 1975, Mathilde Solowey award, 1978, Kayser Internat. award Retina Rsch. Found., 1988, Golden Brain award Minerva Found., 1988, Merit award Nat. Eye Inst., 1990, Alcon Rsch. Inst. award, 1991; Rank Optoelectronics prize Rank Orgn., Eng., 1980; Proctor medal Assn. Rsch. Vision & Ophthalmology, 1986, Von Sallman prize in eye rsch., 1998. Fellow Am. Acad. Arts and Scis.; mem. NAS, Royal Soc. London (fgn.), Phi Beta Kappa, Alpha Omega Alpha. Avocations: jogging, woodworking. Office: Stanford U Sch Med Neurobiology/Fairchild D253 835 Esplanada Way Stanford CA 94305 E-mail: dbaylor@stanford.edu.

BAYLOR, DON EDWARD, former professional baseball manager; b. Austin, Tex., June 28, 1949; s. George Edward and Lillian Joyce B.; m. Rebecca Giles, Dec. 12, 1987; 1 child by previous marriage, Don Edward. Student, Miami-Dade Jr. Coll., Miami, Fla., Blinn Jr. Coll., Brenham, Tex. With Balt. Orioles, 1970-76, Oakland Athletics, 1976, 88, California Angels, 1976-82, N.Y. Yankees, 1983-86, Boston Red Sox, 1986-87, Minnesota Twins, 1987; mem. World Series Championship Team, 1987; mgr. Colorado Rockies, Denver, 1992-98; hitting/batting coach Atlanta Braves, 1999; mgr., coach Chgo. Cubs, 1999—2002. Set new career record for hit by pitches; hit safely in 12 consecutive Am. League Championship Series games. Author: (with Claire Smith) Don Baylor, Nothing But the Truth: A Baseball Life, 1989. Chmn. nat. sports Cystic Fibrosis Found. Recipient Designated Hitter of Yr. award, 1985, 86, Roberto Clemente award, 1985; named Am. League's Most Valuable Player, 1979, Sporting News Player of Yr., 1979; player All-Star Game, 1979; named Nat. League Mgr. of Yr. Sporting News, 1995, Baseball Writers Assn. Am., 1995. Achievements include being a holder of Am. League playoff record most RBI (10), 1982, Am. League single season record most times hit by pitch (35), 1986. Office: Chicago Cubs 1060 W Addison St Chicago IL 60613-4397 also: Major League Baseball Players Assn 805 3d Ave New York NY 10022-7513

BAYLOR, SCOTT ALLEN, chemistry educator; b. Danville, Pa., Sept. 16, 1964; s. Richard Allen and Nancy Lou (Fleming) B.; m. Janelle Denise Reichenbach, Sept. 11, 1993; 1 child, Ethan Scott. Student, Case Western Res. U., 1982-84; BS in Sci. Edn., Bloomsburg U., 1987; MS in Edn., Wilkes U., 2002. Cert. chem. tchr., Pa. Chemistry tchr. Lancaster (Pa.) Cath. H.S., 1987-95, Elizabethtown (Pa.) Area H.S., 1995—, chmn. sci. dept., 1996-99. Lifetouch Enrichment grantee, 1996-97; recipient Cert. of Recognition, Am. Chem. soc., 1994, Commendation, Am. Soc. Microbiology, 1988, Tchr. Recognition, Order of DeMolay, 1996, 97, 2001. Avocations: woodworking, reading, golf. Home: 129 Atkins Ave Lancaster PA 17603

BAYLY, GEORGE V. manufacturing executive; Chmn., pres. & CEO Olympic Packing Inc., Ivex Packaging, Lincolnshire, Ill., 1991—2002; principal Whitehall Investors L.L.C., 2002—. Bd. dir. Carvel Inc., Chicago Stock Exchange, Field Industries, Packaging Dynamics, Roark Capital, Chargeurs Inc., France, Huhtamaki, Finland, U.S. Can Corp., GBC, Miami U. of Ohio, Shedd Aquarium, United Way.*

BAYLY, JOHN HENRY, JR., judge; b. Washington, Jan. 26, 1944; s. John Henry and Salome Carole (Winters) B.; m. Barbara Jean Downey, Feb. 16, 1974 (dec. Jan. 1977); 1 child, Anne Louise; m. Katherine Bridget Kenny, Dec. 1, 1979; children: Johanna, Georgia. AB, Fordham U., 1966; JD, Harvard U., 1969. Bar: U.S. Dist. Ct. D.C. 1969, U.S. Ct. Appeals (D.C. cir.) 1969, D.C. 1971, U.S. Supreme Ct. 1974. Atty., advisor FCC, Washington, 1969-71; asst. atty. Office of U.S. Atty., Washington, 1971-75, 78-85; dep. minority counsel Senate Select Com. on Intelligence, Washington, 1975-76; acting asst. gen. counsel Corp. for Pub. Broadcasting, Washington, 1976-78; gen. counsel Legal Services Corp., Washington, 1985-87, pres., 1987-88; of counsel Stein, Mitchell & Mezines, Washington, 1988-90; judge D.C. Superior Ct., 1990—. Mem. D.C. Bar Assn., John Carroll Soc., Counsellors, Bryant Inn of Ct., Lawyers Club Washington, Phi Beta Kappa. Republican. Roman Catholic. Home: 3512 Runnymede Pl NW Washington DC 20015-2420 Office: DC Superior Ct 500 Indiana Ave NW Ste 1 Washington DC 20001-2131

BAYLY, THOMAS GLEN, minister, publisher religious material; b. Mineola, N.Y., Oct. 14, 1951; s. Thomas G. and Anastasia (Xikes) B.; m. Jennifer Lee Edwards, Sept. 25, 1971; children: Thomas G. III, Douglas E., Michael P., Scott A. BA, U. Calif., Berkeley, 1973. Ordained to ministry Christian and Missionary Alliance Ch. Campus min. Collegiate Encounter, Sacramento, 1971-75; asst. and interim pastor Parkside Alliance Ch., Manassas Pk., Va., 1975-77; founding pastor Staunton (Va.) Alliance Ch., 1977-79, Harrisonburg (Va.) Alliance Ch., 1980-85; chaplain Alliance Christian Fellowship, State College, Pa., 1985-92; pastor Missionary Alliance Ch., Bennington, Vt., 1992—2001, Mifflinburg (Pa.) Allicance Ch., 2001—. Dir. Leadership through Christ Newsletter, Bennington, 1976—; mem. Office Religious Affairs, Pa. State U., State Coll., 1985-92; co-chmn. Penn State Evangelical Ministers, State Coll., 1989-92; dist. exec. com. New England dist. C&MA, Boston, 1995-98; com. mem. Albany (N.Y.) Creation Sci. Seminar, 1995; host radio program Lions Den Univ. Report, 2001--. Bd. dirs. Staunton weekday religious edn., 1978-79; co-founder Harrisonburg Pregnancy Ctr., 1981-85; founding mem. Penn State Christian Faculty/Staff Assn., State Coll., 1985-92; radio program host "Lion's Den Penn State Report", 1992-93; producer (radio program) Lion's Den University Report, 2000—; bd. dirs. Vt. Right to Life, 1996-2001; mem. steering com., co-chmn. Christian Coaliton of Bennington County, 1996-2001; chmn. bd. Christian Coalition Vt., 1997-2001. Avocations: racquetball, tennis, writing. Home: PO Box 226 Millinburg PA 17844 Office: Mifflinburg Alliance Ch RR 4 Box 212 Mifflinburg PA 17844 E-mail: ltcldur@yahoo.com.

BAYM, NINA, English educator; b. Princeton, N.J., June 14, 1936; d. Leo and Frances (Levinson) Zippin; m. Gordon Baym, June 1, 1958; children— Nancy, Geoffrey; m. Jack Stillinger, May 21, 1971 BA, Cornell U., 1957; MA, Harvard U., 1958, PhD, 1963. Asst. U. Calif.-Berkeley, 1962-63; instr. U. Ill., Urbana, 1963-67, asst. prof. English, 1967-69, assoc. prof., 1969-72, prof., 1972—, Jubilee prof. liberal arts and scis., 1989—, dir. Sch. Humanities, 1976-87, sr. Univ. scholar, 1985, assoc. Ctr. Advanced Study, 1989-90, permanent prof. Ctr. Advanced Study, 1997—, Swanlund Endowed chair, 1997—. Author: The Shape of Hawthorne's Career, 1976, Woman's Fiction: A Guide to Novels By and About Women in America, 1978, 2d rev. edit., 1993, Novels, Readers and Reviewers: Responses to Fiction in Antebellum America, 1984, The Scarlet Letter: A Reading, 1986, Feminism and American Literary History, 1992, American Women Writers and the Work of History, 1790-1860, 1995, American Women of Letters and the 19th Century Sciences, 2002; gen. editor: Norton Anthology of American Literature; sr. editor Am. Nat. Biography; also author essays, edits., revs.; mem. editl. bd. Am. Quar., New Eng. Quar., Legacy, A Jour. of 19th Century Am. Women Writers, Jour. Aesthetic Edn. Am. Lit., Tulsa Studies in Women's Lit., Am. Studies, Studies Am. Fiction, Am. Periodicals, Hemingway Rev., Resources for Am. Lit. Study, Am. Lit. History, Cambridge U.P. Studies in Am. Lit. and Culture; mem. editl. adv. bd. PMLA. Guggenheim fellow, 1975-76, AAUW hon. fellow, 1975-76, NEH fellow, 1982-83; recipient Arnold O. Beckman award U. Ill., 1992-93, Hubbell Lifetime Achievement medal, Am. Let. Sect., 2000. Mem. MLA (exec. com. 19th century Am. Lit. divsn., chmn. 1984, chmn. Am. Lit. sect. 1984, Hubbell Lifetime Achievement medal 2000), Am. Studies Assn. (exec. com. 1982-84, nominating com. 1991-93), Am. Lit. Assn., Am. Antiquarian Soc., Mass. Hist. Soc., Nathaniel Hawthorne Soc. (adv. bd.), Western Lit. Assn., Mortar Bd., Phi Kappa Phi, Phi Beta Kappa. Office: U Ill Dept English 608 S Wright St Urbana IL 61801-3630 E-mail: Baymnina@uiuc.edu.

BAYNE, DAVID COWAN, priest, legal scholar, law educator; b. Detroit, Jan. 11, 1918; s. David Cowan and Myrtle (Murray) B. AB, U. Detroit, 1939; LLB, Georgetown U., 1947, LLM, 1948; MA, Loyola U., Chgo., 1946, STL, 1953; SJD (grad. fellow), Yale, 1949; LLD (hon.), Creighton U., 1980. Bar: Fed. and D.C. 1948, Mich. 1960, Mo. 1963. Joined Soc. of Jesus, 1941; ordained priest Roman Catholic Ch., 1952; asst. prof. law U. Detroit, 1954-60; acting dean U. Detroit (Law Sch.), 1955-59, dean, 1959-60; research assoc. Nat. Jesuit Research Orgn., Inst. Social Order, St. Louis, 1960-63; vis. lectr. St. Louis U. Law Sch., 1960-63, prof. law, 1963-67; vis. prof. Mich. Law Sch., 1967, Inst. fur Auslandisches und Internationales Wirtschaftrecht, Frankfurt, 1967; prof. U. Iowa Coll. Law, Iowa City, 1967-88, prof. emeritus, 1988—. Vis. prof. U. Koln, Germany, 1970, 74 Author: Conscience, Obligation and the Law, 1966, 2d edit., 1988; The Philosophy of Corporate Control, 1986; editor legal materials; contbr. articles to profl. jours. Achievements include research in corp. law. E-mail: dcbsj@netzero.net., dcbsj@buckeye-express.com.

BAYNE, JAMES ELWOOD, investor and financial consultant; b. Detroit, May 6, 1940; s. John David and Alice Angie (Davis) Bayne; m. Mary Lee Skinner, May 4, 1963; children: James E. Jr., Laura Lee Poe. BA, Yale U., 1962; MBA, Columbia U., 1967. Investment adminstr. Bankers Trust, N.Y.C., 1962-65; fin analyst Std. Oil, N.Y.C., 1967; sr. fin. analyst Esso Internat., N.Y.C., 1967-70; asst. treas. Esso S.A.P.A., Buenos Aires, 1970-71; treas. Intercol, Bogota, Colombia, 1971-74; asst. treas. Esso InterAm., Coral Gables, Fla., 1974-77; asst. gen. mgr. Esso Ctrl. Am., Coral Gables, 1977-80; mgr. Mexican Bus. Opportunity, Coral Gables, 1980-81; treas. Exxon Chem. Europe, Brussels, 1981-86; mgr., benefits fin. and investment Exxon, Dallas, 1986-99; mgr. benefits fin. and investment Exxon Mobil, Dallas, 1999-2000; cons., advisor to fin. svcs. industry Dallas, 2001—. Exec. com. CIEBA, Washington, 1994—, vice chmn., 1995—96, chmn., 1996—98; pension adv. com. N.Y. Stock Exch., N.Y.C., 1995—99; mem. adv. bd. Wharton Trading Sys., 1993—96. Del. 1st White Ho. Summit Retirement Savs., Washington, 1998; v.p. Incarnation Found., 1996—2003; mem. investment com. Episcopal Found. Dallas; chair Episcopal Renewal Ctr., 1996—2002; dir. Dallas-Ft. Worth Episcopal Renewal Ctr.; mem. steering com. Interforum, 1993—96; bd. dirs.

Fin. Execs. Inst., 1996—98; trustee Ch. Pension Fund, N.Y.C., 2000—; pres. secretariat Dallas-Ft. Worth Cursillo Movement, 1992—96. Fellow: George H. Gallup Internat. Inst.; mem.: Harbor Club (gov. and treas. Seal Harbor, Maine), Yale Club N.Y., Yale Club Dallas, Order St. John. Episcopalian. Avocations: church work, walking, reading, travel. Home: 3401 Lee Pkwy # 1704 Dallas TX 75219

BAYNE, KATHRYN ANN LOUISE, veterinarian; b. Santa Monica, Calif., Feb. 4, 1959; d. Richard Harry and Loretta Mary Bayne; m. Mark Cofer Haines, May 19, 1990. BS cum laude, Calif. State Poly. U., 1979; MS, Wash. State U., 1982, PhD, 1986, DVM, 1987. Vet. behaviorist NIH, Bethesda, Md., 1987-94; assoc. dir Assn. for the Assessment & Accreditation of Lab. Animal Care, Rockville, Md., 1994—. Diplomate Am. Coll. Lab. Animal Medicine, v.p. bd. dirs. Inventor in field; author publs. in field. Comdr. USPHS. Recipient Foster award, USPHS commendaton and achievement awards, Garvey award AALAS; named Alumnus of Yr. award Westlake Sch. Mem.: Scientists Ctr. for Animal Welfare (past v.p. bd. dirs.), DC Vet. Med. Assn. (past pres.), Assn. Primate Vets. (past pres.), Am. Soc. Lab. Animal Practitioners, Animal Behavior Soc., AVMA (chair animal welfare com.). Avocations: gardening, birdwatching. Office: AAALAC International 11300 Rockville Pike Ste 1211 Rockville MD 20852-3040

BAYNES, THOMAS EDWARD, JR., judge, lawyer, educator; b. N.Y.C., Mar. 19, 1940; s. Thomas Edward and Ann Jane (Burke) B.; m. Maija Eva Kokko, Dec. 30, 1963; children: Cynthia Lynn, Barbara Ann. BBA, U. Ga., 1962; JD, Emory U., 1967, LLM, 1972, Yale U., 1973. Bar: Ga. 1968, U.S. Supreme Ct. 1971, Ct. of Mil. Appeals 1978, Fla. 1981. Dir. Legal Assistance to Inmates Program, Emory U., 1968-69; asst. dean, asst. prof. bus. law Ga. State U., 1969-72; acting regional dir. Nat. Ctr. for State Cts., Atlanta, 1973-74; prof. law and public adminstrn. Nova U. Law Ctr., Ft. Lauderdale, Fla., 1974-76, 77-81; jud. fellow U.S. Supreme Ct., 1976-77; speedy trial reporter U.S. Dist. Ct., So. Dist. Fla., 1977-81; ptnr. Peterson, Myers, Craig, Crews, Brandon & Mann, Lake Wales, Fla., 1981-87; U.S. bankruptcy judge for mid. dist. Fla. U.S. Bankruptcy Ct., Tampa, 1987—, chief bankruptcy judge, 2000—03. State chmn., Ga., Nat. Council on Crime and Delinquency, 1971-72; legal counsel Reorgn. Study Commn. Ga., 1971-72 Author: (with W. Scott) Legal Aspects of Laboratory Medicine in Quality Assurance in Laboratory Management, 1978, Eminent Domain in Florida, 1979, Florida Mortgage Law, 1999, (with others) Supreme Court Justices, Illustrated Biographies, 1993; supplement editor Fla. Real Estate Law and Procedure, 1976; contbg. editor Norton Bankruptcy Law and Practice, 1995. Bd. dirs. F. Lee Moffitt Cancer Rsch Hosp., Tampa, 1989-94, 97—. Comdr. JAGC, USNR, 1960-80, ret. Sterling fellow Yale U. Law Sch., 1972-73; Harry J. Loman Found. rsch. fellow, 1979. Mem. Ga. Bar Assn., Fla. Bar Assn. (cert. cir. ct. mediator and arbitrator), Am. Law Inst., Hillsborough Assn. Women Lawyers (bd. dirs. 2001-), Fla. Acad. Profl. Mediators Inc., Supreme Ct. Hist. Soc., Am. Arbitration Assn., Nat. Adv. Com. for Bankruptcy, Ferguson-White Inn (pres. 1992-93, master), Omicron Delta Kappa. Office: US Bankruptcy Ct 801 N Florida Ave Tampa FL 33602-3849

BAYONA, MANUEL, medical educator; MD, Nat. U. Mex., Mexico City, 1977; MSc Biostatistics, Nat. U. Mex., 1979; PhD in Epidemiology, Johns Hopkins U., Balt., 1985. Intern Chihuahua Gen. Hosp., Chihuahua City, Mexico, 1975; med. social svc. intern Nat. U. Mex., Mexico City, 1976; cons. epidemiologist WHO, Ouagadougou, Burkina Faso, 1985—86; cons. pub. health specialist/epidemiologist Westinghouse Corp./Guatemalan Ministry of Health and USAID, Guatemala City, Guatemala, 1986; epidemiologist The Arthritis Rsch. Inst. Am., Clearwater, Fla., 1987; cons. epidemiologist PAHO/WHO and Sch. Malariology and Environ. Sanitation, Min. of Health Venezuela, Maracay, 1987; temp. advisor PAHO/WHO, Washington, 1988; cons. epidemiologist, vis. prof. Min. Health of Venezuela, Maracay, 1988; med. epidemiologist and program dir. UNICEF, Mexico City, 1991—92; acad. coord. Pan Am. Health Orgn. and U. South Fla., Tampa, 1993—95; dir. pub. health program Coll. Allied Health, Nova Southeastern U., Ft. Lauderdale, Fla., 1995—96; and acad. coord. Sch. Malariology and Environ. Health Ministry of Health of Venezuela, Pan Am. Health Orgn. and World Bank, Maracay, 1998—2001; dir. Dr.P.H. program U. North Tex. Health Sci. Ctr., Ft. Worth, 2000—, assoc. prof., dir. Ctr. for Internat. Health and Tropical Diseases, dir. Dr.P.H. Sch. Pub. Health, 2000—. Vis. prof. Ponce Sch. Medicine, Ponce, PR, 1994—, Carabobo U., Maracay, 1997—2001; adj. asst. prof. dept. internal medicine U. South Fla., Tampa, 1994—95; vis. lectr. U. Autonoma de Ciudad Juarez, Mexico, 2003; vis. prof. U. P.R. and Glaxo Wellcome Labs., 1998; cons. epidemiologist in field; vis. prof. numerous colls. and univs.; lectr. in field. Contbr. Recipient numerous rsch. grants, fellowships; grantee, Pan Am. Health Orgn. and World Bank, 1999, Tobacco Rsch. grantee, U. N. Tex. Health Sci. Ctr., 2000. Mem.: APHA, Fla. Pub. Health Assn., Internat. Epidemiol. Assn., Internat. Biometric Soc., Soc. Epidemiologic Rsch. Achievements include invention of method and apparatus for fast and non-invasive diagnosis of malaria; spectrophotometric characterization of human blood; patents for in field. Office: Univ of North Texas Health Sci Ctr EAD 701-A 3500 Camp Bowie Blvd Fort Worth TX 76107-2699

BAYOR, RONALD HOWARD, history educator; b. N.Y.C., Mar. 14, 1944; s. Mac and Lillian Bayor; m. Leslie Steigman, Dec. 24, 1966 (dec. Dec. 20, 2001); children: Jill Cindy, Robin Kim Coe. BA, CCNY, 1965; MA, Syracuse U., 1966; PhD, U. Pa., 1970. Asst. prof. history St. John's U., Jamaica, NY, 1969—73; prof. history Ga. Inst. Tech., Atlanta, 1973—. Founder, editor jour. Am. ethnic history Immigration and Ethnic History Soc., Atlanta, 1981—. Author: (non-fiction) Neighbors in Conflict: The Irish, Germans, Jews and Italians of New York City, 1929-1941, 1978 (outstanding acad. book selection Choice mag., 1978), Fiorello LaGuardia: Ethnicity and Reform, 1993, Race and the Shaping of Twentieth Century Atlanta, 1996 (Outstanding Book award Gustavus Myers Ctr. for Study of Human Rights in N.Am., 1996); editor: Neighborhoods in Urban America, 1982, The New York Irish, 1996 (James S. Donnelly, Sr. prize for best book in history and social scis. Am. Conf. for Irish Studies, 1997); contbr. articles to profl. jours. Lead historian for U.S. Ct. of Appeals case on affirmative action NAACP Legal Def. and Ednl. Fund, Atlanta, 2001—02. Recipient Disting. Svc. award, Immigration and Ethnic History Soc., 1992; fellow, NEH, 1992—93. Mem.: Social Sci. History Assn. (urban network chair 1993—94), Soc. Am. City and Regional Planning History, Orgn. Am. Historians, Urban History Assn. (bd. dirs. 1995—97), Am. Hist. Assn. (chair J. Franklin Jameson Fellowship com. 1987—88), Am. Italian Hist. Assn. (nat. exec. coun. 1977—79), Am. Jewish Hist. Soc. (acad. coun. 1983—2003), Immigration and Ethnic History Soc. (exec. bd. 1987—89), Phi Alpha Theta. Avocation: collecting political campaign memorabilia. Office: Ga Inst Tech Sch of History 685 Cherry St Atlanta GA 30332 E-mail: ronald.bayor@hts.gatech.edu.

BAYRAKDAR, AMMAR ADNAN, endocrinologist; b. Damascus, Syria, Jan. 8, 1966; came to U.S., 1991; s. Adnan and Amira (Reehan) B.; m. Nabeela Humsi, Aug. 27, 1992; children: Keenan, Rahma, Kareem. MD with honors, Damascus U., 1990. Diplomate Am. Bd. Internal Medicine, Am. Bd. Endocrinology, Diabetes and Metabolism; cert. bone densometrist. Intern St. Joseph Hosp., Chgo., 1991-92, resident in internal medicine, 1993-94; fellow in endocrinology and metabolism Loyola U., Maywood, Ill., 1994-96; pvt. practice Chgo., 1996—; med. dir. Diabetes Ctr., Little Company of Mary Hosp. Intensive care com. Roseland Hosp., Chgo., 1996—; clin. asst. prof. medicine Loyola. Author: (Arabic) Textbook of Pathology, 1990. Fellow Am. Assn. Clin. Endocrinologists (cert. thyroid ultrasonography), Am. Coll. Endocrinologists; mem. ACP. Moslem. Avocation: sports. Office: 3830 W 95th St Evergreen Park IL 60805

BAYRAM, ERSIN, electrical engineer, researcher; b. Simav, Turkey, Oct. 19, 1976; s. Hasan and Hafize Bayram. PhD in Biomedical Engring., Wake Forest Sch. of Medicine, 2003; MS in Computer Sci., Wake Forest U., 2000; BS in Elec. and Electronics Engring., Bilkent U., Turkey, 1998. Rsch. asst. Pet Ctr., Wake Forest Sch. of Medicine, NC, 1998—99, Virtual Endoscopy Group, Wake Forest Sch. of Medicine, NC, 1999—2000, Cardiac MRI Rsch. Group, Wake Forest Sch. of Medicine, Winston-Salem, NC, 2000—03; instr. Wake Forest U. Health Scis., 2003—. Cons. Targacept, Inc., Winston-Salem, NC, 2002—02. Contbr. acad. rsch. (Third Pl. in the 23rd Annnual Student Paper Competition, 2001). Fellow Dean's Grad. Fellowship, Wake Forest U. Sch. of Medicine, 1998—2000, Undergraduate Edn. Fellowship, Bilkent U. Bd. of Trustees, 1994—98. Mem.: Internat. Soc. of Magnetic Resonance in Medicine (corr.), The IEEE (IEEE) (corr.), Upsilon Pi Epsilon (life). Office: Wake Forest Sch of Medicine Biomedical Engring Dept MRI Bldg Winston Salem NC 27157 E-mail: ebayram@wfubmc.edu.

BAYS, JOHN THEOPHANIS, consulting engineer; b. Bklyn., July 17, 1947; s. Theophanis A. and Mildred Bays; m. Mindy Giardina, July 8, 1973; 1 dau., Nina. BS, N.Y. Inst. Tech., 1972; BArch, CCNY, 1974; cert. in solar design, Ohio State U., 1975. Cert. energy mgr., energy auditor, asbestos investigator, N.Y. Project mgr., head sys. designer Wormser Sci. Corp., Stamford, Conn., 1975-82, v.p. engring., 1982-85; pres. E.E. Linden Assocs., Cons. Engrs., Norwalk, Conn., 1985—. Recipient wawards in solar design. Mem. ASHRAE. Home: 18 Marion Rd Westport CT 06880-2919 Office: 110 Richards Ave Norwalk CT 06854-1622 E-mail: j.t.bays@eelinden.com.

BAYS, JUNE MARIE, counselor, social worker; b. LaSalle, Ill., Feb. 16, 1941; d. John Frederick and Esther Marie Nielsen; m. James Philip Bays, June 29, 1963; children: Timothy James, Daniel Mark. Diploma in Nursing, Evanston Hosp. Sch. Nursing, 1962; BS, Western Mich. U., 1983, MSW, 1986. Lic. clin. social worker, Ind. Med. surg. nurse Evanston Hosp., 1962-63; psychiat. staff nurse U. Hosp., Madison, Wis., 1963-65, Madison Gen. Hosp., 1965-66; therapist Madison Ctr., South Bend, Ind., 1986-90; social work clin. specialist U. N.C. Hosp., Chapel Hill, 1990-91; therapist Samaritan Counseling Ctr., South Bend, Ind., 1991-95, Bethel Coll. Counseling Ctr., Mishawaka, Ind., 1995—. Mem. NASW, Am. Assn. Christian Counselors. Avocations: reading, sewing, travel, art. Office: Bethel Coll Counseling Ctr 1001 W Mckinley Ave Mishawaka IN 46545-5509

BAYS, MONA RAE, retired librarian; b. Mattoon, Ill., June 16, 1950; d. Alburn Marion and Doris Madeline Reynolds Grafton; m. Michael Allan Bays, Mar. 20, 1999; children: Brent Allan, Clinton Andrew. BA in English, Ea. Ill. U., 1972; MA in Librarianship, U. Denver, 1973. Youth libr. Mattoon (Ill.) Pub. Libr., 1973-75, cataloger, 1975-76, libr., 1976-94, dir., 1994—2002. Author: A House Not Made With Hands, 1981. Elder, bd. dirs. First Christian Ch. of Mattoon. Named Best Boss in Ctrl. Ill. Decatur Herald and Rev., 1987, Young Careerist Bus. and Profl. Women's Assn., 1978. Mem. ALA, Am. Bus. Women's Assn. (Woman of Yr. Mattoon chpt. 1980, 95, Pegtown chpt. 1999), Women of the Moose, Ill. Libr. Assn. Avocations: golfing, traveling. E-mail: mmbays@consolidated.net.

BAYSAL, EDIP, executive; b. Istanbul, Turkey, Aug. 9, 1952; came to U.S., 1997; s. Nushet Zekai and Ayten (Eyinc) B.; m. Sema Semen Dalaman, Apr. 28, 1977; 1 child, Doga. PhD in Geophysics, U. Houston, 1982. Geophysicist Turkish Petroleum Corp., Ankara, 1977-79; rsch. asst. U. Houston, 1980-82; rsch. geophysicist Geophys. Devel. Corp., Houston, 1981-83; assoc. prof. Ankara U., Turkey, 1988-97; deputy exploration mgr. Turkish Petroleum Corp., 1983-97; v.p. rsch. & devel. Seismic Rsch. Corp., Houston, 1997-98; chief geophysicist Paradigm Geophys. Corp., Houston, 1998—. Mem. European Assn. Exploration Geophysicists, Soc. Exploration Geophysicists, Houston Geophys. Soc., Chamber Geophysical Engrs. Turkey. Office: Paradigm Geophys Corp 820 Gessner Ste 400 Houston TX 77024 4313

BAYSINGER, STEPHEN MICHAEL, quality assurance professional; b. St. Louis, May 9, 1954; s. David Richard and Betty I. (Elledge) B.; children: Devin, Derrick, Corey, Jocelyn, Carly. BA in Polit. Sci., U. Denver, 1977; MS in Human Resource Mgmt., Troy State U., 1989. Commd. 2d lt. USAF, 1979, advanced through grades to maj., 1990; maintenance supr. 7th Bombardment Wing, Carswell AFB, Tex., 1979-82, 343d Fighter Wing, Eielson AFB, Alaska, 1982-85; logistics project mgr. Air Force Logistics Mgmt. Ctr., Gunter AFB, Ala., 1985-90; chief maintenance mgmt. 58 Figher Wing, Luke AFB, Ariz., 1990-91, maintenance supr., 1991, chief quality assurance, 1991-92; mgr. quality engring., project officer ISO 9001 K*Tec Electronics divsn., Houston, 1992-94; sr. quality audit engr. Lockheed Martin Manned Space Sys., New Orleans, 1994-96; sr. staff engr. Lockheed Martin Astronautics, Denver, 1996-97; process improvement specialist TeleTech, Denver, 1997-98; quality mgr. Moll Industries, Austin, Tex., 1998-2000; supplier quality engr. Telxon Corp., Houston, 2000, Rtron Electronics, Houston, 2000—02, Guidant Corp., Houston, 2002—. Author: The Complete Guide to the CQA; contbr. articles to profl. jours. Leader Boy Scouts Am., Luke AFB, 1991-92; bd. dirs. Ala. Am. Diabetes Assn., Montgomery, 1985-90. Lt. col. USAFR, 1995—. Mem. Am. Soc. for Quality Control (cert. quality auditor), Soc. Logistics Engrs. Achievements include development of the first-ever automated personnel and equipment performance trend identification and analysis program for USAF, of the automated information center, of the quality division. E-mail: stevebaysinger@hotmail.com.

BAYUZICK, ROBERT J. materials scientist, educator; b. Braddock, Pa., Sept. 6, 1937; s. John and Mary (Holub) B.; m. Jeannette A. Lyle, Apr. 22, 1961; children: Carrie Lynn Hargis, Kellie JoAnn Kidd. BS, U. Pitts., 1961; MS in Phys. Metallurgy, U. Denver, 1963; PhD in Material Sci., Vanderbilt U., 1969. Rsch. metallurgist Battelle Meml. Inst., Columbus, Ohio, 1964—65; instr. Vanderbilt U., Nashville, 1968—69, asst. prof. material sci., 1969—72, program dir. material sci., 1974—75, assoc. prof. material sci., 1972—77, dir. Ctr. for Space Processing of Engring. Materials, 1985—90, prof. material scis., 1977—, dir. material sci., 1993—2002. Vis. rsch. prof. Cambridge (Eng.) U., 1977-78; vis. sr. sci. NASA, Washington, 1991-92; mem. metals and alloys discipline working group NASA, 1986-91, vice chmn. space processing tech. com., 1988-90, chmn. space sta. sci. and applications adv. com. 1989-91, mem. space sta. sci. and applications adv. com. 91-97, mem. space sta. adv. com. 1989-90, mem. Office Comml. Programs adv. com. 1989-90, mem. microgravity sci. and applications adv. com. 1989-91, mem. requirements integration group for space sta., shared lab. support equipment 1990-92, mem. requirements integration group for space sta., microgravity lab. support equipment 1990-92, mem. space sta. customer support team 1991-92, mem. exec. group life and microgravity scis. and applications adv. com. 1994-95; invited lectr. Beijing Rsch. Inst. of Materials and Tech., 1987, Luoyang (China) Inst. Tech., 1987, Northwest Polytechnic Inst., Xian, China, 1987; mem. Internat. Forum for Utilization of Space Sta., 1989-91; mem. com. on microgravity rsch. Space Studies Bd., NRC, 1995-99, mem. com. on internat. progams, 1996-98, mem. task group on instnl. arrangements for space sta. rsch., 1999; spkr. in field. Co-editor: Solidification Processing of Eutectic Alloys, 1988, Space Commercialization: Platforms and Processing, Progress in Astronautics and Aeronautics 127, 1990; patentee in field; contbr. articles and papers to profl. jours. Recipient Pub. Svc. medal NASA, 1992. Mem. AIME Metall. Soc., Materials Rsch. Soc., Sigma Xi. Roman Catholic. Office: Vanderbilt U Olin Hl Rm 303 2400 Highland Ave Nashville TN 37240-0001 E-mail: bayuzick@vuse.vanderbilt.edu.

BAZANT, ZDENEK PAVEL, structural and materials engineering educator, scientist, consultant; b. Prague, Czechoslovakia, Dec. 10, 1937; came to U.S., 1968, naturalized, 1976; s. Zdenek and Stepanka (Curikova) B.; m. Iva Marie Krasna, Sept. 27, 1967; children: Martin Zdenek, Eva Stephanie. Civil Engr., Tech. U., Prague, 1960; PhD in Mechanics, Czechoslovak Acad. Sci., 1963; postgrad. diploma in theoretical physics, Charles U., Prague, 1966; hon. doctorate, Czech Tech. U., Prague, 1991, Karlsruhe (Germany) U., 1998, U. Colo., 2000, Poly. Milan, 2001. Registered structural engr., Ill. Scientist, adj. prof. Bldg. Rsch. Inst., Tech. U., Prague, 1963-67; docent habilitation Tech. U., Prague, 1967; vis. rsch. engr. Centre d'Étude et de Recherche du Bâtiment et des Travaux Publics, Paris, 1967, U. Toronto, 1967—68, U. Calif., Berkeley, 1969; assoc. prof. civil engring. Northwestern U., Evanston, Ill., 1969-73, prof., 1973-90, Walter P. Murphy prof., 1990—, coord. structural engring. program, 1974-78, 92—; founding dir. Ctr. for Concrete and Geomaterials, 1981-86. Cons. Argonne Nat. Lab., many other orgns. Author: Creep of Concrete in Structural Analysis, 1966, Stability of Structures: Elastic, Inelastic, Fracture and Damage Theories, 1991, Concrete at High Temperatures, 1996, Fracture and Size Effect, 1997, Scaling of Structural Strength, 2002, Inelastic Analysis of Structures, 2002; editor 13 books; editor in chief Jour. Engring. Mechanics, 1989-94; regional editor Internat. Jour. Fracture, 1991—; assoc. editor Applied Mechanics Rev., 1987—, Cement and Concrete Research Internat. Jour, 1970—, Materials and Structures, 1979— Solid Mechanics Archives, 1980-91, Materials and Structures, 1981—; mem. editl. bds. of 16 hours.; contbr. (with others) over 350 articles to profl. jours.; patentee in field. Recipient Best Engring. Book of Yr. award Soc. Am. Pubs., 1992, Outstanding New Citizen award Chgo. Citizenship Coun., 1976, A. von Humboldt award, 1990, Šolín medal Czech Tech. U., Prague, 1998, Stodola gold medal Slovak Acad. Scis., 1999, Highly Cited Scientist award Internat. Sci. Index, 2001; grantee NSF, 1970—, Air Force Office Scientific Rsch., 1975—, Los Alamos Sci. Lab., 1978-80, European Power Rsch. Inst., 1980—, Office Naval Rsch., 1990—, Dept. Energy, 1984—; Ford Found. fellow, 1967-68, Guggenheim fellow, 1978-79, Kajima Found. fellow U. Tokyo, 1987, NATO fellow, Paris, 1988, Japan Soc. Promotion of Sci. fellow U. Tokyo, 1995-96. Fellow ASME (Worcester Reed Warner medal 1997), Am. Acad. Mechanics, ASCE (chmn. com. properties of materials 1976-78, 82-84, editor in chief Jour. Engring. Mechanics 1988-94, Walter L. Huber rsch. prize 1976, T.Y. Lin Prestressed Concrete award 1977, Newmark medal 1996, Croes medal 1997), Am. Concrete Inst. (chmn. fracture mechanics com. 1985-92), Internat. Assn. for Fracture Mechanics of Concrete Structures (pres. 1991-93), Internat. Union Testing and Rsch. Labs. Materials Structures (chmn. com. on creep, L'Hermite gold medal 1975), Soc. Engring. Sci. (pres. 1993, Prager medal 1996); mem. NAS, NAE, Academia di Scienze e Lettere Milan, Engring. Acad. Czech Republic (fgn. mem.), Austrian Acad. Scis., U.S. Nat. Com. on Theoretical and Applied Mechanics, Internat. Assn. Structural Mechanics Reactor Tech. (coord. concrete structures divsn.), ASTM (mem. concrete com., skiing com.), Prestressed Concrete Inst., Am. Ceramic Soc. (D.M. Roy award 2001), Internat. Assn. Soil Mech. Found. Engring., Internat. Assn. Bridge and Structural Engring., Soc. Exptl. Mechanics, Am. Soc. Engring. Edn., Bldg. Rsch. Inst. Spain (hon., Torroja Gold medal 1990), Czech Soc. Civil Engring. (hon.), Czech Soc. Mechanics (award of merit 1993), Structural Engrs. Assn. Ill. (Meritorious Paper award 1992). Home: 707 Roslyn Ter Evanston IL 60201-1721 Office: Northwestern Univ Dept Civil Engring Evanston IL 60208-0001

BAZERMAN, STEVEN HOWARD, lawyer; b. N.Y.C., Dec. 12, 1940; s. Solomon and Miriam (Kirschenberg) B.; m. Christina Ann Gray, Aug. 28, 1981 (div. June 1988); m. Beverly Andree, Sept. 9, 2000. BS in Math., BS in Engring., U. Mich., 1962; JD, Georgetown U., 1966. Bar: D.C. 1967, N.Y. 1968, U.S. Dist. Ct. (so. dist.) N.Y. 1970, U.S. Dist. Ct. (ea. dist.) N.Y. 1973, U.S. Claims Ct. 1976, U.S. Ct. Appeals (2d cir.) 1978, U.S. Cts. Customs and Patents Appeals 1981-82, U.S. Ct. Appeals (fed. cir.) 1982. Assoc. Arthur, Dry & Kalish, N.Y.C., 1967-80, Offner & Kuhn, N.Y.C., 1980-83; ptnr., head litigation dept. Kuhn, Muller & Bazerman, N.Y.C., 1983-87; ptnr. Moore, Berson, Lifflander, Eisenberg & Mewhinney, N.Y.C., 1987-88; of counsel Lerner, David, Littenberg, Krumholz & Mentlik, Westfield, N.J., 1988, Sutton, Basseches, Magidoff & Amaral, N.Y.C., 1988-90, Graham, Campaign & McCarthy P.C., N.Y.C., 1990-96, Bazerman & Drangel, P.C., N.Y.C., 1996—. Governing counsel Community Law Offices Legal Aid Soc., N.Y.C., 1974-83, treas., 1979-82. Co-author: Guide to Registering Trademarks, 1999-2003; contbr. articles to profl. jours. Vol. counsel community law offices Legal Aid Soc., N.Y.C., 1974-82, treas., 1979-82. Mem. Assn. of Bar of City of N.Y., Am. Intellectual Property Law Assn., N.Y. Patent, Trademark & Copyright Law Assn. Jewish. Avocation: horses. Office: Bazerman & Drangel PC 60 E 42nd St Rm 820 New York NY 10165-0820 E-mail: sbazerman@nyc.rr.com., bdpc@ipcounsellors.com.

BAZIN, PATRICK, library director; b. Besancon, France, Feb. 23, 1950; s. Joseph Bazin and Louisette (Le Goff) Lazar; m. Denyse Clavel, May 8, 1978; 1 child, Marianne. B in Philosophy, Lyon (France) 2 Univ., 1973, M in Philosophy, 1976; grad., Nat. Upper Libr. Sch., Lyon, 1976. Curator Ecole Nat. des Mines de Paris, Paris, 1976-78, Lyon Pub. Libr., Lyon, 1978-92, dir., gen. curator, 1992—. Tchr. Nat. Upper Sch. Info. Sci. and Librs., Lyon, 1989—; vice-chmn. Rhone-Alpes Agy. for Book and Documentation, Rhone-Alpes Province, 1994—. Mem. Nat. Ctr. of Books. Office: Bibliotheque Municipale 30 blvd VivierMerle 69431 Lyon Cedex 03 France

BAZIRJIAN, ROSANN V. dean, librarian; b. N.Y.C., Sept. 5, 1952; d. Dickran and Rose V. Bazirjian; m. Patrick T. Burger; 1 child, Terence Burger. BA, Lehman Coll., N.Y.C., 1973; MS, Columbia U., 1980; MSSC, Syracuse U., 1993. Acquisitions libr. Syracuse U., NY, 1980—84, head acquisitions dept., 1990—91, head bibliog. svcs., 1991—95; head acquisitions and collections devel. U. West Fla., Pensacola, 1985—90; asst. dir. tech. svcs. Fla. State U., Tallahassee, 1995—99; asst. dean tech. and access svcs. Pa. State U., University Park, 1999 . Contbr. articles to profl. publs., chapters to books. Mem.: ALA (Leadership in Acquisitions award 2002), Assn. Library Collections and Tech. Svcs., Assn. Coll. and Rsch. Libraries, Phi Beta Kappa. Office: Pa State Univ Libr s 507 Paterno Library University Park PA 16802

BAZLER, FRANK ELLIS, retired lawyer; b. Columbus, Ohio, Jan. 17, 1930; s. Frank Hayes and Minnie Maybrum (Rucker) B.; m. Virginia Ann Hutchison, Oct. 17, 1954. BSBA, Ohio State U., 1951, JD, 1953. Bar: Ohio 1953, U.S. Dist. Ct. (we. dist.) Ohio 1956, U.S. Ct. Mil. Appeals 1957, U.S. Supreme Ct. 1957, U.S. Ct. Appeals (6th cir.) 1964. Assoc. Robert S. Miller, Atty., Troy, Ohio, 1955-57; ptnr. Miller, Bazler & Schlemmer, Troy, 1957-71; asst. corp. counsel Hobart Mfg. Co., Troy, 1971-74; corp. atty., asst. sec. Hobart Corp., Troy, 1974-95; ret., 1995; of counsel Dungan & LeFevre, Troy, 1995—. V.p. Bazler Transfer & Storage, Inc., Columbus, Ohio, 1950-58; sec., bd. dirs. Golden Triangle Farms, Inc., Troy, 1972-2001. Pres. Troy United Fund, Inc., 1960, Troy Mus. Corp., 1990; chmn. Miami County chpt. ARC, 1955-59, Miami County (Ohio) Rep. Fin. Com., 1981-84; mem. Miami County Gen. Bd. Health, 1992—, pres. pro-tem, 1998-2001, pres., 2001—; commn. on cert. of Attys. as Specialists of Supreme Ct. of Ohio, 1994-99, chmn., 1994-96. Capt. JAG, USAFR, 1953-61. Named one of Outstanding Young Men in Troy and Ohio, Troy Jaycees, 1957, Ohio Jaycees, 1961; recipient Disting. Citizen award Troy C. of C., 1985, Citizenship award Ohio State U., 1993. Fellow: Ohio State Bar Found. (pres. 1992), Am. Bar Found. (Ohio chair 1995—); mem.: ABA (mem. gen. practice sect. 1967—, coun. 1976—80, ho. of dels. 1984—2000, mem. standing com. on specialization 1999—2002), Nat. Conf. Bar Pres. (exec. coun. 1988—91), Miami County Bar Assn. (pres. 1966, Meritorious Svc. award 1985), Ohio State Bar Assn. (coun. of dels. 1979—88, pres. 1984—85, Ohio Bar medal 1990), Nat. Caucus State Bar Assns. (Ohio rep. 1993—2002, exec com. 1997—2002, pres. 2000—01), Overfield Tavern Mus. (pres. 2001—, bd. trustees 2000—), Indsl. Heritage Mus. of Miami County (trustee, sec. 1997—), Brukner Nature Ctr. (trustee 1998—, pres. 1999—2002), Kiwanis (pres. 1961), Scottish Rite, Masons. Republican. Presbyterian. Avocations: photography, travel, golf. Home: 1156 Premwood Dr Troy OH 45373-3877 Office: Dungan & LeFevre 210 W Main St Troy OH 45373-3287

BAZZY-ASAAD, ALIA, pediatrician, pulmonologist, academic administrator; d. Ralph and Kouther Bazzy; m. Ghazi Asaad, May 17, 1980; children: Dena Asaad, Nadine Asaad, Samer Asaad, Mazen Asaad. MD, Am. U. Beirut, 1978. Assoc. prof. pediat. Yale U. Sch. Medicine, New Haven, 1993—. Dir. asthma program Yale U. Sch. Medicine, 1998—; med. dir. pediatric respiratory care unit Yale New Haven Children's Hosp., 1993—; acting chief, sect. pediatric respiratory medicine Yale U. Sch. Medicine, 2002—. Grantee Ind. Rsch. award, NIH, 1993—2003. Mem.: Soc. Neurosci., Soc. Pediatric Rsch., Am. Physiol. Soc., Am. Thoracic Soc. Office: Yale U Sch Medicine 333 Cedar St New Haven CT 06510

BEACH, ARTHUR O'NEAL, lawyer; b. Albuquerque, Feb. 8, 1945; s. William Pearce and Vivian Lucille (Kronig) B.; m. Alex Clark Doyle, Sept. 12, 1970; 1 child, Eric Kronig. BBA, U. N.Mex., 1967, JD, 1970. Bar: N.Mex. 1970. Assoc. Smith & Ransom, Albuquerque, 1970-74, Keleher & McLeod, Albuquerque, 1974-75, ptnr., 1976-78; shareholder Keleher & McLeod, P.A., Albuquerque, 1978—. Tchg. asst. U. N.Mex., 1970. Bd. editors Natural Resources Jour., 1968-70. Mem. ABA, State Bar N.Mex. (unauthorized practice of law com., adv. opinions com., med.-legal panel, legal-dental-osteo.-podiatry com., jud. selection com., specialization bd.), Albuquerque Bar Assn. (dir. 1978-82). Democrat. Mem. Christian Sci. Ch. Home: 2015 Dietz Pl NW Albuquerque NM 87107-3240 Office: Keleher & McLeod PA PO Box AA Albuquerque NM 87103

BEACH, BARBARA PURSE, lawyer; b. Washington, June 12, 1947; d. Clifford John and Lillian (Natarus) B. BA, U. Ky., 1968; MSW, U. Md., 1972; JD, Am. U., 1980. Bar: D.C. 1980, Va. 1980. Law clk. to presiding justice benefit rev. bd. U.S. Dept. Labor, Washington, 1980; asst. city atty. City of Alexandria, Va., 1981-85; atty. Ross, Marsh, Foster, Myers & Quiggle, Alexandria, 1985-90, Beach, Butt & Assocs., PC, Alexandria, 1990-92; prin. Beach & Assocs., Alexandria, 1992—; town atty. Town of Herndon, Va.,

1992-94. 4th dist. com. disciplinary bd. dirs. Va. State Bd., chmn., 2000-01. Vice-chmn. Va. Health Svcs. Cost Rev. Coun., 1989-92; mem. Va. Commn. on Women and Minorities, 1990-92; bd. dirs. Am. Heart Assn., Alexandria, 1996-2000, divsn. pres., 1998-99. Alexandria Bar Assn. (pres. 1987-88), Kiwanis. Office: Beach & Assocs 416 Prince St Alexandria VA 22314-3114

BEACH, BERT BEVERLY, clergyman; b. Gland, Vaud, Switzerland, June 15, 1928; s. Walter Raymond and Gladys (Corley) B.; m. Eliane Marguerite Palange, Apr. 8, 1954; children: Danielle, Michele. BA, Pacific Union Coll., 1948; postgrad., Stanford U., 1948-49, 51; PhD, U. Paris, 1958; ThD, Christian Theol. Acad., 1986. Prin. West Liberty Union Intermediate Sch., Gridley, Calif., 1949-50, Italian Jr. Coll., Florence, Italy, 1952-58; chmn. history dept. Columbia Union Coll., Takoma Pk., Md., 1958-60; dir. edn. No. Europe-West Africa Div. of SDA, St. Albans, Eng., 1960-75, gen. sec., 1973-80; sec. Conf. of Secs. Christian World Communions, Silver Spring, Md., 1970—2002; dir. pub. affairs Gen. Conf. of Seventh-day Adventists, Silver Spring, Md., 1980-95; gen. sec. Coun. on Inter-Ch. Rels., 1980—; sec. gen. Internat. Religious Liberty Assn., Silver Spring, Md., 1980-95, pres., 1996, 2000. Sec. Internat. Acad. for Freedom of Religion, 1985—; v.p. Internat. Commn. for Prevention of Alcoholism and Drug Dependency, 1980—, pres., 1991, 1997—. Chmn. bd. John H. Weidner Found. Altruism, 1996—; sec. bd. Bridging Boundaries Internat., 2002—. Recipient Citation, Senate of State of Md., 1984; named Paul Harris fellow Rotary Internat., 1984, Order of Bishop Hodura, Polish Nat. Cath. Ch., 1986, Order of St. Magdalene, Polish Orthodox Ch., 1987, Honored Alumnus of Yr. Pacific Union Coll., 1997, Knight's Cross of Order of Merit of Polish Republic, 1998, Human Rights Leadership award Freedom Mag., 1998, Pres. medallion for Leadership Andrews Univ., 1999. Mem. Rotary Club, Cosmos Club, SAR, Md. Assn. Founders and Patriots of Am. (gov. 1998-2000), Polish Bible Soc. (hon.). Adventist. Avocation: prestidigitation. Home: 14508 Cutstone Way Silver Spring MD 20905-7430 Office: 12501 Old Columbia Pike Silver Spring MD 20904-6601 E-mail: 74617.2745@compuserve.com.

BEACH, BETH, elementary educator; b. Binghamton, N.Y., June 5, 1951; d. Martin Patrick and Mildred (Neary) Regan; 1 child, Martin Robert. BA in Elem. Edn., SUNY, Cortland, 1973; MS in Elem. Edn., Binghamton U., 1976. Cert. tchr., N.Y. Kindergarten tchr. Christ the King Sch., Endwell, N.Y., 1973-74, Blessed Sacrament Sch., Johnson City, N.Y., 1974-85, Chenango Forks Schs., Binghamton, 1985-90, 2d grade tchr., 1990-96, 5th grade tchr., 1996-98, 4th grade tchr., 1998—. Lectr. grad. edn. Binghamton U., 1988; mem. adv. bd. Hearts and Hands, Inc., Binghamton; leader workshops in field. Author: (with Muriel Rossie) Discipline and Self-Esteem, 1987. Tchr. safety town program Jr. League of Binghamton, 1982-90. Mem. N.Y. State United Tchrs., Binghamton Area Reading Coun., Binghamton Assn. for Edn. of Young Children (local bd. dirs., publs. com. 1984-86, historian 1986-88, nominating com. 1992). Avocations: sewing, reading. Home: 55 Lathrop Ave Binghamton NY 13905-4224 Office: Chenango Forks Cen Schs 1 Gordon Dr Binghamton NY 13901-5614

BEACH, CHARLES ADDISON, lawyer; b. Albany, N.Y., Apr. 21, 1945; s. Charles A.W. and Eleanor (Johnston) B.; m. Jane L. Shlionsky, June 8, 1968; children: James E. and Jonathan M. BA, Hamilton Coll., 1967; JD, Cornell U., 1973. Bar: N.Y. 1974, U.S. Dist. Ct. (no., ea., we. and so. dists.) N.Y. 1974, U.S. Ct. Appeals (2d and 10th cirs.) 1975, U.S. Supreme Ct. 1982, Tex. 1991, U.S. Dist. Ct. (no. dist.) Tex. 1993, U.S. Ct. Appeals (5th cir.) 1995, U.S. Ct. Appeals (6th cir.) 1998. Assoc. Shearman & Sterling, N.Y.C., 1973-77, 79-81, Paris, 1977-79; sr. counsel, coord. corp. litigation Exxon Mobil Corp., N.Y.C., 1981—90, Irving, Tex., 1990—. Mng. editor: Cornell Internat. Law Jour. Vol. Peace Corps., Libya and Tunisia, 1968-71; adv. coun. Cornell Law Sch. Fellow Tex. Bar Found. (sustaining life); mem. ABA, N.Y. State Bar Assn., Assn. of Bar of City of N.Y., Dallas Bar Assn., Irving Bar Assn., Am. Arbitration Assn. (adv. coun. Dallas chpt.), U.S. Coun. Internat. Bus./Internat. C. of C. (arbitration com., S.W. com. on arbitration), Inst. for Trasnational Arbitration Ctr. for Am. and Internat. Law (adv. bd.), Coll. State Bar Tex. Home: 1431 N Travis Cir Irving TX 75038-6238 Office: Exxon Mobil Corp 5959 Las Colinas Blvd Irving TX 75039-2298 E-mail: charles.a.beach@exxonmobil.com.

BEACH, CHARLES RANDALL, economic developer; b. N.Y.C., Aug. 4, 1947; s. Thomas Coffing and Rose Mary (Randall) B.; m. Lois Stark, Aug. 17, 1969; children: Randall Stark, Jonathan Charles. AA, Pa. State U., 1969; BS, SUNY-Plattsburgh, 1972. V.p. Champlain Valley Fed. S&L, Plattsburgh, 1973-89; pres. Taconic N.W. Properties, Inc., Altona, N.Y., 1989-93; asst. v.p. Adirondack Bank, Saranac Lake, NY, 1993—2001; regional dir. North Country region Empire State Devel. Corp., 2001—. From treas. to pres. Clinton County Hist. Assn., Plattsburgh, 1970-94; mem. bd. Clinton C.C., Plattsburgh, 1982-97, also v.p. and pres.; chmn. bd. Plattsburgh Airbase Redevel. Corp., 1996-2001. Sgt. Army N.G., 1970-76. Mem. North Country C. of C. (chmn., treas.). Republican. Episcopalian. Home: 2251 Rand Hill Rd Altona NY 12910 Office: Empire State Devel 401 West Bay Plz Plattsburgh NY 12901 E-mail: rbeach@empire.state.ny.us.

BEACH, DAVID WILLIAMS, music educator, dean; b. Hartford, Conn., Sept. 5, 1938; s. Raymond Schwarz and Avis (Sugden) B.; m. Marcia Francesca Salemme, June 20, 1964; children: Juliana Williams, Matthew David. BA, Brown U., 1961; MMus, Yale U., 1964, PhD, 1974. Instr. Yale U., New Haven, 1964-67, asst. prof., 1967-71, Bklyn. Coll., CUNY, 1971-72; assoc. prof. Eastman Sch. Music U. Rochester, 1974-85, chair dept. music theory Eastman Sch. Music, 1981-90, 95-96, prof. Eastman Sch. Music, 1985-96, univ. dean grad. studies, 1991-95; dean faculty music U Toronto, 1996—. Translator: The Art of Strict Musical Composition (by J.P. Kirnberger), 1982; editor: Aspects of Schenkerian Theory, 1983, Music Theory in Concept and Practice, 1997; contbr. numerous articles to profl. jours. Mem. Soc. for Music Theory (chair publs. 1979-84, exec. bd. 1984-87), Am. Musicol. Soc., Music Theory Soc. N.Y. State. Democrat. Avocations: golf, hiking.

BEACH, FRANKLIN DARREL, minister; b. South Charleston, W.Va., June 24, 1938; s. Elwood James and Virgie (O'Dell) B.; m. Brenda Pauley, Oct. 4, 1968; children: Frank Jr., Deanna Dawn. Grad. high sch., Alum Creek, W.Va. Ordained min. Bapt. Ch., 1967. Welder, boilermaker Putnam Fabricators, Bandcroft, W.Va., 1972; welder South Charleston, W.Va., 1963-70; assoc. pastor, tchr. Dollie Hill Christian Acad. and God's Ch. Alum Creek, W.Va., 1973-79; min. King (N.C.) Christian Ctr., 1983—; TV min. CAT TV Channel 6, Winston-Salem, N.C., 1994—. Pres. Forsyth County Right to Life, Winston-Salem, 1993-95. With U.S. Army, 1956-61. Recipient award Concerned Citizens of Kanawha County, 1974. Avocations: private pilot, oil painting, auto mechanics. Home: 4673 Hyatt Dr Winston Salem NC 27101-2215 E-mail: darrel_b_27101@yahoo.com.

BEACH, GEO, journalist, poet; b. Boston, Feb. 14, 1957; s. George Richard Plagenz and Faith Hanna-Williams; m. Sydney Liane Webb, March 16, 1991; children: Miranda Rose, Isabel Gallan. Lit., Phillips Exeter Acad., N.H., 1975; Theatre, Yale U., 1979. Dir. commn. Yale U. Tutoring Agency, New Haven, 1979-82; public info. officer Dept. Pub. Safety, Homer, Alaska, 1983-87; columnist, editor Tempest Media Prodn., Acton, Calif., 1988—; editor Marlowe & Co., NY, 1995—; anchor Peninsula Pub. Radio News, Kenai, Alaska, 1997—; commentator TomPaine.com, 2001—. Lectr. U. Alaska, Anchorage, 1997; judge Alaska State Coun. on Arts, Anchorage, 1998—; spokesman Alaska Childrens Trust, Anchorage, 1998; jury chmn. N.Y. Festivals, N.Y.C., 2000—; select reader Play Lab, Last Frontier Theatre Conf., Valdez, Alaska, 2000. Featured essayist Monitor Radio News, Boston, 1993-97, (Pub. Radio Series) Tales of The Great North, 1995, NPR Living on Earth, Boston, 1997—, The Savvy Traveler, L.A., 1997—, PRI Marketplace Bus. Report, 2001—. Trustee, Homer Fire Dept. Inc., 1983-87. Recipient Poetry prize Atlantic Monthly mag., 1975, Rescuer of Yr. award Homer Fire Dept., 1987, Mencken award Free Press Assn., 1994, Davidoff Journalist award, Wesleyan Writers Conf., 1996, Sigma Delta Chi award Radio Commentaries, 1997, Broadcast award AP, breaking news, 1997, live anchoring, 1998, World medal for best writing Internat. Radio Awards, 1999; Murray fellowship Poynter Inst. Media Studies, 1998, guest author, Lila Wallace-Reader's Digest Fund Proj. Common Rhythms: Writing About Work, Wash., 1994. Mem. SAR, Nat. Soc. of Newspaper Columnists, Soc. of Profl. Journalists (sports reporting, 1995, radio commentaries 1997), AIR Assn. Inds. in Radio, Nat. Press Club, Alaska Press Club (columnist, sports analysis, radio essayist, live anchoring 1994-98). Home: Lookout Dr Homer AK 99603-9121 Office: Tempest Media Prodn PO Box 3600 Homer AK 99603-3600 E-mail: tempest@xyz.net.

BEACH, KEVIN SCOTT, marine biologist, educator; b. Nashua, N.H., July 25, 1968; s. Glen Elsworth and Barbara Marion Beach; m. Heidi Beth Slocum Borgeas, Dec. 28, 1999. PhD in Bot. Scis., U. Hawaii, 1996. Instr. marine sci. U. Hawaii, Hilo, 1996; vis. prof. biology Southampton (N.Y.) Coll., LI U., 1996—97; assoc. prof. biology U. Tampa, Fla., 1997—. Grantee, NOAA, 2000—01. Mem.: AAUP, Am. Soc. Limnology and Oceanography, Internat. Coral Reef Soc., Am. Acad. Underwater Scis., Phycological Soc. Am. Achievements include research in coral reef ecology in the Florida Keys including a 10 day saturation mission in the habitat Aquarius. Office: Univ Tampa 401 W Kennedy Blvd Tampa FL 33606 Office Fax: 813-258-7881. E-mail: kbeach@ut.edu.

BEACH, LINDA MARIE, total quality management professional; b. Washington, May 5, 1949; d. Robert L. and Agnes I. (O'Brien) B.; m. Robert L. Riley; 1 child, Grace. AAS in Bus. and Mktg. cum laude, No. Va. Community Coll., 1973; BA cum laude, Luther Rice Coll., 1975; MBPA, Southeastern U., 1977; DBA, Pacific Western U., 1987. Computer systems adminstr. Def. Mapping Agy., Brookmont, Md., 1967-80; mgr. methods and procedures Bur. Nat. Affairs, Inc., Washington, 1980-82; quality and reliability engr. Gen. Electric, Arlington, Va., 1982; sr. product assurance engr. Fairchild Industries, Germantown, Md., 1982-84, CIT-ALCATEL, Reston, Va., 1984-86; software product assurance mgr. Contel, Fairfax, Va., 1986-87; group leader quality engring. Software Productivity Consortium, Reston, 1987-89; dir. quality assurance NYMA, Inc., Greenbelt, Md., 1989—. Product mgr. P4, Inc., Sterling. Va., 1989-92; instr. Learning Tress Internat., Vienna, Va., 1988—; assoc. prof. No. Va. C.C., Sterling, 1984-89; instr. Anne Arundel C.C., 1993—, UMUC, 1996—; adj. faculty Potomac Coll., 1996—. Contbg. editor Info. Mgmt., 1983-85. Mem. IEEE, Am. Soc. for Quality Control, Assn. for Computing Machinery, Internat. Test and Evaluation. Home: 1704 Plane Tree Way Bowie MD 20721-3019 Office: NYMA Inc 7501 Greenway Center Dr Greenbelt MD 20770-3531

BEACH, MILO C. former art museum director; b. Rochester, N.Y., July 12, 1939; m. Robin Cook. BA, Harvard U., 1962, PhD, 1969. With dept. Asiatic art Mus. Fine Arts, Boston, 1963-66, asst. curator dept. Islamic art, 1967; jr. fellow Am. Inst. Indian Art, India, 1967-68; asst. curator dept. Oriental art Fogg Art Mus. Harvard U., 1968-69; mem. faculty dept. art Williams Coll., Williamstown, Mass., 1969-84, chmn. dept. art, 1981-84; asst. dir. Freer Gallery of Art, Arthur M. Sackler Gallery, Washington, 1984-87, acting dir. Freer Gallery of Art, 1987-88, dir., 1988-2001. Adj. prof. art history U. Mich.; mem. adv. coun. dept. art and archaeology Princeton U. Author: The Imperial Image: Paintings for the Mughal Court, 1981, The Adventures of Rama, 1983, Early Mughal Painting, 1987, Mughal and Rajput painting, 1992, King of the World: A Mughal Manuscript from the Royal Library, Windsor Castle, 1997; co-author: (with Glenn D. Lowry) An Illustrated and Annotated Checklist of the Vever Collection, 1989, (with Andrew Topsfield) Indian Paintings and Drawings from the Collection of Howard Hodgkin, 1991, (with Abolala Soudavar) Art of the Persian Courts, 1992. Mem. vis. com. Boston Mus. Fine Arts; mem. dept. of art and archaeology adv. coun. Princeton (N.J.) U. Mem. Am. Fedn. Arts (exhbns. com.).

BEACH, NANCY ANN HELEN, special education educator, educator; b. Kansas City, Kans., Nov. 10, 1944; d. Charles Andrew and Victoria Virginia (Handzel) Nugent; divorced; children: Cathe, Denise, Michelle. AA, East Los Angeles Coll., 1964; BS, Calif. State U., L.A., 1966; postgrad., UCLA, 1966-70. Cert. English teaching credential (life). Tchr. Calif. Pub. Schs., San Gabriel Valley, 1966-77; recreation therapist State of Calif., Pomona, 1966-67; recreation supr. City of Baldwin Park (Calif.), 1967-70; restaurant owner Baldwin Park, 1977; instr. English So. Bay Coll., Baldwin Park, 1984-89; instr. English and success skills Eldorado Coll., West Covina, Calif., 1989-90; tchr. blind and retarded spl. edn. Los Angeles County Schs., 1990—. Author: Reading Skills, 1971. Bd. dirs. pub. rels. com. CAP, El Monte, Calif., 1960-64. Democrat. Avocation: race car driving.

BEACH, REGINA LEE, librarian; b. Georgetown, Ohio, Dec. 22, 1963; d. H. LeRoy and R. Jean (Wardlow) B. BSBA, BA, Ohio No. U., 1987; MLS, Kent State U., 1990; MS in Bus. Adminstrn., Miss. State U., 1999. Serials cataloger, libr. U. Mich., Ann Arbor, 1990-92; libr. Allen Correctional Inst., Lima, Ohio, 1993-94; serials cataloger, libr. Miss. State U., Mississippi State, 1994-99; head info. tech., libr. U. Ark., Little Rock, 1999—2001; head tech. svcs. and systems Tex. A&M U., Kingsville, 2001—. Mem. ALA, ASIS, Southeastern Libr. Assn., Ark. Libr. Assn. Avocations: walking, running, swimming, aerobics, camping. Office: MSC 197 Jernigan Libr Tex A&M U Kingsville TX 78363

BEACH, ROBERT MARK, biologist; b. Athens, Ga., Oct. 7, 1957; s. Robert Ervin and Frances (Myers) B.; m. Catherine Cesaro, Oct. 3, 1987; 2 children: Katelyn Marie, Joseph Mark. BS, Clemson U., 1979; PhD, U. Ga., 1985; MS in Bus., Johns Hopkins U., 1999. Rsch. asst. Clemson (S.C.) U., 1979-81, U. Ga., Athens, 1981-85, 1985-87; scientist Crop Genetics Internat., Columbia, Md., 1987-91, project mgr., 1991-92, dir. bioinsecticides, 1993-94; dir. field sales biosys, Columbia, Md., 1995-97; global project mgr. Abbott Labs., North Chgo., 1997-2000; product devel. Valent Bioscis., Libertyville, Ill., 2000—. Contbr. articles to profl. jours. Mem. Entomol. Soc. Am. Achievements include commercial development of biorational products. Home: 972 Tylerton Cir Grayslake IL 60030-1199 Office: Valent Biosciences 870 Technology Way Libertyville IL 60048-5350 E-mail: Mark.beach@valent.com.

BEACH, STEPHEN HOLBROOK, lawyer; b. Highland Park, Mich., June 3, 1915; s. Stephen Holbrook and Katherine Jean (Campbell) B.; m. Mary Frances Mulvihill, July 6, 1951; children: Jennifer Katherine Beach Buda, Stephen Holbrook III. AB with honors in Polit. Sci, Kalamazoo Coll., 1936; LLB cum laude, U. Detroit, 1941; postgrad., Georgetown U., 1945, Columbia U., 1970. Bar: Mich. 1941, U.S. Dist. Ct. (ea. dist.) Mich., 1941, U.S. Supreme Ct. 1944, N.Y. 1947, U.S. Dist. Ct. (so. dist.) N.Y. 1947, U.S. Dist. Ct. (ea. dist.) N.Y. 1949, D.C. 1949, Conn. 1975. Assoc. Winthrop, Stimson, Putnam & Roberts, N.Y.C., 1946-48, Cann, Lamb & Kittelle, N.Y.C., 1948-56, Willkie, Farr, Gallagher, Walton and Fitzgibbon, N.Y.C., 1956-60; staff atty. IBM Corp., N.Y.C., 1960-61, of counsel supplies div. N.Y.C. and Dayton, N.J., 1961-65; v.p., gen. counsel, sec. The Svc. Bur. Corp., N.Y.C., 1965-75; v.p., gen. counsel Data Svcs. Control Data Corp., Greenwich, Conn., 1976-78, gen. counsel Computer Co. Mpls., 1979-80, v.p., assoc., gen. counsel, 1980-82, sr. v.p. telecommunications policy, corp. sec., 1983-85; of counsel Rogers, Hoge & Hills, White Plains, N.Y., 1985-86; pvt. practice law Greenwich and Stamford, Conn., 1986—. Bd. dirs., corp. sec. Dataware Techs., Inc. Editor-in-chief U. Detroit Law Jour., 1937-41. Capt. U.S. Army, 1943-46. Mem. ABA (sci. and tech. sect., banking and bus. law sect.), Conn. Bar Assn (intellectual property and computer law sects.), N.Y. State Bar Assn. (banking and bus. law sect.), D.C. Bar Assn., Assn. of Data Processing Svcs. Orgns. (v.p. govt. rels., bd. dirs. 1978-84), The Wee Burn Country Club, Ocean Club of Fla. Republican. Episcopalian. Avocation: golf. Home: 52 Brushy Hill Rd Darien CT 06820-6007 Office: PO Box 1202 Darien CT 06820-1202

BEACH, WALTER EGGERT, retired publishing organization executive; b. North Adams, Mass., Aug. 24, 1934; s. W. Edwards and Liselotte Josephine Sophie (von Usedom) B. BA, Dickinson Coll., 1956; MA, George Washington U., 1961. Staff assoc., asst. dir. Am. Polit. Sci. Assn., Washington, 1965-80; sr. staff mem. Brookings Instn., Washington, 1980-90; dir. Heldref Publs. Helen Dwight Reid Ednl. Found., Washington, 1990-97. Treas. D.C. Dem. Party, 1981-84; mem. adv. bd. Hubert H. Humphrey Inst. Pub. Affairs, U. Minn., Mpls., 1990-99; trustee Dickinson Coll., 1984—, Mt. Vernon Coll., 1971-97, Helen Dwight Reid Ednl. Found., 1982—; pres. Internat. Eye Found., 1993-95; mem., bd. dirs. various polit. coms. With U.S. Army, 1956-58. Recipient Disting. Alumni award Dickinson Coll., 1991. Mem. Internat. Polit. Sci. Assn., Am. Polit. Sci. Assn. (Frank Goodnow award 1998), Ctr. Study Presidency, Hist. Soc. D.C., Midwest Polit. Sci. Assn., Nat. Capital Area Polit. Sci. Assn., Policy Studies Orgn., So. Polit. Sci. Assn., UN Assn. Nat. Capital Area, Western Polit. Sci. Assn., Cosmos Club, Pi Sigma Alpha. Democrat. Unitarian Universalist. Home: 5719 Chevy Chase Pky NW Washington DC 20015-2521 Office: Heldref Pubs 1319 18th St NW Washington DC 20036-1826 E-mail: wbeach7421@aol.com.

BEACHLEY, MICHAEL CHARLES, radiologist; b. Harrisburg, Pa., Nov. 14, 1940; s. Kenneth Gumbert and Carolyn Elizabeth (Jones) B.; m. Deborah Rowe Samson, July 27, 1963; children: Kenneth, Barbara, William. AB, Dartmouth Coll., 1962, B.MS, 1963; MD, Harvard U., 1965. Diplomate: Am. Bd. Radiology. Intern in surgery Med. Coll. Va., Richmond, 1965-66, resident in radiology, 1966-69, instr. radiology, 1970, faculty, 1972—, acting chmn. dept. radiology, 1976, prof., 1977-87, chmn. dept. radiology, 1977-82, prof. radiation scis., 1981-87, prof. biophysics, 1980-82, prof. physiology and biophysics, 1982-87, clin. prof., 1987—; clin. prof. radiology U. Pitts., 1988—; chmn. Dept. Radiology St. Margaret Meml. Hosp., Pitts., 1987-97; pres. Three Rivers Imaging Cons., Ltd., 1993-94, Duquesne Imaging Ltd., 1994-2001; med. dir. Radiology Ptnrs.; chmn. dept. radiology U. Pitts. Med. Ctr., Saint Margaret, 1997-99. Cons. McGuire VA Hosp., 1977—; fellow in radiol. pathology Armed Forces Inst. Pathology, Washington, 1969. Contbr. chpt. to book, revs. and med. articles to profl. jours. Vice-pres. College Hills Civic Assn., 1975-77. Served as maj. M.C. U.S. Army, 1970-72. Fellow Am. Coll. Radiology (pres. Va. chpt. 1982-83, chmn. com. on stds. and accreditation 1998—); mem. AMA, Am. Heart Assn., Radiol. Soc. N.Am. (chmn. bylaws com. 1994-96), Am. Roentgen Ray Soc., Pitts. Roentgen Soc. (chmn. com on fellowship nomination 1998-99), Pa. Radiol. Soc., Pa. Med. Soc. (alt. del., mem. med.-legal com.), Allegheny Med. Soc. (peer rev. bd. 1997-99), Pa. Radiol. MSO (chmn. by-laws com., exec. com.), Dartmouth Club Western Pa. (exec. com.), Harvard Club Western Pa. (treas.), Pitts. Field Club. Home: PO Box 331 Bakerstown PA 15007-0331

BEACHLEY, NORMAN HENRY, mechanical engineer, educator; b. Washington, Jan. 13, 1933; s. Albert Henry and Anna Garnet (Eiring) B.; m. Marion Ruth Iglehart, July 18, 1959; children: Brenda Ruth, Rebecca Sue, Barbara Joan. B.M.E., Cornell U., 1956, PhD, 1966. Mem. tech. staff Hughes Aircraft Co., Culver City, Calif., 1956-57; mem. tech. staff Space Tech. Labs., Redondo Beach, Calif., 1959-63; mem. faculty U. Wis., Madison, 1966—, prof. mech. engring., 1978-94, prof. emeritus, 1994—. Cons. numerous orgns., 1967—. Co-author: Introduction to Dynamic System Analysis, 1978. Served with USAF, 1957-59. Sci. and Engring. Research Council Gt. Britain fellow, 1981-82 Fellow Soc. Automotive Engrs.; mem. ASME, Sigma Xi. Achievements include research in field of energy storage powerplants for motor vehicles, 1970—. Home: 2332 Fitchburg Rd Verona WI 53593-9278 Office: U Wis 1513 University Ave Madison WI 53706-1539 E-mail: beachley@facstaff.wisc.edu.

BEADEL, STEPHEN JAY, author; b. Sharpsburg, Iowa, Aug. 5, 1949; s. Walter Reldon and Katherine Margaret (Repplinger) B. BS, Iowa State U., 1971. Owner, mgr. Beadel Lumber, Lenox, Iowa, 1976-83; author, 1985—. Guest on numerous talk shows, 1990. Author: The Prophetic Beast, The Predicted Fall of Berlin Wall, 1989, What the Church Won't Tell You About Christmas, 1989, The Four Horseman of the Apocalypse, 1989, What Do You Mean "Born Again"?, 1990, The Pagan Rituals of Easter, 1990, Where is the True Church, 1990, The Reward for Salvation, 1990. Avocations: photography, painting. Home: 1230 70th St Windsor Heights IA 50311

BEADLE, JOHN GRANT, retired manufacturing company executive; b. Chgo., Dec. 16, 1932; s. John G. and Katharine (Brady) B.; m. Lee Oliver, Apr. 11, 1955; children: Katharine, John. BA, Yale U., 1954. Salesman Pure Oil Co., Jacksonville and Tampa, Fla., 1957-59, Kordite Co., Tampa, New Orleans, 1959-61; with Union Spl. Corp., Chgo., 1961—, exec. v.p., 1972-75, pres., chief operating officer, 1975-76, pres., chief exec. officer, 1976-84, chmn., chief exec. officer, 1984-96. Bd. dirs. Batts, Inc., Oliver Products Co., Woodward Governor Co., William Blair Mut. Funds; past pres., bd. dirs. Juvenile Protection Assn.; past chmn., bd. dirs. Midwest Indsl. Mgmt. Assn.; past chmn. Internat. Coun. Machinery and Allied Products Inst. Trustee, past pres. Castle Park Assn. Served with USAF, 1954-57. Mem. Northwestern U. Assocs., Chgo. Com., Am. Apparel Machinery Mfrs. Assn., Riomar Country Club, Riomar Bay Yacht Club. Clubs: Skokie Country (Glencoe, Ill.), Commonwealth, Comml. Republican. Episcopalian.

BEAGLE, BENJAMIN STUART, JR., columnist; b. Staunton, Va., Apr. 24, 1927; s. Benjamin Stuart Sr. and Mamie Virginia (Smith) B.; m. Mary Ann John, June 25, 1952; children: Ann Beheler, Benjamin III, Lucinda. BA in English, Roanoke Coll., 1952. Reporter Radford (Va.) News Jour.; pub. rels. asst. Roanoke Coll., Salem, Va., 1952-53; reporter Staunton News Leader, 1953-54; sr. writer Roanoke (Va.) Times & World News, 1954-92, columnist, 1957—. Author: The World I Never Made, 1986, El Viejo Writes Again, 1990, J. Lindsay Almond, Virginia's Reluctant Rebel. With U.S. Army, 1945-46, ATO. Named Disting. Alumnus Roanoke Coll., 1992. Avocations: reading, writing, outdoor work, woodworking. Home: 5571 Highfields Rd Roanoke VA 24018-4109 Office: Roanoke Times & World News 201 Campbell Ave SW # 209 Roanoke VA 24011-1100 E-mail: bbeaglejr@aol.com.

BEAGLE, JOHN GORDON, real estate broker; b. Spokane, Wash., Dec. 31, 1943; s. Gordon Avril and Sylvia Alberta (Dobbs) B.; m. Shihoko Ledo, Nov. 14, 1964; children: James, Steven, Kevin, Melanie. BS, Mont. State U., 1970; GRI, Realtors Inst., Helena, Mont. Cert. real estate broker. Instr. Kalispell (Mont.) High Sch., 1970-71; gen. mgr. Equity Coop. Assn., Harlem, Mont., 1971-76; owner, operator Howards Pizza, Livingston, Mont., 1976-79; broker, owner Beagle Properties, Inc., Sidney, Mont., 1979—. Appointed to Mont. Bd. Realty Regulation, 1995. With USN, 1963-67. Mem. Mont. Assn. Realtors (v.p. ea. dist. 1982-84, 90-94), Gateway Bd. Realtors (pres. 1987-88), Assn. Real Estate Lic. Law Ofcls. (elected nat. dir. 1998, regional v.p. 2001), Kiwanis, Masons (past master). Republican. Mem. Ch. of Christ. Avocations: computers, readings, fishing. Office: Beagle Properties Inc 120 2nd Ave SW Sidney MT 59270-4018

BEAGRIE, GEORGE SIMPSON, dentist, educator, dean emeritus; b. Peterhead, Scotland, Sept. 14, 1925; emigrated to Can., 1968, naturalized, 1973; s. George and Eliza Lawson (Simpson) B.; m. Marjorie McVie, Sept. 30, 1950; children: Jennifer, Lesley, Ailsa, Elspeth. LDS, Royal Coll. Surgeons, Edinburgh, Scotland, 1947; DDS, U. Edinburgh, 1966, DDS (hon.), 1987; DSc (hon.), McGill U., Can., 1985; D degree, U. Montreal, Can., 1991. Prof., chmn. dept. restorative dentistry U. Edinburgh Dental Sch., 1963-68; prof., chmn. dept. clin. scis. U. Toronto Dental Sch., 1968-78, dir. postgrad. div., 1974-78; dean faculty dentistry U. B.C., Vancouver, Can., 1978-88, dean emeritus, 1989—. Sci. officer grants com. dental scis. Med. Rsch. Coun. Can., 1971-76, dir. dental tng. grants programme, 1971-78; mem. Nat. Dental Examining Bd. Can.; chmn. written exams com. Nat. Dental Examining Bd., Can., 1984-93; cons. in field. Contbr. over 100 articles to dental jours. Mem. United Ch. Can. Served to flight lt. RAF, 1948-50. Fellow Nuffield Found., 1957-58; grantee Med. Research Council U.K., 1962-64; grantee Med. Research Council Can., 1968; grantee Commonwealth Found., 1973 Fellow Royal Coll. Dentists Can. (pres. 1977-79), Am. Coll. Dentists, Internat. Coll. Dentists; fellow in dental surgery Royal Coll. Surgeons Edinburgh and Eng.; mem. ADA (hon.), Internat. Assn. Dental Research (pres. 1977-78), Fedn. Dentaire Internat. (chmn. commn. on dental edn. and practice 1981-87), Can. Dental Assn. (editor tape cassette program 1972-76), Omicron Kappa Upsilon.

BEAHM, DONALD LEE, political science educator; b. Minden, Nebr., Apr. 18, 1953; s. Merle R. and Mary G. B.; m. Renee L. Beahm, July 28, 1973; children: Tonya L., Jeramie L. BS in Polit. Sci., Black Hills State U., 1980; MA in Polit. Sci., U. Nebr., 1987, PhD in Polit. Sci., 1998. Psych. tech. Hastings (Nebr.) Regional Ctr., 1972-74; orderly St. Johns Hosp., Rapid City, S.D., 1975-78; counselor Rapid City Regional Hosp., 1980-84; tchg. asst., rsch. asst. U. Nebr., Lincoln, 1984-89; adj. prof. Doane Coll., Lincoln, Crete, Nebr., 1989-2001; asst. prof. polit. sci. Dowling Coll., Oakdale, NY, 2001—. Author: Conceptions of and Corrections to Majoritarian Tyranny, 2002. Tchr. Young Scholars Inst., Lincoln, 1996&; commentator Sta. KZUM, pub. radio, Lincoln, 1999-2001. Mem. Am. Polit. Sci. Assn. Democrat. Avocations: playing guitar, hiking, camping, astronomy, travel.

BEAHM, FRANKLIN D. lawyer; b. Independence, Kans., Jan. 18, 1953; s. Edgar Hiram and Dorothy S.; m. Tawny L. McIntyre, Jan. 7, 1994; children: F. David, Patrick Stuart, Kristin Sanders, Stephen McWilliams. BBA, So. Methodist U., 1975; JD, Tulane U., 1977. Bar: La. 1977, Colo. 1993, Tex. 2000, U.S. Dist. Ct. (ea. dist.) La. 1977, U.S. Dist. Ct. (mid. dist.) La. 1980, U.S. Dist. Ct. (we. dist.) La. 1985, U.S. Ct. Appeals (5th cir.), U.S. Tax Ct. 1989, U.S. Supreme Ct. 1993. Assoc. Manard & Scheonberger, New Orleans, 1977-80, Bourgeois, Bennett, Metairie, La., 1980, Hammett, Leake & Hammett, New

Orleans, 1980-83, ptnr., 1983-85, Thomas, Hayes & Beahm, New Orleans, 1985-95, Chehardy, Sherman, Ellis, Breslin, Murray, Metairie, 1995-97, Beahm & Green, New Orleans, 1997—. Mem. Am. Health Lawyers Assn., Am. Soc. Law and Medicine, La. Assn. Def. Counsel, La. Bar Assn. (Interprofl. com. 1997-98, professionalism com. 1999—), La. Med. Soc. (Interprofl. com. 1997-98), La. Soc. Hosp. Attys. of the La. Hosp. Assn., Denver Bar Assn., Def. Rsch. Inst. (med. malpractice com., product liability com.), Beta Alpha Psi. Office: 145 Robert E Lee Blvd Ste 408 New Orleans LA 70124-2581 E-mail: frank@beahm.com.

BEAHM, ROGER, advertising executive; With Kayser-Roth; ptnr. Coyne Beahm Inc., Greensboro, N.C., 1989—, pres., COO. Office: Coyne Beahm Inc 6522 Bryan Blvd Greensboro NC 27409

BEAHRS, OLIVER HOWARD, surgeon, educator; b. Eufaula, Ala., Sept. 19, 1914; s. Elmer Charles and Elsa Katherine (Smith) B.; 1 child, Gean Beahrs Landy; m. Helen Edith Taylor, July 27, 1947; children: John Randolf, David Howard, Nancy Ann Beahrs Oster. BA, U. Calif., Berkeley, 1937; MD, Northwestern U., 1942; MS in Surgery, Mayo Grad. Sch. Medicine, 1949; D of Mil. Medicine honoris causa, Uniform Svcs. U. Health Sci., 1999. Diplomate Am. Bd. Surgery. Fellow surgery Mayo Grad. Sch. Medicine, Rochester, Minn., 1942, 46-49, prof. surgery, 1966-79; Joel and Ruth Roberts prof. surgery Mayo Med. Sch., 1978-79; prof. emeritus Mayo Grad. Sch. Medicine, Rochester, Minn., 1979—; asst. surgeon Mayo Clinic, 1949-50, head sect. gen. surgery, 1950-79, vice-chmn. bd. govs., 1964-75. Bd. dirs. Rochester Meth. Hosp.; trustee Mayo Found.; mem. cancer control and rehab. adv. com. Nat. Cancer Inst., 1975-84; mem. Am. Joint Com. on Cancer, 1975-78, exec. dir., 1980-92. Editor: Surgical Consultations; editorial bd.: Surgery, Surg. Techniques Illustrated; contbr. over 400 articles to profl. jours. Hon. life, bd. dirs. Am. Cancer Soc., 1975—; trustee Rochester Meth. Hosp.; adv. bd. Uniform Svcs. Univ. Health Scis.; med. cons. Pres. and Mrs. Reagan. Capt. USNR, 1942-64, ret. Recipient Leadership and Humanitarian awards Am. Cancer Soc. Fellow Royal Coll. Surgery in Ireland (hon.), Royal Australasian Coll. Surgery (hon.); mem. AMA, ACS (mem. exec. com., bd. govs., chmn. cen. jud. com., long-range planning com., chmn. bd. govs., chmn. bd. regents, pres. 1988-89), Am. Group Practice Assn. (sec.-treas. 1974-75), Minn. Surg. Soc. (pres. 1960-61), Am. Thyroid Assn., James IV Assn. Surgeons, Am. Surg. Assn. (pres. 1979-80, chmn. com. on issues 1980-83), So. Surg. Assn., Cen. Surg. Assn., Western Surg. Assn., Soc. Head and Neck Surgeons (pres. 1966-67), Am. Assn. Endocrine Surgeons (pres. 1986-87), Am. Assn. Clin. Anatomists (pres. 1986-87), Soc. Surgery Alimentary Tract, Soc. Pelvic Surgeons (pres. 1983-84), Soc. Surg. Oncology, Am. Assn. Clin. Anatomists (pres.), Philippine Coll. Surgeons (hon.), Hellenic Coll. Surgery (hon.), Assn. Française de Chirurgie Française, Northwestern U. Alumni Assn. (Merit award), Sigma Xi, Phi Kappa Epsilon, Phi Beta Pi, Theta Delta Chi. Republican. Methodist. Home: 2253 Baihly Ln SW Rochester MN 55902-1023 Office: 200 1st St SW Rochester MN 55905-0001 E-mail: beahrs.oliver@mayo.edu.

BEAIRD, CHARLES T. former publishing executive; b. Shreveport, La., July 17, 1922; s. James Benjamin and Mattie Connell (Fort) B.; m. Carolyn Williams, Feb. 6, 1943; children: Susan, Marjorie, John. BA, Centenary Coll., 1966; PhD in Philosophy, Columbia U., 1972. Vice pres., asst. gen. mgr. J.B. Beaird Corp., Shreveport, 1946-57; cons. in oil and investments Shreveport, 1957-59; pres. Beaird-Poulan Inc., Shreveport, 1959-73; chmn. bd. Beaird-Poulan div. Emerson Electric Co., 1973-76; pres., pub. Shreveport Jour., 1976-99; pres. Beaird Properties LLC, 2000—. Dir. Fed. Res. Bank of Dallas, 1972-78, dep. chmn., 1973-78; dir. Winrock Enterprises, Inc., Little Rock; adj. prof. Centenary Coll., Shreveport, 1969-95, prof. emeritus, bd. dirs. Mem. Caddo Parish Police Jury, 1956-60; bd. dirs. Woodrow Wilson Nat. Fellowship Found., Princeton, N.J., 1975-78 bd. dirs. Community Found. of Shreveport-Bossier, 1975-85, chmn., 1979-80 Served to capt. USMCR, 1943-46. Mem. Shreveport Club, Cambridge Club. Office: 330 Marshall St Ste 1112 Shreveport LA 71101-3015

BEAIRD, JAMES RALPH, law educator, dean; b. 1925. BS, U. Ala., 1949, LLB, 1951; LLM, George Washington U., 1953. Bar: Ala. 1951, D.C. 1973. Atty. U.S. Dept. Labor, 1951-56, asst. solicitor, 1956-59; assoc. gen. counsel NLRB, 1959-60; assoc. solicitor U.S. Dept. Labor, 1960-65; vis. prof. U. Ga., 1965-66, prof. law, 1967-89, prof. emeritus, dean, 1976-87, dean emeritus; John Sparkman Vis. Disting. Prof., U. Ala., 1988—; mem. Sec. Labor's Adv. Council on Welfare and Pension Plans, 1968—. Mem. adv. com. for Ga. SBA, 1969—. Mem. Farrah Order Jurisprudence. Office: U Ga Sch Law Athens GA 30602

BEAK, PETER ANDREW, chemistry educator; b. Syracuse, N.Y., Jan. 12, 1936; s. Ralph E. and Belva (Edinger) B.; m. Sandra J. Burns, July 25, 1959; children: Bryan A., Stacia W. BA, Harvard U., 1957; PhD, Iowa State U., 1961. From instr. to prof. chemistry U. Ill., Urbana, 1961—, Roger Adams prof. chemistry, 1997—2003, Jubille prof. liberal arts and sci., 1990—. Cons. Abbott Labs., North Chicago, Ill., 1964—, Monsanto Co., St. Louis, 1969-99, G.D. Searle Co., Ill., 1987-2001, Pharmacia, 2001-2002. Contbr. articles to profl. jours. A.P. Sloan Found. fellow, 1967-69; Guggenheim fellow, 1968-69 Fellow AAAS (chmn. chemistry sect. 1999); mem. NAS, Am. Chem. Soc. (editl. and adv. bds., sec. and divsn. officer, A.C. Cope scholar 1993, Mosher award 1994, Gilman award 1997, Gassman award 2000). Home: 304 E Sherwin Ave Urbana IL 61802 E-mail: beak@scs.uloc.edu.

BEAL, DENNIS, academic administrator; b. 1942; BA in Acctg., U. Utah; MBA, Westminster Coll., Salt Lake City. With Bushman, Daines, Rasmussan, and Wisan CPAs, 1974—81, Am. Stores Co., 1981—92; v.p., CFO State Bros. Holdings Inc., 1992—98, sr. v.p., CFO, 1998—2000; CFO Stater Bros. Market, Colton, Calif., 2000; exec. v.p., CFO Corinthian Colls., Santa Ana, Calif., 2000—. Recipient INC 500 award, INC Mag., 2001. Office: Corinthian Colls 6 Hutton Centre Dr Ste 400 Santa Ana CA 92707

BEAL, DONNA LEE, association executive; b. Ticonderoga, N.Y., Aug. 22, 1952; d. Donald Lee and Beverley Ann (Burlow) McIntyre; m. Allan Grant Beal, July 15, 1972; children: Andrew, Alison. Assoc., Pierce Coll. for Women, 1972. Office mgr. Med.-Family Practice, Hamilton, N.Y., 1972-74, Gen. Dentistry, Westport, N.Y., 1978-84; sec. The Adirondack Coun., Elizabethtown, N.Y., 1984-85, adminstrv. asst., 1985-86, adminstr., 1986-89, acting co-dir., 1989, adminstr., dir. membership, CFO, 1990-94; v.p. adminstrn. Ecologically Sustainable Devel., Inc., Elizabethtown, 1994-97; dir. devel. Holstein Found., Brattleboro, Vt., 1997-2000, exec. dir., 2000—03. Treas. Environ. Fedn. N.Y., Albany, 1991-94, vice chair Adirondack Centennial Com., Paul Smiths, N.Y., 1990-92; project dir. Conf. Mng. Growth and Devel. in Unique, Natural Settings, Elizabethtown, 1990; trustee Assn. for the Protection of the Adirondacks, 1997-99. Vice chmn. Essex County Sch. Bds. Assn., 1986; bd. dirs. Depot Theatre, Westport, 1988-94, Champlain Health Concerns, Mineville, N.Y., 1980; mem. bd. edn. Westport Ctrl. Sch., 1982-86; mem. pastoral rels. com. Westport Federated Ch., 1990-91, bd. trustees, Ballard Park Found., 1999—, bd. dirs. Westport Chamber Commerce, 1999-2000. Republican. Avocations: golf, reading, exploring the adirondacks. Office: Holstein Found PO Box 816 Brattleboro VT 05302-0816 E-mail: donnabeal@westelcom.com.

BEAL, GRAHAM WILLIAM JOHN, museum director; b. Stratford-on-Avon, Eng., Apr. 22, 1947; came to U.S., 1973; s. Cecil John Beal and Annie Gladys (Barton) Tunbridge; m. Nancy Jane Andrews, Apr. 21, 1973: children: Priscilla Jane, Julian William John. BA, Manchester U., Eng., 1969; MA, U. London, 1972. Acad. asst. to dir. Sheffield City (Eng.) Art Galleries, 1972-73; gallery dir. U. S.D., Vermillion, 1973-74, Washington U., St. Louis, 1974-77; chief curator Walker Art Ctr., Mpls., 1977-83; dir. Sainsbury Ctr. for Visual Arts, Norwich, Eng., 1983-84; chief curator San Francisco Mus. Modern Art, 1984-89; dir. Joslyn Art Mus., Omaha, 1989-96, Los Angeles County Mus. Art, 1996-99, Detroit Inst. Arts, 1999—. Mem. Fed. Adv. Com. on Internat. Exhbns., 1991-94. Author: (book, exhbn. catalog) Jim Dine: Five Themes, 1984; co-author: (book, exhbn. catalog) A Quiet Revolution, 1987, David Nash: Voyages and Vessels, 1994, Sainsbury Collection Catalogue, vol. I, 1997, Joslyn Air Museum: Fifty Favorities, 1994, Joslyn Art Museum: A Building History, 1998, American Beauty: American Paintings and Sculpture from the Detroit Institute of Arts, 2002; contbg. to Apollo Mag., London, 1989-91. Trustee Djerassi Found., Woodside, Calif., 1987-89. Mem.: Assn. Art Mus. Dir. (bd. trustees), Detroit (Mich.) Athletic Club, Century Club. Avocations: history, cooking, music. Office: Detroit Inst Arts 5200 Woodward Ave Detroit MI 48202

BEAL, JASON ELIOT, architect; b. Nashua, N.H., July 2, 1974; s. Eliot Cushman and Constance Crosbie B. BA in Architecture, R.I. Sch. of Design, Providence, 1999. Draftsman Strekalovsky & Hoit, Hingham, Mass.; welder, fabricator Jay Coogan Artist, Providence, R.I.; designer Rockefeller/Hricak, Venice, Calif.; prin. B.O.C. Design, Malibu, Calif. Recipient Merit award Lyceum Fellowship, Boston, 1997. Mem. Am. Inst. Architects. Avocations: motorcycling, fabrication, casting, computers, skate and snow boarding. Office: Rockefeller/Hricak Architects 4052 Del Ray Ave Venice CA 90292 E-mail: jb@rharchitects.com.

BEAL, JOHN EVERETT, composer, conductor; b. Santa Monica, Calif., Jan. 20, 1947; s. Ralph Raymond and Marjory May B.; m. Helene Nina Marie Nielsen, Dec. 12, 2002. Student, San Diego State Coll., UCLA. Composer, pub. Opus Pocus Music, N. Hollywood, Calif., 1978—; pres., sr. composer Reeltime Music, Inc., Beverly Hills, Calif., 1984—. Musician, 1966—; composer (film) Zero to Sixty, 1977, The Funhouse, 1981, Terror in the Aisles, 1984; composer, rec. artist: Coming Soon!, 1998 (Golden Score award 1998). Dir. planned giving Hathaway Children and Family Svcs., 2002—. Sgt. USMC, 1966-72, Vietnam. Decorated Air medal with bronze star, 8 Air medals, Naval Achievement with valor. Mem. ATAS, ASCAP, NARAS (gov. 1984-86), Soc. Composers and Lyricists. Avocations: film, travel, dining. Office: Reeltime Music Inc 9601 Wilshire Blvd Ste 340 Beverly Hills CA 90210-5206 Fax: 818-762-0045.

BEAL, M. FLINT, neurologist; b. London, Nov. 6, 1950; s. Myron C. and Esther (Delong) B.; m. Judy A. Ahlheim, June 12, 1976; children: Bradley, Emily. BA, Colgate U., 1972; MA, U. Va., 1976. Med. resident N.Y. Hosp. Cornell, N.Y.C., 1976-78; neurology resident Mass. Gen. Hosp., Boston, 1978-81, neurology fellow, 1981-83, asst. prof. neurology, 1983-87, assoc. prof. neurology, 1987-95, prof., 1995—98; Ann Parrish Titzell prof., chmn. dept. neurology Cornell U. Weill Med. Coll., N.Y.C., 1998—; neurologist-in-chief N.Y. Presbyn. Hosp., N.Y.C., 1998—. Editorial bd.: Annals of Neurology and Jour. of Neurochemistry; contbr. articles to profl. jours. Fellow Stroke Coun. Am. Heart Assn.; mem. Am. Acad. Neurology, Am. Neurol. Assn. (Derek Denny-Brown award), N.Y. Acad. Sci., Soc. for Neurosci., Internat. Soc. for Cerebral Blood Flow and Metabolism, AAAS, Alpha Omega Alpha. Achievements include delineation of postmortem neurochemistry of neurodegenerative diseases improved animal models of neurodegenerative diseases demonstration of increased lactate in Huntingtons disease cerebral cortex. Office: NY Hosp-Weill Cornell Med Ctr Dept Neurology and Neurosci 525 E 68th St New York NY 10021

BEAL, MERRILL DAVID, conservationist, museum director; b. Richfield, Utah, June 26, 1926; s. Merrill Dee and Bessy (Neill) B.; m. Jean Lorraine Wood, Feb. 24, 1947; children: John David, James Merrill. BA, Idaho State Coll., 1950; MS, Utah State U., 1952. Park ranger, naturalist Yellowstone Nat. Park, 1953-60; chief park naturalist Grand Canyon Nat. Park, 1960-69; asst. supt. Great Smoky Mountains Nat. Park, Gatlinburg, Tenn., 1969-72; assoc. regional dir. Midwest region Nat. Park Service, Omaha, 1972-75, regional dir., 1975-78; supt. Gt. Smoky Mountains Nat. Park, Gatlinburg, Tenn., 1978-83; asst. dir. Ariz.-Sonora Desert Mus., Tucson, 1983-91. Author: Grand Canyon, the Story Behind the Scenery, 1967. Mem. bd. Grand Canyon Sch., 1964-69. Served with USN, 1944-46. Recipient Meritorious Service award U.S. Dept. Interior, 1975 Mem. Wildlife Soc., Gt. Smoky Mountains Natural History Assn. (bd. dirs. 1993-95), S.W. Parks and Monument Assn., Ea. Nat. Park and Monument Assn. (bd. dirs. 1989-95), Sigma Xi. E-mail: jbeal389@msn.com.

BEAL, MYRON CLARENCE, osteopathic physician; b. N.Y.C., Dec. 4, 1920; s. Clarence Joseph and Birdice Elvira (Flint) B.; m. Esther Naomi DeLong, Sept 11, 1948; children: Rebecca Johnson, Myron Flint, Shelley Rees, Julie Wilson, Christina Beal Bailey. AB, U. Rochester, 1942; D.O., Chgo. Coll. Osteo. Medicine, 1945; MS in Physiology, U. Chgo., 1949. Asst. dir. clinics Chgo. Coll. Osteo. Medicine, 1946-49; instr. London Coll. Osteopathy, 1949-51; pvt. practice osteo. medicine Rochester, N.Y., 1951-74; prof. biomechanics Coll. Osteo. Medicine, Mich. State U., East Lansing, 1974-81, prof. family medicine, 1981-89, prof. emeritus, 1989—, acting chmn. biomechanics, 1975-77. Mem. Nat. Bd. Examiners for Osteo. Physicians and Surgeons, 1960-84, cons., 1984-89; mem. N.Y. State Bd. Medicine, 1961-73. Trustee Chgo. Coll. Osteo. Medicine 1969-93, chmn. bd. dirs. 1985-91. Fellow Am. Acad. Osteopathy (editor 1987—); mem. Am. Osteop. Assn., N.Y. State Osteo. Soc., Mich. Assn. Osteo. Physicians and Surgeons, Chgo. Osteo. Health Systems (bd. dirs. 1986-90). Congregationalist. Office: 5873 Seneca Point Rd Naples NY 14512-9763

BEAL, ROBERT LAWRENCE, real estate executive; b. Boston, Sept. 10, 1941; s. Alexander Simpson and Leona M. (Rothstein) B. BS cum laude, Harvard U., 1963, MBA, 1965. Vice pres., ptnr. Beacon Cos., Boston, 1965-76; ptnr. The Beal Cos., Boston; pres. Beal and Co., Inc., Boston, 1976—. Corporator, dir., mem. exec. com., lending com. Provident Instn. Savs., 1975-86; chmn. bd. dirs. Mass. Devel. Fin. Agy., 1976—; instr. real estate Northeastern U., 1969-75; mem. East Cambridge rezoning adv. com., 1989—; dir. Artery Bus. Com., 1989—, chmn., 1995-99, treas., 1989-95. Bd. dirs. Boston Zool. Soc., 1972-86, pres., 1980, chmn., 1981-84, hon. chmn., 1985; mem. vis. com. Sch. Mus. Fine Arts, Boston, 1974-76, 88-89; overseer Boys Club Boston, 1975-93; mem. corp. Belmont Hill Sch.; trustee, overseer Beth Israel Deaconess Med. Ctr., 1981-2001, mem. bldg. and grounds com., 1976-82, 86-90; dir. Harvard Coll. Fund Coun., 1972-73, capital fund dir. Class '63, 1979-85, co-chmn. 25th reunion, co-chmn. 35th and 40th reunions, class gift, class sec., 2000—; exec. bd. Boston chpt. Am. Jewish Com., 1987-96, mem. bd. govs., 1989-92; bd. dirs. Boston Mcpl. Rsch. Bur., 1978—, treas., 1988-89, 92, vice chmn., 1990-93, chmn., 1994-96; bd. dirs. Met. Boston Housing Partnership, Inc., 1983-95; trustee The Partnership, Inc., 1981-89, New Eng. Aquarium, 1987—, bd. govs., 1993-98, 2002—, mem. exec. comm., 2002—, co-chair campaign steering com., 2001—; mem. adv. task force John F. Kennedy Libr., 1982; bd. overseers Mus. Fine Arts, Boston, 1988-97, 98-2001, overseer for life, 2001—; mem. vis. com. Harvard Div. Sch., 1989—, adv. com. Taubman Ctr., John F. Kennedy Sch. Govt., Harvard U., 1989—, chair, 2003—, co-chair campaign steering com., 2001—; co-chair United Way of Massachusetts Bay's Alexis de Tocqueville Soc., 2000, mem. cabinet, 2000, co-chair elect 2003 campaign; bd. overseers Mass. Soc. Prevention Cruelty to Animals, 1988—; chair coun. fellows Angell Meml. Animal Hosp., 1999—. Mem. Nat. Realty Com. (dir., past sec., mem. exec. com. 1974-99, v.p., vice chmn.), Mass. Assn. Realtors (dir. 1979-81), Greater Boston Real Estate Bd. (bd. dir. 1970-72, 76-90, pres. 1978-79), Am. Soc. Real Estate Counselors, Bldg. Owners-Mgrs. Assn. Boston (dir. 1970-72), Ripon Soc. (co-founder, nat. treas. 1968-73, nat. governing bd. 1979-85), Nat. Assn. Real Estate Appraiser (cert.), Mass. Taxpayers Found. (dir. 1980-86), Inst. Property Taxation (affliate), Internat. Assn. Assessing Officers (primary subscribing mem. 1982—), Beacon Hill Civic Assn. (bd. dir. 1975-79), Bostonian Soc. (life), Greater Boston C. of C. (bd. dirs.), The Vault (coord. com. 1978-97), Combined Jewish Philanthropies Greater Boston (exec. com. 1989—, vice chmn. 1992-93, chmn. com. on endowment fund 1999—, chair devel. com. 2001—, chair cmty. capital campaign 2002—), Greater Boston C. of C. (bd. dirs. 1992—). Republican. Jewish. Home: 21 Brimmer St Boston MA 02108-1001 Office: Beal and Co Inc 177 Milk St Ste 2A Boston MA 02109-3410

BEAL, WANDA ELNORA, psychologist, writer, artist; b. Flint, Mich. d. Glenn R. and Nettie (Capron) R.; m. Howard William Beal (div. Feb. 1980); children: Wesley William, Patrice Annette, Cynthia Joan; m. Raymond Mileur, Aug. 30, 1992 (div. 1998). BA in Art Edn. and Psychology, S.W. State U., 1977; MS in Psychology, MS Art Therapy, Emporia State U., 1980; PsyD, Forest Inst. Profl. Psychology, 1995. Writer Denver Post, 1956—70; artist, designer Wanda's Designs, Limon, Colo., 1970—80; psychologist Menard (Ill.) Psychiat. Ctr., 1980—95, Chester (Ill.) Mental Health, 1995—2003; ret., 2003. Freelance writer, Limon, 1960-80; mem. Denver chpt. Fashion Group, 1970-80. Pres. Nat. League Am. Pen Women, 1969, art dir., 1968; bd. dirs. Am. Lung Assn., 1965-70, Colo. chpt. ARC, 1965-70; mem. Nat. Trust Hist. Preservation, 1999, Nat. Mus. Women in Arts, 1999; appointed min. of culture ABI, 2003. Mem. APA, AAUW, Internat. Soc. Photographs, Am. Assn. Correctional Psychologists, Am. Art Therapy Assn. (registered 1981), Mo. Psychol. Assn., Ozark Psychol. Assn., St. Louis Network for Women Psychologists, Psi Chi. Methodist. Avocations: painting, ceramics, tennis, swimming, golf, walking, writing, biking.

BEALE, BETTY (MRS. GEORGE K. GRAEBER), columnist, writer; b. Washington; d. William Lewis and Edna (Sims) B.; m. George Kenneth Graeber, Feb. 15, 1969. AB, Smith Coll. Columnist Washington Post, 1937-40; reporter and columnist Washington Evening Star, 1945-81; weekly columnist North Am. Syndicate (formerly Field Newspaper Syndicate), 1953-89; ret., 1989. Lectr. in field. Author: Power at Play: A Memoir of Parties, Politicians and the Presidents in My Bedroom, 1993; columnist Georgetown and Country, 1998-99. Recipient Freedom Found. award, 1969; named Woman of Distinction, Birmingham So. Coll., 1987. Address: 2926 Garfield St NW Washington DC 20008-3536 E-mail: Gbetg@aol.com.

BEALE, CHRISTOPHER WILLIAM, banker; b. Sydney, New South Wales, Australia, Sept. 13, 1947; s. Jack Gordon Beale and Pamela June Anne (Wallis) Scott; m. Francesca May Macartney, May 6, 1972; children: Julian Macartney, Andrew Macartney. BA, U. Sydney, 1968, LLB, 1971; MBA, Harvard U., 1974. Bar: N.Y. 1975. Atty. Dibbs, Crowther & Osborne, Sydney, 1968-71, Price Waterhouse & Co., Sydney, 1972; assoc. The First Boston Corp., N.Y.C., 1974-77, v.p., 1978-83, mng. dir., 1984-88; chmn. Beale Lynch & Co., N.Y.C., 1988-93; mng. dir. Morgan Stanley & Co., Inc., N.Y.C., 1993-95; mng. dir., global head project structured trade fin. Citigroup Inc., N.Y.C., 1995—. Mem. editl. bd.: Jour. Structured and Project Fin., 2001—. Bd. dirs. Am. Australian Assn., N.Y.C., 1984—, vice chmn., 2002-03, dep. chmn., 2003—; mem. adv. bd. Inst. for Internat. Fin., Washington, 1997—; chmn. Am. Australian Bus. Coun. N.Y., 2002—. Home: 301 E 52nd St New York NY 10022-6319 Office: Citigroup Inc 388 Greenwich St New York NY 10013

BEALE, GEORGIA ROBISON, historian, educator; b. Chgo., Mar. 14, 1905; d. Henry Barton and Dora Belle (Sledd) Robison; m. Howard Kennedy Beale, Jan. 2, 1942; children: Howard Kennedy, Henry Barton Robison, Thomas Wight. AB, U. Chgo., 1926, AM, 1928; PhD, Columbia U., 1938; postgrad., Sorbonne and Coll. de France, 1930-34. Reader in history U. Chgo., 1927-29; lectr. Barnard Coll., 1937-38; instr. Bklyn. Coll., 1937-39; asst. prof. Hollins (Va.) Coll., 1939-41, Wellesley Coll., 1941-42, Castleton (Vt.) State Coll., 1968-70; vis. assoc. prof. U. Ky., Lexington, 1970-72; professorial lectr. George Washington U., 1983-84. Author: Révellère-lépeaux, Citizen Director, 1938, 72, Academies to Institut, 1973, Bosc and the Exequatur, 1978, The Botanophiles of Angers, 1996; contbg. author Historical Dictionary of the French Revolution, 1985; also articles. Mem. Madison (Wis.) Civic Music Assn. and Madison Symphony Orch. League, 1958—; hon. trustee Culver-Stockton Coll., 1974—. Univ. fellow Columbia U., 1929-30. Mem. AAUW (European fellow 1930-31), Am. Hist. Assn., So. Hist. Assn., Soc. French Hist. Studies, Western Soc. French History (hon. mem. exec. coun.), Am. Soc. 18th Century Studies, Brit. Soc. 18th Century Studies, Reid Hall Club (Paris), Brit. Univ. Women's Club (London), Phi Beta Kappa, Pi Lambda Theta, Phi Alpha Theta, Pi Kappa Delta. Office: The Ridge Orford NH 03777

BEALE, JANE GUTHRIE, music publisher, music educator, pianist; b. New Albany, Ind., Aug. 19, 1920; d. John Andrew Smith and Pearl (Hardin) Guthrie; m. James MacArthur Beale, Aug. 18, 1945; children: Eleanor Tappan Beale Harrison, Harriet Guthrie Beale, Sarah B. Phillips. AB in Music, Wellesley Coll., 1943; AM in Music, Harvard U., 1960. Piano instr. U. Louisville, 1945-48; lectr., coach, piano performance Sch. Music Carnegie-Mellon U., Pitts., 1969-70; asst. prof. piano Ctrl. Wash. U., Ellensburg, 1973-74; pvt. studio instr. Seattle, 1985—; pres. Permanent Press Music of Quality, Seattle, 1985—. Program annotator Seattle Symphony Orch., 1960-62; condr. workshops on piano method to Wash. state music tchr. groups, 2001-03. Piano performances include Contemporary Group, U. Wash. Sch. Music, 1960-75, Carnegie-Mellon U., 1969-70, chamber music, cello-piano, solo, Frye Art Mus., 2001—; editor: Northwest Passages, 1994; author, pub.: (piano method books) Keyboard Arithmetic, Scalies, 1990-97. French tutor Franklin H.S., Seattle, 1980-82. Mem. Music Tchrs. Nat. Assn. (music composition adjudicator 1980-2003, worksohps on piano method, 1999—), Western Wash. Radcliffe Club (treas. 1978-79, concert organizer 1984), Western Wash. Wellesley Club (dist. fund chmn. 1981-83). Avocations: swimming, bicycling. Home and Office: 7508 42nd Ave NE Seattle WA 98115-5102

BEALE, ROBERT LYNDON, lawyer; b. Port Angeles, Wash., Sept. 10, 1936; s. Fred G. and Dorothy (Auld) B.; m. Elaine Brown, May 30, 1958 (div. May 1966); children: Tammy, John; m. Marilyn Fijalka, Nov. 4, 1967; children: William, Joseph, Anne. BA, Coll. Puget Sound, 1958; LLB, U. Wash., 1963. Bar: Wash. 1964, U.S. Dist. Ct. (we. dist.) Wash. 1964, U.S. Ct. Appeals (9th cir.) 1989. Assoc. Murray, Scott, McGavick, Tacoma, 1964—66; ptnr., then shareholder McGavick, Graves, P.S., 1966—2002, of counsel, 2002—. Contbr. chpt. to book: Community Property Deskbook, 1977. Bd. dirs. Pacific Harbors coun. Boy Scouts Am., Tacoma, 1984—, pres., 1987-90. Recipient Silver Beaver award Mt. Rainier coun. Boy Scouts Am., 1991. Mem. Wash. State Bar Assn. (bd. bar examiners 1977-91), Tacoma Club (pres. 1990-91), Fircrest Golf Club (bd. dirs. 1988-89), Order of Coif. Avocations: golf, skiing. Office: McGavick Graves PS 1102 Broadway Tacoma WA 98402-3525 Fax: (253) 627-2247. E-mail: rlb@mcgavick.com.

BEALE, SUSAN YATES, social worker; b. Saginaw, Mich., Nov. 17, 1943; d. William Miller and Dorothy LaVerne (Langdon) Yates; m. Henry B.R. Beale, Aug. 27, 1966; children: Andrew, Nathaniel. AB cum laude, Oberlin Coll., 1966; MA, U. Chgo., 1969. Social worker West Side VA Hosp., Chgo., 1969-70, D.C. Dept. Human Resources, Washington, 1970-72, D.C. Pub. Schs., Washington, 1972-73; pvt. practice Washington, 1973-74; dir. social svc. Capitol Hill Hosp., Washington, 1974-80; social worker No. Va. Dialysis Ctr., Alexandria, 1982-87, Vis. Nurse Assn., Rockville, Md., 1987-89; sr. social worker Hospice of Washington, 1989-95; sr. social svcs. analyst Microeconomic Applications, 1982—; pres. Coping Ptnrs., Washington, 1996—; social worker Hospice of Northern Va., 1999—. Tchr. Royal Scottish Country Dance Soc. Mem.: NASW. Avocations: singing, gardening. Office: Coping Ptnrs 4354 Warren St NW Washington DC 20016-2438

BEALER, RICHARD T. social sciences educator; b. Sedalia, Mo., June 3, 1952; s. Raymond Theodore Bealer and Helen Floris Smith; m. Ruth Anne Schiller-Bealer, Dec. 15, 1984; children: Ryan, Zachary; m. Cindy D. Roller (div. Mar. 16, 1983); 1 child, Nicole Bealer-Jacks. BA, George Mason U., Fairfax, Va., 1975; MSc, Ctrl. Mo. State U., Warrensburg, 1977. Instr. psychology So. Ark. U., El Dorado, 1977—80, Barton County CC, Great Bend, Kans., 1980—. Adv. bd. BLINK, Great Bend, 2001—; adv. CKMC Ethics Bd., Great Bend, 1998—2001, New Beginnings, Great Bend, Kans., 1990—94; dist. instr. Barton County CC, Great Bend, 1989. Recipient NISOD Instr., U. Tex., 1987. Mem.: Psychol., Ednl. Rsch. in Kan., Am. Psychol. Soc., Am. Psychol. Assn. divsn. 2. Republican. Lutheran. Avocations: bicycling, target shooting, calligraphy, table tennis. Home: 2924 27th St Great Bend KS 67530 E-mail: rrbealer@hotmail.com.

BEALL, BURTCH W., JR., architect; b. Columbus, Ohio, Sept. 27, 1925; s. Burtch W. and Etta (Beheler) B.; m. Susan Jane Hunter, June 6, 1949; children: Brent Hunter, Brook Waite. Student, John Carroll U., 1943; BArch, Ohio State U., 1949. Draftsman Brooks & Coddington, Architects, Columbus, 1949-51, William J. Monroe, Architects, Salt Lake City, 1951-53, Lorenzo Young, Architect, Salt Lake City, 1953-54; prin. Burtch W. Beall, Jr., Architect, Salt Lake City, 1954—. Vis. lectr. Westminster Coll., 1955; adj. prof. U. Utah, 1955-85, 92-97; treas. Nat. Coun. Archtl. Registration Bds., 1982-84. Restoration architect Salt Lake City and County Bldg; contbr. projects to: A Pictorial History of Architecture in America, America Restored, This Before Architecture. Trustee Utah Found. for Arch., 1985, pres., 1987-91; mem. Utah State Bd. Fine Arts, 1987-95, chmn., 1991-93; chmn. Utah State Capitol Adv. Com., 1986-90, Western States Art Fedn., Bd. trustees, 1991-94; mem. exec. residence com. State of Utah, 1991-97; mem. Utah: A Guide to the State Found. With USN, 1943-45. Recipient several merit and honor awards; Found. fellow Utah Heritage Found., 1985. Fellow AIA (jury mem. 2000-02); mem. Masons, Sigma Alpha Epsilon. Methodist. Home: 4644 Brookwood Cir Salt Lake City UT 84117-4908 Office: Burtch W Beall Jr Arch 2188 Highland Dr Salt Lake City UT 84106-2896

BEALL, CYNTHIA, anthropologist, educator; b. Urbana, Ill., Aug. 21, 1949; d. John Wood and J. Alene (Beachler) Beall. BA in Biology, U. Pa., 1970; MA in Anthropology, Pa. State U., 1972, PhD in Anthropology, 1976. Asst. prof. Case Western Res. U., Cleve., 1976—82, assoc. prof. of anthropology,

1982—87, prof. anthropology, 1987—. Co-editor: Jour. of Cross-Cultural Gerontology, 1986—95; contbr. articles to profl. jours. Active Internat. Rsch. Exch. Program, 1990, 1991. Fellow Nat. Program for Advanced Study and Rsch. in China, NAS, 1986—87, 1997; grantee rsch., NSF, 1981, 1983, 1986, 1987, 1993, 1994, 1995, 1997, 2000, Am. Fedn. for Aging Rsch., 1983, 1986, Nat. Geog. Soc., 1983, 1986—87, 1993, 1995. Fellow: AAAS; mem.: NAS (coun. 2002—), Assn. for Anthropology and Gerontology, Soc. for Study Human Biology, Human Biology Coun. (exec. com. 1989—92, pres. 1992—94), Am. Assn. Phys. Anthropology (exec. com. 1989—92), Am. Anthrop. Assn., Am. Philo. Soc. Achievements include research in in Peru, Bolivia, Nepal, Tibet, Mongolia and Ethiopia. Office: Case Western Res U Dept Anthropology 238 Mather Memorial Bldg Cleveland OH 44106-7125 E-mail: cmb2@po.cwru.edu.

BEALL, DENNIS RAY, artist, educator; b. Chickasha, Okla., Mar. 13, 1929; s. Roy A. and Lois O. (Phillips) B.; 1 son, Garm. Student, Okla. City U., 1950-52; BA, San Francisco State U., 1956, MA, 1958. Registrar Oakland (Calif.) Art Mus., 1958; curator Achenbach Found. for Graphic Arts, Calif. Palace of the Legion of Honor, San Francisco, 1958-1965; asst. prof. art San Francisco State U., 1965-69, assoc. prof., 1969-76, prof. art, 1976-92; prof. emeritus, 1992—. Numerous one-man shows of prints, 1957—, including: Award Exhbn. of San Francisco Art Commn., Calif. Coll. Arts and Crafts, 1978, San Francisco U. Art Gallery, 1978, Los Robles Galleries, Palo Alto, Calif.; numerous group shows 1960— including Mills Coll. Art Gallery, Oakland, Calif., Univ. Gallery of Calif. State U., Hayward, 1979, Marshall-Meyers Gallery, 1979, 80, Marin Civic Ctr. Art Galleries, San Rafael, Calif., 1980, San Francisco Mus. Modern Art, 1985; touring exhibit U. Mont., 1987-91, An Inner Vision, Oysterponds Hist. Soc., Orient, N.Y., 1998, Modernism in Calif. Printmaking, Annex Gallery, Santa Rosa, Calif., 1998, The Stamp of Impulse, Worcester (Mass.) Art Mus., 2001, Palm Springs (Calif.) Desert Mus., 2003; represented in numerous permanent collections including Libr. of Congress, Washington, Mus. Modern Art, N.Y.C., Nat. Libr. of Medicine, Washington, Cleve. Mus., Whitney Mus., Phila. Mus., U.S. embassy collections, Tokyo, London and other major cities, Victoria and Albert Mus., London, Achenbach Found. for graphic Arts, Calif. Palace of Legion of Honor, San Francisco, Oakland Art Mus., Phila. Free Libr., Roanoke (Va.) Art Ctr., Worcester (Mass.) Art Mus., Whitney Mus. Am. Art, Cleve. Mus., various colls. and univs. in U.S. Served with USN, 1947-50, PTO. Office: San Francisco State Univ Art Dept 1600 Holloway Ave San Francisco CA 94132-1722 E-mail: chukar@thegrid.net.

BEALL, FRANK CARROLL, science director and educator; b. Balt., Oct. 3, 1933; s. Frederick Carroll Beall and Virginia Laura (Ogier) McNally; m. Mavis Lillian Holmes, Sep. 7, 1963; children: Amanda Jane Fee, Mark Walter Beall, Alyssa Joan Beall. BS, Pa. State U., 1964; MS, Syracuse U., 1966, PhD, 1968. Rsch. technologist U.S. Forest Products Lab., Madison, Wis., 1966-68; asst., then assoc. prof. Pa. State U., University Park, 1968-75; assoc. prof. U. Toronto, Can., 1975-77; scientist, mgr. Weyerhaeuser Co., Federal Way, Wash., 1977-88; Fred E. Dickinson chair in wood sci. and tech. U. Calif. Forest Products Lab., Richmond, 1997—, prof., dir., 1988—. Contbr. articles in wood and sci. tech.; patentee for wood forming method, method of measuring content of dielectric materials, vertical progressive lumber dryer, bond strength measurement of composite panel products, hybrid pultruded products and method for their manufacture, pultrusion method for condensation resin injection, others. Fellow Acoustic Emission Working Group (chmn. 1996-98), Internat. Acad. Wood Sci. (sec.-treas. 1996-2002, treas. 2002--); mem. ASTM (com. DO7 on wood, chmn. 1994-98), Internat. Union Forestry Rsch. Orgns. (coord. rsch. group physiomech. properties of wood and wood-based materials), Am. Soc. for Nondestructive Testing, Forest Products Soc. (pres. 2001-02), Soc. Wood Sci. and Tech. (pres. 1991-92). Office: U Calif Forest Products Lab 1301 S 46th St Richmond CA 94804-4600 E-mail: frank.beall@ucop.edu.

BEALL, JAMES HOWARD, physicist, educator, public policy analysis; b. Grantsville, W.Va., May 12, 1945; s. Judson Harmon and Mary Lenore (Burns) Beall; m. Mary Ruth Clance; children: Aaron James, Tara Siobhan. BA in Physics, U. Colo., 1972; MS, U. Md., 1975; PhD, U. Md., 1979. Grad. rschr. in astrophysics Goddard Space Flight Ctr., NASA, Greenbelt, Md., 1975—78; Congl. fellow U.S. Congress Office Tech. Assessment, Washington, 1978—79; project scientist sci. and analysis divsn. BKD, Rockville, Md., 1979—81; NAS/NRC resident rsch. assoc. Naval Rsch. Lab., Washington, 1981—83; mem. faculty St. John's Coll., 1983—; sr. cons. E.O. Hulburt Ctr. Space Rsch., Naval Rsch. Lab., Washington, 1983—. Mem. sci. and engring. adv. bd. High Frontier, Arlington, Va., 1991—; prof. space scis., Sch. for Computational Scis. George Mason U., Fairfax, Va., 1992—; project adminstr. black oral history project Folger Shakespeare Libr., Washington, 1981; moderator Libr. of Congress Symposium on Sci. and Lit., 1981. Author: (book) Hickey, the Days, 1980. Dir. edn. Environ. Action Com., U. Colo. Denver, 1971—72; Poets-in-the-Schs. participant Va. Pub. Schs., 1975—; bd. dirs. Partridgeberry Sch., Greenbelt, 1977—78. Served with USAF, 1963—67. Recipient Tchr. Excellent award, Dept. Physics and Astronomy, U. Md., 1974—75; grantee, Nat. Endowment for Humanities, 1976, 1978, NSF, 1991, 1995. Mem.: Md. Writers Coun., Am. Astron. Soc., Am. Phys. Soc., AAAS, Cosmos Club, Sigma Pi Sigma, Sigma Xi, Phi Beta Kappa. Republican. Achievements include research in theoretical and observational astrophysics, renewable energy resources and public policy; discovery of 1st concurrent radio and x-ray variability of active galaxy; made first prediction of inverse compton x-ray emission from supernovae, first prediction of detectable infrared and optical emission from accretion disks around black holes; first detection of a ring of x-ray light around the earth's equator. Office: Naval Rsch Lab Code 7650 Washington DC 20375-0001

BEALL, KENNETH SUTTER, JR., lawyer; b. Evanston, Ill., Aug. 9, 1938; s. Kenneth Sutter and Helen Cantlon (Koenig) B.; m. Blair Hamilton Bissett, May 25, 1975; children: Kevina Anne, Hunter Bissett, Baret Bissett. BA, Washington and Lee U., 1961, LLB, 1963. Bar: Fla. 1964. With Gunster, Yoakley & Stewart, P.A., West Palm Beach, Fla., 1964—, ptnr., 1970—, pres., 1994—. Bd. dirs. The Whitehall Found., The Wells Family Found.; chmn. Palm Beach County Environ. Control Hearing Bd., 1970-92; mem. law coun. Washington and Lee U., 1997-2001; trustee, sec. Caribbean/Latin Am. Action. Served with USMCR, 1963-68. Mem. ABA, Fla. Bar (Pres.'s Pro Bono Svc. award 1983), Palm Beach County Bar Assn., Fed. Bar Assn. (pres. Palm Beach County chpt. 1981). Democrat. Roman Catholic. Office: 777 S Flagler Dr Ste 500E West Palm Beach FL 33401-6121 E-mail: kbeall@gunster.com.

BEALL, PAMELA HONN, therapist, radio talks-show host, writer; b. Mattoon, Ill., Mar. 24, 1955; d. Kenneth Franklin and Dorothy Marie (Linder) Honn; m. Thomas Allen Beall IV, June 23, 1985; children: Christopher Allen, Brittany Alane. BS in Psychology, Evangel Coll., Springfield, Mo., 1976; MS in Edn., Ea. Ill. U., Charleston, 1979. Nat. cert. counselor; lic. clin. profl. counselor. Community care coord. East Ctrl. Ill. Area Agy. on Aging, Bloomington, 1979-80; outpatient therapist Iroquois Mental Health Ctr., Watseka, Ill., 1981-86, 90-91, cons., part-time outpatient therapist, 1987-89, 91-93; program psychologist Paxaton (Ill.) Community Hosp., 1986-87; coord. good beginnings program Ctr. for Children's Svcs., Danville, Ill., 1987-88; psychol. cons., Milford, Ill., 1993—. Instr. psychology Kankakee (Ill.) C.C., 1981-84, 89, Danville Area C.C., 1983-86; cons. evaluator Dept. Rehab. Svcs., Danville, 1981-85; mem. exec. bd. Tgn. and Edn. Coordinating Com., Champaign, Ill., 1985-93. Vol. reading programs sch. sys. Milford; tchr. religion Milford Christian Ch., 1992—2002, vocal soloist, music and drama ministry, 1992—2002. Mem. ACA, Ill. Assn. Mental Health Counselors, Evangel Coll. Alumni Assn. Avocations: hiking, playwriting, costume design, set construction, mentoring. Home: RR 3 Box 52D Milford IL 60953-9431

BEALL, ROBERT MATTHEWS, II, retail chain executive; b. Fresno, Calif., Aug. 7, 1943; s. Egbert Ruffin and Lynda Topp (Matthews) B.; m. Aldona Louise Kupchella, June 15, 1943; children: Jennifer, Lydia, Alexis, Robert. BSBA, U. Fla., 1965; MBA with distinction, NYU, 1969. Asst. buyer Bloomingdale's, N.Y.C., 1969-70; mgr. to CEO/chmn. bd. Beall's, Inc., Bradenton, Fla., 1970—. Bd. Fla. Power & Light Corp., Blue Cross Blue Shield Fla. Divsn. chmn. United Way, Bradenton, 1991; bd. dirs. St. Stephens Sch., Bradenton, 1977-80, Tilton (N.H.) Sch., 1988-92, Fla. Coun. Econ. Edn., 1992—. Capt. U.S. Army, 1965-67. Mem. Nat. Retail Fedn. (bd. dirs. 1982—), Fla. C. of C. (chmn. 1994), Fla. Coun. 100 (bd. dirs., exec. com.), Pi Kappa Phi. Episcopalian. Office: Beall's Inc PO Box 25207 Bradenton FL 34206-5207

BEALS, CLEM KIP, III, dentist; b. Springfield, Ohio, Mar. 7, 1949; s. Clem II and Betty Jane (Epley) B.; m. Mary Elizabeth Barry, June 10, 1974 (div. Feb. 1985); 1 child, Elizabeth Allison; m. Mary Margaret Ewing, June 8, 1985; 1 child, Andrew Jonathan. BS magna cum laude, Urbana (Ohio) Coll., 1971; DDS, Ohio State U., 1974. Resident in dentistry St. Elizabeth Hosp., Youngstown, Ohio, 1975-76; gen. practice dentistry Marion, Ohio, 1976—. Exec. dir. Marion County Dental Clinic, Marion, 1979-94; chmn. dept. dentistry Marion Gen. Hosp., 1984-87. NSF grantee, 1970. Mem. ADA (ho. of dels. 1997-2001), Ohio Dental Assn. (dist. coord. 1994-96, 2002--, ho. of dels. 1986—), Acad. Gen. Dentistry, Ctrl. Ohio Dental Soc. (v.p. 1986-87, pres. 1988-89), Marion Acad. Dentistry (pres. 1977, sec./treas. 1979—), Jaycees (bd. dirs Marion chpt. 1978-79), Kiwanis, Psi Omega (Achievement award 1974). Republican. Methodist. Avocations: flying, skiing. Home: 1025 Brookpark Rd Marion OH 43302-6815 Office: 396 E Church St Marion OH 43302-4106

BEALS, HERBERT KYLE, community planner, historian, consultant; b. Portland, Oreg., July 26, 1934; s. James Herbert and Mae Adelia (Thompson) B.; m. Barbara Carol Brown, Mar. 22, 1957; children: Patricia Louise, Cheryl Ann, Steven Kyle. BA in Social Sci., Portland (Oreg.) State U., 1958, MA in History, 1983. Planner, asst. dir. Clackamas County Planning Dept., Oregon City, 1957-65; planning cons. Bur. of Govt. Rsch., U. Oreg., Eugene, 1965-70; prin. planner Columbia Region Assn. of Govs., Portland, 1970-79; housing planner Met. Svc. Dist., Portland, 1979-80; with spl. projects Oreg. Hist. Soc., Portland, 1983-90; hist. cons. Gladstone, Oreg., 1990-96; ret., 1996. Editor, translator: For Honor and Country, 1985, Juan Pérez on the NW Coast, 1989; editor: Seeking Western Waters, 1995. Vol. Nat. Park Svc., Ft. Vancouver, 1974, USDA Forest Svc., Portland, 1981; commr. City Planning Commn., Gladstone, 1964-67, 72-76; commr. Portland Metro Area Boundary Commn., 1985-88, vice chair 1988; Mem. Pub. Libr. Bd., Gladstone, Oreg., 1996—, chair 1999—; mem. County Hist. Rev. Bd., Clackamas, Oreg., 1990-94, 96—, co-chair 1999—. Recipient John Lyman Book award N.Am. Soc. for Oceanic History, 1990. Mem. Oreg. Archaeol. Soc. (life; pres. 1971, 77), Oreg. Hist. Soc., Hakluyt Soc., Soc. for the History of Discoveries (bd. dirs.), Phi Alpha Theta. Avocation: numismatics. Home: 7005 Valley View Dr Gladstone OR 97027 E-mail: barbherb@aol.com.

BEALS, L(OREN) ALAN, association executive; b. Glens Falls, N.Y., Jan. 10, 1933; s. Edgar Vernon and Ruth (Ackley) B.; m. Sandra Gale Campbell, Feb. 26, 1982; children by previous marriage: Vernon Alan, Catherine Ann, Kimberly Ruth; stepchildren: Vicki Lynn Adair, Steven Montgomery Campbell, Gary Britt Campbell, Toby Lane Poston. BA, Colgate U., 1954; M.P.A., Syracuse U., 1955. Intern, City of Richmond, Va., 1955-56; adminstrv. asst. City of Norfolk, Va., 1956; dir. publs., dir. town affiliations Nat. League of Cities, Washington, 1957-59, dir. congl. relations, 1970, dir. fed. affairs, 1971, dep. dir., 1972-75, exec. dir., 1975-90. Exec. sec. Md. Municipal League, College Park, 1959-65; dir. econ. ops. programs Met. Fund, Detroit, 1965-66; sec. Pub. Ofcls. Adv. Coun., Office Econ. Opportunity, Washington, 1966-67, Great Lakes regional dir., Chgo., 1967-70; lectr. govt. and politics U. Md., 1959-65; chmn. Fed. Regional Coun., Chgo., 1968-69; lectr. U. So. Calif., L.A., 1977-81; founding trustee Cmty. Found., Silver Spring, Md., 1971-75; bd. dirs. Nat. Tng. and Devel. Svc., Washington, 1975-82, chmn., 1976-77; bd. dirs. Nat. Assn. Regional Couns., Washington, 1975-79, Coun. for Internat. Urban Liaison, Washington, 1975-85, chmn., 1980-82; bd. dirs. Pub. Tech., Inc., Washington, 1975-90, chmn., 1978-80, 83-85, 86-90; bd. dirs. Acad. for State and Local Govt., Washington 1975-90, United Way of Coastal Empire, Inc., 1995-98; chmn. Acad. for Contemporary Problems, 1977-78; bd. dirs. Ctr. for Renewal Resources, 1980-83; exec. com. Internat. Union Local Authorities, The Hague, 1985-90; pres., CEO Savannah Area C. of C., 1990-99; mem. Ga. Partnership for Excellence in Edn., 1990-99; exec. com. Savannah Olympic Support Coun., 1991-96; internat. mgmt. cons., 1999-. Contbg. editor: Nation's Cities Weekly, 1970-75, Editor-in-chief, 1975-90; editor: Md. Municipal News, 1959-65. Pres. Savannah Area Conv. and Visitors Bur., 1990-99, mgmt. cons., 1999--. Fellow Nat. Acad. Pub. Adminstrn (trustee 1978-81); mem. Am. Soc. Pub. Adminstrn., Internat. City Mgmt. Assn., City Club of Washington, Savannah Golf Club, Savannah Chatham Club, Savannah Rotary Club. Home: 117 Mcintosh Dr Savannah GA 31406-5245

BEALS, NANCY FARWELL, former state legislator; b. El Paso, July 21, 1938; d. Fred Whitcomb and Katharine Doane (Pier) Farwell; m. Richard William Beals, June 30, 1962; children: Katharine, Robert, Susannah. BA in Polit. Sci., Bryn Mawr Coll., 1960; MA in Teaching, Harvard U., 1961. Group leader Exptl. Internat. Living, Putney, Vt.; jr. high sch. tchr. Wincehster (Mass.) Pub. Schs., 1961-62; high sch. tchr. Hamden (Conn.) Pub. Schs., 1962-64; state rep. Conn. Gen. Assembly, Hartford, 1993—2003. Mem. state adv. coun. on spl. edn., 2000-02. Mem. various local and regional offices PTA, Chgo. and Hamden, 1970-83; local pres., state bd. dirs. LWV, Conn., 1979-92; mem., sec., chmn. Hamden Bd. Edn., 1983-92. Recipient Citizenship award for Conn. Philip Morris Corp., 1992, Hamden Notable award Friends of Hamden Libr., 1986, Children's Hero award Children's Trust Fund, 1995, Disting. Legislator award Conn. Assn. Bds. of Edn., 1998, Master Builder award Habitat for Humanity of Greater New Haven, 2002; named Legislator of Yr. Conn. Libr. Assn., 1994, Caucus of Conn. Dems., 1997, Conn. Coalition on Aging, 2002; Flemming fellow Ctr. for Policy Alternatives, 1995. Democrat.

BEALS, PAUL ARCHER, religious studies educator; b. Russell, Iowa, Feb. 18, 1924; s. Archer Edwin and Myrtle Mae (Kelsey) B.; m. Vivian Brown, Sept. 29, 1945; children: Lois Ruth, Stephen Paul, Samuel Archer, Timothy Joel. AB, Wheaton (Ill.) Coll., 1945; diploma, Moody Bible Inst., Chgo., 1948; ThM with high honors, Dallas Theol. Seminary, 1952, ThD, 1964. Missionary in Cen. African Republic Bapt. Mid-Missions, Cleve., 1952-64; prof. of missiology Grand Rapids (Mich.) Bapt. Seminary, 1964-97, prof. emeritus missiology, 1998—, dir. continuing edn., 1977-90. Theol. cons. Bapt. Mid-Missions, 1969-72, missionary emeritus, 2002--; conf. speaker. Author: A People for His Name, 1985, rev. edit., 1995; contbr. articles to profl. jours. Mem. Evang. Theol. Soc., Evang. Missiological Soc. (pres. 1990-93), Am. Soc. Missiology, Pi Gamma Mu. Home: 2111 Audley Dr NE Grand Rapids MI 49525-1517

BEALS, VAUGHN LE ROY, JR., retired motorcycle manufacturing executive; b. Cambridge, Mass., Jan. 2, 1928; s. Vaughn Le Roy and Pearl Uela (Wilmarth) B.; m. Eleanore May Woods, July 15, 1951; children: Susan Lynn, Laurie Jean. BS, M.I.T., 1948, MS, 1954. Research engr. Cornell Aero. Lab., Buffalo, 1948-52, MIT Aero Elastic and Structures Research Lab., 1952-55; dir. research and tech. N.Am. Aviation, Inc., Columbus, Ohio, 1955-65; exec. v.p. Cummins Engine Co., Columbus, Ind., 1965-70, also dir.; chmn. bd., chief exec. officer Formac Internat., Inc., Seattle, 1970-75; dep. group exec. Motorcycle Products Group, AMF Inc., Milw., 1975-77, v.p. and group exec. Stamford, Conn., 1977-81; chief exec. officer Harley-Davidson, Inc., Milw., 1981-89, chmn., 1981-96, chmn. emeritus, 1996—. Mem. Desert Mountain Club, Desert Forest Golf Club, Forest Highlands Golf Club. Home: PO Box 3260 Carefree AZ 85377-3260 Office: Harley-Davidson Inc Box 653 3700 W Juneau Ave Milwaukee WI 53208-2865

BEAM, CLARENCE ARLEN, judge; b. Stapleton, Nebr., Jan. 14, 1930; s. Clarence Wilson and Cecile Mary (Harvey) Beam; m. Betty Lou Fletcher, July 22, 1951; children: Randal, James, Thomas, Bradley, Gregory. BS, U. Nebr., 1951, JD, 1965. Feature writer Nebr. Farmer Mag., Lincoln, 1951; with sales dept. Steckley Seed Co., Mount Sterling, 1954—58, advt. mgr., 1958—63; from assoc. to ptnr. Chambers, Holland, Dudgeon & Knudsen, Berkheimer, Beam, et al, Lincoln, 1965—82; judge U.S. Dist. Ct. Nebr., Omaha, 1982—87, chief judge, 1986—87; cir. judge U.S. Ct. Appeals (8th cir.), 1987—. Mem. com. on lawyer discipline Nebr. Supreme Ct., 1974—82; mem. Conf. Commrs. on Uniform State Laws, 1979—, chmn. Nebr. sect., 1980—82; mem. jud. conf. com. on ct. and jud. security, 1989—93; chmn., 1992—93. Contbr. articles to profl. jours. Mem. Nebr. Rep. Ctrl. Com., 1970—78. Capt. U.S. Army, 1951—53, Korea. Scholar Regents, U. Nebr., Lincoln, 1947, Roscoe Pound scholar, 1964. Mem.: Nebr. State Bar Assn. Office: US Ct Appeals 8th Cir 435 Federal Bldg 100 Centennial Mall N Lincoln NE 68508-3859

BEAM, JAMES CARROLL (JIM BEAM), retired newspaper editor; b. Cameron, La., Oct. 7, 1933; s. Charles Cleveland and Carrie (Welch) B.; m. Jo Ann Drachenberg, Aug. 20, 1954; children: Jamie Lynn Meek, Bryan Carroll. BA, McNeese State, 1955; MA, La. State, 1962. Tchr. Calcasieu Sch. Bd., Lake Charles, La., 1958-62; reporter Lake Charles (La.) Am. Press, 1962-65, city editor, 1965-81, co-editor, 1981-92, editor, 1992-98, dir. polit. and pub. affairs, 1998-99. Lt. U.S. Army, 1955-57. Recipient 1st place column La. Press Assn., 1979, Hal Boyle award La. Miss AP Assn., 1985-86, 1st place Personal Column, 1997. Mem.: Phi Kappa Phi. Democrat. Methodist. Home: 4824 Gentilly St Lake Charles LA 70607-6341

BEAM, JEFFERY SCOTT, poet, editor; b. Concord, NC, Apr. 4, 1953; s. Robert Wesley and Allie Mae Ervin Beam; m. Debra Jo Bost, Oct. 10, 1971 (div. Apr. 1980); life ptnr.: Stanley Green Finch, May, 15, 1980. B of Creative Arts in Writing, U. N.C., 1975. Editor Sanskrit Lit. Mag., Charlotte, N.C., 1974-75; asst. to biology libr. U. N.C., Chapel Hill, 1983—; poetry editor Oyster Boy Rev., San Francisco, 1997—. Author: (poetry) An Elizabethan Bestiary: Retold, 1999 (Ten Best Books Ind. Pub. award, 50 Books award Am. Inst. for Graphic Arts 1999), Light & Shadow, 1997, little, 1997, Submergences, 1997, Visions of Dame Kind, 1995, The Fountain, 1992, Midwinter Fires, 1990, The Golden Legend, 1981; (CD) What We Have Lost: New and Selected Poems, 1977-2001, 2002, New Growth: New Songs and Poems, 2002; author, librettist: (song cycle) The Life of the Bee, 2000; actor, storyteller, singer, performer Winter Stories for Children of All Ages, 1993--. Vice-chair U. N.C. Employee Forum, Chapel Hill, 1998-99. Recipient Office of Provost Pub. Svc. award U. N.C. Ctr. for Pub. Svc., 2000; grantee Mary Duke Biddle Found., 1998-99, Emerging Artist grantee Orange County Arts Coun., 1991; An Elizabethan Bestiary: Retold exhbn. named Best Art Exhibit During 1998-99 Sch. Yr., Duke U. Chronicle, 1998-99. Mem. N.C. Writers Network, N.C. Writers Conf. Office: Oyster Boy Rev PO Box 83 Chapel Hill NC 27514 E-mail: jeffbeam@email.unc.edu.

BEAM, ROBERT CHARLES, lawyer; b. Phila., Dec. 21, 1946; s. Thomas Joseph and Jeannette Hortense (Templin) B.; m. Maureen McCauley, Aug. 21, 1976.; children: Davis McCauley B., Morgan McCauley B. BS in Commerce and Engring. Scis., Drexel U., 1970; JD, Temple U., 1977. Bar: U.S. Patent Office 1976, Pa. 1977, U.S. Dist. Ct. (ea. dist.) Pa. 1977, N.Y. 1978, D.C. 1979, U.S. Ct. Customs and Patent Appeals 1980, U.S. Ct. Appeals (3d and fed. cirs.) 1982, N.J. 1983, U.S. Dist. Ct. N.J. 1983, Can. Patent Office 1985. Law clk. U.S. Dist. Ct., Phila., 1976-77; assoc. Firzpatrick, Cella, Harper & Scinto, N.Y.C., 1977-79; patent atty. Hercules Inc., Wilmington, Del., 1979-81, CPC Internat. Inc., Englewood Cliffs, N.J., 1981-83; patent counsel and asst. gen. counsel Congoleum Corp., Kearny, N.J., 1983-85, pvt. practice, 1985—. Mem. ABA, Phila. Bar Assn., D.C. Bar Assn., Phila. Patent Law Assn., Am. Intellectual Property Law Assn. Office: U City Sci Ctr Office 3624 Market St Philadelphia PA 19104-2614

BEAM, WILLIAM WASHINGTON, III, data coordinator; b. L.A., Jan. 21, 1960; s. William Washington and Frances (Towler) Beam. BS, UCLA, 1982; MA, U. Wash., 1985. Paralegal Arco, L.A., 1985-88, programmer, 1988-90, data coord., 1990-94, network adminstr., 1994-98; network analyst ARCO IT, L.A., 1998—2000, Brit. Petroleum, L.A., 2000—01, SAIC, L.A., 2001—. Mem.: IEEE, Computer Soc. of IEEE, Am. Econ. Assn. Office: BP 333 S Hope St Ste E212 Los Angeles CA 90071-1406

BEAMAN, ANN THOMSON, volunteer; b. Waukon, Iowa, May 10, 1933; d. Andrew and Ruth Augusta (Ludeking) Thomson; m. Robert L. Beaman, June 25, 1955; children: Roderick Lewis, Alerick Robert, Scott Andrew. BA in Journalism, U. Mont., 1955; postgrad., U. South Fla., autumn 1983, 84. Adminstr. TV programming, radio local news, women's program Bozeman (Mont.) Cable TV, 1955-56; with Sta. KBMN-AM, Bozeman, 1955-56; salesperson Sewing Circle Fabrics, St. Petersburg, Fla., 1978-79, Tall Girl Fashions, St. Petersburg, 1979-80; asst. store mgr. Motherhood Maternity, St. Petersburg, 1980-81; office mgr. Accurate Personnel, St. Petersburg, 1981-82; exec. sec. to State Senator Jeanne Malchon, St. Petersburg, 1982-92; exec. sec. Spkr. Fla. House, Peter Wallace, 1993—96. Den leader, coach Boy/Cub Scouts Am., Woodland Hills, Calif., 1967-71; mem. exec. bd. local PTA, Woodland Hills, 1972-74, St. Petersburg, 1976, Step Ahead, Inc.; pres. Welcome Wagon, St. Petersburg, 1977; sec., mem. newsletter staff Broadwater Civic Assn. Mem. Ord. Ea. Star. Democrat. Presbyterian. Avocations: sewing, skiing. Home: 4348 43rd St S Saint Petersburg FL 33711-4420

BEAMAN, MARY ANINA, psychiatric nurse, educator; b. Alexandria, Va., May 21, 1956; d. Chester Earl and Mary Ruth Beaman; children: Kayla, Bonny, Mary Ruth, Belle, Emily. AA, Luther Rice Coll., 1974; BA with honors, Randolph-Macon U., 1977; AAS in Nursing, John Tyler Sch. Nursing, 1991; MS, Capella U., 2002. RNC, Va.; cert. med. asst.; cert. childbirth educator. Staff nurse Richmond (Va.) Met. Hosp., 1992, Richmond Meml. Hosp., 1992, Medshares Home Care, Richmond and, Charlottesville, 1992-96; adminstr. Comprehensive Home Care, Lovingston, Va., 1996-97; prof. Nat. Bus. Coll., Charlottesville, 1996-98; instr. Fishburne Mil. Sch., Waynesboro, Va., 1997-98; subject area coord. Bryant & Stratton Coll., Richmond, 1993-96, 98—. Owner Positive Transitions, Richmond, 1981—. Contbr. articles, revs. to profl. publs. Disaster health coord. ARC, Charlottesville, 1996—, disaster team leader, Nelson County, 1996-99, health and safety educator, Richmond and Charlottesville, 1993—; medication trainer ARC of the Piedmont Charlottesville, 2000—. Mem.: ACOG (edn. assoc.), Va. Soc. Med. Assts., Am. Assn. Med. Asst. (test writer 1997—), Assn. Women Health Ob/Gyn Neonatal Nurses. Republican. Mem. Ch. of Christ. Avocations: singing, writing, archery, belly dancing. Home: 3242 Rockfish Valley Hwy Nellysford VA 22958-2202 Office: Bryant & Stratton 8141 Hull Street Rd Richmond VA 23235-6411 E-mail: nabeaman@bryantstratton.edu.

BEAMON, GENA R. human resources specialist; b. L.A. d. Robert Beamon Sr. and Shirley J. Lee; m. Moses N. Chenevert, July 1, 1978 (div. Oct. 1986); children: Aisha M. Chenevert, Kaliph C. Chenevert. BA in Mgmt. Human Resources, Spring Arbor Coll., 1996; MS in Gen. Adminstrn., Ctrl. Mich. U., 2000; M in Info. Tech., Am. Intercontinental U., 2002. Admissions and collections clk. Riverside County, 1987-89, group counselor, 1989-90; adminstrv. asst. U. Mich., Flint, 1990-91; recruiter, cons., ptnr. E & G Personnel Svcs., 1994-98; account coord. Temp. Resources Inc., 1996-97; adminstrv. asst. Aramark Corp., 1997; human resources coord. Glovia Internat. LLC, 1997-98; from industry staffing cons. to sch. dir. Advanced Computing Inst., Inc., 1998-99; cons., owner G B Cons. Team, 1998—; human resources generalist prof. HR Only, 1999. Trustee Minority Women's Network, Detroit, 1991-97; liaison Cmty. Found., Flint, 1993; v.p. Palm Desert PTO, 1994. Mem. Soc. Human Resources Mgmt., Toastmasters Internat. Republican. African Methodist. Avocations: hiking, skiing, paintings, sewing, travel. Home: 73700 Hwy 111 # 2111 Palm Desert CA 92260 Office: G B Cons Team 1232 W 109th St Los Angeles CA 90044 E-mail: gbcteam@earthlink.net.

BEAN, BENNETT, artist; b. Cin., Mar. 25, 1941; s. William Bennett and Abigail (Shepard) B.; m. Cathy Bao, Dec. 17, 1966; 1 child, William Bao. Student, Grinnell Coll., 1959-62; postgrad., U. Iowa, 1963, U. Wash., 1963; MFA, Claremont Grad. Sch., 1966. Asst. prof. art Wagner Coll., S.I., N.Y., 1966-79. Trustee Am. Craft Enterprises, New Paltz, N.Y., 1982-85, Am. Craft Coun., N.Y.C., 1980-84; former chmn. bd. dirs. Peters Valley, Layton, N.J. One-man show Royal Marks Gallery, N.Y.C., 1969, Henri Gallery, Washington, 1969; one-person retrospective exhbn. lifetime work Ark. Arts Ctr. Decorative Arts Mus.; exhibited in numerous groups show, including Whitney Mus. Am. Art, 1968-69, Newark Mus., 1968, 80, 89, 91, Am. Craft Mus. II, 1982, 86, N.J. State Mus., 19i4, Newport Art Mus., 1984, Hunter Mus., Chattanooga, 1990; represented in permanent collections Whitney Mus. Am. Art, The White House, Washington, Boston Mus. Fine Arts, Newark Mus., N.J. State Mus., St. Louis Mus. Art, Royal Ont. Mus., Ariz. State U., Grinnell Coll., Milw. Art Mus., Crocker Art Mus., Calif., Toledo Mus. Art, Cin. Art Mus., J.P. Speed Art Mus., Ky., others. Recipient editorial award Met. Home mag., 1990; rsch. grantee Wagner Coll., 1968, 70, 77, 78; fellow N.J. Coun. on Arts, 1978, 88, Nat. Endowment for Arts, 1980. Tibetan Buddhist. Studio: 357 County Road 661 Blairstown NJ 07825-4054

BEAN, BRUCE WINFIELD, lawyer; b. Albany, N.Y., Dec. 19, 1941; s. William Joseph and Ruth Elizabeth (Lafferty) B.; m. Barbara Bryant Hunting; children: Austin Bryant, Ashley Elizabeth. AB, Brown U., 1964; JD, Columbia U., 1972. Bar: N.Y. 1973, Calif. 1981. Law clk. to judge U.S. Ct. Appeals (2d cir.), 1972-73; assoc. Simpson Thacher & Bartlett, N.Y.C., 1973-76, Patterson, Belknap, Webb & Tyler, N.Y.C., 1976-80; counsel fin. and planning Atlantic Richfield, Los Angeles, 1980-85; exec. v.p., gen. counsel AmBase Corp.

(formerly The Home Group Inc.), N.Y.C., 1985-91; ptnr. Coudert Bros., Moscow, 1995—98; ptnr., head corp. dept. Clifford Chance, Moscow, 1998—2002, counsel, 2002—. Col. USAFR, 1964-86. Mem. Calif. Bar Assn., N.Y. State Bar Assn. (former chmn. spl. com. on vets. affairs), City of N.Y. Bar Assn., Am. C. of C. in Russia (bd. dirs. 1996—, chmn. bd. 1998-2000), Russian Inst. of Corp. Law and Governonce (dir.).

BEAN, CRAIG BAYLOR, music educator; b. Middlebury, Vt., Oct. 12, 1951; s. Robert Henry and Emma Baylor Bean; m. Norma M. Mallory, Apr. 18, 1952; children: Victor, Kelly, Norman. Edn. Specialist, Troy State U., 1990. Cert. K-12 music tchr. Ga. Band dir. Deerfield Sch., Albany, Ga., 1973—76, Bacon County Schools, Alma, Ga., 1976—80, Albany (Ga.) H.S., 1980—87, Radium Springs Mid. Sch., Albany, 1987—92, Worth County Mid. Sch., Sylvester, Ga., 1992—. Band dir. Darton Coll., Albany, 1996—2000, Ga. Lions All State Band, 2001—; music dir. Morningside United Meth. Ch., Albany, 1980—. Dir.(band performance): Ga. Music Educators Conf., 1999, 2003, Southeastern U.S. Mid. Sch. Band Clinic, 2000 (Outstanding Svc., 2000), 2003. Recipient Citation of Excellence, Nat. Band Assn., 2003. Mem.: NEA, Music Educators Nat. Conf., Ga. Assn. Educators, Ga. Music Educators Assn. (vice chmn. 1996—98, chmn. dist. 2 1998—2000). Avocations: auto racing, water sports, travel. Home: 168 Berkeley Rd Albany GA 31707 Office: Worth County Mid Sch 1305 North Isabela St Sylvester GA 31791 Home Fax: none; Office Fax: 229-776-8624. Personal E-mail: music_bean@hotmail.com. E-mail: none.

BEAN, FRANK D(AWSON), sociology and demography educator; b. May 20, 1942; s. Frank Dawson and Alta Louzana (Scott) B.; m. Carolyn P. Boyd, Jan. 4, 1975; children: Alan McDavid, Deborah Scott, Peter Justin, Michael Franklin. Student, Oberlin Coll., 1960-62; BA, U. Ky., 1964; MA, Duke U., 1965, PhD, 1970. Asst. prof. sociology U. Tex., Austin, 1968-71, assoc. prof., 1972-78, prof., 1978-85, Ashbel Smith prof. sociology, 1986-99, dept. chmn., 1978-84; asst. prof. Ind. U., Bloomington, 1971-72; dir. Population Rsch. Ctr., U. Tex., Austin, 1995-98; prof. sociology U. Calif., Irvine, 1999—. Dir. Population Studies Ctr., The Urban Inst., Washington, 1988-89. Co-author: (with Marta Tienda) The Hispanic population of the U.S., 1989; editor: (with Jurgen Schmandt and Sidney Weintraub) Mexican and Central American Population: Implications for U.S. Immigration Policy, 1989, (with C. Vernez and C. Keely) Opening and Closing the Doors: Evaluating Immigration Reform and Control, 1989, (with B. Edmonston and J. Passel) Undocumented Migration to the United States: IRCA and the Experience of the 1980s, 1990, (with Stephanie Bell-Rose) Immigration and Opportunity: Race, Ethnicity and Employment in the United States, 1999. Recipient numerous grants. Mem. Am. Sociol. Assn., Population Assn. Am., So. Sociol. Soc., Sociol. Rsch. Assn., Southwestern Social Sci. Assn. Office: U Calif Dept Sociology Irvine CA 92697-0001

BEAN, GLEN ATHERTON, entrepreneur; b. Mpls., Aug. 30, 1962; s. Douglas Atherton Bean and Eleanor Green (Caswell) Nolan; m. Mary Catherine Slingsby, June 16, 1990. BS, Ariz. State U., 1988. Promotion specialist John Deere & Co., Waterloo, Iowa, 1987; regional mgr. Elliott Meat Co., Duluth, Minn., 1989-90; gen. ptnr. No. Star Food Brokerage, Savage, Minn., 1990-92; pres. Rochester (Minn.) Bus. Group, Ltd., 1993-98, Hunter Holdings Ltd., Savage, 1998—. Dir. McGab Agribusiness Scholar., Ariz. State Univ., 1989—. Media coord. U.S. Olympic Festival, Mpls. 1990; vol. Multiple Sclerosis Soc., 1989-2000; founder Ariz. State Univ. Agribus. Speakers Bur., 1987; bd. mem. alumni assn. Phoenix County Day Sch., Phoenix, 1983-89; guarantor Minn. Orch. Mem. Nat. Cattlemens Assn., Ariz. Cattle Growers Assn., Clan MacBean in N.Am., Universidad Iberoamaericana (assoc.), Ducks Unlimited (publicity chmn. Phoenix 1986-88, dinner chmn. Burnsville 1990, 91, zone chmn. 1992-99, dist. chmn. 2000—, state conv. chmn. 1998-99), State Feather Soc. (chair 1999—), Trout Unlimited, T.C. Pub. TV, U.S.A. Shooting, Nat. Geog. Soc., Minn. Waterfowl Assn., Izaak Walton League, Nat. Wild Turkey Fedn., Nat. Sporting Clays Assn., Nat. Skeet Shooting Assn., NRA, PGA Tour/Ptnrs. Club, USGA, Pheasants Forever, D.U. Can. (life), Ariz. State U. Alumni Assn., Mpls. Inst. Arts, Minn. Hist. Soc., Bell Mus. Natural History, Sci. Mus. Minn., Minn. Zoo, Mustang Club Am., Sigma Nu. Republican. Episcopalian. Avocations: hunting, camping, conservation, internat. travel. Office: Hunter Holdings Ltd PO Box 276 Savage MN 55378-0276

BEAN, JUDITH MATTSON, academic administrator, educator; d. Charles Dudley Mattson and Elsie Mae Porter; m. Charles Morris Bean, Dec. 26, 1965 (div. July 1, 1985); children: Margaret Ann, David Austin. BA, Sam Houston State Univ., Huntsville, Tex., 1966, MA, 1988; PhD, Tex. A & M Univ., Coll. Sta., Tex., 1992. Secondary tchr. Buna Ind. Sch. Dist., Buna, Tex., 1962—64, Kirbyville Ind. Sch. Dist., Kirbyville, Tex., 1984—89; prof. Prairie View A & M Univ., Prairie View, Tex., 1993—94, Tex. Women's Univ., Denton, Tex., 1994—2001, asst. v.p. acad. affairs, 2002—. Cons. Univ. Mass. Press, Amherst, Mass., 2001—02. Co-author: Margaret Fuller Critic: Writings from the New York Tribune 1844-1846, 2000; contbr. chapters to books, articles to profl. jour. Bd. mem., newsletter editor League of Women Voters, Denton, Tex., 2003—. Mem.: Margaret Fuller Soc., Phi Kappa Phi. Office: Tex Womens Univ Denton TX 76204

BEAN, MAURICE DARROW, retired diplomat; b. Gary, Ind., Sept. 9, 1928; s. Everett Thomas and Vera Mae (Curry) B.; m. Dolores J. Winston, Apr. 9, 1972; children: Linda D., Karen M., Laura L., James W., Jennifer J. BA in Govt., Howard U., 1950; MA in Social and Tech. Assistance, Haverford Coll., 1953; postgrad., cert., Sch. Advanced Internat. Studies, Johns Hopkins, 1959. With U.S. Bur. Census, 1950-51, AID, 1951-61; with Peace Corps, 1961-66, ops. officer for, 1961-62, regional program officer for, 1962-63, dep. regional dir., 1963-64, dir., 1964-66, Malaysia and Singapore affairs Bur. East. Asian and Pacific Affairs, Dept. State, 1966-70; mem. Sr. Seminar in Fgn. Policy, 1970-71; Am. consul Ibadan, Nigeria, 1971—73; dep. chief mission Am. Embassy, Monrovia, Liberia, 1973-76, sr. fgn. service insp., 1976—77; amb. to Union of Burma, 1977—79; diplomat-in-residence Case Western Res. U., Cleve., 1979-80; State Dept. adv. to comdr. Air U., Maxwell AFB, Ala., 1980-86. Active Neighbors, Inc., Washington; bd. dirs. Watts Health Charities, L.A. Recipient Superior Honor award Dept. State, 1977, Outstanding Service award Gary Host and Hostess Club, 1979, Benjamin Hooks award NAACP, 1980, Meritorious Civilian Svc. award USAF, 1986, Meritorious Svc. award U.S. Dept. State, 1986; Named to Roosevelt High Sch. Hall of Fame, 1980; Christopher Reynolds Found. fellow, 1953; William E. Mosher Meml. scholar, 1961. Mem. Am. Fgn. Svc. Assn., Am. Sch. Assn., Manila, Urban League, Royal Bangkok Club, Sports Club (life), Omega Psi Phi. Home and Office: 285 E California Blvd Apt 308 Pasadena CA 91106-3645 *Opportunity does not knock. It must be sought, pursued, developed and, ultimately, utilized to the fullest.*

BEAN, SUSAN MONTGOMERY, secondary education educator; b. Knoxville, Tenn., Mar. 19, 1928; d. Gerald McCall and Helen Irene (Montgomery) Bean. BS, East Tenn. State U., 1971; MEd, Ga. State U., 1980, EDS in Edn., 1987. English tchr. 7th grade Fountain Jr. High Sch., Forest Park, Ga., 1972-76; English tchr. 8th grade Babb Jr. High Sch., Forest Park, 1976-77; English tchr. 10th, 11th and 12th grades North Clayton High Sch., College Park, Ga., 1977 79; English tchr. Riverdale (Ga.) High Sch., 1979-92. *Susan has worked for years as a tireless feminist for the National Organization for Women, making as many financial contributions as possible. She, as well as her father, were constantly trying to improve the status of women. Susan has considered running for political office herself, for that she believes, is one-way women will finally attain equality. Susan firmly believes that many women to this day do not realize how they are constantly discriminated against in small and enormous ways on a daily basis and has tried to enlighten them to all of there potentialities and possibilities.Served on the CCEA Legislative Committee in 1989, 1990, 1991, 1992. Served as a Lobbyist at the Georgia State Capitol for better working conditions for teachers, plus higher salaries in 1989, 1990, 1991, 1992. NRTA-National Retired Teachers Association 2002- a division of AARP- to present given award for outstanding contributions in making her high school a 1990 Georgia School of Excellence, 1991. Ms. Susan Bean has tirelessly, vigilantly, and persistently, through a plethora of Federal and STATE LEGAL ACTIONS, made available to the disabled and handicapped of the state of Georgia facilities, programs, and services in 1990 until the present that were not present before then. These efforts as the Association Representative for her county Education Association caused Ms. Bean the loss of her career as a teacher in 1993! Nominated by the Faculty of Georgia State University and inducted into Kappa Delta Pi, an international Honor Society for educators who have made outstanding contributions to education. Ms. Bean, for the lack of a better word is called a "Whistleblower," it should be noted here that TIME Magazines Dec. 30th Persons of the Year for 2002 were three female Whistleblowers- (cover Dec. 30th 2002).* Mem. NOW, 1973—, Nat. Women's Polit. Caucus, 1980—, Ga. Women's Polit. Caucus, 1980—, Cumberland Jaycees, 1987, 88. Mem. NAFE, NEA (life, Outstanding Contbns. award 1990), Ga. Assn. Educators (life, Make It Happen award 1988, Outstanding Contbn. award 1989, 91), Clayton County Edn. Assn. (assn. rep. 1986-92, mem. exec. bd. 1989-91, Outstanding Leadership as local assn. rep. award 1987-88, Outstanding Contbns. to exec. bd. award 1989-91), Nat. Coun. Tchrs. English, Kappa Delta Pi. Democrat. Presbyterian. As Ga. Assn. Ed. rep. made services available to disabled and handicapped students through various legal actions. Home: 4247 Laurel Brook Dr Smyrna GA 30082-4318

BEANE, FRANK LLEWELLYN, lawyer; b. Canton, Ohio, Feb. 17, 1943; s. Frank Clarence and Lillian Ruth (Powell) B.; m. Patricia Jean Johnson, Sept. 16, 1967; children— Frank Clarence II, Adam Tyler. B.A., Central State U., Wilberforce, Ohio, 1965; J.D., U. Toledo, 1972. Bar: Ohio 1973, U.S. Dist. Ct. (no. dist.) Ohio 1973, U.S. Ct. Appeals (6th cir.) 1973. Asst. prosecutor Canton Police, 1973-74; pub. defender U.S. Dist. Ct. (no. dist.) Ohio, Cleve., 1974-81; assoc. Matecheck, Ferrero, and Stefanko, Massillon, Ohio, 1981— . Bd. dirs. Urban League, Massillon, 1981—, Boy's Club, Massillon, 1984— . Republican. Home: 1134 3rd St SE Massillon OH 44646-8029 Office: 46 Federal Ave NW Massillon OH 44647-5467

BEANE, JERRY LYNN, lawyer; b. Winnsboro, Tex., Mar. 3, 1944; s. Von Rhea and Charlene (Hawkins) Beane; children: Lucynda, Todd. BA, Baylor U., 1965; JD, 1967. Bar: Tex. 1967, US Dist. Ct. (no. dist.)/Tex. 1968, US Ct. Appeals (5th cir.) 1970, US Dist. Ct. (so. dist.)/Ga. 1971, US Supreme Ct. 1972, US Dist. Ct. (ea. dist.)/Tex. 1972, US Ct. Appeals (10th cir.) 1979, US Ct. Appeals (11th cir.) 1982. Assoc. Strasburger & Price, Dallas, 1967—73; ptnr., 1974; adj. prof. law So. Meth. U. Law Sch., 1989—94; editor in chief Baylor Law Ref., 1967. Contbr. articles. Mem.: Tex. Bar Assn., Baylor Law Sch. Alumni Assn., Baylor Ex-Editors Assn., Dallas Assn. Young Lawyers (pres. 1973, chmn. continuing legal edn. com. 1979, chmn. bar activities com. 1980), ABA, Dallas County Health Com. (mem. 1978), Dallas Commn. on Children and Youth (mem. 1977—78), DAC Country, City. Bapt. Office: Strasburger & Price PO Box 50100 901 Main St Ste 4300 Dallas TX 75202-3724

BEANE, JUDITH MAE, psychologist; b. Durham, N.C., Mar. 28, 1944; d. Joseph William Sr. and Antoinette Gwathmey (Dew) B. BA, Campbell U., 1967; MRE, Golden Gate Bapt. Theol. Sem., Mill Valley, Calif., 1972; PhD, Profl. Sch. of Psychology, San Francisco, 1988. Lic. psychologist, Calif.; mental health therapist II, Northern Neck-Middle Peninsula Cmty. Svcs. Bd., 1995-97; cert. rehab. provider. Home missionary So. Bapt. Home Mission Bd., Atlanta, 1967-69; loan officer Coop Credit Union, Corte Madera, Calif., 1969-70; emergency svcs. specialist Community Action Marin, San Rafael, 1976-78; program coord. Marin Treatment Ctr., San Rafael, Calif., 1980-85; church sec. St. Paul's Episcopal Church, San Rafael, 1979-81; psychol. intern Raleigh Hills Hosp., Redwood City, Calif., 1984; psychol. asst. Lic. Psychologists, San Anselmo, Calif., 1985-92; bd. dirs. The Open Door Ministries, Inc., Sausalito, Calif., 1971—; psychologist Mill Valley, Calif., 1992-93; mng. dir. Ch. Resource Svcs. Inc., Lancaster, Va., 1997-2001; deacon Kilmarnock Bapt. Ch., Lancaster, Va., 1996—99. Cons. Ross (Calif.) Hosp., 1991; guest spkr. Turn on Marin, San Rafael, Calif., 1985; coord. rural domestic violence project MP-NN CSB, 2001—02; outreach therapist Youth and Family Svcs., 2002, mental health therapist II, 2002—. Recipient award Marin County People Speaking, 1985. Mem. APA (assoc.), Calif. State Psychol. Assn., Am. Counseling Assn., Am. Assn. Christian Counselors. Baptist. Avocations: handcrafts, reading. Home: PO Box 172 Lancaster VA 22503-0172

BEAR, DAVID GEORGE, b. Tucson, July 18, 1950; s. Leon and Naomi (Dumes) B.; m. Ruth Elinor Monson, June 29, 1972. BS, U. Ariz., 1972; PhD, U. Calif., Santa Cruz, 1978. Rsch. assoc. U. Oreg., Inst. Molecular Biology, Eugene, 1978-82; asst. prof. cell biology U. N.Mex. Sch. Medicine, Albuquerque, 1982-88, assoc. prof. cell biology, 1988-94, dir. biomed. sci. grad. program, 1990-94, prof. cell biology, 1994-97, prof., chmn. cell biology & physiology, 1997— Cancer ctr. molecular genetics program dir. U. N.Mex., 1988-97; panel mem. biochem. genetics NSF, Washington, 1993-96; program dir. Steve Schiff Ctr. Skin Cancer, 1998-2001. Mem. Am. Soc. Cell Biology, RNA Soc., Microscopy Soc. Am., Am. Chem. Soc. Achievements include research of electron microscopy of gene expression. Office: U N Mex Cancer Ctr 900 Camino De Salud NE Albuquerque NM 87131-0001

BEAR, FREDERICK THOMAS, educator; b. Wilmington, Del., July 31, 1937; s. Frederick Thomas Sr. and Ruth (Kishbach) B.; m. Lynn Everard, Dec. 31, 1960; children: Laura Bear Smith, Wendy. BBA, Westminster Coll., 1959; MBA, U. N.C., 1960; PhD, U. Ga., 1973. Account mgmt. trainee Campbell Soup Co., Camden, N.J., 1961-63; prof. Wesley Coll., Dover, Del., 1963-66, Austin Peay State U., Clarksville, Tenn., 1966-69, 72-76, Western Carolina U., Cullowhee, N.C., 1976-82, Stetson U., DeLand, Fla., 1982—, prof. fin. emeritus, 2000—. Adj. prof. Murray (Ky.) State U., Pace-Priory Sch., Kingston, Jamaica, 1981; cons. Small Bus. Inst., Cullowhee, 1978-82, Ctr. Improving Mountain Living, Cullowhee, 1978-82; rsch. assoc. Bus. Rsch. Mgmt. Ctr., USAF, Dayton, Ohio, 1980. Editl. staff Fin. Edn., 1972-73; reviewer Merrill Pub. Co., Columbus, Ohio, 1989; contbr. articles to profl. jours. Adv. Cumberland Valley Coun. Girl Scouts U.S., Clarksville, 1972-76; pres. PTO, Clarksville, 1975-76; solicitor Heart Fund, DeL an, 1988—. NDEA fellow U. Ga., 1969-72. Mem. So. Fin. Assn., Ea. Fin. Assn., Fin. Mgmt. Assn., Lions (pres. Sylva chpt. 1980-81, treas. DeLand chpt. 1988-90, Man Yr. 1981). Republican. Methodist. Avocations: swimming, model trains, woodworking. Home: 1057 Torchwood Dr Deland FL 32724-9400

BEAR, GERALDINE M. nursing assistant, poet; b. Spartanburg, SC, Mar. 6, 1926; d. Clarence Lee and Lucy Bell Hayes; m. Samuel Sidney Bear, Apr. 8, 1945; children: Diana L., Russell M., Joseph J. Student, Edgecombe Acad., 1943. Cert. nursing asst., CPR, RN home health aide. Author: (poems) Dedications of Love, 1974, The Poetry Seed, 1991. Deacon, mem. choir Grace Presbyn. Ch., Springhill, Fla., 1975—79. Avocations: oil painting, sewing, decorating.

BEAR, GREGORY DALE, writer, illustrator; b. San Diego, Aug. 20, 1951; s. Dale Franklin and Wilma (Merriman) B.; m. Astrid May Anderson, June 18, 1983; children: Erik William, Alexandra. AB in English, San Diego State U., 1973. Tech. writer, host Reuben H. Fleet Space Theater, 1973; freelance writer, 1975—. Author: Hegira, 1979, Psychlone, 1979, Beyond Heaven's River, 1980, Strength of Stones, 1981, The Wind From a Burning Woman, 1983, The Infinity Concerto, 1984, Blood Music, 1985, Eon, 1985, The Serpent Mage, 1986, The Forge of God, 1987, Eternity, 1988, Tangents, 1989, Heads, 1990, Queen of Angels, 1990, Anvil of Stars, 1992, Moving Mars, 1993 (Nebula award 1994), Songs of Earth and Power, 1993, Legacy, 1995, Slant, 1997, Dinosaur Summer, 1998 (Endeavor award 1999), Foundation and Chaos, 1998, Darwin's Radio, 1999 (Endeavor award 2000, Nebula award 2001), Rogue Planet, 2000, Vitals, 2002, Darwin's Children, 2003, Collected Short Stories of Greg Bear, 2003; short stories: Blood Music (Hugo and Nebula awards), 1983, Hardfought (Nebula award), 1993, Tangents (Hugo and Nebula awards), 1987; editor: New Legends, 1995. Cons. Citizen's Adv. Council on Nat. Space Policy, Tarzana, Calif. Mem. Sci. Fiction Writers of Am. (editor Forum 1983-84, chmn. grievance com. 1985-86, v.p. 1987, pres. 1988-90). Avocations: book collecting, science, music, movies, history. Home: 506 Lakeview Rd Lynnwood WA 98037-2141

BEAR, JEFFREY LEWIS, lawyer; b. L.A., Apr. 16, 1947; s. Bernard and Rhoda B.; m. Linda Grodman Bear Snibbe (div.); 1 child, Ryan Steven; m. P. Renee LoCascio, Aug. 9, 1997. BA in Polit. Sci., Calif. State U., Northridge, 1968; JD, Loyola U., 1971. Bar: Calif. 1972, U.S. Dist. Ct. (cen. dist.) Calif. 1972, U.S. Ct. Appeals (9th cir.) 1972. Dep. atty. gen. Calif. Atty. Gen., L.A., 1971-73; dep. pub. defender L.A. County Pub. Defender, L.A., 1973-77; ptnr. Sommer & Bear, Beverly Hills, Calif., 1977—. Mem. arbitrator panel L.A. Superior Ct.; mem. pro tem panel L.A. Mcpl. Ct., Beverly Hills Mcpl. Ct.; spkr. in field. Co-author: Drunk Driving Trial Seminar Syllabus, 1977, 78, 79, Defense of Drunk Driving Cases, 1978—. Fellow Loyola U. Sch. Law, 1968. Mem. State Bar Calif. (mem. litig. sect.), L.A. County Bar Assn. (mem. litig. sect.), Beverly Hills Bar Assn., Consumer Attys. Assn. L.A., Porsche Club Am. (L.A. region), Profl. Assn. Diving Instrs. Office: Sommer & Bear 9777 Wilshire Blvd Ste 512 Beverly Hills CA 90212-1905

BEAR, LARRY ALAN, lawyer, educator; b. Melrose, Mass., Feb. 28, 1928; s. Joseph E. and Pearl Florence B.; m. Rita Maldonado, Mar. 29, 1975; children: Peter, Jonathan, Steven. BA, Duke U., 1949; JD, Harvard U., 1953; LLM, (James Kent fellow), Columbia U., 1966. Bar: Mass. 1953, PR 1963, NY 1967. Trial lawyer Bear & Bear, Boston, 1953-60; cons. legal medicine P.R. Dept. Justice, 1960-65; prof. law sch. U. P.R., 1960-65; legal counsel, then commr. addiction svcs. City of NY, 1967-70; dir. Nat. Action Com. Drug Edn. U. Rochester, NY, 1970-77; pvt. practice NYC, 1970-82; pub. affairs radio broadcaster Sta. WABC, NYC, 1970-82; US legal counsel Master Enterprises of P.R., 1982-90. Vis. prof. legal medicine Rutgers U. Law Sch., 1969; mem. alcohol and drug com. Nat. Safety Coun., 1972—82; cons. in field of substance abuse prevention, edn. programming, 1980—; adj. prof. markets, ethics and law Stern Sch. Bus. NYU, 1986—99; pres. Found. for a Drug Free Pa., 1991—92; mem. Atty. Gen.'s Med./Legal Adv. Bd. on Drug Abuse, Pa., 1992; lectr. in legislation and ethics Wharton Sch. exec. program U. Pa., 1996—2000; vis. prof. legal, social and ethical context of bus. Athens Lab. Bus. Adminstrn., 1996; vis. prof. bus. ethics NYU, 2000—. Author: Law, Medicine, Science and Justice, 1964, The Glass House Revolution: Inner City War for Interdependence, 1990, Free Markets, Finance, Ethics, and Law, 1994; contbr. articles to profl. jour. Adv. com. on pub. issues Advt. Coun., 1972-95; mem.-at-large Nat. coun. Boy Scouts Am., 1972-85; chmn. Bd. Ethics, Twp. of Mahwah (NJ), 1990-91; alumni admissions adv. com. Duke U., 1987—. Mem. ABA, NY State Bar Assn., Forensic Sci. Soc. Great Britain, Acad. Colombiana de Ciencias Medico-Forenses, Harvard Club (N.Y.C.). Home: 95 Tam Oshanter Dr Mahwah NJ 07430-1526 Office: Markets Ethics and Law Program NYU Stern Sch Bus 40 W 4th St Ste 3-305 New York NY 10012-1106 E-mail: lbear@stern.nyu.edu.

BEAR, MARCA MARIE, business educator, management consultant; b. S. Bend, Ind., Nov. 29, 1966; BSBA, Ohio State U., 1989, MA in Bus. Adminstrn., 1991, PhD in Bus. Adminstrn., 1992. Assoc. prof. internat. bus. Rochester (N.Y.) Inst. Tech., 1993-2000; assoc. prof. bus. and mgmt. U. Tampa, Fla., 2000—. Dir. Ctr. Internat. Bus. & Econ. Growth Rochester Inst. Tech., 1996—. Mem. editl. bd. Jour. Tchg. Internat. Bus., 1993—, Competitiveness Rev., 1994—, Ann. Edits. Dushkin/McGraw-Hill, 1996—; contbr. articles to profl. jours. Fellow U.S. Dept. Edn., 1991. Mem. Acad. Internat. Bus., Acad. Mgmt., Internat. Mgmt. Devel. Assn., Beta Gamma Sigma. Avocations: guitarist, lyricist, running, skiing. Home: 7209 Granby Dr Hudson OH 44236-1725 Office: U Tampa 401 W Kennedy Blvd Tampa FL 33606-1450

BEARAK, COREY B(ECKER), lawyer; b. Forest Hills, N.Y., Oct. 7, 1955; s. Stephen Irwin Bearak and Phyllis (Stone) Stark; m. Rachelle Pamela Confino, Mar. 24, 1985; children: Jonathan Marc, Marisa Jean. BA in Polit. Sci., Hofstra U., 1977, JD, 1981. Bar: N.Y. 1982. Asst. to sec. of state N.Y. State, Albany and N.Y.C., 1978; pvt. practice Queens, N.Y., 1982—; counsel, chief staff Councilman Sheldon S. Leffler, N.Y.C., 1982-99; legis. counsel to Bronx Borough Pres. Fernando Ferrer, N.Y.C., 1999—2001; dir. planning policy and budget, legis. counsel to Bronx Borough Pres. Adolfo Carrion Jr., 2002—03; govt. and pub. affairs counselor, 2003—. Mem. bd. edn., chair legal, budget and legis. coms. N.Y.C. Cmty. Sch. Dist. 26, 1989-93. Contbr. publs. to law digest. Mem. Cmty. Planning Bd. 13, Queens, N.Y.C., 1980-88, 2000—; mem. nat. bd. N.Y. State Dem. Action; chmn., mem. Nat. Jewish Dem. Coun., 1994-97; Dem. Liberal candidate for State Assembly from 25th dist., 1988; alt. del. Dem. Nat. Conv., 1984—; bd. dirs. Queens Jewish Cmty. Coun., 1987-94, fin. sec., 1994, v.p., 1995-2001, exec. v.p., 2002—; del. N.E. Queens Jewish Cmty. Coun., 1986, legis. chmn., 1987-95, sec., 1989-91, pres., 1991-98, chair exec. com., 1998—; v.p. Ea. Queens Civic Coun., 1994-97; co-chmn. Cmty. Advocates for Pub. Edn., 1995; founder, v.p. Queens Civic Congress, 1997-99, exec. v.p. 1999—; co-chair Fedn. Civic Councils the Borough Queens, 1995-97; pres. North Bellerose Civic Assn., 1991-97, v.p. 1997—; 1st v.p. Queens County Line Dem. Assn., Glen Oaks, N.Y., 1980-82, pres., 1982-84, 93—, exec. sec., 1985-93; trustee Hofstra Law Sch. Alumni Bd., 1994—, v.p., 1996-98, 1st v.p., 1999-2001. Recipient Cert. of Merit Boy Scouts Am., 1983, Cmty. Svc. award Young Israel New Hyde Park, 1997, Outstanding Svc. to Cmty. N.E. Queens award N.E. Queens Jewish Coun., 1998. Mem. N.Y. State Bar Assn. (legis. policy com., environ. law sect.), Queens Bar Assn. (assoc. editor jour. 1983-86, real property com., legis. and law reform com.). Avocations: family, friends, softball, music, football. Home and Office: 82-35 251st St Bellerose NY 11426-2527

BEARAK, RICHARD LEE, architect, city planner; b. Forest Hills, N.Y., Dec. 6, 1957; s. Stephen and Phyllis Sandra (Stark) Bearak; m. Ellen Susan Schiff, Dec. 3, 1989 (dec. May 1998); 1 child, Douglas Samual; m. Adrianne Ellen Wallace-Bearak, Aug. 28, 2002; stepchildren: Marisa, Mathew. BS, N.Y. Inst. Tech., 1980, BArch, 1987; M.Urban Planning, Hunter Coll., N.Y.C., 1983. Registered architect, N.Y.; cert. planner. Archtl. draftsman Metro. Life Ins., N.Y.C., 1979-80, Sikorski Engring., Mineola, N.Y., 1980-82; planning intern Dept. City Planning, Bronx, 1982-83; site planner Parsons, Bromfield and Redniss, Stanford, Conn., 1983-85; city planner Dept. City Planning, L.I.C., 1985-88; assoc. city planner N.Y.C. Dept. Housing & Devel., 1988-93; dep. dir. land use planning Bklyn. Borough Pres.'s Office, 1993—2001, dep. dir. planning and devel., 2002—. Mem. Am. Planning Assn., Mcpl. Art Soc. Avocations: softball, football. E-mail: rbearak@yahoo.com.

BEARCE, JEANA DALE, artist, educator; b. St. Louis; d. Clarence Russell and Maria Emily Dale; m. Lawrence F. Rakovan, June 7, 1969; children: Barbara Emily, Luke, Francesca. B.F.A., Washington U., St. Louis, 1951; MA, N.Mex. Highlands U., 1954. Vis. artist, various lectureships, India, Pakistan, 1961-62, 93; founder art dept. U. Maine, Portland, 1965, chmn. and dept. rep., 1965-70, asst. prof. art, 1967-70, assoc. prof., 1970-81, prof., 1982—. Reflections South India sabbatical, 1992-93. Exhibited one-woman shows, Portland Mus. Art, Maine, 1958, U. Maine, Orono, 1958, 65, 69, 77, 80, Madras Govt. Mus., India, 1962, Gallery 65, Paris, 1964, Bristol Mus. Art, R.I., 1965, Center Gallery, N.Y.C., 1974, Benbow Gallery, Newport, R.I., 1979, Ctr. for the Arts, Chocolate Ch., Bath, Maine, 1988, USM Gallery, 1991, Main Gallery U. So. Maine, 1991, others, group show, Boston Mus. Art, Library of Congress, Phila. Print Club, Springfield Mus., Mo., Birmingham Mus. Art, Ala., others; represented permanent collection, St. Louis Art Mus., U.S. Edn. Found. in India, New Delhi, U. Maine, Orono and Portland, Bklyn. Mus. Art, Cornell U. Mus. Art, Calif. Coll. Arts and Crafts, Sarasota Art Assn., Fla., Bowdoin Coll., Brunswick, Maine; executed murals, N.Mex. Highlands U., Bowdoin Longfellow-Hawthorn Library, Brunswick, sculpture reliefs, St. Bartholomew, Cape Elizabeth, Maine, St. Charles Ch. Brunswick; retrospective, Maine Ctr. for the Arts, 1988. Mem. artist's com. Maine Art Gallery, 1957-75, 80-87; mem. Maine com. Skowhegan Sch. Painting and Sculpture, 1972— . Recipient various awards; recipient Fannie Cook award People's Competition, 1958, 59; sabbaticals to India: Return to India-Creative Paintings and Printmaking, 1987, South India-Painting and Printmaking, 1993, The Maine to India Series USM Environ. Studies Ctr., 1996, Tibet The Maine Art Gallery, Wiscasset, 1999, Summer Invitational, Ctr. for Maine Contemporary Art, 2002, Maine Coast Artists, Rockport, 2002. Mem. Bowdoin Coll. Mus. Assocs. Home: 327 Maine St Brunswick ME 04011-3310 Office: U So Maine College Ave Gorham ME 04038-1004

BEARD, ANN SOUTHARD, diplomat, government official, travel company executive, oil company executive, consultant, event planner, writer, educator; b. Denver, Jan. 13, 1948; d. William Harvey and Cora Alice Cornelia (Caldwell) Southard; m. Terrill Leon Beard, Dec. 20, 1970 (div. Oct. 1980); 1 son, Jeffery Leon; m. Rainer G. Froehlich, Feb. 12, 1988 (div. 1992). BA, Willamette U., 1970; postgrad., U. Calif., San Diego, 1981-82. Exec. asst. Kidder Peabody & Co., San Francisco, 1970-72; adminstrv. aide Arthur Anderson & Co., Portland, Oreg., 1972-73; owner, mgr. Beard's Frame Shoppes, Inc., Portland, 1973-80; dir. mktg. Multnomah County Fair, Portland, 1979; owner, CEO Ann Beard Spl. Events, San Diego, 1980-82; pres. Frame Affair, Inc., San Diego, 1982-86, Jack Oil Co., Inc., Greeley, 1982—; chancellor Consular Corps. Coll., Phila., 2002—. Co-owner, v.p. Froehlich Internat. Travel, La Jolla, Calif., 1987-92; chief of protocol Mayor Susan Golding's Office, City of San Diego, 1993-2001; pres., CEO, Diplomacy & Internat. Protocol, San Diego, 2001--; chmn. 1st Nat. Protocol Officers Assn. conf. U.S. Dept. State, Washington; chmn. 1st Internat. Protocol Conf., Ottawa, Can.; advisor to Govt. of China in Beijng for 2008

Summer Olympic Games; v.p. 146 Co., Inc., Greeley, pres. 1970-88; mem. San Diego Consular Corps; lectr. World Trade Ctr., Alaska, Consular Corps, Alaska, 2002; cons. SBA, San Diego, 1980-85; facilitator internat. seminars, workshops, and retreats; prof. internat. bus. diplomacy and protocol, San Diego State U., 2002-. Active Civic Light Opera, Old Globe Theatre; bd. dirs. San Diego Master Chorale, 1981-92; mem. state bd. Miss. Calif. Pageant/Miss. Am., 1982-87; citizens adv. bd. Drug Abuse Task Force/Crime Prevention Task Force, San Diego, 1983-87; campaign coord. Bill Mitchell for City Coun., 1985; candidate for Congress; staff aide to dep. mayor, 1987; mem. Lead San Diego Alumni, 1988, Scripps Hosp. Aux., 1992—, Internat. Visitors Coun., 1993—, San Diego County Commn. on the Status of Women, 1993-96; mem. Internat. Affairs Bd., San Diego, 1993—; chancellor, Consular Corps Coll., Phila., 2001—; founder, nat. chmn. Nat. Protocol Resource Bd., USA, 2002—, founder, internat. pres. Protocol and Diplomacy Internat., U.S., 2002—; bd. dirs. La Jolla Rep. Women Fedn., 1992—. Mem. Am. Mktg. Assn., World Affairs Coun., San Diego C. of C., Save Our Heritage Orgn., Charter 100 San Diego, San Diego 1988 Alumna Willamette U., 1909 Univ. Club (bd. dirs. 1992—, pres. 1996—), Univ. Club San Diego (mktg., devel. and social dir. 1987-88), Pres., Protocol and Diplomacy Internat. (founder), Delta Gamma. Home and Office: 597 So Sierra Ave #59 Solana Beach CA 92075-7621

BEARD, AUDREY LUCILLE, artist, art educator; b. Riverside, Calif., Sept. 28, 1928; d. Benjamin Franklin and Mildred Winnefred (Ames) Waters; m. William Gleason Beard, June 2, 1947 (dec. Feb. 15, 1995); 2 children. Student, Riverside Coll., 1947-48, Orange Coast Coll., 1958. Owner, mgr. Waters Galleries, Laguna, Calif., 1962-70, Capistrano, Calif., 1970-78, Beard Art Gallery, Portland, 1979-82; art instr. Art Ctr., Carlsbad, Calif., 1977-78, Performing Arts Ctr., Escondido, Calif., 1991-92, Parks and Recreation, Vista, Calif., 1977-79, Portland, 1981-88, Dana Point, Calif., 1992—. V.p., co-founder Capistrano (calif.) Art Assn., 1978. Author: Sketching through Mexico, 1980; illustrator: To Teachers with Love, 1986; artist various oil and acrylic paintings. Active civic concerts with Laguna Chorale, 1970-74, Saddleback Concert Chorale, Mission Viejo, Calif., 1974-77, Palomar Coll. Chorale, Escondido, Calif., 1977-79, Firehouse Concert Chorale, Portland, 1980-87. Recipient 1st pl. profl. artists Fine Arts Guild, 1988. Fellow, mem. Nat. League Am. Pen Women (membership chmn. 1995, Art scholar 1970), Nigeal Art Assn., San Clemente Arts Assn. (1st pl. oil paintings 1993, 2d pl. 1994, Hon. mention 2003). Avocations: teaching piano, playing piano, composing music, writing, singing.

BEARD, CAROL ELAINE, art educator; b. Boston, May 26, 1945; d. William John and Madolyn Ruth (Johnson) Beard; children from previous marriage: John C. Zajac, Matthew D. Zajac. BSE, Mass. Coll. Art, 1967; student, U. Mass., Dartmouth, 1986, Stonehill Coll., Stoughton, Mass., 1989. Cert. art tchr. Mass., art supr. Mass. Art tchr. Framingham (Mass.) Sch. Dept., 1967—71; art dir. Norfolk (Mass.) Recreation Dept., 1974—83; instr. art Franklin (Mass.) HS Adult Edn., 1986—87; dir. art Norfolk Sch. Dept., 1980—, student coun. advisor, 1993—. Freelance artist graphic designs for various town bds. and orgns., 1967—; collaborator Step-Outside: Cmty.-Based Art Edn., 1994; invited exch. tchr. Wash. Ambassadorship Program, 1994. Author: (poetry) Fallen Requiem, 1964; soft sculptures. Mem. Norfolk Ins. Com., 1989—97, Norfolk Sch. Com., 1990—97; chair Collective Bargaining Com., Norfolk, 1988—96. Mem.: NEA, ASCD, Norfolk County Tchrs. Assn., Mass. Art Edn. Assn., Nat. Art Edn. Assn., Norfolk Tchrs. Assn. (pres. 1988—97, Tchr. of the Yr. 1992), Mass. Tchrs. Assn. Avocations: creative writing, clothes design, golf, photography, toy design. Home: 9 Lincoln St Franklin MA 02038 Office: Centennial Sch 70 Boardman St Norfolk MA 02056-1099 E-mail: beard@norfolk.k12.us.ma.

BEARD, CHARLES EDWARD, library director, consultant; b. New Orleans, July 21, 1940; s. Julius Brown and Lucy Glenn (Dannelly) B.; divorced. BA, U. Ala., 1962; MS in Libr. Sci., Fla. State U., 1964. Adminstrv. officer libr. U.S. Army Command and Staff Coll., Ft. Leavenworth, Kans., 1964-66; head reference dept. Gorgas Libr. U. Ala., Tuscaloosa, 1966-69, head acquisition dept., 1969-70; dir. libr. svc. Judson Coll., Marion, Ala., 1970-71; dir. librs., assoc. prof./coord. edn. libr. media dept. Ga. Coll., Milledgeville, Ga., 1971-78; dir. univ. librs. State U. of West Ga., Carrollton, 1978—. Editor: Solutions to Your Public Relations Problems, 1991, The Ga. Librar., 1975-79; assoc. editor: The Southeastern Libr., 1975-79; contbr. articles to profl. jours. Trustee Freedom to Read Found., Chgo., 1998-2000; co-chair White House Conf. on Librs. and Info. Svc. Task Force, 1991-92; mem. bd. dirs. Positive Response, Inc., Carrollton, 1981—, pres. 1997, 98-2002; v.p. Carrollton County Hist. Soc., 1994-96. Capt. U.S. Army, 1964-66. Recipient Juanita Skelton Disting. Svc. award Ga. Assn. Instrnl. Technologists, 1995, Commendation medal U.S. Army, 1966. Mem. ALA (exec. bd. 1993-97, coun. mem. 1990-97, 1999-2002), Southeastern Libr. Assn. (pres. 1986-88), Ga. Libr. Assn. (exec. bd. 1973-85, 86—, pres. 1981-83, Nix-Jones Disting. Svc. award 1991, Bob Disting. Svc. award 2002), Richardson Libr. (chair), Ga. State Bd. Certification of Librs., Ga. Ctr. for the Book (adv. bd.), Libr. Adminstrn. and Mgmt. Assn. (past mem. exec. com., exec. bd.), Kiwanis (pres. 1975, Outstanding Pres. award 1996), Omicron Delta Kappa (faculty advisor 1990-96), Beta Phi Mu, Phi Alpha Theta. Episcopalian. Avocations: bridge, swimming, gardening, reading. Home: 105 Briarwood Dr Carrollton GA 30117-4104 Office: State U of West Ga Ingram Libr Carrollton GA 30118-0001 E-mail: cbeard@westga.edu.

BEARD, CHARLES JULIAN, lawyer; b. Detroit, Dec. 24, 1943; s. James F. and Ethel W. (Coveney) B.; m. Roslyn M. Watson, June 29, 1974 (div. 1988); m. Vivian C. Male, Aug. 11, 1990; 1 child, James Anthony. AB, Harvard U., 1966, JD, 1969. Bar: Mass. 1969, U.S. Dist Ct. Mass. 1976. Spl. asst. to adminstr. Boston Model City Adminstrn., 1969-70, asst. adminstr. for community svcs., 1970-74; assoc. Foley, Hoag & Eliot, Boston, 1974-78, ptnr., 1979—. Bd. dirs. Blue Cross-Blue Shield Mass., Boston, 1986-. Chmn. bd. trustees Emerson Coll., Boston, 1998—2001; charter trustee Phillips Acad., Andover, Mass., 1997—; trustee WGBH Ednl. Found., 1989—99, 2000—, chmn. bd. trustees, 2003—; trustee Emerson Coll., Boston, 1988—98. Avocations: golfing, sailing, cross-country skiing. Office: Foley Hoag LLP 155 Seaport Blvd Boston MA 02210-2600

BEARD, CRAIG WYETH, librarian; b. Memphis, Dec. 21, 1954; s. Frank Stanley Beard and Lyta Jean Hancock; children: Jason, Jessica. AA, Fla. Coll., 1975; BA, Harding U., 1977, MA in Religion, 1980; MLS, Fla. State U., 1982. Reference libr. Harding U., Searcy, Ark., 1982—90; head reference svcs. Sterne Libr. U. Ala., Birmingham, 1990—94, reference libr. for engring. Sterne Libr., 1994—. Adj. instr. U. Ala. Sch. Libr. and Info. Studies, Tuscaloosa, 1992—94. Vol. So. Bapt. Disaster Relief, Alpharetta, Ga., 1999; lay worker The Ch. at Brook Hills, Birmingham, 1997—. Mem.: Ala. Assn. Coll. and Rsch. Librs. (pres. elect/pres./past pres. 1997—2000), Christian Coll. Librs. (pres. elect/pres./past pres. 1993—98), Am. Soc. for Engring. Edn. Office: Sterne Library U Ala B'ham 917 13th St South Birmingham AL 35294

BEARD, DENNIS ALTON, pastor; b. Overton, Tex., Dec. 21, 1948; s. George Alton and Edna Berneice B.; m. Diane Woodard, July 14, 1969; children: Angela Rochelle, Bradley Alton. AA, Kilgore Coll., 1969; student, Stephen F. Austin State U., 1970. Ins. mgr., Dallas; owner The Am. Agency Ins. and Equities, Dallas, 1975-80; regional v.p. Nat. Assn. Self-employed, Dallas, 1981-83; pastor, evangelist The Testimony of Jesus Christ Ch., Houston, 1985—. Founder OneGodSite.com. Author: The Errors of the Trinity and the Revelation of Jesus Christ, 1998, Behold the Real Jesus, 1999, The Mystery of the Kingdom of God, 2000. Republican. Avocations: playing piano and organ, singing, songwriting. Home: 14525 Main St Houston TX 77035 Office: The Testimony of Jesus Christ Ch 14525 Main St Houston TX 77035 E-mail: MinisterBeard@aol.com.

BEARD, ELIZABETH LETITIA, physiologist, educator; b. New Orleans, Apr. 2, 1932; d. Howard Horace and Irene (Handley) B. BA in Biology, Tex. Christian U., 1952, BS in Med. Tech., 1953, MS in Med. Tech., 1955; postgrad., Smith Coll., 1953-54, Vanderbilt U., 1954-55; PhD in Animal Physiology, Tulane U., 1961. Instr. dept. biol. scis. Loyola U., New Orleans, 1955-58, asst. prof., 1958-62, assoc. prof., 1962-68, prof., 1969—, chmn. premed. com., 1978—; rsch. assoc. dept. physiology Sch. Medicine Tulane U., New Orleans, 1960-63, prof. biology med. reinforcement and enrichment program, 1968-94. Vis. prof. dept. physiology and biophysics Med. Sch. Harvard U., 1983-84, dept. neuropharmacology Scripps Rsch. Inst., La Jolla, Calif., spring 2001; vis. scientist Am. Indian Rsch. Opportunities Programs at Mont. State U., 1994. Contbr. articles on rsch. in physiology to profl. publs. Mem. project rev. com. New Orleans Health Planning Coun., 1974-77, bd. dirs., 1975-78; soprano soloist Holy Name of Jesus Ch., 1978—, pres. sch. bd., 1976-79; mem. grad. rsch. com. La. chpt. Am. Heart Assn., 1970-72, 81-83, mem. undergrad. rsch. com., 1978-81, 89-93; mem. Met. Mus. Art, New Orleans Mus. Art; participant med. mission Christian Med. and Dental Soc., Tepic Navjarit, Mex., 1993, La Esperanza, Honduras, 1994, 95; with Med. Ministry Internat., Muisine, Ecuador, 1996, Tena, Ecuador, 1997, Med. Ministry Internat., San Jose de Los Matas, Domincan Rep., 1998, Riobamba, Ecuador, 1999, Otovalo, Ecuador, 2000, Lima, Peru, 2002, Latacunga, Ecuador, 2003. NIH grantee, 1962-64, 67-69, La. Heart Assn. grantee, 1966-67, Edward Schleider Found. grantee, 1974-77, New Orleans Cancer Assn. grantee, 1962-63; Libby rsch. fellow Sch. Medicine Tulane U., 1961. Mem. AAUP, AAAS, Am. Physiol. Soc., Soc. Exptl. Biology and Medicine, Sigma Xi. Office: 6363 St Charles Ave New Orleans LA 70118-6143 Home: # 22 6363 Saint Charles Ave New Orleans LA 70118-6143 E-mail: Beard@Loyno.edu.

BEARD, EUGENE P. advertising agency executive; b. Pittsburgh, Pa. Grad., Duquesne U., 1959. Exec. v.p., chief fin. officer Interpublic Group of Cos. Inc., N.Y.C., vice chmn. fin. & opers., cfo. Office: Interpublic Group Cos Inc Ste C3-31 1271 Avenue Of The Americas Fl 44 New York NY 10020-1459

BEARD, JANE ALIDA, retired accountant; b. Belton, Tex., Aug. 22, 1920; d. Maurice Doke and Mae Gaynell (Martin) Bryant; m. John Raymond Baugh, Apr. 5, 1940 (div. Nov. 1946); m. Ledford Francis Beard, Apr. 8, 1948; children: John Raymond, Jerome Cater. Student, Southwestern U., 1937-39, Tex. Agr. and Indsl. Coll., 1939-40. Acct. El Paso (Tex.) Nat. Bank, 1947-53; cashier C.R. Anthony Co., El Paso, 1962-80; ret., 1980. Author: Births, Deaths and Marriages from El Paso Newspapers through 1885, 1982, Vol. II 1886-1890, 1992, Vol. III 1891-1895, 1995, vol. IV 1896-1899, 2000. Vol. El Paso Pub. Libr., 1990-96. Mem. DAR, Daus. Rep. Tex., United Daus. Confederacy, Colonial Dames of XVII Century, El Paso County Hist. Soc., El Paso County Geneal. Soc., Zeta Tau Alpha. Anglican. Avocations: family research, bridge, travel, needlepoint, reading. Home: 213 Clairemont Dr El Paso TX 79912-5346

BEARD, KEVIN F. language educator; b. Murray, Utah, Jan. 30, 1962; s. Robert H. Beard and Dorothy Janet McMillan. MA, Brigham Young U., 1989. Prof. U. Nev., Reno, 1989—91; adminstr., fgn. langs. dept. Calif. State U., Chico, Calif., 1991—95; prof. Richland Coll., Dallas, 1995—. Author: (spanish pronunciation guide) Guía a la pronunciación, (learning software) Ahorita. D-Conservative. Avocations: music, travel, tennis, language acquisition. Office: Richland Coll 12800 Abrams Rd Dallas TX 75243 Office Fax: 972-238-6188. E-mail: kbeard@dcccd.edu.

BEARD, LEO ROY, retired civil engineer; b. West Baden, Ind., Apr. 6, 1917; s. Leonard Roy and Barbara Katherine (Frederick) B.; m. Marian Janet Wagar, Oct. 21, 1939 (dec.); children: Patricia Beard Huntzicker, Thomas Edward, James Robert; m. Marjorie Elizabeth Pierce Wood, Aug. 30, 1974. AA, Pasadena City Coll., 1937; BS, Calif. Inst. Tech., 1939. Engr. U.S. Army C.E., Los Angeles, 1939-49; engr. Office Chief of Engrs., Washington, 1949-52; chief of Reservoir Regulation, Sacramento, 1952-64; dir. Hydrologic Engring. Center, Davis, Calif., 1964-72; prof. civil engring. U. Tex., Austin, 1972-87, prof. emeritus, 1987—. Cons. Espey, Huston & Assos., Austin, 1980-92; v.p. Internat. Commn. of Water Resource Sys.; mem. NRC Water Sci. and Tech. Bd. Editor-in-chief: Water International; Editor: Jour. of Hydrology. Served with USNR, 1945-46. Recipient Meritorious Civilian Service award U.S. Army C.E., 1972. Fellow AAAS,. Internat. Water Resources Assn. (exec. bd.), ASCE (water resources exec. com., Julian Hinds award 1981, hon. mem. 1987, Hunter Rouse award 1993, Lifetime Achievement award 2001); mem. Am. Water Resources Assn. (hon.), Am. Geophys. Union (pres. hydrology sect.), Nat. Soc. Profl. Engrs., Internat. Assn. Hydrol. Scis., World Meteorol. Orgn. (chmn. com. on hydrol. design data), U.S. Com. on Irrigation, Drainage and Flood Control, Univs. Council on Water Resources (exec. bd.), Nat. Acad. Engring. *As you spend most waking hours at your work, choose to love it. The key is to select an occupation that serves others.*

BEARD, LILLIAN B. MCLEAN, physician, consultant; b. N.Y. d. Johnie Wilson and Woodie (Durden) McLean; m. Delawrence Beard. BS, Howard U., 1965, MD, 1970. MD, 1970. Pvt. practice pediatrics Lillian M. Beard, Washington, D.C., 1973—; assoc. prof. pediatrics George Washington U., 1983—; asst. prof. community medicine Howard U., 1983—; contbg. editor Good Housekeeping Mag., N.Y., 1989-95; health adv. WUSA-TV, Washington, 1993-95; health and med. contbr. ABC-TV, Washington, 2000—. Communications cons. to industry including: Nestle Nutritional Products; mem. bd. dirs. Nat. Women's Econ. Alliance, 1993-2000; Children's Hosp., 1993-2002. Recipient Disting. Leadership award Nat. Assn. Equal Opportunity in Higher Edn., 1993, Disting. Svc. award Nat. Med. Assn., 1990, Hall of Fame in Medicine award, 1994, Healthy Babies Project "Making a Difference" award, 1995, Howard U. Alumni Achievement award, 1996. Fellow Am. Acad. Pediatrics; mem. Nat. Med. Assn., Am. Acad. Pediatrics (physician recognition awards 1993—). Home: 10517 Alloway Dr Potomac MD 20854-1662 Office: 10801 Lockwood Dr Ste 260 Silver Spring MD 20901

BEARD, RICHARD BURNHAM, engineering educator emeritus, researcher; b. Boston, Dec. 17, 1922; s. Daniel and Anne (Curran) B.; m. Marilyn D. W. Beard, Sept. 18, 1948; children: Beverly, Amy, Adrienne. BSChemE, Northeastern U., 1947; SM in Elec. Engring., Harvard U., 1950; PhD in Elec. Engring., U. Pa., 1965. Chemist Weymouth Artificial Leather, South Braintree, Mass., 1947-48; rsch. engr. Honeywell, Phila., 1950-58; instr. Drexel U., Phila., 1958-60; rsch. assoc. U. Pa., Phila., 1960-65; assoc. prof. elec. engring. Drexel U., Phila., 1965-73, prof. elec. engring., 1973-93, prof. emeritus, 1993—. Dir. biomed. engring. and sci. inst. Drexel U., Phila., 1974-76. Contbr. articles to profl. jours. and procs. including Jour. Applied Polymer Sci., Polymer Bull., Procs. Soc. Photo-Optical Instrument Engrs. Vol. 2309, Vol. 2678. Cpl. U.S. Army, 1943-46. Mem. IEEE (sr.), AAAS, Acoustical Soc. Am., Am. Chem. Soc. Achievements include patents in field. Home: 880 Willow Way Atco NJ 08004-1339

BEARD, RONALD STRATTON, lawyer; b. Flushing, N.Y., Feb. 13, 1939; s. Charles Henry and Ethel Mary (Stratton) Beard; m. Karin Paridee, Jan. 24, 1991; children: D. Karen, Jonathan D., Dana K. BA, Denison U., 1961; LLB, Yale U., 1964. Bar: Calif. 1964, U.S. Ct. Appeals (9th cir.) 1980, U.S. Dist. Ct. (ctrl. dist.) Calif. 1964. Ptnr. Gibson, Dunn & Crutcher, LA, 1964—2001, mng. ptnr., 1991—97, chmn., 1991—2001. Trustee Denison U., Granville, Ohio, 1975—, chmn., 1998—2003; mem. steering com. Calif. Minority Coun. Program, 1991—2001; mem. Constl. Rights Found., 1994—, Orange County Art Mus. Mem.: ABA, LA Bar Assn., Calif. Bar Assn., Coto de Caza Golf Club, Chancery Club, City Club. Avocations: sports, travel, golf. Home: 27442 Hidden Trail Rd Laguna Hills CA 92653-5876 Office: Gibson Dunn & Crutcher 4 Park Plz Ste 1700 Irvine CA 92614-8560

BEARD, THOMAS REX, economics educator; b. Baton Rouge, Aug. 12, 1934; s. Rex and Gertrude Louise (Hampton) B.; m. Sharon Virginia Petty, Dec. 21, 1957; children: Thomas Randolph, Sharon Beard Barber BS, La. State U., 1956, MA, 1958; PhD, Duke, 1963. Asst. prof. La. State U., Baton Rouge, 1961-64, assoc. prof., head econs. dept., 1965-68, prof., head dept. econs., 1969-71, prof., 1972-91, Alumni prof., 1991—97, Alumni prof. emeritus, 1997—. Economist Fed. Res. Bd. of Govs., Washington, 1964-65; 4th Nat. Bank Distinguished prof. Wichita State U., 1968-69; exec. dir. La. Council Econ. Edn., 1972-77; cons. La. Coordinating Council for Higher Edn., 1970, also various fed. govt. agys. Author: U.S. Treasury Advance Refunding, 1966, Financing Government in Louisiana, 1974; Editor: The Louisiana Economy, 1969; assoc. editor: Social Sci. Quar., 1966-70; mem. editorial bd. Pub. Fin. Quar., 1972-74, Rev. Regional Econs. and Bus., 1980-86, Jour. Macroecons., 1987-97; contbr. articles to profl. jours. Chmn. La. Gov.'s Council Econ. Advisors, 1975-77, mem., 1973-80. Earhart Found. fellow, 1957-58; Ford Found. fellow, 1960; James B. Duke fellow, 1958-60; La. State U. Parents Assn. grantee, 1983 Mem. Am. Econ. Assn., So. Econ. Assn. (mem. exec. com. 1967-69), Western Econ. Assn., Southwestern Econ. Assn. (pres. 1969-70), Phi Beta Kappa (pres. La. State U. chpt. 1984-86), Kappa Alpha, Omicron Delta Kappa, Phi Kappa Phi. Methodist. Home: 5952 Hibiscus Dr Baton Rouge LA 70808-8891

BEARDEN, JAMES HUDSON, university official; b. Marion, Ala., Sept. 25, 1933; s. Joseph N. and Lula (Worrell) B.; m. Pauline Larkins, Mar. 31, 1961; children: James Hudson, Jr., Pauline B. Simonowich. BS, Centenary Coll. La., 1956; MA, East Carolina U., 1959; PhD, U. Ala., 1966. Bus. mgr. Marion Inst., 1959; mem. faculty East Carolina U., Greenville, N.C., 1959—, prof. bus. adminstrn., 1964—, dir. bur. bus. research, 1964, dean, 1968-83, dir. BB&T Ctr. for Leadership Devel., 1983—. Author articles in field. Former trustee Campbell U.; pres., trustee N.C. Council Econ. Edn. Served with AUS, 1956-58. Mem. Newcomen Soc. N.Am., Assn. Leadership Educators, Fedn. Bus. Honor Socs. (pres. 1991—), Rotary, Beta Gamma Sigma (pres. 1986-1990), Sigma Beta Delta (pres. 1994-2000). Home: 106 Crown Point Rd Greenville NC 27858-5718 Office: BB&T Ctr for Leadership Devel East Carolina U 1100 Bate Bldg Greenville NC 27858-4353

BEARDEN, THOMAS EUGENE, research scientist, researcher; b. Cheniere, La., Dec. 17, 1930; m. Doris Faye McDonald, 1964. BS in Math., NE La. U., 1953; MS in Nuc. Engring., Ga. Inst. Tech., 1971; PhD in Sci. (hon.), Trinity Coll., U.K., 1999. Commd. U.S. Army, 1954, advanced through grades to lt. col., intelligence specialist air def. and ABM def., 1960—75, ret.; dir. Assn. Disting. Am. Scientists, Huntsville, Ala., 1995—; ceo CTEC, Inc., Huntsville, 1995—. Fellow emeritus Alpha Foundation's Inst. for Advanced Study, 1998—. Author: (scientific book) Energy from the Vacuum: Concepts and Principles; contbr. articles to profl. jours. Mem.: Am. Assn. Physics Tchrs. Achievements include discovery of solution to the problem of the source charge and its associated EM fields and potentials; corrected flaw in 3-law Aristotelian logic to 5-law logic; discovery of proposed mechanism for excess antigravity accelerating expansion of the universe; extension to Becker's model of the cellular regenerative system; thermodynamics of permissible COP over 1.0 electrical power systems; co-inventor of Motionless Electromagnetic Generator; discovery of mechanism for practical antigravity; correction of Second Law of Thermodynamics to include negentropic systems; EM epigenetic reprogramming mechanism in the Priore effect; mechanisms used in advanced Soviet energetics weapons; circuits using the nondiverged Heaviside energy flow component arbitrarily discarded by Lorentz; proposed mechanism for excess gravity holding the arms of spiral galaxies together. Avocations: aikido (retired, sandan), author, consultant. Office: Assn Distinguished Am Scientists PO Box 1472 Huntsville AL 35807

BEARDEN, THOMAS HOWARD, news program producer, correspondent; b. Washington, Feb. 14, 1948; s. Norman C. and Emma Dorothy (Jensen) B.; m. Ruth Ann Harrison, July 12, 1977; children: Jennifer Kate, Emily Jane. BS in Journalism, U. Miss., 1969, MA in Radio and TV, 1971. Reporter, anchorman Sta. WJTV-TV, Jackson, Miss., 1971-72; reporter, anchorman, assignment editor Sta. WHBQ-TV, Memphis, 1972-78; reporter, anchorman Sta. KMGH-TV, Denver, 1978-85; producer, correspondent The NewsHour with Jim Lehrer, Denver, 1985—. Producer/reporter TV news series documentary The Quicksilver Connection, 1984 (Emmy award 1984). 1st lt. U.S. Army, 1971-72. Mem. Sigma Delta Chi. Clubs: Denver Press (news series award 1983). Avocations: computers, photography. Office: The NewsHour with Jim Lehrer 2400 Ulster St Denver CO 80238 E-mail: tbearden@ix.netcom.com., tbearden@newshour.org.

BEARDMORE, HARVEY ERNEST, retired physician, educator; b. Windsor, Ont., Can., Feb. 4, 1921; s. Harold and Marjorie (Harvey) B.; m. Frances Seymour Barnes, Sept. 1, 1945 (dec. Aug. 1996); children: Richard, Anne Beardmore Psaila, Patricia Beardmore Muldoon, Ian, Carol Beardmore Lamb, Diane Beardmore Lobb. BSc, McGill U., Montreal, Can., 1946, MD, CM, 1948. Diplomate Am. Bd. Pediat. Surgery. Intern Montreal Gen. Hosp., 1948-49; resident Queen Mary Vets. Hosp., Montreal, 1949-51; teaching fellow Tufts U., Boston, 1951-52; chief resident Montreal Children's Hosp., 1952-54, staff, 1954-92; practice medicine specializing in pediatric surgery Montreal, 1954-92. Assoc. prof. surgery McGill U., 1954-92. Served with Princess Patricias Canadian Light Inf., 1943-45, Italy, N.W. Europe. Fellow Am. Acad. Pediatrics (chmn. sect. surgery 1972), ACS, Royal Coll. Surgeons Can.; mem. Can. Assn. Paediatric Surgeons (founding pres. 1967-72), Am. Pediatric Surg. Assn. (pres 1974), World Fed. Assn. Pediatric Surgeons (1st pres. 1974-77), Chevalier de la Chaine des Rotisseurs. Home: 4501 Sherbrooke St W Apt 5B Montreal QC Canada H3Z 1E7 E-mail: harvey.beardmore@sympatico.ca.

BEARDSLEY, CHARLES MITCHELL, retired insurance company executive; b. Chgo., Jan. 13, 1921; s. Richard Stanley and Maude Clarice (Mitchell) B.; m. Marjorie Helen Gahan, Feb. 27, 1943; children: Helen Charlene, Karen Jeannette. AB, Depauw U., 1942; MA, U. Wis., 1947. From actuarial student to assoc. actuary Paul Revere Life Ins. Co., Worcester, Mass., 1947-55; from actuary to v.p. Security Life and Trust Co., Winston-Salem, N.C., 1955-63; actuary sr. v.p. H.W. Satchwell & Co., Columbus, Ohio, 1963-67; actuary chmn., chief exec. officer Charles M. Beardsley & Assocs., Columbus, 1967-68; from exec. v.p. to chmn. Booke and Co., Winston-Salem, 1968-85, vice chmn., 1985-91. Author Life Company Annual Statement Handbook and New Items in the Annual Statement for Life Insurance Companies, 1959-2003; contbr. articles to profl. jours. Pres. Wachovia Hist. Soc., Winston-Salem, 1981, Huguenot Soc. N.C., 1987-89; bd. dirs. Moravian Music Found., Winston-Salem. Served to lt. (j.g.) USN, 1943-46. Fellow Conf. of Cons. Actuaries (v.p. 1980-82), Soc. Actuaries (dir. 1983-86); mem. Am. Acad. Actuaries, Internat. Actuarial Assn., Internat. Assn. cons. Actuaries (bd. dirs. 1980-89). Democratic. Clubs: Forsyth Country, Twin City, Piedmont (Winston-Salem). Lodges: Masons, Kiwanis (local pres.). Avocation: music. Home: 341 Muirfield Dr Winston Salem NC 27104-3952 E-mail: cmb2293@yahoo.com.

BEARDSLEY, JACOB EDWARD, retired computer software company executive; b. Bklyn., Dec. 9, 1928; s. David M. and Charlotte C. (Fletcher) B.; m. Annemarie Ludwig, Mar. 11, 1952; children: Barbara, Jacqueline, David. AB, U. Tenn., 1950; MS, Columbia U., 1958. Cert. mgmt. cons. Systems analyst Guardian Life Ins., N.Y.C., 1957-59; mgmt. cons. Fairbanks Assocs., N.Y.C., 1959-65; MIS dir. Billboard Pubs., Cin., 1965-68; sales cons. Honeywell Info. Systems, Waltham, Mass., 1968-74; MIS dir. CBS Mags., N.Y.C., 1974-76; mgmt. cons., 1976-84; pres. Fulfillment Prodn. Systems, Middlesex, N.J., 1984-87, Satisfaction Software, Inc., North Brunswick, N.J., 1988-93. Author: Elements of Subscription Magazine Fulfillment, 1990; contbr. articles to profl. jours. Treas. New Brunswick Presbyn. Ch., 1979-82, pres., trustees, 1982-83, elder, 1974-77, 81-83. With U.S. Army, 1946-48. Mem. Masons (master 1962, 71, 96, 97sec. 1969-78), Pi Kappa Alpha. Avocations: gardening, fishing. Home: 324 Gill Ln Iselin NJ 08830-2836

BEARDSLEY, ROBERT EUGENE, microbiologist, educator; b. Walton, N.Y., June 11, 1923; s. Harrison R. and Margaret (Sliter) B.; m. Philomena E. Pecora, Aug. 28, 1948; children: Luisa M., Margaret R., Robert E. BS, Manhattan Coll., 1950; A.M., Columbia U., 1951, PhD, 1960. Instr. Manhattan Coll., 1951-54, asst. prof., 1954-58, asso. prof., 1958-68, prof., 1968-77; dir. Manhattan Coll. (Lab. Plant Morphogenesis), 1962-69, head dept. biology, 1969-77; prof. Iona Coll., New Rochelle, N.Y., 1977-89, prof. emeritus, 1989—; dean Iona Coll. (Sch. Arts and Sci.), 1977-83. Vis. investigator Inst. Pasteur, Paris, 1966-67; Co-chmn. Scientists Com. Radiation Info., 1960 Contbr. articles to profl. jours. Dist. comdr. U.S. Power Squadrons, 1993. Served with AUS, 1943-46. Guggenheim fellow, 1966 Mem. Am. Pub. Health Assn., Am. Soc. Microbiologists, AAAS, Sigma Xi, Epsilon Sigma Pi. Home: 242 Mountaindale Rd Yonkers NY 10710-3512 Office: Dept Biology Iona Coll New Rochelle NY 10801 E-mail: jasperbs50@yahoo.com. *In retrospect, I find that I have lived with the illusion of being guided by a desire to make some contribution toward a better world for all members of the human family. However, like all other people, I have only done what my unique combination of heredity, environmental programming and ego have compelled me to do.*

BEARDSLEY, THEODORE S(TERLING), JR., professional society administrator; b. East St. Louis, Ill., Aug. 26, 1930; s. Theodore Sterling and Margaret (Kienzle) B.; m. Lenora J. Fierke, May 26, 1955; children: Theodore Sterling III, Mark A., Mary Elizabeth. BS, So. Ill. U., 1952; MA (Max Bryant fellow), Washington U., St. Louis, 1954; postgrad., U. Heidelberg, Germany, 1955-56; PhD, U. Pa., 1961; linguistic rsch., Inst. Caro y Cuervo, Bogota, Colombia, summer 1973. Asst. in English Lycee Wilson, Chaumont, France, 1952-53; mem. faculty Rider Coll., 1957-61, chmn. dept. modern lang., 1959-61; asst. prof. Spanish So. Ill. U., 1961-62, U. Wis., 1962-65. Dir. Hispanic Soc. Am., N.Y.C., 1965-95, pres., 1995—; adj. prof. NYU, 1967-69, 80, Adelphi U., 1966, 68, Columbia U., 1969, Eckerd Coll., 1997—; Fulbright lectr., Ecuador, 1974;

guest lectr. U. Complutense, Madrid, 1990, 94, U. Salamanca, 1994, 99, U. Rábida, Spain, 1996; diss. dir. U. Oviedo, Spain, 1992; vis. prof. U. Wis., 1995; chmn. Museums Coun. N.Y.C., 1972-73; spl. cons. Hispanic bibliography Libr. Congress, fall 1973, N.J. State Dept. Edn., spring 1975, NEH, 1978—. Narrator Spanish lang. recorded tours, Nat. Gallery Art, Met. Mus., Mus. Natural Sci., Boston Sci. Mus., Smithsonian Instn.; continuing series on Caribbean popular music in U.S. WBGO-FM, 1979; Xavier Cugat, 1980, USA Latino, 1981, Enrique Madriguera, Spanish Nat. Radio, 1985; author: Hispano-Classical Translations, 1482-1699, 1970, Tomas Navarro Tomas, A Tentative Bibliography, 1908-1970, 1971; librettist: Ponce de Leon, 1973; also articles; recordings include: Charla con Camilo José Cela, 1966, Visita a la Hispanic Society, 1969; editor: (CD)Enrique Madriguera, 1994, Carlos Molina, 2000, Madriguera II, 2003; co-editor: Celestina: Early Text, 1997; narrator-author: 4 part series Hispanic Immigration to the United States (text pub. 1976), CBS-TV, 1972; narrator: Ponce de Leon, Charlotte Symphony, 2000; master or ceremonies: Conquistador Ball, Punta Gorda, Fla., 1998-03; Introductions for Don Quixote Suite, Charlotte Symphony, 2002; mem. adv. bd.: Hispanic Rev., Studia humanitatis, Boletín de ANLE, Hispanic Sem. of Medieval Studies, Revista Caribe. Served with AUS, 1954-56. Decorated Orden de Mérito Civil, Spain ; Fulbright grantee, 1952-53; Jusserand traveling fellow, 1962; research grantee Am. Council Learned Socs., 1964; travel grantee, 1974; recipient Premio Bibliofilia Barcelona, Spain, 1973, Merit award Noticias de Arte, 1999. Mem. ASCAP, Hispanic Soc. Am., Renaissance Soc. Am. (exec. coun., acting dir. 1981-82), Acad. Norteamericana Lengua Española, Internat. Inst. (Madrid), Internat. Linguistic Assn. (exec. coun.), Hispanic Sem. Medieval Studies (bd. dirs.), Ponce De Leon Conquistadors, Sigma Delta Pi, Sigma Tau Gamma; corr. mem. Royal Spanish Acad., Real Acad. Bellas Artes San Carlos (Valencia), Acad. Guatemalteca de Lengua, Assn. Bibliofilos Barcelona, Fundacion Odón Betanzos (Rociana), Fundacion Santa Maria de la Rabida, Fundacion Universitaria Espanola (Madrid), Inst. Valencia Don Juan (bd. dirs. Madrid). Office: Hispanic Soc Am 613 W 155th St New York NY 10032-7501

BEARE, GENE KERWIN, electric company executive; b. Chester, Ill., July 14, 1915; s. Nicholas Eugene and Minnie Cole (St. Vrain) B.; m. Doris Margaret Alt, Dec. 11, 1943 (dec.); children: Gail Kathryn, Joanne St. Vrain; m. Patricia Pfau Cade, Sept. 12, 1964 (dec.); m. Lee May Hollo, July 29, 1997. BS in Mech. Engring, Washington U., 1937; MBA, Harvard, 1939. Registered profl. engr., Ill. With Automatic Electric Co., Chgo., 1939-58, successively asst. to v.p. and gen. mgr., asst. to pres., mgr. internat. affiliated cos., gen. comml. mgr., 1939-54, v.p. prodn., 1954-58, dir., 1956-61; pres., dir. Automatic Electric Internat., Inc., Chgo., 1958-61; chmn., dir. Automatic Electric (Can.), Ltd., Chgo., Automatic Electric Sales (Can.), Ltd., 1958-61; pres., dir. Sylvania Internat., 1959-60; pres. Gen. Telephone & Electronics Internat., Inc., 1960-61, dir., 1960-72, also dir. numerous subs. in; dir. Am. Research and Devel. Corp., 1967-74, Canadair Ltd., 1972-75. Pres. Sylvania Electric Products, Inc., 1961-69, dir., 1961-72; exec. v.p. mfg., dir. Gen. Telephone & Electronics Corp., 1969-72; exec. v.p., dir. Gen. Dynamics Corp., St. Louis, 1972-77; pres. Gen. Dynamics Comml. Products Co., 1972-77; chmn. Asbestos Corp. Ltd., 1974-77; dir. Arkwright-Boston Mut. Ins. Co., Westvaco Corp., Emerson Electric Co., St. Joe Minerals Corp., Am. Maize-Products Corp., Datapoint Corp., Nooney Realty Trust, Inc. Served to lt. USNR, 1942-45. Mem. Pan Am. Soc., Nat. Elec. Mfrs. Assn. (bd. govs. 1963-72, v.p. 1964, pres. 1965-66), Armed Forces Communications and Electronics Assn., Nat. Security Indsl. Assn. (trustee 1969-72). Clubs: Wee Burn (Darien, Conn.) (gov. 1963-68); Union League (N.Y.C.), Econ. (N.Y.C.); St. Louis (dir., 1979—); Old Warson (Ladue, Mo.) (dir., 1979—), Univ. (St. Louis), The Ocean Club of Fla., Ocean Ridge. Home: 801 S Skinker Blvd Saint Louis MO 63105-3269 Office: Pierre Laclede Center 7701 Forsyth Blvd Ste 1070 Saint Louis MO 63105-1840

BEARE-ROGERS, JOYCE LOUISE, former research executive; b. nr. Pickering, Ont., Can., Sept. 8, 1927; d. Frederick John and Sarah May (Michell) Beare; m. Charles Graham Rogers, Dec. 30, 1961; 1 child, Anne Catherine. BA, U. Toronto, Ont., 1951, MA, 1952; PhD, Carleton U., Ottawa, Ont., 1966; DSc (hon.), U. Man., Winnipeg, Can., 1985, U. Guelph, Ont., Can., 1993. Rsch. assoc. U. Toronto, 1952-54; instr. Vassar Coll., Poughkeepsie, N.Y., 1954-56; chemist Food, Drug Directorate (name now Health Protect Br.), Ottawa, 1956-65, rsch. scientist, 1965-75; rsch. mgr. Bur. Nutritional Scis., Ottawa, 1975-91. Adj. prof. U. Ottawa, 1980-92; cons. Food and Agrl. Orgn. UN, 1992-94; Hilditch lectr. U.K., 1994; trustee Nat. Inst. Nutrition (Can.), 1997-99. Editor: Methods for Nutritional Assessment of Fats, 1985, Fat Requirements for Development and Health, 1988; contbr. articles on dietary fats to profl. jours. Decorated Order of Can.; recipient Queen's Jubilee medal Govt. of Can., 1977, Medaille Chevreul award Inst. Corps Gras, 1984, Crompton award McGill U., 1986, Normann medal German Assn. for Fat Rsch., 1987, Commemorative medal for 125th Anniversary of Fedn. of Can., 1992. Fellow: Am. Inst. Nutrition, Royal Soc. Can. (panelist on food biotechnology 2000—01, hon. treas. 2000—); mem.: Can. Biochem. Soc., Can. Soc. for Nutrition Scis. (pres. 1984—85, Bordon award 1971, McHenry award 1993), Internat. Soc. Fat Rsch. (pres. 1991—92), Am. Oil Chemists Soc. (pres. 1985—86, Lifetime Achievement award Can. sect. 1995, Queen's Golden Jubilee medal 2002). Avocations: hiking, canoeing, cross-country skiing, reading. Home: 41 Okanagan Dr Ottawa ON Canada K2H 7E9 E-mail: jbrogers@sympatico.ca

BEARG, ESTHER MARILYN, retired school counselor, educational consultant; b. N.Y.C., Apr. 8, 1927; d. Frank and Ida D. (Zakim) Becker; widowed; children: Fredrica, Barry, Martin. BA, CUNY, 1947, MS in Edn., 1961; EdD, Fairleigh Dickinson U., 1979; 6th yr. cert., Montclair State U., 1976. Cert. elem. tchr., sch. counselor, prin., sch. social work. Tchr. 4th grade Elmont (N.J.) Bd. of Edn., 1947-50; tchr. 5th grade Woodmere (N.Y.)-Hewlett Bd. of Edn., 1961-63, West Orange (N.J.) Bd. of Edn., 1963-71, sch. counselor, 1971-2000; cons. in edn. and career Caldwell-West Caldwell Adult Sch., 1984-99; freelance counselor, 1999—. Leader numerous summer workshops on new math, child and youth study, career devel.; workshop co-leader NEAT: A Guide for Coll. Admission Counselors, 1985—. Author: Career Planning: Focus on Your Career, 1990, Pointers for Parents: How To Help Your Child Succeed in High School, 2002; contbr. articles to newsletters, newspapers, mags. Pres. local chpt., sec. N.J. region Am. Jewish Congress, 1988—. Named Essex County Counselor of Yr., N.J. Profl. Counseling Assn., 1989. Mem. NEA, N.J. Edn. Assn., N.J. Assn. Coll. Admission Counselors (sec. 1990-92), Essex County Edn. Assn., West Orange Edn. Assn., Essex County Sch. Counselor Assn. (pres., v.p. programming 1981-84, chair nat. sch. counseling week 1984-94). Jewish. E-mail: ebearg@aol.com.

BEARMAN, TONI CARBO See CARBO, TONI

BEARN, ALEXANDER GORDON, physician, retired pharmaceutical executive; b. Surrey, Eng., Mar. 29, 1923; arrived in U.S., 1951; s. Edward Gordon Bearn; m. Margaret Slocum, Dec. 20, 1952; children: Helen B. Pennoyer, Gordon Clarence Frederic. Ed., Epsom Coll.; MB, BS, Guy's Hosp., U. London, Eng., 1945, MD, 1951; MD (hon.), U. René Descartes, Paris, 1974, Cath. U., Korea, 1968. Assoc. Rockefeller Inst., Rockefeller U., NYC, 1951—57; assoc. prof., physician Rockefeller U., NYC, 1957—64, prof., sr. physician, 1964—66, adj. prof., vis. physician, 1966—; prof. medicine Cornell U., 1966—77, Stanton Griffis Distinguished med. prof., 1977—79, chmn. dept., 1966—77; physician-in-chief N.Y. Hosp., 1966—77; sr. v.p. for med. and sci. affairs Merck, Sharp & Dohme Internat., Rahway, NJ, 1979—88; v.p. Am. Philos. Soc., 1990—96, exec. officer, 1997—2002; Disting. vis. fellow Christ's Coll., Cambridge, England, 1996—97, fellow commoner, 1997—. Mem. commn. human resources NAS, 1974—77; chmn. divsn. med. scis. Assembly Life Scis., 1978—79; bd. sci. counselors Nat. Inst. Arthritis, Metabolism and Digestive Diseases, 1976—80; mem. Space Sci. Bd., 1978—79; cons. genetics tng. com., divsn. gen. med. scis. USPHS, 1961—65, cons. genetics study sect., 1966—70; cons. Fogarty Ctr. NIH, 1991—94; pres. Royal Soc. Medicine Found., Inc., 1976—78; bd. sci. overseers Jackson Lab., Bar Harbor, 1969—82. Author: Archibald Garrod and the Individuality of Man, 1993; editor: Am. Jour Medicine, 1971—77; editor-in-chief:, 1977—79; co-editor: Progress in Medical Genetics, 1962—87; assoc. editor: Cecil-Loeb Textbook of Medicine; contbr. articles to profl. jours. Trustee Rockefeller U., 1971—98, trustee emeritus, 1998—; trustee Helen Hay Whitney Found., 1970—97, Macy Found., 1981—98, Howard Hughes Med. Inst., 1987—. Med. officer RAF, 1947—49. Recipient Alfred Benzon prize, Denmark, 1979, Benjamin Franklin medal, 2001, David Rockefeller award, 2002; fellow, Fulbright Found., 1951—52. Fellow: AAAS, Royal Coll. Physicians (London), Royal Coll. Physicians (Edinburgh, Scotland); mem.: Norwegian Acad. Sci. and Letters (fgn. assoc.), Med. Soc. London, Med. Rsch. Soc. Great Britain, Assn. Physicians Great Britain and Ireland, Harveian Soc. London (coun. 1959), Harvey Soc. (pres. 1972—73, Harvey lectr. 1975), Soc. Exptl. Biology and Medicine, Am. Soc. Biol. Chemists, Genetics Soc. Am., Am. Soc. Human Genetics (pres. 1971), Am. Soc. Clin. Investigation, Assn. Am. Physicians, Am. Philos. Soc. (exec. officer 1997—2002, v.p. 1990—96), Inst. Medicine NAS, Century Assn., Misquamicut Club (Watch Hill, R.I.), Knickerbocker Club, Phila. Club, Crail Golf Club (Scotland), Sigma Xi (pres. Rockefeller chpt. 1962—63). Presbyterian. Home: 241 S 6th St Apt 2111 Philadelphia PA 19106-3735

BEARSCH, LEE PALMER, architect, city planner; b. Binghamton, N.Y., July 5, 1942; s. Frederick James and Mildred Jane (Palmer) B.; m. Christine Cromer, Dec. 31, 1972; children: Frederick Cromer, Benjamin Palmer, Peter Furlong. BArch, Clemson U., 1965; M in Planning, Leverhulme Sch. Archtl. Assn., London, 1970. Registered profl. arch., N.Y., Pa., Md., Mass., Wis. Project dir. Llewelyn-Davies Assocs., London, N.Y., Racine, Wis., 1970-75; pres. Bearsch Compeau Knudson, Archs. and Engrs., P.C., Binghamton, 1976—. Mem. N.Y. State Edn. Dept. Bd. for Arch. Lic. Bd., 1997—. Mem. Broome County Planning Adv. Bd., Binghamton, 1978-90, sec., 1986-88; bd. dirs. Broome County Small Bus. Coun., 1979-84, vice chmn., 1981-83; vestryman Christ Episcopal Ch., 1981-84; bd. dirs. Family and Childrens Soc. Broome County Inc., 1982—, pres., 1985-86; bd. dirs. Binghamton Symphony Orch.; mem. adv. bd. Endicott Trust divsn. Mfrs. and Traders Bank; mem. Binghamton U. Coun.; mem. N.Y. State Bd. for Arch. State Licensing Bd. 1995—, chmn., 2002, 03. Fellow AIA (area dir. 1978-79, v.p. 1979-81, chpt. pres. 1981-82, state conv. chmn. 1983, state pres. 1990, nat. bd. dirs. 1990 93, nat. documents com. 1994—, chmn., 1998-2000, nat. conv. chmn. 1996); mem. Am. Inst. Cert. Planners, N.Y. State Assn. Archs. (bd. dirs. 1985—, exec. com. 1987—, pres. 1990, mem. bd. archtl. registration 1995—), Archtl. Assn. (Eng.), Broome County C. of C. (bd. dirs. 1986—, chmn. 1990-91), Leadership Broome (adv. bd. 1988-90), Binghamton City Club (bd. govs. 1995-2000), Binghamton Country Club (bd. govs. 1999—, pres. 2002), Live Wire Club, Nat. Coun. Archtl. Resgistratipn Bds. (chmn. profl. program devel. com. 2002-03). Office: Bearsch Compeau Knndson A&E PC 41 Chenango St Binghamton NY 13901-2901 Home: 1312 Robinson Hill Rd Endwell NY 13760 E-mail: lbearsch@bckpc.com.

BEART, ROBERT W., JR., surgeon, educator; b. Kansas City, Mo., Mar. 3, 1945; s. Robert Woodward and Helen Elizabeth (Wamsley) B.; m. Cynthia Anne, Jan. 23, 1971; children: Jennifer, Kristina, Amy. AB, Princeton U., 1967; MD, Harvard U., 1971. Diplomate Am. Bd. Surgery, Am. Bd. Colon and Rectal Surgery. Intern U. Colo., 1971-72, resident, 1972-76; prof. surgery Mayo Clinic, Scottsdale, Ariz., 1976-87, 1987-92, U. So. Calif., L.A., 1992—. Maj. USMC, 1972-83. Fellow Am. Soc. Colon and Rectal Surgery (pres. 1994). Office: 1450 San Pablo St # 5400 Los Angeles CA 90089-0106

BEARY, JOHN FRANCIS, III, physician, scientist, pharmaceutical executive; b. Melrose, Iowa, Dec. 14, 1946; s. John F. and Dorothy (McGrath) B.; m. Bianca E. Mason, May 6, 1972; children: John Daniel, Vanessa, Webster, Nina. BS summa cum laude, U. Notre Dame, 1969; MD, Harvard U., 1973; MBA, Georgetown U., 1988. Diplomate Am Bd. Internal Medicine, Am. Bd. Rheumatology, Am. Bd. Clin. Pharmacology. Flight surgeon 89th Mil. Airlift Wing (Air Force One), 1974—77; Osler medicine resident Johns Hopkins Hosp., Balt., 1977—78; rsch. fellow Cornell Med. Coll., N.Y.C., 1978—80; from asst. prof. to clin. prof. Georgetown U. Sch. Medicine, Washington, 1980—2000; prin. dept. asst. sec. health affairs Dept. Def., Washington, 1981—83; assoc. dean strategic planning Georgetown U. Sch. Medicine, Washington, 1984—87; sr. v.p. regulatory and sci. affairs Pharm. Rsch. and Mfg. Assn., Washington, 1988—97; sr. med. dir. arthritis rsch. Procter and Gamble Pharma, Cin., 1997—. Steering com. Internat. Conf. on Harmonization of Pharm. Stds., 1990-97; clin. prof. rheumatology and immunology U. Cin., 1997—. Editor: Manual of Rheumatology, 1981, 4th edit., 2000; mem. editorial bd. Jour. Pharm. Medicine, 1990—, Drug Devel. Rsch., 1992-2000. Bd. dirs. Scleroderma Found., Washington, 1982—92. Served to capt. USNR, 1984—99. Recipient disting. pub. service medal Dept. Def., 1983, Navy and Marine Corps Commendation medal, 1997, Georgetown Vicennial medal, 2003. Fellow: ACP, Am. Coll. Rheumatology; mem.: Osteoarthritis Rsch. Soc., Am. Soc. Clin. Pharmacology and Therapeutics, Am. Geriat. Soc., Johns Hopkins Med. and Surg. Assn., Mil. Officers Assn., U.S. Naval Inst., Harvard Club, Notre Dame Club (Cin.), Chevy Chase Club. Office: Procter & Gamble Pharma 8700 Mason Montgomery Rd Mason OH 45040-8006

BEARY, SHIRLEY LORRAINE, retired music educator; b. New Albany, Kans., Feb. 4, 1928; d. Howard Warren and Bertha Adelia (Wilcox) Fogelsanger; children: Stephanie Beary Johnson, Susan Beary Maloney. BA, Andrews U., 1949; MusM, U. Redlands, 1967; D Mus. Arts, Southwestern Bapt. Theol. Sem., 1977. Tchr. music, Nevada, Iowa, 1949-50; prof. music Southwestern Adventist Coll., Keene, Tex., 1959-84, lectr. Christian ethics, 1978-84; prof. music Oakwood Coll., Huntsville, Ala., 1984-94; ret., 1994. Ch. organist Seventh-day Adventist Ch., Kalamazoo, 1951-59, Keene, 1959-80, organist, min. music, 1980-82; adjudicator music Festival of Arts in Bahamas, 1994, 95, 97. Mem. bd. advisors Am. Biog. Inst., Raleigh, N.C. Mem. Coll. Music Soc., Am. Hymn Soc., Internat. Adventist Music Assn. Democrat. Avocations: travel, flower gardening, stamps and records collecting, gospel singing. Home: 215 Mistletoe Ln Keene TX 76059

BEASLEY, AARON BRUCE, football player; b. Pottstown, Pa., July 7, 1973; Student, W.Va. Cornerback Jacksonville Jaguars, 1996—2001; defensive back NY Jets, 2002—. Vol. Clara White Mission, The Bridge of N.E. Fla., 1997; active numerous charity fundraisers; spkr. local elem. schs.; annual participant Navajo Nation Youth Leadership Football Camp; supporter Jaguars Found. Named to 1996 All-Rookie Football News; named first-team All-Pro, Coll. & Pro Football Newsweekly, 1999. Office: 1000 Fulton Ave Hempstead NY 11550

BEASLEY, ALBERT SIDNEY, pediatrician; b. Framingham, Mass., Aug. 2, 1921; s. Albert Sidney and Marion Evans (Wilson) B.; m. Jean Scott Tallman, Aug. 21, 1942 (dec. Jan. 1973); children: Scott Albert, Jean Marion; m. Janet Grybski. BA, Columbia Coll., 1945; MD, NYU, 1947. Cert., Am. Bd. Pediatrics. Intern Queens Gen. Hosp., N.Y.C., 1947-49; pediatric resident Children's Meml. Hosp., Chgo., 1949-51, Larabida Sanitarium, Chgo., 1950; pvt. practice Westport, Conn., 1954-73; pediatric cardiac fellow Yale-New Haven (Conn.) Hosp., 1955-56; pediatrician Willows Pediatric Group, Westport, 1973-99, Bay Street Pediat. Assoc., 1999—2001. Sr. attending pediatrics, chief pediatric cardiology Norwalk (Conn.) Hosp., 1954-2002, emeritus staff in pediats., 2002—; assoc. clin. prof. pediatrics Yale U. Sch. Medicine, New Haven, 1956—. Mem. Youth Adult Coun., Westport, 1973-80; bd. dirs. United Way, Westport, 1988-94; adv. com. Edn. Quality and Diversity Com., Westport, 1993-95; consulting trustee Nature Ctr. Environ. Activities, Westport, 1994—. Capt. USAF M.C., 1951-53. Fellow Am. Acad. Pediatrics; mem. Am. Acad. Pediatrics (Conn. chpt.), Conn. State Med. Soc., Norwalk Med. Soc., Fairfield County Med. Assn. Avocations: music, tennis, home improvement.

BEASLEY, BARBARA STARIN, sales executive, marketing professional; b. Nashville, Dec. 31, 1955; d. Donald Francis and Martha Murry (Bridges) S.; m. Johnny Mark Beasley, Oct. 22, 1983; children: John Thomas, Cara Nicole. BFA, So. Meth. U., 1976. Cert. strategic mktg. mgmt., Harvard Bus. Sch. Producer Bill Stokes Assn., Dallas, 1976-80; Mary Kay Cosmetics, Inc., Dallas, 1980-93; sr. v.p. mktg., 1987-89; exec. v.p. sales divsn., 1990-93; sr. v.p. mktg. Nest Entertainment, Dallas, 1994-99, sr. v.p. sales and mktg., 1999-2000; freelance writer, 2000—. Mem. Leadership Tex., 1986. Avocation: birdwatching.

BEASLEY, BRUCE MILLER, sculptor; b. L.A., May 20, 1939; s. Robert Seth and Bernice (Palmer) B.; m. Laurence Leaute, May 21, 1973; children: Julian Bernard, Celia Beranice. Student, Dartmouth Coll., 1957-59; BA, U. Calif., Berkeley, 1962. One-man shows include Everett Ellin Gallery, L.A., 1963, Kornblee Gallery, N.Y.C., 1964, Hansen Gallery, San Francisco, 1965, David Stuart Gallery, L.A., 1966, Andre Emmerich Gallery, N.Y.C., 1971, DeYoung Mus., San Francisco, 1972, Santa Barbara Mus. Art, 1973, San Diego Mus. Art, 1973, Fuller-Goldeen Gallery, San Francisco, 1981, Hooks-Epstein Gallery, Houston, 1990, 93, 95, 98, Pepperdine U., L.A., 1990, So. Oreg. State U., 1991, Sonoma State U., Rhonert Park, Calif., 1991, Fresno Art Mus., 1992, Oakland Mus., 1992, Utermann Gallery, Dortmund, Germany, 1993, Scheffel Gallery, Bad Homberg, Germany, 1993, Galerie Rudolfinum, Prague, 1994, Kunsthalle Mannheim, Germany, 1994, Harcourts Gallery, San Francisco, 1994, Galerie Wirth, Zurich, Switzerland, 1995, Yorkshire Sculpture Park, Eng., 1995, City Ctr., Dortmund, Germany, 1996, Atrium Gallery, St. Louis, 1997, Purdue U., West Lafayette, Ind., 1997, Solomon-Dubnick Gallery, Sacramento, 1997, Gwenda Jay Gallery, Chgo., 1998, Kouros Gall., N.Y.C., 1999, Math. Scis. Rsch. Inst., Berkeley, Calif., 2000, Gail Severn Gallery, Ketchum, Idaho, 2001, Silicon Valley Art Mus., Belmont, Calif., 2001; exhibited in group shows at San Francisco Mus. of Modern Art, 1961, Mus. of Modern Art, N.Y.C., 1961,62, Dallas Mus. Contemporary Art, 1962, Musee d'Art Moderne, Paris, 1963, U. Art Mus., Berkeley, 1964, Fine Arts Museums, San Francisco, 1965, Guggenheim Mus., 1966, Krannert Art Mus., Ill., 1969, Jewish Mus., N.Y.C., 1970, Milw. Art Ctr., 1970, Expo '70, Osaka, Japan, Stanford Art Mus., 1972, Musee d'Art Moderne, Paris, 1973, Nat. Mus. Am. Art, 1980, Musee d'Art Contemporain Bordeaux, France, 1984, Kunsthalle Mannheim, 1984, Palace of Exhbns., Budapest, Hungary, 1987, Middleheim Sculpture Park, Belgium, 1987, Yorkshire Sculpture Park, Eng., 1984, 87, Hakone Open-Air Mus., Japan, 1993, 95, Landesgartenschau, Germany, 1994, Sculpture '97, Bad Homberg, Germany, Pier Walk '97, 98, 99, 2000, 01, Chgo., Galerie Wirth, Zurich, Switzerland, 1997, Darmstadt (Germany) Sculpture Biennale, 1998, Cairo Biennale, Egypt, 1998, Mus. Modern Art, San Francisco, 2000, Grounds for Sculpture, Hamilton, N.J., 2001, Solomon-Dubnick Gallery, Sacramento, 2002; represented in permanent collections Mus. Modern Art, N.Y.C., Guggenheim Mus., N.Y.C., Musee d'Art, Paris, Nat. Mus. Am. Art, Washington, Kunsthalle Mannheim, Germany, San Franciso Mus. Modern Art, L.A. County Mus. Art, Sheldon Mem. Art Gallery, Lincoln, Nebr., Hood Mus. Art-Dartmouth Coll., Spencer Mus. Art, Lawrence, Kans., Laguna Art Mus., Franklin D. Murphy Sculpture Garden, UCLA, Crocker Art Mus., Sacramento, Seattle Art Mus., Fresno Art Mus., Xantus Janos Mus., Hungary, Fine Art Muss., San Francisco, Oakland Mus. Calif., Santa Barbara Mus. Art, San Jose (Calif.) Mus. Art, Grounds for Sculpture, Hamilton, N.J., Nora Eccles Harrison Mus., Utah State U., Logan; commissions include State of Calif., Oakland Mus., City San Francisco, Miami Internat. Airport, San Francisco Internat. Airport, Fed. Home Loan Bank, San Francisco, Stanford U., City Anchorage, City Salinas, Calif., Fresno Art Mus., Gateway Ctr., Walnut Creek, Calif.; commns. Village of Flossmoor, Ill., City Oakland, Calif., City of Brea, Calif., U. Oreg. Art Mus., Eugene, Miami U., Oxford, Ohio. Bd. dirs. Internat. Sculpture Ctr., Washington. Home: 322 Lewis St Oakland CA 94607-1236

BEASLEY, DAVID MULDROW, former governor, consultant; b. Lamar, S.C., Feb. 26, 1957; s. Richard Lee and Jacqueline Adele (Blackwell) B.; m. Mary Wood Payne. Student, Clemson U., 1976-78; BA, U. S.C., 1979, JD. Mem. Dist. 56 S.C. Ho. Reps., 1979-92, majority leader, 1987, mem. joint legis. com. on edn., vice chmn. joint legis. com. on children, 1987-88; atty., 1992-94; gov. State of S.C., 1995—99; fellow Inst. Politics Kennedy Sch. Govt. Harvard U., 1999; prin. Bingham Cons. Group, 1999—2001; partner Beasley, Ervin & Warr; chmn. Nat. Advisory Com. on Rural Health & Human Svcs., 2001—.

BEASLEY, ERNEST WILLIAM, JR., endocrinologist; b. Atlanta, May 7, 1924; s. Ernest William and Arrinda Elizabeth (Eidson) Beasley; m. Ann Lee Jeffreys, July 1, 1950; children: Janet Ann, Ernest William III, Mary Elizabeth, Barbara Elaine. MD, Georgetown U., 1949. Diplomate Am. Bd. Internal Medicine, Sub-Bd. Endocrinology, Am. Bd. Family Practice Geriatrics. Intern Walter Reed Hosp., Washington, 1949—50; resident in internal medicine VA Hosp.-Grady Meml. Hosp., Atlanta; practice medicine specializing in family practice Atlanta, 1955—65; in internal medicine, 1966—75; in endocrinology, 1975—. Past chief endocrinology and metabolism Ga. Bapt. Med. Center; assoc. dept. internal medicine Emory U.; cons. Ga. Assn. Retarded Children, 1955—65; dir. Diabetes Assn. Atlanta, 1976. Served with AUS, 1943—45, M.C., U.S. Army, 1950—52. Fellow: Am. Coll. Endocrinology; mem.: AMA, Endocrine soc., Med. Assn. Ga., Med. Assn. Atlanta, Am. Assn. Clin. Endocrinologists, Cherokee Country Club. Methodist. Address: #150 5667 Peachtree-Dunwoody Rd Atlanta GA 30342

BEASLEY, JAMES EDWIN, lawyer; s. James Edwin and Margaret Ann (Patterson) B.; children: Pamela Jane, Kimberly Ann, James Edwin, Lynn, Nancy. BS, Temple U., 1953, JD, 1956. Bar: Pa. 1956. Law clk. U.S. Dist. Ct. (ea. dist.) Pa., Phila., 1954-56; prin The Beasley Firm, Phila., 1966—. Instr. law Temple U., 1976-80, adj. prof., 1994; permanent del. 3d Cir. Jud. Conf.; chmn. standard civil jury inst. Pa. Supreme Ct.; Jud. Ct. of Judicial Discipline, Commnwealth of Pa.; bd. dirs. NATA; past trustee Pop Warner Little Scholars. Author: Products Liability and the Unreasonably Dangerous Requirement; contbr. articles to profl. jours. With USN, 1943-45, USAR, 1951-57. Mem.: ATLA, ABA, Union League, Nat. Air Racing Group, Six Diamonds Aerobatic Flight Team, Aircraft Owners and Pilots Assn. (cert. flight instr. single-multi engine airplane and instrument FAA), Pa. Soc., Temple U. Gen. Alumni Assn. (cert. of honor), Am. Bd. Profl. Liability Attys., Inner Cir. Advs., Pa. Trial Lawyers Assn. (pres. 1969—70), Phila. Trial Lawyers Assn. (pres. 1970—71, Justice Michael Musmanno award), Phila. Bar Assn., Pa. Bar Assn., Nat. Transp. Safety Bd. Bar Assn., Am. Bd. Trial Advs., Am. Law Inst., Am. Judicature Soc., Fed. Bar Assn., QB PhL Hanger. Episcopalian. Office: 1125 Walnut St Philadelphia PA 19107-4918 Fax: 215-592-9613. E-mail: jeb@tortlaw.com.

BEASLEY, JAMES W., JR., lawyer; b. Atlanta, July 13, 1943; s. James W. and Sara Capal (Tucker) B.; m. Elizabeth Barno Marshall-Beasley, Nov. 28, 1986. AB cum laude, Davidson Coll., 1965; LLB cum laude, Harvard U., 1968. Bar: N.Y. 1969, D.C. 1971, Fla. 1972, U.S. Supreme Ct. 1973. Assoc. Sullivan & Cromwell, N.Y.C., 1968, Wilmer, Cutler & Pickering, Washington, 1970-72; assoc., then ptnr. Paul & Thomson, Miami, Fla., 1972-78; mng. ptnr. Beasley, Olle & Downs, Miami, 1978-88; ptnr. Tew, Jordan, Schulte & Beasley, Miami, 1988-89, Cadwalader, Wickersham & Taft, Palm Beach, Fla., 1989-94, Tew & Beasley LLP, Palm Beach, 1994-97, Beasley & Hauser, P.A., Palm Beach, 1997—. Author: Florida Corporations, 1985; contbr. articles to profl. jours. Chmn. County Conv. Ctr. Adv. Bd., 1994-96. Capt. U.S. Army, 1968-70. Mem. ABA, ATLA, Fla. Bar Assn. (chmn. securities regulation com. bus. law sect. 1975-77), Acad. Fla. Trial Lawyers. Office: Beasley & Hauser PA 505 S Flagler Dr West Palm Beach FL 33401-5923

BEASLEY, JIM SANDERS See LEE, JACK

BEASLEY, JOHN JULIUS, child and family development educator; b. Raleigh, N.C., July 9, 1947; s. Julius Helland and Ruth Christine (Richardson) B.; m. Mary Sandra Wortham, June 21, 1969; 1 child, Elizabeth. BA, E. Carolina U., 1969; MS, Va. Tech., 1972, PhD, 1978. Extension agent 4-H Va. Tech., Blacksburg, 1971-74, instr. extension, 1974-78, asst. prof. extension, 1978-81; chair Appalachian State U., Boone, N.C., 1981-86, assoc. prof., 1981-88; prof. Ga. So. U., Statesboro, 1988—, chair, 1988-96. Cons. Head Start, Vienna, Va., 1995—; spkr. in field. Editor rsch. sect. Jour. Extension, 1979-81; reviewer Jour. of Family and Consumer Scis., 1994—; contbr. articles to profl. jours. Pres., University Optimist, Statesboro, 1991-92, adv. bd., 1996—; pres. Child Abuse Coun., Statesboro, 1995-97. Grantee Children's Trust Fund, 1991, Ga. Child Care Coun., 1992. Mem. Future Homemakers of Am./HERO (hon.), Am. Assn. Family Consumer Sci. (cert. family consumer scientist), Ga. Family Consumer Scis., Statesboro C. of C., Optimist Internat. (life), Phi Delta Kappa, Phi Kappa Phi, Phi Upsilon Omicron. Episcopalian. Home: 108 Turkey Trl Statesboro GA 30458-8908 Office: Ga So U PO Box 8021 Statesboro GA 30460-1000

BEASLEY, JOHN SNODGRASS, II, university administrator; b. Franklin, Tenn., Oct. 2, 1930; s. Thomas Earl and Elsie (Eggleston) B.; m. Mary D. Allison Tidman, Sept. 4, 1958; children: John III, Eleanor Christensen Beasley Nahley. BA, Vanderbilt U., 1952, JD, 1954. Bar: Tenn. 1954. Atty., Franklin, 1957-58; exec. sec. alumni assn. Vanderbilt U., 1958-61; asst. dean, asst. prof. Vanderbilt Law Sch., 1962-64, assoc. dean, asst. prof., 1964-66, assoc. dean, assoc. prof., 1966-70, assoc. dean, prof., 1970-71; nat. alumni dir. centennial campaign Vanderbilt U., 1980-81, spl. asst. to chancellor, 1981-83, vice chancellor for alumni and devel., 1983-99, vice chancellor emeritus, spl. asst. to chancellor, 1999-2000; vice chancellor emeritus, counselor to chancellor, 2001—; sr. v.p. Commerce Union Bank, Nashville, 1971-74, exec. v.p., 1974-78, vice chmn. trust bd., 1978-80. Founding pres. Heritage Found. of Franklin and Williamson County, 1965-68; bd. dirs. Franklin Spl. Sch. Dist., 1974-76; trustee Battle Ground Acad., Franklin, 1970-74, Tenn. Bot. Gardens

and Fine Arts Ctr. at Cheekwood, Nashville, 1969-75, pres. 1973-75; chmn. bd. Harpeth Hall Sch., Nashville, 1976-81; bd. dirs. Tenn. Performing Arts Ctr., 1986-92, Nashville Symphony Assn., 1958-64, pres., 1962-64; mem. adv. bd. Jr. League of Nashville, 2000—. Mem. Belle Meade County Club (bd. dirs. 1974-80, v.p. 1979-80), Vanderbilt Alumni Assn. (pres. 1979-80), Univ. Club (N.Y.C., Nashville), Order of Coif, Phi Beta Kappa, Omicron Delta Kappa, Sigma Chi, Pi Delta Epsilon, Phi Delta Phi. Republican. Episcopalian. Avocation: piano. Home: 4378 Chickering Ln Nashville TN 37215 Office: Vanderbilt U 102 Alumni Hall Nashville TN 37240 Fax: 615-322-1814. E-mail: John.Beasley@vanderbilt.edu.

BEASLEY, JOSEPH WAYNE, lawyer; b. Sylacauga, Ala, Feb. 10, 1943; s. William Ocie and Alice Lorraine (Blackmon) B.; m. Gerri Gay Aldrich, Aug. 26, 1966. BS in Aerospace Engring., U. Fla., 1966, JD with high honors, 1973; MS in Aeronautics & Astronautics, U. Wash., 1970. Bar: Fla. 1974, U.S. Dist. Ct. (so. dist.) Fla. 1974, U.S. Ct. Appeals (5th cir.) 1981, U.S. Ct. Appeals (11th cir.) 1982, U.S. Dist. Ct. (mid. dist.) Fla. 1982, U.S. Supreme Ct. 2000. From engr. to lead engr. Boeing Aircraft Co., Seattle, 1966-71; instr. legal writing, rsch. U. Fla., Gainesville, 1973-74; assoc. litigator Mershn Sawyer Johnston Dunwoody & Cole, Miami, Fla., 1974-78; ptnr., shareholder Kelly Black Black Byrne & Beasley P.A., Miami, 1978—99; of counsel Josephs, Jack, Miranda, P.A., 2000—. Mem. ABA, Fla. Bar Assn. (environ. com., comml. litigation com., chair 11th judicial cir. grievance com.), Coral Reef Yacht Club, Coconut Grove Civic Club (past bd. dirs.). Republican. Baptist. Avocations: marathon running, snow skiing, handball, sailing, Karate. Office: Josephs Jack Miranda, PA 2950 SW 27th Ave Ste 110 Miami FL 33133

BEASLEY, LEROY B. mathematics educator; b. Shelley, Idaho, July 31, 1942; s. Lawrence Byington Beasley and Grace Vivian (Davis) Orr; m. Debra Ann Schaefer, July 18, 1975; children: Mia L. B. Crossthwaite, Lisa N. BS, Idaho State U., Pocatello, 1964, MS, 1966; PhD, U. B.C., Vancouver, Can., 1969. Cert. secondary tchr., Idaho. Tchr., dept. head Middleton (Idaho) High Sch., Dist. 134, 1972-81; from asst. to prof. math. Utah State U., Logan, 1981—. Vis. prof. U. Coll., Dublin, Ireland, 1987-8, 95, Technin, Israel, 1994-95, Sung Kyun Kwan U, Korea, 1994, U. Lisbon, Portugal, 1995. Contbr. numerous articles to scholarly and profl. jours. Capt. U.S. Army, 1970-71, Vietnam. Grantee NSF, 1979-81, Inst. of Math. and Its Applications, U. Minn., 1991, Korea Rsch. Found., 2003—. Fellow The Inst. Combinatorics and Its Applications; mem. Math. Assn. Am., Internat. Linear Algebra Soc., Irish Math. Soc., Korean Math. Soc. Office: Utah State Univ Dept Of Math And Statistics Logan UT 84322-3900

BEASLEY, MARY CATHERINE, home economics educator, administrator, researcher; b. Portersville, Ala., Nov. 29, 1922; d. Albert Otis and Beulah Green (Killian) Reed; m. Percy Wells Beasley, Dec. 15, 1956 (dec. Dec. 1958). BS in Home Econs., Bob Jones U., 1944; MS, Pa. State U., State College, 1954, EdD, 1968. Tchr. Geraldine and Collinsville (Ala.) High Sch., 1944-45; vocat. home econs. tchr. Glencoe (Ala.) High Sch., 1945-48, Washington County High Sch., Chatom, Ala., 1948-51; home econs. tchr. Homewood Jr. High Sch., Birmingham, Ala., 1958-60; asst. supr. and subject matter specialist Ala. Dept. Edn., Montgomery, 1951-57; asst. prof. Samford U., Birmingham, 1960-62; instr. U. Ala., Tuscaloosa, 1951, asst. prof. then assoc. prof., 1962-68, dir. continuing edn. in home econs., 1968-84, prof., 1984-88, prof. emeritus consumer sci. Coll. Human Environ. Sci., 1988—. Author: (with others) Human Ecological Studies, 1986. Pres. Joint Legis. Coun. of Ala., 1973-75; dir. On Your Own Program, 1970-80; v.p. bd. dirs. Collinsville Cemetery Assn., 2000-02, pres., 2002—. Recipient Creative Programming award Nat. U. Extension Assn., 1979, Women of Achievement award, 2000; named N.E. Ala Woman of Distinction, Girl Scouts North Ala., Inc., 2002. Mem. Am. Home Econs. Assn. (chmn. rehab. com. 1973, 75, leader 1986), Southeastern Coun. on Family Rels. (pres. 1982-84, Disting. Svc. award 1988), Ala. Home Econs. Assn. (pres. 1961-63, leader 1985), Ala. Coun. on Family Rels. (pres. 1981-83, Disting. Svc. award 1987), Altrusa Club of Tuscaloosa (pres. 1988-89, exec. bd. Ft. Payne/DeKalb 1989-93, corr. sec. 1995-96), Collinsville Study Club (v.p. 1992-94, pres. 1996-98, 2002--, reporter 1998-2000, parliamentarian 2000-2002), Ala. Federated Womens Clubs (dir. dist. II 1999-00), Alpha Delta Kappa (treas. Tuscaloosa chpt. 1973-75), Phi Upsilon Omicron, Kappa Omicron Nu. Republican. Baptist. Home: 12860 US Highway 11 Collinsville AL 35961-4321

BEASLEY, MAURINE HOFFMAN, journalism educator, historian; b. Jan. 28, 1936; d. Dimmitt Heard and Maurine (Hieronymus) Hoffman; m. William C. McLaughlin, May 20, 1966 (div. 1969); m. Henry R. Beasley, Dec. 24, 1970; 1 child, Susan Sook. BA in History, U. Mo., 1958; MS in Journalism, Columbia U., 1963; PhD in Am. Civilization, George Washington U., 1974. Edn. editor Kansas City (Mo.) Star, 1959—62; staff writer Washington Post, 1963—73; from asst. prof journalism to prof. U. Md., College Park, 1975—87, prof., 1987—, grad. dir. Coll. Journalism, 2000—02; sr. lectr. Fulbright Jinan U., Guangzhou, China, 2000. Author: Eleanor Roosevelt and the Media: A Public Quest for Self-Fulfillment, 1987; author: (with others) Women in Media, 1977, The New Majority, 1988, Taking Their Place! Documentary History of Women and Journalism, rev., 2002 (Outstanding Acad. Books Choice, 1994); editor: White House Press Conferences of Eleanor Roosevelt, 1983; co-editor: Voices of Change: Southern Pulitzer Winners, 1978, One Third of a Nation, 1981 (hon. mention Washington Monthly Book award, 1982), Eleanor Roosevelt Encyclopedia, 2000 (Editor's Choice award Booklist, 2001); mem. adv. bd. Am. Journalism, 1983—, Jour. Mass Media Ethics, —, Mass Com. Rev., —; corr. editor: Journalism History, 1995—; contbr. articles to profl. jours. Violinist Montgomery County Symphony Orch., 1975—; pres. Little Falls Swimming Club, Inc. 1988-89; bd. dirs. Sino-Am. Ctr. for Media Tech. and Tng., 2000—. Gannett Tchg. Fellowships Program fellow, 1977, Pulitzer Travelling fellow Columbia U., 1963; Eleanor Roosevelt studies grantee Eleanor Roosevelt Inst., 1979-80, Arthur Schlesinger rsch. fellow and grantee Roosevelt Inst., 1998; named one of nation's outstanding tchrs. of writing and editing Modern Media Inst. and Am. Soc. Newspaper Editors, 1981, most outstanding woman U. Md. Coll. Park Pres. Commn. on Women's Affairs, 1993; recipient Haiman award Speech Comm. Assn., 1995, Founders Disting. Sr. Scholar award AAUW Ednl. Found., 1999, Columbia U. Sch. Journalism Alumni award, 2000, Smith-Cotton H.S. Hall Fame award, Sedalia, Mo., 2000. Mem.: AAUW (v.p. Coll. Pk. br. 2002—), Am. Journalism Historians Assn. (pres.-elect 1988—89, pres. 1989—90, Kobre award for lifetime achievement 1997, Rsch. Paper award named in her honor 1998), Internat. Assn. Mass. Comms. Rsch., Soc. Profl. Journalists (chair nat. hist. site com. 1986—87, bd. dirs. Washington chpt. 1988—90, pres. 1990—91, dir. region 2, nat. bd. dirs. 1991—92, Disting. Local Svc. award 1994, First Amendment award with others 1998), Assn. Edn. in Journalism and Mass Comms. (sec. history divsn. 1986—87, vice-head 1987—88, head history divsn. 1988—89, chair profl. freedom and responsibility 1990—91, exec. com. 1990—91, nat. pres. elect 1992, pres. 1993—94, leader People-to-People delegation to China and Hong Kong 1994, exec. com. 1994—95, Outstanding Contbn. to Journalism Edn. award 1994, Disting. Leadership award 2001), Am. Hist. Assn., Am. News Women's Club (bd. govs. 2001—03), Women in Comms., Orgn. Am. Historians, Omicron Delta Kappa, Phi Beta Kappa. Democrat. Unitarian Universalist. Home: 4920 Flint Dr Bethesda MD 20816-1746 Office: U Md Coll Journalism College Park MD 20742 E-mail: mbeasley@jmail.umd.edu.

BEASLEY, ROBERT SCOTT, financial executive; b. Balt., Mar. 17, 1949; s. Robert F. and Marjorie (Scott) B.; m. Susan E. Gibson, Aug. 1, 1978 (div. July 1987); 1 child, Robert W. BS in Bus., Lehigh U., 1971, MBA, 1972; JD, U. Md., 1976; MA Nat. Security Studies, Georgetown U., 1989; cert. in space ops. mgmt., U. Denver, 1990. Bar: Md. 1977; CPA, Md. Audit staff acct. Arthur Young & Co., Balt., 1972—73; pvt. practice Balt., 1973—78; with corp. fin. dept. Merc.-Safe Deposit & Trust, Balt., 1978—80, with asset mgmt. dept., 1980—81; v.p. fin. Broventure Co., Balt., 1981—85, Astrotech Space Ops., LP, Silver Spring, Md., 1985—90; mgr. fin. and strategic analysis Westinghouse Electronic Systems Group, 1990—96, Northrop Grumman, 1996—. Lectr. bus. mgmt. Washington Coll., Chestertown, Md., 1996. Mem. Armed Forces Comms. and Electronics Assn. Republican. Methodist. Avocations: amateur radio, sailing. Home: 17911 Pond Rd Ashton MD 20861-9756 Office: Northrop Grumman PO Box 17319 Mail Stop A-425 Baltimore MD 21297-1319 E-mail: robeasley@comcast.net.

BEASOM, NANCY ANN, occupational therapist, consultant; b. Kansas City, Kans., Nov. 2, 1936; d. Albert Lawrence and Ruth Augusta (Badgley) Hibbs; m. Ronald Lightner Beasom, June 14, 1958; children: Kim Leslie Schwab, Jeffrey Craig Beasom, Bryn Ann Fay. BS, U. Pa., 1958. Registered and lic. occupational therapist, Pa., Fla. Artist/craftsman, West Chester, Pa., 1965-75; occupl. therapy cons. in pvt. practice, 1978-81; occupl. therapist DPW/Embreeville Ctr., Coatesville, Pa., 1975-82, occupl. therapy supr., 1982-85, mental retardation unit mgr., 1982-85, occupl. therapist, 1985-96; occupl. therapy cons. Chester County MH/MR Unit, West Chester, 1988-91, Elwyn, Inc., Pa., 1989-99. Cons. in occupational therapy Brian's House, West Chester, 1978-81, Home Health Care Agy., West Reading, Pa., 1981-82. Mem. Am. Occupational Therapy Assn. Avocations: basketry, gardening, writing poetry, art work, growing orchids. Home: 2085 River Basin Ter Punta Gorda FL 33982-1106

BEATON, HOWARD L. surgeon; b. N.Y.C., Aug. 11, 1950; MD, U. Rochester, 1976. Diplomate Am. Bd. Surgery. Intern N.Y. Hosp.-Cornell Med. Ctr., N.Y.C., 1976-77, resident in surgery, 1977-81; chief of surgery NYU Downtown Hosp., N.Y.C., 1994—; clin. assoc. prof. surgery NYU Sch. Medicine, N.Y.C., 1996—. Fellow ACS; mem. AMA, Assn. Acad. Surgeons, N.Y. Surg. Soc., Soc. Surgery Alimentary Tract. Office: NYU Downtown Hosp 170 William St New York NY 10038-2649

BEATON, MEREDITH, enterostomal therapy clinical nurse specialist; b. Danvers, Mass., Oct. 5, 1941; d. Allan Cameron and Arlene Margaret (Jerue) Beaton; m. William Paul Hollingsworth, Nov. 19, 1983 (div.); 1 stepchild, Brendon R. Diploma, R.I. Hosp. Sch. Nursing, Providence, 1968; BS in Nursing, U. Ariz., 1976; MS in Human Resource Mgmt., Golden Gate U., 1984; postgrad., U. Tex., 1988; EdD, U. N.Mex., 1995; MS in Nursing, U. Phoenix, 1998. Cert. enterostomal therapy nurse, health edn. specialist. Commd. ensign USN, 1968, advanced through grades to lt. comdr., 1979, charge nurse, 1968-88; command ostomy nurse, head ostomy clinic Naval Hosp. Portsmouth, Va., 1985-88; pres., CEO Enterostomal Therapy Nursing Edn. and Tng. Cons. (ETNetc), Rio Rancho, N.Mex., 1989-99; mgr. clin. svcs. western area Support Systems Internat., Inc., Charleston, S.C., 1990-92; pres., CEO, Paumer Assocs. Internat., Inc., Rio Rancho, N.Mex., 1992—2001; sr. cons. enterostomal therapy nursing, edn., & tng. cons.; dir./provost N.Mex. Sch. Enterostomal Nursing, Rio Rancho, 1996-2000; enterostomal therapy nurse, clin. nurse specialist, educator Presbyn. Health Care Svcs., Albuquerque, 1992-95; sr. cons. Enterostomal Therapy Nursing Edn. & Tng. Cons. A Divsn. of Paumer Assocs., Rio Rancho, N.Mex., 1995—2001. Dir./provost N.Mex. Sch. ET Nursing, Rio Rancho, 1995—2000; clin. svcs. mgr. Paper Pak Products Inc., 2000—02; sch. nurse Colinas del Norte Elem. Sch., Rio Rancho Pub. Schs. Sys., N.Mex., 2002—; lectr. in field. Reviewer: RN Mag. Mem. adminstrv. bd. Baylake United Meth. Ch., Virginia Beach, 1980-83; chmn. bd. deacons St. Paul's United Ch., Rio Rancho, moderator, 2001-02, also vice moderator; active Am. Cancer Soc.; mem. adv. bd. Keep Rio Rancho Beautiful, 1998-2003; bd. dirs. Assn. Advancement of Wound Care, 1998-2002. Mem. Wound, Ostomy and Continence Nurses Soc. (nat. govt. affairs com., govt. affairs com. Rocky Mountain region, newsletter editor, pub. rels. com., regional pres. 1989-93, nat. sec. 1994-95), United Ostomy Assn., World Coun. Enterostomal Therapists (mem. editl. bd. 2003-), N. Mex. Health Care Assn., N. Mex. Assn. for Home Care, N.Mex. Assn. Sch. Nurses, N. Mex. Assn. for Continuity of Care, Assn. Advanced Wound Care (bd. dirs.). Republican. Avocations: hot air ballooning, gourmet cooking, flower arranging, interior design. E-mail: meredith60@earthlink.net.

BEATON, REBECCA ANDREA, psychotherapist; b. West Covina, Calif., Dec. 3, 1964; d. Allen Ethan and Joan Delores (Graybill) Brogan; m. Robert Gifford Beaton II, Sept. 4, 1993. BA Human Philosophy & Cultural Geography, U. Calif., Santa Barbara, 1986; MS in Cmty. Counseling, Ga. State U., 1995, specialist in edn., 1996, PhD in Counseling Psychology, 2000. Health counselor Bragg Health Sci., Santa Barbara, Calif., 1986-87; counselor intern Anxiety Disorders Inst./Atlanta Ctr. for Eating Disorders, 1994-95; counselor intern employee assistance program Lockheed Aero. Sys. Co., Marietta, Ga., 1994-95; psychotherapist Anxiety Disorders Inst. Atlanta, 1995-98; pvt. practice Ctr. for Psychotherapy and Healing Arts, 1998-2000; psychology resident Counseling and Testing Ctr. U. Ga., 1999-2000; pvt. practice Atlanta, 2000—. Grad. rsch. asst. Ednl. Rsch. Bur., Ga. State U., Atlanta, 1993-94, dept. counseling and psychol. svcs., 1993-96; therapy group leader Trauma Abuse and Resource Program, Atlanta, 1995-98; psychotherapist Atlanta Ctr. for Eating Disorders, Altanta, 1995-98; growth group leader Ga. State U., Atlanta, 1995-98, adj. faculty counseling and psychol. svcs. dept. and Counseling Ctr., 2000--; trainer Wellness Inst., 1997-2000; process group leader for med. interns Ga. Bapt. Med. Ctr., 1998-99; presenter in field. Contbr. articles to profl. jours. Vol. counselor Ga. Mental Health Inst., Atlanta, 1991-93; vol. rape crisis ctr. counselor, legal liaison Grady Meml. Hosp., Atlanta, 1992-98. Mem.: ACA, APA (divsn. 17, divsn. 38, divsn. 30), Assn. for Transpersonal Psychology, Am. Ednl. Rsch. Assn., Lic. Profl. Counselors Assn. Ga. (licentiate; bd. dirs., ethics chair 2001—). Avocations: wildlife photography, hiking, gardening, mountain bike riding, bird watching. Office: Bdlg 7 Ste 200 1827 Powers Ferry Rd SE Atlanta GA 30339-5621

BEATON, ROY HOWARD, retired nuclear industry executive; b. Boston, Sept. 1, 1916; s. John Howard and Mary Beaton (LaVoie) B.; m. Margaret Marchant, July 22, 1939 (dec. Oct. 4, 1978); m. Leora Lauer Schier, June 26, 1982; children: Constance Beaton Fegley, Roy Howard, Patricia Schier Briselden, Susan Schier Carter, Mary Schier Rieber. BS, Northeastern U., 1939, DSc (hon.), 1967; DEng, Yale U., 1942. Registered profl. engr., Wash., Wis., Fla., Calif. With E.I. DuPont, 1942-46, plant tech. supr. Manhattan (Nuclear Bomb) Project, 1943-44; chief chem. devel., chief engr., gen. mgr. constrn. engring. GE, Richland, Wash., 1946-56, gen. mgr. neutron devices dept. Milw., 1957-63; gen. mgr. Apollo Systems, Daytona Beach, Fla., 1964-68; v.p., gen. mgr. def. electronics systems div. GE, Syracuse, N.Y., 1968-74, v.p., gen. mgr. energy systems and tech. div. Fairfield, Conn., 1974-75; sr. v.p. and group exec. Nuclear Energy Group, San Jose, Calif., 1975-81. Chmn. industry div. United Way Campaign, Santa Clara County, Calif., 1978-79. Fellow Am. Inst. Chemists, AAAS; mem. NSPE, Nat. Acad. Engring., Am. Ordnance Assn., Am. Nuclear Soc., Am. Inst. Chem. Engrs., IEEE, AIAA, Navy League U.S., Air Force Assn., Soc. Mil. Engrs., Santa Clara County Mfg. Group, Sigma Xi, Tau Beta Pi Home: 201 Foursome Dr Sequim WA 98382

BEATRICE, RUTH HADFIELD, hypnotherapist, retired educator, financial administrator; b. Phila., Feb. 6, 1931; d. Claude and Alice Elizabeth (Smith) Hadfield; m. Michael Joseph Beatrice, May 29, 1954 BS, West Chester State U., 1953; MS, Marywood Coll., 1978; postgrad., Temple U., Pa. State U., 1978-80; cert. clinl. hypnotherapist, Phila. Hypnosis Union Inst., 1980. Cert. hypnoanaesthesia therapist Nat. Bd. Hypnotherapy and Hypnotic Anaesthesiology, 1991. Educator Bristol Twp. (Pa.) Sch. Dist., 1953-54, Phila. Sch. Dist., 1954-55; recreation dir. Phila. Dept. Recreation, 1953-57; educator Worcester (Pa.) Sch. Dist., 1958-59, Springford (Pa.) Joint Sch. Dist., 1960-61, Souderton (Pa.) Sch. Dist., 1961-63, Ctrl. Bucks Sch. Dist., Doylestown, Pa., 1970-1993; ret., 1993; clin. hypnotherapist in pvt. practice, 1980—; clin. hypnotherapist, pvt. practice Avalon, N.J., 1980—, Port St. Lucie, Fla., Perkasie, Pa. Bus. adminstr. Beatrice Adminstrs. Co-author books on tutoring for Ptnrs. at Learning Series, 1978, 1979, 1983. Bd. mem. Pierce Free Libr., Hilltown, Pa., 1970-75; union del. Office and Profl. Employees Internat. Union Internat. Conv., Vancouver, B.C., Can., 1995; treas. Newcomers Civic Assn., Perkasie, 1964-85; me. Avalon (N.J.) Civic Assn., avalon Sr. Assn. Mem. NEA (life), Nat. Assn. Profl. Therapists, Am. Legion Aux., Pa. State Edn. Assn. (life), Hypnotism Soc. of Pa. (v.p. Phila. br. 1993-95), Phila. Hypnosis Union Local 476 (v.p. 1993-95), Nat. Guild of Hypnotists, Nat. Bd. for Hypnotherapy and Hypnotic Anaesthesiology. Democrat. Presbyterian. Avocations: biking, fishing, golf, tennis, walking. Home and Office: 3192 Carrick Green Ct Port Saint Lucie FL 34952 also: 3192 SE Carrick Green Ct Port Saint Lucie FL 34952-6042 E-mail: rudibea@yahoo.com.

BEATTIE, ANN, writer; b. Washington, Sept. 8, 1947; d. James and Charlotte (Crosby) B.; m. Lincoln Perry. BA, Am. U., 1969; MA, U. Conn., 1970; L.H.D. (hon.), Am. U., 1983. Vis. asst. prof. U. Va., Charlottesville, 1976-77, vis. writer, 1980; Briggs Copeland lectr. English Harvard U., Cambridge, Mass., 1977. Author: Chilly Scenes of Winter, 1976, Distortions, 1976, Secrets and Surprises, 1979, Falling In Place, 1980, Jacklighting, 1981, The Burning House, 1982, Love Always, 1985, Where You'll Find Me, 1986, Alex Katz, 1987, Picturing Will, 1990, What Was Mine, 1991, My Life Starring Dara Falcon, 1997, Park City: New & Selected Stories, 1998, Perfect Recall, 2000, The Doctor's House, 2002. Recipient Disting. Alumnae award Am. U., 1980, award in lit. Am. Acad. and Inst. Arts and Letters, 1980, PEN/Malamud award for excellence in short fiction, 2000; Guggenheim fellow, 1977. Mem. Am. Acad. and Inst. of Arts and Letters (v.p. lit., 1989-99), PEN, Authors Guild. Office: care Janklow and Nesbit 445 Park Ave New York NY 10022-2606*

BEATTIE, CHARLES ROBERT, III, lawyer; b. Red Wing, Minn., Aug. 25, 1948; s. Charles Robert Jr. and Dorothy Catherine (Shepherd) B.; m. Camilla Lawther Foot, Aug. 26, 1972; children: Virginia, Anne, Charles. BA with honors, U. Mich., 1970; JD, Yale U., 1973. Bar: Minn. 1973, U.S. Dist. Ct. Minn. 1973, U.S. Ct. Appeals (8th cir.) 1975. Assoc. Doherty, Rumble & Butler, St. Paul, 1973-78, ptnr. St. Paul and Mpls., 1978-99, chmn. dept. bus. law, 1987-89, 92-94, dir., 1989-92, 98-99; ptnr. Oppenheimer, Wolff & Donnelly, LLP, Mpls., 1999—2003, mem. mgmt. com., 2003—. Lectr. on partnerships and banking, leasing, comml. law and electronic commerce, 1983—; mem. Minn. Digital Signature Guidelines Task Force, 1997-98. Contbr. articles on ltd. partnerships and electronic commerce to profl. jours. Mem. Citizens League, St. Paul and Mpls., 1979—93; officer Leadership St. Paul, St. Paul, 1981—86; bd. dirs. Civic Symphony Assn., 1976—80; pres., bd. dirs. Valley Chamber Chorale, 1996—99, Afton Citizen's Forum, 2000—03; mem. Gillette Children's Splty. Healthcare Exec. Coun., 1995—; bd. dirs. St. John the Evangelist Episc. Ch., St. Paul, officer, 1981—93. Mem. ABA (uniform comml. code com., com. on cyberspace law 1991—, article 1 task force, subcom. sale of goods 1993—, chair 2000—, co-chair working group on electronic writings and notices 1995-97, bus. law sect. adviser NCCUSL uniform electronic transactions act drafting com. 1997-99), Minn. Bar Assn. (bus. and computer law sects.), Regional Mpls. C. of C. (bd. dirs. 1997—). Avocations: sailing, skiing, choral singing. E-mail: rbeattie@oppenheimer.com.

BEATTIE, DIANA SCOTT, biochemistry educator; b. Cranston, R.I., Aug. 11, 1934; d. Kenneth Allen and Lillian Francis (Barton) Scott; m. Benjamin Howard Beattie, June 30, 1956 (div. 1975); children: Elizabeth, Sara, Rachel, Ruth; m. Robert Nathan Stuchell, Feb. 6, 1976 (div. 1991). BA, Swarthmore Coll., 1956; MS, U. Pitts., 1958, PhD, 1961. Research assoc. U. Pitts., 1961-67, VA Hosp., Pitts., 1967-68; faculty Mt. Sinai Sch. Medicine, N.Y.C., 1968-85, prof. biochemistry, 1976-85; prof., chmn. dept. biochemistry W.Va. U. Sch. Medicine, Morgantown, 1985-2001, chmn. dept. biochemistry and molecular pharmacology, 2001—. Mem. grad. faculty biomed. sci. CUNY, 1968-86, biochemistry, 1971-85, biology, 1974-85; mem. grad. faculty biochemistry W.Va. U. Sch. Medicine, Morgantown, 1985—; vis. prof. U. Louvain, Belgium, 1982, U. Nairobi, Kenya, 1993, Shandong U., China, 2000; mem. ad hoc biochemistry study sect. NIH, 1976-77, 79-81, mem. phys. biochemistry study sect., 1981-85, 1993-97; chmn. phys. biochemistry study sect., 1983-85, 1995-97; mem. metabolic biology panel NSF, 1986-89; mem. basic sci. merit rev. panel VA, 1989-92. Contbr. articles to profl. jours.; mem. editorial bd. Archives of Biochemistry and Biophysics, 1975-78, 85-2000, Jour. Bioenergetics, 1975—. Recipient award Met. N.Y. chpt. Assn. for Women in Sci., 1979; grantee NSF, 1970-92, 97—, NIH, 1966—; Fogarty internat. fellow, 1982, Fulbright fellow, 1993. Mem. Am. Soc. Biol. Chemists (membership com. 1987-89), Am. Soc. Cell Biology, Biophysics Soc., Assn. Med. Sch. Depts. Biochemistry (exec. com. 1989-92, pres.-elect 1995, pres. 1996), Am. Assn. Med. Schs. (coun. acad. socs. 1989-2001, adminstrv. bd. 1994-99, chair 1998), Nat. Bd. Med. Examiners (biochemistry test com. 1991-93, chair 1994-95, cell biology test com. 1998-2001), Nat. Caucus Basic Biomed. Chairs (vice chair 1991—). Home: 324 Dream Catcher Cir Morgantown WV 26508-9473 Office: WVa U Sch Medicine Dept Biochemistry Morgantown WV 26506 E-mail: dbeattie@hsc.wvu.edu.

BEATTIE, DONALD A. energy scientist, consultant; b. N.Y.C., Oct. 30, 1929; s. James Francis and Evelyn Margaret (Hickey) B.; m. Ann Mary Kean, Mar. 27, 1973; children: Thomas James, Bruce Andrew. AB, Columbia U., 1951; MS, Colo. Sch. Mines, 1958. Regional geologist Mobil Oil Co., 1958-63; Apollo lunar expts. program mgr. NASA, 1963-72, dir. NASA energy systems div., 1978-82; v.p. Houston ops. BDM Corp., 1983-84; cons. on energy and space tech., 1984—; pres. Endosat Inc., 1991-96. Dir. advanced energy research and tech. NSF, 1973-75; dep. asst. adminstr. ERDA, 1975-77; acting asst. sec. Dept. Energy, Washington, 1977-78; solar energy coordinator U.S./USSR Coop. in Sci. and Tech.; U.S. rep. Vienna Inst. for Comparative Econ. Studies Workshop on Energy. Author, editor: History and Overview of Solar Heat Technologies, 1997; author: Taking Science to the Moon, 2001; contbr. numerous articles on lunar sci., energy to profl. jours. Active Boy Scouts Am., 1958-71. Served with AC USN, 1951-56. Recipient Exceptional Service medal NASA, 1971, Sr. Exec. Service and Outstanding Performance award, 1980; Superior Achievement award Dept. Energy, 1978 Fellow AAAS; mem. Geol. Soc. Am., Nat. Space Club. Home and Office: 808 Mill Pond Ct Jacksonville FL 32259-3027

BEATTIE, DONALD GILBERT, lawyer; b. Des Moines, Nov. 30, 1947; s. Max and Rowena Jean (Gilbert) B.; divorced; children: Brett Joseph, Ryan Troy, Adam Ross, Nicholas Gilbert. BA, Simpson Coll., 1970; JD, Drake U., 1977. Bar: Iowa 1977, U.S. Dist. Ct. (no. and so. dist.) Iowa 1977. Ptnr. Beattie Law Firm, Pleasant Hill, Iowa, 1975—. City atty. Runnells, Iowa, 1977—. Mem. ATLA, Assn. Trial Lawyers of Iowa, Iowa State Bar Assn., Polk County Bar Assn., Nat. Bd. Trial Advocacy, Drake Law Rev. Alumni Assn. (bd. dirs.), Am. Legion, Order of Coif. Lodges: Masons (master 1980). Democrat. E-mail: beattielaw@aol.com.

BEATTIE, GEORGE CHAPIN, retired orthopedic surgeon; b. Bowling Green, Ohio, Sept. 24, 1919; s. George Wilson and Mary Turner (Chapin) B.; m. Nancy U. Fant, Mar. 1, 1947; children: Michael, Suzanne, Eric. BA, Bowling Green State U., 1939; MD, U. Chgo., 1943. Diplomate Am. Bd. Orthopaedic Surgery. Commd. lt. (j.g.) MC USN, 1943, advanced through grades to lt. comdr., 1951; med. officer, intern U.S. Naval Hosp., Great Lakes, Ill., 1943-44; resident, fellow in orthopaedic surgery Lahey Clinic, Boston, 1944; ward med. officer orthopaedic services Naval Hosp., Guam, 1944-46; sr. med. officer USN, Manus Island, Papua New Guinea, 1946; resident tng. in orthopaedic surgery U.S. Naval Hosp. St. Albans, N.Y.C., 1947-48; resident in orthopaedic surgery Children's Hosp., Boston, 1949; asst. chief orthopaedic surgery U.S. Naval Hosp. Oak Knoll, Oakland, Calif., 1950-52; comdg. officer med. co. 1st Marine Div. Med. Bn., Republic of Korea, 1952-53; chief orthopaedic service Dept. Phys. Medicine and Navy Amputee Ctr. U.S. Naval Hosp., Phila., 1954; resigned USN, 1954; practice medicine specializing in orthopaedic surgery San Francisco, 1954-99; ret., 1999. Co-chmn. handicapping conditions com. Health Action Study San Mateo County, 1965; 1st chmn. orthopaedic sect. surg. dept. Peninsula Hosp. and Med. Ctr., Burlingame, Calif., 1967, chmn. rehab. service, 1967-71, chmn. phys. therapy and rehab. com., 1956—, vice chmn. orthopaedic dept., 1973-76, chmn., 1977-79; med. dir. research and rehab. ctr. San Mateo (Calif.) County Soc. Crippled Children and Adults, 1958-63; mem. exec. com. Harold D. Chope Community Hosp., San Mateo, 1971-76, chief, co-chmn. orthopaedic sect., 1971-76; chief orthopaedic surg. sect. Mills Meml. Hosp., San Mateo, 1976-78; others. Contbr. articles to profl. jours. Active Indian Guides, 1972-77; pres. Calif. Easter Seal Soc., 1969-71. Decorated Bronze Star. Fellow Am. Acad. Orthopaedic Surgeons (exhibit com. 1979-86); mem. AMA (Billings Bronze medal 1954), Internat. Soc. for Prosthetics and Orthotics, Western Orthopaedic Assn. (pres., bd. dirs. 1986), Leroy Abbott Orthopaedic Soc. U. Calif. San Francisco (assoc. clin. prof.), Alpha Omega Alpha.

BEATTIE, GERALDINE ALICE (GERI BEATTIE), advocate; b. Harrisburg, Pa., Jan. 8, 1943; d. John Martin and Marian Pauline (Coulson) Ramsey; m. Robert Bruce Beattie, Nov. 22, 1969; children: Michelle Nichols, Bryan Scott, Todd Alan. Student, U. Pa., 1960-62, Germantown (Pa.) Med. Ctr., 1960-63. Staff nurse Germantown Med. Ctr., Pa., 1963; head nurse Shore Meml. Hosp., Somers Point, NJ, 1964, Children's Hosp., San Diego, 1965-73, nursing supr., 1977-81, founder, supr. child abuse evidentiary program, 1981-93, asst. dir., mgr. Ctr. Child Protection, 1993—2000; dir. Professional Ed., Forensic & Med. Svc., Program Develop., chadwick Ctr. for Children & Families. Bd. supr. Multi-Victim Protocol Task Force, San Diego, 1987-88, Victim Witness Protocol Task Force, San Diego, 1989—; mem. Strategic Plan Task Force, Dept. Social Svc., San Diego, 1996-98; project dir. Calif. Child Sexual Abuse Prevention and Treatment Ctr., Calif. Med. Tng. Ctr.; internat. tng. and tech. assistance expert on multidiscipline investigation of child abuse

and implemt mgmt. of child abuse programs. Author/editor: (protocol manual) Victim Witness Protocol, 1991, 98. Mem. Am. Humane Soc., Am. Profl. Soc. Abuse of Children, Calif. Profl. Soc. Abuse of Children, Calif. Sexual Assault Investigators Assn., Calif. Network Sexual Offending, San Diego Cmty. Child Abuse Coord. Coun. (chair sexual abuse rev. com. 1984-86, Outstanding Svc. to Cmty. award). Republican. Presbyterian. Avocations: crafts, cooking, camping, reading. Home: 2298 Windmill View Rd El Cajon CA 92020-1356 Office: Chadwick Ctr for Children FamiliesChildrens Hosp 3020 Childrens Way San Diego CA 92123-4223

BEATTIE, TED ARTHUR, zoological gardens and aquarium administrator; b. Salem, Ohio, Jan. 13, 1945; s. Don Earl and Frances (Webster) B.; children: Lauralyn, Sean, Kimberly; m. Penelope Johnson, July 13, 1985. BA in Journalism, Ohio State U., 1971, MA in Pub. Rels., 1972. Advt./pub. rels. dir. Shaw-Barton Co., Coshocton, Ohio, 1972-78; mktg. dir. Cin. Zoo, 1978-81; assoc. dir. Brookfield Zoo, Chgo., 1981-87; exec. dir. Knoxville (Tenn.) Zool. Gardens, 1987-92; dir., CEO Ft. Worth Zool. Pk., 1992-94; pres., CEO John G. Shedd Aquarium, Chgo., 1994—. Cons. Zoo Plan Assn., Wichita, Kans., 1981-88; apptd. U.S. Commn. on Ocean Policy, 2001-03. Vice chmn. and chmn. United Way campaign, Coshocton, 1977 78; mem. Leadership Knoxville, 1988. With U.S. Army, 1967-69, Vietnam. Fellow: Am. Assn. Zool. Pks. and Aquariums (bd. dirs. 1989—91, 1994—2002); mem.: Am. Zoo & Aquarium Assn. (v.p. 1998—99, pres. 2000—01), Sawgrass Country Club, Onwentsia Club, Arts Club, Chgo. Econ. Club. Avocations: golf, boating. Home: 260 E Chestnut St Apt 2802 Chicago IL 60611 Office: John G Shedd Aqarium 1200 S Lake Shore Dr Chicago IL 60605-2402

BEATTS, ANNE PATRICIA, writer, producer; b. Buffalo, Feb. 25, 1947; d. Patrick Murray Threipland and Sheila Elizabeth Jean (Sherriff Scott) B. BA with honors, McGill U., Montreal, Que., Can., 1966. Contbg. editor National Lampoon mag., N.Y.C., 1970-74; writer Saturday Night Live NBC, N.Y.C., 1975-80; creator, prodr. Square Pegs CBS, Los Angeles, 1982-83; co-exec. prodr. A Different World NBC, Los Angeles, 1987-88; exec. prodr. The Stephanie Miller Show, 1994-95. Writer, creative cons. Saturday Night Live 25th Ann. Spl., 1999; exec. story cons. (WETV) Committed, 2000-2001. Co-editor: (humorous books) Titters, 1976, Saturday Night, 1977; co-author: (humorous books) Titters 101, 1984, The Mom Book, 1986; author book for Broadway mus. Leader of the Pack, 1985; humor columnist L.A. Times, 1997-98. Mem. AFTRA, SAG, Writers Guild Am. (award 1976, 77, 2001), Dirs. Guild Am., Women in Film, Dramatists Guild, NATAS (2 Emmy awards, 6 Emmy award nominations 1975-80, 2000).

BEATTY, CARL, music educator; b. NYC, Feb. 5, 1956; s. Carl James and Juanita (Hunter) Beatty; m. Jacqueline M. Reid, Mar. 21, 1987; children: Zoe J., Mayrose C.; m. Cynthia Crockford, Sept. 1979 (div. Aug. 1981). BA, C.W. Post Coll., 1977. Rec. engr. Mediasound, NYC, 1979—85; ind. rec. engr., 1985—89; assoc. prof. to prof. Berklee Coll. of Music, Boston, 1989—. Mixing engr. (various performer's recordings albums). Bd. of trustees North Bennet St. Sch., Boston, 1996—2000. Avocations: photography, driving, electronics. Office: Berklee Coll of Music 1140 Boylston St Boston MA 02115

BEATTY, FRANCES, civic worker; b. Chgo., Apr. 17, 1940; d. Pasquale and Rose (Brunetti) Calomeni; m. Robert Alfred Beatty, Aug. 24, 1963; children: Bradford, Roxanna Beatty Goebel. BA, Northwestern U., 1961; MA, U. Chgo., 1967. Tchr. math. Proviso West High Sch., Hillside, Ill., 1961-66. Active Oak Brook Dist. 53 Sch. Bd., 1979-85; mem. women's bd. Field Mus. Natural History, Chgo., 1985—, mem. founders coun., 1988—, treas. women's bd., 1991-93; mem. governing bd. Chgo. Symphony, 1985-92; trustee Chgo. Symphony Orch., 1992—; mem. women's bd. Ravinia Festival, Highland Park, Ill., 1987—, Northwestern U., Evanston, Ill., sec. women's bd., 1999—, mem. libr. bd., 1990-95; mem. women's bd. U. Chgo.; mem. coun. Wellness House, Hinsdale, Ill., 1994; com. mem. Chgo. Humanities Festival, 1999—. Mem.: Merit Sch. Music, Alumnae of Northwestern U. (pres. 1996—98), The Antiquarian Soc. Art Inst. Chgo., John Evans Club, Woman's Athletic Club Chgo. (3d v.p. 1985—87, 1st v.p. 1992—94, pres. 1994—96).

BEATTY, GROVER DOUGLAS, stockbroker; b. Little Rock, Feb. 16, 1952; m. Cheryl Christine Kiecksee, Dec. 1, 1979. BSBA, Lincoln U., Jefferson City, Mo., 1977, MS in Bus. and Fin., 1983. Lic. security dealer Nat. Assn. Securities Dealers. Auditor Mo. Div. Employment Security, Jefferson City, 1979-82; stockbroker Scherck Stein & Franc, Inc., Jefferson City, 1983-86, Stifel Nicolaus & Co., Jefferson City, 1986—, mem. pres.'s coun., 1991—, mem. chmn.'s coun., 1997—. Instr. Lincoln U., 1981-94; apptd. Stifel Nicolaus Brokers Adv. Com., 1996. Fin. chmn. 9th Dist. Ross Perot Campaign. Republican. Baptist. Office: Stifel Nicolaus & Co 222 Madison St Jefferson City MO 65101-3230 E-mail: beattyg@stifel.com.

BEATTY, JOHN CABEEN, JR., judge; b. Washington, Apr. 13, 1919; s. John Cabeen and Jean (Morrison) B.; m. Clarissa Hager, Feb. 8, 1943 (dec. Apr. 4 1996); children: John Cabeen III, Clarissa Jean; m. Virginia R. Campbell, May 10, 1997. AB, Princeton U., 1941; JD, Columbia, 1948. Bar: Oreg. 1948. Practiced law, Portland, 1948-70; ptnr. Dusenbery, Martin, Beatty, Bischoff & Templeton, 1956-70, of counsel, 1985-96; judge circuit ct., 1970-85, sr. judge, 1985—. Mem. Oreg. Bd. Bar Examiners, 1953-54; chmn. legis. com. Oreg. Jud. Conf., 1976-82; mem. Oreg. CSC, 1962-64, Oreg. Law Enforcement Council, 1974-77; vice chmn. Oreg. Commn. Jud. Br., 1979-85; vice chmn. Oreg. Criminal Justice Council, 1985-90. Mem. legis. com. Nat. Sch. Bds. Assn., 1966-68, chmn. coun. large city sch. bds., 1967-68; counsel Dem. Party Oreg., 1956-58; co-chmn. Oreg. for Kennedy Com., 1968; bd. dirs. Portland Pub. Schs., 1964-70, chmn., 1967, 69; chmn. policy adv. com. on hazardous waste Dept. Environ. Quality, 1985-86; mem. Mayor's Spl. Rev. Commn., 1986; chmn. various adv. coms. Dept. Environ. Quality, 1987-89; chmn. tech. adv. com. Willamette River Basin Water Quality Study, 1990-94; chmn. city club study Oreg. Initiative and Referendum, 1994-95; chmn. Oreg. Initiative Com., 1996—. Capt. AUS, 1941-46, ETO. Decorated Bronze Star medal; recipient City Club of Portland award, 1967. Mem. ABA, Oreg. Bar Assn., Multnomah County Bar Assn., Oreg. Hist. Soc. (dir. 1973 92), City Club (past pres., bd. govs.), Racquet Club. Home and Office: 3331 SW Mitchell St Portland OR 97201-1260 E-mail: jcbeatty@comcast.com.

BEATTY, KENNETH ORION, JR., chemical engineer, educator; b. East Lansdowne, Pa., Dec. 18, 1913; s. Kenneth Orion and Ada Pearl (Marshall) B.; m. Mary Catharine Carter, Aug. 8, 1936; children: Susan Jennifer, Prudence Carter, Lucy Margaret. BS, Lehigh U., 1935, MS, 1937; PhD, U. Mich., 1946. Registered profl. engr., N.C. Raybestos-Manhattan fellow Lehigh U., 1935-37; chem. engr. Dow Chem. Co., Midland, Mich., 1937-39; asst. prof. chem. engring. U. R.I., Kingston, 1939-44; rsch. assoc. U. Mich., 1944-46; assoc. prof. N.C. State U., Raleigh, 1946-48, prof., 1948—, acting head dept. chem. engring., 1959-60, R.J. Reynolds Industries prof. chem. engring., 1961—, spl. cons. in forensic engring., 1982—. Dir. Carolina Cons. Scientists and Engrs., 1979-87; vis. prof. chem. engring. Ohio State U., summer 1949; vis. engr. Pratt & Whitney Co., Middletown, Conn., summer 1957; resident cons. engr. Nat. Lead Co. of Ohio, Fernald, summer 1959; mem. Max Jakob Award Com., 1963-67, chmn., 1966; mem. Nat. Heat Transfer Conf. Coordinating Com., 1965-71, chmn., 1967; coordinating chmn. 9th Nat. Heat Transfer Conf., Seattle, 1967; U.S. founding del. Assembly for Internat. Heat Transfer Conf., 1967-72; mem. sci. council Internat. Center for Heat and Mass Transfer, Yugoslavia, 1971-90. Contbr. articles to profl. jours. Mem. N.C. Gov.'s Sci. Adv. Com. Rsch. grantee NASA, NSF, Wright Air Devel. Center, AEC, Am. Soc. Refrigerating Engrs.; Princeton U. fellow, 1967-68. Fellow AIChE; mem. Am. Chem. Soc., University Park Homeowners Assn. Home: 323 Shepherd St Raleigh NC 27607-4031 Office: NC State U Dept Chem Engring Raleigh NC 27695-0001 Fax: 919-515-3465.

BEATTY, PERRIN, business association executive; b. Toronto; married; 2 children. Student, Upper Can. Coll., Toronto, U. Western Ont. Elected mem. Parliament, 1972; cabinet min. Min. of State-Treasury Bd., 1979, Min. of Nat. Revenue, 1984; solicitor gen., 1985; min. of nat. def., 1986; min. of health, 1989; min. of comms., 1991; min. external affairs, 1993; pres., CEO Can. Broadcasting Corp., 1995-1999, Canadian Mfrs. & Exporters, Ottawa, Ont., 1999—. Former hon. vis. prof. dept. polit. sci. U. We. Ont.; former columnist Toronto Sun. Office: CME 1 Nicholas St Ste 1500 Ottawa ON Canada K1N 7B7

BEATTY, RICHARD SCRIVENER, retired lawyer; b. Washington, May 6, 1934; s. John Joseph and Helen Louise (Simpson) B.; m. Barbara Boyd, July 14, 1956; children— Charles, Alexandra, Nicholas. BA, Williams Coll., 1955; LLB, Georgetown U., 1962. Bar: D.C. 1962. Trial atty. Dept. Justice, Washington, 1962-66; assoc. chief counsel Office U.S. Comptroller of Currency, 1966-67; ptnr. firm Alston, Miller & Gaines, Washington, 1968-84; ptnr. Shaw, Pittman, Potts & Trowbridge, Washington, 1985-95, sr. counsel, 1996-99, retired, 1999. Chmn. devel. coun. Williams Coll., St. Patrick's Episcopal Day Sch., 1970—82; sr. warden, Williams Coll., St. Patrick's Episcopal Day Sch., 1980-85; trustee Mt. Vernon Coll., 1985—90; pres. Ho. of Mercy, 1999—; trustee The Key Sch., 1999—; bd. dirs. The Episc. Ch. Found., 1991—99, Sea Web, 1998—. With U.S. Army, 1956—59. Mem.: ABA, Chevy Chase Club, D.C. Bar Assn., Am. Law Inst., Order St. John of Jerusalem, Chevy Chase Club, Met. Club (Washington), Delta Psi. Home: 7001 Glenbrook Rd Bethesda MD 20814-1222

BEATTY, ROBERT CLINTON, religious studies educator; b. Needham, Mass., May 19, 1935; s. Henry Russell and Alice Cornelia (van Schagen) B.; m. Carolyn Phyllis Caton, Oct. 5, 1957; children: Robert Russell, Daniel Clinton, Melissa Lynn, Alicia Felicity. AB in Econs., Northeastern U., 1957; MBA in Mgmt., Fairleigh Dickinson U., 1973; MDiv, Columbia Biblical Sem., 1983, MA in Bible, 1985; DMin in Orgn. Devel., Fuller Theol. Sem., 1993. Ordained to ministry Harmony Ch., 1984. Commd. 2d lt. U.S. Army, 1957, advanced through grades to lt. col., ret., 1980; dir. U.S. extension ctrs. Columbia (S.C.) Internat. U., 1983-89; assoc. prof., chmn. bus. mgmt. Miami Christian Coll., 1989-92, Trinity Internat. U., Miami, 1992-2001, undergrad. program coord., 2001—02; MAR program coord. South Fla. ext. Trinity Evang. Div. Sch., 1994—; prof. Calvary Chapel Bible Inst., 2000—. Lectr. Christian Leadership Tng. Inst., Chisinau, Moldova, 2001—; adj. prof. Embry Riddle Aero. U., Mannheim, Germany, 1976—77, City Colls. of Chgo., Mannheim, 1976—77; bible study tchr. Prison Fellowship, Columbia, 1981—89, Calvary Chapel, Ft. Lauderdale, 1996—2000; ch./ministry bd. cons., 1987—. Author: Extension Coordinator's Handbook, 1984, 1985, 1987, 1989, (student manual) Practical Applications of Biblical Hermeneutics, 1992—94, 2000, 2003, Human Resource Management, 1992, (manual) Business Ethics, 1991, Organization Behavior, 1991, Acts: A Sociological and Cross Cultural Communications Perspective, 1991; editor: Adjunct-Extension Faculty Handbook, 1984, 1985, 1989. Decorated Legion of Merit, Bronze Star with oak leaf cluster, Air medal, Meritorious Svc. medal, Gallantry Cross with Silver Star; recipient Vol. of Yr. award Goodman Correctional Instn., 1985, Broad River Correctional Instn., 1989, Prof. of Yr. award Trinity Internat. U., 2001. Mem.: DAV, Mil. Officers Assn. of Am., AARP. Republican. Avocation: travel. Home: 10500 NW 21st Ct Sunrise FL 33322-3509 Office: Calvary Chapel Bible Inst 2401 W Cypress Creek Rd Fort Lauderdale FL 33309 E-mail: bibleprof@msn.com.

BEATTY, (HENRY) WARREN, actor, producer, director; b. Richmond, Va., Mar. 30, 1937; s. Ira O. and Kathlyn (MacLean) Beaty; m. Annette Bening; 4 children, Kathlyn. Student, Northwestern U., 1956, Stella Adler Theatre Sch., N.Y.C., 1957. Actor films Splendor in the Grass, 1961, The Roman Spring of Mrs. Stone, 1962, All Fall Down, 1962, Lilith, 1963, Mickey One, 1965, Promise Her Anything, 1965, Kaleidoscope, 1966, The Only Game in Town, 1969, McCabe and Mrs. Miller, 1971, Dollars, 1971, The Parallax View, 1974, The Fortune, 1975, Town and Country, 2001; appeared in Broadway play A Loss of Roses, 1960; actor, producer films include Bonnie and Clyde, 1967 (Acad. award nomination for best actor), Ishtar, 1987; producer, co-screenwriter, actor Shampoo, 1975 (Acad. award nomination for best screenplay) ; producer, co-dir., co-screenwriter, actor Heaven Can Wait, 1978 (Acad. award nominations for best actor, best dir. and best screenplay); producer, dir., co-screenwriter, actor Reds, 1981 (Acad. award for best dir.), dir., actor Dick Tracy, 1990; co-producer, actor: Bugsy, 1991; Love Affair (also producer and writer), 1994; Town and Country, 1998; Bulworth (also producer and writer); 1998; actor (TV) A Salute to Dustin Hoffman, 1999; TB guest appearances include Studio One, 1948, What's My Line, 1950, Vibe, 1997. Recipient Irving G. Thalberg Memorial award, 1999, American Soc. of Cinematographers Bd. of Governors award, 2000, BAFTA Fellowship, 2002. Mem. Dirs. Guild Am. Democrat. Office: Creative Artists Agy care Risa Gertner 9830 Wilshire Blvd Beverly Hills CA 90212-1804*

BEATTY, WILBUR C. contract management executive; b. Sparta, N.J., Dec. 8, 1942; s. John Wesley and Bessie May (Sisco) B.; m. Frances Giannone, June 26, 1965; 1 child, Lisa. BBA, Fairleigh-Dickinson U., 1976, MBA, 1982. Cert. purchasing mgr. Various adminstrv. positions Bell Telephone Labs., Murray Hill, N.J., 1961-78, fin. specialist, 1978-79, sr. contract buyer, 1980-83; supr. purchasing AT&T Tech., Short Hills, N.J., 1983-86; procurement mgr. AT&T, Bedminister, N.J., 1986-96; sr. contracts and negotiations specialist Lucent Techs., Warren, 1996-2000, sr. contract mgr., 2000—02; contract mgr. IBM, 2002—. Cons. in field. Served with USAR, 1964-70. Mem. Nat. Assn. Purchasing Mgrs. (v.p. adminstrn. N.J. chpt., nat. ethical stds. com.), Phi Omega Epsilon. E-mail: wcbeatty@us.ibm.com.

BEATTY, WILLIAM GLENN, lawyer; b. Moline, Ill., July 13, 1953; s. Glenn Willard and Mary Frances (Karlson) B.; m. Carla Ann Busse, Feb. 25, 1978; children— Andrew Glenn, Mark William. B.A. cum laude, Augustana Coll., Rock Island, Ill., 1975; postgrad. Creighton U., 1975-76; J.D. with honors, Chgo.-Kent Coll. Law, 1978. Bar: Ill. 1978, U.S. Dist. Ct. (no. dist.) Ill. 1979, U.S. Ct. Appeals (7th cir.) 1979, U.S. Ct. Claims 1979. Assoc. Johnson, Cusack & Bell, Ltd., Chgo., 1978-84, ptnr., 1985— ; asst. instr. Chgo.-Kent Coll. Law, 1978; lectr. in field. Mem ABA, Ill. Bar Assn., Chgo. Bar Assn., Ill. Def. Counsel, Trial Lawyers Club Chgo., Def. Research Inst. Republican. Roman Catholic. Office: Johnson Cusack & Bell Ltd 211 W Wacker Dr Chicago IL 60606-1217

BEATY, JAMES ARTHUR, JR., federal judge; b. 1949; m. Toyoko Christine Beaty; 1 child. BA cum laude, Western Carolina U., 1971; JD, U. N.C., 1974; postgrad., U. Nev., 1985—91; LHD (hon.), Western Carolina U., 2002. With Richard C. Erwin, Winston-Salem, NC, 1974—77; atty. at law Ewrin and Beaty, Winston-Salem, 1977—78, Beaty and Friende, Winston-Salem, 1980—81; pvt. practice Winston-Salem, 1978 79; judge N.C. Superior Ct., 1981—94; dist. judge U.S. Dist. Ct. (mid. dist.) N.C., 1994—. Recipient Disting. Alumni award, Western Carolina U., 1994. Mem.: ABA, NAACP (life), N.C. Assn. Black Lawyers (sec. 1976, v.p. 1978), N.C. Acad. Trial Lawyers (named outstanding trial ct. judge of yr. 1990), Winston-Salem Bar Assn., Forsyth County and 21st Jud. Dist. Bar, N.C. State Bar, Rotary Club, Sigma Pi Phi, Alpha Phi Alpha. Office: 251 N Main St Rm 248 Winston Salem NC 27101-3914*

BEATY, JAMES THOMAS, retired buyer; b. Valdosta, Ga., June 11, 1934; s. James Wilson and Maude Irene (Simpson) B. BBA, Emory U., 1955. Asst. buyer Davisons, Atlanta, 1955-57; with Bruce Clothing Co., Lake City, Fla., 1957-60; owner antique and estate jewelry bus. Alexandria, Va., 1960-84; jr. exec. Marshalls Dept. Stores, Burke, Va., 1984-95. With U.S. Army, 1955-56. Mem. SAR, Sons of Confederate Vets., Magna Charta Barons (Somerset chpt.), Desc. Knights of Bath, Colonial Soc. Am.'s Royal Descent, Colonial Order of Crown, Kiwanis. Democrat. Baptist. Avocations: art, classical music. Home: Culpepper Gardens 4435 N Pershing Dr Apt 600 Arlington VA 22203

BEATY, SANDY, lobbyist, lawyer; b. Kingsport, Tenn., Jan. 7, 1958; d. Elmer and Helen Dodson Johnson. BS, Trevecca Coll., 1982; JD, Nashville Sch. of Law, 1992. Bar: Tenn. Lobbyist, exec. dir. Tenn. State Employees Assn., 1982-92; lobbyist, v.p. Tenn. Assn. of Bus., 1992; lobbyist, atty. Boult, Cummings, Conners & Berry, 1996; lobbyist, dir. govt. rels. Pfizer Inc., Nashville, 1996—. Fundraiser Sen. Ron Ramsey campaign, Nashville, Jay West for Mayor, 1999, Law Mayoral Panel, 1999; citizen adv. panel Saturn GM mfg. plant, 1992; panel mem. Govs. Solid Waste Adv. Panel, 1992-96. Mem. Tenn. Lawyers Assn. for Women (legis. com. chair), Tenn. Lobbyist Assn., Pharm. Rsch. and Mfr. of Am. (taskforce chair). Avocation: jogger. Office: Pfizer Inc 3200 W End Ave Ste 500 Nashville TN 37203-1322

BEAUBIEN, ANNE KATHLEEN, librarian; b. Detroit, Sept. 15, 1947; d. Richard Parker and Edith Mildred Beaubien. Attended, Western Mich. U., 1965-67; BA, Mich. State U., 1969; MLS, U. Mich., 1970. Reference libr., bibliographic instr. U. Mich. Libr., Ann Arbor, Mich., 1971-80, dir. MITS, 1980-85, head coop. access svc., 1985—. Head Business and Cooperative Access Svc., 1995-99; head Cooperative Access Svc. and Grants, 2000—. Author: (booklet) Psychology Bibliography, 1980; co-author: Learning the Library, 1982; contbg. articles to profl. jour., editor, conf. proc., 1987. Mem. vestry St. Clare's Episcopal Ch., Ann Arbor, Mich., 1986—89, 2002—; pres. Ann Arbor Ski Club, Mich., 1978—79. Recipient Woman of Yr. Award, Ann Arbor Bus. and Profl. Women's Club, 1982; Disting. Alumnus Award; Sch. Info. and Libr. Studies, U. Mich., 1987. Mem. ALA; Assn. Coll. and Rsch. Libr. (pres. 1991-92). Avocations: skiing, bicycling, ballroom dancing. Office: U Mich Libr 106 Hatcher Grad Libr Ann Arbor MI 48109

BEAUBIEN, MARK H., JR., state representative; b. Waukegan, Ill., Oct. 30, 1942; m. Dee Beaubien; 2 children. BA, Northwestern U., 1964, JD, 1967. Chmn. State Bank Lake Zurich; ptnr. law firm Palatine, Ill.; chmn. Suburban Bank Barrington; mem. Ill. Ho. of Reps., 1997—. Mem. Lake County Bd., 1992—96; supr. Cuba Twp., 1993—96. Republican. Office: 314 Capitol Bldg Springfield IL 62706 Address: 124-A E Liberty St Wauconda IL 60084 Home: 4 Acorn Ln Barrington IL 60010*

BEAUCHAMP, JOHN JONES, mathematician, educator; s. Robert O. and Ruby Jones Beauchamp; m. Betty Jean Balls, Jan. 20, 1944; children: John A. children: Karen Elaine Beauchamp James. BA, Vanderbilt U., 1959, MAT, 1960; MS, Fla. State U., 1963, PhD, 1966. Asst. prof. math. Birmingham-So. Coll., 1960—61; rsch. statistician Oak Ridge (Tenn.) Nat. Lab., 1967—98; assoc. prof. math. Lipscomb U., Nashville, 1998—. Contbr. articles to profl. jours. Recipient Publ. award, Martin-Marietta Energy Systems, 1989. Mem.: Am. Statis. Assn. Office: Lipscomb University 3901 Granny White Pike Nashville TN 37204 Office Fax: 615-269-1830. E-mail: john.beauchamp@lipscomb.edu.

BEAUCHAMP, MILES PHILIP, newspaper editor, columnist, education consultant; b. L.A., Apr. 17, 1953; s. Henry and Kathrinjo (Shelton) B.; m. Michelle Colleen Ryan, July 1, 1989. BA, San Diego State U., 1993, MA, 1994. V.p. Beauchamp Co. Hotels, San Diego, 1972-84; editor, columnist Asian Jour. newspaper, San Diego, 1985—; instr. U.S. Internat. U., San Diego, 1996—. Instr. Alliant Internat. U., 1996—, Nat. Univ., 1996—; cons. The Writing Ctr., San Diego, 1992—96, Main Street mag., San Diego, 1994—95. Co-author: The Exquisite Cadaver, 1993; author: A New Way of Looking, 1996; editor: Filipinos in America, 1992; columnist Still Amazed, 1985-96. Profl. devel. facilitator Grossmont Coll., San Diego, 1990—; tchr. writing St. Vincent De Paul Shelter, San Diego, 1992; tchr., facilitator Profls. in Schs., San Diego, 1990—. Recipient award of appreciation San Diego Journalism Edn. Assn., 1992, San Diego Pub. Libr., 1994, Georgi awards Writers Fedn. Am., 1993. Mem. Film and Video Artists Assn., Writers Haven, San Diego Press Club. Avocations: travel, boating, photography. Office: Asian Jour Newspaper 550 E 8th St Ste 6 National City CA 91950

BEAUDOIN, GÉRALD A(RMAND), lawyer, educator, senator; b. Montreal, Qué., Can., Apr. 15, 1929; s. Armand and Aldéa (St.-Arnaud) B.; m. Renée Desmarais, Sept. 11, 1954; children: Viviane, Louise, Denise, Françoise. BA summa cum laude, U. Montreal, 1950, LLL magna cum laude, 1953, MA in Law, 1954; postgrad. in comparative law (Carnegie scholar), U. Toronto, 1954-55; DESD cum laude, U. Ottawa, Ont., 1958; LLD, U. Louvain-la-Neuve, Belgium, 1989. Bar: Called to Qué. bar 1954, created queen's counsel 1969. Practiced law with Paul Gérin-Lajoie, Montreal, 1955-56; adv. counsel Dept. Justice, Ottawa, 1956-65, sr. adv. counsel, 1960-65; asst. parliamentary counsel Ho. of Commons of Can., Ottawa, 1965-69; civil law dean Faculty of Law, U. Ottawa, 1969-79, prof. constl. law, 1969-89, dir. Human Rights Ctr., 1986-88; mem. Senate of Can., 1988. Mem. Goldenberg Com. on Constn., 1967, La Commn des Svcs. Juridiques du Quebec, 1972-73, Task Force on Can. Unity, 1977-79; vis. prof. U. Sorbonne, 1985; vis. prof. faculty of law U. Ottawa, 1989-94, prof. emeritus, 1994—; co-chmn. spl. joint com. of Senate and Ho. of Commons. on process for amending Constn. of Can., 1991, on a renewed Can., 1991-92; mem. Senate Spl. Com. on Euthanasia and Assisted Suicide, 1994-95. Author: Essais sur la Constitution, 1979, Le partage des pouvoirs, 1980, 3d edit., 1983, La Constitution du Canada, 1990, Le fédéralisme au Canada, 2000, Les droits et libertés au Canada, 2000; (with others) Mécanismes pour une nouvelle Constitution, 1981; co-editor: La Charte Canadienne des droits et libertés, 3d edit., 1996, Perspectives Canadiennes et Européennes des droits de la personne, 1986; editor: The Supreme Court of Can.-La Cour suprême du Can., 1986, Charter Cases, 1986-87, Your Clients and the Charter, 1988, Vues Canadiennes et Européennes des droits et libertés, 1989, As the Charter Evolves, 1990, The Charter: Ten Years Later, 1992, (with G. Robertson et al) Federalism for the Future: Essential Reforms, 1998; mem. Thémis Law Rev., 1951-52; contbr. numerous articles to Can. and fgn. law revs. Mem. spl. com. to draft Can. Constn. in French, 1985-90. Recipient The Ramon John Hnatyshyn award, 1997, Walter S. Tarnopolsky Human Rights award, 2002. Mem. Royal Soc. Can., Acad. des Lettres du Québec, Can. Bar Assn. (nat. chmn. sect. constl. and internat. law 1971-73, 86-87), Can. Inst. Pub. Affairs, Inst. Pub. Adminstrn. (Can.), Can. Law Deans (chmn. 1972-73), Can. Inst. Inter de Droit d'Expression Française (v.p. 1973—), Que. Law Deans (chmn. 1975-76), Internat. Assn. Comparative Law, Internat. Commn. Jurists (v.p. for Can. 1987-90, pres. for Can. 1990-92), Standing Senate Com. on Legal and Constl. Affairs (chmn. 1993-96, vice chmn. 2001—), Order of Can. Roman Catholic. Home: 4 de la Guadeloupe Gatineau QC Canada J8Y 1L4 Office: Senate of Can Parliament Bldgs Ctr Block Rm 474-F Ottawa ON Canada K1A 0A4 E-mail: beaudg@sen.parl.gc.ca.

BEAUDOIN, ROBERT LAWRENCE, small business owner; b. Newberry, Mich., Nov. 22, 1933; s. Leo Joseph and Edith Wilhelmina (Graunstadt) B.; m. Margaret Cecelia Linck, June 20, 1953; children: Eugene Robert, Kathleen Therese, Annette Marie, Suzanne Margaret. Student, Marquette U., 1952-53. With Fisher plant GM, 1953; dock hand State of Mich., St. Ignace, 1953; sch. bus driver Engadine (Mich.) Consol. Schs., 1957-96; owner, operator Beaudoin's Texaco, Beaudoin's Cafe, Naubinway, Mich., 1956-82, Beaudoin's Cafe and Marathon, Naubinway, 1982-83, Beaudoin's Cafe, Naubinway, 1956—. Bd. dirs. Naubinway Mchts. Inc., 1985—. Mem. Naubinway July 4th Com., 1954—; past mem. Naubinway Port commn., Garfield Twp. Planning and Zoning Commn.; vol. fireman Garfield Twp. Fire Dept., Naubinway, 1980-94; mem. recreation com. Garfield Twp. Bd., Engadine, 1983; support fellow N.G. and Res., support mem. U.S. Army Recruiting Main Sta., Detroit; mem. USAF Ground Observer Corp. Recipient Cert. of Appreciation, U.S. Army Recruiting Main Sta., Detroit, 1971, Statement of Support, N.G. and Res., 1976. Mem. NRA (life; endowment mem.; mem. Golden Eagles), Internat. Platform Assn., West Mackinac C. of C., Nat. Fedn. Ind. Bus. (adv. bd. 1971—, 20 Yr. award 1985), Am. Farmland Trust, Hiawatha Sportsmans Club (bd. govs. Engadine 1965-67, 89-95, apptd. security officer 1996-98, treas. coun. 7472 1998-99), Curtis C. of C., N.Am. Hunting Club (life), Engadine Trap Shooting Club, KC (grand knight 1979-83, 99-2001, coun. 7472 Naubiway membership and program dir. East Marquette diocese 1984-88, 96-98, 2002—, dist. dep. 1988-92, supreme coun. dist. dep. 1988-92, state dir. coun. activities 1992-94, dep. grand knight coun. 7472 1995-96, 2001-2003), Handyman Club Am. (life), Nat. Home Gardening Club (life), NRA Whitttington Ctr. Founders Club, Lions (3d v.p. Engadine club 1970-71), Hiawatha Sportsmans Club. Roman Catholic. Avocations: hunting, fishing. Home: PO Box 143 Naubinway MI 49762-0143 Office: Beaudoins Cafe PO Box 143 US Hwy 2 Naubinway MI 49762

BEAUDRY, DIANE FAY PUTA, medical quality management executive; b. Manitowoc, Wis., Mar. 6, 1947; d. Ruben William and Gertrude Katherine (Novak) Puta. BSN, Alverno Coll., 1971; MS in Ednl. Adminstrn., U. Wis., Milw., 1979, PhD in Urban Edn., 1991. Staff nurse St. Mary's Hosp., Milw., 1971-72, St. Anthony's Hosp., Milw., 1972-74; nurse coord. Pvt. Initiative in PSRO, Wis., 1974-75; insvc. instr. Deaconess Hosp., Milw., 1975-77, insvc. coord., 1977-81; dir. nursing staff devel./quality assurance Good Samaritan Med. Ctr., Milw., 1981-84, dir. quality assurance, 1984-85, dir. utilization mgmt., 1985-88; mgr. quality mgmt. Sinai Samaritan Med. Ctr., Milw., 1988-89, dir. med. staff svcs. and quality mgmt., 1989-97, dir. quality mgmt., 1997—2002, St. Luke's Med. Ctr., 1997—. Author: (with others) Interdisciplinary QA: Issues in Collaboration, 1991; author poem. Mem. Nat. Assn. for Healthcare Quality, Alverno Coll. Alumnae Assn., U. Wis. Alumni Assn., Delta Epsilon Sigma, Kappa Gamma Pi. Avocations: ballroom dancing, motorcycle riding. Home: 11047 N Riverland Ct # 36W Mequon WI 53092-4900 also: St Luke's Med Ctr PO Box 2901 Milwaukee WI 53201-2901 E-mail: diane.beaudry@aurora.org.

BEAUFAIT, FREDERICK W(ILLIAM), civil engineering educator; b. Vicksburg, Miss., Nov. 28, 1936; s. Frank W. and Eleanor Chambliss (Haynes) B.; m. Lois Mary Erdman, Nov. 27, 1964; children: Paul Frederick, Nicole. BSc, Miss. State U., 1958; MSc, U. Ky., 1961; PhD, Va. Poly. Inst., 1965. Structural engr. U.S. Army C.E., Vicksburg, 1958-59; engr. L. E. Gregg & Assocs., Lexington, Ky., 1959-60; vis. lectr. civil engring. U. Liverpool, Eng., 1960-61; prof. civil engring. Vanderbilt U., Nashville, 1965-79; prof., chmn. dept. civil engring. W.Va. U., Morgantown, 1979-83, assoc. dean Coll. Engring., 1983-86; dean Coll. Engring. Wayne State U., Detroit, 1986-95; dir. NSF Greenfield Engring. Edn. Coalition, 1996-98; pres. N.Y.C. Coll. Tech. of the CUNY, 1999—. Vis. prof. civil and structural engring. U. Wales, Cardiff, 1975-76; cons. in field; mem. Engring. Accreditation Commn. Accreditation Bd. for Engring. and Tech., 1988-93, Engring. Manpower Commn., 1988-92; bd. dirs. Ford (Motor) Design Inst., 1991-96. Co-author: Computer Methods of Structural Analysis, 1970; author: Basic Concepts in Structural Analysis, 1977; also over 40 articles to profl. jours. Vice chmn. stewardship com. 1st Presbyn. Ch., Morgantown, 1982, elder, 1983-85, mem. long-range planning com., 1985-86; deacon Southminster Presbyn. Ch., Nashville, 1968-69, elder, 1971-73, 78-79, clk. of session, 1971-73; bd. dirs. Presbyn. Campus Ministry, Nashville, 1972-78, treas., 1972-75, pres., 1976-78; mem. citizens adv. com. Met. Sch. System, Nashville, 1978-79; bd. dirs. Independence Cmty. Found., 2001—. Named Outstanding Vol. of Yr. Mich. Ctr. for High Tech., 1991. Mem. ASCE, NSPE, Mich. Soc. Profl. Engrs. (bd. dirs. Detroit metro chpt. 1987-90, vice chmn. 1991, chmn.-elect 1992, chmn. 1993, pres. profls. in engring. edn. divsn. 1990-93, state bd. dirs., treas. 1995-97, v.p. 1997-98, Outstanding Engr. in Edn. 1994), Am. Soc. Engring. Edn. (chmn. civil engring. divsn. 1992-93, Centennial medallion 1993, George K. Wadlin award of Civil Engring. Divsn. 1994), Engring. Soc. Detroit (Coll. of Fellows 1994, gold award 1997), Order of Engrs. (bd. governance 1989-97), Chevalier dans l'Ordre des Palmes Academiques (France), Chi Epsilon, Tau Alpha Pi, Tau Beta Pi. Home: One Main St Apt 4D Brooklyn NY 11201 Office: NYC Coll Tech CUNY 300 Jay St Brooklyn NY 11201-1909 E-mail: fbeaufait@citytech.cuny.edu.

BEAUFORD, SANDRA, registered nurse, data processing executive; b. N.Y.C., NY, Feb. 7, 1950; d. Ethel Beauford; children: Gary, Michael, David Sumerlin Beauford. AS, Manhattan Cmty. Coll., 1974; BSN, Herbert H. Lehman Coll., 1976. CCRN, cert. parish nurse. Critical care mgr. Botsford Hosp., Farminington, Mich., 1990—92; asst. mgr. Henry Ford Hosp., Detroit, 1992—96; clin. mgr. Taylor Ambulance, Detroit, 1996—98; o.r. quality coord. Oakwood Hosp., Dearborn, Mich., 1999—; parish nurse Oakwood Hosp. Greater Grace Temple, Dearborn, Mich., 2000—01. Author: On The Road to Your New Beginning, 2000 (Bravo award, 2001, 2002). Facilitator customer svc. enhancement program Oakwood Hosp., 2002—. Lt. USAF, 1974—78, Mclaughin Air Force Base. Mem.: American Coll. Cardiology, Soc. Thoracic Surgeons. Pentecostal. Avocations: basketball, photography, reading. Office: 18101 Oakwood Blvd Dearborn MI 48124-4089 Personal E-mail: beaufors@oakwood.org.

BEAUGRAND, KENNETH LOUIS, lawyer, business executive; b. N.Y.C., Oct. 19, 1938; BA, Brown U., 1960; LLB, Columbia U., 1963; LLM, U. London, 1964; m. Augusta Newell Wood Barnard, Nov. 22, 1969; 3 children. Bar: N.Y. 1964, Ont. 1977. Assoc. Willkie, Farr & Gallagher, N.Y.C., 1964-68; solicitor I.O.S. Ltd. Fin. Services, Geneva, 1968-69, sec., 1969-71, v.p., dir., gen. counsel, 1972-73; v.p., dir., gen. counsel Value Capital Services, Amsterdam, 1971-72; assoc. Aird, Zimmerman & Berlis, 1973-77; v.p., sec., gen. counsel Eaton Bay Fin. Services Ltd., Toronto, 1977-79, sr. v.p., gen. counsel, 1979-82, sr. v.p. ins. and fund. divs., 1982-83, sr. v.p. ops., 1983-85; exec. v.p. 1985-86, sr. v.p. investments The Imperial Life Assurance Co. of Can., Toronto, 1986-87, exec. v.p., chief operating officer, 1987—. Bd. dirs. Laurentian Mut. Funds, Viking Mut. Funds, Eaton Funds Mgmt., Ltd., Laurier Life, chmn., chief exec. officer, bd. dirs. Imbrook Properties, Ltd. Avocations: tennis, skiing, sailing. Clubs: University, Toronto Lawn Tennis. Office: The Imperial Life Assurance Co of Can 95 St Clair Ave W Toronto ON Canada M4V 1N7

BEAUJEAN, A. ALEXANDER, researcher; b. Springfield, Ohio, May 25, 1978; s. Lela L. and William E. Beaujean. BA, Cedarville U., Ohio, 1999; MA, U. of Mo., 2003. Lab., rsch. asst. Wright State U., Dayton, Ohio, 1999—2000; rschr. U. of Mo., Columbia, Mo. Home: 605 S 5th St Apt C Columbia MO 65201 Office: U of Mo 205 Lewis Hall Columbia MO 65211 Personal E-mail: abeaujean@ureach.com. E-mail: aab2b3@mizzou.edu.

BEAULIEU, PETER RAYMOND, priest; b. Fitchburg, Mass., May 5, 1951; s. Raymond J. Beaulieu, Pearl M. Prinn. STL, U.of Louvain, Louvain, Belgium, 1987; MA, Loyola U., 1992. Ordained priest Roman Catholic Ch., 83. Assoc. pastor St. Rose of Lima Parish, Northborough, Mass., 1983—86; cath. chaplain Meml. Health Care, Worcester, Mass., 1993—97; dir. pastoral care St. Vincent Hosp. at WMC, Worcester, Mass., 1997—. Mem. ethics com. Meml. Hosp., 1993—97; chmn. ethics com. St. Vincent Hosp. at WMC, 1997—. Roman Catholic. Office: St Vincent Hospital at WMC 20 Worcester Center Blvd Worcester MA 01608

BEAUMONT, PAMELA JO, marketing professional; b. Valentine, Nebr., July 30, 1944; d. William Henry and Phyllis Faye (Zersen) (Mott) Bostrom; m. Fred H. Beaumont, Apr. 17, 1971 (div. May 1981). BS in Bus., U. Colo., 1966, MBA, 1968. Asst. product mgr. Ore-Ida Foods, Boise, Idaho, 1969-71, product mgr., 1971-73, sr. product mgr., 1973-75, gen. mgr. sales and mktg. services, 1975; v.p. consumer affairs Albertson's Inc., Boise, 1975-76, v.p. mktg., 1976-87; ptnr. Forrest/Beaumont & Andrus, Boise, 1987—; chair Garden City Urban Renewal Agy., 1995—. Home: 9304 N Pebble Falls Ln Boise ID 83714 Office: 4948 Kootenai St Ste 201 Boise ID 83705-2082 E-mail: pamb@spro.net.

BEAUPAIN, ELAINE SHAPIRO, psychiatric social worker; b. Boston, Nov. 1, 1949; d. Abraham and Anna Marilyn (Gass) S.; m. Dean A. Beaupain, Feb. 14, 1987; 1 child, Andrew. BA, McGill U., Montreal, Que., Can., 1971, MSW, 1974. Ind. clin. social worker, Mass.; cert. social worker, Maine; cert. social worker with ind. practice lic., Maine; lic. ind. clin. social worker, Mass. Psychiat. social worker Bangor (Maine) Mental Health Inst., 1974-75; outpatient therapist The Counseling Ctr., Bangor, 1975-76, Millinocket, Maine, 1979-86; asst. core group leader adolescent unit Jackson Brook Inst., Portland, Maine, 1986-87; area dir. Cmty. Health and Counseling Svcs., 1981-86; pvt. practice social work, 1987—. Psychotherapy with individuals, couples and families Millinocket and Bangor, 1987—. Mem. AAUW, NASW, Acad. Cert. Social Workers (diplomate 1992). Democrat. Office: 122 Pine St Bangor ME 04401-5216

BEAUPRE, ELAINE MARCIA KENOW, retired chamber of commerce executive; b. Faribault, Minn., Oct. 28, 1942; d. Sylvester John and Marcella Marie (Karp) D.; m. Richard Thomas Kenow, Jan. 25, 1964 (dec.); children: Cheryl Marie, William Richard; m. James Francis Beaupre, Jan. 2, 1988. Student high sch., Bethlehem Acad., 1960. Med. sec. Dr. Paul Bauer, Faribault, Minn., 1956-60; med. asst. Drs. Ersfeld, McGroarty, Shelander, St. Paul, 1960-64; bookkeeper, office mgr. Town & Country Inc., Faribault, 1964-66; sales person Fabric Store, Faribault, Karp's Shoe Store, Faribault, 1968-79; asst. mgr. Nelson's Super Valu Deli, Minn., 1979-84; mgr. pub. rels. Faribault C. of C., 1984-85, exec. asst., 1985-86, exec. dir., 1986-97; part-time pre-sch. tchr. aide Peace Luth. Sch., Faribault, 1997—2001; cons. Mary Kay Cosmetics, 1997—. Cons. Faribault Festivals Inc., 1984-1997; mem. adv. bd. Sales & Mktg. Tech. Inst., Faribault, 1986-97; mem. adv. bd. Small Bus. Devel. Ctr. Faribault, 1986-97, S.E. Minn. Pvt. Industry Coun., 1991-97; mem. planning com. Minn. C. of C. Execs. Bd. dirs. Faribault Regional Ctr. Cmty. Support Employment Adv. Bd., 1987, River Bend Inst. for Art, Faribault, 1988; mem. adv. bd., disaster com. Rice County Child Care, 1998—, Citizens Liaison Coun. for Corrections Facility, Faribault; mem. adv. bd. Downtown Devel. Com., 1994-97; mem. adv. com. Hist. Soc. for Alexander Faribault on hist. register; ret. dir. Chamber and Tourism bur. Faribault C. of C.; mem. Stop Teen Access to Tobacco (STAT) com. Rice County Hosp., 1997-2000; mem. Project SIGHT; mem. TRAM com. Multiple Sclerosis Rideathon Bike, 1999-2000; mem. redistricting com. Faribault Area-Cannon Valley group Girls Scouts U.S., 1998-99. Mem. Mid. Am. Chamber Exec. Exch. Club (pub. rels. sec.), S.E. Minn. Exec. Chamber Assn. (pres. 1994, treas. 1995, 96). Democrat. Roman Catholic. Avocations: sewing, crafts, hiking, canoeing, horseback riding. Home: 37153 Lumberjack Ln Crosslake MN 56442 E-mail: beaup@crosslake.net.

BEAUPREZ, BOB, congressman; b. Lafayette, Colo., Sept. 22, 1948; m. Claudia Beauprez; 4 children. BS, U. Colo., 1970. Ptnr. Boulder Valley Holsteins, Lafayette, Colo., 1970-89; pres. Indian Peaks, Inc., Lafayette, Colo., 1989—; pres., CEO, chmn. Heritage Bank, Louisville, 1990—; state chmn. Rep. State Ctrl. Com. of Colo., 1999—2002; mem. U.S. Ho. Reps. from 7th Colo. dist., 2003—. Pres. Ind. Bankers Colo., 1997-98, chmn. 1998, bd. dirs. 1993-99; vice chmn., policy devel. com. Ind. Com. Bankers of Am., 2000-; mem. Rep. Nat. Com. Western State Chmn. Assn., 1999—. Office: 511 Cannon Ho Office Bldg Washington DC 20515-0607*

BEAUREGARD, ADAM, aerospace engineer; b. Lynchburg, Va., Dec. 6, 1974; s. Richard and Patricia Beauregard; m. Summer McNeal Hillis, July 1, 2000. BS in Aerospace Engring., Va. Tech, 1996. Aerospace engr. Allied Signal (now Honeywell), NASA Goddard Space Flight Ctr., Greenbelt, Md., 1996—99; aerospace engr./sys. analyst Computer Sciences Raytheon, Patrick AFB, Fla., 1999—. Rescued the ERBS satellite from failure; participated in STS-107 Columbia launch debris investigation. Website content developer Adam's Natural Bodybuilding site. Recipient NASA Group Achievement award, NASA, Computer Sciences Raytheon Spec. Achievement award. Mem.: Range Commanders Coun. (assoc., Optical Sys. Group (RCC-OSG)), AIAA (assoc.). Democrat-Npl. So. Bapt. Home: 8758 Ilex Ct Cape Canaveral FL 32920 Office: Computer Sciences Raytheon CSR 7220 PO Box 4127 Patrick AFB FL 32925 Personal E-mail: kissmybasset@juno.com.

BEAUREGARD, JOHN, school librarian, consultant; b. Boston, Jan. 6, 1932; s. Louis D. and Dorothy May (Randall) Beauregard; children: Paul Calvin, Andrew Hudson, Sharon Elizabeth Nichols, Mark Roger. BA, Gordon Coll., Boston, 1953; MDiv, Gordon Div. Sch., Mass., 1956; MLS, U. of Maine, 1969. Prof. Glen Cove Bible Coll. Christian Sch. Inc., Glen Cove, Maine, 1958—69; prof. bibliography, dir. libr. Gordon Coll., Wenham, Mass., 1969—. Dir. Fair Haven Campus, Brooks, Maine, 1959—68; archivist Gordon Coll., Wenham, Mass., 1972—; pres. bd., v.p., treas. North of Boston Libr. Exch., Danvers, 1985—91. Editor: (book) Jour. of Our Journey by Maria H. Gordon, 1989; author: (book index) A School of Christ, (biography index) Adoniram Judson Gordon, (book) William Wilberforce, 1789-1833/ An Annotated Author and Subjuect Bibliography, 2003. Pastor Appleton Bapt. Ch., Maine, 1956; interm pastor 37 Chs. in Maine, Mass., R.I., 1960—2002; elder Calvary Bapt. Ch., Peabody, Mass., 1998—2003. Baptist. Achievements include index to Coll. Records: trustees, pres's. cabinet, acad. com., coll. publs., student publs. Avocations: hockey, book conserver. Home: 132 Burley St Danvers MA 01923-2366 Office: Gordon Coll 255 Grapevine Rd Wenham MA 01984 Personal E-mail: beauregard@hope.gordon.edu.

BEAUREGARD, LUC, public relations executive; b. Montreal, Que., Can., Aug. 4, 1941; s. Francois and Gertrude (Lévesque) B.; m. Michelle Beauregard; children: Valérie, Stéphanie, Francois, Philippe. BA, Coll. Stanislas, Montreal. Reporter, parliamentary corr. in Ottawa, city editor Montreal (Que.) Daily La Presse, Can., 1961-68; press sec. Que. Minister Edn., Quebec City, Que., 1968-69; founding ptnr. Beauregard, Landry, Nantel & Assocs. Pub. Rels. Cons., Montreal; pres., pub. Montreal-Matin Daily Newspaper, 1973-76; chmn., CEO Nat. Pub. Rels., Inc., Montreal, 1976—. Chmn. Amarc, City of Montreal Corp. managing Man and His World (formerly Expo '67), 1982-86; bd. dirs. Molson Inc., St. Hubert Group, 3-Soft. Chmn. Montreal Better Bus. Bur., 1983—84; mem. exec. com. Montreal Mus. Contemporary Art, 1986—97, chmn., 1987—90, Found. Montreal Island Sch. Coun., 1991—97; gov. Conseil du Patronat du Que., 1992—; sec. info. commn. Que. Liberal Party, 1978—79; bd. dirs. Can. C. of C., Nouvelle Compagnie Theatrale, 1984—94, Que. Heart Found., 1983—85; bd. dirs., adv. bd. Montreal Neurological Inst. Decorated mem. Order of Can.; recipient Philip A. Novikoff award Can. Pub. Rels. Soc. Fellow Can. Pub. Rels. soc. (pres. 1984-85, chmn. Cons. Inst. 1982-83); mem. Am. Pub. Rels. Coun. (chmn. 1985-86), Can. C. of C. (bd. dirs.), Club des Quinze, Mt. Royal Club, St. Denis Club, Knowlton Golf Club, Forest and Stream Club. Avocations: golfing, tennis. Office: Nat Pub Rels 2001 McGill Coll Ave Ste 800 Montreal QC Canada H3A 1G1 E-mail: lbeauregard@national.ca.

BEAUREGARD, MICHAEL RAYMOND, engineering executive, consultant; b. Washington, July 1, 1956; s. Raymond L. and Dorothy M. (Drissel) B.; m. Maura B. McGuire, Aug. 25, 1984; children: Kevin, KC. BSChemE, U. Md., 1978. Registered profl. engr., Conn. Shift engr. ICI Americas Inc., Atlas Point, Del., 1978-80; process/project engr. Rogers Corp., Manchester, Conn., 1980-81, process engring. supr., 1981-84, engring. mgr., 1984-87, plant mgr. Willimantic, Conn., 1987-91; dir. technology Resource Engring., Inc., Tolland, Conn., 1987—2003; founder R.E. Consulting, LLC, Manchester, 2003—. Bd. examiners Malcolm Baldrige Nat. Quality Award, NIST, Gaithersburg, Md., 1995, 96, 97, 99, 2000; sr. examiner Conn. Award for Excellence, Hartford, 1993-96, examiner Conn. Quality Improvement Award, Stamford, 1988-93. Author (lead): SPC in Action: Basic Training, 1990, A Practical Guide to Statistical Quality Improvement, 1992, SPC in Action: Exercise Book, 1994, Experimenting for Breakthrough Improvement, 1996; author: The Basics of FMEA, 1996; author: (lead) The Basics of Mistake-Proofing, 1998; co-author: First Class Service, 1991, SPC in Action: Extended Training, 1993, Employee-Driven Quality, 1994, SPC Workout, 1997, FMEA Investigator, 1997, Mistake-Proof It!, 2000, Six Sigma Start-Up, 2001; author: Problem-Solving Techniques, 2002, DOE" Screening Experiments, 2003. Roman Catholic. Avocations: basketball, bicycling, water sports, stamps. Office: R E Consulting LLC 48 Stock Pl Manchester CT 06040 E-mail: mbeauregard@reconsultingllc.com.

BEAUREGARD, RAYMOND A. mathematician, educator; b. New Bedford, Mass., Feb. 10, 1943; s. R. Albert and Adrienne Beauregard; m. Barbara A. Beauregard, Apr. 4, 1964; children: Jacqueline Robbins, David, Stephen. BA, Providence Coll., 1964; MS, U. N.H., 1966, PhD, 1968. Prof. Math. U. R.I., Kingston, 1968—. Author (textbook): Linear Algebra, 3d edit., 1995; contbr. Mem.: Math. Assn. Am. Home: 28 Beechwood Hill Trl Exeter RI 02822 Office: Dept Math Univ Rhode Island Kingston RI 02881

BEAUSOLEIL, DORIS MAE, federal agency housing specialist; b. Chelmsford, Mass., Jan. 9, 1932; d. Joseph Honorious and Beatrice Pearl (Smith) B. Student, State Tchrs. Coll., Lowell, Mass., 1949-51; BA in Sociology and Psychology, Goddard Coll., Plainfield, Vt., 1954; MA in Human Rels., NYU, 1957; postgrad., CUNY, N.Y.C., 1988-97. With div. human rights N.Y. State, N.Y.C., 1960-69, housing dir., 1966-68. Housing cons. Nat. Com. Against Discrimination in Housing, N.Y.C., 1969-70, Edwin Gould Found., N.Y.C., 1970-71; human resources cons. interfaith housing strategy com., housing cons. Fedn. Prot. Welfare Agencies, Inc., N.Y.C., 1971-72; self-employed housing cons., 1972-74; equal opportunity compliance specialist N.Y./N.J. HUD, N.Y.C., 1975-2000, Fed. women's program coord., 1975-79, pub. trust specialist, 2000—; br. chief Title VI Sect. 109 Compliance div. fair housing and equal opportunity Region II, HUD, N.Y.C., 1979-84, sect. III coord. N.Y./N.J., 1998-; founding mem. N.Y. State HUD Com.; adv. panel Housing Mag., 1979; cons., examiner N.Y. State Civil Svc. Commn., 1970-93. Mem. Nat. Assn. Human Rights Workers (Outstanding Svc. award 1974), Citizens Housing and Planning Coun., Goddard Coll. Alumni Assn. (sec. 1988-90), Rep. Bus. Women's Club (pres. 1985-88, bd. dirs. 1989-91). Republican. Unitarian Universalist. Home: 392 Central Park W Apt 14N New York NY 10025-5868 Office: 26 Federal Plz Rm 3532 New York NY 10278-0004 E-mail: doris_m._beausoleil@hud.gov.

BEAUZAY, VICTOR H(ILTON), lawyer; b. Waverly, N.Y., Mar. 28, 1924; s. Eugene Louis and Edith (Peet) B.; m. JoEllen, Apr. 17, 1946; children: Victor H. II, Victoria Ellen Beauzay. Student, Syracuse U., 1947; AB in Polit. Sci., Stanford U., 1948, JD, 1951. Bar: Calif. 1952, U.S. Supreme Ct. 1957. Pvt. practice law, San Jose. Lectr. in workers' compensation law; chmn. Workers' Compensation Adv. Commn., Calif. State Bar Specialization Program; exec. com. State BarCalif., conf. of dels. 1984-87. Served with U.S. Army, 1943-46. Recipient Golden Banana award P & L Seminar Soc., 1979, Gene Marias Lifetime Achievement award. Mem. Santa Clara County Bar Assn. (pres. 1981), Calif. Applicants Attys. Assn. (pres. 1968-69, chmn. legis. com. 1968-71). Clubs: Century (pres.), Masons (San Jose).

BEAVER, BONNIE VERYLE, veterinarian, educator; b. Mpls., Oct. 26, 1944; d. Crawford F. and Gladys I. Gustafson; m. Larry J. Beaver, Nov. 25, 1972 (dec. Nov. 1995). BS, U. Minn., 1966, D.V.M., 1968; MS, Tex. A&M U., 1972. Instr. vet. surgery and radiology U. Minn., 1968-69; instr. vet. anatomy Tex. A&M U., College Station, 1969-72, asst. prof., 1972-76, assoc. prof., 1976-82; prof. Tex A&M U., College Station, 1982-86, prof. vet. small animal medicine and surgery, 1986—, chief medicine, 1990-99. Mem. vet. medicine adv. com. HEW, 1972-74, nat. adv. food and drug com., HEW, 1975, com. on animal models and genetic stocks NAS, 1984-86, 87-89, panel on microlivestock NRC, 1986-87, task force on animal use study Inst. Lab. Animal Resources, 1986, adv. com. for Pew Nat. Vet. Edn. Program, Pew Charitable Trusts, 1987-92, 10th symposium on Vet. Med. Edn. Com., 1988-89. Mem. editl. bd. Applied Animal Ethology, 1981-82, 83-84, VM/SAC, 1982-85, Applied Animal Behavior Sci., 1982-84, 84-86, 86-88, 88-2000, Bull. on Vet. Clin. Ethology, 1994-1999, Jour. Am. Animal Hosp. Assn., 1995—; contbr. articles to profl. jours. Vice pres. Brazos Valley Regional Sci. and Engring. Fair, 1974— 83, dir., 1983-85; bd. dirs. Brazos Valley unit Am. Cancer Soc., 1976-83, v.p., 1976-83. Named Citizen of Week, The Press, 1981, Outstanding Woman Veterinarian of 1982, Disting. Practitioner, Nat. Acads. Practice; Recipient Friskies PetCare award Am. Animal Hosp. Assn., 2001, Bustad Human-Animal Bond award, 2001, Elanco Disting. Lectr. award, 2002. Mem.: AVMA (exec. bd. 1997—2003, chair exec. bd. 2001—02, pres.-elect 2003—04, Animal Welfare award 1996), AAAS, Am. Horse Coun., Am. Quarter Horse Assn., Tex. Palomino Exhibitors Assn., Palomino Horse Breeders Am. (v.p. 1983—88, treas. 1984—85, pres.-elect 1988—89, pres. 1989—90), Nat. Acad. Practice, Am. Coll. Vet. Behaviorists (chair organizing com. 1976—91, pres. 1991—96, charter diplomat 1993—, exec. dir. 1996—), Animal Behavior Soc., Am. Assn. Bovine Practitioners, Am. Assn. Equine Practitioners, Am. Assn. Vet Clinicians, Am. Vet. Soc. Animal Behavior (pres. 1975—80), Am. Animal Hosp. Assn., Brazos Valley Vet. Med. Assn., Tex. Vet. Med. Assn. (3d v.p. 1990, 2d v.p. 1991, 1st v.p. 1992, pres.-elect 1993, pres. 1994), Phi Delta Gamma (pres. 1974—75), Phi Zeta (nat. pres. 1979—81), Sigma Epsilon Sigma, Phi Sigma, Delta Soc. Office: Tex A&M Univ Coll Vet Medicine Vet Small Animal Medicine & College Station TX 77843-4474

BEAVER, DANIEL ROY, history educator; b. Hamilton, Ohio, Sept. 23, 1928; BA, Heidelberg Coll., 1951; MA, U. Cin., 1954; PhD, Northwestern U., 1962. Prof. history U. Cin., 1958—2001, prof. emeritus, 2001—. Cpl. U.S. Army, 1946—47. Mem.: Ohio Acad. History, Interuniv. Seminar for War and Soc., Soc. Mil. History. Democrat. Office: U Cin Dept History Cincinnati OH 45221

BEAVER, FRANK EUGENE, communication educator, film critic and historian; b. Cleve., N.C., July 26, 1938; s. John Whitfield and Mary Louise (Shell) B.; m. Gail Frances Place, June 30, 1962; children: Julia Clare, John Francis, Johanna Louise. BA, U. N.C., 1960, MA, 1966; PhD, U. Mich., 1970. Instr. speech Memphis State U., 1965-66; instr. radio-TV-motion pictures U. N.C., Chapel Hill, 1966-68; asst. prof. speech comm. U. Mich., Ann Arbor, 1969-74, assoc. prof., 1974-79, assoc. prof. comm., 1979-84, prof., chmn. dept. comm., 1987-91, Arthur F. Thurnau prof., 1989-92, dir. grad. program in telecom. arts and film, 1991-96. Advisor Muskegon (Mich.) Film Festival, 2001. Film critic radio Stas. WUOM, WVGR, WFUM, Ann Arbor, Grand Rapids, Mich., 1975-97; author: Bosley Crowther, 1974, On Film, 1983, Dictionary of Film Terms, 1983, 94 (Mandarin-Chinese translation 1993), Oliver Stone: Wakeup Cinema, 1994, 100 Years of American Film, 2001; writer, dir. documentary film Under One Roof, 1967; editor (book series) Framing Film, 98-, gen. editor Twayne Pubs., N.Y., 1987—; editor-in-chief: 100 Years of Cinema, 2000. Bd. dirs. Mich. Theater Found., Ann Arbor, 1977-79, 86—; alumni adv. bd. Lambda Chi Alpha, Ann Arbor, 1989-94; advisor Ann Arbor Film Festival, 1975—, Muskegon Film Festival, 2000-. With M.I. Corps, U.S. Army, 1962-65, Vietnam. Recipient Playwriting award Carolina Playmakers, 1962, Major Hopwood writing awards for drama and essays U. Mich., 1969, Outstanding Teaching award Amoco Found., Ann Arbor, 1985; fellow NEH, 1975. Mem.: Speech Comm. Assn., Soc. Cinema Scholars, Racquet Club, Azazels Club, Phi Kappa Phi, Kappa Tau Alpha. Democrat. Roman Catholic. Home: 1835 Vinewood Blvd Ann Arbor MI 48104-3609 Office: U Mich Film and Video Studios 2512 Frieze Bldg Ann Arbor MI 48109-1285 E-mail: fbeaver@umich.edu.

BEAVER, HOWARD OSCAR, JR., retired alloys manufacturing company executive; b. Lebanon, Pa., May 18, 1925; s. Howard Oscar and Lessie (Yocum) B.; m. Jean Lillian Shollenberger, June 14, 1945; children: Bonne Jean Beaver Riefenstahl, Thomas Arthur. Student, U.S. Naval Acad., 1944; BS in Metallurgy, Pa. State U., 1948; grad. exec. mgmt. program, U. Pitts., 1967; DSc (hon.), Albright Coll., 1982. Metallurgist Carpenter Tech. Corp., Reading, Pa., 1948-51, plant metallurgist, melting, 1951-57, mgr. mill metallurgy, 1957-60, asst. gen. supt., 1960-66, asst. v.p. steel mfg., 1966-68, v.p. prodn., 1968-69, group v.p. steel, 1969-71, dir., 1969-83, chmn. bd., chief exec. officer, 1971-83, bd. dirs.; ret., 1993. Former mem. adv. panel Congl. Office Tech. Assessment, Washington. Contbr. articles to profl. jours.; patentee in field. Past pres. exec. bd. Boy Scouts Am. Hawk Mountain Coun., Reading, Pa.; past pres. adv. bd. Pa. State U., Berks Campus, Reading, gen. chmn. capital campaign; bldg. campaign com. Community Gen. Hosp., Reading; bd. trustees Chit Chat Found., Wernersville, Pa., Pa. State U.; active United Way of Berks County, Pennsylvanians for Effective Govt., Harrisburg, Keystone State Games. Recipient cert. of distinction Fin. World, 1979, Bronze award Fin. World, 1980, Silver award The Wall St. Transcript, 1980, Horatio Alger award, 1981, Humanitarian award B'nai Brith Internat., 1981, Billy Wallis Founders award Elec. Metal Makers Guild Inc., 1982, Disting. Alumnus award Pa. State U., 1991; named Disting. Pennsylvanian William Penn Com., Phila., 1981, Businessperson of Yr., Berks County C. of C., 1982, Wilbur B. Doran award United Way Berks County, 1985, Thun award Meridian Bank, 1990; named to Pa. Hall of Fame, Jr. Achievement Hall of Fame of Reading and Berks County, 1985. Fellow Am. Soc. Metals (Lehigh Valley chpt., Bradley Stoughton award 1967, David Ford McFarland award 1972, medal for advancement of rsch. 1980, Disting. Life Membership award 1988); mem. AIME (Benjamin F. Fairless award 1981), Am. Iron and Steel Inst. (hon. v.p.), Assn. Iron and Steel Engrs., Muhlenberg Lions Club, Berkshire County Club, Skytop (Pa.) Club. Republican. Lutheran. Home and Office: 1954 Meadow Ln Wyomissing PA 19610-2710

BEAVERS, KAREN MARJORIE, small business owner; b. Laurel, Md., Nov. 2, 1947; d. James Walter and Marjorie Lois (Fullerton) McQuaid; m. George Edward Kowalski, Aug. 30, 1969 (div.); children: Eddie, Charlie, Bill; m. Edward George Beavers Jr., Feb. 14, 1991; stepchild, Edward. Student, Art Instrn. Sch., 1970; BS in Behavioral Sci., U. Md., 1994; postgrad., Loyola Coll., 1995. Receptionist Capitol Software, Laurel, 1988-89; new accounts devel. staff Focus Telecom., Burtonsville, Md., 1989-90; CSR & tng. asst. Encore Mktg. Internat., Lanham, Md., 1990-91; office mgr. Computer Image Svc., Laurel, 1991-94; pres., owner Gifts & More, Laurel, 1994-95, Gifts & More, Inc., Laurel, 1993-2000. Author: Tippy and Freckles Great Adventures, 1996; The Development of Children's Behavior, several theories of parenting, author of poetry. Hot-line counselor Domestic Violence Ctr., Howard County, Md., 1993-94; vol. art tchr., playground and lunchroom staff St. Marys of the Mills, Laurel; team mother Prince George Gymnastics, Beltsville, Md.; actress Ann Martin's Drama Guild, Laurel. Mem. APA (grad. affiliate), AAUW, Internat. Soc. Poets, Psi Chi. Roman Catholic. Avocations: gardening, doll collecting, antique shopping.

BEAVERS, ROY LACKEY, retired utility executive, essayist, activist; b. Joplin, Mo., Apr. 24, 1930; s. Roy L. Sr. and Margarette Nellie (Loughlin) B.; m. Valerie Evelyn Gurney; children: Leslie Anne, Brendan G. BS in Bus., U. Mo., 1952; MA in Polit. Sci., U. Md., 1970. Commd. ens. USN, 1952, advanced through grades to comdr., 1966, retired, 1972; agt., broker ins. agy., Lebanon, Mo., 1972-77; field rep. Nat. Rural Electric Coop. Assn., Washington, 1977-84; mgr. pub. info. and legis. liaison wholesale power coop. KAMO Power, Vinita, Okla., 1984-93. Assigned U.S. Arms Control Disarmament Agy. (SALT I strategic arms negotiations), 1970—72; moderator internet discussion list EMF-L concerning electromagnetic field health hazards, 1995—2003; advocate for regulation of electromagnetic radiation. Contbr. polit. and mil. essays to newspapers and other publs. including An Absence of Accountability (U.S. policy failure in Vietnam), 1976. State hdqrs. dir. Va. Com. to Re-elect Nixon, Richmond, Va., 1972; mem. Bd. Mo. Cmty. Betterment Edn. Fund, 1990-93, Bd. Okla. Acad. for State Goals, 1990-93. Decorated Bronze, Silver, and Gold medals U.S. Naval Inst., Pres. Merit Svc. medal, Navy Commendation medal Mem. U.S. Naval Inst., Bioelectromagnetics Soc. Home: Lake Shore Estates 26555 Gene Dr Lebanon MO 65536-5776 E-mail: roy@emfguru.org.

BEAZLEY, HAMILTON SCOTT, writer, educator; b. Houston, Dec. 21, 1943; s. Hamilton and Marjorie Virginia (Yates) B. BA, Yale U., 1966; MBA, So. Meth. U., 1977; PhD, George Washington U., 1998. Founder/exec. com. DyChem Internat. (U.K.) Ltd., Dallas, London, 1970-73; oil and gas industry exec., 1970—80; strategic planning cons., 1980-88; pres. Nat. Coun. on Alcoholism and Drug Dependence, N.Y.C., 1988-90; assoc. prof. orgnl. scis. George Washington U., 1999—2002; scholar-in-residence St. Edward's U., Austin, Tex., 2003—. Co-creator TV series, BBC, Secrets Out, 1984-87; co-author: (with Bishop Payne) Reclaiming the Great Commission, 2000; author: No Regrets, 2003; co-author: Continuity Management, 2002; co-editor: The Servant-Leader Within, 2003. Bd. dirs. Total World Corp., Houston, 1985-97; bd. trustees Ednl. Advancement Found., 1996—; mem. adv. bd. divsn. on addictions Harvard Med. Sch., 1994-98; mem. adv. bd. Discovery Learning Project, U. Tex., Austin, 1996—. Mem. Am. Psychol. Assn., Acad. of Mgmt., Yale Club of N.Y.C. Republican. Episcopalian. Avocation: sailing. Home: 1801 Crystal Dr Apt 615 Arlington VA 22202-4415

BEBB, RICHARD S. lawyer; b. LA, July 22, 1952; s. Robert Stanley and Sue (Williams) B.; m. Christine K. Bebb, June 29, 1974; children: Michelle, David. AB, Stanford U., 1974; JD, U. Calif., San Francisco, 1977. Bar: Calif. 1977. Assoc. Reinjohn, Catlin & Clements, L.A., 1977-79, Ruffo, Ferrari & McNeil, San Jose, Calif., 1979-81, Ferrari Alvarez Olsen & Ottoboni, PC, San Jose, 1981-84, ptnr., 1984-96, Ferrari Olsen Ottoboni & Bebb, PC, San Jose, 1996-98, Ferrari Olsen Ottoboni & Bebb, LLP, San Jose, 1998-2000, Pillsbury Winthrop, LLP, Palo Alto, Calif., 2000—. Mem. Santa Clara County Bar Assn. (past chmn. bus. law sect., exec. com. bus. law sect.). Office: Pillsbury Winthrop LLP 2550 Hanover St Palo Alto CA 94304-1115 E-mail: rbebb@pillsburywinthrop.com.

BEBCHICK, LEONARD NORMAN, lawyer; b. New Bedford, Mass., Dec. 11, 1932; s. Samuel and Frances (Hait) B.; m. Gabriela Meyerhoff, Aug. 31, 1968; children: Ilana, Brian. AB, Cornell U., 1955; LLB, Yale U., 1958. Bar: Mass. 1958, D.C. 1960, Md. 1989. Atty. CAB, Washington, 1958—59; assoc. Ginsburg & Leventhal, Washington, 1960-64; ptnr. Bebchick, Sher & Kushnick, Washington, 1964-74, Martin, Whitfield, Smith & Bebchick, Washington, 1974-82; pres. Leonard N. Bebchick P.C., Washington, 1982-88; ptnr. Leva, Hawes, Mason, Martin & Bebchick, Washington, 1988-89; pvt. practice as lawyer Washington, 1989—. Joint co. sec. Brit Caledonian Airways, Eng., 1963-88; bd. dirs. British Caledonian Group, Eng., 1978-88, London Transport Internat. Cons., U.S., 1990-92; spl. counsel D.C. Pub. Svc. Commn., Washington, 1965-66, V.I. Pub. Utilities Commn., 1967-70. Bd. dirs. Jewish Found. Group Homes, 1992—; pres. Congregation Beth El of Montgomery County, 1993—95; bd. dirs. United Synagogue of Conservative Judaism, 1993—2002, Jewish Fedn. Greater Washington, 1996—2002; bd. govs. coms. Jewish Agy. Israel, 1998—2002; bd. dirs., vice chair, exec. com., Muss H.S., Israel, 1997—; mem. nat. coun. Am. Jewish Com., 2002—. Mem.: ABA (chmn. adv. com. on aero. law 1982—83), Inst. of Dirs. (London), Internat. Assn. Jewish Lawyers and Jurists, U.S. Nat. Student Assn. (v.p. internat. affairs 1953—54). Democrat. Jewish. Home: 6321 Lenox Rd Bethesda MD 20817-6023 Office: 1101 Connecticut Ave NW Washington DC 20036 E-mail: beblaw@erols.com.

BEBER, ROBERT H. lawyer, financial services executive; b. N.Y.C., Aug. 17, 1933; s. Morris and Martha (Pollock) B.; m. Joan Parsons, June 14, 1957; children: Andrea, Judith, Deborah. AB in Econs, Duke U., 1955, JD, 1957. Bar: N.Y., N.C. With Everett, Everett & Everett, N.C., 1957-58; atty. SBA, Washington, 1961-63; with RCA, 1963-81; sr. v.p., gen. counsel, sec. GAF Corp., N.Y.C., 1981-83, exec. v.p., dir., 1983-84, dir. subs.; sr. v.p., gen. counsel, sec. Phlcorp, Inc. (formerly Baldwin United Corp.), Phila., 1984-88; asst. gen. counsel litigation W.R. Grace & Co., N.Y.C., 1988-89, v.p., dir. litigation, 1989-91, sr. v.p., gen. counsel, 1991-93, exec. v.p., 1993-98, ret., 1999, cons., 1999—. Bd. dirs. Advantage Bank. Bd. vis. Sch. Law, Duke U., 1996—; chmn. bd. Health Care Plan N.J., 1975-78; v.p. South Jersey C. of C., 1974-77; dir. Advantage Bank, Palm Beach, Fla., 1999—. Served with U.S. Army, 1958-61. Mem. ABA. Republican. Jewish. Home: 7228 Queenferry Cir Boca Raton FL 33496-5953 Office: WR Grace & Co 5400 Broken Sound Blvd NW Boca Raton FL 33487-3511

BEBO, JOSEPH ANTHONY, counselor, educator; b. Boston, Dec. 31, 1954; s. John Thomas and Leah B.; m. Frances Gail Coker, Oct. 10, 1978 (dec. Aug. 1988); children: Joseph Anthony Jr., John James; m. Patricia Ann Bebo. BA, U. Mass., 1976, MA in Sociology, 1996, postgrad. in edn., 1999—. Cert. substance abuse counselor Mass. Bd. Counselor Certification. Substance abuse counselor Sullivan House Middlesex Human Svcs., Jamaica Plain, Mass., 1993—99; program coord. alcohol and substance abuse studies cert. and grad. cert. forensci svcs. Coll. Arts and Sci. criminal justic program U. Mass., Boston, 1997—99; lectr. U. Mass, 1999—, Rivier Coll., 1999—2000, Fitchburg State Coll., 1999—; vis. lectr. Bridgewater State Coll., 2001—. Treas. Internat. Coalition Addictions Studies Educators, 2000—, convention coord., 2000; alcohol and drug counselor Divsn. Youth Svcs., Phoenix Ctr., Brockton YMCA, Plymouth County Correctional Facility. Contbr. articles to profl. jours. Recipient Cert. Appreciation, Higher Edn. Ctr. Mem.: Acad. Criminal Justice Scis., Nat. Assn. Alcohol and Drug Abuse Counselors, Northeastern Assn. Criminal Justice Scis. (contbr. criminal justice edn. task force), Am. Soc. Criminology, Alpha Kappa Delta. Office: U Mass 100 Morrissey Blvd Boston MA 02125

BEBOUT, ELI DANIEL, oil executive; b. Rawlings, Wyo., Oct. 14, 1946; s. Hugh and Dessie Bebout; m. Lorraine J. Tavares; children: Jordan, Jentry, Reagen, Taggert. BEE, U. Wyo., 1969. With U.S. Energy Co., Riverton, Wyo., 1974-75; field engr. Am. Bechtel Corp., Green River, Wyo., 1975-76; pres. NUPEC Resources, Inc., Riverton, 1976-83, Smith-Collins Pharm. Inc., Riverton, 1976-83; cons. Nucor Inc., Riverton, 1984—2002; v.p. Nucor Drilling, Inc., Riverton, 1987—2001; state legislator Wyo. Assembly; pres. Nucor Oil & Gas, 1993—2002. Past chmn. Wyo. Bus. Alliance; Wyo. Heritage Found.; former mem., mem. rules com. mgmt. coun., majority floor leader, spkr. Wyo. Ho. of Reps.; past chmn. Energy Coun. Republican. Office: Nucor Inc PO Box 112 Riverton WY 82501-0112

BECATTI, LANCE NORMAN, financial consultant; b. Roseland, Ill., Feb. 11, 1959; s. Leroy J. Sr. and Shirley Ann Becatti. CFP, CLTC, Fla. Dist. adminstr. Lanier Bus. Products, Inc., Sarasota and Ft. Myers, Fla., 1976-79; pres. Alpha I Inc. ADC, Ft. Myers, 1979-84; sr. fin. advisor Am. Express Fin. Advisors, Tampa, Fla., 1984—. Mem. adv. bd. Tampa's Downtown Spl. Svcs. Dist., 1993-96; campaign chmn. March of Dimes, Ft. Myers, 1978-79; mem. Tampa Planned Giving Coun. Mem. Internat. Assn. for Fin. Planning (practitioners divsn. 1992—), Tampa Bay Bus. Coun. Avocations: Karate, raquetball, cycling. Home: 201 W Laurel St Apt 203 Tampa FL 33602-2935 Office: Am Express Fin Advisors 2002 E 4th Ave Tampa FL 33605-

BECERRA, XAVIER, congressman, lawyer; b. Sacramento, Jan. 26, 1958; s. Manuel and Maria Teresa B.; m. Carolina Reyes, 1987. AB, Stanford U., 1980, JD, 1984. Atty., 1984—; dir. dist. office State Senator Art Torres, L.A.; dep. atty. gen. dept. justice, Calif., 1987-90; assemblyman, 59th dist. State of Calif., 1990-93; mem. U.S. Congress from 30th Calif. dist., 1993—. Mem. ways and means com.; chmn. Congl. Hispanic Caucus. Mem. Mexican-Am. Bar Assn., Calif. Bar Assn., Assn. Calif. State Attys. and Adminstrv. Law Judges. Democrat. Avocations: reading, carpentry, golf. Office: Ho of Reps 1119 Longworth Bldg Washington DC 20515-0530*

BECH, DOUGLAS YORK, lawyer, resort executive; b. Seattle, Aug. 18, 1945; s. Albert Richard and Vera Evelyn (Peterson) B.; m. Sheryl Annette Tucker, Aug. 9, 1968; children: Kristen Elizabeth, Allison York. BA, Baylor U., 1967; JD, U. Tex., 1970. Bar: Tex. 1970, N.Y. 1993. Ptnr. Andrews & Kurth, Houston, 1970-93, Akin, Gump, Strauss, Hauer & Feld, 1994-97; mng. dir. Raintree Capital Co., Houston, 1994—. Chmn., CEO Raintree Resorts Internat., Inc., Club Regina Resorts, Inc.; bd. dirs. Frontier Oil, Pride Cos., J2 Global Comm. Sgt. USAR, 1968-74. Republican. Baptist. Avocations: running, snowskiing, travel, big game hunting, golf. Office: Raintree Resorts Internat 10000 Memorial Dr Ste 480 Houston TX 77024-3409 E-mail: dybech@raintreeresotrs.com.

BECHAMPS, GERALD JOSEPH, surgeon; b. Flushing, N.Y., 1937; MD, Georgetown U., 1963. Diplomate Am. Bd. Surgery. Intern Meadowbrook Hosp., East Meadow, N.Y., 1963-64, resident in surgery, 1964-65; fellow surgery Mayo Clinic-Found., Rochester, 1965-69; clin. instr. U.Va. Sch. Medicine, 1971—2002; pvt. practice Winchester Surg. Clinic, Ltd., 1971—; asst. clin. prof. Va. Commonwealth U., 2003—. Past pres. Fedn. State Med. Bds. of U.S.; surgeon Winchester Med. Ctr., Surgi-Ctr. of Winchester; mem. Va. State Bd. Medicine, pres., 1985-86, 87-88. Mem. ACS (past pres. Va. chpt.), So. Soc. Clin. Surgeons. Office: Winchester Surg Clinic Ltd PO Box 2698 Winchester VA 22604-1898 Fax: 540-722-4515.

BECHER, WILLIAM DON, electrical engineer, engineering educator, writer; b. Bolivar, Ohio, Nov. 26, 1929; s. William and Eva Vernette (Richardson) Becher; m. Helen Norma Hager, Aug. 31, 1950; children: Eric Alan, Patricia Lynn. BS in Radio Engring., Tri-State U., 1950; MSEE, U. Mich., 1961, PhD, 1968. Registered profl. engr., Mich., N.J. Project engr. Bogue Electric, Paterson, NJ, 1950-53; sr. devel. engr. Goodyear Aircraft Corp., Akron, Ohio, 1953-57; sr. systems engr. Beckman Instruments, Fullerton, Calif., 1957-58; engring. supr. Bendix Aerospace Systems, Ann Arbor, Mich., 1958-63; rsch. engr. U. Mich., Ann Arbor, 1963-68, adj. prof. elec. engring., 1978-79, 81-94, lectr. elec. engring. Dearborn, 1964-68, prof. elec. engring., 1968-78, chmn., 1971-76; engring. dept. mgr. Environ. Rsch. Inst. Mich., Ann Arbor, 1977-79, assoc. dir., 1981-87, tech. cons., 1988-90, engr. emeritus, 1990—; dean elec. engring. Coll. Engring. N.J. Inst. Tech., Newark, 1979-81; cons. Widbec Engr, Ann Arbor, 1978—. Pres. Mich. Computers & Instrumentation, Inc., Ann Arbor, 1983—87; prof., chmn. elec. engring. Calif. State U., Fresno, 1988. Author: (book) Courses in Continuing Education for Electronics Engineers, 1975, 1976, Logical Design Using Integrated Circuits, 1977, An Ocean Between, 2000. With U.S. Army, 1953—55. Fellow GE, 1962—63. Mem.: IEEE (life), Order of Engrs., Am. Soc. Engring. Edn., Tau Beta Pi, Sigma Xi. Achievements include patents in field. Home and Office: Widbec Engring 691 Spring Valley Rd Ann Arbor MI 48105-1060

BECHERER, HANS WALTER, retired agricultural equipment executive; b. Detroit, Apr. 19, 1935; s. Max and Mariele (Specht) B.; m. Michele Beigbeder, Nov. 28, 1959; children: Maxime (dec.), Vanessa. BA, Trinity Coll., Hartford, Conn., 1957; postgrad., Munich U., 1958; MBA, Harvard U., 1962. Exec. asst. office of chmn. Deere & Co., Moline, Ill., 1966-69; gen. mgr. John Deere Export, Mannheim, Germany, 1969-73; dir. export mktg. Deere & Co., Moline, 1973-77, v.p., 1977-83, sr. v.p., 1983-86, exec. v.p., 1986-87, pres., 1987-90, COO, 1987-89, CEO, 1989-2000, chmn., 1990-2000, also bd. dirs. Bd. dirs. Schering-Plough Corp., Honeywell Internat. Inc., Chase Manhattan Corp. and Chase Manhattan Bank; mem. industry sector adv. com. U.S. Dept. Commerce, 1975-81; mem. Bus. Roundtable, 1989—; mem. adv. com. Chase Manhattan Bank Internat., 1990-98; trustee Com. for Econ. Devel., 1990—. Trustee St. Katherine's/St. Mark's Sch., Bettendorf, Iowa, 1983—. 1st lt. USAF, 1958-60. Mem. Coun. on Fgn. Rels., Conf. Bd., Equipment Mfgs. Inst. (bd. dirs. 1987-90), Rock Island (Ill.) Arsenal Golf Club. Republican. Roman Catholic. Office: Deere & Co One John Deere Pl Moline IL 61265-8098

BECHERER, RICHARD JOHN, architecture educator; b. East St. Louis, Ill., Nov. 8, 1951; s. Adam Jacob and Agnes Evelyn (Baker) B.; m. Charlene Castellano, Aug. 13, 1982. Student Courtauld Inst., U. London, 1973; BA, BArch, Rice U., 1974; MA, Cornell U., 1977, PhD, 1981. Archtl. asst. Colin St. John Wilson and Ptnr., London, England, 1972-73; designer The Brooks Assn., Houston, 1973-74; grad. asst. Cornell U., Ithaca, N.Y., 1974-80, asst. prof. architecture, 1981; asst. prof. Auburn (Ala.) U., 1980-82, U. Va., Charlottesville, 1982-86; head grad. architecture program Carnegie Mellon U., Pitts., 1986-90, assoc. prof. architecture, 1987-96; assoc. prof. Cornell U., 1996, Am. U. Beirut, 1999—2001, Iowa State U., 2001—. Presenter seminars NEH, 1982, 88, 89, Am. Collegiate Schs. Architecture, 1988, 93, 97, 2002; lectr. Centre Canadien d'Architecture, Montreal, Carnegie Mus., Pitts., and various colls., univs. and nat. confs.; vis. assoc. prof. U. Pitts., 1997-99; assoc. prof. Am. U. Beirut, 1999—, Iowa State U.; mem. Fulbright Fellowship selection com. Author: Science Plus Sentiment; César Daly's Formula for Modern Architecture, 1984, (mus. catalogue and display) Urban Theory and Transformation, 1976, (tourist guidebook) Canandaigua: A Walking Tour, 1977; contbr. articles to profl. jours.; prin. works include interiors Michael P. Keeley House, Belleville, Ill., 1978, Robert Becherer House, Stonybrook, 1990; selected exhibitor Venice Biennale, Prato della Valle, Padua, 1985; exhibitor Heart of the Park, Houston, 1992. Recipient Design Arts award Nat. Endowment for Arts, 1989-90, Graham Found. award, 1993; grad. fellow Cornell U., 1975-79, Eidlitz fellow, 1978, Soc. for Humanities and Mellon Found. fellow, 1984-85, NEH fellow, 1986, Paul Mellon vis. sr. fellow Ctr. for Advanced Study in Visual Arts, Nat. Gallery of Art; Travel to Collections grantee NEH, 1985. Mem. AAUP, Soc. Archtl. Historians (session chmn. ann. meeting 1989), Coll. Art Assn., Rice U. Alumni Assn. Democrat. Roman Catholic. Avocations: free-hand drawing, ballroom dancing, film. Home and Office: 119 Race St Pittsburgh PA 15218-1337 E-mail: agnes@iastate.edu.

BECHERER, RICHARD JOSEPH, science administrator, physicist; b. Boston, Mar. 19, 1941; s. Edward Charles and Grace Elizabeth (Dalton) B.; m. Kathleen Quinn, June 26, 1965 (div. Aug. 1984) children: Joan Elizabeth, Christine Diane, Carolyn Jean; m. Susan Jaeger, Sept. 30, 1989 (div. Jan. 1999). BS in Physics, Boston Coll., 1962; MS in Physics, U. Ill., Champaign, 1964; NASA trainee, U. Rochester, 1969-71, PhD in Optics, 1972. Scientist Tech. Ops. Inc., Burlington, Mass., 1965-68, EIKONIX Corp., Bedford, Mass., 1968-71; sr. scientist, sect. mgr. Polaroid Research Labs, Cambridge, Mass., 1971-75; mem. tech. staff Lincoln Lab, MIT, Lexington, Mass., 1975-81; dir. optical sys. Sci. Applications Internat. Corp., Lexington, Mass., 1981-91; pres. Delta Sciences, Maynard, Mass., 1991—. Lectr. Northeastern U., Boston, 1966-83, U. Oulu, Finland, 1990, Nat. Tech. U., Ft. Collins, Colo., 1993—; cons. NAS Nat. Rsch. Coun., Washington, 1972-76; mem. Commn. Internat. l'Eclairage, Washington, 1973-76, USN Electro-Optics Working Group, 1977-80, NATO Rsch. Study Group, Munich, 1978-79; Strategic Def. Initiative Experimenters Working Group, 1986-91; instr. SPIE laser radar, sensor sys. courses Nat. Tech. U., 1993—; adj. prof. U. Conn., Storrs, 1992—; dep. dir. CONNECT-New Eng. Alliance Photonics Tech. Deployment, Storrs, 1994—; pres. coun. U. Ill., 1990—. Co-author: Optical Radiation Measurements, Vol. 1: Radiometry, 1979; editor: Adaptive Optics Systems and Technology, 1982, Laser Radar II, 1987, Laser Radar III, 1988, Laser Radar IV, 1989, Laser Radar V, 1990, Laser Radar VI, 1991, Laser Radar VII, 1992, Lidar for Remote Sensing, 1992, Lidar and Atmospheric Sensing, 1995; mem. editl. bd. Laser Focus, 1973-77; patentee optical filtering methods, optical heterodyne detection. Active Conservation Law Found., 1992—; com. mem. Rep. Nat. Com., Washington, 1994; campaign com. Mass. 5th Congl. Dist., Concord, 1994. Presidential scholar Boston Coll., 1962. Fellow Internat. Soc. Optical Engring.; mem. Optical Soc. Am. (chmn. edn. com.), Fides Soc., Pine Tree Soc., Sigma Xi, Sigma Pi Sigma. Roman Catholic. Avocations: history, politics, travel, tennis, skiing.

BECHTEL, RILEY PEART, engineering company executive; BA in Polit. Sci., Psychology, U. Calif., Davis, 1974; JD, MBA, Stanford U., 1979. Bar: Calif. 1979. With Bechtel Group, Inc., San Francisco, 1966—79, 1981—, Thelen, Marrin, Johnson & Bridges, San Francisco, 1979—81; bd. dirs. Bechtel Corp. (formerly Bechtel Group Inc.), 1987—, pres., COO, 1989—90, pres., CEO, 1990—96, chmn., CEO, 1996—. Mem. Bus. Coun., Bus. Roundtable policy com; bd. dirs. J.P. Morgan Chase; adv. com. Stanford U. Grad. Sch. of Bus.; dean's adv. coun. Stanford Law Sch. Trustee Jason Found. for Edn. Fellow: Am. Acad. Arts and Scis.; mem.: Am. Soc. Corp. Execs. (conservation fund corp. coun.), Am. Soc. Civil Engrs. (hon.). Office: Bechtel Group Inc PO Box 193965 San Francisco CA 94119-3965

BECHTEL, ROBERT BERNARD, social sciences educator, consultant; b. Pottstown, Pa., Oct. 19, 1932; s. Leonard Bernard and Helen Ida Bechtel; m. Beverly Smith Bechtel, May 6, 1972; children: Amanda Carolyn Willis, Carrah Elizabeth. BA, Susquehanna U., 1962; MA, U. Kans., 1964, PhD, 1967. Rsch. assoc. Inst. for Cmty. Studies, Kansas City, Mo., 1966-70; sr. rsch. assoc. Greater Kansas City Mental Health Fedn., 1970-74; dir. rsch. Environ. Rsch. Found., Kansas City, 1974-75, exec. dir. Kansas City and Tucson, Ariz., 1975-80; prof. U. Ariz., Tucson, 1976—. Author: Enclosing Behavior, 1977, Methods in Environmentatl Behavioral Research, 1987, Introduction to Environment and Behavior, 1997, Handbook of Environmental Psychology, 2002; editor Environment and Behavior, 1977; contbr. over 15 chpts. to books and over 25 articles and reports to profl. publs. Chmn. Housing Commn., Kansas City, 1974-75, Postal History Found., 1993—. Recipient Career award Environ. Design Rsch. Assn., 1993; grantee Nat. Inst. Mental Health, 1968, HUD, 1970, 76. Mem. Am. Psychol. Assn. (chmn. divsn. 34 1983), Habitat for Humanity. Presbyterian. Avocations: stamp collecting, building houses, ghost towns. Home: 6702 N Nanini Dr Tucson AZ 85704 Office: U Ariz Dept Psychology Tucson AZ 85721 E-mail: bechtel@u.arizona.edu.

BECHTEL, STEPHEN DAVISON, JR., engineering company executive; b. Oakland, Calif., May 10, 1925; s. Stephen Davison and Laura (Peart) Bechtel; m. Elizabeth Mead Hogan, June 5, 1946; 5 children. Student, U. Colo., 1943-44; BS, Purdue U., 1946, D. in Engring. (hon.), 1972; MBA, Stanford U., 1948; DSc (hon.), U. Colo., 1981. Registered profl. engr., N.Y., Mich., Alaska, Calif., Md., Hawaii, Ohio, D.C., Va., Ill. Engring. and mgmt. positions Bechtel Corp., San Francisco, 1941-60, pres., 1960-73, chmn. of cos. in Bechtel group, 1973-80; chmn. Bechtel Group, Inc., 1980-90, chmn. emeritus, 1990—, Fremont Group, 1995—. Former chmn., mem. Bus. Coun. Remington Arms, life-term counselor, past chmn. conf. bd. Trustee, mem., past chmn. bldg. and grounds com. Calif. Inst. Tech., mem. pres.'s coun. Purdue U., mem. adv. coun., bd. visitors Inst. Internat. Studies; former charter mem. adv. coun. Stanford U. Grad. Sch. Bus. With USMC, 1943-46. Decorated officer French Legion Honor; named Man Yr. Engring., News-Record, 1974; recipient Disting. Alumnus award, Purdue U., 1964, Ernest C. Arbuckle Disting. Alumnus award, Stanford Grad. Sch. Bus., 1974, Outstanding Achievement in Constrn. award, Moles, 1977, Disting. Engring. Alumnus award, U. Colo., 1979, Chmn.'s award, Am. Assn. Engring. Soc., 1982, Kenneth Andrew Roe award, 2003, Washington award, Western Soc. Engrs., 1985, Herbert Hoover medal, 1980, Chmn.'s award, Am. Assn. Engring. Soc., 1982, Kenneth Andrew Roe award, 2003, Nat. Medal Tech., Pres. Bush, 1991, Golden Beaver award, 1992, Oxford Cup award, Beta Theta Pi, 1997, Engr. Distinction award, U. Colo., 2000. Fellow AAAS; mem. ASCE (hon., engring. mgmt. award 1979, pres. award 1985, OPAL award for outstanding lifetime achievement in constrn. 2000), Inst. Chem. Engrs. (U.K., hon.); mem. AIME, NSPE (hon. chmn. Nat. Engrs. Week 1990), Nat. Acad. Engring. (past chmn., Founder's award 1999), Calif. Acad. Scis. (hon. trustee), Am. Soc. French Legion Honor (bd. dirs., disting. achievement medal 1994), Royal Acad. Engring. (U.K., fgn. mem.), Pacific Union Club, Bohemian Club, San Francisco Golf Club, Claremont Country Club, Cypress Point Club, Bear River Club (Utah), Wild Goose Club (Calif.), Chi Epsilon, Tau Beta Pi. Office: PO Box 193965 San Francisco CA 94119-3965 Fax: 415-512-1448.

BECHTEL, STEPHEN E. mechanical engineer, educator; BS in Engring. summa cum laude, U. Mich., 1979; PhD in Engring., U. Calif., Berkeley, 1983. Prof. dept. mech. engring. Ohio State U., Columbus, 1983—. Reviewer design, mfg. and computer-integrated engring. divsn., fluid dynamics and hydraulics directorate, thermal transport and thermal processing directorate NSF, 1985—, USDA food characterization, process, product rsch. program; cons. Hoechst Celanese Corp., Los Alamos Nat. Lab., Battelle Meml. Inst., Corning, Inc., Proctor & Gamble. Referee Jour. Rheology, Jour. Applied Mechanics, Jour. Non-Newtonian Fluid Mechanics, others. James B. Angell scholar U. Mich., 1976-79. Mem. ASME (mem. fluid mechanics com., elasticity com., applied mechanics divsn. 1989—, rec. sec. gen. com. 1991-92, rec. sec. exec. com. 1992-93, textile engring. divsn, exec. com., 2002-, Henry Hess award 1990), Am. Acad. Mechanics, Soc. Rheology, Tau Beta Pi. Achievements include research in modeling of industrial polymer processing and fiber manufacturing, viscoelastic fluid flows, free surface flows and instability mechanisms, fundamental modeling of thermal expansion, material characterization, transducer characterization in non-destructive evaluation. Office: Ohio State U Mech Engring 206 W 18th Ave Columbus OH 43210-1189 E-mail: bechtel.3@osu.edu.

BECHTLE, LOUIS CHARLES, lawyer, retired federal judge; b. Phila., Dec. 14, 1927; s. Charles R. and Gladys (Kirchner) B.; m. Margaret Beck, Sept. 7, 1978; children: Barbara, Nancy, Amy; 1 stepchild, Samuel. BS, Temple U., 1951, LL.B., 1954. Bar: Pa. 1954. Asst. U.S. atty. U.S. Dept. Justice, Phila., 1957-59, U.S. atty., 1969-72; pvt. practice law Jacoby & Maxmin, Phila., 1959-62; pvt. practice Wisler, Pearlstine, Talone, Gerber, Norristown, Pa., 1962-69; U.S. dist. judge U.S. Dist. Ct., Phila., 1972—2002; sr. judge U.S. Dist. Ct. (Eastern Dist.), Phila.; atty. Conrad O'Brien Gellman & Rohn, P.C., Phila., 2002—. Adj. faculty Temple U. Law Sch., Phila., 1974-93, Villanova Law Sch., 1985-89; mem. Jud/ Panel on Multidist. Litigation, 1994—. Served with U.S. Army, 1946-47. Mem. Montgomery County Bar Assn., Fed. Bar Assn. Republican. Presbyterian. Office: Conrad O'Brien Gellman & Rohn PC 1515 Market St 16th Fl Philadelphia PA 19102 Office Fax: 215-864-9620.

BECHTOL, LARRY OWEN, pastor; b. Gordon, Ohio, Oct. 14, 1937; s. Owen S. and Maudie B. B.; m. Betty J.; children: Julie, Lori, Stephen, Joan, Melissa, Sean, Tarla. BA, Asbury Coll., 1959; MDiv, United Theol. Sem., 1963. Ordained to ministry, United Ch. of Christ. Pastor Hollansburg (Ohio) UCC Ch., 1961-64, Frankford Congrl. Ch., Phila., 1964-66, Lansdale (Pa.) Schwenkfelder, 1966-68; pastor, counselor First E and R, Vermillion, Ohio, 1976-82; prof. Cin. Christian Coll., 1989-2000, So. State C.C., Sardinia, Ohio, 2000—; pastor, counselor Matthew United Ch., Cin., 1969-76, 82—. Chaplain Boy Scouts Am., Dayton, Ohio, 1960; youth leader Schwenkfelder Youth, 1968; chair Ch. Growth and Devel., Cleve., 1979-81; bd. dirs. CY Inc. Bd. dirs. Winton Place Civic Assn., Cin., 1970-76. Mem. MLA, Am. Assn. Christian Counselors, Christian Educators Assn., Acad. Am. Poets. Avocations: writing, poems, reading, tennis.

BECICH, RAYMOND BRICE, healthcare consultant, mediator, trainer, educator; b. Chgo., Jan. 9, 1945; s. Nicholas Gabriel and Rose Christina (Spillar) B. BA, Ind. U., 1966; MS, Columbia U., 1968. Adminstrv. officer, then hosp. dir. Indian Health Svc., Harlem, Mont., 1968-72, hosp. dir. Rapid City, S.D., 1972-78; hosp. adminstr. St. Elizabeth's Hosp., Washington, 1979-82, exec. officer, 1983-86, NIH Clin. Ctr., Bethesda, Md., 1986-94; healthcare cons., mediator, trainer, educator, 1994—. Adj. faculty Univ. Coll., U. Md., College Park, U. N.Mex., Albuquerque and Los Alamos, Coll. Santa Fe, Ctrl. Mich. U., Mt. Pleasant, U. St Francis, Joliet, Ill., 1995—. Bd. dirs. Ronald McDonald House, Washington, 1986-89; vol. Whitman-Walker Clinic, 1987-95. Fellow Am. Coll. Healthcare Execs. (life). Democrat. E-mail: rbecich@ix.netcom.com.

BECK, AARON TEMKIN, psychiatrist, educator; b. Providence, July 18, 1921; s. Harry S. and Elizabeth (Temkin) B.; m. Phyllis Whitman, June 4, 1950; children: Judith, Daniel, Alice, Roy. BA, Brown U., 1942, Dr.Med.Sci. (hon.), 1982; MD, Yale U., 1946; LHD (hon.), Assumption Coll., 1995. Mem. faculty U. Pa. Med. Sch., 1954—, prof. psychiatry, 1971—, Univ. prof., 1983—; dir. Center Cognitive Therapy, 1965-94; pres. Beck Found. for Cognitive Therapy, 1995—. Mem. rev. panel NIMH, 1965-80, chmn. task force suicide prevention, 1969-80; bd. dirs. West Philadelphia Community Mental Health Consortium, 1975-77. Author: Depression: Causes and Treatment, 1967, Diagnosis and Management of Depression, 1973, Prediction of Suicide, 1973, Cognitive Therapy and the Emotional Disorders, 1976, Cognitive Theory of Depression, 1979, Anxiety Disorders and Phobias: A Cognitive Perspective, 1985, Love is Never Enough, 1988, Cognitive Therapy of Personality Disorders, 1990; co-author: Cognitive Therapy in Clinical Practice, 1989, Cognitive Therapy with Inpatients, 1992, The Integrative Power of Cognitive Therapy, 1997, Scientific Foundations of Cognitive Theory and Therapy of Depression, 1999, Prisoners of Hate, 1999, Bipolar Disorder: A Complete Perspective, 2001. Served as officer M.C. U.S. Army, 1952-54. Recipient rsch. award, R.I. Med. Soc., 1948, ann. award, Phila. Soc. Clin. Psychologists, 1978, Am. Psychopathol. Assn., 1983, Soc. for Psychotherapy Rsch., 1995, Calif. Psychol. Soc., 1996, Belmont Hosp. award, 1996, Disting. Sci. award, APA, 1989, rsch. award, Am. Assn. Suicidology, 1985, Am. Suicide Found., 1991, Albert Einstein Sch. Medicine award, 1992, Nathaniel Winkelman award, 1996, Heinz Found. award for the human condition, 2001. Fellow Royal Coll. Psychiatry, N.Y. Acad. Medicine (Thomas Salmon award 1992), APA (rsch. award 1993); mem. Calif. Psychol. Assn. (lifetime svc. award 1996), So. Psychotherapy Rsch. (pres. 1975-76), Am. Psychiat. Assn. (prize rsch. psychiatry 1979), Am. Assn. Suicidology (rsch. prize 1985), Assn. Advancement of Behavior Therapy, Nat. Acad. Sci. Inst. Medicine. Office: 3600 Market St Ste 754 Philadelphia PA 19104-2641

BECK, ALBERT, manufacturing company executive; b. N.Y.C., Jan. 14, 1928; s. Albert Christian and Mabel Agnes (Dunn) B.; m. Jean Norma Russ, June 16, 1951; children— Nancy, Richard, Douglas BS, Fairleigh Dickinson U., 1950; MS, Rutgers U., 1956. Product line mgr. Tung Sol Electric Inc. div. Wagner Electric, Bloomfield, N.J., 1951-66; dir. quality control IT&T, Brussels, 1966-69, asst. dir. product ops. N.Y.C., 1969-72, dir. N.Am. staff, 1972-73; v.p. ops. Grinnell Fire Protection Co., Providence, 1973-79, exec. v.p., 1979, Grinnell Corp., 1986—2002. Mem. bd. edn. curriculum com. Wayne, N.J., 1964. Served with A.C., USN, 1945-47 Mem. Nat. Fire Sprinkler Assn. (bd. dirs. 1990), Sigma Xi. Republican. Avocations: golf, tennis, bridge, flying.

BECK, ANATOLE, mathematician, educator; b. Bronx, N.Y., Mar. 19, 1930; s. Morris and Minnie (Rosenblum) B.; m. Evelyn Torton, Apr. 10, 1954 (div.); children— Nina Rachel, Micah Daniel BA, Bklyn. Coll., 1951; MS, Yale U., 1953, PhD, 1956. Instr. math. Williams Coll., Williamstown, Mass., 1955-56; Office Naval Rsch. rsch. assoc. Tulane U., New Orleans, 1956-57; traveling fellow Yale U., 1957-58; from asst. to assoc. prof. U. Wis., Madison, 1958-66, prof. math., 1966—; chair of math. London Sch. Econ./U. London, England, 1973-75. Vis. prof. Cornell U., 1960, Hebrew U., Jerusalem, 1964-65, U. Göttingen, Fed. Republic Germany, 1965, U. Warwick, 1968, Imperial Coll., U. London, 1969, U. Erlangen, Fed. Republic Germany, 1969, U. Md., 1971, Tech. U. Munich, Fed. Republic Germany, 1973, London Sch. Econs. and Univ. Coll., U. London, 1985, 91-92, 94-97, 99—; v.p. Wis. Fedn. Tchrs., 1975-83; co-founder Wis. U. Union, 1984, pres., 1988-91. Author: Continuous Flows in the Plane, 1974, (with M.N. Bleicher and D.W. Crowe) Excursions into Mathematics, 1969, 2d edit., 2000, The Knowledge Business, 1997; contbr. articles to profl. jours. Recipient Disting. Alumnus award Bklyn. Coll., 1976 Mem. Am. Math. Soc. (council 1973-75), Math. Assn. Am., AAUP, Sigma Xi, Phi Beta Kappa, Pi Mu Epsilon. Address: 480 Lincoln Dr Madison WI 53706-1325 Office: U Wis 480 Lincoln Dr 721 Van Vleck Hall Madison WI 53706-1329 E-mail: beck@math.wisc.edu., a.beck@lse.ac.uk.

BECK, ANDREW JAMES, lawyer; b. Washington, Feb. 19, 1948; s. Leonard Norman and Frances (Greif) B.; m. Carol Beck, Oct. 13, 2002; children: Carter, Lowell, Justin. BA, Carleton Coll., 1969; JD, Stanford U., 1972; MBA, Long Island U., 1975. Bar: VA. 1972, NY 1973, Pa. 1992. Assoc. Casey, Lane & Mittendorf, N.Y.C., 1972-80, ptnr., 1980-82, Haythe & Curley, N.Y.C., 1982-99, Torys LLP, N.Y.C., 1999—, exec. com., 2000—03. Trustee Bklyn. Heights Synagogue, 1980-81; trustee Bklyn. Heights Montessori Sch., 1988-92, treas., 1990-92. Mem. ABA, Va. State Bar Assn., N.Y. State Bar Assn., Pa. Bar Assn., Assn. of Bar of City of N.Y., Nat. Stroke Assn. (gen. counsel 1992—, sec., bd. dirs. 2000—). Avocation: bridge. Home: 10 East End Ave Apt 10D New York NY 10021 Office: Torys LLP 237 Park Ave New York NY 10017-3142 E-mail: abeck@torys.com.

BECK, ANGEL C. columnist, screenwriter, educator, film director; b. Omaha, Aug. 18, 1951; d. James and Aleane (Fitz) Carter; m. Frank J. Beck, May 7, 1977 (div. May 1988); children: Jaman, Angel Marie, Frank J. BGS, U. Nebr., 1975. Sports reporter Oakland (Calif.) Tribune, 1987-88; reporter Shoreline Times/Ft. Worth, 1988-89, Arlington (Tex.) Citizen Jour., 1989-90; talk show host WNET TV, N.Y.C., 1990-91; tchr. Stamford (Conn.) Pub. Schs., 1990—; syndicated columnist Tribune Media Svcs., Chgo., 1996-97, Zwita Prodns. Syndications, Stamford, Conn., 1997—. Adv. I Have a Dream WCBS-TV, N.Y.C., 1995—. Author: History of Black Golfers, 1989, How To Play Bid Whist, 1995; contbr. Mem.: Nat. Assn. Black Journalists. Avocations: bid whist, jazz. Office: PO Box 112486 Stamford CT 06911-2486

BECK, BARBARA NELL, elementary school educator; b. Corpus Christi, Tex., Oct. 25, 1940; d. Marshall Joseph and Madie Ann (Spence) Robertson; m. Joel J. Beck, June 23, 1973. BA, Baylor U., 1964. Tchr. Killeen (Tex.) Ind. Sch. Dist., 1964-2001. Sunday sch. tchr., 1967—, co-treas., 2000—, ch. clk. First Bapt. Ch. of Nolanville. Mem. NEA, Tex. State Tchrs. Assn. (life), Tex. Assn. for the Gifted and Talented, Killeen Edn. Assn. (treas., past pres., bd. dirs.), Clifton Park PTA (past treas.). E-mail: jbeck1@hot.rr.com.

BECK, BRUCE LENNART, lawyer; b. Harvey, N.D., Dec. 11, 1946; s. Charles Joel and Gertrude A. (Waits) B.; m. Lynne Christine Richards, Oct. 18, 1969; children: Emily, Brian, Lauren. BA, Cornell Coll., Mt. Vernon, Iowa, 1968; JD, U. Minn., 1973. Bar: Minn. 1973, U.S. Dist. Ct. Minn. 1973. Pvt. practice, North St. Paul, Minn., 1973-75; ptnr. Memmer Caswell Parks & Beck, St. Paul, 1975-83, Galena & Beck, Maplewood, Minn., 1983-98; prin. Bruce L. Beck & Assocs., PLLP, Maplewood, 1999—. Author Ramsey County Probate Procedure, 1988. With U.S. Army, 1968-70. Mem. North St. Paul-Maplewood Rotary Club (pres. 1988-89, Dist. 5090 sec. 1989-90, Paul Harris fellow 1991), Minn. Bar Assn. Presbyterian. Avocations: bicycling, book collecting. Home: 5260 Hilltop Ave N Lake Elmo MN 55042-9591 Office: Bruce L Becks & Assocs PLLP 2785 White Bear Ave N Ste 404 Maplewood MN 55109-1307

BECK, BUDDY, systems engineer; BS in Chemistry, Ark. State U.; MS in Sys. Mgmt., U. So. Calif. Pres., CEO Thermo Digital Tech., Arlington, Va.; CEO, pres. Atlantic Sys. Rsch. & Engring Corp., 1984—89; corp. v.p. Coleman Rsch. Corp., 1990—96. Pres. Thermo Washington, Thermo Electron Corp., 1996—. Fellow: Brookings Instn.; mem.: AIChE, AIAA, Am. Def. Preparedness Assn., Assn. U.S. Army, Am. Nuclear Soc., Armed Forces Comm. and Electronics Assn. Office: SAAL-ASB 2511 Jefferson Davis Hwy Arlington VA 22202-3911

BECK, CHARLES MILBURN, II, analytical chemist; b. McKeesport, Pa., July 19, 1941; s. Charles Milburn and Dolly (Hoffman) B.; m. Charlotte Ayres Hastings, Sept. 7, 1968; children: John Charles, Paul Nathan. BS in Chemistry with high distinction, Worcester Poly. Inst., 1963, postgrad., 1978-80; MDiv, Princeton Theol. Sem., 1968. Analytical chemist Water Resources Adminstrn. State of Md., Annapolis, 1970-78; teaching asst. chemistry dept. Worcester (Mass.) Poly. Inst., 1978-80; analytical chemist Luvak Inc., Boylston, Mass., 1980-84; mem. tech. staff materials analysis dept. GTE Labs., Inc., Waltham, Mass., 1984-87; sr. chemist ea. divsn. Wyman-Gordon Co., North Grafton, Mass., 1987-90; rsch. chemist Nat. Inst. Stds. and Tech., Gaithersburg, Md., 1990-95, project mgr., 1995-97, rsch. chemist, 1997—2002; analytical chemist Los Alamos Nat. Lab., N.Mex., 2002—. Contbr. articles to profl. jours. Recipient Edward Condon award for excellence in tech. writing Nat. Inst. Stds. & Tech., 1994. Mem. ASTM (com. on analytical chemistry for metals, ores and related materials, John L. Hague award 1995, Lundell-Bright Meml. award 1999), Am. Chem. Soc. (chmn.-elect Ctrl. Mass. sect. 1988, chmn. 1989), Sigma Xi, Phi Lambda Upsilon. Achievements include research on history and current status of classical analysis; development and preparation of first certified rhodium standard reference material solution; development of analytical methods for certification of standard reference materials; development of chemical separation methods for radionuclides. Office: Los Alamos Nat Lab Mailstop J514 Los Alamos NM 87545 E-mail: cbeck@lanl.gov.

BECK, CHRISTINE SAFFORD, photographer, publisher, volunteer; b. Phila., July 10, 1943; d. Elisha Jr. and Margaret (Tramdack) Safford; m. Leif Christian Beck, Nov. 21, 1964; children: C. Lars, Eric S., Anders. BA in German and French, Queens Coll., 1964; MA in German Lit., Bryn Mawr Coll., 1969; postgrad., N.Y. Inst. Photography. Co-founder, pres. Nat. Jr. Tennis League of Phila., 1969-79; pres., CEO Nat. Jr. Tennis League, N.Y.C., 1979-83; owner, photographer Christine S. Beck Photography, Villanova, Pa., 1990—; pub., owner Prism Light Press, Bryn Mawr, Pa., 1995—; stock photographer Garden Image Agy., Montreal, 1999—2002; v.p. Advisory Publs., 2001—03. Pres. Phila. Tennis Patrons Assn., 1985-95, mem. adv. bd., 1995—; pres. Arthur Ashe Youth Tennis Ctr., Phila., 1985-95; chair adv. coun. Esperanza Health Ctr., Phila., 1994-97. Photographer (books): Beyond Me. Voices of the Natural World, 1993, Spirit of Summit County, Colorado, 1996; producer Broadway Comes to Queens benefit concert, Charlotte, N.C., 1999. Bd. dirs. Habitat for Humanity, Phila., 1988-90; coord. vols. Jimmy Carter Workcamp, North Phila., 1988; chair stewardship campaign Bryn Mawr Presbyn. Ch., 1992; trustee Queens U. Charlotte, N.C., 1995—; trustee Gesu Sch., Phila., 1996—2003, chair devel., 2000-2003, pres., 2003—; chair fundraising campaign Arthur Ashe Youth Tennis Ctr., 2000—; chair alumni phase fundraising campaign Queens U. Charlotte, N.C., 2000-02; trustee Penn Coun. for Relationships, 2000-02. Recipient Kennedy award Robert F. Kennedy Pro Celebrity Tennis Tournament, 1975, Jimmy Carter Hammer award Habitat for Humanity, 1988, Merit award for women Internat. Tennis Hall of Fame, 1988, Svc. Bowl, U.S. Tennis Assn., 1991, Take the Lead award Girl Scouts of Greater Phila., 1992, First Phila. Youth Tennis Jerome Laroque award, 1999. Mem. U.S. Tennis Assn. Middle States (treas. 1986-89, Mangan award 1990, Coren award 1973), N.Am. Nature Photographers Assn. (charter mem.), Nikon Profl. Svcs. Avocations: golf, tennis, hiking. Office: Prism Light Press 224 Broughton Ln Villanova PA 19085-1914

BECK, CRAFTON, music director; b. Memphis, Tenn., Dec. 18, 1956; PhD in conducting, Cincinnati Col. Conserv., 1987. Music dir. Boca Pops, Boca Raton, Fla., 1996—, Miss. Symphony Orch., 2000. Office: Miss Symphony Orch 201 E Pascagoula St, PO Box 2052 Jackson MS 39225-2052

BECK, CURT WERNER, chemist, educator; b. Halle/Saale, Germany, Sept. 10, 1927; came to U.S., 1950, naturalized, 1955; s. Curt Paul and Clara (Fischer) B.; m. Lily Yallourakis, Feb. 10, 1953; children— Curt Peter, Christopher Paul. Student, U. Munich, 1946-48; BS, Tufts U., 1951; PhD, Mass. Inst. Tech., 1955. Instr. Franklin Tech. Inst., Boston, 1955-56; asst. prof. Roberts Coll., Istanbul, Turkey, 1956-57; lectr. Vassar Coll., Poughkeepsie, N.Y., 1957-59, asst. prof., 1959-62, asso. prof., 1962-66, prof. chemistry, 1966-93, Matthew Vassar Jr. prof., 1970-93, rsch. prof., 1993—. Co-editor Art and Archaeology Tech. Abstracts, 1966—; sect. editor Chem. Abstracts, 1967-95; editor: Archaeological Chemistry, 1974; mem. editl. bd. Jour. Field Archaeology, 1975-93, Jour. Archaeol. Sci., 1979-87. Mem. Zoning Bd. Appeals, La Grange, N.Y., 1965-91, chmn., 1974-91; mem. Dutchess County council Boy Scouts Am., 1965-67, Candidate supr., La Grange, 1967. Recipient Rsch. award Mid-Hudson sect. Am. Chem. Soc., 1965, Pomerance award Archaeol. Inst. Am., 2001. Fellow Royal Soc. Arts, Internat. Inst. for Conservation Historic and Artistic Works (London); mem. Am. Chem. Soc. (past sect. chmn.), Royal Soc. Chemistry (London), Gesellschaft Deutscher Chemiker, Archeol. Inst. Am., Internat. Union Prehistoric and Protohistoric Scis. (chmn. com. study of amber, mem. permanent coun., mem. exec. com.), Assn. for Field Archaeology, Sigma Xi. Home: La Grange 149 Skidmore Rd Pleasant Valley NY 12569-5001 Office: Vassar Coll Poughkeepsie NY 12604-0001 E-mail: beck@vassar.edu.

BECK, DAVID EDWARD, surgeon; b. Geneva, Ill., May 1, 1953; s. George R. and Gloria M. (Zesch) B.; m. Sharon Mich, Aug. 30, 1980; children: Allison, Lauren, John. BS, USAF Acad., 1975; MD, U. Miami, Fla., 1979; postgrad., USAF Aerospace Medicine Primary Course, Brooks AFB, Tex., 1978, Combat Casualty Care Course, Ft. Sam Houston, Tex., 1980, Hyperbaric Oxygen CourseB, Brooks AFB, 1982, ATLS Instr. Course, Ft. Sam Houston, 1986, Squadon Officers Sch., 1987-88, Mgmt. for Chief of Hosp. Svcs., Sheppard AFB, Tex., 1988, Sch. Pub. Health, Harvard U., 1990. Diplomate Am. Bd. Colon and Rectal Surgery. Lt. Col. USAF, 1975-93; resident in gen. surgery Wilford Hall USAF Med. Ctr., Lackland AFB, Tex., 1979-84, chief colorectal surgery, 1986-92, staff surgeon, chief colorectal surgery svc., 1986-92, asst. chmn. dept. gen. surgery, 1988, chmn. dept. gen. surgery, residency program dir., 1988-92; staff gen. surgeon Patrick AFB (Fla.) Hosp., 1984-85; fellow in colorectal surgery Cleve. Clinic Found., 1985-86; residency program dir. gen. surgery Joint Mil. Med. Command, San Antonio, 1989-91; clin. assoc. prof. surgery U. Tex. Health Sci. Ctr., San Antonio, 1990-92, F. Edward Herbert Sch. Medicine, U. Health Scis., Bethesda, Md., 1992—; chief surgery 870 USAF Contingency Hosp., RAF Little Rissington, U.K., 1993; staff colorectal surgeon Ochsner Clinic, New Orleans, 1993—, chmn. dept. colon and rectal surgery, 1994—. Cons. USAF Surgeon Gen., Washington, 1986-92. Author chpts. to books; co-editor (textbooks); (with David R. Welling) Patient Care in Colorectal Surgery, 1991, (with Steven D. Wexner) Fundamentals of Anorectal Surgery, 1992, 2nd edit., 1998, (with T.C. Hicks, F.E. Opelka, A.E., Timmcke) Complications of Colon and Rectal Surgery, 1996; editor: Handbook of Colorectol Surgery, 1997, 2d edit., 2002; mem. editl. bd. Current Surgery, 1990—; reviewer Diseases of the Colon and Rectum, 1990—, mem. editl. bd., 1992-98, So. Me. Jour., 1988-92; mem. editl. bd. Perspectives in Colon and Rectal Surgery, 1997-2000; editor-in-chief Clinics in Colon and Rectal Surgery, 2001—; contbr. articles to profl. jours. Decorated Air Force Achievement medal with oak leaf cluster, Air Force Meritorious Svc. medal with oak leaf cluster; recipient Pres. award United Ostomy Assn., 2000. Fellow ACS; mem. AMA, Am. Soc. Colon and Rectal Surgeons (mem. socioecon./legis. com. 1991-94, pub. rels. com. 1993—, chmn. 1996-99, Outstanding Young Investigator award, 1992), Assn. Mil. Surgeons U.S., La. State Med. Soc., Soc. Air Force Clin. Surgeons (treas. 1989-90, v.p. 1990-92, pres. 1992-93, Excalibur award 1992), Soc. Surgery of Alimentary Tract, So. Med. Assn. (mem. colon and rectal sect., sec. 1988-91, v.p. 1990-91, pres. 1991-92), Soc. Med. Cons. to Armed forces, St. Tamminy Parish Med. Soc., Tex. Soc. Colon and Rectal Surgeons (sec. 1991-93), Air force Assn., USAF Acad. Assn. Grads. Avocations: fishing, wood working, gardening. Home: 127 Deloaks Rd Madisonville LA 70447-9597 Office: Oschner Clin Found 1514 Jefferson Hwy New Orleans LA 70121-2429 E-mail: dbeck@ochsner.org.

BECK, DAVID PAUL, biochemist; b. Wilmington, Del., Aug. 3, 1944; s. David Franklin and Mary Jane (Lazar) B.; m. Jeanne Elaine Crawford, Nov. 19, 1966; children: Jennifer Jeanne, David Andrew. AB, Princeton U., 1966; PhD, Johns Hopkins U., 1971. Fellow Harvard U., Cambridge, Mass., 1971-74; staff scientist Md. Psychiat. Rsch. Ctr., Balt., 1974-77; health scientist, adminstr. NIH, Bethesda, Md., 1977-84; assoc. dir., sec. bd. dir. Pub. Health Rsch. Inst., NYC, 1984-91; pres. Coriell Inst. Med. Rsch., Camden, NJ, 1991—, sec. bd. trustees, 1991—. Bd. dir. CorCell, Inc., NJ Tech. Coun., Exec. Svc. Corp. of Delaware Valley, South Jersey C. of C. Contbr. articles to profl. jour. Active Baltimore County Bd. Recreation and Pks., 1977-84; bd. dirs. Hoff-Barthelson Music Sch., Scarsdale, N.Y., 1989-91, West Jersey Chamber Music Soc., Moorestown, N.J., 1992—. Mem. Assn. Ind. Rsch. Insts. (v.p. 1989-92, pres.-elect 1993-95, pres. 1995-97, exec. v.p. 1997-99), NJ Assn. Biomed. Rsch. (bd. dir.), NJ Technology Coun. (bd. dir.), South Jersey Chamber of Commerce (BOD, 2003-), Exec. Svc. Corps. of the Delaware Valley (BOD 2003-) Office: Coriell Inst Med Rsch 403 Haddon Ave Ste 403 Camden NJ 08103-1559 E-mail: dabeck@umdnj.edu.

BECK, DORIS OLSON, retired library media director; b. Kingsville, Tex., June 4, 1930; d. Thomas Leon and Estelle (Fosselman) Olson; m. John Roland Beck, Feb. 9, 1951; children: Elizabeth Joan, Thomas Roland, Patricia Lind, John William. BS in Chemistry, Tex. A & I Coll., 1949, BSChemE, 1950; MLS, Wayne State U., 1975. Cert. secondary educator with libr. endorsement, Ariz. Chemist Patterson's Lab., Harlingen, Tex., 1950-51; asst. libr. Tex. A & I Coll., Kingsville, Tex., 1951; chemist U.S. Geol. Svc., Stillwater, Okla., 1951-53; bookkeeper, nurse's aide McKenzie Co. Hosp., Watford City, N.D., 1953-54; math. tchr. Prescott Jr. High, Corpus Christi, Tex., 1954; chemist U.S. Geol. Svc., Columbus, Ohio, 1957-58; math. tchr. Christiansberg (Va.) High Sch., 1967-69; sci. tchr. East Jr. High Sch., Farmington, Mich., 1969-70; sci./math. tchr. Jane Addams Jr. High Sch., Royal Oak, Mich., 1970-78; math support Oakland Vocat. Sch., Royal Oak, 1978-79; head libr. S.W. Bapt. Coll., Pontiac, Mich., 1977-79; libr. media dir. Humboldt (Ariz.) Jr. High, 1979-87, Bradshaw Mt. Jr. High, Dewey, Ariz., 1987-95; ret., 1995. Site based com. Bradshaw Mt. Jr. High Sch., Dewey, Ariz., 1992-95. Vol. ch. libr., 1994-2002, Park View Middle Sch., Prescott Valley, Ariz., 1999—. Mem. Ariz. Libr. Assn., Alpha Delta Kappa. Republican. Baptist. Avocations: reading, needlework, travel. Home: PO Box 26566 3829 N Valorie Dr Prescott Valley AZ 86312

BECK, ELAINE KUSHNER, elementary and secondary school educator; b. Phila., May 31, 1942; d. Joseph and Emma Kushner; m. Stuart Edwin Beck, June 20, 1964; children: Adam, Barry, Caroline. BS, Drexel U., 1963; Masters equivalent, Temple U., Pa. State U., West Chester U., 1984. Cert. tchr., Pa. Tchr. grades 4, 5, 6 Upper Darby (Pa.) Sch. Dist., 1963-64; tchr. high sch. Francis Hammond-Alexandria (Va.) Sch. Dist., 1964-65; tchr. adult edn. YMCA, Alexandria, 1966-67; tchr. mid. sch. Haverford Sch. Dist., Havertown, Pa., 1980—. Bus. owner Lady Elaine Creations, Havertown, 1976-80. Contbg. editor: Passoverama, 1979-80; author (teaching program) The Equipment Scavenger Hunt, 1989. Mem. strategic plan com. Haverford Sch. Dist., Havertown, 1995-96; organizer sr. citizen dances, Havertown, 1992, 93, 94; pres., v.p., mem. adv. bds. sisterhood Temple Beth Hillel/Beth El, 1980-81. Recipient Dominick Recchiuti Humanitarian award, 1992; named one of Top 5 Home Econs. Tchrs. in U.S., Home Baking Assn., 1994; Ptnr. in Edn. grantee Sun Oil Co., 1989. Mem. NEA, Pa. Edn. Assn., Nat. Audubon Soc., Nature Conservancy, World Wildlife Fund, Sierra Club, Key and Triangle, Omicron Nu, Phi Sigma Sigma (honored Drexel U. chpt. 1998). Avocations: exotic bird training, wild bird watching, sailing, environmentalism, biking. Home: 624 Greythorne Rd Wynnewood PA 19096-2509 Office: Haverford Sch Dist 1701 Darby Rd Havertown PA 19083-3738

BECK, GEORGE PRESTON, anesthesiologist, educator; b. Wichita Falls, Tex., Oct. 21, 1930; s. George P. and Amanda (Wilbanks) Beck; m. Constance Carolyn Krog, Dec. 22, 1953; children: Carla Elizabeth, George P., Howard W. BS, Midwestern U., 1951; MD, U. Tex., 1955. Diplomate Am. Bd. Anesthesiology. Intern John Sealy Hosp., 1955—56; resident in anesthesiology Parkland Meml. Hosp., Dallas, 1959—62, vis. staff, 1964—; pvt. practice Lubbock, Tex., 1964—. Asst. prof. anesthesiology U. Tex. Southwestern Med. Sch., Dallas, 1962—64, asst. clin. prof., 1964—71, prof., 1996—; assoc. clin. prof. anesthesiology U. Tex. Med. Br., Galveston, 1971—; pres. Gt. Plains Ballistics Corp., 1967—; clin. prof. Tex. Tech U. Sch. Medicine, Lubbock, 1986—. Pres. coun. Luth. Ch., 1965—66. With USAF, 1956—59. Fellow: Am. Coll. Anesthesiologists; mem.: Lubbock Surg. Soc., Lubbock County Med. Soc., Tex. Soc. Anesthesiologists (pres. 1974), Tex. Med. Soc., Am. Soc. Anesthesiologists. Achievements include invention of Beck Airway Airflow Monitor. Home: 4601 18th St Lubbock TX 79416-5713 Office: PO Box 16385 Lubbock TX 79490-6385

BECK, GEORGE WILLIAM, retired industrial engineer; b. Dayton, Ohio, Aug. 31, 1921; s. George A. and Florence I. (Hosket) B.; m. Elizabeth A. Thatcher, Apr. 14, 1945 (died Nov. 8, 1992); children: Bruce, Christine, William. B.Indsl. Engring., Gen. Motors Inst., 1946. Registered profl. engr., Ohio. Sales rep. Inland Mfg. div. Gen. Motors Corp., Dayton, 1946-53, sr. project engr., 1953-56, staff engr., 1956, asst. chief engr., 1956-62, chief engr., 1962-80, dir. engring., 1980-85; ret., 1985. Trustee Met. YMCA, 1964-71; chmn. bd. mgmt. Kettering YMCA, 1966-70; mem. Centerville City Sch. Dist. bd. edn., 1968-74, v.p., 1973-74. Served to lt. (j.g.) USNR, 1943-45. Mem. Soc. Automotive Engrs., Dayton C. of C., Aircraft Owners and Pilots Assn. (lic. pilot). Clubs: MVMA, Sycamore Creek Country, Mission Valley Country. Lutheran. Achievements include the invention of automotive products; holder of 10 patents in field. Home: 2120 Timucua Trl Nokomis FL 34275-5306

BECK, GREGORY MICHAEL, lawyer; b. San Diego, Aug. 31, 1952; s. Francis Joseph and Dora Louise (Youman) Beck; m. Jennifer Hunter; children: Mallory, Allison, Mackenzie, Jonathan. BS in Acctg. and Econs., Loyola U., L.A., 1974; JD, U. Calif., 1978. Prin. Beck & Christian, APC, Laguna Hills, Calif. Mem. YMCA, Mission Viejo, 1997. Roman Catholic. Avocations: mountain biking, swimming, camping, skiing. Office: Beck & Christian 23041 Mill Creek Dr Laguna Hills CA 92653-1257

BECK, GUSTAV JULIUS, retired pulmonologist, allergist, immunologist; b. Vienna, May 7, 1920; came to U.S., 1938; BS, Columbia U., 1941; MD, NYU, 1944. Diplomate Am. Bd. Allergy & Immunology. Intern Bellevue Hosp., N.Y.C., 1944-45; resident Goldwater Meml. Hosp., N.Y.C., 1945-48; fellow in pulmonary medicine Presbyn. Hosp., N.Y.C., 1948-54; chief pulmonary diseases Lenox Hill (N.Y.) Hosp., 1968-92, emeritus chief, 1992; prof. clin. medicine N.Y. Med. Coll., 1984-91. Asst. prof. clin. medicine NYU Med. Coll., 1972-94, clin. prof. medicine, 1994-99. Fellow Am. Coll. Chest Physicians, Am. Coll. Physicians, Am. Coll. Allergy & Immunology (disting.), Am. Thoracic Soc.

BECK, IRENE CLARE, educational consultant, writer; b. N.Y.C., Dec. 18, 1944; d. James E. and Helen (Carroll) Clare; m. William J. Beck, Aug. 9, 1986; children: Daniel, James Chesire. BA, St. Mary's Coll., 1966; MA, Fairfield U., 1977; EdD, U. Rochester, 1982; Grad. Cert. Women's Studies, DePaul U., 1998. Cert. tchr., N.Y. Tchr. Elem. Sch., N.Y.C., 1966-68, Montessori Acad. N.Y., Bklyn., 1968-73; faculty Housatonic Community Coll., Bridgeport, Conn., 1975-77, Nazareth Coll., Rochester, N.Y., 1977-83; faculty dir. Sheppard Pratt Nat. Ctr. Human Devel., Balt., 1983-91; exec. dir. William & Irene Beck Found., 1987—. Cons. Headstart Programs, Rochester, 1980-83, Family Day Care Tng., Rochester, 1980-83; mem. women's studies faculty program DePaul U., 1999—; presenter workshops and seminars. Author: Expect Respect, Let Me Tell You (manuals), (No Hang Ups (telephone audiotape), 1987, In Tune With Teens (booklet), 1990; weekly news col. Parents and Teens, 1987-90; freelance writer, 1986—; contbr. articles to profl. jours.; sr. editor What's Working for Girls in Illinois, 1996-99. Mem. AAUW, Assn. Childhood Edn. Internat. Avocations: hiking, swimming, biking.

BECK, JAMES DAVID, lawyer; b. Troy, Mo., Sept. 3, 1968; s. James Noel and Susan Ellyn (White) B. BS, Lindenwood Coll., 1990; JD, Washington U., 1993. Bar: U.S. Dist. Ct. (ea. and we. dists.) Mo. Asst. pub. defender Mo. State Pub. Defender, St. Joseph, 1993-94, dist. pub. defender Troy, 1994-97; ptnr. Mueller, Suddarth & Beck, Troy, 1997—2002, Mueller, Beck & Meyer, 2002—. Mem. Lincoln County Reps., Troy, 1993—; campaign mgr. for Candidate for State Rep., Citizens for Michael Schaper, Troy, 1994. Recipient Kiwanis Renaissance Medal of Honor, Circle K, 1989, Lt. William C. Ewbank Meml. scholarship, 1991, Pres.'s Outstanding Bd. Mem. award, 1993; named W. Dean Moore Outstanding Circle K Mem., 1992, Al F. Sullivan Outstanding Dist. Officer, 1991, 92, Jay N. Emerson Disting. Lt. Gov., 1991, R.P. "Reg" Merridew Disting. Dist. Sec., 1992. Mem. ABA, ATLA, Nat. Lawyers Assn., Nat. Assn. Criminal Def. Lawyers, Mo. Bar Assn., Mo. Assn. Criminal Def. Lawyers, Lincoln County Bar Assn., Mo. Bar Leadership Acad., Mo. Juvenile Justice Assn., Nat. Acad. Elder Law Attys., Circle K Internat. (dist. lt. gov. 1989-90, dist. sec. 1990-91, internat. trustee 1991-92, internat. pres. 1992-93), Kiwanis Internat. (asst. dist. adminstr. for Circle K Internat. 1994-95, 1998—, dist. adminstr. for Circle K Internat. 1995-96, regional counselor for Key Club Internat. 1995-96, v.p. 1997-98, pres. 1998-99), Christian Legal Soc., Soc. Disting. Collegians, Troy C. of C. (bd. dirs. 1997-98). Republican. Avocations: biking, reading, sports, baseball collecting, singing. Home: 1060 Huntington Dr Troy MO 63379-2254 E-mail: msb@nothnbut.net.

BECK, JAMES HAYES, lawyer; b. Canton, Ohio, Aug. 29, 1935; s. Harry W. and Helen (Hayes) B.; m. Denise, Dec. 22, 1995; children: Barbara Elizabeth, James Rolf. AB, Wittenberg U., 1956; LLB, U. Va., 1959, JD, 1970. Bar: Ohio 1959, U.S. Dist. Ct. (no. dist.) Ohio 1960, U.S. Supreme Ct. 1971. Pvt. practice, Cleve., 1959-63; jr. ptnr. Leanza, Longano, Farina & Mendelson, Cleve., 1963-66; assoc. Nadler & Nadler, Youngstown, Ohio, 1966-73; ptnr. Beck & Tyrrell, Canfield, Ohio, 1973-83; sr. ptnr. Beck & Vaughn, Canfield, 1984-87; pvt. practice Canfield, 1987—. V.p. Canfield Civic Assn., 1972-74; mem. Better Bus. Bur. of Mahoning Valley. Mem. Am. Arbitration Assn., Assn. Trial Lawyers Am., Mahoning County Bar Assn. (chmn. profl. econs. com. 1979-82, chmn. unauthorized practice of law com. 1976-79, grievance com. 1983-84, ins. com. 1984-85, inquiry com. 1987-99), Ohio State Bar Assn., ACLU, Youngstown Power Squadron (comdr. 1985, exec. com. 1983-95), Canfield Lions Club (bd. dirs. 1978-79), Point Yacht Club, Boardman Tennis Ctr. Democrat. Lutheran. Avocations: boating, tennis, bridge, gourmet cooking. Office: James H Beck Olde Courthouse Bldg Canfield OH 44406-1407 Fax: 330-533-0896.

BECK, JAN SCOTT, lawyer; b. Newark, May 5, 1955; s. Robert William and Dorothy (Warhaftig) B.; m. Marla Terri Klein, Sept. 27, 1981; children: Jamie Kyle, Bryan Michael, Sean Jason. BA in Acctg., Rider Coll., 1977; JD, Villanova U., 1980, LLM in Taxation, 1985. Bar: N.J. 1980, U.S. Dist. Ct. N.J. 1980, N.Y. 1981, U.S. Tax Ct. 1981, D.C. 1985, U.S. Supreme Ct. 1986. Pvt. practice, Westfield, N.J., 1980-86; atty. Inspiration Resources Corp., N.Y.C., 1986-88; dir. taxation ADT Inc., Boca Raton, Fla.; 1988-89, v.p., gen. counsel, 1989-96; sr. v.p., dir. ADT Security Svcs., Inc., 1996-97; mng. dir., CEO The Turbary Group, Boca Raton, Fla., 1997—2002; CFO, StarCapital Corp., 2002—. Atty. Laventhol & Horwath, Phila., 1979-80, Touche Ross & Co., N.Y.C., 1980-86; dir. taxation Inspiration Resources Corp., N.Y.C., Monsoon Internat. LLC, 2000-02. Author: The Strike: Student Involvement, 1975. Mem. ABA, N.Y. State Bar Assn., N.J. Bar Assn., AICPA, N.J. Soc. CPAs, Tax Exec. Inst., Omicron Delta Epsilon, Delta Epsilon Kappa. Avocations: camping, backpacking, mountain climbing, writing, skiing. Home: 20988 Solano Way Boca Raton FL 33433-1621 Office: StarCapital 3320 Fairlane Farms Rd Ste 12 Wellington FL 33414-8764 E-mail: jbeck@starcapital.net.

BECK, JAY M. gynecologist; b. Dallas, May 23, 1932; Student, Rice Inst.; MD, U. Tex., 1956. Diplomate Am. Bd. Ob-Gyn. Intern Lisbon VA Hosp., Dallas, 1956-57; resident Baylor U. Med. Ctr., Dallas, 1957-60, obstetrician-gynecologist; clin. prof. Health Sci. Ctr. U. Tex.; pvt. practice, ptnr. Ob-gyn. Specialists of Dallas. Fellow ACOG; mem. Am. Fertility Soc., Tex. Assn. Obstetrician-Gynecologists, Tex. Med. Assn., Dallas/Ft. Worth OB Gyn Soc. Office: Drs Beck Branning Wilkerson & Assocs 3600 Gaston Ave #601 Dallas TX 75246-1540

BECK, JEAN MARIE See WIK, JEAN MARIE

BECK, JEFF L. music educator; b. Kansas City, Kans., Apr. 24, 1952; s. Ernest Lee Beck, LeNora Elaine Beck. B in Music Edn., Kans. U., 1974, M in Music Edn., 1984. Tchr. Argentine Mid. Sch., Kansas City, Kans., 1974—78, Sumner Acad., Kansas City, Kans., 1978—82, Arrowhead Sch., Kansas City, 1982—86, Eisenhower Sch., Kansas City, 1986—. Founder, condr. Kansas City Cmty. Orch., 2000—. Recipient Outstanding Mid. Sch. Band Dir. award, Kans. Music Educators Assn., 2000—01. Mem.: NEA, Music Educators Nat. Conf. Avocations: cooking, gardening, weightlifting, piano. Home: 6410 Roundtree St Shawnee KS 66226

BECK, JOHN CHRISTIAN, b. Audubon, Iowa, Jan. 4, 1924; s. Wilhelm and Marie (Brandt) Beck. MD, McGill U., 1947, MSc, 1951, DSc (hon.), 1994; PhD (hon.), Ben Gurion U. of the Negev. Diplomate Am. Bd. Internal Medicine (chmn., dir.). Intern Royal Victoria Hosp., Montreal, 1947—48, sr. asst. resident, 1948—49, physician-in-chief, endocrinologist, 1964—74, chmn. dept. medicine and dir. Univ. Clinic McGill U., 1964—74; prof. medicine U. Calif., San Francisco, 1974—79; dir. Robert Wood Johnson Clin. Scholars Program, 1973—78; prof. geriat. medicine and gerontology UCLA, 1979—, dir. academic geriat. resource ctr., 1984—90; dir. long term car gerontology ctr. UCLA/U. So. Calif., 1980—85; dir. Calif. Geriatric Edn. Ctr., 1987—97, emeritus dir., 1993—; dir. multicampus program in geriat. medicine and gerontology UCLA, 1979—93. Pres. Am. Bd. Med. Spltys.; vis. prof. numerous univs.; Simeonè lectr. Brown U., 1977; John McCreary Meml. lectr. U. B.C., 1985; Bruce Hall Meml. lectr. Garvan Inst. Med. Rsch., U. NSW, Sydney, 1989; Allen T. Bailey Meml. lectr. U. Sask., Canada, 1989. Editl. bd. Jour. Clin. Endocrinology and Metabolism, Current Topics in Exptl. Endocrinology, Psychiatry in Medicine, Health Policy and Edn., Jour. Am. Bd. Family Practice, cons. editor Roche Lab. Series on Geriatrics and Gerontology. Recipient Lifetime award, Ben Gurion U. of Negev, Israel, 1985, Ann. Gerontology award in edn., Jewish Homes for the Aging, 1994, commendation, City of L.A., 1994. Master: ACP; fellow: AAAS, Am. Fedn. on Aging Rsch. (Irving S. Wright award 1991), Gerontol. Soc. Am. (mem. editl. bd. jour., Joseph T. Freeman award 1990, Donald P. Kent award 2001), Am. Geriat. Soc. (Milo F. Leavitt Meml. award 1988), Soc. Exptl. Biology and Medicine (mem. editl. bd. jour.), Can. Med. Protective Assn., Am. Clin. and Climatol. Assn., Laurentian Hormone Conf. (bd. dirs.), Montreal Physiol. Soc., Can. Diabetes Assn., Royal Coll. Physicians London, Royal Soc. Can., Inst. Medicine, Internat. Soc. Endocrinology (sec.-gen.), Can. Soc. Clin. Investigation (pres.), Endocrine Soc. (v.p., chmn. postgrad. assembly), Am. Fedn. Clin. Rsch. (coun. East divsn.), Can. Med. Assn. (postgrad. edn. com.), Am. Diabetes Assn., Royal Coll. Physicians Can. (mem. coun., Duncan Graham award 1990), McGill Osler Reporting Soc. (sec.), Can. Physiol. Soc., Can. Assn. Profs. Medicine (Ronald V. Christie award 1987), Assn. Am. Med. Colls., Internat. Soc. Neuroendocrinology, Western Assn. Physicians, Alpha Omega Alpha, Sigma Xi; mem.: Assn. for Gerontology in Higher Edn. (Disting. Svc. Recognition award 2001). Office: 1562 Casale Rd Pacific Palisades CA 90272-2714 Fax: 310-454-1944. E-mail: egebjcb@ucla.edu.

BECK, JOHN ROBERT, pathologist, information scientist; b. Cleve., Sept. 8, 1953; s. John Edward and Maralyn Janet (Smith) Beck; children: John Benjamin, Stefan Andrew, Meredith Louise; m. Marjorie Callahan Ritchie, July 20, 2002. AB, Dartmouth Coll., 1974; MD, Johns Hopkins U., 1978. Diplomate Am. Bd. Pathology. Intern, then resident in pathology Dartmouth-Hitchcock Med. Ctr., Hanover, N.H., 1978-80, dir. bloodbank, 1984-89, dir. clin. pathology, 1987-89; fellow, clin. decision making New Eng. Med. Ctr., Boston, 1981; from asst. to assoc. prof. pathology Dartmouth Med. Sch., Hanover, 1982-89; prof., dir. biomed. info. communication ctr. Oreg. Health Scis. U., Portland, 1989-92; prof., v.p. info. tech. Baylor Coll. Medicine, Houston, 1992—2001; exec. dir. Houston Acad. Medicine-Tex. Med. Ctr. Libr., 1999—2001; v.p. Infotech Fox Chase Cancer Ctr., Phila., 2001—. Editor-in-chief Med. Decision Making, 1989-94. Active United Way, Burlington County, NJ, 2003—. Recipient Rsch. Career Devel. award Nat. Libr. Medicine, 1986. Fellow: Coll. Am. Pathologists (com. vice-chair 1997—2000), Am. Coll. Med. Informatics; mem.: Leadership of Phila., Group on Info. Resources (exec. com. 1997—2000), Am. Assn. Med. Colls., Acad. Clin. Lab. Physicians and Scientists (exec. councilor 1989—91, Young Investigator award 1981), Soc. for Med. Decision Making (sec.-treas. 1985—87, v.p. 1987—88, pres. 1995—96). Republican. Avocations: golf, bridge, trumpet. Office: 7701 Burholme Ave Philadelphia PA 19111

BECK, LELAND S. lawyer; b. Newark, May 6, 1931; s. Stanely S. and Jennie Beck; m. Phyllis Mae Krawitz, Aug. 21, 1954; children: Hillary, Matthew, Susan, Joan. BA, Cornell U., 1953, JD, 1955. Bar: N.Y., 1955, U.S. Dist. Ct. (so. and ea. dists.) N.Y., 1956, U.S. Cir. Ct. (2nd cir.), 1975, U.S. Claims Ct., 1994. Trial lawyer Liberty Mut. Ins. Co., N.Y.C., 1955-57; ptnr. Whiting & Beck, N.Y.C., 1957-60; pvt. practice Mineola, N.Y., 1960-63; ptnr. Rothenberg & Beck, Mineola, 1963-68, Cooperstein & Beck, Garden City, N.Y., 1973-95, Beck & Rubin, Garden City, Beck, Salvi, Gewurz & Strauss, Garden City, 1995-2000, Beck Gewurz Strauss, Garden City, 2000—02, Uniondale, NY, 2002—. Mem. ABA, N.Y. State Bar Assn., N.Y. St. Assn. Trial Lawyers, Nassau County Bar Assn. (bd. dirs. 1991-92, 98-2001). Office: Beck Gewurz & Strauss 50 Charles Lindberg Blvd Uniondale NY 11553

BECK, LOIS GRANT, anthropologist, educator, author; b. Bogota, Colombia, Nov. 5, 1944; d. Martin Lawrence and Dorothy (Sweet) Grant; m. Henry Huang; 1 dau., Julia. BA, Portland State U., 1967; MA, U. Chgo., 1969, PhD, 1977. Asst. prof. Amherst (Mass.) Coll., 1973-76, Univ. Utah, Salt Lake City, 1976-80; from asst. to assoc. prof. Washington U., St. Louis, 1980-92, prof., 1992—. Author: Qashqa'i of Iran, 1986, Nomad, 1991; co-editor Women in the Muslim World, 1978, Women in Iran from the Rise of Islam to 1800, 2003, Women in Iran from 1800 to the Islamic Republic, 2004. Grantee Social Scis. Rsch. Coun., 1990, NEH, 1990-92, 98, Am. Philos. Soc., 1998. Mem. Mid. East Studies Assn. (bd. dirs. 1981-84), Soc. Iranian Studies (exec. sec. 1979-82, edit. bd. 1982-91, coun. 1996-98). Office: Washington U Dept Anthropology 1 Brookings Dr Saint Louis MO 63130-4899

BECK, MARILYN MOHR, columnist; b. Chgo, Ill, Dec. 17, 1928; d. Max and Rose (Lieberman) Mohr; m. Roger Beck, Jan. 8, 1949 (div. 1974); children: Mark Elliott, Andrea; m. Arthur Levine, Oct. 12, 1980. AA, U. So. Calif., 1950. Free-lance writer nat. mag. and newspapers, Hollywood, Calif., 1959-63; Hollywood columnist Valley Times and Citizen News, Hollywood, Calif., 1963-65; West Coast editor Sterling Mag., Hollywood, Calif., 1963-74; free-lance entertainment writer LA Times, Calif., 1965-67; Hollywood columnist Bell-McClure Syndicate, 1967-72; chief Bell-McClure Syndicate (West Coast bur.), 1967-72; Hollywood columnist NANA Syndicate, 1967-72; syndicated Hollywood columnist NY Times Spl. Features, 1972-78, NY Times Spl. Features (United Feature Syndicate), 1978-80, United Press abroad, 1978-80, Internat. Editors News and Features, Chgo. Tribune/NY Daily News Syndicate, 1980-97; Grapevine columnist TV Guide, 1989-92; creators syndicate, 1997—. Creator, host Marilyn Beck's Hollywood Outtakes spls. NBC, 1977, 78; host Marilyn Beck's Hollywood Hotline, Sta. KFI, LA, 1975-77; Hollywood reporter Eyewitness News, Sta. KABC-TV, LA, 1981, (TV program) PM Mag., 1983-88; on-air corr. E! TV, 1993-99, CompuServe Entertainment Authority, 1994-96, eDrive Internet Authority, 1996-97, e!online Internet Hollywood Authority, 1997—, Compuserve, 2000—, aeNTV.com, 2001-02; author: (non-fiction) Marilyn Beck's Hollywood, 1973, (novel) Only Make Believe, 1988; co-author: Unfinished Lives, What If...?, 1996. Recipient Citation of Merit LA City Coun., 1973, Press award Pub. Guild Am., 1974, Bronze Halo award So. Calif. Motion Picture Coun., 1982. Address: 4926 Delos way Oceanside CA 92056 *Being the best isn't everything; it's the only thing. "Life is too short to be little" (Disraeli).*

BECK, MATTHIAS, mathematician, educator; b. Erbach, Hessen, Germany, Nov. 14, 1970; s. Hermann and Elisabeth Beck; m. Tendai Chitewere, Apr. 29, 1999. Diploma, Universitat Wursburg, Wurzburg, Germany, 1997; PhD, Temple U., Philadelphia, PA, 2000; Staatsexamen, Universitat Wurzburg, Wurzburg, Germany, 1997. Vis. asst. prof. State U. NY Binghamton, Binghamton, NY, 2000—. Atheist. Office: SUNY Binghamton Dept Math Scis Binghamton NY 13902 Office Fax: 607-777-2450.

BECK, MORRIS, allergist; b. Miami, Fla., Oct. 12, 1927; s. Max and Anna (Luks) B.; m. Hollis Schwartz, Aug. 6, 1960; children: Gayle Beck Finan, Anne Lin. BA, UCLA, 1949; MD, U. Zurich, Switzerland, 1957. Diplomate Am. Bd. Allergy and Immunology, Am. Bd. Pediatrics. Intern Queens Hosp. Ctr., 1958, resident in pediatrics, 1959-60; preceptor in allergy U. Miami (Fla.) Med. Sch., 1961-77; pvt. practice pediatrician Miami, 1961—78; pvt. practice allergist, 1979—; chief dept. allergy Miami Children's Hosp., 1986—2003; clin. prof. pediatrics Nova U. Southeastern Med. Sch., 1998—; clin. asst. prof. U. Miami Med. Sch. With U.S. Army, 1950-52. Fellow: Am. Assn. Cert. Allergists, Am. Acad. Pediatrics, Am. Acad. Asthma, Allergy and Immunology, Am. Coll. Allergy and Immunology; mem.: Am. Coll. Chest Physicians. Republican. Jewish. Avocations: photography, fishing, travel. Office: 7800 SW 87th Ave # C-340 Miami FL 33173-3570 E-mail: beckmd123@aol.com.

BECK, PAUL ALLEN, political science educator; b. Logansport, Ind., Mar. 15, 1944; s. Frank Paul and Mary Elizabeth (Flanegin) B.; m. Maria Teresa Marcano, June 10, 1967; children: Daniel Lee, David Andrew. AB, Ind. U., 1966; MA, U. Mich., 1968, PhD, 1971. Asst. prof. U. Pitts., 1970-75, assoc. prof., 1976-79; prof. Fla. State U., Tallahassee, 1979-87, chmn. dept., 1981-87; prof. Ohio State U., Columbus, 1987—, chmn. dept., 1991—. Co-author: Political Socialization Across the Generations, 1975, Individual Energy Conservation Behaviors, 1980, Electoral Change in Advanced Industrial Democracies, 1984, Party Politics in America, 10th edit., 2003. Chmn. coun. Inter-Univ. Consortium for Polit. and Social Research, 1982-83, mem., 1980-83; mem. NSF polit. sci. panel, 1988-89. Recipient Disting. Svc. award Ohio State U., 2000. Mem. Am. Polit. Sci. Assn. (exec. coun. 1981-82, 93-94, book rev. editor 1976-79, program chair 1994, chair strategic planning com. 1999-2000), Midwest Polit. Sci. Assn. (exec. coun. 1987-90, mem. editl. bd. 1988-90, program chair 1991, v.p. 1996-98), So. Polit. Sci. Assn. (mem. editl. bd. 1982-87), Pi Sigma Alpha (exec. coun.). Democrat. Home: 7003 Perry Dr Columbus OH 43085-2815 Office: Ohio State U Dept Polit Sci Columbus OH 43210-1373 E-mail: beck.9@osu.edu.

BECK, PHILIP S. lawyer; b. Chgo., Apr. 30, 1951; BA, U. Wis., 1973; JD, Boston U., 1976. Bar: Ill. 1977. Clerk U.S. Ct. Appeals DC Cir., 1976-77; ptnr. Bartlit Beck Herman Palenchar & Scott, Chgo. Office: Bartlit Beck Herman et al 54 W Hubbard St Chicago IL 60610-4645 E-mail: philip.beck@bartlit-beck.com.

BECK, PHYLLIS WHITMAN, judge; b. N.Y.C. d. Irving and Dora (Sugar) Whitman; m. Aaron T. Beck; children: Roy, Judith, Daniel, Alice. AB magna cum laude, Brown U.; JD, Temple U., 1967, hon. degrees (2), 1997. Bar: Pa. 1967. Pvt. practice law, Phila., 1967-74; assoc. prof. Temple U. Law Ctr., Phila., 1974-76; vice dean U. Pa. Law Sch., Phila., 1976-81; judge Superior Ct. Pa., 1981—. Chmn. Pa. Gov.'s Commn. on Jud. Reform, 1987—88; Phi Beta Kappa lectr. Brown U., Providence; Lindbach lectr. Bryn Mawr Coll.; bd. dirs. Mann Ctr. for Performing Arts, WHYY--Pub. Broadcasting Corp. Contbr. articles to profl. jours. Pres. Found. Cognitive Therapy, 1974—; chair bd. Independence Found.; bd.dirs. Temple Law Sch., Free Libr. of Phila., Jewish-Am. History Mus.; mem. Joint State Govt. Commn. on Domestic Rels. Law, 1995—; mem. Pennsylvanians for Modern Cts.; mem. bd. consultors Villanova Law Sch.; mem. bd. overseers U. Pa. Sch. Nursing. Named a Disting. Dau. of Pa.; recipient Leadership award, Med. Coll. Pa., Phila., William Brennan award, Phila. Bar Assn., 1997. Mem. Am. Law Inst., Am. Bar Found., Am. Judicature Soc. (bd. dirs., Herbert Harley award 1995), Pa. Bar Assn. (Jud. award 1990, Anne Alperin award 1997), Women in the Profession, Nat. Assn. Women Judges (Murray award 1998), Disting. Dau. of Pa. 2000. Office: Pa Superior Ct GSB Bldg Ste 800 Bala Cynwyd PA 19004 E-mail: phylliswbeck@yahoo.com.

BECK, RALPH, financial consultant; BA, Beloit Coll., 1977; MBA, Wash. U., St. Louis, 1981. Admissions officer Beloit Coll., Wis., 1977—79; comml. banker Am. Nat. Bank, Chgo., 1981—87, sr. lender Libertyville, Ill., 1987—91; credit adminstr. comml. banking MAB-First Colonial Bank, Chgo., 1991—92; sr. lender First Colonia -Rosemont/EG, Rosemont, Ill., 1992—94, ABOP-First Colonial, Oak Park, Ill., 1994—95, Firstar Ill., Chgo., 1995—97, divsn. head comml. banking Rosemont, 1997—98; prin. The RPMB Co., L.L.C., Wilmette, Ill., 1998—, Principle Advisors, L.L.C., Wilmette, 2002—. Pres. Colo. Rocky Mountain Sch., 2001—03, trustee, 1997—. Office: Principle Advisors LLC 444 Skokie Blvd Ste 360 Wilmette IL 60091

BECK, RHONDA JOANN, paramedic, educator, writer; b. Hawkinsville, Ga., Apr. 20, 1965; d. Franklin Lamar and Ida (Scarborough) Woodard; m. Gary Wendell Bramlett, Apr. 9, 1983 (div. May 1995); 1 child, Gary Michael Bramlett; m. Kenneth Steve Beck, June 8, 1997. Gen. Banking Degree, Am. Inst. Banking. Cert. BTLS, CPR, PHTLS, ACLS, BLS instr. trainer, emergency med. technician-paramedic, instr. Collateral clk. Bank South, N.A., Perry, Ga., 1986-94; emergency med. technician Taylor Regional Hosp., Hawkinsville, 1993-94; paramedic Med. Ctr. Ctrl. Ga., Macon, 1994-99; emergency med. technician instr., paramedic instr. Ctrl. Ga. Tech. Coll., Macon, 1997—; paramedic Houston Med. Ctr., Warner Robins, Ga., 1997—. Instr. ACLS, Pediat. Life Support, PreHosp. Trauma Life Support, Basic Trauma Life Support, Am. Heart Assn.; reviewer Delmar Thomson, 1999—, Jones & Bartlett, 2000-, GEMS Faculty, 2003-present, Am. Geriatric Soc.; Brady, 2001—. Author: Emergency Care and Transportation of the Sick and Injured, student workbook, AAOS, 8th edit., 2001; pub. author, reviewer: Jones & Bartlett. Vol. firefighter Houston County Vol. Fire Dept., Hayneville, Ga., 1986-95. Recipient Heartsaver award Laerdal Med. Corp., 1994, Vol. Svc. award Am. Lung Assn. Ga., 1995. Democrat. Baptist. Avocations: reading, swimming, exercise, writing, coin collecting. Office: Houston County EMS Warner Robins GA 31093 E mail: takai_scnsci@yahoo.com.

BECK, RICHARD THOMAS, scientific facility administrator; BS, SUNY, Albany, 1978, MPA, 1981; PhD, George Mason U., 1993. Rsch. asst. Marine Scis. Rsch. Ctr., Stony Brook, N.Y., 1978-79, N.Y. State Energy Office, Albany, 1980-81; program analyst NASA/Space Sci. and Applications, Washington, 1981-88, program analysts br. chief, 1988-90; program control mgr. NASA Earth Observing System, Washington, 1990-93; program mgr. NASA Environ. Monitoring Satellites, Goddard Space Flight Ctr., 1993-96; dep. dir. resources Earth Sci. Systems program office NASA, Goddard Space Flight Ctr., 1997-99; bus. divsn. dir. NASA Office of Earth Sci., 1999-2000; dir. resources analysis divsn. NASA, 2000—. Presdl. Mgmt. Intern, U.S. Govt., Washington, 1981-83; James E. Webb Space Adminstrn. fellow NASA/Nat. Space Club, Washington, 1992; V.p.'s Nat. Performance Rev. Hammer award, 1995. Avocations: horseback riding, photography, bicycling. Office: NASA Headquarters Office Of CFO Washington DC 20546 0001

BECK, ROBERT ALFRED, hotel administration educator; b. Boston, Nov. 1, 1920; s. Alfred and Laura Martha (Reissman) B.; m. Mary Kathryn Murray, Nov. 5, 1944; children: Susan Jane, Janice Barbara, Robin Maria. BS, Cornell U., 1942, MS in Edn., 1952, PhD, 1954. Food technologist, pers. mgr. Quincy Market Co., Boston, 1945-50; mem. faculty Sch. Hotel Adminstrn., Cornell U., 1954-84, prof., 1960-84, dean, 1961-81; dir. Internat. Inst. Hotel Mgmt., Cergy-Pontoise, France, 1981-84; prof., disting. scholar in residence Fla. Internat. U., 1984—. Vis. lectr. USAF in PTO and ETO, U.S. Army in Europe, others; bd. dirs. Carrolls Devel. Corp., Consulan AG, Switzerland; mgmt. cons. U.S. Dept. Commerce, USAF, U.S. Army, USN, Govt. of Jamaica, Govt. of Barbados, Govt. of Bahama Is., Nat. Restaurant Assn., others. Contbr. articles to trade publs. Trustee, v.p. Ednl. Inst. Am. Hotel and Motel Assn.; v.p. Nat. Inst. Foodservice Industry; trustee Caribbean Hotel Tng. Inst., Ithaca (NY) Coll.; bd. adv. Nova U., Ft. Lauderdale, Fla.; bd. dirs. Culinary Inst. Am., Internat. Hotel and Tourism Tng. Inst., Basel, Switzerlandgov. bd. East-West Coll. Natural Medicine, Sarasota, Fla., 2000—. 1st lt. F.A., AUS, 1942-45, ETO. Decorated Purple Heart. Mem. AAUP, Croix de Guerre, Phi Kappa Phi, Phi Delta Kappa. Home: 1255 N Gulfstream Ave Apt 805 Sarasota FL 34236-8929

BECK, ROBERT BERYL, real estate executive; b. Dalton, Ga., Feb. 25, 1935; s. Carson W. and Gladys (Gray) B.; m. Martha Lucinda Cone, June 14, 1957; children: Perkie Cone Beck Cannon, Robert B. Jr., Carson W. Student, Vanderbilt U., 1953-57; LLB, JD, Nashville Sch. Law, 1964. Salesman Southeastern Inc., Nashville, 1957-64; purchasing agt. Nashville Bd. Edn., 1965-66; pres. Beck & Beck Realty, Nashville, 1967—, Beck & Beck Ins. Co., Nashville, 1967-78, v.p., 1978—; pres. Tri-County Builders, Nashville, 1974—. Editor Grace Bapt. Monthly, 1985, real estate newsletter, 1986-87. Mem. Nashville Bd. Realtors, Lodges: Masons. Democrat. Avocations: fishing, hiking, cycling. Home: 3500 Brick Church Pike Nashville TN 37207-2002 Office: Beck & Beck 4205 Gallatin Rd Nashville TN 37216-2111

BECK, ROBERT EDWARD, computer scientist, educator; b. Denver, June 7, 1941; s. Arthur Walter and Caroline Adelheid (Petrie) B.; m. Barbara Ruth Pennell, Aug. 21, 1965; children: Philip Arthur, Christopher William, Jennifer Grove. BS in Math., Harvey Mudd Coll., Claremont, Calif., 1963; PhD in Math., U. Pa., 1969. Instr. Villanova (Pa.) U., 1966-69, asst. prof., 1969-74, assoc. prof., 1974-78, prof. computer sci., 1978—, dept. chair, 1992—. Team chair computing accreditation commn. ABET, 1986—. Author: Elementary Linear Programming, 2d edit., 1995; editor: Computers in Nonassociative Rings and Algebras, 1978. Fulbright Exchange fellow, 1981-82. Mem. AAUP, ACM (chair computer sci. conf. 1995, 96, chair preparing future faculty program 1998-2002), Am. Math. Soc., Sigma Xi. Office: Villanova U Dept Computing Sci Villanova PA 19085 E-mail: robert.beck@villanova.edu.

BECK, ROBERT JAMES, editor, energy economist, author, consultant; b. Milw., Nov. 21, 1938; s. Walter John and Evelyn Barbara (Bigus) B.; m. Mary Ellen Drew, Jan. 20, 1968 (div. Aug. 1978); m. Connie Sue Sparling, Apr. 2, 1988 (div. May 1994). BS in Econs. with honors, U. Wis., Milw., 1961; MS in Internat. Econs., U. Wis., 1965; postgrad., Wharton Sch., U. Pa., 1967, U. Okla., 1981. Actuarial asst. Milliman & Robertson, Milw., 1963-64; rsch. asst. U. Wis., Milw., 1964-65; economist, statistician Wis. Telephone Co., Milw., 1965-68; dir. econ. rsch. Mackay Shields Econs., N.Y.C., 1968-69; head oper. planning Oil Svc. Co. Iran, Ahwaz, 1969-79; econs. editor Oil & Gas Jour., Tulsa, 1979-2000; developer, mgr. Oil & Gas Jour. Energy Database, Tulsa, 1984—; cons. Oil & Gas Jour., 2000—, Robert J. Beck & Assocs., 2000—; contract mgr. Oil & Gas Jour. Energy Database Online, 2001—. Cons. Oil and Gas Jour. Online Rsch. Ctr. for the Oil and Gas Industry, 1994—, Altec Energy, Centralia, Ill., 1986-90, Rainbow Petroleum, N.Y.C., 1986, Farrar and Assocs., Tulsa, 1985 86, Internat. Soc. Energy Advocates, 2002—; mem. Tulsa Com. on Fgn. Rels. Author: Oil Industry Outlook, 1983, 20th edit., 2003; developer Energy Statistics Sourcebook, 15 edits., 1986—; editor: International Energy Statistics Sourcebook, 10 edits., 1991—, Natural Gas Statistics Sourcebook, 7 edits., 1993—, Refining Statistics Sourcebook, 7 edits., 1993—, Price Statistics Sourcebook, 6 edits., Company Performance Statistics Sourcebook, 5 edits., 1966—; contbr. articles to mags. and newspapers. Active Wis. Gov.'s Commn. on Econ. Indicators, 1967, Philbrook Mus. Art, Tulsa, 1989—, Nature Conservancy, Tulsa, 1988—, Tulsa Zoo, 1991—, Mus. Fine Arts, Houston, 1999—, Tulsa (Okla.) Mayor's Energy Adv. Com., 2002—, Tulsa Com. Fgn. Rels., 2002—; pres. Young Dems., West Allis, Wis., 1960-62, Energy Literacy Project, 1996—; bd. dirs., pres. Energy Literacy Project Inc., 1996—. Mem. Internat. Assn. Energy Econs. (coun.), Internat. Assn. Energy Advocates, Nat. Assn. Bus. Econs., Assn. Petroleum Writers, U.S. Assn. Energy Economics, Ind. Petroleum Assn. Am. (mem. supply and demand com., cost study com.), Mus. Fine Arts (Houston), Gilcrease Mus., Philbrook Art Mus. Avocations: biking, hiking, cinema, tennis, golf. Office: PO Box 35723 Tulsa OK 74153-0723

BECK, ROBERT N. nuclear medicine educator; b. San Angelo, Tex., Mar. 26, 1928; married, 1958. AB, U. Chgo., 1954, BS, 1955. Chief scientist Argonne Cancer Rsch. Hosp., 1957-67, assoc. prof., 1967-76; prof. radiological sci. U. Chgo., 1976; dir. Franklin McLean Inst., 1977-94, dir. Ctr. Imaging Sci., 1986-98; prof. emeritus U. Chgo., 1998—. Cons. Internat. Atomic Energy Agency, 1966-68; mem. Internat. Com. on Radiation Units, 1968—, Nat. Coun. on Radiation, Protection & Measurements, 1970—. Recipient Aebersold award FDR, 1991. Mem. IEEE (Med. Imaging Sci. award 1996), Soc. Nuclear Med., Am. Assn. Physicists in Medicine, Soc. Magnetic Resonance. Achievements include research in development of a theory of the process by which images can be formed of the distribution of radioactive material in a patient in order to diagnose his disease. Office: U Chgo (MC 2026) 5841 S Maryland Ave Chicago IL 60637-1463

BECK, ROBERT RANDALL, investment management executive; b. San Francisco, July 2, 1940; s. Lester L. and Eunice (Hague) B. AB with cert. in pub. affairs, Woodrow Wilson Sch. Princeton U., 1962; MBA, Harvard U., 1967. Prodr., dir. Les Films Numero Uno, Paris, 1963-65; with State St. Rsch. and Mgmt. Co., Boston, 1967—, ptnr., 1973-85; mng. ptnr. Marble Arch Ptnrs., 1985-89; mng. dir. The Putnam Cos., 1989—; chmn., pres. Am. Mobile Systems, 1987-90; bd. dirs. Charlesbridge Pub., Inc., 1970—. Mem. bd. overseers Beth Israel-Deaconess Hosp. Lt. USN, 1962-64. Mem. Assn. for Investment Mgmt. and Rsch., Boston Soc. Security Analysts. Home: 867 Forest Rd Alstead NH 03602-7705 Office: The Putnam Cos PO Sq Boston MA 02109 E-mail: robert_beck@putnam.com.

BECK, ROBERT RAYMOND, priest; b. Waterloo, Iowa, Aug. 28, 1940; s. Paul Clayton and Mildred Anne (Klein) B. BA, Loras Coll., Dubuque, Iowa, 1962; ThM, Aquinas Inst. Theology, Dubuque, 1965; cert. of study, Ecole Biblique, Jerusalem, 1978; DMin, Cath. U., 1983. Assoc. pastor St. Columbkille Parish, Dubuque, 1966-71; with campus ministry U. No. Iowa, Cedar Falls, 1971-73; instr. of Scripture Aquinas Inst. Theology, 1973-81; prof. religious studies Loras Coll., 1981—, chair dept. religious studies, 1992—2001, John Cardinal O'Connor endowed chair in Cath. thought, 1999-2000. Co-founder, bd. dirs. Cath. Worker, Dubuque, 1976-94; co-founder, pastor Anawim Faith Community, Dubuque, 1981—; founder, dir. Ray Herman Peace Ctr., Dubuque, 1983-86. Author: Nonviolent Story: Narrative Conflict Resolution in the Gospel of Mark, 1996; composer: (rock opera) Mark, A Pop Opera 1975, 87, 99, Our Father, 1968; columnist: Sunday's Word, 1982-87; editor: Loras Faculty Review, 1989 1999; contbr. articles to profl. jours. Mem. Soc. Bibl. Lit., Am. Acad. Religion, Cath. Theol. Soc. Am. Democrat. Home: 1220 N Booth St Dubuque IA 52001

BECK, ROSEMARIE, artist, educator; b. N.Y.C., July 8, 1924; d. Samuel and Margit (Weisz) B.; m. Robert Phelps, Sept. 15, 1945 (dec.); 1 child, Roger Phelps. AB, Oberlin Coll., 1944; student, Inst. Fine Arts, 1944-45, Columbia U., 1945, Atelier Robert Motherwell, 1950. Instr. Vassar Coll., Poughkeepsie, N.Y., 1956-57, 60-61, 63-64, Middlebury (Vt.) Coll., 1958, 59, 62, Parsons Sch. Design, N.Y.C., 1965-69; instr. to prof. Queens Coll., N.Y.C., 1968-91, prof. emeritus, 1991—. Lectr. Columbia U., N.Y.C., 1972, U. Pa., Phila., 1971, New Studio Sch., N.Y.C., 1991—; artist-in-residence Dartmouth Coll., N.H., 1992. One-person shows include Allen Art Mus., Oberlin, Ohio, 1944, Maverick Concert Hall, Woodstock, N.Y., 1948, Woodstock Artists Assn., 1948, Peridot Gallery, N.Y.C., 1953, 55, 56, 59, 60, 63, 65, 66, 68, 70, 72, Vassar Coll., 1957, 61, Wesleyan U., Middletown, Conn., 1960, SUNY, New Paltz, 1962, Kirkland Coll., Clinton, N.Y., 1971, Duke U. Mus., 1971, Zachary Waller Gallery, L.A., 1971, Washburn Gallery, 1972, Paul Klapper Libr., 1975, Poindexter Gallery, N.Y.C., 1975, 80, Mari Galleries, Westchester, N.Y., 1979, Middlebury Coll., 1980, Weatherspoon Gallery, Greensboro, N.C., 1980, Cornell U., 1980, Ingber Gallery, N.Y.C., 1980, 85, 89, N.Y. Studio Sch., 1992, N.Y. Mus. Annex, Bklyn., 1985, Am. U., Washington, 1990, Dartmouth Coll., 1992, Swarthmore Coll., 1996, Smith Coll., 1997, Queens Coll., 1999; group shows include Kootz Gallery, N.Y.C., 1951, Stable Gallery, 1954, 55, 56, Pa. Acad. Fine Arts, Phila., 1954, 66, Art Inst. Chgo., 1955, 57, 60, 62, Whitney Mus., N.Y.C., 1955, 57, 58, U. Wis., 1956, U. Mich., 1956, Martha Jackson Gallery, 1956, Woodstock Artists Assn., 1958, Tate Gallery, London, 1958, Butler Inst. Am. Art, Cin., 1962, Felix Landau Gallery, L.A., 1962, Wadsworth Atheneum, 1964, Kansas City Art Inst., 1964, Walters Art Gallery, Balt., 1965, Nat. Inst. Arts and Letters, 1968, 69, 73, 75, 78, 79, Bowery Gallery, 1970, Nat. Arts Club, 1970, Deutsch Gallery, N.Y.C., 1982, 83, Moorhead Gallery, Greensboro, N.C., 1982, Nat. Acad. Design, 1985, Joel Becker Gallery, Provincetown, Mass., 1987, 88, Am. U., Washington, 1990, Nat. Acad., 1991, 92, 93. Recipient Altman Figure prize NAD, 1986, 89; grantee Woodstock Found., 1951, Ingram Merrill, 1967, 78, Rockefeller Found., 1983, NEA, 1986-87. Office: 6 E 12th St New York NY 10003-4447

BECK, STEPHANIE G. lawyer; b. Endicott, N.Y., Jan. 10, 1964; d. Ray A. and Donna E. (Geesey) B. BA with honors, SUNY, Binghamton, 1986; JD, Syracuse U., 1989. Bar: N.Y. 1990, U.S. Dist. Ct. (no. dist.) N.Y. 1990. Atty. Young & Paniccia, Binghamton, 1990—. Advisor/vol. Drama Club for Mentally and Physically Impaired, Binghamton, 1992—96; asst. coach Boys and Girls Club, Endwell, 1986—91; mem. ch. coun. Our Saviour Luth. Ch., Endwell, NY, 1990—94, 1996, Our Savior Luth. Ch., Endwell, NY, 2003—; mem. pers. com. Broome County Coun. Chs. Mem. N.Y. State Bar Assn., Broome County Bar Assn. (bd. dirs.). Democrat. Lutheran. Avocations: softball, volleyball. Office: Young and Paniccia 22 Riverside Dr Binghamton NY 13905-4612

BECK, STUART EDWIN, lawyer; b. Phila., Aug. 12, 1940; s. Louis M. and Anna (Cooper) B.; m. Elaine Kushner, June 20, 1964; children: Adam, Barry, Caroline. BSME, Drexel U., 1964; JD, George Washington U., 1968. Bar: Va. 1968, U.S. Dist. Ct. D.C. 1969, Pa. 1970, U.S. Dist. Ct. (ea. dist.) Pa. 1971, U.S. Ct. Appeals (3d cir.) 1971, U.S. Supreme Ct. 1980, U.S. Ct. Appeals (4th cir.) 1989, U.S. Patent and Trademark Office. Assoc. Seidel, Gonda & Goldhammer, Phila., 1969-73; atty. pvt. practice, Phila., 1974-79, 91—; ptnr. Trachman, Jacobs & Beck, Phila., 1979-88, Weinstein, Trachtman, Beck & Kimmelman, Phila., 1988-91. Adj. prof. patent law Rutgers U. Law Sch., Camden, N.J.; instr. patent, trademark and copyright law The Phila. Inst.; lectr. patent, trademark and copyright law Newmann Coll., 1999, lectr. U.S. trademark prosecution, seminar on U.S. trademark practice for paralegals, Phila., 2003; lectr. trademark law Halfmoon LLC, 2003. Capt. Am. Cancer Soc., 1974, 75; bd. dirs. Jewish Family and Children Svc. Phila., 1973-89, legal, fin. and budget com., 1979—, spkrs. com., 1979—, bldg. and grounds com., 1980-82, trustee, 1989; bd. dirs., by-laws revision com., bldgs. and grounds com., edn. com. Temple Beth Hillel; bd. dirs. Phila. Vol. Lawyers for Arts, 1980-84, treas., 1980-82. Mem. ABA (patent trademark and copyright law sect., litigation sect., antitrust law sect.), Am. Intellectual Property Law Assn. (com. patent contracts other than govt. 1971-75), Pa. Bar Assn., Phila. Bar Assn. (com. profl. responsibility 1975-93, com. election procedures 1976-84, com. law and arts 1976-80), Phila. Patent Law Assn. (com. ethics 1977-83, com. pub. rels. 1974-77, com. profl. responsibility 1975-79). Avocations: sailing, travel.

BECK, SUSAN J. school librarian; b. Norwalk, Ohio, Nov. 4, 1953; d. Kenneth R. Beck and Patricia Nabring Brady; m. James A. Benson, 1984. AB, Ea. Ky. U., 1975; MA, Miami U., 1977; MLS, Kent State U., 1980. Reference libr., instr. U. Ala., Tuscaloosa, 1980—83; reference libr., head pub. svcs. Rutgers U., Camden, NJ, 1983—. Vis. program officer Assn. of Rsch. Libraries, Washington, 2002—; vis. prof. U. Ala. Grad. Sch. Libr. Svc., Tuscaloosa, 1986, Rutgers U. Sch. Comm., Info. & Libr. Studies, New Brunswick, NJ, 1998—2000. Recipient More Than 500 Hours Svc. award, ARC, 1976; fellow, Kent State U., 1979—80, Miami U., 1976—77, 1977, Assn. of Rsch. Libraries, 2002; grantee Rsch. Coun. grantee, Rutgers U., 2001—02. Mem.: ALA (com. mem. in RUSA 1981—2002), Mgmt. and Operation of User Services (fee-based reference services & rsch. & stats. com. 1996—2002, mgmt. of reference com. 1996—2002), Assn. Coll. and Rsch. Librs., RUSA Machine Assisted Reference Sect. (chair measurement & evaluation com. 1986—87). Presbyterian. Achievements include research in Impact on Assessment in Decision Making in Academic Libraries in the United States and Canada. Avocations: gardening, swimming, travel. Home: One Hanover Ct Princeton NJ 08540 Office: Paul Robeson Library Rutgers University 300 North 4th Street Camden NJ 08101 Office Fax: 856-225-6428.

BECK, TIMOTHY DANIEL, human resources specialist, consultant; b. Santa Monica, Calif., Mar. 21, 1953; s. James Daniel and Bettye June (Cisler) B.; m. Marcia Ann Smith, Jan. 16, 1977; children: Tracy Beth and Erica Brandy (twins), Jenna Michelle. AA, El Camino Community Coll., 1974; BA, Calif. State U., Northridge, 1979. Registered health underwriter, registered employee benefits cons. Candidate cert. employee benefit specialist, group claims supr. Prudential Ins. Co. Am., L.A., 1973-79; employee benefits cons. Olanie, Hurst & Hemrich, L.A., 1979-81; v.p. policyholder svc. dept. Health Maintenance Life Ins. Co., Fountain Valley, Calif., 1981; v.p. Robert E. French Ins. Svcs., Inc., Huntington Beach, Calif., 1981-85; v.p., mng. cons. employee benefits Warren, McVeigh & Griffin, Inc., Newport Beach, Calif., 1985-91; mng. cons. employee benefits A. Foster Higgins and Co., Inc., 1991-96; prin. Buck Cons., Inc., L.A., 1996—. Mem. Kaiser Permanente Orange County Consumer Coun., 1987—; mem. pub. edn. com. Calif. Health Decision, 1988—; mem. bus. and health adv. panel Am. Health Pub.; speaker to confs. and profl. socs.; cons. Healthnet Adv. Coun., 1996—, Orange County Bus. Coun., Town Hall, 1996—; mem. Healthnet Cons. Adv. Coun., 1997—. Creator, contbg. editor Employee Benefits Mgmt. Letter, 1985-91; contbr. articles to profl. publs. Mem. Internat. Found. Employee Benefits, Nat. Assn. Health Underwriters, Calif. Assn. Health Underwriters, Employee Benefit Planning Assn. So. Calif. (bd. dirs. 1992-93), So. Calif. Assn. Benefit Plan Adminstrs., Orange County Assn. Health Underwriters (founder, 1st v.p. 1987-88), Orange County Bus. Coun., Orange County Employee Benefit Coun., Calif. State U. Northridge Alumni Assn. Avocations: fishing, hiking, backpacking, rock climbing.

BECK, TOM, state legislator, rancher; b. Deer Lodge, Mont., Nov. 14, 1939; m. Kay Beck. Student, Mont. State U. Rancher; mem. Mont. Senate, Dist. 28, Helena, 1987—; chair legis. adminstrn. com.; mem. fin. and claims com., rules com., fish and game com.; mem. agr., livestock and irrigation com.; majority whip Mont. Senate, 1995. Chmn. Powell Hosp. Bd.; former Powell County Commr. Mem. Mont. Assn. Counties (pres.). Republican. Home: 792 Yellowstone Trl Deer Lodge MT 59722-8704 Office: Capitol Sta Helena MT 59620

BECK, WILLIAM G. lawyer; b. Kansas City, Mo., Mar. 4, 1954; s. Raymond W. Beck and Wanda Williams; m. Cheryl A. Beck; children: Collin M., Sergei M., Valentina M., Kseniya M. BA in Econs., U. Mo., Kansas City, 1974, JD, 1978. Bar: Mo. 1978, U.S. Dist. Ct. (we. dist.) Mo. 1978, U.S. Ct. Appeals (5th cir.) 1988, U.S. Dist. Ct. (ea. dist.) Mich. 1991, U.S. Dist. Ct. (no. dist.) Ill. 1992, U.S. Ct. Appeals (6th cir.) 1992, U.S. Dist. Ct. (ea. dist.) Wis. 1997, U.S. Ct. Appeals (2d cir.) 1997, U.S. Ct. Appeals (10th cir.) 1997, U.S. Supreme Ct. 1997, U.S. Ct. Appeals (1st cir.) 1998, U.S. Ct. Appeals (7th cir.) 1999, U.S. Dist. Ct. Colo. 2000, U.S. Dist. Ct. Rhode Island 2002, U.S. Dist. Ct. Mass. 2002. Shareholder Field, Gentry, Benjamin & Robertson, P.C., Kansas City, 1978-89; ptnr. Lathrop & Norquist, Kansas City, 1989-95, Lathrop & Gage, L.C., Kansas City, 1996—. Commr. Human Rels. Commn., Jackson County, Mo., 1985-89; chmn. Citizens Assn., Kansas City, 1991-92, 95-96; mem. Pub. Improvement Adv. Com., Kansas City, 1991-2001, vice chmn., 1995-98, chmn. 1998-2001, fin. chmn. cmty. infrastructure com., 1996-1997; mem. Waste Minimization Com., Kansas City, 1990-91; bd. mem. Regional Transit Authority, 2001--. Office: Lathrop & Gage LC 2345 Grand Blvd Ste 2800 Kansas City MO 64108-2684

BECK, WILLIAM HAROLD, JR., lawyer; b. Clarksdale, Miss., Aug. 18, 1928; s. William Harold and Mary (McGaha) B.; m. Nancy Cassity House, Jan. 30, 1954; children: Mary, Nancy, Katherine. BA, Vanderbilt U., 1950; JD, U. Miss., 1954. Bar: Miss. 1954, La. 1960. Atty., Clarksdale, 1954-57; asst. prof. Tulane U., 1957-59; ptnr. Foley & Judell, New Orleans, 1959-88, of counsel, 1988—. Capt. AUS, 1951-53. Mem. La. Bar Assn., Miss. Bar Assn., SAR, Soc. Colonial Wars, S.R., Mil and Hospitaller Order of St. Lazarus of Jerusalem, Huguenot Soc., Mil. Order Fgn. Wars. Office: Foley & Judell LLP 1 Canal Pl 365 Canal St Ste 2600 New Orleans LA 70130-1138 E-mail: wandnbeck@aol.com

BECK, WILLIAM SAMSON, hematologist, educator, biochemist, writer; b. Reading, Pa., Nov. 7, 1923; s. Myron Paul and Gertrude (Harris) B.; m. Helene Samuels, Oct. 24, 1947; children: Thomas Russell, Peter Dean; m. Hanne Troedsson, July 20, 1964; children: John Christopher, Paul Brooks BS in Chemistry, U. Mich., 1943, MD, 1946; AM (hon.), Harvard U., 1971. Diplomate Am. Bd. Internal Medicine. Instr., asst. prof. medicine UCLA, 1950—57; fellow in biochemistry NYU Coll. Medicine, 1955—57; faculty dept. medicine Harvard U., Boston, 1957—, prof., 1979—96, emeritus, 1996—, tutor in biochem. scis., 1957—. Prof. div. health sci. and tech. Harvard-MIT, 1971—, chmn. admissions com., 1977-88; dir. clin. labs. Mass. Gen. Hosp., Boston, 1957-75, chief hematology unit, 1957-72, dir. hematology rsch. lab., physician, 1957-96; mem. adv. coun. Nat. Inst . Arthritis, Metabolism and Digestive Diseases, NIH, 1971-74; mem. hematology study sect. NIH, 1967-71; Austin S. Weisberger vis. prof. medicine, CWRU, 1996. Author: Modern Science and the Nature of Life, 1957, Life: An Introduction to Biology, 3d edit., 1991; (with K.F. Liem, G.G. Simpson), Human Design, 1971, Hematology, 5th edit., 1991 (CD-ROM) Hemavid, 1995; contbr. articles to profl. jours. With AUS, 1943-46. Fellow AAAS; mem. Am. Soc. Biochemistry and Molecular Biology, Am. Soc. Hematology (exec. com. 1979-84), Assn. Am. Physicians, Am. Soc. Clin. Investigation, Am. Assn. Cancer Rsch. Home: 85 Arlington St Winchester MA 01890-3734 E-mail: william_beck@hms.harvard.edu.

BECKEL, CHARLES LEROY, physicist, educator; b. Phila., Feb. 7, 1928; s. Samuel Mercer and Katherine (Linsky) Beckel; m. Josephine Ann Beck, June 27, 1958; children: Amanda S., Sarah Beckel Lentz, Timothy C. Lentz, Andrea C. Lentz. BS, U. Scranton, 1948; PhD, Johns Hopkins U., 1954. Asst. prof. physics Georgetown U., 1953-59, assoc. prof., 1959-64; rsch. staff mem. Inst. Def. Analyses, Arlington, Va., 1964-66; assoc. prof. U. N.Mex., Albuquerque, 1966-69, prof., 1969-94, prof. emeritus, 1995—, asst. dean, 1971-72, acting v.p. rsch., 1972-73. Cons. Ballistics Rsch. Lab., Aberdeen Proving Ground, Md., 1955—57, Inst. Def. Analyses, 1962—64, 1966—69, Dikewood Corp., Albuquerque, 1967—72, Albuquerque, 1974—80, Albuquerque Urban Obs., 1969—71, U.S. ACDA, 1981—84; Fulbright lectr. U. Peshawar, Pakistan, 1957—58, Cheng Kung U., Tainan, Taiwan, 1963—64; acting dir. Inst. Social R & D, 1972; vis. prof. theoretical chemistry Oxford U., 1973; vis. prof. chemistry and molecular scis. U. Sussex, England, 1987; phys. sci. officer U.S. Arms Control and Disarmament Agy., 1980—81; vis. prof. physics U. Scranton, 1995. Pres. Nat. Kidney Found. N.Mex Inc., 1968—72, del. trustee, 1972—73, 1976—80, mem. exec. com., 1974—80, 1983—86, v.p., 1982—83, trustee, 1987—93, 2002—; bd. dirs. Nat. Capital Area Nat. Kidney Found., 1965—66, N.Mex Combined Health Appeal, 1972—73. Recipient Vol. award, Nat. Kidney Found. N.Mex, 1988, Frank J. O'Hara award for Disting. Achievement in Sci., U. Scranton Nat. Alumni Soc., 1988, award in solic state physics materials scis., U.S. Dept. Energy, 1988, Outstanding Tchg. award, Burlington No. Found., 1989. Mem.: Biolectromagnetics Soc., Am. Phys. Soc., Nat. Eagle Scout Assn. Office: U NMex Dept Physics And Astronomy Albuquerque NM 87131-0001 E-mail: clbeckel@unm.edu.

BECKEN, BRADFORD ALBERT, engineering executive; b. Providence, Oct. 5, 1924; s. Albert R. and Ruth M. (Stephenson) B.; m. Gaynelle M. Lane, Nov. 30, 1946; children: Bradford Albert, Brian A., Christian L., Anne Tracey. Student, U. R.I., 1942-43; BS, U.S. Naval Acad., 1946; BS in Electronics, U.S. Naval Postgrad. Sch., 1952; MS, UCLA, 1953, PhD, 1961. Commd. officer USN, advanced through grades to comdr.; cons. Airtronics-Spl. Warfare Lab., 1967; mgr. systems engring. lab. submarine signal div. Raytheon Co., Portsmouth, R.I., 1967-70, mgr. engring., 1970-82, dir. tech. Portsmouth Engring. Lab., 1982-94; cons., 1994—97. Author: Advances in Hydroscience, 1964. Trustee Newport Hosp., 1977, chmn. bd., 1979-84; chmn. bd. dirs. Newport Health Care Corp., 1984-93; treas. Newport Hist. Soc., 1993-94, pres., 1994-2001. Recipient Asst. Chief Bur. Ships award, 1963, Am. Def. Preparedness Assn. Gold medal, 1995, Navy Undersea Warfare Ctr. Decibel award, 1997, Capt. George W. Ringenberg award, 1999. Fellow Acoustical Soc. Am.; mem. Nat. Def. Indsl. Assn., Naval War Coll. Found., U.S. Naval Inst., U.S. Naval Acad. Alumni Assn. Episcopalian. Home: 260 Fischer Cir Portsmouth RI 02871-5400

BECKENSTEIN, MYRON, journalist; b. Cleve., Mar. 11, 1938; s. Irwin and Rachel (Miller) B.; 1 child, Stacey Amanda. BS, Northwestern U., 1959, MS, 1960. Mem. staff Chgo. Daily News, 1959-78, Balt. Sun, 1978—2002. Served with AUS, 1961-64. Mem. Upper Patuxent Archeol. Group, Archeol. Soc. Md., Soc. Profl. Journalists. Home: 9256 Feathered Head Columbia MD 21045-5306

BECKER, ANNE MARGARET, neonatal nurse, clinical nurse specialist; b. San Rafael, Calif., Sept. 4, 1953; d. Robert E. and Helen (Grondorf) Spitzer; m. Michael Becker, Nov. 21, 1973; children: Miriam, Davina. Diploma, St. Luke's Sch. Nursing, San Francisco, 1974; AS, San Francisco Community Coll., 1974; BS, U. Calif., San Francisco, 1984, MS, 1986. RN, Calif.; cert. high-risk perinatal nurse; cert. CNS, Calif. Staff nurse II Children's Hosp. Med. Ctr., Oakland, Calif., 1974-86; outreach educator Children's Hosp., San Francisco, 1986; staff nurse Med. Personnel Pool, San Francisco, 1986-87; staff nurse II-IV Stanford (Calif.) U. Hosp., 1987-91; staff nurse IV Lucile Salter Packard Children's Hosp. at Stanford, Palo Alto, Calif., 1991-97, acting clin. nurse specialist, 1993-97, neonatal clin. nurse specialist, 1997-99, staff nurse IV, 1999—2002, acting clin. nurse specialist, 2000-2001, cons., 2002—. Cons. E.I. duPont Co., 2002, Lucile Salter Pakard Children's Hosp., Stanford, Calif., 2003—. Mem. editl. bd., contbr. Neonatal Network Jour., Petaluma, Calif., 1987—; peer reviewer Jour. Am. Acad. Nurse Practitioners, Pitts., 1990-92; author (poetry) Waiting, 1989; contbr. chpt. to book. Treas. St. Christopher's Epis. Ch., San Lorenzo, 2002—. Mem. ANA (state bd. dirs. 2002--, exec. com. Calif. chpt. coun. on maternal-child nursing 1993-94, exec. com. mem. coun. for acute care nursing practice 1994-98, chair 1996-98), ANCC (perinatal nurse test devel. com. 1989-92, bd. on cert. for maternal-child nursing 1989-91, mem. Calif. chpt. founding bylaws com. 1995-96), Calif. Nurses Assn. (chair nursing practice commn. 1991-93, commr. 1991-94, co-founder, vice chair coun. on children and families 1991-94), Acad. Neonatal Nursing, U. Calif. San Francisco Nursing Alumni Assn. (editl. cons. grad. nursing students 1991-92), Sigma Theta Tau (cmty. mem., continuing edn. reviewer online program 2000—). Republican. Episcopalian. Avocations: reading, choral singing, poetry writing, needlework. Home: 15309 Edgemoor St San Leandro CA 94579 E-mail: ambecker@msn.com.

BECKER, BARBARA ANN STULAC (BOBBIE BECKER), small business owner; b. Chgo., Sept. 29, 1938; d. Josef Florian and Dagmar Adrienne Pakonen Stulac; m. Raymond August Becker (div. 1980); children: Raymond August, Jr., Renay Dagmar. AA, Florissant Valley (Mo.) C.C., 1980; BA, U. Mo., St. Louis, 1981. Pvt. instrumental music instr., St. Louis, 1977-80, Dallas, 1981-83, Columbia, Mo., 1984—, Boonville, Fayette, Mo., 1987—; owner Bobbie Becker Music, Franklin, Mo., 1992—, piano tuner, instrument repair profl., 1992—. Mem. Mid-Mo. Music Tchrs. Assn., Mo. State Old Time Fiddlers Assn., Mo. Folklore Soc. Avocations: painting, travel, violin, guitar, piano. Office: Bobbie Becker Music 3764 State Route J Franklin MO 65250-9592

BECKER, BRENDA L. federal agency administrator; Degree, Mich. State U.; MBA, Ctrl. Mich. U. Former v.p. congl. comm. Blue Cross Blue Shield Assoc.; asst. sec. legis. and intergovt. affairs U.S. Dept. of Commerce, Washington, 2001—. Office: US Dept of Commerce Legis and Intergovt Affairs 14th and Constitution Ave NW Washington DC 20230 Office Fax: 202-482-4420.

BECKER, BRUCE ALAN, music educator, director; b. Ill., Sept. 11, 1968; MusB in Music Edn., U. Fla., 1992. Exec. dir. Sizzling Strings, Inc., Charlotte, NC, 1994—; orch. tchr. Charlotte-Mecklenburg Schools, Charlotte, NC, 1993—2002. Dir. Temple Israel Youth Band, Charlotte, 2001—. Personal E-mail: sizzledude@aol.com. E-mail: sizzledude@aol.com.

BECKER, BRUCE CARL, II, physician, educator, health facility administrator; b. Chgo., Sept. 8, 1948; s. Carl Max and Lillian (Podzamski) B.; m. Irene Stepien-Thibault, 1991; 1 child, Joseph. BS in Aero. and Astron. Engring., U. Ill., 1970; MSME, Colo. State U., 1972; postgrad., Wright State U., 1973-74; MD, Chgo. Med. Sch., 1978; MS in Health Svcs. Adminstrn., Coll. of St. Francis, Joliet, Ill., 1984; Diploma in Spanish, U. Chgo., 1988; Diploma in Polish, Coll. of Du Page, 1989. Diplomate Am. Bd. Med. Mgmt., cert. physician exec. Resident in surgery U. N.C., Chapel Hill, 1978-79; resident in family practice St. Mary of Nazareth Hosp. Ctr., Chgo., 1979-81, chmn., program dir. dept. family practice, 1985-90, asst. dir. med. edn., 1981-82, dir. family practice residency, 1983-90, chief Family Practice Ctr., 1983-85, chmn. dept. family practice, 1985-90, med. dir. home health svc., 1985-2001, med. dir. HMO-III., 1985-2001, mem. planning and devel. com. governing bd., 1987-91, v.p. med. affairs, 1989-2001; clin. instr. Chgo. Med. Sch., 1982, affiliate instr., 1982-83, asst. prof., 1983, vice chmn. dept. family medicine, 1983-91; chief med. officer Med. Ctr. Hosp., Odessa, Tex., 2002—. Mem. family practice residency act Adv. Com. Ill. Dept. Pub. Health, 1991-2002. Mem. editl. rev. bd. Postgrad. Medicine, 1987-89; contbr. articles to med. jours. Mem. pub. health adv. network HHS, 1990-91; bd. dirs. Midwest region Inn Care Am., 1991—; mem. dinner com. Ill. chpt. Lupus Found. Am., 1991. Capt. USAF, 1970-75. Fellow Am. Acad. Family Physicians (rep. to accrediation rev. com. for physician assts. 1989-94, chmn., 1991-93), Am. Coll. Physician Execs., Am. Coll. Health Care Execs. (regents adv. coun. 1996-2000), Inst. of Medicine Chgo.; mem. AMA, Ill. Acad. Family Physicians (commn. on internal affairs 1986, commn. pub. and govt. policy 1987-89, chmn. 1989-90, bd. dirs. 1988-92, chmn. pub. rels. and info. com. 1988-92, state rep. family practice res. act com. 1990-92, vice spkr. 1991-92), Soc. Tchrs. Family Medicine, Assn. Am. Med. Colls., Alliance Continuing Med. Edn., Am. Coll. Occupl. Medicine, Am. Acad. Med. Adminstrn., Chgo. Med. Soc. (councilor for Chgo. Med. Sch. 1986-91, alt. councilor 1991-95, mem. physicians stress ad hoc com. 1989-90, vice chmn. 1990-91, adv. com. on pub. health policy 1990-2001, presdl. adv. com. 1991-2001), Ill. Med. Soc. (coun. on edn. and manpower 1986-96, chmn. com. on CME activities 1991-96, chmn. subcom. physician placement and practice issues 1986-90, third party payment and processes com., Ill. Acad. Family Physicians rep. 1990-92), Phi Delta Epsilon. Roman Catholic. E-mail: bbecker@echd.org.

BECKER, BRUCE WARREN, music educator; b. St. James, Minn., Aug. 31, 1952; s. Marvin W. and Gladys A. Becker; m. Paula Noel Mott, July 30, 1983; 1 child, Joshua Aaron. BA, Augustana Coll., 1974; MA, U. St. Thomas, 1982. Dir. choirs Apollo H.S., St. Cloud, Minn., 1974—75, Sr. H.S., New Ulm, Minn., 1975—78, Irondale H.S., New Brighton, Minn., 1978—85, Robbinsdale Armstrong H.S., Plymouth, Minn., 1985—86, Apple Valley (Minn.) H.S., 1986—. Dir. music Cross View Luth. Ch., Edina, Minn., 1978—85; min. music Christ Meml. Luth. Ch., Plymouth, 1985—86; dir. music Prince of Peace Luth. Ch., Burnsville, Minn., 1986—. Composer: (hymn tune) Evan. Lutheran Hymnary-ELS, 1996, Hymnal Supplement-LCMS, 1998, (worship setting) Victory Feast, 1989. Named Outstanding Young Man of Am., U.S. Jaycees, 1982. Mem.: Minn. Music Educators Assn. (cons. 1983—85, Tchr. of the Yr. 1991), World Choral Symposium (bd. mem., program chair 1998—), Am. Choral Dirs. Assn. (divsn. pres. 1994—96). Democrat. Lutheran. Home: 12027 Gantry Ln Apple Valley MN 55124 Office: Apple Valley HS 12027 Gantry Ln Apple Valley MN 55124

BECKER, CARL FREDERICK, judge; b. Endicott, NY, Jan. 31, 1948; m. Christine Hill, July 6, 1974; children: Valeria, Jonathan. BS in Indsl. Mgmt., Clarkson Coll., 1970; JD, Albany Law Sch., 1973. Bar: N.Y. 1974. Ptnr. Govern, McDowell & Becker, Stamford, NY, 1973—2002; county judge Del. County Ct. House, Delhi, NY, 2002—. Social svcs. atty. Del. County Dept. Social Svcs., Delhi, 1974—2002; village atty. Village of Hobart, NY, 1976-2002, Village of Stamford, NY, 1989-2002. Mem. N.Y. State Bar Assn., Delaware County Bar Assn. (pres. 2001—), N.Y. State Pub. Welfare Assn. (v.p. atty.'s sect. 1989-92, pres. 1993), Rotary (pres. Stamford 1978-79, chair dist. 7170 youth exch. com. 1999-2001). Republican. Presbyterian. Office: Del County Ct House Delhi NY 13753

BECKER, CATHERINE HICKEY HANDY, retired librarian; b. Holyoke, Mass., May 10, 1932; d. Cornelius Joseph and Mary Agnes (Collins) Hickey; m. Wallace H. Handy, Nov. 1955 (dec. Nov. 1961); children: Cornelia and Roberta (twins), Mary; m. Bernhard H. Becker, Sept. 1992. BA, U. Mass., 1953; MS in LS, So. Conn. State Coll., 1965. Tchr. New Salem (Mass.) Acad., 1953-54, Londmeadow (Mass.) Jr. High Sch., 1954-56; libr. Wilson Jr. High Sch., Windsor, Conn., 1965-69; reference libr. Westfield (Mass.) State Coll., 1969-92, ret., 1992. Abstractor Libr. Currents, 1984-86. Vol. Noble Hosp., Westfield, 1977-80, LifeLink of S.W. Fla., 1996—, Venice Hosp., 1997—. Mem. AAUW, ALA (cert. sch. and acad. libr., reviewer RQ 1980-92, Choice 1984-92), Assn. Coll. and Rsch. Librs., New Eng. Libr. Assn., NEA, Mass. Tchrs. Assn., Mass. State Coll. Assn., Venice Area Audubon Soc., U. Mass. Alumni Assn., Sigma Kappa. Roman Catholic. Avocations: reading, biking, bird watching. Home: 5815 Buchanan Rd Venice FL 34293-6864

BECKER, CHARLES MCVEY, economics and finance educator; b. Cleve., Nov. 13, 1937; s. William Nevison and Helen (McVey) B.; m. Natalie Sage Slaughter, July 25, 1964; children: William Nevison II, James Pahl. BA cum laude, U. Ariz., 1960, MA, 1962, PhD, 1966. Chartered fin. analyst. Asst. prof. fin., econs. Nev. So. U., Las Vegas, 1965-67; asst. prof. Tex. Christian U., Ft. Worth, 1967-70, assoc. prof., 1970—2002, assoc. prof. emeritus, 2003—. Asst. dir. Am. Free Enterprise Inst. Contbr. articles to 50 profl. jours. Mem. Southwestern Econs. Assn. (pres. 1990-91), Southwestern Soc. Economists (pres. 1992-93), N.Am. Econs. and Fin. Assn. (adv. bd.), Assn. for Investment Mgmt. and Rsch., Am. Econ. Assn. (life), Alpha Kappa Psi, Beta Gamma Sigma, Phi Alpha Theta, Alpha Sigma Phi, Omicron Delta Epsilon, Order of Omega. Avocations: tennis, golf.

BECKER, DAVID, artist, educator; b. Milw., Aug. 16, 1937; s. Walter Gustav and Fern Bertha (Raddatz) B.; m. Catherine Claytor, Aug. 27, 1960 (div. 1981); children: Sarah Lynne, Amelia Elisabeth; m. Patricia Ann Fennell, Nov. 13, 1988; 1 child, Sloane Fennell. Student, Layton Sch. Art, 1956-58; BS, U. Wis., Milw., 1961; MFA, U. Ill., 1965. Asst. prof. Wayne State U., Detroit, 1965-71, assoc. prof., 1971-80, prof., 1980-85; assoc. prof. U. Wis., Madison, 1985-87, prof., 1987—. Vis. prof. U. Wis., Madison, 1985—87; vis. artist Utah State U., Logan, 1981; art lectr. in field; rep. by Ann Nathan Gallery, Chgo. Exhbns. include Mus. Fine Arts, Boston, 1965, 75, Butler Inst. Am. Art, Youngstown, Ohio, 1967, 68, 72, Lawrence Stevens Gallery, Detroit, 1968, Detroit Inst. Arts, 1971, 77, 86, 91, Richard Nash Gallery, Seattle, 1974, Franz Bader Gallery, Washington, 1974, 77, 80, Madison (Wis.) Art Ctr., 1975, 79, Libr. of Congress, Washington, 1975, Honolulu Acad. Arts, 1975, 83, ADI Gallery, San Francisco, 1975, London Arts Gallery, Detroit, 1976, Boston Ctr. Arts, 1976, 78, Museo de Arte Moderno, Cali, Colombia, 1976, 77, 81, Bawag Found., Vienna, Austria, 1976, Bklyn. Mus., 1976, 84, Met. Mus., Miami, Fla., 1977, 80, Habatat Galleries, Dearborn, Mich., 1977, Visual Arts Ctr. Alaska, Anchorage, 1978, 86, Cranbrook Acad. Art, Bloomfield Hills, Mich., 1980, Associated Am. Artists Gallery, Phila., 1980, Phila. Art Alliance/Phila. Print Club, 1980, Kalamazoo (Mich.) Inst. Arts, 1980, 86, Nat. Mus. Am. Art, Washington, 1982, DeCordova Mus., Lincoln, Mass., 1982, 86, USIA, 1983, Saginaw (Mich.) Mus. Art, 1984, Brockton (Mass.) Mus. Art, 1984, Mich. Gallery, Detroit, 1986, Neville-Sargent Gallery, Chgo., 1986, Intergrafic, East Berlin, 1984, 87, 9th Brit. Internat. Print Biennale, Bradford, 1986, Jane Haslem Gallery, Washington, 1987, 90, 92, 93, John Szoke Graphics, N.Y.C., 1988, Silvermine Gallery, Stamford, Conn., 1988, Elvehjem Mus. Art, Madison, 1989, Boston Printmakers 42d and 43d Nat. Print Exhbn., 1993, Fitchburg (Mass.) Mus. Art, 1990, New Orleans Mus. Art, 1990, NAD, N.Y.C., 1986, 87, 90, 91, 92, 93, 94, The Hoyt Inst. Fine Arts, New Castle, Pa., 1992, Sodarco Gallery, Montreal, 1993, Davidson Galleries, Seattle, 1993, Galleria Mesa, Mesa, Ariz., 1993, Intergrafia, Katowice, Poland, 1994, Sapporo Internat. Print Biennale, Japan, 1993, Maastricht Internat. Print Biennale, The Netherlands, 1993, Outside Art Fair, N.Y.C., 2002, Arch Chgo., Navy Pier, 2002, 03; permanent collections include: Libr. of Congress, Washington, Art Inst. Chgo., Rose Art Mus., Waltham, Mass., Elvehjem Mus. Art, Madison, Wis., Butler Inst. Am. Art, Minot (N.D.) Art Assn., Silvermine Guild Arts, New Canaan, Conn., Honolulu Acad. Arts, N.Y. Pub. Libr., Detroit Inst. Art, Museo de Arte Moderno, Bklyn. Mus., Met. Mus., Miami, Nat. Mus. Am. Art, Washington, Portland (Oreg.) Art Mus., Art Ctr., South Bend, Ind., USIA, Prague, Czech Republic, and numerous colls. and univs. 1st lt. U.S. Army, 1961-63. Creative Artist grantee Mich. Coun. Arts, 1982; NEA Visual Arts fellow, 1993-94. Fellow The MacDowell Colony; mem. NAD (nat. academician). Home: 2512 Lunde Ln Mount Horeb WI 53572-2440 Office: U Wis Art Dept 6241 Humanities Bldg Madison WI 53706 E-mail: dhbecker@facstaff.wisc.edu.

BECKER, DAVID MANDEL, law educator, author, consultant; b. Chgo., Dec. 31, 1935; m. Sandra Kaplan, June 30, 1957; children: Laura, Andrew, Scott. AB, Harvard Coll., 1957; JD, U. Chgo., 1960. Bar: Ill. 1960. Assoc. Becker and Savin, Chgo., 1960-62; instr. law U. Mich., Ann Arbor, 1962-63; from asst. prof. law to prof. Washington U., St. Louis, 1963—93, Joseph H. Zumbalen prof. law, 1993—, assoc. dean external rels., 1998—. Author: (with David Gibberman) Legal Checklists, 1968, and ann. supplements; Legal Checklists-Specially Selected Forms, 1977, and ann. supplements; Perpetuities and Estate Planning: Potential Problems and Effective Solutions, 1993; contbr. numerous articles to profl. jours. Recipient Founders Day award Washington U. Alumni Assn., 1973, Tchr. of Yr. award Washington U., 1980, 89, Disting. Tchr. award Washington U. Sch. Law Alumni, 1988. Home: 843 Woodmoor Dr Saint Louis MO 63132-3518 Office: Washington U Sch Law Saint Louis MO 63130

BECKER, DOUGLAS WESLEY, lawyer; b. St. Louis, July 12, 1950; s. Donald William and Joetta Lea (Greer) B.; m. Deborah Ackerman, June 10, 1972 (div. Oct. 1985); 1 child, Laura Marie; m. Kimberly Dinsdale, Apr. 30, 1989; children: MacKenzie Brooke, Mallory Greer. BBA, So. Meth. U., 1972,

JD, 1976. Bar: Tex. 1976, U.S. Supreme Ct. 1979; cert. residential and comml. real estate law Tex. Bd. Legal Specialization. Ptnr. Gresham, Davis, Gregory, Worthy & Moore, San Antonio, 1976—82; mem. Kaufman, Becker, Reibach & Richie, Inc., San Antonio, 1983—94, Cauthorn, Hale, Hornberger, Fuller, Sheehan, Becker & Beiter, San Antonio, 1994—2003; closing atty. Chgo. Title Ins. Co., San Antonio, 2003—. Contbr. articles to profl. jours. Pres. Vis. Nurse Assn., San Antonio, 1982; trustee, chmn. San Antonio Regional Hosp., 1993-94. Staff sgt. USAR, 1971-77. Mem.: San Antonio Real Estate Coun. (chmn. govt. affairs com. 1993—94, sec. 1994—95, v.p. 1995—96, bd. dirs. 2003—), San Antonio Bd. Realtors (bd. dirs. cert. comml. investment mem. chpt. 1992—93, 1998—2002), Am. Coll. Real Estate Lawyers, San Antonio Young Lawyers Assn. (pres. 1984), Tex. Assn. Bank Counsel, Tex. Coll. Real Estate (bd. dirs.), State Bar Tex. (coun. real estate, probate and trust law sects. 1993—97, treas. 2002—03, chmn.-elect 2003—), Oak Hills Country Club (bd. dirs. 1993—97). Avocations: golf, skiing, trivia, reading, real estate. Office: Chgo Title Ins Co 755 E Mulberry Ste 125 San Antonio TX 78212 E-mail: beckerd@ctt.com.

BECKER, DWIGHT LOWELL, physician; b. Mercer County, Ohio, July 21, 1918; s. George and Maude R. (Purdyzz) B.; m. Mary Lauer, Sept. 6, 1942; children— Lawrence, Judith, George Edward. BA, Ohio State U., 1940, MD, 1943. Intern Christ Hosp., Cin., 1943-44; gen. practice medicine Lima, Ohio, 1946-65; emergency room practice, 1965-87; mem. staff Lima Meml. Hosp.; med. dir. Blue Cross of Lima, 1970-87; past student health dir. Ohio No. U.; med. dir. Auglaize County Health Dept., Wapakoneta, Ohio, 1994—; ret., 1999. Past chmn. bd. Ohio Med. Indemnity, Inc., Worthington; field med. cons. Ohio Vocat. Rehab.; past bd. dir. Met. Bank, Lima. Mem. Allen County Bd. Health, 1952-55; past v.p. bd. dirs. Allen County Coun. on Aging; past med. advisor Lima and Allen County Vis. Nurses Assn.; past bd. dirs. Sta WIMA, Lima. Served to capt. M.C. AUS, 1944-46. Mem. Am. Coll. Emergency Physicians, AMA, Ohio Med. Assn., Phi Beta Kappa. Clubs: Masons, Shawnee Country, Elks. Republican. Home and Office: 1 Galvin Ln Lima OH 45805-3870 E-mail: dlbmkl@wcoil.com.

BECKER, EDWARD A. accounting educator, consultant; b. Phila., Jan. 9, 1938; s. Henry L. and Anne M. (Miller) B.; m. Esther Lipson, Aug. 23, 1959 (div. Oct. 1970); children: Felisa R., Jacki M. BS in Acctg., Temple U., 1959; MBA, Drexel U., 1967; PhD, Pa. State U., 1984. CPA, Washington, Pa., N.C. Sr. staff acct. Jack H. Felzer & Co., CPA, Bala Cynwyd, Pa., 1960-67; sr. corp. staff auditor Radio Corp. of Am., N.Y.C., 1967-68; regional controller Laventhol & Horwath, CPA, Phila., 1968-70; treas., controller Scanforms, Inc., Bristol, Pa., 1970-72; controller Empire Assocs., Inc., Phila., 1972-76; sr. staff acct. Friedlander Dunn & Co., CPA, Jenkintown, 1976-77; asst. prof. Bucknell U., Lewisburg, Pa., 1977-83, Va. Commonwealth U., Richmond, 1983-84; assoc. prof. U. N.C., Wilmington, 1984-86; prof., dir. master acctg. program Nova U., Ft. Lauderdale, Fla., 1986-92; cons., Lauderhill, Fla., 1986—. Mem. New Hanover (N.C.) County Commrs.' Performance Adv. Task Force, 1985-86; frequent speaker for profl. orgns. Reviewer Acad. Accounting Historians Working Paper series, 1982—; editorial bd. Pa. CPA Spokesman/Pa. CPA Jour., 1980-82, 84-85; contbr. articles to profl. jours. Recipient Legion of Honor Chapel of the Four Chaplains, Temple U., 1982. Mem. Beta Gamma Sigma. Home: 792 NW 84th Ln Coral Springs FL 33071-7126 E-mail: EdBeckeratHome@aol.com.

BECKER, EDWARD ROY, judge; b. Phila., May 4, 1933; s. Herman A. and Jeannette (Levit) Becker; m. Flora Lyman, Aug. 11, 1957; children: James Daniel(dec.), Jonathan Robert, Susan Rose, Charles Lyman. BA, U. Pa., 1954; LLB, Yale U., 1957; LLD (hon.), Temple U., 2003. Bar: Pa. 1957. Ptnr. Becker, Becker & Fryman, Phila., 1957—70; U.S. Dist. Judge, 1970—82; judge U.S. Ct. Appeals (3d cir.), 1982—98, chief judge, 1998—2003, sr. judge, 2003—. Counsel Rep. City Com., Phila., 1965—70; mem. task force on implementation of new jud. article Joint State Govt. Commn., 1969; lectr. law U. Pa. Law Sch., 1978—83; mem. edn. adv. com. concerning Comprehensive Crime Control Act Fed. Jud. Ctr., 1981—90, Fed. Jud. Ctr. Com. on Sentencing, Probation and Pretrial Svcs., 1985—90; bd. dirs. Fed. Jud. Ctr., 1991—95; mem. faculty sr. appellate judges seminar Inst. Jud. Adminstrn., N.Y.C., 1992—94. Bd. editors: Manual for Complex Litigation, 1981—90; contbr. articles to profl. jours. Trustee Magna Carta Found., Phila.; vis. com. U. Chgo. Law Sch., 1988—91; chair Rhodes Scholarship Selection Com. Dist. II (Pa., N.Y., Vt., N.H.), 1996—98; bd. mem. Historic Phila., Inc., 2001—; bd. mem., adv. bd. Am. Soc. of Internat. Law, 2000. Mem.: ABA (jud. rep. antitrust sect. 1983—86), Jud. Conf. U.S. (com. on adminstrn. probation sys. 1979—87, chmn. com. on criminal law and probation adminstrn. 1987—90, com. on long range planning 1991—96, exec. com. 1998—2003), Am. Law Inst. (mem. ALI-ABA com. 1992—, chmn. program subcom. 1996—99, adv. com. restatement conflict of laws 2d), Am. Judicature Soc. (Devitt award 2001), Phila. Bar Assn., Phi Beta Kappa. Jewish. Home: 936 Herbert St Philadelphia PA 19124-2417 Office: US Ct Appeals 19613 US Courthouse 601 Market St Philadelphia PA 19106-1713

BECKER, ELIZABETH ANNE, secondary education educator; b. Winston-Salem, N.C., Aug. 27, 1959; d. Byron Gustav Becker and Shirley Anne Howard; m. Duane Allen Johnson, June 27, 1981 (div. 1991); children: Christopher, Matthew; m. Thomas Everett Edmonds, Aug. 17, 1991; stepchildren: Jacob, Sarah. AAS, Sauk Valley Coll., Dixon, Ill., 1979; BS in Biology summa cum laude, Radford U., 1998; postgrad. in neurobiology and anatomy, Wake Forest U., 1998-99; MS in Edn., Radford U., 2000. Registered clin. lab. scientist; lic. collegiate profl., Va. Med. lab. technician St. Joseph Hosp., Belvedere, Ill., 1980-88, Pulaski (Va.) Hosp., 1988-90; clin. lab. scientist Giles Meml. Hosp., Pearesburg, Va., 1990-95; biology tchr. Carroll County H.S., Hillsville, Va., 2000—; sci. rschr. Radford U., 1996—99. Vol., Spl. Olympics, Radford, Va., 1998; cub scout leader, Cub Scouts A., 1990, 91; coord. infant and child support group, SHARE, Belvedere, 1986, 87, 88; ednl. advisor Nat. Youth Leadership Forum Medicine, 2002. Mem. AAAS, Nat. Sci. Tchrs. Assn., Nat. Cert. Agy. for Clin. Scientists, Beta Beta Beta (pres. Sigma Rho chpt. 1997-98, Excellence in Rsch. award 1998), Omicron Delta Kappa (life). Achievements include research in desert funnel-web spiders courtship behavior; discovery of male pheromone transmission. Avocations: sculpting, pen and ink, hiking, remodeling, behavior research. Home: 286 Huddle Rd Wytheville VA 24382 Office: Carroll County High Sch Rt 58 Hillsville VA 24343

BECKER, ELIZABETH WALLACE, elementary school guidance counselor; b. Charleston, W.Va., Apr. 14, 1972; d. Harry Alvin III and Mary Merrill Wallace; m. Frank Joseph Becker, June 6, 1998. Bachelor's, Conn. Coll., 1994; Master's, U. Va., 1996. Cert. nat. counselor. Sch. guidance counselor Charlottesville (Va.) City Schs., 1996-99, Hanover (Va.) County Schs., 1999—. Mem. Am. Counseling Assn.

BECKER, FRAWLEY, film company executive; s. Arthur A. and Mildred (Cohen) Becker. BA, U. Pa., 1950; postgrad., Oxford (Eng.) U., 1956. Asst. entertainment dir. Spl. Svcs. Hdqrs. Dept. of the Army, Paris, 1958—61; mng. dir. Paris Playhouse, 1961—63; dialogue coach, dialogue dir. various film cos., Paris, 1964—72; asst. to prodr. (film) Weingarten Prodns., L.A., 1973—74; rsch. writer (t.v.) Columbia Pictures, Burbank, Calif., 1974—75; location mgr. (film) various film cos., Calif., 1976—; prodn. exec. (film) Disney Studios, Burbank, 1990—91. Founder, dir. Studio 128, Paris, 1957—61, Harlequin Guild, Paris, 1959—61; founder, dir., mng. dir. Paris Playhouse, 1961—63; French interpreter Olympic Games, 1984. Author: (screenplays) But Not A Drop to Drink, 1973, Columbo Stories, 1975, On The Way Out, 1976, The Strike, 1976, Behold the Evening Spider, 1980, The Gang's All Where?, 1989, Bonjour Homicide, 1995, (plays) Dreamhouse, 1987, The Picture They Never Made, 1987, Bashing, 1990, 411 Joseph, 1998, Never Fall in Love with A Fireman, 2001, Tiger by the Tail, 2003, (novels) Tittyboo For President, 1984, (memoirs) Seeing Stars, 2001, short stories. French interpreter 1984 Olympics Games. Cpl. U.S. Army, 1951—53, Korea. Avocations: cooking, travel. Home: 15016 Archwood St Van Nuys CA 91405

BECKER, FRED REINHARDT, JR., association executive, lawyer, retired military officer; b. Louisville, June 14, 1949; s. Fred Reinhardt and Olivia (Nicklies) B.; m. Barbara Lee Sheinhouse, Sept. 8, 1973; children: Kimberly Lee, Lori Michelle, Melissa Olivia, Ashley Nicole. BS, U.S. Naval Acad., 1971; JD, Coll. William and Mary, 1979; MBA, Va. Tech. U., 1998. Bar: Va. 1979, U.S. Ct. Appeals (4th cir.) 1979. Commd. ensign USN, 1971, capt., 1992; aide-de-camp Jr. Armed Forces Staff Coll., Norfolk, Va., 1974-76; from pros. atty. to head pros. atty. Naval Legal Service Office, Norfolk, 1979-81, exec. officer, 1981-83; head procurement and plans div. Office of JAG, Alexandria, Va., 1983-85; atty. office of legis. affairs USN, Washington, 1985-87, mil. advisor to assoc. dir. Nat. Security and Internat. Affairs, Office of Mgmt. and Budget, Exec. Office of Pres., 1987-89, asst. fleet legal advisor comdr.-in-chief U.S. Pacific Fleet Pearl Harbor, Hawaii, 1989-90, fleet judge adv., comdr. 3d fleet San Diego, 1990-92; legal counsel Bur. Naval Personnel, Washington, 1992-94; dir. legis. Navy Office Legis. Affairs, Washington, 1994-96; naval affairs dir. Res. Officers Assn., Washington, 1996-2000; pres., CEO Nat. Assn. Fed. Credit Unions, Arlington, Va., 2000—. Adj. instr. bus. mgmt. dept. U. Md., College Park, 1982-94. Bd. dirs. Consumer Fedn. Am., Nat. Coop. Bus. Assn., Nat. Assn. Fed. Credit Unions Svcs. Corp. Recipient Exemplary Svc. medal Surgeon Gen., 1999, Meritorious Pub. Svc. award USCG, 1999. Mem.: ABA (award of profl. merit 1979), Va. Bar Assn., Order of Coif, Beta Gamma Sigma, Phi Alpha Delta. Democrat. Mem. Christian Ch. (Disciples Of Christ). Home: 7606 Maritime Ln Springfield VA 22153-1627 Office: Nat Assn Fed Credit Unions 3138 Tenth St N Arlington VA 22201-2149 E-mail: fbecker@nafcu.org.

BECKER, GAIL ROSELYN, museum director; b. Long Branch, N.J., Oct. 22, 1942; d. Joseph and Adele (Michelsohn) B. BA, Vassar Coll., 1964. Exhibit project officer U.S. Info. Agy., Washington, 1967-87, chief devel. and prodn. exhibits, 1987-91; exec. dir. Louisville Sci. Ctr. (formerly Mus. History and Sci.), 1991—. Bd. dirs. Louisville Advanced Tech. Coun., 1993-2000, Louisville Com. Fgn. Rels., Main St. Assn., 1998—, Arts and Cultural Attractions Coun., 1999 ; active Leadership Louisville. Recipient Presdl. Design awards Nat. Endowment for the Arts, Washington, 1984, 88, 92, Special Achievement award U.S. Info. Agy., Washington, 1988. Mem. Am. Assn. Mus. (bd. dirs. 1994-97), Assn. Sci.-Tech. Ctrs. (bd. dirs. 1992—, pres. 1999-2001), Vassar Coll. Alumnae Assn., Rotary. Office: Louisville Sci Ctr 727 W Main St Louisville KY 40202-2681

BECKER, GARY STANLEY, economist, educator; b. Pottsville, Pa., Dec. 2, 1930; s. Louis William and Anna (Siskind) Becker; m. Doria Slote, Sept. 19, 1954 (dec.); children: Judith Sarah, Catherine Jean; m. Guity Nashat, Oct. 31, 1979; children: Michael Claffey, Cyrus Claffey. AB summa cum laude, Princeton U., 1951, PhD (hon.), 1991; AM, U. Chgo., 1953, PhD, 1955, Hebrew U., Jerusalem, 1985, Knox Coll., 1985, U. Ill., Chgo., 1988, SUNY, 1990, U. Palermo, Buenos Aires, 1993, Columbia U., 1993, Warsaw (Poland) Sch. Econs., 1995, U. Econs., Prague, Czech Republic, 1995, U. Miami, 1995, U. Rochester, 1995, Hofstra U., 1997, U. d'Aix-Marselles, 1999, U. Athens, 2002, Harvard U., 2003. Asst. prof. U. Chgo., 1954—57; from asst. prof. to assoc. prof. Columbia U., N.Y.C., 1957—60, prof. econs., 1960—68, Arthur Lehman prof. econs., 1968—70; prof. econs. U. Chgo., 1970—83, Univ. prof. econs. and sociology, 1983—2002, chmn. dept. econs., 1984—85, Univ. prof. econs., sociology, and Grad. Sch. Bus., 2002—. Ford Found. vis. prof. econs. U. Chgo., 1969—70; assoc. Econs. Rsch. Ctr. Nat. Opinion Rsch. Ctr., Chgo., 1980—; mem. domestiv adv. bd. Hoover Instn., Stanford, Calif., 1973—91, sr. fellow, 1990—; mem. acad. adv. bd. Am. Enterprise Inst., 1987—91; rsch. policy advisor Ctr. for Econ. Analysis Human Behavior Nat. Bur. Econ. Rsch., 1972—78; mem. and sr. rsch. assoc. Monetary Policy, Min. Fin., Japan, 1988—; bd. dirs. Unext.com, 1999—; affiliate Lexecon Corp., 1990—2002. Author: The Economics of Discrimination, 1957, (2d edit.), 1971, Human Capital, 1964, (3d edit.), 1993, (Japanese transl.), 1975, (Spanish transl.), 1984, (Chinese transl.), 1987, (Romanian transl.), 1997, Human Capital and the Personal Distribution of Income: An Analytical Approach, 1967, Economic Theory, 1971, (Japanese transl.), 1976; author: (with Gilbert Ghez) The Allocation of Time and Goods Over the Life Cycle, 1975; author: The Economic Approach to Human Behavior, 1976, (German transl.), 1982, (Polish transl.), 1990, (Chinese transl.), 1993, (Romanian transl.), 1994, (Italian transl.), 1998, A Treatise on the Family, 1981, (expanded edit.), 1991, (Spanish transl.), 1987, (Chinese transl.), 1988, 2000, Accounting for Tastes, 1996, (Czech transl.), 1998, (Chinese transl.), 1999, (Italian transl.), 2000; author: (with Guity Nashat Becker) The Economics of Life, 1996, (Chinese transl.), 1997, with Guity Nashat Becker: The Economics of Life, 1998, (Spanish transl.), 2002; author: (in German) Family, Society and State, 1996; author: (in Italian) L'approccio Economico al Comportamento Umano, 1998; author: (with Kevin M. Murphy) Social Economics, 2000; editor: Essays in Labor Economics in Honor of H. Gregg Lewis, 1976; co-editor (with William M. Landes): Essays in the Economics of Crime and Punishment, 1974; columnist: Bus. Week, 1985—; contbr. articles to profl. jours. Recipient W.S. Woytinsky award, U. Mich., 1964, Profl. Achievement award, U. Chgo. Alumni Assn., 1968, Frank E. Seidman Disting. award in Polit. Economy, 1985, merit award, NIH, 1986, John R. Commons award, Omicron Delta Epsilon, 1987, Nobel prize in Econ. Sci., 1992, award, Lord Found., 1995, Irene Taueber award, 1997, Nat. medal Sci., 2000, Phoenix award, U. Chgo., 2000, award, Am. Acad. Achievement, 2001, Heartland prize, 2002. Fellow: Am. Econ. Assn. (Disting., v.p. 1974, pres. 1987, John Bates Clark medal 1967), Am. Acad. Arts and Scis., Nat. Assn. Bus. Economists, Econometic Soc., Am. Statis. Assn.; mem.: NAE, NAS, Nat. Assn. Bus. Economists, Econ. History Assn., Pontifical Acad. Scis., Western Econ. Assn. (v.p. 1995—96, pres. 1996—97), Mont Pelerin Soc. (exec. bd. dirs. 1985—96, v.p. 1989—90, pres. 1990—92), Internat. Union for Sci. Study Population, Am. Philos. Soc., Nat. Assn. Bus. Economists, Phi Beta Kappa. Office: U Chgo Dept Econs 1126 E 59th St Chicago IL 60637-1580

BECKER, GEORGE, labor union administrator; b. Madison, Ill. Staff rep. United Steelworkers of Am., Ill., 1965-75, safety and health technician, 1975-85, internat. v.p. adminstrn., 1985-94, internat. pres., 1994—2001. V.p. exec. coun., chmn. econ. policy com. AFL-CIO; mem. exec. com. Internat. Metalworkers Fedn., Geneva; chmn. world rubber coun. Internat. Fedn. Chem., Energy, Mine and Gen. Workers' Unions, Brussels; apptd. by Pres. Clinton to Pres.'s Export Coun.; confirmed by congress to U.S. Trade and Environ. Policy Adv. Com., Washington. Office: United Steelworkers of America 5 Gateway Ctr Pittsburgh PA 15222-1214

BECKER, GERALD ARTHUR, publisher; b. Elyria, Ohio, Sept. 29, 1941; s. Louis A. and Eleanor (Phillipson) B.; m. Ryna L. Trope, Nov. 27, 1965; children: David, Adam. BS in Journalism, Ohio U., 1963. Asst. to pub. Penton Publ., Inc., Cleve., 1964-69; editorial dir. CRC Press, Cleve., 1969-77; v.p., assoc. pub. Oster Communications, Chgo., 1977-84; pub. Commodity Perspective div. Knight Ridder, Inc., Chgo., 1984-91, Commodity Research Bur. div. Knight Ridder, Inc., N.Y.C., 1984-91; pub. fin. publishing group Knight-Ridder, Inc., 1991-93; v.p. mktg. Knight-Ridder Fin. Americas, Chgo., 1993-94; v.p. global product mktg.-commodities Knight-Ridder Fin., Inc., Chgo., 1995-96; pres. The Insight Group, Inc., Arlington Heights, Ill., 1996—2000; pub. Candy Industries Mag. divsn. Stagnito Comms., Deeerfield, Ill., 2001—. Served with USCGR, 1963-69. Mem. Futures Industry Assn. (pres., sec. mktg. div.). Avocations: tennis, bowling, reading, music, swimming. Home: 3270 N Windsor Dr Arlington Heights IL 60004-1615 Office: Stagnito Comms 155 Pfingsten Rd Ste 205 Deerfield IL 60015 E-mail: jbecker@stagnito.com.

BECKER, HAROLD, film director, producer; b. New York, NY, 1950; Prodr., dir. films The Ragman's Daughter, 1972, Malice, 1993 (winner audience award best and best dir. award Cognac Festival du Film Policier), City Hall, 1996, Domestic Disturbance, 2001; dir. The Onion Field, 1979, Taps, 1981, The Boost, 1988, Vision Quest, 1985, Sea of Love, 1989, Bodily Harm, 1993, Mercury Rising, 1998, Solo, 1999, others. Office: c/o Jim Wiatt William Morris Agy 151 El Camino Dr Beverly Hills CA 90212

BECKER, HERBERT LAWRENCE, writer, accountant; b. Hollywood, Fla., Aug. 12, 1956; s. Jack and Lorraine (Abrams) B.; m. Malka Gasner, Jan. 1, 1977 (div. Jan. 1990); children: Randi, Adam, Brian; m. Shelly Basser, Nov. 8, 1992; children: Gillah, Dovid, Nehemiah, Ezra. BBA, Roosevelt U., Belgium, 1983, MBA, 1984; DBA, Columbia U., 1997. CPA, Belgium; cert. mgmt. acct., Soc. Pub. Accts. Dist. mgr. Coles Book Stores, U.S. and Can., 1976-83; pub. acct., U.S. and Can., 1983-87; sr. fin. mgr. Video One, Can., 1987-90; pres. Postal Plus Svcs., Can., 1990-93; CEO BEE Multimedai, Montreal, 1995—2000; pres., CEO EnterVision, Inc., 2001—. Author: All the Secrets of Magic, 1994, Magic Secrets, 1996,, So That's How They Do It, 1996, Magic Secrets, 1997-98; (tv spls.) World's Greatest Magic Secrets . . . Revealed, More Magic Secrets, 1997, World's Greatest Magic Secrets, 1999, 101 Greatest Magic Secrets Exposed, 2002. Democrat. Avocations: writing, magic, Karate. Office: BEE Multimedia 78541 CP Wilderton Montreal QC Canada H3S 2W9

BECKER, HERMAN ELI, retired pharmacist; b. N.Y.C., Mar. 27, 1910; s. Abraham Jacob and Esther (Sabin) B.; m. Mina Becker, Sept. 13, 1936; children: Jerome David, Stanley Harold (dec. 1996). Degree in pharmacy, Med. Coll. Va., 1931. RPh, Va. Pharmacist, asst. mgr. Peoples Drug Stores, Richmond, Va., 1931-38; pharmacist Grant Drug Store, Richmond, 1938-40; co-owner, mgr. Blvd. Grant Drug Co., Richmond, 1940-48; pharmacist, asst. mgr. Meadowbridge Pharmacy, Richmond, 1948-67; pharmacist, asst. drug buyer Gem Drug Co., Richmond, 1967-69; pharmacist St. Mary's Hosp., Richmond, 1969-71; pharmacist, asst. mgr. various pharmacies, Richmond, 1971-89. V.p., chmn. bd. Temple Beth El, Richmond, 1963-64, lay reader evening svcs.; bd. dirs. Beth Sholom Home for Aged, Richmond, 1979-84; active Richmond Jewish Ctr., 1990. Recipient Disting. Worker award Temple Beth El, 1965, Samuel Gerson award, 1978, Methuselah award Beth Sholom Home for Aged, 1984. Mem. Richmond Pharm. Assn. (pres. 1957-58, dist. pres. svc. award 1957, human rels. award 1962), Va. Pharm. Assn., Am. Acad. Gen. Pharmacy Practice, B'nai Brith, Masons, Omega Chi. Republican. Home: 5108 Downy Ln # 101 Richmond VA 23228-3950

BECKER, ISIDORE A. business executive; b. N.Y.C., May 10, 1926; s. Max and Eva (Chester) B.; m. Adele Sandler, Dec. 20, 1947; children: Steven Richard, Carol Ann. BA, Bklyn. Coll., 1949. Partner Herbert D. Silver & Co., N.Y.C., 1956-63; fin. v.p., chmn. financial com. Rapid-Am. Corp., N.Y.C., 1966-72, vice chmn. bd., 1967-72, 76-82, dir., 1964-82, pres., 1972-76; chief financial officer, treas. McCrory Corp., N.Y.C., 1964-70, dir., 1964-82; vice chmn. bd., dir. Glen Alden Corp., N.Y.C., 1967-72; chmn. bd., dir. Schenley Industries, Inc., 1968-82; pres. Riviera Hotel, Inc., 1973-83; chmn. bd. Shaw-Ross Internat. Importers, Inc., 1983—, Southern Wine & Spirits, 1983—. Vice chmn. bd. Boys Town Jerusalem; founder Albert Einstein Coll. Medicine; asso. chmn., bd. govs. Anti Defamation League B'nai B'rith. Served with USMCR, 1944-46. Home: 10155 Collins Ave Bal Harbour FL 33154-1655 Office: 15960 NW 15th Ave Miami FL 33169-5608

BECKER, JAMES MURDOCH, surgeon, educator; b. Cleve., Jan. 7, 1949; s. Norman O. and Mildred Edith (Murdoch) B.; m. Christine Louise Lohmann, Dec. 30, 1972; children: Alexander, Selby, Catherine, Anne. BA in Biology, Yale U., 1971; MD, Case Western Res. U., 1975. Diplomate Nat. Bd. Med. Examiners, Am. Bd. Surgery; lic. surgeon, Minn., Utah, Mo., Mass. Intern in surgery U. Utah Hosps., Salt Lake City, 1975-76, resident in gen. surgery, 1976-79, chief resident in surgery, 1979—80; research fellow in surgery U. Utah Sch. Medicine, 1977-78, asst. prof. surgery, 1982-86; NIH rsch. fellow digestive diseases Mayo Clinic, 1980-82; mem. surg. staff VA Hosp., Salt Lake City, 1982-86, chief green service, 1983-86, head nutritional support team, 1983-86; mem. cons. staff Intermountain Unit Shriners Hosps. for Crippled Children, Salt Lake City, 1984-86; assoc. prof. surgery, dir. gastrointestinal surgery Washington U. Sch. Medicine, 1986-89; assoc. prof surgery, chief divsn. gen. and gastroint. surg. Harvard Med. Sch./Brigham and Women's Hosp., Boston, 1989-94; James Utley prof. and chmn. surgeon-in-chief Boston U. Sch. Medicine/Boston Med. Ctr., 1994—. Contbr. articles to profl. jours., chpts. to books. NIH fellow, Mayo Clinic, 1980-82; grantee Johnson & Johnson Products, Inc., 1985, NIH, 1985—, Sandoz Corp., 1985-87, Ethicon, Inc., 1985-86. Mem. ACS, AMA, Am. Gastroenterol. Assn., Am. Motility Soc., Am. Pancreatic Assn., Assn. Acad. Surgery, Am. Soc. Parenteral and Enteral Nutrition, Internat. Biliary Assn., Collegium Internat. Chirurgiae Digestivae (Grassi prize 8th World Congress 1984), Soc. for Surgery Alimentary Tract, Soc. Univ. Surgeons, Yale U. Alumni Assn., Am. coll. Surgeons, Am. Surg. Assn., We. Surg. Assn., Cen. Surg. Assn., New Eng. Surg. Assn., Am. Soc. Colorectal Surgeons, Soc. Internat. Chirugiae, Soc. Surg. Oncology, Alpha Omega Alpha. Office: Boston Med Ctr 88 E Newton St Boston MA 02118-2308

BECKER, JAMES RICHARD, lawyer; b. San Juan, P.R., Sept. 25, 1954; s. John Joseph and Patricia (Doherty) B.; m. Mary E. McGurk; children: Colette Anne, Robert Charles II. BA in English, Va. Tech., 1977; JD, George Mason Law Sch., 1982. Bar: Va. 1982, U.S. Dist. Ct. (ea. and we. dists.) Va. 1982, U.S. Ct. Appeals (4th cir.) 1982. Atty. pvt. practice, Middleburg and Chantilly, Va., 1982-93; assoc. atty. Nichols, Bergere & Zauzig, P.C., Woodbridge, Va., 1993-94, Joel Atlas Skirble and Assocs., Falls Church, Va., 1994-98, Anderson & Corrie, Fairfax, Va., 1998-2000; atty. pvt. practice, Chantilly, 2000, 2003—; assoc. John A. Boneta & Assocs., Falls Church, 2001—03. Editor Law Rev., 1980-82. Mem. Fairfax Bar Assn. Avocations: computers, software development. Home: 4515 Fillingame Dr Chantilly VA 20151-2820 Office: 12600 Fair Lakes Cir Ste 220 Fairfax VA 22033-4904 E-mail: JamesRBecker@juno.com.

BECKER, JANET SUE, musician; b. Barberton, Ohio, Feb. 25, 1957; d. Eugene John Becker and Alice Janell (Keister) Kersker; m. Joseph Andrew Zolyak, Oct. 10, 1987; children: Andrew, James. BM, Cleve. Inst. of Music, 1979; MM, U. Akron, 1982; DM, Northwestern U., 1993. Instr. Cleve. Music Sch. Settlement, 1983-85, 86-90, Cleve. Inst. of Music, 1986-90, Malone Coll., Canton, Ohio, 1987—2001; gen. mgr. The Emerald Winds, Norton, Ohio, 1995—; musician Ohio, 1979—. Judge for competitions; lectr. in field. Contbr. articles to profl. jours. Flutist Watercolors Emsemble, Akron, 1987—. Recipient Performance Incentive grant Am. Composer's Forum, 1996. Mem. Ohio Music Tchrs. Assn. (state chair of student chpts. 1993—), Nat. Flute Assn., Coll. Music Soc., Am. Fedn. of Musicians, Pi Kappa Lambda, Mu Phi Epsilon (Musicological Rsch. award 1994). Home: 3614 Greenwich Rd Norton OH 44203-5523 E-mail: jbecker1@neo.rr.com.

BECKER, JEROME DAVID, writer; BA, U. Richmond, Va., 1965; MA, Pa. State U., State Coll., 1967; PhD, Am. U., Washington, 1974. Sports writer Hopewell (Va.) News, 1964-65; columnist, editl. writer Cin. Enquirer, 1974-84; editor, writer USA Today, Rosslyn, Va., 1984-86; assoc. dir. pub. affairs The White House, Washington, 1986-89; dep. dir. speechwriting Dept. Health and Human Svcs., Washington, 1989-91; speech writer to dir. Office Thrift Supervision, Washington, 1991-93; pub. affairs analyst, speechwriter Am. Petroleum Inst., Washington, 1993-99; sr. writer America's Cmty. Bankers, Washington, 1999—. Office: 900 19th St NW Ste 400 Washington DC 20006-2105

BECKER, JON ANDREW, arts and education consultant; b. Milw., Aug. 9, 1953; s. Raymond Matthias and Adeline (Yellen) B. BMus, Lawrence U., 1975; MS in Music Edn., U. Ill., 1987. Cert. K-12 music tchr. life Wis., N.J., K-12 music, Mich., supervision N.J. Tchr. Oconomowoc (Wis.) Public Schs., 1976-84; prof. Ripon (Wis.) Coll., 1987-88, Westminster Choir Coll., Princeton, N.J., 1988-91; arts edn. cons. Traverse City, Mich., 1991-99, Madison, Wis., 1999—. Cons. Ednl. Testing Svc., Princeton, 1989-91, Madison (Wis.) Symphony Orch., 2000, Wis. Edn. Assn. Coun., 1999, Edward Collins Fund Am. Music, 1999—, others; co-founder, coord. Watershed Suite Project, 1996—; founder Earth/Art Resources, 2001. Prodr. (CDs) Dancing Bear Music, 1998, NMC Music Department Presents!, 1998. Bd. dirs. Traverse Area Arts Coun., Traverse City, 1993-99, Mich. Assn. Cmty. Arts Agys., Southfield, Mich., 1995-99; pres.-elect Grand Traverse County Planning Commn., 1995. U. Ill. fellow, 1984-86. Mem. ASCD, Internat. Soc. of Music Educators (lect. 1990, St. Petersburg, Russia), Am. Fedn. of Musicians, Internat. Trombone Assn., Soc. of Music Tchr. Educators. Democrat. Avocations: environmental advocacy, outdoor activities.

BECKER, JULIA MARGARET, artist, educator; b. Cin., July 12, 1957; d. Flavian Thomas Becker and Peggy Becker Jackson; m. Daniel Shaw Biehl; 1 child, Eula Viva Becker Biehl. Student, Edgecliff Coll., 1976, U. Mont., 1977-79, Art Acad. Cin., 1975, 80; BA, Evergreen State Coll., 1985; MFA, Mont. State U., 1993. Tchr. Art for Kids Cin. Art Mus., 1987-90, Beall Park Art Ctr., Bozeman, Mont., 1994-96; facilitator, instr. Very Spl. Arts Mont., Bozeman, 1995-97, Great Falls, 1998—; adj. prof. Mont. State U., Bozeman, 1994-99, Great Falls, 1997—; artist-in-residence Great Falls Sch. Dist., 1996-98; asst. prof. art, dept. head U. Great Falls, 1998—2003, assoc. prof. art, dept. head, 2003—. Vis. lectr. Mont. State U., Bozeman, 1993-97; featured artist Festival of the Dead, Missoula, Mont., 1997; juror Sweet Pea Festival of the Arts, Bozeman, 1994; participant, artist The Caravan Project, Mont., 1995—. Artist numerous exhbns.; contbr. articles to profl. jours. Grantee Beall Park Art Ctr. and Mont. Arts Coun., 1994, P.E.O. Sisterhood, 1993, Mont. State U., 1994, Helena Presents and Colo. Dance Festival, 1995; Travel scholar grantee to South India, 2002, Svc. Learning Faculty fellow, 2002-03. Mem. Coll. Art Assn., Internat. Film and Video Assn., Rural Inst. on Disabilities. Democrat. Avocations: education, health, world ecology, disability studies, cultural studies, creative arts, world travel, endurance swimming. Office: U Great Falls Dept Art 1301 20th St S Great Falls MT 59405-4934 E-mail: jbecker@ugf.edu.

BECKER, JULIETTE, psychologist, marriage and family therapist; b. LA, Sept. 22, 1938; d. Louis Joseph and Elissa Cecelia (Bevacqua) Cevola; m. Richard Charles Sprenger, Aug. 13, 1960 (div. Dec. 1984); children: Lisa Anne, Stephen Louis, Gina Marie, Paul Joseph, Gretchen Lynette; m. Vance Benjiman Becker, Nov. 7, 1986. BA in Psychology, Calif. State U., Fullerton, 1983; M in Marriage and Family Therapy, U.S. Internat. U., 1985; PhD in Clin. Psychology, William Lyon U., 1988. Therapist Villa Park (Calif.) Psychol. Svcs., 1985-88, psychologist, 1988—. Owner, editor-in-chief Postcards from Your Mindseye Publs; prodr. audio books on stress mgmt. Mem. APA, Am. Assn. Marriage, Family and Child Therapists, Calif. Assn. Marriage, Family and Child Therapists. Avocations: painting, opera, classical piano, interior design, writing. Office: Becker Psychol Svcs 1451 Quail St #102 Newport Beach CA 92660 Fax: 714-283-3701; Office Fax: 949-757-1114. E-mail: juliettebecker@cox.net.

BECKER, KARL MARTIN, lawyer; b. Glenridge, N.J., May 30, 1943; s. Alfred Martin and Helen K. (Gramse) B.; m. Barbara A. Benton, Feb. 19, 1966; children— Glenn M., Mark W. AB, Yale U., 1965; JD, U. Chgo., 1968. Bar: Ill. 1968, S.C. 1994. Assoc. Vedder Price Kaufman Kammholz, Chgo., 1968-75, ptnr., 1975-78; asst. gen. counsel Esmark, Inc., Chgo., 1978-83, assoc. gen. counsel, 1983-84; v.p., gen. counsel, sec. Swift Ind. Corp., Chgo., 1985-86, sr. v.p., gen. counsel, sec., 1986; sr. v.p., gen. counsel Beatrice Cos., Inc. and BCI Holdings Corp., Chgo., 1986-87, E-II Holdings, Inc., Beatrice Co., Chgo., 1987-88, Beatrice Co., Chgo., 1988-90; dir. Mathers Fund, Inc., Bannockburn, Ill., 1991-98. Mem. ABA, S.C. Bar Assn. Avocations: skiing, sailing. Home: 31 Hearthwood Dr Hilton Head Island SC 29928-2906 E-mail: KBecker1@aol.com.

BECKER, KARLA LYNN, systems analyst; b. West Point, N.Y., Nov. 3, 1956; d. Fred D. and Margaret Erika (Buckmann) Spinks; m. Eric Louis Becker; children: Erika Margaret Augusta Ashmore, Eric Robert. BA, Ind. U.-Purdue U. at Indpls., 1982; MS, Ind. U., 1986. Cert. software quality engr. Mgr. Eastside Chiropractic Clinic, Indpls., 1978-80; English tutor univ. div. Ind. U.-Purdue U. at Indpls., 1980-82, composition instr. English dept., 1982-83, tech. writer computing services, 1983-84; tech. writer Ind. U. Adminstrv. Computing, 1984-87; mgmt. info. svcs. cons., writer, support adminstr. Simon Property Group, Indpls., 1987-97; sys. cons. KFORCE.COM, Indpls., 1997-99, sr. sys. analyst Eli Lilly & Co., Indpls., 1999—. Author: Composing Technical Documents, 2000; contbr. articles, book revs., poems to various publs.; editor: Lit. Jour., Genesis, All-Am. Mag., Am. Collegiate Press Assn., 1983. Mem. Am. Soc. Quality, Soc. Tech. Communication (Cert. of Achievement 1985), Sigma Delta Chi, Pi Lambda Theta. Democrat. Roman Catholic. Avocations: singing, yoga. Office: Eli Lilly & Co Lilly Corp Ctr Drop Code 3118 Ctr Indianapolis IN 46285-0001 E-mail: karla11@hotmail.com.

BECKER, KENNETH H. physician; b. Oct. 2, 1957; MD, Ross U., Rosseau, Dominica, 1984. Physician in pvt. practice, East Setauket, NY, 1987—; attending physician St. Charles Hosp. and Rehab. Ctr., Port Jefferson, N.Y., 1987—, John T. Mather Meml. Hosp., Port Jefferson, 1987—; physician Suffolk County Correctional Facility, Yaphank, N.Y., 1987-89; clin. assoc. prof. dept. family medicine SUNY, Stony Brook, 1988—. Maj. U.S. Army Res., 1989-97. Mem. Three Village Kiwanis. Office: 12 Brewster Ln Setauket NY 11733-3224

BECKER, LAWRENCE CARLYLE, philosopher, educator, writer; b. Lincoln, Nebr., Apr. 26, 1939; s. Albert Carlyle and Harriette (Toren) B.; m. Charlotte Ann Burner, June 10, 1967. BA in History, Midland Coll., 1961; MA in Philosophy, U Chgo., 1963, PhD in Philosophy, 1965; LHD (hon.), Midland Luth. Coll., 1994. Instr. philosophy Hollins Coll., Roanoke, Va., 1965-67, asst. prof. philosophy, 1967-71, assoc. prof., 1971-78, prof., 1978-89, fellow of coll., 1989—, dir. summer inst. for ethics and pub. policy, 1990-92; prof. philosophy, William R, Kenan, Jr. prof. humanities Coll. William and Mary, Williamsburg, Va., 1989-2001, acting chair, 1992-93; pres. Bookwork, L.L.C., 2000—. Mem. summer conf. in metaphysics Coun. for Philos. Studies, 1968, mem. summer conf. on moral problems in medicine, 1974; vis. fellow in philosophy Harvard U., Cambridge, Mass., 1975-76; invited lectr. in field. Author: On Justifying Moral Judgments, 1973, Property Rights: Philosophic Foundations, 1977, Reciprocity, 1986, A New Stoicism, 1998; editor: (with Kenneth Kipnis) Property: Cases, Concepts and Critiques, 1984 (with Charlotte B. Becker) A History of Western Ethics, 1992, Encyclopedia of Ethics, 2 vols., 1992, 2d edit., 3 vols., 2001; mem. editl. bd. Ethics, 1979-85, 2000, assoc. editor, 1985-2000, acting editor, 1994-95, book rev. editor, 1998-2000; contbr. over 70 articles and book revs. to profl. jours. Woodrow Wilson grad. fellow, 1961-62, Danforth grad. fellow, 1961-65, Woodrow Wilson dissertation fellow (hon.), 1964-65, fellow NEH, 1971-72, 93-94, Oxford (Eng.) U., 1971-72, Harvard U., 1975-76, Am. Coun. Learned Socs., 1975-76, humanities fellow Rockefeller Found., 1982-83, Ctr. for Advanced Study in Behavioral Scis., 1983-84. Mem. Am. Philos. Assn. (com. on philosophy and law 1984-87, adv. com. to program com. ethics divsn. 1989-92, com. on status and future of profession 1993-96), Am. Soc. for Legal and Polit. Philosophy, Va. Philos. Assn. (sec. 1978-79, v.p. 1979-80, pres. 1980-81).

BECKER, LORNE ARTHUR, family physician; b. Kitchener, Ont., Can., Mar. 6, 1945; s. Percy Lorne Becker and Katie Klassen; m. Elizabeth Joy Wonnacott, June 1, 1968; children: Andrew James, Doug Scott, Lynn Marie. MD, U. Western Ont., London, Can., 1969. Diplomate Am. Bd. Family Practice. Asst. prof. U. Rochester, N.Y., 1977-79; assoc. prof. Temple U., Phila., 1979-83, U. Okla., Oklahoma City, 1983-88, dir. family health program, 1983-88; assoc. prof. U. Toronto, Ont., 1988-94, chief family medicine, 1988-93; prof. dept. family medicine SUNY, Syracuse, 1994—, chair dept. family medicine, 1997—. Contbr. chpts. to books; author, mem. rev. bd. Jour. Family Practice. Fellow Coll. Family Physicians Can., Am. Acad. Family Physicians; mem. Soc. Tchrs. Family Medicine (chair rsch. com. 1985-89, Curtis Hames Rsch. award 2001), Ambulatory Sentinel Practice Network (bd. dirs. 1979-93), Cochrane Collaboration (coord. primary care 1998—); Member Inst. of Med. Panel on the Gulf War & Health, 2002-2003. Avocations: sailing, handheld computers. Office: SUNY Dept Family Medicine 475 Irving Ave Ste 200 Syracuse NY 13210-1529 E-mail: beckerla@upstate.edu.

BECKER, MARK PAUL PAUL, statistics and sociology educator, consultant; s. Alvin John and Mildred Theresa (Hines) B.; m. Laura Lynn Voisinet, July 16, 1983; children: Matthew Brian, Julia Marie. BS in Math., Towson State U., 1980; PhD in Stats., Pa. State U., 1985. Asst. prof. U. Fla., Gainesville, 1985-89; sr. fellow U. Wash., Seattle, 1987-89; asst. prof. U. Mich., Ann Arbor, 1989-92, assoc. prof., 1992-98, assoc. dean, 1997—, prof., 1998—. Cons. Am. Coll. Emergency Physicians, 1991, Kellogg Co., Battle Creek, Mich., 1993-96, Pa. State U., 1999; mem. spl. study sect. NIH, Bethesda, Md., 1994-97. Editor Sociol. Methodology jour., 1998—; assoc. editor Biometrics Jour., 1998-2000; contbr. articles to profl. jours. Recipient Fellow, Am. Statis. Assn., 1999, Hon. Mem., Honor Soc. of Phi Kappa Phi, Mary Hudson Scarborough Award for Excellence in Math., Towson State U., 1980; fellow Postdoctoral Rsch. Fellowship, NIH, 1987-1989. Fellow Royal Statis. Soc., Am. Statis Assn.; mem. Population Assn. Am., Am. Sociol. Assn., Internat. Biometric Soc., Inst. Math. Stats., Phi Kappa Phi (hon.). Office: U Mich Dept Biostatistics Ann Arbor MI 48109-2029

BECKER, MARVIN BURTON, historian, educator; b. Phila., July 20, 1922; s. Benjamin and Florence (Wachs) B.; m. Beatrice Lapayowker, Jan. 16, 1944; children: Wendy, Dana. BS, U. Pa., 1946, MA, 1947, PhD, 1950. Asst. prof. history U. Ark., 1950-52, Baldwin-Wallace Coll., Berea, Ohio, 1952-56; asso. prof. Western Res. U., 1957-63; prof. U. Rochester, N.Y., 1964-73; from prof. history to prof. emeritus U. Mich., Ann Arbor, Mich., 1973—95, prof. emeritus, 1995—. Seminar presenter Spelman Villa of Johns Hopkins U., Florence, Italy, 1995. Author: Florence in Transition, 2 vols., 1967-68, (published on web site www.Questia.com), Medieval Italy: Constraints and Creativity, 1981, transl. into Italian, 1986, Civility and Society in Western Europe, 1300-1600, 1988, The Emergence of Civil Society in the 18th Century: A Privileged Moment in the History of England, Scotland, and France, 1994, An Essay on the Vicissitudes of Civil Society in Scotland, 18th Century, Indiana Law Jour., vol. 72, 1997, Florentine Essays: Selected Writings of Marvin B. Becker, 2002; series gen. editor Studies in Medieval and Early Modern Civilization for U. Mich. Press, 17 vols., 1990—. Served with AUS, 1944. Fulbright fellow, 1953-55; fellow Guggenheim Found., 1956-57; fellow Am. Council Learned Socs., 1963-64; fellow Inst. Advanced Study, Princeton, N.J., 1968-69; Harvard fellow I Tatti, 1963-64; sr. fellow Humanities Inst., Johns Hopkins U., 1966-67; hon. mem. Deputazione di Storia Patria per la Toscana, 1976. Mem. Medieval Acad., Renaissance Soc. Am., Am. Hist. Assn., Nat. Humanities Faculty, Soc. Scholars (Johns Hopkins U. 1992). Jewish. Home: 2335 Hill St Ann Arbor MI 48104-2651 Office: 4609 Haven Hall Ann Arbor MI 48109

BECKER, MARY DRUKE, anthropologist, researcher; b. Townshend, Vt., July 19, 1951; d. Bernard William and Elizabeth Eva (Robinson) Druke; m. Charles Adrian Becker, Sept. 5, 1981; children: Adrian B.D., Sara M.D. BA, Wellesley Coll., 1973; MA, U. Chgo., 1974, PhD, 1981. Assoc. dir. Hist. of Iroquois Newberry Libr., Chgo., 1978—82; rsch. cons. Yager Mus. Hartwick Coll., Oneonta, NY, 1982—84; instr. Grad. and Continuing Studies Union Coll., Schenectady, NY, 1986; rsch. cons. Iroquois Indian Mus., Howes Cove, NY, 1987—89, 1990—, bd. dir. Rsch. cons. Hearts and Hand Media, San Francisco, 1997. Assoc. editor: microfilm Iroquois Indians: A Documentary History, 1984, The History & Culture of Iroquois Diplomacy, 1985. Mem. leadership team Alliance of Children and Families, Schenectady, 2001—; bd. dir. Am. Diabetes Assn., Albany, NY, 1982—84, United Way Schenectady (N.Y.) County, 1997, 2000—, Iroquois Indian Mus., 1996—99, 2002—. Recipient Vol. of Yr. award, Am. Diabetes Assn., 1987, Cmty. Hero award, Arthritis Found., 1998, Anthony Salerno award for volunteerism, United Way Schenectady County, 2001. Mem.: Assn. Documentary Editing, Am. Soc. Ethnohistory (chmn. Robert Heizer award com. 1992—93), Am. Anthrop. Assn., Phi Beta Kappa. Democrat. Roman Cath. Avocations: reading, scrapbooks, travel. Office: Iroquois Indian Museum PO Box 7 Howes Cave NY 12092

BECKER, MARY LOUISE, political scientist; b. St. Louis; d. W. R. and Evelyn (Thompson) Becker; divorced; children: James, John. BS, Washington U., St. Louis, 1949, MA, 1951; PhD, Radcliffe Coll., 1957; postgrad., U. Karachi, Pakistan, 1953-54. Intelligence rsch. analyst Dept. State, Washington, 1957-59; internat. rels. officer AID, Washington, 1959-64, community rels. officer, 1964-66, sci. rsch. officer, 1966-71, UN rels. officer, 1971-91; pres. Internat. Devel. Enterprises, Washington, 1992—. Adviser U.S. dels. 19th, 21st, 23d, 24th, 26th, 28th, 30th, 32d, 34th Governing Coun. sessions UN Devel. Program; adv. U.S. del. 3d prep. com. meeting World Conf. UN Decade for Women; adviser U.S. dels. UNICEF exec. bd. sessions, 1987—91; mem. U.S. Com. for UN Fund for Women; lectr. internat. rels. civic orgn., student groups 1954—. Author: Muhammed Iqbal, 1965; contbg. editor: Concise Ency. of Mid. East, 1973; contbr. articles to profl. jours. Mem. adv. bd. chmn. internat. student placement Washington Citizenship Seminar Nat. YMCA-YWCA, Washington, 1961—71. Named Blewett fellow, Washington U., 1951, Resident fellow, Radcliffe Coll., 1952—56, Fulbright scholar, U. Karachi, 1953—54. Mem.: AAUW, Nat. Press Club, Mo. Soc. Washington (sec. 1959—60), S. Asian Muslim Studies Assn. (v.p. 1992—), UN Assn. (bd. dirs. Nat. Capital area 1991—), Mid. East Inst., Asia Soc., Assn. Asian Studies, Soc. Internat. Devel., Am. Polit. Sci. Assn., Harvard Club (Washington), Chimes, Mortar Bd., Pi Sigma Alpha, Eta Mu Phi, Beta Gamma Sigma, Alpha Lambda Delta. Presbyterian. Home: 2301 E St NW Washington DC 20037-2829 Office: North Bldg Ste 700 601 Pennsylvania Ave NW Washington DC 20004-2601

BECKER, MATTHEW LEE, religious studies educator, minister; b. Salem, Oreg., Sept. 10, 1962; s. David Lee and Glenys Mae Becker; m. Detra Renee Crunk, June 5, 1993; 1 child, Jacob David. BA, Concordia Coll., 1980—84; MDiv, Concordia Sem., 1984—88; MA, U. of Chgo., 1988—90, PhD, 1991—2001. Pastor Bethlehem Luth. Ch., Dundee, Ill., 1989—94; asst. prof. of religion and humanities Concordia U., Portland, Oreg., 1994—98, assoc. prof. of religion and humanities, 1998—; sec. NW Dist. of the Luth. Ch.-Mo. Synod, Portland, 1997—. Guest pastoring Luth. Ch., Portland, 1994—. Editor: (history book) God Opens Doors (Commendation (maj. publications) by Concordia Hist. Inst., 2001); contbr. articles to profl. jours. Mem.: Soc. of Bibl. Lit., Luth. Hist. Conf., Am. Soc. of Ch. History, Am. Acad. of Religion. Luth. Home: 6454 NE 38th Ave Portland OR 97211 Office: Concordia University 2811 NE Holman St Portland OR 97211

BECKER, MICHAEL ALLEN, physician, educator; b. N.Y.C., Oct. 3, 1940; s. David S. and Sylvia M. (Salomon) B.; m. Mary E. Baim; children: David, Jonathan, Abigail, Arielle, Daniel. BA, U. Pa., Phila., 1961, MD, 1965. Diplomate Am. Bd. Internal Medicine, Am. Bd. Rheumatology. Intern Barnes Hosp., Washington U., St. Louis, 1965-66, resident, 1969-70; asst. prof. U. Calif., San Diego, 1972-77, assoc. prof., 1977-80; prof. medicine U. Chgo. Pritzker Sch. Medicine, 1980—. Mem. biochemistry study sect. NIH, Bethesda, Md., 1991-95. Contbr. numerous rsch. articles to med. publs. Sr. asst. surgeon USPHS, 1966-69. Fellow John Simon Guggenheim Meml. Found.; mem. Am. Soc. Clin. Investigation, Assn. Am. Physicians, Am. Coll. Rheumatology. Office: U Chgo Med Ctr MC0930 Chicago IL 60637 E-mail: mbecker@medicine.bsd.uchicago.edu.

BECKER, MICHAEL ANTHONY, osteopathic family physician, educator; b. Phila., Apr. 30, 1962; s. John T. and Marie A. (Levito) B.; m. Barbara Ann Carney, Sep. 18, 1988; children: Christopher Michael, Katelyn Rose, Claire Elizabeth. BA in Biology, LaSalle U., 1983; DO, Phila. Coll. Osteo. Medicine, 1987; MS in Health Adminstrn., St. Joseph's U., Phila., 1999. Diplomate Nat. Bd. Osteo. Med. Examiners; bd. cert. family medicine. Intern Met. Hosp., Phila., 1987-88; resident in ob-gyn. Phila. Coll. Osteo. Medicine Hosp., 1988-89; resident in family medicine Suburban Gen. Hosp., Norristown, Pa., 1989-91; attending in family medicine Gen. Practice Assocs., Phila., 1991-92, Upper Chesapeake Health Svc., Havre de Grace, Md., 1992-93, Phila. Coll. Osteo. Medicine, Phila., 1993—2001, asst. prof. family medicine, 1997—; med. dir. Phila. Coll. Osteo. Medicine Roxborough Healthcare Ctr., 1991—2001; assoc. program dir. family medicine residency program Mercy Suburban Hosp., 2001—; med. dir. Mercy Suburban Hosp. Family Practice Ctr., Norristown, 2001—. Recipient Disting. Physician award Overbrook Friedlander Program, Phila., 1995, Grad. award in health adminstrn. St. Joseph's U., Phila., 1999; named Ambulatory Care Physician of Yr., Phila. Coll. Osteo. Medicine, 1999. Mem.: AMA, Phila. County Med. Soc., Pa. Med. Soc., Pa. Osteo. Med. Assn., Am. Coll. Healthcare Execs., Am. Acad. Family Physicians, Osteo. Family Physicians, Am. Coll., Am. Osteo. Assn. Democrat. Roman Catholic. Avocations: music, swimming. Office: Mercy Suburban Hosp Family Practice Ctr 530 Church St Norristown PA 19401 E-mail: mabdoc@aol.com.

BECKER, MURRAY LEONARD, corporate financial consultant, consulting actuary; b. Phila., July 30, 1933; s. Simon and Bertha B. (Berlin) B.; m. Anita Goodman, Apr. 3, 1955; children: Mark, Lynn, Donna (dec.). BS in Econs., U. Pa., 1955. Actuary Mutual of N.Y., N.Y.C., 1955-70; v.p., cons. actuary Johnson & Higgins, N.Y.C., 1970-88; pres. Becker & Rooney, Inc., Teaneck, N.J., 1988-95; pres. Becker & Rooney divsn. Kwasha Lipton, Ft. Lee, N.J., 1995-97; v.p. J.P. Morgan Investment Mgmt., N.Y.C., 1997-98. Mem. actuarial adv. com. N.Y.C. Retirement System, 1990. Named Advisor of Yr., Pension World Mag., 1986; voted by his peers for the Investment Mgmt. Inst.'s 1996 most respected GIC/Stable Value profl. award. Fellow Soc. of Actuaries; mem. Am. Acad. Actuaries, Actuarial Soc. N.Y. (pres. 1982-83). Home: 631 James Ln Rivervale NJ 07675

BECKER, NANCY ANNE, state supreme court justice; b. Las Vegas, May 23, 1955; d. Arthur William and Margaret Mary (McLoughlin) Becker. BA, U.S. Internat. U., 1976; JD, George Washington U., 1979. Bar: Nev. 1979, D.C. 1980, Md. 1982, U.S. Dist. Ct. Nev. 1987, U.S. Ct. Appeals (9th cir.) 1987. Legis. cons. D.C. Office on Aging, Washington, 1979—83; assoc. Goldstein & Ahalt, College Park, Md., 1980—82; pvt. practice Washington, 1982—83; dep. city atty., prosecutor criminal div. City of Las Vegas, 1983; judge Las Vegas Mcpl. Ct., 1987—89, Clark County Dist. Ct., Las Vegas, 1989—99; now assoc. state supreme ct. justice Nev. Supreme Ct. Cons. MADD, Las Vegas, 1983—87. Contbr. articles to profl. jours. Pres. Clark County Pro Bono Project, Las Vegas, 1984—95. Mem.: NCCJ, Am. Businesswomen's Assn. (treas. Las Vegas chpt. 1985—86), Southern Nev. Assn. Women Attys. (past officer), Soroptimist Internat., Vietnam Vets. Am., Las Vegas and Latin C. of C. Office: Nevada Supreme Court Capital Complex 316 Bridger Ave Las Vegas NV 89101-5906

BECKER, NANCY S. retired real estate broker, retired shop owner; b. Erie, Pa., June 14, 1928; d. Raymond Joseph and Anna Marie (Bechtold) Sanner; m. Eugene Thomas Becker, Nov. 1, 1947; children: Douglas, Kim, Jeffrey, Amy. Student, U. Maine, 1976—78. Lic. real estate salesperson and broker Fla. Owner Irish Import & Antique Shop, Bar Harbor, Maine, 1972—74, Irish Import Shop, Bar Harbor, Maine, 1972—74; asst. libr. St. Andrews, Canada, 1974—76; salesperson DeSantis Real Estate, Stuart, Fla., 1978—79; broker, owner Becker Real Estate, Stuart, 1980—84; proprietor Capt.'s House B & B, Thomaston, Maine, 1985—87; libr. Pittsfield, Maine, 1987—88, Holmes Beach, Fla., 1995—97. Active PTA, 1953—84; leader Girl & Boy Scouts, 1959—75; vol. ARC, 1955—72; asst. coach, supporter Little League, Pony League, 1955—65. Recipient Civic award, NATO, Izmir, Turkey, 1964, Papal Citation, Vatican City, 1964. Mem.: St. Petersburg (Fla.) Art Mus., Ringling Mus. of Art, Audubon Soc., Nat. Geog. Soc., Smithsonian Assocs., Art League (Bradenton, Fla.). Roman Catholic. Avocations: painting, gardening, sewing, fishing, cooking. Home: Bradenton, Fla. Died Feb. 28, 2001.

BECKER, PAUL ALBERT, investment executive; b. Evansville, Ind., Jan. 20, 1939; s. Roger Kenneth and June (Scheller) B.; m. Jayne Ann Wanamaker, Sept. 11, 1965; children: David K., Michael J. BSE, U. Mich., 1960; MBA, Harvard U., 1962. Cert. fin. analyst. Staff asst. FMC Corp., San Jose, Calif., 1962-66; asst. v.p. Waddell & Reed, Kansas City, Mo., 1966-68; v.p. Baker Weeks & Co., N.Y.C., 1968-76, Wall, Patterson, McGrew & Richards, Atlanta, 1976-78; mng. dir. Mitchell Hutchins Asset Mgmt., N.Y.C., 1978-98; mng. ptnr. Summit Investors, 1982—. Bd. dirs. PlanetJam Media Group, Atlanta. Trustee Bravo! Vail Valley Music Festival, Vero Beach Mus. Art. E-mail: pbecker@attglobal.net.

BECKER, PHYLLIS, systems analyst; b. Plainfield, N.J., Nov. 9, 1963; d. Stephen and Jean Mae Potasky; m. Andrew D. Becker, Feb. 14, 1993; 1 child, Samuel. BS in Computer Sci., Kean U., 1986; MS, Stevens Inst., 1998. Programmer ITT Def. Comms., Nutley, N.J.; sys. analyst AT&T, Somerset, N.J., CSC, Somerset. Republican. Jewish. Avocations: cat and dog care, sewing, needlework. Office: CSC 500 Atrium Dr Somerset NJ 08873 E-mail: pbecker@csc.com.

BECKER, QUINN HENDERSON, orthopedic surgeon, army officer; b. Kirksville, Mo., June 11, 1930; s. Quinn Henry B. and Sarah Lucille (Henderson) Finley; m. Gladys Marie Roussell, Aug. 11, 1951; children: Quinn E., Terri K., Paul Eric. Grad., N.E. La. State Coll., 1952; MD, La. State U., 1956; student, Armed Forces Staff Coll., 1969-70, Command and Gen. Staff Coll., 1971, U.S. Army War Coll., 1974-75. Diplomate Am. Bd. Orthopedic Surgery. Commd. 2d lt. U.S. Army, advanced through grades to lt. gen., 1985; intern Tripler Gen. Hosp., 1956-57; resident in orthopedic surgery Confederate Meml. Med. Ctr., Shreveport, La., 1958-61; orthopedic surgeon Ft. Gordon, Ga., 1962-63; chief orthopedic service Ft. Rucker, Ala., 1963-64; comdg. officer 5th Surg. Hosp. (Mobile Army), Heidelberg, W. Ger., 1964-65; surgeon 3d Inf. Div., Wurzburg, W. Ger., 1965-66; chief orthpedic surgery 33d Field Hosp., Wurzburg, 1965; asst. chief orthopedic service Walter Reed Gen. Hosp., 1966-69; chief profl. services 85th Evacuation Hosp., Vietnam, 1970; div. surgeon and bn. comdr. 15th Med. Bn. 1st Cavalry Div., Vietnam, 1970-71; chief orthopedic service and orthopedic residency tng. Tripler Army Med. Ctr., 1971-74; surgeon 18th Airborne Corps., Ft. Bragg, 1975-77; comdr. Med. Activity Womack Army Hosp., Ft. Bragg, 1976-77; dir. health care ops. Office Surgeon Gen., 1977-80; comdt. Acad. Health Scis., U.S. Army, Ft. Sam Houston, Tex., 1980-81; dep. surgeon gen. Washington, 1981-83; comdr. 7th Med. Command, Heidelberg, 1983-85; Surgeon Gen. Dept. Army, 1985-88, ret., 1988. Asst. prof. orthopedic surgery Howard U., Washington, 1967-69; clin. assoc. prof. Sch. Medicine U. Hawaii, Honolulu, 1973-74; chief of staff VA Hosp., Asheville, N.C., 1989-92, ret. 1992; mem. Congl. Commn. on Svc. Mems. and Vets. Transition Assistance, 1998. Contbr. papers to publs. and confs. in field. Decorated Legion of Merit, Meritorious Service medal, Bronze Star, Air medal, Disting. Service medal. Fellow Am. Acad. Orthopedic Surgeons (chmn. mil. affairs com. 1981-85), ACS, Am. Coll. Physician Execs. (disting.); mem. AMA (ho. of dels.), Am. Orthopaedic Assn., Masons (33d degree, Grand Cross 1993), Civitan (pres. Asheville club 1992, chmn. internat. rsch. com. 1996-98). Home: PO Box 2388 Dillon CO 80435-2388 E-mail: mqbecker@vail.net.

BECKER, RALPH LEONARD, psychologist; b. Cin., July 15, 1927; s. Morris and Sarah Ruth B.; m. Evelyn Zeifman, Aug. 15, 1976. BA in Sci., Ohio State U., 1958, BS in Edn., 1960, MA in Psychology, 1961, PhD in Psychology, 1979. Lic. psychologist, Ohio; cert. counselor, Ohio. Spl. tchr. Columbus (Ohio) City Schs., 1962-64; staff psychologist Ohio Dept. Mental Retardation/Devel. Disabilities, Columbus, 1964-68, research scientist, 1968-72, research assoc., 1972-82; research dir. Elbern Pubs., Columbus, 1982—. Author: Reading-Free Vocational Interest Inventory, 1981, rev. edit. 2000, Occupational Title List, 1984, rev. edit. 2001, Becker Work Adjustment Profile, 1989; contbr. articles to profl. jours. Grantee State of Ohio, 1966, 67, U.S. Office of Edn., 1968. Fellow Am. Assn. on Mental Retardation; mem. Coun. for Exceptional Children, Ohio Psychol. Assn., Ohio State Alumni Assn., Am. Psychol. Assn. Avocations: carpentry, elec. wiring, gardening, woodcraft. Office: Elbern Publs PO Box 09497 Columbus OH 43209-0497 E-mail: ebecker@insight.rr.com.

BECKER, RAY EVERETT, management consultant; b. Grand Rapids, Mich., Jan. 14, 1937; s. Lawson Everett and Virginia Jane (Shellman) B.; m. Mary Rita Warren, Aug. 18, 1960 (div. 1972); children: Elizabeth Anne, Catherine Virginia; m. Arlyss Ellen Roeber, Aug. 17, 1974. AB in Engring., Dartmouth Coll., 1959, MS in Engring and Bus. Adminstrn., 1960; MS in Mgmt., MIT, 1974. Project adminstr. Astro Electronics div. RCA, Hightstown, N.J., 1961-65; bus. mgr.radar lab. Missile Systems div. Raytheon Corp., Bedford, Mass., 1965-68, mgr. mgmt. systems, 1968-70, mgr. adminstrn. and data processing, 1970-73, program mgr. Lowell, Mass., 1981-85; mgr. comml. svcs. Raytheon Svc. Co., Burlington, Mass., 1974-75, dir. mktg., 1975-80; v.p., mgr. Mideast area Raytheon Overseas Ltd., Riyadh, Saudi Arabia, 1980-81; v.p., gen. mgr. Info. Svcs. div. Keane Inc., Boston, 1985-95; mgmt. cons. to info. svcs. cmty., 1995—. Avocations: skiing, reading. Home and Office: 785 Lamoine Beach Rd Ellsworth ME 04605-4748 E-mail: raybecker@acadia.net.

BECKER, REX LOUIS, architect; b. St. Louis, May 20, 1913; s. Louis Herman and Elsie (Schroeder) B.; m. Ada Sylva Schmidt, Nov. 20, 1937; children: Susan (Mrs. Robert L. Barley), Kathryn (Mrs. Russell Kisling), Rex Louis, Roger G. B.Arch., Washington U., St. Louis, 1934, M.Arch., 1935. With archtl. firm Johnson & Maack, St. Louis, 1935-42; ptnr. Froese, Maack & Becker, St. Louis, 1946-73; pres. Becker & Flowers, St. Louis, 1973-81. Cons., mem. architects com. Luth. Ch.-Mo. Synod, 1980-96, chmn. 1986-87. Works include: Luth. Hosp., St. Louis, Civil Engring. Bldg., Math & Computer Bldg U. Mo. at Rolla, over 150 ch. projects. Pres. Council Luth. Chs. Greater St. Louis, 1960-61. Served with C.E. U.S. Army, 1942-45. Recipient Disting. Alumni award Washington U., 1995. Fellow AIA (pres. St. Louis 1956, regional dir. 1966-69, treas. 1969-71, Gold Medal award St. Louis chpt. 1998), Mo. Assn. Registered Architects (pres. 1955), Guild Religious Architecture, Scarab. Clubs: Mo. Athletic (St. Louis) (gov. 1973-76, treas. 1975-76), Engrs. (St. Louis). Home: Apt G02 701 S Laclede Station Rd Webster Groves MO 53119

BECKER, RICHARD CHARLES, retired college president; b. Chgo., Mar. 1, 1931; s. Charles Beno and Rose Mildred (Zak) B.; m. Magdalene Marie Kypry, June 19, 1954; children: Richard J., Daniel P., Douglas F., Steven G., Pamela J. BS in Elec. Engring, Fournier Inst. Tech., 1953; MS in Elec. Engring, U. Ill., 1954, MS in Math., 1956, PhD in Elec. Engring, 1959; postgrad., Harvard Inst. Ednl. Mgmt., 1976. Engr. Ill. Bell Tel. Co., Chgo., 1952, Andrew Corp., Chgo., 1953; rsch. asst. U. Ill., Urbana, 1954-58, asst. prof., 1959; sr. staff engr. Amphenol Corp., Chgo., 1959-60, sr. rsch. scientist, 1961-64, dir. program mgmt., 1965-67; dir. Amphenol Corp. (Far Eastern ops.), 1968; group v.p., corporate dir. adminstrn. Bunker Ramo Corp., Oak Brook, Ill., 1968-73; chief exec. officer and chmn. bd. Fortune Internat. Enterprises, Inc., Oak Brook, 1973-76; pres. Benedictine Univ. (formerly Ill. Benedictine Coll.), Lisle, 1976-95, pres. emeritus, 1995—. Trustee, prof. Midwest Coll. Engring., Lombard, Ill., 1968—86; trustee Ill. Benedictine Coll., Lisle, 1973—76; bd. dirs. Amphenol Tyree Proprietary, Ltd., Australia, Amphetronix, Ltd., India, Oxbow Resources, Ltd., Canada; v.p. Bonita Springs Incorporation Com., Inc., 1998—99, pres., 1999—2000; bd. dirs. Arthur J. Schmitt Found., 1970—, pres., 1995—; mem. exec. adv. bd. Internat. Engring. Consortium. Contbr. articles and chpts. to profl. jours. and books. Gov. Brook Forest Community Assn., 1971-74; del. Oak Brook Caucus, 1970; trustee, pres. Arthur J. Schmitt Found., Ill. Benedictine Coll.; chmn. Coun. West Suburban Colls., Chgo. Met. Higher Edn. Coun., officer Fedn. Ind. Ill. Colls. and Univs.; chmn. Associated Colls. of Ill., West Suburban Regional Acad. Consortium. Named Disting. Eagle Scout, 1989,

Regent Nat. Eagles Scout Assn.; Arthur J. Schmitt fellow U. Ill., 1953-56. Mem. Am. Phys. Soc., Nat. Assn. Ind. Colls. and Univs. (bd. dirs.), Albertus Magnus Guild, Rotary (Paul Harris fellow), Equestrian Order of the Holy Sepulchre of Jerusalem (knight commdr.), KC (4th deg), Sigma Xi, Eta Kappa Nu, Tau Beta Pi. Home: 25761 Creek Bend Dr Bonita Springs FL 34135-9523 E-mail: rpapinani@aol.com.

BECKER, RICHARD STANLEY, music publisher; b. Hillside, N.J., Nov. 9, 1934; s. Nat Edward and Hattie Adele (Perkel) B. Student, U. Miami, Fla., 1953. Pres. Richie Becker's Music, Inc. Pub. Music pub.: Moody River (No. 1 song in nation), Pat Boone, 1961, Anna, Beatles, 1963 (million selling album), You Better Move On, Rolling Stones, 1966 (Gold Record award), December's Children album, Moody River, Frank Sinatra, 1969 (Gold Record award), Cycles album, You Better Move On, Dean Martin, 1974, Moody River, Readers Digest, 1975, mgr., Alex Bradford, star of Broadway show, Don't Bother Me, I Can't Cope, 1975; pub.: musical Your Arm's Too Short to Box with God, 1975; dir. first country music show in history, Madison Sq. Garden, 1964; Contbr.: Moody River to, Colliers Yearbook, 1961, Anna to, Ency. Brit., 1963. Recipient Broadcast Music award, 1961, Key to City Memphis, 1973, Ark. Traveler award, 1973; named Hon. Citizen Tenn., 1973, Hon. lt. col. aide-de-camp George C. Wallace, 1973; Alex Bradford Meml. Music scholar Spelman Coll., 1996; Richard S. Becker collection of Alex Bradford Gospel. Music Materials Archives Collection at Smithsonian Nat. Mus. Am. History. Mem. Friars Club, Broadcast Music, Inc. Achievements include establishing Richard S. Becker scholarship Juilliard Sch. Music, 1976. Office: PO Box 144 Deal NJ 07723-0144

BECKER, ROBERT A. advertising executive; b. Mar. 3, 1920; s. William and Eva (Kats) B.; m. Pearl Pehr, Aug. 22, 1948; son, David Jonathan; m. Nancy Gibbs, 1977. BS in Mktg., NYU, 1941; BS in Pharmacy, L.I. U., 1949; DCS (hon.), St. John's U., 1989. Copywriter Plough Inc., Memphis, 1941-42, Murray Breese Assocs., N.Y.C., 1944-48; copywriter, product mgr. Squibb, N.Y.C., 1949-52, profl. advt. mgr., 1955-57; advt. dir. Nepera Pharm. Co., Yonkers, N.Y., 1953-54; v.p. Burdick & Becker Inc., N.Y.C., 1957-61; pres. Robert A. Becker, Inc., N.Y.C., 1961-88, chmn. bd. emeritus, 1988—; pres. Hosp. Publs., Inc., 1963-84. Bd. visitors Fordham U. Sch. Law, 1987—; trustee George London Found. for Singers, N.Y.C., 1993—, Guild Hall Mus., East Hampton, N.Y., 1995-97, Collegiate Chorale, N.Y.C., 2000-; founder, pres. The Beethoven Soc., N.Y.C., 1976-90. Recipient Decoration of honor in Gold, Govt. Austria; officer's cross Order of Merit, Fed. Republic Germany, 1985; Distinction of Merit in Gold, City of Vienna; elected to Med. Advt. Hall of Fame, 1997. Mem. Lotos Club. Home: 875 Park Ave New York NY 10021-0341

BECKER, ROBERT ALLEN, data processing executive; b. Chgo., June 27, 1942; s. Sig Herman and Dorothy (Shaw) B.; m. Babs Lee Hefter, Dec. 24, 1964; children: David, Edie. BS in Indsl. Mgmt., Purdue U., 1964. Programmer analyst Standard Oil Co. (Amoco), Chgo., 1964-67, R.R. Donnelley & Sons, Chgo., 1967-68, project leader, 1968-71, supr. computer ops., 1971-72, supr. tech. svcs., 1972-79; mgr. data. ctr. ops. Chic Merc. Exch., Chgo., 1979-82; dir. info. resources Richard D. Irwin, Homewood, Ill., 1982-87; dir. sys. svcs. Holy Cross Health Sys., South Bend, Ind., 1987-89; dir. info. systems and comm. Elkhart (Ind.) Gen. Hosp., 1989-92; dir. info. systems Mt. Sinai Hosp. Med. Ctr., Chgo., 1992—2002, Schwab Rehab. Hosp., Chgo., 1994—2002, dir. hosp. info. sys., 1996—2002, St. Alexius Med. Ctr., Hoffman Estates, 2003—. Instr., Thornton Community Coll., South Holland, Ill., 1970-71, Prairie State Coll., Chicago Heights, Ill., 1982-87. Asst. cub master, Boy Scouts Am., Homewood, Ill., 1976; mgr. Homewood Little League. Mem. Guide Internat. (bd. dirs. 1971-80), Computer Ops. Mgmt. Assn., Data Processing Mgmt. Assn., (bd. dirs. 1984-88, pres. Calumet chpt. 1987-88, Individual Performance award 1988), Soc. Info Mgmt., Healthcare Info. and Mgmt. Sys. Soc. (sec.-treas. region III med. users software exchange, 1994-95, treas. med. users software exchg. internat., 1996—), Purdue Alumni Assn. (dir. Region 17, 1997-2000), Purdue Club (bd. dirs. 1987, treas. 1989—), Alpha Epsilon Pi. Home: 12996 Pierce Ct Crown Point IN 46307-9255 Office: Mt Sinai Hosp Med Ctr California 15th Chicago IL 60608 E-mail: bobpu@aol.com.

BECKER, ROBERT ALLEN, economist, educator; b. St. Louis, July 30, 1950; s. M. William and Marguerite (Meyer) Becker; m. Karen Gernsbacher, Nov. 27, 1977; 1 child, Adam David. AB, Washington U., St. Louis, 1972; MA, U. Rochester, N.Y., 1975, PhD, 1978. Lectr. econs. Ind. U., Bloomington, 1976—78, asst. prof. econs., 1978—83, assoc. prof. econs., 1983—87, prof. econs., 1987—, chair, dept. econs., 1996—2002. Co-author: Capital Theory of Equilibrium Analysis and Recursive Utility, 1997; contbr. articles to profl. jours. Grantee NSF, 1986—88, Resources for the Future, Washington, D.C., 1979. Mem.: Am. Econ. Assn., Econometric Soc. (assoc. editor 1999—). Achievements include proved form of Ramsey's Conjecture on long-run steady states of growth models; development of indirec method for solving tax-distorted dynamic equilibrium models; formal linkages between descriptive and optimal growth theories. Avocations: reading, golf. Office: Ind U Dept Econs Wylie Hall 214 Bloomington IN 47405 E-mail: becker@indiana.edu.

BECKER, ROBERT CLARENCE, retired clergyman; b. N.Y.C., June 19, 1927; s. Clarence Henry and Lillian (Butler) B.; m. Harriet Louise Egland, June 23, 1951; children: John, Ruth, Paul, Carol, Joel. Student, Providence Bible Inst., 1944-47, Gordon Coll. Theology and Missions, 1947-48; BA, Upsala Coll., 1951. Ordained to ministry Baptist Ch., 1951; pastor First Bapt. Ch., Sedgwick, Maine, 1952-54, Ticonderoga, N.Y., 1954-58, Garden View Bapt. Ch., Williamsport, Pa., 1958-67, First Bapt. Ch., Clayton, N.J., 1967-73, sr. minister Bloomfield, N.J., 1973-97. Pres. Conservative Bapt. Assn. Am., 1979-82; chmn. Am. Council, Africa Evangelical Fellowship, 1981-86; pastoral mentor Vision New England, 2000—. Bd. dirs. Denver Conservative Bapt. Theol. Sem., 1972-84, Eastern Conservative Bapt. Sem., 1982-84, Northeastern Bible Coll., 1983-86, Conservative Bapt. Fgn. Mission Soc., 1988-94. Mem. Nat. Assn. Evangelicals, Conservative Bapt. Fgn. Mission Soc., Conservative Bapt. Home Mission Soc., Conservative Bapt. Assn. (eastern v.p. 1984) Home: PO Box 57 Sedgwick ME 04676-0057 E-mail: rcbecker@acadia.net.

BECKER, ROBERT JEROME, allergist, health care consultant; b. Milw., May 29, 1922; s. Jacob and Sarah (Saxe) B.; m. June Granof, June 25, 1950; children: Scott M., Jill Becker Wilson, Jon G. BS, U. Wis., Milw., 1943; MD, Med. Coll. Wis., 1949. Intern Michael Reese Hosp., Chgo., 1949-50; resident in internal medicine VA Hosp., Wood, Wis., 1950-53; resident in allergy Roosevelt Hosp., N.Y.C., 1955-56; pvt. practice specializing in allergy Joliet, Ill., 1956-82; founder, chmn. bd. dirs. HealthCare COMPARE, 1982-90, chmn. bd. dirs. emeritus, 1990—98; cons. health care utilization co., 1982-90; founder, pres. Becker Cons. Corp., 1990—; founder, chmn. bd. dirs. Healthcare Comm. Mgmt. Corp., 1990-93. Med. dir. Quad river Found. Med. Care, 1976-84; pres. Am. Assn. Profl. Stds. Rev. Orgns., 1980-82; exec. v.p. Joint Coll. Allergy and Immunology, 1978-86; mem. adv. coun. Nat. Inst. Environ. Health Scis., 1984-88, bd. dirs. Impac Corp., Am. Psych Sys.; vice chmn, bd. dirs. Madison Info. Technologies, Inc.; bd., 1995-2002, bd. dirs. CPR Corp., 2001; chmn. Utilization Rev. Accreditation Commn., 1991-94, bd. dirs., 1994-96. Author articles in field. Pres. bd. edn. Joliet Twp. H.S. Dist. 204, 1969-70, 75-76; mem. bus. adv. com. U. Ill. Sch. Bus., Chgo., 1987—. Recipient Clemens von Pirquet award Georgetown U. Internat. Interdisciplinary Ctr. Immunology, 1978, Alumni Merit award Marquette U., 2003; named Entrepreneur of Yr. Arthur Young/Venture Mag., 1988. Fellow ACP, Am. Acad. Allergy, Am. Coll. Allergists (pres. 1987), Am. Coll. Chest Physicians; mem. Ill. Soc. Internal Medicine (pres. 1984-86), Asthma and Allergy Assn. Am. (bd. dirs. 1987—), Asthma and Allergy Found. Am. (bd. dirs. 1990-94), Am. Managed Care and Rev. Assn. (bd. dirs. 1989-95), Am. Assn. Preferred Providers Assn. (bd. dirs. 1989—), Utilization Rev. Accreditation Commn. (chair 1991-94, bd. dirs. 1991-96), Am. Assn. Preferred Provider Orgns. (bd. dirs. 1988-93), Am. Psychiat. Sys. (bd. dirs. 1994—), Alpha Omega Alpha, Alpha Sigma Nu. Office: 1S 045 Spring Rd Oakbrook Terrace IL 60181 E-mail: wsimed@aol.com. *Whatever success I have achieved has occurred with the following rules of my life: 1) Individual and public accountability for decisions made; 2) Kindness to all persons in my sphere of contact; 3) Hard work; 4) Humility, truth, and respect for human dignity have been uppermost elements in my interpersonal relations; and, 5) I have accepted my humanness when I fall short of these rules.*

BECKER, ROBERT JOSEPH, database consultant, computer science specialist, database software developer and educator; b. Grand Rapids, Mich., Apr. 22, 1946; s. Leon Joseph and Alfreda Mary (O'Rielly) B.; m. Kathleen Zbikowski, Jan. 16, 1970; children: Steven, Michael, Kimberly, John. BS in Computer Sci., Mich. State U., 1970. Computer sci. specialist Wolverine World Wide, Rockford, Mich., 1970-73; data base adminstr. Foremost Ins. Co., Grand Rapids, 1973-80, with data base, data communications, 1980-86, mgr. data base adminstrn., 1986-88, cons. of tech. directions, 1988—; prin. info. tech. cons., 2000—. Keynote data base performance speaker U.S. and European Software AG Confs., 1973—; tchr. computer basics to elem. sch. students, 1988-93; actor cmty. theater, 1995—. Editor (data base products) Software Ag Connections, 1987-98, author performance courses, 1993—; contbr. articles to profl. jours. Community edn. instr., Wyoming, Mich., 1974-80; vol. examiner FCC, Grand Rapids, 1975-85; vol. religious edn. instr., 1980—. Mem. Software AG Internat. Users Group (cert., chmn. performance spl. interest group 1978—, tech. rep. 1983-85, data base products rep. 1987-94, chmn. data base future directions 1989-99, comm. and client-server software rep. 1994-96, bd. dirs. 1996—, v.p. software exec. bd. 2002—, best presentation award 1978, 82, best speaker award 1979), Am. Radio Relay League, Nat. Train Collectors Assn. Republican. Roman Catholic. Avocations: amateur radio, commercial broadcasting, community and semi-professional theater. Home: 4560 Bremer St SW Grandville MI 49418-2238 Office: Foremost Ins Co PO Box 1233 Grand Rapids MI 49501-1233 E-mail: bob.becker@foremost.com., bob.becker@grnet.com.

BECKER, ROBERT OTTO, orthopedic surgery educator; b. River Edge, N.J., May 31, 1923; s. Otto and Elizabeth (Blank) B.; m. Lillian J. Moller, Sept. 6, 1946; children: Lisa, Michael, Adam. BA, Gettysburg Coll., 1946; MD, NYU, 1948. Am. Bd. Orthopedic Surgery Nat. Bd. Med. Examiners. Intern Bellevue Hosp., N.Y.C., 1948-49; resident Mary Hitchcock Meml. Hosp., Hanover, N.H., 1950-51, SUNY Downstate Med. Ctr., 1953-56; practice medicine specializing in orthopedic surgery, 1956—; prof. orthopedics SUNY Upstate Med. Ctr., Syracuse, 1966—; clin. prof. orthopedics La. State Coll. Medicine, Shreveport, 1980—; v.p. rsch. Becker Biomagnetics, 1992—. Author: Electromagnetism and Life, 1982, The Body Electric, 1985, Cross Currents, 1990; editor: Mechanisms of Growth Control, 1981; patentee electric stimulation of growth, iontophoretic method for tissue healing and regeneration. Served to 1st lt. USMC, 1951-53. Faculty exchange scholar SUNY, 1979; recipient Middletown research award VA, 1960, disting. alumnus award NYU Coll. Medicine, 1966, Nicolas Andry award Assn. Bone and Joint Surgery, 1979, Albert Einstein Internat. Acad. award 2000. Mem. AAAS, N.Y. Acad. Scis., Bioelectronics Soc., Internat. Soc. for Bioelectricity. Republican. Home: 6802 Erie Canal Rd Lowville NY 13367 Office: Becker Biomagnetics Star Route Lowville NY 13367 *Any success I have enjoyed in research has been due to the fact that it has been the most exciting and all-consuming endeavor I ever engaged in.*

BECKER, RONALD LEONARD, archivist; b. N.Y.C., Feb. 16, 1950; s. Bernard and Frieda (Miller) B.; m. Christine Lee Johnsen, Jan. 6, 1974; children: Nathan James, Bernard William. AB in History, Duke U., 1971; AM in History, Rutgers U., 1972, MLS, 1973. Cataloger, bibliographer N.J. Hist. Soc., Newark, 1973-74; curator manuscripts Rutgers U., New Brunswick, N.J., 1974—, head spl. collections, 1991—. Grant reviewer NEH, 1977—, U.S. Dept. Edn., 1992-94; program evaluator N.J. Com. for Humanities, Trenton, 1983—; mem. N.J. State Hist. Records Adv. Bd., 1997—; adv. bd. Ctr. Jewish History, 2001-. Author: Checklist of New Jersey Periodicals, 1982; co-author: Union List of New Jersey Annual Publications, 1977, History of the Jewish Community in Newark, N.J., 1995; editor Mid-Atlantic Archivist, 1983-92. Mem., v.p. bd. trustees Metuchen (N.J.) Pub. Libr., 1977-82. Mem. Soc. Am. Archivists, Mid-Atlantic Regional Archives Conf. (pres. 1975-77), Fedn. Jewish Men's Clubs (v.p. 1986-88, trustee 1988-92). Democrat. Jewish. Home: 84 Highland Ave Metuchen NJ 08840-1913 Office: Spl Collections Univ Archives Rutgers U Libr 169 College Ave New Brunswick NJ 08901-1163 Fax: (732) 932-7012. E-mail: rbecker@rci.rutgers.edu.

BECKER, SEYMOUR, hazardous materials and wastes specialist; b. Bronx, N.Y., Feb. 14, 1924; m. Ruth Schmitt, Aug. 30, 1958. MS, U. Wis., 1949; PhD, Pacific Western U., 1981. Nationally cert. hazardous materials mgr. and hazardous control mgr. Radiation control insp. Suffolk County Dept. Health Svcs., Hauppauge, N.Y., 1960-81; tech. cons., 1981-83; hazardous materials and wastes cons. Environ. Svcs., Portland, Maine, 1983-85; hazardous materials and wastes cons., safety/environ. specialist Mercy Hosp., Portland, 1985—. Del. to China, People to People, Spokane, Wash., 1987, del. to Russia and Ukraine, 1992; advisor and cons. State of Maine Hosp. Assn., Augusta, 1988-90, Low Level Radioactive Wastes Authority, Augusta, 1989-93, Dept. Environ. Protection, Augusta, 1989-93. Contbr. articles to profl. jours. Cons. Emergency Mgmt. Agy., Windham, Maine, 1983—, Local Emergency Planning Com., Windham, 1989—, chair Cumberland, Maine, 1996—2001; rep. State Emergency Response Commn., Maine, 1998—. Mem. APHA, Acad. Hazardous Materials Mgmt., Health Physics Soc., N.Y. Acad. Scis., Maine Pub. Health Assn. Achievements include development of N.Y. State radiation code; initiation of radiation control program in Suffolk County, N.Y. Home: 169 High St Apt 312 Portland ME 04101-2852 Office: Mercy Hosp 144 State St Portland ME 04101-3795

BECKER, SEYMOUR, history educator; b. Rochester, N.Y., Sept. 15, 1934; s. Aaron P. and Lena (Saperstone) B.; m. Alla Zeide, Oct. 23, 1981; children: Geoffrey Mark, Susan Elizabeth. AB, Williams Coll., 1956; AM, Harvard U., 1958, PhD, 1963. From asst. to full prof. Rutgers U., New Brunswick, NJ, 1962—2002, prof. emeritus, 2002—. Author: Russia's Protectorates in Central Asia: Bukhara & Khiva, 1865-1924, 1968, Nobility & Privilege in Late Imperial Russia, 1985; author: (with others) The Nationality Question in Soviet Central Asia, 1973, Russian Colonial Expansion to 1917, 1988, Central Asia: Its Strategic Importance & Future Prospects, 1994; contbr articles to profl. jours. Mem. Am. Hist. Assn., Am. Assn. Advancement of Slavic Studies (bd. dirs. 1979-82), Assn. Study of Nationalities (v.p. 1990-94), Mid-Atlantic Slavic Conf. (pres. 1979-80). Home: 245 W 104th St Apt 9D New York NY 10025-4279 E-mail: sybecker@rci.rutgers.edu.

BECKER, STEPHEN A. physicist, designer; b. Evanston, Ill., Sept. 11, 1950; s. John N. and Irene A. (Wlodarski) B.; m. Wendee M. Brunish, May 30, 1980. BA, Northwestern U., 1972; MS, Case Western Res. U., 1974; PhD, U. Ill., 1979. Rsch. and teaching assoc. U. Ill., Champaign, 1979-80; postdoctoral fellow Calif. Inst. Tech., Pasadena, 1980-82; dep. group leader Los Alamos (N.Mex.) Nat. Lab., 1983—. Contbr. articles to Astrophys. Jour. Recipient Recognition of Excellence award U.S. Dept. Energy, 1999, R&D 100 award, 1999. Mem. Am. Astron. Soc., Internat. Astron. Union. Roman Catholic. Office: Los Alamos Nat Lab PO Box 1663 Mail Stop T085 Los Alamos NM 87545 E-mail: sab@lanl.gov.

BECKER, STEPHEN BRADBURY, fraternal organization administrator; b. Toronto, Can., Aug. 17, 1947; s. Jack and Anne (Havill) B.; m. Trudy Ann Gaar, Dec. 27, 1968; two children. BSc, U. Fla., 1969; MEd in Human Resources Devel., Xavier U., 2002. Asst. mgr. distbn. Composers Authors & Publs. Can., Toronto, 1969-71; employee rels. adminstr. Can. Imperial Bank Commerce, Toronto, 1971-80; dir. pers. & mgmt. tng. Mother's Restaurants, Inc., Burlington, Canada, 1980-83; dist. mgr. Radio Shack, Toronto, 1983-85; mgr. devel. & cmty. rels. Oakville (Can.)-Trafalgar Meml. Hosp., 1985-88; v.p. Navion Fund Raising Cons., Toronto, 1988-92, v.p., prin., 1995-97; dir. advancement Beta Theta Pi Found., Oxford, Ohio, 1992-94; assoc. adminstr. sec. Beta Theta Pi Frat., Oxford, 1997-98; admin. sec. Beta Theta Pi, Oxford, 1998—. Fellow Inst. Canadian Bankers; mem. Nat. Soc. Fund Raising Execs. (cert.), Fraternity Execs. Assn. Home: 10 University Ave Oxford OH 45056-1348

BECKER, SUSAN KAPLAN, management and marketing communication consultant, educator; b. Newark, Jan. 4, 1948; d. Charles and Janet Kaplan; m. William Paul Becker, 1969 (div. 1977). BA in English cum laude, with distinction, U. Pa., 1968, MA, 1969, PhD, 1973, MBA in Fin., 1979. Instr. English Bryn Mawr (Pa.) Coll., 1972-74; assoc. editor U. Pa., Phila., 1975, asst. dir., lectr. urban studies, 1975-77; fin. analyst Phila. Nat. Bank, 1979-82; asst. v.p. Chem. Bank, N.Y.C., 1982-84; v.p. Bankers Trust Co., N.Y.C., 1984-85; prin. Becker Cons. Svcs., N.Y.C., 1985—; adj. assoc. prof. mgmt. comm. Stern Sch. Bus. N.Y.U., 1990—. Cons./evaluator Pa. Humanities Council, Phila., 1977-78; mem. editorial bd. Mgmt. Comm. Quar., 1993-97. Author: How to Develop Profitable Financial Products for the Institutional Marketplace, 1988; contbr. articles and revs. to profl. jours. Vol. N.Y. Cares, 1989-92, N.Y.C. affiliate Am. Heart Assn., 1995-97. U. Pa. fellow, 1968-72; E.I. DuPont de Nemours fellow, 1979, N.Y. Regents Coll. Teaching fellow, 1968-70. Mem. Internat. Comm. Assn. (reviewer tech. and comm. divsn. 1991), Fin. Women's Assn. N.Y. (profl. devel. com. 1995—), Profl. Assn. Investment Comm. Resources. Democrat. Avocations: painting and drawing, swimming. Office: 155 E 29th St New York NY 10016-8173 E-mail: susan.kaplan.becker.wg79@wharton.upenn.edu.

BECKER, TAMARA SUE, nursing administrator; b. Jerome, Idaho, June 18, 1955; d. Robert Howard and Dorothy Ineas Carson; m. Theron Daniel Becker, Dec. 27, 1975; children: Troy Daniel, Trent Anthony, Tawna Malee, Telcia Diane. AS, Coll. So. Idaho, Twin Falls, 1975; BS, Boise State U., 1999; MS U. Wyo., 2003—. RN, Idaho. Staff nurse Twin Falls (Idaho) Clinic and Hosp., 1975-83; charge nurse ICU, Magic Valley Regional Med. Ctr., Twin Falls, 1983-85; charge nurse emergency room St. Benedicts Family Med. Ctr., Jerome, 1985-91; patient care coord. Magic Valley Regional Med. Ctr., Twin Falls, 1991—2001, basic EKG class instr., 1997—, instr. ACLS, 1993—, instr. BLS, 1986-98, mgr. unit support team, 2001—. Mem. Golden Key, Phi Kappa Phi, Sigma Theta Tau. Avocations: bible study, swimming, white-water rafting. Home: 372 N 100 W Jerome ID 83338-5408 Office: Magic Valley Regional Med Ctr PO Box 409 Twin Falls ID 83303-0409

BECKER, TERESA ANN, neonatal nurse practitioner; b. Bangor, Maine, Apr. 22, 1957; d. George Robert and Marlene Ellen (Mueller) B. BSN, East Tenn. State U., 1980; cert. nurse practitioner, Georgetown U., 1988; MSN, U. Tenn., 1995. RN, Tenn.; cert. nurse practitioner NNP, PNP Nat. Cert. PNP/N, regional instr. neonatal resuscitation, pediatric advanced life support instr. Charge nurse newborn Johnson City (Tenn.) Med. Ctr., 1980-82, staff nurse SCN, 1982-84, staff nurse NICU, 1984-85, charge nurse NICU, 1985-88, mem. neonatal transport team, 1987—, neonatal nurse practitioner, 1989—. Regional instr. neonatal resuscitation AAP, Johnson City, 1989—; instr. PALS Am. Heart Assn., Johnson City, 1991—. Bd. dirs. March of Dimes, Johnson City, 1992-93; chmn. Health Profl. Adv. Com. Mem. Nat. Assn. Neonatal Nurses, Nat. Assn. Pediatric Nurse Assocs. and Practitioners, Sigma Theta Tau. Roman Catholic. Avocations: water skiing, swimming, reading, gardening. Home: 4117 Aztec Dr Johnson City TN 37604-1144 Office: Johnson City Med Ctr 400 N State Of Franklin Rd Johnson City TN 37604-6094

BECKER, THOMAS BAIN, lawyer; b. St. Charles, Mo., Sept. 3, 1944; s. John Bruere and Marie Louise (Denker) B.; m. Linda Ann Flynn, May 25, 1974; children: Thomas Bain Jr., Shannon Flynn. BSBA, Georgetown U., 1966; MBA, U. Mo., Columbia, 1968, JD, 1976. Bar: Mo. 1976. Acct. Kerber, Eck & Braeckel, St. Louis, 1966, Rothaus, Bartels & Earley, St. Louis, 1968; acctg. analyst U.S. Dept. Commerce, Washington, 1971-73; shareholder Stinson, Mag & Fizzell, Kansas City, 1976-98, Gilmore & Bell, P.C., Kansas City, 1998—. Bd. dirs., v.p., pres. Westport Citizens Action Coalition, Kansas City, 1987—; bd. dirs. Hist. Kansas City Found., 1981-89, Kansas City Union Sta., Inc., 1988-97; bd. commrs., vice chair Mo. Housing Devel. Commn., 1995-98; mem. task force Mayor's Odyssey 2000, Kansas City, 1993; bd. dirs., vice chmn. Citizens Assn. Kansas City, 1996—. Recipient Community Svc. award Westport Coop. Svcs., 1991. Mem. ABA, Nat. Assn. Bond Lawyers, Rockhill Tennis Club (pres., bd. govs., treas. 1999—). Democrat. Roman Catholic. Avocations: sports, politics, reading, travel. Home: 816 Gleed Ter Kansas City MO 64109-2617 Office: Gilmore & Bell PC 2405 Grand Blvd Ste 1100 Kansas City MO 64108-2521

BECKER, WALTER HEINRICH, vocational educator, planner; b. St. Louis, Mar. 20, 1939; s. Anthon and Maria (Fleischman) B.; m. Ayse Nur Alpyoruk, Aug. 3, 1971; children: Volkan P., Kristal S. BS, S.E. Mo. State U., 1963; MS, U. Mo., Columbia, 1969; PhD, St. Louis U., 1978; MS, Fontbonne Coll., 1989. Cert. tchr. Secondary tchr. Sch. Dist. of Hancock Pl., Lemay, Mo., 1963-64, Mascoutah (Ill.) Sch. Dist., 1964-65, U.S. Dept. of Def., Japan, Turkey, Philippines, 1965-70; vocat. edn. supr. Mo. Divsn. of Mental Health, Farmington, Mo., 1971-79; program analyst Arabian Am. Oil Co., Dhahran, Saudi Arabia, 1979-80, planning and programs analyst, 1981-85; vocat. edn. supr. Mo. Dept. of Corrections, Jefferson City, 1990-93.

BECKER, WENDY JEANNE, music and drama educator, songwriter, singer; b. Milw., July 26, 1956; d. Arthur Becker and Muriel Jeanne (Mark) Sweet; m. Rik Howard. BFA, U. Wis., 1979. Registered music therapist. Music dir. Camp Hess Kramer, L.A., 1976-81; music tchr., dir. schs. and synagogues, L.A., 1981-90; music and choir dir. Stephen Wise Cmty. H.S., L.A., 1987-94; drama dir. Milken Cmty. H.S., L.A., 1992-97; v.p. Merrie Way Cmty., non-profit org.; producer Morphing of Am. Actress: Days of Our Lives, My Work is Blessed, Getting Back, Blithe Spirit; performances include (with Barbara Streisand) Dem. Nat. Conv., Barbara Streisand Farewell Tour Concert, L.A.; performer various benefits and charities; editor, sub-pub.: Jean Davoust. Music specialist Congregation Ohr Ha Torah, 1997-2003, Petite Amie Music. Recipient Tchr. of the Yr. award Morphing of Am., 1997. Mem. Nat. Assn. Music Therapy, SAG, AFTRA, Actors Equity Assn., Songwriters Guild of Am., Nat. Acad. Recording Arts and Scis., Delta Omicron. Avocations: singing, dancing, violin. E-mail: wendybecker@adelphia.net.

BECKER, WENDY S. educator; Bachelors, Pa. State U., 1980, Masters, 1984, PhD, 1999. Instr. Pa. State U., University Park, 1996—2000; asst. prof. SUNY, Albany, 2000—. Faculty Rsch. grantee, SUNY, Albany, 2002. Mem.: APA, SIOP, Acad. Mgmt. Office: SUNY Albany Washington Ave Albany NY 12222

BECKER-KLICKER, MARGARET CHAN, library director; b. Tronoh, Perak, West Malaysia; came to U.S., 1972; d. Chan Heong and Ng Tai; m. Millage W. Becker, Oct. 10, 1972 (dec. Sept. 1984); m. Alfred Klicker, June 19, 1991. Degree in bus., Bus. Inst., Ipoh, West Malaysia. Cert. libr., N.Mex. Sec. dist. and land office Malaysian Govt., Batu Gajah, 1963-72; health and social coord. Migrant Coun., Burley, Idaho, 1977-78; clk. Deming (N.Mex.) Pub. Libr., 1979-87, asst. dir., 1987-92, acting dir., 1992, dir., 1993—. Mem. N.Mex. Libr. Assn. Home: PO Box 745 Deming NM 88031-0745 Office: Deming Pub Libr 301 S Tin St Deming NM 88030-3698

BECKERMAN, DALE LEE, lawyer; b. Omaha, Feb. 7, 1949; s. Harold Frank and Marjorie Jane (Butler) B.; m. Kathryn Jane Barr, Nov. 20, 1971; children: Clare, Harold. BA, Amherst Coll., 1971; JD with honors, George Washington U., 1975. Bar: D.C. 1976, Mo. 1976, U.S. Dist. Ct. (we. dist.) Mo. 1976, U.S. Ct. Appeals (8th cir.) 1979, U.S. Ct. Appeals (10th cir.) 1990, Kans. 1993. Assoc. Deacy & Deacy, Kansas City, Mo., 1975-80, ptnr., 1980—. Mem. Cir. Ct. Bench Bar Com., Kansas City, 1985, advisor, 1986. Mem. ABA, Mo. Bar, Kansas City Met. Bar Assn., Lawyers Assn. Kansas City, Internat. Assn. Def. Counsel, Johnson County Kans. Bar Assn. Home: 4509 W 82d St Prairie Village KS 66208 Office: Deacy & Deacy Ten Main Ctr 920 Main St Ste 1900 Kansas City MO 64105-2010 Fax: 816 421-7880. E-mail: dlb@deacylaw.com.

BECKERS, JACQUES MAURICE, astrophysicist; b. Arnhem, The Netherlands, Feb. 14, 1934; came to U.S., 1962; s. Wilhelmus B.H. and Maria H. (Hermans) B.; m. Gerda M. Van Vuurden, Mar. 24, 1959 (div. Aug. 1995); children: Christina M., Michael P. PhD, U. Utrecht, The Netherlands, 1959. Astrophysicist Sacramento Peak Obs., Sunspot, N.Mex., 1962-79; astrophysicist, dir. Multiple Mirror Telescope Obs., Tucson, 1979-84, Advanced Devel. program Nat. Optical Astronomy Observatories, Tucson, 1984-88; astrophysicist European So. Obs., Garching, Fed. Republic of Germany, 1988-93, VLT Program Scientist, 1991-93; dir. Nat. Solar Observatory, Tucson, 1993-98, astronomer, 1998—2001; sr. scientist U. Chgo., 2001—. Mem. Norwegian Acad. Scis. (fgn.), Royal Netherlands Acad. Scis. (corr.). Office: Dept Astronomy and Astrophysics U Chgo Chicago IL 60637

BECKETT, JOSHUA PATRICK, baseball player; b. Spring, Tex., May 15, 1980; Baseball player Fla. Marlins, 2001—. Supporter Fla. Marlins-Josh Beckett Baseball Tournament, Adopt-A-Classroom program. Nominee Sporting News Good Guy award, 2002; named 2001 Marlins Rookie of Yr., Baseball Writers Assn. Am. So. Fla. chpt., 2001, Marlins Orgnl. Pitcher of Yr., Pitcher of Yr., Sportsticker Minor League, Player of Yr., USA Today Minor League, Pitcher of Yr., Baseball Weekly Minor League, Baseball Am. Player of Yr., Player of Yr., Sporting News Minor League, Fla. State League All-Star, top

prospect in 1999 Draft, Baseball Weekly, Ea. League Pitcher of Week, Fla. State League Pitcher of Week, Marlins' Orgnl. Pitcher of Month, Marlin's Top prospect, No. 3 prospect in overall, Baseball Am., Ea. League, Fla. State League best pitching prospect, Baseball Am. ; recipient 3 Player of Week awards. Office: Fla Marlins 2269 Dan Marino Blvd Opa Locka FL 33056 Office Fax: 305-624-6403.

BECKETT, JOYCE, educator, social worker; b. Norfolk, Va., Aug. 2, 1945; d. William James and Bettye Mae (Bailey) B.; m. John C. Purnell, Jr. AB, Temple U., 1967; MSS, Bryn Mawr (Pa.) Coll., 1969, PhD, 1977. Lic. clin. social worker. Psychiat. social worker Ea. Pa. Psychiat. Inst., Phila., 1969-71; lectr., counselor Bryn Mawr Coll., 1971-75; from asst. to assoc. prof. U. Mich., Ann Arbor, 1975-85; prof. Va. Commonwealth U., Richmond, 1985—. Pvt. practice, Phila., 1973-75, Richmond, 1985-90; spl. asst. to commr. Va. Dept. Mental Health, Mental Retardation and Substance Abuse Svcs., Richmond, 1993-94. Mem. editorial bd. Social Work, Smith Coll. Studies in Social Work; contbr. chpts. to books and articles to profl. jours. Trustee William Byrd Community Ctr., Richmond, 1988-91; agy. evaluation com. United Way, Richmond, 1986-87; bd. dirs. Octagon House, Ann Arbor, 1979-81; bd. dirs. Va. Alliance for the Mentally Ill, 1994-96. Named one of Outstanding Young Women Am., 1979; Ford Found. fellow, 1983-84; recipient Rsch. award Ford Found., 1977-78, Individual Rsch. award NIMH, 1984-85, curriculum devel. award Nat. Inst. Alcohol Abuse & Alcoholism, 1991-95. Mem. NASW (chair leadership identification com. state chpt. 1995-97, bd. dirs. state chpt. 1987-91, nat. book com. 1997-2000), Nat. Assn. Black Social Workers (chpt. v.p. 1983-85), Coun. on Social Work Edn., Acad. Cert. Social Workers, Gerontol. Soc. Am., Phi Kappa Phi. Democrat. Office: Va Commonwealth U PO Box 842027 Richmond VA 23284-2027

BECKETT, THEODORE CHARLES, lawyer; b. Boonville, Mo., May 6, 1929; s. Theodore Cooper and Gladys (Watson) B.; m. Daysie Margaret Cornwall, 1950; children: Elizabeth Gayle, Theodore Cornwall, Margaret Lynn, William Harrison, Anne Marie. BS, U. Mo., Columbia, 1950, JD, 1957. Bar: Mo. 1957. Of counsel Baker, Sterchi, Cowden & Rice, LLC; instr. polit. sci. U. Mo., Columbia, 1956-57; asst. atty. gen. State of Mo., 1961-64. Mem. City Plan Commn., Kansas City, 1976-80; bd. curators U. Mo., 1995-2001, pres. 1998. 1st lt. U.S. Army, 1950-53. Mem. ABA, Mo. Bar, Kansas City Bar Assn., Lawyers Assn. Kansas City, Newcomen Soc. N.Am., SAR, Order of Coif, Sigma Nu, Phi Alpha Delta. Clubs: Kansas City (Kansas City, Mo.), Blue Hills Country (Kansas City, Mo.). Presbyterian. Office: 2400 Pershing Rd Ste 500 Kansas City MO 64108

BECKETT, VICTORIA LING, physician; m. Peter G.S. Beckett, 1954 (dec. 1974); 1 child, Paul T. (dec.); m. Joseph C. Sharp, 1996. BA, Mt. Holyoke Coll., 1945; MD, U. Mich., 1949; MA, St. Mary's U., 1995. Intern Mpls. Gen. Hosp., 1949-50; fellow Mayo Grad. Sch., 1951-55; clin. instr. Wayne State U. Sch. Medicine, Detroit, 1956-67; staff cons. internal medicine oncology svc. Henry Ford Hosp., Detroit, 1957-60; rsch. physician Darling Meml. Ctr., Detroit, 1965-69; rsch. assoc. rheumatology Wayne State U. Sch. Medicine, 1970-72, postgrad. tutor, 1972-73, dir., 1973-76; med. dir. Rochester (Minn.) Health Care Ctr., 1985—90; cons. physician in rheumatology Federated Dublin Vol. Hosps., 1973-76; staff cons. rheumatology Mayo Clinic, 1976-90, emeritus staff, 1990—; asst. prof. medicine Mayo Med. Sch., 1976-90. Fellow ACP; mem. Mayo Med. Alumni Assn., Am. Coll. Rheumatology (ret. mem.), Minn. State Med. Assn., Zumbro Valley Med. Soc., Phi Beta Kappa, Sigma Xi. Methodist. Avocations: teaching exercise class, creative writing.

BECKETT, WILLIAM HENRY MILLER, lawyer; b. Newton, Mass., May 3, 1940; s. Ralph G. and Elizabeth (Bartlett) B.; m. Sally Wadsworth, Jan. 25, 1963 (dec.); children: William H.M. Jr., Alexander F.W., Elizabeth B.; m. Virginia Morgan, June 15, 1997. BA, Harvard U., 1962; JD, Boston U., 1965. Bar: Mass. 1965, N.H. 1966, U.S. Dist. Ct. N.H. 1966, U.S. Dist. Ct. Mass. 1966, U.S. Ct. Appeals (1st cir.) 1966, U.S. Supreme Ct. 1966. Law clk. to chief justice and judges Superior Ct. of the Commonwealth of Mass., Boston, 1965—66; assoc. Perkins, Holland and Donovan, Exeter, NH, 1966—70; ptnr. Holland, Donovan, Beckett, Hermans & Davison, P.A., Exeter, 1970—2001; pvt. practice William H.M. Beckett, P.A., Portsmouth, NH, 2001—. Bar examiner N.H. Com. of Bar Examiners, Concord, 1978-88; master N.H. Superior Ct., Concord. Mem. Exeter Sch. Bd., 1971-74; trustee Exeter Hosp., 1987—, N.H. Hosp. Assn., Concord, 1990—, Seacoast Hospice, 1999—. Mem. ABA, Assn. Trial Lawyers Am., N.H. Bar Assn., Mass. Bar Assn., U.S. Supreme Ct. Hist. Soc. (N.H. chairperson). Avocations: sailing, tennis, golf, squash. Office: William HM Beckett 104 Congress St Ste 304 Portsmouth NH 03801 Fax: 603-766-1687. E-mail: attorneybeckett@yahoo.com.

BECKHAM, EDGAR FREDERICK, educational consultant; b. Hartford, Conn., Aug. 5, 1933; s. Walter Henry and Willabelle (Hollinshed) B.; m. Ria Haertl, Aug. 16, 1958; 1 child, Frederick Hollinshed. BA, Wesleyan U., 1958; MA, Yale U., 1959, postgrad., 1959-61; DHL, Olivet Coll., 1997, Clark U., 2000. Instr. German Wesleyan U., Middletown, Conn., 1961-66, dir. lang. lab., 1963-66, lang. lab. dir., lectr. German, 1967-69, assoc. provost, 1969-73, dean, 1973-90, dean emeritus, 1996—; program officer The Ford Found., N.Y.C., 1990-96; coord. Campus Diversity Initiative, 1996-98; sr. fellow Assn. Am. Colls. and Univs., 1998—. Lectr. English U. Erlangen, Germany, 1966-67; cons. Nat. Endowment for Humanities; mem. Commn. on Instns. of Higher Edn., 1981-84; pres. Rockfall Corp., 1985-86; bd. dirs. Assn. Am. Colls., 1985-90. Chmn. Conn. Humanities Coun., 1979-80, Conn. Com. on Edn. Equity and Excellence, 1994-95, Conn. State Bd. Edn., 1993-95; mem. Dem. Town Com., Middletown, 1972-90; pres. bd. dirs. Conn. Housing Investment Fund, 1981-83; chmn. bd. dirs. Middlesex Hosp., 1983-85, dir. emeritus; trustee emeritus Vt. Acad.; chmn., bd. dirs. Conn. Pub. Broadcasting, 1990-92; chmn. bd. trustees Donna Wood Found.; trustee Mt. Holyoke Coll.; bd. dirs. NAFSA; mem. adv. coun. Appalachian Coll. Assn. Inst., mem. Future of Higher Edn. Project. With AUS, 1954-57. Recipient Outstanding Contbn. to Higher Edn. award Nat. Assn. Student Pers. Adminstrs., 1997, Raymond E. Baldwin medal Wesleyan U. Alumni Assn., 1991, Outstanding Svc. award, 1998. Mem. MLA, Am. Assn. for Higher Edn., Am. Assn. Tchrs. German. Office: Assn Am Colls and Univs 1818 R St NW Washington DC 20009-1604

BECKHAM, WALTER HULL, JR., lawyer, educator; b. Albany, Ga., Apr. 18, 1920; m. Ethel Koger, Mar. 13, 1943; children: Barbara, Walter III, James K. AB, Emory U., 1941; LLB cum laude, Harvard U., 1948. Bar: Fla. 1949, U.S. Supreme Ct. 1956, D.C. 1978. Assoc. prof. law U. Miami, Fla., 1948-49; ptnr. Nichols, Gaither, Beckham et al, 1950-67; of counsel Podhurst, Orseck, Josefsberg, Eaton, Meadow, Olin & Perwin P.A., Miami, 1967—. Prof. law U. Miami, 1967-82, prof. emeritus, 1982—. Editor Harvard Law Rev. Pres. Greater Miami YMCA, 1963-68, Crippled Children's Soc. Dade County, 1968-69; mem. Dade County Mental Health Bd., 1971-73; chmn. bd. trustees YMCA Blue Ridge Assembly, 1977-79; trustee Nat. Jud. Coll., 1990-96, trustee, chmn., 1995-96, chmn. emeritus, 1996—. With USNR, 1941-46; capt. USNR, ret. Recipient The Perry Nichols award, Acad. Fla. Trial Lawyers, 1984. Mem. ABA (spl. com. on tort liability system 1979-84, spl. commn. on assn. governance 1983-84, chmn. tort and ins. practice sect. 1974-75, Ho. of Dels. 1979-85, 87-95, sec.-elect 1986-87, sec. 1987-90), Am. Bar Found., Am. Coll. Trial Lawyers, Am. Law Inst., Assn. Trial Lawyers Am. (chmn. aviation sect. 1966-68), Fla. Bar Assn. (past mem. bd. of govs. jr. bar sect.), Dade County Bar Assn. (pres. jr. bar sect. 1952-53, exec. com. 1953-54), Internat. Acad. Trial Lawyers (pres. 1973), Internat. Acad. Law and Sci., Law Sci. Inst., Maritime Law Assn. U.S., Nat. Inst. Trial Adv. (trustee 1976-86, chmn. 1983-85), Inner Circle of Advs., Med. Inst. for Attys. (dir. 1968-83), Nat. Bd. Trial Adv. (founding mem.), Phi Beta Kappa, Omicron Delta Kappa, Phi Alpha Delta, Chi Phi, Kiwanis. Office: Podhurst Orseck Josefsberg Eaton Meadow Olin Perwin City Nat Bank Bldg 25 W Flagler St Ste 800 Miami FL 33130-1720

BECKHAM, WALTER HULL, III, lawyer; b. Boston, Feb. 12, 1948; s. Walter Hull Beckham Jr. and Ethel Brooks (Koger) Beckham. BA, Emory U., 1970, JD, 1977; MBA, U. Mich., 1972. Bar: Ga. 1977, U.S. Dist. Ct. (no. dist.) Ga. 1978, U.S. Dist. Ct. (so. dist.) Ga. 1980, U.S. Dist. Ct. (mid. dist.) Ga. 1988, U.S. Ct. Appeals (11th cir.) 1982. Investment analyst, portfolio mgr. Life of Ga., Atlanta, 1972-74; assoc. Jessee, Ritchie & Duncan, P.C., Atlanta, 1977-81, ptnr., 1981-82; pvt. practice, Atlanta, 1982—. Bd. dirs. Cmty. Outreach YMCA, Atlanta, 1973—75; Brookhaven Boys Club Atlanta, 1976; pres. Sr. Hon. Soc. Emory U., Atlanta, 1984—85, mem. Law Sch. Coun., 1993—2001, mem. bd. govs., 2001—. Mem.: ABA (tort and ins. practice sect., long range planning com. 1986—90, chmn. satellite seminars and videotapes com. 1990—92, coun. 1990—93, chmn. pub. rels. com. 1993, com. coord. 1993, sect. chmn. 1995—96), Ga. Trial Lawyers Assn. (long range planning com. 1982—86), Internat. Acad. Trial Lawyers, Atlanta Bar Assn. (state ct. com. 1985), Ga. Bar Assn. (co-chmn. com. on professionalism 1997—2000, jud. procedure and adminstrn. com. 2000—), Kappa Alpha (Hardeman Province Ct. of Honor). Avocations: hunting, fishing, skiing. Home: 1208 Village Run NE Atlanta GA 30319-5303 Office: Ste 2600 75 14th St Atlanta GA 30309

BECKHOLT, ALICE, clinical nurse specialist; b. N.Y.C., Aug. 7, 1941; d. Julius and Mary (Katz) Kalkow; m. Richard H. Polakoff, Aug. 12, 1962 (div. 1984); children: Katherine, Michael, Matthew; m. Kenneth Eugene Beckholt, Feb. 3, 1990. BA, Syracuse U., 1962; ADN, El Centro Coll., 1977; BSN, U. Tex., Arlington, 1980; MS, Tex. Women's U., 1988. RN, Tex., Ohio. Staff nurse, outpatient mgr. Irving (Tex.) Cmty. Hosp., 1977-86; staff nurse Meth. Hosp., Dallas, 1986-89, U. Tex. S.W. Med. Ctr., Dallas, 1989-90; pediat. home care nurse various agys., Columbus, Ohio, 1990-94; advanced practice nurse, pub. speaking, preceptor Columbus Health Dept., 1994—. Med. advisor Ohio Support HELP. Sec., 2nd v.p., 1st v.p., pres. Am. Cancer Soc., 1971-76, bd. dirs. Irving, Tex., 1971-90, BSE instr., nurse's com., 1990-97, triple touch coord., 1991-97, BSE faculty, 1986-90; vol., auction subchair Sta. KERA-TV, Dallas, 1972-84; CPR instr. Am. Heart Assn., 1984-98; med. adv. Ohio Support HELP. Recipient Outstanding Svc. award Am. Cancer Soc. Columbus chpt., 1992-93; named Outstanding Vol., Am. Cancer Soc., Irving, Tex., 1973, 74, 76. Mem.: APHA, Ohio Assn. Advanced Practice Nurses, Ohio Pub. Health Assn., Sigma Theta Tau. Avocations: gourmet cooking, classical music, travel. Home: 2605 Brookwood Rd Columbus OH 43209-2904 Office: Columbus Dept Health 240 S Parsons Ave Columbus OH 43215-4022

BECKJORD, ERIC STEPHEN, nuclear engineer, energy researcher; b. Evanston, Ill., Feb. 17, 1929; s. Walter Clarence and Mary Amelia (Hitchcox) B.; m. Caroline Wendell Gardner, Feb. 28, 1953; children: Eric H., Amy W., Charles A., Sarah H. AB cum laude, Harvard U., 1951; MS in Elec. Engring., MIT, 1956; MBA, U. Chgo., 1984. Devel. engr. GE, San Jose, Calif., 1956-60, project engr. Pleasanton, Calif., 1960-63; engring. mgr. Westinghouse Electric Corp., Pitts., 1963-70, project dir., mgr. strategic planning-nuclear, 1973-75; v.p. Westinghouse Nuclear Europe, Brussels, 1970-73; dep. dir. FEA, Washington, 1975; dir. div. reactor devel. and demonstration ERDA, Washington, 1976-77; dir. nuclear power devel. Dept. of Energy, Washington, 1977-78, coordinator internat. nuclear study, 1978-80; dep. dir. Argonne Nat. Lab., Ill., 1980-84; vis. prof. nuclear engring. MIT, Cambridge, 1984-86, exec. dir. nuclear energy study, 2002—03; dir. rsch. U.S. Nuclear Regulatory Commn., Washington, 1986-95, cons., 1995—; chmn. com. safety of nuclear installations NEA-DECD, Paris, 1995. Author: Boiling Water Reactor Design, 1962; contbr. articles to profl. jours. Mem. vis. com. for nuclear engring. dept. MIT, 1992-98; mem. bd. visitors dept. materials and nuclear engring. U. Md., 1995—. Lt. (j.g.) USNR, 1951-54. Recipient Presdl. Meritorious award, 1992. Fellow Am. Nuclear Soc. (bd. dirs. 1995-98, chair nuclear installations safety divsn. 2000-01); mem. IEEE (sr.), Sigma Xi. Avocation: history.

BECKLAKE, MARGARET RIGSBY, physician, educator; b. London, May 27, 1922; d. James Thomas and Dorothy Mabel (Mills) B.; m. Maurice McGregor, Mar. 20, 1948; children: James, Margaret. MBBCh, U. Witwatersrand, 1944, MD, 1951, MD (hon.), 1974. Lectr. U. Witwatersrand, 1950-57; asst. prof. exptl. medicine McGill U., 1961-65, prof., 1967-96, prof. epidemiology and medicine, 1973-96, prof. emeritus, 1996—. Career investigator Med. Rsch. Coun. Can., 1968-93. Contbr. 160 articles to med. jours. Named hon. prof., U. Witwatersrand, 1984-85. Fellow Royal Coll. Physicians, Royal Soc. (Can.); mem. Am. Thoracic Soc. (Disting. Achievement award 1997, World Lung Health award 2001), Can. Thoracic Soc., Am. Physiol. Soc. Home: 532 Pine Ave W Montreal QC Canada H2W 1S6 Office: McGill Univ Dept Epidem 1110 Pine Ave W Montreal QC Canada H3A 1A3 E-mail: margaret.becklake@mcgill.ca.

BECKLER, DAVID ZANDER, government official, science administrator; b. June 29, 1918; s. William J. and Thekla (Levy) B.; m. Harriet Levy, Aug. 1, 1943; children: Stephen, Paul, Rochelle. BSChemE, U. Rochester, N.Y., 1939; JD, George Wash. U., 1943. Bar: D.C. 1942. Patent atty. Pennie, Davis, Marvin & Edmonds, Washington, 1939-42; tech. aide fgn. liaison office Office Sci. R & D Exec. Office of Pres., Washington, 1942-45; patent atty. Eastman Kodak Co., Rochester, N.Y., 1946; dep. tech. historian Ops. Crossroads Joint Chiefs of Staff, Washington, 1946; chief tech. intelligence br., exec. dir. atomic energy R & D Bd. Office of Sec. of Def., Washington, 1947—52; mem. internat. sci. policy survey group Dept. of State, Washington, 1949-50; asst. dir. office indsl. devel. AEC, Washington, 1952-53; exec. officer Pres. Sci. Adv. Com., Washington, 1953—73; spl. asst. to dir. Office of Def. Mobilization, Washington, 1954—57; asst. to spl. asst. to pres. for sci. and tech. The White House, 1957—62; asst. to dir. Office Sci. and Tech. Exec. Office of Pres., Washington, 1962—73; asst. to pres. NAS, Washington, 1973-76; dir. sci. tech. and industry OECD, Paris, 1976-83; assoc. dir. Carnegie Commn. on Sci. Tech. and Govt., 1988—93. Cons. sci. and tech. policies, 1983-88, 94—. Recipient cert. of appreciation War and Navy Depts., Washington, 1945. Fellow AAAS; mem. Coun. Fgn. Rels., Cosmos Club (Washington). Home: 8709 Duvall St Fairfax VA 22031-2711 E-mail: dzbeckler@aol.com.

BECKLEY, DAVID LENARD, academic administrator; b. Shannon, Miss., Mar. 21, 1946; s. George and Georgianna (Fields) B.; m. Gemma Douglas, June 1, 1968; children: Jacqueline, Lisa. BA, Rust Coll., 1967; MEd, U. Miss., 1975, PhD, 1986. Dir. advancement Rust Coll., Holly Springs, Miss., 1967-87; pres. Wiley Coll., Marshall, Tex., 1987-93, Rust Coll., Holly Spring, Miss., 1993—. Mem. NAACP (life). Named Outstanding Alumni, U. Miss., Oxford, 1989; recipient Silver Beaver award, Yocona Area coun. Boy Scouts Am., 2002. Mem. Tex. Assn. Developing Colls. (chmn. 1991-93), Edn. Ins. Assn. (bd. dirs. 1988-93), United Negro Coll. Fund (bd. dirs. 1990—), Omega Psi Phi (Citizen of Yr. award 1986, Man of Yr. award 1984). Democrat. Methodist. Avocations: reading, traveling, collecting antiques. Office: Rust Coll 150 E Rust Ave Holly Springs MS 38635-2330 E-mail: dbeckely@rustcollege.edu.

BECKLEY, ROBERT MARK, architect, educator; b. Cleve., Dec. 24, 1934; s. Mark Ezra and Marie Elizabeth (Kuhl) Beckley; m. Jean Dorothy Love, Feb. 26, 1956 (div. May 1988); children: Jeffery, Thomas, James; m. Jytte Dinesen, Oct. 24, 1990. BArch, U. Cin., 1959; MArch, Harvard U., 1961. Registered architect, Mich., Ohio, Ill., Wis. From asst. to assoc. prof. U. Mich., Ann Arbor, 1963—69, dean, prof., 1987—97, prof., 1997—2002, prof., dean emeritus, 2002—; from assoc. prof. to prof. U. Wis., Milw., 1969—86. Prin. Beckley-Myers, Architects, Milw., 1980—91. Prin. works include Theater Facilities, 1980—81 (award, 1983), Theater Dist., 1981—82 (award, 1984), Bellevue Downtown Park, 1985 (1st place award, 1985). Recipient Distinction award, Milw. Art Mus., 1986. Fellow: Graham Found., Inst. Urban Design, Am. Inst. Architects (Mich. Pres.'s award 1994). Home: 1016 Scott Pl Ann Arbor MI 48105-2585 Office: U Mich Coll Arch 2000 Bonisteel Dr Ann Arbor MI 48109-2069

BECKMAN, FRANK SAMUEL, computer science educator, researcher; b. NYC, Apr. 10, 1921; s. Morris and Esther (Newburgh) B.; m. Shirley Cooperblum, Mar. 18, 1951; children: Susan, Denise, Jonathan. BS, CCNY, 1940; AM, Columbia U., 1947, PhD, 1965. Asst. prof. maths. Pratt Inst., 1947-51; mgr. univ. rels., assoc. dir. IBM Systems Rsch. Inst. IBM Corp., Yorktown Heights, NY, 1951-71; chmn. dept. computer sci. Bklyn. Coll. CUNY, NYC, 1971-85, exec. officer PhD program in computer sci. Grad. Ctr., 1985-88, prof. PhD program in computer sci. Grad. Ctr., 1988-93; prof. emeritus, 1993—. Cons. rsch. div. IBM Corp., Yorktown Heights, 1983-84, IBM Corp., White Plains, NY, 1989-90. Author: Mathematical Foundations of Programming, 1980. Sgt. US Army, 1944-46. Grantee HEW, 1974, Exxon Edn. Found., 1975, NSF, 1984-85, IBM, 1984-86, John Ben Snow Found., 1987. Mem. Am. Math. Soc., Math. Assn. Am., Soc. for Indsl. and Applied Math., Assn. for Computing Machinery, AAAS, Sigma Xi. Home: # 126-101 14095 Royal Vista Dr Delray Beach FL 33484-1828

BECKMAN, JAMES WALLACE BIM, economist, marketing executive, educator; b. Mpls., May 2, 1936; s. Wallace Gerald and Mary Louise (Frissell) B. BA, Princeton U., 1958; PhD, U. Calif., 1973. Ordained elder Presbyterian Ch. Pvt. practice, Berkeley, Calif., 1962-67; cons. Calif. State Assembly, Sacramento, 1967-68; pvt. practice Laguna Beach, Calif., 1969-77; cons. Calif. State Gov.'s Office, Sacramento, 1977-80; pvt. practice real estate cons. L.A., 1980-83; v.p. mktg. Gold-Well Investments, Inc., L.A., 1982-83; pres. Beckman Analytics Internat., econ. cons. to bus. and govt., L.A. and Lake Arrowhead, Calif., 1983—, East European/Middle East Bus. and Govt., 1992—. Adj. prof. Calif. State U. Sch. Bus., San Bernardino, 1989—, U. Redlands, 1992—, U. Calif., 1998—; cons. European environ. and development issues. Contbr. articles to profl. jours. Maj. USMC, 1958-67. NIMH fellow, 1971-72. Fellow Soc. Applied Anthropology; mem. Am. Econs. Assn., Am. Statis. Assn., Am. Mktg. Assn. (officer, Nat. Assn. Bus. Economists (officer). Democrat. Home and Office: Beckman Analytics Internat PO Box 1753 Lake Arrowhead CA 92352-1753 E-mail: bimbhappy@aol.com.

BECKMAN, JOHN, literature educator, novelist; b. Dubuque, Iowa, Dec. 30, 1967; s. Jerome and Ann Beckman; 1 child, Katy Raine. PhD, U. Calif., Davis, 2000. Lectr., English U. of Bordeaux, France, 1998—2000; asst. prof., English U.S. Naval Acad., Annapolis, Md., 2001—. Author: (novel) The Winter Zoo (NY Times Notable Book, 2002). Mem.: MLA. Green Party. Office: English Dept US Naval Academy Annapolis MD 21402 E-mail: beckman@usna.edu.

BECKMAN, L. DAVID, university chancellor; b. Denver, Aug. 21, 1926; BA, Wheaton Coll., 1947; MTh, Dallas Theol. Sem., 1952, ThD, 1956; MA, Columbia U., 1962; DD, Colo. Christian Coll., 1987. Instr. Dallas Bible Inst., 1952-55, London (Ont., Can.) Bible Inst. and Theol. Sem., 1955-61; chmn. Bible dept. The King's Coll., Briarcliff Manor, N.Y., 1961-63; pres. Rockmont Coll., Longmont/Denver, Colo., 1963-81, pres. emeritus Lakewood, Colo., 1981-83, 1983-85; pres. Colo. Christian Coll./Colo. Christian U., Lakewood, 1985-91, Colo. Christian U., Lakewood, 1991-93, chancellor, 1993-95, pres. emeritus, 1995—. Home: Heritage Eagle Bend 7775 S Biloxi Way Aurora CO 80016

BECKMAN, MICHAEL, lawyer; b. N.Y.C., Oct. 8, 1945; s. Albert Beckman and Cecille Bronson; m. Susan Liebowitz, June 26, 1970 (separated Dec. 1987); children: Andrew D., Jason D. Bar: N.Y. 1969, U.S. Dist. Ct. (so. dist.) N.Y. 1972. Atty. Gordon Brady Keller & Ballen, N.Y.C., 1969-71; ptnr. Wolkowitz & Beckman, N.Y.C., 1971-74; sr. ptnr. Bell Kalnick Beckman Klee & Green, N.Y.C., 1974-88; sole practice N.Y.C., 1988-92; sr. ptnr. Beckman & Millman PC, N.Y.C., 1992-96, Beckman Millman & Sanders LLP, N.Y.C., 1996—2000, Beckman, Millman, Barandes, & Douglass, LLP, N.Y.C., 2000—. Adj. prof. law NYU, 1981-93. Dir. N.Y. Jr. Tennis League, N.Y.C., 1986-95, Sports & Arts in Schs. Found. Mem. West Side Tennis Club. Avocations: tennis, skiing. Home: 437 W 24th St New York NY 10011-1253 Office: Beckman Millman & Sanders LLP 116 John St Rm 1313 New York NY 10038-3303

BECKMAN, THOMAS J. physician; MD, U. Iowa, 1992. Diplomate Am. Bd. of Internal Medicine, 1999. Fellowship advanced gen. internal medicine Mayo Clinic, Rochester, Minn., 1999—2000, sr. assoc. cons. divsn. gen. internal medicine, 2000—. Contbr. articles. Lt. comdr. USN, 1993—97, Pearl Harbor, Hawaii. Msg George Schulte scholar, Loras Coll., 1988. Fellow: Am. Coll. Physicians; mem.: Americal Med. Assn., Internat. Assn. Med. Sci. Educators, Undersea and Hyperbaric Med. Soc., Soc. Gen. Internal Medicine, Delta Epsilson Sigma. Office: Mayo Clinic 200 First St SW Rochester MN 55905

BECKMANN, CHARLES HENRY, cardiologist, educator; b. N.Y.C., July 18, 1930; s. William and Margaret (Wellershaus) B.; m. Ardith Clara Kuehm, June 9, 1956; children: David, Eric, Diana. BS, MIT, 1952; MD, Cornell U., 1956. Diplomate Am. Bd. Internal Medicine, Am. Bd. Cardiology. Entered USAF, 1957, advanced through grades to col., 1971; asst. chief cardiology USAF Willford Hall Med. Ctr., San Antonio, 1965-70; chmn. dept. medicine Clark AFB Hosp. USAF, Philippines, 1970-73, chief cardiology Wilford Hall Med. Ctr., 1973-83; dir. med. ctr. San Antonio (Tex.) State Hosp., 1983-84; cardiologist Skinner Clinic, San Antonio, 1984—; clin. prof. medicine U. Tex., San Antonio, 1983—; prof. medicine Uniformed Svcs. U. Health Scis., Bethesda, Md., 1982-83. Nat. cons. to surgeon gen., USAF, 1979-83, chief cardiology Bapt. Meml. Hosp. System, San Antonio, 1992-93, chmn. dept. medicine, mem. exec. bd., 1993-94; chmn. ethics com. Baptist Meml. Hosp., 1993-94,; chmn. dept. cardiology Bapt. Hosps. Sys., San Antonio, 1996-98. Mem. editl. bd. Heart Smart mag., contbr. articles to Am. Jour. Cardiology, Jour. Nuclear Medicine, Archives Internal Medicine, Jour. Cardia Rehab., Circulation, Jour. Allergy and Clin. Immunology. Pres. Helotes (Tex.) Park Civic Assn., 1965-67, Helotes Elem. PTA, 1968-70; mem. exec. bd. So. Region Boy Scouts Am., Atlanta, 1989—; bd. dirs. San Antonio dvsn. Am. Heart Assn., 1989-92. Recipient Award of Merit Boy Scouts of Am., San Antonio, 1976, Silver Beaver medal, 1977. Fellow ACP, Am. Coll. Cardiology (bd. govs. 1979-83), Am. Coll. Preventive Medicine, Coun. Clin. Cardiology, Am. Heart Assn., N.Y. Acad. Sci., San Antonio Cardiology Soc. (pres. 1989-90), Am. Fed. Clin. Rsch. (sr.), Masons, Shriners. Lutheran. Home: 14802 Circle A Trl Helotes TX 78023-4023 Office: Skinner Clinic 124 Dallas St San Antonio TX 78205-1288

BECKMANN, JON MICHAEL, publishing company executive; b. N.Y.C., Oct. 24, 1936; s. John L. and Grace (Hazelton) B.; m. Barbara Ann Efting, June 26, 1965. BA, U. Pa., 1958; MA, NYU, 1961. Sr. editor Prentice-Hall Inc., Englewood Cliffs, N.J., 1964-68; v.p., editor Barre Pubs., Mass., 1970-73; pub. Sierra Club Books, San Francisco, 1973-94; pres. Beckmann Assocs. and Millennium Press, Sonoma, Calif., 1994—. Author: After-Dinner Drinks, 1998. Mem. Book Club of Calif. Office: Beckmann Assocs & Millennium Press 18185 7th St E Sonoma CA 95476-4797 E-mail: jonnytheb@aol.com.

BECKMANN, MARTIN JOSEPH, retired economics educator; b. Ratingen, Germany, July 5, 1924; came to U.S., 1950; s. Josef Beckmann and Katharina Linnartz; m. Gloria Gronna Rice, Dec. 31, 1956; children: Sybilla, Carl, Chantal, Gwendolyn. BA in Math., U. Göttingen, Germany, 1947; diploma, U. Freiburg, Germany, 1949; D of Polit. Sci., U. Freiburg, 1950; PhD (hon.), U. Umeå, Sweden, 1980, U. Karlsruhe, Germany, 1982, Bundeswehrhochschule, Hamburg, Germany, 1984. Rsch. assoc. Cowles Commn. U. Chgo., 1951-56; asst. prof. Yale U., New Haven, 1956-59; assoc. prof. Brown U., Providence, 1959-61, prof., 1962—89, U. Bonn, Germany, 1962-69, Tech. U., Munich, 1969-89. Cons. GM, 1969-89. Author: Location Theory, 1959, Dynamic Programming, 1969, Tinbergen Lectures in Organization Theory, 1983, Lectures on Location Theory, 1999; co-author: Studies in the Economics of Transportation, 1956. Recipient Herman award Ops. Rsch. Soc., 1995. Fellow Econometric Soc., Regional Sci. Assn. (pres. 1975, Founder's medal 1970), Western Regional Sci. Assn. (pres. 1970). Achievements include creation of assignment problem (with T.C. Koopmans). Home: 77 Arlington Ave Providence RI 02906 Office: Dept Econs Brown U Providence RI 02912 Fax: 401-863-1970.

BECKMEYER, HENRY ERNEST, anesthesiologist, medical educator, pain management specialist; b. Cape Girardeau, Mo., Apr. 13, 1939; s. Henry Ernest Jr. and Margaret Gertrude (Link) B. BA, Mich. State U., 1961; DO, Des Moines U., 1965. Diplomate Am. Bd. Med. Examiners, Am. Acad. Pain Mgmt.; cert. Am. Osteo. Bd. Anesthesiology. Chief physician migrant worker program and op. head start Sheridan (Mich.) Community Hosp., 1967-69; resident in anesthesia Bi-County Community Hosp./DOH Corp., Detroit, 1969-71, chief resident, 1968-69; staff anesthesiologist Detroit Osteo. Hosp./BCCH, 1971-75; founding chmn. dept. anesthesia Humana Hosp. of the Palm Beaches, West Palm Beach, Fla., 1975-79; assoc. prof. Mich. State U., East Lansing, 1979-88, prof. anesthesia, 1988—, chmn. dept. osteo. medicine, 1985-96; chmn. dept. osteo. surg. specialities, 1996-97; chief staff Mich. State U. Health Facilities, 1988-90, chmn. med. staff exec. and steering coms., 1988-90; chmn. of anesthesia St. Lawrence Hosp., Lansing, Mich., 1984-90, adminstrv. dir. dept. anesthesia and pain mgmt., 1994-98. Chief of staff Sheridan Cmty. Hosp., 1968-69; adminstrv. coun. Mich. State U., 1988-97, acad. coun., 1992-96, faculty coun., 1992-96, U. hearing bd., 2000-, bylaws com., 2000-, clin. practice bd., bd. dirs. sports medicine; internal mgmt. com. Mich. Ctr. for Rural Health; cons. Ministry Health, Belize C.A., 1993-97; amb. Midwestern U. Consortium Internat. Activities, 1993; chmn. com. student performance, 2002-03, com. on acad. policy, 2000—, admissions com., 2000-2002, chmn. admissions com., 2003—, athletic coun., 2003—; adv. com. on pain mgmt. State of Mich., 1999-2001; program chmn. Am. Russian Med. Exch., 1993-97; bd. dirs. Belize Med. Partnership. Spkr. Sta. WKAR, Mich. State U.; bd. dirs. Boy Scouts Am., W. Bloomfield, Mich., 1973-74, Palm Beach Mental Health, 1977-79, Care Choices HMO, Lansing, 1987-88; mem. adv. com. pain and symptom mgmt.

State of Mich., 1999-2002; mem. athletic coun. Mich. State U., 2003--. Fellow Am. Coll. Osteo. Anesthesiologists; mem. AMA, Am. Osteo. Coll. Anesthesiology (chmn. commn. on colls. 1988-89), Soc. Critical Care Medicine, Internat. Anesthesiology Rsch. Soc., Am. Coll. Physician Execs., Am. Osteo. Assn. (spkr., mem. evaluators registry), Am. Acad. Pain Mgmt., Am. Arbitration Assn., Mich. State Med. Soc., Mich. Pain Soc., Mich. Peer Rev. Orgn., Mich. Osteo. Assn. (edn. com.), Ingham County Med. Soc. (edn. com.), Am. Soc. Regional Anesthesia, Soc. Security Disability Evaluation, Soc. Internat. Scholars, Phi Beta Delta. Office: Mich State U West Fee Hall East Lansing MI 48824

BECKNER, EVERET HESS, federal agency administrator; b. Clayton, N.Mex., Feb. 24, 1935; s. Elmer Hess and Ursla (Brown) B.; m. Claudia Lee Garrett, Aug. 12, 1955 (div. Aug. 1983); children: Gregory Mitchell, Lee Elizabeth Strouse, Matthew Hess; m. Mary Caroline Allen, Feb. 16, 1984. BS, Baylor U., 1956; MA, Rice U., 1959, PhD in Physics, 1961. Staff engr. Lockheed Missiles and Space Co., Sunnyvale, Calif., 1956-57; staff mem. Sandia Nat. Labs., Albuquerque, 1961-65, research and device devel. div. supr., 1965-69, plasma research dept. mgr., 1969-74, phys. research dir., 1974-83, energy programs v.p., 1983-86, def. programs v.p., 1986—91; dep. adm. defense prog. U.S. Dept. Energy, Washington, 2002—. Bd. dirs. N.Mex. Dept. Econ. Devel. Tourism, Santa Fe, 1985—, N.Mex. Energy Research and Devel. Inst., 1983-85. Fellow Am. Phys. Soc.; mem. AAAS. Office: US Dept of Energy Defense Programs 1000 Independence Ave SW Washington DC 20585-0001

BECKSON, MACE, psychiatrist; b. N.Y.C., Aug. 6, 1959; s. Karl and Estelle B.; m. Ann Marie Davis, June 16, 1989. AB magna cum laude, Harvard U., 1980; MD, Cornell U., 1985. Diplomate forensic psychiatry and addiction psychiatry Am. Bd. Psychiatry and Neurology, cert. addiction medicine Am. Soc. Addiction Medicine. Intern N.Y. Hosp.-Payne Whitney Clinic, N.Y.C., 1985—86; resident UCLA Neuropsychiatric Inst., L.A., 1986—89; neurobehavior fellow UCLA Sch. Medicine, L.A., 1989—91, assoc. clin. prof., 2000—; rsch. psychiatrist NIDA-VA Med. Devel., L.A., 1991—97; program chief alcohol and drug treatment VA Med. Ctr., L.A., 1992—95, chief intensive OPT treatment of addictions, 1995—97; med. dir. PICU VA Greater L.A. Healthcare Sys., 1998—. Cons. Sexual Recovery Inst., L.A., 1998—2001, Aim Healthcare Found., L.A., 1998—2001, Didi Hirsh Cmty. M.H.C., L.A., 1998—98. Contbr. articles. Fellow: Am. Psychiat. Assn. (disting. fellow); mem.: Nat. Coun. Sexual Addiction, Am. Acad. Psych & Law, Am. Soc. for Addiction Medicine. Office: PO Box 84507 Los Angeles CA 90073 Office Fax: 310-477-0661. E-mail: becksonmd@becksonmd.com.

BECKSTROM, CHARLES G. lawyer; b. Jamestown, N.Y., July 14, 1940; s. Charles Wilbert and Dorothy Helen (Carlson) B.; m. Marie Jane Trebilcock, Nov. 28, 1964; children: Kimberly Leigh, Erika Lynne, Kristyn Marie, Stephanie Rae. BA, Mich. State U., 1962; MBA, Wayne State U., 1966; JD, SUNY-Buffalo, 1969. Bar: Mich. 1969, N.Y. 1971, Pa. 1997. Ptnr. Johnson, Peterson, Tener & Anderson, Jamestown, 1970-89, Beckstrom & Plumb, Jamestown, 1989—2001, of counsel, 2001—. Fin. analyst Fisher Body div. Gen. Motors Corp., Warren, Mich., 1963-66; lawyer Ernst & Ernst, Detroit, 1969-70; town atty. Town of Ellery, N.Y., 1972-83; bd. dirs. Dowcraft Corp.,1990-2001; bd. dirs., asst. sec. Bur. Veritas Quality Internat. (N.Am.) Inc., 1995-2001; bd. dirs., sec. Ellison Bronze, Inc., 2001—. Trustee, chmn. 1st Covenant Ch. Jamestown, 1976-82; chmn., bd. pensions Evangelical Covenant Ch. Nat. Pension Plan, Chgo., 1979-84; mem. exec. bd. Evangelical Covenant Ch., 1986-92. Served with U.S. Army, 1963-64. Mem. Jamestown Bar Assn., N.Y. Assn. Sch. Attys., Jamestown Estate Planning Coun. (pres., v.p., sec.), Internat. Found. Employee Benefit Plans, Norden Club. Republican. Home: 125 Westminister Dr Jamestown NY 14701-4438 Office: PO Box 579 Jamestown NY 14702-0579 E-mail: beckplum@netsync.net., cbeck@netsync.net.

BECK-VON-PECCOZ, MICHELE, retired secondary school educator, writer; b. Phila., Pa., July 12, 1939; d. William Wallace Perry and Margaret Kenny; m. Stephen Beck-von-Peccoz, Jan. 8, 1972; 1 child, Lisa Michele Beck-von-Peccoz. MD. BA, Trinity Coll., 1958—62. Eng./art tchr. San Dieguito Union H.S. Dist., Encinitas, Calif., 1971—2003. Author: (teachers manual) Holt Handbook, 2001. Mem.: Trinity Coll. Alumnae Orgn. (pres. 1988—90). Achievements include invention of a method of grammar instruction copyrighted 2000: Sentence Surgery: A Systematic and Graphic Method of Grammar Instruction, based on the consistent use of eight symbols to identify grammar concepts. Avocations: e-mail Scrabble, bronze casting sculpture. Home: 636 Nardito Ln Solana Beach CA 92075-2306 Personal E-mail: michelebvp@cox.net.

BECK-VON-PECCOZ, STEPHEN GEORGE WOLFGANG, artist; b. Munich, Oct. 18, 1933; came to U.S., 1937; s. Wolfgang Anton Willibald Maria and Martha Jeanette (Morse) Beck-von-P.; m. Dorothy Ann Freytag, June 16, 1956 (div. 1971); m. Michele Marie Perry, Jan. 8, 1972; children: Stephen Jr., David, Kenneth (dec.), Lisa. BEE, Cornell U., 1956; MA in Art, Calif. State U., San Diego, 1974. Electronic engr. Stromberg Carlson Co., San Diego, 1958-60; project mgr. Control Data Corp., San Diego, 1960-65, Digital Devel. Corp., San Diego, 1965-66; project engr. Stromberg Datagraphix, Inc., San Diego, 1966-69; project mgr. Digital Sci. Corp., San Diego, 1969-71; artist San Diego, 1974—. Cons. elec. engring., San Diego, 1974-78. Served to 2d lt. USAF, 1956-58. Mem. Internat. Sculpture Ctr., Kappa Alpha Soc. Avocations: art, travel. Home: 636 Nardito Ln Solana Beach CA 92075-2306 E-mail: sgb9@cornell.edu.

BECKWITH, BARBARA JEAN, journalist; b. Chgo., Dec. 11, 1948; d. Charles Barnes (dec.) and Elizabeth Ann (Nolan) Beckwith. BA in Journalism, Marquette U., 1970. News editor Lake Geneva (Wis.) Regional News, 1972-74; asst. editor St. Anthony Messenger, Cin., 1974-82, mng. editor, 1982—. Mem. Cath. Conf. Comm. Com., 1990—92. Mem.: Cath. Journalism Scholarship Fund (bd. dirs. 1993—, v.p. 1995—96, pres. 1996—99, 2001—), Nat. Cath. Assn. for Broadcasters and Communicators (bd. dirs. 1989—96, 1997—98), Fedn. Ch. Press Assns. of Internat. Cath. Union of the Press (3d v.p. 1989—92, pres. 1992—), Cath. Press Assn. (bd. dirs. 1986—96, v.p. 1988—90, pres. 1990—92, best interview 1982, best photo story 1985, St. Francis de Sales award for outstanding contbn. to Cath. journalism 1994, best poetry 1997). Office: St Anthony Messenger 28 W Liberty St Cincinnati OH 45202-6498

BECKWITH, EDWARD JAY, lawyer; b. Paterson, N.J., July 18, 1949; s. David and Beverly Beckwith; m. Iris Kailo; children: Jessica, Jason, Jenna. BS, Pa. State U., 1971; JD, Georgetown U., 1974, ML in Taxation, 1983. Bar: D.C., U.S. Supreme Ct., U.S. Ct. Appeals (fed. cir.), U.S. Ct. Appeals (D.C. cir.), U.S. Dist. Ct. D.C., U.S. Tax Ct., U.S. Claims Ct. Staff asst. Coun. on Environ. Quality Exec. Office of Pres., Washington, 1973; assoc. Fried, Frank, Harris, Shriver & Kampelman, Washington, 1974-82, Baker & Hostetler, Washington, 1982-83, ptnr., 1984—. Adj. prof. law Georgetown U. Law Ctr., Washington, 1984—; bd. advisors Jour. Taxation Trusts and Estates, 1989-92; mem. Greater Washington Bd. Trade. Contbr. articles to profl. publs. Mem. steering com. sect. on trusts and probate law D.C. Bar, 1985-87; chmn. planned giving adv. coun. Pa. State U., 2000—. Alumni fellow honoree Pa. State U., 1998. Fellow: Am. Bar Found., Am. Coll. Trust and Estate Counsel (state chair D.C. 1998—2003, state chmn. D.C. 1998—2003, state chmn. 1998—2003, chmn. philanthropy study com. 2000—03, regent 2002—, chmn. charitable planning and exempt orgns. com. 2001—); mem.: ABA, Am. Law Inst. (Estate Planning Coun. Washington chpt.), Pa. State U. Alumni Assn., Omicron Delta Kappa. Office: Baker & Hostetler LLP 1050 Connecticut Ave NW Washington DC 20036-5304 E-mail: beckwith@bakerlaw.com.

BECKWITH, F. WILLIAM, food products executive; CEO Fareway Stores, Boone, Iowa, chmn. bd., 1998—. Office: Fareway Stores Inc 2300 E 8th St Boone IA 50036

BECKWITH, JOHN, musician, composer, educator; b. Victoria, B.C., Can., Mar. 9, 1927; BMus, U. Toronto, 1947, MMus, 1961; DMus (hon.), Mt. Allison U., Sackville, N.B., 1974, McGill U., Montreal, 1978, U. Guelph, Ont., 1995, U. Victoria, B.C., 1999; LLD (hon.), Queen's U., Kingston, Ont., 1998. Pvt. piano studies Alberto Guerrero, Royal Conservatory of Music, Toronto, 1945-50; pvt. composition studies Nadia Boulanger, Paris, 1950-51; pub. relations dir. Royal Conservatory of Music, Toronto, 1948-50; staff writer for radio music continuity Can. Broadcasting Corp., Toronto, 1953-55; freelance radio programmer and writer, 1955-70; spl. lectr. U. Toronto, 1952-53, lectr., 1954-60, asst. prof. music, 1960-66, assoc. prof., 1966-70, dean, 1970-77, prof., 1977-90, 1st holder Jean A. Chalmers chair in Can. music, 1984-90. Debut: Toronto, 1950; over 130 compositions including 4 operas, works for orch., chorus, etc.; 30 works published including: 4 songs to poems by E.E. Cummings, 1950; Fall Scene and Fair Dance, 1956; Music for Dancing, 1959; Jonah, 1963; Sharon Fragments, 1966; Circle, with Tangents, 1967; Gas, 1969; Taking a Stand, 1972; Musical Chairs, 1973; 3 Motets on Swan's China, 1981; Sonatina in 2 Movements, 1982; Harp of David, 1985; recorded compositions include: Music for Dancing; The Trumpets of Summer; Sharon Fragments; Circle, with Tangents; Quartet; Keyboard Practice; 3 Motets on Swan's China; Upper Can. Hymn Preludes; Taking a Stand, Etudes, Arctic Dances, Harp of David, On the Other Hand..., A Concert of Myths, Synthetic Trios, Stacey, Round and Round; recordings.: Music at Sharon, 1982; Musical Toronto, 1984, à la claire fontaine, 2000; arranger, dir. of instrumental ensemble; editor: The Modern Composer and His World, 1961; Contemporary Canadian Composers, 1975; Canadian Composer series, 1975-90, Musical Canada, 1988; Canadian Consultant, The New Grove, London, 1980; author: Music Papers, 1997; contbr. articles to profl. jours. Recipient Can. Music Coun. ann. medal, 1972, Arts Found. of Greater Toronto ann. music award, 1994; named to Order of Can., 1987. Mem. Can. League of Composers (former sec.), Ency. of Music in Can. (bd. dirs. 1972-94), Can. Musical Heritage Soc. (editl. bd. 1981-2003). Office: 121 Howland Ave Toronto ON Canada M5R 3B4 E-mail: j.beckwith@utoronto.ca.

BECKWITH, JOHN BRUCE, pediatric pathologist; b. Spokane, Wash., Sept. 18, 1933; s. John Keith Beckwith; m. Nancy Gay Browning, June 21, 1984; m. Lorna Glen Gourlay, Sept. 10, 1954 (dec. May 23, 1983); children: Deborah, Sarah, Lorna. BA, Whitman Coll., 1954; MD, U. Wash., 1958; ScD (hon.), Whitman Coll., 1980. Diplomate Am. Bd. Pathology. From asst. prof. to assoc. prof. U. Wash. Sch. Medicine, Seattle, 1964—74, prof. pathology and pediats., 1974—85; head labs. Children's Hosp., Seattle, 1964—85, chair pathology Denver, 1985—91; prof. pathology U. Colo. Sch. Medicine, Denver, 1986—91; head divsn. pediat. pathology Loma Linda (Calif.) U. Sch. Medicine, 1991—99, prof. pathology and human anatomy, 1991—99, prof. emeritus, 1999—. Head Nat. Wilms Tumor Study Pathology Ctr., various locations, 1969—99. Contbr. papers to profl. jours.; co-author: Sudden Infant Death Syndrome, 1969, Tumors of the Kidney, Renal Pelvis and Ureter, 1975, Anencephaly, 1978; author: Tumors of the Kidney, Bladder and Related Structures, 1994. Recipient Astute Clinician award, NIH, 1998. Fellow: Royal Coll. Pathologists U.K. (hon.); mem.: Soc. for Pediat. Pathology (pres. 1994—95). Democrat. Achievements include co-discovery of Beckwith-Wiedemann Syndrome; named Sudden Infant Death Syndrome; discovery of several newly recognized renal tumors including Rhabdoid Tumor and Clear Cell Sarcoma of Kidney. Avocations: collecting antiquarian books on congenital malformations, collecting Christmas seals, fly fishing, birding. Home: 88 Brookside Way Missoula MT 59802 Fax: 406-829-1624. E-mail: beckwithbrowning@earthlink.net.

BECKWITH, JONATHAN ROGER, geneticist; b. Cambridge, Mass., Dec. 25, 1935; s. Manuel and Mildred B.; m. Barbara Shutt, Dec. 26, 1960; children— Benjamin Hunter, Anthony Rhys. BA, Harvard U., 1957, PhD, 1961. Mem. faculty Harvard U. Med. Sch., 1965—, prof. microbiology, 1969—, Am. Cancer Soc. prof., 1971—. Mem. Nat. Acad. Scis., 1984— Recipient Eli Lilly award, 1970, Genetics Soc. Am. medal, 1993. Fellow AAAS; mem. Am. Acad. Arts and Scis., European Molecular Biology Orgn. (assoc.), Am. Soc. Exptl. Biologists, Am. Soc. Microbiology, Genetics Soc. Am. Achievements include research and publs. in bacterial genetics and social implications of genetics. Home: 8A Appleton Rd Cambridge MA 02138-2226 E-mail: jbeckwith@hms.harvard.edu.

BECKWITH, LARRY EDWARD, mechanical engineer; b. Pierre, S.D., Oct. 21, 1943; s. Charles Edward and Junebelle Ann (Robley) B.; m. AnhTuyet Thi Pham, Mar. 3, 1970. BSME, S.D. Sch. Mines Tech., Rapid City, 1966. Mil. engring. officer USACE, 1967-69; from mech. engr. to ptnr. Dunham Assocs., Bloomington, Minn., 1966, 1970—2003. Bd. dirs. Beckwith Hardware, Inc., Presho, S.D., 1977-92. State chmn. S.D. Coll. Reps., 1965-66; life mem. Rep. Nat. Com., 1994—; bd. govs. Walden Assn., 1994-96, pres., 1996. Capt. U.S. Army, 1967-69, Vietnam. Decorated Bronze Star with oak leaf cluster. Mem. VFW (life), Am. Legion. Avocations: chess, music (clarinet, piano), golf. E-mail: leb@larrybeckwith.com.

BECKWITH, LEWIS DANIEL, lawyer; b. Indpls., Jan. 30, 1948; s. William Frederick and Helen Lorena (Smith) B.; m. Marcia Ellen Ride, June 27, 1970; children: Laura, Gregory. BA, Wabash Coll., 1970; JD, Vanderbilt U., 1973. Bar: Ind. 1973, U.S. Dist. Ct. (so. dist.) Ind. 1973. Assoc. Baker & Daniels, Indpls., 1973-80, ptnr., 1981—. Articles editor Vanderbilt Law Rev., 1972-73. Mem. ABA (assoc. editor occupational safety & health law 2002), Ind. Bar Assn., Indpls. Bar Assn., Ind. C. of C. (com. occupational safety and health law 1982—), Associated Gen. Contractors of Ind. (com. occupational safety and health 1988—, safety and health counsel), Indpls. Athletic Club, ORder of Coif, Eta Sigma Phi, Beta Theta Pi. Republican. Lutheran. Avocation: sports. Office: Baker & Daniels 300 N Meridian St Ste 2700 Indianapolis IN 46204-1782 E-mail: ldbeckwi@bakerd.com.

BECKWITH, PETER HESS, bishop; b. Battle Creek, Mich., Sept. 8, 1939; s. Robert Edgar Sr. and Florence Cathryn (Hess) Beckwith; m. Melinda Jo Foulke, July 10, 1965; children: Peter H. II, Michael J. AB, Hillsdale (Mich.) Coll., 1961, ThD (hon.), 1988; MDiv, U. of the South, 1964, DD (hon.), 1999; STM, Nashotah Ho., 1974, LHD (hon.), 1992. Ordained deacon Episc. Ch., 1964, ordained priest Episc. Ch., 1965, ordained bishop Episc. Ch., 1992; cert. marriage counselor Mich. Asst. rector St. John's Episcopal Ch., Plymouth, Mich., 1964—66, St. Paul's Episcopal Ch., Jackson, Mich., 1966—70; rector St. Matthew's Episcopal Ch., Saginaw, Mich., 1970—78, St. John's Episcopal Ch., Worthington, Ohio, 1978—92; bishop Episcopal Diocese of Springfield, Ill., 1992—. Chaplain USNR, 1972—99; instr. Sch. of Theology Diocese of Mich., Saginaw, 1975; res. instr. Navy Chaplains Sch., Newport, RI, 1979; chaplain to Episcopal inmates So. Mich. State Prison, Jackson, 1966—70; nat. chaplain Navy League of U.S., Washington, 1992—; chaplain Marine Corps Res. Assn., Washington, 1994—96, Ill. State Police, 1995—. Chair Jackson County Cancer Crusade, 1967. Rear adm. USNR, 1996—99, dep. chief of chaplain for total force USNR. Named Hon. Seabee, U.S. Naval Constrn. Force, Washington, 1992; named to Hillsdale Coll. Athletic Hall of Fame, 2002; recipient Alumni Achievement award, Hillsdale Coll., 1982. Mem.: Am. Anglican Coun. (bd. dirs. 2000—), Navy League (pres. Columbus coun. 1990). Republican. Avocations: golf, skiing, gardening. Home: 400 Clipper Rd Springfield IL 62707-8010 Office: Episcopal Diocese of Springfield 821 S 2d St Springfield IL 62704-2694 Fax: 217-525-1877. E-mail: phbxebs@midwest.net.

BECKWITH, RODNEY FISK, management consulting firm executive; b. Passaic, N.J., Oct. 24, 1935; s. Raymond Fisk and Nancy Angel (Oberdorf) B. m. Elizabeth Ann Wedemann, July 23, 1960; children: Allison B. Melson, Kimberly Hall. BME with distinction, Cornell U., 1958; MBA with distinction, Harvard U., 1963. Plant engr. Western Electric Co., Kearny, N.J., 1960-61; sr. assoc. Cresap, McCormick and Paget, Inc., N.Y.C., 1963-68, prin., 1968-72, v.p. Melbourne, Australia, 1972-77, v.p., dir., exec. com. N.Y.C., 1977-83; v.p., dir. Fin. Instns. Svcs., 1983-84, v.p., dir. internat., 1984-90, v.p., chief adminstrv. officer, 1990—. Bd. dirs. Am. C. of C., Australia, 1975-77. With USN, 1958-60, lt. USNR, 1960-65. Baker scholar, Harvard U., 1963. Mem. Inst. Mgmt. Cons. (founding), Harvard Club N.Y.C., Wee Burn Country Club, Glenmore Country Club, Delta Upsilon, Tau Beta Pi. Presbyterian. Home: 3156 Prestwick Pl Keswick VA 22947-9114 Office: 335 Madison Ave New York NY 10017-4605

BECKWITH, SANDRA SHANK, judge; b. Norfolk, Va., Dec. 4, 1943; d. Charles Langdale and Loraine (Sterneberg) Shank; m. James Beckwith, Mar. 31, 1965 (div. June 1978); m. Thomas R. Ammann, Mar. 3, 1979. BA, U. Cin., 1965, JD, 1968. Bar: Ohio 1969, Ind. 1976, Fla. 1979, U.S. Dist. Ct. (so. dist.) Ohio 1971, U.S. Dist. Ct. Ind. 1976, U.S. Supreme Ct. 1977. Sole practice, Harrison, Ohio, 1969-77, 79-81; judge Hamilton County Mcpl. Ct., Cin., 1977-79, 81-86, commr., 1989-91; judge Ct. Common Pleas, Hamilton County Divsn. Domestic Rels., 1987-89; assoc. Graydon, Head and Ritchey, 1989-91; judge U.S. Dist. Ct. (so. dist.) Ohio, 1992—. Mem. Ohio Chief Justice's Code of Profl. Responsibility Commn., 1984, Ohio Gov.'s Com. on Prison Crowding, 1984-90, State Fed. Com. on Death Penalty Habeas Corpus, 1995—; pres. 6th Cir. Dist. Judges Assn., 1998-99; chair So. Dist. Ohio Automation Com., 1997—. Bd. dirs. Tender Mercies. Mem. Fed. Judges Assn., Am. Judges Assn., Am. Judicature Soc., Fed. Bar Assn. (exec. com.), Fed. Cir. Bar Assn. Office: Potter Stewart US Courthouse Ste 810 Cincinnati OH 45202

BECKWITH, SIDNEY JOHNSON, director special programs, curriculum administrator; b. East Grand Rapids, Mich., Dec. 30, 1947; d. William Judson and Betty Dame (Bonisteel) Johnson; m. James Luther Beckwith, Aug. 17, 1974; children: Crystina Ann, Betty Bonisteel-Chaffee, William James. BS, Western Mich. U., 1969; MS in Guidance and Counseling, Boston State Coll., 1974, cert. advanced grad. studies, 1976; adminstrv. cert., Syracuse U., 1981. Cert. tchr. reading and English, N.Y.; cert. guidance counselor, Mass. Tchr. English and reading Boston Pub. Schs., 1970-76; coord. K-12 reading, lang. arts, and compensatory program Union Springs (N.Y.) Cen. Schs., 1976-91, 99, chair com. spl. edn., 1984-2001, dir. spl. programs and curriculum, 1990-2001, cons. K-12 program cons.; dir. nat. difusion network IPIMS Reading Ctr. Union Springs Cen. Schs., 1984-90. Co-dir. Wellsprings Leadership Summer Camp, 1993-2001; co-founder, co-dir. Wellsprings Leadership Curriculum and Summer Camp. Mem. Cayuga County children's com. United Way, 1983-89; bd. dirs. YMCA-WEIU, 1978-81. Grantee NDN, N.Y. State ESEA. Mem. ASCD, Midlakes Reading Coun. (pres. 1978-79), Cayuga County Prins. Assn. (sec. 1986-87), Regional Com. for Reading, Spl. Edn., Gifted and Talented, Fingerlakes Reading Assn., Phi Delta Kappa.

BECKWITT, RICHARD DAVID, biology educator, researcher; b. Detroit, Apr. 25, 1949; s. Morris Colton and Ellen (Gottesman) B.; m. Gloria Jean Kaminski, June 22, 1974; children: Katherine Ilana, Emily Celeste. BA in Zoology with honors, U. Calif., Berkeley, 1970; PhD in Biology, U. So. Calif., L.A., 1979. Rsch. assoc. Occidental Coll., L.A., 1978-85; asst. prof. Framingham (Mass.) State Coll., 1985-90, assoc. prof., 1990-94, prof., 1994—. Rsch. cons. in biotech. rsch., devel. and engring. ctr. U.S. Army, Natick, Mass., 1989-96. Contbr. articles to Jour. Genetics, Zool. Jour. Linnean Soc., Jour. Exptl. Marine Biology and Ecology, and others. Mem. AAAS, Am. Soc. Zoologists, Genetics Soc. Am. Office: Framingham State Coll Dept of Biology Framingham MA 01701

BECOFSKY, ARTHUR LUKE, arts administrator, writer; b. N.Y.C., Sept. 17, 1950; s. Arthur and Frances (Oliva) B. BA in Polit. Sci., Duke U., 1972; MA in Polit. Sci., Columbia U., 1974. Adminstr. Cunningham Dance Found., N.Y.C., 1974-79, exec. dir., 1980-94; pres. Art Becofsky Associates, 1994—. World booking agt. Merce Cunningham Dance Co., N.Y.C., 1976-94; cons. Found. for Ext. and Devel. of Am. Profl. Theatre, N.Y.C., 1985, Found. for Dance Promotion, 1995-2000, Ringside/Elizabeth Streb, 1995-2001, The Armitage Found., 1995, 2002—, Cross Performance, Inc., 1995-98, Stephen Petronio Dance Co., 1995-2002, Gotham Dance, Inc., 1995, ODC/San Francisco, 1995—, Twyla Tharp, 1996, David Dorfman Dance, 1996-2001, Ballet Hispanico, 1996-2001, David Rousseve/Reality, 1996-2001, Susan Marshall Dance Co., 1996-2001, Rena Shagan Assocs., 1996-2001, Margaret Jenkins Dance Co., 1997—, Bill Young and Dancers, 1997—, Bridgehampton Chamber Music Assocs., 1997, Ananda Shankar Dance Co., Calcutta, 1997—, Nest/Tokyo, 1997—, Garth Fagan Dance, 1998—, Moving Education, 1998—, Richard Alston Dance Co., London, 1998—, Grupo Corpo/Brazil, 1998—, Rosy Co./Tokyo, 1998—, Siobhan Davies Dance Co., London, 1998-99, Lines Contemporary Ballet, 1998-2000, Joe Goode Performance Group, 1999-2001, Compagnie Jant-Bi, 1999—, Pentacle Help Desk, 1999-2003, Art Plus Care to Dance, 1999—, Expressions Dance Co., Brisbane, 1999-2002, Uno Man, Tokyo, 1999—, Kazco Takemoto, Tokyo, 1999—, Kenichi Tanno & Numbering Machine, Tokyo, 1999—, Jose Limon Dance Co., 1999-2002, Daniel Yeung, Hong Kong, 1999—, Compagnie Marie Chouinard, 2001—, Chunky Move, 2001-, Armitage Gone Dance, 2002—, Dance Works Rotterdam, 2002—, Compagnie Flak/Jose Navas, 2002—, Pappa Tarahumara, Tokyo, 2002—; mem. dance panel NEA, 1983-94. Guitarist with Rhys Chatham & The Din, 1981; composer: Secretarial Suite, 1980, Track, 1983, Get Real, Cassandra, 1985, Space Into Action, 1986; author: The Road Show Abroad, 1985, On Commissioning New Art, 1989, MMerce, 1991, Lar Lubovitch: The Company We Keep, 1999. Bd. dirs. Dancing for Life, 1987; U.S. Performing Arts subcom. CULCON for U.S.-Japan cultural exch., 1989-93. Mem. Dance/U.S.A. (bd. dirs. 1983-88, 91-98, treas. 1983-86, vice chair 1993-96), World Dance Alliance (bd. dirs. 1993-97), Am. Arts Alliance (bd. dirs. 1983-87). Democrat. Avocation: photography. Office: 46 Barkit Kennel Rd Pleasant Valley NY 12569 Home: 46 Barkit Kennel Rd Pleasant Valley NY 12569-7210 E-mail: ckdance@aol.com.

BECRAFT, STEPHEN JAY, accountant; b. Middletown, Ohio, June 13, 1941; s. Stephen Roe and Mildred Becraft; m. Sandra Moore, Aug. 13, 1965; children: Felicia Lyn, David Scott. BS, U. Ariz., 1965; MS, U. No. Colo., 1979. Sr. auditor Ernst & Ernst, CPA, Denver, 1969-72; dir. auditing Jefferson Bank & Trust, Lakewood, Colo., 1972-75; prin. Becraft & Assocs., Aurora, Colo., 1975-85; CFO James Dobson, Inc., Colorado Springs, Colo., 1986-92; acct. II City of Riverside (Calif.) Fin., 1993-94; sr. mgmt. analyst Riverside Redevel. Agy., 1994-97; CFO Charo Cmty. Devel. Co., L.A., 1997-98; dir. acctg. Alpert & Alpert Iron & Metal, L.A., 1998—. V.p. Rheam Life Fellowship, Aurora, 1986—2000; pres. Word of Life Ministry, Inc., LaVerne, Calif., 1997—2000. Com. mem. Arapahoe County Rep. Ctrl. Com., Aurora, 1980-85. Capt. USAF, 1964-69. Avocations: genealogy research, music, sports. Home: 1529 Carnation Way Upland CA 91786-2210 Office: Alpert & Alpert Iron and Metal 1815 S Soto St Los Angeles CA 90023-4210

BECTON, HENRY PRENTISS, JR., broadcasting company executive; b. Englewood, NJ, Oct. 16, 1943; s. Henry Prentiss and Jean Sprague (Coggan) B.; m. Jean Campbell Redpath, Sept. 28, 1968; children: Sara Campbell, Wilson Prentiss, Elizabeth Campbell BA magna cum laude, Yale U., 1965; JD cum laude, Harvard U., 1968. Tchr. Cambridge Sch., Weston, Mass., 1968-69; tel. producer WGBH Ednl. Found., Boston, 1970-73, program mgr., 1974-78, v.p., gen. mgr., 1978-84, pres., 1984—. Bd. dirs. Becton, Dickinson & Co., Pub. Broadcasting Svc., 1988—2001, Banff Internat., TV Festival, Pub. Radio Internat.; trustee Scudder Funds, Conn. Coll., 1992—97; with Com. for Econ. Devel., 1992—2002, Ethics Resource Ctr., 1994—97; bd. dir. Am. Pub. TV, 1997—2003. Bd. dirs. Mass. Com. for Prevention of Child Abuse, 1979-81; trustee Boston Ballet, 1976-78, Met. Cultural Alliance, Boston, 1974-76, New Eng. Aquarium, 1981-2003, Boston Mus. Sci., 1984—, Wang Ctr. for Performing Arts, 1985-93, 99, Concord Acad., 1993—, v.p., 1994-2002, pres., 2002-; bd. overseers Boston Mus. Fine Arts, 1990-98, New Eng. Aquarium, 2003. Mem. NATAS (bd. dir. New Eng. chpt. 1980-84), Mass. Bar Assn., Kollegewidgwok Yacht Club (Blue Hill, Maine), Phi Beta Kappa. Office: Sta WGBH-TV & WGBH-FM 125 Western Ave Allston MA 02134-1008

BEDARD, EMIL R. career officer; b. Argyle, Minn., Dec. 3, 1943; m. Linda Kathleen Deck; children: Jason, Jordan, Camille. Grad., Univ. N.D., 1967. 2nd lt., 1967; rifle plt. cdr. 2/27, comp xo 3/3; lt. col., asst. ops. officer MAF-G3; col. Twentynine Palms, Calif.; asst. G-3 for ops. 7th Marine Expeditionary Brigade, 1991-93; asst. divsn. commander 1st Marine Div., Camp Pendleton, Calif., 1993; pres. Marine Corps. Univ., Quantico, 1994; major gen. CG 2d Marine div., CG II MEF, 1997; lt. gen. dep. comdt. plans, policies, ops. USMC, Washington, 2000—. Decorated Def. Superior Svc. medal, Legionof Merit with gold star, Bronze star with Combat V, Navy Commendation medal with Combat V, two gold stars, Def. Meritious Svc. medal, Meritorious Svc. medal, Navy and Army Achievement medals, Air Medal with numeral 16, Combat Action Ribbon with Gold star, Vietnam Cross of Gallantry with Silver Star. Office: DC PP&O HOMC 2 Navy Annex Washington DC 20380

BÉDARD, ÉRIC, Olympic athlete; b. Ste-Thècle, Que., Can., Dec. 17, 1976; Profl. speed skater, Canada, 1997—. Can. record holder 3000m. Recipient 1st pl. 777m, 1000m, 1500m, relay, Can. Games, 1995, 1st pl. relay, World Championships, 1998, 1st pl., World Team Championships, 1998, 2000, Gold medal relay, Olympic Games, 1998, Bronze medal 1000m, 1998, 1st pl., World Team Championships, 2001, 1st pl. relay, Goodwill Games, 2000, 1st pl. 500m, World Championships, 2000, 1st pl. relay, World Cup, 2001, 2002, Gold medal 5000m short track men's relay, 2002 Olympic Games. Avocations: baseball, golf, movies. Office: Speed Skating Can 2781 Lancaster Rd Ste 402 Ottawa ON K1B 1A7 Canada

BEDARD, PATRICK JOSEPH, editor, writer, consultant; b. Waterloo, Iowa, Aug. 20, 1941; s. Gerald Joseph and Pearl Leona (Brown) B. BS in Mech. Engring, Iowa State U., 1963; M.Automotive Engring., Chrysler Inst. Engring., 1965. Product engr. Chrysler Corp., Highland Park, Mich., 1963-67; tech. editor Car and Driver mag., N.Y.C., 1967-69, exec. editor, 1969-78, editor-at-large, 1978—. Race driver, cons. in field; freelance writer mags. and TV films. Author: Expert Driving, 1987. Mem. Soc. Automotive Engrs., U.S. Ultralight Assn., Aero Sports Connection, Sports Car Club Am., Pi Tau Sigma. Roman Catholic. Achievements include first driver to win profl. road race in N.Am. in Wankel-powered car, 1973; raced at Indpls. 500, 1983-84; 1st driver to go 200 miles per hour at Indpls. in Stockblock-powered car, 1984. Home: Rt 1 Box 779 Port Saint Joe FL 32456 Office: Car and Driver 2002 Hogback Rd Ann Arbor MI 48105-9795

BEDAU, HUGO ADAM, philosophy educator; b. Portland, Oreg., Sept. 23, 1926; s. Hugo Adam and Laura (Romeis) B.; m. Jan Lisbeth Peterson Mastin, 1952 (div. 1988); children— Lauren, Mark Adam, Paul Hugo, Guy Antony; m. Constance Elizabeth Putnam, 1990. Student, U. So. Calif., 1944-45; BA summa cum laude, U. Redlands, 1949; MA, Boston U., 1951, Harvard, 1953, PhD, 1961. Instr. Dartmouth, 1953-54; instr. Princeton, 1954-57, lectr., 1958-61; assoc. prof. Reed Coll., 1962-66; prof. philosophy Tufts U., 1966-72, Austin Fletcher prof. philosophy, 1972—97, Romanell-Phi Beta Kappa prof. philosophy, 1994-95, prof. emeritus, 1997—. Vis. prof. law faculty U. Natal, South Africa, 1981, U. Westminster, London, 1994; vis. life fellow Clare Hall, Cambridge U., 1980; vis. fellow Wolfson Coll., Oxford, 1988; hon. rsch. fellow Bentham Project, U. London, 1997-99, 2003—. Author: The Courts, The Constitution and Capital Punishment, 1977, Death is Different, 1987, Thinking and Writing About Philosophy, 2d edit., 2002; co-author: Victimless Crimes, 1974, Current Issues and Enduring Questions, 1987, 6th edit., 2002, In Spite of Innocence, 1992, Critical Thinking, Reading, and Writing, 4th edit., 2002; editor: Death Penalty in America, 1964, 4th edit., 1997, Civil Disobedience, 1969, Justice and Equality, 1971, Civil Disobedience in Focus, 1991; co-editor: Capital Punishment in the US, 1976; contbr. articles and essays on social, polit., and legal philosophy to books and profl. jours. Bd. dirs. Am. League Abolish Capital Punishment, 1959—72, pres., 1969—72; bd. dirs. ACLU, Mass., 1984—87, 1988—93, 1995—98, v.p., 1987; chmn. Nat. Coalition Against Death Penalty, 1990—93. Danforth fellow, 1957-58, Liberal Arts fellow in law and philosophy Harvard U. Law Sch., 1961-62. Mem. Am. Philos. Assn., AAUP, Am. Soc. Polit. and Legal Philosophy (v.p. 1981), Phi Beta Kappa. Office: Tufts U Dept Of Philosophy Medford MA 02155

BEDDALL, THOMAS HENRY, lawyer; b. Pottsville, Pa., Apr. 24, 1922; s. Thomas and Martha Roberta (Gallagher) B.; m. Priscilla Kimball, July 26, 1956 (dec.); children: Laurence, Frederic, Margaret, and Katherine; m. Catherine C. Larmore, May 2, 1994. AB, Yale U., 1943; LL.B., U. Va., 1950. Bar: N.Y. 1951, D.C. 1968. Assoc. Sullivan & Cromwell, N.Y.C., 1950-57, Paul Mellon Interests, Washington, 1957-89. Dir. Carborundum Co., Niagara Falls, N.Y., 1960-78; lectr. U. Va., 1976-79 Chmn. bd. trustees Sheridan Sch., Washington, 1972-74; trustee Va. Mus. and Found., 1984-99, Nat. Mus. of Racing, 1988-2001, The Textile Mus., 1990-92, Va. State Parks Found., 1992-96. Mem. Bar Assn. City N.Y., Mil. Order World Wars, Order of Coif, Raven Soc., Metropolitan Club, Va. Tech. Equine Rsch. Sta. (chmn. 2000-), Phi Delta Phi, Omicron Delta Kappa, Pi Delta Epsilon, Chi Psi. Office: PO Box 914 Middleburg VA 20118-0914

BEDDOW, RICHARD HAROLD, judge; b. Springfield, Mass., Jan. 3, 1932; s. Richard Harold and Elizabeth Christine (Geehern) B.; m. Trudy C. Howells, Jan. 14, 1967; children: Catherine Elizabeth Almand, Elissa Christine. BS, U. Mass., 1953; LLB, Boston Coll, 1959. Bar: Mass. 1960. Atty. ICC, Washington, 1959-69, mem. rev. bd., 1969-73, adminstrv. law judge, 1973-81, NLRB, Washington, 1981—2002, ret., 2002—. With USN, 1953-55. Roman Catholic. Avocation: landscape gardening. Home: 2406 Rockwood Rd Accokeek MD 20607-9584

BEDEIAN, ARTHUR GEORGE, business educator; b. Davenport, Iowa, Dec. 22, 1946; s. Arthur and Varsenick (Donjoian) B.; m. Lynda L. Kennon, June 29, 1968; children: Katherine Nicole Kingsmill, Thomas Arthur. BBA, U. Iowa, 1967; MBA, Memphis U., 1968; DBA, Miss. State U., 1973. Instr. mgr. Miss. State U., Mississippi State, 1969-71; asst. prof. Ga. So. Coll., Statesboro, 1971-73; adj. asst. prof. Boston U., 1973-74; Edward L. Lowder prof. mgmt. Auburn (Ala.) U., 1974-85; Ralph and Kacoo G. Olinde Disting. prof. mgmt. La. State U., Baton Rouge, 1985-96, Boyd prof., 1997—. Dir. Found. for Adminstrv. Rsch., 1982-93, pres., 1989-90; cons. in field. Author: Organizations: Theory and Design, 1991, Management Laureates, 1992, 5th edit., 2002; Standardization of Selected Management Concepts, 1986, Management, 3d edit., 1993, Management in Extension, 3d edit., 1995; editor Jour. of Mgmt., 1977-79. With USAR, 1968-73. Fellow Acad. Mgmt. (pres. 1987-89, dean 1997-99), Internat. Acad. Mgmt., So. Mgmt. Assn.; mem. APA, Inst. Decision Scis. (nat. coun. 1976-79), Southeastern Inst. Decision Scis. (pres. 1978-79), So. Mgmt. Assn. (pres. 1982-83), Am. Sociol. Assn., Beta Gamma Sigma, Delta Mu Delta, Phi Kappa Phi, Sigma Iota Epsilon. Armenian Orthodox. Home: 838 High Plains Ave Baton Rouge LA 70810-4349 Office: La State U Dept Mgmt Baton Rouge LA 70803-6312 Fax: 225-578-6140. E-mail: abede@lsu.edu.

BEDELIA, BONNIE, actress; b. N.Y.C., Mar. 25, 1948; d. Philip and Marian (Wagner) Culkin; m. Kenneth Luber, Apr. 15, 1969; children: Yuri, Jonah. Student, Hunter Coll., N.Y.C.; studied with Uta Hager, Herbert Berghof studios; studied with Lee Strasberg, Actors Studio. Stage appearances include The Glass Menagerie, 1970, The Sea Gull, 1970, As You Like It, 1970, Midsummer Night's Dream, 1970; Broadway appearances include Isle of Children, 1960, Enter Laughing, 1963, The Playroom, 1965, Happily Never After, 1966, My Sweet Charlie, 1967 (Theatre World award 1967)); film appearances include Gypsy Moths, 1969, They Shoot Horses, Don't They?, 1969, Lovers and Other Strangers, 1970, Rosalie, 1972, Between Friends, 1973, The Big Fix, 1978, Heart Like a Wheel, 1983, Death of an Angel, 1986, The Boy Who Could Fly, 1986, Violets are Blue, 1986, The Stranger, 1987, Die Hard, 1988, Prince of Pennsylvania, 1988, Fat Man & Little Boy, 1989, Presumed Innocent, 1990, Die Hard II, 1990, Needful Things, 1993, Speechless, 1994, Judicial Consent, 1994, Homecoming, 1996, Any Mother's Son, 1997, Bad Manners, 1998; TV series Love of Live, 1961-67, The New Land, 1974, mini-series Salem's Lot, 1979, A Season in Purgatory, 1996; TV films Then Came Bronson, 1969, Sandcastles, 1972, Hawkins on Murder, 1973, A Message to My Daughter, 1973, A Time for Love, 1973, Heatwave, 1974, A Question of Love, 1978, Walking Through the Fire, 1979, Fighting Back, 1980, Million Dollar Infield, 1982, Memorial Day, 1983, The Lady from Yesterday, 1985, Alex, The Life of a Child, 1986, When the Time Comes, 1987, Somebody Has to Shoot the Picture, 1990, Switched At Birth, 1991, A Mother's Right: The Elizabeth Morgan Story, 1993, The Fire Next Time, 1993, Fallen Angels (The Quiet Room), 1993 (Emmy nomination, Guest Actress - Drama, 1994), Shadow of a Doubt, 1995, Legacy of Sin: The William Coit Story, 1995, Her Costly Affair, 1996, To Live Again, 1998. Recipient Golden Globe award, 1983. Office: care ICM c/o Michael Black 8942 Wilshire Blvd Beverly Hills CA 90211-1934

BEDELL, BARBARA LEE, journalist; b. Annapolis, Md., July 10, 1936; d. Royal Lee and Kathryn Rosalee (Alton) Sweeney; m. Raymond Lester Bedell, July 1, 1955 (div. 1979); children: Patricia Bedell Pulito, Barbara Ann Bedell Porrini, Raymond, Robert. DHL (hon.), Mt. St. Mary Coll., 2000. Dir. woman's programming, host daily talk show Sta. KLME, Laramie, Wyo., 1962-68, Sta. WKIP, Poughkeepsie, N.Y., 1968-70; asst. soc. editor, feature writer Poughkeepsie Jour., 1968-70; dir. comm. and publs. Spackenkill Sch. Dist., Poughkeepsie, 1970-73; columnist, reporter Times Herald-Record Newspaper, Middletown, N.Y., 1973—. Bd. dirs. Middletown Day Nursery, 1988—; mem. steering com. Dr. Martin Luther King Jr. Cmty. Wide Celebration, 1992—; lectr. on various topics to civic, polit., religious, social orgns., 1961—. Mem. 75th Anniversary Com., Cheyenne, Wyo., 1965; mem. Rep. Precinct Com., 1961-68, Albany County Bd. Electors, 1966-68; mem. com. history and heritage collection Orange County C.C., Middletown, 1984; mem. 100th Anniversary Com., Middletown, 1983-88; bd. dirs. divsn. marshal 1988 Parade; apptd. del. Gov. Mario Cuomo's N.Y. State Conf. on Librs., 1981; campaign chair United Way, 1996; bd. dirs. Literacy Vols. of Am.; kettle chmn. Salvation Army, 1999. Recipient 1st in N.Y. feature writing award Am. Cancer Soc., 1973, Disting. Svc. award NAACP, 1980, 96, Hadassah Myrtle Wreath award, 1979, Cmty. Svc. award Boy Scouts Am., 1990, Humanitarian award Human Rights Commn., 1997, Orange County Agr. Soc. award, Svc. awards from numerous svc. clubs and lodges, chs., assns.; named Mrs. Wyo., Mrs. Am. Pageant, 1967, N.Y. State All-Am. Family, 1972, Lions Knight of the Blind award, 1999, Pinnacle award U.S. Harness Racing Hall of Fame, 2002, Masonic DeWitt Clinton award, 2002. Mem. Nat. Fedn. Press Women (8 awards for feature writing 1967-70, top Wyo. state award for radio script writing 1966), Elks (Mother of Yr. award 1989), SAR (Woman of Yr. award 1991), Kiwanis, Lions, Rotary. Home: PO Box 458 Walker Valley NY 12588-0458 Office: Times Herald-Record PO Box 2046 Middletown NY 10940-0558 E-mail: bbedell@th-record.com.

BEDELL, ELIZABETH SNYDER (BETTY BEDELL), editor-in-chief, marketing professional; b. Jacksonville, Fla., Mar. 26, 1940; d. Ralph Edward and Elizabeth Follin Snyder; m. David Thorpe Bedell, June 16, 1961 (div. Aug. 1974); children: Charles, Elizabeth Bedell Coyle, George. Student, Hollins U.; BA, U. North Fla. Founding editor Kalliope, A Jour. of Women's Lit. and Art, 1978—81; tchr. Stanton Coll. Prep., Venetia Elem., 1981—84; freelance writer, editor, 1984—93, 1997—; program developer St. Vincent's Found., Inc., 1993—98; editor Betty Snyder Bedell Editl. Svcs., Jacksonville, 1999—. Chmn. garden and grounds Ximenez-Fatio Mus. House, St. Augustine, Fla.; bd. dirs. Jr. League, Jacksonville. Mem.: Colonial Dames, Fla. Yacht Club Jacksonville. Democrat. Episcopalian. E-mail: ebedell@bellsouth.net.

BEDELL, GEORGE CHESTER, retired publisher, educator, priest; b. Jacksonville, Fla., May 13, 1928; s. Chester and Edmonia (Hair) B.; m. Elizabeth Reed Phillips, Jan. 22, 1983; children: George Chester III, Frank Moor, Nathan Gale. BA, U. of South, Sewanee, Tenn., 1950; MDiv, Va. Theol. Sem., Alexandria, 1953; MA, U. N.C., 1966; PhD, Duke U., 1969; DCL (hon.), U. of South, 1991. Ordained priest Episcopal Ch.; parish priest Episc. Ch., Lake City, Panama City and Tallahassee, Fla., 1953-64; asst. prof. religion Fla. State U., Tallahassee, 1967-73, assoc. prof., 1973-74; dir. humanities and fine arts State U. System of Fla., 1971-72, dir. pers. and faculty rels., 1972-76, assoc. vice chancellor, 1976-77, exec. asst. to chancellor, dir. pub. affairs, 1977-79, vice chancellor, 1979-80, interim chancellor, 1980-81, exec. vice chancellor, 1981-86, vice chancellor for adminstrv. affairs, 1986-87; dir. U. Press of Fla., 1987-94. Mng. editor AAR Studies in Religion, 1970-76, historiographer Episc. Diocese of Fla., 1968-76 Author: Kierkegaard and Faulkner: Modalities of Existence, 1972, Religion in America, 1975, 82. Mem. Tallahassee City Park Bd., 1972—76; mem. jud. nominating commn. Fla. Supreme Ct., 1990—94; mem. fee arbitration com. Fla. Bar, 1994—98; mem. Leon County Dem. Exec. Com., 1970—74; trustee Jessie Ball du Pont Fund, 1985—98, chmn., 1988—89, 1993—95, 1997—98; trustee Newberry Libr., 1995—2002; bd. dirs. Episcopal Relief Devel., 1996—2001. Arthur N. Morris fellow, 1964-67; Duke-Danforth fellow, 1965-67 Mem. MLA, Fla. Hist. Soc., Nat. Trust for Hist. Preservation, Rotary. Democrat. Episcopalian. Home: 2810 NW 38th Dr Gainesville FL 32605-2680 E-mail: gbedell@ufl.edu.

BEDELL, GEORGE NOBLE, physician, educator; b. Harrisburg, Pa., May 1, 1922; s. George Harold and Elsie Clair (Noble) B.; m. Betty Jane Goldzier, Nov. 4, 1950 (dec. Mar. 1970); children: David, Mark, Barbara, Bruce; m. Mirriel Shields Hummel, Oct. 17, 1970; step-children: Judy, Jeffrey, Eric, Deborah, Andrew. BA, DePauw U., 1944; MD, U. Cin., 1946. Intern U. Iowa, 1946-47, resident in pathology, 1947-48, resident in internal medicine, 1950-52, research fellow in internal medicine, specializing in cardiology, 1952-54; research fellow physiology Postgrad. Sch. Medicine, U., Pa., 1954-55; asst. prof. dept. medicine Coll. Medicine, U. Iowa, 1955-59, asso. prof. dept. medicine, 1959-68, prof., 1968—; dir. Pulmonary Disease div. Dept. Medicine, 1968-81. Cons. VA Hosp., Iowa City, 1954— ; mem. staff U. Hosps., Iowa City Contbr. articles to profl. jours. Mem. Johnson County Democratic Central Com., 1956-69, treas., 1958-64. Served with AUS, 1948-50. NIH Spl. fellow, 1954-55; recipient Career Devel. award, 1960-70, Walter L. Bierring award Am. Lung Assn. Iowa, 1973 Mem. ACP, Am. Lung Assn. (dir. 1972-80), Am. Lung Assn. Iowa (dir. 1971-81), Am. Fedn. Clin. Research, Am. Thoracic Soc., Iowa Thoracic Soc. (v.p. 1960-61, pres. 1962-63), Iowa Tb and Health Assn. (dir. 1961-65, 67-71), AMA (vice chmn. sect. council on diseases of chest 1971-73, chmn. sec. council diseases of chest 1974-76, Am. Thoracic Soc. del. to AMA 1979-85), Iowa, Johnson County med. socs., Soc. Exptl. Biology and Medicine, Iowa Clin. Soc. Internal Medicine, Central Soc. Clin. Research, Am. Coll. Chest Physicians, Am. Physiol. Soc., Am. Soc. Clin. Investigation, A.C.P., Central Clin. Research Club. Democrat. Unitarian Universalist. Home: 903 Highwood St Iowa City IA 52246-3807 E-mail: george-bedell@uiowa.edu.

BEDELL, JAY DEE, educator, writer; b. Monterey, Calif., Oct. 20, 1946; s. John Dewhirst and Lucille (Huffman) Bedell. BA, U. Calif., Davis, 1968. Tchr. Antioch Schs., Calif., 1969-84; v.p., dir. Credit Union, 1979-81; owner Bedell Enterprises, 1986—; supr. security Chevron U.S.A., 1988-90. Mem. Adv. Coun. for Spl. Edn., Antioch, Calif., 1979-81; mem. State Dept. Conf. on Spl. Edn., 1978; staff devel. com. Office of Supt. of Schs., Contra Costa County, Calif., 1979-81; cons. in field. Author numerous poems. Deacon Adventist Ch., Antioch, Calif.; sch. bd. Hilltop Christian Sch., Antioch; honor guard Vets. Home Calif. With US Army, 1971-75. Recipient Golden Poet award, World of Poetry Press, 1985—92. Fellow Am. Biog. Inst. Rsch. Assn. (life); mem. NRA (cert. asst. rifle instr.), Sierra Club, Nature Conservancy, Internat. Platform Assn., Wilderness Soc., Libr. of Congress (assoc.), Smithsonian (assoc.), Knight Sovereign Mil. Templar Order, Delta Upsilon. Democrat. Address: Vets Home of Calif PO Box 1200 Yountville CA 94599

BEDENBAUGH, ANGELA LEA OWEN, chemistry educator, researcher; b. Seguin, Tex., Oct. 6, 1939; d. Wintford Henry and Nelia Melanie (Fischer) Owen; m. John Holcombe Bedenbaugh, Dec. 27, 1961; 1 child, Melanie Celeste. BS cum laude, U. Tex., 1961; PhD in Organic Chemistry, U. S.C., 1967. Geol. mapping asst. Roland Blumberg Assocs., Seguin, summer 1958, 59; chemistry lab. instr. U. Tex., Austin, 1960-61; rsch. assoc. chemistry U. So. Miss., Hattiesburg, 1966-80, rsch. assoc. prof. chemistry, 1980—, bd. mem. women's studies program, 1996-97. Co-prin. investigator Bell South Found. grant, 1998; dir. website NASA grant, 1999-00. Author: Nomenplayture, 1998; co-author: (with John H. Bedenbaugh) Handbook for High School Chemistry Teachers, 1985, (with John H. Bedenbaugh) Teaching First Year Chemistry, 4th edit., 1993; patentee in field. Adminstrv. bd. Parkway Heights United Meth. Ch., 1974-75, women's unit leader, 1973-75, women's unit treas., 1977, Wesleyan Svc. Guild v.p., 1970, Sunday Sch. tchr., 1973-74; bd. dirs. Forrest Stone Area Opportunity Inc., 1970-72, bd. dirs. exec. com., 1972, mem. com. to rewrite pers. policies and procedures, 1971, mem. Headstart monitoring com., 1971-72, mem. pers. screening com., 1971; mem. nat. Women's Polit. Caucus, 1976—; mem. Toastmasters Internat., 1986—, club. pres., 1993, area gov., 1994; adminstr., dir. Tchr. Mentoring Initiative through Bell South Found. Grant, 1998-2000; Miss. state coord. Bldg. a Presence for Sci. Recipient John and Angela Bedenbaugh award Coastal Miss. Assn. H.S. Chemistry Tchrs., 1996—; Rsch. grantee U.S. Dept. Energy, U. So. Miss., 1980, NSF, U. So. Miss., 1985, Adminstrv. Dir. Rsch. grant, 1988-91, 1993-96, 2001-04, NSF, 2000—, others. Mem. NSTA (nat. resource rev. panel for rev. of instrnl. materials), LWV, AAUW, Am. Chem. Soc. (chmn. 1984-85, program chmn. 1983-84, exec. bd. 1983—, Chemist of Yr. award 1991), Miss. Sci. Tchrs. Assn. (exec. bd. 1994—, pres.-elect 1998-2000, pres. 2000-02, state bldg. a presence for sci. coord. 2002—, Disting. Sci. Tchr. award 1994), Delta Kappa Gamma (pres. Miss. br. 1989-91, chmn. internat. rsch. com. 1980-82, chmn. internat. computer share fair at internat. conv. 1994, editor U.S. Forum Connection 2000-), Sigma Xi (charter, sec.-treas. 1967-69, treas. 1970, pres. 1973-74, program chmn. 1972-73). Democrat. Methodist. Home: 63 Suggs Rd Hattiesburg MS 39402-3639 Office: Univ So Miss PO Box 8466 Hattiesburg MS 39406-1000

BEDERMAN, GAIL, education educator, historian; b. Evanston, Ill., Oct. 20, 1952; d. Alfred N. Bederman, Henriet T. Bederman. BFA, NYU, 1978; MA, Brown U., R.I., 1984, PhD, 1992. Asst. prof. U. of Notre Dame, Notre Dame, Ind., 1992—98, assoc. prof., 1998—. Author: (book) Manliness and Civilization: A Cultural History of Gender and Race in the United States 1877-1917, (article) Radical History Review, American Quarterly. Sr. Fellow, Stanford Humanities Ctr., 2002—03. Mem.: Nat. Assn. for Women in Cath. Higher Edn., Am. Studies Assn., Orgn. of Am. Historians, Am. Hist. Assn. Office: U of Notre Dame History Dept Notre Dame IN 46556

BEDERSON, BENJAMIN, physicist, educator; b. NYC, Nov. 15, 1921; s. Abraham Michael and Lena (Waxlowsky) B.; m. Betty Weintraub, Jan. 20, 1956; children: Joshua Benjamin, Geoffrey Adam, Aron Gregory, Benjamin Boris. BS, CCNY, 1946; MS, Columbia U., 1948; PhD, NYU, 1950. Rsch. scientist MIT, Cambridge, 1950-52; faculty dept. physics NYU, 1952-92, prof., 1967-92, prof. emeritus, 1992—, chmn. dept., 1973-76, spl. advisor for sci. to dean Faculty Arts and Scis., 1983-86, dean Grad. Sch. Arts and Scis., 1986-89. Chmn. Internat. Conf. Physics of Electronic and Atomic Collisions, 1983-85; chmn. vis. panel Ctr. for Absolute Phys. Quantities, Nat. Bur. Standards, 1980-83. Editor-in-chief Am. Phys. Soc., 1992-96; editor Phys. Rev. A, 1978-91; assoc. editor Atomic Data and Nuclear Data Jour., 1969-98; editor (with Herbert Walther) Advances in Atomic, Molecular, and Optical Physics, 1974—; contbr. articles to profl. jours.; patentee in field. With U.S. Army, 1942-46, PTO. Fellow: APS (chair forum history physics 2001—02), AAAS. Home: 60 E 8th St Apt 24K New York NY 10003-6522 Office: NYU Physics Dept 4 Washington Pl New York NY 10003-6621 E-mail: ben.bederson@nyu.edu.

BEDFORD, AMY ALDRICH, public relations executive; b. Pendleton, Oreg., July 13, 1912; d. Edwin Burton and Elsie (Conklin) Aldrich; m. J.M. Bedford (wid.); 1 child, Jacqueline Bedford Brown. BS, Oreg. State U., 1933. Mgr. comml. dept. East Oregonian, Pendleton, 1950-75, mgr. pub. rels., 1975—; corp. sec. East Oregonian Pub. Co., Pendleton, 1950-2000. Bd. dirs. Oreg. Status of Women Com., 1972-75, Oreg. Law Enforcement Commn., 1975-82; active Arts Coun. Pendleton. Recipient Pendleton First Citizen award C. of C., 1962, Gov.'s award for the Arts, 1988, Woman of Achievement award Oreg. Commn. for Women, 1998, Paul Harris award Rotary, 1993. Mem. Women in Communications, Oreg. Press Women, AAUW (pres. 1956-58, grantee 1965), LWV, Pendleton River Parkway Found., World Affairs Coun. Oreg., Altrusa. Avocations: reading, travel, music, theatre. Home: PO Box 1456 Pendleton OR 97801-0360 Office: East Oregonian Pub Co PO Box 1089 Pendleton OR 97801-1089 E-mail: jacbrown@eastoregonian.com.

BEDFORD, ANNE MARIE, musician, educator, insurance agent; b. N.Y.C., Sept. 22, 1938; d. David Nathaniel and Solveig (Johansen) Dattelbaum; children: Charles Andrew, Stephanie Anne Nelson. AB (magna cum laude), Mount Holyoke Coll., Hadley, Mass., 1960; MS, The Juilliard Sch., N.Y.C., 1965; CLU, ChFC, The Am. Coll., Bryn Mawr, Pa., 1982. Writer, sec. The Univ. Soc., N.Y.C., 1962—65; head of piano, lectr. in music Immaculata Coll., Malvern, Pa., 1969—74; asst. prof. piano Duquesne U., Pitts., 1974—75; ins. and fin. agt. Conn. Mutual, Hartford, 1978—98, Mass. Mutual, Springfield, Mass., 1978—, broker, 1998—; piano faculty Settlement Music Schs., Phila., 1992—; mem. piano faculty Bryn Mawr Conservatory Music, Pa., 1998—. Asst. prof. music West Chester U., Pa., 1968—74; adj. prof. music Germantown Acad., Ft. Washington, Pa., 2000—; mem. Tri County Concerts Assn., Inc., 1986—; performer (solo and in chamber orchs.) various locations, Pa., 1965—, dir. student recitals, Pa., 1960—. Democrat. Home: 9 Grubb Rd Malvern PA 19355

BEDFORD, BARBARA J. Olympic athlete; b. Hanover, N.H., Nov. 9, 1972; Recipient Gold medal 4 x 100-meter medley (team) Sydney Olympics, 2000, 100-meter backstroke U.S. nats., Mpls., 1999; 3d pl. 100-meter backstroke Pan Pacific Championships, Gold medley relay, 1999, 7 time US Nat. Champion 5-100 backstroke, 1-200 backstroke, 1-50 free, Olympic Trials Champion, 2000, Pan Pacific Champion, 200-meters backstroke, 1993, Pan Am. Champion, 100-meter backstroke, 200-meter backstroke, 4X100 medley relay, 1995, World Championships 3d pl. 100-meter backstroke, 4th pl. 200-meter backstroke, 1994, Goodwill Games Champion 200-meter backstroke, 2nd pl. 100 backstroke, Gold winner on medley relay, 1994, World U. Games champion, 1st pl. 100-meter backstroke, 1st pl. 4X100 medley relay, 1991, 1st pl. 100-meter backstroke, 1st pl. 4X100 medley relay, 1993, World Championships Gold on free realy, Gold Preliminary Medley, 1998. Office: USA Swimming 1 Olympic Plz Colorado Springs CO 80909-5746

BEDFORD, FELICE L. psychologist, educator; b. Manhatten, N.Y., Dec. 9, 1960; d. Pauline (Allalouf) and Donald Bedford. BA, U. Pa., 1982, MA, 1983, PhD, 1988. Asst. prof. U. Ariz., Tucson, 1988—94; vis. scholar U. Calif., Berkeley, 1995—96, assoc. prof. Tucson, 1994—2002; rsch. fellow cognitive sci. program U. Ariz., Tucson, 2000—. Grant reviewer NSF, The Israel Sci. Found., and U.S. Air Force, 1990—; cons. USAF, 1993—95; chair undergrad. psychology curriculum U. Ariz., Tucson, 1997—; cons. Pub. Defender's Office and Dist. Attorney's Office, Tucson, 1997—; organizer cognitive sci. lectures series U. Ariz., Tucson, 1999—2000. Contbr. articles. Grantee, NSF, 1989—93, U. Ariz. Found., 2000—01, Social and Behavioral Sciences Rsch. Inst., 1994—95, 1998—99. Mem.: Rocky Mountain Psychol. Assn., Brain and Behavioral Sci., Am. Psychol. Soc., Sephardic Brotherhood Am., Phi Beta Kappa (life inducted 1982). Liberal. Avocations: dogs, genealogy, hiking, birdwatching. Office: Univ Ariz Dept Psychology Rm 312 Tucson AZ 85721 Office Fax: 520-621-9306. Business E-mail: bedford@u.arizona.edu.

BEDFORD, ROBERT FORREST, anesthesiologist; b. Boston, Oct. 6, 1942; s. Nathaniel Forrest and Roberta Lelia (Skinner) B.; m. Faith Goodwin Andrews, Dec. 28, 1963; children: William, Eleanor, Sarah. AB in Biology, Princeton U., 1964; MD, Cornell U., 1968. Diplomate Am. Bd. Anesthesiology (assoc. examiner 1987-90). Intern Va. Mason Hosp., Seattle, 1968-69; resident/fellow anesthesiology U. Pa. Hosp., Phila., 1969-72; chief anesthesiology, operating svcs. U.S. Walson Army Hosp., Ft. Dix, N.J., 1972-74; asst. clin. prof. anesthesiology Columbia U. Coll. Physicians and Surgeons, N.Y.C., 1974-77; from asst. prof. to prof. anesthesiology U. Va. Sch. Med., Charlottesville, Va., 1977-86; chmn. dept. anesthesiology Meml. Sloan-Kettering Cancer Ctr., N.Y.C., 1986-90; clin. prof. anesthesiology U. Va. Sch. Med., Charlottesville, 1990-96, 99—; prof. anesthesiology U. South Fla., Tampa, 1996—; chief anesthesiology svc. James Haley VA Med. Ctr., Tampa, 1996-99, cons., 1999—. Spl. govt. employee anesthetic and life support drug adv. com. FDA, Rockville, Md., 1991-94, 96—, acting dir. pilot drug divsn. 1994-95, divsn. anesthetics, 1995-96. Contbr. over 200 published articles and abstracts to profl. jours., over 20 chpts. to books. Maj. USAR, 1972-74. Grantee Found. Anesthesia Edn./Rsch., 1981; recipient Univ. Bordeaux II medal, 1988, Physician Recognition award AMA, 1991—. Mem. Soc. Neurosurg. Anesthesia (sec., treas., v.p., pres.), Va. Soc. Anesthesiologists (sec., treas., v.p., pres.), Am. Soc. Anesthesiologists (chair neurosci. com. 1986-88, resident rsch. essay award, 1973). Presbyterian. Avocations: sailing, fishing, skiing. Home: 5311 Ambrose Ct Tampa FL 33647-1010 Office: James Haley VA Med Ctr Anesthesiology Svc 123 13000 Bruce B Downs Blvd Tampa FL 33612-4745

BEDIAN, MARAL PAPAZIAN, civil and geotechnical engineer; b. Aleppo, Syria, Sept. 11, 1953; came to U.S., 1979, naturalized, 1986; d. Hovanes and Lucine Bedian; m. Artur Papazian, Apr. 5, 1986. BSc, Aleppo U., 1978; MSc, N.J. Inst. Tech., 1981, postgrad., 1982—. Registered profl. engr., N.J., N.Y., Mass., Pa. Civil engr. Syrian Arab R.R.s, Aleppo, 1978-79; geotech. engr. Converse Cons., Parsippany, N.J., 1981-84; sr. geotech. engr. Storch Engrs., Florham Park, N.J., 1984-87, geotech. project mgr., 1987-90, geotech. dept. head, 1990-92; sr. geotech. engr. Dames & Moore, Inc., Cranford, N.J., 1992-96; design mgr., chief geotech. engr. Perini Corp., Hawthorne, N.Y., 1996—. Rsch. grantee N.J. Inst. Tech., 1981. Mem. ASCE, Deep Foundations Inst., Can. Geotechnical Soc., Internat. Soc. Soil Mechanics and Found. Engrs. Achievements include research on laterally loaded caissons and shear strength of stiff clays and value engineering during construction. Home: 200 Winston Tower # 2311 Cliffside Park NJ 07010

BEDIKIAN, AGOP Y. internist, oncologist, educator; b. Lebanon; arrived in U.S., 1972, naturalized, 1978; BS, Am .U. Beirut, 1967; MD, Am. U. Beirut, 1971. Diplomate Am. Bd. Internal Medicine, Am. Bd. Med. Oncology. Intern St. Louis City Hosp., 1972—73; resident Barnes Hosp., St. Louis, 1973—75; fellow U. Tex. M.D. Anderson Hosp. and Tumor Inst., Houston, 1975—77, clin. instr., faculty assoc. dept. devel. therapeutics, 1977—78; asst. prof. medicine, assoc. internist U. Tex. M.D. Anderson Hosp. Cancer Ctr., Houston, 1978—82; cons. oncologist, dep. chmn. oncology dept. King Faisal Specialist Hosp. and Rsch. Ctr., Riyadh, Saudi Arabia, 1981—91; assoc. prof. medicine dept. melanoma/sarcoma med. oncology U. Tex. M.D. Anderson Cancer Ctr., Houston, 1991—97, internist dept. melanoma/sarcoma med. oncology, 1991—2000, prof., 1997—2000, dep. dir. Melanoma and Skin Ctr., 1997—, prof. dept. melanoma med. oncology, 2000—, ad interim chmn. dept. melanoma

med. oncology, 2000—. Presenter numerous papers at profl. conf.s. Contbr. over 95 articles to profl. jours., 13 chpts. to books; reviewer (jours.) Cancer, Jour. Clin. Oncology, Annals Saudi Medicine, Melanoma Rsch. Grantee, Rhone-Poulenc Rorer Pharms. Inc., 1992—93, UpJohn, 1993—94, Sanofi Winthrop, 1994—95, 1996—97, Schering Plough, 1996—, Ligand Pharms., 1997—98, NaPro Biotherapeutics, 1998—2000, Supergen, 1999—2000, Agouron Pharms. Inc., 2000—02, Bristol-Myers Squibb Co., 2000—, Genta, Inc., 2000—, Vical Inc., 2001, Cell Therapeutics, 2002—, Protarga, Inc., 2002—, INEX, 2002—, Celgenes, 2003—, Med Immune, 2003—, Astrazeneca, 2003—. Mem.: AAAS, ACP, Harris County Med. Soc., Tex. Med. Assn., N.Y. Acad. Scis., Am. Soc. Clin. Oncology, Am. Assn. Cancer Rsch. Home: 5661 Piping Rock Houston TX 77056 Office: U Tex MD Anderson Cancer Ctr 1515 Holcombe Blvd Box 430 Houston TX 77030 Fax: 713-745-1046. E-mail: abedikia@mdanderson.org.

BEDINI, SILVIO A. historian, author; b. Ridgefield, Conn., Jan. 17, 1917; s. Vincent and Cesira (Stefanelli) B.; m. Gerda Hintz, Oct. 20, 1951; children: Leandra, Peter. Ed., Columbia U., 1935-42; LLD, U. Bridgeport, 1970. Curator divsn. mech. and civil engring. U.S. Nat. Mus., Smithsonian Instn., Washington, 1961-65; from asst. dir. to dep. dir. Mus. History and Tech., 1965-78, keeper rare books, 1978-87; historian emeritus Smithsonian Inst., 1987—. Author: Ridgefield in Review, 1958, The Scent of Time, 1963, Early American Scientific Instruments and Their Makers, 1964; (with F.R. Maddision) Mechanical Universe, 1966; (with W. Von Braun and F.L. Whipple) Moon, Man's Greatest Adventure, 1970, The Life of Benjamin Banneker, 1972, rev. and expanded edit., 1999; (with others) The Unknown Leonardo, 1974, Thinkers and Tinkers, Early American Men of Science, 1975, The Spotted Stones, 1978, Declaration of Independence Desk: Relic of Revolution, 1981, Thomas Jefferson and His Copying Machines, 1984, At the Sign of the Compass and the Quadrant, 1984, Clockwork Cosmos, 1985, Thomas Jefferson Statesman of Science, 1990, The Pulse of Time, 1990, The Trail of Time, 1993, Science and Instruments in Seventeenth Century Italy, 1994, The Pope's Elephant, 1997, The Mace and the Gavel: Symbols of Government in America, 1997, The Jefferson Stone, 1999, Patrons, Artisans and Instruments of Science, 1999, The Life of Benjamin Banneker, The First African American of Science, rev. and expanded edit., 1999, With Compass and Chain, Early American Surveyors and Their Instruments, 2000, Jefferson and Science, 2002. Fellow Washington Acad. Scis.; mem. Am. Philos. Soc., Am. Antiquarian Soc., Soc. Am. Historians, History Sci. Soc., Soc. for History Tech., Astrolabe Soc. Home: 4303 47th St NW Washington DC 20016-2449 E-mail: sbedini@ATT.net.

BEDJAOUI, M. MOHAMMED, former judge International Court of Justice; b. Sidi Bel Abbes, Sept. 21, 1929; s. Benali and Fatima El-Oukili); m. Leila Francis, Oct. 21, 1962; children: Amal, Assia. Doctorate in Law, Grenoble U., France; diploma, Polit. Studies Inst. Lawyer Appeal Ct., Grenoble; attache researches internat. law sect. Nat. Ctr. Sci. Rsch., Paris; jur. counsellor provisional govt. of Algeria; dir. Cabinet Pres. Nat. Constituent Assembly, Algiers, Algeria, 1962, gen. sec. govt., 1962-64; pres. dir. Nat. Rys. Soc. Algeria, 1964; dean Faculty Law, Algiers, 1964-65; min. of justice Govt. of Algeria, 1964-70; amb. to France, Algerian Embassy, Paris, 1970-79; amb. to UN N.Y.C., 1979-82; judge Internat. Ct. Justice, The Hague, 1982—2001, pres., 1994-97; mem. exec. bd. UNESCO, 2002—. Mem. Internat. Law Commn., UN, 1965-82. Author: International Civil Service, 1956. Fonction Publique internationale et influences nationales, 1958; La Revolution Algerienne et le Droit, 1961; Problèmes récents de Succession d'Etats, 1970; Non-alignement et droit international, 1976; Pour un nouvel ordre economique international, 1978; contbr. articles to profl. jours. Recipient decorations UAR, France, Morocco, Algeria, Mali. Mem. Assn. Acad. Internat. Law. Office: UNESCO 7 place de Fontenoy 75352 Paris France

BEDKE, ERNEST ALFORD, retired air force officer; b. Oakley, Idaho, Oct. 16, 1934; s. Herschel McIntosh and Ethel Marie (Alford) B.; m. Marilyn Meils, June 8, 1955; children: Curtis, Michael. BSBA, U. Idaho, 1955; grad., Air Command and Staff Coll., 1967, Air War Coll., 1973. Commd. 2d lt. U.S. Air Force, 1955, advanced through grades to maj. gen., 1977; instr. pilot Reese AFB, Tex., 1957-62; air ops. officer Chaumont Air Base, France, 1962; fighter pilot Phalsbourg Air Base, France, 1962-63, Holloman AFB, N.Mex., 1963-66, Da Nang Air Base, Vietnam, 1966; air liaison officer, forward air controller Cat Lai, Vietnam, 1967-68; ops. staff officer NATO, Ramstein Air Base, Fed. Republic Germany, 1968-71; chief Europe-NATO, plans & policy, Hdqrs. U.S. Air Force, Wash., 1971-72; dep. comdr. ops. Eglin AFB, Eglin, Fla., 1973-74; comdr. 56 Tactical Fighter Wing Macdill AFB, Fla., 1975-77; dep. comdr. tng., testing and range facilities Nellis AFB, Nev., 1977-79; insp. gen. Tactical Air Command Langley AFB, Va., 1979-80; dep. chief staff ops. and intelligence Hdqrs. Pacific Air Forces Hickam AFB, Hawaii, 1980-83; ret., 1983; mgmt. cons. Decorated AF Disting. Svc. medal, Legion of Merit (2), D.F.C. (2), Air medal (20), M.S.M., Air Force Commendation medal. Mem. Air Force Assn., Order of Daedalians. Home: 18509 Turtle Dr Lutz FL 33548-4461

BEDNAR, CHARLES SOKOL, political scientist, educator; b. N.Y.C., Nov. 3, 1930; s. Karel and Anna (Tomcala) B.; m. Beluse Alzbeta Pokorny, Aug. 31, 1959. AB, Rutgers U., 1951, MA, 1952; PhD, Columbia, 1960. Asso. prof. Lynchburg Coll., 1958-62; prof., chmn. dept. polit. sci., asso. dean of coll. Muhlenberg Coll., 1962-99, Eve Elizabeth Muhlenberg Disting. Svc. prof., 1989-99, prof. emeritus; adj. prof. grad. program in gen. edn., chmn. social sci. panel Temple U., 1963-86. Author: Transforming the Dream: Ecologism and the Shaping of an Alternative American Vision, 2003; contbr. articles to profl. jours. Chmn. Lehigh Valley Citizens for Progress, 1972-75; pres. Allentown YMCA, 1979-80. Recipient award Lindback Found., 1965, Paul E. Empie Meml. award, 1983. Mem. Czechoslovak Acad. Arts and Scis., AAUP, Phi Beta Kappa, Delta Phi Alpha, Tau Kappa Alpha, Omicron Delta Kappa, Pi Sigma Alpha. Home: 1285 Sheridan Rd Coopersburg PA 18036-1816

BEDNAR, MICHAEL JOHN, architecture educator; b. Cleve., Mar. 19, 1942; s. Peter and Mary (Rohal) B.; m. Mary Kathryn Gillman; children: Richard Earl, Matthew Scott, Rachel Catherine; m. Elizabeth Waddel Lawson. BArch, U. Mich., 1964; MArch, U. Pa., Phila., 1967. Registered architect, Pa., N.Y., Va. Jr. designer I.M. Pei & Ptnrs., N.Y.C., 1965-66; project architect Geddes, Brecher, Qualls, Cunningham, Phila., 1967-68; asst. prof. Rennselaer Polytech. Inst., Troy, N.Y., 1968-72; assoc. prof. U. Va., Charlottesville, 1972—, co-chmn. div. of architecture, 1976-81, assoc. dean for academics, 1992-95. Prin. Michael Bednar, FAIA Architect, Charlottesville, 1973-90, Bednar Lawson Architects, 1990—. Author: Architecture for Handicapped, 1973, The New Atrium, 1986; Interior Pedestrian Places, 1989; editor: Barrier-Free Environment, 1977. Mem., chair City Planning Commn., Charlottesville, 1982—; chmn. Urban Design Task Force, Charlottesville, 1985-88; mem. Bd. of Architectural Review, Charlottesville, 1983-86. Booth fellow U. Mich., 1972, NEA fellow, 1984, Graham Found. fellow, 1988-2003; recipient Nat. Book award Am. Assn. of Publ., 1986, Nichols award Preservation Alliance Va., 1997, Cmty. Svc. award AIA Ctrl. Va., 1997. Fellow Am. Inst. Architects (Disting. Achievemnt award 1997). Assn. for the Preservation of Va. Antiquities (bd. dirs. Jefferson chpt. 1999-2000). Avocations: jazz music, tennis, travel. photography. Home: 1201 E Jefferson St Charlottesville VA 22902-5414

BEDNAR, R. CRAIG, magazine and book publisher; b. Hancock, Mich., June 19, 1963; s. David Henry and Marie Claire Bednar. BA in Econs., BA in Fin., U. Minn., 1985; MBA in Fin. and Mktg., U. Notre Dame, 1986. Corp. fin. analyst Cowles Media Co., Mpls., 1987-89; sr. fin. analyst Star Tribune newspaper, Mpls., 1989-92; pres. Tiger Oak Publs., Inc., Mpls., 1992—. Adj. prof. Concordia Coll., St. Paul, 1989—91; adj. prof. MBA program U. St. Thomas, 2001—; cons. U. Minn., Mpls., 1998, Minn. Orch., Mpls., 1997—98, Arts Midwest, Mpls., 1995—96. Pub., Minn. Bride, 1993—; pub. mags. Seattle Bride, 1997—, Seattle Mag., 1995-98, Minn. Law and Politics, 1992, Minn. Meetings and Events, 2001, San Francisco Bride, 2000, Twin Cities Parent, 1999, Northwest Home and Garden, 2001. Mem. fin. com. Gov. Arnie Carlson, Mpls., 1994-95. Named to 40 Under 40, Mpls., 1999. Avocations: golf, cooking, biking. Office: Tiger Oak Publs 251 1st Ave N Ste 401 Minneapolis MN 55401-1669 E-mail: rcbednar@tigeroak.com.

BEDNAR, RICHARD JOHN, lawyer, law educator; b. Omaha, Oct. 30, 1931; s. John Stanley and Frances Julia (Zikas) B.; m. Judith Ann Jaudon, Feb. 8, 1969; children— Linda, Elizabeth, John, Paul. LL.B., Creighton U., 1954; LL.M., George Washington U., 1969. Bar: Nebr. 1954, D.C. 1985. Commd. 2d lt. U.S. Army, 1954, advanced through grades to brig. gen., 1979; staff judge adv., Ft. Leavenworth, Kans., 1971-72; exec. to Judge Adv. Gen., Dept. Army, 1973-75, chief trial atty., 1975-76, chief litigation div., 1976-77, judge adv. U.S. Forces, Korea, 1977-79; asst. judge adv. gen. for civil law Dept. Army, 1979-81; judge adv. U.S. Army Europe, 1981-83; asst. judge adv. gen. for civil law Dept. Army, 1983-84, ret., 1984; dir. govt. contracts program George Washington U., Nat. Law Ctr., Washington, 1984— . Decorated Bronze Star, Legion of Merit with 2 oak leaf clusters, D.S.M. Mem. Assn. U.S. Army (past. pres. European dept.), ABA, Fed. Bar Assn., Nebr. Bar Assn., Nat. contract Mgmt. Assn. Republican. Episcopalian. Club: Army-Navy Country (Arlington, Va.). Home: 3805 Ft Worth Ave Alexandria VA 22304-1708 Office: Nat Law Ctr Washington DC 20052-0001

BEDNAR, RUDY, television producer, director; b. Palmerton, Pa., May 31, 1951; s. Rudolph and Rita (Colan) Bednar. BA, Marquette U., 1973. Producer, dir. various TV stas., 1973—79; prodr., dir. ABC, N.Y.C., 1980—84, Good Morning Am., ABC, N.Y.C., 1984—88, 20/20 ABC, N.Y.C., 1989; prodr. Prime Time Live ABC, N.Y.C., 1990—92; sr. prodr. Turning Point ABC News, N.Y.C., 1993—98; exec. prodr. ABC News Long Form Unit, 1999—. Recipient 9 Emmy awards, Monitor award, Investigative Reports & Editors award, 3 Dupont awards. Mem.: Dirs. Guild Am. Office: ABC News 147 Columbus Ave New York NY 10023-5999

BEDNASH, GERALDINE POLLY, association executive; b. San Antonio, May 6, 1943; d. David Anthony and Bernice (Brewer) Parrott; m. Thomas Francis Bednash, June 24, 1967, children: Thomas F. Jr., Joseph Andrew. B of Nursing, Tex. Women's U., 1965; M of Nursing, Cath. U. Am., 1977; PhD, U. Md., 1989. Cert. nurse practitioner. Nurse Binghamton (N.Y.) Gen. Hosp., 1967-69; instr. Broome County Community Coll., Binghamton, 1967-71; asst. prof. No. Va. Community Coll., Annandale, 1977-78, George Mason U., Fairfax, Va., 1978-86; dir. govt. rels. Am. Assn. Coll. Nursing, Washington, 1986-89, exec. dir., 1989—. Co-chmn. Nat. Com. Nursing Implementation Project, Washington, 1990-91; cons. in field. Contbr. articles to profl. jours. Polit. action chmn. Va. Nurses Assn., 1979-83; nurse clinician So Others Might Eat, Washington, 1981-83. Capt. U.S. Army, 1963-67. Primary Care fellow Robert Wood Johnson Found., U. Md., 1981-82, Nat. Rsch. Svc. fellow, Washington, 1983-87. Fellow Am. Acad. Nursing; mem. ANA, Sigma Theta Tau. Roman Catholic. Avocations: skiing, horticulture. Office: Am Assn Coll Nursing 1 Dupont Cir NW Ste 530 Washington DC 20036-1135

BEDNOFF, STUART LEON, obstetrician, gynecologist, educator; b. NYC, Aug. 31, 1936; MD, SUNY, 1961. Diplomate Am. Bd. Ob/gyn. Intern L.I. Jewish Hosp., N.Y.C., 1961-62; resident in ob/gyn. North Shore U. Hosp., Manhasset, N.Y., 1962-66, mem. staff, 1965; pvt. practice, Gt. Neck, N.Y., 1968. Clin. assoc. prof. dept. ob-gyn. NYU Sch. Medicine. Fellow ACOG, ACS; mem. Nassau Obstetricians/Gynecologists.

BEDRICK, ANTHONY EDWARD, oral surgeon, educator; b. Fall River, Mass., Jan. 29, 1918; s. Samuel and Ida (Snyder) Bedrick; m. Rachel Libbian Rubinstein, Jan. 21, 1945; 1 child, Jeffrey David. Grad., Durfee Tech. Inst., Fall River, Mass., 1935—37; pre-dental, Providence Coll., R.I., 1941; DDS, St. Louis Sch. of Dentistry, 1954. Textile chemist/colorist, Fall River/New Bedford, Mass., 1937—42; staff mem. Beekman Downtown Hosp., NYC, 1959—65; instr. NYU Sch. of Dentistry, NYC, 1960—2002; attending Met. Hosp., NYC, 1959—. Author: (jour.) Pharmacology, 1979. With U.S. Army, 1942—45. Fellow: Royal Soc. of Health; mem.: Am. Dental Assn., Rsch. Soc. of Am. Achievements include research in A.A.A.S. - rsch. histological staining of benign and malignant human tissues with textile dyes not previously used for staining tissue. Avocation: sci. reading. Home: 345 Webster Ave Apt 4-H Brooklyn NY 11230

BEDRICK, BERNICE, retired science educator, consultant; b. Jersey City, Sept. 29, 1916; d. Abraham Lewis and Esther (Cowan) Grodjesk; m. Emanuel Arthur Bedrick, Dec. 25, 1938 (dec. 1967); children: Allen Paul, Jane Bedrick Abels; m. Samuel Milberger, Sept. 23, 1984 (dec. 1984); stepchildren: Susan Milberger Rafael, Stanford. BS, U. Md., 1938; MA, NYU, 1952. Cert. tchr., N.J. Tchr. Linden (N.J.) Pub. Sch. System, 1950-69, supr. sci. curriculum, 1969-79, sch. prin., 1979-87; ret., 1987. Co-author: A Universe to Explore, 1969; developer program of safety and survival N.J. Dept. Edn., 1975. Founder, mem., bd. dirs., v.p. edn. Temple Mekor Chayim, Linden; pres. bd. trustees Linden Pub. Libr., 1989-90, v.p., 1991; pres. Friends of Linden Libr., 1987-92, 95-97, coord. used books sales, 1990—, founder, 1987; bd. trustees Temple Beth-El Mekor Chayim, Cranford, N.J., 1999—, bd. edn., 1999—. Recipient Cmty. Vol. Svc. award B'Nai B'Rith, 1993, Outstanding Sr. Citizen of Yr., City of Linden, 1996; honored with Bernice Bedrick rm. at Sunnyside br. Linden Pub. Libr., 2001. Mem.: NEA (life), Nat. Sci. Tchrs. Assn., N.J. Sci. Tchrs. Assn., N.J. Prins. and Suprs. Assn., N.Y. Acad. Scis., Linden Edn. Found. (bd. dirs.), Am. Fedn. Sch. Adminstrs. (chpt. pres. 1984—86), Nat. Coun. Jewish Women (life), N.J. PTA (life), N.J. Edn. Assn. (life), Linden Ceramics Club (life; sec. 1991—92, 1995—99, pres. 2000—), Hadassah (life), Phi Kappa Phi, Alpha Lambda Delta, Alumni Assn. U. Md. (life). Home: 2016 Orchard Ter Linden NJ 07036-3719

BEDRIJ, OREST, investment banker, scientist; b. Ukraine, May 24, 1933; arrived in U.S., 1949, naturalized, 1955; s. Eustachy and Olha (Banach) B.; m. Oksana Cymbalista, Nov. 10, 1956; children: Orest W., Roksana Bedrij Arpa, Chrystyna Bedrij Stecyk. BSEE, Rochester Inst. Tech., 1956, MS in Humanities; PhD in Physics, Columbia Pacific U., 1986. Various positions IBM Corp., Poughkeepsie, N.Y. and Los Angeles, 1956-68; IBM tech. dir. Space Flight Ops. Facility, Jet Propulsion Lab., Calif. Inst. Tech., 1962-63; founder, pres., dir. Securities Coun., Inc., 1965-83, Profit Tech., Inc., 1983-89, Griffin Capital Mgmt. Corp., N.Y.C., 1989-97. Co-founder, dir. Advance Memory Sys. Inc. (merged with GE) as Intersil, Inc., Sunnyvale, Calif., 1968—72, Inst. Math. Physics, 1972—, Internat. Jour. Nonlinear Math. Physics, Kiev, 1992; with Griffin Securities, Inc., N.Y.C., 1997—; mem. exec. com., treas., dir. Ukranian Studies Fund Harvard U., 1959—72. Author: Yes, It's Love: Your Life Can Be a Miracle, 1974, One, 1977, You, 1988, La preuve scientifique de l'existence de Dieu (Scientific Proof of the Existence of God), 2000; contbr. articles to profl. jours.; patentee in field. Trustee, treas. John E. Fetzer Found., 1987-89. With USAR, 1954-60. Recipient Outstanding Contbn. award, IBM, 1967. Mem.: Am. Inst. Physics, Sci. and Med. Network London, Shevchenko Sci. Soc., NY Acad. Arts and Scis., Internat. Soc. for Study of Human Ideas on Ultimate Reality and Meaning (dir.). Achievements include research in physics and philosophy of ultimate reality and meaning.

BEDROSIAN, EDWARD, electrical engineer; b. Chgo., May 22, 1922; s. Charles and Hazel (Najarian) B.; m. Evelyn Patricia Gardner, Apr. 16, 1971; children— William C., Barbara A., Charles E., Edward G., Victoria G. BS, Northwestern U., 1949, MS, 1950, PhD, 1953. Aero. engr. Convair, San Diego, 1942, Hughes Aircraft Co., Culver City, Calif., 1943-44; elec. engr. Motorola, Chgo., 1953-57; sr. scientist Rand Corp., Santa Monica, Calif., 1957-98. Adj. prof. U. So. Calif., 1968 71 Contbr. articles to profl. jours. Served with USMC, 1944-46. Fellow IEEE, Inst. Advancement Engring.; mem. Sigma Xi, Eta Kappa Nu, Tau Beta Pi. Home: 3923 Sierks Way Malibu CA 90265-5214 Fax: 310-456-1777. E-mail: bedrosian@charter.net.

BEDROSIAN, GREGORY RONALD, investment banker; b. Phila., Sept. 14, 1966; s. Samuel D. and Agnes Bedrosian; m. Elena V. Mayorova; 1 child, Nicholas G. BS in Econs., U. Pa., 1988; MBA, Harvard U., 1992. Investment banker Salomon Bros., Inc., N.Y.C., 1988-90; investment banker Credit Suisse First Boston Ltd., London, Moscow, 1992-95; co-founder, mng. dir. Sputnik Funds (Renaissance Capital), Moscow, 1995-99; co-founder, pres., CEO InVentures, London, 2000; co-CEO Redwood Ptnrs. Internat., London, 2001—. Mem.: Royal Inst. Internat. Affairs, Inst. Dirs. (London), Coun. on Fgn. Rels., Penn Club N.Y., Met. Club, Harvard Club of N.Y. Republican. Home: 35 Bryan Ave Malvern PA 19355-3007

BEE, ANNA COWDEN, dance educator; b. Feb. 17, 1922; d. Porter Guthrie and Marion Irene (McCurry) Cowden; m. Alon Wilton Bee, Oct. 21, 1942; children: Anna Margaret Bee Foote, Alon Wilton. AB, Samford U., 1944; student, Chalif Sch. Dance, N.Y.C., 1950-54. Mem. faculty Byram H.S., JAckson, 1945-52, Hinds Jr. Coll., Raymond, Miss., 1952—. Dir. Hi-Steppers, girls' precision dance group; chaperone Miss Mississippi to Miss Am. Pageant; condr. charm clinics for teenagers; judge beauty pageants. Prodr. half-time shows for Gator Bowl, 1958, 64, 81, Sugar Bowl, 1960, Hall of Fame Bowl, 1977-79, Mid-Am. Bowl, 1988, Sr. Bowl, 1988. Bd. dirs. Multiple Sclerosis Soc., Jackson, 1966-72; state chmn. Miss. Easter Seals Soc. campaign, 1966, 79; chmn. women's divsn. United Way, Jackson, 1973; commencement spkr. Hinds C.C., 1999. Recipient Hinds C.C. Svc. award, 1993, Miss Miss. Vol. of Yr. award, 1995, Miss Am. Vol. of Yr. award, 1995, Dance Tchrs. Unlimited Lifetime Achievement award, 1996, Dance Tchrs. United Achievement award in dance, 1996; named Woman of Achievement, Jackson Bus. and Profl. Women's Club, 1967-78, Outstanding Vol. Goodwill Industry Miss., 1997, Golden Isles Bowl Classic, 1997; Miss. Legislature commendation for contbn. to youth, 1981; Anna Cowden Bee Hall named in her honor Hinds C of C., bd. trustees, 1993; named Ageless Hero, Blue Cross/Blue Shield, 2001, Hometown Hero, WJTV, 2000; honored Legis., 2003. Mem. Nat. Faculty Dance Educators Am., Dance Masters Am., Miss. Edn. Assn., Miss. Assn. Health and Phys. Edn., Beta Sigma Omicron. Baptist. Home: 256 Azalea Ct Brandon MS 39047-7264 Office: Hinds Cmty Coll Box 10415 Raymond MS 39154

BEE, ROBERT NORMAN, banker; b. Milw., Mar. 4, 1925; s. Clarence Olson and Norma Pern (Pitt) B.; m. Dolores Marie Cappelletti, Apr. 23, 1955; children: Diane, John, Leslie. Ph.B., Marquette U., 1949; BS in Fgn. Service, Georgetown U., 1950, MA, 1955. With Dept. Treasury, various locations, 1950-65; fin. attache Stockholm, 1952-54, Ankara, Turkey, 1956-60; chief fin. affairs Am. embassy, Bonn, Germany, 1960-65; dep. dir. AID, Karachi, Pakistan, 1965-67; 1st. v.p. 1st Wis. Nat. Bank, 1967-71; sr. v.p. Wells Fargo Bank; also pres. Wells Fargo Internat. Investment Corp., San Francisco, 1971-78; mng. dir., chief exec. officer London Interstate Bank Ltd., Eng., 1978-87; mng. dir. TSB Pvt. Bank Internat. SA, London, 1987-90; chmn. U.S. Fin. Adv. Svc., London, 1990-91, SAJ Investments Ltd., London, 1991-95; sr. advisor Porvenir Inc., San Francisco, 1998-2000. Sr. fellow Ctr. Internat. Banking Studies, Charlottesville, Va. Chmn. World Affairs Coun. Milw., 1970-71; bd. dirs. Adam Smith Inst., London, chmn., 1985-87; chmn. Am. Soc. in London, 1986-87. With AUS, 1943-46. Recipient Bronze Star, 1945. Mem. Bankers Assn. for Fgn. Trade (pres. 1977-78) Home and Office: 1940 Vallejo St Apt 5 San Francisco CA 94123-4918

BEE, SUSAN, artist, editor, designer; b. N.Y.C., Jan. 14, 1952; d. Sigmund and Miriam (Ickowitz) Laufer; m. Charles Kegel Bernstein, Aug. 17, 1977; children: Emma Bernstein, Felix Bernstein. BA, Barnard Coll., 1973; MA, Hunter Coll., 1977. Co editor, designer, pub. M/E/A/N/I/N/G mag., N.Y.C., 1986-96; co-editor M/E/A/N/I/N/G: An Anthology of Artists' Writing, Theory, and Criticism, 2000. One-woman shows at Virginia Lust Gallery, N.Y.C., 1992, Granary Books, N.Y.C., 1997, A.I.R. Gallery, N.Y.C., 1998, 2000, 03. Recipient Pub. grant Nat. Endowment for Arts, 1992, 93, 94, 95, 96, Pub. grant N.Y. State Coun. of Arts, 1989-96. Home and Office: 215 W 92nd St Apt 5F New York NY 10025-7476

BEEBE, GRACE ANN, retired special education educator; b. Wyandotte, Mich., Feb. 16, 1945; d. Cecil Vern and Elizabeth Lucille (Tamblyn) B. BA, Ea. Mich. U., 1967; MEd, Wayne State U., 1970; postgrad., U. Mich., 1973-78; student, Meth. Theol. Sch., Ecumenical Theol. Sem. Cert. spl. edn. tchr., Mich. Tchr. POHI 1st grade Grand Rapids (Mich.) Pub. Schs., 1967-69; tchr. title VI Taylor (Mich.) Pub. Schs., 1970-73, tchr. Physically or Otherwise Health Impaired pre-kindergarten, 1973-79, tchr. POHI 1st-3rd grades, 1979-81, tchr. POHI pre-kindergarten, 1981-84, tchr., cons. POHI, 1984-2000; ret., 2000. Sem. student Ecumenical Theol. Sch., Detroit, 2000—01, Meth. Theol. Sch., Delaware, Ohio, 2001—. Area coord. Indian Trails Camp, Grand Rapids, 1979-97; Brownie troop leader Girl Scouts U.S., 1997-98. Recipient Recognition award 4-H Wayne County Handicapped Riding, 1986, Indian Trails Camp, 1990; Ronald McDonald Children's Charities grantee, 1990; State of Mich. Spl. Edn. scholar, 1966-67, Vocat. Rehab. scholar, 1969-70. Mem. SCADS (alt. rep.), N.Am. Riding for the Handicapped Assn., Mich. Fedn. Tchrs., Physically Impaired Assn. Mich., Taylor Fedn. Tchrs. (ancillary v.p. 1990-92), Taylor Handicapped Assn., Allen Park Assn. for Handicapped, Trenton Hist. Soc. (exec. bd. 1988-97), Coun. for Exceptional Children, Phi Delta Kappa, Alpha Delta Kappa. Democrat. United Methodist. Avocations: horseback riding, gardening, walking. Home: 2225 Emeline St Trenton MI 48183-3653 E-mail: Beebega@aol.com.

BEEBE, JAMES, leadership studies educator; b. New Orleans, La., Oct. 26, 1946; m. Maria Africa, July 1, 1970; children: David, Ligaya. MA in Anthropology, MA Food Rsch., Stanford U., 1976, PhD in Internat. Devel. Edn., 1978. Vol. U.S. Peace Corps, Philippines, 1968—73; prin. investigator and project dir. u.s. dept of labor gran Filipino Assn. of Mountain View, Mountain View, Calif., 1977—78; cons. and planning specialist Cmty. Assn. for Retarded, Palo Alto, Calif., 1978—79; asst. prof. of edn. Monterey Inst. of Fgn. Studies, Monterey, Calif., 1977—78; fgn. svc. officer US AID, Washington, 1979—96, devel. officer Khartoum, Sudan, 1979—83, chief, agrl. devel. and project officer Manila, Philippines, 1983—87, dir., office of resource devel. Monrovia, Liberia, 1987—90, dir., office of econ. devel. Pretoria, South Africa, 1994—96; prof. Oreg. State U., Corvallis, 1990—92; prof. leadership studies Gonzaga U., Spokane, Wash., 1996—, dir. Inst. for Action Against Hate, 2001—02. Author: (book) Rapid Assessment Process: An Introduction, 2001; contbr. articles to profl. publs., chpt. to book. Fellow: Soc. Applied Anthropology; mem.: Am. Anthrop. Assn. Democrat. Unitarian Universalist. Avocation: theology. Home: 1249 S Wall St Spokane WA 99204 Office: Gonzaga U 502 E Boone Spokane WA 99258 Office Fax: 509-323-5964. E-mail: beebe@gonzaga.edu.

BEEBE, MARY LIVINGSTONE, curator; b. Portland, Oreg., Nov. 5, 1940; d. Robert and Alice Beebe. BA, Bryn Mawr Coll., 1962; postgrad., Sorbonne, U. Paris, 1962-63. Curatorial asst. Fogg Art Mus., Harvard U., Cambridge, Mass., 1966-68; apprentice Portland Art Mus., 1963-64, Boston Mus. Art, 1964-65; exec. dir. Portland Ctr. for Visual Arts, 1973-81; dir. Stuart Collection U. Calif., San Diego, 1981—. Cons. in field; mem. art steering com. Portland Devel. Commn., 1977-80; bd. dirs. Henry Gallery, U. Wash., Seattle, 1977-80; project cons. Nat. Rsch. Ctr. for Arts, N.Y.C., 1978-79; bd. dirs. Western Assn. Art Museums, Art Mus. Assn. San Francisco, 1978-84; bd. dirs., trustee Art Matters Inc., 1985—; trustee Russell Found., 1982-94; hon. mem. bd. dirs. Portland Ctr. for Visual Arts, 1984-91; mem. arts adv. bd. Centre City Devel. Corp., San Diego, 1982-94, art adv. bd. U. Calif. San Francisco Mission Bay, 1999—; panel mem., cons. Nat. Endowment Arts; juror numerous art exhbns. Nat. Endowment Arts fellow, 1979. Author: Landmarks: Sculpture Commissions for the Stuart Collection at the University of California, San Diego, 2001; contbr. articles to profl. jours. Recipient Allied Professions award AIA, 1992. Office: U Calif San Diego Stuart Collection 9500 Gilman Dr La Jolla CA 92093-0010

BEEBE, MIKE, state attorney general; b. Amagon, Ark., Dec. 28, 1946; s. Lester Kendall and Meadean Louise (Quattlebaum) B.; m. Ginger Croom, Mar. 2, 1979; 1 child, Kyle. BA, Ark. State U., 1968; JD, U. Ark., 1972. Bar: Ark. 1972. Ptnr. Lightle, Beebe, Raney, Bell & Simpson, Searcy, Ark., 1972—2003; mem. Ark. Senate, 1983—2003; pres. Ark. Senate, 2001—03; atty. gen. State of Ark., 2003—. Editor (in-Chief): U. Ark. Sch. of Law, 1972. Trustee Ark. State U., Jonesboro, 1974-79, chmn. bd. trustees, 1977-79; chmn. Ctrl. Ark. Gen. Hosp., Searcy, 1985-93. Named Outstanding Trial Lawyer, Ark., 1982. Mem. Ark. Mcpl. League (dist. svc. award 1985), Searcy C. of C. Democrat. Episcopalian. Avocation: golf. Office: Atty Gen 200 Tower Bldg 323 Center St Little Rock AR 72201

BEEBE, SUSAN JANE, English language educator; b. Sacramento, Calif., Nov. 20, 1952; d. William Herbert and Janie Lou (Jennings) Dye; m. Steven A. Beebe, May 25, 1974; children: Mark, Matthew. BSE in Comm., Ctrl. Mo. State U., 1973; MA in English Lit., U. Miami, Coral Gables, Fla., 1979. Cert. secondary edn. tchr., Mo. Tchr. English, debate coach Moberly (Mo.) H.S., 1974-76; tchr. English Deerborne Sch., Coral Gables, 1977; lectr. Sch. Comm., U. Miami, 1980-86; coord. of vols. San Marcos (Tex.) Consol. Ind. Sch. Dist., 1989-93, mem. ednl. improvement coun., 1995-2001, trustee, 2000-01; lectr., assoc. dir. first-year English, dept. English, S.W. Tex. State U., San Marcos, 1988—. Co-author: (textbook) Interpersonal Communication: Relating to Others, 1996, 3d edit., 2002, Public Speaking: An Audience-Centered Approach, 5th edit., 2003, Communication: Principles for a Lifetime, 2001, 2d edit., 2004; (manual) Instructor's Manual for Communicating in Small Groups:

Principles and Practices, 2d edit., 1986. Bd. dirs. Tex. Assn. Ptnrs. in Edn., 1992-93; founding coord. Volunteers in Pub. Schs., San Marcos, 1987—; mem. San Marcos Sch. Bd., 2000-2001; active Cmty. of Christ Ch. Recipient Gov.'s Ednl. Excellence award, Tex., 1991, pvt. citizen award Tex. Classroom Tchrs. Assn., 1993. Mem. Conf. of Coll. Tchrs. of English, Tex. Coun. Tchrs. of English, Nat. Coun. Tchrs. of English. Democrat. Avocations: reading, music. Office: SW Tex State U Dept English San Marcos TX 78666

BEEBER, MARSHALL LAWRENCE, sales executive; b. Dayton, Ohio, Jan. 29, 1950; s. Joseph Reuben and Yetta Beeber; m. Lynne Gail Pepper; 1 child, Elizabeth. BA in Biology, Temple U., 1982. Rsch. biologist DuPont-Merck Pharm., Wilmington, Del., 1996—97; biotechnology Sales rep. Amersham Bioscis., Piscataway, NJ, 1997—. Author poetry and religious lit. With USN, 1973—74. Messianic Jew. Avocations: poetry, photography. Personal E-mail: mbeeber@att.net.

BEECH, JOHNNY GALE, lawyer; b. Chickasha, Okla., Sept. 18, 1954; s. Lovell Gale and Lucille L. (Phillips) B.; m. Judy Carol Schroeder, Dec. 31, 1977. BS, Southwestern Okla. State U., 1977; JD, U. Ark., Little Rock, 1980; LLM in Energy-Environment, Tulane U., 1985. Bar: Okla. 1980, U.S. Dist. Ct. (we. dist.) Okla. 1982, U.S. Dist. Ct. (no. dist.) Tex. 1983, U.S. Dist. Ct. (no. dist.) Okla. 1986, U.S. Dist. Ct. (ea. dist.) Okla. 1997. Assoc. Meacham, Meacham and Meacham, Clinton, Okla., 1980-84, Ford & Brown, Enid, Okla., 1985-86, Wright & Sawyer, Enid, 1986-88, Phillips, McFall, McCaffrey, McVay, Sheets and Lovelace, Oklahoma City, 1988-90; ptnr., mng. dir. Lester & Bryant, Oklahoma City, 1990-96; mgr. Beech Edwards and Percival PLLC, 1996—2001; of counsel Mulinix, Ogden, Hall, Andrews & Ludlam, PLLC, 2002—. Bd. dirs. Proserv Basketball; mcpl. judge Town of Arapaho, Okla., 1982-84; assoc. gen. counsel Proserv Basketball, 1996—. Bd. dirs. Jr. Achievement Garfield County, Enid, 1986-88; commr. Little League Baseball; bd. dirs., treas. Edmond All Sports, Inc., 1999; mem. Bus. Sch. adv. coun. Southwestern U. Mem. ABA (real property, probate and trusts sect.), ATLA, Okla. Bar Assn. (law sch. com. 1989-91, uniform laws com. 1994-96, chmn. desk manual com. young lawyers div., uniform laws com. 1994—), Okla. Assn. Def. Counsel, Garfield County Bar Assn. (treas. 1988-89), Am. Bus. Club, Southwestern Okla. State U. Alumni Assn. (pres. 1983-86, parliamentarian 1992, exec. counsel 1986—, pres. 1997—), Southwestern Sch. Bus. Alumni Assn. (v.p. 1980-92, pres. 1992-93), Jaycees, Am. Bus. Club, Phi Alpha Delta (sec. 1979). Democrat. Methodist. Avocations: reading, bike racing. Home: 702 N Cook St Cordell OK 73632-3002 Office: Mulinix Ogden Hall Andrews & Ludlam 204 N Robinson Ste 3100 Oklahoma City OK 73102 E-mail: jgblaw@hotmail.com.

BEECHAN, CURTIS MICHAEL, science educator; b. Loma Linda, Calif., Sept. 19, 1947; s. Michael and Anna Beechan. PhD, Stanford, Palo Alto, CA, 1970—77. Prof. of chemistry Mt. St. Mary's Coll., Los Angeles, Calif., 1984—86, Sterling Coll., Sterling, Kans., 1986—; postdoctoral rsch. chemist U. of Calif., La Jolla, Calif., 1982—84; organic chemist Ultrasystems, Irvine, Calif., 1981—82; organic chemist and supr. Rachelle Laboratories, Long Beach, Calif., 1979—81; postdoctoral rsch. chemist U. of Calif., Riverside, Calif., 1978—79. E-5 California N.G., 1971—77, San Mateo, California. Recipient McCreery Tchg. Award, Sterling Coll., 1995-1996. Mem.: Am. Chem. Soc. Conservative. Avocations: photography, fishing. Home: 714 N Broadway Sterling KS 67579 Office: Sterling College PO Box 98 Sterling KS 67579 Office Fax: 620-278-4414. E-mail: cbeechan@sterling.edu.

BEECHER, GRACIELA FERNANDEZ, language educator, writer; b. Havana, Cuba, Jan. 16, 1927; arrived in U.S., 1961; d. Manuel S. Fernandez and Maria Teresa del Cueto. BS, Memphis State U.; Ed.D., cert. lang. proficiency, U. Havana; student in linguistics, Columbia U. Instr. U. St. Francis, Ft. Wayne, asst. prof., assoc. prof., chmn. modern lang. dept.; exec. dir. Ednl. Opportunity Ctr., Ft. Wayne, Ind. Bd. dirs. Nat. Coun. Vocat. Edn., Washington, Nat. Coun. Sch. Desegregation, N.Y.C. Spanish corr.: Today's Cath. Newspaper. Bd. dirs. Am. by Choice, N.Y.C.; chmn. Midwest Hispanic Repulicans. Mem.: MLA, AAUP, Ind. State Tchrs. Assn.

BEECHER, JONATHAN FRENCH, history educator; b. Boston, Mass., Apr. 26, 1937; s. HenryKnowles Unangst and Margaret Swain Beecher; m. Merike Lepasaar, Aug. 24, 1974; children: David Ilmar, Daniel Lembit. BA magna cum laude, Harvard U., 1959; postgrad., Ecole Normale Superieure, Paris, 1962-64; PhD, Harvard U., 1968. Seaman Sailors Union of the Pacific, San Francisco, 1957-58; instr. history Harvard U., Cambridge, Mass., 1967-69; asst. prof. U. Calif., Santa Cruz, 1970-76, assoc. prof., 1976-86, prof., 1986—. Fgn. corr. Revue D'Histoire Du XIXe Siècle, Paris, 1986—. Author: Charles Fourier: The Visionary and His World, 1986, Victor Considerant and the Rise and Fall of French Romantic Socialism, 2001. Fulbright fellow, 1959-60, ACLS fellow, 1976-77, Guggenheim fellow, 1988-89; recipient Bowdoin prize, 1959, Palmes Acad., Govt. of France, 1998. Mem. Assn. D'Etudes Fouriéristes, Am. Histo. Assn., Acad. Des Sciences, Belles Lettres et Arts de Besancon (assoc.), Melville Soc., Phi Beta Kappa. Avocations: hiking, soccer, reading, book collecting. Home: 401 Pine Flat Rd Santa Cruz CA 95060 Office: U Calif Stevenson Coll Santa Cruz CA 95064 E-mail: jbeecher@cats.ucsc.edu.

BEECHER, WILLIAM MANUEL, government official; b. Framingham, Mass., May 27, 1933; s. Samuel and Gertrude (Kradelman) B.; m. Eileen Brick, June 8, 1958; children: Debbie, Diane, Lori, Nancy. BA, Harvard U., 1955; MS, Columbia U., 1956. Reporter St. Louis Globe-Democrat, 1956-59; corr. Fairchild Pubs., Washington, 1959-60, Wall Street Jour., Washington, 1960-66, N.Y. Times, Washington, 1966-73; asst. sec. def. U.S. Dept. Def., Washington, 1973-75; corr. Boston Globe, Washington, 1975-87; Washington bur. chief Mpls. Star Tribune, Washington, 1987-92; pub. affairs dir. U.S. Nuclear Regulatory Commn., Washington, 1993—; mem. U.S. Sr. Exec. Svc., 1993—. Author: Mayday Man, 1990; co-author: (newspaper study) U.S.-Soviet Relations, 1983 (Pulitzer prize 1983); bd. of editors Foreign Svc. Jour. 2d lt. U.S. Army, 1956. Recipient Disting. Pub. Svc. medal Dept. of Def., 1975, Excellence awards Overseas Press Club, N.Y.C., 1975, 79, 86, Weintal award Georgetown U., Washington, 1983, Presdl. medal Y2K conversion, 2000; named Knight, Order of St. John of Medina, 2003. Mem. Internat. Inst. for Strategic Studies, State Dept. Corrs. Assn. (pres. 1982), Overseas Writers Assn. (pres. 1978-79), Aviation/Space Writers Assn. (pres. 1970-71), Coun. Fgn. Rels., Gridiron Club, Army and Navy Club. Home: 7911 Robison Rd Bethesda MD 20817-6928 Office: US Nuclear Regulatory Commn 02-H1 1 White Flint N # 02-h1 Washington DC 20555-0001

BEEDLE, DENNIS DEAN, psychiatrist, educator; b. Aberdeen, Md., Mar. 20, 1956; s. Harvey Dean and Sharon Elaine Beedle; m. Margaret Mary Baumann, Aug. 11, 1979; children: Robert, Catherine, James. BS, Creighton U., 1978, MD, 1982. Asst. on faculty Rush U., Chgo., 1982-86; psychiatry instr. Med. Sch. Harvard U., Cambridge, Mass., 1986-90; asst. prof. clin. psychiatry Coll. Medicine U. Ill., Chgo., 1990—. Author: (with others) Principles and Practice of Addictions in Psychiatry, 1997, Advances in Somatic Therapies Update, Principles and Practices of Psychopharmacotherapy, 1998. Mem. ad hoc com. to revise Ill. Mental Health Code, Kane County Alliance for Mentally Ill., Chgo., 1998-99. Recipient citation Mass. Senate, 1990. Mem. AMA, Am. Psychiat. Assn. (Disting. fellow). Avocations: woodworking, gardening. Office: U Ill Chicago 912 S Wood St Chicago IL 60612-7325

BEEDLE, LYNN SIMPSON, civil engineering educator; b. Orland, Calif., Dec. 7, 1917; s. Granville L. and Carol (Simpson) B.; m. Ella Marie Grimes, Oct. 20, 1946; children: Lynn, Helen, Jonathan, David, Edward. BS, U. Calif., 1941; MS, Lehigh U., 1949, PhD, 1952. Cert. U.S. Postgraduate Sch., Annapolis, 1942. With Todd-Calif. Shipbldg. Corp., Richmond, Calif., 1941; instr. Postgrad. Sch., U.S. Naval Acad., 1941-42; officer-in-charge Underwater Explosions Research div. Norfolk Naval Shipyard, Va., 1942-47; dir. Lehigh U. Fritz Engring. Lab., Bethlehem, Pa., 1960-84; prof. civil engring. Lehigh U., 1958-77, Univ. Disting. prof., 1978—, prof. emeritus, 1988—, dir. High-Rise Inst., 1983-89. Coord., chair Fazlur Rahman Khan, 1983—2001. Author: Plastic Design of Steel Frames, 1958, (with others) Structural Steel Design, 2d edit., 1974, Tall Buildings of the World, 1987; editor-in-chief: Planning and Design of Tall Buildings, 5 vols., 1978-81, Recent Developments in Tall Buildings, 1983, Advances in Tall Buildings, 1986, High-Rise Buildings-Recent Progress, 1986, Second Century of the Skyscraper, 1988, Tall Buildings: 2000 and Beyond, 1990, Cast-in-Place Concrete in Tall Building Design and Construction, 1992, Cladding, 1992, Building Design for Handicapped and Aged Persons, 1992, Fire Safety in Tall Buildings, 1992, Semi-Rigid Connections in Steel Frames, 1992, Cold-Formed Steel in Tall Buildings, 1993, Structural Systems for Tall Buildings, 1995, Architecture of Tall Buildings, 1995, Habitat and the High-Rise, 2 vols., 1995, Tall Building Structures--A World View, 1996, Structural, Design, Codes and Special Building Projects, 1997, (with others) 100 of the World's Tallest Buildings, 1998; contbr. (with others) articles to profl. jours. Served with USNR, 1941-47. Recipient Robinson award Lehigh U., 1952, Hillman award, Lehigh U. 1973, Silver medal Am. Welding Soc., 1957, Lynn S. Beedle Disting. Civil Environl. Engring. award, Lehigh U., 2003, Regional Tech. Mfg. award Am. Iron and Steel Inst., 1958, Constrn. award Engring. News Record, 1965, 73, Engr. of Yr. award Lehigh Valley sect. NSPE, 1977, Internat. Contbns. award Japan Soc. Civil Engrs., 1994, John Fritz medal by various profl. engring. assns., 1994; named Acad. Specialist U. Jordan, 1987, Bangladesh U. Engring. and Tech., 1988, one of 125 top people since 1874 who has contbd. most to the constrn. industry Engring. News-Record, 1999. Fellow: ASCE (hon.; bd. dirs. 1974—77, bd. dis. Lehigh Valley sect. 1979—82, past chmn. structural sivsn. exec. com., past mem. rsch. com., Rsch. prize 1956, E.E. Howard award 1963, Shortridge Hardesty award 1993, OPAL award for lifetime achievement in mgmt. 2002), Royal Soc. Arts; mem.: AIA (liaison mem. regional and urban design com. 1973—76), Coun. Tall Bldgs. and Urban Habitat (dir. 1976—99, dir. emeritus 1999—, chmn. 1970—76, Lynn S. Beedle award 2002), Fritz Engring. Rsch. Soc., Nat. Acad. Engring., Structural Stability Rsch. Coun. (life; exec. com. 1947—, chmn. 1966—70, dir. 1970—93, dir. emeritus 1993—, Lifetime Achievement award 2000, Lynn S. Beedle award 2001), Internat. Assn. Bridge and Structural Engring. (hon.), Am. Inst. Steel Constrn. (T.R. Higgins Lectureship award 1973, Spl. Citation award 1991, Lifetime Achievement award 2000, Geerhardt Haaijer Edn. award 2003, Acerband Haaijer Edn. award 2003), Welding Rsch. Coun. (Disting. Engring. Alumnus award 2000). Presbyterian (elder 1957—). Home: 102 Cedar Rd Hellertown PA 18055-2303 Office: Lehigh U 117 Atlss Dr Bethlehem PA 18015-3101 E-mail: lsb0@lehigh.edu.

BEEDLES, WILLIAM LEROY, finance educator, financial consultant; b. Independence, Kans., Apr. 9, 1948; s. Roy William Beedles and Opal Irene (Connor) Hunter; m. Margaret Ann Vanderlip, Dec. 21, 1974; children: Margaret Micaela, Patricia Opal, Cyrus Dean. BS, Kans. State U., 1970, MS, 1971; PhD, U. Tex., 1975. Asst. prof. Ind. U., Bloomington, 1975-78; vis. prof. Monash U., Melbourne, Victoria, Australia, 1984, U. NSW, Sydney, Australia, 1985; assoc. prof. to prof., dir. Masters program U. Kans., Lawrence, 1978—. Vis. rsch. fellow Pub. Utilities Commn., Austin, Tex., 1981 Contbr. articles to profl. jours. Capt. U.S. Army, 1970-78 Mem. Am. Fin. Assn., Western Fin. Assn., So. Fin. Assn. (assoc. editor jour. 1979-84), Fin. Mgmt. Assn. Congregationalist. Avocation: raquetball. Office: U Kans Summerfield Hall Lawrence KS 66045-7585 E-mail: wbeedles@ku.edu.

BEEHLER, BRUCE MCPHERSON, research zoologist, ornithologist, conservationist; b. Balt., Oct. 11, 1951; s. William Henry Jr. and Cary (Baxter) B.; m. Carol Hare, June 7, 1982; children: Grace Bryant, Andrew McPherson, Cary Elizabeth Selden. BA, Williams Coll., 1974; MA, Princeton U., 1978, PhD, 1983. Sci. asst. to sec. Smithsonian Instn., Washington, 1981-84, sci. asst. to sec. emeritus, 1984-88, zoologist, 1988-91; assoc. rsch. zoologist N.Y. Zool. Soc., Washington, 1991-93; sr. ecologist Conservation Internat., 1993-95; natural resource mgmt. officer U.S. Dept. State, Washington, 1995-97; dir. environ. conservation Counterpart Internat., 1997-99, v.p. environ. and nat. resources, 1999-2001; sr. rep. Melanesia Conservation Internat., 2001—02, sen. dir. Melanesia, 2002—03, v.p. Melanesia, 2003—. Leader expdns. to Papua New Guinea, 1975-76, 78-84, 86-87, 89, 91-93, to India, 1983, 85-86, 88; rsch. assoc. dept. vertebrate zoology Nat. Mus. Natural History, 1985—. Author: Birdlife of the Adirondack Park, 1978, Upland Birds of Northeastern New Guinea, 1978, A Naturalist in New Guinea, 1991; sr. co-author: Birds of New Guinea; jr. co-author: The Birds of Paradise, 1998; contbr. articles to sci. jours. Thomas J. Watson Found. fellow, 1974; rsch. grantee Nat. Geog. Soc., 1980, 86, 89, 94, N.Y. Zool. Soc., 1986. Fellow Am. Ornithologists Union (elective). Democrat. Avocations: hiking, tennis. Co-discoverer with John P. Dumbacher of toxicity in the Pitohui, a genus of bird that uses as a chemical defense the alkaloid homobatrachotoxin. Home: 6421 Broad St Bethesda MD 20816-2607 Office: Conservation Internat 1919 M St NW Ste 600 Washington DC 20036

BEEKMAN, WILLIAM BEDLOE, lawyer; b. N.Y.C., July 8, 1949; s. Robert Struthers and Mary (Marckwald) B.; m. Helen Hinckley, June 7, 1980; children: Izaak, Hugo. BA magna cum laude, Harvard U., 1971; JD, Yale U., 1980. Bar: N.Y. 1981. Assoc. Debevoise & Plimpton, N.Y.C., 1980-89, ptnr., 1989—. Bd. dirs. Lafayette Studios Corp., N.Y.C. Bd. dirs. Ice Theatre of N.Y., Inc. Mem. ABA, Assn. of Bar of City of N.Y.., Am. Coll. Investment Counsel, N.Y. Hist. Soc. (bd.dirs.), Century Assn. Grolier Club. Democrat. Episcopalian. Home: 284 Lafayette St Apt 4B New York NY 10012-3303 Office: Debevoise & Plimpton 929 3rd Ave 2d fl New York NY 10022-6225

BEEKS, CHERYL ELAINE, elementary school educator; b. Concord, NC, Aug. 28, 1946; d. Ray Edward and Maxine (Peterson) Barringer; m. Raymond Neil Beeks, July 12, 1971; 1 child, Alison Elaine Rios. B in Music Edn., So. Meth. U., Dallas, 1968. Tchr. Lamesa (Tex.) Ind. Sch. Dist., 1968—69, 1970—73, Loraine (Tex.) Ind. Sch. Dist., 1976—77, Highland Ind. Sch. Dist., Roscoe, Tex., 1980—. Coach 5th grade events Univ. Interscholastic League, Roscoe, 1980—, elem. poetry judge, 1995—. Pianist, organist Hermleigh (Tex.) United Meth. Ch., 1990—, treas., 1995—98; lay delegate United Meth. Northwest Conf., Lubbock, Tex., 1999—. Mem.: Tex. Assn. Cmty. Schs., Tex. Music Edn. Assn., Nat. Assn. Music Edn. Home: 206 Lowe Hermleigh TX 79526 Office: Highland Ind Sch Dist 6625 FM608 Roscoe TX 79545 Business E-Mail: cbeeks@highland.esc14.net.

BEEKS, DELISCO JAMES (DELISCO), vocalist, actor, poet; b. Jacksonville, Fla., June 7, 1972; s. Barbara Ann Edwards. Student, Jacksonville U., Valencia C.C., Orlando, Fla., King's Coll. Actor: (Broadway plays) Aida, 2002—, Ragtime, Smokey Joe's Café; (plays) The Wild Party. Founder Lil' Angel Project for Underprivileged Children, N.Y.C., 1999. Mem.: AFTRA, Actors Equity Assn. Republican. Methodist. Avocations: rollerblading, weightlifting. Home: 41-15 50th St # 6F Woodside NY 11377

BEELER, DONALD DARYL, retired retail executive; b. Hettinger, N.D., Nov. 13, 1935; s. Earl Aaron and LaVera Grace (Krause) B.; m. Laurice Marianne Fisk, May 23, 1954; children: Jillayne Marianne, Jacalyn Faye, Donald Earl. Grad. high sch., Lemmon, S.D. Owner, operator Lemmon (S.D.) Recreation, 1954-55; owner D&M Gifts, Lemmon, 1956-57; mgr. trainee to store mgr. Snyder Drug Stores, Inc., Hopkins, Minn., 1964-67, dist. mgr. to dir. of franchise ops., 1967-77, v.p. franchise ops. to v.p. gen. mgr., 1977-82, sr. v.p., gen. mgr., 1982, pres., 1982-86, chmn., pres., chief exec. officer, 1986-94, chmn., CEO, 1994-99, ret., 1999. Bd. dirs. Variety Club Children's Hosp., U. Minn., 1991-99, Christopher & Banks, 1992—; mem. U.S. Olympic Com., Minn., 1986-98; vis. exec. United Fund, Mpls., 1988, sect. chmn., 1989; pres. Food, Drug and Liquor Coun., City of Hope, Mpls., 1984-87; exec. coun., 1987-99. Served with U.S. Army, 1957-64. Recipient Spirit of Life award City of Hope, 1984. Mem. Nat. Assn. of Chain Drug Stores (bd. dirs. 1990-2000, exec. com. 1996-99), So. Drug Stores Assn., Minnetonka Country Club (bd. govs. 1988-92, v.p. 1991, pres. 1992). Republican. Presbyterian. Avocations: golf, sports fan. Home: 4450 Manitou Rd Excelsior MN 55331-9447

BEELER, MARGERY D. librarian; b. Troy, N.Y., Oct. 9, 1940; d. John Franklin and Mildred Brownhardt Donk; m. Richard M. Beeler, Jan. 10, 1965 (dissolved June 2001); children: Susan J. Queary, Wendy R. AB with honors, Cornell U., 1962; MLS, SUNY, 1973. Cert. libr. N.Y., 1973. Tchr. English Peace Corps, Visiakhapatnam, India, 1963—65; ref. libr. Schenectady County Pub. Libr., NY, 1973—85, head tech. svcs., 1985—89, asst. dir., 1989—97; libr. coord. Audubon Fla., Naples, 1998—2002. Bd. dirs. Literacy Vols. Am., Schenectady, 1995—96, pres., 1996—97. Mem.: Fla. Librs. Assn., Phi Beta Kappa. Avocations: birdwatching, cooking, quilting. Home: #6-104 2323 9th Ave SW Olympia WA 98502

BEELER, PATRICIA, court administrator; b. Troy, N.Y., June 25, 1955; d. Andrew John and Virginia Ann (Catone) Beeler. AAS in Criminal Sci., Hudson Valley C.C., Troy; BA, Coll. St. Rose, Alabny, N.Y., MA in Comm. Arts. Lt. in charge of security Burns Security Svcs., Albany, 1973-75; chief clk. Rensselaer County Family Ct., Troy, 1975—. Bd. dirs. The Next Step, Inc., Albany, 1994—; mem. Dist. Atty.'s Task Force on Violence, Troy, 1995—; mem. City of Troy Mayor's Task Force. Mem. Family Ct. Clks. Assn. (bd. dirs., sec.), Women's Bar Assn. N.Y., Single Ski Club Albany. Avocations: running, alpine and cross-country skiing. Office: Rensselaer County Family Ct 1504 5th Ave Troy NY 12180-4192 Home: 107 Fernbank Ave Delmar NY 12054-4222

BEEM, JACK DARREL, lawyer; b. Chgo., Nov. 17, 1931; AB, U. Chgo., 1952, JD, 1955. Bar: Ill. 1955. Assoc. firm Wilson & McIlvaine, Chgo., 1958-63; ptnr. firm Baker & McKenzie, Chgo., 1963—. Mem. vis. com. Ctr. for East Asian Studies U. Chgo. Decorated Order of the Sacred Treasure gold rays with rosette Japan. Mem. ABA, Chgo. Bar Assn., Japan-Am. Soc. Chgo. (pres. 1988-92), Am. Fgn. Law Assn. (chmn. Chgo. br.), Univ. Club of Chgo., Tokyo Club, Tokyo Am. Club, Sons Am. Revolution, Phi Beta Kappa, Alpha Delta Phi. Home: 175 E Delaware Pl Apt 8104 Chicago IL 60611-7746 Office: Baker & McKenzie 1 Prudential Plz 130 E Randolph St Ste 3700 Chicago IL 60601-6342

BEEM, JOHN KELLY, mathematician, educator; b. Detroit, Jan. 24, 1942; s. William Richard and June Ellen (Kelly) B.; m. Eloise Masako Yamamoto, Mar. 24, 1964; 1 child, Thomas Kelly AB in Math., U. So. Calif., 1963, MA in Math., 1965, PhD in Math., 1968. Asst. prof. math. U. Mo., Columbia, 1968-71, assoc. prof., 1971-79, prof., 1979—2002; ret., 2002. Author: (with P. Y. Woo) Doubly Timelike Surfaces, 1969, (with P. E. Ehrlich) Global Lorentzian Geometry, 1981, (with P.E. Ehrlich and K.L. Easley), 2d edit., 96; condr. research in differential geometry and gen. relativity. Recipient Kemper Tchg. award, 1996; NSF fellow, 1965, 68. Mem. Math. Assn. Am., Am. Math. Soc., Phi Beta Kappa Home: 5204 E Tayside Cir Columbia MO 65203-5191

BEEMAN, DAVID GERARD, psychologist; b. Des Moines, June 23, 1964; s. Richard Lee and Geraldine Laura Beeman; m. Linda Jane Beeman, Feb. 7, 1998; children: Anne Margaret, Luke Frederick. BA, U. Notre Dame, 1986; MS, Iowa State U., 1989, PhD, 1992. Lic. psychologist, Iowa. Psychologist Iowa Luth. Hosp., Des Moines, 1991-98; pvt. practice Des Moines, 1998—; psychologist State of Iowa Disability Determination Svcs., Des Moines, 1998—, Innovative Learning Profls., Des Moines, 1998—. Author: (with others) Issues in Clinical Psychology, 1993. Bd. dirs. Child Abuse Prevention Coun., Des Moines, 1994-99; vol. Ch. Youth Group Leader, Des Moines, 1994-99. Mem. Iowa Psychol. Assn., Am. Psychol. Assn. Roman Catholic. Avocations: canoeing, reading, camping. Office: 4715 Grand Ave Des Moines IA 50312-2074

BEEMAN, JOSIAH HORTON, diplomat; b. San Francisco, Oct. 8, 1935; s. Josiah Horton and Helen Virginia (Hooper) B.; m. Susan Louise Sturman, Oct. 28, 1995; children: Olivia Louise, Josiah Horton. BA, Calif. State U., 1957. Adminstrv. asst. Congressman Phillip Burton, Washington, 1964-66; mem. San Francisco Bd. Suprs., 1967-68; sec. internat. affairs Presbyn. Ch., N.Y.C., 1969-70, dir. Washington Office, 1970-75; staff dir. Democratic Caucus U.S. Ho. of Reps., Washington, 1975; chief dep. dir. fin. State Calif., Washington, 1975-80; polit. and legis. dir. Am. Fedn. State, County and Mcpl. Employees, Washington, 1980-83; dir. Dem. Nat. Conv., San Francisco, 1983-84; pres. Beeman and Assocs., Washington, Sacramento, 1983-94; U.S. amb. to New Zealand and Samoa, 1994-99; chief of staff U.S. Broadcasting Bd. Govs., 2000-2001. Bd. dirs. Presbyn. Pub. Corp. Democrat. Presbyterian. Office: 3036 Beechwood Ln Falls Church VA 22042-3138

BEEMAN, RICHARD ROY, historian, educator; b. Seattle, May 16, 1942; m. Pamela Jane Butler, Dec. 26, 1964; children: Kristin Dowds, Joshua Douglas. AB in History, U. Calif., Berkeley, 1964; MA in History, Coll. of William and Mary, 1965; PhD in History, U. Chgo., 1968. Asst. prof. history U. Pa., 1968-73, assoc. prof., 1973-82, prof., 1982—, acting chmn. dept., 1986-87, chmn., 1987-91, assoc. dean, 1991-96; vis. prof. Am. studies U. Hull, Eng., 1976-77; dean Coll. Arts and Scis. U. Pa., 1998—2003; William R. Kenan prof. history, chmn. Colby Coll., 1979-80; Vyvian Harmsworth prof. Am. history Oxford U., 2003—. Dir. Phila. Ctr. for Early Am. Studies, 1980-85. Author: The Old Dominion and the New Nation, 1788-1801, 1972, Patrick Henry: A Biography, 1974, The Evolution of the Southern Backcountry, 1984; editor: Beyond Confederation: The Origins of the American Constituion and National Identity, 1987, The Varieties of Political Experience in Eighteenth Century America, 2003; also articles and book revs. Dept. of History fellow Coll. William and Mary, 1964, Univ. fellow U. Chgo., 1966-67, Newberry Library jr. fellow, Chgo., 1967-68, U. Pa. summer research grants, 1969, 71, Am. Philos. Soc. research grants, 1971, 76, 89, Social Sci. Research Council post-doctoral fellowship, 1972-73, Nat. Book Award nominee, 1974, Fulbright sr. lectr., U.K., 1976-77, NEH basic research grant, 1983-84, summer seminar grant, 1986, sr. fellow, 1989—; fellow Inst. Advanced Study, 1989-90, Huntington Libr., 1997. Home: 301 Glenwood Ave Media PA 19063-4131 Office: U Pa 120 Logan Hall Philadelphia PA 19104 E-mail: rbeeman@sas.upenn.edu.

BEEMER, JOHN BARRY, lawyer; b. Scranton, Pa., Sept. 4, 1941; s. Ellis and Rose Mary (Costello) B.; m. Diane Montgomery Fletcher, July 18, 1964 (dec. July 1999); children: David, Bruce. BS, U. Scranton, 1963; LL.B., George Washington U., 1966. Bar: Pa. 1966, U.S. Supreme Ct. 1980; cert. civil trial adv. Nat. Bd. Trial Advocacy. Law clk. U.S. Ct. Claims, 1966-67; clk. to judge U.S. Dist. Ct. (mid. dist.) Pa., 1967-68; assoc. Warren, Hill, Henkelman & McMenamin, Scranton, 1968-72; ptnr. Beemer, Brier, Rinaldi & Fendrick, 1972-77; pres. Beemer, Rinaldi, Fendrick & Mellody, P.C., Scranton, 1977-83; ptnr. Beemer & Beemer, Scranton, 1984—. Lectr. in law U. Scranton, 1969-70. Chmn. com. constn. and by-laws revision Lackawanna (county Pa.) United Fund., 1971; nat. chmn. U. Scranton Alumni Fund Drive, 1972. Mem. ABA, Pa. Bar Assn., Lackawanna Bar Assn. (bd. dirs. 1988—), Assn. Trial Lawyers Am., Pa. Trial Lawyers Assn., Phi Delta Phi. Office: 114-116 N Abington Rd Clarks Summit PA 18411 E-mail: bbeemer123@aol.com.

BEEMSTER, JOSEPH ROBERT, risk management consultant; b. Chgo., Nov. 11, 1941; s. Joseph Z. and Emily (Dehaus) B.; m. Judith L. Scheffers, Sept. 7, 1963; children: David, Susan. BA, DePaul U., 1962; postgrad., Ill. Inst. Tech., 1976, 77, U. Minn., 1979, 80. Mfg. mgr. Johnson & Johnson, Chgo., 1967-71, mgr. safety and security, 1971-78; corp. dir. safety and health Pacific Dunlop GNB Inc., St. Paul, 1978-88; sr. loss control cons. Willis of Ill., 1988—. Author: Safe Work Practices for Workers Exposed to Lead; prodr. videotapes on health and safety tng. Chmn. Bolingbrook (Ill.) Human Rels. Commn., 1971-77. Mem. Am. Soc. Safety Engrs., Am. Indsl. Hygiene Assn. Home: 1606 Hadley Ct Wheeling IL 60090-6916 Office: 10 S LaSalle St Ste 3000 Chicago IL 60603

BEER, BARRETT LYNN, historian; b. Goshen, Ind., July 4, 1936; s. Peter J. and Mabel M. Beer; m. Jill Parker, 1965. BA, DePauw U., 1958; MA, U. Cin., 1959; PhD, Northwestern U., 1965. Instr. history Kent State U., Ohio, 1962-65, assoc. prof., 1968-76, prof., 1976—; asst. prof. U. N.Mex., Albuquerque, 1965-68, asst. dean Coll. Arts and Scis., 1966-68; Fulbright prof. U. Tromso, Norway, 1983. Author: Northumberland: The Political Career of John Dudley, Earl of Warwick and Duke of Northumberland, 1973, Rebellion and Riot: Popular Disorder in England during the Reign of Edward VI, 1982, (with others) Recent Historians of Great Britain, 1990, Tudor England Observed: The World of John Stow, 1998; editor (with S.M. Jack) The Letters of William, Lord Paget of Beaudesert, 1547-1563, 1974, The Life and Raigne of King Edward the Sixth (John Hayward), 1993. Am. Philos. Soc. grantee, 1966; Am. Council Learned Socs. grantee, 1973; fellow Newberry Libr., 1991, Folger Shakespeare Libr., 1997. Fellow Royal Hist. Soc.; mem. Conf. on Brit. Studies, Ohio Acad. History, Phi Beta Kappa. Episcopalian. Home: 445 Dansel St Kent OH 44240-2626 Office: Kent State U Dept History Kent OH 44242-0001 E-mail: bbeer@kent.edu.

BEER, CLARA LOUISE JOHNSON, retired electronics executive; b. Bisbee, Ariz., Jan. 14, 1918; d. Franklin Fayette and Marie (Sturm) Johnson; m. Philip James McElmurry, May 15, 1937 (div. July 1944); children— Leonard Franklin, Philip James Jr.; m. William Sigvard Beer, July 15, 1945 (dec. Aug. 1977); 1 son, Douglas Lee; m. Kenneth Christy Huntwork, May 1, 1982 (dec. Jan. 2003). Student, Merritt Bus. Sch., Oakland, Calif., 1935, Bus. Instrn. Sch., Palo Alto, Calif., 1955. Sec., artist M.R. Fisher Studios, Oakland, 1936-40; piano, organ instr. Anna May Studios, Palo Alto, 1948-50; pvt. piano, organ instr. Palo Alto, 1949-56; sec. Stanford Electronics Labs., Stanford U., 1955-58; corporate sec. and exec. sec. to chmn. bd. Watkins-Johnson Co., Palo Alto,

1958-88. Dir., sec. Watkins-Johnson Internat., 1968-88, Watkins-Johnson Ltd., 1971-88, Watkins-Johnson Assocs., 1977-88. Mem. Nat. Secs. Assn., Christian Bus. and Profl. Women's Coun. (sec. 1966-67, adviser 1968) Home: 24157 Hillview Rd Los Altos CA 94024-5222

BEER, DAVID WELLS, architect; b. N.Y.C., June 29, 1934; s. Walter Eugene Jr. and Florence Louise (Fay) B.; m. Laura Decay Houghton (div. 1979); children: Elizabeth Amory, Andrew David. Student, Philip's Exeter Acad., 1952; BArch, Harvard Coll., 1956; MArch, Harvard Grad. Sch. Design, 1959. Registered architect, N.Y., N.J., Ga., Fla., Conn., Va., D.C. Designer Sakallarios Assoc., Athens, 1959-60, Pederson and Tilney, N.Y.C., 1960-62; assoc. designer Hoberman and Wasserman, N.Y.C., 1962-65; design dir. Welton Becket Assoc., N.Y.C., 1965-74, sr. v.p. design, 1974-84; founding ptnr. Brennan Beer Gorman / Architects, N.Y.C., Washington, Hong Kong, 1984—; ptnr. Brennan Beer Gorman Monk/Interiors, N.Y.C., Washington, Hong Kong, 1986—. Trustee N.Y. State Preservation League, N.Y.C., 1991—. Prin. works include St. Regis Hotel restoration, 1991—. Sec., vol. Momentum Project, N.Y.C., 1985—; mem. Save Venice, Inc., N.Y.C. and Venice, 1984—. Recipient 1st prize FDR Meml. Competition, 1962, Office Bldg. of Yr. award Bldg. Owners and Mgrs. Assn., 1986, 87, 88, 93, 95, Platinum Circle Award, 1996. Fellow AIA; mem. Century Assn., Met. Opera Club, Delphic Club (Harvard), Traveller's Club (Paris), Knickerbocker Club. Avocations: opera, theatre, fundraising, international travel. Office: Brennan Beer Gorman/Architects Brennan Beer Gorman Monk/Interiors 515 Madison Ave New York NY 10022-5403

BEER, FRANCIS ANTHONY, political science educator; b. N.Y.C., Feb. 5, 1939; s. William Joseph and Anne (Benedikt) B.; m. Diana Darnall, June 12, 1965; children: Omar, Marie, Jeremy. AB cum laude, Harvard U., 1960; MA, U. Calif., Berkeley, 1963, PhD, 1967. Asst. prof. dept. govt. U. Tex., Austin, 1967-70, assoc. prof. dept. govt., 1970-75; prof. dept. polit. sci. U. Colo., Boulder, 1975—. Author: Integration and Disintegration in NATO: Processes of Alliance Cohesion and Prospects for Atlantic Community, 1969, Peace Against War: The Ecology of International Violence, 1981, Meanings of War and Peace, 2001; editor Alliances: Latent War Communities in the Contemporary World, 1970; co-editor: (with Ted. R. Gurr) Conflict, Violence, Peace: An International Series of Books, 1990-93, (with R. Hariman) Post-Realism: The Rhetorical Turn in International Relations, 1996; asst. editor Jour. Politics, 1968-71; contbr. articles to profl. jours. Lt. USNR, 1960-62. Fulbright fellow, 1965-66, 71, Mershon fellow, 1966-67, NEH fellow, 1990; grantee Earhart Found., 1972, Inst. World Order, 1974-77. Mem. Internat. Polit. Sci. Assn., Internat. Soc. Polit. Psychology, Am. Polit. Sci. Assn., Internat. Studies. Assn. Office: U Colo Polit Sci Dept PO Box 333 Boulder CO 80309-0333

BEÉR, JANOS MIKLOS, engineering educator; b. Budapest, Hungary, Feb. 27, 1923; s. Sandor and Gizella (Trismai) B.; m. Marta Gabriella Csato, Oct. 27, 1944. Dipl. Ing., Jozsef Nador U. Tech., Budapest, 1950; PhD, U. Sheffield, Eng., 1960, DSc, 1968; Dr honoris causa, U. Miskolc, Hungary, 1987, U. Tech. Scis., Budapest, Hungary, 1997. Research engr. Heat Research Inst., Budapest, 1949-56, head combustion div., 1952-56; prin. lectr. combustion Budapest Tech. U., 1953-56; research engr. Babcock & Wilcox Ltd., Renfrew, Scotland, 1956-57; head research sta. Internat. Flame Research Found., Ijmuiden, Holland, 1960-63; prof. fuel sci. Pa. State U., 1963-65; Newton Drew prof., head dept. chem. engring. and fuel tech. U. Sheffield, 1965-76, dean engring., 1973-75; prof. chem. and fuel engring. MIT, 1976-93, prof. emeritus, 1993—, sci. dir. MIT Combustion Rsch. Facility, 1976—93. Vis. fellow Australian Commonwealth, 1972; mem. joint com. Internat. Flame Research Found., 1972-89, supt. research, 1972-89 ; bd. dirs. Combustion Inst., Pitts., 1974-86; adv. council research and devel. fuel and power U.K. Dept. Energy, 1973-76; mem. Clean Air Council, Dept. Environ., U.K., 1974-76; mem. chem. tech. com. U.K. Sci. Research Council, 1972-75; mem. combustion sci. com. Italian Nat. Research Council, 1974—; chmn. clean coal utilization project NAS, 1987-88; mem. adv. coun. U.S. Sec. Energy Nat. Coal Coun., 1994—. Co-author: Combustion Aerodynamics, 1972; editor: Fuel and Energy Science Monograph Series, 1972; co-editor: Heat Transfer in Flames, 1972, Industrial Flames, 1972, Combustion Technology, 1974; author articles; patentee in field. Recipient BCURA Coal Sci. gold medal, 1986, Alfred Egerton gold medal Combustion Inst., 1986, Axel Axelson Johnson medal Swedish Acad. Engring. Scis., 1995, AIAA Energy Sys. award, 1998, George Westinghouse gold medal ASME Internat., 2001; named Hon. Supt. Rsch., Internat. Flame Rsch. Found., 1991. Fellow ASME (Moody award 1964, Percy Nicholls award 1988, Internat. George Westinghouse Gold medal 2001), Inst. Energy (sr., Melchett medal 1985), Royal Acad. Engring. U.K.; mem. Am. Inst. Chem. Engrs., Inst. Chem. Engring., Hungarian Acad. Scis. (hon.), Hungarian Nat. Acad. Engring. (hon.), Finnish Acad. Tech. (fgn.). Office: MIT 66-548 Dept Engring Cambridge MA 02139 E-mail: jmbeer@mit.edu.

BEER, JANUSZ ZYGMUNT, radiation and photo biologist, scientist; b. Warsaw, Apr. 18, 1930; came to U.S., 1978; s. Zygmunt Wlodzimierz and Maria (Zyskowska) B.; m. Zofia Stefania Olempska, May 5, 1960; children: Tomasz Michal, Kasia Barbara. MS, Warsaw Poly. and U. Warsaw, 1952; PhD, U. Warsaw, 1964, DSc, 1976. From tech. asst. to asst. U. Warsaw, 1951-59; from sr. asst. to lab. head Inst. Nuclear Rsch., Warsaw, 1959-78; vis. scientist Bur. Radiol. Health FDA, Rockville, Md., 1978-84; sr. scientist Ctr. Devices and Radiol Health FDA, 1989—; branch chief Ctr. Devices and Radiol. Health, 1984-89. Sr. scientist Biomed. Rsch. Svc., 1996—; vis. scientist Chester Beatty Rsch. Inst., London, 1962-63; reviewer NIH and EPA grant proposals and sci. papers for several profl. jours.; lectr. numerous nat. and internat. sci. meeting.; cons. if field. Contbr. articles to profl. jours.; patentee in field. Mem. adv. bd. Advances Radiation Biology, 1979-90; rsch. adviser Nat. Rsch. Coun.; resident Rsch. Associateship Program, 1988—, Oak Ridge Associated Univs./Food and Drug Adminstrn. Rsch. Program, 1990—. Recipient several sci. awards Polish Biochem. Soc., Polish Coun. for Atomic Energy Devel., FDA, Marie Curie medal for sci. achievements, 1992; Internat. Atomic Energy Agy. fellow, 1962; travel grantee Internat. Assn. for Radiation Rsch. 1970, 74. Mem. Polish Assn. for Radiation Rsch. (hon. sec. 1968-74, award), U.K. Assn. for Radiation Rsch., European Soc. for Radiation Biology (mem. coun. 1976-84), Radiation Rsch. Soc. U.S., Am. Soc. Photobioloby, European Soc. Photobiology, Am. Conf. Govtl. Indsl. Hygienists, Polish Acad. Sci. (radiobiol. com. exec. sec. 1974-76), Photomedicine Soc., Union Polish Tchrs. (chpt. chmn. 1956-57), N.Y. Acad. Scis., Sigma Xi. Roman Catholic. Avocations: photography, biking, hiking. Home: 2 Lorre Ct Rockville MD 20852-4103 Office: FDA Ctr Devices Radiol Health HFZ-114 5600 Fishers Ln Rockville MD 20857-0001 E-mail: jzb@cdrh.fda.gov.

BEER, JOHN R. poet, educator; b. New Bedford, Mass., Aug. 28, 1969; s. Roger J. and Patricia Foster Beer; m. Paula Virginia Diaz, Aug. 29, 1998. BA in Philosophy, Princeton U., 1991; MFA in Poetry, U. Iowa, 1996. Lit. asst. Robert Lax, Patmos, Greece, 1996—98; prof. Robert Morris Coll., Chgo., 1998—. Editor: (book) Journal F (Robert Lax), 1998, Moments (Robert Lax), 2000; contbr. poems to publs., rev. articles to newspapers. Fellow Nat. Mellon, Woodrow Wilson Found., 1991. Roman Catholic. Office: Robert Morris Coll 401 S State St Chicago IL 60605 Personal E-mail: jbeer@smtp.rmcil.edu.

BEER, JOHN VINCENT, pathologist, consultant; b. Newbury, Eng., May 3, 1928; s. Harold Vincent and Henrietta Elizabeth (Andow) B. BSc, U. Reading, U.K., 1948, Diploma in Gen. Bacteriology, 1950; PhD, U. Bristol, U.K., 1960. Microbiologist Howards of Ilford Ltd., England, 1949-53, Boots Ltd., Nottingham, England, 1953-54; pathologist Wildfowl Trust, Slimbridge, England, 1954-69; rsch. dir. Oiled Seabird Rsch. Unit, Newcastle, England, 1969-70; sr. pathologist The Game Conservancy Trust, Fordingbridge, England, 1971-93; cons. Gamebird Consultancy, Salisbury, England, 1993—. Author: Diseases of Gamebirds and Wildfowl, 1988, Egg Production and Incubation, 1982. Fellow The Wildfowl and Wetlands Trust, Zool. Soc. London; mem. Inst. Biology, Brit. Vet. Poultry Assn. (assoc.), Brit. Vet. Zool. Soc (assoc.), Wildlife Diseases Assn., World Assn. Wildlife Vets. (assoc.), Incubation and Fertility Rsch. Group, World's Poultry Sci. Assn. U.K., World Phesant Assn., Australian Assn. Vet. Conservation Biologists (assoc.). Avocations: photography, amateur dramatics, hill walking, natural history, amateur radio, travel, astronomy. Home: Hillside Combe Hill Combe St Nicholas Chard Somerset TA20 3NW England

BEER, PAMELA JILL PORR, writer, retired vocational school educator; b. Denver, Sept. 23, 1941; d. Wyeth Wittwer and Mary Porr (DuReece) Beer; m. Calvin George Beer, Dec. 25, 1968. BS, Pittsburg State U., Kans., 1963; MBE, 1979. Clk. Bookkeeper Hubbard Auto Supply, Pitts., 1960—63; tchr. bus. edn. Sabetha HS, Kans., 1963—65, Nevada HS, Mo., 1965—71; head bus. dept. Nev. Vocat. Area Sch., 1971—93; ret., 1993; freelance writer, 1993; instr. continuing edn. Mo. Southern State Coll., Joplin, 1987—. Instr. 4-H, 1987. Contbr. articles. Named Nev. R-5 Tchr. of Yr., 1992, Bus. Edn. Tchr. of Yr., Mo. Southwest Dist., 1993, Tchr. of Yr., Mo. Bus. Edn. Assn. SW Dist. Mem.: Alpha Gamma Delta, Nev. C. of C. (Area Educator of Yr. 1987), Am. Vocat. Assn., Nat. Bus. Edn. Assn., Roxburg Pub. Co. (mem. editorial adv. bd. 1984), articulation com., Delta Kappa Gamma. Meth. Avocations: bowling, swimming, bridge, tennis. Home: 1827 F Kennedy Pittsburg KS 66762

BEER, PETER HILL, federal judge; b. New Orleans, Apr. 12, 1928; s. Mose Haas and Henret (Lowenburg) B.; children: Kimberly Beer Bailes, Kenneth, Dana Beer Long-Innes; m. Marjorie Barry, July 14, 1985. BBA, Tulane U., 1949, LLB, 1952; LLM, U. Va., 1986. Bar: La. 1952. Successively assoc., ptnr., sr. ptnr. Montgomery, Barnett, Brown & Read, New Orleans, 1955-74; judge La. Ct. Appeal, 1974-79, U.S. Dist. Ct. (ea. dist.) La., New Orleans, 1979—. Vice chmn. La. Appellate Judges Conf.; apptd. by chief justice of U.S. to state-fed. com. Jud. Conf. U.S., 1985-89; apptd. by chief justice of U.S. to Nat. Jud. Coun. State and Fed. Cts., 1993—. Mem. bd. mgrs. Touro Infirmary, New Orleans, 1969-74; mem. exec. com. Bur. Govtl. Rsch., 1965-69; chmn. profl. divsn. United Fund New Orleans, 1966-69; mem. New Orleans City Coun., 1969-74, v.p., 1972-74. Capt. USAF, 1952-55. Decorated Bronze Star. Mem. ABA (mem. ho. dels.), Am. Judicature Soc., Fed. Bar Assn., La. Bar Assn., Nat. Lawyers Club, So. Yacht Club, St. John Golf Club. Jewish. Home: 133 Bellaire Dr New Orleans LA 70124-1008 also: 204 3rd Ave Pass Christian MS 39571-3214 Office: US Dist Ct US Courthouse 500 Camp St New Orleans LA 70130-3313

BEER, REINHARD, atmospheric scientist; b. Berlin, Nov. 5, 1935; came to U.S., 1963, naturalized, 1979; s. Harry Joseph and Elizabet Maria (Meister) B.; m. Margaret Ann Taylor, Aug. 11, 1960. B.Sc. with Honors, U. Manchester, Eng., 1956, PhD, 1960. Rsch. asst. physics U. Manchester, 1956-60, sr. asst. astronomy, 1960-63; sr. scientist Jet Propulsion Lab., Pasadena, Calif., 1963-70, group supr. tropospheric sci., 1970-90, sr. rsch. scientist, 1985—, mgr. atmospheric and oceanographic scis. sect., 1990-92, flight team leader, 1997—, prin. scientist, 1999—. Vis. assoc. prof. anstronomy U. Tex., Austin, 1974; vis. astronomer Kitt Peak Nat. Obs., 1979-81, Mauna Kea Obs., 1982-86; prin. investigator tropospheric emission spectrometer NASA Earth Observing System, 1989—, airborne emission spectrometer program NASA, 1992—; co-investigator NASA Atlas 1 mission, 1992, Atlas 2, 1993. Author: Remote Sensing by Fourier Transform Spectrometry, 1992; contbr. articles to profl. jours. Hon. Turner and Newall fellow, 1961; recipient medal for exceptional sci. achievement NASA, 1974; NASA group achievement award for Pioneer Venus, 1980, Spacelab 3 ATMOS experiment and sci., 1986. Mem. AAAS, Am. Geophys. Union, Optical Soc. Am. Achievements include discovery of extra-terrestrial deuterium (heavy hydrogen), 1972, of carbon monoxide in Jupiter, 1975. Office: 183-601 Jet Propulsion Lab Pasadena CA 91109

BEERBOWER, CYNTHIA GIBSON, lawyer; b. Dayton, Ohio, June 25, 1949; d. Charles Augustus and Sarah (Rittenhouse) Gibson; m. John Edwin Beerbower, Aug. 28, 1971; children: John Eliot, Sarah Rittenhouse. BA, Mt. Holyoke Coll., 1971; JD, Boston U., 1974; LLB, Cambridge (Eng.) U., 1976. Bar: N.Y. 1975. Assoc. Cadwalader, Wickersham & Taft, N.Y.C., 1975-76, Simpson, Thacher & Bartlett, N.Y.C., 1977-81, ptnr., 1981-93; internat. tax counsel, dept. asst. sec. Dept. Treasury, Washington, 1993-96; chmn., CEO Reeve Ct. Ins. Ltd., 1997—2001; prin. The Quellos Group, N.Y.C., 2001—. Mem. ABA, Assn. Bar City N.Y., N.Y. State Bar Assn. (com. co-chmn. 1987-93). Presbyterian. Home: 720 Park Ave New York NY 10021-4954 Office: 667 Madison Ave New York NY 10021

BEERBOWER, JOHN EDWIN, lawyer; b. Columbus, Ohio, Jan. 7, 1948; m. Cynthia Gibson, Aug. 28, 1971; children: John Eliot, Sarah Rittenhouse. BA, Amherst Coll., 1970; JD, Harvard U., 1973; student, Trinity Coll., Cambridge (Eng.) U. Bar: N.Y. 1975. Mem. Cravath, Swaine & Moore, LLP, N.Y.C., 1980—. Bd. govs. Mannes Coll. Music, 1993—, vice chmn., 2000—02, chmn., 2002—; com. on instl. policy New Sch. U., 2003—; trustee Madison Ave. Presbyn. Ch., 1995—2001, pres. bd. trustees, 2000—01. Mem. ABA, N.Y. State Bar Assn., N.Y. Law Inst. (mem. nominating com.), Assn. of Bar of City of N.Y. (chmn. profl. and jud. ethics com. 1990-93), Soc. of Alumni Amherst Coll. (pres. 1994-95), Union Internat. Advocats, Am. Econ Assn., Phi Beta Kappa. Office: Cravath Swaine & Moore LLP Worldwide Plz 825 8th Ave Fl 40 New York NY 10019-7416

BEERING, STEVEN CLAUS, academic administrator, medical educator; b. Berlin, Aug. 20, 1932; arrived in U.S., 1948, naturalized, 1953; s. Steven and Alice (Friedrichs) Beering; m. Catherine Jane Pickering, Dec. 27, 1956; children: Peter, David, John. BS summa cum laude, U. Pitts., 1954; DSc (hon.), Ind. Cen. U., 1983; MD, U. Pitts., 1958; DSc (hon.), U. Evansville (Ind.), 1984; ScD (hon.), U. Pitts., 1998; DSc (hon.), Ramapo Coll., 1986, Anderson Coll., 1987; ScD (hon.), Ind. U., 1988; LLD (hon.), Hanover Coll., 1986; DsC (hon.), Purdue U., 2000; LLD (hon.), Tex. Wesleyan, 2001. Intern Walter Reed Gen. Hosp., Washington, 1958—59; resident Wilford Hall Med. Center, San Antonio, 1959—62, chief internal medicine, edn. coordinator, 1967—69; prof. medicine Ind. U. Sch. Medicine, Indpls., 1969—, asst. dean, 1969—70, assoc. dean, dir. postgrad. edn., 1970—74, dir. statewide med. edn. system, 1970-83, dean, 1974—83; chief exec. officer Ind. U. Med. Center, Indpls., 1974—83; pres. Purdue U. and Purdue U. Rsch. Found., West Lafayette, Ind., 1983—2000, pres. emeritus, 2000—; chmn. Purdue Rsch. Found., West Lafayette, 2000—. Prof. pharmacology and toxicology Purdue U.; bd. dirs. Eli Lilly Co., NISource, Inc., Am. United Life; cons. Indpls. VA Hosp., St. Vincent Hosp.; chmn. Med. Edn. Bd. Ind., 1974—83, Liaison Com. Med. Edn., 1976—81, Ind. Commn. Med. Edn., 1978—83. Contbr. articles to sci. jours. Sec. Ind. Atty. Gen.'s Trust, 1974—83; regent Nat. Libr. Medicine, 1987—91; trustee U. Pitts. Lt. col. M.C. USAF, 1957—69. Fellow: ACP, Royal Soc. Medicine; mem.: Nat. Sci. Bd., Ind. Acad., Nat. Acad. Sci. Inst. of Medicine, Assn. Am. Univs. (chair 1995—96), Coun. Med. Deans (chmn. 1980—81), Assn. Am. Med. Colls. (chmn. 1982—83), Endocrine Soc., Am. Diabetes Assn., Am. Fedn. Med. Rsch., Meridian Hills Club, Skyline Club, Phi Rho Sigma (U.S. v.p. 1976—85), Alpha Omega Alpha, Sigma Xi, Phi Beta Kappa. Presbyterian. Home: 10487 Windemere Dr Carmel IN 46032 Office: Purdue U Office of Pres Emeritus Rm 218 Memorial Union West Lafayette IN 47906-3584 Fax: 765-496-7561. E-mail: scb@purdue.edu.

BEERMAN, MIRIAM, artist, educator; b. Providence; d. William and Rose (Nochemsohn) B.; m. Julian F. Jaffe (dec. 1973); 1 child, William Jaffe. Student, Atelier 17, Paris, 1953; BFA, R.I. Sch. Design, 1945; postgrad., Art Students League, N.Y.C., 1945-46, New Sch. for Social Rsch., NYU. Prof. painting and drawing Queensborough C.C., CUNY, 1972—95; instr. Jersey City State Coll., 1973—75, Montclair (N.J.) Art Mus. Art Sch., 1974—90; resident Montclair Art Mus. Art Sch., 1980—90; instr. Montclair State Coll., 1980—89. Artist-in-residence MacDowell Colony, 1959, Ossibaw Island, Ga., 1974, Camargo Found., Cassis, France, 1980—, Va. Ctr. for Creative Arts, Sweet Briar, 1983, 84, 86, 89, 90, 91, 92, 93, 94, 97, 98, Leighton Artist's Colony, Banff Ctr., Alta., Can., 1986-87, Blue Mountain Ctr., N.Y., 1988, 93, 95, 97, Millay Colony for Arts, 1976, 91, Camargo Found., 1980, Mid-Atlantic Arts Found., 2000, Women's Studio Workshop, 2000. One-woman shows include Bklyn. Mus., 1971, Montclair Art Mus., 1974, 87-88, Graham Gallery, N.Y.C., 1972, 78, Mus. of St. John the Divine, N.Y.C., 1978, N.J. State Mus., Trenton, 1991, Klarfeld Perry Gallery, N.Y.C., 1993, Suffolk C.C., N.Y., 1993, Bergen Mus., Paramus, N.J., 1996, Jersey City Mus., 1997-98, Priebe Gallery, U. Wis., 2002, also others; exhibited in group shows Inst. Contemporary Art, New Orleans, 1986, Newark Mus., 1985-86, Roanoke Mus. Fine Art, 1985, Bayly Mus., 1985, Corcoran Gallery of Art, Washington, 1994, Bergen Mus., Paramus, N.J., 1996, Montclair Mus., N.J., 1997, Ctr. for Book Arts, N.Y.C., 1996, 98, Women of the Book, 1997-2002, Bristol Meyers-Squibb Gallery, Lawrenceville, N.J., 2000, others; represented in permanent collections U. Del., Sterling Art Libr., Yale U., New Haven, Nat. Mus. Women in Arts, Washington, Israel Mus., U. Oreg., Newark Mus., Whitney Mus., Am. Art, Bklyn. Mus., Montclair Art Mus., Arnot Art Mus., Morris Mus., Met. Mus. Art, Mus. of Art, RISD, Queens Mus., N.Y., Jersey City Mus., Jewish Mus., N.Y.C., Rosendale, N.Y., Allen Meml. Art Mus., Oberlin, Ohio, Skirball Mus., L.A., Spertus Mus., Chgo., Neuberger Mus., Purchase, N.Y., others. Recipient numerous awards including Childe Hassam Purchase award AAAL, 1977, prize 11th R.I. Arts Festival, 1969, Ives prize RISD, Disting. Artist award N.J. Coun. on Arts, 1987; grantee N.Y. State Coun. on Arts, 1971, Womens Rsch. and Devel. Fund, CUNY, 1986, N.J. Coun. on Arts, 1978, 83, 87, Rutgers Ctr. for Innovative Printmaking, 1987, 97, Joan Mitchell Found., 1994, Mid Atlantic NEA, 1996, Dodge Found. grantee for residency, 1998, 2000, 02, Pollock/Krasner Found., 2000, Artist as Catalyst grant Midatlantic Arts Found., 2000, Womens Studio Workshop, Rosendale, N.Y., 2000, E.D. Found.; Fulbright fellow, Paris, 1953-55, Forest fellow Millay Colony, 1992, others. Home: 6 Macopin Ave Montclair NJ 07043-2002

BEERMANN, ALLEN J. former state official; b. Sioux City, Iowa, Jan. 14, 1940; BA, Midland Lutheran Coll., Fremont, Nebr., 1962; JD, Creighton U., Omaha, 1965; LLD (hon.), Midland Luth. Coll., 1995. Bar: Nebr. 1965. Legal counsel, adminstrv. asst. to sec. state, State of Nebr., 1965-67; dep. sec. state, 1967-71; sec. of state, 1971-95. Mem. Fed. Election Commn. adv. panel. Bd. dirs. NebraskaLand Found.; exec. bd. Cornhusker coun. Boy Scouts Am.; state chair N.E. Commn. Employer Support for Guard and Res., 1997-2002. Lt. col. U.S. Army, ret. Recipient Disting. Svc. plaque Omaha Legal Aid Soc., 1964, Silver Beaver award Boy Scouts Am., 1979, Fgn. Svc. Medallion Rep. of China, 2001, Homeland Def. Ribbon, 2001; named Outstanding Young Man Lincoln Jaycees, 1975, Outstanding Young Man Nebr. Jaycees, 1975 Mem. ABA, Nat. Assn. Secs. State (pres. 1976-77), Nebr. Bar Assn. (exec. dir. 1995—), Nebr. Press Assn., Am. Legion (fed. election commn. adv. panel, Cert. Appreciation). Republican. Lutheran. Office: Nebr Press Assn 845 S St Lincoln NE 68508-1226 E-mail: nebpress@nebpress.com.

BEERS, CHARLOTTE LENORE, federal agency administrator; b. Beaumont, Tex., July 26, 1935; d. Glen and Frances (Bolt) Rice; m. Donald C. Beers, 1971; 1 dau., Lisa. BS in Math. and Physics, Baylor U., Waco, Tex., 1958. Group product mgr. Uncle Ben's Inc., 1959-69; sr. v.p., dir. client services J. Walter Thompson, 1969-79; chief operating officer Tatham-Laird & Kudner, Chgo., from 1979, mng. ptnr., chmn. and chief exec officer; vice chmn. RSCG Group Roux Seguela, Cayzac & Goudard, France; chmn., CEO Ogilvy & Mather Worldwide, N.Y.C., Ogilvy Group Inc., N.Y.C., chmn. emeritus, 1997-99; chmn. J. Walter Thompson, N.Y.C., 1999-2000; under sec. for public diplomacy U.S. Dept. State, Washington, Conn., 2001—. Named Nat. Advt. Woman of Yr. Am. Advt. Fedn., 1975 Mem. Am. Assn. Advt. Agencies (chmn. from 1987), Women's Advt. Club Chgo., Chgo. Network. Republican. Episcopalian. Office: US Dept State Public Diplomacy & Public Affairs 2201 C St NW Washington DC 20520

BEERS, DEBORAH YARDLEY, musician; b. N.Y.C., Oct. 28, 1954; d. L. Yardley and Dorothy (Sands) B.; m. James Leo Jones, Aug. 26, 1989. MusB, Fla. State U., 1976; MusM, U. Mo., Kansas City, 1978; postgrad., Staatliche Hochschule Musik, Hanover, Germany, 1978-80; D Musical Arts, U. Colo., 1984. Mem. faculty Dean Jr. Coll., Franklin, Mass., 1985-91; mem. piano faculty Longy Sch. Music, Cambridge, Mass., 1988—, assoc. chair dept. piano, 1996—. Composer: Sweet Sixteenths, 1996, others; soloist with Atlanta Symphony, 1973, Denver Symphony, 1982, several others. Mem. New England Piano Tchrs. Assn. (treas. 1987-91), Mass. Music Tchrs. Assn. (v.p. 1985-87) Democrat. Unitarian Universalist. Office: Longy Sch Music 1 Follen St Cambridge MA 02138-3599

BEERS, FREDERICK GORDON, writer, retired corporate communications official; b. Perry, Okla., Aug. 19, 1924; s. Frederick William and Ivy Isabel (Bucklin) B.; m. Laura Belle Thomas, May 2, 1954; children: Kathleen Faye Beers Lindsey, Susan Gail Beers Bieberdorf. Student, St. Bonaventure U., 1943-44. City editor Perry Daily Jour., 1941-43; copy editor Mid-Pacific edit. Stars & Stripes, 1945-46; mng. editor, columnist Perry Daily Jour., 1946-69; mem. advt. and pub. rels. staff Charles Machine Works, Inc., Perry, 1969-89, cons. in corp. graphics, 1990-95; freelance writer, Perry, 1990—. Lab. instr. Journalism Sch., Okla. State U., 1968. Author: The First Generation, 1991, History of the Paul W. Cress Family, 1993, Perry Tales, 1995, Dedicated to Excellence, 2000; free-lance columnist Perry Daily Jour., 1994—; contbr. numerous hist. articles to newspaper. Sec. Noble County Rep. Com., Perry, 1950-52; pres., mem. Perry Bd. Edn., 1973-83, Stagecoach Community Theatre, Perry, 1975—; bd. dirs. Perry Hist. Preservation Com., 1992—; ruling elder 1st Presbyn. Ch., Perry, 1949—; mem. Perry Libr. Bd. Staff sgt. AUS, 1943-46, PTO. Mem. Soc. Profl. Journalists, Perry C. of C. (pres. 1959, Outstanding Citizen award 1992), Rotary (pres. Perry 1949, Paul Harris fellow). Avocations: travel, reading, community theatre, music, grandchildren. Home: 1715 Parklane St Perry OK 73077-1213 E-mail: fbeers@perryisp.net.

BEERS, MAYRA E. academic administrator; b. Havana, Cuba, July 3, 1952; m. Randy M. Beers, Apr. 29, 1972; children: Jonathan, Joshua. BA in Biblical Studies, Miami Christian Coll., 1992; MA in History, Fla. Internat. U, 1995, ABD in History, 2000. Tchr. mid. sch. King's Christian Sch., Miami, Fla., 1991—94; adj. lectr. Trinity Internat. U, Miami, 1996; rsch. assoc. Office of the Pres. Fla. Internat. U, Miamai, 1995—. Bd. trustees Fla. Internat. U, Miami, 2001—; lectr. in field. Contbr. articles. Recipient Jay. I Kislak Found. Prize in History and Anthropology, 1997, James R. Scovie Memorial Award, 2000; grantee Mellon Doctoral Fellow, 1996—98. Avocations: piano, costume design. Office: Floridat International U University Park Campus Miami FL 33199-0001

BEERS, R. RAND, former narcotics and law enforcement administrator; married; 2 children. BA in History, Dartmouth U., 1964; MA in History, U. Mich., 1971. With Fgn. Svc., Washington, 1971; dep. for strategy, ops. coord. regional affairs and security Dept. of State, Washington, dir. Office of Security Analysis, Office of Internat. Security Policy, dep. dir. Office of Policy Analysis, dep. polit. advisor to Supreme Allied Comdr., Europe, dep. asst. sec. regional affairs and export control Bur. Polit. Mil. Affairs, asst. sec. Internat. Narcotics and Law Enforcement Affairs, 1998—2002, special asst. to the Pres. & Sr. Dir. for combating terrorism, 2002—03. Dir. global issues NSC, Washington, spl. asst. to Pres., sr. dir. for intelligence programs. With USMC.

BEERS, V(ICTOR) GILBERT, publishing executive; b. Sidell, Ill., May 6, 1928; s. Ernest S. and Jean B.; m. Arlisle Felten, Aug. 26, 1950; children: Kathleen, Douglas, Ronald, Janice, Cynthia. AB, Wheaton Coll., 1950; M.R.E., No. Baptist Sem., 1953, M.Div., 1954, Th.M., 1955, Th.D., 1960; PhD, Northwestern U., 1963. Prof. No. Baptist Sem., Chgo., 1954-57; editor Sr. High Publs., David C. Cook Pub. Co., Elgin, Ill., 1957-59, exec. editor, 1959-61, editorial dir., 1961-67; pres. Books for Living Inc., Elgin, 1967—; editor Christianity Today, 1982-85, sr. editor, 1985-87; pres. Scripture Press Publs. Inc., Wheaton, Ill., 1990-96, Scripture Press Ministries, 1990—. V.p. ministry devel. Cook Cmty. Ministries, 1996—2000. Author: more than 150 books, including: Family Bible Libr., 10 vols., 1971, The Book of Life, 23 vols., 1980. Bd. dirs. Christian Camps Inc., N.Y., Wheaton (Ill.) Youth Symphony, 1961-63, pres. 1962-63; trustee Wheaton Coll., 1975-92, adv. life trustee, 1992—; trustee Scripture Press Ministries, 1973—. Office: Scripture Press Ministries 250 Pennsylvania Ave Glen Ellyn IL 60137-4327 E-mail: gil3319@aol.com. *True strength for success or adversity is the practice of the presence of God daily.*

BEERY, BARBARA FAYE, secondary school educator; b. Flint, MI, Nov. 6, 1937; d. Ralph Lester and Anne Louise Rose; m. Carl Leonard Beery, Jan. 10, 1966 (dec. Sept. 1987); stepchildren: Julieanne, Elizabeth, Mary June, Deborah, John. BA in History, MA in Spl. Edn., Ariz. State U., 1971, DEd, 1992. Cert. paralegal Ariz., 1994. Tchr., coach Glendale (Ariz.) Union Sch. Dist., 1974—84, human resources adminstr., 1984—94. Adj. prof. No. Ariz. U., Flagstaff, Ottawa U., Phoenix.

BEESLEY, H(ORACE) BRENT, bank executive; b. Salt Lake City, Jan. 30, 1946; s. Horace Pratt and Mary (Brazier) B.; m. Bonnie Jean Matheson, Dec. 20, 1980; children: Laura Jean, Sarah Janice, Mary Roslyn, Amy Elizabeth, David Brent, Katherine Ann, Daniel Pratt. BA, Brigham Young U., 1969; MBA, JD, Harvard U., 1973. Bar: Utah 1973. Instr. U. Utah, Salt Lake City, 1973-81; ptnr. Ray, Quinney & Nebeker, Salt Lake City, 1977-81; dir. Fed. Savs. and Loan Ins. Corp., Washington, 1981-83; chmn., chief exec. officer Charter Savs. Corp., Jacksonville, Fla., 1983-86; pres., chief exec. officer Farm Credit Corp. Am., Denver, 1986-88; chmn., chief exec. officer Heritage Bank, St. George, Utah, 1988—. Bd. dirs. Fed. Home Loan Bank, Seattle, 1992-95, Savs. and Cmty. Bankers Am., 1992-96, Utah Heritage Found., 1978-81, Utah Arthritis

Found., 1978-81; trustee So. Va. Coll., 1998-2002. Mem. Utah State Bar Assn., Alta Club, Entrada at Snow Canyon Country Club. Home: 1492 Kristianna Cir Salt Lake City UT 84103-4221 Office: 95 E Tabernacle St Saint George UT 84770-2307

BEESON, JACK HAMILTON, composer, educator, writer; b. Muncie, Ind., July 15, 1921; children: Christopher Sigerist (dec.), Miranda. Student, U. Rochester, Columbia U.; studied with, Béla Bartók; Mus D (hon.), Columbia U., 2002. Tchr. Juilliard Sch. Music; former chmn. dept. music, assoc. dir. opera workshop Columbia U., N.Y.C., MacDowell prof. emeritus. Former sec. Alice M. Ditson Fund; former chmn. music publ. com. Columbia U. Press.; bd. dirs. Composers Recs., Inc., others. Composer: (operas) Jonah, Hello Out There, The Sweet Bye and Bye, Lizzie Borden (commd. by Ford Found.), My Heart's in the Highlands (commd. by NET), Captain Jinks of the Horse Marines (commd. by Nat. Endowment of Arts), Dr. Heidegger's Fountain of Youth (commd. Nat. Arts Club), Cyrano, Sorry, Wrong Number, Practice in the Art of Elocution, (for orch.) Hymns and Dances, Symphony in A, Transformations, Interludes and Arias from Cyrano (for baritone and orchestra), Two Concert Arias (for soprano and orch.), (chamber music) Sonata for Viola and Piano, Interlude, Song, 4th and 5th Piano Sonatas, Two Diversions, Round and Round, Sonata Caronica, Old Hundredth for Organ, (vocal works) Six Lyrics, Five Songs, Eldorado, Piazza Piece, Big Crash Out West, Indiana Homecoming, Margret's Garden Aria, To a Sinister Potato, (cycles) From a Watchtower, Two by Betjeman, A Rupert Brooke Cycle, (countertenor and chamber ensemble) The Daring Young Man on the Flying Trapeze, (mezzosoprano and chamber ensemble) Ophelia Sings, (soprano, tenor and chamber ensemble) The Equilibrists, others, works for voice and string quartet, (choral works) Knots, Magicke Pieces, Epitaphs, In Praise of Singing, Summer Rounds and Canons. Recipient Rome prize, City of Rochester prize, Marc Blitstein Mus. Theatre award Nat. Inst. Arts and Letters, Gold medal for music Nat. Arts Club, 1976, Gt. Tchrs. award Columbia U., 1979, Alumni Achievement award U. Rochester, 1985, award for Lifetime Achievement award Nat. Opera Assn., 1998; Guggenheim fellow, Fulbright fellow to Italy. Mem. ASCAP (bd. dirs. 1991-95), AAAL (treas., v.p. for music), Phi Beta Kappa. Home: 18 Seaforth Ln Huntington NY 11743-9714 also: 404 Riverside Dr New York NY 10025-1861 Office: Columbia U Dept Music New York NY 10027

BEESON, PAUL BRUCE, physician; b. Livingston, Mont., Oct. 18, 1908; s. John Bradley and Martha Gerard (Ash) Beeson; m. Bartara Neal, July 10, 1942; children: John, Peter, Judith. Student, U. Wash., 1925—28; MD, CM, McGill U., 1933, DSc (hon.), 1971, Emory U., 1968, Albany Med. Coll., 1975, Yale U., 1975, Med. Coll. Ohio, 1979. Asst. Rockefeller Inst., 1937—39, Harvard Med. Sch., 1939—40; asst. prof. medicine Emory U. Med. Sch., 1942—46, prof., chmn. dept., 1946—52; Ensign prof. medicine, chmn. dept. internal medicine Yale Med. Sch., 1952—65; physician-in-chief univ. service Grace-New Haven Community Hosp., 1952—65; Nuffield prof. clin. medicine Oxford (Eng.) U., 1965-74; prof. medicine U. Wash., Seattle, 1974—81. Named Alumnus Summa Laude Dignatus, U. Wash., 1968, hon. knight comdr. Brit. Empire, 1973; recipient 50th Anniversary Gold medal, Peter Bent Brigham Hosp., 1962, Bristol award, Infectious Diseases Soc. Am., 1972, Kober medal, Assn. Am. Physicians, 1973, Abraham Flexner award, Assn. Am. Colls., 1977, Willard Thompson award, Am. Geriat. Soc., 1984, Founders award, So. Soc. Clin. Rsch., 1982, Paul Beeson Scholarship in Aging Rsch., 1995; fellow Berkeley Coll., Yale U., Magdalen Coll. (hon.), Green Coll. (hon.), Oxford U. Master: ACP (John Phillips Meml. award 1976, Disting.Tchr. award 1990); fellow: Royal Coll. Physicians (London), Royal Soc. Medicine (hon.); mem.: NAS, Assn. Physicians Gt. Britain and Ireland, Assn. Am. Physicians (pres. 1967), Am. Soc. Clin. Investigation, Soc. Exptl. Biology and Medicine, Am. Acad. Arts and Scis. Episcopalian. Home: Unit F125 7 Riverwoods Dr Exeter NH 03833-4376*

BEETON, ALFRED MERLE, laboratory director, limnologist, biologist, educator, environmentalist; b. Denver, Aug. 15, 1927; s. Charles Frederick and Edna F. (Smith) B.; m. Mary Eileen Wilcox, July 20, 1945; children: Maureen Ann, Heather Ann, Celeste Nadine; m. Ruth Elizabeth Holland, June 4, 1966; children: Jonathan Eugene, Daniel Paul. BS, U. Mich., 1952, MS, 1954, PhD, 1958; DSc (hon.), U. Wis., Milw., 1996. Fishery biologist U.S. Bur. Comml. Fisheries, Ann Arbor, Mich., 1957-65, chief environ. research, 1960-65; prof. zoology U. Wis.-Milw., 1965-76; asst. dir. U. Wis.-Milw. (Center for Gt. Lakes Studies), 1965-69, assoc. dir., 1969-73; assoc. dean U. Wis.-Milw. (Grad. Sch.), 1973-76; dir. Gt. Lakes and Marine Waters Ctr., Mich. Sea Grant; prof. engring. and natural resources U. Mich., Ann Arbor, 1976-86; dir. Gt. Lakes Environ. Research Lab., Nat. Oceanic and Atmospheric Adminstrn. Dept. Commerce, Ann Arbor, 1986-96, emeritus, 2002—, acting chief scientist Nat Oceanic & Atmospheric Adminstrn. Washington, 1996-97, sr. sci. advisor, 1998—2002. Instr. biology Wayne State U., 1956—57, lectr. biology, 1957—61; lectr. civil engring. U. Mich., 1961—65; U.S. chmn. Sci. Adv. Bd. Internat. Joint Commn., 1986—91; mem. Mich. Toxic Substance Control Commn., 1987—89; mem. rsch. adv. coun. Wis. Dept. Natural Resources; mem. water quality criteria com. Nat. Acad. Scis.; cons. U.S. Army C.E., 1967—73, Met. San. Dist. Chgo., 1968—76, EPA, 1973—83; adviser on projects in Ghana, Laos and Yugoslavia Smithsonian Instn., 1972—82; adviser WHO/Pan Am. Health Orgn., Venezuela, 1978; mem. environ. program com. NRC, 1976—82, internat. environ. program com., 1977—82, mem. environ. studies bd.; adj. vis. prof. Oreg.State U., 1982; mem. Coun. Great Lakes Rsch. Mgrs., 1995—97; chmn. sci. adv. bd. NOAA, 1998—2002; mem. Ocean Rsch. Adv. Panel/Nat. Oceanographic Partnership Program, 2000—02. Contbr. chpts. to books; articles Ency. Brit. Mem.: Mich. Acad. Sci., Arts and Letters, Internat. Assn. Gt. Lakes Rsch., Am. Soc. Limnology and Oceanography (treas. 1962—81), Internat. Assn. Theoretical and Applied Limnology (nat. rep. for U.S. 1976—95), Detroit Audubon Soc. (bd. dirs. 2002—). Home: 2761 Oakcleft St Ann Arbor MI 48103-2247 E-mail: abeeton@netzero.net.

BEEVER, JAMES WILLIAM, III, biologist; b. Balt., Aug. 17, 1955; s. James William Jr. and Virginia Irene (Ruhlmann) B.; m. Lisa Britt Dodd, May 26, 1990. BS, Fla. State U., 1977, MS, 1979; postgrad., U. Calif., Davis, 1984. Environ. specialist Fla. Dept. of Environ. Regulation, Ft. Myers, 1984-88; resource mgmt. and rsch. coord. South West Fla. Aquatic Preserves, Bokeelia, Fla., 1988-90; biol. scientist III, Fla. Game and Fresh Water Fish Commn., Punta Gorda, 1990-98; biol. scientist IV Fla. Fish and Wildlife Conservation Commn., Punta Gorda, 1998—. Adj. faculty biology Edison C.C., Charlotte County; mem. tech. adv. bd. Sarasota Bay and Tampa Bay Nat. Estuary Program, Sarasota, 1989—, mem. policy com. and tech. adv. com. Charlotte Harbor Nat. Estuary Program; chair sci. com. on Mangrove Tech. Adv. Com. Fla. Dept. Environ. Protection, 1994-95; chair Fla. com. on rare and endangered plants and animals, 1994-96; expert witness in field, 1986—; coord. Conservation Plan for the Hillsborough River Greenway Area, 1995; founder Frog Listening Network, 1997; chair Estero Bay Agy. on Bay Mgmt., 1999—. Author: Lemon Bay Aquatic Preserve Management Plan, 1988, The Cedar Point Study, 1992, Hydric Pine Flatwoods of Southwest Florida, 1994, (computer database) Resource Inventory of Species in S.W. Fla., Coastal Conservation Corridor Plan, 1999—; contbr. articles to profl. jours. Chair Grad. Student Assn., Davis, 1981-83. Regents fellowship U. Calif, 1983-84; recipient Grad. Rsch. award, 1982-83, Outstanding Profl. Achievements award Fla. DNR, 1989, Spl. Chmn.'s award Fla. Wildlife Fedn./Nat. Wildlife Fedn., 2000, Guy Bradley award, 2001. Mem. Fla. Acad. Sci., Estuarine Rsch. Fedn., Soc. Wetland Scientists, Soc. for Conservation Biology, Ecol. Soc. Am., Phi Beta Kappa, Sigma Xi. Achievements include rsch. on mangrove tree crab and arboreal folivore, mangrove cutting, endangered species protection, red cockaded woodpeckers; hydric pine flatwoods, xeric oak scrub, regional wildlife habitat/wildlife corridor planning; designation Fla. ecosystems, hydrogeomorphic method for the Everglades. Office: Fla Fish & Wildlife Conservation Commn 29200 Tuckers Grade Punta Gorda FL 33955-2207 E-mail: beeverjw@aol.com.

BEEVER, LISA BRITT-DODD, transportation and environmental planner, researcher; b. Alton, Ill., Apr. 16, 1960; d. Ralph Everett and Martha Guinilda (Ebbersten) D.; m. James William Beever III, May 26, 1990. BS in Landscape Architecture, Tex. A&M, 1982, PhD, 1987; MLA, N.C. State U., 1983. Registered landscape architect; cert. planner. Landscape designer Dave Bost Group, Round Rock, Tex., 1983-84; teaching asst. Tex. A&M U., College Station, 1984-85; landscape planner Richardson-Verdoorn, Austin, Tex., 1985; planner Austin Parks and Recreation Dept., 1985-88; prin. planner divsn. planning Lee County, Ft. Myers, Fla., 1988-89, dir. environ. scis., 1989-92; dir. Charlotte County-Punta Gorda (Fla.) Met. Planning Orgn., 1993—2002, Charlotte Harbor Nat. Estuary Program, 2002—. Adj. faculty Barry U., 1994—2002. Author several environ. regulations and transp. tech. reports, Lee County Wildlife Corridor Plan, Charlotte County Long Range Transp. Plan; contbr. articles to profl. jours. Mem., vol. landscape architect Calusa Land Trust, Pine Island, Fla., 1990—; vol. Children's Sci. Ctr., N. Ft. Myers, Fla., 1992. Recipient County Achievement award Nat. Assn. Counties, 1990, 91, 92, award of excellence Fla. Planning Assn., Nat. award for outstanding met. transp. planning Assn. Met. Planning Orgns., 1997, award of environ. excellence Fed. Hwy. Adminstrn., 1999. Mem. Am. Planning Assn., Fla. Native Plant Soc. (Landscape Design award), Inst. Transp. Engrs. (Fla. chpt., Transp. Profl. of Yr. 1999), Am. Inst. Cert. Planners, Fla. Acad. Scis. (chair urban and regional planning sect. 1991-94, pres. 1995-96). Democrat. Unitarian Universalist. Avocations: gardening, art, travel, dachshunds, hiking. Home: 306 Little Grove Ln Fort Myers FL 33917-3929 Office: Charlotte Harbor Nat Estuary Program 4980 Bayline Dr 4th Fl Fort Myers FL 33917

BEEVERS, HARRY, biologist, educator; b. Shildon, Eng., Jan. 10, 1924; came to U.S., 1950, naturalized, 1958; s. Norman and Olive (Ayre) B.; m. Jean Sykes, Nov. 19, 1949; 1 child, Michael BSc, U. Durham, Eng., 1945, PhD, 1947; DSc, U. Newcastle-on-Tyne, 1974, Purdue U., 1972, Nagoya U., 1986. Rsch. fellow Oxford U., England, 1946-50; asst. to prof. Purdue U., West Lafayette, Ind., 1950-69; prof. biology U. Calif., Santa Cruz, 1969-90, prof. emeritus, 1990—. Fellow Crown Coll. U. Calif., Santa Cruz, 1969— Author: Respiratory Metabolism in Plants, 1961; contbr. articles to profl. jours. Recipient von Humboldt Sr. Scientist award, 1987. Mem. NAS, Am. Soc. Plant Physiologists (Stephen Hales award 1970, pres. 1960, Barnes award 1999), Am. Soc. Biol. Chemists, Am. Acad. Arts and Scis., Accademia Nazionale dei Lincei, Deutsche Botanische Gesselschaft (hon.), Academia Europaea (fgn.), Bayerische Akademie der Wissenschaften (corr.). Home: 57 Del Mesa Carmel CA 93923 Office: U Calif Santa Cruz Dept Biology Santa Cruz CA 95064 E-mail: hbeevers@webtv.net.

BEEZER, ROBERT RENAUT, federal judge; b. Seattle, July 21, 1928; s. Arnold Roswell and Josephine (May) B.; m. Hazlehurst Plant Smith, June 15, 1957; children: Robert Arnold, John Leighton, Mary Allison. Student, U. Wash., 1946-48, 51; BA, U. Va., 1951, LLB, 1956. Bar: Wash. 1956, U.S. Supreme Ct. 1968. Ptnr. Schweppe, Krug, Tausend & Beezer, P.S., Seattle, 1956-84; judge U.S. Ct. Appeals (9th cir.), Seattle, 1984-96, sr. judge, 1996—. Alt. mem. Wash. Jud. Qualifications Commn., Olympia, 1981-84 1st lt. USMCR, 1951-53 Fellow Am. Coll. Trust and Estate Counsel, Am. Bar Found.; mem. ABA, Seattle-King County Bar Assn. (pres. 1975-76), Wash. Bar Assn. (bd. govs. 1980-83) Clubs: Rainier, Tennis (Seattle). Office: US Ct Appeals 802 US Courthouse 1010 5th Ave Seattle WA 98104-1195 E-mail: judge_beezer@ca9.uscourts.gov.

BEFU, HARUMI, anthropology educator; b. L.A., Mar. 20, 1930; s. Juma Befu and Komaki Shimizu; m. Kei Tomita, Aug. 23, 1959; 2 children. BA, UCLA, 1954; MA, U. Mich., 1956; PhD, U. Wis., 1962. Asst. prof. to assoc. prof. anthropology Stanford (Calif.) U., 1995—96; asst. prof. Kyoto Bunkyo U., Uji, Japan, 1996-2000; ret., 2000. Asst. prof. U. Nev., Reno, 1961—62, U. Mo., Columbia, 1962—64; vis. assoc. prof. U. Mich., Ann Arbor, 1964—65; external examiner U. Hong Kong, 1998—2000, assoc. editor, Thunderbird Internat. Bus. Rev., Phoenix, 1991—. Assoc. editor: Thunderbird Internat. Bus. Rev., 1991—. Co-organizer Japanese-Am. Environ. Conf., 1976-96; bd. dirs. Post-Adoption Ctr. for Edn. and Rsch., Palo Alto, Calif., 1982-85, Ben Lomond (Calif.) Quaker Assn., 1986-88, Asian Mgmt. Inst., Sunnyvale, Calif., 1986-88. Rsch. grantee NSF, 1966-67, 69-75, 79-81, NEH, 1983-87, Guggenheim grantee, 1971-72, Fulbright grantee, 1978-79, also 22 other grants and fellowships. Mem. Am. Anthrop. Assn. (life, nominating com. 1973-76), Assn. for Asian Studies (life, bd. dirs. 1975-76, 81-83, various offices 1973-83), Japanese Soc. for Ethnology, European Assn. for Japanese Studies. Avocations: reading, camping, hiking. Office: Stanford U Dept Cultural-Social Anthro Stanford CA 84305-2145 Fax: 650-725-0605.

BEGALA, JOHN ADELBERT, human service administrator; b. Akron, Ohio, Nov. 29, 1950; s. Joseph William and Harriet (Kilb) B.; m. Carole Tate, Dec. 18, 1981; 1 child, Stephen T. BA, Kent State U., 1972, MA, 1975. Councilman-at-large City of Kent, 1973-76; mem. Ohio Ho. of Reps., Columbus, 1977-82; dep. dir. Ohio Dept. Mental Retardation/Developmental Disabilities, Columbus, 1983-85; v.p. Greater Cin. Hosp. Coun., 1986-90; assoc. v.p. U. Cin. Med. Ctr., 1991-94; sr. v.p. MetroHealth Sys., Cleve., 1994-97; exec. dir. Fedn. Cmty. Planning, Cleve., 1998—. Adj. faculty U. cin., 1986—94. Columnist Planning & Action, 1998—. Avocation: music. Office: Fedn Cmty Planning 1226 Huron Rd E Cleveland OH 44115-1702

BEGAM, ROBERT GEORGE, lawyer; b. N.Y.C., Apr. 5, 1928; s. George and Hilda M. (Hirt) B.; m. Helen C. Clark, July 24, 1949; children— Richard, Lorinda, Michael. BA, Yale U., 1949, LL.B., 1952. Bar: N.Y. bar 1952, Ariz. bar 1956, U.S. Dist. Ct. Ariz. 1957, U.S. Ct. Appeals (9th cir.) 1958, U.S Supreme Ct. 1973. Assoc. firm Cravath, Swaine & Moore, N.Y.C., 1952-54; spl. counsel State of Ariz., Colorado River Litigation in U.S. Supreme Ct., 1956-58; pres. Begam, Lewis Marks & Wolfe, P.A., Phoenix. Author: Fireball, 1987. Pres. Ariz. Repertory Theater, 1960—66; trustee Atla Roscoe Pound Found.; bd. dirs. Boys Clubs of Met. Phoenix; bd. govs. Welzmann Inst. Sci., Rehovot, Israel; pres. Am. Com. for Welzmann Inst. of Sci., 1996—98, chmn. fin. resource devel., 2000—; bd. dirs. Phoenix Theater Ctr., 1955—60, 1987—92, Ariz. Theatre Co., 2001—, Shakespeare-Sedona Theatre Co. Fellow: Internat. Soc. Barristers; mem.: State Bar Ariz. (cert. specialist in injury and wrongful death litication), Am. Bd. Trial Advocates (bd. dirs.), Western Trial Lawyers Assn. (pres. 1970), ATLA (pres. 1976—77, chmn. polit. action com. 1979—86), Phoenix Country Club, Yale Club (N.Y.C.). Avocations: writing, theater, golf. Office: Begam Lewis Marks & Wolfe 111 W Monroe St Ste 1400 Phoenix AZ 85003-1787 E-mail: begam@fastq.com.

BEGANDO, JOSEPH SHERIDAN, retired university chancellor, educator; b. Roseland, Kans., Jan. 7, 1921; s. James and Bessie (Barcus) B.; m. Virginia DeVillo Suttee, Aug. 6, 1943; children: DeVillo Begando Janecek, Dana Ann Begando Rodziewicz, Darcy V. BS, Pittsburg (Kans.) State U., 1942; MS, U. Ill., 1947, PhD, 1951. Asst. in mktg. U. Ill., 1946-47, instr., 1948-51; instr. commerce Pittsburg State U., 1947-48, asst. prof. econs., summer 1951; asst. prof. mktg. U. Kans., 1951-53; asst. dean, asso. prof. pharmacy adminstrn. U. Ill., Chgo., 1953-58, asst. to pres., 1958-61, v.p univ., 1961-66; chancellor U. Ill. Med Center, Chgo., 1966-83, chancellor emeritus, 1983—, prof. health resources mgmt. Sch. Pub. Health, 1982-95. Citizen fellow Inst. Medicine, Chgo., 1985. Served to lt. (s.g.) USCG, 1942-45. Recipient Meritorious Achievement award Pittsburg State U., 1959, Disting. Service award U. Ill. Alumni Assn., 1983 Mem. Assn. Acad. Health Centers (pres. 1976-77), Assn. Am. Med. Colls., Pi Omega Pi, Beta Gamma Sigma, Alpha Kappa Psi, Rho Chi, Delta Kappa Sigma, Phi Delta Chi. Clubs: Univ. (Chgo.). Home: 842 Washington St Elmhurst IL 60126-4841

BEGELL, WILLIAM, publisher; b. Wilno, Poland, May 18, 1928; came to U.S., 1947, naturalized, 1953; s. Ferdinand and Liza (Kowarski) Beigel; m. Esther Kessler, May 27, 1948; children: Frederick Paul (dec.), Alissa Maya (dec.). BChemE, CCNY, 1953; MChemE, Poly. Inst. Bklyn., 1958; postgrad., Columbia U., 1958-59; DSc, Acad. Sci. BSSR, Minsk, 1984. Engring. mgr. heat transfer research facility dept. chem. engring. Columbia U., 1953-59; co-founder, exec. v.p. Scripta Technica, Inc., Washington, 1959-74; founder, pres. Hemisphere Publishing Corp., Washington, 1974-91, Begell House, Inc., Pubs., N.Y.C., 1991—; pres., chief scientist Byelocorp Sci., Inc., 1991—; dir. Supco Internat. Engring. Corp., Milan, 1994—. Lectr. pub. George Washington U., Washington, also N.Y. U.; cons. Heat Transfer Research Lab., Columbia U.; cons. in field. Editor 7 books; contbr. numerous articles on heat transfer to profl. jours.; patentee in field. Mem. nat. adv. bd. ctr. for the Book, Libr. of Congress; chmn. exec. coun. Profl. and Scholarly Pubs.; bd. dirs. Am. Fedn. for the Blind. Recipient Benjamin Gomez award book pub. div. Anti-Defamation League, 1984 Mem. AAAS, Am. Inst. Chem. Engrs., Am. Soc. for Engring. Edn., ASME (communications bd. Fellow, 1996, Disting. Svc. award 1992), Assn. Am. Publishers (dir.), N.Y. Acad. Scis. (publs. bd.), Internat. Centre for Heat and Mass Transfer, Washington Book Publishers (founder), Am. Assn. Engring. Socs. Jewish. Home: 46 E 91st St New York NY 10128-1350 Office: Begell House Inc Pubs 145 Madison Ave New York NY 10016-7802

BEGELMAN, KENNETH MARC, cardiovascular surgeon; b. N.Y.C., Dec. 8, 1946; m. Helen A. Leibowitz, Sept. 17, 1968; children: Rebecca, Rachel, Benjamin. BS, Pa. State U., 1967; MD, U. Chgo., 1971. Cert. Am. Bd. Surgery, Am. Bd. Thoracic Surgery. Intern, then resident in gen. surgery U. Fla., Gainesville, 1971-76; resident in thoracic surgery U. Wis., Madison, 1976-78; staff cardiac surgeon Guthrie Clinic Ltd., Sayre, Pa., 1980-83; chief cardiovasc. surgery Everett (Wash.) Clinic, 1983-85, Delray Med. Ctr., Delray Beach, Fla., 1985—, pvt. practice, 1985—2002; chief surgeon South Palm Cardiovasc. Surgery, 1985—2002; Emeritus Staff Delray Med. Ctr., Delray Beach, 2002—. Visiting prof. Univ. of Chgo., Chgo., 2002—. Comdr. USNR, 1978-80. Fellow, Harvard Med. Sch., 1972—73. Fellow ACS, Am. Coll. Cardiology; mem. Soc. Thoracic Surgery, So. Thoracic Assn., Fla. Thoracic Surgery Soc. Avocation: fly fishing. Office: PO Box 764 Jackson WY 83001

BEGELMAN, MITCHELL CRAIG, astrophysicist, educator, writer; AB, AM, Harvard U., 1974; PhD, U. Cambridge, Eng., 1978. Asst. prof. dept. astrophys., planetary and atmospheric scis. U. Colo., Boulder, 1982-87, assoc. prof., 1987-91, prof., 1991—, assoc. chair, 1992-95, chmn., 1995-98, fellow Joint Inst. for Lab. Astrophysics, 1984—. Recipient Presdl. Young Investigator award, 1984, Sci. Writing award Am. Inst. Physics, 1996; Alfred P. Sloan Found. rsch. fellow, 1987-91; John Simon Guggenheim fellow, 1998-99. Fellow Royal Astron. Soc., Cambridge Phil. Soc.; mem. Am. Astron. Soc. (Helen B. Warner prize 1988). Office: U Colo Joint Inst Lab Astrophysics PO Box 440 Boulder CO 80309-0440

BEGERT, WILLIAM J. lieutenant general United States Air Force; BS, U.S. Air Force Acad., 1968; grad., Squadron Officer Sch., Maxwell AFB, Ala., 1974; MPA, U. Colo., 1980; student, Air Command and Staff Coll., Maxwell AFB, Ala., 1981, Nat. War Coll., Ft. Lesley J. McNair, Washington, 1985; Mgmt. Program for Execs., U. Pitts., 1990; Program for Sr. Execs. in Nat. Security, John F. Kennedy Sch. Govt., Harvard, 1995. Pilot, aircraft comdr. 20th Mil. Airlift Squadron USAF, Dover AFB, Del., 1969-71; combat crew tng. USAF, Hurlburt Field, Fla., 1971; forward air controller, flight examiner pilot 20th tactical support squadron USAF, DA Nang Air Base, Vietnam, 1972-73; pilot, flight examiner 9th mil. airlift squadron 436th Airlift Wing, Dover AFB, Del., 1973-77; mil. instr. U.S. Air Force Acad., Colorado Springs, 1977-78, air officer commanding Cadet Squadron 20, 1978-80; comdr. and wing exec. officer 436th Mil. Airlift Wing, Dover AFB, Del., 1981-82, squadron comdr. 3d Mil. Airlift Squadron, Dover AFB, Del., 1983-84; from mobility forces programmer to chief mobility forces divsn., directorate of programs Hdqtrs. USAF, Washington, 1985-88; vice comdr. then comdr. 436th Mil. Airlift Wing USAF, Dover AFB, Del., 1988-90; comdr. 60th Mil. Airlift Wing USAF, Travis AFB, Calif.; chief of staff Hdqtrs. U.S. Transp. Command, Scott AFB, Ill., 1992-94; comdr. USAF Mobility Warfare Ctr., Air Mobility Command, McGuire AFB, N.J., 989-90; dir. ops. and logistics Hdqtrs. U.S. Transp. Command, Scott AFB, Ill., 1995-97; vice comdr. Hdqtrs. U.S. Forces in Europe, Ramstein Air Base, Germany. Decorated Defense Disting. Svc. medal, Defense Superior Svc. medal, Legion of Merit with oak leaf cluster, Disting. Flying Cross with oak leaf cluster, Meritorious Svc. medal with oak leaf cluster, Air medal with 11 oak leaf clusters. Office: USAFE/CV Unit 2050 Box 1 Apo AE 09094-0501

BEGGAN, ROBERT M. non-profit executive; s. Thomas Franklin and Ethel Veronica Beggan; m. Pamela M. Hudson, Sept. 28, 1968; children: Blair, Brendan, Kyle, Neil. BA scholastic philosophy, Stonehill Coll., North Easton, Mass., 1966; M in social work, Rutgers U., New Brunswick, NJ, 1968. Planning dir. United Cmty. Svc., New Brunswick, NJ, 1968—70; campaign dir. United Way of Dade County, Miami, 1970—74; sr. v.p. United Way of Am., Alexandria, Va., 1970—87; pres., CEO United Way Internat., Alexandria, Va., 1997—. Bd. mem. Cmty. Anti Drug Coalition of Am., Alexandria, Va., 1983—87, Nat. Com. to End Homelessness, Washington, 1984—88, Good Shepherd Housing, Alexandria, Va., 1990—93, Nat. Health Coun., Washington, 1991—94. Mem.: Mount Vernon Yacht Club. Avocations: sailing, skiing, cmty. svc..

BEGGS, WILLIAM H. microbiologist, researcher; b. Ft. Dodge, Iowa, Feb. 19, 1935; s. Harold William and Bliss Jewel (Swanstrom) Beggs; m. Nancy Florence Ost, Sept. 14, 1957 (dec. June 1995); children: John W., Margaret B. BA, U. Minn., 1956; PhD, U. Cin., 1964. Rsch. microbiologist Dept. Vets. Affairs Med. Ctr., Mpls., 1965—. Bd. dirs. Minn. Vets. Rsch. Inst., Mpls. Contbr. articles to profl. jours. and conf. procs. 1st lt. U.S. Army, 1956—58, Tex., Kans., La. Mem.: Am. Soc. Microbiology. Achievements include research in chemical properties, biological activities, modes of action and chemotherapeutic potentials of antituberculosis and antifungal drugs. Avocations: tennis, travel, hiking, music.

BEGHE, RENATO, federal judge; b. Chgo., Mar. 12, 1933; s. Bruno and Emmavve (Frymire) B.; m. Bina House, July 10, 1954; children: Eliza Ashley, Francesca Forbes, Adam House, Jason Deneen. BA, U. Chgo., 1951, JD, 1954. Bar: N.Y. 1955. Practiced in, N.Y.C.; assoc. Carter, Ledyard & Milburn, 1954-65, ptnr., 1965-83, Morgan, Lewis & Bockius, 1983-89; judge U.S. Tax Ct., Washington, 1991—. Lectr. N.Y. U. Fed. Tax Inst., 1967, 78, U. Chgo. Fed. Tax Conf., 1974, 80, 86, also other profl. confs. Mng. editor U. Chgo. Law Rev., 1953-54; contbr. articles to profl. jours. Mem. ABA, Internat. Bar Assn., N.Y. State Bar Assn. (chmn. tax sect. 1977-78), Assn. of Bar of City of N.Y. (chmn. art law com. 1980-83), Am. Law Inst., Internat. Fiscal Assn., Am. Coll. Tax Counsel, America-Italy Soc. Inc. (bd. dirs. 1980-92), Phi Beta Kappa, Order of Coif, Phi Gamma Delta. Home: 633 E St SE Washington DC 20003-2716 Office: US Tax Ct 400 2nd St NW Washington DC 20217-0002

BEGLEITER, MARTIN DAVID, law educator, consultant; b. Middletown, Conn., Oct. 31, 1945; s. Walter and Anne Begleiter; m. Ronni Ann Frankel, Aug. 17, 1969; children: Wendy Cara, Hilary Ann. BA, U. Rochester, 1967; JD, Cornell U., 1970. Bar: N.Y. 1970, U.S. Dist. Ct. (ea. dist.) N.Y. 1971, U.S. Ct. Appeals (2d cir.) 1975. Assoc. Kelley Drye & Warren, N.Y.C., 1970—77; assoc. prof. Law Sch., Drake U., Des Moines, 1977—80, prof., 1980—87, 1993—, Richard M. and Anita Calkins disting. prof. law, 1987—93. Contbr. articles to legal jours. Mem. ABA (com. on estate and gift taxes, taxation sect. 1980—, com. malpractice, real property, probate and trust law sect. 1999—, com. on tax legislation and regulations, lifetime transfers, real property, probate and trust law sect. 1980-2002, study com. law reform 1996-2002, chmn. task force on spl. use valuation 1988-93, advisor Nat. Conf. Commns. on Uniform State Laws 1988-93), Iowa Bar Assn. (adviser, resource person, probate, trust sect. 1983-89, 93—), Am. Law Inst. (adviser restatement 3d trusts 1994—). Jewish. Avocations: science fiction, golf. Office: Drake U Sch Law 2507 University Ave Des Moines IA 50311 E-mail: martin.begleiter@drake.edu.

BEGLEITER, MICHAEL L. genetic counselor; b. Bklyn., Mar. 26, 1948; s. Albert and Beverly Begleiter; m. Linda R. Negron; 1 child, Ben. MS, Rutgers U., New Brunswick, NJ, 1973. Genetic Counseling Am. Bd. of Med. Genetics/Md., 1982. Genetic counselor Children's Mercy Hosp., Kans. City, Mo., 1974—96, sr. genetic counselor, 1996—. Instr. of pediat. & genetics U. Mo.-Kans. City Sch. of Medicine, Kans. City, Mo., 1974—92, asst. prof. of pediat. and genetics, 1992—2001, assoc. prof. of pediat. and genetics, 2001—. Office: Children's Mercy Hosp 2401 Gillham Rd Kansas City MO 64108

BEGLEITER, RONNI FRANKEL, lawyer; b. Tupper Lake, NY, July 7, 1948; d. Samuel and Ruth (Kaplan) Frankel; m. Martin David Begleiter, Aug. 17, 1969; children: Wendy Cara, Hilary Ann. BA, Cornell U., 1969; MLS, Columbia U., 1971; JD, Drake U., 1982. Bar: Iowa 1983, U.S. Tax Ct. 1987. Libr. Fried Frank Harris Shriver & Jacobson, N.Y.C., 1971-74, Proskauer Rose Goetz & Mendelsohn, N.Y.C., 1974-77; reference libr. Drake U. Law Libr., Des Moines, 1977-81; clk. Iowa Supreme Ct., Des Moines, 1983-84; assoc. Davis, Hockenberg, Wine, Brown & Koehn, Des Moines, 1984-87; assoc., shareholder Pingel & Templer PC, West Des Moines, Iowa, 1987-2000; ptnr. Brown Winick, Graves, Gross, Baskerville & Schoenebaum, Des Moines, Iowa, 2000—. Adj. prof. Drake U. Law Sch., Des Moines, 1992, 95, 97. Chmn. Clive (Iowa) Mayor's Libr. Com., 1995-98; trustee Clive Pub. Libr., 1999-2001; bd. dirs. Iowa Libr. Assn. Found., 2002—; active Clive City Coun., 2002—. Nominated for Clive Citizen of Yr., 1999. Mem. ABA, Am. Coll. of Trusts and Estates Council, Iowa State Bar Assn., Mid Iowa Estate Planners, Iowa Libr. Assn. Found. (dir. 2002—), Polk County Bar Assn., ERISA Forum. Office: Brown Winick Graves Gross Baskerville & Schoenebaum Ste 2000 666 Grand Ave Des Moines IA 50309 E-mail: begleiter@ialawyers.com.

BEGLEY, ED, JR., actor; b. Hollywood, Calif., Sept. 16, 1949; s. Edward James and Allene Jeanne Begley; m. Ingrid Margaret Taylor (div.); children: Amanda, Nicholas, Hayden; m. Rachelle Carson-Begley.. Student, Los Angeles Valley Coll. Actor (theatre) Love Letters, The Cryptogram, The Old Neighborhood, (films) including Showdown, 1973, Citizen's Band, Stay Hungry, 1976, Blue Collar, 1978, Goin' South, 1978, The In-Laws, 1979, The One and Only, Airport 79, 1979, TPrivate Lessons, 1981, Buddy Buddy, 1981, Cat People, 1982, Protocol, 1984, Transylvania 6-5000, 1985, The Accidental Tourist, 1988, Scenes from The Class Struggle in Beverly Hills, 1989, She Devil, 1989, Meet The Applegates, 1991, Dark Horse, 1992, Mastergate, 1992, Page Master, 1994, Even Cowgirls get the Blues, 1993, Cooperstown, 1993, Sensations, Renaissance Man, Greedy, 1994, Renaissance Man, 1994, Batman Forever, 1995, Santa With Muscles, 1996, Lay of the Land, 1997, Ms. Bear, 1997, Joey, 1997, I'm Losing You, 1998, Addams Family Reunion, 1998, Best in Show, 2000, Anthrax, 2001, Bug, 2002, Ragged Point, Mighty Wind, 2003, others; (TV movies) A Shining Season, Elvis, Amateur Night at the Dixie, Dead of Night, Rascals & Robbers, Hot Rod, An American Love Affair, Spies, Lies and Naked Thighs, The Incredible Ida Early, Roman Holiday, Home, In the Best Interest of the Child, Not a Penny More, Not a Penny Less, 1990, A Change of Heart, Story Lady, Stand Off At Marion, Exclusive, World War II: When the Lions Roared, Jacks, The Late Shift, Alone, Not in This Town, Murder She Purred: A Mrs. Murphy Mystery; (TV series) Homicide: The Movie, Tale of Two Freedoms, The Practice, Mary Hartman, Mary Hartman, Battlestar Galactica, Roll Out, Room 222, St. Elsewhere, Parenthood, Winnetka Road, Todays Environment, Meego, Maggie Day, Meego, 7th Heaven, 1999 , The Web, Six Feet Under, 2001, Providence, The West Wing, Gideon's Crossing; also numerous TV commls., night club performances, dir. Enemies of Laughter, 1999; TV guest appearances include Quincy, The Love Boat, Touched by an Angel, 3rd Rock from the Sun, Star Trek: Voyager, Sabrina, The Teenage Witch, The Drew Carey Show, Ellen, The Simpsons, The Agency Titus, others. Chmn. Santa Monica Mountains Conservancy; commr. environ. affairs, L.A. Democrat. Roman Catholic. Avocations: carpentry, organic gardening, environmental concerns.*

BEGLEY, LOUIS, novelist, retired lawyer; b. Stryj, Poland, Oct. 6, 1933; came to U.S., 1948, naturalized, 1953; s. Edward David Begley and Frances Hauser; m. Sally Higginson, Feb. 11, 1956 (div. May 1970); children: Peter Higginson, Amey B. Larmore, Adam C.; m. Anne Muhlstein Dujarric de la Riviere, Mar. 30, 1974. AB summa cum laude, Harvard U., 1954, LLB magna cum laude, 1959. Bar: N.Y. 1961. Assoc. Debevoise & Plimpton, N.Y.C., 1959-67, ptnr., 1968—. Author: Wartime Lies, 1991, The Man Who Was Late, 1993, As Max Saw It, 1994, About Schmidt, 1996, Mistler's Exit, 1998, Schmidt Delivered, 2000, Das Gelobte Land, 2001, Shipwreck, 2003; author: (with Anka Muhlstein) Venedig unter vier Augen, 2003; contbr. articles and revs. to newspapers and periodicals. With U.S. Army, 1954-56. Recipient Irish Times-Aer Lingus Internat. Fiction Prize, 1991, PEN/Hemingway Found. award, 1992, Prix Medicis Etranger, 1992, Harold U. Ribalow prize, 1992, award in Lit., Am. Acad. Arts and Letters, 1995, Jeanette Schocker prize, 1995, Konrad-Adenauer-Stiftung Literaturpreis, 2000, Chevalier de l'Ordre des Arts et Lettres. Mem. Am. Philos. Soc., PEN Am. Ctr. (pres. 1993-95, trustee 1995-2001), Coun. Fgn. Rels., Century Assn. Democrat. Office: Debevoise & Plimpton 919 3rd Ave 46th Fl New York NY 10022-3904

BEGUHN, SANDRA E. poet, author; b. Kirksville, Mo., Nov. 3, 1942; d. Charles Elwin and Loeta Elaine (Payton) Funk; m. Lynn L. Beguhn, June 29, 1963; children: Kelly Lyn Beguhn Simpson, John Christopher. Student, MaryCrest Coll., Davenport, Iowa, 1962-63. Contbr. poetry to Capper's Weekly, Lyrical Iowa, Nat. Libr. of Poetry, Creative Arts and Enterprises. Mem.: Poetry Guild, Durango Colo. Poetry Gathering, Famous Poets Soc., Sparrowgrass Poetry Forum, Illiad Press, Mu Chi Sigma Soc. (pres.). Methodist. Avocations: travel, photography, writing. Home: 2115 W 34th St Davenport IA 52806-5301 E-mail: xalthim@mchsi.com.

BEGUM, MOMOTAZ, medical researcher, consultant, educator; b. Dhaka, Bangladesh, Oct. 7, 1960; came to U.S., 1994; d. Mohammad and Begum Jahanara Ali; m. Hashib Deen Faruque, June 24, 1984; 1 child, Munim Hasib Deen. MB, BChir in Med. Scis., U. London, Dhaka, Bangladesh, 1984; MPH in Health Edn. and Promotion, U. Okla., 1997. Lic. to practice medicine, Bangladesh. Med. officer Rushmono Gen. Hosp., Dhaka, 1985-88, Iran, 1988-91; resident med. officer Dhaka Med. Coll. Hosp., 1993-94; sr. med. officer, counselor maternal and child health and family planning New Al-Rajhi Hosp., Dhaka, 1994; staff physician, physician mgr. Internat. Ctr. Diarrhoeal Diseases Rsch., Dhaka, 1994; grad. rsch. asst. dept health promotion scis. U. Okla. Med. Ctr., Oklahoma City, 1995-96, grad. rsch asst. urinary incontinence project col. pub. health, 1996, grad. rsch asst. Ctr. Prevention Rsch. Native Ams., 1996-97, rsch asst. II Ctr. Am. Indian Health Rsch., 1997-98. Pub. health educator, prodn. editor newsletter Okla. State Dept. Health, Oklahoma City, 1998-99, also edn. rsch. specialist maternal and infant health family planning divsn., 1997; extern Birth and Beyond, Okla. State Med. Assn., Oklahoma City, 1999; cons. Johnson & Johnson, 1996, Worksite Health Screening Programs, Oklahoma City, 1996-97; rschr., cons. Ctr. Am. Indian Health Rsch., 2000—. Organizer Multicultural Social, Internat. Students spring Activity Day, Grad. Studnet Orientation, Internat. Student Awareness Day, Multicultural Award Banquet, mistress of ceremony, Internat. Student Assn., Coll. Pub. Health, U. Okla. Med. Ctr., Oklahoma City, 1996, rep., pres., 1995-97, v.p. Internat. Student Orgn., 1995-97; vol. Carter Hospice Care, Oklahoma City, 1995-97; alumni rep. Faculty-Student Task Force Reaccreditation Self-Study, Coll. Pub. Health, 1998—99. Recipient All-Am. Scholar Collegiate award, U.S. Achievement Acad., 1997, Outstanding Health Edn. Student award, Okla. Pub. Health Assn., 1996. Mem. Bangladesh Med. Assn., Dhaka Med. Coll. Student Orgn. (Patient Welfare Soc. and Blood Donation chpt.), Internat. Student Assn. U. Okla. Med. Ctr.(pres., Outstanding Internat. Student award 1996-97), Alpha Epsilon Lambda (U. Okla. chpt.). Avocations: organizing activites, meeting people with diverse backgrounds, travel, music, cooking.

BEHBEHANI, ABBAS M. clinical virologist, educator; b. Iran, July 27, 1925; came to U.S., 1946, naturalized, 1964; s. Ahmad M. and Roguia B. (Tasougi) B.; married; children— Ray, Allen, Bita BA, Ind. U., 1949; MS, U. Chgo., 1951; PhD, Southwestern Med. Sch., U. Tex., 1955. Asst. prof. Baylor U. Coll. Medicine, Houston, 1960-64; assoc. prof. pathology U. Kans. Sch. Medicine, Kansas City, 1967-72, prof., 1972-90, prof. emeritus, 1990—. Author three books, 5 chpts. in books, more than 70 articles. Fellow Am. Acad. Microbiology; mem. AAAS, Am. Soc. Microbiology, Soc. Exptl. Biology and Medicine Moslem. Achievements include current research on history of smallpox, history of yellow fever and Persian founders of Islamic medicine during middle ages. Home: 5415 Hazen Ave Kansas City KS 66106-3229 Office: U Kans Med Ctr Dept Pathology & Lab Med Kansas City KS 66160-0001 E-mail: kulgener@kumc.edu.

BEHL, WISHVENDER KUMAR, research chemist; b. Dhariwal, Punjab, India, Dec. 26, 1935; arrived in U.S., 1962; s. Amar Nath and Vidya Wati (Trehan) B.; m. Ravi K. Sharma, Feb. 15, 1977; children: Vikas, Renuka. BSc in Chemistry with honors, U. Delhi, India, 1955, MSc in Phys. Chemistry, 1957, PhD in Phys. Chemistry, 1962; postdoctoral rsch. scientist, NYU, 1962-64, Postdoctoral rsch. assoc. Brookhaven Nat. Lab., Upton, N.Y., 1964-67; jr. chem. asst. Govt. Test House, Calcutta, India, 1957-58; rsch. chemist U.S. Army Rsch. Lab., Adelphi, Md., 1967—. Contbr. over 60 articles to profl. jours. Recipient Rsch. and Devel. Achievement award, Dept. of Army, 1999, 2001. Fellow Am. Inst. Chemists; mem. Am. Chem. Soc. (mem. exec. com. Monmouth County sect. 1971-74), Electrochem. Soc. Achievements include inventor and holder of 28 U.S. patents in area of ambient temperature lithium and lithium-ion batteries and high temperature molten salt batteries.

BEHLAR, PATRICIA ANN, political science educator; b. New Orleans, Jan. 16, 1939; d. James Edward and Maude Albertine (Davis) B. BA, U. New Orleans, 1966; MA, La. State U., 1968, PhD, 1974. Instr. Northwestern State U. of La., Natchitoches, 1971-72; instr. Pan Am. U., Edinburg, Tex., 1974-76, asst. prof., 1976-77, U. Ark., Pine Bluff, 1977-84, Pittsburg (Kans.) State U., 1986-92, assoc. prof., 1992—2003, ret., 2003. Mem. U. Ark. Pine Bluff Winthrop Rockefeller lectures steering com., 1980-82; referee Ark. Polit. Sci. Jour., 1983-84; alt., edit. com. Univ. Press of Kans., 1991-93; mem., edit. com. Univ. Press of Kans., 1993-95; book rev. editor, The Midwest Quarterly, 1994-03; faculty cons. Ednl. Testing Svc., 1999. Contbg. author ref. books. Audio reader for the blind, Pittsburg, 1992; vol. March of Dimes, 2003. Recipient La. State U. fellowship, 1970-71. Mem. Am. Polit. Sci. Assn., Sou. Polit. Sci. Assn., Kans. Polit. Sci. Assn., Southwestern Social Sci. Assn., Phi Kappa Phi. Democrat. Roman Catholic. Avocations: reading, walking, bird watching. Home: 508 Hobson Dr Pittsburg KS 66762-6315

BEHLEN, CHARLES WILLIAM, poet, consultant; b. Slaton, Tex., Jan. 29, 1949; s. Stinson Robert and Oleta Elizabeth B. Poet-in-the-schs. Tex. Commn. on the Arts, Austin, 1984—. Poet-in-the-schs. N. Mex. Arts Divsn., Santa Fe, 1985, Ark. Arts Coun., Little Rock, 1986; judge Louzelle Rose Barclay Lit. Contest, Belton, Tex., 1978, Univ. Tex., San Antonio, 1983, 86; coord. Tex. Cir., Austin, 1978. Author: Perdition's Keepsake, 1978, Dreaming at the Wheel, 1988. Dobie-Paisano fellow Univ. Tex., Austin, 1995-96, Frank Waters fellow Frank Waters Found., Taos, N. Mex., 1996. Unitarian Universalist. Avocations: book collecting, fine cigars, gourmet coffees. Home: 503 W Industrial Dr Apt B Sulphur Springs TX 75482 E-mail: cwbehlen@yahoo.com.

BEHLING, CHARLES FREDERICK, psychology educator; b. St. George, S.C., Sept. 8, 1940; s. John Henry and Floy (Owings) B.; m. Jennifer Crocker; children: John Charles, Andrew Crocker. BA, U. S.C., 1962, MA, 1964, Vanderbilt U., 1966, PhD, 1969. Asst. dean of students U. S.C., Columbia, 1962-63; asst. state news editor The State Newspaper, Columbia, 1963-64; asst. prof. psychology Lake Forest (Ill.) Coll., 1968-74; assoc. prof. Lake Forest Coll., 1974-88, chmn. dept., 1977-84; pvt. practice psychotherapy Lake Bluff, Ill., 1970-88, Buffalo, 1988-95; clin. assoc. prof. SUNY, Buffalo, 1988-95; dir. of undergraduate studies, 1989-95; adj. prof. U. Mich., Ann Arbor, 1995—; dir. intergroup rels., conflict and cmty., 1995—. Contbr. articles to profl. jours. Bd. dirs. Nat. Abortion Rights Action League, Planned Parenthood; mem. long-range planning com. Lake Bluff Bd. Edn. Named Outstanding Prof., Underground Guide to Colls., 1971, Birnbaum Guide, 1992, Outstanding Tchr., Lake Forest Coll., 1981, SUNY, Buffalo, 1991; NASA fellow. Mem. Am. Psychol. Assn., Soc. Psychol. Study of Social Issues, Assn. Humanistic Psychology, AAUP, Univ. S.C. Alumni Assn., Psi Chi, Sigma Delta Chi. Democrat. Office: U Mich Dept Psychology Ann Arbor MI 48109 Address: 1325 Wynnstone Dr Ann Arbor MI 48105-2894

BEHLMAR, CINDY LEE, business manager, consultant, speaker; b. Smyrna, Tenn., July 4, 1959; d. James Wallace and Barbara Ann (Behlmar) Gribble. BBA, Coll. William and Mary, 1981; MBA, Old Dominion U., 1995. Cert. mgmt. acct. Adminstrv. extern Hampton (Va.) Gen. Hosp., 1981-82; from mktg. rep. to supr. mktg. svcs. PruCare of Richmond, Va., 1983-85; exec. dir. PhysicianCare, Inc., Newport News, Va., 1986-89; provider rels. cons. Va. Health Network, Richmond, 1989-91; ind. cons. Tidewater Health Care, Virginia Beach, Va., 1991-92; COO Tidewater Phys. Therapy, Inc., Newport News, 1993-95; ind. cons. Yorktown, Va., 1996-97; contract mgr. Sentara Health Mgmt., Virginia Beach, 1998-99; state mgr. managed care Va. Oncology Assocs., 1999—. Sec., bd. dirs. Greater Peninsula Area Med.-Bus. Coalition, Newport News, 1987-89; symposium faculty mem. Am. Hosp. Assn., Orlando, Fla., 1987, Washington, 1988; profl. spkr. in field. Mem. ch. coun. St. Mark Luth. Ch., Yorktown, Va., 1988-91. Fin. Exec. Inst. scholar, 1993. Mem. Inst. Mgmt. Accts., Toastmasters Internat. (club pres. 1997-98, area gov. 1998-99, Club Toastmaster of Yr. 1997-98, Dist. Spirit Success award 1998, Dist. Area Gov. of Yr. 1998-99, Disting. Toastmaster 1999), Phi Kappa Phi, Beta Gamma Sigma. Avocations: reading, music theory and piano, art and fashion. Home: 922 Hanson Dr Newport News VA 23602-8910 Office: Va Oncology Assocs Bldg 200 895 Middle Ground Blvd Newport News VA 23606-4250 E-mail: CiLeBe@aol.com., cindy.behlmar@usoncology.com.

BEHLMER, RUDY H., JR., director, writer, film educator; b. San Francisco, Oct. 13, 1926; s. Rudy H. and Helen Mae (McDonough) B.; 1 child by previous marriage, Curt; m. Stacey Endres, Oct. 1992. Student, Pasadena Playhouse Coll., 1946-49, Los Angeles City Coll., 1949-50. Dir. Sta. KLAC-TV, Hollywood, Calif., 1952-56; network TV dir. ABC-TV, Hollywood, 1956-57; TV comml. producer-dir., exec. Grant Advt., Hollywood, 1957-60; exec. producer-dir. Sta. KCOP-TV, Hollywood, 1960—63; v.p., TV comml. producer-dir. Hollywood office Leo Burnett USA, 1963-84; lectr. film Art Ctr. Coll. of Design, Pasadena, Calif., 1967-92, Calif. State U., Northridge, 1984-92, UCLA, 1988. Author: Memo from David O. Selznick, 1972, (with Tony Thomas) Hollywood's Hollywood, 1975, America's Favorite Movies-Behind the Scenes, 1982, Inside Warner Bros., 1985, Behind the Scenes: The Making of..., 1990, Memo From Darryl F. Zanuck, 1993, W.S. Van Dyke's Journal-White Shadows in the South Seas, 1996, Henry Hathaway (a Directors Guild of Am. Oral History), 2001; co-author: The Films of Errol Flynn, 1969; text on Warner Bros. Fifty Years of Film Music, 1973; editor: The Adventures of Robin Hood, 1979, The Sea Hawk, 1982 (Wis./Warner Bros. screenplay series), Warner Bros. 75 Years of Film Music, 1998; contbr. articles on film history, booklets for film music CDs; writer, narrator and on camera participant for DVD's, laserdiscs, and video documentaries. Served with AC, USNR, 1944-46. Mem. Dirs. Guild Am.

BEHM, FORREST EDWIN, glass manufacturing company executive; b. Lincoln, Nebr., July 31, 1919; s. Forrest E. and Lisle (Jacobson) B.; m. Ethel E. Groth, Aug.11, 1943; children: Courtney Ann, Douglas, Brian, Gregory. BS, U. Nebr., 1941, LL.D., 1965, LHD, 1991. Foreman to plant mgr. Corning (N.Y.) Glass Works and affiliates, 1946-55; div., sales and mfg. mgr. Corning Glass Works, 1955-61, v.p., 1961-65; pres., bd. dirs. Corning Internat. Corp., 1965-75; sr. v.p., mem. mgmt. com., bd. dirs. Corning Glass Works, 1975-82, sr. v.p. ops., 1982-83, dir. quality, 1983-87; pvt. practice, 1987—. Bd. examiners Malcolm Baldridge Nat. Quality award, sr. examiner, 1989, 90, judge for N.Y. State Quality award, 1991, 92. Author: Saving a Great Company, 2001. Served to maj. AUS, 1942-46. Mem. All Am. Football at Nebr., 1940, Nebr. Football Hall of Fame; elected to Nat. Coll. Football Hall of Fame, 1988. Mem. Beta Gamma Sigma. Clubs: Corning Country. Republican. Presbyterian. Home: 3 Briarcliff Dr Corning NY 14830-3328 Office: 80 E Market St Ste 303 Corning NY 14830-2722

BEHM, MARK EDWARD, university administrator, consultant; b. Balt., Apr. 21, 1945; s. Carl and Margaret Anderson (Weichman) B.; m. Linda Ann Walker, Oct. 9, 1976; children: Scott Anderson, Craig Redgwick. BS, U. Md., 1967, MBA, Loyola Coll., Balt., 1980. Co-owner Applied Light Tech. Co., Silver Spring, Md., 1968-69; product area adminstr. Singer Co., Link Div., Silver Spring, Md., 1969-73; asst. comptroller U. Md. Balt. County (UMBC), 1973-75, dir. fin. planning, 1976-85, dir. planning and budget, 1986-88, v.p. for adminstrv. affairs, 1988—, also mem. adv. bd. Tech. Enterprise Ctr. Founding mem., bd. dirs. Grant-a-Wish Found., Balt., 1979-87, Baltimore County Govt. Econ. Devel. Commn., BWI Partnership Bd.; steering com. Md. Ctr. for Indsl. Energy Efficiency; econ. devel. subcom. Md. Info. tech. Bd.; chmn. Troop 880 com. Boy Scouts Am. Mem. Assn. Univ. Rsch. Parks, Ea. Assn. Coll. and Univ. Bus. Officers (bd. dirs.). Home: 13809 Princess Anne Way Phoenix MD 21131-1521 Office: U Md Baltimore County (UMBC) 1000 Hilltop Cir Baltimore MD 21250-0001

BEHNER, ELTON DALE, dentist; b. Oberlin, Ohio, Sept. 6, 1952; s. Wayne Edwin and Velma Jean (Sevison) B.; m. Brenda Kay Crabtree, Aug. 18, 1974 (div. July 1982); m. Annette Lynn Brunst, Oct. 27, 1984: children: Nicolas, Ryan, Tadd. Student, Andrews U., 1971-74; BS, Loma Linda U., 1976; DDS, Ind. U., 1984. Diplomate Am. Bd. Dental Examiners, cert. Invisalign tech., 2002. Staff technologist clin. lab. Loma Linda (Calif.) U. Hosp., 1976-77, rsch. technologist, 1977-79; sr. technologist Ind. U. Hosp., Indpls., 1982-84; asst. prof. sch. dentistry Ind. U., Indpls.; grad. residency Ind. U. Med. Ctr., Indpls., 1984; pres. Dental Care Today, PC, Indpls., 1985—. Coord., cons. dental svc. Am. Surgery Ctr., Indpls., 1987—; active mem. staff dental svc. Wishard Meml. Hosp., Indpls. Fellow Acad. Gen. Dentistry; mem. ADA, Am. Acad. Cosmetic Dentistry, Ind. Dental Assn., Indpls. Dist. Dental Soc., Crown Coun. Avocations: flying, model bldg., restoring sport cars, skiing, boating. Office: Dental Care Today PC 9744 Lantern Rd Fishers IN 46038-9612 E-mail: dbehner@prodigy.net.

BEHNEY, CHARLES AUGUSTUS, JR., veterinarian; b. Bryn Mawr, Pa., Nov. 30, 1929; s. Charles Augustus and Victoria Parks (Wythe) B.; m. Joan M. Langdon, Nov. 15, 2000; children: Charles Augustus III, Keenan F. BS, U. Wyo.; DVM, Colo. State U., 1961. Owner Cochise Animal Hosp., Bisbee, Ariz., 1961—; veterinarian, dir. S.W. Traildust Zoo, Bisbee, 1966—; owner Ultra Mini Ranch, Bisbee, 1969—. Assoc. prof. Cochise Coll.; chmn. Comprehensive Health Planning, Cochise County, Ariz., 1968. Mem. Ariz. Coun. for the Hearing Impaired, 1999. Mem. Am. Vet. Med. Assn., Soc. for Breeding Soundness, Internat. Platform Assn., Rotary, Elks. Republican. Episcopalian. Achievements include patents in ultrasound device and eye cover for treating infections, apparatus to alter equine leg conformation, external vein clamp, equine sanitation instrument; development of ear implant instrumentation system; patent for Farrier's rasp with measure. Home and Office: PO Box 4337 Bisbee AZ 85603-4337 E-mail: dodeeclare@aol.com.

BEHNEY, CLYDE JOSEPH, health policy researcher; b. Williamstown, Pa., May 19, 1946; s. Clyde J. Behney and Gladys Yvonne (Host) Williams; m. Nancy L. Kenney, Sept. 12, 1981; children: Lindsay, Fletcher, Taylor. BS, Lehigh U., 1968; MBA, U. Md., 1972; postgrad., George Washington U., 1975-82. Staff asst. U.S. Dept. Health, Edn., & Welfare, Washington, 1972-74, mgmt. intern, 1974-77; analyst/project dir. Office Tech. Assessment U.S. Congress, Washington, 1977-81, health program mgr. Office Tech. Assessment, 1981-93, asst. dir. Office Tech. Assessment, 1993-96; dir. divsn. health care svcs. Inst. Medicine, NAS, 1996-97, dep. dir., 1997—, interim exec. officer, 1998. Exec. dir. The Sorcerer's Apprentice Network, Washington, 1981—85, 1998—; mem. steering com. Nat. Health Policy Forum, 1998—2000; mem. quality awards adv. bd. Health Improvement Inst., 1998—; adv. com. mem. George Washington Univ. Pub. Health Program, 1999—; mem. tech. adv. bd. Millbank Meml. Fund, N.Y.C., 1998—. Co-author: Toward Rational Technology in Medicine, 1981; author/co-author chpts. in 9 books; editor: (newsletter) The Sorcerer's Apprentice, 1981-85; mem. editl. bd. Internat. Jour. Tech. Assessment in Health Care, 1985-98; contbr. articles to profl. jours. Treas. Glebe Elem. PTA, Arlington, Va., 1990—94, Swanson Mid. Sch. PTSA, Arlington, 1994—96, Yorktown H.S. PTA, 2001—02. Sgt. U.S. Army, 1969—71. Home: 2515 N Vermont St Arlington VA 22207-4125 E-mail: cbehney@nas.edu.

BEHNKE, DOLEEN, computer and environmental specialist, consultant; b. Alameda, Calif., Sept. 23, 1950; d. Charles Joseph Ziegler and Dola Faye (Cushing) Peterson; m. Glen A. Pellett, June 26, 1971 (div. 1986); children: Mark Dolan Pellett, Michael Jay Pellett; m. Danny L. Carr, Dec. 29, 1986 (div. 1996); m. Jon T. Behnke, June 28, 1996. BA, U. Wis., Madison, 1973. Notary pub. Mich. Budget analyst Ednl. Testing Svc., Princeton, N.J., 1979-80; tech. recruiter Uniforce Svcs., Inc., Rock Hill, S.C., 1983-84; mgr. tng. and documentation Electronic Data Systems Corp., Troy, Mich., 1985-87; tech. writer, trainer, analyst cons. CES, Inc., Troy, 1989-92; pres. D'Carr Co., Inc., Roseville, Mich., 1988-93; tech. writer, trainer, cons. Eaton Corp., Southfield, Mich., 1988-93; pres., CEO Carr-Ben Tech Ltd., Lake Orion, Mich., 1996—97, bd. dirs. Cons. Hazardous Materials Info. Exch., Washington, 1989—; installer, instr. Gt. Plains Acctg., Fargo, ND, 1990—; cons., tech. writer Saturn Corp., 1991—92, Blue Cross Blue Shield, Southfield, Mich., 1992—93, Southfield, 1995—96; tech. writer FANUC Robotics, N.A., Inc., Auburn Hills, Mich., 1993—95. Co-author: CIW-Weld Monitor, 1990, 1993. Mem.: AARP, NAFE, AAUP, Greater Trenton Musicians Union, Key Club (mktg. dist. chair 2002—, dist. chair 2002—, dist. adminstr. 2003—), Oxford-Orion Kiwanis, Kiwanis Internat. (internat. com. K-Kids 2001—), Roseville Kiwanis (pres. 1995, lt. gov. elect 1996—97, lt. gov. 2001—02, cert. Kiwanis instr. 2002—), Am. Legion. Republican. Roman Catholic. Avocations: piano, swimming, computers, politics. E-mail: dfb876@charter.net.

BEHNKE, ELIZABETH DOELKER, community volunteer, retired nurse; b. Sheboygan, Wis., Oct. 4, 1926; d. Adolf Gustav and Gertrud Anna (Geissler) Doelker; m. Leroy J. Behnke, Nov. 2, 1963. RN, Mercy Hosp. Sch. Nursing, Oshkosh, Wis., 1954; BS in Pub. Health Nursing, U. Minn., 1960. RN, Wis. Dir. nursing Vis. Nurse Assn., Oshkosh, 1954-56; staff nurse Kanton Hosp, Zurich, Switzerland, 1956-57; pub. health nurse Washington County, West Bend, Wis., 1957-58; dir. nursing Manitowoc County Pub. Health Nurses, Manitowoc, Wis., 1960-63, Calumet County Pub. Health Nursing, Chilton, Wis., 1964-74; nurse supr. for health svc. Lakeshore Tech. Coll., Cleveland, Wis., 1974-88. Bd. dirs. Planned Parenthood Assn., Manitowoc, 1978-80; mem. Commn. on Aging, Manitowoc, 1988-89; past bd. dirs. Manitowoc County Cancer Soc., Mental Health Assn., Easter Seal Soc.; vol. Mobile Meals of Manitowoc, 1988—. Mem. Wis. Nurses Assn. (hon. life; bd. dirs., program com. chair). Lutheran. Avocations: reading, walking. Home: 3206 Wildwood Dr Manitowoc WI 54220-2343

BEHNKE, HENRYK JORG, marketing and fundraising executive; b. Berlin, Mar. 24, 1968; came to U.S., 1995; s. Henning Kurt Behnke and Angelika Dietz. MBA, Tech. U. Berlin, 1995, Fla. Atlantic U., 1998. Small bus. exec. Car-Rental H. Behnke, Berlin, 1987-91; mktg. mgr. Bekum Maschinenfabriken GmbH, Berlin, 1988-90; corp. rels. mgr. Bund fur Umwelt und Naturschutz e.V., Bonn, Germany, 1994-95; fundraising assoc. Fla. Atlantic U. Found. Inc., Boca Raton, Fla., 1996-98; membership assoc. Am. Ballet Theatre, N.Y.C., 1998; dir. mktg. and devel. LSA Social Svcs., N.Y.C., 1999-2000; v.p. devel. Staten Island (N.Y.) Inst. Arts and Scis., 2000—03; bd. mem. ARTS Inc., N.Y.C., 2002—; v.p. mktg. and devel. Staten Island Inst. Arts and Scis., NY, 2003—. Cons. ARTS Inc., N.Y.C., 1998—. Mem.: Assn. Fundraising Profls. Avocations: classical music, scuba diving, eco-travel. Home: 334 Ogden Ave Apt 2 Jersey City NJ 07307 Office: Staten Island Inst Arts & Scis 75 Stuyvesant Pl Staten Island NY 10301 E-mail: emailhenryk@aol.com.

BEHNKE, WALLACE BLANCHARD, JR., consultant, engineer, retired utility executive; b. Evanston, Ill., Feb. 5, 1926; s. Wallace Blanchard and Dorothea (Bull) B.; m. Joan F. Murphy, Sept. 24, 1949; children: Susan F., Ann B., Thomas W. BS, Northwestern U., 1945, BSEE, 1947. Registered profl. engr., Ill. With Commonwealth Edison Co., Chgo., 1947-89, dist. supt. Crystal Lake, Ill., 1956-58, div. engr. Joliet, Ill., 1958-60, area mgr. Mount Prospect, Ill., 1960-62, div. v.p. Chgo., 1962-66, asst. to pres., 1966-69, v.p., 1969-73, exec. v.p., 1973-80, vice chmn., 1980-89. Hon. dir. Northwestern Meml. Hosp.; mem. U.S. Nat. Com. Cigrè; bd. dirs. IEEE Found. Lt. USNR, 1943-56. Fellow IEEE (bd. dirs. 1990-91; mem. NAE, IEEE Power Engring. Soc. (pres. 1987-89), Am. Nuclear Soc., Western Soc. Engrs. (pres. 1975-76), Comml. Club Chgo., Kiawah Island Club, Country Club of Lexington. Phi Delta Theta. Home and Office: 323 Glen Eagle Ct Johns Island SC 29455-5728 E-mail: wbehnkejr@aol.com., w.behnke@ieee.org.

BEHNKE, WILLIAM ALFRED, landscape architect, planner; b. Cleve., Jan. 7, 1924; s. Walter William and Constance Helen (Ireson) B.; m. Virginia E. Woolever, Sept. 18, 1948; children: Lee, Deborah, Mitchel, Mark. B.Landscape Architecture, Ohio State U., 1951. Designer Grier Riemer Assos., Cleve., 1951-55; prin. William A. Behnke, Cleve., 1955-57; asso. Charles L. Knight, Cleve., 1957-58; partner Behnke, Szynyog & Ness, Cleve., 1958-61, Behnke, Ness & Litten, Cleve., 1961-70; mng. partner William A. Behnke Assoc., Cleve., 1970-89; ret. Assoc. prof. Kent State U., 1973-74; pres. Ohio State Bd. Landscape Archtl. Examiners, 1973; vice-chmn. Ohio Bd. Unreclaimed Strip Mined Lands, 1973-74; bd. dirs. Landscape Architecture Found., 1981-85, pres., 1983; mem. adv. bd. Trust for Pub. Lands, 1988—. Mem. Ohio Arts Coun., 1983-84; pres. metro bd. Lake County YMCA, 1989-90; bd. dirs. Ohio Presbyn. Retirement Svcs., Breckenridge Village, 2002. Served with USNR, 1943-46. Named Distinguished Alumnus Ohio State U., 1978; inductee Willoughby-Eastlake Sch. Dist. Hall of Fame, 1999. Fellow Am. Soc. Landscape Architects (v.p. 1977-79, pres. 1980-81). Home: 37334 Harlow Dr Willoughby OH 44094-5758 Office: William Behnke Assocs Inc 700 St Clair Ave W # 416 Cleveland OH 44113-1230 E-mail: wbehnke@earthlink.net. *I am gratified with the knowledge that my livelihood is achieved from a profession that has as its goal the betterment of mankind.*

BEHNKEN, WILLIAM JOSEPH, art educator, artist; b. N.Y.C., Mar. 29, 1943; s. William Henry and Margaret Mary (Hoolan) B. BA, CCNY, 1968, MA, 1995. Dir. art sch. Provincetown (Mass.) Art Assn. Mus., 1984-93; prof. art Bronx (N.Y.) C.C., 1973-83, CCNY, 1970—; instr. studio art Art Students League, N.Y.C., 1998—; instr. printmaking Sch. Fine Arts Nat. Acad. Design, 2001—. Artist print edits. lithographs, aquatints, mezzotints; represented in permanent collections at Met. Mus. Art, N.Y.C., Fitzwilliam Mus., Cambridge, Eng., Brit. Mus., N.Y. Pub. Libr. Print Divsn., Bklyn. Mus., Bowdoin Coll. Mus., Indpls. Mus. Fine Arts, Mus. Nat. Acad. Design, Jane Voorhees Zimmerli, Mus. Rutgers U., Mus. City N.Y., New Orleans Mus. Recipient Luis Lozowick awards Audubon Artists Soc., N.Y.C., 1991, 92. Mem. Soc. Am. Graphic Artists

(pres. 1998-2002), NAD (graphics prize 1992, Ralph Fabri Graphics prize 2003, instr. 2001—), Boston Printmakers, Phi Beta Kappa (pres. CCNY Gamma chpt. 2001). Democrat. Home: 3415 Fort Independence St Bronx NY 10463-4507

BEHR, ALAN ANDREW, lawyer, writer, photographer; b. Paterson, N.J., Aug. 18, 1954; s. Ludwig Louis B. and Sary Behr Fox; m. Julie Lyn Hackett, Sept. 24, 1994. BA cum laude, U. Pa., 1976; JD, Columbia U., 1979, postgrad., 1980. Bar: N.Y., U.S. Ct. Appeals (2d cir.), U.S. Dist. Ct. (so. and ea. dists.) N.Y. Assoc. Dreyer and Traub, N.Y., 1985-86, Newman, Tannenbaum, Helpern, Syracuse & Hirschtritt, N.Y., 1986-87; atty. intellectual property and corp. Met. Life Ins. Co., N.Y.C., 1987-95; v.p. legal and bus. affairs GT Interactive Software Corp., N.Y.C., 1995-2000; gen. counsel w-Trade Technologies, Inc., N.Y.C., 2000; counsel N.Y. office Alston & Bird, 2000—. Spkr. in field. Author: Once Around the Fountain, 2001; contbr. numerous articles and photographs to profl. jours., newspapers, mags., and lit. revs.; photo exhbns. include Leica Gallery, N.Y.C., 2001; group shows include Leica Gallery, N.Y.C., 2002. Mem. Am. Intellectual Property Law Assn., Copyright Soc. U.S.A. (program com. N.Y. chpt.), Assn. of Bar of City of N.Y., N.Y. New Media Assn., Christian Den Fjerdes Laug, Penn Club. Republican. Avocations: opera/concerts, mus., lit., theatre, skiing. Home: 190 E 72nd St New York NY 10021-4370 Office: Alston & Bird 90 Park Ave New York NY 10016-1387

BEHR, DONALD JAY, retired internist, cardiologist, educator; b. N.Y.C., Feb. 3, 1927; s. Siegfried S. and Beatrice F. (Joachimson) B.; m. Barbara R. Price, Dec. 19, 1950; children: Bruce M., Jill Behr Medved, Eric H. BA, NYU, 1949; BM, MD, Chgo. Med. Sch., 1953. Diplomate Am. Bd. Internal Medicine. Intern Queens Gen. Hosp., Jamaica, N.Y., 1953-54; resident Kings County Hosp., Bklyn., 1954-57; pvt. practice, Oceanside, N.Y., 1957-90; sr. phys. cons. Island Peer Rev. Orgn. Inc., Lake Success, N.Y., 1990—. Assoc. vis. physician Kings County Hosp., Bklyn., 1957-80, physician cardiac clinic, 1957-76; clin. asst. prof. medicine SUNY Downstate Med. Ctr., Bklyn., 1973-97; asst. prof. clin. medicine SUNY Coll Medicine, Stony Brook, 1978-99; electrocardiographer South Nassau Cmtys. Hosp., Oceanside, 1966-88, pres. med. bd., 1986-88. Contbr. articles to med. jours. With USN, 1945-46. Fellow Am. Coll. Chest Physicians, Nassau Acad. Medicine; mem. ACP, Nassau County Med. Soc. (peer rev. com. 1974-90). Avocations: tennis, photography. Home: 3404 Tull Rd Oceanside NY 11572-5632

BEHR, MARION RAY, artist, writer, business executive; b. Rochester, N.Y., Sept. 12, 1939; d. Justin Max and Sophie Gusta (Koffler) Rosenfeld. B.Art Edn., Syracuse U., 1961, M.F.A., 1962; m. Omri Marc Behr, June 24, 1962; children: Dawn Marcy Yael, Darrin Justin Mason, Dana Marisa Jana. Contbr. publs. for stories, crafts, mag. covers and toy designs to nat. mags. including McCall's, Good Housekeeping, Lady's Circle, 1962-77; one-woman shows include Douglas Coll., 1983, Pargot Gallery, 1989, Eldorado Gallery, 1992, Beamsderfer Gallery, 1992, Hunterdon Art Gallery, 1993; Hunterdon Mus. Art, 1998; Inst. Cultural Peruano Norteamericano, 1999, Johnson Gallery, 2002; exhibited in group shows at Contemporary Am. Artists, Scarsdale, N.Y., 1964, Douglass Coll., 1977, John Szoke Gallery, 1989, Kanagawa Prefectual Gallery, Yokohama, Japan, 1989, 80 Washington Sq. East Gallery, N.Y.C., 1990, Juniper Gallery, Napa, Calif., 1991, Eldorado Gallery, Colorado Springs, Colo., 1992, B. Beamsderfer Gallery, Highland Park, N.J., 1992, Artsquad Gallery, Easton, 1993, Lever House, 1995, Audubon Artists, 1995, 97, 99, Cork Gallery, 1996, Cheltenham Ctr. for Arts, 1996, Krasdale Gallery, 1998, Nat. Acad. Mus., 1998, Stark & Stark, 1998, Grounds for Sculpture, 2001, Zimmerli Art Mus., Rutgers U., New Brunswick; permanent print collection Smithsonian Instn. Nat. Mus. Art History, 1995, Jane Voorhees Zimmerli Art Mus., 1993, 96, 2002, Thai Royal Art Collection, Bangkok, 1995, Inst. Cultural Peruano Norteamericano, Peru, 1999; creator survey Women Working Home-the Invisible Workforce, 1978; pres. Women Working Home, Inc., Edison, N.J., 1980—; condr. workshops; author: (with others) Women Working Home: The Homebased Business Guide and Directory, 1981, 2nd edit., 1983; contbr. articles to popular mags., 1988-89, popular art jours., 1991-98, numerous articles to profl. jours.; illustrator Jewish Holiday Book, 1977; inventor (with Omri Behr) acid free, environmentally safe graphic etching process; installed Electrotech processor and taught first non toxic intaglio etching class at Stanford U., 1999; installed electroetch and established non-toxic etching in the Inuit Artists Holman Eskimo Co-op Art Center, Holman Island, NWT, Canada, 1999, U. Al Moutamid IBN Abbad, Asilah, Morocco, 2000, Howard U., Washington, Syracuse U., N.Y., 2001, U. Alaska, Juneau, U. Alaska, Fairbanks, 2001; extensive radio and TV appearances rep. Nat. Alliance Homebased Businesswomen. Mem. Kean for Gov. campaign, 1981; mem. White House Conf. on Free Enterprise Zones, 1982, Nat. Assn. of Women Artists, 1992, Soc. Am. Graphic Artists, So. Graphics Coun., 1992, Print Coun. N.J., 1993; trustee Women's Bus. Ownership Ednl. Conf., Inc., N.J., 1985; apptd. to N.J. Devel. Authority for Small, Minority and Women's Bus. Commn., 1986; Presdl. del. White House Conf. on Small Bus., 1986. Recipient N.J. Women in Bus. Advocate of the Yr. award SBA, 1984, Merit award Am. Artist Profl. League, Woman of Yr. in Bus. and Industry award, 1985, Audubon Artists Merit award, 1995; Syracuse U. alumni grantee, 1957; Arts and Humanities grantee Charles E. Lindbergh Fund, 1993-94. Mem. Nat. Alliance Homebased Businesswomen (pres. 1980-82, legis. chair 1982-85; originator, founder), Women's Caucus for Art, Audubon Artists. Jewish. E-mail: eee@electroetch.com., electroetch@prodigy.net. *Father Justin Rosenfeld, born 1901 in Schopfloch, Bavaria. Studied law and economics, 1926, employed by bankers Wilhelm Vogt & CO., full responsibility for stories, casting, advertising, licensing, production and distribution of films for German speaking and foreign countries, film producer, president Orbis Film, Berlin.1936, very successfully produced film Razzia in St. Pauli and Mademoiselle Josette, Ma Femme. 1937, compelled by Nazi laws to cease operations completely. Fled to United States in 1938 with wife, Sophie Koffler Rosenfeld. Died in 1947 at 47. Mother- Sophie Koffler Rosenfeld Lustik-teacher and translator of fine languages lived to be 92.*

BEHR, OMRI M. lawyer; m. Marion Behr. BA in Chemistry with honors, Oxford U., 1956, BSc in Organic Chemistry, 1958, MA in Chemistry, 1960; PhD in Organic Chemistry, U. Glasgow, 1961; NIH postdoctoral fellow, Columbia U., 1960-61; LLB/JD, Seton Hall U., 1966. Bar: N.J. 1967, N.Y. 1968, U.S. Dist. Ct. N.J. 1967, U.S. Patent and Trademark Office 1966, U.S. Ct. Customs and Patent Appeals, 1977, U.S. Supreme Ct. 1977; chartered chemist U.K., European chemist. Rsch. chemist U.S. Rubber Co., Inc., Wayne, N.J., 1961-63; patent trainee, agent, atty. Merck & Co., Rahway, N.J., 1963-67; assoc. Ostrolenk, Faber, Gerb & Soffen, N.Y.C., 1967-68; ptnr. Lerner, David & Behr, Newark, 1968-69, Cifelli & Behr, Newark, 1969-72, Omri M. Behr, Newark, 1972-74, Behr & Woodbridge, Princeton, N.J., 1974-76, Omri M. Behr, Princeton, 1976-81, Behr & Adams, Edison, N.J., 1981—. Contbr. articles to profl. jours.; inventor (with Marion Behr) new acid free, environ. safe graphic etching process (patent of week N.Y. Times, May 2, 1992). Del. N.J. White House Confs Small Bus., 1986; moderator N.J. Gov. Conv. Small Bus., 1986; lectr. U.S. Dept. Energy Licensing Seminars, 1983-87; legis. co-chair, mem. nom. com. Nat. Assn. Homebased Bus.; mem. N.J. Small Bus. Devel. Adv. Bd., 1988—; mem. Edison Twp. Rent Control Bd., 1984-94; committeeman Rep. County Middlesex County, N.J., 1989-94. Charles E. Lindbergh Fund: Arts and Humanities co-grantee, 1993-94. Fellow Royal Soc. Chemistry, Royal Inst. Chemistry (U.S. sect., hon sec. 1968-74); mem. ABA, N.J. Bar Assn., Middlesex County Bar Assn., Internat. Fedn. Counsels in Indsl. Property, Am. Indsl. Property Law Assn., Raritan Valley C. of C. (small bus. coun.), Phi Lambda Upsilon. Home: 325 Pierson Ave Edison NJ 08837-3123*

BEHR, RAYMOND ANTHONY, psychiatrist; b. Johannesburg, May 26, 1948; came to U.S., 1976; s. David Chone and Joan Roxanna (Lazarus) B.; m. Avril Pera Galasko; children: Gerald, Nadia, Warren. MD, U. Pretoria, South Africa, 1973. Diplomate Am. Bd. Psychiatry and Neurology (gen. psychiatry and child psychiatry). Intern Pretoria Acad. Hosp., 1974-75; resident in psychiatry L.I. Jewish Med. Ctr., New Hyde Park, N.Y., 1976-78, fellow in child psychiatry, 1978-80, med. dir. project outreach, 1980-81, psychiat. cons. child devel. clinic, 1985-87, dir. adolescent day hosp., 1987-88; coord. law and psychiatry program L.I. Jewish Med. Ctr., Schneider Children's Hosp., New Hyde Park, 1988-93; psychiat. cons. Peninsula Counselling Ctr., Woodmere, N.Y., 1981-85; pvt. practice Great Neck, N.Y., 1980—. Asst. clin. prof. psychiatry Albert Einstein Coll. Medicine Yeshiva U. Fellow Am. Psychiat. Assn. (disting.); mem. AMA, Am. Acad. Child and Adolescent Psychiatry, Am. Soc. Clin. Psychopharmacology. E-mail: raybehr@mail.com.

BEHREND, ALBERT JAMES, surgeon; b. Phila., Nov. 18, 1946; MD, Jefferson Med. Coll., 1972. Cert. surgery. Intern Vanderbilt U. Hosp., Nashville, 1972-74; resident in surgery La. State U. Med. Ctr., New Orleans, 1974-76, Albert Einstein Med. Ctr., Phila., 1976-79; fellow in vascular surgery U. Ill., Chgo., 1981-82; with Grossmont Hosp., La Mesa, Calif. Vol. asst. clin. prof. surgery U. Calif., San Diego. Mem. ACS, AMA, So. Calif. Vascular Soc., Soc. Clin. Vascular Surgery. Office: 5525 Grossmont Center Dr La Mesa CA 91942-3009 E-mail: ajjeff2@juno.com.

BEHREND, DONALD FRASER, environmental educator, university administrator; b. Manchester, Conn., Aug. 30, 1931; s. Sherwood Martin and Margaret (Fraser) B.; m. Joan Belcher, Nov. 9, 1957; children: Andrew Fraser, Eric Hemingway, David William. BS with honors and distinction, U. Conn., 1958, MS, 1960; PhD in Forest Zoology, SUNY, Syracuse, 1966. Forest game mgmt. specialist Ohio Dept. Natural Resources, Athens, 1960; res. asst. Coll. Forestry, SUNY, Newcomb, 1960-63, res. assoc., 1963-67; dir. Adirondack ecol. ctr. Coll. Environ. Science and Forestry, SUNY, Newcomb, 1968-73; acting dean grad. studies Syracuse, 1973-74; asst. v.p. research programs, exec. dir. Inst. Environ. Program Affairs, 1974-79; v.p. acad. affairs, prof., 1979-85; prof. emeritus, 1987—; asst. prof. wildlife mgmt. U. Maine, Orono, 1967-68; provost, v.p. acad. affairs U. Alaska Statewide System, Fairbanks, 1985-87, exec. v.p., provost, 1988; chancellor U. Alaska, Anchorage, 1988-94, chancellor emeritus, 1994—. Mem. patent policy bd. SUNY, 1983-85, chmn. Res. Found. com. acad. res. devel., 1984-85; chmn. 6-Yr. planning com. U. Alaska, 1985-86; bd. dirs. Commonwealth North, 1991-92, Alaska Internat. Ednl. Found., 1997; mem. selection com. Harry S. Truman Scholarship Found.; mem. Pres.'s Commn., NCAA, 1992-95; chmn. spl. com. on student athlete welfare access and equity, 1993-95; chmn. 20th Great Alaska Shootout, 1997. Contbr. numerous articles and papers to profl. jours. Mem. Newcomb Planning Bd., 1967-69; mem., pres. Bd. Edn. Newcomb Cent. Sch., 1967-73; chmn. governing bd. N.Y. Sea Grant Inst., 1984-85; trustee U. Ala. Found., 1990-94. Served with USN, 1950-54. Mem. Alaska Internat. Edn. Found. (bd. dirs. 1997—), Wildlife Soc., Soc. Am. Foresters, AAAS, Phi Kappa Phi (hon.), Sigma Xi, Gamma Sigma Delta, Sigma Lambda Alpha (hon.). Lodges: Rotary (bd. dirs. Fairbanks club 1985-86), Lions (bd. dirs. Newcomb club 1966-67). Avocations: reading, writing, photography, fly fishing, bagpiping. Home: 222 M St Apt #407 Anchorage AK 99501-1907

BEHRENDT, DAVID FROGNER, retired journalist; b. Stevens Point, Wis., May 25, 1935; s. Allen Charles and Vivian (Frogner) B.; m. Mary Ann Weber, Feb. 4, 1961 (dec. Sept 1998); children: Lynne, Liza, Sarah. BS, U. Wis., 1957, MS, 1960. Reporter Decatur (Ill.) Review, 1957-58; reporter Milw. Jour., 1960-70, copy editor, 1970-71, editorial writer, 1971-84, editorial page editor, 1984-95; Crossroads sect. editor Milw. Jour. Sentinel, 1995-98. Home: 1522 N Prospect Ave #1402 Milwaukee WI 53202

BEHRENDT, JOHN CHARLES, geophysicist researcher, writer; b. Stevens Point, Wis., May 18, 1932; s. Allen Charles and Vivian Eulaine B.; m. Donna Ebben, Oct. 6, 1961 (div.); children: Kurt Allen, Marc Russell. Student, Cen. State Coll., Stevens Point, 1950-52; BS in Physics, U. Wis., Madison, 1954, MS in Geology, 1956, PhD in Geophysics, 1961. Cert. geophysicist, Calif. Asst. seismologist Arctic Inst. N.Am., Ellsworth Sta., Antarctica, 1956-58; rsch. assoc. U. Wis., Madison, 1958-64; rsch. geophysicist U.S. Geol. Survey, Denver, 1964-72, Liberia, West Africa, 1968-70, Denver, 1970-72; chief br. of Atlantic-Gulf of Mex. marine geology Woods Hole, Mass., 1974-77; research geophysicist, Antarctic coordinator U.S. Geol. Survey, 1977-95, geophysicist emeritus, 1995—; fellow Inst. Arctic and Alpine Rsch U. Colo., Boulder, 1996—, rsch. scientist, 1996—. Frequent pub. spkr. on Antarctica and other rsch.; advisor U.S. Depts. State and Interior, Washington, 1977—; mem. U.S. del. to Antarctic Treaty Meetings, various countries, 1977-95, various working groups NAS-NRC; rsch. on Antarctic, earthquakes in ea. U.S., Rocky Mountain tectonics, Gt. Lakes geologic structure, Atlantic continental margin of N.Am. and West Africa. Author: Innocents on the Ice: A Memoir of Antarctic Exploration, 1957, 1998 (Colo. Book award for non-fiction 1999); contbr. over 275 articles to sci. jours. Recipient Antarctic Svc. medal U.S. Dept. Def., 1966, Meritorious Svc. award Dept. Interior, 1992, Filice Ippolito Gold medal for Antarctic Rsch., Italian Antarctic Rsch. Program and Acad. Nazionale dei Linceia, 1999. Fellow: AAAS, Geol. Soc. Am., Explorers Club; mem.: Soc. Exploration Geophysicists, Am. Geophys. Union. Avocations: photography, outdoor activities, music. E-mail: behrendj@stripe.colorado.edu.

BEHRENDT, RICHARD LOUIS, academic administrator; BA in Secondary Edn., U. Pitts., 1964, MEd in Secondary Edn., 1965; PhD in Higher Edn., U. Mich., 1980. Tchr. Mt. Lebanon (Pa.) High Sch., 1963, Hempfield Area High Sch., Greensburg, Pa., 1965; departmental asst. U. Mich., Ann Arbor, 1965-66; dir. instnl. rsch. Washtenaw Community Coll., Ypsilanti, Mich., 1967; asst. to pres. Ind. State U., Terre Haute, 1967-68, dir. student rsch., 1968-69; dir. instnl. rsch. Hagerstown (Md.) Jr. Coll., 1969-74, dir. instl. rsch. and dir. personnel svcs., 1974-76, dean of supportive svcs., 1976-81; dean of coll. svcs. Clark County Community Coll., North Las Vegas, Nev., 1982-84; pres. Lincoln Trail Coll., Robinson, Ill., 1984-86, Sauk Valley Community Coll., Dixon, Ill., 1986—. Instr. bus. and speech U. Pitts., 1964; assoc. prof. mgmt. Frostburg (Md.) State Coll., 1971-74; mem. master planning com. Clark County Sch. Dist.; chmn. Washington County (Md.) Bd. Edn. Open versus Traditional Schs. Study Commn.; mem. Employment and Tng. Coun., Clark County, Nev., Pvt. Industry Coun., Nev., steering com. Correctional Ctr. Location, Ill. Contbr. articles to profl. jours. Bd. dirs. Community Theatre of Terre Haute, Family Svc. Agy. of Washington County (Md.), Big Bros. of Washington County, Crawford County (Ill.) Opportunities; v.p. bd. Potomac Playmakers, Md.; gen. vice chmn. United Way of Sterling-Rock Falls, 1988-89, chmn., 1989-90. Mem. Am. Assn. Higher Edn., Coll. and Univ. Pers. Assn., Assn. Instl. Rsch., Nat. Coun. on Community Svcs. and Continuing Edn., Md. Community Coll. Rsch. Group, Md. Community Coll. and Bus. Pers. Officers Assn., Nev. Assn. for Community Edn., Ill. Coun. Pub. Community Colls., Ill. Pres.'s Coun. (chmn. profl. devel. com.), Coun. North Cen. Community Jr. Colls. (sec., treas. 1987-88, 2d v.p. 1988-89, pres. 1989-90), Jaycees (Sterling, Ill. chpt.), Rotary (bd. dirs., pres.), Greater Sterling Area C. of C. (bd. dirs., v.p., pres.), Phi Delta Kappa. Home: 805 E 19th St Sterling IL 61081-1334 Office: Sauk Valley Community Coll 173 Ill Route 2 Dixon IL 61021 E-mail: behrenr@svcc.edu.

BEHRENS, BEREL LYN, physician, academic and healthcare administrator; b. New South Wales, Australia, 1940; MB, BS, Sydney (Australia) U., 1964. Cert. pediatrics, allergy and immunology. Intern Royal Prince Alfred Hosp., Australia, 1964; resident Loma Linda (Calif.) U. Med. Ctr., 1966-68; with Henrietta Egleston Hosp. for Children, Atlanta, 1968-69, T.C. Thompson Children's Hosp., Chattanooga, 1969-70; instr. pediatrics Loma Linda U., 1970-72, with dept. pediatrics, 1972—, dean Sch. Medicine, 1986-91, pres., 1990—; pres., CEO Loma Linda U. Med. Ctr., 1999—. Office: 11175 Campus St Loma Linda CA 92354 E-mail: myhanna@ahs.llumc.edu.

BEHRENS, BRIAN CHARLES, lawyer, associate; b. St. Louis, Sept. 9, 1969; s. Kenneth Charles Behrens and Patricia Ann Osterberg; m. Laura Lee Sak, June 29, 1996. BSBA, U. Mo., Columbia, 1991; MBA, JD, St. Louis U., 1995. Bar: Mo. 1995, Kans. 1996, U.S. Dist. Ct. (we. dist.) Mo. 1995, U.S. Dist. Ct. Kans. 1996. Assoc. Wallace, Saunders, Austin, Brown & Enochs, Overland Park, Kans., 1995-97, Suelthaus & Walsh, P.C., St. Louis, 1997—. Contbr. articles to profl. jours.; staff mem. St. Louis U. Pub. Law Rev., 1993-94. Mem. ABA, Mo. Bar, Kans. Bar Assn. Roman Catholic. Avocations: travel, golf, hockey. Office: Suelthaus & Walsh PC 7733 Forsyth Blvd Fl 12 Saint Louis MO 63105-1817

BEHRENS, ELLEN ELIZABETH COX, writer, counselor, educator; b. Fremont, Ohio, July 25, 1957; d. William Luther and Dorothy Cox. BA in English, Denison U., 1979; MFA in Creative Writing, Bowling Green State U., 1990. Writer in residence Ohio Arts Coun., 1991-94; ednl. devel. counselor Sch. Social Work Delphi Chassis Sys. facility U. Mich., Sandusky, Ohio and Flint, Mich., 1994-2000; mgr. instrnl. design and project mgr. Novations Learning Technologies, Lansing, Mich., 2000—. Adj. faculty Firelands Coll., Terra Tech. Coll., 1988-94; cons. Bowling Green State U., 1991-94. Author: None But the Dead and Dying, 1996; asst. editor: Mid-American Review, 1988-90, fiction editor, 1990-94, advisory editor, 1994—; contbr. short stories to anthologies, Wastelands Rev., Descant, Fiction, Echoes, Paragraph, other literary mags. Individual Artist fellow Ohio Arts Coun., 1992. Mem. Bowling Green State U. Creative Writing Alumni Assn. (bd. dirs. 1990—), Ohioana Lib. Assn. Office: Novations Learning Technologies MSU Rsch Park 3245 Technology Blvd Lansing MI 48910-8546 E-mail: ebehrens@novations.com.

BEHRENS, JAMES WILLIAM, physicist, administrator, author; b. Litchfield, Ill., Apr. 29, 1947; s. George William and Norma Clara Marie (Boeker) B.; m. Pamela Jane Breese, July 7, 1973 (div. Jan. 1980); 1 child, Jaime Rhea; m. Linda Sue Lawrence, July 5, 1984. BS in Engring. Physics, U. Ill., 1970; MS in Engring and Applied Sci., U. Calif., Davis, 1976, postgrad., 1976-78. Physicist Lawrence Livermore (Calif.) Nat. Lab., 1969-78, U.S. Dept. Commerce, Nat. Bur. Stas., Gaithersburg, Md., 1978-89; sci. tech. advisor Joint Chiefs of Staff, U.S. Dept. Def. Joint Staff, Washington, 1989-91; asst. exec. program mgr. Office Asst. Sec. Def. U.S. Dept. Def., Washington, 1991-92; sr. spl. projects mgr. U.S. Dept. Def., USN, Indian Head, Md., 1992-93; asst. dir. U.S. Dept. Def., Interagy. Tng. Ctr., Ft. Washington, Md., 1993-95; dep. dir. Interagy. Tng. Ctr. U.S. Dept. Def., Ft. Washington, Md., 1995-97; dir. U.S. Dept. Def. Ft. Washington Facility, 1997-99; sr. rsch. scientist, engr. U.S. Dept. Def., Naval Rsch. Lab., Washington, 1999—2000. Tech. cons., pres. I.Q. in Nuc. Electronics Sys. & Tech., Inc., Rockville, Md., 1983-89; guest scientist Commissariat à l'Energie Atomique (CEA), Bruyere-le-Chatel, France, 1984. Author: Symbols and Fragments, 1993, Record of the House of Braunschweig-Illinois-Hannover, 1995, The 1995 Behrens Chronicle: A Complete Work, 1996, The 1995 Boeker Chronicle: A Complete Work, 1996, The 1996 Behrens-Boeker Chronicles: A Combined Work, 1997; co-editor: Fifty Years with Nuclear Fission, 1989; contbr. tech. articles to profl. pubs. Mem. Nat. Geneal. Soc., Nat. Writers Assn., Internat. Platform Assn., Nat. Audubon Soc., Nat. Wildlife Fedn., Am. Nuc. Soc. (cert. Appreciation 1989). Independent. Lutheran. Achievements include investigation of fast neutron-induced fission cross section measurements of the actinide elements, improvement of accuracy of neutron-induced fission cross section values which are used in broad areas of applied nuclear physics. Home: 1 Spa Creek Lndg Unit A2 Annapolis MD 21403-2330

BEHRENS, JOHN (JACK), editor, writer, columnist, educator; b. Lancaster, Ohio, Feb. 7, 1933; s. Charles H. and Dorothy Margaret (Pairan) Behrens; m. Patricia Ann Beaty; children: Cynthia Sue Daugherty, Mark Andrew. BS in Journalism, Bowling Green State U., 1955, MA in Journalism History, Pa. State U., 1956. Corr. Korea Bur. Pacific Stars and Stripes, 1957—58; sports editor SAC Times, Korea, 1957—58; sports and wire editor Lancaster (Ohio) Eagle-Gazette, 1958—62; instr., chmn. dept. journalism Ohio Wesleyan U., 1962—63; interim mng. editor Marysville (Ohio) Jour.-Tribune, 1962—63; asst. prof. dept. journalism Marshall U., Huntington, W.Va., 1963—65; summer desk editor Ashland Daily Ind., Ky., 1963—65; asst. prof., publs. editor Utica Coll. Syracuse U., 1965—86; adminstrv. asst. on media rels. to Rep. Walter H. Moeller, 1965—68; Reader's Digest Found. prof. mag. journalism Utica Coll. Syracuse U., 1969—97; adminstrv. aide to Dr. Virgil Crisafulli, del. to N.Y. Constnl. Conv., 1969—85; editor UC Pioneer Mag., 1969—85; editing cons., 1985—2001; dir. pub. rels./journalism programs Utica Coll. Syracuse U., 1986—92; editor Commerce Commentary Quar., 1969—; bus. columnist The Elks Mag., 1976—; assoc. editor Am. Printer Mag., 1978—2000; editor HomeBus. Jour. Mag., 1995—2001. Curator CMA Student Press Archives, 1968—; host, founder CBS/WIBX/Utica Coll. Roundtable Sunday, 1994—; assoc. editor Coll. Press Review, Am. Journalism History, 1970—89; editor Laubach's Literacy Advance Mag., 1984—86. Author: The Writer's Handbook, 1968; author: (with Allan Neuharth) Reporting Worktext, 1974; author: The Typewriter Guerrillas, 1977; author: (with Alex Haley) The Writing Business, 1992; author: Pioneering Generations, 1946-1997, 1997, The Big Band Days: A Memoir and Source Book, 2003; editor: Wood and Stone: Landmarks of the Mohawk Valley, 1972, School of Art: The First Fifty Years, 1991; contbr. (over 11,000 articles to profl. jours. and mags.). Trustee Village of Clinton, 1992—; mem. Village Planning Bd., Clinton, 1980—92. With U.S. Army, 1956—58, Korea. Named Journalist of Yr., Fairfield County (Ohio) Friends of Libr., 1984; named to Hall of Fame, Lancaster (Ohio) H.S., 1995; recipient Outstanding Writer award, Nazareth Coll., 1971, Outstanding Comm. award, St. Bonaventure, 1972, Nat. Disting. Svc. award, NCCPA, 1975, Gold Key award, Columbia U. Scholastic Press Assn., 2000. Mem.: Am. Soc. Journalists and Authors, Oneida County Hist. Soc. (bd. dirs., chmn. membership com. 1998—), Mohawk Valley Inst. of Learning in Retirement. Avocations: big band historian, power cruiser enthusiast. Home: 57 Stebbins Dr Clinton NY 13323

BEHRENS, MYLES MICHAEL, neuro-ophthalmologist; b. N.Y.C., Oct. 26, 1938; s. Alvin Behrens and Anne Beth (Sleppin) Figman; m. Roberta Alice Kinstler Jaeger, Aug. 23, 1964 (div. 1967); m. Susan Ruth Page, Nov. 20, 1970 (div. 1976); m. Marsha Carole Miller, June 7, 1981; 1 child, Adam James. BA, Yale U., 1958; MD, Columbia U., 1962, D in Med. Sci., 1970. Diplomate Nat. Bd. Med. Examiners, Am. Bd. Ophthalmology. Intern and resident in medicine Columbia-Presbyn. Hosp., N.Y.C., 1962-64; clin. assoc. NIH-NIAID, Bethesda, Md., 1964-66; resident in ophthalmology Columbia-Presbyn. Hosp., 1966-70; Heed fellow in neuro-ophthalmology U. Calif. Med. Ctr., San Francisco, 1970-71; attending in ophthalmology, chief neuro-ophthalmology clinic Columbia-Presbyn. Hosp., 1971—; prof. clin. ophthalmology Columbia U., 1987—. Contbr. over 90 articles to profl. jours.; mem. editl. bds. major ophthalmol. and neurol. jours. Mem. adv. bd. Heed Found. Lt. comdr., USPHS, 1964-66, Bethesda. Recipient Lucien Howe prize N.Y. State Med. Soc., 1989, Philip Knapp Meml. tchg. award Harkness Eye Inst., 1992, Heed Found. award, 1986. Fellow Am. Acad. Ophthalmology (sr. honor award 1990), N.Am. Neuro-Ophthalmology Soc., N.Y. Acad. Medicine (chmn. sect. ophthalmology 1996-97). Jewish. Office: Columbia-Presbyn Med Ctr 635 W 165th St New York NY 10032-3701

BEHRENS, RICHARD JAMES, language educator; b. Chateroux, France; s. Clifford Hiram and Lidia Carmen Carlota B.; m. Monika Hill, May 20, 1989; children: Joshua, Jessica, Ryker. MS in Human Resource, U. Ctrl. Tex., 1990; MEd in Counseling, U. Hawaii, 2001. Legal rschr. Corp. Counsel, Honolulu, 1979-80; asst. mgr. Foodland, Honolulu, 1980-81; mgr. Sam's Hawaiian Shop, Waikiki, Hawaii, 1981-83; commd. 2nd lt. U.S. Army, 1983, advanced through grades to lt. col., 2002, resigned, 1995; resident mgr. Hawaiiana Property Mgmt., Inc., Honolulu, 1995—; counselor Nanaikapono Elem. Sch., Waianae, Hawaii, 2001—02; instr. English, counselor St. John Berchmans Sch., San Antonio, 2002—. Counselor State Dept. Edn., Pearl City, Hawaii, 2000. Contbr. articles to profl. jours. Constl. conv. candidate Rep. Com., Honolulu, 1978; lay eucharistic min., 1991—. Lt. col. U.S. Army Res., 1995—. Decorated Meritious Svc. ribbons, Army Commendation medals. Mem. Hell on Wheels 2nd Armored Divsn. (life), Am. Counseling Assn., K. of C. (3rd order knight), 3rd Order of Mary (life). Republican. Roman Catholic. Avocations: surfing, swimming, biathalons, running, body building, writing. Office: Saint John Berchmans Sch 1147 Cupples Rd San Antonio TX 78226 E-mail: harrypotter.3@netzero.net.

BEHRENS, WILLIAM BLADE, television program syndication executive; b. Burlington, Vt., Oct. 17, 1956; s. Robert Allen and Elizabeth (Husk) B. BA in Psychology, Emory U., 1978. Video/audio tech. WXII-TV, Winston-Salem, 1979-80; v.p. sales Behrens Co.-Behrens Prodns., Miami, Fla., 1980-87; S.E. sales mgr. Access Syndication, Studio City, Calif., 1987-88, The Great Entertainment Co., N.Y.C., 1988-90; dir. syndication World Sports Syndication, Atlanta, 1988-91; S.E. sales mgr. Colbert TV Sales, L.A., 1988—; v.p. Litton TV Syndications, Balt., 1989-94; pres. Show Bus., Inc., Atlanta, 1989—; dir. southeast sales Polygram Television/ITC, Beverly Hills, Calif., 1994-98; v.p. Nat. Wrestling Alliance, 1998—2002, bd. dirs. Music editor Emory Wheel, 1977-78; contbr. articles to profl. jours. Mem.: Nat. Assn. TV Program Execs., Nat. Assn. TV Arts and Scis., Am. Film Inst. Avocations: collecting films, animation cells, records and comic books, fishing. Home: PO Box 941787 Atlanta GA 31141-0787

BEHRING, DANIEL WILLIAM, educational and business professional, consultant; b. Sheboygan, Wis., Jan. 9, 1940; s. Melvin William and Frieda (Ostwald) B.; m. Nancy Jean Steeno, July 28, 1962; children: Deanna, Shelley, Tanya, Jonathan. BA, Ripon Coll., 1962; MA, Ohio U., 1964, PhD, 1969. Tchg. fellow Ohio U., Athens, 1965-66, acting instr., 1966; asst. prof. So. Ill. U., Edwardsville, 1968-71; dean students, asst. prof. Monmouth Coll., Ill., 1971-76; assoc. prof., v.p. Alma Coll., Mich., 1976-86; v.p. acad. affairs Adrian (Mich.) Coll., 1986-91, interim pres., 1988-89; v.p., dir. schs. Cranbrook Edn. Cmty., 1991-95; pres. SQT Sys., 1995—. Assoc. prof. DeVos Grad. Sch. Mgmt., 1998-2000, prof., 2000-; cons. colls., high schs., mental health orgns., busi-

nesses, mfrs. and C. of C. Contbr. articles to profl. jours. Bd. dirs. Hoogerland Meml. Workshop, St. Louis, Mich., 1977-86, Lenawee Tomorrow Econ. Devel. Assn., 1989-91, Lenawee Symphony, 1986-91, Farm Credit Svcs., 1990-94; reviewer United Way, Alma, 1983, 84; bd. dirs. Prodn. Credit Assn., 1990-94. Capt. U.S. Army, 1966-68. Grantee Kellogg Found., 1976-80, U.S. Office Edn., 1977, 78, 79, Lilly, 1988, Towsely Found., 1989, State of Mich., 1989, 91. Mem. APA, Am. Assn. Higher Edn., Rotary (pres. 1983-84, bd. dirs. Adrian chpt.), Oakland County Bus. Roundtable, Sigma Xi, Sigma Chi (Grand Consul Merit award 1984). Avocations: numismatics, studebaker automobiles, model trains, science, sailing. Home and Office: 3695 Lakeshore Dr Manistee MI 49660-9760

BEHRINGER, SAMUEL JOSEPH, JR., lawyer; b. Detroit, Oct. 6, 1948; s. Samuel Joseph and Evania Theresa (Cherry) B.; m. Linda Suzanne Gross, Sept. 7, 1979; 1 child, Kathryn Elizabeth. BS in Labor & Indsl. Rels., Mich. State U., 1970; JD, U. Detroit, 1973. Bar: Mich. 1974, U.S. Dist. Ct. (ea. dist.) Mich. 1974, U.S. Ct. Claims 1975, U.S. Tax Ct. 1975, U.S. Ct. Appeals (6th cir.) 1974, U.S. Supreme Ct. 1980. Asst. U.S. atty. Ea. Dist. Mich., Detroit, 1974-80; group v.p., gen. counsel Mich. Nat. Bank, Detroit, 1980-83; atty. pvt. practice, Grosse Pointe Farms, Mich., 1983—. Chmn. young lawyers sect. 6th cir. admission ceremony State Bar Mich., 1975-83. Contbr. articles to profl. jours. Recipient Merit commendations U.S. Dept. Justice, 1977, 78, Spl. commendation Outstanding Svc. U.S. Atty. Gen., 1979. Mem. NRA, ABA, Fed. Bar Assn. (chmn. chpt. host. com. of nat. conv. Detroit 1985, mem. exec. bd. Detroit chpt. 1979-81), Detroit Bar Assn., Comml. Law League Am., Oakland County Bar Assn., Am. Corp. Counsel Assn., Assn. Trial Lawyers Am., Elks, Phi Kappa Tau, Gamma Eta Gamma. Home: 333 McKinley Ave Grosse Pointe MI 48236-3420

BEHRMAN, BRUCE WARD, social sciences educator; b. Peoria, Ill., Sept. 15, 1934; s. Carl Martin and Elwin Ward Behrman; m. Rileyne Elizabeth Brown; children: Zachary, Matthew. BA, Bradley U., 1956, MA, 1957; JD, Northwestern U., 1962; PhD, Purdue U., 1967. Asst. prof. Calif. State U., Sacramento, 1967—70, assoc. prof., 1970—77, prof., 1978—. Cons. in field, 1980—. Contbr. articles to profl. jours. Mem.: Am. Psychology & Law Soc., Am. Psychol. Soc., Phi Kappa Phi. Independent. Presbyterian. Office: Calif State U Dept Psychology 6000 J St Sacramento CA 95819

BEHRMAN, EDWARD JOSEPH, biochemistry educator; b. N.Y.C., Dec. 13, 1930; s. Morris Harry and Janet Cahn (Solomons) B.; m. Cynthia Fansler, Aug. 29, 1953; children: David Murray, Elizabeth Colden, Victoria Anne. BS, Yale, 1952; PhD, U. Calif. at Berkeley, 1957. Research asso. biochemistry Cancer Research Inst., Boston, 1960-64; bd. tutors biochem. scis. Harvard, 1961-64; asst. prof. chemistry Brown U., Providence, 1964-65; mem. faculty Ohio State U., Columbus, 1965—, asso. prof. biochemistry, 1967-69, prof., 1969—. Rschr. in peroxydisulfate and nucleotide chemistry. Contbr. articles to profl. jours. USPHS fellow, 1955-56, 57-60; NSF grantee, 1966-73; NIH grantee, 1973-81 Mem. Am. Chem. Soc., Royal Soc. Chemistry, Phi Beta Kappa, Sigma Xi. Home: 6533 Hayden Run Rd Hilliard OH 43026-9642 Office: Ohio State U Dept Biochemistry Columbus OH 43210 E-mail: behrman.1@osu.edu.

BEHRMAN, HAROLD RICHARD, endocrinologist, physiologist, educator; b. Sask., Can., Nov. 26, 1939; s. Henry Fred and Minnie Alice (Waslenko) B.; m. Carol Hope O'Rourke, Aug. 8, 1981; children: Tracy Lee, Terri Lynne, Russell Norman, Kevin Michael, Kathleen Hope. BS, U. Man., (Can.), 1962, MA, 1965; PhD, N.C. State U., 1967; MS (hon.), Yale U., 1982. Research fellow Harvard U. Med. Sch., Boston, 1967-71, asst. prof., 1971-72; dir. reproductive biology Merck Inst., Rahway, N.J., 1972-75; assoc. prof. gynecology and pharmacology Yale U., New Haven, 1975-81, prof. ob-gyn. and pharmacology, 1981—, dir. reproductive biology sect., 1975—. Cons. NIH, 1978-83, 91-95, USDA, 1985, NSF, 1985, Med. Rsch. Coun. Can., 1990-91. Recipient Research award Lalor Found., 1971-72; Fulbright-Hays Disting. prof., 1978; MRC Can. fellow, 1967-70; recipient Alta. Heritage Vis. Prof. award, 1983 Mem. AAAS, Am. Physiol. Soc., Endocrine Soc., Soc. Study of Reprodn., Soc. Endocrinology, Can. Physiol. Soc. Home: 790 Green Hill Rd Madison CT 06443-2404 Office: Yale U Dept Ob-Gyn 1303A Yale Sta New Haven CT 06520

BEHRMAN, RICHARD ELLIOT, pediatrician, neonatologist, university dean; b. Phila., Dec. 13, 1931; s. Robert and Vivian (Keegan) Behrman; m. Ann Nelson, Aug. 14, 1954; children: Amy Jane, Michael Jameson, Carolyn Ann, Hillary. AB, Amherst Coll., 1953; JD, Harvard U., 1956; MD, U. Rochester, 1960; DSc (hon.), Med. Coll. Wisc., 2000. Diplomate Am. Bd. Pediat. (examiner). Intern Johns Hopkins Hosp., Balt., 1960—61, resident in pediat., 1963—65; asst. prof. pediat. U. Oreg. Sch. Medicine, Portland, 1965—67, assoc. prof., 1967—68; prof. U. Ill. Coll. Medicine, Chgo., 1968—71; prof., chmn. dept. pediat. Columbia U. Coll. Physicians and Surgeons, N.Y.C., 1971—76; prof., chmn. dept. Case Western Res. U. Sch. Medicine, Cleve., 1976—81, dean Sch. Medicine, 1980—89, v.p. med. affairs, 1987—89; dir. dept. pediat. Rainbow Babies and Children's Hosp., Cleve., 1976—81; dir. Ctr. for Future of Children, 1989—99; sr. v.p. med. affairs Lucile Packard Found. for Children's Health, Palo Alto, Calif., 1999—2002, chmn. bd., 1996—99; dir. Lucile S. Packard Children's Hosp./Stanford Health Svcs., Stanford, UCSF-Stanford Health Care; exec. chair pediat. edn. steering com. Fedn. Pediat. Orgns., 2002—. Author: Neonatology: Diseases of the Fetus and Infant, 1973, Neonatal-Perinatal Medicine, 1977; editor: Nelson's Textbook of Pediatrics, 1978, 1983, 1987, 1992, 1995, 2000, 2003, Essentials of Pediatrics, 1989, 1993, 1997, 2001; editor-in-chief: The Future of Children, 1990, mem. editl. bd., sect. editor fetal and neonatal medicine: Jour. Pediat., 1970—85, assoc. editor, mem. editl. bd., cons. editor: Pediat. Rsch. Jour., 1971—80. With USPHS, 1961—63. Fellow, Wyeth pediat., 1963—65; scholar, Whipple, 1960—61, Univ., U. Rochester, 1960. Fellow: Am. Acad. Pediat.; mem.: Soc. Gynecol. Investigation, Perinatal Rsch. Soc. (coun. 1970—73), Inst. Medicine of NAS, Soc. Pediat. Rsch. (v.p. 1976—77), Century Assn., Sigma Xi. Episcopalian. Home: 15 Crest Rd Belvedere Tiburon CA 94920-2433 E-mail: rbehrman@jopo.org.

BEHRMANN, JOAN GAIL, newspaper editor; b. N.Y.C. d. Jerome and Jeanette (Silberman) Metzner; m. Larry Jinks, Oct. 2, 1960 (div. 1970); children: Laura Jinks Kastigar, Daniel Carlton; m. Nicolas Lee Behrmann, Dec. 21, 1972. BA, Queens Coll., 1956; MS, Columbia U., 1958. Reporter Charlotte (N.C.) Observer, 1958-60, Miami (Fla.) Herald, 1960-64, Miami News, 1965-66; asst. prof. Miami Dade C.C., 1968-72; assoc. prof. Boston U., 1975-78; Sunday editor The Saratogian, Saratoga Springs, NY, 1979-80; editor Gannett Westchester, Westchester County, N.Y., 1981-83; page one editor, entertainment editor USA Today, Rosslyn, Va., 1983-87; exec. editor The Desert Sun, Palm Springs, Calif., 1987-95; arts editor The Detroit News, Detroit, 1996-2000; ret., 2000; freelance writer Trash or Treasure column, theater revs. Detroit News, Detroit, 2001—. Co-author: Questioning Media Ethics, 1978. Bd. dirs. Coll. of the Desert Found., Palm Desert, 1993-95, Jewish Family Svcs., Palm Springs, 1994-95, Palm Springs Opera Guild, 1989-91, Adult Well-Being Svcs., Detroit, Mich., 1997-2000, Mich. Opera Theatre, 2000—; founder Every Women's Coun., Glens Falls, N.Y., 1978-80. Recipient Athena award Palm Springs C. of C., 1991. Mem. Assn. Press Mng. Editors Orgn. (bd. dirs. 1991-96, com. chair 1996-97), Am. Soc. Newspaper Editors. Avocations: travel, reading. E-mail: jbehrmann@aol.com.

BEHUNIAK, PETER, psychometrician, educational psychologist, educational consultant; b. Derby, Conn., Feb. 11, 1950; s. Peter and Stella (Spak) Behuniak; m. Gail Ann Tomala, Mar. 8, 1986; 1 child, Alexander T. BS with high honors, U. Conn., 1971, MA, 1973, PhD in Ednl. Psychology, 1981; postgrad., U. Mass., 1975-77. Cert. tchr. Conn. Tchr. Glastonbury (Conn.) Pub. Schs., 1971-78; rsch. asst. U. Conn. Bur. Ednl. Rsch., Storrs, 1979-80; pres. Edn. Resource Assocs., Glastonbury, 1980-83; edn. cons. Conn. Dept. Edn., Hartford, 1983-89, coord. student assessment, 1989-91, chief Bur. Evaluation and Student Assessment, 1991-92, dir. student assessment and testing, 1992—2002, chief bur. cert. and profl. devel., 2002—03; pres. Criterion Consulting, LLC, 2001—; prof. in residence, dept. ednl. psychology U. Conn., Storrs, 2002—. Lectr. U. Conn., Storrs, 1980—85, U. Bridgeport, Conn., 1982—83, Ea. Conn. State U., 1987—89; adj. faculty U. Hartford, dir. student assessment, 1988—2001; mem. validity panel Nat. Assessment Ednl. Progress, 2000—; prof. ednl. psychology U. Conn., 2003—. Contbr. articles to profl. jours. Mem. evaluation com. Cmty. Coun. Capital Region, Hartford, 1984—87; bd. overseers N.E. Regional Labs.; pres. Edn. Adminstrs. Union, Conn. State Dept. Edn.; chmn. tech. guidelines for performance assessment Coun. Chief State Sch. Officers; Nat. Coun. Measurement Edn. rep. Joint Com. Testing Practices; bd. dirs. S.E. Conn. Civil Liberties Union, Windham, 1977—80, Mem.: Am. Evaluation Assn. (presenter), Nat. Coun. Measurement Edn. (presenter), Am. Ednl. Rsch. Assn. (presenter), Phi Delta Kappa. Avocation: photography. Office: Conn State Dept Edn PO Box 2219 Hartford CT 06145-2219 E-mail: PeterBehuniak@cox.net.

BEIDLER, MARSHA WOLF, lawyer; b. Bridgeton, N.J., Feb. 29, 1948; d. Benjamin and Esther (Lourie) Wolf; m. John Nathan Beidler, Aug. 18, 1974; children: Dora E., Evan A. BA, Dickinson Coll., Carlisle, Pa., 1969; JD, Rutgers U., Camden, N.J., 1972; LLM in Taxation, NYU, 1979. Bar: Pa. 1972, Fla. 1973, N.J. 1975; Fla. bar bd. cert. tax lawyer. Estate and gift tax atty. IRS, Phila., 1972-74, Trenton, N.J., 1974-76; atty. McCarthy & Hicks, Princeton, N.J., 1976-81; ptnr. Pinto & Beidler, Princeton, 1981-83; prin. Smith, Lambert, Hicks & Miller, Princeton, 1983-88; ptnr. Drinker, Biddle & Reath, Princeton, 1988—. Sec. Mercer County Estate Planning Council, 1977-86; prof. paralegal studies Rider Coll., Trenton, 1982; lectr. estate planning various corps. and univs. Bd. dirs. Birth Alternatives, Princeton, 1980; bd. dirs. Mercer Council on Alcoholism, Trenton, 1985-86. Fellow Am. Coll. Trusts and Estate Counsel; mem. ABA (taxation sect., real property, probate and trust sect.), Fla. Bar Assn., N.J. Bar Assn. (taxation sect.). Office: Drinker Biddle & Reath 105 College Rd E PO Box 627 Princeton NJ 08542-0627 E-mail: beidlemw@dbr.com.

BEIDLER, PETER GRANT, English educator; b. Bethlehem, Pa., Mar. 13, 1940; s. Paul Henry and Margaret (Grant) B.; m. Anne E. Gilbert, June 15, 1963; children: Paul, Kurt, Gretchen, Nora. BA, Earlham Coll., 1962; MA, Lehigh U., 1965, PhD, 1968. Asst. prof. English Lehigh U., Bethlehem, Pa., 1968-72, assoc. prof., 1972-77, prof., 1977—, Lucy G. Moses Disting prof. English, 1978—, acting v.p. for student affairs, 1982-83; Robert Foster Cherry disting. tchg. prof. Baylor U., 1995-96. Author: Fig Tree John: An Indian in Fact and Fiction, 1977; co-author: (bibliography) The Indian in American Short Fiction, 1979; editor: John Gower's Literary Transformations, 1982, Ghosts, Demons and Henry James, 1989, Writing Matters, 1992, Henry James's The Turn of the Screw: Case Studies in Contemporary Criticism, 1995, Geoffrey Chaucer's The Wife of Bath: Case Studies in Contemporary Criticism, 1996, Masculinities in Chaucer, 1998, Chaucer's Wife of Bath: Prologue and Tale: An Annotated Bibliography, 1990-1995, 1998, A Reader's Guide to the Novels of Louise Erdrich, 1999, Native Americans in the Saturday Evening Post, 2000, The Native American in Short Fiction in the Saturday Evening Post, 2001, Why I Teach, 2002. Served with USAF, 1962-68. Named Nat. Prof. of Yr. Coun. for Advancement and Support of Edn., 1983; Fulbright lectr. Sichuan U., Chengdu, Peoples Republic of China, 1987-88; recipient Robert Foster Cherry Disting. Teaching chair Baylor U., 1995-96. Mem. MLA, New Chaucer Soc., Medieval Soc. Am., Phi Beta Kappa, Phi Beta Delta. Office: Lehigh U English Dept 35 Sayre Dr Bethlehem PA 18015-3116 E-mail: pgb1@lehigh.edu.

BEIGHEY, LAWRENCE JEROME, packaging company executive; b. Akron, Ohio, June 24, 1938; s. Jac Laverne and Martha Rose (Vestal) B.; m. Carole Anne LaFlamme, Dec. 11, 1970; children: Basil, Susan, Thomas, Timothy, Elizabeth, Anne. BS in Indsl. Engring., Pa. State U., 1960. Registered profl. engr., Pa.; cert. data processor. Mgr. internat. div. Brockway (Pa.), Inc., 1968-76, mgr. energy div., 1976-78, project mgr., 1978-79, plant mgr., 1979-81, mfg. staff and services, 1981-83; exec. v.p. Brockway Standard, Atlanta, 1983-86, pres., 1986-89; v.p. Brockway, Inc., Jacksonville, Fla., 1986-89; pres. Transition Mgmt. Resources, Atlanta, 1989; v.p., gen. mgr. All-Pak, Inc., Decatur, Ga., 1990; pres. Plastite Corp., 1990-95; mfg. cons., 1995—. Bd. dirs. Boy Scouts Am., DuBois, Pa., 1978-80, YMCA, DuBois, 1981-83; mem. sch. bd. Brockway Area Sch. Dist., 1981-83; pres. Jaycees, DuBois, 1964. Mem. Steel Shipping Container Inst. (bd. dirs. 1986), Data Processing Mgmt. Assn. (bd. dirs. 1966-68), Alpena Country Club, Amelia Island (Fla.) Ocean Club. Avocations: golf, tennis. E-mail: LJBeighey@aol.com.

BEIGHLE, DOUGLAS PAUL, aerospace industry executive, retired; b. Deer Lodge, Mont., June 18, 1932; s. Douglas Paul Beighle and Clarice Janice (Driver) Kiefer; m. Gwendolen Anne Dickson, Oct. 30, 1954 (dec. Jan. 1996); children: Cheryl, Randall, Katherine, Douglas J. BS in Bus. Adminstrn., U. Mont., 1954; JD, U. Mont., 1958, LL.M., Harvard U., 1960. Bar: Mont. 1958, Wash. 1959, U.S. Supreme Ct. 1970. Assoc. Perkins & Coie, Seattle, 1960-67, ptnr., 1967-80; v.p. contracts Boeing Co., Seattle, 1980-81, v.p. contracts, gen. counsel, sec., 1981-86, sr. v.p., 1986-97; chief legal counsel Puget Energy, Inc., Bellevue, Wash., 1970-80; also bd. dirs. Puget Sound Energy Co., Bellevue, Wash., 1981—; chair Puget Sound Energy, Inc., 2002—; exec. dir. Wash. State, U.S. West Comm., Denver, 1990-95, ret., 1995. Bd. dirs. Washington Mut. Inc., Seattle, 1989—, Simpson Investment Co., Seattle, Active Voice Corp., Seattle, Infrastrux Group, Bellevue, Wash.; bd. dirs. KCTS-9 TV, chair 1996—. Nat. bd. dirs. Jr. Achievement, Colorado Springs, 1981-95; bd. dirs. Greater Puget Sound Jr. Achievement, 1983—, Intiman Theatre, Seattle, 1991-93; trustee Mcpl. League Seattle, 1983-88, U. Mont. Found., Missoula, 1983-91, Mansfield Found., Missoula, 1990-95, Pacific Sci. Ctr., Seattle, 1992—, pres. 1996; trustee Corp. Coun. for the Arts, Seattle, 1994—, chair, 1995-96. 1st lt. USAF, 1954-56. Harvard U. Law Sch. fellow, 1959 Mem. Wash. State Bar Assn. (chmn. adminstrv. law sect. 1979-80), Nat. Assn. Mfrs. (bd. dirs., regional vice chmn. 1988-93), Greater Seattle C. of C. (chair 1994-95), Rainier Club Seattle, Seattle Yacht Club. Republican. Presbyterian. Office: 1000 2nd Ave Ste 3700 Seattle WA 98104-1053

BEIGHTOL, SCOTT CHRISTOPHER, lawyer; b. Sioux City, Iowa, May 16, 1963; s. Richard Eugene and JoAnn (Lichty) B.; m. Desiree Kristin Erickson, June 29, 1991; children: Quinn, Ari. BA in English, Holy Cross Coll., 1985; JD, U. Wis., 1988. Bar: Wis., U.S. Dist. Ct. (ea. and we. dists.) Wis. 1988, U.S. Dist. Ct. (so. dist.) Ind. 1998, U.S. Ct. Appeals (7th cir.) Ill. 1988. Assoc. U.S. Dept. Justice, Washington, summer 1987; atty. Michael, Best & Friedrich, Milw., 1988—. Dir. Nat. Worksite Benefits, LLC, Mequon, Wis., 1996—. Sr. editor Wis. Law Review, 1986-88. Dir. Friends of Milw. Pub. Mus., 1994-98, Guest House, 1995-98; mem. Milw. Curling Club, 1994—; trustee Village of Whitefish Bay, Wis., 1998—. Mem. Wis. State Bar (dir. employment sect. 1996—). Republican. Roman Catholic. Avocations: distance running, reading. Office: Michael Best and Friedrich LLP 100 E Wisconsin Ave Ste 3300 Milwaukee WI 53202-4108

BEIGL, WILLIAM, physician, hypnotist, acupuncturist, consultant; b. Chgo., July 9, 1950; s. William C. Beigl and Mary Tomlinson; m. Mavis Johnson, Aug. 5, 1977. BA in Elem. Edn., U. South Fla., 1971; D of Natural Medicine, Acad. Sci. of Man, Sussex, Eng., 1979. Founder "You Too Can Choose Happiness" System, 1975; pvt. practice hypnotherapy Chgo., 1977—; pvt. practice naturopathic medicine, acupuncture and oriental natural medicine, 1979—. Mem. rsch. team Donsbach U., 1980; chief rschr. disease prevention B.P.H. Corp.; bd. dirs. Mid-West Hypnosis Conv.; cons. in field; 1st syndicated hypnosis columnist, 1982; CEO Bill Beigl Enterprises, Inc., 1992, World Hypnosis Orgn., Inc., 1992; guest presenter Paramedics 25th Anniversary Celebration, Phila., 1993, (with Lee Ramsey) Blair Cheese Fest, 1994; devised lowered casino game tables; expert witness on hypnosis Cook County Ct. Sys. Editor, pub. Portage Park News, 1980; originator Paramedic System, 1968 (honored by Pres. Johnson 1968, Pres. Nixon 1969, Pres. Reagan 1985); responsible for Ramped Curbs, Braille Markings on Elevators and Monuments, Handicapped Parking Space, Licence Plates and Pub. Accessibility for Wheelchairs, Lowered Casino Gaming Tables, licensing of naprapaths and naturopaths in Ill., 1994, licensing acupuncturists in Ill., 1997; author: Adventures in Hypnosis, 1990, 2d edit., 1991; contbg. author: Think & Grow Breasts, 1994; contbr. articles on natural healing and hypnosis to newspapers and mags.; patentee in field. Mem. trauma unit Operation Desert Storm, 1991, Infinite Justice & Enduring Freedom, 2001; assoc. bd. mgrs. Robert R. McCormick chpt. Chgo. Boy's Club, 1973; vol. with Hurricane Andrew victims, 1992, Mississippi River flood victims, 1993; summer Centennial Olympics physicians Atlanta, 1996; bd. dirs. Kids Internat., 1996; mem. trauma unit Operation Desert Thunder, 1998; with Small Bus. Nonprofit Orgn. Credit Cards, 1998, Acceptance of Alternative Med. Fees by HMOs, 1999; physician Summer Olympics, Sydney, 2000; involved in passage of Med. Privacy Act, 2001; triage cons. for govt. regarding terrorist Attack on America, 2001. Recipient award Congressman Sidney Yates, 1971, Disease Prevention award Better Positive Health Found., 1979, Pen and Quill award Nat. Bd. for Hypnotherapy and Hypnotic Anesthesiology, 1991, Excellence award Honeywell, 1994, N.Y.C. Humanitarian award for efforts on 9/11/01; named Chicagoan of Yr., Mayor Richard J. Daley, 1968, Chgo. Cath. of Yr., Cardinal John Cody, 1968, Illinoisan of Yr., Gov. Richard B. Ogilvie, 1968, One of 10 Outstanding Young Citizens, Chgo. Jaycees, 1980, Inspirational Mind of Four Profl. Championship Sports Teams, 1983-84, Citizen of Week, Sta. WBBM, 1984; appeared in Ripley's Believe It Or Not, 1984; honored by Gov. James R. Thompson, 1985, U.S. Senator Charles H. Percy, 1986; featured on CBS-TV Portrait Series, 1985, Cablevision's Good Neighbors, 1987; inducted into Internat. Hypnosis Hall of Fame, 1989. Mem. Internat. Naturopathic Assn. (cert., Naturopathic Physician Yr. 1985), Nat. Assn. Naturopathic Physicians (cert.), Nat. Guild Hypnotists (cert.), Assn. Advance Ethical Hypnosis (cert., past v.p., past sec. Ill. chpt., bd. dirs. 1986, participant the biggest hypnosis conv. 1988, co-chmn. world's largest and friendliest 1987-88, 89), World Hypnosis Orgn. (cert.), Am. Naturopathic Assn., Am. Soc. Clin. Hypnosis, Minn. Assn. Naturopathic Physicians (cert.), Hemlock Soc., Chgo. Meml. Assn., Boys Clubs Am. (life, Boy of Yr. 1968), Hospice, Midwest Pain Soc., Pain Clinic Physicians. Lodges: Moose. Office: 2521 W Montrose Ave Chicago IL 60618-1505

BEIHL, FREDERICK, lawyer; b. St. Joseph, Mo., Jan. 26, 1932; s. Ernst F. and Evelyn E. (Kline) B.; m. Lillis Prater, Mar. 3, 1962. AB, U. Mo., 1953, LLB, 1955. Bar: Mo. 1955, U.S. Supreme Ct. 1968. With Shook Hardy & Bacon, Kansas City, 1955-99, ptnr., 1961-99, shareholder, 1992-99. Chmn. bd. dirs. UMKC Conservatory of Music, Kansas City, 1988-91, Visiting Nurses Assn., Kansas City, 1977-79; pres. Heart of Am. Family and Children Svcs., Kansas City, 1982-84, Friends of Art Nelson Mus., Kansas City, 1979-81. Avocations: tennis, skiing, art collecting. Office: Shook Hardy & Bacon 1200 Main St Ste 3000 Kansas City MO 64105-2122 E-mail: fbeihl@shb.com.

BEIK, WILLIAM H. education educator, writer; b. N.Y.C., NY, June 28, 1941; s. Paul H. and Doris Humphrey Beik; m. Mildred Alice Allen, Aug. 15, 1975; children: John Eric Kauffman, Carl Vincent Kauffman. BA, Haverford Coll., 1959—63; MA, Harvard U., 1963—66, PhD, 1966—68. Asst. prof. No. Ill. U., 1969—84, assoc. prof., 1984—90, Emory U., 1990—97, prof., 1997—. Series editor Cambridge U. Press, Cambridge, 1988—. Author: (scholarly study) Absolutism and Soc. in Seventeenth-Century France: State Power and Provincial Aristocracy in Languedoc (Herbert Baxter Adams Prize, 1986), Urban Protest in Seventeenth-Century France: the Culture of Retribution, (collection of docs.) Louis XIV and Absolutism: a Study with Docs. Recipient Herbert Baxter Adams Prize, Am. Hist. Assn., 1986; fellow Woodrow Wilson Fellow, Woodrow Wilson Found., 1963-64, Woodrow Wilson Dissertation Fellowship, 1966-67, Fellow Shelby Cullom Davis Ctr., Princeton U., 1974, NEH Fellow, NEH, 1974-75, ACLS Summer Fellow, Am. Coun. of Learned Societies, 1974, 1984, APS Fellow, Am. Philos. Soc., 1987. Mem.: Soc. for French Hist. Studies (co-president, mem. of bd. 1994—96), Am. Hist. Assn. (mentioned above Herbert Baxter Adams Prize 1986), Phi Beta Kappa. Avocation: maintain historical web site. Office: Dept of History Emory U 561 Kilgo Cir Atlanta GA 30322 Office Fax: 404-727-4959.

BEILENSON, PETER LOWELL, public health official; b. L.A., Feb. 6, 1960; s. Anthony Charles and Dolores (Martin) B.; m. Christina Weininger; children: Valerie, Alex, Jane, Jack. AB, Harvard U., 1981; MD, Emory U., 1987; MPH, Johns Hopkins U., 1990. Family practice intern U. Md., Balt., 1987-88; resident in preventive medicine Johns Hopkins U., Balt., 1989-91, chief resident, 1991-92; commr. Balt. City Health Dept., 1992—. Mem. AMA, APHA (Milton and Ruth Roemer award for creative pub. health 1996). Avocations: sports, coaching youth sports. Office: Balt City Health Dept 210 Guilford Ave Baltimore MD 21202-3621 E-mail: pbeilenson@baltimorecity.gov.

BEILSTEIN, HENRY RICHARD, microbiologist, educator; b. Phila., Dec. 2, 1920; s. Henry Nicholas and Anna Elizabeth (Binder) B.; m. Grace Alta Marple, June 8, 1946; children: Janet Lee Bittner, Richard Alan (dec.), David Richard. BS in Bacteriology, Phila. Coll., 1943, MS in Microbiology, 1961, PhD in Microbiology, 1970. Registered microbiologist Nat. Registry Microbiologists, registered specialist microbiologist. Analytical chemist Merck Sharp & Dohme, Glenolden, Pa., 1943-45; biol. processor, sr. microbiologist Pub. Health Labs., City of Phila., 1945-61; asst. dir. pub. health lab. Health Dept., City of Phila., 1961-70; dir. Pub. Health Labs., Phila., 1970-78; dir. MLT program Manor Coll., Jenkintown, Pa., 1978-86, dir. med. lab. tech. program, 1978-86; assoc. prof. microbiology and immunology Temple U. Sch. Podiatric Medicine, Phila., 1974—; adj. assoc. prof. microbiology and immunology Temple U. Sch. Medicine, Phila. Adj. prof. biology Beaver Coll., Glenside, Pa., 1986-91; assoc. prof. dept. microbiology MCP/Hahnemann Med. Coll., 1970—, adj. assoc. prof. microbiology and immunology, 1995—; adj. faculty microbiology Montgomery County C.C., Pa. State U., Abington, Gwynedd-Mercy Coll., Gwynedd, Pa. Co-author: (book chpt.) Current Diagnosis, 1974, 77 (cassette tapes) Topics in Clinical microbiology, 1972; co-author publ. on microbiology of gonorrhea, pub. by Am. Soc. Microbiology; contbr. articles and reports to profl. publs. Bd. dirs., chmn. Child Evangelism Fellowship of Phila., 1980—, Child Evangelism Fellowship, State of Pa., Harrisburg, 1992. Recipient Legion of Honor award Chapel of 4 Chaplains, 1978, Scientist of the Year, Am. Soc. Microbiology (ea. Pa. br.), 2001. Fellow APHA, Am. Acad. Microbiology Christian Med. and Dental Soc. (exec. coun. 1982—, pres. 1982-84); mem. Am. Sci. Affiliation, Am. Soc. for Microbiology (bd. dirs. Ea. Pa. br. 1980--, pres. 1981-83, Scientist of Yr. Ea. Pa. br. 2001). Avocations: music, photography, stamp collecting, bible study and teaching, travel. Home: 1032 E Mount Pleasant Ave Philadelphia PA 19150-3421 E-mail: beilstein2@juno.com.

BEIM, DAVID ODELL, investment banker, educator; b. Mpls., June 2, 1940; s. Raymond Nelson and Moana (Odell) B.; m. Elizabeth Lucile Artz, Aug. 29, 1964; children— Amy Marie, Nicholas Frederick. BA with honors, Stanford U., 1963; MPhil (Rhodes scholar), Oxford (Eng.) U., 1965. With First Boston Corp., N.Y.C., 1966-75, v.p., 1971-75, head project finance, 1973-75; exec. v.p. Export-Import Bank U.S., Washington, 1975-77; head corp. fin. Bankers Trust Co., N.Y.C., 1978-87, sr. v.p., 1978-79, exec. v.p., 1979-86, mem. mgmt. com., 1986-87; mng. dir. Dillon Read & Co., 1987-89; prof. Bus. Sch. Columbia U., N.Y.C., 1990—. Chmn. Wave Hill, Inc.; trustee Phillips Exeter Acad., Outward Bound, Inc. Mem. Coun. Fgn. Rels. Home: 4684 Dodgewood Rd Bronx NY 10471-3604 Office: Columbia U Uris Hall 711 New York NY 10027

BEIM, NORMAN, playwright, actor, theater director, writer; b. Newark; s. Herman and Frieda (Thau) B.; m. Virginia Rapkin (div.). Student, Ohio State U., Hedgerow Theatre Sch., Phila., Inst. Contemporary Art, Washington. Appeared in Broadway play Inherit the Wind, 1956-58, off-Broadway play Coriolanus, 1953, Black Visions, 1973; nat. touring prodn. Tribute, 1980; plays include The Deserter, (Samuel French award) 1979, Success, 1983, Pygmalion and Galatea, 1984, Archie's Comeback, 1986, Jewel Thieves, 1990, On a Darkling Plain (James Ellis Meml. award 1992), Death Amid the Rich and Famous, 1991, Cri de Coeur, 1991, Dreams (No Empty Theater New Play award 1993), Shakespeare Revisited (Maxim Mazumdar New Play award 1993); author: Six Award Winning Plays, Plays at Home and Abroad, My Family, The Jewish Immigrants, 1997, (novel) Hymie and the Angel, 1998, Giants of the Old Testament, 2001. Mem. Bronx Coun. of the Arts. Served with U.S. Army. Mem. SAG, AFTRA, Dramatists Guild Am., Actors Equity Assn. Home: 425 W 57th St New York NY 10019-1764 E-mail: normanbeim@aol.com.

BEIMERS, GEORGE JACOB, financial executive; b. Grand Rapids, Mich., Dec. 30, 1930; s. Jacob Beimers and Betty Marie (Ashby) Gerold; m. Susannah Shrack, June 5, 1952 (div. 1972); m. Gertrude Hii, Apr. 5, 1986; children: Linda Sue Barrie, Mark George, Pamela Ann. BS in Edn., Western Mich. U., 1952; MEd in Adminstrn., U. Ariz., 1960, MEd in Psychology, 1976; degree in internat. rels., Johns Hopkins U., Bologna, Italy, 1970. Instr. polit. sci. Tucson Pub. Schs., 1957-87; instr. psychology and sociology U. Ariz., Tucson, 1972-87; v.p. New Era Corp., Tucson, 1970-71; pres. Beimers Properties and Investment Co., Tucson, 1972—. Author: Luck, the Human Factor, 1983, Never Kiss a Chinese Dragon, 1992, Gift From the Gods, 1993, 2000, Out of the Mouth of a Chinese Dragon, 1996, Additional Gifts From the Gods, 2000, The Buryat Princess and little America, 2003; editor: Blackboard mag., 1960. With U.S. Army, 1953-55. Recipient Golden Poet award World of Poetry, 1987, 91, award of merit, 1987, 90. Mem. U.S. Boat Owners Assn., Sierra Club, Met. Yacht Club. Republican. Avocations: sailing, photography, scuba diving, tennis, golf. Office: Beimers Properties & Investments PO Box 2667 Port Aransas TX 78373-2667 Home: 12 La Playa Port Aransas TX 78373

BEINECKE, FREDERICK WILLIAM, investment company executive; b. Stamford, Conn., June 3, 1943; s. William S. and Elizabeth (Gillespie) B.; m. Candace Krugman, Oct. 2, 1976; children— Jacob Sperry, Benjamin Barrett BA, Yale U., 1966; JD, U. Va., 1972; P.MD, Harvard U., 1977. Bar: N.Y. 1973. Assoc. firm Hughes Hubbard & Reed, N.Y.C., 1972-73; gen. counsel South Street Seaport Mus., N.Y.C., 1973-75; with Sperry and Hutchinson Co., N.Y.C., 1975-82; pres. Gunlocke Co. subs., 1979-80, corp. v.p., 1977-80, pres., 1980-82, dir., 1977-82; pres. Antaeus Enterprises, Inc., 1982—, also bd. dirs. Bd. dirs. Catalina Mktg. Corp. Trustee Phillips Acad., Andover, Mass., 1980—2000, Wildlife Conservation Soc., 1984—, Outward Bound USA, 1987—2000; pres. Close Encounters with Music, 1995—2003; trustee Sterling and Francine Clark Art Inst., 2000—, Trudeau Inst., Saranac Lake, NY, 1971—98, chmn., 1984—91, 1995—97, chmn. emeritus, 1998—; bd. dirs. Prospect Hill Found., 1962—, Samuel H. Kress Found., 1997—, N.Y.C. Ballet, 1978—88, 1992—2000, 2001—, Sperry Fund, 1977—, pres., 1982—; bd. visitors Yale Sch. Music, New Haven, 1997—; pres. N.Y.C. Ballet, 2003—. Capt. USMC, 1966—69. Decorated Bronze Star. Mem. Assn. Bar City N.Y., River Club, Sky Club, Yale Club, Hollenbeck Club, Clove Valley Club, Knickerbocker Club. Office: Antaeus Enterprises Rm 2200 99 Park Ave New York NY 10016-1601

BEINECKE, WILLIAM SPERRY, corporate executive; b. N.Y.C., May 22, 1914; s. Frederick William and Carrie (Sperry) B.; m. Elizabeth Barrett Gillespie, May 24, 1941; children: Frederick W. II, John B., Sarah S., Frances G. BA, Yale U., 1936, MA (hon.), 1971; LL.B., Columbia U., 1940; LL.D. (hon.), Southwestern U., 1967, Cath. U. Am., 1972, Yale U., 1986. Former asso. firm Chadbourne, Wallace, Parke & Whiteside; co-founder firm Casey, Beinecke & Chase; became gen. counsel The Sperry and Hutchinson Co., N.Y.C., 1952, v.p., 1954-60, pres., 1960-67, chmn. bd., chief exec. officer, 1967-80. Bd. dirs. Antaeus Enterprises, Inc. Pres., bd. dirs. The Prospect Hill Found.; chmn. emeritus Hudson River Found. for Sci. and Environtl. Rsch.; dir. The Sperry Fund; hon. trustee Am. Museum of Natural History, The Pingry Sch.; life trustee Ctrl. Park Conservancy. Served to comdr. USNR, World War II. Recipient Alumni medal Alumni Fedn. Columbia U., 1971, Yale medal, 2000, Frederick Law Olmsted award, 1986. Mem. Yale U. Club, Sky Club, Baltusrol Golf Club, Eastward Ho Country Club, Gulf Stream Golf Club, Ocean Club, Little Club. Home: 21 E 79th St New York NY 10021-0125 Office: Antaeus Enterprises Inc 99 Park Ave #2200 New York NY 10016-1601

BEINEKE, LOWELL WAYNE, mathematics educator; b. Decatur, Ind., Nov. 20, 1939; s. Elmer Henry and Lillie Agnes (Snell) B.; m. Judith Rowena Wooldridge, Dec. 23, 1967; children: Jennifer Elaine, Philip Lennox. BS, Purdue U., 1961; MA, U. Mich., 1962, PhD, 1965. Asst. prof. Purdue U., Ft. Wayne, Ind., 1965-68, assoc. prof., 1968-71, prof., 1971-86, Jack W. Schrey prof., 1986—. Tutor Oxford (Eng.) U., 1974, The Open U., Milton Keynes, England, 1974, 75; vis. lectr. Poly. North London, 1980—81; vis. scholar Wolfson Coll., Oxford U., 1993—94, 2000—01; mem. SCR Keble Coll., 2000—01. Co-author, co-editor Selected Topics in Graph Theory, 3 vols., 1978, 1983, 1988, Applications of Graph Theory, 1979, Graph Connections, 1997, mem. editl. bd., assoc. editor Jour. Graph Theory, 1977—80, editl. bd., 1977—, mem. editl. bd. Internat. Jour. Graph Theory, 1991—95; co-editor: Congressus Numerantium, Vols., 1963—64, 1988; editor-elect The Coll. Math. Jour.; contbr. numerous articles to profl. jours. Corp. mem. Bd. for Homeland Ministries, United Ch. of Christ, N.Y., 1988-91, del. Gen. Synod, 1989, 91. Recipient Outstanding Tchr. award AMOCO Found., 1978, Friends of the Univ., 1992, Outstanding Rsch. award Ind. U.-Purdue U. Ft. Wayne, 1999; Fulbright Found. grantee London, 1980-81, rsch. grantee Office Naval Rsch., Washington, 1986-89; fellow Inst. Combinatorics and its Applications, 1990—. Mem. AAUP, Math. Assn. Am. (chairperson Ind. sect. 1987-88, bd. govs. 1990-93, Disting. Tchg. award Ind. Sect. 1997, Disting. Svc. award Ind. sect. 1998), Am. Math. Soc., London Math. Soc., Common Cause, Amnesty Internat., Summit Book Club, Internat. Affairs Forum, Sigma Xi (club pres. 1984-86, chpt. pres. 1997-98), Phi Kappa Phi (chpt. pres. 1993), Pi Mu Epsilon. Achievements include characterization of line graphs and thickness of complete graphs; enumeration of multidimensional trees. Home: 4529 Bradwood Ter Fort Wayne IN 46815-6028 Office: Ind U-Purdue U Dept of Math Scis 2101 E Coliseum Blvd Fort Wayne IN 46805-1445 E-mail: beineke@ipfw.edu.

BEINERT, HELMUT, biochemist; b. Lahr, Germany, Nov. 17, 1913; came to U.S., 1947; m. Elisabeth Meyhoefer, 1955; 4 children. Dr rer nat, U. Leipzig, 1943; DSc, U. Wis., Milw., 1987, U. Konstanz, Germany, 1994. Rsch. assoc. Kaiser Wilhelm Inst. Med. Rsch., Germany, 1943-45; biochemist Air Force Aeromed Ctr., Germany, 1946, USAF, Sch. Aviation Medicine, 1947-50; postdoctoral rschr. U. Wis., Inst. Enzyme Rsch., Madison, 1950, rsch. assoc., 1951-52, asst. prof. to prof. enzyme chemistry, 1952-84, chmn. section III, 1958-84, prof. biochemistry, 1967-84, emeritus prof. enzyme chemistry and biochemistry, 1984—. Prof. biochemistry, dist. scholar residence Med. Coll. Wis., 1985-94; permanent guest prof. U. Konstanz, Germany, 1967. Recipient Rsch. Career award NIH, 1963, Sr. Scientist award Alexander von Humboldt Found., 1981, Keilin medal Biochem. Soc. London, 1985, Krebs medal Fed. European Biochem. Soc., 1989, Warburg medal German Soc. Biochem. and Molecular Biology, 1994, Lipmann plaque Am. Soc. Biol. Chem. Molecular Biology, 1993. Fellow Am. Acad. Arts and Sci., Wis. Acad. Scis. Arts and Letters; mem. NAS, Internat. EPR Soc., Am. Chemical Soc., Am. Soc. Biol., Chemistry and Molecular Biology, Soc. Biol. Inorganic Chemistry. Office: Univ Wis Inst Enzyme Rsch 1710 University Ave Madison WI 53726-4087

BEIRIGER, EUGENE EDWARD, historian, educator, dean; b. Evergreen Park, Ill., Oct. 18, 1958; s. Edward Raymond Beiriger and Lorraine A. Fletcher; m. Antonia Beiriger, Aug. 16, 1981; children: Alexandra, Anastasia. BA, Northwestern U., Evanston, Ill., 1980; MA, U. Ill., 1981; PhD, U. Ill., Chgo., 1992. Instr. history Roycemore Sch., Evanston, 1985—90; lectr. history Barat Coll., Lake Forest, Ill., 1986—90, instr. history, 1990—92, asst. prof. history, 1992—96, assoc. prof. history, 1996—, assoc. dean acad. affairs, 2001—. Vis. prof. history U. Ill., Chgo., 1997. Author: (book) Churchill, Munitions and Mechanical Warfare, 1998. V.p. Friends of the Pub. Libr., Waukegan, Ill., 1992—94, pres., 1994—96; rep. Chgo. Ctr. for Peace Studies, 1990—94. Recipient Award for Tchg. Excellence, Barat Coll. Bd. Trustees, 1997. Mem.: Chgo. Coun. on Fgn. Rels., N.Am. Conf. on Brit. Studies, Am. Hist. Assn. Avocations: reading, collecting books, baseball, music. Office: Barat Coll of DePaul Univ 700 E Westleigh Rd Lake Forest IL 60045

BEIRNE, MARTIN DOUGLAS, lawyer; b. N.Y.C., Oct. 24, 1944; s. Martin Douglas and Catherine Anne Beirne; m. Kathleen Harrington; children: Martin, Shannon, Kelley. BS, Spring Hill Coll., 1966; JD with honors, St. Mary's U., 1969. Bar: Tex. 1969, U.S. Dist. Ct. (ea. dist.) Tex. 1972, U.S. Dist. Ct. (so. dist.) Tex. 1971, U.S. Dist. Ct. (no. dist.) Tex., U.S. Dist. Ct. (we. dist.) Tex., U.S. Ct. Appeals (5th and 11th cirs.) 1974, U.S. Dist. Ct. (ea. dist.) Calif., U.S. Supreme Ct. 1975. Ptnr. Fulbright & Jaworski, Houston, 1971-85; mng. ptnr. Beirne, Maynard & Parsons, Houston, 1985—. Editor-in-chief St. Mary's Law Rev. Bd. dirs. St. Thomas U., Houston Law Rev. Found., NCCJ. Capt. U.S. Army, 1969-71. Fellow Am. Bar Found., Tex. Bar Found.; mem. ABA, Tex. Bar Assn., Houston Bar Assn., Coronado Club, The Houstonian Club, Legatus-U. Houston Law Sch. Found. Am. Law Inst., Inst. for Transnat. Arbitration. Roman Catholic. Office: Beirne Maynard & Parsons LLP 1300 Post Oak Blvd Fl 25 Houston TX 77056-3028

BEISNER, JOHN HERBERT, lawyer; b. Salina, Kans., Feb. 24, 1953; s. Herbert J. and Matilda (Cordel) B.; m. Diane G. Klinke, Apr. 26, 1980; 1 child, Laura Ann. BA, U. Kans., 1975; JD, U. Mich, 1978. Bar: Calif. 1978, D.C. 1980. Assoc. O'Melveny & Myers, Washington, 1978-85, ptnr., 1985—, mng. ptnr. Washington office, 2000—. Mem. State Colls. Coord. Com. Kans. Bd. Regents, 1974-75. Mem. ABA, Am. Law Inst., Fed. Comm. Bar Assn. Office: O'Melveny & Myers 555 13th St NW Ste 500W Washington DC 20004-1159 E-mail: jbeisner@omm.com.

BEISNER, RALPH ANDREW, judge; BA, Wagner Coll., 1964; JD, Bklyn. Law Sch., 1968. Bar: N.Y. 1968, U.S. Dist. Ct. (so. and ea. dists.) N.Y. 1971, U.S. Ct. Appeals (2d cir.) 1971. Asst. dist. atty. Queens County, N.Y., 1969-73; asst. N.Y. State atty. gen., Poughkeepsie, 1973-79; asst. counsel N.Y. State Legislature, Albany, 1979-80; pvt. practice Clinton Corners, N.Y., 1979-83; judge 9th Jud. Dist. Supreme Ct., Poughkeepsie, 1984—2002.

BEISNER, ROBERT LEE, historian; b. Lexington, Nebr., Mar. 8, 1936; s. Elmer John and Charlene Day Beisner; m. Valerie French, Mar. 6, 1976; children: John Brinton, Katharine Lee, Signe Ann Linscott, John French Allen. Student, Hastings (Nebr.) Coll., 1956; MA, U. of Chgo., 1960, PhD, 1965. Instr. of the social scis. U. of Chgo., 1962—63; instr. of history Colgate U., Hamilton, NY, 1963—65; from asst. prof. to prof. emeritus Am. U., Washington, 1965—98, prof. emeritus, 1998—. Dir. gen. edn. Am. U., 1993—97. Author: Twelve Against Empire: The Anti-Imperialists, 1898-1900, From the Old Diplomacy to the New, 1865-1968, 1975; editor: American Foreign Relations since 1600: A Guide to the Literature, 2003. Recipient Allan Nevins prize, 1966, John H. Dunning prize, 1968. Mem.: Soc. for Historians of Am. Fgn. Rels. (pres. 2002—02). Home: 3851 Newark St NW Washington DC 20016 Personal E-mail: huskerindc@rcn.com.

BEISTLINE, EARL HOOVER, mining consultant; b. Juneau, Alaska, Nov. 24, 1916; s. Ralph H. and Catherine (Krinach) B.; m. Dorothy Ann Hering, Aug. 24, 1946; children— Ralph Robert, William Calvin, Katherine Noreen, Lynda Marie. B. Mining Engring., U. Alaska, 1939, E.M., 1947, LL.D. (hon.), 1969. Mem. faculty U. Alaska, 1946-82, dean Sch. Mines, 1949-61, dean Coll. Earth Sci. and Mineral Industry, 1961-75, provost Coll. Earth Sci. and Mineral Industry, 1970-75, exec. officer no. region, 1970-73, dean Sch. Mineral Industry, 1975-82, dean emeritus, prof. mining engring. Sch. Mineral Industry, 1982—; mining cons. Served to maj. AUS, 1941-46. Fellow AAAS, Explorers Club; mem. NSPE, Am. Inst. Mining and Metall. Engrs., Mining and Metall. Soc. Am., Arctic Inst. N.Am., Am. Soc. Engring. Edn., N.W. Mining Assn., Alaska Mining Assn., Pioneers of Alaska. Home and Office: PO Box 80148 Fairbanks AK 99708-0148

BEISWANGER, GARY LEE, lawyer; b. Billings, Mont., May 31, 1938; BA in Philosophy, History-Polit. Sci., U. Mont., 1960, LLB, 1963. Bar: Mont. 1963, U.S. Dist. Ct. Mont. 1963, U.S. Ct. Appeals (9th cir.) 1987. Pvt. practice, Billings, 1965—. Mem. ABA, ATLA, State Bar Mont., Mont. Trial Lawyers Assn., Yellowstone County Bar Assn. Office: Rocky Village Ctr I 1500 Poly Dr Billings MT 59102-1748 E-mail: garylbeiswanger@lawyer.com.

BEITLER, STEPHEN, private equity and venture capital executive; b. N.Y.C., Oct. 1956; s. Stanley and Arline Beitler; m. Deborah, Jan. 1982; children: Grace, Elinore. BA, cert. of Asian Study, Am. U. Sch. Internat. Studies, Washington, 1977; postgrad., U. Chgo., 1977-78; MS, Def. Intelligence Coll., 1986. Legis. aide U.S. Ho. of Reps., Washington, 1975-77; commd. 2d lt. U.S. Army, 1977, advanced through grades to maj., 1989; intelligence briefing officer to Sec. Def. and Chmn. Joint Chiefs of Staff, Washington, 1984-86; asst. to asst. sec. of def. Office Sec. Def., Washington, 1987-88, asst. to undersec. of def., 1988-89; resigned U.S. Army, 1989; mgr. ops. devel. Helene Curtis, Inc., Chgo., 1989-90, corp. mgr. strategy and devel., 1990-92, dir. strategy and devel., 1993; nat. mgr. operational planning and info. Sears Merchandise Group, Hoffman Estates, Ill., 1993-95; sr. dir. fin. processes and systems Sears, Roebuck and Co., Hoffman Estates, Ill., 1995-97, asst. corp. contr., 1997-98; mng. dir., gen. ptnr. Trident Capital, Chgo., 1998—2002; mng. gen. ptnr., sr. mng. dir. Dunrath Capital, Chgo., 2002—. Comdr. 305th psychol. ops. bn. USAR, Arlington Heights, Ill., 1992-96; comdr. 16th psychol. ops. bn. USAR, Ft. Sheridan, Ill., 1996-98; cons. MGA, Inc., Chgo., 1985—; founding chmn. Conf. Bd. Coun. Competitive Analysis; bd. dirs. Brightroom, Inc.; bd. adv. ARXAN, Inc., Imaging Portals, Inc., Zonetrader Inc., Salon 123 Inc., Queston Inc.; former bd. observer The Revere Group, Ltd; entrepreneurial adv. bd. Grad. Sch. Bus., Univ. Chgo., 2003—. Contbg. author: The Military Intelligence Community, 1986; contbr. articles to profl. publs. Bd. dirs. United Way of Highland Park-Highwood, 1999-2002; vol. Bus. Vols. for the Arts, Chgo., 1991-94; bd. dirs. Spl. Ops. Warrior Found., 2001—. Lt. col. USAR, ret. 1998. Decorated Green Beret for valor and svc. Fellow Inter-univ. Seminar on Armed Forces and Soc., Soc. Competitive Intelligence Profls. (bd. dirs. 1991-94); mem. Ill. Venture Capital Assn. (founding mem., bd. dirs. 2000—, sec. 2001, vice chmn. 2002, chmn. 2003), Spl. Forces Club, Army and Navy Club, Union League Club of Chgo., The Execs. Club of Chgo., Fin. Execs. Inst., The Birchwood Club, Carleton Club, Met. Club City of Washington D.C. Office: Dunrath Capital 1 N Franklin Ste 750 Chicago IL 60606 Office Fax: 888-287-3459. E-mail: steve@dunrath.com.

BEITO, DAVID TIMOTHY, humanities educator; b. Mpls., Mar. 8, 1956; s. Rangvald Conrad Beito and Doris Ethelyn (Quale) Betio; m. Linda Gail Royster, June 11, 1997. BA, U. Minn., 1980; MA, U. Wis., 1983, PhD, 1986. Rsch. fellow Inst. Human Studies, Fairfax, Va., 1986—89, 1993—94; instr. U. Nev., Las Vegas, 1989—93; asst. prof. U. Ala., Tuscaloosa, 1994—2000, assoc. prof., 2000—. Author: Taxpayers in Revolt, 1989, From Mutual Aid to the Welfare State, 2000; co-editor: Voluntary City, 2002. Recipient Best Scholarly Jour. award, Urban History Assn., 1991, Ellis Hurley prize, 1995. Mem.: Nat. Assn. Scholars, Ala. Scholars Assn. (pres. 2002—). Office: Univ Ala Dept History Box 870212 Tuscaloosa AL 35487 E-mail: dbeito@history.as.ua.edu.

BEIZER, LANCE KURT, lawyer; b. Hartford, Conn., Sept. 8, 1938; s. Lawrence Sidney and Victoria Merriam (Kaplan) B. BA in Sociology, Brandeis U., 1960; MA in English, San Jose State U., 1967; JD, U. San Diego, 1975. Bar: Calif. 1975. Selective svc. affairs coord. U. Calif., 1969-73, vet. affairs coord., 1973-75; vet. outreach coord. San Diego Community Coll. Dist., 1975-76; dep. dist. atty. Santa Clara County, Calif., 1976—2002. Bd. mgrs. Santa Clara Valley S.W. YMCA, Saratoga, Calif., 1988-, chair, 1991-93; bd. dirs. The Lumen Found., San Francisco, 1985—; bd. dirs. Fedn. Cmty. Ministries, Calif., 1992—, chmn., 1996—; bd. dirs. Apostolic Cath. Orthodox Ch., 1997—. Lt. USNR, 1961-65. Mem. Nat. Assn. Counsel for Children, Am. Weil Soc., Mensa, Commonwealth Club. Republican. Episcopalian. Office: PO Box 1121 Campbell CA 95509-1121 E-mail: lbeizer@yahoo.com.

BEIZER, ROBERT A. lawyer; b. Hartford, Conn., Dec. 13, 1939; AB, Harvard U., 1961; LLB, Yale U., 1964. Bar: Conn. 1964, D.C. 1965. Law clerk U.S. Ct. Appeals 2d cir., 1964-65; ptnr. Sidley & Austin, Washington, 1994; with Venable, Baetjer, Howard & Civiletti, 1994—. Tutor law Yale U., 1964-65; lectr. comm. law U. Va. Law Sch., 1968-84; v.p. law & devel. Gray Comm. Sys., Inc., 1996—. Named Disting. Practitioner Residence Comms. Law Inst. Cath. U. Law Sch., 1994. Mem. Fed. Comm. Bar Assn. (exec. com. 1979-81, pres. 1992-93). Office: Venable, Baetjer, Howard & Civiletti 1201 New York Ave NW Washington DC 20005-3917

BEJ, EMIL, economics educator, researcher, journalist; b. Stryj, Ukraine, Apr. 26, 1925; came to U.S., 1949; m. Vera A. Szwabiuk, Oct. 7, 1961; children: Mark D., Andrew E. LLB, Ukrainian Free U., Munich, 1949; B Comml. Sci., Detroit Bus. Inst., 1957; MA in Econ., U. Detroit, 1966; D in Econ., Ukrainian Free U., 1970. From asst. to full prof. Shippensburg (Pa.) U., 1969-98; assoc. dean faculty of law and econ. Ukrainian Free U., 1995-97. Vis. prof. U. Manitoba, Winnipeg, Canada, 1976, Ukrainian Free U., 1974, 79, 81, 1994—98, Dickinson Coll., Carlisle, Pa., 1983, Lviv (Ukraine) Inst. Mgmt., 1992. Author: (textbooks) Theory of International Integration, 1985, Political Economy of European Communities, 1992, International Economics Theory, 1995; mem. editl. bd. Studien zu Nationalitatenfragen, 1986-94; contbr. articles to profl. jours. Recipient fellowship Shippensburg U., 1992. Mem. Ukrainian Acad. Arts and Scis., Internat. Social Sci. Honor Soc. (life). Home: 9730 Alvin Dr Shippensburg PA 17257-9228

BEJ, SHYAMAL K, chemical engineer, researcher; b. Midnapur, West Bengal, India, July 5, 1961; arrived in U.S., 2000; s. Radhagobinda and Sadhanabala Bej; m. Sudipta Sahu, July 8, 1966; 1 child, Shouvik. B.Sc Hons. in Chemistry, U. of Calcutta, India, 1981—81, B.Tech. in Chem. Tech. (Petroleum), 1985; M.Tech. in Chem. Engring., Indian Inst. of Tech., Kharagpur, Kharagpur, India, 1987; PhD in Chem. Engring., Indian Inst. of Tech., Kanpur, India, 1991. Sr. engr. - r & d Reliance Silicones (India) Ltd., Mumbai, India, 1991—92; sr. officer - rsch. Associated Cement Cos., Ltd., Mumbai, India, 1992—94; asst. mgr. - rsch. Montari Industries Ltd., New Delhi, 1995—97; asst. dir. Indian Inst. of Petroleum, Dehra Dun, India, 1997—99; postdoctoral rsch. fellow Dept. of Chem. Engring., Saskatoon, Canada, 1999—2000; rsch. fellow Dept. of Chem. Engring., U. of Mich., Ann Arbor, Mich., 2000—. Contbr. articles to profl. jours. Mem.: AIChE, N.Am. Catalysis Soc. Home: 1069 Barton Dr # 209 Ann Arbor MI 48105 Office: Dept Chem Engring Univ Mich 3230 HH Dow Bldg, 2300 Hayward Ave Ann Arbor MI 48109 Office Fax: 734-763-0459. Business E-Mail: shyamal@engin.umich.edu.

BEJA, MORRIS, English literature educator; b. N.Y.C., July 18, 1935; s. Joseph and Eleanor (Cohen) B.; children: Andrew Lloyd, Eleni Rachel; m. Ellen Carol Jones, 1990. BA, CCNY, 1957; MA, Columbia U., 1958; PhD, Cornell U., 1963. From instr. to prof. English Ohio State U., Columbus, 1961-2000, prof. emeritus, 2001—. Vis. prof. U. Thessaloniki, Greece, 1965-66, Univ. Coll. Dublin, 1972-73. Author: Epiphany in the Modern Novel, 1971, Film and Literature, 1979, Joyce the Artist Manqué and Indeterminacy, 1989, James Joyce: A Literary Life, 1992; editor: Virginia Woolf's Mrs. Dalloway, 1996, Joyce in the Hibernian Metropolis, 1996, Perspectives on Orson Welles, 1995, Samuel Beckett: Humanistic Perspectives, 1983, James Joyce Newestlatter, 1977—, James Joyce's Dubliners and Portrait of the Artist, 1973, 5 other books. Pres. Internat. James Joyce Found., 1982-90, sec. 1990—; dir. Internat. James Joyce Symposia, 1982, 86, 92. With USAR, 1958-63. Guggenheim fellow, 1972-73; Fulbright lectr., 1965-66, 72-73. Mem. MLA, Internat. Virginia Woolf Soc. (trustee 1976-84), Am. Conf. Irish Studies. Jewish. Avocations: photography, travel, cycling. Home: 1135 Middleport Dr Columbus OH 43235-4060 Office: Ohio State U Dept of English 164 W 17th Ave Columbus OH 43210-1326 E-mail: beja.1@osu.edu.

BEJARANO, PABLO A. physician, consultant, medical educator; b. Bogota, Colombia, Dec. 15, 1960; s. Pablo Anania Bejarano and Marina Hernandez. MD, Universidad Javeriana, 1985. Lic. MD and surgeon Govt. of Colombia, 1986, ECFMG ECGMG, 1988, Anatomic Pathology Am. Bd. of Pathology, 1993. Asst. prof. U. of Cin., 1993—99; assoc. prof. U. of Miami Sch. of Medicine, 1999—. Mem. South Fla. Soc. of Pathologists, 2001—. Contbg. editor: Year Book Of Pathology And Lab Medicine; contbr. articles to profl. jours. Surg. Pathology fellow, Wash. U. Sch. of Medicine, 1992—93. Mem.: U.S. and Can. Acad. of Pathology (assoc.). Office: University of Miami School of Medicine 1611 NW 12th Ave Miami FL 33143 Office Fax: 305-326-9523. E-mail: pbejaran@med.miami.edu.

BEJCZY, ANTAL KAROLY, research scientist, research facility administrator; b. Ercsi, Hungary, Jan. 16, 1930; came to U.S., 1966; s. Jenö and Erzsébet (László) B.; m. Margit Tóth, Oct. 12, 1957. BSEE, Tech. U., Budapest, Hungary, 1956; PhD in Physics, Sci. U., Oslo, 1963. Univ. lectr. Sci. U., Oslo, 1963-66; rsch. scientist Norwegian Rsch. Coun., Oslo, 1963-66; sr. rsch. fellow Calif. Inst. Tech., Pasadena, 1966-69; mem. tech. staff Jet Propulsion Lab., Pasadena, 1969-79, tech. mgr., 1979-85, sr. rsch. scientist, 1985—2001, ret., 2001; cons., 2001—. Bd. dirs. Zoltán Bay Applied Scis. Found., Budapest, Hungary, 1993-98; affiliate prof. Washington U., St. Louis, 1983—. Contbr. articles on robotics and telerobotics to profl. jours.; assoc. editor Automatic Control Trans., 1982-85; mem. editl. bd. Jour. Robotic Sys., 1983—; patentee in field. Recipient Jean Vertut award Robotics Internat., 1987; NASA Exceptional Svc. medal, 1991. Fellow IEEE (Third Millenium Medal award 2000); mem. Robotics and Automation Soc. of IEEE (pres. 1986-87, adminstrv. com. 1991-99). Avocations: tennis, gardening, music. Office: Jet Propulsion Lab MS 198-219 4800 Oak Grove Dr Pasadena CA 91109-8001

BEJJANI, BASSEM A, molecular researcher; b. Beirut, Mar. 31, 1962; MD, Am. U. of Beirut, 1987. Medical Diploma Lebanon, 1987. Med. dir., kleberg cytogenetics lab. Baylor Coll. of Medicine, Houston, 1997—2002; dir., molecular diagnostic lab. Sacred Heart Med. Ctr., Spokane, Wash., 2002—. Achievements include research in Genetics of Glaucoma.

BEKAERT, GEERT, finance educator; b. Zottegem, Belgium, Oct. 3, 1964; arrived in U.S., 1987; s. Jules Bekaert and Denise De Paepe. BA in Econs., U. Gent, Belgium, 1986; PhD in Econs., Northwestern U., 1992. Asst. prof. fin. Stanford (Calif.) U., 1992—96, assoc. prof. fin., 1996—2000; Leon Cooperman prof. fin. and econs. Columbia Bus. Sch., N.Y.C., 1999—. Rsch. assoc. Nat. Bur. Econ. Rsch., Cambridge, Mass., 1999—; advisor Fin. Engines, Palo Alto, Calif., 1997—; mem. sci. coun. Tilburg U., 2001—, vis. scholar, 1996—97, 1998, U. Limburg, 1997, 98, IMF, 1996; cons. Price Waterhouse, 1997—98, World Bank, 1993, 1994—95, Catalyst Inst., 1994; tech. advisor Nikko Securities, 1993—95; mem. econ. rsch. dept. Kredietbank, Belgium, 1986—87; bd. dirs. Fin. Econs. Network, mem. adv. bd. jour.; presenter in field. Contbr. articles to profl. jours.; assoc. editor Pacific Basin Fin. Jour., 1997—, Jour. Fin. and Quantitative Analysis, 1998—, Emerging Markets Quar., 1997—2001, Rev. Fin. Studies, 1996—2000, Jour. Empirical Fin., 1993—97; Jour. Fin., 2003—; editor: Jour. Empirical Fin., 1998—; editor, reviewer jours. in field, patentee pricing module for fin. adv. sys. Named Internat. Rsch. fellow, Kiel Inst. World Econs., 2000—; recipient Zellmer award for best doctoral thesis, European Fin. Assn., 1994, Best Paper award, 1995, NYSE Best paper award in equities, Western Fin. Meetings, 2000, 1st prize, Chgo. Quantitative Alliance Acad. Paper Competition, 2001, Crowell Meml. prize paper competition, 2001; grantee, Inst. Quantitative Investment Rsch., 2001, NSF, 1994—96, 1996—99, 2000—02, William Davidson Inst., 1996—97. Mem.: Soc. Fin. Studies, Am. Fin. Assn. Avocations: basketball, squash. Office: Columbia U Uris Hall Rm 802 3022 Broadway New York NY 10027 Office Fax: 212-662-8474. Business E-Mail: gb241@columbia.edu.

BEKAVAC, NANCY YAVOR, academic administrator, lawyer; b. Pitts., Aug. 28, 1947; d. Anthony Joseph and ELvira (Yavor) Bekavac. BA, Swarthmore Coll., 1969; JD, Yale U., 1973. Bar: Calif. 1974, U.S. Dist. Ct. (cen. dist.) Calif. 1974, U.S. Dist. Ct. (no. dist.) Calif. 1975, U.S. Ct. Appeals (9th cir.) 1975, U.S. Dist. Ct. (so. dist.) Calif. 1976, U.S. Surpeme Ct. 1979, U.S. Ct. Appeals (8th cir.) 1981. Law clk. at large U.S. Ct. Appeals (D.C. cir.), Washington, 1973-74; assoc. Munger, Tolles & Rickershauser, L.A., 1974-79, ptnr., 1980-85; exec. dir. Thomas J. Watson Found., Providence, 1985-87, cons., 1987-88; counselor to pres. Dartmouth Coll., Hanover, N.H., 1988-90; pres. Scripps Coll., Claremont, Calif., 1990—. Adj. prof. law UCLA Law Sch., 1982—83; mem. Calif. Higher Edn. Roundtable, 1996—; trustee Am. Coun. Edn., 1994—97. Bd. mgrs. Swathmore Coll., 1984—; trustee Wenner-Gren Found. Anthrop. Rsch., 1987—94; bd. trustees Am. Coun. Edn., 1994—97; chair Assn. Ind. Colls. and Univs., 1996—97. Recipient Human Rights award, L.A. County Commn. Civil Rights, 1984; fellow Woodrow Wilson fellow, Thomas J. Watson fellow, 1969. Mem.: Am. Assn. Ind. Calif. Colls. and Univs. (chair 1996), Sierra Club. Avocations: hiking, reading, travel. Office: Scripps Coll Office of Pres 1030 Columbia Ave Claremont CA 91711-3986*

BEKER, BERNARDO ENRIQUE, anesthesiologist; b. Montevideo, Uruguay, Nov. 4, 1951; came to U.S., 1979; s. Moses and Pola (Lewkowicz) B.; m. Martha K. Bennett, Jan. 3, 1983. MD, U. Uruguay, 1978. Diplomate Am. Bd. Anesthesiology. Resident in anesthesiology U. Chgo. Hosp. Clinic, 1979-82, intern, 1980-81, fellow in cardiovascular anesthesiology, 1982-83; pvt. practice. Staff anesthesiologist St. Joseph Regional Med. Ctr., South Bend, Ind., 1990—. Vol. The Dian Fossey Gorilla Fund, Atlanta, 1991—. Mem. Am. Soc. Anesthesiologists, Internat. Anesthesia Rsch. Soc., Ind. Soc. Anesthesiologists. Address: 15628 Baintree Way Mishawaka IN 46545-1537 Office: St Joseph Regional Med Ctr Dept Anesthesia 801 E LaSalle Ave South Bend IN 46617 E-mail: dabek@earthlink.net.

BEKES, GREGORY E. lawyer; b. Phila., Feb. 15, 1950; s. Walter Thomas and Ethel Florence (Finger) B.; m. Kathleen Robin Moore, Feb. 12, 1972; children: Jason, Matthew, Melissa. BA, Glassboro State Coll., 1971; MBA, So. Ill. U., 1978; JD with honors, U. Louisville, 1988. Bar: Ind. 1988, U.S. Dist. Ct. (no. and so. dists.) Ind. 1988, U.S. Ct. Appeals (7th cir.) 1988, Ky. 1989, U.S. Dist. Ct. (we. dist.) Ky. 1989. Prodn. supr. Campbell Soup Co., Camden, N.J., 1971-78; quality control supr. William Underwood Co., Hannibal, Mo., 1978-79; pers. mgr. Orville Redenbacker Popcorn, Valparaiso, Ind., 1979-81; pers. assoc. Gen. Foods, Inc., Chgo., 1981-85; dir. human rels. Ferraley, Salem, Ind., 1985-88; assoc. Rogers Fuller & Pitt, Louisville, 1988-90; ptnr. Grotke & Bekes, Greenwood, Ind., 1990—. Mem. Ind. Bar Assn., Ky. Bar Assn., Washington County Bar Assn. Avocation: astronomy. Office: Grotke & Bekes PC 748 S State Road 135 Greenwood IN 46143-9410 E-mail: gbpc@attnet.net.

BEKEY, GEORGE ALBERT, computer scientist, educator, engineer; b. Bratislava, Slovakia, June 19, 1928; arrived in U.S., 1945, naturalized, 1956; s. Andrew and Elizabeth Bekey; m. Shirley White, June 10, 1951; children: Ronald Steven, Michelle Elaine. BS with honors, U. Calif., Berkeley, 1950; MS, UCLA, 1952, PhD, 1962. Rsch. engr. UCLA, 1950-54; mgr. computer ctr. Beckman Instruments, LA and Berkeley, Calif., 1955-58; mem. sr. staff, dir. computer ctr. TRW Systems Group, Redondo Beach, Calif., 1958-62; mem. faculty U. So. Calif., LA, 1962—, prof. elec. and biomed. engring. and

computer sci., 1968—, chmn. dept. elec. engring. systems, 1978-86, dir. Robotics Lab., 1983-98, chmn. computer sci. dept., 1984-89, dir. Ctr. for Mfg. and Automation Rsch., 1987-94, assoc. dean Sch. Engring., 1996-2001. Chair computer sci. Gordon Marshall, 1990—2002; cons. to govt. agys. and indsl. orgns. Author (with W. J. Karplus): (book) Hybrid Computation, 1968; author: (with K. Goldberg) Robotics and Neural Networks, 1994; editor: 6 books; mem. editl. bd.: 3 profl. jours., founding editor: IEEE Trans. Robotics and Automation; editor: Autonomous Robots; contbr. articles to profl. jours. With U.S. Army, 1954—56. Recipient Disting. Faculty award, 1977, Sch. Engring. Svc. award, U. So. Calif., 1990, Presdl. medallion, 2000, Engelberger prize in robotics, 2001, Pioneer in Robotics and Automation award, IEEE Robotics and Automation Soc., 2002. Fellow: IEEE (3d Millennium medal 2000), AAAS, Am. Assn. Artificial Intelligence, Am. Inst. Med. and Biol. Engring.; mem.: NAE, World Affairs Coun., Biomed. Engring. Soc., Neural Network Soc., Soc. Computer Simulation, Assn. Computing Machinery, IEEE Robotics and Automation Soc. (pres. 1996—97), Eta Kappa Nu, Tau Beta Pi, Sigma Xi. Achievements include patents in field. Office: U So Calif Computer Sci Dept Los Angeles CA 90089-0781

BEKEY, SHIRLEY WHITE, psychotherapist; b. L.A. d. Lawrence Francis and Alice (King) White; m. George Albert Bekey, June 10, 1951; children: Ronald S., Michelle E. BA in Psychology, Occidental Coll., L.A., 1949; MSW in Psychiat. Social Work, UCLA, 1954; PhD in Edn. Psychology, U. So. Calif., 1980. Lic. clin. social worker, Calif.; cert. in pupil pers., parent-child edn. Caseworker outpatient svcs. Calif. State Dept. Mental Health, Montebello; caseworker Lowman Sch. for Handicapped, L.A. Unified Sch. Dist., North Hollywood, Calif., 1971-72; psychotherapist Hofmann Psychiat. Clinic, Glendale (Calif.) Adventist Hosp., 1973-75; pvt. practice Encino, Calif., 1980—2002; pvt. practice cons. Gifted and Talented Relationship Counseling, Arroyo Grande, Calif., 2002—. Sprk. in field.; TV expert on children's emotional problems. 1st hosp. vol. candystriper in U.S., Hollywood Hosp, L.A., 1942; mem. World Affairs Coun., 1960—. Fellow Soc. for Clin. Social Work; mem. NASW, APA, Am. Ednl. Rsch. Assn., Nat. Assn. Gifted Children, Assn. Transpersonal Psychology, Inst. Noetic Sci., Assn. Ednl. Therapists, So. Calif. Soc. for Clin. Hypnosis, Analytical Psychology Club L.A., Nat. Assn. Poetry Therapy, Calif. Assn. for Gifted. Avocations: clinical hypnosis, gifted and talented, learning disabilities. Home and Office: 612 Via Belmonte Arroyo Grande CA 93420

BEKIR, NAGWA ESMAT, electrical engineer, educator, consultant; b. Cairo, Dec. 31, 1944; came to U.S., 1972; s. Mohammed Ragab Shalaby and Kamla (Abdel Megeed) Mahmood; m. Esmat Chibl, Sept. 23, 1971; children: Ahmad C., Badr E. BSEE, Cairo U., Egypt, 1966; MSEE, U. So. Calif., 1975, PhD in EE, 1978. Rsch. and hardware engr. Egyptian Indsl. Rsch. Inst., Cairo, 1966-69; quality control engr. Nat. Egyptian Co. for TV and Electronics, Cairo, 1969-72; mem. tech. staff Axiomatics, L.A., 1978; sr. staff engr. Hughes Aircraft Co., Canoga Park, Calif., 1985, mem. tech. staff, 1978-80; assoc. prof. elec. and computer engring. dept. Calif. State U., Northridge, 1980-83, prof., 1984—, chair elec. and computer engring. dept., 1997—. Mem. tech. staff ITT Gilfillan, Van Nuys, Calif., 1984; cons. aircraft divsn. Northrop Co., El Segundo, Calif., 1987; cons. Budlong & Assocs., Inc., Agoura Hills, Calif., 1992-93; rschr. Northrop Grumman Co., El Segundo, 1994-95. Contbr. articles to profl. jours. Recipient Engring. Merit award, 1999, Meritorious Performance and Profl. Promise award Calif. State U., Northridge, 1989, Outstanding Faculty awards Sch. of Engring. and Computer Sci., 1990, Dist. Engring. Educator of Yr. award Engr's Coun., 2003. Mem. IEEE (sr.), Eta Kappa Nu, Tau Beta Pi. Avocations: swimming, racquet ball. Office: Calif State U 18111 Nordhoff St Northridge CA 91330-0001

BEKKEDAHL, BRAD DOUGLAS, dentist; b. Williston, ND, Nov. 23, 1957; s. Oliver Lawrence Jr. and Gudrun Joan (Sundby) B. BA, Jamestown (N.D.) Coll., 1979; BS, U. Minn., 1982, DDS, 1984. Gen. practice dentistry, Williston, 1984—. Chmn. dental staff Mercy Med. Ctr., 1991-93. Scoutmaster Boy Scouts Am., Williston, 1984-86, mem. exec. bd. no. lights coun., 2002—; pastoral com. Gloria Dei Luth. Ch., Williston, 1986-88, coun. mem., 1993-96, congregation pres., 1995; pres. Am. Legion Drum and Bugle Corps, Williston, 1986; edn. officer Luth. Brotherhood br. 8334, 1989-93; mem. exec. com. Raymond Family Cmty. Ctr., 1988-96; city commr. Williston, 1996—; mem. Williston Pk. Bd., 1988-96, pres., 1988-92; mem. exec. com. N.D. Oil and Gas Counties; MinnKota dist. dir. USA Hockey, 1999—. Capt. Dental Corps, USAR. Recipient Williston Western Star award, Williston Area C. of C., 2003. Mem. ADA, N.D. Dental Assn. (New Dentist of Yr. 1997), N.W. Dist. Dental Assn., Williston Dental Soc. (sec.-treas.), N.D. Amateur Hockey Assn. (v.p. 1990-93, cmty. rep., pres. 1986-90, pres. 1993-99). Avocations: youth coaching, camping, woodworking, sports. Home: PO Box 2443 Williston ND 58802-2443 Office: 2204 2D Ave W PO Box 2443 Williston ND 58802-2443

BEKKERS, JOHN, food products company executive; b. Arnhem, The Netherlands; arrived in U.S., 1962, naturalized, 1983; Student, The Netherlands, Harbor Jr. Coll., San Pedro, Calif.; grad., Duke U. Dir. Poultry Group Mgmt. Sys., Atlanta, 1985-87; mgr. N.E. Ala. Poultry divsn. Boaz, 1987-94, exec. v.p., 1994-95; exec. v.p., mem. exec. com. Gold Kist Inc., Atlanta, pres., COO, 1995—. With U.S. Army, Vietnam. Office: Gold Kist Inc 244 Perimeter Ctr Pkwy NE Atlanta GA 30346

BEKRENEV, ANATOLIY, physicist; b. Shuya, Russia, Feb. 24, 1944; s. Nikolai and Anna Bekrenev; m. Ludmila Kudysh, Sept. 16, 1972; children: Vlada, Serge. MS, Petrozabodsk State U., Russia, 1966; PhD, Kharkov State U., Ukraine, 1971; DSc, Materials Sci. Inst., Ukraine, 1985. From asst. prof. to prof. Samara State Tech. U., 1970—96; instr. Nat. Am. U., 1999—. Cons. Phys. Tech. Co., 1996—99. Author: Small-angle X-ray Scattering, 1991, Post Deformation Processes, 1992, Physics for Martieulates, 1996, Diffusion Along Dislocations, 1996. Mem.: Internat. Higher Edn. Acad. Scis., St. Petersburg Acad. Sci. for Strength Problems, N.Y. Acad. Scis. Avocations: singing, gardening. Home: 13951 Wellington Dr Eden Prairie MN 55347 Office: Nat Am Univ W112 W Market Bloomington MN 55425-5521 E-mail: bekrenev@prons.net.

BELAFONTE, HARRY (HARRY GEORGE BELAFONTE JR.), singer, concert artist, actor; b. Harlem, N.Y.C., Mar. 1, 1927; s. Harold George and Melvine (Love) B.; m. Marguerite Byrd, 1948 (div. 1957); m. Julie Robinson, Mar. 8, 1957; children— Adrienne, Shari, David, Gina. Student pub. schs.; LHD (hon.), Park Coll., Mo., 1968; HHD (hon.), Park Coll.; Doctorate Liberal Arts (hon.), ArtsD (hon.), New Sch. Social Research; MusD (hon.), Morehouse Coll., 1987; DFA (hon.), SUNY, Purchase, 1987, Spelman Coll., 1990; DHL (hon.), CCNY, 1990, Columbia U., 1993; DSc (hon.), Tufts U., 1991, Brandeis U., 1991, Long Island U., 1991; DA (hon.), Bard Coll., 1993; DLitt, U. West Indies, Kingston, Jamaica, 1996; hon. degree, U. Mass., 1996; LLD(hon.), McMaster U., Hamilton, Ont., Can., 1996; D (hon.) in Civil Law, U. Newcastle, Britain, 1998; LHD (hon.), Bklyn. Coll., 1998. Pres. Belafonte Enterprises, Inc., N.Y.C. Singer, actor in Broadway shows John Murray Anderson's Almanac (Tony award 1953); Three for Tonight, 1955; motion pictures: Bright Road, 1952, Carmen Jones, 1954, Island in the Sun, 1957, The World, the Flesh and the Devil, 1958, Odds Against Tomorrow, 1959, The Angel Levine, 1969, Buck and the Preacher, 1971, Uptown Saturday Night, 1974, White Man's Burden, 1995, Kansas City, 1996; prodr. stage play To Be Young Gifted and Black, 1969; appeared in TV movies Grambling's White Tiger, 1981, Swing Vote, 1999; prodr. TV spls. A Time for Laughter, 1967, Harry and Lena, 1969; TV program Tonight with Belafonte, 1960 (Emmy award); appeared on German TV spl. I Sing What I See, 1980; concert performances in Cuba, Jamaica, Europe, 1980, Australia, N.Z., U.S., Europe, 1981, Can., 1982, U.S., Europe and with Can. symphony orchs., 1983, U.S., 1985, U.S., Can., Japan, Europe, 1986; prodr. Strolling Twenties-TV, Parting the Waters, (miniseries), 2000; co-prodr. Beat Street, 1984; appeared at Golden Nugget, Atlantic City and Las Vegas, 1985, 86; initiator, performer rec. We Are the World, 1985 (Grammy award 1985); performer concert tours, U.S., Can. and Europe including 60 city tour, 1988, concerts in U.S., Europe, Can., 1989, 90, 93, concerts in U.S., Japan and Can., 1991, concert tour U.S., 1992, concerts U.S., Can. and Europe, 1995, U.S., Can., Europe and Far East, 1996, 50-city European tour, 1998; 1st N.Y. appearance in 30 yrs. Avery Fisher Hall, Lincoln Ctr., 1993; albums: The Long Road to Freedom, 2001, Island in the Sun, 2002. Chmn. Martin Luther King., Jr. Holiday Commn., 1987; goodwill amb. UNICEF, 1987; bd. dirs. N.Y. State Martin Luther King, Jr. Inst. for Nonviolence, 1989—; N.Y. State Employees Brotherhood com. (Benjamin Potocker brotherhood award 1993). Recipient award of appreciation for initiation of and work for USA for Africa, Am. Music, 1986, Leader for Peace award Peace Corps, 1988, Danny Kaye award U.S. Com. for UNICEF, 1989, Africa's Future award, 1994, Whitney M. Young Jr. Svc. award Boy Scouts Am., 1989, Golden Acorn award Bronx Community Coll., 1989, Kennedy Ctr. honors, 1989, Mandela Courage award (inaugural presentation), 1990, Tribute to a Black Am. award Nat. Conf. Black Mayors, Inc., 1991, Bill of Rights award ACLU So. Calif., 1991, Internat. House Berkeley award, 1994, Food and Hunger Hotline award, 1994, Humanitarian award N.Y. Assn. New Americans, 1994, Brotherhood award 100 Black Men, 1994, Children's Champion award UNICEF Com. Greater Boston-joint award with Julie Belafonte, 1994, Nat. Medal of the Arts, 1994, Letelier-Moffitt Human Rights award, 1994, Best Supporting Actor (Kansas City), 1996, N.Y. Film Critics Cir., Jesse Owens Humanitarian award, 1996, Man of the Yr. award N.Y. chpt. Hadassah, 1996, Hadassah Internat. First Citizen of the World award, 1996, Medal of Distinction, Lenox Hill Hosp., N.Y.C., 1996, South African-Am. Orgn. Leadership award, 1996, Florinda Lasker Civil Liberties award, 1997, Living Landmark award N.Y. Landmarks Conservancy, 1997, Humanitarian of Yr. award WLIW/21, 1997, William Moses Kunstler Racial Justice award, 1997, N.Y. Arts & Bus. Coun. award, 1997, Chmn.'s award NAACP Image Awards, 1999, Ronald H. Brown award Nat. Child Labor Com., 1999; inducted into Miami Children's Hosp. Internat. Pediat. Hall of Fame, 1996.*

BELAG, ANDREA SUSAN, artist; b. N.Y.C., Nov. 21, 1951; d. Julius Belag and Harriet (Goldberg) Belag-Lange; m. James Cole Bowness, Apr. 20, 1980 (div. Aug. 1989). Student, N.Y. Studio Sch., 1971-74. Lectr. visual arts program Princeton (N.J.) U., 1995; instr. Sch. Visual Arts, 1995—, SUNY., Purchase, 1992, Md. Inst. Coll. of Art, Baltimore, 1993; resident Bellagio Study Ctr. Curator Eight Painters, Jersey City Mus., 1980, 1981 Invitational, Selected Drawings, 1983, Ralph Hilton 1946-84, 1985, Mystery Show, 1985, The Mirror in Which Two Are Seen as One, 1989, Drawn Out, Kansas City (Mo.) Art Inst., 1987.; vis. artist N.Y. Studio Sch., 1983, Bard Coll., 1984, N.J. Coun. of Arts (fellowship juror), 1985, Kansas City Art Inst., 1987, N.Y. Feminist Art Inst., 1989, RISD, Providence, 1993, Hampshire Coll., 1999, Concordia U., Montreal, Que., Can., 1999. One-person shows include Jersey City Mus., 1979, N.J. State Mus., Trenton, 1984, John Davis Gallery, Akron, 1985, N.Y.C., 1987, 88, David Beitzel Gallery, N.Y.C., 1991, (monotypes), Richard Anderson Fine Arts, N.Y.C., 1992, 93, 94, Rutgers U., New Brunswick, N.J., 1995, Littlejohn Contemporary Art, N.Y.C., 1996, Bill Maynes Gallery, N.Y.C., 1998, 2000, 02, Galerie Heinz Holtmann, Cologne, Germany, 1998, 2000, 02, Bill Maynes Gallery, N.Y.C., N.Y., 2003; numerous group shows include Graham Modern, N.Y.C., 1991, Tibor de Nagy Gallery, N.Y.C., 1992, Galerie Bernhard Steinmetz, Bonn, Germany, 1992, 93, Newhouse Ctr. for Contemporary Art, Snug Harbor, N.Y., 1997, Michael Schneider Zeitgenossische Kunst, Bonn, 1997, 99, Rhona Hoffman Gallery, Chgo., 1997, Pratt Inst., Bklyn., U. Mich., Ann Arbor; represented in mus. collections including Newark Mus., N.J. State Mus., Moriss Mus. of Arts and Scis.; work represented in numerous publs. Fellow N.J. Coun. for Arts, 1984, Nat. Endowment for Arts, 1987, Mariposa Found. fellow Corp. of YADDO, 1994; grantee Blue Mountain Ctr., 1993; Guggenheim fellow, 1999, Bellagio Study Ctr. fellow Rockefeller Found., 2003. Home: 7 Harrison St Apt 4D New York NY 10013-2834 Studio: 137 W Broadway New York NY 10013 E-mail: abelag@aol.com.

BELAK, MICHAEL JAMES, information systems executive; b. Cleve., Nov. 26, 1961; s. John James and Violet Mae (Yamek) B.; children: Michael James II, Nathaniel Hinds; m. Monica Vidal: children: Nils, Vidal, Jean Paul Vidal. BS in Computer Engring., Ohio State U., 1985; MBA in Info. Systems Mgmt., George Washington U., 1990; postgrad., U. Md., 2003—. Application programmer, office of registrar Ohio State U., Columbus, 1984-85; project leader database adminstrn. IBM, Gaithersburg, Md., 1985-88; cons. svcs. mgr. Gen. Electric, Rockville, Md., 1988-91; dir. fleet svcs. devel. PHH Corp., Hunt Valley, Md., 1991-94; dir. data quality mgmt. Nat. Assn. Securities Dealers, Rockville, Md., 1994-97; sr. dir. data mgmt. Marriott Internat., Bethesda, Md., 1998—2001; chief info. officer Dept. of Pub. Works, Washington, 2001—. Contbr. articles to profl. jours. Allocation panel United Way, 1993-94; tech. and innovation com. City of Gaithersburg, Md., 2001—. Named to Premier 100 IT Leaders Computerworld, 2000. Mem. Internat. DB2 Users Group (conf. com. 1990-92), Washington Case Users Group (sec. 1991), Assn. for Computing Machinery (profl. devel. com. 1989-91), Soc. Info. Mgmt. (East Coast working group on client server tech.; bd. dirs. D.C. chpt. 1997). Republican. Avocations: weight training, golf. Home: Kentlands 301 Ridgepoint Pl Gaithersburg MD 20878-5704 Office: Dept Pub Works DC 2000 14th St NW Washington DC 20009 E-mail: mbelak@comcast.net.

BELAND, CHARLET SUE, secondary school educator; b. Sheridan, Wyo., Sept. 24, 1942; d. Charles Edward and Doris Leona (Hanson) Ridgway; m. Rodney Glen Beland, Aug. 22, 1964; children: Mark Thomas, Mikeal Paul. BS, Mont. State U., 1964, MS, 1969, postgrad., 1970—. Cert. in secondary adminstrn., high sch. bus. Tchr. Lompoc (Calif.) City Schs., 1964-65, Santa Barbara (Calif.) City Schs., 1965-69, Bozeman (Mont.) Sr. H.S., 1970-71; instr. Linn Benton C.C., Albany, Oreg., 1972; tchr. bus. Park H.S., Livingston, Mont., 1973—. Instr. Vo-tech, Bozeman, 1969-70, Mont. State U., Bozeman, 1969-75, adult edn. instr., 1965-2001, Mont. State U. No. instr., 1995-97; pvt. computer cons., Livingston, 1989—; organizer Tchrs. Credit Union, Livingston, 1980. Adult leader 4-H, 1992-2002, parent com. chair, parent vol. Boy Scouts Am., 1994-2000, Bus Profls. Am., 1975-2000. Recipient grants and scholarships. Mem. NEA, Mont. Edn. Assn. (del. assembly 1978-88, 94, state retirement com. 1985-90), Livingston Edn. Assn. (prse., negotiator 1974-80, 93-2000), Bus. and Profl. Women (treas. 1975), DAR, Delta Kappa Gamma, Chi Omega (pres. 1963). Democrat. Lutheran. Avocations: sewing, reading, horseback riding, boating, camping. Home: 209 Arbor Dr Livingston MT 59047-9251 Office: Park High Sch 102 View Vista Dr Livingston MT 59047-3597

BELANGER, CHERRY CHURCHILL, elementary school educator; b. Berea, Ky., May 14, 1923; d. David Carroll and Anna Eleanor (Franzen) Churchill; m. Paul Adrien Belanger, Oct. 15, 1950 (dec. Feb. 1987); children: Peter Carroll, Karen Michelle Belanger-Magon. BA, Pomona Coll., Claremont, Calif., 1944; MA in Elem. Edn., Calif. State U., Northridge, 1983. Cert. tchr. early childhood edn. Actress Actor's Equity Assn., 1944-49; retail promotion asst. Bloomingdale's, N.Y.C., 1948-52; editor Living for Young Homemakers, N.Y.C., 1953-54, Bride-To-Be Mag., N.Y.C., 1955; off-camera editor NBC Home Show, N.Y.C., 1955-56; publicist home furnishing Alfred Auerbach, Bell & Stanton, N.Y.C., 1956-61; retail rep. Betsy Ross Martin Assocs., L.A., 1961-66; exec. sec. So. Calif. Assn. Bedding Mfrs., L.A., 1966-70; retail rep. Hercules Corp., L.A., 1971; tchr. early childhood edn. Carthay Nursery, Beverly Hills, Calif., 1971-78, L.A. Unified Sch. Dist., 1976-79, tchr. kindergarten and 1st grade, 1979-99. Den mother, treas., chmn., inst. rep. Boy Scouts Am., Beverly Hills, 1961-85; troop leader Brownies, Girl Scouts U.S., 1968-83. Recipient Silver Fawn award Boy Scouts Am., L.A., 1972, Elizabeth H. Brady Tchr. award So. Calif. Kindergarten Assn., 1997; honored Cherry Belanger Day in Beverly Hills, City Coun., 1976. Mem. DAR, AAUW, United Tchrs. of L.A. Avocations: drama, music, camping.

BELANGER, GERARD, economics educator; b. St. Hyacinthe, Que., Can., Oct. 23, 1940; s. Georges and Cecile (Girard) B.; 1 child, Marie-Jose. BA, U. Montreal, 1960; B.So.Sc., Laval U., 1961, M.So.Sc., 1967; MA, Princeton U., 1966. Asst. prof. econs. Laval U., 1967-71, assoc. prof., 1971-77, prof. econs., 1977—; research coordinator Howe Inst., Montreal, 1977-79; mem. fin. com. Council Univs., Que., 1971-73. Co-author: The Price of Health, 1974, Le Prix du Transport au Quebec, 1978; author: L'economique du secteur public, 1981, Croissance du secteur public et fédéralisme, 1988. Woodrow Wilson scholar, 1964-65; Walter N. Rothchild scholar, 1965-66 Fellow Royal Soc. Can. Office: Université Laval Dept D'eco Pav Desêve Quebec QC Canada G1K 7P4 E-mail: gebe@ecn.ulaval.ca.

BELANGER, KENNETH DOUGLAS, cell and molecular biologist, educator; b. Rochester, Minn., July 27, 1967; s. Kenneth Douglas and Karen Ann B.; m. Karyn Goudie, July 17, 1993; children: Bryce, Karley. BA, Luther Coll., 1990; PhD, Duke U., 1996. Postdoctoral rsch. fellowship U. N.C., Chapel Hill, 1996-98; asst. prof. biology U. Scranton, Pa., 1998—2001, Colgate U., Hamilton, NY, 2001—. Contbr. articles to profl. jours. including Protoplasma, Current Opinion in Plant Biology, Jour. of Biol. Chemistry, Jour. of Cell Biology, others. Postdoctoral rsch. fellowship NIH, 1996-98; grantee NIH, 2001—. Mem.: Soc. Devel. Biology, Am. Soc. of Cell Biology, Coun. on Undergrad. Rsch., Sigma Xi. Avocations: hiking, camping, nature photography, running, basketball. Office: Colgate U 13 Oak Dr Hamilton NY 13346 Home: 2385 Brookview Dr Hamilton NY 13346-2243

BELANGER, PAUL, director; b. Ont., Can. BA, U. Victoria, B.C., Can., 1992; MA, U. Ky., 1994; PhD, SUNY, Buffalo, 2002. Mktg. database specialist Molson Breweries Can., Toronto, 1997—99; ops. dir. REDD Inst. Local Governance and Regulatory Growth SUNY, Buffalo, 1999—. Office: Inst for Local Governance & Reg Growth 3435 Main St Buffalo NY 14214 Office Fax: 716-829-3776. Business E-Mail: pxbelang@acsu.buffalo.edu.

BELANGER, WILLIAM JOSEPH, chemist, polymer applications consultant; b. Chgo., Mar. 20, 1925; m. Keltah Long, Feb. 1, 1947; children: William Joseph, Thomas, Kathryn, Michael, Jeanne, Judith, Elizabeth, John, Anne. BS in Chemistry, St. Louis U., 1948; PhD in Organic Chemistry, Notre Dame U., 1951. Research chemist duPont Co., 1951-53; research chemist, then tech. service mgr. Devoe & Reynolds Co., 1953-60; tech. mgr. resin devel. Celanese Coatings & Specialties Co., Louisville, 1960-69; v.p. tech. and engring. Celanese Polymer Specialties Co., Jeffersontown, Ky., 1970-79; v.p. Specialties Group, Celanese Plastics & Specialties Co., 1979-82; Splty. polymer applications cons., 1982—. Tchr. polymer chemistry U. Louisville, 1957; tchr. organic chemistry Ind. Univ. Southeast, 1986. Patentee in field. Vice chmn. Jefferson County Housing Authority, 1975-78; trustee Audubon Hosp., 1979-82. Served with USNR, 1943-45. Mem. Am. Chem. Soc., Nat. Paint and Coatings Assn. Home and Office: 1208 Creighton Hill Rd Louisville KY 40207-2244 E-mail: bllbel@juno.com.

BELARBI, ABDELDJELIL, civil engineering educator, researcher; b. Tlemcen, Algeria, Apr. 21, 1959; came to US, 1983; s. Sid-Ahmed and Rabia (Benchouk) B.; m. Samira Bereksi, Aug. 14, 1986; children: Sihem L., Hishem I., Yasmine E. BSc, U. Oran, Algeria, 1983; MSc, U. Houston, 1986, PhD, 1991. Rsch. asst. U. Houston, 1984-90, tchg. fellow, 1990-91; asst. prof. civil engring. U. Mo., Rolla, 1991-97, assoc. prof., 1997—2003, prof., 2003—. Rsch. investigator Grad. Ctr. for Materials Rsch., Intelligent-Systems Ctr.; proposal and jour. reviewer. Contbr. articles to profl. jours. Recipient Outstanding Tchr. award U. Houston, 1991, U. Mo.-Rolla., 1995, 96, 97, 98, 99, 2000, 02; Faculty Excellence award 1995-2003; Algerian Govt. scholar, 1984-90; NSF rsch. grantee, 1992, 98-2001, Outstanding Paper award Earthquake Spectra Jour., 1995, Disting. Young Alumnus award U. Houstn, 1999. Fellow Am. Concrete Inst.(bd. dir., pres. Mo. chpt.); mem. ASCE, Am. Soc. Engring. Edn., Earthquake Engring. Rsch. Inst., Masonry Soc., Transp. Rsch. Bd.Sigma Xi (scholar 1986), Tau Beta Pi, Chi Epsilon (Excellence in Tchg. award ctrl. dist. 2001). Islamic. Achievements include rsch. on shear, torsion and in-plane forces on reinforced concrete, nonlinear modelling of reinforced concrete, performance and durability of archtl. glazing systems under wind and earthquake effects, smart structures and smart sensors as applied to civil infrastructures. Home: 11110 Breeden Dr Rolla MO 65401-9313 Office: Univ Mo - Rolla Dept Civil Engring Rolla MO 65401

BELAVEK, DEBRA LOUISE, school psychologist; b. Detroit, Mar. 22, 1959; d. Richard Frank and Patricia Ann (Mitchell) Czerw; m. John Frank Belavek, June 29, 1985; children: Cameron, Trevor. BA, Mich. State U., 1982; MA, Gallaudet U., 1985, cert of advanced grad. studies, 1986. Nat. cert. sch. psychologist; cert. sch. psychologist, Mich. Tchr. Muskegon (Mich.) Pub. Schs., 1983-84; sch. psychologist Bloomfield Hills (Mich.) Sch. Dist., 1986—. Ind. evaluator, expert on deafness, presenter workshops various sch. dists., Mich., 1986—. Mem. Nat. Assn. Sch. Psychologists. Avocations: reading, gardening, walking, swimming, crafts. Office: 1101 Westview Bloomfield Hills MI 48304 E-mail: dbelavek@bloomfield.org.

BELAY, HALEFOM, economist, educator; b. Mekelle, Tigray, Ethiopia, Oct. 5, 1959; s. Belay Asres, Emabaynesh Sebhatu (Stepmother). PhD, Binghamton U., Binghamton, N.Y., 1996. Lectr. Kotebe Tchrs. Coll., Addis Ababa, Ethiopia, 1987—89; assoc. prof. econs. Whitman Coll., Walla Walla, Wash., 1996—. Author: (outstanding feature article of the year) Bayesian VAR forecasts fail to live up to their promise, 2000; contbr. articles. Recipient Abramson Scroll award, Nat. Assn. Bus. Econs., 2000. Mem.: Am. Econ. Assn. Office: Whitman College 345 Boyer Ave Walla Walla WA 99362 Home Fax: 509-527-5026; Office Fax: 509-527 5026. Personal E-mail: belayh@whitman.edu. Business E-Mail: belayh@whitman.edu.

BEL BRUNO, JOSEPH JAMES, chemistry educator; b. Passaic, N.J., June 30, 1952; s. Joseph and Carmella (Nicastro) Bel B.; m. Kathleen B. Cassidy, Aug. 10, 1980; children: Joseph Hugh, Elizabeth Kelly. BS, Seton Hall U., 1974; PhD, Rutgers U., 1980. Rsch. assoc. chemistry Princeton (N.J.) U., 1980-82; asst. prof. chemistry Dartmouth Coll, hanover, N.H., 1982-88; assoc. prof. chemistry Dartmouth Coll., Hanover, N.H., 1988-93, prof. chemistry, 1994—, chair dept. chemistry, 1998—2001. Feature editor Jour. Chemistry Edn.; mem. editl. bd. Heteroatom Chemistry; contbr. over 90 articles to profl. jours. Bd. dirs. Cradle and Crayon Child Devel. Ctr., Hanover, 1991-95. Alexander von Humboldt Found. fellow, 1988, Dartmouth Humanities Rsch. Inst. fellow, 1998. Mem. Am. Chem. Soc., Am. Phys. Soc., Inst. for Main Group Chemistry, Material Rsch. Soc., Sigma Xi. Office: Dartmouth Coll Burke Laboratory Hanover NH 03755 E-mail: jjbchem@dartmouth.edu.

BELCASTRO, PATRICK FRANK, pharmaceutical scientist; b. Italy, June 3, 1920; came to U.S., 1927, naturalized, 1943; s. Samuel and Sarah (Mosca) B.; m. Hanna Vilhelmina Jensen, July 6, 1963; children— Helen Maria, Paul Anthony. BS, Duquesne U., 1942; MS (Am. Found. Pharm. Edn. fellow), Purdue U., 1951, PhD in Pharmacy and Pharm. Chemistry (Am. Found . for Pharm. Edn. fellow), 1953. Instr. pharmacy Duquesne U., 1946-49; asst. prof. pharmacy Ohio State U., 1953-54; prof. indsl. pharmacy Purdue U., 1954-90, prof. emeritus, 1990—. Author: Physical and Technical Pharmacy, 1963; contbg. editor: (with others) Pharm. Tech, 1977— ; contbr. to: (with others) Jour. Pharm. Scis. Served with U.S. Army, 1942-46. Mem. Am. Pharm. Assn., Rho Chi, Phi Lambda Upsilon. Roman Catholic. Home: 327 Meridian St West Lafayette IN 47906-2603 Office: Purdue U Sch Pharmacy and Pharm Scis West Lafayette IN 47907 E-mail: pbelcas1@purdue.edu.

BELCHAK, FRANK ROBERT, computer technologist; b. Chgo., June 21, 1943; s. Paul and Marion (Vrba) B. BS, Roosevelt U., 1969; MBA, Ill. Inst. Tech., 1990. Computer tech. capacity planner, systems developer, dealer support analyst Navistar Internat. Corp., Oakbrook Terrace, Ill., 1969—, also mgr., sales mktg. tng., mem. council future employee recognition program. Chief fin. officer, systems. cons. Innovative Software Solutions, Inc., Lombard, Ill. Mem. keystone council John G. Shedd Aquarium. Recipient Gen. Robert E. Wood Citizenship award, 1965. Mem. Computer Measurement Group, Assn. Individual Investors, Art Inst. Chgo., Chgo. Zool. Soc., Edward J. Sparling Soc., Keystone Coun., Internat. Platform Assn., Ill. High Sch. Athletic Assn. Roman Catholic. Office: Navistar Internat Corp 4201 Winfield Rd Warrenville IL 60555 *Personal philosophy: We were put on this planet for two purposes: to improve ourselves and to help others.*

BELCHER, CAROLYN R. state representative; b. Lexington, Ky, Dec. 11, 1953; m. Danny Belcher. BS, Univ. of Ky, 1986. State Rep. House of Rep., Dist. 72, 1998—; Cert. Pub. Act. (CPA), 1991. Mem. State Gov., Econ. Devel. & Tourism; Vice chair Licensing & Oc.; mem. Sr., Mil. Affairs and Pub. Safety, Budget Rev. Subcommittee, Pub. Safety Subcommittee, Tobacco Task Force. Mem.: Chamber of Commerce (past pres.), DAV Aux., AICPA, KSCPA, KY Farm Bur., Christian Soc. Svc. Ctr. (past chair and current bd. mem.), Bath Co. Salvation Army (chair), Owingsville Woman's Club (past pres.), Kiwanis Club (pres. elect), Phi Kappa Phi Nat. Hon. Soc. Democrat. Christian. Office: Capitol Capitol Annex, Rm 351E Frankfort KY 40601 also: Dist PO Box 44 Preston KY 40366*

BELCHER, CHARLES WILLIAM, education educator; b. Independence, Mo., Sept. 29, 1954; s. Daniel Marvin and Florence Marie Belcher; m. Rebecca Sue Newcom, May 10, 1985. AA in Music, Nebr. Western Coll., 1974; B Music Edn., Park U., 1985; MA in Ednl. Adminstrn., postgrad., N.Mex. State U., 1992—. Cert. music tchr., spl. edn. tchr. Mo., N.Mex., profl. spl. educator Coun. Exceptional Children, 1998. Part-time faculty mem. N.Mex. State U., Las

Cruces, 1991—92, grad. asst., 1992—94; spl. edn. tchr. Las Cruces Pub. Schs., 1994—99, head spl. edn. dept., 1995—96; dir. spl. svcs. Cole County R-II Schs., Jefferson City, 1999—2000; instr. William Woods U., Fulton, Mo., 2000—. Cons. Cmty. Tutors, Jefferson City, 2002—. Bd. dirs. Mo. Impact, 2001—. Mem.: Mo. Coun. Exceptional Children (v.p. tchr. edn. divsn. 2001—). Mem. Community Of Christ. Avocations: reading, music performance, music composition.

BELCHER, DENNIS IRL, lawyer; b. Wheeling, W.Va., Aug. 24, 1951; s. Finley Duncan Belcher and Ellen Jane (Huffman) Good; m. Vickie Marie Early, Aug. 2, 1975; children: Sarah Anne, Matthew Irl, Benjamin Scott. BA, Coll. William and Mary, 1973; JD, U. Richmond, 1976. Bar: Va. 1976, U.S. Tax Ct. 1978. Assoc. McGuire, Woods, Battle & Boothe, Richmond, Va., 1976-83, ptnr., 1983—, mem. exec. com., 1996—2001. Adj. prof. taxation Va. Commonwealth U., Richmond, 1985-88. Co-author: Business Tax Planning Forms for Businesses and Individuals, 1985. Chmn. Richmond chpt. Am. Heart Assn., 1984-85; trustee St. Christopher's Sch., 1993-2003. Fellow Am. Coll. Trust and Estate Counsel (bd. regents 1999—); mem. ABA (real property and probate sect., sec. 1997-98, chmn. marital deduction com., vice chmn. lifetime transfers com., ho. of dels. 1998-99, vice chair probate divsn. 1999-2001, chair 2002-03), Va. Bar Assn. (wills and trusts and taxations sects.), Bull and Bear Club, Country Club of Va., Kinloch Golf Club. Presbyterian. Avocations: golf, farming. Office: McGuire Woods 1 James Ctr 901 East Cary St Richmond VA 23219 E-mail: dbelcher@mcguirewoods.com.

BELCHER, DOROTHY S. state correctional department administrator; b. Macon, Ga., Sept. 3, 1954; d. Lawyer B. Stanley and Lena Mae Montgomery; divorced; children: Ayotunde Ronke Ware, Aziza Asha Belcher. BA, U. Wis., 1976. Cert. correctional probation officer, correctional officer inspector, Fla. Probation and parole officer I State of Fla. Dept. of Corrections, Miami, 1978-80, probation and parole officer II, 1980-83, pub. svc. officer, 1983-87, gold program coord., 1987-89, probation and parole supr., 1989-90, correctional probation sr. supr., 1990-91, correctional officer, sr. inspector, 1991-97, correctional probation sr. supr. Ft. Lauderdale, 1997-98, correctional probation dep. adminstr. Miami, 1998-99, correctional probation sr. cir. adminstr., 1999—. Fellow Eta Phi Beta; mem. 100 Black Women, Fla. Coun. on Crime and Delinquency, Criminal Justice Inst. (hon.). Democrat. Pentecostal. Avocations: reading, writing, singing, playing piano, gardening. Home: 17731 NW 32d Ave Opa Locka FL 33056 Office: State of Fla Dept Corrections Probation and Parole 3552 Okeechobee Rd Fort Pierce FL 34947-4597

BELCHER, LA JEUNE, automotive executive; b. Chgo., Nov. 16, 1960; d. Lewis Albert and Dorthy (Brandon) B. BA, Northwestern U., 1982; postgrad., Am. Inst. of Banking, 1983-84; cert. paralegal, Roosevelt U., 1998. Notary pub.; securities lic.; ins. lic., Ill. Securities processor Am. Nat. Bank, Chgo., 1983, divisional asst., 1983-84; mgmt. trainee Toyota Motor Distbrs., Carol Stream, Ill., 1984-85, dist. parts mgr., 1985-90, sr. customer rels. adminstr., 1990-99; fin. rep. Waddell and Reed, 1992; from wholesale specialist, parts cons. to retail ops. cons. Toyota Motor Distbr., Aurora, Ill., 1998—2001, signature process mgr., 2002—. Rep. to Japan-U.S. Toyota Dealer Meeting, Tokyo, 1985; owner Crystal Clear Concepts. Author: (booklet) The Cutting Edge: 127 Tips to Improve Your Professional Image. Mem. alumnni admissions coun. Northwestern U., Evanston, Ill.; bd. dirs. Boys and Girls Club; comty. docent Art Inst. Chgo. Mem. NAFE, NAACP, Northwestern Club Chgo., Toastmasters (edn. v.p. 1988, 94, 95, advt. v.p. 1989, pres. 1990-93), Delta Sigma Theta. Office: Toyota Motor Distbrs 2350 Sequoia Dr Aurora IL 60506-6211

BELCHER, LOUIS DAVID, marketing and operations executive, former mayor; b. Battle Creek, Mich., June 25, 1939; s. Louis George and Josephine (Johnson) B.; children: Debora Louise, Sheri Lynn, Stacy Elizabeth; m. Jane Elisabeth Dillon, May 8, 1987. Student, Kellogg Community Coll., 1959; BS, Eastern Mich. U., 1962. With Gen. Motors Corp., Livonia, Mich., 1962; adminstr. U. Mich., Ann Arbor, 1962-63; with NCR, Lansing, Mich., 1963-69, Veda, Inc., Ann Arbor, 1969-72; owner, v.p., treas. First Ann Arbor Corp., 1972-83; owner, chief fin. officer Third Party Services, Inc. and Data Scan, Inc., Ann Arbor, Mich., 1983-84; pres., chief exec. officer Data Scan, Inc., Ann Arbor, 1984-86, Ann Arbor Rod & Gun Co., 1986-88; ptnr. Shipman, Corey, Belcher, Ann Arbor, 1984-86; sr. asst. to pres. and dir. tech. svcs. Environ. Rsch. Inst. Mich., Ann Arbor, 1988-93; owner, prin. L. D. Belcher and Assocs. Mgmt. Cons., Ann Arbor, 1993—; v.p. Cybernet Syss. Corp., Ann Arbor, 1996-97; v.p., owner, dir. Innovative Rsch. Corp., Ann Arbor, 1999—. Bd. dirs. The Geosat Com., Inc., Washington; corp. dir. M.W. Microwave, Inc., Ann Arbor, Environment Tech. Corp., Ann Arbor, Innovative Rsch. & Svcs., Inc.; adv. bd. dirs. Mich. Consol. Gas Co.; mem. exec. com. Ann. Conf. Earth Observations and Decision Making - A National Partnership, Washington, 1988—, Ann. Internat. Symposium on Remote Sensing of Environment, 1990—, Thematic Conf. Geol. Remote Sensing, 1990, Ann. Thematic Conf. Coastal and Marine Environment, 1992—; co-founder, dir. Ann Arbor IT Zone, 1999. Mem. City Coun., Ann Arbor, 1974-78, mayor pro tem, Ann Arbor, 1976-78, mayor, 1978-85; mem. adv. coun. region 5 SBA, Detroit, 1982-86; pres. bd. dirs. U. Mich. Theatre, 1983-85; bd. dirs. Marcel Marceau World Ctr. for Mime, Inc., Ann Arbor, 1986-89, Mich. Theatre Found., Ann Arbor, 1986-92; mem. nat. Rep. campaign team, 1980. Served to capt. Air N.G., 1956-70. Recipient Outstanding Alumni awards Kellogg C.C., Outstanding Alumni awards Ea. Mich. U. Coll. Bus., Silver Elephant award Rep. Party, Commendation Adminstr. Vets. Affairs, Commendation Ann Arbor Vets. Hosp.; Bügermedaille, City of Tübingen, Fed. Republic Germany; elected Mayor's Hall of Fame, 1995. Mem. Air Force Assn., U.S. Conf. Mayors (past pres.), Mich. Conf. Mayors (chmn.), Am. Soc. for Photogrammertry and Remote Sensing, Ann Arbor Club. Republican. Mem. Ch. of Christ. Home: 1352 Cobblestone Ct Ann Arbor MI 48108-9553 Office: IRIS Corp 1350 Highland Dr Ste E Ann Arbor MI 48108-2263 *I have had incredible luck - I was born an American and given the opportunity and freedom to chase my dreams.*

BELCHER, MAX, social services administrator, college dean; b. East Lynn, W.Va., Mar. 16, 1942; s. George H. and Ella D. (Dickerson) B.; m. Linda L. Frey, Aug. 8, 1964; children: Kipling, Babbette, Andrew, Raleigh, Perry. BA, Berea (Ky.) Coll., 1969; ThM, Trinity Coll., 1972; ThD, Trinity Theol. Sem., 1973; MA, Liberty (Va.) U., 1994; DD, LLD (hon.), Internat. Free Prof. Episc. U., London, 1966; PhD, U. San Jose, 1996. Cert. cognitive behavorial therapist, rational marriage and family therapist, rational sex therapist. From caseworker to dist. mgr. Mich. Dept. Social Svcs., Flint, 1964-97, dist. mgr., 1992-97; mem. faculty dept. psychology Baker Coll., Flint, 1987-98, 99—, dean for gen. edn., 1998-99. Bd. dirs. Consortium on Child Abuse and Neglect, Flint, 1993-97, 99. Recipient Cert. of Merit in Youth Employment, Genesee Intermediate Sch. Dist., 1979, Cert. of Appreciation, Health Care Access Project, 1990. Mem. Nat. Assn. Cognitive Behavioral Therapists, Am. Assn. Christian Counselors, Intercollegiate Studies Inst. (faculty advocate), Mich. County Social Svcs. Assn. (life). Home: 9421 McAfee Rd Montrose MI 48457-9123 Office: Baker Coll 1050 W Bristol Rd Flint MI 48507-5508 E-mail: max.belcher@baker.edu.

BELCO, KAREN MARIE, cardiology nurse; b. Cleveland, Ohio, Oct. 24, 1953; d. Arthur W. and Daniella E. (Lokar) Schultz. m. Joseph E. Belco, Nov. 24, 1979. BSN, St. John Coll., 1975. Staff nurse cardiac surgery Cleve. Clinic, 1976-79, 81, clin. instr. cardiac surgery, 1982-85, nurse clinician dept. cardiology, 1985-92, mgr. electro physiology, 1989-92; sr. clin. electrophysiology specialist, mgr. Baylor Coll. Medicine, Houston, 1993—98, rsch. assoc., 1993-98; cardiac electrophysiology and device specialist Houston VA Med. Ctr., Houston, 1995-98; mgr. cardiac electro physiology and device specialist Cardiology Assoc. of Lubbock, Tex., 1998—2002; mgr., cardiac electro physiology and device specialist practice mgr. Cardiac Arrhythmia Svc., Lubbock, Tex., 2002—. Mem. writing com. NASPEXAM; Medtronic Patient Edn. adv. bd.; Guidant nurse adv. bd.; lectr. in field. Author book chapters and abstracts; contbg. to abstracts and manuscripts. Active in The Woodlands Symphony Chorus. Mem.: North Tex. EP Soc., Am. Heart Assn., Am. Coll. Cardiology (coalition for collaborative cardiology practice 1999—, allied health profls. coms. 2001—), North Am. Soc. Pacing and Electro Physiology (CAP exec. com. 1989—96, trustee 1992—94, CAP chair 1992—94, writing com. 1995—, publs. com. 1996—, credentialing com. 1997—99, data base com. 1998—2000, history com. 1998—). Avocations: boating, golf. E-mail: KBelco@aol.com.

BELDA, ALAIN J. P. metal products executive; b. Meknes, Morocco; Degree in bus. adminstrn., MacKenzie U. With Alcoa Aluminio, Brazil, 1969—79, pres., 1979—94; v.p. Alcoa Inc., 1982—94, pres. Latin Am., 1991, exec. v.p., 1994—97, vice chmn., 1995—97, pres., COO, 1997—99; CEO Alcoa, Inc., Pitts., 1999—, chmn. bd. dirs., 2001—. Bd. dirs. Citigroup, Coopers Industries. Office: Alcoa Inc 201 Isabella St Pittsburgh PA 15212-5858

BELDEN, DAVID LEIGH, professional association executive, engineering educator; b. Mpls., Min., Jan. 9, 1935; m. Lois Marion Lind, June 14, 1956; children: Richard Alan, Grant David. B in Gen. Edn., U. Omaha, 1961; MS in Indsl. Engring., Stanford U., 1963, PhD, 1969; grad., Indsl. Coll. Armed Forces, 1973; DSc (hon.), Manhattan Coll., 1992. Registered profl. engr., Calif. rated navigator, aviator. Enlisted U.S. Air Force, 1954, commd. 2d lt., 1956, advanced through grades to col., 1973; served Thailand; asst. for procurement mgmt. to Sec. Air Force, Washington; ret., 1976; exec. dir. Inst. Indsl. Engr., Norcross, Ga., 1976-87, ASME, NYC, 1987—2002, United Engring. Found., 2003—. Adj. prof. Far East divsn. U. Md., 1970; asso. prof. George Washington U., 1974 Author articles in field. Bd. dirs. NYC Indsl. Tech. Assistance Corp. Decorated Legion of Merit, Meritorious Svc. medal, Commendation medal (3); recipient Nat. Engring. Leadership award Ariz. State U., 2000. Fellow ASME, Instn. of Engrs. of Ireland, Hong Kong Instn. of Engrs., Inst. Indsl. Engrs., Inst. Prodn. Engrs. (Eng., life); mem. Am. Assn. Engring. Socs. (bd. govs. 1980-2002, Kenneth Andrew Roe award), Coun. Engring. and Sci. Soc. Execs. (pres. 1984-85, Leadership award), Am. Soc. Engring. Edn., NY Soc. Assn. Execs. (bd. dirs. 1996-2000, vice chair 2000-01, chair 2002—, Outstanding Assn. Exec. award), Am. Soc. Assn. Execs. (found. bd. 1992-94, bd. dirs. 1994-97), United Engring. Found. (bd. dirs. 1998-2002, pres. 2002), Australian Inst. Indsl. Engrs. (hon.), Japan Mgmt. Soc. (assoc.), Israeli Soc. Mech. Engrs. (hon.), Nat. Eagle Scout Assn., Alpha Pi Mu, Tau Beta Pi. Republican. Office: United Engring Found Three Park Ave New York NY 10016-5990 E-mail: beldend@asme.org.

BELDEN, URSULA, set designer; b. Weimar, Fed. Rep. Germany, Sept. 27, 1947; came to U.S., 1949; d. Ernest J. and Edith G. (Pütter) Mugdan; 1 child, Willow Allegra. MA, U. Mich., 1972; MFA in Design, Yale U., 1976. Prof., chair design dept. Sch. Theatre Ohio U., 1996, Disting. Prof., 2000. Designer Broadway, Off-Broadway, and internat. plays, including: The Mikado, 1977, The Eastern Opera Theatre, 1977, Patience, 1977, Where Memories are Magic and Dreams Invented, 1978, The Importance of Being Ernest, 1979, At Her Age, 1979, Galileo, 1979, Shortages, 1979, Dark Ages, 1980, A Dream Play, 1980 (Villager award for outstanding scene design 1981), Amadeus, 1980, 82, I Can't Keep Running in Place, 1981, Living Quarters, 1983, Weekend, 1983, Quilters, 1984, Pieces of Glass, 1987, A Murder of Crows, 1988 (Peggy Ezekiel award U.S. Inst. Theatre Tech. 1989), Spare Parts, 1989, Waitin' in the Wings, 1990, Trinity, 1991, Night of the Iguana, Cleve., 1993 (Peggy Ezekiel award U.S. Inst. Theatre Tech. 1993), Lay of the Land, Edmunton, Can., 1994, Edith Stein, 1994, Awake and Sing, 1995, Conversations with My Father, 1993 (Peggy Ezekiel award 1995); (films) Pasta Paolo, 1997, You're Gonna Pass, 1999, (play) How the Other Half Loves, 2001, The Dybbuk, 2002, USA Exhibit Installation, Prague Quadrennial, 2003. Recipient Prague Quadrenial award, 1987, 95, 99. Mem. United Scenic Artists (local 829). Office: 84 Prospect Ave Flushing NY 11363-1370

BELDOCK, DONALD TRAVIS, corporate financial executive; b. N.Y.C., May 29, 1934; s. George and Rosa (Tribus) B.; m. Lucy Geringer, Apr. 23, 1971; children: John Anthony, Gwen Ann, James Geringer. BA, Yale U., 1955. Mdse. and fin. exec. R. H. Macy & Co., N.Y.C., 1955-60; mng. ptnr., fin. cons., chmn. D. T. Beldock & Co., N.Y.C., 1961-66; pres., chief exec. officer, chmn. fin. com. BASIX Corp. (formerly Basic Resources Corp.), N.Y.C., 1966-69, chmn. bd., pres., chief exec. officer, 1970-88; chmn., dir. White Shield Greece Oil Corp., N.Y.C., 1969—98; chmn., chief exec. officer Fundamental Properties, Inc., N.Y.C., 1989—, also bd. dirs.; chmn., pres., chief exec. officer Primavera Labs, 1989—; also bd. dirs. CRA Inc, Phoenix, 1982-89. Chmn., CEO Packard Press Corp., Phila., 1987-88, bd. dirs., 1977-88; founding ptnr. Transp. Infrastructure Adv. Group; mng. dir. Hellenic Oil Co., 1989—; chmn., CEO AGB2, Inc., 1999—. Patentee in field. Chmn. bd. trustees Strang Cancer Rsch. Ctr.-Preventive Medicine Inst., 1985-89, chmn. emeritus, 1989—, chmn. investment com., 1996-; mem. bd. advisors Chem. Bank, 1983-88; bd. dirs. Renewable Energy Inst., 1981-86; trustee Am. Symphony Orch., 1979-96; chmn. bd. dirs. Teamwork Found., 1980-89, trustee, 1989—; mem. com. Nat. UN Day, 1978-87; mem. N.Y. Gov.'s Commn. on Voluntary Enterprise, 1985-88; chmn. N.Y. Gov.'s Commn. Subcom. on Foster Care, 1986-88, Foster Care Ind. Living, 1986-89; bd. advisers Free Fellowship program U. Hawaii, 1982-86; mem. pvt. sector adv. panel on infrastructure financing of budget com. U.S. Senate, 1984-88; mem. devel. bd. Yale U., 1983-93, mem. exe. com., 1984-88. Honoree testimonial dinner United Jewish Appeal, 1960. Mem. Am. Mgmt. Assn., Fgn. Policy Assn., Assn. Yale U. Alumni (nat. class rep. 1983-86, bd. govs. 1986-89), Alumni Assn. N.Y. (hon., bd. dirs.), Yale Club, Westchester Country Club, Lotos Club. Office: Fundamental Properties Inc Red Oak Ctr 70 W Red Oak Ln White Plains NY 10604

BELDOCK, MYRON, lawyer; b. N.Y.C., Mar. 27, 1929; s. George J. and Irene (Goldstein) B.; m. Elizabeth G. Pease, June 28, 1953 (div. 1969); children: David, Jennifer, Hannah, Benjamin, Adam Schmalholz; m. Karen L. Dippold, June 19, 1986. BA, Hamilton Coll., 1950; LLB, Harvard U., 1958. Bar: (N.Y.) 1958, N.Y. (U.S. Dist. Ct. (ea. and so. dists.)) 1960, (U.S. Ct. Appeals (2d cir.)) 1960, (U.S. Supreme Ct.) 1973. Asst. U.S. Atty. U.S. Atty's Office, Eastern Dist., N.Y., 1958-60; assoc. Geist, Netter & Marx, N.Y.C., 1960-62; sole practice N.Y.C., 1962-64; ptnr. Beldock Levine & Hoffman LLP, N.Y.C., 1964—. Bd. dirs., v.p. Brotherhood-In-Action, N.Y.C., 1972—; bd. dirs. Brookdale Revolving Fund., N.Y.C., 1973-76. Served with U.S. Army, 1951-54. Mem. Assn. of Bar of City of N.Y. (spl. com. penology 1974-80, com. on judiciary 2000-2003), N.Y. County Lawyers Assn., Bklyn. Bar Assn., Kings County Criminal Bar Assn., N.Y. County Criminal Bar Assn., N.Y. State Assn. Criminal Def. Lawyers, Nat. Assn. Criminal Def. Lawyers, Nat. Lawyers Guild.

BELDON, SANFORD T. publisher; b. Scranton, Pa., Nov. 9, 1932; s. Benjamin and Evelyn (Jacobson) B.; m. Jeanne Sherman, June 25, 1967 (dec. Nov. 1992); m. Patricia Wood, Feb. 4, 1995; children: Mary, Kenneth, Emily. BBA, CCNY, 1955; postgrad., NYU Grad. Sch. Bus., 1956-57. Publicist Prentice-Hall, Inc., N.Y.C., 1956-59; publicity dir. Fawcett Publs., Inc., N.Y.C., 1959-62; asst. dir. public relations Crowell-Collier-Macmillan, N.Y.C., 1963-65; dir. advt. and public relations, edn. group Litton Industries, White Plains, N.Y., 1966-68; dir. promotion Baker & Taylor divsn. W.R. Grace Co., 1968-71; dir. mktg. book div. Rodale Press, Inc., Emmaus, Pa., 1971-74; dir. advt. Organic Gardening mag., Emmaus, 1974-78, v.p., 1974-82, pub., 1978-86, group v.p., 1982-91, sr. v.p., 1991-98. Pub. New Shelter mag., 1984-86, Pub. Prevention Mag., 1986-91, sr. v.p., 1991-99; bd. dirs. Second Harvest Food Bank of Lehigh Valley, 1996—, chmn., 2002—. Pres. ecology adv. com. Allentown (Pa.) City Coun., 1972-75; bd. dirs. Lehigh Valley Child Care, Allentown, 1974-82, pres. bd., 1976-80; bd. dirs. Lehigh Valley Conservancy, Allentown, 1976-77, Planned Parenthood Lehigh County, Pa., 1977-78, Lehigh County Youth and Childrens Office, 1999-2002, Jewish Family Svc. Lehigh Valley, 2000-2003; mem. bd. assocs. Cedar Crest Coll., 1985—; trustee, mem. corp. com., chmn. mktg. coms. Allentown Art Mus., 1992—, pres. bd. trustees, 1997—; mem. Pa. Housing Adv. Commn., 1997-2002. Democrat. Jewish.

BELEFANT, ARTHUR, engineer; b. N.Y.C., June 17, 1927; s. Benjamin and Lena Helen (Roth) B.; m. Rita Myra Sinclair, July 29, 1958; children: Helen Miller, Brian, Sterling. BEE, CCNY, 1949; BA in Mgmt., U. Md., 1964; MS in Mgmt., Fla. Inst. Tech., 1969. Profl. engr. D.C. Fla., Ga., Md., N.Y., Tex. Pres. Belefant Assocs., Inc., Cocoa Beach, Fla., 1966-79; chief electrical engr. Louis Berger Internat., Tel Aviv, 1979-81; dir. ops. Frank E. Basil, Inc., Washington, 1981-84; asst. project mgr. TRW, Omaha, 1984-87, sr. staff engr. Redondo Beach, Calif., 1987-90; prin. project engr. Walt Disney Imagineering, Glendale, Calif., 1990-91; cons. engr. in forensics Melbourne Beach, Fla., 1991--; instr. Facilities Engring. FIT, 1993—94. Mem. Canaveral Coun. Tech. Soc., Cape Canaveral, Fla., chmn. 1977; lt. gov. com. on the Space Shuttle, Kennedy Space Ctr., 1970. Contbr. articles to profl. jours. Mem. Bd. Adjustment, Melbourne Beach, 1992-95, GSA Citizens Adv. Bd., Atla., 1978. With U.S. Army, 1947-48. Recipient Spl. Commendation award Balistic Missile Office, 1989. Mem. ASME, IEEE (sr., chmn. SBIR chpt. 1995-96), Soc. Am. Mil. Engrs. (pres. Canaveral post pres. 1972, Engr. of Yr. 1971), Illuminating Engring. Soc. (emeritus, Award for Libr. light 1970), Fla. Engring. Soc. (Outstanding Civic Contbn. award 1977, Engr. of Yr. Indian River chpt. 1971). Office: 305 Oak St Melbourne Beach FL 32951-2035

BELENKY, ALEXANDER SOLOMONOVICH, mathematician, consultant, researcher; b. Moscow, Mar. 16, 1946; came to the U.S., 1993; s. Solomon Yosefovich Belenkii and Sofia Meerovna Belenkaia. MS in Automation, Moscow Inst. of Chem. Engring., 1967; MA in Piano, Gnesyn's Coll. Music, Moscow, 1968; MS in Math. summa cum laude, Moscow State U., 1974; PhD in Math., Russian Acad. Scis., 1981, DSc in Math. Method Applications, 1995, Prof. Math. Method Applications, 1997; Academician, Russian Acad. Transport, 1996. Lectr. All Union Soc. Znanie, Moscow, 1981-89; vis. rschr. MIT, Boston, 1991-92, 93-94; leading rschr. Inst. of Control Scis., Moscow, 1995-99; cons. Vis. lectr. U. Udina, Italy, Ecole Central, France, 1992-94. Author: Computer-Aided Systems for Container Transportation, 1981, Economics-Mathematical Methods of Planning Publishing Activities, 1983, Applied Mathematics in National Economy, 1985, Mathematical Models of Optimal Planning in Transportation Systems, 1988, Methods of Optimal Planning in Transport, 1988, Perfecting of Planning in Transportation Systems, 1988, Operations Research in Transportation Systems: Ideas and Schemes of Optimization Methods for Strategic Planning and Operations Management, 1998, others, (scenarios of documentaries) Transport in the USSR, 1985, Engineer of a Nuclear Power Station, 1986, Oil-well Drilling Technology, 1987, Technology of Processing Waste Products, 1988, (scenario of an advertising film) Water-Pipe Faucet, 1988, Extreme Outcomes of U.S. Presidential Elections: The Logic of Appearance, Examples, Approaches to Eliminating (The logical analysis of the U.S. presidential elections system), 2003; exec. editor Jour. Transport, Sci., Tech., Mgmt., 1990-94; contbr. articles on optimization methods and their applications in strategic mgmt. to profl. publs. Mem. Moscow House of Scientists. Home and Office: Nistraman Consulting PO Box 1314 Brookline MA 02446-0010 E-mail: alex_belenky@lycos.com.

BELETZ, ELAINE ETHEL, nurse, educator; b. N.Y.C., Jan. 5, 1944; d. Harry and Rose (Friedman) Beletz. RN, Mt. Sinai Hosp., N.Y.C., 1968; BSN, Fairleigh Dickinson U., 1970; MA, NYU, 1974; MEd, Columbia U., 1978, EdD, 1979. Staff nurse ICU Mt. Sinai Hosp., 1968-70, asst. head nurse, 1970, adminstrv. supervisory relief nurse, 1973-74, 77-78; clin. instr. Roosevelt Hosp. Sch. Nursing, N.Y.C., 1970-73; nurse gerontologist St. Luke's Hosp. Ctr., N.Y.C., 1974; asst. dir. nursing Bklyn. Hosp., N.Y.C., 1975-77; asst. prof. nursing Hunter Coll. CUNY, 1978-81; v.p. nursing Mt. Sinai Hosp. Med. Ctr., Chgo., 1982-83; assoc. prof. nursing Villanova (Pa.) U., 1983—. Lectr.; cons. nursing adminstrn., labor rels. in health care; mem. task force on block grants Ill. Dept. Health. Contbr. articles to profl. jours.; internat. cons. and lectr. Bd. dirs. Hadassah Nurses Coun., Phila., 1993-94; pres.-elect, 1994-96, pres. 1996-98; Midatlantic Reg. v.p. nat. bd. Zionist Orgn. Am., 1998-2000, del. 91st nat. conv., 1998, nominating com., 1998; mem. religious affairs and fgn. rels. com. Am. Jewish Com., 1997-2000; mem. investment com. of bd. trustees Villanova U., 2001—. Recipient Disting. Achievement award Columbia U. Nursing Edn. Alumni Assn., 1989; named to Hall of Fame, Columbia U. Nursing Edn. Alumni Assn., 1999. Fellow Am. Acad. Nursing; mem. Am. Nurses Assn. (bd. dirs. 1982-87, mem. polit. action com. 1982-86), N.Y. State Nurses Assn. (treas. 1977-78, pres.-elect 1978-79, pres. 1979-81, bd. trustees, cert. of appreciation 1981, hon. recognition award 1987), Pa. Nurses Assn. (nominating com. 1985-86, chair polit. action com. 1990-92), N.Y. Counties Registered Nurses Assn. (nominating com. 1973, dir. 1975-78, Amanda Silvers award 1981), Shershower Benevolent Assn., Nursing Edn. Alumni Assn. (Leadership award 1989), Sigma Theta Tau, Phi Kappa Phi, Phi Beta Delta (co-founder 1998). Jewish. Office: Villanova U Grad Program Nursing Health Care Adminstrn Coll Nursing Villanova PA 19085

BELEU, STEVE (DAN BELEU), librarian; b. Shawnee, Okla., June 6, 1952; s. Dan Lewis and Ann Beleu; m. Debbie Dougherty, June 7, 1977 (div. Jan. 1991). BA, Okla. Bapt. U., 1975; MLS, U. Okla., 1977. Ref. libr. Okla. Dept. Librs., Oklahoma City, 1979-86, regional depository libr., head U.S. govt. info. divsn., 1986—. Fellow Nat. Ctr. for Edn. Stats., 2002—. Author: Yoga Asanas for the Relief and Prevention of Carpal Tunnel Syndrome, 2001; compiler: Forty-Six Important Federal Publications About Oklahoma, the 46th State, 2001, American Indian Materials in the Federal Depository Libraries of Oklahoma, 2002, Oklahoma Directory of Depositories for United States and State of Oklahoma Government Publications, 2002, Yoga in Norman--A Guide to Yoga Teachers and Classes in Norman, Oklahoma, 2003; contbr. poetry to small press periodicals; author various musical compositions; contbr. articles to profl. jours. Mem. Ctrl. Okla. Grotto (sec. 1994—), Metrodocs (coord. 1986—). Democrat. Avocations: writing poetry, composing music, teaching yoga, caving, backpacking. Home: 1609 E Boyd St Norman OK 73071 Office: Okla Dept Libraries 200 NE 18th St Oklahoma City OK 73105-3298 E-mail: sbeleu@oltn.odl.state.ok.us.

BELEW, JOHN SEYMOUR, academic administrator, chemist; b. Waco, Tex., Nov. 3, 1920; s. George H. and Mary (Seymour) B.; m. Ruth Edna McAtee, June 3, 1944; children— James Seymour, Janet Elizabeth. BS, Baylor U., 1941; MS, Wichita State U., 1947; PhD, U. Wis., 1951; LLD, Hong Kong Bapt. U., 1995. Instr. U.S. Army Air Corps Tech. Tng. Command, 1941-43; rsch. assoc. Brown U., Providence, 1951-53; acting. asst. prof. U. Va., 1953-56; asst. prof., then assoc. prof. and prof. chemistry Baylor U., Waco, Tex., 1956-91, prof. emeritus, 1991—, assoc. dean Coll. Arts and Scis., 1973-74, dean Coll. Arts and Scis., 1974-79, chief acad. officer, 1979-91, Jo Murphy chair in internat. edn., 1990-96, provost emeritus, 1991—. Vis. fellow Manchester Coll., Oxford U., summer 1995; mem. team advs. to Tech. U. Liberec, Czech Rep., 1999. Mem. various cmty. bds.; trustee Midway Ind. Sch. Dist., Waco, 1962-72; bd. dirs. Tex. High Speed Rail Authority, 1992—; del. Nat. Dem. Conv., 2000. With USAAF, 1943-46. Wilton Park fellow, 1976; recipient Disting. Alumnus award Baylor U., 1993. Mem.: Royal Soc. Chemistry, Am. Chem. Soc., Turner Soc. London, Grolier Club, Sigma Xi. Office: Provost Emeritus Baylor Univ Waco TX 76798-7121 E-mail: john_belew@baylor.edu.

BELFIGLIO, VALENTINE JOHN, political science educator, pharmacist; b. May 28, 1934; s. Edmond Liberato and Mildred Elizabeth (Sherwood) B.; 1 child by previous marriage, Valentine Edmond; m. Ellie K. Belfiglio; stepchildren: Andy, Kevian Navid. BS, Union U., 1956; MA, U. Okla., Norman, 1967; PhD, U. Okla., 1970. Registered pharmacist, Fla., Okla., Tex. Grad. asst., instr. U. Okla., 1967-70; prof. polit. sci. Tex. Woman's U., Denton, 1970—. Author: The United States and World Peace, 1971, American Foreign Policy, 1979, The Italian Experience in Texas, 1983, The Best of Italian Cooking, 1985, Alliances, 1986, Go for Orbit, 1987, Pride of the Southwest, 1991, Italian Experience in Texas: A Closer Look, 1994, Honor, Pride, Duty: A History of the State Guard, 1995, They Came from the Sea, 2000, A Study of Ancient Roman Amphibious and Offensive Sea=Ground Task Force Operations, 2001; contbr. numerous articles on internat. rels., Asian politics to profl. jours., as well as extensive rsch. and publs. about ancient Roman amphibious warfare; reviewer textbooks in internat. politics Holbrook Press, Boston, 1973-75. With USAF, 1959-67. Decorated knight Order of Merit, Republic of Italy; recipient Guido Dorso prize U. Naples, 1985, C.K. Chamberlain award East Tex. Hist. Assn., 1990; Tex. Woman's U. Instnl. Rsch. grantee, 1973-74, 76-77, NEH grantee, 1978; postdoctoral fellow Republic of South Africa, 1976; sabbatical leave, Rome, 2001. Mem. AAUP, Internat. Studies Assn. (sec.-treas. region 1974-76), Am. Polit. Sci. Assn., Am. Italian Hist. Assn., Fourth degree Knight of Columbus, Mensa, Kappa Psi. Republican. Roman Catholic. Avocations: chess, dancing, gourmet cookery. Office: Tex Woman's U PO Box 425889 Denton TX 76204-5889 Home: 11505 Sonnet Dr Dallas TX 75229-2629 E-mail: f.belfiglio@venus.twu.edu.

BELFIORE, PHILLIP JOSEPH, education educator, researcher; b. Canonsburg, Pa., Jan. 6, 1960; s. Philip Joseph Belfiore and Yvonne Tauzel; m. Nancy Lou Pierce, Aug. 1, 1987; children: Emily Pierce, Elisa Pierce, Angelea Pierce. PhD, Lehigh U., Bethlehem, Pa., 1985—91. Assoc. prof. Purdue U., West Lafayette, Ind., 1991—95, Mercyhurst Coll., Erie, Pa., 1995—. Dir. Edn. Leadership Forum, Erie, Pa., 1998—. Contbr. articles to profl. jours. Edn. and curriculum Greater Erie Cmty. Action Com. Charter Sch., Erie, Pa., 2000—03. Mem.: Assn. for Behavior Analysis. Office: Mercyhurst Coll 501 E 38th St Erie PA 16546 Office Fax: 814-824-2438. E-mail: belfiore@mercyhurst.edu.

BELFORT, DAVID ERNST, lawyer; b. Newport Beach, Calif., July 6, 1970; s. Georges and Marlene Belfort. BA, Hobart Coll., 1992; JD, Franklin Pierce Law Ctr., 1996; cert. internat. law, Sheffield U., 1997. Bar: Mass. 1996, U.S. Dist. Ct. Mass. 1996, U.S. Ct. Appeals (D.C. cir.) 1998. Ptnr. Carrigan, Bennett and Belfort, Cambridge, 1996—. Mem. Mass. Employment Lawyers Assn., Mass. Bar Assn., Health Care for All (vol., network atty.). Avocations: outdoor activities, politics, chess, basketball, travel. Office: Corrigan Bennett and Belfort One Kendall Sq Bldg 300 2d Fl Cambridge MA 02139 E-mail: DBelfort@corgenbel.com.

BELFORT, GEORGES, chemical engineering educator, consultant; b. Johannesburg, Transvaal, Republic of South Africa, May 8, 1940; came to U.S., 1964; s. Nathan Leveen and Sophie (Konviser) Belfort; m. Marlene Bertha Stern, Dec. 28, 1967; children: David, Gabriel, Jonathan. BScChemE, U. Capetown, 1963; MS in Engring., U. Calif., Irvine, 1969, PhD in Engring., 1972. Rsch. engr. Astropower Labs., McDonnel Douglas Corp., Newport Beach, Calif., 1964-70; acting instr. U. Calif., Irvine, 1971-72; sr. lectr. Hebrew U., Jerusalem, 1973-77; vis. assoc. prof. Northwestern U., Evanston, Ill., 1977-78; assoc. prof. Rensselaer Poly. Inst., Troy, NY, 1978-82, prof., 1982—, Russell Sage prof. chem. engring, 2003—. Chair Gordon Rsch. Conf. on Membranes, Materials and Processes, 1977; cons. in field. Co-editor (author (with others): Fundamentals of Adsorption, 1984, Advanced Biochemical Engineering, 1987; contbr. articles. Fellow Japanese Soc. for Promotion Sci., 1981, 96; rsch. grantee U.S. Dept. Energy, 1994—, USN, 1990-94, NSF, 1995—; elected Nat. Acad. Engring., 2003; apptd. to Russel Sage Endowed chair chem. engring., 2003. Mem. NAE, AIChE (Sci. and Tech. award 2000), Am. Chem. Soc. (Award in Separations Science and Technology 1995), N.Am. Membrane Soc. (pres. 1995, bd. of dirs. 1993—), European Membrane Soc. Office: Rensselaer Poly Inst Chem Engring Dept Troy NY 12180-3590 E-mail: belfog@rpi.edu.

BELFORTE, DAVID ARTHUR, business executive; b. Framingham, Mass., Oct. 25, 1932; s. Arthur David and Jean Louise (Purcell) B.; m. Virginia Elizabeth Crowley, Aug. 2, 1958; 1 child, Steven, David. BS, Northeastern U., 1963, MS, 1970. Staff scientist Raytheon Co., Waltham, Mass., 1957-65; v.p. Thomson Gen. Corp., Lynn, Mass., 1965-70; dir. mktg. Am. Optical Corp., Southbridge, Mass., 1970-73; mgr. Ferranti Elec. Inc., Sturbridge, 1973-76; dir. mktg. Avco Everett Metal Working Lasers, Somerville, Mass., 1976-81; pres. Belforte Assocs., Sturbridge, 1982—. Pub., editor-in-chief: Industrial Laser Handbook, 1986-92; editor Indsl. Laser Rev., 1986-98; pub., editor-in-chief Indsl. Laser Solutions, 1999—. Recipient Arthur L. Schawlow award Laser Institute of America, 1995. Fellow Laser Inst. Am. (Pres.'s award 1988, Arthur L. Schawlow Award, 1995); mem. Am. Welding Soc. (life), Soc. Mfg. Engrs., Ukranian Acad. Engring. Scis. Office: Belforte Assocs PO Box 245 Sturbridge MA 01566-0245

BELFOUR, ED, hockey player; b. Carman, Man., Can., Apr. 21, 1965; Student, U. N.D. Goalie Chgo. Blackhawks, 1988—97, Dallas Stars, 1997—2002, Toronto Maple Leafs, 2002—. Mem. NCAA All AM. West 2d Team, 1986—87, mem. tournament team, 1986—87, WCHA All-Star 1st Team, 1986—87; players NHL All Star Game, 1992—93. Co-recipient Garry F. Longman Meml. Trophy, 1987—88; named Rookie of Yr., 1990—91, All-Star 2d Team, The Sporting News, 1992—93, All-Am. 2d Team, NCAA, 1986—87, All-Rookie Team, NHL, 1990—91, All-Star 1st Team, 1990—91, 1992—93; recipient Vezina Trophy, 1990—91, 1992—93, Calder Meml. Trophy, 1990—91, William M. Jennings Trophy, 1990—91, 1992—93, Trico Goaltender award, 1990—91. Office: Toronto Maple Leafs Air Canada Ctr 40 Bay St Ste 300 Toronto ON Canada M5J 2X2

BEL GEDDES, JOAN, writer; b. L.A. d. Norman and Helen (Sneider) Bel G.; m. Barry Ulanov, Dec. 16, 1939 (div. 1968); children: Anne, Nicholas, Katherine. BA, Barnard Coll. Columbia U., 1937. Researcher and theatrical asst. to Norman Bel Geddes, Inc., N.Y.C., 1937-41; publicity dir. Compton Advt., Inc., N.Y.C., 1942, new program mgr., 1943-47; pub. info. officer UNICEF, N.Y.C., 1970-76, chief editl. and publs. svcs., 1976-79, cons. devel. edn., promoter Universal Children's Day (over 100 countries), 1979-85, editor Almanac World's Children, 1985-90; editor Pate Inst. Bull., 1988-94. Tchr. drama Birch Wathen Sch., N.Y.C., 1950; mem. faculty Inst. Man and Sci., Rensellaerville, N.Y., 1969. Interviewer-hostess: weekly radio program Religion and the Arts, NBC, 1968; author: Small World: A History of Baby Care from the Stone Age to the Spock Age, 1964, How to Parent Alone: A Guide for Single Parents, 1974, To Barbara With Love--Prayers and Reflections by a Believer for a Skeptic (Catholic Press Assn. award 1974), Are You Listening, God?, 1994, Childhood and Children, a Compendium of Customs, Superstitions, Theories, Profiles, and Facts, 1998, Children Praying, Why and How to Pray with Your Children, 1999, (with others) Art, Obscenity and Your Children, 1969, American Catholics and Vietnam, 1970, The Future of the Family, 1971, Holiness and Mental Health, 1972, The Children's Rights Movement, 1977, And You, Who Do You Say I Am?, 1981; translator: (with Barry Ulanov) Last Essays of Georges Bernanos, 1955; editor: Magic Motorways (Norman B. Geddes), 1940, Earth: Our Crowded Spaceship (Isaac Asimov), 1974; editor in chief: My Baby mag, 1954-56, Congratulations mag, 1954-56. Rep. Balkan-Ji-Bar Internat. Orgn. for Child and Youth Welfare of the World, UN. Mem. Authors League Am., Assn. Former Internat. Civil Servants, The Coffee House, Teilard de Chardin Assn., Mcpl. Arts Soc. N.Y., Internat. Inst. Rural Reconstrn. (mem. internat. coun.), Thomas More Soc. (pres. 1966), Barnard Coll. Alumnae Assn. (class v.p. 1972-76, 92—, pres. 1976-82), N.Y. City Mission Soc., Guilford Friends of Music, Pate Inst. Human Survival (bd. dirs. 1989-95, editor bi-monthly bull. 1990-93), The Charles A. and Anne Morrow Lindbergh Fund, Citizens Against Govt. Waste. Roman Catholic. Home and Office: 60 E 8th St New York NY 10003-6514 Office: 60 E 8th St New York NY 10003-6514 *The longer I live the more I relish life. People praise and envy youth but, to my great surprise, I find that growing older is even better than being young. Pleasures taken for granted before become valued, enlarged, prolonged. Like a baby chortling joyfully at seeing things for the first time, I marvel at seeing things for the hundredth or last time. I don't think of life as a right one can in any way earn or deserve but as an inexplicably, unbelievably amazing gift to enjoy and to use and to learn from — so each day is, to me, wondrous, surprising, full of unimagined possibilites.*

BELIAVSKY, YURI, violinist, educator; b. Moscow, Feb. 15, 1932; s. Lazar Beliavsky and Dalila Peltzer; m. Eleonora Beliavsky, July 7, 1955; children: Alexander, Ninah Beliavsky-Twersky, Daniel. Master's degree, Moscow State Music Inst., 1956. Cert. diploma of soloist. Mem. faculty music dept. U. Wis., Milw., 1989-98, Music Inst. Chgo., 1982—. 1st violinist, soloist Moscow Radio, Grand Symphony Orch. of Moscow Radio & TV, 1962-71; asst. concermaster Jerusalem Symphony Orch., 1972-76; 1st violinist Milw. Symphony, 1975—; author: (radio programs) Sta. WFMR, 1986; musician, violinist, soloist recs. with Jerusalem Symphony, 1972; other recordings include Mozart's Concerto N3 K-216, Bartok's Concerto N1 op posth., Bruch's Kol Nidre with Jerusalem Symphony, L. Harrison's concerto for violin with percussion orch. Home: 8574 N Manor Ln Fox Point WI 53217 Office: Milw Symphony Orch Ste 900 330 E Kilbourne Ave Milwaukee WI 53202 E-mail: artofviolin@artofviolin.com.

BELICH, JOHN PATRICK, SR., journalist; b. Peekskill, N.Y., Dec. 6, 1938; s. John Andrew and Iris Patricia (Brown) B.; m. Louise Daniel, June 4, 1971; children: Mary Louise, John P., Andrew J. Student, N.Y. Inst. Photography, St. Petersburg Jr. Coll. Staff news photographer UPI, 1963-69; So. div. photo mgr. Atlanta, 1969-72; photo editor, dir. photography St. Petersburg Times and Evening Independent, 1972-87, mgr. newsroom projects, 1987-94, asst. to pres., 1994—. V.p., bd. dirs. N.W. Fla. Little Maj. League Assn.; mem. photography adv. com. St. Petersburg Vocat. Tech. Inst.; guardian ad litem 6th Jud. Ctr., Fla.; Skywarn vol. Amateur Radio Emergency Svc. Corp., Nat. Weather Svc.; bd. advisors Coll. Comm., Fla. State U. Recipient Pres.'s medal Nat. Press Photographers Assn., 1978, citation of excellence, 1979 Mem. Nat. Press Photographers Assn. (bd. dirs., chmn. info. com. 1978), Atlanta Press Photographers Assn. (past treas., v.p.), Fla. News Photographers Assn., Nat. Press Photographers Found., Am. Meteorol. Soc., Nat. Weather Assn., Am. Radio Relay League, Amateur Radio Satellite Corp., NRA, Wyo. Antelope Club, St. Petersurg Police Pistol Club, Skyway Trap and Skeet Club, Clearwater Amateur Radio Soc., Soc. Newspaper Design, Bass Anglers Sportsman Soc., Fla. Assn. Lic. Investigators, Am. Soc. Indsl. Security, Computer Security Inst., INfo. Sys. Security Assn., Sigma Delta Chi. Office: 490 1st Ave S Saint Petersburg FL 33701-4204 E-mail: jbelich@sptimes.com.

BELICHENKO, PAVEL VASILIEVICH, neuroscientist, researcher; b. Torez, USSR, Sept. 6, 1953; came to U.S., 1999; s. Vassili Pavlovich and Nadejda Vasilievna Belichenko; m. Elena Marcovna Volkova, Mar. 1, 1980; children: Alexandra, Vassili, Nadejda. MD, 2d Med. Inst., Moscow, 1976; PhD, Acad. Med. Scis., Moscow, 1981. Sr. lab. technician 2d Med. Inst., Moscow, 1975-76; scientist Brain Rsch. Inst., Moscow, 1990-99; postdoctoral fellow Stanford (Calif.) U., 1999-2000, basic life sci. rsch. assoc., 2000—. Author: Comparative Cytoarchitectonic Atlas of the C57BL/6 and 129/SV Mouse Brains, 2000. Fellow Max-Plank Inst. Rsch., 1988, Swedish Med. Rsch. Coun., 1992, Royal Med. Soc. Rsch., 1997; Fribourg Canton Rsch. fellow, 1996. Mem. Soc. Neuroscience, Internat. Rett Syndrome Assn., German Neuropathology Soc. Mem. Green Party. Achievements include research in neuronal alteration in the brain of patients with epilepsy; in neuronal alteration in the brain of Rett syndrome patients; in study of brain structures in AIDS vicitims; in study of brain structure in mouse model of Down syndrome. Office: Stanford U 1201 Welch Rd Rm P 220 Stanford CA 94305-5489 Office Fax: 650-498-6262. E-mail: pavel_belinchenko@yahoo.com.

BELICHICK, BILL, professional football coach; b. Nashville; m. Debbie Belichick April 30, 1977; Children: Amanda, Stephen. BA, Wesleyan U. Asst to the coaching staff Baltimore Colts, 1975; asst. Detroit Lions, 1976-78, Denver Broncos, 1978-79; special teams coach N.Y. Giants, 1979-85; defensive coord. N. Y. Giants, 1985-91; head coach Clevc. Browns, 1991-95; asst. head coach New England Patriots, Foxboro, Mass., 1996-97; asst. head coach defensive backs N.Y. Jets, 1997-99; head coach New England Patriots, Foxboro, 2000—. Office: New England Patriots One Patriots Pl Foxboro MA 02035-1388

BELIĆ WEISS, ZORAN, artist, designer, educator; b. Beograd, Srbija, Yugoslavia, Apr. 24, 1955; arrived in U.S., 1989, naturalized, 2000; s. Milan and Ljubinka (Vidosavljević) Belić; m. Mila Djermanović, 1999. BFA in Painting/Mixed media, U. Arts, Belgrade, Yugoslavia, 1981; BA in Philosophy, U. Belgrade, 1985; MFA in Multi-media, Rutgers U., 1991. Pvt. practice, Irvine, Calif.; art dir. D'Arcy, Masius, Benton & Bowles, Inc., N.Y.C., 1991-93; prof. Miss. State U., 1993-96, U. Denver, 1996-97, Laguna Coll. Art and Design, 1997—; chair design program Laguna Coll. of Art and Design, Laguna Beach, 2001—; prof. U. Calif., Irvine, 1997—; dir. gen. Imperium deSign, Irvine, Calif., 1998—. Tchr. Internat. Aikido Fedn., Irvine, 1988—; juror numerous exhbns., art event proposals for art programs; curator, co-curator 11 exhbns.; lectr. in field. *His scholastic research focuses on axiological (aesthetic, cognitive and ethical) issues and cultural, historical and technological conditions that influence visual artists and designers, as well as their methods of articulating ideas and visions in their attempt to respond to a specific communication requirement or to fulfill a specific purpose. In design, his electric background enabled him to transcend the need for an individual style and to develop passion for progressive and innovative visual communication solutions. Hence he believes in the multi-faceted and polyglotic nature of contemporary design culture, and cognizant of many voices that echo and grow in a rhizomatic sense out of the historic and cultural heritage of the humanity. As an artist, Zoran Belic has been exploring mythical, cosmological and cosmological archetypes via the ephemeral, symbolic, quite frequently hermetically encrypted and abstractly staged visual constructs.* Author: Academy of Arts and Sciences Dictionary of Visual Arts, 1989; editor: Mental Space, 1983—87, Dragon Series, 1988—89; one-man shows include SKC, Belgrade, 1977, 1978, 1979, 1980, 1984, 1994, New Gallery, Zagreb, Yugoslavia, 1979, Gallery Rhinoceros, Novi Sad, Yugoslavia, 1984, Collegium Artisticum, Sarajevo, Yugoslavia, 1984, Gallery AUT, Groznjan, Yugoslavia, 1989, Jewish Hist. Mus., Belgrade, 1989, Rutgers U., New Brunswick, NJ, 1990, 1991, Gallery Sebastian, Belgrade, 1994, McCommas Gallery, Miss. State U., 1996, Asbury Gallery, Denver, 1997, OCCCA Gallery, Santa Ana, Calif., 2002, exhibited in group shows at White Palace, Genoa, Italy, 1979, The Apple, Amsterdam, Holland, 1979, Paris. 1980, Wroclaw, Poland, 1981, Bilbao, Spain, 1982, Mus. Modern Art, Brussels, 1982, Mus. Contemporary Art, Belgrade, 1983, Mimar Sinan U., Istanbul, Turkey, 1983, Modern Mus., Stockholm, 1983, Art Space, Hamburg, Germany, 1985, Skenderija, Sarajevo, 1989, Franklin Furnace, N.Y.C., 1989, Mus. Modern Art, Tampere, Finland, 1989, Gallery ULUS, Belgrade, 1990, Zimmerly Mus., New Brunswick, 1991, Gallery V, N.Y.C., 1991, Anthology Film Archives, 1992, Art in Gen., 1993, Sherry Frumkin Gallery, Santa Monica, Calif., 1995, Barutana, Belgrade, 1997, Seven Degrees, Laguna Beach, 2003, others, Represented in permanent collections Mus. Contemporary Art, Belgrade, ULUS, Nat. Mus., Wroclaw, Poznan, Poland, others; contbr. over 55 articles to profl. jours. Recipient 2d award Internat. Drawing Triennial, Wroclaw, Poland, 1981, 4th award Internat. Drawing Biennial, Rijeka, Yugoslavia, 1988; Robert Watts Meml. scholar, 1989; ULUS fellow Beograd, Yugoslavia, 1986-87; rsch. grantee U.S. Dept. Interior, Washington, 1995. Mem. Internat. Assn. Aesthetics, Internat. Assn. Philosophers, Internat. Aikido Fedn., Coll. Art Assn., Udruzenje Likovnih Umetnika Srbije (v.p. 1987-89, pres. expanded media chpt. 1986-89, cons. program bd. 1987-89), Serbian Assn. Aesthetics, Assn. Spacial Rsch. (Belgrade). Avocation: Aikido (2d degree black belt). Home: 2253 Martin St # 204 Irvine CA 92612 Office: Imperium Design Ste 204 2253 Martin St Irvine CA 92612 E-mail: zbelic@imperiumdesign.com.

BELINFANTE, ALEXANDER ERIK ERNST, economist, statistician; b. Leiden, Netherlands, Mar. 12, 1944; came to U.S., 1948; s. Frederik Jozef and Wilhelmina (Beukers) B. BA, Purdue U., 1963; PhD, U. Calif., Berkeley, 1969. Rsch. asst. U. Calif., Berkeley, 1963-67; lectr. NYU, 1967-69, asst. prof., 1969-70, U. Wis., Oshkosh, 1970-76; visiting assoc. prof. U. New Orleans, 1976-78; industry economist FCC, Washington, 1978—. Editor: Monitoring Report, 1987—; contbr. articles to profl. jours. Recipient Flood fellowship, U. Calif., Berkeley, 1964-65. Mem. Am. Econ. Assn., Am. Statis. Assn., Econometric Soc., Assn. for Cultural Econs., Mensa, Delta Rho Kappa, Omicron Delta Epsilon. Avocations: music, art. Home: 2575 Rittenhouse St NW Washington DC 20015-1100 Office: FCC 445 12th St SW Washington DC 20554-0001

BELINFANTE, GEOFFREY WARREN, television producer; b. Brookline, Mass., Oct. 9, 1947; s. Louis and Charlotte (Williams) B.; m. Judy Lee Shapiro; children: Carrie Rachael, Lacey Beth. BA, Brandeis U., 1969, MFA, 1971. TV producer Kenyon and Eckhardt Advt., N.Y.C., 1972-78, Major League Baseball Prodns., N.Y.C., 1978—; sr. v.p., exec. producer Phoenix Communications Group, 1985—; exec. producer Nat. Hockey League Prodns., 1988-97, Hockey Week, 1988-97. Producer: (TV shows) This Week in Baseball, 1977-78, Race for the Pennant, 1978, Baseball Bunch, 1983-84; exec. prodr. numerous TV and radio shows and home video prodns, 1985—, including Play It Up, Live Broadway USA, Play It Up children's sports show, 1996—; founder Sports NewSatellite Daily Sports News Feed, 1985—. Recipient Gold award, Internat. Film and TV Festival, N. Y., 1983, 1984, 1985, 1990, Monitor award, Internat. Teleprodn. Soc., 1985, Emmy award, Sport Century 50 Greatest and Beyond, 2001. Mem. Radio and TV New Dirs. Assn., NATAS, Nat. Cable TV Assn., Nat. Acad. Cable Programming, Internat. Radio and TV Soc. Office: Phoenix Communications Group Major League Baseball Prodns 3 Empire Blvd South Hackensack NJ 07606-1806 E-mail: geoffbell@phoenixcomm.com.

BELINGER, HARRY ROBERT, retired business executive; b. Phila., Sept. 16, 1927; s. Harry and Florence (McGovern) B.; m. Jean Marie O'Neill, Nov. 30, 1957 (dec. Aug. 1998); 1 child, Lizanne. BS, Temple U., 1957. Reporter UPI, Phila., 1957-62, Phila. Daily News, 1962-63, asst. city editor, 1963-66, city editor, 1966-68, 70-71, Phila. Inquirer, 1968-70; city rep., dir. commerce City of Phila., 1972-76; v.p. pub. affairs ARAMARK Inc., Phila., 1976-95; ret., 1995. Pres. Great Flag Gateway, Inc., 2002. Former ex-officio mem. City Planning Commn.; former v.p. Phila. Indsl. Devel. Corp.; past dir., mem. exec. com. Phila. Port Corp.; former mem. sch. bd. Archdiocese of Phila.; past bd. dirs., mem. exec. com. Conv. and Tourist Bur., Phila.; past bd. dirs. Phila. Civic Ctr., Mercy Fitzgerald Hosp. With inf., AUS, 1950-52. Mem. Phila. Press Assn. (bd. dirs. 1964-66). Home: 830 Strawberry Ln Wynnewood PA 19096-1644

BELINSKY, ILENE BETH, lawyer; b. Boston, Jan. 30, 1956; d. Harry Lewis and Ann Natalie (Rubin) B. BA., Simmons Coll., 1977; J.D. cum laude, New Eng. Sch. Law, Boston, 1980. Bar: Mass. 1980, U.S. Dist. Ct. Mass. 1981, U.S. Ct. Appeals (1st cir.) 1981, U.S. Supreme Ct. 1984. Reservitz, Steinberg & Belinsky P.C., Brockton, Mass., 1980-85; ptnr., 1985— ; bd. dirs. Southeastern Mass. Legal Assistance Corp., New Bedford, 1982-86. Bd. dirs. Brockton unit Am. Cancer Soc., 1983, 84. Mem. Mass. Bar Assn. (dir. young lawyers div. 1984-86), Mass. Women's Bar Assn., ABA, Plymouth County Bar Assn., Assn. Trial Lawyers Am., Mass. Acad. Trial Lawyers. Republican. Jewish. Office: 528 Pleasant St Brockton MA 02301 2515

BELINSKY, RACHEL, mathematician, educator; b. St. Petersburg, Russia; arrived in U.S., 1992; d. Mendel and Polina Yekhilevsky; children: Natalia Cohen, Velvel. BS, MS, Leningrad U., PhD, 1971. Lectr., asst. prof., assoc. prof. Leningrad Naval Tech. U., St. Petersburg, 1971—92; assoc. prof. Morris Brown Coll., Atlanta, 1993—. Adj. prof. Ga. State U., Atlanta, 1996—. Contbr. articles to profl. jours.

BELINSKY, STEVEN ALAN, health science association administrator; m. Kathleen Conley, July 15, 1991. PhD, UNC, 1984. Sr. scientist Lovelace Respiratory Rsch. Inst., Albuquerque, 1998—, dir., lung cancer program, 1997—, scientist, 1990—98; sr. staff fellow Nat. Inst. of Environ. Health Sciences, Research Triangle Park, NC, 1986—90; scientist Lovelace Respiratory Rsch. Inst., Albuquerque, 1990—98; sr. staff fellow Nat. Inst. of Environ. Health Scis., Research Triangle Park, NC, 1986—90. Clin. prof. Coll. of Pharmacy, Univ. N.Mex, Albuquerque, 2001—; assoc. scientist U. of N.Mex, Albuquerque, 1991—; adj. assoc. prof. Purdue U., West Lafayette, Ind., 1992—, U. of N.Mex, Albuquerque, 1997—, Albuquerque, 1997—, Purdue U., West Lafayette, Ind., 1992—; assoc. scientist Cancer Ctr., U. of N.Mex, Albuquerque, 1991—. Contbr. articles. Mem.: Internat. Assn. Study of Lung Cancer, Am. Assn. Cancer Rsch. Office: Lovelace Respiratory Rsch Inst 2425 Ridgecrest Dr SE Albuquerque NM 87108

BÉLISLE, PAUL C. Canadian government official; b. St. Joachim, Ont., Can., Nov. 14, 1950; m. Danielle Parent; children: Ariane, Alexia. B in Social Sci. (hon.), U. Ottawa, Ont., 1974, cert. in pub. adminstrn., 1975, LLL, 1980. Bar: Que. Clk. Coms. and Pvt. Legis. Directorate, 1979-84, asst. dir., 1984-94; sec. gen. Can.-France Interparliamentary Assn., 1989-91; clk. of the Senate, clk. of the Parliaments Senate of Canada, Ottawa, Ont., 1994—. Mem. editl. bd. Can. Parliamentary Rev. Recipient l'Ordre de la Pleiade award. Mem. Assn. Clks.-at-the-Table Can., Commonwealth Parliamentary Assn. (exec. sec. treas.), Assn. of Secs. Gen. of Parliaments. Office: Senate of Canada Parliament Bldgs Centre Block Rm 185-S Ottawa ON Canada K1A 0A4 Fax: 613-992-7959.

BELITZ, PAUL EDWARD, lawyer; b. Omaha, July 11, 1951; s. Edward Paul and Jo Anna Beverly (Brown) B.; m. Joanne Deborah Nilson, June 9, 1973; children: Nicholas P., Christopher T. BS with high distinction, U. Nebr., 1973; JD magna cum laude, Creighton U., 1976. Bar: Nebr. 1976, Colo. 1982. Assoc., then ptnr. Kutak Rock LLP, Omaha, 1976-81, ptnr. Denver, 1982—. Bd. dirs. Fleischer Found., Scottsdale, Ariz., 1986—, Fleischer Mus., Scottsdale, 1989—. Mem.: ABA, Denver Bar Assn., Colo. Bar Assn., Nebr. Bar Assn., Glenmoor Country Club. Avocations: reading, skiing, golf. Office: Kutak Rock LLP 1801 California St Ste 3100 Denver CO 80202 E-mail: paul.belitz@kutakrock.com.

BELIVEAU MUCHNICKI, MARGARET ANNE, television producer; b. Milford, Conn., July 23, 1954; d. Jean Paul and Dorothy Anne (Zender) Beliveau; m. John Robert Muchnicki, Oct. 8, 1983. BA, Fairleigh Dickinson U., 1976. Program budget coord. daytime series D'Arcy, Maisius, Benton & Bowles, N.Y.C., 1976-80, supr. program budgets daytime series, 1980-86, assoc. daytime mgr., 1986-91; assoc. producer Another World, Bklyn., 1991-93; supervising producer Procter & Gamble Prodns., N.Y.C., 1993-95; freelance producer and designer, 1996—. Mem. Milford Hosp. Aux. Mem. NATAS. Roman Catholic. Home: 155 Cat Rock Rd Cos Cob CT 06807-1305

BELJAN, JOHN RICHARD, university administrator, medical educator; b. Detroit, May 26, 1930; s. Joseph and Margaret Anne (Brozovich) B.; m. Bernadette Marie Marenda, Feb. 2, 1952; children: Ann Marie, John Richard, Paul Eric. BS, U. Mich., 1951, MD, 1954. Diplomate: Am. Bd. Surgery. Intern U. Mich., Ann Arbor, 1954-55, resident in gen. surgery, 1955-59; dir. med. services Stuart div. Atlas Chem. Industries, Pasadena, Calif., 1965-66; from asst. prof. to assoc. prof. surgery U. Calif. Med. Sch., Davis, 1966-74, from asst. prof. to assoc. prof. engring., 1968-74, from asst. dean to assoc. dean, 1971-74; prof. surgery, prof. biol. engring. Wright State U., Dayton, Ohio, 1974-83, dean Sch. Medicine, 1974-81, vice provost, 1974-78, v.p. health affairs, 1978-81, provost, sr. v.p., 1981-83; prof. arts and scis., assoc. v.p. med. affairs Cen. State U., Wilberforce, Ohio, 1976-83; provost, v.p. acad. affairs, dean Sch. Medicine Hahnemann U., Phila., 1983-85, prof. surgery and biomed. engring., 1983-86, spl. adviser to pres., 1985-86; v.p. acad. affairs Calif. State U., Long Beach, 1986-89, prof. anat., physiology and biomed. engring., 1986-91, provost, 1989-91; pres. Northrop U., L.A., 1989-93, pres. emeritus, 1993—. Trustee Cox Heart Inst., 1975-77, Drew Health Ctr., 1977-78, Wright State U. Found., 1975-83, CSULB Found., 1986-89, 49er Athletic Found., 1986-89; trustee, regional v.p. Engring. and Sci. Inst. Hall of Fame, 1983—; bd. dirs. Miami Valley Health Sys. Agy., 1975-82, UCI Ctr. for Health Edn., 1987-90, Long Beach Rsch. Found., 1989-94; cons. in field. Author articles, revs., chpts. in books. Served with M.C. USAF, 1955-65. Decorated Commendation medal; Braun fellow, 1949; grantee USPHS, NASA, 1968—. Fellow A.C.S.; mem. Los Angeles County Med. Assn., Mich. Alumni Club (Dayton, Outstanding Alumnus award 1976), Oakwood Fur Club, Fin and Feather Club, Phi Beta Delta, Phi Beta Kappa, Alpha Omega Alpha, Phi Eta Sigma, Phi Kappa Phi, Alpha Kappa Kappa. Home and Office: 1671 Mission Hills Rd Apt 501 Northbrook IL 60062-5735

BELK, JOAN PARDUE, English language and literature educator; b. Lancaster, S.C., Oct. 4, 1933; d. William Hazel and Alfleda Steele Pardue; m. Joe Harvey Belk, Sr.; children: Joe Harvey Jr., Jennifer Elizabeth. Degree, Winthrop U., 1954; BA summa cum laude, U. Houston, 1957. Cert. tchr. Tex. asst. to dir. librs. U. Houston, Houston, 1957—61; tchr. English Galena Park HS, Galena Park, Tex., 1961—62; tchr. English (advanced placement) Meml. HS, Houston, 1962—96; instr. English Houston C.C., Houston, 1996—2003. Musician, piano accompanist, piano tchr. Editor articles for profl. pubs. Mem. chancel choir Spring Branch (Tex.) Presbyn. Ch., accompanist children's choir, elder; mem. Royal Spring Civic Assn., Houston, 1989—, newsletter editor, 2002—; mem. Happy Hide-a-Way Civic Assn., Crosby, 1972—, Cancer Fighters Houston, Inc., Houston, 1998—, bd. dirs., 2003—; chmn. evaluations com. Expanding Your Horizons (conf. jr. HS girls), Houston, 1997—. Recipient Friedheim Found. award, Winthrop U., 1954, Mrs. James P. Houstoun Found. award, U. Houston, 1957, Excellence in Tchg. award, So. Meth. U., 1992. Mem.: AAUW (com. chair 1997—), NEA, Delta Kappa Gamma (rsch. com. chair 1998—2002), Spring Br. Ind. Sch. Dist. Minority Lit. Reading and Discussion Group (discussion leader 1990—96), U. Houston Reading and Discussion Group (sec. 1990—), Tex. Coun. Tchrs. English, Nat. Coun. Tchrs. English, Outstanding Lit. Book Club, Les Belles Lettres Club (pres. 1967—68), En Amie Book Rev. Club, Shadow Oaks Garden Club (v.p. 1958—60, pres. 1960—61), Phi Mu (award 1957), Kappa Delta Pi (award 1957), Phi Kappa Phi (treas. 1958—60, award 1957). Presbyterian. Avocations: piano, bridge, travel, crocheting. Home: 2014 Southwick Dr Houston TX 77080 Office: Houston CC 1010 West Sam Houston Parkway North Houston TX 77043 Home Fax: 713-465-9535. Personal E-mail: joebelksr@aol.com.

BELK, JOHN MONTGOMERY, retail company executive; b. Charlotte, N.C., 1920; Student, Davidson Coll., 1943. Mayor City of Charlotte, NC, 1969—77; CEO, chmn. Belk Stores Svcs., Inc. and Belk, Inc. Bd. dirs. Bros. Investment Co., Chaparral Steel Co., Coca Cola Bottlin Co. Consolidated. Mem. Nat. Retail Fedn. (bd. dirs.). Office: Belk Stores Svcs Inc 2801 W Tyvola Rd Charlotte NC 28217-4500*

BELK, LEOTIS S. language educator; b. Lancaster, SC, Jan. 8, 1934; s. Samuel David and Mabel Cora Belk; m. Johnnie Ruth Alexander (div.); 1 child, Shayila Nicole Adela. BA, Queens Coll., 1955; MDiv, Va. Union U., 1958; MA, U. San Carlos, 1963; PhD, Temple U., 1975. Instr. J.C. Smith U., Charlotte, NC, 1958—63, Bishop Coll., Dallas, 1963—69; chair, philosophy of religion Colgate-Rochester Divsn. Sch., NY, 1969—75; pastor New Hope Bapt. Ch., Niagara Falls, 1977—80; assoc. prof. Shaw U., Raleigh, NC, 1991—93; adj. prof. Campbell U., Buies Creek, NC, 1998—2000; asst. prof. St. Augustines

Coll., Raleigh, 2000—. Bd. mem. Charlotte symposium of World Affairs, NC, 1962—63; chmn. Colgate-Rochester Div. Sch., Philos. Religion Dept., 1971—72; cons. NY State Correctional Sys., Albany, NY, 1974—75; vice-chair Love Canal Revitalization Agy., Niagara Falls, 1980—90. Author: Outstanding Black Sermons, 1976, A Record of the Carey Mungo Family and Kin Families of SC. Exec. dir. HUD of Niagara Falls, 1982—83; bd. mem. Criminal Justice Task Force, Niagara County, NY, 1978—79. Grantee Study grant for Mex., J.C. Smith U., 1956. Mem.: NAACP, Raleigh Area Theo. Soc., Martin Luther King Fellows Inc. Democrat. Baptist. Avocations: genealogy, badminton, languages, anthropology, second hand books. Office: St Augustines Coll 1315 Oakwood Ave Raleigh NC 27610 E-mail: belkleo@aol.com.

BELKIN, BORIS DAVID, violinist; b. Sverdlovsk, USSR, Jan. 26, 1948; s. David Boris and Anna Alexandre Belkin; children: Alexander, Maïa. Student, Central Music Sch., Moscow, 1969, Moscow Conservatory, 1969-74; studied with, Yankelevitch and Andrievsky. Violinist; appeared with orchs. throughout world, including, N.Y. Philharm., Israel Philharm., Chgo. Symphony Orch., Los Angeles Philharm., Cleve. Symphony Orch., Boston Symphony Orch., Berlin Philharm., Royal Philharm., Phila. Symphony Orch., Paris National, Vienna Symphony, London Philharm., Pitts. Symphony Orch., Concertgebouw, Tokyo Philharm., Phila. Orch.; recs. include Prokofiev Concertos, Brahms, Sibelius, Strauss, Paganini, Shostakovich, Bruch, Glazunov. Recipient 1st prize Nat. Violin Competition USSR, 1973 Office: care Terry Harrison Artists Mgmt The Orchard Market St Charlbury 0X7 3PJ England E-mail: artists@terryharrison.force9.co.uk.

BELKNAP, JERRY P. lawyer; b. Napoleon, Ohio, Aug. 22, 1917; s. Nathaniel J. and Mary E. (Ragan) B.; m. Maryellen Pilliod, Nov. 29, 1945; children: Nathaniel J., Raymond V., Caroline M. Belknap Russell, Mary Elizabeth Belknap Brann, Sarah A. Belknap Boonstra. AB, U. Mich., 1939, JD, 1941. Bar: Ohio 1941, Ind. 1942, U.S. Ct. Appeals (7th cir.) 1942, U.S. Supreme Ct. Ptnr. Barnes, Hickam, Pantzer & Boyd, and successor firm Barnes & Thornburg, Indpls., 1941—; chmn. Ind. Supreme Ct. com. on rules and practice, 1981-93. Mem. Indpls. Sch. Bd., 1968-72; bd. dirs. Episcopal Diocese of Indpls., 1964-71. Served with USAAF, 1942-45. Decorated Bronze Star, Air medal. Mem. Ind. State Bar Assn., ABA, Indpls. Bar Assn., Bar Assn. 7th Fed. Cir. Republican. Contbr. articles to legal jours. Home: 9539 Cedar Spring Dr Indianapolis IN 46260-1282 Office: 11 S Meridian St Merchants Bank Bldg Ste 1313 Indianapolis IN 46204-3506

BELKNAP, JODI PARRY, graphic designer, writer, business owner; b. New Canaan, Conn., June 4, 1939; d. Corliss Lloyd and Joan (Pike) Parry; m. William Belknap III, Feb. 20, 1970 (div. Nov. 1982). AB in English and Writing, Barnard Coll., 1962; MA in Drama and Theater, U. Hawaii at Manoa, Honolulu, 1988. Life elem. tchr. credential, Calif. Tchr. grade 6 Ruth Fyfe Sch., Las Vegas, Nev., 1963-64; tchr. grades. 2,3 Schilling Sch., Hayward, Calif., 1964-69; master tchr. U. Calif., Hayward, 1967-69; editor Island Heritage Ltd., Honolulu, 1970-73; Pacific bur. chief OAG Publs. (Dun and Bradstreet), Honolulu, 1972-82; freelance writer, columnist various mags. and publs., 1976-88; owner Belknap Pub. and Design, Honolulu, 1987—. Author: Majesty, The Exceptional Trees of Hawaii, 1982, Kaanapali, 1981, Halekulani, 1982, (children's book) Felisa and the Magic Tikling Bird, 1973; book designer: How the B-52 Cockroach Learned to Fly, 1995, Hula Is Life, 1998, Ko Olina, Place of Joy, 2002; prin. design projects for Sheraton Hotels in Hawaii, 1988—, others. Bd. dirs. Hawaii Vocal Arts Ensemble. Recipient Gold award Hospitality Mktg. Assn. Internat., 1995, award Hawaii chpt. Pub. Rels. Soc. Am., 1993, 94, Ilima award of excellence Internat. Assn. Bus. Communicators, 1989, 90. Mem. Soc. Children's Book Writers, Nat. League Am. Pen Women. Avocations: swimming, hiking, family trips. Address: Belknap Pub PO Box 22387 Honolulu HI 96823-2387

BELKNAP, MARIA ANN, writer; b. Portland, Oreg., Mar. 28, 1958; d. Russell Lee B. BS in Resource Mgmt., U. Oreg., 1980. Buyer Splendiferous Inc., L.A., 1982-83; v.p. Am. Croissant, L.A., 1983-90; owner Marbel Coneptz, Inc., Beverly Hills, Calif., 1999—. Author: The Horseman's Spanish/English Dictionary, 1991, The Horseman's German-English Dictionary, 1994, The Horseman's English/Spanish Dictionary, 3d edit., 2000, The Equine Dictionary, 1997, 2d edit., 2000, Immigrant, An American Portrait, 2000, Bar and Restaurant English/Spanish Dictionary, 2002. Democrat. Avocation: adventure sports. Office: PO Box 15452 Beverly Hills CA 90209-1452 E-mail: mabe1@earthlink.net.

BELKNAP, MICHAEL H. P. real estate developer; b. South Bend, Ind., Oct. 27, 1940; s. Paul E. and Mary Elizabeth (Gibb) B.; m. Dorothy Callaway, Aug. 12, 1967 (div. Dec. 1989); children: Michael, Jenny Warner, Matthew Gibb; m. Martha Burke-Hennessy, May 25, 1996; stepchildren: Hélène Lesterlin, Roland Lesterlin. BA, Harvard U., 1963, JD, 1967; LLB, Cambridge (Eng.) U., 1965. Bar: N.Y. 1969. Assoc. Sullivan & Cromwell, N.Y.C., 1967-70; dir. Coun. on Environment, Office of Mayor City of N.Y., 1970-72; v.p., gen. counsel Corp. Property Investors, N.Y.C., 1972-75; v.p. Levitt & Sons Inc., Greenwich, Conn., 1975-78; pres. Belknap Co. Ltd., Canaan, N.Y., 1978—. Adj. prof. Western New Eng. Coll. Sch. Law. English Speaking Union fellow, 1963-64. Mem. Berkshire Natrual Resources Coun. (trustee), Harvard Club. Democrat. Episcopalian. also: 45 E End Ave New York NY 10028-7953 Office: 41 Warner Crossing Rd Canaan NY 12029-2807

BELKNAP, NORTON, petroleum company consultant; b. Topeka, June 17, 1925; s. Paul Edward and Twila Norton Belknap; m. Mary Lonam, June 7, 1950; children: Paula Belknap Reynolds, David Barrett, Randall Page. BS, MIT, 1950, MS, 1951. Various tech. and supervisory positions Exxon, 1951-60; v.p., dir. Esso Japan, 1961-65; chmn., mng. dir. Esso Australia, 1966-69; v.p., exec. v.p., dir. Esso Europe, 1969-73; v.p. corporate planning Exxon Corp., N.Y.C., 1973-79; sr. v.p. Exxon Internat., N.Y.C., 1979-82; trustee Carnegie Hall, N.Y.C., 1974—, mng. dir., 1983-88. Petroleum cons., 1982—; bd. dirs., pres. So. Pacific Petroleum USA; dir. So. Pacific Petroleum NL. Pres. dirs. Paul Taylor Dance Co. 1st lt. USAAF, 1943—46. Decorated Air medal with oak leaf cluster. Mem. Tau Beta Pi. Clubs: Union, Century Assn., Metropolitan Opera (N.Y.C.). Home: 563 Park Ave New York NY 10021-7314 E-mail: nbelknap@aol.com.

BELL, ALBERT LEO, retired lawyer; b. Columbus, Ohio, May 22, 1930; s. Jerome E. and Elizabeth Mary Bell; m. Jean M. DiFino, Aug. 22, 1959; children: Albert, Kathleen, Paul. BA in Journalism, Ohio State U., 1956, JD, 1958. Bar: Ohio 1959. Cert. assn. exec. Ptnr. Walter & Bell, Columbus, Ohio, 1959-64; referee Franklin County Probate Ct., Columbus, 1964-65; ptnr. Maguire and Bell, Columbus, 1965-71; gen. counsel Ohio State Bar Assn., Columbus, 1971-87, 89-97; ret. Judge Franklin County Common Pleas Ct., Columbus, 1988; adj. prof. law Capital U., Columbus, 1986-88. Contbr. articles on legal ethics to profl. jours. Chair Ohio Elections Com., 1990-92. Sgt. U.S. Army, 1948-52. Mem. ABA, Ohio State Bar Assn., Ohio Soc. Assn. Exec. (pres. 1995), Columbus Bar Assn., Nat. Orgn. Bar Counsel (pres. 1975-76), Am. Soc. Assn. Execs. (cert. assn. exec.), Am. Legion, U.S. Power Squadron, Ohio State U. Alumni Assn., Sigma Delta Chi, Phi Delta Phi. Home and Office: 1103 Bryan Dr Westerville OH 43081-1904 Fax: (614) 899-6174. E-mail: alleobell@aol.com.

BELL, ALLEN ANDREW, JR., lawyer; b. Paris, Ill., June 23, 1951; s. Allen Andrew and Mary Elizabeth (Charley) B.; m. Carol Anne Larson, June 15, 1974; children: Sara Elizabeth, Emily Anne, David Allen, Elizabeth Anne. BA, DePauw U., 1973; JD cum laude, Ind. U. - Indpls., 1980. Bar: Ill. 1980, Ind. 1980, U.S. Dist. Ct. (so. dist.) Ind. 1980, U.S. Dist. Ct. (ctrl. dist.) Ill. 1980, (so. dist.) Ill. 1990, U.S. Ct. Appeals (7th cir.) 1988, U.S. Supreme Ct., 1994. Underwriter Am. States Ins. Co., Indpls., 1973-80; assoc. Dillavou Overaker Asher & Smith, Paris, Ill., 1980-85; ptnr. Ruff, Garst & Bell, Paris, 1985-87, Ruff & Bell, 1987-94, Jones & Jones Law Office, P.C., 1994-2000; asst. state's atty. Edgar and Clark Counties, 1987, Edgar County, 2000—; pub. defender Edgar and Clark Counties, 1982-84, 87-91; pvt. practice, 2000—. Mem. City of Paris Planning Commn., 1985-94, City of Paris Police Pension Bd., 1988-93; treas. Edgar County Hist. Soc., 1984-87; mem. Wabash Valley coun. Boy Scouts Am., 1994-2001. Mem. Ill. State Bar Assn., Ind. State Bar Assn., Edgar County Bar Assn. (pres. 1982-83, v.p. 2000, sec. 2001—), Comml. Law League, KC. Republican. Roman Catholic. Office: PO Box 725 209 N Central Paris IL 61944-0725

BELL, ALLEN D. art director, writer; b. Decatur, Ga., Jan. 12, 1973; s. Ronald A. and Shirley J. Bell. BA with honors, Berry Coll., Rome, Ga., 1995; MA, Binghamton U., 1998. Exec. dir. Rome Area Coun. for Arts, Ga., 1999—. Bd. dirs. Ga. Assembly of Cmty. Arts Agencies, Cordele, Ga.; mem. panel Ga. Coun. for Arts, Atlanta, 2001—. Sec. bd. dirs. Ga. Citizens for Arts, Atlanta, 1999—. Recipient Outstanding Young Alumni award, Berry Coll., 2001. Mem.: Nat. Creative Soc., High Mus. Art, Friends of Sara Hightower Libr. Avocations: rock climbing, darts, chess, billiards, running. Office: Rome Area Coun for Arts PO Box 203 Rome GA 30162

BELL, ANDREW C. music educator; b. New Orleans, Oct. 9, 1964; s. Clark B. and Maxine P. Bell; m. Angela W. Bell, June 3, 1989; children: Andee, Alayna. B in Music Edn., Glenville State Coll., 1987; M in Music Edn., VanderCook Coll. Music, 1997. Band dir. Washington Middle Sch., Cairo, Ga., 1987—93, Screven County H.S., Sylvania, Ga., 1993—2000, Ctrl. H.S., Macon, Ga., 2000—; prof. Ga. Mil. Coll., Warner Robins. Mem.: Music Educators Nat. Conv., Condrs. Guild, Ga. Music Educators Assn. (dist. band chair 1997—2000, state rsch. and advocacy chmn. instrumental 1999—2002), Nat. Band Assn. Avocations: movies, reading, Star Trek. Home: 865 Malwood Dr Macon GA 31204 Office: Ctrl High Sch Band 2155 Napier Ave Macon GA 31204 Business E-mail: abell.central@bibb.k12.ga.us.

BELL, BRYAN, real estate and oil investment executive, educator; b. New Orleans, Dec. 15, 1918; s. Bryan and Sarah (Perry) Bell; m. Rubie S. Crosby, July 15, 1950; children: Rubie Perry Gosnell, Bettina Bell Larson, Bryan, Beverly Saunders, Barbara Bell Barrett. BA, Princeton U., 1941; MA, Tulane U., 1962. Pres. Tasso Plantation Foods, Inc., New Orleans, 1945—66; ptnr. Bell Oil Cos., New Orleans, 1962—; gen. ptnr. 26 ltd. partnerships in oil, real estate and venture capital, 1962—. Instr. econs. of real estate devel. Sch. Architecture, Tulane U., New Orleans, 1967—; instr. entrepreneurship Univ. Coll. Author: Lessons in Lifemanship. Chmn. Human Talent Bank Com., New Orleans, 1969—; mem. City Planning Commn., New Orleans, 1956—58; mem. bd. Met. Area Com., 1968—, pres., 1971—; mem. Episcopal Ch., mem. vestry, 1960—, jr. warden, 1968—70, sr. warden, 1970—72; bd. dirs. Christ Spirit of 76 Com., Fedn. Chs., 1975—, pres., 1984; bd. dirs. Trinity Episc. Sch., chmn., 1958—68, Trinity Christian Cmty., 1975—79; bd. dirs. St. Martin's Protestant Episc. Sch., 1964—68; sr. counsellor Episcopal Ch., 1972; bd. dirs. United Fund for Greater New Orleans Area, 1964—71, pres., 1968—69; bd. dirs. aux. Lighthouse for Blind; trustee Alton Ochsner Med. Found., 1983—; bd. dirs. Metairie Park Country Day Sch., 1967—71, Bur. Govtl. Rsch., 1966—, pres., 1971—; bd. dirs. Family Svc. Soc., 1951—58, pres., 1956—58; chmn. com. Met. Leadership Forum, 1969—. Served to 1st lt. AUS, WWII. Recipient Benemerenti Papal honor from Pope John Paul II, Weiss Brotherhood award, NCCJ, 1983, Times Picayune Loving Cup, City of New Orleans, 1985. Mem.: Fgn. Rels. Assn., Princeton Alumni Assn. La. (pres. 1962—63), Garden Dist. Assn., New Orleans C. of C., New Orleans Country Club, Pickwick Club, Wyvern Club, Boston Club. Address: 1331 3rd St New Orleans LA 70130-5743

BELL, BURWELL BAXTER, III, general United States Army; b. Oak Ridge, Tenn., Apr. 9, 1947; BS in Bus. Adminstrn., U. Tenn.; MS in Systems Mgmt., U. So. Calif.; grad. armor officer advanced course, U.S. Army Armor Sch, Fort Knox, Ky., 1976; student, Army Command, Gen. Staff Colls, Fort Leavenworth, Kans., 1980-81, Nat. War Coll., Fort McNair, N.J., 1987-88. Commd. 2d lt. U.S. Army, 1969, advanced through grades to gen., 2002; from platoon leader to exec. officer Troop M, 14th Cavalry U.S. Army Europe and Seventh Army, Germany; comdr. L troop, 3d Reconnissance Squadron, 14th Cavalry U.S. Army Europe and Seventh Army, Germany, 1971-72; comdr. D troop 5th Cavalry Squadron 1st Indivual Tng. Brig. U.S. Army Armor Sch., Ft. Knox, Ky., 1974-75; chief individual tng. dept. U.S. Army Armor Ctr., Ft. Knox, Ky., 1975-76; staff officer modernization coord. office Chief of Staff, Army, Washington, 1981-83; cmmdr. 2d squadron, 9th cavalry, 24th infantry divsn. U.S. Army, Ft. Stewart, Ga., 1984-87; exec. officer to cmdr.-in-chief U.S. Ctrl. Command Operation Desert Shield/Desert Storm, Saudi Arabia, 1990-91; comdr. 24th infantry divn., 2nd brigade, Ft. Stewart, Ga., 1991—93; chief of staff 3d infantry divsn. U.S. Army Europe and Seventh Army, Germany, 1993-94; asst. div. comdr. 1st infantry divn. (mech.), Bamberg, Germany, 1995—96; chief of staff V Corps U.S. Army Europe and Seventh Army, Germany, 1996-97, dep. chief of staff for ops., 1997-98, chief of staff, 1998-99; comdg. gen. U.S. Army Armor Ctr., and Ft. Knox, Ft. Knox, Ky., 1999—2001, III Corps. and Fort Hood, Ft. Hood, Tex., 2001—02, U.S. Army, Europe & 7th Army, Heidelberg, Germany, 2002—. Decorated Legion of Merit with 2 Oak Leaf Clusters, Bronze Star medal, Army Commendation medal with 2 Oak Leaf Clusters, Defense Superior Svc. medal, Meritorious Svc. medal with 2 Oak Leaf Clusters.

BELL, CARL COMPTON, psychiatrist, researcher; b. Chgo., Oct. 28, 1947; s. William Yancy and Pearl Louise (Debnam) Bell; m. Joanne Scott, Jan. 1, 1969 (div. Apr. 1971); 1 child, Cristin Carol; m. Dora Dixie, Dec. 1984 (div. May 1989); m. Tyra Taylor, Mar. 19, 1991; children: Briatta Honore, William Yancy Bell IV. BS in Biology, U. Ill.-Chgo., 1967; MD, Meharry Med. Coll., 1971. Diplomate Am. Bd. Psychiatry and Neurology (examiner). Intern Ill. State Psychiat. Inst., Chgo., 1971-72, resident, 1972-74; pvt. practice medicine specializing in psychiatry Chgo., 1974—; dir. psychiat. emergency svcs. Jackson Park Hosp., Chgo., 1976-77, assoc. dir. divsn. behavioral and psychodynamic medicine, 1979-82, mem. staff, 1972—; staff psychiatrist Human Correctional and Svcs. Inst., Chgo., 1977-78, Chgo. Bd. Edn., 1977-79, Chatham Avalon Mental Health Ctr., Chgo., 1977-79, Cmty. Mental Health Coun., Chgo., 1977-79, med. dir., 1983-87, exec. dir., 1987—; pres., CEO Cmty. Mental Health Coun. and Found., 1993—; assoc. prof. to prof. clin. psychiatry U. Ill., 1983—, prof. pub. health, 1993—. Cons. Cmty. divsn. Lilly Endowment; cons. editl. bd. Jour. Prison and Jail Health, 1990-92, Cmty. Mental Health Jour., 1989—, Jour. Hosp. and Cmty. Psychiatry, 1990-94, Jour. Nat. Med. Assn., 1994-98, Psychiat. Svcs., 1994-98, Jour. Correctional Health Care, 1997-2000, Jour. Health Care to Poor and Underserved, 1991—, Jour. Infant, Child and Adolescent Psychotherapy, 1997—, Clin. Psychiatric News, 2000—; cons. in field. Prodr.(creator animation): Book Worm, 1984; author: Psychiatric Aspects of Violence: Issues in Prevention and Treatment, 2000, Getting Rid of Rats: Reflections of a Community Psychiatrist, 2003; co-author: Suicide and Homicide Among Adolescents, 1994; mem. editl. bd.: Am. Psychiat. Pub., Inc., 2001—; contbr. articles to profl. jours.; prodr.(creator): (video) Eight Pieces of Brocade, 2000—; talk show host : Sta. WVON-AM, 1987—90; Sta. WJPC-FM, 1992—93. Profl. adv. panel Mental Health Assn. Greater Chgo., 1983—; adv. com. funded grant on Aggressors, Victims and Bystanders, 1989-92; bd. dirs. Ill. Coun. Against Handgun Violence, 1990—, Nat. Commn. on Correctional Health Care, 1983—, chmn. 1992; lectr. U. Chgo., 1986—, Chgo. Med. Sch., 1987—; tchr. martial arts, 1973—; apptd. to violence against women adv. coun., 1995-2000; mem. White House strategy session on Children, Violence and Responsibility, 1999; mem. surgeon gen. report on mental health-Culture, Race and Ethnicity Working Group, 2000; mem. Surgeon Gen. report on youth violence working group, 2000—; mem. Chgo. Bd. Health, 2002—. Lt. comdr. USN, 1974-76. Named Top Doctor, Chgo. mag., 1997, 2001; recipient plaque in recognition and appreciation, Chatham-Avalon Mental Health Ctr., 1979, Div. Behavioral Medicine, 1982, Social Action award, Chgo. chpt. Black Social Workers, 1988, Mental Health award, Englewood Cmty. Health Orgn., 1988, Scholastic Achievement award, Chgo. chpt. Nat. Assn. Black Social Workers, 1980, Ellen Quinn Meml. award, 1986, Monarch award, Alpha Kappa Alpha, 1986, Alumnus of Yr. award, Meharry Med. Coll., 1991, Cmty. Psychiatry award, Am. Assn. Cmty. Psychiatrists, 1992, Lifetime Achievement award, Black Psychiatrists of Am., 1994, Freddye Smith award, Cmty. Mental Health Coun., 1997, Blanche F. Ittleson award Lifetime Contbns., Am. Ortho Psychiatric Assn., 2000, Lifetime Achievement award, Cmty. Behavioral Healthcare Assn. Ill., 2001, Living Legacy award, Provident Found., 2001, Dr. Jeanne Spurlock Lectr. award, Am. Acad. Child and Adolescent Psychiatrists, 2002; grantee, NIMH, 2001—; Goldberger fellow, 1969, Dr. Martin Luther King Jr. fellow, 1970—71. Fellow Am. Coll. Psychiatrists (com. Laughlin fellows 1989-92, com. on fins. 1993-96, com. on pub. edn. 1994-96, com. membership devel. 1996-2000, com. strategic planning 2000—, Bowis Disting. Svc. award 2002); mem. APA (Falk fellow 1972-73, task force-delivery psychiat. svcs. to proverty areas 1972-73, com. black psychiatrists, 1988-90, chmn. black caucus 1990-92, vice chair task force psychiat. aspects of violence 1997—, joint commn. on pub. affairs 2000—, Spl. Presdl. Commendation 1997), Nat. Med. Assn. (local chmn. sect. on neurology and psychiatry 1983, conv., nat. chmn. sect. on psychiatry and behavioral scis. 1985-86, E. Y. Williams Disting. Sr. Clin. scholar psychiatry sect. 1992), Black Psychiatrists Am. (editor Bottom Line newsletter 1977-82, v.p. 1980-82), Cook County Physicians Assn., Prairie State Physicians, Ill. Psychiat. Soc., Am. Assn. Cmty. Mental Health Ctr. Psychiatrists (bd. dirs. 1985-89), Am. Coll. Psychiatry, Nat. Coun. Cmty. Health Ctrs. (sec. bd. dirs. 1986, sec., treas. 1987), Underwater Explorers Soc., Shorei Goju Karate Soc. (6th degree Black Belt), Marial Arts Karate Assn., Alpha Omega Alpha. Office: Community Mental Health Coun 8704 S Constance Ave Chicago IL 60617-2756 also: Jackson Park Hosp 7531 S Stony Island Ave Chicago IL 60649-3993

BELL, CHARLES EUGENE, JR., industrial engineer; b. N.Y.C., Dec. 13, 1932; s. Charles Edward and Constance Elizabeth (Verbella) Bell; m. Doris R. Clifton, Jan. 14, 1967; 1 child, Scott Charles. B.Engring., Johns Hopkins U., 1954, MS in Engring., 1959. Registered Calif. Indsl. engr. Signode Corp., Balt., 1957—61, asst. to plant mgr., 1961—63, plant engr., 1963—64, divsn. indsl. engr. Glenview, Ill., 1964—69, asst. to divsn. mgr., 1969—76, engring. mgr., 1976—93; cons., 1993—. Host committeeman Internat. Indsl. Engring. Conf., Chgo., 1984, Chgo., 92. With U.S. Army, 1955—57. Mem.: NSPE, Soc. Plastics Engrs., Ill. Soc. Profl. Engrs., Indsl. Mgmt. Club Ctrl. Md. (pres. 1964), Am. Inst. Indsl. Engrs. (pres. 1981), Druid Hills Country Club. Republican. Roman Catholic. Home: 207 Markham Ln Crossville TN 38558

BELL, CHESTER GORDON, computer engineering company executive; b. Kirksville, Mo., Aug. 19, 1934; s. Roy Chester and Lola Dolph (Gordon) Bell; m. Gwendolyn Kay Druyor, Jan. 3, 1959; children: Brigham Roy, Laura Louise. BSEE, MIT, 1956, MSEE, 1957; DEng (hon.), Worcester Poly. Inst., 1993. Engr. Speech Communication Lab., MIT, Cambridge, 1959—60; mgr. computer design Digital Equipment Corp., Maynard, Mass., 1960—66, v.p. engring., 1972—83; prof. computer sci. Carnegie-Mellon U., 1966—72; vice chmn. Encore Computer Corp., Marlboro, Mass., 1983—86; asst. dir. NSF, Washington, 1986—87; v.p. R & D Stardent Computer, Sunnyvale, Calif., 1987—89; cons. The Bell-Mason Group, 1989—. Bd. dirs. Cradle Tech., Caspian Networks; bd. dirs., trustee Computer Mus., 1982—90, trustee, 2000—; sr. rschr. Microsoft Corp., 1995—. Co-author (with Newell): (novels) Computer Structures, 1971; co-author: (with Grason, Newell) Designing Computers and Digital Systems, 1972; co-author: (with Mudge, McNamara) Computer Engineering, 1978; co-author: (with McNamara) High Tech Ventures, 1991; actor:. Recipient 6th Mellon Inst. award, 1972, Nat. medal Tech., U.S. Dept. Commerce Tech. Adminstrn., 1991, award for greatest econ. contbn. to region, Am. Electronics Assn., 1993, MCI Smithsonian award for Innovation, 1995. Fellow: Assn. for Computing Machingery, Am. Acad. Arts and Scis., IEEE (McDowell award 1975, Eckert-Mauchly award 1982, von Neumann medal 1992); mem.: NAE, AAAS, Eta Kappa Nu (Karapetoff and Emminent mem. awards 2001). Office: c/o Microsoft 455 Market Ste 1690 San Francisco CA 94105

BELL, CHRIS See **BELL, ROBERT CHRISTOPHER**

BELL, CHRISTINE MARIE, secondary educator; b. Bluefield, W.Va., Nov. 5, 1961; d. Robert Warren and Therese (Wolinski) Stroh; m. Harlin Lindel Bell, Aug. 3, 1991; children: Shelby Katherine. BA, Mary Washington Coll., Fredericksburg, Va., 1983; MEd, U. Va., 1986. Cert. history and social studies tchr., Va. Adminstrv. asst. U. Va. Hosp., Charlottesville, 1984-85; tchr., counselor Oakland (Va.) Residential Sch., 1986-87; tchr. social studies Hopewell (Va.) High Sch., 1987—, coord. computers for edn. program, 1991-93. (workshops) Va. Gov. Best Practice Ctr., 2001; (documentaries) Dept. of Edn. Hour, 2001. Advisor model exec. br. YMCA, Richmond, Va., 1991-92, advisor model gen. assembly, 1991—. Recipient YMCA service to youth award, YMCA, 1996, Resolution of Appreciation, Va. Dept. of Edn. Sch. Bd., 2001, Tchr. of the Yr., Hopewell City Sch., 2001. Mem. APA (affiliate), ASCD, Nat. Coun. for Social Studies, Va. Geog. Soc., New Va. Dept. of Edn. Database ofexemplary educators, Avocations: politics, reading, travel, swimming, jogging. Home: 96 Sand Hill Rd Williamsburg VA 23188-6600 Office: Lafayette High Sch Williamsburg VA 23188

BELL, CORINNE REED, psychologist; b. Holly Springs, Miss., July 6, 1943; d. Robert Norris and Laura Kathleen (Robinson) Reed; children: Jeffrey Kenneth Bell, Jennifer Bell Monroe. BA with highest honors, U. Tenn., 1976, MA, 1978, PhD, 1985. Lic. psychologist, Tenn. Rsch. asst. Lakeshore Mental Health Inst., Knoxville, 1976; instr. psychology dept. Roane State C.C., Harriman, Tenn., 1978; cons., sch. psychologist dept. spl. edn. U. Tenn., Knoxville, 1979-80; pvt. practice psychology Knoxville, 1979—; founder, psychologist, ptnr. Clin. & Sch. Assocs., Knoxville, 1985-96; v.p. mktg. Lark Industries, Inc., Knoxville, 1994-95, also bd. dirs.; founder, adminstr., psychologist Behavioral Health Ctr. Child & Adult Svcs., Knoxville, 1996—. Cons. social svcs. Dept. Human Svcs., Tenn., 1985—. Contbr. articles to profl. jours. Mem. adv. bd. John Tarleton Children's Home, Knoxville, 1987-93, Florence Crittendon Agy., 1994—; bd. dirs. Sexual Assault Crisis Ctr., Knoxville, 1987-94, Children's Ctr. Knoxville, 1995-98; mem. Big Bros. Big Sisters, 1999—, bd. dirs., 1999-; mem., cons. Knox County Child Abuse Rev. Team, Knoxville, 1982-2000; vol. Knox County Mental Health Assn., 1991-95, Interfaith Health Clinic, 1990-96. Acad. scholar U. Tenn., 1974; rsch. grantee Knox County Children's Fund, 1979. Mem.: APA, Exec. Women's Assn., Knoxville Assn. Women Execs. (programs chair 2001), Mortar Bd., Unified Psychology Coalition (co-founder, legis. chair/spokesperson 1989—92), Knoxville Area Psychol. Assn. (treas. 1986—88, pub. rels. chair 1989—90, pres. 1990—91), Tenn. Psychol. Assn. (pub. rels. chair 1992—94, v.p. East Tenn. 1999—2000), Phi Beta Kappa, Phi Kappa Phi. Episcopalian. Avocations: performing arts, piano, creative writing, physical fitness, gardening. Office: Behavioral Health Ctr Child and Adult Svcs 3624 Vandeventer Ave Knoxville TN 37919-4578

BELL, DANIEL CARROLL, realtor, community association, ranch and land manager; b. Chgo., July 17, 1940; s. Daniel Gregory and Inez Margarite (Carroll) B.; m. Elaine Paula Rhody, Feb. 1, 1960; children: Tana Lou, Daniel Arden, Andrea Jane. Student, Colo. State U., 1958-62, Reisch Coll. Auctioneering, Mason City, Iowa, 1983. Cert. assn. mgmt. specialist, ind. cmty. mgr. Mgr. ptnr. Three Bell Ranch, Ft. Collins, Colo., 1958-69; sales rep. Pacific Vegetable Oil Co., San Francisco, 1969-70; mng. dir. Paveocor A.G. subs. PVO Internat., Rotterdam, Netherlands, 1970-71; nat. sales mgr. PVO Internat., San Francisco, 1971-72; v.p. commodity trading San Pablo Mfg. Co. subs. PVO Internat., Manila, Philippines, 1972-74; v.p. Rothschild Brokerage Co., San Francisco, 1975-76; owner, prin. Feed, Etc., Harbor, Oreg., 1976-79; commodity specialist Shearson Loeb Rhodes, Medford, Oreg., 1979-80; exec. v.p., gen. mgr. Superior Credit Assocs., Inc., Medford, 1981-86; mng. ptnr. Three Bell Land Co., Pierce, Colo., 1986—; ptnr. Legacy Transp. Co., 1986-93; CEO Bell & Assocs. Ltd., 1993—; gen. mgr. Greenfield Village RV Resort Assn., 1994-98; exec. dir. Sun Village HOA, 1999. Mem. Medford (Oreg.) Planning Commn., 1981-84, Medford Sister Cities Commn., 1984; treas. Jackson County Rep. Ctrl. Com., Medford, 1982-84; arbitrator Better Bus. Bur., Medford and Ft. Collins, Colo., 1984-89; candidate Oreg. Ho. Reps., 1984; mem. Mesa (Ariz.) Human Svcs. Adv. Bd., 1994-95; grad. Mesa Citizens Police Acad., 1995, v.p., 1996, pres., 1998—, facilitator, 1997-98; mem. Civilian Res. Ariz. Dept. Pub. Safety; mem. Housing and Human Svcs. Adv. Bd., Mesa, 1998-99; mem. Camp Verde Bd. Adjustments, 1999-2000; mem. Town Camp Verde Civil Enforcement Hearing Officer, 2000—; mcpl. judge pro tem, 2000—. With USAR, 1958-63, Colo. Air N.G., 1963-65. Mem. NRA, Cmty. Assn. Inst. (cert. assn. mgmt. specialist), Inst. Cmty. Mmgt. (cert. ind. cmty. mgr.), Ariz. Travel Parks Assn. (bd. dirs. 1997-99, treas.), Ariz. Magistrates Assn., Elks. Republican. Presbyterian. Avocations: fishing, golf. Office: 2034 Rustler Trail Camp Verde AZ 86322-7536 E-mail: deb5434@aol.co,.

BELL, DANIEL MARK, music educator; b. Omaha, Aug. 17, 1962; s. Rance and Nancy Bell; 1 child, Ryan. MusB, U. Iowa, 1985; MusM, Colo. State U., 1988. Tchr. Ft. (Colo.) Lupton HS, 1988—94, Rangeview HS, Aurora, Colo., 1994—97, Cheyenne Mt. Jr. HS, Colo. Springs, Colo., 1997—; freelance musician Colo., 1985—. Band dir. Colo. Music Educators Conf., 2000—03. Avocation: skiing.

BELL, DAVID ARTHUR, advertising agency executive; b. Mpls., May 29, 1943; s. Arthur E. and Frances (Tripp) B.; m. Gail G. Galvani; children: Jennifer L., Jenny L., Jeffrey D., Ashley Tripp, Andrew Joseph. BA in Polit. Sci., Macalester Coll., 1965. Account exec. Leo Burnett, Chgo., 1965-67; pres. Knox Reeves, Mpls., 1967-74; pres. Atlantic div. Bozell & Jacobs, 1974-85; pres. Bozell, Jacobs, Kenyon & Eckhardt, 1986-92; chmn., CEO Bozell Worldwide

Inc., 1992-96, True North Comm., Inc., 1996—2001; vice chmn. Interpublic Group of Companies, Inc., N.Y.C., 2001—03, chmn., CEO, 2003—. Bd. dirs. Bus. Publs. Audit, Primedia, Inc.; chmn. Am. Advt. Fedn. Nat. com. coord. United Way Am., Minn., 1975—; trustee Macalester Coll., 1986—88, trustee emeritus, 1998—, Sacred Heart Acad., NY; chmn. Advt. Ednl. Found., Ad Coun., 2002—; bd. dirs. True North, 1998—2001, Nat. Forest Fedn., 2002—. Recipient charter centennial medallion Macalester Coll., 1974; named disting. alumnus Macalester Coll., 1978; recipient Minn. Airman of Yr. award, 1967 Mem. Am. Advt. Fedn. (chmn. nat. bd. dirs. 1988-91), Am. Assn. Advt. Agys. (chmn. 1996-97. Republican. Presbyterian. Office: Interpublic Group of Companies Inc 1271 Avenue of the Americas New York NY 10020*

BELL, DAVID GUS (BUDDY BELL), professional baseball manager; b. Pitts., Aug. 27, 1951; s. Gus B.; m. Gloria Bell; children: David, Michael, Ricky, Kristi Marie, Tracy. Player in minor leagues, 1969-71; outfielder, 3d baseman Cleve. Indians, 1972-78, minor league hitting instr., 1990, coach, 1994-95; 3d baseman Tex. Rangers, 1979-85, 89; with Cin. Reds, 1985-88; player Houston Astros, 1988; dir. minor league instrn. Chgo. White Sox, 1991-93; mgr. Detroit Tigers, 1996-98, Colo. Rockies, Denver, 1999—. Mem.: Am. League All-Star Team, 1973, 80-82, 84. Recipient Gold Glove award, 1979 84. Address: Colorado Rockies 2001 Blake St Denver CO 80205-2008

BELL, DAVID MAXWELL, music educator, consultant; b. Waukehsa, Wis., Nov. 8, 1954; s. Vernon Leigh Bell and Enid Ruth Morrison-Bell; m. Lois Jean Tams, May 30, 1979; children: Lauren Elizabeth, Amanda Leigh, Eric William. BA, No. Ill. U., 1975; MusM, U. of Cin., 1979. Cert. tchr. Ohio Dept. of Edn., 1979. Fine arts facilitator and head choral dir. Winton Woods City Schools, Cin., 1982—; guest clinician College-Conservatory of Music U. of Cin., Cin., 2002—02; guest clinician Miami U. of Ohio, Oxford, Ohio, 2001—01; founding music dir. Sing Cin.! Cin. Arts Festival, Cin., 1994; music dir. Dayton (Ohio) Liederkranz-Turner Soc., 1979—87; vocal music tchr. Dayton (Ohio) City Schs., 1979—82. Bd. mem. Ohio Alliance for Arts Edn., Columbus, Ohio; mem. arts edn. adv. com. Ohio Dept. of Edn., Columbus, Ohio, 1997—99, mem. adv. bd. state content standards for fine arts, 2001—; co-chmn. ednl. leadership team Winton Woods HS, Cin., 2000—; arts in edn. partnerships adv. panel Ohio Arts Coun., Columbus, 2000—01; adv. panel fine arts field test Nat. Coun. of Exec. State Sch. Officers, Washington, 1998—98; adv. panel Ohio dept. of edn. Ednl. Testing Svcs., Princeton, NJ, 1999—99; cons. WLWT TV, Cin., 1996; founding adv. com. May Festival Youth Honors Chorus, Cin., 1988—88, Muse Machine Youth Arts Orgn., Dayton, 1981—82. Contributing conductor: TV series Cin, Pops Holiday: Fourth of July from the Heartland; contributing conductor (TV series) Cin. Olympic Torch Ceremony, (albums) Cin. Pops Mega Movies (Premiered at number fourteen on the Billboard Mag. classical-crossover charts, 2000), (TV series) Tall Stacks Farewell Ceremony (Emmy award, 1995); singer: (albums) Verdi's Requiem with Chicago Symphony and Symphony Chorus (Grammy award, 1978), Beethoven's Missa Solemnis with Chicago Symphony and Symphony Chorus (Grammy award, 1979), Verdi's Four Sacred Pieces with Chicago Symphony and Symphony Chorus (Grammy award, 1980); contbr. articles to profl. jours. Scholar, U. of Cin. College-Conservatory of Music, 1977—79. Mem.: Winton Woods Teachers Assn. (bldg. rep. 1984—86), Ohio Music Edn. Assn. (choral affairs chair for state conf. 1992—93), Ohio Choral Dirs. Assn. (pres. 1999—2001), Pi Kappa Lambda (hon.). Avocations: family, reading, golf. Home: 7695 Chelsea Court Hamilton OH 45011 Office: Winton Woods City Schools 1231 West Kemper Road Cincinnati OH 45240

BELL, DAVID SAMUEL HENRY, medical educator; b. Armagh, Northern Ireland, Jan. 13, 1944; came to U.S., 1975; s. James Smyth and Violet (Burgess) B.; m. Jocelyn Anne Johnson, Nov. 20, 1971; children: James, Michael, Andrew. MB, BCh, BAO, Queens U., Belfast, 1976. Diplomate Am. Bd. Internal Medicine. Fellow in Endocrinology U. Saskatchewan, Saskatoon, 1974-75; fellow in Endocrinology Greater Balt. Med. Ctr., Balt., 1975-76; cons. Georgetown (Ont.) Hosp., 1976-78; dir. internal medicine Connemaugh Hosp., Johnstown, Pa., 1978-80; assoc. prof. U. Ala., Birmingham, 1980-87, prof. medicine, 1987—, dir. diabetes program, 1985—. Contbr. numerous articles to profl. jours. Fellow ACP, Royal Coll. Physicians (Edinburgh), Royal Coll. Physicians (Can.), Am. Coll. Endocrinology. Avocations: golf, power walking. Office: U Ala Sch Medicine 702 FOT 510 S 20th St Birmingham AL 35294-3407

BELL, DEAN PHILLIP, dean; b. Erie, Pa., Aug. 17, 1967; BA, U. Chgo., 1989; MA, PhD, U. Calif., Berkeley, 1995. Assoc. dean Spertus Inst. of Jewish Studies, Chgo., 1998—2001, dean, chief acad. officer, 2001—. Author: (scholarly book) Sacred Communities: Jewish and Christian Identities in Fifteenth-Century Germany; editor: (publn. of scholarly lectrs.) The Solomon Goldman Lectures, Volume VII, (spl. issue of scholarly jour.) Historical Memory and the State of Jewish Studies in Germany, 1997; assoc. editor: Shofar: An Interdisciplinary Jour. of Jewish Studies, 1998—2001. Recipient dissertation fellowship, Mellon Found., 1994—95, pre-dissertation fellowship, Ctr. for German and European Studies, 1992, German Lang. fellowship, U.S. Fgn. Lang. and Area Studies, 1991. Mem.: Sixteenth Century Studies Assn., Assn. for Jewish Studies, Midwest Jewish Studies Assn. (pres. 2001—03), Phi Beta Kappa. Office: Spertus Inst Jewish Studies 618 S Michigan Ave Chicago IL 60605 Office Fax: 312-922-6406. E-mail: dbell@spertus.edu.

BELL, DELORIS WILEY, physician; b. Solomon, Kans., Sept. 30, 1942; d. Harry A. and Mildren H. (Watt) Wiley; children: Leslie, John. BA, Kans. Wesleyan U., 1964; MD, U. Kans., 1968. Diplomate Am. Bd. Ophthalmology. Intern St. Luke's Hosp., Kansas City, Mo., 1968-69; resident U. Kans. Med. Ctr., Kansas City, 1969-72; practice medicine specializing in ophthalmology Overland Park, Kans., 1973—. Mem. AMA, Kans. Med. Soc. (pres. sect. ophthalmology 1985-86, spkr. house 1994-97), Am. Acad. Ophthalmology (councillor 1988-93, chmn. state govtl. affairs 1993-97, bd. trustees 2000-03), Kans. Soc. Ophthalmology (pres. 1985-86), Kansas City Soc. Ophthalmology and Otolaryngology (sec. 1984-86, pres.-elect 1988, pres. 1989). Avocations: photography, travel. Office: 7000 W 121st St Ste 100 Shawnee Mission KS 66209-2010 E-mail: cd2c@aol.com.

BELL, DENISE LOUISE, newspaper reporter, photographer, paralegal, librarian, life agent; b. Washington, Nov. 27, 1967; d. Richard Keith Bell and Kay Lorraine (Sutherland) Reynolds. Student, Inst. Adventiste du Saleve, Collonges, France, 1988; BA in French, Loma Linda U., 1990. Yearbook editor Loma Linda U., La Sierra, Calif., 1989-90, desk technician Loma Linda, Calif., 1990-92; staff writer Inland Empire Cmty. Newspapers, Colton, Calif., 1990-91, city editor San Bernardino, Calif., 1991-94; asst. circ. supr. Del Webb Meml. Libr. Loma Linda (Calif.) U., 1994-2000; reporter City Newspaper Group, Colton, Calif., 1995-99; life agt. Denise Bell Life Agt., Redlands, Calif., 2000—01; paralegal Law Offices Don Featherstone, Corona, Calif., 2001—. Asst. leader Girl Scouts U.S., Walla Walla, Wash., 1986; co-leader Girl Scouts Switzerland, Geneva, 1987, Girl Scouts U.S., Loma Linda, 1988-93. Mem.: San Bernardino County Bar Assn. Avocations: photography, writing, archery. Home: 391 N Main St Ste 204 Loma Linda CA 92880 E-mail: natashabelle@lycos.com.

BELL, DEREK, professional baseball player; b. Tampa, Fla., Dec. 11, 1968; With Toronto Blue Jays, 1991—92, San Diego Padres, 1993—95; outfielder Houston Astros, 1995—99, N.Y. Mets, 1999—. Named Nat. League Player of the Week, 1995, 1997. Office: New York Mets 12301 Roosevelt Ave Flushing NY 11368-1699

BELL, DERRICK ALBERT, law educator, author, lecturer; b. Pitts., Nov. 6, 1930; s. Derrick Albert and Ada Elizabeth (Childress) B.; m. Jewel Allison Hairston, June 26, 1960 (dec. Aug. 1990); m. Janet Dewart, June 28, 1992; children: Derrick Albert III, Douglass Dubois, Carter Robeson. AB, Duquesne U., 1952; LLB, U. Pitts., 1957; hon. degree in law, Toogaloo Coll., 1983, Northeastern U., 1985, Mercy Coll., 1988, Allegheny Coll., 1989, Howard U., 1995, Bates Coll., 1997, Medgar Evers Coll., 1998; degree in law (hon.), Metro. Coll. N.Y., 2003. Bar: DC 1957, Pa. 1959, NY State 1966, Calif. 1969. Atty. civil rights div. Dept. Justice, Washington, 1957-59; 1st asst. counsel NAACP Legal Def. Edn. Fund, NYC, 1960-66; dep. dir. Office Civil Rights, HEW, Washington, 1966-68; exec. dir. Western Ctr. on Law and Poverty, 1968-69; lectr. law Harvard U., Cambridge, Mass., 1969-71, prof. law, 1971-80, 86-92; dean U. Oreg. Law Sch., 1981-85;, 1991-93. Vis. prof. NYU Sch. Law, 1991—. Author: Race, Racism and American Law, 1973, 4th edit., 2000, Constitutional Conflicts, 1992, Shades of Brown: New Perspectives on School Desegregation, 1980, And We Are Not Saved: The Elusive Quest for Racial Justice, 1987, Faces at the Bottom of the Well: The Permanence of American Racism, 1992, Confronting Authority: Reflections of an Ardent Protester, 1994, Ethical Ambition: Living a Life of Meaning and Worth, 2002. Gospel Choirs Psalms of Survival in an Alien Land Called Home, 1996, Afro/antica Legacies (1998), Ethical Ambition: Living a Life of Meaning and Worth, 2002; 1st lt. USAF, 1952-54. Grantee Ford Found., 1972, 75, 91, 93, 94-96, NEH, 1980-81. Home: 444 Central Park W Apt 14B New York NY 10025-4358 Office: NYU Sch Law 40 Washington Sq S New York NY 10012-1005

BELL, DON ANTONIO, neuroradiologist; b. Yadkinville, N.C., Feb. 11, 1958; s. Joseph Luther and Jeanette (Bruner) B.; m. Amelia Fort, May 19, 1984; children : Ryan Tierney, Riley Katherine, Joseph Regan. BS, U. N.C., 1980, MD, 1984. Diplomate Am. Bd. Internal Medicine, Am. Bd. Diagnostic Radiology. Instr. radiology U. Utah, Salt Lake City, 1993-94; asst. prof. radiology Wake Forest U., Winston-Salem, N.C., 1994-97; clin. prof. radiology U. N.C., Chapel Hill, 1997-2000, Med. U. S.C., Charleston, 2000—. Scientific adv. bd. Cordis Endovasc. Sys., Miami, 1999—, Datascope, Inc., Islen, N.J., 1998—, Siemens Med. Sys., Erlangen, Germany, 1999—, GE Med. Sys., Milw., 1996-98. NSF fellow, 1978-80, Nat. Cancer Inst. fellow, 1986-87. Mem. World Fedn. Intvl. Neuroradiology, Radiol. Soc. N.Am., Am. Roentgen Ray Soc., Am. Soc. Neuroradiology, Am. Soc. Intvl. Therapeutic Neuroradiology. Democrat. Unitarian Universalist. Avocations: running, rock climbing, mountaineering, golf, gardening. Office: Presbyn Hosp Dept Radiology 200 Hawthorne Ln Charlotte NC 28204-2515

BELL, DOROTHY FRANCES, nurse, educator; b. Milw. m. Daniel J. Bell, 1970; 5 children. BS, Coll. St. Teresa, Winona, Minn., 1969; postgrad., U. Md., 1969-70; MS, Winona State U., 1973. RN, Minn. Staff nurse pediatrics U. Md. Hosp., Balt., 1969-70; staff nurse psychiatry St. Marys Hosp., Rochester, Minn., 1970-71, staff nurse pediatrics, pediatric ICU, 1974-75; instr. pub. health Coll. St. Teresa, Rochester, 1971-73; mem. nursing edn. staff Rochester Meth. Hosp., 1977-85, staff devel./continuing edn. coord., 1985-91; nursing edn. specialist Mayo Found., Rochester, 1991—. Editorial bd. Jour. Nursing Staff Devel., 1991-98; contbr. articles to profl. publs. Vol. Rochester Parochial Schs., 1980—, Am. Cancer Soc., Rochester, 1989, 91, 92; mem. Rochester Ctrl. Cath. Sch. Bd. Edn., 1994—, treas., 1995—, v.p., 1996-97; mem. Am. Nurses Credentialing Commn. on Accreditation, 1997-2003, vice chair, 1998-99, chair, 1999-2003, bd. dir. 1999-2003; bd. dir. Lourdes Found., Inc. Mem. ANA (at-large exec. com., coun. continuing edn. and staff devel.), APHA, Nursing Continuing Edn. Consortium S.E. Minn. (sec.-treas. 1987-91, pres. 1994-95, chmn. 1993-95), Minn. Nurses Assn. (vice chmn. continuing edn. approval program 1993-95, chmn. 1995-96), Nat. Nursing Staff Devel. Orgn. (charter), Sigma Theta Tau (charter Kappa Mu chpt., sec. 1989-91. Republican.

BELL, EDWARD ALLEN, pharmacy educator; b. Harve DeGrace, Md., Oct. 17, 1959; s. Raymond and Evelyn Bell; m. Myndell L. Nussbaum, Oct. 3, 1992; children; Aaron, Sarah. BS in Pharmacy, U. Md., 1982, D Pharmacy, 1988. Cert. Bd. Pharmacol. Specialties. Pharmacist Wyman Park Health Sys., Balt., 1982-86; asst. prof., then assoc. prof. Coll. Pharmacy Drake U., Des Moines, 1989—. Mem. editl. rev. bd. Jour. Pediat. Pharmacy Practice, 1999—; contbr. articles to profl. jours., column to Infectious Diseases in Children, 1999—. Named Big Brither of Yr., Jewish Big Bros./Sister League of Balt., 1985. Mem. Am. Soc. Colls. Pharmacy, Am. Coll. Clin. Pharmacy, Iowa Pharmacy Assn., Iowa Soc. Hosp. Pharmacists (treas. 1991-93). Home: 2011 Country Club Blvd Clive IA 50325-8597 Office: Drake U Coll Pharmacy Des Moines IA 50311

BELL, ELVA GLENN, retired secondary school educator, retired counseling administrator, interpreter; b. Phila., Sept. 3, 1922; d. Arthur Edward Glenn, Ruth Ann Marie Demby Glenn; m. Howard Wesley Bell, Sr.; children: Howard Bell, Jr., Linda Bell-Powell. BS in Edn., Cheyney State Coll., 1945; MS in Edn., Temple U., 1970. Case worker Dept. Pub. Assistance, Phila., 1945—51; tchr., guidance counselor Phila. Sch. Dist., 1956—71; guidance counselor Abington (Pa.) Sch. Dist., Pa., 1971—82; interpreter at Clivden - Hist. Mansion Nat. Trust Property, Germantown, Pa., 1987—. Sch./cmty. rep. human rels. adv. coun. Abington Sch. Dist., 1974—. Mem., chairperson ways and means com. United Neighbors, Willow Grove, 1975—; mem. Abington Coalition of Civics - Abington Township, 1996—; bd. mem., Unity Day chairperson, life mem. NAACP - Willow Grove, 1939—; Congl. sr. intern CLOSE-UP, Washington, 1997—. Recipient Cmty. Svc. and Leadership award, Citizens for Progress, 1976, Trailblazer award, Willow Grove NAACP, 1985, Cmty. Svc. and Leadership award, Optimist Club Lower Montgomery County, 1986, Ho. of Reps. citation, Pa., 1987, 1999, Martin Luther King award, Abington Twp., 1988, Svc. award, Willow Grove NAACP, 2001. Mem.: AAUW, Black Women's Ednl. Alliance (treas., fin. sec. 1980—86, newsletter editor, Svc. award 1986, Cmty. Svc. and Leadership award 1986), Zeta Phi Beta Sorority - Beta Delta Zeta Chpt. (vol.). Lutheran. Avocations: travel, church activities, community activist.

BELL, ERNEST LORNE, III, retired lawyer; b. Boston, June 12, 1926; s. Ernest L. and Ellamay (Currier) B.; m. Margaret Van Nostrand Depue, Apr. 14, 1951 (dec. Oct. 1988); children: David E., Robin E., Roseanne Margaret; m. Sally Leavitt Cheney, Nov. 25, 1989. BA cum laude, Harvard Coll., 1949; JD, U. Mich., 1952. Bar: N.H. 1952, U.S. Supreme Ct. 1962. Pvt. practice, Keene, N.H., 1952; ptnr. firm Bell & Falk, P.A., 1972-99; sole practice law Keene, NH, 1999—2003; ret., 2003, 2003. Author: An Initial View of Ultra as an American Weapon in World War II. Mem. exec. bd. Daniel Webster coun. Boy Scouts Am., 1970-79, 93—; chmn. bd. advisers Colony House Mus., 1984-91; trustee, treas. Keene Pub. Libr.; del. N.H. Constl. Conv., 1964, 74; mem. World War II Studies Assn.; mem. N.H. Aero. Commn., 1980-86. Recipient Silver Beaver award Fellow Am. Bar Found. (N.H. chair 1993-99); mem. ABA, N.H. Bar Assn (pres. 1978-79), N.H. Bar Found. (sec., bd. dirs. 1985-90, chmn. 1991-93), Cheshire County Bar Assn., Lawyer Pilots Bar Assn. (founding dir. 1962-68), Def. Rsch. Inst. (v.p. 1969-73, sec. 1973-76), Am. Kennel Club (del. 1979-81), Std. Schnauzer Club Am., Harvard Club (Boston). Episcopalian. Home: 35 Felt Rd Keene NH 03431-2103 E-mail: tuttfelteen@monad.net.

BELL, FRANCES LOUISE, medical technologist; b. Milton, Pa., Apr. 28, 1926; d. George Earl and Kathryn Robbins (Fairchild) Reichard; m. Edwin Lewis Bell II, Dec. 27, 1950; children: Ernest Michael, Stephen Thomas, Eric Leslie. BS in Biology cum laude, Bucknell U., 1948; MT, Geisinger Meml. Hosp., 1949. Registered med. technologist. Med. technologist Burlington County Hosp., Mt. Holly, N.J., 1949-50, Robert Packer Hosp., Sayre, Pa., 1950, Carle Hosp./Clinic, Urbana, Ill., 1951-52, St. Joseph Hosp., Reading, Pa., 1972-83. Vol. Crime Watch, City Hall, Reading, 1985-90, Am. Heart Assn., Reading, 1956-2000, March of Dimes, Reading, 1956-72, Am. Cancer Soc., Reading, 1956-71, Multiple Sclerosis, Reading, 1956-72, Reading Musical Found., 1985-90, Hist. Soc. Berks County; corr. sec. women's aux., 1986-90; fin. sec. aux. Albright Coll., 1988-95; hospitality co-chmn. women's com. Reading Symphony Orch., 1985 90, editor yearbook women's com., 1992-96; editor yearbook Reading Symphony Orch. League, 1996-2003; chmn. hospitality Reading-Berks Pub. Librs., 1988-91; mem. Friends Reading Mus., Berks County Conservancy. Mem. AAUW (assoc. editor bull. 1961-63, cultural interests rep. 1967-68), Woman's Club of Reading (treas. 1986-88, fin. sec. 1991—), United Meth. Women, World Affairs Coun. Berks County, Libr. Soc. Albright Coll., Phi Beta Kappa. Republican. Methodist. Avocations: music appreciation, photography, postcard art prints. Home: 1454 Oak Ln Reading PA 19604-1865 *Life and grace are cherished gifts to each one of us from our creator. We are spiritual beings, so our nature is to be loving, kind, understanding, forgiving and compasssionate in all our relations with others.*

BELL, FRANK JOSEPH, III, architect; b. Paterson, N.J., Sept. 30, 1955; s. Frank Joseph and Evelyn Dorothy (Nemeth) B.; m. Greta Eichlin, Sept. 13, 1987; children: Marjorie Blair, Caroline Frances. Student, U. Miami, Coral Gables, Fla., 1976-78; BArch, N.J. Inst. Tech., 1981. Registered architect, N.J., N.Y., Pa.; cert. profl. planner, N.J. Staff architect Houghton-Quarty-Warr, Architects, 1981-86; prin. Frank Joseph Bell, Architect, Branchville, N.J., 1986—. Apptd. county architect County of Hunterdon, 1990—; bd. dirs. constrn. housing Hunterdon County Housing Corp. Secretary, chmn. bd. dirs. Highlands Workshop/Easter Seal Soc., Franklin, N.J., 1981—; chmn. bldg. and grounds com. St. Joseph's Ch., Newton, 1984—; mem. Franklin Twp. Sch. Bd. Mem. AIA, N.J. Soc. Architects, Bldg. Ofcls. Code Adminstrn. Avocations: photography, water skiing, fly fishing. Office: PO Box 314 Pittstown NJ 08867-0314

BELL, FRANK OURAY, JR., lawyer; b. San Francisco, Aug. 13, 1940; s. Frank Ouray Sr. and Clara Belle (McClure) Bell; m. Sherrie A. Levie, Mar. 29, 1981; children: Aimee, David;children from previous marriage: Carin, Laurie. AB, San Francisco State U., 1963; JD, U. Calif., San Francisco, 1966. Bar: Calif. 1966, U.S. Dist. Ct. (no. dist.) Calif. 1967, U.S. Ct. Appeals (9th cir.) 1967, U.S. Supreme Ct. 1973. Dep. atty. gen. Calif. State's Atty.'s Office, Sacramento, 1966-68; ptnr. Goorjian & Bell, San Francisco, 1968-70; chief asst. Fed. Pub. Defender's Office, San Francisco, 1970-82; dir. Calif. State Pub. Defender's Office, 1984-87; pvt. practice law San Francisco, 1982-84; sr. litig. assoc. Olimpia, Whelan & Lively, San Jose, Calif., 1987-89; pvt. practice San Mateo, Calif., 1989—. Mem.: Calif. Pub. Defenders Assn. (bd. dirs. 1986—87), San Mateo County Bar Assn. Democrat. Jewish. Office: 303 Bradford St Ste C Redwood City CA 94063 E-mail: FrankBell@FrankBellLaw.com.

BELL, GARY LYNN, owner production company, video and audio producer; b. Coffeyville, Kans., Oct. 11, 1949; s. Robert Hayes Bell and Nadine Owens; m. Karen Elizabeth Miller, Feb. 1, 1997; 1 child, Eric; m. Bertha Ruth May (div. Sept. 0, 1978); children: Gregory, Jeremy. Sonar technician USN, Long Beach, Calif., 1969—73; ind. prodr., musician L.A., 1973—92; news cameraman, editor Jones Intercable TV, Palmdale, Calif., 1997—99; owner, CEO Gig 2 Me Music & Video, Lancaster, Calif., 1999—2002. Prodr. Dabany Productions, Hollywood, Calif., 1986—94. Prodr.: (musical composition) I'm Telling You, 1998 (named most popular song on Indie.com, 2000). Com. mem. Lancaster C. of C., 1999—2002, Palmdale C. of C., 2000—02; mem. Quartz Hill Chamber Of Commerce, 2001—02. Recipient appreciation award, Palmdale C. of C., 2001. Office: Gig 2 Me Music & Video 43568 Yaffa St Lancaster CA 93535 Business E-Mail: gary@gig2me.com.

BELL, GENE, newspaper publishing executive; Pres., CEO San Diego Union-Tribune, 1992—. Office: San Diego Union-Tribune 350 Camino De La Reina San Diego CA 92108-3003

BELL, GREGORY KNOX, management consultant; b. La Ronge, Saskatchewan, Can., Aug. 16, 1960; s. Robert Douglas and Catharine Elizabeth (Tate) B.; m. Marie Madelene Ducluzeau, May 2, 1981; children: Andrea Marie, Kristen Robin. BA with honors, Simon Fraser U., Vancouver B.C., 1982; MBA with honors, Harvard U., 1987, PhD in Bus. Econs., 1992. Chartered acct., Can. Acct. Pannell, Kerr, MacGillivray, Victoria, B.C., Can., 1982-85; asst. prof. Northeastern U., Boston, 1991-92; lectr. Harvard U., Boston, 1991-92; group v.p., practice leader pharm. and intellectual property Charles River Assocs., Boston, 1992—. Lectr. in field. Recipient Gov. Gen.'s gold medal Simon Fraser U., 1982, bronze medal B.C. Chartered Accts., Vancouver, 1983; named Knox fellow Harvard Bus. Sch., 1985-87, Dean's Doctoral fellow, 1987-90, Baker scholar Harvard Bus. Sch., 1987, John Thayer scholar Harvard U., 1987. Home: 1 Apple Hill Ln Lynnfield MA 01940-1127 Office: Charles River Assocs 200 Clarendon St Fl 33 Boston MA 02116-5092 E-mail: gkb@crai.com.

BELL, GRIFFIN B. lawyer, former attorney general; b. Americus, Ga., Oct. 31, 1918; s. A.C. and Thelma (Pilcher) B.; m. Mary Foy Powell, Feb. 20, 1943 (dec.); 1 son, Griffin B.; m. Nancy Duckworth Kinnebrew, June 8, 2001. Student, Ga. Southwestern Coll.; LL.B. cum laude, Mercer U., 1948, LL.D., 1967. Bar: Ga. bar 1947. Practice in, Savannah and Rome, 1947-53; partner firm King & Spalding, Atlanta, 1953-59, mng. partner, 1959-61; U.S. judge 5th Circuit, 1961-76; sr. partner firm King & Spalding, Atlanta, 1976, 79—; atty. gen. U.S., 1977-79; served chief of staff Gov. Vandiver of Ga., 1959-61; chmn. Atlanta Commn. on Crime and Delinquency, 1965-66. Mem. vis. com. Law Sch., Vanderbilt U.; trustee Mercer U.; bd. dirs. Fed. Jud. Center, 1974-76; chmn. Madrid Conf. on Security and Cooperation in Europe, 1980; co-chmn. Nat. Task Force on Violent Crime, 1981 Co-chmn. Pres. Bush's Com. on Fed. Ethics, 1989. Served to maj. AUS, 1941-46. Mem. ABA (chmn. divsn. jud. adminstrn. 1975-76), Am. Coll. Trial Lawyers (past pres.), Am. Law Inst., Order of Coif. Baptist. Office: King & Spalding LLP 191 Peachtree St NE Atlanta GA 30303-1740 E-mail: gbell@kslaw.com.

BELL, HANEY HARDY, III, lawyer; b. Staunton, Va., Aug. 20, 1944; s. Haney Hardy Jr. and Maud (Deekens) B.; m. Alice Tester, Feb. 17, 1968; 1 child, Landon D. BA, U. Va., 1966; JD cum laude, U. Wis., 1973. Bar: Va. 1974. Group ins. rep. Prudential Ins. Co. Am., Milw., 1969-70; assoc. Woods, Rogers & Hazelgrove, Roanoke, Va., 1973-78; assoc. counsel R.J. Reynolds Industries, Inc., Winston-Salem, N.C., 1978-79; sec., gen. counsel RJR Foods, Inc., 1979-80; sr. internat. counsel R.J. Reynolds Tobacco Internat., Inc., 1980-87; assoc. gen. counsel Fieldcrest Cannon Inc., Eden, N.C., 1987-95, Lorillard Tobacco Co., Greensboro, 1996—2002, Santa Fe (N.Mex.) Natural Tobacco Co., 2002—. Lt. AUS, 1967-69. Mem. Va. State Bar, Order of Coif.

BELL, HARRY FULLERTON, JR., lawyer; b. Charleston, W.Va., Nov. 17, 1954; s. Harry Fullerton and Kathryn Laura (Lewis) B. BS in Econs. cum laude, W.Va. U., 1977, JD, 1980. Bar: W.Va. 1980, U.S. Dist. Ct. (so. dist.) W.Va. 1980, U.S. Dist. Ct. (no. dist.) W.Va. 1986, U.S. Ct. Appeals (4th cir.) 1986. Asst. pros. atty. Kanawha County, Charleston, 1980-82; assoc. Kay, Casto, Chaney, Love & Wise, Charleston, 1982-85, ptnr., 1986-92, Bell and Bands, PLLC, Charleston, 1992—. Instr. Marshall U., Huntington, W.Va., 1984-86. Contbr. articles to profl. jours. Pres. fireman's civil svc. commn. City of Charleston, 1985-86; mem. adminstrv. bd. Christ Meth. Ch., Charleston, 1985-87, bd. trustees, 1986-87; bd. dirs. Charleston Civic Ctr., 1987-91, 2003—, chmn., 1989-91. Mem. W.Va. Bar Assn. (vice chmn. com. on lawyers profl. liability ins. 1984-85, 90—, chmn. 1985-87, young lawyers bd. 1985, cert. merit 1985, young lawyers sect. 1985), Kanawha County Bar Assn. (chmn. courthouse renovation com. 1984-85), Def. Trial Counsel of W.Va., Def. Rsch. Inst., W.Va. U. Alumni Assn. (treas. 1985, v.p. Kanawha County chpt. 1986, pres. 1986-88), Berry Hills Country Club, Beta Gamma Sigma, Omicron Mu Epsilon. Republican. Avocations: sports car racing, flying, golf, tennis, skiing. Home: 1235 Upper Ridgeway Rd Charleston WV 25314-1427 Office: Bell & Bands PLLC PO Box 1723 Charleston WV 25326-1723

BELL, ISAAC, JR., music educator; b. Brighton, Ala., May 7, 1965; s. Isaac and Mary Louise Bell; m. Zenzi Jones, Nov. 10, 1991; children: Isaac III, Jamillah Mary. BA, Ala. State U., 1989, MA in music, 1999. Trombonist/pianist Air U. Band, Maxwell Air Force Base, Ala., 1990—91; trombonist, pianist, arranger Command Band of the Air Force Res., Robins Air Force Base, Ga., 1991—94; choral music dir. Selma City Schs., Ala., 1995—96; grad. tchg. asst. Ala. State U., Sch. of Music, Montgomery, 1996—98; music arranger Clark-Atlanta U., 1998—2000; low-brass instr. Morris Brown Coll., Atlanta, 1998—2000; asst. dir. of bands, brasswinds instr. Benedict Coll., Columbia, SC, 2000—. Mem.: Internat. Trombone Assn. Office: Benedict Coll 1600 Harden St Columbia SC 29204 E-mail: belli@benedict.edu.

BELL, JACQUELINE MICHELLE, marketing professional, public relations executive; b. Dallas, Oct. 3, 1961; d. Robert Moore Sr. and Rebecca Jane Bell; 1 child, Malcolm Bell-Yeldell. BFA, So. Meth. U., 1985; MS, Amber U., 1990. Min. of music Mt. Calvary Missionary Bapt. Ch., Dallas, 1980—; owner It Must Be Jamm!, Dallas, 1996—; grants writer Dallas Mus. Art, 1990-93; dir. devel., mktg. and edn. Jr. Black Acad. of Arts and Letters, Dallas, 1993; coord. fed. and found. rels. Paul Quinn Coll., Dallas, 1993-96; pub. info. officer North Cen. Tex. Coun. of Govts., Arlington, 1997-2000; dir. of mktg. The Women's Mus., Dallas, 2000—. Devel. chair Family Outreach So. Dallas. Mem. Class of 2000, Leadership S.W., Dallas, 1999-00. Mem. Dallas-Ft. Worth Assn. Black Communicators, Internat. Assn. Bus. Communicators, Pub. Rels. Soc. Am., Delta Sigma Theta (Golden Life mem., chpt. pres., corr. sec., collegiate advisor, Outstanding Young Delta 1986, named one of Dallas Shakers and Movers, 2001, Amerigroup Healthy Heros award 2001). Democrat. Baptist. Avocations: reading, piano, gardening.

BELL, JAMES EDWARD, psychologist, educator; b. Chgo., May 12, 1941; s. Codie Dee and Clara (Reynolds) B.; m. Ruth Wilder, Sept. 5, 1964; children: Carl Dougias, Sara Wilder. BA, U. Minn., 1963, PhD, 1967. Asst. prof. Hanover (Ind.) Coll., 1966-68, Elmira (N.Y.) Coll., 1968-71; asst. prof., assoc. prof.

Howard C.C., Columbia, Md., 1971-82, prof. psychology, 1982—. Author: Evaluating Psychological Information, 3d edit., 1999, A Guide to Library Research in Psychology, 1971; editor: Ideas and Issues in Psychology, 8th edit., 2003. Mem. APA (Tchg. award 1982), Assn. for Advancement of C.C. Tchg. Md. Methodist. Home: 5411 Storm Drift Columbia MD 21045 Office: Howard Cmty Coll 10901 Little Patuxent Pkwy Columbia MD 21044 E-mail: jbell@howardcc.edu.

BELL, JAMES THOMAS, housing authority official; b. N.Y.C., Oct. 17, 1949; m. Leslie Toombs, June 25, 1977; children: Guy K., Colin J., Kate E. BA in English Edn. cum laude, Boston Coll., 1971; MPA, L.I. U., 1985. Cert. tchr., N.Y., Conn., Mass. With pers. office Nassau County Dept. Recreation and Parks, N.Y., 1971-72; with pub. info. office Town of Oyster Bay, N.Y., 1972-76, dir. cmty. rels., 1977-80, founding mem., vice chmn. Indsl. Devel. Agy., 1980-82, exec. asst. to town supr., 1980-82, dep. town supr., 1982-87, comptr., 1988-97, chmn. town geog. info. sys. commn., 1995-97, dep. town supr., 1998—2002; exec. dir. Town of Oyster Bay Housing Authority, 2002—. Instr. L.I. U.-C.W. Post, 1998—, mem. adv. coun. health care and pub. adminstrn. dept. Exec. com. Sea Cliff (N.Y.) Rep. Com.; N.Y. State rep. com. 15th A.D., 1996-2002; del. 10th Jud. Dist. Rep. Conv.; trustee Inc. Village Sea Cliff, 1978-80. Recipient Fin. Reporting Achievment award Govt. Fin. Officers Am. and Can., 1996. Mem. Am. Soc. for Pub. Adminstrn. (exec. coun. L.I. chpt.), Sea Cliff Civic Assn., Met. Boston Coll. Club N.Y., North Shore Kiwanis, Pi Alpha Alpha Home: 9 Leonard Pl Sea Cliff NY 11579-2011 Office: Town of Oyster Bay Housing Authority 115 Central Park Rd Plainview NY 11803

BELL, JAMES WINFRED, retired publishing executive; b. Little Rock, Sept. 27, 1929; s. Thacher Winfred and Edna Hafner; m. Ruth Naomi Fletcher, July 1, 1951; children: Susan, Anne, Elizabeth, Charlotte. BS in Bus. Adminstrn., Northwestern U., 1951. V.p Bush-Caldwell Co., Little Rock, 1961—72; pres. Pub. Bookshop, Inc., Little Rock, 1972—94; ret. Moderator Word Spinners Ink-Mainstream, 2000—02. Author: Pulaski County Handbook, 1980; editor: (newsletter) Toast of the South, 1994—95; assoc. editor: Ink Spin Ezine, 2002—03. Pres. Hi-Noon Toastmasters Club, Little Rock, 1994—95. Named Hi-Noon Toastmaster of the Yr., Hi-Noon Toastmasters Club, 1991—92. Mem.: Fiction Writers Ctr. Ark. (treas. 2002—03), Pulaski County Hist. Soc. (past pres. 1998, 1999), Little Rock Toastmaster Club (divsn. gov. 1995—96, Dist. 43 Toastmaster of the Yr. 1995—96, Divsn. Gov. of the Yr. 1995—96). Unitarian Universalist. Avocation: writing historical fiction. Home: 7611 Briarwood Cir Little Rock AR 72205-4810

BELL, JASON CAMERON, lawyer; b. Danville, Ill., Dec. 14, 1963; s. Lamont Bell and Marion (Turner) Butler; m. Yolanda Scott, June 19, 1992; children: Maurice, Ricky Scott, Marcus, Charles, Natalie. BS, Fla. A&M U., 1987; JD, Ill. Inst. Tech., 1997. CPA, Ill. Dir. after-sch. program Frontline Outreach, Orlando, Fla., 1987-88; acct. Washington, Pittman & McKeever, Chgo., 1989-91; acct., founder J. Cameron Bell & Assocs., Chgo., 1991—; atty. Law Offices of Jason Bell, South Holland, Ill., 2002—. Founder East Oak Accessories, 1994—, Creative Career Design, 1999, The Everest Inst., 1999, The Fin. Freedom Forum, 1999; co-founder Adjetey & Bell, Ltd., 2000, Law Offices of Jason Bell, 2002; founder Care Med. Staffing. Bd. dirs. Black Ensemble Theatre Co., Chgo., 1991-93, Phoebe's Place Sr. Ctr., Chgo., 1994—. Named one of Outstanding Young Men Am., 1990. Mem. AICPA, Nat. Assn. Black Accts. (Outstanding Svc. award Chgo. chpt. 1990, 92), Ill. CPA Soc. Avocation: sailing. Office: 500 W Taft Dr South Holland IL 60473

BELL, JEANNE VINER, public relations counselor; b. L.A., Feb. 27, 1923; d. Herman and Mary (Kaufman) Spitzel; m. Melvin A. Viner, Feb. 1, 1942 (dec.); children: Michael Viner, Karen Viner Fawcett; m. J. Raymond Bell, Dec. 15, 1974 (dec.). Student, UCLA, George Washington U. Prin. Jeanne Viner Spl. Svcs., Washington, 1958-61, Jeanne Viner Assocs., Washington, 1961-82; pub. rels. counselor, 1982—2003. Bd. dirs., vice-chair Independence Fed. Bank, Washington, Independence Fed. Fin. Corp., 1969-2003. Contbr. articles to profl. jours., mags., books. Presdl. appointee to adv. coun. SBA, 1983—, Pres.'s Com. People with Disabilities, 1982-96; bd. dirs. Arthritis Found. Met. D.C., 1982-95; mem. D.C. Adv. Com. Resources and Budget, 1981-90, D.C. Pvt. Industries Coun., 1983-97; bd. visitors U. Md. Coll. Journalism, 1989—; trustee U. Bridgeport, Conn. Recipient Outstanding Leadrship and Achievement award State Bus. and Profl. Women's Clubs, Washington, 1981, Met. Washington Women Bus. Advocate of Yr. award, 1996. Fellow Pub. Rels. Soc. Am.; mem. Capital Press Women (pres. 1980-82, Woman of Achievement 1982, Communicator of Achievement 1983), Am. News Women's Club (bd. govs. 1969-70, 97-98, pres. 1988-90), Nat. Press Club. Address: 3506 Winfield Ln NW Washington DC 20007-2344 Fax: (202) 298-5963. E-mail: jvb223@aol.com.

BELL, JERRY ALAN, science education association administrator; b. Davenport, Iowa, June 28, 1936; s. Walter Samuel and Lilah Mae (Mergy) B.; m. Dorothy Alice Rodgers, June 10, 1961 (div. Dec. 1981); children: Allan Tracy (dec.), John Leonard; m. Mary Ann Stepp, Mar. 21, 1984; children: Christina Marie, Allison Rachel. AB, Harvard U., 1958, PhD, 1962. Asst. prof. U. Calif., Riverside, 1962-67; assoc. prof., prof. Simmons Coll., Boston, 1967-92; dir. sci. edn. program AAAS, Washington, 1992—99; Sr. Scientist, Edn. & Internat. Activities Div. Am. Chem. Chem. Soc., Washington, 1999—. Mem. adv. bd. Merck Inst. for Sci. Edn., Newark, 1993-99. Author: Chemical Explorations, 1993; editor, author: Chemical Principles in Practice, 1967. Recipient Catalyst award Mfg. Chemists Assn., 1977, John Timm award New Eng. Assn. Chemistry Tchrs., 1986. Fellow AAAS, Am. Chem. Soc. (sec. div. chem. edn. 1977-82, chmn. 1988, councilor 1992—, vis. scientist western Conn. sect. 1979, Norris award northeastern sect. 1992, George C. Pimentel award in Chem. Edn., 2000). Avocations: carpentry, gardening. Office: Am Chem Soc 1155 16th St NW Washington DC 20036

BELL, JOHN ALTON, lawyer, judge; b. Greer, S.C., Dec. 1, 1958; s. Dallas Frank Sr. and Una Merle (Gay) B.; m. Vida Ivy, June 30, 1984; children: Luke, Meredith. BA, Carson-Newman Coll., 1980; JD, Memphis State U., 1982. Bar: Tenn. 1983, U.S. Dist. Ct. (we. dist.) Tenn. 1983, U.S. Army Ct. Mil. Rev. 1984, U.S. Ct. Mil. Appeals 1987, U.S. Dist. (ea. dist.) Tenn. 1988. Assoc. Litigation Support, Inc., Memphis, 1983; officer ops. and tng. U.S. Army, Ft. Knox, Ky., 1983-84, legal assistance atty., 1984-86, defense counsel, 1986-87; assoc. King & King, Greeneville, Tenn., 1987-89; ptnr. King, King & Bell, Greeneville and Newport, Tenn., 1989-90, Bell & Bell P.C., Newport, 1990-98; judge Cocke County Sessions and Juvenile Ct., Newport, 1998—. Instr. bus. law Sullivan Jr. Coll., Ft. Knox, 1986-87; adj. prof. bus. law Walter State C.C., 1989-90, 97—. Columnist It's The Law, Newport Plain Talk, 1984-85, 89-98. Bd. dirs. Extended Sch. Program, Greeneville, 1988; co-vice chmn. Rep. Com. Cocke County, Tenn., 1989-95. Lt. comdr. USAR, 1986—. Named Ky. Col., Gov. Ky., 1986. Mem. ABA, Fed. Bar Assn., Tenn. Bar Assn., Assn. Trial Lawyers Am., Judge Advocate Gen.'s Assn. Republican. Baptist. Avocations: sports, church activities. Office: Cocke County Sessions Ct 111 Court Ave Newport TN 37821-3102

BELL, JOHN PERRY, minister, religious organization administrator; b. Columbia, La., Feb. 8, 1948; s. John Dixon and Laverne (Beck) B.; m. Gwendolyn Jean McKay, Dec. 18, 1971; children: Felicia, Peter, Rachel. BA, N.E. La. U., 1970, MA, 1971; ThM, Southern Meth. U., 1973; DMin, Garrett Evang. Sem., 1989. Ordained to ministry United Meth. Ch., 1974. Min. youth United Meth. Ch., Athens, Tex., 1972, pastor Argyle, Wis., 1973-76, Sheboygan Falls, Wis., 1976-84, Waupaca, Wis., 1984-91; assoc. conf. min. United Ch. of Christ, 1991-97; exec. dir. United Meth. Found., 1998-2000. Bd. dirs. Bell Press, Waupaca, 1990—; sec. Coun. on Fin. Adminstrn., Sun Prairie, Wis., 1984-92; del. World Meth. Conf., Honolulu, 1981, Nairobi, 1986, New World Mission, Bangalore, India, 1989, UNCED, Rio de Janeiro, 1992, UN Conf. on Population, Cairo, Egypt, 1994. Pres. Am. Cancer Soc., Waupaca, 1988-90, Mental Health Assn., Waupaca, 1988-91. Recipient Superior award Am. Cancer Soc., 1989-90. Mem. World Future Soc., Kiwanis (local pres. 1983). Democrat. Home: 2212 Stockton Dr Springfield IL 62703-5268 E-mail: gnanny50@aol.com. *Life is both internal and external. We have to place equal emphasis on both. Our internal life needs as much care as any other part of life. How we think and feel will determine what we do and say. Faith, then, is the foundation for life.*

BELL, JONATHAN ROBERT, lawyer; b. Bklyn., Oct. 2, 1947; s. Saul A. and Hope R. (Rosenblat) B.; children: Gabriel J., Nicholas R.; m. Catherine Janow, May 5, 1989. BA, Yale U., 1969; JD, Harvard U., 1973. Bar: Mass. 1974, U.S. Tax Ct. 1977, N.Y. 1978, U.S. Dist. Ct. (so. dist.) N.Y. 1980. Assoc. Nutter, McClennen & Fish, Boston, 1973-77, Debevoise & Plimpton, N.Y.C., 1977-83, ptnr., 1984-93, Paul. Weiss, Rifkind, Wharton & Garrison, N.Y.C., 1993—2001, Duane Morris, N.Y.C., 2002—. Bd. dirs. United Way, N.Y.C., 1984-95, N.Y.C. Ballet, 1995-2003; bd. dirs. Studio in A School, 1988—, vice chair, 2003—. Fellow Am. Coll. Trust and Estate Counsel; mem. N.Y. State Bar Assn. (trusts and estates law sect.), Assn. Bar City N.Y. (chair trusts, estates and surrogate cts. com. 1995-98). Home: 99 Jane St New York NY 10014-7221 Office: Duane Morris LLP 380 Lexington Ave New York NY 10168 E-mail: jrbell@duanemorris.com.

BELL, JOSEPH JAMES, lawyer; b. Kansas City, Mo., Sept. 30, 1947; s. James Joseph and Mary Beatrice (O'Rourke) B. BA in Polit. Sci., U. Nev., Reno, 1969; JD, New Coll. of Calif., San Francisco, 1979. Bar: Calif. 1980, U.S. Dist. Ct. (no.dist.) Calif. 1980, U.S. Dist. Ct. (ea. dist.) Calif. 1981, U.S. Dist. Ct. (ctrl. dist.) Calif. 1988, U.S. Ct. Appeals (9th cir.) 1988. Law clk. Pub. Advocates, Inc., San Francisco, 1977-79, San Francisco Neighborhood Legal Assistance Found. Litigation unit, San Francisco, 1977-79, Law Offices of Thomas E. Horn, 1979-80; supervising atty. Nevada County Legal Assistance, Inc. and Lawyer Referral Svc., 1980-81; pvt. practice Grass Valley, Calif., 1982—. Pro tem judge Nevada County Superior Ct., Nevada City, Calif., 1988-91, Nevada County Small Claims Ct., 1989—; lectr. Sierra Coll., Grass Valley, 1997—; bd. govs. dist 1 State Bar of Calif., 1994; mem. family adv. com. Calif. Jud. Coun., 1998—. Bd. dirs. Legal Svcs. No. Calif., Inc., Sacramento, 1981-84; mem. Dem. Ctrl. Com., Nevada County, Calif., 1982-86; vol. firefighter Ophir Hill Fire Dept., pres., 1991-92, bd. dirs., 1993-94. Recipient Pro Bono award State Bar Calif., 1982, 87-88, Law Day award ABA, 2001 Mem. Nevada County Bar (pres. 1986-87, family law sect., pro tem judge fee arbitration com. 1988—), Sacramento County Bar, Placer County Bar, Sierra Club (Sierra Nevada Group, officer Mother Lode chpt., Conservationist award 1991), Kiwanis. Democrat. Avocations: travel, rafting, skiing, biking, piano. Office: 350 Crown Point Cir Ste 250 Grass Valley CA 95945-9524 Fax: 530-272-7340. E-mail: attorney@bellslaw.com.

BELL, JOSHUA, musician; b. Ind., Dec. 6, 1967; Vis. prof. Royal Acad. Music. Youngest guest soloist Phila. Orch. Subscription concert, 1982; participant European tour St. Louis Symphony, 1985, German tour Indpls. Symphony, 1987; guest soloist with numerous orchs., U.S.A., Can., Europe; recitalist U.S.A., Europe, Far East; recs. include Mendelssohn and Bruch concertos with Acad. St. Martin-in-the-Fields, Sir Neville Marriner, Tchaikovsky and Wieniawski concertos with Cleve. Orch. and Vladimir Ashkenazy, (recital album) Brahms, Paganini, Sarasate, Wieniawski with Samuel Sanders, Lalo Symphonie Espagnole and Saint-Saens Concerto with Montreal Symphony Orch. and Charles Dutoit, Franck, Fauré and Débussy, Chausson Concerto for violin, piano, string quartet with Thibaudet and Isserlis, Poème with Royal Philharmonic Orch. and Andrew Litton, Mozart Concertos 3 and 5 with English Chamber Orch. and Peter Maag, Prokofiev violin concertos with Montreal Symphony Orch. and Charles Dutoit, Barber and Walton concertos, Bloch Baal Shem, with Balt. Symphony and David Zinman; Sibelius and Goldmark concerti with L.A. Philharm and Esa-Pekka Salonen; Gershwin Fantasy with London Symphony Orch., others. Avocations: chess, computers, golf, tennis, baseball. Address: care IMG Artists, Lovell House, 616 Chiswick High Rd Chiswick London W4 5RX England

BELL, KAREN JUNE, critical care nurse; b. Forsyth County, N.C., Aug. 28, 1954; d. James Cecil and Margaret (Vaughn) B. Student, Rex Hosp. Sch. Nursing, Raleigh, N.C.; BSN, East Carolina U., 1983; MBA, MHA, Pfeiffer U., 1999. Asst. clin. mgr., staff RN med. ICU Rex Hosp., Raleigh, 1977-91; staff nurse ICU Western Wake Med. Ctr., Cary, 1992-93; nurse cons. Divsn. of Facility Svc., State of N.C., 1993-94; staff RN ICU Moses H. Cone Meml. Hosp., 1994-95; med. policy analyst, Medicare adminstr. CIGNA Healthcare, 1995-97; policy analyst Medicare Fiscal Intermediary-N.C., 1997-98; health care coord. QualChoice of N.C., 1998-99; nurse reviewer Medicare adminstrn. CIGNA Health Care, NC, 2000—02; mgr. Med. Rev. of N.C., 2002. Recipient Great 100 Nurse Excellence award, N.C., 1990.

BELL, KEVIN J. zoological park administrator; b. N.Y., Aug. 14, 1952; s. Joseph L. and Muriel E. (Beck) B.; m. Catharine Kleiman, Sept. 8, 1991. BS in Biology, Syracuse U., 1974; MS Zoology, SUNY, Brockport, 1976. Rsch. asst. Nat. Audubon Soc., Ea. Egg Rock, Maine, 1975; curator of birds Lincoln Park Zoological Gardens, Chgo., 1975-92, dir., 1993—; pres., CEO Lincoln Park Zool. Soc., Chgo., 1995—. Leader Zoo Soc. Tours to Africa, India, Nepal and Thailand. Contbr. articles to jours. in field. Office: Lincoln Pk Zool Gardens 2001 N Clark St Chicago IL 60614-4712 also: PO Box 14903 Chicago IL 60614-0903

BELL, LARRY STUART, artist; b. Chgo., Dec. 6, 1939; s. Hyman David and Rebecca Ann (Kriegmont) B.; three children. Student, Chouinard Art Inst., L.A., 1957-59. One man exhbns. include Stedelijk Mus., Amsterdam, 1967, Pasadena (Calif.) Art Mus., 1972, Oakland (Calif.) Mus., 1973, Ft. Worth Art Mus., 1975, Santa Barbara (Calif.) Mus. Art, 1976, Washington U., St. Louis, 1976, Art Mus. So. Tex., Corpus Christi, 1976, Erica Williams, Anne Johnson Gallery, Seattle, 1978, Hayden Gallery, MIT, Cambridge, Mass., 1977, Hudson River Mus., Yonkers, N.Y., 1981, Newport Harbor Art Mus., 1982, Marian Goodman Gallery, N.Y.C., 1982, Ruth S. Schaffner Gallery, Santa Barbara, Calif., Arco Ctr. Visual Arts, L.A., 1983, Unicorn Gallery, Aspen, Colo., 1983, Butler Inst. Am. Art, Youngstown, Ohio, 1984, Leigh Yawkey Woodson Art Mus., Wausau, Wis., 1984, Colorado Springs, Colo. Fine Arts Ctr., 1987, Cleve. Ctr. for Contemporary Art, Ohio, 1987, Mus. Contemporary Art, L.A., 1987, Am. Acad. and Inst. Arts and Letters, N.Y.C., 1987, Boise (Idaho) Gallery Art, 1987, Gilbert Brownstone Gallery, Paris, 1987, Braunstein/Quay Gallery, San Francisco, 1987, 89, Fine Arts Gallery, N.Mex. State Fairgrounds, 1987, Laguna Art Mus., Laguna Beach, Calif., 1987, High Mus. Art, Atlanta, 1988, Sena Galleries West, Santa Fe, 1989, Kiyo Higashi Gallery, L.A., 1989, 90, 94, 2002, Musee D'Art Contemporain, Lyon, France, 1989, Contemporary Art Ctr., Kansas City, Mo., 1989, San Antonio Art Inst., 1990, New Gallery, Houston, 1990, Braunstein/Quay Gallery, San Francisco, 1990, Galerie Rolf Ricke, Koln, Fed. Republic Germany, 1990, Galerie Montenay, Paris, 1990, 95, The Works Gallery, L.A., 1990, Galerie Kammer, Hamburg, Germany, 1990, Tony Shafrazi Gallery, N.Y.C., 1991, Tucson Mus. Art, 1991, New Gallery, Houston, 1991, Janus Gallery, Santa Fe, 1992, Kiyo Higashi Gallery, L.A., 1992, 93, New Gallery, Houston, 1992, Tampa Mus. Art, 1992, Kiyo Higashi Gallery, L.A., 1993, 94, New Directions Gallery, Taos, N.M., 1993, Dartmouth St. Gallery, Albuquerque, 1994, Braunstein/Quay Gallery, San Francisco, 1994, Leedy/Voulkos Gallery, Kansas City, 1994, Kiyo Higashi Gallery, L.A., 1994, U. Wyo. Art Mus., Laramie, 1995, Denver Art Mus., 1995, Indigo Gallery, Boca Raton, Fla., 1995, Harwood Mus. U. N. Mex., Taos, 1995, Galerie Montenay, Paris, 1995, Joy Tash Gallery, Scottsdale, Ariz., 1996, Kiyo Higashi Gallery, L.A., 1996, Boulder Mus. Contemporary Art, 1996, Braunstein/Quay Gallery, San Francisco, 1996, Art et Industrie Gallery, N.Y.C., 1996, The Albuquerque Mus., 1997, The Reykjavik Mcpl. Art Mus., Iceland, 1997, Bergen (Norway) Kunstmus., 1998, Seljord (Norway) Art Assn., 1998, Wood Street Galleries, Pitts., 1999, Mus. Moderner Kunst Landkreis Cuxhaven, Otterndorf, Germany, 1999, Kiyo Higashi Gallery, 1999, Center Galleries, Detroit, 2000, Larry Bell Studio Annex/New Directions Gallery, Taos, N.Mex., 2000, Mus. Moderner Kunst Landkreis Cuxhaven, Otterndorf, Germany, 2000, New Gallery, Houston, 2001, Gallery Gan, Tokyo, 2001, Skovridder AS, Oslo, Norway, 2001, Roswell Mus. and Art Ctr., 2002, New Gallery, Houston, 2002, Off Main Gallery, Santa Monica, Calif., 2003; group exhbns. include Mus. Modern Art, N.Y.C., 1965, 79, Jewish Mus., N.Y.C., 1966, Whitney Mus. Am. Art, 1966, Guggenheim Mus., N.Y.C., 1967, Tate Gallery, London, 1970, Hayward Gallery, London, 1971, Detroit Inst. Arts, 1973, Nat. Collections Fine Arts, 1975, San Francisco Mus. Modern Art, 1976, Museo de Arte Contemporaneo de Caracas, Venezuela, 1978, Aspen Ctr. for Visual Arts, 1980, Fruit Market Gallery, Edinburgh, Scotland, 1980, Albuquerque Mus., 1980, Art Inst. Chgo., 1982, Santa Barbara Art Mus., 1984, The Rufino Tamayo Mus., Mexico City, 1985, Colorado Springs Fine Art Ctr., 1986, Mus. Contemporary Art, 1986, AAAL, 1986, Ariz. State U., Tempe, 1987, Phoenix Art Mus., 1987, Braunstein/Quay Gallery, 1987, The Works Gallery, Long Beach, 1987, Davis/McClain Gallery, Houston, 1987, Basel (Switzerland) Art Fair, 1989, Galerie Joan Prats, Barcelona, Spain, 1989, Musee d'Art Contemporain, Lyon, 1989, Harcus Gallery, Boston, 1989, Colorado Springs Gallery Contemporary Art, 1990,Mus. Contemporary Art, L.A., 1990, Musee de Grenoble, France, 1990, L.A.County Mus. Art, 1991, U. So. Calif. Fisher Gallery, L.A., 1991, Espace Lyonnais d'Art Contemporain, France, 1991, Galerie Montenay, Paris, 1991, Galerie Rolf Ricke, Köln, Germany, 1991, Arolsen, Germany, 1992, Leedy/Voulkos Gallery, Kansas City, Mo., 1993, Musee du Palais du Luxembourg, Paris, 1993, Denver Art Mus., 1993, New Gallery, Houston, 1993, Whitney Mus. Am. Art, N.Y.C., 1993, Conn., 1994, Parrish Art Mus., Southampton, N.Y., 1994, Kiyo Higashi Gallery, L.A., 1994, Madison (Wis.) Art Ctr., 1994, Whitney Mus. Am. Art, 1995, Galerie Ncht St. Stephen, Vienna, 1995, Galerie Rolf Ricke, Cologne, 1996, Colorado Springs Fine Art Ctr., 1996, Mus. N.Mex., Santa Fe, 1996, Orange County Mus. Art, Newport Beach, Calif., 1997, Harwood Mus. U. N.Mex., Taos, 1997, Louisiana Mus. Modern Art, Humlebaek, Denmark, 1997, Milw. Art Mus., 1997, Whitney Mus. Am. Art, N.Y., 1997, San Jose (Calif.) Mus. Art, 1997, Grounds for Sculpture, Mercerville, N.J., 1998-99, Frederick R. Weisman Mus. Art, Pepperdine U. Malibu, Calif., 1998, Calif. Ctr. Arts, Escondido, Calif., 1999, P.S.1 Contemporary Art Ctr., Long Island City, N.Y., 1999, Seattle Art Mus., 1999, Norton Simon Mus., Pasadena, Calif., 1999, Seljord Kunstforening, Norway, 1999, U. Art Mus., U. N.Mex., Albuquerque, 1999, Orange County Mus. Art, Newport Beach, Calif., 1999, Orange County Mus. Art, Newport Beach, Calif., 2000, Palos Verdes Art Ctr., Rancho Palos Verdes, Calif., 2000, Peggy Guggenheim Collection, Venice, Italy, 2000, Guggenheim Mus. Bilbao, Spain, 2000, La. Mus. Art, Humlebaek, Denmark, 2000, L.A. County Mus. Art, 2000, Solomon R. Guggenheim Mus., N.Y., 2001, Bernard Jacobson Gallery, London, 2001, Museu Serralves, Porto, Portugal, 2002, The Contemporary Mus., Honolulu, 2002, Yale U. Art Gallery, New Haven, Conn., 2002, Denver Art Mus., 2002, Gagosian Gallery, N.Y.C., 2002, Franklin Parrasch Gallery, N.Y.C., 2003, Gagosian Gallery, N.Y.C., 2002, Stephen Stux Gallery, N.Y.C., 2002, others; represented in permanent collections including Nat. Collection Fine Arts, Musee de Art Contemporaine, Lyon, France, Mus. of Fine Arts, Santa Fe, N.Mex., Whitney Mus. Am. Art, N.Y.C., 1994, Laguna Gloria Mus., Austen, 1994, H & W Bechtler Gallery, Charlotte, 1994, Calif. Crafts Mus., San Francisco, 1994, Parrish Art Mus., Southampton, 1994, Tate Gallery, London, Gallery New South Wales, Australia, Albright-Knox Gallery, Buffalo, Art Inst. Chgo., Denver Art Mus., Dallas Mus. Fine Arts, Guggenheim Mus., Houston, L.A. County Mus., Victoria and Albert Mus., London, San Antonio Mus. Art, The Menil Collection, Houston, Mpls. Inst. Arts, Mus. Ludwig, Koln, Albuquerque Mus., Mpls. Inst. Arts, others; instr. sculpture, U. South Fla., Tampa, U. Calif., Berkeley, Irvine, 1970-73, So. Calif. Inst. of Architecture, 1988, Taos (N.Mex.) Inst. of Art, 1989-94, City of Albuquerque, Art in Pub. Places, 1999, Myers Devel. Co., 1999, Billingsley Co., Carrolton, 2001, Mus. Abteiberg, Monchengladbach, Germany, 2002. Copley Found. grantee, 1962; Guggenheim Found. fellow, 1970; Nat. Endowment Arts grantee, 1975; recipient Gov.'s award for excellence in visual arts, N.Mex., 1990. Office: Box 4101 Taos NM 87571-9998

BELL, LAURA JEANE, retired nurse; b. Chgo., Mar. 11, 1922; d. Harold Elwood and Mary Etta (Sprague) Downey; m. David Hoge Bell, Feb. 21, 1943; children: David, Roy, Thomas, John, Ruth, Keith, Mary, Richard, Howard. AA, Blackburn Coll., 1941; diploma in nursing, St. Elizabeths Hosp., Washington, 1946; BS in Nursing, Washington U., St. Louis, 1962; MS in Edn., St. Louis U., 1969. RN, Mo. Relief supr. St. Vincent's Hosp., St. Louis, 1949-58; staff asst. head nurse, head nurse Barnes Hosp., St. Louis, 1958-61, instr., coord. Sch. Nursing, 1962-67; instr. Jefferson Barracks VA Hosp., St. Louis, 1967-70, asst. chief nursing svc. for edn., 1970-71; instr. Jefferson Barracks div. St. Louis VA Med. Ctr., 1971-73, med. supr. John Cochran div., 1973-81, supr. ambulatory care Jefferson Barracks div., 1981-84; ret., 1984. Dist. rep. intercultural programs Am. Field Svc., St. Louis, 1983-91; rec. sec. Overland (Mo.) Hist. Soc., 1988-89, pres., 1990-92; pres. United Meth. Women, Stephan Meml. Ch., Charlack, Mo., 1988-92; mem. Women's Polit. Caucus, St. Louis, 1987—; v.p. St. Louis North Dist. United Meth. Women, 1992-95; sec. Mo. Ch. Women United, 1992-95, pres., 1996-980; chair Commn. on Status and Role of Women, Mo. East Conf., U. Mo., 1992-96; bd. dirs. Wesley Found., St. Louis, 1992—; pres. Met. St. Louis Ch. Women United, 1993-97; pres. Mo. Ch. Women United, 1996-98. Recipient Alumni Achievement award Blackburn Coll., 1995, Valiant Woman award Mo. State Bd. Ch. Women United, 1999; named Fed. Employee of Yr., Fed. Exec. Bd., 1970; named to Ritenour H.S. Hall of Fame, 1998. Mem. ANA (accreditation com. cen. region 1984-88), Mo. League for Nursing (pres. 1978-80, chmn. bylaws 1985-92), Mo. Nurses Assn. (continuing edn. and bylaws com., chmn. nominating com., 3d dist. 1988, regional bd. dirs. 1988-90, Pres.'s award 1989, 3d Dist. Mem. of Yr. 2000), Mo. Student Nurses Assn. (hon., scholarship named in her honor 1982, chair nominations com. 3d dist. 1999-2000, sec. 3d dist. 2001—). Home: 2450 Ashland Ave Saint Louis MO 63114-5002 E-mail: Hogebell@aol.com.

BELL, LEE PHILLIP, television personality, television producer; b. Chgo. d. James A. and Helen (Novak) P.; m. William Joseph Bell, Oct. 23, 1954; children: William J., Bradley, Lauralee. BS in Microbiology, Northwestern U., 1950. With CBS-TV, Chgo., 1952-86; pres. Bell-Phillip TV Prodns., 1985—. Bd. dirs. William Wrigley, Jr. Co., Chgo. Bank Commerce, Phillips Flowers Inc. TV and radio shows include Lee Phillip Show, Chgo., from 1952, Lady and Tiger Show WBBM Radio, from 1962, WBBM TV from 1964; hostess Noon Break, numerous TV Spls. including Forgotten Children, The Rape of Paulette (nat. Emmy award, duPont Columbia award); Children and Divorce (Chgo. Emmmy award) co-creator: (with William Bell) The Young and the Restless CBS-TV daytime drama, 1973 (Emmy award); co-creator, exec. producer The Bold and the Beautiful, 1987—. Bd. dirs. United Cerebral Palsy, Chgo. Unlimited, Northwestern U. Hosp., Chgo. Heart Assn., Nat. Com. Prevention of Child Abuse, Mental Health Assn., Children's Home and Aid Soc., Salvation Army, Chgo., Family Focus; mem. Chgo. Maternity Ctr.; life mem. Northwestern U. Bd. Trustees. Recipient 16 Chgo. Emmys; Top Favorite Female award TV Guide mag., 1956, Outstanding Woman of Radio and TV award McCall's mag., 1957-58, 65, bd. govs. award Chgo. chpt. Nat. Acad. TV Arts and Scis., 1977, William Booth award for community svc. Salvation Army, 1990; named Person of Yr. Broadcast Advt. Club, Chgo., 1980. Mem. Am. Women Radio and TV (Golden Mike award 1968, Broadcaster of Yr. 1993), Acad. TV Arts and Scis. (bd. dirs.), Chgo. chpt. Acad. TV Arts and Scis., Women's Athletic Club of Chgo., Comml. Club, Delta Delta Delta. Office: CBS c/o Bold and Beautiful 7800 Beverly Blvd Los Angeles CA 90036-2188 E-mail: dianemoss@boldandbeautiful.tv.

BELL, LEO S. retired physician; b. Newark, N.J., Nov. 7, 1913; s. Alexander M. and Marie (Saxon) B.; m. Edith Lewis, July 3, 1938; children; Jewyl Linn, David Alden. AB, Syracuse U., 1934, MD, 1938. Diplomate Am. Bd. Pediatrics. Intern N.Y.C. Hosp., 1938, Bklyn. Hosp., 1939-40; resident Sea View Hosp., N.Y.C., 1940-41, N.Y.C. Hosp., 1941-42; pediatrician pvt. practice, San Mateo, Calif., 1946-84. Staff mem. Mills Meml. Hosp., San Mateo, Peninsula Hosp. & Med. Ctr., Burlingame, Children's Hosp., San Francisco; assoc. clin. prof. pediatrics U. Calif. Med. Sch., San Francisco; prof. clin. emeritus Stanford Med. Sch., Palo Alto; mem. curriculum & ednl. affairs com. U. San Francisco Med. Sch., adminstrv. coun. Columnist San Mateo Times; contbr. articles to profl. jours. Bd. dirs. Mills Hosp. Found., San Mateo, U. Calif. San Francisco Hosp., San Mateo County Heart Assn., Hillsborough Schs. Found. (Calif.), 1980-83. Capt. USAAF, 1942-46. Recipient bronze and silver medals Am. Heart Assn. Fellow Am. Acad. Pediatrics, Am. Pub. Health Assn.; mem. AMA (alt. del. to ho. of dels), U. Calif. San Francisco Clin. Faculty Assn. (pres.), Calif. Fedn. Pediatric Socs. (pres.), Am. Fedn. Pediatric Socs. (pres.), Calif. Med. Assn., Am. Pub. Health Assn., Air Force Assn., Calif. Med. Assn. (ho. of dels.), San Mateo County Med. Assn. (vice chmn. quality assurance com. San Mateo county health plan), Internat. Snuff Bottle Soc., Hong Kong Snuff Bottle Soc., San Francisco Gem and Mineral Soc., World Affairs Coun. San Francisco, U. San Francisco Med. Sch. Clin. Faculty Assn. (coun., pres.), Peninsula Golf & Country Club, Commonwealth Club. Office: PO Box 1877 San Mateo CA 94401-0946

BELL, LEWIS CLAY, economics educator, government administrator; b. New Dorp, S.I., N.Y., Mar. 29, 1928; s. Samuel Virgil and Ruth Bell; m. Dolores Eva Bell, Dec. 19, 1951; children: Brent, David, Daniel. BA in Econs., Berea Coll., 1953; postgrad., Emory U., 1953—54; PhD in Econs., U. Ky., 1957. Rsch. asst. Bur. Bus. Rsch. U. Ky., 1954—55, rsch. assoc., 1956—57; asst. dir. purchases Commonwealth of Ky., 1957, dir. purchases, 1957—60; assoc. prof. U. Miss., 1960—63, assoc. prof. econs., econs. rsch. analyst, 1963—64, prof. econs., sr. rsch. analyst, 1964, prof. econs., 1964—65; dir. Tax Rsch. Ctr., prof. econs.

Western Ky. U., 1965—66, dir. Tax Rsch. Ctr., Office of Rsch. and Svcs., prof. econs., 1966—68; prof. econs. fiscal cons. to W.Va. Legis., 1968—70; dir. legis. fiscal studies W.Va. U., 1969—70, prof. econs., 1969—88, dir. grad. programs econs., 1978—83, prof. emeritus, 1988—; exec. dir. W.Va. Coun. Econ. Edn., 1985—87; prof. econs. Christian Sci. Practitioner, 1988—. Author (with D.H. McKinney): The Role of Third-Structure Taxes in the Highway-User Tax Family, 1968; contbr. articles to profl. jours., chapters to books. Mem. Ky. Efficiency Task Force, 1966—68; Ky. col.; treas. Support Our Schs., Morgantown, 1971; mem. com. on publ. for W.Va. Christian Sci., 1975—91; counsel, advisor Christian Sci. Coll. Orgn. W.Va. U., chmn. bd.; 1st reader, Sunday sch. supt. Christian Sci. Ch.; advisor Sch. Bonds. Com., Morgantown, 1971. Mem.: Mountain State Econ. Assn. (pres. 1980), W.Va. Tax Inst. (pres. 1973), So. Econs. Assn., Tax Inst. Am., Nat. Tax Assn., Am. Econ. Assn., Rotary (pres. 1983—84), Beta Gamma Sigma, Phi Kappa Phi. Democrat. Christian Scientist. Home and Office: 1287 Colonial Dr Morgantown WV 26505-2437

BELL, LINDA GREEN, psychology educator, therapist; b. Austin, Tex., July 12, 1944; d. Leslie Mason and Anna Violet Weber Green; m. David Chalres Bell, Dec. 27, 1965; children: Michael James, Eric Matthew, Claire Toshiko Ishikawa. BA, Oberlin (Ohio) Coll., 1967; MA, U. Tex., 1968; PhD, Duke U., 1973. Postdoctoral rsch. fellow U. Chgo., 1974-76; rsch. asst. Scientific Methods Inc., Austin, 1964-67; vis. rschr. Nat. Inst. of Mental Health, Ichikawa, Chiba, Japan, 1985-87; prof. psychology and family therapy U. Houston-Clear Lake, 1976—. Rchr. in field; presenter and workshops in family rsch. and family therapy. Contbr. articles to profl. publs. Vol. Peace Corps, Senegal, Liberia, 1968-70. Grantee, NIMH, 1976—77, 1977—83, Hogg Found. for Mental Health, 1978 82, Tex. Coord. Bd. for Higher Edn., 1998—2002. Fellow Am. Assn. for Marriage and Family Therapy, Am. Psychol. Assn., Am. Family Therapy Acad., Nat. Coun. on Family Rels., Japan Family Therapy Assn. Democrat. Mem. Soc. Of Friends. Avocation: music.

BELL, LORI JO, crisis counselor, psychiatric nurse; b. Pitts., Dec. 16, 1960; d. John Spencer and Nancy Carol (Schleicher) B. ADN, C.C. Allegheny Co., Pitts., 1987; BS in Devel. Psychology, U. Pitts., 1984; MSEd in Cmty. Counseling, Duquesne U., 1996, postgrad.; MSN, Indiana U. of Pa. Nat. cert. counselor, cert. in adult psychiat./mental health nursing, crisis intervention specialist, cert. critical incident stress debriefing, cert. pre/post HIV counseling. Primary counselor Mon Yough Mental Health/Mental Retardation, McKeesport, Pa., 1984; residential advisor Chartiers Mental Health/Mental Retardation, Bridgeville, Pa., 1985-87; counselor, 1985-87; psychiat. nurse in acute/admissions bldg. Eastern State Hosp., Williamsburg, Va., 1987; psychiat. nurse St. Francis Med. Ctr., Pitts., 1987-90, Mercy Psychiat. Inst., Pitts., 1990-92; coord. emergency outpatient psychiat. svcs. Meadville Med. Ctr., 1997-99; shift nursing supr. U. Pitts. Med. Ctr., Western Psychiat. Inst. & Clinic, 2003—; night nursing supr. U. Pitts. Med. Ctr./We. Psychiat. Inst. and Clinic, 2003—. Cmty. HIV/AIDS educator; microbiology tutor Duquesne U., 1994. Contbr. articles to profl. jours. Vol. disaster mental health svcs., disaster health svcs., disaster action team Southwestern Pa. chpt. ARC, 1996—; hotline vol. Women's Ctr. and Shelter of Greater Pitts., 1995-96. Mem.: Am. Psyc. Nurses Assn., ACA, Am. Nurses Assn., Psychiat Nurses Assn., Pa. State Nursing Assn. (polit. action com.), Am. Mental Health Counseling Assn., Am. Mental Health Assn., Internat. Critical Incident Stress Found., Crisis Intervention Assn. Pa., Assn. Traumatic Stress Specialists, Am. Assn. Suicidology, United Animal Nations Emergency Disaster Svc., U.S. Humane Soc., Sigma Theta Tau, Chi Sigma Iota. Home: 337 Shadowlawn Ave Pittsburgh PA 15216-1239

BELL, M. JOY MILLER, financial planner, real estate broker; b. Enid, Okla., Dec. 29, 1934; d. H. Lee and M.E. Madge (Hatfield) Miller; m. Richard L.D. Berlemann, July 21, 1957 (div. Nov. 1974); children: Richard Louis, Randolph Lee; m. Donald R. Bell, Aug. 17, 1996; children: Jeri, Johnna, Nolan, Charles, Mary. BSBA, N.Mex. State U., 1956. CFP; grad. Realtors Inst.; fellow Life Underwriting Tng. Coun. Tchr. bus. and math. Alamogordo (N.Mex.), Las Cruces (N. Mex.) and Omaha Pub. Schs., 1956-63; tchr., dir. Evelyn Wood Reading Dynamics So. N.Mex. Inst., 1967-68; registered rep. Westamerica Fin. Corp., Denver, 1968-76; gen. agt. Security Benefit Life, Topeka, 1969—, Delta Life & Annuity, Topeka, Kans., 1969—; registered rep. AGF Sponsors, Inc., Denver, 1976—; pres., broker Fin. Design Corp. R.E. (name changed to Bell, Inc. 1997), Las Cruces, 1977—; with Allianz L.I. Co. N.Am., 2000—. Mrs. U.S. Savings Bonds ofcl. goodwill amb. U.S. Treasury, U.S. Savs. Bond Divsn., Washington, 1968-70. Contbr. articles to profl. jours. Vice pres. Dona Ana County Fedn. Rep. Women. Recipient Top Sales Person award Investment Trust and Assurance, 1976-77; named Outstanding Young Woman of N.Mex., 1970, Outstanding Young Women of Am., 1970. Mem. Nat. Assn. Realtors, Nat. Assn. Ins. and Fin. Advisors, Nat. Assn. Ret. Fed. Employees (v.p. programs local chpt.), Internat. Assn. Registered Fin. Planners, S.W. N.Mex. Assn. of Ins. and Fin. Advisors (treas. 1990-91, pres.-elect 1991-92, pres. 1992-93), Las Cruces City Alumnae Panhellenic, Altrusa, Order Ea. Star, Delta Zeta. Presbyterian. Home: 4633 Lamar Rd Las Cruces NM 88005-3558 Office: Bell Inc PO Box 577 Las Cruces NM 88004-0577 E-mail: joybell@bellinc.com.

BELL, MARTIN ALLEN, investment company executive; b. N.Y.C., Apr. 29, 1951; s. Bernard B. and Helene (Spiro) Bell; m. Alison D. Brown, Dec. 1, 2002; 1 child, Olivia Joan;children from previous marriage: Daniel Warren, Frances Annelies. BA, U. Mich., 1974; JD, NYU, 1977. Bar: N.Y. 1978. Ptnr. Finley, Kumble, Wagner, Heine, Underberg, Manley & Casey, N.Y.C., 1977-85; pres. Svc. Resources Corp., N.Y.C., 1985-90; gen. counsel D.H. Blair Investment Banking Corp., N.Y.C., 1991—, vice chmn., 1995—. Bd. dirs. Venus Exploration Corp., Rand Pub. Corp., News Comm., Inc. Democratic. Jewish. Home: 1035 5th Ave New York NY 10028-0135 Office: D H Blair Investment Banking Corp 44 Wall St New York NY 10005-2401

BELL, MARVIN HARTLEY, poet, English language educator; b. N.Y.C., Aug. 3, 1937; s. Saul and Belle (Spector) B.; m. Mary Mammosser, 1958 (div.); m. Dorothy Murphy; children: Nathan Saul, Jason Aaron. BA, Alfred U., 1958, LHD (hon.), 1986; MA, U. Chgo., 1961; MFA, U. Iowa, 1963. Mem. faculty, Writers' Workshop U. Iowa, Iowa City, 1965—, Flannery O'Connor prof. of letters, 1986—. Vis. lectr. Goddard Coll., 1970; disting. vis. prof. U. Hawaii, 1981; vis. prof. U. Wash., 1982; Lila Wallace-Reader's Digest Writing fellow U. Redlands, 1991-92, 92-93; Woodrow Wilson vis. fellow St. Mary's Coll. of Calif., 1994-95, Nebr. Wesleyan U., 1996-97, Pacific U., 1996-97, Hampden-Sydney Coll., 1998-99, W.Va. Wesleyan Coll., 2000-2001, Birmingham So. U., 2000-2001, Ill. Coll., 2002-03; judge Lamont Award-Acad. Am. Poets, 1989-91, Pushcart Prizes, 1991, 97, Western Book Awards-Western States Arts Fedn., 1991, Nat. Poetry Series, NEA, N.C. Arts Coun., Coordinating Coun. Lit. Mags., Discovery Contest-Poetry Ctr. of 92nd St Y, N.Y.C., Poetry Soc. Am., Hopwood Awards, Tulsa Arts Coun., Anhinga Poetry Prize-Fla. State U. Press, numerous others. Author: (poems) Things We Dreamt We Died For, 1966, A Probable Volume of Dreams, 1969 (Lamont award Acad. Am. Poets 1969), The Escape into You, 1971, 94, Residue of Song, 1974, Stars Which See, Stars Which Do Not See, 1977 (Nat. Book award finalist 1977), 92, These Green-Going-To-Yellow, 1981, Drawn by Stones, by Earth, by Things That Have Been in the Fire, 1984, New and Selected Poems, 1987, Iris of Creation, 1990, The Book of the Dead Man, 1994, Ardor: The Book of the Dead Man, vol. 2, 1997, Wednesday: Selected Poems, 1998, Poetry for a Midsummer's Night, 1998, Nightworks: Poems 1962-2000, 2000, Ashes Poetica, 2002; (essays) Old Snow Just Melting: Essays and Interviews, 1983; (anthology) A Marvin Bell Reader, 1994; co-author: Segues: A Correspondence in Poetry, 1983, Annie-Over, 1988, editor, pub. Statements, 1959-64; poetry editor The Iowa Rev., 1969-71, guest poetry editor, 1980; poetry editor The Pushcart Prize, vol. XXI, 1996-97, editor-at-large vol. series, 1994-96, series editor, poetry, 1997—; columnist The Am. Poetry Rev., 1975-78, 90-92; contbr. and commd. poetry to numerous mags. and anthologies. Fellow Guggenheim Found., 1977, NEA, 1978, 84; Sr. Fulbright scholar to Yugoslavia, 1983, Sr. Fulbright scholar to Australia, 1986; recipient Bess Hokin award Poetry, 1969, Emily Clark Balch prize Va. Quar. Rev., 1970, Am. Poetry Rev. prize, 1982, Lit. award Am. Acad. Arts and Letters, 1994; named Poet Laureate of Iowa, 2000. Home: 1416 E College St Iowa City IA 52245-4409 also: PO Box 1759 Port Townsend WA 98368-0180 Office: U Iowa Writer's Workshop Dey House Iowa City IA 52242

BELL, MARY E. BENITEAU, accountant; b. San Antonio, Dec. 20, 1937; d. Thomas Alfred and Mary Elizabeth (McMurrain) Beniteau; m. William Woodward Bell, May 31, 1969; children: Susan Elizabeth, Carol Ann. BBA, Baylor U., 1959; MBA, U. Tex., 1960. CPA, Tex. Tchg. asst. U. Tex., Austin, 1959-60; prin. Deloitte & Touche CPA, Dallas, 1960-69; county auditor Brown County, Tex., 1972-78; pvt. practice acctg. Brownwood, Tex., 1969-95; ptnr. Bell & Isbell LLP, CPA, 1996—; acct. Brownwood Regional Med. Ctr. Aux., 1969—. Mem. bus. and audit com. Bapt. Gen. Conv. Tex., 1985-90, 97-2002, vice chmn., 1987-88, chmn., 1988-89; bd. dirs., sec. Brownwood Civic Improvement Found., Inc., 1991-2001, pres., 1993-95, treas., 1995-2001. Recipient W.R. White Meritorious Svc. award Baylor U., 1996; named Outstanding 4-H Leader, Dist. 8, Tex., 1992, Outstanding Woman Over 35, Brownwood Jaycees, 1986, Outstanding Com. Chmn., Dallas chpt. CPA, 1968-69. Mem. Brownwood C. of C. (dir. 1979-82, sec.-treas. 1981-82), Tex. Soc. CPAs (dir. 1979-82, 99-2002, chair rels. with AICPA com. 1988-89, trustee found. 1981-89, sec.-treas. 1982-84, pres. 1984-86, Kenneth W. Hurst fellow 1990, peer rev. com. 1993-96, CPA helping Schs. Com. 1994-95), AICPA, Nat. Soc. DAR (Mary Garland chpt., vice regent 1994-98, regent 1998-2000), Tex. Soc. DAR (treas. 2003—), Abilene Chpt. CPA (dir. 1984-85, 87-88, CPA of Yr. 1984-85), Brownwood Com. CPA (pres. 1987-88), Pi Beta Phi, Baylor U. Alumni Assn. (dir. 1979-82), Brownwood Woman's Club (pres. 1980-84), Rotary Ann of Brownwood (pres. 1983-84, 2000-01). Baptist. Home: PO Box 1564 Brownwood TX 76804-1564 Office: 109 N Fisk Ave Brownwood TX 76801-8207

BELL, MELODIE ELIZABETH, artist, massage therapist; b. Long Beach, Calif., Apr. 21, 1958; d. Robert I. and Bettymay (Shelley) Bell; m. Timothy Monroe Roach, Feb. 4, 1993; children: Chelsea Ann Bell, Rory Michael Bell. Student, Calif. State U., Long Beach, 1976-78, Humboldt State U., 1978-79; BA in Art (Photography), Calif. State U., Fullerton, 1981. Cert. massage therapist, L.A. Coll. Massage and Phys. Therapy. Owner Mel's Place, Cypress, Calif., 1982—91; mgr. George Galanoudes Apts., Garden Grove, Calif., 1991-93; massage therapist Office of Stephen Waldman, MD, Fullerton, Calif., 1992-97, drug study site coord., 1996-98; freelance portrait artist, photographer, 1984—; buyer Pegasus Rsch. Corp., Santa Ana, Calif., 1998-99; regional sales mgr. Discovery Med., Inc. (formerly TZT Internat. Inc.), Anaheim, Calif., 1999-2000, corp. acct. specialist, 2000-01; pvt. practice massage therapist, 2001—; owner Mel's Plance, 1999—2000. One-woman shows include Calif. State U., Fullerton, 1979, 84, Rossmoor Pub. Libr., Seal Beach, Calif., 1992, Six Flags Magic Mountain, Saugus, Calif., 1983-85; exhibited in group shows at Tutu Tango Cafe, Orange, Calif., 2001-02, Toscany Pizza, Huntington Beach, Calif., 2002—, Artworks NYC, N.Y., 2003; represented in numerous pvt. collections; illustrator: It's All About Me, 2002. Cubscout leader Boy Scouts Am., Garden Grove, 1994-95; vol. Thanksgiving for the Homeless, Santa Ana, Calif., 1996, Fryberger Elem. Sch., Westminster, Calif., 1995-96, Choc Walk, 1995, 99, 2002, AIDS Dance-a-Thon, 1997. Mem. Humboldt State Alumni Assn., Calif. State U. Fullerton Alumni Assn. Democrat. Jewish. Avocations: camping, fine furniture repair and restoration, ceramics, fine art. Home and Office: 601 S Paula Dr Fullerton CA 92833 E-mail: melobellgg@aol.com.

BELL, MELVIN, management consultant; b. East Chicago, Ind., Jan. 3, 1915; s. Abram and Lillian (Goldenson) B.; m. Lillian Bodnar, 1949 (div. 1969); children: Douglas, Janet; m. Kathy Naylor, 1971. BSME, Purdue U., 1939; MS in Pub. Adminstrn., George Washington U., 1956; PhD in Pub. Adminstrn., Am. U., 1960. With Office of the U.S. Sec. of Def., Washington, 1949-70, dir. Office of Ordnance and Guided Missiles (R&E), ret. 1970; pvt. cons. Lake Worth, Fla., 1970—. Exec. v.p. Rhodes Lewis Co., L.A. Contbr. articles to profl. jours. Mem. staff R & D bd. Pentagon, Washington. Lt. comdr. USN, 1942-46, col. USAR, 1958-75, ret. Mem. ASME (life), Ret. Officers Assn. (life), Nat. Def. Industry Assn., Purdue Alumni Assn. (life). Achievements include research in military equipment. Home and Office: 894A Worcester Ln Lake Worth FL 33467-2726

BELL, MICHAEL G. trade association administrator; b. Atlantic City, May 1, 1954; s. Daniel and Bertha (Zaleski) B.; m. Monica Piaskowski, June 9, 1979 (div. 1997); children: Melissa S., Maria D. B Liberal Studies in Econs. Bus. Adminstrn., Hillsdale Coll., 1976; Grad., N.Y. Inst. Photography, 1991. Account exec. Mgmt. Recruiters, Southfield, Mich., 1978-80; mgr. profl. interests Soc. Mfg. Engrs., Dearborn, Mich., 1980-91; dir. ednl. svcs. Fedn. of Socs. for Coatings Tech., Blue Bell, Pa., 1991-98; dir. continuing edn. Inst. Mgmt. Accts., Montvale, N.J., 1999-2000; comm. cons. Harleysville, Pa., 2000—01; exec. dir. Fernley & Fernley, Phila., 2001—. Guest columnist Indsl. Finishing Mag., 1985-86, Coatings Mag., 1995; contbg. writer Assn. Educator, 1995. Mem. indsl. adv. bd. Ea. Mich. U., Ypsilanti, 1984-87; mem. Greater Detroit Econ. Devel. Task Force, 1988; mem. Rep. Presdl. Task Force, Washington, 1984-89. Recipient Outstanding Photograph award Mich. Renaissance Festival, Holly, 1988-89. Mem. Am. Soc. Assn. Execs. (edn. tech. subcom. 1994-95), Am. Mgmt. Assn., Intersoc. Polymer Edn. Coun. (treas. 1997—, bd. dirs. 1997—), Hillsdale Coll. Alumni Assn. (pres. Detroit area 1989-91), Ancient Order of Hibernians. Roman Catholic. Avocation: photography. Home: 92 Montgomery Dr Harleysville PA 19438-2130

BELL, NORMAN HOWARD, physician, endocrinologist, educator; b. Gainesville, Ga., Feb. 11, 1931; s. Kenneth Rush and Henrietta Maria (Howard Rankin) B.; m. Claude Handy, June 27, 1959 (dec. 1967); children: Douglas Howard, Julianne Rankin; m. Mary Virginia Baughman, Aug. 24, 1968 (div. July 1972); m. Ledlie Laird Dinsmore, Dec. 16, 1972; 1 child, Bayard Gardiner. AB, Emory U., 1951; MD, Duke U., 1955. Intern Duke U. Med. Ctr., Durham, N.C., 1955-56, resident, 1956-57; clin. assoc. Nat. Inst. Allergy and Infectious Diseases, NIH, Bethesda, Md., 1957-59; mem. staff clin. endocrinology br. Nat. Heart, Lung and Blood Inst., NIH, Bethesda, 1959-63, assoc. in medicine, 1963-65; asst. prof. medicine Northwestern U. Sch. Medicine, Chgo., 1965-68; assoc. prof. Ind. U. Med Sch., Indpls., 1968-71, prof., 1971-79; prof. medicine and pharmacology Med. U. S.C., Charleston, 1979—, disting. univ. prof., 1998—. Mem. gen. medicine B study sect. NIH, Bethesda, 1982-86, chmn., 1985-86; trustee Nat. Osteoporosis Found., Washington, 1984-88, chmn. sci. adv. bd., 1985-88; mem. spl. grants rev. com. Nat. Inst. Arthritis, Musculo-Skeletal and Skin Diseases, NIH, 1990-95, chmn., 1993-94. Edit. bd. Calcified Tissue Internat., 1978-83, 94—; Jour. Clin. Endocrinology and Metabolism, 1982-87, Jour. Bone and Mineral Rsch., 1989-93, Italian Jour. Mineral and Electrolyte Metabolism, 1990—, Revs. in Endocrinology and Metabolism, 1999—, Current Drug Targets—Immune, Endocrine and Metabolic Disorders, 2000—. Served with USPHS, 1957-63. Recipient Career Devel. award USPHS, 1963-68, VA med. investigator award, 1979, 81-87, Thomas A. Roe Found. award S.C. Med. Assn., 1982; William S. Middleton VA award, 1983; Frederic C. Bartter award Am. Soc. Bone and Mineral Rsch., 1992, Career Recognition award Vitamin D Workshop, 1997. Mem. Am. Soc. Clin. Investigation, Am. Soc. Bone and Mineral Rsch. (sec.-treas. 1978-85, pres. 1986-87, Shirley Hohl Svc. award 1998), Am. Soc. Pharmacology and Exptl. Therapeutics, Assn. Am. Physicians, Assn. Osteobiology (councillor 1997-98, sec.-treas. 1999, pres. 2000-02), Endocrine Soc., Alpha Omega Alpha Democrat. Episcopalian. Home: 1 Johnson Rd Charleston SC 29407-7514 Office: Strom Thurmond Rsch Bldg 114 Doughty St Charleston SC 29425 E-mail: belln@musc.edu.

BELL, PAUL ANTHONY, II, lawyer; b. Latrobe, Pa., Mar. 12, 1954; s. Paul Anthony and Marcia Chloe (Martin) B.; m. Arlene Rotella, Aug. 19, 1978; children: Montgomery Vincent, Elyse Maureen, Alexa Marie. AB cum laude, Princeton U., 1975; JD, U. Pitts., 1978. Bar: Pa. 1978, U.S. Dist. Ct. (we. dist.) Pa. 1978. Assoc. Scales and Shaw, Greensburg, Pa., 1978, Laurel Legal Services, Indiana, Pa., 1978-81; sole practice Blairsville, Pa., 1981-88; asst. public defender Indiana County, Pa., 1982-85, asst. dist. atty., 1985-87; ptnr. Simpson, Kablack & Bell, Indiana, Pa., 1987—. Bd. dirs. Laurel Legal Services. Pres. Saints Simon and Jude Council, Blairsville, 1982-85; dir. rights com. Torrance (Pa.) State Hosp., 1984-86; dir. Blairsville-Saltsburg Sch. Dist., 1996—, pres., 1997—. Mem. ABA, Pa. Bar Assn., Indiana County Bar Assn. (dir. 1995—). Lodges: Rotary. Republican. Roman Catholic. Avocations: golf, bridge, reading, basketball. Office: Simpson Kablack & Bell 834 Philadelphia St Indiana PA 15701-3908 E-mail: pbell@skblawyers.com.

BELL, PAUL BUCKNER, lawyer; b. Charlotte, N.C., July 29, 1922; s. George Fisher and Carrie (Savage) B.; m. Betty Sue Trulock, May 3, 1952; children: Paul B., Morris Trulock, Betty Fisher, Douglas Savage. BS, Wake Forest U., 1947, JD cum laude, 1948. Bar: N.C. 1948. Pres. Bell, Seltzer, Park & Gibson, Charlotte, 1948-97; of counsel Alston & Bird LLP, 1998—; dir. Southland Investors Inc., Idlewild Farms, Inc. Pres., dir. Charpat Investment Corp.; lectr. Practising Law Inst., 1974, N.C. Bar, 1985; adj. prof. patent law Wake Forest U. Sch. Law, 1974—2002; prof. patent law U. N.C. Sch. Law, 1995—2002. Trustee Mecklenburg Presbytery, Alexander Children's Ctr., Presbyn. Home of Charlotte, Mountain Retreat Assn.; chmn. Presbyn. Ch. Found. Served to 1st lt. USAAF, 1943-46. Mem. ABA, N.C. Bar Assn. (v.p. 1988—), Mecklenburg Bar Assn., Am. Intellectual Property Assn., Licensing Execs. Soc., Federation Internationale Des Conseils Propriete Industrielle (pres. U.S.A.), Charlotte City Club (past pres.), Charlotte Country Club, Charlotte Textile club (past pres.), Grandfather Golf and Country Club, Union League (N.Y.C.), Sigma Phi Epsilon, Phi Alpha Delta. Presbyterian. Home: 322 S Canterbury Rd Charlotte NC 28211-1838 Office: Bank of Am Plz 101 S Tryon St Ste 4000 Charlotte NC 28280-4000

BELL, PAUL R. pharmaceutical executive; BA, MA with honors, U. Canterbury, New Zealand. With IBM New Zealand Ltd., 1968—73; personnel dir. Merck Sharp & Dohme, New Zealand, 1973—78; personnel mgr. MSD Internat. Divsn. Hqrs., 1978—79; personnel dir. Latin Am./Far East Merck Sharp & Dohme Internat. Divsn., 1979—81, dir. adminstr. Far East, 1981—83; asst. to mng. dir. Merck Sharp & Dohme Australia, 1983—86, dir. bus. devel., 1986—88, mng. dir., 1988—93, v.p., mng. dir., 1993—94; v.p. Merck Sharp & Dohme Australia and New Zealand, 1994—97; pres. human health Asia-Pacific Merck & Co., Inc., Whitehouse Station, NJ, 1997—. Mem. APMA Com., 1988—94, vice chmn., 1993—94; mem. Industry/Govt. Consultative Forum, Prime Min.'s Sci. Coun. Working Party on Pharm. Industry. Office: Merck and Co Inc One Merck Dr Whitehouse Station NJ 08889-0100

BELL, PHILIP WILKES, accounting and economics educator; b. N.Y.C., Oct. 24, 1924; s. Samuel Dennis and Miriam Ball (Wilkes) B.; m. Katherine Elizabeth Hubbard, June 16, 1945 (div. May 1980); children: Susan, Geoffrey, Mary Ellen, James; m. Virginia Wood Crozier, June 14, 1980 (dec. Nov. 1998); stepchildren: Thomas, Steven, Peter; m. Jean Grady Wyeth, Oct. 24, 1999. BA, Princeton U., 1947; MA, U. Calif., Berkeley, 1949; PhD, Princeton U., 1954. Instr. Princeton (N.J.) U., 1948-51; rsch. assoc. Inst. for Advanced Study, Princeton, 1951-52; asst. prof. Haverford (Pa.) Coll., 1952-56, assoc. prof., then prof., 1960-68; assoc. prof. U. Calif., Berkeley, 1957-60; prof. Merrill Coll., U. Calif., Santa Cruz, 1968-79, provost, 1968-72; William A. Kirkland prof. Rice U., Houston, 1979-89; prof. acctg. and econs. Boston U., 1989-92. Assoc. dir. Rockefeller Found., 1963-68; dir. Edn. Abroad Program U. Calif., Kenya, 1972-74; vis. prof. Univ. Sains Malaysia, Penang, 1976-77, Norges Handelshoyskole, Bergen, Norway, spring 1982, U. Pa., Phila, fall 1982. Author: Sterling Area in the Postwar World, 1956, Toward Greater Logic and Utility in Accounting: The Collected Writings of Philip W. Bell, 1997; co-author: Theory and Measurement of Business Income, 1961, Accounting for Economic Events, 1979, Financial Accounting: Principles and Issues, 1992; contbr. articles to profl. jours. 2d lt. USAF, 1943-45. Rsch. fellow Social Sci. Rsch. Coun., London, 1956-57, Ford Found. fellow, Berkeley, 1959. Mem. Am. Acctg. Assn., Brit. Acctg. Assn., European Acctg. Assn., Royal Econ. Soc. (U.K.), Acctg. Assn. Australia and New Zealand. Mem. Soc. Of Friends. Home: 30 Lonsdale Ln Cartmel Kennett Square PA 19348-2045 E-mail: philjean@kennett.net.

BELL, REBECCA, psychotherapist, journalist; b. N.Y.C., Dec. 20, 1942; d. Hiram Charles Bluming and Mildred Ann Good; m. Martin Bell, Feb. 7, 1986 (div. Apr. 1993); children: Michael Sobel, Jessica Sobel. BA, UCLA, 1993, MSW, 1995. Lic. clin. social worker. Reporter Hollywood Citizens News, L.A., 1969-70; news writer Sta. KTLA-TV, L.A., 1970-71; assignment editor Sta. KHJ-TV, L.A., 1971-72; anchor, reporter Sta. WXYZ-TV, Detroit, 1972-76; reporter Sta. WCAU-TV, Phila., 1976-78; anchor Sta. WNET-TV, N.Y.C., 1978; corr. NBC, N.Y.C., 1978-86; corr. war coverage, White House reporter NBC Network, London, N.Y., Washington, 1978-86; pvt. practice as psychotherapist Beverly Hills, Calif., 1995—. Author: (book) The Strange Disappearance of Jimmy Hoffa, 1974. Recipient Emmy award Am. Fedn. Radio and TV Artists, 1983, Deadline award, 1978, Golden Mike award, 1974. Mem. NASW. Avocations: painting, horseback riding.

BELL, REGINA JEAN, corporate consulting company executive; b. Lebanon, Mo. d. Stephen S. and Ida M. (Reaves) B. BA, Draughens U.; postgrad., Butler U., Ind.-Purdue U., Indpls., 1968. Prodn. mgr. Howe Mfg. Co., Inc., Indpls., 1958-64; v.p. budgetary control Howe Engring. Co., Inc., Indpls., 1964-67; mgr. material control Nat. Aluminum Div., Indpls., 1968-84; owner Brown County Letter Shop, Nashville, Ind., 1985-89; pres. Trend 90's Corp. Cons. Co., Venice, Fla., 1993—.

BELL, ROBERT, orchestra executive; Ops. & pers. mgr. Toledo Symphony Orch., mng. dir., pres., CEO, 1984—. Office: Toledo Symphony Orch 1838 Parkwood Ave Ste 310 Toledo OH 43624-2502

BELL, ROBERT BROOKS, lawyer; b. Norman, Okla., Aug. 31, 1953; m. Susan F. Krause, Apr. 15, 1989. BA, Dartmouth Coll., 1975; MA, Cambridge U., 1977; JD, Stanford U., 1980. Bar: U.S. Dist. Ct. D.C. 1981, U.S. Ct. Appeals (D.C. cir.) 1981, U.S. Dist. Ct. Md. 1985; N.Y. 1987. Law clk. to judge U.S. Dist. Ct. D.C., 1980-81; law clk. to Justice Byron White U.S. Supreme Ct., Washington, 1981-82; assoc. Sullivan & Cromwell, Washington, 1982-88; of counsel Gibson, Dunn & Crutcher, Washington, 1988-90; ptnr. Wiley, Rein & Fielding, Washington, 1990-99, Wilmer, Cutler & Pickering, Washington, 1999—. Contbr. articles to profl. jours. Deacon Georgetown Presbyn. Ch., 1983-85, trustee, 1987-88, pres. bd. trustees, 1989, elder, 1991-93; trustee Nat. Capital Chpt. Trout Unltd., Washington, 1984-86. Mem. ABA (litigation, antitrust sects.), Order of the Coif, Phi Beta Kappa. Democrat. Office: Wilmer Cutler & Pickering 2445 M St NW Washington DC 20037-1420 E-mail: Robert.Bell@Wilmer.com.

BELL, ROBERT CHRISTOPHER (CHRIS BELL), congressman; b. Abilene, Tex., Nov. 23, 1959; s. Peter Frank Arundel and Dorothy (Hyde) B.; m. Burkely Wells, July 13, 1987 (div. apr. 1988); m. Alison Ayres, Nov. 14, 1992; children: Atlee Christopher, Connally Ayres. BJ in Journalism, U. Tex., 1982; JD, South Tex. Coll. Law, 1992. Bar: Tex. 1992, U. S. Dist. Ct. (so. dist.) Tex. 1992. Reporter, photographer Sta. KXII-TV, Ardmore, Okla., 1982-83; reporter, anchorperson Sta. KVII-TV, Amarillo, 1983-88; reorter Sta. KTRH Radio, Houston, 1989-91; law clk. Hinton, Sussman & Bailey, Houston, 1991-92; assoc. Alexander & McEvily, Houston, 1992-93; pvt. practice Houston, 1993-95; ptnr. Bell & Henry LLP, Houston, 1995—; mem. U.S. Ho. of Reps. from 25th Tex. dist., 2003—. Mem. govt. rels. bd. United Way, Houston, 1998—; mem. adv. bd. Trees for Houston, Houston, 1997—; mem. Houston City Coun., 1997-2001; vol. Houston Taping for the Blind, 1991—; bd. dirs. Big Bros./Big Sisters, Houston, 1996—. Democrat. Episcopalian. Avocations: tennis, running, writing, reading. Office: 216 Cannon Ho Office Bldg Washington DC 20515-4325

BELL, ROBERT DANIEL, religious studies educator; b. Fresno, Calif., July 11, 1942; s. Oran Robert and Arshaloos (Bedrosian) B.; m. Kathryn L. Kruse, July 29, 1967; children: Jonathan Adam, David Benjamin. BA, Bob Jones U., 1964, MA, 1966, PhD, 1970. Prof. Bible and Hebrew Bob Jones U., Greenville, S.C., 1968—, chmn. divns. grad. sch. of religion and seminary, 1979-2000. Asst. editor (jour.) Bibl. Viewpoint, 1979—; contbr. articles to profl. jours. Republican. Ind. Bapt. Avocations: computers, baseball, stamp collecting. Office: Bob Jones U Greenville SC 29614-0001 Home: 26 Prof's Place Greenville SC 29609-5107 E-mail: rdanbell@yahoo.com.

BELL, ROBERT EUGENE, anthropologist educator; b. Marion, Ohio, June 16, 1914; s. Harry Thew and Clara (Stouffer) B.; m. Emily Virginia Merz, Aug. 31, 1938; children— Patricia (Mrs. Paul Lindsey), David Eugene. Student, Ohio State U., 1936-38; BA with honors, U. N.M., 1940; MA, U. Chgo., 1943, PhD, 1947. Asst. prof. anthropology U. Okla., 1947-51, assoc. prof., 1951-55, prof., 1955-69, George L. Cross Research prof., 1969-80, emeritus, 1980—. Chmn. dept., 1947-55, 61-64; head curator Stovall Mus., 1947-85; dir. Mississippi Valley Dendochronology Lab. U. Chgo., 1942-43, 46-47, Oklahoma River Basin Salvage Lab., 1962-78 Author: Oklahoma Archaeology: an Annotated Bibliography, 1969, 2d edit., 1978, The Harlan Site, CK-6, A Prehistoric Mound Center in Cherokee County, Eastern Oklahoma. Archaeol. investigations at site of El Inga, Ecuador; Editor: Am. Antiquity, 1966-70, Bull. Okla. Anthrop. Soc, 1963-66, Prehistory of Oklahoma, 1984. Served with M.C. AUS, 1943-46. Recipient Clarence H. Webb award Outstanding Contbns. to Caddoan Archeology, 1985, Presentation in Recognition of Outstanding Contbn. to Ecuadorian Archeology, Govt. of Ecuador, 1986; subject of Festschrift Okla. Anthrop. Soc., Okla. Archeol. Survey, 1983, Shirk Meml. award for Hist. Preservation, 1987;

named to Okla. Hist. Soc.'s Hall of Fame, 1994, Plains Anthropol. Soc. Disting. Svc. award 1994; Fulbright fellow, New Zealand, 1955-56. Mem. Am. Anthrop. Assn., Am. Assn. Phys. Anthropology, AAAS, Okla. Hist. Soc., Am. Ethnol. Soc., Soc. for Am. Archaeology (50th Anniversary award 1985), Mo., Ark., Tex., Kans. archaeol. socs., Inst. Gt. Plains, Southeastern Archaeol. Conf., Polynesian Soc., Soc. for Hist. Archaeology, Soc. for Conservation Archaeology, Explorers Club, Phi Beta Kappa (hon.), Sigma Xi. Home: 1120 Berry Cir Norman OK 73072-6307

BELL, ROBERT HOLMES, district judge; b. Lansing, Mich., Apr. 19, 1944; s. Preston C. and Eileen (Holmes) B.; m. Helen Mortensen, June 28, 1968; children: Robert Holmes Jr., Ruth Eileen, Jonathan Neil. BA, Wheaton Coll., 1966; JD, Wayne State U., 1969. Bar: Mich. 1970, U.S. Dist. Ct. (we. dist.) Mich. 1970. Asst. prosecutor Ingham County Prosecutor's Office, Lansing, Mich., 1969-72; state dist. judge Mich. State Cts., 1973-78, state cir. judge, 1979-87; judge U.S. Dist. Ct. Mich., Grand Rapids, Mich., 1987-2001, chief judge, 2001—. Office: US Dist Ct 402 Fed Bldg 110 Michigan St NW Grand Rapids MI 49503-2363 E-mail: kim@miwd.uscourts.gov.

BELL, ROBERT LLOYD, retired neurosurgeon; b. McKeesport, Pa., Sept. 3, 1923; s. Samuel Lowry and Nellie Pearl Bell; m. Helen Louise Matthews, Oct. 13, 1951; children: Robert Matthews, Louise Helen. BS, Washington and Jefferson Coll., 1944; MD, U. Pitts., 1947. Jr. intern Shady Side Hosp., Pitts., 1945—47; intern Western Pa. Hosp., Pitts., 1947—48; surg. resident Aspin Wall Pa. Hosp., Pitts., 1948—49; neurosurg. resident Bklyn. Hosp., 1949—50, Kings County Hosp., Bklyn., 1950—51, chief neurosurg. resident, 1953—54; chief neurosurgery 98th GH Hosp., Munich, 1951—53; from instr. to assoc. prof. SUNY, Bklyn., 1954—59; chief neurosurgery Wadsworth (Kans.) VA Hosp., 1959—64, Coatesville (Pa.) VA Hosp., 1964—69, Chester County Hosp., West Chester, Pa., 1969—83; chair nuc. medicine VA Hosp. Coatesville, 1983—91. 1st lt. col. USMC, 1951—53. Fellow: ACS, Am. Coll. Nuc. Medicine (gold medal 1989); mem.: AMA, SAR (compatriot), Chester County Med. Soc., Pa. Med. Soc., Am. Legion. Presbyterian. Home: 51 S 12th St Coatesville PA 19320

BELL, ROBERT M. state supreme court justice; b. Rocky Mount, N.C., July 6, 1943; AB with honors, Morgan State Coll., 1966; JD, Harvard U., 1969. Bar. Md. 1969. Judge Md. Dist. Ct. Dist. 1, Balt., 1975-79; former judge Cir. Ct. Md. 8th Jud. Cir.; assoc. judge Md. Ct. Spl. Appeals, 1980-91, Md. Ct. Appeals, Balt., 1991-96, chief judge, 1996—. Mem. ABA, Nat. Bar Assn., Md. State Bar Assn., Inc., Bar Assn. Balt. City, Monumental City Bar Assn. Office: Court of Appeals 634 Courthouse East 111 N Calvert St Baltimore MD 21202-1904 also: Court of Appeals 361 Rowe Blvd Annapolis MD 21401-1672*

BELL, ROBERT MATTHEW, pharmaceutical company consultant; b. London, Dec. 3, 1932; came to U.S., 1972; s. George Frederick and Patricia (Brusso) B.; m. Jeanette Edna Head, Sept. 17, 1955; children: Adrian R., Colette M. Pharm. diploma, Portmouth Coll., England, 1954; MB,ChB, Birmingham U., Eng., 1968. Diplomate Am. Bd. Family Practice. Relief mgr. Boots Chemists, Eng., 1955-57; owner Bell's Pharmacy, Rhodesia, 1958-61; joint owner Strachan's Pharmacy, Rhodesia, 1962-69; asst. lectr. Godfrey Huggins Sch. Medicine, Rhodesia, 1970-72; clin. project dir. Sterling Winthrop Rsch. Inst., Renesselaer, 1973-75; chief clin. pharmacology ICI Americas, Wilmington, Del., 1975-78; pres., owner RAMA Med. Clinic, Charlotte, N.C., 1980-86; from assoc. dir. to sr. dir. healthcare info. svcs. Searle, Inc., Skokie, Ill., 1986-96; prin. Bell and Assocs., Sedona, Ariz., 1996—. Mem. drug rev. com. Drugs Control Coun. of Rhodesia, Salisbury, 1971—72; mem. adv. bd. Upjohn Healthcare Svcs., Charlotte, NC; chmn. adv. bd. med. office asst. program Piedmont C.C., Charlotte, NC; chief dept. family practice Charlotte Meml. Hosp., 1983—84; trustee Am. Acd. Pharm. Physicians, Raleigh, NC, 1995—96; mem. Pharm. Soc. of Great Britian, 1955—72. Co-author: (book) The Practical Management of Renal Failure, 1969; co-editor: (book) The Endorphins, Marcel Dekker, N.Y., 1982. Grantee Malvern Trust, Rhodesia, 1963; named Metrolina Vol. of Yr., Am. Lung Assn., N.C., 1985. Mem. AMA, Drug Info. Assn.(Outstanding Svc. award 1997), Am. Acad. Pharm. Physicians (Life Hon. Membership award 2002, Certs. of Appreciation 1999, 2000), Am.-Zimbabwe Med. Assn. (chmn. 1996-98). Avocations: postal history, reading, exercising. Office: Bell & Assocs PO Box 3668 Sedona AZ 86340-3668 E-mail: rmsbell@aol.com.

BELL, ROBERT MORRALL, lawyer; b. Graniteville, SC, Feb. 15, 1936; s. Jonathan F. and Ruby Lee (Carpenter) B.; m. Cecelia Richardson Coker, June 11, 1965 (dec.). AB, U. S.C., 1958, LLB, 1965. Bar: S.C. 1965, U.S. Dist. Ct. S.C. 1965, U.S. Ct. Appeals (4th cir.) 1970. With Watkins, Vandiver, Kirven & Long, Anderson, S.C., 1965-67; sr. law clk. to chief judge U.S. Dist. Ct. S.C., Greenville, 1967-69; mem. Abram. Bowen & Townes, Greenville, 1969-71, Bell, Surasky and Brown, P.A., Langley, S.C., 1971-76, sr. ptnr., 1976—. County atty. Aiken County (S.C.), 1982—. Mem. SC Hwy Commn., 1982-86; state exec. committeeman SC Dem. Com., 1980-86; active SC Bd. Chiropractic Examiners, 1978-80, Svc. Coun. of Aiken County, 1976-82, Aiken County Planning Commn., 1976-80; chmn. Aiken County Transp. Com., 1993-96; bd. dirs. Aiken County Crippled Children's Soc., 1976-82, Beech Island Agrl. Club, 1978-; bd. dirs. Gregg-Graniteville Found., 1984—, chmn., 1998—; del. gen. and jurisdictional confs. United Meth. Ch., 1988-92; mem. SC Midlands Citizens Com. on Jud. Qualifications, 1996—. With USAR, 1959-60. Named to Order Ky. Cols., 1989—. Mem. ABA, ATLA, Aiken County Bar Assn., S.C. Bar Assn., S.C. Trial Lawyers Assn., Masons, Shriners, Am. Legion, Beech Island Agrl. Club, Kappa Sigma Kappa, Tau Kappa Alpha, Phi Delta Phi, Chi Psi. Democrat. Office: Bell Surasky and Brown PA PO Box 1890 2625 Jefferson Davis Hwy Langley SC 29834 E-mail: psichi7@cs.com.

BELL, RONALD MACK, university foundation administrator, consultant; b. Atlanta, Mar. 4, 1937; m. Deborah Jean Slaton, Dec. 28, 1989. BS in Indsl. Mgmt., Ga. Inst. Tech., 1959; MBA, U. Mich., 1965; attended, Cornell U., 1980. Commd. USN, 1959, advanced through grades to capt., 1979, ret., 1985; assoc. dir. rsch. contracts Ga. Inst. Tech., Atlanta, 1985-88; v.p., gen. mgr. Ga. Tech. Rsch. Corp., Atlanta, 1988-97; exec. dir. S.C. Rsch. Inst., Columbia, 1997-2001; v.p., bd. dirs. Pisgah Astrol. Rsch. Inst., 1999—; pres., CEO UCRF Support Assoc., St. Simons Island, Ga., 1998—. Bd. dirs., past pres., now dir. emeritus Nat. Supply Corps. Assn.; cons. Wesvaco/Post, Buckley, Coastal Cons., Inc., also others, 1985—; expert witness ELSCO, U. Tenn., others, 1987-90; nat. chmn. Univ. Connected Rsch. Found., 1990-91. Past chmn., dir. emeritus Naval Supply Corps. Sch. Mus. Com., Athens, mem., 1983—; mem. Exec. Roundtable, Atlanta, 1985-97; resource staff Gov.'s Com. Tech. & Devel., Atlanta, 1992-97; bd. dirs. Ga. Tech. Sch. Mgmt., 1995-98. Decorated Legion of Merit (2), Meritorious Svc. medal (2), Navy Commendation medal (2). Mem. Soc. Rsch. Adminstrs. (nat. coms., chair regional com. 1985-2002), Licensing Execs. Soc., Nat. Coun. Univ. Rsch. Adminstrs. (chair regional com., nat. panelist 1985-2001), Coun. Rsch. and Tech. (dir. workshop, tax com. 1986-92), Ga. Tech. Nat. Alumni Assn. (various coms.), Nat. Conf. on the Advancement of Rsch. (conf. com. 2000), Assn. Univ. Tech. Mgrs., Theta Chi (past chpt. pres.), Phi Kappa Phi, Beta Gamma Sigma. Avocations: golf, woodworking. Home: 113 Thompson Cv Saint Simons GA 31522-3768 Office: UCRF Support Assoc PO Box 20272 Saint Simons GA 31522 E-mail: bellssi@earthlink.net.

BELL, ROSONALD RENAE, toxicologist; b. Gainesville, Fla., July 8, 1959; s. Gerome Bell, Sarah Dollie Stewart; m. Michelle Angela Crane; children: Maya, Sharon. MS, PhD, Fla. A&M U., 1992. Diplomate Am. Bd. of Toxicology 1996. Bil. lab. technigian insects affecting man and animals rsch. lab. USDA/Agrl. Rsch. Svc., Gainesville, Fla., 1981—86; grad. rsch. asst. toxicology lab. Fla. A&M U., 1986—92; grad. summer intern new molecule rsch. divsn., pulmonary pharmacolog 3M Pharms., St. Paul, 1989, profl. intern new drug discovery rsch. divs., 1990—91; postdoctoral rsch. scientist Pharmacia Corp., Kalamazoo, 1992—94; study dir. reproductive and gen. toxicology Novartis Pharms. Corp., Summit, NJ, 1994—96; study dir. gen. toxicology Novartis Pharms. Corp.Ciba Pharms., East Hanover, NJ, 1997—98; sr. toxicologist Pharmacia Corp./GD Searle, Skokie, Ill., 1998—. Contbr. Fellow Patricia Robert Harris fellow, Patricia Robert Harris Found., 1991—92, Doctoral fellow, McKnight Found.-Fla. Endowment Fund, 1988—91, inority Biomed. Rsch. Support fekkiw, Fla. A&M U., 1986—88; scholar 3M Scholarship, 3M Pharms., 1990—92. Mem.: Mid-West Teratology Assn., Soc. of Toxicology, Nat. Soc. of Toxicology, Teratogy Soc., Kappa Psi, Rho Chi (VP 1990—91, National Honor Society 1988), Alpha Kappa Mu (National Honor Society, Highest GPA - Graduate Student 1991-1992). Avocations: basketball, softball, travel, exercise. Office: Pharmacia Corporation 4901 Searle Pkwy Rm J203A Skokie IL 60077 Office Fax: 847-982-4799. Business E-Mail: rosonald.r.bell@pharmacia.com.

BELL, RUDOLPH, historian, educator; b. N.Y.C., Nov. 5, 1942; s. Rudolph Albert Bell and Amy Thienpont; m. Laura Tomici; children: Tara, Alessia. BA, Queen's Coll., N.Y.C., 1963; PhD, CUNY, 1969. Instr. history Rutgers U., New Brunswick, NJ, 1968—69, asst. prof. history, 1964—73, assoc. prof. history, 1973—79, prof. history, 1979—. Vis. prof. history U. Colo., Boulder, 2002, U. Ariz., Tucson, 1979; Fulbright scholar U. Genoa, Italy, 1971—72. Mem.: Am. Hist. Assn. (nom. com. 1992—94). Office: Rutgers U History Dept 16 Seminary Pl New Brunswick NJ 08901

BELL, SAMUEL H. federal judge, educator; b. Rochester, N.Y., Dec. 31, 1925; s. Samuel H. and Marie C. (Williams) B.; m. Joyce Elaine Shaw, 1948 (dec.): children: Henry W., Steven D.; m. Jennie Lee McCall, 1983 BA, Coll. Wooster, 1947; JD, U. Akron, 1952. Pvt. practice, Cuyahoga Falls, Ohio, 1956-68; asst. pros. atty. Summit County, Ohio, 1956-58; judge Cuyahoga Falls Mcpl. Ct., Ohio, 1968-73, Ct. of Common Pleas, Akron, Ohio, 1973-77, Ohio Ct. Appeals, 9th Jud. Dist., Akron, 1977-82, U.S. Dist. Ct. (no. dist.) Ohio, Akron, 1982-2000, sr. status, 1996; sr. judge. Adj. prof. Coll. Wooster, 1987—; adj. prof., adv. bd. U. Akron Sch. Law, past trustee Dean's club; bd. dirs. Jos. R. Miller Found. Co-author: Federal Practice Guide 6th Cir., 1996. Recipient Disting. Alumni award U. Akron, 1988, St. Thomas More award, 1987. Fellow Akron Bar Found. (trustee 1989-94, pres. 1993-94); mem. Fed. Bar Assn., Akron Bar Assn., Akron U. Sch. Law Alumni Assn. (Disting. Alumni award 1983), Charles F. Scanlon Akron Inn Ct. (pres. 1990-92), Akron City Club, Masons, Phi Alpha Delta. Republican. Presbyterian. Office: US Dist Ct 433 US Court House Fed Bldg 2 S Main St Akron OH 44308-5836

BELL, SANDRA CHEEVER, artist; b. Cambridge, Mass., Apr. 11, 1932; d. Sumner Cheever and Dora Rioeux Andrews; m. Robert Kittredge Bell, Nov. 22, 1952; children: Sumner, Elizabeth Bell Darby, Gregory K. Grad., Boston Mus. Sch.; postgrad., George Aarons Inst., Brookline, Mass. Cert. nurses aide. Nurses aide Essex (Mass.) Agrl., 1981-82, Essex Hall, Beverly, Mass.; occupl. therapy asst. Beverly, Mass., 1987-89. One woman show at Gabor Gallery, Vero Beach, 1972, Maine Gallery, Wiscassett, 1978, 80, 82, Coconut Grove, Miami, Fla; sculptures (1st pl. award for stone sculpture 1972). Mem. vol. bd. Mary Allen Hosp., Marblehead, Mass., 1954-56; vol. aide North Conway (N.H.) Hosp., 1964-65; vol. Sr. Home Care Svcs., Inc., Salem, Mass., 1994; nutrition vol. North Shore Elder Svcs., Danvers, Mass., 1993. Recipient Cert. Appreciation, North Shore Elder Svcs., 1993, Silver Dove award Sec. Elder Affairs, Mass., 1994, Excellence award Sr. Home Care Svcs., 1994. Mem. Nat. League Am. Pen Women (1st Pl. award for oil painting 1998). Republican. Congregationalist. Avocations: sailing, swimming, reading, painting amateur theatrical sets, golf. Home: 9751 Conservation Dr New Port Richey FL 34655-6025 E-mail: SandraBellAries@aol.com.

BELL, SCOTT WILLIAM, private school educator, principal; b. Aurora, Ill., Aug. 7, 1961; s. William Laurence and Violet Annabelle (Miller) B.; m. Jill Robin Burton, July 26, 1986; 1 child, Seth Andrew Thomas. BA in Edn., Concordia Coll., River Forest, Ill., 1985; MA in Ednl. Leadership, Marian Coll., Fond du Lac, Wis., 1999. Cert. tchr., Ill. Min. of music, tchr. Peace Luth. Sch., Ft. Lauderdale, Fla., 1985-86; music tchr. St. Paul Luth. Sch., Boca Raton, Fla., 1986-88; min. of music, tchr. Immanuel Luth. Ch., Houston, 1988-92; prin. St. Peter Luth. Sch., Hilbert, Wis., 1992-96, St. John Luth. Sch., Mayville, Wis., 1996—2001, Trinity Luth. Sch., Mequon, Wis., 2000—. Firefighter Hilbert Vol. Fire Dept., 1992-96, Mayville Vol. Fire Dept., 1997-2000; mem. South Wis. Dist. Supts. Cabinet, 1994-97, 2000—; bd. dirs. Wis. Non-pub. Schs. Accreditation Assn., 2001—; commr. Nat. Luth. Sch. Accreditation Dist., 2002—. Mem. ASCD, NAESP, Luth. Edn. Assn. Office: Trinity Luth Sch 10729 W Freistadt Rd Mequon WI 53092 Home: 11915 N Ridgeway Ave Mequon WI 53097-3022 E-mail: sbell@trinityfreistadt.com.

BELL, SHARON KAYE, small business owner; b. Lincoln, Nebr., Sept. 14, 1943; d. Edwin B. and Evelyn F. (Young) Czachurski; m. James P. Kittrell (div. Sept. 1974); children: Nathan James, Nona Kaye; m. Joseph S. Bell, June 5, 1976; stepchildren: Eugene, Patricia, Bobbie, Linda. Continuing edn./active tax preparer/interviewer assoc., H&R Block, Laguna Hills, 1987—. Various positions mgmt., bookkeeping, 1961-71; bookkeeper Internat. Harvester, Chesapeake, Va., 1971-73, Cheat'AH Engring., Santa Ana, Calif., 1973-74, Fre Del Engring., Santa Ana, Calif., 1974-75; bookkeeper/mgr. Tek Sheet Metal Co., Santa Ana, Calif., 1975-79; owner, bookkeeper Bell's Bookkeeping, Huntington Beach, Calif., 1979-86, Fountain Valley, Calif., 1986—, Laguna Hills, Calif., 1986—; tax preparer H.R. Block, 1989-2000, Bell's Bookkeeping, Laguna Hills, 1998—. Mem. Inst. Mgmt. Accts. (bd. dirs. 1985-86, sec. 1986-87, v.p. 1987-90, dir. manuscripts 1990-91), Nat. Notary Assn., NAFE, Wives of Submarine Vets. World War II (v.p. L.A. chpt. 1986-87, treas. 1990-92), Nat. Soc. Pub. Accts., Internat. Platform Assn. Republican. Avocations: gardening, dancing, grandchildren and great grandchildren, rv travel. Office: Bells Bookkeeping PO Box 5883 Oceanside CA 92052-5883

BELL, STEPHANIE, economics educator; b. Salt Lake City, Oct. 10, 1969; d. Jerald Ray and Marlene Raye Bell. BA, BS, Calif. State U., Sacramento, 1995; MPhil, Cambridge (Eng.) U., 1997; PhD, New Sch. for Social Rsch., 2001. Vis. rsch. scholar Jerome Levy Econs. inst., Annandale-on-Hudson, N.Y., 1997-98; rsch. assoc. Ctr. for Full Employment and Price Stability, Kansas City, Mo., 1999—; asst. prof. econs. U. Mo., Kansas City, 1999—. Bd. editors. Jour. Econ. Issues. Editor: The State, the Market, and the Eruo, 2003; contbr. articles to profl. jours. Cambridge U. vis. scholar's fellow Jerome Levy Econs. Inst., 1997-98. Mem.: Ea. Econs. Assn., Assn. for Instnl. Thought, Assn. for Social Econs., Am. Social Sci. Assn. Office: U Mo-Kansas City 211 Haag Hall 5100 Rockhill Rd Kansas City MO 64110 Fax: (816) 235-5263. E-mail: bellsa@umkc.edu.

BELL, STEPHEN ROBERT, lawyer; b. Menominee, Mich., July 10, 1942; s. John Martin and Catherine Irene (Goodman) B.; m. Linden Tucker, May 22, 1976. AB, Georgetown U., 1964; JD, U. Wis., 1967. Bar: D.C. 1971, Minn. 1967, Wis. 1967, U.S. Ct. Appeals (4th and 5th cirs.), U.S. Supreme Ct. Assoc. Dorsey & Whitney, Mpls., 1967—68; ptnr. Wilkinson, Cragun & Barker, Washington, 1971—82, Squire, Sanders & Dempsey, Washington, 1982—96, Willkie, Farr & Gallagher LLP, Washington, 1996—. Contbr. article to profl. jours. Lt. USNR, 1968-71. Mem. ABA, D.C. Bar Assn., Fed. Communications Bar Assn., Computer Law Assn. (bd. dirs. 1987-93), Order of Coif. Office: Willkie Farr & Gallagher LLP 1875 K St NW Washington DC 20006-1238 E-mail: sbell@willkie.com.

BELL, STEPHEN SCOTT (STEVE BELL), journalist, educator; b. Oskaloosa, Iowa, Dec. 9, 1935; s. Howard Arthur and Florance (Scott) B.; m. Joyce Dillavou, June 16, 1957; children: Allison Kay, Hilary Ann. BA, Central Coll., Pella, Iowa, 1959, PhD (hon.), 1969; MS in Journalism, Northwestern U., 1963. Announcer Radio Sta. KBOE, Oskaloosa, 1955-59; reporter WOI-TV, Ames, Iowa, 1959-60; news writer WGN Radio-TV, Chgo., 1960-61; reporter, anchorman WOW-TV, Omaha, 1962-65; anchorman Radio Sta. WNEW, N.Y.C., 1965-66; corr. ABC News, 1967-86, assignments include corr., 1970-71, polit. corr., 1968, 72, chief Asia corr., 1972-73, White House corr., 1974-75; news anchorman World News This Morning and Good Morning Am., 1975-86; news anchor KYW-TV, Phila., 1987-91, USA Network Updates, 1989-92; prof. telecomm. Ball State U., Muncie, Ind., 1992—. Recipient Emmy nominations, 1965, 73, Overseas Press Club award, 1969, Headliner award, 1975 Mem. AFTRA, Council Fgn. Relations. Presbyterian (elder). Office: Ball State U Dept Telecommunications Muncie IN 47306-0001 *As a journalist, the older I get, the less inclined I am to "play God."*

BELL, STEWART LYNN, judge; b. L.A., Feb. 6, 1945; s. Jack C. and Kathryn Arline (Winn) B.; m. Karen Virginia Davis, Dec. 23, 1966 (div. Feb. 1974); 1 child, Linda Marie; m. Jeanne Dorothy Brick, June 8, 1974; children: Kristin Denise, Stephen Jeffrey, Gregory Matthew. BS, U. Nev., Las Vegas, 1967; JD, UCLA, 1970. Bar: Calif. 1970, Nev. 1971, U.S. Dist. Ct. Nev. 1971, U.S. Dist. Ct. (cen. dist.) Calif. 1973, U.S. Supreme Ct. 1976, U.S. Ct. Appeals (9th cir.) 1990. Legal asst. to Hon. Judge Howard W. Babcock 8th Judicial Dist. Ct., Nev., 1970-71; lawyer Clark County Pub. Defender's Office, Nev., 1971-72; sr. ptnr. Bell, Leavitt & Green, Chtd., 1974-83, Stewart L. Bell, Chtd., Las Vegas, Nev., 1983-89, Bell & Davidson, Nev., 1990-94; dist. atty. Clark County Dist. Atty. Office, Nev., 1995—2003; dist. judge U.S. Dist. Ct. (8th dist.), 2003—. Alt. judge City of North Las Vegas, 1981-88; coroner's inquest judge Clark County, 1979-94; referee Juvenile Ct., 1988-94; mental commitment judge, 1981-94; small claims judge, 1990-94; trial judge 8th Judicial Cir. Ct., 2003-. Vol. Clark Cty. Med./Legal Malpractice Screening Panel, 1974—75; vol. sec. Clark County Bar Assn., 1978, vol. v.p., 1979; vol. State Bar of Nev. Ethics and Atty. Discipline Com., 1980, Dis. court Adv. Com., 1980—82, State Bar of Nev. Bd. of Governor, 1981—92, Pro Bono Project, 1985—94. Recipient Dist. Men in Southern Nev., Asian Pacific Am. Advovate Champion of Excellence, 1995, Amigo award, Hispanics in Politics, 1996, Broche de Oro award, 1998, Stop DUI Appercation award, 1997, Families of Murder Victims award, 1997, Cir. of Excellance award, Las Vegas C. of C. Com., 1999, Louis Weiner Citizen of the Yr. award, 2001, Nat. Multiple Sclerosis Soc. Hope award for Com. Achievement, 2002. Mem. ABA, Assn. Trial Lawyers Am., Nev. Bar Assn. (bd. govs. 1981-92, v.p. 1989-90, pres. elect 1990-91, pres. 1991-92), Nev. Trial Lawyers Assn., Clark County Bar Assn. (sec. 1978, v.p. 1979, pres. 1980), State Bar Calif., Nat. Dist. Atty's Assn. (bd. dirs. 1995—, co-chair met. prosecutors com. 1996-2000, Nev. Dist. Atty's Assn. (v.p. 2000, pres. 2001), Nev. Adv. Coun. Prosecuting Atty's. Lodges: Elks. Democrat. Office: Clark County Dist Ct 200 S 3rd St #700 Las Vegas NV 89155

BELL, STOUGHTON, computer scientist, mathematician, educator; b. Waltham, Mass., Dec. 20, 1923; s. Conrad and Florence Emily (Ross) Bell; m. Mary Carroll O'Connell, Feb. 26, 1949 (div. 1960); children: Karen, Mark; m. Laura Joan Bainbridge, May 24, 1963 (div. 1979); children: Nathaniel Stoughton, Joshua Bainbridge. Student, Harvard U., 1946-49; AB, U. Calif., Berkeley, 1950, MA, 1953, PhD, 1955. Mem. staff Sandia Corp., Albuquerque, 1955-66, div. supr., 1964-66; vis. lectr. U. N.Mex., 1957-66, dir. computing center, 1966-79, assoc. prof. math., 1966-71, prof. math. and computer sci., 1971-92, prof. emeritus, 1992—. Vis. lectr. N.Mex. Acad. Scis., 1965—. Co-author: (book) Linear Analysis and Generalized Functions, 1965, Introductory Calculus, 1966, Modern University Calculus, 1966, Mathematical Analysis for Modeling, 1999. With AUS, 1943—44. Mem.: Ops. Rsch. Soc. Am., Am. Statis. Assn., Soc. Indsl. and Applied Math., Math. Assn. Am., Am. Math. Soc., Assn. Computing Machinery (nat. lectr. 1972—74). Office: U NMex Computer Sci Dept Albuquerque NM 87131-1386 E-mail: sto@cs.unm.edu.

BELL, SUE ELLEN, research analyst, administrator, nursing educator; b. Parkston, S.D., Dec. 24, 1951; d. Jay Quentin and Dorothy Rose (Topping) B.; m. James Richard Hulbert, Aug. 12, 1978. BA, De Pauw U., 1974; BSN, U. Iowa, 1979; MA, Iowa State U., 1984; PhD, U. Minn., 1998. Rsch. analyst Starr & Assocs. Inc, Des Moines, 1985-86; rsch. asst. Coll. Medicine, U. Iowa, Iowa City, 1986-87, project coord. Ctr. for Health Svcs. Rsch., 1987-90; devel. assoc. Macalester Coll., St. Paul, 1990-92; rsch. analyst Health Risk Mgmt., Mpls., 1992—93; mgr. Practice Guideline Development Health Risk Mgmt., Mpls., 1993—2000; rsch. coord. U. Minn., Mpls., 2000—01; nursing Wayne State U., Detroit, 2001—. Co-editor spl. issue Practicing Anthropology; contbr. articles to profl. jours. Mem. Soc. for Med. Anthropology, Soc. for Applied Anthropology, APHA, Am. Soc. Bioethics and Humanities, Sigma Theta Tau. Office: Wayne State Univ 5557 Cass Ave Rm 238 Cohn Detroit MI 48202

BELL, SUSAN JANE, nurse; b. Columbus, Ohio, July 24, 1946; d. Donald Richard Bell and Martha Jane (McDowell) Nichols; m. Robert Earlin Ward, Oct. 24, 1964 (div. 1984); children: Duane Allen Ward, Melissa Jane Ward, Bryan Thomas Ward. Degree in nursing, Columbus Sch. Practical Nursing, 1986; ADRN, Columbus State C.C., 1989; student, Franklin U., 1993—. RN, Ohio; cert. CPR. Nurse's asst. Riverside Meth. Hosp., Columbus, 1970-80, Norworth Convalescent Ctr., Columbus, 1980-86; nurse, charge nurse Heartland Thurber Care Ctr., Columbus, 1986-89; staff nurse Am. Nursing Care, Columbus, 1989—; medicare home visitation, staffing and pvt. duty nurse Telemed, Columbus, 1989—; asst. head nurse Northland Terr., Columbus, 1989; supr. Elmington Manor, Columbus, 1989; staff nurse cardiac step down unit Grant Hosp., Columbus, 1989-92; nurse med. ICU, CCU and pediatric ICU, 1992-93; charge nurse critical-skilled unit first Cmty. Village Health Care Ctr., Columbus, 1992-95; supr., charge nurse St. Rita's Home. Pres. Bell Mktg. Distbrs., pvt. duty ALS ventilator patients Med. Pers. Poole. Mem. NAFE, ASPCA, World Wildlife Found., Nature Conservancy, Ohio Hist. Found. (archives/libr. divsn.), Nat. Audubon Soc., Environ. Def. Fund, Nat. Wildlife Fedn., Humane Soc. U.S., Am. Assn. Individual Investors, Columbus Met. Mus. Art (supporting), Internat. Assn. Global Execs., Nat. Notary Assn., Nat. Mus. of Women in the Arts, Ohio Hist. Soc.-Archives Libr., Omtermat/ Exec. Guild, Rotary. Avocations: body building, power lifting, swimming, music, crocheting.

BELL, SUSAN KOELLE, paleontologist; b. St. Louis, Aug. 17, 1939; d. Arthur Ernst and Anne Bowman (Kinnaird) K.; m. Byron Bell, May 6, 1972. AB, Vassar Coll., 1961; MA, NYU, 1989. Mem. staff paleontology divsn. Am. Mus. Natural History, N.Y.C., 1966—. Fellow Explorers Club; mem. Am. Anthropol. Assn., Soc. Vertebrate Paleontology. Office: Am Mus Natural History Central Park W at 79th St New York NY 10024

BELL, THEODORE AUGUSTUS, advertising executive; b. Tampa, Fla., July 3, 1946; s. Theodore A. and Mary Trice (Howell) B.; m. Evelyn Byrd Lorentzen, Mar. 31, 1978; 1 child, Evelyn Byrd. BA in English, Randolph-Macon Coll., 1969; DFA (hon.), Kendall Coll., 1990. Copywriter Wilson, Haight, Welsh Advt., Hartford, Conn., 1970-71, Tinker, Dodge & Delano, N.Y.C., 1971-72; v.p., creative dir. Doyle Dane Bernbach, N.Y.C., 1972-82; pres., chief creative officer Leo Burnett USA, Chgo., 1982-93; vice-chmn., worldwide creative dir. Young & Rubicam, N.Y.C., 1993 . Creative cons. Heart of Am. America's Cup Challenge, Chgo., 1985-86. Bd. dirs. Lincoln Park Zoo, 1988—, Prentice Women's Maternity Ctr. Northwestern Meml. Hosp., Chgo., 1981—. Recipient Gold Lion award Cannes (France) Internat. Festival du Film Publicitaire, 1988. Mem. Racquet Club (Chgo. and N.Y.C.), Field Club (Greenwich, Conn.). Republican. Episcopalian. Avocations: sailing, golf, screenwriting, gamebird hunting.

BELL, THOMAS DEVEREAUX, JR., communications company executive; b. Niagara Falls, Nov. 2, 1949; s. Thomas Devereaux and Lenore (Chisholm) B.; m. Margaret McDaniel, Jan. 17, 1975 (div.); 1 child, Thomas Devereaux III; m. Jennifer Holtzman, Dec. 27, 1987; children: Kevin Holtzman Bell, Hannah Holtzman Bell. Student, U. Tenn., 1967-70, George Washington U., 1973, NYU, 1984-88. Exec. dir. Presdl. Inaugural Ball Com., Washington, 1972; dep. div. dir. Com. to Reelect the Pres., Washington, 1971-72; adminstrv. asst. U.S. Senator William Brock, Washington, 1973-75; pres., CEO Bell and McDaniel, Washington, 1975-76, Holder, Kennedy, Dye & Bell, Nashville, 1976-79, Creative Com. Corp., Washington, 1979-82, Hudson Inst., Indpls., 1982-87; exec. v.p. Ball Corp., Muncie, Ind., 1987-89; vice chmn., COO Burson-Marsteller, 1989-94; vice chmn. Gulfstream Aerospace Corp., Savannah, Ga., 1994-95; pres., CEO Burson-Marsteller, N.Y.C., 1995-98; also bd. dirs. Gulfstream Aerospace Corp., Savannah, Ga.; chmn., CEO Young & Rubicam Advt., N.Y.C., 1998-99; pres., CEO Young & Rubicam Inc., N.Y.C., 2000—. Bd. dirs. Lincoln Nat. Corp., Ft. Wayne, Ind., Young & Rubicam Inc., N.Y.C., Hudson Inst., Indpls., Lincoln Life & Annuity Co. N.Y. Mem. Transition Team for Pres. Ronald Reagan, Washington, 1981; ptnr. N.Y.C. Partnership. Mem. U.S. C. of C. (bd. dirs. Washington chpt.), Skyline Club, Univ. Club (Indpls.), Econ. Club (N.Y.), Burning Tree Club (Bethesda, Md.), Arthur Page Soc., Union League Club (N.Y.C.), Georgetown Club (Washington), Field Club (Greenwich, Conn.), Blind Brook Club (Harrison, N.Y.), Gold Club of Purchase (N.Y.). Republican. Office: Young & Rubicam Advt 285 Madison Ave New York NY 10017-6486

BELL, TONYA LYNN, auditor; b. Evanston, Wyo., Dec. 30, 1973; d. Johnnie Kennith and Sherrylee Ramey; m. Brian Wyane Bell, May 23, 1997. BS, St. Mary's of Minn. U., 1996. Mfg. quality assurance auditor Abbott Labs., Abbott Park, Ill., 1996—97; tech. svcs. and devel. coatings technician Allied Colloids (Ciba), Suffolk, Va., 1997—98; sr. quality assurance auditor Cytogen Corp., Princeton, NJ, 1998—99, Clin. Rsch. Labs., Piscataway, NJ, 1999—2001; quality assurance auditor Merial Ltd., 2001—. Mem. Am. Soc. for Quality, Soc. Quality Assurance. Avocations: outdoor sports, reading. Home: 3501 Lynley Mill Ln Dacula GA 30019-5054 Office: 3239 Satellite Blvd Duluth GA 30096

BELL, VICKI P. music educator, organist; b. Harrodsburg, KY, Apr. 19, 1954; d. Llewellyn J. and Betty Jo Peavler; m. Donald Paul Bell, Aug. 5, 1977 (div. 1991); 1 child, Cully; m. Francois Daniel Botha, June 5, 1993. BME, Univ. KY, 1976, MusM, 1989, PhD, 1998. Assoc. prof. Asbury Coll., Wilmore, Ky., 1993—. Organist, choirmaster Trinity Episcopal Church, Danville, Ky., 1996—. Vol. Habitat for Humanity, Danville. Mem.: Am. Guild Organists, Coll. Music Soc., Soc. Music Theory. Avocations: travel, hiking, reading. Office: Asbury Coll 1 Macklem Dr Wilmore KY 40390 Business E-Mail: vicki.bell@asbury.edu.

BELL, WAYNE S. lawyer, state agency official; b. L.A., June 24, 1954; s. Joseph and Jane Barbara (Barsook) B.; m. M. Susan Modzelewski, Apr. 1, 1989; 1 child, Seth Joseph Bell. BA magna cum laude, UCLA, 1976; JD, Loyola U., L.A., 1979; Advanced Mgmt. Program, Rutgers U., 1992. Bar: Calif. 1980, U.S. Dist. Ct. (cen. dist.) 1981, U.S. Tax Ct. 1981, U.S. Ct. Appeals (9th cir.) 1981, U.S. Dist. Ct. (so. and no. dists.) Calif. 1983, U.S. Supreme Ct. 1984, D.C. 1986, Tex. 1995; lic. real estate broker, Calif. Intern office of gov. State of Calif., Sacramento, summer 1976; assoc. Levinson, Rowen, Miller, Jacobs & Kabrins, L.A., 1980-82; sr. assoc. Montgomery, Gascou, Gemmill & Thornton, L.A., 1982-84; counsel, project developer Thomas Safran & Assocs., L.A., 1984-85; of counsel Greenspan, Glasser & Medina, Santa Monica, Calif., 1984-86; assoc. gen. counsel Am. Diversified Cos., Costa Mesa, Calif., 1985-88; legal cons. Project Atty., L.A., 1988-89; sr. counsel, asst. sec. Ralphs Grocery Co., L.A., 1989-99, v.p., sr. counsel, asst. sec., 1999; dep. sec., gen. counsel Calif. Bus., Transp. and Housing Agy., Sacramento, 1999—, spl. counsel to Gov.'s Legal Affairs Sec., 1999—. Judge pro tem Mcpl. Ct. South Bay Jud. Dist., 1987, L.A. Superior Ct., 1991, 94, 97; settlement officer L.A. Mcpl. Ct., Settlement Officer Program, 1990-92; spl. master State Bar Calif., 1991-92. Chief note and comment editor Loyola U. Law Rev., 1978-79; contbr. articles to profl. jours. and gen. pubs. Vol. atty. Westside Legal Svcs., Santa Monica, 1982-87; legal ombudsman Olympics Ombudsman Program L.A. County Bar Assn., 1984; gov. apptd. mem. Calif. adv. coun. Legal Svcs. Corp., 1982-88, Autism Soc. Am., Amnesty Internat.; contbg. mem. Dem. Nat. Com.; mem. leadership coun. So. Poverty Law Ctr.; charter mem. presdl. task force Ams. for Change; bd. dirs. Am. Theatre Arts, Hollywood, Calif., 1983-84; pres., exec. com., bd. dirs. Programs for the Developmentally Handicapped, Inc., L.A., 1987-92; chmn. bd. appeals handicapped accommodations City of Manhattan Beach, 1986-88; bd. dirs. The Foodbank of So. Calif., 1991-94, sec., 1993; legal oversight com. Legal Corps L.A., 1995-97; sec. bd. trustees The Ralphs/Food 4 Less Found., 1995-99; vol. L.A. County Bar Assn., Barristers Homeless Shelter Advocacy Project, 1996-99, exec. com. labor and employment law sect., 1997-99; mem. coordinating com. Lake Tahoe Interagy Coun., 2001—; mem. San Francisco Bay Conservation and Devel. Commn., 2002-. Mem. Calif. Bar Assn. (legal svcs. sect. standing com. legal problems of aging 1983-86, chmn. legis. subcom. 1984-86, conf. dels. alternate 1987), D.C. Bar Assn. (real estate sect. com. on comml. real estate), Legal Assistance Assn. Calif. (bd. dirs., mem. exec. com., legis. strategy com. 1984-86), Loyola Law Sch. (advocate), Sacramento County Bar Assn. (pub. and adminstrv. law sects.). Democrat. Avocations: sailing, hiking, human behavior study, photography, travel. Office: Calif Bus Transp and Housing Agy 980 9th St Ste 2450 Sacramento CA 95814-2742

BELL, WENDELL, sociologist, educator, futurist; b. Chgo., Sept. 27, 1924; s. Wendell and Blanche (Leiferman) B.; m. Lora-Lee Edwards, June 15, 1947; children: Karen Ann, Sharon Lee (dec. 2001), David Howard. BA with highest honors, Calif. State U., Fresno, 1948; MA, UCLA, 1951, PhD, 1952; MA (hon.), Yale U., 1963. Asst. prof. sociology, acting dir. survey rsch. facility Stanford U., 1952-54; assoc. prof. sociology Northwestern U., 1954-57; from assoc. prof. to prof. sociology, dir. West Indies study program UCLA, 1957-63; prof. sociology Yale U., New Haven, 1963-95, chmn. dept., 1965-69, dir. comparative sociology tng. program, 1969-77, dir. undergrad. studies, 1976-83, dir. grad. studies, 1984-89, 94; prof. emeritus, 1995—. Sr. rsch. scientist, Yale Ctr. for Comparative Studies, 2000—; mem. exec. com. div. behavioral scis. NRC, 1968-69; tng. grant dir. NIMH, 1969-77; vis. fellow Inst. Advanced Studies, The Australian Nat. U., 1985. Author: (with E. Shevky) Social Area Analysis, 1955; (with R.J. Hill and C.R. Wright) Public Leadership, 1961; (with I. Oxaal) Decisions of Nationhood, 1964, Jamaican Leaders, 1964, Foundations of Futures Studies, Vol. I. History, Purposes, and Knowledge, paperback edit., 2003, Vol II Values, Objectivity, and the Good Society, 1997; editor, contbr.: The Democratic Revolution in the West Indies, 1967; (with James A. Mau) The Sociology of the Future, 1971; (with Walter Freeman) Ethnicity and Nation-Building, 1974; editor Internat. Studies in Polit. and Social Change, 1966-76; assoc. editor Am. Sociol. Rev., 1958-61; mem. editl. adv. bd. Sage Profl. Papers in Internat. Studies, 1972-84, Sage Rsch. Papers in Social Sci., Series Social Orgn. of Cmty., U. Iowa, 1974-84, Futurics, 1976—, Cultural Futures Rsch., 1976-87, Technological Forecasting and Social Change, 1995-96; editl. cons. Sociometry, 1959-61; mem. editl. bd. Internat. Studies Quar., 1970-80, Plantation Soc. in the Americas, 1978-90, Political Behavior, 1978-80, Jour. Conflict Resolution, 1980-97, Futures Rsch. Quar., 1992—, The Jour. of Contingencies and Crisis, 1992-97, Jour. Futures Studies, 2000—, Foresight, 1998—; cons. editor D.C. Heath and Co., 1971-84, cons., U.S. Commn. on National Security/21st Century, 1999. Gov.'s appointee Commn. on Conn.'s Future, 1987-89; mem. adv. coun. Inst. for Global Ethics, 1990—. Aviator USNR, 1943-46, CBI. Recipient Disting. Alumnus award Calif. State U., Fresno, 1988, W. Bloomberg award for promoting a vision of future based on social justice, 2000; rsch. tng. predoctoral fellow Social Sci. Rsch. Coun., 1951-52, faculty fellow, 1956-59, fellow Ctr. for Advanced Study Behavioral Scis., 1963-64; rsch. grantee, Soc. Sci. Rsch. Coun., 1978, grantee Carnegie Corp. N.Y., 1960-63, NSF, 1969-70. Mem. AAUP, Internat. Sociol. Assn., Am. Sociol. Assn., Eastern Sociol. Soc., Pacific Sociol. Assn. (v.p. 1960-61), Sociol. Rsch. Assn., Internat. Studies Assn. (v.p. 1970-71), Caribbean Studies Assn. (v.p. 1978, pres 1979, Meritorious Service award 1985, mem. coun. 1988-89), World Future Soc., World Futures Studies Fedn. Home: 364 Sperry Rd Bethany CT 06524-3542 Office: Yale U Dept Sociology PO Box 208265 New Haven CT 06520-8265 E-mail: wendell.bell@yale.edu.

BELL, WILLIAM LYNN, neurologist, researcher; b. Waco, Tex., Apr. 25, 1951; s. Elmo Lynn and Lois Margaret (Davies) Bell; m. Rhonda Sue Robson, June 19, 1982 (dec. Mar. 1984); 1 child, Robert (dec.); m. Judith Helene Suskind, June 18, 1989; children: Jonathan, Kyle Anne. BS in Biology, Baylor U., 1973; MD, Wake Forest U., 1977. Diplomate Am. Bd. Internal Medicine, Am. Bd. Psychiatry and Neurology, Am. Bd. Clin. Neurophysiology, Am. Bd. Psychiatry and Neurology with added qualifications in clin. neurophysiology, Am. Bd. Sleep Medicine, lic. physician, N.C., physician, Tex. Intern N.C. Bapt. Hosp., Winston-Salem, 1977-80; resident in neurology U. Tex., Dallas, 1980-83, asst. prof., 1989-93; fellow in neurology Duke U., Durham, N.C., 1987-89; asst. prof. neurology and neurosurgery Wake Forest U. Sch. Medicine, Winston-Salem, 1993—, dir. Comprehensive Epilepsy Ctr., asst. prof. neurology and neurosurgery, 1995—. Contbr. Maj. USAF, 1963—87. Fellow: ACP, Am. Electroencephalographic Soc., Am. Acad. Sleep Medicine; mem.: AMA, AAAS, Dallas Epilepsy Assn. (profl. adv. bd. 1992—93), Nat. Assn. Epilepsy Ctrs., Christian Med. and Dental Soc., Am. Sci. Affiliation, Am. Epilepsy Assn., Am. Acad. Neurology, Omicron Delta Kappa. Baptist. Home: 7925 Lasley Forest Rd Lewisville NC 27023-8244 Office: Wake Forest U Sch Medicine Dept Neurology Medical Ctr Blvd Winston Salem NC 27157-0001 E-mail: wbell@wfubmc.edu.

BELL, WILLIAM WOODWARD, lawyer; b. May 15, 1938; s. Charles Smith and Janie Mae (Woodward) B.; m. Mary Elizabeth Beniteau, May 31, 1969; children: Susan Elizabeth, Carol Ann. BBA, Baylor U., 1960, JD, 1965. Bar: U.S. Dist. Ct. (we. dist.) Tex. 1967, U.S. Dist. Ct. (no. dist.) Tex. 1993, U.S. Supreme Ct. 1971. Ptnr. Sleeper, Boynton, Burleson, Williams & Johnson, Waco, Tex., 1965-68, Holloway, Slagle & Bell, Brownwood, 1968-71, Johnson, Slagle & Bell, Brownwood, 1971-74; pvt. practice Brownwood, 1974—. Capt. USMC, 1960-63. Named Vol., 1991, Developer of Yr., Tex. Indsl. Devel. Coun. Fellow Tex. Bar Found.; mem. ATLA, ABA, Tex. Bar Assn., Brown County Bar Assn., Am. Judicature Soc., Phi Alpha Delta. Baptist. Home: PO Box 1564 Brownwood TX 76804-1564 Office: PO Box 1726 115 S Broadway Brownwood TX 76804-1726

BELLA, DANTINA CARMEN QUARTAROLI, human services consultant; b. Providence, May 11, 1922; d. Bernardo and Jennie (Zinno) Quartaroli; m. Salvatore J. Bella, Dec. 30, 1946; children: Theresa, Joseph, Jennifer. BA, Bryant Coll.; MA in Psychology, Alfred U., 1952; MS in Adminstr., U. Notre Dame, 1973; postgrad., U. Mich., 1977. Cert. social worker. Rehab. counselor R.I. Dept. Edn., 1942-46; admission counselor Coll. Bus. Adminstrn., Boston U., 1946-49; asst. to dean Coll. of Ceramics, Alfred U., 1949-53; dir. pupil personnel svcs., asst. prin. Marian H.S., Mishawaka, Ind., 1968-74; registrar, admissions officer Ind. Vocat. Tech. Coll., South Bend, 1974-76; resident counselor, dir. Forever Learning Inst., Harvest House, South Bend, 1977-84; pres., owner Potentials for Greying Ams., Notre Dame, Ind., 1981—; exec. dir. Battell Sr. Workers, Inc., Mishawaka, 1985—97. Textbook cons. South Bend Community Sch. Corp., 1974-77; lectr., workshop coordinator, 1974-80. Writer, prodr. TV series Pub. Broadcasting System; Better Understanding of Self Through Literature, 1978, Mothers of the Depression, 1979. Columnist Sr. Life, 1987—; therapist older adult specialist Cath. Social Svc., 1989—; bd. dirs. Cath. Social Svc. Ctr., 1968-90, Women Career Ctr., 1974; pres. South Bend Commn. on Status of Women, 1975-78; mem. Older Adult Legislature, Ind., 1995-96. Named to, South Bend Cmty. Hall of Fame, 2001. Mem. AACD, AAUW, Beta Gamma Sigma. Democrat. Roman Catholic. Home: 1029 Clermont St South Bend IN 46617-1801

BELLA, GIOVANNI, shipping agent; b. Catania, Italy, Aug. 24, 1964; s. Salvatore and Tina B (Sirugo) Bella; life ptnr. Angela De Martino; children: Salvatore, Teo. Cert. shipping agt, forwarding agt. Dir. dept. water SE.A.MAR. Srl, Augusta, Italy, 1985-91; sales mgr. Eliades Paschalides and Co., Nicosia, Cyprus, 1991-94; mng. dir. Besamar Lines, Valletta, Malta, 1994-97; CEO Bella Giovanni Shipping and Trading, Augusta, 1997—. Consul Consulate Republic of Cyprus, Augusta; dir. for Europe Drug Testing Internat., N.Y.C.; dir. for Mediterranean, Black and Caspian Sea region Marine Pollution Control, Detroit. Mem.: Consul Cyprus Sicily, Drug and Alcohol Testing Indust Asn, Italian Cypriot CofC (dir), Int Bunker Indust Asn, Baltic and Int Maritime Coun, Baltic Exchange. Office: Bella Giovanni Shipping & Trading SRL Via F Caracciolo 118 96011 Augusta Italy Fax: 0931-523490. E-mail: main@gbella.it., gbella@gbella.it.

BELLA, JONATHAN NORIEGA, cardiologist; b. Cotabato City, The Philippines, Apr. 12, 1965; came to U.S., 1991; s. Primitivo Jr. and Patrocinio (Noriega) B. BA in Humanities, U. of Philippines, Manila, 1985; MD, U. of East, Manila, 1989. Cert. Am. Bd. Internal Medicine, Am. Bd. Cardiovasc. Disease. Intern Atlantic City Med. Ctr., N.J., 1991-92; resident Montefiore Med. Ctr., N.Y.C., 1992-94; fellow in cardiology N.Y. Hosp.-Cornell Med. Ctr., 1994-97; instr. medicine Weill Med. Coll. Cornell U.; fellow in echocardiography N.Y. Hosp.-Cornell Med. Ctr., 1997-98; instr. Weill Med. Coll. Cornell U.; dir. echocardiology Louis Stokes Cleve. VA Med. Ctr., 1998-2000; asst. prof. medicine Sch. Medicine Case Western Res. U., Cleve., 1998-2000; dir. echocardiology Bronx-Lebanon Hosp. Ctr., Bronx, N.Y., 2000—; asst. prof. medicine Albert Einstein Coll. Medicine, 2000—. Fellow Am. Coll. Cardiology; mem. Am. Heart Assn., Am. Soc. Echocardiography. Roman Catholic. Office: Bronx-Lebanon Hosp Ctr 1650 Grand Concourse Bronx NY 10457

BELLAC, PATRICIA SHARMAN, lawyer; b. N.Y.C., May 8, 1961; d. Alphonse Heinz and Doreen (Prete) B.; m. Jonathan L. Kates, May 26, 1990; children: Benjamin, Daniel, Gregory. BA, McGill U., 1983; JD, Fordham U., 1991. Bar: N.J. 1991, Colo. 1993. Paralegal Proskaver, Rose, Goetz & Mendelsohn, N.Y.C., 1987-89; summer assoc. atty. Carpenter, Bennett & Morrissey, Newark, 1990, atty., 1991-93, Berenbaum, Weinshienk & Eason, P.C., Denver, 1993-98, Jung & Assocs., P.C., Boulder, 1998-99, Law Offices of Patricia S. Bellac, Boulder, 1999—. Bd. dirs. NOW (dir. fundraising and programs, N.Y.C., 1986-91), Sage Elem. Sch., 2001, Boulder County Parents of Twins and More, 2001-02. Mem. Colo. Bar Assn. (event co-chair 2003—), Denver Bar Assn., Colo. Women's Bar Assn. Avocations: skiing, hiking, swimming, running. Home: 4566 Robinson Pl Boulder CO 80301-3143 E-mail: tbellac@prodigy.net.

BELLACK, ALAN SCOTT, clinical psychologist; b. N.Y.C., Nov. 27, 1944; s. Jack and Yetta B.; m. Barbara Bartlett, Nov. 16, 1969; children: Jonathan, Adam. BS, CCNY, 1965; MS, St. John's U., 1967; PhD, Pa. State U., 1970. Diplomate Am. Bd. Profl. Psychology. Asst. prof. psychology Pa. State U., 1970; mem. faculty U. Pitts., 1971-82, prof. psychology and psychiatry, 1980-82; prof. psychiatry Med. Coll. Pa., Phila., 1982-95, U. Md., 1995—; vice chmn., dir. clin. psychology Med. Coll. Pa., Phila.; dir. VA Capitol Health Care Network MIRECC. Chmn., dir. clin. psychology; prof. psychiatry U. Md. Sch. Medicine, dir. VISN5 Mental Illness Rsch., Education and Clinical Ctr.; cons. in field. Author: Behavioral Assessment: A Practical Handbook, 1976, 2nd edit., 1981, 3rd edit., 1988, Behavior Modification: An Introduction, 1977, Introduction to Clinical Psychology, 1980, The Clinical Psychology, Handbook, 1983, 2nd edit., 1991, others; editor: Clin. Psychology Rev., 1981—, Behavior Modification, 1977— ; contbr. articles to profl. jours. USPHS fellow, 1968-70 Mem. Am. Psychol. Assn., Assn. Advancement Behavior Therapy Office: Univ of Maryland at Balt Dept Psychiatry 737 W Lombard St Fl 5 Baltimore MD 21201-1009

BELLACOSA, JOSEPH W. retired state supreme court justice; b. Bklyn., Sept. 1, 1937; s. Frank and Antoinette Bellacosa; m. Mary Bellacosa; children: Michael, Peter, Barbara. BA in English, St. John's U., 1959, LLB, 1961. Bar: N.Y. 1961. With N.Y. Life Ins. Co., 1961-63; law asst., law sec. to Hon. Marcus G. Christ N.Y. Cts. Appellate Divsn., 1963-70; assoc. prof. law St. John's U., 1970-75, asst. dean academics and admissions, 1970-73; prof. law, dir. govt. law ctr. Union U., 1970-75, 83-85; chief clk., counsel N.Y. Ct. Appeals, 1975-83; judge N.Y. Ct. Claims, 1985-87; chief adminstrv. judge N.Y. State Cts., 1985-87; assoc. judge N.Y. Ct. Appeals, Albany, 1987—2000. Vis. prof. St. John's U., 1979-83; chmn. N.Y. State Sentencing Guidelines Com., 1983-85; mem. Chief Judge's Media Adv. Com. on TV and Cts. Author: Criminal Procedure Law of the State of New York, 1974-85; assoc. editor St. John's Law Rev. Mem. Albany chpt. Fund for Modern Cts. Bd. and Strategic Planning Com. City of Albany; communicant, law scripture reader, lay eucharistic min. St. Madeleine Sophie, Guilderland, N.Y. Mem. Am. Law Inst., Assn. of Bar of City of N.Y. (arbitration com. 1965-69, ethics com. 1969-73), N.Y. State Bar Assn. (criminal justice sect., Outstanding Contbn. to Criminal Justice Edn. criminal justice sect. 1981).

BELLAH, KENNETH DAVID, lawyer; b. Aug. 17, 1955; s. Virgil and Joyce (Allen) B.; m. Dana Mills Bellah, Aug. 19, 2000. BA, Augustana Coll., 1977; JD, Chgo. Kent Coll. Law, Ill. Inst. Tech., 1980. Bar: Ill. 1980, U.S. Dist. Ct. (no. dist.) Ill. 1980, U.S. Ct. Appeals (7th cir.) 1980, Tex. 2000. Assoc. Matthias & Matthias, Chgo., 1980-83; ptnr. Matthias & Bellah, Chgo., 1983-99, Fox and Grove, Chartered, Chgo., 1999-2001; sole practice Law Offices of Kenneth D. Bellah, Chgo., 2001—. Republican. Methodist. Office: 222 S Riverside Plz 1410 Chicago IL 60606 E-mail: KenBellah@aol.com.

BELLAH, LISA DANIELLE, psychologist, educator; b. El Paso, Tex., Feb. 5, 1973; d. Luis Alfonso and Josefita Velarde; m. Christopher Garth Bellah, Oct. 26, 2001. BA, St. Mary's U., San Antonio, 1991—95; MA, U. Tex., El Paso, 1995—97; PhD, La. Tech U., Ruston, 1997—2001. Psychology intern Fed. Bur. of Prisons, Butner, NC, 2000—01, staff psychologist Oakdale, La., 2001—; adj. faculty Northwestern State U., Natchitoches, La., 2001—. Contbr. articles to profl. jours. Mem.: APA. Roman Catholic. Avocations: reading, travel. Office: Fed Correctional Instn PO Box 5050 East Whatley Rd Oakdale LA 71463 Office Fax: 318-215-2553. Personal E-mail: lisavelar@yahoo.com. E-mail: lvelarde@bop.gov.

BELLAH, ROBERT NEELLY, sociologist, educator; b. Altus, Okla., Feb. 23, 1927; s. Luther Hutton and Lillian Lucille (Neelly); m. Melanie Hyman, Aug. 17, 1949; 4 children. BA, Harvard U., 1950, PhD, 1955. Rsch. assoc. Inst. Islamic Studies, McGill U., Montreal, Can., 1955-57; with Harvard U., Cambridge, Mass., 1957-67, prof., 1966-67; mem. faculty dept. sociology U. Calif., Berkeley, 1967-97, Elliott prof. emeritus, 1997—. Author: Tokugawa Religion, 1957, Beyond Belief, 1970, The Broken Covenant, 1975 (Sorokin award Am. Sociol. Assn. 1976), (with Charles Y. Glock) The New Religious Consciousness, 1976, (with Phillip E. Hammond) Varieties of Civil Religion, 1980, (with others) Habits of the Heart, 1985, (with others) The Good Society, 1991, Imagining Japan, 2003. With U.S. Army, 1945-46. Fulbright fellow, 1960-61; recipient Harbison award Danforth Found., 1971, Nat. Humanities medal, 2000. Mem. Am. Acad. Arts and Scis., Am. Sociol. Assn., Am. Acad. Religion, Am. Philos. Soc. Episcopalian. Office: U Calif Dept Sociology Berkeley CA 94720-1980

BELLAMY, CAROL, international organization executive; b. Plainfield, N.J., 1942; BA with honors, Gettysburg Coll., 1963; JD, NYU, 1968. Asst. commr. Dept. Mental Health and Mental Health Retardation Svc., N.Y.C.; with Peace Corps.; dir. U.S. Peace Corps, 1963—65; assoc. Cravath, Swaine & Moore, N.Y.C.; mem. N.Y. State Senate; prin. Morgan Stanley & Co., N.Y.C.; mng. dir. Bear Stearns, N.Y.C.; dir. Peace Corps., Washington, 1993-95; exec. dir. UNICEF, 1995—. Office: UNICEF Office of Exec Director 3 United Nations Plz New York NY 10017-4486

BELLAMY, JAMES CARL, retired insurance company executive; b. Detroit, Oct. 15, 1926; s. Robert Maxwell Belllamy and Mamie (Moery) B.; m. Marie Alice Brakebill, Jan. 20, 1951; children: James Carl, Janet Marie. BS, U. Tenn., 1950. C.L.U. Agt., asst. mgr. Nat. Life & Accident Ins. Co., Chattanooga, Louisville, 1950-58, dist. mgr. Little Rock, Nashville, 1958-73, 2d v.p. Nashville, 1973-78, v.p., 1978-82; sr. v.p., dir. Am. Gen. Life & Accident Ins. Co., Nashville, 1982-87; sr. v.p. mktg. Southlife Holding Co., Nashville, 1987-91, ret., 1991. Exec. v.p. mktg. Pub. Savs. Life Ins. Co., Charleston, S.C.; vice chmn. Security Trust Life Ins. Co., Macon, Ga., bd. dirs.; pres. Southlife Gen. Agys., Nashville; bd. dirs. Pub. Savs. Life Ins. Co., Charleston. Solicitor United Way, Nashville, 1968-74; solicitor Boy Scouts Am., 1968-74. Served with USNR, 1944-46, PTO. Mem. Nat. Assn. Life Underwriters, Nashville Assn. Life Underwriters (pres. 1970-71), Nashville Gen. Agts. and Mgrs. Assn. (pres. 1967), Ins. Mktg. Research Assn. (exec. com.), Hillwood Country Club (bd. dirs.), Univ. Club, Kiwanis, Sigma Chi. Republican. Baptist. E-mail: jasbellamy@aol.com.

BELLAMY, JENNIFER WIGGINS, artist; b. Clio, S.C., Aug. 9, 1944; d. Leland and Myrtle Lee (Wise) Wiggins; married; 1 child, Audrey Katherine Rollins. BA in Art & Performance magna cum laude, U. Tex., 1989, postgrad., 1992-93, 95-99. Cert. interior decorator 2002. Dist. sec. Corning Glass Works, Richardson, Tex., 1977-80; adminstrv. asst. The Chase Manhatten Bank, Dallas, 1981-85; owner The Bellamy Studio, Richardson, Tex., 1990—, Interiors by Jennifer Rachelle Wiggins, 2003—. Recipient tchg. assistantships U. Tex., Dallas, 1993. Mem. Phi Theta Kappa. Avocations: writing, gardening, cooking, walking. E-mail: jennw24121@cs.com.

BELLAMY, JOHN CARY, civil engineer, meteorologist; b. Cheyenne, Wyo., Apr. 18, 1915; s. Benjamin Charles and Alice Elizabeth (Cary) B.; m. Josephine Marie Johnston, Sept. 21, 1940; children: John Cary, Agnes Louise, Charles Fulton, William Delaney, Mary Elizabeth. BCE, U. Wyo., 1936; PhM, U. Wis., 1938; PhD in Meteorology, Chgo. U., 1947. Registered profl. engr., Wyo. Ptnr. Bellamy & Sons Engrs., Lamont, Wyo., 1938-42; asst. prof. U. Chgo., 1942-47; assoc. dir. Cook Rsch. Labs., Chgo., 1947-60; dir. NRRI U. Wyo., Laramie, 1960-73, prof. civil engring., 1973-81; prin. Bellamy & Sons Engrs., Laramie, 1981—. Dir. Inst. Tropical Meteorology, U. P.R., 1943-44; spl. cons. U.S. Army Air Corps, Washington, 1944-45; mem. Western Interstate Nuclear Bd., Denver, 1964-75. Contbr. articles to profl. jours.; contbr. to books; patentee in field. Recipient Losey award, Inst. Aero. Sci., 1944, Medal of Freedom, Pres. U.S.A., 1946, Thurlow award Inst. Navigation, 1946. Fellow NSPE (chpt. pres. 1976), Am. Meteorol. Soc. (dir. 1948-52), Inst. Navigation (pres. 1962), Am. Geophys. Union; mem. Wyo. Engring. Soc., Lions (chpt. pres. 1981, 84). Avocations: golf, bowling, computer programming. Home and Office: 2308 Holliday Dr Laramie WY 82070-4847

BELLAMY, JOHN STARK, II, librarian; b. Cleve. s. Peter and Jean (Dessel) B.; m. Laura A. Serafin, Aug. 9, 1996; children: Sarah, Catherine. BA, Goddard Coll., Plainfield, Vt., 1971; M.History, U. Va., 1977; MLS, Case Western Res. U., 1978. Pub. svcs. libr. Cuyahoga County Pub. Libr., Beachwood, Ohio, 1982-89, subject specialist libr. Fairview Park, Ohio, 1989—. Angels on the Heights, 1991; author: They Died Crawling, 1995, The Maniac in the Bushes, 1997, The Corpse in the Cellar, 1999, By the Neck Until Dead, 2000, The Killer in the Attic, 2002. Roman Catholic. Office: Cuyahoga County Pub Library 21255 Lorain Rd Fairview Park OH 44126-2120 E-mail: jstarkbII@aol.com.

BELLAMY, WALTER, retired basketball player; Student, Ind. U., 1957-61. With Chgo. Packers, 1961-62, Balt. Bullets, 1963-66, N.Y. Knicks, 1966-68, Atlanta Hawks, 1970-74. Mem. U.S. Olympic Basketball Team, 1960. Mem. Atlanta Police Athletic League; trustee Gate City Day Nursery Assn.; bd. dirs. S.W. Youth Bus. Orgn.; founder, 1st pres. Men of Tomorrow, Inc., Md.; membership chmn. Campbelltown/Cascade YMCA Men internat. Club; chmn. Atlanta Labor Day Weekend Football Classic; vice chmn. College Park Bus. and Devel. Authority. Named Rookie of Yr., 1962, Basketball Hall of Fame, 1993; winner Gold medal U.S. Olympics, 1960; named to U.S. Olympic Hall of Fame, N.C. Sports Hall of Fame, 100% Wrong Club Atlanta Hall of Fame, Ind. U. Sports Hall of Fame, NBA Hall of Fame. Mem. Ind. U. Alumni Club, Alpha Phi Alpha, Alpha Phi Omega. Achievements include mem. gold-medal-winning U.S. Olympic Team, 1960, holds single-season record for most games played-88, 1969. Address: PO Box 42751 Atlanta GA 30311-0751

BELLANCA, JOSEPH PAUL, engineering construction executive; b. Rochester, N.Y., Nov. 25, 1936; s. Sam and Anna (Cani) B.; m. Joy Eleanor Gaston, Dec. 5, 1964 (dec.); children: Joseph Jr., Victoria Ann Gordon, Lizabeth Ann Wilbur, Lorraine Thacker. BSCE, Purdue U., 1958. Registered profl. engr., D.C. and 10 states. Assoc./project mgr. TAMS Cons., Dallas/Ft. Worth, 1968-73, assoc./resident mgr. Washington, 1973-77; pres. Bellanca Engring. Cons., Atlanta, 1977-85; dir. Schal Assocs., Chgo., 1985-86; v.p. Greiner, Inc., Orlando (Fla.), Denver, 1986-88, Bechtel Internat. Inc., Vienna, Va., 1988-92, Turner Constrn. Co., Atlanta, 1992-98; exec. v.p. Bovis Lend Lease, Atlanta, 1998—2002; v.p. Heery Internat., 2002—. Lobbyist Airport Cons. Coun. Editor Airports--Challenges of the Future, 1973; (design compendium) World Travel Center--Detroit Met. Airport (Design award for $1 billion new air terminal complex). Named Young Engr. Yr. Mid-Cities chpt. Tex. Soc. Profl. Engrs., 1971. Mem. ASCE (sec. 1973, vice-chmn. 1979, exec. com., air transport divsn.), NSPE, Tex. Soc. Profl. Engrs. (pres. Mid-Cities chpt. 1972-73). Achievements include aifield pavement design for future 2 million pound aircraft at Dallas-Ft. Worth airport; executive-level involvement in airport development programs for Dallas-Ft. Worth, Atlanta, Chicago, Denver, Barcelona, 2-Jordan, 4-Saudi Arabia, New Seoul, and Detroit Downtown People Mover. Home: 9295 Heatherton Walk Duluth GA 30097-2492 Office: Heery Internat 999 Peachtree St Atlanta GA 30309 E-mail: jbellanca@mindspring.com.

BELLAND, BRIAN ROBERT, language educator; b. Columbus, Ohio, Jan. 27, 1977; s. John Clarke and Elizabeth Ann Belland. BA, Coll. Wooster, 1995—99; MA, Ohio State U., 1999—2001. Lic. Accident and Health, Life and Variable Annuities Ohio, 2001. Tchg. assoc. Ohio State U., Columbus, Ohio, 1999—2001; assoc. AFLAC, Columbus, Ohio, 2001—02; lectr. fgn. lang. Purdue U., West Lafayette, Ind., 2002—03, computer ops. supr., 2003—. Recipient Sci. and Math Scholarship, Coll. Wooster, 1995—99, Eagle Scout, Boy Scouts Am., 1992. Mem.: Nat. Geog. Soc.

BELLANGER, BARBARA DORIS HOYSAK, biomedical research technologist; b. Syracuse, N.Y., Oct. 24, 1936; d. Edward George and Bernardine Elizabeth (Blaney) Hoysak; m. Ronald Patrick Bellanger, July 1, 1961; children: Laura Jeanne, Andrea Lynne, Janis Anne. BS, Syracuse U., 1958. Cert. lab. animal technician. Tech. asst. Bur. of Labs., Syracuse, 1958; rsch. scientist Bristol Labs., Syracuse, 1958-63; chief rsch. assoc., facility supr. Syracuse Cancer Rsch. Inst., 1973—. Pres. CNS Northstars Band Parents, Inc., Cicero-North Syracuse, N.Y., 1986-87. Mem. Am. Assn. Lab. Animal Sci. (cert. and registered lab. animal technician, sec. Upstate N.Y. br. 1990—, Technician of Yr. award 1992, Harlan Teklad award 1998, Charles E. Schadler award 2000), N.Y. Acad. Scis., Alpha Gamma Delta (pres. Alpha alumnae chpt. 1959-60, treas. 1989—). Home: 410 David Dr North Syracuse NY 13212-1929 Office: Syracuse Cancer Rsch Inst Presdl Plz Med Bldg Ste 130 600 E Genesee St Syracuse NY 13202-3111

BELLANGER, SERGE RENÉ, bank executive; b. Vimoutiers, France, Apr. 30, 1933; s. René Albert and Raymonde Maria (Renard) Bellanger. MBA, Paris Bus. Sch., 1957. With Citibank, 1966-73, mem. Paris br., 1966-69, world corp. rels. officer for Europe N.Y.C., 1969-73, asst. v.p., 1969-71, v.p., 1972-73; sr. v.p., gen. mgr. Crédit Industriel et Commercial, N.Y.C., 1974-79, exec. v.p., gen. mgr., 1979—; U.S. gen. rep. CIC Group, N.Y.C., 1973—, mem. exec.

com., 1998—. Prof. banking French Banking Inst., 1961—64; mem. adv. com. French Ho. Columbia U., 1976—, chmn., 1996—, mem. internat. adv. bd. Inst. Study Europe, 2002—; mem. Nat. Com. Fgn. Trade Advisors France, 1978—, exec. v.p. U.s. nat. com., 1985—93, bd. dirs. nat. com., 1987—2002, v.p. U.S. nat. com., 1992—93, mem. Paris exec. com., 1994—95; chmn. internat. banking course New Sch. Social Rsch., N.Y.C., 1981—83; dir. Am. Ctr. Paris, 1985—93; mem. adv. com. Ctr. Study French Civilization and Culture NYU, N.Y.C., 1988—2000; mem. adv. bd. French Inst. Culture and Tech. U. Pa., 1992—, chmn. adv. bd., 1992—95; mem. adv. bd. Lycée Francais, NY, 2000—; mem. Adv. Coun. French Abroad, 2000; mem. exec. com. Fedn. French Vets., 2001—; bd. dirs. Ubifrance, French Ctr. Fgn. Trade, Banque Transatlantique. With French Air Force, 1958—60. Decorated Algeria Commemorative medal Officer Legion of Honor, Comdr. Nat. Order of Merit. Mem.: Bank Adminstrn. Inst. (mem. editl. bd. World Banking Mag. 1981—87, columnist Banker's Mag. 1986—96), N.Y. Cotton Exch. (bd. dirs. fin. instrument exch. divsn. 1985—95), N.Y. Futures Exch. (dir. 1980—87, chmn. fgn. exch. com. 1981—82), Banque de l'Union Européenne (bd. dirs. 1989—90), Assn. Promotion French Sci., Industry and Tech. (pres. 1986—91), Lyonnaise de Banque (bd. dirs. 1986—89), Inst. Internat. Bankers (trustee 1975—77, v.p. 1977—79, chmn. legis. and regulatory com. 1977—79, chmn. 1979—80), French Overseas Assn., European-Am. Bus. Coun. (bd. dirs. Washington 1991—), Food and Wine France (bd. dirs. 1983—93), N.Y.C. Partnership and C. of C. (ptnr. 1991—), Assn. French C. of C. and Industry Abroad (adminstr. 1984—, v.p. 1989—95, 1st v.p. 1995—99, pres. 1999—), N.Y. C. of C. (mem. internat. bus. initiative 1994—95), French-Am. C. of C. (councillor 1973—74, mem. exec. com. 1974—80, v.p. 1980—82, exec. v.p. 1982—83, nat. pres. 1983—, pres. N.Y. chpt. 1983—), European-Am. C. of C. (pres., CEO 1990—96, hon. chmn. 1996—), Automobile Club de France, River Club, Univ. Club. Home: 860 U N Plz Apt 23/24C New York NY 10017-1810 Office: 520 Madison Ave New York NY 10022-4213

BELLANTONI, MAUREEN BLANCHFIELD, manufacturing and retail executive; b. Warren, Pa., Mar. 18, 1949; d. John Joseph and Patricia Anne (Southard) Blanchfield; m. Michael Charles Bellantoni, Aug. 12, 1972; children: Mark Christopher, Melissa Catherine. BS in Fin., U. Bridgeport, 1976; MBA, U. Conn., Stamford, 1070. Fin. analyst Dictaphone Corp., Rye, N.Y., 1970-73, Gen. Telephone & Electronics, Stamford, 1973-74, Smith Kline Ultrasonic Products, now Branson, Danbury, Conn., 1974-77; fin. mgr. Gen. Foods, White Plains, N.Y., 1977-80; contr. Branson Ultrasonics Corp. div. Emerson Electric, Danbury, Conn., 1980-88, v.p. fin., 1988-90; v.p. fin., CFO Automatic Switch Co. divsn. Emerson Electric, Florham Park, NJ, 1990-93, PYA/Monarch, Inc. divsn. Sara Lee Corp., Greenville, SC, 1993-94; v.p. fin. CFO Meat Group Sara Lee Corp., Cordova, Tenn., 1994-97; pres., COO BilMar Foods divsn. Sara Lee Corp., 1997-98; exec. v.p., CFO Rohn Industries Inc., Peoria, Ill., 1999-2000; CFO divsn. Diageo Burger King Corp., Miami, Fla., 2000—01, sr. v.p. fin., 2001—02; sr. v.p., CFO CP Kelco, Chgo., 2003—. Vice chair Nat. Legacy Campaign Cancer Fund, Franciscan Sister of Poor Found. Mem. Fin. Execs. Inst., S.C. C. of C., Danbury C. of C. (leadership program 1989), Beta Gamma Sigma. Avocations: golf, tennis, racquetball. Office: 311 S Wacker Dr Chicago IL 60606 Business E-Mail: maureen.bellantoni@cpkelco.com.

BELLAS, ALBERT CONSTANTINE, investment banker, advisor; b. Steubenville, Ohio, Sept. 15, 1942; s. Constantine Michael and Kiki (Michalopoulos) B.; m. Kay Mazzo, Dec. 21, 1978; children: Andrew James, Kathryn Kiki. BA, Yale U., 1964; JD, U. Chgo., 1967; MBA, Columbia U., 1968. Summer intern The White House, 1963; assoc. Dillon, Read & Co., Inc., N.Y.C., 1968-72; v.p. Goldman Sachs & Co., N.Y.C., 1973-76; gen. ptnr. Loeb Rhoades & Co., N.Y.C., 1976-78; sr. exec. v.p. Shearson Lehman Bros., NYC, 1979—90, Lehman Bros., Inc., NYC, 1990—91; mng. dir. Offitbank, NYC, 1992—2000; chmn., CEO Neuberger Berman Trust Co., N.Y.C., 2000—; mng. dir. Neuberger Berman, LLC, NYC, 2000—. Allied mem. N.Y. Stock Exch., 1976-92; bd. dirs. 1128 Park Ave. Corp. Trustee St. Mary's Found. for Children, 1999—2002, Lenfest Found., 2000—, Statue of Liberty-Ellis Island Found., 2002—, investment com., 2002—; day sch. com. Brick Ch., N.Y.C., 1985—88; bd. regents, investment com. Mercersburg Acad., Pa., 1992—, exec. com., 1993—, chmn. fin. com., 1994—; bd. dirs. Lincoln for Performing Arts, N.Y.C., 1987—, audit com., 1989—, investment com., 1990—93; bd. dirs. Sch. Am. Ballet, N.Y.C., 1975—85, chmn., 1987—; bd. dirs. Guild Hall, East Hampton, NY, 1990—96, 1998—, fin. com., 1998—. McKinsey scholar, 1968. Mem.: ABA, Ohio Bar Assn., Brook Club, Univ. Club, India Ho., Century Assn., Yale Club, Maidstone Club. Avocation: tennis. Home: 1130 Park Ave New York NY 10128-1255 Office: 605 Third Avenue 44th Fl New York NY 10158

BELLATTI, LAWRENCE LEE, lawyer; b. Oklahoma City, Apr. 19, 1944; s. Lawrence Fitzhugh and Esther Lee (Swank) B.; m. Barbara Gail Wolfinger, June 25, 1977; children: Julie M., Jenny E., Jill N. BS, Okla. State U., 1966; JD, Okla. U., 1969. Bar: Okla. 1969, Tex. 1974, U.S. Dist. Ct. (so. dist.) Tex. 1975, U.S. Ct. Mil. Appeals 1978, U.S. Dist. Ct. (ea. dist.) Tex. 1979, U.S. Ct. Appeals (5th cir.) 1979, U.S. Ct. Appeals (11th cir.) 1981, U.S. Ct. Appeals (10th cir.) 1982, U.S. Dist. Ct. (we. dist.) Tex. 1983, U.S Dist. Ct. (we. dist.) Okla. 1983, U.S. Dist. Ct. (no. dist.) Tex., 1984, U.S. Dist. Ct. (no. dist.) Okla., 1992, U.S. Dist. Ct. (ea. dist.) Okla. 1994. Assoc. Andrews, Kurth, Campbell & Jones, Houston, 1974-80; ptnr. Andrews & Kurth LLP, Houston, 1980—. Bd. dirs. Samaritan Counseling Ctrs., Inc., Houston, 1984—2001. Mem. Harris County Flood Control Dist. Task Force, Houston, 1984. Lt. comdr. JAGC, USNR, 1969-74. Mem. Tex. Bar Assn., Okla. Bar Assn., Houston Bar Assn., Order of Coif, Phi Kappa Phi, Sigma Chi, Phi Delta Phi. Republican. Baptist. Office: Andrews & Kurth LLP 600 Travis St Ste 4200 Houston TX 77002-2910

BELLAVANCE, MARIA ISABEL, librarian; b. Lisboa, Portugal, July 24, 1946; came to U.S., 1966; d. Adriao Garcia and Maria de Lourdes (Serrao) B.; m. David Walter Bellavance, Sept. 28, 1969 (div. Aug. 1999); 1 child, Angela Maria Bellavance. BS in Elec. Engring., Brown U., Providence, R.I., 1969; MLS, North Tex. U., Denton, 1985. Tech. staff Bell Lab., Murray Hill, N.J., 1970-72; parish libr. All Saints Cath. Ch., Dallas, 1985—; libr. specialist Ctr. Info. Processing Southern Meth. Univ., Dallas, 1996—. Part-time staff dir. All Saints Parish Resource Libr., Dallas. Mem. Ch. and Synagogue Libr. Assn. (Outstanding Congl. Libr. award 1993), Tau Beta Pi. Roman Catholic. Avocations: reading, sewing, knitting, bible study, travel. Home: 1225 Danville Dr Richardson TX 75080-5809 Office: So Meth U Ctrl U Librs Ctr Info Processing PO Box 750135 Dallas TX 75275-0135

BELLE, ALBERT JOJUAN, professional baseball player; b. Shreveport, La., Aug. 25, 1966; Student, La. State U. With Cleve. Indians, 1987—96, Chgo. White Sox, 1997—99, Balt. Orioles, 1999—. Named Player of Yr., Sporting News, 1995; named to All-Star Game, Am. League, 1993—96, Silver Slugger Team, 1993—95, Am. League All-Star Team, Sporting News, 1993—94. Achievements include being ranked1st in Am. League for runs batted in, 1993; leading the Maj. League in home runs, 1995; being a mem. of Am. League Champions, 1995. Office: Balt Orioles Oriole Park at Camden Yards 333 W Camden St Baltimore MD 21201-2435

BELLEAU, LEISA A. English educator; b. Evansville, Ind., Nov. 13, 1951; d. Billy Joe and Patsy Joyce Below; m. Terry David Appel, July 1, 1995; children: R. Caroline Simpson, S. Zachary Simpson, Hannah L. Broshears. BS in Lit., U. So. Ind., 1993; MA in Fiction, So. Ill. U. Instr. English U. So. Ind., Evansville, 1996—. Contbr. Co-founder 4-H Club, Newburgh, Ind., 2000. Scholar Rope-Walk Writers Retreat scholar in fiction, nonfiction and poetry, 1994, 1995, 1997. Mem.: AAUP, Pinnacle Honor Soc., Coll. English Assn., Nat. Coun. Tchrs. English, Sigma Tau Delta. Methodist. Avocations: reading, writing, needlecrafts, travel, gardening. Home: 312 W Main Newburgh IN 47630

BELLEMARE, DAVID JOHN, architectural designer; b. Waterbury, Conn., Dec. 25, 1960; s. John Arthur and Lucille (Cianciolo) B. Student, Boston Archtl. Ctr., 1984-89. Drafter Monacelli Assocs., Inc., Cambridge, Mass., 1984-85; designer, drafter The Architects Group, Boston, 1986-89; fed. regulations coord. John Errichetti Assocs., Waterbury, Conn., 1989—. Served with USMC, 1980-84. Mem. Boston Soc. Architects. Avocations: running, football, movies, cars, dancing. Home: 90 Frost Rd Waterbury CT 06705-2103 Office: John Errichetti Assocs 34 Prospect St Waterbury CT 06702-1310

BELLENGER, GEORGE COLLIER, JR., physics educator; b. Gadsden, Ala., Oct. 15, 1926; s. George Collier Sr. and Corrie Anna (Sitz) B.; m. Anna Conwell Hubbard, July 4, 1959; children: Baily, George III, James Thomas. B in Indsl. Engring., Ga. Inst. of Tech., 1952. Constrn./indsl. engring. E.I. DuPont Co., Augusta, Ga., 1952-54, Richmond, Va., 1955-58, ops. rsch. Wilmington, Del., 1958-63, group supr.-engring. Chattanooga, 1963-65, sr. supr. systems Wilmington, 1965-67, chief supr. Deep Water, N.J., 1967-70, systems mgr. Wilmington, 1970-78, mgr. project devel., 1978-87; math/physics educator Wilmington Coll., New Castle, Del., 1987-91, chair gen. studies divsn., 1991—, chair faculty senate, 1998-2000. PTA pres. Mt. Pleasant Sch. Dist., Wilmington, 1972-76; commr. North Brandywine Youth Baseball, Wilmington, 1974-77; head coach Mt. Pleasant Youth Football, Wilmington, 1977-79. Lt. U.S. Army, 1944-47. Named Disting. ROTC Mil. Grad.; recipient Disting. Mil. Student award, Ga. Inst. of Tech., 1952. Mem. Rotary Internat. (pres. 1983-84, Paul Harris fellow 1987), Nat. Norwich/Norfolk Terrier Assn. (pres. 1993-96), Army and Navy Club, Phi Delta Theta. Achievements include research on a micro/macro production and inventory system based on a stochastic deterministic, partial differential set of equations, a manufacturing capacity expansion plan based on combining a unique LP model and computer simulation methods. Home: PO Box 449 Unionville PA 19375-0449 Office: Wilmington Coll 320 Dupont New Castle DE 19720

BELLER, GARY A. lawyer, insurance company executive; b. N.Y.C., Oct. 16, 1938; s. Charles W. and Jeanne A. B.; m. Carole P. Wrubel, Nov. 22, 1967; 1 child, Jessie Melissa. BA, Cornell U., 1960; LLB, NYU, 1963, LLM, 1971. Bar: N.Y. 1963. Various positions gen. counsel's office Am. Express Co., N.Y.C., 1968-82, exec. v.p. and gen. counsel, 1983-94; exec. v.p., chief legal officer Met. Life Ins. Co., N.Y.C., 1995—. Bd. dirs. Lenox Hill Neighborhood Assn.; bd. dirs., chmn. Citizens' Crime Commn. N.Y. Mem. ABA, Assn. Bar City N.Y. Office: Met Life Ins Co 1 Madison Ave # Area11G New York NY 10010-3603

BELLER, GEORGE ALLAN, medical educator; b. N.Y.C., 1940; MD, U. Va., 1966. Diplomate Am. Bd. Internal Medicine. Intern U. Wis. Hosp., Madison, 1966-67, resident, 1967-68; resident in medicine Boston Med. Svc., 1968-69; fellow in cardiology Thorndike Meml. Lab. Harvard Med. Unit/Boston City Hosp., 1969-70; mem. staff cardiac unit Mass. Gen. Hosp., Boston, 1973-77; instr. medicine Harvard U., Boston, 1974-75, asst. prof., 1975; prof. medicine U. Va., Charlottesville, 1977—, chief cardiovascular divsn., 1977—, vice-chmn. dept. medicine, 1997-99, pres. med. staff, 1998—. Maj. M.C., U.S. Army, 1970-73. Mem. Am. Soc. Clin. Investigation, Am. Fedn. Clin. Rsch., Assn. Am. Physicians, Am. Coll. Cardiology (chmn. bd. govs. 1994-95, pres. 2000), Assn. Profs. Cardiology (pres. 1995). Office: U Va Med Ctr Dept Cardiology PO Box 800158 Charlottesville VA 22908-0158

BELLER, GERALD STEPHEN, professional magician, former insurance company executive; b. Phila., Aug. 6, 1935; s. Nathan and Adelaide B. (Goldfarb) B.; m. Nancy R. Nelson, June 8, 1968; children: Fay A., Mark S., Royce W., Merrilee A., Marie A., Frank A. CLU, Am. Coll., Bryn Mawr, Pa., 1972. Spl. agt. Prudential Ins. Co., San Bernardino, Calif., 1959-62, div. mgr., 1962-66; agy. supr. Aetna Life & Casualty, L.A., 1966-69, gen. agt., 1969-77; rsch. analyst Investigative Svcs. Bur. San Bernadino County Sheriff's Dept., 1991-95; capt. specialized svcs. bur. San Bernardino County (Calif.) Sheriff's Dept.; profl. magician, 1982—. Mem. Magician Magic Castle, Hollywood, Calif. Mem. sheriff's coun. San Bernardino County Sheriff's Dept., Apple Valley sheriff's adv. bd. Served with USAF, 1953-57. Recipient Man of Year award, 1961; Manpower Builders award, 1966-69; Agy. Builders award, 1970-72; Pres.'s Trophy award, 1973-74 Mem. Am. Soc. CLUs, Golden Key Soc., Internat. Exec. Svc. Corps. (vol.), Acad. Magical Arts, Internat. Brotherhood of Magicians (Outstanding Magic Lectr. of Yr. 1989-90, Aldini Meml. award 1990), Soc. Am. Magicians. Home: 20625 Tonawanda Rd Apple Valley CA 92307-5736

BELLER, HERBERT N. lawyer; b. Ill., 1943; BSBA, Northwestern U., 1964, JD cum laude, 1967. Bar: Ill. 1967, D.C. 1969; CPA, Ill. Law clk. to Hon. Theodore Tannenwald, Jr. U.S. Tax Ct., 1967-68; ptnr. Sutherland, Asbill & Brennan, Washington. Adj. prof. law Georgetown U., Washington, 1972-81. Editor-in-chief: The Tax Lawyer, 1993-96. Mem. ABA (mem. sect. taxation, vice chair 1993-96, chair, 2002—, mem. coun. 1989-92, liaison to AICPA tax div. 1998-2000, chmn. govt. submissions com. 1988-89, chmn. closely held corps. com. 1981-83), Am. Coll. Tax Counsel (regent), D.C. Bar Assn., Ill. State Bar Assn., Nat. Conf. Lawyers and CPAs. Office: Sutherland Asbill & Brennan LLP 1275 Pennysylvania Ave NW Washington DC 20004

BELLER, LUANNE EVELYN, accountant; b. Ft. Dodge, Iowa, Feb. 5, 1950; d. Gerald L. and Evelyn E. (Liston) Heyl; m. Stephen M. Beller, June 28, 1970; children: Clancy Dee, Corby Lu. BA, Oreg. State U., 1977; MBA, Rochester Inst. Tech., 1981. CPA, Ill. Plant acct. DuBois Plastic Products, Avon, N.Y., 1977-79; coll. acct. SUNY, Geneseo, 1979-81; gen. acctg. supr. M&M/Mars, Inc., Cleveland, Tenn., 1981-83, Hackettstown, N.J., 1983-84, sales rep. Jacksonville, Ill., 1984-86, terr. sales supr., 1986-88; gen. acctg. coord. Master Foods USA (formerly Kal Kan Foods, Inc.), Columbus, Ohio, 1988-90, fin. info. coord., 1990-92, gen. acctg. supr., 1992-97, site svc. and fin. mgr., 1997—. Vol. Girl Scouts U.S.A., Jacksonville, 1985—88, Bexley, Ohio, 1988—; mem. sound control com. Bexley United Meth. Ch., 1989—2001, chair edn. com., 1998—2001, mem. edn. com., 1996—2003, LOGOS vol., 1996—2002, mem. diversity team, 2001—02; com. mem. Meth. Theol. Sch. Ohio Partnership, 2001—02. Mem. Phi Kappa Phi, Beta Gamma Sigma, Beta Alpha Psi. Democrat. Avocations: children, pets, reading. E-mail: lbeller@columbus.rr.com.

BELLER, MARTIN LEONARD, retired orthopaedic surgeon; b. N.Y.C., Apr. 30, 1924; s. Abraham Jacob and Ida (Fishkin) B.; m. Wilma Gertrude Kjelgaard, June 29, 1947; children: Alan Lewis, Beatrice Ann Beller Foreman Heck, Peter James. AB with honors, Columbia U., 1944, MD, 1946. Diplomate Am. Bd. Orthopaedic Surgery. Intern Mt. Sinai Hosp., N.Y.C., 1946-47; resident in orthopaedic surgery Hosp. Joint Diseases, N.Y.C., 1949-52; pvt. practice Phila., 1952-87; asst. prof. orthopaedic surgery U. Pa. Sch. Medicine, Phila., 1967-72, assoc. prof., 1972-80, clin. prof., 1980-87. Attending orthopaedic surgeon Hosp. U. Pa., 1963-87; assoc. attending orthopaedic surgeon Albert Einstein Med. Center, Phila., 1960-70; chmn. dept. orthopaedic surgery Albert Einstein Med. Center (Daroff divsn.), 1970-79. Author: (with I. Stein and R. O. Stein) Living Bone in Health and Disease, 1955, (with I. Stein) Clinical Densitometry of Bone, 1970. Vestryman Episcopal Ch., 1966—87, 1990—93, 1996—99, 2002—; trustee St. Paul's Episcopal Ch., Wellsboro, Pa., 1999—. Am. Orthopaedic Assn. exchange fellow Gt. Britain, 1963. Fellow ACS, Am. Acad. Orthopaedic Surgeons (bd. councilors 1978-81, Pa. rep. commn. on trauma 1984-87), Internat. Soc. Orthopaedic Surgery and Traumatology; mem. Am. Orthopaedic Assn., Pa. Orthopaedic Soc. (pres. 1975-77), Orthopaedic Rsch. Soc., Am. Coll. Rheumatology, N.Y. Acad. Sci., Phi Beta Kappa, Alpha Omega Alpha, Phi Delta Epsilon (nat. pres. 1975-76, chmn. bd. trustees 1984-85, assoc. exec. sec. 1991-95, exec. com. 1995—), Union League Phila. (life), Tyoga Country Club (Wellsboro, Pa.). Republican. Home: RR 1 Box 256-B Gaines PA 16921-9768

BELLER, STEPHEN MARK, university administrator; b. Chgo., Aug. 14, 1948; s. I.E. and De Vera (Jameson) B.; m. Luanne Evelyn Heyl, June 28, 1970; children: Clancy Dee, Corby Lu. BS, U. Ill., 1970; MS, Western Ill. U., 1972; PhD, Oregon State U., 1977. Asst. head ed. Awards of Rotary Found., Evanston, Ill., 1972-73; asst. dean of students SUNY, Geneseo, N.Y., 1977-81; dean of student svcs. Tenn. Wesleyan Coll., Athens, 1981-83, MacMurray Coll., Jacksonville, Ill., 1984-88, Capital U., Columbus, Ohio, 1988-99, vice pres., dean of student svcs., 1999—2003, v.p. emeritus, 2003—. Mem. Nat. Assn. Student Pers. Adminstrs., Am. Coll. Personnel Assn., Phi Kappa Phi, Phi Delta Kappa. Methodist. Avocations: railroading, photography. Home: 2474 Seneca Park Pl Bexley OH 43209-1750 E-mail: sbeller@capital.edu.

BELLES, DONALD ARNOLD, pastoral therapist, mental health counselor; b. Sayre, Pa., Mar. 7, 1948; s. William and Alice (Arnold) B.; m. Linda Scheel, July 9, 1981. BA, St. Martin's U., 1973; MDiv, Fuller Theol. Sem., 1977; PhD, Calif. Grad. Sch. Theology, 1981; MBA, City U. Bellevue, 1994; postdoctoral, Seattle Pacific U., 1997—. Lic. amateur radio operator; ordained to ministry Worldwide Congl. Fellowship, 1989; cert. c.c. tchr., Calif., mental health counselor, Wash., profl. stage hypnotist. Chaplain Vols. of Am., L.A., 1976-78; therapist Greater life Found., Seattle, 1979-81; industrial engr. commercial airplane divsn. Boeing, 1979-80, program planner aerospace divsn., 1980-86, sr., lead program planner electronics divsn., 1986-89, systems analyst, contract tech. mgr., 1989-92, analyst software engring. practices, mgr. total quality improvement project, 1992-95, lead, mgr. computing infrastructure archtl. design team, 1995-98, sr. analyst/architect IT/bus. sys. integration, 1998—; therapist, dir. clinic Creative Therapies, Seattle, 1982-83; clin. dir. Applied Hypnosis, Tacoma, 1984-87; dir. Active Therapy Assoc., Tacoma, 1988-89; dean of students Coll. Therapeutic Hypnosis, Tacoma, 1989-93. Cons. theological issues, abduction rsch., psychic phenomena, paranormal events; adult edn. instr. Tacoma C.C., 1987-88, Pierce Coll., 1990-92; mem. U.S. Acad. Team to CIS, acad. team Seattle Pacific U. to Moscow and Shuya, U. St. Petersburg, Russia, 1994; presenter, lectr. in field; instr. Olympia Diocese Sch. of Theology, 1995; adv. bd. mem. Software Support Profls. Orgn.; cons. Wash. State Offices Supr. of Pub. Instrn.; mem. faculty U. Phoenix, 1999—. Contbr. articles to profl. jours., prodr. hypnosis, mental health videos in field. Exec. dir. Nat. Assn. to Prevent and Eliminate Child Abuse, Tacoma, 1987-89; active Light of the Hill Ch. Maj. U.S. Army, 1969-75, USAR, 1975-92. Fellow Am. Assn. Profl. Hypnotherapists; mem. Nat. Assn. Clergy Hypnotherapists (bd. dirs. 1987-88, editor jour. 1987), Internat. Med. Dental Hypnotherapy Assn., Wash. State Head Injury Found. Avocations: backpacking, swimming, reading, amateur radio. E-mail: dbelles@technologist.com.

BELLES, MARTIN RUSSEL, manufacturing engineer; b. Ft. Wayne, Ind., Sept. 4, 1952; s. Russel Elwin and Irene (Crossley) B. Student, U. Calif., Berkeley, 1970-72; BS in Computer Sci., Armstrong Atlantic State U., Savannah, Ga., 1999. Aircraft assembler Rockwell Internat., Bethany, Okla., 1974-83; process planner Gulfstream Aerospace, Bethany, 1984-85, mfg. engr. Savannah, 1985—. Contbg. author: Stupid Windows Tricks, 1992. Mem. Ga. Hist. Soc., Historic Savannah Found., Telfair Acad. of Arts and Scis. Mem. IEEE, Assn. Computing Machinery, Epsilon Data Pi, Upsilon Pi Epsilon. Avocation: computer programming. Office: Gulfstream Aerospace 500 Gulfstream Rd Savannah GA 31407-9643 E-mail: martybelles@csi.com.

BELLEVILLE, PHILIP FREDERICK, lawyer; b. Flint, Mich., Apr. 24, 1934; s. Frederick Charles and Sarah (Adelaine) B.; m. Geraldean Bickford, Sept. 2, 1953; children— Stacy L., Philip Frederick II, Jeffrey A. BA in Econs. with high distinction and honors, U. Mich., 1956, JD, 1960, MS in Psychology CCU, 1997. Bar: Calif. 1961. Assoc. Latham & Watkins, LA., 1960-68, ptnr. L.A. and Newport Beach, Calif., 1968-98, chmn. litigation dept., 1973-80, ptnr. L.A., Newport Beach, San Diego, Washington, 1980-98, Chgo., 1983-98, N.Y.C., 1985-98, London and San Francisco, 1990-98, Moscow, 1992-98, Hong Kong, 1995-98, Tokyo, 1995-98, Singapore, 1997-98, Silicon Valley, 1997-98. Past mem. So. Calif. steering com. NAACP Legal Def. Fund, Inc.; past mem. cmty. adv. bd. San Pedro Peninsula Hosp., Calif., 1980—88; mem. Harbor Interfaith Bd. James B. Angell scholar U. Mich., 1955-56 Mem. ABA, L.A. County Bar Assn., Assn. Bus. Trial Lawyers, Order of Coif, Portuguese Bend (Calif.) Club, Palos Verdes (Calif.) Golf Club, Caballeros, Phi Beta Kappa, Phi Kappa Phi, Alpha Kappa Psi. Republican. Avocations: antique and classic autos, public service, sports, art, antiques.

BELLEW, JAMES WILLIAM, JR., physical therapist, educator; b. Owensboro, Ky., Apr. 1, 1968; s. James William Sr. and Elizabeth Flora Bellew; m. Mary Helen Gruber, Sept. 5, 1992. BS, Marquette U., 1990; MS, U. Ky., 1995, EdD, 2000. Cert. phys. therapist Am. Phys. Therapy Assn. Asst. prof. La. State U. Med. Ctr., Shreveport, La., 2000—. Contbr. (chpt.) Isokinetics in Human Performance; author: (textbook) Orthopedic and Sports Physical Therapy. Mem.: La. Phys. Therapy Assn. (dist. rep. to govt. affairs), Am. Phys. Therapy Assn., Nat. Strength and Conditioning Assn., Am. Coll. Sports Medicine. Office: La State U 1501 Kings Hwy Shreveport LA 71130

BELLHOUSE, CAROL, lawyer; b. Brantford, Ont., Can., Oct. 14, 1953; came to U.S., 1960, naturalized, 1980; d. Gerald LaVerne and Irma (Vansickle) Bellhouse; m. James K. Horstman, July 2, 1980 (div.); children: Whitney Sarah, Michael Andrew. BA, Wesleyan U., 1976; JD, Washington U., St. Louis, 1980. Bar: Ill. 1981, U.S. Dist. Ct. (cen. dist.) Ill. 1981, Colo. 1991. Assoc. Costello, Young & Metnik, Springfield, Ill., 1980-82; sole practice Springfield, Leadville, 1982—. Office: PO Box A Leadville CO 80461-1017

BELLIN, HOWARD, management consultant company executive; b. N.Y.C., Oct. 30, 1933; arrived in Australia, 1961; s. Paul and Anna (Sterner); m. Barbara Ann Box, May 12, 1962; children: Sara Lea, Paul. BSMetE, Carnegie Mellon U., 1955. Trainee Great Lakes Steel Corp., Detroit, 1955; dept. mgr. Kelsey Hayes Corp., Detroit, 1955-57; from indsl. engr. to dept. mgr. Gillette Co., Boston, 1957-64; factory mgr. Allied Corp., Richmond, Va., 1964-65, Sydney, Australia, 1966-67; mng. dir. Avin Plating, Melbourne, Australia, 1967-69; founder, chmn. IF Cons., Melbourne, Australia, 1969—. Presenter in field. Mem. editl. bd. Jour. Mktg. Channels; contbr. articles to profl. jours. Active franchise divsn. Singapore Productivity Bd. With U.S. Army, 1957. Mem. Am. Club. Liberal. Jewish. Avocations: exercise, jogging, photography, reading, history. Home: 17 Moule Ave, Brighton 3186 Victoria Australia Office: I F Cons 390 St Kilda Rd 3004 Melbourne Victoria Australia E-mail: hbellin@i-f.com.

BELLIN, HOWARD THEODORE, plastic surgeon; b. N.Y.C., Apr. 8, 1936; s. Maurice and Etta (Rosenbloom) B.; m. Christina Paolozzi, Oct. 27, 1964 (dec. Apr. 27, 1988); children: Marco, Andy. BA, Amherst Coll., 1957; MD, N.Y. Med. Coll., 1962. Diplomate Am. Bd. Plastic Surgery. Intern U. Calif. Hosp., San Francisco, 1962-63; resident Met. Hosp., N.Y.C., 1963-66; resident in plastic surgery Columbia Presbyn. Med. Ctr., N.Y.C., 1968-70; instr. in surgery Columbia Coll. Physicians and Surgeons, N.Y.C., 1968-70; asst. clin. prof. surgery N.Y. Med. Coll., N.Y.C., 1970-84, asst. clin. prof. demratology, 1975-83; chief plastic surbery Cabrini Med. Ctr., N.Y.C., 1973-80; pres. Cosmedica Plastic Surgery Ctr., N.Y.C., 1980—. Pres. Cortec, Inc., N.Y.C., 1983—, Life Signs, Inc., N.Y.C., 1989—, Motor Vehicle Protection Systems, Inc., N.Y.C., 1993—, also chmn. bd.; bd. dirs. Novamed, Inc.; mem. sci. adv. com. Inst. Ecosystem Studies, 1998—; chmn. of bd. PerfectYourself.com. Author: Dr. Bellin's Beautiful You Book, 1981, Beauty Science: Advice from One of the World's Leading Plastic Surgeons, 2000; patentee on cardiac monitoring system, 1991, portable EKG monitoring device, 1985, system for subliminal signals, 1992, systems for cancellation...artifacts, 1992, auto theft prevention system, 1995, patient monitor sheets, 1995, automobile security device, 1998. Capt. USAF, 1966-68. Fellow N.Y. Acad. Medicine; mem. AAAS, Am. Soc. Plastic and Reconstrv. Surgeons, Explorers Club (nominating com. 1985). Avocations: auto racing, helicopter flying, archaeology, computer programming. Office: Cosmedica 105 E 73rd St New York NY 10021-3502

BELLINGER, EDGAR THOMSON, lawyer; b. N.Y.C., Sept. 23, 1929; s. John and Margaret (Thomson) B.; children from previous marriage: Edgar Jr., Robert, Margaret; m. Ann Clark, Feb. 25, 1989. BA, Haverford Coll., 1951; JD with honors, George Washington U., 1955. Bar: D.C. 1955, Md. 1955. Law clk. to chief judge U.S. Dist. Ct. D.C., 1955-57; asst. U.S. aty for Washington, 1957-59; ptnr. Pope, Ballard & Loos, Washington, 1959-81, Zuckert, Scoutt and Rasenberger, Washington, 1981-94, Bellinger & Assocs., Washington and Md., 1995—. Chmn. unauthorized practice com. D.C. Ct. Appeals, 1972-78; mem. D.C. jud. conf., 1972-90; bd. mgrs. Chevy Chase Village, 1983-86. Mem. ABA (mem. fidelity and surety com., mem. forum on constrn. industry, past chmn. bonds, liens and ins. divsn.), Am. Arbitration Assn. (panel of arbitrators), D.C. Bar Assn. (D.C. Ct. Appeals orgn. com. 1972), Md. Bar Assn., Talbot County Bar Assn., Nat. Assn. Securities Dealers (panel of arbitrators), Met. Club, Chevy Chase Club (bd. govs. 1972-77, pres. 1976-77). Home: 27497 West Point Rd Easton MD 21601-8439 Office: 888 17th St NW Washington DC 20006-3939 also: PO Box 739 Easton MD 21601-8914

BELLINGER, JOHN BELLINGER, III, lawyer, government official; b. Paris, Mar. 28, 1960; s. John B. Bellinger Jr. and Anne Taliaferro (Tynes) B.; m. Caroline Dawn Renzy, June 9, 1984; children: Catharine Meade, Ann Thomson. AB, Princeton U., 1982; JD, Harvard U., 1986; MA, U. Va., 1991. Assoc. Shaw, Pitman, Potts & Trowbridge, Washington, 1986-88; spl. asst. to dir. CIA, Washington, 1988-91; assoc., then spl. counsel Wilmer, Cutler & Pickering, Washington, 1991-95; gen. counsel, commn. on the roles and capabilities of U.S. Intelligence Cmty., Washington, 1995-96; spl. counsel senate select com. on intelligence U.S. Senate, Washington, 1996; sr. counsel for nat. security matters criminal divsn. Dept. Justice, Washington, 1997-2001; sr. assoc. counsel

to Pres., Exec. Office of the Pres., Washington, 2001—, legal adviser to Nat. Security Coun., 2001—. Vestryman St. Mary's Episcopal Ch., Arlington, Va., 1991-94, sr. warden, 1993-94; bd. govs. St. Albans Sch., Washington, 1997—; mem. Coun. on Fgn. Rels., Am. Coun. on Germany. Fellow, Brit.-Am. Project. Office: The White House EEOB Rm 348 Washington DC 20504

BELLINGER, MARK FREDERICK, urology educator; b. Syracuse, NY, Apr. 20, 1948; s. Richard F. and Nancy K. Bellinger; m. Catherine Irene Mahardy, June 14, 1969; children: Deborah, Michael, Todd, Karen. BS, Lemoyne Coll., 1970; MD, SUNY, Syracuse, 1974. Diplomate Am. Bd. Urology. Intern Med. Coll. Va., Richmond, 1974-75, resident in surgery, 1975-76, resident in urology, 1976-79; fellow pediatric urology Children's Hosp., Phila., 1979-80; asst. prof. Pa. State U. M.S. Hershey Med. Ctr., 1980-85; prof. dept. pediatric urology U. Pitts., 1985—. Fellow Am. Acad. Pediat.; mem. Am. Urol. Assn. Northeastern Sect. Am. Urol. Assn. (sec. 1997—). Avocation: rowing. Office: Pediat Urology Assoc 128 N Craig St Pittsburgh PA 15213-2744 Business E-Mail: bellinger@pediatricurologyassociates.com.

BELLINGHAM, ROGER GERRY, librian, researcher, consultant; b. Cin., Aug. 10, 1945; s. Charles Albert and Helen Mildred (Weiss) Bellingham. BS, U. Cin., 1973; MEd, Xavier U., 1975; MS, U. Cin., 1983; MLS, U. Ky., 1989; M in environ. sci., Miami U., 1990. Chemist DuBois Chem. Co., Cin., 1967—74; rsch. assoc. U. Cin., 1978—84; cons. Foto Technicks Group, Cin., 1983—2002; libr. dir. Margrave Rsch. Libr., Cin., 1992—. Mem.: Am. Assn. Advancement Sci., N.Y. Acad. Sci. Achievements include consulting expertise in light microscopy-quantitive color work. Avocation: history. Office: Margrave Rsch Libr 8307 Jadwin St Cincinnati OH 45216 E-mail: toa1775@nyas.org.

BELLIS, ARTHUR ALBERT, financial executive, government official; b. Worcester, Mass., June 16, 1928; s. Frank Clayton and Ruth Porter (Gordon) B.; m. Barbara Swift, Feb. 22, 1952 (div. 1969); children: Bradford, Susan; m. E. Deborah Shea, May 28, 1972 (div. 1997); children: Cynthia, Michael. BSBA, Boston U., 1952. Asst. credit mgr. Procter & Gamble, N.Y.C., 1955-56; asst. supr. capital budget Western Union, N.Y.C., 1956-58; corp. budget analyst CBS, N.Y.C., 1958-64; account exec. Edwards & Hanley, N.Y.C., 1964-66, Spencer Trask, Worcester, 1966-70; sr. securities compliance examiner SEC, Boston, 1970-90; retired, 1990; treas., CFO, chief compliance officer Burlington Securities Corp., Chatham, Mass., 1993-97. Advisor Explorer program Mohegan council Boy Scouts Am., 1966-70; mem. Worcester Rep. Com., 1952-53, Rep. Presdl. Task Force, 1984-85; mem. fin. com. Town of Yarmouth, 1982-86; v.p. Sheriff's Cmty. Patrol, 1997. Recipient Superior Performance award SEC, 1976, 1986; Medal of Merit, Pres. of U.S., 1985. Mem. Masons (treas. Howard lodge 1988-91, trustee 1992-97), Pine Run High Twelve Club (sec. 2003, leader cmty. emergency response team, 2003—). Roman Catholic. Avocations: flying, hiking, camping. Address: 9701 e Highway 25 #32 Belleview FL 34420 E-mail: lebtra@CS.com.

BELLIS, CARROLL JOSEPH, surgeon, educator; b. Shreveport, La. s. Joseph and Rose (Bloome) B.; m. Mildred Darmody, Dec. 26, 1939; children: Joseph, David. BS summa cum laude, U. Minn., 1930, MS in Physiology, 1932, PhD in Physiology, 1934, MD, 1936, PhD in Surgery, 1941. Diplomate Am. Bd. Surgery, cert. Internat. Bd. Proctology, Internat. Bd. Surgery. Fellow in physiology U. Minn., Mpls., 1930-34; resident in surgery U. Minn. Hosps., Mpls., 1937-41; pvt. practice surgery Long Beach, Calif., 1945-95. Prof., chmn. dept. surgery Calif. Coll. Medicine, 1962—; surg. cons. to surgeon gen. U.S. Army; adj. prof. surgery U. Calif. Author: Fundamentals of Human Physiology, A Critique of Reason, Lectures in Medical Physiology; contbr. numerous articles on surgery and physiology to profl. jours. Served to col. M.C. AUS, 1941-46. Recipient Charles Lyman Green prize in physiology, 1934, prize Mpls. Surg. Soc., 1938, ann. award Mississippi Valley Med. Soc., 1955; Alice Shevlin fellow U. Minn., 1932-34. Fellow: ACS, Peripheral Vascular Soc. Am. (founding), Internat. Acad. Proctology, Nat. Cancer Inst., Phlebology Soc. Am., Gerontol. Soc., Am. Med. Writers Assn., Internat. Coll. Surgeons, Royal Soc. Medicine, Am. Coll. Gastroenterology, Internat. Coll. Angiology (sci. coun.), Am. Soc. Abdominal Surgeons; mem.: AAAS, Pan Am. Med. Assn. (diplomate), Indsl. Med. Assn., Pan Pacific Surg. Assn., Am. Assn. History Medicine, Irish Med. Assn., Am. Geriatrics Soc., Hollywood Acad. Medicine, N.Y. Acad. Scis., Miss. Valley Med. Soc., Am. Assn. Study Neoplastic Diseases, Alpha Omega Alpha, Sigma Xi, Phi Beta Kappa. Home: PMB 808 904 Silver Spur Rd Rolling Hills Estates CA 90274

BELLIVEAU, GERARD JOSEPH, JR., librarian; b. Waltham, Mass., May 27, 1940; s. Gerard Joseph and Mary Teresa (Reilly) B. BA in English Lit., Boston Coll., 1963; MA in Philosophy, Boston U., 1972; MLS in Libr. Svc., Rutgers U., 1973. Lectr. U. Rouen (France), 1965-66; philosophy bibliographer Boston Pub. Libr., Boston, 1967-68; asst. libr. Racquet & Tennis Club: Libr. of Sport, N.Y.C., 1971-78, head libr., 1979—; libr. gen. rsch. div. N.Y. Pub. Libr., N.Y.C., 1973-79, libr. in charge gen. rsch. div., 1980-81, asst. chief pub. catalog sect. gen. rsch. div., 1981-88, asst. chief libr. gen. rsch. div., 1988-95. Mem. coop. acquisitions program com. METRO Ref. and Rsch. Libr. Agy., N.Y.C., 1984-88, chair coop. acquisitions program com., 1985-86, mem. resources devel. com., 1986-89. Bd. dirs. Peabody-Mason Music Found., Boston, 1972-87. Mem. Williams Club. Democrat. Avocations: architecture, travel, french medieval history. Office: Racquet & Tennis Club Libr 370 Park Ave New York NY 10022-5968

BELLIZZI, JOHN J. law enforcement association administrator, educator, pharmacist; b. N.Y.C., July 26, 1919; s. Francis X. and Carmela (Bruno) B.; m. Celeste Morga, Sept. 1, 1942; children: John J. Jr., Robert F. PhG, St. John's U., N.Y.C., 1939; LLB, Albany Law Sch., 1960; JD, Union U., 1968; LLD, St. John's U., 1981. Pharmacist St. Luke's Hosp., N.Y.C., 1939-44; police officer N.Y.C. Police Dept., 1944-53; narcotics agt. N.Y. Bur. Narcotics Enforcement, N.Y.C., 1953-59, dir. Albany, 1959-81; exec. dir. N.Y. State Drug Abuse Commn., Albany, 1981-84, Internat. Narcotics Enforcement Assn., Albany, 1984—. Prof. pharmacy law St. John's U., N.Y.C., 1962-76; lectr. in field. Contbr. articles to profl. jours. Recipient Papal medal Vatican, 1965. Mem. Internat. Narcotics Enforcement Officers Assn. (pres. 1960-62, Anslinger medal 1979, chmn. law enforcement com. Paramount Pictures, 1972-75, Svc. award 1975), Ft. Orange Club, Albany Country Club, Univ. Club (Albany), Am. Friends of Law Enforcement Found. (bd. dirs., sec. Japanese), Phi Alpha Delta, Phi Sigma Chi (pres. 1939), Sigma Chi (fellow). Office: Internat Narcotics Enforcement Officers Assn 112 State St Albany NY 12207-2005

BELL-JACKSON, MARIANNE JEANNE, elementary and secondary education educator; b. Chgo., Feb. 13, 1944; d. David Vincent and Jeanne Elizabeth Bell; m. Michael Ross Jackson, Aug. 12, 1989; m. Roscoe Edward Mitchell; 1 child, Atala-Nicole Mitchell; m. Jerry Alan Levy. B Art History, U. Chgo., 1967; M Elem. Edn., U. Wis., Platteville, 1985. Lic. tchr. 1st - 8th grades. Sec. The Filter People, Chgo., 1960-66; office mgr. U. Chgo. Maroon, 1966-68; asst. program dir. Emerson & Taylor House Community Ctrs., Chgo., 1968-71; child advocate Lawndale Day Care Ctr., Chgo., 1971-73; potter, owner Burnt Earth Pottery, Hollandale, Wis., 1973-85, Token Creek, Wis., 1998—; tchr. Madison (Wis.) Met. Sch. Dist., 1985—. Cons. Ednl. Devel. Ctr., Newton, Mass., 1991-92; Search for Extra Terrestrial Intelligence pilot program tchr., 1993-94; resource agt. Am. Astron. Soc., 1994—. Author: Model for a 4th Grade Curriculum, 1990 (with Larry Johns) Proposal for Construction of an Effigy Mound, 1990, The Swan Twins, ColorAnDraw 1, 1999; contbr. to Poetry Out of Wisconsin, 1982; inventor ColorAnDraw Books, 1995. Recipient 1st pl. for pottery, 1st pl. for hand painted ceramics Cambridge (Wis.) Art Fair, 1979; named to Golden Apple Club Madison Met. Sch. Dist., 1993. Mem.: Physician's Com. for Responsible Medicine, Farm Sanctuary, Wis. Earth Sci. Tchrs., Madison Tchrs., Inc., Amnesty Internat. Lutheran Buddhist. Avocation: writing, drawing, running, astronomy.. Home: 6251 Portage Rd De Forest WI 53532-2900 Office: Madison Met Sch Dist 545 E Dayton St OCP Office Madison WI 53703-1967 E-mail: mariannejbell@aol.com.

BELLM, JOAN, civic worker; b. Alton, Ill., June 20, 1934; d. Harvey Jacob and Alma Lorene (Roberts) Goldsby; m. Earl David Bellm, Oct. 1, 1955; children: David, Lori, Michael. Bd. dirs. Drug Watch Internat., 1991-02, lifetime hon. dir., 1998—; exec. dir. Ctr. for Drug Info., 1998—. Editor Best of IDEA newsletter, 1991-96, Drug Watch World News, 1996-02; chmn. Drug Watch Internat. editl. rev. com., 1996-02; columnist weekly newspaper, 1998—. Organist, dir. jr. choir St. Mary's Cath. Ch., 1958-78; mem. adv. bd. Carlinville (Ill.) Area Hosp., 1981-86; trustee Blackburn Coll., Carlinville, 1983-86; bd. dirs. Cath. Children's Home, Diocese of Springfield, Ill., 1986—; founder, bd. dirs., state networker Ill. Drug Edn. Alliance, 1982-86, pres., 1987-89; bd. dirs., nat. networker Nat. Fedn. Parents for Drug-Free Youth, Washington, 1984-86; mem. Ill. Gov.'s Adv. Coun. on Alcoholism and Substance Abuse, 1989-93; dir. Ctr. for Drug Info., 1998—; founder Drug Watch Internat., 1991, Internat. Drug Strategy Inst., 1993, invited participant Internat. Private Sector Conf. on Drugs, Seville, 1993, advisor U.N. Internat. Drug Ctrl. Program, 1994 ; numerous others. Recipient letter of endorsement Pres. of U.S., 1981, citation of recognition Ill. Dept., Am. Legion, 1981, Meritorious Svc. award, 1982, award Ill. Drug Edn. Alliance award, 1984, Southwestern Ill. Law Enforcement Commn., 1984, Carlinville Sch. Bd., 1985, Outstanding Svc. award Nat. Fedn. Parents, 1986, award Ill. Alcohol and Drug Dependence Assn., 1986, Optimist Internat., 1987, Ill. Drug Edn. Alliance, 1988, Outstanding Citizen award Blackburn U., 1989, Citizen of Yr. award, Carlinville, 1990; Leadership award Drug Watch Internat., 2001. Home: PO Box 227 Carlinville IL 62626-0227

BELLMORE, LAWRENCE ROBERT, JR., financial planner; b. Flint, Mich., May 1, 1947; s. Lawrence R. and Vaneta O. (Wortz) B.; m. Patricia Antonopolos, Dec. 27, 1969; (div. 1973); 1 son, Lawrence Robert III; m. Susan Marie Thompson, Aug. 1979 (div. July 2002); children: Samuel Ryan, Stuart Logan; 1 stepchild, Stacy Marie Thompson. BS in Mech. Engring., Gen. Motors Inst., 1970; MBA, U. Pitts., 1987; JD, Widener U., 2000. CFP. Engr. in tng. Gen. Motors Inst., Flint, Mich., 1969-70; dist. service and parts mgr. Detroit Diesel Allison div. Gen. Motors, ... zone Buick Motor Div., Flint, Mich., 1970-72; mgr. fleet maintenance N.Am. Van Lines, Ft. Wayne, Ind., 1972-74, Eazor Express, Pitts., 1974-75; asst. br. mgr. Pullman Trailmobile, Inc., Jersey City, Pa., 1974-75, br. mgr., 1976-77, Balt., 1977-79; pres. Lyco Truck Sales & Svc., Inc. and Lyco Leasing, Inc., Montoursville, Pa., 1979-81, L.R. Bellmore & Assocs., Montoursville, Pa., 1981-89; registered rep. Waddell & Reed, Inc., 1981-84, FSC Securities Corp., 1984-87; nat. sales mgr. R. Dummont & Co., GMBH W.Ger. in U.S., 1982-84; mktg. dir. DKM Bldg. Enterprises, 1989-90, v.p. sales, 1990-92, v.p. adminstrn., corp. planning, 1993—; branch mgr. Am. Home Loans Mortgage Bankers, 1997—; reg. rep. Tower Equities, Inc., 2001—02. Founder LRBA Advisory Inc., Bus. Brokers, Mortgage Brokers & Investment Mgmt., 1987—; mng. exec. Integrated Resources Equity Corp., Montoursville, 1987-89; mktg. dir. Muncy Homes Inc.; mng. exec. Royal Alliance Assocs. Bd. dirs. Black Hawk Home Owners Assn., 1972-74. Mem. Internat. Assn. Cert. Fin. Planners, Full Gospel Bus. Men's Fellowship, Internat. Republican. Home and Office: 1685 Rte 405 Hwy Hughesville PA 17737

BELLO, JUDITH HIPPLER, lawyer; b. Alexandria, Va., May 31, 1949; BA in History summa cum laude, U. N.C., 1971; JD, Yale U., 1975. Bar: D.C. 1975. Office legal adviser Dept. State, Washington, 1977-82; dep. to dep. asst. Sec. Commerce for Import Adminstrn., Washington, 1982-84, from dep. gen. counsel to gen. counsel, U.S. trade rep. and chmn. Sect. 301 Com., 1985-89; ptnr. Sidley & Austin, Washington, 1989-96; exec. v.p. policy and strategic affairs Pharm. Rsch. and Mfrs. of Am., Washington, 1996-2001, sr. advisor, 2002. Lectr. internat. trade seminar Yale Law Sch., 1984-85, 85-86, 2001-02, Woodrow Wilson Sch., 2002; mem. Pres. Commn. on Fed. Ethics Law Reform, 1989; mem. adv. bd. Corp. Counsel's Internat. Adviser, 1985-96; adj. prof. Georgetown U. Law Ctr., 1989-90; mem. adv. com. Export-Import Bank, 1990-92. Author: (with Alan F. Holmer) The Antidumping and Countervailing Duty Laws: Key Legal and Policy Issues, 1987, Guide to U.S.-Can. Free-Trade Agreement, 1990; editor: North American Free Trade Agreement, 1994; contbr. numerous articles to profl. jours. Bd. dirs. Atlantic Coun. of U.S., 2001—; mem. adv. coun. on pub. policy and edn. Brookings Inst.; mem. adv. bd. Maxwell Sch. Citizenship and Pub. Affairs Syracuse (N.Y.) U., 1993-98, G.W.J. Internat. Law and Econs., 1984-97, Georgetown J.L. & Poly Internat. Bus., 1993-98, also corporate counsel; mem. Aspen Strategy Group, 2001. Recipient Overall Excellence award D.C. Bar Com., 1985, Meritorious Pub. Svc. award USCG, 1978. Mem. ABA (internat. sect. co-chmn. trade com. 1986-90, couns. 1987-90), D.C. Bar (internat. sect., chmn. steering com. 1987-88; co-chmn. trade com. 1983-86), Am. Soc. Internat. Law (editl. adv. bd. 1982-89, coun. 1994-96, bd. dirs. 1995-2000), Coun. on Fgn. Rels., Phi Beta Kappa. Home: 1710 Chesterbrook Vale Ct Mc Lean VA 22101-3244 Office: PhRMA 1100 15th St NW Ste 900 Washington DC 20005-1763 E-mail: jbello@phrma.org.

BELLOCK, PATRICIA RIGNEY, state legislator; b. Chgo., Oct. 14, 1946; d. John Dungan and Dorothy (Comiskey) Rigney; m. Charles Joseph Bellock, Nov. 8, 1969; children: Colleen, Dorothy. BA, St. Norbert Coll., 1968. With customer rels. 3M Corp., Chgo., 1968-69; tchr. jr. h.s. Milw. and Fairbanks, Alaska, 1970-72; v.p. sports corps. Dor-Mor-Pat Corp., River Forest, Ill., 1976-84; mem. DuPage County Bd. from Dist. 3, Wheaton, Ill., 1992-98, Ill. Ho. of Reps., Springfield, 1999—. Asst. treas. DuPage County Forest Preserve Dist. Mem. sch. bd. St. Isaac Jogues Sch., Hinsdale, Ill., 1989-91; bd. dirs. Hinsdale Cmty. House, 1987-89, U. Ill. Gerontology Rsch., 1988-91, Hinsdale Youth Ctr., 1987-90, DuPage County Bd. Health, Wheaton, 1990—, Care and Counseling Ctr., Downers Grove, 1977—, pres., 1986-89. Recipient award Ill. Health Dept., 1992, Woman of Yr. award Serenity House, Addison, Ill. Roman Catholic. Office: 6301 S Cass Ave Westmont IL 60559-3277 Home: 431 Canterbury Ct Hinsdale IL 60521-2825*

BELLOHUSEN, RONALD MICHAEL, orthodontist, educator; b. McKeesport, Pa., July 25, 1947; s. Michael and Ann (Montrenes) B.; m. Gail Jean Davies, Nov. 22, 1969; children: Michael, Beth. BS, U. Pitts., 1968, MS in Organic Chemistry, 1974, DMD, 1978. Cert. in splty. of orthodontics. Rschr. NIH/Nat. Cancer Inst., Bethesda, Md., 1971-72; clin. instr. Eastman Dental Ctr., Rochester, N.Y., 1994—; orthodontist Orthodontic Assocs. of So. Tier, Elmira, N.Y., 1994—. Lt. USN, 1969-72. Recipient Pierre Fauchard Acad. award, 1992; NESO rsch. grantee on asymmetry in cleft palate, 1993. Fellow Internat. Coll. Dentists; mem. ADA, Am. Assn. Orthodontists, Am. Bd. Orthodontists (bd. eligible). Avocations: flying, sailing, kayaking, skiing. Office: Orthodontic Assoc So Tier 440 E Water St Elmira NY 14901-3411 E-mail: ortho1@infoblvd.net.

BELLON, MICHAEL KENNETH, director, music educator; s. Dom and Lucy Bellon. MusB, Furman U., 1991; MusM in Edn., Fla. State U., 1993. Band dir. Dreher H.S., Columbia, SC, 1993—. Golf coach Dreher H.S., 2001—. Mem.: S.C. Athletic Coaches Assn., Nat. Band Assn., S.C. Band Dirs. Assn., Northwoods Golf Club. Office: Dreher High School 701 Adger Rd Columbia SC 29205 Office Fax: 803-253-7007. E-mail: mbellon@richlandone.org.

BELLO-REUSS, ELSA NOEMI, physician, educator; b. Buenos Aires, May 1, 1939; came to U.S., 1972; naturalized, 1989; d. Jose F. and Julia M. (Hiriart) Bello; m. Luis Reuss, Apr. 15, 1965; children: Luis F., Alejandro E. BS, U. Chile, 1957, MD, 1964. Intern, then resident in internal medicine U. Chile, Santiago, 1964-66; pvt. practice medicine/nephrology Santiago, 1967-72; prof. pathophysiology Sch. Nutrition U. Chile, 1970-72; Internat. NIH fellow U. N.C., Chapel Hill, 1972-74; mem. faculty Jewish Hosp., St. Louis, 1976-83; asst. prof. medicine, physiology and biophysics Washington U. Sch. Medicine, St. Louis, 1976-86, assoc. prof. physiology dept. cell biology and physiology, 1986; assoc. prof. medicine U. Tex. Med. Br., Galveston, 1986-94, prof. dept. internal medicine and dept. phys. and biophys., 1994—, area med. dir. renal clinic, 1995-98, 2001—, dir. divsn. nephrology dept. internal medicine, 2001—. Vis. asst. prof. physiology U. N.C., Chapel Hill, 1974-75; Louis Welt fellow U. N.C.-Duke U. Med. Ctr., 1975-76; chair Women's Coun. Internat. Medicine U. Tex. Med. Bd. chpt., 1993-97, mem. rsch. coun.; mem. gen. medicine B sect. NIH, 1987-91, mem. reviewers res. study sect., 1991-95, mem. study sect. NIDDKD, 1997-2001. Author: (with others) The Kidney and Body Fluids in Health and Disease, 1983, Handbook of Signaling a Kidney, 2003; contbr. articles on nephrology and epithelial electrophysiology to med. and physiology jours. Mem. Internat., Am. Socs. Nephrology, Royal Soc. Medicine, Nat. Kidney Found. of S.E. Tex. (med. adv. bd., chairperson med. adv. bd., bd. dirs. 1994-95), Coun. of Women in Nephrology, Tex. Med. Assn., Am. Fedn. Clin. Rsch., Am. Soc. Renal Biochemistry and Metabolism, Internat. Soc. Renal Nutrition and Metabolism, Am. Physiology Soc., Am. Heart Assn., Kidney Coun., Soc. Gen. Physiologists, Math. Assn. Am., Gt. Houston and Gulf Coast Nephrology Assn., Sigma Xi. Office: U Tex Med Br Dept Medicine Nephrology 4 200 John Sealy Annex Galveston TX 77555-0001 E-mail: ebellore@utmb.edu.

BELLOW, ALEXANDRA, mathematician, educator; b. Bucharest, Romania, Aug. 30, 1935; d. Dumitru and Florica Bagdasar; m. Cassius Ionescu Tulcea, Apr. 1956 (div. 1969); m. Saul G. Bellow, Oct. 1974 (div. 1986); m. Alberto P. Calderon, Sept., 1989 (dec. 1998). MS in Math, U. Bucharest, 1957; PhD in Math., Yale U., 1959. Research assoc. Yale U., New Haven, Conn., 1959-61, U. Pa., Phila., 1961-62, asst. prof., 1962-64; assoc. prof. U. Ill., 1964-67; prof. Northwestern U., Evanston, Ill., 1967-96, prof. emeritus, 1996—. Emmy Noether lectr., 1991. Author: (with C. Ionescu Tulcea) Topics in the Theory of Lifting, 1969; assoc. editor: Annals of Probability, 1979-83, Advances in Math., 1979— . Recipient Sr. Disting. Scientist award Alexander von Humboldt Found., 1987; Fairchild Disting. scholar Calif. Inst. Tech., 1980; NSF grantee Mem. Sigma Xi. Office: Northwestern U Dept of Math 2033 Sheridan Rd Evanston IL 60208-2730 E-mail: a_bellow@math.northwestern.edu.

BELLOW, DONALD GRANT, mechanical engineering educator; b. Winnipeg, Man., Can., Aug. 5, 1931; s. Walter William and Lillian Christine (Hnappdal) B.; m. Jean Marion Daye, May 18, 1956; children: Jonathan Mark, Denise Gisele. BASc in Applied Sci., U. B.C., 1956; MS, U. Alta, 1960; PhD, U. Alta., 1963. Registered profl. engr., Alta., Can. Project engr. Can. Industries Ltd., Kingston, Ont., 1956-57, Gen. Motors Diesel Ltd., London, Ont., Can., 1957-58; lectr., asst. prof., assoc. prof., prof. U. Alta., Edmonton, Can., 1958—, chmn. dept., 1975-84, assoc. v.p. facilities, 1989-94, spl. asst. to v.p. fin. and adminstrn., 1994-96, ret., 1996. Recipient L.C. Charlesworth award Assn. Profl. Engrs., Geologists and Geophysicists of Alta., 1982; Cert. of Recognition, Alta. Soc. Engring. Technologists, 1986. Fellow Can. Acad. Engring., Can. Soc. Mech. Engrs.; mem. ASME, Soc. for Exptl. Mechanics, Assn. Profl. Engrs., Geologists and Geophysicists of Alta. (2d v.p. 1983-84, 1st v.p. 1984-85, pres. 1985-86, hon. life mem. 1987-93), Assn. Profs. Emeriti U. Alta. (pres.). Conservative. Anglican.

BELLOW, SAUL C. writer, educator; b. Lachine, Que., Can., June 10, 1915; s. Abraham and Liza (Gordin) Bellow; m. Susan Glassman, 1961 (div.); 1 child, Daniel; m. Alexandra Tschacbasov, 1956 (div.); children: Gregory, Adam; m. Susan Glassman, 1961 (div.); m. Alexandra Ionesco Tuleca, 1974 (div.); m. Janis Freedman, Sept. 1989; 1 child, Naomi Rose. Student, U. Chgo., 1933—35; BS, Northwestern U., 1937, LittD, 1962, Bard Coll., 1962, NYU, 1970, Harvard U., 1972, Yale U., 1972, McGill U., 1973, Brandeis U., 1974, Hebrew Union Coll.-Jewish Inst. Religion, 1976, Trinity Coll., Dublin, Ireland, 1976. Instr. Pestalozzi-Froebel Tchrs. Coll., Chgo., 1938—42; mem. editl. dept. "Great Books" project Ency. Brit., Inc., Chgo., 1943—46; mem. English dept. U. Minn., Mpls., 1946, asst. prof., 1948—49, assoc. prof. English, 1954—59; vis. lectr. NYU, 1950—52; creative writing fellow Princeton (N.J.) U., 1952—53; faculty mem. Bard Coll., Annandale-on-Hudson, NY, 1953—54; vis. prof. English U. P.R., Rio Piedras, 1961; celebrity in residence U. Chgo., 1962, Grunier Disting. Svcs. prof., 1962—, mem. com. on social thought, 1962—, chmn. com. on social thought, 1970—76. Tanner lectr. Oxford U.; Romanes lectr., 1990. Author: (novels) Dangling Man, 1944, The Victim, 1947, The Adventures of Augie March, 1953 (nat. Book award, 1954), Seize the Day, 1956, Henderson the Rain King, 1959, Herzog, 1964 (Prix Internat. de Litterature, 1965, Nat. Book award, 1970, Soc. Midland Authors Fiction award, 1976), Mr. Sammler's Planet, 1970 (Nat. Book award, 1970), Humboldt's Gift, 1975 (Pulitzer prize for fiction, 1976), The Dean's December, 1982, More Die of Heartbreak, 1986, The Theft, 1989, The Bellarosa Connection, 1989, The Actual, 1997, (short stories) Mosby's Memoirs, and Other Stories, 1968, Him with His Foot in His Mouth, and Other Stories, 1984, Something to Remember Me By: Three Tales, 1991, Occasional Pieces, 1993, (plays) The Wrecker, 1954, The Last Analysis, 1964, Under the Weather, 1966, (non-fiction) To Jerusalem and Back: A Personal Account, 1976, It All Adds Up: From the Dim Past to the Uncertain Future, 1994, Ravelstein, 2000; contbr. . Recipient Croix de Chevalier, France, 1968, comdr., Legion of Honour, France, 1983, Order of Arts and Letters, France, 1985, O. Henry prize for the Gonzaga Manuscripts, 1956, O. Henry prize for the A Silver Dish, 1980, Friends of Lit. Fiction award, 1960, James L. Dow award, 1964, Jewish Heritage award, B'nai B'rith, 1968, Formentor prize, 1970, Nobel prize for lit., 1976, Gold medal, Am. Acad. Arts and Letters, 1977, Brandeis U. Creative Arts award, 1978, Medal of Honor for lit., Nat. Arts Club, 1978, Malaparte Lit. award, 1984, Premio Scanno Lit. award, Italy, 1988, Nat. Medal of Arts, 1988, Lifetime Achievement award, Nat. Book Club, 1990, Lifetime Cultural Achievement award, YIVO Inst. for Jewish Rsch., 1996; Guggenheim fellow, 1948, Neil Gunn Internat. fellow, 1977, Nat. Inst. Arts and Letters grantee, 1952, Ford Found. grantee, 1959—61. Mem.: Am. Philos. Soc., Am. Acad. Arts and Scis. (Emerson-Thoreau medal 1977).*

BELLOWS, A. ROBERT, ophthalmologist, surgeon; b. Manchester, N.H., May 14, 1937; s. Arnold Leo and Eleanora Bellows; m. Jean Blunt Farley, May 30, 1964; children: Matthew, Kristen, Nathaniel. BA, Brown U., 1959; MD, Boston U., 1963. Diplomate Am. Bd. Ophthalmology. Intern Univ. Hosp., Boston, 1963-64; asst. resident in internal medicine VA Hosp., Boston, 1964-65; opthal. resident Yale New Haven (Conn.) Hosp., 1967-70, chief resident, 1970; W.M. Grant MD Glaucoma Fellowship Mass. Eye and Ear Infirmary, Boston, 1971-72; partner Ophthalmic Consultants of Boston, Inc., 1974—; surgeon Mass. Eye & Ear Infirmary, 1990—. Instructor in ophthal. surgery, Yale U., 1969-70; asst. clin. prof. ophthal. Harvard U., 1972-92, assoc. prof., 1992-97, lectr., 1997—; asst. clin. prof. Tufts U., 1992—. Capt. USAF, 1965-67, Libya. Fellow Am. Acad. Ophthal. (Hon. award 1984, Sr. Hon. award 1996); mem. ACS, Mass. Med. Soc., Ophthal. Assn. in Rsch. to Prevent Blindness, Mass. Soc. Eye Physicians and Surgeons, Assn. for Rsch. in Vision and Ophthal., New Eng. Ophthal. Soc., Am. Glaucoma Soc., Am. Eye Study Club, Chandler Great Glaucoma Soc. (pres. 1995-97). Home: 327 Commonwealth Ave Boston MA 02115-1900 Office: Ophthalmic Cons of Boston 50 Staniford St Ste 600 Boston MA 02114-2587 also: 88 Ansel Hallet Rd West Yarmouth MA 02673-2556

BELLOWS, HOWARD ARTHUR, JR., marketing research executive; b. N.Y.C., Mar. 10, 1938; s. Howard Arthur and Rita Jennie (Maffitt) B.; m. Mary Josephine Boyd, Sept. 7, 1968; children— Maffitt Vodrey, Alexander Scott, Hillary Newland, Jennifer Pacheteau. BA, Princeton U., 1960; MBA, Harvard U., 1964. Dir. mktg. Olga Co., Van Nuys, Calif., 1964-66; chmn. bd., co-chief exec. officer Triangle Corp., Stamford, Conn., 1967-71, chmn. bd., pres., chief exec. officer, 1971-95; pres. Audits & Surveys Worldwide, Inc., N.Y.C., 1995—, also bd. dirs., cons., dir. Bd. dirs. Audits and Surveys Worldwide, Inc., Tools Ins. co. Ltd., Trustee Western Res. Acad., Hudson, Ohio, dir., Boys and Girls Club of Greenwich and Arch St. Teen Ctr., Served to lt. (j.g.) USNR, 1960-62. Mem. Links Club, Blind Brook Club, Racquet and Tennis Club, Round Hill Club, Eagle Springs Golf Club. Office: Audits & Surveys Worldwide 650 Avenue Of The Americas Fl 6 New York NY 10011-2098

BELLOWS, LAUREL GORDON, lawyer; b. Chgo., Apr. 9, 1948; d. Michael M. Gordon and Lois (Loren) Gross; m. Joel J. Bellows, June 9, 1978. BA, U. Pa., 1969; JD, Loyola U., Chgo., 1974. Bar: Ill. 1974, Fla. 1975, U.S. Dist. Ct. (no. dist.) Ill. 1975, U.S. Dist. Ct. (no. dist.) Ga. 1980, Calif. 1981, U.S. Dist. Ct. (cen. dist.) Calif. 1980. Ptnr. Bellows and Bellows, Chgo., 1975—. Editor Loyola U. Law Rev., 1973-74; co author: Trial Techniques in Business and Commercial Cases, 1988-2000. Past pres. women's bd. Traveller's Aid Soc., Chgo.; past chmn. Chgo. Network, 1992—; mentor Woman of Destiny program, 1990-91. Mem. ABA (bd. govs. 2001—, sec.-treas. 1991-92, past chmn. commn. on women 1993-95, mem. fed. jud. com. 1999—), Ill. Bar Assn., Chgo. Bar Assn. (bd. mgrs. 1983-85, sec. 1987-89, pres. 1991-92), Women's Bar Assn. Ill., Women's Bar Assn. Ill. Found. (bd. dirs. 1988—), Am. Arbitration Assn. (arbitrator 1976—, award 1990). Clubs: The Arts. Office: Bellows and Bellows 79 W Monroe St Ste 800 Chicago IL 60603-4906 E-mail: lbellows@bellowspc.com.

BELLOWS, MICHAEL DONALD, foreign service officer; b. Spirit Lake, Iowa, Mar. 7, 1952; s. Donald Morris and Dolores Elizabeth (Thiesen) B.; m. Toni Leder, July 27, 1974; 1 child, Melissa Elizabeth. BA in History, Morningside Coll., Sioux City, Iowa, 1974; diploma, Nat. Def. U., 1990. Vice consul U.S. Embassy, Manila, 1975-77, U.S. Consulate Gen., Frankfurt, Germany, 1978-80, dep. prin. officer Halifax, Can., 1980-82; consul U.S. Embassy, Suva, Fiji, 1982-84, polit. officer, 1985-87; polit. and econ. officer U.S. Dept. State, Washington, 1987-89; consul gen. U.S. Consulate Gen., Auckland, New Zealand, 1990-93; dean Auckland Consular Corps, 1992-93; dir. Office Pub. and Diplomatic Liaison Dept. State, Washington, 1994-96; spl. asst. Bur. of Consular Affairs Dept. State, Washington, 1996—; min.-counselor U.S. Embassy, Ottawa, Can., 1997—; sr. advisor Bur. Consular Affairs, Dept.

State, Washington, 2001—. Vis. fellow Inst. Nat. Strategic Studies, Nat. Def. U., 1993-94. Editor: Asia in the 21st Century: Evolving Strategic Priorities, 1994. Mem. Am. Fgn. Svc. Assn., Am. Defenders of Bataan and Corregidor. Avocations: reading, music. Office: US Dept State Fgn Svc Lounge Washington DC 20520-0001

BELLOWS, THOMAS JOHN, political scientist, educator; b. Chgo., Aug. 15, 1935; s. Charles Everett and Dorothy (Morrison) B.; m. Marilyn Denise Corbell; children: Scott Anthony, Justin Thomas, Trevor Cullen, Ethan Forrest; children by previous marriage: Roderick Alan, Adrienne Marie, Jeannine Louise, Derek John, Marshall Everett. Student, Am. U., 1956, UCLA, 1956-57; BA, Augustana Coll., 1957; MA, U. Fla., 1958, Yale U., 1960, PhD, 1968. Asst. prof. polit. sci. West Ga. Coll., Carrollton, 1962-64, 66; from asst. prof. to prof. polit. sci. U. Ark., Fayetteville, 1967-81, chmn. dept., 1971-78; dir. divsn. social policy scis. U. Tex., San Antonio, 1981-88, prof. polit. sci., 1981—. Vis. lectr. depts. history, polit. sci. Nanyang U., Singapore, 1965; vis. prof. Nat. Chengchi U., Taiwan, 1979. Author: The People's Action Party of Singapore: Emergence of a Dominant Party System, 1970, (with S. Erikson and H. Winter) Political Science: Introductory Essays and Readings, 1971, Taiwan's Foreign Policy in the 1970's, 1976, (with H. Winter) People and Politics: An Introduction to Political Science, 1985, Bridging Tradition and Modernization: The Singapore Bureaucracy, 1989, (with H. Winter) Conflict and Compromise, 1992; Taiwan and Mainland China, 2000, (with Felix Almaraz) Modern Texas, 2003; editor: Am. Jour. Chinese Studies, 1999—. Mem.: Am. Assn. for Chinese Studies (pres. 1998—2000), Assn. Asian Studies, S.W. Conf. Asian Studies (pres. 1995), Phi Beta Kappa, Phi Kappa Phi. Methodist. Office: U Tex Dept Polit Sci San Antonio TX 78249 E-mail: TBellows@Lonestar.UTSA.edu.

BELLUOMINI, FRANK STEPHEN, accountant; b. Healdsburg, Calif., May 19, 1934; s. Francesco and Rose (Giorgi) B.; m. Alta Anita Gifford, Sept. 16, 1967; 1 child, Wendy Ann. AA, Santa Rosa Jr. Coll., 1954; BA with honors, San Jose State U., 1956. CPA, Calif. Staff acct. Hood, Gire & Co., CPA's, San Jose, Calif., 1955-60, ptnr., 1960-66, Touche Ross & Co., CPA's, San Jose, 1967-89, ptnr.-in-charge San Jose office, 1971-85, sr. ptnr., 1985-89; ptnr. Deloitte & Touche, San Jose, 1989-95. Bd. dirs. Santa Clara Valley chpt. ARC, 1993-99, 2000—, chmn. bd. dirs. 1995-97; mem. adv. bd. Salvation Army, San Jose, 1979-83, San Jose Children's Coun., 1982-85, mem. citizens adv. coun. Via Rehabiliation Svcs., Inc., 1989-94, bd. dirs., 1995-2002, sec./treas., 1996-98, vice chair, 1998-99, chair, 1999-2000; trustee Santa Clara County (Calif.) United Way, 1979-95, v.p. planning and allocations, 1981-83, vice chmn., 1985-87, chmn. 1987-89; bd. dirs. San Jose Mus. Art, 1984-86; mem. Presentation High Sch. Devel. Bd., 1989-92; mem. dean's adv. coun. San Jose State U. Bus. Schl., 1990-95, mem. adv. bd. The Acad. of Fin., 1992-94. Named Disting. Alumnus, San Jose State U. Sch. Bus., 1978. Mem. AICPA (chmn. state and local govt. com. 1976-79), Santa Clara County Estate Planning Coun. (pres. 1979-80), Calif. Soc. CPA's (pres. chpt. 1968-69, state v.p. 1976-77), San Jose State Alumni Assn. (treas. 1960-61, dir. 1961-62, exec. com. 1961-62), San Jose State Acctg. Round Table (bd. dirs., treas. 1982-87, 92-97, pres. 1994-95), Beta Alpha Psi (San Jose State U. Outstanding Alumnus award 1986), Rotary (dir. 1979-81, dir. San Jose Rotary Endowment 1976-83, 2000-01, pres. 2001-03).

BELLUOMINI, RONALD JOSEPH, secondary education educator, poet; b. Chgo., July 19, 1946; m. Marilyn Lucille Naselli, Sept. 27, 1969; children: Thomas, Marc. BS in Edn., Chgo. State U., 1968, MA in Geography, 1971. Cert. 6-12 Tchr., ILL. Tchr. St. Basil Sch., Chgo., 1968-71, Northbrook (Ill.) Dist. II 28, 1971—2003; ret., 2003. Author: The Thirteenth Labor, 1985 (Robert and Hazel Ferguson Meml. award for poetry Friends of Lit. Chgo. 1986); contbr. to lit. revs. Mem. Poetry Soc. Am. Home: 2179 Spruce Pointe Ct Gurnee IL 60031

BELLUOMINI, WENDY, microprocessor design researcher; b. San Jose, Calif., June 8, 1972; d. Frank and Anita Belluomini; m. Chandler McDowell, Sept. 11, 2001. BS in Computer Sci., Calif. Inst. of Tech., 1994; MS in Computer Sci., U. of Wash., 1996; PhD in Computer Sci., U. of Utah, 1999. Rsch. staff mem. IBM, Austin, Tex., 1999—. Achievements include research in Developed new algorithms for analyzing timing dependant systems; Developed new circuit design aproaches for microprocessor design.

BELLUS, RONALD JOSEPH, marketing and communications executive; b. Travis AFB, Calif., Feb. 25, 1951; s. Vincent Joseph and Katherine Veronica (Giudice) B.; m. Beth Ann Johnson, June 26, 1976 (div.); children: Veronica Lee, Joseph Vincent, Kenneth James; m. Gina Jean Prom, Aug. 9, 1990; children: Anthony Taylor, Andrew Tyler. BA in Communications, Brigham Young U., 1977. Lic. FCC radio telephone operator, 1979. Sports dir. Sta. KGUY-AM, Palm Desert, Calif., 1979; news, sports dir. Sta. KBLQ-AM/FM, Logan, Utah, 1979-80; gen. sales mgr. Sta. KSTM-FM/KVVA-AM, Phoenix, 1980-84, Sta. KLFF-AM/KMZK-FM, Phoenix, 1984-85; media cons. Mediacorp Planning & Buying, Phoenix, 1985-86; press sec. Gov. of Ariz., Phoenix, 1986-87; asst. dir. Ariz. Office of Tourism, Phoenix, 1987-88; media cons. Bellus Media, Phoenix, 1988-93; pres. Taska Ltd. (formerly Bellus Media), Phoenix, 1993—; ptnr. Desertwest Media Group, Inc., Phoenix, 1988-96; v.p. Nat. Restaurant Group, Inc., Phoenix, 1990-91. Media cons. Mecham for Gov. com., Glendale, Ariz., 1986; host cable TV show Arizona-Now and Then, Cox Cable, 1990-2000; v.p. Infosystems, Tempe, 1991-94, Green Valley Health Group, Phoenix, 1992-98; co-founder Cinema Concepts Found., Scottsdale, 1994—; co-founder, CEO Bronze Memories Ltd., Phoenix, 1994—; co-founder, pres. Taurus, Inc., 1998—; assoc. dir. Southwest Ctr. for Ethics, Scottsdale C. C., 1999. Author: Mecham: Silence Cannot Be Misquoted, 1988, Ariz. Tourism Travel Planner, 1988. Comm. mem. Phoenix Boys Choir, 1988; precinct committeeman Rep. State Com., Phoenix, 1987-89, 2001—, del., 1988; candidate for state senate, Phoenix, 1988; bd. dirs. Cinema Concepts Found., 1994—; mem. Gilbert Anti-Gang Task Force, 1994—, Gilbert Action Inter-Faith Network, 1994—; chmn. adv. bd. Original Kids TV, Inc.; candidate for Ariz. State Senate, Gilbert, 2000; vice-chair, Gilbert Human Rel. Commn., 2001—. Named one of Outstanding Young Men Am., 1987. Mem.: Gilbert C. of C. (pub. policy com. 2002—03), Kiwanis, Phoenix Press Box Assn. (treas. 1984—85, exec. dir. 1985—86). Ch. of Latter Day Saints. Avocations: golf, travel, reading. Office: 15812 N 32d St Ste 9 Phoenix AZ 85032-3857

BELLUSCHI, ANTHONY C. architect; b. Portland, Oreg., Aug. 2, 1941; s. Pietro and Helen (Hemila) B.; m. Helen Risom, June 25, 1966 (div. 1975); children: Pietro Antonio, Catharine Camilla; m. Martha Mull Page, July 17, 1992. BArch, R.I. Sch. Design, 1966. Lic. arch. 28 states including N.Y., Mass., R.I., Calif., N.J., Oreg., Ill., Fla., Ga. Draftsman Ernest Kump Assocs., San Francisco, 1964; designer Zimmer-Gunsel-Frasca, Portland, 1965; assoc. Jung/Brannen Assocs., Boston, 1968-73; prin., treas. Belluschi/Daskalakis Inc., Boston, 1973-77; sr. v.p. Charles Kober Assocs., L.A., 1977-84; mng. ptnr. Kober/Belluschi Assocs., Chgo., 1984-87; pres. Anthony Belluschi Assocs. Inc., 1984-87; founder Anthony Belluschi Archs., Ltd., Chgo., 1988-2000; pres. Belluschi-OWP&P Arch. INc., Chgo., 2000—. Archtl. cons. U.S. Peace Corps, El Salvador, 1966-68; trustee R.I. Sch. Design, 1986—, vice chmn., 1995-2000, chair bd., 2000—. Bd. adv. Inland Arch. Mag., 1992-95. Bd. dirs. Friends of the Park, Chgo., 1993—. Recipient First prize sculpture contest RKO & Redevel. Agy., Boston, 1973, award of merit Mass. Commn. Housing, 1975, Alumni of Yr. award RISD, 1982-83. Mem. AIA (award of excellence 1997), Urban Land Inst. (award of excellence 1997), Internat. Coun. Shopping Ctrs. (design awards for Erieview Galleria, Clevel., Bridgewater Commons, N.J., 1989, Sportsgirl Office/Retail Hirise Bldg., Melbourne, Australia, 1991, Park Meadows Retail Resort, Denver, Univ. Retail Ctr., Tampa, Fla., 1996, The Falls, Miami, 1996, Northwood Cafe, Appleton, Wis., 1999), RISD Alumni Assn. (founder Chgo. chpt.). Avocation: collecting stamps and coins, automobiles, skiing, hunting.. Home: The Coach House 119 W Chestnut St Chicago IL 60610-3254 Office: Belluschi-OWP&P Arch Inc 111 W Washington St Ste 2100 Chicago IL 60602-2783

BELLUSSI, GIUSEPPE CARLO, research manager; b. Cremona, Italy, Feb. 25, 1953; s. Paride and Angela Rosa (Serafini) B.; m. Maria Grazia Sabini, July 20, 1980; children: Brando, Dario. Undergrad. Degree in Agrl. Scis., U. Parma, Italy, M in Chemistry, 1978. Researcher Duco S.p.A., Fombio, Italy, 1980-81, Assoreni, S. Donato, Italy, 1981-85, Eniricerche S.p.A., S. Donato, Italy, 1986-89, sr. scientist, 1989-90, head catalytic processes dept., 1991-98, head Rsch. Ctr. for Catalysis and Process Techs., 1998—. Cons. UN Ind. Devel. Orgn., Pune, India, 1989. Contbr. over 50 articles to profl. jours. Recipient D. Breck award Internat. Zeolite Assn., 1992, Disting. Svc. award Japan Gas Assn., 1996, Federchimica award, 1998. Mem. Catalysis Group of Italian Chem. Soc. (mem. coun.), European Fedn. Catalysis Socs. (mem. coun.). Achievements include 60 patents in field. Home: Via Millo 14 29100 Piacenza Italy Office: EniTecnologie Via F Maritano 26 20097 San Donato Italy E-mail: gbellussi@enitecnologie.emi.it.

BELLUZZO, RICK, information technology executive; BS in Acctg., Golden Gate U. Various positions including gen. mgr. Laser Jet Divsn., Hewlett-Packard, exec. v.p.; CEO Silicon Graphics Inc.; group v.p. Personal Svcs. and Devices Group Microsoft, Redmond, Wash., 1999—2001, pres., COO, 2001—. Mem. Sr. Leadership Team, Bus. Leadership Team, Microsoft. Avocations: running, scuba diving, skiing. Office: Microsoft One Microsoft Way Redmond WA 98052-6399

BELL WILSON, CARLOTTA A. state official, consultant; b. Detroit, Dec. 7, 1944; d. Albert Powell (dec.) and Elfrieda (Bertram) Bell; divorced; children: Lizette C. Wilson, SaMia M. Wilson, Shira M. Ingram. AA, Wayne County C.C., Detroit, 1975; BS, Wayne State U., 1979; MEd, Bowling Green State U., 1983. Dental asst. Fred Colvard, DDS, Detroit, 1968-73; edn. coord. Merrill Palmer Inst., Detroit, 1979-81; head start evaluator Cmty. Devel. Inst., Wayne County, 1981; grad. asst. Bowling Green (Ohio) State U., 1981-83; child care worker Meth. Children's Village, Detroit, 1984-85; tchr. New Calvary Head Start, Detroit, 1985; child welfare specialist Mich. Dept. Social Svcs., Detroit, 1985-93; resource program analyst teen parent program Family Independence Agy., Lansing, Mich., 1993—2002. Conf. presenter U. Mich., Ann Arbor, 1995, Mich. Assn. Cmty. and Adult Edn., Bellaire, 1995, Baker Coll., Flint, Mich., 1996. Mem. Mich. Profl. Soc. on Abuse of Children, Internat. Assoc. Infant Massage (cert. infant massage instr.). Roman Catholic. Avocations: gardening, pottery, cultural activities, travel. Home: 2110 Chene Detroit MI 48207

BELMAN, MURRAY JOEL, lawyer; b. Omaha, June 11, 1935; s. Hymen Belman and Margarette (Margolin) Yudelson; m. Laura Haines, Aug. 20, 1966; children— John Chase, Owen Wolcott AB, Cornell U., 1957; JD cum laude, Harvard U., 1960. Bar: D.C. 1960. Dep. legal adviser, asst. legal adviser Dept. State, Washington, 1961-69; gen. counsel IOS Devel. Co., Geneva, 1969-70; sole practice Washington, 1972-77; ptnr. Pepper, Hamilton & Scheetz, Washington, 1977-84, Thompson Coburn (formerly Thompson & Mitchell), Washington, 1984—. Professorial lectr. law George Washington U., Washington, 1972-74; adj. prof. Georgetown U. Sch. Law, Washington, 1975-76. Trustee St. John's Child Devel. Ctr., Washington, 1984-92, v.p., 1987-90, pres. 1990-92. Mem. ABA, D.C. Bar Found. (adv. bd. 1991—), Am. Soc. Internat. Law, Internat. Law Inst. Democrat. Jewish. Office: Thompson Coburn 1909 K St NW Ste 600 Washington DC 20006-1167

BELMONT, BARBARA S. association executive; b. Sharon, Pa., Aug. 4, 1941; d. Albert Belmont and Ruth Helen Strifling; (stepfather) Herman Miles Strfling; m. Robert M. Borschow, July 10, 1963 (div. 1979); children: Erin Ranee, Jennifer Lauren. BA, U. Colo., 1964, MA, 1966. Tchr. history Ritnour H.S., Overland, Mo., 1966-68; assoc. editor Nat. Assn. Home Builders, Washington, 1978-81, staff v.p., 1982-89; sr. v.p. mktg. Smart House, Upper Marlboro, Md., 1989-92; exec. dir., CEO Am. Sch. Food Svc. Assn., Alexandria, Va., 1993—. Bd. dirs. Friends of the World Food Program, 1999—. Recipient 2001 Winner of Fame award for Friend of Child Nutrition; named Assn. Trends 2002 Assn. Exec. of Yr. Fellow Am. Soc. Assn. Exec. (bd. dir. 1996—, vice chmn. 1999-2001, sec., treas. 2001, 02, chmn.-elect 2002-03), chmn. bd., 2003-04. Home: 228 South Alfred Alexandria VA 22314

BELMONT, LARRY MILLER, retired public health executive; b. Reno, Apr. 13, 1936; s. Miller Lawrence and Madeline (Echante) B.; m. Laureen Metzger, Aug. 14, 1966; children: Miller Lawrence, Rebecca Madeline, Amie Echante, Bradley August. BA in Psychology, U. Nev., 1962; MPH, U. Mich., 1968; cert. in environ. mgmt., U. So. Calif., 1978; MPA, U. Idaho, 1979. Rep. on loan to city health depts. USPHS, Los Angeles and Long Beach, 1962-63, advisor pub. health on loan to Alaska dept. health & welfare Anchorage, 1963-64, Juneau and Anchorage, 1964-67; dep. dir. Wash./Alaska Regional Med. Program, Spokane, Wash., 1968-71; dir., sec.-treas. bd. of health Panhandle Health Dist., Coeur d'Alene, Idaho, 1971-98; ret., 1998. Past adj. faculty Whitworth Coll., Spokane; presenter in field. Contbr. articles to newspapers. Chmn. nominating com. Kootenai Econ. Devel. Coun., Idaho, 1985, bd. dirs. 1981-86; mem. adv. com. Kootenai County Coun. Alcoholism, 1979-80; regional coord. Gov.'s Com. Vol. Svcs., Idaho, 1979-80; chmn. Montessori Adv. Bd., Idaho, 1975-79; chmn. pers. com. North Idaho Hospice, 1985-88, bd. dirs. 1985-88; bd. dirs. North Idaho Spl. Svcs. Agy., 1972-76; bd. dirs., vice-chmn. Pub. Employees Credit Union, 1990-95; bd. dirs. United Way of Kootemai County, Inc., 1990-91; mem. nat. steering com. APEX/PH, 1987-91; others; treas. Friends of Head Start Bd. Area Aging Agy. Legis. Com.; mem. Newspaper Adv. Coun., 1998-2002, tactical chair, cmty. svc. coun.; congl. dist. II coord. AARP; treas. Friends of Head Start. USPHS trainee U. Mich., 1967-68, EPA trainee U. So. Calif., 1978. Mem. APHA, AARP (chair comty. svcs. network, mem. state legis. com.), Nat. Assn. Home Health Agys. (chmn. legis. com. 1979-82, bd. dirs. 1978-81), Nat. Assn. County Health Ofcls. (bd. dirs. 1986-88, registry com. 1990), Idaho Pub. Health Assn. (bd. dirs. 1998-2002, treas. 1973-77, 98-00, 00—, Award of Merit 1999), Idaho Conf. Dist. Health Dirs. (bd. dirs. 1998, vice-chmn. and chmn. 1993-95), Idaho Forest Owners Assn. (tree farmer), Kootenai County Environ. Alliance, Idaho Conservation League, Area Agy. on Aging (legis. com., adv. coun.), Newspaper Adv. Coun., Idaho Rural Health Coalition, The Nature Conservancy, Ducks Unltd., Dem. Club (natural resources com.), Senior Coalition. Democrat. Avocations: hunting, fishing, wood carving, music, camping.

BELMONTE, STEVEN JOSEPH, hotel chain executive; b. Oak Park, Ill., Aug. 25, 1952; s. Silvio J. and Vilma (Giannini) B.; m. Dwyonia Conrad; children: Gino Anthony, Kellie Rose, Michael Steven. BA in Hotel Mgmt., Wright Coll., Chgo., 1974; student, Holiday Inn U., Memphis, 1974; BM in Innkeeping, Harper Coll., Rolling Meadows, Ill., 1981; D Applied Pub. Svc. (hon.), Hocking Coll., 1993. Gen. mgr., regional dir. Holiday Inns, Chgo., 1972-84; pres., CEO Equity Hotel Corp., Rolling Meadows, 1984-91, Ramada Franchise Sys., Inc., 1991—. Chmn. Ramada Inns Nat. Assn.; founding sponsor Childreach; speaker Ill. Budget for Tourism, 1978-81. Bd. advisors Wright Jr. Coll.; mem. Joint Civic Com. Italian Ams.; hon. chmn. Childreach Plan Internat., 1996; bd. dirs. Chgo. chpt. Inner City Games, 1998—, chmn., 2000—; active fund raiser for various charities and retirement homes; chmn., lodging chair Am. Hotel Found., 2000—. Recipient citation Italo-Am. War Vets, U.S., 1980, Humanities award PLAN Internat. Charities, 1994, Ambassador of Peace Humanitarian award Am. Friends of Neve Shalom/Wahat-Al-Salam, 1999. Fellow Hotel and Catering Internat. Mgmt. Assn. (hon.); mem. Am. Soc. Travel Agts., Am. Hotel and Motel Assn. (bd. trustees ednl. inst.), Am. Hotel Fedn., Hotel Sales Mgmt. Assn., Soc. Mng. Execs., Chgo. Innkeepers Assn. (v.p. 1979-81), Am. Hotel Found. (exec. com. 1997—, chmn. devel. com. 1997-2000). Office: Ramada Franchise Sys Inc 1 Sylvan Way Parsippany NJ 07054-3878

BELMONTEZ, DEBORAH LYNN GROVES, poet, editor; b. Newark, May 14, 1955; d. Howard and Edna (Loveday) Groves; m. Samuel Belmontez, Aug. 27, 1983; 1 adopted child, Maryann Rose. Grad., Heritage Bible Inst., 1982; leadership tng., WCTU, Evanston, Ill., 1982. English tchr. Heritage Acad., N.J., 1980-81; editor White Ribbon News, WCTU, N.J., 1980-82, 91—. Contbr. poems to a dozen poetry anthologies. Recipient WCTU Nat. Reading award, N.J., 1981, Writing Appreciation award, Am. Rescue Workers, 1982, Publisher's Choice award, Watermark Press, 1990. Mem. WCTU (editor White Ribbon News). Republican. Avocations: writing, traveling, collecting paintings and santini's statues. Mailing: 21 Almond Pass Dr Ocala FL 34472-8729

BELNAP, DAVID F. journalist; b. Ogden, Utah, July 27, 1922; s. Hyrum Adolphus and Lois Ellen B.; m. Barbara Virginia Carlberg, Jan. 17, 1947. Student, Weber Coll., Ogden, 1940. Asst. city editor Seattle Star, 1945-47; bur. chief UP Assns., Helena, Mont., 1947-50, Honolulu, 1950-52; regional exec. Pacific N.W., 1952-55, dir. Latin Am. services, 1955-67; Latin Am. corr. L.A. Times, 1967-80, asst. fgn. news editor, 1980-93. Recipient Overseas Press Club Am. award for best article on Latin Am., 1970, Maria Moors Cabot prize, 1973 Mem. Overseas Press Club Am., Greater Los Angeles Press Club, Audiophile Soc. Clubs: Am. of Buenos Aires; Phoenix of Lima (Peru). Home and Office: 1134 W Huntington Dr Arcadia CA 91007-6308

BELOFF, ZOE, artist, educator; Student, Edingburgh (Scotland) U.; MFA in Film, Columbia U. Tchr. digital media Pratt Inst., City Coll. N.Y. Prodr. (CD-ROM) Beyond (First prize QuickTime VR Competition), Where There There There Where, (film) Life Underwater, Lost. Found. Contemporary Arts grantee, 1997.

BELONGIA, CHRISTINE GIESE, education educator, director; b. Wis. d. Milton George Giese and Christine Sheldon; m. Douglas Wayne Belongia. AS in Tchr. Edn. and Liberal Arts, Genesee C.C., Batavia, N.Y., 1990; BS in Psychology, SUNY, Brockport, 1992; MA in Psychology, SUNY, Buffalo, 1997. Instr./adj. faculty psychology Genesee C.C., Batavia, 1998—2002, Genesee inst. coord., 2001—, instr./tchr. edn. coord., 2002—. Policy bd. mem. Genesee Region Tchr. Ctr., NY, 2002—; faculty advisor Genesee C.C. Edn. Club, Batavia, NY, 2002—. Contbr. articles to profl. ours. Paraprofessional program facilitator Genesee C.C., Batavia, 2002—03. Recipient Excellence in Tchg. award, Nat. Inst. for Staff and Orgnl. Devel. (NISOD), 2000. Mem.: APA, Americal Psychol. Soc. Avocations: gardening, music, reading. Home: 36 Webber Ave Oakfield NY 14125 Office: Genesee Cmty Coll One College Rd Batavia NY 14020 Personal E-mail: cbelongia@genesee.edu. E-mail: cbelongia@genesee.edu.

BELONICK, CYNTHIA ANN, psychiatric-mental health nurse; b. New Britain, Conn., Mar. 21, 1957; d. Steven and Anne (Kochanowski) B. Diploma, St. Francis Hosp. Sch. Nursing, Hartford, Conn., 1982; BA cum laude, U. Conn., 1979; MSN, Yale U., 1992. Cert. clin. specialist in adult psychiat. and mental health, advanced practice RN. Nurse educator The Inst. of Living, Hartford, Conn., 1993—. Contbr. Psychiat. Nursing Diagnoses: A Comprehensive Manual of Mental Health Care. Mem.: Conn. Nurses Assn., Delta Mu, Sigma Theta Tau.

BELOT, GORDON, philosophy; b. Ontario, Canada, July 12, 1968; arrived in USA, 1991; s. Donald Edward and Audrey Laura Belot. BS, U of Toronto, Toronto, Can., 1991, MS, 1993; PhD, U. Pitts., 1996. Post-doctoral fellowship, ctr. for philos. of sci. U of Pitts., Pitts., 1996—97; asst. prof., dept. of philos. Princeton U, Princeton, NJ, 1997—99; assoc. prof., dept. of philos. NYU, NY, NY. Contbr. articles to profl. jours. Fellow Social Sci. and Humanities Rsch., Pitts., Pa., 1996—97, fellowship Nat. Sci. Found., 2002—03. Office: NYU Dept of Philosophy 100 Washington Sq E New York NY 10003

BELOTSERKOVSKY, MAXIM, dancer; b. Kiev, Ukraine; m. Irina Dvorovenko. Student, Sch. of Dance, Kiev, Ukraine. Prin. dancer Nat. Opera of Bulgaria, 1990—91; leading soloist Nat. Opera of Ukraine, 1991—94; mem. Am. Ballet Theatre, 1994—95, soloist, 1995—2000, prin. dancer, 2000—; prin. guest artist Hawbury Ballet, 1993—99. Dancer (ballets) Cinderella, Giselle, The Legend of Love, The Nutcracker, The Sleeping Beauty, La Bayadère, Le Corsaire, Don Quixote, La Sylphide, Swan Lake, Coppélia, Am. Ballet Theatre, Le Corsaire, Jardin aux Lilas, The Snow Maiden, La Sylphide, Variations for Four, Bruch Violin Concerto No. 1, Diversion of Angels, Études, Sinfonietta, Spring and Fall, Anastasia, Ballet Imperial, The Leaves are Fading, Push Comes to Shove, created leading roles Baroque Game, The Brahms-Haydn Variations, The Elements, created featured role Known by Heart, Romeo and Juliet. Office: Am Ballet Theatre 890 Broadway New York NY 10003

BELOVARSKI, BORIS V. (MORRIS BOLIVAR), writer, producer; b. Sofia, Bulgaria, May 9, 1961; s. Vassil B. and Tania Dakova Belovarski; m. Radostina Kozarova Belovarski, Dec. 8, 1982 (dec. Dec. 30, 1985); children: Emanuela, Bojana; m. Viktoria D. Archimedes Belovarski, Aug. 20, 1990; children: Ioan, David, Joshua. PhD in Metaphysics and Biblical Lit., Am. Coll. Metaphys. Theology, Golden Valley, Minn., 1999—. Artist, asst. producer Nat. Radio TV Ctr., Sofia, Bulgaria, 1980-87; INDIE prodr. Inri Films, Sofia, Bulgaria, 1992-95, Inri Comm., Johannesburg, '1995-97; writer, scriptwriter pvt. practice, Albuquerque, 1997—. Author: The Deathmakers of Happiness, 1980, The Unearthly, 1982, Air Mail, 1983, Timeship, 1997—99; prodr.: New Life, 1989, I Was Psychic, I Saw Him, 1993, By Faith, 1994, He, 1996, If I Could Only, 1997. Avocations: digital video, animation, radio drama, music composing. Home: 6091 Jack Rabbit Rd Rio Rancho NM 87144 E-mail: boris@timeshipstudio.com.

BELSER, HOWARD MCGRIFF, JR., lawyer; b. Decatur, Ala., June 19, 1947; s. Howard McGriff and Geneva (Beard) B.; m. Suzanne F. Belser, Aug. 15, 1969; children: Howard M. III, Crawford Patterson. BA, Athens Coll., 1970; JD, Sanford U., 1973. Bar: Ala. 1983. Law clk. to Justice James W. Bloodworth Supreme Ct. Ala., Montgomery, 1973-74; atty. Hutson, Elrod, and Belser, Decatur, 1974-79, Hardwick, Knight & Belser, Decatur, 1979-81; pvt. practice Decatur, 1981—. Mem. Ala. State Bar Assn., Morgan County Bar Assn. Democrat. Methodist. Avocations: golf, duck hunting. Office: PO Box 2126 Decatur AL 35602-2126

BELSHAW, GEORGE PHELPS MELLICK, bishop; b. Plainfield, N.J., July 14, 1928; s. Harold and Edith (Mellick) B.; m. Elizabeth Wheeler, June 12, 1954; children: Richard, Elizabeth, George. BA, U. of South, 1951; STB, Gen. Theol. Sem., N.Y.C., 1954, STM, 1959, DD (hon.), 1975, U. of South, 1994, Hamilton Coll., 2003. Ordained to ministry, Episcopal Ch., consecrated bishop. Vicar St. Matthew's Ch., Waimanalo, Hawaii, 1954-57; fellow, tutor Gen. Theol. Sem., N.Y.C., 1957-59; rector Christ Ch., Dover, Del., 1959-65, St. George's Ch., Rumson, N.J., 1965-75; suffragan bishop Diocese of N.J., Trenton, 1975-83, bishop of N.J., 1983-94. Vis. lectr. Gen. Theol. Sem., 1969, 70; governing bd. Episc. Urban Caucus, 1982—, pres., 1986-89; mem. Commn. Peace of Episc. Ch., 1979-85, Econ. Justice Implementation Com., Episc. Ch., 1988-95. Editor: Lent with Evelyn Underhill, 1964, Lent with William Temple, 1966; contbr. articles to theol. jours. Trustee Gen. Theol. Sem., 1975—, chmn. 1992-2000, acting dean, pres., 1997-98; trustee Westminster Choir Coll., 1976-82. Mem. Am. Teilhard de Chardin Assn. (bd. dirs. 1976—), N.J. Coalition Religious Leaders (pres. 1986), Bd. Anglican Theol. Rev. (1993—), Coalition for Peace Action (chmn. 1999—). Episcopalian. Home: 15 Boudinot St Princeton NJ 08540-3007 E-mail: gpmbelshaw@aol.com.

BELSKY, MARTIN HENRY, law educator, lawyer; b. May 29, 1944; s. Abraham and Fannie (Turnoff) Belsky; m. Kathleen Waits, Mar. 9, 1985; children: Allen Frederick, Marcia Elizabeth. BA cum laude, Temple U., 1965; JD cum laude, Columbia U., 1968; cert. of study, Hague Acad. Internat. Law, The Netherlands, 1968; diploma in Criminology, Cambridge U., England, 1969. Bar: Pa. 1969, Fla. 1983, N.Y. 1987, U.S. Dist. Ct. (ea. dist.) Pa. 1969, U.S. Ct. Appeals (3d cir.) 1970, U.S. Supreme Ct. 1973. Chief asst. dist. atty. Phila. Dist. Atty.'s Office, Pa., 1969—74; assoc. Blank, Rome, Klaus & Comisky, Phila., 1975; chief counsel U.S. Ho. of Reps., Washington, 1975—78; asst. adminstr. NOAA, Washington, 1979—82; dir. ctr. for govtl. responsibility, assoc. prof. law U. Fla. Holand Law Ctr., 1982—86; dean Albany Law Sch., 1986—91, dean emeritus, prof. law, 1991—95; dean U. Tulsa Coll. of Law, Okla., 1995—. Chmn. Select Commn. on Disabilities, NY, Spl. Commn. on Fire Svcs.; bd. advs. Ctr. Oceans Law and Policy; mem. corrections task force Pa. Gov.'s Justice Commn., 1971—75; adv. task force on cts. Nat. Adv. Commn. on Criminal Justice Standards and Goals, 1972—74; mem. com. on proposed standard jury instrns. Pa. Supreme Ct., 1974—81; lectr. in law Temple U., 1971—75; mem. faculty Pa. Coll. Judiciary, 1975—77; adj. prof. law Georgetown U., 1977—81. Author (with Steven H. Goldblatt): (non-fiction) Analysis and Commentary to the Pennsylvania Crimes Codes, 1973; author: Handbook for Trial Judges, 1976, Law and Theology, 2003, (non-fiction) Rehnquist Court: A Retrospective, 2002; editor (in chief): (jour.) Jour. Transnat. Law, Columbia Law Sch., 1968; editor: The Rehnquist Court: Farewell to the Old Order in the Court, 2002; contbr. articles to legal pubs. Chmn. N.Y. region, mem. D.C. bd. Anti-Defamation League, 1977—78, chmn. N.Y. region, mem. nat. leadership coun.; exec. v.p. Urban League Northeastern N.Y. and Tulsa Urgan League; state chair exec. com. Okla. Anti-Defamation League; pres.-elect Tulsa (Okla.) Metro. Ministry; bd. dir. Coun. on Aging & Disability; pres. Jewish Fedn.; mem. exec. com. NCCJ, Okla. Ethics Commn. Fellow Intenat., Columbia U. Law Sch.; scholar Stone. Mem.: ABA (bd. young lawyers sect. exec. bd. 1973—75), Fund for Modern Cts. (bd. dirs.), Am. Law Inst., Am. Arbitration Assn. (referee N.Y. State Commn. on Jud. Discipline), Am. Soc. Internat. Law, Nat. Dist. Attys. Assn., Am. Judicature Soc., Fed. Bar Assn., Fla. Bar Assn., Pa. Bar Assn. (exec. com. young lawyers sect. 1973—75), Phila. Bar Assn. (chmn. young lawyers sect. 1974—75), Albany County Bar Assn., N.Y. State Bar Assn., United Jewish Fedn. Northeastern N.Y. (v.p., pres. elect), Cardoto Soc., B'nai

B'rith (v.p. lodge 1973—75), Sword Soc., Hudson-Mohawk Assn. Coll. and Univs. (v.p.), Temple U. Liberal Arts Alumni Assn. (v.p. 1971—75). Office: U Tulsa Coll Law 3120 E 4th Pl Tulsa OK 74104-2418

BELSOLE, ROBERT JOHN, surgeon; MD, N.Y. Med. Coll., 1969. Intern Cleve. Clinic Found., 1969-70; resident in gen. surgery NYU-Bellevue Hosp., N.Y.C., 1970-71, resident in orthopaedic surgery, 1971-74; postgrad. fellow U. Louisville Sch. Medicine, 1976-77; prof. orthopaedic surgery and plastic surgery/assoc. dean clin. affaris U. South Fla. Coll. Medicine, Tampa, dir. divsn. orthopaedic surgery, dir. hand surgery fellowship, assoc. dean clin. affairs. Mem. Am. Soc. for Surgery of the Hand, Am. Acad. Orthopaedic Surgeons, Am. Orthopaedic Assn. Office: U South Fla Coll Medicine Harborside Med Tower Ste 650 4 Columbia Dr Tampa FL 33606-3589 E-mail: rbelsole@hsc.usf.edu.

BELSOM, JOHN ANTON (JACK BELSOM), writer, researcher; b. Roaring Spring, Pa., June 21, 1933; s. John and Mary Ottilia (Schiele) B. BA, Tulane U., 1955; MA, La. State U., 1972. Personnel technician Dept. Civil Svc., New Orleans, 1957-70, personnel divsn. chief, 1970-76, dir. personnel, 1976-88. Archivist New Orleans Opera Assn., 1974—. Author: (monograph) Opera In New Orleans, 1993, Celebrating 200 Years of Opera in New Orleans, 1998; contbr. articles to publs. Pres. Lower Quarter Crime Watch Assn., New Orleans, 1981-82; pres. Cath. Bookstore Found., New Orleans, 1984-85, recording sec., 1995—; recording sec. Vieux Carré Property Owners Assn., New Orleans, 1989-91. With U.S. Army, 1955-57. Mem. Internat. Personnel Mgmt. Assn. (L.A. chpt., chpt. treas. 1977—), Geneal. Rsch. Soc. New Orleans (pres. 1984-1986, 2002-2004). Democrat. Roman Catholic. Avocations: genealogy, opera, traveling, music, writing. Home: 721 Barracks St New Orleans LA 70116-2516

BELSON, ABBY AVIN, writer; b. Bklyn., Apr. 1, 1935; d. Raphael and Molly Avin; m. Joel Jay Belson, June 17, 1956; children: Gabrielle Belson Rattner, Nicole Belson Goluboff. BA, Barnard Coll., N.Y.C., 1956; MA, Columbia U., N.Y.C., 1959. Tchr. N.Y.C. Sch. Sys., 1956—59; adj. lectr. Queens Coll., CUNY, 1961—64; freelance writer, 1970—83; editor med. pubs. Mount Sinai Med. Ctr., N.Y.C., 1983—94; freelance writer, 1994—. Bd. dirs. Conservative Synagogue of Jamaica Estates, Jamaica, NY, 1993—96. Recipient MacEachern award, Pub. Rels. Soc. Am., 1989, Med. Journalism award 1st prize, Sandoz Pharms., 1989, Med. Journalism award, 1991. Mem.: Nat. Assn. Sci. Writers. Avocations: gardening, swimming.

BELSON, JAMES ANTHONY, judge; b. Milw., Sept. 23, 1931; s. Walter W. and Margaret (Taugher) B.; m. Rosemary P. Greenslade, Jan. 11, 1958; children: Anthony James, Marie Taylor, Elizabeth Ann, Stephen Griffin. AB cum laude, Georgetown U., 1953, JD, 1956, LLM, 1962. Bar: D.C. 1956, Md. 1962. Law clk. U.S. Ct. Appeals (D.C. cir.), 1956-57; assoc. Hogan & Hartson, Washington, 1960-67, ptnr., 1967-68; trial judge D.C. Superior Ct., 1968-81, presiding judge civil divsn., 1978-81; assoc. judge D.C. Ct. Appeals, Washington, 1981-91, sr. judge, 1991—. Faculty Nat. Jud. Coll., 1973-80; bd. dirs. Coun. for Ct. Excellence, 1981—; bencher Am. Inn of Ct. VI, 1983-90. Bd. editors Georgetown Law Jour., 1955-56. Bd. dirs. Project SHARE D.C., Inc., 1992—, chmn., 1997-99; bd. dirs. Cath. Legal Immigration Network, 1994-98. With JAGC, U.S. Army, 1957-60. Mem. ABA, Bar Assn. of D.C. (bd. dirs. 1966-67, chmn. jr. bar 1965-66), Am. Judicature Soc. (bd. dirs. 1980-85), Am. Bar Found., John Carroll Soc. (bd. govs. 1978-85, 1st v.p. 1989-91), Sovereign Mil. Order of Malta Fed. Assn. (pres. 1991-94, bd. dirs. 1988-95, 97—, chmn. task force on Cuba 1994-2000). Home: 12 W Severn Ridge Rd Annapolis MD 21401-5844 Office: DC Ct Appeals 500 Indiana Ave NW Washington DC 20001-2131 E-mail: jbelson@dcca.state.dc.us.

BELSON, PATRICIA A. artist; b. San Francisco, Apr. 5, 1932; d. Joseph Patrick and Norma Stephanie (Bole) Gleeson; m. Dogan E. Belson, Sept. 2, 1961 (dec. July 1991); children: Linda, Susan. Office mgr. Psychiat. Group Offices, Seattle, 1958-63; pub. rels., brochure designer, English sec. Istanbul Hilton Hotel, Turkey, 1963-64; office mgr. Psychiat. Outpatient Facility, San Francisco, 1973-76; owner Wadyacallit, Sequim, Wash., 1980-85; corp. ptnr., mktg. dir. Fantasy Prodns., Inc., Seattle, 1985-90; self employed fine artist Seattle, Sequim, 1990—. Vol. treas. Blue Whole Gallery, Sequim, 1997—98; charter mem. Artist's Coop., 1997—99, 2001—02; publicity chmn. Sequim Arts, 2003; program chmn. Clallam Art League, 2003; art judge Sequim Arts Scholarships, 2001—02; art judge Juan de Fuca Festival of Arts Greywolf Sch., 2002—03. Solo exhbns. include Istanbul (Turkey) Intercontinental Hotel, 1978, Galerie du Soleil, Sequim, 1996, Gallery at the Fifth, Sequim, 2000, Mus. and Arts Ctr., Sequim, 2001-2002; exhbns. include Bechtel Corp., 1976 (3d place award), A Contemporary Theater Gallery, Seattle, 1992, Reigning Visions Artwork Gallery, Sequim, The Acorn Gallery, Sequim, 2001-, Port Angeles Fine Arts Ctr.'s Strait Art 2001: Silver Waters Show, 2001-2002, Juan de Fuca Festival of Arts, 1994, (hon. mention), Clallam Art League, Port Angeles, 1994 (2d place watercolor), 95, Northwest Watercolor Soc., 1994 (hon. mention), Juan de Fuca Festival Arts, 1995 (1st place watercolor), Clallam Art League Sr. Show, 1995 (Best of Show award), 98 (Best Still life winner), 1999 (Best Seascape), Sequim Arts Mem. Show, 1997 (1st place mems. choice, 2d place pub. choice), Blue Whole Gallery, Sequim, 1997-99, Olympic Nat. Resource Ctr. U. Washington, Forks, 1997-2000, Clallam Art League Gallery, 1999-2001, Frye Art Museum, Seattle, 2000, Port Angeles Fine Arts Ctr., 2001-02; also pvt. galleries, Calif., Hawaii, Oreg. and Washington, others. Vol. tourist info. ctr. Sequim/Dungeness Valley C. of C., 1994-96; pub. rels. vol. Sequim Arts, 1996-97; vol. tutor Seattle Sch. Dist., 1991-92; vol. Sequim Arts Treas., 1997-99. Recipient Best of Show award, Clallam Art League Sr. Show, 1995, Best Landscape award, 2001, Best Seascape award, 1999, 2d pl. watercolor, 2002, 1st Pl. award, Sequim Arts Mem. Show, 1995, Daler-Rowney Mdse award, N.W. Watercolor Soc., 2000, hon. mention watercolor, Sequim Arts Ann. Juried Show, 2002. Avocations: sailing, canoeing, tennis, skiing, hiking. Home: 101 Wilcox Ln Sequim WA 98382-8904 E-mail: pen4pat2@hotmail.com.

BELTH, JOSEPH MORTON, retired business educator; b. Syracuse, N.Y., Oct. 22, 1929; s. Irving and Helen Rose (Bright) B.; m. Marjorie Helen Lavine, June 12, 1955; children: Ann Irene, Michael Irving, Jeffrey Edward. AAS., Cayuga Community Coll., 1958; BS summa cum laude, Syracuse U., 1958; PhD, U. Pa., 1961. C.L.U., C.P.C.U. Asst. purchasing agt. Onondaga Supply Co., Syracuse, N.Y., 1947-53; agt. Continental Am. Life Ins. Co., Syracuse, 1953-58; asst. dir. continuing edn. Am. Soc. Chartered Life Underwriters, Bryn Mawr, Pa., 1961-62; asst. prof. Ind. U., Bloomington, 1962-65, assoc. prof., 1965-68, prof., 1968-93, prof. emeritus, 1993—. Author: Participating Life Insurance Sold by Stock Companies, 1965, The Retail Price Structure in American Life Insurance, 1966; Life Insurance: a Consumer's Handbook, 1973, 2d edit., 1985, The A.L. Williams Replacement Empire, 1987, 2d edit., 1989, Viatical Transactions, 2000; editor newsletter The Ins. Forum, 1974— (George Polk award 1990). Mem. Am. Risk and Ins. Assn. (pres. 1973-74, Elizur Wright award, 1966, Jour. Risk and Ins. awards 1962,64,67,71,79), Huebner Gold medal, 1999, AAUP, Beta Gamma Sigma, Phi Kappa Phi. Democrat. Jewish. Home: 5125 N Starnes Rd Bloomington IN 47404-9358

BELTHOFF, RICHARD CHARLES, JR., lawyer; b. Denville, N.J., Jan. 28, 1958; s. Richard Charles and Barbara Ann (Erdmann) B.; m. Vicki Shannon Alligood, June 13, 1981; children: Ashley Nicole, Jason Michael. BSP, East Carolina U., 1980; JD, U. N.C., 1984. Bar: N.C. 1984, U.S. Dist. Ct. (we. dist.) N.C. 1984, U.S. Ct. Appeals (4th cir.) 1987. Assoc. Grier & Grier, Charlotte, N.C., 1984-89; ptnr. Grier Belthoff & Furr PA, Charlotte, N.C., 1989-98; chief ops. counsel, dir. real estate, asst. sec. Compass Group USA, Inc., Charlotte, NC, 1998—2002; v.p., asst. gen. counsel Wachovia Corp., Charlotte, 2002—. Contbr. articles to legal jours. Mem. N.C. State Bar, Mecklenburg County Bar Assn. Home: 426 Shasta Ln Charlotte NC 28211-4054 Office: Wachovia Corp Legal Div 310 S College St NC0630 Charlotte NC 28288-0630 *Notable cases include: Raritan River Steel Co. vs. Cherry, Bekaert & Holland, 1986, the first case in N.C. determining accountant's liability for negligently prepared audits.*

BELTON, JOHN THOMAS, lawyer; b. Yonkers, N.Y., Feb. 24, 1947; s. Harry James and Anne Marie (Kupko) B.; m. Linda Susanne Cheugh, jan. 6, 1973; 1 child, Joseph Timothy. BA, Ohio State U., 1972; postgrad. in bus. adminstrn., Xavier U., 1972-73; JD, Ohio No. U., 1976. Bar: Ohio 1977, U.S. Ct. of Claims. Sole practice, Columbus, Ohio, 1976-83; ptnr. Belton & Marlin, and predecessor firm Belton, Golowin & Cheugh, Columbus, 1983—; arbitrator Franklin County Ct. Common Pleas, 1983—; dir. Weeks-Finneran Inc. Rep. precinct chmn., 1983. V.p. Far Northwest Coalition, 1984. Mem. ch. coun. St. Peter's Parish, 1984—, Dublin Pub. Bd. Zoning Appeals, 1991—; pres. Dublin Youth Athletics, 1985—. With USAF, 1968-71. Mem. ABA, ATLA, Columbus Bar Assn. (com. chmn. 1976—), U.S. Dist. Ct. Fed. Bar, U.S. Supreme Ct. Bar, Ohio Bar Assn. (bd. govs. 1993—), Dublin Jr. C. of C., The Pres. Club. of Ohio State U., Ohio State Alumni, Republican Glee, Columbus Shamrock, K.C., Order of Barristers, Omicron Delta Kappa, Phi Alpha Delta (justice 1975). Roman Catholic. Avocations: reading, chess, golfing, racquetball, recreational activities. Home: 8649 Dunsinane Dr Dublin OH 43017-8757 Office: Belton & Marlin 2066 Henderson Rd Columbus OH 43220-2452 E-mail: lsbjtb@cs.com.

BELTON, ROBERT, law educator; b. 1935; BA, U. Conn., 1961; JD, Boston U., 1965. Bar: N.Y. 1966, N.C. 1970, Tenn. 1980. Asst. counsel legal def. fund NAACP, N.Y.C., 1966-70; ptnr. Chambers, Stein, Ferguson & Lanning, Charlotte, N.C., 1970-75; lectr., dir. fair employment clinic Vanderbilt U., Nashville, 1975-77, assoc. prof., 1977-82, prof., 1982—. Vis. prof. Harvard U. Law Sch., Cambridge, Mass., 1986-87, U. No. Car., 1990-91, Charles Hamilton Houston Disting. vis. prof. N.C. Ctrl. Law Sch., 1997. Author: Remedies in Employment Discrimination Law, 1992; co-author Casebook on Employment Discrimination Law, 1999; contbr. articles to profl. jours. Fellow Coll. Labor and Employment Lawyers, Inc.; mem. ABA, Nat. Bar Assn., Am. Assn. Law Schs. (exec. com. 1991-94), Am. Law Inst., Nat. Employment Lawyers' Assn. (exec. bd. 1996—). Office: Vanderbilt U Sch Law 131- 21st Ave S Nashville TN 37203-1181

BELTRAMO, MICHAEL NORMAN, management consultant; b. L.A., Feb. 9, 1942; s. Blase and Violette (Murphy) B.; m. Susan Annette Lawton, Dec. 24, 1969 (div. 1980); m. Jane Sinden Spiegel, Apr. 21, 1984; children: Helen Weedon, Anna Sinden, Emily Murphy. AB, UCLA, 1964; MPA, U. So. Calif., 1967; PhD, Rand Grad. Inst., Santa Monica, Calif., 1983. Cert. cost estimator/analyst. Mem. tech. staff The RAND Corp., Santa Monica, 1969-75; dep. mgr. Sci. Applications Internat. Corp., L.A., 1975-80; pres. Beltramo and Assocs., L.A., 1980—. Author: LA County Economic Adjustment Strategy for Defense Reduction; contbr. articles to profl. publs. Named Ky. Col. Commonwealth of Ky., 1973. Mem. Soc. Cost Estimating and Analysis (cert., bd. dirs. 1987-88). Republican. Methodist. Avocations: fly fishing, surfing. Home and Office: 13039 Sky Valley Rd Los Angeles CA 90049-1037

BELTRAN, ANTHONY NATALICIO, non-commissioned officer, deacon; b. Flagstaff, Ariz., Aug. 17, 1938; s. Natalicio Torres and Mary Mercedes (Sandoval) B.; m. Patricia Emily Cañez, Nov. 18, 1962; children: Geralyn P., Bernadette M., Albert A., Catherine M., Elizabeth R., Michael J., Theresa R., Christopher M. AA, Phoenix Jr. Coll., 1971, C.C. of Air Force, 1992; grad., Def. Equal Oppty. Mgmt. Inst., 1991. Gen. clk. Blue Cross Blue Shield, Phoenix, 1958-61; enlisted Air N.G., advanced through ranks to chief master sgt.; unit clk. Ariz. Air N.G., Phoenix, 1961, personnel technician, 1962-65, adminstrv. supr., 1965-81, support services supr., 1981-88, equal employment specialist, 1988-95, state sr. enlisted advisor, 1995-98, ret., 1998. With St. Matthew Cath. Ch., Phoenix. Bd. dirs. Friendly House, Phoenix, 1982-86, mem. aux. bd., 1989-97; mem. Alma de la Gente, Phoenix, 1982-92, Chiefs Police Cmty. Adv. Group, Phoenix, 1984-85, Mayor's Task Force on Juvenile Crime, Phoenix, 1979-81; pres. IMAGE de Phoenix, 1985-87. Staff sgt. USAF, 1961-62. Recipient Community Service award Phoenix C. of C., 1982. Mem.: Ariz. ANG Copperhead Retiree Assn. (v.p. 2000—02, pres. 2002—), Non-Commd. Officers Acad. Grad. Assn. (chpt. 46 v.p. 1992—94), Enlisted Assn. N.G. Ariz. (pres. Copperhead chpt. 1987—90), Ariz. Hispanic Employment Program Mgrs. (treas. 1980—81, v.p. 1981—82, pres. 1982—84, named Outstanding Mem. of Yr. 1981, 1983), Am. GI Forum (sec. Sylvestre Herrera chpt. 1995—96, comdr. 1996—, state comdr. 2000—), Fed. Exec. Assn. (sec.-treas. Phoenix chpt. 1985—86, 1st v.p. 1987, pres. 1987—88, Cmty. Svc. award 1986). Democrat. Avocations: permanent Deacon Roman Cath. Diocese assigned to ministry for the Spanish speaking. Home: 4109 W Monte Vista Rd Phoenix AZ 85009-2005 also: St Matthew Cath Ch 320 N 20th Dr Phoenix AZ 85009-3819

BELTRAN, EUSEBIUS JOSEPH, archbishop; b. Ashley, Pa., Aug. 31, 1934; s. Joseph C. and Helen Rita (Kozlowski) Beltran. Grad., St. Charles Sem., Overbrook, Pa. Ordained priest Roman Cath. Ch., 1960. Consecrated bishop, 1978; pastor various chs., Atlanta and Decatur, Ga., 1960; notary, then vice officialis Atlanta Diocesan Tribunal, 1960—62; vice chancellor Archdiocese Atlanta, 1962; officialis Archdiocesan Tribunal, 1963—74; pastor various chs., Atlanta and Rome, Ga., 1963—66; vicar gen. Archdiocese of Atlanta, 1971—78; pastor St. Anthony's Ch., Atlanta, 1972—78; bishop of Tulsa, 1978—92; archbishop of Oklahoma City Archdiocese of Okla., 1992—. Liturgy com. Nat. Conf. Cath. Bishops; com. mem. Am. Coll., Louvain, Belgium; bd. regents Conception Sem.; bd. dirs. St. Gregory's Coll., Shawnee, Okla. Mem.: NCCJ, Equestrian Order Holy Sepulchre, K.C. Office: Archdiocese of Oklahoma City 7501 NW Espressway Oklahoma City OK 73132-2180*

BELTZ, CHARLES ROBERT, retired engineering executive; b. Pitts., Feb. 23, 1913; s. Charles Fred and Ester (Johnston) B.; m. Amy Margaret Ferguson, Oct. 23, 1935; children: Charles R., A.M. Bonnie Beltz Hatch, Homer F., William T., Carol E. Beltz Marks, M. Joy Beltz O'Keefe. Student, Greenbrier Mil. Sch., 1930-33; MSE, Cornell U., 1934; MS in Aero. Engring., U. Pitts., 1937. Engr. Crane Co., 1937-39; design engr. Stout Skycraft Corp., 1939-43; project engr. Cycle-Weld Labs., 1943-44; project engr., mgr. Fairchild E&A Corp., Roosevelt Field, 1944-46; corp. engr. Chrysler Corp., 1946-47; pres. Charles R. Beltz & Co., Detroit, 1947-85, Beltz Engring., 1950-2001, Beltemp, Inc., 1969-81. Author: Ice Skating, Skating Weather or Not, ABC's Air-conditioning, Roatable Aircraft; designer in field. Mem. Nat. Aero. Assn. (past pres.), Air Conditioning Inst. (past pres.), Inst. Aero. Scis. (vice chmn.), ASHRAE (contbg. author), Engring. Soc. Detroit, Air Force Assn., Grosse Pointe Hist. Soc., English Speaking Union, Air Force Found., Yankee Air Force, Toledo Zool. Soc., Am. Philatelic Soc., Aero Club (bd. dirs.), Econ. Club, Curling Club (Detroit), Grosse Pointe Yacht Club, Lost Lake Woods Club. Address: 500 Lakeland St Grosse Pointe MI 48230-1655

BELTZ, HOMER FERGUSON, radiologist, healthcare executive; b. Detroit, Apr. 21, 1944; s. Charles R. and Amy F. Beltz; m. Linda P. Beltz; children: Christine, M. Scott, Eric, Nicolle. BS, Alma (Mich.) Coll., 1966; MD, U. Mich., 1970. Pres., CEO N.W. Radiology Network, Mpls., 1997—; chmn. radiology St. Vincent Hosp. and Healthcare, Indpls., 1997—; intern St. Joseph Hosp., Ann Arbor, Mich., 1970—71; resident Ind. U. Med. Ctr., 1971—72, 1974—76. CMO bd. St. Vincent Hosp. and Health Care. Lt. comdr. USN, 1972-74. Home: 1510 Prestwick Cir Carmel IN 46032-9551 Office: NW Radiology Network 5756 W 71st St Indianapolis IN 46278-1750

BELTZ, WILLIAM ALBERT, publisher; b. Meriden, Conn., Aug. 24, 1929; s. Albert Henry and Marie Adelade (Heusel) B.; m. Beverly Sawyer, May 31, 1958; children— John, Jane, Kurt, Adam. AB, Tufts U., 1951. With Bur. Nat. Affairs, Inc., Washington, 1956—; assoc. editor, then exec. editor Nat. Affairs, Inc., 1965-79; pres., editor in chief Bur. Nat. Affairs, Inc., 1979-96, chief exec. officer, 1980-96; chmn. Nat. Affairs, Inc., 1991—. Bd. dirs. McArdle Printing Co., Silver Spring, Md. Trustee The Washington Opera Co., 1989-91, The Shakespeare Theater, 1991-99; Washington trustee Fed. City Coun., 1992—. Mem.: Wash. Theater Awards Soc. (dir. 1986—, pres. 1988—98), Info. Industry Assn. (dir.), The White House Corrs. Assn., Nat. Press (Washington). Democrat. Episcopalian. Office: Bur Nat Affairs Inc 1231 25th St NW Washington DC 20037-1197 E-mail: bbeltz@bna.com.

BELTZNER, GAIL ANN, music educator; b. Palmerton, Pa., July 20, 1950; d. Conon Nelson and Lorraine Ann (Carey) Beltzner. BS in Music Edn. summa cum laude, West Chester State U., 1972; postgrad., Kean State Coll., 1972, Temple U., 1972, Westminster Choir Coll., 1972, Lehigh U., 1972. Tchr. music Drexel Hill Jr. H.S., 1972-73; music specialist Allentown (Pa.) Sch. Dist., 1973—; tchr. Corps Sch. and Cmty. Devel. Lab., 1978-80, Corps Cmty. Resource Festival, 1979-81, Corps Cultural Fair, 1980, 81. Mem. bd. assocs. Lehigh Valley Hosp. and Health Network. Mem. Mus. Fine Arts, Boston, aux. Allentown Art Mus., aux. Allentown Hosp.; mem. woman's com. Allentown Symphony, The Lyric Soc. of the Allentown Orch.; mem. Allentown 2nd and 9th Civilian Police Acads.; bd. dirs. Allentown Area Ecumenical Food Bank, Allentown Arts Commn; mem. Growing with Sci. partnership—Air Products and Chems., Inc. and Allentown Sch. Dist., Good Shepherd Home Aux.; bd. assoc. Lehigh Valley Hosp. and Health Network. Decorated Dame Comdr., Ordre Souverain et Militaire de la Milice du St. Sepulcre; recipient Cert. of Appreciation, Lehigh Valley Sertoma Club; Excellence in the Classroom grantee Rider-Pool Found., 1988, 91-92. Mem. AAUW, NAFE, ASCD, Am. String Tchrs. Assn., Am. Viola Soc., Internat. Reading Assn., Internat. Platform Assn., Allentown Edn. Assn., Music Educators Nat. Conf., Pa. Music Educators Assn., Am. Orff-Schulwerk Assn., Orgn. Am. Kodaly Educators, Am. Recorder Soc., Phila. Area Orff-Schulwerk Assn., Soc. Gen. Music, Am. Assn. Music Therapy, Internat. Soc. Music Edn., Internat. Tech. Edn. Assn., Assn. for Tech. in Music Instrn., Civil War Roundtable Ea. Pa., Choristers Guild, Lenni Lenape Hist. Soc., Lehigh Valley Arts Coun., Allentown Symphony Assn., Midi Users Group, Pa.-Del. String Tchrs. Assn., Nat. Sch. Orch. Assn., Lehigh County Hist. Soc., Confedn. Chivalry (life mem. of merit, grand coun.), Maison Internat. des Intellectuels Akademie, Order White Cross Internat. (apptd. dist. comdr. for Pa./U.S.A. dist., nobless of humanity), Airedale Terrier Club of Greater Phila., Kappa Delta Pi, Phi Delta Kappa, Alpha Lambda. Republican. Lutheran. Home: PO Box 4427 Allentown PA 18105-4427

BELUSHI, JAMES A. actor; b. Chgo., June 15, 1954; s. Adam and Agnes Belushi; children: Robert, Jamison. Student, Coll. DuPage; grad., So. Ill. U. Mem., musician James Belushi & The Sacred Hearts, Blues Brothers Band. Mem. Second City comedy troupe, 1977-78, 80. Actor: (plays) Under Milkwood, Born Yesterday, Dubwaiter, Sexual Perversity in Chicago, 1979, Baal in the Twenty-first Century, 1980, Pirates of Penzance, 1982, True West, 1983, Moon Over Miami, 1987; (films) About Last Night, 1986—, Little Shop of Horrors, 1986—, K-9, 1989—, Taking Care of Business, 1990—, Mr. Destiny, 1990—, Only the Lonely, 1991, Curly Sue, 1991, Diary of a Hitman, 1991, Once Upon a Crime, 1992, Trace of Red, 1992, Separate Lives, 1995—, Race the Sun, 1996—, Gang Related, 1997—, Angel's Dance, 1999—, The Florentine, 1999—, Made Men, 1999, K-911, 1999, Return to Me, 2000; (TV series) According to Jim, 2001—; actor (voice) (films) Nuttiest Nutcracker, 1999, Snow Dogs, 2002; voice overs : (TV series) Bad Baby; Mighty Duck's Duckman; Ahh, Monsters; Animaniacs; Superman; Pinky and the Brain; 3 Little Pigs; Real Monsters; Looie and Louie; Cow & Chicken; voiceovers (TV series) Legend of the Lost Tribe, 2002; voice overs : (TV series) Life with Louie; (films) The Pebble and the Penguin, 1995; Dog's Best Friend, 1997; Babes In Toyland, 1997; Hey Arnold!, 1997; Gargoyles; Felix the Cat; Timon and Pumbaa; The Tick; Bruno the Kid; Hercules; Greedy Show; voiceover (films) Pinocchio, 2002; co-author: (films) Number One With a Bullett; writer: TV series Saturday Night Live, 1983—85, TV films Birthday Boy, 1986, films Greedy Show, 2001. Mem. Actors Equity Assn., Screen Actors Guild, AFTRA, Writers Guild Am., Acad. Motion Picture Arts and Scis., Acad. TV Arts and Scis. Office: care ICM 8942 Wilshire Blvd Beverly Hills CA 90211-1934

BELYAKOV, IGOR M. immunologist, researcher; b. Tallinn, Russia, July 13, 1960;, U.S.1993; s. Mikhail V. Belyakov and Maria N. Belyakova; m. Irina M. Baulina-Belyakov, July 12, 1998; children: Anastasia, Catherine. MD with honors, North-Osetian State Med. Inst., Russia, 1983; PhD in Immunology, Chelyabinsk State Med. Inst., Russia, 1986; ScD in Immunology and Medicine, Inst. Immunology of Moscow, 1993. FellowChelyabinsk Med. Inst., 1983—86; assoc. prof. North Osetian Med. Inst., Vladikavkaz, 1986—90; rsch. scientist Inst. Immunology, Moscow, 1990—93; postdoctoral fellow dept. microbiology U. Ala., Birmingham, 1993—95; postdoctoral fellow molecular immunogenetics and vaccine sect. Nat. Cancer Inst.-NIH, Bethesda, Md., 1996—2001, sr. staff scientist, 2001—. Contbr. Recipient Fellowship Advancement award, NIH, 2000, Tech. Trainer award, 2001, Immunology Interest Group award, 2000, Honor award, USSR Soc. Radiobiology, 1992. Mem.: Am. Assn. Immunologists. Achievements include research in cytotoxic T lymphocytes, viral immunology, mucosal immunity and mucosal vaccines, especially for HIV, smallpox and other viral infection. Home: 10230 Wild Apple Cir Gaithersburg MD 20886 Office: NIH Metabolism Br Bethesda MD 20892-0001

BELYEA, KARLENE BOYES, professional association executive; b. Lansing, Mich., Jan. 4, 1962; d. Rodney L. Boyes and Sharon Lynn Britton; m. Allen Ross Belyea, Sept. 10, 1988; children: Tyler Ross, Kelsey Lynn Belyea. BA in Telecomm., Mich. State U., 1984; MBA in Fin., U. Mich., 1988. Mktg. program dir. Am. Collegiate Mktg., Lansing, Mich., 1984-86; fin. analyst BOC Powertrain-GM, Brighton, Mich., 1987; COO Mich. Nurses Assn., Okemos, Mich., 1988—. Mem. Am. Soc. Assn. Execs. Avocations: musician, stained glass making, roller blading. Office: Mich Nurses Assn 2310 Jolly Oak Rd Okemos MI 48864-3546

BELYN, DAVID NEVES, journalist, editor; b. St. Christianstad, Virgin Islands, Apr. 7, 1971; s. Stephen Newton and Virgina Anne (Reynolds) B. Student, U. Iowa, 1989-94, U. San Francisco, 1998—. Assignment editor KION-KCBA, Salinas, Calif., 1996-98, Hearst-Argyle KSBW, Salinas, 1998-99, Hearst-Argyle KCRA, Sacramento, 1999—. Author: The Missing Man, 1995, Grey Matters, 1999. Office: Hearst-Argyle KCRA 3 Television Cir Sacramento CA 95814-0750 E-mail: dbelyn@hearst.com.

BELYTSCHKO, TED, civil and mechanical engineering educator; b. Proskurov, Ukraine, Jan. 13, 1943; came to U.S., 1950; s. Stephan and Maria (Harpinak) B.; m. Gail Eisenhart, Aug. 1967; children: Peter, Nicole, Justine. BS in Engring. Sci., Ill. Inst. Tech., 1965, PhD in Mechanics, 1968; PhD (hon.), U. Liege, 1997. Asst. prof. structural mechanics U. Ill., Chgo., 1968-73, assoc. prof., 1973-76, prof., 1976-77; Walter P. Murphy prof. civil and mech. engring. Northwestern U., Evanston, Ill., 1977—, chair mech. engring., 1998—2002. Editor (assoc.): (journals) Computer Methods in Applied Mech. and Engring., 1977—, Jour. Applied Mechanics, 1979—85; editor: Nuclear Engring. and Design, 1980—88, Engring. with Computers, 1984—98, Internat. Jour. Numerical Methods in Engring., 1998—. NDEA fellow, 1965-68; recipient Thomas Jaeger prize Internat. Assn. Structural Mechanics in Reactor Tech., 1983, Japanese Soc. Mech. Engrs. Computational Mechanics award, 1993, Gold medal Internat. Conf. on Computational Engring. and Scis., 1996, Computational Mechanics award Internat. Assn. for Computational Mechanics, 1998, Gauss-Newton medal, 2002. Fellow: ASME (chmn. applied mechanics divsn. 1991, Pi Tau Sigma Gold medal 1975, Timoshenko medal 2001), Am. Acad. Arts and Scis.; mem.: NAE, ASCE (chmn. engring. mechanics divsn. 1982, Walter Huber Rsch. prize 1977, Structural Dynamics and Materials award 1990, Theodore von Karman medal 1999), Shock and Vibration Inst. (Baron medal 1999), U.S. Assn. for Computational Mechanics (pres. 1992—94, von Neumann medal 2001, Computational Structural Mechanics award 1997). Office: Northwestern Univ Mech Engring Dept 2145 Sheridan Rd Evanston IL 60208-3111 E-mail: t_belytschko@northwestern.edu.

BELZ, JULIE ANNE, language educator; b. Ill. BS, U. of Ill., 1986; MA, U. of Calif., 1990, PhD, 1997. English instr. Fulbright Tchg. Fellowship, Vienna, 1987—88; german instr. U. of Calif., Berkeley, 1988—93; rschr. Berkeley (Calif.) Lang. Ctr., 1996—97; dir. german lang. program U. of Ariz., Tucson, 1997—98; asst. prof. of applied linguistics and german Pa. State U., U. Pk., Pa., 1998—. Rschr. Ctr. for Lang. Acquisition, U. Pk., 2000—; rschr. Ctr. for Advanced Lang. Proficiency Edn. and Rsch. Pa. State U., 2002—. Guest editor: Lang. Learning and Tech.: Telecollaboration, 2003; author: Foreign Language Play and the Discursive Construction of Identity; contbr. articles to profl. jours.; editor volumes. Fellow Fgn. Lang. and Area Studies fellowship, U.S. Dept. of Edn., 1991—92, U. of Calif. at Berkeley, 1996, Instrnl. Devel. fellowship, Berkeley (Calif.) Lang. Ctr., U. of Calif., 1996—97; grantee Internat. Studies and Rsch. grant, U.S. Dept. of Edn., 2000—03, Nat. Fgn. Lang. Rsch. Ctr. grant, 2002—; scholar, The Rotary Found. Internat., 1986—87, Fulbright Found., 1987—88, Deutscher Akademischer Austauschdienst, 1995. Mem.: MLA (exec. com. of the divsn. on applied linguistics 2001—), Am. Assn. for Applied Linguistics, Am. Assn. of Tchrs. of German, Phi Beta Kappa. Office: Penn State University 311 Burrowes Building University Park PA 16802 E-mail: jab63@psu.edu.

BELZER, ELLEN J. editor, negotiations and communications consultant; b. Kansas City, Mo., May 22, 1951; d. Meyer Simmon and Fay (Weinstein) B. Student, U. Okla., 1969-70, U. Ibero-Americana, Mexico City, 1971; BA, Northwestern U., 1973; MPA, U. Mo., Kansas City, 1976. Rsch. asst. dept. polit. sci. Northwestern U., Evanston, Ill., 1970-73; adminstrv. asst. Ctrs. for Regional Progress Midwest Rsch. Inst., Kansas City, 1974; various positions to dir. socioecons. div. Am. Acad. Family Physicians, Kansas City, 1974-86; pres. Belzer Seminars and Cons., Kansas City, 1986—, Healthcare Collaborator, Inc., Kansas City, 2000—. Instr. communication Avila Coll., Kansas City, 1987-92,

dept. continuing edn. U. Kans., Lawrence, 1989-92; spkr. on negotiation strategies, conflict resolution techniques, communication skills, 1986—; mediator for hosps., physician groups, state health depts., cmty. health ctrs., others. Contbr. articles to profl. publs., also monographs. Campaign vol. for local candidate, Kansas City, 1970, 82, 99. Democrat. Home and Office: 21 W Bannister Rd Kansas City MO 64114-4009

BELZUNG, PAUL EDWARD, engineering executive; b. San Antonio, Oct. 27, 1934; s. Oscar Albert and Melinda Wilimina (Keller) B.; m. Dylece LaNore Sherbondy, Sept. 19, 1952 (div. Sept. 1969); children: Brenda Belzung Holder, Gary Wayne Belzung, Wanda Belzung Sheetz; m. Teresa Galvan, Aug. 26, 1983; stepchildren: DiAnna VanNess Chavez, Dominic A. VanNess, Jaki VanNess Frost. Student, U. Tex., San Antonio Coll. Various positions Dept. Def.-USAF, Kelly AFB, Tex., 1952-90; gen. mgr. GM15 San Antonio Air Logistics Ctr., Kelly AFB, Tex., 1990; ret., gen. mgr. Dept. Def.; officer, pres. Kelly Mgmt. Assoc., San Antonio, 1975-76; v.p. Sunset Resources, Inc., San Antonio, 1992-94; v.p. govt. svcs. Karta Tech. Inc., San Antonio, 1995, v.p., 1996-97; assoc. Pinnacle Solutions, Inc., San Antonio, 1997-99; v.p. Classic Choice, Inc., New Braunfels, Tex., 2001—. Dir. Medina Lake Betterment Assn., Lakehills, Tex., 1988-91, pres., 1991-93; dir. Lakewood Owners Assn., v.p., 1994-96, pres., 1997-98; cert. lay spkr., dist. coord. Meth. Ch. Kerrville dist., Tex., 1992-2000. Mem. Soc. Logistics Engrs. (committeeperson 1992-94), Masons (jr./sr. warden San Antonio lodge 1964-65), Shriners. Republican. Avocations: fishing, camping, horseback riding. Home: 417 Ogden Ln New Braunfels TX 78130-2980 Office: Classic Choice Inc 417 Ogden Ln New Braunfels TX 78130-2980 E-mail: pbelzung@aol.com.

BEMENT, ARDEN LEE, JR., engineering educator; b. Pitts., May 22, 1932; s. Arden Lee and Edith Ardelia (Bigelow) B.; m. Mary Ann Baroch, Aug. 24, 1952 (dec.); children: Kristine, Kenneth, Vincent, Cynthia, Mark, David, Paul, Mary; m. Louise Coquestrain, June 15, 2001. Degree of Engr. in Metallurgy, Colo. Sch. Mines, 1954; MSMetE, U. Idaho, 1959; PhD, U. Mich., 1963; PhD honoris causa, Cleve. State U., 1997, Case Western Res. U., 2002. Rsch. metallurgist Hanford Labs., GE, Richland, Wash., 1954-65; sr. rsch. mgr. Pacific N.W. Lab., Battelle Meml. Inst., Richland, 1965-70; prof. nuc. materials MIT, 1970-76; dir. Def. Advanced Rsch. Projects Agy. Office Materials Sci., DARPA, DOD, Washington, 1976-79, dep. undersec. rsch. and advanced tech., 1979-80; v.p. tech. resources TRW, Lyndhurst, Ohio, 1980-89, v.p. sci. and tech., 1990-92; Basil S. Turner disting. prof. engring. Purdue U., West Lafayette, Ind., 1992-98, head sch. nuc. engring., 1998—2001; dir. Nat. Inst. Standards & Tech., Dept. Commerce, Gaithersburg, Md., 2001—. Tech. assistance expert to Mexico UNIAEA, 1974-76; cons. NRC, Taiwan, 1975; mem. Nat. Sci. Bd., 1988-94; mem. sci. adv. com. Electric Power Rsch. Inst., 1987—, Advanced Tech. Inc., 1993—. Author publs. in field; editor: Biomaterials: Structural and Biomedical Bases for Hard Tissue and Soft Tissue Substitutes, 1971; co-editor: Dislocation Dynamics, 1968, Creep of Zirconium Alloys in Nuclear Reactors, 1983; mem. editl. bd. Jour. Nuclear Materials, 1970-77, Materials Tech., 1987-99; contbr. articles to profl. jours. Chmn. bd. health Mental Health/Mental Retardation, Benton-Franklin Counties, Wash., 1968-70; mem. Richland, Wash. city coun., 1968-70; pres. Arts Coun., Richland, Pasco and Kennewick, Wash., 1968-70; bd. dirs. Cleve. Opera Bd., treas., 1982-86, v.p., 1986-91, nat./internat. bd. mem., 1992—; bd. dirs. LaFayette Symphony, 1998—; bd. overseers Fermi Nat. Accelerator Lab., 1999—. Lt. col. USAR, 1954-79. Recipient Outstanding Achievement award Colo. Sch. Mines, 1984, Melville F. Coolbaugh award, 1991, Disting. Engr. award UCLA, 1987, Honor Roll award U. Idaho Alumni Assn., 1991, Engring. Alumnus of Yr. award U. Mich. Alumni Assn. (Cleve. br.), 1992, Merit award U. Mich. Alumni Assn., 1993, Nat. Mats. Adv. award Fedn. of Mats. Socs., 1997. Fellow Am. Nuclear Soc., Am. Soc. Metals (Disting. Life mem. 1998), Am. Inst. Chemists; mem. Nat. Acad. Engrs., ASTM, AIME, Metals Soc. of AIME (Leadership award 1988, life mem. 2000), Sigma Xi, Tau Beta Pi, Sigma Gamma Epsilon. Republican. Roman Catholic. Home: 4027 Falconswalk Ct Stow OH 44224 Office: Dept Commerce Nat Inst Stds and Tech 100 Bureau Dr MS 1000 Gaithersburg MD 20899 E-mail: arden.bement@nist.gov.

BEMIS, MARY FERGUSON, magazine editor; b. N.Y.C., Dec. 28, 1961; d. Edmund Augustus and Anne Adoian (Nalbandian) Bemis. BFA in Writing, Johnson State Coll., 1983. Co-editor, co-pub. Ave. Literary Rev. Ave. Publs. Inc., Burlington, Vt., 1983-85; editor Unique Hair and Beauty Mag., 1994; editor Lady's Circle Mag. Lopez Publs., N.Y.C., 1987-94, editor, 1989-94; freelance editor, writer Mus. Sci., Boston, 1991-93; freelance editor Woman's Day Spl. Interest Publs., 1996—98; sr. editor Am. Salon and Am. Spa Mags., 1988—; editor-in-chief Am. Spa Mag., 1998—; bd. dirs. Internat. Spa Assn., 2003. Co-editor: The Green Mountain Rev., 1982—83, Nature Through Her Eyes: Art and Literature by Women, 1994, Journey Into the Wilderness, 1994. Mem.: Am. Soc. of Mag. Editors. Democrat. Unitarian Universalist. Home and Office: 127 East 28 St Ste 3R New York NY 10016 E-mail: MFBEMIS@aol.com.

BEN, MANUEL, chemist; b. Syracuse, N.Y., July 30, 1916; s. David and Sarah (Slakter) B.; m. Evelyn Ben, July 14, 1940 (dec. Mar. 1988); children: Allan Wayne Ben, Francine Adele Savin. BS, U. Mich., 1939, postgrad., 1939-40. Cert. electroplater finisher. Sr. rsch. chemist AC Spark Plug divsn. GM Corp., Flint, Mich., 1940-53; supr. electrochemistry dept. GM Rsch. Labs., Warren, Mich., 1953-67; sr. chem. engr./supr. GM Mfg., Warren, 1967-72; sr. design engr./plating specialist Chevrolet divsn. GM Corp., Warren, 1972-74; staff devel. engr. GM Mfg. Staff, Warren, 1974-81. Cons. in field. Contbr. articles to profl. jours.; patentee in field. Vol. counselor Svc. Corps of Ret. Execs., Detroit, 1983— (Platinum award 1998). Fellow Am. Electroplaters and Finishers Soc. (Saginaw Valley br. pres. 1954, Detroit br. pres., Charles Henry Proctor Meml. award 1964); mem. Electrochemistry Soc. (Detroit chmn., emeritus mem.), Inst. Metal Finishing (England chpt., emeritus). Avocations: music, travel, counseling, volunteering. Home: Apt 444 25800 W Eleven Mile Rd Southfield MI 48034-6181

BENACERRAF, BARUJ, pathologist, educator; b. Caracas, Venezuela, Oct. 29, 1920; arrived in US, 1939, naturalized, 1943; s. Abraham and Henriette (Lasry) Benacerraf; m. Annette Dreyfus, Mar. 24, 1943; 1 child, Beryl. B es L, Lycee Janson, 1940; BS, Columbia U., 1942; MD, Med. Sch. Va., 1945; MA, Harvard U., 1970; MD (hon.), U. Geneva, 1980; DSc (hon.), NYU, 1981, Va. Commonwealth U., 1981, Yeshiva U., 1982, U. Aix-Marseille, 1982, Columbia U., 1985, Adelphi U., 1988, Weizmann Inst., 1989, Harvard U., 1992, U. Bordeaux, 1993, U. Vienna, 1995. Intern Queens Gen. Hosp., N.Y.C., 1945—46; rsch. fellow dept. microbiology Med. Sch. Columbia U., 1948—50; charge de recherches Centre Nat. de Recherche Scientique Hosp. Broussais, Paris, 1950—56; asst. prof. pathology Sch. Medicine NYU, 1956—58, assoc. prof. Sch. Medicine, 1958—60, prof. Sch. Medicine, 1960—68; chief immunology Nat. Inst. Allergy and Infectious Diseases NIH, Bethesda, Md., 1968—70; Fabyan prof. comparative pathology, chmn. dept. Med. Sch. Harvard U., 1970—91; ret. Med. Sch., Harvard U., Cambridge, Mass., 1991. Pres, CEO Dana-Farber Cancer Inst, 1980—91, Dana-Farber Inc, 1990—95; mem immunology study sect NIH; pres Fedn Am Socs Experimental Biol, 1974—75; chmn sci adv comt Centre d'Immunologies de Marseille, France. Bd govs Weizmann Inst Med; mem sci adv comt Children's Hosp, Boston; mem award comt GM Cancer Research Found, chmn selection comt Sloan Prize, 1980. Capt MC AUS, 1946—48. Recipient T Duckett Jones Meml Award, Helen Hay Whitney Found, 1976, Rabbi Shai Shacknai Lectr and Prize, Hebrew Univ Jerusalem, 1974, Waterford Award, 1980, Nobel Prize, 1980, Corr, Emerite de l'Institut de la Sante et de la Rcherche Scientifique, Nat Medal Sci, NSF, 1990. Fellow: Am Acad Arts and Scis; mem.: NAS, Int Union Immunology Socs (pres 1980—83), French Soc Biol Chemistry, Brit Asn Immunology, Am Asn Immunologists (pres 1973—74), Nat Inst Med. Home: 111 Perkins St Jamaica Plain MA 02130-4313 Office: Dana-Farber Cancer Inst 44 Binney St Boston MA 02115-6084

BENADA, JAROSLAV, research scientist, consultant; b. Mikulcice, Moravia, Czech Republic, Mar. 13, 1928; s. Frantisek and Hedvika Benada; children: Stanislav, Vladimir. Engr. in agronomy, Mendel U. Agr. and Forestry, Brno, Czech Republic, 1951. Lectr. Mendel U. Agr. and Forestry, Brno, 1955-60; rsch. plant pathology Agrl. Rsch. Inst., Kromeriz, Czech Republic, 1960-93, cons. plant pathology and biology, 1993—. Editor, co-author (ency.) Agrl. Plant Pathology, Vols. 1-4, 1962 (Czech Agrl. Acad. award 1965); contbr. articles to profl. jours. Home: Vrchlicky Str 2650 76701 Kromeriz Czech Republic Office: Agrl Rsch Inst Havlickova Str 2787 76741 Kromeriz Czech Republic Fax: 420 573 339725. E-mail: benada@vukrom.cz.

BEN-AKIVA, MOSHE EMANUEL, civil engineering educator; b. Tel Aviv, June 11, 1944; came to U.S., 1968; s. Eliezer and Rivka (Reiner) B.A.; children: Ori, Lea, Danna, Elana, Erez. BSCE, Technion-Israel Inst. Tech., Haifa, 1968; MSCE, MIT, 1971, PhD in Transp. Systems, 1973; docteur honoris causa, U. Lumiere Lyon, France, 1992; Docterate (hon.), U. of the Aegean, 2000. Registered profl. engr., Israel. Edmund K. Turner prof. civil engring. MIT, Cambridge, Mass., 1973-96. Vis. prof. Technion-Israel Inst. Tech., Haifa, 1978—79, Haifa, 1981—82, Tel Aviv, 1981—82; vis. scholar NTT Rsch. Labs., 1988; cons. Am. Airlines, 1987; Atty. Gen. Mass., Boston, 1985—88, The Hague Cons. Group, 1985—2000, Cambridge Systematics, Inc., 1972—, RAND, 2001—. Editor-in-chief: Transport Policy; assoc. editor: Intelligent Transportation Systems Jour. and Transp. Sci.; mem. editl. bd. Jour. Transp. and Statistics. Lady Davis fellow Technion-Israel Inst. Tech., 1978. Mem. Transp. Rsch. Bd., Transp. Rsch. Forum, Regional Sci. Assn., Ops. Rsch. Soc. Am. (award 1973), World Conf. on Transp. Rsch. Soc. Office: MIT 77 Massachusetts Ave Rm 1-181 Cambridge MA 02139-4307 E-mail: mba@mit.edu.

BENAMATI, DENNIS CHARLES, librarian, editor, consultant; b. Orlando, Fla., Oct. 30, 1948; s. Thomas Guy and Ann (Clements) B.; m. Evelina Estella Lemelin, Aug. 19, 1983; children: Suzette, Alicia, Marcus. BA, St. Francis Coll., Loretto, Pa., 1970; MA, Fordham U., 1974; MLS, So. Conn. State U., 1975. Law libr. Conn. State Libr., Stamford, 1976-78; reference libr. U. Bridgeport (Conn.) Sch. Law, 1979; asst. law libr. for tech. svcs. U. Maine Sch. Law, Portland, 1979-83; asst. law libr. Aetna Life & Casualty Co., Hartford, Conn., 1983-84; head cataloging U. Conn. Sch. Law, Hartford, 1984-88; dir. The Dewey Grad. Libr. SUNY, Albany, 1988-93; adj. faculty Sch. Criminal Justice, SUNY, Albany, 1993—95; vis. elec. info. svcs. libr., instr. advanced legal rsch. U. S.C. Sch. Law, 1995—97; asst. libr. dir. Marist Coll., 1997—2002, adj. instr. criminal justice dept., interim libr. dir., adj. instr. Sch. Mgmt., 2000—02; libr. Sacred Heat U., Fairfield, Conn., 2002—. Ptnr. Lemelin & Benamati; cons., Kinderhook, N.Y., 1985—; cons. to various law firms, Lawyers Coop. Pub. Co., European Inst. for Crime Prevention and Control. Co-author: Publication Opportunities for Law Librarians, 1995, Criminal Justice Information: How to Find It, How to Use It, 1998; rapporteur World Criminal Justice Libr. Network Conf., 1997, 99, 2001; contbr. articles to profl. jours. Mem. ALA, Assn. Coll. & Rsch. Librs., Am. Assn. Law Librs., Law Librs. New England (bd. dirs. 1985-87). Roman Catholic. Home: 26 Hawthorne Dr Valatie NY 12184-5004 E-mail: benamatid@sacredheart.edu.

BENAMOU, CATHERINE LAURE, filmmaker, educator; b. Paris, June 13, 1956; d. Jean Michel Benamou and Gerane (Siemering) Heinreich; m. Agustin Lao Montes, May 1, 1993 (div.); children: Aiyana Maya Lao, Emma Ursula Lao. Student, Reed Coll., 1974—75; BA, U. Wis., 1978; MA, NYU, 1982, MA, 1988, PhD, 1997. Asst. rsch. scientist N.Y. Rsch. Program in Inter-Am. Affairs NYU, 1984—86; adj. lectr. CUNY, S.I., 1992—96; vis. asst. prof. Duke U., Durham, NC, 1996—98; asst. prof. Film and Video Studies U. Mich., Ann Arbor, 1998—. Curator Latin Am. Film and Video, N.Y.C., 1983—92; adv. panelist Film and Media Grants N.Y. Coun. for Humanities, 1988; cons., rsch. coord. Film and Video Ctr. Nat. Mus. Am. Indian, N.Y.C., 1993—95. Co-prodr.: Latinos en Accion, 1990—92; contbr. Bd. dirs. Alafia Arts Orgn.; co-founder Women Make Movies, Inc., N.Y.C., 1983—85. Recipient Recognition of Spl. Achievement, Smithsonian Instn., 1996; grantee, U. Mich., 2002. Mem.: Soc. Cinema and Media Studies (co-chair Latino Caucus 1999—2001), Latin Am. Studies Assn., Phi Beta Kappa. Avocations: photography, poetry, bicycling, piano, sailing. Office: Univ Mich Film and Video Studies 105 S State St #2512 Ann Arbor MI 48109*

BENARDE, ANITA ESTELLE, artist; b. Oct. 11, 1927; Student, Bklyn. Coll., St. Martins Sch., London. Curator program in women's studies Princeton U., NJ. Solo exhbns. include Turkish Consulate Gallery, N.Y.C., 1986, AT&T Corp. Edn. Ctr., Princeton, N.J., 1989, 2000, Johnson & Johnson World Headquarters, New Brunswick, N.J., 1993; group exhbns. include Hunterdon Art Mus., Clinton, N.J., 1988-91, Newark Mus., 1988, Milberg Gallery, Princeton Univ., 1988, Rider U., Lawrenceville, N.J., 1990, Soviet Art Exch., Moscow, 1990, The Scanticon, Princeton, 1990-94, The Bianco Gallery, Doylestown, Pa., 1996, The Lobby Gallery, N.Y.C., 1996, Gratella Gallery, Princeton, 1998, Bristol-Myers-Squibb, 1999, Home Box Office, N.Y.C., 1999; represented by Art Bank, Phila., Emmie Gallery, Marleton, N.J., Wenniger Gallery, Rockport, Mass. Home: 6 Thorngate Ct Princeton NJ 08540-7807 Fax: 609-951-8652. E-mail: abartist@comcast.net.

BEN-ARIE, JEZEKIEL, electrical engineer, computer scientist, educator; m. Ronit Peleg Popovitch, Nov. 17, 1983. BSc, Technion, Haifa, 1967, MSc, 1971, ScD, 1986. Cert. elec. and computer engring., Israeli Engring. Orgn., 1967. Chief engr. Technion Rsch. Lab, Haifa, Israel, 1971—89; asst. prof. Ill. Inst. of Tech., Chgo., 1989—94, assoc. prof., 1994—95, U. Ill., Chgo., 1995—2001, prof. elec. and computer engring., 2001—. Contbr. articles to profl. jours. Grantee Rsch., Darpa, 1993—97, Whitaker Found., 1992—96, U.S. Army Rsch. Office, 1998—99, NSF, 1992, 1996—97, 1999—2000, 2002. Mem.: IEEE. Jewish. Achievements include research in The Probabilistic Peaking Effect of Angles and Distances - A novel probabilistic model of viewed angles and distances of objects; Affine Invariant Spectral Signatures (AISS) - A novel method for object recognition that is robust in affine trnsformations of the image; Expansion Matching Method (EXM) - A novel method to match templates using signal expansion instead of the prevalent matching by correlation; Volumetric Frequency Representation (VFR) - a novel method to represent 3D objects in the frequency domain; Reconition by Indexing and Sequencing (RISq) - A novel method for recognition of vector sequences especially applied for human activity recognition and speech recognition. Office: U Ill Chgo 851 S Morgan St ECE Dept M/C154 Chicago IL 60601 Office Fax: 312-996-6465. Personal E-mail: jbenarie@yahoo.com.

BENARIO, HERBERT WILLIAM, classicist, educator; b. N.Y.C., July 21, 1929; s. Frederick and Ilse (Kessler) Benario; m. Janice M. Martin, Dec. 23, 1957; children: Frederick M., John H. BA, CCNY, 1948; MA, Columbia U., 1949; PhD, Johns Hopkins U., 1951. Instr. Greek and Latin Columbia U., 1953-58; asst. prof. Greek and Latin Sweet Briar Coll., 1958-60; mem. faculty Emory U., Atlanta, 1960—, prof. classics, 1967-87, chmn. dept., 1968-73, 76-78, prof. emeritus, 1987, disting. fellow emeritus, 2001—02. Dir. Vergilian Soc. Summer Sch., Italy, 1963, Italy, 67, Italy, 73, Italy, 81, asst. dir., Italy, 57, Italy, 59; dir. Roman Britain Tour, 1977, 86, Roman Germany Tour, 1981, 88, Rome and North Italy, 1982, Roman Germany Tour Mediterranean Soc., 1998, North Italy Tour Mediterranean Soc., 1999; vis. prof. Intercollegiate Ctr. Classical Studies, Rome, 1967, co-prof. in charge, 1984—85; vis. prof. U. Colo., 1969, Brigham Young U., 1999; Fulbright Sr. prof. U. Passau, Germany, 1990; co-exec. sec. Vergilian Soc., 1992—93; mem. Latin achievement test com. Coll. Entrance Exam. Bd., 1963—66. Author: (book) Tacitus, Agricola, Germany, Dialogue on Orators, 1967, Tacitus, Agricola, Germany, Dialogue on Orators, rev. edit., 1991, An Introduction to Tacitus, 1975, A Commentary on the Vita Hadriani in the Historia Augusta, 1980, Tacitus Annals 11 and 12, 1983, The Classical Association of the Middle West and South, 1989, Caesaris Augusti Res Gestae et Fragmenta, 1990, Thusnelda: A German Princess in Ancient Rome, 1993, Tacitus Germany, 1999; co-editor: Basil Lanneau Gildersleeve: An American Classicist, 1986. With AUS, 1951—53. Fellow Am. Coun. Learned Soc., 1978, Heilbrun, Emory U., 2002; grantee Fulbright, 1956, Rsch., Am. Philos. Soc. Mem.: Classical Soc. Am. Acad. Rome (pres. 1965), Am. Classical League, Vergilian Soc. Am. (trustee 1960—65, 1969—73, pres. 1980—82), Classical Assn. Midwest and South (pres.so. sect. 1968—70, pres. 1971—72), Am. Philos. Soc., Phi Beta Kappa (pres. Emory U. chpt. 1968—69). Office: Emory U Classics Dept Atlanta GA 30322-0001 Home: 1717 N Decatur Rd NE #119 Atlanta GA 30307 E-mail: hbenari@emory.edu.

BENARIO, JANICE MARTIN, retired classics educator; b. Feb. 19, 1923; m. Herbert W. Benario, Dec. 23, 1957; children: Frederick M., John H. AB in Latin, Goucher Coll., 1943; AM in Classical Lit., Johns Hopkin's U., 1949, PhD in Classical Lit., 1952. Teaching intern St. John's Coll., 1953-54; from instr. to asst. prof. Sweet Briar Coll., 1954-60; asst. prof. classics Ga. State U., 1960—62, assoc. prof., 1962-84, assoc. prof. emerita fgn. langs., 1989; co-prof. in charge Intercollegiate Ctr. for Classical Studies, Rome, 1984-85; assoc. prof. Emory U., 1989-94, Agnes Scott Coll., 1997, ret., 1997. Editor: Vergilius, 1960-63, 73-79, mem. editorial bd., 1963-73; book rev. editor: Arch, 1964-69; editor: Ga. Classicist, 1981-83. Lt. (j.g.) USNR, 1943—46. Ford Found. grantee 1953-54, Fulbright grantee, 1957. Mem. Classical Soc. of Am. Acad. in Rome (treas., v.p., pres. 1963-69), Classical and Modern Fgn. Lang. Assn. (pres. 1969-71), Atlanta Soc. Archaeol. Inst. Am. (pres. 1979-80), Ga. Classical Assn. (pres. 1985-87), Vergilian Soc. Am. (co-exec. sec. 1992-93).

BENAROYA, HAYM, aerospace engineer, educator, researcher; b. May 12, 1954; BE in Civil Engring., The Cooper Union, 1976; MS, U. Pa., 1977, PhD in Probabilistic Structural Dynamics, 1981. Sr. rsch. engr. Weidlinger Assoc., N.Y.C., 1981-89; prof. dept. mech. and aerospace engring. Rutgers U., Piscataway, N.J., 1989—. Rsch. on lunar structures, vortex-induced oscillations, probabilistic mechanics, and offshore structural dynamics; founder, dir. Lab. for Extraterrestrial Structures Rsch., Rutgers U., 1990—. Founder, mng. editor (2 e-jours.on space and engring.). Avocations: mathematics, science, history and policy. Office: Rutgers U Sch Engring 98 Brett Rd Piscataway NJ 08854-8058 E-mail: benaroya@rci.rutgers.edu.

BEN-ASHER, DANIEL LAWRENCE, legislative researcher, writer; b. Newark, Apr. 15, 1946; s. Jerry and Florence (Tasoff) B.; m. Michele Lauren Cohn, July 16, 1978; children: Sarah, Joshua. AB, Rutgers Coll., 1968; MA, U. Minn., 1970. Plant pers. adminstr. Tanatex Chem. Co. div. Sybron Corp., Lyndhurst, N.J., 1970-71; rsch. asst. Office Legis. Svcs. N.J. State Legislature, Trenton, 1971-76, rsch. assoc., 1976-87, sr. rsch. assoc., 1987-98, sr. rsch. analyst, 1999—. Staff N.J. Assembly Labor Com., 1974-81, Assembly Commerce and Industry Com., 1981-82, Alcoholic Beverage Control Study Comm., 1986-88, Assembly Drug and Alcohol Abuse Policy Com., 1990-91, Assembly Housing Com., 1995; mem. N.J. Tobacco Age-of-Sale Enforcement Task Force, 1994-96; mem. politics and govt. judges panel The Best in America spl. edit. U.S. News and World Report, 1990. Mem. Ewing Twp. (N.J.) Rent Control Bd., 1976-77; fin. coord. Lawrence Twp. (N.J.) Hist. Preservation Adv. Com., 1985-92; twp. chmn. A Guide to Lawrenceville's Historic Landmarks, 1991-93; chmn. Mason Gross Presdl. Meml., Rutgers-New Brunswick, 1992-94; mem. nat. alumni adv. com. on admissions Rutgers U., 1992-94; Rutgers Alumni Admissions Rep., 1994-2001. Recipient Loyal Son award for extraordinary svc. to alma mater Rutgers Alumni Assn., 1995. Home: 11 Bonnington Dr Lawrenceville NJ 08648-1536 Office: NJ Office Legis Svcs PO Box 68 Trenton NJ 08625-0068 E-mail: Legisdan@aol.com.

BEN-ASHER, M. DAVID, physician; b. Newark, June 18, 1931; s. Samuel Irving and Dora Ruth (Kagan)B.; m. Bryna S. Zeller, Nov. 22, 1956 BA, Syracuse U., 1952; MD, U. Buffalo Sch. Med., 1956. Intern E.J. Meyer Mem. Hosp., Buffalo, N.Y., 1956-57; resident Jersey City Med. Ctr., 1957-58; asst. chief med. service U.S. Army Hosp., Ft. McPherson, Ga., 1958-60; resident Madigan Gen. Hosp., Tacoma, Wash., 1960-62; chief gen. med. service Walson Army Hosp., Ft. Dix, N.Y., 1962-64; attending staff St. Mary's Hosp., Tucson, Ariz., 1964—; pvt. practice Tucson, 1964—. Bd. dirs. Tucson Symphony, 1971-73; mem. Ariz. State Bd. Med. Examiners, 1978-88, joint bd. for regulation of physicians' assts., 1990-97; bd. trustees United Synagogue Am., 1981-87, nat. adv. bd., 1987-91. Fellow ACP; mem. AMA, Pima County Med. Soc. (bd. dirs. 1971-77, pres. 1976), Ariz. Med. Assn., Am. Soc. Nephrology. Democrat. Avocations: health club, music, computers. Home: 3401 N Tanuri Dr Tucson AZ 85750-6735 Office: So Ariz Med Specialists 4711 N 1st Ave Tucson AZ 85718-5610

BENAVENTE, DIEGO T. lieutenant governor; Lt. gov. Commonwealth of No. Marianas Islands. Office: Office of the Gov Caller Box 10007 Saipan MP 96950

BENAVIDES, FORTUNATO PEDRO (PETE BENAVIDES), federal judge; b. Mission, Tex., Feb. 3, 1947; BBA, U. Houston, 1968, JD, 1972. Atty. Rankin, Kern & Martinez, McAllen, Tex., 1972—74, Cisneros, Beery & Benavides, McAllen, 1974, Cisneros, Brown & Benavides, McAllen, 1975, Cisneros & Benavides, McAllen, 1976; pvt. practice McAllen, 1977; judge Hidalgo County Ct.-at-Law # 2, Edinburg, Tex., 1977—79; prin. Law Offices of Fortunato P. Benavides, McAllen, 1980—81; judge 92nd Dist. Ct. of Hidalgo County, Tex., 1981—84, 13th Ct. Appeals, Corpus Christi, Tex., 1984—91, Tex. Ct. Criminal Appeals, Austin, 1991—92; atty. Atlas & Hall, McAllen, 1993—94; judge U.S. Ct. Appeals (5th cir.), Austin, 1994—. Commr. Tex. Juvenile Probation Commn., 1983—89; vis. judge to cts. in Tex., 1993. Active Mustangs of Corpus Christi, 1990—91, hon. mem., 1992; active Mex.-Am. Dems. of Tex., 1990—92; mem. St. Michael Episc. Ch., Austin, 1992—. Mem.: ABA, Hidalgo County Bar Assn., State Bar Tex. Office: US Ct Appeals 5th Cir Homer Thornberry Judicial Bldg 903 San Jacinto Blvd Rm 450 Austin TX 78701

BENBOW, CAMILLA PERSSON, psychology educator, researcher; b. Lund, Sweden, Dec. 3, 1956; came to U.S., 1965, naturalized, 1985; m. David Lubinski; children: Wystan R., Bronwen G., Trefor A., Evan M., Lovisa D., G. Byron, Lena C. BA in Psychology with honors, Johns Hopkins U., 1977, MA in Psychology, 1978, MS in Edn. of the Gifted, 1980, EdD with distinction in Edn. of Gifted, 1981. Dir. Office of Precollegiate Programs for Talented & Gifted Iowa State U., 1987-98, Johns Hopkins U., Balt., 1977-79, asst. dir. Study of Mathematically Precocious Youth, 1979-81, assoc. dir., 1981-85, co-dir., 1985-86, dir., 1986—, assoc. rsch. scientist dept. psychology, 1981-86, asst. prof. sociology, part-time, 1983-86; assoc. prof. psychology Iowa State U., Ames, 1985-90, prof. psychology, 1990-95, chair dept. psychology, 1992-98, disting. prof., 1995-98, interim dean coll. edn., 1996-98; dean Peabody Coll. of Edn. and Human Devel., Vanderbilt U., Nashville, 1998—. Sr. editor: Academic Precocity: Aspects of Its Development, 1983, Intellectual Talent: Psychometric and Social Issues, 1996; contbr. articles to profl. jours. Recipient John curtis gowan prize Nat. assn. Gifted children, 1980, 81; Rsch. award Am. Ednl. Rsch. Assn., 1982; Spencer fellow, alt., 1984, 85, 86, Rsch. paper award Mensa, 1985, 86, 89, 94, 95; Early Scholar award Nat. Assn. Gifted Children, 1985, Disting. Scholar award 1992, George A. Miller award, APA, 1999. Mem. Johns Hopkins Soc. Scholars, Phi Beta Kappa, Sigma Xi. Office: Vanderbilt Univ Peabody Coll Edn/Human Devel Deans Office Box 329 Peabody Sta Nashville TN 37203 E-mail: camilla.benbow@vanderbilt.edu.

BENBOW, CHARLES CLARENCE, retired writer, critic; b. Moore Haven, Fla., Feb. 23, 1929; s. Clarence Oliver and Rosalie Florence (King) B.; m. Lois Chandler, Oct. 10, 1954; children— Margot Britton, Claudia King. B. Applied Arts, U. Fla., 1951; MS in Art Edn., Fla. State U., 1961, postgrad., 1965-66. Art dir. sta. WJXT-TV, Jacksonville, Fla., 1955-58; tchr. art Duval County (Fla.) Pub. Schs., 1958-62; instr. humanities U. Fla., 1962-65; writer-critic St. Petersburg (Fla.) Times, 1966-86. Co-author Fla. state guide for art in secondary schs.; Contbr. articles to profl. jours. Mem. City St. Petersburg Arts Commn. Served with USN, 1951-55. Named Best Architecture Critic in Fla. Fla. Assn. Am. Inst. Architects, 1978, 80 Mem. Fla. Art Edn. Assn. (v.p., treas. 1958-63, Disting. Service award 1989). Democrat. Presbyterian. Home: 255 21st Ave SE Saint Petersburg FL 33705-2828

BENBOW, RICHARD ADDISON, psychological counselor; b. Las Vegas, Dec. 27, 1949; s. Jules Coleman and Bonnie Ray B. BBA, U. Nev., 1972, MS in Counseling, 1974; AAS in Bus. Mgmt. & Real Estate, Clark County C.C., 1980; PhD in Clin. Psychology, U. Humanistic Studies, 1986. Cert. tchr., Nev.; cert. clin. mental health counselor, secondary sch. counselor, Nev., substance abuse counselor, Nev., substance abuse program adminstr., Nev.; nat. cert. counselor. Jud. svcs. officer Mcpl. Ct. City of Las Vegas, 1983-88, pretrial program coord., 1988—. Inmate classification technician Detention and Correctional Svcs., 1982-83; stress mgmt. cons. Mem. biofeedback Soc. Am., Assn. Humanistic Psychology, Nat. Assn. Psychotherapists, Am. Counseling Assn., Am. Mental Health Counselors Assn., Am. Acad. Crisis Interveners, Jr. C. of C., U.S. Jaycees (presdl. award of honor 1978-79), Delta Sigma Phi. Democrat. Christian Scientist.

BENCHERIF, MEROUANE, medical researcher, business executive; b. Djelfa, Algeria, Dec. 25, 1954; s. Abdelmalek and Fatihat-el-kheir Bencherif; m. Amel Bouhired, May 15, 1995; children: Yasmine Sarah, Samy Adel. MD, PhD, U. Va., Charlottesville, Va., 1987. Dir. and sr. mgr. Targacept, Winston-Salem, NC, 1997—2000; v.p. Targacept Inc, Winston-Salem, NC, 2000—. Adj. assoc. prof. physiology and pharmacology Wake Forest U. and Med. Sch., Winston-Salem, NC, 1996—, Winston-Salem, NC, 2002—. Contbr. scientific papers

to profl. jour. (Golden Eagle Award; Vision award, 1997). Grantee, Ariz. Disease Control Rsch. Commn., 1992-1995. Achievements include more than 30 issued patents. Home: 104 Brampton Ct Winston Salem NC 27106 Office: Targacept Inc 200 East First St Ste 300 Winston Salem NC 27101-4165 Office Fax: 336-480-2107. E-mail: merouane.bencherif@targacept.com.

BENCHLEY, PETER BRADFORD, author; b. N.Y.C., May 8, 1940; s. Nathaniel Goddard and Marjorie Louise (Bradford) Benchley; m. Winifred B. Wesson, Sept. 19, 1964; children: Tracy, Clayton, Christopher. BA cum laude, Harvard U., 1961. Gen. assignment reporter Washington Post, 1963; assoc. editor Newsweek mag., N.Y.C., 1963—67; staff asst. to Pres. White House, Washington, 1967—69; freelance writer, 1969—. Mem. Nat. Coun. Environ. Def.; mem. bd. advisors Bermuda Underwater Exploration Inst. Author: (books) Time and a Ticket, 1964, Shark Trouble, 2002, (novels) Jaws, 1974, The Deep, 1976, The Island, 1978, The Girl of the Sea of Cortez, 1982, Q Clearance, 1986, Rummies, 1989, Beast, 1991, White Shark, 1994; author: (with others) (screenplays) Jaws, 1975 (Brit. Acad. Award nomination), The Deep, 1977, The Island, 1979; co-author Ocean Planet, 1995; writer, narrator, host (episodes) The Am. Sportsman TV show, 1974—83, Galapagos TV spl., 1987, host, narrator Expedition Earth TV series, 1990—93, co-creator Dolphin Cove TV series, 1989, exec. prodr. Beast miniseries, 1996, host, narrator Ocean Reports pub. radio series, 1997—2000, creator, co-exec. prodr. (syndicated TV series) Peter Benchley's Amazon, 1999—2000, co-creator, co-prodr., co-writer, narrator New Eng. Aquarium's World of Water film series, 1998—; contbr. articles to newspapers and mags., including Nat.Geographic, N.Y.Times. With USMCR, 1962—63. Recipient Diver of Yr. award, Sea Rovers Assn., 2002. Office: care ICM 40 W 57th St New York NY 10019-4001

BENCHOFF, JAMES MARTIN, manufacturing company executive; b. Hagerstown, Md., May 18, 1927; s. J. Thompson and Marie (Hickey) B.; m. Brigitte R. Puhringer, July 1, 1978 (div.); children by previous marriage—Helen Marie, James Martin II. Student, U. Pa., 1944-45. With Grove Mfg. Co. div. Hanson Industries, Shady Grove, Pa., 1954—, v.p., 1962-66, 1st v.p., 1966, 1st v.p., asst. gen. mgr., 1966-68, exec. v.p., gen. mgr., 1968-69, pres., chief exec. officer, 1969-80, chmn., chief exec. officer, 1980-88, chmn. emeritus, 1988—. Pres. Monta Vista Inc., Waynesboro, Pa., 1959—; pres., chmn. Ben Mar Holdings Ltd., Waynesboro, 1970—. Mem.: Waynesboro Country; Fountain Head Country (Hagerstown, Md); Met. (N.Y.C.). Office: PO Box 308 Waynesboro PA 17268-0308

BENCINI, SARA HALTIWANGER, concert pianist; b. Winston Salem, N.C., Sept. 2, 1926; d. Robert Sydney and Janie Love (Couch) Haltiwanger; m. Robert Emery Bencini, June 26, 1954; children: Robert Emery, III, Constance Bencini Waller, John McGregor. Mus. B., Salem Coll., 1947; postgrad. grad. Juilliard Sch. Music, 1948-50; M.A., Smith Coll., 1951; D In Mus. Arts, U. N.C., Greensboro, 1989. Head piano dept. Mary Burnham Sch. for Girls, Northampton, Mass., 1949-51; pianist, composer dance and drama dept. Smith Coll., 1951-52; head music dept. Walnut Hill Sch. for Girls, Natick, Mass., 1952-54; pvt. piano tchr., High Point, N.C., 1954-66; concert pianist appearing in Am. and Europe, 1948—; duo-piano performances with PBS-TV, Columbia, S.C., 1967, Winston Salem Symphony, N.C., 1964-68, Ea. Mus. Festival, Greensboro, N.C., 1969. Democrat. Presbyterian.

BENCSATH, KATALIN A. mathematician; b. Szeged, Hungary, May 24, 1945; arrived in U.S., 1973; d. Aladár Bencsáth and Ilona Hajós; m. Mihaly Mezei. Diplomate Cert. Mathematician, Eötvös L. U., Budapest, 1968; MA in Math., CUNY, N.Y.C., 1976; PhD in Math., CUNY, 1983. Sys. analyst Közti Inst. Arch., Budapest, 1968—69; ops. rschr. Infelor Sys. Engring. Inst., Budapest, 1969—72; instr., grad. fellow Hunter Coll., N.Y.C., 1976—81; instr., asst. prof. Manhattan Coll., Riverdale, Bronx, NY, 1981—94, prof. math., 1994—. Cons. FÜTI Data Processing Inst., Budapest, 1969; assoc. NYU Faculty Resource Network, N.Y.C., 1986—98; reviewer math. rev. Am. Math. Soc., 1993—; vis. rsch. scholar Grad. Sch. CUNY, 1996—97; lectr. in field. Mem. editl. bd. (jour.) CARUS, 1993—97; editor: (Springer-Verlag book series) Problem Books in Mathematics, 1997—. Recipient Achievement award, CUNY PhD Alumni Assn., 1999; Mina Rees fellow, Grad. Sch. CUNY, 1975—76, Scholar-in-residence, NYU Faculty Resource Network, Courant Inst., 1989, 1993, 1997. Avocations: birdwatching, swimming, classical music, roof-top gardening. Office: Manhattan Coll Dept Math and Computer Sci RLC 201D Riverdale NY 10471

BEN DANIEL, DAVID JACOB, entrepreneurship educator, consultant; b. Phila., Nov. 10, 1931; s. Daniel and Rosella (Soffian) Berkowitz; m. Judith Milgram, June 3, 1957 (div. Nov. 1975); children: Matthew, Elisabeth; m. Claire S. Berman, Nov. 19, 1991. BA with honors, U. Pa., 1952, MS in Physics, 1953; PhD in Engring., MIT, 1960. Physicist GE, Schenectady, N.Y., 1961-67, mgr. advanced programs R & D Ctr., 1967-70, mgr. tech. ventures ops., 1970-76; area mgr. advanced energy Exxon Corp., Florham Park, N.J., 1976-79; group v.p. Exxon Enterprises Co., Florham Park, 1979-81; sr. v.p. Am. R & D, Boston, 1981-83; exec. v.p. Genesis Venture Capital, Boston, 1983-84; Berens prof. entrepreneurship Johnson Grad. Sch. Mgmt., Cornell U., Ithaca, N.Y., 1984—. Cons. Venture Capital Partnerships, 1984-89; vis. prof. Keio U., Japan, 1997-98. Co-editor Handbook of International Mergers and Acquisitions, 1991, Internat. M&A, Jt. Ventures and Beyond, 1997; contbr. articles to profl. jours. Chmn. Human Rights Commn., Schenectady, 1970-73; trustee Union Am. Hebrew Congregations, N.Y.C., 1972-80. Lt. USN, 1953-56. Recipient Disting. Svc. award Jaycees of Am., 1968; vis. fellow Harvard Bus. Sch., 1970. Mem. Harvard Club (Boston), Cornell Club (N.Y.C.), Sigma Xi. Republican. Jewish. Avocation: mathematical foundations. Home: 111 Kelvin Pl Ithaca NY 14850-2319 Office: Johnson Grad Sch Mgmt Cornell U Ithaca NY 14853

BENDELAC, ROGER E. investment executive, financial consultant; b. Oct. 5, 1956; s. David and Marie Bendelac; married; 2 children. Diplome, Institut D'Etudes Politiques, Paris, France, 1978; MBA, Columbia U., 1980. Lic. securities and commodities registered rep. Acct. exec. Oppenheimer & Co., Inc., N.Y.C., 1980-83, v.p. retail sales dept., 1983-84, sr. v.p. retail sales dept., 1984-85; sr. v.p. internat. br. Shearson Lehman Hutton, Inc., N.Y.C., 1985-87; pres., CEO REB Futures, Inc., N.Y.C., 1987-90; investment exec. Westminster Securities Corp., N.Y.C., 1988—; CEO Generis Capital Corp., N.Y.C., 1990-91; mng. dir. Genersis Assocs., Inc., N.Y.C., 1991—; mng. dir. internat. instnl. sales Laidlaw Global Securities, N.Y.C., 1997-98; pres., COO, dir. Laidlaw Global Corp., N.Y.C., 1998—, Global Electronic Exch., Inc., N.Y.C., 1998—; chmn., CEO Laidlaw Global Corp., N.Y.C., 2003—. Editor bus. rev. Columbia U., 1979. Mem. N.Y. Acad. Scis. (elected mem.), Columbia Bus. Sch. Club. Avocations: running, team hand ball, readings in economics and history. Office: Laidlaw Global Corp 575 Madison Ave New York NY 10022

BENDELE, NICHOLE A. public relations executive, writer; b. Fredericksburg, Tex., Mar. 24, 1972; d. Charles Allen and Meta Kathleen Bendele. BA in English, Tarleton State U., 1994. Co-editor J-TAC; Stephenville, Tex., 1994; pub. rels. coord. Becker Vineyards, Stonewall, Tex., 1996—. Mem.: Tex. Wine and Grape Growers, Soc. Profl. Journalists, Resident Advisors Assn., Student Programming Assn., Tarleton Alumni Assn. (chpt. sec. 2001—). Home: PO Box 274 Stonewall TX 78671

BENDELIUS, ARTHUR GEORGE, engineering firm executive; b. Passaic, N.J., May 21, 1936; s. Arthur Leopold and Lydia Ella (Flach) B.; m. Virginia Brown, June 21, 1958; children: Linda Ellen Newlin, Bonnie Sue, Heidi Ann. BE, Stevens Inst. Tech., 1958, MMS, 1966. Registered profl. engr., N.Y., N.J., Mich., Minn., Ga., Fla., Tex. Ala., Ky., N.c., S.c., Miss., Tenn., La., Ohio, Ark., Okla., Md., Utah, Colo., Wyo., W.Va., Pa. Engr. Syska & Hennessey, N.Y.C., 1958-60, Parsons Brinckerhoff Quade & Douglas, Inc., N.Y.C., 1960-62, asst. dept. head, 1963-68, dept. head, 1968-70, project mgr., 1970-73, regional mgr. Atlanta, 1973-76, asst. v.p., 1976-78, v.p., 1978-82, sr. v.p., 1982-89; regional mgr. Energy Systems Group, N.Y.C., 1989-93, prin. profl. assoc., 1991—, sr. v.p., 1989—, tech. dir., 1992—. Engr. Nat. Biscuit Co., N.Y.C., 1962-63; divsn. mgr. PBES, N.Y.C., 1994-96, PBQD, N.Y.C., 1996—; condr. seminars, moderator forums in computer usage and environ. design Co-author: Tunnel Engineering Handbook, 1982, 2d edit., 1995, ASHRAE Handbook Applications, 1978, 82, 95; contbr. articles to profl. jours. Pres. Brookside Home Sch. Orgn., Westwood, N.J., 1972-73; co-v.p. Dunwoody Band Booster Club, Ga., 1975-76, co-pres. 1976-77. Named Atlanta Engr. of Yr. in Pvt. Practice, 1978; recipient Harold R. Fee Alumni award, 1978 Fellow Soc. Am. Mil. Engrs. (pres. Atlanta chpt. 1978-79, nat. bd. dirs. 1983-86), ASHRAE (chmn. tech. com. 1975-79, rsch. promotion com. 1980-82, tech. com. 1982—); mem. NSPE, Ga. Soc. Profl. Engrs. (bd. dirs. 1976-78), Nat. Coun. Examiners Engring. and Surveying (cert.), Ga. Engring. Found. (life, bd. dirs. 1977-89, sec. 1979, v.p. 1980, pres. 1982, 83), Steven's Alumni Assn., ASME, Australian Inst. Refrigerating and Air Conditioning, Brit. Tunneling Soc., Transp. Assn. S.C. (bd. dirs. 1987, treas. 1987-89), Nat. Fire Protection Assn. (mem. tech. com. 130, 1992—, mem. task group ventilation, mem. tech. com. 502 1993—, chair NPPA 502 subcom. 1994-97, mem. smoke control Working Group-PIARC, 1993—, chair com. on motor vehicles 1997—), Permanent Internat. Assn. Road Congresses (mem. Com. on Fire & Smoke 1992—), Electric Railroaders Assn., Aircarft Owners and Pilots Assn., Ansley Golf Club, Atlanta Stevens Club (pres. local chpt. 1974-90), Tau Beta Pi, Sigma Nu (pres. alumni assn. 1966-70, comdr. 1971-73). Clubs: Ansley Golf, Atlanta Stevens (pres. 1974-90). Lutheran. Office: Parsons Brinckerhoff 3340 Peachtree Rd Ste 2400 Tower 100 Atlanta GA 30326 E-mail: Bendelius@pbworld.com., dnhmitch@bellsouth.net.

BENDER, BETTY WION, librarian; b. Mt. Ayer, Iowa, Feb. 26, 1925; d. John F. and Sadie A. (Guess) Wion; m. Robert F. Bender, Aug. 24, 1946. BS, N.Tex. State U., Denton, 1946; MA, U. Denver, 1957. Asst. cataloger N. Tex. State U. Library, 1946-49; from cataloger to head acquisitions So. Meth. U., Dallas, 1949-56; reference asst. Ind. State Library, Indpls., 1951-52; librarian Ark. State Coll., 1958-59, Eastern Wash. Hist. Soc., Spokane, 1960-67; reference librarian, then head circulation dept. Spokane (Wash.) Public Library, 1968-73, library dir., 1973-88. Vis. instr. U. Denver, summers 1957-60, 63, fall 1959; instr. Whitworth Coll., Spokane, 1962-64; mem. Gov. Wash. Regional Conf. Libraries, 1968, Wash. Statewide Library Devel. Council, 1970-71 Bd. dirs. N.W. Regional Found., 1973-75, Inland Empire Goodwill Industries, 1975-77, Wash. State Library Commn., 1979-87, Future Spokane, 1983-88, vice chmn., 1986-87, pres., 1987-88. Recipient YWCA Outstanding Achievement award in Govt., 1985 Mem. ALA (mem. library adminstrn. and mgmt. assn. com. on orgn. 1982-83, chmn. nominating com. 1983-85, v.p./pres.-elect. 1985-86, pres. 1986-87), Pacific N.W. Library Assn. (chmn. circulation div. 1972-75, conv. chmn. 1977), Wash. Library Assn. (v.p./pres.-elect 1975-77, pres. 1977-78), AAUW (pres. Spokane br. 1969-71, rec. sec. Wash. br. 1971-73, fellowship named in honor 1972), Spokane and Inland Empire Librarians (dir. 1967-68), Am. Soc. Pub. Adminstrn. Clubs: Zonta (pres. Spokane chpt. 1976-77, dist. conf. treas. 1972). Republican. Lutheran. Home: 221 E Rockwood Blvd Apt 504 Spokane WA 99202-1274

BENDER, BOB, advertising executive; Grad., Columbus Coll. Art & Design. With Lord, Sullivan & Yoder Inc., Worthington, Ohio, 1965—, mem. exec. com., bd. dirs., 1984—, pres., CEO, 1997—. Work included in publs. N.Y. Illustrators Ann., Creativity Ann., Advt. Age, Print, Graphis, Comm. Arts. Recipient N.Y. Art Dir.'s Gold award, 3 Silver awards. Office: Lord Sullivan & Yoder Inc 250 Old Wilson Bridge Rd Worthington OH 43085

BENDER, BRUCE F. book publishing executive; b. Toledo, Ohio, Oct. 4, 1949; s. Richard S. and Joan B. Bender; m. Margaret Norris, Sept. 4, 1971; children: Courtney, Meghan. BA, Musklingum Coll., 1971; MBA, Rutgers U., 1972. Supr. Coopers & Lybrand CPA's, N.Y.C., 1972-76; pres. Lyle Stuart, inc., Secaucus, N.J., 1989—; also bd. dirs.; pres. Carol Pub. Group, N.Y.C., 1989-2000; mng. dir. Citadel Press, N.Y.C., from 2000, Kensington Pub. Corp., N.Y.C., 2000—. Pres. Brightwood Assn.; bd. dirs. Westfield Symphony. Mem. AICPA, Pub. Fin. Round Table, N.J. Inst. CPAs, Echo Lake Club, Royal Poinciana Club. Office: Kensington Pub Corp 850 3d Ave New York NY 10022

BENDER, BYRON WILBUR, linguistics educator; b. Roaring Spring, Pa., Aug. 14, 1929; s. Ezra Clay and Gertrude Magdalene (Kauffman) B.; m. Lois Marie Graber, Aug. 25, 1950; children: Susan Alice, Sarah Marie, Catherine Anne, Judith Lee, John Richard. BA, Goshen Coll., 1949; MA, Ind. U., 1950, PhD, 1963. Edn. specialist Trust Terr. of Pacific Islands, Majuro, Marshall Island, 1953-59, Saipan, Marianas Island, 1962-64; asst. prof. Goshen Coll., Ind., 1960-62; assoc. prof. linguistics U. Hawaii at Manoa, Honolulu, 1964-69, prof., 1969-99, chmn. dept., 1969-95, prof. emeritus, 2000—. Bd. dir. U. Hawaii Profl. Assembly, Honolulu, 1978-88, 92-98, pres., 1982-88. Author: Spoken Marshallese, 1969, Linguistic Factors in Maori Education, 1971, (with others) Marshallese-English Dictionary, 1976; editor Oceanic Linguistics Spl. Publ., 1965—, Studies in Micronesian Linguistics, 1984, Oceanic Linguistics, 1991—; mng. editor Oceanic Linguistics, 1965-90. Trustee Hawaii Pub. Employees Health Fund Bd., 1987-95; Regent, U. Hawaii Bd. of Regents, 2003-. Recipient Merit awards U. Hawaii 1971, 76, 86. Mem. NEA (standing com. higher edn. 1985-89), Linguistic Soc. Am. (dir. Linguistic Inst. summer 1977, program com. 1987-89, parliamentarian 1994-97). Mem. Soc. Of Friends. Home: Apt 1504 6710 Hawaii Kai Dr Honolulu HI 96825-1559 Office: U Hawaii Dept Linguistics 1890 E West Rd Honolulu HI 96822-2318 E-mail: bender@hawaii.edu., bender@hawaii.rr.com.

BENDER, CARL MARTIN, physics educator, consultant; b. Bklyn., Jan. 18, 1943; s. Alfred and Rose (Suberman) B.; m. Jessica Dee Waldbaum, June 18, 1966; children— Michael Anthony, Daniel Eric AB summa cum laude with distinction, Cornell U., 1964; AM, Harvard U., 1965, PhD, 1969. Mem. Inst. for Advanced Study, Princeton, N.J., 1969-70; asst. prof. math. MIT, Cambridge, 1970-73, assoc. prof., 1973-77; prof. physics Washington U., St. Louis, 1977—; research assoc. Imperial Coll., London, 1974. Cons. Los Alamos Nat. Lab., 1979—; vis. prof. Imperial Coll., London, 1986-87, 95-96, Technion Israel Inst. of Technology, Haifa, Israel, 1995; fellow Engring. and Phys. Scis. Rsch. Coun., U.K., 2003—. Author: Advanced Mathematical Methods for Scientists and Engineers, 1978; editor: Am. Inst. Physic series on math. and computational physics; mem. editl. bds. Jour Math. Physics, 1980-83, Advances in Applied Math., 1980-85, Jour. Physics A, 1999-2003; editor-in-chief, Jour. Physics A, 2004—; contbr. more than 200 articles to sci. jours. Trustee Ctr. for Theoretical Study of Phys. Sys., Clark Atlanta U. Recipient Burlington No. Found. Faculty Achievement award, 1985, Fellows award Acad. Sci. St. Louis, 2002; Telluride scholar, 1960-63, NSF fellow, 1964-69, Woodrow Wilson fellow, 1964-65, Sloan Found. fellow, 1973-77, Fulbright fellowship to U.K., 1995-96, Lady Davis fellowship to Israel, 1995, Rockefeller Found. grantee to visit Bellagio Study and Conf. Ctr., 1999; Guggenheim Fellow, 2003—, fellow Engring. and Physical Scis. Rsch. Coun., London, 2003—. Fellow: St. Louis Acad. Sci., Am. Phys. Soc. (vice chmn. Danny Heineman prize selection com., chmn. Danny Heineman prize selection com.); mem.: Phi Kappa Phi, Phi Beta Kappa. Home: 509 Warren Ave Saint Louis MO 63130-4155 Office: Washington U Dept Physics Saint Louis MO 63130

BENDER, CHARLES CHRISTIAN, retail home center executive; b. Bklyn., July 4, 1936; s. Charles C. and Virginia R. (Rahlfs) B.; m. Jean Ann Couper; children: Lori Ann Grenier, Hallie Couper. BA, Hillsdale Coll., 1959; MBA, U. Mich., 1960. Buyer Target, Detroit, 1962-69; v.p., gen. mdse. mgr. Wickes Lumber, Saginaw, Mich., 1969-81; gen. mgr. Wickes B.V., Utrecht, Netherlands, 1981-84; pres., CEO, owner Busy Beaver Bldg. Ctrs., Pitts., 1984—, also chmn. bd. dirs. Mem. adv. bd. Home Ctr. Industry Pres. Coun., 1986—; mem. Coun. of Exec. Officers; chmn. bd. dirs. Home Ctr. Inst., 1998. With U.S. Army, 1960—61. Mem.: Coun. Exec. Officers Group, Pitts. Field Club, Rotary. Republican. Presbyterian. Avocations: golf, sailing. Home: 310 Buckingham Rd Pittsburgh PA 15215-1527 Office: Busy Beaver Bldg Ctrs Inc 3130 William Pitt Way Pittsburgh PA 15238-1360

BENDER, CHARLES WILLIAM, lawyer; b. Cape Girardeau, Mo., Oct. 2, 1935; s. Walter William and Fern Evelyn (Stroud) Bender; m. Carolyn Percy Gavagan, June 20, 1961 (div. 1983); children: Theodore Marten, Christopher Percy; m. Betty Lou Port, May 5, 1983; stepchildren: Courtney Elizabeth, Cameron Ann. AB magna cum laude, Harvard U., 1960, LLB magna cum laude, 1963. Bar: Calif. 1965, U.S. Dist. Ct. (ctrl. dist.) Calif. 1965, U.S. Ct. Appeals (9th cir.) 1969, U.S. Supreme Ct. 1979, DC 1984. Assoc. O'Melveny & Myers, LA, 1965—71, ptnr., 1972—84, mng. ptnr., 1984—92, chmn., 1993—2001. Editor: Harvard U. Law Rev., 1961—62; articles editor:, 1962—63. Trustee LA Legal Aid Found., 1971, Lawyers' Com. for Civil Rights Under Law, Washington, 1985—2001; advisor campaign Alan Cranston for Senator, Calif., 1968, 1974, 1980; mgr. campaign Jess Unruh for Gov., Calif., 1970. Served with U.S. Army, 1956—57. Fellow Sheldon Traveling, Harvard U., 1963—64. Democrat. Home: 2831 The Strand Hermosa Beach CA 90254-2400 Office: O'Melveny & Myers 400 S Hope St Los Angeles CA 90071-2899

BENDER, DANIEL F. chemist, education educator; b. Cin., Mar. 22, 1936; s. Henry A. and Dorothy Bender; m. M. Grace Haeufle, June 13, 1959; children: Pete, Tim, Greg, Mary, Sue, Jenny, Jill. BS in Chemistry, Xavier U., 1959, MS in Chemistry, 1963; PhD in Chemistry, U. of Cin., 1967. Grad. asst. Xavier U., Ohio, 1959—60; rsch. chemist U.S. DHEW, Cin., 1960—72, U.S. EPA, Cin., 1972—; adj. prof., chemistry U. of Cin., 1988—. Contbr. scientific papers. Mem.: Am. Chemical Soc. Avocations: sports, winemaking, exercise. Office: US Environmental Protection Agency 26 W Martin Luther King Dr Cincinnati OH 45268

BENDER, DAVID RAY, library association executive; b. Canton, Ohio, June 12, 1942; s. John Ray and Mary Elizabeth (Witmer) B.; children: Robert Ray, Scott David, Lori Jo Ryan. BS, Kent State U., 1964; MS in LS, Case Western Res. U., 1969; PhD, Ohio State U., 1977. Librarian South High Sch., Willoughby, Ohio, 1964-68; cons. sch. library services Ohio Dept. Edn., Columbus, 1969-70; grad. research asso. Ohio State U., Columbus, 1970-72; br. chief sch. library media services Md. Dept. Edn., Balt., 1972-79; exec. dir. Spl. Librs. Assn., Washington, 1979-2001, exec. dir. emeritus, 2001—. Lectr. Rutgers U., New Brunswick, N.J.; vis. prof. Towson State U., Balt.; cons., project dir. various state depts. edn. and colls. and univs., profl. assns. also internat., state and local orgns.; mem. adv. com. on naval history, USN, 1991-95. Author: Learning Resources and the Instructional Program in Community College, 1980, Library Media Programs and the Special Learner, 1981; co-author (with others). Nat. Information Policies: Strategies for the Future, 1991; contbr. numerous articles to profl. jours. Mem. adv. coun. Kent (Ohio) State U. Sch. of Libr. and Info. Sci., 1991-99, Washington Nat. Cathedral Fund Com., 1998—; CWRU Libr. ann. gift fund chair, 1999-2002; bd. dirs. Dresden Condominium, 2002-03. Recipient award for outstanding svc. Md. Ednl. Media Orgn., 1980, H.W. Wilson Co. award, 1989. Mem. Spl. Librs. Assn. (President's award 1986, John Cotton Dana award 2001, David R. Bender Endowment Fund for Internat. Devel. 2001), Nat. Libr. and Info. Assns. (chmn. 1990-91), Internat. Fedn. Libr. Assns. and Instns. (chmn. round table for Mgmt. of Libr. Assn. 1993-99), Am. Soc. Assn. Execs. Found. (chmn. 1988), Greater Wash. Soc. Assn. Execs. (chair CEO adv. coun. 2000-2001, Five Smart Assn. CEO's 2001), Kappa Sigma. Republican. Episcopalian. Home: Unit 34 2126 Connecticut Ave NW Washington DC 20008-1729 Office: Spl Librs Assn 1700 18th St NW Washington DC 20009-2506

BENDER, HOWARD JEFFREY, software engineering consultant; b. Phila., Dec. 18, 1946; s. Irving Monroe and Ethel (Hellman) B.; m. Randi Laine Anderson, May 22, 1971 (div. 2003); children: Rebecca Jennifer, Heidi Julia (dec.). BS, Pa. State U., 1969; MS, Polytech. Inst. N.Y., 1980; PhD, U. Md., 1992. Sr. programmmer, analyst ITEL Corp., White Plains, N.Y., 1977-80; computer scientist CSTA, Greenbelt, Md., 1980-82; systems engr. Lockheed Corp., Greenbelt, Md., 1982-85, CTA, Inc., Rockville, Md., 1985-93; instr. U. Md., College Park, 1981-85, adj. asst. prof., 1986-94, assoc. dir., 1994-98, cons., 1994—. Pres. Edn. Process Improvement Ctr., Hyattsville, Md., 1995—; chmn. Any-Lang. Comms. Inc., 2001—. Author tech. articles; programmer (software) Personal Computing to Aid the Handicapped, 1981. Welcome wagon host University Park Civic Assn., 1989—. Mem. ASCD, Assn. for the Advancement of Computing in Edn., Computer Profls. Social Responsibility. Avocations: tennis, bridge, banjo. Home: 4200 Sheridan St Hyattsville MD 20782-2137 E-mail: hjbender@epi-center.net.

BENDER, HY, writer; b. Bronx, N.Y., May 14, 1958; BA, NYU, 1981. Author: Excel Quick Reference, 1990, PC Tools Deluxe: The Complete Reference, 1990, PC Tools: The Complete Reference, 2nd Edition, 1991, Essential Software for Writers, 1994, Getting Started with Windows 95, 1995, Students 2004 Survival Guide: College Edition, 2003; co-author: (with M. Young) Dummies 101: The Internet for Windows 95, 1996, (with M. Young) Dummies 101: Netscape Navigator, 1996, (with M. Young, J. Levine and C. Baroudi) The Internet for Dummies, Starter Kit Edition, 1997, Dummies 101: Netscape Communicator 4, 1997, Dummies 101: The Internet for Windows 98, 1998, The Sandman Companion, 1999, (with others) The Mad Bathroom Companion, 2000; contbr. nat. mags., including PC Week, PC Mag., Am. Film, Advt. Age, Spy, Mad Mag., PC World, Folio: The Mag. for Mag. Mgmt., Bottom Line/Personal, and Yahoo! Internet Life. E-mail: hybender@aol.com.

BENDER, JEFF BLAINE, epidemiologist, veterinarian; b. Bismarck, N.D., Aug. 30, 1961; m. Debra Jean Bender, Dec. 5, 1989; children: Megan June, Clare Noel, Jan Christopher. BS in Biology, Calif. Polytech., San Luis Obispo, 1985; DVM, U. Minn., 1989, MS, 1995. Diplomate Am. Coll. Vet. Preventive Medicine, lic. veterinarian Calif., Wis., Minn. Vet. Minn. Vet. Hosp., St. Paul, 1989-95; rsch. assoc. U. Minn., St. Paul, 1992-95; epidemiologist Minn. Dept. Health, Mpls., 1995—. Cons. Judicon Antibiotic U., 1998—, Generic Environ. Impact Study, 1999. Contbr. articles to profl. jours. Mem.: AVMA, Infectious Disease Soc. Am., Coun. for State and Terr. Epidemiologists, Nat. Assn. State Pub. Health Vets., Minn. Vet. Med. Assn. Office: U Minn 136F ABLMS 1354 Eckles Ave Saint Paul MN 55108

BENDER, JOHN CHARLES, lawyer; b. N.Y.C., May 17, 1940; s. John H. and Cecilia B.; m. Helen Hadjiyannakis; 1 child, Marianna Celene. BSME, Northea. U., 1964; JD, NYU, 1968, LLM, 1971. Bar: N.Y. 1968, U.S. Dist. Ct. (so. dist.) N.Y. 1972, U.S. Supreme Ct. 1997. Atty. Marshall, Bratter, Greene, Allison and Tucker, 1968-69; asst. dir, NYU Ctr. for Internat. Studies, N.Y.C., 1969-71; atty. Poletti Freidin Prashker Feldman & Gartner, N.Y.C., 1971-75; spl. counsel Moreland Act Commn. on Nursing Homes and Residential Facilities, N.Y.C., 1975-76; gen. counsel N.Y. State Fin. Control Bd., N.Y.C., 1976-80; v.p., gen. counsel News Am. Pub. Inc., N.Y.C., 1980-85; group v.p., gen. counsel Simon & Schuster Inc., N.Y.C., 1985-90; sr. v.p., dir., gen. counsel Maxwell Macmillan Group, 1991-95; dir. Black Book Mktg. Group, Inc., 1994-96. Chmn., trustee Trust for Cultural Resources of City of N.Y., 1981-99; chmn., trustee Mary McDowell Ctr. for Learning, 1993—. Mem. ABA, Assn. of Bar of City of N.Y. (mem. com. on comm. law 1981-85, mem. spl. com. on edn. and the law 1982 85). Home: 27 W 67th St New York NY 10023-6258 Office: 708 3d Ave New York NY 10017-4201

BENDER, JOHN HENRY, JR., (JACK BENDER), editor, cartoonist; b. Waterloo, Iowa, Mar. 28, 1931; s. John Henry and Wilma (Lowe) B.; divorced; children: Thereza, John Henry IV, Anthony; m. Carole R. Suggs, 1995. BA, U. Iowa, 1953; MA, U. Mo., 1962; postgrad., Art. Inst. Chgo., 1956, Washington U., St. Louis., 1957. Art dir., asst. editor Commerce Pub. Co., St. Louis, 1953-54, 56-58; editor Florissant Reporter, 1958-61; editl. cartoonist Waterloo Courier, 1962-84, assoc. editor, 1975-83; art. dir., editor Alpha VII Corp., Tulsa, 1984-87; head dept. prodn. art Platt Coll., Tulsa, 1987-92; cartoonist Don Martin Studio, Miami, Fla., 1989-92; artist Alley Oop comic strip United Media Syndicate, N.Y.C., 1991—; artist, writer, 2001—. Sports cartoonist Basketball Weekly, Baseball Digest Mag., U. Iowa, others. Author: Pocket Guide to Judging Springboard Diving, (with Dick Smith) Inside Diving, (with Ed Gagnier) Inside Gymnastics; career retrospective exhibit Grout Mus., Waterloo, Iowa, 2002. With USAF, 1954-56, col. USAFR, ret. Recipient Best Editl. award Mo. Press Assn., 1960, Grenville Clark Editl. Page award, 1968, Freedoms Found. award, 1969, 71, 75, Ignatz award Orlandocon, 1992, Air Force Commendation medal, 1981; named to Hall of Fame East H.S., Waterloo, Iowa, 1972, Names on Main, Cedar Falls, Iowa, 1997. Mem. Assn. Am. Editl. Cartoonists, Nat. Cartoonists Soc., Comic Art Profl. Soc., Sigma Chi. Home: RR 1 Box 540 Terlton OK 74081-9740 Office: 7220 E 32 Pl Tulsa OK 74145

BENDER, LARRY WAYNE, vocational educator; b. Indpls., May 23, 1942; s. Wayne Crawford and Margaret Dell (Ramer) B.; m. Barbara Agnes Kroll, Aug. 26, 1967; children: Anissa Gayle, Timothy Alan. BS in Indsl. Edn., Purdue U., 1967, MS in Indsl. Edn., 1972. Tchr. South Newton Sch. Corp., Kentland, Ind., 1967-81; tchr. tech. edn. Franklin (Ind.) Community Schs., 1981—. Recipient IPALCO Golden Apple award 1997, Newmast award 1997; Eli Lilly Found. grantee, 1999. Mem. Internat. Tech. Edn. Assn. (Outstanding Program of Yr. award 1987), Tech. Educators of Ind. (Meritorious Tchr. award 1987). Episcopalian. Avocations: photography, computers, bowling, golf, woodworking. Home: 4215 North Graham Rd Whiteland IN 46184-9326 Office: Custer Baker Middle Sch 101 W State Road 44 Franklin IN 46131-8936 E-mail: lbender@netdirect.net., benderl@fcsc.k12.in.us.

BENDER, PAUL, lawyer, educator; b. 1933; AB, Harvard U., 1954, LLB, 1957. Law clk. to Judge Learned Hand, 1958-59; law clk. to Justice Felix Frankfurter, U.S. Supreme Ct., 1959-60; asst. to Solicitor Gen., Dept. Justice, 1964-66; asst. prof. U. Pa. Law Sch., Phila., 1960-63, assoc. prof., 1963-66, prof., 1966-84; dean Coll. Law, Ariz. State U., Tempe, 1984-89, prof., 1989—; of counsel Meyer & Klipper, Washington D.C., 2001—. Prin. dep. solicitor gen. U.S., 1993-96; gen. counsel Nat. Commn. on Obscenity and Pornography, 1968-70; reporter UN Assn. Panel on human rights, Am. fgn. policy, 1978; justice Supreme Ct. of the Ft. MacDowell Yavapai Nation, 2000—. Author: (with Dorsen and Neuborne) Political and Civil Rights in the United States, 1976, 78. Recipient Cert. of Merit, ABA, 1973. Office: Coll Law Ariz State U Tempe AZ 85287 E-mail: paul.bender@asu.edu.

BENDER, PAUL EDWARD, lawyer; b. Decatur, Ill., Dec. 5, 1951; s. Kenneth Donald and Martha Rosalin (Heinzelmann) B.; m. Anne Marie Scartabello, Dec. 31, 1976 (div. 1978). BA, Millikin U., 1973; JD cum laude, Hamline U., 1976; MBA, U. Phoenix, 1997. Bar: Minn. 1976, Ill 1977, U.S. Dist Ct. (cen. dist.) Ill. 1982. Assoc. Halloran & Alfuby, Mpls., 1976-77; sole practice Bender Law Office, Arthur, Ill., 1977-79; sr. title atty Chgo. Title Ins. Co., Peoria, Ill., 1979-82; ptnr. Cordis & Bender, Princeville, Ill., 1982-84; sr. title atty. Chgo. Title Co., Champaign, Ill., 1984-88, asst. v.p., mgr., 1990-92, resident v.p., Champaign County mgr., 1992-96; mgr. McLean County Title Co., 1996—, Decatur Title, 1997—. Mem. ABA, Peoria Bar Assn. (chmn. real estate com. 1983-84, mem. continuing legal edn. 1981-83), McLean County Bar Assn., Ill. Bar Assn., Optimist Club (Peoria chpt., prs. 1981-82, lt. gov. zone 6 Ill. 1982-83), Champaign C. of C. (zoning com. 1990-96), Mason, Shriners. Republican. Methodist. Home: 303 N Cottage Ave Normal IL 61761-4264 E-mail: benderpa@ctt.com.

BENDER, PEGGY WALLACE, charitable gift planning consultant; b. Athens, Ohio, Apr. 29, 1957; d. Allen Riley and Carol Jean (Jago) Wallace; children: Meghan Elizabeth, Erin Michelle. AS, Ohio U., 1986, BA, 1988. Cert. Fund Raising Exec., 1988. Asst. to dean Ohio U. Col. Bus. Admin., Athens, 1981-86; asst. dir. planned giving U. Cin. Fed., 1986-88; dir. planned/major gifts Western Md. Col., Westminster, 1988-89; dir. planned giving Am. Red Cross, Cleve., 1991-93; pres. Strategies for Planned Giving, Cleve., 1993—. Bd. dirs. Nat. Com. Planned Giving, Indpls. Mem. Kindergarten Curriculum Com. Family Life Ctr., Berea, Ohio, 1996-97; bd. dirs. Nat. Com. Planned Giving, 1998-2000. Named Outstanding Fund Raising Exec. No. Ohio Planned Giving Coun./NSFRE Cleve./Ohio Coun. Fundraising Execs., 1997. Mem. Northern Ohio Planned Giving Council (pres., 1993-96, bd. dirs.), Nat. Soc. Fund Raising Execs. (v.p., 1992), Ohio Council Fund Raising Execs., Ohio Assn. Healthcare Philanthropy. Avocations: reading, travel, boating. Office: Strategies Planned Giving 15300 Pearl Rd Cleveland OH 44136-5091 E-mail: giftplan@aol.com.

BENDER, ROSS THOMAS, minister; b. Tavistock, Ont., Can., June 25, 1929; came to U.S., 1960, naturalized, 1966; s. Christian and Katie (Bender) B.; m. Ruth Eileen Steinmann, Dec. 22, 1950 (dec. Dec. 1997); children: Ross Lynn, Elizabeth, Michael, Deborah, Anne. BA, Goshen Coll., 1954, BD, 1956; MA, Yale U., 1961, PhD, 1962. Ordained to ministry Mennonite Ch., 1958. Prin. Rockway Mennonite sch., Kitchener, Ont., 1956-60; prof. Christian edn. Associated Mennonite Bibl. Sem., Elkhart, Ind., 1962-96, dean, 1964-79, dean emeritus, 1996; dir. Inst. Mennonite Studies, 1990-97. Pres. Mennonite World Conf., 1984-90. Author: The People of God, 1969, Christians in Families, 1982, Education for Peoplehood, 1997; co-editor: Baptism, Peace and the State in the Reformed and Mennonite Traditions, 1991. Rockefeller doctoral fellow, 1960-61; Am. Assn. Theol. Schs. fellow, 1961-62; NIMH postdoctoral fellow U. Pa., 1970-71 Mennonite.

BENDER, SHEILA SUE, essayist, poet, author; b. Richmond, Va., Mar. 6, 1948; d. Bertrand J. Lillian and Arline Lillian; m. Kurt C. Vandersluis, Nov., 24, 1986; children: Emily Ruth, Seth Michael (dec.); m. Arthur J. Bender, Aug., 21, 1969 (div. May, 1980). BA in English, U. Wis., 1970; MAT, Keane Coll., 1972; MA in Creative Writing, U. Wash., 1981. Tchr. Matawan N.J. Sch. Dist., 1970-72; day care dir./program coord. Temple Day Care, Seattle, 1972-75; instr. Shoreline Comm. Coll., Seattle, 1982-95; vis. writer Seattle U., 1996-97, U. Ariz. and Pima C. C., Tucson, 1995—. Instr. Pima Writer's Conf., Tucson, 1997, Soc. S.W. Authors, 1999—, Colo. Mountain Writers Workshop, 1999-, La Jolla Writer's conf., 2003, Whidben Island Writer's conf., 2001, 03; critic Seattle Times, 1996-98, The World, 1996-2000. Author: (books) Love From the Coastal Route, 1991, Writing Personal Essays, 1995, Sustenance, 1999, Writing Personal Poetry, 1999; co-author: Writing in a New Convertible with the Top Down, 1997; editor Writer's Journal, 1997, A Year in the Life: Journaling for Self-Discovery, 2000, Keeping a Journal You Love, 2001; contbg. editor Writer's Digest mag., 2000-; pub. www.writingitreal.com. Recipient fellowship Residency Centrum Found., Port Townsend, Wash., 1994.

BENDER, THOMAS, history and humanities educator, writer; b. Redwood City, Calif., Apr. 18, 1944; s. Joseph Charles and Catherine Frances (McGuire) B.; m. Sally Hill, June 8, 1966 (div. 1983); 1 child, David William; m. Gwendolyn Wright, Jan. 14, 1984; 1 child, Sophia Wright BA, U. Santa Clara, 1966; MA, U. Calif.-Davis, 1967, PhD, 1971. Asst. prof. history and urban studies U. Wis., Green Bay, 1971-74; asst. prof. history NYU, N.Y.C., 1974-76, assoc. prof. history, 1976-77, prof. history, 1977—, Samuel Rudin prof. humanities, 1977-82, Univ. prof. humanities, 1982—, dean for the humanities, 1995-98, dir. Internat. Ctr. for Advanced Studies, 1996—. Rsch. planning com. N.Y.C. Social Sci. Rsch. Coun., 1985-88. Author: Toward an Urban Vision, 1975 (Frederick Jackson Turner prize 1975), Community and Social Change in America, 1978, (with Edwin Rozwenc) The Making of American Society, 1978, New York Intellect, 1987, Intellect and Public Life, 1993, The Unfinished City: New York and the Metropolitan Idea, 2002; editor: Democracy in America, 1981, Intellectual History Group Newsletter, 1978-85, The University and the City, 1988, The Anti-Slavery Debate: Capitalism and Abolitionism as a Problem in Historical Interpretation, 1992; co-editor: (with Carl Schorske) Budapest and New York: Studies in Metropolitan Transformation 1870-1930, 1994, (with Carl Schorske) The Tranformation of American Academic Culture, 1998, (with Michael Peter Smith) City and Nation: Rethinking Identity and Place, 2001, Rethinking American History in a Global Age, 2002; cons. editor New Studies in American Intellectual and Cultural History, 1981-94; mem. editl. bd. Readers Encyclopedia of American History, 1988-91, Am. Hist. Rev., 1991-94, Modern Intellectual History, 2002—; assoc. editor Am. Nat. Biography, 1990-97. Bd. dirs. Mcpl. Art Soc. N.Y., N.Y.C., 1983-84, N.Y. Coun. for the Humanities, 1989-96, chair, 1992-95; mem. gov. coun. Rockefeller Archives Ctr., Pocantico Hills, N.Y., 1987-92; trustee Grace Sch., N.Y.C., 1987-94. N.Y. Inst. Humanities fellow, 1977-88; Guggenheim fellow, 1980-81; Rockefeller Found. fellow, 1984-85; Getty scholar Getty Ctr. for Study of Art and Humanities, 1992-93; Mel and Lois Tukman fellow Cullman Ctr. for Scholars and Writers, N.Y. Pub. Libr., 2002-2003. Fellow Am. Acad. Arts and Scis.; mem. Am. Hist. Assn., Orgn. Am. Historians, Soc. Am. Historians, Writers Guild, PEN. Democrat. Home: 54 Washington Mews New York NY 10003-6608 Office: NYU Dept History 53 Washington Sq S New York NY 10012-1098

BENDER, VIRGINIA BEST, computer scientist, educator; b. Rockford, Ill., Feb. 10, 1945; d. Oscar Sheldon and Genevieve Best; m. Robert Keith Bender, July 19, 1969; children: Victoria Ruth, Christopher Keith. BS in Chemistry, Math., No. Ill. U., 1967; postgrad., U. Ill., 1967-69; MBA, Loyola U., Chgo., 1973. Cert. computer profl. Sr. sys. rep. Burroughs Corp., Chgo., 1969-73; sys. analyst Marshall Field & Co., Chgo., 1973-74; project leader Fed. Home Loan Bank, Chgo., 1974-76; sr. sys. analyst United Air Lines, Elk Grove Village, Ill., 1976-78; supr. Kemper Group, Long Grove, Ill., 1978-82; prof. computer info. sys., coord. computer info. sys. William Rainey Harper Coll., Palatine, Ill., 1982—2002, prof. emeritus, 2002—. Spkr. Midwest Computer Conf., DeKalb, Ill., 1988, moderator, 91; exch. prof. Maricopa CC, Mesa, Ariz., 1990, rsch. sabbatical, 93, 98; spkr. conf. info. tech. League for Innovation, Kansas City, Mo., 1995; steering com. Midwest Computer Conf., 1995—99; facilitator ToolBook User's Conf., Colo. Springs, Colo., 2000, presenter, Colorado Springs, 2001—03; adj. prof. SUNY/Westchester CC, Valhalla, 2003—. Nat. chief mother-dau. group Indian Maidens YMCA, Des Plaines, 1982—83; mem. Vols. Pks. Environ. Edn. Westchester County Dept. Pks., Recreation and Conservation, NY, 2002—; mem. choir Kingswood United Meth. Ch., Buffalo Grove, Ill., 1982—2002, asst. organist, 1982—89; mem. choir 1st Congl. Ch., Chappaqua, NY, 2002—, mem. bell choir, 2003—. Named Tchr. of the Month, Burroughs Corp., Chgo., 1972. Mem.: No. Ill. Computer Soc., Ill. Assn. Data Processing Instrs., Inst. Cert. Computer Profls. (life), No. Ill. Alumni Assn. (life), Mortar Bd., Sigma Zeta, Phi Theta Kappa. Avocations: swimming, sewing, needlecrafts, reading, playing piano. Office: William Rainey Harper Coll 1200 W Algonquin Rd Palatine IL 60067-7373 E-mail: vbender@hotmail.com.

BENDERSKY, LEONID A. metallurgist, researcher; b. Tiraspol, Moldova, Dec. 24, 1948; s. Arkady and Rosa Bendersky; children: Gabriel, Naomi. PhD, Technion, Israel, 1982. Metallurgist NIST, Gaithersburg, Md., 1983—. Achievements include discovery of of a decagonal phase with two-dimensional quasiperiodicity; 3 Patents Of High-Strength High Temperature Light Intermetallic Alloys; discovery of icosahedral twins in Al-based alloys; research in High-temperature Ti-based intermetallics. Office: NIST 100 Bureau Dr Gaithersburg MD 20899 Home Fax: 301-975-4553; Office Fax: 301-075-4553. Personal E-mail: leoben@highstream.net. E-mail: leoben@nist.gov.

BENDIG, WILLIAM CHARLES, editor, artist, publisher; b. Corry, Pa., Dec. 1, 1927; s. William Charles and Hazel Grace Mae (Dailey) B. BA with honors, Trinity Coll., 1953; postgrad., U. London, 1955-56. Founding editor Erie (Pa.) Tribune, 1944-48; mgr. Nat. Symphonic Choir, Erie, 1946-49; program mgr. Erie Philharmonic Orch., 1947-49; instr. Cheshire (Conn.) Acad., 1953-54, Brunswick Sch., Greenwich, Conn., 1954-55; editor in chief, pub. theARTgallery Mag., Ivoryton, Conn., 1957-84; prin., pub. Hollycroft. Pubs., Ivoryton, 1987—; editor in chief Botswana Rev., Ivoryton and Gaborone, 1988-90; curator, archivist theARTgallery Archive, 1990—; pres. Hollycroft Found., 1992—; cons. Kuwait Info. Office, Washington, 1993-96; chief curator Madison (Conn.) Mile, 2001—. Cons. Submarine Force Libr. & Nautilus Mus., Groton, Conn., 1994—; dep. dir. U.S.-Africa Arts Found., Gaborone, 1988-93, life trustee; trustee Contemporary Sculptors Guild, 1994-95; dep. dir. Sculptors Guild, N.Y.C., 1997—; juror nat. art exhbns.; lectr. univs. and mus. Designer, fabricator Pentecost rose window All Sts.' Episcopal Ch., Ivoryton, 1988; contbr. works in various art exhbns. V.p. Essex Art Assn., 1960-62; founding v.p. Ivoryton Village Assn.; mem. Essex Landmark Commn., 1981-82; trustee Ivoryton Pub. Libr., Ivoryton Playhouse Found. (founding); dir. art seminar program. Episcopal Conf. Ctr., Ivoryton, 1982-92. Mem. Mediaeval Acad. Am., Africa Studies Assn., Friends of Trinity Libr., Naval Submarine League, Trinity Coll. Alumni Assn. (pres. New London chpt. 1963-67), Grad. Club, New Haven Club. Episcopalian (vestryman 1970-92). Home and Office: Hollycroft Found Main St Ivoryton CT 06442-0278

BENDINER, ROBERT, writer, editor; b. Pitts., Dec. 15, 1909; s. William and Lillian (Schwartz) B.; m. Kathryn Rosenberg, Dec. 24, 1934; children: David, William (dec.), Margaret. Student, CCNY, 1928-33; LHD (hon.), L.I. U., 1994. Mng. editor The Nation, N.Y.C., 1937-44, assoc. editor, 1946-50, free-lance writer, 1951-68, 78—. Lectr., program chmn. Wellesley Summer Inst. Social Progress, 1946-53; mem. faculty Salzburg Sem. in Am. Studies, 1956; vis. lectr. journalism Wesleyan U. (Conn.), 1983 Contbg. editor The Reporter, N.Y.C., 1956-60; U.S. corr. New Statesman, London, 1959-61; mem. editorial bd. N.Y. Times, 1969-77; author: The Riddle of the State Department, 1942, White House Fever, 1960, Obstacle Course on Capitol Hill, 1964, Just Around the Corner, 1967, The Politics of Schools, 1969, The Fall of the Wild, The Rise of the Zoo, 1981, TV documentary NBC White Paper, The Man in the Middle, The State Legislator, 1961. Served with AUS, 1944-45. Guggenheim fellow, 1962-63; grantee Carnegie Fund; recipient Benjamin Franklin Mag. award U. Ill., 1955, NEA award, 1960 Mem. Nat. Press Club. Clubs: Coffee House (N.Y.C.). Home and Office: Southampton Estates 238 Street Rd Apt A202 Southampton PA 18966-3128

BENDITT, THEODORE MATTHEW, humanities educator, educator; b. Phila., Oct. 23, 1940; m. Anne Rosamond Shaw, Feb. 3, 1968; 1 child, David Shaw. AB, U. Pa., 1962, JD, 1965, MA, 1967; PhD, U. Pitts., 1971. Instr. Duke U., Durham, N.C., 1970-71, asst. prof., 1971-75, U. So. Calif., Los Angeles, 1975-78; assoc. prof. U. Ala., Birmingham, 1978-83, prof., 1983—, dean, Sch. Arts and Humanities, 1984-98. Author: Law as Rule and Principle, 1978, Rights, 1982, Modest Judicial Restraint, 1999. Recipient Younger Humanist Fellowship, NEH, 1974-75. Mem. Am. Philos. Assn., Am. Soc. for Polit. and Legal Philosophy, Amintaphil. Office: Univ of Ala at Birmingham Dept Philosophy Birmingham AL 35294-1260

BENDITZSON, DAVID JEROME, physician, educator; b. Chgo., June 14, 1938; s. Eser and Pearl Linn Benditzson; m. Ruth Joyce Benditzson, July 2, 1966. BSBA, Roosevelt U., 1959; MD, Chgo. Med. Sch., 1965. Diplomate Am. Bd. Internal Medicine. Resident, fellow Northwestern U. Med. Sch., Chgo., 1968-72, clin. instr., 1972—; pvt. practice Chgo., 1972—; clin. instr. U. Ill., Chgo., 1972-90, U. Chgo., 1990-99. Capt. USAF, 1966-68. Mem. AMA, Am. Soc. Internal Medicine, Ill. Med. Assn., Chgo. Med. Assn., Chgo. Soc. Internal Medicine. Home: 260 E Chestnut # 4107 Chicago IL 60611 Office: 55 E Washington Ste 2903 Chicago IL 60602

BENDIX, HELEN IRENE, lawyer; b. N.Y.C., July 24, 1952; d. Gerhard Max and Eva Gabriela (Sternberger) B.; m. John A. Kronstadt, Nov. 29, 1974; children: Jessica Claire Kronstadt, Erik Bendix Kronstadt, Nicola Eva Kronstadt. BA, Cornell U., 1973; JD, Yale U., 1976. Bar: Calif. 1976, D.C. 1978, U.S. Dist. Ct. D.C. 1980, U.S. Dist. Ct. (ctrl. dist.) Calif. 1986, U.S. Ct. Appeals (D.C. cir.) 1981, U.S. Ct. Appeals (9th cir.) 1987, U.S. Dist. Ct. (so. dist.) Calif. 1990. Law clk. to Hon. Shirley M. Hufstedler U.S. Ct. Appeals (9th cir.), L.A., 1976-77; assoc. Wilmer Cultler & Pickering, Washington, 1977-79; asst. prof. law UCLA, 1979-80; from assoc. to ptnr. Leva Hawes Symington Martin & Oppenheimer, Washington, 1980-85; of counsel Gibson Dunn & Crutcher, L.A., 1986-89; ptnr. Heller Ehrman White & McAuliffe, L.A., 1989-96; sr. v.p., gen. counsel KCET Cmty. TV of So. Calif., 1996—; judge Mcpl. Ct. L.A. Jud. Dist., 1997-2000, Superior Ct. L.A., 2000—. Vis. prof. law UCLA, 1985-86. Co-author: Moore's Federal Practice, Vols. X and XI, 1976, Vols. XII and XIII, 1979; contbr. articles to profl. jours. Violinist Palisades Symphony, Pacific Palisades, Calif., 1989—. Mem. European Union Ctr. of Calif., (mem. exec. adv. bd., 2003—), D.C. Bar Assn., Calif. State Bar Assn. (chairperson internat. law sect. 1990-91), Calif. Judges Assn., L.A. County Bar Assn. (past pres. dispute resolution svcs.), Jud. Coun. Calif. (mem. ad hoc com. on canon 6D 1998, working group on mediator ethics 2000, mem. access and fairness adv. com.), Nat. Charity League (past chmn. 12th grade class), Chancery Club, Phi Beta Kappa. Office: Dept 18 111 N Hill St Los Angeles CA 90012-3014 E-mail: hbendix@lasuperiorcourt.org.

BENDIX, JANE, artist, author, anthropological illustrator; b. Lansing, Mich., Oct. 20, 1920; d. Helmer and Violet Walstrum; m. Reinhard Bendix, July 5, 1940 (dec. Feb. 1991); children: Karen, Erik, John. BA, U. Chgo., 1941; postgrad., Art Inst. Chgo., 1941-43. Freelance artist, 1941—. Author: Mi'ca, 1987 (Kinderbuch prize 1987), Mi'ca, Buffalo Hunter, 1992, Türkishöhle, 1990, Chaco. The Anasazi Mystery, 1997, The Secret Map, 2000; exhbns. San Francisco, 1988, Oakland, Calif., 1979, Goldern, Switzerland, 1965, Oxford, Eng., 1966, Washington, 1975, Berlin, Germany, 1990. Mem. Calif. Watercolor Assn. Home: 3 Orchard Ln Berkeley CA 94704-1821

BENDOR, SUSAN JULIA, social worker, educator; b. Budapest, Feb. 5, 1937; arrived in U.S., 1959, naturalized, 1968; d. David and Elizabeth Blum; m. Edgar Bendor, Nov. 29, 1959; children: Jane Melissa, Catherine Anne. BS in Math. and Physics, Bishops U., Lennoxville, Que., Can., 1968; M in Social Svc., Adelphi U, 1962; PhD in Social Welfare, CUNY, 1986. Caseworker Jewish Childcare Assn., NYC, 1962—64; psychiat. social worker Mt. Sinai Hosp., NYC, 1964—65; chief psychiat. social worker Nassau County Med. Ctr., East Meadow, NY, 1968—75; assoc. dir. field devel. SUNY, Stony Brook, NY, 1971—75; dir. social work Molloy Coll., Rockville Centre, NY, 1977—81; assoc. dir. social svcs. dept Montefiore Med. Ctr., Bronx, NY, 1981—86; assoc. prof., dir. gerontology program Yeshiva U., NYC, 1988—. Co-chair Coun. On Aging, NYC, 1994—; head start cons. OEO, DC, 1966—68; sr. tng. cons. sch. social work Hunter Coll., NYC, 1977—80; adv. social work com. Am. Ctr. South. Contbr. articles to profl. jours. Chair social action com., mem. bd. dirs. Temple Isaiah, Great Neck, NY, 1995. Master: NASW (licentiate; exec. bd. 2001—03, chair 1999—2001, Citations from County Execs. 2001, Social Worker of Yr. 1975). Avocations: folk dancing, swimming. Home: 38 Allenwood Road Great Neck NY 11023-2127 Office: Wurzweiler School Of Social Work-Yeshiva 2495 Amsterdam Avenue New York NY 10033 Office Fax: 212-960-0822.

BENEDETTO, ANTHONY DOMINICK See BENNETT, TONY

BENEDETTO, LORRAINE ANN, computer scientist; b. Newark, Oct. 17, 1949; d. Frank and Hilda May (Holt) Vanna; m. William Robert Benedetto, Sept. 12, 1970; children: Annemarie Lyn, William Francis. BA, Newark State Coll., 1972. Secondary tchr. St. Casimir's Sch., Newark, 1972-73; substitute tchr. various schs., NJ, 1975-86; mgr. Burger King, Hazlet, NJ, 1979-81; computer operator Miller-Wohl Corp., Secaucus, NJ, 1981-83, supr. computer ops., 1983-84, mgr. computer ops., 1984-86; tech. support computer ops. Petrie Stores Corp., Secaucus, 1986—; tchr. Queen of Peace Sch., North Arlington, NJ, 1990—, social studies dept. chmn. Organizer Local Neighborhood Improvement, Union Beach, NJ, 1977—80. Mem.: NAFE. Roman Catholic. Avocations: reading, collecting music, computers. Home: 144 Arlington Blvd North Arlington NJ 07031-5733 E-mail: ibenedet@verizon.net.

BENEDICK, JAMES MICHAEL, psychotherapist; b. Winston Salem, N.C., Dec. 16, 1942; s. Michael Anthony and Isla May (McSperrin) B.; m. Janice Yantzer-Benedick, Sept. 15, 1978; children: Jesse Mathew, Jason Kirk. BA, Coll. William and Mary, 1975; MSW, Norfolk State Coll., 1977; EdD, U. Sarasota, 2001. Bd. cert. diplomate in clin. social work, in clin. sexology, in clin. forensic counseling; lic. clin. social worker, Fla. Staff social worker Peninsula Group Home, Hampton, Va., 1977-78; sch. social work supr. Mandan (N.D) Pub. Sch., 1978; clin. social worker S.E. Human Svc. Ctr., Fargo, N.D., 1978-84, Coastal Recovery Ctrs., Sarasota, Fla., 1989-90; mgr. community svcs. div. Red River Human Svcs. Found., Fargo, 1984-89; psychotherapist Lifestyle Profl. Ctr., Sarasota, 1990-92; pvt. practice Sarasota, 1992—; psychotherapist Neurobehavioral Medicine Ctr., Sarasota, 1997, 99. Adj. faculty Argosy U., 2003. With U.S. Army, 1960-63. Fellow Am. Acad. Clin. Sexologists; mem. NASW, APA, Acad. Cert. Social Workers, Register Clin. Social Workers Avocations: physical fitness, jogging, reading, study. Office: 1620 Main St Ste 8 Sarasota FL 34236-5824 E-mail: jbenedic@tampabay.rr.com

BENEDICK, RICHARD ELLIOT, diplomat; b. N.Y.C., May 10, 1935; s. Lester and Jean (Shamski) B.; m. Hildegard K.G. Schulz, 1957 (div.); children: Andreas Peter Anselm, Julianna Valeska.; m. Helen Ruth Freeman, 1983 (div.); m. Irene E. Federwisch, 1997. AB summa cum laude, Columbia U., 1955; MA, Yale U., 1956; postgrad., Oxford U., 1956; DBA, Harvard U., 1962. Program economist AID U.S. Dept. State, Washington, 1958, Tehran, Iran, 1959-61, Karachi, Pakistan, 1962-64; economist OECD, Paris, 1964-66; 1st sec. Am. Embassy, Bonn, Germany, 1966-71; dir. Office Devel. Fin., Washington, 1971-75; counselor for econ. and comml. affairs Am. Embassy, Athens, Greece, 1975-77; mem. sr. seminar Dept. State, Washington, 1977-78; coord. population affairs with rank amb. U.S. Dept. State, Washington, 1979-84, dep. asst. sec. for environ., health and natural resources, 1984-87; sr. fellow World Wildlife Fund, 1987-98; dep. dir. Battelle Pacific N.W. Nat. Lab., 1998—; sr. adv. Battelle/Joint Global Change Rsch. Inst./U. Md., 2001—. Spl. advisor to sec. gen. UN Conf. on Environ. and Devel., 1990-92, Internat. Conf. on Population and Devel., 1993-94; pres. Nat. Coun. for Sci. and Environ., 1994—; vis. prof. Academie Internationale de l'Environnement, Geneva, 1992-96; lectr. in field; head U.S. del. to numerous confs.; chief U.S. negotiator Montreal Protocol on protection of ozone layer, 1985-87; bd. dirs. Population Resource Ctr., 1984—, Pacific Inst., 1990—, Transparency Internat., 1994-97, Environ. and Energy Study Inst., 1994—; mem. internat. adv. bd. Battelle, 1994-97, Environ. Tech. Ctr., Berlin, 1996; v.p. OECD Environ. Com., 1984-87; v.p. Transboundary Air Pollution Conv., Econ. Commn. for Europe, 1985-87; vis. fellow Nat. Ctr. Atmospheric Rsch., 1988, 89, Ostwestwirtschafts Akademie, Berlin, 1991-96, Wissenschaftszentrum Berlin, 1995—; Stimson fellow Yale U., 2001; adj. faculty Fgn. Svc. Inst., U.S. Dept. State, 1999. Author: Industrial Finance in Iran, 1964, The High Dam and the Transformation of the Nile, 1979, Ozone Diplomacy, 1991, 2d edit., 1998; contbr. articles to profl. jours. Recipient Presdl. Meritorious Svc. award, 1984, 90, Superior Honor medal Dept. State, 1985, 87, John Jacob Rogers award, 1993, Presdl. Disting. Svc. award, 1988, ann. award Climate Inst., 1988, UN Global Ozone award, 1997; Evans fellow Oxford U., 1956, Population Ref. Bur. hon. fellow, 1986. Fellow World Acad. of Art and Sci. (elected 1991), Am. Acad. Diplomacy (elected 2002); mem. Toenissteiner Kreis (Germany), Phi Beta Kappa. Home: 4111 27th St N Arlington VA 22207-5211 Office: Joint Global Change Rsch Inst 8400 Baltimore Ave College Park MD 20470 E-mail: richard.benedick@battelle.org.

BENEDICT, A. JOAN, music educator; b. Findlay, Ohio, Sept. 6, 1933; d. James E. Grauel and Alice Caroline Leiter Grauel; m. John E. Benedict, June 26, 1954; children: Julia Lynne Bauer, Jeffrey James, Joel Edward, Jay Douglas. Student, Toledo U., 1951, Findlay Coll. Tchr. piano, organ, theory Groman's Music Store, Findlay, Ohio; organist Coll. First Ch. of God, 1952—53. Program chair, sec.-treas., v.p., pres. Ohio Music Tchrs. Assn., Findlay; adj. Am. Coll. Musicians, Nat. Guild Auditions, Guild Ctr., Mich., Ind., Ky. Mentoring in Pedagogy with Dr. Coral Martin, Findlay Coll., 1948—51; mem., pianist St. John Mennonite Ch. Mem.: Ohio Music Tchrs., Findlay Cptr. (v.p.), Nat. Guild Piano Tchrs., Christian Women's Club. Republican. Achievements include development of choir at Toledo Hosp. Sch. of Nursing for Sunday morning ch. svcs., 1951. Avocations: reading, crossword puzzles, lighthousing. Home: 3204 St Andrews Ct Findlay OH 45840

BENEDICT, ANTHONY WAYNE, lawyer; b. Perry, Okla., Aug. 18, 1956; s. Billy Lee and Kathryn Enola (Dowell) Benedict. BA in Polit. Sci., Sul Ross State U., 1981; JD with honors, U. Tex., 1984. Bar: Tex. 1984, U.S. Dist. Ct. (no. dist.) Tex. 1984, Okla. 1998, U.S. Ct. Appeals (5th cir.) 1989, U.S. Dist. Ct. (we. dist.) Tex. 2001. Atty. Phillips Petroleum Co., Amarillo, Tex., 1984-99; asst. atty. gen. State of Tex., 1999—. Republican. Avocations: golf, travel, computers. Home: 5903 Kayview Austin TX 78749 E-mail: abenedict@rr.austin.com., anthony.benedict@oag.state.tx.us.

BENEDICT, BURTON, retired museum director, anthropology educator; b. Balt., May 20, 1923; s. Burton Eli Oppenheim and Helen Blanche (Deiches) B.; m. Marion MacColl Steuber, Sept. 23, 1950; children: Helen, Barbara MacVean AB cum laude, Harvard U., 1949; PhD, U. London, 1954. Sr. rsch. fellow Inst. Islamic Studies, McGill U., Montreal, Que., Can., 1954-55; sociol. rsch. officer Colonial Office, London and Mauritius, 1955-58; sr. lectr. social anthropology London Sch. Econs., 1958-68; prof. anthropology U. Calif., Berkeley, 1968-91, prof. emeritus, 1991—, chmn. dept., 1970-71, dean social scis., 1971-74, dir. Hearst Mus. Anthropology, 1989-94; dir. emeritus Hearst Mus. Anthropology, 1994—. Dir. U. Calif. Study Ctr. for U.K. and Ireland, London, 1986-88 Author: Indians in a Plural Society, 1961; author and editor: Problems of Smaller Territories, 1967, (with M. Benedict) Men, Women & Money in Seychelles, 1982, The Anthropology of World's Fairs, 1983; contbr. numerous articles to profl. jours. Trustee East Bay Zool. Soc. Sgt. USAF, 1942-46. Recipient Western Heritage award Nat. Cowboy Hall of Fame, 1984; rsch. fellow Colonial Office, 1955-58, 60, U. Calif., Berkeley, 1974-75; grantee NEH, 1981-83. Fellow Royal Anthrop. Inst. (mem. coun. 1962-65, 67-68, 86-89), Am. Anthrop. Assn.; mem. Assn. Social Anthropologists of Brit. Commonwealth, Athenaeum Club (London) Avocations: museums, zoos, bird watching, postcards, world's fairs. Office: U Calif Berkeley Dept Anthropology Berkeley CA 94720-0001

BENEDICT, CHUCK (CHARLES J. BENEDICT JR.), writer, broadcaster, editor, producer; b. Silver Spring, Md., Apr. 17, 1919; s. Charles J. and Margaret (Olds) B.; m. Elsie Nelson, Feb. 6, 1944 (div. Jan. 1958); children: Charles J. III, LeAnne Karolyn Dann; m. Frances Frey, Dec. 30, 1960; children: Steven Robert, Richard Rodgers. Grad., Orangeburg (S.C.) H.S., 1935. Staff announcer Sta. WSPA-AM, Sta. WORD-AM, Spartanburg, S.C., 1941; prodr. Armed Forces Radio Svc. Hdqs., L.A., 1945-48, sports dir.., 1951-55; asst. prodr. Std. Program Libr., 1949-51; with L.A. Rams, 1953-92; sports anchor Sta. KTTV (11), L.A., 1963-70, color commentator, 1967-70; sports dir. Sta. KLAC, L.A., 1965-70. Prodr., announcer Game of the Day, 1952-55; writer, prodr. L.A. Rams pre-game and post-game shows, 1953, Sports Challenge, 1970-75; sports dir., sta. mgr. Sta. KOLD-AM, Yuma, Ariz., 1955-57; football play-by-play announcer Ariz. State, 1957; creator, editor-in-chief Petersen Pub. Co., 1970-80; mng. editor Football Today, 1976-77; talk show host Sta. KGIL-AM, 1976-77,

Sta. KIEV-AM, 1977-79; columnist Glendale News-Press, 1990—; host one man stage show, 1996-2000. Far west dir. Heisman Trophy electors, 1996—. Staff sgt. USAF, 1942-45. Republican. Episcopalian. Deceased.

BENEDICT, Mrs. COLEMAN HAMILTON See WOLFE, ETHYLE

BENEDICT, DOROTHY JONES, genealogist, researcher; b. Bronxville, N.Y., Mar. 23, 1916; d. Harry Edwin and Katherine Jones; m. Mark Charles Benedict; children: Ann Benedict Johnson, Sharon Benedict Bash, Gail Benedict Bain, Faye. BA, Goucher Coll., 1938. Statistician E.W. Axe Co., N.Y.C., 1938; with Nat. Labor Rels. Bd., N.Y.C., 1938-39. Leader Girl Scouts of Am., Glastonbury, Conn., 1957-64; creator convalescent homes Sunday mini-svc. Asbury Ch., Glastonbury, 1960-70. Mem. Nat. Soc. Magna Carta Dames, Arts Soc. Orlando Mus., DAR, Delta Delta Delta, Phi Beta Kappa. Methodist. Avocations: golf, walking, art. Home: 100 S Interlachen Ave Winter Park FL 32789-4438

BENEDICT, GAIL CLEVELAND, music educator; b. Rockville Ctr., N.Y., Dec. 15, 1942; d. Walter Charles and Louise Cleveland; m. Donald Alexander Davis, July 4, 1967 (div. Apr. 14, 1980); 1 child, Scott Paul Davis; m. Robert Lorin Benedict, July 6, 1983. BS in Music Edn., SUNY, Fredonia, 1964; MS in Adminstrn. and Supervision, Nova U., 1980; EdD, U. Sarasota, Fla., 1982. Cert. tchr. Fla., N.Y. Music tchr., dept. chair North Country Elem. Sch., Stony Brook, NY, 1964—66; music tchr., chorus dir. Narimasu Elem. Sch., Tokyo, 1966—67; vocal music tchr. Mineral Wells (Tex.) H.S., 1967—68; music tchr., chorus dir. Park Ave. Elem. Sch., Amityville, NY, 1968—70; music tchr., resource tchr. Magruder Elem. Sch., Newport News, Va., 1970—72; music specialist Skyview Elem. Sch., Pinellas Park, Fla., 1979—; adj. instr. Nova Southea. U., Tampa, Fla., 1991—. Gen. mgr. V.I. Properties, St. Petersburg, Fla., 1989—. Author: (book) Cruzan Child, 2002. Grantee, Pinellas County Arts Coun., 2001. Mem.: Pinellas Co. Music Educators Assn. (vocal chair 1980—83), Fla. Elem. Music Educators Assn. (chair Dist. III 1979—84), Music Educators Nat. Conf. Avocations: travel, reading, history, writing. Home: 6712 Cardinal Dr S Saint Petersburg FL 33707 Office: Skyview Elem Sch 8601 60th St N Pinellas Park FL 33782 E-mail: drmommusic@aol.com.

BENEDICT, JAMES NELSON, lawyer; b. Norwich, N.Y., Oct. 6, 1949; s. Nelson H. and Helen (Wilson) B.; m. Janet E. Fagal, May 8, 1982. BA magna cum laude, St. Lawrence U., 1971; JD, Albany Law Sch. of Union U., 1974. Bar: N.Y. 1975, U.S. Dist. Ct. (no., ea. and so. dists.) N.Y. 1975, U.S. Ct. Appeals (2d cir.) 1975, U.S. Ct. Appeals (8th cir.) 1977, U.S. Ct. Appeals (10th cir.) 1978, U.S. Ct. Appeals (11th cir.) 1982, U.S. Supreme Ct. 1978. Assoc. Rogers & Wells, N.Y.C., 1974-82; ptnr. Clifford Chance, N.Y.C., 1982—. Mem. bd. contbg. editors and advisors The Corp. Law Rev., 1976-86; contbr. articles to profl. jours. Bd. dirs. Reece Sch., N.Y.C., 1984-89, Stanley Isaacs Neighborhood Ctr., N.Y.C., 1984-89; trustee St. Lawrence U., Canton, N.Y., 1985-91. Mem. ABA (chmn. securities litigation subcom. on 1940 Act matters 1984-86, 96—), Fed. Bar Coun. N.Y. State Bar Assn., Assn. Bar City N.Y. (com. on securities regulaton, fed. legislation com., fed. cts. com.), Am. Soc. Writers on Legal Subjects, Sky Club (N.Y.C.), Scarsdale Golf Club, Phi Beta Kappa. Home: 26 Kensington Rd Scarsdale NY 10583-2217 Office: Clifford Chance 200 Park Ave51st Fl New York NY 10166-0800

BENEDICT, JOHN ANTHONY, II, army officer; b. Morgantown, W.Va., July 24, 1970; s. John Anthony Benedict and Diana Lynn (Pennington) Jones. BA, Va. Tech. U., 1992. Commd. 2d lt. U.S. Army, 1992, advanced through grades to maj., 2003; platoon leader, ops. officer 257th Signal Co., Camp Humphreys, Republic of Korea, 1993—94; platoon leader, co. exec. officer 82d Signal Battalion, Ft. Bragg, NC, 1995—96; dep. sec. gen. staff 82d Airborne Divsn., Ft. Bragg, 1995—96; squadron signal officer 17th Cav., Ft. Bragg, 1996—97; brigade signal officer 69th Air Def., Giebelstadt, Germany, 1997—99; co. comdr. 17th Signal Bat., Kitzingen, Germany, 1999—2001; mgr. HDQA Spectrum Mgmt. Office, Alexandria, Va., 2001—02; command, control and comms. sys. evaluator Army Evaluation Ctr., Alexandria, 2002—. Mem. Assn. U.S. Army, Armed Forces Comm.-Elect Assn., 82d Airborne Divsn. Assn., Am. Legion, Signal Corps Regimental Assn., VFW. Republican. Roman Catholic. Avocations: reading, hiking, golf, travel, football. E-mail: johnbenedict2@hotmail.com.

BENEDICT, JOSEPH HAROLD, JR., academic administrator, management consultant; b. Albany, N.Y., Aug. 13, 1941; s. Joseph Harold Sr. and Frances Ellen (Long) B.; m. Elizabeth Ann Roberts, July 8, 1968 (div.); children: Brian Arthur, Timothy Joseph. BS in Edn., SUNY, Brockport, 1965; MS in Edn. Adminstrn., SUNY, Albany, 1967; MS in Pub. Adminstrn., L.I. U. C.W. Post Campus, Brookville, 1985. Coord. student activities Rockland (N.Y.) Cmty. Coll., 1966-67; assoc. dir. student activities SUNY, Farmingdale, 1967-72; dir. student life L.I. U., 1972-90; mgmt. cons. Henn & Green Assocs. Inc., Williston Park, N.Y., 1984—; exec. dir. Bklyn. Coll. Student Svcs. Corp., Bklyn., 1990—. Mem. Assn. Coll. Unions Internat. (pres. 1986, v.p. regional affairs 1981-84, regional rep. 1984-85, Butts-Whiting award 1992), Nat. Assn. Campus Activities (chair commn. for vols. 1987-88). Democrat. Roman Catholic. Avocations: boating, bicycling, cross-country skiing. Home: Apt 511 140-18 Burden Crescent Briarwood NY 11435

BENEDICT, KENNETTE MARI, foundation executive, researcher; b. NYC, Jan. 19, 1948; d. Donald LaVerne Benedict and Ann Kennette Cnare; m. Jonathan David Casper, Aug. 2, 1980 (div. 2002); 1 child, Sarah Casper. AB, Oberlin Coll., 1971; PhD, Stanford U., 1981. Rschr. Gov.'s Com. Law Enforcement/Adminstrn. Criminal Justice, Boston, 1971; asst. prof. Rutgers U., New Brunswick, N.J., 1980-81, U. Ill., Urbana-Champaign, 1981-85; dep. dir. peace and internat. cooperation MacArthur Found., Chgo., 1989-92, dir. internat. peace and security, 1992—, sr. advisor on philanthropy, 2002—. Cons. Compton Found., Menlo Park, 1998-2000, bd. dirs.; adv. coun. Stanley Found., Muscatine, Iowa, 2001-, Ctr. for Effective Philanthropy, 2003—; advisor Rockefeller Bros. Fund, NYC, 1996-97, com. mem. Leonard Rieser Prize, Chgo., 2000— Contbr. articles to profl. jours. Bd. dirs. Compton Found., 2003— Lena Lake Forrest fellow Bus. and Profl. Women's Found., 1977 78. Mem. Coun. on Fgn. Rels., Internat. Inst. Strategic Studies, Chgo. Coun. on Fgn. Rels. Avocations: hiking, music. Office: MacArthur Found 140 S Dearborn St Chicago IL 60603

BENEDICT, LAWRENCE NEAL, foreign service officer; b. Independence, Mo., Dec. 17, 1942; s. Albert Michael and Audentia Elizabeth (Thomas) B.; m. Gloria Kay Bruning, July 2, 1966. BA, Calif. State U., Long Beach, 1974. V.p. A.M. Benedict & Assocs., Long Beach, Calif., 1966-72; vice consul Am. Embassy, Dahka, Bangladesh, 1974-77; comml. officer Am. Consulate Gen., Rio de Janeiro, 1977-79; desk officer for Bangladesh U.S. Dept. of State, Washington, 1979-80, desk officer for Turkey, 1980-82, dep. dir. devel. fin., 1986-89; fin./devel. officer Am. Embassy, Ankara, Turkey, 1982-86, counselor econ. affairs Islamabad, Pakistan, 1989-92, dep. chief of mission Khartoum, Sudan, 1992-95, amb. Praia, Cape Verde, 1996—. Staff sgt. USANG, 1963-69. Mem. Am. Fgn. Svc. Assn. Avocations: tennis, reading, collecting books and wine. Address: PO Box 1217 Pearblossom CA 93553

BENEDICT, MANSON, chemical engineer, educator; b. Lake Linden, Mich., Oct. 9, 1907; s. C. Harry and Lena I. (Manson) Benedict; m. Marjorie Oliver Allen, July 6, 1935 (dec. 1995); children: Mary Hannah (Mrs. Myran C. Sauer, Jr.), Marjorie Alice (Mrs. Martin Cohn). B in Chemistry, Cornell U., 1928; MS, MIT, 1932, PhD, 1935. NRC fellow chemistry, 1935—36; rsch. assoc. geophysics Harvard, 1936—37; rsch. chemist M.W. Kellogg Co., 1938—43; in charge process design gaseous diffusion plant for uranium-235 Kellex Corp., 1943—46; dir. process development Hydrocarbon Rsch., Inc., 1946—51; tech. asst. to gen. mgr. AEC, 1951—52; prof. nuclear engring. MIT, 1951—69, Institute prof., 1969—73, prof. emeritus, 1973—, head dept. nuclear engring., 1958—71; dir. Burns & Roe, Inc., 1979—85. Sci. advisor Nat. Rsch. Corp., 1951—58, dir., 1962—67; mem. gen. adv. com. AEC, 1958—68, chmn., 1962—64; dir. Atomic Indsl. Forum, 1966—72; mem. energy R & D adv. coun. FEA, 1973—75. Co-editor: Engineering Developments in the Gaseous Diffusion Process, 1949; co-author: Nuclear Chemical Engineering, 1981. Recipient Indsl. and Engring. Chemistry award, Am. Chem. Soc., 1962, Perkin medal Soc. Chem. Industry, Robert E. Wilson award in nuclear chem. engring., Fermi award, AEC, 1972, John Fritz medal, Engring. Founder Socs., 1974, Nat. Medal Sci., 1975, Henry D. Smyth Nuclear Statesman award, Atomic Indsl. Forum, 1979, Washington award, Western Soc. Engrs., 1982. Fellow: AIChE (William H. Walker award 1947, Founders award 1965), Am. Philos. Soc., Am. Acad. Arts and Scis., Am. Nuclear Soc. (pres. 1962—63, Arthur H. Compton award); mem.: NAS, Nat. Acad. Engring. (Founders award 1976), Country Club Naples (Fla.), Weston Golf Club (Mass.), Sigma Xi. Office: MIT Nuclear Engng Dept 77 Mass Ave Cambridge MA 02139-4307

BENEDICT, MARK J. government analyst, marketing executive, lawyer, real estate investment consultant; b. San Antonio, Oct. 1, 1951; s. Irvin J and Loraine H. (Layer) B. AA cum laude, San Antonio Coll., 1970; BA summa cum laude, Trinity U., 1973; JD, U. Tex., 1977. Bar: Tex. 1978, U.S. Dist. Ct. (we. dist.) Tex. 1979, U.S. Ct. Appeals (5th cir.) 1980, U.S. Supreme Ct. 1980; lic. real estate salesperson, Tex., Va. Legis. aide Tex. State Rep., San Antonio, 1977-79; law ptnr. Nowlin and Benedict, San Antonio, 1977-79; atty., owner Law Offices of Benedict, San Antonio, 1980-86; sr. mgmt. Rasamny Group, N.Y.C., 1986-87; residential and comml. broker Shannon and Luchs, Washington, 1987-88; v.p. mktg. Microlaw/MLX, Washington, 1987-88; comml. broker Century 21 Real Estate, Fairfax, Va., 1988-91; v.p. mktg. Shared Equity Cons., Annandale, Va., 1988-91; owner, pres. PreMar Cons., Austin, Tex., 1986—, PreMar Internat., Fredericksburg, Tex., 1990—; exec. v.p. Equity Ventures Group, Inc., Washington, San Francisco, 1990-91. Cons. Resolution Trust Corp., Washington, 1989-91; mktg. aide Fairfax C. of C., 1988-91; mem. No. Va. Bd. Realtors, Fairfax, 1987—; sr. analyst U.S. Presdl. Com. for Disabled, Washington, 1991-2001; policy analyst USDA/Food Safety Inspection Svc., Washington, 2001—; v.p. programs Assoc. People with Disabilities in Agr. Rsch. editor Tex. Internat. Law Jour., 1972-73, Am. Jour. Criminal Law, 1972-73; contbr. articles to jours. and newspapers. Active Big Bros. and Sisters, San Antonio, 1979-80, Young Republicans. Benedict fellow, 1973; named one of Outstanding Young Men of Am., 1980, Top Broker, U.S. C. of C., 1979. Mem.: ABA, Tex. State Soc., Tex. Soc. City Attys., USDA Toastmasters (pres. 2003—), Optimist Club San Antonio, U. Tex. Ex-Student Assn. (life), Phi Alpha Delta, Phi Theta Kappa, Phi Beta Kappa. Republican. Lutheran. Avocations: chess, travel, tennis, sailing, food and wine. Office: 477 Summit Cir Fredericksburg TX 78624-5042

BENEDICT, MARY-ANNE, nursing educator, consultant; b. Cambridge, Mass., Apr. 14, 1944; d. Preston E. and Mary Rose (Murphy) Woodward; m. Charles A. Benedict, Sept. 20, 1969; children: Annmarie, Helene, Laura. BS in Nursing, Boston Coll. Sch. Nursing, 1967; MSN, Salem State Coll., 1995. Cert. orthopedic nurse. Instr. Sch. Nursing New Eng. Bapt. Hosp., Boston, 1969-79, edn. specialist, 1979-96; coord. edn. and tng. Emerson Hosp., Concord, Mass., 1997-99; ednl. accreditation cons., 1999—. Lt. (j.g.) USN, 1966-69. Mem. Nat. Assn. Orthopedic Nurses, Sigma Theta Tau (Alpha Chi chpt.), Am. Nurses Credentialling Ctr. Com. on Accrediatation, 2003. Home: 84 Rockland Pl Newton MA 02464-1234 E-mail: maryannebenedict@aol.com.

BENEDICT, PETER BEHRENDS, lawyer; b. Pittsfield, Mass., Feb. 28, 1951; s. Bruce Merrill and Eleanor Jean (Hamel) B.; m. Jan Elizabeth Roina, May 20, 1972; children— Seth Behrends, Sarah Krapf. B.A. in English, Central Conn. State Coll., New Britain, 1973; J.D. cum laude, New Eng. Sch. Law, Boston, 1976. Bar: Conn. 1976, U.S. Dist. Ct. Conn. 1978, Mass. 1977, U.S. Supreme Ct. 1980. Atty., R. Richard Roina, Norwalk, Conn., 1976-78, Roina & Benedict, Norwalk, 1978, Roina, Benedict & Fiore, Norwalk, 1979, Rapaport & Manheim, Stamford, Conn., 1979-83, Rapaport, Manheim & Benedict, Stamford, 1983— . Bd. dirs. Norwalk YMCA, 1979-82, Literacy Vols. of Stamford, 1981— . Mem. ABA, Conn. Bar Assn., Stamford Bar Assn., Assn. Trial Lawyers Am., Conn. Trial Lawyers Assn. Independent. Congregational. Clubs: Bridgeport Rifle, Greenwich Boat and Yacht. Home: 33 Sachem Ln Greenwich CT 06830-7229 Office: Rapaport & Benedict PC 750 Summer St Stamford CT 06901-1020

BENEDICT, STEWART H. writer, playwright; Author (editor): (book) Tales of Terror and Suspense, 1963, Harper's English Grammar, 1954, The Crime Solvers, 1966, A Teacher's Guide to Senior High School Literature, 1966, Famous American Speeches, 1967, A Teacher's Guide to Modern Drama, 1967, A Teacher's Guide to Poetry, 1969, Blacklash: Black Protest in Our Time, 1970, Twelfth Night and Your Own Thing, 1970, Making a Difference, 1971, A Teacher's Guide to Contemporary Teenage Fiction, 1973, A Teacher's Guide to Jonathan Livingston Seagull, 1973, A Teacher's Guide to Fireweed, 1973, A Teacher's Guide to the Faraway Lurs, 1973, The Literary Guide to the United States, 1981, Street Beat, 1982, Curtain Going Up, 2002; contbr. chapters to books; author: (plays) One Day in the Life of Ivy Dennison, 1967, The Puppeteer, 1967, Not Guilty, 1967, Dance of Life, 1981, Bad Guy, 1972, Judgment Day, 1971, Count That Day Lost, 1971, Going Up, 1971, Red, 1972, Busy, Busy, Busy, 1975, A Crime, 1977, Floored, 1979, It's the Rhinoceros Man's Life, 1983, Down Home, 1984, Gift of Tongues, 1984, Dead Center, 1984, City Desk, 1985, The Wild West: A Liberated Look, 1987, St. Patrick's Day, 1987, Frissons, 1989, I Have Seen the Future..., 1989, Out of the Frying Pan, 1990, Gone to the Dogs, 1994, Left Face, 1994, Right Face, 1994, Family Values, 1994, Dr. Hyde and Mr. Jekyll, 1994, The Bargain, 1995, The Mother, 1995, The People Store, 1995, Tomorrow the World, 1995, The Robbery, 1996, Absolutely Fabulous Fairy Tales, 1996, Fancy Bread, 1996, Be Still My Liver, 1996, Yuletide Treasure, 1996, The Hero, 1999, Homicidal Murders, 2002; contbr. articles to profl. jours.

BENEDYK, MIKA ONO, editor, writer; b. Palo Alto, Calif., Jan. 21, 1963; d. Hiroshi Ono and Jenny Ono Suttaby. BA, Reed Coll., 1985; MA in Law and Diplomacy, The Fletcher Sch., Tufts U., 1988. Spl. programs and comm. mgr. EF Internat., Cambridge, Mass., 1989—90; pub. rels. writer Geto & deMilly, N.Y.C., 1990—91; editor The Rockefeller U., N.Y.C., 1991—94; editl. svcs. mgr. The Rockefeller Group, N.Y.C., 1994—95; sr. editor The Scripps Rsch. Inst., San Diego, 2000—. Cons. in field, 1995—2000. Editor (writer): (online publ.) News & Views (Internat. Assn. Bus. Communicator's Gold Quill award, 2002); author (editor): Rockefeller Center's Center Magazine; contbr. articles to jours. Pub. rels. com. mem. First Unitarian Universalist Ch., San Diego, 2000—01. Mem.: San Diego Profl. Editors Network, Nat. Sci. Writers Assn., Am. Med. Writers Assn., Internat. Assn. Bus. Communicators. Office: The Scripps Rsch Inst 10550 N Torrey Pines Rd TPC-20 San Diego CA 92037

BENEKE, MILLIE STONG, civic worker, author; b. Prairie City, Iowa; d. Rueben Ira and Lillian (Garber) Stong; m. Arnold W. Beneke, Aug. 10, 1939; children: Bruce Arnold, Paula Rae, Bradford Kent, Cynthia Jane, Lisa Patrice. Student, Washington U., 1942-43, Mankato State Coll., 1951, 67. Exec. sec. chmn. vol. svcs. ARC, St. Paul, 1940-41; v.p. Pi House, St. Paul, 1972-77; founder, bd. dirs., chmn. Project Interaction Boutique Minn. Correctional Instn. for Women, Shakopee, 1971—; supervising vol., 1970—. Republican chairwoman McLeod County (Minn.), 1969-73; mem. Rep. Minn. Platform com., 1970; McLeod County del. Rep. Minn. Central Com., 1969— ; mem. Rep. Feminist Caucus; alderman Glencoe City Council, 1974-80. Author: (play) The Garage Sale, 1978, Politics Unusual, 1979, The Househusband and the Working Wife, 1982, also children's pays. V.p. Friends of Libr., 1975—; bd. dirs. Buffalo Creek Palyers, 1976—, v.p., 1980—; bd. dirs. Mpls. Children's Theatre Co., Housing for elderly named in her honor. Mem. Glencoe Bus. and Profl. Women (Woman of Yr. 1975), Dramatists Guild. Lutheran. Home: Glenview Woods Box 215 330 Scout Hill Dr Glencoe MN 55336-3137

BENEKOHAL, RAHIM FARAHNAK, civil engineering educator, researcher, consultant; b. Tabriz, Iran;, naturalized, U.S. s. Mohammed and Batol (Farahnak) Benekohal. BS in Agrl. Engring., U. Rezaieh, 1977; BSCE, MSCE, Ohio State U., 1981, PhD in Civil Engring., 1986. Tchg. asst. Ohio State U., Columbus, 1981-86, instr., 1986; traffic engr. RKA, Inc., Tarrytown, N.Y., 1986-87; asst. prof. civil engring. U. Ill., Urbana, 1987—92, assoc. prof., 1993—2000, prof., 2001—. Transp. cons.; dir. Ill. Traffic and Safety Conf., Champaign, 1987—; chmn. Traffic Congestion and Traffic Safety in 21st Century Conf., 1997. Editor: Traffic Congestion and Traffic Safety in the 21st Century, 1997; contbr. articles to profl. jours. Mem. ASCE (Arthur M. Wellington prize, chair traffic ops. com.), Tranp. Rsch. Bd., Inst. Transp. Engrs. (Past Pres. award Ill. sect.), Phi Kappa Phi (hon., faculty), Chi Epsilon (hon., faculty). Home: 2719 Lakeview Dr Champaign IL 61822-7532 Office: U Ill 205 N Mathews Ave Urbana IL 61801-2350

BENENSON, CLAIRE BERGER, investment and financial planning educator, finance educator; b. NYC; d. Nathan H. and Alice E. (Zeisler) B.; m. Lawrence A. Benenson: children: Harold, Gary. BA, Wellesley Coll.; postgrad., N.Y. Inst. Fin., New Sch. Social Rsch., 1965-69. Security analyst Merrill Lynch, N.Y.C., 1940-43; rsch. assoc. Conn. Coll., 1943-45; lectr. NYU Mgmt. Inst., N.Y.C., 1960-68, New Sch. for Social Rsch., N.Y.C., 1963-86, dir. ann. conf. Wall St. and Economy, 1967-87, dir. ann. conf. Futures and Options, 1979-86, chmn. dept. investment and fin. planning, 1974-86. Adv. bd. The First Women's Bank, N.Y.C., 1984-86; bd. trustees Burnham Investors Trust, Phoenix Trust; trustee Simms Global Fund, 1987-89, Phoenix-Euclid Mkt. Neutral Fund, 1998—; pres. Money Marketeers, NYU, N.Y.C., 1979-80; cons. in field. Contbg. editor Exec. Jeweler, 1981-83; creator, moderator NBC-TV series, Wall St. for Everyone, 1967-78. Bd. overseers Parsons Sch. Design, N.Y.C., 1974-93; coun. conservaters N.Y. Pub. Libr., 1990—, chair SIBL com., 1994—; bus. leadership coun. Wellesley Coll., 1991—, bd. dirs. Ctrs. for Women, 1998-2002; v.p. 92d St. YMHA & YWHA, N.Y.C., lectr. com., co-chair planned giving com. Named Disting. Alumna Wellesley Coll., 1968, Durant Scholar, Wellesley Coll.; Alt. fellow in econs. Columbia U., 1938-39. Mem. Fin. Women's Assn. (bd. dirs., chair dirs. resource adv. com., co-chair program com. 1988 89), Nat. Assn. Bus. Econs., Women's Econ. Roundtable, Econ. Club N.Y., N.Y. Assn. Bus. Economists, Money Marketeers NYU, Durant Soc. Wellesley Coll., Women's Bond Club, Harmonie Club (bd. mem., chair forum com.), Cosmopolitan Club (investment and fin. com.), Phi Beta Kappa. Jewish.

BENENSON, EDWARD HARTLEY, realty company executive; b. N.Y.C., Mar. 27, 1914; s. Robert C. and Nettie B.; m. Gladys Steinberg, Apr. 5, 1962; 1 dau., Lisa; children by previous marriage: Thomas Hartley, James Stuart, Amy Roberta. BA, Duke, 1934. Chmn. Benenson & Co., Benenson Funding Corp., Benenson Investment Corp., Greenwich Devel. Corp., Sedgefield Realty N.C., Thomas James Corp., Arbee Properties of Fla. Author: The Benenson National Restaurant Guide, 1985-94, The Benenson Guide (Manhattan), 1991, 93, 95, 97, 98. Host Hiroshima Maidens, 1955-56; chmn. Urban-Patron Redevel. Commn., Stamford, Conn., 1957-58; mem. N.Y.C. Mayor's Youth Adv. Group, 1956-58; chmn. Friends Duke U. Mus. Art; bd. dirs. Duke Med. Ctr.; trustee emeritus Duke U.; bd. overseers Albert Einstein Coll. Medicine; trustee, mem. governing bd. Am. Ballet Theatre; mem. Rep. Nat. Com.; pres. YM-YWHA, 1958-63, now bd. dirs.; donor Benenson Arts awards Duke U.; univ. rep. com. Corp. Support for Pvt. Univs.; mem. President's Citizens Com.; donor Benenson Scholar award for Duke U. Lt. 77th inf. div. AUS, 1939-43. Decorated officer Ordre de Merite, Legion of Merit (France), knight Order St. John of Malta; recipient gold medal Renaissance Francaise, bronze medal City of Paris; Donor-Benenson scholar. Mem. Confrerie des Chevaliers du Tastevin (Grand Camerlingue d'Amerique), Culinary Inst. Am. (co-founder and trustee), Les Amis d'Escoffier Soc., Grand Jury Assn., Commerce and Industry Assn. N.Y., Nat. Bd. Realtors, Internat. Real Estate Fedn. (charter), Order of Lafayette, Fedn. War Vets. (France), Chaine des Rotisseurs (former chmn., Chaine Man of Yr. award 1991), Conseil d'Honneur, Am. Soc. Italian Legions Merit (Cavaliere d'Italia), Les Chevaliers de la Croix de Lorraine, Commanderie de Bordeaux, Res. Officers Assn., Conseil de la Croix du Combattant de l'Europe, Les Vingt-Six Soc. (founder), Presidents Club, Paris Am. Club, Wine and Food Soc., Century Country Club, Noyac Country Club, Palm Beach Country Club, Southampton Golf Club, Princeton Club, Army-Navy Club. Office: 445 Park Ave New York NY 10022-2606

BENENSON, JAMES, JR., manufacturer; b. Moultrie, Ga., Mar. 9, 1936; s. James and Mary (Camp) B.; m. Sharen Statler, Aug. 28, 1966; children: James, Clement. BS, MIT, 1958. With F. Eberstadt & Co., N.Y.C., 1960-65, Walker, Hart & Co., N.Y.C., 1965-68, James Benenson & Co., Inc., N.Y.C., 1968—; CEO, Vesper Corp., Newtown Square, Pa., 1978—; chmn. bd. Arrowhead Holdings Corp., Cleve., 1983—. Served with U.S. Army Chem. Corps, 1959. Woodrow Wilson scholar, 1959-60; Andover Teaching fellow, 1958-59 Mem. Hort. Soc. N.Y., N.Y. Bot. Garden (dir.), Soc. of Cincinnati, Century Assn., Racquet Club (Phila.), Buck's Harbor Yacht Club (Brooksville, Maine), N.Y. Yacht Club. Episcopalian. Office: care Vesper Corp 3400 W Chester Pike Newtown Square PA 19073-4638

BENENSON, MARK KEITH, lawyer; b. N.Y.C., Oct. 13, 1929; s. Aaron and Luba (Stein) B.; m. Letizia Pitigliani, Dec. 29, 1959; children: Alexander, Daniela. BSS., CCNY, 1951; JD, Columbia U., 1956. Bar: N.Y. 1956. Atty. Dept. Labor, Washington, 1957-58; practiced in N.Y.C., 1958—. Bd. dirs. Amnesty Internat. U.S.A., 1966-80, sec., 1966-67, chmn., 1968-71, vice chmn., 1972-73, gen. counsel, 1972-80; pres. Vanguard Found., Inc., 1962— Contbr. articles to profl. jours., mags. and newspapers. Exec. sec. Nat. Found. for Firearms Edn., 1983-91, Pres. 1991—. With U.S. Army, 1951-53. Recipient John Amber Gun Digest Writing award, 1998. Home and Office: 585 W End Ave New York NY 10024-1715

BENENSON, MICHAEL WILLIAM, physician, epidemiologist; b. N.Y.C., Mar. 31, 1941; s. Abram Salmon and Regina B.; m. Martina Muriel Srichandra, Jan. 19, 1974; children: Gabrielle Amie, Jonathan David. BA, Cornell U., 1963; MD, U. Md., 1968; MPH, Johns Hopkins Sch. of Hygiene, 1975. Diplomate Am. Bd. Preventive Medicine. Commd. 2nd lt. U.S. Army, 1967, advanced through ranks to col., 1983; epidemiologist Med. Rsch. Team/Republic of Vietnam, Saigon, 1970-71, SEATO Med. Lab., Bangkok, 1971-74; chief dept. epidemiology Walter Reed Army Inst. of Rsch., Washington, 1976-79; dir. Armed Forces Rsch. Inst. of Med. Scis., Bangkok, 1980-84; chief preventive medicine 7th Med. Command, Heidelberg, Germany, 1984-95; comdr., rear 30th Med. Brigade, Heidelberg, 1995-96; chief dept. preventive health svcs. Acad. Health Sci., Ft. Sam Houston, Tex., 1996-98; sr. scientist Henry M. Jackson Found., Bangkok, Thailand, 1998—. Preventive medicine cons. U.S. Army, Europe, Heidelberg, 1984-95; surgeon Operation Provide Comfort, U.S. Army, Incirlik, Turkey, 1991. Decorated Bronze Star, Order of Mil. Med. Merit, Legion of Merit (2); recipient Gorgas medal Assn. Surgeons of the U.S. Fellow Am. Coll. Preventive Medicine; mem. Am. Pub. Health Assn., Am. Soc. Tropical Medicine, Am. Coll. Epidemiology, AAAS. Avocations: sailing, skiing. Office: USACM-AFRIMS Apo AP 96546 E-mail: benenson@inet.co.th.

BENENSON, WALTER, nuclear physics educator; b. N.Y.C., Apr. 27, 1936; s. Charles and Sylvia (Ogush) B.; m. Antje Semsrott, Dec. 4, 1969; children: Arleigh Ann, Tanya. BS, Yale U., 1957; MS, U. Wis., 1959, PhD, 1962. Rsch. assoc. U. Strasbourg, 1962-63; asst. prof. nuclear physics Mich. State U., East Lansing, 1963-68, assoc. prof., 1968-72, prof., 1972-97; u. disting. prof. Nat. Superconducting Cyclotron Lab., 1997—, assoc. dir., 1980-82, 90-95. Vis. fellow Australian Nat. U., 1968; vis. prof. U. Grenoble, 1970; vis. lectr. Inst. for Nuclear Sci., Moscow, 1975; cons. Lawrence Berkeley Lab., 1979; participation profl. confs.; mem. nuclear sci. adv. com. U.S. Govt., 1993—. Assoc. editor: Phys. Rev. C; contbr. articles to profl. jours., mags. and newspapers. Bd. dirs. Happendance Dance Co., 1994-96. Nat. Acad. Scis. fellow, 1974; A.V. Humboldt Sr. Scientist award Fed. Republic of Germany Govt., 1988, Eminent Scientist award Riken, Japan, 1997. Fellow Am. Phys. Soc. (chmn. 6th Internat. Conf. on Atomic Masses 1979, mem. exec. com. divsn. nuclear physics); mem. Lansing Sailing Club (commodore 1987), Univ. Club, Golden Key Hon. Soc. (hon.). Home: 6111 Skyline Dr East Lansing MI 48823-1604 E-mail: benenson@nscl.msu.edu.

BENERIA, LOURDES, economist, educator; b. Boi, Lleida, Spain, Oct. 8, 1939; came to U.S., 1964; d. Agusti Beneria and Josepa Farre; children: Jordi, Marc. Licenciatura, U. Barcelona, Spain, 1961; MPhil, Columbia U., 1974, PhD in Econs., 1975. Coord. program on rural women ILO, Geneva, 1977-79; asst. prof. Rutgers U., New Brunswick, N.J., 1975-81, assoc. prof., 1981-86; prof. city and regional planning and women's studies Cornell U., Ithaca, NY, 1987—, dir. program on gender and global change, 1987—92, 2000—03, dir. Latin Am. studies program, 1993—97; pres. Internat. Assn. for Feminist Economy, 2003—. Recipient Narcis Monrutiol award for rsch. in the social scis., Barcelona. Office: Cornell Univ CRP W Sibley Hall Ithaca NY 14853-2148

BENERITO, RUTH ROGAN (MRS. FRANK H. BENERITO), chemist; b. New Orleans, Jan. 12, 1916; d. John Edward and Bernadette (Elizardi) Rogan; m. Frank Henshaw Benerito, Aug. 22, 1950. BS, H. Sophie Newcomb Coll., 1935; postgrad., Bryn Mawr Coll., 1935-36; MS, Tulane U., 1938, DSc (hon.), 1981; PhD, U. Chgo., 1948. Instr. chemistry Randolph-Macon Woman's Coll., Lynchburg, Va., 1940-43; Newcomb Coll., New Orleans, 1943-47; asst. prof. chemistry Tulane U., New Orleans, 1947-53, mem. grad. faculty, 1945—86,

adj. prof. dept. biochemistry Med. Sch., 1960-86, prof. emeritus, 1986; phys. chemist fat emulsion program So. Regional Lab., USDA, New Orleans, 1953-58, supervisory phys. chemist, head phys. chem. investigations natural polymers lab., 1958-86; cons. phys. chemistry of cellulose, adj. prof. chemistry U. New Orleans, 1986-96. Contbr. articles to profl. publs. Recipient Disting. Svc. USDA award, 1970, New Orleans Fed. Exec. Assn., 1967, Fed. Woman's award U.S. CSC, 1968; named one of 75 Most Important Women in U.S., Ladies Home Jour., 1971. Fellow Am. Inst. Chemists (Honor Scroll L.A. chpt. 1977); mem. AAAS, Am. Chem. Soc. (So. Chemist award 1968, Garvan medal 1970, S.W. Regional award 1972, Lemelson MIT Lifetime Achievement award 2002), Am. Oil Chem. Soc., Am. Assn. Textile Chemists and Colorists, Sci. Rsch. Soc. Am., Sigma Xi, Sigma Delta Epsilon, Delta Kappa Gamma (hon.), Iota Sigma Pi (hon.). Home: 4733 Marigny St New Orleans LA 70122-5020 Office: USDA PO Box 19687 New Orleans LA 70179-0687 *Happiness comes only by contributing to the development and happiness of others; it abounds with selflessness and can be found without travelling to far off places.*

BENES, FRANCINE M. neuroscientist, psychiatrist; b. N.Y.C., May 8, 1946; d. Joseph William and Emma Mary B. BA in Biology, St. John's U., 1967; PhD in Cell Biology, Yale U., 1972, MD, 1978. Lic. med. Mass. Lectr. in neuroanatomy Yale Sch. of Medicine, New Haven, 1975-77; asst. prof. psychiatry Harvard Med. Sch., Boston, 1982-87, assoc. prof., 1987-97, prof., 1997—; dir. program in structural and molecular neurosci. McLean Hosp., Belmont, Mass., 1982—, dir. Harvard Brain Tissue Resource Ctr., 1996—; dir. clin. neurosci. tng. program in psychiatry Harvard Med. Sch., 1994-99. Mem. bd. sci. counselors Nat. Inst. Mental Health, Bethesda, Md., 1994-98; mem. sci. adv. bd. Internat. Congress Schizophrenia Rsch., 1994—, Schizophrenia Bull., Calif. Neuro-Aids Tissue Network, San Diego, 2000—; cons. WHO, Paris, 1999. Neuropsychiatry editor Current Opinion in Psychiatry, 2000—; mem. editl. bd. Biotechniques, 1990-96, Devel. and Psychopathology, 1991—, Synapse, 1995—, Neuropsychopharmacology, 1997-2001, Schizophrenia Rsch., 1998—; contbr. articles to profl. jours. Bd. dirs. Waldon Pond Reservation Trust, Concord, Mass., 2001—; mem. Nat. Wildlife Fedn., Humane Soc. of U.S.; chair affirmative action com., McLean Hosp., Belmont, 1993-94. Recipient Shervert S. Frazier Lifetime Achievement award, 1999, Merit award NIMH, 2000-2002. Mem. Soc. for Neurosci., Am. Coll. Neuropsychopharmacology, World Fedn. Socs. of Biol. Psychiatry (co-chair task force on brain pathology 2001—), Nat. Assn. for Rsch. on Schizophrenia and Depression (mem. sci. adv. bd., Lieber prize 2002). Avocations: sailing, reading, creative writing. Office: McLean Hosp 115 Mill St Belmont MA 02478

BENES, SOLOMON, biomedical scientist, physician; b. Iasi, Romania, Mar. 28, 1925; came to U.S., 1978; s. Moritz and Cecilia (Abramovici) B.; m. Liudmila Topor, Mar. 27, 1954. MD, U Bucharest, Romania, 1952. Intern microbiology lab. Mil. Hosp., Bucharest, 1949-50, fellow microbiology lab., 1950-51, dir. clin. lab. outpatient dept., 1951-52; dir. rsch. lab. Ctr. for Radiobiology Rsch., Bucharest, 1953-57, 59-66; chief physician microbiology lab. Mil. Hosp., Bucharest, 1967-73; chief physician clin. lab. Ctr. of Haematology, Bucharest, 1973-76; assoc. in medicine Havard Med. Sch., Boston, 1978-81; asst. rsch. scientist, asst. prof. SUNY Downstate Med. Ctr., Bklyn., 1982-95; sr. rsch. scientist, asst. prof. SUNY Rsch. Found., Bklyn., 1995-98; ret., 1998. Author: (with others) Seminars in Infectious Diseases, 1983; contbr. articles to Sexually Transmitted Diseases, Antimicrobial Agts. and Chemotherapy, Jour. Clin. Microbiology, Proceedings of the 6th Internat. Symposium on Human Chlamydial Infections. Col. Romanian Army Med. Svc., 1946—73. Achievements include discovery that the Trachoma biovar of Chlamydia trachomatis is able to achieve intercellular propagation in cell culture and that, in a proper cell setting, this bacterium spreads from cell to cell in cell culture, contrary to what was generally believed. Home: 2421 Shellpot Dr Wilmington DE 19803-2547 E-mail: lands280@cs.com.

BENESCH, KATHERINE, lawyer; b. Balt., Jan. 18, 1946; d. Isaac and Jane (Van Praag) B.; m. Thomas Romer, Oct. 21, 1977. BA, Wheaton Coll., Norton, Mass., 1968; MPH, Yale U., 1970; JD, Duquesne U., 1979. Bar: Pa., 1980, U.S. Ct. Appeals (3rd cir.) 1981, U.S. Supreme Ct. 1985, N.J. 1991, U.S. Dist. Ct. Pa. 1980, U.S. Dist. Ct. N.J. 1991, U.S. Dist. Ct. (no. dist.) N.Y., 2000, U.S. Ct. Appeals D.C. 1992. Assoc. Dickie, McCamey and Chilcote, Pitts., 1979-80; asst. exec. dir., legal counsel Presbyn. U. Hosp., Pitts., 1980-81; assoc. Specter & Buchwach PC, Pitts., 1982-84; atty. Mellon Bank Corp., Pitts., 1984-86; pvt. practice Pitts., 1986-88; prin. Katherine Benesch & Assoc., Pitts., 1989-91; ptnr. Hannoch Weisman, Trenton, N.J., 1991-93; prin. Law Offices of Katherine Benesch, Princeton, 1994-96, 98; ptnr. Benesch & Obade, Princeton, 1997, Archer & Greiner, Princeton, 1999-2001, Duane Morris LLP, Princeton, 2001—. Adj. asst. prof. anesthesiology and critical care sch. medicine U. Pitts., mem. ctr. med. ethics; advisor Princeton U. Bioethics Forum. Editor: Medicolegal Aspects of Critical Care, 1986; contbr. chpts. to books and articles to profl. jours. Fellow: Am. Bar Found.; mem.: ATLA, ABA, Princeton Bar Assn. (past pres.), Mercer County Bar Assn., N.J. Bar Assn. (health and hosp. law sect., past pres.), Pa. Trial Lawyers Assn., Allegheny County Bar Assn. (bd. govs.), Pa. Bar Assn. (del.), Am. Health Lawyers Assn., Am. Arbitration Assn. Office: Duane Morris LLP 100 College Rd W Ste 100 Princeton NJ 08540-6604

BENESH, SARA C. adult education educator; b. Marinette, Wis., Aug. 26, 1973; d. Gregory J and Jayne C Benesh; m. Donald V Pashak, May 25, 2002. PhD, Mich. State U., 1999. Asst. prof. U. New Orleans, 1999—2001, U. Wis.-Milw., 2001—. Author: (book) The U.S. Courts of Appeals and the Law of Confessions: Perspectives on the Hierarchy of Justice. Grantee Grant for Creation of a Database, NSF, 1999. D-Liberal. Roman Catholic. Office: U Wis-Milwaukee PO Box 413 Milwaukee WI 53201 Office Fax: 414-229-5021. E-mail: sbenesh@uwm.edu.

BENESH, WILLIAM STEPHEN, lawyer, partner; b. San Antonio, July 24, 1961; s. G. A. and Betty Jo (Humphries) B.; m. Jennifer Loraine Kulcak, Apr. 27, 1985; children: William Stephen, Jr., Austin Humphries. BBA, U. Tex., 1984, JD, 1987. Bar: Tex. 1988, U.S. Ct. Appeals (5th cir.) 1989, U.S. Dist. Ct. (so. dist.) Tex. 1988, U.S. Dist. Ct. (ea. dist.) Tex. 1992, U.S. Dist. Ct. (no. dist.) Tex. 1993, U.S. Dist. Ct. (we. dist.) Tex. 1997. Assoc. Bracewell & Patterson, L.L.P., Houston, 1988-96, ptnr., 1996—. Fellow Tex. Bar Found., Houston Bar Found., Travis County Bar Assn. Republican. Avocations: scouting, camping, college sports. Home: 479 Tom Sawyer Rd Dripping Springs TX 78620 Office: Bracewell & Patterson LLP 111 Congress Ave Austin TX 78701-4043 E-mail: sbenesh@bracepatt.com.

BENESTAD, KELLY ANN, secondary school educator; d. Joyce Ann and William Gerald Myers; m. Christopher Thomas Benestad, Aug. 4, 2001. B in Polit. Sci., U. of Scranton, 1995—99; EdM, Worcester State Coll., 2000—03. Seconday schools provisional certification Mass. State Bd. Edn., 2000, cert. tchr. Mass. State Bd. Edn., 2002. Spl. edn. teacher's aid West Boylston H.S., Mass., 2000, social studies tchr., 2000—. Social studies dept. program leader West Boylston H.S., 2002—, nat. honor soc. advisor, 2002—. Mem.: Orgn. of Am. Historians. Avocations: running, bicycling, conducting historical research. Office: West Boylston HS 125 Crescent St West Boylston MA 01583

BENET, CAROL ANN LEVIN, journalist, teacher; b. Albany, N.Y., Mar. 21, 1939; d. Morton Harold and Ethel Leona (Maitland) Levin; m. Leslie Z. Benet, Sept. 8, 1960; children: Reed Michael, Gillian Vivia. AB, U. Mich., 1961, MA, 1964; PhD, U. Calif., Berkeley, 1987. Freelancejournalist, arts critic Ark newspaper, Belvedere, Calif., 1975—; book seminar tchr. U. Calif. Extension, Berkeley, in San Francisco, 1991-98; book group leader Marin County, San Francisco, 1987—; PhD career advisor/counselor U. Calif., Berkeley, 1993-97; journalist, arts critic Bay City News Svc., San Francisco, 1993—2000, Ind. Jour. newspaper, Marin, Calif., 1993—2002; theater critic ARTSF.com, San Francisco, 2000—. Adj. prof. Antioch Coll., Yellow Springs, Ohio, 1995-96, lectr. grad. humanities program, Dominican Coll, San Rafael, Calif., 1996-97; instr. lit. seminars San Franciso and Marin Counties. Author: The German Reception of Sam Shephard, 1990. Docent Asian Art Mus., San Francisco, 1987, De Young Mus., San Francisco, 1984. Jewish. Avocations: swimming, travel, gardening, hiking/walking, reading. Home: 53 Beach Rd Belvedere CA 94920-2364

BENET, LESLIE ZACHARY, pharmacokineticist, educator; b. Cin., May 17, 1937; s. Jonas John and Esther Racie (Hirschfeld) Benet; m. Carol Ann Levin, Sept. 8, 1960; children: Reed Michael, Gillian Vivia. AB in English, U. Mich., 1959, BS in Pharmacy, 1960, MS in Pharm. Chemistry, 1962; PhD in Pharm. Chemistry, U. Calif., San Francisco, 1965; PharmD (hon.), Uppsala U., Sweden, 1987; PhD (hon.), Leiden U., The Netherlands, 1995; DSc (hon.), U. Ill., Chgo., 1997, Phila. Coll. Pharm. and Sci., 1997, L.I. U., 1999. Asst. prof. pharmacy Wash. State U., Pullman, 1965—69; asst. prof. pharmacy and pharm. chemistry U. Calif., San Francisco, 1969—71, assoc. prof., 1971—76, prof., 1976—, vice chmn. dept. pharmacy, 1973—78, chmn. dept. pharmacy, 1978—96, dir. drug studies unit, 1977—, dir. drug kinetics and dynamics ctr., 1979—98, chmn. dept. biopharm. scis., 1996—98. Mem. pharmacology study sect. NIH, Washington, 1977—81, chmn., 1979—81, mem. pharmacol. scis. rev. com., 1984—88, chmn., 1986—88; mem. generic drugs adv. com. FDA, Washington, 1990—94; mem. Sci. Bd., 1992—98; chair external rev. com. CBER, 1998, chair expert panel on individual equivalence, 1998—2000; mem. sci. adv. bd. SmithKline Beecham Pharms., 1989—92, Pharmetrix, 1989—92, Alteon, Inc., 1993—. TheraTech, Inc., 1993—96, Roche Biosci., 1998—2001, Pain Therapeutics, Inc., 1999—, UMD, Inc., 1999—, Silico Insights, Inc., 2000—, InforMedix, 2001—; chmn. bd. AvMax, Inc.; bd. dirs. OxoN Medica, Inc., InforMedix, Inc., Josman Labs., Inc., Impax Pharmas., One World Health; chair com. on accelerating rsch., devel. and acquisition of med. countermeasures against biol. warfare agents Inst. Medicine and NRC, 2002—. Editor Jour. Pharmacokinetics and Biopharmaceutics, 1976—98, assoc. editor Pharmacology and Therapeutics, 1995—2000, editl. bd. The Effect of Disease States on Drug Pharmacokinetics, 1976, Pharmacology, 1979—, Pharmacy Internat., 1979—82, Pharm. Rsch., 1983—95, Pharmacokinetic Basis for Drug Treatment, 1984, Pharmacokinetics: A Modern View, 1984, ISI Atlas of Sci.: Pharmacology, 1988—89, Pharm. News, 1994—98, AAPS PharmSci, 1999—, Chemistry and Pharm. Bull., 2000—, Molecular Interventions, 2000—, Integration of Pharmacokinetics, Pharmacodynamics and Toxicokinetics in Rational Drug Development, 1992, Clinical Applications of Mifepristone (RU486) and Other Antiprogestins, 1993, Drug Metabolism and Pharmacokinetics, 2002—, contbr. more than 400 articles to profl. jours. Apptd. Forum on Drug Devel. and Regulation, 1988. Fellow: AAAS (mem.-at-large exec. com. pharm. scis. sect. 1978—81, 1991—95, chair 1996—97), Am. Assn. Pharm. Scientists (pres. 1986, treas. 1987, bd. dirs. 1988—93, Disting. Pharm. Scientist award 1989, Disting. Svc. award 1996, Wurster rsch. award in pharmaceutics 2000), Acad. Pharm. Scis. (chmn. basic pharmaceutics sect. 1976—77, mem.-at-large exec. com. 1979—83, pres. 1985—86, Rsch. Achievement award 1982), mem.: [illegible] (councillor 1992—96, treas. 1998—99), AAUP, Inst. Medicine Nat. Rsch. Coun., Am. Assn. Colls. Pharmacy (bd. dirs. 1992—95, pres. 1993—94, Volwiler Rsch. Achievement award 1991), Am. Coll. Clin. Pharmacy, Drug Info. Assn., Internat. Pharm. Fedn. (bd. pharm. scis. 1988—, chair 1996—2000, Host-Madsen medal 2001), Generic Pharm. Industry Assn. (mem. blue ribbon com. on generic medicines 1990), Am. Soc. for Pharmacology and Exptl. Therapeutics, Am. Soc. Clin. Pharmacology and Exptl. Therapeutics (Rawls-Palmer award and lectureship 1995), Am. Pharm. Assn. (Higuchi Rsch. prize 2000), Am. Coll. Clin. Pharmacology (Disting. Svc. award 1988), Am. Found. for Pharm. Edn. (bd. dirs. 1987—, Disting. Svc. "Profile" award 1993), Inst. Medicine NAS (forum on drug devel. and regulation 1988—94, chmn. com. on antiprogestins 1993, membership com. 1994—97, chmn. other health profns. sect. 1995—97, chmn. com. pharmacokinetics and drug interactions in elderly 1996—97, mem. Round Table R & D Drugs, Biologics & Med. Devices 1997—2000, bd. on health scis. policy 1999—), Sigma Xi, Phi Lambda Sigma, Rho Chi (Ann. Lecture award 1990). Home: 601 Van Ness Ave Apt 451 San Francisco CA 94102-3259 Office: U Calif San Francisco Dept Biopharm Scis 533 Parnasus Rm U68 San Francisco CA 94143-0446 E-mail: benet@itsa.ucsf.edu.

BENETTI, LYNN, music educator; b. Hanover, NH, May 21, 1960; d. Frederick Loren and Joan Doten Staples; m. J. Christopher Benetti, Sept. 26, 1981; children: Kate, Daniel. MusM, Rhode Island Coll., Providence, RI, 1996, MusB, 1982. Cert. Life profl. tchr. RI. Music tchr., grades k-5 Glocester Sch. Dept., Chepachet, RI, 1990—; adj. faculty RI Coll., Providence, 2000—. Bd. of Trustees N. Smithfield Pub. Libr., Slatersville, RI; treas. Friends of Linda T., N. Smithfield, RI. Mem.: Music Ed. Nat. Conf., Glocester Tchr. Assoc. (pres. elect). Independent. Congregationalist. Avocation: knitting. Home: 45 Mechanic St North Smithfield RI 02896 Office: W Glocester Elem Sch 111 Reynolds Rd Chepachet RI 02814

BENEWITZ, MAURICE CHARLES, labor arbitrator, educator; b. Hartford, Conn., Nov. 16, 1923; d. Doris L. Benewitz; m. Lesley Frank Alan Benewitz. AB in Econs., Harvard U., 1947; PhD in Econs., U. Minn., 1954. From asst. prof. to prof., dept. chair Baruch Coll., N.Y.C., 1955-75; arbitrator Manhasset, N.Y., 1958—. Dir. Nat. Ctr. for the Study of Collective Bargaining in Higher Edn., N.Y.C., 1970-73. Author: Higher Education Arbitration, 1988. Mem. Am. Arbitration Assn. (panel mem.), Fed. Mediation and Conciliation Svc. (panel mem.), N.Y. State Pub. Employee Rels. Bd. (panel mem.), N.Y.C. Office Collective Bargaining (panel mem.), N.J. State Med. Bd., Nat. Acad. Arbitrators, Phi Beta Kappa. Home and Office: 261 Thompson Shore Rd Manhasset NY 11030-2240

BENFER, DAVID WILLIAM, hospital administrator; b. Toledo, Ohio, May 28, 1946; s. Wilson L. and Marjorie (Baringer) B.; m. Mary Sturner, Sept. 5, 1970; children: Emily, Matthew, Andrew. BA, Wittenberg U., 1968; MBA in Hosp. Adminstrn., Xavier U., 1970. Asst. admintrn. Med. Coll., Ohio Hosp., Toledo, 1971-76, exec. dir., CEO, 1976-81, Bon Secours Hosp., Grosse Pointe, Mich., 1982-84, Henry Ford Hosp., Detroit, 1985-92; pres., CEO, St. Joseph Med. Ctr., Joliet, Ill., 1992-99; CEO St. Raphael Healthcare System, New Haven, 1999—. Dir. Merchants and Mfrs. Bank; fellow Berkeley Coll. Yale U., 2002—. Co-author: Issues in Health Care Management, 1982; contbg. author: Sisters of Bon Secours Centennial, 1982. Trustee, chmn. Family Svcs., Detroit and Wayne County, 1982-92; chmn. AIDS Consortium Southeastern Mich., Toledo, 1988-92l v.p. Med. Value Plan, Inc., 1986-91; chmn. S.E. Mich. Hosp. Coun.; bd. dirs. U. St. Francis, Joliet, 1993-2002; vice chmn. New Ctr. Area Coun., 1991-92; mem. Mich. Tastefest, 1996; bd. dirs., chmn. Ctr. Econ. Devel., Will County C. of C., Ill., New Haven Symphony. Recipient Commendation 114th Ohio Gen Assembly, 1981; Berkeley Fellow, Yale U., 2003. Fellow Am. Coll. Health Care Execs. (coun. regents 1989-92, bd. govs. 1992—2000, Robert S. Hudgens award 1982, chair 1998-99); mem. Am. Hosp. Assn., Conn. Hosp. Assn. (bd. dirs.), Cath. Health Assn. (bd. dirs.), Quinnipiack Club (New Haven), Country Club Detroit (Grosse Pointe), Pine Orchard (Conn.) Yacht and Country Club, New Haven Country Club. Roman Catholic. Avocations: jogging, golf. Office: St Raphael Healthcare System Hosp of St Raphael 659 George St New Haven CT 06511-5324

BENFIELD, ANN KOLB, lawyer; b. Reading, Pa., May 1, 1946; d. Curtis Kepler and Stella (Kolb) B. BA, George Washington U., 1969, MA, 1974; JD, U. Ky., 1983. Ky. 1983, U.S. Ct. Appeals (6th cir.) 1985, U.S. Supreme Ct. 1987; cert. mental health consumer cons./educator; cert. trained mediator. Probation officer Superior Ct. of D.C., Washington, 1973-78; jud. law clk. to chief judge U.S. Dist. Ct. (we. dist.) Ky., Louisville, 1983-86, jud. atty. to fed. sr. judge, 1989-95; trial atty. Ogden, Welsh and Newell (formerly Ogden & Robertson), Louisville, 1986-89; pvt. practice Louisville, 1995—2001; ret., 2001. Adj. prof. U. Louisville Sch. Law, 1993. Mem. exec. com., bd. dirs. Ky. chpt. ACLU, 1988-89, 91—, nat. bd. dirs., 1992-94, sec., 1995-96, treas., 1996-98, mem. legal panel, 1988-2002; mem. Reproductive Freedom Adv. Com., 1994-2001; mem. steering com. Fellowship Reconciliation, Louisville, 1997-2002; mem. governing coun. U. Louisville Women's Ctr., 1998-2001; rape crisis advocate Ctr. for Women and Families, 1997—, domestic violence advocate, 1998-; bd. dirs., gen. counsel Depressed Self-Help Svcs., Inc., 1998-2000. Fellow: Ky. Bar Found. (charter mem., bd. dirs. 1994—96); mem.: Louisville Women's Law Assn., Louisville Bar Assn., Ky. Bar Assn. (Donated Legal Svcs. Recognition award 2000, 2001), Ky. Paso Fino Horse Assn. (sec. 2000—01), Phi Beta Kappa, Order of Coif. Home and Office: 1113 Holly Springs Dr Louisville KY 40242-7762 E-mail: akbenfield@msn.com.

BENFIELD, JOHN RICHARD, surgeon, educator; b. Vienna, June 24, 1931; came to U.S., 1938, naturalized, 1945; s. Richard and Charlotte Lola Benfield; m. Joyce A. Cohler, Dec. 22, 1963; children: Richard L., Robert E., Nancy J. AB, Columbia U., 1952; MD, U. Chgo., 1955. Diplomate Am. Bd. Surgery, Am. Bd. Thoracic Surgery (bd. dirs. 1982-88). Intern Columbia-Presbyterian Hosp., N.Y.C., 1955-56; E.H. Andrews fellow in thoracic surgery U. Chgo., 1956-57; chief resident and instr. in surgery U. Chgo. Clinics, 1962-64, resident in surgery, 1956-57, 59-63; asst. prof. surgery U. Wis., 1964-67; asst. prof. UCLA, 1967-69, assoc. prof., 1969-73, prof., 1973-77, clin. prof., 1978-88; prof. surgery, chief cardiothoracic surgery, vice chmn. surgery U. Calif. Davis Med. Ctr., Sacramento, 1988-95, prof. surgery, chief thoracic surgery, 1995-98, prof. emeritus, 1998—; attending surgeon V.A. Martinez Med. Ctr., 1988-98; courtesy staff Kaiser Permanente Med. Ctr., Sacramento, 1988-98. James Utley prof. surgery, chmn. dept. surgery Boston U., 1977; chmn. surgery City of Hope Nat. Med. Ctr., Duarte, Calif., 1978-87; bd. dirs. Am. Bd. Thoracic Surgery, 1982-88; cons. U.S. Naval Med. Ctr., San Diego, 1968-88; mem. sr. staff VA Wadsworth Med. Ctr., L.A., 1978-88. Editor Current Problems in Cancer, 1975-86; mem. editl. bd. Annals Thoracic Surgery, 1979-2001, assoc. editor, 1987-2001; mem. editl. bd. Annals Surg. Oncology, 1994-2000; contbr. articles to profl. jours., chpts. to books. Sec., trustee Univ. Synagogue, Los Angeles. Served as capt. M.C. U.S. Army, 1957-59, Korea. Grantee Life Ins. Med. Rsch., 1962-66, Am. Heart Assn., 1968-71; USPHS, 1971-92. Mem. ACS (bd. govs. 1982-88, 92-98), Am. Surg. Assn., Am. Assn. Thoracic Surgery, Am. Assn. Cancer Rsch., Am. Med. Writers Assn., Internat. Assn. Study Lung Cancer, Internat. Soc. Surgery, Calif. Med. Soc., Ctrl. Surg. Assn., L.A. Acad. Medicine, The Royal Soc. Medicine (Gt. Britain), The Transplantation Soc., Soc. Thoracic Surgeons (v.p. 1994-95, pres. 1995-96), Soc. Univ. Surgeons, Pacific Coast Surg. Assn. (v.p. 1995-96), Soc. Surg. Oncology, Am. Coll. Chest Physicians (pres. Calif. chpt. 1996-97), Western Thoracic Surgeons Assn. (pres. 1989-90), Internat. Surg. Soc., Thoracic Surgery Dirs. Assn. (pres. 1995-97), Thoracic Surgery Found. for Rsch. and Edn. (pres. 2003—). E-mail: jbenfield@verizon.net.

BENFIELD, MARION WILSON, JR., law educator; b. Belwood, N.C., July 26, 1932; s. Marion Wilson and Gazzie Cleo (Martin) B.; m. Dalida Quijada, Feb. 21, 1964; children: Marion, Steve, Robin, Rosalina, Christopher, Jeanette, Antonio, Maria. AA, Gardner-Webb Coll., Boiling Springs, N.C., 1951; AB in English, U. N.C., 1953; LLB, Wake Forest U., 1959; LLM, U. Mich., 1965. Bar: N.C. 1959. Asst. dir. Inst. Govt. U. N.C., 1959-61; individual practice law Hickory, N.C., 1961-63; asst. prof. law U. Ga., 1963-65; assoc. prof. Case Western Reserve U., 1965-66, U. Ill., 1966-68, prof., 1968-88, Albert E. Jenner, Jr. prof. law, 1988-90, assoc. dean, 1980-85; disting. chair law Wake Forest U., 1990-97, adj. prof., 1997-98; vis. prof. U. Tex., 1998—. Vis., prof. U. Houston, 1976-77, Duke U., 1979, NYU, 1984, Peking U., 1985, Shenzhen U., China, 1986, Loyola U., L.A., 1995, U. Tex., 1990-2001, U. Milan, 2001; mem. Nat. Conf. of Commrs. on Uniform State Laws, 1973—. Reporter, draftsman: The Uniform Land Transactions Act and Uniform Simplification of Land Transfers Act, 1970-77, Revised Uniform Commercial Code, Article 2A, 1995-98; author: Social Justice through Law-New Approaches in the Law of Contracts, 1970, (with W.H. Hawkland) Cases and Materials on Sales, 1979, 3d edit., 1992, (with Peter Alces) Commercial Paper and Alternative Payment Systems, 1987, (with Peter Aces) Payment Systems, 1993; mem. editl. bd.: Uniform Commercial Code, 1974—, Uniform Land Transactions Act and Uniform Simplification of Land Transactions Act, 1982-93. Served with U.S. Army, 1954-56. Mem. Am. Law Inst., ABA. Home: 10 Overlook Cir New Braunfels TX 78132-4728 E-mail: mbenfield@compuvision.net.

BENFORADO, DAVID M. environmental engineer; b. N.Y.C., Nov. 17, 1925; s. Mark Joseph and Mathilde (Abraham) B.; m. Ruthann Martin, May 5, 1950; children: Mark Andrew, Marcia Ann, David Dean. BS in Chem. Engring., Columbia, 1948; student, CCNY, 1942-44. Registered profl. engr., N.Y. Engr., Skelly Oil Co., Eldorado, Kans., 1948-53; applied research engr. Walter Kidde Nuclear Labs., Garden City, N.Y., 1953-56; heat transfer specialist Trane Co., La Crosse, Wis., 1956-61; mgr. application engring. Penn Brass & Copper, Erie, Pa., 1961-65; product mgr. air pollution control equipment Air Preheater Co., Wellsville, N.Y., 1965-69; sr. environ. engring. specialist 3M, St. Paul, 1969-94. Cons. control odorous indsl. emissions; mem. com. odors from stationary and mobile sources NRC, 1978; gen. conf. chair nat. meeting Air Pollution Control Asns., 1986; cons. for subcom. on pollution prevention EPA Sci. Adv. Bd. Environ. Engring. Com., 1991. Mem. City of Woodbury (Minn.) Solid Waste Adv. Commn., 1987-95; apptd. pub. mem. Minn. Emergency Response Commn., 1991; active Boy Scouts Am., 1937—; mem. Am. Inst. Pollution Prevention, 1990-96; pres. BMD Environ. Vols., Woodbury, Minn. Fellow Air and Waste Mgmt. Assn. (dir. 1968—, pres. 1972-73, hon. mem. 1981—, chmn. gen. conf. ann. nat. meeting 1986); mem. Am. Inst. Chem. Engrs., Am. Acad. Environ. Engrs. (diplomate, trustee 1981-84, pres. 1990), Woodbury Lions Club (sec. 1970, bd. dirs. 1971—, pres. 1978). Home: 7100 Glenross Rd Woodbury MN 55125-1624

BENFORD, ANNE MICHELE (ANNE SASS), pediatric nurse practitioner, clinical nurse specialist; b. N.Y.C., Apr. 17, 1965; d. William Kenneth and Panthie (Hopper) S.; m. Maurice R. Benford; children: Jade Clarice, Delaney Brooke. BSN, SUNY, Buffalo, 1989; MSN, Emory U., 1995. RN, Ga.; cert. pediatric nurse practitioner. Staff nurse orthopedics Buffalo Gen. Hosp., 1989; charge nurse gen. surgery Millard Fillmore Hosp., Buffalo, 1990; staff nurse newborn nursery, postpartum unit USAF Wilford Hall Med. Ctr., Lackland AFB, Tex., 1990-94. Childbirth educator Wilford Hall, 1993-94. 1st lt. USAF, 1990-94. Mem. Nat. Assn. Pediat. Nurse Practitioners, Internat. Nursing Honor Soc., Sigma Theta Tau. Avocations: performing African, modern and jazz dance, aerobics, reading,. E-mail: benford@peoplepc.com.

BENFORD, GREGORY ALBERT, physicist, writer; b. Mobile, Jan. 30, 1941; s. James Alton and Mary Eloise (Nelson) Benford; m. Joan Abbe, Aug. 26, 1967; children: Alyson Rhandra, Mark Gregory. BS, U. Okla., 1963; MS, U. Calif., San Diego, 1965, PhD, 1967. Research asst. U. Calif., San Diego, 1964—67; postdoctoral fellow Lawrence (Calif.) Radiation Lab., 1967—69, research physicist, 1969—71; prof. physics U. Calif., Irvine, 1971—. Cons. in field. Author: (novels) If the Stars are Gods, 1977, In the Ocean of Night, 1977, The Stars in Shroud, 1978, Find the Changeling, 1980, Timescape, 1980 (Nebula award), Against Infinity, 1983, Across the Sea of Suns, 1984, Artifact, 1985, Heart of the Comet, 1986, In Alien Flesh, 1986, Great Sky River, 1987, Tides of Light, 1989, Beyond the Fall of Night, 1990, Chiller, 1993, Furious Gulf, 1994, Sailing Bright Eternity, 1995; author: (with Mark O Martin) A Darker Geometry, 1996; author: Foundation's Fear, 1997, Cosm, 1998, The Martian Race, Eater, 2000; author: (collections) Matter's End, 1994; editor: Far Futures, 1995; editor: (with Martin H. Greenburg) The New Hugo Winners Volume IV, 1997; editor: Nebula Awards Showcase 2000: The Year's Best SF and Fantasy Chosen by the Science Fiction and Fantasy Writers of America, 2000; editor: (with George Zebrowski) Skylife: Space Habitats in Story and Science, 2000; editor: Worlds Vast and Various, 2000, Deep Time, 1999, Cosm, 1999, Eater, 2000. Recipient Brit. Sci. Fiction award, 1981, Australian Ditmar award for internat. novel, 1981, John Campbell award for best novel, 1981, UN medal in Lit., 1993, Lord prize in Sci., 1994, Lord Found. prize, 1995; fellow Woodrow Wilson, 1963—64; grantee Office Naval Rsch., 1975—, 1982—, Army Rsch. Orgn., 1977—82, Air Force Office Sci. Rsch., 1982—, Calif. Space Office, 1984—85. Mem.: NASA Sci. Adv. Bd., Soc. Sci. Exploration, Sci. Fiction Writers Am. (Nebula award 1975, 1981), Royal Astron. Soc., Am. Phys. Soc., Phi Beta Kappa. Home: 84 Harvey Ct Laguna Beach CA 92651 Business E-Mail: gbenford@uci.edu.

BENFORD, HARRY BELL, naval architect; b. Schenectady, Aug. 7, 1917; s. Frank Albert and Georgia (Rattray) B.; m. Edith Elizabeth Smallman, Apr. 26, 1941; children— Howard Lee, Frank Alfred, Robert James. BSE. in Naval Architecture and Marine Engring, U. Mich., 1940. With Newport News Shipbldg. Co., Va., 1940-48; mem. faculty U. Mich., Ann Arbor, 1948-59, 60-83, prof. naval architecture, 1959-83, prof. emeritus, 1983—, chmn. dept. naval architecture and marine engring., 1967-72. Exec. dir. maritime rsch. adv. com. NRC, 1959-60 Author 4 books, 150 tech. papers. Fellow Soc. Naval Architects and Marine Engrs. (hon. mem., pres.'s award 1957, Linnard prize 1962, Taylor medal 1976), Royal Instn. Naval Architects; mem Tau Beta Pi, Phi Kappa Phi. Home: 6 Westbury Ct Ann Arbor MI 48105-1411 Office: U Mich Dept Naval Architecture Ann Arbor MI 48109-2145 E-mail: harben@engin.umich.edu.

BENFORD, ROBERT DEE, sociology educator, editor; b. Akron, Ohio, July 22, 1951; s. Robert Dee Benford, Sr. and Carolyn Sue Benford; m. Michelle Hughes Miller, Aug. 17, 1990; children: Kiri Elaine Miller, Cambra Rae Benford-Miller. BA, U. Tex., Arlington, 1981; MA, U. Tex., 1984, PhD, 1987. CEO Benford and Assocs., Inc., Houston, 1969—85; social sci. rsch. assoc. III Hogg Found. for Mental Health, U. of Tex., Austin, 1986—87; prof. dept. sociology U. Nebr., 1987—2000; prof., chair dept. sociology So. Ill. U.,

Carbondale, Ill., 2000—. Editor Jour. of Contemporary Ethnography, Thousand Oaks, Calif., 2000—; series editor Twayne's Social Movements Past and Present, N.Y.C., 1995—99. Editor: (ency.) Compendium of Social Issues; contbr. articles to profl. jours. Exec. coun. The Drake Group, Des Moines, 1999—2001; peacekeeping coord./trainer Red River Peace Network, Austin, 1984—85; del., peace rsch. del. to Cuba Pastors for Peace, Mpls.; vol. coord. Austin Peace and Justice Coalition, 1983—84; co-founder gun tree zone movement U. of Nebraska, 1994—96. Recipient People Who Inspire award, Black Masque chpt. Mortarboard Nat. Honor Soc., 1998, U. Grad. fellowship, U. of Tex. at Austin, 1982—85. Mem.: So. Sociol. Soc., Soc. for the Study of Symbolic Interaction, Soc. for the Study of Social Problems, Midwest Sociol. Soc., Am. Sociol. Assn. (chair peace, war, and social conflict sect. 1998—99), Phi Kappa Phi, Alpha Chi, Alpha Kappa Delta (pres.Gamma chpt. 1984—85). Achievements include research in social movements, peace movements, Chinese democracy movement, environmentalism, nuclear politics, political discourse. Home: 45 Hillcrest Dr Carbondale IL 62901 Office: So Ill U 3426 Faner Hall Carbondale IL 62901-4524 Office Fax: 618-453-8926. E-mail: rbenford@siu.edu.

BENGE, RAYMOND DOYLE, JR., astronomy educator; b. Houston, Oct. 10, 1961; s. Raymond Doyle and Gladys Jean (Patrick) B. BS, Duke U., 1983; MS, Tex. A&M U., 1988. Tchg. asst. Tex. A&M U., College Station, 1984-88; tchg. fellow U. N. Tex., Denton, 1988-94; part-time faculty mem. Tarrant County Jr. Coll., Ft. Worth, 1994-97; assoc. faculty Collin County C.C., Plano, Tex., 1994-97; assoc. prof. physics Tarrant County Coll., Hurst, Tex., 1997—. Adj. faculty Richland Coll., Dallas, 1994-98, Tex. Christian U., Ft. Worth, 2002; astronomy lab. coord. Tex. A&M U., College Station, 1986-88; observatory dir. U. N. Tex., Denton, 1991-94; SPICA agt. Harvard-Smithsonian Ctr. for Astrophysics, Cambridge, 1993-95. Author, editor: (lab. manual) Experiments on Stars and the Universe, 1994, asst. publ. Star Watch Nights, Tex. Dept. Pks. and Wildlife; contbr. articles to profl. jours. Dorm rep. Baldwin Fedn., Duke U., 1985; organizer pub. observation nights U. N. Tex., Denton, 1991-94; asst. pub. planetarium shows Richland Coll. Mem. Am. Astron. Soc., Astron. Soc. Pacific, Royal Astron. Soc. Can., Am. Assn. Variable Star Observers., Tex. Astron. Soc. Republican. Achievements include measurement of period changes in the eclipsing binary star GK Cephei; establishment of undergrad. rsch. program in astronomy at the U. N. Tex.; development of several astronomy workshops for pre-college tchrs. Office: Tarrant County Coll Dept Natural Scis 828 W Harwood Rd Hurst TX 76054-3219

BENGHIAT, RUSSELL, advertising agency executive; b. N.Y.C., July 10, 1948; s. Isaac and Pearl (Feld) B.; m. Nancy Joseph, Nov. 8, 1987; children: Joshua Laurence, Gabriel William. BA in English Lit., Swarthmore Coll., 1970; MS in Advt., U. Ill., 1972. Copywriter Kight, Cowman, Abram, Columbus, Ohio, 1972-73; assoc. creative dir. Johnson & Dean, Grand Rapids, Mich., 1973-76; mktg. analyst FTC, Cleve., 1976-81; v.p. Nicholes & Benghiat Advt., Cleve., 1981-83; pres. Benghiat Mktg. and Comm., Inc., Cleve., 1983—. Pres. bd. dirs. Cleve. Dancers, 1983; del. Dem. Nat. Convention, San Francisco, 1984. Recipient Nat. Addy award Am. Advt. Fedn., 1974. Mem. Greater Cleve. Growth Assn. (com. chmn., COSE Vol. of Month 1989). Office: 3628 Walnut Hills Ave Ste 200 Cleveland OH 44122-4484

BENGSTON, BILLY AL, artist; b. Dodge City, Kans., June 7, 1934; Exec. dir. Westfall Art, Venice, Calif., 1996-98. Founder Artist Studio, Venice, Calif., 1960; aesthetic cons., co-designer Disneyland Call Ctr., Anaheim, Calif., 1998; established Pelican Club Prodns., Ltd., 1982. One-man shows include Galerie Neuendorf, Frankfurt, Germany, 1993, Rosamund Felsen Gallery, Santa Monica, Calif., 2000, Danese Gallery, N.Y.C., 2001, exhibited in group shows at Art Inst. Chgo., 1963, 1972, Sao Paolo, Brazil, 1965, Gagosian Gallery, N.Y.C., 2002, one-man shows include Whitney Mus. Am. Art, 1967—69, Biennial Exhbn., 1979, retrospective, L.A. County Mus. Art, 1968, 1988, Stedelijk van Abbemuseum, Eindhoven, The Netherlands, 1969, retrospective, Contemporary Arts Mus., Houston, 1988, Oakland (Calif.) Mus., 1988, The Contemporary Mus., Honolulu, 1988, Represented in permanent collections Mus. Modern Art, N.Y.C., Art Inst. Chgo., L.A. County Mus. Art, Whitney Mus. Am. Art, Ft. Worth Art Ctr. Mus., Guggenheim Mus., Beauborg, Paris, N.Y.C., Nat. Gallery, Washington, commd., Calif. State Office Bldg., L.A., 1990; contbr. articles to art jours. Nat. Found. Arts grantee, 1967, Ford Found. grantee Tamarind Lithography Workshop, 1968, 87; Guggenheim fellow, 1975. Home: 805 Hampton Dr Venice CA 90291-3020

BENGSTON, DAVID NEIL, economist, educator; b. St. Peter, Aug. 4, 1956; s. Roger E. and Marjorie M. Bengston; m. Cheryl M. Kane. BS, U. Minn., 1978, MS, 1982, PhD, 1986. Market rschr. Bengston Market Rsch., Minnetonka, Minn., 1979—84; prin. ecol. economist North Ctrl. Rsch. Sta., USDA Forest Svc., St. Paul, 1984—. Dep. coord. ecologic econs. rsch. group Internat. Union of Forestry Rsch. Orgns., Vienna, 2000—; cons. UN Devel. Project, N.Y.C., 1992—93; sec. Tech. Assessment and Futures Analysis Working Group, Soc. Am. Foresters, Bethesda, Md., 1991—92; adj. prof. Coll. Natural Resources, U. Minn., St. Paul, 1986—, Conservation Biology Grad. Program, U. Minn., St. Paul, 1996—; cons. Internat. Union of Forestry Rsch. Orgns. Spl. Program for Developing Countries, Vienna, 1992—93, Food and Agr. Orgn. for UN, Rome, 1989—90. Bd. dirs., mem. World Population Balance, Mpls., 1997—2001. Mem.: U.S. Soc. for Ecological Econs. Avocations: bicycle design and framebuilding, jazz piano. Office: North Ctrl Rsch Sta 1992 Folwell Ave Saint Paul MN 55108 Office Fax: 651-649-5285.

BENGTSON, RICHARD LEE, agricultural engineer, educator; b. Clinton, Iowa, Dec. 23, 1942; s. Robert Eino and Helen Carolyn (Piper) B.; m. Neveena Jean Lee, June 27, 1970; children: Robert Lee, Rhonda Joy. BS in Agrl. Engring., U. Wyo., 1966; MS in Agrl. Engring., U. Ill., 1967; PhD in Agrl. Engring., Okla. State U., 1980. Registered profl. engr., La. Rsch. asst. dept. agrl. engring U. Ill., Urbana, Ill., 1966-67; commd. 2d. lt. U.S. Army, 1967, advanced through grades to capt., 1968; rsch. assoc. dept. agrl. engring. Okla. State U., Stillwater, Okla., 1977-80; from asst. prof. to prof. La. State U., Baton Rouge, La., 1980-92, prof. dept. biol. and agrl. engring, 1992—. Adv. council Scotlandville High Sch. for Engring., Baton Rouge, 1991-94, 99—; cons. Baton Rouge (La.) Green, 1996. Contbr. articles to Transactions of the Am. Soc. Agrl. Engrs., Jour. Soil and Water Conservation, Jour. Irrigation and Drainage; assoc. editor Am. Soc. Agrl. Engrs. Recipient Tchg. award Nat. Assn. Coll. and Tchg. Agr., 1995, First Miss. Corp. award La. Agr. Experiment Station, Baton Rouge, 1995, Outstanding Advising award Nat. Acad. Advising Assn., 1995, Excellence in Environ. Rsch. award U.S. EPA, 1996, Sedberry award for Outstanding Undergrad. Tchg., 1999, Disting. Faculty award La. State U., 2000. Mem.: La. State U. Faculty Senate (v.p. 1999—2000), Soil Water Conservation Soc., Am. Soc. Agrl. Engrs. (divsn. chair 1995—96, La. Sect. Engr. of Yr. 2001), Sigma Xi (chpt. pres. 1992—93), Gamma Sigma Delta (chpt. sec. 1996—98). Methodist. Achievements include development of subsurface drainage designs for Southern Louisiana, management practices for improved surface runoff water quality from sugarcane, GLEAMS-WT model to simulate water quality from different management practices. Assisted in the development of a new biological engineering curriculum. Office: Biol and Agrl Engring Dept Louisiana State Univ Baton Rouge LA 70803-4505 E-mail: bengtson@bae.lsu.edu.

BENGTSON, ROGER DEAN, physicist, department chairman; b. Wausa, Nebr., Apr. 29, 1941; s. Fridolph M. and Edith E. (Pearson) B.; m. Billie A. Spies, June 15, 1963; children— Nissa C., Hans E. BS, U. Nebr., 1962; MS, Va. Poly. Inst. and State U., 1964; PhD, U. Md., 1968. Aerospace engr. NASA-Langley Research Ctr., Hampton, Va., 1962-67; research assoc. U. Tex., Austin, 1968-70, asst. prof. physics, 1970-75, assoc. prof., 1975-81, prof., 1981—, chmn. dept., 1984-88. Mem. Am. Phys. Soc., AAAS, Sigma Xi Home: 411 Honeycomb Rdg Austin TX 78746-5324 Office: U Tex Dept Physics C-1600 Austin TX 78712

BENGTSSON, ERLING BLÖNDAL, classical cellist, educator; b. Copenhagen, Mar. 8, 1932; s. Valdemar and Sigridur (Nielsen) Bengtsson; m. Merete Bloch-Jørgensen, Oct. 19, 1958; children: Henrik Bløndal, Stefan Bløndal. Diploma, Curtis Inst. Music, Phila., 1950. Asst. tchr. cello Curtis Inst. Music, 1949—50, tchr. cello, 1950—53; prof. music Royal Danish Conservatory of Music, Copenhagen, 1953—90; tchr. cello Swedish Radio's Inst. Advanced String Studies, Stockholm, 1958—78; prof. music Staatliche Hochschule für Musik, Cologne, Germany, 1978—82, U. Mich. Sch. Music, Ann Arbor, 1990—. Tchr., cello master classes conservatories and univs., throughout Europe and U.S., 1953—. Performer: numerous LPs and CDs, 1949—, worldwide concerts, 1950—. Named knight 1st class, Order of Dannebrog, Queen of Denmark, 1972, grand knight, Order of Falcon, Pres. Iceland, 1970, chevalier du violoncello, Ind. U. Eva Janzer Meml. Cello Ctr., 1993; recipient award of distinction, Manchester (Eng.) Internat. Cello Festival, 2001. Avocation: collecting modern Scandinavian art. Home: 1217 Westmoorland Ypsilanti MI 48197 Office: U Mich Sch Music 1100 Baits Dr Ann Arbor MI 48109 E-mail: cellist@erlingbb.com.

BENHABIB, JESS, adult education educator; b. Istanbul, Turkey, June 9, 1948; s. Jack and Nelli Benhabib; m. Madeline Jennifer Blum, May 12, 1950; children: Nicole, Michael Eric. PHD, Columbia U., 1976. Paulette Godard prof. polit. economy NYU, 1991—, dean of social scis., 1997—2000, dean of arts and sci., 1998—2000. Editor: Jour. of Econ. Theory, 1992, (book) Cycles and Chaos in Economic Equilibrium, 1992. 2d lt. Ordinance-Turkish Army, 1974, Balikesir, Turkey. Fellow: Econometric Soc. Home: 37 Washington Sq W #16A New York NY 10011 Office: NYU 269 Mercer St 7th Fl New York NY 10003 Home Fax: 212-995-4186; Office Fax: 212-995-4186. Personal E-mail: jess.benhabib@nyu.edu. E-mail: jess.benhabib@nyu.edu.

BEN-HAIM, ZIGI, artist; b. Baghdad, Iraq, Nov. 28, 1945; came to U.S., 1970; s. Jacob and Violet (Halawe) B.-H.; m. Tsipi Inberg, July 28, 1980; 1 child, Yori Lee. Diploma, Avni Inst. Fine Arts, Tel Aviv, 1970, Calif. Coll. Arts and Crafts, 1971; MFA, San Francisco State U., 1974. Guest artist fellow Artists Union, Russia, 1992. Prin. works include sculptures Bklyn. Mus., Buscaglia-Castellani U. Mus., Ghent (Belgium) Mus., Israel Mus., Jerusalem, Malmo Mus., N.Y.C., Jewish Mus., N.Y.C., Tel Aviv Mus., U. Md., College Park, Westminster Bank, N.Y.C., Chelouche Gallery, Tel Aviv, Herbert Johnson Mus., Cornell U., Ithaca, N.Y., Jewish Mus., N.Y.C., Baumgartner Gallery, Washington, Art Gallery Hamilton, Ont., Can., Munro Gallerie, Hamburg, Germany, Cleve. Mus. Art, Jersey City Mus., Touchstone Gallery, N.Y.C., Las Vegas Art Mus. N.Y. State Coun. on Arts grantee, 1983, NEA grantee, 1984, Pollock Krasner Found. grantee, 1990, 96; recipient Achievement award Israel Ministry Culture, 1971. Home: 94 Mercer St New York NY 10012-4425 E-mail: zigi126@aol.com.

BENHAM, HELEN, music educator; b. N.Y.C., Dec. 4, 1941; d. Charles Mead and Dorothea Wheaton Benham; m. Samuel S. Kim, June 12, 1965; 1 child, Sonya Wheaton Kim Guardo. MusB, Oberlin Conservatory Music, 1962; BA, Oberlin Coll., 1963; MS, The Juilliard Sch., 1965; PhD, Rutgers U., 2001. Music faculty Diller-Quaile Sch. Music, N.Y.C., 1964-75, Mannes Coll. Music, N.Y.C., 1966-82, Monmouth Conservatory Music, Red Bank, N.J., 1967—; prof. music Brookdale C.C., Lincroft, N.J., 1973—. Concert artist, piano and harpsichord. Author: Piano for the Adult Beginner Books I and II, 1977. Trustee, sec. A. Louis Scarmolin Trust. Named Outstanding Young Women of Am., 1978. Mem. Music Tchrs. Nat. Assn., Nat. Guild Piano Tchrs., Am. Musicological Soc., Composers Guild N.J., Shore Music Educators Assn. Avocations: swimming, walking. Home: 960 Elberon Ave Long Branch NJ 07740-4709 Office: Brookdale CC Music Dept 765 Newman Springs Rd Lincroft NJ 07738-1597

BENHAM, LELIA, small business owner, social and political activist; b. Cartersville, Ga., July 15, 1945; d. Emory and Nellie Pearl (Carson) Benham; children: Gary K., Margo L., Berrie E. Student, North Cen. State Coll., Mansfield, Ohio, 1981-83, 91—, Mansfield Bus. Coll., 1964-66, 84-85. Bookkeeper/sec. M-R-M Cmty. Action Program, 1970-72; with The Tappan Co., 1972-81; sec., bookkeeper daycare ctr. Mansfield Opportunities Industrialization Ctr., 1983-84; office svcs. contractor FSC Ednl., Inc., Mansfield, 1988-89; pres., dir. Benham & Co., Mansfield, 1988—. Home health habilitation aide, waiver/supportive living provider Ohio Dept. Mental Retardation and Developmentally Disabled, 1992—, Richland Newhope Ctr., Mansfield, 1992—; nurse asst. Mansfield Meml. Geriatric Ctr., 1994; nat. and internat. cons. in field; dir. orgnl. sales, reltail sales meetings and workshops, 1988-90. Editor Richland NOW News, 1985-87, 91-92. Cand. Mansfield Sch. Bd. and City Coun., 1987, 89, 91; founding mem. adv. bd., bd. dirs. Litter Prevention and Recycling/KAB (Mid-Ohio Clean Scene), 1982-96; v.p., founding treas. Sister Cities Assn., Mansfield, 1986-94; active various charitable orgns.; bd. dirs. Ohio Women Inc.; mem. alumni bd. Ohio Dept. Adminstrv. Svcs. Minority Bus. Enterprise, 1989-96, others; adv. bd. mem. Keep Yourself Alive, 1992, 93. Recipient 10 billboard advt. awards Cleve. Regional Transit Authority Community Minority Taskforce, 1989-96, Keeper of the Flame Proclamation award Ohio Sec. of State, 1990, award AFrican Am. Women Agenda of Ohio,. 1991, others. Mem. NOW (Richland County founder, pres. 1985-96, Scholarship award 1987, task force chair state bd. racial and ethnic diversity 1993—), NAACP (Ohio rep. to state orgns. 1989—, Pres.'s award 1982, Cmty. award 1988). Democrat. Ch. of God in Christ. Avocations: reading, sewing, travel. Home and Office: Benham & Co 12 Bonaire St Cartersville GA 30120

BENHAM, LINDA SUE, civil engineer; b. Toledo, Oct. 31, 1954; m. William H. Benham; children: William H. IV, Katherine L. BS in Civil Engring., U. Toledo, 1977. Structural engr. Itil and Assocs., Toledo, 1977-78; environ. design mgr., assoc. Finkbeiner, Pettis and Strout, Inc., Toledo, 1978—. Pres. A Mind's Eye Photography, Sylvania, 1997—; part-time instr. civil engring. U. Toledo, 1999-2001. Trustee Huntington Community Ctr., Sylvania, Ohio, 1990-92; mem. coun., sec. St. Joseph Sch., 1999-2002; mem. parish bldg. com. St. Joseph Ch., 2002-. Recipient Spirit of Am. Woman in Bus. award, 1990. Mem. Tech. Soc. Toledo, Kiwanis (past pres.). Republican. Avocations: private pilot, writer, canoeing, camping, pianist. Office: Finkbeiner Pettis Strout Inc One Lake Erie Ctr 600 Jefferson Ave Ste 400 Toledo OH 43603-1808 E-mail: linda.benham@fpsengineering.com.

BENHAM, ROBERT, state supreme court justice; m. Nell (Dodson) B.; children: Corey Brevard, Austin Tyler. BS in Polit. Sci. with honors, Tuskegee U.; JD, U. Ga.; LLM, U. Va. Judge Ga. Ct. Appeals, Ga., 1984-89; justice Supreme Ct., State of Ga., Atlanta, 1989—, presiding justice, chief justice. Mem. adv. bd. 1st So. Bank. Chmn. Gov.'s Commn. on Drug Awareness and Prevention, State of Ga.; mem. Ga. Hist. Soc.; trustee Fa. Legal Hist. Found.; bd. dirs. Cartersville (Ga.) Devel. Authority, Cartersville-Bartow C. of C.; deacon, former Sunday Sch. supt. The Greater Mt. Olive Bapt. Ch.; notably one of first black individuals elected to a statewide position in the history of Ga. Mem Atlanta Bar Assn. (bd. dirs. jud. sect.), Ga. Bar Found., Lawyers Club Atlanta, Masons, Shriners, Elks. Office: Ga Supreme Ct 244 Washington St SW Rm 572 Atlanta GA 30334-9007 Fax: (404) 657-4329.

BENHAMOU, ERIC A. computer company executive; MSEE, Stanford U.; diplome d'Ingenieur, Ecole Nationale Superieure d'Arts et Metiers, Paris; doctorate (hon.), Ben Gurion U. of Negev, Widener U., Western Govs. U., U. S.C. Project mgr., software mgr., design engr. Zilog, Inc.; v.p. Bridge Comm., 1981—87; CEO 3Com Corp., Santa Plz., Calif., 1990—2000, chmn., 1990—. Bd. dirs. Smart Valley Inc., Cypress Semiconductor, Legato, Santa Clara U. Sch. Bus., New Am. Found., Intransa, Atrica, INSEAD Sch. Bus., Stanford U. Sch. Engring., Ben Gurion U. of Negev; chair Am. Electronics Assn. Nat. Info. Infrastructure Task Force; apptd. to Pres. Info. Tech. Advisory Com., 1997. Recipient Pres. Environ. and Conservation Challenge award, 1992, Fgn. Investment Jubilee award Israeli Prime Min. Benjamin Netanyahu, 1998, Ellis Island medal honor, 1998. Office: 3COM Corp 5400 Bayfront Plz Santa Clara CA 95054-3601*

BEN-HUR, EHUD, research scientist, researcher; b. Tiberias, Israel, Dec. 24, 1940; came to U.S., 1993; s. David and Miriam (Singer) Ben-H.; m. Dina Fuhrman, Apr. 14, 1965; children: Asa, Adi. BS, Hebrew U., Jerusalem, 1965; MS, Technion, Haifa, Israel, 1967, PhD, 1970. Rsch. assoc. Brookhaven Nat. Lab., Upton, N.Y., 1970-73; asst. prof. Hebrew U., Jerusalem, 1973-75; sr. scientist Nuclear Rsch. Ctr., Beer-Sheva, Israel, 1975-92; assoc. mem. Head, Virus Inactivation Lab. N.Y. Blood Ctr., N.Y.C., 1993-96; dir. photobiology and virus inactivation lab. V.I. Techs., Inc., N.Y.C., 1996-99; cons. photomedicine and blood safety N.Y.C., 1999—. Regional editor Lasers in Life Sci., 1985—; editor: Photomedicine, 1987; contbr. over 150 articles to profl. jours. and books. Office: 160 W End Ave Apt 24P New York NY 10023-5614 E-mail: ehudbenhur@yahoo.com.

BENI, GERARDO, electrical and computer engineering educator, robotics scientist; b. Florence, Italy, Feb. 21, 1946; came to U.S., 1970; s. Edoardo and Tina (Bazzanti) B.; m. Susan Hackwood, May 24, 1986; children: Catherine Elizabeth, Juliet Beatrice. Laurea in Physics, U. Firenze, Florence, Italy, 1970; PhD in Physics, UCLA, 1974. Research scientist AT&T Bell Labs., Murray Hill, N.J., 1974-77, Holmdel, N.J., 1977-82, disting. mem. tech. staff, 1982-84; prof. elec. and computer engrng. U. Calif., Santa Barbara, 1984—91, dir. Ctr. for Robotic Systems in Microelectronics, 1985—91, prof. elec. engring. Riverside, 1991—, dir. multimedia lab. and studio, 1991—94, chmn. elec. engring. dept., 1997—98. Dir. Multimedia Lab & Studio, 1991—94. Founder, editor: Jours. Robotic Systems, 1983 (Jour. of Yr. award 1984); editor: Recent Advances in Robotics, 1985, Vacuum Mechatronics, 1990; contbr. more than 140 articles to tech. jours.; 16 patents in field. Fellow AAAS, Am. Physics Soc. Office: U Calif-Riverside Coll Engring Riverside CA 92521-0001 *Produce in freedom; give in freedom; and in freedom enjoy.*

BENIGNO, THOMAS DANIEL, lawyer; b. Queens, N.Y., July 29, 1954; s. John Baptiste and Ernesta Mary (Yannaco) B.; m. Maria Angelica Vasquez, Jan. 26, 1980; children: Diana Maria, Laura Michelle, John Frederick. BA with honors, Hofstra U., 1976; JD, Benjamin Cardozo Law Sch., 1979. Bar: N.Y. 1981, U.S. Dist. Ct. (so. and ea. dists.) N.Y. 1985. Atty. Legal Aid Soc., Bronx, N.Y., 1979-84; ptnr. Benigno, Cassisi & Casissi, Floral Park, N.Y., 1984-87; mng. ptnr., gen. counsel Benigno/Gurrieri Real Estate Mgmt. and Devel., Bklyn., 1984-95. Pres. Gurben Properties, Inc., Floral Park, 1987-88, Movies for Kids Inc., Valley Stream, N.Y., 1989 90; gen. counsel Our Gang Assocs. Inc. (dba Thin White Line), Cedarhurst, N.Y., 1988-90. Mem. N.Y. Bar Assn., Rotary Internat. Office: 269 Hempstead Ave Ste 2 Malverne NY 11565-1224

BENING, ANNETTE, actress; b. Topeka, May 29, 1958; m. Steven White, 1984 (div. 1991); m. Warren Beatty, 1992; children: Kathlyn Bening Beatty, Benjamin Beatty, Isabel Ashley Ira Beatty, Ella Corinne Beatty. Student, Mesa Coll.; theatre degree, San Francisco State U.; studied at, Am. Conservatory Theatre. Films include The Great Outdoors, 1988, Valmont, 1989, The Grifters, 1990 (Acad. award nomination best supporting actress 1990), Postcards from the Edge, 1990, Guilty by Suspicion, 1991, Regarding Henry, 1991, Bugsy, 1991, Love Affair, 1994, Richard III, 1995, The American President, 1995, Mars Attacks!, 1996, The Siege, 1998, American Beauty, 1999 (Acad. award nom. best actress), In Dreams, 1999, What Planet Are You From, 2000, Open Range, 2003; stage appearances Coastal Disturbances, 1986, (Tony award nomination 1986, Clarence Derwin award 1987, Theatre World award 1987), Spoils of War, 1988, Hedda Gabler, 1999; TV movies: Manhunt for Claude Dallas, 1986, Hostage, 1988; TV series: Liberty's Kids (voice only); TV appearances: Sesame Street, 1969, Miami Vice, 1987, Wiseguy, 1987. Avocation: scuba diving. Office: Creative Artists Agy c/o Kevin Huvane 9830 Wilshire Blvd Beverly Hills CA 90212-1804*

BENITEZ, JOHN GRISWOLD, medical toxicologist; b. St. Louis, July 1, 1957; s. Vicente and Jane (Griswold) B.; m. Linda Gail Allison, May 2, 1982. BA, So. Ill. U., 1978, MD, 1981; MPH, U. Pitts., 1995. Diplomate Am. Bd. Med. Toxicology, Am. Bd. Emergency Medicine, Am. Bd. Preventive Medicine with spl. qualifications in med. toxicology, Am. Bd. of Preventative Medicine in Occupl. Medicine. Intern surgery Southwestern Mich. Area Health Edn. Ctr., Kalamazoo, 1981-82; fellow in hyperbaric medicine St. Luke's Hosp., Milw., 1988; emergency med. svcs. project med. dir. Bromenn Med. Ctr., Normal, Ill., 1988-89; instr., fellow in clin. toxicology Vanderbilt U. Med. Ctr., Nashville, 1989 91; clin. toxicology fellowship dir., asst. prof. U. Pitts., 1991-2000; chmn. adverse drug reaction com. U. Pitts. Med. Ctr., 1991-95; med. dir. Pitts. Poison Ctr., 1993-2000; Intox Project Internat. Programme on Chemical Safety World Health Orgn., 1995—; dir. toxicology treatment program U. Pitts., 1996-99; dir. multidisciplinary MPH and MD/MPH programs Grad. Sch. Public Health, U. Pitts., 1997-2000; mng. dir., assoc. med. dir. Finger Lakes Regional Poison and Drug Info. Ctr., 2000—; assoc. prof. U. Rochester, 2000—. Emergency medicine edn. chmn. St. John's Hosp., Springfield, Ill., 1984-88; clin. assoc. Dept. Surgery So. Ill. Sch. Medicine, 1986-89; affiliate faculty, mem. AHA Ill. affiliate, Normal, 1988-89; asst. state dir. basic trauma life support, Normal, Ill., 1988-89. Med. cons. disaster svcs. ARC, Springfield, Ill., 1987-88. Recipient Am. Acad. Clin. Toxicology Rsch. award, 1990; fellow Legis. Office of Rsch. Liaison, Ho. of Reps., Commonwealth Pa., 1998. Fellow Am. Coll. Med. Toxicology, Am. Coll. Preventive Medicine; mem. Am. Coll. Sports Medicine, Soc. Acad. Emergency Medicine, Am. Acad. Clin. Toxicology, Am. Coll. Med. Toxicology, Wilderness Med. Soc. Avocations: astronomy, sailing, cross country skiing, backpacking, amateur radio. Office: Finger Lakes Regional Poison & Drug Info Ctr U Rochester 601 Elmwood Ave Box 321 Rochester NY 14642 E-mail: john_benitez@urmc.rochester.edu.

BENITEZ, JORGE ANTONIO, microbiology educator; b. N.Y.C., July 9, 1949; s. Jose Antonio Benitez and Athala Mercedes Robles; m. Anisia Silva Cabrera, Oct. 23, 1951; children: Blanca Elena, Jorge Enrique. BS, U. Havana, Cuba, 1973, PhD, 1983. Asst. prof. Havana Higher Poly. Inst., 1973-79; rsch. scientist Nat. Ctr. Sci. Rsch., Havana, 1979-98; assoc. dir. U. Mo. Protein Core, 1998; asst. prof. Calif. State U., Fresno, 1999—2002; asst. prof. microbiol. biochem. immunology Morehouse Sch. Med., Atlanta, 2002—. Adj. assoc. prof. Havana Higher Poly. Inst., 1979-98, U. Havana, 1988-98. Rsch. grantee Internat. Found. for Sci., Sweden, 1979, 80; rsch. fellow Alexander von Humboldt Found., Germany, 1986. Mem. Am. Soc. for Microbiology. Home: 7600 Cole Ln Atlanta GA 30349 Office: Morehouse Sch Med 720 Westview Dr Atlanta GA 30310 E-mail: Jorge_Benitez@msm.edu.

BENITEZ, JUAN CARLOS, federal agency administrator; b. P.R. BA in Jud. Sys., Sacred Heart U., San Juan, P.R.; JD cum laude, Inter-Am. U. Bar: Supreme Ct. P.R., U.S. Dist. Ct. P.R., U.S. Ct. Appeals (D.C. cir.), U.S. Ct. Fed. Claims, U.S. Supreme Ct. Law clk. Judge Raymond L. Acosta Fed. Dist. Ct.; labor assoc. Fiddler, Gonzalez and Rodriguez, 1993—95; assoc. gen. counsel, legis. dir. P.R. Fed. Affairs Adminstrn., Washington, 1995—99; of counsel Long Aldridge and Norman, 1999—2001; spl. counsel Office Immigration-Related Unfair Employment Practices U.S. Dept. Justice, Washington, 2001—. Mem.: ABA (spl. com. on govtl. affairs), Hispanic Nat. Bar Assn. (White House liaison, legis. affairs dir., regional pres.). Office: US Dept Justice Civil Rights Divsn 950 Pennsylvania Ave NW Washington DC 20530-0001

BENITEZ, ROBERT MICHAEL, medical educator, cardiologist; b. Baltimore, Sept. 12, 1960; s. Eugenio E. and Betty Stewart Benitez; m. Pamela Jean Wilson. BA, McDaniel Coll. (formerly Western Md. Coll.), Westminster, Maryland, 1978—82; MD, U. Md. Sch. Medicine, 1982. Asst. prof. of medicine U. of Md. Sch. of Medicine, Baltimore, 1992—2002, assoc. prof. of medicine, 2002—. Dir. of cardiology fellowship program U. of Md. Sch. of Medicine, 2002—. Mem.: Am. Coll. of Cardiology (assoc.), Am. Heart Assn. (assoc.). Office: University of Maryland School of Medicine 22 South Greene St Baltimore MD 21201 Home Fax: 410-328-4382; Office Fax: 410-328-4382. Personal E-mail: mbenitez@medicine.umaryland.edu. E-mail: mbenitez@medicine.umaryland.edu.

BENIVEGNA, VITO NICHOLAS, language educator; b. Hamden, Conn., Apr. 29, 1935; s. Frank and Louise Benivegna; m. Maria Theresa Narcisi, June 25, 1966; children: Andrea Smith, Michael. BA, Fairfield U., 1957; MA, U. Ill., 1964. Spanish tchr. West Haven (Conn.) H.S., 1958—61, North Haven (Conn.) Jr. H.S., 1961—62; grad. tchg. asst. U. Ill., Urbana, 1962—65; instr. Spanish U. Dayton, Ohio, 1965—66; grad. tchg. assoc. U. Ariz., Tucson, 1967—69; prof. Spanish Belleville (Ill.) Area Coll., 1969—98; adj. prof. Southwestern Ill. Coll., Belleville, 1998—. Avocations: volunteer work, reading, traveling.

BENJAMIN, ADELAIDE WISDOM, community volunteer and activist, retired lawyer; b. New Orleans, Aug. 23, 1932; d. William Bell and Mary (Freeman) Wisdom; m. Edward Bernard Benjamin Jr., May 11, 1957; children: Edward Wisdom, Mary Dabney, Ann Leith, Stuart Minor. Student, Hollins Coll., 1950-52; BA in English, Newcomb Coll., 1954; JD, Tulane U., 1956; student, Loyola U., New Orleans, 1980-81; grad. extension program Sewanee Theol. Sch., U. South, 1982. Assoc. Wisdom, Stone, Pigman and Benjamin, New Orleans, 1956-58; tchr. ext. courses Sewanee Theol. Sem., 1984-88; ret. attorney; ret., 1959. Spkr., panelist on sch. issues various local and nat. groups. Mem. Tulane Law Rev., 1954-56; compiler, editor, pub. Trinity Ch. supplemental songbook, 1980. Trustee Mary Freeman Wisdom Charitable Found., sec., 1987—92, pres., 1990—94, treas., 1994—, pres., 2000—; sec. bd. dir.

YWCA, New Orleans, 1967—68, 1st v.p., 1968—69; bd. dir. Kingsley House, New Orleans, 1971—77; trustee Metairie Pk. Country Day Sch., 1971—79, sec., 1976—79; mem. adv. bd. Tulane Summer Lyric Theatre, Tulane U., 1972—, pres. adv. bd., 1977—79; pres. PTA, 1975—76; bd. dir. Children's Hosp., New Orleans, 1976—79; mem. adv. bd. Pub. Radio Sta. WWNO, 1980—; bd. dir. Parenting Ctr., 1981—; pres. E&A Charitable Found., New Orleans, 1983—; pres. bd. New Orleans Symphony, 1984—89; mem. Loving Cup selection com. New Orleans Times Picayune, 1985; bd. dir. La. Mus. Found., New Orleans, 1989—, S.E. La. coun. Girl Scouts US, New Orleans, 1989—97, Loyola U., New Orleans, 1989—99, mem. exec. com., 1996—99, hon. bd. mem., 2003; bd. dir. Louise S. McGehee Sch., New Orleans, 1990—97, v.p., 1991—97, hon. bd. dir., 1991; pres. New Orleans Mus. Art Fellows Forum, 1991—; mem. exec. com. La. Mus. Found., New Orleans, 1991—; bd. dir. Newcomb Children's Ctr., New Orleans, 1991—94; mem. adv. bd. dept. psychiatry La. State U. Med. Ctr., 1992—; mem. exec. bd. La. Philharm. Orch., 1992—; mem. Newcomb Dean's Coun., 1997—, pres., 2002—; bd. dir. Nat. D-Day Mus., New Orleans, 1998—2002; sec. parish coun. Trinity Episc. Ch., New Orleans, 1973—75, sec. vestry, 1975—79, active, leader Trinity Quartet, 1979—84. Recipient Weiss Brotherhood award Nat. Conf. Christians and Jews, 1986, Outstanding Philanthropist, Nat. Soc. Fund-raising Exec., 1986, Volunteer Activist Award, St. Elizabeth Guild, 1986, Jr. League Sustainer award, 1987, Disting. Alumna award McGehee Sch., 1987, George Washington Honor Medal for Individual Achievement, Freedom Found. at Valley Forge, 1988, Living and Giving award Juvenile Diabetes Found. 1991, Outstanding Citizen New Orleans award La. Colonials, 1994, Jacques Yenni award Outstanding Cmty. Svc. Sch. Bus. Adminstrn. Loyola Univ., 1994, Integritas Vitae award for outstanding cmty. svc. Loyola U., 1994, Classical Arts Patron award Tribute to the Classical Arts, 1998; named Goodwill Ambassador for Louisiana Gov.'s Commn. Internat. Trade, Industry and Tourism, 1987, Sweet Art, Contemporary Arts Ctr., 1988, Significant Role Model, Young Leadership Coun., 1988, Woman of Distinction S.E. La. Girl Scout Coun., 1992. Mem. ABA, LWV, La. Bar Assn., New Orleans Bar Assn., Jr. League New Orleans (exec. com. 1971-72, bd. dir. 1967-72), Ind. Women's Orgn., Com. 21, Am. Symphony Orch. League, Quarante Club (2d v.p. 1978-79), Debutante Club, Le Debut des Jeunes Filles Club, New Orleans Town Gardners (pres. 1979-80), Thomas Wolfe Soc. (life mem.). Home: 1837 Palmer Ave New Orleans LA 70118-6215

BENJAMIN, ARLIN JAMES, physicist; b. Guthrie, Okla., Oct. 9, 1933; s. Harold Dinsmore and Lula Martha (Black) Benjamin; m. Patricia Ann Crabb, Oct. 10, 1964; children: Arlin James, Cynthia Denise, Deborah Dawn. BS, Sam Houston State Coll., 1955; MS, Okla. State U., 1957; postgrad., MIT, 1959, Wichita U., 1959-60. Rsch. engr. Boeing Co., Wichita, Kans., 1956-63; lead nuc. engr. LTV Corp., Dallas, 1963-64; ops. rsch. analyst Research Triangle Inst., Research Triangle Park, NC, 1964-66; sr. ops. rsch. analyst Gen. Dynamics Corp., Ft. Worth, 1966-68; mgr. Control Data Corp., Honolulu, 1968-70; sr. scientist S.W. Rsch. Inst., San Antonio, 1970-78; prin. scientist Hittman Assocs. Inc., Sacramento, 1978-81; mgr., sr. staff mem. BDM Corp., Hawthorne, Calif., 1981-86; prin. engr. Northrop Grumman Corp., Midwest City, Okla., 1995—, Pico Rivera, Calif., 1986-95. Contbr. articles to profl. jours. Mem.: Inst. Mgmt. Sci., European Phys. Soc., Inst. of Physics and the Phys. Soc. (London), Am. Phys. Soc., Am. Nuc. Soc., Am. Geophys. Union, Pi Gamma Mu, Alpha Chi.

BENJAMIN, BARBARA BLOCH, writer, editor; b. May 26, 1925; d. Emil William and Dorothy (Lowengrund) B.; m. Joseph B. Sanders, Aug. 3, 1944 (div. 1961); children: Elizabeth Sanders, Ellen Janice Benjamin; m. Theodore S. Benjamin, Sept. 20, 1964 (dec.). Student, NYU, 1943-45, New Sch. Social Rsch., 1966. Office mgr. Writers War Bd., N.Y.C., 1943-45, Westchester Dem. Com., White Plains, N.Y., 1955-56; mgr. Westchester Symphony Orch., 1957-62; mng. editor, Cooking Ency. Rutledge Books, N.Y.C., 1970-71; pres. Internat. Cookbook Svcs., White Plains, 1978—. Columnist House Beautiful, 1984-87; cookbook editor Benjamin Co., 1990-97; cons. in field; tchr. cooking classes White Plains, 1975-80; lectr. in field. Author: Anyone Can Quilt, 1975; Meat Board Meat Book, 1977; If It Doesn't Pan Out, 1981; Garnishing Made Easy, 1983, Microwave Party Cooking, 1988, A Little Jewish Cookbook, 1989, A Little New England Cookbook, 1990, A Little Southern Cookbook, 1990, A Little New York Cookbook, 1990, The Little Book of Chocolate, 2003; editor/author: All Beef Cookbook, 1973; In Glass Naturally, 1974; Fresh Ideas with Mushrooms, 1977; Holly Farms Complete Chicken Cookbook, 1984; Gulden's Cookbook, 1985, A Centennial Celebration of Recipes from Solo, 1988, Salute to the Great American Chefs, 1988, TCBY and More, 1989, GoldStar Micro-Convection Cookbook, 1991, Healthy Cooking with Amway Queen Cookware, 1993, McCormick/Schilling's New Spice Cookbook, 1994, Simply the Best Chicken, 1997, Fabulous Things To Do With Chocolate, 1998, The Pasta Pack, 1998; Am. adapter The Cuisine of Olympe, 1983, Baking Easy and Elegant, 1984, series of 3 English cookbook mags., 1984-87, Best of Cold Foods, 1985, Cakes and Pastries, 1985, series of 12 Creative Cuisine books, 1985, The Art of Cooking, 1986, The Art of Baking, 1987, Perfect Pasta, 1992, Rocky Food, 1994; columnist Westfair Comm., 2000—; editor, contbr. various books; contbr. articles to profl. jours. Nat. bd. dirs. Encampment for Citizenship, N.Y.C., 1966-72; bd. dirs. YWCA Ctrl. Westchester, 1965-71, Westchester Ethical Humanist Soc., 1968—; exec. com., pres. Internat. Student Exch. of White Plains, 1955-70; bd. dirs. Westchester Chamber Music Soc., 1986—: chmn. Concerned Citizens for Open Space, 1997—. Jewish. Home and Office: Internat Cookbook Svcs 21 Dupont Ave White Plains NY 10605-3537 Fax: 914-997-7214. E-mail: bbenj2626@aol.com.

BENJAMIN, BEZALEEL SOLOMON, architecture and architectural engineering educator; b. Anand, India, Feb. 21, 1938; came to U.S., 1971; s. Solomon and Penninah (Ellis) B.; m. Nora Jacob David, Feb. 25, 1962; children— Ashley Bezaleel, Jennifer Elana B.E. in Civil Engring., Bombay U., India, 1957; D.I.C., Imperial Coll., London, 1958; MS in Engring., London U., 1959, PhD, 1965. Design engr. M.N. Dastur & Co., Bombay, 1961-63; postdoctoral fellow U. Surrey, Eng., 1965-66; prin. lectr. Hatfield Poly., Eng., 1966-71; asst. prof. archtl. engring. U. Kans., Lawrence, 1971-72, assoc. prof., 1972-76, prof., 1976—. Vis. Fulbright prof. Technion, Haifa, Israel, 1987-88. Author: The Analysis of Braced Domes, 1963, Structural Design with Plastics, 1969, Structures for Architects, 1975, Building Construction for Architects and Engineers, 1978, Structural Evolution: An Illustrated History, 1990, Statics, Strengths and Structures for Architects, 1992; children's book) Susan Altencroft, 1976; (novels) Rampaging Lovers, 1988, A Nazi Among Jews, 1990, Bene Israel Tales, 1991, The Jewish Amendment, 1992, David Rahabi, 1993. Jewish. Avocation: writing. Office: U Kans Sch Architecture Lawrence KS 66045-0001 E-mail: benj@ukans.edu.

BENJAMIN, DAVID NICHOLAS, architect, researcher; b. Cleve., Mar. 18, 1957; arrived in Norway, 1984; s. Stanley Solomon and Jeanne Ruth Benjamin. BA, Washington U., St. Louis, 1979, MArch, 1982; PhD, Norwegian Inst. Tech., 1993. Architect trainee Stewart Farnet Architect, New Orleans, 1982, Planned Expansion Group, White Plains, N.Y., 1983; architect Richard Fleischman Architects, Cleve., 1984, Per Knudsen Arkitekt, Trondheim, Norway, 1984-85, Trond Thommesen Arkitekt, Trondheim, Norway, 1985-88; rschr. The Norwegian Inst. of Tech., Trondheim, 1988-93; prin. Environ. design Ptnrs., Inc., 1998—. Pvt. cons. in architecture and cultural heritage mgmt., 1994—; cons. Lejre Hist. Archaeol. Rsch. Ctr., UN Spl. Commns. of Experts on War Crimes Geneva, 1993-94. Pres. Third Planet. Mem. Norske Arkitekters Landsforbund. Avocation: music.

BENJAMIN, EDWARD BERNARD, JR., lawyer; b. New Orleans, Feb. 11, 1923; s. Edward Bernard and Blanche (Sternberger) B.; m. Adelaide Wisdom, May 11, 1957; children: Edward Wisdom, Mary Dabney, Ann Leith, Stuart Minor. BS, Yale U., 1944; JD, Tulane U., 1952. Bar: La. 1952. Practiced in, New Orleans, since 1952; ptnr. Jones, Walker, Waechter, Poitevent, Carrere & Denegre, New Orleans, 1967—. Pres. Am. Coll. Probate Counsel, 1986-87, Internat. Acad. Estate and Trust Law, 1976-78; vice chmn. bd. trustees Southwestern Legal Found., 1980-88, bd. dirs., 1988-90; chmn. bd. Starmount Co., Greensboro, N.C., 1968-88, chmn. emeritus, 1988—. Editor-in-chief Tulane U. Law Rev., 1951-52; mem. editl. bd. Cmty. Property Jour., 1974-89. Trustee Hollins Coll., 1966-87; chancellor Episcopal Diocese of La., 1984-2003, Trinity Episcopal Ch., New Orleans, 1974-92; mem. adv. bd. CCH Estate & Fin. Planning Svc., 1982-88; chmn. Salvation Army City Commd. Adv. Bd., 1965-68; pres. New Orleans Jr. C. of C., 1953. 1st lt., F.A. pilot, U.S. Army, 1943-46. Mem. Am. Coll. Tax Counsel, Am. Law Inst., ABA (sec. taxation sect. 1967-68, coun. 1976-79, coun. real property, probate and trust law sect. 1978-81), La. Bar Assn. (chmn. taxation sect. 1959-60), La. Law Inst., La. Bar Found. (trustee 1998-99), New Orleans Country Club, Southern Yacht Club, New Orleans Lawn Tennis Clu Home: 1837 Palmer Ave New Orleans LA 70118-6215 Office: Jones Walker Waechter Poitevent Carrere & Denegre 201 Saint Charles Ave Fl 51 New Orleans LA 70170-1000

BENJAMIN, GEORGES CURTIS, emergency physician, consultant; b. Chgo., Sept. 28, 1952; s. George and Tessie Cozie (Edwards) B.; m. Yvette Josphanie Janisse; children: Stephanie, Kali. BS, Ill. Inst. Tech., 1973; MD, U. Ill., 1978. Diplomate Am. Bd. Internal Medicine, Am. Bd. Med. Examiners. Intern and resident internal medicine Brooke Army Medical Ctr., San Antonio, 1978-81; dept. emergency medicine Madigan Army Medical Ctr., Tacoma, 1981-83; chief emergency medicine Walter Reed Army Med. Ctr., Washington, 1983-87; chair. dept. com. health & ambulatory care Dist. Columbia Gen. Hosp., Washington, 1987-90; commr. pub. health Dist. Columbia, 1990-91; health policy cons., 1992-95; emergency physician Holy Cross Com. Hosp., Silver Spring, Md., 1991-95; dep. sec. Pub. Health State of Md., Balt., 1995-99; sec. Dept. Health and Mental Hygiene, Balt., 1999—2002; exec. dir. Am. Pub. Health Assn., 2002—. Emergency physician Patuxent Naval Air Station, Patuxent River, Md., 1989, Nisqually Clinic, Yelm, Wash., 1981-82, Allenmore Com. Hosp., Tacoma, 1981-82; house internist Greater Southeast Com. Hosp., Washington, 1985-87; clinical instr. emergency medicine, Georgetown U., 1988-95; adj. prof. Health Care Scis., 1993, asst. prof. medicine Uniformed Svcs. U. Health Scis., Bethesda, Md., 1984-87. Editorial bd. Jour. Nat. Medical Assn., 1986-93; reviewer Am. Coll. Physician Execs., 1989—, Am. Jour. Emergency Medicine, 1986-94, Military Medicine, 1983-87; contbr. articles to profl. jours. Bd. dirs. Hosp. Sock Children, Boarder Baby Project, Inc. Whiteman Walker Clinic Inc.; adv. bd. D.C. Commn. Pub. Health Disability and Injury Prevention Program, 1993, Montgomery County HIV/AIDS Citizens, 1992-93; bd. trustees Am. Cancer Soc.; bd. govs. Medico Chirurgical Soc. D.C.; mem. D.C. Emergency Med. Svcs. Com., 1990-91, D.C. State Health Coord. Coun., 1990-91; gov. commn. Welfare Policy State of Md., 1993. With M.C. U.S. Army, 1978-87, USAR, 1974-78. Recipient Cert. Recognition, 1993, Com. Govs. Svc. award, 1991, Disting. Pub. Svc. award, 1991, Cert. Appreciation Best Friends of D.C., 1991, Cert. Appreciation D.C. Pub. Schs., 1991, Svc. award Medico Chirurgical Soc., 1990, Recognition award D.C.G.H. Medical/Dental staff, 1990; decorated Army Commendation medal, 1983, Commanders award, 1981, Eisenhower Proclamation medal, 1970. Fellow ACP, Am. Coll. Emergency Physicians (Nat. Key Contact 1987-90, 92-95, gov. affairs com. 1993, D.C. chpt. v.p. 1988-90, D.C. chpt. pres. 1989-90, liaison rep. emergency nurses assn. 1992-95, nat. health policy com. Dallas 1992-93); mem. APHA, AMA, Nat. Med. Assn. (mil. and aerospace medicine sect. sec. 1983, nat. co-chmn. 1985, 86, nat. chmn. 1987, emergency medicine nat. chmn. 1990-93), Medico Chirurgical Soc. (violence task force chmn. 1992-94), Am. Coll. Physicians Execs., Assoc. State Territorial Health Ofcls. (sec./treas. 1999-2000, pres. 2001-02). Office: APNA 800 I St NW Washington DC 20001-3710

BENJAMIN, GILBERT LEON, career counselor; b. Bklyn., Dec. 28, 1936; s. Carl and Esther (Tuvim) B.; m. Joan Warshaw, Apr. 15, 1962; children: Marc, Daniel. BA, Bklyn. Coll., 1958; MS, Columbia U., 1960; cert. advanced study, NYU, 1969. Nat. cert. career counselor, lic. career counselor, N.J.; nat. cert. counselor; master career counselor. Employment interviewer, vocat. counselor Hotel Placement office/Youth Placement Svc., N.Y.C., 1960-63; sr. counselor B'nai B'rith Career Counseling Svc., N.Y.C., 1963-68; asst. prof., dir. career devel. and placement Coll. S.I., N.Y., 1968-96; pres. N.Y. Career Devel. Assoc., 1990-92, trustee, 1992—2002. Adj. asst. prof., career counselor Coll. S.I., 1996—; Golden Group dir./mem. N.Am. adv. bd. Sunrider Internat., 1997-99. Vice-pres. Pied Piper Playhouse Nursery Sch., Englishtown, N.J., 1974-93, Iron Ore Realty Co., Englishtown, 1974-93. Mem. N.J. Counseling Assn., Met. N.Y. Coll. Placement Officers Assn. (dir. continuing edn. 1990-93, dir. 1995-97), Nat. Career Devel. Assn., N.Y. Career Devel. Assn. (pres. 1990-92, trustee 1992-2002), N.J. Career Devel. Assn., Mid. Atlantic Career Counseling Assn., World Futurist Soc. Jewish. Avocations: camping, genealogy, travel, photography. Home: 7 Mccue Rd Morganville NJ 07751-1642 Office: College Staten Island 2800 Victory Blvd Staten Island NY 10314-6600 E-mail: Gilben@att.net.

BENJAMIN, JANICE YUKON, development executive; b. Kansas City, Mo., Aug. 12, 1951; d. Stanley and Frances (Weneck) Yukon; m. Bert Lyon Benjamin, June 14, 1975; children: Brett David, Blair Yukon. AS, Bradford Coll., 1971; BA, Newcomb Coll., 1973; MA, U. Mo., 1978. Tchr. secondary, dept. chmn. Shawnee Mission (Kans.) Sch. Dist., 1973-80; career counselor Career Mgmt. Ctr., Kansas City, 1980-82, pres., owner, 1982-97; v.p., chief devel. officer Menorah Med. Ctr. Found., 1997—2001; dir. devel. KU Endowment Assn. for U. Kans. Hosp., 2001—. Ptnr. Career Mgmt. Press, Kansas City, 1983-97, The MBL Human Resources Cons. Group, 1989-91. Co-author: How to Be Happily Employed, 1983, 2d edit., 1995; contbr. articles to profl. jours. Bd. dirs. Cmty. Jr. League, Kansas City, 1988-89, v.p., 1989-90, pres.-elect, 1990-91, pres., 1991-92; bd. dirs. Menorah Med. Ctr., Overland Park, Kans., 1995-97, gen. chair grand hosp. opening, 1996; bd. dirs. Menorah Med. Ctr. Aux., 1984-97, auditor, 1990-92, v.p., 1994-96; bd. dirs. Health Partnership Clinic of Johnson County, 1997-2001, sec., 2000-01; bd. dirs. Women's Found. Greater Kansas City, 1991-96, chair bd. devel., 1993-95; bd. dirs. Kansas City Friends of Alvin Ailey, 1992-94, co-chair planning com.; bd. dirs. Ctrl. Exch., Kansas City, vice-chair comms., 2000-01, co-chair capital campaign, 1999-2000, chair-elect, 2001-03, bd. chair 2003—; adv. bd. women's coun. U. Mo. Kansas City, 1988-89; initiator, sponsor Kansas City Youth Vol. Svc. awards United Way, 1989-90, adv. com. Heart of Am. United Way, 1994-97; mem. Promise Project steering com. Kansas City Consensus, 1994-96; co-chmn. Youth Declaration; adv. com. Vol. Connection, 1998; bd. dirs. The New Reform Temple, 1999-2002; active Kans. Pub. Employee Rels. Bd., 2000-2003; mem. adv. bd. Health Partnership Clinic, 2001-, mem. med. adv. bd., First Nat. Bank, 2002—. Recipient Miss T.E.E.N. Encouraging Excellence award, 1990; named one of 25 Up and Comers award Jr. Achievement of Mid. Am., 1994, a woman to watch in 2002, Kansas City Star. Mem. Greater K.C. Coun. Philanthropy. Republican. Jewish. Office: KU Med HEO 1215 3901 Rainbow Blvd Kansas City KS 66160 Address: 4000 W 101 Terrace Overland Park KS 66207

BENJAMIN, JEFF, lawyer, pharmaceutical executive; b. Bklyn., Dec. 28, 1945; s. Haskell and Lillian (Sikofski) B.; m. Betty Gae Meckler, Mar. 21, 1971; children: Lily Meckler, Ross Meckler. BA, Cornell U., 1967; JD cum laude, NYU, 1971. Bar: N.Y. 1971, U.S. Dist. Cts. (so. and ea. dists.) N.Y. 1972. Assoc. Kronish, Lieb, Shainswit, Weiner & Hellman, N.Y.C., 1971-74; atty. Ciba-Geigy Corp., Ardsley and Tarrytown, N.Y., 1974—, counsel for regulatory affairs, 1976—, divsn. counsel, 1978—, asst. gen. counsel, 1985—, dir. legal dept., assoc. gen. counsel, 1986-89, v.p., gen. counsel, 1996-97; assoc. gen. counsel, ethics and law compliance officer Novartis Corp., N.Y.C., 1997—2001, v.p. dep. gen. counsel, ethics and law compliance officer, 2001—. Mem. adv. bd. Brennan Ctr. for Justice, 2002—; lectr. in field. Contbr. articles to law jours. Mem. Citizens Adv. Com., Ramapo, N.Y. With USAR, 1969-74. Mem. ABA, Ethics Officer Assn., Cornell U. Alumni Assn. (admissions amb.), Order of Coif. Home: 13 Park Ave New City NY 10956-1107 Office: Novartis Corp 608 Fifth Ave 10th Fl New York NY 10020-2305

BENJAMIN, KARL STANLEY, artist, art educator; b. Chgo., Dec. 29, 1925; s. Eustace Lincoln and Marie (Klamsteiner) B.; m. Beverly Jean Paschke, Jan. 29, 1949; children: Beth Marie, Kris Ellen, Bruce Lincoln. Student, Northwestern U., 1943, 46; BA, U. Redlands, 1949; MA, Claremont Grad. Sch., 1960. With dept. arts Pomona Coll., Claremont, Calif., 1979-97, Loren Barton Babcock Miller prof., artist-in residence, 1978-94, prof. emeritus, 1997—; prof. art Claremont Grad. Sch. Traveling exhbns. include New Talent, Am. Fedn. Arts, 1959, 4 Abstract Classicists, Los Angeles and San Francisco museums, 1959-61, West Coast Hard Edge, Inst. Contemporary Arts, London, Eng., 1960, Purist Painting, Am. Fedn. Arts, 1960-61, Geometric Abstractions in Am, Whitney Mus., 1962, Paintings of the Pacific, U.S., Japan and Australia, 1961-63, Artists Environment, West Coast, Amon Carter Mus., Houston, 1962-63, Denver annual, 1965, Survey of Contemporary Art, Speed Mus., Louisville, 1965, The Colorists, San Francisco Mus., 1965, Art Across Am, Mead Corp., 1965-67, The Responsive Eye, Mus. Modern Art, 1965-66, 30th Biennial Exhbn. Am. Painting, Corcoran Gallery, 1967, 35th Biennial Exhbn. Am. Painting, 1977, Painting and Sculpture in California: The Modern Era, San Francisco Mus. Modern Art, 1976-77, Smithsonian Nat. Collection Fine Arts, Washington, 1976-77, Los Angeles Hard Edge: The Fifties and Seventies, Los Angeles County Mus. Art, 1977, Corcoran Gallery, Washington, Cheney Cowles Mus., Spokane, 1980, Calif. State U., Bakersfield, 1982, Henry Gallery, U. Wash., 1982, U. Calif., Santa Barbara, 1984, L.A. Mcpl. Art Galleries, Barnsdall Park, 1986, Turning the Tide: Early Los Angeles Modernists, Santa Barbara Mus. Art, Oakland Mus., others, 1989-91, l.A. County Mus. Art, 1996; rep. permanent collections, Whitney Mus., L.A. County Mus. Art, San Francisco Mus. Art, Santa Barbara (Calif.) Mus. Art, Pasadena (Calif.) Art Mus., Long Beach (Calif.) Mus. Art, La Jolla (Calif.) Mus. Art, Fine Arts Gallery San Diego, U. Redlands, Mus. Modern Art, Israel, Pomona Coll., Scripps Coll., Univ. Mus., Berkeley, Calif., Wadsworth Atheneum, Nat. Collection Fine Arts, Seattle Mus. Modern Art, Newport Harbor Mus., U. N.Mex. Mus. Art, Wash. State U., L.A. Mus. Contemporary Art; retrospective exhbn. covering yrs. 1955-87 Calif State U. at Northridge, 1989, retrospective exhbn. 1979-94, Pomona Coll., 1994, 450 year survey Calif. art Orange County Mus. Art, Newport Beach, 1998-99. Served with USNR, 1943-46. Visual Arts grantee NEA, 1983, 89. Office: Pomona Coll Dept Arts 333 N College Way Dept Arts Claremont CA 91711-4429 also: Claremont Grad U Art Dept 251 E 10th St Claremont CA 91711-3913

BENJAMIN, LAURA J. management consultant, speech professional; d. Robert J. and Marilyn J. Schickler; children: Wilder Anthony, Brett James, Kimberly Victoria. BA, Calif. State U., 1988. Enlisted USAF, 1974, hon. discharge, 1981; sr. benefits specialist Rochester (N.Y.) Inst. Tech., 1988—92; sales team mgr. Current Inc., Colorado Springs, Colo., 1994—97; owner Laura Benjamin Internat., Colorado Springs, Colo., 1997—. Co-author: Safety, Health and Asset Protection Management Essentials, 2d edit., 2002. Bd. dirs. Boy Scouts Pikes Peak Coun., Colorado Springs, 1999. Mem.: Nat. Spkrs. Assn., Colo. Springs Soc. for Human Resource Mgmt. (v.p. 2000, pres. 2001). Avocations: hiking, writing, horseback riding. Business E-Mail: Laura@LauraBenjamin.com.

BENJAMIN, LAWRENCE, food service executive; Pres., CEO Specialty Foods Corp., Deerfield, Ill., 1997—. Office: Specialty Foods Corp PO Box 3400 Saint Charles IL 60174-0002

BENJAMIN, LENI BERNICE, elementary education educator; b. Durham, N.C., Aug. 15, 1945; d. Irving Jack and Svea Elisabeth (Wohlers) Kruger; m. Stuart Dychtwald, Sept. 21, 1968 (div. May 1985); children: Dana Kyle, Scott Eric, Rachel Ann; m. Wellington Leon Benjamin, Nov. 30, 1985. BA, Newark (N.J.) State Coll., 1967; MA, NYU, 1969; postgrad., Drake U., 1980-81, Kean Coll., 1984-85. Cert. reading tchr., N.J., Iowa, elem. tchr., N.J., Iowa, Mass., prin./supr., N.J. Tchr. Elizabeth (N.J.) Bd. Edn., 1967-69, 84-85, Diocese of Green Bay, Wis., 1977-79, Diocese of Des Moines, 1979-81; acting dept. mgr., sales assoc. Lord & Taylor, Northbrook, Ill., 1981-82; tchr. Diocese of Metuchen-St. Helena's, Edison, N.J., 1982-83; instr. Edison Job Corps Ctr., 1983-84; tchr. Plainfield (N.J.) Bd. Edn., 1985-87, Pleasantville (N.J.) Bd. Edn., 1987—; team leader mid. level, tchr. 8th grade; coord. PRISM math. project Pleasantville (N.J.) Bd. Edn., career awareness specialist elem. sch., 1995—2000, HSPA math. prep. tchr., 2000—; adminstr. Night H.S., 2002—. Chair Reading Curriculum Com., Green Bay, 1978-79; mem. English Curriculum Com., Des Moines, 1979-81, Family Life Edn. Curriculum Com., Plainfield, 1985-86, Dist. Test Com., Pleasantville, 1987—. Treas. Boy Scouts Am., Green Bay, 1977. Elizabeth Edn. Assn. scholar, 1963. Mem. NEA, ASCD, N.J. Edn. Assn., Nat. Reading Assn., Nat. Coun. Tchrs. Math., N.J. Tchrs. Math., Nat. Reading Assn., Kean Coll. Alumni Assn., NYU Alumni Assn. Democrat. Jewish-Christian. Avocations: reading, needlework. Home: 39 Masters Cir Marlton NJ 08053-3745

BENJAMIN, LORNA SMITH, psychologist; b. Rochester, N.Y., Jan. 7, 1934; d. Lloyd Albert and Esther Smith; children: Laureen, Linda. AB, Oberlin Coll., 1955; PhD, U. Wis., 1960. NIMH fellow dept. psychiatry U. Wis., 1958-62, clin. psychology intern, 1960-64, asst. prof., 1966-71, assoc. prof., 1971-77, prof. psychiatry, 1977-88; prof. psychology U. Utah, 1988—. Research asso. Wis. Psychol. Inst., Madison, 1962-66 Contbr. articles to profl. jours. Mem.: APA, Soc. Psychotherapy Rsch., Phi Beta Kappa. Office: Univ Utah Dept Psychology 390 S 1530 E Salt Lake City UT 84112-8934 E-mail: lsb_3@msn.com. *I attribute my success to a high energy level, and to some teachers and friends who supported me in times and places women were unwelcome.*

BENJAMIN, MICHAEL ANTHONY, engineer; b. London, July 27, 1962; s. Joseph and Sylvia Benjamin; m. Felicity Jane Hill, Jan. 19, 1991; children: Tristan Edward Benjamin Hill, Miles Alexander Benjamin Hill. BS in Mech. Engring. with honors, U. Fla., Gainesville, 1987, MS in Mech. Engring., 1990, PhD, 1994. Sr. support engr. Parker Hannifin Corp. Gas Turbine Fuel Systems Divsn., Cleveland, 1994—96, tech. support engr. Mentor, Ohio, 1996—97, tech. team leader, 1997—. Mem. adv. com. Ohio Aerospace Inst., Cleveland, 1997—2003, mem. core rsch. program rev. bd., 1998—; chair mech. engring. adv. com. Cleve. State U., Ohio, 1999—. Keynote speaker (conference) Fuel Atomization for Next Generation Gas Turbine Combustors. Fellow Fla. Grad. Scholars' Fund, State Fla., 1989-1990. Mem.: ASME (combustion and fuels com. 1998—), AIAA, Inst. Liquid Atomization and Spray System-Americas (co-chair rocket and air breathing power atomization com. 1997—2003, dir. 2000—03). Achievements include patents pending for Hybrid Atomizing Fuel Nozzle; patents for Pure Airblast Nozzle; Stable pre-mixer for lean burn composition; patents pending for Injector with Active Cooling; patents for Fuel atomization method for turbine combustion engines having aerodynamic turning vanes; patents pending for Injector with active cooling. Office: Parker Hannifin Corp 9200 Tyler Blvd Mentor OH 44060 Office Fax: 440-954-8111. Personal E-mail: drmbenj@aol.com. E-mail: mbenjamin@parker.com.

BENJAMIN, PEGGY-ANN BIEL, artist; b. N.Y.C., May 15, 1927; d. Edward J. and Joan (Ascheim) Biel; m. Alan K. Benjamin, Dec. 20, 1947 (dec.); children: Ellen Jane, Alan K. Jr. BA in Econ., Smith Coll., 1948; postgrad., U. Mo., 1954. Artist, Westwood, 1948—. Home: 5500 W 123d St # 206 Overland Park KS 66209

BENJAMIN, THERESA MARY, psychotherapist, writer; b. Boston, July 27, 1926; d. Vincenzo James and Maria (Morelli) Cardinale; children: Richard, Lorri, Denise. PhD, 1982. Psychotherapist Living Your Way, Oceanside, Calif., 1978—88; pvt. practice Carlsbad, Calif., 1988—. Cons. Mgmt. Plus, Oceanside; lectr. U. So. Calif., L.A., Carlsbad (Calif.) HS, Carlsbad. Author: What's The Meta, 1982, I'd Rather Be Right Than Happy, 1995, The Courage To Live And Love, 2003. Grantee, Social Work Advancement Assn., 1997. Mem.: Sierra Club. Home and Office: 4809 Kelly Drive Carlsbad CA 92008 Fax: 760-734-7333. E-mail: drtmbenjamin@msn.com.

BENJAMIN, THOMAS EDWARD, music educator, composer, conductor; b. Bennington, Vt., Feb. 17, 1940; s. Paul Alfred and Frances (Stern) B.; m. Elizabeth Klein, Aug. 25, 1963 (div. 1986); children: Matthew, Sarah; m. Carol Jean Russell, May 28, 1994. BA, Bard Coll., 1961; MA, Harvard U., 1963; PhD, Eastman Sch. Music, 1968. Prof. U. Houston, 1968-87; tchr. Nat. Music Camp, Interlochen, Mich., 1969-71, 77-83; prof. music theory Peabody Conservatory, Balt., 1987—. Author: The Craft of Modal Counterpoint, 1978, Counterpoint in the Style of Bach, 1986; co-author: Techniques and Materials of Tonal Music, 4th edit., 1992, Music for Analysis, 4th edit., 1996; mem. editl. bd. Jour. Music Theory Pedagogy, 1989-96; 40 published compositions. Resident fellow MacDowell Colony, 1982, 83, 96; composer grantee Meet-the-Composer, 1980, 86, 88; Composer award NEA, 1978; resident fellow Yaddo, 1978, 80, 84. Mem. ASCAP (Std. Music award 1975-97), Am. Soc. Univ. Composers, Nat. Coun. Coll. Music Soc. Avocations: gardening, sailing. Home: 4093 Fragile Sail Way Ellicott City MD 21042-5018 E-mail: tben1@attglobal.net.

BENJAMIN, WILLIAM CHASE, lawyer; b. Glen Cove, N.Y., Dec. 2, 1947; AB, Princeton U., 1969; postgrad., Grad. Inst. Internat. Affairs, Geneva, 1969-70; JD, Harvard U., 1973. Bar: N.Y. 1974, U.S. Tax Ct. 1978, Mass. 1983. Assoc. Cleary, Gottlieb, Steen & Hamilton, Brussels, 1975-78, N.Y.C., 1978-82; assoc. Hale and Dorr, Boston, 1982-84, jr. ptnr., 1984-86, sr. ptnr., 1986—.

Fulbright scholar, 1969-70. Mem. ABA, Internat. Bar Assn., Mass. Bar Assn., Boston Bar Assn., Internat. Fiscal Assn. Avocations: skiing, tennis, swimming. sailing. Office: Hale and Dorr LLP 60 State St Boston MA 02109-1816 E-mail: william.benjamin@haledorr.com.

BENJAMIN, YUKHANAN, physician; b. Tashkent, Uzbekistan, Oct. 2, 1937; arrived in U.S., 1982; s. Meyer Benjamin and Zina Ykubova; m. Leonora Iuzaylov Banjamin; children: Arthur, Ilya. MD, Tashken State Med. Sch., Uzbekistan, 1960—66; PhD, Tashuet-Mocow U., 1968—73. Pvt. practice 167 St. Med. Ctr., Miami, 1987—2003. Mem.: Am. Acad. of Family Physicians, N.Y. Acad. of Sciences. Republican. Jewish. Avocations: reading, theater, travel. Office: 167 St Med Ctr 909 N Miami Beach Blvd North Miami Beach FL 33162

BENKARD, JAMES W. B. lawyer; b. N.Y.C., Apr. 10, 1937; s. Franklin Bartlett and Laura Derby (Dupee) B.; m. Margaret Walker Spofford, Dec. 12, 1964; children: Andrew Minturn, James Robinson, Margaret Mercer. AB, Harvard U., 1959; LLB, Columbia U., 1963. Bar: N.Y. 1963. Assoc. Davis Polk & Wardwell, N.Y.C., 1963-73, ptnr., 1973—. Trustee Vassar Coll., Poughkeepsie, N.Y., Tchrs. Coll., N.Y.C., Environ. Def. Fund, N.Y.C., St. Mark's Sch., Southborough, Mass, Columbia Law Sch. Alumni Assn., Scenic Am. Mem. Am. Coll. Trial Lawyers, Knickerbocker Club, River Club (N.Y.C.), Fishers Island Country Club. Home: 1192 Park Ave Apt 11A New York NY 10128-1314 Office: Davis Polk & Wardwell 450 Lexington Ave Fl 31 New York NY 10017-3982

BENKE, PAUL ARTHUR, academic administrator; b. Michigan City, Ind., May 27, 1921; s. Paul Rol and Virginia (Peterson) B.; m. Beverly Anne Benke, Mar. 14, 1982; children: Janet, Eric. Student, Ind. U., 1941-42; AB, Ind. State U., Terre Haute, 1948; MA, U. Chgo., 1951, MBA, 1954. Gen. mgr. war prodn. div. Cline Electric Mfg. Co., Chgo., 1951-55; gen. mgr. Paasche Airbrush Co., Chgo., 1955-58; asst. to pres. H.K. Porter Co., 1956-57; gen. mgr. div. Coldform, 1957-58, Coldform (Thermoid div.), 1958-63; pres. (Colt's Firearms Div.), Hartford, Conn., 1963-73; v.p. Colt Industries Inc., 1969-73; group exec., marine products group, v.p. AMF Inc., White Plains, N.Y., 1973-81; pres. Jamestown (N.Y.) Community Coll., 1981-91; pres./CEO Metacomet; Ltd. Cons., 1996—. Bd. dirs. Bush Industries, Inc.; mem. regional adv. bd. HSBC Bank (USA). Pres., CEO Roger Tory Peterson Inst. Natural History, 1982-96. 1st lt. Ordnance Corps U.S. Army, 1942-45, CBI. Pres., exec. dir. Roger Tory Peterson Inst. Natural History, 1982-96. Served to 1st lt. Ordnance Corps. U.S. Army, 1942-45, CBI. Mem. Blue Key, Beta Gamma Sigma, Alpha Phi Gamma, Pi Gamma Mu. Office: Metacomet Ltd 3270 Gerry Levant Rd Falconer NY 14733-9639 E-mail: pab5279@netsync.net.

BENKERT, MARY RUSSELL, pediatrics nurse, researcher; b. Boston, Aug. 27, 1961; d. Charles Edward and Ann Russell (Schork) Doherty. BS in Nursing, St. Anselm Coll., Manchester, N.H., 1983; MS in Nursing, U. Colo., Denver, 1993. Cert. pediatric nurse. Clin. nurse III, preceptor pediatric med. unit Children's Hosp. Nat. Med. Ctr., Washington, 1983-87; staff nurse pediat. ICU The Children's Hosp., Boston, 1987-88, flex team nurse Denver, 1992-96; sr. staff nurse pediatric clin. rsch. ctr. U. Colo. Health Scis. Ctr., Denver, 1988-90; asst. nursing dir. The Children's Hosp., Denver, 1990-91, clin. nurse IV, 1991-92; neurology nurse health care program for children spl. needs Colo. Dept. Health, Denver, 1995; nurse care coord. Denver Health Children & Families Program, 1996—. Mem.: Soc. Pediatric Nurses (co-chair program com. 1995—96, mem.-at-large chpt. 2000—01, pub. policy com. 2001—). Home: 5655 S Routt St Littleton CO 80127-1900

BENKO, LINDSAY, Olympic athlete; b. Elkhart, Ind., Nov. 29, 1976; Degree in comms., U. So. Calif., 1999. Recipient Gold medal 4 x 200-meter freestyle (team) Sydney Olympics, 2000, Silver medal 4 x 200-meter relay (team) World Championships, 1998, 200-meter backstroke, 400-meter freestyle summer nats., 1999, Silver medal 200-meter and 400-meter freestyle Pan Pacific Championships, 1999, gold medal 200m free at Pan Pacific Championships, 2002; winner NCAA title in 500-meter freestyle and 200-meter backstroke, 1996, 97, 500-meter freestyle; broke world record in 400m freestyle for short course meters at the World Cup stop in Berlin, 2003, broke world record in 200m at Short course World Championships; also won gold 200m back and swam on 3 Am. record breaking relays; world record holder in 200m and 400m free; Kiputh award winner, Spring Nat., 2003; inducted into Ind. swimming Hall of Fame, 2003 Spring Nat. Avocations: surfing, basketball, volleyball, reading, skiing. Office: USA Swimming 1 Olympic Plz Colorado Springs CO 80909-5746

BENKOVIC, STEPHEN JAMES, chemist; b. Orange, N.J., Apr. 20, 1938; s. Stephen and Mary (Zamadics) Benkovic; m. Patricia Doran, June 10, 1961. AB in English Lit., BS in Chemistry, Lehigh U., 1960; PhD in Organic Chemistry (NIH fellow 1961-63. Teeple fellow 1960-61), Cornell U., 1963. Rsch. assoc. U. Calif., Santa Barbara, 1964—65; asst. prof. chemistry Pa. State U., University Park., 1965—67, assoc. prof., 1967—70, prof., 1970—, Evan Pugh prof., 1977, univ. chair in biol. scis., 1984, Univ. prof., Eberly chair in chemistry, 1986—. Contbr. articles to profl. jours. Recipient NIH career devel. award, 1969—74, Pfizer award in enzyme chemistry, Pa. State U., 1977, Gowland Hopkins award, 1986, Arthur Cope Scholar award, 1988, NIH Merit award, 1988, Alfred R. Bader award, Am. Chem. Soc., 1995; fellow Alfred P. Sloan Found., 1968—70, Guggenheim, 1976. Mem.: NAS, Inst. Medicine, Am. Chem. Soc., Am. Acad. Arts and Scis., Fedn. Am. Biologists, Phi Beta Kappa, Sigma Xi. Home: 771 Teaberry Ln State College PA 16803-3183 Office: Pa State U 414 Wartik Laboratory University Park PA 16802-6300

BENKOWSKI, ANN MARIE, writer; b. Marion, Ohio, Dec. 7, 1965; d. Ronald Mel and Patricia Ann (Wakely) Richie; m. Timothy Jay Benkowski; children: Corrina, Alyssa, Courtney, Thomas. Diploma, Writer's Digest Sch., Cin., 2000, diploma, 2001. Cashier Burger King, Marion, 1982—84; sec., bookkeeper Rotary Towers, Marion, 1984—85; clk., bookkeeper Western & So. Life, Marion, 1985 88; computer programmer Fullfillment Corp., Marion, 1989—95; sec., bookkeeper Northfield, Minn., 1997—. Author: (novels) Accidents Can Happen; contbr. poetry to anthologies (Editor's Choice award, 2002, Internat. Poet of Merit award, 2002, Commemorative award, 2002). Mem.: Internat. Soc. of Poets (hon.). Avocations: reading, cross stitch, crocheting, gardening. Home: 9260 310th St W Northfield MN 55057 Home Fax: 507-663-7920. Personal E-mail: act@ll.net.

BEN-MENACHEM, DAVID, religious studies educator; b. Tel Aviv, Israel, Sept. 27, 1950; s. Mordechai Menachem and Naomi-Esther Shabetai; m. Chana Eichemzweig, Apr. 12, 1981; children: Aviv-Moshe, Ilan Menachem, Raya Rachel, Yosef Haim, Tehilla Yehudit, Yehuda Binyamin. BA in Hebrew Lang./Bible, Tel Aviv U., 1972—75; MA in Nr. Ea. Languages, UCLA, 1982—85, PhD in Nr. Ea. Languages, 1985—87. Tchr. cert. in Bible/Hebrew lang. U. of Tel Aviv, 1979. H.S. tchr. Ministry of Edn., Tel Aviv, 1974—79; tchr. of Hebrew Yeshiva Gedola of LA H.S., LA, Calif., 1979—82; sr. lectr., Judaic studies UCLA, 1982—90; lectr./prof. of Hebrew LA City Coll., 1987—92; prof. of Judaic studies, dept. modern languages/lit. Pomona Coll., 1990—94; prof., chmn. Bible/Judiac studies dept. Achva Coll., Beer Tuvya, Israel, 1994—2001; prof. of Bible Lifshitz Coll., Jerusalem, 1996—2001; prof. of Hebrew Yeshiva U., NYC, 2001—; tchr. of Hebrew/Bible Yeshiva of Flatbush, Bklyn, 2001—02; tchr. of Hebrew lang. Schechter H.S. of NY, 2002—. Com. mem. Ednl. Testing Svc., Princeton, NJ, 1987—94; prof. Ministry of Edn., Jerusalem, 1995—2001, Givat Wash. Coll., Ashdod, Israel, 1994—96, Levinsky Coll., Tel Aviv, 1994—96. Author: (books) Hibbur Ha-Qonim by R. Shimshon Hanakdan, 1987, The Commentary on the Creation of the World by Nachmanedes, 1995, Sefer Ha-Isbel by R. Isaac Ben Yehuda, 2000; contbr. essays to profl. jours. With Israeli Army, 1979—82. Recipient, Rotary Club, Tel Aviv, 1974, Lavon Found., Tel Aviv, 1975, Meml. Found. of Jewish Culture, NY, 1987, Am. Acad. for Jewish Rsch., 1989. Jewish. Avocations: reading, lecturing for cmty., watching polit. shows. Home: 939 E 13th St Brooklyn NY 11230

BENMOSCHE, ROBERT H. insurance company executive; BA in Math., Alfred U., 1966. With Chase Manhattan Bank, Paine Webber, 1982, sr. v.p. mktg., 1984-86, CFO retail bus., 1986-87, dir. securities ops., 1987, exec. v.p.; exec. v.p. individual bus. dept. Met. Life Ins. Co., 1995—97, pres., CEO, 1997—98, chmn., CEO, 1998—2000, MetLife Inc., 2000—. Bd. dirs. N.Y. Philharm. Lt. U.S. Army Signal Corps, 1966-68. Mem. Life Ins. Mktg. and Rsch. Assn. (bd. trustees). Office: Met Life 1 Madison Ave New York NY 10010-3603

BENN, DOUGLAS FRANK, information technology and computer science executive; b. Detroit, May 8, 1936; s. Frank E. and Madeline (Pond) B.; m. Shirley M. Flanery, July 16, 1955; children: Christopher, Susan, Kathy. BS in Math., Mich. State U., 1960, MA, 1962; cert. data processing (NSF scholar), Milw. Inst. Tech., 1965; postgrad., U. Wis., 1965-66; Ed.Adminstrn., Washington U., 1972; MS in Computer Sci., So. Meth. U., 1982, D of Engrng. in Computer Sci., 1990. Tchr. math. and sci. Lansing (Mich.) Public Schs., 1960-64; chmn. computer sci. dept. Kenosha (Wis.) Area Tech. Inst., 1964-67, mgr. data processing, 1965-67; sr. project leader Abbott Labs., North Chicago, Ill., 1967-68, world-wide sr. IT cons. (67 countries), 1968-69; dir. data processing div. St. Louis Public Schs., 1969-74; dir. info. systems div. mental health State of Ill., Springfield, 1974-78; v.p., chief info. officer Med. Computer Systems, Inc., Dallas, 1978; dir. bus. adminstrn. Dallas County Mental Health Center, 1979-80; prof. computer sci. So. Meth. U., Dallas, 1979-82, 89-96; sr. dir. corp. research and devel. Blue Cross & Blue Shield of Tex., Dallas, 1980-83; v.p., chief info. officer svcs. Western States Adminstrs., Fresno, Calif., 1984—88; chmn., pres. D.F. Benn & Assocs. Inc., 1989—; prof. Info. Tech. U. Tex., Dallas, 1990-92, 2000—; exec. U. Tex. Digital Forensics and Emergency Preparedness Inst., Dallas, 2002—; chief info. officer Tex. Natural Resource Conservation Commn., 1996-98. Exec. dir. for tech. Corpus Christi Ind. Sch. Dist., 1998-99; lectr. and adv. coun. Great Cities Pub. Sch. Sys., 1969-74; chief info. officer Ill. Dept. Mental Health and Developmental Disabilities, 1974-78, Wis. Bd. Vocat. Tech. and Adult Edn., 1964-67; co-dir. mgmt. adv. group Ill. Dept. Mental Health, 1974-78; mem. adv. group Tex. Gov.'s Task on Mental Health, 1980; adj. prof. computer info. sys. Wash. U., 1972-74; expert witness/software appraisal svcs. U.S. Tax Ct., 1995; chief info. officer State of Tex., 1997-99, Strategic Planning Coun., 1997, Geog. Info. Sys. Coun., 1997—, Nat. Gov.'s Assn./EPA Joint Task Force Electronic Commerce, 1997-99; project mgr. EPA E-Plan, 2000-; faculty sen. U. Tex., 2002—. Contbr. articles on info. techs., engring. mgmt., and software valuation to profl. jours. Arbitrator computer and bus. contract cases, 1976—. Mem. Data Processing Mgmt. Assn., Assn. for Sys. Mgmt. (Disting. Svc. award 1980, Merit award 1976, Achievement award 1978, chpt. pres. 1976-77, dist. dir. 1976-78), Am. Arbitration Assn., Data Processing Mgmt. Assn. (bd. dirs. 1987-89), Am. Soc. Engring. Mgmt., Telecom Corridor Tech. Club (founder, bd. dirs., officer 2002—), Sigma Xi (chpt. officer 2002—). Presbyterian. Home and Office: 3417 Mount Vernon Way Plano TX 75025-3611 E-mail: dfbenn@attbi.com.

BENN, T(HEODORE) ALEXANDER (ALEC BENN), writer; b. London, July 10, 1918; came to U.S., 1925, naturalized, 1933; s. Theodore and Beatrice Alice (Martin) B.; m. Ethel Borner, June 14, 1940 (div.); 1 child, Theodore A. Jr.; m. Caroline Meredith Whittingham, Dec. 31, 1959; children: Alexander W., Richard R. ScB in Engring., Brown U., 1939; postgrad., NYU, 1939-40, 83-87, Columbia U., 1946-56. Exec. Aluminum Co. Am., Edgewater, N.J., 1939-44, 46-48; writer Merrill Lynch Pierce Fenner and Smith, N.Y.C., 1948-51, McGraw Hill, N.Y.C., 1952; copy dir., v.p., creative dir. Doremus & Co., N.Y.C., 1953-64; v.p. Kudner Agy., N.Y.C., 1964-65, J.M. Mathes, N.Y.C., 1965-66, Bozell & Jacobs, N.Y.C., 1966-67; pres. Benn & MacDonough, Inc., N.Y.C., 1967-87, Short Hills, N.J., 1987-88. Columnist Money and Power, 1988; author: 27 Most Common Mistakes in Advertising, 1978, 23 Most Common Mistakes in Public Relations, 1982, Advertising Financial Products and Services, 1986, The Unseen Wall Street of 1968-1975 and Its Significance For Today, 2000; contbr. articles to profl. jours. Lt. (s.g.) USN, 1944-46. Recipient awards for advt. Mem.: Deep Canyon Tennis Club, Racquets Club Short Hills, Univ. Club. Avocation: tennis. Home: 63 Great Oak Dr Short Hills NJ 07078-3426 Address: 73224 Bill Tilden Ln Palm Desert CA 92260

BENNACK, FRANK ANTHONY, JR., publishing company executive; b. San Antonio, Feb. 12, 1933; s. Frank Anthony and Lula W. Bennack; m. Luella M. Smith, Sept. 1, 1951; children: Shelley, Laura, Diane, Cynthia, Julie. Student, U. Md., 1954—56, St. Mary's U., 1956—58. Advt. account exec. San Antonio Light, 1950—53, 1956—58, adv. mgr., 1961—65, asst. pub., 1965—67, pub., 1967—74; gen. mgr. newspapers Hearst Corp., N.Y.C., 1974—76, exec. v.p., COO, 1975—78, pres., CEO, 1978—2002, vice chmn. bd. dirs., chmn. exec. com., 2002—. Chmn. Mus. of TV and Radio, N.Y.C., 1991—; dir. Mfrs. Hanover Trust Co., N.Y.C., Am. Home Products Corp. Chmn. bd. San Antonio Symphony, 1973—74; trustee Our Lady of Lake Coll.; hon. trustee Witte Meml. Mus.; bd. govs. N.Y. Hosp., N.Y.C. With U.S. Army, 1954—56. Mem.: Am. Newspaper Pubs. Assn. (dir.), Tex. Daily Newspaper Assn. (pres. 1973—), Greater San Antonio C. of C. (pres. 1971—), Rotary Club (pres. 1974—75).*

BENNER, CHARLES HENRY, retired music educator; b. Fort Recovery, Ohio, Feb. 4, 1912; s. Henry Farraday and Ida Matilda (Denney) B.; m. Mary Arbutus Kautz; children: Charles Jonathan, Susan Elizabeth, Daniel Farraday. BS in Edn., Wittenberg U., 1935; MEd, U. Cinn., 1947; PhD, Ohio State U., 1963. Tchr. music, gen. subjects Pub. Schs., Butler County, Ohio, 1934-42; prin. Lemon-Monroe Sch., Ohio, 1946-48; tchr. music, math. Wyoming Schs., Ohio, 1948-58; mem. faculty Sch. Music Ohio State U., Columbus, 1958-68; mem. faculty Coll. Conservatory Music U. Cinn., 1968-79, ret., 1979, prof. emeritus, 1979—. Pres. N. Ctrl. Divsn. Music Educators Nat. Conf., 1965-67; U.S. del. internat. symposium October-Art-Children, Moscow, 1977; cons. to Australia Coun. and Australia Soc. Music Edn., Canberra, 1980; vis. prof. music edn. Cath. U., Washington, 1981-82; mem. faculty Brigham Young U., Provo, Utah, summer 1974. Author: From Research to the Classroom: Teaching Performing Groups, 1972; co-author: Music in General Education, 1965. Reader Radio Reading Svc., Cinn., 1990—. With USCG, Maryland, 1942-43, Deck Ofcr., Lt. jg., PTO, 1944-46. Recipient Disting. Svc. award Ohio Music Edn., 1971, Canticum Novum award Wittenberg U., Springfield, Ohio, 1973, U. Cincinnati Coll., Conservatory of Music, Dist. Svc. Awd., 1979. Mem. Ohio Music Edn. Assn. (pres. 1958-60, disting. svc. award 1971), Internat. Soc. Music Edn. (bd. dirs. 1974-76), Music Educators Nat. Conf. (life, pres. 1974-76).

BENNER, RICHARD BYRON, philosophy educator; b. Somers Point, NJ, Dec. 6, 1936; s. Theodore Roosevelt and Carolyn Mildred (Wilkinson) B.; m. Ethel Barbara Blair, June 7, 1958 (div. Oct. 1996); children: Richard Byron Jr., Kathryn Lynn, Cheryl Susan; m. Linda Jean Foster, Dec. 24, 1996; 1 stepchild, Genevieve Lynn Fox. BA, Villanova U., 1969; MS, Fla. State U., 1972; postgrad., U. Pa., 1972-77. Clin. lab. chief Shore Meml. Hosp., Somers Point, N.J., 1961-62; med. rschr. Bryn Mawr (Pa.) Hosp., 1962-71; office mgr. O.C. Plumbers, Inc., Ocean City, N.J., 1972-79; plumbing contractor Doctor's Plumbing and Heating, Ocean City, 1979-85; hist. preservationist R.B. Benner and Son, Ocean City, 1985-93; animal care specialist Wildlife Aid, Inc., English Creek, N.J., 1993-95; instr. philosophy Atlantic Cape C.C. (formerly Atlantic C.C.), Mays Landing, NJ, 1995-99, asst. prof. philosophy and religion, 1999—. Adj. asst. prof. philosophy Ocean County Coll., Toms River, NJ, 1998—99, 2002—03; gen. edn. project task force NJ County Coll.; spkr. in field. Contbr. articles, photographs to profl. publs. Founder, pres. Ocean City Hist. Preservation Soc., 1986-90. With U.S. Army, 1958-61; vol. U.S. Dept. Interior, N.J. Divsn. Fish and Game. Recipient 1st place photo award Egg Harbor Twp., 1995, 96, cert. of recognition Exch. Club, 1991. Mem. AAUP, NEA, Am. Philos. Assn., Philosophy Edn. Soc., Nature Conservancy, Def. Wildlife, Environ. Def. Fund., Earth Justice Legal Def. Fund, Natural Resources Def. Coun., World Wildlife Fund, Mensa. Avocations: outdoor and wildlife photography, conservation. Home: 6037 Main St Mays Landing NJ 08330-1896 Office: 5100 Black Horse Pike Mays Landing NJ E-mail: rbenner@atlantic.edu.

BENNER, RICHARD EDWARD, JR., community service volunteer, investor; b. Jersey City, Dec. 7, 1932; s. Richard E. and Dorothy (Linstead) B.; m. Virginia Hart; children: Linda, Richard III, Christopher. BS, Lehigh U., 1954; postgrad., NYU, 1959-63. Sales exec. IBM Corp, Norwalk, Conn., 1955-58; with Avon Products, Inc., N.Y.C., 1959-78, group v.p. mktg. and internat., 1972-78; exec. v.p. The Fuller Brush Co., Kansas City, Mo., 1979-86; mktg. cons. Kansas City, 1987—. Bd. dirs. Game Hill, Inc., Weston, Mo., exec. com., chmn., bd, dirs., cons. Exec. Svc. Corp., 1993—; LINC, Local Investment commn., 21st Century Initiative; mentor Helzberg Entrepreneurial Mentoring Program, 1998—. Bd. dirs., pres. Northland Homes Partnership for the Homeless, 1988-94; active Eccumedia, 1987-89; maj. corp. com. chmn. United Way, N.Y.C., 1976; Rep. committeeman, Bergan County, 1973; mem. SCORE, 1990—, vice chmn., 1991-92; vice chair cmty. rels. Exec. Svc. Corps, 1990—, chmn., 1993-97, dir., 1997—; trustee Shepherd Ctr. North, 2000—; Stephen minister, 1998—. Mem. Direct Selling Assn. Edn. Found. (bd. dirs. 1982-84). Clubs: Beaverkill Trout (Livingston Manor, N.Y.) (bd. dirs. 1975-78); Old Pike Country (bd. dirs. 1987-90). Lodges: Rotary (bd. dirs., Polio Plus area coord., pres.). Lutheran. Avocations: fly fishing, investing, gardening. Home and Office: 4404 NW Normandy Ln Kansas City MO 64116-1553

BENNER, RICHARD WALTER, oil company executive, geologist, engineer; b. Dayton, Ohio, June 2, 1922; s. Frederick and Edna Marie B.; m. Parnel Gillilan, Mar. 19, 1949 (dec. Apr. 1970); m. Donna Tschappat, Nov. 24, 1978 (dec. Sept. 1995). BS in Geology, U. Mich., 1947, MS in Geology, 1948. Registered profl. engr., Colo. Photo geologist Texaco, Inc., Lewistown, Mont., 1947-48, field geologist, 1948-59, dist. geologist Denver, 1959-66, spl. projects geologist, 1966-77; v.p. Kissinger Petroleum Corp., Englewood, Colo., 1977-81, Kissinger Drilling & Exploration, Englewood, 1981-86; pres. Kissinger Exploration, Inc., Denver, 1981-86; cons. Corpus Christi, Tex., 1987—; ret., 2003. Author, co-author: Ann. Field Book Publs., Rocky Mountain Geol. Soc. and Montana Geol. Soc., 1949-77; co-author Geological Atlas of Rocky Mountain Region, Wind River Basin, Wyo., 1970, U.S. Geol. Bull., Reserves of Oil and Gas in Rocky Mountain Region, 1977. With U.S. Coast Guard, 1943-44, lt. U.S. Navy, 1944-46, ETO, PTO. Named Hon. Alumnus, William Woods U., 2002. Mem. Am. Assn. Petroleum Geologists, Sigma Gamma Upsilon. Home and Office: 5206 Wooldridge Rd Corpus Christi TX 78413-3823

BENNET, DOUGLAS JOSEPH, JR., university president; b. Orange, N.J., June 23, 1938; s. Douglas Joseph and Phoebe (Benedict) B.; m. Susanne Klejman, June 27, 1959 (div. 1995); children: Michael, James, Holly; m. Midge Bowen Ramsey, July 27, 1996. BA, Wesleyan U., Middletown, Conn., 1959; MA, U. Calif., Berkeley, 1960; PhD, Harvard, 1968. Asst. to econ. adv. AID, New Delhi, 1963—64; spl. asst. to Am. ambassador to India, 1964—66; asst. to Vice Pres. Hubert H. Humphrey, 1967—69; adminstrv. asst. to U.S. Senator Thomas Eagleton, 1969—73, to U.S. Senator Abraham Ribicoff, 1973—73; staff dir. com. budget U.S. Senate, 1974—77; asst. sec. state congressional relations, 1977—79; adminstr. AID, Washington, 1979—81; pres. Roosevelt Ctr. for Am. Policy Studies, 1981—83; pres., CEO Nat. Pub. Radio, Washington, 1983—93; asst. sec. state Internat. Orgnl. Affairs Dept. State, Washington, 1993—95; pres. Wesleyan U., Middletown, Conn., 1995—. Mem. Coun. Fgn. Rels., Cosmos Club. Democrat. Home: 269 High St Middletown CT 06457-3208 Office: Office of Pres Wesleyan U 229 High St Middletown CT 06459-3208

BENNETT, ALAN JEROME, electronics executive, physicist; b. Phila., June 13, 1941; s. Leon Martin and Reba (Perry) B.; m. Frances Kitey, June 16, 1963; children: Sarah, Rachel, Daniel. BA, U. Pa, 1962; MS, U. Chgo., 1963, PhD, 1965. Physicist R & D ctr. GE, Schenectady, N.Y., 1966-74, br. mgr. R & D ctr., 1975-79; dir. electronics lab. Gould Inc., Rolling Meadows, Ill., 1979-84; v.p. R & D Varian Assocs., Palo Alto, Calif., 1984-91; dir. program devel. Lawrence Livermore Nat. Lab., Livermore, Calif., 1992-96, dir. indsl. partnerships and commercialization, 1997—, mgr. program devel. Contbr. articles to profl. jours. Fellow NSF, 1963-65, 66. Mem. Phi Beta Kappa, Sigma Xi. Avocations: linguistics, amateur radio. Home: 233 Tennyson Ave Palo Alto CA 94301-3737 Office: Lawrence Livermore Nat Lab PO Box 808 Livermore CA 94551-0808 E-mail: Abennett@llnl.gov.

BENNETT, ALEXANDER ELLIOT, lawyer; b. Houston, Aug. 9, 1940; s. William Ernest and Verna Evelyn (Donelan) B.; m. Marilyn A. Bennett, June 6, 1960 (div. 1981); children: Andrew, Laura, Peter; m. Brooksley Born, Oct. 9, 1982; children: Nicholas Landau, Ariel Landau. BA, U. Mich., 1961, JD, 1963. Bar: D.C. 1964. Assoc. Arnold & Porter, Washington, 1966-70, ptnr., 1971—. Editor U. Mich. Law Rev., 1963. Mem. ABA, D.C. Bar Assn., Order of Coif. Democrat. Avocations: sailing, tennis. Home: 2319 Tracy Pl NW Washington DC 20008-1640 Office: Arnold & Porter Thurman Arnold Bldg 555 12th St NW Washington DC 20004-1206 E-mail: alexander_bennett@aporter.com.

BENNETT, AMANDA, editor; m. Terence Foley; 2 children. Grad. cum laude, Harvard U., 1975. Reporter Wall St. Jour.; mng. editor projects The Oregonian, 1998—2001; editor, v.p. Lexington Herald-Leader, 2001—03; editor, exec. v.p. Phila. (Pa.) Inquirer, 2003—. Mem. Pulitzer Prize Bd., 2002—. Author: In Memoriam, 1998; co-author: (with Terence B. Foley) The Man Who Stayed Behind, (with Sidney Rittenberg) Death of the Organziation Man, 1991. Recipient Pulitzer prize, The Oregonian, 2001. Mem.: Pulitzer Prize Bd. Office: Philadelphia Inquirer PO Box 8263 400 N Broad St Philadelphia PA 19101

BENNETT, ANNA DELL, minister, religion educator, retired elementary school educator; b. Cobb Hill, Ky., Jan. 11, 1935; d. James Edison Shoemaker and Chrystal (Abney) Shoemaker-Hurst; m. Stanley Bennett, Oct. 7, 1950 (dec. Jan. 1987); children: Eddie Wayne, James Lloyd, Kathryn Melissa. BS, U. Dayton, 1966; MS in Elem. Classroom Teaching, Wright State U., 1974, M in Gifted Teaching, 1980; Assoc. Bibl., Centerville Bible Coll., 1985, degree in theology, 1987. Lic. minister, Ohio; ordained minister Open Bible Standard Chs., 1992. Tchr. West Carrollton (Ohio) Bd. Edn., 1966-86; dir. Christian edn., Way of the Cross Ch., Dayton, Ohio, 1989-96; retired, 1996. Founder, adminstr. Noah's Ark Pre-Sch., 1994; adj. prof. Mt. St. Joseph Coll., Cin., 1981-85. Recipient plaque Mt. St. Joseph Coll., Cin., 1985. Republican. Home: 1916 Hickory Ridge Dr Beavercreek OH 45432-4036

BENNETT, ARLIE JOYCE, clinical social worker emeritus; b. Central Lake, Mich., Nov. 22, 1921; d. Charles Herbert and Bernice Evelyn (Miller) B. Student, Alma (Mich.) Coll., 1946-48; BA, U. Mich., 1950, MSW, 1955. Bd. cert. diplomate emerita Am. Bd. Examiners in Clin. Social Work. Social worker Ypsilanti (Mich.) State Hosp., 1950-54; staff social worker Kalamazoo Child Guidance Clinic, 1955-67, chief social worker, 1967-71; clin. social worker State Tech. Inst. Rehab. Ctr., Plainwell, Mich., 1971-90; pvt. practice, Kalamazoo, 1991-92. Field instr. Mich. State U., 1959-76, Western Mich. U. Sch. Social Work, Kalanazoo, 1971-90, U. Mich., 1967-71. Author: Pie Is in the Eye of the Beholder, 1980, War and Memory, 1991; editor newsletter Late Show Connection, 1993—; also articles. Vol. record reviewer Cath. Family Svcs. Agys., Kalamazoo; bd. dirs. Youth Opportunities Unltd., Kalamazoo, 1968—. Tech. sgt. WAC, AUS, 1944-46, ETO. Mem. NASW (past chmn. and officer), AAUW (legis. chmn. Kalamazoo br. 1985-89, 93-95, pres. 1991-93, pub. policy chmn. 1999-), Mensa (local coord. 1990—), Loners Am. (pres. Mich. chpt. 1990-92, 97-98), U. Mich. Alumnae Club (past pres. and officer), Phi Kappa Phi. Avocations: poetry, writing, camping, seat weaving, upholstery. Home: 1110 W Maple St Kalamazoo MI 49008-1846

BENNETT, BARBARA VIRGINIA, fashion consultant, concert pianist; b. St. Louis, May 26, 1940; d. Thomas Charles Rostron and Virginia Balmer; m. James Marvin Bennett Ph.D., July 2, 1965; children: J. Justin, Bradley A. Music performance, Juilliard, N.Y., N.Y., 1967. Exec. dir. Bennett Piano Studios, N.Y., N.Y., 1982-96; pres., CEO Chic Boutique Ltd., N.Y., 1996—. Office: Chic Boutique Ltd 211 E 53rd St New York NY 10022-4803 E-mail: jmb.bennettenvmgt@msn.com.

BENNETT, BETTY T. English literature educator, university dean, writer; b. N.J. children: Peter, Matthew. BA, Bklyn. Coll., 1962; MA, NYU, 1963, PhD, 1970. Adj. asst. prof. dept. English and comparative lit. SUNY, Stony Brook, 1970-75, asst. chmn. comparative lit., 1971-72, asst. to dean Grad. Sch., 1970-79, adj. assoc. prof., 1975-79; assoc. prof. English and humanities Pratt Inst., Bklyn., 1979-81, prof., 1981-85, dean Sch. Liberal Arts and Scis., 1979-85; dean Coll. Arts and Scis. Am. U., Washington, 1985-97, disting. prof. lit., 1997—. Fellowship reader Danforth Found., 1978-79; edn. liaison officer N.Y. State, 1977-80; co-dir. NEH Inst., 1989-90. Author: British War Poetry in the Age of Romanticism: 1793-1815, 1976, The Letters of Mary Wollstonecraft Shelley, Vol. I, 1980, The Letters of Mary Wollstonecraft Shelley, Vol. II, 1983, The Letters of Mary Wollstonecraft Shelley, Vol. III, 1988, Mary Diana Dods: A Gentleman and a Scholar, 1991, Mary Diana Dods: A Gentleman and a Scholar, paperback edit., 1994, Mary Wollstonecraft Shelley: An Introduction, 1998; editor (with Donald H. Reiman and Michael Jaye): The Evidence of the Imagination, 1978; editor: (with Charles Robinson) The Mary Shelley Reader, 1990; editor: Proserpine and Midas and Relation of the Cenci, 1992, The Selected Letters of Mary Wollstonecraft Shelley, 1995, Lives of the Great

Romantics III: Mary Shelley, 1999; editor: (with Stuart Curran) Mary Shelley in Her Times, 2000; cons. editor and author gen. intro.: The Novels and Selected Works of Mary Wollstonecraft Shelley, 1996, book rev. editor: Keats-Shelley Jour., 1976—94. Keats-Shelley Assn. Am. Disting. scholar, 1992; NEH fellow, 1974-75, Henry E. Huntington Libr. fellow, 1976, Am. Coun. Learned Socs. fellow, 1977-78; Am. Philos. Soc. grant, 1980-81, NEH grant, 1984-87. Mem. MLA, Byron Assn., Keats-Shelley Assn. Am. (bd. dirs.), Soc. for Textual Scholarship (exec. com. 1993—), NYU Alumni Assn., Phi Beta Kappa (founding pres. Zeta chpt. of D.C.). Office: Am U Dept Lit Coll Arts and Scis 4400 Massachusetts Ave NW Washington DC 20016-8001 E-mail: bbennet@american.edu.

BENNETT, BIANCA CHERIE, lawyer; b. Washington, May 14, 1971; d. Carl Roosevelt and Barbara Jean (Pope) B. Grad., Princeton U., 1993; JD, U. Va., 1996. Bar: D.C., 1997. Assoc. Zuckert, Scoutt & Rasenberger, Washington, 1996—; mgr. Law Dept. General Dynamics Corp., Falls Church, Virginia, 1998-2000; dir. business affairs Paramount Pictures, Hollywood, Calif., 2000—02; prin. Bennett & Assoc., LA, 2003—. Mem. Washington Bar Assn., Black Entertainment and Sports Lawyers' Assn., Washington Area Lawyers for the Arts, Delta Sigma Theta Sorority, Inc. Avocations: photography, music, foreign travel, films, running. Office: Bennett Entertainment Inc 4440 Finley Ave Ste 101 Los Angeles CA 90027 E-mail: Bianca@bennettentertainment.com.

BENNETT, BRADLEY FREDERICK, retired military officer, science association director; b. New Milford, Conn., Aug. 29, 1911; s. Frederick Lum and Florence Kay Bradley; m. Eunice Gwendolyn Meissner (div. 1933); m. Virginia White, Dec. 22, 1956; children: Bradley Robert, Bruce Roy. MS, MIT, 1940, MS in Physics, 1953. Commd. ensign USN, 1935, advanced through grades to capt., 1983; asst. planning officer Norfolk Navy Yard, Portsmouth, Va., 1940—43; hull supt. Pearl Harbor (Hawaii) Navy Yard, 1943—47; engring. svc. officer US Naval Rsch. Labs., Washington, 1947—50, dir. adminstrn., 1960—63, dir., 1963—65; repair supt. US Fleet Repair Facility, Yokuska, Japan, 1950—51; dir. materials rsch. divsn. Bur. Ships Navy Dept., Washington, 1951—57; commdg. officer U.S. br. office Office Naval Rsch., London, 1957—60; v.p. Univ. Rsch. Assn. Washington, 1967—77. Hydropneumatic explosion rschr. USN, Washington, 1953—55. Capt. USN, 1954—65. Decorated Bronze star USN. Fellow: Royal Instn. Eng.; mem.: Philos. Soc. of Washington (pres. 1973), Brit. Royal Soc. Medicine, Am. Geophys. Union, Am. Soc. Metals, N.Y. Acad. Scis., Cosmos Club (chmn. program com. 1965—73, Washington). Achievements include research in metallurgical factors affecting cavitation damage; Rayleigh scattering of gamma rays. Avocation: ancient numismatics. Home: 750 S La Pasada Cir # 18 Green Valley AZ 85614

BENNETT, BROOKE, Olympic athlete; b. Tampa, Fla., May 6, 1980; Grad., Durant HS, Plant City, Fla., 1998. Swimmer; winner gold and silver medals Pan-Am Games, 1995; winner gold medal Pan Pacific Games, 1995, 97; gold medalist 800m freestyle Olympic Summer Games, 1996; sponsor swim team Brower Aquatic Suns, Davie, Fla.; gold medalist 400m freestyle, Sydney, 2000, 800m freestyle, Sydney, 2000. Recipient Spring Nationals Kiphuth award, 1996, Spring Nationals Phillips Performance award, 1996, USOC Sports Woman of the Yr. for swimming, 1995. Avocation: horseback riding. Office: c/o USA Swimming 1 Olympic Plz Colorado Springs CO 80909-5746

BENNETT, BRUCE ANTHONY, civil engineer; b. Providence, Nov. 8, 1950; s. George Sr. and Anne (Rominyk) B.; m. Patricia Anne Matteson, May 29, 1971; children: Paul Jason, Susan Lynn. BSCE, U. R.I., 1973; MSCE, Northeastern U., 1981. Sr. engr. Stone & Webster Engring. Corp., Boston, 1973-81; project mgr. Nat. Hydro Corp., Boston, 1981-86; sr. engr. Heat Exch. Systems, Boston, 1986-89; project mgr. Stowe Engring. Corp., Norwell, Mass. Conf. com. Nat. Sci. Found., Amherst, Mass., 1988. Editor: Pipeline Infrastructure, 1988. Com. mem. Pub. Works Study, Duxbury, Mass., 1985, Solid Waste Study, Duxbury, 1986, Nuclear Matters, Duxbury, 1987. Recipient Cert. of Appreciation ASME, 1994. Mem. ASCE (divsn. chmn. 1981—, conf. chmn. 1988, exec. com. 1994, Award of Excellence, 1994), Tau Beta Pi. Achievements include inventionr of generator cooling system, condenser perf. monitor, most recent discovery proving that substitution of a chilled water process facilitates the achievement of higher electric power generator output. Home: PO Box 387 Westport Point MA 02791-0387

BENNETT, BRUCE W. construction company executive, civil engineer; b. St. Joseph, Mo., Dec. 24, 1930; s. Bruce W. and Laura Louella (Clark) B.; m. Barbara Gail Haase, July 26, 1957; children: Stacy Suzanne, Bruce W. BS in Civil Engring., U. So. Calif., 1954. Project mgr. George A. Fuller & Co., Chgo., 1956-61; contract mgr. Huber, Hunt & Nichols, Indpls., 1961-70, v.p., 1970-82, exec. v.p., 1982-84, pres., 1984-95, ret., 1995. Pres. Hunt Corp., 1988-95, bd. dirs. Served to capt. USAF, 1954-57 Mem. Archimedes Circle, David Wilson Assocs., Newcomen Soc. Clubs: Indpls. Athletic, Skyline (Indpls.). Republican. Avocations: tennis; golf. Home: 437 Seville Ave Newport Beach CA 92661-1528

BENNETT, C. LEONARD, consulting engineer; b. Lowell, Mass., Oct. 5, 1939; s. C. Leonard and Ruth E. (Glow) B.; m. Patricia Ann Derival, Aug. 22, 1966; children: Craig, Dawn Marie. BS in Elec. Engring., Lowell Tech. Inst., Mass., 1961; MS, N.C. State U., Raleigh, 1964; PhD, Purdue U., 1968. Registered profl. engr., Mass. Research engr. Purdue U., 1968; mem. tech. staff Sperry Research Ctr., Sudbury, Mass., 1968-73, mgr. systems applications, 1973-83; cons. engr. Raytheon, Marlboro, Mass., 1983—; lectr. in field. Contbr. chpts. to books, articles to profl. jours.; patentee field. Chmn. Groton Fin. Com., Mass., 1970-76; treas. Groton Ctr. for the Arts, 1976-78; coach Groton Jr. Hockey, 1979-86, Groton Little League Baseball, 1981-84; mem. com. local troop Boy Scouts Am., 1983—; bd. dirs. Groton Dunstable Soccer Club, 1981-92, Nashoba Valley Youth Soccer League, 1986—; soccer referee U.S. Youth Soccer Assn., 1987—. Fellow IEEE (assoc. editor Trans. on Antennas and Propagation 1983-96); mem. Internat. Union of Radio Scis., Eta Kappa Nu, Tau Beta Pi, Phi Kappa Phi, Sigma Pi Sigma. Home: 304 Reedy Meadow Rd Groton MA 01450-1408 Office: Raytheon 1001 Boston Post Rd E Marlborough MA 01752-3789

BENNETT, CARL, retired discount department store executive; b. Greenwich, Conn., Jan. 27, 1920; s. Mayer and Rebecca (Lipsky) B.; m. Dorothy Becker, June 24, 1951; children: Marc Mitchell, Robin Cheryl Bennett Kanarek, Bruce Kenneth. Student, NYU, 1937-38. Wholesale liquor salesman, Conn., 1940-51; founder, ret. chmn. bd., chief exec. officer Caldor, Inc., Norwalk, Conn., 1951-84; ptnr. DorCal Assocs., Norwalk, Conn., 1984—. Chmn. Bi-Cultural Day Sch., Stamford, Conn., 1965-67, treas., 1967-68; bd. dirs. Stamford Hosp., nat. bd. dirs. NCCJ; mem. Am. com., internat. bd. govs. Weizmann Inst. Served with AUS, 1942-45. Recipient Amudin award outstanding work Hebrew day schs., 1965, disting. service award Prime Minister Israel, 1973; named Retailer of Yr., 1982; named to Retailers Hall of Fame, 1983 Mem. World Bus. Council (charter), Nat. Retail Mchts. Assn. (bd. dirs.) Clubs: Sailfish Point Country (Stuart, Fla.); Quaker Ridge Country (Scarsdale, N.Y.). Home: Windrose Way Greenwich CT 06830 Office: DorCal Assocs 607 Main Ave Norwalk CT 06851-1058

BENNETT, CAROL(INE) ELISE, retired reporter, retired actress; b. New Orleans, Dec. 27, 1938; d. Gerald Clifford Graham and Edna Doris (Toennies) Kerr; m. Ralph Decker Bennett, Jr., Feb. 27, 1966; children: Ralph Decker III, Katherine Elise. BA, U. B.C., Vancouver, Can., 1960; BLS, McGill U., Montreal, Que., Can., 1962. Libr. various locations, 1962-76; reporter TV/radio Washington-Ala. News Report, Washington, 1981-2001; ret., 2001. Actor: (plays) Girl in My Soup, 1978; (films) Prime Risk, 1984; host (TV series) Modern Maturity, 1986—88. Vol. reader Rec. for Blind, Washington, 1985—. Mem.: AAUW, AFTRA, SAG, Nat. Press Club, Soc. Profl. Journalists. Avocation: tennis. Home: 115 Southwood Ave Silver Spring MD 20901-1918

BENNETT, CARRIE, retired chemical company executive; b. Huger, S.C., Oct. 26, 1955; d. Henry and Christine Bennett; 1 child, Larry. BS, Johnson C. Smith U., 1978; MBA, The Citadel, 1983. Tchr. N.W. Jr. H.S., Charlotte, N.C., 1977-78; acct. Huger Constrn. Co., Mt. Pleasant, S.C., 1980; subcontractor for Amoco Small Loading Co., Huger, S.C., 1980; with Morris Small & Co., Huger, S.C., 1979; mfg. exec. Amoco, Mt. Pleasant, 1981-91, ret., 1991. Author: How Big is the Cat, The Carrie Bennett Story; poet: poems published since. Active PUSH Rainbow Coalition, People United for Justice, Charlotte, N.C.; mem. YWCA; guardian Good Parent; Sunday sch. tchr. Mem. NAACP, Alpha Kappa Alpha. Democrat.

BENNETT, CATHERINE JUNE, information technology executive, educator, consultant; b. Augusta, Ga., June 19, 1950; d. Robert Stogner and Catherine Sue (Jordan) Robinson; m. Danny Marvin Bennett, Sept. 5, 1971; children: Timothy Jordan, Robert Daniel. BS in Stats., U. Ga., 1971, MA in Bus., 1973. Cert. project mgmt. profl. Project Mgmt. Inst., rational cert. cons., fellow Life Mgmt. Inst. Programmer William M. Shenkel & Assocs., Athens, Ga., 1971-73; sys. analyst U. Ga., Athens, 1973-76; product cons. ISA/SUNGUARD, Atlanta, 1976-78, mgr. product support, 1980-85, hotline mgr., sr. fin. specialist, 1986-88, mem. edn. staff Investment Client Support, 1988-90, mgr. investment reporting, 1991-93, mgr. devel., 1993-95; dir. Fin. Reporting Solutions, 1998-99; project mgr. CGI, Atlanta, 1999, dir. cons. svcs., 1999—2002, dir. outsourcing svcs., 2002—. Presenter in field. Den leader Cub Scouts, 1989-90, treas., 1990-95; head ofcl. Duluth Thunderbolts, 1994; mem. Gwinnett Swim League (sec. 1995-2003). Avocations: bridge, swimming, travel. Office: CGI 3740 Davinci Ct # 400 Norcross GA 30092-2670 E-mail: cathieben@worldnet.att.net., cathie.bennett@cgi.com.

BENNETT, CHARLES ANDREW, economics educator; b. N.Y.C., Feb. 8, 1943; s. Joseph C. and Catherine F. (Gallagher) B.; divorced; 1 child, William C.B. BA in Econs. with honors, St. Francis Coll., Bklyn., 1965; MA in Econs., Fordham U., 1968; student, 1968. Grad. asst., teaching fellow Fordham U., Bronx, N.Y., 1965-68; instr. econs. Gannon U., Erie, Pa., 1968-76, asst. prof., 1976—, dir. Ctr. for Econ. Edn., 1977—, chmn. dept. econs. and fin., 1986—97. Author: Principles of Microeconomics Manual for External Study Courses, 1977, 12th edit., 2003; mem. bd. editors Worth Pub., N.Y.C., Harper & Row, N.Y.C., Wadsworth Pubs., N.Y.C., Dryden Press, N.Y.C., McGraw Hill Pub. Co. Mem. Erie Mayor's Office Community Affairs; mem. microcomputer com. Fairview (Pa.) Sch. Dist., mem. resource com. strategic planning action group, mem. tech. edn. task force; mem. steering com. Family Support Svcs., Erie; mem. task force on citizenship Pa. Dept. Edn.; mem. strategic planning com. Dahlkemper Sch. Bus. Adminstrn. Recipient award for meritorious support of free enterprise BP Oil, 1980, Leavey award for excellence in econ. edn. Freedoms Found., 1984, Internat. Paper award Joint Coun. on Econ. Edn., 1988, Com. to Excellence award in econ. edn., 1989. Mem. Pa. Coun. Econ. Edn., Nat. Fedn. Ind. Bus. (mem. adv. panel), Nat. Assn. Econ. Educators, Nat. Coun. Econ. Edn., Econ. Am., Assn. for Pvt. Edn. Avocations: biking, swimming. Home: 5570 Sebago Dr Fairview PA 16415-2223 Office: Gannon U 109 Univ Sq Erie PA 16541

BENNETT, CHARLES FRANKLIN, JR., biogeographer, educator; b. Oakland, Calif., Apr. 10, 1926; s. Charles Franklin and Charlotte Louise (Normand) B.; m. Carole Ann Messenger, Nov. 30, 1947; 1 child, Ashley Lynn. PhD, UCLA, 1959. Instr. UCLA, 1959-60, asst. prof., 1960-65, assoc. prof., 1965-69, prof. biogeography, 1969—; prof. emeritus, 1993—. Cons. in field. Author: Human Influence on Zoogeography of Panama, 1968, Man and Earth's Ecosystems, 1976, Conservation of Natural Resources, 1983; contbr. articles to profl. jours. Guggenheim fellow, 1970-71. Fellow AAAS, Royal Geog. Soc.; mem. Ecol. Soc. Am., Brit. Ecol. Soc., Assn. Tropical Biology, Soc. for Conservation Biology, Fauna and Flora Preservation Soc., Am. Inst. Biol. Scis. Avocation: collecting natural history books. Home: 317 S Anita Ave Los Angeles CA 90049-3805 Office: UCLA Dept Geography 405 Hilgard Ave Los Angeles CA 90095-9000 E-mail: chasben@ucla.edu.

BENNETT, CHARLES LEON, vocational and graphic arts educator; b. Salem, Oreg., Feb. 5, 1951; s. Theodore John and Cora Larena (Rowland) B.; m. Cynthia Alice Hostman, June 12, 1976 (div.); m. Lynn Marie Toland, Aug. 12, 1977 (div.); children: Mizzy Marie, Charles David.; m. Christina M. Crawford, Dec. 19, 1987 (div.); m. Iris J. Perrigo, Mar. 17, 2001. AS in Vocat. Tchr. Edn., Clackamas C.C., 1977; AS in Gen. Studies, Linn Benton C.C., 1979; BS in Gen. Studies, Ea. Oreg. State Coll., 1994. Tchr. printing Tongue Point Job Corps, Astorial, Oreg., 1979-80; tchr., chmn. dept. Portland (Oreg.) Pub. Schs., 1980—; owner, mgr. printing and pub. co. Portland, 1981-87. With AUS, 1970-72. Mem. NRA, Oreg. Vocat. Trade-Tech. Assn. (cept. chmn., pres. graphic arts divsn., Indsl. Educator of Yr. 1981-82), Oreg. Vocat. Assn. (Vocat. Tchr. of Yr. 1982-83), Graphic Arts Tech. Found., In-Plant Printing Mgmt. Assn., Internat. Graphic Arts Edn. Assn. (v.p. N.W. region VI), Oreg. Assn. Manpower Spl. Needs Pers., Oreg. Indsl. Arts Assn., Internat. Platform Assn., Nat. Assn. Quick Printers, Am. Vocat. Assn., Pacific Printing and Imaging Assn., Inplant Printing Mgmt. Assn., Portland Club Lithographers and Printing House Craftsmen. Republican. Home: 20295 S Unger Rd Beavercreek OR 97004-8884 Office: 546 NE 12th Ave Portland OR 97232-2719 E-mail: cbennett@aracnet.com., cbennett@pps.k12.or.us.

BENNETT, CLAY, cartoonist; b. Clinton, S.C., Jan. 20, 1958; B in Art and History, U. North Ala., 1980. Artist Pitts. Post-Gazette, Fayetteville Times, Fayetteville, NC; editl. cartoonist St. Petersburg Times, 1981—94, Christian Sci. Monitor, Boston, 1998—. Editl. cartoonist King Features Syndicate, 1994—. Named Editl. Cartoonist of Yr., Editor & Pub. Mag., 2001; recipient Nat. Headliner award, 1999, 2000, John Fischetti award, 2002. Office: Christian Sci Monitor 1 Norway St Boston MA 02115

BENNETT, CORNELIUS, retired professional football player; b. Birmingham, Ala., Aug. 25, 1965; m. Tracey Bennett. Student, U. Ala. With Buffalo Bills, 1987—95, Atlanta Falcons, 1996-98; linebacker Indianapolis Colts, 1999—2000. Named to Pro Bowl team, 1988, 90-93, Sporting News All-Pro team, 1988, Sporting News Coll. All-Am. team, 1984-86; recipient Lombardi award, 1986.

BENNETT, DICK, college basketball coach; b. Pitts., Apr. 20, 1943; m. Anne; children: Kathi, Amy, Tony. BS in phys. edn., Ripon Coll., 1965; MEd, UW-Stevens Point. Basketball coach West Bend (Wis.) H.S., 1965-66; coach various Wis. H.S. teams, 1966-76, UW-Stevens Point, 1976-85, UW-Green Bay, 1985-95, U. Wis., Madison, 1995—. 1st team at U. Wis. (17-15) appeared in 1996 N.I.T.; 2d team (18-10) made 2d U. Wis. appearance in N.C.A.A. tournament in 50 yrs., put together sch.'s 1st 6-game winning streak since 1951. Named WSUC Coach of Yr., 1982, 1985, NAIA Coach of Yr., 1984, NAIA Area IV Coach of Yr., 1985, Mid-Continent Coach of Yr., 1990, 1992, NABC Dist. 11 Coach of Yr., 1992, 1994, Basketball Times Midwest Coach of Yr., 1994. Achievements include 21-yr. collegiate coaching record, 395-214 (.649). Office: U Wis 1440 Monroe St Madison WI 53711-2051

BENNETT, DICK, advertising executive; V.p., assoc. creative dir. J. Walter Thompson, N.Y.C.; v.p. McCann Erickson; sr. v.p. pres., creative dir. Young & Rubicam; chmn. Bennett Kuhn Varner Inc., Atlanta. Office: Bennett Kuhn Varner Inc Ste 700 2964 Peachtree Rd Atlanta GA 30305

BENNETT, DOUGLAS MARSHALL, construction and marketing executive; b. Schenectady, Sept. 15, 1947; s. Benjamin Floyd and Constance (Rice) B. BArch. with honors, N.C. State U., 1970; MBA, Harvard Bus. Sch., 1976. Architect Wallace Floyd Ellenzweig Moore Assocs., Cambridge, Mass., 1974; asst. supt. Chgo., 1976-78; asst. to regional sr. v.p. Turner Constrn. Co., Chgo., 1978-80; dir. corp. mktg. Turner Corp., N.Y.C., 1981-88, dir. corp. planning and communications, 1989-92; dir. finance Turner Steiner Internat. SA, 1992-96; with office of the chmn. Turner Corp., 1996—, dir. mktg., 1997-98; consect exec. Turner Steiner Internat., LLC, 1989; cons., 1989—; sr. v.p. strategic mktg. Dick Corp., Pitts., 1999—. Instr. Boston Archtl. Ctr., Cambridge, Mass., 1971-75; pres. N.C. State U. Sch. of Design Found., 1992; cons. in field. Contbr. articles to profl. jours. Exec. com. Coun. on Tall Bldgs. and Urban Habitat. Lt. Civil Engr. Corp USNR, 1970 Mem. Urban Land Inst., Soc. for Mktg. Profl. Services. Clubs: Harvard Bus. of N.Y., Harvard of N.Y.C. Home: 1411 Grandview Ave #303 Pittsburgh PA 15211 Office: Turner Corp 375 Hudson St Rm 700 New York NY 10014-3667

BENNETT, EDITH LILLIAN, lay church worker, radio personality; b. Livermore, Ky., June 21, 1931; d. Dorsey Slade and Isa Carey (Taylor) B. AS, Owensboro (Ky.) Bus. Coll., 1950; student, Mid Continent Bible Coll., Owensboro, Ky., 1991-96; Assoc in Bible, Moody Bible Inst., 2001. Various positions including sec., office mgr., writer-dir. Sta. WOMI, Owensboro, 1950—; fin. sec. Third Bapt. Ch., Owensboro, 1981—. Pres. West Central Kentucky Fam. Research Assn. Radio personality 4-VOC, Haiti, WOMI Radio weekly; author, compiler, editor numerous publs. on Livermore history, genealogy and slavery, McLean County in the Civil War. Sunday sch. tchr. Third Bapt. Ch.; 2d v.p. Hunt Family Found., Ky., 1958—; instr. AARP 55-Alive Dirving, started video sect. (with DAR) in new Livermore Libr.; mem. McLean County Museum Com., Saving Our Heritage; clk. of Daviess McLean Bpat. ASsn. of 60 chs. in we. Ky., 1999--. Named to Honorable Order of Ky. Cols., 1969, Someone Spl., Owensboro, 1984, honored for 50 years in radio with keys to cities, Livermore and Owensboro, 1999, two bricks Dollywood Music Hall of Fame, Edith Bennett Day in Owensboro, 52 Yrs. of Tchg. Sunday Sch. 3rd Bapt. Ch.; named Citizen of Yr., Livermore, 1999. Mem. Owensboro Choral Soc. (48 yr. honoree, co-chmn., presenter MESSIAH benefits 1941—), DAR (local officer 1960—, state officer 1989—), Ky. Hist. Soc. Home: 324 W 15th St PO Box 1414 Owensboro KY 42302-1414 Office: Third Bapt Ch PO Box 808 527 Allen St Owensboro KY 42302 also: WOMI Radio 3301 Frederica St Owensboro KY 42301 E-mail: edithwomi@juno.com.

BENNETT, EDWARD JAMES, lawyer; b. Newton, Iowa, Dec. 27, 1941; s. Erskine Francis and Malvina Esther (Goodhue) B.; m. Virginia Lee Cook, Jan. 30, 1965; children: Susan Elizabeth, Edward James. BA, U. Iowa, 1964, JD, 1966. Bar: Iowa 1966, U.S. Dist. Ct. (so. dist.) Iowa 1967. Atty. Diehl, Clayton & Cleverley, Newton, 1966-70, The Maytag Co., Newton, 1970-74, sr. atty., 1974-80, assoc. counsel, 1980-85, asst. sec., asst. gen. counsel, 1985-86, Maytag Corp. (formerly The Maytag Co.), Newton, 1986-90; sec., asst. gen. counsel Maytag Corp., Newton, 1990-99. Sec. The Hoover Co., 1990-99, Dixie-Narco Inc., 1990-99, Maytag Internat. Inc., 1990-99, Hoover Holdings Inc., 1990-99, Maytag Fin. Svcs. Corp., 1990-99, Maytag Corp. Found., 1990-99; dir. Progress Industries, 1993—, sec., 1994—. Mem. Civil Svc. Commn., Newton, 1980-86; mem. Newton Zoning Bd. Adjustment, 1978-96, chmn., 1978-85; sec., trustee Newton Cmty. Ctr., Inc., 1976-94; trustee Newton Cmty. Schs. Found., 1994-99, v.p., 1996, pres., 1997; bd. dirs. Des Moines Metro Opera, 1998—, sec. 1998-99, pres. 2001-02; bd. dirs. Des Moines Metro Opera Found., 2000—, pres. 2002—; bd. dirs. Calvin Cmty., 2002—. Mem. ABA, Iowa State Bar Assn. (mem. trade regulation com. 1981-92, 93-97, 99—), Iowa Assn. Bus. and Industry (chmn. unemployment compensation com. 1976-94), Assn. Home Appliance Mfrs. (mem. product safety com. 1975-92). Republican. Methodist. Home and Office: 203 Foster Dr Des Moines IA 50312-2539

BENNETT, EDWARD VIRDELL, JR., surgeon; b. Nashville, July 17, 1947; s. Edward Virdell and Florence Elaine (Nelson) B. BA in Biology, Fisk U., 1969; MD cum laude, Ohio State U., 1973. Fellow in surgery Johns Hopkins U., Balt., 1973-75; intern, then resident Johns Hopkins Hosp., Balt., 1973-75; resident in surgery and cardiothoracic surgery Albany Med. Ctr. Hosp., N.Y., 1975-80, instr. in surgery, 1976-80; asst. prof. surgery Health Ctr. U. Tex.-San Antonio, 1980-83; practice medicine specializing in cardiothoracic surgery Sayre, Pa., 1983-91; chief cardiac surgery Guthrie Clinic Ltd., Sayre, 1990-91; mem. Staff Robert Packer Hosp., Sayre, 1983-91; mem. Guthrie Clinic, Ltd., Sayre, 1983-91; cardiac surgeon Albany Cardiothoracic Surgeons, P.C., 1991—; pres., 2000—; mem. staff Albany Med. Ctr. Hosp., 1991—, St. Peters Hosp., Albany, 1991—; clin. asst. prof. Albany Med. Coll., 1991—; chief cardiac surgery St. Peter's Hosp., Albany, 1997—. Contbr. articles to med. jours. Producer med. motion picture. Mem. N.Y. State Cardiac Adv. Com., 1995—. Fellow ACS, Am. Coll. Chest Physicians, Am. Coll. Cardiology; mem. Soc. Thoracic Surgeons, Upstate Soc. Thoracic Surgeons (pres. 2000—), Internat. Soc. for Heart Transplantation, Sigma Xi, Alpha Omega Alpha, Omega Psi Phi. Republican. Episcopalian. Avocations: sailing, scuba diving, skiing. Office: Albany Cardiothoracic Surgeons 116 Everett RD Albany NY 12205

BENNETT, SISTER ELSA MARY, retired secondary education educator; b. Muskegon, Mich., Dec. 13, 1930; d. Thomas B. and Elsa (Koelbel) B. BS, Our Lady of Lake Coll., San Antonio, 1955, MEd, 1971. Registered massage therapist, Tex.; Reiki master. Tchr. phys. edn. parochial schs., Abilene, Tex., Tulsa, San Antonio, Houston, Ennis, Tex., Alexandria, La., 1954-69, tchr., coach San Antonio, 1969-74, 86-87, pub. schs., Mich., 1974-78; tchr. St. Augustine Sch., Laredo, Tex., 1978-79; adminstr., coach Our Lady of Lake U., 1979-86; phys. therapy aide Warm Springs Rehab., San Antonio, 1989-90; tchr. San Antonio Ind. Sch. Dist., 1990-2000; ret., 2000. With pub. rels. dept. San Antonio City Parks and Recreation Dept., 1987-89. Instr. ARC, San Antonio, 1952. Mem. AAHPER and Dance, Tex. Assn. Health, Phys. Edn., Recreation and Dance. Avocations: golf, swimming, sailing, bowling, travel. Home: 2318 Town Grove Dr San Antonio TX 78238-5023

BENNETT, FRED GILBERT, lawyer; b. May 28, 1946; HBA magna cum laude, U. Utah, 1970; JD, U. Calif., 1973. Bar: Calif. 1974. Ptnr. Gibson, Dunn & Crutcher, L.A., 1980-98; sr. ptnr. Quinn Emanuel Urquhart Oliver & Hedges, 1998—. Mem. nat. com. on arbitration U.S. Coun. for Internat. Bus., 1984—, chmn. western subcom., 1989—; comml. and constrn. arbitrator Internat. C. of C./Am. Arbitration Assn. Large Complex Case Panel; chmn. continuing edn. com. Am. Arbitration Assn. Large Complex Case Panel; bd. dirs. Am. Arbitration Assn. Mng. editor UCLA Law Rev., 1972-73. Named Outstanding U.S. Lawyer, Chambers U.S.A., 2003. Mem. ABA, Internat. Bar Assn., L.A. County Bar Assn., Phi Beta Kappa. Office: Quinn Emanuel Urquhart Oliver & Hedges 865 S Figueroa St Los Angeles CA 90017-2543

BENNETT, GENEVIEVE, artist; b. Chgo., Feb. 11, 1927; d. Joseph and Mary Sieczka; m. William A. Bennett, Jan. 31, 1953; children: William George, J. Daniel, Gordon Dean. BA, Calif. State U., Fullerton, 1974; MA, Calif. State U., Long Beach, 1978. Artist, Anaheim, Calif. Tchr. art Ebell Club Anaheim, 1985-97, Whittier and Anaheim, Calif.; lectr. N.Am. temple mound builders. One-woman shows include Calif. Poly. U., Pomona, 1995, Orange County Fair, Calif., 1995, Anaheim Mus., 1997, exhibitions include Hotel-Restaurant La Musardiere, Giverny, France, 2002. Recipient Grumbacher Gold medal, 1999, Celebrating Remarkable Women Among Us award Orange County chpt. Nat. Assn. Women Bus. Owners, 1999, Cert. Spl. Congl. Recognition, Loretta Sanchez, 1999, Beyond the Call award Anaheim (Calif.) Arts Coun. and Arts in Pub. Places, 2002. Mem. Am. Internat. Culture and Art Assn., Nat. League Am. Pen Women (state v.p. 1997-98, Am. Internat. Culture and Art Assn., Orange County br. pres. 1997-98, recipient State Women of Achievement award, 1998), Calif. State U. Art Alliance, So. Calif. Women's Caucus for Art, Orange County Fine Arts, Phi Delta Gamma (Phi chpt.). Avocations: archaeology, piano, music, travel, art meetings. Home: 2026 W Judith Ln Anaheim CA 92804-6511

BENNETT, GEORGE FREDERICK, investment manager; b. Quincy, Mass., Aug. 16, 1911; s. Wallace Cherrington and Lois E. (Williams) B.; m. Helen F. Brigham, Oct. 25, 1935; children— Peter C., George Frederick, Robert B. AB cum laude, Harvard, 1933. With First Boston Corp., Boston, 1934-37, Newton, Abbe & Co., Boston, 1937-43; with State Street Research & Mgmt. Co., Boston, 1943—, partner, 1946—. Chmn. State St. Exchange Fund, Boston; pres. State St. Investment Corp., Boston, Fed. St. Fund, Inc., Boston; dir. Campbell Taggert, Inc., Dallas, Middle South Utilities, Inc., N.Y.C., N.E. Electric System, Hewlett Packard Co., Palo Alto, Calif., Fla. Power & Light Co., Miami, Ford Motor Co., Detroit, John Hancock Mut. Life Ins. Co., Boston, Hanna Mining Co., Cleve. Treas. Harvard U., Harvard-Yenching Inst.; trustee Wheaton (Ill.) Coll., Rockefeller U., Gordon Conwell Theol. Sem., Com. Econ. Devel., Washington. Mem. Pi Eta. Clubs: Harvard (Boston and N.Y.C.); Union (Boston); Links (N.Y.C.). Home: 712 Main St Hingham MA 02043-3327 Office: State Street Rsch & Mgmt Co One Financial Ctr Boston MA 02111

BENNETT, GERALDINE EUDORA (JERRIE BENNETT), mental health services professional, nursing educator; b. Creighton, Pa., Apr. 23, 1921; d. Harry Curtin and Ellnora Mira (Guyer) Baish; m. Donald Patrick Bennett, Aug. 10, 1953 (div. 1971); children: Brent Norman, Terrance Patrick(dec.), Patricia Eileen Bennett Wilson(dec.). RN, Sewickley Valley Sch. Nursing, 1942; BS, U. So. Calif., 1953; MA, Kent State U., 1969. RN Pa., Calif., Mich., Ohio, Fla. Asst. supr. oper. rm. Merrit Hosp., Oakland, Calif., 1947-48; surg. asst. Robert Foote, MD, Bakersfield, Calif., 1949-51; adminstrv. asst. Permanente Found. Hosp., L.A., 1953; mem. faculty surgery, oper. rm. Queen of Angels Coll. Nursing, L.A., 1954-55; tchr. exceptional edn. Canton (Ohio) Pub. Schs., 1967-69; nurse ICU Naples (Fla.) Cmty. Hosp., 1970-71; tchr. exceptional edn., guidance counselor Collier County Schs., Naples, 1971-86; psychiat. crisis

counselor David Lawrence Mental Health Ctr., Naples, 1987-96. Founder, 1st coord. Collier County Spl. Olympics, Naples, 1971—77; dir. S. Fla. dist. Spl. Olympics, Tallahassee, 1977—80; chmn. Selective Svcs. Bd., Naples, 1981—2002; capt. CAP Squadron 8, Naples, 1990—; bd. dirs. Founding First Charter Sch. Collier County, 1997—98, Gabriel Ho. for Children, 1998—99, Naples Ret. Inc., 1989—98; sr. intern adv. bd. 14th Congl. Dist., Ft. Meyers, Fla., 1990—93; mem. Lay Assn. Sisters of Charity, NJ, 2001—. With USN, 1942—45, PTO. Named Hon. U.S. Olympian, 1983. Mem.: AAUW, Navy League Coun., Am. Legion, Alpha Eta Rho, Phi Delta Kappa. Republican. Roman Catholic. Avocations: swimming, painting, volunteer work, travel. E-mail: jbdora@aol.com.

BENNETT, HAROLD EARL, physicist, optics researcher; b. Missoula, Mont., Feb. 25, 1929; s. Edward Earl and Linda Queen (McCoy) B.; m. Jean Louise McPherson, Aug. 17, 1952 (div. Nov. 1984); m. Dorothy Jean Searles, Nov. 17, 1984; children: Jeanie Nybo, Dorothy Anne Picking. BA, U. Mont., 1951; MS, Pa. State U., 1953, PhD, 1955. Instrument-rated pilot. Grad. asst. Pa. State U., State College, 1951-55; physicist Wright Air Devel. Ctr., Dayton, Ohio, 1955-56, Naval Air Warfare Ctr. (name Naval Weapons Ctr. 1964-93), China Lake, Calif., 1956-62, rsch. physicist, 1962-95, ret., 1995, assoc. head rsch. dept. physics div., 1972-91; cons. optical physics Quoin Inc., Ridgecrest, Calif., 1995-96; pres. Bennett Optical Rsch. Inc., Ridgecrest, 1995—; chair Space Applications Com., IWV 2000 Orgn., Ridgecrest, Calif., 1996—. Co-chmn. Laser Induced Damage in Optical Materials Conf., Boulder, Colo., 1979-96. Adv. editor Optics Communications, 1969-86; contbr. over 100 articles on optics to profl. jours., chpts. to books; holder 12 patents on optical instruments and systems. Pres. Indian Wells Valley Community Concert Assn., Ridgecrest, Calif., 1974-75; sr. fellow Naval Weapons Ctr., 1990; former mem. Calif. Rep. State Ctrl. Com. Recipient LTE Thompson award Naval Weapons Ctr., 1974, Tech. Dir.'s award, 1983; Capt. Robert Dexter Conrad award Dept. Navy, 1979, Dep. Comdr.'s award for R & D, 1995, Tech. Leadership award Navy High Energy Laser Project, 1995, Navy Meritorius Civilian Svc. award, 1995. Fellow Optical Soc. Am. (assoc. editor Jour. 1968-79, bd. dirs. 1972-75), Internat. Soc. for Optical Engring. (bd. dirs. 1985-87, v.p. 1987, pres. 1988, Tech. Achievement award 1983, organizer and chair Laser Power Beaming II Conf. 1995, chair Free Electron Laser Challenges Conf. 1997, chair Free Electron Laser Challenges II 1999), Maturango Mus. (life). Republican. Achievements include development of polishing techniques for reducing scattered light from resting, thim film optics, laser power beaming to space and fabrication of large weight low scatter adaptive optic mirrors. Home: 916 N Randall St Ridgecrest CA 93555-3007 Office: 201 N Sanders St Ridgecrest CA 93555-3867 E-mail: bennett@bennettopticalresearch.com.

BENNETT, HARRIET COOK, social worker, educator; b. Aug. 3, 1945; d. Harry A. and Amy H. Cook; children: Amy, Andrew. BA, LaGrange (Ga.) Coll., 1967; MSW, U. Ga., Athens, 1969; postgrad., Tulane U., 1970. LCSW. Med. social reviewer state rev. team Dept. Family and Children Svcs., Atlanta, 1969-71; social worker/instr. U. Mo. Med. Ctr., Columbia, 1971-73; social worker Easter Seal Rehab. Ctr., Tampa, Fla., 1978-79, Children's Home Soc. Fla., St. Petersburg, 1984-95; dir. LaPetite Acad., Tampa, 1980, tchr. kindergarten, 1981-84; social worker Hillsborough County Pub. Sch. Sys., 1995—. Vol. cons. Desenzano, Italy, 1976-78; vol. Nat. Kidney Found., Arthritis Found., Boy Scouts Am.; mem. Northdale Civic Assn. Mem. NASW, Acad. Cert. Social Workers, Fla. Assn. Sch. Social Workers. Methodist.

BENNETT, HARRY LOUIS, history educator; b. Ansonia, Conn., Dec. 22, 1923; s. Louis and Florence (Swole) B.; m. Claire Davis, July 2, 1949; 1 dau., Lisa Brierley. BA, Yale U., 1944, MA, 1948, PhD, 1954. Welfare investigator, Conn., 1950-51; mem. faculty Quinnipiac Coll., Hamden, Conn., 1951—, prof. history, dean coll., 1956-67, v.p. acad. affairs, 1967-69, 72-90, prof., chmn. history, 1969-72, provost, 1972-90, acting pres., 1978-79, provost emeritus, 1990, emeritus prof. history, 1992—. Sec.-treas. Conn. Conf. Community and Jr. Colls., 1955-62, v.p., 1962-64, pres., 1964-65; chmn. standing com. accreditation Conn. Council Higher Edn., 1964-65, vice chmn., 1985-86; chmn. Conn. Adv. Com. on Accreditation, 1986-88. 1st lt., inf. AUS, 1944-46, MTO. Mem. Am. Hist. Assn., Am. Cath. hist. Assn., New Eng. Hist. Assn., Orgn. Am. Historians, Assn. Study Conn. History, Conn. Hist. Soc., New Haven Colony Hist. Soc. Roman Catholic. Home: 21 Knollwood Rd North Haven CT 06473-4328

BENNETT, HELEN, social worker; b. Antwerp, Belgium, Sept. 7, 1937; came to U.S., 1946; d. Emil and Maria (Klein) Fruchter; m. Ronald Sanford Bennett, 1956 (div. 1976); children: Denice, Miriam (dec. 1996), Sharon, Ruth. BA, Wayne State U., 1978, MSW, 1980. Lic. clin. social worker, Mich. Social worker Pontia Mental Hosp., Mich., 1978-79, Cath. Social Svcs., Mich., 1979-80; head of mental health Fathers for Equal Rights of Am., Southfield, Mich., 1980—. Cons. Sid Young's Retailers, Jackson, Mich., 1990—; divorce therapist, mediator, 1980—. Editor Father's Jour. Mem. NASW, World Fedn. Mental Health. Mem. World Fedn. Mental Health, Women's Freedom Network. Avocations: oil painting on canvas, sculpture, composer, poetry, voice. Home and Office: 25440 Lois Lane Dr Southfield MI 48075-6160

BENNETT, JACK FRANKLIN, oil company executive; b. Macon, Ga., Jan. 17, 1924; s. Andrew Jackson and Mary Eloise (Franklin) B.; m. Shirley Elizabeth Goodwin, Sept. 17, 1949; children: Jackson Goodwin, Philip Davies, Hugh Franklin, Elizabeth Fraser. BA, Yale U., 1944; MA, Harvard U., 1949, PhD, 1951. Negotiator Joint U.S.-U.K. Export Import Agy., Berlin, Germany, 1946-47; teaching fellow finance Harvard, 1949-51; spl. asst. to adminstr. Tech. Assistance Program, U.S. Dept. State, Washington, 1951-52; economist U.S. Mut. Security Agy., Washington, 1952-53, sr. economist Presdl. Commn. on Fgn. Econ. Policy, 1954; sr. fgn. exch. analyst Exxon Corp., N.Y.C., 1955-58, dep. European fin. rep. London, 1958-60; treas. Esso. Petroleum Co., Ltd., London, 1960-61; asst. treas. Exxon Corp., N.Y.C., 1961-65, mgr. gen. econs. dept., 1965-66, mgr. coordination and planning dept., 1966-67; gen. mgr. supply dept. Exxon Co., U.S.A., Houston, 1967-69; v.p., dir. Exxon Internat., N.Y.C., 1969-71; sr. v.p. Exxon Corp., N.Y.C., 1975-89, also bd. dirs., ret., 1989. Dep. undersec. for monetary affairs U.S. Dept. Treasury, Washington, 1971-74, undersec. for monetary affairs, 1974-75. Contbr. articles to profl. jours. Trustee Com. Econ. Devel. With USNR, 1943-46. Mem. Stanwich Club (Greenwich, Conn.), York (Maine) Club, Blind Brook Club, John's Island Club (Fla.). Republican. Office: 141 Taconic Rd Greenwich CT 06831-3113 E-mail: jbnt@aol.com.

BENNETT, JACQUELINE BEEKMAN, school psychologist; b. Santa Paula, Calif., Sept. 4, 1946; d. Jack Edward and Margaret Blanche (MacPherson) Beekman.; m. Thomas LeRoy Bennett Jr., Aug. 5, 1972; children: Shannon, Brian, Laurie. BA, U. Calif., Davis, 1968; MS, Colo. State U., 1975, PhD, 1984. Histologist Sch. Veterinary Medicine, Davis, 1969-71; sch. psychologist Poudre Sch. Dist. R-1, Ft. Collins, Colo., 1983-95, Ctr. Neurorehabilitation Svcs., Ft. Collins, 1995—. Mem. augment panel Colo. State Grievance Bd., 1988-94; nominating cmn. United Presbyn. Women, Timnath, Colo., 1982, pres., 1986; mem. Women and the Ch. com. Boulder Presbytery, Colo., 1985-86; elder Timnath Presbyn. Ch., 1985—. Mem. Colo. Soc. Sch. Psychologists (cert.), Nat. Assn. Sch. Psychologists (cert.), NEA, Am. Psychol. Assn., Ft. Collins Parents of Twins (pres. 1977-78), Sigma Xi, Phi Kappa Phi. Clubs: Squaredusters (Ft. Collins) (v.p. 1977-78). Democrat. Avocations: camping, gardening, swimming, cooking. Home: 213 Camino Real Fort Collins CO 80524-8907 Office: Ctr for Neurorehab Svcs 1049 Robertson St Fort Collins CO 80524-3926

BENNETT, JAMES DAVISON, lawyer; b. Mineola, N.Y., Dec. 2, 1938; BA, Cornell U., 1960, JD, 1963. Bar: N.Y. 1963. Of counsel Farrell, Fritz, P.C., Uniondale, NY, 2001—. Councilman Town of Hempstead, 1968-87, supr., 1978-87; active Nassau County Bd. Suprs., 1978-87, L.I. Power Authority, 1995-98; commr. N.Y.S. Pub. Svc. Commn., 1998—; apptd. to N.Y. State Conservation and Wildlife Fund, 1975-78; chmn. L.I. Area Devel. Agy., 1988-90, L.I. Regional Export Coun., 1988-90. Recipient citation Practising Law Inst., 1982-73, others. Mem. ABA, N.Y. State Bar Assn. (jud. conf. 1989, lectr. 1990), Nassau County Bar Assn. Home: 34 Hilton Ave Garden City NY 11530-4414 Office: EAB Plz Uniondale NY 11556-0120 E-mail: jbennett@farrellfritz.com.

BENNETT, JAMES EDWARD, retired plastic surgeon, educator; b. Burlington, Wis., May 19, 1925; s. John Francis and Florence (Mauer) B.; m. Ellen MacPherson, June 18, 1956; children: David, Martha, Thomas, Jonathan. Student, Notre Dame U., 1943-44, Mass. Inst. Tech., 1944-45; MD, Northwestern U., 1950. Diplomate Am. Bd. Plastic Surgery (dir. 1978-84, chmn. 1983-84, chmn. residency rev. com. 1978-79), Am. Bd. Surgery. Intern Milw. County Hosp., 1949-50; resident in surgery U. Mich. Hosp., 1953-58; gen. practice medicine Burlington, 1950-51; exchange fellow in plastic surgery, 1956-57; resident in plastic surgery U. Tex. Sch. Medicine, Galveston, 1958-61; asst. prof. surgery, dir. plastic surgery Ohio State U. Sch. Medicine, 1961-64; prof. surgery, dir. plastic surgery Ind. U. Med. Center, 1964-91, Willis D. Gatch prof. surgery, 1981-91, Willis D. Gatch prof. emeritus, 1991—. Lt. (j.g.) USNR, 1951—53. Fellow ACS (2d v.p. 1991-92); mem. Plastic Surgery Rsch. Coun. (chmn. 1970), Frederick A. Coller Surg. Soc. (councillor 1981-83), Am. Soc. Plastic and Reconstructive Surgeons, Am. Assn. Surgery Trauma, Am. Assn. Plastic Surgeons (sec. 1978-81, v.p. 1981-82, pres. 1983-84), Am. Surg. Assn., Ind. Trotting and Pacing Horse Assn. (chmn. 1993-94), Ind. Standardbred Assn. (bd. dirs. 1994-95), Phi Rho Sigma. Home: 8174 N Kivett Rd Monrovia IN 46157-9260

BENNETT, JAMES MARVIN, consulting company executive; b. St. Louis, June 28, 1939; s. Marvin L. and Florence Anntonette (Rumph) B.; m. Barbara Virginia Rostron, July 2, 1965; children: J. Justin, Bradley Alexander. BS, Washington U., St. Louis, 1963, PhD in Botany, 1968. Prof. biology NYU, 1968-70; Ford Found. lectr. New Sch. Social Rsch., 1968-70; dir. environ. affairs Joseph Schlitz Brewing Co., Milw., 1970-75, dir. environ. and indsl. affairs, 1975-78, dir. govt. rels., 1978-82; exec. v.p., gen. mgr. Consultancy Internat., N.Y.C., 1984-86; pres., CEO Bennett & Assocs. (name now Bennett Environ. Mgmt., Inc.), N.Y.C., 1982—. Assoc. prof. environ. engring., N.Y.I.T., 1994—; cons. A.T. Kearney, Inc., N.Y., 1986—, Castlton Environ. Contractors, 1998-2001, exec. v.p. mktg., sales, adminstrn., sr. fin. rep., NMFN, 2001- NSF fellow, 1965-68. Mem. AAAS, N.Y. Acad. Scis. Office: 420 Lexington A New York NY 10170-8505

BENNETT, JAMES RONALD, state official; b. Red Oak, Iowa, Jan. 3, 1940; s. George T. and Florence B. (Olson) B.; m. Luan Atkins, June 11, 1989; children: Donald B., Tara L.; 1 stepchild, Megan L. Scott. BS, Jacksonville State U., 1961; MA, U. Ala., 1980. Mem. Ala. Ho. of Reps., 1978-83; senator State of Ala., 1983-93, sec. of state, 1993—2003. Chmn. bd. trustees Jacksonville State U.; bd. dirs. Tannehill Ironworks Hist. State Park, 1970. Mem. Nat. Assn. Secs. of State (pres. 1999 2000). Republican. Office: Commr Dept Labor 100 N Union St Montgomery AL 36130-3500 E-mail: alsecst@alalinc.net.*

BENNETT, JAMES THOMAS, economics educator; b. Memphis, Oct. 19, 1942; m. Sara Ellen Dorman, Sept. 2, 1967. BS in Ops. Research magna cum laude, Case Inst. Tech., 1964, MS in Mgmt. Sci., 1966; PhD in Econs., Case Western Res. U., 1970; student Grad. Sch. Bus., Columbia U., 1964-65. Teaching fellow Case Inst. Tech., 1968-69; instr. bus. Cleve. State U., 1967-68; asst. prof. econs. George Washington U., Washington, 1970-75; assoc. prof. econs. George Mason U., Fairfax, Va., 1975-77, Eminent Scholar and William P. Snavely prof. polit. economy and pub. policy, 1975—. Dir. John M. Olin Inst. for Employment Practice and Policy; chmn. faculty senate George Mason U., 2002-. Co-author: The Political Economy of Federal Government Growth: 1958-1978, 1980; Better Government at Half the Price, 1981; Deregulating Labor Relations, 1981; Underground Government: The Off-Budget Public Sector, 1983; Destroying Democracy: How Government Funds Partisan Politics, 1985, Unfair Competition: The Profits of Nonprofits, 1989, Patterns of Corporate Philanthrophy: Ideas, Advocacy and the Corporation, 1989, Health Research Charities: Image and Reality, 1990, Health Research Charities II: The Politics of Fear, 1991, Official Lies: How Washington Misleads Us, 1992, Unhealthy Charities: Hazardous to Your Health and Wealth, 1994, Cancer Scam: The Diversion of Federal Cancer Funds to Politics, 1998, The Food and Drink Police: America's Nanies, Busybodies, and Petty Tyrants, 1999, From Pathology to Politics: Public Health in America, 2000, Public Health Profiteering, 2001, The Future of Private Sector Unionism in the United States, 2002, Tax-Funded Politics, 2004; contbr. chpts. to books, articles to profl. jours.; editor Jour. Labor Rsch. Ford Found. scholar, 1960-64; Continental Grain Corp. fellow; McKinsey scholar; Case Inst. fellow, 1965-67; Fed. Res. Bank Cleve. fellow, 1969-70 Mem. Am. Econ. Assn., So. Econ. Assn., Pub. Choice Soc., Western Econ. Assn., Am. Statis. Assn., Phila. Soc., Mont Pelerin Soc., Phi Beta Kappa, Sigma Xi, Tau Beta Pi, Alpha Lambda Delta, Phi Theta Kappa. Office: George Mason U Dept Econs Fairfax VA 22030 E-mail: jbennett@gmu.edu.

BENNETT, JANICE LYNN, publisher, educator; b. Chgo., Jan. 31, 1951; d. Harry Albert and Dorothy Marie Goodman; m. James Stephen Bennett, Oct. 6, 1973; children: Scott James, Anne Christine. BA in Graphic Design, No. Ill. U., 1973; BA in Spanish, Met. State Coll. of Denver, 1993; MA in Spanish Lit., U. Colo., 1997. Graphic artist Montgomery Ward, Chgo., 1973-74; asst. prodn. mgr., art dir. Crow Publs., Denver, 1977-80; owner, graphic artist, typographer Charter Graphics, Classic Typography, Denver, 1980-89; Spanish instr. Met. State Coll. of Denver, 1995—2000; pub., editor, author Libri de Hispania, Littleton, Colo., 2000—. Translator Denver Pub. Schs., Greenlee Elem., Denver, 1993-94; translator, interpreter World Youth Day, Denver, 1993; bilingual tchg. asst. Knapp Elem., Denver, 1990-91; freelance writer Denver Cath. Register. Author: Guia práctica a la literatura, el análisis y la redacción, 1998; author, pub., editor: Sacred Blood, Sacred Image: The Sudarium of Oviedo, New Evidence for the Authenticity of the Shroud of Turin, 2001, St. Laurence and the Holy Grail: The Story of the Holy Chalice of Valencia, 2002. Mem. MLA, Altar and Rosary Soc. (pres. 2000-01, 2002-03), Am. Assn. of Tchrs. of Spanish and Portuguese, Pub. Mktg. Assn., Cath. Book Pub. Assn., Spanish Ctr. for Sindonology, Sigma Delta Pi, Phi Sigma Iota. Avocations: traveling, photography, piano, biblical studies, drawing and painting. Office: Libri de Hispania PO Box 270262 Littleton CO 80127-0005 Fax: 303-973-3014. E-mail: acbc@sprintmail.com.

BENNETT, JAY BRETT, healthcare industry executive; b. Durham, N.C., Dec. 13, 1961; s. James Leonard Jr. and Yoalder Kathleen (Brunson) B.; m. Trisha Helen Folds, Feb. 3, 1990; children: Lydia Helen, William Chisholm. BA in Econs., Wake Forest U., 1984; M Health Adminstrn., Duke U., 1986. Sr. cons. Ernst and Whinney (now Ernst and Young), Charlotte, NC, 1986—89; assoc. dir. strategic planning SSI Med. Svcs., Inc., Charleston, SC, 1989—92, dir. strategic planning, 1992—94; dir. planning and bus. devel. Hill-Rom, Inc., Charleston, 1994—96, bus. unit dir., 1996—99, v.p., 1999—2001, Nuesoft Techs., Inc., Atlanta, 1999—2001, Healthcare Informatics Premier, Inc., Charlotte, 2001—. Adj. prof. bus. and econs. Coll. Charleston, 1995—; bd. dirs. Nuesoft Techs., Inc., Atlanta. Mem. alumni coun. Fuqua Sch. Bus., Duke U.; mem. Leadership Charleston '99. Mem. Am. Coll. Healthcare Execs., Nat. Soc. SAR, Ducks Unltd., Quail Unltd., Trout Unltd. Avocations: outdoors, history of American South, photography.

BENNETT, JAY D. lawyer; b. Albany, Ga., June 3, 1952; s. J. Donald and Clara Louise (Jordan) B.; m. Susan Parker, June 9, 1974; children: Summer, Lillian, Sky. BA with honors, U. N.C., 1974; JD cum laude, Harvard U., 1977. Bar: U.S. Dist. Ct. (no. and mid. dist.) Ga., U.S. Ct. Appeals (4th, 5th, 9th and 11th cirs.), U.S. Supreme Ct. Assoc. Alston & Bird, Atlanta, 1977-83, ptnr., 1983—. Morehead scholar Morehead Found. 1970-74. Mem. State Bar Ga., Atlanta Bar Assn., Lawyers Club Atlanta, Phi Beta Kappa. Avocations: flying, skydiving, motorcycling, fishing. Office: Alston & Bird LLP One Atlantic Ctr 1201 W Peachtree St Atlanta GA 30309-3424

BENNETT, JEAN LOUISE MCPHERSON, physicist, research scientist; b. Kensington, Md., May 9, 1930; d. Archibald Turner and Margaret Fitch (Willcox) McPherson; m. Harold Earl Bennett, Aug. 17, 1952 (div. Nov. 1984). BA summa cum laude, Mt. Holyoke Coll., 1951, DSc (hon.), 1992; MS, Pa. State U., 1953, PhD in Physics, 1955. Physicist Wright Air Devel. Ctr., Dayton, Ohio, 1955-56, Naval Ordnance Test Sta. (now Naval Air Warfare Ctr. Weapons Div.), China Lake, Calif., 1956-85, sr. research scientist, 1987-93, 95; vis. prof. U. Ala., Huntsville, 1986-87, Mt. Holyoke Coll., South Hadley, Mass., 1994-95; ret., 1996—. Mem. NRC Evaluation Panel Nat. Bur. Stds., Ctr. for Radiation Rsch., 1979-85, Nat. Inst. Stds. and Tech. Mfg. Engring. Lab., 1988-94, U.S. Nat. Com. for Internat. Commn. for Optics, 1984-85, 88-95; vis. scientist Inst. Optical Rsch., Royal Inst. Tech., Stockholm, Mar.-Sept., 1988, 98, 99, 2000, 01. Author: (with Lars Mattsson) Introduction to Surface Roughness and Scattering, 1989, revised 1999; author: Surface Finish and Its Measurement, 1992; contbr. sci. articles to profl. jours.; patentee in field. Recipient Tech. Achievement award Soc. Photo-Optical Instrumentation Engrs., 1983, L.T.E. Thompson award Naval Weapons Ctr., 1988, Women in Sci. and Engring. Lifetime Achievement award, 1993, Outstanding Sci. Alumni award Pa. State U., 1999; named sr. fellow Naval Weapons Ctr., 1989, Disting. Fellow, 1994. Fellow Optical Soc. Am. (v.p. 1984, pres.-elect 1985, pres. 1986, past pres. 1987, chmn. book publ. com. 1991-94, David Richardson medal 1990); mem. Am. Inst. Physics (subcom. on books 1990-94), Phi Beta Kappa, Sigma Xi, Sigma Delta Epsilon, Iota Sigma Pi, Pi Mu Epsilon, Sigma Pi Sigma. Achievements include being the first woman to receive PhD in Physics at Pa. State U., 1955; first woman pres. Optical Soc. of Am. Home: 1275 Sage Ct Ridgecrest CA 93555-2622 Office: Code 4T41A0D Michelson Lab Naval Air Warfare Ctr Stop 6302 1900N Knox Rd China Lake CA 93555 E-mail: jbennett@ridgenet.net.

BENNETT, JESSIE F. lawyer; b. Bridgeport, Conn. d. Cornelius T. and Jessie F. (Sutcliffe) B.; m. Ronald J. Canuel, Nov. 3, 1990. BS in Fin. with honors, Fairfield U., 1980; JD magna cum laude, Quinnipiac U., 1986. Bar: Conn., 1986; U.S. Dist. Ct. Conn., 1987, U.S. Dist. Ct. (so. and ea. dists.) N.Y. 1989, U.S. Ct. Appeals (2d cir.) 1989, D.C. Ct. of Appeals, 1989, U.S. Supreme Ct., 1989. Jud. clk. to Judge Ellen Bree Burns U.S. Dist. Ct., New Haven, 1986; atty. Cohen & Wolf, Danbury, Conn., 1987-88, Davidson & Naylor, Norwalk, Conn., 1988-92; law clk. State of Conn., Jud. Dept., Waterbury, 1992-96; asst. state's atty. State of Conn. Divsn. Criminal Justice, 1996—. Recipient Am. Jurisprudence awards in Remedies and Family Law, Kristin Ann Carveth Meml. Scholastic award. Mem.: ATLA, ABA, D.C. Bar Assn., Conn. Trial Lawyers Assn., Nat. Dist. Attys. Assn., Conn. Bar Assn., Phi Alpha Delta (Code Enforcement Ofcl. of Yr. 1999, Pres. award 1999, Cert. of Appreciation award 1999, Svc. in Excellence award 2001, Pub. Svc. Star award 2002, Am. Registry Outstanding Profls. 2002—03), Phi Delta Phi. Roman Catholic. Avocations: exercise, music, cooking, travel. Office: States Attys Office 80 Washington St Hartford CT 06106-4405

BENNETT, JOE CLAUDE, pharmaceutical executive; b. Birmingham, Ala., Dec. 12, 1933; s. Claude and Clara Lucille (Clark) B.; m. Nancy Miller, June 17, 1958; children: Katherine Diane, Miller, Clark Barton. AB, Samford U., 1954; MD, Harvard U., 1958; DSc (hon.), U. Ala., 1992. Diplomate Am. Bd. Internal Medicine (governing bd. 1987—, cert. exam. com. for 1989, ind. com. R & D, 1988—), Am. Bd. Rheumatology, Nat. Bd. Med. Examiners. Intern Univ. Ala. Hosp., Birmingham, 1958-59, resident, 1959-60; rsch. assoc. molecuar biology NIH, Bethesda, Md., 1962-64; sr. rsch. fellow dlv. biology Calif. Inst. Tech., Pasadena, Calif., 1964-65; asst. prof. dept. medicine, assoc. prof. dept. microbiology, asst. dir. div. clin. immunology and rheumatology U. Ala. Med. Sch., Birmingham, 1965-70, dir. div. clin. immunology and rheumatology, 1970-83, prof., chmn. dept. microbiology, 1970-82, prof., chmn. dept. medicine, 1982-92, Spencer Prof. Med. Sci., 1992—, dir. multipurpose arthritis center, 1977-84, disting. faculty lectr., 1979; pres. U. Ala., Birmingham, 1993-96; pres., COO BioCryst Pharms., Birmingham, 1996—. Physician in chief U. Ala. Hosp.; vis. prof. U. Mo.-Columbia Sch. Medicine, 1987, U. Leiden, The Netherlands, 1988, Baylor U. Coll. Medicine, Houston, 1989, others; invited lectr. various univs., confs. including IX Pan-Am. Congress Rheumatology, Buenos Aires, 1986, U. Mo.-Columbia Sch. Medicine, 1987, Cornell Med. Sch., 1986, U. Colo., 1986; mem. sci. adv. bd. Merck Sharp & Dohme Rsch. Labs., 1987-89, Gorgas Meml. Inst. Tropical and Preventive Medicine, 1985—, others; mem. bd. health sci. policies, NIH, NAS, 1988—. Editor: Vistas in Connective Tissue Diseases, 1968; co-editor: Rheumatology and Immunology, 2d edit., 1986, Cecil Textbook of Medicine, 1988—, Cecil Essentials of Medicine; editor-in-chief Am. Jour. Medicine, 1986-97, Arthritis and Rheumatism, 1975-80; mem. editorial bd. Protein and Peptide Revs., 1980—, Current Opinion in Rheumatology, 1988—, Arthritis and Rheumatism, 1969-75; contbr. numerous articles, papers, book revs., abstracts to profl. publs. Recipient Ala. Acad. Honor award, 1987, Seale Harris award So. Med. Assn., 1987; John and Mary R. Markle Found. scholar in acad. medicine, 1965-70; recipient Rsch. Career Devel. award NIH, 1965-75; fellow Arthritis and Rheumatism Found., Harvard Med. Sch., Mass. Gen. Hosp., 1960-62 Fellow AAAS (sec. N. Med. scis. nominating com. 1989—); mem. Am. Bd. Internal Medicine (exec. com. 1992), Federated Coun. of Internatl Medicine, Assn. of Am. Med. Colls. (adv. panel on biomed. rsch. 1991-92), Inst. Medicine NAS, ACP (master 1990), Am. Assn. Immunologists, Am. Fedn. Clin. Rsch., Am. Coll. Rheumatology (pres. 1981-82, bd. dirs. planning group 1986-87), Am. Soc. Biol. Chemists, Am. Soc. Clin. Investigation, Am. Soc. Microbiology, more. Home: 3520 River Bend Rd Birmingham AL 35243-4832 Office: BioCryst Pharms 2190 Parkway Lake Dr Birmingham AL 35244-1879

BENNETT, JOEL HERBERT, construction company executive; b. Chgo., Nov. 7, 1936; m. Seraphima H. Lamb, 1999; children: Evan Alan, Julie Andrea. BSChemE, U. So. Calif., L.A., 1958, MSChemE, 1962; MBA in Ops. Rsch., UCLA, 1960. Chem. process engr. C. F. Braun & Co., Alhambra, Calif., 1960-65, with bus. devel., 1965-73; v.p. Arthur G. McKee & Co., Cleve., 1973-78, Parsons Engring. Sci., Inc., Pasadena, Calif., 1978-81; sr. v.p. Santa Fe Braun Inc., Alhambra, 1981-89; exec. v.p. The Parsons Corp., Pasadena, 1989-92, 96—; pres. Parsons Environ. Svcs. Inc., Pasadena, 1992-96, Harland Bartholomew & Assocs., 1992-95; exec. v.p. The Parsons Corp., 1995-96; sr. v.p. Parsons Brinckerhoff, Inc., N.Y.C., 1996—, also mem. bd. dirs.; chmn. PB Power Inc., NYC, 1998—2000, PB Power, 1998—; chmn., pres. Parsons Brinckerhoff Internat., Inc., 2001—. Bd. dirs. Inst. Redesign Lng.; co-chair environ. mgmt. adv. bd. U.S. Dept. Energy, 1994—. Author: (with others) Project Management, 1989. Dir. Calif. State U. L.A. Found.; mem. bd. advisors The Asian Am. Architects/Engrs. Assn. Mem. Am. Inst. Chem. Engrs., Jonathan Club (L.A.). Avocations: skiing, jogging, tennis, music. Home: 30 W 61st St Apt 9D New York NY 10023-7619 Office: Parsons Brinckerhoff Inc One Penn Plz New York NY 10119

BENNETT, JOHN J. writer, publisher; b. Bklyn., Aug. 8, 1938; s. John Judson and Margaret Elisabeth Bennett. Editor, pub. Vagabond Press, Ellensburg, Wash., 1966—. Author: Bodo, 1995, (translated to Czech), 1997; Names We Go By, 1993, The Adventures of Achilles Jones, 1979. Recipient D.B. Houston award Tom Robbins Com., 1988, William Wantling award, Second Coming Press, 1987. Home: 605 E 5th Ave Ellensburg WA 98926 E-mail: dasleben@eburg.com.

BENNETT, JOHN JOSEPH, professional services company executive; b. Camden, N.J., Sept. 4, 1923; s. John Henry and Margaret Katherine (Bloxsum) B.; m. Dolores Florence Griffiths, June 17, 1943; children: Jill, T. Robert, T. Richard. Student, Centenary Coll., 1951-55; MBA, Mich. State U., 1961; DBA, George Washington U., 1974. Commd. 2d lt. USAAF, 1943; advanced through grades to col. USAF, officer various operational and mgmt. jobs, 1942-60; asst. comptroller Hdqrs. AFSC, Washington, 1961-66; asst. to Asst. Sec. Air Force and dep. chief staff, Personnel Hdqrs. USAF, Washington, 1967-69; ret. USAF, 1969; exec. dir. Mauchley Edn. Inst., Washington, 1969-70; pres. Sycom, Inc., Washington, 1969-70; mgr. aerospace def. practice Peat, Marwick, Mitchell & Co., Washington, 1970-74; prin. dep. asst. U.S. Sec. of Def., Washington, 1975-76, Asst. Sec. of Navy, Washington, 1976-77; dir., exec. office pres. Fed. Acquisition Inst., Washington, 1977-79; chief exec. officer ANADAC, Inc., Washington, 1979-88, chmn. bd., 1988-92, chmn. emeritus, 1992-96. Lectr. George Washington U., 1979-89; chmn. bd. dirs. TBG Reliance Corp., 1997—. Author: The Next Generation Management Systems for Systems Management, 1967, Department of Defense Systems Acquisition Management, 1974, Program Management Principles and Practices, 1994; author: (with others) Systems Concepts for Human Resources Management, 1968. Decorated Legion of Merit, D.F.C., Air medal with 4 oak leaf clusters; recipient Disting. Civilian Svc. award, 1976, Disting. Pub. Svc. award, 1977. Methodist. Home: 343 Bayshore Dr Palm Harbor FL 34683-5482 Office: TBG Reliance 465 Orange St Palm Harbor FL 34683-5449 E-mail: jbennett@wewatch.net.

BENNETT, JOHN K. lawyer; b. Newark, N.J., Apr. 4, 1955; BA magna cum laude, Lafayette Coll., 1977; JD cum laude, Seton Hall U., 1980; LLM in Labor Law with honors, NYU, 1988. Bar: N.J. 1980, U.S. Dist. Ct. N.J., U.S. Dist. Ct. N.Y. (ea., so. and no. dists.), U.S. Ct. Appeals (2d and 3d cirs.), U.S. Supreme Ct. Law sec. to Hon. Robert L. Clifford Supreme Ct. N.J., 1980—81; assoc. to sr. ptnr. Carpenter, Bennett & Morrissey, Newark, 1981—98; ptnr., chair labor and employment law practice Connell Foley LLP, 1998—. Articles editor Seton Hall Law Rev., 1979-80; contbr. articles to profl. jours. Mem. ABA (litigation

and labor and employment law sects., state labor law devel. com.), N.J. State Bar Assn. (exec. com. labor and employment law sect.), Essex County Bar Assn. Office: Connell Foley LLP 85 Livingston Ave Roseland NJ 07068-3702 Fax: 973-535-9217. E-mail: jbennett@connellfoley.com.

BENNETT, JOHN MORRISON, hematologist and medical oncologist; b. Boston, Apr. 24, 1933; s. Theodore and Gladys B.; m. Carol F. Rosenblum, Dec. 22, 1957; children: Robert, Elizabeth, Douglas. AB cum laude, Harvard U., 1955; MD cum laude, Boston U., 1959. Intern Mass. Meml. Hosp., Boston, 1959-60; resident Beth Israel Hosp., Boston, 1960-62; instr. medicine Harvard Med. Sch., 1965-66; head morphology and histochem. sect. clin. pathology dept. NIH, 1966-68; asst. prof. medicine Sch. Medicine Tufts U., 1966-69; dir. outpatient labs. Boston City Hosp., 1968-69; dir. hematology and med. oncology Highland Hosp., Rochester, N.Y., 1969-74; prof. oncology in medicine, pathology and lab. medicine U. Rochester Sch. Medicine, 1976-98; prof. medicine emeritus, 1999—; assoc. dir. clin. affairs U. Rochester Cancer Ctr., 1978-94; head med. oncology unit Strong Meml. Hosp., Rochester, 1974-95. Editor: Leukemia Research, 1993; contbr. more than 400 articles to profl. jours. Chmn. Myelodysplastic Syndromes Founds., 1996—. With USPHS, 1966-68. Mem. ACP, AMA, Am. Soc. Clin. Oncology, Am. Soc. Hematology, Internat. Soc. Hematology, European Soc. Oncology. Home: 335 Avalon Dr Rochester NY 14618-2731 Office: 601 Elmwood Ave Rochester NY 14642-0001 E-mail: j.bennett2@rochester.rr.com., John_Bennett@urmc.rochester.edu. *The major principle that has guided my academic career has been to treat patients with compassion but also in a setting of clinical trials research. Participation of patients in innovative studies and randomized trials offers the best opportunity for quality care and improved results in the field of oncology. My research has focused on classifcation of leukemias and establishing clinical correlations.*

BENNETT, JOHN O. state legislator; b. Long Branch, N.J., Aug. 6, 1948; m. Margaret Meier, 1977; children: Meghan, Caitlin, Mairin. BA, W.Va. U., 1970; JD, Seton Hall Law Sch., 1974. Mem. N.J. Gen. Assembly, 1980-89; mem., co-pres. N.J. Senate, Dist. 12, Trenton, 1989—; mng. ptnr. Dilworth Paxson, LLP, Wall Twp., NJ. N.J. Nat. Guard, 1970-76; com. to study sex discrimination in the statutes N.J. Assembly, 1983-89, legis. svc. commn., 1986-89, chmn. assembly environ. quality com., 1986-89, select com. on ocean & beach protection, 1987-89; Supreme Ct. task force on drugs and the courts N.J. Senate, 1991—, judiciary com., 1992—, legis. oversight com., 1994—, urban policy planning com., 1994—, dep. majority leader, 1992-93, majority leader, 1994—2001; Rep. Pres. 2002-; environ. com., exec. com. Eastern Regional Conf. Coun. State Govt., 1992—; mng. ptnr. satellite office Dilworth Paxson, L.L.P.; asst. county counsel bd. chosen freeholders, 1977-79; atty. Borough of Keansburg Bd. Edn., 1978—; planning bd. Borough of Roosevelt, 1981; zoning bd. adjustment Marlboro, 1982-90; bd. dirs. Freehold Savings & Loan Assn. Mem. Little Silver Bd. Edn., 1978-81; citizen's adv. bd. Jersey Shore Addiction Svc., 1986—. Mem. Trial Lawyers Assn., ABA, Monmouth County Bar Assn., N.J. Inst. Mcpl. Attys, Intergovt'l Rels. Commn., Legis. Svcs. Commn. Republican. Office: 41 Center St Freehold NJ 07728

BENNETT, JUNE NEWTON, interior designer; b. Windsor, Colo., June 17, 1926; d. Arthur Arnaud and Irma Mae (Wilkinson) Newton; m. Thomas Willard Bennett, Aug. 14, 1948; children: Polly Alison Bennett, Susan Jane Bennett Mallory. BA, U. Denver, 1948. Pvt. sec. to univ. dean Northwestern U., Evanston and Chgo., Ill., 1948-52; interior designer Bowling's Furniture, Ft. Collins, Colo., 1963-65; owner, designer Bennett-Raetzman Interior Design, Ft. Collins, 1965-67; owner, pres., designer June Newton Bennett Interior Design, Ft. Collins, 1967—. Water color artist, 1992—. Sec., founder Ft. Collins Coun. Arts-Humanities, 1963; chairperson, founder Ft. Collins Hist. Landmarks Commn., 1968; project mgr. Avery House Restoration, 1974-79; mem. design com. Lincoln Ctr. for Performing Arts, Ft. Collins, 1982—; pres. bd. Ft. Collins Symphony, 1987-88; trustee Ft. Collins Symphony Orch., 1990—. Mem. No. Colo. Interior Design Guild (sec. 1986-88). Republican. Episcopalian.

BENNETT, KATHLEEN MAROURNEEN, elementary school educator; b. Harlingen, Tex., Jan. 26, 1943; d. Owen James Bennett and Betty Margaret Bell. BS, No. Mich. U., 1966. Cert. elem. edn. Mich. Tchr. Head Start, Iron Mountain, Mich., 1966, Iron Mountain Pub. Schs., 1966, Gladstone (Mich.) Area Schs., 1967. Chair Sch. Improvement Team, Gladstone, Mich., 1988—90; dir. musicals various elem. schs. Actor: Area Children's Theatre. Active Recreation Adv. Bd., Escanaba, Mich., 1980—82; dir. children's musicals; actor children's theater. Named Disting. Alumni, No. Mich. U., 1988. Mem.: AAUW (pres., Outstanding Educator Escanaba br. 1980), Mich. Edn. Assn. (sec. 1977—79, Outstanding Person in Edn. award 2003). Democrat. Episcopalian. Avocations: reading, walking, movies, interior decorating, travel. Home: 321 S 6th St Escanaba MI 49829

BENNETT, KENNETH ALAN, retired biological anthropologist; b. Butler, Okla., Oct. 3, 1935; s. Kenneth Francis and Lillian Imogene (McDaniel) B.; m. Helen Lucille Maze, Sept. 6, 1959; children: Letitia Arlene, Cheri Lynn. AS, Odessa Coll., 1956; BA, U. Tex., 1961; MA, U. Ariz., 1966, PhD, 1967. Asst. prof. anthropology U. Oreg., 1967-70; assoc. prof. U. Wis., Madison, 1970-75, prof., 1975-97, ret., 1997. Author: The Indians of Point of Pines, Arizona, 1973, Fundamentals of Biological Anthropology, 1979, Skeletal Remains from Mesa Verde National Park, 1975, A Field Guide for Human Skeletal Identification, 1987, 2nd edit., 1993; editor Yearbook of Phys. Anthropology, 1976-81; contbr. editor Social Biology, 1981-87; mem. editl. com. Ann. Revs. in Anthropology, 1987-91; contbr. articles to profl. jours. Mem. Wis. Burial Sites Preservation Bd., 1988. With U.S. Army, 1956-58. NIH fellow, 1964-67 Mem. Am. Assn. Phys. Anthropologists, Am. Soc. Naturalists, Human Biology Council, Soc. for Study Evolution, Am. Acad. Forensic Scis., Soc. for Study Human Biology, Soc. Systematic Zoology, Am. Assn. Physical Anthropologists (exec. com. 1976-81), Sigma Xi. Home: 5718 Hammersley Rd Madison WI 53711-3450

BENNETT, KENNETH R. oil company executive, state legislator; b. Tucson, Aug. 1, 1959; s. Archie Roy and Donna Lucille (Bulechek) B.; m. Jeanne Tenney Bennett, Mar. 13, 1982; children: Ryan, Dana, Clifton. BS, Ariz. State U., 1984. Ceo Bennett's Oil Co., 1984—; mem. Ariz. Senate, Tucson, 1998—, Ariz. St. Bd. Education, 1992-1999; councilman Prescott City, 1985-89; pres. Ariz. Senate, 2003—. Mem. Ariz. State Bd. Edn., Phoenix, 1992—, pres., 1996-97; Ariz. State Bd. for Charter Schs., Phoenix, 1994—, Governor's Task Force Edn. Reform, Phoenix, 1991-92. Mayor Pro Tempore City of Prescott (Ariz.), 1988; councilman City of Prescott (Ariz.), 1985-89; scoutmaster Boy Scouts of Am., 1993—. Mem., Education Leaders Council, Washington; Ariz. St. Charter Sch. Bd. Republican. Mem. Lds Ch. Office: Bennett Oil Co 810 E Sheldon St Prescott AZ 86301-3214*

BENNETT, KEVIN RAY, music educator, musician; b. Vandenberg AFB, Calif., July 21, 1976; s. Dennis and Betty Bennett; m. Amy Hargis, July 28, 2001. MusB in Music Edn. Instrumental, U. Idaho, 1999. Cert. tchr. Idaho, Ariz. Music tchr. Gilbert (Ariz.) Pub. Schs., 1999—. Profl. musician, Mesa, Ariz., 2000—. Mem.: NEA, Music Educators Nat. Conf. (v.p. U. Idaho collegiate chpt. 1996—97), Internat. Jazz Educators Assn., Internat. Trombone Assn., Phi Eta Sigma, Beta Theta Pi. Office: Highland HS 140 S Gilbert Rd Gilbert AZ 85296

BENNETT, LAWRENCE ALLEN, psychologist, criminal justice researcher; b. Selma, Calif, Jan. 4, 1923; s. Allen Walter and Eva Eleanor (Hall) B.; m. Beth J. Thompson, Aug. 14, 1948; children: Glenn Livingston, Yvonne Irene Solis. BA, Fresno State Coll., 1949; MA, Claremont Grad. Sch., 1954, PhD, 1968. Supervising psychologist Calif. med. facility Calif. Dept. Corrections, Vacaville, Calif., 1955-60, deptl. supr. clin. psychology Sacramento, 1960-67, chief rsch., 1967-76; dir. Ctr. for Study Crime, Delinquency and Corrections, So. Ill. U., Carbondale, Ill., 1976-79; dir. Office Program Evaluation, 1979-84; dir. crime prevention and enforcement divsn. Nat. Inst. Justice, Wash., DC, 1985-86, dir. adjudication and corrections divsn., 1987-88; criminal justice cons., Sacramento, 1988—; practice clin. psychology, 1988-99. Mem. part-time faculty U. Calif., Davis and Berkeley, 1959-76, Calif. State U., Sacramento, 1988—; mem. bd. Calif. Crime Technol. Rsch. Found., 1970-75; mem. Calif. Interdeptl. Coordinating Coun., 1967-76, chmn., 1970; bd. dir. Am. Justice Inst., Sacramento, 1970-79, 88—, v.p., 1989-90, pres., 1991-2003; project dir. San Francisco Project, 1999-2002; mem. juvenile adv. bd. State of Ill., 1977-79; mem. Calif. Blue Ribbon Commn. on Inmate Population Mgmt., 1988-90. With US Army, 1942-45, 49-50. Author: (with Thomas S. Rosenbaum and Wayne R. McCollough) Counseling in Correctional Environments, 1978; contbr. articles to profl. jours. Decorated Bronze Star with oak leaf cluster. Mem. APA, Acad. Criminal Justice Scis., Am. Soc. Criminology, Am. Correctional Assn. (rsch. coun. 1992-95), Evaluation Rsch. Soc., Assn. for Correctional Rsch. and Info. Mgmt. (pres. 1989-90). Unitarian Universalist. Office: Am Justice Inst 1129 Rivara Cir Sacramento CA 95864-3720 E-mail: flylarry@cwnet.com.

BENNETT, LAWRENCE HERMAN, physicist; b. Bklyn., Oct. 17, 1930; s. Harold and Irene (Kamel) B.; m. Devora Mae Spintman, Mar. 22, 1953; children: Claire Ann Bennett Freeland, Charles Leonard, Craig David. BA cum laude, Bklyn. Coll., 1951; MS, U. Md., 1955; PhD, Rutgers U., 1958. Physicist Naval Ordnance Lab., White Oak, Md., 1950-58, Nat. Bur. Stds., Gaithersburg, Md., 1958-96. Adj. prof. physics U. Md., College Park, 1959-94, rsch. prof. Inst. for Magnetics Rsch. The George Washington U., Washington, 1995—. Author: (with G.C. Carter and D.H. Kahan) Metallic Shifts in NMR, 1977; editor: Theory of Alloy Phase Formation, 1980, Computer Modeling of Alloy Phase Diagrams, 1986, High Temperature Superconductors: Magnetic Interactions, 1989, Magnetic Multilayers, 1994; contbr. articles to profl. jours. Recipient Gold medal Dept. Commerce, 1971. Fellow Am. Phys. Soc. (chair magnetism group 1999-2000), Am. Soc. for Metals (Burgess Meml. award 1964); mem. IEEE Magnetics Soc., AIME Metall. Soc., Phi Beta Kappa, Sigma Xi (pres. bur. of stds. 1987). Home: 6524 E Halbert Rd Bethesda MD 20817-5414 Office: George Washington U Inst Magnetic Rsch Ashburn VA 20147 E-mail: lbennett@gwu.edu.

BENNETT, LERONE, JR., retired magazine editor, author; b. Clarksdale, Miss., Oct. 17, 1928; s. Lerone and Alma (Reed) Bennett; m. Gloria Sylvester, July 21, 1956; children: Alma Joy, Constance, Courtney;1 child, Lerone III. BA, Morehouse Coll., 1949, LittD (hon.), 1966; HHD (hon.), Wilberforce U., 1977; DLitt (hon.), Marquette U., 1979, Voorhees Coll., 1981, Morgan State U., 1981; LHD (hon.), U. Ill., 1980, Lincoln Coll., 1980, Dillard U., 1980; LittD (hon.), Howard U., 1982; LHD (hon.), Boston U., 1987; DLitt (hon.), Tuskegee U., 1989. Reporter Atlanta Daily World, 1949—51, city editor, 1952—53; assoc. editor Ebony mag., Chgo., 1953—58, sr. editor, 1958—87, exec. editor, 1987—2003. Vis. prof. hist. Nothwestern U., 1968—69. Author: Before the Mayflower: A History of Black America, 1619-1964, 1962, 3d edit., 1987, The Negro Mood, 1964, What Manner of Man, A Biography of Martin Luther King, Jr., 1964, Confrontation: Black and White, 1965, Black Power U.S.A., 1968, Pioneers in Protest, 1968, The Challenge of Blackness, 1972, The Shaping of Black America, 1975, Wade in the Water, 1979, Forced Into Glory: Abraham Lincoln's White Dream, 2000; contbg. author: New Negro Poets: USA, 1964, American Negro Short Stories, 1966. Trustee Morehouse Coll., Columbia Coll.; mem. Pres.'s Com. Arts and Humanities. Recipient Patron Saints award, Soc. Midland Authors, 1965, Book of the Yr. award, Capital Press Club, 1963, AAAL Acad./Inst. lit. award, 1978. Mem.: Sigma Delta Chi, Kappa Alpha Psi, Phi Beta Kappa.*

BENNETT, MARGARET AIROLA, lawyer; b. San Francisco, Calif; AB cum laude, U. Calif., Berkeley, 1972; JD, U. San Francisco and Loyola U., 1976. Bar: Ill.1976, US Dist. Ct. (no. dist.) Ill. 1977, US Ct. Appeals (7th cir.) 1983. Intern Cook County State's Atty.'s Office, Chgo., 1975-76; assoc. Dunlap, Thompson & Boyd, Ltd., Libertyville, Ill., 1977-79; ptnr. Bennett & Bennett, Ltd., Oak Brook, Ill., 1980-96; pvt. practice The Law Offices of Margaret A. Bennett, Oak Brook, Ill., 1997. Atty. rep. McDonald's Corp., Oak Brook, 1982—, County of DuPage, Wheaton, Ill., 1990-95. Counsel fo DuPage Ill. Fair and Exposition Authority, County of DuPage, 1991-95, co-chmn. next generation com.; mem. devel. coun. Good Samaritan Hosp., 1988-92. Mem. DuPage County Bar Assn. (chmn. real estate law com. 1994-95, Cert. of Appreciation 1989, Bd. Dir. award 1998, chmn. profl. responsibility com. 1996-97, chmn. family law com. 1997-98), Ill. State Bar Assn. (assembly mem., 1996-2000, Cert. of Appreciation 1990, real estate sect. council 1996-2002, jud evaluation com. 1998—), Womens Bar Assn. DuPage County, Evang. Health Found. (bd. sponsors 1988-92). Republican. Episcopalian. Avocations: golf, reading, skiing, travel. Office: Ste 718 1200 Hanger Rd Oak Brook IL 60523-1908

BENNETT, MARGUERITE HILDRETH, college administrator, mathematics educator; b. Mar. 17, 1945; MEd, U. Ill., 1971, PhD, 1976. Dir. instnl. rsch. and planning, math. prof. Mt. Vernon Nazarene U., 1976—. Cons.-evaluator North Ctrl. Assn. Colls. and Schs., 1989—. Mem. Mt. Vernon City Schs. Bd. Edn. 1, 1988—2003; v.p. Knox County Career Ctr. Bd. Edn., 1992—2003. Mem. Mt. Vernon-Knox County C. of C. Office: 800 Martinsburg Rd Mount Vernon OH 43050-9509 E-mail: mbennett@mvnu.edu.

BENNETT, MARK J. state attorney general; m. Patricia Tomi Ohara. BA in Polit. Sci. summa cum laude, Union Coll., 1976; JD magna cum laude, Cornell U., 1979. Law clk. to Hon. Samuel P. King, Chief Judge U.S. Dist. Ct. Hawaii; asst. U.S. atty. Washington, 1980—82, Honolulu, 1982—90; litig. ptnr. McCorriston Miller Mukai MacKinnon LLP, Honolulu, 1991—2002; spl. dep. atty. gen., spl. asst. proc. atty. Hawaii. Instr. criminal and civil trial advocacy Atty. Gen.'s Adv. Inst., Washington; instr. U. Hawaii Sch. Law. Republican. Office: 425 Queen St Honolulu HI 96813

BENNETT, MAXINE TAYLOR, lawyer; b. Owensboro, Ky., Apr. 6, 1938; d. John Clevis and Alice Elizabeth (Siebe) Taylor; m. Wilford Thomas Bennett, Jan 19. 1957 (div. Dec. 1976); children: Cynthia Bennett Radseck, Jonathan Taylor Bennett; m. Edwin R. Druker, May 13, 1978. BA, Ky. Wesleyan Coll., 1959; MA, Western Ky. U., 1967; JD, Ind. U., Indpls., 1977. Bar: Ind. 1977, U.S. Dist. Ct. (so. and no. dists.) Ind. 1977, U.S. Ct. Appeals (7th cir.) 1984, U.S. Supreme Ct. 1986. Clk. Indpls. Corp. Counsel, 1975-77; atty. Commodities Dealers Licensing Bur. State of Ind., Indpls., 1977-78; sole practice Indpls., 1977—; assoc. Buck, Berry, Landau & Breunig, Indpls., 1984—. Bd. dirs. Women's Haven, Indpls., 1981-82, Indpls. Hebrew Congregation Found., 2002-; trustee E.A. Block Charitable Trust, Indpls., 1982-2002. Recipient Nat. Career Woman of Yr. award Women's Expo, 1988-89. Mem. ABA, Ind. State Bar Assn., Indpls. Bar Assn. (Disting. fellow 1993), Columbia Club. Republican. Avocations: world travel, reading, creative needlework, gourmet cooking. Office: Buck Berry Landau & Breunig 302 N Alabama St Indianapolis IN 46204-2166 Fax: 317-264-0819. E-mail: MAXBEN302@aol.com.

BENNETT, MICHAEL VANDER LAAN, neuroscience educator; b. Madison, Wis., Jan. 7, 1931; s. Martin Toscan and Cornelia (Vanderlaan) B.; m. Ruth Berman, July 19, 1963 (div. 1993); children: Nicholas Toscan, Elena Paula; m. R. Suzanne Zukin Nov. 19, 1997. BS, Yale U., 1952; DPhil, Oxford U., Eng., 1957. Research worker Coll. of Physicians and Surgeons Columbia U., N.Y.C., 1957-58, rsch. assoc., 1958-59, asst. prof. neurology, 1959-61, assoc. prof. neurology, 1961-66; co-dir. neurobiology Marine Biol. Lab., Woods Hole, Mass., 1970-74; prof. anatomy Albert Einstein Coll. Medicine, Bronx, N.Y., 1967-74, prof. neurosci., 1974-96, chmn. neurosci., 1982-96, Sylvia and Robert S. Olnick Prof. of Neurosci., 1986—. Editor rev. jours.; contbr. articles to profl. jours. Hon. Pepsi Cola scholar, 1948, Rhodes scholar, 1952; Grass Fellow, 1958. Fellow AAAS; mem. NAS, Am. Physiol. Soc., Am. Soc. Cell Biology, Biophys. Soc., Soc. Neurosci., N.Y. Road Runners Club, Phi Beta Kappa. Avocations: running, skiing, scuba, science. Office: Albert Einstein Coll of Medicine Dept Of Neurosci Bronx NY 10461 E-mail: mbennett@aecom.yu.edu.

BENNETT, OLGA SALOWICH, civic worker, graphic arts researcher, consultant; b. Detroit, June 30, 1925; d. Nicholas Stefanovich and Maria Elarionovna (Mikuliak) Salowich; m. Robert William Bennett, Dec. 20, 1947; 1 child, Susan Roberta. Student, U. Mich., 1943-45, Parsons Sch. Design, 1948, U. Md., Nagoya, Japan, 1959; BA, NYU, 1975. Graphic artist Silver & Co., N.Y.C., 1948-50; editor, pub. Bull., organizer radio series LWV, Pitts., 1950-55; instr. Nanzan U., Nagoya, 1959; aide, cons. to U.S. hon. consul, Safi, Casablanca, Morocco, 1962-65; chmn. internat. affairs LWV, Montclair, N.J., 1966-73; conf. coord. UN Assn., Madison, N.J., 1974; weekly broadcaster LWV, San Juan, P.R., 1979-81; lectr. color theory Cunard, Ltd., London, Miami, Fla., 1985-88. Bd. dirs., docent Ctr. Fine Arts, Miami, 1990-92; docent Bass Mus. Art, Miami Beach, Fla., 1990-92, Vizcaya Mus. Art, Miami, 1983—; cons. on corp. overseas placement. Author artist brochures, ednl. pamphlets; translator Russian-Am. Conf., Miami, 1990. Mem. panel theater award com. New Theater, Miami, 1991; mem. Nat. Mus. of Women in the Arts; bd. dirs. Kings Creek South Condominium Assn., 1996-99. Mem. AAUW, LWV, UN Assn., NYU Alumni Assn., New Sch. Alumni Assn., Fgn. Policy Assn., Great Decisions Program. Democrat. Russian Orthodox. Home: Kings Creek S Apt A1-402 7727 SW 86th St Miami FL 33143-7283

BENNETT, PAUL B. brokerage house executive, economist; BA in econ., U. Chgo.; PhD in econ., Princeton U. Various positions Fed. Reserve Bank of N.Y., 1978—93, sr. v.p. rsch. group, 1994—99, sr. v.p. capital markets rsch., 1999—2001; sr. v.p. and chief economist N.Y. Stock Exch., 2001—. Office: NY Stock Exch 11 Wall St New York NY 10005

BENNETT, PETER BRIAN, researcher, hyperbaric medicine; b. Portsmouth, Hampshire, Eng., June 12, 1931; s. Charles Risby and Doris Isobel (Peckham) B.; m. Margaret Camellia Rose, July 7, 1956; children: Caroline Susan, Christopher Charles BSc, U. London, 1951; PhD, U. Southampton, 1964, DSc, 1984; Dr. honoris causa, U. de la Mediterranean, France, 2001. Asst. head surg. sect. Royal Navy Physiol. Lab., Alverstoke, Eng., 1953-56, head inert gas narcosis sect., 1953-66; dep. dir., prin. sci. officer, head pressure physiology sect. Royal Naval Physiol. Lab., Alverstoke, 1968-72; head pressure physiology group Can. Def. and Civil Inst. for Environ. Rsch., Toronto, Ont., 1966-68; prof. biomed. engring. Duke U., Durham, N.C., 1972-75, assoc. prof. physiology, 1975—, prof. anesthesiology, 1972—, dir. rsch. dept. anesthesiology Med. Ctr., 1973-84, dir. Nat. Divers Alert Network, 1980—; dep. dir. F.G. Hall Lab. Environ. Rsch., 1973-74; co-dir. F.G. Hall Lab. Environ. Research, 1974-77, dir., 1977-88; sr. dir. Hyperbaric Ctr., 1988—. Cons. in field Author: The Aetiology of Compressed Air Intoxication and Inert Gas Narcosis, 1966; author, editor: The Physiology and Medicine of Diving and Compressed Air Work, 1969, Russian edit., 1987, 4th edit., 1993; contbr. over 200 articles to profl. jours. With RAF, 1951-53. Recipient Letter of Commendation, Pres. Ronald Reagan, 1981, Sci. award Underwater Soc. Am., 1980, Leonard Greenstone Safety award Nat. Assn. Underwater Instrs., 1985, 1st Prince Tomohito of Mikasa Japan prize, 1990, Craig Hoffman Meml. award, 1992, Dan Seap Mentor award, 1998, Ernst & Young Entrepreneur of Yr. in Life Scis. award, NC and SC, 2002, Reaching Out award Diving Equipment Mfrs., 2002. Fellow Nat. Underwater Explorers Club; mem. Undersea Med. Soc. (pres. 1975-76, mem. exec. com. 1972-75, editor jour. 1976-79, 1st Oceaneering Internat. award 1975, Albert R. Behnke award 1985), Am. Physiol. Soc., European Undersea Biomed. Soc., Russian Acad. Sci. (fgn. mem., Pavlov medal 2001), Aerospace Med. Soc., Marine Tech. Soc., Croatian Undersea and Hyperbaric Med. Soc. (hon.), Nat. Acad. Scuba Educators (Meritorious Svc. award 1997). Avocations: gardening, swimming, boating. Home: 213 Lancaster Dr Chapel Hill NC 27517-3430 Office: Duke U Med Ctr Divers Alert Network 6 W Colony Pl Durham NC 27705

BENNETT, PETER DUNNE, retired marketing educator; b. Mt. Pleasant, Tex., Feb. 19, 1933; s. Alvin Lowell and Jessie Lorene (Wintz) B.; m. Mary Lou Sanders, Aug. 23, 1953; children— Bonnie Kathleen, Blythe Allison BBA, U. Tex., Austin, 1955, MBA, 1961, PhD, 1965. Mktg. rep. IBM Corp., Lubbock, Tex., 1957-60; lectr. U. Tex., Austin, 1961-63; vis. researcher U. Chile, Santiago, 1963-64; prof., chmn. dept. mktg., assoc. dean, bus. Pa. State U., University Park, 1964-97; gen. contractor State College, Pa., 1997—. Bd. dirs. Walshire Asurance; cons. and lectr. in field. Author: Consumer Behavior, 1973, Marketing, 1988, Dictionary of Marketing Terms, 1989, 2d edit. 1995; editor numerous books in field; contbr. chpts. to books. Mem. Habitat for Humanity. Served to capt. USAF, 1955-57 Named Disting. Visitor, U. Tex., 1979. Mem. Assn. Consumer Research, Am. Mktg. Assn. (v.p. mgmt. 1983-85, editor 1982-84) Democrat. Presbyterian. Avocations: golf, sailing, water skiing, house building, wood working. E-mail: pdb1@psu.edu.

BENNETT, R. DAWN, social worker; b. Roanoke, Va., Nov. 16, 1937; d. Robert Lee and Pearl Lucille (Webber) Moore; m. Charles Peter Bennett, June 16, 1961; children: Michael Charles, Laura Dawn. BA, Baylor U., 1960; MSW, Norfolk State U., 1979. Lic. clin. social worker, Va. Clinician Cath. Family and Children's Svc., Norfolk, Va., 1979-83; social worker Multimodal Therapy, Norfolk, 1983-86; pvt. practice social work Virginia Beach, Va., 1986—. Vol. Results, Domestic Hunger Lobby, 1998-2002. Mem. Nat. Assn. Social Workers, Va. Soc. Clin. Social Workers. Avocations: oil painting, golf, bridge, spiritual support and leadership activities.

BENNETT, RICHARD A. state senator; b. Portland, Maine, May 24, 1963; m. Karen Bennett; 2 children. BA, Harvard U., 1986; postgrad. in Bus. Adminstrn., U. So. Maine. Exec. dir. Maine Rep. Party, 1986-88, vice chair, 1989-94; sales mgr., rep. Burlington Homes of Maine, 1989-92, 95-96; propr. Bennett Devel. Co., 1992—; with Lens Investment Mgmt., LLC, 1997—; del. Rep. Nat. Conv., 1996—; mem. Dist. 25 Maine Senate, Augusta, 1990-94, 96—, pres. pro tempore, 2001, pres., 2002. Corporator Western Maine Health Care Corp., Norway Savs. Bank; chair Western Maine Vets. Home Com., 1992-93; asst. minority leader Maine State Senate, mem. joint select com. on R&D. Mem. NRA Maine, Sportsmans Alliance Maine, Appalachian Mountain Club. Republican. Home: 413 Norway Center Rd Norway ME 04268-4436 Office: Senate Minority Office 3 State House Sta Augusta ME 04333-0003 E-mail: rbenett@megalink.net., rbennett@maine.com.

BENNETT, RICHARD CARL, social worker; b. Eau Claire, Wis., July 25, 1933; s. Ira Anthony and Marion Rhoda (Johnson) Bennett; m. Patricia Ann Work, Oct. 27, 1972; children: Matthew, Elizabeth, Kimberly, Timothy. BA, Hamline U., St. Paul, 1955; MS, George Williams Coll., 1957, U. Chgo., 1962; postgrad., Loyola U., Chgo., Roosevelt U., Forest Inst., 1998, Capella U., Mpls.; grad., Ind. Family Meditation Tng., 1992; PhD, Clayton Sch., Birmingham, Ala., 1997; Paralegal Diploma, Kaplan Coll., 2001. LCSW, lic. marriage and family counselor, profl. counselor. Caseworker Rock County Welfare Dept., Janesville, Wis., 1957-61; area dir. Luth. Family Svc. Oreg., Eugene, 1962-67; exec. dir. Family Svc. Travelers Ald, Ft. Worth, 1967-70; mgr. agy. ops. Tarrant County United Way, Ft. Worth, 1970-73; mile coord. Hands Across Am., 1986; coord. Porter County Share Food, 1986-87; exec. dir. Luth. Family Svc. N.W. Ind., Merrillville, 1973-80; exec. v.p. Listening Inc., Gary, Ind., 1979—; clin. dir. Oasis Ctr., Gary, 1999—2001; substance abuse profl. Dept. Transp. Mem. clin. staff Midwest Ctr. Children and Families, 1998—99, Kouts, Inc., 1998—99; exec. dir. Inst. for Family Life Porter County, 1982—93; CEO Environtech, 1988—94; instr. Ind. U.; coord. of telecourses Calumet Coll., 1989—97; instr. Davenport Coll., 1998—2000; cons. internat. bd. Parents without Ptnrs.; cons. Support Group Adult Attention Deficit Disorder, 1992, 98; appt. by gov. Ind. Social Work, Marriage and Family Therapist and Mental Health Counselor Licensing Bd., 1991—99, chmn., 1995, 98; field instr., 1964—70, 2001. Author: Second Opinion: A Hollistic Approach to Treating Adults with ADD, 1994, Reversing Attention Deficit Disorder in Adult, 1996, Brief Therapy Treatment Planner, 1996, Due Process and Professional Licensing, 2001, divorce mgmt. materials, newspaper column, profl. manuals; Step Families and Beyond, 1979—89; editor: (jours.) The Business of Social Work, 1983—84, ADD-Up Newsletter for ADD-Adults, 1995—98, The Violence Chronicles, 1998—; host : (TV series) Life's Dimensions, 1985—90. Founding bd. mem. Dunes Shakespeare Repertory Theatre, 1998. With USAR, 1958—62. Mem.: NASW (dir. Ind. chpt.), Acad. Cert. Social Workers, Nat. Coll. Forensic Examiners, Am. Coll. Forensic Examiners, Acad. Cert. Social Works (diplomate in clin. social work), APA (assoc.), Delta Epsilon Tau. Home and Office: 8716 Pine Ave Gary IN 46403-1441

BENNETT, RICHARD CLARK, fundraising consultant; b. Pitts., Aug. 5, 1941; s. Abram Clark and Sara (Jones) B.; children: Elizabeth Anne, Jordan, Ronald. BA, Duquesne U., 1964. With Boy Scouts Am., 1964—; executive Pitts., 1964-67; dist. exec. Reading, Pa., 1967-70; dir. of camping Lehigh Valley, Pa., 1970-77; devel. dir. N.Y.C., 1977-81; exec. dir. Chester County, Pa., 1981-88, Boy Scouts Am., Reading, Pa., 1988—. Author: Historic Trails of Lehigh Valley, 1976 (state citation), Lunch-O-Ree Guidebook (manual), 1979, Guide to Fund Raising (manual), 1983. Dir. Boyertown Mus. Historic Vehicles; pres. Reading Rotary Found. Recipient of citation Commonwealth of Pa., 1977. Mem. Nat. Soc. Fund Raising Execs., Jaycees (Pitts. chpt. pres.), Rotary (pres. Reading chpt.), Masons (royal arch mason 32 degree), Shriners. Republican. Episcopalian. Home: 1926 Meadow Ln Reading PA 19610-2707 Office: Hawk Mountain Coun Boy Scouts Am 5027 Pottsville Pike Reading PA 19605-9713 E-mail: RCB1926@comcast.net.

BENNETT, RICHARD THOMAS, retired manufacturing executive; b. Trenton, N.J., Jan. 7, 1930; s. George and Gladys (Burgess) B.; m. Bertha B. Wilson, Jan 24, 1958; children: Sandra, Richard, Terri, David. BS in Chemistry, Yale U., 1952; MS in Organic Chemistry, Rutgers U., 1954, PhD in Organic Chemistry, 1956. Rsch. chemist E.I. duPont de Nemours & Co., Wilmington, Del., 1956-58, Phila., 1958-59, tech. rep. Wilmington, 1959-62; tech. dir. Am. Bag and Paper Corp., Phila., 1962-64; rsch. assoc. Allied Chem. Corp., Morristown, NJ, 1964-66, tech. supr., 1966-67, product mgr., 1967-70, bus. mgr., 1970-73, asst. to pres., 1973-74, mem. of task force, 1975-76, gen. mgr. Toledo, 1974-79; pres. Plaskon Products, Inc., Toledo, 1979-84, PLK Corp., Toledo, 1984-86, Congoleum Corp., Kearny, N.J., 1986-88; plastic cons. Hillside Capital, N.Y.C., 1988-91. Bd. dirs. Ohio Chem. Coun., 1978-86, pres. 1981. Vestryman St. Michael's Episc. Ch., Toledo, 1979-81; sr. warden St. Michael's Ch., Toledo, 1980-81; bd. dirs. United Way, Toledo, 1981-86, vice chmn. spl. gifts, 1978-86, chmn., 1983; vice chmn. Toledo Council Boy Scouts Am., 1981-83; chmn. Blue Guardian Corp. of Blue Cross, 1984-86; trustee Blue Cross of Northwest Ohio, 1981-86, Med. Coll. Ohio at Toledo Found., 1983-86; past vice chmn. and bd. dirs. Toledo Area C. of C. Mem. Ohio Mfrs. Assn. (vice chmn. 1983-86), Am. Mgmt. Assn., Pres.'s Assn.

BENNETT, ROBERT F. senator; b. Salt Lake City, Utah, 1933; s. Wallace F. Bennett; m. Joyce McKay; 6 children. BS, U. of Utah, 1957. Various staff positions U.S Ho. of Reps., U.S. Senate, Washington; CEO Franklin Quest, Salt Lake City, 1984-90; senator from Utah, U.S. Senate, Washington, 1993—. Chmn. agr. subcom., instns. subcom., mem. banking, housing, urban affairs com., appropriations com., joint econ. ic com., small bus. com.; mem. Rep. high tech. task force, gov. affairs com.; lobbyist various orgns., Washington; head Dept. Transp.'s Congl. Liaison. Author: Gaining Control. Chmn. Education Strategic Planning Commn. Utah State Bd. Edn. (mem. Edn. Strategic Planning Com.). Recipient Light of Learning award for Outstanding Contbns. to Utah edn., 1989; named Entrepreneur of Yr. for Rocky Mtn. region INC. magazine, 1989. Republican. Office: US Senate 431 Dirksen Senate Ofc Bldg Washington DC 20510-0001*

BENNETT, ROBERT LEROY, computer software development company executive; b. Salt Lake City, May 16, 1937; s. Edward L. and Helen (Hofheins) B.; m. Linda Lou Anderson, Aug. 25, 1961; children: Keri Lynn, Troy, Nicole, Jessica, Candice, Chelsea. BA, Brigham Young U., 1962; JD, UCLA, 1965. Bar: Calif. 1966, U.S. Supreme Ct. 1969. Atty., advisor CIA, Washington, 1965-70; exec. v.p., chief operating officer Mead Data Central, Inc. (now Lexis-Nexis), Washington and N.Y.C., 1970-81; assoc. Heidrick and Struggles, Inc., N.Y.C., 1982-83; pres., chief exec. officer Mirror Systems, Inc., Cambridge, Mass., 1983—93; prin. Bennett, Fisher, Giuliano and Gottsman: The Electronic Publishing Group, N.Y.C., 1993—2000. Mem.: ABA. Mem. Lds Ch. E-mail: RLBepg@earthlink.net.

BENNETT, ROBERT MENZIES, retired gas pipeline company executive; b. Louisville, Oct. 24, 1926; s. Donald Menzies and Irene Marie (Schubring) B.; m. Elizabeth Lois Sherman, June 11, 1949; children: James, Elizabeth, Emily, Robert Jr. BEE, U. Louisville, 1950. Registered profl. engr., W.Va. Engr. Louisville Gas and Electric, 1950-55, Columbia Gas div. United Fuel Gas Co., Charleston, W.Va., 1955-61, supervisory engr., 1961-71; mgr. Columbia Gas W.Va., Charleston, 1971-73; dir. planning Columbia Gas Transmission Corp., Charleston, 1973-80, v.p. gas procurement, 1980-85, sr. v.p. mktg., 1985-87, pres., 1987-88, vice chmn., 1988-90, also bd. dirs.; co-owner Enerco Oil and Gas Corp., Charleston, 1990—. Served with U.S. Army, 1945-46, PTO. Mem. IEEE (chmn. W.Va. sect. 1972). Clubs: Kanawha Country. Lodges: Rotary. Republican. Episcopalian. Avocations: golf, hiking. Home: 5120 Kanawha Ave SE Charleston WV 25304-2114 Office: Enerco Oil and Gas Corp PO Box 4296 Charleston WV 25364-4296

BENNETT, ROBERT THOMAS, lawyer, accountant; b. Columbus, Ohio, Feb. 8, 1939; s. Francis Edmund and Mary Catherine (Weiland) B.; B.S., Ohio State U., 1960; J.D., Cleve. Marshall Law Sch., 1967; m. Ruth Ann Dooley, May 30, 1959; children— Robert Thomas, Rose Marie. Admitted to Ohio bar, 1967; C.P.A., Ernst and Ernst, Cleve., 1960-63; with tax assessing dept. Cuyahoga County (Ohio) Auditor's Office, Cleve., 1963-70; mem. firm Bartunek, Bennett, Garofoli and Hill, Cleve., 1975-79; mem. firm Bennett & Klonowski, Cleve., 1979-83; mem. firm Bennett & Harbarger, Cleve., 1983-88. Exec. vice chmn. Cuyahoga County Rep. Orgn., 1974-88; state chmn. Ohio Rep. Orgn., 1988—; mem. Rep. Nat. Com., 1988—; bd. dirs. Univ. Hosp. of Cleve. and S.W. Gen. Health Ctr. Republican. Roman Catholic. Mem. Citizens League Club, Capitol Hill Club (Washington). Contbr. articles to profl. pubs. Home: 4800 Valley Pky Cleveland OH 44126-2847 Office: Ohio Rep Party 211 S 5th St Columbus OH 43215-5203*

BENNETT, ROBERT WILLIAM, law educator; b. Chgo., Mar. 30, 1941; s. Lewis and Henrietta (Schneider) Bennett; m. Harriet Trop, Aug. 19, 1979. BA, Harvard U., 1962, LLB, 1965. Bar: Ill. 1966. Legal asst. FCC commr. Nicholas Johnson, 1966-67; atty. Chgo. Legal Aid Bur., 1967-68; asso. firm Mayer, Brown & Platt, Chgo., 1968-69; faculty Northwestern U. Sch. Law, Chgo., 1969—, prof. law, 1974—, dean, 1985-95, Nathaniel L. Nathanson prof., 2002—. Author (with LaFrance, Schroeder and Boyd): (book) Handbook on Law of the Poor, 1973; author: Talking it Through: Puzzles of American Democracy, 2003. Knox Meml. fellow, London Sch. Econs., 1965-66. Fellow: Am. Bar Found. (pres., bd. dirs.); mem.: ABA, Am. Law Inst., Chgo. Coun. Lawyers (pres. 1971—72). Home: 2130 N Racine Ave Chicago IL 60614-4002 Office: Northwestern U Sch Law 357 E Chicago Ave Chicago IL 60611-3059

BENNETT, RONALD THOMAS, photojournalist, government official; b. Portland, Oreg., Nov. 6, 1944; s. E.E. Al and Donna Mae Bennett; 2 children. Student, Portland State U., 1964-67; student in photojournalism, U. Wash., 1965; student pre-law and bus. mgmt, Multnomah Coll., Portland, 1963—64; BA. Lab. technician, photographer Sta. KATU-TV, Portland, 1963-65; staff photographer Oreg. Jour., Portland, 1965-68, UPI Newspictures, L.A., 1968-70; staff photojournalist UPI at White House, 1970-88; sr. photo editor The San Diego Union, 1988-89; owner, CEO Capital TV, La Jolla, Calif., 1989-97; graphic artist, illustrator, 1997—. Internat. launch svcs. mission integrator, 1997-99; instr. photojournalism Portland State U., 1967; mem. standing com. U.S. Senate Press Photographers Gallery, 1980-89, sec.-treas.; CEO, Ronald T. Bennett Photography Frameable Original Photos & Note Cards, 1995—; dir. photography HUD, Washington, 1999—. Photographer: Assassination, 1968; one-man show Lake Oswego, Oreg., 1979; group exhbns. Libr. of Congress, 1971-89; exhibited in juried art shows in Calif. and Ariz., show photography, Offtrack Gall. Mem. coun. Town of La Jolla, Calif., Assic, Vol. Buyers, chmn. Brown Goods. Recipient 1st prize World Press Photo Assn., 1969, Calif. Press Photographers, 1968, 69, Gold Seal competition, 1968, 69; nominated for Pulitzer prize, 1968, 76, 77, 78, first prize, Internatl. Exhibition of Photography, 1996-99. Mem. White House News Photographers (bd. dirs. photo exhbn. com. 1974-78, 1st prize 1976, 77, 78, 80, 84, 86, 87), Nat. Headliner Club (1st prize 1969, 78), Nat. Press Photographers Assn. (1st prize 1972), San Diego Art Guild and Colo. Art Assn., Calif. Press Photographers Assn., Rotary (staff photographer La Jolla chpt., Achievement award Am. Project 1992, 93), German Shepherd Dog Club.

BENNETT, RONDI KIM ALBRECHT, financial services executive; b. Holloman AFB, N.Mex., July 9, 1971; d. Ronald Lewis and MiKyong (Kim) A. BS, U. Maine, 1993. Adminstrv. asst. A.G. Edwards, Bangor, Maine, 1992-93; mktg. rep. Fidelity Investments Instl. Svcs., Boston, 1993-94; nat. sales rep. Boston Capital, 1994-95; fin. svcs. exec. Commonwealth Fin. Network, Bangor, 1995—. Bd. dirs. YWCA, Bangor, pub. rels. com., fin. com., 1999—, ann. fund com., 2000—. Fellow Internat. Assn. Fin. Planning, Ea. Maine Assn. Life Underwriters; mem. Alpha Phi (treas. 1996—, fin. advisor 1995—). Avocations: hiking, skiing, reading, biking. Office: Commonwealth Fin Network 23 Water St Key Plaza Bangor ME 04401

BENNETT, SAUL, public relations agency executive; b. N.Y.C., Oct. 21, 1936; s. Philip and Ruth (Weinstein) Ostrove; m. Joan Marian Abrahams, Aug. 15, 1965; children: Sara (dec.), Charles, Elizabeth. BS in Journalism, Ohio U., Athens, 1957. Engaged in pub. rels., 1963—; from acct. supr. to v.p. Rowland Co., N.Y.C., 1965—74; from v.p. to sr. v.p. Robert Marston and Assocs., N.Y.C., 1974—78, exec. v.p., 1978—86, ptnr., 1979—, sr. exec. v.p., 1986—; pres. Robert Marston Mktg. Communications Inc., 1996—. Cons. in field. Author: (poems) New Fields and Other Stones, Jesus Matinees and Other Poems, 1998, Harpo Marx at Prayer, 2000. With USAR, 1958-59, 61-62. Mem. Pen Am. Ctr. E-mail: saulben@aol.com.

BENNETT, SCOTT BOYCE, retired librarian; b. Kansas City, Kans., July 22, 1939; s. Preston Theodore Bennett and Viola Louise (Scott) Mayberry; m. Carol Jean Glass, June 20, 1960; children: Beth Louise, Theodore David, Myron Richard, Kristellen Anne. AB magna cum laude, Oberlin Coll., 1960; MA in English, Ind. U., 1966, PhD in English, 1967; MS in Libr. Sci., U. Ill., 1976. Woodrow Wilson teaching intern St. Paul's Coll., Lawrenceville, Va., 1964-65; asst. prof. English U. Ill., Urbana-Champaign, 1967-74, from instr. to asst. prof. to assoc. prof. libr. adminstrn., 1974-81; asst. libr. collection mgmt. Northwestern U., Evanston, Ill., 1981-89; dir. Milton S. Eisenhower Libr. Johns Hopkins U., Balt., 1989-94; univ. libr. Yale U., New Haven, 1994-2001; project worker Coun. Ind. Colls. and Coun. on Libr. and Info. Resources, 2001—. Contbr. articles to profl. jours. Adv. panel library and archival preservation Ill. State Libr., adv. bd. Ill. State Archives; rev. panelist NEH; chair project Rsch. Librs. Group; prin. state-wide preservation planning Md. Woodrow Wilson Nat. fellow 1960-61, Ind. U. Dissertation Yr. fellow, Haskell fellow, 1966-67, U. Ill. Faculty fellow, 1969, Hon. Vis. Rsch. fellow Victorian Studies Ctr. U. Leicester, Eng., 1979, Am. Coun. Learned Socs. fellow, 1978-79. Mem. AAUP (pres., sec. Urbana-Champaign chpt. 1975-78, various other offices), Rsch. Soc. Victorian Periodicals (exec. bd. 1971-73, pres. 1977-82). Address: 711 S Race Urbana IL 61801-4132

BENNETT, SCOTT LAWRENCE, lawyer; b. N.Y.C., July 8, 1949; s. Allen J. and Rhoda Bennett. BA with high distinction, U. Mich., 1971; JD, Cornell U., 1974. Bar: NY 1975, U.S. Ct. Appeals (2d cir.) 1975, U.S. Dist. Ct. (so. and ea. dists.) N.Y. 1975, U.S. Supreme Ct. 1976. Assoc. Donovan, Leisure, Newton & Irvine, N.Y.C., 1974—79; sr. v.p., assoc. gen. counsel, sec. The McGraw-Hill Cos., Inc., N.Y.C., 1979—. Mem.: ABA, Assn. Am. Pubs. (lawyers com.), Assn. Bar City N.Y., N.Y. State Bar Assn., Phi Beta Kappa. Office: The McGraw Hill Co Inc Fl 48 1221 Avenue Of Americas New York NY 10020-1095 E-mail: Scott_Bennett@Mcgraw-Hill.com.

BENNETT, SONJA QUINN, administrative assistant; b. Dallas, Sept. 27, 1942; d. Cabe Terrell and Iva Pearle (McAuley) Quinn; m. Thomas Rae Bennett, May 27, 1961 (div. Dec. 1980); children: Richard James, Gary Don, Regina Anne. Student, U. Ark., 1983—. Tchr. Springdale (Ark.) Schs., 1975-80; adminstrv. asst. U. Ark., Fayetteville, 1980—; attendance office Springdale Pub. Schs., Ark., 2001—. Mem. exec. bd. U. Ark., 1998—. Mem. exec. bd. West Ark Area coun. Boy Scouts Am., Ft. Smith, 1972-90; EYC youth min. St. Thomas Episcopal Ch., Springdale, 1975-89; house mother internat. students Spring Internat., 1993—. Recipient Silver Beaver award Boy Scouts Am., 1976. Mem. Nat. Thespian Soc., Order Eastern Star, Elks. Republican. Home: 2060 N Juneway Ter Fayetteville AR 72703-2737 E-mail: sbennett@uark.edu.

BENNETT, STEPHEN M. computer company executive; b. Madison, Wis., Mar. 8, 1954; BA in Fin. and Real Estate, U. Wis., 1976. Various mgmt. positions GE Appliances, GE Med. and GE Supply; v.p. of Ams. GE Elec. Distbn. and Control; pres., CEO Vendor Fin. Svcs., GE Capital e-Business; exec. v.p., CEO GE Capital subsidiary of GE Corp.; CEO, pres. Intuit, 2000—. Office: Intuit Inc 2535 Garcia Ave Mountain View CA 94043-1111

BENNETT, STEVEN ALAN, lawyer; b. Rock Island, Ill., Jan. 15, 1953; s. Ralph O. and Anne E. B.; m. Jeanne Aring; children: Preston, Spencer, Hunter, Whitney. BA in Art History, U. Notre Dame, 1975; JD, U. Kans., 1982. Bar: Tex. 1983, Ohio 1995, U.S. Dist. Ct. (no. dist.) Tex. 1983, U.S. Ct. Appeals (5th cir.) 1983, U.S. Supreme Ct. 1995. Atty. Freytag, Marshall et al, Dallas, 1982-84, Baker, Mills & Glast, Dallas, 1984-87; ptnr. Shank, Irwin, Conant et al, Dallas, 1987-89; gen. counsel Bank One, Tex., N.A., Dallas, 1989-94; sr. v.p., gen. counsel, sec. Banc One Corp., Columbus, Ohio, 1994-99; exec. v.p., chief legal officer, sec. Cardinal Health, Inc., Dublin, Ohio, 1999-2001; pvt. practice Columbus, 2001—. City councilman, Mesquite, Tex., 1984-86, mayor pro tem, 1995; trustee Meadowview Sch., Mesquite, 1985-92; chair fin. com. St. Brendan Ch., Hilliard, Ohio, 1998—; pres., bd. dirs. Dallas Dem. Forum, 1993-94; bd. dirs. Ohio Hunger Task Force, Columbus; trustee Woodrow Wilson Internat. Ctr. for Scholars, Washington, 1996—, vice-chmn., 1999—; bd. dirs. Capital U. Law Sch., Columbus, Ctr. for Thomas More Studies, Dallas. Fellow Am. Bar Found., Ohio State Bar Found.; mem. ABA, Dallas Bar Assn., Ohio State Bar Assn., Columbus Bar Assn., St. Thomas More Soc. (Dallas bd. dirs. 1990-94), Am. Corp. Counsel Assn. (sec. 1999-2000, bd. dirs. 1996-2002, chair policy com. 1997-99), Phi Beta Kappa. Avocation: landscape photography. E-mail: sbennett@columbus.rr.com.

BENNETT, THOMAS, orchestra executive; Exec. dir. S.D. Symphony Orch., Sioux Falls, 1996—. Office: SD Symphony Orch Ste 112 300 N Dakota Ave Sioux Falls SD 57104

BENNETT, THOMAS B. federal judge; b. Phila., Jan. 6, 1949; BS, W.Va. U., 1970, MA, 1973, JD, 1976. Bar: W. Va., 1976, Tex., 1979. Instr. econs. W.Va. U., 1971-76; law clk. hon. John R. Brown U.S. Ct. Appeals 5th Cir., 1976-77; assoc. Bowles, Rice, McDavid, Graff & Love, 1977-79, ptnr., 1980-95; judge US Bankruptcy Ct. for Northern Dist. of Alabama, Birmingham, 1995—. Office: 1800 5th Ave N Rm 128 Birmingham AL 35203-2111 Fax: 205-714-3882.

BENNETT, THOMAS LEROY, JR., clinical neuropsychology educator; b. Norwalk, Conn., Sept. 25, 1942; s. Thomas LeRoy and Gertrude Upson (Richardson) B.; m. Jacqueline Beekman, Aug. 5, 1972; children: Dean, Shannon, Brian, Laurie. BA, U. N. Mex., 1964, MS, 1966, PhD, 1968. Diplomate Am. Bd. Profl. Neuropsychology (examiner, treas. 1993-96, 2001--, pres.-elect 1995-97, pres. 1997-99), Am. Bd. Forensic Examiners, Am. Bd. Profl. Disability Cons., Am. Bd. Profl. Psychology. Asst. prof. Calif. State U., Sacramento, 1968-70; assoc. prof., then prof. psychology and physiology Colo. State U., Ft. Collins, 1970-98, coord. exptl. psychology sect., 1978-81, 92-95, prof. emeritus, 1998—; pvt. practice neuropsychology Ft. Collins, 1981—. Mem. allied health staff Poudre Valley Hosp., Ft. Collins; clin. dir. Ctr. for Neurorehab. Svcs., Ft. Collins. Author: Brain and Behavior, 1977, The Sensory World, 1978, The Psychology of Learning and Memory, 1979, Exploring the Sensory World, 1979, Introduction to Physiological Psychology, 1982, The Neuropsychology of Epilepsy, 1992, Brainwave-R: Cognitive Strategies for Brain Injury Rehabilitation, 1997, Mild Traumatic Brain Injury, 1999, Psychology Video Teaching Modules: The Brain, 2d edit., 1997, Psychology Video Teaching Modules: The Mind, 2000; also articles and book chpts.; assoc. editor Rehab. Psychology, Archives of Clinical Neuropsychology; mem. editl. bd. Cognitive Rehab., Archives Clin. Neuropsychology, Jour. Head Injury, Bull. of Nat. Acad. Neuropsychology, Neuropsychology Rev., others. Elder Timnath Presbyterian Ch. Named Outstanding Grad. Educator for Coll. Natural Scis., 1998. Fellow APA, Nat. Acad. Neuropsychology (editl. bd. Bull., bd. dirs. 1993-95, conv. chmn. 1993, 94), Am. Psychol. Soc., Am. Coll. Profl. Neuropsychology (pres. 1997-99); mem. Am. Coll. Forensic Examiners, Psychonomic Soc., Rocky Mountain Psychol. Assn., Soc. for Cognitive Rehab., Nat. Head Injury Found. (provider's coun.), Colo. Head Injury Found. (provder's coun.), Internat. Neuropsychol. Soc., Colo. Neuropsychol. Soc., Sigma Xi (named Colo. State U. Honored Scientist 1996). Home: 213 Camino Real Fort Collins CO 80524-8907 Office: Colo State U Dept Psychology Fort Collins CO 80523-0001 E-mail: brain1@frii.com., benny@frii.com. *Always look for something good in everyone you meet.*

BENNETT, TONY (ANTHONY DOMINICK BENEDETTO), entertainer; b. Astoria, N.Y., Aug. 3, 1926; s. John and Anna (Suraci) Benedetto; m. Patricia Beech, Feb. 12, 1952 (div. 1971); children: D'Andrea, Daegal; m. Sandra Grant, Dec. 29, 1971 (div. 1984); children: Joanna, Antonia. Ed., Am. Theatre Wing, N.Y.C.; MusD, U. Berkeley. Ofcl. artist Ky. Derby, 2001. Classic pop vocalist, entertainer (frequent appearances on TV, in concert); singer: (albums) Treasure Chest of Songs, 1955, Tony, 1957, Count Basie Swings, Tony Bennett Sings, 1958, Blue Velvet, 1959, To My Wonderful One, 1960, Bennett and Basie Strike Up the Band, 1961, I Left My Heart in San Francisco, 1963 (Grammy award album of the year, 1962), I Wanna Be Around, 1963, Love Story, 1971, Summer of '42, 1972, Sunrise, Sunset, 1973, 16 Most Requested Songs, 1986, The Art of Excellence, 1986, Bennett/Berlin, 1987, The Movie Song Album, 1989, Astoria, 1990, Forty Years: The Artistry of Tony Bennett, 1991, Perfectly Frank, 1992 (Grammy award best traditional vocal performance, 1992), Steppin' Out, 1993 (Grammy award, Best Traditional Pop Vocal, 1993), The Essence of Tony Bennett, 1993, In Person! With Count Basie and His Orchestra, 1994, MTV Unplugged, 1994 (Grammy award Album of the Year, Best Traditional Pop Vocal), Here's to the Ladies, 1995, Tony Bennett on Holiday, 1997, Tribute to Billie Holiday, Bennett Sings Ellington-Hot and Cool, 1999, The Ultimate Tony, 2000, Playin' With My Friends: Bennett Sings The Blues, 2001 (Grammy award best traditional pop vocal album, 2003), The Essential Tony Bennett, 2002, A Wonderful World, 2002; owner, rec. artist Improv Records; exhibitions include Butler Inst. of Am. Art, Youngstown, Ohio, 1994, Nat. Arts Club, N.Y.C.; appeared in : The Scout, 1994; appeared in (TV films) Men, Movies & Carol, 1994, The Scout, 1994, Sinatra: 80 Years My Way, 1995, (TV series) The Simpsons, 1989, Muppets Tonight, 1996, (TV spl.) Tony Bennett on Holiday: A Tribute to Billy Holiday, 1997, Analyze This, 1999, TV guest appearances The Andy Williams Show, 1966, The Jackie Gleason Show, 1969, Space Ghost Coast to Coast, 1994, Suddenly Susan, 1997; author: The Good Life: The Autobiography of Tony Bennett. Served with inf. AUS, World War II. Named to Star on Hollywood Walk of Fame; recipient Gold records for recs., Because of You, I Left My Heart in San Francisco, Best Male Vocalist award, Cash Box mag., 1951, Grammy lifetime achievement award, Salute to Greatness award Martin Luther King Ctr., Atlanta. Office: c/o Columbia Records 550 Madison Ave New York NY 10022*

BENNETT, VELMA JOYCE (JOYCE WILLIAMS), writer, poet; b. Chgo., Mar. 25, 1941; d. Floyd Theodore and Willie Belle (Williams) B. BA in Secondary Edn., Western Mich. U., 1964; MEd, Loyola U., 1975. Cert. secondary and elem. edn., coll. counseling. Tchr. English and social studies Wendell Phillips H.S., Chgo., 1964-65; editor Follett Pub. Co., Chgo., 1965-66; tchr. Bryant Elem., Chgo., 1966-72; H.S. tchr. Outward Bound, Grand Rapids, Mich., 1979-81; pvt. practice writer, poet Allegan, Mich., 1990—. Author: Everybody's Poetry, 1994. Past pres. NAACP, Allegan. Avocations: reading, listening to music, nature watching, people watching, spirits.

BENNETT, WILLIAM LEO, JR., management consultant; b. Bklyn., Nov. 7, 1921; s. William L. and Anna Christine (Lawless) B.; m. Mary Louise Short, Aug. 18, 1948 (div. 1971); children: Mary Christine Bennett Cooke, Elizabeth Nancy Bennett Payne (dec.), Susan Laura Bennett Smith, William Leo III; m. Mary-Louise Aspinwall, Nov. 23, 1972; children: Lucy Knapp Richardson, Molly Knapp Gloss, John F. Knapp, Jr. BS in Naval Sci., U.S. Navl Acad., 1943; postgrad., Test Pilot Sch., 1950, Armed Forces Staff Coll., 1954. Commd. ensign USN, 1943, advanced through grades to capt., ret., 1972; project mgr. ENSCO, Inc., Springfield, Va., 1972-76; dir. quality div. Nat. R.R. Passenger Corp., Washington, 1976-81; v.p. ops. Intertek Svcs. Corp., Fairfax, Va., 1981-88; pvt. practice cons. Falls Church, Va., 1988-94. Mem. Fairfax County Rep. Com., 1981-84. Decorated Legion of Merit. Mem. Early and Pioneer Naval Aviators Assn., Am. Soc. Quality Control, Am. Helicopter Soc., The Retired Officers Assn., U.S. Naval Acad. Alumni Assn., U.S. Naval Acad. Athletic Assn., USS Yorktown Assn. (v.p., bd. dirs.), Army-Navy Country Club., VFW, Am. Legion, Disabled Am. Vets. Episcopalian. Avocation: golf. Home: 46910 Grissom St Sterling VA 20165-3576

BENNETT, WILLIAM MICHAEL, internist, nephrologist, educator; b. Chgo., May 6, 1938; s. Harry H. and Helen A. (Kaplan) B.; m. Sandra S. Silen, June 12, 1977; four children. Student, U. Mich., 1956-59; BS, Northwestern U., 1960, MD, 1963. Diplomate Am. Bd. Internal Medicine, Am. Bd. Nephrology, Am. Bd. Clin. Pharmacology. Intern U. Oreg., 1963-64; resident Northwestern U., 1964-66; practice medicine specializing in internal medicine Portland, Oreg. and; Boston; mem. staff Mass. Gen. Hosp., 1969-70; asst. prof. medicine U. Oreg. Health Scis. Center, 1970-74, asso. prof., 1974-78, prof. medicine and pharmacology, 1978-2000, ret., 2000. Author: Pharmacology and Management of Hypertension, 1994, Manual of Nephrology, 1990, Drug Therapy in Renal Failure, 1994; contbr. articles to med. jours. Served with USAF, 1967-69. Fellow ACP; mem. Am. Soc. Nephrology (pres. 1998-99), Transplantation Soc., Internat. Soc. Nephrology, Am. Soc. Pharmacology and Exptl. Therapeutics. Office: Legacy Good Samaritan Hosp NSC 430 1015 NW 22d St U Portland OR 97210 also: NW Renal Clinic 1130 NW 22d St Ste 640 Portland OR 97210 E-mail: bennettw@lhs.org.

BENNETT, WILLIAM PERRY, lawyer; b. Inglewood, Calif., Aug. 28, 1938; s. George William and Lenora (Perry) B.; m. Linda L. Schneider, Aug. 19, 1961; children: Greg, Mark, Carin; m. Hilda Rodriguez, Dec. 29, 2000. BA, Calif. State U., Long Beach; MA in Specialized Ministry, Grace Theol. Sem.; JD, U. So. Calif.; DMin, Reformed Theol. Sem. Bar: Calif. 1965, U.S. Ct. Appeals (9th cir.) 1965, U.S. Supreme Ct. 1993; lic. real estate broker; cert. real estate investment specialist, real estate mgmt. specialist, family law specialist; lifetime tchg. credential specialized subject; ordained to ministry Reformed Ch. Am. Ptnr. Powars, Tretheway & Bennett Law Corp., 1965-78; sr. ptnr. William P. Bennett Law Corp., 1978-01; sr. real estate atty. Wise, Wiezorek, Timmons & Wise, 1991-94; owner, broker Century 21 Pacific Coast Realty, 1979-88, Pacific Coast Properties, Long Beach, 1988—; assoc. prof. bus. and real estate law Calif. State U., Long Beach, 1965-86; exec. dir. Grandparents Rights Ctr., 1998—2001. Gen. counsel Campus Crusade for Christ, 1991-93, Crystal Cathedral Ministries, 1995—; alumni pres., adv. bd. Calif. State U., Long Beach; arbitrator Am. Arbitration Assn. Panel, 1965—, L.A. County Superior Ct. Arbitrator/Pro Tem Judge, Christian Conciliation Svc., L.A. and Orange Counties; bus. adv. bd. Long Beach City Coll.; spl. counsel Chs. Uniting in Global Mission, Calvary Chapel; adj. prof. law Simon Green Leaf/Trinity U. Bd. dirs., legal advisor Long Beach Area March of Dimes, 1973-90; exec. dir. Legal Ministry Campus Crusade for Christ, dir. property mgmt. Campus Crusade, exec. mgmt. team Arrowhead Springs Conf Ctr., 1991-94; dir. Grandparents Rights Ctr.; adminstr. Reformed Ch. in Am., Calif., 1999-2000. Maj. USAR. Mem. Long Beach Bar Assn. (bd. govs. 1970-76), Long Beach Area C. of C. (bd. dirs. 1985-86, Bus. Person of Yr. award 1987), Seal Beach C. of C. (pres. 1985-86, 89-90), Kiwanis Internat. (pres., lt. gov., Kiwanian of Yr.), Century 21 Orange County Brokers Coun. (pres. 1984), So. Calif. Investment Soc. (pres. 1988). Republican. Avocations: academics, speaking, religion, hiking. Home and Office: 425 A N Bloomberry Orange CA 92869

BENNETT, WILLIAM RALPH, JR., physicist, educator; b. Jersey City, Jan. 30, 1930; s. William Ralph and Viola (Schreiber) B.; m. Frances Commins, Dec. 11, 1952; children: Jean, William Robert, Nancy. AB, Princeton U., 1951; MA, PhD, Columbia U., 1957; MA (hon.), Yale U., 1965; D.Sc. (hon.), U. New Haven, 1975. Rsch. asst. physics Columbia Radiation Lab., 1952-54; mem. Pupin Cyclotron Group, 1954-57; mem. faculty Yale U., New Haven, 1957-59, 62—, prof. physics and applied sci., 1965-72, Charles Baldwin Sawyer prof. engring. and applied sci., prof. physics, 1972-98, prof. emeritus, 1998—, fellow Berkeley Coll., 1963-81, master Silliman Coll., 1981-87, life fellow Silliman Coll., 1981—. Tech. staff Bell Telephone Labs., Murray Hill, NJ, 1959—62; cons. Tech. Rsch. Group, Melville, NY, 1962—67, Inst. Def. Analysis, Washington, 1963—70; vis. scientist Am. Inst. Physics Vis. Scientist Program, 1963—64; vis. prof. Brandels Summer Inst. Theoretical Physics, 1969; cons. mem. bd. dirs. Laser Scis. Corp., Bethel, Conn., 1968—71; mem. adv. panels atomic physics and astrophysics Nat. Bur. Stds., 1964—69; cons. CBS Labs., Stamford, Conn., 1967—68, AVCO Corp., 1978—81, Reeves Sci. Co., New Haven, 1989—91, Oak Ridge Assn. Univs., Washington, 1991—92, MCG Internat., New Haven, 1992—93, Kahn Electronics, NY, 1998—2000, Premier Heart, 1999, U. Cin., 2000; mem. lab. adv. bd. for rsch. Naval Rsch. Adv. Com., 1968—78; guest Soviet Acad. Scis., 1967, 69, 79; rschr. gas lasers and atomic physics, gravitational physics, applications of computers to med. diagnostics. Author: Introduction to Computer Applications, 1976, Scientific and Engineering Problem Solving With the Computer, 1976, The Physics of Gas Lasers, 1977, Atomic Gas Laser Transition Data: A Critical Evaluation, 1979, Health and Low Frequency Electromagnetic Fields, 1994; editl. adv. bd. Jour. Quantum Electronics, 1965-69; guest editor Applied Optics, 1965. Recipient Western Electric Fund award for outstanding tchg. Am. Assn. Engring. Educators, 1977, Outstanding Patent award R & D Coun. N.J., 1977, Eli Whitney Patent award Conn. Patent Lawyers Assn., 1994, DeVane medal Phi Beta Kappa, 2000; fellow Alfred P. Sloan Found., 1967, Guggenheim Found., 1967, John Fenders fellow, 1987. Fellow IEEE (life, Morris Liebmann award 1965), Am. Phys. Soc., Optical Soc. Am.; mem. Sigma Xi.

BENNETT-KASTOR, TINA LYNNE, linguist, educator; b. La Mesa, Calif., Feb. 8, 1954; d. Clayton Leon and Patricia Jean (Billups) Bennett; m. Frank Sullivan Kastor, Oct. 28, 1979; children: Kristina, Patrick, Liam, Mary Elisabeth, Caroline. BFA, Calif. Inst. Arts, 1973; AM, U. So. Calif., 1976, PhD, 1978. Rsch. assoc. John Tracy Clinic, L.A., 1977; asst. prof. Wichita State U., 1978-87, assoc. prof., 1987-97, prof., 1998—. Vis. scholar Linguistics Inst. Ireland, Dublin, 1995; rsch. cons. Rehab. Ctr., UCLA, 1976; humanities cons. Children's Audio Svcs., Columbia, S.C., 1979-86. Editor: Discourse Across Time and Space, 1977; author: Analyzing Children's Language, 1988; contbr. chpt. to Repetition in Discourse, 1995; contbr. articles to mags. and profl. jours., including Jour. Child Lang., First Lang., Am. Speech, Functions of Lang., Bilingualism: Lang. & Cognition, Irish Life, Vocabula Review; editl. cons. (jour.) Lang., Speech, and Hearing Svcs. in the Schs., 1998—2001. Pres. Little Red Wagon Child Care, Inc., Wichita, 1985; v.p. Celtic Cir./Irish-Am. Cultural Inst., Wichita, 1994-2001. Hall fellow Hallmark Found., U. Kans., 1987; rsch. grantee Wichita State U., 1979, 81, 88, 99. Mem. Am. Speech, Lang., and Hearing Assn., Linguistic Soc. Am., N.Y. Acad. Sci., Irish-Am. Cultural Inst., Irish-Am. Partnership. Democrat. Roman Catholic. Avocations: folk music, photography. Home: 115 N Fountain St Wichita KS 67208-3831 Office: Wichita State U 1845 Fairmount St # 14 Wichita KS 67260-0014

BENNEY, DOUGLAS MABLEY, direct marketing executive, consultant; b. Cold Spring Harbor, N.Y., Aug. 7, 1922; s. William Mabley and Wilhelmina (Walters) B.; m. Eugenia Sammis, Sept. 30, 1944 (div. Jan. 1980); children: William Douglas, Barbara Gates, Robert Scott; m. Barbara Mueller, July 8, 1983; stepchildren: Gregory Carmichael, Andrew Carmichael. Navy air cadet, U. N.C.-Chapel Hill, 1943, Cornell U., 1943; student in engring., Purdue U., 1939-41; AB, Colgate U., 1946-49; postgrad., Columbia U., 1951-52. With Curtis Publs., Phila., 1950-63; editor, assoc. pub. Jack & Jill, 1960-63; mktg. mgr. edn. div. Doubleday & Co., N.Y.C., 1963-67; advt. and sales mgr. Hearst Book div., N.Y.C., 1967-68; v.p. creative svcs. Nat. Liberty Corp., Valley Forge, Pa., 1968-72; v.p. mktg. Gerber Life Ins. Co., N.Y.C., Pa., 1972-75; sr. mktg. officer Internat. Group Plans, Washington, Pa., 1975-78; v.p. mktg. Maxon Adminstrs., Inc., Irvington, N.Y., 1978-89; pres. A&B Advt., Inc., Springdale, Md., 1989—. Patentee newspaper inserts, self-mailers. Lt. (j.g.) AC, USN, 1943-46; PTO. Recipient award Artists Guild Delaware Valley, 1969, Direct Mail Mktg. Assn., 1965, Myasthenia Gravis Found., 1985, Profl. Ins. Mass Marketers Assn., 1992, 94, 96. Mem. Direct Mktg. Assn. Washington, Greater Washington Soc. Assn. Execs., Mt. Vernon Country Club (Alexandria, Va.). Avocations: woodworking, sailing, photography, scuba diving.

BENNING, JOSEPH RAYMOND, principal; b. Streator, Ill., May 23, 1956; s. Joseph Charles and Shirley Ann (Smith) B.; m. Katherine Marie Turner, Apr. 24, 1976; children: Jennifer Nichole, Joseph Donald. BA, Augustana Coll, 1978; MS in Edn., No. Ill. U., 1988. Cert. state supr., teaching, Ill. Tchr., coach Fulton (Ill.) High Sch., 1978-79; recreation dir. Fulton Recreation Corp., 1979; tchr., coach Streator (Ill.) High Sch., 1979-80, Woodland High Sch., Streator, 1980-83; program dir. Ill. State Bd. Edn., Ottawa, 1983-85; prin. St. Mary Grade Sch., Streator, 1985-89; assoc. supt. schs. Cath. Diocese Peoria, Ill., 1989-91, supt. schs., 1991-94; prin. St. Bede Acad., Peru, Ill., 1994-99, St. Columba Sch., Ottawa, Ill., 1999—. Pres. Streator Youth Football League, 1984-90; adv. bd. Streator High Sch., 1985-89; prins. adv. bd. Cath. Diocese Peoria, 1987-89. Recipient CJ McDonald award Streator Youth Football League, 1989. Mem. ASCD, Nat. Cath. Edn. Assn., Nat. Assn. Secondary Sch. Prin., Nat. Assn. Elem. Sch. Prin., Ill. Elem. Sch. Assn., Cath. Conf. Ill., KC. Roman Catholic. Avocations: sports, music. Office: St Columba Schd 1110 Lasalle Ottawa IL 61350 E-mail: benningjr@hotmail.com.

BENNING, MARY ETZOLD, interior designer; b. El Paso, Mar. 8, 1957; d. David Enberg and Mary (Francis) Etzold; m. George Henry Benning III, Nov. 2, 1985; children: Mary Francis, Lucy Alexander. AA, Stephens Coll., 1977, BFA, 1979. Lic. interior designer Tex. Designer Bus. Products & Svcs., Inc., El Paso, 1979-80; display designer Popular Dept. Store, El Paso, 1980-83; residential designer Reinharts Fine Furniture, El Paso, 1983-85; comml. designer FLooring Systems, Inc., El Paso, 1985-86, Charlotte's Comml. Interiors, El Paso, 1986-88; comml. interior designer N.Mex. State U., Las Cruces, 1988-94, Henry Benning Assocs., Inc., El Paso, 1994—. Cons. in field. Bd. dirs. Epilepsy El Paso, 1987-90. Mem.: AIA, Tex. Assn. Interior Designers, Am. Soc. Interior Designers, Pan Am. Soc. Am., El Paso Symphony Guild, Jr. League El Paso, Magna Carta Dames Am. (life), Colonial Dames Am. (life). Republican. Epsicopalian. Episcopalian. Avocations: reading, sewing, walking, gourmet cooking, travel. Office: 1205 Myrtle Ave El Paso TX 79901

BENNINGER, MICHAEL STEPHEN, otolaryngologist; BA, Harvard U., 1977; MD, Case Western Reserve U., 1983. Intern, resident Cleve. Clinic Found., 1983—88; chmn. Dept. Otolaryngology Henry Ford Hosp., Detroit, 1992—; Cummings Brush chmn. surg. edn. Henry Ford Health Sys., Detroit, 1998—2002; prof. of otolaryngology Case Western Reserve U., Cleve., 1998—. Chmn. bd. dirs. Sinus and Allergy Health Partnership, Washington. Author 3 books and a monograph; editor-in-chief: Otolaryngology-Head and Neck Surgery, 2000—02; contbr. over 80 articles to profl. jours. Fellow: Am. Laryngologic Soc., Am. Rhinologic Soc. (pres. 1997—98, Goldon Head Mirror award 2000); mem.: AMA (bd. dels. 1997—), Internat. Assn. of Phonosurgeons (bd. mem. 2000—02), Triologic Soc. (bd. dirs. 2001—), Am. Head and Neck Soc., Mich. State Med. Soc. (Pres.'s award 1998), Mich. Otolaryn. Soc. (pres. 1995), Am. Acad. of Otolaryngology-Head and Neck Surgery (bd. dirs. 1994—, vice-president 1997—2000, Honor award 2000). Office: Henry Ford Hospital 2799 West Grand Blvd Detroit MI 48202

BENNINGFIELD, CAROL ANN, lawyer; b. San Antonio, Dec. 8, 1952; d. Gordon Lane Benningfield and Ann Benningfield McCraw. BA in Polit. Sci., S.W. Tex. State U., 1975; JD, U. Tex., 1979. Bar: Tex. 1979, U.S. Dist. Ct. (so. dist.) Tex. 1995. Staff atty. Tex. Dept. Labor and Stds., Austin, 1979; staff counsel Tex. Chem. Coun., Austin, 1979-80; assoc. Wiley, Garwood, San Antonio, 1981-83; account exec. Dean-Witter Reynolds, San Antonio, 1983-89; pvt. practice, Rockport, Tex., 1990—. Gala com. San Antonio Stock Show and Rodeo, 1981-83; mem. Target 90 Goals for San Antonio, 1984-85; deacon First Presbyn. Ch., Rockport, 1992-95, choir, 1990-96; active Rockport Art Assn., 1990—; trustee Aransas County Ind. Sch. Dist., Rockport, 1993-96, sec., 1993-96. Fellow Tex. Bar Found. Tex.; mem. San Antonio Young Lawyers (membership chmn. 1982), Rockport Fulton C. of C. (dir. 1992-94, awards com. chmn., v.p. 1993), Rotary. Office: 614 E Market Street Rockport TX 78382 E-mail: ladylawyer@sbcglobal.net.

BENNINGTON, LESLIE ORVILLE, JR., insurance agent; b. Sedalia, Mo., Dec. 29, 1946; s. Leslie Orville Sr. and Eunice May Marguerite (Cole) B.; m. Susan Frances Grotha, June 1, 1968; children: Leslie O. III, Jeremy Lawrence. BSME, U. Mo., Rolla, 1968; postgrad., U. Tenn. Space Inst., 1969; ChFC, Am. Coll., 1988. CLU; chartered fin. cons.; registered profl. engr., Wyo. Design engr. Arnold Research Orgn., Tullahoma, Tenn., 1968-70; engr. Pacific Power & Light, Glenrock, Wyo., 1973-75; agt., asst. gen. agt. Am. Nat. Ins. Co., Casper, Wyo., 1975-85; gen. agt. Ins. Sales, Glenrock, 1985—. Pres. Ctrl. Wyo. Estate Planning Coun., Casper, 1985-86. Mem. Glenrock Vol. Fire Dept., 1973—, asst. chief, 1982, pres., 1993-97; pres., v.p. Converse County Recreation Bd., Douglas, Wyo., 1980-90; judge dist. h.s. speech contests, Glenrock; bd. dirs. Converse County Sch. Dist. 2, 1976; bd. dirs. Glenrock Cmty. Recreation Dist., 1990-97, pres., 1992-94; guide Helluva Hunt for physically disabled hunters, 1986—, bd. dirs., 1991—; bd. dirs. Nat. Bow Hunt, Glenrock, 1994-98; baseball coach Little League and Babe Ruth, 1983-93; trustee St. Louis Cath. Ch., 1999—. Mem. Nat. Assn. Ins. and Fin. Advisors (Nat. Quality award, Health Ins. Quality award, Nat. Sales Achievement award), Ctrl. Wyo. Assn. Ins. and Fin. Advisors (pres. 1978-80), Wyo. Assn. Ins. and Fin. Advisors (chmn. membership com. 1985-87, nat. com. 1982-87, v.p. 1986-87, bd. dirs. 1980-90, Ins. Agt. of Yr., 1980, pres. 1988-89), West Cen. Wyo. CLUs (pres. 1986-88), Million Dollar Round Table, Nat. Pony Express Assn. (pres. Ea. Wyo. div. 1985—, v.p. Wyo. divsn. 1989-97, pres. 1997—, exec. bd. dirs. 2001—), KC (grand knight, faithful navigator). Republican. Roman Catholic. Avocations: cattle, livestock. Home: 6 Shannon Dr Glenrock WY 82637 Office: PO Box 757 1260 E US Hwy # 20-26 Glenrock WY 82637-0757

BENNINK, JACK RICHARD, microbiologist, researcher; b. Corry, Pa., Feb. 18, 1953; s. Ivan Guy and Mary Lou (Hurlbert) B.; m. Cindi Sue Merkle, May 29, 1976; children: Nathanael Scott, Tara Susanne. BA, Asbury Coll., 1975; PhD, U. Pa., 1978. Staff mem. Basel (Switzerland) Inst. for Immunology, 1980-82; asst. prof., assoc. prof. Wister Inst., Phila., 1982-87; sr. investigator NIH, Bethesda, Md., 1987—. Contbr. articles to profl. jours. Recipient Pub. Health Svc. award, 1990, 94, 95, 96, 99, 2000. Mem. Am. Soc. Virology, Am. Assn. Immunologists. Office: NIH Rm 213 Bldg 4 Bethesda MD 20892-0440

BENNION, JOHN WARREN, urban education educator; b. Salt Lake City, Nov. 25; s. M. Lynn and Katherine Bennion; m. Sylvia Lustig; children: Philip, Stanford, David, Bryan, Grant, Andrew. BS in Philosophy, English, U. Utah, 1961, MA in Edn. Adminstrn., 1962; PhD in Edn. Adminstrn., Ohio State U., 1966. Tchr. Granite High Sch., Salt Lake City, 1961-63; asst. instr. Ohio State U., Columbus, 1963-64, adminstrv. asst., 1965-66; adminstrv. intern Parma (Ohio) Sch. Dist., 1964-65; asst. supt. Elgin (Ill.) Pub. Schs., 1966-68; asst. prof. edn. adminstrn. Ind. U., Bloomington, 1968-69; supt. Brighton Cen. Schs., Rochester, N.Y., 1969-79, Bloomington (Minn.) Pub. Schs., 1979-80, Provo (Utah) Sch. Dist., 1980-85, Salt Lake City Schs., 1985-94; prof. urban edn., dir. Utah Edn. Consortium U. Utah, Salt Lake City, 1994—. Dir. Utah Urban Sch. Alliance, Salt Lake City; ednl. cons. Comprehensive Sch. Reform, Salt Lake City. Mem. ASCD, Assn. Early Childhood Edn., Am. Assn. Sch. Adminstrs. (Nat. Superintendent of Yr. award 1992, Disting. Svc. award 2002), Phi Delta Kappa, Rotary. Home: 1837 Harvard Ave Salt Lake City UT 84108-1804 Office: Utah Urban Sch Alliance 1865 S Main St Ste 22 Salt Lake City UT 84115-2045

BENNION, SCOTT DESMOND, physician; b. Casper, Wyo., July 26, 1948; s. Desmond and Wanda Bennion; m. Mary Marie Blanton; children: Scott, Beau, Brandon. BS summa cum laude, U. Wyo., 1970, MS, 1972; MD, U. Utah, 1975. Diplomate Nat. Bd. Med. Examiners, Am. Bd. Internal Medicine, Am. Bd. Dermatology, Am. Bd. Dermatologic Immunology/Diagnostic and Lab. Immunology. Intern U. Rutgers Med. Sch., 1975-76, resident in internal medicine, 1976-78, chief resident dept. medicine, 1978; commd. 2d lt. U.S. Army, 1976, advanced through grades to col., 1991; resident in dermatology Fitzsimons Army Med. Sch., Denver, 1981-84, chief resident dermatology svc., 1984, chief dept. clin. investigations, 1994-96, chmn. lab. animal use and care com., 1994-96; asst. chief dermatology svc. 98th Gen. Hosp., Nuremburg, Germany, 1986, chief dept. health clinics, 1987-88; chief immunodermatology sect. dermatology svc. Fitzsimons Army MC, Aurora, Colo., 1989—96; command surgeon ARTASK, Kuwait, 1992; command surgeon joint task force Kuwait and Army Ctrl. Command-Forward, 1992; dermatology cons. to the Army Surgeon Gen., 1996-99; chief Troop Med. Clin. Fitzsimmons Army Garrison, 1996-99. Asst. clin. prof. dept. dermatology U. Colo. Health Sci. Ctr., 1992—99, assoc. prof. clin. dermatology, 1999—; assoc. prof. clin. medicine U. Wash. Med. Ctr. Contbr. chpts. to books: Military Dermatology, 1994, Secrets of Dermatology, 1996, 2d edit., 2000, Dubois Lupus, 1997, also articles to profl. publs. Pres. Nuremburg Elem. Sch. PTSA; asst. cubmaster, cubmaster, chmn. Volksmarch com. Boy Scouts Am., 1986; pres. Foxridge Improvement Assn., 1992—, pres., 1994-2001; bd. dirs. Wyo. Make a Wish Found., 2000—; mem. Alcova Lake Area Bd., 2001—; trustee Casper Coll., 2000—, sec. to bd., 2002—; trustee Anam Chara Hospice, Denver, 2001. Named to Order of Mil. Med. Merit, 1987; named Cubmaster of Yr. Bavaria dist. Boy Scouts Am., 1987; recipient Legion of Merit award, 1999. Fellow: ACP, Am. Acad. Dermatology (mem. govt. medicine task force 1996—2000, Colo. Dermatology Soc. rep. to adv. bd. 1997—); mem.: Dermatology Found. Leadership Soc. (chmn. Wyo.), Ctrl. Wyo. Skin Clinic, Wyo. Acad. Dermatology (sec. 1999—, rep. to AAD adv. bd.), Soc. for Investigative Dermatology, Assn. Mil. Dermatologists (sec.-treas. 1990—96, guest editor jour. 1991, pres. 1998—99, Residents award 1984), Assn. Mil. Surgeons, Phi Kappa Phi. Avocations: skiing, diving. Home: 1604 S Sycamore St Casper WY 82604 Office: 2241 Farnum St Ste 204 Casper WY 82609-4108

BENNIS, WARREN GAMELIEL, business administration educator, writer, consultant; b. N.Y.C., Mar. 8, 1925; s. Philip and Rachel (Landau) B.; m. Clurie Williams, Mar. 30, 1962 (div. 1983); children: Katharine, John Leslie, Will Martin; m. Mary Jane O'Donnell, Mar. 8, 1988 (div. 1991); m. Grace Gabe, Nov. 29, 1992. AB, Antioch Coll., 1951; hon. cert. econs., London Sch. Econs., 1952; PhD, MIT, 1955; LLD, Xavier U., Cin., 1972, George Washington U., 1977; LHD (hon.), Hebrew Union Coll., 1974, Kans. State U., 1979; DSc (hon.), U. Louisville, 1977, Pacific Grad. Sch. Psychology, 1987, Gov.'s State U., 1991; LHD (hon.), Doan Coll., 1993. Diplomate Am. Bd. Profl. Psychology. Asst. prof. psychology MIT, Cambridge, 1953-56, prof., 1959-67; asst. prof. psychology and bus. Boston U., 1956-59; prof. Sloan Sch. Mgmt., 1959-67; provost SUNY-Buffalo, 1967-68, v.p. acad. devel., 1968-71; pres. U. Cin., 1971-77; U.S. prof. corps. and soc. Centre d'Etudes Industrielles, Geneva, Switzerland, 1978-79; exec.-in-residence Pepperdine U., 1978-79; George Miller Disting. prof.-in-residence U. Ill., Champaign-Urbana, 1978; Disting. prof. Bus. Adminstrn. Sch. Bus., U. So. Calif., L.A., 1980-88; univ. prof., disting. prof. bus. adminstrn. U. So. Calif., L.A., 1988—. Vis. lectr. Harvard U., 1958-59, Indian Mgmt. Inst., Calcutta; vis. prof. U. Lausanne (Switzerland), 1961-62, INSEAD, France, 1983; bd. dirs. The Foothill Group. Author: Planning of Change, 4th edit., 1985, Interpersonal Dynamics, 1963, 3d and 4th edits., 1975, Personal and Organizational Change, 1965, Changing Organizations, 1966, repub. in paperback as Beyond Bureaucracy, 1974, The Temporary Society, 1968, Organization Development, 1969, American Bureaucracy, 1970, Management of Change and Conflict, 1972, The Leaning Ivory Tower, 1973, The Unconscious Conspiracy: Why Leaders Can't Lead, 1976, Essays in Interpersonal Dynamics, 1979; (with B. Nanus): Leaders, 1985, On Becoming a Leader, 1989, (with I. Mitroff) The Unreality Industry, 1989, Why Leaders Can't Lead, 1989, Leaders on Leadership, 1992, An Invented Life: Reflections on Leadership and Change, 1993, Beyond Bureaucracy, 1993, (with J. Goldsmith) Learning to Lead, 1994, (with M. Mische) Reinventing the 21st Century, 1994, Beyond Leadership, 1994, Herding Cats: Bennis on Leadership, 1996, Organizing Genius, 1997, The Temporary Society, 1998, Co-Leaders, 1999, Old Dogs, New Tricks, 1999, (with G. Heil and D. Stephens) Douglas McGregor Re-Visited, 2000; co-leaders, 1999, Managing the Dream, 2000; co-author: Geeks & Geekers, 2002, On Becoming a Leader, 2003; cons. editor Calif. Mgmt. Rev., Mgmt. Series Jossey-Bass Pubs. Mem. Pres.' White House Task Force on Sci. Policy, 1960-70; mem. FAA study task force U.S. Dept. Transp., 1975; mem. adv. com. N.Y. State Joint Legis. Com. Higher Edn., 1970-71; mem. Ohio Gov.'s Bus. and Employment Coun., 1972-74; mem. panel on alt. approaches to grad. edn. Coun. Grad. Schs. and Grad. Record-Exam Bd., 1971-73; chmn. Nat. Adv. Commn. on Higher Edn. for Police Officers, 1976-78; adv. bd. NIH, 1978-84; trustee Colo. Rocky Mountains Sch., 1978-82; bd. dirs. Am. Leadership Forum, 1984-89; mem. vis. com. for Humanities MIT, 1975-81; trustee Antioch Coll., Salk Inst. Capt. AUS, World War II. Decorated Bronze Star, Purple Heart; recipient Dow Jones award, 1987, McKinsey Fedn. award, 1967, 68. Mem. Am. Acad. Arts and Scis. (co-chmn. policy coun. 1969-71), Am. Mgmt. Assn. (dir. 1974-77), U.S. C. of C. (adv. group scholars). Office: U So Calif Sch Bus University Park Los Angeles CA 90089-0001

BENNISON, ALLAN PARNELL, geological consultant; b. Stockton, Calif., Mar. 8, 1918; s. Ellis Norman Lambly and Cora Mae (Parnell) B.; m. DeLeo Smith, Sept. 4, 1941; children: Victor, Christina, Mary. BA, U. Calif., Berkeley, 1940. Cert. petroleum geologist, cert. profl. geologist. Geology fellow Antioch Coll., Yellow Springs, Ohio, 1940-42; photogrammetrist U.S. Geol. Survey, Arlington, Va., 1942-45; stratigrapher, asst. chief geologist Companias Unidas de Petroleos, Cartagena, Colombia, 1945-49; staff stratigrapher Sinclair Oil & Gas Co., Tulsa, 1949-69; geol. cons. Tulsa, 1969—. Cons. in field. Editor: Tulsa's Physical Environment, 1973; compiler maps; contbr. articles to profl. jours. Fellow AAAS, Geol. Soc. Am., Explorers Club; mem. Am. Assn. Petroleum Geologists (hon., trustee assoc., Disting. Svc. award 1986), Soc. Econ. Paleontologists and Mineralogists (Disting. Svc. award 1990), Tulsa Geol. Soc. (pres. 1965), Tulsa Astronomy Club (v.p. 1965), Explorers Club, Sigma Xi. Republican. Episcopalian. Avocations: photography, astronomy, reading, travel. Home and Office: 11200 Butler Rd Grass Valley CA 95945-6917

BENOH, IBRAHIM, artist, art educator; arrived in U.S., 1977; s. Hasan Benoh and Afifa Haj; m. Andrea Sara Akel, Jan. 21, 1995. Diploma in fine arts, Acad. of Fine Arts, Rome, 1977; MFA, RISD, 1980; ArtsD, NYU, 1993. Tchg. asst. RISD, Providence, 1978, instr., summer program, 1979—81; prof. art Coll. of Basic Edn., Kuwait, Kuwait, 1994—96, United Arab Emirates U., Al-Ain, 1996—98, Broome C.C., Binghamton, NY, 1999—. Exhibitions include Palazzo Pemma Gallery, Venice, Italy, 1986, Istituto Universitario di Architettura di Venezia, Venice, 1985, Museum RISD, 1980, Jack Tilton Gallery, 1983, Betty Parsons Gallery, 1980, Roberson Museum of Art, Binghamton, 2002, Avenue Art Gallery, Endicott, NY, Marywood U., Scranton, Pa., 2000, Gallery X, N.Y.C., 1999, Dubai International Arts Ctr., Dubai, United Arab Emirates, 1997, Tossan-Tossan Gallery, 1984—87, book cover, Water Runs to What is Wet (by Heather SJ Steliga), monoprint used as cover and chapter image, Educating the Deaf (by Donald F. Moores). Fellow Artist in Residence, Arts Coun. of Norwalk, Inc., Norwalk, CT, 1981. Mem.: Art Mission, Coll. Art Assn. Avocations: tae kwondo, writing poetry. Home: 3901 Connecticut Ave NW #200 Washington DC 20008

BENOIT, JOHN, state official; m. Sheryl Benoit; children: Benjamin, Sarah. AA, Riverside City Coll.; BS, Calif. State U., 1978; MA in Pub. Adminstrn., U. Calif., San Bernardino, 1993. Law enforcer; state assembly mem. Dist. 64 Calif. State Assembly, 2002—. Mem. Desert Sands Unified Sch. Dist. Bd. Edn.; mem. budget com.; mem. rules com.; mem. ins. com.; mem. transp. com. Mem. United Way, 1989—. Republican. Roman Catholic. Mailing: Rm 4144 PO Box 942849 Sacramento CA 94249 Office: Ste 230 1223 University Ave Riverside CA 92507

BENOIT, PHILIP GROSVENOR, communications executive, educator, writer; b. Syracuse, N.Y., June 11, 1944; s. Paul Grosvenor and Doris Louise (Pond) B.; m. Candace Gail Blohm, Sept. 11, 1971; children: Kimberly Whitney, Marie Suzanne. BA, St. Lawrence U., 1966; MA, SUNY-Oswego, 1973. Asst. prof. communications SUNY-Oswego, 1971-79; dir. pub. rels. Hartwick Coll., Oneonta, N.Y., 1979-84; dir. comms. Dickinson Coll., Carlisle, Pa., 1984-96; dir. pub. affairs Middlebury Coll., Vt., 1996—. Chmn. bd. dirs. Ctr. Media Pub. Interest, New Canaan, Conn., 1993—. Author: (with Carl Hausman) Do Your Own Public Relations, 1983, Radio Station Operations, 1989, Positive Public Relations, 1990, (with O'Donnell and Hausman) Announcing: Broadcast Communicating Today, 5th edit., 2003, Modern Radio Production, 6th edit., 2003. Served to capt. U.S. Army, 1966-69. Decorated Bronze Star. Avocations: photography, music. Home: 517 High St Bridport VT 05734-9500 Office: Middlebury Coll Munford Hse Office Pub Affairs 139 S Main St Middlebury VT 05753-1442 E-mail: benoit@middlebury.edu.

BENOIT, RICHARD ARMAND, retired police chief, lawyer; b. Oliver Maurice and Delina Marie Benoit; m. Elizabeth Benoit, Nov. 17, 1962; children: Karen Marie, Richard Michael. AS, Bristol Community Coll., Fall River, Mass., 1972; BS, Salve Regina U., 1975, MS, 1979; JD, So. New Eng. Sch. Law, New Bedford, 1989. Bar: Mass. 1990. Police officer New Bedford Police Dept., 1967-71, sgt., 1971-75, lt., 1975-82, capt., 1982-86, chief of police, 1986—; pvt. practice law New Bedford, 1990-97; ret., 1997; pvt. practice law, 1997—. Mem. Mayor's Task Force on Drug Free Community, New Bedford, Neighborhood Crime Watch, New Bedford, YMCA, New Bedford. With U.S. Army, 1959-62. Mem. ABA, Mass. Bar Assn., New Bedford Bar ASsn., Bristol County Bar Assn. Avocations: swimming, golf, reading. Home: 209 Maywood St New Bedford MA 02745-5108

BENOLIEL, JOEL, lawyer; b. Seattle, June 11, 1945; s. Joseph H. and Rachel (Maimon) B.; m. Maureen Alhadeff, Mar. 1971; 1 child, Joseph D. BA in Polit. Sci., U. Wash., 1967, JD, 1971. Bar: Wash., US Dist. Ct. (we. dist.) Wash., US Ct. Appeals (9th cir.), US Mil. Ct. Appeals. Assoc. atty. MacDonald, Horgue & Bayless, Seattle, 1971-73, ptnr., 1973-78; v.p., gen. counsel Jack A. Benaroya Co., Seattle, 1978-84; ptnr. Trammell Crow Co., Seattle, 1985-87, Spieker Ptnrs., Bellevue, Wash., 1987-92; sr. v.p. law and real estate, gen. counsel Price Costco, Inc., Issaquah, Wash., 1992—. Bd. dir. Overlake Sch., Redmond, Wash., 1995—, Congregation Ezra Bessaroth, Seattle, 1992-95. With US Army, 1968-74. Avocations: tennis, boating, skiing, reading fiction. Office: Price Costco Inc 999 Lake Dr Issaquah WA 98027-5367

BENOVITZ, MADGE KLEIN, civic volunteer; b. Wilkes-Barre, Pa., Nov. 26, 1934; d. Nathan and Esther (Miller) Klein; m. Burton S. Benovitz, Sept. 5, 1954; 1 child, Jane. Student, Cornell U., 1952-54, U. Pa., 1955; AB, Wilkes U., 1956. Bd. dirs. King's Coll., Wilkes-Barre, Pa., exec. com. mem., acad. and profl. affairs com. mem., chmn. phys. plant com., 1980-86, chmn. acad. affairs com., 1995-98; bd. dirs. Leadership Wilkes-Barre, 1981-83, organizing com. mem., 1981, mentor, 1984, 86, 87; mem. exec. com. Econ. Devel. Coun. Northeastern Pa., 1971-78, tax task force mem., 1978-79; state bd. mem. Pa. Crime Stoppers, 1986-88; mem. organizing bd. Pa. Women's Campaign Fund, 1982. Various coms., dir. Nat. Assn. State Bds. Edn., 1984-89, Pa. State Bd. Edn., 1974-94; site rev. team mem. So. Regional Edn. Bd., 1993; nat. orgn. com. mem. LWV, 1971-73, Pa. pres., 1971-73, 1st v.p. and bd. dirs., 1967-71, chair, bd. trustees edn. fund, 1971-73; bd. trustees United Way Pa., 1983, Gold award, 1980; pres. bd. United Way Wyoming Valley, 1980-82, bd. dirs., 1976-83, chmn. planning, allocations, and resources devel. com., 1977-80, chmn. needs assessment com., 1977, chmn. recreation com., 1976; sec. Kingston Borough Civil Svc. Commn., 1997—; trustee Temple Israel, 1986-92, chair endowment allocations com., 1992—. Recipient Disting. Svc. award Wyoming Sem., 1992, Pathfinder award Wyoming Valley Women's Network, 1986, Cmty. Svc. award S.J. Strauss Lodge B'nai B'rith, 1983, Disting. Pennsylvanian award William Penn Com., 1982, Recognition award Penn's Woods Girl Scout Coun., 1977; named Disting. Dau. Pa., 1989, Hon. Order Ky. Cols., 1987. Mem. Hadassah, Jr. League Wilkes-Barre, Women's Aux. Wyoming Valley Health Care Sys., Wilkes-Barre Gen., Women's Aux. Luzerne County Med. Soc., Disting. Daus. of Pa. (area dir. 1995-97, v.p. 1997-99, pres., 1999-2001), Columbine Codominium Assn. (bd. dirs. 2000—), Health and Tennis Club (bd. dirs. 2002—), Huntsville Golf Club, Women's Golf Assn. (co-chair 2003—). Home: 840 Nandy Dr Kingston PA 18704-5608

BENOWITZ, JUNE MELBY, historian, educator; b. Portland, Oreg., Mar. 8, 1949; d. Harold Eugene and Peggy Terry Melby; m. Elliot Benowitz, Sept. 29, 1979. AA in History, Portland C.C., 1979; BA in History, Portland State U., 1981, MA in History, 1988; PhD in History, U. Tex., Austin, 1996. Adj. history instr. Portland State U., 1991—93, Portland C.C., 1994—95, Keiser Coll., Sarasota, Fla., 1997—2002, Manatee C.C., Bradenton, Fla., 2001—02; history instr. U. South Fla., Sarasota/Manatee, 2002—. Author: Days of Discontent, 2002, Encyclopedia of American Women and Religion, 1998 (Choice Mag. award, 1999); contbr. chapters to books. Mem.: Am. Hist. Assn., Orgn. Am. Historians. Evangelical Lutheran. Avocations: hiking, swimming, bird study and care, reading, theater. Office: U South Fla 5700 N Tamiami Trail Sarasota FL 34243

BENSCH, KLAUS GEORGE, pathology educator; b. Miedar, Germany, Sept. 1, 1928; married; 3 children. MD, U. Erlangen, Germany, 1953. Diplomate: Am. Bd. Pathology. Intern U. Hosps. of Erlangen, 1953-54; resident in anat. pathology U. Tex. and; M.D. Anderson Hosp., Houston, 1954-56, Yale, 1956-57; instr. pathology Yale Med. Sch., 1958-61, asst. prof., 1961-64, assoc. prof., 1964-68; prof. pathology Stanford Med. Sch., 1968—, acting chmn. dept. pathology, 1984-85, chmn. dept. pathology, 1985-99, prof. emeritus, 2001—. Office: Stanford U Med Sch Dept Pathology 300 Pasteur Dr Palo Alto CA 94304-2203

BENSCHIP, GARY JOHN, manufacturing company executive; b. Chgo., Aug. 27, 1947; s. Melville John and Eleanor (Melin) B.; m. Susan Diane Mattson, Sept. 19, 1970; 1 child, Jaclyn. BS in Fin., U. Ill., Chgo., 1969; MBA, DePaul U., 1971. Budget analyst R.R. Donnelly & Sons, Chgo., 1969-73; rep. DuPont Walston, Chgo., 1973-74; mgr. fin. ops. Sun Electric Corp., Crystal Lake, Ill., 1974-78; dir. fin. analysis Cenco, Inc., Oak Brook, Ill., 1979-83; treas. Amerace Corp., Hackettstown, N.J., 1983-91, Curtiss-Wright, Lyndhurst, N.J., 1991—. Mem. Beta Gamma Sigma, Delta Mu Delta. Avocations: running, golf, coaching athletic youth teams. Office: Curtiss-Wright Corp 1200 Wall St W Lyndhurst NJ 07071-3677

BENSE, CHARLES JAMES, English educator; b. Sacramento, June 17, 1948; s. Charles Augustus and Joan Marie Bense; m. Susan Jane Pengray, 1966 (div. 1970); 1 child, Heidi Susan; m. Caroline Collins, Dec. 2, 1988. BA in English, Calif. State U., Sacramento, 1970, MA in English, 1973, U. Calif., Davis, 1984, PhD in English, 1989. Cert. secondary tchr., Mont. Tchr. reading Hellgate H.S., Missoula, Mont., 1975-78; lectr. European div. U. Md., Heidelberg, Germany, 1978-81; tchg. asst. English U. Calif., Davis, 1982-85, assoc. English, 1985-89, lectr. English, 1989-90; asst. prof. Moorhead (Minn.) State U., 1990-95, assoc. prof., 1995-2001; prof. Minn. State U., Moorhead, 2001—. Interim chair dept.

English Moorhead State U., 1997. Assoc. editor Jour. Mind and Behavior, 1980-93, assessing editor, 1993—; panel reviewer Am. lit. younger scholars program NEH, 1993; contbr. articles to profl. jour. Faculty Rsch. grantee Moorhead State U., 1995. Mem. MLA (mem. Am. lit. sect.), Minn. State Univ. Inter Faculty Orgn., Ralph Waldo Emerson Soc., 2002-, Nathaniel Hawthorne Soc., 2002-. Office: Dept English Minn State U Moorhead MN 56563-0001

BENSEL, CAROLYN KIRKBRIDE, psychologist; b. Orange, N.J., Sept. 21, 1941; d. William Everitt and Margaret Mary (McGlynn) B.; A.B. with honors in Psychology, Chestnut Hill Coll., 1963; M.S., U. Mass., 1964, Ph.D. (Univ. fellow), 1967. Teaching asst. U. Mass., Amherst, 1963-64, research asst., 1964-66; human factors psychologist Grumman Aerospace Corp., Bethpage, N.Y., 1967-71; chief human factors group U.S. Army Natick (Mass.) Research, Devel. and Engring. Ctr., 1971—. Lic. psychologist, Mass. Fellow Human Factors Soc., APA; mem. Ergonomics Soc., Soc. Engring. Psychologists, Internat. Ergonomics Assn., AAAS, Sigma Xi. Editor: Proc. 23d Ann. Meeting of Human Factors Soc., 1979. Office: Sci & Advanced Tech Directorate Army Natick Research Devel Engring Ctr Kansas St Natick MA 01760

BENSEL, RICHARD FRANKLIN, political science educator; b. Pendleton, Oreg., Nov. 13, 1949; s. John Gordon B. and Dorothy Lois (Carey) Bohlender; m. M. Elizabeth Sanders, Jan. 1, 1979; 1 child, Seth Joseph Bensel. BA, U. Chgo., 1971; MA, Cornell U., 1976, PhD in Polit. Sci., 1978. Asst. prof. Tex. A & M U., College Station, 1977-82, U. Tex., Dallas, 1982-84; prof. New Sch. Social Rsch., N.Y.C., 1984-93, Cornell U., Ithaca, N.Y., 1993—. Author: Sectionalism and American Polit. Devel., 1880-1980, (Mark Ingraham prize U. Wis. 1984), 1984, Yankee Leviathan: The Origins of Central State Authority in America, 1859-77, 1991, The Political Economy of American Industrialization, 1877-1900, 2000 (Greenstone prize 2002). Mem.: Econ. History Assn., Agrl. History Assn., Orgn. Am. History, Am. Polit. Sci. Assn., Am. Hist. Assn. Home: 16 The Byway Ithaca NY 14850-2719 Office: Cornell U Dept Govt White Hall Ithaca NY 14853 E-mail: rfb2@cornell.edu.

BENSELER, DAVID PRICE, foreign language educator; b. Balt., Jan. 10, 1940; s. Ernest Parr and Ellen Hood Escar (Turnbaugh) B.; m. Suzanne Shelton, May 25, 1985; children: James Declan, Derek Justin. BA, West Wash. U., 1964; MA, U. Oreg., 1966, PhD, 1971. Prof. german, dept. chair Ohio State U., 1977—91; chair dept. modern langs and lits. Case Western Reserve U., 1991-98, Louis D. Beaumont U. Prof. Humanities, 1991-98, Emile B. de Sauzé prof. modern lang. and lit., 1998—. Disting. vis. prof. fgn. langs. U.S. Mil. Acad., West Point, N.Y., 1987-88, N.Mex. State U., Las Cruces, 1989; founding dir. German Studies program Case Western Reserve U. and Max Kade Ctr. for German Studies; mem. numerous coms. Case Western Res. U., U.S. Military Acad., U.S. Naval Acad., U. Akron, Ohio State U., Wash. State U., Ind. U., Emory U., U. Md., U. Cin., U. Wis., Pa. State U., U. Va., U. Mich., various others; lectr., panel mem., workshop condr., cons. in field. Compiler, editor: (with Suzanne S. Moore) Comprehensive Index to the Modern Language Journal, 1916-1996, MLJ Electronic Index, 1997—; author/editor 50 books, bibliographies, jours.; contbr. chpts. to books and articles to profl. jours. With USN, 1957—63. Decorated Bundesverdienstkreuz I. Klasse (Germany); recipient Army Commendation medal for disting. civilian svc. U.S. Mil. Acad., 1988; Lilly Found. Faculty Renewal fellow Stanford U., 1975, Fulbright grad. fellow, 1967-68, NDEA fellow, U. Oreg., 1964-67; various other grants, fellowships, scholarships. Mem. MLA, TESOL, Am. Assn. Applied Linguistics, Am. Assn. Tchrs. of German, Am. Assn. Univ. Profs., Am. Goethe Soc., Am. Soc. for 18th Century Studies, German Studies Assn., Lessing Soc., Soc. German-Am. Studies, Phi Sigma Iota, Sigma Kappa Phi, Delta Phi Alpha. Office: Case Western Res U Dept Modern Langs and Lits Cleveland OH 44106-7118 E-mail: dpb5@cwru.edu.

BENSEN, ANNETTE WOLF, graphic art company consultant; b. Bklyn., Aug. 7, 1938; d. Isidor and Sylvia Wolf; m. Gene Bensen, Oct. 14, 1979. AAS, N.Y.C. C.C., 1958; postgrad., Pratt Inst., 1974-75, Sch. Visual Arts, N.Y.C. With Wagner-Ellsberg, Inc., N.Y.C., 1958-62; art dir. Island Pen Mfg. Inc., Stacie Pen, Curtis Rand Industries, Inc., N.Y.C., 1962-68; with G.S. Lithographers, Inc., N.Y.C., 1968-70; ptnr., pres. Rembrandt's Mother, Inc., N.Y.C., 1970-72; co-owner, pres. Film Comp., Inc., N.Y.C., 1972-75; mgr. Expertype, N.Y.C., 1975-90, Expertype & The Graphic Word Co., N.Y.C., 1990-92; sr. v.p. Expertype divsn. JCH Group Ltd., N.Y.C., 1992-93; v.p. prodn. Metro Creative Graphics, Inc., N.Y.C., 1993-97; v.p. ops. Digital Ops. Tech. Svcs., Inc., N.Y.C., 1997-98; owner, mgr. AnGen Svcs., N.Y.C., 1999—. Adj. lectr. N.Y.C. C.C., 1971—75, 1998—, Baruch Coll., 1999—; adv. commn. dept. graphic arts and advtg. tech. Coll. Tech./CUNY, 1994—; adv. commn. H.S. Graphic Comm. Arts, 1999—, H.S. Art and Design, N.Y.C., 2002—; chmn. curriculum com., adv. com. graphic comms. H.S. Graphic Comm. Arts. Mem. Found. for Graphic Arts, Inc., 1994—; mem. Graphic Arts Ednl. Commn.; chair curriculum com. Bd. Edn., N.Y.C.; mem. adv. commn. Bushwick H.S. Recipient Gamma Gold Key award Gamma Epsilon Tau, 2001, Bus. and Industry Partnership award H.S. of Graphic Comm. Arts, 2002, Svc. to Industry award Navigators, 2003; N.Y. Club of Printing House Craftsmen fellow, 1996. Mem. Assn. Publ. Prodn. Mgrs., Assn. Graphic Comm. (Outstanding Instr. Recognition award 1999, Cert. Appreciation 2001, Outstanding Contbn. to Graphic Industry 2001, Arthur Meyer Meml. award 2003), Graphic Arts Profls., Women in Prodn., Printing Women N.Y. (pres.), Printing Tchrs. Guild N.Y. (Contbn. to Edn. award 2001), Mid-Hudson Graphic Art Assn. Address: AnGen Svcs 585 C Heritage Hills Dr Somers NY 10589-1908 Fax: 914-276-0666. E-mail: angen@rcn.com.

BEN SHAUL, YOCHANAN MENASHSHEH See MISHLER, JOHN

BEN-SHIR, RYA HELEN, medical librarian; b. Ottawa, Ont., Can., 1955; came to U.S., 1981; m. Alan H. Peres, June 26, 1977. BA, McGill U., Montreal, 1977; MLS, McGill U., 1979. Med. librarian Jewish Rehab. Hosp., Montreal, 1979-81; mgr. health sci. resource ctr. MacNeal Hosp., Berwyn, Ill., 1981— . Author (software package and manual): Fast Inter-Library Loan and Statistics, 1984, 85; contbr. articles to profl. jours. Recipient John Cotton Dana Spl. award for pub. rels. and mktg. ALA, 1992. Recipient John Cotton Dana Spl. award ALA, 1992. Office: Takeda Pharmaceuticals North America, Inc 475 Half Day Rd Lincolnshire IL 60069

BENSINGER, DAVID AUGUST, dentist, university dean; b. St. Louis, May 14, 1926; s. William and Esther (Lissner) B.; m. Myra Blass, Dec. 24, 1944 (div. June 1972); children: Judith Ann (Mrs. William Thomas Haynes), Scott David; m. Susan Cohn Hartman, May 31, 1975. BA, Washington U., St. Louis, 1944; D.D.S., St. Louis U., 1948; postgrad. health systems mgmt, Harvard U. Sch. Bus. Adminstrn., 1977. Mem. faculty, adminstrn. Sch. Dentistry Washington U., St. Louis, 1949—, assoc. prof. dept. periodontics, 1956-76, prof., 1976-90, assoc. dean, 1970-76, acting dean, 1976-83, exec. assoc. dean, 1983-87; dean Washington U. Sch. Dental Medicine, 1987-90, dean, prof. emeritus, 1990; practice dentistry, specializing in periodontics St. Louis, 1949-90; mem. staff Barnes, Jewish hosps., both St. Louis; mem. deans com. VA Hosp.; mem. nat. adv. com. Dental Edn. Rev. Com., NIH, 1969-72. Cons. Scott AFB, St. Louis, 1956-62; mem. adv. coun. SBA, 1975. Editor: Jour. Greater St. Louis Dental Soc, 1963-70; asso. editor: Jour. Mo. Dental Assn, 1966-73. Mem. exec. bd. Ladue (Mo.) Sch. Sys., 1964-67; chmn. bd. counselors U. Calif. Med. Ctr., San Francisco, 1995-98; chmn. regional cabinet Wash. U., San Francisco, 1996—; elected trustee Coll. of Notre Dame, Belmont, Calif., 1998—, chmn. fin. and investment com. Lt. M.C., U.S. Army, 1948-49, capt. med. dept. USAF, 1955-56. Fellow Am. Coll. Dentists, Internat. Coll. Dentists; mem. ADA (ho. of dels.), Mo. Dental Assn. (pres. 1973-74, jud. coun.), Greater St. Louis Dental Soc. (bd. dirs. 1963-70, Svc. award 1971), Am. Acad. Periodontology, Internat. Assn. Dental Rsch., Midwest Soc. Periodontology (pres. 1972-73), Pierre Fouchard Acad., Royal Soc. Medicine (Eng.), Inst. Internat. Edn. (vice chmn. bd. dirs., chmn. exec. com. 1996-98), Washington U. Alumni Assn. (Alumnus of Yr. 1968), Univ. Club (St. Louis), Harvard Club (Boston and N.Y.C.), Omicron Kappa Upsilon. Home: 2100 Pacific Ave San Francisco CA 94115-1585

BENSINGER, PETER BENJAMIN, consulting firm executive; b. Chgo., Mar. 24, 1936; s. Benjamin Edward and Linda Elkus (Galston) B.; m. Judith S. Bensinger; children: Peter Benjamin, Jennifer Anne, Elizabeth Brooke, Virginia Brette. Grad., Phillips Exeter Acad., 1954; BA, Yale, 1958; hon. degree, San Marcos U., Peru, 1978; LLD (hon.), Dan Kook U., Seoul, Republic of Korea, 1980. Various mktg. positions Brunswick Corp., Chgo., 1958-65, new products mgr., 1966-68; gen. sales mgr. Brunswick Internat., Europe, 1965-66, spl. products mgr., 1966-68; chmn. Ill. Youth Commn., 1969-70; dir. Ill. Dept. Corrections, Chgo., 1970-73; exec. dir. Chgo. Crime Commn., 1973; adminstr. Drug Enforcement Adminstrn., Washington, 1976-81; pres. Bensinger, DuPont & Assocs., Chicago, 1982—. Chmn. Ill. Criminal Justice Info. Authority, 1991—; cons. various orgns.; del. White House Conf. on Corrections, 1971, Drug Abuse, 1988, U.S. Del. to Interpol, 1978. Pres. Lincoln Park Zool. Soc., Chgo., 1962-63; governing life mem., also mem. men's council Chgo. Art Inst.; mem. Ill. Alcoholism Adv. Council, Ill. Law Enforcement Commn., Ill. Council on Diagnosis and Evaluation Criminal Defendants, Ill. Narcotics Adv. Council; adv. com. Center for Studies in Criminal Justice, So. Ill. U., Center for Studies in Criminal Justice, U. Chgo.; vice chmn. ad hoc adv. com. U.S. Dept. Justice Nat. Inst. Corrections; mem. exec. com. Am. Bar Assn. Nat. Commn. Corrections; chmn. Ill. Task Force on Corrections, 1969; mem. bd. Fed. Prison Industries, Inc., 1973-85; bd. dirs. Jewish Fedn. Met. Chgo., Council Community Services Met. Chgo., Ill. Commn. on Children, Children's Meml. Hosp., Chgo., 1988—; bd. dirs., mem. exec. council Anti-Defamation League; regional bd. dirs. NCCJ; trustee Phillips Exeter Acad.; chmn. nat. law enforcement explorers conf. Boy Scouts Am., 1981, U.S. del. to, Interpol, 1978. Recipient Young Leadership award Jewish Fedn.-Welfare Bds. Met. Chgo., 1969, award for excellence John Howard Assn., 1972, Disting. Svc. award Govt. of Peru, 1978, U.S. Dept. of Justice award, EEO award, 1979, Disting. Svc. medal USCG, 1981, John Phillips award Phillips Exeter Acad., 1990, Lincoln medal Lincoln Acad., 1998. Mem. Am. Correctional Assn. (bd. dirs.), Assn. State Correctional Adminstrs. (sec. 1971-72, pres. 1972-73), Internat. Assn. Chiefs of Police (mem. exec. com.), Nat. Sheriffs Assn. (life), Chgo. City Club (bd. dirs.), Arts Club, Comml. Club Chgo., Yale Club (N.Y.C.), Shoreacres Club (Lake Bluff), Casino Club (Chgo.). Office: 20 N Wacker Dr Chicago IL 60606-2806

BENSMAIA, REDA, French studies educator, researcher; b. Kouba, Algeria, Oct. 15, 1944; arrived in U.S., 1979; s. Kaddour and Saleha (Benouniche) Bensmaia; m. Joelle Proust, Feb. 2, 1947 (div. June 1989); children: Sliman, Djamel; m. Maurizia Natali, Oct. 22, 1995. Licence es-lettres, Facultes des lettres, Aix-En-provence, France, 1969, MPhil, 1971; BA, Ecole Pratique, Paris, France, 1977, PhD, 1981. Asst. prof. Institut d' Etudes Politiques, Algiers, Algeria, 1973-74, U. Algiers, Algeria, 1974-76; prof. philosophy Lycée Français, San Francisco, 1979-81; assoc. prof. U. Minn., Mpls., 1981-85; dir. Paris Ctr. for Critical Studies, 1985-88; assoc. prof. U. Minn., Mpls., 1988-89; prof. U. Va., Charlottsville, Va., 1989-91, Brown U., Providence, 1991—. Author: The Barthes Effect, 1987, The Year of Passages, 1995, Alge ou la maladie de la mémoire, 1997, Experimental Nations of the invention of the Maghreb, 2003; editor: On Gilles Deleuze, 1989; contbr. Recipient award, Am. Inst. for Maghrebi Studies, 1995; grantee, NEH, 1983, Chevalier des Palmes Academiques, French Min. of Culture, 2001; EDP grant, U. Minn., 1989. Mem.: MLA, Coun. for Internat. Ednl. Exch. (steering com., adv. bd. curriculum), Sites (adv. bd.), Lendemains (adv. bd.), Continuum (adv. bd.). Avocations: writing poetry and fiction, music, hiking. Office: Brown U Dept French Studies PO Box 1961 Providence RI 02912-1961

BENSMAN, STEPHEN J. school librarian, researcher; b. Sheboygan, Wis., Aug. 26, 1938; s. Solomon and Leah Z. Bensman; m. Miriam Roza, July 9, 1936. MLS, U. Wis., 1975, PhD in History, 1977. Fgn. law libr. U. Wis., Madison, 1975—78; libr. La. State U., Baton Rouge, 1978—. Contbr. articles to profl. jours. Specialist 6 U.S. Army, 1963. Mem.: ALA, Am .Soc. Info. Sci. and Tech., Beta Phi Mu, Phi Beta Kappa, Phi Eta Sigma. Home: 724 Shady Lake Pky Baton Rouge LA 70810-4328 Office: LSU Librs La State Univ Baton Rouge LA 70803-3300 Office Fax: 225-578-6535. Personal E-mail: bensmans@bellsouth.net. Business E-Mail: notsjb@lsu.edu.

BENSON, BETTY JONES, retired school system administrator; b. Barrow County, Ga., Jan. 11, 1928; d. George C. and Bertha (Mobley) Jones; m. George T. Benson; children: George Steven, Elizabeth Gayle, James Claud, Robert Benjamin. BS in Edn., N. Ga. U., Dahlonega, 1958; MEd in Curriculum and Supervision, U. Ga., Athens, 1968, edn. specialist, 1970. Tchr. Forsyth County (Ga.) Bd. Edn., Cumming, 1956-66, curriculum dir., 1966—; asst. supt. for instrn. Forsyth County Schs., 1981—2003; ret., 2003. Mem. media com. Lanier Tech. Inst. Active Alpine Ctr. for Disturbed Children; chmn. Ga. Lake Lanier Island Authority; mem. North Ga. Coll. Edn. Adv. Com., Ga. Textbook Com.; adv. Boy Scouts; Sunday Sch. tchr. 1st Bapt. Ch. Cumming; active Forsyth County Substance Abuse Commn., Forsyth County Drug Task Force, Forsyth County Vision 20/20 Com., Forsyth County Drug Commn., Forsyth County Interagy. Coun. for Children and Youth, Forsyth County Health Dept. Bd., local coord. coun. Family and Children Svcs., Blue Ridge Cir. Ct.-Cherokee/Forsyth County Youth Shelter Com.; mem. literacy com. Forsyth County, Ptnrs. in Edn. program. Mem. NEA, ASCD, Am. Heart Assn., Ga. Assn. Educators (bd. dirs.), Ga. Assn. Supervision and Curriculum Devel. (pres.), Assn. Childhood Edn. Internat., Bus. and Profl. Women's Club, Internat. Platform Assn., Ga. Future Tchrs. Adv. Assn. (pres.), Profl. Assn. Ga. Educators, Ga. Assn. Ednl. Leaders (bd. dirs.). Headstart Dirs. Assn., Forsyth County Hist. Soc., Forsyth County Youth Shelter, Sawnee Mt. Cmty. Ctr. Assn., Ga. Cumming/Forsyth County C. of C. (edn. com.), Mt. Local Coord. Coun. Home: 1235 Dahlonega Hwy Cumming GA 30040-4525 Office: 101 School St Cumming GA 30040-2427 E-mail: bettybenson@adelph.net.

BENSON, BRIAN JOSEPH, English language educator, author; b. San Diego, Aug. 6, 1941; s. Harry Land and Maude Frances (Walker) B.; m. Heli Koppel, 1993; 1 child, Eleanor Blair. BA, Guilford Coll., 1964; MA, U. N.C., Greensboro, 1967; PhD, U. S.C., 1972. Tchr. English Page High Sch., Greensboro, 1966-67; instr. English A&T State U., Greensboro, 1968-69, assoc. prof., 1972-76, prof., 1977—. Writing cons. Magic Gardens Landscape Co., Greensboro, 1988-91. Co-author: Jean Toomer, 1980; asst. (Kenneth Kinnamon, editor) A Richard Wright Bibliography, 1990; contbr. articles to profl. jours. Bd. dirs. Creative Renewal Inc., Greensboro, 1986-89. NDEA fellow, 1969; grantee NEH, 1974, N.C. Humanities Coun., 1982, 83. Mem. N.C. Writers Network. Avocations: tennis, charity work. Home: 1222 Onslow Dr Greensboro NC 27408-6021 Office: A&T State U 1601 E Market St Greensboro NC 27401-3209

BENSON, BRUCE LOWELL, economics educator; b. Havre, Mont., Mar. 18, 1949; s. Russell Lowell and Cora Mae (Emerson) B.; m. Terrie LaVerne Johnson, Aug. 25, 1973; children: Lacey Jean, Kaitlin Bree. BA in Econs., U. Mont., 1973, MA in Econs., 1975; PhD in Econs., Tex. A&M U., 1978. Vis. asst. prof. Pa. State U., University Park, 1978-79, 1979-82; assoc. prof. Mont. State U., Bozeman, 1982-85; prof. Fla. State U., Tallahassee, 1987, disting. rsch. prof., 1993—, DeVoe Moore prof., 1997—; Fulbright sr. specialist in Econ. to the Czech Republic, 2003—04. Assoc. Polit. Economy Rsch. Ctr., Bozeman, 1982—; rsch. fellow Pacific Rsch. Inst., San Francisco, 1982—90; mem. adv. bd. James Madison Inst., Tallahassee, 1987—; grant reviewer Fla. State U., Earhart Found., Social Sci. and Humanities Rsch. Coun. Can., NSF; fellowships reviewer Inst. for Humane Studies, Fairfax, Va., 1989—; fellow Ind. Inst., Oakland, 1990—97, sr. fellow, 1997—; mem. adv. bd. Econ. Jour. Watch, 2001—; co-editor Jour. Watch, 2001—; mem. sci. com. Jour. Economistes et des Etudes Humaine, 2002—; adj. scholar Ludwig von Mises Inst., 1995—; adv. coun. Friedrich A. Von Hayek Found., Buenos Aires, 2001—; adj. fellow Enterprise Prison Inst., 1998—; assoc. Inst. Econ. Affairs, London, 1999—. Co-author: (books) Am. Antitrust Laws, 1989, The Econ. Anatomy of a Drug War, 1994; author: The Enterprise of Law, 1990, To Serve and Protect, 1998 (Sir Antony Fisher Internat. Meml. award, 2000); assoc. editor: Jour. Reg. Sc., contbg. editor The Ind. Rev.; assoc. editor: Jour. Drug Issues, assoc. editor: Rev. Austrian Econs., editl. bd.: Quar. Jour. Austrian Econ.; contbr. articles to profl. jours., chapts. to books; mem. editl. bd.: Jour. Libertarian St., —. Sgt. U.S. Army, 1969-70, Vietnam. Recipient Ludwig von Mises prize, 1992, F. Leroy Hill faculty fellow, Inst. for Humane Studies, 1985—86, Earhart fellow, 1991—92, 1995, 2002, Salvatori fellow, Heritage Found., 1992—94, Best Paper award, Jour. Pvt. Enterprise, 1999—. Mem.: Soc. for Legal and Econ. Studies, Franz Oppenheimer Soc. (bd. cons. 1999—), Soc. for Devel. of Austrian Econ., European Soc. for Social Drug Rsch., Assn. Pvt. Enterprise Edn. (exec. com. 1999—2001, v.p. 2001—02, pres. 2002—03, exec. com. 2003—04, Disting. Scholar award 2001), Am. Law and Econ. Assn., Inst. for Humane Studies (charter), Free Nation Found., Pub. Choice Soc., Western Econ. Assn., So. Econ. Assn. (trustee 1995—97, Georgescu-Roegen prize 1989), Am. Econ. Assn. Home: 2007 Chimney Swift Holw Tallahassee FL 32312-3501 Office: Fla State U Dept Econs Tallahassee FL 32306

BENSON, CAROL KAY CANTRELL, English and Latin educator; b. Dallas, Sept. 12, 1938; d. Walter A. Gatlin and Peggy Joan Harris Gatlin Elrod; children: James Lee, Gary Don, Calvin Dean, Sherry Kay. BA, Baylor U., 1961; MA, U. Tex., Arlington, 1985. Tchr. English and Latin Irving (Tex.) H.S., 1961-62, Grand Prairie (Tex.) H.S., 1963-67, 73-99; tchr. English Jackson Jr. H.S., Grand Prairie, 1968-69; ret., 1999. Proof reader Ct. Reporters, Arlington, 1990-99; tchr. latin Grand Prairie H.S., Tex., 1999-2000. Mem. Grand Prairie Fedn. Tchrs., Order Ea. Star, Order of Rainbow Girls (advisor 1988-89). Democrat. Baptist. Avocations: reading, movies, geneology, travel. Home: 1613 Dorothy Dr Grand Prairie TX 75051

BENSON, CRAIG ROBERT, governor; b. NY, Oct. 8, 1954; m. Denise Benson; 2 children. B in Fin., Babson Coll., 1977; MBA, Syracuse U., 1979. With Teradyne Inc., Boston, 1979—81, Inetlan, Chelmsford, Mass., 1981—83; co-founder Cabletron, 1983, dir. ops., 1984—89, chmn., COO, treas., 1989—97, pres., CEO, chmn., treas., 1998—99; dir. bd. dirs. Enterasys, Rochester, NH; gov. State of N.H., Concord, 2003—. Adj. prof. entrepreneurship Babson Coll., 2000. Office: Office of the Governor 25 Capitol Street Concord NH 03301*

BENSON, D(AVID) MICHAEL, plant pathologist; b. Dayton, Ohio, Aug. 28, 1945; s. Phillip Wayne and Edna Mae (Yowler) B.; m. Patricia D. Miller, Jan. 28, 1967; children: Julie Ann, Jeremy M., Jamie M. BS, Earlham Coll., Richmond, Ind., 1967; MS, Colo. State U., 1968, PhD, 1973. Postdoctoral fellow U. Calif., Berkeley, 1973 74; prof. plant pathology N.C. State U., Raleigh, 1974—. Editor: Phytopathology, 1988-90, Crop Prot., 1993-96, Can J. Microbiology, 1993-96, APS Press, 1998-2001; contbr. articles to profl. jours. Fellow Am. Phytopathol. Soc.; mem. Sigma Xi (v.p. 1987, Young Rschr. award 1980), Gamma Sigma Delta (treas. 1991-93, pres. 1994-95). Office: N C State Univ Dept Plant Pathology Campus Box 7629 Raleigh NC 27695-7629

BENSON, DONALD ERICK, holding company executive; b. Mpls., June 1, 1930; s. Fritz and Annie (Nordstrom) B.; children: Linda K., Nancy A., Stephen D.; m. Roberta Mann, 1992. BBA in Acctg., U. Minn., 1955. CPA, Minn. From staff to partnership Arthur Andersen & Co., Mpls., 1955-68, MEI Corp., Mpls., 1968-86; pres. MEI Diversified Inc., Mpls., 1986-94; exec. v.p. Marquette Fin. Companies, Mpls., 1992—; also bd. dirs. Bd. dirs. Mesaba Holdings, Inc., Champion Air, Minn. Twins Baseball Club, Mass. Mut. Corp. Investors, Mass. Mut. Participation Investors, Capital Cargo Holdings, Inc., Delta Beverage Group, Inc., Nat. Merc. Bancorp.; dir. Swedish Coun. Am. and its Royal Round Table. Chmn. Bethel Coll. Found., St. Paul; past chmn. Pk. Nicollet Med. Services, Mpls.; past pres. Boys and Girls Clubs, Mpls., Minn. Mem. AICPA, Minn. CPA Soc., Mpls. Club, Interlachen Country Club. Office: Marquette Financial Companies 3900 Dain Rauscher Plz Minneapolis MN 55480-1000

BENSON, ELIZABETH POLK, art specialist; b. Washington, May 13, 1924; d. Theodore Booton and Rebecca Dean (Albin) Benson. BA, Wellesley Coll., 1945; MA, Cath. U. Am., 1956. Mus. aide, curator Nat. Gallery of Art, Washington, 1946-60; curator Pre-Columbian Collection Dumbarton Oaks, Washington, 1962-79, dir. Ctr. for Pre-Columbian Studies, 1971-79; rsch. assoc. Inst. Andean Studies, Berkeley, Calif., 1980—. Lectr. Cath. U. Am., Washington, 1968—69; adj. prof. Columbia U., N.Y.C., 1973; sr. lectr. U. Tex., Austin, 1985; Andrew S. Keck disting. vis. prof. Am. U., Washington, 1987; cons. Montreal Mus. Fine Arts, 1980—84, 1990—92; mem. adv. bd. L.Am. Indian Lits. Jour., Pitts., 1989—; co-curator traveling exhbn. Birds and Beasts of Ancient L.Am., 1995—98. Author: The Maya World, 1967, 1972, 1977, The Mochica, 1972, Birds and Beasts of Ancient Latin America, 1997; co-editor: Olmec Art of Ancient Mexico, 1996, Ritual Sacrifice in Ancient Peru, 2001. Mem.: Coll. Art Assn., L.Am. Indian Lits. Assn. (v.p. 1989—), The Lit. Soc., Soc. Women Geographers (co-chair mus. com. 1994—). Home and Office: 8314 Old Seven Locks Rd Bethesda MD 20817-2005

BENSON, ELLEN MARIE, elementary school educator; b. Albuquerque, Sept. 27, 1975; d. John Thomas and Patricia Louise Sandager; m. George Walton Benson, June 1, 2001. BS in Elem. Edn., U. N.Mex., 1998, MA in Elem. Edn., 1999. Tchr. elem. Albuquerque Pub. Schs., 1998—2000, Sunset Mesa Schs., Albuquerque, 2000—01; instr. We. Mich. U., Kalamazoo, 2002—. Grantee, AIAA, 2000. Mem.: Phi Delta Kappa (advisor 2002—03). Avocations: camping, hiking, photography, rollerblading, snowboarding.

BENSON, FRANCES GOLDSMITH, publishing executive; b. Orange, N.J., Oct. 27, 1945; BA, Wells Coll., 1967. Dir. ILR Press Cornell U., Ithaca, NY, 1982-95; editor-in-chief ILR Press Cornell U. Press, Ithaca, NY, 1995—2002, editl. dir. ILR Press, 2002—. Mem. adv. bd. Ctr. Study of Working Class Life, 2002—03; mem. Rutgers U. Press Coun., 2003—. Mem. Indsl. Rels. Rsch. Assn. Office: Cornell U Press Ithaca NY 14850 E-mail: fgb2@cornell.edu.

BENSON, GORDON D. gastroenterologist, medical educator, dean; b. Sharon, N.D., Apr. 13, 1931; m. Frances Ahart; children: James G., G. Brinkley, Mark S. Student, Drake U., 1949—50, U. Minn., 1950—52; MD, Duke U., 1956. Diplomate Am. Bd. Internal Medicine, Am. Bd. Gastroenterology. Intern medicine N.Y. Hosp.-Cornell Med. Ctr., 1956—57, asst. resident medicine, 1957—58, trainee gastroenterology, 1958—59, fellow gastroenterology, 1959—60; fellow liver study unit dept. medicine Yale U. Sch. Medicine, 1962—63; asst. prof. medicine Rutgers Med. Sch., 1963—65, assoc. prof. medicine, 1965—70; prof. medicine Jefferson Med. Coll., Thomas Jefferson U., 1970—78, UMDNJ-Robert Wood Johnson Med. Sch., 1978—2003; emeritus prof. med. UMDNJ-Robert Wood Johnson Med Sch., New Brunswick, NJ, 2003—; assoc. dean UMDNJ-Robert Wood Johnson Med. Sch., 1989—2000; head sect. liver disease divsn. gastroenterology Thomas Jefferson U. Hosp., 1970—78; chief dept. medicine Middlesex Gen.-U. Hosp., New Brunswick, NJ, 1978—80, chief divsn. gastroenterology, 1980—83; chief divsn. gastrointestinal and liver disease Cooper Hosp./Univ. Med. Ctr., Camden, NJ, 1983—90, attending med. staff, 1983—. Cons. physician medicine gastroenterology VA Hosp., Lyons, NJ, 1965—70, cons. physician, East Orange, NJ, 1969—70, U.S. Naval Hosp., Phila., 1974—80; vis. prof. biochemistry UMDNJ-Rutgers Med. Sch., 1977, chief divsn. liver disease, 1978—83; vis prof. medicine U. Calif., Davis, 2001; cons. staff St. Peter's Med. Ctr., New Brunswick, NJ, 1979—; adj prof. Coriell Inst. for Med. Rsch., 1997—; presenter in field. Assoc. editor Gastroenterology Abstracts and Citations, NIAMDD, 1972-79, editl. advisor, 1979-80; contbr. articles to profl. jours. including Am. Jour. Med. Sci., Med. Sci., Jour. Clin. Investigation, Medicine, Jour. Acad. Medicine, New Eng. Jour. Medicine, Jour. Parasitology, Sci., Life Scis., Gastroenterolgoy, others. Mem. Nat. Digestive Disease adv. bd. U.S. Dept. HHS/PHS/NIH, Washington, 1992-95. Capt. USAF, 1960-62. Recipient Disting. Achievement and Med. Edn. award Delaware Valley/Am. Liver Found., 1994. Fellow ACP; mem. Internat. Assn. for the Study of Liver, Am. Assn. for the Study of Liver Disease, Alpha Omega Alpha. Office: UMDNJ-Robert Wood Johnson Med Sch 401 Haddon Ave Ste 292 Camden NJ 08103-1505 E-mail: benson@umdnj.edu.

BENSON, IRENE M. nurse; b. Chgo. BSN, Loyola U., 1980; MS, Saint Xavier U., 1993. RN Ill., cert. critical care nurse, emergency room nurse, trauma nurse specialist, med. surg. nursing, clin. nurse specialist. Staff nurse hematology/oncology unit Michael Reese Hosp. and Med. Ctr., Chgo., 1980-86, operating rm. nurse, 1980—86; staff nurse trauma ICU Loyola U., Maywood, Ill., 1986-87; staff nurse telemetry U. Ill., Chgo., 1987-88; staff nurse Cook County Hosp., Chgo., 1988—, tour supr. emergency rm., 1990—91, clin. nurse specialist med.-surg. nursing, 1993—; staff nurse emergency rm. St. Francis Hosp., Blue Island, Ill., 1991-94, U. Ill., Chgo., 1992—98; clin. instr. Triton Coll., River Grove, Ill., 1998—, clin. cons. trainer, 2000—. Trauma nurse instr. USAF, 1990—. Maj. USAF Res., 1982—. Mem.: Am. Assn. Critical Care Nurses, Nat. Assn. Clin. Nurse Specialists, Internat. Assn. of Forensic Nurses, Ill. Nurses Assn., Acad. of Med.-Surg. Nurses, Emergency Nurses Assn., Res. Officers Assn. (life), Sigma Theta Tau Internat. Roman Catholic. Avocations: reading, sky diving, traveling. Office: Cook County Hosp 1835 W Harrison St Chicago IL 60612-3785

BENSON, JERRY KENNETH, sociologist; b. Winters, Tex., Feb. 1, 1937; s. George Alvin and Gladys Virginia (Green) Benson; m. Norma Sue Ainsworth, Aug. 30, 1958; children: Lisa Virginia, Kathryn Neal, David Kenneth, Michael Ainsworth. BA, Baylor U., 1959; MA, U. Tex., 1963; PhD, 1965. Instr. U. Tex. State U., Denton, 1964-65; asst. prof., 1965-66; from asst. prof. to prof. U. Mo.,

Columbia, 1966-85, prof., 1986—, chair dept. sociology, 1984—85, 1986—88, 1999—2002. Vis. prof. Gothenburg (Sweden) U., 1985-86; treas. local chpt. Nat. Edn. Assn., Columbia, early 1970's. Co-author: Coordinating Human Services, 1973; editor (assoc.): The Sociol. Quarterly; contbr. articles to profl. jours. Coach, umpire Daniel Boone Little League, Columbia, 1970's. Fellow, Fulbright Found., 1985—86. Mem. Am. Sociol. Assn., Midwest Sociol. Soc., Soc. Study Social Problems. Democrat. Baptist. Avocations: music, chess, fishing. Home: 4 Mumford Dr Columbia MO 65203 E-mail: bensonjk@missouri.edu.

BENSON, JERYL DISANTI, occupational therapist; b. Tarentum, Pa., Aug. 14, 1965; d. Joseph Richard and Constance Ann (Grebeck) Disanti; m. Troy Bartholomew, Mar. 28, 1987. BS, U. Pitts., 1987, MS, 1995; postgrad., Duquesne U. Registered occupl. therapist; cert. neurodevel. treatment, infant massage instr.; cert. to administer Sensory Integration and Praxis Test; bd. cert. in pediatrics. Occupl. therapist United Cerebral Palsy Assoc., Nassau County, N.Y., 1987-88; occupl. therapist, coord. equipment clinic Nat. Ctr. for Disability Svcs., Albertson, N.Y., 1989-91, reah. tech. cons., 1990-91; occupl. therapist, clin. edn. coord. DT Watson Ednsl. Svcs., Sewickley, Pa., 1991-98; faculty Duquesne U., 1998—. Mem. Internat. Med. Assistance Team, 1994. Mem. com. NFL Childrens Charities, N.Y.C., 1987-91, Nat. Ctr. for Disability svcs./Sports Night Fundraiser, Albertson, N.Y., 1988-91; cmty. rep. Am. Cancer Assn., L.I., 1990; mem. Midwestern Intermediate Unit Task Force, Lawrence County, Pa., 1993. Mem. Am. Occupl. Therapy Assn., Neurodevel. Treatment Assn. (state rep. 1993—), Pa. Occupl. Therapy Assn., Sensory Integration Internat. Roman Catholic. Avocations: skiing, reading, cross-stitching, biking. Home: 1038 Victoria Pl Gibsonia PA 15044-9200 Office: Duquesne U Occpl Therapy Dept 226 Health Scis Bldg Pittsburgh PA 15282-0001 E-mail: benson@duq.edu.

BENSON, JIM, finance company executive; Chmn., pres., chief exec. MetLife affiliate New Eng. Fin.; pres. individual svc. MetLife; chmn., pres., CEO GenAm. Fin. Corp., 2002—. Office: 700 Market St Saint Louis MO 63101

BENSON, JOHN ALEXANDER, JR., physician, educator; b. Manchester, Conn., July 23, 1921; s. John A. and Rachel (Patterson) B.; m. Irene Zucker, Sept. 29, 1947; children: Peter M., John Alexander III, Susan Leigh, Jeremy P. BA, Wesleyan U., 1943; MD, Harvard Med. Sch., 1946. Diplomate Am. Bd. Internal Medicine (mem. 1969-91, sec.-treas. 1972-73, pres. 1973-91, pres. emeritus 1991—), Subsplty. Bd. Gastroenterology (mem. 1961-66, chmn. 1965-66). Intern Univ. Hosps., Cleve., 1946-47; resident Peter Bent Brigham Hosp., Boston, 1949-51; fellow Mass. Gen. Hosp., Boston, 1951-53; rsch. asst. Mayo Clinic, Rochester, Minn., 1953-54; asst. in medicine Mass. Gen. Hosp., 1954-59; instr. medicine Harvard U., 1956-59; head divsn. gastroenterology U. Oreg. Med. Sch., Portland, 1959-75, prof. medicine, 1965-93; prof. emeritus Oreg. Health Sci. U., Portland, 1993—, interim dean Sch. Medicine, 1991-93, dean emeritus, 1993—; asst. dir. Oreg. health Sci. U. Ctr. for Ethics in Health Care. Cons. VA Hosps., Madigan Gen. Army Hosp., John A. Hartford Found. Editorial bd.: Am. Jour. Digestive Diseases, 1966-73, The Pharos, 2000—; contbr. articles to profl. jours. Mem. Oreg. Med. Ednl. Found., 1967-73, dir., 1967-73, pres., 1969-72; bd. dirs. N.W. Ctr. for Physician-Patient Comm., 1994-99, Am. Acad. on Physician and Patient, 1994-99; bd. dirs. Found. for Med. Excellence, 1996—, pres., 1998-2000; trustee Oreg. Health Scis. Found., 1999—. With USNR, 1947-49. Mem. AAS, AMA, ACP (master), Am. Gastroenterol. Assn. (sec. 1970-73, v.p. 1975-76, pres.-elect. 1976-77, pres. 1977-78), Am. Clin. and Climatol. Assn. (v.p. 1997), Am. Soc. Internal Medicine, Western Assn. Physicians, North Pacific Soc. Internal Medicine, Am. Fedn. Clin. Rsch., Federated Coun. for Internal Medicine, Am. Assn. Study Liver Disease, Western Soc. Clin. Investigation, Soc. Health and Human Values, Assn. Health Svcs. Rsch., Inst. Medicine NAS (sr.), Phi Beta Kappa, Sigma Xi, Alpha Omega Alpha. Office: Oreg Health and Sci U Sch Medicine L102 Portland OR 97239 E-mail: bensonj@ohsu.edu.

BENSON, JOHN STEVEN, education educator; b. Moline, Ill., Aug. 19, 1958; s. John Stanley and Marie Schafer Benson; m. Cynthia Ruth Benson, Aug. 14, 1982; children: Claire Ruth, John Samuel. BA in Geography, Gustavus Adolphus Coll., 1980; BS in Elem. Edn., Mankato State U., 1982; MA in Geography, U. Minn., 1990, PhD in Geography, 1996. 6th grade tchr. Laredo (Tex.) Ind. Sch. Dist., 1982-83, Tex. history tchr., 1983-84; tchr.'s aide/long-term substitute Wilson Ctr., Faribault, Minn., 1984-85; 6th grade tchr. Columbus Sch., Medellin, Colombia, 1985-88; asst. prof. elem. edn. Minn. State U., Moorhead, 1994—. Democrat. Lutheran. Home: 1321 5th Ave S Moorhead MN 56560 Office: Minn State U Moorhead Dept Edn Moorhead MN 56563 E-mail: bensonj@mnstate.edu.

BENSON, JOSEPH FRED, journalist, legal historian; b. St. Louis, Dec. 14, 1953; s. Max and Addie Marie (Klein) B.; m. Sandra Ann Mears, Oct. 29, 2000. AA, St. Louis C.C., 1974; AB cum laude, St. Louis U., 1976, AM, 1977, JD, 1985. Legal historian, archivist Cir. Ct. St. Louis County, Clayton, Mo., 1978-85; columnist St. Louis Daily Record and St. Louis Countian, 1987—2000, spl. corres., 1989—2000, editl. writer, 1990—2000, cons. in constl. law, 1995—2000; editl. writer St. Peters Courier, 1998—2000; jud. asst. Supreme Ct. Mo., Jefferson City, 2000—. Asst. law libr. St. Louis County Ct. House Law Libr., 1979-85; adj. instr. Am. history Harris-Stowe State Tchrs. Coll., St. Louis, 1987; adj. asst. prof. bus. law Lincoln U., Jefferson City, Mo., 2002—; rsch. cons. law firm David C. Godfrey, Clayton, 1981—, Zwibelman, Edelman & Walter, Clayton, 1989-95, Law Firm of Scott E. Walter, P.C., 1997—; friend of the ct. 21st cir. Cir. Ct. St. Louis County, Mo., 1993-94; instr. Am. history Van Buren (Mo.) R-1 Pub. Schs., 1994-95; instr. Am. history and Am. govt. East Carter County R-II Pub. Schs., Ellsinore, Mo., 1995, U. City (Mo.) H.S., 1995-96; cons. in field. Author newspaper column Law In History, 1987—; contbr. Wentzville Union (Mo.) Legal Newspaper, 1995—; contbr. articles on internat. law to profl. jours. including Mo. Lawyers Weekly. Judge St. Louis County Bd. Elections, Clayton, 1978-84, supr., 82-84; incorporator Hist. Soc. St. Louis County, 1978, exec. dir., asst. sec., 1979-87, comm. Bicentennial U.S. Constn., 1983-91; sexton, prayer leader Shaare Zedek Synagogue, University City, Mo., 1998—. Sam. A. Kessler Meml. scholar, 1981, Project '87: Bicentennial scholar, 1985-91; faculty fellow St. Louis U., 1983, 84. Mem. Am. Soc. Legal History, Supreme Ct. Mo. Hist. Soc., U.S. Supreme Ct. Hist. Soc., B'nai B'rith, Rotary, Phi Alpha Theta, Phi Theta Kappa. Democrat. Jewish. Avocations: cooking, tennis, gardening. Home: 726 Kevin Dr Jefferson City MO 65109

BENSON, KENNETH VICTOR, manufacturing company executive, lawyer; b. New Lisbon, Wis., Aug. 2, 1929; s. Carl W. and Ottilia (Olson) B.; m. Alice May Drewry, June 23, 1951; children: Jennifer, Elizabeth, Kenneth, Jonathan, Nathan. BBA, U. Wis., 1951, JD, 1957. Bar: Wis. 1957. Sales trainee, sales corr. Marathon Corp., Menasha, Wis., 1953-54; practice law with Benson & Day, Marshfield, Wis., 1957-58; sr. v.p., dir., exec. com. Kohler Co., Wis., 1959-81; pres., mem. exec. com., dir. Vollrath Co., Sheboygan, Wis., 1982-89; ptnr. Benson, Zufelt & Donohue, Sheboygan, 1990-92. Bd. dirs. Sheboygan United Fund, 1969-75, Wis. 4-H Found., Inc., 1988-92, Sheboygan YMCA, 1971-79, sec., 1975-76, v.p., 1977-79; pres. Sheboygan Comty. Players and Civic Orch., 1967-69, bd. dirs., 1963-76; bd. dirs. Sheboygan Retirement Home, 1976-85, v.p., 1979-80, pres., 1980-81; trustee Lakeland Coll., 1978-92. With AUS, 1951-53. Mem. Home: 125 White Ash Dr Pine Knoll Shores NC 28512-6218

BENSON, KIMBERLY DAWN, paralegal; d. Randall Joel and Barbara Ann Jones; m. Shane Karl Benson, July 25, 1992 (div. May 9, 1999). AA, Casper Coll., Wyo., 2000. Cert.: Nat. Assn. of Legal Assistants 2001. Paralegal intern Williams, Porter, Day & Neville, Casper, Wyo., 1999—2000; paralegal Schwartz, Bon, Walker & Studer, Casper, Wyo., 2000—. Mem.: Legal Assistants of Wyo., Nat. Assn. of Legal Assts., Parent Autism Group, Phi Theta Kappa. Conservative. Avocations: triathlon, travel, reading, sewing. Office: Schwartz Bon Walker & Studer 141 S Ctr Ste 500 Casper WY 82609 Office Fax: 307-234-5099. Personal E-mail: kibenson2@yahoo.com. E-mail: kimcla@hotmail.com.

BENSON, LOYD, retired state legislator; BA in Govt. and Econs., Okla. U., JD, 1965. Bar: Okla. Ptnr. firm McBee & Benson, Inc., Frederick, Okla.; mem. Okla. Ho. of Reps., 1984—, majority leader, 1991-97, speaker, 1997—. Contbr. articles to profl. jours. Capt. U.S. Army. Decorated Army Commendation medal; recipient disting. svc. awards Okla. Hosp. Assn., Okla. Dist. Attys. Assn., Okla. Rural Water Assn., Okla. Cattlemen's Assn., Okla. Farmers Union, Okla. Credit Union League, Okla. Dental Assn., others, Kate Barnard Youth Advocate award. Mem. Okla. Bar Assn. (vice chair real property sect.), Okla. Mcpl. Attys. Assn. (past pres.), Nat. Conf. State Legislators (mem. law and justice com.).

BENSON, LUCY WILSON, political and diplomatic consultant; b. N.Y.C., Aug. 25, 1927; d. Willard Oliver and Helen (Peters) Wilson; m. Bruce Buzzell Benson, Mar. 30, 1950 (dec. Mar. 1990). BA, Smith Coll., 1949, MA, 1955; LHD (hon.), Wheaton Coll., Norton, Mass., 1965; LLD (hon.), U. Mass., 1969; LHD (hon.), Bucknell U., 1972; LLD (hon.), U. Md., 1972; LHD (hon.), Carleton Coll., 1973; LLD (hon.), Amherst Coll., 1974, Clark U., 1975; HHD, Springfield Coll., 1981; L.H.D. (hon.), Bates Coll., 1982; L.L.D. (hon.), Lafayette Coll., 1999. Mem. jr. exec. tng. program Bloomingdale's, N.Y.C., 1949-50; asst. dir. pub. rels. Smith Coll., 1950-53; rsch. asst. dept. Am. studies Amherst Coll., 1956-57; pres. Amherst LWV, Mass., 1957-61, pres. Mass., 1961-65, nat. pres., 1968-74; mem. Gov.'s cabinet and sec. human svcs. Commonwealth of Mass., 1975; mem. spl. commn. on adminstrv. rev. U.S. Ho. of Reps., Washington, 1976-77; under sec. State Security Assistance, Sci. and Tech. U.S. Dept. State, Washington, 1977-80; cons. U.S. Dept. State and SRI Internat., Washington, 1980-81; pres. Benson and Assocs., Amherst, 1981—. Vice-chair Citizen Network for Fgn. Affairs; bd. dirs. Dreyfus Fund and other Dreyfus mut. funds, Internat. Exec. Svc. Corps. Steering com. Urban Coalition, 1968, exec. com., 1970-75, 80-84, co-chair, 1973-75; mem. Gov. Mass. Spl. Com. Rev. Sunday Closing Laws, 1961; mem. spl. commn. Mass. Legislature to Study Budgetary Powers of Trustees U. Mass., 1961-62; mem. Gov. Mass. Com. Rev. Salaries State Employees, 1963, Mass. Adv. Bd. Higher Ednl. Policy, 1962-65, Mass. Bd. Edn. Adv. Com. Racial Imbalance and Edn., 1964-65, Mass. adv. com. U.S. Commn. Civil Rights, 1964-73; vice-chair Mass. Adv. Coun. Edn., 1965-68; mem. Mass. Com. Children and Youth Com. to Study Report by U.S. Children's Bur., Mass. Youth Svc. Div., 1967; mem. pub. adv. com. U.S. Trade Policy, 1968; vis. com. John F. Kennedy Sch. Govt.; mem. Trilateral Commn., Coun. Fgn. Rels.; mem. town meeting, Amherst, 1957-74, 2000, mem. fin. com., 1960-66; trustee Edn. Devel. Center, Newton, Mass., 1967-72, Nat. Urban League, 1974-77, Smith Coll., 1975-80, Brookings Instn., 1974-77, Alfred P. Sloan Found., 1975-77, 81-2000, Bur. Social Sci. Rsch., Inc., 1985-87; bd. dirs. Catalyst, 1972-90, Atlantic Coun. of U.S., 1988—, vice-chair, 1990-2000, former bd. govs. Am. Nat. Red Cross, Common Cause, Women's Action Alliance; bd. govs. Internat. Ctr. on Election Law and Adminstrn., 1985-87; trustee Lafayette Coll., 1985-2000, vice-chair, 1990-2000, trustee emeritus, 2000—. Recipient Achievement award Bur. Govt. Research, U. Mass., 1963; Distinguished Service award Boston Coll., 1965, Smith Coll. medal, 1969, Distinguished Civil Leadership award Tufts U., 1965, Distinguished Service award Northfield Mount Hermon Sch., 1976; Radcliffe fellow Radcliffe Inst., 1965-67. Mem. NAACP, ACLU, Nat. Acad. Pub. Adminstrn., UN Assn., Urban League, Assn. Am. Indian Affairs, East African Wildlife Soc., Jersey Wildlife Preservation Trust Channel Islands, Internat. Inst. Strategic Studies. Home and Office: 46 Sunset Ave Amherst MA 01002-2097

BENSON, MARY ETTA, English educator; b. Washington, Pa., July 24, 1943; d. James Archer and Blanche Naomi (Speicher) Scott; m. Donald L. Benson, June 20, 1998. BA, Westminster Coll., 1965; MA, Miami U., Oxford, Ohio, 1969, PhD, 1975. Tchr. Berlin (Pa.) Brothersvalley Schs., 1965-67; from grad. asst. to assoc. Miami U., Oxford, 1967-70; from instr. to asst. prof. Behrend Coll., Erie, Pa., 1970-81; from assoc. prof. to prof. Tarkio (Mo.) Coll., 1981-91; prof. Avila U., Kansas City, Mo., 1991—. Fellow Nat. Def. Edn. Act, 1967-70. Mem. MLA, Nat. Coun. Tchrs. English. Presbyterian. Avocations: reading, travel. Office: Avila University 11901 Wornall Rd Kansas City MO 64145

BENSON, MORGAN, energy engineer, military officer; b. Washington, Sept. 20, 1948; s. Wilmer Kersey and Virginia Cabell Benson; m. Elaine Rae Page, Oct. 26, 2000; children: Jennifer R., Jason C. Gaskill, Karen L., Matthew E. Gaskill, Erik P. Gaskill. BS, U. Del., 1972; MBA, U. Scranton, 1984. Cert. energy engr., Assn. Energy Engrs., 2000, registered profl. engr., Ky., 1974. Facilities engr. Scranton (Pa.) Army Ammunition Plant, 1979—86; chief environ. br. U.S. Army Tobyhanna (Pa.) Army Depot, 1986—88; energy mgr. HQs, US Army, Europe / 7A, Heidelberg, Germany, 1988—94; chief of utilities U.S. Army 26th Area Support Group, Heidelberg, 1994—99; project mgr. Walter Reed Army Med. Ctr., Washington, 1999—2000; installation energy mgr. U.S. Army Dugway (Utah) Proving Ground, 2000—. Ops. officer HQs, U.S. Army 21st TAACOM, Kaiserslautern, Germany, 1988—94, HQs, U.S. Army V Corps, Heidelberg, 1994—96. Contbr. Lt. col. Ordnance Corps U.S. Army, 1972—97, Germany. Decorated Meritorious Svc. medal HQs, U.S. Army, Europe /7A, Army Commendation medal, 7th Oak Leaf Cluster; recipient Fed. Energy and Water Mgmt. award, Dept. of Energy, 1998, Energy Mgmt. award, Sec. of the Army, 2002. Fellow: Soc. Am. Mil. Engrs. (life; post pres. 1997—99, Silver medal 1994, Paul W. Thompson medal 1996, Regional Vice President's medal 1994); mem.: CAP (lt. col. 1999—2002), ASME, Ret. Officers Assn. (life). Avocations: military history, genealogy, travel. Office: US Army Dugway Proving Ground Building 5330 Dugway UT 84022-5000 E-mail: bensonm@dpg.army.mil.

BENSON, ROBERT A. photojournalist; b. Minn., 1968; Schooled photojournalism, SI Newhouse Sch. of Pub. Commn. (Syracuse Univ. Photojournalist US Navy; freelance Virginian Pilot, Assoc. Press. Recipient Two-time Military Photographer of the Yr., 1998—99, DoD Print Journalist of the Yr., 1995, 1999, Eddie Adams Barstorm Workshop selectee. Achievements include co-founder of www.americanphotojournalist.com. Home: 251 Lake Dr Virginia Beach VA 23451

BENSON, ROBERT CRAIG, III, business consultant; b. Waukegan, Ill., May 27, 1944; s. Robert Craig II and Leona (Pollard) B.; m. Ree Ann Christensen, June 3, 1961; children: Bradley, Barry. BA in Bus. Adminstrn. and Math., Dakota Wesleyan U., Mitchell, S.D., 1967. CPA, Cert. Mgmt. Cons. Supervising sr. Broeker Hendrickson & Co., St. Paul, 1967-70; ptnr. Sands Benson & Weinberg, St. Paul, 1970-73; mgr. Miller, McCollom & Co., Denver, 1973-74; mng. ptnr. Benson Wells & Co., Denver, 1974-84; pres. Am. Bus. Advisors, Denver, 1984—. Lectr. Ctr. for Leadership Devel., Kiev, Ukraine, 1998—; Opperman disting. alumni lectr. Dakota Wesleyan U., 2002. Contbr. articles to profl. jours. Bd. mem., chair Denver Youth for Christ, 1975-85; elder Cherry Hills Cmty. Ch., Highlands Ranch, Colo., 1982-87; bd. mem. COMPA Food Bank, Denver, 1986-93, Global Connections Internat., 2000-2003, Project C.U.R.E., 2000—. Mem.: AICPA (mgmt. cons. divsn.), Inst. Mgmt. Cons., Colo. Soc. CPAs (co-chmn. profession practice bd. 1981—82). Avocations: golf, snow skiing, teaching about god. Office: Am Bus Advisors Inc 8400 E Prentice Ave Ste 215 Englewood CO 80111-2926 E-mail: bob@abadvisors.com.

BENSON, ROBERT EUGENE, lawyer; b. Red Oak, Iowa, Apr. 7, 1940; s. Paul J. and Frances (Sever) B.; m. Ann Marie Lucke, July 20, 1968; children: Steven J., Robert J., Katherine A. BA, U. Iowa, 1962; LLB, U. Pa., 1965. Bar: Colo. 1965. Assoc. Holland & Hart, Denver, 1965-71, ptnr., 1971—. Adj. faculty U. Denver Coll. Law, 1992. Author: The Power of Arbitrators and Courts to Order Discovery in Arbitration, 1996, Application of the Pro Rata Liability, Comparative Negligence and Contribution Statues, 1994; co-author: How to Prepare For, Take and Use a Deposition, 5th edit., 1994; mng. editor: Colorado Construction Law, 1999, 2003; contbr. articles to profl. jours. Capt. USAF, 1965-73. Mem. ABA, Colo. Bar Assn., Denver Bar Assn. Avocations: golf, skiing. Home: 5454 Preserve Pky N Greenwood Village CO 80121-2185 Office: Holland & Hart LLP 555 17th St Ste 3200 Denver CO 80202-3950

BENSON, ROBERT JOHN, physical therapist, department chairman, massage therapist; b. Crosby, Minn., Dec. 20, 1958; s. Matthew Edward Benson, Gertrude Marian Benson; m. Ruth Linda Mahder; children: Geoffrey, Hannah, Teresa. MEd, Marian Coll., Fond Du Lac, Wis., 1987—89; AAS, Williston State Coll., Williston, N.D., 2000—01; B in Phys. Therapy/Natural Sci., Coll. St. Scholastica, Duluth, Minn., 1977—83. Cert. Phys. Therapy 1983, Massage Therapy 2001. Dir. phys. therapy Cuyuna Reg. Med. Ctr., Crosby, Minn., 1983—86; dir. rehab. Beaver Dam Cmty. Hosp., Beaver Dam, Wis., 1987—92; dept. chair Williston State Coll., Williston, ND, 1992—2003. Bd. mem. Basin United Way, Williston, ND, 1994—99. Mem.: Natl. Strength and Conditioning Assn., Am. Massage Therapy Assn., Am. Phys. Therapy Assn. Home: 1201 E Hillcourt Williston ND 58801-4454 Office: 1410 University Ave Williston ND 58801-4464 Home Fax: 701-774-4265; Office Fax: 701-774-4265. Personal E-mail: robert.benson@wsc.nodak.edu. Business E-Mail: robert.benson@wsc.nodak.edu.

BENSON, SARA ELIZABETH, real estate broker, real estate appraiser; b. Columbia, S.C., Nov. 29, 1960; d. Herbert Lankford Benson and Anna Marian (Stanley) Tucker; m. Donald Joseph DeBat, Aug. 20, 1994; children: D. Edward, Herbert L. Benson IV. Student, U. S.C., 1977, Am. Conservatory Music, Chgo., 1978-81. Lic. real estate broker, Ill., S.C.; designated cert. real estate brokerage mgr.; approved ind. fee appraiser; cert. real estate appraiser, Ill. Pres., owner Benson Stanley Realty, Chgo., 1990—; owner Sara Benson Cons., Inc., Chgo., 1992—. Fee appraiser FHA, HUD, Chgo., 1986—; speaker, author in field. Bd. dirs. Chgo. Child Care Soc. Mem. NAFE, Nat. Assn. Realtors, Assn. Fed. Appraisers, Real Estate Buyer's Agt. Coun., Ill. Assn. Realtors, Chgo. Assn. Realtors (chair profl. standards com.), North Shore Bd. Realtors, Real Estate Brokerage Mgrs. Coun., MLS No. Ill., Nat. Assn. Ind. Fee Appraisers, Bus. Execs. Assn. Chgo., Chgo. Child Care Soc. (bd. dirs. 1997—). Avocations: piano, literature, interior design. Office: Benson Stanley Realty 980 N Michigan Ave Ste 1400 Chicago IL 60611-7500

BENSON, SCOTT MICHAEL, lawyer; b. West Bend, Wis., Apr. 28, 1963; m. Lisa Louise Autio, Oct. 3, 1987; children: Sarah M., Scott M. II, Joseph E. BA, Carroll Coll., 1985; JD, Marquette U., 1991. Bar: Wis.; U.S. Dist. Ct. (ea. and we. dists.) Wis., U.S. Ct. Appeals Fed. Cir. Assoc. Gutglass, Erickson & Bonville, Milw., 1991-92, Law Offices of Robert L. Pavlic, S.C., Brookfield, Wis., 1993-95; shareholder Hutchison & Benson, S.C., Brookfield, 1996—. Mem. ABA, State Bar of Wis., Waukesha County Bar Assn. Republican. Lutheran. Office: Hutchison & Benson SC 1025 S Moorland Rd Ste 500 Midway Office Ctr Brookfield WI 53005

BENSON, SIDNEY WILLIAM, chemistry researcher; b. N.Y.C., Sept. 26, 1918; m. Anna Bruni, 1986; 2 children. AB, Columbia Coll., 1938; A.M., PhD, Harvard U., 1941; Docteur Honoris Causa, U. Nancy, France, 1989. Rsch. asst. Gen. Electric Co., 1940; rsch. fellow Harvard U., 1941-42; instr. chemistry CCNY, 1942-43; group leader Manhattan Project Kellex Corp., 1943; asst. prof. U. So. Calif., 1943-48, assoc. prof., 1948-51, prof. chemistry, 1951-64, 76-89, disting. prof., 1986—, Disting. prof. emeritus, 1989—, dir. chem. physics program, 1962-63; dir. dept. kinetics and thermochemistry Stanford Rsch. Inst., 1963-76; sci. dir. Hydrocarbon Rsch. Inst. U. So. Calif., 1977-90, sci. dir. emeritus, 1991—; rsch. assoc. dept. chemistry and chem. engrng. Calif. Inst. Tech., 1957-58; vis. prof. UCLA, 1959, U. Ill., 1959; hon. Glidden lectr. Purdue U., 1961; vis. prof. chemistry Stanford U., 1966-70, 71, 73; mem. adv. panel phys. chemistry Nat. Bur. Standards, 1969-72, chmn., 1970-71; hon. vis. prof. U. Utah, 1971; vis. prof. U. Paris VII and XI, 1971-72, U. St. Andrews, Scotland, 1973, U. Lausanne, Switzerland, 1979. Frank Gucker lectr. U. Ind., 1984—; Brotherton prof. in phys. chemistry U. Leeds, 1984; cons. G.N. Lewis; lectr. U. Calif., Berkeley, 1989. Author: Foundations of Chemical Kinetics, 1960, rev. edit. 1982, Thermochemical Kinetics, 1968, 2d edit., 1976, Critical Survey of the Data of the Kinetics of Gas Phase Unimolecular Reactions, Reactions, 1970, Chemical Calculations, 3d edit., 1971, Atoms, Molecules and Chemical Reactions, 1972; founder, editor-in-chief Internat. Jour. Chem. Kinetics, 1967-83; mem. editl. adv. bd. Combustion Sci. and Tech., 1973-94, Oxidation Comms., 1978—, Revs. of chem. Intermediates, 1979-87, Hydrocarbon Letters, 1980-81, Jour. Phys. Chemistry, 1981-85; sci. adv. coun. Annales Medicales de Nancy, 1993—. Recipient Polanyi medal Royal Soc. Eng., 1986; faculty rsch. award U. So. Calif., 1984, Presdl. medal, 1986, Peter Kapitsa Gold Medal award Russian Acad. Natural Sci., 1997; Guggenheim fellow, 1950-51, Fulbright fellow, France, 1950-51, fellow NSF, 1957-58, 71-72; recipient citation Chem. Rev., 2000; nominated for Scientist of Yr. Internat. Biog. Ctr., Cambridge, Eng., 2002. Fellow AAAS, Am. Phys. Soc.; mem. NAS, Am. Chem. Soc. (Tolman medal 1977, Hydrocarbon Chem. award 1977, Langmuir award 1986, Orange County award 1986), Faraday Soc., Indian Acad. Sci., Phi Beta Kappa, Sigma Xi, Pi Mu Epsilon, Phi Lambda Upsilon, Phi Kappa Phi Home: 1110 N Bundy Dr Los Angeles CA 90049-1513 Office: U So Calif University Pk Mc 1661 Los Angeles CA 90089-0001

BENSON, STEVEN CLARK, management and engineering executive; b. Chillicothe, Ohio, Sept. 27, 1954; s. Myron Clark and Velma Lucille (Dye) B.; married; children: Michael Lee, Kelly Dawn. BSCE, Ohio U., 1976. Registered profl. engr., Ohio, Ky., Pa., Va., W.Va., Fla. Project engr. McNally Pittsburg, Inc., Wellston, Ohio, 1976-87; pres. SBA Cons., Inc., Jackson, Ohio, 1995—97, SBA Assocs., Inc., Jackson, 1989—, also bd. dirs. City engr., asst. svc., safety dir. City of Jackson, Ohio. Mem. NRA (life), NSPE, Ohio Soc. Profl. Engrs., Ohio Design Profls. and Code Analysts, Ohio Gun Collectors Assn., Aircraft Owners and Pilots Assn., Cousteau Soc., Exptl. Aircraft Assn. Avocations: flying, scuba diving, camping, travel, hunting. Home: 54399 Benson Rd Ray OH 45672-8947 Office: SBA Inc PO Box 962 Jackson OH 45640-0962

BENSON, STEVEN DONALD, sheet metal research and marketing executive, sheet metal mechanic, programmer, author; b. Longview, Wash., Oct. 11, 1953; s. Steven Hughes Benson and Donna Ruth (Johnson) McKinney; m. Patricia Joyce Krauss, Feb. 14, 1982; children: Steven William, Patricia Ann. AA in Drafting, Merit Davis, 1973; AA in Robotics, AMADA Sch., Buena Park, Calif., 1997. Precision sheet metal mechanic Ariz. Precision Sheet Metal, Phoenix, 1980-86, Neilson Mfg. Inc., Salem, Oreg., 1986—92; owner, operator Time Honored Gifts, Salem, 1988—94; pres. Advanced Sheet Metal Applications, Salem, 1986—; co-owner A-Cab Taxi and Transp. Svcs. LCC, Salem, Gizmo Med. Transport Inc., 2003. Instr. Oreg. Advanced Tech. Consortium, Wilsonville, 1990—; sheet metal instr. Clackamas C.C., Oregon City, Oreg., 1997—; editor, pub. Precision Sheet Metal Chronicle, electronic mag., 1998—; pres. Brake Tng. & Cons. Author: (textbooks) Introduction to Precision Press Brake, 1991, Intermediate Press Brake, 1992, Advanced Precision Press Brake, 1994, Press Brake Technology, 1997, Lasers, Punches, PressBrakes & Shears, 2001, Darkness to Light, 2002, (software) Advanced Sheet Metal Applications (ASMA 4.0), 1982, 90, 92, 95, 97; contbr. articles to profl. jours. Sec., treas. Bike PAC of Oreg., Salem, 1988-2001, lobbyist, 1992; mem. A Brotherhood Against Totalitarian Enactments (ABATE), Oreg., Inc.; chief petitioner Statewide Initiative Petition, Oreg.; hon. chmn. Oreg. chpt. Nat. Rep. Congl. Com., 2002. Named Businessman of Yr., NRCC, 2003; recipient Edn. award, Fabricators and Mfg. Assn. Internat., 1999, Article of the Yr. award, Croydon/FMA, 2001, Congl. Leadership award, 2002, Freedom isn't Free award, Bike PAC of Oreg., 1997, Legends of BikePac award, 2001. Mem. Fabricators and Mfrs. Assn. (adv. com. precision sheet metal adv. 1997—, coun.), Soc. Mfg. Engrs., Internat. Sheet Metal Workers (local 16), Masons (master, 33 deg.). Avocations: family activities, children, politics, indian moto-cycles, british sports cars. Home: 395 23d St NE Salem OR 97301-4440 Office: Advanced Sheet Metal Applications 398 Rose St NE Salem OR 97301-4468 Fax: 206-727-8729. E-mail: steve@asmachronicle.com.

BENSON, STUART WELLS, III, lawyer; b. Sewickley, Pa., Jan. 6, 1951; s. Stuart Wells and Rosalie (Sassin) B.; m. Ruthanne Ackerman, July 15, 1978; children: Kate Eileen, Laura Elizabeth, Sarah Wells. BA, Northwestern U., 1972; JD, U. Pitts., 1975. Bar: Pa. 1975, U.S. Dist. Ct. (we. dist.) Pa. 1975, U.S. Supreme Ct. 1982. Assoc. Brandt McManus Brandt & Malone, Pitts., 1975-80; ptnr. Dickie, McCamey & Chilcote, P.C., Pitts., 1980—96, Pietragallo, Bosick & Gordon, Pitts., 1996-2002, Dapper, Baldasare, Benson & Kane, PC, Pitts., 2002—. Contbr. articles to profl. jours. Bd. dirs. North Hills YMCA, Pitts., 1981-84. Mem. ABA, Am. Arbitration Assn. (Appreciation award 1980), Pa. Def. Inst., Pa. Claims Assn., Pitts. Claims Assn., Allegheny County Bar Assn., Pa. Bar Assn., Internat. Assn. Indsl. Accident Bds. and Commns., Oakmont Country Club, Wildwood Golf Club, Rotary (bd. dirs. 1979-87, pres. 1985, parliamentarian 1985—, found. chmn. 1999—) Republican. Episcopalian. Home: 2116 Grandeur Dr Gibsonia PA 15044-7498 E-mail: sbenson@dbbk.com.

BENSON, THOMAS LUTHER, academic administrator; b. White Plains, N.Y., Mar. 2, 1940; s. Wilbert Ernest and Elaine Dorothy Benson; m. Eleanor Jo Rodger, June 14, 1964 (div. Dec. 1975); 1 child, Anders. BA, Augustana Coll., 1962; BD, Harvard U., 1966; PhD, MA, Johns Hopkins U., 1975. Assoc. prof. philosophy, dir. hons. program U. Md., Balt., 1969-86; v.p., provost St. Andrew's Coll., Laurinburg, N.C., 1986-94; pres. Green Mountain Coll., Poultney, Vt., 1994—. Contbr. Ency. Religion, 1987, Interdisplinary: Essays

from the Literature, 1998; contbr. articles to profl. jours. including Issues in Integrative Studies, ASIANetwork Exch. Bd. dirs. Isle La Motte Preservation Trust, Isle La Motte, Vt., 1998—, Vt. World Trade Orgn., Burlington, Vt., 1996-2000; mem. adv. bd. Dorset (Vt.) Theatre Festival, 1999—; mem. alumni bd. dirs. Harvard Divinity Sch., 1995-98. Recipient Francis Asbury award United Meth. Bd. Higher Edn,. 1997; named Disting. Alumnus of Yr. Augustana Coll., 2001. Mem. Assn. for Integrative Studies (pres. 1983-85), ASIANetwork (adv. coun. 1993-95), Jefferson Legacy Fond. (dir. 1998—), Vt. Assn. Ind. Colls. (v.p. 1998—), Phi Beta Kappa. Lutheran. Avocations: tennis, swimming, hiking, reading, travel. Home: 323 Main St Poultney VT 05764 Office: Green Mountain Coll 1 College St Poultney VT 05764 E-mail: bensont@greenmtn.edu.

BENSON, VALERIE A. artist, writer; b. Elmhurst, Ill., Aug. 11, 1949; Student, Art Inst. Chgo., 1963; student in art, No. Ill. U., 1971; BA, MA in Fine Arts, Columbia Pacific U., 1981; grad., Guatemalan Airborne Sch., 1993. Freelance illustrator, 1960—; instr. in art history and art appreciation Waubonsee Cmty. Coll., 1986; with Harry Claflin Group. Author: I've Never Been to Sweden, 1990, Swedish Cookbook; cartoon, U.S. on Warpath. U.S. del. Creative Art Commn.; mem. Eckankar. With G-2 Forces Honduras Army, 1993. Finalist Strange Universe, Better Homes and Gardens Recipe contest, Century Standouts ; recipient Sesquicentennial Mural award, Chgo. Art Review. Mem.: Am. Ctr. Internat. Leadership, Internat. Airborne Soc., Warrenville Hist. Soc. (hon.; life). Achievements include First woman to jump with elite G-2 Forces Honduras, 1993. Office: 9306 Poplar Spring Ct Warrenville IL 60555-3302 : 9306 Poplar Spring Ct Burke VA 22015-3455

BENSON, WARREN FRANK, composer, educator; b. Detroit, Jan. 26, 1924; s. Fred William and Ella Alma (Hermenau) B.; m. Patricia Louise Vander Velde, Nov. 19, 1949; children: Erika, Dirk, Kirsten, Sonja. MusB in Theory, U. Mich., 1949, MusM in Theory, 1951. Timpanist Detroit Symphony Orch., 1946, Ford Sunday Evening Hour Orch., 1946, Brevard Music Ctr. Orch., 1949, 53, 54; Fulbright tchr. music Anatolia Coll., Salonica, Greece, 1950-52; dir. orch. and band Mars Hill Coll., 1952-53; prof. music, composer in residence Ithaca Coll., 1953-67; prof. composition Eastman Sch. of Music U. Rochester, NY, 1967-93, Kilbourn prof. composition, 1980-93, prof. emeritus, 1994—. Disting. vis. prof. Meadows Sch. Arts, So. Meth. U., Dallas, 1986-88; guest condr., lectr. at festivals and ednl. ctrs., US, Can., Mex., S.Am., Europe; mem. MacDowell Colony, 1955, 63. Author: Creative Projects in Musicianship, 1967, ...And My Daddy Will Play the Drums, 1999; compositions include Concertino for Alto Saxophone, 1954, Trio for Percussion, 1956, Psalm XXIV for womens voices and string orch., 1957, Symphony for Drums and Wind Orch., 1962, The Leaves are Falling for wind ensemble, 1963, The Solitary Dancer for wind ensemble, 1966, Helix for tuba and wind ensemble, 1966, The Mask of Night for wind ensemble, 1968, Shadow Wood, song cycle for soprano and orch. or wind ensemble, 1968, String Quartet, 1969, The Dream Net for alto saxophone and string quartet, 1972, Five Lyrics of Louise Bogan for mezzo-soprano and flute, 1977, Largo Tah for bass trombone and marimba, 1978, Songs For The End of the World, for mezzo-soprano, horn and chamber ensemble, 1980, The Man With The Blue Guitar, for orch., 1980, Beyond Winter: Sweet Aftershowers for string orch., 1981, Moon Rain and Memory Jane for soprano and two cellos, 1981, Hills, Woods, Brook: Three Love Songs for soprano and chamber ensemble, 1982, Symphony II-Lost Songs, 1982, Wings for wind ensemble, 1984, The Hearth Within for a cappella chorus, 1985, Steps for brass quintet, 1987, Dawn's Early Light for band, 1987, The Red Lion for vibraphone and piano, 1988, Still for solo clarinet, 1989, Still, A Love Song for solo cello, 1990, Meditation on I Am For Peace for band, 1990, Danzon-Memory for band, 1991, Trio Tertulio for clarinet, violin and cello, 2001, Adagietto for wind ensemble, 1992, Shadow Wood for soprano and wind ensemble, 1992, Divertissement I, 1993, Aurora Morning for organ, 1994, String Quartet III-Cat's Cradle, 1995, The Drums of Summer for winds and voices, 1997, Daughter of the Stars for wind ensemble, 1998, Songs and Asides About Love, baritone, viola and guitar, 1999, Love and the Lady, mezzo-soprano and oboe and cello, 2000, The Roswell Set, piano, 2000, The Alexandria Set, piano, 2000, Aurora Morning II, for two violas, 2000, Still Dancing, wind ensemble, 2001, Scherzo, Chorale & Aria, wind ensemble, 2002; recs. include Gasparo CD, Centaur CD, Nonesuch CD, CRI, Golden Crest, Orion, Coronet, USAF and USMC bands CD, Nanset (Norway) CD, Kosei, Japan CD, Albany CD, Crystal CD, Musical Heritage Soc. CD; commns. include Nat. Endowment for Arts, NY State Coun. on Arts, Ohio Music Educators Assn., Charlotte Symphony Orch., Internat. Horn Soc., Baldwin-Wallace Conservatory, Am. Wind Symphony Orch., Rochester Philharm. Orch., Mich. State U., U. Conn., The Cantata Singers, U. MIT, USAF Band, Chestnut Brass Company, Cricklade Music Festival (Eng.), Kronos Quartet, US Marine Band, Emory U., Uster Festival of Switzerland, So. Meth. U., West Point Band. Named to PAS Hall of Fame; recipient Diploma de Honor Argentina, 1970, Lillian Fairchild Meml. prize in arts, U. Rochester, 1971, Citation of Excellence, Nat. Band Assn., 1976, Warren Benson Disting. Tchr. award established at Ithaca Coll., 1965; grantee, Ford Found., 1963, 1965; Guggenheim fellow, 1981—82. Mem. ASCAP (Serious Music awards 1960—), Am. Bandmasters Assn., Pi Kappa Lambda, Phi Mu Alpha (nat. hon. mem. Orpheus award), Kappa Kappa Psi. Home: 10 Reitz Pkwy Pittsford NY 14534-2206 *My goal is to write music worthy of the best in the art which speaks to the best in people of my time.*

BENSON, WILLIAM EDWARD (BARNES), geologist; b. West Haven, Conn., May 15, 1919; s. John Edward and Lucia Purdy (Barnes) B.; m. Mary Freda Hill, July 11, 1944; children— Sharon (Mrs. J.G. Rachel), Lynn (Mrs. J.D. Walker), William Edward. BA, Yale, 1940, MS, 1942, PhD, 1952. Geologist Conn. Geol. and Natural History Survey, 1940-42; geologist U.S. Geol. Survey, 1942-54, br. chief, 1953-54; exec. sec. div. earth sci. Nat. Acad. Scis./NRC, 1954-55; chief geologist Manidon Mining Inc., N.D., 1955-56; program dir., sect. head NSF, 1956-75, chief scientist earth sci. div., 1975-79; sci. advisory to Office of Pres., Washington, 1976-77; pvt. cons., 1980—. Vis. prof. U. Hawaii, 1980; sr. staff assoc. NAS, 1980-99. Contbr., editor profl. jours. Served with USNR, 1944-45. Yale fellow, 1940-42 Fellow Geol. Soc. Am., Am. Geophys. Union, AAAS (sec. sect. E 1969-73, chmn. sect. E 1974-75); mem. Geol. Soc. Washington (v.p. 1958), Pick and Hammer Soc. (chmn. 1970-73), Phi Beta Kappa, Sigma Xi (lectr. 1980-81). Home: 7531 Parish Ln Falls Church VA 22042-3521

BENSUR, BARBARA JEAN, art educator, researcher; b. Erie, Pa., Feb. 11, 1950; d. Jean Elizabeth and Durker William Braggins; children: Adele, Rebecca. BA, Mercyhurst Coll., 1972; MA, U. Md., 1992, PhD, 1995. Cert. art tchr. grades K-12, adminstrv. endorsement. Art tchr. St. Mary's County Pub. Schs., Leonardtown, Md., 1989—98; instr. Frostburg (Md.) State U., 1996—98; asst. prof. Millersville (Pa.) U., 1998—. Exhibitions include Delaware County C.C., 2001 (Purchase award, 2001), 30th Ann. Spring Arts Festival, 2001, Lancaster Open Award Exhibit, 2001, Millersville Faculty Art Show, 2001; contbr. articles to profl. jours. Cons. Demuth Found., Lancaster, 2000—01. Mem.: Am. Edn. Rsch. Assn., Pa. Art Edn. Assn., Nat. Art Edn. Assn. Roman Catholic. Avocation: jogging. Home: 743 Steeplechase Rd Landisville PA 17538 Office: Millersville Univ Art Dept PO Box 1002 Millersville PA 17551 Home Fax: (717) 871-2004; Office Fax: (717) 871-2004. Personal E-mail: barbara.bensur@millersville.edu. Business E-Mail: barbara.bensur@millersville.edu.

BENT, ALAN EDWARD, political science educator, administrator; b. Shanghai, June 22, 1939; s. Walter J. and Tamara (Rocklin) B.; m. Dawn Bickler, Aug. 13, 1977; 1 son by previous marriage, Ronald Geoffrey. BS, San. Francisco State U., 1963; MA, U. So. Calif., 1968, Claremont Grad. Sch., 1970, PhD, 1971; MBA, Xavier U., 1985. Instr. polit. sci. Chapman Coll., Orange, Calif., 1969-70; research assoc. Mcpl. Systems Research, Claremont Grad. Sch., 1970-71; asst. prof. polit. sci., assoc. dir. Inst. Govtl. Studies and Research Memphis State U., 1971-74; assoc. prof., chmn. dept. pub. adminstrn. Calif. State U., Dominguez Hills, 1974-77; prof. polit. sci. U. Cin., 1977-81, 82-92, head dept. polit. sci., 1977-81; dean Coll. Arts and Scis. U. No. Colo., Greeley, 1981-82, prof. polit. sci., 1981-82; prof. pub. adminstr. Troy State U., Europe, 1989-92. Cons. police agys., govtl. and pvt. instns. Author: Escape from Anarchy: A Strategy for Urban Survival, 1972; The Politics of Law Enforcement: Conflict and Power in Urban Communities, 1974, 2d edit., 1976; co-author: Police, Criminal Justice and the Community, 1976, Collective Bargaining in the Public Sector: Labor-Management Relations and Public Policy, 1978; co-editor, contbr. Urban Administration: Management, Politics and Change, 1976, 2d edit. 1977; contbr. articles to profl. jours.; bd. editors: Rev. Pub. Personnel Adminstrn., 1980-89, Spectrum, A Jour. of Comparative Politics and Devel., New Delhi, 1984-92. Served to capt. USAF, 1964-69. NASPAA fellow, 1981-82 Home: 1006 Oro St Laguna Beach CA 92651-3534

BENTAS, LILY HASEOTES, retail executive; Chmn, pres. Cumberland Farms, Canton, Mass., 1989—, pres., CEO, 1991—. Office: Cumberland Farms Inc 777 Dedham St Canton MA 02021-1484*

BENTEL, CAROL RUSCHE, architect; m. Paul Bentel, 1987. BArch, Washington U., St. Louis, 1979; MArch (with hons.), NC State U., 1981. Registered Mass., NY. Asst. prof. architecture Ga. Inst. Tech., 1984—85; ptnr. Bentel & Bentel, Locust Valley, NY, 1987—. Tchg. asst. NC State U., 1980—81; vis. assoc. prof. NY Inst. Tech., 1999—; juror architecture Fulbright Found., 1996—98; vis. adj. prof. City Coll. NY, 1997; lectr. in field. Recipient First prize, Mcpl. Arts Soc., 1985, Disting. Alumni award, Washington U . St. Louis, 1999; fellow, Partitions, Inc., 1980, Samuel Kress Found., 1993—94, Am. Acad. Rome, 1993—94; grantee, Fulbright-Hays, 1985—86; scholar, Washington U., 1974—79, Fulbright scholar, U. Venice, 1985—86. Fellow: AIA (nat. com. design, chair Rome conf. 2001, scholar 1977—81), mem.. Soc. Archl. Historians, NY State Assn. Archs. Office: 22 Buckram Rd Locust Valley NY 11560*

BENTEL, FREDERICK RICHARD, architect, educator; b. N.Y.C., Jan. 2, 1928; s. Carl August and Mary (Muller) B.; m. Maria L. R. Azzarone, Aug. 16, 1952 (deceased Nov. 8, 2000); children: Paul Louis, Peter Andreas, Maria Elisabeth. BArch., Pratt Inst., 1949; grad. fellow, Mass. Inst. Tech., MArch., 1950; DArch., Technische Hochschule, Graz, Austria, 1953. Registered architect, N.Y., 1956, N.J., 1960, Va., 1958, Vt., 1970, Conn., 1985, Mo., 2001, Del., 1998, Mass., 2001, profl. planner, N.J., 1967. Architect, partner Bentel & Bentel (AIA), Locust Valley, N.Y., 1957—; pres. Correlated Designs Inc., Locust Valley, 1961—; ptnr. Old Path Realty, Cobblestone Enterprises. Prof. Sch. Architecture, Pratt Inst., 1955-70; prof. Sch. Architecture, N.Y. Inst. Tech., 1969—. Author publs. in field. Founding mem. com. Locust Valley Bus. Dist. Planning; adv. bd. Oyster Planning and Hist. Preservation Commn., 1970-73; mem. Oyster Bay Hist. Preservation Commn., 1975-91; alt. APD panel N.Y. State Coun. on Arts, 1985-86, St. Joseph's Coll. Libr. Arch., L.I., chpt. AIA, 1990, St. Stephen's Ch., Warwick, N.Y., L.I. chpt. AIA, 1991, Pavilion, Old Westbury, N.Y. Fulbright scholar, 1952-53; recipient awards in field including 1st pl. commn. Islip Bay Shore downtown redevel. competition, 1976, Suffolk County Ct. Complex, 1985. Fellow AIA (task force for archtl. graphic stas., St. Joseph's Coll. Libr. Arch. L.I. chpt. 1990, St. Stephen's Ch., Warwick, N.Y., L.I. chpt. 1991, Pavilion, Old Westbury, N.Y., Gramercy Tavern, N.Y.C., L.I. chpt. 1996, Nat. Design award, 2003); mem. N.Y. Soc. Architects (numerous awards), Am. Italy Soc., MIT Alumni Assn. (ednl. coun.), Home: 23 Frost Creek Dr Locust Valley NY 11560-1029 Office: Bentel & Bentel Architect & Planner 22 Buckram Rd Locust Valley NY 11560-1928

BENTEL, PAUL L. architect, educator; m. Carol Rusche, 1987. BA in Visual Studies (magna cum laude), Harvard Coll., 1979, M in Architecture (with hons.), 1982; student, Swiss Fed. Inst. Tech., Zurich, 1981—82; PhD in History Theory, Criticism, MIT, 1992. Ptnr. Bentel & Bentel, Locust Valley, NY, 1985—; asst. prof. history, preservation and design Columbia U., 1993—. Bd. advisors Buell Ctr. Study Am. Architecture; dir. Am. archl. design studio Swiss Fed. Inst. Tech., 1988—90; lectr. MIT, 1986, Harvard U., 1991. Fellow: AIA; mem.: USICOMOS, Soc. Archl. Historians. Office: Sch Arch Planning Preservation Columbia U 400 Avery 2960 Broadway New York NY 10027-6902 also: Bentel & Bentel 22 Buckram Rd Locust Valley NY 11560*

BENTER BROCK, TERESA ANN, health facility administrator; b. Seymour, Ind., July 3, 1965; d. Alvin Willis and Wilma Ann (Tormoehlen) Benter. Student, Ivy Tech., Columbus, Ind., 1997—. Cert. med. mgr. Ins. clk. Weir, Bevers, Baxter, Seymour, Ind., 1984—; office mgr. Rosemary Weir, MD, Seymour, 1994—2002, Legacy Primary Care Physicians, P.C., 2002—. Leader 4-H Club, Seymour, 1984-2001; Sunday sch. tchr. St. Paul Luth. Ch., Brownstown, 1986-2002. Mem. Assn. Health Care Mgrs., Phi Theta Kappa. Avocation: cross stitching. Office: PO Box 427 120 Saint Louis Ave Seymour IN 47274-2304

BENTHEIM, WENDY J. municipal official; b. Phoenix, Nov. 2, 1972; d. Charles A. and Judith K. Bentheim. BA in Polit. Sci., Ariz. State U., 1998; MPA, Western Internat. U., Phoenix, 2002. Asst. supr. Phoenix Mcpl. Ct., 1996—2002; customer svc. supr. Neighborhood Svcs. City of Phoenix, Phoenix, 2002—. Sec. Laveen Village Planning Com., City of Phoenix, 2002—. Mem.: ASPA. Republican. Lutheran. Office: Phoenix City Hall 200 W Washington St Phoenix AZ 85003 Fax: 602-495-5567. Personal E-mail: Winnep101@aol.com. Business E-Mail: wendy.bentheim@phoenix.gov.

BENTLEY, ALFRED YOUNG, JR., information technology and education consultant; b. Boston, Dec. 22, 1943; s. Alfred Young Bentley and Virgina (Ellis) Rhone; m. Geraldine Giaccone, Apr. 21, 1968; children: Alfred Young III, Suzanne Kathleen. BE, Stevens Inst., 1965. Systems engr. data processing div. IBM Corp., Newark, 1965-73, cons. systems and programming corp. hdqrs. Armonk, N.Y., 1973-76, mgr. market requirements office products div. Franklin Lakes, N.J., 1976-81; dir. product mgmt. Exxon Office Systems Co., Stamford, Conn., 1981-83, v.p. product mgmt., 1983-85; exec. dir. AT&T Info. Systems, Morristown, N.J., 1985-88, AT&T Systems Integration Div., Bridgewater, N.J., 1988-91; v.p. tech. svcs. Beneficial Data Processing Corp. (subs. of Beneficial Corp.), Peapack, N.J., 1991-92, sr. v.p. tech. svcs., 1992-94; sr. v.p. tech. requirements and architecture Beneficial Tech. Corp. (subs. Beneficial Corp.), Peapack, N.J., 1994-95; founder, pres. A and S Tech. Svcs., Inc., West Caldwell, N.J., 1995—. Science To Go, Inc., West Caldwell, 1997—. Mem. IEEE Computer Soc., Assn. Computing Machinery. Roman Catholic. Avocations: personal computing, hiking, carpentry, gourmet cooking, boy scout leadership. Home: 243 Central Ave West Caldwell NJ 07006-6907 Office: A and S Tech Svcs Inc 243 Central Ave West Caldwell NJ 07006-6907 also: Sci to Go Inc 243 Central Ave West Caldwell NJ 07006 6907 E mail: al@aands.com.

BENTLEY, CHARLES RAYMOND, geophysics educator; b. Rochester, N.Y., Dec. 23, 1929; s. Raymond and Janet Cornelia (Everest) B.; m. Marybelle Goode, July 3, 1964; children: Molly Clare, Raymond Alexander. BS, Yale U., 1950; PhD, Columbia U., 1959. Rsch. geophysicist Columbia U., 1952-56; Antarctic traverse leader and seismologist Arctic Inst. N.Am., 1956-59; project assoc. U. Wis., 1959-61, asst. prof., 1961-63, assoc. prof., 1963-68, prof. geophysics, 1968-98, A.P. Crary prof. geophysics, 1987-98, prof. emeritus, 1998—. Recipient Bellingshausen-Lazarev medal for Antarctic rsch. Acad. Scis. USSR, 1971; NSF sr. postdoctoral fellow, 1968-69; NAS-USSR Acad. Sci. exch. fellow, 1977, 90 Fellow AAAS, Am. Geophys. Union, Arctic Inst. N.Am., Am. Polar Soc. (hon., bd. dirs.); mem. AAUP, Soc. Exploration Geophysicists, Internat. Glaciological Soc. (Seligman Crystal award 1990), Am. Quaternary Assn., Oceanography Soc., Am. Geol. Inst., Geol. Soc. Am., Phi Beta Kappa, Sigma Xi. Achievements include research on Antarctic glaciology and geophysics, satellite studies of geomagnetic anomalies, magnetotelluric exploration of Earth structure, satellite radar and laser altimetry, ice coring and drilling services. Home: 5618 Lake Mendota Dr Madison WI 53705-1036 Office: U Wis Geophys & Polar Rsch Ctr Weeks Hall 1215 Dayton St Madison WI 53706 E-mail: bentley@geology.wisc.edu.

BENTLEY, CLARENCE EDWARD, savings and loan executive; b. Ranger, Tex., Oct. 9, 1921; s. Clarence Edward and Rosa Estelle (Bryant) B.; m. Gloria Gill, Oct. 9, 1943; children: Jon, Kitty, Perry (dec.). Student, McMurry U., Abilene, Tex., 1939-42. Pres. Abilene Savs. Assn., 1944-77, Southwestern Group Fin. Co., Houston, 1976-77; pres. United Savs. Assn. Tex., Houston, 1977-80, chmn. bd., 1980-85; dir., chmn. bd. Sandia Fed. Savs. & Loan, Albuquerque, 1986-89; dir. Kaneb Pipeline Partners, 1990—. Chmn. bd. dirs. United Fin. Mortgage Co., Dallas, United Fin. Group, Inc., Houston, 1980-86; bd. dirs. Kaneb Services Inc., Investors Mortgage Ins. Co., Boston. Contbr. articles to profl. publns. Pres. Abilene Indsl. Found., 1970, United Fund Abilene, 1962; mem. bd. Tex. State Hosps., 1962-64; mem. Tex. Fin. Commn., 1964-76, chmn., 1971. Served with USAAF, 1942-43. Recipient Outstanding Citizen award City of Abilene, 1964, Disting. Alumnus award McMurry U., 1971 Mem. Nat. Savs. and Loan League (pres. 1970-71), Tex. Savs. and Loan League (pres. 1970-71), Assn. Thrift Holding Cos. (chmn. bd. 1985-87), Abilene C. of C. (pres. 1964). Clubs: Abilene Country (pres. 1951). Episcopalian. Home: 52 Rue Maison St Abilene TX 79605-4710

BENTLEY, FRED DOUGLAS, SR., lawyer; b. Marietta, Ga, Oct. 15, 1926; s. Oscar Andrew and Ima Irene (Prather) B.; children from previous marriage: Fred Douglas, Robert Randall; m. Jane Morrill McNeel, Nov. 7, 1997. BA, Presbyn. Coll., 1949; JD, Emory U., 1948; HHD (hon.), PhD (hon.), LHD (hon.), Kennesaw State U., 2000. Bar: Ga. 1948. Sr. mem. Bentley & Dew, Marietta, 1948-51; ptnr. Bentley, Awtrey & Bartlett, Marietta, 1951-56, Edwards, Bentley, Awtrey & Parker, Marietta, 1956-75, Bentley & Schindelar, Marietta, 1975-80, Bentley, Bentley & Bentley, Marietta, 1975—. Pres. Beneficial Investment Co., Newmarket, Inc., Happy Valley, Inc., Bentley & Sons, Inc.; founder, chmn. emeritus bd. Charter Bank and Trust Co.; founder, trustee emeritus Kennesaw Coll. Mem. Ga. Ho. Reps., 1951-57, Ga. Senate, 1958; past pres. Cobb County (Ga.) C. of C.; founder, hon. curator Bentley Rare Book Galleries-Brenau U., Kennesaw State U.; mem., past chmn. Ga. Coun. Arts, 1976-89; mem. Gov.'s Fine Arts Com., 1990-92, Cummer Mus. of Art (hon. life); attache Ghana Olympic Com.; founder Cobb Emergency Svc.; fell. US Supreme Ct. Museum Acquisition Com., US Constitution Museum; Served with USN. Recipient Blue Key Cmty. Svc. award, Founder's award, 1992, Clarisse Baquell award for outstanding svc., First GEM award, Spl. Svc. award Kennesaw State U., Robert Cleveland award for lifetime achievement in law, Extra Mile award; named Citizen of Yr., C. of C., 1951, Leader of Tomorrow, Time mag., 1953, Vol. Citizen of Yr., Atlanta Jour./Constn., 1981, Kennesaw Hist. Soc. Man of Yr., 1996, Brenau U.. Man of Yr. award, 1996, President's award Kennesaw State U., 1999, Disting. Alumna Marietta HS, Bus. Assoc. of Yr. award ABWA, 2002, First Go to the Last Mile trphy, 2003; fellow J. Pierpont Morgan Libr., Oct. 15 Fred Bentley Day City & Coun.; Bridge named in his honor, 2000. Fellow Am. Trust Brit. Libr.; mem. Ga. Bar Assn., Ga. Mus. Art (bd. advisors, hon. life mem.), Nat. PTA (hon. life), Supreme Ct. Hist. Soc., Cobb Landmarks Soc. (founder), Kennesaw Mountain Jaycees (founder), Rotary (hon. life), Georgian Club (bd. dir.), The Grolier Club (hon.), Fellows of Marietta Cobb Mus. of Art (founder). Republican. Presbyterian. Home: 1441 Beaumont Dr Kennesaw GA 30152-3201 Office: 241 Washington Ave NE Marietta GA 30060-1958

BENTLEY, GREGORY W. literature educator; b. Brawley, Calif., Apr. 20, 1949; s. Robert Paul and Nina Esther Bentley; BA, Calif. State U., Fresno, 1975, MA, 1977; PhD, U. Calif., Davis, 1986. Prof. Miss. State U., Starkville, 1986—. Vis. lectr. Gutenberg U., Mainz, Germany, 1980—81, Meisei U., Tokyo, 1991—92. Author: (book) Shakespeare and the New Disease, 1989. Mem.: MLA, Lit. and Film Soc., S.-Ctrl. Renaissance Assn. Democrat. Avocations: jogging, gardening. Home: 203 Seville Pl Starkville MS 39759 Office: Miss State U Mississippi State MS 39762 Business E-Mail: greg@english.msstate.edu.

BENTLEY, JAMES LUTHER, former journalist; b. Panama City, Fla., Jan. 24, 1937; s. Thomas Pierce and Sara Pope (Woodruff) B.; m. Patricia Ann Daniel, July 30, 1965. Student Ga. Inst. Tech, Ga. State U., 1958-61, N.C. State U., 1962. Reporter Atlanta Constitution, 1958-64, asst. city editor, 1964-66, night city editor, 1966-71, city editor, 1971-79; corr. Reuters Ltd., 1967-79; dir. info. TVA, 1979; mng. editor Cox News Svc., Washington, 1979-98. Bd. dirs. Friends of Jekyll Island, Hofwyl Plantation. Served with U.S. Army, 1961-63. Mem. Rotary. Lutheran. Home: 317 Old Plantation Rd Jekyll Island GA 31527-0857 E-mail: bentley@thebest.net.

BENTLEY, JAMES ROBERT, association curator, historian, genealogist; b. Louisville, Feb. 14, 1942; s. Francis Getty and Katharine Elizabeth (Wescott) B. BA, Centre Coll. Ky., 1964; MA, Coll. William and Mary, 1971. Research asst. Colonial Williamsburg (Va.), 1966-68; asst. to curator Filson Club, Louisville, 1964-65; curator, 1968-83; sec., 1972-84; acting dir., 1983-84; dir., 1984-92, G.R. Clark Press, Louisville, 1974—. Mem. adv. com. to photograph archives U. Louisville, 1971-72; mem. Hist. Zoning Task Force Louisville and Jefferson County, 1971-73; mem. hist. protection and preservation com. Bd. Aldermen Louisville, 1972-73; mem. Mayor's Com. Public Amenities, 1991—; mem. Jefferson County Comm. Ky. Bicentennial Comn., 1991-92; commr. Hist. Landmarks and Preservation Dists. Commn., Louisville, 1973-79. Editor, pub. Ky. Genealogist, 1979-86. Mem. SAR (registrar 1970-93, library com.), Ky. Soc. Mayflower Descs. (historian, librarian 1970-78, gov. 1978-84, dep. gov. gen. 1981-87, 5 generation project com. 1979-80), Ky. Soc. Colonial Wars (councillor 1971-76, registrar 1976—), Jeffersontown Hist. Soc. (dir. 1972-73, v.p. 1974-76, pres. 1976-78), Soc. Am. Archivists, Manuscript Soc., Hist. Homes Found. Louisville, Vt. Hist. Soc. (life), New Eng. Hist. Geneal. Soc., Nat. Geneal. Soc. (life), Vt. Geneal. Soc., Ind. Hist. Soc., Vt. Old Cemetery Assn., Louisville Hist. League, Alden Kindred Am., Soc. Stukely Westcott Descs., Edmund Rice 1638 Assn., Soc. Descs. Robert Bartlett of Plymouth Colony, Harleian Soc., Order Ky. Cols., Sigma Chi. Clubs: Pendennis (Louisville), Filson (life). Episcopalian. Home: 1048 Cherokee Rd Louisville KY 40204-1231

BENTLEY, JEFFREY, performing company executive; Grad., U. Wash. Ballet dancer, N.Y.C.; from asst. to producing dir. to adminstrv. dir. Seattle Repertory Theatre, 1973-81; exec. dir. Northlight Theatre Co., Evanston, Ill.; mng. dir. dance ctr. Columbia Coll., Chgo., 1983-85; exec. dir. Eugene Ballet Co., Oreg.; dir. DanceAspen Festival and Sch., Aspen, Colo.; exec. dir. Royal Winnipeg Ballet, 1993-96, State Ballet of Mo. (now Kansas City Ballet), Kansas City, Mo., 1998—. Panelist, site visitor NEA, Colo. Coun. Arts, Ill. Arts Coun.; cons. Western States Art Fedn., Santa Fe, Found. Ext. and Devel. Am. Profl. Theatre. NEA fellow Wash. State Arts Commn. Office: Kansas City Ballet 1601 Broadway Kansas City MO 64108

BENTLEY, JOHN R. language educator; s. Russell Gordon and Armina Nadine Bentley; m. Chiemi Sato, June 10, 1982; children: Jennifer S., Michelle A., Stephen T. PhD, U. of Hawaii at Manoa, Honolulu, Hawaii, 1996—99. Assoc. prof. No. Ill. U., DeKalb, Ill., 2000—. Author: (linguistic) A Descriptive Grammar of Early Old Japanese, (historiographical) Historiographical Trends in Early Japan. Local ch. leader Ch. of Jesus Christ of Latter-day Saints, Sycamore, Ill., 2000—03. Mem.: Mokkan Gakkai (mem. 2003). Office: Northern Illinois Univ Foreign Languages Dept DeKalb IL 60115-2828

BENTLEY, KENNETH CHESSAR, oral and maxillofacial surgeon, educator; b. Montreal, Que., Can., Sept. 22, 1935; s. Albert Edwin and Lilian Beatrice (Hoare) B.; m. Jean Wadsworth, Aug. 19, 1961; children: Douglas, Margaret. DDS, McGill U., 1958, MD, CM, 1962. Intern, then resident Montreal Gen. Hosp. and Bellevue Hosp., N.Y., 1962-66; from asst. prof. to assoc. prof. McGill U., 1966-67, prof. dentistry, 1975-98, prof. emeritus, 1998; dean McGill U. Sch. Dentistry, 1977-87; jr. asst. dental surgeon Montreal Gen. Hosp., 1966, assoc. dental surgeon, assoc. dir. dentistry, 1968, dental surgeon-in-chief, 1970-2000. Cons. oral and maxillofacial surgery Royal Victoria Hosp.; v.p. Thistle Coun. Quebec, pres, bd dirs. Griffith-McConnell Residence. Co-author: Advanced Oral Radiographic Interpretation, 1979. Named Decorated Hospitaller, Order St. John Jerusalem; recipient Queen's Golden Jubilee medal, 2002. Fellow Am. Coll. Dentists, Internat. Coll. Dentists, Royal Coll. Dentists Can., Pierre Fauchard Acad., Academie Dentaire Du Quebec; mem. Assn. Oral and Maxillofacial Surgeons Que., Bellevue Soc. Oral Surgeons, Can. Dental Assn. (chmn. council hosp. services 1971-75, council edn. 1982-85), Can. Assn. Oral and Maxillofacial Surgeons (sec.-treas. 1970-71), Internat. Assn. Study Pain, Internat. Assn. Oral Surgeons, Montreal Dental Club (sec. 1968, pres.1992), Nat. Dental Examining Bd. Can., Order Dentists Que., St. Andrew's Soc. Montreal (1st v.p.). Avocations: music, pipe organ, scottish country dancing. Office: B3-149 1650 Cedar Ave Montreal QC Canada H3G 1A4

BENTLEY, KIA JEAN, social worker, educator; b. Mineola, NY, June 17, 1956; d. William Gerald and Zilpha Ann (Draper) B. BA, Auburn U., 1978; MSSW, U. Tenn., 1979; PhD, Fla. State U., 1987. Diplomate in Clin. Social Work; lic. clin. social worker. Social worker East Ala. Med. Ctr., Opelika, 1979-84; asst. prof. La. State U. Sch. Social Work, Baton Rouge, 1987-89; prof., dir. PhD program Va. Commonwealth U. Sch. Social Work, Richmond, 1989—. Chair human rights com. Ctrl. State Hosp.; mem. commn. on accreditation Coun. on Social Work Edn., 2003—. Co-author: The Social Worker and Psychotropic Medication, 2d edit., 2001; editor: Social Work Practice in Mental Health, 2002; cons. editor: Jour. Social Work Edn., 2003—.

Active St. Paul's Episcopal Ch. Mem. NASW, Coun. on Social Work Edn. (mem. commn. on accreditation), Nat. Alliance for the Mentally Ill. Democrat. Avocations: wine, movies, cooking, golf. Office: Va Commonwealth U Sch Social Work 1001 W Franklin St Richmond VA 23284-2027

BENTLEY, LISA, publisher; BA in Engliish, U. Iowa. Acct. exec. Bozell; with SW Media Corp., Dallas, NY; sales exec. People and Life mag., L.A., NY; regional mgr. info. tech. Time mag., 1992—99; founding pub. Bus. 2.0 Mag. (formerly eCompany Now); with Time Inc.; pub. Bus. 2.0 mag., San Francisco, 2002—. Office: One California St 29th Fl San Francisco CA 94111*

BENTLEY, MARGARET ANN, librarian; b. Tawas City, Mich., June 13, 1956; d. Rupert A. and Joy A. (Bills) B. AB in English, Gordon Coll., 1978; MA in Libr. Sci., U. Mich., 1979. Cert. libr., Mich. Adult svcs. libr., asst. dir. Shiawassee Dist. Libr. (formerly Owosso Pub. Libr.), Owosso, Mich., 1979—. Mem.: AAUW (treas. 1984—2003), Mich. Libr. Assn., Phi Alpha Chi, Lambda Iota Tau, Beta Phi Mu. Avocations: reading, crafts, camping. Office: Shiawassee Dist Libr 502 W Main St Owosso MI 48867-2607

BENTLEY, PETER, lawyer; b. Jersey City, Sept. 1, 1915; s. Peter and Emma (Patterson) B.; m. Signe Von Krusenstierna, Apr. 15, 1944 (dec. Mar. 1984); 1 child, Frederique Bentley Boire; m. Jane Morfoot Chapman, Apr. 19, 1986. BA, Princeton U., 1938; JD, Yale U., 1941. Bar: N.Y. 1942, U.S. Ct. Appeals (2d cir.) 1943, U.S. Dist. Ct. (so. dist.) N.Y. 1944, Conn. 1952, U.S. Dist. Ct. Conn. 1954. Assoc. Simpson, Thacher & Bartlett, N.Y.C., 1941—52, Maguire, Cole, Bentley & Babson (and predecessors), Stamford, Conn., 1952—81; mem. Bentley, Mosher, Babson & Lambert, P.C. and predecessors, Stamford, 1981—99; of counsel Bentley, Mosher, Babson, & Lambert P.C., Greenwich, Conn., 1999—2002. Rep. Greenwich Town Meeting, 1966—68; bd. dirs., pres. The Carl J. Herzog Found. Inc., 1978—; bd. dirs. Feris Found. Am. Inc., 1983—90, The Royal Soc. of Medicine Found., Inc., 1991—96. Mem. ABA, Conn. Bar Assn., Stamford Bar Assn. (pres. 1971-72, bd. dirs.), Am. Skin Assn. (bd. dirs., chmn. 1988-96). Mem. Soc. Of Friends. Home: Crawford 232 7 Riverwoods Dr Exeter NH 03833-4374 Office: Bentley Mosher Babson & Lambert PC 321 Railroad Ave Greenwich CT 06830-0788

BENTLEY, RICHARD NORCROSS, regional planner, writer, educator; b. Chgo., Mar. 17, 1937; s. Richard and Phoebe Wrenn (Norcross) B.; m. Carolyn Stiglic, Sept. 10, 1977; children: Nicholas Northrup, Julia Wrenn. BA, Yale U., 1959; MFA, Norwich U., 1992; writers workshop, U. Iowa, 1995. Chief project mgr. Kate Maremont Found., 1965-70, Rose Assocs., N.Y.C., 1973-75, Adv. Svcs. for Better Housing, N.Y.C., 1975-78, Mass. Dept. Community Affairs, Boston, 1978-83; chief planner Mayor's Office Housing, Boston, 1983-86; planning dir. Boston Housing Authority, 1986-87; sr. planning mgr. Pioneer Valley Planning Commn., West Springfield, Mass., 1987-88. Instr. Internat. City Mgmt. Assn., Washington, 1982-90; instr. creative writing U. Mass., 1992—, Cambridge Coll., 1994-2000, Mass. Coll. Liberal Arts, 1995-99, Holyoke C.C., 1997-99; instr. MFA program Vt. Coll., 1997, 99; adj. prof. Western New England Coll., 2000—. Author: Post-Freudian Dreaming, 2002; mng. editor Peregrine Mag., 1991-93. Bd. govs. Groton (Mass.) Sch., 1990-95; gov.'s appointee Mass. Mortgage Rev. Bd., 1984—; del. Dem. State Conv., Mass., 2000. Served with U.S. Army, 1960-62. Recipient Internat. Fiction award Paris Writers' Workshop, 1994. Mem.: Am. Planning Assn., Mass. Housing and Redevel. Ofcls., Assn. Yale Alumni Assembly (del. 2000—), Soc. Mayflower Descs., Assn. Personal Historians (founding), Harvard Club (Boston), Yale Club (Conn. Valley), Amherst Yacht Club. Home: 24 N Prospect St Amherst MA 01002-2014 E-mail: rbentley@acad.umass.edu.

BENTLEY, THOMAS ROY, English language educator, writer, consultant, professor emeritus; b. Belfast, No. Ireland, June 5, 1931; s. Thomas and Anne (Hill) B.; m. Joan M. Williams, Dec. 24, 1955; children: Kimberley, Shannon, Carolyn. M.A. U. Toronto, 1960, MA, 1966; EdB, Ont. Coll., 1961; PhD, Meml. U., Nfld., Can., 1970. Assoc. dean edn., 1979-81, prof. lang. edn., 1983-96, prof. emeritus, 1996—. Cons. to maj. cos. on comml. and transp. issues; co-founder Internat. Lifewriting Network. Author 4 books on English comms.; editor 12 books on Can. lit.; contbr. articles to profl. jours.; broadcaster numerous programs on radio and TV. Mem. Nat. Assn. Tchrs. English (chmn. internat. assembly 1981), Assn. Profs. Emeriti, Nat. Conf. for Rsch. in English, Can. Coun. Tchrs. English (editor, bd. dirs., 1975-78), Vancouver Club. Office: 5529 University Blvd Vancouver BC Canada V6T 1K5 E-mail: raybentley@ubc.ca.

BENTLEY-SCHECK, GRACE MARY, artist; b. Troy, N.Y., Apr. 20, 1937; d. John Franklin and Gladys Serena B.; m. George Frederick Scheck, July 22, 1967. BFA, SUNY, Alfred, 1959, MFA, 1960. Tchr. art Riverhead (N.Y.) Jr. High Sch., 1963-67, North Colonie Ctrl. Schs., Latham, N.Y., 1967-72; artist, printmaker Oswego, NY, 1972—83. Narragansett, RI, 1983—. Chair art scholar Wickford (R.I.) Art Assn., 1986—; graphic designer, fundraiser South County Cmty. Action, Wakefield, R.I., 1996, 97, 98. Mem. Soc. Am. Graphic Artists (Paul Cadmus Meml. award 1997, Robert Conover Meml. award 2002), Printmakers Network So. New England, Boston Printmakers, 19 on Paper (treas. 1994—), Fla. Printmaking Soc., Art League R.I. Avocations: cooking, literature, gardening, German Shepherds. Home and Office: 63 Sassafras Trl Narragansett RI 02882-2503 E-mail: gbentleyscheck@msn.com.

BENTLY, DONALD EMERY, electrical engineer; b. Cleve., Oct. 18, 1924; s. Oliver E. Bently and Mary Evelyn (Conway) B.; m. Susan Lorraine Pumphrey, Sept. 1961 (div. Sept. 1982); 1 child, Christopher Paul. BSEE with distinction, U. Iowa, 1949, MSEE, 1950; DS (hon.), U. Nev., 1987. Registered profl. engr., Calif., Nev. Pres. Bently Nev. Corp., Minden, 1961-85, chief exec. officer, 1985—2002, Bently Rotor Dynamics and Research Corp., Minden, 1985—2002; also chmn. bd. dirs. Bently Nev. Corp., Minden; chief exec. officer and chmn. Nat. Tribology Svcs., Inc., 2001—. Chief exec. officer Gibson Tool Co., Carson City, Nev., 1978—; bd. dirs. Sierra Pacific Resources, 1982-83. Contbr. articles to profl. jours.; developer electronic instruments for the observation of rotating machinery, and the algorithm for rotor fluid-induced instability; inventor in field. Trustee Inst. World Politics. With USN, 1943-46, PTO. Named Inventor of Yr., State of Nev. Innovation and Tech. Coun., 1983; recipient first Decade Decade award, Vibration Inst., 1992, Myklestad award; inducted to Jr. Achievement of Northern Nev. Bus. Leaders' Hall of Fame. Mem. ASME (industry adv. bd.), Am. Petroleum Inst., St. Petersburg (Russian Fedn.) Acad. Engring., Sigma Xi, Eta Kappa Nu, Tau Beta Pi, Sigma Alpha Epsilon. Episcopalian. Avocations: skiing, hiking, biking. Office: Bently Nev Corp 1711 Orbit Way Minden NV 89423-4114

BENTMAN, JULIUS, periodontist; b. Phila., Sept. 26, 1919; s. Isadore and Gertrude (Schipior) B.; m. Ada Ruth Kaplan, Nov. 22, 1944; children: Adrienne Lynn. BA, U. Pa., 1943, MScD, 1947. Diplomate Am. Bd. Periodontology. Practice periodontology, Lancaster. Mem. faculty U. Pa., 1947-74; asst. prof., 1964-67, asst. prof., dir. divsn. advanced dental edn., 1964-74; cons. VA Med. Ctr., 1948-90, U.S. Navy Hosp., Phila., 1951-60, Lancaster Gen. Hosp., 1949-90, St. Joseph Hosp., 1950-90; cons. Lancaster Cleft Palate Clinic, 1952-2000, also adv. com., 1980-2000, chmn. investigation review bd., adv. com., 1994-2000; preparator Smithsonian Instn., 1987-91. Chmn. Lancaster County Fluordation Com., 1950-59. Capt. AUS, 1941-46. Fellow Am. Coll. Dentistry; mem. ADA, Royal Soc. Health, Pa. Soc. Periodontists (pres. 1973), Am. Acad. Periodontology (chmn. com. dental care programs 1980-82), Am. Assn. Dental Cons., Ret. Officers Assn. (sec. Lancaster chpt. 1999-), Omicron Kappa Upsilon, Cryer Hon. Dental Soc., Mil. Officers Assn. Am. (sec. Lancaster chpt. 1999—). Home: 383 Blossom Hill Dr Lancaster PA 17601-3249

BENTON, ALLEN HAYDON, biology educator; b. Ira, N.Y., Sept. 4, 1921; s. Haydon Willey and Pearl Amelia (Diddy) B.; m. Marjorie Louis Hall, Aug. 16, 1947; children: Thomas Hall, Christopher Allen, Holly Anne. BS, Cornell U., 1948, MS, 1949, Ph.D. 1952. Jr. wildlife biologist U.S. Fish and Wildlife Service, 1949-57; asst. prof. biology SUNY-Albany, 1949-57, assoc. prof., 1957-62; prof. biology SUNY-Fredonia, 1962-73, disting. teaching prof., 1973-84, faculty exchange scholar, 1975-84, prof. emeritus, 1984—. Vis. prof. Stephen F. Austin Coll., 1957, Concord Coll., Athens, W.Va., 1969-70, U. Minn. Biol. Sta., 1970; cons. Nuclear Fuel Services Inc., Fla. Arthropod Collection, Roger Tory Peterson Inst. for the Study of Natural History. Author: (with W.E. Werner Jr.) Field Biology and Ecology, 3rd edit., 1974, Atlas of Fleas of the Eastern United

States, 1980, Manual for Field Biology and Ecology, 6th edit., 1983. Wild Worlds, 1988, Light and Natural, 1992; columnist Dunkirk (N.Y.) Evening Observer, Albany (N.Y.) Knickerbocker News, Jamestown (N.Y.) Post Jour.; freelance writer on nature and sci.; contbr. articles to profl. jours. Served with cav. U.S. Army, 1942-46. Decorated Bronze Star; grantee Research Found. SUNY, 1963, 83; NSF grantee, 1972; E.N. Huyck Found. grantee, 1976-78 Mem. Am. Ornithologists Union, Am. Soc. Mammalogists, Wilson Ornithol. Soc., Fedn. N.Y. State Bird Clubs (pres.), PTA (life), Sigma Xi, Phi Kappa Phi. Home: 292 Water St Fredonia NY 14063-2025

BENTON, ANDREW KEITH, university administrator, lawyer; b. Hawthrone, Nev., Feb. 4, 1952; s. Darwin Keith and Nelda Lou Benton; m. Deborah Sue Strickland, June 22, 1974; children: Hailey Michelle, Christopher Andrew. BS in Am. Studies, Okla. Christian Coll., 1974; JD, Oklahoma City U., 1979. Bar: Okla. 1979, U.S. Dist. Ct. (we. dist.) Okla. (admitted to) 1982. Sole practice, Edmond, Okla., 1979-81, 83-84; ptnr. Benton & Thomason, Edmond, 1981—83; asst. v.p. Pepperdine U., Malibu, Calif., 1984—85, v.p., 1985—87, v.p. adminstrn., 1987—89, v.p. univ. affairs, 1989—91, exec. v.p., 1991—2000, pres., 2000—. Chmn. precinct, state conv. del. Okla. Reps., 1980. Mem.: Okla. Bar Assn. (contbr. articles to ednl. community), ABA (chmn. subcom. emerging land use trends 1987—88, chmn. subcom. decisional trends 1988—90). Republican. Mem. Ch. Of Christ. Office: Pepperdine U 24255 Pacific Coast Hwy Malibu CA 90263-0002*

BENTON, ANTHONY STUART, lawyer; b. Decatur, Ill., Jan. 28, 1949; s. Paul Stewart and Allene Juanita (Jones) B.; m. Peggy Ann Miller, Aug. 6, 1977; children: Allison Renee, Emily Elizabeth, Anne McKinley. BA cum laude, U. Ill., 1971; JD summa cum laude, Ind. U., 1976. Bar: Ill. 1976, Ind. 1976, U.S. Dist. Ct. (so. and no. dists.) Ind. 1976, U.S. Ct. Appeals (7th cir.) 1978, U.S. Supreme Ct. 1993. Assoc. Stuart & Branigin, Lafayette, Ind., 1976-80, ptnr., 1980—; chief legal counsel Purdue U., 2000—. Prof. in environ. Purdue U. Sch. Civil Engring., 1993-2000. Bd. dirs. Lafayette C. of C., 1993-2003, treas., 1998, chair-elect, 1999, chmn. 2000-01; bd. dirs. New Directions, Lafayette, 1978-80, Clegg Found., Lafayette, 1988-93, Wabash Ctr., Lafayette, 1984-86, Greater Lafayette CDC, 2001—, exec. com.; mem. pres. coun. Purdue U., 1990—, convocations bd. dirs., 1991-97. With USNR, 1971-77. Fellow Ind. Bar Found. (bd. dirs 1998-0); mem. Nat. Assn. R.R. Trial Counsel, Ind. State Bar Assn. (sec. sect. on environ. law 1992), Ill. State Bar Assn., Am. Judicature Soc., Environ. Law Inst., Masons. Office: Stuart & Branigin PO Box 1010 Lafayette IN 47902-1010 E-mail: asb@stuartlaw.com

BENTON, AUBURN EDGAR, lawyer; b. Colorado Springs, Colo., July 12, 1926; s. Auburn Edgar and Ella Dot (Heyer) B.; m. Stephanie Marie Jakimowitz, June 8, 1951; children: Margrit Laura, Mary Ellen BA, Colo. Coll., 1950; LLB, Yale U., 1953. Bar: Colo. 1953, U.S. Dist. Ct. Colo. 1953, U.S. Ct. Appeals (10th cir.) 1954. Assoc. Holme Roberts & Owen, Denver, 1953-57, ptnr., 1957-91, of counsel, 1992—. Mem. Bd. Edn. Denver Pub. Schs., 1961-69; mem. Colo. Commn. Higher Edn., Denver, 1975-85; mem. Colo. Bd. Ethics, Denver, 1975-98; mem. Nat. Common Cause Bd., Washington, 1975-85; dir. soc. sci. found. U. Denver. Mem. Colo. Bar Assn., Denver Bar Assn., Cactus Club (Denver), Phi Beta Kappa. Democrat. Home: 901 Race St Denver CO 80206-3735 Office: Holme Roberts & Owen 1700 Lincoln St Ste 4100 Denver CO 80203-4541

BENTON, DONALD MARK, state legislator, political organization chairman; b. Agua Dulce, Calif., Apr. 8, 1957; s. Arlis Redford and Dorothy Helen B.; m. Mary E. Enders, Nov. 6, 1982; children Jennifer Marie, Adam Carson, Bradly, Austin. AS, Coll. of the Canyons, Valencia, Calif.; BS in Bus. Mgmt. & Comm., Concordia U., Portland, Oreg. Founder, chief exec. officer Santa Clarita Temporaries, Inc., Newhall, Calif., 1979-83; dist. mgr. Farmers Ins. Group, L.A., 1983-88; nat. sales trainer, speaker Nat. Cons. Svcs., Vancouver, Wash., 1988; founder, chief exec. officer The Benton Grp., 1988—; mem. Wash. Ho. of Reps., Olympia, 1994-96, Wash. Senate, Dist. 17, Olympia, 1996—; chair. Wash. Republican Party, 1998—2001; senator State of Wash. from 17th Dist., 1996—. Author: How To Start a Temporary Service, 1981; inventor aerovane. Clk., trustee Santa Clarita Community Coll. Dist., Valencia, Calif., 1981-88, pres. bd. trustees, 1985; pres. Santa Clarita Valley Jaycees, 1981-82; chmn. bd. dirs. Santa Clarita Valley unit ARC, 1983-86. Recipient resolution Calif. Assembly, 1981, ofcl. resolution L.A. County Bd. Suprvs., 1982, spl. recogition U.S. Congress, 1982, Outstanding Young Man award Santa Clarita Valley Jaycees, 1982. Republican. Home: 121 NE 117th Ave Vancouver WA 98684-5019 Address: Wash Senate 109-B Irving R Newhouse Bldg PO Box 40417 Olympia WA 98504-0417

BENTON, DONALD STEWART, publishing company executive, lawyer; b. Marlboro, N.Y., Jan. 2, 1924; s. Fred Stanton and Agnes (Townsend) B. Student, U. Leeds, Eng., 1945; BA, Columbia U., 1947, JD, 1949; LLM, NYU, 1953. Bar: N.Y. 1953. Practiced in N.Y.C., 1953-56; atty. N.Y. State Banking Dept., 1954-55; v.p. Found. Press, Inc., Bklyn., 1957-60; exec. asst. to exec. v.p. N.Y. Stock Exchange, 1960-61; dir. reference book dept. and spl. projects editor Appleton Century Crofts, N.Y.C., 1962-71; sr. editor Matthew Bender & Co., Inc., N.Y.C., 1974-77; sr. legal editor Warren, Gorham & Lamont, Inc., N.Y.C., 1977-89. Author: Thorndike Encyclopedia of Banking and Financial Tables, 3rd edit., 2000 yearbook, Federal Banking Laws, 3rd edit., 2000, Real Estate Tax Digest, 1984, Criminal Law Digest, 3rd edit., 1983, Modern Real Estate and Mortgage Checklists, 1979. Mem. Cresskill (N.J.) Zoning Bd. Adjustment, 1969-71, 82-83, 86—, Cresskill Planning Bd., 1971-74; councilman City of Cresskill, 1972-74. With AUS, 1943-46, 50-52. Decorated Bronze Star. Mem. Phi Delta Phi. Mem. Reformed Ch. in Am. Home: 117 Heatherhill Rd Cresskill NJ 07626-1020 Office: AS Pratt & Sons- Warren Gorham & Lamont 395 Hudson St New York NY 10014-3669

BENTON, JACK MITCHELL, management consultant; b. Bakersfield, Calif., July 15, 1941; s. James Edwin and Alice Kathryn (Hawthorne) B.; m. Suzanne Wilken, June 14, 1964; children: Mitchell Brian, Andrea Katherine. BS in Acctg., Calif. State U., Chico, 1964. CPA, Calif., N.Y. Acct. Arthur Young & Co., Los Angeles, 1964-68; chief fin. officer Newport Nat. Bank, Newport Beach, Calif., 1968-70; mng. dir. human resources Chase Manhattan Bank & Chase Manhattn Capital Markets Corp., N.Y.C., 1970-87; sr. v.p., mgr. human resources Bank Tokyo, Ltd.-N.Y Agy. Bank Tokyo Trust Co., N.Y.C., 1987-93; mng. dir. Alec Peters Assoc., N.Y.C., 1993-95, Cromwell Ptnrs., Inc., N.Y.C., 1995-96, Ward Howell Internat., N.Y.C., 1996-98; v.p. Mitsubishi Materials U.S.A., N.Y.C., 1998-2000; v.p. gen. affairs Mitsubishi Silicon Am., Salem, Oreg., 2000—02, Sumco, U.S.A., 2002—. Served with USCG, 1960-61, USCGR, 1961-68. Mem. AICPA, Soc. Human Resource Mgmt., Calif. Soc. CPAs, N.Y State Soc CPAs, Shek-O Country Club, Hong Kong. Home: 2328 NW Gusan St #9 Portland OR 97210 Office: Sumco Oreg Corp 1351 Tandem Ave NE Salem OR 97303-4105 E-mail: jackbentonx@comcast.net.

BENTON, LEE F. lawyer; b. Springfield, Ohio, Feb. 18, 1944; AB, Oberlin Coll., 1966; JD, U. Chgo., 1969. Bar: Calif. 1970. Mng. ptnr. Cooley Godward LLP, Palo Alto, Calif. Teaching fellow Stanford Law Sch., 1969-70. Mem. Order Coif, Phi Beta Kappa. Office: Cooley Godward LLP 5 Palo Alto Sq 3000 El Camino Real Palo Alto CA 94306-2120

BENTON, NICHOLAS, theater producer; b. Boston, Oct. 18, 1926; s. Jay Rogers and Frances (Hill) B.; m. Kate Lenthal Bigelow, June 5, 1954; children: Frances Hill, Kate, Emily Weld, Louisa Barclay. *Nicholas Benton's daughter Frances Hill married David Edward Nallett, the son of Edward Joseph Nallett and Clara Ellis in Spring Bay, Virgin Gorda (BVI) on February 27, 2002. His daughter Kate married James Francis Doughan, the son of Leo Doughan and Nancy Berry, in Wareham, Massachusetts on August 27, 1988. They have two sons, Charles Benton Dougham born in Los Angeles, California on April 22, 1991, and Henry Leo Bigelow Doughan, born in Los Angeles, California on December 1, 1993. His daughter Emily Weld Benton married John Francis Morgan, son of James Paul Morgan and Joan Margaret Fitzgerald, in Wareham, Massachusetts on August 29, 1998. They have one adopted son, August Yong-Kee Morgan, born in Taegu Korea on May 24, 2002.* Grad. Phillips Exeter Acad., 1945; AB, Harvard U., 1951. Promotion writer Life mag., N.Y.C., 1951-55; Fortune mag., N.Y.C., 1955-56; staff writer Time Mag., N.Y.C., 1956-57; advt. promotion mgr. Archtl. Forum, N.Y.C., 1957-64; gen. promotion mgr. Time-Life Books, Alexandria, Va., 1965-68, dir. pub. rels. 1968-83, v.p., 1977-83; lectr. pub. procedures course Radcliffe Coll., 1976-82;

producing dir. Am. Kaleidoscope Theatre, 1983-85; pub., editor Middlesex House Press, N.Y., 1999—. Mem. Nat. Book Awards Com., 1971; co-chmn. Nat. Book Awards Book Awards Com., 1975-79; vice-chmn. Am. Book Awards, 1981-82. Author: A Benton Heritage, 1964, The Call of the Weld, 1999; co-producer musical Phoenix '55, 1955, Salad Days, 1958, The Golden Age, 1984, the Perfect Party, 1986, Love Letters, 1989, The Heart's a Wonder, 1990; author, dir. (play) Not So Long Ago, 1995. Pres. East 69th St. Assn., 1963-64; 1st v.p. Soc. Meml. Sloan-Kettering Cancer Ctr., 1963-64, asst. treas., 1964-66, treas., 1967-68; exec. com. Friends of the Theatre Collection, Mus. of City of N.Y., 1983-86; pres. Land Owners Assn. Indian Neck, Wareham, Mass., 1993-95; chmn. tutoring program Harvard U., NY H.S., 1991—. With AUS, 1945-46. Recipient Opera Vol. Yr., Opera Guild Internat., 2000. Mem. Pubs. Publicity Assn. (pres. 1970-71), New Eng. Historic Geneal. Soc. (trustee 1979-95, corr. sec. 1982-88, v.p. 1988-93), N.Y. Geneal. and Biog. Soc., Assn. Am. Pubs. (freedom to pub. com. 1979-82), Time-Life Alumni Soc. (bd. dirs. 1994—), Soc. of Colonial Wars, Harvard Club (bd. mgrs. N.Y.C. chpt. 1971-73), Bourne Cove Yacht Club (commodore Wareham, Mass. chpt. 1988-91), N.Y. City Opera (bd. dirs. 1995-99, guild pres. 1995-99, editor Tempo newsletter 1993-00). Home and Office: 129 E 82nd St New York NY 10028-0836 Home (Summer): Indian Neck Wareham MA 02571

BENTON, NICHOLAS FREDERICK, publisher; b. Ross, Calif., Feb. 9, 1944; s. Frederick C. H. and Jeanne Emma (Brun) B.; m. Donna Carley, Apr. 15, 1979 (div. Oct. 1984); m. Janine Schollnick, Oct. 20, 1985. AA, Santa Barbara City Coll., Calif., 1963; BA, Westmont Coll., 1965; MDiv cum laude, Pacific Sch. Religion, Berkeley, Calif., 1969. Reporter Santa Barbara News Press, 1961-66; dir. Christian edn. Plymouth Ch., Oakland, Calif., 1966-69; chief corr. Berkeley Barb, 1970-72; dir. advt. display Syufy Enterprises, San Francisco, 1973-76; regional dir. Exec. Intelligence Rev., Washington, 1976-87; chief Washington corr. Century News Svc., Falls Church, Va., 1987—2002, chmn., chief exec. officer, 1987—2002; owner, editor Falls Church News Press, 1991—; pres., CEO Benton Comms., Inc., 2002—. Pres. Falls Church Baseball, Inc., 1991—; clk. Emmaus Ch., 1989-92; bd. dirs. Arlington (Va.) Symphony, 1992-93, Falls Church Edn. Found., 2003—. Recipient Bus. of Yr. award Falls Church City Coun., 1991, Bus. Contbn. to Cmty. award, 1997, Bus. of Yr. award Fall Church City Coun., 2001, Grand Marshall Falls Church Meml. Day Parade, 2001; named to Media Honor Roll, Va. Sch. Bd., 1998. Mem. Greater Falls Church C. of C. (bd. dir. 1991—, pres. 1993-94, Pillar of Cmty. award 1995), LWV of Falls Church, mem. Falls Church City Dem. Com., Optimists Club, White Ho. Corr. Assn., Nat. Press Club (Washington). Mem. United Ch. Christ. Office: Falls Church News Press 929 W Broad St Ste 200 Falls Church VA 22046-3121

BENTON, STEPHEN RICHARD, civil and mechanical engineer; b. Brawley, Calif., Aug. 26, 1952; s. Homer Grabill and Blanche Carolyn (Saxe) B.; m. Diane Gordon Brooks, June 19, 1976; children: Matthew Richard, Sarah Ruth, Carolyn Brooks. BS, U.S. Mil. Acad., 1974; MSCE, MSME, Stanford U., 1982. Registered prof. engr., Va. Commd. 2d lt. U.S. Army, 1974, advanced through grades to lt. col., 1991; exch. officer Sch. Mil. Engring., Casula, New South Wales, Australia, 1988-90; mil. planning officer Office of Chief Engrs., Washington, 1990-92; dept. dist. engr. U.S. Army C.E., San Juan, P.R., 1992-95; engr. staff officer U.S. Army Space and Strategic Def. Command, Arlington, Va., 1995-97; dir. mgmt. devel. Centennial Contactors Enterprises, Inc., Vienna, Va., 1997—99, v.p., 1999—2000, sr. v.p., 2000—. Assoc. editor Jour. Mgmt. Engring., 1998—, Leadership and Mgmt. in Engring., 2001-. Decorated Legion of Merit; recipient Bronze de Fleury medal Army Engr. Assn., 1992, Silver de Fleury medal, 1997. Fellow ASCE; mem. ASME, Soc. Am. Mil. Engrs., Phi Kappa Phi. Office: Centennial Contractors Enterprises Inc 8500 Leesburg Pike Ste 500 Vienna VA 22182-2412

BENTON, W. DUANE, judge; b. Springfield, Mo., Sept. 8, 1950; s. William Max and Patricia F. (Nicholson) B.; m. Sandra Snyder, Nov. 15, 1980; children: Megan Blair, William Grant. BA in Polit. Sci. summa cum laude, Northwestern U., 1972; JD, Yale U., 1975; MBA in Accounting, Memphis State U., 1979; student Inst. Jud. Adminstrn., NYU, 1992; LLD (hon.), Ctrl. Mo. State U., 1994; LLM, U. Va., 1995; LLD (hon.), Westminster Coll., 1999. Bar: Mo. 1975; CPA, Mo. Ensign USN, 1972; advanced through grades to capt., 1993; judge advocate USN, Memphis, 1975-79; chief of staff for Congressman Wendell Bailey, Washington, 1980-82; pvt. practice Jefferson City, Mo., 1983-89; dir. revenue Mo. Dept. of Revenue, Jefferson City, 1989-91; judge Mo. Supreme Ct., Jefferson City, 1991—, chief justice, 1997-99. Adj. prof. Westminster Coll., U. Mo.-Columbia Sch. Law. Contbr. articles to profl. jours.; mng. editor Yale Law Jour., 1974-75 Chmn. Multistate Tax Commn. Washington, 1990-91; chmn. Mo. State Employees Retirement System, Jefferson City, 1989-93; regent Ctrl. Mo. State U., 1987-89; dir. Coun. for Drug Free Youth, Jefferson City, 1989-97; mem. Mo. Mil. Adv. Com., 1989-91; mem. Mo. Commn. Intergovernmental Coop., Jefferson City, 1989-91; trustee, deacon 1st Bapt. Ch., Jefferson City. Danforth fellow JFK Sch. Govt. Harvard U., 1990. Mem. AICPA (tax com. 1983—), Mo. Bar Assn. (tax com. 1975—), Mo. Soc. CPA's (tax com. 1983—), Navy League, Mil. Order of World Wars, Vietnam Vets of Am., VFW, Am. Legion, Phi Beta Kappa, Beta Gamma Sigma, Rotary. Baptist. Lt. USN, 1975-80. Capt. JAGC USNR, 1993-2002. Office: Supreme Court PO Box 150 Jefferson City MO 65102-0150 E-mail: dbenton@osca.state.mo.us.

BENTSEN, KENNETH E., JR., congressman; b. Houston, June 3, 1959; m. Tamra Bentsen; children: Louise, Meredith. BA, U. St. Thomas, Houston, 1982; M in Pub. Adminstrn., Am. U., 1985. Mem. staff Congressman Ronald D. Coleman, 1983-87; assoc. staff U.S. House Appropriations Com., 1985-87; chair Harris County Dem. Party, 1990-93; investment banker Houston, 1987-94; mem. 104th-107th Congresses from 25th Tex. dist., 1995—. Democrat. Presbyterian. Office: US House Reps 405 Cannon House Ofc Bldg Washington DC 20515-0001

BENTSEN, KENNETH EDWARD, architect; b. Mission, Tex., Nov. 21, 1926; s. Lloyd Millard and Edna Ruth (Colbath) B.; m. Mary Dorsey Bates, Dec. 3, 1953; children: Molly Bates, Elizabeth Jean, Kenneth Edward Jr., William Lloyd. BS, U. Houston, 1951, BA, 1952. Pvt. practice architecture, prin. Kenneth Bentsen Assocs., Houston, 1958-91. Projects include Baylor Coll. Medicine, Jones and Anderson Med. Research Tower, M.D. Anderson-R. Lee Clark Clinic Bldg., West Tower, Clin. Care Ctr., Tex. Children's Hosp., Houston, Tex. Med. Ctr., Agnes Arnold Hall, Philip Hoffman Hall, U. Houston, M.D. Anderson Library, U. Houston, Pan Am. U., Grad. Sch. Bus., U. Tex, M.D. Anderson Environ. Rsch. Ctr., U. Tex, Learning Ctr., Allied Health Sci. & Nursing, U. Tex. Med. Br., Galveston, Compaq Ctr., Houston State Law Ctr., Austin, Tex., Harris County Adminstrn. Bldg., Houston, Tex. Commerce Bldg. Complex, McAllen, Tex. Bd. dirs. Tex. Children's Hosp., Cultural Trust Coun. Tex.; past bd. dirs. Tex. Commn. on the Arts, Mayor's Com. Bd. Appeals, Mus. Fine Arts, Blaffer Gallery; past mem. adv. coun. U. Tex. Sch. Architecture Pres.'s Adv. Com. Recipient numerous design awards. Mem. AIA, Tex. Soc. Architects, Houston C. of C. Office: Kenneth Bentsen FAIA 12 E Greenway Plz Ste 1100 Houston TX 77046-1201

BENTSEN, LLOYD, former government official, former senator; b. Mission, TX, Feb. 11, 1921; s. Lloyd M. and Edna Ruth (Colbath) B.; m. Beryl Ann Longino, Nov. 27, 1943; children: Lloyd M. III, Lan, Tina. JD, U. Tex., 1942. Bar: Tex. 1942. Practice law, McAllen, Tex., 1945-48; judge Hidalgo County, Tex., (hdqs. Edinburg), 1946-48; mem. 80th-83d congresses from 15th Tex. Dist.; pres. Lincoln Consol., Houston, 1955-70; U.S. Senator from Tex., 1971-93; chmn. senate fin. com.; mem. senate commerce, sci., transp. and joint com. on taxation and congl. joint econ. com.; sec. Dept. Treasury, Washington, 1993-94; ptnr. Verner, Liipfert, Bernhard, McPherson and Hand. Democratic nominee for Vice Pres. U.S., 1988. Served to maj. USAAF, 1942-45. Decorated D.F.C., Air Medal with 3 oak leaf clusters; recipient Presdl. medal of Freedom, 1999.

BENTZ, DALE MONROE, librarian; b. York County, Pa., Jan. 3, 1919; s. Solomon Earl and Mary Rebecca (Wonders) B.; m. Mary Gail Menius, June 13, 1942; children: Dale Flynn, Thomas Earl, Mary Carolyn. AB, Gettysburg Coll., 1939; BSL.S., U. N.C. Chapel Hill, 1940; MS, U. Ill., 1951. With Periodicals dept. U. N.C. Library, Chapel Hill, 1940-41, Serials Dept., Duke U. Library, Durham, N.C., 1941-42; asst. librarian E. Carolina Tchrs. Coll., Greenville, N.C., 1946-48; head processing dept. U. Tenn. Library, Knoxville, 1948-53; assoc. dir. libraries U. Iowa, Iowa City, 1953-70, univ. librarian, 1970-86, univ.

librarian emeritus, 1986—. Editor U. Tenn. Library Lectures, 1952; contbr. articles to profl. jours. Pres. Iowa City Bd. Edn., 1962-63 Mem. Iowa Library Assn. (pres., 1959-60), ALA (pres. resources and tech. services div. 1975-76), AAUP, Assn. Coll. and Research Libraries, Beta Phi Mu (pres. 1966-67) Clubs: Triangle (pres. 1958-59), Univ. Athletic (sec. 1979-80). Lutheran. Home: 701 Oaknoll Dr # 430 Iowa City IA 52246-5168 E-mail: dalembentz@hotmail.com.

BENTZ, EDWARD JOSEPH, JR., energy, environment and transportation management consulting firm executive; b. N.Y.C., May 17, 1945; m. Carole. BS in Physics, Rensselaer Poly. Inst., 1966; vis. fellow Rockefeller Inst., 1966-67; MPhil., Yale U., 1969, PhD, 1971. Danmark-Amerika Fondet George C. Marshall fellow Neils Bohr Inst., Copenhagen, 1971-72; vis. fellow USSR Acad. Scis., 1972, mem. tech. staff David Sarnoff Research Center, RCA, Princeton, N.J., 1972-74; mem. policy staff EPA, Washington, 1974-77; Congl. fellow U.S. Senate com. Commerce, sci. and transp., Washington, 1976-77; dir. impact analysis Presidential-Congl. Nat. Transp. Policy Study Commn., Washington, 1977-79; exec. dir. Presidential-Congl. Nat. Alcohol Fuels Commn., Washington, 1979-80; pres. E.J. Bentz & Assocs., Inc., Springfield, Va., 1980—. appointed mem. Fairfax County Va. Wetlands Bd., 1986—, vice-chmn., 1988—. Author books; contbr. articles to profl. jours. Mem. NAS (transp. rsch. bd. rail tank care design com. 1992—), N.Y. Acad. Scis., Transp. Research Bd., Va. Acad. Scis., Soc. Govt. Regulatory Economists, Sigma Xi, Sigma Pi Sigma. Office: EJ Bentz & Assocs Inc 7915 Richfield Rd Springfield VA 22153-2324

BENTZ, MICHAEL LLOYD, plastic and reconstructive surgeon; b. Pitts., May 9, 1958; s. Joe Denton and Ida Mae (Troxell) B.; m. Kim Marie Livingstone, Nov. 19, 1988. BA, Ind. U., 1980; MD, Temple U., 1984. Diplomate Am. Bd. Surgery, Am. Bd. Plastic Surgery, Nat. Bd. Med. Examiners. Resident in gen. surgery Temple U. Hosp., Phila., 1984-89; rsch. fellow U. Pitts., 1989-90, resident in plastic and reconstructive surgery, 1990-92, asst. prof. surgery and pediat., 1992-99, assoc. prof. surgery and pediat., 1999; prof., chmn. plastic and reconstructive surgery U. Wis., Madison, 1999—. Instr. advanced trauma life support U. Pitts., 1989-95. Contbr. articles to profl. jours. Rsch. grantee Am. Soc. for Surgery of Hand, 1990-91, Plastic Surgery Ednl. Found., 1991-92, 92-93; recipient 1st prize rsch. Ohio Valley soc. Plastic and Reconstructive Surgeons, 1990, Ivy Soc., 1991, Clin. Tour award Coller Soc., 1989, Humaneness in Medicine award Philadelphia County Med. Soc., 1989. Fellow ACS, Am. Acad. Pediatrics; mem. Am. Cleft Palate-Craniofacial Assn., Am. Soc. Plastic and Reconstructive Surgeons, Plastic Surgery Rsch. Coun. Republican. Presbyterian. Home: 9029 Settlers Rd Madison WI 53717-2730 Office: G5/361 Clinical Sci Ctr 600 Highland Ave Madison WI 53792-0001 E-mail: bentz@surgery.wisc.edu.

BENUSSI, ELENA, financial consultant; d. Lucie and Matthew Benussi. BA, NYU, N.Y.C., 1982. V.p. sales Bellmarc Downtown L.L.C, N.Y.C., 1985—2000; fin. advisor pvt. client group UBS Fin. Svcs. Inc., N.Y.C., 2001—. Author: Process of Studying for Certified Financial Planner Certificate. Recipient Baush and Lomb award, 1978; scholar Undergrad. scholar, NYU, 1978—82. Christian. Avocations: tennis, swimming, writing poetry, digital photography, guitar.

BENVENISTE, JACOB, retired physicist; b. Portland, Oreg., Dec. 21, 1921; s. Nissim Aslan and Boule (Capeluto) B.; m. Lucie Almeleh, Apr. 23, 1944; children: Richard Nissim, David Mark, Daniel Stephen. BA, Reed Coll., 1943; PhD, U. Calif., Berkeley, 1952. Physicist Lawrence Livermore (Calif.) Nat. Lab., 1950-63; dir. nuclear effects subdiv. Aerospace Corp., San Bernardino, Calif., 1963-68; v.p., dir. research Physics Internat. Corp., San Leandro, Calif., 1968-72; sr. staff scientist Aerospace Corp., El Segundo, Calif., 1972-82; chief scientist Northrop Research and Tech. Ctr., Palos Verdes, Calif., 1982-88. Mem. adv. rsch. panel Def. Nuclear Agy., Washington, 1965-68; chmn. adv. tech. panel USAF, El Segundo, 1973-77. Patentee in field; contbr. articles to profl. jours. Chmn. Livermore Joint Union High Sch. Dist., 1955-63. Served with USNR, 1944-45. KERR Scholar, Reed Coll., 1941. Mem. AAAS, Am. Phys. Soc., Phi Beta Kappa, Sigma Xi. Jewish. Avocations: auto mechanics, needlepoint. Home: 4458 170th Ave SE Bellevue WA 98006-6500 E-mail: luciejack@webtv.net.

BEN-YAACOV, GIDEON, computer systems designer; b. Bney Brack, Israel, July 26, 1941; arrived in U.S., 1979; s. Abraham and Henda (Natel) Ben-Yaacov; m. Miriam R. Schultz, May 11, 1967; children: David, Saul. BSEE, Technion Israel Inst. Tech., Haifa, 1966. R&D engr. Israeli Ministry of Def., Haifa, 1967-69; sci. asst. U. of the Witwatersrand, Johannesburg, Republic of South Africa, 1969-71; head office engr. ESCOM, Johannesburg, 1971-79; staff engr. Gibbs & Hill, Omaha, 1979-82; head process computer engring. HDR, Omaha, 1982-83; cons. engr. Power Utility Process Computer Engring., Omaha, 1983-92; sr. engr. advanced transp. techs. MFS Network Techs., Omaha, 1992-96; mgr. proposal engring. Adesta Transp., Mt. Laurel, NJ, 1996—2002; cons. engr. Toll Collection Sys. Engring., Omaha, 2002—. Contbr. articles to profl. jours.; author: tech. papers. Mem.: IEEE (sr.), Instrument Soc. Am. (sr. Philip P. Sprague Application award for devel. advanced operator interface 1980). Achievements include research in on human-factors in power and transportation industries; development of of operator interface terminals for power plant computer systems, sound verification and validation procedures to enhance software QA process; technical and administrative leadership for the design of more than 30 advance computer systems for the process industries; introduction of application of distributed controls for electrostatic preciptators. Home: 1870 Mayfair Dr Omaha NE 68144-1050 E-mail: gideonby@yahoo.com.

BENYEI, CANDACE REED, psychotherapist; b. N.Y.C., Feb. 25, 1946; d. Harlow John and Jacqueline de la Valtaire (Smyth) Reed; m. Curt Christian Benyei, July 1, 1967; children: Tara Elaine, Christian Harlow. BA in Chemistry, Colo. Coll., 1967; MS in Sch. Psychology, So. Conn. State U., 1985; MS in Marriage and Family Therapy, U. Bridgeport, Conn., 1987; PhD in Clin. Psychology, Union Inst., Cin., 1988; MPS, N.Y. Theol. Sem., 1994. Lic. marriage and family therapist, Conn. Rsch. assoc. Cornell U., Ithaca, N.Y., 1967-68; rsch. asst. Yale-New Haven Hosp., 1968-70, Clairol, Inc., Stamford, Conn., 1970-71; asst. chaplain So. Conn. State U., New Haven, 1984-85; adj. prof. U. Bridgeport, 1988-89, cons. family svcs. div. Danbury (Conn.) Superior Ct., 1990-91; mgr., pres. Whimsy Brook Farm, Ltd., Redding, Conn., 1972—; dir. Inst. for Human Resources, Redding, 1985—. Lectr. So. Conn. State U., 1990—97; adj. prof. Fairfield U., 1990—97; acting exec. dir. Burning Tree, Inc., 1998—; founder, tchg. elder Congregation of the Way, 2000—; adminstr. Schulhof Animal Hosp., 1999—. Author: Called to Be Lonely: A Company of Clowns, 1984, A Cape Cod Journal, 1985, Understanding Clergy Misconduct in Religious Systems: Scapegoating, Family Secrets and the Abuse of Power, 1998, How to Get There From Here: Creating God Among Us, 2002; contbr. poetry to jours. Pres. Fairfield Coop. Ext. Coun., 1975-78; mem. Redding Bd. Edn., 1978-86; lic. lay reader Episc. Diocese Coun., 1982-91, mem. diocesan com. on spiritual direction, 1985-87; assoc. Order of Holy Cross, 1986—; mem. adv. com. Ellis Clark Regional Agri-Sci. and Tech. Ctr. Mem.: Spiritual Emergence Network (counselor, spiritual dir.), Nat. Ctr. Homeopathy, Conn. Group Therapy Assn., Conn. Assn. Marriage and Family Therapists (clin mem., approved supr.), Am. Assn. Marriage and Family Therapists (approved supr.), Conn. Psychol. Assn., Conn. Farm Bur. (bd. dirs.), Am. Quarter Horse Assn. Democrat. Avocations: photography, gardening, writing poetry. Office: Inst Human Resources 29 Giles Hill Rd Redding CT 06896-2511

BENZ, DANIEL ARTHUR, animal scientist; b. Carrollton, Ill., Aug. 26, 1957; s. Arthur J. and Theresa M. B.; m. Sharon A., Nov. 1990; 1 child, Emily. BS, U. Ill., 1979; MS, Colo. State U., 1982; PhD, Tex. A&M U., 1987. Animal scientist U.S. FDA, Rockville, Md., 1987—. Mem. Am. Soc. Animal Sci., Am. Registry Profl. Animal Scientists. Office: USFDA 7500 Standish Pl Rockville MD 20855 Fax: 301-594-0688.

BENZ, EDWARD JOHN, SR., clinical pathologist; b. June 11, 1923; s. Henry John and Gertrude Nora (Heffernan) B.; m. Verna Marie Cuddyre, June 20, 1945; children: Edward John, Thomas James, Gregory Paul, Mary Louise. BS, U. Pitts., 1943, MD, 1946; MS, U. Minn., 1952. Intern St. Joseph's Hosp., Pitts., 1946-47; resident, fellow Mayo Found., Mayo Clinic, 1949-53; pathologist, dir. labs. St. Luke's Hosp., Bethlehem, Pa., 1953-84, v.p. med. affairs, 1984-89; med. dir. utilization rev. Sacred Heart Hosp., Allentown, Pa., 1990-98. Adj. prof. microbiology Lehigh U., Bethlehem, 1956-64; pres. Lab. Clin. Pathology, Bethlehem, 1956-88, ret., 1988; cons. Palmerton (Pa.) Hosp., Allentown (Pa.) State Hosp.; past dir. Miller Meml. Blood Bank, Bethlehem Mem. adv. com. Pa. Sec. Health on Clin. Labs., 1973-89; mem. health sci. adv. com. Lehigh U., 1973-89. Contbr. articles to profl. publs. Trustee St. Luke's Hosp., 1968-71; pres. Pa. Assn. Clin. Pathologists, 1966-67. Capt. M.C., AUS, 1947-49. Fellow Coll. Am. Pathologists (past chmn. anat. path. commn., past del. from Pa.), Am. Soc. Clin. Pathologists; mem. Internat. Acad. Pathology, Am. Assn. Pathologists and Bacteriologists, Am. Assn. Blood Banks, Am. Coll. Physician Execs., Saucon Club, Valley Country Club, Sigma Xi, Alpha Omega Alpha. Home and Office: 1564 Saucon Valley Rd Bethlehem PA 18015-5260

BENZ, EDWARD JOHN, JR., physician, educator; b. Pitts., May 22, 1946; s. Edward John and Verna Marie (Cuddyre) B.; m. Margaret A. Vettese; children: Timothy Edward, Jennifer Kirsten. AB in Biology cum laude, Princeton U., 1968; MD magna cum laude, Harvard U., 1973. Diplomate Am. Bd. Internal Medicine, Am. Bd. Hematology. Resident Peter Bent Brigham Hosp., Boston, 1973-75; fellow pediatric hematology Children's Hosp. Med. Ctr., Boston, 1974-75; fellow adult hematology Yale U. Sch. of Medicine, New Haven, 1978-79, asst. prof. internal medicine, 1979-82, assoc. prof. internal medicine, human genetics, 1982-87, prof. internal medicine, human genetics, 1987-92, chief sect. hematology, 1987-92, chmn. dean's curriculum task force, 1987-88, assoc. chmn. dept. internal medicine, 1988-92; Jack D. Myers prof., chmn. dept. medicine U. Pitts. Sch. Medicine, 1993-95; Sir William Osler prof., dir. dept. medicine Johns Hopkins U. Sch. Medicine., Balt., 1995-2000; physician-in-chief Johns Hopkins Hosp., Balt., 1995-2000; prof. molecular biology and genetics Johns Hopkins U. Sch. of Medicine, 1995-2000; pres., CEO Dana Farber Cancer Inst., Boston, 2000—; Richard & Susan Smith prof. medicine, prof. pediat. and path Harvard Med. Sch., Boston, 2000—. CEO Dana Farber Ptnrs. Cancer Care, Boston, 2000—; dir. Dana Farber Harvard Cancer Care, Boston, 2000—; rsch. assoc. molecular hematology Nat. Heart, Lung, Blood Inst., Bethesda, Md., 1975—78; chmn. curriculum com. Yale Sch. of Medicine, New Haven, 1985—88; prof. pro-tem, hon. vis. chief of svc. Brigham & Women's Hosp., 1997; surgeon USPHS, 1975—78; adj. prof. biol. scis. Carnegie Mellon U., 1993—95; Howard Hiatt vis. prof. Harvard Med. Sch., 1998; Clement Finch prof. U. Wash., 1998; Bulfinch vis. prof. medicine Mass. Gen. Hosp., Harvard Med. Sch., Boston, 2000; Haynes disting. vis. prof. medicine Duke U., 2000; Franz Inglefinger vis. prof. Boston U., 2001; Litchfield lectr. Oxford U., 1999; lectr. in field. Author: Molecular Genetics Methods, 1987; co-editor: Hermatology, Principles and Practice, 1990, Hermatology, Principles and Practice, 3d edit., 1999; mem. editl. bd. Blood, 1988—94, New Eng. Jour. Medicine, 2002—; assoc. editor: New Eng. Jour. Medicine, —; contbr. articles to profl. jours. Recipient Career Devel. award nat. Inst. Health, 1982, Edward Paradiso Research award Cooley's Anemia Found., N.Y.C., 1985, Basil O'Connor award March of Dimes, 1980. Fellow: Molecular Med. Soc., ACP; mem.: Inst Medicine, Assn. Profs. Medicine, Am. Soc. Human Genetics, Am. Clin. and Climatological Soc., Am. Soc. Hematology (exec. coun. 1994, v.p. 1998, pres.-elect 1999, pres. 2000), Am. Fedn. Clin. Rsch., NIH (study sect. 1984—, chmn. 1993—95), Assn. Am. Physicians, Am. Soc. Clin. Investigation (nat. coun. 1987—91, pres. 1991—92), Md. Club, Johns Hopkins Club, Princeton Elm Club, Interurban Clin. Club, St. Botoph's Club, Alpha Omega Alpha, Sigma Xi, Phi Beta Kappa. E-mail: Edward_Benz@dfci.harvard.edu.

BENZ, GEORGE ALBERT, economist, consultant, retired economist educator; b. St. Louis, Mo, Feb. 21, 1926; s. George and Genevieve Beatrice (Klueg) B.; m. Dorris Jean Tabor, Apr. 14, 1951; 1 dau., Lynda Kaye. BBA, North Tex. State U., 1953, MS, 1955; PhD, U. Okla., 1969. Mgmt. trainee Montgomery Ward, 1953-54; tchr. social studies, coach Bryson HS, Tex., 1954-55; tchr. math., coach Grapevine HS, Tex., 1955-56; instr. social studies N.W. Mo. State Coll., Maryville, 1956-57; grad. asst. U. Okla., Norman, 1957-59; asst. prof. econs. and sociology Central State Coll., Edmond, Okla., 1959-66; asso. prof. econs. St. Mary's U., San Antonio, prof. econs., 1979-93; dir. Univ. Rsch. Ctr., 1979-93, chmn. dept. urban studies; retired, 1993. Cons. in field; econ. advisor Greater San Antonio C. of C.; bus. advisor, various small bus. loan org.; research dir. Scientific Profit Analysis for Restaurants, 1979-99 ; dir. Urban Adv. Group, 1990-99 ; econ. expert witness in loss of income and anti-trust cases, 1973-99 ; mem. Tex. State adv. com. US Civil Rights Com., 1969-77 Contbr. articles to profl. jours. Campaign treas. various local and nat. candidates. Served with US Army, 1943-49. Decorated Bronze Star, Purple Heart.; named Tchr. of Yr. St. Mary's U.; recipient KBAT Tex. Star award Sta. KBAT, Outstanding Centennial Alumnus U. North Tex., 1990. Mem. Am. Econ. Assn., Southwestern Social Sci. Assn., So. Econ. Assn., Assn. for Evolutionary Econ., AAUP, San Antonio Bus. and Econ. Soc. Democrat. Unitarian Universalist. Home: San Antonio, Tex. Died Feb. 9, 2003.

BENZ, MAUDY LOUISE, writer, educator; b. Ann Arbor, Mich., June 24, 1951; d. Carl Alfred and Jeanne Louise (Stevens) B.; m. Dennis John Zaborowski (div. 1999); children: Daphne Elizabeth, Conrad William; m. Ronald Christopher Wells. BSN magna cum laude, U. Mich., 1974; MSN, U. N.C., 1977; MFA, Bennington Coll., 1996. Instr. Duke U., Durham, N.C., 1995—. Fellow Wesleyan U. Writers' Conf., Middletown, Conn., summer 1998; instr. U. Iowa, Iowa City, July 1999; vis. writer St. Andrews Coll., Laurinburg, N.C., 1998, Louisburg (N.C.) Coll., 2000, Applalachian State U., Feb. 2001; tour dir. of Provence, www.provenceforaweek.com., 2001—; vis. writer, spkr., lectr. various colls. and univs.; freelance writer, condr. freelance workshops, 1996—. Author: Oh, Jackie, 1998; contbr. numerous short stories and poems to lit. jours., revs. to pubs. Sunday sch. tchr., Chapel of the Cross, Chapel Hill, N.C., 1993-2001. Mem. Authors Guild N.Y., N.C. Writers Network, Carolina Club, U. N.C. Alumni Assn., U. Mich. Alumni Assn. Episcopalian. Avocations: swimming, dancing, kayaking, gardening, sailing.

BENZAN, JOHN PATRICK, lawyer; b. Cambridge, Mass., Dec. 12, 1963; s. Rafael and Grace Beatrice Benzan; m. Kimberly Henrietta Kelley, May 30, 1992; children: Patrick, Katharine. BA, Coll. Holy Cross, Worcester Mass., 1985; JD, Suffolk U., 1989. Bar: Mass., 1990, R.I., 1990, U.S. Dist. Ct. Mass., 1990. Asst. atty. gen. Atty. Gen.'s Office, Boston, 1994-96; asst. dist. atty. Middlesex County Dist. Atty.'s Office, Cambridge, Mass., 1996-98; assoc. Lane, Altman & Owens, Boston, 1998—2000. Bd. dirs. YMCA, 1994—2000. Mem. ABA (mem. criminal litig. sect. coun. 1998—99), Holy Cross Gen. Alumni Assn. Roman Catholic. Avocations: physical fitness, reading. Office: Ste 8 70 Warren St Roxbury MA 02119-3208 E-mail: johnbenzan@msn.com.

BENZER, SEYMOUR, neuroscience educator; b. NYC, Oct. 15, 1921; s. Mayer and Eva (Naidorf) Benzer; m. Dorothy Vlosky, Jan. 10, 1942 (dec. 1978); children: Barbara Ann Benzer Freidin, Martha Jane Benzer Goldberg; m. Carol A. Miller, June 11, 1980; 1 child, Alexander Robin. BA, Bklyn. Coll., 1942; MS, Purdue U., 1943, PhD, 1947, DSc (hon.), 1968; DSc, Columbia U., 1974, Yale U., 1977, Brandeis U., 1978, CUNY, 1978, U. Paris, 1983, Rocketeller U., N.Y.C., 1993, Cold Spring Harbor Watson Sch. of Biol. Scis., 1999. Mem. faculty Purdue U., 1945—67, prof. biophysics, 1958—61, Stuart disting. prof. biology, 1961—67; prof. biology Calif. Inst. Tech., 1967—75, Boswell prof. neurosci., 1975—; biophysicist Oak Ridge Nat. Lab., 1948—49; vis. assoc. Calif. Inst. Tech., Pasadena, 1965—67. Contbr. articles to profl. jour. Recipient award of honor, Bklyn. Coll., 1956, Sigma Xi rsch. award, Purdue U., 1957, Ricketts award, U. Chgo., 1961, Gold medal, N.Y. City Coll. Chemistry Alumni Assn., 1962, Gairdner award of merit, 1964, McCoy award, Purdue U., 1965, Lasker award, 1971, T. Duckett Jones award, 1975, Prix, Leopold Mayer French Acad. Scis., 1975, Louisa Gross Horwitz award, 1976, Harvey award, Israel, 1977, Warren Triennial prize, Mass. Gen. Hosp., 1977, Dickson award, 1978, Rosenstiel award, 1986, T.H. Morgan medal, Genetics Soc. Am., 1986, Karl Spencer Lashley award, 1988, Gerard award, Soc. Neurosci., 1989, Helmerich award, 1990, Wolf Found. prize in medicine, Israel, 1991, Bristol-Myers Squibb Neurosci. award, 1992, Crafoord prize, Royal Swedish Acad. Scis., 1993, Mendel award, Brit. Genetical Soc., 1994, Alberto Feltrinelli prize, Accademia dei Lincei, Italy, 1994, Internat. prize for biology, Japan, 2000, Passano award, 2001, Neurosis. award, Acad. Sci. USA, 2001, March of Dimes prize, 2002, Pasarow award, 2002; fellow Rsch. fellow, Calif. Inst. Tech., 1949—51, Fulbright rsch. fellow, Pasteur Inst., Paris, 1951—52, sr. NSF postdoctoral fellow, Cambridge, Eng., 1957—58. Fellow: Indian Acad. Sci. (hon.); mem.: AAAS, NAS (Neurosci. award 2001, Passano award 2001), Acad. des Sci. France (fgn. mem.), Royal Acad. Sci. Spain (fgn. mem.), Royal Soc. London (fgn. mem.), NY Acad. Sci., Harvey Soc., Am. Philos. Soc. (Lashley award 1988), Am. Acad. Arts and Sci. Home: 2075 Robin Rd San Marino CA 91108-2831

BENZI, MICHELE, mathematics educator, researcher, consultant; b. Bologna, Italy, Oct. 1, 1962; s. Valerio Benzi and Annamaria Leccis; m. Carol Louise Cox, June 13, 1992; children: Joyce Anne, Carlo Valerio, Sofia Margherita. PhD, NC State U., 1989—93. Assoc. prof. Emory U., Atlanta, 2000—, Winship disting. rsch. prof., 2003—; adj. assoc. prof. Old Dominion U., Norfolk, Va., 2001—. Cons. Los Alamos Nat. Lab., 2001—. Recipient SIAM Outstanding Paper prize, Soc. for Indsl. and Applied Math., 2001. Mem.: SIAM, Unione Matematica Italiana. Achievements include research in numerical linear algebra, sparse matrices. Office: Emory U 400 Dowman Dr Atlanta GA 30322 Office Fax: 404-727-5611. E-mail: benzi@mathcs.emory.edu.

BENZING, CYNTHIA DELL, economics educator; b. Upper Darby, Pa., Oct. 23, 1951; d. Martin Paul and Alyce (Chapman) Dell; m. William Thomas Benzing, Oct. 21, 1972; children: William, Daniel, Edward, James. BS in Psychology, Pa. State U., 1972; MBA, Drexel U., 1977, PhD in Bus., 1987. Asst. contr. Parade Publs., Inc., Phila., 1972-76; teaching asst. Drexel U., Phila., 1976-77; acctg. instr. St. Joseph's U., Phila., 1977-80; tchg. fellow Drexel U., Phila., 1983-87; prof. West Chester (Pa.) U., 1987—, chair, 1996-2000, assoc. dean, 2001—. Editor-in-chief Pa. Econ. Rev., 1991-94; contbr. articles to profl. jours. Instr. Thresholds Vols. in Prison, Delaware County, Pa., 1989; foster parent Children and Youth Svcs., Delaware County, 1986-88, 90-98; bd. dirs. West Chester Area Sch. Bd., 1999 , Mem. Pa. Econ. Assn. (bd. dirs. 1989-91, treas. 1991-93, v.p. 1994-95, pres. elect 1996, pres. 1997), Ea. Econ. Assn. (bd. dirs. 2000—, Internat. Atlantic Econ. Soc. Avocations: camping, reading. Home: 331 Caswallen Dr West Chester PA 19380-4119 Office: West Chester U Dept Econs And Fin West Chester PA 19383-0001 E-mail: cbenzing@wcupa.edu.

BENZING, DAVID WARREN, semiconductor equipment company executive; b. Perth Amboy, N.J., Feb. 11, 1953; s. Walter Charles and Ruth E. (McBride) B.; m. Pamela Jean Drummond, Dec. 28, 1972 (div. 1982); 1 child, Thor A.; m. Cathleen Lynn Hays, Sept. 12, 1985 (div. 1988); 1 child, Allison G. BSChemE, U. Calif., Berkeley, 1974; PhD in Chem. Engring., Princeton U., 1978. Sr. engr. Signetics Corp., Sunnyvale, Calif., 1978-81, Applied Materials, Inc., Santa Clara, Calif., 1981-82; dir. R&D, Anelva Corp., San Jose, Calif., 1982-84; pres., founder Benzing Technologies, Inc., Santa Clara, 1984-2000; pres. Innovative Silicon Systems, San Jose, 2000—. V.p., gen. mgr. Direction Inc., Sunnyvale, 1994-97; lectr. Sci. and Tech. Inst., Mountain View, Calif., 1981-83; cons. Ube Industries, Ltd., Tokyo, 1984-87, Plasma Sys. Corp., Tokyo, 1993-96, Lam Rsch. Corp., Fremont, Calif., 1999—. Contbr. articles to profl. jours.; patentee in field. Mem. Electrochem. Soc., Thin Film Soc., Semiconductor Equipment and Materials Inst. Republican. Avocations: wine, home remodeling, gardening. Office: Innovative Silicon Systems 1203 Foxworthy Ave San Jose CA 95118-1212 E-mail: dbenzing@ix.netcom.com.

BENZLE, CURTIS MUNHALL, artist, art educator; b. Lakewood, Ohio, Apr. 20, 1949; s. Arthur George and Martha (Munhall) B; m. Suzan Scianamblo, Feb. 6, 1972 (div. 1995); children: Elliott, Kyle, Marisa; m. Sally Jo Havas, Aug. 28, 1996 (div. 1999). Student, Hillsdale Coll., 1967-69; BFA, Ohio State U., 1972; postgrad., Rochester Inst. Tech., 1973; MA, No. Ill. U., 1978. Owner, mgr. Oz Crafts, Hilton Head, S.C., 1973-76, Benzle Porcelain Co., Columbus, Ohio, 1980—, Benzle Applied Arts, Hilliard, Ohio, 1988—. Owner Creative Spirit Workshop; exec. dir. Ohio Designer Craftsmen, 1996—99; instr. U. S.C., Beaufort, 1978—79; prof., chair dept. dimensional studies Columbus Coll. Art and Design, 1982—, dir. com. art project; pres. Japan-USA Exch. Exhbn., 1988—92; bd. overseers Am. Crafts Assn., 1991—96; trustee Am. Crafts Coun., 1992—96. One-man show U. S.C., 1979, Indpls. Mus. Art, 1984, Lawrence Gallery, Portland, Oreg., 1986, Running Ridge Gallery, Santa Fe, 1986, Akasaka/Green Gallery, Tokyo, 1987, 90, Zanesville Art Ctr., 1988, Swidler Gallery, 1990, Tsukushi Gallery, Kitakyushu, Japan, 1991, del Mano Gallery, 1998, also others; exhibited in numerous group shows, 1971—, including Smithsonian Instn., 1980, 83, Suntory Art Mus., Tokyo, 1984, Cermaic Nat. Everson Mus., Syracuse, 1988, Internat. Competition of Ceramics, Mino, Japan, 1989, Seto (Japan) Ceramic and Glass Ctr., 2001 21st Century Ceramics, Canzani Gallery, Columbus, Ohio; represented in numerous permanent collections, including Smithsonian Instn., Everson Mus. Art, Los Angeles County Mus. Art, Cleve. Mus. Art., White House Collection Contemporary Craft. Mem. Ohio Citizens Com. for Arts, 1986—. Nat. Endowment for Arts fellow, 1980, Ohio Arts Coun. fellow, 1981, 83, 84, 86, 88, Greater Columbus Arts Coun. fellow, 1987. Mem. Am. Crafts Coun. (bd. overseers 1991-96, trustee 1992-96), Nat. Coun. on Edn. in Ceramic Art, Ohio Designer Craftsmen (bd. dirs. 1984-88, pres. 1985-87). Avocation: gardening. E-mail: cbenzle@ccad.edu.

BENZO-BONACCI, ROSEMARY ANNE, health facility administrator; b. Utica, N.Y., Apr. 28, 1955; d. Rocco Anthony and Grace Lillian (Maggi) B.; m. Michael V. Bonacci. AAS, Mohawk Valley C.C., 1988; BS, New Sch. for Social Rsch., 1992; postgrad. in Comm., SUNY, Albany. With Mohawk Valley C.C., Utica, 1977-89, alumni asst., 1989-93; dir. cmty. rels. Charles T. Sitrin Health Care Ctr., New Hartford, N.Y., 1993—. Program dir. Youth Mentorship Activities Program in Health Care Svcs. Dept. Health N.Y. Pres. Vol. Horizons, 1993—, Coalition for Tobacco Control, 1994; bd. dirs., mem. task force pub. edn. sector Utica Coalition for a Smoke-Free Cmty., 1989-93, chair ann. coalition meeting, 1990-91; chair search com. for tech. asst. Mohawk Valley C.C., 1990; vol. Small Paws Rescue. Mem. Mohawk Valley C.C. Alumni Assn. (bd. dirs. 1991-93). Democrat. Roman Catholic. Avocations: writing short stories, reading, weight training. Home: 16 Symphony Pl Whitesboro NY 13492-2227 Office: Charles T Sitrin Health Care Ctr Box 2050 Tilden Ave New Hartford NY 13413

BENZON, HONORIO TABAL, anesthesiologist; b. Ilocos Sur, The Philippines, Sept. 12, 1946; came to U.S., 1972; s. Alejo Gonzales and Concepcion Tacto (Tabal) B.; m. Julieta Palpal-latoc, May 30, 1970; children: Barbara Hazel, Hubert Anthony. BS, Far Eastern U., Manila, Philippines, 1966, MD, 1971. Diplomate Am. Bd. Anesthesiology, Am. Bd. Pain Medicine. Intern Overlook Hosp., Summit, N.J., 1972-73; resident in anesthesia U. Cin. Med. Ctr., 1973-75, Northwestern U. Affil. Hosps., 1975-76; instr. Med. Sch. Northwestern U., Chgo., 1976-80, asst. prof. anesthesia, 1980-85, assoc. prof., 1985-94, prof. anesthesiology, 1994—, chief sect. pain medicine, 1990—, program dir. pain mgmt. fellowship program; assoc. staff Northwestern U. Meml. Hosp., 1976-82, attending staff, 1982—, VA Lakeside Hosp., 1976—, Brigham and Women's Hosp., 1985-86. Instr. dept. anesthesia Harvard Med. Sch., 1985-86; cons. staff Rehab. Inst. Chgo. Editor: Regional Anesthesia and Pain Medicine; chief editor book: Essentials of Pain Medicine and Regional Anesthesia; sect. editor: (book) Practical Management of Pain, Textbook of Regional Anesthesia; mem. editl. bd. Clin. Jour. Pain, Consult Pain Medicine; contbr. numerous articles to profl. jours. and book chpts. Fellow Am. Coll. Anesthesiologists; mem. AMA, Am. Soc. Anesthesiologists, Internat. Anesthesia Rsch. Soc., Am. Soc. Regional Anesthesia, Am. Pain Soc., Midwest Pain Soc. (pres. 2002-). Roman Catholic. Home: 161 E Chicago Ave #48F Chicago IL 60611-6681 Office: Northwestern U Med Sch Dept Anes Feinberg 5-704 251 E Huron St Chicago IL 60611-2908 E-mail: hbenzon@nmff.org.

BEOHM, RICHARD THOMAS, safety engineering consultant; b. Youngstown, Ohio, Nov. 15, 1943; s. John and Eleanor (Leverence) B.; m. Rose Elizabeth Ralston, Oct. 25, 1968; children: Michael F., Eric R. B.E.E.T., Devry Inst. Tech., Chgo., 1969. Registered profl. engr., Ga., Fla., Mass. Asst. engr. North Electric Co. (ITT), Galion, Ohio, 1966-69; engr. Gen. Dynamics, Ft. Worth, 1969-71; fire protection engr. State of Ga. Self Ins. Program, Atlanta, 1971-80, acting dep. dir., 1980; fire protection cons. State of Ga. Risk Mgmt. Svc., Atlanta, 1981-87, acting field support supr., 1987-88, sr. loss control engring. cons., 1988-97; consulting engr. Atlanta, 1997—; consulting engr., fire marshal Ga. Tech., 2001—. Cartoonist Upson Home Jour., 1986-88; creator several safety coloring books; editor ASSE Refresher Guide for the Bd. Cert. Safety Profls. Safety Fundamentals Exam., 2002; contbr. articles to profl. jours. Past mem. Fire Safe Ga. Commn.; vol. safety engr. and fire marshall Olympics and Paralympics, 1996; Ga. state games risk mgr. Mem.: NSPE, Soc. Fire Protection Engrs. (chpt. pres. 1998—99, nat. FPE-PE lic. com. problem review chair, S.E. chpt. Person of Yr. 1992, Nat. Hats Off award), Fed. Criminal

Investigation Assn. (sec. Atlanta chpt. 1989), Am. Soc. Safety Engrs. (adminstrv. engring. divsn. 1997—99, editor 3rd edit. Safety Engring. 2000, past pres. Ga. chpt., past chair com. safety engring. tech. gorup engring divsn., editor refresher guide for BCSP Safety Fundamentals Exam. 2002, Engring. Divsn. Safety Profl. of Yr. 1996, cert. safety profl.). Democrat. Avocations: bird watching, butterfly collecting, illustrating, german language, church trustee. Home and Office: 981 Waymanville Rd Thomaston GA 30286-4759

BEPKO, GERALD LEWIS, university administrator, law educator, lecturer, consultant, lawyer; b. Chgo., Apr. 21, 1940; s. Lewis V. and Geraldine S. (Bernath) B.; m. Jean B. Cougnenc, Feb. 24, 1968; children: Gerald Lewis Jr., Arminda B. BS, No. Ill. U., 1962; JD, Ill. Inst. Tech.-Chgo. Kent Coll. Law, 1965; LLM, Yale U., 1972. Bar: Ill. 1965, U.S. Supreme Ct. 1968, Ind. 1973. Assoc. Ehrlich, Bundesen, Friedman & Ross, Chgo., 1965; spl. agt. FBI, 1965-69; asst. prof. law Ill. Inst. Tech.-Chgo. Kent Coll. Law, 1969-71; prof. Ind. U., Indpls., 1972-86, assoc. dean acad. affairs, 1979-81, dean, 1981-86, v.p., 1986—2002, interim pres., 2003. Vis. prof. Ind. U.-Bloomington, summers, 1976, 77, 78, 80, U. Ill., 1976—77, Ohio State U., 1978—79; cons. and reporter Fed. Jud. Ctr.; bd. dirs. First Ind. Bank/Corp., Ind. Energy Inc. & Ind. Gas Co., Inc., 1989—97, Lumina Found. for Edn., Indpls. Life Ins. Co.; mem. Conf. Commrs. on Uniform State Laws, 1982, Permanent Editl. Bd. for the Uniform Comml. Code, 1993—; mem. Ind. Lobby Registration Commn., 1992—, vice chair, 1992—96, chair, 1996—2000. Author: (with Boshkoff) Sum and Substance of Secured Transactions, 1981; contbr. articles on comml. law to profl. jours. Indpls. Chgo. Title and Trust Co. Found. scholar 1962-65; Ford Urban law fellow, 1971-72. Fellow Am. Bar Found., Ind. State Bar, Indpls. Bar Found.; mem. ABA, Ind. State Bar Assn., Indpls. Bar Assn., Country Club Indpls., Rotary. Methodist. Office: Ind U 355 Lansing St Indianapolis IN 46202-2815

BERACHA, BARRY HARRIS, retired food products executive; b. Bronx, NY, Feb. 28, 1942; s. Nissim Macy and Celia Grace (Sides) B.; m. Barbara Marie Capobianco, Dec. 23, 1967; children: Brian, Bradley, Bonnie. BChE, Pratt Inst., 1963; MBA, U. Pa., 1965. Ops. researcher Celanese Corp., 1965-67; tech. economist Sun Oil Co., 1964-65; with Anheuser-Busch Cos., Inc., 1967-96, v.p. corp. planning, 1974-76, v.p., group exec., 1976-96; chmn., CEO Earthgrains Co., Clayton, Mo., 1996—2001; exec. v.p. Sara Lee Corp., Clayton, 2001—; CEO Sara Lee Bakery Group, Clayton, 2001—03; ret., 2003.

BERALL, FRANK STEWART, lawyer; b. N.Y.C., Feb. 10, 1929; s. Louis J. and Jeannette F.; m. Christiana Johnson, July 5, 1958 (dec. July 1972); children: Erik Dustin, Elissa Alexandra; m. Jenefer M. Carey, Sept. 1, 1980. BS, Yale U., 1950, JD, 1955; LLM in Tax, NYU, 1959. Bar: N.Y. 1955, Conn. 1960; accredited estate planner. Assoc. firm Mudge, Stern, Baldwin & Todd, N.Y.C., 1955-57, Townley, Updike, Carter & Rodgers, N.Y.C., 1957-60; atty. Conn. Gen. Life Ins. Co., Bloomfield, Conn., 1960-65; atty. trust dept. Hartford Nat. Bank & Trust Co., Conn., 1965-67; assoc. Cooney & Scully, Hartford, Conn., 1968-70; ptnr. Copp & Berall and predecessors, Hartford, 1970—. Asst. in instrn. Yale U. Law Sch., 1954—55; lectr. U. Conn. Sch. Ins., 1964—72, U. Conn. Law Sch., 1972—73; instr. estate planning Am. Coll. Life Ins., 1968—69; v.p., sec., gen. counsel John M. Blewer, Inc., Essex, Conn., 1969—86; counsel Conn. Gov.'s Strike Force for Full Employment, 1971—72, Conn. Gov.'s Commn. on Tax Reform, 1972—73, State Tax Commr.'s Commn., 1972—75, Com. on Tax Law Clarification, 1984—88; adj. asst. prof. grad. tax program U. Hartford, 1973—74; trustee Culver Ednl. Found., 1997—99; estate tax planning advisor; lectr., spkr. in field. Co-author: A Practitioners Guide to the Tax Reform Act of 1969, 1970, Estate Planning and the Close Cooperation, 1970, Planning Large Estates, 1970, Revocable Inter Vivos Trusts, 1985, The Migrant Client: Tax, Community Property, and Other Considerations, 1994; sr. editor Conn. Bar Jour., 1969—, mem. editl. bd. Estate Planning mag., 1973—, Practical Tax Lawyer, 1988—, Jour. Taxation of Trusts and Estates, 1988—92, Estate Tax Planning Advisor. Bd. dirs. Bloomfield Interfaith Homes, 1967—71; adv. coun. U. Hartford Tax Inst., 1970—82; trustee Culver Ednl. Found., 1997—99; co-chmn. adv. coun. Hartford Tax Inst., 1986—94; co-chmn. Notre Dame Estate Planning Inst., 1977—. 1st lt., F.A. U.S. Army, 1951—52. Fellow: Am. Coll. Trust and Estate Counsel (Conn. chpt. chmn. 1975—81, mem. editl. bd. 1975—87); mem.: ABA, Internat. Acad. Estate and Trust Law, Am. Law Inst., Hartford County Bar Assn. (chmn. com. liaison with IRS 1972—74, com. charter and by-laws 1975), Conn. Bar Assn. (chmn. tax sect. 1969—72, exec. com. 1969—, exec. com., estates and probate sect. 1973—, vice chmn. com. on specialization 1974—77, chmn. 1984—86), Am. Coll. Tax Counsel, Culver Summer Schs. Alumni Assn. (v.p. 1975—85, bd. dirs. 1985—91, 1993—, pres. 1997—99), Yale Club of Harford (dir. 1998—, pres. 1999—), Culver Club Ctrl. New Eng. (pres. 1996—), Tax Club of Hartford (pres. 1975—76). Home: 9 Penwood Rd Bloomfield CT 06002-1520 Office: Copp & Berall LLP 864 Wethersfield Ave Hartford CT 06114-3184 *As a tax lawyer, I view my job as helping to keep the system going by seeing to it that my clients pay the government all it is legally entitled to receive in taxes, but no more, and doing pro bono work for the improvement of the entire federal and state tax law system.*

BERAN, DENIS CARL, publisher; b. Apr. 14, 1935; s. Carl Earl and Jessica Mary (Bogue) B.; m. Virginia Martha Knox, Feb. 20, 1960; children: Michael Knox, Elizabeth Virginia. BA in Econs., U. Mich., 1958; postgrad. in mktg. mgmt., Harvard Bus. Sch., 1976; Internat. Strategies Program, Columbia U., 1984. With McGraw-Hill Pubs. Co., N.Y.C., 1962—, advt. sales trainee, 1962, dist. mgr. nucleonics, 1962-65; dist. mgr. Business Week, 1965-70, sales devel. mgr., 1970-72, mktg. dir., 1972-76, asst. pub., 1979, internat. pub. dir., 1980-85, v.p. Europe McGraw-Hill, 1976-79; v.p. advt. Gannett Internat., 1986-87, v.p. mktg., 1988-89. Chmn. New Canaan Am. Cancer Soc., 1973-75; dir. So. Fairfield County Am. Cancer Soc., 1972-76, 80-90, 1st v.p., 1975-76. 1st lt. USMC, 1958-61. Mem. Internat. Periodical Pubs. Assn. (exec. com.), Aircraft Owners and Pilots Assn. (v.p. 1990-2000), New Canaan Country Club, Grand Harbor Club. Republican. Roman Catholic. Home: 5550 N Harbor Village Dr Vero Beach FL 32967-7268

BERAN, GEORGE WESLEY, veterinary microbiology educator; b. Riceville, Iowa, May 22, 1928; s. John and Elizabeth (Buresh) B.; m. Janice Ann Van Zomeren, Dec. 21, 1954; children: Bruce, Anne, George. DVM, Iowa State U., 1954; PhD, Kans. U., 1959; LHD, Silliman U., Philippines, 1973. Diplomate Am. Coll. Vet. Preventive Medicine, Am. Coll. Epidemiology. Epidemic intelligence officer USPHS, 1954-56; asst. prof. biology Silliman U., Dumaguete City, Philippines, 1960-63, chmn. dept. agr., 1962-71, assoc. prof. microbiology, 1963-67, prof. microbiology, 1967-73; prof. vet. microbiology and preventive medicine Iowa State U., Ames, 1973-93, disting. prof. vet. microbiology, immunology-preventive med., 1993—; dir. WHO Collaborating Ctr. in Food Safety, 1994—. Cons. WHO, Belize, Ecuador, Mex., India, Laos, Malaysia, Philippines, Jamaica, Surinam, Barbados; rsch. del. USSR/Iowa State U. exch. program, Moscow, 1989-90, Latvia, 1993; rsch. cons., Taiwan, 1983, 96, 98, Hungary, 1988, 90, U. Yucatan, 1989-90, 97, 98, 2003, Ukraine, 1996, Japan, 1998; vis. lectr. Nat. Inst. Vet. Bioproducts and Pharms., Beijing, Faculty Vet. Medicine, Huazhong Agrl. U. Wuhan, Peoples Republic of China, 1988; cons. Pan Am. Health Orgn., 1979, 85, 93, 95, 96, 98, 99, 2000, 02; cons., mem. WHO Expert Panel on Zoonoses, 1980-99; mem. expert panel on risk assessment WHO-FAO; Fulbright prof. Ahmadu Bello U., Zaria, Nigeria, 1980; mem. subcom. on drug use in animals NRC, 1993-98, mem. nat. adv. com. on microbiol. criteria for foods, 1997-99; adv. com. Wellcome Trust, 1998-99; mem. Food Safety and Inspection Svc. Task Force for Veterinarians, 1999-2000; mem. HACCP Based Inspection Models Project, 1999-2000 Editor, co-editor books on zoonoses; contbr. articles to profl. jours., chpts. to books. Active Ames Humane League, Ames chpt. Ptnrs. of Ams., UN Assn.; election supr. OSCE, Bosnia, 1998, Kosovo, 2000; mem. adv. com. Nat. Cath. Rural Life Ctr., 2001. Recipient James H. Steele award World Vet. Epidemiology Soc., 1979, Nat. Meritorious Svc. award Livestock Conservation Inst., 1989, Gold Head Cane award Am. Vet. Epidemiology Soc., 1993. Mem. AVMA (mem. coun. pub. health and regulatory vet. medicine, Internat. Svc. award 1996, Pub. Svc. award 1999), Am. Coll. Vet. Preventive Medicine (pres.), Conf. Pub. Health Veterinarians (pres.), Am. Assn. Food Hygiene Veterinarians (Outstanding Tchr. award 1978), Assn. Tchrs. Vet. Pub. Health and Preventive Medicine, Iowa Vet. Med. Assn. (chair pub. health com.), Iowa Pork Producers Assn. (pseudorables com.), Practical Farmers Iowa (Svc. to Agr. award), U.S. Animal Health Assn. (com. on pseudorables, pub. health, food safety, chair com. on feral swine), Cardinal Key, Sigma Xi, Phi Beta Delta, Phi Kappa Phi (pres.), Gamma Sigma Delta (Svc. to Agr. Merit award 1995), Phi Zeta, Alpha Zeta, Phi Eta Sigma. Home: 304 24th St Ames IA 50010-4834 Office: Coll Vet Medicine Iowa State U Rm 2134 Ames IA 50011-0001 E-mail: gberan@iastate.edu.

BERAN, MICHAEL JAMES, research psychologist, primatologist; b. Middlefield, Ohio, Aug. 11, 1973; s. Robert and Ellen Beran; m. Mary M. Beran, July 12, 1972. BA, Oglethorpe U., Atlanta, 1995; MA, Ga. State U., 1997, PhD, 2002. Rsch. assoc. Lang. Rsch. Ctr., Ga. State U., Atlanta, 1998—. Author: (jour.) Psychol. Sci., Jour. of Comparative Psychology, Jour. of the Exptl. Analysis of Behavior, Animal Cognition, Animal Learning and Behavior, Jour. of Gen. Psychology, Psychol. Record, Internat. Jour. of Comparative Psychology, Devel. Psychobiology, Evolution of Commn., Fgn. Psychology. Mem.: Internat. Soc. for Comparative Psychology, Comparative Cognition Soc., Animal Behavior Soc., Am. Soc. of Primatologists, Internat. Primatological Soc., Southeastern Psychol. Assn., Am. Psychol. Soc., APA, So. Soc. for Philosophy and Psychology (assoc. Richard M. Griffith Meml. Award 1999), Psi Chi, Pi Gamma Mu. Office: Language Rsch Ctr 3401 Panthersville Rd Decatur GA 30034 Office Fax: 404-244-5752. E-mail: mjberan@yahoo.com.

BERAN, SAMUEL JONATHAN, plastic surgeon; b. Phila., June 5, 1966; s. Irving Nathan and Phyllis Elaine Beran; m. Nancy Reisman, Aug. 25, 1996; children: Jacob Alexander, Rachel Elizabeth. BS, Union Coll., 1988; MD, Albany Med. Coll., 1990. Diplomate Am. Bd. Plastic Surgery, Am. Bd. Surgery. Resident in gen. surgery Thomas Jefferson Hosp., Phila., 1990-95; resident in plastic surgery U. Tex. Southwestern, Dallas, 1995-97, asst. prof. plastic surgery, 1997-99; plastic surgeon White Plains, N.Y., 1999—. Mem. staff No. Westchester Hosp. Ctr., United Hosp. Med. Ctr., White Plains Hosp. Ctr.; presenter in field. Author: Ultrasound-Assisted Liposuction, 1998; author chpts. to books; mem. editl. bd. Selected Readings in Plastic Surgery, 1997—; contbr. more than 25 articles to profl. jours. including Plastic and Reconstructive Surgery, Clin. Plastic Surgery. Mem. organizing staff Phila. chpt. Am. Cancer Soc., 1990-95. Grantee NIH, 1988. Mem. AMA, Am. Soc. for Laser Medicine and Surgery, Am. Soc. Plastic and Reconstructive Surgeons, Am. Soc. for Aesthetic Plastic Surgery, Med. Soc. State N.Y. (rep. Albany Med. Coll. 1987-90), Plastic Surgery Rsch. Coun., Westchester County Med. Soc., Alpha Omega Alpha. Avocations: scuba diving, traveling, roller blading. Office: 10 Chester Ave White Plains NY 10601-5112

BERANBAUM, JOHN A. lawyer; b. N.Y.C., Feb. 9, 1955; s. Samuel Louis and Betty (Samson) B.; m. Nancy Coates, Jan. 16, 1994; 1 child, Sarah Elizabeth Fuller. BA magna cum laude, Yale U., 1977; JD, NYU, 1981. Bar: N.Y. 1982, N.J. 1983, Pa. 1989, U.S. Dist. Ct. (so. and ea. dist.) N.Y., U.S. Dist. Ct. (ea. dist.) Pa., U.S. Ct. Appeals (2d and 3d cirs.), U.S. Supreme Ct. Atty. Hunterdon County Legal Svcs., Flemington, N.J., 1981-85, N.J. Dept. Pub. Advocate, Trenton, 1985-89; assoc. Galfand, Lurie & March, Phila., 1989-92, Vladeck, Waldman, Elias & Engelhard, N.Y.C., 1992-95; ptnr. Law Office of John A. Beranbaum, N.Y.C., 1995-98, Beranbaum & Menken, N.Y.C., 1998—. Mediator U.S. Dist. Ct. for Ea. Dist. N.Y., 1994—. Mem. ABA, N.Y. State Bar Assn., Assn. Bar City N.Y., Nat. Employees Lawyers Assn. Office: Beranbaum Menken Et Al 3 New York Plz New York NY 10004-2442 E-mail: jberanbaum@bmbf.com.

BERANEK, LEO LEROY, acoustical consultant; b. Solon, Iowa, Sept. 15, 1914; s. Edward Fred and Beatrice (Stahle) B.; m. Phyllis Knight, Sept. 6, 1941 (dec. Nov. 1982); children: James Knight, Thomas Haynes; m. Gabriella Sohn, Aug. 10, 1985. AB, Cornell Coll., 1936, D.Sc. (hon.), 1946; MS, Harvard U., 1937, D.Sc., 1940; D.Eng. (hon.), Worcester Poly. Inst., 1971; D.Comml. Sci. (hon.), Suffolk U., 1979; LL.D. (hon.), Emerson College, 1982; Dr. Pub. Service (hon.), Northeastern U., 1984. Instr. physics Harvard U., 1940-41, asst. prof., 1941-43; dir. Electro-Acoustics and Systems Rsch. Labs., 1941-46; assoc. prof. communications engring. MIT, 1947-58; pres., dir., chief exec. officer Bolt Beranek & Newman, Cambridge, Mass., 1953-69, chief scientist, 1969-71, dir., 1953-84; pres., chief exec. officer, dir. Boston Broadcasters, Inc., 1963-79, chmn. bd., 1980-83; pres. Am. Acad. Arts and Scis., Cambridge, 1989-94. Part-owner WCVB-TV, Boston, 1972-82; chmn. bd. Mueller-BBM GmbH, Munich, 1962-86; bd. dirs. Tech. Integration Inc., Bedford, Mass. Author: Acoustic Measurements, 1949, 2d edit., 1986, Music, Acoustics and Architecture, 1962, Noise Reduction, 1960, Noise and Vibration Control, 1971, 2d edit., 1988, Noise and Vibration Control Engineering, 1992, Concert and Opera Halls: How They Sound, 1996, Concert Halls and Opera Houses: Music, Acoustics and Architecture, 2003. Charter mem. bd. overseers Boston Symphony Orch., 1968-80, chmn., 1977-80, trustee, 1977-87, chmn. bd. trustees, 1983-86, hon. chmn., 1987, life trustee 1994-; mem. bd. overseers Harvard U., 1984-90; mem. coun. for arts MIT, 1972—; life trustee Cornell Coll., 1998—; others in past. Guggenheim fellow, 1946-47; recipient Presdl. certificate of merit, 1948, Abe Lincoln TV award So. Bapt. Conv., 1976, Lord Rayleigh award Mex. Inst. Acoustics, 2002. Fellow NAE (bd. dir, marine bd., com. pub. engring. policy, aeros. and space engring. bd.), AAAS, IEEE (chmn. profl. group audio 1950-51), Am. Phys. Soc., Am. Acad. Arts and Scis. (Scholar-Patriot Disting. Svc. award 2000), Audio Engring. Soc. (pres. 1967-68, Gold medal 1971, gov. 1966-71), Acoustical Soc. Am. (mem. coun. 1944-47, v.p. 1949-50, pres. 1954-55, Bienniel award 1944, Sabine award 1961, Gold medal 1975, Hon. mem. 1994); mem. Inst. Noise Control Engring. (charter pres. 1971-73, dir. 1973-75, 1st Disting. Noise Control Engr. 1997), Internat. Inst. Acoustics (hon. fellow 2000), Am. Inst. Archs. (hon.), Mass. Broadcasters Assn. (bd. dirs. 1973-80, pres. 1978-79, Disting. Svc. award 1980), Acad. Disting. Bostonians, Greater Boston C. of C. (dir. 1973-79, v.p. 1976-79, Disting. Cmty. Svc. award 1980, 83), Phi Beta Kappa, Sigma Xi, Eta Kappa Nu (eminent mem. 2000). Episcopalian. Home and Office: 975 Memorial Dr Ste 804 Cambridge MA 02138-5755

BERARDELLI, CATHERINE MARIE, women's health nurse, nurse educator; b. Portland, Oreg., Aug. 22, 1949; d. Francis Lawrence and Jean Carolyn (Petersen) Ison; m. Victor Francis Berardelli Jr., May 28, 1988. BSN, U. Oreg., 1972; MSN, U. So. Maine, Portland, 1985; PhD, Adelphi U., 1994, FNP, 1995. RN; cert. family nurse practitioner. Night staff nurse Dornbecker Childrens Hosp., Portland, Oreg., 1972-73; night charge nurse Maine Med. Ctr., Portland, 1973-78; evening supr. St. Andrews Hosp., Boothbay Harbor, Maine, 1978-82, DON, 1982-85; instr. nursing Cen. Maine Med. Ctr. Sch. Nursing, Lewiston, 1985-88, U. So. Maine Sch. Nursing, Portland, 1986-90; clin. nurse specialist Long Island Jewish Med. Ctr., New Hyde Park, N.Y., 1990-92; clin. learning lab. coord. Adelphi U., Garden City, N.Y., 1991-94; dir. nursing programs U. New Eng., Westbrook Coll. Campus, 1995—99; RN studies coord. U. Maine, Orono, 2000—. Adj. assoc. prof. Simmons Coll., 1995—; expert witness Kelly Remmel & Zimmerman, Portland, 1989-92; test item writer Nat. League Nursing, N.Y.C., 1991; vis. prof. Sch. Nursing Adelphi U., 1993-95. Co-author patient edn. brochure. Mem. New Eng. Women's Studies Assn., 1987; bd. dirs. Kaler Vaill Home for Older Women, 1996, Park Danforth, 1997, Vis. Nurse Svc. So. Maine, 1997. U. So. Maine rsch. grantee, 1989. Mem. ANA, Assn. Women's Health Obstetrics and Neonatal Nurses, Nat. League Nursing, Maine Nursing Honor Soc. (charter), Maine Nurse Practitioners Assn., Sigma Theta Tau. Home: 435 Mudgett Rd Newburgh ME 04444

BERARDI, JORGE ENRIQUE, economist; b. Buenos Aires, June 8, 1937; s. Francisco and Ofelia Beatriz (Pinasco) B.; m. Maria Dolores de las Mercedes Lopez Narvaja; children: Fabiana Beatriz, Gabriela Leonor. Degree in pub. acctg., Buenes Aires U., 1960, lic. in econs., 1969, D in Econs., 1973. Min. economy Provincia de Santa Fé, Argentina, 1976-78; sec. of treas. Govt. of Argentina, Buenos Aires, 1981; econ. adviser Buenos Aires Stock Exch., 1982-85, sec., 1990-92, v.p., 1992-93, pres., 1993-94; adviser Inst. Argentino Mercado de Capitales, Buenos Aires, 1985-89. Pres. InverPlus Diagonal Mut. Fund, Buenos Aires, 1993-95; pres. MBK Bursatil, 1994-99; v.p. Provincia Bursatil S.A., 2000-2001; owner Jorge Berardi Econ. Advisor, Buenos Aires, 1982-90; trustee Acindar, S.A., Buenos Aires, 1983—; bd. dirs. Consultora Este Asiatico. Author: La Crisis del Mercado de Valores Argentino en la Capitalizacion Empresaria, 1974; contbr. more than 200 articles to profl. jours. Fellow Internat. Bank, 1963. Mem. Circulo de Armas, Consejo Argentino para las Relaciones Internacionales. Roman Catholic. Avocation: jogging. Office: Jorge Berardi Econ Adviser Avda Corrientes 980 7oB 1043 Buenos Aires Argentina E-mail: jeberardi@cscom.com.ar.

BERARDINO, JOSEPH FRANCIS, accounting company executive; b. N.Y.C., Dec. 29, 1950; s. Joseph John and Gloria (Gerace) B.; m. Gail Therese Hamilton, May 7, 1977; children: Andrea, Allison. BS, Fairfield U., 1972. CPA, N.Y. Staff mem. Arthur Andersen & Co., N.Y.C., 1972-76, mgr., 1976-82, ptnr., 1982—2002, CEO, 2001—02. Contbr. articles to profl. jours. Mem. Fairfield U. Alumni Assn. (v.p., treas. 1973, pres.). Clubs: Burnee Tree Country, N.Y. Athletic. Roman Catholic. Home: 4 Avon Ln Greenwich CT 06830-3926 Office: Arthur Andersen 33 W Monroe Chicago IL 60603

BERARDUCCI, ADRIENNE, nursing educator, researcher; d. Anthony Frank and Josephine Gertrude Berarducci. PhD, U. of South Fla., 2001, MS, 1989; BS summa cum laude, Daemen Coll., 1987. Cert. bd. cert. adult nurse practitioner, ANCC, RN N.Y. Charge nurse Sisters of Charity Hosp., Buffalo, 1976—79; staff nurse, rsch. coord. VA Med. Ctr., Buffalo, 1979—87; staff nurse Sarasota Meml. Hosp., 1988—89; nurse practitioner Sarasota Palms Hosp., 1989—90; nursing instr. U. of Tampa, Fla., 1991—92, So. Coll., Orlando, Fla., 1994—94; nurse practitioner Internal Medicine Assocs., Sarasota, 1990—95; pvt. practice nurse practitioner in internal medicine Sarasota, 1996—2001; asst. prof. U. of South Fla., Tampa, 2001—; nurse practitioner Bayview Med. Assocs., Sarasota, Fla., 2002—. Sci. cons. Alliance for Better Bone Health, Mason, Ohio, 2003—; med.-legal cons. pvt. law firms, Sarasota, 2001—; parenteral/enteral therapy cons. U.S. Ethicare Corp., Buffalo, 1983—85. Author: (clin. monograph) Osteoporosis: Clinical Issues, Detection, and Treatment Strategies, (rsch. presentation) Osteoporosis-related, health-promoting practices of primary care providers (Grad. Student Rsch. award, 1999), Development and testing of an instrument to measure women's knowledge of osteoporosis (Grad. Student Rsch. award, 2000); contbr. articles to profl. jours. Recipient Meritorious Svc. award, VA Rsch. Ctr., 1985, rsch. study grants (2), Merck & Co., Inc, 1999, rsch./ednl. grants (2), Alliance for Better Bone Health, 2001; grantee, Bur. of Health Professions, 2000—03. Mem.: ANA (assoc.), Fla. Nurses Assn. (assoc.; treas. dist. 20 2003—), Fla. Osteoporosis Bd. (assoc.; bd. dirs. 2003), Sigma Theta Tau (hon.), Phi Kappa Phi (life). Liberal. Roman Catholic. Achievements include research in osteoporosis; development of psychometric instruments for osteoporosis-related research; nationally recognized for osteoporosis and women's health research and education. Avocations: dog and cat care and training, gourmet cooking, antique and art glass collecting, antique children's literature collecting. Office: U South Florida MDC Box 22 12901 Bruce B Downs Blvd Tampa FL 33612 Home Fax: 813-974-5418; Office Fax: 813-974-5418. Personal E-mail: aberardu@hsc.usf.edu. E-mail: aberardu@hsc.usf.edu.

BERBARY, MAURICE SHEHADEH, physician, military officer, hospital administrator, educator; b. Beirut, Jan. 14, 1923; arrived in US, 1945, naturalized, 1952; s. Shehadeh M. and Marie K. Berbary; children: Geoffrey Maurice, Laura Marie. BA, Am. U., Beirut, 1943; MD, U. Tex., Dallas, 1948; MA in Hosp. Adminstrn., Baylor U., 1970; diploma, Army Command and Gen. Staff Coll., Leavenworth, Kan., 1963, Air Force Sch. Aerospace Medicine, San Antonio, 1964, Army War Coll., Carlisle, Pa., 1969. Diplomate Am. Bd. Ob-Gyn., Am. Coll. Healthcare Execs. Intern Parkland Meml. Hosp., Dallas, 1948-49, resident in ob-gyn., gen. surgery and urology, 1949-53; resident in ob-gyn. Walter Reed Army Hosp., Washington, 1955-57; fellow in obstetric and gynecologic pathology Armed Forces Inst. Pathology, Washington, 1959-60; practice clin. medicine in ob-gyn., 1953—; capt. MC U.S. Army, 1952, advanced through grades to col., 1968, sr. flight surgeon, 1970; chief dept. ob-gyn. U.S. Army Hosp., Ft. Polk, La., 1957-59, Womack Army Hosp., Ft. Bragg, N.C., 1960-62; div. surgeon 1st. inf. div., Ft. Riley, Kans., 1963-64, 3d. Armored div., Germany, 1964-65; corps surgeon V. Corps, Germany, 1965-67, 24th Army Corps, S. Vietnam Theater of Operation, 1970; comdr., hosp. adminstr. U.S. Army Hosp., Teheran, Iran, 1954-55; comdr. 43d Hosp. Group Complex, Vietnam, 1969-70; command surgeon U.S. Armed Forces Command and U.S. Army South, U.S. C.Z., Panama, 1970-73; comdr. 5th Gen. Hosp., Stuttgart, West Germany, 1973-77, Munson Army Hosp., Ft. Leavenworth, Kans., 1977-81; sr. staff officer dept. ob-gyn William Beaumont Army Med. Ctr., Ft. Bliss, Tex., 1981-83; ret., 1983; cons. health care adminstrn. and med.-legal affairs, 1984—. Vis. lectr. ob-gyn. pathology Duke U. Med. Ctr., Durham, N.C., 1960-62; clin. instr. dept. ob-gyn. U. Kans. Coll. Medicine, Kansas City, 1963-80, advanced to clin. asst. prof., 1980—; instr. 5th Army NCO Acad., Fort Riley, Kans., 1963-64. Decorated Legion of Merit with three oak leaf clusters, Bronze Star medal, Meritorious Svc. medal, Army Commendation medal, Combat Air medal, Sr. Flight Surgeon's badge, Expert Field Med. badge. Fellow: ACS, Am. Coll. Health Care Execs., Am. Coll. Ob-Gyn.; mem.: AMA, Dallas County Med. Assn., Tex. State Med. Assn., Am. Hosp. Assn., Soc. U.S. Army Flight Surgeons, Am. Occupl. Med. Assn., Assn. Mil. Surgeons, Internat. Platform Assn., N.Y. Acad. Scis. Avocation: languages. Home and Office: 7923 Abramshire Ave Dallas TX 75231-4712

BERBERICH, PATRICIA LOUISE, librarian; b. Norwalk, Conn., Nov. 2, 1928; d. Thomas Edward and Theresa A. (Nesline) B. BS in English Lit., St. Joseph Coll., West Hartford, Conn., 1949; MLS, Rutgers U., 1966. Contract writer group ins. The Travelers Ins. Co., Hartford, Conn., 1950-55; editorial asst. The Catholic Transcript, Hartford, 1955-59; libr. asst. Pope Pius X Libr. St. Joseph Coll., West Hartford, 1961-65; head libr. Blue Hills br. Hartford Pub. Libr., 1966-69, head libr. Camp Field br., 1969-77, adminstrv. asst. to chief libr., 1977-82, assoc. libr., 1982-91, chief libr., 1991-94. Coord. ext. svcs. Hartford Pub. Libr., 1974-82; bd. dirs. Capitol Region Libr. Coun., 1979-85. Named Disting. Alumna St. Joseph Coll., 1992. Home: 22 Southbridge Ct Simsbury CT 06070-2349

BERC, KENNETH MYLES, psychiatrist; b. N.Y.C., May 7, 1942; s. Ira Lee and Viola Helene (Lebowitz) B. BA cum laude, Colgate U., 1963; MD, Harvard U., 1967. Diplomate Am. Bd. Psychiatry and Neurology. Intern St. Luke's Hosp. Center, N.Y.C., 1967-68, resident in psychiatry, 1968-71, chief resident, 1972; cons. rapid intervention project Family Ct. N.Y. State, 1972-74; emergency room psychiatrist St. Luke's Hosp. Center, N.Y.C., 1974-76; acting dir. psychiat. in-patient services St. Luke's Hosp., 1974-76, assoc. attending psychiatrist, 1972-83; attending psychiatrist Gracie Sq. Hosp., N.Y.C., 1983-94, Mt. Sinai Hosp., N.Y.C., 1994—. Assoc. clin. instr. Columbia Coll. Phys. and Surgs., N.Y.C., 1972-83; med. dir. N.Y.C. Service Program for Older People, 1975-81; sr. med. cons. Staff Builders, Inc., 1984-86; faculty Brookdale Center on Aging, Hunter Coll., N.Y.C., 1977-89, 96-97, Mt. Sinai Med. Sch., 1994—; practice psychiatry, N.Y.C., 1972—; pres. Am. MedRisk, Inc., 1993—; sr. cons. psychiatrist Equitable Life Assn. Soc., 1981-94; cons. N.Y. Life Ins. Co., 1992—, UNUM, 1993-98, Tchrs. Ins. Assn. Am./CREF Ins. Co., 1993—; lectr. in field. Served in U.S. Army, 19690-70. With U.S. Army, 1969—70. NIMH grantee, 1974; recipient Audi Math. prize Colgate U., 1963, Physics prize, 1963. Mem. AMA (Physicians Recognition award 1972), Am. Psychiat. Assn., N.Y. Acad. Scis. (life), N.Y. Acad. Medicine, Am. Geriatrics Soc., Boyleston Soc. Clubs: Harvard of N.Y. Office: 155 E 76th St New York NY 10021-2810

BERCAW, ROY, freelance/self-employed writer; b. Passaic, N.J., Sept. 5, 1942; s. Samuel Howard and Faye (Schweitzer) B. Student, Rutgers U., Newark, 1959-64; BA in Philosophy, Columbia U., 1970; law student, Boston U., 1970-71. Radio helicopter traffic announcer, news writer Bergen Broadcasting Corp.-WJRZ, Newark, 1961-62; substitute tchr. Rutherford (N.J.) H.S., 1964-65; systems analyst Chase Manhattan Bank, N.Y.C., 1965-66; sr. programmer Computer Usage Co., N.Y.C., 1966-68, Cybernetics Internat., N.Y.C., 1969; programmer, analyst Automated Concepts Inc., N.Y.C., 1970; substitute tchr. Arlington (Mass.) H.S., 1971-72; programmer Softec Inc., Waltham, Mass., 1972; freelance writer N.J., 1979-88, 1988—. Lawyer pro se Wash. State Cts., Spokane, 1975-76, N.J. State and Fed. Cts., Newark, Paterson, Trenton, Passaic, Clifton, Phila., Washington, 1983-88, Mass. State Cts., Cambridge, 1990-94; petitioner U.S. Supreme Ct., Washington, 1987, 88; pres., founder Anti-Censorship and Deception Union, Cambridge, 1990. Author: I'm Alive, 1996; pub. newsletter Enough Room, 1996—; prodr., editor, host (TV news show) Enough Room, 1999—; prodr., videomaker, VHS & digital NLE, video editor Cambridge Cmty. TV, 1999—; writer (9 bills) for Mass. Ho. of Reps., 2000; contbr. 250 letters, articles, essays to periodicals including N.Y. Times, N.Y. Post, Boston Globe, Boston Herald, The Humanist, Chronicle of Higher Education, Village Voice, Cambridge TAB, Passaic Citizen, Boston Phoenix, Cambridge Chronicle, Arlington Advocate. Vol. sch. com. video cameraman, Arlington, 1992, book restoration Robbins Pub. Libr., Arlington, 1993; vol. cameraman Arlington cable TV, 1993, event coord. Fox Br. Libr., Arlington, 1995. With USN Air Res., 1965-67. Univ. restructuring grantee Columbia U. Trustees, N.Y.C., 1968-69; recipient Avellone award for tech. accomplishment

Cambridge Cmty. TV, 2000. Mem. Columbia U. Alumni Assn., Am. Legion. Office: Anti Censorship & Deception Union PO Box 400297 Cambridge MA 02140-0003 E-mail: bercaw@alumni-mail.gs.columbia.edu.

BERCEL, NICHOLAS ANTHONY, neurologist, neurophysiologist; b. Budapest, Hungary, Aug. 20, 1911; came to U.S., 1940; s. Desiré and Julia (Kapos) B.; m. Eva Mindszenti, Mar. 25, 1982; children: Diana, Anthony, Christopher, Patrick, Yvette. MD, U. Rome, 1936., 1940; resident U. Rome, 1936-38, U. Paris, 1938-40; intern Swedish Hosp., Mpls., 1958—; assoc. prof. in physiology U. So. Calif., L.A., 1948-67; mem. staff St. John Hosp., Santa Monica, 1954-84; mem. staff dept. neurodiagnosis Queen of Angels Hosp., L.A., 1960-80. Neuro-psychiat. cons. Social Security Adminstrn., West Los Angeles, 1958— Author: Textbook on Etiology of Schizophrenia, Psychopathology, 1959; contbr. numerous articles to profl. publs., including Diseases of the Nervous System, Jour. of Neuropsychiatry, Jour. AMA, Calif. Medicine, Am. Jour. Med. Scis., others. Republican. Achievements include research on experimental epilepsy for testing the comparative activity of anticonvulsants; schizophrenic serum influence on spider beahvior; schizophrenic model psychoses induced with LSD-25. E-mail: drnickb@earthlink.net.

BERCH, REBECCA WHITE, state supreme court justice, lawyer; b. Phoenix, June 29, 1955; d. Robert Eugene and Janet Kay (Zimmerman) White; m. Michael Allen Berch, Mar. 9, 1981; 1 child, Jessica. BS summa cum laude, Ariz. State U., 1976, JD, 1979, MA, 1990. Bar: Ariz. 1979, U.S. Dist. Ct. Ariz., U.S. Ct. Appeals (9th cir.), U.S. Supreme Ct. Assoc., ptnr. McGroder, Tryon, Heller, Rayes & Berch, Phoenix, 1979-85; dir. legal rsch. and writing program Ariz. State U. Coll. Law, Tempe, 1986-91, 94-95; solicitor gen. State of Arizona, Phoenix, 1991-94, 1st asst. atty. gen., 1996—98; judge Ariz. Ct. Appeals, 1998—2002, Ariz. Supreme Ct., Phoenix, 2002—. Co-author: (Book) Introduction to Legal Method and Process, 1985, 2002, Teacher's Manual for Introduction to Legal Method and Process, 1992, 2002, Handling Complex Litigation, 1986; Bd. editors Jour. Legal Writing Inst., 1993—2002; contbr. articles to profl. jours. and newspapers. Bd. dirs. Tempe-Mesa chpt. ACLU, 1984—86, Homeless Legal Assistance Project, Phoenix, 1990—98. Mem. Ariz. Women Lawyer's Assn., Ariz. State Bar Assn. Republican. Methodist. Avocations: reading, travel. Office: Ariz Supreme Ct 1501 W Washington St Phoenix AZ 85009-3831

BERCHEM, ROBERT LEE, SR., lawyer; b. Milford, Conn., Aug. 17, 1941; s. Robert W. and Barbara (Maher) B.; m. Lee Contrucci, Feb. 19, 1966; children: Kerry, Robert L. Jr., Jonathan. AB, Fairfield U., 1962; LLB, Villanova U., 1965; LLM, U. Mich., 1967. Bar: Conn. 1965. Law clk. U.S. Dist. Ct., Conn., 1965-66; prin. Berchem, Moses & Devlin, P.C., Milford, 1967—. Trustee Fairfield (Conn.) U.; chmn. Milford Hist. Dist. Commn., 1976—. Mem. ABA, Conn. Bar Assn., New Haven County Bar Assn., Milford Bar Assn. Democrat. Roman Catholic. Avocations: golf, skiing. Home: 125 W River St Milford CT 06460-3420 Office: Berchem Moses & Devlin PC 75 Broad St Milford CT 06460-3331

BERCK, PETER, agricultural economics educator; b. N.Y.C., Apr. 26, 1950; s. Joseph and Sharon Berck; m. Cyndi Ann Spindell; children: David, Michelle, Joseph. BA, U. Calif., Berkeley, 1971; PhD, MIT, 1976; Dr. honoris causa (hon.), U. Umea, Sweden, 2002. Prof. U. Calif., Berkeley, 1976—. Author: Economists Mathematical Manual, 2000; editor: Nat. Resource Modelling, 1991—95, Am. Jour. Agrl. Econs., 1999—2003. Mem.: Assn. Environ. and Resource Econs. (bd. dirs. 1986—87), Am. Agrl. Econs. Assn. Office: U Calif Dept Agrl and Resource Econs Berkeley CA 94720-3310 E-mail: pberck@uclink.berkeley.edu.

BERCOVITCH, SACVAN, English language professional, educator; b. Montreal, Que., Can., Oct. 4, 1933; s. Alexander and Brytha (Avrutick) B.; m. Susan L. Mizruchi; children: Eytan, Alexander. BA, Sir George William Coll., 1961; MA, Claremont (Calif.) Grad. Sch., 1963, PhD, 1965; LittD (hon.), Concordia U., 1993. Asst. prof. English and Am. lit. Brandeis U., 1966-68; asso. prof. U. Calif., San Diego, 1968-70; prof. English and Am. Lit. Columbia U., 1970-83; Powell M. Cabot rsch. prof. Am. lit. Harvard U., 1983—. Lectr., Kyoto, Tokyo, Shanghai, Beijing, Amsterdam, Frankfurt, Konstanz, Lisbon, Jerusalem, Tel Aviv, Salzburg, Coimbra, Montreal, Rome, Budapest, Paris, Venice, Bologna, Toronto, Oxford, Berlin, Moscow, Prague, Olomouc, Ostrava, Brno, Yale U., Princeton U., U. Pa., U. Calif., Berkeley, L.A., San Diego, Irvine, Cornell U., Dartmouth Coll., Concordia Coll., Claremont Grad. Sch., many others; advisor, cons. in field. Author: Typology and Early American Literature, 1972, The American Puritan Imagination, 1974, The Puritan Origins of the American Self, 1975, The American Jeremiad, 1978, Reconstructing American Literary History, 1986, Ideology and Classic American Literature, 1986, The Office of the Scarlet Letter, 1991, The Rites of Assent: Transformations in the Symbolic Construction of America, 1992; gen. editor: Cambridge History of American Literature (8 vols.); author more than 100 essays and revs. Am. Philos. Soc. fellow, 1968-69, Guggenheim fellow, 1969-70, Am. Coun. Learned Socs. fellow, 1971-72, Nat. Humanities Inst. fellow, 1975-76, Ctr. for Advanced Study in Behavioral Scis. fellow, 1978-79, NEH fellow, 1978-79, 86-87, Woodrow Wilson Ctr. fellow, 1990-91, Time-Life fellow Huntington Libr., 1994—, Cabot fellow for achievement in humanities; recipient James Russell Lowell prize for scholarship, 1992, Disting. Scholar award for extraordinary lifetime contbns. in Early Am. Lit., 2003, Award for Excellency in Tchg. Fellow Am. Acad. Arts and Scis.; mem. MLA (mem. exec. com. Am. sect. 1976-78), English Inst., Am. Studies Assn. (pres. 1982-84) E-mail: bercovit@fas.harvard.edu.

BERCU, BARRY BERNARD, pediatric endocrinologist; b. Montreal, Aug. 10, 1944; m. Sandra Bercu, 2 children. BS, U. Md., 1965, MD, 1969. Diplomate Nat. Bd. Med. Examiners, Am. Bd. Pediatrics, Am. Bd. Pediatric Endocrinology; lic. physician, Mass., Md., Fla. Med. intern V and VI Med. Svc. Boston City Hosp., 1969—70; asst. and sr. resident pediat. Mass. Gen. Hosp., Boston, 1970—72; clin. and rsch. fellow pediatric endocrinology & metabolism Harvard Med. Sch., Boston, 1974—77; clin. and rsch. fellow endocrinology dept. internal medicine Tufts U. Med. Sch., New Eng. Med. Ctr., Boston, 1974—77; clin. assoc. Nat. Inst. Child Health and Human Devel., NIH, Bethesda, Md., 1977—79, head pediatric endocrine unit neonatal & pediatric med. br., 1979—82, head pediatric endocrine unit, pregnancy rsch. br., 1982—84; assoc. prof. pediat. Uniformed Svcs. U., Bethesda Naval Ctr., 1980—84; assoc. rsch. prof. child health and devel. George Washington U. Sch. Medicine and Health Scis., Washington, 1983—84; prof. pediat., prof. pharmacology and therapeutics U. South Fla. Coll. Medicine, Tampa, 1984, pres. faculty coun., 1998—99. Grant reviewer various orgns.; chmn. U. IRB Com.; mem. Dir.'s Conf. on Uses and Abuses of Growth Hormone in Children, Nat. Inst. Child Health and Human Devel., NIH, 1983-; mem. med. adv. bd. Parent Coun. Growth Normality, 1985—; mem. pediatric clin. oncology group Clin. Oncology Program, 1989-, Magic Found., 1995-; mem. staff All Children's Hosp., St. Petersburg, 1984-, Shriner's Hosp., Tampa, 1985-, Tampa Gen. Hosp., 1986-, others; chmn. Internat. Symposium on Growth Hormone, Tampa, 1985, Perinatal Thyroidology, Longboat Key, Fla., 1990, Growth Hormone, Tarpon Springs, Fla., 1992, Internat. Symposium on Growth Hormone Releasing Secretagogues, 1994, Second Internat. Symposium on Growth Hormone Secretagogues, 1997, Therapeutic Outcome of Endocrine Disorders: Efficacy, Innovation and Quality of Life, 1997, 4th Internat. Symposium Growth Hormone Secretagogues, 2002, Internat. Symposium on Endocrine and Molecular Interventions in Aging, 1998, Forum on Drug and Hormone Interventions in Aging, 1998, Endocrinology of Aging, 1999, 3d Internat. Symposium Growth Hormone Secretagogues, 2000, Symposium Cultural Diversity Clin. Rsch., 2000, Symposium Instnl. Rev. Bds. and Human Subject Rsch., 2000, 3d Internat. Symposium on Endocrinology of Aging: Growth Hormone, 2001, Advances in Pituitary Disease: Metabolic, Neuroendocrine and Psychosocial Issues, 2001, 3d Nat. Symposium: Bioethical Issues in Human Subject Rsch., 2002, 4th Internat. Symposium on Growth Hormone Secretagogues, 2002; instr. online courses Theraputic Intervention in Aging: Growth Hormone, 2002, Bioethical Considerations in Human Subject Rsch., 2003, Bioethical Issues in Sex Assignment, 2003. Mem. editorial bd. Jour. Clin. Endocrinology and Metabolism, 1986-89, Jour. Anti-Aging Medicine, 1998—; editorial manuscript reviewer Acta Endocrinologica, Am. Jour. Nutrition, Biol. Psychiatry, Biology of Reprodn., Clin. Endocrinology, Clin. Pediatrics, Endocrine Jour., Endocrine Revs., Endocrinology, European Jour. Pediatrics, Hormone and Metabolic Rsch., Jour. AMA, Jour. Clin. Endocrinology and Metabolism, Jour. Clin. Investigation, Metabolism, Advances in Pituitary Disease: Metabolic, New England Jour. Medicine, Neuroendocrine and Psychosocial Issues, 2001, others; contbr. articles to profl. jours.; patentee in field. Bd. dirs. Birth Defects Found., Fla. Bay Area chpt., 1991—, chmn. med. adv. com., 1991; mem. expert divsn. vaccine injury compensation and mem. bd. dirs. USF Divsn. Sponsored Rsch., 1994-95. Grantee NIH, NIDA, BioNebr., Eli Lilly and Co., Genentech Corp., Daniel Pharm. Corp., Serono Labs., Am. Cancer Soc. Fla., ICN Pharms., Merck & Co., Novo Nordisk, Pharmacia Peptides, Inc., Pharmacia & Upjohn, Wyeth-Ayerst, Alkermes, Astra Zeneca, Infimed. Mem. AMA, Am. Acad. Pediatrics (endocrinology sect.), Am. Assn. Clin. Endocrinologists, Am. Fedn. Clin. Rsch., Am. Pediatric Soc., Am. Pituitary Assn., Endocrine Soc., Fla. Endocrine Soc., Fla. Med. Assn., Hillsborough County Med. Assn., Hillsborough County Pediatric Soc., Lawson Wilkins Soc. Pediatric Endocrinology, Soc. Pediatric Rsch., So. Soc. Pediatric Rsch., Tampa Bay Area Soc. Neurosci. Office: All Children's Hosp USF Coll Medicine 801 6th St S Saint Petersburg FL 33701-4899

BERCZI, ANDREW STEPHEN, academic administrator, educator; b. Budapest, Hungary, Aug. 15, 1934; s. Stephen Andrew and Iren Maria (Bartha) B.; m. Susan Bartok, Aug. 30, 1958; children— Thomas Edgar, Peter Alexander. EE, U. Tech. Scis., Budapest, 1956; BSc, Sir George Williams U., 1961, BA, 1963; MBA, McGill U., 1965, PhD, 1972. Engr. Bell Telephone Co., Montreal, 1956-59, mem. hdqrs. staff acctg., 1959-62, supr. computer systems, 1962-65; prof. quantitative methods, chmn. dept. quantitative methods Sir George Williams U., 1965-71; dean Faculty of Commerce and Adminstrn. Concordia U., Montreal, 1971-77; dean Faculty of Grad. Studies Wilfrid Laurier U., Waterloo, Canada, 1978-87, v.p. fin. and adminstrn., 1987-98, prof. mgmt. scis. and decisions scis., 1999—. Cons. govtl. agys., pvt. industry; lectr. U. Calif. at Berkeley, U. Va., U. Chgo. Author: Exercises in Management Science, 1968, Problems in Managerial Operations Research, Vol. I and II, 1969, The Stock Exchange - A Total System Approach, 1970; contbr. over 80 articles and papers to profl. jours. and assns. McConnell fellow, 1965-66; Canada Council fellow, 1966-67; Quebec Province scholar, 1967-68 Fellow AAAS.; mem. IEEE, Operations Research Soc. Am., Canadian Operations Research Soc., Inst. Mgmt. Scis., Assn. Systems Mgmt., Fin. Execs. Inst., Acad. of Mgmt., Am. Statis. Assn. Home: 76 McCarron Crescent Waterloo ON Canada N2L 5N1 Office: Wilfrid Laurier U 75 University Ave W Waterloo ON Canada N2L 3C5 E-mail: aberczi@wlu.ca.

BERDAHL, ROBERT MAX, academic administrator, historian, educator; b. Sioux Falls, S.D., Mar. 15, 1937; s. Melvin Oliver and Mildred Alberta (Maynard) B.; m. Margaret Lucille Ogle, Aug. 30, 1958; children— Daphne Jean, Jennifer Lynne, Barbara Elizabeth. BA, Augustana Coll., 1959, MA, U. Ill., 1961; PhD, U. Minn., 1965. Asst. prof. history U. Mass., Boston, 1965—67; asst. prof. history U. Oreg., Eugene, 1967—72, assoc. prof., 1972—81, prof., 1981—86; dean U. Oreg. (Coll. Arts and Scis.), 1981—86; prof. U. Ill., 1986—93, vice chancellor academic affairs, 1986—93; pres. U. Tex., Austin, 1993—97; chancellor U. Calif., Berkeley, 1997—. Research asso. Inst. for Advanced Study, Princeton, 1972-73 Author: The Politics of Prussian Nobility, 1988; (with others) Klassen und Kultur, 1982; contbr. articles to profl. jours. Fulbright fellow, 1975-76; Nat. Endowment Humanities fellow, 1976-77 Office: U Calif at Berkeley 200 California Hall Spc 1500 Berkeley CA 94720-1500*

BERDICK, LEONARD STANLEY, insurance broker; b. New Rochelle, N.Y., Aug. 13, 1938; s. Julius and Fay (Jaffe) B.; m. Arlene Jean Kaufman, Oct. 31, 1968. BA, Colgate U., 1960; MA, Columbia U., 1963; student, U. N.C. Law Sch., 1960-61. Mem. Nat. Assn. Life Underwriters, Acad. Polit. Sci., Colgate U., Columbia U., U. N.C. alumni assns. Clubs: Colgate Univ. Jewish. Home: 80 Richmond Hill Rd Staten Island NY 10314-7581 Office: 5 E 41st St # 129 New York NY 10017-6205

BERDON, ROBERT IRWIN, judge trial referee, retired state supreme court justice; b. New Haven, Dec. 24, 1929; s. Louis J. and Jean (Cohen) B.; m. Nancy Tarr, Aug. 30, 1964 (dec. Mar. 1992); 1 child, Peter A. BS, Duke U., 1951; JD, U. Conn., 1957; LLM in Jud. Process, U. Va., 1988. With Bank of Manhattan, 1953-54; pvt. practice New Haven, 1957-73; treas. State of Conn., 1971-73; judge Superior Ct., State of Conn., New Haven, 1973-91; justice Supreme Ct., State of Conn., 1991-99, ret., 1999—99, judge trial referee, 2000—. Adj. prof. law U. Bridgeport Sch. Law, 1986-91; lectr. in law U. Conn. Sch. of Law, 1993; assoc. fellow Saybrook Coll., Yale U., 1986—; lectr. Am. Bd. Trial Advs., 1986; mem. Conn. Bd. Pardons, 1991-92. Contbr. articles to profl. jours. Recipient Judiciary award Conn. Trial Lawyers Assn., 1976, Disting. Alumni award U. Conn., 1977, Outstanding State Trial Judge in U.S. award Assn. Trial Lawyers in Am., 1982, Pub. Svc. award U. Conn. Sch. Law Alumni Assn., 1989, Judiciary award Conn. Bar Assn., 1991, Hartford Neighborhood Housing Coalition award, 1992, RosCossi - Koskoff Justice award Conn. Trial Lawyers Assn., 1999, Jud. Recognition award Conn. Def. Lawyers Assn., 1999. Home: 245 Pleasant Point Rd Branford CT 06405-5609 Office: Superior Ct 235 Church St New Haven CT 06510

BEREK, JONATHAN SAMUEL, writer, educator, dean, surgeon, gynecologist; b. Sioux City, Iowa, Apr. 21, 1948; s. Samuel I. and Janet (Graetz) Berek; m. Deborah L. Jones, June 6, 1970; children: Micah, James, Jessica. AB, Brown U., 1970, MMSc, 1973; MD, Johns Hopkins U., 1975; postgrad., Harvard U., 1979. Diplomate in ob-gyn. and gynecol. oncology Am. Bd. Ob-Gyn. Intern and resident Brigham and Women's Hosp. Harvard U. Med. Sch., Boston, 1975-79; fellow UCLA Sch. Medicine, 1979-81, prof., 1981—2003, prof., exec. vice chair dept. ob-gyn., chair gynecologic oncology, chair Coll. Applied Anatomy, 1992—. Author: Practical Gynecologic Oncology, 1989, 3d edit., 2002, Novak's Gynecology, 1996, 2d edit., 2002; contbr. articles to profl. jours. Fellow: ACOG, ACS. Office: UCLA David Geffen Sch Medicine 24-137 CHS Los Angeles CA 90095-1740

BEREK, PETER, English educator; b. Bklyn., June 20, 1940; s. Leo and Ida (Kantrowitz) B.; m. Ellen H. Stark, June 10, 1962; children— Rachel, Martha, Elizabeth BA, Amherst Coll., 1961; MA, Harvard U., 1963, PhD, 1967. Instr. English, Hamilton Coll., Clinton, N.Y., 1965-67; asst. prof. English, Williams Coll., Williamstown, Mass., 1967-72, assoc. prof., 1972-77, prof., 1977-90, dept. chmn., 1980-86, Morris prof. rhetoric, 1984-90, dean of coll., 1975-78, spl. asst. to pres., 1987-90, prof. English Mt. Holyoke Coll., South Hadley, Mass., 1990—, dean faculty, provost, 1990-98, interim pres., fall 1995. Cons. NEH, Washington, 1973-76, 86-87, 89. Contbr. articles to profl. jours. Woodrow Wilson Found. fellow, 1961-62; NEH fellow, 1971-72, 82-83. Mem. MLA, Shakespeare Assn. Am., AAUP. Jewish. Home: 87 Woodlot Rd Amherst MA 01002-3452 Office: Mt Holyoke Coll Dept English South Hadley MA 01075 E-mail: pberek@mtholyoke.edu.

BERENATO, AGNUS MCGLADE, women's basketball coach; b. Dec. 9, 1956; m. Jack Berenato; children: Theresa Marie, Andrew, Joey, Clare, Christina. Student, U. N.C., 1976-77; BA in Sociology, Mt. St. Mary's Coll., Emmitsburg, Md., 1980, DHL (hon.), 1995. Profl. basketball player Entente Senonaise, Sens, France, 1975-76; head coach Rider Coll., 1981-85; asst. coach Ga. Tech U., 1986-88, head coach women's basketball, 1988—; lead coach women's basketball U. Pitts., 2003—. Recipient Disting. Alumni award Mt. St. Mary's Coll., 1984; named Ga. Win Coll. Coach of Yr., 2000, Divsn. I Ga. Coach of Yr., 2002, Coach WBCA All Star Challenge, 2002; Sports Ethics fellow Inst. Internat. Sports, 1996; inducted into Rider Coll. Hall of Fame, 2002. Mem. Atlanta Tip-Off Club (nat. adv. bd.), Atlanta Women's Network Inc., Women's Basketball Coaches Assn., Ga. Women's Intersport Network, Atlanta Women in Sports, Naismith Hall of Fame. Office: U Pitts PO Box 7436 Pittsburgh PA 15213 Business E-Mail: aberenato@at.gtaa.gatech.edu.

BERENATO, ANTHONY FRANCIS, financial executive; b. Phila., Dec. 3, 1922; s. Frank A. and Eleanor A. (Siderio) B.; m. Dena Marie Marchione, Sept. 5, 1946; children: Anthony Francis Jr., Mark Anthony. BS in Econs. and Acctg., Villanova U., 1949; postgrad., Am. U., Biarritz, France, 1945-46; student-philosophy and art appreciation, Barnes Found., 1966-68. C.P.A., Pa. Ptnr. Steinberg, Spiegel & Berenato, Springfield, Pa., 1956-91; pres. Roger Fin. Corp., Phila., 1961-63, Sure Loan Corp., Phila., 1961-65, Cobbs Fla. Cupboard Inc., Bala Cynwyd, Pa., 1965-67, Phila. Arena Corp., 1961-65; chmn. Crescent Iron Works, Phila., 1974-85; chmn., chief exec. officer Custom Art Metals, Inc., Barrington, N.J., 1967-89; co-founder, mng. dir. OSA Environ. Svcs., Southampton, N.J., 1996. Founder, chmn. Crescent Cab Co., Phila.; pres., CEO Custom Art Metals P.R. Inc., 1987-90. Trustee Anthony F. and Dena Marie Berenato Charitable Trust. Served with U.S. Army, 1942-46, ETO, active Res. 1946-49. Fellow Am. Inst. Mgmt., Navy League of U.S. (life mem.), Pa. Soc., AICPA, Pa. Inst. CPAs, U.S. Naval Inst. (life), Am. Sec. Coun., Bala Golf Club (treas. 1974-76), Rio Mar Country Club (P.R.), Greate Bay Country Club, Rolling Green Golf Club, Hamilton Club. Republican. Roman Catholic. Home: 550 Bay Ave Apt 702 Somers Point NJ 08244-2547 Home (Winter): Cecilia's Pl #207 Isla Verde PR 00979

BERENATO, MARK ANTHONY, lawyer, insurance executive; b. Lansdowne, Pa., Feb. 24, 1958; s. Anthony Francis and Dena Marie (Marchione) B.; m. Linnie Louise Swineford, Sept. 9, 1989. Diploma, Episcopal Acad., 1976; BS in Acctg., Villanova U., 1980; JD, Am. U., 1983; postgrad., Temple U., 1984. Bar: Pa. 1984, U.S. Dist. Ct. (ea. dist.) Pa. 1987. Tax lawyer Deloitte, Haskins & Sells, N.Y.C., 1984-85; pvt. practice Law Offices of Mark A. Berenato, Phila., 1985—. Counsel Custom Art Metals, Inc., Barrington, N.J., 1985-91; pres. Cumberland Devel. Corp., Voorhees, N.J., 1989-95; sec., gen. counsel Sterling Metal Fabricators, Inc., Barrington, N.J., 1985-93; prin. Mark A. Berenato Ins. Agy., Media, Pa., 1993—. Mem. ABA, Pa. Bar Assn., Phila. Bar Assn., Rolling Green Golf Club, Vesper Club, Phi Alpha Delta. Republican. Roman Catholic. Avocations: golf, literature, antique collecting. Home: 740 Iris Ln Media PA 19063 Office: 2 Penn Ctr Ste 200 Philadelphia PA 19102-1754 E-mail: markberenato@earthlink.net.

BERENBAUM, MICHAEL GARY, theology educator; b. Newark, July 1, 1945; s. Saul Berenbaum and Rhea Kass; m. Linda Bayer, Aug. 25, 1968 (div. July 1992); children: Ilana, Lev; m. Melissa Patack, June 25, 1995; children: Joshua, Mira. Student, Jewish Theol. Sem., 1963—67, Hebrew U., 1965—66; AB in Philosophy, Queens Coll., 1967; postgrad., Boston U., 1967—69; PhD in Religion and Culture, Fla. State U., 1975; DD (honoris causa), Narazeth Coll., Rochester, N.Y., 1995; LHD (hon.), Dennison U., 2000. Instr. dept. philosophy and religion Colby-Sawyer Coll., 1969—71; adj. asst. prof. religion, Jewish chaplain Wesleyan U., 1973—80; assoc. professorial lectr. dept. religion George Washington U., 1981—83; opinion page editor Washington Jewish Week, 1983—86, acting editor, 1985; sr. scholar Religious Action Ctr., 1986—88; Hymen Goldman prof. theology Georgetown U., 1983—97; rsch. fellow U.S. Holocaust Meml. Mus., 1987—88, project dir., 1988—93, dir. U.S. Holocaust Rsch. Inst., 1993—97; pres., CEO Survivors of Shoah Visual History Found., 1997—99; prof. theology U. Judaism, 1998—; Ida E. King disting. vis. scholar of the Holocaust Richard Stockton Coll., 1999—2000; pres. Berenbaum Group, 1999—; dir. Sigi Ziering Inst.: Exploring Ethical and Religious Implications of the Holocaust, 2002—. Adj. prof. Judaic studies Am. U., 1987; assoc. dir.-Zachor Holocaust Resource Ctr., 1978; dep. dir. Pres. Commn. on Holocaust, 1979—80; vis. prof. Hebrew Studies U. Md., 1983; assoc. Gannett Ctr. Media Studies Columbia U. Author: The Vision of the Void: Theological Reflections on the Works of Elie Wiesel, 1979, reprinted as Elie Wiesel: God, The Holocaust and the Children of Israel, 1994, The World Must Know: The History of the Holocaust as Told in the U.S. Holocaust Museum, After Tragedy and Triumph, 1990, A Promise to Remember: The Holocaust in the Words and Voices of the Survivors, 2003; editor: From Holocaust to New Life, 1985, Witness to the Holocaust, 1997, The Holocaust and History: The Known, The Unknown, The Disputed and The Reexamined, 1998; co-editor: Holocaust: Religious and Philosophical Implications, 1989, Anatomy of the Auschwitz Death Camp, 1996, What Kind of God?, 1997, The Bombing of Auschwitz: Should the Allies Have Attempted It, 2001; mem. editl. bd.: Tikkun, Jour. Holocaust and Genocide Studies; contbg. editor: Sh'ma; editor: Together, 1986—89; : The Holocaust and History, 1998. Recipient Simon Rockower Meml. award in Jewish journalism for Disting. Editl. Writing, Am. Jewish Press Assn., 1986, Disting. Coverage of Arts, 1987, Outstanding Informational Emmy award for One Survivor Remembers, 1995, Cable Ace award for One Survivor Remembers, 1996; fellow Ezra Styles, Yale U., 1979, Danforth Found. Underwood, 1976—77, George Wise, Tel Aviv U., 1974, Charles E. Merrill, Fla. State U., 1972—73. Fellow: Soc. Values in Higher Edn. Democrat. Jewish. Home: 1124 S Orlando Los Angeles CA 90035 E-mail: michael@berenbaumgroup.com.

BERENBEIM, JANE ROSEN, not-for-profit developer; d. Murray and Sylvia (Reiter) Rosen; m. Ronald Everett Berenbeim, Mar. 25, 1979; children: Jessica Lucy, Sarah Katherine. AB cum laude, Vassar, 1960—64; AM, Harvard, 1964—66; MA, Brandeis, 1970. Asst. v.p. Personal Fin. Planning, E.F. Hutton & Co., NY, 1975—81; devel. dir. Fund for Artist Colonies, N.Y., 1984—86; assoc. dir. found. rels. Columbia U., N.Y., 1986—90, sr. devel. officer, major gifts, 1990—91; dir. found. & corp. rels. Mt. Sinai Med. Ctr., N.Y., 1991—92; dir. devel. Riverdale Country Sch., N.Y., 1993—96; chief devel. officer Jewish Bd. Family & Children's Svc., N.Y., 1996—. Bd. mem. Saeko Ichinohe Co. Modern Dance Co., N.Y., 1981—. E-mail: peartreejr@aol.com.

BERENBEIM, RONALD EVERETT, business writer, educator; b. Denver, May 5, 1944; s. Samuel Leonard and Joan Madelon (Goodney) B.; m. Jane Susan Rosen, Mar. 25, 1979; children: Jessica Lucy, Sarah Katherine. AB cum laude, Cornell U., 1966; BA, Oxford (Eng.) U., 1968, MA, 1971; JD, Harvard U., 1971. Bar: Wash. 1973, Mass. 1974. Atty. Nat. Labor Rels. Bd., Seattle, 1971-73; bus. rep. Motion Picture and TV Union, N.Y.C., 1975-77; rsch. assoc. The Conf. Bd., Inc., N.Y.C., 1977-80; dir. Guaranty Nat. Corp., 1977-88; sr. rsch. assoc. The Conf. Bd., Inc., N.Y.C., 1980-97; dir. Working Group of Bus. Ethics Prins., N.Y.C., 1997—; prin. rschr. The Conf. Bd., Inc., N.Y.C., 1998—. Prof. NYU, N.Y.C., 1990, Stern Sch. Bus. Adminstrn., 1995; dir. Working Group on Global Bus. Ethics Principles, N.Y.C., 1997—; vis. fellow New Zealand Ctr. for Bus. Ethics, 2000; project dir. East Asia Pacific pvt. sector anti-corruption project The World Bank, 2001; mem. exec. adv. panel Open Compliance and Ethics Group, 2002. Author: (with Jean-Francois Arvis) Fighting Corruption in East Asia: Solutions from the Private Sector, 2003; contbr. articles to profl. jours., chpts. to books. Keasbey Meml. scholar Balliol Coll., Oxford U., 1966; grantee John D. and Catherine T. MacArthur Found., 2000. Mem.: Inst. of Mgmt. Cons. U.S. (ethics com. 2002—), Nat. Assn. Corp. Dirs. (blue ribbon commn. on profl. bd. 1996), Transparency Internat. Soc. Accountability Internat. (steering com. to devel. bus. prin. for countering bribery 2000—). Home: 172 E 95th St New York NY 10128-2511 Office: The Conf Bd 845 3rd Ave New York NY 10022-6601 E-mail: ronald.berenbeim@conference-board.org., peartreeJR@aol.com.

BERENDI, ERLINDA BAYAUA, physician surgeon; b. Santiago, Isabela, The Philippines, Oct. 31, 1947; came to U.S., 1972; d. Jeremias Carreon and Amanda (Florentin) Bayaua; m. S. Alexander Berendi, Jan. 2, 1981. BS, U. Santo Tomas, Manila, 1966, MD, 1971. Med. dir. Great Pacific Life Ins. Co., Manila, 1971-72; intern, resident Michael Reese Hosp., Chgo., 1973-77; pres., physician, surgeon Consultative Exams., Inc., Chgo., 1980—; med. dir. Intracorp. Med. Rev. Svcs., Arlington Heights, Ill., 1987-89. Pres. Finnegan's Choice, Inc., Chgo., 1985—; med. cons. Dept. Health and Human Svcs., Chgo., 1977-83, State of Ill., Dept. Rehab. Svcs., Chgo., 1981—; acting chmn. med. quality rev. com. Bur. of Program Integrity, Ill. Dept. Pub. Aid, Chgo., 1977—; physician cons. Comprehensive Health Svcs, Inc., Chgo., 1978-79; chief med. cons. U.S. R.R. Retirement Bd., 1981-95. Mem. AMA, Am. Acad. Family Physicians, Nat. Assn. Disability Examiners, N.Y. Acad. Scis. Avocations: running, weightlifting, piano. Home: 6666 N Tower Circle Dr Lincolnwood IL 60712-3221 Office: Consultative Exams Inc 55 E Washington St Ste 2101 Chicago IL 60602-2219

BERENDT, JOHN LAWRENCE, writer, editor; b. Syracuse, N.Y., Dec. 5, 1939; s. Ralph Sidney and Carol (Deschere) B. AB, Harvard U., 1961. Assoc. editor Esquire mag., N.Y.C., 1961-69, sr. staff editor Holiday mag., N.Y.C., 1969; assoc. prodr. David Frost Show, N.Y.C., 1969-71; writer Dick Cavett Show, N.Y.C., 1973-75; editor N.Y. Mag., N.Y.C., 1977-79; columnist Esquire mag., N.Y.C., 1982-94. Author: Midnight in the Garden of Good and Evil, 1994 (Pulitzer prize finalist for gen. non-fiction 1995); contbr. articles to profl. jours. Mem. PEN, Century Assn. Office: c/o William Morris Agy 1325 Ave of the Americas New York NY 10019-0002

BERENDT, PAUL, political organization worker; b. July 16, 1956; m. Beth Berendt. BA, Evergreen State Coll., 1987. Chmn. Wash. State Dem. Party, 1995—. Roman Catholic. Home: 1702 Sulenes Dr SE Olympia WA 98501-7042 Office: PO Box 4027 Seattle WA 98104-0027 also: Democratic Party 616 First Ave Ste 300 PO Box 4027 Seattle WA 98104*

BERENDT, ROBERT TRYON, lawyer; b. Chgo., Mar. 8, 1939; s. Alex E. and Ethel L. (Tryon) B.; m. Sara Probert, June 15, 1963; children: David, Elizabeth, Katherine. BA, Monmouth Coll., 1961; JD with distinction, U. Iowa, 1965. Bar: Iowa 1965, Ill. 1968, U.S. Dist. Ct. (no. dist.) Ill. 1968, U.S. Ct. Appeals (7th cir.) 1968, Mo. 1979, U.S. Dist. Ct. (ea. dist.) Mo. 1979. Assoc. Schiff Hardin & Waite, Chgo., 1968-73, ptnr., 1973-78; litigation counsel Monsanto Co., St. Louis, 1978-83, asst. gen. counsel, 1983-85, assoc. gen. counsel, 1986-96; of counsel Thompson Coburn, St. Louis, 1996—. Disting. Neutral, Ctr. for Pub. Resources; editl. adv. bd. Alternatives, Inside Litigation, Product Safety and Liability Reporter-Bur. Nat. Affairs. Contbr. articles to profl. jours. Lt. USNR, 1965-68. Mem. ABA (litigation sect., coun. mem. 1993-96), Mo. Bar Assn., Ill. Bar Assn., Iowa Bar Assn., Bar Assn. Met. St. Louis, Product Liability Adv. Coun. (bd. dirs., exec. com., Inst. for the Judiciary, pres.-trustee Found. 1992-98). Avocations: golf, tennis, reading. Office: Thompson Coburn 1 Mercantile Ctr Ste 3400 Saint Louis MO 63101-1643

BERENDZEN, RICHARD, astronomer, educator, author; b. Walters, Okla., Sept. 6, 1938; s. Earl Emmanuel and Florine Adora (Harrison) B.; m. Gail Anita Edgar, Nov. 26, 1964; children: Deborah Carol, Natasha Karina. BS, MIT, 1961; MA, Harvard U., 1967, PhD, 1969; LLD (hon.), W.Va. Wesleyan U., 1979; LHD (hon.), Bridgewater Coll., 1983; LLD (hon.), Kean Coll. of NJ, 1984, Seton Hall U., 1985; DS (hon.), U. Columbo, Sri Lanka, 1985; LLD (hon.), U. Charleston, 1986, U. Balt., 1990. Staff scientist Geophysics Corp. Am., 1959-64, Ling-Temco-Vought, 1961-62; lectr. Harvard U., 1964, 66; mem. staff Project Physics, 1965; mem. faculty Boston U., 1965-73, assoc. prof. astronomy, 1971-73, acting dept. chmn., 1971-72; prof. physics, dean Coll. Arts and Sci., Am. U., Washington, 1974-76; univ. provost Am. U., Washington, 1976-79, pres., 1980-90, prof., 1990—; commentator on edn. and astronomy Stat. WUSA-TV/WTOP, Washington, 1984-90; cons. NASA, 1991, 98. Commentator on NASA for NBC-TV, 2003; cons. space sci. bd. NAS, 1973-74, mem. panel astron. survey com., 1971-73; cons. acad. affairs Am. Coun. on Edn., 1973-74; cons. to pub. cos.; holder numerous lectureships; Am. specialist in Asia Am. Council Edn. and Dept. State; adv. Am. Inst. Physics, Library of Congress, Internat. Communication Agy., UNESCO, Smithsonian Instn., NSF; univ. evaluator Commn. Higher Edn. Middle States Assn. Colls. and Secondary Schs.; chmn. priorities and planning com. Assn. Am. Colls., 1978-80, chmn. pres.'s adv. com., 1977-79; program evaluator US Armed Forces Inst.; mem. rev. panel human resources NRC; lectr. USIA; host spls. on astronomy and higher edn. NBC-TV, 1976-77; organizer Space 2000 Symposium, 1998; frequent guest radio and TV shows; researcher on cosmology, history of astronomy, sci. and soc., Am. and internat. edn. Author: Education in and History of Modern Astronomy, 1972, Life Beyond Earth and the Mind of Man, 1973, Man Discovers the Galaxies, 1976, Is My Armor Straight? A Year in the Life of a University President, 1986, Come Here: A Man Overcomes the Tragic Aftermath of Childhood Sexual Abuse, 1993, Pulp Physics: Humankind in Space & Time Audio Series, 2000; founding editor Jour. Coll. Sci. Teaching; contbr. numerous articles and revs. to profl. jours. Bd. dirs. Bus. Coun. for Internat. Understanding, 1980-84, Assn. Am. Colls., 1981-83, European Inst., Group Hospitalization Med. Svc. Inc., Nat. Network for Youth, Inc., 1994-97; chmn. Com. on Fng. Students and Instl. Policy, 1981-82; chmn. Employment/Edn. Bur. Greater Washington Bd. Trade, 1989; co-chmn. AIDS project Meyer Found., 1988-90; mem. DC Com. on Pub. Schs., 1988-90; chmn. DC Commn. on Budget and Fin. Priorities, 1989-90, 94; mem. NASA Exploration Adv. Task Force, 1988-91; chmn. bd. dir. Orphan Found. Am., 1996-97; dir. NASA's DC Space Grant Consortium, 2000—. Named one of Top Young Educators Change: Mag. of Learning, 1978; recipient Mortar Bd. Faculty award, 1977, Freedoms Found. Valley Forge award, 1982, Glenn T. Seaborg award Internat. Platform Assn., 1997; fellow com. Scientists Investigating Claims of the Paranormal, 1977-78. Fellow AAAS; mem. Internat. Astron. Union, Internat. Assn. Univ. Pres., Am. Astron. Soc., Am. Assn. U. Adminstrs., Am. Assn. for Higher Edn., Internat. Assn. Univs., NY Acad. Scis., Am. Assn. Physics Tchr., Astron. Soc. Pacific, History of Sci. Soc., Nat. Sci. Tchrs. Assn., Am. Assn. Higher Edn., Am. Conf. Acad. Deans, Washington Inst. Fgn. Affairs, Cosmos Club, Sigma Xi, Kappa Mu Epsilon, Phi Eta Sigma, Phi Kappa Phi. Home: 1300 Crystal Dr Arlington VA 22202-3234 Office: Am U Dept Physics Washington DC 20016-8058

BERENFELD, MARK M. chemist; b. Moscow, Aug. 14, 1940; s. Moisey I. Berenfeld and Fanya I. Prosmushkina; m. Genya Berenfeld, Oct. 9, 1971; children: Benjamin, Sonya. BS, Engring. Inst., Moscow, 1965; MS, Lomonossov U., Moscow, 1970; PhD, Karpoff Sci. Inst. Physics, Moscow, 1974. Sr. scientist Pigment and Varnishes Co., Moscow, 1971-77, Dyestuff Co., Moscow, 1977-89; R&D chemist Fabricolor, Inc., Paterson, N.J., 1991-95; sr. sci. chemist Jos. H. Lowenstein, Inc., Bklyn., 1996—. Mem. Am. Chem. Soc. Home: 688 Mill St Belleville NJ 07109- E-mail: mberenfeld@msn.com.

BERENS, MARK HARRY, lawyer; b. St. Paul, Aug. 4, 1928; s. Harry C. and Gertrude M. (Scherkenbach) B.; m. Barbara Jean Steichen, Nov. 20, 1954; children: Paul J., Joseph F. (dec.), John M., Stephen M., Thomas M., Michael M., Lisa B. Moran, James M., Daniel M. BS in Commerce (Acctg.) magna cum laude, U. Notre Dame, 1950, JD magna cum laude, 1951; postgrad., U. Chgo., 1951-53. Bar: Ill. 1951, D.C. 1955, U.S. Supreme Ct. 1971; CPA, Ill. Assoc. Mayer, Brown and predecessors, Chgo., 1956-61, ptnr., 1961-96; chmn., CEO Attys.' Liability Assurance Soc., Inc., Chgo., 1987-95; ptnr. Altheimer & Gray, Chgo., 1996—2003, Bell, Boyd & Lloyd, Chgo., 2003—. Chmn. bd. dirs. Attys.' Liability Assurance Soc. (Bermuda) Ltd., 1979-95; bd. dirs. Accts. Liability Assurance Co.; nat. chmn. Nat. Assn. Law Rev. Editors, 1950-51. Editor-in-chief Notre Dame Law Rev., 1950-51; contbr. articles to profl. jours. 1st lt. JAGC U.S. Army, 1953-56. Mem. ABA, D.C. Bar Assn., Chgo. Bar Assn., Am. Law Inst., The Comml. Bar Assn. (London), Am. Assn. Atty.-CPAs, Union League Club, Lawyers Club of Chgo., Met. Club, Sunset Ridge Country Club (Northbrook). Republican. Roman Catholic. Home: 1660 North Ln Northbrook IL 60062-4708 Office: Bell Boyd & Lloyd LLC 70 W Madison St Chicago IL 60602

BERENS, WILLIAM JOSEPH, lawyer; b. New Ulm, Minn., Dec. 12, 1952; s. Robert J. and Lorraine M. (O'Brien) B.; m. Janet Christiansen, June 13, 1975; children: Margaret, Elizabeth, Catherine. BA, Coll. St. Thomas, 1975; JD, U. Minn., 1978. Bar: Minn. 1978. Assoc. Dorsey & Whitney, LLP, Mpls., 1978-83, ptnr., 1984—. Adj. prof. William Mitchell Coll. of Law, St. Paul, 1981-84. Fellow: Am. Coll. Trust and Estate Counsel. Home: 1601 Beechwood Ave Saint Paul MN 55116-2409 Office: Dorsey & Whitney LLP 50 S 6th St Minneapolis MN 55402-1498

BERENSON, GERALD SANDERS, physician; b. Bogalusa, La., Sept. 19, 1922; s. Meyer A. and Eva (Singerman) B.; m. Joan Seidenbach, Mar. 7, 1951; children— Leslie, Ann, Robert, Laurie. BS, Tulane U., 1943, MD, 1945. Intern U.S. Navy Hosp., Great Lakes, Ill., 1945-46; practice medicine specializing in cardiology New Orleans; mem. staff Charity Hosp., Hotel Dieu; instr. dept. medicine Tulane U., 1949-52, prof. epidemiology Sch. Pub. Health, 1992—; asst. prof. medicine La. State U. Med. Sch., 1954-58, assoc. prof., 1958-63, prof., 1963-92, Boyd prof., 1988-92, prof. emeritus, 1992—; prof. medicine, biochemistry and pediatrics Tulane U. Sch. Medicine, New Orleans, 1992—. Dir. Specialized Ctr. Rsch. Arteriosclerosis, New Orleans, 1972-87, Nat. Rsch. and Demonstration Ctr. in Arteriosclerosis, 1984-87, Nat. Ctr. Cardiovascular Health, Sch. Pub. Health and Tropical Medicine Tulane U., 1992—; sr. vis. physician Charity Hosp. La., New Orleans, 1948—; cons. Touro Infirmary, 1967—; cons. medicine Hotel Dieu, 1962—. Contbr. articles to profl. jours. Served with USNR, 1945-48. USPHS fellow U. Chgo., 1952-54 Mem. Am. Coll. Cardiology (gov. La. 1985-88, trustee 1988, chmn. prevention com. 1990-93), So. Soc. Clin. Investigation (pres. 1969), La. Heart Assn. (pres. 1971), New Orleans Acad. Internal Medicine (pres. 1966), Musser-Burch Soc. (pres. 1981), Soc. Geriatric Cardiology (pres. 1999-00), Sigma Xi, Alpha Omega Alpha. Home: 505 Northline St Metairie LA 70005-4435 Office: Tulane Sch Pub Health Nat Ctr Cardiovascular Health 1440 Canal St Ste 1838 New Orleans LA 70112-2750 E-mail: berenson@tulane.edu.

BERENSON, PAUL STEWART, advertising agency executive; b. Boston, Aug. 28, 1944; s. Joseph and Estelle Ada (Isenberg) B.; m. Tilly Lemler, Nov. 19, 1966 (div. 1984). AAS in Nuclear Engring., Wentworth Inst., 1964; Diploma in Bus. Adminstrn., Northeastern U., 1968. Editor Sylvania Electric Systems, Waltham, Mass., 1965-67; editor, writer Honeywell EDP, Newton, Mass., 1967-69; ptnr., writer Waldon Assocs., Newton, 1969-71; ptnr. Insight Advt., Boston, 1971-73; chmn., CEO Berenson and Isham, Inc. (merged with Snyder Comm.), Boston, 1973—98; chief mktg. officer, ptnr. Colony Mill Marketplace, Keene, NH, 2001—. Chmn. New Market Ventures, Boston, 1995, Data Applications Inc., Boston, 1995; instr. direct mktg. mgmt. Bentley Coll., 1989-99; advt. cons. Silver Edits., Larkspur, Calif., 1985-86; cons. divsn. extended edn. Boston U., 2000—, v.p. mktg. tng. track divsn., 2000—; cons. various mktg. groups, 1973—. Author: Venture Capital and Management, 1971; writer, editor computer course, 1987. Dir. Mass. Found. for Children, 1993-94. With Army N.G., 1964-70. Recipient Tchr. of Yr. award Advt. Club Greater Boston, 2000, Art Dirs. Club, Good Samaritans, Bus./Profl. Advt. Assn., Addy award. Mem. Am. Mktg. Assn., New Eng. Direct Mktg. Assn. (pres. 1995-96), Art Dirs. Club, Advt. Club (trustee), Direct Mktg. Club, Gt. Dane of N.E. Club (pres. 1979-82). Avocations: fishing, boating, collecting stamps and coins. Office: Colony Mill Marketplace 222 West St Keene NH 03431

BERENSON, ROBERT LEONARD, advertising agency executive; b. Chgo., Nov. 14, 1939; s. James Morton and Harriet Ruth (Fisher) B.; m. Terry Reiner, Nov. 14, 1993; 1 child, Cindy Elizabeth. BA, Syracuse U., 1961; MS in Journalism, Northwestern U., 1962. Mgmt. trainee Grey Advt., Inc., N.Y.C., 1964-67, v.p., account supr., 1967-70, v.p., mgmt. supr., 1970-71, sr. v.p., mgmt. rep., 1971-77, exec. v.p., 1977-82, exec. v.p. adminstrn. and account mgmt., 1982-92, pres., 1993-2000; vice chmn. Grey Global Group, N.Y.C., 2000—. Guest lectr. mktg. U. Conn., Syracuse U., Northwestern U., St. John's U., 1974-88; bd. dirs. Burgundy Wine Co. Bd. dirs. BBB; chmn., bd. dirs. Fed. Law Enforcement Found.; trustee Culinary Inst. Am.; nat. bd. dirs. Steppenwolf Theater. 1st lt. U.S. Army, 1962-64. Jewish. Office: Grey Global Group 777 3d Ave New York NY 10017-1401 E-mail: bberenson@grey.com.

BERENSON, WILLIAM KEITH, lawyer; b. Nashville, Nov. 23, 1954; s. Leon and Lorraine Florence (Keiles) B; m. Mara Lynn Rubinton; 1 child, Marissa Laurel. BA with honors, U. Tex., 1976; JD, So. Meth. U., 1979. Bar: Tex. 1979, U.S. Dist. Ct. (no. dist.) Tex., U.S. Ct. Appeals (5th and 11th cirs.), U.S. Supreme Ct.; cert. personal injury trial law, Tex. Bd. Legal Specialization. Mem. Supreme Ct. Jury Task Force. Author: Evaluating Settlement Offers, 1990, Texas Automobile Injury Guide, 1993, Trying the Automobile Injury Case in Texas: Plaintiff's Perspective, 1995, Automobile Injury Cases in Texas, 1996, Quantification of Personal Injury Claims, 1997; mem. editl. bd. Ins. Settlement and Litigation Reporter, Ins. Issues Annotated. Chmn. Longhorn coun. Boy Scouts Am., Ft. Worth; bd. dirs. So. Meth. U. Alumni Assn., AIDS Interfaith Network; bd. dirs. Regional Coun. Parents and Alumni, So. Meth. U.; vol. atty. Animal Rescue Orgn. Fellow Tarrant County Bar Found.; mem. ABA, ATLA (sustaining mem. pub. interest group com.), State Bar Tex., Tex. Bar Assn., Tarrant County Bar Assn. (jud. evaluation com., fee arbitration com.), Tarrant County Lawyrs Assn. (bd. dirs. 1994-2003), Tex. Trial Lawyers Assn., Coll. State Bar Tex., Nat. Coll. Advocacy, Roscoe Pound Found., Phi Alpha Delta. Avocations: golf, snow skiing. Office: 900 River Plaza Tower 1701 River Run Fort Worth TX 76107-6579

BERENT, IRWIN MARK, writer, software executive; b. Norfolk, Va., Feb. 10, 1958; s. Nathan and Selma Faye (Caplan) B. BA in History, Old Dominion U., 1980; MA in Am. History, East Carolina U., 1982. Dir. Monitor Rsch. and Recovery Found., Norfolk, 1980-82; exec. dir. The Speakers' Agy., Norfolk, 1988—; v.p. StoryCraft Corp., Norfolk, 1994—2002; pres. WritersSuperCenter.com, 2002—. Speaker in field. Author: Fundamentalism, 1988, The Crew of the USS Monitor: A Biographical Directory, 1981, The Right Words, 1992, Drug Legalization: For and Against, 1992, Getting Your Words Worth, 1993, Jewish Genealogy, 1984, The Monuments and Statues of the Capitol Square of North Carolina, 1985, Weird Words, 1995, More Weird Words, 1995, History of Tidewater Jewry: 1900-1950, 1986, The Quotable Conservative, 1996, ABC of Cat Trivia, 1996, The Dictionary of Highly Unusual Words, 1997, Norfolk Virgina: A Jewish History, 2001; developer: StoryCraft Fiction Writer's Software, designer: StarCross Ecumenical Sculpture. Avocations: philosophy, literature, ham radio, tennis. Home: 560 Roland Dr Norfolk VA 23509-1554 Office: Writers SuperCenter 560 Roland Drive Norfolk VA 23509-1554 E-mail: ibstory@exis.net.

BERENT, STANLEY, psychologist, educator, researcher, consultant; b. Norfolk, Va., Mar. 10, 1941; s. David and Esther (Laibstain) B.; m. Joy McKeever; children: Melissa Virginia, Alison Reneé, Rachel Irene. BS, Old Dominion U., 1966; MS, Va. Commonwealth U., 1967; PhD, Rutgers U., 1972. Diplomate Am. Bd. Profl. Psychology. Prof. U. Va., Charlottesville, 1972-79, U. Mich., Ann Arbor, 1979—. Chief of psychology, VA Med. Ctr., Ann Arbor, 1979-85, U. Mich., 1993-01; vis. prof. U. London, 1988-89, China Rehab. Rsch. Ctr., Beijing, 1998—; pres., CEO, bd. dirs. NeuroBehavioral Resources, Inc., 1998—, founder and dir. of neuropsychology divsn., U. Mich., 1979-2001 Author 4 books, 20 book chpts.; contbr. more than 200 articles to profl. jours. Bd. dirs. Arbor Hills Assn., 1986-88. Served with USMC, 1959-63. Fellow Am. Psychol. Assn.; mem. Assn. Advancement Sci., Neurosci. Soc., Am. Epilepsy Soc., Am. Acad. Neurology. Office: U Mich Hosps Box 0840 Med Inn Bldg Suite 480 Ann Arbor MI 48109-0840 E-mail: sberent@umich.edu.

BERENTSEN, KURTIS GEORGE, music educator, choral conductor; b. North Hollywood, Calif., Apr. 22, 1953; s. George O. and Eleanor J. (Johnson) B.; m. Jeanette M. Sacco, Aug., 1975 (div. 1977); m. Floy I. Griffiths, March 17, 1984; 1 child, Kendra Irene. MusB, Utah State U., 1975; MA in Music, U. Calif., Santa Barbara, 1986; cert. colloguy, Concordia Coll., 1996. Cert. cmty. coll. tchr., Calif., pub. tchr., Calif.; commd. minister Luth. Ch., Mo. Synod, 1996. Dir. music Hope Luth. Ch., Daly City, Calif., 1975-81; gen. mgr. Ostara Press, Inc., Daly City, Calif., 1975-78; condr. U. Calif., Santa Barbara, 1981-86; dir., condr. Santa Barbara oratorio Chorale, 1983-85; dir. music 1st Presbyn. Ch., Santa Barbara, 1983-84, Goleta (Calif.) Presbyn. Ch., 1984-85; minister music Trinity Luth. Ch., Ventura, 1985-92, Christ Luth. Ch. & Sch., Little Rock, Ark., 1992-98; dir. choral music Concordia U., Portland, Oreg., 1998—; instr. Ventura Coll., 1987-88; music dir., condr. Gold Coast Community Chorus, Ventura, 1988-92. Choir dir. Temple Beth Torah Jewish Community, Ventura, 1982-87; adj. prof. Pepperdine U., Malibu, Calif., 1988; chorus master Ventura Symphony Orch., 1987. Condr. oratorios Christus Am Oelberg, 1983, Elijah, 1984, Hymn of Praise, 1988, cantata Seven Last Words, 1979, 84, Paukenmesse, 1989, Mozart's Requiem, 1990, Requiem-Fauré, 1991, 2002, Judas Maccabaeus-Handel, 1992; soloist 15 major oratorio and opera roles, 1971-92, Nat. Anthem, L.A. Dodgers, 1989; dir. (with John Rutter) Gold Coast Community Chorus, Carnegie Hall, N.Y.C., 1991, Tribute to America, Lincoln Ctr. Concert, N.Y.C., 1991. Min. music, tchr. Christ Luth. Ch. and Sch., Little Rock, 1992—. First place winner baritone vocalist Idaho Fedn. Music Clubs, 1971, recital winner Utah Fedn. Music Clubs, 1974. Mem. Choral Condrs. Guild, Assn. Luth. Ch. Musicians, Am. Guild of English Handbell Ringers, Am. Choral Dirs. Assn., Music Educators Nat. Conf., Sigma Nu (sec., song leader 1973-75). Home and Office: 2811 NE Holman St Portland OR 97211-6067 E-mail: Kberentsen@cu-portland.edu.

BERENZWEIG, JACK CHARLES, lawyer; b. Bklyn., Sept. 29, 1942; s. Sidney A. and Anne R. (Dubowe) B.; m. Susan J. Berenzweig, Aug. 8, 1968; children: Mindy, Andrew. B.E.E., Cornell U., 1964; JD, Am. U., 1968. Bar: Va. 1968, Ill. 1969. Examiner U.S. Pat. Off., Washington, 1964-66; pat. adviser U.S. Naval Air Systems Command, Washington, 1966-68; ptnr. Brinks, Hofer, Gilson & Lione and predecessor firm, Chgo., 1968—. Editorial staff Am. U. Law Rev., 1966-68; contbr. articles to profl. jours. Mem. ABA, Chgo. Bar Assn., Ill. State Bar Assn., Bar Assn. 7th Fed. Cir., Va. State Bar, Internat. Trademark Assn. (bd. dirs. 1983-85), Brand Names Edn. Found. (bd. dirs. 1993-2000), Meadow Club (Rolling Meadows, Ill.), Miramar Club (Naples, Fla.), Delta Theta Phi. Home: 127 W Oak St Apt A Chicago IL 60610-5422 Office: Brinks Hofer Gilson & Lione Ltd Ste 3600 455 N Cityfront Plaza Dr Chicago IL 60611-5599 E-mail: jcb@brinkshofer.com.

BERES, MARY ELIZABETH, management educator, organizational consultant; b. Birmingham, Ala., Jan. 19, 1942; d. John Charles and Ethel (Belenyesi) Beres. BS, Siena Heights Coll., Adrian, Mich., 1969; PhD, Northwestern U., 1976. Joined Dominican Sisters, 1960. Tchr. St. Francis Xavier Sch., Medina, Ohio, 1962-64, St. Edward Sch., Medina, Ohio, 1964-67. Our Lady of Mt. Carmel Sch., Temperance, Mich., 1967-69, asst. prin., 1968-69; tchr. math. St. Ambrose H.S., Detroit, 1969-70; vis. instr. Cornell U., 1973-74; assoc. prof. orgn. behavior Temple U., Phila., 1974-84; assoc. prof. mgmt. Mercer U., Atlanta, 1984-91; founder, sr. assoc. Leadership Sys., Atlanta, 1988—. Mem. World Pilgrims, 2002—; bd. dirs. Aquinas Ctr. Theology, 2001—. Contbr. chpts. to books; organizer of symposia in areas of corp. leadership, orgn. change and cross-cultural comm. Bd. dir. Ctr. for Ethics and Social Policy, Phila., 1980—84, Assn. Global Bus., 1989—91; mem. program planning com. of interdepartmental group in bus. adminstrn. U. Ctr. in Ga., 1987—91, chair, 1988—90; trustee Adrian Dominican Ind. Sch. Sys., Adrian, Mich., 1971—79; pres. bd. dirs. New Ventures Network, 1998—2001; mem. Atlanta Clergy and Laity Concerned, 1986—95; econ. pastoral imlementation com. Archdiocese of Atlanta, 1988—89, Atlanta Archdiocesan Planning and Devel. Coun., 1991—93; episcopal moderator women Religious Archdiocese of Atlanta, 1993—97, Atlanta Conf. Sisters, 1984—, pres., 1993—97, 2001—; vicar Religious Archdiocese of Atlanta, 2001—. Recipient Legion of Honor membership Chapel of the Four Chaplains, Phila., 1982, Disting. Tchg. award Lindback Found., 1982, Cert. for Humanity Mercer U, 1985. Mem. NAFE, Acad. of Mgmt., Dominican Sisters of Adrian, Mich. (strategic planning com. 2000-01). Democrat. Roman Catholic. Office: Leadership Sys PO Box 76475 Atlanta GA 30358-1475 E-mail: LeadSys@aol.com.

BERES, MICHAEL JOHN, plant engineer; b. Gary, Ind., June 26, 1950; s. Edward Kenneth and Joan Marie (Petrovich) B.; m. Susan Eileen Heminger, Oct. 26, 1973; children: Amanda Eileen, Matthew James. AAS, Purdue U., 1972, BS, 1973. Registered profl. engr., Ill. Estimator, field engr. J.M. Foster, Inc., Gary, 1973-74; civil engr. Brown & Root, Inc., Oakbrook, Ill., 1974-76; field piping engr. Dedelow, Inc., Gary, 1977; plant facilities engr. Reynolds Metals Co., McCook, Ill., 1977-88; constrn. mgr. midwest region Waste Mgmt. of N.Am., Inc., Westchester, Ill., 1988-91; project supt. Exec. Constrn., Inc., Downers Grove, Ill., 1992—; pres. Beres Engring., Downers Grove, 1993—; plant engr. Heinemann's Bakeries, Inc., 1994—. Team leader Dupage County Pub. Action to Deliver Shelter, Downers Grove, Ill., 1983-92. Recipient Cert. of Recognition Gov. James R. Thompson. Mem.: Waste Mgmt., Inc. Midwest Region Golf League (pres. 1989-90), Reynolds Golf League (McCook, pres. 1981-87). Roman Catholic. Avocation: golf. Home and Office: 4210 Highland Ave Downers Grove IL 60515-2133

BERES, MILAN, surgeon; b. Trebisov, Slovak Republic, Jan. 13, 1936; came to U.S., 1968, naturalized, 1974; s. Juraj and Barbara (Hrinova) B.; m. Terezia Marcinova, Nov. 17, 1962; children: Stephen, Milan Jr. Grad., Slovak U., 1955; MD, P.J. Safarik U., Slovak Republic, 1959. Otolaryngologist Univ. Hosp., Kosice, Slovak Republic, 1962-68; fellow in otolaryngology Cleve. Clin. Ednl. Found., 1970-71; resident physician in otolaryngology and facial plastic and reconstructive surgery U. Conn. Health Ctr., Farmington, 1971-74, sr. attending physician, 1974-00, chief otolaryngology sect., 1987-96, Bridgeport (Conn.) Hosp., 1987-96. Clin. asst. divsn. otolarynology Sch. of Medicine, U. Conn., Farmington, 1974—. Ontbr. articles to med. jours. Elected pres. Sloval Cultural Ctr., 1991-94. Served with Czechoslovakian Army, 1960-61. Recipient Presdl. medal in recognition of svcs. rendered to Slovakia Pres. of the Slovak Republic, 1998. Fellow ACS; mem. AMA (Physicians Recognition awards), Conn. Med. Assn., Fairfield County Med. Assn., Greater Bridgeport Med. Assn., Am. Acad. Otolaryngology, ACS, Internat. Corr. Soc. Ophthalmologists and Otolaryngologists, New England Otolaryn. Soc., Pan Am. Assn. Oto-rhino-laryngology Head and Neck Surgery, New Eng. States Slovak League Am. (v.p.). Roman Catholic. Home: 31 Isinglass Terr Trumbull CT 06611-4038 E-mail: milanbe@earthlink.net.

BERESFORD, ANNETTE DIANA, researcher; b. Bethesda, Md., Feb. 26, 1958; d. Spencer Moxon and Ann Lincoln Beresford; children: Conner Crossman, Mekha Schmidt. BS summa cum laude, U. So. Miss., 1991; M Pub. Policy and Adminstrn., Jackson State U., 1997; PhD in Pub. Adminstrn., Fla. Atlantic U., 2002. Analyst Hancock Bank, Gulfport, Miss., 1985-93; program mgr., planner Bd. Trustees of State Instns. of Higher Learning, Jackson, Miss., 1993—97; fin. specialist divsn. securities and investor protection Office of Contr., West Palm Beach, Fla., 1997—2002; vis. instr. Fla. Atlantic U., Jupiter, Fla., 2002—03; rsch. assoc. Nat. White Collar Crime Ctr., Morgantown, W.Va., 2003—. Bd. dirs. Mayan Towers, Palm Beach Shores. Contbr. articles to profl. jours. Named to Am. Acad. Disting. Students, Am. Ctr. for Grad. Edn., 1996-97; Breland scholar U. So. Miss., 1990-91; Newell doctoral fellow Fla. Atlantic U., 2000-2001. Mem. Am. Soc. for Pub. Adminstrn., Pub. Adminstrn. Theory Network, Phi Kappa Phi, Pi Alpha Alpha. Office: Nat White Collar Crime Ctr 12 Roush Dr Morgantown WV 26505

BERESFORD, DOUGLAS LINCOLN, lawyer; b. Washington, June 1, 1956; s. Spencer Moxon and Ann (Lincoln) B.; m. Lori Anne Mainous, Sept. 22, 1990; children: Alexander Gould, Erik Mainous. AB cum laude, Harvard U., 1978; JD, Georgetown U., 1982. Bar: D.C. 1982, U.S. Ct. Appeals (D.C. cir.) 1984, U.S. Supreme Ct. 1986. Assoc. Morgan, Lewis & Bockius, Washington, 1982-83, Newman & Holtzinger, P.C., Washington, 1983-89, ptnr., 1989-94, Long, Aldridge & Norman, Washington, 1994-2000, Hogan & Hartson LLP, Washington, 2000—. Office: Hogan & Hartson LLP 555 13th St NW Ste 700E Washington DC 20004-1161 E-mail: dlberesford@hhlaw.com.

BERESIN, MARTA ILENE, lawyer; b. Phila., July 27, 1965; d. Carl Morris and Constance (Goldman) Beresin; m. William Jacob Scher, July 9, 1995; 1 child, Razi Esther Beresin Scher. BA, Pa. State U., 1987; JD with honors, George Washington U., 1991. Bar: Md. 1991, D.C. 1998, U.S. Dist. Ct. Md. Law clk. Women's Legal Def. Fund, Washington, 1990, ACLU, Washington, 1990; assoc. Mitterhoff & Henrichsen, Washington, 1991-92; staff atty. Legal Aid Bur., Inc., Hughesville, Md., 1992-95, acting chief atty., 1995; staff atty. Homeless Persons Representation Project, Balt., 1995-97. Vol. HIV counselor Washington Free Clinic, 1992-97, bd. dirs., 1994, sec. bd. dirs., 1995; vol. shelter atty. Homeless Persons Representation Project, Bethesda, Md., 1999. Equal Justice Found. grantee, 1990. Mem. Law Assn. for Women (exec. bd. 1990-91). Democrat. Jewish. Avocations: yoga, running, photography. E-mail: berscher@erols.com.

BEREUTER, DOUGLAS KENT, congressman; b. York, Nebr., Oct. 6, 1939; s. Rupert Wesley and Evelyn Gladys (Tonn) B.; m. Louise Meyer, June 1, 1962; children: Eric David, Kirk Daniel. BA, U. Nebr., 1961; M in City Planning, Harvard U., 1966, MPA, 1973. Urban planner HUD, San Francisco, 1965-66; dir. div. state and urban affairs Nebr. Dept. Econ. Devel., 1967-68, state planning dir., 1968-70; coord. fed.-state relations Nebr. State Govt., 1967-70, urban planning cons., 1971-78; assoc. prof. U. Nebr., 1971—73, Kansas St. Univ., 1971—78; mem. Nebr. Legislature, 1974-78, U.S. Ho. Reps. from 1st Nebr. Dist., 1979—; mem. fin. svcs. com., vice chmn. internat. rels. com., mem. intelligence com., mem. transp. and infrastructure com. Mem. Nebr. State Crime Commn., 1969-71; chmn. standing com. on urban devel. Nat. Conf. State Legislatures, 1977-78; mem. Nat. Agrl. Export Commn., 1985-86. Served as officer U.S. Army, 1963-65. Mem. Am. Planning Assn., Phi Beta Kappa, Sigma Xi. Republican. Lutheran. Office: Ho of Reps 2184 Rayburn Ofc Bldg Washington DC 20515-2701*

BEREZIN, SERGEI, hockey player; b. Voskresenska, Russia, Nov. 5, 1971; Mem. Toronto Maple Leafs, 1994—. Mem. Russian Hockey Team, 1994. Named to All-Star Team, 1996; recipient Silver medal, World Jr. Championships, 1991. Office: Toronto Maple Leafs Air Canada Ctr 40 Bay St Ste 300 Toronto ON Canada M5J 2X2

BEREZIN, TANYA, acting coach, educator, actress; b. Phila., Mar. 25, 1941; d. Maurice and Bettye (Shifrin) Berezin; m. Robert Leeming Thirkield, June 29, 1969 (div. June 1977); children: Lila Joy, Jonathon Schuyler; m. Mark Beers Wilson, Oct. 18, 1987. Student, Boston U., 1959-63. Co-founder Circle Repertory Co., N.Y.C., 1969, artistic dir., 1986-94, pvt. coach, studio class, seminars, 1994—; resident acting coach All My Children, One Life to Live ABC, N.Y.C., 1994-99; resident acting coach Another World NBC, N.Y.C., 1997-98; resident acting coach As the World Turns CBS, N.Y.C., 1998-99. Actor: (TV shows) St. Elsewhere, 1984, Law and Order, 1992—94, 2000—02; (plays) Angels Fall, 1983, Moundbuilders, 1975 (Obie award), Sympathetic Magic, 1997; (films) Awakenings, 1993; prodr.: Prelude to a Kiss, Destiny of Me, Three Hotels, Baltimore Waltz. Avocation: gardening. E-mail: berezin@bellatlantic.net.

BEREZNEY, RONALD, molecular biologist; b. N.Y.C., Dec. 25, 1943; s. Michael and Marie Berezney; m. Linda A. Buchholtz, Nov. 27, 1982; children: John Paul, James Robert. BS magna cum laude, Fairleigh Dickinson U., 1966; PhD, Purdue U., 1971. NIH internat. fellow U. Freiburg, 1971—72; postdoctoral fellow Johns Hopkins Sch. Medicine, Balt., 1972—75; asst. prof. U. Buffalo, 1975—81, assoc. prof., 1981—85, full prof., 1986—, chmn. dept. biol. scis., 1996—99. Ad hoc reviewer, panel mem. NIH, 1979—; bd. mem. Jour. Cellular Biochemistry, 1994—; organizer various sci. meetings; spkr. in field. Author, editor: Nuclear Matrix, 1995; editor: Critical Reviews in Eukaryotic Gene Expression, 1999—2000; contbr. articles to profl. jours. Grantee, NIH, 1977—. Mem.: AAAS, Am. Soc. for Biochemistry and Molecular Biology, Am. Soc. for Cell Biology. Office: Dept Biol Scis Univ Buffalo Buffalo NY 14260

BERG, ALAN, lawyer, arbitrator; b. Scranton, Pa., June 5, 1947; s. Donald and Lucile (DeLugo) Berg; m. Rita A. Samin, June 15, 1975 (dec. Feb. 20, 2001); children: Thomas M., Matthew P., Andrew J. BA, Hartwick Coll., Oneonta, N.Y., 1969; JD, St. John's U., 1972; LLM in Labor Law, NYU, 1975. Bar: N.Y. 1973, U.S. Dist. Ct. (dists. N.Y.) 1973, U.S. Ct. Appeals 1973, U.S. Supreme Ct. 1976. Atty. N.Y. State Labor Rels. Bd., 1972—79, adminstrv. law judge, 1979—80, chief judge, 1980—84, gen. counsel, 1984—91, N.Y. State Employment Rels. Bd., 1991—2003, arbitrator, 2003—. Judge N.Y. Law Sch. Wagner Moot Ct.; advisor NYU Law Sch. student adv. program. Trustee Freeport Meml. Lib., NY, 1976—81; coach Freeport H.S. summer basketball team, 1973—; N.Y. all-star team N.Y.-Phila. basketball festival, 1985—86, 1988—97; arbitrator Better Bus. Bur. Recipient George Emma Meml. Sportsmanship award, 1986, Citizen award, Freeport Boosters Club, 1987. Mem.: Indsl. Rels. Rsch. Assn., N.Y. State Bar Assn., St. John's Law Sch. Alumni Assn. Home: 108 Delaware Ave Freeport NY 11520-1313

BERG, A(NDREW) SCOTT, author, biographer; b. Conn., 1949; Grad., Princeton U., 1971. Author: Lindbergh, 1999 (Pulitzer prize for biography 1999 Ernest Hemingway Found. award), Goldwyn: A Biography, Max Perkins: Editor of Genius (Nat. Book award), Kate Remembered, 2003; (films) Making Love, 1982; co-prodr., co-writer Goldwyn, 2001. Guggenheim fellow, 1996. Office: Janklow & Nesbit Assocs 445 Park Ave 13th Fl New York NY 10022*

BERG, BARBARA ANN COWAN, corporate workshops consultant, critical incident consultant; b. New Brunswick, N.J., Aug. 24, 1953; d. Milton Howard and Marie Ina (Mackay) Cowan; 1 child, Brittany Alise. BS, Rutgers U., 1975; MSW, Va. Commonwealth U., 1980; postgrad., West End Family Counseling Ctr, Ontario, Calif., 1988-92. With child care ctr. Zale Diamond Corp., Dallas, 1980-83; dir. Zale Corp., 1980-83; cons. mktg. child care related svcs. and workshops, 1985—; lectr. child care and group work at corps. Calif. State U. Extended Edn., Fullerton, 1986-88; pediatrics social worker Suspected Child Abuse and Neglect White Meml. Med. Ctr., L.A., 1986-87, team coord. on child abuse reporting, 1986-87; lectr., cons. for workshops; assoc. Haven Psychol. Assocs., Rancho Cucamonga, Calif., 1992—. Mental health sch. site counselor, clin. intern, 1988-91, clin. intern, 1989-92; educator Calif. State U., Fullerton; presenter in field. Author: What To Do When Life is Driving You Crazy!, 1997; contbr. articles to profl. jours. Calif. State grant co-mgr. Mem. NASW. Home: 6899 Charloma St Alta Loma CA 91701 Office: PMB 116 2058 N Mills Ave Claremont CA 91711-2812

BERG, BARBARA KIRSNER, health education specialist; b. Cin., Dec. 6, 1954; d. Robert and Mildred Dorothy (Warshofsky) Kirsner; m. Howard Keith Berg, Apr. 8, 1984; children: Arielle, Allison, Stacy. BA, Brandeis U., 1976; MEd, U. Cin., 1977. Cert. health edn. specialist Nat. Commn. for Health Edn. Credentialing, Inc., Mass. Health educator S.W. Ohio Lung Assn., Cin., 1977-79; coord. adminstrv. edn. N.E. Regional Med. Edn. Ctr., Northport, N.Y., 1979-81; patient health edn. coord. VA Med. Ctr., Buffalo, 1981-87; clin. asst. prof. SUNY, Buffalo, 1982-87; dir. comty. health edn. N.W. Hosp. Ctr., Balt., 1987-89; coord. law and health care program U. Md. Sch. Law, Balt., 1989-90; med. mgmt. cons. Dr. Howard K. Berg, Owings Mills, Md., 1990—. Cons. health edn. Edward Bartlett, Assoc., Rockville, Md., 1987-88; mem. adult edn. com. Chizuk Amuno Congregation, Balt., 1993-99, mem. bd. dirs., 1996-98, chair cultural arts com., 1996-98. Bd. dirs., mem. Am. Lung Assn. Western N.Y., Buffalo, 1983-86, Pumpkin Theater, Balt., 1990-91; chair domestic concerns com. Balt. Jewish Coun., 1994-96, chair govt. rels. com., 1996-98, sec., bd. dirs., 1996-98, 2d v.p. 1998-2000; sec. women's dept. Associated Jewish Charities, Balt., 1994-97; mem. sch. bd. nominating conv. Baltimore County, 1995—; pres. Pikesville Mid. Sch. PTA, 1998-2001. Mem. APHA, Soc. for Pub. Health Edn., Am. Jewish Com., Balt. Brandeis Alumni Assn. (pres.), Phi Delta Kappa. Jewish. Avocations: reading, travel, advocacy. Home and Office: 12116 Heneson Garth Owings Mills MD 21117-1629

BERG, BRUCE JEFFREY, psychiatrist; b. Wilmington, Del., Oct. 13, 1956; s. Howard Michael and Sandra Joy (Fine) B.; m. Fanny Jove, Mar. 27, 1982; children: David Edward, Erica Susan. BA, Emory U., 1978, MD, 1983. Diplomate Am. Bd. Psychiatry and Neurology, Nat. Bd. Med. Examiners. Intern in psychiatry U. Ill., Chgo., 1983-84; resident in psychiatry Michael Reese Hosp., Chgo., 1984-87; clin. asst. prof. psychiatry U. Pa. Sch. Medicine, 1991—; med. dir. treatment rsch. unit U. Pa., Phila., 1990-91; med. dir. Career Intensive Outpatient Program, 1987-90; unit dir. acute care and intermediate care units Albert Einstein Med. Ctr., 1990; assoc. unit dir. Substance Abuse Treatment Unit Phila. VA Med. Ctr., 1991-92; medical dir. N.J. Div. The Counseling Program Penn. Hosp., 1992-93; dir. substance abuse svcs. 8th St. divsn. Pa. Hosp., 1993-97; v.p. med. svcs. Magellan Behavioral Health, 1998—2001; chief addiction psychiatry, active med. staff dept. psychiatry Crozer-Chester Med. Ctr. and Cmty. Hosp., 2002—. Attending psychiatrist Phila. Psychiat. Ctr., Belmont Ctr., 1987-98; active med. staff Hosp. The U. Pa., assoc. psychiatrist The Inst. Pa. Hosp., profl. staff Pa. Hosp., 1992-98; psychiat. cons. Sexual Dysfunction Clinic, Loyala U. Med. Ctr., Maywood, Ill., 1986, Dwight (Ill.) Correction Ctr., 1986-87, Lower Merion Sch. Dist., 1988-90; cons. in self-psychology, 1990—; physician advisor Green Spring Health Svcs., Inc., 1994-97, Magellan Behavioral Health, 1997—; physician cons./cons. med. dir. Human Affairs Internat., Inc., 1997-98; attending psychiatrist addiction recovery unit U. Pa./Phila. VA Ctr. for the Study of Addiction, 1990-97; psychiat. cons. Northeast Treatment Ctr., 1995-97. Clin. fellow in forensic psychiatry U. Pa., 1987-88. Mem. Am. Psychiat. Assn., Psychiat. Physicians Pa., Phila. Psychiat. Soc., AMA, Pa. Med. Soc., Am. Acad. Psychiatry and the Law, Am. Acad. Addiction Psychiatry, Am. Soc. for Adolescent Psychiatry. Jewish. Avocations: photography, skiing, golf, tennis, traveling. E-mail: bjbergmd@aol.com.

BERG, BRUCE O. child neurologist, educator; b. St. Paul, Jan. 2, 1931; s. Oscar A. and Olga Marie (Palmquist) B.; m. Linda E. Berg, Nov. 23, 1962; children: Katherine E., Sarah M. BA, BS, U. Minn., 1951, MD, 1955. Intern Fitzsimons Gen. Hosp., Denver, 1955-56; resident in pediatrics Letterman Gen. Hosp., San Francisco, 1957-59; chief pediatrics USA Hosp., Nurnberg, Germany, 1959-62; registrar neurology and child neurology Nat. Hosp. for Nervous Diseases/Queen Square, London, 1962-64; resident in neurology, fellow in child neurology U. Calif. Med. Ctr., San Francisco, 1964-66, prof. neurology and pediat., dir. child neurology, 1968—. Cons. Letterman Hosp., Oak Knoll Hosp., Oakland, Calif., 1968-92, Calif. Children's Svcs., 1968—, Shriners Hosp., San Francisco, 1968-72. Author: Child Neuro-Clinical Manual, 1984, 2d edit., 1994, Neuro Aspects of Pediatrics, 1992, Principles of Child Neurology, 1996. Col. U.S. Army. Recipient Ogden Bruton award, J. Elliot Royer award, Hower award. Democrat. Episcopalian. Avocations: reading, photography, electronics. Office: U Calif Med Ctr Depts Neurology And Pediatri San Francisco CA 94143-0001 E-mail: bobcns@itsa.ucsf.edu.

BERG, CHARLES G. insurance company executive; BA in Polit. Sci., Macalester Coll., St. Paul; degree in Law, Georgetown U. Founder, CEO Health Ptnrs., Inc.; exec. v.p. med. delivery Oxford Health Plans, Inc., 1998—2000, v.p. claims and info. sys., 2000—01, pres., COO, 2001—02, pres., CEO, 2002—. Office: Oxford Health Plans Inc 48 Monroe Turnpike Trumbull CT 06611*

BERG, DANIEL, science and technology educator; b. N.Y.C., June 1, 1929; s. Jack and Hattie (Tannenbaum) B.; m. Frances Helena Ely, Aug. 18, 1956; children: Brian, Laura, Meredith. BS, CCNY, 1950; MS, Yale U., 1951, PhD, 1953; grad. execs. program, Carnegie-Mellon U., 1972. With Westinghouse Electric Corp., Pitts., 1953-77, research div. mgr., then tech. dir., 1976-77; prof. sci. and tech. Carnegie-Mellon U., 1977-83, dean Mellon Coll. Sci., 1977-81, univ. provost, 1981-83; v.p. acad. affairs, provost, Inst. prof. sci. and tech. Rensselaer Poly. Inst., Troy, N.Y., 1983-85, pres., 1985-87, Inst. prof., 1987—. Bd. dirs. Hy-Tech. Machine Co., Inc.; chmn. bd. Crystek Inc.; mem. Pa. Sci. and Engring. Found., 1975-76; mem. vis. coun. sci. and engring. CCNY, 1980-84; mem. vis. coun. Sch. Computer Sci., Carnegie-Mellon U., 1992—; mem. Yale U. Coun., 1981-85; assoc. fellow Jonathan Edwards Coll., 1982—; cons. to industry and govt. Author, editor, patentee in field. Fellow IEEE, AAAS, INFORMS, Am. Inst. Chemists, N.Y. Acad. Scis.; mem. Nat. Acad. Engring. (coun. 1985-88), Am. Chem. Soc., Am. Phys. Soc., Cosmos Club of Washington, Rivers Club of Pitts., Century Club N.Y.C., Phi Beta Kappa, Sigma Xi, Alpha Chi Sigma, Tau Beta Pi. Home: 12 The Crossways Troy NY 12180-7263 Office: Rensselaer Poly Inst 5015 CII Troy NY 12180-3522

BERG, DAVID HOWARD, lawyer; b. Springfield, Ohio, Mar. 4, 1942; s. Nathan Stewart Berg and Mildred (Besser) Berg-Filion; children: Geoffrey Alan, Gabriel Adam, Caitlin Hannah; m. Kathryn Page, July 10, 1994. Student, Tulane U., 1963; BA in English, U. Houston, 1964, JD, 1967. Bar: Tex. 1967, U.S. Dist. Ct. Tex. 1967, N.Y. 1989, U.S. Dist. Ct. (so. dist.) N.Y. 1990, U.S. Ct. Appeals (2d, 4th, 5th, 8th and 11th cirs.) 1990, U.S. Supreme Ct. 1990. Law clk. NLRB, Washington, 1967-68; ptnr. David Berg & Assocs., Houston, 1968-77, Berg & Androphy, 1977—. Mem. fed. ct. lawyers adv. com. U.S. Dist. Ct. (so. dist.) Tex.; mem. U. Houston Law Found., 1996—; spl. counsel commn. on lawyer discipline, Tex. State Bar, 1996—. Contbr. articles and essays to mags. Adviser Jimmy Carter Transition Govt., Washington, 1976; adviser Mayor Kathy Whitmire campaigns, 1980-91; patron Friends of Menil Collection, 1990-91; adviser campaign Mayor Bob Lanier, 1991; chmn. City of Houston's "Imagine Houston"; mem. adv. bd. Camp for All; bd. dirs. U. Houston Law Ctr, Law Found., 1996, Houston Shakespeare Festival, 1997, Anti-Defamation League, 2002, Houston Holocaust Mus.; chmn. bd. Houston Area Water Corp., 2001--. Recipient 1st pl. for best feature article in a scholarly jour. Nat. Assn. Publ., 1991. Fellow Internat. Acad. Trial Lawyers, Houston Bar Found.; mem. ATLA, Tex. Bar Assn. (chmn. grievance com. 1984-85), Tex. Bar Found., N.Y. State Bar Assn., Tex. Trial Lawyers Assn., Houston Trial Lawyers Assn., U. Houston Law Alumni Assn. (bd. dirs. 1992-95), Am. Bd. Trial Advocates (assoc.). Democrat. Jewish. Avocations: writing, running, fishing. Home: 16 Sunset Blvd Houston TX 77005-1838 Office: Berg & Androphy 3704 Travis St Houston TX 77002-9550

BERG, DORIS VERON (DORIS VERON MCKINSTRY), musician, educator; b. Vista, Calif., Apr. 21, 1932; d. Verne Watson and Doris Mary (Hedge) McKinstry; m. Jon Daniel Berg, June 29, 1956; children: Erik Vern, Karin Diane. MusB, U. So. Calif., 1955, MusM, 1968. Cert. secondary tchr. Calif. Music tchr. various elem. schs., Calif., 1957-59, Millican Jr. HS, Calif., 1959-61; freelance musician various orgns., L.A., 1964—89; music instr. Immaculate Heart Coll., Hollywood, Calif., 1962-67, El Camino Coll., Torrance, Calif., 1967-71, L.A. Coll., 1972-82, Santa Monica (Calif.) Coll., 1972-84; harpsichord instr. Loyola Marymount U., Westchester, Calif., 1972-82; freelance music tchr., musician L.A., Pacific Palisades, 1972-89; freelance music tchr., 1990—96; freelance musician, 1990—. Musician: Harpsichordist Monday Evening Concerts, 1968, Mammoth Festival, 1974, others. Scholar, U. So. Calif., 1953—55. Mem.: Calif. Music Tchrs. Assn. (bd. dirs., sec.), Am. Fedn. Musicians, Mu Phi Epsilon. Democrat. Home: 1394 E Manor Way Freeland WA 98249-9625

BERG, G. VIVIAN, artist; b. Worcester, Mass., Feb. 28, 1932; d. Emil Mauritz Mattson and Gunhild Maria Israelson; m. Kenneth George Berg, May 10, 1957; children: Donna Maria, Leah Christine. Tng. cert., Ward Sch. Airline Tng., Worcester, 1951; diploma, Worcester Sch. Bus., 1951. Sec. Ea. Airlines, N.Y.C., 1951-52; legal sec. Office of Russell W. Anderson, Worcester, 1953-61; tchr. art Worcester, 1976-2000. One woman shows include Ogunquit (Maine) Art Ctr., Shore Road Gallery, Boston, Harrison Conf. Ctr., Marlboro, Mass; group shows include Cultural Assembly Portrait Show, UN Conf. Women in Nairobi, 1985; represented in permanent collecions including Milford (Mass.) Fed. Bank, Milford Savs. Bank, 1st Svc. Bank, Pepperell, Mass., Merrimac Valley Credit Union, North Andover, Mass., Spencer Savs. Bank, Medway (Mass.) Nat. Bank, Unibank for Savs., Hoosac Savs. Bank North Adams, Mass., Medway Co-Operative Bank, Methuen (Mass.) Co-Operative Bank, Am. Eagle Credit Union, Manchester, Conn., TruNorth Fin., North Adams, N.E. Cmty. Credit Union, Haverhill, Mass., Haverhill Co-Op Bank, New Eng. Design Assocs., Worcester, Oxford (Mass.) Free Pub. Libr. Mem. Am. Soc. Marine Artists, Am. Mensa Ltd., Nat. Mus. Women in the Arts. Episcopalian. Studio: 8 Inwood Rd Auburn MA 01501-1115

BERG, GALE DIANE, lawyer; b. Bklyn., June 24, 1951; d. Sidney and Evelyn (Schulman) B.; m. Joel Hochdorf, Feb. 8, 1981; children: Jillian, Rachel. BA, Am. U., 1972; JD, Vt. Law Sch., 1976. Bar: N.Y. 1977, D.C. 1978, U.S. Dist. Ct. (so. and ea. dists.) N.Y. 1978, U.S. Ct. Appeals (2d cir.) 1978. Asst. atty. gen. N.Y. State Dept. Law, N.Y.C., 1977-80; assoc. Fischbein, Olivieri, Rozenholc & Badillo, N.Y.C., 1980; pvt. practice, N.Y.C., 1981-84; asst. counsel N.Y. State Racing and Wagering Bd., N.Y.C., 1984—; asst. adj. prof. bus. contract law Baruch Coll., 1982, asst. adj. prof. domestic relations, 1983; arbitrator N.Y.C. Civil Ct., 1983-84. Vol. Friends of Mario Cuomo, N.Y.C., 1984. Mem. ABA (chmn. subcom. on atty.'s fees of com. sole practitioners and small firms 1981-84, N.Y. State Bar Assn., N.Y. State Women's Bar Assn. (chmn. membership 1981-82). Office: NY State Racing and Wagering Bd 400 Broome St New York NY 10013-3238

BERG, IVAR ELIS, JR., social science educator; b. Bklyn., Jan. 3, 1929; s. Ivar Elis and Hjordis (Holmgren) B.; m. Calli J. Smallwood, Feb. 16, 1991; 1 child, Geoffrey Sverre; stepchildren: James and Timothy Smallwood. AB, Colgate U., 1954; postgrad., U. Oslo, Norway, 1954-55; PhD, Harvard U., 1959; MA (hon.), U. Pa., 1979. Asst. prof. to prof. sociology Columbia U., N.Y.C., 1959-75, dean faculties, 1969-71; prof. sociology Vanderbilt U., Nashville, 1975-79, Justin Potter prof. bus., 1983-84; prof. and chmn. dept. sociology U. Pa., Phila., 1979-83, prof. sociology/dean of coll., 1984-89, dean social sci., 1989-91; prof. sociology, 1979—. Cons. Chancellor of Higher Edn., Trenton, N.J., 1982-89, Pres.'s Commn. on crime, Washington, 1966-67; chmn. coll. svcs. Coll. Bd., N.Y.C., 1989-91; chmn. com. on coll. edn. Coll. Entrance Exam. Bd., 1985-89. Author: Great Training Robbery, 1970, 2d edit., 2002, Managers and Work Reform, 1978, Work and Industry, 1987; co-editor, co-author: Sourcebook on Labor Markets, 2001, co-author: Education and Jobs: The Great Training Robbery, 1970, rev. edit., 2003; contbr. articles to profl. jours. and encys. Conciliator Ad Hoc Com. on Pub. Edn., Hastings-on-Hudson, N.Y., 1967-69. Maj. USMC, 1946-65; ATO. Guggenheim fellow, 1973-74, Rockefeller fellow, 1975-76, Woodrow Wilson fellow, 1954-55, Chester Hastings Arnold fellow Harvard U., 1959 Fellow AAAS, N.Y. Acad. Sci., Internat. Acad. Mgmt.; mem. Am. Sociol. Assn. (coun. 1989-91), Ea. Sociol. Soc. (v.p. 1989-90), Harvard Club (N.Y.C.), Pres.'s Club of Colgate U., Phi Beta Kappa. Presbyterian. Avocations: tennis, stamp collecting. Home: RR 1 Box 176 Harveys Lake PA 18618-9738 Office: U Pa Dept Sociology 113 McNeil Philadelphia PA 19104 E-mail: ivberg@sas.upenn.edu.

BERG, JEFFREY SPENCER, talent agency executive; b. L.A., May 26, 1947; BA in English with honors, U. Calif., Berkeley, 1969. Vice pres., head lit. div. Creative Mgmt. Assocs., Los Angeles, 1969-75; v.p. motion picture dept. Internat. Creative Mgmt., Los Angeles, 1975-80, pres., 1980-85, chmn., chief exec. officer, 1985—. Dir. Josephson Internat., Inc., Marshall McLuhan Ctr. of Global Communication. Trustee U. Berkeley Found.; bd. govs. Music Ctr. L.A. County; pres. letters and sci. exec. bd. U. Calif. Berkeley; co-chmn. Calif. Info. Tech. Coun.; bd. vis. Anderson Grad. Sch. of Mgmt., UCLA. Mem. U. Calif. Berkeley Alumni Assn. Office: Internat Creative Mgmt 8942 Wilshire Blvd Beverly Hills CA 90211-1934

BERG, JOHN CONRAD, political science educator; b. Louisville, Nov. 19, 1943; s. William G. and Mary E. (DeBardeleben) B.; m. Emily S. Perkins, Nov. 29, 1969; children: Andrew C., Thomas W., Katherine M. BA in English, U. Wis., 1964; PhD in Polit. Sci., Harvard U., 1975. Instr. govt. Suffolk U., Boston, 1974-75, asst. prof. govt., 1975-80, assoc. prof. govt., 1980-85, prof. govt., 1985—. Mem. liaison adv. bd. The Washington Ctr., 1988-95; chair spl. projects com. Boston-Cambridge Ministry in Higher Edn., 1988-92; acting chair dept. govt. Suffolk U., 1989; book rev. editor New Polit. Sci., 1994—2003; vis. fellow Australian Nat. U., 1994, Oxford U., 2003. Author: Unequal Struggle: Class, Gender, Race, and Power in the U.S. Congress, 1994; editor: Teamsters and Turtles? Progressive U.S. Political Movements in the 21st Century, 2003; contbr. articles to profl. jours. Grantee Everett McKinley Dirksen Congl. Leadership Rsch. ctr., 1988-89. Mem. AAUP, New Eng. Polit. Sci. Assn. (John Donovan award), Northeastern Polit. Sci. Assn. (program chair 2003), N.Y. State Polit. Sci. Assn. (award 1989), Am. Polit. Sci. Assn. (chair, sect. internships and experiential edn., 1993-95), Am. Soc. Pub. Adminstrn., Nat. Soc. Internships and Experiential Edn. (chair New Eng. regional conf. planning com. 1986, mem., chair faculty spl. interest group 1985-88), Caucus for a New Polit. Sci. (treas., newsletter editor, chair), Internat. Polit. Sci. Assn. (chair rsch. com. Socialism, Capitalism and Democracy 1994—). Home: 93 Lyndhurst St Dorchester MA 02124-2213

BERG, JONATHAN ALBERT, investment company executive; b. San Francisco, Nov. 13, 1943; s. Daniel and Noyon (Blanchard) B.; m. Susan Ann Reiner, May 14, 1988; 1 child, Jackson Augustus. BS, U. Calif., Berkeley, 1965; MBA, U. Pa., 1970. Portfolio mgr. Standard & Poor's Counseling Corp., N.Y.C., 1970-71; v.p., portfolio mgr. Oppenheimer Capital Corp., N.Y.C., 1971-83; pres., founder Berg Capital Corp., N.Y.C., 1983—; founder, pres. Precision Trading, Inc., N.Y.C., 1992—, Jackson Strategic, Inc., 1995—. Founder, pres. Jackson Strategic, Inc. Bd. dirs. Phoenix Theatre, N.Y.C., 1976-83. 1st lt. U.S. Army, 1966-68, Vietnam. Mem. Calif. Soc. Pioneers, Calif. Tennis Club, Delta Kappa Epsilon Club. Avocations: fly fishing, skiing. Home: 222 W 23rd St New York NY 10011-2301 Office: Berg Capital Corp 10 E 23rd St New York NY 10010-7108

BERG, KARL, real estate company executive; Gen. ptnr. Berg & Berg Developers, 1979—; chmn., CEO Mission West Properties, Inc., Cupertino, Calif., 1997—. Bd. dirs. Focus Enhancements, Inc., Valence Tech., Inc., Sys. Integrated Rsch., Ltd. Office: Mission West Properties 10050 Bandley Dr Cupertino CA 95014-2188

BERG, KATHY RAE, public relations consultant; b. Cleve., June 20, 1948; d. Austin Alexander and Dorothy Winifred Johnston; m. Thomas Clair Berg; 1 child, Thomas Clair Berg, Jr. BA in Journalism, Baylor U., 1970. Acct. exec. The View (newspaper), Rancho Palos Verdes, Calif., 1979-80; asst. mktg. dir. Peninsula Shopping Ctr., Rolling Hills Estates, Calif., 1980-82; pres., pub. rels. cons. Kathy Berg Pub. Rels., Rancho Palos Verdes, Calif., 1983—. Host TV talk show Cox Comms., Rolling Hills Estates, 1997-2000; mktg. dir. Peninsula Shopping Ctr., Rolling Hills Estates, 1999-2002. Adv. bd. Flossie Lewis Ctr., Long Beach, Calif., 1998—, Palos Verdes Peninsula, C. of C., 1993-99, pres. coord. coun., 1999-2001, bd. dirs., v.p. programs, 2001-03; bd. worship Neighborhood Ch. Recipient Outstanding Woman for 2001, City of Rancho Palos Verdes, State Senator Betty Karnette. Mem. AAUW (bd. dirs., v.p. programs 1989-90), Palos Verdes Peninsula C. of C. (Grand prize bus. winner 2000), Baylor Alumni Assn. Republican. Mem. Church Of Christ. Avocations: ballroom dancing, travel, reading. Home and Office: 26621 Hawkhurst Dr Palos Verdes Peninsula CA 90275-2443

BERG, LEONARD, retired neurologist, educator, researcher; b. St. Louis, July 17, 1927; s. Jacob and Sara (Kessler) B.; m. Gerry Saltzman, Mar. 25, 1948; children: Kathleen, John, Nancy. AB cum laude, Washington U., St. Louis, 1945, MD cum laude, 1949. Diplomate: Am. Bd. Psychiatry and Neurology (dir. 1978-85, pres. 1985). Intern Barnes Hosp., St. Louis, 1949-50, resident, 1950-51, Neurol. Inst., N.Y.C., 1951-53; clin. assoc. Nat. Inst. Neurol. Diseases and Blindness, NIH, 1953-55; mem. faculty Washington U. Med. Sch., 1955—98, prof. clin. neurology, 1972-89, prof. neurology, 1989-98, prof. emeritus neurology, 1998—; ret., 1998. Attending neurologist Barnes Hosp., Jewish Hosp., St. Louis; dir. Alzheimer's Disease Rsch. Ctr., Washington U., 1985-97; expert U.S. FDA, 1992-96; mem. U.S. Congress Adv. Panel on Alzheimer's Disease, 1993-96, Leonard Berg Annual Symposiums Nat. Spkrs. Co-author: Atlas of Muscle Pathology in Neuromuscular Diseases, 1956. Bd. dirs. Temple Israel, St. Louis, 1972-74, Jewish Center for Aged, 1981-98, hon. dir., 1999—. With USPHS, 1953-55. Recipient Lifetime Disting. Rsch. on Alzheimer's Disease and Related Disorders award, 7th World Alzheimer's Congress, 2000, Robert E. Schlueter Leadership award, St. Louis Met. Med. Soc., 2001, 2d Century award, Washington U. Mem. AMA, Am. Acad. Neurology, Am. Neurol. Assn. (1st v.p. 1988-89), Soc. for Neurosci., Alzheimer's Assn. (Chgo.) (bd. dirs. 1989-95, 96-98, chair med. and sci. adv. bd. 1991-95), Phi Beta Kappa, Sigma Xi, Alpha Omega Alpha. Home: 816 S Hanley Rd Apt 7D Saint Louis MO 63105-2678 Office: Washington U Alzheimer's Disease Rsch Ctr 4488 Forest Park Ave Ste 130 Saint Louis MO 63108-2212

BERG, LORINE MCCOMIS, retired guidance counselor; b. Ashland, Ky., Mar. 28, 1919; d. Oliver Botner and Emma Elizabeth (Eastham) McComis; m. Leslie Thomas Berg, Apr. 27, 1946; children: James Michael, Leslie Jane. BA in Edn., U. Ky., 1965; MA, Xavier U., 1969. Tchr. A.D. Owens Elem. Sch., Newport, Ky., 1963-64, 6th dist. Elementary Schs., Covington, Ky., 1965-69; guidance counselor Twenhofel Jr. H.S., Independence, Ky., 1969-78, Scott H.S., Taylor Mill, Ky., 1978-84. Bd. dirs. Mental Health Assn., Covington, Ky, 1970-76, v.p., 1973 (valuable svc. award 1973); mem. Lakeside Christian Ch., Ft. Mitchell, Ky. Named to Honorable Order of Ky. Colonels, Hon. Admissions Counselor U.S. Naval Acad.; cited by USN Recruiting Command for Valuable Assistance to USN, 1981. Mem. Am. Assn. of Univ. Women, Covington Art Club, Retired Tchrs. Assn., Kappa Delta Pi, Delta Kappa Gamma, Phi Delta Kappa. Democrat. Avocations: oil painting, dancing, reading, arts and crafts. Home: 11 Idaho Ave Covington KY 41017-2925

BERG, LOUIS LESLIE, investment executive; b. Vienna, Austria, Dec. 27, 1919; s. Gustav and Hedwig (Kohn) B.; came to U.S., 1938, naturalized, 1943; student U. Vienna, 1937-38, Coll. City N.Y., 1941-43; m. Minnette Whitman, Aug. 28, 1959; children: Sharon, Randee, Michel. Pres., Gt. Empire Corp., N.Y.C., 1946—, Bendalou Real Estate Corp., N.Y.C., 1950-60, Netherlands Securities Co., Inc., N.Y.C., 1959-62, Imported Automotive Parts, Ltd., L.I. City, N.Y.; chmn., bd. dirs. IAP Inc., Avenel, N.J., IAP West Inc., Los Angeles; bd. dirs., exec. com. Auto Internat. Assn.; advisor U.S. Congl. Adv. Bd. dir. Internat. Aviation Corp., Cosmos Industries, Kane-Miller Corp., Knickerbocker Toy Co., Inc., Vernitron Corp., Jet Aero Corp., Fidelity Am. Finance Corp., S.W. Fla. Enterprises, Sulray Inc., U.S. Airlines, Commuter Airlines, Aviation Equipment. Mem. Am. Mgmt. Assn. Club: Wings. Office: IAP Inc 26 Engelhard Ave Avenel NJ 07001-2217 also: IAP West Inc 2939 Bandini Blvd Los Angeles CA 90023-4508

BERG, SISTER MARIE MAJELLA, president emerita; b. Bklyn., July 7, 1916; d. Gustav Peter and Mary Josephine (McAuliff) B. BA, Marymount Coll., 1938; MA, Fordham U., 1948; DHL (hon.), Georgetown U., 1970, Marymount Manhattan Coll., 1983. Registrar Marymount Sch., N.Y.C., 1943-48; prof. classics, registrar Marymount Coll., N.Y.C., 1948—57; registrar Marymount Coll. of Va., Arlington, 1957-58, Marymount Coll., Tarrytown, N.Y., 1958-60; pres. Marymount U., Arlington, Va., 1960-93, chancellor, 1993—2001, pres. emerita, 2001—. Pres. Consortium for Continuing Higher Edn. in Va., 1987-88; mem. com. Consortium of Univs. in Washington Met. Area, 1987-93, chmn., 1992-93. Contbr. five biographies to One Hundred Great Thinkers, 1965; editor Otherwords column of N.Va. Sun newspaper, Arlington, College to University: A Memoir, 1999. Bd. dirs. Internat. Hospice, 1984-96, Ballston Partnership, 1992—, Hope, SOAR, 10th Dist. Congl. Award Coun., No. Va.; vice chmn. bd. Va. Found. Ind. Colls., 1992-93; cmty. advisor Jr. League No. Va., 1992—; mem. Friends of TACT, 1994—. Recipient commendation Va. Gen. Assembly, Richmond, 1990, 93, Elizabeth Ann Seton award, 1991, Arlington Notable Women award Arlington Commn. on Status of Women, 1992, Voice and Vision award Arlington Cmty. TV Channel 33, 1993, Pro Ecclesia et Pontifice medal Holy See, 1993; elected to Va. Women's Hall of Fame, 1992; named Washingtonian of Yr., Washingtonian mag., 1990, Arlington Cmty. Hero award, 1999; named to Washington Bus. Hall of Fame, Washingtonian mag. 1998, Jr. Achievement, 1998. Roman Catholic. Avocations: sewing, crocheting, reading. Home and Office: Marymount U Pres Emerita 2807 N Glebe Rd Arlington VA 22207-4224

BERG, MARY JAYLENE, pharmacy educator, researcher; b. Fargo, N.D., Nov. 7, 1950; d. Ordean Kenneth and Anna Margaret (Skramstad) B. BS in Pharmacy, N.D. State U., 1974; PharmD, U. Ky., 1978. Lic. pharmacist, N.D., Ky., Iowa. Fellow in pharmacokinetics Millard Fillmore Hosp./SUNY, Buffalo,

1978-79; asst. prof. U. Iowa, Iowa City, 1980-85, assoc. prof., 1985-95, prof., 1995—; with dept. clin. rsch., clin. pharmacology/pharmacokinetics F. Hoffmann-La Roche, Ltd., Basel, Switzerland, 1992; with Office of Rsch. on Women's Health NIH, 1999. Bd. dirs. Soc. for Women's Health Rsch., 1998—; mem. adv. com. rsch. on women's health NIH, 1995-99, mem. task force rsch. on women's health NIH, 1997-99; mem. adv. bd. Pfizer Women's Health, 1998—; mem. adv. com. on pharm. scis. FDA, 1999-2002. Reviewer Cin. Pharmacy, 1984—, Epilepsia, 1987—, Annals of Pharmacotherapy, 1997—; editor: (med. symposia) Internat. Leadership Symposium, The Role of Women in Pharmacy, 1990, Women-A Force in Pharmacy Symposium, 1992, Gender Related Health Issues: An International Perspective, 1996, Global Visions of Women Pharmacists, 1998; assoc. editor: XX vs XY: The Internat. Jour. of Sex Differences in the Study of Health Disease and Aging, 2003—, mem. editl. adv. bd.: The Internat. Jour. of Applied and Basic Nutritional Scis., 1998, Jour. Gender Specific Medicine, 1998—2001; mem. editl. bd. Jour. Women's Health, 2003—; contbr. articles to numerous med., pharmacy and nutrition jours. Advisor Kappa Epislon, Iowa City, 1980-94; pres. Mortar Bd. Alumnae, Iowa City, 1986-88. NIH grantee, 1984, Nat. Insts. on Drug Abuse grantee, 1986; recipient Career Achievement award Kappa Epsilon, 1985, Vanguard award Kappa Epsilon Merck, 1999, Master award N.D. State U., 2000; named to Iowa Women's Hall of Fame, 1999. Mem.: Leadership Internat-Women for Pharmacy (bd. dirs. 1991—), Fedn. Internat. Pharmaceutique (del. World Health Assembly 1992, pres. acad. sect. 2000—02), Internat. Forum of Women for Pharmacy (U.S. contact) (U.S. contact 1988—), Am. Pharm. Assn., Am. Epilepsy Soc., Am. Soc. Hosp. Pharmacists (chair spl. interest group clin. pharmokinetics 1987—89), Am. Assn. Pharm. Scientists, Phi Beta Delta, Kappa Epsilon, Rho Chi, Sigma Xi. Lutheran. Achievements include research in multiple doses of oral activated charcoal to clear totally absorbed drug, pharmacokinetics of drug-nutrient interaction between phenytoin and folic acid, also on both national and international levels, pharmacological differences between men and women (gender analysis of medications) and among ethnic groups for prescription medicines, over-the-counter medications and alternative natural drugs, research on the interrelations among folic acid, vitamin B6, vitamin B12 and zinc in diet and vitamin supplementation in pregnant and non-pregnant women with and without epilepsy; initiating graduate program in clinical pharmaceutical sciences at the U. Iowa College of Pharmacy. Office: U Iowa Coll of Pharmacy Iowa City IA 52242

BERG, MIRIAM ROSEMARY, association executive; b. N.Y.C., Jan. 9, 1948; d. Edgar Marion and Rosemary (Shafer) Villchur. BA, Barnard Coll., 1968. Pres. Coun. on Size & Weight Discrimination, Mt. Marion, N.Y., 1990—. Contbr. articles to Healthy Weight Jour., 1990—. Bd. dirs. Ulster County Coalition for Free Choice, Bearsville, N.Y., 1980—; pres. Planned Parenthood of the Mid Hudson Valley, Poughkeepsie, N.Y., 1984-86. Recipient Margaret Sanger award Planned Parenthood of the Mid-Hudson Valley, 1998. Avocation: singer of medieval and renaissance music. Office: Coun on Size & Weight Discrimination PO Box 305 Mount Marion NY 12456 E-mail: miriam@cswd.org.

BERG, PATRICIA ELENE, molecular biologist; b. Dubuque, Iowa, Sept. 17, 1943; d. Clifford Jay and Dorothy Ruth (McKibben) Emerson; 1 child, Bridget K. Mora; m. Robert S. Weiner. SB in Math., U. Chgo., 1965; PhD in Microbiology, Ill. Inst. Tech., 1973. Postdoctoral fellow U. Chgo., 1973-78; dir. genetic engring. Bethesda Rsch. Labs., Rockville, Md., 1978-80; expert NIH, Bethesda, 1980-82, sr. staff fellow, 1982-85, Nat. Inst. Digestive Diseases and Kidney, 1985-91; assoc. prof. divsn. of pediatric hematology/oncology Sch. Medicine U. Md., Balt., 1991-98; assoc. prof. dept. biochem. and molecular biology George Washington U. Med. Sch., Washington, 1999—. Contbr. articles to profl. jours. Scholar U. Chgo., 1961-65. Mem. AAAS, Am. Soc. Microbiology, Am. Soc. Hematology, Am. Assn. Cancer Rsch., Sigma Xi. Democrat. Methodist. Achievements include discovery of BP1, new gene expressed in over 80 percent of breast cancer patients. Office: George Washington U Med Sch Dept Biochem/Molecular Biol 2300 Eye St NW Washington DC 20037-2336

BERG, PATTY, state legislator; b. Eureka, Calif. 2 children. BA in Sociology and Social Welfare, UCLA, 1967. Social worker; mem., dist. 1 Calif. State Assembly, 2002—. Mem. Agriculture Com., Appropriations Com., Higher Edn. Com., Water, Parks, and Wildlife Com.; vice-chair Aging and Long-Term Care Com. Democrat. Mailing: PO Box 942849 Rm 2137 Sacramento CA 94249 Office: 235 4th St Ste C Eureka CA 95501*

BERG, PAUL, biochemist, educator; b. N.Y.C., June 30, 1926; s. Harry and Sarah (Brodsky) Berg; m. Mildred Levy, Sept. 14, 1947; 1 child, John. BS, Pa. State U., 1948; PhD (NIH fellow 1950-52), Western Res. U., 1952; DSc (hon.) (hon.), U. Rochester, 1978, Yale U., 1978, Washington U., St. Louis, 1986, Oreg. State U., 1989, Pa. State U., 1995. Postdoctoral fellow Copenhagen (Denmark) U., 1952—53; postdoctoral fellow Sch. Medicine, Washington U., 1953—54, Am. Cancer Soc. scholar cancer research dept. microbiology sch. medicine, 1954—57, from asst. to assoc. prof. microbiology, 1955—59; prof. biochemistry Sch. Medicine, Stanford (Calif.) U., 1959—, now prof. emeritus, Sam, Lulu and Jack Willson prof. biochemistry, 1970—94, Robert W. Cahill prof. cancer rsch., 1994—2000, chmn. dept. sch. medicine, 1969—74. Dir. Stanford U. Beckman Ctr. for Molecular and Genetic Medicine, 1985—2000, Affymetrix, 1993—, Nat. Found. Biomed. Rsch., 1994—; non-resident fellow Salk Inst., 1973—83; adv. bd. NIH, NSF, MIT; vis. com. dept. biochemistry and molecular biology Harvard U. ; bd. sci. advisors Jane Coffin Childs Found. Med. Rsch., 1970—80; chmn. sci. adv. com. Whitehead Inst., 1984—90; bd. sci. adv. DNAX Rsch. Inst., 1981—; internat. adv. bd. Basel Inst. Immunology ; chmn. nat. adv. com. Genome Project, 1990—92. Editor: Biochem. and Biophys. Research Communications, 1959—68; editl. bd.: Molecular Biology, 1956—69; contbr. Trustee Rockefeller U., 1990—92. Lt. (j.g.) USNR, 1943—46. Named Calif. Scientist of Yr., Calif. Museum Sci. and Industry, 1963, Lynen lectr., 1977, Priestly lectrs., Pa. State U., 1978, Dreyfus Disting. lectrs., Northwestern U., 1979, Lawrence Livermore Dir.'s Disting. lectr., 1983, Linus Pauling lectr., 1993; recipient Eli Lilly prize biochemistry, 1959, V.D. Mattia award, Roche Inst. Molecular Biology, 1972, Henry J. Kaiser award for excellence in teaching, 1969, Disting. Alumnus award, Pa. State U., 1972, Sarasota Med. awards for achievement and excellence, 1979, Gairdner Found. annual award, 1980, Lasker Found. award, 1980, Nobel award in chemistry, 1980, N.Y. Acad. Sci. award, 1980, Sci. Freedom and Responsibility award, AAAS, 1982, Nat. Medal of Sci., 1983, numerous disting. lectureships including Harvey lectr., 1972. Fellow: AAAS; mem.: NAS, Royal Soc. (elected fgn. mem. 1992), French Acad. Sci. (elected fgn. mem. 1981), Japan Biochem. Soc. (elected fgn. mem. 1978), Internat. Soc. Molecular Biology, Am. Philos. Soc., Am. Soc. Microbiology, Am. Soc. Cell Biology (chmn. pub. policy com. 1994—), Am. Soc. Biol. Chemists (pres. 1974—75), Am. Acad. Arts and Scis., Inst. Medicine. Office: Stanford Sch Medicine Beckman Ctr B-062 Stanford CA 94305-5301 E-mail: pberg@cmgm.stanford.edu.*

BERG, ROBERT LEWIS, physician, educator; b. Spokane, Wash., Sept. 10, 1918; s. Evan and Rachel Myfanwy (Lewis) B.; m. Florence Mitcham Foster, June 18, 1943 (dec. 1985); children— Erik Christian, Astri Maren. BS, Harvard, 1940, MD, 1943. Successively intern, resident, chief med. resident Mass. Gen. Hosp., Boston, 1944-46, 50, asst. to dir. rsch. and edn., 1951-54, asst., then assoc. physician, 1951-58; Moseley travelling fellow Royal Caroline Inst., Stockholm, 1948-49; from instr. to asst. prof. medicine Harvard Med. Sch., 1951-58, Albert D. Kaiser prof., also chmn. dept. preventive, family and rehab. medicine, 1958-89; assoc. dean planning Univ. Rochester, 1982-89, assoc. prof. medicine, 1958-69, prof. medicine, 1969-89, prof. emeritus, 1989—; sr. assoc. physician Strong Meml. Hosp., 1958-69, physician, 1969-89. Acting adminstr., 1960-61; mem. NIH Epidemiology and Biometry Tng. Com., 1962-66, 67-71, chmn., 1969-70; mem. U.S. Com. Vital and Health Statistics, 1965-69, chmn., 1967-69 Author: (with M. Roy Brooks Jr. and Miomir Savicevic) Health Care in Yugoslavia and the United States, 1976; editor: Health Status Indexes, 1973, (with Joseph S. Cassells) The Second Fifty Years: Promoting Health and Preventing Disability, 1990. Trustee Eastman Dental Center, 1971-97, chmn., 1975-79; mem. Governors commn. on domestic violence, 1982-88, Ednl. Commn. for Fgn. Med. Grads., 1983-91. Recipient George Washington Goler award, NY Pub. Health Assn., 1986, David Kaiser award, Rochester Acad. Medicine, 2002, Alumni Gold Medal, U. Rochester Sch. Medicine & Dentistry, 2002. Mem. Am. Pub. Health Assn., Assn. Tchrs. Preventive Medicine (treas. 1963-69, v.p. 1969-70, pres. 1970-72), Internat. Epidemiological Assn. Home: 45 Songbird Ln Rochester NY 14620-3174 Office: Box 644 601 Elmwood Ave Rochester NY 14642-0001

BERG, ROBERT RAYMOND, geologist, educator; b. St. Paul, May 28, 1924; s. Raymond F. and Jennie (Swanson) B.; m. Josephine Finck, Dec. 22, 1946; children: James R., (dec.), Charles R., William R. BA, U. Minn., 1948, PhD, 1951. Geologist, Calif. Co., Denver, 1951-56; cons. Berg and Wasson, Denver, 1957-66; prof. geology, head dept. Tex. A&M U., 1967—, Michel T. Halbouty prof. geology, 1982-2001, prof. emeritus, 2001—; dir. univ. research Tex. A & M U., 1972—. Cons. petroleum geology, 1959— Contbr. papers in field. Served with AUS, 1943-46. Recipient Disting. Achievement award U. Minn., 1992. Fellow Geol. Soc. Am.; mem. Am. Assn. Petroleum Geologists (disting. lectr. 1972, hon. mem. 1985, Sidney Powers Meml. award 1993, Disting. Educator award 2000), Am. Inst. Profl. Geologists (pres. 1971, hon. mem. 1988), Nat. Acad. Engring. Home: 414 Brookside Dr E Bryan TX 77801-3701 Office: Tex A&M U Dept Geology College Station TX 77843-3115

BERG, STANTON ONEAL, firearms and ballistics consultant; b. Barron, Wis., June 14, 1928; s. Thomas C. and Ellen Florence (Nedland) Silbaugh; m. June K. Rolstad, Aug. 16, 1952; children: David M., Daniel L., Susan E., Julie L. Student, U. Wis., 1949-50; LLB, LaSalle Ext. U., 1951; postgrad., U. Minn., 1960-69. Claim rep. State Farm Ins. Co., Mpls., Hibbing and Duluth, Minn., 1952-57, claim supt., 1957-70; regional mgr. State Farm Fire and Casualty Co., St. Paul, Minn., 1970-84; firearms cons. Mpls., 1961—. Bd. dirs. Am. Bd. Forensic Firearm and Tool Mark Examiners; instr. home firearms safety, Mpls., 1975—; cons. to Sporting Arms and Ammunition Mfrs. Inst., 1974-84; internat. lectr. on forensic ballistics Adv. Bd. Milton Helpern Internat. Ctr. for Forensic Scis., 1975—; mem. bd. cons. Inst. Applied Sci., Chgo., 1974—; cons. for re-exam. of ballistics evidence in Robert Kennedy assassination/Sirhan case Superior Ct. L.A., 1975; ct. expert witness in most state cts., Mil. Gen. Ct. Martial Territorial Ct. at V.I. and U.S. Dist. Cts., Supreme Ct. of Ont., Can.; mem. Nat. Forensic Ctr., 1979-98, internat. study group in forensic scis., 1985—; chmn. internat. symposiums on forensic ballistics, Edinburgh, Scotland, 1972, Zurich, 1975, Bergen, Norway, 1981, Dusseldorf, Germany, 1993. Contbg. editor: Am. Rifleman mag., 1973—84, mem. editl. bd.: Internat. Microform Jour. Legal Medicine and Forensic Scis., 1979—, Am. Jour. Forensic Medicine and Pathology, 1979—91; contbr. articles to profl. jours.; presenter : Forensic Firsts, History Channel, 2001. With U.S. Army Counter Intelligence Corp., 1948-52. Fellow Am. Acad. Forensic Sci., Am. Coll. Forensic Examiners (life, bd. cert. forensic examiner and diplomate); mem. ASTM (criminalistics subcom. 1989—, non powder guns subcom. 1990—, paintball guns and sys. subcom. 1994—), NRA, Assn. Firearms and Tool Mark Examiners (life, charter mem., exec. coun. 1970-71, editl. com. AFTE jour., 1989-92, Disting. Mem. and Key Man award 1972, exam. and standards com. 1975-76, Spl. Honors award 1976, nat. peer group on cert. of firearms examiners 1978—), Forensic Sci. Soc., Internat. Assn. forensic Scis., Internat. Assn. for Identification (life, disting. mem., firearms subcom. of sci. and practice com. 1961-74, 86-2000, chmn. firearm subcom. 1964-66, 69-70, 91-95, lab. rsch. and techniques subcom. 1980-81, life charter mem. Minn. divsn.), Internat. Wound Ballistics Assn., Western. Conf. Criminal and Civil Problems (sci. adv. com.), Am. Gunsmithing Assn. (life), Am. Legion (life), Army Counter-Intelligence Corp. Vets. Assn. (life), Browning Arms Collectors Assn. (life), Am. Ordnance Assn. (life), Minn. Weapons Collectors, Internat. Cartridge Collectors Assns. (life), Internat. Reference Orgn. Forensic Medicine and Scis., Internat. Assn. Bloodstain Pattern Analysts. Address: 6025 Gardena Ln NE Minneapolis MN 55432-5840 E-mail: forensicb@msn.com., forensicb@aol.com.

BERG, STEPHEN WARREN, government official; b. Washington, Jan. 21, 1948; s. Isidore and Dorothy (Faust) B.; children: Ashley Michelle, Marcus Alan. BA, Tulane U., 1970; MS, Shippensburg U., 1976. Program analyst Dept. Army, New Cumberland, Pa., Ft. Monmouth, N.J., Chambersburg, Pa., 1972-75; program mgr. Army Officer Environ. Program, Washington, 1975-76; chief, directorate support br. Army Corps Engrs., Washington, 1976-78; chief coord. & support br. Pub. Bldgs. Svc., Washington, 1978-79, chief mgmt. control & analysis br., 1979-82, sr. planner policy & planning office, 1982-86; operational dir. Office Assoc. Adminstr. for Ops., GSA, Washington, 1986—. Exec. officer Coop. Adminstrv. Support Program, 1987—, Pres.'s Coun. Mgmt. Improvement, 1987-94; realty specialist Office Bus., Industry & Govt. Affairs, 1990—; spl. asst. to dir. mgmt. & adminstrn. svcs. ctr. Info. Tech. Svc., Washington, 1995-96; dir. investment analysis staff Office of Chief Info. Officer, 1996-98, dir. Ctr. Info. Tech., Acquisition Office of CIO, dir. GSAITA Svcs. Ctr. Fed. Tech. Svc., 1999—, dir. Fed. Computer Acquisition Ctr., 1999—. Mem. Nat. Contract Mgrs. Assn. Home: 10626 Tuppence Ct Rockville MD 20850-3930 Office: 18th And F Sts NW Washington DC 20405-0001 E-mail: steve.berg@gsa.gov., steveb218@yahoo.com.

BERG, THOMAS KENNETH, lawyer; b. Willmar, Minn., Feb. 10, 1940; s. Kenneth Q. and Esther V. (Westlund) B.; m. Margit Kathryn Larson, July 31, 1965; children: Erik, Jeffrey. BA, U. Minn., 1962, LLB, 1965. Bar: Minn. 1965, U.S. Dist. Ct. Minn. 1968, U.S. Ct. Appeals (8th cir.) 1974, U.S. Supreme Ct. 1980. Atty. Dept. Navy, Washington, 1965-67; assoc. Carlsen, Greiner & Law, Mpls., 1967-79; state rep. Minn. Ho. of Reps., St. Paul, 1970-78; U.S. atty. Dept. of Justice, Mpls., 1979-81; ptnr. Popham, Haik, Schnobrich & Kaufman, Mpls., 1981-97, Hinshaw & Culbertson, Mpls., 1997—. Treas. Moe for Gov. com., 2002. Chair Gov.'s Re-election Com., St. Paul, 1984-86, Gov.'s Commn. for Drug Abuse, Mpls., 1989; U.S. Senate candidate for endorsement Dem. Farmer Labor Party, Mpls., 1994; chmn. bd. dirs. St. Paul Rehab. Ctr., 1995-97. Recipient Outstanding Narcotics Prosecution award U.S. Drug Enforcement Adminstrn., 1981. Mem. Am. Health Lawyers Assn. Office: Hinshaw & Culbertson 3100 Campbell Mithun 222 S 9th St Minneapolis MN 55402-3389

BERG, WARREN STANLEY, retired banker; b. Lynn, Mass., Jan. 17, 1922; s. Carl W. and Gladys (Colburn) B.; m. Marjorie E. Coleman, Mar. 25, 1944; children— Peter C., Carolyn (Mrs. John Spengler), Dana S. BS, Harvard U., 1943; grad. exec. devel. program, Cornell U., 1944. Player Boston Red Sox, 1946; farm sys. coach MIT Baseball Team, 1948-50; Dir. pub. relations and sales promotion Arthur D. Little, Inc., Cambridge, Mass., 1951-65; with Shawmut Bank of Boston (N.A.), 1965-87, sr. v.p., 1969-87. Author: History of Harvard Baseball, 1964, History of Massachusetts Institute of Technology Athletics, 1950. Trustee, pres. Museum of Sci.; chmn. bd. dirs. Freedom House, Freedom Trail; pres. Freedom Trail Found.; chmn. Freedom Trail Commn.; exec. com. Wang Ctr. for Performing Arts. Served to capt. USMCR, 1943-46. Named to Harvard U. Athletic Hall of Fame (baseball). Mem. Pub. Relations Soc. Am. (presdl. citiation for meritorious service 1962), Assoc. Grantmakers of Mass. (v.p.) Clubs: Harvard (Boston), Harvard Varsity (Boston); Perry Hollow Country Club. Home: 635 Witchtrot Rd Sanbornville NH 03872-4224

BERG, WILLIAM JAMES, French language educator, writer, translator; b. Dunkirk, N.Y., Oct. 26, 1942; s. Francis John and Adalyn Huldah (Goodwin) B.; m. Verity Anne Fry, July 2, 1966 (div. 1985); children— Jennifer Anne, Jessica Lyn; m. Laurey Kramer Martin, Feb. 1, 1986; stepchildren: Stirling Brooke Martin, Hunter Kirk Martin. Cert. pratique, Sorbonne, Paris, 1962-63; BA, Hamilton Coll., 1964; MA, Princeton U., 1966, PhD, 1969. NDEA inst. asst. Hamilton Coll., Clinton, N.Y., 1964; teaching asst. Princeton (N.J.) U., 1966; instr. French U. Wis., 1967-68, asst. prof., 1968-73, assoc. prof., 1973-79, prof., 1979—, assoc. chmn. French dept., 1974-75, 78-79, 79-80, 90-92, 99-2000, chmn. dept. French and Italian, 1982-85, 2002; dir. Acad. Yr. Abroad, Paris and N.Y.C., 1973-74. Outside examiner Swarthmore Coll., 1978, No. Ill. U., 1985, 86; outside program evaluator U. Mich., 1979; tenure reviewer Swarthmore Coll., 1982, Tulane U., 1985, Marquette U., 1992, 2000, U. Calif., Riverside, 2002; invited lectr. Rice U., 1985, U. Tenn., 1993; full prof. reviewer Georgetown U., 1984, Swarthmore Coll., 1992, U. Mich., 1994, Northwestern U., 1996, U. Colo., 1997, Va. Tech., 1999, U. Mich., 2001, NYU, 2002; U. Oklahoma, 2002. editl. bd. Summa Publs., Birmingham, Ala., 1983—; reviewer panel for travel and collections NEH, 1989. Author: (with P. Schofer and D. Rice) Poèmes, Pièces, Prose, 1973, (with G. Moskos and M. Grimaud) Saint/Oedipus. Psychocritical Approaches to Flaubert's Art, 1982, (with L. Martin) Images, 1989, The Visual Novel, 1992, (with L. Martin) Emile Zola Revisited, 1992, Gustave Flaubert, 1997, (with S. Magnan, Y. Ozzello and L. Martin-Berg) Paroles, 1999, 2d edit., 2002; author study guides on Twain's Huckleberry Finn, 1986, Tom Sawyer, 1987, (with L. Martin) Flaubert's Madame Bovary, 1989, Zola's Germinal, 1989, Maupassant's Short Stories, 1992; translator: (with P. Scott) Graphics and Graphic Information-Processing, 1981; Semiology of Graphics (design award Midwest Books Competition 1983), 1983-84; mem. editl. bd. Substance, 1971-79; contbr. articles to profl. jours. Travel grantee Am. Philos. Soc., 1969, rsch. grantee U. Wis., 1969, 75, 81-82, 86, 87; Vilas assoc., 1991-93, honors fellow, 1994—; Halverson-Bascom professorship, 1995-2000; recipient U. Wis. Chancellor's award for excellence in tchg., 1995. Mem. MLA, Am. Coun. Tchrs. of Fgn. Langs., Phi Beta Kappa. Home: 5201 Pepin Pl Madison WI 53705-4724 Office: U Wis Dept French and Italian Madison WI 53706

BERGA, SARAH LEE, women's health physician, educator; b. San Benito, Tex., May 22, 1954; d. John Orrin and Nancy Estelle (Michael) B.; m. Frederick S. Sherman, Sept. 26, 1981 (div. 1994); children: Alexis Estelle, Nathaniel Abbott; m. Lockwood Hoehl, Oct. 28, 1995. BA, U. Va., 1976, MD, 1980. Diplomate Am. Bd. Ob-Gyn., Am. Bd. Reproductive Endocrinology and Infertility. From asst. to assoc. prof. U. Pitts., 1988-2001; dir. reproductive endocrinology and infertility divsn. U. Pitts. Sch. Medicine, 2000; prof. U. Pitts., 2001—03; prof., chair, dept. gynecology and obstetrics Emory U., Atlanta, 2003—. Med. dir. menopause ctr. Magee-Womens Hosp.; assoc. med. dir. Gen. Clin. Rsch. Ctr. Mem. Soc. Gynecologic Investigation (coun. mem. 1999-2002), Am. Soc. Reproductive Medicine (bd. dirs. 2002-). Home: 5432 Northumberland St Pittsburgh PA 15217-1129 Office: Emory U Sch of Medicine Dept OBGYN Atlanta GA 30322 E-mail: sberga@emory.edu.

BERGAMO, RON, marketing executive; b. Palm Springs, Calif., Nov. 26, 1943; s. Ralph and Dorothy (Johnson) B.; m. Jane E. Reed; children: Brad, Doug, Steve. BS, U. Ariz., 1965; MBA, Northwestern U., 1972. With Leo Burnett, 1966-68, NBC Network, 1968-69, AVCO TV Sales, 1969-72, Eller Outdoor, 1972-74, Sta. KMBC-TV Sales, 1974-77, LSM Sta. WFAA-TV, 1977-80; gen. mgr. Sta. KFDM-TV, Beaumont, Tex., 1980-82, Sta. KWCH-TV, Wichita, Kans., 1983-88; pres., gen. mgr. KSAZ-TV, Phoenix, 1988-95; exec. v.p., gen. mgr. KWBA TV58, Tucson, 1997—2001; v.p., gen. mgr. KAZ-TV, Phoenix, 2002—. Bd. dirs. Kartchner Caverns, Ariz. Arts Commn., UA Eller Sch. Bd., Boys/Girls Club, Fiesta Bowl. With U.S. Army NG, 1965-71. Recipient Gen. Mgr. of Yr. award Am. Women in Radio and TV, 1990, Phoenix award Pub. Rels. Soc. Am., 1992, Tucson Ad Fed. Silver medal award, 2001; named Wichita Ad Person of Yr., 1985, Person of Yr. Phoenix Ad Club, 1993. Mem. Ariz. Broadcasters Assn. (pres. 1993), Ariz. C. of C. (bd. dirs.), Hispanic C. of C. (mem. bd.), Sigma Chi. Republican. Methodist. Avocations: reading, travel, porsches, vintage racing. Home: 5901 E Stella Ln Paradise Valley AZ 85253-4276 Office: KAZ-TV 4343 E Camelback Phoenix AZ 85018 E-mail: rbergamo@aol.com.

BERGAN, EDMUND PAUL, JR., lawyer; b. N.Y.C., May 6, 1950; s. Edmund Paul and Alice (Gordon) P. B.; m. Patricia Ann Gallagher, Jan. 31, 1987; children: Annabel (dec.), Caroline. BA, Holy Cross Coll., 1971; JD, Fordham U., 1975. Bar: N.Y. 1976. Staff atty. SEC, Washington, D.C., 1975-77; v.p., assoc. gen. counsel Securities Industry Assn., N.Y.C., 1977-81; v.p., asst. gen. counsel Alliance Capital Mgmt. LP, N.Y.C., 1981-88; v.p. gen. counsel Alliance Fund Distbrs., N.Y.C., 1988-94; v.p., gen. counsel Alliance Fund Svc. Subs., N.Y.C., 1988-94; sr. v.p., gen. counsel Alliance Fund Distbrs. and Alliance Fund Svcs., N.Y.C., 1994—. Mem. ABA (mem. fed. securities com. 1982—, investment advisers and cos. subcom. 1999—), Investment Co. Inst. (SEC rules com. 1986—, closed-end fund com. 1989—, chmn. 1992-97, various subcoms.), Bar Assn. City N.Y. (investment mgmt. com. 1999—). Republican. Roman Catholic. Avocations: historical studies, athletics. Office: Alliance Capital Mgmt LP 1345 Ave of Americas New York NY 10105-3198

BERGAN, WILLIAM LUKE, lawyer; b. Auburn, N.Y., Sept. 3, 1939; s. Luke Joseph and Mary Beatrice (Twyne) B.; m. Marilyn Terese Meister, Aug. 8, 1964 (dec. May 1990); children: William Luke, Elizabeth M., Ann G.; m. Frances Maureen West, Jan. 2, 1993. BA summa cum laude, Niagara U., Niagara Falls, N.Y., 1961; JD magna cum laude, Syracuse U., 1964. Bar: N.Y. 1964, U.S. Dist. Ct. (we. dist.) N.Y. 1977, U.S. Dist. Ct. (no. dist.) N.Y. 1968, U.S. Ct. Appeals (2d cir.) 1970. Sr. ptnr. Bond, Schoeneck & King, Syracuse, 1966—. Trustee, past pres. parish coun. St. John the Evangelist Ch., Syracuse, 1993—. Capt. U.S. Army, 1964-66. Fellow Am. Bar Found., Coll. Labor and Employment Lawyers; mem. ABA, N.Y. State Bar Assn. (chmn. labor and employment law sect. 1981-82, exec. com. 1976—), Onondaga County Bar Assn., Nat. Assn. Coll. and Univ. Attys., Am. Arbitration Assn. (bd. dirs. 1984-2000), Greater Syracuse C. of C. (bd. dirs. 1992-96), Niagara U. Alumni Assn., Century Club Syracuse. Democrat. Roman Catholic. Avocation: tennis. E-mail: wbergan@bsk.com.

BERGAU, FRANK CONRAD, real estate, commercial and investment properties executive; b. N.Y.C., Sept. 17, 1926; s. Frank Conrad and Mary Elizabeth (Davie) B.; m. Rita I. Korotkin; children: Mary, Rita, Francis, Theresa, Veronica. BA in English, St. Francis Coll., Loretto, Pa., 1950; MS in Edn. and English, Potsdam (N.Y.) State U., 1969. Cert. tchr., supr., adminstr., N.Y.; cert. comml. investment mem. Tchr. English, Gouverneur (N.Y.) Schs., 1962-81, dir. continuing edn., 1968-81, summer prin., 1974-80; project dir. St. Lawrence County (N.Y.) Bd. Co-op Ednl. Svcs., Canton, 1974; pres. Irenicon Assocs., Clermont, Fla. Bd. dirs. St. Lawrence County Assn. Retarded Children, 1965—; pres. bd. dirs. Gouverneur Libr.; mem. Family Care Coun., Fla. Dist. 13. Mem.: KC (fin. sec. coun. 13240), NEA, N.Y. Assn. Continuing Edn. (dir.), South Lake County Devel. Coun. (pres.), Lake County Bd. Realtors, Nat. Assn. Realtors, Gouverneur C. of C. (bd. dirs. 1963—66), Kiwanis, Gouverneur Luncheon Club.

BERGÉ, CAROL, writer; b. N.Y.C., 1928; d. Albert and Molly Peppis; m. Jack Bergé, June 1955; 1 child, Peter. Asst. to pres. Pendray Public Relations, N.Y.C., 1955; disting. prof. lit. Thomas Jefferson Coll., Allendale, Mich., 1975-76; instr. adult degree program Goddard Coll., 1976; tchr. fiction and poetry U. Calif. Extension Program, Berkeley, 1976-77; assoc. prof. U. So. Miss., Hattiesburg, 1977-78; vis. prof. Honors Ctr. and English dept. U. N.Mex., 1978-79, 87; vis. lectr. Wright State U., 1979, SUNY, Albany, 1980-81; tchr. Poets and Writers, Poets in the Schs. (N.Y. State Council on Arts), 1970-72, Poets in the Schs. (Conn. Commn. Arts). Summer writing confs. Squaw Valley, Ind. U., U. Calif., Santa Cruz, 1975-1980; propr. Blue Gate Gallery of Art and Antiques, 1988-2003. Author: (fiction) The Unfolding, 1969, A Couple Called Moebius, 1972, Acts of Love: An American Novel, 1973 (N.Y. State Coun. on Arts CAPS award 1974), Timepieces, 1977, The Doppler Effect, 1979, Fierce Metronome, 1981, Secrets, Gossip & Slander, 1984, Zebras, or, Contour Lines, 1991; (poetry) The Vulnerable Island, 1964, Lumina, 1965, Poems Made of Skin, 1968, The Chambers, 1969, Circles, as in the Eye, 1969, An American Romance, 1969, From a Soft Angle: Poems About Women, 1972, The Unexpected, 1976, Rituals and Gargoyles, 1976, A Song, A Chant, 1978, Alba Genesis, 1979, Alba Nemesis, 1979, (reportage) The Vancouver Report, 1965; editor CENTER Mag., 1970-84, pub., 1991—; editor Miss. Rev., 1977-78, Subterraneans, 1975-76, Paper Branches, 1987, LIGHT YEARS: The N.Y.C. Coffeehouse Writers and Multimedia Artists of the 1960s, 2003; contbg. editor Woodstock Rev., 1977-81, Shearsman mag., 1980-82, S.W. Profile, 1981; editor, pub. CENTER Press, 1991-93; pub.: Medicine Journeys (Carl Ginsburg), Coastal Lives (Miriam Sagan), 1991; co-pub.: Zebras (Carol Berge). Nat. Endowment Arts fellow, 1979-80 Mem. Authors' League, Poets and Writers, MacDowell Fellows Assn., Nat. Press Women Home: 2070 Calle Contento Santa Fe NM 87505-5406

BERGEL, ERNEST WALTER, psychiatrist, educator; b. Vienna, Nov. 9, 1930; came to U.S., 1938; s. Egon Ernst and Emma Joan Bergel; divorced; 1 child, Marguerite. BA, Columbia U., N.Y.C., 1951, AM, 1952; MD, Harvard Med. Sch., 1956. Diplomate Nat. Bd. Med. Examiners, Am. Bd. Psychiatry and Neurology; lic. physician, Mass.; cert. child psychiatrist, Am. Assn. Psychiat. Clinics for Children. Intern N.C. Meml. Hosp., Chapel Hill, 1956-57; staff psychiatrist Med. Ctr. for Fed. Prisoners, Springfield, Mo., 1957-59; resident in psychiatry Mass. Mental Health Ctr., Boston, 1959-61; asst. in psychiatry Peter Bent Brigham Hosp., Boston, 1961-62; resident in child psychiatry James Jackson Putnam Children's Ctr., Boston, 1962-63, Judge Baker Guidance Ctr., Boston, 1963-64, staff psychiatrist, 1964-99, psychiat. supr., 1966-98; resident in psychiatry Children's Hosp. Med. Ctr., Boston, 1963-64, asst., then assoc. in psychiatry, 1964—99; pvt. practice adult, child, family psychiatry, 1964—.

Founding mem., asst. dir., then co-dir. family therapy unit Judge Baker Guidance Ctr., 1966-83, co-founder/co-leader family therapy seminars, 1968-83; supr., classroom cons. Manville Sch., 1979-99; teaching fellow Med. Sch. Harvard U., 1959-61, 63-64, rsch. fellow, 1961-62; clin./rsch. fellow Mass. Gen. Hosp., 1962-63, asst. in psychiatry, 1964-69, clin. instr., 1969—; mem. intake redesign task force Mass. Divsn. Social Svcs., 1979; cons. Mass. Dept. Vocat. Rehab., 1964-96, divsn. of child guardianship Mass. Dept. Pub. Welfare, 1964-72, Family Soc. Cambridge, 1967-70, Consulate Gen., Germany, 1973—, Human Resource Inst., 1977-80; presenter in field. Contbr. chpt. to: Progress in Group and Family Therapy, 1972; contbr. articles to sci. jours. and profl. procs. Mem. Mass. Med. Soc., New Eng. Coun. Child and Adolescent Psychiatry, Phi Beta Kappa. Avocations: music, reading, chess. Office: 33 Pond Ave Ste 104B Brookline MA 02445-7163

BERGELT, PHILIP ROBERT, JR., printer, antiques dealer; b. Tampa, Fla., Dec. 3, 1962; s. Philip Robert and Honora Ann (Carey) B. Student, U. South Fla., 1980-82, Fla. Keys C.C., 1988-89. Mgr. Dunderbaks, Tampa, Fla., 1981-84; dir. purchasing Hyatt Hotels & Resorts, Tampa, 1984-92; pub. Oblivion Mag., Palm Desert, Calif., 1992-93; prodn. mgr. Kinko's, Palm Springs, Calif., 1993-95; printer Triangle Reprographics, Orlando, Fla., 1996—; antiques wholesaler self-employed, St. Cloud, Fla., 1995—; rep. Primerica Fin. Svcs., 2003—. Recipient Eagle Scout award, Boy Scouts Am., St. Cloud, 1980. Mem. Sons Union Vetrans Civil War. Republican.

BERGEMAN, GEORGE WILLIAM, mathematics educator, software author; b. Ft. Dodge, Iowa, July 16, 1946; s. Harold Levi and Hilda Carolyn (Nuhn) B.; m. Clarissa Elaine Hellman, Oct. 24, 1968; 1 child, Jessica Ann. BA, U. Iowa, 1970, MS, 1972; postgrad., Va. Inst. Tech., 1978-83. Teaching asst. U. Iowa, Iowa City, 1970-72; coll. instr. Peace Corps, Liberia, 1972-75; asst. prof. math. No. Va. C.C., Sterling, 1975—; software author George W. Bergeman Software, Round Hill, Va., 1984—. Cons. Excel Corp., Reston, Va., 1983-84; developer software including graphics and expert systems. Author: (software, book) 20/20 Statistics, 1985, 2nd edit., 1988 (software) MathCue, 1987, 2nd edit., 1991, Graph 2D/3D, 1990, 93, MathCue Solution Finder, 1991, 2nd edit., 1992, F/C Graph, 1993, F/C.P Graph, 1995-96, MathCue Practice, 1994, 95-96, MathCue Business, 1997, 2000, 02, MathCue, 1998, 2000, MathCue Course Management, 1999, 2000, MathCue Express, 2001, IVSB/MathCue, 2003. Cmty. worker VISTA, Ctrl. Fla., 1968-69. Named Outstanding Educator Phi Theta Kappa, 1987. Mem. Math. Assn. Am., Am. Math. Soc., Am. Math. Assn. Two-Yr. Colls., Phi Kappa Phi. Home: 35441 Williams Gap Rd Round Hill VA 20141-2231

BERGEN, CANDICE, actress, writer, photojournalist; b. Beverly Hills, Calif., May 9, 1946; d. Edgar and Frances (Westerman) B.; m. Louis Malle, Sept. 27, 1980 (dec. 1995); 1 dau., Chloe; m. Marshall Rose, 2000. Ed., U. Pa. Model during coll. Films include The Group, The Sand Pebbles, 1966, The Day the Fish Came Out, Live for Life, 1967, The Magus, 1968, Soldier Blue, The Executioner, The Adventurers, Getting Straight, 1970, The Hunting Party, Carnal Knowledge, T.R. Baskin, 1971, 11 Harrowhouse, 1974, Bite the Bullet, The Wind and the Lion, 1975, The Domino Principle, The End of the World in Our Usual Bed in a Night Full of Rain, Oliver's Story, 1978, Starting Over, 1979, Rich and Famous, 1981, Gandhi, 1982, Stick, 1985, Miss Congeniality, 2000, Sweet Home Alabama, 2002, View from the Top, 2003, The In-Laws, 2003; TV appearances include What's My Line, 1965, Coronet Blue, 1967, The Muppet Show, 1976, The Way They Were, 1981, 2010 (voice), 1984, Trying Times, 1987, Seinfeld, 1990, Images of Life: Photographs that have Changed the World, 1996, The Human Face (miniseries), 2001, Murphy Brown: TV Tales, 2002, Sex and the City, 2002, TV series: Murphy Brown, 1988-98 (Emmy award, Leading Actress in a Comedy Series, 1989, 90, 92, 94, 95); TV films Arthur the King, 1985, Murder by Reason of Insanity, 1985, Mayflower Madam, 1987, Shelley Duvall's Bedtime Stories, Vol. 7, 1993, Mary and Tim, 1996; TV miniseries Hollywood Wives, 1985, Trying Times, Moving Day; author Knockwood; photojournalist credits include articles for Life, Playboy; dramatist: (play) The Freezer (included in Best Short Plays of 1968).

BERGEN, CHRISTOPHER BROOKE, opera company administrator, translator, editor; b. L.A., Jan. 11, 1949; s. Edward Grinnell Bergen and Alvina Ellen (Temple) Stevens; m. Mary Novella Tilman, Apr. 11, 1998. BA, UCLA, 1971; MA, Yale U., 1977. Conf. officer IAEA, Vienna, Austria, 1973-75, data analyst, 1979-81; import mgr. COBEC Trading Corp., N.Y.C., 1978-79; assoc. Geissler Engring. Co., Oakland, Calif., 1982-83; dir. Yale Cons. Assocs., San Francisco, 1983-84; editor INPUT, Mountain View, Calif., 1984; adminstr. surtitles San Francisco Opera, 1985-98. Editor profl. jours.; translator operatic texts for projection during performances at San Francisco Opera, Santa Fe Opera, Met. Opera, Lyric Opera of Chgo., Washington Opera, many other opera cos., symphonies and conservatories in U.S., abroad. Avocations: literature, rowing. Home: 16 La Salle Rd Upper Montclair NJ 07043 E-mail: chrisbergen@supertitles.net.

BERGEN, DORIS, psychologist, educator; b. St. Louis, Mo., Feb. 11, 1932; m. Joel S. Fink; m. James Sponseller (div.); children: Ellen Creager, Holly Andrecheck, Gail Burnett. Student, Heidelberg Coll., 1949—51; BS, Ohio State U., 1953; MA, Mich. State U., 1970, PhD, 1974. Instr., asst. prof., assoc. prof. Oakland U., Rochester, Minn., 1970—80; dean grad. sch. Wheelock Coll., Boston, 1980—84; dean grad. studies and rsch. Pittsburg State U., Pittsburg, Kans., 1984—88; prof., chair Ednl. Psychology Dept. Miami U., Oxford, Ohio, 1988—98, prof., dir. Ctr. for Human Devel., Learning and Tchg., 1998—. Assoc. dean Oakland U., Rochester, 1979—80; vis. scholar Com. Scholarly Comm. with China NAS, 1989—91; cons. Fisher-Price, Inc., 2000—; trainer Heads Up Network, 1998—99; cons. PBS TV program, Dooley and Pals, 1995—99; cons. Mayerson Found., 1994—95; cons. High/Scope, 1990—91. Author: Assessment Methods for Infants and Toddlers: Transdisciplinary Team Approaches, 1994; co-author (with J.M. Coscia): Brain Research and Childhood Education: Implications for Educators, 2001; co-author: (with R. Reid, L. Torelli) Educating and Caring for Infants and Toddlers: A Comprehensive Curriculum, 2000; editor: Play as a Learning Medium, 1974, Play as a Learning Medium, 2d printing, 1976, Play as a Learning Medium, 3d printing, 1978, Play as a Learning Medium, 4th printing, 1982, Play as a Medium for Learning and Development: A Handbook of Theory and Practice, 1988, Readings from Play as a Medium for Learning and Development, 1998; co-editor (with D. Fromberg): Play from Birth to Twelve and Beyond: Contexts, Perspectives and Meanings, 1998; contbr. . Grantee Rsch. on Rescue Heroes, Fisher-Price, Inc., 2001—02, Evaluation of Dragonfly Sci. Inquiry Tng., Eisenhower Grant, 1996—99, Evaluation of Oxford/Talawanda Family Resource Ctr., Oxford/Talawanda Cmty. Svcs., 1999, Evaluation of RISE Winning Teams Early Childhood Tng., Ohio Dept. Edn., 1996—98, Evaluation of Butler County Early Intervention Tracking Program, Civitan Svc. Club, 1996—98, Instl. Devel. Grant, U.S. Dept. Edn., 1986—89, Birth through Seven: Early Intervention and Preschool Spl. Needs, U.S. Dept. Spl. Edn., 1981—84, Day Care Policy: Views of Parents and Practitioners in Mich., NSF, 1979—80. Fellow: Am. Orthopsychiatric Soc., Am. Psychol. Soc.; mem.: Nat. Assn. Early Childhood Tchr. Educators (sec. 2000—02, Found. bd. dirs.), Jean Piaget Soc., Coun. Exceptional Children (divsn. Early Childhood), Soc. Rsch. Adminstrs., Am. Evaluation Soc., Assn. for Study of Play, Nat. Assn. for Edn. Young Children (governing bd. 1996—), Soc. Rsch. in Child Devel., Am. Ednl. Rsch. Assn. (Early Childhood sect., bd. dirs. 1998—2000), Assn. Childhood Edn. Internat., Internat. Humor Soc., Phi Delta Theta, Phi Kappa Phi. Office: Miami Univ 201 McGuffey Hall Oxford OH 45056

BERGEN, JOHN DONALD, communications, public affairs executive; b. Bronx, N.Y., Sept. 16, 1942; s. John D. and Alice Jean (Almand) B.; m. Linda L. Rosewall, Nov. 21, 1964; children: John M., Michael L. BS in Engring., U.S. Mil. Acad., 1964; MA in English, Ind. U., 1971. Commd. 2d lt. U.S. Army, 1964, advanced through grades to lt. col., 1968; battalion advisor Vietnam, 1968-69; comdr. U.S. Army, Republic of Korea, 1974-76; prof. U.S. Mil. Acad., West Point, N.Y., 1971-74; strategic planner Dept. Def., Washington, 1976-81; dir. speechwriting and issue mgmt. Office of Sec. Def., Washington, 1981-84; v.p., corp. affairs RCA, N.Y.C., 1984-86; mgr. corp. affairs Gen. Electric Corp., Fairfield, Conn., 1986; sr. v.p., chief adminstrv. officer Hill & Knowlton, Inc., N.Y.C., 1987, exec. v.p., gen. mgr. ea. region, 1988-90, also bd. dirs.; pres., COO, Hill and Knowlton USA, N.Y.C., 1990-91; pres., CEO, GCI Group, N.Y.C., 1991-96; sr. v.p. corp. rels. Westinghouse/CBS, N.Y.C., 1996-98; pres. Coun. of PR Firms, 1998—2001; sr. v.p. corp. affairs and mktg. Siemens Corp., 2001—. Author: Military Communications: A Test for Technology, 1987; contbr. articles to profl. and tech. jours. Chmn. Inst. of Pub. Rels. Named Outstanding Young Am., Jaycees, 1973. Mem. Pub. Rels. Soc. Am., Pub. Rels. Seminar, Arthur W. Page Soc. Roman Catholic. Avocations: tennis, soccer, sports officiating. Home: 1789 Wrightstown Rd Newtown PA 18940-2603 Office: Siemens Corp 153 E 53rd St New York NY 10022 E-mail: jack.bergen@siemens.org.

BERGEN, POLLY, actress; b. Bluegrass, Tenn. d. William and Lucy (Lawhorn) Burgin; m. Freddie Fields, Feb. 13, 1956 (div. 1976); children: Kathy, Pamela, Peter. Pres. Polly Bergen Cosmetics, Polly Bergen Jewelry, Polly Bergen Shoes. Author: Fashion and Charm, 1960, Polly's Principles, 1974, I'd Love To, But What'll I Wear, 1977; author, producer for TV: Leave of Absence, 1994; Broadway plays include Champagne Complex, John Murray Andersons' Almanac, First Impression, Plaza Suite, Love Letters, Follies (Best Supporting Actress Tony and Drama Desk nominee), The Vagina Monologues, Cabaret; films include Cape Fear, Move Over Darling, Kisses for My President, At War with the Army, The Stooge, That's My Boy, The Caretakers, A Guide for the Married Man, Making Mr. Right, Cry-Baby, 1990, Dr. Jekyll and Ms. Hyde, When We Were Colored, 1994; performed in one woman shows in Las Vegas, Nev., and Reno; albums: Bergen Sings Morgan, The Party's Over, All Alone By the Telephone, Polly and Her Pop, The Four Seasons of Love, Annie Get Your Gun and Do Re Mi, My Heart Sings, Act One Sing Too; numerous TV appearances including star of The Polly Bergen Show, NBC-TV; other TV appearances include The Helen Morgan Story, 1957 (Emmy award as best actress), To Tell the Truth, The Lightning Field, The Surrogate, For Hope; miniseries include The Winds of War (Emmy nomination), 79 Park Ave, War and Remembrance, 1988 (Emmy nomination); writer, prodr. NBC movie Leave of Absence, 1994. Bd. dirs. Martha Graham Dance Ctr., The Singer Co., Soc. Singers, Calif. Abortion and Reproductive Rights Action League, Show Coalition; hon. canister campaign chairperson Cancer Care, Inc., Nat. Cancer Found.; founder Nat. Bus. Coun. for ERA; mem. Planned Parenthood Fedn., Am. Bd. Advs.; mem. nat. adv. com. NARAL, Hollywood Women's Polit. Com. Recipient Fame award Top Ten in TV, 1957-58, Troupers award Sterling Publs., 1957, Editors and Critics award Radio and TV Daily, 1958, Outstanding Working Woman award Downtown St. Louis, Inc., Golden Plate award Am. Acad. Achievement, 1969, Outstanding Mother's award Nat. Mothers' Day Com., 1984, Best Achievement in New Jewelry Design award, 1986, Cancer Care award, 1989, Woman of Achievement award LWV, 1990, Extraordinary Achievement award Nat. Women's Law Ctr., 1991, Freedom of Choice award Calif. Abortion and Reproductive Rights Action League, 1992; Polly Bergen Cardio Pulmonary Rsch. Lab., Children's Rsch. Inst. and Hosp., Denver dedicated, 1970. Mem. AFTRA, AGVA, SAG, Actors Equity. Office: Apt 15C 136 E 56th St New York NY 10022-3620

BERGEN, ROBERT LUDLUM, JR., retired materials scientist; b. Islip, N.Y., Oct. 29, 1929; s. Robert Ludlum and Alice (D'Oench) B.; m. Grace-Elizabeth Field, June 11, 1951; children: Beryl F., Alice D'Oench, Robert Ludlum III, Jennifer U. AB cum laude, Williams Coll., 1951; MS, Cornell U., 1953, PhD, 1955. Various tech. assignments Uniroyal Chem. div. Uniroyal, Inc., Naugatuck, Conn., 1955-68; mgr. plastics and fibers rsch. corp. R&D Uniroyal, Inc., Wayne, N.J., 1969-72; various mgmt. assignments Uniroyal Chem. div. Uniroyal, Inc., Naugatuck, 1972-75; mgr. elastomers R & D Uniroyal Chem. Divsn., Uniroyal Inc., Naugatuck, Conn.; group mgr. chems. and polymers R & D Uniroyal Chem. div. Uniroyal, Inc., Naugatuck, 1975-79; dir. corp. R & D Uniroyal, Inc., Middlebury, Conn., 1979-81, dir., rsch., devel. and engring., Engineered Products Group, 1981-84, dir. corp. engring., 1985; adj. prof. math. U. New Haven, 1986-97; cons. Bethany, Conn., 1986-2000. Mem. adv. bd. Inst. Materials Sci., U. Conn., 1979-97; adj. prof. chemistry U. New Haven, 1964-69; chmn. Soc. Plastic Engrs., Engring. Properties, 1970-71. Author: Testing of Polymers-Stress Relaxation Tests, 1966, various publs., 1954-68. Pres. Bethany Conservation Trust, 1979-82; moderator New Haven Assn. United Ch. Christ, 1991-93; bd. dirs. Conn. conf. United Ch. Christ, 1993-97, mem. investment com., 1994-97; moderator First Ch. Christ, Bethany, 2000—; chmn. Com. on Sr. Housing, Bethany, 2002—. Fellow AAAS; mem. Am. Chem. Soc., Sigma Xi. Achievements include patents on improving stress cracking resistance of plastics; development of specialized impact test for plastics, of correlations between long term mech. properties of plastics and environ. stress cracking. Home and Office: 79 Lebanon Rd Bethany CT 06524-3033

BERGEN, STANLEY SILVERS, JR., retired university president, physician; b. Princeton, N.J., May 2, 1929; s. Stanley Silvers and Leah (Johnson) B.; m. Suzanne E. Miller, Nov. 16, 1965; children: Steven Richard, Victoria Elizabeth, Stuart Vaughn; children by previous marriage: Stanley Silvers III, Amy Dorle. AB, Princeton U., 1951; MD, Columbia U., 1955; hon. degrees, Bloomfield Coll., 1972, Stevens Inst., 1985; LLD (hon.), Princeton U., 1995; DSc Patterson (N.J.) State U. (hon.), 1997; DSc (hon.), Ramapo Coll. N.J., 1997, N.J. Inst. Tech., 1998; DHL (hon.), Univ. Medicine Dentistry N.J., 2002. Resident St. Luke's Hosp., N.Y.C., 1955-58, chief resident, Francis Zabriskie fellow, 1958-59, asst. chief dept. medicine, 1959-60, asst. attending physician, 1962-64; med. dir. Convalescent and Research Unit, Greenwich, Conn., 1962-64; chief medicine Cumberland Hosp., Bklyn., 1964-68; asst. dir. dept. medicine Bklyn.-Cumberland Med. Center, 1964-68, chief community medicine, 1968-70; sr. v.p. N.Y.C. Health & Hosps. Corp., 1970-71; instr. medicine Columbia, 1959-64; asso. prof. medicine Downstate Med. Sch., Bklyn., 1964-71; pres. U. Medicine and Dentistry N.J., Newark, 1971-98, founding pres. emeritus, 1998—. Prof. medicine N.J. Med. Sch., Robert Wood Johnson Med. Sch., Sch. Osteo. Medicine; prof. cmty. dentistry N.J. Dental Sch.; attending med. staff Univ. Hosp., Newark, 1971—, VA Hosp., East Orange, 1972-98, Robert Wood Johnson U. Hosp., 1981-98; trustee Univ. HealthCare Corp., 1993-99; chair bd. trustees Univ. Health Plans N.J., 1994-99; trustee University Heights Sci. Park, 1995—, chmn. bd., 1996—. Author articles in field. Mem. Mayor's Commn. Health and Hosps., N.Y.C., 1969-70; mem. N.J. Comprehensive Health Planning Coun., 1971-91; chmn. N.J. Commn. to Study Structure and Function N.J. Dept. Health, 1973, N.J. Abortion Commn., 1975, Adv. Coun. Grad. Edn. N.J., 1978-98; adv. com. mcpl. health svc. program R.W. Johnson, also, Nat. Conf. Mayors, 1980-85; mem. Bd. Comprehensive Health, Newark, 1976-81, treas., 1972-80; bd. dirs. Cancer Inst. N.J., 1974-98; bd. dirs. Ednl. Commn. Fgn. Med. Grads., 1982-91, sec., vice chmn., 1985-86, chmn., 1986-91; bd. dirs., mem. exec. com. Hastings Ctr. on Biomed. Ethics, 1976-, chmn. devel. com., 1980-95, mem. governance com., 1995-, chmn. elect, 1997, chmn., 1998-; bd. dirs., mem. exec. com. Art Center No. N.J., 1978-82; chmn. N.J. Blood Banks Task Force, 1980-90; trustee Robert Wood Johnson U. Hosp., 1985-98, exec. com. 1987-98; trustee Hackensack Med. Ctr., 1990-99, exec. com., 1992-99; bd. joint mgrs. Cancer Inst. N.J., 1991-98, trustee 1998-2002; trustee Bergen Pines County Hosp., 1994-98, exec. com. 1994-98, trustee Univ. Healthcare Corp. of N.J., 1993-97, Gilda's Club No. N.J., 1997-2000, treas., mem. exec. com., 1998-2000, Kessler Med. Rehab. Rsch. Edn. Corp., 1998-2003, Matheny Sch. and Hosp., 1998-2000, Internat. Ctr. Pub. Health Inc., 1999-; treas. Pres.'s Coun. N.J. Commn. Higher Edn., 1996-98; chmn. bd. trustees U. Health Plan N.J., 1997-99; chair bd. mgrs. N.J. Ctr. Biomaterials, 1997-02; bd. trustees University Heights Sci. Park, 1989-, chair, 1995-; bd. dirs. Blue Hill Meml. Hosp., 2000-, vice chmn. bd., 2001 , Eastern Maine Healthcare Sys., 2002-; bd. dirs. Blue Hill Meml. Hosp. Found., 2000-, vice chmn. bd., 2001-; chair bd. dirs. MedTower, 2000-; trustee Ea. Maine Health Sys., 2002-. First recipient Woodrow Wilson medal for pub. svc. leadership Gov. of N.J., 1987, Univ. medal UMDNJ, 1995. Fellow ACP, Assn. Am. Med. Colls., Am. Fedn. Clin. Rsch., Endocrine Soc., Clin. Soc. N.Y., Diabetes Assn. (v.p. 1969-70, chmn. clin. soc. 1968-69), N.Y. Acad. Scis., Am. Inst. Nutrition; mem. AMA (ho. dels. sect. on med. schs. 1978-98), Assn. Acad. Health Ctrs., Am. Diabetes Assn. (bd. dirs. N.J. affiliate), Am. Soc. Clin. Nutrition, Am. Coll. Healthcare Execs. (hon. fellow), Essex County Med. Soc., Med. Soc. N.J., Am. Hosp. Assn. (trustee 1992-94, chmn. com. grad. med. edn. 1974-76, mem. coun. profl. svcs. 1973-76, mem. governing coun. sect. met. hosps. 1984-87, com. med. edn. 1984-91, ad hoc com. on AIDS 1987-91, chmn. tech. com. biomed. ethics 1986-91, alt. del. Ho. Dels., 1991, mem. AHA regional policy bd., 1988-94, mem. internat. med. scholars program 1987-92, mem. com. to study single pathway to nat. med. licensure 1987-90, mem. com. to study clin. med. skills assessement 1988-92, trustee 1991-94, trustee regional plan commn. 1995-98), Greater Newark C. of C. (dir. 1978-84), Nat. Assn. Pub. Hosps. (trustee 1982-88), State N.J. Health Coord. Coun., Univ. Health System N.J. (trustee, exec. com. 1987-98), Univ. Hosp. Consortium (trustee 1988-92, exec. com. 1990-92), N.Y. Acad. Scis., Opera House Arts (mem. bd. advisors, 2002-, chair facilities com., 2003-). Home: 164 Glenwood Rd Englewood NJ 07631-1951 Office: U Medicine & Dentistry NJ 100 Bergen St Newark NJ 07103-2407 E-mail: sasbergen@aol.com. *My career has taken many significant turns, most of which have improved my ability to lead efforts toward better and more accessible health services. I have been fortunate in the opportunity to lead a variety of activities and to express creativity through institutions and individuals. My successes are due to the extent to which this nation still rewards those willing to work hard and learn from experience, as well as to the many intelligent, compassionate mentors with whose guidance I have been blessed.*

BERGENDOFF, ROBERT PERRY, retired civil engineer; b. Omaha, May 3, 1935; s. Ruben Nathaniel and Dorothy Alice (Lindgren) B.; m. Mary Gwen Erickson, Apr. 13, 1957; children: Lisa Diane Anderson, Lori Sue Haberman, Linda Jo Weber. BSCE, U. Colo., 1957. Registered profl. engr., Mo., Ill., Ind. Engr. Howard, Needles, Tammen & Bergendoff, Kansas City, Mo., 1957-67, project mgr. Chgo., 1967-88; mgr. transp. projects Fluor Daniel, Chgo., 1988-92; civil engring. cons. Chgo., 1992-94; ret., 1994. Chmn. Ill. Architect Engr. Coun., Chgo., 1988-89. Trustee Village of Inverness, Ill., 1979-85, 89-94; bd. dirs. Meth. Manor Retirement Cmty., 2000—. Fellow ASCE; mem. NSPE, Ill. Soc. Profl. Engrs. (pres. 1982-83, Ill. award 1990), Storm Lake C. of C. (pres. 1998). Home: 118 Scott St Storm Lake IA 50588-7712

BERGER, ANITA HAZEL, psychotherapist, adult educator, organizational consultant; b. N.Y.C., Mar. 27, 1930; d. Harry William and Sadye (Lauzar) Fink; m. Ramon Francis Berger, May 6, 1951, (dec.); children: Elizabeth Harrie, Gideon Samuel. BA cum laude, Bklyn. Coll., 1951; MSW, U. Pa., 1953; postgrad., Postgrad. Ctr. for Psychotherapy. Cert. social worker, N.Y.; lic. ind. clin. social worker R.I., Mass. Psychotherapist Jewish Cmty. Svcs. L.I., N.Y.C., 1953-57; psychotherapist, field work instr. Jewish Family Svc., Columbia U., NYU, N.Y.C., 1957-60; supr. lower Manhattan social svc. dept., dir. student unit N.Y.C. Housing Authority, 1972-74; asst. prof. SUNY Grad. Sch. Social Work, Buffalo, 1974-75; psychotherapist Ch. Mission of Hope Family Svc., Erie County Mental Health Svcs., Buffalo, 1975-77; pvt. practice Providence, 1978—; instr. Brown Learning Community Brown U., 1988-92, 98—; cons. orgnl. and leadership devel., career performance Quest for Excellence, Providence, 1992-94, staff assoc., 1992-94; cons. Non-Profit Resources, 1996-98. Cons. orgnl. and bd. devel. Bus. Vol. for the Arts (now Arts and Bus. Coun. R.I.), Greater Providence C. of C.; cons. orgnl. dynamics/design various cos., 1997—; lectr. workplace learning, 2000—. Coord. Community Ctr. Art Show, N.Y.C., 1964; rep. community planning bd. 2 Congressman Koch's, N.Y.C., 1968-71; mem. adv. com. to bd. dirs. Mental Health Clinic, Buffalo, 1976-77; bd. dirs., chmn. tng. and edn. com., trainer Vols. in Action, Providence, 1979-85; mem. R.I. adv. com. U.S. Commn. on Civil Rights, 1981-85; rep. R.I. Coalition Against Bigotry, 1982-85; mem. allocations and budget com. United Way Southeastern New Eng., Providence, 1981-84; mem. R.I. Gov.'s Adv. Commn. on Women, 1982-85, mem. subcom. on the family; vol. Greater Providence C. of C., Cmty. Svcs. Coun., R.I., Options for Working Parents, 1997-2000. Recipient Woman of Yr. award Providence Bus. and Profl. Women's Orgn., 1984, Vol. of Yr. R.I. Bus. and Arts Coun., Bus. Vols. for the Arts, 2003. Fellow N.Y. State Soc. Clin. Social Work Psychotherapists; mem. ASTD, Nat. Assn. Social Workers, R.I. Group Psychotherapy Assn. (pres. 1988-89), Alpha Kappa Delta. Jewish.

BERGER, ARTHUR SEYMOUR, organization executive, city official; b. N.Y.C., Sept. 19, 1920; m. Joyce Berger. JD cum laude, NYU. Bar: N.Y. 1949. Mcpl. atty. State of N.Y., 1963-71; pres. Survival Rsch. Found., Miami, Fla., 1981—; dir. Internat. Inst. for Study of Death, 1985—; instr. Inst. for Ret. Profls., U. Miami, 1999; instr. Lifelong Learning Soc., Fla. Atlantic U.; vice mayor City of Aventura. Instr. Acad. for Lifelong Learning, Fla. Internat. U., adj. prof., 1996-97; instr. Fla. Atlantic U. Lifelong Learning Soc., Inst. for Ret. Profls., U. Miami, Nova Southeastern U.; adj. prof. Broward Coll., 1989-94, Union Inst., 1990-92; cons. Readers Digest; former commr. City of Aventura, Fla. Author: Liberation of the Person, 1964, Aristocracy of the Dead, 1987, Lives and Letters in American Parapsychology, 1988 (outstanding acad. book list), Evidence of Life After Death: Casebook for Tough-Minded, 1988, Dying and Death in Law and Medicine, 1993, When Life Ends, 1995; co-author: The Encyclopedia of Parapsychology and Physical Research, 1991, Fear of the Unknown, 1995; co-editor: Religion and Parapsychology, 1989, Perspectives in Death and Dying, 1989, To Die or Not to Die?, 1990; mem. NYU Law Rev. Mem. Aventura (Fla.) City Commn.; mem. ethics com. Columbia Aventura Hosp. and Med. Ctr.; narrator reading program for blind Libr. of Congress. 1st lt. U.S. Army, 1942-46, 50-52. Recipient Ashby Meml. award Acad. Religion, grantee, 1985, Phys. Rsch. Found., 1984, Fla. Endowment of the Arts, 1989. Mem. DAV (life), Soc. for Sci. Exploration, Am. Soc. for Psychical Rsch., Soc. for Psychical Rsch., Parapsychol. Assn. E-mail: srf5@juno.com.

BERGER, BARBARA PAULL, social worker, marriage and family therapist; b. St. Louis, June 18, 1955; d. Ted and Florence Ann (Vines) Paull; m. Allan Berger, Dec. 27, 1980 (dec.); children: Melissa Dawn, Tammi Alyse, Jessica Lauren. BS, U. Tex., 1977; MSSW, U. Wis., 1978. Diplomate Am. Bd. Clin. Social Work; lic. social worker, Tex., Ky., Ind.; lic. marriage and family therapist. Clin. social worker Child and Family Svcs., Buffalo, 1980-81, United Cerebral Palsy Assn., St. Louis, 1982-83; clin. social worker/coord. Jewish Family Life Edn. Jewish Family Svc., Dallas, 1984-85, 88-90; instr. Miss. Delta C. C., Greenville, 1991; child and adolescent therapist United Behavioral Systems, Louisville, 1993-94; therapist Inpsych, Louisville, 1994-98, Beacon Behavioral Health Group, Louisville, 1998-2000, Louisville Behavioral Health Sys., 2000—. Mem. NASW, Acad. Cert. Social Workers, Am. Assn. Marriage and Family Therapy, Phi Kappa Phi, Pi Lambda Theta, Omicron Nu. Home: 2719 Avenue Of The Woods Louisville KY 40241-6281 E-mail: bepberger@hotmail.com.

BERGER, BARRY STUART, lawyer; b. Houston, May 22, 1942; s. Herman and Anna (Seidler) B. BS, U. Houston, 1964, JD, 1967; LLM, Georgetown U., 1969. Bar: Tex. 1967, U.S. Ct. Appeals (D.C. cir.) 1971, U.S. Supreme Ct. 1973, U.S. Dist. Ct. (so. and ea. dists.) Tex., U.S. Ct. Appeals (5th cir.). Asst., then assoc. prof. law U. Balt., 1969-72; counsel select com. on crime U.S. Ho. of Reps., Washington, 1972-73; gen. counsel, asst. v.p. Green Internat., Balt., 1973-75; gen. atty. Dresser Industries, Inc., Houston, 1976-81; assoc. gen. counsel Geosource Inc., Houston, 1982-84; pres. Barry S. Berger, P.C., Houston, 1984—. Cons. Jud. Conf. D.C., Washington, 1968-69, Jud. Conf. Md., Balt., 1970-72; instr. S.W. Legal Asst. Inst., Houston, 1980-81 Ford Found. fellow, 1967-69. Mem. ATLA, Tex. Bar Assn., Houston Bar Assn., Tex. Trial Lawyers Assn., Houston Trial Lawyers Assn. (bd. dirs. 1996-97), Phi Beta Kappa, Phi Kappa Phi, Omicron Delta Kappa, Phi Delta Phi. Avocations: golf, tennis, fishing, reading. Office: 1863 Post Oak Park Dr Houston TX 77027-3303

BERGER, BONNIE G. sport psychologist, educator; b. Champaign, Ill., May 20, 1941; d. Bernard G. and Mildred W. Berger; 1 child, Stephen Casher. BS, Wittenberg U., 1962; MA, Columbia U., 1965, EdD, 1972. Tchr. George Rogers Clark Jr. H.S., Springfield, Ohio, 1962-64; supr. phys. edn. Agnes Russell Elem. Sch., N.Y.C., 1964-65; asst. prof. SUNY, Geneseo, 1965-66, Dalhousie U., Halifax, N.S., Can., 1969-71, Bklyn. Coll., 1971 77, assoc. prof., 1978-82, prof., 1982-93, dir. Sport Psychology Lab., dep. chair dept. phys. edn., 1989-93; prof., assoc. dean Sch. Phys. and Health Edn. U. Wyo., Laramie, 1993-96, prof., assoc. dean Coll. Health Scis., 1996-99; prof., dir. Sch. Human Movement, Sport and Leisure Studies, Bowling Green (Ohio) State U., 1999—. Cons. in field. Author: Free Weights for Women, 1984, Foundations of Exercise Psychology, 2002; contbr. chpts. to books, articles to profl. jours. Fellow Assn. for Advancement of Applied Sport Psychology (exec. bd.) Am. Acad. Kinesiology and Phys. Edn.; mem. APA, AAHPERD, Internat. Soc. Sports Psychology, N.Am. Soc. Psychology and Phy. Activity. Home: 640 Pine Valley Dr Bowling Green OH 43402

BERGER, BRUCE WARREN, physician, urologist; b. Auburn, N.Y., Sept. 25, 1942; m. Toni M. LeRoy, Aug. 27, 1966; children: Jill, David. BA, Cornell U., 1964; MD, Upstate Med. Ctr., 1968. Diplomate Am. Bd. of Urology, Nat. Bd. of Med. Examiners. Surg. intern Hosp. U. of Pa., Phila., 1968-69; surgery resident NYU Hosp.-Bellevue (N.Y.) Med. Ctr., 1969-70; resident in urology Johns Hopkins Hosp., Balt., 1972-76; urologist Chesapeakd Urology Assocs., Balt., 1976—. Assoc. prof. clin. surgery urology U. Md., Balt., 1976—; attending, pres. med. staff Sinai Hosp., 1989-90, 94, 95; attending Northwest Hosp., Greater Balt. Med. Ctr.; bd. dirs. Life Bridge Health System. Maj.

USAR, 1970—72, Vietnam. Named One of Balts. Best Urologists Balt. mag., 1997, 2000. Mem. AMA, Balt. Med. Soc., Am. Assn. Clin. Urologists, Md. Urologists Assn. (pres. 1995-96), Am. Urologists Assn., The Associate Jewish Cmty. Fedn. (chmn. physicians divsn. 1991), Alpha Omega Alpha. Avocations: tennis, golf, skiing. Office: Chesapeake Urology Assocs PA 2411 W Belvedere Ave Ste 305 Baltimore MD 21215-5230

BERGER, CAROLYN, judge; BA, U. Rochester, 1969; MEd, Boston U., 1971, JD, 1976. Bar: Del. 1976, U.S. Dist. Ct. Del. 1976, U.S. Ct. Appeals (3d cir.) 1981, U.S. Supreme Ct. 1981. Dep. atty. gen. Del. Dept. Justice, Wilmington, 1976-79; assoc. Prickett, Ward, Burt & Sanders, Wilmington, 1979, Skadden, Arps, Slate, Meagher & Flom, Wilmington, 1979-84; vice-chancellor Ct. of Chancery, Wilmington, 1984-94; justice Del. Supreme Ct., 1994—. Mem. ABA, Del. Bar Assn. Office: Carvel State Office Bldg 820 N French St Fl 11 Wilmington DE 19801-3509*

BERGER, CHARLES LEE, lawyer; b. Evansville, Ind., Oct. 14, 1947; s. Sydney L. and Sadelle (Kaplan) B.; m. Leslie Lilly, Apr. 20, 1973; children: Sarah, Rebecca, Leah. BA, U. Evansville, 1969; JD (cum laude), Ind. U., 1972. Bar: Ind. 1972, U.S. Dist. Ct. (so. dist.) Ind. 1972, U.S. Ct. Appeals (7th cir.) 1972, U.S. Ct. Appeals D.C. 1975, U.S. Supreme Ct. 1977, U.S. Dist. Ct. (we. dist.) Ky. 1981, U.S. Ct. Appeals (6th cir.) 1984. Ptnr. Berger & Berger, Evansville, 1972—. Mem. study com. Ind. Supreme Ct. Rules of Evidence, 1993—; mem. Ind. Jud. Qualifications Disciplinary Commn., 1998—. $Den—Sarah, Rebecca, Leah. B.A., U. Evansville, 1969; J.D. cum laude, Ind. U., 1972. Bar: Ind. 1972, U.S. Dist. Ct. (so. dist.) Ind. 1972, U.S. Ct. Appeals (7th cir.) 1972, U.S. Ct. Appeals D.C. 1975, U.S. Supreme Ct. 1977, U.S. Dist. Ct. (we. dist.) Ky. 1981, U.S. Ct. Appeals (6th cir.) 1984. Ptnr., Berger & Berger, Evansville, 1972—; mem. study com. Ind. Supreme Ct. Rules of Evidence, 1993—; mem. Ind. Jud. Qualifications Disciplinary Commn., 1998—. Bd. dirs. Leadership Evansville, 1977. Fellow Ind. Bar Found.; mem. Ind. Bar Assn. (chmn. trial lawyers sect. 1982-83), Am. Bd. Trial Advocates, Ind. Trial Lawyers Assn. (bd. dirs. 1973-77, 77-84, v.p. 1984—). Bd. dirs. Leadership Evansville, 1977. Fellow Ind. Bar Found.; mem. Ind. Bar Assn. (chmn. trial lawyers sect. 1982-83), Am. Bd. Trial Advocates, Ind. Trial Lawyers Assn. (bd. dirs. 1973-77, 77-84, v.p. 1984—). Jewish. Home: 7408 E Sycamore St Evansville IN 47715-3762 Office: Berger & Berger 313 Main St Evansville IN 47708-1485 E-mail: cberger@bergerlaw.com.

BERGER, CHARLES MARTIN, lawn and garden company executive; b. Wilkes-Barre, Pa., May 2, 1936; s. Edward and Sadie (Zwass) B.; m. Jane Elrod Purdy, June 5, 1960; children: Cary John Aaron, Elizabeth Anne, Valerie Ann. AB, Princeton U., 1958; MBA, Harvard U., 1960. Mktg. mgmt. Procter and Gamble Co., Cin., 1960-64; with H.J. Heinz Co., 1964-96, gen. mgr. mktg. U.S.A. div., 1964-69, dir. corp. planning world hdqrs., 1969-70; mktg. dir. Heinz-London, 1970-72; mng. dir. Plasmon SpA, Milan, 1972-78; pres., CEO, chmn. Weight Watchers Internat. Inc., Jericho, N.Y., 1978-94; chmn., CEO Heinz India Pvt. Ltd., Bombay, 1994-96; chmn., pres. and CEO The Scotts Co., Columbus, Ohio, 1996—2001, chmn., 2001—03. Philharmonic Ctr. for the Arts, Naples Fl, North Shore Hosp. Sys., Manhasset, NY. Chmn. bd. dirs. Am. Sch. Milan, 1975-78; bd. dirs. Buckley Country Day Sch., Manhasset, N.Y., 1983-89, Columbus Symphony Orch.; exec.-in-residence Ohio Wesleyan U., Delaware, Ohio. Mem. World Pres'. Orgn. (bd. dirs.), Princeton Club, Village Club of Sands Point (N.Y.), Columbus Club, Capital Club (bd. gov.'s), Port Royal Club. Republican. Jewish. Office: 2455 Lantern Ln Naples FL 34102

BERGER, DANIEL, retired newswriter; b. N.Y.C., June 4, 1932; s. Louis S. and Henriette (Fischkin) Berger; m. Elena L. Plotnikoff, Mar. 16, 1968; children: Juliet D., Joseph R. BA in History, Oberlin Coll., 1954. Reporter, copy reader Cleve. Press, 1954-60; chief editl. writer Indpls. Times, 1960-65; copy editor N.Y. Herald Tribune, N.Y.C., 1965-66; editl. writer Evening Sun-Balt. Sun, 1967-69; London corr. Sun-Balt. Sun, 1969-72, editl. writer, 1973—2002; ret., 2002. Author: Bergerisms. With U.S. Army, 1956—58. Recipient Headline Writing award, Cleve. Newspaper Guild, 1959, Editl. Writing award, Indpls. Press Club, 1963, Front Page award, Washington Balt. Newspaper Guild, 1981, Opinion Writing award, Edn. Writers Assn. U.S., 1986, Editl. award, Md.-Del. DC Press Assn., 1997, 1998; Nieman fellow, Harvard U., 1962—63. Mem.: 14 W. Hamilton St. Club. Avocations: U.S. history, walking. Home: 310 Edgevale Rd Baltimore MD 21210-1914

BERGER, DAVID, lawyer; b. Archbald, Pa., Sept. 6, 1912; s. Jonas and Anna (Raker) B.; m. Barbara Simmons Wainscott, Nov. 5, 1997; children: Jonathan, Daniel. AB cum laude, U. Pa., 1932, LLB cum laude, 1936. Bar: Pa. 1938, D.C., N.Y. Asst. to prof. U. Pa. Law Sch., Phila., 1936-38, spl. asst. to dean; law clk. Pa. Supreme Ct., Phila., 1939-40; spl. asst. to dir. enemy alien identification program U.S. Dept. Justice, Washington, 1941-42; law clk. U.S. Ct. Appeals, 1946; pvt. practice Phila., Washington and N.Y.C.; city solicitor Phila., 1956-63; founder, chmn. Berger & Montague, P.C., Phila. Former counsel Sch. Dist. Phila.; former chmn. adv. com. Pa. Superior Ct.; mem. drafting com. fed. rules evidence U.S. Supreme Ct.; lectr. on legal subjects. Author numerous articles on law. Nat. commr. Anti-Defamation League; assoc. trustee U. Pa., mem. bd. overseers Law Sch.; Presdl. appointee U.S. Holocaust Meml. Coun.; dir. Internat. Tennis Hall of Fame; bd. dirs. ARC, Palm Beach, Fla.; founder, mem. Friends of Art and Preservation in Embassies. Decorated Silver Star and Presdl. Unit Citation; Fellow Duke of Edinburgh's Award World Fellowship; David Berger chair of law for the improvement of the adminstrn. of justice established at U. Pa. Law Sch.; enshrined in U. Pa. Tennis Hall of Fame, 1997. Fellow Am. Coll. Trial Lawyers, Internat. Acad. Trial Lawyers, Internat. Soc. Barristers; mem. ABA (vice-chair tort and ins. practice sect. com. on comml. torts 1988-89), Phila. Bar Assn. (pres., bd. govs., chancellor), Phila. Bar Found. (past pres.), The Athenaeum Phila., Penn Club (N.Y.C., founder), Order of Coif, The Queens Club (London), Royal Ascot Racing Club (Ascot, Eng.). Home: Elephant Walk 109 Jungle Rd Palm Beach FL 33480-4809 Office: Berger & Montague PC 1622 Locust St Philadelphia PA 19103-6305

BERGER, DAVID, history educator; b. Bklyn., June 24, 1943; s. Isaiah and Shirley (Kravitz) B.; m. Pearl Rabinowitz, June 14, 1965; children: Miriam, Yitzhak, Gedalyah. BA, Yeshiva Coll., 1964; MA, Columbia U., 1965, PhD, 1970. Ordained rabbi, 1967. Instr. Yeshiva Coll., N.Y.C., 1968-70; asst. to assoc. prof. Bklyn. Coll., 1970-80; prof. Bklyn. Coll. and the Grad. Sch., CUNY, 1980—. Author: The Jewish-Christian Debate in the High Middle Ages, 1979 (John Nicholas Brown prize 1983), The Rebbe, the Messiah, and the Scandal of Orthodox Indifference, 2001; co-author: Judaism's Encounter with other Cultures: Rejection or Integration?, 1997, Jews and "Jewish Christianity", 1978; editor: History and Hate: The Dimensions of Anti-Semitism, 1986; The Legacy of Jewish Migration: 1881 and Its Impact, 1983. Bd. trustees Beth Din of Am., N.Y.C., 1995—. Recipient Bernard Revel Meml. award Yeshiva Coll. Alumni Assn., 1990. Fellow Am. Acad. for Jewish Rsch.; mem. Am. Hist. Assn., Medieval Acad. Am., Assn. for Jewish Studies (pres. 1998-2000), Internat. Assn. of Socs. for the Study of Jewish History (chair Am. sect. 1991—), Nat. Found. for Jewish Culture (vice-chair acad. adv. bd. 1996-2002, co-chair 2002—), Am. Acad. for Jewish Rsch. (exec. com. 1992—). Office: Dept History Brooklyn Coll Brooklyn NY 11210 E-mail: dberger@gc.cuny.edu.

BERGER, DEBORAH KORNBLUTH, educator, educational consultant; b. Chgo., Oct. 10, 1968; d. Ralph Ross and Anita Dubow Kornbluth; m. Burman Aaron Berger, Mar. 14, 1992; children: Benjamin Adam, Eli Matthew, Ezra Bruce. BA, Emory U., 1990; MEd, Loyola U., Balt., 1993; Certificate, AMI Assn. Montessori Internat., Washington, 1993. Cert. tchr., Md. Youth advisor B'nai B'rith Youth Orgn., Rockville, Md., 1990-93; spl. asst. ABRH Cons., Washington, 1990-91; youth dir. Kadima Orgn., Rockville, 1991-93; tchr. Hebrew B'nai Shalom, Alexandria, Va., 1991-94, Kehilat Shalom, Gaithersburg, Md., 1992-94; ednl. cons., tchr. Jefferson Montessori, Gaithersburg, 1995-96; elem. directress, tchr. Manor Montessori Internat., Potomac, Md., 1993-98; ednl. tutor, cons., owner Tutoring & Test Preparation by Deborah K. Berger, North Potomac, Md., 1992—. Ednl. cons. Flower Hill Sch., Gaithersburg, Butler Sch., 1999—; mem. adv. bd. B'nai Israel, Rockville, 1998-2001; tutor, ednl. cons. Butler Sch., 1999-2002. Mem. nursery bd. B'nai Israel, 1998-2001; mem. leadership com. United Jewish Appeal, 1994-95; mem. Jones Cane PTA. Recipient Internat. Gold Star award B'nai B'rith Orgn., 1986, Nat. Leadership Orgn. award of Honor, 1985. Mem. Hadassah, Potomac Chase Women's Assn., Bunco Club, Reading Club. Jewish. Avocations: reading, writing, skiing, dancing, volunteering at schools. E-mail: tutoringdeb@earthlink.net.

BERGER, FRANK STANLEY, management executive; b. N.Y.C. s. Ernest A. and Anna Berger; m. Judith Berger; children: Evan, Stacey. BA, Queens Coll.; MBA, NYU; postgrad., N.Y. Law Sch., IBM Edn. Center. Supr. dept. mktg. and fin. analysis Lever Bros.; v.p. fin. and adminstrn. Pacific Enterprises; mem. corp. mktg. staff Joseph E. Seagram & Sons, Inc.; mktg. asst. to mgr. cen. div. Calvert Distillers, asst. mgr. Fla. region, mgr. N.J. region, asst. mgr. ea. div., mgr. so. div.; v.p., gen. sales mgr. Frankfort Distillers, exec. v.p. mktg. and fin.; pres. Gen. Wine & Spirits Co., N.Y.C.; pres. and dir. Seagram Distillers Co.; pres., CEO House of Seagram; dir. Joseph E. Seagram & Sons, Inc.; chmn. bd. Quadrillon Investments Inc., 1980-86; chmn. bd., pres. Viceroy Imports, Inc., 1981-86; chmn., CEO Hazel Bishop Cosmetics Inc., 1981-87; dir. Majestic PLC, 1988-89; chmn. bd. dirs., pres. CII, Inc., 1990-95; chmn., pres., CEO Naturally Scientific Inc., 1996—. Trustee N.Y. Hall of Sci.; chmn. N.Y. Lunch-o-Ree Boy Scouts Am., United Jewish Appeal, Gaucho Basketball Assn., Cystic Fibrosis Soc.; exec. com. wine and spirits div. Anti-Defamation League, Pro-Am. tennis sponsor Cerebral Palsy; bd. dirs. Bronfman Found. With AUS. Mem. AIM, Nat. Assn. Chain Drug Stores, Am. Mgmt. Assn., Am. Mktg. Assn, N.Y. C. of C., Young Pres.' Orgn., Quality and Productivity Mgmt. Assn., Conf. Bd. (CEO program). Clubs: Advt. of N.Y, N.Y. Sales Execs.

BERGER, FRANK MILAN, biomedical researcher, scientist, former pharmaceutical company executive; b. Pilsen, Czech Republic, June 25, 1913; came to U.S., 1947, naturalized, 1953; s. Otto and Martha (Weigner) B.; m. Bozena Jahodova, Mar. 15, 1939 (dec. Nov. 1972); children: Franklin Milan, Thomas Jan; m. A. Christine Spade, May 21, 1975. MD, U. Prague, Czechoslovakia, 1937, SUNY, 1948; D.Sc. (hon.), U. of the Scis. in Phila., 1966. Rsch. fellow physiology U. Prague, 1934-36, rsch. asst. bacteriology, 1936-38; bacteriologist Czechoslovak State Inst. Health, 1938-39; sr. resident Monsall Hosp. Infectious Diseases, Manchester, Eng., 1941-43; chief pharmacologist Brit. Drug Houses, London, 1945-47; asst. prof. pediatrics U. Rochester, 1947-49; dir. rsch. Carter-Wallace Inc., 1949-55, v.p., 1955-58; pres. Wallace Labs. div. Carter-Wallace Inc., Cranbury, N.J., 1958-73; mem. adv. coun. dept. biology Princeton U., 1961-74, lectr., prof., 1969-74; mem. sci. adv. com. Waksman Inst. Microbiology, Rutgers U., 1960-67; cons. Surgeon Gen., Walter Reed Army Med. Ctr., Washington, 1974-80; pres. Mario Negri Inst. Found. for Biomed. Rsch., Inc., 1973—; prof. psychiatry U. Louisville Med. Sch., 1974-90; hon. prof. microbiology Waksman Inst. Microbiology, Rutgers U., 1982. Chmn. Ad Hoc Study Group on Clin. and Preclin. Pharmacology, 1977-80. Fellow N.Y. Acad. Scis., Am. Coll. Neuropsychopharmacology, AAAS; mem. AMA, AAUP, Am. Pharm. Soc., Brit. Pharm. Soc., Can. Pharm. Soc., Am. Bacteriol. Soc., Soc. Exptl. Biology and Medicine, Am. Chem. Soc., Biometric Soc., Cosmos Club (Washington), Princeton Club (N.Y.C.), N.Y. Athletic Club, Sigma Xi. Achievements include discovering tranquilizer meprobamate, muscle-relaxant mephenesin, pain reliever carisoprodol, antiepileptic felbamate; also method purification penicillin. Office: 200 E 72nd St New York NY 10021-4537 *Concentrate on the important, rather than the urgent; try not to do what everybody else is doing; and remember that within limits of reason and decency, it is better to do what you like rather than what is expected of you.*

BERGER, FREDERICK JEROME, electrical engineer, educator; b. Szatmar, Hungary, Nov. 26, 1916; came to U.S. 1929; s. Joseph and Goldie (Weiss) B. BS, CCNY, 1959, BEE, 1961; MEE, NYU, 1964; LLD, Frank Ross Stuart U., 1981; DSc, Capitol Coll., Laurel, Md., 1986. Tool and die maker Brewster Aero. Co., 1935-39, chief tool, gauge and plant engr., 1939-45; process engr. Arma Co., 1946-51; entrepreneur Elec. Electronic Communication Systems and Machine Shop Equipments, 1952-61; prof., dep. chmn., chmn. and engring. sci. coord. CUNY, 1962-82. Evaluator Accrediting Bd. Engring., 1962-81; cons. NSF, 1969-80. Editor Jour. of Tau Alpha Pi, 1975-95. With U.S. Army, WWII. Recipient Letter of Recognition for Outstanding Contbn. to Edn. Pres. Ronald Regan, 1987, Pres. William Clinton, 1993. Fellow Am. Soc. Engring. Edn. (Frederick J. Berger ann. scholarship award 1990—, James H. McGraw award in Engring. Tech. Edn. 1992, Centennial cert. and medallion 1993); mem. IEEE (life, Engring. Svc. award 1964-81), Am. Nuclear Engring. Soc., Instrument Soc. Am. (life), Masons, Tau Alpha Pi (founding exec. dir. 1973—), Tau Beta Pi.

BERGER, GEORGE, lawyer; b. N.Y.C., Jan. 21, 1936; BA summa cum laude, NYU, 1957, JD, 1960. Bar: N.Y. 1960, U.S. Dist. Ct. (so. dist.) N.Y. 1961, U.S. Ct. Appeals (2nd cir.) 1963, U.S. Supreme Ct. 1971, U.S. Ct. Appeals (5th cir.) 1974, U.S. Dist. Ct. (ea. dist.) N.Y. 1975, U.S. Dist. Ct. (we. dist.) 1980, U.S. Ct. Appeals (D.C. cir.) 1977, U.S. Ct. Appeals (10th cir.) 1985. Assoc. Phillips, Nizer, LLP, N.Y.C., 1960-67, ptnr., 1967—. Disting. neutral, N.Y. panel, Ctr. for Pub. Resources, 1992-93. Editor: Hazardous Waste and Toxic Torts: Law and Strategy, 1987-92. Mem. ABA, Assn. of Bar of City of N.Y. Office: Phillips Nizer LLP 666 5th Ave New York NY 10103-0001 E-mail: gberger@phillipsnizer.com.

BERGER, H. JEAN, retired physical education educator; b. Broken Bow, Nebr., Apr. 14, 1924; d. Stuart Albert Berger and Harriet Eglantine Bolles. BS in Edn., State Tchrs. Coll., Buffalo, N.Y., 1945; MA in Edn., NYU, 1949, EdD in Camping Edn., 1958. Phys. edn. tchr. various pub. schs., N.Y.; assoc. prof. women's phys. edn., chair dept. NYU; assoc. prof. women's phys. edn. SUNY, Cortland. Vis. prof., U. R.I., Kingston, U. B.C., Vancouver, Ea. Wash. Coll., Cheney; athletic coord. girls interscholastic sports, Ward Melville H.S., Three Village schs., Setauket, N.Y.; exec. for Camp Fire Girls, Butte, Montana; owner Cones 'n' Things. Author Inspirational Poetry for Youth and Camp Groups, Program Activities for Camps; contbr. numerous articles to jours., mags. and bulls. Three-term pres., founder, Retirees Assn. Three Village Ctrl. Sch. Dist., editor newsletter; rep. ch. and sch. youth groups in Three Village area, 1966—; former sec., Lending Aids Soc., Three Villages. Mem. Am. Assn. Health, Phys. Edn. and Recreation (pres. ea. dist. 1971-72, Honor award 1973), N.Y. State Assn. Health, Phys. Edn. and Recreation (pres. 1975-76, sec.-treas. 1969-72, svc. award 1974), Assn. Women in Phys. Edn. in N.Y. State (pres. 1964-65), DAR, Pi Lambda Theta. Avocations: knitting, gardening, sailing, yard work, cone crafts. Home: # 129 1 Jefferson Ferry Dr South Setauket NY 11720-4707

BERGER, HAROLD, lawyer, electrical engineer; b. Archbald, Pa., June 10, 1925; s. Jonas and Anna (Raker) Berger; m. Renee Margareten, Aug. 26, 1951; children: Jill Ellen, Jonathan David. BSEE, U. Pa., 1948, JD, 1951. Bar: Pa. 1951. Practiced in, Phila.; judge Ct. of Common Pleas, Phila. County, 1971-72; chmn., moderator Internat. Aerospace Meetings Princeton U., 1965-66; chmn. Western Hemisphere Internat. Law Conf., San Jose, Costa Rica, 1967; chmn. internat. Confs. on Aerospace and Internat. Law, Coll. William and Mary; permanent mem. Jud. Conf. 3d Circuit Ct. of Appeals; mem. County Bd. Law Examiners, Phila. County, 1961-71; chmn. World Conf. Internat. Law and Aerospace, Caracas, Venezuela, Internat. Conf. on Environ. and Internat. Law, U. Pa., 1974, Internat. Confs. on Global Interdependence, Princeton U., 1975, 79; mem. Pa. State Conf. Trial Judges, 1972-80, Nat. Conf. State Trial Judges, 1972—; chmn. Pa. Com. for Independent Judiciary, 1973—. Adv. coun. Biddle Law Libr. U. Pa., 1991—, mem. bd. overseers Sch. Engring. and Applied Sci., 1998—. Mem. editl. adv. bd.: Jour. Space Law, U. Miss. Sch. Law, 1973—; contbr. articles to profl. jours. Mem. We the People 200 Com. for Constn. Bicentennial, 1991. With Signal Corps, AUS, 1944—46. Recipient Alumnus of the Yr. award, Thomas McKean Law Club, U. Pa. Law Sch., 1965, Space award, GE, 1966, Nat. Disting. Achievement award, Tau Epsilon Rho, 1972, Spl. Pa. Jud. Conf. award, 1981, Special National Distinguished Svc. Award, 1978. Mem.: ABA (past chmn. aerospace law com., mem. state and fed. ct. com., nat. conf. state trial judges, Spl. Presdl. Program medal 1975), Internat. Acad. Astronautics, Assn. U.S. Mems. Internat. Inst. Space Law Internat. Astronautical Fedn. (former bd. dirs.), Phila. Bar Assn. (past chmn. jud. liaison com. 1975, chmn. internat. law com. 1977), Fed. Bar Assn. (past nat. chmn. com. aerospace law, pres. Phila. chpt. 1983—84, chmn. class action and complex litig. com. 3d cir. 1990—, nat. chmn., alt. dispute resolution com. 1992—95, pres. eastern dist. Pa. chpt. 1996—, mem. nat. exec. coun., past chmn. fed jud. com., chair spl. bench bar liason com. eastern dist. Pa. chpt. 2001—, nat. com. 1987 bi-centennial of U.S. Constn., Presdl. award 1970, Spl. Disting. Svc. award ea. dist. chapter 2002), Inter-Am. Bar Assn. (past chmn. aerospace law com.). Office: 1622 Locust St Philadelphia PA 19103-6305

BERGER, HAROLD RICHARD, physician; b. Elizabeth, N.J., Oct. 31, 1914; s. Abraham and Frances (Herfield) B.; m. Minna Constance Wolfson, Aug. 22, 1943; children: Brian, Andrew, Alan, James. AB, Cornell U., Ithaca, N.Y.; MD, NYU Sch. Medicine. Diplomate Am. Bd. Pediatrics. Intern Elizabeth (N.J.) Gen. Hosp., 1940-41; maj. U.S. Med. Corp., 1941-46; resident in pediatrics Jersey City (N.J.) Med. Ctr., 1951-53; pvt. practice, 1946—. Mem. child health program Elizabeth Bd. of Health, Hillside Bd. of Health; sch. physician Elizabeth Bd. Edn. Recipient award Am. Bd. Pediatrics, 1954. Mem. AMA, N.J. Med. Soc., Union County Med. Soc. Avocations: golf, reading, traveling. Home: 987 Harding Rd Elizabeth NJ 07208-1047 Office: 987 Harding Rd Elizabeth NJ 07208-1047

BERGER, HARVEY ROBERT, psychologist; b. Quincy, Mass., Nov. 3, 1927; s. Joel Joseph and Helen Esther (Stone) B.; m. Thelma Lee Cohen, July 11, 1954. BA, Tufts U., 1949, MA, 1950; PhD, U. Mo., 1953. Diplomate Am. Bd. Examiners Profl. Psychology, Am. Bd. Psychol. Specialties, Am. Bd. Forensic Examiners, Prescribing Psychologists Register, cert. fellow; cert. fellow Am. Coll. Forensic Exam.; cert. prescribing psychologist Am. Psychologist Physicians' Register. Psychologist Marblehead (Mass.) Pub. Schs., 1953-79; dir. psychol. svcs. federally assisted programs Salem (Mass.) Pub. Schs., 1967-76; cons. Revere (Mass.) Pub. Schs., 1979-90; nat. svc. officer Jewish War Vets. U.S.A., 1984-2000, Mil. Order of the Purple Heart, 2000—. Assoc. prof. Salem State Coll., 1963; clin. dir. North Shore Psychol. Counseling and Testing Ctr., 1963-75; pres. Paul Revere Savs. & Loan Assn., 1971-76, William Dawes Realty Corp.; with U.S. Dept. Commerce, 1983-84. Mem. Nat. Commn. on Safety Edn., 1952-54; capt., Mass. comdt. U.S. Naval Cadet Program, 1966-86; col. Gov.'s staff Ky. N.G.; pres. Area Bd. on Mental Health and Retardation, 1975-78; vice chmn. Greater Lynn (Mass.) Coun. for Children, Mass. Office for Children, 1977-78; mem. governance bd. Greater Lynn Cmty. Mental Health Ctr., 1977-90; auditor Rep. City Com., Lynn, 1970-75; pres. Mass. Am. Legion Coll., 1964-66; pres. NEA Mut. Fund; chmn. bd. NEA Income Fund; trustee Ida C. Romanow Fund, Jewish Cmty. Rels. Coun. of Greater Boston; pres. Congregation Chevra Tehillim; pres. coun. World Jewish Congress; mem. Jewish Inst. for Nat. Security affairs, Friends of the Israel Def. Forces, Friends of Israel Disabled War Vets. With U.S. Army, 1945-47. Sch. Alcohol Studies fellow Yale U., 1957, John F. Kennedy Libr. fellow. Fellow APA, Am. Coll. Advanced Practice Psychologists; mem NASP (life), NEA (life, Disting. Svc. award), VFW (life), DAV (life, past comdr.), Am. Assn. Mental Retardation, Am. Orthopsychiat. Assn., Royal Soc. Health, Am. in Torah (life, patron, benefactor, pillar), Soc. for Personality and Social Psychology, Internat. Assn. for the Scientific Study of Intellectual Disabilities, Nat. Assn. Sch. Counselors, Mass. Schoolmasters Club (life). Am. Psychology-Law Soc., Soc. for Advancement Social Psychology, Soc. for Psychol. Study Social Issues, Am. Security Coun. Found. (congl. adv. bd.), USN Meml. Found. (mem. nat. adv. coun.), Soc. Behaviorists, Religious Zionists Am. (life), Mass. Bar Assn., Am. Legion (life, past comdr.), Def. of Washington Garrison, Army and Navy Union USA, Bay State Camp, Sons Union Vets. of the Civil War (comdr.), Mil. Order of the Loyal Legion of the U.S.A., Ohio Commandery, Mil. Order Purple Heart (life, comdr. Dept. Mass.), Navy League (life), U.S. Naval Inst. (life, Silver Citation award), Orders and Medals Soc. Am., Nat. Soc. Profs. (life), Am. Assn. Higher Edn. (life), Jewish War Vets (life, nat. svc. officer 1984-2000, Disting. Svc. award), Soc. Supporters of the Ho. of Sages, Am. Jewish Congrees, Am. Jewish Com.Tufts Jumbo Club, Charles Tufts Soc., Nat. Eagle Scout Assn., Masons (32 degree), Shriners (fire brigade chaplain), Legion of Honor, Supreme Grand Royal Arch Chpt. State Israel, Order Ea. Star (worthy patron), Order of Amaranth (trustee), Phi Beta Kappa, Phi Delta Kappa. Home: 31 Tudor St Lynn MA 01902-4617 Office: John F Kennedy Federal Bldg Boston MA 02203-0002

BERGER, HARVEY JAMES, pharmaceutical company executive, physician, educator; b. N.Y.C., June 6, 1950; s. Howard H. and Edith E. (Muskat) B.; m. Wendy S. Wolk, May 16, 1976; children: Eric Michael, Mark Phillip. Grad., The Hotchkiss Sch., 1968; AB magna cum laude, Colgate U., 1972; MD, Yale U., 1977. Diplomate Am. Bd. Nuclear Medicine. Resident Yale-New Haven (Conn.) Hosp., 1977-81, dir. cardiovascular imaging, 1981-84; asst. prof. radiology and medicine Yale U., New Haven, 1981-83, assoc. prof., 1983-84; prof. radiology and assoc. prof. medicine Emory U., Atlanta, 1984-86; dir. Divsn. Nuclear Medicine Emory U. affiliated hosps., Atlanta, 1984-86; sr. v.p. med. affairs Centocor, Inc., Malvern, Pa., 1986—87; sr. v.p., R&D Centacor, Inc., Malvern, Pa., 1987—89; pres. R&D div., exec. v.p., med. dir. Centocor, Inc., Malvern, Pa., 1989-91; chmn., chief exec. officer, founder ARIAD Pharms., Inc., Cambridge, Mass., 1991—; chmn., CEO, founder ARIAD Gene Therapeutics, Inc., Cambridge, Mass., 1993—; chmn. ARIAD Inst. Biomed. Rsch., 1993—. Bd. dirs. Centocor Devel. Corp. I, PTC Therapeutics, Inc.; lectr. divsn. health scis. and tech. MIT, 1992-97, Harvard Med. Sch., 1992-97; adj. prof. U. Pa., Phila., 1986-92; mem. adv. study sects. Nat. Heart, Lung and Blood Inst., Washington, 1984-90; advisor Office of Dir. NIH, Washington, 1984-87; mem. panel on govt. role in civilian tech. NRC/NAS, 1989-92. Founding editor Am. Jour. of Cardiac Imaging, 1985-89; editor Nuclear Medicine Communications, 1985-88; mem. editorial bds. Investigative Radiology, 1984-88; contbr. numerous articles to profl. jours.; patentee in field. Cline Fixott award Am. Acad. Dental Radiologists, 1984. Mem. ACP, Soc. Nuclear Medicine (com. chmn., nat. trustee, Tetalman award 1982), Am. Coll. Cardiology (editl. bd. jour. 1983-88), Am. Coll. Chest Physicians, Am. Heart Assn. (established investigator 1981, cardiovascular radiology/circulation couns.), Am. Coll. Radiology, Am. Fedn. Clin. Rsch., Assn. Univ. Radiologists (Young Investigator award 1979), N.Am. Soc. Cardiovascular Radiology, Soc. Thoracic Radiology, Soc. Exptl. Biology and Medicine, Harvard Club of Boston, Yale Club of N.Y., Phi Beta Kappa. Office: ARIAD Pharmaceuticals Inc 26 Landsdowne St Cambridge MA 02139-4216

BERGER, IVAN BENNETT, magazine editor, writer; b. July 9, 1939; s. Leynard and Celia (Berlin) B.; m. Roberta Thumim, Sept. 13, 1985 (dec. Oct. 27, 1995). Electronics and camera editor Popular Mechanics mag., N.Y.C., 1972-77; sr. editor Popular Electronics mag., N.Y.C., 1977-79; tech. editor Audio mag., N.Y.C., 1982-2000; freelance mag. and tech. writer, 2000—. Author: The New Sound of Stereo, 1985. Mem. Am. Soc. Journalists and Authors, Nat. Writers Union, Internat. Motor Press Assn. Avocations: poetry, cooking, photography. Home: 459 La Grande Ave Fanwood NJ 07023-1732 E-mail: audioib@comcast.net.

BERGER, JAMES CHARLES, computer consultant and systems educator; b. Wilmington, Del., Nov. 9, 1941; s. Theodore and Grace (First) B.; m. Linda Simon, Oct. 24, 1975. BA, U. Del., 1965; MA, U. Mass., 1968; PhD, U. Conn., 1973; Diploma, Chubb Inst., 1988. Asst. prof. Newton (Mass.) Coll., 1972-75; research assoc. Fairleigh Dickinson U., Teaneck, N.J., 1975-76; research dir. John Jay Coll. Criminal Justice, N.Y.C., 1976-88; computer cons. Morristown, N.J., 1988-89; computer cons. and systems educator M.I.S.I. Co., Ltd., N.Y.C., 1989-96, M.I.S.I. Co. Ltd., Mesa, Ariz., 1996—; computer cons., and systems educator Mesa, Ariz., 1996—. Cons. Nat. Orgn. Black Law Enforcement Execs., Washington, 1977, Nat. Assn. Legal Assts., Tulsa, 1981, Ctr. Applied Research and Analysis in the Social Scis., Bklyn., 1981-88. Author: Criminal Justice Education, 1980; contbr. articles to profl. jours.; mem. U.S. News and World Report Sci. and Tech. Panel for spl. edition "The Best of America," 1990. Cons. Jewish Family Service of Del., Wilmington, 1974-75. Grantee NSF, 1974, Conn. Research Found., 1971-72; hon. mem. research bd. advisors Am. Biographical Inst., 1988. Mem.: Pi Alpha Alpha, Pi Sigma Alpha. Jewish. Avocations: music, reading, swimming, tennis, handicrafts. Home and Office: 323 N Williams Mesa AZ 85203-8207

BERGER, JAMES HANK, business broker; b. Lakewood, Ohio, July 27, 1951; s. James Henry and Joan Marie (Wertz) B.; m. Rochelle Anne Kiehl, Apr. 29, 1977; children: Justin Henry, Max Albert. Degree, Cooper Sch. Art, 1972. Owner H.M.S. Titanic Art Studio, Cleve., 1971-73; mgr. various rock groups Cleve., 1972-73; exec. producer TV show Music Your'e My Mother, 1975-76; owner Club Roundtable, Cleve., 1976, Deja Vu, Cleve., 1977-78, Club Traxx, Hanks Cafe, Cleve., 1976-88, Club Metropolis, 1988-90; Club U41A; owner Berger Bus. Brokerage, Bay Village, Ohio, 1990—. Owned and marketed sections of original Hollywood (Calif.) Sign, 1980-82; owner The Probe-Disco, Hollywood, 1983-85; sold more than 400 bars, nightclubs and liquor permits; cons. in field. Author screen play When The Music's Over, 1980. Coach Rocky River Little League, 1990-95, Rocky River Recreation, 1994-95. With USN, 1969-71, Vietnam. Recipient High Pope of Pub. Rels., The Ch. of Sub Genius, 1983; named 78 Most Ineresting People Cleve., Cleve. mag., 1978; Club Probe

voted # 1 disco So. Calif. D.J. Assn., 1984; featured in People mag., 1979, 80. Democrat. Roman Catholic. Avocations: interior designing, literature, gardening. Home and Office: 24446 Lake Rd Bay Village OH 44140-2959 Fax: 440-835-9421. E-mail: hashell@comcast.net.

BERGER, JEROME MORRIS, communications executive; b. Cleve., Dec. 7, 1951; s. Jack and Beatrice Berger; m. Francine Ellis, Oct. 9, 1977. BA, Boston U., 1973; MS in Journalism, Columbia U., 1976. Editor, reporter Marlboro (Mass.) Enterprise, 1977-82; reporter UP Internat., Boston, 1982-87, statehouse bur. chief, 1987-90; asst. prof. Sch Journalism Northeastern U., Boston, 1990-96; comms. dir. com. on ways and means Mass. Senate, Boston, 1996-98; comms. dir. Mass. Cultural Coun., Boston, 1998-2001; dir. media rels. Beth Israel Deaconess Med. Ctr., Boston, 2001—. Developer, cons. Nat. Polit. Awareness Test, Project Vote Smart, Boston, 1993-96. Media columnist The Middlesex News, 1996; editor-in-chief: Insuring American Health for the Year 2000, 1992; contbr. articles to profl. publs. Mem. adv. network State Fiscal Analysis Initiative, Boston, 1993-94; media cons. Graduated Income Tax Campaign, Boston, 1994. Mem. Soc. Profl. Journalists. Avocations: reading, walking. Office: 330 Brookline Ave Boston MA 02215 E-mail: jfberger@world.std.com.

BERGER, JERRY ALLEN, museum director; b. Buffalo, Wyo., Oct. 8, 1943; BA in Psychology, U. Wyo., 1965, BA in Art, 1971, MA in Art History, 1972. Curator collections U. Wyo. Art Mus., Laramie, 1972-88, asst. dir., 1980-83, 87-88, acting dir., 1984-86; dir. Springfield (Mo.) Art Mus., 1988—. Office: Springfield Art Mus 1111 E Brookside Dr Springfield MO 65807-1829 E-mail: jerry_berger@ci.springfield.mo.us.

BERGER, JOHN TORREY, JR., lawyer; b. St. Louis, Apr. 14, 1938; s. John Torrey Sr. and Maud Alice (Beattie) B.; m. Helen Lee Thompson, Aug. 26, 1961; children: John Torrey III, Helen E. JD, Washington U., 1963. Bar: Mo. 1963. Assoc. Lewis, Rice & Fingersh, L.C., St. Louis, 1963-70; mem. Lewis & Rice, St. Louis, 1971—, chmn. real estate sect. Bd. dirs. Carr Lane Mfg. Co., St. Louis, St. Louis Audubon Soc., Logos Sch., St. Louis; adv. bd. dirs. St. Louis Screw & Bolt Co. Deacon, elder, trustee Presbyn. Ch., St. Louis, 1970-75, 75—. Mem. ABA (corp. sect., real estate sect.), Mo. Bar Assn. (real estate sect., banking and securities com.), Bar Assn. Met. St. Louis, Internat. Conf. Shopping Ctrs., SAR, Phi Delta Phi. Avocations: fishing, birding, photography. Home: 1257 Takara Ct Saint Louis MO 63131-1013 Office: Lewis Rice & Fingersh 500 N Broadway Ste 2000 Saint Louis MO 63102-2147 E-mail: jberger@lewisrice.com.

BERGER, JOSEPH, author, educator, counselor; b. Bklyn. s. Harry and Rose (Diner) Berger; m. Margaret Smith, July 9, 1966; children: Adam, Rachel, Gideon. AB magna cum laude, Bklyn. Coll., 1949; MA, Harvard U., 1952, PhD in Sociology, 1958. Lic. counselor. Instr. sociology Dartmouth, 1954-56, asst. prof., 1956-59, Stanford, 1959-62, assoc. prof., 1962-68, prof. sociology, 1968-95; prof. emeritus, 1995—; dir. Lab. for Social Research, 1968-70, 71-74, chmn. dept. sociology, 1977-83, 85-89; sr. fellow by courtesy Hoover Instn., 1984-86, 91—, sr. rsch. fellow, 1986-91. Author (with others): Types of Formalization in Small Groups Research, 1962, Expectation-States Theory: A Theoretical Research Program, 1974, Status Characteristics and Social Interaction: An Expectation-States Approach, 1977, Status, Power and Legitimacy, 1998; editor, contbr.: Sociological Theories in Progress Vol. I, 1966, Sociological Theories in Progress Vol. II, 1972, Sociological Theories in Progress Vol. III, 1989, Status, Rewards, and Influence: How Expectations Organize Interaction, 1985, Theoretical Research Programs: Studies in the Growth of Theory, 1993, Status, Network, and Structure: Theory Development in Group Processes, 1997, New Directions in Contemporary Sociological Theory, 2002; contbr. articles and papers to profl. jours. and books. 1st lt. AUS, 1943—46, ETO. Decorated Bronze Star medal, Army Commendation medal; spl. postdoctoral fellow, NIMH, 1964, 1970—71. Mem.: Propylea, Am. Assn. for Marriage and Family Therapy, Pacific Sociol. Assn., Am. Sociol. Assn. (Cooley-Mead award Social Psychology sect. 1991). Home: 955 Mears Ct Stanford CA 94305-1041

BERGER, JOYCE MURIEL, foundation executive, author, editor; b. N.Y.C., Oct. 20, 1924; d. Samuel and Daisy (Lichtenstein) Zeitlin; m. Arthur Seymour Berger, Feb. 11, 1946. BA magna cum laude, N.Y. U., 1944, MA, 1946. Editor Theta Psychical Rsch. Found., Durham, N.C., 1978-80; sec.-treas., libr. Survival Rsch. Found., administr. Internat. Inst. for Study of Death, Miami, Fla., 1980—. Convener confs. Internat. Inst. Study of Death, Miami, 1985, 87, Survival Rsch. Found., Miami, 1986. Co-author: Reincarnation Fact or Fable, 1991, Encyclopedia of Parapsychology, 1991, Fear of the Unknown, 1995; co-editor: To Die or Not to Die, 1990, Perspectives on Death and Dying, 1989; lectr. and seminar coord. in field. Right to Die conf. grantee Fla. Endowment of the Humanities, Tampa, 1987. Mem. Am. Soc. for Psychical Rsch., Soc. for Psychical Rsch., The Book Group of South Fla., Phi Beta Kappa. Avocations: bridge, tennis, travel, recording for the blind.

BERGER, LAWRENCE HOWARD, lawyer; b. Phila., May 19, 1947; s. Howard Merrill Berger and Doris Eleanor Cummins; m. Julie Mitchell Collins, Aug. 8, 1970; children: Colby Shaw, Ryan Lawrence, Lindsey Wade. BS, Mich. State U., 1969; JD, U. Va., 1972. Bar: Pa. 1972, U.S. Dist. Ct. (ea. dist.) Pa. 1973, U.S. Ct. Appeals (3d cir.) 1986. Assoc. Morgan, Lewis & Bockius LLP, Phila., 1972-79, ptnr., 1979—. Bd. dirs. US Lacrosse, 2000—, chmn., 2002—. Trustee Agnes Irwin Sch., 1984-86, 1984—86, Naomi Wood Charitable Trust-Woodford Mansion Mus., 1986—, Fairmount Park Coun. for Hist. Sites, 1989—95, Fairmont Park Hist. Trust, 1993—95; dir. Phila. Lacrosse Assn., 1992—2000. Recipient Frank Carr Community Svc. award, 1991. Fellow Am. Bar Found.; mem. ABA (sec. com. on nonprofit corps. 1980-90), Pa. Bar Assn. (chmn. com. on uniform comml. code 1978-80), Phila. Bar Assn., Pa. Bar Inst., Banking Law Inst. (lectr. 1985), Pa. Bankers Assn. (lectr. 1980, 89), Martins Dam Club, Blue Key, Omicron Delta Kappa. Home: 360 Pond View Rd Devon PA 19333-1732 Office: Morgan Lewis & Bockius LLP 1701 Market St Philadelphia PA 19103-2903

BERGER, LEV ISAAC, physicist, educator; b. Rostov, USSR, June 23, 1929; came to U.S., 1978; s. Isaac Mark and Sara (Poltevsker) B.; m. Ninelle Rossine, July 2, 1956; 1 child, Yuri. MS in Physics, State U., Moscow, 1955; PhD in Physics, State U., Minsk, USSR, 1959; PhD in Tech. Scis., U. Steel and Alloys, Moscow, 1968. Lectr. physics U. Nonferrous Metals, Moscow, 1956-60; docent Physics U. Metallurgy, Moscow, 1960-62; prof. Poly. Inst., Moscow, 1962-77; sr. scientist New Eng. Research Ctr., Sudbury, Mass., 1979-81; lectr. physics San Diego State U., 1981-89, U. San Diego, 1989-98; pres. Calif. Inst. Electronics & Materials Sci., Hemet, 1981—. Dir. divsn. Inst. Spl. Purity Substances, Moscow, 1962-71, Introscopy Research Inst., Moscow, 1971-77. Author: Ternary Diamond-like Semiconductors, 1969, Semiconductor Materials, 1997; contbr. articles to profl. jours.; patentee in field. San Diego State U. grantee, 1983. Mem. ASTM (com. electronics, thermal measurements), Soc. for Advancement of Material and Process Engrng. (exec. bd.), Am. Phys. Soc., Am. Assn. Crystal Growth, Materials Rsch. Soc., Nat. Assn. Scholars. Home: 2115 Flame Tree Way Hemet CA 92545-7803 Office: Calif Inst Electronics & Materials Sci PO Box 832 Hemet CA 92546-0832 E-mail: berger@ciems.com.

BERGER, LINDA FAY, writer; b. Ft. Worth, Mar. 12, 1943; d. Walter Bob and Bertha Fay (Christensen) B. AA, Tarrant County Jr. Coll., Ft. Worth, 1976; BBA, U. Tex., Arlington, 1981; MBA, North Tex. U., 1987. Cert. profl. sec. Profl. Sec. Assn. Internat. With Tex. Refinery Corp., Ft. Worth, 1961-91, file clk., telex operator, departmental sec., exec. sec., asst. pers. dir., pers. dir. Co-author: A Joyful Journey, 1995. Mem. Profl. Secs. Internat. (sec. 1969-79), Tex. Assn. Bus. (sec. 1990), Order Ea. Star (Riverside chpt. 834). Mem. Unity Ch. Avocations: travelling, yoga, reading, cooking. E-mail: linda@dns-tx.com.

BERGER, MARC JOSEPH, lawyer; b. Chgo., June 28, 1947; s. Lawrence and Esther Berger; m. Eileen Neiberg, Aug. 29, 1971. MA in Music Theory, U. Chgo., 1973; MusD, Northwestern U., 1984; JD, Southwestern U., 1989. Bar: Calif. 1989, U.S. Dist. Ct. (ctrl. dist.) Calif. 1989, U.S. Ct. Appeals (9th cir.) 1989. Prof. music Am. Conservatory Music, Chgo., 1973-79; assoc. Yusim Stein & Hanger, Encino, Calif., 1989-91, Howarth & Smith, L.A., 1991-97, Théver & Assocs., L.A., 1999—2001, Beam, Brobeck, West & Sullivan, Santa Ana, Calif., 2001—02, Michael P. Stone P.C., Pasadena, Calif., 1997-99, 2003—. Composer (opera) Der Gruftwächter, 1998. Wildman scholar Southwestern U., 1985-89. Avocations: music, theater, chess.

BERGER, MARVIN, medical educator; b. Bronx, N.Y., July 22, 1936; s. Jack and Hannah Berger; m. Roslynn Berger, June 26, 1965; children: David, Kenneth. BA, Ohio U., 1957; MD, Chgo. Med. Sch., 1961. Diplomate Am. Bd. Internal Medicine, Am. Bd. Cardiovascular Disease. Intern Beth Israel Med. Ctr., N.Y.C., 1961-62, resident in internal medicine, 1962-64, dir. echocardiography lab., 1975—, assoc. chief of cardiology, 1981—; fellow in cardiology Mt. Sinai Med. Ctr., N.Y.C., 1964-65; asst. prof. clin. medicine Mt. Sinai Sch. of Medicine, N.Y.C., 1976-81, assoc. prof. clin. medicine, 1982-90, assoc. prof. medicine, 1990-94, Albert Einstein Coll. Medicine, Bronx, 1994—, prof. clin. medicine, 1999—. Editor: Doppler Echocardiography in Heart Disease, 1987; contbr. numerous articles to profl. jours. Capt. U.S. Army, 1965-67. Fellow ACP, N.Y. Cardiol. Soc., Am. Coll. Chest Physicians, Am. Coll. Cardiology; mem. AMA, Am. Heart Assn. Avocations: reading, classical music, dixieland jazz, sports. Office: Beth Israel Med Ctr 1st Ave and 16th St New York NY 10003 E-mail: mberger@bethisraelny.org.

BERGER, MELVIN, allergist, immunologist; b. Phila., Mar. 7, 1950; MD, PhD in Biochemistry, Case Western Res. U., 1976. Internship, resident pediatrics Children's Hosp. Med. Ctr., Boston, 1976-78; fellow allergy & immunology Nat. Inst. Allergy & Infectious Diseases, Bethesda, Md., 1978-81; pediatrician, chief Immunology-Allergy Divsn. Rainbow Babies and Children's Hosp., Cleve., 1984—. Prof. peds. & pathology Case Western Res. U. USPHS, 1978-81, col. U.S. Army Res., 1981—. Fellow Am. Acad. Pediatrics. Office: Rainbow Babies Hosp Div Pediatrics/Immunology Cleveland OH 44106 E-mail: mxb12@po.cwru.edu.

BERGER, MIRIAM ROSKIN, creative arts therapy director, educator, therapist; b. N.Y.C., Dec. 9, 1934; d. Israel and Florence Roskin; m. Meir Berger, July 16, 1967; 1 child, Jonathan Israel. Student, Barnard Coll., 1952-53; BA, Bard Coll., 1956; postgrad., CCNY, 1956-58; Dr. Arts, NYU, 1998. Alumni dir. Bard Coll., Annandale-on-Hudson, N.Y., 1958-59; dance therapist Manhattan Psychiatric Ctr., N.Y.C., 1959-60; performer, educator Jean Erdman Theater of Dance, N.Y.C., 1959-62; dir. adult program Hebrew Arts Sch., N.Y.C., 1981; faculty Dance Notation Bur., N.Y.C., 1974-75, 77; asst. prof. dance therapy program NYU, 1975—, acting dir. dance therapy program, 1991, dir. dance edn. program, 1993—2002; dir. creative arts therapies Bronx Psychiatric Ctr., N.Y.C., 1970-90. Workshop leader in field. Prodr. off-Broadway The Coach with the Six Insides, 1962-63; author, prodr. Non-Verbal Group Process, 1978; co-editor Am. Jour. Dance Therapy, 1991-94; led dance therapy session Senate hearing on Aging, 1992; contbr. articles to profl. jours.; editl. bd. Arts in Psychotherapy, Jour. Dance Edn. Chair Nat. Coalition of Creative Arts Therapies Assns., 2002—; bd. dirs. Theater Open Eye, 1978—82, v.p. bd. trustees, 1982—89, pres., 1989—94. Recipient NYU scholarship, 1981, Best Paper award Med Art World congress on Arts and Medicine, 1992. Mem.: Acad. Registered Dance Therapists, Am. Dance Therapy Assn. (founder, bd. dirs. 1967—76, v.p. 1974—76, 1992, credential com. 1976, 1982, keynote speaker at nat. conf. 1991, pres. 1994—98), Dance Libr. Israel (v.p.). E-mail: miriam.berger@nyu.edu.

BERGER, MORRIS ISAIAH, humanities educator; b. N.Y.C., Aug. 5, 1928; s. Victor and Minnie (Waltzer) B.; m. Sheila B. Berger, June 12, 1957; 1 child, Jamie. BA, SUNY, Albany, 1950, MA, 1952; PhD, Columbia U., 1956. Project dir., advisor to Min. Edn. A.I.D., Somalia, 1987-90; prof., chair SUNY, Albany, 1956-2000, svc. prof., 2000—. Author: The Settlement, The Immigrant and the Public School, 1980; contbg. editor The Rev. Edn., 1977-80. Chair, bd. dirs. Capital dist. ACLU, 1971-75. Fulbright scholar, 1984; rsch. fellow SUNY Albany, 1969. Home: 222 Heritage Rd Guilderland NY 12084 E-mail: mberger@nycap.rr.com.

BERGER, NATHAN ALLEN, academic administrator; b. Phila., July 8, 1940; s. Meyer and Lillian (Salko) B.; m. Sosamma John, June 23, 1968; children: Joshua S., Ravi B., Sarina H. AB, Temple U., 1962; MD, Hahneman U., 1966. Intern Michael Reese Med. Ctr., Chgo., 1967-68; rsch. assoc. NIH, Balt., 1968-71; assoc. prof. Washington U. Sch. Medicine, St. Louis, 1971-82; prof. medicine, biochemistry, and oncology Case Western Res. U., Cleve., 1983-95, dir. cancer ctr., 1985-95, interim dean, v.p. med. affairs, 1995-96, dean, v.p. med. affairs, 1996—2002, dir. Ctr. for Sci., Health and Soc., 2002—. Bd. trustees Edison Biotech. Am. Cancer Soc., U. Hosp. Cleve., Henry Ford Health System, Menorah Park, Ohio Biomed. Rsch. and Tech. Task Force. Contbr. articles to profl. jours.; mem. editl. bd. Jour. Clin. Investigation, Jour. Biol. Chemistry, Cancer Rsch.; others. Lt. comdr. USPHS, 1968-71. Fellow Washington U. Sch. Medicine, 1971-82; Leukemia Soc. Am. scholar. Mem. Am. Soc. Hematology, Am. Soc. Biol. Chemists, Am. Soc. Clin. Oncology, Am. Soc. Cancer Rsch., Am. Soc. Clin. Investigation, Am. Assn. Physicians. Office: Case Western Res U 10900 Euclid Ave Cleveland OH 44106-1712 E-mail: nab@po.cwru.edu.

BERGER, NEWELL JAMES, JR., retired security professional; b. Pitts., Oct. 26, 1926; s. Newell James and Marjorie Ikler (Herndon) B.; m. Darlene Ingram, Sept. 6, 1950 (dec. Nov. 1990). BS, Mich. State U., l958; grad., U.S. Army Command and Gen. Staff Coll., l963, U.S. Army War Coll., l972; MA, Webster U., 1993. Enlisted man U.S. Army, 1944, advanced through grades to staff sgt., 1948, commd. 2d lt., 1948, advanced through grades to col., 1970, chief corrections hdqrs., 1970-72, dir. security Office Surgeon Gen., 1972-73, dir. security Health Svcs. Command Ft. Sam Houston, Tex., 1973-78, ret., 1978; security cons. Phoenix and San Diego, 1979-84; chief plant security Teledyne Ryan Aero. Co., San Diego, 1985-86; dep. dir. security BAE Sys. Mission Solutions, San Diego, 1986-99; ret., 1999. Decorated Legion of Merit with two oak leaf clusters. Mem. Internat. Assn. Chiefs Police (life), Am. Soc. for Indsl. Security (life cert. protection profl.). Republican. Episcopalian. Avocations: music, history. Home: 11872 Caminito Corriente San Diego CA 92128-4550 Fax: 858-485-6247. E-mail: bergernj@aol.com.

BERGER, PATRICIA WILSON, retired librarian; b. Washington, May 1, 1926; d. Thomas Decatur Wood and Nina Hughes; m. George Hamilton Combs Berger, May 20, 1970. BA, George Washington U., 1965; MSLS, Cath. U. Am., 1974. Asst. libr., ops. rsch. office Johns Hopkins U., Chevy Chase, Md., 1949-51, asst. ops. rsch. analyst, 1951-54; head libr. CEIR, Washington, 1954-55; chief, tech. info. and libr. svcs. Human Rels. Area Files Yale U., Washington, 1955-57; tech. info. officer, chief libr. Inst. for Def. Analyses, Washington, Arlington, Va., 1957-67; dir. tech. info. and security programs Lambda Corp., Arlington, 1967-71; chief libr. U.S. Commn. on Govt. Procurement, Washington, 1971-72; head gen. ref. br., later dep. chief libr. U.S. Patent and Trademark Office, Arlington, 1972-76; chief libr. divsn. U.S. Nat. Bur. Stds., Gaithersburg, Md., 1976-78; dir. info. resources and svcs. U.S. EPA, Washington, 1978-79; chief libr. and info. svcs. U.S. Nat. Bur. Stds., Washington, 1979-83, chief info. resources and svcs., 1983-91, dir. Office Info. Svcs., 1990-92; ret., 1992. Cons. libr., info. and security matters, 1965-95; del. 1st White House Conf. on Librs. and Info. Svc., 1979; bd. dirs. Universal Serial and Book Exch., 1983-84; chmn. Nat. Info. Std. Orgn., Am. Nat. Std. Inst., 1981-83, elected Nat. Info. Std. Orgn. fellow, 1989. Mem. editl. bd. Sci. and Tech. Librs., 1979-92; contbr. articles to profl. jours. Apptd. by Govs. of Va. to Libr. of Va. Bd., 1986-90, 90-95, vice chair, 1992-93, chair, 1993-94; bd. dirs. Va. Commn. for Reenactment of Battle First Bull Run, 1960-61; bd. dirs. Freedom to Read Found., 1988-90, 92-94; apptd. U.S. Postmaster Gen's. Commn. Lit., 1990-92. Recipient Internat. Women's Yr. award Dept. Commerce, 1976, Bronze medal, 1980, Silver medal, 1984, Outstanding Adminstrv. Mgr. award, 1985, H.W. Wilson Pub. Co. award, 1980, Disting. Svc. award U. Richmond Librs., 1989, Cert. of Recognition, Gov. State of Va., 1989, Resolution of Esteem, Va. State Libr. Bd., 1988, award Coun. Libr. and Media Technicians, 1989; named Outstanding Alumnus in Libr. and Info. Sci., Cath. U. Am., 1988, 20th Century Nat. Libr. Adv., Am. Libr. Assn./Am. Libr. Trustees Assn. Nat. Adv. Honor Roll, 2000; Cert. of appreciation Martin Luther King Jr. Fed. Holiday Commission, 1996. Mem AAAS (elected assn. fellow 1992), Spl. Librs. Assn. (exec. bd. Washington chpt. 1970-71, pres. Washington chpt. 1977, elected assn. fellow 1987), ALA (coun. 1984-88, exec. bd. 1986-90, v.p./pres.-elect 1988-89, pres. 1989-90, immediate past pres. 1990-91), D.C. Libr. Assn. (Ainsworth Rand Spofford Pres.'s award 2001), Fed. Librs. Roundtable (pres. 1982-83, Achievement award 1985), Cosmos Club, Chi Omega, Beta Phi Mu. Episcopalian. Home: 105 Queen St Alexandria VA 22314-2610 E-mail: pberger@his.com.

BERGER, PAUL ERIC, artist, photographer; b. The Dalles, Oreg., Jan. 20, 1948; s. Charles Glen and Virginia (Nunez) B. BA, UCLA, 1970; M.F.A., SUNY-Buffalo, 1973. Vis. lectr. U. Ill., 1974-78; prof. art U. Wash.-Seattle, 1978—. Exhibited one-man shows, photographs, Art Inst. Chgo., 1975, Light Gallery, N.Y.C., 1977, Seattle Art Mus., 1980, Light Gallery, N.Y.C., 1982, Univ. Art Mus., Santa Barbara, Calif., 1984, Cliff Michel Gallery, 1989, Seattle Art Mus., 1990, Fuel Gallery, 1993, Galerie Lichtblick GFFK, Cologne, Germany, 1996, SOHO Photo, N.Y.C., 1999. NEA Photographer's fellow, 1979, NEA Visual Artist's fellow, 1986; recipient Artist's Commn., Wash. State Arts Commn., 1990. Mem. Soc. Photographic Edn., Mus. of Contemporary Photography. Office: U Wash Sch Art PO Box 353440 Seattle WA 98195-3440 E-mail: peberger@u.washington.edu.

BERGER, PEARL, library director; b. N.Y.C., Nov. 30, 1943; d. Baruch Mayer and Tova (Brandwein) Rabinowitz; m. David Berger, June 14, 1965; children: Miriam Esther, Yitzhak, Gedalyah Aaron. B in Religious Edn., Yeshiva U.; BA, Bklyn. Coll., 1965; MLS, Columbia U., 1974. Diploma tchr. Hebrew. Tchr. Hebrew & Jewish studies Yeshiva of Crown Heights, Bklyn., 1963-65; asst. libr. YIVO Inst. Jewish Rsch., N.Y.C., 1976-80; head tech. svcs. Librs. Yeshiva U., N.Y.C., 1980-81, head libr. Pollack Libr., 1981-83, head libr. main ctr. librs., 1983-85, dean librs., 1985—. V.p. Coun. Archives and Rsch. Librs. in Jewish Studies, 1984-86, pres. 1986-89. Assoc. editor: Jour. Judaica Librarianship, 1983—; first v.p. Met. Reference and Rsch. Libr. Orgn., 1996-99; contbr. articles to profl. jours.; compiler catalog Guide to Yiddish Classics on Microfiche, 1980. Recipient Benjamin Gottesman Libr. Chair Yeshiva U. Mem. Am. Libr. Assn., Metro. Ref. Rsch. Libr. Agency (trustee 1991—, sec. 1993-99, 1st v.p. 1996-99), Assn. Jewish Librs. (rsch., spl. librs. divsn., v.p. 1982-84, pres. 1984-86, voting rep. Nat. Info. Stds. Orgn. 1995-2000, v.p., pres.-elect 2000-01, pres. 2002-). Office: Yeshiva U Dean of Libraries 500 W 185th St New York NY 10033-3299

BERGER, PHIL, musician; b. Chgo., Aug. 31, 1963; s. Sheldon and Cyrena Berger. BA in Comm., U. Iowa, Iowa City, 1985. Intern CBS, Chgo, 1986; pianist Nordstrom, Glendale, Calif., 1986—88; accompanist, performer, singer freelance, Woodland Hills, Calif., 1987—; sales mgr. Mattress Discounters, West L.A., 1999—2001. Mem. MADD; mem. and vol. performer City of Hope, Duarte, Calif., 2002—03; campaign vol. Mayor Tom Bradley. Mem.: Sierra Club, Alpha Epsilon Pi. Avocations: guitar, piano, tennis, working out. Home and Office: 6301 Glade Ave Woodland Hills CA 91367 Fax: 818-595-2240. E-mail: chitownphil@creativewc.com.

BERGER, P(HILIP) JEFFREY, animal science educator, quantitative geneticist; b. Newark, June 28, 1943; s. Philip Graham and Jean Bar (Weller) B.; m. Frances Ann Williams, June 25, 1965; children— Sarah Katherine, Philip Calvin BS, Delaware Valley Coll., 1965; MS, Ohio State U., 1967, PhD, 1970. Research and teaching asst. Ohio State U., Columbus, 1965-70; mem. faculty Iowa State U., Ames, 1972—, prof. animal sci., 1982—. Cons. computer applications, animal prodn. div. FAO, Rome, 1979; vis. coop. scientist Bet Dagan, Israel, 1980; participant 1st Animal prodn. Conf., San Jose, Costa Rica, 1981; developer mixed model animal prediction programs, 1972—; participant tech. transfer project to develop genetic evaluation program for dairy cattle in tunisia, 1988, Sabbatical Wageningen Agrl. U., The Netherlands, 1994. Contbr. articles to profl. jours. Mem. Am. Dairy Sci. Assn., Am. Soc. Animal Sci., Sigma Xi, Delta Tau Alpha Republican. Methodist. Home: 2518 Kellogg Ave Ames IA 50010-4863 Office: Ia State U Dept Animal Sci 225 Kildee Hl Ames IA 50011-0001

BERGER, REENA, musician, music educator; arrived in U.S., 2000; d. Ben Berger and Anita Landa. MusB, Tel Aviv U., 1989; MusM, New Eng. Conservatory Music, 1992; D in Music, U. Montreal, 1999. Grad. tchg. asst. piano dept. New Eng. Conservatory Music, Boston, 1990—92; lectr. piano U. Montreal, Canada, 1994—99; asst. prof. piano, head piano dept. Pittsburg (Kans.) State U., 2000—. Musician: (concert appearances) U.S. and Israel. Named winner, Que. Festival Competition, 1981, Assn. Music Tchrs. Que. Competition, 1982, Tel Aviv U. Piano Competition, 1989; grantee, U. Montreal, 1994—97, The Que. Govt., 1996, Conseil des Arts et des Lettres du Que., 1997; scholar, Rubin Acad. Music, 1987—89; Pulver scholar, Tel Aviv U., 1985—89. Mem.: Coll. Music Soc., Kans. Music Tchrs. Assn., Music Tchrs. Nat. Assn., Nat. Fedn. Music Clubs, Pi Kappa Lambda. Office: Pittsburg State Univ 1701 S Broadway Pittsburg KS 66762

BERGER, RICHARD STANTON, dermatologist; b. Flint, Mich., July 30, 1940; s. Frederick S. and Millicent (Petschau) B.; m. Brenda Gorne (div.); children: Adam, Lauren; m. Janice Marie Berger, Feb. 10, 1978. MD, U. Mich., 1965. Intern Walter Reed Gen. Hosp., Washington, 1965-66; resident U. Mich., Ann Arbor, 1968-71; asst. prof. medicine and dermatology U. Mo., Columbia, 1971-73; assoc. dir. clin. rsch. Johnson & Johnson, New Brunswick, N.J., 1973-78; clin. asst. prof. medicine and dermatology Rutgers Med. Sch., New Brunswick, N.J., 1973-77; assoc. prof. medicine and dermatology U. Medicine and Dentistry of N.J., New Brunswick, 1977-87, clin. prof., 1987—, chief dermatology, 1979-95, Robert Wood Johnson Univ. Hosp., New Brunswick, 1979-95; pvt. practice Kendall Park, N.J., 1983—. Cons. for several cos. and hosps., including Rutgers Cmty. Health Plan, New Brunswick, 1976-89, Personal Products Rsch. Divsn., Milltown, N.J., 1978-95, Chicopee Mfg. Co., Rsch. Divsn., Milltown, 1978-94, VA Hosp., Lyons, N.J., 1978—, Greenbrook Regional Ctr., Green Brook, N.J., 1980—; med. dir. Hilltop Rsch., East Brunswick, N.J., 1979—. Contbr. more thean 130 articles to profl. jours. Capt. Med. Corps, U.S. Army, 1966-68. Fellow: Am. Acad. Dermatology (Silver award for Tchg. Value 1985); mem.: Dermatol. Soc., Middlesex County Med. Soc. Avocation: swimming. Office: 3270 State Route 27 Kendall Park NJ 08824-1458

BERGER, ROBERT BERTRAM, lawyer; b. N.Y.C., Sept. 1, 1924; s. Edward William and Sophie (Berkowitz) B.; m. Phyllis Ann Korona, June 14, 1947; children: Barry Robert, Mark Alan, Karen Elizabeth Berger Adametz, James Michael; m. 2d, Arlene Kidder Wills, Dec. 27, 1980; 1 stepchild, Kimberly Kidder Wills Campbell. BS, Georgetown U., 1948; JD, U. Conn., 1952. Bar: Conn. 1952, U.S. Dist. Ct. Conn. 1953, U.S. Tax Ct. 1967, U.S. Ct. Appeals (2d cir.) 1968. Sole practice law, 1952-56; ptnr. Berger & Alaimo, Enfield, Conn., 1956-82, Berger, Alaimo, Santy & McGuire, Enfield, Conn., 1982-91, Berger, Santy & McGuire, Enfield, 1991-94, Berger & Santy, Enfield, 1994—2001, Berger, Santy & Barbieri, Enfield, 2001—. Judge Probate Dist. of Enfield, 1989-94; dir. Enfield Vis. Nuses Assn., 1993-96; bd. dirs., mem. exec. com. Conn. Attys. Title Ins. Co., Rocky Hill, 1980-2003. Chmn. Enfield Dem. Town Com., 1979-87, Conn. Psychiat. Security Review Bd., 1985—; bd. dirs. Catic Fin. Inc. Contbr. monthly polit. column Enfield Press, 1980-84. Pres. United Way North Ctrl. Conn., 1981-84; trustee St. Bernard's Roman Cath. Ch., 1977-90, 99-2000; trustee, exec. bd. mem. Johnson Meml. Hosp., Johnson Meml. Corp., Stafford, Conn.; bd. dirs. United Way of Capitol Area, 1981-85, United Way North Ctrl. Conn., 1977—. With USMCR, 1942-45. Decorated Purple Heart; recipient disting. svc. award Enfield Jr. C. of C., 1955, Clayton Frost award U.S. Jr. C. of C., 1959-60. Mem. ABA, Conn. Bar Assn., Hartford County Bar Assn., Enfield Lawyers Assn. (pres. 1973-74), Am. Judicature Soc., Enfield Rotary (pres. 1970-71, Paul Harris fellow 1984). Office: PO Box 1163 Enfield CT 06083-1163

BERGER, ROBERT LEWIS, retired biophysicist, researcher; b. Omaha, Sept. 2, 1925; BS, Colo. State U., Ft. Collins, 1950; MS, Pa. State U., 1953, PhD, 1956. Instr. Park Coll., Parkville, Mo., 1950-51; postdoctoral fellow Cambridge U., Eng., 1956-57; asst. prof. Utah State U., Logan, 1957-60, assoc. prof., 1960-62; sr. investigator Nat. Heart Inst., Bethesda, Md., 1962-77; chief biophysics sect. Nat. Heart, Lung and Blood Inst., NIH, Bethesda, Md., 1977-96; sr. sci. advisor Blood Rsch. Detachment Walter Reed Army Inst. Rsch., Washington, 1994—96; pvt. cons. Bethesda, 1996—; emeritus sr. investigator Walter Reed Army Inst. Rsch., 1998—. On-loan sci. exec. EEG, Inc., Las Vegas, Nev., 1959-60; vis. scientist dept. chemistry U. Calif., San Diego, 1969-71; organizer med. and biol. sect. 4th Internat. Conf. on Temperature, Washington, 1971; invention devel. coord. Nat. Heart Lung Blood Inst., 1990-94. Author over 100 sci. articles and book chpts. on fast reaction methods,

calorimetry, mixing, computer and protein chem. reactions; mem. editorial bd. J. Biochem. and Biophys. Methods, 1982-96; inventor Berger Ball Mixer. Pres., chief exec. officer, fund raiser Karma House Inc., Rockville, Md., 1974-77; bd. dirs., fund raiser Protestant Student House, Utah State U., Logan, 1958-62; advisor Bd. Christian Edn., United Presbyn. Ch, 1960-68. Lt. (j.g.) USCG, 1943-45, PTO. Recipient Comdrs. award for Pub. Svc. Legion of Merit Equin, 1994-96, Disting. Svc. award Eberely Coll. of Sci. and PSH Alumni Soc., 1998. Fellow Am. Phys. Soc., AAAS; mem. Biophys. Soc. (chmn. discussions com. 1976-92), Soc. for Gen. Physiology, Am. Soc. Molecular Biology and Biochemistry. Democrat. Episcopalian. Home: 4503 Avamere St Bethesda MD 20814-3930 E-mail: rlberger@comcast.net.

BERGER, ROBERT MARTIN, urologist; b. N.Y.C., Aug. 28, 1950; s. Samuel and Pearl Anna Berger; m. Amy Gail Dwork, June 16, 1974; children: Randy, Daniel, Seth. BA, SUNY, Binghamton, 1972; MD, SUNY Upstate Med. Ctr., Syracuse, 1976; postgrad., Children's Meml. Hosp., Chgo., 1982. Diplomate Am. Bd. Urology. Intern in gen. surgery George Washington U. Hosp., Washington, 1976-77, resident in gen. surgery, 1977-78, resident in urology, 1978-81; pediat. urology fellow Children's Meml. Hosp., Chgo., 1981-82; clin. instr. in urology Northwestern U., Chgo., 1981-82, George Washington U., Washington, 1982-84, asst. clin. prof., 1984—; pvt. practice pediatric urology Fairfax, Va., 1982-98; pediat. urologist Kaiser Permanente, Fairfax, 1998—; clin. asst. prof. dept. surgery (urology) Georgetown U. Med. Ctr., 1998—2003. Owner, cons. Med. Products Internat., Ltd., Bethesda, Md., 1995—, Berger Internat., Ltd., Great Falls, Va., 1996—; mem. exec. com. Fairfax Hosp., Falls Church, Va., 1987-90, mem. credentials com., 1987, chmn. med. records com., 1988-90; mem. credentials com. Reston (Va.) Hosp., 1987. Contbr. numerous articles to profl. publs., chpt. to book; rschr. in field FDA, 1989. Named one of Top Washington Drs., Washingtonian Mag., 1991, 93, 95, 99, 2002, one of Top Urologists in Washington, Washington Checkbook, 1993, one of Outstanding Physician Specialists, Washington Consumer Checkbook, 1998. Fellow ACS; mem. Am. Urol. Assn., No. Va. Pediatric Soc. Avocations: collecting marine fish, beekeeping, swimming, tennis. Office: Penderbrook Med Ctr Dept Urology 12011 Lee Jackson Hwy Fairfax VA 22033-3310 Fax: 703-383-5547.

BERGER, ROBERT MICHAEL, lawyer; b. Chgo., Jan. 29, 1942; s. David B. and Sophia (Mizock) B.; m. Joan B. Israel, Aug. 16, 1964; children: Aliza, Benjamin, David. AB, U. Mich., 1963; JD, U. Chgo., 1966. Bar: Ill. 1966, U.S. Supreme Ct. 1975. Law clk. to cir, judge Henry J. Friendly U.S. Ct. Appeals, 2d Circuit, N.Y.C., 1966-67; atty. Chgo. Legal Aid Bur. Law Reform Unit, 1967-68; mem. firm Mayer, Brown & Platt, Chgo., 1968-72, ptnr., 1972-2001; adjunct prof. Northwestern U. Law Sch., 1997—; exec. v.p., gen. counsel, sec. Capri Capital LP, 2001—; sr. counsel Krasnow, Saunders, & Cornblath, 2001—. Lectr. Northwestern U. Law Sch., 1973; adj. prof. grad. program in real estate law John Marshall Law Sch., 1995-97; summer inst. faculty mem. Nat. Inst. Law-Focused Edn., Chgo., 1969-74; mem. hearing bd. Ill. Supreme Ct. Atty. Disciplinary Sys., 1973-79; mem. Ill. Sec. State Adv. Com. on Revised Uniform Ltd. Partnership Act, 1984-88, mem. spl. tax adv. commn. to Ill. Dept. Ins., 1972; bd. dirs., legal counsel Consumer Fedn. Ill., 1967-71; mem. regional consumer adv. coun. coun. FTC, 1969; bd. dirs., chmn. program com. Legal Assistance Found., Chgo., 1975-78; mem. Highland Park (Ill.) Zoning Bd. Appeals, 1984-86; chmn. blue ribbon com. Cook County Recorder, 1989-92; mem. real estate adv. bd. Dai-Ichi Kangyo Bank, Chgo., 1988-93; lectr. continuing legal edn. seminars. Comment editor: U. Chgo. Law Rev, 1965-66; author: Law and the Consumer, 1969, 74; author 500 page chpt. Lending, Finance and Banking, Construction Law, 1986, 92, ann. supplements; reporter Revised Uniform Ltd. Partnership Act, 1984-88; adv. com. Restatement of the Law of Property 3d-Mortgages; contbr. articles to law jours. Trustee Am. Friends of Hebrew U., bd. dirs., Primo Ctr. for Women and Children. Mem. ABA (chmn. subcom. on rev. uniform ltd. partnership act 1981-85, chmn. com. on partnerships and unincorporated bus. orgns. 1985-88), Am. Law Inst. (consultative group), Am. Coll. Real Estate Lawyers (bd. govs. 1995-98, nominating com., vice chmn. program com.), Chgo. Bar Assn. (bd. mgrs. 1970-72, chmn. com. on real estate fin. 1984-86, chmn. real property law com. 1987-88), Chgo. Coun. Lawyers (founder, bd. govs. 1969-71), Am.-Israel C. of C. (1st vice-chmn.), Order of Coif, Phi Beta Kappa, Phi Kappa Phi. Office: Capri Capital LP Ste 3430 875 N Michigan Ave Chicago IL 60611 E-mail: rberger@capricap.com.

BERGER, ROGER ALAN, social sciences educator; b. Chgo., Apr. 9, 1953; s. Marvin Joseph and Elaine Scherba Berger; m. Eileen Deirdre Simmons, June 7, 1986; 1 child, Patrick Ryland Burkett. BA, Syracuse U., 1974; MA, U. Wis., 1976, PhD, 1984. Vis. asst. prof. Wabash Coll., Crawfordsville, Ind., 1984—87, Grand Valley State U., Allendale, Mich., 1987—88, 1989—90; sr. Fulbright prof. Fourah Bay Coll.-Univ. Sierra Leone, Freetown, 1988—89; assoc. prof. Wichita (Kans.) State U., 1990—99; instr. Everett (Wash.) C.C., 1999—. Adv. editor Coll. Lit., Pa., 2001—. Contbr. articles to profl. jours. Fellow, NEH, 1987, 1993, 1996; scholar, Sch. Criticism and Theory, 1990. Mem.: MLA, Mid-Am. Assn. for African Studies (exec. com. mem. 1996—99). Avocations: travel, reading. Home: 3524 Federal Ave Everett WA 98201 Office: Everett Community College 2000 Tower St Everett WA 98201 Personal E-mail: rberger25@hotmail.com. E-mail: rberger@evcc.ctc.edu.

BERGER, SAMUEL MARTIN, physician; b. N.Y.C., Aug. 3, 1938; MD, Chgo. Med. Sch., 1964. Diplomate Am. Bd. Ob-Gyn. Intern Brookdale Hosp., N.Y.C., 1964-65, resident in ob-gyn., 1965-69; resident in psychiatry Creedmoor Psychiat. Ctr., N.Y.C., 1974-78; fellow Cornell U., N.Y.C., 1977-78; mem. staff Brotman Med. Ctr., Culver City, Calif.; instr. UCLA; ptnr. So. Calif. Med. Group of Kaiser Permanente, 1987—. Fellow Am. Coll. Ob-Gyn.; mem. APA.

BERGER, SANFORD JASON, lawyer, securities dealer, real estate broker; b. Cleve., June 29, 1926; s. Sam and Ida (Solomon) Berger; m. Bertine Mae Benjamin, Aug. 6, 1950 (div. Dec. 1977); children: Bradley Alan, Bonnie Jean. BA, Case Western Res. U., 1950, JD, 1952. Bar: Ohio 52, U.S. Supreme Ct. 79, U.S. Ct. Appeals 81. Field examiner Ohio Dept. Taxation, Cleve., 1952; pvt. practice law Cleve., 1952—. Real estate cons., Cleve., 1960—; investment cons., Cleve., 1970—. Contbg. author Family Evaluation in Child Custody Litigation, 1982, Child Custody Litigation, 1986, The Parental Alienation Syndrome and the Differentiation Between Fabricated and Genuine Child Sex Abuse, 1987, Family Evaluation in Child Custody Mediation, Arbitration and Litigation, 1989; copyright 10 songs:. Candidate police judge, East Cleveland, 1955; mem. Bd. Edn., Beachwood, Ohio, 1963; judge ct. common pleas Cuyahoga County, Ohio, 1986; judge Ct. Appeals, 1988, 1990, 1992, 1994; mayor Beachwood, 1967. With USMC, 1944—45, PTO. Recipient Cert. Appreciation, Phi Alpha Delta, 1969, Healer award, U.S. Supreme Ct. Chief Justice Warren Burger, 1987; Outstanding Ohio Citizen award, Ohio Gen. Assembly, 1987. Mem.: B'nai B'rith (editor 1968—70). Republican. Jewish. Achievements include being a successful lawyer in U.S. Supreme Ct. Case of Cleveland Bd. of Edn. vs. Loudermill, 1985; 17 appeals to Supreme Court. Avocations: writing poetry, writing lyrics, legal writing, drag racing, scuba diving. Home: 1032 Som Center Rd Cleveland OH 44143-3527 Office: Sanford J Berger 1836 Euclid Ave # 305 Cleveland OH 44115-2234

BERGER, SEYMOUR MAURICE, social psychologist; b. Bklyn., Jan. 7, 1928; s. Leo and Bessie Ida (Okun) Berger; m. Sara Marilyn Nappen, Sept. 7, 1952; children: Evelyn Joyce, Nancy Faith. BS, Okla. A&M Coll., 1949; MA, Columbia U., 1950; PhD, Cornell U., 1959. Instr. Trinity Coll., Hartford, Conn., 1958-59; from instr. to assoc. prof. Ind. U., Bloomington, 1959-69; prof. social psychology U. Mass., Amherst, 1969-95, prof. emeritus, 1995—, acting dean social and behavioral scis., 1991-92, dean social behavioral scis., 1992-95. Contbr. articles on social psychology to profl. jours.; mem. editorial bd. Jour. Personality and Social Psychology. Served with USNR, 1945-46; served with USAF, 1951-55. Fulbright sr. research scholar, 1975-76,83; spl. fellow NIH, 1965-66 Democrat. Jewish. Home: 459 Flat Hills Rd Amherst MA 01002-1219 E-mail: berger@psych.umass.edu.

BERGER, STANLEY ALLAN, mechanical and biomechanical engineering educator; b. Bklyn., Aug. 9, 1934; s. Jack and Esther (Bernstein) B.; m. Anna Ofman, Jan. 30, 1966 (div. Aug. 1984); children: Shoshana, Maya. BS, Bklyn. Coll., 1955; PhD, Brown U., 1959. Rsch. assoc. Princeton U., N.J., 1959-60; from lectr. to prof. U. Calif., Berkeley, 1961—. Cons. IBM, The Rand Corp., Lockheed Missiles and Space Co., Sci. Applications, Inc., Aluminum Co. Am. Author: Laminar Wakes, 1971; editor: Introduction to Bioengineering, 1996; contbr. articles to profl. jours. Fellow: AIAA, ASME (chair applied mechanics divsn. 1997—98), AAAS, Am. Inst. Med. and Biol. Engring., Am. Phys. Soc. (chair divsn. fluid dynamics 2001—02). Home: 899 Arlington Ave Berkeley CA 94707-1926 Office: U Calif Dept Mech Engring Berkeley CA 94720-1740 E-mail: saberger@me.berkeley.edu.

BERGER, STEPHEN, financial services company executive; b. N.Y.C., July 11, 1939; s. Saul and Paula (Rosenzweig) B.; m. Cynthia C. Wainwright, Sept. 24, 1977. BA, Brandeis U., 1959. Editor Crowell-Collier Publs., N.Y.C., 1961-62; exec. asst. to Rep. Jonathan Bingham N.Y.C., 1964-68; pres. PCM Corp., N.Y.C., 1969-73; exec. dir. N.Y. Study Commn. on N.Y.C., 1972-73; dir. Studies Commn. on Critical Choices for Americans, N.Y.C., 1973-74; commr. N.Y. Dept. Social Svcs., Albany, 1975-76; dir. N.Y. Office Planning Svcs., Albany, 1975; exec. dir. N.Y. Emergency Fin. Control Bd., N.Y.C., 1976; mem. N.Y. Bd. Social Welfare, 1977; dir. corp. devel. Oppenheimer & Co., Inc., N.Y.C., 1981-82; investment banker Odyssey Ptnrs., N.Y.C., 1983-85; chmn. U.S. Ry. Assn., Washington, 1980-87; prof. pub. adminstrn. N.Y.U., 1977-85; bd. dirs., chmn. fin. com. N.Y. Met. Transp. Authority, 1979-85; exec. dir. Port Authority, N.Y., N.J., 1985-90, Intergovtl. Policy Adv. Com. (office U.S. trade rep.), 1988-90; chmn., chief exec. officer Fin. Guaranty Ins. Co., N.Y.C., 1990-92; exec. v.p. GE Capital Corp., 1992-93; ptnr. Odyssey Ptnrs., L.P., N.Y.C., 1993—. Chmn. Odyssey Investment Ptnrs., LLC, 1997—; bd. dirs. Trans-Digm Inc., Dayton Superior. Co-chair Gov.'s Com. on Scholastic Achievement; trustee Brandeis U., 1994—2001. Democrat. Jewish. Office: Odyssey Investment Ptnrs 280 Park Ave Fl 38 New York NY 10017-1216 E-mail: sberger@odysseyinvestment.com.

BERGER, THOMAS LOUIS, author; b. Cin., July 20, 1924; s. Thomas Charles and Mildred (Bubbe) Berger; m. Jeanne Redpath, June 12, 1950. BA with honors, U. Cin., 1948; postgrad., Columbia U., 1950—51; LittD (hon.) (hon.), L.I.U., 1986. Librarian Rand Sch. Social Sci., N.Y.C., 1948—51; staff mem. N.Y. Times Index, 1951—52; assoc. editor Popular Sci. Monthly, 1952—53. Disting. vis. prof. Southampton Coll., 1975—76; vis. lectr. Yale U., 1981—82; Regent's lectr. U. Calif., Davis, 1982. Author: (books) Crazy in Berlin, 1958, Reinhart in Love, 1962, Little Big Man, 1964, Killing Time, 1967, Vital Parts, 1970, Regiment of Women, 1973, Sneaky People, 1975, Who is Teddy Villanova?, 1977, Arthur Rex, 1978, Neighbors, 1980, Reinhart's Women, 1981, The Feud, 1983 (Pulitzer Prize nomination, 1984), Nowhere, 1985, Being Invisible, 1987, The Houseguest, 1988, Changing the Past, 1989, Orrie's Story, 1990, Meeting Evil, 1992, Robert Crews, 1994, Suspects, 1996, The Return of Little Big Man, 1999, (plays) Other People, 1970, (novels) Best Friends: A Novel, 2003, The Tree That Grew Through the Roof, 2000, Crafts Through the Year, 2000. With U.S. Army, 1943—46, ETO. Recipient Rosenthal award, Nat. Inst. Arts and Letters, 1965, Western Heritage award, 1965, Ohioana Book award, 1982; Dial fellow, 1962. Office: Don Congdon Assocs 156 Fifth Ave New York NY 10010-7002 *In my work I try to compete with that reality to which I must submit in life.**

BERGER, TOBY, electrical engineer, educator; b. Sept. 4, 1940; s. Henry and Doris L. (Goldstein) B.; m. Florence Cohen, Aug. 27, 1961; children: Elizabeth, Lawrence. BS, Yale U., 1962; MS, Harvard U., 1964, PhD, 1966. Assoc. scientist Raytheon Co., Wayland, Mass., 1962-66, sr. scientist, 1966-68, cons., 1968-75; asst. prof. elec. engring. Cornell U., Ithaca, N.Y., 1968-72, prof., 1977-88, J. Preston Levis prof. engring., 1988-98, Irwin and Joan Jacobs prof. engring., 1998—, acting dir. dept. elec. engring., 1988—. Cons. IBM, Owego, N.Y., 1975-94, Bell Labs., Murray Hill, N.J., 1987-97, TCSI, Berkeley, Calif., 1986-96, Sight Speed Tech., Berkeley, Calif., 2003—; vis. prof. ENST, Paris, 1986, Princeton U., 1989-90, Northeastern U., 1990, U. Va., 1997. Author: Rate-Distortion Theory, 1971, Digital Compression for Multimedia, 1998, Information Measures for Discrete Random Fields, 1998; contbr. articles to profl. jours. Fellow Guggenheim Found., 1975-76, Japan Soc. for Promotion of Sci., 1980-81, Peoples Republic of China Ednl. Ministry, 1981, Fulbright Travel fellow, 1987; recipient Shannon award, IEEE Information Theory Soc., 2001. Fellow: IEEE (pres. info. theory group 1979, editor-in-chief Transactions on Info. Theory 1987—89, Frederick E. Terman award 1982); mem.: AAAS, Info. Theory Soc. of IEEE (Shannon award 2002), Am. Soc. Engring. Tech., Tau Beta Pi, Sigma Xi. Home: 422 Highland Rd Ithaca NY 14850-2216 Office: Cornell U Sch Elec & Computer Engring Ithaca NY 14853

BERGER, WOLFGANG H. oceanographer, marine geologist; b. Erlangen, Germany; came to U.S., 1961; MS in Geology, U. Colo., 1963; PhD in Oceanography, U. Calif., San Diego, 1968. Asst. prof. Scripps Inst. Oceanography U. Calif., La Jolla, 1971-74, assoc. prof., 1974-80, prof. oceanography, 1980—; dir. Calif. Space Inst. U. Calif., San Diego, 1998—. Co-editor: Abrupt Climatic Change, 1987, Ocean Productivity, 1989, co-author: The Sea Floor, 1993. Co-chief scientist, Ocean Drilling Prog., Leg 130 (1990), Leg 175 (1997). Recipient Bigelow medal Woods Hole (Mass.) Oceanographic Inst., 1979, Huntsman medal Bedford Oceanographic Inst., Can., 1984, Humboldt award German Sci. Found., Bonn, Germany, 1986, Albert I medal, Paris, 1991, Balzan prize, 1993, Steinmann medal Geol. Vereingung, 1998, Francis P. Shepard medal, Soc. for Sedimentary Geology, 2001; Lady Davis fellow Hebrew U., 1986. Fellow AAAS, Am. Geophysical Union (Ewing medal 1988), Geol. Soc. Am.; mem. European Geophysical Soc., Academia Europaea (fgn.). Avocation: water color. Office: U Calif San Diego Scripps Inst Oceanography Dept 0524 La Jolla CA 92093 E-mail: wberger@ucsd.edu.

BERGER-KNORR, LAWRENCE, education educator, information technology manager; s. Lawrence D and Emily F Knorr; m. Ann L Berger-Knorr, Nov. 5, 1994; children: Taylor, Abbey. BA Bus./Economics in bus. and economics (summa cum laude), Wilson Coll., 2000—01; MBA, The Pa. State U., 2001—02. Cert. Computing Profl. Inst. for the Cert. of Computing Professionals, 2001. Ind. computer cons. Knorr Software Systems, Wyomissing, Pa., 1983—94; pres./ceo NorSoft, Inc., Camp Hill, 1994—2000; ind. computer cons. IT Analytics, Inc., Carlisle, 2000—02; edi mgr. Exel Logistics, Mechanicsburg, 2002—; adj. prof. of computer sci. Wilson Coll., Chambersburg, 2002—; grad. tutor The Pa. State U., Harrisburg, 2001—. Cons. Exel Logistics, Mechanicsburg, Pa., 1991—2002. Author: (book) Seventy-One Years of Marriage: The Ancestors, Descendents & Relations of George and Alice Knorr of Reading, PA. Registrar Harris Ferry Chpt. - SAR, Harrisburg, Pa., 2002—02; pres. & treas. The Ridings Homeowners Assn., Carlisle, Pa., 1999—2002. Recipient 50 Fastest Growing Companies in Ctrl. PA (NorSoft, Inc.), Ctrl. Penn Bus. Jour. & KPMG, 1999. Mem.: Am. Fin. Assn. (assoc.), Orgn. of Am. Historians (assoc.), The Am. Numis. Assn. (assoc.), Coun. on Logistics Mgmt. (assoc.), Palatines to Am. (assoc.), Soc. for the History of Tech. (assoc.), Nat. Geneal. Soc. (assoc.), Pa. Heritage Soc. (assoc.), Berks County Geneal. Soc. (assoc.), The Pa. German Soc. (assoc.), The Oxford Club (life), Penn State Alumni Assn. (assoc.), Beta Gamma Sigma (assoc.). Avocations: genealogy, photography. Personal E-mail: bergerknorr@comcast.net.

BERGER-KRAEMER, NANCY, speech and language pathologist, artist; b. N.Y.C., Aug. 15, 1941; d. George G. and Ruth (Kirsch) Berger; m. Aaron Kraemer, July 10, 1966; children: Lea, Steven. BA, Adelphi U., 1963; MS in Edn., Queens Coll., 1968; cert. clin. competency in speech pathology. Lic. and cert. speech and lang. pathologist, N.Y., N.J.; permanent cert. speech and hearing for handicapped, N.Y. Speech therapist Dist. # 24 Sch. Sys., Valley Stream, L.I., 1962-64; dir. speech and lang., hearing/speech pathologist Port Chester Sch. Dist., Rye, N.Y., 1965-66; speech and lang. pathologist Roselle Park (N.J.) Sch. Sys., 1966-67, Willis Sch. for Educationally Handicapped, Plainfield, N.J., 1967-68, St. Barnabas Med. Ctr., West Orange, N.J., 1971-97; pvt. practice Maplewood, N.J., 1968—, Andover Twp., 1998—. Lectr., spkr. in field; cons. in field. One-woman shows include Romano Gallery, Blairstown, N.J., 2001, exhibited in group shows at N.J. Ctr. Visual Arts, Summit, City Without Walls, Newark, Bergen Mus., Jersey City Mus., Trenton City Mus., N.J. State Mus., Montclair Art Mus., Noyes Mus., Phoenix Gallery, Veridian Gallery, Newark Mus., Pindar Gallery, Gallerie Ambiente, Germany, William Carlos Williams Ctr. Arts, N.J., San Diego Art Inst., Stedman Art Gallery, New Brunswick, N.J., Fordham U.-Lowenstein Libr., N.Y.C., Johnson & Johnson, N.J., Cali Assocs., Bellemead Devel. Corp., AT&T, Nabisco Brands, Beneficial Ins. Co., Prudential Ins. Co., Pleiades Gallery, N.Y.C., Art Ctr. No. N.J., Art Assn. Harrisburg, Pa., Stamford Art Assn., Conn., Princeton (N.J.) Art assn., Bucknell U. Ctr. Gallery, Art Alliance 13th Ann. N.J. Statewide Exhibit, Skylands Ann. Art Exhibit, Sussex Arts, Heritage Coun., Sparta, N.J., Ceres Gallery, N.Y.C., Romano Gallery, Blair Acad., Blairstown, N.J., Gaelen Gallery, Whippany, N.J., Sussex C.C., Newton, NJ, Faith Ringgold Salon Exhibit, Englewood, NJ, ACA Gallery, N.Y.C., Anyone Can Fly Found., Inc., others. Mem. Am. Speech Lang. Hearing Assn., Auditory Verbal Internat. (charter, lectr. 1975-2000), Alexander Graham Bell Assn., N.J. Speech and Hearing Assn., Sussex Co. Judicial Ctr., Newton, N.J.

BERGERON, CLIFTON GEORGE, ceramic engineer, educator; b. Los Angeles, Jan. 5, 1925; s. Lewis G. and Rose C. (Dengel) B.; m. Laura H. Kaario, June 9, 1950; children— Ann Leija, Louis Kaario. BS, U. Ill., 1950, MS, 1959, PhD, 1961. Sr. ceramic engr. A. O. Smith Corp., Milw., 1950-55; staff engr. Whirlpool Corp., St. Joseph, Mich., 1955-57; research asso. U. Ill., Champaign-Urbana, 1957-61, asst. prof., 1961-63, asso. prof., 1963-67, prof., 1967-78, head dept. ceramic engring., 1978-86, prof. emeritus, 1988—. Cons. A. O. Smith Corp., Whirlpool Corp., Ingraham Richardson, U.S. Steel Corp., Pfaudler Corp., Ferro Corp. Editor, Ann. Conf. on Glass Problems. Served in U.S. Army, 1943-46, ETO. Recipient Everitt award for tchg. excellence U. Ill., 1975; NSF grantee, 1961-82. Fellow Am. Ceramic Soc. (Outstanding Educator award 1988); mem. AAAS, Nat. Inst. Ceramic Engrs. (Friedberg lectr. 1986), AAUP, KERAMOS, Am. Soc. Engring. Edn., Sigma Xi. Achievements include research in crystallization kinetics in glass; high temperature reactions. Home: 208 W Michigan Ave Urbana IL 61801-4944 Office: 105 S Goodwin Ave Urbana IL 61801-2901 E-mail: clifcraft@aol.com.

BERGERON, EARLEEN FOURNET, actress; b. New Orleans, Aug. 7, 1938; d. Earl Joseph Fournet and Lucia (Cuccia) Wadsworth; m. James Ronald Bergeron Sr., June 17, 1961; children: Blanche Theresa, Michele Yvette, James Ronald Jr. B in Social Sci. in Theatre and Speech, Loyola U., 1960. Actor: (plays) The Secret Affairs of Mildred Wilde, 1977, The Boyfriend, 1977, The Shadow Box, 1979, California Suite, 1980, Hay Fever, 1985, Brighton Beach, 1986, Beyond Therapy, 1987, Steel Magnolias, 1988, 1989, Nunsense, 1990, Broadway Bound, 1991, The Women, 1993, Nunsense II, 1995, Stomping Grounds, 1995, 1996, Angels in America, Part I: Millenium Approaches, Part II: Perestroika, 1997, Spareribs, 1998, Come Back Little Sheba, 1999, The Cripple of Inishmann, 2001, Ancestral Voices, 2002, Our Town, 2002, (comml.) Goodwill, 1988, Schumpert Medical Center, 1991, Cunningham and McDonald, Plastic Surgeons, 1991, JB Cable Ads, 1995, Pierre Bossier Mall, 1996; (films) Man in the Moon, 1990, (TV series) Rescue 911, 1991. Bd. dirs. Port Players, Shreveport, La.; assoc. mem. Co. Repertory Theatre, Inc., Project Shakespeeare in Schs.; active Shreveport Med. Aux., 1968—97, mem. exec. bd., 1976—78; mem. Shreveport Opera Guild, 1972—97; area leader fund dr. Am. Cancer Soc., Shreveport, 1985—89. Named one of Outstanding Team Capts., United Way Fund, 1969. Mem.: Shreveport Little Theatre Guild (bd. dirs. 1985—86), Strand Theatre, Majorie Lyons Playhouse, Shreveport Little Theatre. Roman Catholic.

BERGERON, ELMO P. chemical engineer, consultant; b. Gray, La., Dec. 18, 1936; s. Elmo P. and Estelle F. Bergeron; m. Carolyn Gaudet, Nov. 30, 1963; 1 child, Ann Michele. BS in Chem. Engring., La. State U., Baton Rouge, 1960, MS, 1961, PhD, 1963. Registered profl. engr., La. Devel. engr. Allied Chem., Morristown, N.J., 1963-66; sys. engr., process specialist Dow Chem., Plaquemine, La., 1966-74, process cons. Terneuzen, Netherlands, 1974-76, process cons., project mgr. Plaquemine, 1977-93; cons., 1993—. Contbr. articles to profl. jours.; patentee in fields of math. modeling, control of chem. processes and vapor deposition. Named to Outstanding Young Men of Am., 1970. Mem. AIChE, La. Soc. Profl. Engrs. Republican. Roman Catholic. Avocations: reading, photography, woodworking.

BERGERON, ROBERT FRANCIS, JR., (TERRY BERGERON), software engineer; b. Gloucester, Mass., Jan. 23, 1942; s. Robert Francis and Jean Ann (Francis) B.; children: Robert, Karin, Kristin; m. Marion Louise Pisarchuk, July 14, 1979; children: Steven, Tanya. ScB summa cum laude, Brown U., 1964; PhD math., MIT, 1968. Rsch. assoc. Bolt Beranek & Newman, Cambridge, Mass., 1968; instr. math MIT, Cambridge, 1969; mem. tech. staff Bell Lab., Whippany, N.J., 1969-72, supr., 1972-84; tech. mgr. AT&T Bell Lab., Warren, N.J., 1984-95; cons., sr. mgr. Cotelligent, Liberty Corner, N.J., 1996-2000; cons. Smithville, N.J., 2001—. Patentee in field; contbr. articles to profl. jours. Home and Office: 102 Southhampton Dr Smithville NJ 08205

BERGERON, WILTON LEE, physician; b. Scott, La., Feb. 13, 1933; s. Lee and Ida (Duhon) B.; m. Juanita Marie Landry, Aug. 3, 1957; children: David, Marcel, René, Jeanne. BS, U. South La., 1956; MD, La. State U., 1958. Diplomate Am. Bd. Allergy and Immunology. Intern Confederate Meml. Med. Ctr. (now La. State U. Med. Sch.), Shreveport, 1958-59; resident Lafayette (La.) Charity Hosp., 1959-60; fellow in allergy Tulane U. Med. Sch., New Orleans, 1968-70; pvt. practice Lafayette and Scott, La., 1960—; allergist, 1970—. Pres. Secular Franciscan Order, 1990-93. Mem. La. Allergy Soc. (former pres.). Republican. Roman Catholic. Avocations: fishing, computers. Home and Office: PO Box 98 # 90 Scott LA 70583-0098

BERGERSON, DAVID RAYMOND, lawyer; b. Mpls., Nov. 23, 1939; s. Raymond Kenneth and Katherine Cecille (Langworthy) Bergerson; m. Nancy Anne Heeter, Dec. 22, 1962; children: W. Thomas C., Kirsten Finch, David Raymond. BA, Yale U., 1961; JD, U. Minn., 1964. Bar: Minn. 1964. Assoc. Fredrikson Law Firm, Mpls., 1964-67; atty. Honeywell Inc., Mpls., 1967-74, asst. gen. counsel, 1974-82, v.p., asst. gen. counsel, 1983-84, v.p., gen. counsel, 1984-92; pvt. practice law Mpls., 1992-94; v.p., sec. Telcom Sys. Svcs., Inc., Plymouth, Minn., 1994-96, dir., cons., 1996-97; v.p. bd. dirs. Hogan Bergerson, Inc., Mpls., 1997—. Mem. city coun. Minnetonka Beach, Minn., 2001—; bd. dirs. Pillsbury Neighborhood Svcs., Inc., Mpls., 1983—92. Republican. Avocations: scuba diving, bird-hunting. Home: 2303 Huntington Point Rd E Wayzata MN 55391-9740 Office: Hogan Bergerson Inc 4040 IDS Ctr Minneapolis MN 55402 E-mail: dbergerson1@mchsi.com.

BERGERSON, NANCY DAHL, life and health underwriter, paralegal; b. Waco, Tex., Sept. 18, 1954; d. Howard Edward and Gladys Marie (Haynes) Dahl; children: Russell Edward Johnston, Dennis Aaron Johnston. Student, U. So. Maine, Portland; cert., Nat. Acad. Paralegal Studies, 1991. Exec. sec. to state court adminstr. State of Maine, Portland, Maine, 1993-95; risk mgmt. technician UNUM Corp., Portland, Maine, 1996-99; life and health ins. underwriter, 1999—. Vol. Maine Audubon Soc. Mem. Greenpeace. Avocations: camping, winter sports. Home and Office: 302 Plaza Dr Apt 5 Dover NH 03820-2446

BERGESEN, ROBERT NELSON, transportation consultant; b. Phila., Pa., Nov. 1, 1937; s. Bernhard E. and Carol Pearl (Nelson) B.; m. Jean Nicol, Apr. 23, 1966; children: Susan, Jean, Jeffrey. BA, Cornell U., 1959, MBA, 1961. With Price Waterhouse and Co., NYC, 1961-63; sys. analyst Warner-Lambert, Morris Plains, NJ, 1963-66; asst. contr. C.T.I., NYC, 1970-71; contr. Flexi-Van Leasing, NYC, 1971-75; from controller to gen. mgr. Vt. Transit Co., Inc., Burlington, Vt., 1977-2000. Mem. New Eng. Bus. Assn. (bd. dir. 1993-2000). Lutheran. Home: 182 Morningside Dr Middlebury VT 05753-1074 E-mail: rbergesen@hotmail.com.

BERGESON, MARVIN ERNEST, pediatrician; b. Seattle, Feb. 28, 1950; s. Ernest Axel Eugene and Martha Bergeson; m. Cindy Lewanne Little, Aug. 21, 1971; children: Bo Eric, Jon Carl, Will Ernst. BA, Augustana Coll., 1972; MD, U. Ill., Peoria, 1977. Diplomate Am. Bd. Pediat.; lic. physician, Wash., Alaska. Tchg. asst. biol. scis. U. Ill., 1972-73; intern, then resident in pediat. Madigan Army Med. Ctr., Tacoma, 1977-80; fellow in developmental pediat. Med. Sch. Harvard U., Boston, 1982; pvt. practice Tanana Valley Clinic, Fairbanks, Alaska, 1984—, also bd. dirs., mem. exec. com., 1986-93, 99—. Chmn. dept. pediat. Fairbanks Meml. Hosp., 1985-87; mem. drug utilization rev. State of Alaska, 1992-98. Co-contbr. articles to profl. jours. Bd. dirs. Alaska Crippled Children's Assn., 1983-89, v.p., 1984-85, 87, pres., 1985-87, 87-89; bd. dirs. Fairbanks Counseling and Adoption, 1985-93, v.p., 1986-87, pres., 1990-92, treas., 1992-93; mem. exec. com. Fairbanks Child Sexual Abuse Task Force, 1985-87, Midnight Sun coun. Boy Scouts Am., 1989-92; founding mem. Youth at Risk Multidisciplinary Team, 1990-93, Super Substance Use, Pregnancy, Edn. and Resources, 1990-2000; hon. bd. dirs. Resource Ctr. for Parents and Children, 1987—; pres. bd. dirs. Samaritan Counseling Ctr., 1996-2003; bd. dirs. Alaska Health Care Network, 1997—, v.p., 1999—; treas. Christ Luth. Ch.,

1981-88, mem. ch. coun., 1982-85. Maj. U.S. Army, 1977—84. Recipient Leadership award Ill. Alumni Assn., 1977, Granville A. Bennett award for contbns. to med. edn., 1977, Pediat. award for Excellence, Ross Labs., 1977, Friends of Edn. award Beta chpt. Delta Kappa Gamma, 1988, award for Outstanding Cmty. Work, Resource Ctr. for Parents and Children, 1988, award for Vol. Svc. to Fairbanks Cmty., Arctic Alliance for People, 1988, Parent Support Group Cert. of Svc. award City of Fairbanks, 1993. Fellow Am. Acad. Pediat.; mem. AMA, North Pacific Pediat. Soc., Alaska State Med. Assn. (councilor 1989-91), Fairbanks Counseling and Adoption-Bishop Whelan Soc., Omicron Delta Kappa, Beta Beta Beta. Home: 1621 Gonzaga Way Fairbanks AK 99709-6764 Office: Tanana Valley Med Clinic 1001 Noble St Fairbanks AK 99701-4977

BERGESON, SCOTT D. education educator; PhD, U. of Wis. at Madison, 1990—95. Asst. prof. Brigham Young U., Provo, Utah, 1998—; nrc postdoctoral fellow Nat. Inst. of Standards and Tech., Gaithersburg, Md., 1996—98. Fellow NRC Postdoctoral Fellowship, NRC, Nat. Inst. of Standards and Tech., 1996-1998. Mem.: Optical Soc. of Am. (topical editor 2000—03), Am. Phys. Soc. Mem. Lds Ch. Avocation: running. Office: Brigham Young U N-283 Esc Provo UT 84602 E-mail: scott.bergeson@byu.edu.

BERGETHON, KAARE ROALD, retired college president; b. Tromso, Norway, June 8, 1918; arrived in U.S., 1926, naturalized, 1930; s. Maximilian and Petra Ruud (Olsen) B.; m. Katherine Lind, Apr. 4, 1942; children: Bruce L., Peter R. AB, DePauw U., 1938; MA, Cornell U., Ithaca, N.Y., 1940, PhD, 1945; Litt.D., Brown U., 1959, Franklin and Marshall Coll., 1959, New England Coll., 1998; LL.D., Rutgers U., 1959, Muhlenberg Coll., 1959, Lehigh U., 1959, Waynesburg Coll., 1960, DePauw U., 1961, Gannon Coll., 1978, Lafayette Coll., 1978, Temple U., 1978, Allegheny Coll., 1979, Bloomfield Coll., 1980. With Walter Kidde Constructors Inc., N.Y.C., 1938-39, 41-44; instr. German Syracuse (N.Y.) U., 1945-46, Brown U., 1946-47, asst. prof. German, asst. to chmn. divsn. modern langs., 1947-52, assoc. dean, 1952-55, assoc. prof. German, 1953-58, dean, 1955-58, prof. German, 1958; pres. Lafayette Coll., Easton, Pa., 1958-78, pres. emeritus, 1978—; interim chief exec. and cons. Bloomfield (N.J.) Coll., 1979-80, interim pres., cons., 1986-87; vice chmn. Econ. Devel. Coun. of N.Y.C., Inc. and; exec. dir. Nat. Alliance of Bus. of N.Y.C., 1980-81; interim pres. New Eng. Coll., Henniker, N.H., 1981-82, pres., 1982-85; ednl. cons. Easton, 1985-95; interim pres., cons. Wells Coll., Aurora, N.Y., 1987-88. Author: Grammar for Reading German, 1950, alt. edit., 1963, rev. edit., 1979, also articles in profl. publs. Past pres. Presbyn. Coll. Union; past pres. Middle States Assn. Colls. and Secondary Schs.; trustee Charlotte W. Newcombe Found., Princeton, N.J.; bd. dirs. Presbyn. Housing & Svcs. Corp., Camp Hill, Pa. Mem. Phi Beta Kappa, Phi Eta Sigma, Phi Kappa Phi, Beta Theta Pi, Sigma Delta Chi, Alpha Phi Omega. Unitarian Universalist. Home: 1312 Kirkland Village Cir Bethlehem PA 18017-4759

BERGEVIN, V. RÉAL, customer relationship management executive; b. Oshawa, Mar. 9, 1963; Bus. degree Sir Wilfrid Laurier U., 1986. With General Motors, 1984—88; with Wardair Airlines, 1988—90; with Rogers Cablesystems, 1990—92; founder John Moss Assoc., 1992—96; founder, pres. NuComm Internat., 1991—. Pub. (other) 23 Steps to an Effective Call Centre, 2000. Recipient Niagara Entrepreneur Yr. Award. Mem.: Can. Mktg. Assn., Direct Mktg. Assn. Office: NuComm Internat Corbloc Bldg 80 King St 3d Fl Saint Catharines ON Canada L2R 7G1

BERGEY, GREGORY KENT, neurology educator, neuroscientist; b. Bryn Mawr, Pa., Nov. 9, 1949; s. Robert Harr and Kathryn (Schmidt) B.; m. Stefanie Friday Antonakos, Aug. 27, 1972; children: Alyssa Noelle, Alexander Christian. AB, Princeton U., 1971; MD, U. Pa., 1975. Diplomate Am. Bd. Psychiatry and Neurology, diplomate internal medicine. Intern internal medicine Yale U., New Haven, 1975-76, resident internal medicine, 1975-77; fellow neurophysiology Lab. Devel. Neurobiology Nat. Inst. Child Health and Human Devel., NIH, Bethesda, Md., 1977-79, 82; resident neurology Johns Hopkins, Balt., 1979-83; assoc. prof. U. Md. Sch. Medicine, Balt., 1989-96, prof. neurology and physiology, 1996-99; dir. Md. Epilepsy Ctr. Md. Epilepsy Ctr., Balt., 1988-99; prof. neurology Johns Hopkins Sch. Medicine, Balt., 1999—; dir. Johns Hopkins Epilepsy Ctr., Balt., 1999—, vice chmn. for neurol. labs., 2002—. Contbr. articles to med. jours. Lt. cmdr. USPHS, 1977-79, 81-82. Mem. Soc. for Neurosci., Am. Acad. Neurology, Am. Epilepsy Soc. (bd. dirs. 1999-2002. Office: 5207 Springlake Way Baltimore MD 21212-3421 also: Johns Hopkins Hosp Dept Neurology Meyer 2-147ogy 600 N Wolfe St Baltimore MD 21287-0005

BERGFIELD, GENE RAYMOND, engineering educator; b. Granite City, Ill., July 11, 1951; s. Walter Irvin Bergfield and Venie Edith (Sanders) Bennett; m. Juanita Pauline Kapp, Sept. 19, 1970; children: Gene Raymond Jr., Timothy Shawn. BA in Applied Behavioral Scis., Nat. Coll. Edn., Chgo., 1988. Field engr. Westinghouse PGSD, St. Louis, 1979-81, instr. Phila., 1982-84, asst. resource mgr. Chgo., 1984-89; power plant instr. Westinghouse PGPD, Orlando, Fla., 1989-93; ops. and maintenance supr. Edison Mission O&M Inc., Auburndale, Fla., 1993-97; power plant cons. PenPower, Auburndale, Fla., 1997-99; ind. power plant cons., 1999—. With USN, 1971-79.

BERGFORS, CONSTANCE MARIE, artist, educator; b. Quincy, Mass., Feb. 8, 1931; d. Fred Eric Bergfors and H. Margaret Sandberg; m. Andrew E. Rice, Dec. 2, 1972; children: Stefan Andrej, Brandt Eric. BA, Smith Coll., 1952; postgrad., Concoran Coll. Art, Washington, D.C., 1956, postgrad., 1957, postgrad., 1981, postgrad., 1982, Acad. di Belle Arte, Palermo, Naples, and Rome, Italy, 1957—60. Dir. Cabin John Visual Studies Workshop, Cabin John, Md., 1970—75; founding mem. Gallery 10, Washington, 1974—78; tchr. sculpture dept. Corcoran Sch. Art, Washington, 1991—95. Judge art scholarships for h.s. srs., 1981—2001. One-woman shows include Peabody, Rivlin, Gore, Caldouhos and Lambert Law Firm, Washington, 1970, Gallery Modern Art, Fredericksburg, Va., 1974, Gallery 10, Washington, 1974, 1976, U.S. Govt., 1978, Langley, Va., 1985, Galleria Editalia, Rome, 1980, Strathmore Hall Arts Ctr., Rockville, Md., 1984, Capital Ctr. Gallery, Landover, Md., 1984, Plum Gallery, Kensington, Md., 1986, 1988, 1991, Cmty. Gallery Lancaster, Pa., 1988, South Shore Art Ctr., Cohasset, Mass., 1988, Urban Inst., Washington, 1996, Workshop Gallery, Cabin John, Md., 1997, Temple Sinai Commn., Washington, 1998, Renwick Alliance visits the Workshop Gallery, 2000, Arts Coun. of Montgomery County, 2000, exhibited in group shows at 14 Sculptors Gallery, N.Y.C., 1977, Art Barn, Washington, 1983, Georgetown Ct. Artists' Space, 1984, Arlington Arts Ctr., Va., 1984, 1985, Three Rivers Arts Festival, Pitts., 1984, Sculpture 84 Washington Square, Washington, 1984, Washington Women's Art Ctr., 1985, Audubon Naturalist Soc. Sculpture Show, Washington, 1985, Brandeis Coll. Art Exhibit, Rockville, Md., 1986, D.C. Sculpture Now Show Summer Sch. Mus., Washington, 1989, Bldg. Mus., 1989—90, Montgomery County Art Exhibit, Rockville, Md., 1990, Internat. Sculpture 90 Montgomery Coll., 1990, Washington Sculpture Group Show Summer Sch., Washington, 1990, Mus. Nat. de Belas Artes, Rio de Janeiro, 1991—92, Oxon Hill Manor Found., Oxon Hill, Md., 1992, Fairfax County Coun. Arts Northern Va. C.C., Annandale, Va., 1992, Washington Sculptors Group Exhbn., Bethesda, Md., 1992, Fairfax County Coun. Arts Northern Va. C.C., 1993, The Cutting Edge: 20 Years at Gallery 10, Washington, 1994, Corcoran Sch. Art Washington Square, 1994, Washington Sculptors Group Show Washington Square, 1995, Arts 901, 1996, Bldg. Mus., 1999—2000, Represented in permanent collections. Recipient Mary Lay Thom award for Outstanding Achievement in Sculpture, Washington, 1983, Montgomery County Purchase prize, Exec. Office Bldg, Rockville, Md., 1987, 3rd prize, Montgomery County Art Exhibit, Strathmore Hall, Rockville, Md., 1990. Avocations: travel, architecture, archaeology. Home: 6517 80th St Cabin John MD 20818-1208 Home Fax: 301-229-4293.

BERGGREN, DICK, editor; b. Westerly, R.I., May 27, 1942; s. Richard and Lorraine Berggren; m. Kathy Berggren, July 19, 1964. BS, So. Conn. State, 1964; MS, Tufts U., 1967, PhD, 1970. Editor Performance Media, Ipswich, Mass., 1977—. TV personality Stas. Fox, Speed Channel, Fox Sports Net, FX. Recipient Deery award Race Promoters Am., 1986, Frank Blunk award Ea. Motorsport Press Assn., 1979, McLemore award, Unocal Corp., 1983, Don Martin award, 1998; named to Dirt Motorsports Hall of Fame, Sprint Car Hall of Fame. Mem. Am. Automobile Racing Writers and Broadcasters Assn., Ea. Motorsport Press Assn., Nat. Motorsports Press Assn. Office: Speedway Ill Mag 107 Elm St Salisbury MA 01952-1803 E-mail: dberggren@speedwayillustrated.com.

BERGGREN, JEAN R. psychiatrist; b. Feb. 5, 1941; BA, Radcliffe Coll., 1962; MD, Case Western Res. U., 1966, MA in Bioethics, 1997. Divsn. chief cons./liaison psychiatry Mt. Sinai Med. Ctr., Cleve., 1994-97, interim dept. dir. psychiatry, 1997-99, dept. dir. psychiatry, 1999-2000; asst. prof. dept. psychiatry Case Western Res. U. Sch. Medicine, Cleve. Asst. prof. dept. bioethics Case Western Res. U., 2002—; co. dir. clin. ethics U. Hosps. of Cleve., 2002—. Office: 2460 Fairmount Blvd Ste 320 Cleveland OH 44106-3164

BERGGREN, WILLIAM ALFRED, geologist, research micropaleontologist, educator; b. N.Y.C., Jan. 15, 1931; s. Wilhelm Fritjof and Lilly Maria (Skog) B.; m. Lois Albee, June 19, 1954 (div. July 1981); children: Erik, Anna Lisa, Anders, Sara Maria; m. Marie Pierre Aubry, June 19, 1982 BS, Dickinson Coll., 1952; M.Sc., U. Houston, 1957; PhD, U. Stockholm, 1960, D.Sc., 1962; doctorate (hon.), U. Utrecht, 2001. Research micropaleontologist Oasis Oil Co., Tripoli, Libya, 1962 65; asst. scientist Woods Hole Oceanographic Inst., Mass., 1965-68, assoc. scientist, 1968-71, sr. scientist, 1971-98, sr. scientist emeritus, 1998—; Disting. vis. prof. Rutgers U., New Brunswick, N.J., 2001—. Adj. prof. Brown U., Providence, 1968-93. Editor: Catastrophes and Earth History, 1984, Late Eocene-Early Oligocene Climatic and Biotic Change, 1992, Geochronology Time-Scales and Global Stratigraphic Correlation, 1995, Late Paleocene-Early Eocene Climate and Biotic Events, 1998; contbr. articles to sci. jours. Recipient Cushman Found. award for foraminiferal rsch., 1995, Raymond C. Moore medal in paleontology Soc. of Sedimentary Geology, 1997. Fellow Geol. Soc. Am., Geol. Soc. London (hon.); mem. NAS (Mary Clark Thompson medal 1982), Am. Assn. Petroleum Geologists, Soc. Econ. Paleontologists and Mineralogists (hon.), Paleontol. Soc. Am. (co-editor jour. 1980-84), Am. Geophys. Union, Geol. Soc. Switzerland. Avocation: skiing. Office: Woods Hole Oceanographic Inst 22 Water St Woods Hole MA 02543-1024

BERGGREN-MOILANEN, BONNIE LEE, education educator; b. L'Anse, Mich., June 2, 1940; d. Alvin Carl and Emma Leola (Wandell) Lydman; m. Grant Lorns Berggren, Jr., Aug. 22, 1959; children: Grant Victor Berggren, Rex Alvin Berggren, Konnie Kay Berggren; m. Glenn Moilanen, 2003. BA, U. Hawaii, 1961; MA, Ea. Mich. U., 1988; MA in Ednl. Adminstrn., No. Mich. U., 1991. Tchr. home econs. Baraga (Mich.) Twp. Schs., 1960-61, L'Anse Twp. Schs., 1963-65, Spencerport (N.Y.) Cen. Schs., 1979-84; presch. tchr. NCA Sch., Cmty. Action Agy., Hermansville, Mich., 1971-73; circulation supr. Spring Arbor (Mich.) Coll. Libr., 1985-87; adj. prof., supr. student tchrs. No. Mich. U., Marquette, 1989—96; co-owner, co-mgr. Menominee (Mich.) Floral, 1993-96; curriculum and tng. coord./spl. project coord. Campus Crusade for Christ, Children of The World Dept., San Clemente, Calif., 1997-2000; sr. staff Internat. Student Resources Campus Crusade for Christ, Madison, Wis., 2000—. Tchr. trainer Negaunee Pub. Schs., Negaunee, Mich., 1988—90; leader workshop Republic-Michigamme Schs., Republic, Mich., 1989—90; mem. evaluation team Marquette Pub. Schs., 1991; mem. tchr. edn. adv. coun. No. Mich. U., Marquette, 1991—96, mem. Hoppes award com., 1990—92, mem. pers. com., 1992. Libr. bd. Republic-Michigamme Schs., 1988—91; spkr. Christian Women's Club, 1989—90; bd. regents Liberty U., 1990—91; active Operation Carelift to Russia, 1997, Operation Sunrise to Africa, 2002. Fellow: Roberts Wesleyan Coll.; mem.: AAUW, DAV Aux. (life; Mich. historian 1975), AAUP, Concerned Women Am., U. Hawaii Alumni Assn., Ea. Mich U. Alumni Assn., Univ. Women No. Mich. U., Phi Delta Kappa, Phi Kappa Phi. Baptist. Avocations: reading, travel, writing, crafts. Home: 10 Oakbridge Ct Madison WI 53717 E-mail: bonnielb@chorus.net.

BERGHAHN, KLAUS LEO, German and Jewish studies educator; b. Duesseldorf, Germany, Aug. 5, 1937; arrived in U.S., 1967; s. Wilhelm and Anna (Bong) B.; m. Doris E. Beyer, Aug. 10, 1966; 1 child, Marcus J. Student, U. Cologne, Germany, 1957-59; Staatsexamen, U. Muenster, Germany, 1963, Dr phil, 1967. Tutor, asst. U. Muenster, 1963-67; asst. prof. German studies U. Wis., Madison, 1967-71, assoc. prof., 1971-73, prof., 1973—, chmn. German dept., 1994-97, mem. senate, 1974-78, 85-87, dir. ctr. German European studies, 1998—, Weinstein-Bascom prof. German and Jewish studies, 1999—. Vis. prof. Free U. Berlin, 1978, U. Bielefeld, Germany, 1980-81, U. Giessen, Germany, 1983, 92, U. Mich., Ann Arbor, 1984, U. Calif., Davis, 1989, Hebrew U., Jerusalem, 1993; mem. adv. bd. German Am. Art Found., Chgo., 1995-99; mem. German sect. Fulbright Commn., 1995-98; mem. adv. bd. German dept. Harvard U., 1994-95, 96-97; organizer spl. sessions, confs. and symposia, 1983—. Author: Formen der Dialogführung in Schillers klassischen Dramen, 1970, Friedrich Schiller: Vom Pathetischen und Erhabenen, 1970, Friedrich Schiller: Kallias oder über die Schönheit, 1971, Briefwechsel zwischen Schiller und Körner, 1973, Schillers Gedichte, 1980, G.E. Lessing: Hamburgische Dramaturgie, 1981, Schiller Ansichten eines Idealisten, 1986, (with Beate Pinkerneil) Am Beispiel Wilhelm Meister, 2 vols., 1980, Grenzen der Toleranz, 2000; editor: (with Reinhold Grimm) Schiller Zur Theorie und Praxis der Dramen, 1972, Wesen und Formen des Komischen im Drama, 1975, Utopian Vision Technological Innovation Poetic Imagination, 1990, (with Hans Ulrich Seeber) Literarische Utopien von Morus bis zur Gegenwart, 1983, 2d edit., 1985, (with Holub and Scherpe) Responsibility and Committment. Ethische Postulate der Kulturvermittlung. Festschrift für Jost Hermand, 1996; editor: Schiller Zur Geschichtlichkeit seines Werkes, 1976, The German-Jewish Dialogue-Reconsidered, 1996, Friedrich Schiller: Ueber die aesthetische Erzhiehung des Menschen, 2000, Goethe in German-Jewish Culture, 2001, Friedrich Y. Schiller: Ueber naire und sentimentalische Dichtung, 2002, Cultural Representations of the Holocoust in Germany, 2002; mem. editl. bd. Monatshefte, 1975, Mich. Germanic Studies, 1985, Goethe Yearbook, 1985, German Politics and Society, 2000; contbr. articles and revs. to profl. jours., chpts. to books. Fellow VW-Found., Germany, 1965-67, Am. Philos. Soc., 1969, 73, Inst. for Rsch. in Humanities, U. Wis., 1972, 89-94, Ctr. for Interdisciplinary Rsch., Bielefeld, 1980-81, German Acad. Exch. Svc., 1990, 99, also others; 14 summer rsch. grants U. Wis. Grad. Sch. Mem. MLA (19th and early 20th century German lit. divsn. exec. com. 1974-78, chmn. 1977, mem. 18th and early 19th century German lit. divsn. 1983-88, chmn. 1987, mem. adv. bd. MLA Profession 1997-99), Am. Assn. Tchrs. German (program and selection com. 1990), Internat. Union Germanists (program com. 1995), Lessing Soc., Schiller Soc. (medal 1984), Goethe Soc. Avocations: reading, writing, music, theater, chess. Home: 2908 Oxford Rd Madison WI 53705-2220 Office: U Wis Dept German 860 Van Hise Hall 1220 Linden Dr Madison WI 53706-1525

BERGHAHN, VOLKER ROLF, history educator; b. Berlin, Feb. 15, 1938; came to U.S., 1988; s. Alfred and Gisela (Henke) B.; m. Marion Ilse Koop, Dec. 29, 1969; children: Sascha, Vivian, Melvin. MA, U. N.C. Chapel Hill, 1961; PhD, U. London, 1964; Habil., U. Mannheim, 1966-69. Sr. scholar St. Anthony's Coll., Oxford, Eng., 1964-66; rsch. fellow U. Mannheim, 1966-69; lectr. U. East Anglia, Norwich, 1969-71; reader U. E. Anglia, Norwich, 1971-75; prof. U. Warwick, Coventry, 1975-88, Brown U., Providence, 1988-97, Columbia U., N.Y.C., 1998—. Author: Der Stahlhelm, 1966, Der Tirpitz Plan, 1970, Germany and the Approach of War, 1973, Modern Germany, 1982, The Americanization of West German Industry, 1945-1973, 1986, Otto A. Friedrich, 1902-1975, 1992, Imperial Germany, 19871-1914, 1995, America and the Intellectual Cold Wars in Europe, 2001, Europa im Zeitalter der Weltkriege, 2002. Various grants and fellowships. Fellow Royal Hist. Soc.; mem. German History Soc. (pres. 1986-88), Am. Hist. Assn., German Studies Assn. Avocations: tennis, walking. Office: Columbia U Dept History New York NY 10027 E-mail: vrb7@columbia.edu.

BERGHOFF, PAUL HENRY, lawyer; b. Chgo., Aug. 25, 1956; s. John Colerick Sr. and Doris Margaret (Anderson) B.; m. Kathryn Elaine Thompson, May 30, 1981. BA cum laude in Chemistry, Lawrence U., 1978; JD cum laude, U. Mich., 1981. Bars: Ill. 1981, U.S. Dist. Ct. (no. dist.) Ill. 1981, U.S. Ct. Appeals (fed. cir.) 1983, U.S. Supreme Ct. 1986. Assoc. Allegretti & Witcoff, Ltd., Chgo., 1981-85, ptnr., 1985-96; founding ptnr. McDonnell Boehnen Hulbert & Berghoff, Chgo., 1996—. Mem. Intellectual Property Owners, Am. Intellectual Property Law Assn. Mem. United Ch. of Christ. Avocation: music. Office: McDonnell Boehnen Hulbert & Berghoff 300 S Wacker Dr Ste 3200 Chicago IL 60606-6709 E-mail: berghoff@mbhb.com.

BERGIA, ROGER MERLE, school system administrator; b. Peoria, Ill, Nov. 26, 1937; s. Merle Frederick and Doris Ann (Markham) B.; m. Valerie Jean Lane, Oct. 16, 1960; children: Lori, Amy, Beth. BA, Eureka Coll., 1960; MA, Bradley U., 1967, postgrad., 1968—. Tchr., coach jr. h.s. Peoria Hts. (Ill.) Sch., 1960-65; prin. Kelly Ave Grade Sch., Peoria Hts., 1965-74; supt. Peoria Hts. Schs., 1974—. Adminstrv. agt. Ill. State Bd. Early Childhood Edn. Early Childhood Exemplary Program. Named Sch. Adminstr. of Yr., Ill. Bd. Edn., 1981-82; recipient Exemplary Practices award, 1992. Mem. Phi Delta Kappa, Lambda Chi Alpha. Republican. Presbyterian. Home: 6723 N Gem Ct Peoria IL 61614-2901 Office: 500 E Glen Ave Peoria Heights IL 61616

BERGIN, ALLEN ERIC, clinical psychologist, educator; b. Spokane, Wash, Aug. 4, 1934; s. Bernard F. and Vivian Selma (Kullberg) B.; m. Marian Shafer, June 4, 1955; children: David, Sue, Cyndy, Kathy, Eric, Ben, Patrick, Daniel, Michael. BS, Brigham Young U., 1956, MS, 1957; PhD, Stanford U., 1960. Diplomate Am. Bd. Profl. Psychology, 1969. Fellow U. Wis., Madison, 1960-61; prof. psychology and edn. Tchr. Coll., Columbia U., NYC, 1961-72; prof. psychology Brigham Young U., Provo, Utah, 1972-99, prof. emeritus, 1999—, dir. Values Inst., 1976-78, dir. clin. psychology, 1989-93. Assessment officer Peace Corps, Washington, 1961-66; cons. NIMH, Rockville, Md., 1969-75, 90. Co-author: Changing Frontiers in Psychotherapy, 1972, A Spiritual Strategy for Counseling and Psychotherapy, 1997; co-editor: Handbook of Psychotherapy, 1971, 4th edit., 1994 (citation classic 1979), Handbook of Pyschotherapy and Religious Diversity, 2000; author: Eternal Values and Personal Growth, 2002. Bishop LDS Ch., Emerson, NJ, 1970-72, Provo, 1981-84, stake pres., Church Ed. Mission, San Diego, 1992-95, 2002-03; mem. steering com. Utah Gov.'s Conf. on Families, Salt Lake City, 1979-80. Recipient Biggs-Pine award Am. Assn. Counseling and Devel., 1986, Maeser rsch. award Brigham Young U. Alumni Assn., 1986, exemplary paper award Templeton Found., 1996, Am. Psychiat. Assn. (Pfister award 1998). Fellow APA (Disting. Contbn. to Knowledge award 1989, William James award div. 36 1990); mem. Soc. for Psychotherapy Integration, Soc. for Sci. Study Religion, Soc. for Psychotherapy Rsch. (pres. 1974-75, Disting. Career award 1998), Assn. Mormon Counselors (pres. 1979-80). Republican. Avocations: world travel, writing.

BERGLEITNER, GEORGE CHARLES, JR., investment banker; b. Bklyn., July 16, 1935; s. George Charles and Marie (Preitz) B.; m. Betty Van Buren, Oct. 29, 1966; children: George Charles III, Michael John, Stephen William. BBA, St. Francis Coll., Bklyn., 1959; MBA, CCNY, 1961; PhD in Bus. Adminstrn. (hon.), Colo. State Christian Coll. Dir. instl. sales A.T. Brod & Co., N.Y.C., 1965-66; dir. instl. sales Weis, Voisin & Cannon, Inc., N.Y.C., 1966-67, C.B. Richard, Ellis & Co., N.Y.C., 1967 68; pres. Stamford (N.Y.) Fin. Co., also bd. dirs. Pres. M.J. Manchester & Co., Fashion & Time, Inc., B.J.B. Graphics, Inc., First Coinvestors, Inc., Smart Fit Foundations, Inc., Jay Co., Computer Holdings Corp., Ltd., Delhi Mfg. Corp., Delhi Industries, Delhi Mfg., Inc., Delhi Internat., Inc., Luxemborg; bd. dirs. Alpha Capital Corp., Am. Energy Mgmt. Corp., Stamford Fin., Electronic Tax Ctrs., Inc., L.I.U.G., L.I. Venture Capital Group, L.I. Venture Group, Del. County Indsl. Devel.; sponsor N.Y. Venture Group; bd. dirs. Indsl. Devel. Agy., Delaware County, N.Y. Chmn. Franciscan fathers Devel. Program, 1967-71; mem. Pres.'s Econ. Coun., Franciscan Spirit award, 1959-, Knight of Malta, 2001; pres. South Kortright Ctrl. Sch.; chmn. No. Catskills Econ. Devel. Coun., Econ. Devel. Coun. Stamford, Econ. Devel. Coun. Delaware County; regent St. Francis Coll.; bd. dirs. Econ. Devel. Coun., Printing Trade Sch., Cmty. Hosp. Stamford, N.Y., Stamford Econ. Devel. Coun., Delaware County Indsl. Devel. Authority County, 1999—, ECO Devel. Coun. Delaware County; sec. Delaware County Econ. Devel. Agy., 2000—; co-chair Project Strive, Albany, N.Y.; fin. com. Sacred Heart Roman Cath. Ch.; pres. Otsego Delaware Bd. Realtors, 2000; v.p. bd. dirs. Cath. Charities, 1999-2004, pres., 1999-2000; Delaware County Indsl. Devel. sec., 2000—. Paul Harris fellow Rotary Internat.; Internat. Rotary Benefactor; recipient St. Francis Coll. Alumni Fund award, 1965, Del. County Youth award, 1991, John F. Kennedy Meml. award, 1972, Internat. award for Svc. to Investment Commn., 1982, Youth Bur. award, 1991, St. Francis Prep Sch. Alumni Achievement award, 1993; named Stamford Citizen of Yr., 1992, Realtor of Yr., 1992, Col. Harper Grange Citizen of Yr., 1993. Mem.: Alumni Assn. St. Francis Coll., Am. Inst. Mgmt., Stamford C. of C. (pres. 1991—92), Otsego- Delaware Bd. Realtors (P.A.F. chmn., bd. dirs., pres.), Assn. Investment Bankers, Venture Assn. NJ (bd. dirs.), Conn. Venture Capital Assn., NY State Realtors Assn. (polit. action dir. 1999, trustee 2000—, bd. dirs., chmn. polit. action), CCNY Alumni Assn., Am. Legion, Honor Legion N.Y.C. Police Dept., Cath. War Vets., Univ. Club of Albany, KC (4th deg.), Knights of Malta, Moose, Elks. Republican. Home: Red Rock Rd Stamford NY 12167 Office: Stamford Fin Bldg Off Bd Dirs Stamford NY 12167 *With all affluence, accomplishment, and success goes the responsibility of assistance; economic, social, and physical to the less fortunate of the world.*

BERGLES, ARTHUR EDWARD, mechanical engineering educator; b. N.Y.C., Aug. 9, 1935; s. Edward H. and Victoria (Winkelmann) B.; m. Priscilla Lou Maule, June 19, 1960; children: Eric, Dwight. SB, SM, MIT, 1958, PhD, 1962; DEng (hon.), U. Porto, Portugal, 1998, Rand Afrikaans U., Johannesburg, S. Africa, 1999. Registered profl. engr., Mass. Research staff Nat. Magnet Lab., Cambridge, Mass., 1962-69; asst. prof. to assoc. prof. mech. engring. MIT, Cambridge, 1963-69, assoc. dir. heat transfer lab., 1966-69; prof. mech. engring. Ga. Inst. Tech., Atlanta, 1970-72; prof., chmn. dept. mech. engring. Iowa State U., Ames, 1972-83, prof., dir. heat transfer lab., 1983-86; Clark and Crossan prof. engring., dir. heat transfer lab. Rensselaer Poly. Inst., Troy, N.Y., 1986-97, dean of engring., 1989-92, Clark and Crossan prof. emeritus, 1997—; Martin Inst. prof. engring. U. Md., College Park, 1999—; sr. lectr. MIT, 1999—. Chmn. U.S. group heat transfer U.S./USSR Agreement, Washington, 1979-82; cons. to industry, mem. numerous adv. groups.; hon. prof. Beijing Polytechnic U. Co-author: Two-Phase Flow and Heat Transfer in the Power and Process Industries, 1981; co-editor: Two-Phase Heat Exchangers, 1988, Heat Transfer Enhancement of Heat Exchangers, 1999, others; editor: Heat Transfer in Electronic and Microelectronic Equipment, 1990; mem. editl. adv. bd. 13 jours.; contbr. numerous articles to tech. jours. Scoutmaster Boy Scout Am., Ames, 1976-84; bd. dirs. Ames Soc. for Arts, 1975-79. Recipient U.S. Sr. Scientist award Alexander von Humboldt Found., U. Hanover, Fed. Republic Germany, 1979-80, Tech. U., Munich, 1996-97, Faculty Achievement award in research Iowa State U., 1986, Nusselt-Reynolds prize Assembly Internat. Conf. on Exptl. Heat Transfer, 2001; named Anson Marston Disting. prof. engring., Iowa State U., 1981. Fellow AIAA (assoc.), ASHRAE (Edn. and Rsch. award N.E. chpt. 1993, Disting. Svc. award 1996, Anderson award 2000, Holladay award 2002), AAAS, NAE, ASME (hon. mem. 1996, v.p. 1981-85, chmn. heat transfer divsn. 1982-83, bd. govs. 1985-89, pres. 1990-91, Heat Transfer Meml. award 1979, Dedicated Svc. award 1984, Max Jakob Meml. award AIChE and ASME 1995, ASME medal 2000), Internat. Ctr. Heat and Mass Transfer (exec. com. 1984-2000, chmn. exec. com. 1996-98, Luikov medal 1998), Am. Soc. Engring. Edn. (Lamme award 1987, Centennial cert. and medal 1993); mem. AIChE (Donald Q. Kern award 1990), Soc. Automotive Engrs. (Ralph R. Teetor award 1987), Union Mech. and Elec. Engrs. and Technicians Yugoslavia (hon.), Acad. Scis. and Arts Slovenia (fgn.), Italian Nat. Acad. Scis. (fgn.), Polish Soc. Theoretical and Applied Mechanics (fgn.), Royal Acad. Engring. U.K. (fgn.), Rotary (Paul Harris fellow), Theta Chi. Republican. Lutheran. Office: Rensselaer Poly Inst Mech Aeronautical and Nuc Engring Troy NY 12180-3590 E-mail: abergles@aol.com. *My personal philosophy is to do as many things as I can, always striving for excellence and professionalism.*

BERGLUND, ROBIN G. child psychiatrist, former corporate executive; b. Milw., Oct. 12, 1945; s. Gunnar E. and V. June (Huebsch) B.; children: Victoria S., Christopher F.; m. Akiko Haraguchi, Oct., 2000; 1 child, Liri Haraguchi. BS in Biochemistry magna cum laude, Mich. State U., 1967; MBA, Harvard U., 1971; MD, Med. Univ. S.C., 1995. Engr. Eastman Kodak Co., Rochester, N.Y., 1967-69; v.p. The First Nat. Bank of Chgo., 1971-75, Wells Fargo Bank, N.A., L.A., 1975-77; exec. v.p. Ponderosa Homes, Newport Beach, Calif., 1977-84; chmn., CEO Glenfed Devel. Corp., Encino, Calif., 1984-88; pres. Lowe Enterprises Northwest, Seattle, 1988-89, Met. Homes Inc., Portland, Oreg., 1989-90; pediatrician UCLA-Cedars Sinai Med. Ctr., L.A., 1995-96; psychiatrist UCLA Neuropsychiatric Inst. and Hosp., 1996-98, child psychiatrist, 1998-2000; pvt. practice child and adult psychiatry, 2000—. Bd. dirs. United Svc. Orgn., Hollywood, Calif., 1975-80, Am. Youth Soccer Orgn., Newport Beach, Calif., 1980-84, Waring Libr. Soc., Charleston, 1992-95; scoutmaster Boy Scouts of Am., San Marino, Calif., 1984-89; vol. Children's Hosp., Seattle, 1990-91. Nat. Merit and Nat. Honor Soc. scholar, Mich. State U., 1964-67.

Mem. Am. Psychiatric Assn., Am. Acad. Child & Adolescent Psychiatry, Young Pres.'s Orgn., Blue Key, Phi Kappa Phi, Phi Eta Sigma, Delta Phi Epsilon, Omicron Delta Kappa. Avocations: travel, sailing.

BERGMAN, ALAN, lyricist, writer; b. Bklyn., Sept. 11, 1925; s. Samuel and Ruth (Margulies) Bergman; m. Marilyn Keith Bergman, Feb. 9, 1958; 1 child, Julie Rachel. Grad., Ethical Culture Sch.; BA, U. N.C.; MA, UCLA; Doctorate (hon.), Berklee Coll. Music, 1995. TV dir. CBS, Phila., 1949-53; ind. lyricist, collaborator with Marilyn Bergman, 1956—. Including TV themes Bracken's World, 1969—70, The Sandy Duncan Show, 1972, Maude, 1972—78, Good Times, 1974—79, The Nancy Walker Show, 1976, The Dumplings, 1976, Alice, 1976—82, In the Heat of the Night, 1988—84, Brooklyn Bridge, 1991—93, The Powers That Be, 1993, TV film lyrics The Hands of Time, from Brian's Song, 1971, Queen of the Stardust Ballroom, 1975 (Emmy award best dramatic underscore, 1975, score only), Sybil, 1976 (Emmy award best dramatic underscore, 1976), Too Many Springs, from Hollow Image, 1979, theatrical scores Something More, 1964, Ballroom, 1978 (Grammy award nominee for best cast show album, 1979), The Lady and the Clarinet, 1980, The Marriage-Go-Round, from The Marriage-Go-Round, 1960, Any Wednesday, from Any Wednesday, 1966, Make Me Rainbows, from Fitzwilly, 1967, feature film songs (score) In the Heat of the Night, 1967, The Windmills of Your Mind, from the Thomas Crown Affair, 1968 (Acad. award for best song, 1968, Golden Globe award for best original song, 1969), His Eyes, Her Eyes, 1968, You Must Believe in Spring, from Young Girls at Rochefort, 1968, Maybe Tomorrow, from John and Mary, 1969, Tomorrow Is My Friend, from Gaily, Gaily, 1969, There's Enough to Go Around, from Gaily, Gaily, 1969, A Smile, A Mem'ry and an Extra Shirt, from A Man Called Gannon, 1969, Sugar in the Rain, from Stiletto, 1969, What Are You Doing the Rest of Your Life?, from The Happy Ending, 1969 (Acad. award nominee for best song, 1969), I Was Born in Love With You, from Wuthering Heights, 1970, Sweet Gingerbread Man, Nobody Knows, from The Magic Garden of Stanley Sweetheart, 1970, Move, from Move, 1970, Pieces of Dreams (AKA Little Boy Lost), from Pieces of Dreams, 1970 (Acad. award nominee for best song, 1970), The Costume Ball, from Doctors' Wives, 1971, All His Children, from Sometimes a Great Notion, 1971 (Acad. award nominee for best song, 1971), Rain Falls Anywhere It Wants To, from The African Elephant, 1971, The Summer Know, from Summer of '42, 1971 (Grammy award nominee for song of the year, 1972), A Face in the Crowd, from Le Mans, 1971, Marmalade, Molasses and Honey, from The Life and Times of Judge Roy Bean, 1972 (Acad. award nominee for best song, 1972), Love's the Only Game in Town, from Pete and Tillie, 1972, Molly and Lawless John, 1972, The Way We Were, from The Way We Were, 1973 (Grammy award for song of the year, 1973, Acad. award for best song, 1973, Golden Globe award for best original song, 1974, Grammy award for best original score, 1974), Breezy's Song, from Breezy, 1973, In Every Corner of the World, from Forty Carats, 1973, Summer Wishes, Winter Dreams, from Summer Wishes, Winter Dreams, 1973, Easy Baby, from 99 and 44/100%, 1974, There'll Be Time, from Ode to Billy Joe, 1975, Evening Sun, Morning Moon, from The Yakuza, 1975, I Believe in Love, from A Star is Born, 1976 (Grammy award nominee for best original score, 1977), I'm Harry, I'm Walter, from Harry and Walter Go to New York, 1976, Hello and Goodbye, from Noon to Three, 1976, Bobby Deerfield, from Bobby Deerfield, 1977, The Last Time I Felt Like This, from Same Time Next Year, 1978 (Acad. award nominee for best song, 1978), The One and Only, from The One and Only, 1978, There's Something Funny Goin' On, from ...And Justice For All, 1979, I'll Never Say Goodbye, from The Promise, 1979 (Acad. award nominee for best song, 1979), Where Do You Catch the Bus for Tomorrow, from A Change of Seasons, 1980, Ask Me No Questions, from Back Roads, 1981, How Do You Keep the Music Playing?, from Best Friends, 1982 (Acad. award nominee best song, 1982), Think About Love, 1982, Comin' Home to You, from Author! Author!, 1982, Tootsie, from Tootsie, 1982, It Might Be You, 1982 (Acad. award nominee for best song, 1982, Grammy award nominee for best original score, 1983), If We Were in Love, from Yes, Giorgio, 1982 (Acad. award nominee for best song, 1982), Never Say Never Again, from Never Say Never Again, 1983; feature film songs Papa, Can You Hear Me?, from Yentl, 1983 (Acad. award nominee best song, 1983); feature film songs The Way He Makes Me Feel, from Yentl, 1983 (Acad. award nominee for best song, 1983), Will Someone Ever Look at Me That Way?, 1983 (Acad. award for best original score, 1983, Grammy award nominee for best original score, 1984), Little Boys, from The Man Who Loved Women, 1983, Something New in My Life, from Mickey and Maude, 1984, The Music of Goodbye, from Out of Africa, 1985, I Know the Feeling, from The January Man, 1989; feature film songs The Girl Who Used to Be Me, from Shirley Valentine, 1989 (Acad. award nominee for best song, 1989, Golden Globe nominee for best original, 1990, Grammy award nomination, 1990); feature film songs Welcome Home, from Welcome Home, 1989, Most of All You, from Major League, 1989, Dreamland, from For the Boys, 1991; feature film songs Places That Belong to You, from The Prince of Tides, 1991; feature film songs It's All There, from Switch, 1991, Moonlight, from Sabrina, 1995 (Acad. award nominee for best original song, 1996), Bogus, 1996, pop songs You Don't Bring Me Flowers (Grammy award nominee for song of the year, 1978), In the Heat of the Night, The Summer Knows, Nice 'N' Easy (Grammy award nominee for song of the year, 1960), Someone in the Dark, L.A. Is My Lady, After the Rain, I Was Born in Love With You, That Face, Look Around, I Love to Dance Like They Used to Dance, What Matters Most, One Day, A Child Is Born, Sleep Warm, Sentimental Baby, Live It Up, If I Close My Eyes, Yellow Bird, Like a Lover, Where Do You Start?, On My Way to You, Ordinary Miracles (Ace award and Emmy award for best original song), albums Never Be Afraid for Bing Crosby, The Ballad of the Blues for Jo Stafford, writer Barbra Streisand: The Concert, 1995 (Ace nominee for writing of a spl., Emmy award for Best Music & Lyrics). Served with AUS, 1943—45. Named to Songwriters Hall of Fame, 1980; recipient Singers Salute to Songwriter award, Clooney Foundation, 1986, Aggie award, Songwriter's Guild, 1987; grantee Am. Film Inst., 1976. Mem.: Motion Picture Acad. Arts and Scis. (gov.), ASCAP. Office: Gorfaine-Schwartz 13245 Riverside Dr Ste 450 Sherman Oaks CA 91423-2172

BERGMAN, ANNE NEWBERRY, civic leader; b. Weatherford, Tex., Mar. 12, 1925; d. William Douglas and Mary (Hunter) Newberry; m. Robert David Bergman, Aug. 17, 1947; children: Elizabeth Anne Bozzell, John David, William Robert. BA, Trinity U., San Antonio, 1945; postgrad., UCLA, 1946-47. Councilperson City of Weatherford, 1986-91, mayor pro tem, 1990-91; pres. Weatherford Libr. Found., 1987-97, bd. dirs., 1987—. Mem. heritage gallery com. Weatherford Pub. Libr. (Mary Martin collection), 1993-98. Founder Hist. Home Tour, Weatherford, 1972; co-chair Spring Festival Bd., 1976, Weatherford Planning and Zoning Commn., 1980—85; fundraising chair Weatherford Libr. Found., 1985—86; chair Tex. State Rev. Com. Cmty. Devel. Block Grants, 1987—91; pres. Tex. Fedn. Rep. Women, 1975—77; del.. Nat. Rep. Conv., 1988; pres. Episcopal Churchwomen's Cabinet, Diocese of Ft. Worth, 1999—2001; del. Episcopal Ch. Women Triennial, Episcopal Ch. U.S.A., 1997, 2000. Named Outstanding Rep. Woman, Tex. Fedn. Rep. Women, 1981. Mem. Parker County Rep. Women, DAR (Weatherford chpt.), Weatherford C. of C. (Outstanding Citizen of the Yr. 1988), Friends of Weatherford Pub. Libr. (life, charter pres. 1959-61, pres. 1973-74). Avocations: sailing, bridge. Home: 609 W Josephine St Weatherford TX 76086-4055

BERGMAN, BRUCE E. municipal official; m.; 2 children. BA, Simpson Coll., 1970; JD, U. Houston, 1972. Clk. to Hon. M.E. Rawlings Iowa Supreme Ct., 1973-74; assoc. Williams, Hart, Lavorato & Kirtley, West Des Moines, Iowa, 1974-78, ptnr., 1978-79, Davis, Baker & Bergman, Des Moines, 1980-85, Isaacson, Clarke & Bergman, P.C., Des Moines, 1985-89; asst. city atty. City of Des Moines Legal Dept., 1989-90, solicitor, 1990-91, chief solicitor, 1991-96, corp. counsel, 1996—. Mem.: ABA, Iowa Mcpl. Attys. Assn. (bd. dir. 1996—99, 2002—, sec., treas. 2003), Polk County Bar Assn., Iowa State Bar Assn. Home: 4508 49th St Des Moines IA 50310-2970 Office: Office of the Corp Counsel City of Des Moines City Hall 400 E 1st St Des Moines IA 50309 E-mail: bebergman@dmgov.org.

BERGMAN, BRUCE J. lawyer; b. N.Y.C., May 15, 1944; s. Lawrence A. and Myrna (Coe) B.; m. Linda A. Cantor, May 30, 1971; children: Jennifer Dana, Jason Cole. BS, Cornell U., 1966; JD, Fordham U., 1969. Bar: N.Y. 1970, D.C. 1987, U.S. Dist. Ct. (so. dist.) N.Y. 1971, U.S. Supreme Ct. 1973, U.S. Dist. Ct. (ea. dist.) N.Y. 1973, U.S. Ct. Appeals (2d cir.) 1973. Assoc. law firm Jarvis, Pilz, Buckley & Treacy, N.Y.C., 1970-76; ptnr. law firm Pedowitz & Bergman, Garden City, N.Y., 1976-80; dep. county atty. Nassau County, Mineola, N.Y., 1980-84; counsel Jonas Libert & Weinstein, Garden City, 1981-84; ptnr. Roach & Bergman, 1984-90; counsel N.Y. State Senate, 1988—; ptnr. Certilman Balin Adler & Hyman, East Meadow, N.Y., 1991—. Adj. assoc. prof. NYU Real Estate Inst., N.Y.C., 1981—; faculty mem. Mortgage Bankers Assn. Am. Sch. of Mortgage Banking, 1994—; special lectr. Hofstra Law Sch., 1998—. Author: Bergman on New York Mortgage Foreclosures, vols. 1-3, 1990; rev. edit. 2003; contbr. numerous articles to legal jours. Councilman City of Long Beach, N.Y., 1980-88. Mem. ABA, N.Y. State Bar Assn., Nassau County Bar Assn. (dir., chmn. real property law com.), Am. Coll. Real Estate Lawyers, Scribes, Am. Soc. Writers on Legal Subjects, Cornell Club (past pres.). Republican. Home: 12 Hawthorne Ln Lawrence NY 11559-2521 Office: Certilman Balin Adler & Hyman 90 Merrick Ave East Meadow NY 11554-1571 E-mail: bbergman@certilmanbalin.com.

BERGMAN, CHARLES CABE, foundation executive; b. May 1, 1933; s. Sidney Meyer and Esther Rachel (Cabe) B. AB, Harvard U., 1954. Account asst. Ketchum, MacLeod & Grove, Inc., Pitts., 1955-57; assoc. dir. devel. and alumni affairs Browne & Nichols Sch., Cambridge, Mass., 1957-59; assoc. v.p. Lavin Co., Inc., Boston and NYC, 1959-61; v.p. People to People Health Fedn., Washington, 1962-63, Inter-Am. Found. for the Arts, NYC, 1963-65; exec. v.p., treas., trustee Acad. Religion and Mental Health, NYC, 1965-72; exec. v.p., COO, dir. Inst. Religion and Health, 1972-78; sr. assoc. Jeffcoat Schoen & Morrell, 1981-82; exec. v.p., COO Pollock-Krasner Found., Inc., NYC, 1985-99, chmn. bd., CEO, 1999—. Cons. UN Ctr. on Transnat. Corps., 1979-80; dir. George Nelson & Co., N.Y.C. Cons. Adminstrv. Psychiatry Program, Yale Med. Sch., New Haven, 1971, NIMH, Argentina, 1969, Ctr. for Studies Child and Family Mental Health, NIMH, Washington, 1971; spl. adviser Pres.'s Com. on Mental Retardation, Washington, 1971, White House Conf. on Children and Youth, Washington, 1970, Maurice Falk Med. Fund, 1971; vis. lectr. U. Colo.; Presdl. fellow Aspen Inst. Humanistic Studies; mem. cultural adv. commn. N.Y.C. Dept. Cultural Affairs. Chmn. internat. coun. Am. Field Svc. Internat. Intercultural Programs; bd. dirs. The Alliance for Young Artists and Writers, Inc., NY, VSA Arts, Washington, Delfina Studios Trust, London, The Nat. Found. for Advancement in the Arts, Miami, Fla.; mem. bd. advisors Fund for Arts and Culture in Cen. and East Europe; bd. artistic advisors Creative Artists Network; former panelist NY State Coun. on Arts Visual Arts Program; mem. N.Y. State Coun. on Arts, 1999—; sr. advisor Foursome Investments, Ltd., London; adv. bd. Lucy Daniels Found., Raleigh, NC; mem. overseers' com. to visit Harvard U. Art Mus.; mem. NYC Cultural Affairs Adv. Com. Home: 24 E 82nd St # 4C New York NY 10028-0344 Office: 863 Park Ave New York NY 10021-0342

BERGMAN, DANIEL CHARLES, county official, lawyer, environmental manager; b. Corpus Christi, Tex., Aug. 18, 1943; s. Benjamin and Pearl H. B.; m. Susan Lee Axall, Aug. 15, 1965 (div. 1987); children: Erica Catherine, Kelli Lorraine. B.S. in Biology, San Diego State U., 1965, M.S., 1971; J.D., U. San Diego, 1975. Bar: Calif. 1976, U.S. Dist. Ct. (so. dist.) Calif. 1976, U.S. Ct. Appeals (9th cir.) 1977; registered environ. health specialist Calif., Ill.; cert. community coll. tchr., vector ecologist, 1971-72, supervising environ. health specialist Dept. Health Services, 1972-79, chief div. environ. health mgr., 1979-81; environ. health cons. Contra Costa (Calif.) Dept. Health Services, 1981, asst. health services dir. Div. Environ. Health, 1981-89; pres., CFO Pyrite Canyon Group, Inc., 1991—; sole practice law, San Diego and Danville, Calif., 1976— ; lectr. in field. Recipient Am. Jurisprudence awards. Mem. Am. Pub. Health Assn., Nat. Environ. Health Assn. (Presdl. citation 1977), Calif. Environ. Health Assn. (Presdl. citation 1977, 78), ABA, Calif. State Bar Assn. Office: 3200C Pyrite St Riverside CA 92509-1109

BERGMAN, DONALD ARTHUR, endocrinologist; b. Bklyn., Apr. 6, 1946; s. Joseph and Clara Bergman; m. Susan Menin, June 23, 1970; 1 child, Melissa. AB, Dartmouth Coll., 1967; MD, Jefferson Med. Coll., 1971. Diplomate: Am. Bd. Endocrinology, Am. Bd. Internal Medicine. Ob-gyn. resident Mt. Sinai Hosp., N.Y.C., 1971—72, med. resident, 1973—75, endocrinology fellow, 1975—77; asst. clin. prof. medicine Mt. Sinai Sch. Medicine, N.Y.C., 1984—97, assoc. clin. prof., 1997—; med. intern NYU Hosps., 1972—73; pvt. practice N.Y.C., 1977—. Contbg. author: Mount Sinai Book of Nutrition; contbr. articles to profl. jours.; assoc. editor (jour.) Endocrine Practice, 1996-99; co-author: Clinical Practice Guidelines for Physicians-Thyroid Cancer, 2000. Bd. dirs. N.Y. Menopause Ctr., 1997—. Capt. U.S. Army Res., 1971-77. Fellow: ACP, Am. Coll. Endocrinology (sec.-treas. 2000—01, bd. trustees 2000—01, pres.-elect 2002, pres. 2003—); mem.: Endocrine Soc., Am. Assn. Clin. Endocrinologists (bd. dirs. 1993—, chair practice stds. com. 1995—97, state chpts. 1997—2002, sec. 1999—2000, treas. 2000—01, v.p. 2001—02, co-chmn. corp. adv. bd. 2002—03, pres. 2003—, co-chmn. ann. meeting 2003). Office: 1199 Park Ave Apt (1f) New York NY 10128-1713

BERGMAN, EDWARD JONATHAN, lawyer, educator; b. Jersey City, Aug. 10, 1942; s. Abe and Ethel (Leitner) B.; m. Jennifer Shapiro, Feb. 1, 1969 (div.); children: Peter Jeremy, Jennifer Amy. BA, U. Pa., 1963; JD, Columbia U., 1966. Bar: N.J. 1974, U.S. Dist. Ct. N.J. 1974, U.S. Supreme Ct. 1989. Ptnr. Bergman & Barrett, Princeton, N.J., 1975—; pub. defender Princeton Borough, 1986—, Princeton Twp., 1988—; fed. mediator U.S. Dist. Ct., N.J., 1992—; mediator N.J. Superior Ct., 1995—. Lectr. Woodrow Wilson Sch., Princeton U., 1990-92, dept. politics, 2003-; affiliated faculty U. Pa. Wharton Sch. of Bus. Dept. of Legal Studies, Phila., 1995—; vis. lectr. U. Calif. at Berkeley, St. Petersburg U. Joint Mgmt. Program, Russia, 1995-99; offcl. dispute resolver NHLA/AAHA; acad. dir. negotiation workshops IGE Ltd., India, 1999-2000; cert. comml. mediator NJ Assn. Profl. Mediators. Author: (with J. Bickerman) Court-Annexed Mediation: Perspectives on Selected State & Federal Programs, 1998; contbr. articles to profl. jours. Trustee Princeton Ballet, 1984-92, Arts Coun. Princeton, 1998-2003. Mem. ABA (sec. on dispute resolution, mediation com., vice-chmn. subcom. on ct.- annexed dispute resolution, mem., sec. dispute resolution publs. bd.), N.J. Bar Assn., Mercer County Bar Assn., Princeton Bar Assn. (pres. 1986-87), Penn Basketball Club (exec. bd. 1995—), Penn Club N.Y. Avocations: wine, food, travel, sports, art and architecture. Home: 95 Wilson Rd Princeton NJ 08540-2601 Office: Bergman & Barrett PO Box 1273 Princeton NJ 08542-1273 E-mail: ejb@gear3.com.

BERGMAN, EMILY ANNE, librarian; b. Tulsa, July 24, 1953; d. Arthur L. and Jean Lucy (Anson) B.; m. Mark Andrew Allen, June 20, 1982; children: Philip Isaac Allen, Brian Anson Allen. BA, Goucher Coll., 1975; MLS, U. Tex.-Austin, 1976; student Wroxton Coll., Banbury, Eng., 1974. Research librarian Tracy-Locke Advt., Dallas, 1977-78; cataloger Dallas Pub. Library, 1978-80, head spl. collections, 1980-81; info. specialist, Dallas, 1978-81; asst. library dir. Calif. Sch. Profl. Psychology, Los Angeles, 1981-90; catalog libr. Gene Autry Western Heritage Mus., L.A., 1990-92, head libr., 1992-96, curator rare books, 1996—. Mem. ALA (coms.), Spl. Library Assn., So. Calif. Spl. Library Assn., Calif. Acad. and Research Libraries, Libr. Instruction Round Table (vice treas., 1992-93, treas. 1993-94), Mental Health Librarians (v.p., pres.-elect 1987-88, pres. 1988-89). Democrat. Jewish. Home: 1001 Geneva St Glendale CA 91207-1709 Office: Autry Mus Western Heritage 4700 Western Heritage Dr Los Angeles CA 90027-1462

BERGMAN, GEORGE MARK, mathematician, educator; b. Bklyn., July 22, 1943; s. Lester V. and Sylvia G. (Bernstein) B.; m. Mary Frances Anderson, Dec. 26, 1981; stepsons: Jeff Elam, Michael L. Anderson; children: Clifford I. and Rebecca N. Anderson-Bergman (twins). BA, U. Calif., Berkeley, 1963; PhD, Harvard U., 1968. Asst. prof. Dept. Math. U. Calif., Berkeley, 1967-72, assoc. prof., 1972-78, prof., 1978—. Contbr. articles to profl. jours. Mem. AAUP, Am. Math. Soc. Democrat. Avocations: linguistics, folk-dancing. Office: U Calif Dept Math Berkeley CA 94720-3840

BERGMAN, HERMAS JOHN (JACK BERGMAN), retired college administrator; b. May 3, 1926; s. Ruebin Eric and Esther (Schierman) Bergman; m. Jeanne Louise Culton, 1946 (div. 1961); children: Stephen, Kathleen, Marsha; m. Evelyn Alice Templeman, Apr. 6, 1963; children: Kristin, Robert. BA, Walla Walla Coll., 1948; MA, U. Puget Sound, 1963; PhD, Wash. State U., 1967. Tchr. Wash. Pub. Schs., Wenatchee and Tacoma, 1948—58, 1961—64; bus. mgr. Totem Plywood, Inc., Tacoma, 1958—61; prof. history Western Oreg. U., Monmouth, 1966—79, dean Liberal Arts and Scis., 1980—85; pres. Walla Walla Coll., College Place, Wash., 1985—90; ret., 1990. Author: The Religious Fringe; contbr. articles to profl. jours. Chmn. bd. commrs. Polk County Parks and Recreation Commn., Dallas, Oreg., 1977—80; nat. adv. coun. Am. United for Separation of Ch. and State, 1992—2001; bd. trustees Walla Walla Gen. Hosp., 1985—; chmn. bd. Internat. Children's Care Inc., Vancouver, Wash., 1981—89; bd. dirs. Walla Walla Symphony, 2003—; mem. exec. com. Oreg. Conf. Seventh-day Adventists, 1981—85; v.p. Wash. State Religious Liberty Assn. of Pacific N.W., 1991—2001; bd. dirs. Portland Adventist Med. Ctr., 1972—78, 1985—90, Ind. Colls. of Wash., Seattle, 1985—90, United Way of Walla Walla, 1988—91, Wash. Friends of Higher Edn., Seattle, 1985—90. Avocations: photography, geology, stamps, lapidary.

BERGMAN, JERRY RAE, science educator; b. Detroit, May 30, 1946; s. Ernest R. and Irene (Buck) B.; m. Marie Fox, June 20, 1970; children: Aeron, Mishalea; m. Dianne Haldiman, Dec. 28, 1985; stepchildren: Chris, Scott. BS, Wayne State U., 1969, MEd, 1971, PhD, 1976; MA, Bowling Green State U., 1986; PhD, Columbia Pacific U., 1992; MSBS, Med. Coll. Ohio, 1999, MS in Occupl. Health, 2003; MPH, N.W. Ohio Consortium for Pub. Health, 2001. Lic. profl. clin. counselor. Prof. Bowling Green State U., Bowling Green, Ohio, 1973-80, U. Toledo, Toledo, Ohio, 1981-86, Northwest Coll., Archbold, Ohio, 1987—. Dir. Soc. for Study of Male Psychology and Physiology, Montpelier, Ohio, 1974—; rsch. assoc., adj. instr. Med. Coll. of Ohio, Toledo. Author: 22 books and monographs; contbr. 550 articles (trans. into 14 langs.) to profl. jours. Founder, 1st pres. Bowling Green State U. Friends of the Libr. Recipient Langsford award for excellence in writing, 1998, Paul C. Krouse Tchg. award, 2000. Fellow Am. Sci. Affiliation; mem. AAAS, Am. Chem. Soc. Office: Northwest State Cmty Coll 22-600 State Rt 34 Archbold OH 43502 E-mail: jerryber@nscc.cc.oh.us.

BERGMAN, MARILYN KEITH, lyricist, writer; b. Bklyn. d. Albert A. and Edith (Arkin) Katz; m. Alan Bergman, Feb. 9, 1958; 1 child, Julie Rachel. BA, NYU; MusD (hon.), Berklee Coll. Music, 1995, Trinity Coll., 1997. Lyricist, collaborator (with Alan Bergman) (numerous pop, theatrical and film score songs, TV themes) Bracken's World, 1969—70, The Sandy Duncan Show, 1972, Maude, 1972—78, Good Times, 1974—79, The Nancy Walker Show, 1976, The Dumplings, 1976, Alice, 1976—82, In the Heat of the Night, 1988—94, Brooklyn Bridge, 1991—93, The Powers That Be, 1993, TV film lyrics The Hands of Time (from Brian's Song), 1971, Queen of the Stardust Ballroom, 1975 (Emmy award for best dramatic underscore and best musical material, 1975, score only), Sybil, 1976 (Emmy award for best dramatic underscore 1976, 1976), Too Many Springs (from Hollow Image), 1979, theatrical scores Something More, 1964, Ballroom, 1978 (Grammy award nominee for best cast show album, 1979), The Lady and the Clarinet, 1980, feature film songs The Marriage Go-Round, from The Marriage Go-Round, 1960, Any Wednesday, from Any Wednesday, 1966, Make Me Rainbows, from Fitzwilly, 1967, (score) In the Heat of the Night, 1967, The Windmills of Your Mind, from the Thomas Crown Affair, 1968 (Acad. award for best song, 1968, Golden Globe award best original song, 1969), His Eyes, Her Eyes, from The Thomas Crown Affair, 1968, You Must Believe in Spring, from Young Girls of Rochefort, 1968, Maybe Tomorrow, from John and Mary, 1969, Tomorrow Is My Friend, from Gaily, Gaily, 1969, There's Enough to Go Around, 1969, A Smile, A Mem'ry and an Extra Shirt, from A Man Called Gannon, 1969, Sugar in the Rain, from Stiletto, 1969, What Are You Doing the Rest of You Life?, from The Happy Ending, 1969 (Acad. award nominee for best song, 1969), I Was Born in Love With You, from Wuthering Heights, 1970, Sweet Gingerbread Man, from The Magic Garden of Stanley Sweetheart, 1970, Nobody Knows, 1970, Move, from Move, 1970, Pieces of Dreams (Little Boy Lost), from Pieces of Dreams, 1970 (Academy award nominee for best song, 1970), The Costume Ball, from Doctors' Wives, 1971, All His Children, from Sometimes a Great Notion, 1971 (Acad. award nominee for best song, 1971), Rain Falls Anywhere It Wants To, from the African Elephant, 1971, The Summer Knows, from Summer of '42, 1971 (Grammy award nominee for song of the year 1972, 1972), A Face in the Crowd, from Le Mans, 1971, Marmalade, Molasses and Honey, from The Life and Times of Judge Roy Bean, 1972 (Acad. award nominee for best song, 1972), Love's the Only Game in Town, from Pete and Tillie, 1972, Molly and Lawless John, 1972, The Way We Were, from The Way We Were, 1973 (Grammy award for song of the year, 1973, Acad. award for best song, 1973, Golden Globe award for best original song, 1974, Grammy award for best original score, 1974), Breezy's Song, from Breezy, 1973, In Every Corner of the World, from Forty Carats, 1973, Summer Wishes, Winter Dreams, from Summer Wishes, Winter Dreams, 1973, Easy Baby, from 99 and 44/100%, 1974, There'll Be Time, from Ode to Billy Joe, 1975, Evening Sun, Morning Moon, from The Yakuza, 1975, I Believe in Love, from A Star is Born, 1976 (Grammy award nomination best original score, 1977), I'm Harry, I'm Walter, from Harry and Walter Go to New York, 1976, Hello and Goodbye, from Noon to Three, 1976, Bobby Deerfield, from Bobby Deerfield, 1977, The Last Time I Felt Like This, from Same Time Next Year, 1978 (Acad. award nominee for best song, 1978), The One and Only, from The One and Only, 1978, There's Something Funny Goin' On, from ...And Justice For All, 1979, I'll Never Say Goodbye, from The Promise, 1979 (Acad. award nominee for best song, 1979), Where Do You Catch the Bus for Tomorrow, from A Change of Seasons, 1980, Ask Me No Questions, from Back Roads, 1981, How Do You Keep the Music Playing?, from Best Friends, 1982 (Acad. award nominee for best song, 1982), Think About Love, 1982, Comin' Home to You, from Author! Author!, 1982, Tootsie, from Tootsie, 1982, It Might Be You, 1982 (Acad. award nominee for best song, 1982, Grammy award nominee for best original score, 1983), If We Were in Love, from Yes, Giorgio, 1982 (Acad. award nominee for best song, 1982), Never Say Never Again, from Never Say Never again, 1983, Papa, Can You Hear Me?, from Yentl, 1983 (Academy award nomination best song, 1983), The Way He Makes Me Feel, 1983 (Acad. award nominee for best song, 1983), Will Someone Ever Look at Me That Way?, 1983 (Acad. award best original score and Grammy award nomination for best original score, 1984, Acad. award nominee for best original song, 1983), Yentl, 1983 (Acad. award for best original score, 1983), Little Boys, from The Man Who Loved Women, 1983, Something New in My Life, from Mickey and Maude, 1984, The Music of Goodbye, from Out of Africa, 1985, I Know the Feeling, from The January Man, 1989, The Girl Who Used to Be Me, from Shirley Valentine, 1989 (Acad. award nominee for best song, 1989, Golden Globe nominee for best original song, 1990, Grammy award nominee, 1990), Welcome Home, from Welcome Home, 1989, Most of All You, from Major League, 1989, Dreamland, from For the Boys, 1991, Places That Belong to You, from The Prince of Tides, 1991, It's All There, from Switch, 1991, Moonlight, from Sabrina, 1995 (Acad. award nominee for best original song, 1996, Golden Globe nominee, Grammy nominee), The Best of Friends, from Bogus, 1996, Love is Where You Are, from At First Sight, pop songs You Don't Bring Me Flowers, 1978 (Grammy award nominee for song of the year, 1978), In the Heat of the Night, The Summer Knows, Nice 'N' Easy (Grammy award nominee for song of the year, 1960), Someone in the Dark, L.A. Is My Lady, After the Rain, I Was Born in Love With You, That Face, Look Around, I Love to Dance Like They Used to Dance, What Matters Most, One Day, A Child Is Born, Sleep Warm, Sentimental Baby, Live It Up, If I Close My Eyes, Yellow Bird, Like a Lover, Where Do You Start?, On My Way to You, Ordinary Miracles (Cable Ace award and Emmy award for best original song), A Ticket to Dream (Emmy Awd. for best song), albums Never Be Afraid for Bing Crosby, The Ballad of the Blues for Jo Stafford, 1999, Barbra Streisand: The Concert (Ace nominee for writing of a spl.). Named to songwriters hall of Fame, 1980; recipient singers salute to songwriter award, Clooney Found., 1986, Aggie award, Songwriter's Guild, 1987; grantee Am. Film Inst., 1976. Mem.: ASCAP (pres., chmn. bd. dirs. 1994—). Office: ASCAP 7920 Sunset Blvd Ste 300 Los Angeles CA 90046

BERGMAN, MARK STEVEN, lawyer; b. Washington, June 27, 1956; s. Paul M. and Arlene (Stern) B.; m. Susan E. Gibson, Apr. 14, 2001. BA, Bowdoin Coll., 1978; MA, U. Va., 1979; JD with honors, Am. U., 1982. Bar: N.Y. 1983, DC 1991. Assoc. Paul, Weiss, Rifkind, Wharton & Garrison, N.Y.C., 1982-90, ptnr., 1991—; head Paul Weiss Securities Group, London, 1997—; resident corp. ptnr. Paul, Weiss Paris, London, 2001—. Frequent panelist corp. governance and securities law issues. Contbr. articles to profl. jours. Mem. ABA, Assn. of Bar of City of N.Y. Office: Paul Weiss Rifkind Wharton & Garrison 10 Noble St London EC2V 7JU England E-mail: mbergman@paulweiss.com.

BERGMAN, NANCY PALM, real estate investment company executive; b. McKeesport, Pa., Dec. 3, 1938; d. Walter Vaughn and Nellie (Sullivan) Leech; m. Donald Bergman; 1 child, Tiffany Palm Taylor. Student, Mt. San Antonio Coll., 1970, UCLA, 1989-93. Corporate sec. U.S. Filter Corp., Newport Beach, Calif., 1965—. Pres. Jaguar Research Corp., Los Angeles and Atlanta, 1971—; owner Environ. Designs, Los Angeles, 1976—; pres. Prosher Corp., Los Angeles., 1978-83; now pres., dir. Futura Investments, L.A.; CEO Rescor, Inc.

Author: Resident Managers Handbook. Home: 1255 Benedict Canyon Dr Beverly Hills CA 90210 also: 23540 Tapatia Rd Homeland CA 92548 Office: PO Box 15246 Beverly Hills CA 90209

BERGMAN, RICHARD ISAAC, health information company executive; b. Bklyn., Jan. 18, 1934; s. Joseph and Clara (Menchel) B.; m. Judith Hyman, June 24, 1956 (div. 1974); children: Deborah Jill, Susan Bergman Hackett; m. Victoria Smalley, June 9, 1987. SB, MIT, 1955, SM, 1956. Devel. engr. Exxon Rsch., Linden, N.J., 1956-60; mem. adj. faculty N.J. Inst. Tech., Newark, 1957-58; dir. engring. Princeton (N.J.) Chem. Rsch., 1960-67; exec. v.p. Systemedics, Inc., Princeton, 1967-80; pres. Savant Assocs., Inc., Princeton, 1980-98; exec. dir. White House Task Force on Workplace Safety and Health, Washington, 1977-78; pres. Project Masters, Inc., Princeton, 1980—. Mem. vis. com. med. dept. MIT, Cambridge, Mass., 1973-83, 86-88; Whitaker Coll., 1979-85, dir. Response Analysis Corp., Princeton, 1970-77; pres., dir. CWW, Inc., Princeton, 1998—. Contbr. articles to profl. jours.; patentee in field. Mem. AIChE (past chmn. N.J. sect.), Am. Chem. Soc., N.Y. Acad. Scis., MIT Alumni/ae Assn. (dir. 2000-03). Home: 134 Leabrook Ln Princeton NJ 08540-3622 Office: Project Masters Inc PO Box AG Princeton NJ 08542-0872 E-mail: richard.bergman@verizon.net.

BERGMAN, ROBERT GEORGE, chemist, educator; b. Chgo., May 23, 1942; s. Joseph J. and Stella (Horowitz) Bergman; m. Wendy L. Street, June 17, 1965; children: David R., Michael S. BA cum laude in chemistry, Carleton Coll., 1963; PhD (NIH fellow), U. Wis., 1966; PhD (hon.), Carleton Coll., 1995. NATO fellow in chemistry Columbia U., N.Y.C., 1966-67, Arthur Amos Noyes instr. chemistry Calif. Inst. Tech., Pasadena, 1967-69, asst. prof. chemistry, 1969-71, assoc. prof. chemistry, 1971-73, prof., 1973-77; prof. chemistry U. Calif. at Berkeley, 1977—; asst. dean Coll. Chemistry U. Calif., Berkeley, 1987-91, 96, Miller Rsch. prof., 1982-83, 93, 2003. Sherman Fairchild Disting. scholar Calif. Inst. Tech., 1984; mem. panel bioinorganic and metallobiochemistry study sect. NIH, 1977—80; cons. Union Carbide Corp., 1977—81, 1990—2001, E. I. DuPont de Nemours, 1982—85, Chevron Rsch. Co., 1983—89, Dow Chem. Co., 2001—02; disting. vis. prof. U. N.C., Chapel Hill, 1999. Mem. editl. bd.: Chem. Revs., Jour. Am. Chem. Soc., Organometallics, Tetrahedron Publs., European Jour. Inorganic Chemistry; contbr. articles to profl. jours. Recipient Tchr. Scholar award, Camille and Henry Dreyfus Found., 1970—75, Excellence in Tchg. award, Calif. Inst. Tech., 1978, Merit award, NIH, 1991, E. O. Lawrence award for Chemistry, Dept. Energy, 1993, Chem. Pioneer award, Am. Inst. Chemists, 2000; fellow Alfred P. Sloan Found., 1970—72, Guggenheim, 1999. Mem.: NAS, AAAS, Am. Chem. Soc. (Organometallic Chemistry award 1986, Arthur C. Cope scholar 1987, Edward Fahs Smith award Pa. sect. 1990, Ira Remsen award Balt. sect. 1990, Arthur C. Cope award 1996, Edward Leete award 2001, James Flack Norris award 2003), Phi Beta Kappa, Phi Lambda Upsilon, Sigma Xi (Monie Ferst award 2003). Home: 501 Coventry Rd Kensington CA 94707-1316 Office: U Calif Dept Chemistry Berkeley CA 94720-0001

BERGMAN, ROBERT IRA, laywer; b. N.Y.C., May 9, 1954; s. Morris and Frances R. BA, Bklyn. Coll., 1977; JD, Bklyn. Law Sch., 1980. Bar: N.Y. 1981, Fla. 1982, U.S. Dist. Ct. (so. and ea. dists.) N.Y. 1982. Assoc. Isaacson Robustelli Fox et al, N.Y.C., 1980-87, ptnr., 1987-92, Fogelgaren and Bergman, N.Y.C., 1992-98, Fogelgaren, Forman & Bergman LLP, N.Y.C., 1998—. Mem. N.Y. State Bar Assn., Workers Compensation Bar Assn. (bd. dirs. 1988—). Home: 5 Horizon Rd Fort Lee NJ 07024-6651 Office: Fogelgaren Forman & Bergman LLP 277 Broadway New York NY 10007-2001

BERGMAN, VICTORIA BESTERMAN, small business owner, consultant; b. Covington, Ky., Aug. 22, 1944; d. John Joseph and Marion Julia (Schlueter) Besterman; m. Ralph D. Smalley, June 6, 1966 (div. Sept. 1975); m. Richard I. Bergman, June 9, 1987. BA in Polit. Sci., U. Cin., 1966, MA in Pub. Adminstrn., 1969. Adminstr., organizer state and local govt., Cin., 1966-72; project coord., planner Health Svcs., Atlantic County, N.J., 1972-73; program and budget analyst, spl. asst. to Asst. Commnr. N.J. State Govt., Trenton, 1973-77; pub. affairs officer, staff spl. reorgn. project, adminstr. U.S. Govt., EOP, Washington, 1977-81; v.p. Savant Assocs., Inc., Princeton, NJ, 1981—98. Adj. faculty in pub. adminstrn. Trenton State Coll., 1973-77; v.p. Project Masters, Inc., 1981—. Founder Princeton Cmty. Without Walls; past co-chair Princeton U. Summer Chamber Concerts Com.; founder Women's PAC of N.J., past co-chair; founder N.J. Women's Network, past trustee; mem. Princeton Twp. Zoning Bd. Adjustment, 1989—96, chair, 1995—96; mem. Regional Planning Bd. Princeton, 2000—, chair, 2001—. Mem.: Am. Soc. Pub. Adminstrn. (past bd. dirs. sect. women in pub. adminstrn., regions I and II liaison, coun. and coms. mem. N.J. chpt., natural resources sect. environ. adminstrn. sect.), World Future Soc., U. Cin. Alumni Assn. (Outstanding Disting. Alumna award). Avocations: reading current fiction, singing, walking, hiking. Office: Project Masters Inc PO Box AG Princeton NJ 08542-0872

BERGMANN, ARTHUR M. writer, former county official, former newspaperman; b. N.Y., Nov. 24, 1927; s. Augustus H. Bergmann. BS in Polit. Sci. and Pub. Adminstrn., Empire State Coll., SUNY, Old Westbury, 1974; M in Pub. and Gen. Adminstrn., L.I.U., 1979. Cert. arbitrator. With N.Y. Herald Tribune, 1945-63; asst. news editor Riverhead News, 1949-50; Suffolk County (N.Y.) corr. for N.Y.C. newspapers, 1949-63; news editor Moriches (N.Y.) Tribune, 1950-51; mem. staff Newsday, 1951-71, Suffolk County polit. editor, columnist, 1965-71; chief dep. Suffolk County Exec., Hauppauge, N.Y., 1972-79. Chmn. Suffolk Criminal Justice Coordinating Coun., 1975-79, Arson Action Com.-Suffolk Arson Task Force, 1975-77, MTA Permanent Citizens Adv. Com., 1978-79; adv. coun. N.Y. State Crime Victims Compensation Bd., 1978-79; trustee Suffolk Acad. Medicine, 1974. Served with USAAF, 1946-47. Recipient Disting. Svc. award United Jewish Appeal, 1976; Pub. Adminstrn. award C. W. Post Coll., 1977; Disting. Svc. plaque L.I. Assn. Commerce & Industry, 1977; Exemplary Svc. award Empire State Coll., SUNY, 1981; nominated for Pulitzer prize (2). Mem. Acad. Polit. Sci., Soc. Silurians, Am. Legion, Moriches Yacht Club (past commodore, Center Moriches, N.Y.), Pi Alpha Alpha. Address: 2403 24th Way West Palm Beach FL 33407

BERGMANN, BARBARA ROSE, economics educator; b. N.Y.C., July 20, 1927; d. Martin and Nellie Berman; m. Fred H. Bergmann, July 16, 1965; children: Sarah Nellie, David Martin. BA, Cornell U., 1948; MA, Harvard U., 1955, PhD, 1959; PhD (hon.), De Montford U., 1996, Muhlenberg Coll., 2000. Economist U.S. Bur. Labor Stats., N.Y.C., 1949-53; sr. staff economist, cons. Council Econ. Advisors, Washington, 1961-62; sr. staff Brookings Inst., Washington, 1963-65; sr. econ. advisor AID, Washington, 1966-67; assoc. prof. U. Md., College Park, 1965-71, prof. econs., 1971-88; disting. prof. econs. Am. U., Washington, 1988-97, prof. emeritus, 1997—. Author: (with Chinitz and Hoover) Projection of a Metropolis, 1961; (with George W. Wilson) Impact of Highway Investment on Development, 1966; (with David E. Kaun) Structural Unemployment in the U.S., 1967; (with Robert Bennett) A Microsimulated Transactions Model of the United States Economy, 1985, The Economic Emergence of Women, 1986, Saving Our Children from Poverty: What the United States Can Learn from France, 1996, In Defense of Affirmative Action, 1996, Is Social Security Broke? A Cartoon Guide to the Issues, 1999, (with Suzanne W. Helburn) America's Child Care Problem: The Way Out, 2002; mem. editl. bd. Am. Econ. Rev., 1970-73, Challenge, 1978—, Signs, 1978-85; columnist econ. affairs N.Y. Times, 1981-82. Mem. Economists for McGovern, 1977; mem. panel econ. advisors Congl. Budget Office, Washington, 1977-87; mem. price adv. com. U.S. council on Wage and Price Stability, 1979-80. Mem. AAUP (coun. 1980-83, pres. 1990-92), Am. Econ. Assn. (v.p. 1976, adv. com. to U.S. Census Bur. 1977-82), Ea. Econ. Assn. (pres. 1974), Internat. Assn. for Feminist Econs. (pres. 1999), Soc. for Advancement of Socio-Econs. (pres. 1995-96). Democrat. Home: 5430 41st Pl NW Washington DC 20015-2911 E-mail: bbergman@wam.umd.edu.

BERGMANN, CARL ADOLF, chemical engineer, researcher; b. Concordia, Mo., Mar. 27, 1932; s. Theodore H. and Clara A. (Brandenberg) B.; m. Elizabeth C. Moran, Apr. 16, 1960; children: Beverly E. Bergmann Hammer, William C. BS in Chem. Engring., U. Mo., 1954; MBA, U. Pitts., 1968. Sr. engr. Bettis Atomic Power Lab., Pitts., 1963-74; prin. engr. Westinghouse Electric Co., Pitts., 1975-96; cons. Pitts., 1996—. Mem. com. Electric Power Rsch. Inst., Palo Alto, Calif., 1986-96; mem. indsl. adv. com. Brookhaven Nat. Lab. Alara Ctr., L.I., N.Y., 1987-96. Contbr. articles to profl. jours.; co-inventor process to inhibit corrosion in a nuclear reactor, 1992. Chmn. traffic bd. Mt. Lebanon (Pa.) Twp., 1978-79. Capt. USAF, 1955-58. Mem. Am. Nuclear Soc. Democrat. Unitarian-Universalist. Avocations: gardening, stamp collecting, walking. Home: 638 Briarwood Ave Pittsburgh PA 15228-2552

BERGMANN, DONALD GERALD, pharmaceutical company executive; b. Aug. 13, 1949; s. Edgar Frank and Dorothy Bertha Bergmann; m. Kathy Jeanne Dumont, Sept. 4, 1976; children: Karen Ann, Kim Jeanne. BS, Mich. State U., 1972; PhD, Ohio State U., 1978. Rschr. UCLA, 1978-81; project leader Burroughs-Wellcome Co., Kansas City, Kans., 1981-83; scientist Genentech, Inc., South San Francisco, Calif., 1983, ops. mgr., 1983-87, sr. project mgr., 1987-88; dir. biopharm. mfg. SmithKline Beecham Pharms., Phila., 1988-91, group dir. biopharm. tech. ops., 1991-95, gen. mgr. biopharms., 1995-2000; gen. mgr. global biopharms. GlaxoSmithKline Pharms., Phila., 2001—. Contbr. articles to profl. jours. and publs. Fellow Nat. Cancer Inst., 1978-80; grantee Nat. Cancer Inst., Am. Cancer Soc. Mem. Internat. Soc. Pharm. Engring. (lectr.), Pharm. Rsch. and Mfrs. Assn. (lectr., com. chair, steering com.). Avocations: skiing, wine collecting.

BERGMANN, STEVEN ROBERT, medical educator, physician; b. N.Y.C., Feb. 4, 1951; m. Joanne L. Rubin. BA, George Washington U., 1972; PhD, Hahnemann Med. Coll., 1978; MD, Washington U., St. Louis, 1985. Diplomate Am. Bd. Internal Medicine, Am. Bd. Nuclear Cardiology. NIH postdoctoral fellow cardiovasc. divsn., dept. internal medicine Washington U. Sch. Medicine, St. Louis, 1977—80; asst. prof. medicine Washington U., St. Louis, 1980—89, assoc. prof. medicine, 1989—95, prof. medicine and radiology, 1995—96, dir. nuc. cardiology, 1994—96; intern in internal medicine program, dept. medicine Barnes-Jewish Hosp., St. Louis, 1986—88, fellow in cardiovasc. disease, cardiovasc. divsn. dept. internal medicine, 1988—90, resident in internal medicine, 1994—96; prof. medicine and radiology Coll. Physicians and Surgeons Columbia U., N.Y.C., 1996—2003, Margaret Milliken Hatch prof. medicine, 2002—03; dir. nuc. cardiology Columbia Presbyn. Ctr., N.Y.C., 1996—2003; chief cardiology Beth Israel Med. Ctr., N.Y.C., 2003—. Fellow Am. Coll. Cardiology, N.Y. Acad. Medicine; mem. Am. Soc. Nuclear Cardiology (bd. dirs. 2000), Soc. Nuclear Medicine. Avocation: boating. Office: Cardiology Beth Israel Med Ctr 16th St and 1st Ave New York NY 10003

BERGMANN, WILLIAM J. personnel director; b. Dubuque, Iowa, Apr. 5, 1939; s. George John Bergmann and Martha Brehm; m. Karen Ann Kreps, Dec. 26, 1964; children: Kathleen S., John W. BA, Loras Coll., 1963; MSIR, Loyola U., Chgo., 1964. Group human resource mgr. Clow Corp., Oak Brook, Ill., 1968—78; mgr. human resources Lifetime Foam, North Lake, Ill., 1978—79; mgr. employee rels. Sara Lee Corp., Chgo., 1979—81; safety mgr. NIPSCO, Hammond, Ind., 1981—83; dir. employee rels. Am. Bakeries, N.Y.C., 1983—88; pers. dir. Stroehman Bakeries, Horsham, Pa., 1988—95; human resources dir. Perdue Farms, Milford, Del., 1995—. Mem. steering com. Project Impact, Milford United Way, Transitions; mem. Govs. Welfare Employment Com. Served with USNR, 1956—62. Mem.: Delmarva Human Resource Mgmt., Soc. Human Resource Mgmt. Avocations: golf, tennis. Home: 730 Bicentennial Blvd Dover DE 19904 Office: Perdue Farms 255 N Rehoboth Blvd Milford DE 19963 Business E-Mail: bill.bergman@perdue.com.

BERGNER, JANE COHEN, lawyer; b. Schenectady, N.Y., Apr. 6, 1943; d. Louis and Selma (Breslaw) Cohen; m. Alfred P. Bergner, May 30, 1968 (dec. Sept. 24, 2002); children: Lauren, Justin. AB, Vassar Coll., 1964; LLB, Columbia U., 1967. Bar: D.C. 1968, U.S. Dist. Ct. D.C. 1968, U.S. Ct. Appeals (D.C. cir.) 1968, U.S. Ct. Fed. Claims 1969, U.S. Ct. Appeals (fed. cir.) 1969, U.S. Tax Ct. 1979, U.S. Supreme Ct. 1992. Trial atty. tax divsn. U.S. Dept. Justice, Washington, 1967-74; assoc. Arnold & Porter, Washington, 1974-76, Rogovin, Huge & Lenzner, Washington, 1976-83; of counsel Arter & Hadden, 1983-86; ptnr. Spriggs & Hollingsworth, 1986-89, Feith & Zell, P.C., 1989-93; pvt. practice Washington, 1993—. Mem. jud. confs. U.S. Ct. Fed. Claims, U.S. Tax Ct. Contbr. articles to profl. jours. Bd. dirs. Jewish Social Svc. Agy., Washington; former mem. cmty. adv. bd. Sta. WAMU-FM, Washington. Fellow Am. Coll. Tax Counsel; mem. ABA (sect. taxation, govt. rels. com., ct. procedure com., civil and criminal penalties com., chmn. subcom. important devels. 1991-93, chmn. regional liaison meetings com. 1993-95, sect. litigation); Vassar Coll. Class Alumnae (chair spl. gifts com. 25th reunion), D.C. Bar (chair taxation sect. 1985-90, chair tax audits and litigation com. 1990-93, Outstanding Sect. award 1986, Cmty. Outreach award 1993), Fed. Bar Assn., Women's Bar Assn. D.C., Washington Estate Planning Coun., Women's Tax Luncheon Group, Columbia U. Law Sch. Alumni Assn., Svc. Guild Washington, Vassar Club. Home: 5659 Bent Branch Rd Bethesda MD 20816-1049 Office: Ste 650 1615 L Street NW Washington DC 20036 E-mail: jbergnerlaw@abanet.org.

BERGONIA, RAYMOND DAVID, venture capitalist; b. Spring Valley, Ill., May 21, 1951; s. Raymond A. and Elva M. (Bernadini) B.; m. Linda Goble, Dec. 31, 1988; children: Alexandra, Andrew, Caroline, Margot. BBA, U. Notre Dame, 1973; JD, Harvard U., 1976. Bar: Ill. 1976, U.S. Dist. Ct. (no. dist.) Ill. 1976, U.S. Tax Ct. 1977; C.P.A., Ill. Assoc. Winston & Strawn, Chgo., 1976-79; legal counsel, v.p. adminstrn. Heizer Corp., Chgo., 1979-86; v.p. corp. fin. Chgo. Corp., 1986-89; exec. v.p., prin. N.Am. Bus. Devel. Co. L.L.C., Chgo., 1989—. Bd. dirs. numerous pvt. cos. Recipient Elijah Watts Sells award Am. Inst. C.P.A.s, 1973 Mem. ABA, Chgo. Bar Assn. Home: 605 Essex Rd Kenilworth IL 60043-1129 Office: NAM Bus Devel Co LLC 135 S La Salle St Chicago IL 60603-4159 E-mail: dbergonia@northamericanfund.com.

BERG ORAM, STEPHANIE, music educator; b. Peoria, Ill., May 22, 1949; d. Glen Virgil and Margaret Eaton Berg; m. Roger Oram, May 19, 1990. BA in Linguistics, U. Mich., 1970, MA in Linguistics, 1972; MMus, Peabody Conservatory, Balt., 1981; DMA, U. Colo., 1990. Tchg. fellow U. Mich., Ann Arbor, 1970-72; vis. faculty ESL Jundi Shapur U., Ahwaz, Iran, 1972-76; tchr. ESL Baltimore County Adult Edn., Balt., 1976-81; ESL program coord. The Stratford Schs., Towson, Md., 1981-84; faculty ESL Econs. Inst., Boulder, Colo., 1984; adj. faculty ESL Colo. Sch. Mines, Golden, 1984-86; asst. dir. English Studies Inst. Teikyo Loretto Heights U., Denver, 1990-91; adj. faculty music Red Rocks C.C., Lakewood, Colo., 1992—2000, asst. prof., 2000—, arts dept. chair, 2002—. Adj. faculty music Metro. State Coll. Denver, 1997-2000; pvt. music tchr. voice, piano, Balt., then Denver, 1981—; guest spkr. Colo. Music Festival, Boulder, 1997, 98, 99, 2000, 01. Soprano soloist Ch. of the Holy Ghost, Denver, 1994-97, Basilica of the Immaculate Conception, Denver, 1997-98. Mem. Nat. Assn. Tchrs. Singing, Colo./Wyo. Nat. Assn. Tchrs. Singing, Coll. Music Soc.,Rocky Mt. Coll. Music Soc. (v.p. 2002—), Music Tchrs. Nat. Assn., Colo. State Music Tchrs. Assn., Foothills Music Tchrs. Assn. Office: Red Rocks CC Arts Dept 13300 W 6th Ave Lakewood CO 80228-1225 E-mail: stephanie.berg@rrcc.edu.

BERGOUST, ERIC, Olympic athlete; Olympic athlete aerials, 1994, 1998. Named World Aerial Champion, 1999; recipient Gold medal Aereals Competition, Nagano Olympics, Japan, 1992, World Cup, 1992, Silver medal, World Championships, 1997. Achievements include 9 time World Cup aerial event champion; 2 time U.S. Nat. champion.

BERGQUIST, GENE ALFRED, farmer, rancher, county commissioner; b. Paynesville, Minn., Aug. 5, 1927; s. Albin and Viola (Heinrich) B.; m. Ann Dorothy Corwin, Aug. 2, 1958; children: Wayne A., Viola M. Grad. high sch., Rhame, N.D. Self-employed farmer-rancher, Rhame, 1948—; Slope County commr. Amidon, ND, 1982—2003; ret., 2003. Bd. dirs. Rhame, N.D. Cenex, 1970-82; bd. dirs. Harper Twp. Rhame; com. mem. Slope County Agrl. Stabilization and Conservation Svc.-USDA Commn., Amidon, 1968-84. Bd. dirs. Rhame Rural Fire Dept., 1976—, Bowman-Slope Social Svc. Bd., Bowman, N.D., 1991—, Deep Creek Twp., 1958-64, Richland Center Twp. Bd., 1952-57; elder Lyle Presbyn. Ch.; youth leader 4-H Slope County, 1950-57; mem. Bowman-Slope Revolving Loan Fund Com., 1998—; mem. job devel. bd. Slope and Bowman Counties, 1999—. Mem. Nat. Assn. Counties, N.D. Assn. Counties. Presbyterian. Avocations: reading, painting, fishing, riding, gardening. Office: Courthouse Amidon ND 58620

BERGQUIST, JAMES MANNING, history educator; b. Council Bluffs, Iowa, Feb. 1, 1934; s. Reuben Neil and Irene Mary (Norton) B.; m. Joan Marie Solon, May 17, 1969; children: John Norton, Charles James. BA, U. Notre Dame, 1955; MA in History, Northwestern U., 1956, PhD in History, 1966. Instr. history Coe Coll., Cedar Rapids, Iowa, 1961-63, Villanova (Pa.) U., 1963-66, asst. prof., 1966-69, assoc. prof., 1969-86, prof., 1986—2002, prof. emeritus, 2002. Contbr. articles on Am. social history and immigration to profl. jours., chpts. to books. Trustee Balch Inst. for Ethnic Studies, Phila., 1988—92, 1994—2001; mem. Pa. Task Force on Diversity in Higher Edn., 1991—94. Fellow, NEH, 1967, 1977, 1980. Mem.: AAUP (pres. Pa. divsn. 1988—90, nat. coun. 1995—2001), Ethnic Studies Assn. Phila. (pres. 1980—82), Hist. Soc. Pa., Am. Assn. State and Local History, Immigration and Ethnic History Soc. (bd. dirs. 1995—), Am. Studies Assn., Orgn. Am. Historians, Am. Hist. Assn. Democrat. Roman Catholic. Avocations: swimming, travel. Home: 217 Devon Blvd Devon PA 19333-1616 Office: Villanova U History Dept Villanova PA 19085

BERGQUIST, PETER, music educator emeritus; b. Sacramento, Aug. 5, 1930; s. Ed Peter and Margaret (Rogers) B.; m. Dorothy Catherine Clark, June 16, 1956; children: Carolyn, Emily (dec.). Student, Eastman Sch. Music, Rochester, N.Y., 1948-51; BS, Mannes Coll. Music, N.Y.C., 1958; MA, Columbia U., 1960, PhD, 1964. Asst. prof. Sch. Music, U. Oreg., Eugene, 1964-69, assoc. prof., 1969-73, prof., 1973-95, prof. emeritus, 1995—. Editor: Orlando di Lasso, Samtliche Werke neue Reihe, vol. 22-25, 1992—93, Orlando di Lasso: The Complete Motets, 18 vols., 1995—, Orlando di Lasso Studies, 1999; music reviewer Eugene Register Guard; contbr. articles. Sr. warden, jr. warden, vestryman St. Mary's Episcopal Ch., Eugene. With USAF, 1951-55. Recipient Ersted award for disting. teaching U. Oreg., 1973; Fulbright sr. rsch. awardee, 1985; Nat. Endowment for Humanities grantee, 1994-98; rsch. and travel awardee DAAD, ACLS. Mem. AAUP, Am. Musicol. Soc., Internat. Musicol. Soc., Soc. for Music Theory, Music Libr. Assn., Coll. Music Soc. Democrat. Home: 3195 Portland St Eugene OR 97405-5140 Office: Sch Music 1225 U Oreg Eugene OR 97403-1225 E-mail: pbergq@darkwing.uoregon.edu.

BERGQUIST, SANDRA LEE, medical and legal consultant, nurse; b. Carlton, Minn., Oct. 13, 1944; d. Arthur Vincent and Avis Lorene Portz; m. David Edward Bergquist, June 11, 1966; children: Rion Eric, Taun Erin. BSN, Barry U., 1966; MA in Mgmt., Central Mich. U., 1975; student U. So. Calif., 1980-82. RN, advanced registered nurse practitioner; cert. physician asst. Commd. 2nd lt. USAF, 1968, advanced through grades to lt. col., 1985; staff and charge nurse USAF, 1968-76, primary care nurse practitioner, McConnell AFB, Kans., 1976-79, officer in charge Wheeler Med. Facility, Wheeler AFB, Hawaii, 1979-83, supr. ambulatory care services, Elgin AFB, Fla., 1983-84; med.-legal cons., Pensacola, Fla., 1985—; risk mgr., quality assurance coordinator HCA-Twin Cities Hosp., Niceville, 1986-88. Bd. dirs. Elder Svcs. of Okaloosa County, Fla., 1984—; mem. adv. bd. Advanced Home Health, 1990—; chairperson Niceville/Valparaiso Task Force on Child Abuse Prevention, Fla., 1985-88; chmn. home and family life com. Twin Cities Women's Club, Niceville, 1985-88; chmn. advancement com. Gulf Coast coun. Boy Scouts Am., 1985-87; instr. advanced and basic cardiac life support Hawaii Heart Assn. and Tripler Army Med. Ctr., 1981-83. Decorated Commendation medal with 1 oak leaf cluster, USAF Meritorious Svc. medal, Air Force Commendation medal. Mem. AACN, Am. Assn. Physician Assts., Assn. Mil. Surgeons U.S., Soc. Ret. Air Force Nurses, Soc. Air Force Physician Assts., Twin Cities Women's Club. Lutheran. Avocations: computer programming, reading, handicrafts.

BERGQUIST, TIMOTHY M. business educator, researcher; b. Portland, Oreg., May 13, 1949; married, May 15, 1971. BS in Math., U. Portland, 1971; MS in Stats., U. La., 1972; MBA, Santa Clara U., 1975; MS in Ops. Rsch., Oreg. State U., 1986; PhD in Decision Scis., U. Oreg., 1996. Commd. 2d lt. USAF, 1971, advanced through ranks to maj., 1983, ret., 1991; grad. tchg. fellow U. Oreg., Eugene, 1991—96; prof. bus. and mgmt. NW Christian Coll., Eugene, Oreg., 1996—. Pres. Statis. Quality Consulting, Eugene, 1994—; dir. info. sys. NW Christian Coll., Eugene, 1998—2001, dir. instl. rsch., 2001—. Mem.: Inst. for Ops. Rsch. and Mgmt. Sci., Am. Prodn. and Inventory Control Soc., Am. Soc. for Quality, Am. Statis. Assn., Decision Scis. Inst. Office: NW Christian Coll 828 E 11th Ave Eugene OR 97401 Office Fax: 541-349-5260. E-mail: timberg@nwcc.edu.

BERGREN, SCOTT C. career officer; b. Mineola, N.Y. BA in Econ., Clemson U., 1970; student navigator tng., Mather AFB, Calif., 1970-71; student, Squadron Officer Sch., 1974; M in Polit. Sci., Auburn U., 1981; student, Air Command and Staff Coll., 1981, Air War Coll., 1990, Harvard U., 1996. Commd. 2d lt. USAF, 1970, advanced through grades to maj. gen., 1999, various F-4 Phantom assignments, 1971-76; air staff ops. officer programs and resources Air Staff Tng. program, Hdqs. USAF, Pentagon, Washington, 1976-77, asst. exec. officer to dep. chief staff programs/resources, 1976-77; instr., navigator and exchange officer 237th Operational Conversion Unit, RAFB Honington, Eng., 1977-80; dir. ops. force analysis div. then spl. asst. comdr. Hdqs. Tactical Air Command, Langley AFB, Va., 1981-85; comdr. 325th Tactical Tng. Wing's Aircraft Generation Squadron, Tyndall AFB, Fla., 1985-87, asst. dep. comdr. maintenance, 1985-87; dep. comdr. maintenance 33rd Tactical Fighter Wing, Eglin AFB, Fla., 1987-89; Air Univ. chair for chief staff of Air Force Maxwell AFB, Ala., 1990-91; various comdr. positions Nellis AFB, Nev., 1991-93; stationed at U.S. Ctrl. Command, MacDill AFB, Fla., 1994-96; vice comdr. San Antonio Air Logistics Ctr., Kelly AFB, Tex., 1996-97; comdr. 82d Tng. Wing, Sheppard AFB, 1997-99; dir. maintenance, dep. chief staff installations & logistics HQ/USAF, 1999-2000; comdr. Ogden Air Logistics Ctr., Hill AFB, Utah, 2000—. Decorated Silver Star, D.F.C. with silver oak leaf cluster, Purple Heart, Air medal with three silver oak leaf clusters and bronze oak leaf cluster, Small Arms Expert Marksmanship Ribbon, Rep. Vietnam Gallantry Cross with Palm, Rep. Vietnam Campaign medal. Office: Hill AFBM OO-ALC/CC 7981 Georgia St Hill Air Force Base UT 84056-5824

BERGSCHNEIDER, DAVID PHILIP, legal administrator; b. Springfield, Ill., Nov. 19, 1951; s. Fred J. and Ruby A. (Martin) B.; m. Dawn E. Combes, Sept. 23, 1989; children: Alec, Bryant, Cale. Student, Bradley U., 1969-71; BA, Ill. Coll., 1973; JD, Marquette U., 1976. Bar: Ill. 1976, Wis. 1976, U.S. Ct. Appeals (7th cir.) 1990, U.S. Supreme Ct. 1980. Mem. legis. staff Ill. Gen. Assembly, Springfield, 1976-77; asst. defender Office State Appellate Defender, Springfield, 1977-93, legal dir., 1993—. Mem. governing bd. Ill. Integrated Justice Info. Sys. Co-author: Defending Illinois Criminal Cases, 1988, 2003, Illinois Criminal Practice, 1980, Brief Writing and Oral Argument Handbook, 1988, 94, 97; author: Illinois Handbook of Criminal Law Decisions, 1993, 2d edit., 1998, supplement, 2003; also articles. Recipient Award of Excellence Ill. Pub. Defender Assn., 1989. Mem. ABA, Ill. Bar Assn. (criminal justice sect. coun. 1987-91, 94-98, sec. 1995-96, chmn. 1996-97), Ill. Attys. for Criminal Justice, Aircraft Owners and Pilots Assn. Office: Office State Appellate Def PO Box 5780 Springfield IL 62705-5780

BERGSMAN, KENNETH LLOYD, hematologist, oncologist; b. Cleve., 1938; s. Alexander Bergsman and Eleanor Levey; m. Janet Anne Bolek, July 25, 1964; children: Cheryl, Christopher, Jeffrey, Jennifer, Todd. BS, U. Dayton, 1962; MD, Ohio State U., 1964. Cert. in internal medicine, specialty in oncology, specialty in hematology. Intern Detroit Receiving Hosp.-Wayne State U., 1964-65, resident in internal medicine, 1964-66, 68-69; fellow in hematology Henry Ford Hosp., Detroit, 1969-70; fellow in hematology, chief med. resident Detroit Receiving Hosp.-Wayne State U., 1970-71; v.p. med. affairs Sinai-Grace Hosp., Detroit; prof. medicine Wayne State U., Detroit, 1991—. Fellow ACP; mem. Assn. Program Dirs. in Internal Medicine, Am. Soc. Clin. Oncology, Am. Soc. Hematology, Detroit Acad. Medicine. E-mail: KBergsma@dmc.org.

BERGSMARK, EDWIN MARTIN, mortgage bank executive; b. July 14, 1941; married; 2 children BBA, U. Cin., 1964; postgrad. in mgmt., U. Colo.; JD, U. Toledo, 1972; postgrad. in banking, U. Wis. Bar: Ohio 1972, U.S. Dist. Ct. Ohio, U.S. Tax Ct., Ct. Customs and Patent Appeals, U.S. Supreme Ct. 1975. Indsl. rels. pers. dir. Textileather div. Gen. Tire and Rubber, 1967-70; exec. v.p., gen. counsel TrustCorp, Inc., Toledo, 1970-89. Chmn., CEO Cavista Corp.; chmn. Vista Capital Group Inc., Cavalear Corp., Cavalear Realty Co., Cavalear Ins.; bd. dirs. Unimast Corp., Vista Devel. Inc., Gen. Aluminum and Chem. Corp., N.Am. Travel Corp. Past chmn. Sta. WGTE-TV (PBS); past pres., trustee Toledo Zool. Soc.; trustee Lourdes Coll.; chmn., trustee Toledo Mud Hens Baseball Club; pres. bd. trustees Lucas County Recreation Ctr.; past pres. Kidney Found. Northwestern Ohio, Toledo Neighborhood Housing Svcs.; vice chmn., treas., commr. Ohio Turnpike Commn. Served to capt. U.S. Army,

Vietnam. Named Toledo's Outstanding Young Man of Yr., 1972 Mem. ABA, Toledo Bar Assn., Fed. Bar Assn. (trustee), Legal Inst. of Gt. Lakes, Am. Econ. Coun., Burning Tree Golf Club, Inverness Country Club. Office: Vista Capital Group Inc 6444 Monroe St Ste C Sylvania OH 43560-1430

BERGSON, HENRY PAUL, professional association administrator; b. Boston, Dec. 22, 1942; s. Harry Jr. and Elizabeth (Paul) B.; m. Jacqueline Hope Wilson, June 11, 1966; children: Susan Elizabeth, Abigail Anne. BS, U. N.H., 1966. Various mgmt. positions Fed. Signal, Blue Island, Ill., 1970-78; dir. mktg. Tork, Mt. Vernon, N.Y., 1978-83; v.p. ops. G.C.S. Svc., Chappaqua, N.Y., 1983-85; exec. v.p. Nat. Elec. Mfrs. Reps. Assn., Armonk, N.Y., 1985-93, pres., 1994—, also bd. dirs. Bd. dirs. Elec. Industry Joint Bus. Productivity Coun.; fire commr. Katonah Fire Dist., 1992—; vice chmn. bd. fire commrs., Katonah, 1996—; mem. fire adv. bd. Westchester County, N.Y., 2001—. Contbr. articles to profl. jours. Elder 1st Presbyn. Ch. of Katonah, N.Y., 1991-94; chief Katonah Vol. Fire Dept., 1980-84, v.p., 1984-87, pres., 1987-90, bd. dirs., 1990—, chmn. bd. dirs., 1995—; mem. Bedford Transp. Com., 1984-86; cmty. adv. bd. Taconic and Bedford Hills Correctional Facilities, N.Y. State Dept. Corrections. Capt. U.S. Army, 1967-70. Decorated Bronze Star for Valor with two oak leaf clusters, Air medal with three oak leaf clusters, Purple Heart, Army Commendation medal for Valor, Vietnam Medal of Honor. Mem. Nat. Elec. Mfrs. Assn. (assoc.), Nat. Assn. Elec. Distribrs. Republican. Avocation: collecting firematic antiques. Home: PO Box 182 Katonah NY 10536-0182 Office: NEMRA 660 White Plains Rd Fl 6 Tarrytown NY 10591-5147

BERGSTEIN, ELEANOR, filmmaker, writer; b. N.Y.C., Apr. 17, 1938; d. Joseph and Sarah (Rein) B.; m. Michael Goldman, Jan. 17, 1965. BA, U. Pa., 1958. Author (novel) Advancing Paul Newman, 1973, Ex-Lover, 1989; screenwriter (film) It's My Turn, 1980; screenwriter, co-prodr. (film) Dirty Dancing, 1987; screenwriter, dir. (film) Let It Be Me, 1996; writer, dir., prodr. (film) Starry Night with Sprinkles, (stage musical) The Baby and Johnny Project. Creative Arts Pub. Svc. fellow, 1973. Mem. PEN, Acad. Motion Pictures Arts and Scis., Writers Guild Am., Dirs. Guild Am. Democrat. Jewish. Office: Magic Hour Prodns 210 Central Park S New York NY 10019-1428

BERGSTEIN, JACK MARSHALL, surgeon; b. Duluth, Minn., Apr. 21, 1955; s. Sherman and Muriel (Gilder) Bergstein; m. Amber C. Bergstein, June 15, 2002; children: Lauren, Julianstepchildren: Samara, Baye. BA in Journalism, U. Minn., 1978, MD, 1982. Diplomate Am. Bd. Surgery with added qualifications in surg. critical care; diplomate Am. Bd. Forensic Examiners, Am. Bd. Forensic Medicine. Resident surgery U. Minn., Charlotte Med. Ctr., 1982-85, 85-87; surg. critical care fellow Lincoln Med. and Mental Health Ctr., Bronx, N.Y., 1987-88; sr. attending surgeon Froedert Hosp., Milw., 1988-97; dir. trauma and surg. critical care St. Francis Med. Ctr., Peoria, 1997-99; assoc. prof. surgery U. Ill. Coll. Medicine, Peoria, 1997-99; dir. surg. critical care, assoc. dir. trauma Jon Michael Moore Trauma Ctr. W.Va. U. Hosp., Morgantown, 1999—2003; prof. surgery W.Va. Sch. Medicine, Morgantown, 1999—2003. Active staff St. Francis Hosp., Peoria, 1997—99. Dir. at large Peace Studies Ctr., Milw., 1995-97; adv. bd. Peoria Safe Cmtys., 1997-99. Fellow ACS (chmn. Wis. com. on trauma 1995-97); mem. Am. Trauma Soc. (pres. Wis. 1992-97), Am. Assn. Surgery of Trauma, Ea. Assn. for the Surgery of Trauma (dir.-at-large 1999—2002, chmn. violence prevention task force, 1999—2002, vice chair violence prevention task force, 1994-99), Assn. Tchrs. Preventive Medicine, Midwest Surg. Assn., Nat. Network Violence Prevention Practitioners, Surg. Infection Soc., Am. Soc. Bariatric Surgery. Avocations: bonsai, watercolor painting, gardening. Home: Box 3300 Lindell Rd Russell PA 16345 Office: 103 W St Clair St Ste 2D Warren PA 16365

BERGSTEIN, JERRY MICHAEL, pediatric nephrologist; b. Cleve., June 26, 1939; s. Sol R. and Hilda (Nittscoff) B.; m. Renee M. Hillman, July 7, 1963; children: Stephanie, Michael, Jeffrey. BA, UCLA, 1961; MD, U. Minn., 1965. Diplomate Nat. Bd. Med. Examiners, Am. Bd. Pediat., Am. Bd. Pediat. Nephrology; lic. physician, Ind. Intern in pediat. U. Minn., Mpls., 1965-66, jr. pediat. resident, 1966-67, chief pediat. resident, 1969-70, postdoctoral fellow in pediat. nephrology, 1970-73; asst. prof., head pediat. nephrology UCLA, 1973-77; assoc. prof. Ind. U. Sch. Medicine, Indpls., 1977-82, head pediat. nephrology, 1977—, prof., 1982—. Mem. adv. bd. Nat. Kidney Found. Ind., 1980—; mem. adv. coun. Am. Heart Assn., 1988—. Mem. editl. bd. Child Nephrology and Urology, 1980-90, Pediat. Nephrology, 1995—; contbr. chpts. to books. Lt. comdr. USN, 1967-69. Recipient Fellowship USPHS, Washington, 1970; grantee Thrasher Fund, 1980, Amgen, 1990. Mem. Am. Soc. Nephrology, Am. Soc. Pediat. Nephrology, Am. Soc. Investigative Pathology, Soc. Exptl. Biology and Medicine. Achievements include research on the role of the fibrinolytic inhibitor plasminogen activator inhibitor-1 in the pathogenesis and outcome of the hemolytic-uremic syndrome; development of anti-tubular basement membrane antibody disease; development of radiation nephritis in bone marrow transplant patients. Office: James Whitcomb Riley Hosp for Children 702 Barnhill Dr Indianapolis IN 46202-5128 E-mail: jbergste@iupui.edu.

BERGSTEN, JAMES ROBERT, computer technology architect; b. N.Y.C., May 21, 1954; s. Robert Frederick and Jean Laura B.; m. Mary Elizabeth, July 20, 1980; children: Sarah Margaret, Carl Alexander. Student, Cooper Union, 1972-74. System developer NASA, N.Y.C., 1974-77; software mgr. Amdahl Corp., Sunnyvale, Calif., 1977-81; founder, pres./CEO Kolinar Corp., Santa Clara, Calif., 1981-90; v.p. engr. Andor Systems, Cupertino, Calif., 1990-94; founder, pres. ARK Rsch. Corp., San Jose, Calif., 1995—; dir. LSI Logic, Milpitas, Calif., 2000—. Bd. dirs. Ark Rsch., Kolinar, Santa Clara; owner CTHIA Prodns.; chmn., CEO Ark Storage Systems Corp., 2003—. Author: (operating system) Arts, 1995, (software) Xmenu, 1991 (ICP award 1995); co-author: (software) Kprobe, SQ Lexec, SQ Lmenu, 1995; contbr. articles to profl. jours.; patentee in field. Mem. computer adv. bd. KTEH TV, San Jose, 1985. Mem. IEEE, Assn. Computing Machinery, Audio Enging. Soc. Avocations: composing, arranging, and producing music. Home: 8 Brightwood Way Danville CA 94506 E-mail: jim@thegergstens.com.

BERGSTRESSER, PAUL RICHARD, dermatologist, educator; b. Ottawa, Kans., Aug. 24, 1941; s. Karl Samuel and May (Holmes) B.; m. Rebecca Louise Baird, Jan. 4, 1969; children: Daniel Baird, Laura Suzanne. AB, Coll. of Wooster, 1963; MD, Stanford U., 1968. Diplomate Am. Bd. Dermatology (dir. 1996—). Asst. prof. dept. dermatology U. Miami (Fla.), 1975-76; asst. prof. to prof. Southwestern Med. Ctr. U. Tex., Dallas, 1976—, chmn. dept., 1986—. Mem. dermatologic drugs adv. com., FDA, 1986-88; mem. gen. medicine study sect. GM1A, NIH, 1989-93; mem. adv. coun. Nat. Inst. Arthritis and Musculoskeletal and Skin Disease, 2000—. Editor Photodermatology, Photoimmunology and Photomedicine, 1990-99; contbr. numerous articles to profl. jours. Maj. U.S. Army, 1970-72. Fellow AAP, AAAS, ACP, Am. Acad. Dermatology; mem. Am. Assn. Immunologists, Assn. Am. Physicians, Soc. Investigative Dermatology (bd. dirs. 1987-92, sec.-treas. 1999—), Am. Assn. Tissue Banks, Am. Dermatol. Assn., Assn. Profs. Dermatology (bd. dirs. 1990-95, pres.-elect 1998-2000, pres. 2000-2002). Democrat. Methodist. Avocations: choral music, running. Home: 3758 Pallos Verdas Dr Dallas TX 75229-2740 Office: U Tex Southwestern Sch Med Dept Dermatology 5323 Harry Hines Blvd Dallas TX 75390-7208 E-mail: paul.bergstresser@utsouthwestern.edu.

BERGSTROM, ALBION ANDREW, military officer, educator; b. Salem, Mass., Sept. 2, 1947; s. Eric Hjalmar and Helen Lawrence (Andrew) Bergstrom; m. Angela Jane Feyerabend, May 11, 1997; children: Victoria Helen, John Albion. Student, Boston U., 1965-67; BA, Colo. State U., 1969; MA, Ctrl. Mich. U., 1978; grad., Command and Gen. Staff Coll., 1982; MA, Naval War Coll., 1998. Cert. fed. ofcl. Commd. 2d lt. U.S. Army, 1969, advanced through grades to col., 1991, platoon leader, aide de camp, 1970-71, co. comdr., 1974-75; br. exec. officer I-35 Armor, Erlangen, Germany, 1980-81; assignment officer Armor Br. U.S. Army, 1983-85, bn. comdr. 1-35 Armor, 1986-88, cols. assignment officer Pers. Command, 1988-89, chief, officer divsn. DCS pers., The Pentagon Washington, 1990-92; dep. comdr. U.S. Army Phys. Disability Agy., Washington, 1992-96; prof. jt. mil. ops., chief regional contingency planning and war fighting divsn. Naval War Coll., Newport, RI, 1996-99, prof. electives program, CCE, 2000—. Program chmn. Abrams Ch. Armor Assn., 1982—85. Del. N.H. Rep. Convs., 1966, 1968. Decorated Legion of Merit (3), Bronze Star, Purple Heart, Bronze medal, Silver medal, Order St. George; Nat. Security fellow, John F. Kennedy Sch. Govt., Harvard U., 1988—90. Mem.: VFW, Boston U. Alumni Assn., Ctrl. Mich. U. Alumni Assn., Colo. State U. Alumni Assn., 1st Cav. Divsn. Assn., Armor Assn., Assn. U.S. Army, U.S. Naval Inst., Naval War Coll. Found., U.S. Army War Coll. Alumni Assn., Order Ky. Cols., Mil. Order Purple Heart, Shriners, Masons, Am. Legion, Nat. Sojourners, Zeta Beta Tau, Phi Sigma Delta. Congregationalist. Avocations: photography, cross-country skiing. Home: 19 Madison Way Portsmouth RI 02871-2249 E-mail: bergstra1@aol.com.

BERGSTROM, BETTY HOWARD, consulting executive, foundation administrator; b. Chgo., Mar. 15, 1931; d. Seward Haise and Agnes Eleanor (Uek) Guinter; m. Robert William Bergstrom, Apr. 21, 1979; children: Bryan Scott, Cheryl Lee, Jeffrey Alan, Mark Robert, Philip Alan. BS in Speech, Northwestern U., 1952, postgrad., 1983, U. Nev., Reno, 1974. Dir. sales promotion and pub. rels. WLS-AM, Chgo., 1952-56; account exec. E.H. Brown Advt. Agy., Chgo., 1956-59; v.p. Richard Crabb Assocs., Chgo., 1959-61; pres., owner Howard Assocs., Calif. and Chgo., 1961-76; v.p. Chgo. Hort. Soc., 1976-90; pres. Bergstrom Assoc., Chgo. and Carefree, Ariz., 1990—; exec. dir. Ariz. Found. for Women, 1996-98. Mem. editl. bd. Garden mag., 1977-84, Glenview Cmty. Ch., 1977-89, Fourth Presbyn. Ch., 1990—, trustee, 1994-97; editor Garden Talk, 1976-86; contbr. articles on fund devel., horticulture, edn. advt. and agr. to profl. jours.; editor Ill. AAUW Jour., 1966-67. Del. Ill. Constl. Conv., 1969-70, mem. com. legis. reform, 1973-74, cts. and justice com., 1971-74; apptd. mem. Ill. Hist. Libr. Bd., 1970, Ill. Bd. Edn., 1971-74. AAUW fellowship grant named in her honor; recipient Communicator of Yr. award Women in Comm., 1983; named Outstanding Fundraising Exec., 1997. Mem.: LWV (state v.p. Ariz. 1999), AAUW (Pres.'s award 1988), Assn. Fund Raising Profls. (bd. dirs. 1983—92, sec. 1986, v.p. 1990—92, nat. bd. dirs. 1990—92, bd. dirs. 1996—, pres.-elect 1997, nat. del. assembly 1997—99, pres. 1999, internat. bd. dirs. 2000—, vice chmn. 2002—03, cert. fund raising exec., Outstanding Fund Raising Exec.-Ariz. 1997), U. So. Calif. Alumni Assn., Am. Assn. Bot. Garden and Arboreta, Ariz. Women's Coun. (pres. 1999), Nat. Women's History Mus. (chmn. nat. bd. dirs. 2000—02, nat. adv. coun.), Charter 100, Am. Assn. Museums, Garden Writers Am., Northwestern U. Alumni, Fortnightly Club (bd. dirs. 1994—96). Office: 111 E Chestnut St Apt 42H Chicago IL 60611-6020 also: PO Box 5253 Carefree AZ 85377-5253 E-mail: b.bergstrom@worldnet.att.net.

BERGSTROM, DEDRIC WALDEMAR, retired paper company executive; b. Neenah, Wis., Aug. 21, 1919; s. D. Waldemar and Agnes (Forsythe) B.; m. Jane Katherine Gibson, June 14, 1941; children— Dedric Waldemar IV, John F., Richard A., Jennifer M., William L. Grad., Northwestern Mil. and Naval Acad., Lake Geneva, Wis., 1936; student, Lawrence Coll., Appleton, Wis., 1936-38, U. Minn., 1939. With Bergstrom Paper, Neenah, Wis., 1936-84, successively gen. mill, office work, purchasing agt., 1945-50, treas., 1950-56, dir., 1950—, dir. purchases, 1950-71, dir. prodn. planning and scheduling, 1957-71, v.p., sec., 1956-62, exec. v.p., 1962-75, pres., chief operating officer, 1975-79; pres. Bergstrom divsn. P.H. Glatfelter Co., 1979-84. Bd. dirs. Twin City Savs. and Loan Assn., 1951-90. Vice pres. Bergstrom Found., 1962-80, pres., 1980—; bd. regents Campion High Sch., 1968-72. Served to maj. AUS, 1942-45. Mem. Wis. Paper & Pulp Mfrs. Traffic Assn. (dir. 1967-72) Clubs: Bergstrom Paper Management. Roman Catholic. Home: 835 River Ln Neenah WI 54956-2931

BERGSTROM, DONALD E. medical educator; b. Tacoma, Wash., Oct. 9, 1943; s. Robert E. and Betty M. Bergstrom; m. Eva Ng, Aug. 28, 1970; children: John E., Robert C., Christina N. PhD, U. Calif. Berkeley, 1940; BS, U. Wash., 1965. Asst. prof. Rockefeller U., New York, NY, 1972—74, U. Calif., Davis, Calif., 1974—79; prof. U. N.D., Grand Forks, 1980—89; Walther prof. Medicinal Chemistry Purdue U., West Lafayette, Ind., 1989—. Sci. adv. bd. mem. Oridigm Corp., Seattle, 1994—, Koronis Pharm., Redmond, Wash., 2001—. Grantee NIH rsch. awards, NIH, 1976—2002. Mem.: Am. Assn. of Sci., Am. Chem. Soc. (chmn., red river valley sect. 1983—83). Achievements include invention of Universal Base; first to Development of synthetic technologies for chemically reengineering DNA. Home: 3416 Hamilton St West Lafayette IN 47906 Office: Dept Medicinal Pharm Purdue University West Lafayette IN 47907 Personal E-mail: bergstrom@purdue.edu. E-mail: bergstrom@purdue.edu.

BERGSTROM, RICHARD WILLIAM HOULDER, SR., information technology executive; b. Chgo., Dec. 25, 1949; s. Will Houlder Bergstrom and Vivian Elaine Lake; m. Vicky Costanza, Nov. 24, 1968; children: Richard Jr., Michelle, Christopher. BS summa cum laude, Troy State U., 1974; MBA, Lake Forest Grad. Sch. Mgmt., 1992; M Computer Info. Sys., M. Telecomms., U. Denver, 1996; D of Mgmt., Colo. Tech. U., 1998. Mgr. tech. support Internat. Harvester, Broadview, Ill., 1980-82; sr. sys. analyst Tandem Computers, Inc., Itasca, Ill., 1982-84, sr. mgr. Santa Clara, Calif., 1984-87; sr. software mgr. Motorola Inc., Schaumburg, Ill., 1990-92, product mgr. Arlington Heights, Ill., 1992-93, sr. program mgr. Denver, 1993-95; program mgr. U.S. West Comms., Inc., Denver, 1997-98; v.p. devel. Summit Info. Sys., Corvallis, Oreg., 1998—2001; asst. prof. bus. Am. Intercontinental U., 2002—. Sr. cons. Westhaven Group, Wheaton, Ill., 1987-90; adj. prof. computer sci. Colo. Tech. U., Denver, 1997-98. Pres., bd. dirs. Danada West Homeowners Assn., Wheaton, Ill., 1988-90. Sgt. USAF, 1970-74. Mem. Project Mgmt. Inst.

BERGSTROM, STIG MAGNUS, geology educator; b. Skovde, Sweden, June 12, 1935; s. Axel Magnus and Karin Margareta (Engberg) B.; m. Disa Birgitta Kullgren Fil. lic., Lund U., Sweden, 1961, hon. doctorate, 1987. Amanuensis Lund U., 1958-62, asst. lectr., 1962-68; asst. prof. geology Ohio State U., Columbus, 1968-70, assoc. prof., 1970-72, prof., 1972—2002; dir. Orton Geol. Mus., 1968—2002. Contbr. numerous articles to profl. jours. Served with Swedish Army, 1955—56. Recipient Assar Hadding prize 1995, Raymond C. Moore medal, 1999, Golden medal Faculty of Sci., Charles U., Czech Rep., 1999, Pander Soc. medal, 2001; Am.-Scandinavian Found. fellow, 1964; Fulbright scholar, 1960; grantee numerous orgns., 1958—. Fellow Geol. Soc. Am., Ohio Acad. Sci.; mem. Royal Physiographic Soc. Office: Ohio State U Orton Geol Mus 155 S Oval Mall Columbus OH 43210-1308

BERGSTROM, TERRY JOSEPH, medical educator, physician; s. Willard Joseph and Ruth Alene Bergstrom; m. Anne Cecile Plamondon, Aug. 26, 1961; children: Tracy Alene Pantuso, Martha Anne Chapman, David Allen, Elizabeth Marie. BS, Mich. State U., 1955; MS, U. Mich., 1969, MD, 1965. Diplomate Am. Bd. of Ophthalmology, 1971. Commd. 2d lt. USAF, 1955, advanced through grades to col., pilot, 1955—60; med. intern David Grant USAF Hosp., Fairfield, Calif., 1965—66; cons. ophthalmology USAF, Riverside, Calif., 1970—73, Wiesbaden, Germany, 1973—77, cons. glaucoma San Antonio, ret., 1980; cons. glaucoma U. Mich., Ann Arbor, Mich., 1980—, program dir. ophthalmology. Contbr. chapters to books, articles. Coach Ann Arbor Sch. Dist., 1980—98; cmty. glaucoma screening U. Mich. Med. Sch-AMSA, Ann Arbor, 1997—2002; lay min. St. Thomas the Apostle Ch., Ann Arbor, 1980—2002. Fellow: Am. Acad. Ophthalmology (assoc.; com. chair 1984—87, Honor award 1985, Sr. Honor award 1998); mem.: Am. Eye Study Club (pres. 1990—91), Mich. State Med. Soc., Assn. U. Prof. Ophthalmology (assoc.), AMA (life), Am. Bd. of Ophthalmology (assoc.), Am. Glaucoma Soc. (assoc.), Assn. for Rsch. in Vision and Ophthalmology (assoc.). Avocations: gardening, coaching. Office: Kellogg Eye Ctr 1000 Wall St Ann Arbor MI 48105 Office Fax: 734-936-2340. E-mail: bergy@umich.edu.

BERGT, GREGORY PAUL, chemist, consultant; b. West Point, Nebr., Nov. 20, 1948; s. Lowell Duane and Elaine Angela (Schula) B.; m. Diann Helen Stigge, May 6, 1972; children: Matthew, Lisa, Troy, Ross. BS, Nebr. Wesleyan U., 1971; postgrad., U. Minn., 1974. Chemist Wendt Labs., Belle Plaine, Minn., 1971-77, dir. sci. and regulatory affairs, 1978-87; v.p. Eudaemonic Corp., Omaha, 1987—; dir. regulatory affairs I.D. Russell Co., Longmont, Colo., 1989-95; dir. R&D Pennfield Animal Health, Omaha, 1995—. Cons. VA Hosp., Mpls., 1977. Patentee in field. Pres., St. John's Luth. Ch., Belle Plaine, 1981, Bethlehem Luth. Ch., Longmont, 1993-94; sponsoring liaison Boy Scouts Am., Belle Plaine, 1980-84; county del. Republican Party, Scott County, Minn., 1982. Recipient award Chemistry Tng. Program, NSF, 1967. Mem. Parenteral Drug Assn., Generic Pharm. Industry Assn./Animal Drug Alliance (treas., dir. Rocky Mountain Biomed. Devel. Forum 1990-95), Am. Dairy Sci. Assn., Am. Chem Soc., Am. Inst. Chemists, Am. Fedn. Ind. Pharm. Mfrs. (sec.-treas., dir. 1979—), Coun. Agrl. and Sci. Tech., Tiger Booster Club (pres. 1973-75), Rotary (pres. 1984-85). Home: 335 S 124th Cir Omaha NE 68154-2319 Office: Pennfield Animal Health 14040 Industrial Rd Omaha NE 68144-3351 E-mail: staff@pennfieldanimalhealth.com.

BERGTRAUM, HENRY M. minister; b. N.Y.C., Nov. 5, 1955; s. Stanley and Bernice Natalie Bergtraum. BA, Yale U., 1977; postgrad., Yale/Union Theol. Sem., N.Y.C., 1999—. Social scis. asst. dept. polit. affairs UN Hdqrs., N.Y.C., 1978—95; resident chaplain St. John's Episcopal Hosp., N.Y.C., 1997—98; chaplain Ronald McDonald House, N.Y.C., 2000—. Elder Ch. of the Covenant, N.Y.C., 1992—. Presbyterian. Avocations: writing, poetry, swimming. Office: Ronald McDonald House 405 E 73rd St New York NY

BERGTRAUM, HOWARD MICHAEL, lawyer; b. N.Y.C., Jan. 8, 1946; s. Murry and Edith (Katz) B.; m. Susan Levitan, July 27, 1969; children: Jordan, Matthew, Andrea. BS, Queens Coll., 1966; JD, Cornell U., 1969; LLM, Georgetown Law Ctr., 1972. Bar: N.Y. 1970. Atty. adviser SEC, Washington, 1969-72; ptnr. O'Sullivan LLP, N.Y.C., 1975—2002, O'Melveny & Myers LLP, N.Y.C., 2002—. Mem. ABA, N.Y. State Bar Assn. Home: 10 I U Willets Rd Old Westbury NY 11568-1519 Office: O'Melveny & Myers LLP 30 Rockefeller Plz Fl 24 New York NY 10112-0198 E-mail: hmb@omm.com.

BERICK, JAMES HERSCHEL, lawyer; b. Cleve., Mar. 30, 1933; s. Morris and Rebecca Alice (Gerdy) B.; m. Christine Berick; children: Michael, Daniel, Robert, Joshua. AB, Columbia U., 1955; JD, Case Western Res. U., 1958. Assoc. Burke, Haber & Berick, Cleve., 1958-60, ptnr., 1960-86, mng. ptnr., 1968-83; chmn. Berick, Pearlman & Mills Co. L.P.A., 1986-99; ptnr. Squire, Sanders & Dempsey, LLP, 2000—02, ret. ptnr., 2003—. Bd. dirs. MBNA Corp., MBNA Am. Bank, N.A., MBNA Europe Bank, Ltd., The Town and Country Trust, The Town and Country Funding Corp.; sec. A. Schulman, Inc., 1973—; lectr. law Case Western Res. U., 1969—78; sec. Cleve. Browns Football Co. LLC; bd. vis. Case Western Res. U. Sch. Law, 1998—. Life trustee Rock and Roll Hall of Fame and Mus.; mem. Shaker Heights (Ohio) Bd. Edn., 1980-83; bd. visitors Columbia Coll., 1981-87, 90-96, emeritus, 2000—; bd. dirs. Univ. Circle Inc., 1994—; trustee Arthritis Found. of N.E. Ohio, chmn. major gifts com., mem. med. and sci. com. Mem.: Soc. of Benchers, Ct. of Nisi Prius, Seagate Beach Club, Union Club (Cleve.), Shoreby Club, Order of Coif. Home: 14 W Mather Ln Bratenahl OH 44108-1158 Office: Squire Sanders & Dempsey LLP 4900 Key Tower 127 Public Sq Cleveland OH 44114-1216

BERING, EDGAR ANDREW, III, physicist, educator; b. N.Y.C., Jan. 9, 1946; s. Edgar Andrew and Harriet Crocker (Aldrich) B.; m. Stacie Eden Cherniack, June 27, 1971 (div. 1979); m. Barbara Adele Clark, May 11, 1985; children: Edgar Andrew IV, Janet Ilse. BA, Harvard U., 1967; PhD, U. Calif., Berkeley, 1974. Tchg. asst. U. Calif., Berkeley, 1967-69, rsch. assoc., 1969-74; rsch. scientist physics dept. U. Houston, 1974—75, asst. prof., 1975—81, assoc. prof., 1981—89, prof., 1989—99, prof. physics, ECE, 1999—. Ptnr. I.F.&G. Tech. Cons., Bellaire, Tex., 1984—. Contbr. articles to profl. jours. Pres. Festival Angels, Inc., Houston, 1984, treas., 1983; bd. dirs. Gulf Coast World Affairs Coun., Houston, 1982-98. Recipient Antarctica Svc. medal NSF, 1981. Mem. AIAA, Am. Geophys. Union (editor EOS 1992-94), N.Y. Acad. Scis., Internat. Union Radio Sci., Sigma Xi. Home: 119 Warrenton Dr Houston TX 77024-6223 E-mail: eabering@uh.edu.

BERINGER, MICHAEL PENNELL, public relations executive; b. Boston, Sept. 22, 1944; s. Edward Robert and Ruth Kaolin (McVeigh) B.; m. H. Joy Zammito, Apr. 23, 1946. BS in Broadcasting magna cum laude, Boston U., 1967; MA in Communications, Fairfield U., 1986. Radio announcer various radio stas., Conn., Mass., Pa., Md., 1969-72, 81-86; dir. Conn. Sch. Broadcasting, Stratford, 1972-81; publicist Dept. on Aging, Hartford, 1986-88; pub. info. dir. State Libr., Hartford, 1988-92; sr. comms. officer State Tourism Office, Rocky Hill, Conn., 1992-95; comms. specialist Dept. Social Svc., Hartford, 1995—2003; pres. Hattie Comms., 2003—. Author: (with others) Front & Center, 1991. Recipient Army Commendation medal U.S. Army, 1969; named Outstanding Sr., Alumni Assn., 1967, Excellent Mgr., State of Conn., 1991. Mem. Assn. U.S. Army, Pub. Rels. Soc. Am., Soc. 5th Divsn., Mensa. Avocations: pysanky (ukranian easter eggs), travel. Home: 65 Pinecrest Rd Orange CT 06477-1221

BERINGER, WILLIAM ERNST, mediator, arbitrator, lawyer; b. Madison, Wis., Oct. 24, 1928; s. William and Martha M. Beringer; m. Marilyn J. Walter, Aug. 4, 1984; children: Amy, Julia, Barry, Thomas, Maureen. BA summa cum laude, Lawrence Coll., 1950; JD with distinction, U. Mich., 1953. Bar: Mich. 1953, Wis. 1953, Ill. 1955. Assoc. Vedder, Price, Kaufman & Kammholz, Chgo., 1953-56; atty. law dept. Swift & Co., Chgo., 1956-71; dir. gen. law dept. Allis-Chalmers Corp., Milw., 1971-77; v.p., gen. counsel, sec. Siemens Energy & Automation, Inc., Alpharetta, 1978-94; assoc. gen. counsel Siemens Corp., 1987-94. Bd. dirs. corp. banking and bus. law sect. Wis. Bar, 1976-78; mem. antitrust and corp. policy com. U.S. C. of C., 1974-80; mem. panels Am. Arbitration Assn., Resolution Resources Corp., NASD Regulation, N.Y. Stock Exch., EEOC. Editorial bd. Mich. Law Rev, 1952-53. Bd. dirs. Hinsdale (Ill.) Community Concert Assn., 1969-71, Dupage County (Ill.) Girl Scouts U.S., 1969-71, Clarendon Hills (Ill.) Community Chest, 1968-70; vice chmn. Clarendon Hills Human Relations Commn., 1968-70; mem. Chgo. study team Nat. Commn. on Causes and Prevention Violence, 1968; chmn. MAPI Law Coun. II, 1992-94. Mem. ABA, Am. Corp. Counsel Assn. (bd. dirs. Ga. chpt. 1985-88), Atlanta Bar Assn., Assn. Conflict Resolution, Lawrence U. Alumni Assn. (bd. dirs. 1998-2002), Order of Coif, Cherokee Town and Country Club, Rotary. Republican.

BERINSKY, ADAM JEREMIAH, political scientist, educator; b. N.Y.C., Oct. 4, 1970; s. Burton and Helene Berinsky; m. Deirdre Logan, June 9, 2002. BA, Wesleyan U., 1992; PhD, U. of Mich., 2000. Asst. prof. Princeton (N.J.) U., 1999—. Author: Silent Voices; contbr. articles to profl. jours. Mem.: Am. Polit. Sci. Assn. Office: Pinceton University 041 Corwin Hall Department of Politics Princeton NJ 08544 E-mail: berinsky@princeton.edu.

BERINSTEIN, WILLIAM PAUL, business executive; b. Elmira, N.Y., Dec. 25, 1935; s. Benjamin M. and Ann (Newhouse) B.; m. Phyllis Altman, Aug. 22, 1964; children: Benjamin M., Dorothy C. BA, U. Mich., 1957. Pres. Polk Properties, Inc., Syracuse, N.Y., 1960-89; ptnr. HLB Assocs. Investments, Syracuse, 1973—, ANB Assocs. Investments, Syracuse, 1964—; pres. Cortland Cinema Corp., Syracuse, 1967—, Cornell Theatres, Inc., Syracuse, 1973—; owner Euclid Enterprises, Syracuse, 1973—; pres. Bendor Mgmt. Ltd., 1992—. Pres. 715 Realty Corp., 1990—. Trustee Temple Soc. of Concord, Syracuse, 1968-74, 90-92, treas, 1992-96, pres., 1997-2001; pres. Syracuse Jewish Cemetery Assn., 1998—; dir. Syracuse Jewish Childrens Fund, 2001—. Named to Hall of Fame, Syracuse Men's Bowling Assn., 1990. Mem. Onondaga County Bowling Coun. (sec. 1985—), N.Y. State Bowling Proprs. Assn. (bd. dirs. 1958-65), Bowling Proprs. Assn. Am. (bd. dirs. 1958-64). Jewish. Avocations: genealogy, travel. Home: 5166 Pointe East Dr Jamesville NY 13078-8798 Office: 1067 W Genesee St Syracuse NY 13204-2244

BERK, ALAN S. law firm executive; b. N.Y.C., May 11, 1934; s. Phil and Mae (Buchberg) B.; m. Barbara Binder, Dec. 18, 1960; children— Charles M., Peter M., Nancy M. BS in Econs., U. Pa., 1955; MS in Bus., Columbia U., 1956. CPA N.Y., 1960. Staff acct. Arthur Young & Co., N.Y.C., 1956-62, mgr., prin., 1962-67; sr. v.p. Avco Corp., Greenwich, Conn., 1967-75; dir. Arthur Young & Co., 1975—, ptnr., 1976—, chief fin. officer, 1979-89; nat. dir. fin., treas. Ernst & Young, 1989-92; exec. dir. Kelley, Drye & Warren, N.Y.C., 1993-94. Mem. nat. adv. group Nat. Tech. Inst. for the Deaf, Rochester, N.Y.; chmn. bd. dirs. Jewish Home for the Elderly of Fairfield County, Inc., 1997-99, vice chmn., 2002—; 1st v.p., treas. Bruce Mus., Greenwich, Conn.; mem. golf bd. Town of Greenwich, Conn.; commn. on aging Town of Greenwich. With U.S. Army, 1957. Mem. AICPA, N.Y. State Soc. CPAs, Fin. Execs. Inst., Landmark Club, Stockbridge (Mass.) Golf Club, Lake Dr. Homeowners Assn. (pres.), Stockbridge Bowl Assn. (1st v.p.). Home: 14 Cornelia Dr Greenwich CT 06830-3906

BERK, GEORGE ELLIS, cardiologist; b. N.Y.C., May 4, 1942; s. Samuel and Muriel Berkowitz; m. Noel Nelkin, Oct. 7, 1967 (div.); children: Matthew Adam, Bradley Tyler; m. Penelope Susan Smith, Apr. 25, 1998. AB, Princeton U., 1964; MD, Cornell U., 1968. Diplomate Am. Bd. Internal Medicine. Intern Cornell Cooperating Hosps., 1968—69, resident, 1969—70; cardiology fellow North Shore Univ. Hosp., 1973—75; resident Cornell Cooperating Hosps., 1972—73; pvt. practice cardiology No. Westchester Cardiology, Yorktown Heights, NY, 1975—; attending physician Westchester Med. Ctr., 1975—, No. Westchester Hosp. Ctr., 1975—. Chief divsn. cardiology No. Westchester

Hosp., Mt. Kisco, NY, 1994—98; med. dir. Imaging for Life, LLC, N.Y.C. and White Plains, 1999—. Adv. bd. Free Romania Relief Fund, N.Y.C., 1992—95, Albanian Relief Assn., N.Y.C., 1992—97; bd. dirs. Westchester/Putnam divsn. Am. Heart Assn., Purchase, NY, 1981—; pres. Westchester/Putnam chpt. Am. Heart Assn., 1996—98. Maj. USAF, 1970—72. Decorated Air Force Commendation medal; recipient Congl. Proclamation, Congresswoman Nita Lowey, 2000. Fellow: Am. Coll. Cardiology (assoc.). Avocations: Oriental carpets, collecting vintage photography, art glass, pottery, running, mountaineering. Home: 181 Hook Rd Bedford NY 10506 Office: Northern Westchester Cardiology 1888 Commerce St Yorktown Heights NY 10506

BERK, HAROLD, dentist, consultant, educator; b. Mpls., July 27, 1917; s. Wolf and Jennie (Sachs) B.; m. Helen Ruth Levin, Aug. 2, 1942; children: Kenneth Joel, Fredrick Matthew, Donald Allan. Student, Loras Coll., 1935-37; DDS with honors, Northwestern U., 1941; DSc (hon.), Loras Coll., 2000. Intern, resident Forsyth Dental, Boston, 1941-43; asst. chief clinic Forsyth Dental Infirmary, Boston, 1943-44, chief clinic, 1944-46; asst. clin. prof. Tufts U. Dental, Boston, 1946-50, clin. prof., 1950-90, clin. prof. emeritus, 1990—. Pres. Pulpdent Corp., Watertown, Mass., 1950-95, cons. 1995—. Pres. coun. Bradeis U., Waltham, Mass. Lt. Comdr. USPHS, 1955-57. Recipient Harold Berk Rsch. Lab award, Tufts U. Dental Alumnus Faculty award, 1996, Alumnus Merit award Northwestern U. Dentistry, 1998; Rsch. award named in his honor. Fellow Am. Coll. Dentists, Internat. Coll. Dentists, Acad. Pediat. Dentistry, Acad. Dentistry for persons with Disabilities (founder); mem. G.V. Black Soc. (life) Fed. Dentaire Internat. (life), Am. Assn. Endodontics (life), ADA (life), Mass. Dental Soc. (life), Pierre Fauchard Acad. (life), Soc. Dentistry for Children (past pres. Mass. chpt.), Greater Boston Dental Soc. (past pres.), Internat. Assn. Dental Rsch., Sigma X, Omicron Kappa Upsilon. Jewish. Achievements include discovery of calcium hydroxide suspended in Aqueous methyl Cellulose, its affect on the dental Pulp-Apexification-Remineralization. Home: 369 Dudley Rd Newton Center MA 02459-2832 Office: Pulpdent Corp PO Box 780 80 Oakland St Watertown MA 02471

BERK, JACK EDWARD, gastroenterologist, educator; b. Phila. s. Samuel and Esther B.; m. Adeline Elizabeth Alberts, June 26, 1937; children: Philip Howard (dec.), Richard Hanna. BA, U. Pa., 1932, MSc in Medicine, 1939, DSc in Medicine, 1943; MD, Jefferson Med. Coll., 1936; postgrad., Grad. Sch. Medicine, U. Pa., 1937-38. Diplomate Am. Bd. Internal Medicine, Am. Bd. Gastroenterology. Intern Walter Reed Gen. Hosp., Washington, 1936-37; resident in medicine No. divsn. Albert Einstein Med. Ctr., Phila., 1938-39; fellow gastroenterology Grad. Hosp., U. Pa., 1939-40; Ross V. Patterson fellow physiology Jefferson Med. Coll., Phila., 1940-41; instr. gastroenterology U. Pa., 1941-46; asst. prof. medicine Sch. Medicine, Temple U., 1946-54; asst. dir. Fels Research Inst., 1946-54; assoc. prof. clin. medicine Coll. Medicine, Wayne State U., 1954-62, prof. clin. medicine, 1962-63; prof. medicine Coll. Medicine, U. Calif., Irvine, 1963-79, Disting. prof. medicine, 1979—, chmn. dept. medicine, 1963-79, head div. gastroenterology, 1963-79, asst. dean, 1979-90. Cons. VA Hosp., Long Beach, Calif., 1963-97, Cedars-Sinai Med. Ctr., 1963—, Meml. Hosp., Long Beach, 1964-97. Contbg. author: Bockus Gastroenterology, 1st and 2d edits.; assoc. editor: Bockus Gastroenterology 3d edit., 1974, editor-in-chief 4th edit., 1985, cons. editor 5th edit., 1994; editor: Developments in Digestive Diseases, Vol. 1, 1977, Vol. 2, 1979, Vol. 3, 1980; co-editor: Gastrointestinal Symptoms: Clinical Interpretation, 1991; mem. editl. bd. 13 med. jours., various times, 1959—; delivered 14 named lectureships; contbr. 200 articles to med. jours., 108 chpts. in more than 60 books. U.S. Dept. State rep. to S.Am. countries Cultural Exch. Program, 1961. Served to maj. M.C. AUS, 1941-46. Recipient Disting. Svc. award Mich. Med. Soc., 1959, Faculty Cmty. Svc. award U. Calif.-Irvine Alumni Assn., 1971, also Faculty Univ. Svc. award, 1976, Disting. Achievement award Jefferson Med. Coll. Alumni Assn., 1977, Maimonides award Maimonides Soc., 1984, Centennial award N.E. High Sch., Phila., 1990, Aldrich Disting. Univ. Svc. award U. Calif., Irvine, 1993, Bockus medal World Orgn. Gastroenterology, 1994; named Disting. Physician Nat. Found. for Ileitis and Colitis, 1980; J. Edward Berk Lectr. established U. Calif. Irvine Gastroenterology Alumni Assn., Aug., 1991, J. Edward Berk Lectr. established U. Calif. Irvine Vol. Clin. Faculty, 1991, J. Edward Berk Alumni Med. Edn. Ctr. dedicated U. Calif., Irvine, May 30, 1996. Master ACP (gov. So. Calif. region II 1976-80, Laureate award So. Calif. region 1990), Am. Coll. Gastroenterology (pres. 1975-76, Rorer award 1970, 74, 78, 79, Disting. Sci. Achievement award 1982, Clin. Achievement award 1988, Samuel Weiss award 1995); mem. AMA (chmn. sect. gastroenterology 1965-66), Am. Gastroent. Assn. (Disting. Educator award 1992), Am. Soc. Gastrointestinal Endoscopy (pres. 1958-59, Rudolf Schindler award 1966), Am. Fedn. Clin. Rsch. (chmn. Ea. sect.), Bockus Internat. Soc. Gastroenerology (pres. 1967-71), Detroit Gastroent. Soc. (pres. 1960-61), So. Calif. Soc. Gastroenterology (pres. 1967-68), L.A. Acad. Medicine (gov. 1981-84), So. Calif. Soc. Gastrointestinal Endoscopy (hon.), Orange County Acad. Medicine, Orange County Gastroenterology Soc. (founding pres.), Interam. Gastroent. Assn. (life, hon. pres. 1981—), Fgn. Med. Soc., Acad. Med. Ecuador, Peruvian and Cuban Soc. Gastroenterology (hon.), Gastroenterology Socs. Colombia, Gastrointestinal Endoscopy Soc. Colombia, Ecuador, Venezuela and Brazilian Soc. of Gastroenterology and Nutrition, Sigma Xi, Alpha Omega Alpha. Home: 894 Ronda Sevilla Unit C Laguna Woods CA 92653-4796 E-mail: jeberk@uci.edu.

BERK, PAUL DAVID, physician, scientist, educator; b. Bklyn., Apr. 3, 1938; s. Charles and Helen (Goell) B.; m. Aviva Ancona, July 4, 1965 (div. Aug. 1990); children: Claire, Philip, Edward; m. Nicole Polak, 1991. BA, Swarthmore Coll., 1959; cert., U. St. Andrews, Scotland, 1960; MD, Columbia U., 1964. Diplomate Am. Bd. Internal Medicine, Am. Bd. Hematology. Intern Columbia-Presbyn. Med. Ctr., N.Y.C., 1964-65, resident, 1965-66, fellow in hematology, 1969-70; clin. assoc. metabolism br. Nat. Cancer Inst., Bethesda, Md., 1966-69, sr. investigator, 1970-73; clin. asst. prof. medicine Georgetown U., Washington, 1971-75, clin. assoc. prof., 1975-77; chief sect. on diseases of the liver Nat. Inst. Arthritis, Metabolism and Digestive Diseases, NIH, Bethesda, 1973-77; prof. medicine Mt. Sinai Sch. Medicine, N.Y.C., 1977—, Albert and Vera List prof. medicine, 1980-89, prof. biochemistry, 1987-99, Henry and Lillian Stratton prof. molecular medicine, 1989—, chief divsn. hematology, 1977-89, acting chief, 1989-90, chief divsn. liver disease, 1989-01. Prof. biochemistry and molecular biology Mt. Sinai Sch. Medicine, 1999—; adj. prof. Rockefeller U., 1987-89; cons. in liver disease NIH, 1977-80, mem. adv. coun. Nat. Inst. Diabetes and Digestive and Kidney Diseases, 1990-94. Editor: (with others) Chemistry and Physiology of the Bile Pigments, 1977, Frontiers in Liver Disease, 1981, Myelofibrosis and the Biology of Connective Tissue, 1984, Hans Popper: A Tribute, 1992, Hepatic Transport and Bile Secretion, 1993, Polythemia Vera, 1994; editor in chief Seminars in Liver Disease, 1981-90, 96—, Hepatology, 1991-96; mem. editorial bd. Artificial Organs, 1979-92, Liver, 1980-93; contbr. articles to profl. jours. Served as sr. surgeon USPHS, 1966-69, 75-77. Recipient Merck award Columbia U., 1964; Fulbright scholar, 1959 Fellow ACP, Am. Coll. Gastroenterology; chmn., bd. dirs. Am. Liver Found., 2000—; mem. Am. Soc. Clin. Investigation, Assn. Am. Physicians, Am. Assn. Study of Liver Disease (councillor 1985-93, v.p. 1988, pres. 1989), Internat. Assn. Study of Liver (councillor 1988-91), Am. Soc. for Hematology, Am. Clin. and Climatological Assn., Nat. Polycthemia Vera Study Group (vice chmn. 1978-95), Soc. Exptl. Biol. Medicine (councillor 1993-96), N.Y. Soc. Study of Blood (pres. 1982-83), Sigma Xi, Phi Deta Kappa, Alpha Omega Alpha. Office: Mt Sinai Sch Medicine Box 1039 1 Gustave L Levy Pl New York NY 10029-6500 E-mail: paul.berk@mssm.edu.

BERK, PHILIP WOOLF, journalist; b. Cape Town, South Africa, Feb. 13, 1933; arrived in U.S., 1952; s. Benjamin and Rebecca (Brenner) Berk; m. Ruth Greenberg, June 20, 1954; children: Benjamin, Alexander, Ann, Melanie. BA, UCLA, 1955; gen. secondary life tchg. credential, Calif. State U., Northridge, 1963—63; MA, Calif. State U., 1965. With The Argus Group, Johannesburg, 1974—83; pres. Hollywood Fgn. Press Assn., 1989—92; internat. freelancer. Mem.: Hollywood Fgn. Press Assn. (pres. 1990—92), Phi Eta Sigma. Home: 6829 Mclennan Ave Van Nuys CA 91406-4530 Office: The Argus Group PO Box 1014 Johannesburg South Africa 2000

BERKA, MARIANNE GUTHRIE, health and physical education educator; b. Queens, N.Y., Dec. 25, 1944; d. Frank Joseph and Mary (DePaul) Guthrie; m. Jerry George Berka, June 1, 1968; children: Katie, Keri. BS, Ithaca Coll., 1966, MS, 1968; EdD, NYU, 1990. Tchr. Northport H.S., 1966—67; prof. Health, Phys. Edn. and Recreation Nassau C.C., Garden City, NY, 1968—. Adj. assoc. prof. Hofstra U., Hempstead, NY, 1998—. Mem.: AAHPER, AAHPERD, Am. Coll. Sports Medicine (cert. health/fitness instr.), Am. Assn. Sex Educators, Counselors and Therapists (cert. sex educator), N.Y. State Assn. Health, Phys. Edn., Recreation and Dance (J.B. Nash scholarship com. 1983—2000, Nassau Zone Disting. Svc. award 1988, Disting. Svc. award, Nassau zone 1988, Higher Edn. Tchr. of Yr. (Nassau Zone) 2003), Assn. Women Phys. Educators N.Y. State (chpt. chmn. 1973—74, chpt. treas. 1980—84). Roman Catholic. Home: 90 Bay Way Ave Brightwaters NY 11718 2012 Office: P226 HPER Nassau Community Coll Garden City NY 11530

BERKE, AMY TURNER, health science association administrator; b. Cleve., Oct. 27, 1942; d. Elliott L. and Evelyn (Silverman) Glicksberg; m. Donald Alan Turner, Dec. 16, 1962 (div. 1979); children: Matthew, Kelli; m. Joseph Jerold Berke, June 21, 1981; children: Richard, Rachel, Jason. Student, Ohio State U., 1960-63; BS, Wayne State U., 1965, MA, 1966. Tchr. Waterford (Mich.) Sch. System, 1965-67; v.p. Apt. Referral Service, Oak Park, Mich., 1970-73; instr. Detroit Coll. Bus., Dearborn, Mich., 1975-79; exec. dir. Detroit Neurosurgical Found., 1979—. Past bd. dirs. Internat. Mus. Surg. Sci., Friends of Belle Isle; bd. dirs. Goodwill Industries Found.; sec. bd. dirs. Jewish Home for Aged; mem. Citizens Adv. Wayne County Youth; commr., vice chair Detroit Recreation Adv. Commn.; commr. Youth Sports and Recreation Commn. Mem. Coun. Mich. Founds., Wayne State U. Alumni Club, Ohio State U. Alumni Club, Coun. of Mich. Founds., Detroit Area Grantmakers. Avocations: reading, hiking, aerobics, traveling. Office: Detroit Neurosurg Found 3333 E Jefferson Ave Detroit MI 48207

BERKE, IRVING, obstetrician-gynecologist, military officer; b. Bklyn., June 21, 1924; s. Abraham and Adela (Soffer) Berkowitz; m. Ruth E. Miller, Dec. 28, 1947 (dec. Feb. 1996); children: David, Laura, Nancy; m. Teresa A. Sears, Apt. 19, 1997. Student, U. Wis., 1943; MD, Case Western Res. U., 1949. Cert. in obstetrics and gynecology; recert. Commd. 1st lt. U.S. Army, 1949, advanced through grades to col., 1972; ret., 1984; med. dir. U.S. Army M.C., 1949-56; pvt. practice Youngstown, Ohio, 1956-63; med. officer USAR, Youngstown and L.A., 1956-84; pvt. practice Long Beach, Calif., 1963-83; physician Long Beach Dept. Health and Human Svcs., 1992-99. Med. advisor Calif. Blue Shield, L.A., 1967-73, Med. Bd. Calif., L.A., 1985-93; expert witness in ob-gyn., L.A., 1985—; asst. clin. prof. ob-gyn. Sch. Medicine, U. Calif., Irvine, 1977-83. Fellow ACOG, Internat. Coll. Surgeons; mem. Am. Acad. Anti Aging Medicine. Avocations: tennis, jogging, alternative medicine. Home and Office: 6430 E Mantova St Long Beach CA 90815-4658 E-mail: longfinger@prodigy.net.

BERKE, JUDIE KLEYMAN, publisher, editor; b. Mpls., Apr. 15, 1938; d. Maurice M. and Sue (Supak) Kleyman. Student, Mpls. Sch. Art, 1945-59, U. Minn., 1956-60. Freelance illustrator and designer, 1959—; pres. Berke-Wood, Inc., N.Y.C., 1971-80, Manhattan Rainbow & Lollipop Co. subs. Berke-Wood, Inc., 1971-80, Get Your Act Together, N.Y.C., 1971-80, Coord. Pubs., Inc., 1982-87; pres., CEO Health Market Comm., 1987—. Pres. Pub. and Media Svcs., Burbank, Calif., 1987—; pub., editor Continuing Care Coord., Health Watch mags.; pres. Continuing Care Coord. Convs. and Seminars; pres. Rainbow and Lillipop Prodns., 1994—; cons. to film and ednl. cos.; guest lectr. various colls. and univs. in Calif. and N.Y., 1973—; cons., designer Healthy Lifestyle mag. Writer, illustrator, dir. numerous ednl. filmstrips, 1972—including Focus on Professions, 1974, Focus on the Performing Arts, 1974, Focus on the Creative Arts, 1974, Workstyles, 1976, Wonderworm, 1976, Supernut, 1977; author, illustrator film Fat Black Mack, 1970 (San Francisco Ednl. Film Festival award, part of permanent collections Mus. Modern Art, N.Y.C.); designer posters and brochures for various entertainment groups, 1963—; composer numerous songs including Time is Relative, 1976, Love Will Live On in My Mind, 1976, My Blue Walk, 1976, You Make Me a Baby, 1982, Let's Go Around Once More, 1983, Anytime Anyplace Anywhere, 1987, Bittersweet, 1987, Sometimes It Pays, 1987, Gimme Back My Money Blues, Everybody Wants Me But the One I Love, Skin to Skin, It's Your Turn to Sing the Blues, Deny Till You Die, Men Just Call It Woman Talk, Poor Me, Women's Work is Never Done, 1993; composer, author off-Broadway musical Street Corner Time, 1978; prodr.: The Real Estate TV Shows, 1988-89; contbr. children's short stories to various publs., also articles. Trustee The Happy Spot Sch., N.Y.C., 1972-75. Mem. NAFE, Nat. Fedn. Bus. and Profl. Women, Am. Acad. Polit. and Social Sci., Women in Animation. E-mail: Judieberke@earthlink.net.

BERKEBILE, CHARLES ALAN, geology educator, hydrogeology researcher; b. Queens, NY, Mar. 4, 1938; s. Charles Dean and Bernice (Manlove) B.; children: Patricia Berlowe. BS, Allegheny Coll., 1960; MA, Boston U., 1961, PhD, 1964. Mem. rsch. staff MIT, Cambridge, 1963-64; asst. prof. Southampton (N.Y.) Coll. L.I. U., 1964-67, assoc. prof., dept. chair Southampton (N.Y.) Coll., 1969-75, prof., assoc. dir. Southampton (N.Y.) Coll., 1975-81; rsch. mineralogist Corning (N.Y.) Glass Works, 1967-69; prof., dept. chair Corpus Christi (Tex.) State U., 1981-91; prof., dir. Tex. A&M U., Corpus Christi, 1991—, prof., asst. dean, 1994-98, Regents prof., 2001. Vis. assoc. chemist Brookhaven Nat. Lab., Upton, N.Y., 1966-67; vis. sr. rsch. geologist Princeton (N.J.) U., 1979-80. Contbr. articles to profl. jours. Mem. Regional Stormwater Master Plan Adv. Com., Corpus Christi, 1989-90, Mayor's Adv. Com. on Water Issues, Corpus Christi, 1991-92; treas., bd. dirs. Rockport (Tex.) Country Club Estates Homeowners Assn., 1991-94. Named Outstanding Educator, Koch Industries, 2001. Fellow Geol. Soc. Am.; mem. Assn. Ground Water Scientists and Engrs., Nat. Ground Water Assn., Nat. Assn. Geology Tchrs., Tex. Ground Water Assn. (bd. dirs. 1990—, v.p. ground water sci. 1994, pres. 1995-96), Corpus Christi Geol. Soc. Avocations: golf, music. Home: 314 Champions Dr Rockport TX 78382-6906 Office: Tex A&M U 6300 Ocean Dr Corpus Christi TX 78412-5503 E-mail: alanb@falcon.tamucc.edu., alanb@pyramid3.net.

BERKEL, EDWIN MARTIN, fire marshal; b. Washington, Mo., Oct. 8, 1949; s. Edward Frederick and Verna Victoria (Pinkley) B.; m. Reba R. Maupin, June 2, 1979; 1 child; Brian Edwin. A in Applied Sci., East Central Coll., 1980. Fire inspector Mehlville Fire Protection Dist., St. Louis, Mo., 1981-85, fire marshal, 1985—. Dir. Bldg. Ofcls. and Code Adminstrs., Inc., Country Club Hills, Ill, 1995-2002, sec.-treas., 2002-03; dir. St. Clair Fire Protection Dist., St. Clair, Mo., 1990-99, 2002—, Internat. Code Coun., Fairfax, Va.. Mem. Fire Marshals Assn. Mo. (pres. 1995-99, sec. 1987-95). St. Louis Met. Area Fire Marshals Assn. (pres. 1992-95). Baptist. Avocation: golf. Office: Mehlville Fire Protection Dist 11020 Mueller Rd Saint Louis MO 63123-6943 Fax: 314-894-3964. E-mail: eberkel@mehlvillefire.gen.mo.us.

BERKELEY, EDMUND, JR., retired archivist, educator; b. Charlottesville, Va., Apr. 1, 1937; s. Edmund and Dorothy A. Berkeley; m. Elizabeth Makaritis, June 9, 1963; children: Maria Randolph, Edmund III. BA, U. South, 1958; MA in Am. History, U. Va., 1961. Prep. sch. tchr., 1961-63; asst. archivist Archives divsn. Va. State Libr., 1963-65; sr. asst., asst. curator Manuscripts divsn. U. Va., Charlottesville, 1965-69, univ. archivist, 1976-87, curator manuscripts, 1970-87, records adminstr., 1976-99, dir. spl. collections dept., 1987-93, sr. curator, 1994, univ. archivist, sr. assoc. dir., 1995-99, assoc. prof. Coll. Arts and Scis., 1976-99, assoc. prof. emeritus, 1999—. Cons. U. Ga. Library, George C. Marshall Library, SUNY-Stony Brook. Nat. Hist. Publs., Ashantilly Press. Editor: Autographs and Manuscripts: A Collector's Manual, 1978; author, editor articles to profl. jours. Commn. grantee Dept. Edn. Fellow Soc. Am. Archivists (coun. 1977-81); mem. Soc. Am. Architects, Mid-Atlantic Regional Archives Conf., Assn. Documentary Editing, Va. Hist. Soc. Episcopalian. Home: 2403 Bennington Rd Charlottesville VA 22901-2205 E-mail: eb2c@virginia.edu.

BERKELEY, FRANCIS LEWIS, JR., retired archivist; b. Albemarle County, Va., Apr. 9, 1911; s. Francis Lewis and Ethel (Crissey) B.; m. Helen Wayland Sutherland, June 12, 1937. BS, U. Va., 1934, MA, 1940. Tchr. Va. pub. schs., 1934-38; curator manuscripts U. Va. Libr., Charlottesville, 1938-41, curator and univ. archivist, 1946-63, assoc. libr., 1957-63, sec. of Rector and Visitors, 1953-58, exec. asst. to pres., 1963-74, archivist emeritus, prof. emeritus, 1974—. Coun. Inst. Early Am. History and Culture. Editor, compiler: Dunmore's Proclamation of Emancipation, 1941, Annual Reports on Historical Collections, University of Virginia Library, 1945-50, with cumulative indexes, 1945, 50, Jefferson Papers of the University of Virginia, 1950, Papers of John Randolph of Roanoke, 1950, John Rolfe's True Relation, 1951, Introduction to Thomas Jefferson's Farm Book, 1953; mem. editl. bd. Va. Quar. Rev., 1961-74; contbr. to Dictionary of Biography, Ency. Brit., Collier's Nat. Am. Cyclopedia, other reference works. Sec. of navy adv. com. on naval history, 1958-74; trustee Thomas Jefferson Meml. Found.; mem. adv. com. Papers of Thomas Jefferson, Papers of James Madison, Papers of George Washington; mem. Va. Com. on Colonial Records, 1955-71, Va. Commn. on Hist. Records, 1976—. Served with USNR, 1942-46, capt. ret. Fulbright rsch. fellow U. Edinburgh, 1952-53, Guggenheim fellow U. London, 1961-62. Fellow Soc. Am. Archivists; mem. Am. Antiquarian Soc., Mass. Hist. Soc., Va. Hist. Soc. (v.p. 1970-78, trustee 1979—), Colonial Soc. Mass, Walpole Soc., Raven Soc., Colonnade Club (Charlottesville), Century Club (N.Y.), Phi Beta Kappa, Omicron Delta Kappa. Democrat. Episcopalian. Home: 2610 Barracks Rd Apt H226 Charlottesville VA 22901-2121

BERKELEY, SEAMUS OSBORNE, artist; b. Mar. 26, 1955; BA, Salem State Coll. Freelance artist and portrait painter, Taos, N.Mex. Represented by Gallery A, Taos. Home: 223 Victor Ct 4198 NDCBU Taos NM 87571 E-mail: seamus@sbart.com.

BERKELHAMER, JAY ELLIS, pediatrician; b. Tuscaloosa, Ala., Apr. 8, 1942; s. Louis H. and Belle F. B.; m. Jacqueline Beth Colman, June 12, 1966; children: Beth Carolyn, Sara Kay, Adam Colman. BS, U. Mich., 1963, MD, 1967. Resident U. Chgo., 1967-70, asst. prof., 1972-78, assoc. prof., 1978-84, prof., 1984-93, assoc. chair, dir. residency program, 1986-93, assoc. dean ambulatory care, 1983-88; chair pediatrics Henry Ford Health Sys., Detroit, 1993-99. Prof. pediatrics Case Western Res. U., Cleve., 1994-99; clin. prof. pediatrics and communicable diseases U. Mich., Ann Arbor, 1994-99; sr. v.p. for med. affairs Children's Healthcare of Atlanta, 1999—; clin. prof. pediats. Emory U., Atlanta, 1999—. Lt. comdr. USPHS, 1970-72. Robert Wood Johnson Health Policy fellow NAS, Washington, 1978-79. Mem. Am. Acad. Pediatrics (pres. Ill. chpt. 1992), Chgo. Pediatric Soc. (pres. 1987, Archibald L. Hoyne award 1993), Ambulatory Pediatric Assn. (pres. 1986). Office: 1600 Tullie Circle Atlanta GA 30329

BERKELHAMMER, ROBERT BRUCE, lawyer; b. Providence, Oct. 27, 1949; s. Cyril Lester and Anne Louise (Rossman) B.; m. Miriam June Finkelstein, Mar. 9, 1975; children: Jessi, Max, Abby. BA, U. Rochester, 1971; JD, Boston U., 1974. Bar: R.I. 1975, U.S. Dist. Ct. R.I. 1977, Mass. 1998, Conn. 2001. Atty. NLRB, Pitts., 1974-77; ptnr. Licht & Semonoff, Providence, 1977-97, Chace Ruttenberg & Freedman, LLP, Providence, 1997—. Pres. Jewish Family Service, Inc., Providence, 1988-91. Mem.: ABA, RI Jewish Hist. Assn. (pres. 2000—02), R.I. Bar Assn. Jewish. Home: 131 Laurel Ave Providence RI 02906-4622 Office: Chace Ruttenberg & Freedman 1 Park Row Ste 300 Providence RI 02903-1235 E-mail: rberkelhammer@crfllp.com.

BERKELMAN, KARL, physics educator; b. Lewiston, Maine, June 7, 1933; s. Robert George and Yvonne (Langlois) B.; m. Mary Bowen Hobbie, Oct. 10, 1959; children: Thomas, James, Peter. BS, U. Rochester, N.Y., 1955; PhD, Cornell U., 1959. From asst. prof. to prof. physics Cornell U., Ithaca, N.Y., 1961—, dir. lab. nuclear studies, 1985-2000; sci. assoc. DESY, Hamburg, Fed. Republic of Germany, 1974-75, CERN, Geneva, 1967-68, 81-82, 91-92, 2000-2001. Office: Cornell U Newman Lab Ithaca NY 14853

BERKENBLIT, SCOTT IRA, orthopaedic surgeon; b. Bklyn., Jan. 3, 1964; s. Ronald Henry and Sarita (Daniels) B.; m. Gail Benson, Oct. 19, 1997. BS, MIT, 1986, MS, 1990, PhD, 1996; MD, Harvard U., 1996. Diplomate Nat. Bd. Med. Examiners; lic. in Md. Intern in gen. surgery Johns Hopkins Hosp., Balt., 1996-97, resident in orthopaedic surgery, 1997-01. Author: (with others) Advances in Osteoarthritis, 1998; contbr. articles to profl. jours. Exec. bd. Roland Springs Cmty. Assn., Balt., 1999, chmn. residential issues com., 1999. NSF fellow 1987-90. Mem. AMA, Am. Acad. Orthopaedic Surgeons, Orthopaedic Rsch. Soc., Sigma Xi, Phi Beta Kappa, Tau Beta Pi. Jewish. Avocations: playing the trumpet, skiing, hiking, classical music, strategic games. Home: 4313 Roland Springs Dr Baltimore MD 21210-2756 Office: 7350 Van Dusen Rd Ste 110 Laurel MD 20707 E-mail: bblit@alum.mit.edu.

BERKENES, JOYCE MARIE POORE, social worker; b. Des Moines, Aug. 29, 1953; d. Donald Roy and Thelma Beatrice (Hart) Poore; m. Robert Elliott Berkenes, Jan. 3, 1976; children: Tiffany Noelle, Cory Matthew. BA in Social Work and Biology, Simpson Coll., Indianola, Iowa., 1975. Resident counselor and group home mgr. Chaddock Boys Home, Quincy, Ill., 1976-78; social service dir. North Adams Nursing Home, Mendon, Ill., 1978; home tchr. Head Start, Camp Point, Ill., 1978-79, home tchr. supr./edn. and parent involvement coordinator, 1979-82; family counselor Iowa Children's and Family Services, Des Moines, 1982-85; family counselor and vol. coordinator Luth. Social Services, Des Moines, 1985-89; coordinator/educator/social worker Parent-Infant Nurturing Ctr., Meth. Med. Ctr., Des Moines, 1989-95; social worker The Homestead, 1995-97; state program mgr. Healthy Families Iowa Projects of Home Care Iowa, Des Moines, 1997-01, Healthy Families Am. Trainer, 1998—; program dir. HOPES/ Healthy Families Iowa Prevent Child Abuse Iowa, 2001—03; rep. State Domestic Violence Response Tng. Team Iowa Dept. Pub. Health, 2003—. Mem. Greater Des Moines Child Abuse and Neglect Coun. Bd.; cons. in field, 1975-76. Mem. infant mortality prevention/health start consortium; mem. Prevent Child Abuse Iowa. Mem. Internat. Assn. Infant Massage, Abbie Gardner Questers. Democrat. United Ch. Christ. Avocations: collecting antiques, reading, playing piano, ballet, church work. Home: 2901 NE 80th St Altoona IA 50009-9423

BERKENKAMP, FRED JULIUS, management consultant; b. Alma, Wis., Oct. 19, 1925; s. Julius Henry and Elisabeth Helen Berkenkamp; m. Ruth Ethelyn Taylor; children: Linda Birch, Vicki Fitzgerald, Thomas, JoAnne. BS in Electron Engring, U. Wyo., 1948; postgrad., U. Syracuse, N.Y., 1951. Quality control mgmt. Gen. Electric Co., Syracuse, 1948-55, corporate cons. mfg. mgmt. N.Y.C., 1955-65, mgr. planning jet engines Cin., 1966-68, mgr. nuclear fuels mfg. Wilmington, N.C., 1969; corp. exec. v.p., pres. Appliance Group, Roper Corp., Kankakee, Ill., 1970-80; pres., chief exec. officer, dir. Allied Structural Steel Co. subs. MSL Industries/Alleghany Corp., Chicago Heights, Ill., 1980-83; pres. Berkenkamp & Co. Inc., mgmt. cons., 1984—; pres., CEO FMH, Inc., Newport Beach, Calif., 1988-91. Trustee Community Coll., 1974-80. Served with USNR, 1944-46. Mem. Assn. Home Appliance Mfrs. (chmn. bd. dirs.), Gas Appliance Mfrs. Assn. (dir.), Sigma Chi. Home: 14216 W Cavalcade Dr Sun City West AZ 85375-5624

BERKENSTADT, JAMES ALLAN, lawyer; b. Chgo., June 26, 1956; s. Edward Jules and Lois Marion (Solomon) B.; m. Holly Lynn Cremer, Aug. 3, 1985; children: Rebecca, Bradley. BA, Northwestern U., 1978; JD, So. Ill. U., 1981. Bar: Ill., Wis. Litigation atty. Pollina & Phelan, Chgo., 1982-85; atty. for security dept. Chgo. Cubs Nat. League Ball Club, Chgo., 1982-84; litigation atty. Axley & Brynelson, Madison, Wis., 1986-87; v.p., corporate counsel The Wisconsin Cheeseman, Inc., Madison, 1987—. Author: Black Market Beatles: The Story Behind The Lost Recordings, 1995, Nevermind: Nirvana, 1998; prodr. The Beatles Tapes CD, 1994—, Live At The Edgewater: vol. 1 and 2 CD; hist. cons. for The Beatles, 2002; contbr. articles to Musician mag. Bd. dirs. Cremer Charitable Found., Madison, 1989—, Alliant Energy Ctr. Bd. Dave County; Transport 20/20 Dave County; historian/archivist for rock band Garbage, Estate of George Harrison. Mem. NARAS. Avocations: golf, writing. Office: The Wisconsin Cheeseman Inc 301 Broadway Dr Sun Prairie WI 53590-1799

BERKETT, MARIAN MAYER, lawyer; b. Mar. 29, 1913; d. Maurice J. and Beulah (Lob) Mayer; m. George David B., Jan. 26, 1943. BA, La. State U., 1933, MA, 1935; LLB, Tulane U., 1937. Bar: La. 1937. Assoc. firm Deutsch, Kerrigan & Stiles, New Orleans, 1937—61, ptnr., 1961—. Bd. dir. New Orleans Lawyer Referral Svc. Author: (non-fiction) Workmen's Compensation Law in Louisiana, 1937; contbr. articles to Tulane Law Rev. Mem. charter commn., Jefferson Parish, La., 1953; vice chmn. La. Civil Svc. Commn., Baton Rouge, 1963—75; mem. adv. com. on charter reform Jefferson Parish; bd. dir., officer Family Svc. Soc. of New Orleans; mem. budget com. Cmty. Chest of New Orleans; emeritus mem. Bur. Govtl. Rsch. New Orleans Met. Area Com. ACLU; bd. dir., officer, hon. pres. La. Civil Svc. League; bd. dir. New Orleans chpt. NCCJ. Recipient Monte Lemann award, La. Civil Svc. League, 1973, award, Am. Coun. for Career Women, 1989, Disting. Grad. award, Tulane Law Sch., Lifetime Achievement award, La. Civil Svc. League. Mem.: ABA (vice chmn. fidelity and surety com. ins. sect., governing com. forum on constrn. industry,

Cornerstone award), New Orleans Bar Assn. (award of spl. distinction), La. Bar Assn., Am. Law Inst., Order of Coif. Home: 332 Iona St Metairie LA 70005-4140 Office: Deutsch Kerrigan & Stiles 755 Magazine St New Orleans LA 70130-3698

BERKEY, DENNIS D. mathematics educator; b. Wooster, Ohio, May 27, 1947; s. William Bruce and Mary Louise (Schrock) B.; m. Catherine Grooms, Aug. 24, 1974; children: Cristin, Aaron, Jessica. BA, Muskingum Coll., New Concord, Ohio, 1969; MA, Miami U., Oxford, Ohio, 1971; PhD, U. Cin., 1974. Lectr. U. Cin., 1972-73; instr. Miami U., Oxford, Ohio, 1973-74; asst. prof. math. Boston U., 1974-79, assoc. prof. math., 1979-93, prof. Math., 1993—, dean grad. sch., 1987—2002, dean arts and scis., 1987—2002, provost, 1987-91, 96—. Author: Calculus, 1983, 3d edit., 1992, Applied Calculus, 1986, 3d edit., 1994, Calculus for Management, 1986, 3d edit., 1994. Recipient Metcalf Award for Excellence in Teaching, Boston U., 1978. Mem. Am. Math. Soc., Math. Assn. Am., Soc. for Indsl. and Applied Math. Home: 30 Nobscot Rd Weston MA 02493-1147 Office: Boston U One Sherborn St Boston MA 02215 E-mail: berkey@bu.edu.

BERKEY, DONALD FREDERICK, counseling administrator; b. E. Cleveland, OH, Feb. 17, 1954; s. Fred Henry and Doris Mae (Oestreich) Berkey; m. Barbara Jean Cartmell, May 7, 1977; children: Lauren Ashley, Matthew Owen. BA, Coll. of Wooster, Wooster, OH, 1976; EdM, Cleveland State U, Cleveland, OH, 1984. Cert. guidance couns. State of OH, elementary ed. State of OH, psycology State of OH, speech State of OH. Driver ed. tchr. Strongsville City Schools, Strongsville, Ohio, 1976—78; elem. sch. tchr. Columbia Local Sch., Columbia Sta., Ohio, 1978—83, mid. sch. tchr., 1983—85; guidance coun. Strongsville City Sch., Strongsville, Ohio, 1985—. H.s. and coll. basketball referee, 1981—; volleyball ofcl., 1997—; elder Presbyn. ch., Berea, Ohio, 1982—. Recipient hon. scholar, Martha Holden Jennings Foundation, 2000. Mem.: Who's Who among Am. Tchr. (hon.), Ohio Sch. Coun. Assoc. (assoc.), Ohio Ed. Assoc. (assoc.), Parent Tchr. Assoc. (life). Presbyterian. Achievements include presented at state and nat conv. on middle sch. orgn. and devel. Avocations: sports, travel. Home: 335 Bonds Pkwy Berea OH 44017 Office: Albion Middle Sch 11109 Webster Rd Strongsville OH 44136-3723

BERKEY, JEFFREY ALAN, project manager; b. Danville, Ind., Oct. 3, 1963; s. Donald Lloyd and Judith Ann Berkey; m. Lisa Marie Durham, July 21, 1963. BA, Bob Jones U., 1987; postgrad., U. Indpls. Dept. supr. Zacson/IBM, Indpls., 1991—95; account mgr. Vanstar, Inc., Indpls., 1995—97; dept. mgr. Conseco, Carmel, Ind., 1997—99; project mgr. S.G.I., Indpls., 1999—. Nursing home ministry Brownsburg Health Care, Ind., 2001—03; adult Sunday sch. tchr. Bethesda Bapt. Ch., Brownsburg, Ind., 1988—2003. Mem.: U.S. Parachute Assn., Toastmasters Internat. (club officer 1993—95, Able Toastmaster 1995). Conservative. Baptist. Avocations: public speaking, marathons, triathlons, skydiving, scuba diving. Home: 17 Ashwood Cir Brownsburg IN 46112 Office: SGI 8350 Allison Ave Indianapolis IN 46268 Personal E-mail: jberkey@sgi-net.com. Business E-Mail: jberkey@sgi-net.com.

BERKHOFER, ROBERT FREDERICK, JR., retired history educator; b. Teaneck, N.J., Nov. 20, 1931; s. Robert Frederick and Elsa Berkhofer; m. Genevieve Zito, June 9, 1962; 1 child, Robert Frederick III. BA, SUNY, Albany, 1953; MA, Cornell U., 1955, PhD, 1960. Instr. Ohio State U., Columbus, 1959-60; from instr. to assoc. prof. U. Minn., Mpls., 1960-69; prof. U. Wis., Madison, 1969-73, U. Mich., Ann Arbor, 1973-91; grad. rsch. prof. U. Fla., Gainesville, 1984-85; prof. history U. Calif., Santa Cruz, 1991-97; ret., 1997. Author: Salvation and the Savage, 1965, A Behavioral Approach to Historical Analysis, 1969, The White Man's Indian, 1978, Beyond the Great Story, 1995. Recipient fellowships Social Sci. Rsch. Coun., 1957-59, Nat. Endowment for Humanities, 1973-74, John Simon Guggenheim Found., 1978-79, Stanford Humanities Ctr., 1987-88. Mem. Am. Studies Assn. (pres. 1980-82), Orgn. Am. Historians (exec. bd. 1981-84), Am. Hist. Assn. E-mail: berkhof@urcad.org.

BERKHOUT, BJORN HALDANE, composer, music educator; b. L.A., Sept. 25, 1969; s. Jan and Barbara Berkhout; life ptnr. Todd Nickow. MusB, U. Minn., 1991, MusM, 1994; MusD, Northwestern U., 2003. Lectr. Northwestern U., Evanston, Ill., 1998—2001, Loyola U., Chgo., 1998—. Composer: Visual Sound, 2000 (William T. Faricy award, 1998, nominee Gaudeamus prize, 2000), Zapstar, 2003. Treas. Golden Valley (Minn.) Orch., 1995—96; judge PTA Reflections Program, Chgo. Grantee, N.Y. Art Ensemble, 1998. Mem.: Composers' Forum. Office: Loyola U 6525 N Sheridan Rd Chicago IL 60626-5311

BERKLAND, JAMES OMER, geologist; b. Glendale, Calif., July 31, 1930; m. Janice Lark Keirstead, Dec. 19, 1966; children: Krista Lynn, Jay Olin. AA, Santa Rosa Jr. Coll., 1951; AB, U. Calif., Berkeley, 1958; MS, San Jose State U., 1964; postgrad., U. Calif., Davis, 1969-72. Registered geologist, Calif.; cert. engring. geologist, Calif. Psychiat. tech. Sonoma State Hosp., 1951-57; with U.S. Geol. Survey, 1958-64; engring. geologist U.S. Bur. Reclamation, 1964-69, cons. geologist, 1969-72; asst. prof. Appalachian State U., Boone, N.C., 1972-73; county geologist Santa Clara County, San Jose, Calif., 1973-94; ret., 1994. Mem. geotech. adv. com., San Jose; adj. prof. San Jose State U., 1973—75; lectr. Gen. Edn. Conf. Sci. and Tech. Soc., 1985—89, coord. com. Calif. Conv., 1978; mem. evening faculty San Jose City Coll.; mem. West Valley Legis. Com., 1979—90; lectr. ann. deposit recipt seminar San Jose Real Estate Bd., 1980—85; discoverer in field; featured spkr. Keynote Spkrs., Inc.; role model San Jose Sch. Dist., 1995—97; geology tchr. Sonoma High Sch. Adult Edn., 2001—03. Contbr. numerous articles to profl. jours.; originator seismic window theory for earthquake prediction, 1974; TV and radio appearances including PBA, Frontline, Evening Mag., People are Talking, 48 Hours, Sightings, You Bet Your Life, Science Faction, Science Fiction Cable, Two on the Town, In Search of CNN News, WGN, KIRO, KSL, KIEV, KGO, KCBS, KNYV, KOA, KOGO, KVEN, KSCO, KOMO, KPFK, Two at Noon, KPFA-FM Radio, The Other Side, Northwest Afternoon, Art Bell's Coast to Coast, Town Meeting, Ron Owens Show, Laura Lee Show, Art Bell Show, Kathi Gori Show, Extra, Strange Universe; articles on work featured in OMNI, STERN, Wall St. Jour., Bergen's Tidende, San Francisco Examiner, San Francisco Chronicle, L.A. Times, Nat. Geog., Am. Health, The Astrology Ency., Old Farmers Almanac, 1991, Gilroy Dispatch, Bakersfield Californian, San Jose Mercury News, Sonoma Index Tribune, Intuition, Farmers Almanac, others; editor, pub.: SYZYGY-An Earthquake Newsletter, 1990—; co-founder Quakeline. Treas. Creekside/Park Pl. Homeowners Group; mem. various city and county adv. bds.; mem. legis. com. Route 85 Task Force, Earthquake Watch, 1979—82, New Weather Observer, Nat. Wildlife Fedn.; active Statue of Liberty Found.; mem. tech. and soc. San Jose Sch. Dist., 1980—, mem. role model program, 1996—97; mem. Sonoma Land Trust; bd. dirs. Glen Ellen Cmty. Ch., 2001—; v.p. West Coast Aquatics, Creekside/Park Pl. Swim Team; mem. Ctr. Study Early Man East Valley WMCA; mem. legis. com. West Valley YMCA, 1980—; mem. Found. for the Study of Cycles, invited lectr. monthly and ann. meeting.; mem. The Nature Conservancy; Nat. Wildlife Fedn.; charter mem. The Dolphin Inst.; docent Bouverie Nature Preserve, 1999—; mem. Jack London Found. Recipient Resolution of Commendation Santa Clara Bd. Suprs., 1994; Dwight E. Stanford fellow A.J. Robinson Found. Mem. Smithsonian Inst. (assoc.), Ret. Pub. Employee Assn. Calif., Alumni Assn. San Jose State U., Sons of Norway, Sonoma Hist. Soc., Jack London Reading Group, Lions Club (various offices and awards, including pres. Valley of the Moon Lions, 2002-03, Lion of Yr. awards 1990-91, 93-94). Home: 1175 Chauvet Rd # 1926 Glen Ellen CA 95442-1926 Fax: (707) 935-6639. E-mail: syzygyjob@aol.com.

BERKLEY, BURTON, federal judge; b. Chgo., May 10, 1934; s. Ralph Albert and Frieda (Fleischman) Berkowitz; m. Carol Grace Goldberg, Dec. 22, 1955; children: David Saul (dec.), Florence Melissa Berkley-Yokie. AB, Harvard U., 1955, JD, 1958. Bar: Ill. 1958, U.S. Supreme Ct. 1962, N.Y. 1969, D.C. 1978. Asst. atty. gen. Ill. Atty. Gen.'s Office, Chgo., 1958-59; asst. U.S. atty. Dept. of Justice, Chgo., 1959-61, appellate trial atty. Tax Div., Washington, 1961-67; dep. tax counsel GE, N.Y.C., 1967-70; legal advisor NIH, HEW, Washington, 1971-72, dep. gen. counsel, 1972-77; spl. counsel to assoc. commr. Office of Hearings and Appeal, Social Security Adminstrn., Arlington, Va., 1977-80, dep. chmn. appeals coun. Office of Hearings and Appeals, 1980-88, chief adminstrv. law judge Hearing Office, Washington, 1988-97, adminstrv. law judge, 1997—. Co-editor: Ethical Issues in Human Genetics, 1973. Avocations: reading, music, theatre, travel. Office: Social Security Adminstrn Office Hearings and Appeals 820 1st St NE 8th Fl Washington DC 20002-4243 E-mail: burton50@msn.com.

BERKLEY, EMILY CAROLAN, lawyer; b. Richmond, Va., Mar. 2, 1950; d. Charles Garvice and Edna Gray (Berkley) Broom; m. Richard E. Bird, Sept. 6, 1969 (div. Mar. 1988); children: Jessica A. Bird, Martel J. Bird. Student, Coll. of William and Mary, 1968-70; BS in Psychology cum laude, Tufts U., 1972; JD magna cum laude, Temple U., 1977. Ptnr. Ballard Spahr Andrews & Ingersoll LLP, Phila., 1977—. Seminar panelist Pa. Bar Inst., 1992, 98-2003, Practicing Law Inst., 1993-2003. Long range planning com. Performing Arts for Tredyffrin-Easttown Sch. Dist., Berwyn, Pa., 1989, chair subcom. on creativity, futures com., 1990; active United Way, 1989-91; bd. dirs. Devon-Strafford Little League, 1992-95. Fellow: Am. Bar Found. (life); mem.: ABA (chair task force on exporation of Uniform Comml. Code 1995—97, vice chair internat. comml. law subcom. 1997—99, bus. law sect. liaison U.S. Sec. of State's adv. com. on pvt. interest 1998—2001, vice chair com. on legal opinions 2002—, mem. Uniform Comml. Code com.), N.Y. TriBar Opinion Com., Phila. Bar Assn., Pa. Bar Assn. (bus. law sect., chair legal opinion task force, chair article 9 task force, treas.), Am. Law Inst., Am. Coll. Comml. Fin. Lawyers (bd. regents 1993—2001, pres. 2000). Office: Ballard Spahr Andrews et al 1735 Market St Ste 5100 Philadelphia PA 19103-7599 E-mail: berkley@ballardspahr.com.

BERKLEY, ERMA VAN METER, retired librarian; b. Thayer, Kans., Nov. 18, 1922; d. George William and Elizabeth (Hamill) Van Meter; m. Donald William Berkley, May 28, 1944 (dec. 1980); children: Ann Elizabeth, James Donald. BA in Bus. Edn. magna cum laude, Western Wash. U., 1964; MLS, U. Wash., 1973. Cert. profl. libr., 1976. Sec., bookkeeper Blue Ribbon Growers, Inc., Yakima, Wash., 1941-44; aircraft communicator CAA, Kodiak, Alaska, 1944-47; libr., sec., tchr. Crescent Consol. Sch., Joyce, Wash., 1965-66; asst. libr., reference libr. Port Angeles (Wash.) High Sch., 1966-68, secretarial tchr., 1968-75, head libr., 1975-86; ret., 1986. Bd. dirs. exec. com. Wash. Libr. Network, 1979-81; N.W. rep.-at-large Washington Libr. Media Assn., 1983-84; del. Gov.'s Conf. on Libr. and Info. Svcs., Olympia, 1979; sec. Western Wash. Bus. Edn. Assn., 1973-74. Mem. AAUW (treas. 1966-67, pres. 1982-84, v.p. 1988-90), PEO, Nat. Ret. Tchrs. Assn., Am. Philatelic Soc., Phi Theta Kappa, Beta Phi Mu. Avocations: travel, philately, golf, hiking, gardening.

BERKLEY, EUGENE BERTRAM (BERT BERKLEY), envelope company executive; b. Kansas City, Mo., May 8, 1923; s. Eugene Bertram (Bert) Berkowitz and Caroline Newman (Newburger) B.; m. Joan Meinrath, Sept. 1, 1948; children: Janet Lynn Berkley Dubrava, William (Bill) Spencer, Jane Ellen Berkley Levitt. BA, Duke U., 1948; MBA, Harvard U., 1950. Pres., CEO Tension Envelope Corp., Kansas City, Mo., 1962-88, chmn. bd., 1967—. Patentee in field. Bd. dirs. The Inst. for Ednl. Leadership Inc., Washington; trustee, chmn. U. Kansas City, 1983-85, vice chmn., 1981-83, North Campus Devel. Com., policy bd., charter mem. Univ. Assocs.; chmn. bd. dirs. Minority Supplier Coun., 1986-88, bd. dirs. Ewing Marion Kauffman Found., Ctr. for Entrepreneurial Leadership, 1991—; chmn. Ctr. for Bus. Innovation, 1987-89; bd. dirs. Nat. Youth Info. Network, 1997—; mem. adv. bd. Nat. Coun. Econ. Edn., 1993-95, human resources com. Heart of Am. United Way, 1983, chmn. Comprehensive Needs and Svc. Survey Com., 1971; pres. Civic Coun. of Greater Kansas City, 1967-68, charter mem., bd. dirs. 1982-83; pres. C. of C. of Greater Kansas City, 1968-69; bd. dirs. Menorah Med. Ctr. Bd., 1980-94; mem. Kitchen Cabinet, Kansas City, Mo. Sch. Dist., 1990-92; chmn. adv. com., bd. dirs. Ctr. for Workplace Preparation, U.S. C. of C., 1989-91; trustee Midwest Rsch. Inst., exec. com., 1969-72; bd. dirs. Kansas City Area Health Planning Coun., Inc., 1982-83, Nat. Minority Supplier Devel. Coun., 1989-98; chmn. bd. dirs. Human Svcs. Testing and Retng. Coun., 1983-90; active Bus. Roundtable Dept. Social Svcs. State of Mo., 1989—; adv. bd. U. Kans. Natural History Mus., 1994-2000, Nat. Parks and Conservation Assn., 1986—; bd. dirs. Can. Cellulose Co., Vancouver, BC, 1973-80, founder, LINC, 1992; chmn. local investment commn. LINC Mo. Dept. Social Svcs., 1992-95, exec. comm., 1992—; mem. exec. com. Ctr. for Mgmt. Assistance, 1980-83; mem. Mayor's Prayer Breakfast Com., 1964-84; mem. exec. com., met. chmn. Nat. Alliance of Businessmen of Met. Kansas City, 1973; chmn. bd. dirs. Decorated Bronze Star; recipient Brotherhood award NCCJ, 1968, numerous other awards, including Mr. Kansas City award C. of C. of Greater Kansas City, 1972, Disting. Svc. award Johnson County Friends of the Libr. (Johnson County, Kans.), 1982, Chancellor's medal U. Mo.-Kansas City, 1989. Mem. Envelope Mfrs. Assn. (exec. com. 1960-63, 67-70, 76-79, vice chmn. exec. com. 1981-83, v.p. 1981-83, pres. 1983-85), Flexographic Tech. Assn. (bd. dirs. 1993-97), Oakwood Country Club, Homestead Country Club. Avocations: flyfishing, race walking, camping, white water rafting, backpacking. Office: Tension Envelope Corp 819 E 19th St Kansas City MO 64108-1781 E-mail: BertBerkley@tension.com.

BERKLEY, GAIL WINNICK, psychotherapist; b. Detroit, Feb. 21; d. Lawrence C. Winnick and Helen M. Caner Leytus; m. Daniel Theodore Berkley, Jan. 22, 1966 (div. Feb. 1989). MA in Orgn. and Leadership, U. San Francisco; MS in Psychology, San Francisco State U.; PhD in Psychology, Kensington U. Lic. marriage, family, child therapist. With San Francisco Unified Sch. Dist., 1971-81, Belmont (Calif.) Hills Psychiat. Hosp., Cmty. Counseling Ctr. San Mateo County, East Palo Alto, Calif.; pvt. practice Berkley Therapy & Mediation Ctr., San Mateo, Calif., 1981—. ASID allied designer Berkley Goods, San Mateo and San Francisco, 1969—; design cons. interior residential/comml. properties designer. Author: (book) Financial Planner, 1988, (manual) How to Handle Probate, 1988; pub. quar. mag. People in Transition, 1989. Commr., chair San Mateo County Juvenile Justice and Delinquency Prevention, San Mateo; commr. San Mateo Maternal Child and Adolescent Bd., Mem. AAUW (bd. dirs., women comty. rels.), San Francisco Legal Aux. (bd. dirs., charity), Peninsula Humane Soc. (chair fundraising, spl. events chair), San Francisco Zool. Soc. (guardian mem. fundraising). Avocations: animal rights, children, humanitarian rights advocate.

BERKLEY, JAMES DONALD, clergyman; b. Yakima, Wash., May 19, 1950; s. Donald William and Erma Ercile (Van Meter) B.; m. Deborah Milam, Aug. 18, 1974; children: Peter James, Mary Milam. BS, U. Wash., 1972; MDiv, Fuller Theol. Seminary, 1975, D Ministry, 1980. Intern First Presbyn. Ch., Yakima, Wash., 1971-73, Bel Air Presbyn. Ch., L.A., 1973-75; asst. pastor Community Presbyn Ch., Ventura, Calif., 1975-78; sr. pastor Dixon (Calif.) Community Ch., 1978-85; sr. assoc. editor Leadership jour. Christianity Today Inc., Carol Stream, Ill., 1985-90, editor Your Church, 1990-94; sr. assoc. pastor First Presbyn. Ch., Bellevue, Wash., 1994—2002; nat. issues ministry dir. Presbyns. for Renewal, Bellevue, 2002—. Author: Making the Most of Mistakes, 1987, Called into Crisis, 1988, The Dynamics of Church Finance, 2000, Essential Christianity, 2001; gen. editor: Preaching to Convince, 1986, Leadership Handbooks of Practical Theology, Vol. I, 1992, Vols. II and III, 1994; editor reNEWS, 1999—. Recipient 1st place award interview Evangelical Press Assn., 1991, 92. Republican. Avocations: bagpipes, hiking, tennis, golf, music. Home: 304 128th Ave NE Bellevue WA 98005-3242 Office: Presbyns for Renewal 304 128th Ave NE Bellevue WA 98005

BERKLEY, JOHN L. geology educator, meteoriticist; b. Lawrence, Kans., May 17, 1948; s. Robert Harris and Margaret (Lyons) B.; m. Mira Tetkowski, Oct. 9, 1977; children: Jory William, Alexander Donald. BS, U. Minn., Duluth, 1970; MS, U. Mo., 1972; PhD, U. N.Mex., 1977. Rsch. asst. U. N.Mex., Albuquerque, 1973-77; postdoctoral fellow Inst. of Meteoritics, Albuquerque, 1977-79; rsch. assoc. Lunar and Planetary Lab., Tucson, 1979-82; asst. prof. geology SUNY Coll. at Fredonia, 1982-88, assoc. prof., 1988-2000, prof., 2000—, interim dean, 1990-93, chair dept. geoscis., 1997—. Mem. Pres.'s Adv. Bd., Fredonia, 1998—. Author: In the Defense of This Flag, 1993; contbr. articles to profl. jours. Mem. Dunkirk-Fredonia Peace and Justice, 1984—. Meteorite Rsch. grantee NASA, 1984-92, NASA/Am. Assn. Engring. Educators, 1998-99. Mem. Geol. Soc. Am. (Penrose grantee 1975), Mineral. Soc. Am., Am. Geophys. Union, Meteoritical Soc., Phi Kappa Phi. Democrat. Avocations: photography, gardening, ice hockey. Home: 348 Temple St Fredonia NY 14063-1020 Office: SUNY Coll at Fredonia Geoscis Dept Fredonia NY 14063

BERKLEY, PETER LEE, lawyer; b. Newark, N.J., Mar. 10, 1939; s. Irving S. and Goldie A. (Karp) B.; m. Nancy R. Margolis, Aug. 2, 1964; children: James, Alison, John. BA, Williams Coll., 1960; JD, Harvard U., 1963. Bar: N.J. 1963, U.S. Dist. Ct. N.J. 1963. Assoc. Riker, Danzig, Scherer & Brown, Newark, 1963—68; ptnr. Riker, Danzig, Scherer & Hyland, Newark and Morristown, N.J., 1969-83; mng. ptnr. Riker, Danzig, Scherer, Hyland & Perretti, L.L.P., Morristown, 1984—95; ptnr. Riker, Danzig, Scherer, Hyland & Perretti, LLP, Morristown, 1996—99, of counsel, 1999—. Trustee Livingston (N.J.) Symphony Orch., 1975-89. Mem. ABA, N.J. State Bar Assn., Am. Coll. Real Estate Lawyers, Harvard Law Sch. Alumni Assn. N.J. (pres. 1980-81), Williams Coll. Alumni Assn. Ctrl. N.J. (pres. 1986-89), Phi Beta Kappa. Home: 16 Fordham Rd Livingston NJ 07039-5507 Office: Hdqrs Plz 1 Speedwell Ave Morristown NJ 07962-1981 E-mail: pberkley@riker.com.

BERKLEY, ROBERT JOHN, retired federal agency professional; b. Albion, Mich., Oct. 2, 1933; s. Paul Clifford and Ina Muriel (Burroughs) B.; m. Sharon Irene Haynes, Sept. 9, 1955 (div. 1965); children: Thomas Alan, Richard Jon, Luann Michele; m. Jacquelyn Jane (Lewis) Ballou, Jan. 14, 1966. AA, Jackson (Mich.) Jr. Coll., 1953; BS in Police Adminstrn., Calif. State U., L.A., 1962. Police officer City of Claremont, Calif., 1959-62, 63-66; investigator U.S. Civil Svc. Commn., Washington and L.A., 1962-63, 66-72; spl. agt. FAA, Seattle, 1972-99, office mgr., 1973-99, ret., 1999. Local chmn. Selective Svc. Bd., Wash., 1981-2001. Sgt. USMC, 1953-56, Korea. Mem. SAR (chpt. pres. 1989-90, state sec. 1989-91, state pres. 1992, Patriots medal 1990, Law Enforcement medal 1991, 92), Am. Legion, Eastern Star (patron 1989-90), Masons (master 1984, life), Scottish Rite, Shriners. Avocations: computers, photography, camping, travel. Home: 644 Briarwood Ter East Wenatchee WA 98802-8326

BERKLEY, SHELLEY, congresswoman; b. N.Y.C., Jan. 20, 1951; BA, U. Nev., 1972; JD, U. San Diego, 1976. Mem. U.S. Congress from 1st Nev. dist., 1999—; mem. transp. and infrastructure com., internat. affairs com., vet. affairs com. Democrat. Office: US Ho Reps 439 Cannon House Office Bldg Washington DC 20515-0001 also: 2340 Paseo Del Prado Ste D-106 Las Vegas NV 89102*

BERKLEY, STEPHEN MARK, computer industry entrepreneur and investor; b. N.J., 1944; s. Irving S. and Goldie A. Berkley; children: David, Michael. Student, London Sch. Econs., 1964-65; BA in Econs., Colgate U., 1966; MBA, Harvard U., 1968. Mgmt. cons. Boston Cons. Group, 1968, 71-73; mgr. strategic planning Potlatch Corp., 1973-77; v.p. bus. devel. Qume Corp. subs. ITT, Hayward, Calif., 1977-80, v.p., gen. mgr. memory products divs., 1980-81; v.p. mktg. Quantum Corp., Milpitas, Calif., 1981-83, chmn., CEO, 1987-92, chmn., 1992-93, 95-98; pres. Plus Devel. Corp. (Quantum subs.), 1983-87, chmn., CEO, 1987-92; pres. The Rosewood Found., 1991—. Bd. dirs. Quantum Corp., Edify Corp., Coactive Computing Corp.; instr. bus. and econs. E. Carolina U., 1969-71. Served to lt. USNR, 1968-71. Mem. Corp. Planners Assn. (dir.), Harvard Bus. Sch. Club No. Calif., Los Altos Golf and Country Club, The Reserve Golf Club, Phi Beta Kappa. Avocations: golf, modern art, travel.

BERKLEY, WILLIAM ROBERT, insurance holding company executive; b. Oct. 31, 1945; m. Marjorie Adnepos, June 19, 1971; children: Lisa A., W. Robert Jr., Lauren E. BS, NYU, 1966; MBA, Harvard U., 1968. Founder, chmn., chief exec. officer W. R. Berkley Corp., 1967—; pres. W.R. Berkley Corp., 2000—. Officer and/or dir., chmn. Assoc. Cmty. Bancorp, Inc., Strategic Distbn., Inc.; officer and/or dir. Atlee of Del., Inc., Berkley Group Inc., FLOORgraphics, Inc., Interlaken Capital, Inc. and affiliates, The First Marblehead Corp., Greenwich Bank & Trust Co., W.R. Brokerage, Inc., Westport Nat. Bank; bd. dirs. Kiln Plc, Five Mile Capital Ptnrs., LLC. Co-chmn. Sabin Vaccine Inst.; chmn. bd. overseers Stern Sch. Bus., NYU; vice chmn. bd. trustees, mem. exec. com. U. Conn.; trustee, mem. exec. com. NYU; bd. dirs., mem. exec. com. Georgetown U. Office: W R Berkley Corp 475 Steamboat Rd Greenwich CT 06830-6608

BERKMAN, CLAIRE FLEET, psychologist; b. New Orleans, Dec. 5, 1942; d. Joel and Margaret Grace (Fishler) Fleet; m. Arnold Stephen Berkman, Apr. 27, 1975; children: Janna Samantha, Micah Seth Siegel. BA, Boston U., 1964; EdM, Harvard U., 1966; EdD, Boston U., 1970. Asst. prof. Counseling Ctr. Mich. State U., East Lansing, 1971-75, assoc. prof., 1975-78, assoc. prof. dept. psychiatry, 1975-82, clin. assoc. prof., 1986-87; pvt. clin. practice, 1975—. Cons. Cath. Family Social Service, Lansing, 1979-83; mem. adv. bd. Cir. Ct. Family Counseling Program, 1982-88. V.p. Kehillat Israel Synagogue, 1975-76, pres., 1992-94; bd. dirs. Jewish Welfare Fedn., Lansing, 1974-75, 84-87; mem. children's task force State Bar Mich., 1993-95. NDEA fellow, 1968-70. Mem. APA, Mich. Psychol. Assn., Mich. Soc. Forensic Psychologists, Nat. Soc. Arts and Letters (pres. Mid-Mich. chpt. 2000-02). Office: 4084 Okemos Rd Okemos MI 48864-3258

BERKMAN, MICHAEL G. lawyer, chemical consultant; b. Poland, Apr. 4, 1917; came to U.S., 1921; s. Harry and Bertha (Jay) B.; m. Marjorie Edelstein, Nov. 28, 1941; children— Laurel, William BS, U. Chgo., 1937, PhD, 1941; JD, DePaul U., 1958; LLM in Intellectual Property, John Marshall Law Sch., 1962; spl. courses, Harvard U., 1943, MIT, 1943. Bar: U.S. Patent Office 1960. Research chemist Argonne Nat. Lab., 1946-51; assoc. dir., chief chemist Colburn Labs., Chgo., 1951-59; instr. chemistry Roosevelt U., Chgo., 1946-49; patent lawyer Mann, Brown & McWilliams, Chgo., 1959-63; ptnr. Kegan, Kegan & Berkman, Chgo., 1963-84, Trexler, Bushnell, Giangiorgi & Blackstone, Chgo., 1984-91; pvt. practice law Glenview, Ill., 1991—. Chem. cons.; expert witness in patent law. Contbr. articles to profl. jours. Served to 1st lt. Signal Corps, U.S. Army, 1942-46. Mem. Am. Chem. Soc., ABA, Patent Law Assn., Chgo., Sigma Xi. Home and Office: 939 Glenview Rd Glenview IL 60025-3172

BERKMAN, RICHARD LYLE, lawyer; b. Pitts., Sept. 4, 1946; s. Allen H. and Selma (Wiener) B.; m. Toni Seidl, June 7, 1998; children: Benjamin, Lisa, Daniel. AB magna cum laude, Harvard U., 1968, JD cum laude, 1973. Bar: Pa. 1973, U.S. Dist. Ct. (ea. dist.) Pa. 1973, U.S. Ct. Appeals (3d cir.) 1975, U.S. Dist. Ct. (mid. dist.) Pa. 1979, U.S. Supreme Ct. 1986. Asst. to dir. Office Emergency Preparedness Exec. Office of U.S. President, Washington, 1970; law clk. to Hon. Edward R. Becker U.S. Dist Ct., Phila., 1973-74; ptnr. Dechert LLP, Phila., 1974—. Adj. prof. Temple Law Sch. Co-author: Damming the West, 1971, Pennsylvania Evidence, 1974; contbr. articles to profl. jours. Bd. govs. Am. Jewish Com., Hebrew Union Coll.; officer, bd. dirs. Congregation Rodeph Shalom; active Salzberg Seminar on AIDS. Lt. (j.g.) USN, 1968-70. Mem. ABA, Phila. Bar Assn., Am. Law Inst. Avocations: reading, charities, sports. Office: Dechert LLP 4000 Bell Atlantic Tower 1717 Arch St Philadelphia PA 19103-2793

BERKMAN, SAMUEL, materials scientist; m. Virginia Berkman, Aug. 2, 1964; 2 children. BS in Physics, Fairleigh Dickinson U., 1965. Various to mem. tech. staff David Sarnoff Rsch. Ctr., Princeton, NJ, 1975—90; v.p. Nu-Tec Corp., Point Pleasant, NJ, 1990—2002. Co-author: (Book) Heteroepitaxial Semi-Conductors for Electronic Devices, 1978; patentee (patents) 21 in field. Recipient Achievement awards, NASA, 1979, 1980. Achievements include development of and applications of boundary layer theory for the design and operation of chem. vapor deposition (CVD) reactors; devel. of systems for bulk and shaped crystal growth. Avocation: boating, fishing, hiking, art. Office: Nu-Tec Corp 1818 Boat Point Dr Point Pleasant NJ 08742

BERKMAN, WILLIAM ROGER, lawyer, army reserve officer; b. Chisholm, Minn., Mar. 29, 1928; s. Carl Emil and Millie (Mikkelson) B.; m. Betty Ann Klamt, Dec. 17, 1950. AB, U. Calif., Berkeley, 1950, JD, 1957. Bar: Calif. 1957, D.C. Ct. Appeals 1957, D.C. 1957. Law clk. to judge James Alger Fee, U.S. Ct. Appeals 9th cir., 1957-58; assoc. Morrison & Foerster, San Francisco, 1958-67, mem. firm, 1967-79; comdg. gen. 351st Civil Affairs Command, Mountain View, Calif., 1975-79; chief Army Res., Dept. of Army, Washington, 1979-86; mil. exec., Res. Forces Policy Bd., Office Sec. Def. Dept. of Def., Washington, 1986-92. Mng. editor: Calif. Law Rev, 1956-57. Pres. Sausalito (Calif.) Bd. Libr. Trustees, 1976-78; pres. Civil Affairs Assn., 1979-80, 93-99; bd. dirs. Army Distaff Found., 1988-92; dir. Sausalito-Marin City Sanitary Dist., pres., 2002—. Maj. gen. U.S. Army, 1979—. Decorated DSM with oak leaf cluster, Def. DSM, Def. Superior Svc. medal, S. Order of Calif., U.S. Spl. Ops. command medal U.S. Army, USN, C.G., Legion of Merit medal, Army Commendation medal; named to Hall of Fame Sr. Army Res. Comdrs. Assn.; recipient Meritorious Svc. medal, Army Outstanding Civilian Svc. medal. Mem.: ABA (chmn. standing com. on lawyers in armed svcs. 1988—91), Civil

Affairs Assn. (pres. 1992—99, pres. emeritus 1999—, chief civil affairs corps), Res. Officers Assn., Assn. U.S. Army, State Bar Calif., Army and Navy Club, Lions (dir. Sausalito Marin City san. dist., pres.). Home: 33 Atwood Ave Sausalito CA 94965-2245

BERKOBEN, JOHN PERRI, physician; b. Lakewood, N.J., 1947; BA, Cornell U., 1969; MD, U. Pa., 1973. Intern Montefiore Hosp., Bronx, 1973-74, resident, 1974-76. Cardiology fellow Boston U. Med. Ctr., 1976-78. Mem. Am. Coll. Physicians, Am. Coll. Cardiology, N.Am. Soc. Pacing & Electrophysiology, Mass. Med. Soc. Office: Lahey-Arlington Symmes Hosp Arlington MA 02474

BERKOFF, CHARLES EDWARD, pharmaceutical executive; b. London, Sept. 29, 1932; came to U.S., 1963; naturalized, 1976; s. Maurice and Dora (Landy) B.; children: Timothy, David, Kevin; m. Heide-Gisela Triesch, 1997. BS in Chemistry (1st class honors), U. London, 1956, DIC, 1958; PhD, Imperial Coll., U. London, 1959. Chartered chemist. Dir. GlaxoSmithKline, Phila., 1964-83; exec. v.p. ImuTech, Inc., Huntingdon Valley, Pa., 1983-84; pres., CEO Antigenics, Inc., Horsham, Pa., 1984-89; pres., chief exec. officer Creative Licensing Internat., Inc., Sarasota, Fla., 1987—, CEBRAL, Inc., 1987—. Research fellow Johns Hopkins U., Balt., 1959-60; sr. research fellow Southampton U., Eng., 1960-61; mem. Adv. Council Smithsonian Sci. Info. Exchange, Washington, 1976-82. Contbr. articles to profl. jours.; patentee numerous U.S. and fgn. patents. Monsanto Research fellow Imperial Coll. Sci. and Tech., 1956-59; Fulbright scholar, 1959-60; recipient Statue of Victory World Culture prize Centro Studi e Ricerche Delle Nazioni, 1985. Fellow Am. Chem. Soc., Royal Soc. Chemistry; mem. Am. Arbitration Assn., Entomol. Soc., Am. Inst. Chem. Engrs., Licensing Execs. Soc. Clubs: Engrs. Club of Phila. Republican. Unitarian Universalist. Avocations: writing scientific humor, competitive tennis and swimming, classical guitar, bridge. Office: CEBRAL Inc PO Box 5850 Sarasota FL 34277-5850 E-mail: cebral@comcast.net.

BERKOFF, MARSHALL RICHARD, lawyer; b. Milw., Apr. 10, 1937; s. Louis S. and Edith E. (Cohen) B.; m. Bebe R. Brandwein, June 19, 1960; children: Mark Andrew, Jonathan Hale, Adam Todd. BA, U. Wis., 1959; LLB, Harvard U., 1962. Bar: Wis. 1962, U.S. Dist. Ct. (we. and ea. dists.) Wis. 1962. Ptnr. Michael, Best & Friedrich, Milw., 1962—. Co-author: Employment Law Challenges of 1987, 1987, Labor Relations: The New Rules of the Game, 1984, The Legal Issues of Managing Difficult Employees, 1987; author/editor Currier and Ives "The New Best 50", 1991. Chmn. Charles Allis and Villa Terrace Art Mus., Milw., 1983-96; chmn. Milw. County War Meml. Corp., 1989-94, bd. dirs., 1983; chmn. bd. dirs. St. Michael Hosp., Milw., 1988-89; bd. dirs. Covenant Health Care, 1993-95. Mem. ABA (labor and employment sect., hosp. and health care law sect.), Wis. Bar Assn., (chmn. labor law sect. 1977-78), Milw. Bar Assn., Am. Hist. Print Collector Soc. (pres. 1987-90, bd. dirs. 2002—). Avocations: collecting, speaking, writing, restoring and cataloguing antique Am. lithographs, fishing. Office: Michael Best & Friedrich 100 E Wisconsin Ave Ste 3300 Milwaukee WI 53202-4108

BERKON, MARTIN, artist; b. Bklyn., Jan. 30, 1932; s. Samuel F. and Sara (Hodes) B.; m. Eileen Phyllis Eichel, July 10, 1960. Student, Pratt Inst., 1952; BA, Bklyn. Coll., 1954; MA, NYU, 1959. Mem. adj. faculty Fairleigh Dickinson U., 1966, Nassau C.C., 1966-67; lectr. City Coll., CUNY, 1968-69; guest lectr. Middlebury Coll., 1977, Nassau C.C., 1982, St. Thomas Aquinas Coll., 1995; interviewed L.I. Art Scene TV, 1986. One-man shows include Smolin Gallery, N.Y.C., 1962, 20th Century West Gallery, N.Y.C., 1967, Soho Ctr. for Visual Artists, N.Y.C., 1974, Genesis Galleries, N.Y.C., 1978, Adelphi U., Garden City, N.Y., 1983, Blue Hill Cultural Ctr., Pearl River, N.Y., 1995, Schering Plough Corp. Gallery, Madison, N.J., 2001; exhibited in group shows at Bklyn. Mus., 1958, Silvermine (Conn.) Guild Artists, 1963, Ohio U. Gallery, 1964, Ball State U., 1965, Wesleyan Coll. at Ga., 1965, Butler Inst. Am. Art, 1965, 67, 69, Aldrich Mus. Contemporary Art, Ridgefield, Conn., 1974, 75, 82, New Britain (Conn.) Mus., 1974, Am. Fedn. Arts traveling show, 1975-77, Meadowbrook Art Gallery Oakland U., Rochester, Mich. and Flint (Mich.) Inst. Art, 1974-76, Firehouse Gallery, Garden City, 1982, Barbara Walter Gallery, N.Y.C., 1982, Spaceport USA, Kennedy Space Ctr., 1985, 87, NASA collection traveling exhbn. Visions of Flight, 1988-91, Ctr. for Arts The Abstract Image, Vero Beach, Fla., 1996, Blue Hill Cultural Ctr., Pearl River, N.Y., 1997-98; represented in permanent collections Aldrich Mus. Contemporary Art,, Ridgefield, Conn., Texaco Inc., White Plains, N.Y., Pepsico Inc., Somers, N.Y., Pfizer Inc., Rye Brook, N.Y.; commd. NASA, 1984, 87, NASA Gallery of Art, Kennedy Space Ctr., Ctr. for Arts, Vero Beach, Fla. Home: 503 Devries Ct Piermont NY 10968-1068

BERKOVITZ, LEONARD DAVID, mathematician, educator; b. Chgo., Jan. 24, 1924; s. Judea and Esther (Trop) B.; m. Anna Whitehouse, June 18, 1953; children Dan M., Kenneth E. BS, U. Chgo., 1946, MS, 1948, PhD, 1951. AEC postdoctoral fellow Stanford (Calif.) U., 1951-52; rsch. fellow Calif. Inst. Tech., Pasadena, Calif., 1952-54; mathematician Rand Corp., Santa Monica, Calif., 1954-62; prof. math. Purdue U., West Lafayette, Ind., 1962—2003, prof. emeritus, 2003—. Author: Optimal Control Theory, 1974, Optimization and Convexity in Rn, 2002; mem. editl. bd. Soc. for Indsl. and Applied Math. Jour. on Control, 1970-89, Optimization Theory and Applications, 1983-2001, Jour. Math Analysis and Applications; mem. editl. com. Math. Reviews, Am. Math. Soc., 1985-92; contbr. articles to profl. jours. 1st Lt. USAAF, 1943-46.

BERKOW, IRA HARVEY, author, journalist; b. Chgo., Jan. 7, 1940; s. Harold Grosswald and Shirley (Halperin) B.; m. Dolores Case, Apr. 18, 1978. BA, Miami U., Oxford, Ohio, 1963; MS in Journalism, Northwestern U., 1964. Reporter Mpls. Tribune, 1965-67; sports columnist, sports editor Newspaper Enterprise Assn., N.Y.C., 1967-76; sports columnist, feature writer N.Y. Times, N.Y.C., 1981—. Author: (with Oscar Robertson) Golden Year, 1971, (with Walt Frazier) Rockin' Steady, 1974 (Am. Libr. Assn. Best Books of Yr. 1975), Beyond the Dream, 1975, Maxwell Street, 1977, The DuSable Panthers, 1978, (with Rod Carew) Carew, 1979, Red: The Biography of Red Smith, 1986, The Man Who Robbed the Pierre, 1987, Pitchers Do Get Lonely and Other Sports Stories, 1988; editor: Hank Greenberg: The Story of My Life, 1989, (with Jackie Mason) How to Talk Jewish, 1991, (with Jim Kaplan) The Gospel According to Casey, 1992, To the Hoop: The Seasons of a Basketball Life, 1997, Court Vision, 2000, The Minority Quarterback, and Other Lives in Sports, 2002, Playwright: The Shakespeare of the Press Box, 2003. Recipient Page One award Newspaper Guild, Mpls., 1966, Scripps-Howard Feature award N.Y.C., 1969, N.Y. Pub. Libr. commendation, 1978, AP Sports Editors award, 1982, 93, 94, 95, 96, Disting. Achievement medal Miami U., 1988, Feature Reporting award Deadline Club, 1994, award N.Y. State Newspaper Pubs., 1990; nominee ACE awards, 1983, Edgar award, 1988; finalist Pulitzer prize for commentary, 1988, Harold Washington Achievement award Roosevelt U., 2003; named to Hall of Achievement, Northwestern U. Medill Sch. of Journalism, 1997; mem. N.Y. Times Pulitzer-Prize-Winning Team for Nat. Reporting, 2001. Mem. Baseball Writers Assn. Am., Authors Guild, PEN, Mystery Writers Am. Office: NY Times 229 W 43rd St New York NY 10036-3959

BERKOWITZ, BRAD ALAN, stock analyst; b. Woodmere, NY, May 5, 1964; s. Morton Michael and Barbara Judith Berkowitz. BS in Econs., U. Pa., 1986; MBA in Fin., NYU, 1993. Investment analyst Integrated Resources, N.Y.C., 1986—89; fixed income sales Lehman Bros., N.Y.C., 1989—94; fin. cons., prin. AXA Advisors, N.Y.C., 1995—2000; stock analyst Cramer, Berkowitz, N.Y.C., 2001—. Adv. bd. mem. Smartix, Internat., N.Y.C., 2002—. Author: (Book) The 21st Century Guide to Bachelorhood, 1999, The Iran Barkley Story: The Rise and Fall of a Boxing Champion, 2001; co-author: Natural Disaster, 2001. Mem.: AFTRA, Am. Mensa. Jewish. Avocations: golf, sports, movies, theater, acting. Home: Apt 30A 1520 York Ave New York NY 10028 Office: Cramer Berkowitz 14th Fl 909 Third Ave New York NY 10022 Personal E-mail: berkathome@aol.com.

BERKOWITZ, HERBERT MATTIS, lawyer; b. N.Y.C., June 23, 1947; m. Gloria E. Deems, June 16, 1968; 1 child, Peter Aaron. BA, Bklyn. Coll., 1967; JD, U. Wis., 1971. Bar: Wis. 1971, Ohio 1972, Fla. 1979, U.S. Supreme Ct. 1974, U.S. Ct. Appeals (D.C. cir. 1974), U.S. Ct. Appeals (6th cir.) 1976, U.S. Ct. Appeals (5th cir.) 1981, U.S. Ct. Appeals (11th cir.) 1981. Law clk. Ohio Ct. Appeals, Cleve., 1971-73; atty. antitrust div. U.S. Dept. Justice, Cleve., 1973-74, asst. U.S. Atty., 1975-78, atty. organized crime strike force Tampa, 1978-80; assoc. Levine, Freedman, Hirsch & Levinson, Tampa, 1980-84; ptnr. Oster & Berkowitz, Tampa, 1984-90; mng. sr. ptnr. Berkowitz & Almerico, Tampa, 1990-94, Berkowitz & Assocs., Tampa, 1994-2000; of counsel Clark, Charlton & Martino, P.A., Tampa, 2000—. Mem. ABA, Fla. Bar Assn., Hillsborough County Bar Assn. (In the Trenches award 1997), ATLA (sustaining), Fla. Trial Lawyers Assn., Am. Bd. Trial Advocates, Am. Inns of Ct. Office: Clark Charlton & Martino PA 3407 W Kennedy Blvd Tampa FL 33609

BERKOWITZ, LAWRENCE M. lawyer; b. Leavenworth, Kans., Nov. 29, 1941; s. Barney and Sarah (Kramer) B.; m. Ursula Lustenberger, Sept. 2, 1969; children: Lizbeth Berkowitz, Leslie Berkowitz. BA Polit. Sci., U. Mich., 1963, JD, 1966. Bar: Mo. 1966. Law clerk U.S. Dist. Ct., Kansas City, Mo., 1966-68; assoc., ptnr. Stinson, Mag & Fizzell, P.C., Kansas City, Mo., 1968-97; ptnr. Berkowitz, Stanton, et al, Kansas City, Mo., 1997—. Mng. ptnr. Stinson, Mag & Fizzell, Kansas City, 1991-92. Bd. dirs. Nelson Gallery Bus. Coun., Kansas City, 1989—, Downtown coun., Kansas City, 1992-93; trustee Kansas City Art Inst., 1994—. Fellow Am. Coll. Trial Lawyers, Am. Bar Found.; mem. ABA, Am. Judicature Soc., Kansas City Met. Bar Assn., Lawyers Assn. Kansas City, Mo. Bar Assn., Am. Coll. Trial Lawyers (state bd. 1989—). Avocations: tennis, hiking, skiing, history, reading. Office: Berkowitz Stanton et al Two Emanuel Cleaver Blvd Ste 500 Kansas City MO 64112

BERKOWITZ, ROBERT ARI, neurobiologist; b. Harvey, Ill., Oct. 30, 1961; s. Joseph and Nina (Kessler) B.; m. Marshall Kathleen Cheney, May 2, 1992; children: Rachel Ilana, Dalya Ruth. AB in Chemistry with honors, U. Chgo., 1984; PhD in Neurosci., Washington U., 1993. Grad. rsch. asst. Washington U., St. Louis, 1987-93; rsch. fellow Calif. Inst. Tech., Pasadena, 1993-96; postdoctoral fellow UCLA, 1996-97, asst. prof. U. Okla., Norman, 1997—2003, assoc. prof., 2003—. Contbr. articles to profl. jours. Mem., speaker New Jewish Agenda, St. Louis, 1991-93; co-chair chpt. Interreligious Com. for Peace in the Mid. East, St. Louis, 1992. Grantee NSF, 1998—; recipient Nat. Rsch. Svc. award NIH, 1994-96, predoctoral fellowship NSF, 1987-90. Mem. Am. Physiol. Soc., Soc. for Neurosci., Internat. Soc. for Neuroethology, Phi Beta Kappa. Achievements include research on mechanisms used by nervous systems to select and produce an appropriate behavior for each circumstance. Office: U Okla Dept Zoology 730 Van Vleet Oval Norman OK 73019-6120 E-mail: ari@ou.edu.

BERKOWITZ, STEPHEN DAVID, sociologist, educator; b. N.Y.C., N.Y., Nov. 26, 1943; s. Bernard and Sylvia (Coplan) B.; m. Harriet Bertha Friedmann, Sept. 1, 1968 (div. Jan. 1974); m. Teresa Norma Traynor, Jan. 8, 1974; children: Shawn Daniels, Colin Daniels. AB, U. Mich., 1965, grad. study in sociology, 1965—67; PhD, Brandeis U., 1975. Tchg. fellow, asst. U. Mich., Brandeis U., 1965—68; joint rsch. fellow Edn. Devel. Ctr./Stanford Rsch. Inst., 1969—71; asst. prof. dept. social studies U. Sask., Regina, Canada, 1971—73; lectr. dept. sociology U. Toronto, 1973—75, asst. prof. dept. sociology, 1976—81; from asst. prof. to fellow New Coll., U. Toronto, 1976—81; rsch. assoc. Inst. for Quantitative Analysis of Social and Econ. Policy, U. Toronto, 1974—81; asst. prof. dept. sociology U. Vt., 1980—87; prof. dept. sociology U. Ft. Hare, Alice, South Africa, 1997—99; assoc. prof. dept. sociology U. Vt., 1987—96, prof. dept. sociology, 1996—2001, prof. emeritus sociology, 2002—; CEO Am. Protective Devices, Inc., 2002; mng. dir. Inst. for Study in South Africa, 2002—. Vis. asst. prof. dept. sociology Meml. U. Nfld., 1978; vis. scholar dept. sociology Harvard U., 1987—88; chief scientist OMNIDAT, LLC, 2001; mem. adv. com. Internat. Network for Social Network Analysis, 1977—83; mem. adv. com. on sci. and edn. Contact Can., Ottawa, 1977—80. Author: (book) Death Before Honor, 2003; author: (with R. Logan) Canada's Third Option, 1978; author: An Introduction to Structural Analysis: The Network Approach to Social Research, 1982, Models and Myths in Canadian Sociology, 1984; author: (with B. Wellman) Social Structures: A Network Approach, 2d edit., 1997; author: (with Howard Ball and Mbulelo Mzamane) Multicultural Education in Colleges and Universities: A Transdisciplinary Approach, 1998; author: (with Mbulelo Mzamane) The Mbeki Turn: South Africa After Mandela, 2002; contbr. articles to profl. and scholarly jours., chpts. to books; assoc. editor: Can. Jour. Sociology, 1980—83. Mem. program com. Chavurah, 1981—82; v.p. non-partisan com. Can. Unity Through Diversity, 1978—80; mem. adv. bd. B'Nai Brith Hillel Found., Toronto, 1979—80. Recipient NIMH trainee and fellowship, Ctr. for Rsch. on Social Orgn., U. Mich., 1965—66, tchg. fellowship in sociology, U. Mich., 1966—67, Brandeis fellowship in sociology, 1967—68, NIMH Advanced Field Tng. fellowship, Brandeis U., 1968—69, Brandeis fellowship in sociology, 1969—70. Mem.: ASA (mem. exec. adv. bd. sect. on math. sociology 1999—, steering com. sect. on math. sociology 1997—, steering com. sect.-in-formation math. sociology 1995—97), Internat. Network for Social Network Analysis, Alpha Kappa Delta. Avocations: writing detective fiction, listening to classical music, collecting rare and out-of-print books, Go. Office: Dept Sociology 31 S Prospect St Burlington VT 05405 also: Inst for Study in South Africa PO Box 44 Underhill VT 05489

BERKOWITZ, WILLIAM R. psychologist, writer, consultant; b. Albany, NY, Sept. 21, 1939; s. Leon and Ethel Berkowitz; m. Madelon H. Helfer; children: Daniel, Rachel. BA with honors, Cornell U., 1961; PhD, Stanford U., 1965. Lic. psychologist 1973. Chief psychologist Solomon Mental Health Ctr., Lowell, Mass., 1973—92; writer and cons. Self-employed, Arlington, Mass., 1988—97; assoc. prof. of psychology Univ. of Mass. Lowell, 1997—2002. Editor and cons. Cmty. Tool Box, 1995—2002. Author: (book) Community Impact, 1982, Community Dreams, 1984 (Disting. Contributions to Practice in Cmty. Psychology, 1995), Local Heroes, 1987, The Spirit of the Coalition, 2000; contbr. over 50 articles to profl. jours. Town meeting mem. (elected) Town of Arlington, 1982—2002. Recipient Cmty. Tool Box (with colleagues), Robert Wood Johnson Found., 1996—, Cmty. Partners (with Tom Wolff), W. K. Kellogg Found., 1990—95; Fellow, Am. Psychol. Assn., 1990. Home: 12 Pelham Ter Arlington MA 02476 Office: Dept of Psychology U of Mass 870 Broadway St Lowell MA 01854 Business E-Mail: Bill_Berkowitz@uml.edu.

BERKOWSKY, PETER ARTHUR, lawyer, retired military officer; b. Cornwall, NY, Mar. 29, 1942; s. Samuel Nathan and Sydell Berkowsky; m. Dolores Ethel Finder, Aug. 3, 1980; children: Daniel Benjamin, Jesse Samuel. AB in History, Brandeis U., 1964; JD, Cornell U., 1967; grad., Air War Coll., 1992. Bar: NY, U.S. Dist. Ct. (so. and ea. dists.) NY, U.S. Ct. Appeals (2d cir. and Armed Forces), U.S. Supreme Ct. Spl. agt., Office Spl. Investigations USAF, Beale AFB, Calif., 1967-71; asst. atty. gen., Dept. Law NY State, N.Y.C., 1972-77; prin. ct. atty. Appellate Divsn. 1st dept. Supreme Ct., N.Y.C., 1977-79, 87-91, prin. law clk. to Hon. Justice Arnold L. Fein, 1979-86, prin. law clk. to Hon. Justice Richard W. Wallach, 1991—2003. Intelligence officer, USAFR, McGuire AFB, NJ, 1973-75; asst. staff judge advocate, McGuire AFB, Hanscom AFB, Mass., Pentagon, Washington, 1975-98; admissions liaison officer U.S. Air Force Acad., 1992—; mem. law dept. adv. panel for bus. sch. Baruch Coll., N.Y.C., 1998—. Founder, dir. Internat. Minyan for N.Y.C. Marathoners, 1983—. Served to col. USAF, 1967-71, USAFR, 1971-98, returned to active duty Desert Storm, 1991. Decorated Legion of Merit. Mem. Am. Assn. Jewish Lawyers and Jurists, NY County Lawyers' Assn. (law-related edn. com.), Civil Svc. Employees Assn. (AFSCME local 1000, AFL-CIO), Cracow Soc. (2d generation), Soc. Am. Baseball Rsch., Jewish War Vets of U.S. (life mem.), NY Road Runners Club. Democrat. Jewish. Avocation: running. Home: 16 Fredon Dr Livingston NJ 07039-3136 Office: Supreme Ct Appellate Divsn 1st Dept 27 Madison Ave New York NY 10010-2201 E-mail: fud42@comcast.net.

BERKSON, JACOB BENJAMIN, lawyer, author, conservationist; b. Washington County, Md., Dec. 6, 1925; s. Meyer and Ida Evelyn (Berman) B.; m. Ann Goldstein, June 25, 1955 (div.); children: Daniel Jeremy, Susan Kay, James Meyer. BA, U. Va., 1947, LLB, 1949, JD, 1970; grad., US Naval Sch., Naval Justice, Newport, RI, 1952, Fed. Exec. Inst., Charlottesville, Va., 1972, USNR Midshipmen's Sch., Columbia U., NY; attended, Naval Sch. Oriental Langs. (Japanese). Bar: Md. 1949, Va. 1949, U.S. Supreme Ct. 1965, Calif. 1975. Sole practice, Hagerstown, Md., 1949-52, 54-64; ptnr. McCauley, Cooey, Berkson & Wright, Hagerstown, 1964-70; dep. gen. counsel U.S. GSA, Washington, 1970-76; pvt. practice law Hagerstown, 1976—. Instr. Law Hagerstown Bus. Coll., 1986; trial magistrate, Hagerstown and Washington County, Md., 1951-52; mem. Legis. Coun. Md., 1955-58; del. Md. Legislature, 1955-58; trial magistrate, Hagerstown, 1958-59. Recipient commendation for svc. to U.S. Naval Acad. and pub. interest Chief of Naval Personnel, 1956. Author: Shingahi Saburo and Short Stories, 1978, Comin' Home, 1993, A Canary's Tale, 1996; case editor, co-founder Va. Law Weekly, 1948; contbr. articles to profl. jours., address to Congrl. Record. Scoutmaster local coun. Boy Scouts Am.; organizer, dir. County Youth Conservation Corps; active Big Bros.; bd. dirs. Doub's Woods County Park, Devil's Backbone County Park; assisted in establishment of C&O Canal Nat. Histo. Park, 1954-70; camp sponsor YMCA; adv. Model Youth Legis.; pres. PTA; chmn. Washington County Park Commn., 1961-66; bd. dirs. Rachel Carson Coun., Inc., Chevy Chase, Md., 1996-2003. WWII USNR V12 program line officer UVA, 1944, Commissioned Ensign, 1945, ordered to staff Comdr. Naval Base, Saipan, Marianas I., staff legal officer, 1945—46, Judge Advocate General Courts Martial, recalled, 1952, Korean War, Lt. USNR, ordered to Pusan, Korea, ordered to Comdr. Naval Forces, Far East, Yokosuka, Japan, staff legal, trial counsel, 1952—53, Defense Counsel before General Courts Martial, ordered to serve as staff legal officer to Comdr. Destroyer Divsn. 322 on Round the World Mission, 1953—54, aboard USS Healey DD 672, Navy JAG duties. Mem. ABA, Calif. Bar Assn., Va. Bar Assn., Md. Assn. County Civil Attys. (pres., award for svc. as pres. 1966), Washington County Bar Assn. (pres.), Am. Legion, Hagerstown Club, Lions (pres.), Speakers Soc., Elks, Torch Club (Hagerstown), Thomas Jefferson Soc. Alumni, Lile Law Soc. Republican. Jewish. Home and Office: 1419 Potomac Ave Hagerstown MD 21742-3315

BERKUS, DAVID WILLIAM, venture capitalist; b. Los Angeles, Mar. 23, 1941; s. Harry Jay and Clara S. (Widess) B.; m. Kathleen McGuire, Aug. 6, 1966; children: Eric, Matthew, Amy. BA, Occidental Coll., 1962. Pres. Custom Fidelity Inc., Hollywood, Calif., 1958-74, Berkus Compusystems Inc., Los Angeles, 1974-81; pres., CEO, Computerized Lodging Systems Inc. and subs., Los Angeles, 1981-93; pres. Berkus Tech. Ventures, venture capital, L.A., 1993—; mng. dir. worldwide lodging Sulcus Computer Corp., 1998-99; mng. ptnr. Kodiak Ventures, LP, L.A., 1999—. Chmn., bd. dirs. seven private and one pub. corps. Author: Better Than Money, 1994; author software Hotel Compu-system, 1979; creator 1st artificial intelligence-based yield mgmt. sys., 1987. Chmn. bd. Boy Scouts Am., San Gabriel Valley, 1986, v.p. area IV, 1993-94, pres. 1995-98, v.p. western region, 1998—; trustee Occidental Coll., L.A. Lt. USNR, 1963-72. Recipient Disting. award of Merit, Boy Scouts Am., 1986, INC. mag. 500 award, 1986, Silver Beaver award Boy Scouts Am., 1988, Silver Antelope award, 1997, Dir. of Yr. award Forum for Corp. Dirs., 1999, Alumni Seal award Occidental Coll., 2000; inducted into hospitality industry Hall of Fame, 1998. Mem. Am. Hotel-Motel Assn., Audio Engring. Soc. (chmn. L.A. sect. 1973-74), Tech. Coast Angels (chmn. 2002--). Office: 1430 Glencoe Dr Arcadia CA 91006-1909

BERKUS, JAMES, talent agent; Pres. United Talent Agy., Beverly Hills, Calif., chmn., 1997—. Office: United Talent Agy 9560 Wilshire Blvd Fl 5 Beverly Hills CA 90212-2400

BERKWITS, LELAND, physical medicine and rehabilitation physician; b. Chgo., Jan. 25, 1957; s. Edward and Gloria (Kozin) B.; m. Barbara D. Hall, Feb. 28, 1987. BS magna cum laude, Rensselaer Poly. Inst., 1979; MS, U. Ill., 1980; MD, Northwestern U., Chgo., 1984. Diplomate Am. Bd. Phys. Medicine and Rehab. Intern and resident Rehab. Inst. Chgo., 1985-88; sr. tech. assoc. E.I. DuPont DeNemours & Co., Inc., Wilmington, Del., 1988-90; resident Johnson/JFK Rehab., Edison, N.J., 1991-92; staff physician Bryn Mawr Rehab. Hosp., Malvern, Pa., 1992—, pres. of med. staff, 1996-97; pvt. practice Rehab. Assocs. of the Main Line, P.C., Malvern, Pa., 1992—. Chief phys. medicine and rehab. Jennersville Regional Hosp., West Grove, Pa., 1994—; dir. phys. medicine and rehab Paoli (Pa.) Hosp., 2001—, v.p. med. staff, 2003—04. Contbr. articles to profl. jours. Avocations: piano/music, computer science, architecture. Office: Rehab Assoc of Main Line PC 414 Paoli Pike Malvern PA 19355-3311

BERL, JOSEPH M. lawyer; b. Bklyn., Oct. 1, 1942; AB, Columbia U., 1964; JD with honors, George Washington U., 1967. Bar: N.Y. 1968, D.C. 1972, U.S. Supreme Ct. 1972. Law clk. to Hon. Frank H. Myers D.C. Ct. Appeals, 1967-68; trial atty. Div. Trading and Markets, SEC, Washington, 1968-70, br. chief, 1970-71; ptnr. Fortas & Koven, Washington, 1971-83, Stroock and Stroock and Lavan, Washington, 1984-86, Baker & Hostetler, Washington, 1986-98, Powell, Goldstein, Frazer & Murphy LLP, Washington, 1998—. Mem. ABA (mem. corp., banking and bus. law sect.), D.C. Bar. Office: Powell Goldstein Frazer & Murphy LLP 6th Flr 1001 Pennsylvania Ave NW Fl 6 Washington DC 20004-2505 E-mail: jberl@pgfm.com.

BERLAGE, GAI INGHAM, sociologist, educator; b. Washington, Feb. 9, 1943; d. Paul Bowen and Grace (Artz) Ingham; m. Jan Coxe Berlage, Aug. 7, 1965; children: Jan Ingham, Cari Coxe. BA, Smith Coll., 1965; MA, So. Meth. U., 1968; PhD, NYU, 1979. Tchr. math. Piner Jr. High Sch., Sherman, Tex., 1968-69; asst. prof. sociology Iona Coll., New Rochelle, N.Y., 1971-83, assoc. prof., 1983-88, chmn. dept., 1981—90, 1993—2003, prof., 1988—. Coord. urban studies program, 1984-90, gerontology program, 1984-90, NCAA faculty athletic rep., 1996—. Author: Experience with Sociology: Social Issues in American Society, 1983, Understanding Social Issues: Sociological Fact Finding, 1987, 2d edit., 1990, 3d edit., 1993, Women in Baseball: The Forgotten History, 1994, Understanding Social Issues: Critical Thinking and Analysis, 1996, 6th edit., 2003; mem. editl. bd. Jour. Sport and Social Issues, 1990-94; contbr. articles to profl. jours. Commr. Wilton Commn. on Aging and Social Svcs., 1980-88, chmn., 1982-88; co-chmn. Wilton Task Force on Youth Coun., 1988; chmn. Wilton Task Force Com. for Outreach Program, 1981-82, Wilton Task Force on Day Care, 1983-88; mem. Wilton Task Force for Pub. Health Nursing Assn., 1981-82, Wilton Sport Coun., 1985-88; bd. dirs. Wilton Meals on Wheels, 1983-88; fellow N.Am. Faculty Network of Northeastern Univs. Ctr. for Study of Sport in Soc. Recipient Best Profl. Paper award Third Annual Cooperstown Symposium on Baseball and the Am. Cultre; named to Iona Coll. Women of Achievement, 1993. Mem. Am. Sociol. Assn., N.Am. Soc. Sociology of Sport (treas. 1992-93), Wilton Assn. for Gifted Edn. (pres. 1980-81), N.Am. Soc. for Sports History, Soc. for Am. Baseball Rsch., Women's Sport Found. (resources coun.). Office: Iona Coll Dept Sociology New Rochelle NY 10801

BERLAGE, JAN INGHAM, lawyer; b. Lewiston, NY, Nov. 17, 1969; s. Jan Coxe and Gai Elizabeth (Ingham) B. BA, Wesleyan U., Middletown, Conn., 1992; postgrad., Oxford U., 1992; JD, U. Va., 1995. Law clk. to Hon. E. Stephen Derby U.S. Bankruptcy Ct. Dist. Md., Balt., 1995-96; assoc. Day, Berry & Howard, Hartford, Conn., 1996-2001, Ballard Spahr Andrews & Ingersoll, Balt., 2001—. Exec. editor Jour. Law and Politics, Charlottesville, 1994-95, mem. editl. bd., 1993-94; author: Aguilar Expression, 1990; contbr. articles to profl. jours. Deacon Avon Congl. Ch., 1997-2001; mem. Rep. Town Com., Avon, 1998-2001; mem. Avon Zoning Bd. Appeals, 1999-2001; exec. adv. bd. Heroes-Helping-Heroes, Inc., 2003—. Mem. ABA (vice chmn. young lawyers divsn. individual rights and responsibilities sect. 2001-2002, chmn. 2002—, vice chmn. young lawyers divsn. bankruptcy sect. 2002-03, chmn. 2003—), Md. State Bar Assn. (chmn. young lawyers divsn. edn. com. 2003—), Federalist Soc. (pres. U. Va. chpt. 1994-95, co-chmn. Hartford chpt. 1997-2001, bd. dirs. Chesapeake chpt. 2001—), Conn. Young Lawyers Assn. (co-chmn. comml. law and bankruptcy sect. 1997-2000, co-chmn. civil rights sect. 2000-01), N.Y. Bar Assn. (comml. law and fed. litigation sects., intellectual property subcom. 1998-2001), Jefferson Literary and Debating Soc., N.Am. Securities Adminstrn. Assn. (task force mem. 1994), Oxford U. Legal Soc., United Oxford/Cambridge U. Club, Phi Delta Phi, Psi Upsilon, Phi Beta Kappa. Office: Ballard Spahr Andrews & Ingersoll 300 E Lombard St Baltimore MD 21202-3268 Home: 16422 J M Pearce Rd Monkton MD 21111 E-mail: Berlageji@ballardspahr.com.

BERLAND, DAVID I. psychiatrist, educator; b. St. Louis, Aug. 1, 1947; s. Harry I. and Mildred (Cornblath) B.; m. Elaine Prostak, May 22, 1977; children: Katharine J., Rachel P. BA, U. Pa., 1969; MD, U. Mo., 1973. Diplomate Am. Bd. Psychiatry and Neurology. Resident psychiatry Menninger Found., Topeka, Kans., 1973-78, staff child and adolescent psychiatrist, 1978-83; dir. div. child and adolescent psychiatry St. Louis U. Med. Sch., 1983-93; with dept. adolescent psychiatry St. Luke's Hosp., Chesterfield, Mo., 1993-97; pvt. practice St. Louis, 1997—. Contbr. articles to profl. jours. Fellow Am. Acad. of Child and Adolescent Psychiatry; mem. AMA (rotating seat relative value update com. 1996-99), Soc. of Profs. of Child and Adolescent Psychiatry,. Jewish. Office: 7700 Clayton Rd Ste 103 Saint Louis MO 63117

BERLAND, SANFORD NEIL, lawyer; b. N.Y.C., Aug. 12, 1950; s. Stephen Isaiah and Alice Lydia (Greenfield) B.; m. Susan A. Winston, Nov. 4, 1989; children: Laurence, Noah, Stephanie, Alexander, Schuyler, Grant. BA magna cum laude, SUNY, Buffalo, 1972, JD magna cum laude, 1977. Bar: N.Y. 1978, U.S. Ct. Appeals (2d, 10th and 11th cirs.), U.S. Dist. Ct. (ea., so. and no. dists.) N.Y., U.S. Supreme Ct. Law clk. to Hon. E.R. Neaher U.S. Dist. Ct. (ea. dist.) N.Y., 1977-79; assoc. Dewey, Ballantine, Bushby, Palmer & Wood, N.Y.C., 1979-83; assoc., ptnr. Law Offices of Russel H. Beatie, Jr., N.Y.C., 1983-88; counsel Kellner, Chehebar & Deveney, N.Y.C., 1988-90; corp. counsel-litigation Pfizer Inc., N.Y.C., 1990-93, sr. corp. counsel, 1993-99, dir. corp. risk mgmt., asst. sec., 1999—2001, asst. gen. counsel, 2000—, sr. dir. corp. risk mgmt. and ins., 2000—, sr. dir. corp. risk mgmt., asst. gen. counsel, 2001—. Tchg. fellow Washington U., St. Louis, 1973-74; guest lectr. Pace U. Law Sch., 1989. Editor-in-chief Buffalo Law rev., 1976-77; contbr. articles to profl. jours. Mem. Huntington (N.Y.) Town Dem. Com., 1996—, mem. exec. com., 2002—; mem., bd. dirs. House Beautiful at Dix Hills Civic Assn., 2002—. Mem. ABA, N.Y. Bar Assn., Assn. Bar City N.Y., Phi Beta Kappa. Avocations: tennis, cycling. Home: 16 Wildwood Dr Dix Hills NY 11746-6041 Office: Pfizer Inc 235 E 42nd St New York NY 10017-5755

BERLANDT, HERMAN JOSEPH, editor, publisher; b. Chelm, Poland, May 7, 1923; s. Saul and Eva Dorscytz B.; m. Elisa Elliott, May 12, 1946 (div. June 1953); 1 child, Nicola Walker; m. Gloria Martine, Sept. 2, 1967; 1 child, Spring. AA, U. Calif., Berkeley. Chmn. Nat. Poetry Assn., San Francisco, 1975-92; tchr. Word Magic and the Power of Lang., San Francisco, 1987-92; prodr. Nat. Poetry Week Fort Mason, San Francisco, 1987-92; editor, pub. Mother Earth Internat. Jour., Bolinas, 1990—. Program dir. Internat. Guitar Festivals, Lake Geneva, Wis., 1965-66; lectr. in field. Author: Poens for Laughs and Snickers, 1999, The Last Decade, Mother Earth Anthology, 1989-99, Neither Ryyme Nor Reasonr, 1998, Sea Poems, 1998, Good Riddance: Farewell Poems for a Catastrophic Century, 1997, 32 Variations on a Much-Abused Metaphor, 1996, Suicide Mediations, 1995, In Praise of the Muses, 1994, A Spring Bouquet: The Hippie Garden of Verses, 1991, A Musical Offering, 1990, others; prodr.: 17 poetry film festivals; filmmaker :. Radio interviewer Ch. of the Muses. Grantee Marin Arts Coun., 1997. Mem.: Nat. Poetry Assn. (cons., advisor, bd. dirs.). Mem. Green Party. Episcopalian. Home: Box 886 Bolinas CA 94924 Office: Nat Poetry Assn 934 Brannan St San Francisco CA 94103

BERLE, PETER ADOLF AUGUSTUS, lawyer, media director; b. N.Y.C., Dec. 8, 1937; s. Adolf Augustus and Beatrice (Bishop) B.; m. Lila Sloane Wilde, May 30, 1960; children: Adolf Augustus, Mary Alice, Beatrice Lila, Robert Thomas. BA (Knox fellow), Harvard U., 1958, LLB, 1964; LLD (hon.), Hobart Smith Coll., 1977, L.I. U., 1993, So. Vt. Coll., 1996; LLB (hon.), North Adams Tchrs. Coll., 1988. Bar: N.Y. 1964, U.S. Dist. Ct. (so. and ea. dists.) N.Y. 1966, U.S. Ct. Appeals (2d cir.) 1966, U.S. Supreme Ct. 1973. Assoc. Paul, Weiss, Rifkind, Wharton & Garrison, N.Y.C., 1964-71; ptnr. Berle, Butzel & Kass, N.Y.C., 1971-76; N.Y. state commr. environ. conservation, 1976-79; ptnr. Berle, Kass & Case, 1979-85; pres., CEO (pub. Audubon mag.) Nat. Audubon Soc., 1985-95; dir., host The Environment Show N.E. Pub. Radio, 1995—2001; trustee Twentieth Century Fund, Inc., 1971—, chmn., 1982-87. Tchg. fellow econs. Harvard Coll., Cambridge, Mass., 1963-64; assoc. adj. prof. Sch. Urban Affairs Hunter Coll., 1974, 84; vis. prof. environ. sci. and forestry SUNY, 1980. Author: Does the Citizen Stand a Chance, 1974. Mem. N.Y. State Assembly, 1968-74; chmn. N.Y. Gov.'s Transition Task Force on Environment, 1974-75; commr. N.Y. State Moreland Act Commn. on Nursing Homes, 1975-77; bd. dirs. Clean Sites, Inc., 1986-93; chmn. Commn. on the Adirondacks in the 21st Century, 1989-90; mem. EPA adv. group on biotech., 1989-92, EPA adv. grout air quality; mem. nat. com. environ., 1991-92, nat. commn. superfund, 1992-94; mem. joint pub. adv. com. N.Am. Commn. on Environ. Coop., 1994-2002; dir. N.Y. Ind. Sys. Operator, 1999—; adv. bd. Harvard U. Com. on Environment; mem. commn. internat. environ. law World Conservation Union; pres. Stockbridge Land Trust, 2001—. 1st lt. USAF, 1959-61. Decorated Commendation medal; named Outstanding Legislator Eagleton Inst. Politics, 1971 Mem. ABA, N.Y. State Bar Assn., Assn. of Bar of City of N.Y. (environ. law com., profl. responsibility com., energy policy com., internat. human rights com., internat. environ. law com.). Episcopalian. E-mail: pberle@audubon.org.

BERLEANT, ARNOLD, philosopher; b. Buffalo, Mar. 4, 1932; s. Bernard and Elizabeth (Barkun) B.; m. Riva Schiller, Aug. 1, 1958; children: Daniel, Andrea, Anne Nicole. Student, SUNY, Fredonia, 1949-51; MusB, Eastman Sch. Music; BM, U. Rochester, 1953, MA, 1955; PhD, SUNY, Buffalo, 1962. Teaching fellow SUNY, Buffalo, 1958-60, instr., 1960-61, lectr., 1961-62; asst. prof. philosophy C.W. Post Campus, L.I.U., 1962-65; asso. prof. C.W. Post Center, L.I.U., 1965-70, prof., 1970-92, prof. emeritus, 1992—. Bingham prof. humanities U. Louisville, 1994; vis. assoc. prof. San Diego State Coll., 1966; mem. social sci. faculty Sarah Lawrence Coll., 1966-68 Author: The Aesthetic Field, 1970, Art and Engagement, 1991, The Aesthetics of Environment, 1992, Living in the Landscape: Toward an Aesthetics of Environment, 1997; editor: Environment and the Arts, 2002; founding editor online jour. Contemporary Aesthetics, 2003; contbr. articles to profl. jours. Served with U.S. Army, 1954-56. Am. Council Learned Socs. grantee, 1972, 76 Mem. AAUP, Internat. Assn. Aesthetics (sec.-gen. 1987-95, pres. 1995-98), Am. Soc. Aesthetics (sec.-treas. 1978-88), Internat. Inst. Applied Aesthetics (Lahti, Finland), Finnish Soc. Aesthetics (hon.), Sydney Soc. Lit. and Aesthetics (hon.), French Soc. Aesthetics (mem. com. of honor), Internat. Assn. Aesthetics (hon. life). Home: PO Box 52 Castine ME 04421-0052 E-mail: aberleant@yahoo.com.

BERLEW, FRANK KINGSTON, lawyer; b. Bangor, Maine, Apr. 9, 1930; s. Herman David and Lillian (Kingston) B.; m. Jeanne Cadigan, Aug. 16, 1952; children: Derek K., Sarah. AB, Conn. Wesleyan U., 1951; JD, Harvard U., 1954. Bar: Mass. 1954, U.S. Dist. Ct. Mass. 1954, Maine 1980. Law clk. Hon. Bailey Aldrich U.S. Dist. Ct. Mass., Boston, 1956-57; assoc. Ropes & Gray, Boston, 1957-61; regional legal counsel U.S. AID, Washington, 1961-62; dir. U.S. Peace Corps, Lahore, Pakistan, 1962-64, assoc. dir. Washington, 1964-66; legal dir., exec. v.p. ITT Africa and Mid. East, London, 1966-70; asst. group dir. consumer svcs. ITT, N.Y.C., 1970-72; pres. Canteen Internat., London, 1972-76, Berlew Bus. Devel. Internat., Boston, 1977-83; ptnr. Goldstein & Manello, Boston, 1984-88, Palmer & Dodge, Boston, 1988-98, internat. legal cons., 1999—. Contbr. articles to profl. jours. Trustee Conn. Wesleyan U., Middletown, 1978-81; pres. World Law Group, 1987-90; chmn. bd. trustee Meth. Ch. York and Ogunquit, Maine, 1986-88, 2002—. With U.S. Army, 1954-56. Mem. French-Am. C. of C. New Eng. (dir., pres. 1987-90), Japan Soc. Boston (dir. 1992-94). Avocations: guitar, singing, sports, wine. Home and Office: 130 Cider Hill Rd York ME 03909-5205 E-mail: kingbee@rcn.com.

BERLEY, MARC S. foundation administrator, English educator; b. N.Y.C., Apr. 14, 1963; s. David I. and Madaleine B.; m. Vered Rachel Sussman, June 22, 1997. BA in English, Columbia Coll., 1985; MA in English, Columbia U., 1988, PhD in English and Comp Lit., 1993. Prof. English Lawrence U., Appleton, Wis., 1993-94, Rutgers U., Newark, 1995, Columbia U., N.Y.C., 1996-98; pres. Found. Acad. Stds., N.Y.C., 1996—; prof. English Barnard Coll., 2000—. Author, editor: The Diversity Hoax, 1999, After the Heavenly Tune, 2000, Reading the Renaissance, 2003; book reviewer; contbr. articles to profl. jours. and major newspapers. Pres. fellow Colubmia U., 1990-93; Salvatori fellow Salvatori Found., 1999. Mem. MLA, Nat. Assn. Scholars, Assn. Lit. Scholars and Critics, Milton Soc. Am. E-mail: msb4@columbia.edu.

BERLIANT, MARCUS CRAIG, economist; b. Chgo., July 16, 1956; s. Kenneth and Esther B.; m. Clara Frances Asnes, Sept. 16, 1984. BA, Cornell U., 1977; MA in Stats., U. Calif., Berkeley, 1981, PhD in Econ., 1982. From asst. to assoc. prof. econ. U. Rochester, NY, 1982-94; prof. econ. Washington U., St. Louis, 1994—. Assoc. editor Regional Sci. and Urban Econ., 1989—, Jour. Pub. Economic Theory, 1997—, Papers in Regional Sci., 1999—, Jour. Regional Sci., 2000—; contbr. numerous articles to profl. publ., including Jour. Econ. Theory, Jour. Math. Econ., others. Fulbright fellow Erasmus U., Rotterdam, The Netherlands, 1984, vis. fellow Australian Nat. U., Canberra, 1995, S.W. Brooks vis. fellow U. Queensland, Brisbane, Australia, 1995, fellow Ctr. Polit. Economy, Washington U., 1994—, Vis. assoc. in econ., Calif. Inst. Tech., 2002-2003; Sabbatical fellow Am. Philos. Soc., 2002-03; vis. scholar U. Calif., Berkeley, 1988-89; grantee NSF, 1984, 86, 90, 93, 95, NATO, 1985; recipient Outstanding Faculty Mentor award Washington U., St. Louis, 2000, 02. Mem. Am. Econ. Assn., Assn. Pub. Policy Analysis and Mgmt., Econometric Soc., Nat. Tax Assn., Regional Sci. Assn. Internat. Office: Washington U Dept Econ CB 1208 1 Brookings Dr Saint Louis MO 63130-4899 E-mail: berliant@wueconc.wustl.edu.

BERLIN, ALAN DANIEL, lawyer, international energy and legal consultant; b. Bklyn., Oct. 20, 1939; s. Joseph Jacob and Rose (Smith) B.; m. Renee Wellinger, Dec. 22, 1962; children— Nicole Suzanne, Allison Leigh. BBA, CCNY, 1960; LLB, NYU, 1963, LLM, 1968. Bar: N.Y. 1963. Assoc. Aranow, Brodsky, Bohlinger, Einhorn & Dann, N.Y.C., 1965-68; asst. counsel Gen. Electric Co., N.Y.C., 1968-70; tax counsel Norton Simon Inc., N.Y.C., 1970-77; asst. prof. Pace U. Grad. Sch. Bus., 1977-85; pres. Belco Petroleum Corp., N.Y.C., 1977-88, The Crown Group, White Plains, N.Y., 1988-95; ptnr. Aitken Irvin Berlin & Vrooman L.L.P., 1995—. Spl. cons. to UN Dept. Tech. Cooperation for Devel., 1989—, UN Ctr. for Transnat. Corps., 1990—; hon. assoc. Ctr. for Petroleum and Mineral Law and Policy, U. Dundee, Scotland, 1993—. Author monographs on fed. income tax. With U.S. Army, 1963-65. Mem. ABA, Internat. Bar Assn., N.Y. State Bar Assn., Assn. of Bar of City of N.Y., Inter-Am. Bar Assn., Assn. Internat. Petroleum Negotiators. Lodges: Masons. Office: Aitken Irvin Berlin & Vrooman LLP 2 Gannett Dr White Plains NY 10604-3403 E-mail: aberlin273@aol.com., aibvlaw@yahoo.com.

BERLIN, CHESTON MILTON, JR., pediatrician, educator; b. Pitts., Mar. 28, 1936; s. Cheston Milton and Gladys Irene (Vance) B.; m. Anne Risher, July 9, 1960; children: Jean Vance, Douglas Cheston, Alexander Lindsay, Gordon Johnston. BA, Haverford (Pa.) Coll., 1958; MD, Harvard U., 1962. Intern Boston Children's Hosp., 1962-63, resident in pediatrics, 1965-67; asst. prof. pediatrics U. Ala. Sch. Medicine, Birmingham, 1967-68, George Washington U. Sch. Medicine, Washington, 1968-71; assoc. prof. pediatrics Pa. State U. Coll. Medicine, Hershey, 1971-75, prof. pediatrics and pharmacology, 1975-86, univ. prof. pediatrics, prof. pharmacology, 1986—. Pediat. panel U.S. Pharmacopeia, Rockville, Md., 1970—75, Rockville, 1980—2000. Contbr. articles to profl. jours. Sr. asst. surgeon USPHS, 1963-65. Markle Found. scholar, 1969, 74; recipient Cheston M. Berlin Alumni Svc. award Pa. State U. Coll. Medicine, 1987. Mem. Am. Acad. Pediatrics, Am. Soc. Exptl. Pharmacology and Therapeutics, Am. Soc. Clin. Pharmacology and Therapeutics, Am. Pediatric Soc., Am. Soc. Nutrition Sci., Phi Beta Kappa, Alpha Omega Alpha, Alpha Epsilon Delta. Episcopalian. Office: MS Hershey Med Ctr Dept Pediatrics PO Box 850 Hershey PA 17033-0850 E-mail: cmb6@psu.edu.

BERLIN, DONALD ROBERT, rabbi; b. Montreal, Que., Can., June 30, 1936; came to U.S., 1959; s. Saul Schnair Berlin and Isabel (Riven) Levy; m. Norma Brass, Nov. 26, 1959; children: Seth Daniel, Sharon Leah Berlin Kollender. Student, U. Toronto, Ont., Can., 1955-57; BA in Philosophy, U. Cin., 1961; B Hebrew Letters, Hebrew Union Coll.-Jewish Inst. Religion, Cin., 1963, MA in Hebrew Letters, 1965, D Divinity, 1990. Prin. Hebrew Sch. Temple Sinai, Toronto, Ont., Can., 1957-59; rabbi Temple Emanuel, Roanoke, Va., 1965-71, Congregation Keneseth Israel, Allentown, Pa., 1971-76; sr. rabbi Temple Oheb Shalom, Balt., 1976-99, rabbi emeritus, 1999—; acting regional dir. Mid-Atlantic coun. Union of Am. Hebrew Congregations, 1999-2001; rabbi-in-residence Washington Hebrew Congregation, 2001—02. Instr. Goucher Coll., Towson, Md., 1977—98, St. Mary's Sem. and U., Balt., 1983—93; mem. rabbinic cabinet World Union for Progressive Judaism, United Jewish Appeal, State of Israel Bonds; chmn. Rabbinical Placement Commn., 1992—2001; interim regional dir. Great Lakes Coun., Chgo. Fedn. Union of Am. Hebrew Congregations, 2003—04. Founding mem., trustee Inst. Christian and Jewish Studies, Balt., 1987-94; trustee Mental Health Assn. of Balt., 1979-83, Associated Jewish Fedn. of Balt., 1981-83, 86-88, Balt. Coun. on Fgn. Affairs, 1989-95; pres. Balt. Jewish Coun., 1986-88; mem. nat. rabbinic exec. coun. Jewish Nat. Fund; past chmn. coun. of clergy State of Md. Dept. Health and Mental Hygiene; past pres., founding mem. BL-EWS Balt. Blacks & Jews Dialogue Forum; bd. dirs., past chair Jewish addictions svcs. com. Jewish Big-Brother, Big Sister League; leader tour missions to Israel; del. World Zionist Congress, 1987; mem. adv. bd. Balt. Zionist Dist. Recipient Brotherhood Citation award NCCJ, 1970, Legion of Honor Chapel of the Four Chaplains, 1975, 30th Anniversary award State of Israel Bonds, 1981, Golden Shofar award State of Israel Bonds, 1998, Shofar award Boy Scouts Am., 1983, Good Scout award Boy Scouts Am., 1995. Mem. Balt. Bd. Rabbis (pres. 1983-85), Ctrl. Conf. Am. Rabbis (nat. exec. bd., pres. mid-Atlantic region 1980, nat. membership sec. 2003—), Assn. Reform Zionists Am. (nat. bd. dirs. 1980-86, exec. com. 1988-94, rabbinic advisor Balt. region 1984-88), Union Am. Hebrew Congregations (commn. on Jewish edn.) Avocations: classical music, professional ice hockey, overseas travel, antiques, crafts. Home: PO Box 898 Saint Michaels MD 21663-0898 E-mail: osdrb@aol.com.

BERLIN, DORIS ADA, psychiatrist; b. Newark, May 23, 1919; d. Samuel and Fanny (Lippman) B.; m. Saul R. Kelson (div.); children: Joel, Tamar. BS in Pharmacy, Columbia U., 1940; MD, Med. Coll. Va., 1948; MPH in Community Mental Health, U. Mich., 1966. Cert. Am. Bd. Psychiatry and Neurology; lic. psychiatrist N.Y., Va., Ohio, Mich., Tex., Calif. Intern Beth Israel Hosp., N.Y.C., 1948-49; resident in psychiatry Bellevue Hosp., N.Y.C., 1949-52; pvt. practice N.Y.C., 1952-57, Toledo, 1957-66, Fishkill and Poughkeepsie, N.Y., 1984—. Clin. asst. in psychiatry NYU Coll. Medicine, 1952-57; asst. in psychiatry U. Hosp., N.Y., 1952-53; clin. asst. vis. neuropsychiatrist Bellevue Hosp., N.Y., 1954-57; lectr. mental health Sch. Pub. Health U. Mich., 1966-68; dir. profl. edn. Toledo State Hosp., 1969-70; clin. assoc. prof. N.Y. Sch. Psychiatry, 1970-81; dir. residency program Hudson River Psychiat. Ctr., Poughkeepsie, 1970-83, others. Mem. citizen's adv. bd. Lucas County (Ohio) Welfare Dept., 1963-67, chair, 1965-66; bd. dirs. Jewish Family Svc., Toledo, 1969-70; mem. policy coun., rehab. com. Toledo Area Program on Drug Abuse, 1970; bd. dirs. Dutchess County Assn. for Sr. Citizens, 1993-96. Grantee NEH, 1979. Fellow Am. Psychiat. Assn. (chair editl. bd. Hosp. and Cmty. Psychiatric Jour., 1979-80, task force on cmty. mental health ctrs., 1983-88, com. on advertisers and exhibitors 1989-92, vice-chair lifers caucus, 1990-91, chair lifers orgn. 1992), Am. Coll. Psychiatrists (Laughlin fellowship com. 1976-79); mem. Am. Acad. Psychoanalysis (com. on psychoanalysis and cmty. mental health 1967-68), Dutchess County Med. Soc. (psychiatrists' rep. to coun. 1985-95, treas. 1987). Home and Office: 66 Mitchell Ave Poughkeepsie NY 12603-3423

BERLIN, EDWARD ALAN, musicologist, writer, retired application developer; b. N.Y.C., June 26, 1936; s. Milton and Sadie Berlin; m. Andree de Plata, Sept. 7, 1958; children: Michele Andree, Stephanie Jacqueline Caputo, Kim Elizabeth. BA, Queens Coll., 1959; MA, Hunter Coll., 1965; PhD, CUNY, 1976. Author: (book) Ragtime: A Musical and Cultural History, 1980, Reflections and Research on Ragtime, 1987 (ASCAP-Deems Taylor, 1989), King of Ragtime: Scott Joplin and His Era, 1994; dir.: (exhbn.) Duke Ellington - Love You Madly. Personal E-mail: edberlin06@hotmail.com.

BERLIN, HOWARD RICHARD, investment advisory company executive; b. White Plains, N.Y., Dec. 30, 1935; s. Simon and Frances (Held) B.; m. Joy Monte Shortino, June 10, 1961; children: Howard R. Jr., Asa Ward, Carter Franklin. BS in Econs., U. Pa., 1957; postgrad., NYU, 1962-63. Security analyst Merrill Lynch, N.Y.C., 1961-69, v.p. capital markets, 1969-86; sr. portfolio mgr. Neuberger & Berman, N.Y.C., 1986—2001, prin. ptnr., mem. exec. com., 1990—2001; ret., 2001; mng. mem. The Maverick Group, LLC. Hon. nat. campaign chmn. Uriah P. Levy Ctr., US Naval Acad.; scholarship co-chmn. Inst. Am. Indian Arts. Cmdr. USN, 1957—59. Mem. Fin. Analyst Fedn., N.Y. Soc. Security Analysts, Naval Res. Assn., Ret. Officers Assn., Boulders Club (Carefree, Ariz.). Avocations: land development, small business development.

BERLIN, KENNETH DARRELL DARRELL, chemistry educator, consultant, researcher; b. Quincy, Ill., June 12, 1933; s. Kenneth Marion Fischer and Mary Esther (Beckley) B.; m. Grace Frances Smith, Apr. 3, 1937; children: Grace Esther, James Darrell. BA cum laude, North Cen. Coll., Naperville, Ill., 1955; PhD, U. Ill., 1958. Postdoctoral fellow U. Fla., Gainesville, 1958-60; asst. prof. chemistry Okla. State U., Stillwater, 1960-63, assoc. prof., 1963-66, prof., 1966-71, Regents prof., 1971—. Spl. cons. Nat. Cancer Inst., Bethesda, Md., 1969—; cons. E.I. DuPont Co., Wilmington, Del., 1969-70, Am. Heart Assn., Oklahoma City, 1983-86, Ariz. Disease Control Commn., 1989—. Co-author: Organic Chemistry, 1972, Phosphorous Stereochem, 1977; contbr. rsch., articles. Recipient Regents Disting. Tchg. award, 1998, Sigma Xi rsch. award Okla. State U., Stillwater, 1969, Okla. Chemist of Yr. award, 1977, Okla. Medallion Found. for Excellence in Coll./Univ. Tchg., 2003. Fellow Okla. Acad. Sci. (scientist of yr. 1976), Burlington No. Faculty Achievement award 1988, Eminent Faculty award 1998, Okla. medallion Excellence in Tchg. at Coll./Univ. Regents Disting. Rsch. award 2003); mem. Am. Chem. Soc. (sr.), Internat. Soc. Hetercyclic Chemists, Alpha Chi Sigma. Assembly of God. Office: Okla State Univ Dept Chemistry Ps I Stillwater OK 74078-0001 E-mail: kdberlin@bmb-fs1.biochem.okstate.edu.

BERLIN, MEREDITH RISE, editor; b. Bronxville, N.Y., Nov. 22, 1955; d. Marvin and Seena (Goldsmith) Brown; m. Jordan Stuart Berlin, Aug. 13, 1988; children: Gregory Samuel, Lauren Julia, Connor David. BS, Emerson Coll., 1976. With circulation-subscription World Bus. Weekly, N.Y.C., 1978-79; feature editor Soap Opera Digest, N.Y.C., 1979-82, editor-in-chief, 1982-91; editor-at-large, 1991-96, Soap Opera Digest, N.Y.C., 1999—; editor-in-chief Seventeen Mag., N.Y.C., 1997-99; dir. devel. Promedia Consumer Magazines, 1999—. Exec. producer Soap Opera Awards NBC-TV, L.A., 1988-91; commentator WCBS-TV Noon News, 1987-96; commentator NBC's House Party; producer, journalist Afternoon TV Show, 1982. Columnist N.Y. Post, 1994-96. Recipient 3 Emmy nominations, 1988, 89; named N.Y. Alumni of Yr. Emerson Coll. Mem. NOW, AFTRA, Am. Soc. Mag. Editors.

BERLIN, ROBERT HARRY, military studies educator; b. Pitts., Oct. 24, 1946; s. Abraham Maurice and Betty W. Berlin; children: Jessica Sabrina, Leslie Farrah. BA, Rockford Coll., 1968; PhD in History, U. Calif., Santa Barbara, 1976. Vis. prof. Mansfield (Pa.) State Coll., 1976—77; instr. Allan Hancock C.C., Lompoc, Calif., 1976—79; assoc. prof. U.S. Army Command and Gen. Staff Coll., Ft. Leavenworth, Kans., 1979—90; prof. and dir. academic affairs Sch. of Advanced Mil. Studies, Ft. Leavenworth, 1991—; adj. prof. Benedictine Coll., Atchison, Kans., 2003. Exec. dir. Soc. for Mil. History, Lexington, Va., 1999—; vis. prof. summer program Oxford (England) U., 2003—. Author: (history booklet) U.S. Army World War II Corps Commanders (The Journal of Military History, 53), 1989 (Moncado Prize Award, 1990). Decorated Superior Civilian Svc. award Dept. of the Army. Mem.: Soc. for Mil. History, Orgn. Am. Historians (life). Jewish. Avocations: travel, hiking, biking, military poetry, oneology. Home: 3119 Lakeview Cir Leavenworth KS 66048 Office: Sc Advanced Mil Studies 250 Gibbon Ave Fort Leavenworth KS 66027 Office Fax: 913-758-3309. Personal E-mail: rhberlin@aol.com.

BERLIN, STEVEN RITT, oil company executive; b. Pitts., July 1, 1944; s. Sidney D. and Pauline (Ritt) B.; children: Leslie, Jessica, Loren. BBA, Duquesne U., 1967; MBA, U. Wis., 1969. Prof. U. Houston, 1070-72; various fin. positions Cities Svc. Co., Tulsa, 1973-83; v.p. fin. Citgo Petroleum, Tulsa, 1983-85, gen. mgr., 1985-86, CFO, 1986-97; prof., assoc. dean U. Tulsa, 1997-99; chief fin. officer Kaiser-Francis Oil Co., Tulsa, 1999—. Speaker various industry, profl. seminars; mem. Acctg. Edn. change Commn. Mem. bd. visitors U. Wis.; sec.-treas. Green T Club of Tulsa. Mem. AICPA, Am. Acctg. Assn., Okla. Soc. CPAs, Stanford U. Alumni Assn., Beta Gamma Sigma. Avocations: jogging, reading. Office: Kaiser-Francis Oil Co 6733 S Yale Ave Tulsa OK 74136-3302 Home: 1243 E 32d St Tulsa OK 74105 E-mail: cfo@berlin.com.

BERLINCOURT, MARJORIE ALKINS, government official, retired; b. Toronto, Ont., Can., June 2, 1928; came to U.S., 1950, naturalized, 1956; d. Herbert John and Ellen Florence (Barker) Alkins; m. Ted Gibbs Berlincourt, Feb. 28, 1953; 1 child, leslie Berlincourt Yale. BA, U. Toronto, 1950; MA, Yale U., 1951, PhD, 1954. Editl. dir. tech. publs. Rocketdyne, 1956-59; lectr. classics U. So. Calif., 1959-61; assoc. prof. classical history Calif. Luth. Coll., 1961-67, Calif. State U., Northridge, 1967-71; prof. Met. State Coll., Denver, 1971-72; program dir. div. fellowships for summer sems., fellowships NEH, Washington, 1972-78, dir. state programs, 1983—91, dir. divsn. fellowships, seminars, 1991-94; ret., 1995. Vis. lectr. Georgetown U., 1972 Author: De Surprise en Surprise, 1953, Entrez Petits Amis, 1954, Victory as a Coin Type, 1973; contbr. articles to profl. jours. Sterling fellow Yale U., 1950-53; recipient Calif. Faculty Rsch. award, 1970. Mem. Am. Assn. Ancient Historians. Episcopalian.

BERLIND, BRUCE PETER, poet, educator; b. Bklyn., July 17, 1926; s. Peter Sydney and Mae (Miller) B.; m. Doris Lidz, 1947 (div. 1950); m. Mary Elizabeth Dirlam, 1954 (div. 1983); children: Lise, Anne, John, Paul, Alexandra; m. Jo Anne Pagano, 1985. Student, Mercersburg Acad., 1941-43; AB, Princeton U., 1947; MA, Johns Hopkins U., 1950, PhD, 1958. Instr. English Colgate U., Hamilton, N.Y., 1954-58, asst. prof., 1958-63, assoc. prof., 1963-66, prof., 1966-80, Charles A. Dana prof. English, 1980-88, prof. emeritus, 1988—, chmn. dept. English, 1967-72, 80-83; poet in residence U. Rochester, 1966. USIS lectr., Germany, 1963, with Hungarian P.E.N. Translation Program, Budapest, 1977, 79, 86, 88, 91. Author: (poems) Ways of Happening, 1959, Companion Pieces, 1971; translator: (poems) Selected Poems of Agnes Nemes Nagy, 1980, Birds and Other Relations: Selected Poetry of Dezso Tandori, 1987, When You Became She by Imre Oravecz, 1994, The Journey of Barbarus by Ottó Orbán, 1997, Charon's Ferry: Fifty Poems of Gyula Illyés, 2000; assoc. editor: (poems) The Hopkins Rev., 1949-53; contbr. poems, essays, revs. to mags. 1st lt. AUS, 1945-46, 50-52. Recipient Meml. medal Hungarian PEN, 1986; Fulbright grantee, Hungary, 1983-84. Mem. PEN Am. Ctr., Poetry Soc. Am., Am. Lit. Translators Assn., AAUP (mem. council, past pres. N.Y. State Conf.) Home: PO Box 237 Hamilton NY 13346-0237 E-mail: bberlind@mail.colgate.edu.

BERLIND, ROBERT ELLIOT, artist, educator; b. N.Y.C., Aug. 20, 1938; s. Peter Sidney Berlind and Mae (Miller) Bach; m. Dorothy Welch, June 1963 (div. 1974); 1 child, Alexey Fuller; m. Nancy Lee Hubbard, June 17, 1978 (div. 1993); 1 child, Gabriel Peter; m. Mary Lucier, June 7, 1997. BA, Columbia U., 1960; BFA, Yale U., 1962, MFA, 1963. Assoc. prof. art N.S. Coll. of Art and Design, Halifax, Can., 1974-76; prof. SUNY, Purchase, 1979—. One man exhbns.: Alexander Milliken Gallery, N.Y.C., 1981, 82, Tomasulo Gallery, Union Coll., 1983, Ruth Siegel Gallery, N.Y.C., 1984, 86, 88, 90, Gallery One, Toronto, Can., 1985, Warren Wilson Coll., Swananoa, N.C., 1986, St. Peter's Ch., N.Y.C., 1988, Delaware Valley Arts Alliance, Narrowsburg, N.Y., 1992, Tibor de Nagy Gallery, N.Y.C., 1994, 96, 98, 2001, Hampshire Coll. Main Gallery, Amherst, Mass., 1995, Reynolds Gallery, Richmond, Va., 1996, Wright State U., Dayton, Ohio, 1997, Newberger Mus. Art, Purchase, N.Y., 1998; group shows: N.Y. Studio Sch., 1986, The Bronx Mus. of the Arts, 1987, Sherry French Gallery, N.Y.C., 1987, One Penn Pla., N.Y.C., 1988, Fay Gold Gallery, 1988, Art Mus. Fla. Internat. U., 1989, Meml. Art Gallery U. Rochester, 1989, Found. Mona Bismarck, Paris, 1991, Am. Acad. and Inst. Arts and Letters, 1992, Neuberger Mus., Purchase, N.Y., 1994, Maier Art Mus., Lynchburg, Va., others. Recipient award in painting Am. Acad. Inst. Arts and Letters, 1992, Pollock-Krasner award, 1997; NEA fellow in painting, 1993. Mem. Coll. Art Assn., Internat. Assn. Art Critics, Nat. Acad. Design. Home: 215 W 20th St Apt 4W New York NY 10011-3552 E-mail: berlind4@aol.com.

BERLIND, ROGER STUART, stage and film producer; b. N.Y.C., June 27, 1930; s. Peter Sydney and Mae (Miller) B.; m. Helen Polk Clark, July 7, 1962 (dec.); 1child, William Polk; m. Brook Wheeler, May 19, 1979. AB, Princeton U., 1952. Account exec. Eastman Dillon, Union Securities & Co., N.Y.C., 1956-60; gen. ptnr. Carter, Berlind & Weill, N.Y.C., 1960-65; chmn. exec. com. Cogan, Berlind, Weill & Levitt, Inc., N.Y.C., 1965-69; chief exec. officer Shearson Lehman Bros., N.Y.C., 1969-73, vice chmn. bd., 1974-75. Bd. dirs. Lehman Bros. Prodr.: (films) Beyond Therapy, 1987; (plays) Rex, Music Is, Diversions and Delights, The Merchant, The 1940's Radio Hour, Passione, The Lady from Dubuque, Amadeus, Sophisticated Ladies, Lydie Breeze, Nine, All's Well that Ends Well, The Real Thing, The Rink, Joe Egg, After the Fall, Precious Sons, Big Deal, Long Day's Journey into Night, Ain't Misbehavin', Jerome Robbins' Broadway, City of Angels, Artist Descending A Staircase, Lettice and Lovage, Death and The Maiden, Guys and Dolls, Passion, Indiscretions, Hamlet, Getting Away with Murder, A Funny Thing Happened on the Way to the Forum, Skylight, Steel Pier, The Life, A View from the Bridge, The Judas Kiss, The Blue Room, Closer, Amy's View, Kiss Me Kate (Tony award, 2000), Copenhagen (Tony award, 2000), Proof (Tony award, 2001), Dance of Death, Medea. Hon. trustee Am. Acad. Dramatic Arts. With CIC, U.S. Army, 1952-54. Mem. League Am. Theatres and Producers (gov.), Princeton Club (N.Y.C.), Univ. Club, River Club, Century Assn.

BERLINE, JAMES H. advertising executive, public relations executive; b. Youngstown, Ohio, Aug. 6, 1946; s. James Howard and Eloise Blanche (Smith) Berline; children: Erin Michele, Jess Brandon, Quincy Blaine. BA in Econs., U.

Mich., 1968; MS in Advt., U. Ill., 1971. V.p. Campbell-Ewald Co., Detroit, 1971-76; sr. v.p. Batten Barton Durstine & Osborn Inc., Troy, Mich., 1976-78, exec. v.p. Southfield, Mich., 1984-85; pres. Yaffe Berline Inc., Southfield, 1980-82; pres., CEO Berline Group, Birmingham, Mich., 1982—. Bd. dirs. Leadership Detroit Alumni; pres. MAGNET (Mktg. and Advt. Global Network). Program chmn. United Found., Detroit, 1984; mem. adv. bd. Jr. League; founder Winning Futures; trustee Detroit Sci. Ctr., 1985—, Juvenile Diabetes Found., 1994; chmn. comm. com. Leadership Detroit, 1993; bd. dirs. Make-A-Wish Found., chmn., 2001—03; trustee CATCH, mem. exec. com. Mem.: Young Pres. Orgn. (chair office commn. 1994, trustee, com. chmn. Ea. Mich. chpt.), World Pres. orgn., Detroit C. of C. (mktg. com. 1987—88), Greater Detroit Alliance Bus. (bd. dirs. 1984—86), Bingham Athletic Club (pres.), U. Mich. Grad. M Club (bd. dirs. 1986), U. Mich. Club Detroit (past bd. govs.), Adcraft Club (bd. dirs. 1980—99, pres. 1988). Avocations: squash, travel, golf. Office: The Berline Group 6001 N Adams Rd Bloomfield Hills MI 48304-1566

BERLINER, ALLEN IRWIN, dermatologist; b. N.Y.C., Apr. 18, 1947; s. Joseph Benjamin and Ruth (Kaplan) B.; m. Edwina BA, Queens Coll., 1967; MD, SUNY, Buffalo, 1971. Diplomate: Am. Bd. Dermatology. Intern Nassau County Med. Ctr., East Meadow, N.Y., 1971-72; resident in dermatology Boston U. Med. Ctr., 1974-76, chief resident, 1976-77; practice medicine specializing in dermatology Norwood, Mass., 1977—; asst. clin. prof. Tufts U., 1980-90, assoc. clin. prof., 1990—; chief dermatology sect. Norwood Hosp., 1986—; assoc. staff Boston U. Hosp., Tufts-New Eng. Med. Ctr. Bd. dirs. Mass. Acad. Dermatology. Served as surgeon USPHS, 1972-74. Mem. Am. Acad. Dermatology, New Eng. Dermatol. Soc., Mass. Acad. Dermatology (pres. 1994-95). Office: 95 Chapel St Norwood MA 02062-3161

BERLINER, ERNST, chemistry educator; b. Kattowitz, Germany, Feb. 18, 1915; came to U.S., 1940, naturalized, 1949; s. Joseph and Lucy (Selinger-Ehrenhaus) Berliner; m. Frances Jean Bondhus, Sept. 11, 1947 (dec. Jan. 2002); 1 child, Susan Lucy. Student univs., Breslau and Freiburg, Germany, 1935—38; MA, Harvard U., 1941, PhD, 1943. Mem. faculty Bryn Mawr Coll., Pa., 1944—, chmn. dept. chemistry, 1951-76, 80-82, prof., 1953-85, prof. emeritus, 1985—. Contbr. articles profl. jours.; Bd. editors: Jour. Organic Chemistry, 1963-68. Recipient Coll. Chemistry Tchr. award Mfg. Chemists Assn., 1963; Disting. Teaching award Lindback Found., 1975; Guggenheim fellow, 1962 Fellow AAAS; mem. Am. Chem. Soc. (Phila. Sect. award 1971), Chem. Soc. (London, Eng.), Sigma Xi. Home: Rosemont Plz 1062 Lancaster Ave Apt 214 Rosemount PA 19010 E-mail: eberline@brynmawr.edu.

BERLINER, EVE, writer, editor, publishing executive; d. Herman and Doris (Samowitz) Berliner; m. Dennis Patrick Carey, Nov. 26, 1983 (dec. Oct. 29, 1990). BA magna cum laude, CUNY, Bklyn., 1964. Asst. to the editor, editor of letters to the editor N.Y. Post, N.Y.C., 1965—71; feature writer Bklyn. Heights Press, N.Y.C., 1979—81, N.Y. Arts Weekly, N.Y.C., 1981—83; sr. writer The Silurian News, N.Y.C., 1983—90; editor-in-chief Silurian News, N.Y.C., 1990—; editor and pub. Eve's Mag., N.Y.C., 1998—. Author: (electronic book) Jack Nicholson: Auspicious Beginnings, 1998; editor: The Journalist, 2003—. Tchr. children's lit. arts project Bklyn Pub. Libr., 2000—03. Mem.: The Soc. of the Silurians (pres. 1988—89), Phi Beta Kappa. Home: Ste LB1 7401 Shore Rd Brooklyn NY 11209-1953 Office: Eve's Magazine Ste LB1 7401 Shore Rd Brooklyn NY 11209-1953 Home Fax: 718-238-8445; Office Fax: 718-238-8445. Personal E-mail: evesmag@aol.com. E-mail: evesmag@aol.com.

BERLINER, HERMAN ALBERT, university provost and officer, economics educator; BA, CCNY, 1965; PhD, CUNY, 1970. Assoc. prof. econs. Hofstra U., Hempstead, N.Y., 1970-85, assoc. dean advisement, 1975-76, assoc. provost, 1976-83, dean Sch. Bus., 1980-82, 83-90, prof. econs., 1985—, provost, dean faculties, 1989-2001, Lawrence Herbert disting. prof., 1996—, provost, sr. v.p., 2001—. Mem. External Periodic External Review Evaluator, Mid. States, 2003, Health and Welfare Coun., LI, NY, 1997—, Nassau County Assessments Improvement Commn., NY, 1999-2000. Assoc. editor Am. Economist, 1975-80, 83—. Periodic rev. report external reviewer Middle States Commn., 2003—. Home: 93 Plymouth Dr N Glen Head NY 11545-1126 Office: Hofstra U Office of Provost Hempstead NY 11550 E-mail: herman.berliner@hofstra.edu.

BERLINER, RUTH SHIRLEY, real estate company executive; b. N.Y.C., June 20, 1928; d. Irving William and Florence (Tomback) Blum; m. Arthur Ivan Berliner, Sept. 23, 1948; children: Daniel Scott, Michael Robert, Eric Lance. BA, Empire State Coll., Westbury, N.Y., 1974; diploma, Wilsey Sch. Interior Design, Hempstead, N.Y., 1975; MBA, Adelphi U., 1980. Lic. real estate broker, N.Y. Sec. to dir. librs. NYU, N.Y.C., 1948-50; sec. Paragon Mut. Syndicates Inc., N.Y.C., 1958-72; v.p. Paragon Mut. Investors Svcs., N.Y.C., 1972-78; pres. Ruth S. Berliner, Inc., N.Y.C., 1978—. Pres. Irmed Corp., 1983—; cons. E. 59th St. Assocs., N.Y.C., 1962-70, Amrep Corp., N.Y.C., 1968-75, FKBA Assocs., N.Y.C., 1974-78; mem. stores com. Real Estate Bd. N.Y., 1984-96. V.p. NYU Dental Sch. Parents Assn., 1974-76; bd. dirs. Hadassah, Hewlett, N.Y., 1978-87; advisor Citizens for Charter Change, N.Y.C., 1987—. Mem. Nat. Assn. Realtors, Real Estate Bd. N.Y. (store com. 1984-98, econ. devel. com. 1994-99), Inwood Club, Nat. Realty Club, Williams Club, N.Y. Athletic Club. Avocations: tennis, swimming, dancing, painting.

BERLINGER, WARREN, actor; b. Bklyn., Aug. 31, 1937; s. Elias and Frieda (Shapkin) B.; m. Betty Lou Keim, Feb. 18, 1960. Student, Profl. Children's Sch., 1952-55, Columbia, 1958. Broadway appearances include Annie Get Your Gun, 1946, Happy Time, 1950, Take a Giant Step, 1951, Anniversary Waltz, 1955, Roomful of Roses, 1957, Blue Denim, 1958 (Theatre World award 1959), Come Blow Your Horn, 1960, Bernardine, 1953; London appearance in How to Succeed in Business Without Really Trying, 1963-64; film appearances include The Long Goodbye, Spinout, The World According to Garp, My African Adventure, Outlaw Force, Hero, 1992, Crime and Punishment, 1994, Feminine Touch, 1994, Dear God, 2000, The Great John Rexx, 2002, Time and Again, 2002, So They Call Him Sasquatch, 2002, 2003; TV appearances on Secret Storm, 1955-57, The Funny Side, 1971-72, Touch of Grace, 1973, My African Adventure, 1986, Take Two, 1987, Agatha Christie's Death on Safari, (TV series) Shades of L.A., 1991, Picket Fences, 1993; films include Hero, That Thing You Do!, Dear God, T.O. Friends, November Conspiracy; plays include Lend Me a Tenor. Named hon. mayor of Chatsworth Calif., 1968, hon. sheriff, 1975; recipient Theatre World award, 1958.

BERLINSKI, EDWARD GERARD, writing educator, writer; b. Spokane, Wash., Apr. 18, 1961; s. Edward Joseph and Dorothy Florence (Chojnowski) B. BA in History, Cath. U., Washington, 1984; MFA in Creative Writing, Am. U., Washington, 1990; PhD in Rhetoric and Composition, Cath. U., 1997. Writer/editor Naval Surface Warfare Ctr., Silver Spring, Md., 1984-90; writing instr. Cath. U., 1990-96; adj. prof. humanities Strayer U., Takoma Park, Md., 1993-97; lectr. profl. writing program U. Md., College Park, 1996—. Specialities include: medical, bus., tech., and creative writing (poetry). Avocation: writing poetry. Home: PO Box 11038 Takoma Park MD 20913-1038 Office: Univ Md Profl Writing Program 3119 Susquehanna Hl College Park MD 20742-0001 E-mail: eb127@umail.umd.edu.

BERLOW, ROBERT ALAN, lawyer; b. Detroit, Feb. 11, 1947; s. Henry and Shirley (Solovich) B.; m. Elizabeth Ann Goldin, Sept. 20, 1972; children: Stuart, Lisa. BA, U. Mich., 1968; JD, Wayne State U., 1971. Bar: Mich. 1971, U.S. Supreme Ct. 1978. Asst. to dean, instr. law sch. Wayne State U., Detroit, 1971-72, mem. Radner, Radner, Shefman, Bayer and Berlow, P.C., Southfield, Mich., 1972-78; gen. counsel Perry Drug Stores, Inc., Pontiac, Mich., 1978-80, gen. counsel, sec., 1980-82, v.p., gen. counsel, sec., 1982-88, sr. v.p., gen. counsel, sec., 1988-93, sr. v.p., chief adminstrn. officer, gen. counsel, sec., 1993-94, exec. v.p., gen. counsel, sec., 1994-95; sr. mem. Dykema Gossett, PLLC, Bloomfield Hills, Mich., 1995—, also chmn. retail practice group. Pres. Agy. for Jewish Edn., Metro Detroit, 1993-95, v.p., 1987-93; bd. dirs. Jewish Cmty. Ctr. Met. Detroit, 1989-2003, v.p., 1992-93, treas., 1996-97, sec., 1997-98. Mem. ABA, Mich. Bar Assn. (chair comml. leasing and mgmt. of real estate com. of real property law sect. 1993-98, chmn. real property law sect. 2001-2002). Avocations: sports, photography. Office: Dykema Gossett PLLC 39577 N Woodward Ave Bloomfield Hills MI 48304-2837 E-mail: r.berlow@dykema.com.

BERLYN, SHELDON, art educator, artist; b. Worcester, Mass., Sept. 6, 1929; m. Diane C. Satterfield. Diploma, Worcester Art Mus. Sch., 1951; student, Yale-Norfolk Summer Sch. Art, 1949-50, Art Acad. Cin., 1954-55, SUNY Buffalo, 1959-62. Instr. drawing Worcester (Mass.) Art Mus. Sch., 1957-58; assoc. prof. painting (emeritus) SUNY Buffalo, 1962-99; ret., 1999—. With U.S. Army, 1951-53, Korea. Home: 4598 Vine Rd Penn Yan NY 14527

BERMAN, ARIANE R. artist; b. Danzig, Mar. 27, 1937; m. Mario La Rossa, 1965. B.F.A., Hunter Coll., N.Y.C., 1959; M.F.A., Yale, 1962; AAUW and Found. des Etats-Unis fellow, U. Paris, 1962-63. Juror nat. screening com. Fulbright grants, 1976-77, chmn. screening com., 1977-78. One man shows at Center Gallery, Conn., 1963, Harry Salpeter Gallery, N.Y.C., 1966, Brentano's Art Gallery, N.Y.C., 1973, Graphic Art Gallery, Tel Aviv, 1973, Galleria San Sebastianello, Rome, 1973, Eileen Kuhlik Gallery, N.Y.C., 1971, 73, Pub. Mus., Oshkosh, Wis., 1974, Wustum Mus. Fine Arts, Racine, Wis., 1974, Fontana Gallery, Pa., 1963, 71, 74, Galleria d'Arte Helioart, Rome, 1974, Munson Gallery, Conn., 1975, Ward-Nasse Gallery, N.Y.C., 1975, 77, 80, Phila. Art Alliance, 1980, Silvermine Guild Artists, Conn., 1976, Kornblee Gallery, N.Y.C., 1982, Babson Coll., Mass., 1983, Northwood Inst., Mich., 1983, Westenhook Gallery, Mass., 1984, Phoenix Gallery, N.Y.C., 1985, 87, Concordia Coll., Bronxville, N.Y., 1989, Gallery 84 Inc., N.Y.C., 1992, L'Artisanat, Mass., 1992, others; exhibited in group shows at Galerie Atrium Artis, Geneva, Switzerland, 1975, F 15 Gallery, Norway, 1974, Galeries Raymond Duncan, Paris, 1964, Asso. Am. Artists, N.Y.C., 1971, Circle Galleries Ltd., N.Y.C., 1974, Margo Feiden Galleries, N.Y.C., 1972, Gallery 500, Pa., 1973, Van Straaten Gallery, Chgo., 1974, Genesis Gallery, N.Y.C., 1978, Marymount Coll., N.Y.C., 1983, NYU, 1982, Fairleigh Dickenson U., 1982, Allentown Art Mus., Pa., 1982, numerous others; represented in permanent collections at Am. Petroleum Inst., Israel Ministry of Tourism, USIA, McGregor-Doniger, Inc., Shipley Sch., Bryn Mawr, Pa., Readers Digest, N.J. Bd. Edn., Athena Gallery, New Haven, Charles E. Ellis Coll., Newton Square, Pa., Hearst Corp., Met. Mus. Art, Phila. Mus. Art, Phila. Art Alliance, Ms. mag., Seventeen, Redbook, Feminist Press, Duke U., Newspaper Advt. Bur., Purdue U., Phila. Child Guidance Ctr., others. Recipient Yale Painting prize, 1960, Purchase award Purdue U., 1964, Stella Drabkin Meml. award, ACPS Purchase prize, 1973, Catherine Lorillard Wolfe Arts Club Gold medal, 1973, Hon. mention Hudson River Mus., 1974, Artists Equity award, 1985. Mem. Am. Color Print Soc., Nat. Assn. Women Artists, Yonkers Art Assn., Women's Caucus for Art, Met. Painters and Sculptors, Pen and Brush, League of Present Day Artists, Sheffield Art League, Silvermine Guild of Artists, Soc. Women Artists (past corr. sec.), Hunter Coll. Alumni Assn. (Hall of Fame 1974) Home: 161 W 54th St New York NY 10019-5322 *I use art as a means of communicating to people. My work is representational and tries to depict life in all its humor, sorrow, satiric aspects, and dream-like qualities of humanity as I see it. I particularly use color for emphasis in everything I do— paintings, graphics, plastics, and sculpture.*

BERMAN, ARTHUR LEONARD, retired state senator; b. Chgo., May 4, 1935; s. Morris and Jean (Glast) B.; m. Barbara Dombeck; children: Adam, Marcy Padorr. BS in Commerce & Law, U. Ill., 1956; JD, Northwestern U., 1958. Bar: Ill. 1958. Atty. pvt. practice, Chgo.; ptnr. White, White & Berman, Chgo., 1958-74, Maragos, Richter, Berman, Russell & White, Chtd., 1974—81, Chatz, Berman, Maragos, Haber & Fagel, Chgo., 1981-82, Berman, Fagel, Haber, Maragos & Abrams, Chgo., 1982-86, Karlin & FLeisher, Chgo., 1986-99; dir. labor mediations svcs. Chgo. Bd. Edn., 2000—. Spl. atty. Bur. Liquidations, Ill. Dept. Ins., 1962-67; spl. asst. atty. gen. Ill., 1967-68; mem. Ill. Ho. of Reps., 1969-76, Ill. Senate, 1977-99. Pres. 50th Ward Young Dems., 1956-60; v.p. Cook County Young Dems., 1956-60, 50th Ward Regular Dem. Orgn., 1955-99; active 48th Ward Regular Dem. Orgn., 1967-99; exec. bd. Dem. Party, Evanston, Ill., 1973-99; bd. govs. State of Israel Bonds. Mem. ABA, Ill. Bar Assn., Chgo. Bar Assn. (bd. mgrs. 1988-89), Nat. Assn. Jewish Legislators (pres. 1987-89), Am. Trial Lawyers Assn., U. Ill. Alumni Assn., Phi Epsilon Pi, Tau Epsilon Rho. Office: 6007 N Sheridan Rd Chicago IL 60660-3039

BERMAN, BARBARA, educational consultant; b. N.Y.C., Oct. 15, 1938; d. Nathan and Regina (Pasternak) Kopp; children: Adrienne, David. BS, Bklyn. Coll., 1959, MS, 1961; adminstrv./supervision cert., Coll. S.I., 1971; EdD, Rutgers U., 1981. Tchr. N.Y.C. Pub. Schs., 1959-70; project coord., dir. fed. projects Rutgers U., New Brunswick, N.J., 1976-80; math. cons. B&F Cons., S.I., NY, 1978—2003, BB Consulting, S.I., NY, 2003—; dir. fed. math. project Ednl. Support Systems, Inc., S.I., 1981-94; dir. Foresight Sch., S.I., 1985—. Great Beginnings Infant and Toddler Ctr., 1989—; cons. B&F, 1985—2003. Cons. to sch. dists. for restructuring/sch. reform and math. staff devel. Co-author of many books and articles on teaching mathematics for elem. and jr. h.s. tchrs. Mem. Nat. Coun. Tchrs. Math., Nat. Staff Devel. Coun., N.Y. Acad. Scis., Nat. Coun. Suprs. Math. Avocations: reading, travel, theatre. Office: BB Consulting 446 Travis Ave Staten Island NY 10314-6149 E-mail: BarbBerman@aol.com.

BERMAN, BERNARD MAYER, lawyer; b. Phila., May 9, 1940; s. Henry and Mildred (Ginsburg) B.; m. Mona Halpern, June 7, 1964; children: Minda, Kyle, Joshua. BA, Swarthmore (Pa.) Coll., 1962; LLB, Columbia U., 1965, JD, 1969. Bar: Pa. 1965, U.S. Dist. Ct. (ea. dist.) Pa. 1966, U.S. Ct. Appeals (3d cir.) 1966, U.S. Supreme Ct. 1969. Jud. law clk. Ct. of Common Pleas, Phila., 1965-66; pvt. practice Phila., 1965-66; pub. defender trial atty. Delaware County, 1966-77; jud. law clk. Ct. of Common Pleas, Delaware County, Pa., 1967-74; pvt. practice Delaware County, 1966-89; ptnr. Scallan, March, Berman & Hurwitz and predecessor firms, Media, Pa., 1966-88, Scallan and Berman, Media, 1988-89, Bernard M. Berman and Assocs., Media, 1989-97; mng. ptnr. Berman Asbel & Berman, 1997—. Mem. Spl. Com. to Revise Rules of Civil Procedure, Delaware County, 1974-75; arbitrator Am. Arbitration Assn., 1968—; mediator Fee Dispute Resolution Com., Delaware County, 1987—. Mem., Guy G. DeFuria Amer. Inn of Ct., 1997—, sec. young men's com. Phila. Fedn. Jewish Agys., 1966, 67; pres. B'nai B'rith Simon Wolf Lodge, Wallingford, Pa., 1978-80, Southeastern Pa. and Del. coun., 1984-86, bd. govs. dist. 3, Phila., 1984-89. Mem. ABA, Pa. Bar Assn., Delaware County Bar Assn., Rose Valley Chorus (parliamentarian 1986-87), Phi Sigma Kappa Found. (trustee 1995—, investment com. 1998—), Phi Sigma Kappa (grand coun. 1983-91, grand pres. 1991-95, Ct. of Honor, 1995—). Avocations: tennis, sailing, amateur theater, gardening, singing. Office: Berman Asbel & Berman LLP 20 W Third St Media PA 19063-2824 E-mail: bmb@BermanLaw.com.

BERMAN, BRUCE, entertainment company executive, television producer; b. N.Y.C., Apr. 25, 1952; Grad., Calif. Inst. Arts Film Sch.; grad. magna cum laude in history, UCLA, 1975; JD, Georgetown U., 1978. Bar: Calif. 1978. Asst. to Jack Valenti Warner Bros., Burbank, Calif.; asst. to Peter Guber Casablanca Filmworks, 1979; asst. to Sean Daniel and Joel Silver Universal Pictures, 1979, v.p. prodn., 1982, Warner Bros., 1984, sr. v.p. prodn., 1988, pres. theatrical prodn., 1991-96, chmn., CEO Village Roadshow Pictures, 1998; pres. Worldwide Prodn., 1991-96. Founder Plan B Entertainment, 1996—. Office: Village Roadshow Pictures care Warner Bros Studios 3400 W Riverside Dr Ste 900 Burbank CA 91505-4639

BERMAN, BRUCE JUDSON, lawyer; b. Roslyn, N.Y., Oct. 9, 1946; s. Howard M. Berman and Soosha T. (Draizen) Hurwitz; children: Daniel H., Ann N., Andrew J., Josie A.; m. Susan Leigh Readinger, Dec. 29, 1991. BA, Williams Coll., 1968; MBA, Columbia U., 1972; JD, Boston U., 1972. Bar: Fla. 1973, U.S. Dist. Ct. (so. dist.) Fla. 1980, U.S. Dist. Ct. (mid. dist.) Fla. 1990, U.S. Ct. Appeals (5th cir.) 1980, U.S. Ct. Appeals (11th cir.) 1981, U.S. Supreme Ct. 1976. Assoc. Guggenheimer & Untermyer, N.Y.C., 1973-79; from assoc. to ptnr. Myers, Kenin, Levinson, Frank & Richards, Miami, Fla., 1979-85; ptnr. Weil, Gotshal & Manges LLP, Miami, 1985-2000, McDermott, Will & Emery, Miami, 2000—. Spl. ad hoc trial com. to Dade County (Fla.) Cir. Ct., 1988—; apptd. Fla. Supreme Ct. ct. reporter cert. planning com., 1995, Supreme Ct. Com. on Std. Jury Instrns. in Civil Cases, 2000, 03, Fla. Supreme Ct. workgroup on access to pub. records, 2000. Author: Florida Civil Procedure, 1998—99, 2001—03. Mem. New World Symphony Cmty. Bd., Miami Beach, Fla., 1991-2000; bd. dirs., Daily Bread Food Bank, 2002—. Mem. Fla. Bar (civil procedure rules com. 1984-2003, chmn. 1988-90, jud. adminstrn. rules com. 1988-2002, chmn. 1993-94), Dade County Bar. Office: McDermott Will & Emery 201 S Biscayne Blvd Miami FL 33131 E-mail: bberman@mwe.com.

BERMAN, CAROL, commissioner; b. Bklyn., Sept. 21, 1923; d. Hyman and Sarah (Levy) B.; m. Seymour Jerome Berman, May 19, 1944; children: Elizabeth, Charles. BA, U. Mich., 1943. Trustee Bd. Edn., Lawrence, N.Y., 1973-77; senator State of N.Y., Albany, 1978-84; spl. rep. State Divsn. for Housing, Hempstead, N.Y., 1985-86; commr. N.Y. State Commn. on Lobbying, Albany, 1988-92, N.Y. State Commn. of Elections, Albany, 1992—. N.Y. co-chair Nat. Jewish Dem. Coun., 1988—, Met. Airport Noise Mitigation Rev. Commn., 1992—; del. Dem. Nat. Conv., N.Y., 1992; vice-chair Nassau Dem. County Com., Mineola, N.Y., 1970-72. Mem. Phi Beta Kappa, Phi Kappa Phi. Jewish. Avocations: grandchildren, golf. Home: 42 Lord Ave Lawrence NY 11559-1324 Office: NY State Bd Elections 40 Steuben St Albany NY 12207

BERMAN, CASSIA, writer, educator; b. Bronx, N.Y., Apr. 5, 1949; d. Samuel Yitzhaak and Anna Berman. BA, Sarah Lawrence Coll., 1970; postgrad., Chinese Healing Arts Ctr., N.Y.C., 1991. cert. Qi Gong therapist, Qi healer. Poet CETA artists project Cultural Coun. Found., N.Y.C., 1978-90; tchr. T'ai Chi and Qi Gong Divine Mother Comms., Woodstock, N.Y., 1991—; spiritual corr. Woodstock Times, Kingston, N.Y., 1991—; poet-in-residence Woodstock Jewish Congregation, 1998—. Editor Golden Quest Pubs., N.Y.C., 1988-95, Chinese Healing Arts Ctr., N.Y.C., 1988-98, SMVA Trust, N.Y.C., 1999—; literary asst. Lex Hixon, N.Y.C., 1991-95. Author: Divine Mother Within Me; contbr. articles, poems to profl. jours., mags. Recipient 1st prize Glascock Poetry contest, Mt. Holyoke Coll. Mass., 1970. Mem. Sri Sarada Soc. (bd. dirs. 2000—), Chinese Healing Arts Ctr. (bd. dirs. 1988—), SRV Retreat Ctr. (bd. dirs. 1995—), People for Ethical Treatment of Animals, Nat. Qigong Assn. Avocations: meditation, t'ai chi, qi gong, spiritual development, healing. Home and Office: 11 1/2 Tannery Brook Rd Woodstock NY 12498

BERMAN, CHERYL R. advertising company executive; b. Chgo. BA in Journalism, U. Ill., Urbana. Copywriter, various positions Leo Burnett Co., Chgo., 1974-99, chief creative officer, chmn. U.S. bd. dirs., 1999—. Composer advt. music for McDonald's, Hallmark, Kraft, Walt Disney World. Named Ad Woman of Yr. Women's Advt. Club Chgo., 1997. Office: Leo Burnett Co 35 W Wacker Dr Ste 3710 Chicago IL 60601-1648 E-mail: cheryl.berman@chi.leoburnett.com.

BERMAN, DANIEL K(ATZEL), educational consultant, university official; b. Detroit, Nov. 17, 1954; s. Louis Arthur and Irene (Katzel) B. BS, Northwestern U., 1976, MS, 1977; AM, Harvard U., 1983; MA, U. Calif., Berkeley, 1984, PhD, 1991; cert. study, U. Paris, 1973, Peking (China) Normal U., 1981, Nat. Taiwan U., 1982. Subscription mgr. The N.Y. Times, 1983-84; editorial and rsch. asst. Inst. for Contemporary Studies, San Francisco, 1984-85; lang. cons. Berlitz Translation Svcs., San Francisco, 1986-89; v.p. Golden Gate Investment, San Francisco, 1985-87; lectr. St. Mary's Coll., Moraga, Calif., 1987; instr. U. Calif., Berkeley, 1984-90; chief exec. officer Pacific Fin. Svcs., San Francisco, 1987-92; editor Credit Report Newsletter for Consumer Edn., San Francisco, 1989-92; sales and mktg. cons. The Deerwood Corp./MRI, San Ramon, Calif., 1989-91; lectr. dept. mass comm. Calif. State U., Hayward, 1993-94; lectr. dept. elec. engring. San Jose State U., 1997-98; founder/dir. Acad. Cons. Internat., San Francisco, 1993—; assoc. provost Summit U. La., New Orleans, 1995—. Author: The Hottest Summer in Peking, 1982, The Credit Power Handbook for American Consumers, 1988, 89, Words Like Colored Glass: The Role of the Press in Taiwan's Democratization Process, 1992; co-author: Proverb Wit & Wisdom, 1997; editor, translator: The Butterfly's Revenge and Other Chinese Mystery Stories, found. CyberTip4theDay.com, 1998—. Edn. scholar Rep. of China Ministry of Edn., 1979-82; rsch. grantee Pacific Cultural Found., 1981; fgn. lang. and area studies fellow in Chinese U. Calif., 1983-84. Fellow John F. Kennedy Libr. Found.; mem. The Harvard Club of San Francisco, Soc. of Profl. Journalists, Acad. of Polit. Sci., Nat. Ctr. for Fin. Edn. (profl. sponsor), Kappa Tau Alpha (grantee). Jewish. Avocations: computers, foreign languages, piano, t'ai-chi-ch'uan, tennis. Office: Acad Cons Internat PO Box 4489 Foster City CA 94404-0489

BERMAN, DANIEL LEWIS, lawyer; b. Washington D.C., Dec. 14, 1934; s. Herbert A. and Ruth N. (Abramson) B.; children: Priscilla Decker, Jane, Katherine Ann, Sara Mark, Heather, Melinda. BA, Williams Coll., 1956; LLB, Columbia U., 1959. Bar: N.Y. 1960, Utah 1962. Assoc. Chadbourne, Parke, Whiteside & Wolff, N.Y.C., 1959-60; asst. prof. law U. Utah, 1960-62; pvt. practice Salt Lake City, 1962—; sr. ptnr. Berman, Tomsic & Savage, Salt Lake City, 1981—. Vis. prof. U. Utah, 1970, 74, 77; mem. Utah Coordinating Coun. Higher Edn., 1965-68, Salt Lake County Merit coun., 1974-80; mem. nominating commn. Utah Appellate Ct., 1999—. Trustee Salt Lake Art Ctr., 1978-80; Dem. candidate for U.S. Senate from Utah, 1980; mem. Utah Transit Authority, 1992-97. Mem. Am. Law Inst., Salt Lake Area C. of C. (bd. govs. 1976-79). Democrat. Jewish. Office: Berman Tomsic & Savage 50 S Main St Ste 1250 Salt Lake City UT 84144-2073 E-mail: dlb@btslaw.net.

BERMAN, DAVID, lawyer, poet; b. N.Y.C., Sept. 11, 1934; s. Joseph and Sophie (Hersh) B. BA with honors, U. Fla., 1955; postgrad. Johns Hopkins U., 1955-56; JD, Harvard U., 1963. Bar: Mass. 1963. Tchg. fellow Harvard Coll., 1962-63, 66-67; law clk. to justice Mass. Supreme Ct., 1963-64; asst. atty. gen. Commonwealth of Mass., 1964-67; assoc. Zamparelli & White, 1967, ptnr., 1968-74; pvt. practice, 1974-82, 1990—; ptnr. Berman & Moren, Medford, Mass., 1982-89. Author: Future Imperfect, 1982, Slippage, 1996, Early Mandamus in Massachusetts, Massachusetts Legal History, 1998, David Berman Greatest Hits, 1965-2002, 2003. Trustee Cantata Singers, 1981—. Mem. ABA, Mass. Bar Assn., Mass. Bar Found., Middlesex Bar Assn. (Most Outstanding Trial Lawyer Appelate award, 1998), Harvard Club (Boston), Signet Soc., Confrerie de la Chaine des Rotisseurs, Ordre Mondial, Masons. Republican. Unitarian. Home: 33 Birch Hill Rd Belmont MA 02478-1729 Office: 100 George P Hassett Dr Medford MA 02155-3264

BERMAN, ELEANORE, artist; b. N.Y.C., Sept. 2, 1928; d. Isidor and Elsie (Goldstein) Berman; children: Deborah Nicholas, Jan Nicholas, Anthony Nicholas, David Lazarof. BA, UCLA, 1950. One-woman shows include Kirk De Gooyer Gallery, L.A., 1982, Kouros Gallery, N.Y.C., 1982, L.A. City Hall, 1984, Stuhr (Nebr.) Mus., 1984, U. Wyo. Art Gallery, 1984, U. Minn., Duluth, 1984, Gallery X Brussels, 1985, New Eng. Ctr. for Contemporary Art, Mass., 1985, Mcpl. Gallery, Kampen, The Netherlands, 1986, Mcpl. Gallery, Amstelveen, The Netherlands, 1986, Lisa Kurts Gallery, Memphis, 1989, Boritzer/Gray Gallery, Santa Monica, Calif., 1991, L.A. Art Core, 1996, Cruz L.A., Venice, Calif., 2000, Don O'Melveny Gallery, L.A., 2003; exhibited in group shows: LAART, N.Y.C., 1986, U. Hawaii, Hilo, 1986, L.A. County Mus. Art, 1981, Boston Ctr. for the Arts, 1981, Wesleyan Coll., Conn., 1980, Newport (R.I.) Harbor Mus., 1977, Nat. Acad. Western Art Traveling Exhbn., 1988, L.A.-U.K. Print Connection, 1989, Bonnie Fridholm Gallery, Asheville, N.C., 1989, San Bernardino County Mus., Calif., 1994, Wichita Falls (Tex.) Mus., 1995, No. Calif. Arts Ann. INternat., 2000, 8th Ann. Gt. Plains Nat., Hays, Kans., 2001, Calif. Poly. Pomona, 2003; represented in permanent collections: L.a. County Mus. Art, Bklyn. Mus., Milw. Art Ctr., Grunwald Graphic Art Ctr., UCLA, others. Mem. Nat. Assn. of Women Artists, So. Calif. Women's Caucus for the Arts, L.A. Printmaking Assn., Nat. Watercolor Soc., Artists Equity Assn. E-mail: eberman718@earthlink.net.

BERMAN, ELLEN SUE, energy and telecommunications executive, theatre producer; Student, U. N.C., Greensboro, 1960-62, U. N.C., Chapel Hill, summer 1961, U. Calif., Berkeley, summer 1962; BA in Russian, Barnard Coll., 1964. Legis. asst. Senator Joseph Tydings, 1965-66; rsch. assoc. Washington Poverty Program United Planning Orgn., 1966-70; pres. Consumer Energy Coun. Am. Rsch. Found., Washington, 1973—. Mem. Office Tech. Assessment Residential Energy Conservation Adv. Com., 1976-77, Magnetic Fusion Adv. Com., 1986-87, Aspen Inst. Energy Policy Forum; mem. coun. for the Arts MIT, 1995—; mem. Com. on Energy and Econ. Devel. NAACP; mem. German Marshall Fund Adv. Com. on Energy Efficiency in Swedish Bldgs. Co-author: A Decade of Despair, A Compendium of Utility-Sponsored Appliance Rebate Programs, Transportation, Energy and Environment: Balancing Goals and Identifying Policies, 1995, Restructuring the Electric Utility Industry: A Consumer Perspective, 1998; author: Equity and Energy: Rising Energy Prices and the Living Standards of Lower Income Americans, 1983, Oil, Gas or ..? A Guide to Saving Heating Dollars, The Consumer and Energy Impacts of Oil Exports, Operating Costs of Refrigerators/Freezers and Room Air Conditioners, If You Want to Lower Your Heating Bill, It's Time to Raise the Roof, A Comparative Analysis of Utility and Non-Utility Based Energy Services

Companies, A State by State Compendium of Energy Efficiency Programs Using Oil Overchange Funds; (reports) The Consumer and Energy Impacts of Oil Exports, 1984, A Comprehensive Analysis of a Crude Oil Import Fee: Dismantling a Trojan Horse, 1982, A Comparison of Crude Oil Decontrol and Natural Gas Deregulation: An Analysis of the Impract of Immediate Decontrol of Crude Oil and Related Products on End Use Consumers, Natural Gas Deregulation: A Case of Trickle Up Economics, 1982; pub. The Quad Report, 1993—. Bd. dirs. Barnard in Washington, 1994—; bd. trustees Wider Opportunities for Women; bd. mgrs. Adas Israel Congregation, 1996—; chmn. bldgs. and gounds com. Woodley Park Towers condominium. Named Woman of the Eighties, Ladies Home Jour., 1979; grantee German Marshall Fund. Mem. Barnard Coll. Washington Alumnae Assn. (bd. dirs.), Cosmos Club. Home: 2737 Devonshire Pl NW Washington DC 20008-3479 Office: Consumer Energy Coun Am Rsch Found 2000 L St NW Ste 802 Washington DC 20036-4913

BERMAN, GARRETT L, education educator; m. Jamie Berman, June 20, 1999; children: Madison, Jacob, Victoria. PhD, Fla. Internat. U., 1990—95. Prof. Broward C.C., Ft. Lauderdale, Fla., 1993—, Roger Williams U., Bristol, RI, 1995—. Recipient Presdl. Scholar, Roger Williams U., 1998. Mem.: Phi Kappa Phi, Psi Chi. Achievements include research in. Office: Roger Williams University One Old Ferry Rd Bristol RI 02809-2921 E-mail: gberman@rwu.edu.

BERMAN, GEOFFREY LOUIS, management company executive; b. L.A., July 15, 1953; s. Geoffrey M. and Patricia A. (Meyer) B.; m. Autumn Joy Patton, Mar. 26, 1983; children: Arielle Louise, Michelle Elise. BA/BS in Bus. Adminstrn., U. of the Pacific, 1975; JD, Southwestern U., 1985. Loan officer Union Bank, L.A., 1975-80; adminstrv. asst. Credit Mgrs. Assn., L.A., 1980-82; asst. v.p. Mitsui Mfrs. Bank, L.A., 1982-86; asst. sec., mgr. adjustment bur. Credit Mgrs. Assn., Burbank, Calif., 1986-97; v.p. turnaround management Devel. Specialists, Inc., L.A., 1997—. Dir. Comml. Fin. Conf. Calif., L.A., 1978-80; co-chair insolvency laws com. Am. Bankruptcy Inst., Alexandria, Va., 1994—, dir., 2002--; mem. panel of mediators Ctrl. Dist. Bankruptcy Ct., L.A., 1995—; chmn. Task Force on Gen. Assignments for Benefit of Creditors, 1995-2000. Author: (manual) ABI Creditor's Com. Manual, 1995, ABI General Assignments for the Benefit of Creditors, A Practical Guide, 2000; contbg. editor Am. Bankruptcy Inst. Jour., 1996—, Fed. CT Receiver 1999-2000; contbr. articles to profl. jours. Mem. task force City of Buena Park (Calif.) Investment Policy Rev. Com.,, 1995. Recipient Recognition award Fed. Bar Assn., L.A., 1986. Mem. L.A. Bankruptcy Forum, Bay Area Bankruptcy Forum, Orange County Bankruptcy Forum. Office: Devel Specialists Inc 333 S Grand Ave Ste 2010 Los Angeles CA 90071-1524 E-mail: gberman@dsi.biz.

BERMAN, HENRY STEPHEN, lawyer; b. N.Y.C., Aug. 5, 1942; s. Bernard Barry and Julia (Friedman) B.; children from previous marriage: Daniel, Elissa; m. Ronnie Parker Gouz, Dec. 6, 1992. BA, CUNY, 1964; JD, St. John's U., 1967; LLM, NYU, 1968. Bar: N.Y. 1967, U.S. Dist. Ct. (so. dist.) N.Y. 1969. Atty. U.S. Fed. Trade Commn., N.Y.C., 1967; law asst. Appellate divsn. 2d dept., Monroe Pl., Brooklyn, 1967-74; sec. Hon. Morrie Slifkin, Westchester City, 1974-77; ptnr. Fink, Weinberger, Fredman, Berman & Lowell, P.C., White Plains, N.Y., 1981-93, Hall, Dickier, Kent, Friemdna & Wood, 1993-96, Beiman, Bavero, Frucco & Govz, P.C., White Plains, 1996—. Contbr. articles to profl. jours. Fellow Am. Acad. Matrimonial Lawyers; mem. N.Y. State Bar Assn. (fin. officer family law sect. 1982-84, sec. family law sect. 1984-86, chmn. family law sect. 1988-90, co-chair CLE com. 1985—), Westchester County Bar Assn. (editor domestic law rev. family law sect. 1982-90, chair 1990-92). Home: 81 Boulder Rdg Scarsdale NY 10583-3152 Office: 123 Main St White Plains NY 10601-3104

BERMAN, HOWARD LAWRENCE, congressman; b. L.A., Apr. 15, 1941; m. Janis Schwarz Berman. BA, UCLA, 1962, LLB, 1965. Bar: Calif. 1966. Vol. VISTA, Balt., San Francisco, 1966-67; assoc. Levy, Van Bourg & Hackler, L.A., 1967-72; mem. Calif. State Assembly from 43d dist., 1972-82 (majority leader), U.S. Congress from 28th Calif. dist., Washington, 1983—. Mem. jud. com., immigration and claims sub com.; ranking mem. on courts, the Internet, and intellectual property subcoms.; mem. internat. rels. com., Middle East and Ctrl. Asia subcom. Pres. Calif. Fedn. Young Democrats, 1967-69 (budget com.); mem. adv. bd. Jewish Fund for Justice. Democrat. Office: US Ho Reps 2221 Rayburn Ho Office Bldg Washington DC 20515-0528*

BERMAN, JAMES H. pediatrician, gastroenterologist, educator; b. Pitts., Nov. 26, 1955; s. Howard and Barbara Berman; m. Caryn Hirsh Hirsh, May 20, 1984; children: Andrew, Emily. BA/BS, U. Pa., 1977; MD, U. Pitts., 1981. Cert. pediat. gastroenterology Am. Bd. Pediat., 1990. Pediat. resident Children's Hosp. of Pitts., 1981—84; fellow in pediat. gastroenterology Children's Hosp. of Boston; instr. pediat. Harvard Med. Sch., Boston, 1987—88; asst prof. pediat. Chgo. Med. Sch., North Chicago, Ill., 1990—97; asst prof., sect. chief Loyola U. Sch. Medicine, Maywood, Ill., 1998—. Chief sect. pediat. gastroenterology Ronald McDonald Children's Hosp., Maywood, 1998—. Office: Loyola Univ Dept Pediatrics 2160 S First Ave Maywood IL 60153 Office Fax: 708-327-9160.

BERMAN, JEFFREY, language educator; b. N.Y.C., Jan. 16, 1945; s. Isadore and Roslyn (Dranoff) B.; m. Barbara Kozinn, Aug. 11, 1968; children: Arielle, Jillian. BA, SUNY, Buffalo, 1967; MA, Cornell U., 1968, PhD, 1971. Asst. prof., assoc. prof. English U. Albany, N.Y., 1973-86, prof. English, 1986—. Author: Joseph Conrad: Writing as Rescue, 1977, The Talking Cure, 1985, Narcissism and the Novel, 1990, Diaries to an English Professor, 1994, Surviving Literary Suicide, 1999, Risky Writing: Self-Disclosure and Self-Transformation in the Classroom, 2001; editor lit. and psychoanalysis NYU Press, 1993—; rev. psychoanalytic books, N.Y.C., 1993—. Home: 137 Mohawk Dr Schenectady NY 12303-5732 Office: Univ Albany English Dept Albany NY 12222-0001 E-mail: jberman@albany.edu.

BERMAN, JOEL DAVID, mathematics educator; b. Mpls., Feb. 2, 1943; s. Morris and Hilda Berman. BA, U. Minn., 1965; PhD, U. Wash., 1970. Asst. prof. U. Ill., Chgo., 1970—75, assoc. prof., 1975—82, prof., 1982—. Office: Univ of Ill at Chgo MSCS Dept 851 S Morgan St Chicago IL 60607

BERMAN, JOSHUA MORDECAI, lawyer, manufacturing company executive; b. Rochester, N.Y., Aug. 4, 1938; s. Jeremiah Joseph and Rose (Rappaport) B.; m. Ruth Freed, Mar. 17, 1996; children: Marc Ethan, Eve. BBA summa cum laude, CCNY, 1958; JD cum laude, Harvard U., 1961. Bar: Mass. 1961, N.Y. 1984. With Goodwin, Procter & Hoar, Boston, 1961-80, ptnr., 1969-80; pres. Berman Engel P.C., 1980-85; counsel Kramer, Levin, Naftalis & Frankel, 1985—. Chmn. bd.. CEO Tyco Internat. Ltd., 1970—73; adviser Fidelity Investments, 1971—, Rank Group Ltd., Auckland, New Zealand, 1996—, Med. Info. Tech., Inc., 1970. Founder, pres. Boston Children's Sch., 1965-66. Home: Alexandra La Frasse 1660 Chateau d'Oex Switzerland

BERMAN, KEITH, solicitor, lawyer; b. Liverpool, Eng., Dec. 23, 1942; came to U.S., 1980; s. Joseph and Gerty Berman; children; Chloé Jo, Jade Kara, Kate Alexis. LLB with honors, U. Liverpool, 1963. Admitted as solicitor Supreme Ct. Eng. and Wales, 1966; bar: N.Y. 1980, U.S. Dist. Ct. (so. and ea. dists.) N.Y. 1982, U.S. Ct. Internat. Trade 1992, U.S. Ct. Appeals (fed. cir.) 1992. Founding ptnr. Bermans English Solicitors, Liverpool, Manchester, 1970—, N.Y.C., 1980—. Trustee Fifth Ave Synagogue, N.Y.C., 1986—. Mem. ABA, Law Soc. Eng. and Wales, Comml. Law League Am., Internat. Bar Assn. Jewish. Office: Bermans 1775 Broadway #608 New York NY 10019-1903

BERMAN, LAURA, journalist, writer; b. Detroit, Dec. 8, 1953; d. Seymour Donald and Rose (Mendelson) B. AB, U. Mich., 1975. Writer, reporter Detroit Free Press, 1976-86; columnist The Detroit News, 1986-93; freelance writer, 1994—; sr. writer The Detroit News, 1995-98; columnist Detroit News, 1998—. Mem. Soc. Profl. Journalists. Office: The Detroit News 999 Haynes St Ste 260 Birmingham MI 48009 E-mail: lberman@detnews.com.

BERMAN, LEWIS PAUL, financial executive; b. Cape Town, South Africa, Jan. 28, 1937; came to U.S., 1959, naturalized, 1969; s. Joshua Z. and Gertrude Berman; m. Karen Scott Dunlap, Oct. 18, 1969; children: Joshua Evans, Caroline Isabel. BCom, U. Cape Town, 1956, MCom, 1958; MBA with high distinction, Harvard U., 1961. V.p. Mgmt. Analysis Ctr., Cambridge, MAss., 1964-66; with Irwin Mgmt. Co. Inc., Columbus, Ind., 1966-68; asst. to chmn. Cummins Engine Co., Inc., Columbus, 1968-70; pres. Cummins Internat. Fin. Corp., Columbus, 1970-76; dir. fin. svcs. Cummins Engine Co., Inc., Columbus, 1976-80, treas., 1980-87; sr. v.p. Reams Asset Mgmt. Co., Columbus, 1987-99; ret. Chmn. Am. Fletcher Bank Suisse S.A., Geneva, Switzerland, 1970-82. Contbr. to textbooks. Trustee Columbus (Ind.) Regional Hosp., 1982-93; bd. dirs. Bartholomew County Hosp. Found., 1977-81; co-chmn. Uncommon Cause, Columbus, 1984-85; pres. Columbus Disting. Visitors, 1967. Baker scholar Harvard Bus. Sch., 1961. Home: 1301 N Tamiami Tr Apt 413 Sarasota FL 34236-2423

BERMAN, MARLENE OSCAR, neuropsychologist, educator; b. Phila., Nov. 21, 1939; d. Paul Oscar and Evelyn (Hess) Oscar; m. Michael Brack Berman, June 23, 1963 (div. Feb. 1980); 1 son, Jesse Michael. BA, U.Pa., 1961; MA, Bryn Mawr Coll., 1964; PhD, U. Conn., 1968; postgrad., Harvard U., 1968-70. Research assoc. Boston VA Med. Ctr., 1970-72, clin. investigator, 1973-76, research psychologist, 1976—; assoc. prof. neurology Boston U. Sch. Medicine, 1975-82, prof. neurology and psychiatry, 1982—, dir Neuropsychology Lab. dept. psychiatry, 1981—. Mem. Com. for Protection Human Participants in Rsch., 1979-82, 98—, chmn., 1983-85; affiliate prof. psychology Clark U., Worcester, Mass., 1975—; mem. biomed. rsch. initial rev. group Nat. Inst. Alcohol Abuse and Alcoholism, 1987-91, chmn. 1990-91; mem. initial rev. group Nat. Inst. Drug Abuse, 1996-97. Contbr. articles to profl. jours. Coordinator Newton Community Schs. (Mass.), 1978-80. Recipient Rsch. Scientist awards, Nat. Inst. Neurol. and Communicative Disorders and Stroke, 1976—81, Nat. Inst. Alcohol Abuse and Alcoholism, 1981—, Method to Extend Rsch. in Time award, 1996—, clin. investigator award, VA, 1973—76, Rsch. Career Scientist award, 2001—. Fellow Mass. Psychol. Assn., Am. Psychol. Assn. (sec.-treas. 1981-83); mem. Acad. Aphasia, Soc. Neurosci., Internat. Neuropsychol. Soc., Psychonomic Soc., Huntington's Disease Soc. Am., New Eng. Psychol. Assn., Mass. Neuropsychol. Soc., N.Y. Acad. Scis., Eastern Psychol. Assn., Fulbright Found. Democrat. Jewish. Office: Boston U Lab Neuropsych Dept Psychiatry L-815 715 Albany St Roxbury MA 02118-2526 *The four most significant helpers in my career have been hard work, luck, mentors, and a sense of humor.*

BERMAN, MARSHALL FOY, lawyer; b. Portsmouth, Va., Aug. 27, 1939; s. Israel and Etta (Fox) B.; m. Barbara Pressner, Aug. 29, 1965 (dec. Feb. 1993); m. Karen Orloff Kaplan, Nov. 18, 1996; children: Richard Joseph, Deborah Lynn. BA, U. Va., 1961, postgrad. in rhetoric, 1961-62; JD, Am. U., 1967; LLM in Labor Law with highest honors, George Washington U., 1970. Bar: Va. 1967, D.C. 1971, U.S. Supreme Ct. 1971. Tchr. reading pub. schs., Washington, 1965-66; staff D.C. Minimum Wage and Indsl. Safety Bd., 1966-67; atty. NLRB, Washington, 1968-71; assoc. Gall, Lane & Powell, Washington, 1971-75; ptnr. Dow, Lohnes & Albertson, Washington, 1975-91, Epstein, Becker and Green, Washington, 1992-98, Hewes, Gelband, Lambert and Dann, Washington, 1999—2000, Ruben & Aronson, Washington, 2000—; spl. master for labor and employment cases U.S. Dist. Ct. D.C., 2001—. Co-author: Aviation Drug Testing Handbook, 1989, Aviation Drug Testing Operating Manual, 1990. Mem. ABA, Fed. Bar Assn., D.C. Bar Assn., Va. Bar Assn. Home: 7732 Canal Ct Mc Lean VA 22102-1406 Office: 3299 K St NW # 403 Washington DC 20007-4415

BERMAN, MICHAEL, vice president, chief medical officer; b. Brooklyn, N.Y. MD, State U. N.Y., 1967; postgrad in pediatrics, Johns Hopkins Sch. Medicine. Exec. v.p., dir. N.Y. Presbyterian Hosp., 1999—, sr. v.p., 1997, chief med. officer, 1997; prof. Maryland Sch. Medicine, chmn. dept. pediatrics; pediatric cardiologist Nat. Inst. of Health; chief clinical pediatric cardiology Yale U. Sch. Medicine. Office: NY Presbyterian Hosp Herbert Irving Pavilion 161 Fort Wash Ave 14th Fl New York NY 10032

BERMAN, MICHAEL BARRY, lawyer; b. NYC, Apr. 10, 1942; s. Mark S. and Roslyn (Roberts) B.; m. Rochelle Holland, June 7, 1969 (dec. Jan. 2002); 1 child, Michele. BA, Iowa Wesleyan U., 1964; MAT, Trenton State Coll., 1973; MA in Indsl. Rels., Rutgers U., 1977; JD, Cardozo Sch. Law, N.Y.C., 1984. Bar: N.J. 1985, D.C. 1985, U.S. Ct. Appeals (3d cir.) 1985, U.S. Ct. Appeals Vets. Claims 1999, U.S. Supreme Ct. 1989. Assoc. Jerome A. Gertner, Lakewood, N.J., 1984-86; staff atty. Ocean-Monmouth Legal Svcs., Toms River, N.J., 1986-87; assoc. Cohen, Meshulam & Cohen, Verona, N.J., 1987-89, Krieger & Ferrara, Jersey City, 1989; pvt. practice Lakewood, N.J., 1989-90; ptnr. Collins & Berman, Toms River, NJ, 1990—2001; sole practitioner Toms River, 2001—. Asst. to chmn. N.J. Pub. Employment Rels. Com., Trenton, 1973-81; gen. counsel Nat. Mus. Am. Jewish Mil. History, 1992-98, 2000--. V.p. Lakewood Cmty. Sch. Bd., 1984-87; active Lakewood Bd. Edn., 1984-87, 89, Rep. Cen. Com., Lakewood, 1987-88; pres. Lakewood Rep. Club, 1992-93; adv. bd. Ocean County Cath. Charities; pres. Congregation Ahavat Shalom, 1993-95. With U.S. Army, 1968-70. Mem. Ocean County Bar Assn., N.J. Bar Assn. (subcom. alimony support 1987), Jewish War Vets (state comdr. N.J. chpt. 1985-86, nat. com. 1985-89, nat. judge advocate 1992-98, nat. quartermaster 1996-98, nat. comdr. 1998-99), Vietnam Vets Am. (v.p. N.J. chpt. 1990-92, gen. counsel 2000--), Masons. Office: 18A Robbins St Toms River NJ 08753-7629

BERMAN, MICHAEL LEONARD, gynecologic oncologist; b. Washington, Mar. 11, 1942; s. Ben I. and Sylvia (Rogers) B.; m. June 21, 1964; children: Mara, Lisa, Deborah, Vicki. BS in Phys. Scis., U. Md., 1963; MD, George Washington U., 1967. Diplomate Am. Bd. Obstetrics and Gynecology; lic. physician, Nev., Calif. Resident in ob-gyn. George Washington U., Washington, 1968-69, Harbor Gen. Hosp., Torrance, Calif., 1971-74; NICHD clin. assoc. UCLA Sch. Medicine, 1969-71, acting asst. prof. ob-gyn., 1974-75, asst. prof. ob-gyn., 1975-77; asst. prof. and dir. divsn. gynecologic oncology U. Pitts./Magee Women's Hosp., 1977-81; assoc. prof. U. Calif.-Irvine Coll., Orange, 1981-90; prof. divsn. gynecologic oncology U. Calif.-Irvine Coll. Medicine, Orange, 1990—; dir. divsn. gynecologic oncology U. Calif.-Irvine Med. Ctr., Orange, 1981—; clin. assoc. prof. U. Nev., Las Vegas, 1983-99. Cons. med. staff St. Paul Mary Med. Ctr., Long Beach, Calif., 1988-99, Saddleback Meml. Hosp., Laguna Hills, Calif., 1988—, U. Nev., Las Vegas, 1985-99, City of Hope Nat. Med. Ctr., Duarte, Calif., 1983-94; fellow in gynecologic oncology City of Hope Nat. Med. Ctr., Duarte, and UCLA Med. Ctr., 1974-76; attending physician Long Beach Meml. Med. Ctr./Women's Hosp., 1981—; lectr. in field; mem. carrier adv. com. Medicare, State of Calif., 1993—; cons. Health Care Fin. Adminstrn., others. Co-editor: Med. Tribune News, 1994—99; mng. editor: SGO Issues, 1990—91; reviewer Am. Jour. Obstetrics and Gynecology, Cancer, Gynecologic Oncology, Obstetrics and Gynecology, reviewer PDQ External Adv. Bd NIH, Nat. Cancer Inst., 1994—96; co-author: Bibliography of Chemical Kinetics and Collision Processes, 1969; contbr. numerous articles and abstracts to profl. jours., chapters to books. Mem. comms. com. Gynecologic Cancer Found., 1994—, membership dr. com., 1994—; bd. dirs. Orange County unit Am. Cancer Soc. Recipient Physician's Recognition award AMA, 1990-93; Am. Cancer Soc. 2d yr. faculty clin. fellow, 1977-78, 1st yr. faculty clin. fellow, 1976-77, 2d yr. fellow, 1975-76, 1st yr. fellow, 1974-75; rsch. grantee NIH, 1987-90, 89-94, U.S. Biosci., 1989-91, Cetus, 1989-92, Gynecologic Oncology Group, 1989-94, Nat. Cancer Inst., 1991—. Fellow: ACOG (health econs. com. 1992—, mem. com. on coding and nomenclature 1997—99, chair com. coding and nomenclature 1999—2001); mem.: AMA, ACS, Gynecologic Oncology Group, Long Beach Obstetrics and Gynecology Soc., Internat. Gynecologic Cancer Soc., Am. Soc. Clin. Oncology, Am. Radium Soc., Western Assn. Gynecologic Oncologists (sec.-treas. 1981—86, pres. 1987), Soc. Gynecologic Oncologists (chair com./govt. rels. com. 1991—94, chair govt. rels. com. 1994—97, chair coding com. 1997—2000, pres.-elect 1999—2001, pres. 2001—02, past pres. 2002—), Dan Morton Soc., Phi Delta Epsilon, Alpha Omega Alpha. Office: Univ of Calif-Irvine Med Ct Dept Ob-Gyn 101 The City Dr S Bldg 23 Orange CA 92868-3201 E-mail: mberman@uci.edu.

BERMAN, MILTON, history educator; b. N.Y.C., Apr. 18, 1924; s. Morris and Ida (Epstein) B.; m. Barbara Ann Roesch, Aug. 18, 1968. BA, Hofstra Coll., 1953; A.M., Harvard U., 1954, PhD, 1959. Instr. history Harvard U., 1959-61, vis. assoc. prof., summer 1963; fellow Charles Warren Ctr., 1968-69; asst. prof. history U. Rochester, N.Y., 1961-63, assoc. prof., 1963-70, prof., 1970-89, prof. emeritus, 1989—, assoc. chmn. dept., 1966-68. Author: John Fiske: The Evolution of a Popularizaer, 1961; contbr. articles to profl. jours., biographical articles and supplements. Served with U.S. Army, 1949-50. Mem.: Orgn. Am. Historians, Am. Hist. Assn. Democrat. Jewish. Home: 16 Ranch Village Ln Rochester NY 14624-2857 Office: Univ Rochester Dept History Rochester NY 14627

BERMAN, MIRIAM NAOMI, librarian; b. Phila., May 27, 1929; d. Max Isaac and Sonia Leona (Brown) Mosevitzky; m. Aaron Arthur Berman, July 4, 1955; children: David Hirsh, Raphael Judah, Michael Jonah. BA, CUNY, 1950, MA, 1952; MLS, Pratt Inst., 1975. Lic. profl. librarian, N.Y.; lic. elem and secondary tchr., N.Y. Tchr. Crown Heights Yeshiva, Bklyn., 1950-52, Pub. Sch. 26/N.Y.C. Bd. Edn., Bklyn., 1952-64; exec. Aaron Berman Gallery, N.Y.C., 1976-77; librarian Bklyn. Pub. Library, 1977-79, Aviation High Sch., L.I., N.Y., 1979-89, Sheepshead Bay High Sch., Bklyn., 1989-96; ret., 1996. Juror Art Auction Com., N.Y.C., 1972-77. Mem. N.Y.C. Library Assn. (treas. 1985-87). Avocations: music, art, theater, ballet.

BERMAN, MITCHELL A. orchestra executive; Gen. mgr. Wichita (Kans.) Symphony Orch. Office: Wichita Symphony Orch 225 W Douglas Ste 207 Wichita KS 67202

BERMAN, MONA S. actress, playwright, theatrical director and producer; b. Jersey City, 1925; d. Edward and Mary (Auster) Solomon; m. Carroll Z. Berman; children: Marcie S. Berman Ries, Laura Jane. BA, Beaver Coll., 1945; postgrad., Columbia U.; MFA, Boston U., 1957. Tchr. English, drama Jersey City High Schs.; actress indsl., stage, TV, Valley Players Holyoke, Mass.; actress The Millbrook Playhouse, Mill Hall, Pa., 1991; owner, dir. The Theater Sch. and Producing Co., Maplewood, NJ. Chmn. drama edn. YM-YWHA of Met. N.J. Cons., Clark Ctr. for Performing Arts, N.Y.C., 1965-66; instr. South Orange, Maplewood Adult Sch., 1967; artistic dir. Children's Theatre Co. Inc., Maplewood, 1968-70; cons. The Whole Theater Co.; dir. pub. rels. Co. 3 by 2; cons. new plays City Theatre, Miami, Fla., 2000. Playwright: Hello Joe, That Ring in the Center, The Big Show, Interim, Who Can Belong?, Sudden Changes, Without Malice, Interim 2; prodr., dir., A Night of Stars; guest theater reviewer El Paso Herald Post, 1980-82; mem. artistic steering com. Women's Theatre Project. Active Boston United Fund, 1955—59, chmn. Boston residential area, 1957; active S. Fla. Theater League, City Theatre, Miami, Fla.; mem. artistic steering com. Womens Theatre Project South Fla.; bd. dirs. Greater Boston Girl Scouts Am., 1956—58, Tufts Med. Faculty Wives, 1956—58. Mem. Dramatist Guild, Actors Equity Assn., Profl. Actors Assn. Fla., The Creative Alliance, Women's Theatre Project (artistic steering com.). Address: Women's Theatre Project of South Fla 8925 Collins Ave Miami FL 33154-3530

BERMAN, MURIEL MALLIN, optometrist, humanities lecturer; b. Pitts. d. Samuel and Dora (Cooperman) Mallin; m. Philip I. Berman, Oct. 23, 1942; children: Nancy, Nina, Steven. Student, U. Pitts., 1943, Carnegie Tech. U., 1944-45; BS, Pa. State Coll. Optometry, 1948; postgrad., U. Pitts., 1950, Muhlenberg Coll., 1954, Cedar Crest Coll., 1953, DFA (hon.), 1972; hon. degree, Hebrew U., Israel, 1982; DHL (hon.), Ursinus Coll., 1987, Lehigh U., 1991. Lic. Pa., N.J. Practice optometry, Pitts.; sec.-treas., dir. Philip and Muriel Berman Found.; underwriting mem. Lloyd's of London, 1974—94. Lectr. on travels, art, UN activities, women's status and affairs. Producer: (TV) College Speakout, 1967-77; producer, moderator: (TV) Guest Spot. Active in UNICEF, 1959—, ofcl. non-govtl. orgns., 1964, 74; U.S. State Dept. del. UN Internat. Women's Yr. Conf., Mexico City, 1975; mem. State Dept. Arts and Humanities Com. Nat. Commn. on Observance of Women's Yr., 1975; adv. com. U.S. Ctr. for Internat. Womens Yr., Washington; founder, donor Carnegie-Berman Coll. Art Slide Library Exchange; mem. Aspen (Colo.) Inst. Humanistic Studies, 1965, Tokyo, 1966; chmn. exhibits Great Valley council Girl Scouts U.S.A., 1966; adminstrv. head, chmn. various events Allentown Bicentennial, 1962; vice-chmn. Women for Pa. Bicentennial, 1976; co-chmn. Lehigh County Bicentennial Bell-Trek, 1976; patron Art in Embassies Program, Washington, 1965— ; chmn. Lehigh Valley Ednl. TV, 1966— ; program chmn. Fgn. Policy Assn. Lehigh County, 1965-67; treas. ann. ball Allentown Symphony, 1955— ; mem. art adv. com. Dieruff High Sch., Allentown, 1966— ; co-chmn. art. com. Episcopal Diocese Centennial Celebration, 1971; mem. Pa. Council on Status of Women, 1968-73; reappointed Pa. Gov.'s Commn. on Women, 1984; chmn. numerous art shows; mem. Art Collectors Club Am., Am. Fedn. Art, Friends of Whitney Mus., Mus. Modern Art, Mus. Primitive Art, Jewish Mus., Kemmerer Mus., Bethlehem, Pa., Univ. Mus., Phila., Archives of Am. Art, Met. Opera Guild, others; ofcl. del. Dem. Nat. Conv., 1972, 76, mem. Democratic Platform Com., 1972; mem. Pa. Humanities Coun., 1979—; bd. dirs. Heart Assn. Pa., Allentown Art Mus. Aux., Phila. Chamber Symphony, Baum Art Sch., Lehigh County Cultural Ctr., Heart Assn. Pa., Baum Art Sch., Young Audiences, Israel Mus., Hadassah Womens Orgn.; bd. govs. Pa. State System of Higher Edn., 1986—; trustee Kutztown State Coll., 1960-66, vice-chmn. bd., 1965; trustee, sec. bd. Lehigh Community Coll.; mem. nat. bd. UN-U.S.A., 1977— ; trustee Pa. Council on Arts, Pa. Ballet, Smithsonian Art Council, Bonds for Israel, Hadassah (nat. bd. with portfolio), Am. Friends Hebrew U., 1984; bd. regents Internat. Ctr. for Univ. Teaching of Jewish Civilization, Israel, 1982—; fine arts chmn. Women's Club; mem. com. on Prints, Drawings, & Photography Pa. Mus. Art, 1984; hon. chmn. Bucks County Coillectors Art Show; hon. bd. dirs., trustee Phila. Mus. Art, 1997—. Named Woman of Valor State of Israel, 1965; recipient Centennial citation Wilson Coll., 1969, Henrietta Szold award Allentown chpt. Hadassah, Outstanding Woman award Allentown YWCA, 1973, George Washington Honor medal Freedoms Found. at Valley Forge, 1985, Hazlett award Outstanding Svc. to Arts Pa., Outstanding Citizen award Boy Scouts Am., 1982, Myrtle Wreath award Pa. Region Hadassah, Mt. Scopus award State of Israel Bonds, 1984, Woman of Yr. award Am. Friends Hebrew U., Phila., 1984, Arts Ovation award, 1989, Cmty. Spirit award City of Allentown, 1990, Pres.' Medallion award West Chester U., 2002, Eberly award Pa. State Sys. Higher Edn., 2002, Am. Coun. Jewish Mus. award, 2003, others; hon. fellow Hebrew U., 1975. Mem. LWV, NOW, Am. Fedn. of Art., Pa. Hist. Soc. (life), Jewish Publ. Soc. Am. (former pres., chmn. bd. 1984), Disting. Daus. Pa., Art Collector's Club Am., Wellesley Club. Jewish. Avocation: american and english sculpture art. Address: 2000 Nottingham Rd Allentown PA 18103

BERMAN, MYLES LEE, lawyer; b. Chgo., July 11, 1954; s. Jordan and Eunice (Berg) B.; m. Mitra Moghimi, Dec. 19, 1981; children: Elizabeth, Calvin, Justin. BA, U. Ill., 1976; JD, Chgo.-Kent Coll. of Law, 1979. Bar: Ill. 1980, Calif. 1987, U.S. Dist. Ct. (no. dist.) Ill. 1980, U.S. Dist. Ct. (cen. dist.) Calif. 1988, U.S. Supreme Ct. 1992. Asst. state's atty. Cook County State's Atty.'s Office, Chgo., 1980-82; pvt. practice Offices of Myles L. Berman, Chgo., 1982-91; pvt. practice, L.A., 1988—. Founder Nat. Drunk Driving Def. Task Force; traffic ct. judge pro tem Beverly Hills Mcpl. Ct., 1990—; traffic ct. judge pro tem adminstr. Culver Mcpl. Ct., 1991—; probation monitor State Bar Calif., 1992—. Editor: Century City Lawyer, 1992—. Mem. ABA, Santa Monica Bar Assn., Los Angeles County Bar Assn., Calif. Attys. for Criminal Justice, Nat. Assn. Criminal Def. Lawyers, Beverly Hills Bar Assn., Century City Bar Assn. (chmn. criminal law sect. 1989—, bd. govs. 1991—, Outstanding Svc. award 1990, 92, 93, 94, Spl. Recognition 1994, treas. 1994, sec. 1995, v.p. 1996, pres.-elect 1997, pres. 1998), Criminal Cts. Bar Assn. (evaluation profl. stds. and state bar com. 1996-97), Century City Bar Assn. (pres. 1998-99, criminal law award 2001-02), Orange County Bar Assn., South Orange County Bar Assn., Cyberspace Bar Assn. Avocations: family, sports. Office: 9255 Sunset Blvd Ste 720 Los Angeles CA 90069-3304 also: #9 3075 E Thousand Oaks Blvd Westlake Village CA 91362 also: 4665 MacArthur Ct Ste 240 Newport Beach CA 92660

BERMAN, NEIL SHELDON, chemical engineering educator; b. Milw., Sept. 21, 1933; s. Henry and Ella B.; m. Sarah Ayres, June 3, 1962; children: Jenny, Daniel. BS, U. Wis., 1955; MS, MA, U. Tex., Austin, 1961, PhD, 1962. Engr. Standard Oil Co. Calif., Los Angeles, 1955-62; research engr. E.I. DuPont Co., Wilmington, Del., 1962-64; from asst. prof. to prof. chem. engring. Ariz. State U., 1964-2000; prof. emeritus, 2000—; Grad. Coll. Disting. Rsch. prof. Ariz. State U., 1984-85. Cons. air pollution, fluid dynamics; mem. Phoenix Air Quality Maintenance Area Task Force, 1976-77 Contbr. articles on fluid dynamics of polymer solutions, air pollution, thermodynamics and chem. engring. edn. to profl. jours. Served to capt. M.S.C. USAR, 1956-58. Recipient numerous grants for research in fluid dynamics and air pollution. Fellow Am. Inst. Chem. Engrs. (chmn. Ariz. sect. 1978-79), AAAS, Ariz.-Nev. Acad. Sci. (corr. sec. 1981-88, pres.-elect 1988-89, pres. 1989-90). mem. ASME, Am. Chem. Soc., Am. Phys. Soc., Ariz. Council Engring. and Sci. Assns. (chmn.

1980-81), Soc. Rheology, Am. Soc. Engring. Edn., Am. Acad. Mechanics, Nat. Assn. State Acads. Sci. (mem.-at-large bd. dirs.), Sigma Xi, Tau Beta Pi, Phi Kappa Phi. Home: 418 E Geneva Dr Tempe AZ 85282-3731 Office: Ariz State U Dept Chem Engring Tempe AZ 85287-6006

BERMAN, RICHARD ANGEL, health and educational administrator; b. Cin., Jan. 23, 1945; s. Isidore Alexander and Cecilia (Angel) B.; m. Jean Berman; 1 child, Joshua BBA with distinction, U. Mich., 1966, MBA with distinction, MHA, U. Mich., 1968. Spl. asst., asst. sec. health, dir. health policy Econ. Stblzn. Program, HEW, Washington, 1972-74; sr. program cons. Robert Wood Johnson Found., Princeton, N.J., 1974-77; asst. dean, assoc. hosp. dir. N.Y. Hosp.-Cornell Med. Ctr., N.Y.C., 1974-77; dir. N.Y. State Office Health Sys. Mgmt., Albany, 1977-80; commr. N.Y. State Divsn. Housing and Cmty. Renewal, 1981-83; exec. v.p. NYU Med. Ctr., N.Y.C., 1983-86; prof. health care mgmt. NYU Sch. Medicine, 1983-86; candidate for U.S. Congress 1986, 1986; spl. cons. McKinsey and Co., N.Y.C., 1987-90; v.p. Korn/Ferry Internat., N.Y.C., 1990-91; pres. N.Am. Howe-Lewis Internat., N.Y.C., 1991-92, pres., CEO, 1992-94; pres. Manhattanville Coll., Purchase, N.Y., 1995—. Cons. in field; bd. dirs. Health Ins. Plan Greater N.Y., NCAA-Divsn. III Pres.'s Coun., 2002—. Contbr. articles to profl. jours. Chmn. N.Y. State Bldg. Code Coun., 1981-83; mem. N.Y. State Housing Fin. Agy., 1981-83, N.Y. Statewide Health Coord. Coun.; adv. bd. Ctr. Hosp. Fin. and Mgmt.; bd. dirs. N.Y.C. Pub. Devel. Corp., 1985-90; mem. Prospective Payment Assessment Commn., 1989-95; exec. com. N.Y. March of Dimes Bd., 1980-95; mem. Mayor's Mgmt. Adv. Task Force, 1991-93; nat. adv. coun. Nat. Inst. for Nursing Rsch., NIH, 1991-94; trustee SUNY, 1993-95; bd. dirs. Inst. for Student Achievement, Manhasset, N.Y., 199-2001, Today's Students Tomorrow's Tchrs., Yorktown Heights, N.Y., 1998—, Westchester Med. Ctr., Valhalla, N.Y. Recipient Horace M. Kallen Disting. Cmty. Svc. award Am. Jewish Congress, 1981, Brotherhood award NCCJ, 1985, Disting. Achievement award B'nai B'rith, 1997, award of honor Westchester Holocaust Edn. Ctr., 2002. Fellow Am. Coll. Health Care Execs., N.Y. Acad. Medicine (assoc.); mem. APHA, Am. Hosp. Assn., Pub. Health Assn. N.Y., Nat. Acad. Sci. Inst. Medicine. E-mail: bermanr@mville.edu.

BERMAN, RICHARD KEITH, television producer, film producer; b. N.Y.C., Dec. 25, 1945; BA in Speech, U. Wis., Madison, 1967. Prodr., writer (story): Star Trek: Generations, 1994, Star Trek: First Contact, 1996, Star Trek: IMAX, 1998, Star Trek: Insurrection, 1998; prodr., writer (story), (TV): Star Trek: Deep Space Nine-Emissary/Emissary, 1993, Star Trek: Voyager-Caretaker, 1995; supervising prodr.: Star Trek: The Next Generation-Encounter at Farpoint, 1987, -All Good Things, 1994, (series) Star Trek: The Next Generation, 1987; creator (TV series) Star Trek: Deep Space Nine/DS9, 1993; co-creator (TV series) Star Trek: Voyager, 1995; creative cons. Star Trek: The Experience, 1998. Office: c/o Paramount Television Grp Bun Cooper 232 5555 Melrose Ave Los Angeles CA 90038-3112

BERMAN, RICHARD MILES, judge; b. N.Y.C., Sept. 11, 1943; s. Samuel and Sophie Berman; m. Emily Krasna, May 29, 1979 (div. Nov. 1983). BS, Cornell U., 1964; JD, NYU, 1967; diploma in comparative law, U. Stockholm, 1968, diploma in internat. law, 1970; MSW, Fordham U., 1996. Bar: N.Y. 1971. Assoc. Davis, Polk & Wardwell, N.Y.C., 1970-74; exec. asst. Senator Jacob K. Javits, N.Y.C., 1974-78; gen. counsel, exec. v.p., dir. Warner Cable Comm. Inc., N.Y.C., 1978-86; gen. counsel, sec. MTV Networks, Inc., N.Y.C., 1983-86; ptnr. LeBoeuf, Lamb, Greene & MacRae, N.Y.C., 1986-95; mng. ptnr. L.A., 1989-91; judge Family Ct. State of N.Y., 1995-98, U.S. Dist. Ct. (so. dist.) N.Y., 1998—. Exec. dir. N.Y. State Alliance Save Energy, Inc., N.Y.C., 1977—78; mem. N.Y.C. Child Abuse Task Force, 1995, N.Y. State Permanent Commn. Justice Children, 1996—; chmn. collegiality com. U.S. Dist. Ct. (so. dist.) N.Y., 2000—. Judge Valente, Clarence Palitz and Jacob Levy Found. scholar, NYU Sch. Law, 1964—67, Thord-Gray fellow, Am.-Scandinavian Found., 1967—68, Donald Frank Sussman Meml. scholar, Cornell U. Mem.: U.S. Jr. Davis Cup Squad (met. N.Y.C.). Avocations: tennis, horseback riding, house restoration. Office: US Dist Ct 40 Centre St New York NY 10007-1502 E-mail: Richard_Berman@nyds.uscourts.gov.

BERMAN, ROBERT S. marketing consultant; b. N.Y.C., Apr. 13, 1932; s. Sydney and Beatrice (Lipman) B.; m. Eleanor Rae Greenwald, June 16, 1956 (div. 1973); children: Thomas, Eric, Terry; m. Sherry Rona Frawley, May 29, 1975 (div. 1994); m. Sharon Louise Erbe, Oct. 5, 1996. BA, Cornell U., 1953, MA, 1954; advanced mgmt. certificate, Harvard U., 1964. Vice pres. Marschalk, Inc., N.Y.C., 1962-64; exec. v.p. DeGarmo, Inc., N.Y.C., 1964-70, 1970-80; exec. v.p., gen. mgr. D'Arcy MacManus & Masius, N.Y.C., 1980-83; chmn. exec. com. Margeotes Fertitta & Weiss, 1984-88; ptnr. Ber/Cam Ptnrs., 1987-89; pres. Berman Mktg. Network, Naples, 1983—. Instr. dept. communications Parsons Sch., 1968-70, Pratt Inst., 1974-76; columnist Madison Ave. Mag., N.Y.C., 1968-72. Dir. Collier County Spl. Olympics Internat. Served to 1st lt. U.S. Army, 1954-56. Named Advt. Accountman of the Yr. N.Y. Advt. Council, 1969 Mem. Unity of Naples (bd. dirs.), The Conservancy, Civil War Roundtable N.Y., Komos Aiden Theatrical Assn., Quill and Dagger Club, Cornell Club, The Vineyards Golf Club, Naples Bath and Tennis Club.

BERMAN, RONALD CHARLES, lawyer, accountant; b. Chgo., July 7, 1949; s. Joseph and Helen Berman; m. Kristine K. Topp, May 1, 1993; children: Daniel J. Lohr, Joseph James. BBS with highest honors, U. Ill., 1971, JD with honors, 1974. Bar: Ill. 1974, Wis. 1976; CPA, Wis. Mem. tax staff Grant Thornton, Chgo., 1974-76, tax supr. Madison, Wis., 1976-78, tax mgr., 1978-81, ptnr. tax dept., 1991-94; assoc. Neider & Boucher, Madison, 1995, shareholder, 1996—. Lectr. cont. legal edn. U. Wis., 1999—. Mem. editl. adv. bd. Physician's Tax Advisor Newsletter, 1986-89, Physician's Tax and Investment Advisor, 1989-93. Scoutmaster Boy Scouts Am., Middleton, Wis., 1978—; fin. chmn. Mohawk Dist. Four Lakes Coun., Madison, 1981—85, chmn. endowment fund, 1984—92, v.p. fin., 1992—94, mem. exec. bd., 1982—, treas., 1994—96, nat. rep., 1996; cubmaster Boy Scouts Am., Middleton, 2001—02, asst. cubmaster, 2002—; v.p. Scouts on Stamps Soc. Internat., 1996—2002, bd. dirs., 1986—96, Madison Pension Coun., 1986—98, pres., 1988—89. Recipient Silver Beaver award Boy Scouts Am., 1981, Middleton Good Neighbor award Middleton Good Neighbor Festival, 2000. Mem. ABA (employee benefits com. taxation sect.), AICPA, Wis. Soc. CPAs (chmn. fed. tax com. 1990-92), State Bar Wis., Ill. Bar Assn., Madison Estate Coun. (bd. dirs. 1991-97, pres. 1995-96), Wis. Planned Giving Coun., Nat. Com. Planned Giving, Web Network Benefits Profls., Optimists, Order of Coif, Alpha Pi Omega, Phi Kappa Phi, Phi Alpha Delta. Avocations: photogrphy, philately, camping. Home: 3906 Rolling Hill Dr Middleton WI 53562-1224 E-mail: rberman@neiderboucher.com.

BERMAN, SIEGRID VISCONTI, interior designer; b. May 22, 1944; came to U.S., 1951, naturalized, 1956; d. Walter L. and Annegrete M. (Wolf) Knapp. Designer Shepard Martin Assocs., N.Y.C., 1970-78. Dir. interiors DAT Cons., N.Y.C., 1980-83; dir. design Ralph Mancini Assocs., N.Y.C., 1983-85; sr. designer Karco-Davis, 1985-91; sr. mng. dir. Meli Borrelli Assocs., Architects and Designers, 1991-95, John Francis Borrelli, Architect, P.C., 1996—. Composer songs; illustrator book. Bd. dirs. Temple Spiritual Rsch. and Learning, 1981-82; reader Lighthouse for Blind. Colo. State Coll. scholar, 1962. Mem. AFTRA, SAG, Vanguard Soc. of Peta.

BERMAN, STANLEY ZISSMAN, allergist, immunologist, internist, educator; b. New Orleans, June 17, 1941; s. Herman Zissman and Golda (Kleinfeldt) Feir; adopted s. Leo Berman; m. Leslie Dale Miller, July 7, 1968; children: Jason Lee, Laura Elizabeth. Student, Tulane U., 1959-62; BSM, Northwestern U., Evanston, Ill., 1963; MD, Northwestern U., Chgo., 1966. Diplomate Am. Bd. Internal Medicine, Am. Bd. Allergy and Immunology. Intern Chgo. Wesley Meml. Hosp., 1966-67; med. resident Mayo Grad. Sch. Medicine, Rochester, Minn., 1969-71; fellow in allergy and immunology Scripps Clinic and Rsch. Found., La Jolla, Calif., 1971-73; chmn. allergy Lovelace Clinic now Lovelace Health Sys., Albuquerque, 1973—99, ret., 1999; clin. asst., assoc. prof. dept. medicine U. N.Mex. Sch. Medicine, Albuquerque, 1973—98, clin. prof. dept. medicine, 1998—2000. Spkr. in field. Co-author, reviewer, contbr. articles to profl. jours. Lt. comdr. M.C., USNR, 1967-73, U.S. Submarine Svc., USS Nathanael Greene, 1967-69. Fellow ACP, Am. Coll. Chest Physicians, Am. Acad. Allergy, Asthma and Immunology (emeritus); mem. Am. Thoracic Soc. (pres. N.Mex. chpt. 1977-78), N.Mex. Lung Assn. (bd. dirs. 1977-78). Avocations: jogging, travel, history. Office: 7416 Vista Del Arroyo Ave NE Albuquerque NM 87109-2941

BERMAN, STEVEN ERIC, audiologist; b. Newark, N.J., July 4, 1948; s. Milton and Maxine Berman; m. Shirley Ann Sviben, May 23, 1992; children: Stacy Beth, Daniel Max. BEd, U. Miami, 1972; MA, Kean Coll., 1975; PhD, Fla. state U., 1978. Dir. spl. edn. Colquitt County Sch. Sys., Moultrie, Ga., 1975—78; dir. Audiology Med. Coll. Pa., Phila., 1978—98; v.p. Eartech Inc., Cherry Hill, NJ, 2001—. Cons. Speech Pathology Salem Home Care, Salem, NJ, 1980—; dir. Speech and Hearing Ctr. So. Ocean County Hosp., Manahawkin, NJ, 1995—; pres. Coastal Audiology, Toms River, NJ, 2002—; cons. Ga. Basket and Crate, Thomasville, 1979—81, Voorhees Pediat. Hosp., Voorhees, NJ, 1998—. Author (internat. lectr.): Vibrotactile Stimulation, 1977. Assoc. M'Kor Shalom, Voorhees, 2002. Grantee, State Ga., 1978. Mem.: Pa. Speech Lang. Hearing Assn., N.J. Speech Lang. Hearing Assn., Am. Speech Lang. Hearing Assn. (cert. audiology and speech pathology). Avocations: golf, tennis, travel. Home: 22 Nolen Cir Voorhees NJ 08043 Office: EARTECH Barclay Pavilion Rt 70 Ste 13 Cherry Hill NJ 08034

BERMAN, STEVEN RICHARD, computer company executive; b. N.Y.C., Dec. 30, 1947; s. Harold and Norma (Bystock) B.; m. Susan Segall, Aug. 3, 1969; 1 child, Russell T. BS in Meteorology, CCNY, 1968; postgrad., U. Chgo., 1968-69; MS in Tech. Mgmt., Pepperdine U., 1993. Programmer, analyst Logicon, Inc., San Pedro, Calif., 1970-73, 75-78, Hughes Aircraft Co., Culver City, Calif., 1973-75; sr. analyst Argosystems, Inc., Sunnyvale, Calif., 1978-80; mgr. software support Ultrasystems, Inc., Irvine, Calif., 1981-86; sr. rsch. engr. Northrop Grumman Inc., Hawthorne, Calif., 1986-98; software project mgr. TRW Inc., L.A., 1998—. Author (computer programs) Recording Input-Output, 1983, Batch Jobs from Fortran, 1988, Marking Files No Backup, 1988. NDEA Title IV fellow, Chgo., 1968. Mem. Am. Contract Bridge League, Mensa. Avocations: bridge, travel. Home: 17336 Flame Tree Cir Fountain Valley CA 92708-3522

BERMAN, WESLEY R. minister, retired social worker; b. Hartford, Conn., Sept. 11, 1933; s. Jacob and Anna (Woike) Berman; m. Doris Pauline Abrahamson; children: George David(dec.), Sonya Jeanne Tirado-Berman. Student, Gordon Coll., 1950—52; BA, Wheaton Coll., 1955; B of Divinity, Gordon-Conwell Theol. Sem., Wenham, Mass., 1958. Recipient award for cmty. svc., Peekskill (N.Y.) NAACP, 2002. Democrat. Mem. Ame Zion Ch. Home: 6255 Broadway Apt 1C Bronx NY 10471-3140

BERMAN, WILLIAM H. publishing company executive; b. Stamford, Conn., 1936; Grad., U. of Pa., 1959. Exec. v.p. Houghton Mifflin Co., Boston, Md., retired, 1993.

BERMAN, WULFRED, pediatrician; b. Paarl, Rep. South Africa, Jan. 12, 1935; s. Barney Berman and Bella Kvasnik; m. Geertruda R. Van Rhyn, Sept. 29, 1964; children: Eytan, Avishai, Micha. MBChB, U. Capetown, 1958; DTM&H, U. Liverpool, 1962. Diplomate Am. Bd. Pediatrics, Am. Bd. Disability Analysts. Intern. Govt. Hosp., Tel Hashomer, Israel, 1959; house physician Royal Liverpool Children's Hosp., England, 1960; registrar in pediatrics Kind Edward VIII Hosp., Durban, South Africa, 1961-62; house physician Tropical Disease Unit Liverpool Sch. Medicine, 1962-63; resident in pediatrics Govt. Hosp., Tel Hashomer, 1963-67; pediatrician Dept. Pub. Health, Hadassah Hosp., Tel Aviv, 1969-70; fellow in devel. pediats. Johns Hopkins U., Balt., 1970-72, sr. fellow epilepy clin., 1972-73; rsch. assoc. Livingston Epilepsy Treatment Ctr., Balt., 1973-74; dir. epilepsy clinic Rosewood State Hosp., Owings Mills, Md., 1974-75; assoc. dir. neuropediat. ctr. Levenstein Hosp., Raanana, Israel, 1975-76; acting med. dir. Rosewood State Hosp., 1986-88, med. dir., 1994—. Cons. in epilepsy Md. State Health Dept., Balt., 1972-75; instr. pediatrics Johns Hopkins U., Balt., 1973-74; asst. prof. pediatrics U. Md., 1974-86. Fellow: Internat. Coll. Pediat., Soc. Devel. Pediat.; mem.: Pharmacy and Therapeutics Soc., Harriet Lane Alumni Soc., JFK Fellow Soc. Office: Rosewood Ctr Rosewood Ln Owings Mills MD 21117-2999

BERMAN-HAMMER, SUSAN, public relations executive; b. Buffalo, Sept. 12, 1950; d. Leonard and Judith H. (Goldenberg) Berman; m. Tony Hammer, Aug. 17, 1975; 1 child, Erik Jason. BA, Northwestern U., 1972, MS, 1975. Pub. info. asst. Sta. WBBM-TV, Chgo., 1972; news asst. exec. trailer Dem. Nat. Conv. ABC-TV News, Miami, Fla., 1972; writer Chgo. Conv. and Visitors Bur., 1973-75; Washington corr. Sta. WYEN, Des Plaines, Ill., 1975; sr. v.p. Herbert H. Rozoff Assocs., Inc., Chgo., 1976-82; pres., owner Susan L. Berman Assocs., Inc., Highland Park, Ill., 1982—; v.p. corp. communications Sheldon Good & Co., Chgo., 1988-89; exec. v.p. client svcs. On Deck Execs.com, Highland Park, Ill., 2003—. Chair Chgo. Comm./10, 1982-83; media rels. dir. Chris Cohen for Congress Campaign, 1999; exec. v.p. clinet svcs Ondeckexecs.com, Highland Park, 2003—. Asst. regional dir. Nat. Movement for Student Vote, Chgo., 1972; bd. dirs. Chgo. Women in Broadcasting, 1972-76, Younger Set Jewish Fedn., Dallas, 1985-87; chair, spokesperson North Shore Sch. Dist. 112 Edn. Found., Highland Park, Ill., 1995-2002, bd. advisor, 2002-; mem. North Shore Sch. Dist. 112 Caucus, 1995; exec. bd., chair Safe Home, liaison to North Shore Sch. Dist. 112, 1995-96, Edgewood Mid. Sch. PTA, Highland Park, 1995-97; also Dist. 112 crisis intervention team advisor, 1997-98; founder, chair, exec. com. Safe Home program North Shore Sch. Dists. 112 & 109, 1994-99; Sherwood Sch. PTO liaison to North Shore Sch. Dist. 112 & CIC Legis. Com., Highland Park, 1994-95; young women's exec. bd., v.p. cmty. devel., co-chair Trendsetter luncheon, co-chair Insights com., nominating com., Shalom Chgo. com., mem. campaign cabinet Jewish United Fund Chgo., 1991-96; bd. dirs. nat. women's com. North Shore chpt. Brandeis U., 1991-93; exec. bd., v.p. programming, reenrollment and membership, nominating com. Tamarisk chpt. ORT, Deerfield, Ill., 1990-95; chair comm. com. North Shore Congregation Israel, Glencoe, Ill., 1993-94; spokesperson, co-leader Parents Against Proposed Annexation of Deerfield subdivsns. from North Shore Sch. Dist. 112 into Deerfield Sch. Dist. 109, 1993-94. Recipient Recognition award City Coun. of Highland Park, Ill. Avocations: aerobics, tennis. E-mail: sbhsba@aol.com.

BERMANN, NANCY STEWART, artist; b. Chgo., Oct. 26, 1957; d. John Stewart and Carolyn Jean (Kurt) G. BA in Internat. Bus., Carthage Coll., Kenosha, Wis., 1982. Ski instr., race coach Wilmot Mt. (Wis.), Inc., 1979—97; leader div. clinic Profl. Ski Instrs. of Am., Milw., 1986-88; asst. dir. Ski Sch., Wilmot Mt., 1980-82; regional mgr. Carrol Corp., Chez Chocolat, Arlington Heights, Ill., 1982-84; area sales mgr. Unitog Bus. Clothing, Kansas City, Mo., 1985—98; decorative painter, 1998—. Mem. NAFE, NOW, Profl. Ski Instrs. of Am., Internat. Ski Instrs. Fedn., Chgo. Met. Ski Coun., Alpha Kappa Psi. Republican. Avocations: skiing, golf, guitar, windsurfing, bicycling, running.

BERMANN, SANDRA LEKAS, English language educator; b. Chgo., Mar. 30, 1947; d. Clarence and Theria Belle (Pollard) Lekas; m. George Alan Bermann, Dec. 28, 1969; children: Sloan Douglas, Suzanne Evelyne, Grant Alexander. AB, Smith Coll., 1969; MA, Columbia U., 1971, PhD, 1976. Asst. prof. Princeton (N.J.) U., 1976-83, assoc. prof., 1983-94, prof., 1994—, chmn. comparative lit. dept., 1998—. Dir. undergrad. studies dept. comparative literature Princeton U., 1978-82, 83-84, master of Stevenson Hall, 1984-92, dir. grad. studies dept. comparative literature, 1993-95; visitor Inst. for Advanced Study, Princeton, fall 2001; fellow Columbia U. Inst. for Scholars at Reidl Hall, Paris, 2002. Author: The Sonnet Over Time, 1988; translator, introducer: Manzoni's On the Historical Novel, 1984; contbr. articles to profl. jours. Fellow Fulbright Commn., Italy, 1969-70, Mrs. Giles Whiting Found., Columbia U. and Paris, 1974-75. Mem. MLA, Internat. Comparative Literature Assn., Am. Comparative Literature Assn. (chair undergrad. com. 1987-90, adv. bd. 1989-92, chair constitution 1991-93). Avocations: dance, music. Office: Princeton Univ Dept Comparative Literature 325 E Pyne Princeton NJ 08544-0001 E-mail: sandralb@princeton.edu.

BERMANT, GORDON, psychologist, lawyer, consultant, writer; b. L.A., Oct. 10, 1936; s. Ira George and Josephine (Wilson) B.; m. Roberta Mae Woolever, June 1958 (div. July 1975); children: Laura Diane, Daniel Bennett, Jennifer Wilson; m. Geri Lorraine Lincoln, Aug. 20, 1983. BA, UCLA, 1957; PhD, Harvard U., 1961; JD, George Mason U., 1991. Bar: Va. 1991, U.S. Ct. Appeals (4th cir.) 1991. Assoc. prof. U. Calif., Davis, 1964-69; fellow Battelle Seattle Rsch. Ctr., Seattle, 1969-76; sr. rsch. psychologist Fed. Jud. Ctr., Washington, 1976-82, dir. innovations and sys. dept., 1982-86, sr. rsch. advisor, 1986-91, dir. planning and tech., 1992-97; cons. Burke, Va., 1997—. Bd. dirs. Doar Comms., Inc., Rockville Center, N.Y., Justice Web Collaboratory, Chgo.; sec., bd. dirs. Internat. Jud. Acad., Washington; lectr. U. Penn., Phila., 1994—. Author: Biological Bases of Sexual Behavior, 1974; editor: Ethics of Social Intervention, 1977, Markets and Morals, 1977, Psychology and Law, 1976. V.p. Buddhist Chs. Am., San Francisco, 2000-01. Grantee NSF, 1965-68, NIH, 1968-69. Fellow APA, Am. Psychol. Soc.; mem. ABA, Am. Jud. Soc., Law and Soc. Assn., Am. Bankruptcy Inst. Avocations: hiking, skiing. Office: 5603 Tilia Ct Burke VA 22015 E-mail: gordon.bermant@verizon.net.

BERMAS, STEPHEN, lawyer; b. N.Y.C., Apr. 27, 1925; BS, Cornell U., 1949, JD, 1950; LLM, NYU, 1957. Bar: N.Y. 1950. Assoc. Wagner, Quillinan, Wagner & Tennant, N.Y.C., 1950-51; law sec. to chief justice U.S. Dist. Ct. (so. dist.) N.Y., N.Y.C., 1951-55; assoc. Gordon, Brady, Caffrey & Keller, N.Y.C., 1955-59; ptnr. Medine & Bermas, N.Y.C., 1959-63, Feltman & Bermas, N.Y.C., 1964-66; sr. atty. Columbia Gas System Corp., N.Y.C., 1966-69; asst. gen. counsel Continental Group Inc., N.Y.C., 1970-77, assoc. gen. counsel, 1978-82; v.p., gen. counsel Continental Can Co. Inc., Norwalk, Conn., 1982-86, exec. v.p., gen. counsel, 1987-91; v.p., gen. counsel Continental Plastic Containers, Inc., 1991—2001; gen. counsel Lockwood, Kessler and Bartlett, Inc., 1998—. Instr. law Queen's Coll, N.Y.C., 1964-68; adminstrv. law judge Office Profl. Med. Conduct N.Y. State Dept. Health, N.Y.C., 1993—. Mem. ABA. Office: 1 Aerial Way Syosset NY 11791-5501

BERMES, EDWARD WILLIAM, JR., biochemist, educator; s. Edward William and Magdelen Bermes; m. Patricia Ann Skokan, Oct. 19, 1957; children: Kathleen Lynn Onori, Edward William Bermes,III, Mark Lawrence, Alicia Marie Joebgen, Christopher John. BS, St. Mary's Coll., 1950—54; MS, Loyola U., 1954—56, PhD, 1957—59. Asst. prof. Loyola U. Med. Ctr., 1959—69; dir. of biochemistry St. Francis Hosp., Evanston, 1961—69; assoc. prof. Loyola U. Med. Ctr., 1969—74, prof., 1975—99, prof. emeritus, 1999—. Dir. of clin. chemistry Loyola U. Med. Ctr., 1969—97, dir. of clin. lab., 1981—97, acting chmn., pathology, 1982—86, assoc. chmn, pathology, 1986—96; chmn., editl. rev. group Doody's Health Sci. Book Rev., 1993—2000. Author: (exhibition) Effect of Hemolysis on Serum Chemistry Values (Gold Medal: ASCP/CAP Meeting, 1978); contbr. chapters to books; mem. editl. bd. Clin. Chem., 1981—90, Clinical and Applied Hemostasis, 1994—2002, Annals of Clinical Laboratory Science, 1978—82, 1990—2000; author: of over 100 articles published in profl. jours. including the Annals of Clinical Laboratory Science, Blood Coagulation and Fibrinolysis, British Journal of Experimental Pathology, Clinical Chemistry, et. al. Recipient Natelson award, Chgo. Sect., Am. Assoc. for Clin. Chemistry, 1976, Diploma of Honor, Assn. of Clin. Scientists, 1980, Edn. award;Outstanding Efforts in Edn. and Tng., Am. Assn. for Clin. Chemistry, 1983, Presdl. Citation, 1998. Fellow; Nat. Acad. of Clin. Biochemistry; mem.: Commn. on Accreditation in Clin. Chemistry (bd. dirs. 1981—), Assn. of Clin. Scientists, Am. Assn. of Pathologists, Am. Chem. Soc., Commn. on Edn. in Clin. Chemistry (pres. 1989—96), Am. Assn. for Clin. Chemistry (sec. 1978—80, mem. fin. com, exec. com., bd. dir. 1978—80, chmn., commn. on edn. and science 1985—87), Sigma Xi. Home: 1907 Sunnyside Circle Northbrook IL 60062 Office: Loyola University Medical Center 2160 So First Ave Maywood IL 60153 E-mail: ebermes@lumc.edu.

BERMUDEZ, EUGENIA M. See DIGNAC, GENY

BERMUDEZ, RUDY, state official; m. Nancy Bermudez; children: Rudy, Nicolas. BA in Sociology, UCLA, 1983. Coun. mem., Norwalk, Calif.; state assembly mem. Dist. 56 Calif. State Assembly, 2002—. Parole agt. Mem. Parent Tchr. Assn. Mem.: League of United Latin Am. Citizens, Calif. Correctional Peace Officers Assn., Norwalk KC. Democrat. Mailing: Rm 5135 PO Box 942849 Sacramento CA 95814 Office: 2d Fl 16600 Civic Center Bellflower CA 90706

BERMÚDEZ, SILVIA, literature educator; arrived in US, 1983; d. Salvador Bermúdez and Marta Rosell. Licenciatura, U. de Barcelona, Spain, 1982; PhD, U. So. Calif., 1991. Lectr., asst. prof. Colby Coll., Waterville, Maine, 1989—92; asst. prof. to assoc. prof. U. Calif., Santa Barbara, 1992—; vis. prof. Duke U., Durham, NC, 1995, U. Calif., Irvine, 1998, U. de Navarra, Pamplona, Spain, 1999; scholar in residence Aberdeen U., Scotland, 2002. Dir. U. Calif., Latin Am. Iberian Studies Program, 1992—2002. Author: Las dinámicas del deseo, 1997, La esfinge de la escritura: la poesía ética de Blanca Varela, 2004. Grantee Seminar fellowship, NEH, Cornell U., 1992. Mem.: Latin Am. Studies Assoc., Modern Lang. Assn. Am. (chair, 20th century Spanish lit. 2002). Office: U Calif Phelps Hall Mesa Rd Santa Barbara CA 93106-4150 Fax: 805-893-8341. E-mail: bermudez@spanport.ucsb.edu.

BERN, DORRIT J. apparel company executive; BSc in Bus., U. Wash. Mem. staff Sears, Roebuck & Co.; pres., CEO Charming Shoppes, Inc., Bensalem, Pa., 1995—, Chmn., 1997—. Bd. dirs. So. Co. Atlanta. Mem. Active Keeping Kids Warm, Bensalem, Pa. Mem.: Atlanta C. of C. (bd. dirs.). Office: Charming Shoppes Inc 450 Winks Ln Bensalem PA 19020-5993

BERN, HOWARD ALAN, science educator, research biologist; b. Montreal, Que., Can., Jan. 30, 1920; m. Estelle Bruck, 1946; children: Alan, Lauren. BA, UCLA, 1941, MA, 1942, PhD in Zoology, 1948; D (hon.), U. Rouen, France, 1996; LLD (hon.), U. Hokkaido, Japan, 1994; DPhil (hon.), Yokohama City U., 1997; DSc (hon.), Toho U., Japan, 2001. Nat. Rsch. Coun. predoctoral fellow in biology UCLA, 1946—48; instr. in zoology U. Calif., Berkeley, 1948-50, asst. prof., 1950-56, assoc. prof., 1956-60, prof., 1960-89, prof. integrative biology, 1989-90, prof. emeritus, 1990—; rsch. endocrinologist Cancer Rsch. Lab., U. Calif., Berkeley, 1960—; chair group in endocrinology U. Calif., Berkeley, 1962-90, faculty rsch. lectr., 1988. Rsch. prof. Miller Inst. for Basic Rsch. in Sci., 1961; vis. prof. pharmacology U. Bristol, 1965-66, U. Kerala, India, 1967, Ocean Rsch. Inst., U. Tokyo, 1971, 86, U. P.R., 1973 74, U. Tel Aviv, 1975, Nat. Mus. Natural History, Paris, 1981, Toho U., Funabashi, Japan, 1982-84, 86-89, U. Hawaii, 1986, 91-93, Hokkaido U., 1992, 94, U. Fla., 1991, 92; James vis. prof. St. Francis Xavier U., Antigonish, N.S., 1986; Walker-Ames prof. U. Wash., 1977; disting. visitor U. Alta., Edmonton, Can., 1981; John W. Cowper Disting. vis. lectr. SUNY, Buffalo, 1984; Watkins vis. prof. Wichita (Kans.) State U., 1984; vis. scholar Meiji U., Tokyo, 1986; internat. guest prof. Yokohama City U., Japan, 1988, 95; adv. com. on instl. rsch. grants Am. Cancer Soc., 1967-70; adv. com. Nat. Cancer Inst., 1975-79; adv. com. in endocrinology and metabolism NIH, 1978-79; mem. GM Cancer Rsch. Found., Sloan Medal Selection Com., 1984-85, Japan Internat. Prize in Biology Selection Com., 1987, 92, 96; guest of honor Internat. Symposium Amphibian and Reptilian Endocrinology and Neurobiology, Camerino, Italy, 2001, Jeju, Korea, 2003; lectr., spkr. in field Mem. editl. bd. Endocrinology, 1962-74, Gen. and Comparative Endocrinology, Revs. in Fish Biology and Fisheries, Jour. Exptl. Zoology, 1965 69, 86-89, Internat. Rev. Cytology, Neuroendocrinology, 1974-80, Cancer Rsch., 1975-78, Jour. Comparative Physiology B, 1977-84, Am. Zoologist, 1978-83, Acta Zoologica, 1982-96, Zool. Sci., Tokyo, 1984-2002; contbr. articles to profl. jours. Assoc. Nat. Mus. Natural History, Paris, 1980; adv. com. Contra Costa Cancer Rsch. Fund, 1984-98, Stazione Zoologica Anton Dohrn di Napoli, 1987-92. Recipient Disting. Tchg. award U. Calif., Berkeley, 1972, The Berkeley Citation, 1990, Disting. Svc. award Soc. Adv. Chicanos and Native Americans in Sci., 1990, Hatai medal Sci. Coun. Japan, 1998, Beverton medal Fisheries Soc. Brit. Isles, 2001, Outstanding Achievement award Am. Inst. Fishery Rsch. Biologists, 2003; Guggenheim fellow, 1951-52, NSF fellow U. Hawaii, 1958-59, fellow Ctr. for Advanced Study in Behavioral Scis., Stanford, 1960, NSF fellow Stazione Zoologica, Naples, 1965-66, Japan Soc. Promotion of Sci. Rsch. fellow U. Toyama, Japan, 1993. Fellow NAS, AAAS, Am. Acad. Arts and Scis., Indian Nat. Sci. Acad. (fgn.), Società Nazionale di Scienze Lettere e Arti Napoli (fgn.), Calif. Acad. Sci., Accademia Nazionale dei Lincei (fgn.), Am. Inst. Fishery Rsch. Biologists; mem. Soc. Integrative Comparative Biology (hon.; pres. 1967, Howard A. Bern Disting. Lectureship in comparative endocrinology 2002—), Am. Assn. Cancer Rsch., Am. Physiol. Soc., Endocrine Soc., Internat. Soc. Neuroendocrinology (coun. 1977-80), Exptl. Biology and Medicine (coun. 1980-83), Am. Soc. Molec. Marine Biol. Biotech., Western Soc. Naturalists, Japan Soc. Zootech. Sci. (hon.), Am.

Fisheries Soc., Japan Soc. Comparative Endocrinology (hon.), Cosmos Club. Home: 1010 Shattuck Ave Berkeley CA 94707-2626 Office: U Calif Dept Integrative Biology Berkeley CA 94720-3140 Fax: 510-643-6264. E-mail: bern@socrates.berkeley.edu.

BERN, LYNDA KAPLAN, women's health and pediatric nurse; b. NYC, Apr. 17, 1960; d. Melvin and Marilyn Kaplan; m. Jay Bern, June 1986. BSN, SUNY, Binghamton, 1981. RN, N.Y., Md., D.C., Va., N.J. Clin. nurse Gt. Neck (N.Y.) Pediatrics, 1981-82, North Shore Ob-Gyn, Bayside, N.Y., 1982-84; clin. ladder level three nurse North Shore U. Hosp., Manhasset, N.Y., 1981-88; breast feeding cons., instr. childbirth preparation Shady Grove Adventist Hosp., Rockville, Md., 1989-90, 91-92; relief nurse Md. Profl. Staffing Svc., Bethesda, Md., 1989-92; staff nurse St. Peter's Med. Ctr. (now St. Peter's U. Hosp.), New Brunswick, NJ, 1993—. Instr. maternal-child series St. Peter's Med. Ctr. (now St. Peters U. Hosp.), 1994-96, cert. preceptor, 1997—; nurse cons. Sons of Israel, Manalapan, N.J., 1998-2000, Pied Piper, Manalapan, 2000—; mgr. nursing hon. com. SUNY, mem. hosp. stds. of care com., nursing preceptor Adelphi Sr. Nursing Students, Vol. March of Dimes/Health Screening Fair. Nursing scholar, Good Citizenship League.

BERN, MURRAY MORRIS, hematologist, oncologist; b. Montgomery, Ala., Feb. 26, 1944; s. Hymie and Ruth Edith (Schaeffer) B.; m. Nancy Frazee, Nov. 23, 1967; 1 child, Alan. BA, Vanderbilt U., 1966; MD, Tulane U., 1970. Diplomate Am. Bd. Internal Medicine, Am. Bd. Hematology, Am. Bd. Oncology. Intern, then resident New Eng. Deaconess Hosp., Boston, 1970-72; resident in medicine Boston City Hosp., 1972-73; fellow in hematology & oncology New Eng. Deaconess Hosp.; Am. Cancer Soc. fellow Ctr. for Blood Rsch., Boston, 1973-75; sect. chief hematology New Eng. Deaconess Hosp., Boston, 1975-86; co-founder Cancer Ctr. of Boston, 1986; lab. dir. bone marrow transplantation Cancer Ctr. Boston, Boston and Plymouth, Mass., 1986-90; chmn. transfusion com., chmn. cancer care com., sect. chief hematology, oncology New Eng. Bapt. Hosp., 1999—. Dir. Cancer Ctr. of Boston and its stem cell support care, 1990-97; asst. prof. medicine Harvard U., 1987-94, asst. clin. prof. medicine, 1978-87, instr. medicine, 1999—. Author, editor: Urinary Track Bleeding, 1985, Hematologic Disorders in Maternal and Fetal Medicine, 1990. Mem. bd. med. advisors Am. Cancer Soc., Mass., 1976-80, fellow, 1973-75; bd. dirs. med. adv. com. N.E. region ARC, 1994—. Recipient Tullis award for rsch. Fellow: ACP (jr. faculty fellow 1975—77), mem.: Mass. Soc. Clin. Oncologists (bd. dirs. 2003—), Am. Soc. Clin. Oncology, Am. Soc. Hematology (clin. practice com. 1996—2000, govt. affairs com. 2000—). Avocations: camping, fishing. Office: Cancer Ctr Boston 125 Parker Hill Ave Boston MA 02120-2847 E-mail: murraybone@aol.com.

BERN, PAULA RUTH, columnist; b. Pitts. children: Bruce, Caryn, Marshall, Samuel, Rona. BA, Pa. State U., 1956; MA, U. Pitts., 1978, PhD, 1980. Editor-in-chief Jaffe Pub. Co., L.A., 1958-63; on-air producer Sta. WQED-TV, Pitts, 1963-65; dir. univ. rels. and devel. Robert Morris U., Pitts. and Coraopolis, 1965-69, Point Park Coll., Pitts, 1969-72; pres. Bern Asocs., Inc., 1972—; CEO The Exec. TV Workshop, Pitts., 1987—. Tchr. sr. exec. seminars grad. sch. Urban and Pub. Affairs, Carnegie Mellon U., 1985-90; trustee Ptts. Ballet Theatre, Inc., 1973-95 Contb. editor New Women mag., 1988—; syndicated columnist Scripps Howard NewsSvc., Washington, 1988—; Author: Point Park College: A History, 1980; How to Work for a Woman Boss (Even if You'd Rather Not)., 1987. Bd. dirs. council for Internat. Visitors, 1975-91; Exec. Women's Council, 1980—; adv. council Internat. Poetry forum, 1979—, Pa. Comn. for Women; bd. dirs. Assn. Commns. Women, bd. dirs. Conflict Resolution Ctr. Internat., Inc., 1998—, bus. dispute resolution alliance. Recipient Am. Coun. on Edn. awad, 1982 Mem. Women in Comm., Pub. Rels. Soc. Am., Press Club Western Pa., Delta Sigma Rho, Phi Beta Kappa. Office: Scripps Howard News Svc Ste 1000 1090 Vermont Ave NW Washington DC 20005-4906 E-mail: paularbern@aol.com.

BERN, RONALD LAWRENCE, consulting company executive; b. Anderson, SC, Aug. 23, 1936; s. Samuel Harris and Minnie (Siegel) B.; m. Elaine Kay Lefkowitz, Dec. 25, 1960; children: Brett Alan, Melissa Lynn. BA in Journalism, U. S.C., 1958, MA in Journalism, 1961. Writer William Barton Marsh Co., NYC, 1958-59; editor, writer Univac div. Sperry Rand, NYC, 1959-60; editor, mgr. Bell Tel. Labs., NYC, 1961-63; pres. Ronald Bern Co., NYC, 1990-2000; corp. sr. v.p. The LVI Group, Inc., NYC, 1985-90. Cons. AT&T Co., NY, NJ, 1966-85, The LVI Group, Lehr Constrn.; bd. dir. Talon Corp., The Bern Cos., Inc., Healing Images Inc., Riverstone Svc., Inc. Author: An American in the Making, 1960, The Successful Salesman, 1972, The Legacy, 1975; Gone Fishin': The 100 Best Spots in New Jersey, 1998, Gone Fishin': The 100 Best Spots in New York, 1999; contbr. articles to profl. publ. Bd. dir. North Brunswick Little League, NJ, 1975-79; mem. North Brunswick Planning Commn., 1984. With US Army, 1958-59, 61-62. Fellow SC Press Assn., 1960. Mem. South Caroliniana Soc. Democrat. Jewish. Avocations: fishing, reading, travel. Home: 37 Hidden Lake Dr North Brunswick NJ 08902

BERNA, MARIE-ROSE, international organization executive; b. Luxembourg; Dep. sec.-gen. Benelux Econ. Union, Brussels. Office: Benelux Econ Union 39 rue de la Régence B-1000 Brussels Belgium

BERNABEI, LYNNE ANN, lawyer; b. Highland Park, Ill., Apr. 11, 1950; d. Guy and Anna (Tamarri) B. BA, Harvard U., 1972, JD, 1977. Bar: D.C. 1977, U.S. Supreme Ct. 1988, U.S. Dist. Ct. D.C. 1977, U.S. Ct. Appeals (D.C. cir.) 1979, U.S. Ct. Appeals (3d cir.) 1985, U.S. Ct. Appeals (fed. cir.) 1988, U.S. Ct. Appeals (4th cir.) 1992, U.S. Ct. Appeals (6th cir.) 1990. Clk. U.S. Dist. Ct. Judge William Bryant, Washington, 1977-78; assoc. Tigar & Buffone, Washington, 1978-80; clin. instr. Georgetown U., Washington, 1980-81; gen. counsel Govt. Accountability Project, Washington, 1981-85; ptnr. Newman, Sobol, Trister & Owens, Washington, 1985-87, Bernabei & Katz, Washington, 1987—. Co-author: The High Citadel: On the Influence of Harvard Law School, 1978; author articles. Recipient Achievement award Lambda Legal Defense and Edn. Fund, Washington, 1990. Mem. ABA, ATLA, Nat. Lawyers Guild (bd. dirs. D.C. chpt. 1992-95). Office: Bernabei & Katz 1773 T St NW Ste 100 Washington DC 20009-7139 E-mail: lbernabei@aol.com.

BERNABEI, RAYMOND, management consultant; b. New Castle, Pa., Nov. 26, 1925; s. Leo and Maria Bernabei; m. Rosella E. Taucher, May 4, 1946; children: Raymond L., Alan J., Rosemary, Leo J., Lori J. BS in Math. and Geography, Indiana U. of Pa., 1947; MEd in Ednl. Adminstrn., U. Pitts., 1950; cert. in guidance and counseling, Duquesne U., 1960; DEd, Western Res. U., 1966. Math. tchr., head basketball coach Clymer (Pa.) H.S., 1947-50; math. tchr. Tarentum (Pa.) H.S., 1950-54; dir. guidance and testing, head football coach Tarentum Sch. Dist., 1954-61; asst. jr.-sr. H.S. prin. Hampton Twp. (Pa.), 1961-63; grad. asst. Western Res. U., Cleve., 1963-64; dir. secondary edn. Mentor Pub. Schs., Ohio, 1964-65, asst. supt., 1965, supt., 1965-67; asst. exec. dir. Bucks County (Pa.) Schs., 1967-80; mgmt. cons. I.E. Banreb Assocs., Longwood, Fla. Vis. tchr. John Carroll U., Cleve., 1965, Bowling Green (Ohio) U., 1966, N.S. Summer Sch./Dalhousie U., Halifax, Can., 1967, Wis. State U., Eau Claire, 1968, U. Ala., University, 1969, 71, U. Nev., Las Vegas, 1970, 72, 93, Cleve. State U., 1970, Laurence U., Sarasota, Fla., 1971, 72, 73; adj. prof. U. Ala., 1974, 75, 76, Lehigh U., Bethlehem, Pa., 1978, 80, 81, 82, Rollins Coll., Winter Park, Fla., 1983—; presenter in field. Recipient Disting. Prof. award Nat. Acad. Sch. Execs., 1973, Recognition award Nat. Soccer Coaches Athletic Assn., 1983, Bill Jeffrey award, 1985, Honor award Nat. Soccer Coaches Assn. Am., 1991, Honor award Nat. Intercollegiate Soccer Ofcls. Assn., 1975, Disting. Svc. award Pa. State Athletic Dirs. Assn., 1987, Nellie DelCamp Excellence in Tchg. award Rollins Coll., 1995, 2002; named to Western Pa. Hall of Fame, 1977, Nat. Soccer Hall of Fame, 1978, Allegheny-Kiski Valley Hall of Fame, 1979, Nat. Assn. Intercollegiate Athletics Hall of Fame, 1994, Ind. U. Pa. Hall of Fame, 1996. Home and Office: 541 Woodview Dr Longwood FL 32779-2614

BERNACCHI, RICHARD LLOYD, lawyer; b. Los Angeles, Dec. 15, 1938; s. Bernard and Anne B. BS with honors in Commerce (Nat. Merit Found. scholar), U. Santa Clara, 1961; LL.B. with highest honors (Legion Lex scholar, Jerry Geisler Meml. scholar), U. So. Calif., 1964. Bar: Calif. 1964. Assoc. Irell and Manella, L.A., 1964-70, ptnr., 1970—; lectr. Am. Law Inst., 1972-73; lectr. data processing contracts and law U. So. Calif., L.A., 1972, 78, 81. Co-chmn. Regional Transp. Com., 1970-72; mem. adv. bd. U. So. Calif. Computer Law Inst., 1979—, Ariz. Law and Tech. Inst., 1982-86; U. Santa Clara Computer and High Tech. Law Jour., 1982-90. Author: (with Gerald H. Larsen) Data Processing Contracts and the Law, 1974, (with Frank and Statland) Bernacchi on Computer Laaw, 1986; editor-in-chief U. So. Calif. Law Rev., 1962-64; adv. bd. Computer Negotiations Report, 1983-95, Computer and Tech. Law Jour., 1984-93, Computer Law Strategist, 1984-94. Capt. AUS, 1964-66, PTO. Mem. ABA (mem. adv. com. on edn. 1973-74, chmn. subcom. taxation computer sys. of sect. sci. and tech. 1976-78), L.A. Bar Assn., Computer Law Assn. (bd. dirs. 1973-86, chmn. preconf. symposium on law and computers 1974-75, West Coast v.p. 1976-79, sr. v.p. 1979-81, pres. 1981-83, adv. bd. 1986—), Internat. Bar Assn. (co-chmn. sect. on bus. law mem. com. on internat. tech. and e-commerce law 1995-98, steering com. 1998—), Am. Fedn. Info. Processing Socs. (mem. spl. com. electronic funds transfer sys. 1974-78), Order of Coif, Scabbard and Blade, Beta Gamma Sigma, Alpha Sigma Nu. Office: Irell & Manella 1800 Avenue Of The Stars Los Angeles CA 90067-4276

BERNAL, VICTORIA, anthropologist, educator; b. N.Y.C., Apr. 5, 1954; d. Arthur William and Barbara Brönte Bernal; m. Tekle Woldemikael, Sept. 15, 1979; children: Olivia Woldemikael, Eve Woldemikael. BA, SUNY, Buffalo, 1976; MA, Northwestern U., 1977, PhD, 1985. Asst. prof. Bates Coll., Lewiston, Maine, 1985—87, Hamilton Coll., Clinton, NY, 1987—91; assoc. prof. U. Calif., Irvine, 1991—, acting chair anthropology dept., 2000—01. Rschr. Social Sci. Rsch. Coun. & NSF, Sudan, 1980—82, Fulbright, Tanzania, 1999. Author: Cultivating Workers, 1991. Fellow, Rockefeller Found., Harvard U., 1990—91; grantee, Wenner-Gren Found., Tanzania, 1999, Inst. on Global Conflict and Cooperation, Eritrea, 2001. Fellow: Am. Anthropol. Assn.; mem.: Phi Beta Kappa. Office: U Calif Irvine Anthropology Dept Jamboree Rd Irvine CA 92617

BERNAL-LABRADA, EMILIO, writer, poet, translator; b. Havana, Cuba; came to U.S., 1956; s. Emilio Labrada Bernal and Sofia Escobar; m. Margaret Tijerina (div. Apr. 1976); children: Sophia, Hilda, Emily. Student, U. Havana. Sr. Spanish reviewer Orgn. Am. States, Washington, 1962-89; chief Office Pub. Info., N.Am. Acad. Spanish Lang., N.Y.C., 1996—. Dir. Labrada Lang. Svcs., Sterling, Va. Author: La prensa LiEbre, 2001; columnist: Nuestro Idioma de Cada Dia; Language, Our Daily Fiesta; editor: Emilia Bernal: su Vida y su obra. Mem. Real Acad. Española. Avocations: tennis, table tennis, photography. Home and Office: 20804 Great Falls Forest Dr Sterling VA 20165-2428 Fax: 703-406-1299.

BERNARD, ALEXANDER, protective services official; b. LA, Apr. 23, 1952; s. Louis and Hannah (Bergman) Bernard; m. Diana LoRee Winstead, Dec. 17, 1976; children: Michael Alexander, Andrew Alexander. AA magna cum laude, L.A. Valley Coll., 1976; BS summa cum laude, Calif. State U., L.A., 1989. Parking meter collector L.A. City Clk.'s Office, 1973-79; police officer L.A. Airport, Ontario, Calif., 1979-95, sgt. police svcs. divsn., 1995—. Mem. adv. com. Calif. Commn. Peace Officer Stds. and Tng., 1999—, vice chmn., 2001, chmn., 02. Contbr. articles to profl. jours. Active Boy Scouts Am. Mem.: NRA (life), L.A. Airport Peace Officers Assn. (pres. 1981—89, bd. dirs. 1992—94, pres. 1994—95), Fraternal Order Police, L.A. Airport Police Suprs. Assn. (bd. dirs., v.p. 1997—98, pres. 1999—2003, v.p. 2003—), Balloon Fedn. Am., So. Calif. Balloon Assn., Peace Officers Rsch. Assn. Calif. (chpt. pres. 1982—84, state bd. dirs. 1984—85, chpt. pres. 1985—87, state bd. dirs., ethnic rels. com. 1993—94, exec. com. 1994—, sec. 1999—), Calif. Peace Officers Assn., Indsl. Rels. Rsch. Assn., Law Enforcement Alliance Am. (life), Internat. Police Assn. (life), Calif. Rifle and Pistol Assn. (life), Golden Key (life), Phi Kappa Phi (life). Democrat. Avocations: travel, record collecting, hot air ballooning. Office: Police Svcs Divsn Ontario Internat Airport 1070 S Vineyard Ave Ontario CA 91761-8007

BERNARD, ANDRÉ PHILIPPE, publishing executive, writer; b. Newton, Mass., Apr. 15, 1956; s. Albert Yves and Ethel Potts Bernard; m. Jennie F. McGregor, June 16, 1990; children: Lucia McGregor, Elizabeth Eustis. BA, Franklin and Marshall Coll., 1979. Asst. editor Viking Penguin, N.Y.C., 1985—87; exec. editor David R. Godine, Boston, 1987—89; sr. editor Simon & Schuster, N.Y.C., 1989—91, Book of Month Club, N.Y.C., 1991—93, dir. acquisitions, 1993—96; exec. editor Harvest Books/Harcourt Brace, N.Y.C., 1996—98, editor-in-chief, 1998—2001; v.p., pub. Harcourt Brace, N.Y.C., 2001—. Bd. trustees PEN, N.Y.C., 2003—, chair forums com., 2003—; bd. dirs. German Book Office, N.Y.C.; mem. internat. freedom to publish com. Assn. Am. Publishers, N.Y.C., 1992—98. Author: Rotten Rejections: A Literary Companion, 1990; author: (with Bill Henderson) The Complete Rot, 1993; author: Now All We Need is a Title: Famous Book Titles and How They Got That Way, 1996; author: (with Clifton Fadiman) Bartlett's Book of Anecdotes, 2000; author: Madame Bovary C'est Moi!: The Great Characters of Literature and Where They Came From, 2003; contbg. editor: The American Scholar, 1998—. Bd. dirs. Mercantile Libr., N.Y.C., 1992—96. Jerusalem fellow, Jerusalem Book Fair, 2000. Mem.: Ye Buz Fuz, Miami Valley Hunt and Polo Club, Mahkeenac Boat Club, Century Assn. Office: Harcourt Brace 15 E 26th St New York NY 10010

BERNARD, BRUCE WILLIAM, lawyer; b. Erie, Pa., Feb. 3, 1951; s. Barney and Barbara Jean (Wurst) B.; m. Valerie Jean Noziglia, June 2, 1978 (div.); children: Elizabeth Anne, Brandon Wallace, Brittany Lynn; m. Catherine Ann Blore, May 4, 1984. BA, Case Western Res. U., Cleve., 1972; JD, Case Western Res. U., 1975. Bar: Pa. 1975, U.S. Dist. Ct. (we. dist.) Pa. 1975, U.S. Supreme Ct. 1980, U.S. Ct. Fed. Claims 1989. Assoc. Silin, Eckert & Burke, Erie, 1975-77; ptnr. Ely & Bernard, Erie, 1978-85, Bernard, Stuczynski & Bonanti, Erie, 1985—. Instr. Am. Inst. Banking, Erie, 1981-82. Bd. dirs. Erie Civic Music Assn., 1976-83, Florence Crittendon Svcs., Erie, 1978-84, Meth. Towers, Erie, 1979—. Named Vol. of Yr., Erie chpt. ARC, 1982. Mem. ATLA, Pa. Bar Assn., Pa. Trial Lawyers Assn., Erie County Bar Assn., Kiwanis (bd. dirs. 1978-81, 90-91, Disting. Svc. award 1976, 79), Phi Delta Phi. Republican. Methodist. Home: 6720 Manchester Farms Rd Fairview PA 16415-1649 Office: Bernard Stuczynski & Bonanti 234 W 6th St Erie PA 16507-1319 E-mail: bbernard@erie.net.

BERNARD, CATHY S. management corporation executive; b. Bronx, N.Y., Nov. 13, 1949; d Burton and Norma (Ebb) B. BBA, George Washington U., 1971, M of Pub. Adminstrn., 1978; MA, U. Miami, 1972. Cert. property mgr. Staff asst. HEW, Washington, 1970-74; evaluation specialist OEO, Washington, 1974; tchr. St. Patrick's Acad., Washington, 1975; asst. prof. No. Va. C.C., Woodbridge, 1976-78; adj. prof. Prince George's CC, 2002; staff dir. Dem. Nat. Conv., N.Y.C., 1976; pres., chief exec. officer CSB Assocs. Mgmt. Corp., Riverdale, Md., 1977—. Mem. Housing Opportunities Commn., Kensington, Md., 1979-93, chmn., 1988, vice chair, 1980, 87, chair pro tem, 1986, chair housing honor roll, 1985-88, Moderate Priced Dwelling Unit Commn.; mem. exec. coun. Inst. Real Estate Mgmt., Washington, 1982-87, cert. property mgr.; adj. prof. bus. Prince Georges C.C., 2002. Adv. coun. Suburban Hosp., Bethesda, Md., 1984-89; bd. dirs. Ivymount Sch. for Handicapped, Potomac, Md., 1984—, chmn. bd. dirs., 2003, chair property com., chair bldg. expansion project, 1999-2002; treas. Jewish Coun. on Aging, 1988; bd. dirs., chair property com. Jewish Found. for Group Homes, Rockville, Md., 1989-91; bd. dirs. Roundhouse Theatre, Wheaton, Md., 1994—, treas., 1995—; bd. dirs. McLean Sch. Md., 2001, trustee 2001—03, vice chmn., asst. sec., site com. chair, 2002; trustee Temple Emanuel, Kensington, Md., 1994-97; candidate Md. State Legislature, 1986; pres. Cmty. Housing Res. Bd., 1985. Recipient Hughes award for property mgmt., 1980, Jewish Coun. award, 1989. Mem. Montgomery County C. of C. (bd. dirs., v.p. housing com. 1981-82), Apt. and Office Bldg. Assn. (bd. dirs., chmn. affordable housing com. 1990—). Office: CSB Assocs Mgmt Corp PO Box 647 Riverdale MD 20738-0647

BERNARD, DAVID GEORGE, retired management consultant; b. Cambridge, Mass., Oct. 30, 1921; s. Frederick and Fayetta (Smith) B.; m. Edith Barnes, Dec. 10, 1960; 1 child, Andrew; children by prior marriage: Jeffrey, Frederick, Joan, Peter. BS, Harvard U., 1943, MBA, 1947. Gen. sales mgr. Am. Can. Co., N.Y.C., 1958-61; sr. v.p. Medusa Corp., Cleve., 1961-63; v.p. Internat. Paper, N.Y.C., 1968-78, Nat. Can Corp., Chgo., 1978-81; exec. v.p. Fischbach Corp., N.Y.C., 1981-83; pres. Delta Marine Supply Corp., N.Y.C., 1983-84. Bd. dirs. Trojan Techs. Inc. Bd. dirs. S.C.A.N. Served to lt. USN, 1943-46, PTO. Mem. Newcomen Soc., Bay Head Yacht Club (N.J.). Democrat. Episcopalian. Home: 254 E 68th St Apt 27E New York NY 10021-6017

BERNARD, DAVID KANE, minister, writer, editor; b. Baton Rouge, Nov. 20, 1956; s. Elton David and Loretta (Artigue) B.; m. Connie Jo Sharpe, June 6, 1981; children: Jonathan David, Daniel Kent, Lindsey Renee. BA magna cum laude, Rice U., 1978; JD with honors, U. Tex., 1981. Ordained to ministry United Pentecostal Ch. Internat., 1981—; bar: Tex. 1981. Dean of students Jackson Coll. Ministries, Miss., 1981-82, asst. v.p., 1982-86; assoc. editor United Pentecostal Ch. Internat., Hazelwood, Mo., 1986-2000; pastor New Life United Pentecostal Ch., Austin, 1992—; pres. Urshan Grad. Sch. of Theology, 2000—. Author: In Search of Holiness, 1981, The Oneness of God, 1983, 19 others, also author booklets. Supt. South Tex. dist. United Pentecostal Ch., 2002—. Named Writer of the Yr., Word Aflame Press, Hazelwood, Mo., 1987. Mem. State Bar Tex., Order of the Coif, Phi Beta Kappa. Avocations: reading, travel, racquetball, swimming. Home: 3603 Del Robles Austin TX 78727 Office: New Life Ch 4001 Adelphi Ln Austin TX 78727-5319 E-mail: newlife@onr.com.

BERNARD, DONALD RAY, law educator, international business counselor; b. San Antonio, June 5, 1932; s. Horatio J. and Amber (McDonald) B.; children: Doren, Kevin, Koby; m. Elizabeth Priscilla Gilpin, 1986. Student, U. Mich., 1950-52; JD, U. Tex., 1958, BA, 1954, JD, 1958, LLM, 1964. Bar: Tex. 1958, U.S. Ct. Mil. Appeals, 1959, U.S. Supreme Ct. 1959; lic. comml. pilot. Commd. ensign U.S. Navy, 1954, advanced through grades to commdr., 1956-75, retired, 1975; briefing atty. Supreme Ct. Tex., Austin, 1958-59; asst. atty. gen. State of Tex., Austin, 1959-60; ptnr. Bernard & Bernard, Houston, 1960-80; pvt. practice law Houston, 1980-94; prof. internat. law U. St. Thomas, Houston, 1991-94; guest lectr. Sch. Bus. Mont. State U., 1995-96. Mem. faculty S.W. Sch. Real Estate, 1968-77. Author: Origin of the Special Verdict As Now Practiced in Texas, 1964; co-author: (novel) Bullion, 1982. Bd. dirs. Nat. Kidney Found., Houston, 1960-63; chmn. Bd. Adjustment, Hedwig Village, Houston, 1972-76; bd. regents Angeles U. Found., The Philippines; chmn. of the bd. Metro Verde Devel. Corp., The Philippines;; bd. dirs. Gloria Dei Luth. Ch., Endowment Found. Comdr. USN, 1950-92; ret., air show pilot Confederate Air Force, 1970-80. Mem. Lawyers Soc. Houston (pres. 1973-74), Houston Bd. Realtors, ABA, Inter-Am. Bar Assn., Tex. Bar Assn. (com. liaison Mex. legal profession), Houston Bar Assn. (chairperson emeritus internat. law sect.), Internat. Bar Assn. (del. to 1st seminar with Assn. Soviet Lawyers, Moscow, 1988), Assn. Soviet Lawyers, Lawyer-Pilot Bar Assn., Sons of the Republic of Tex., Lic. Execs. Soc., St. James's Club, Masons, Shriners, Alpha Tau Omega, Phi Delta Phi. Lutheran. Home: 14 Scenic Dr Whitehall MT 59759-9789 E-mail: donbernard@msn.com.

BERNARD, EDDIE NOLAN, oceanographer; b. Houston, Nov. 23, 1946; s. Edward Nolan and Geraldine Marie (Dempsey) B.; m. Shirley Ann Fielder, May 30, 1970; 1 child, Elizabeth Ann BS, Lamar U., 1969; MS, Tex. A&M U., 1970, PhD, 1976. Geophysicist Pan Am. Petroleum Co., 1969; rsch. asst. oceanographic rsch. Tex. A&M U., College Station, Tex., 1969-70; rschr. NOAA, 1970-73, dep. dir. pacific marine environ. lab., 1980-82; rschr. Joint Tsunami Rsch. Effort, 1973-77; dir. Nat. Tsunami Warning Ctr., 1977-80, Pacific Marine Environ. Lab., Seattle, 1982—, chmn. Nat. Tsunami Hazard Mitigation Program, 1997—. Dir. NOAA hydrothermal vents program, fisheries oceanography program; exec. com. Coop. Inst. for Marine Resource Studies and adv. bd. for Coll. of Oceanic and Atmospheric Rsch., Oreg. State U.; adminstrv. bd. Joint Inst. Marine and Atmospheric Rsch. U. Hawaii; mem. Washington Sea Grant Steering Com., 1987—; mem. sci. coun. Joint Inst. for Marine Observations, Scripps Instn. of Oceanography, 1992—; exec. com. Cooperative Inst. for Arctic Rsch. U. Alaska; advisor Japan Marine Sci. and Tech. Ctr., 2000—; adv. Coll. Oceanic and Atmospheric Scis., Oregon State U., 2002—. Editor: Tsunami Hazard: A Practical Guide for Tsunami Hazard Reduction, 1991; contbr. articles to profl. jours. Recipient Best of New Generation award, Esquire Mag., 1984, Meritorious Presdl. Rank award, Pres. Clinton, 1993, Pres. G.W. Bush, 2002. Mem. Internat. Union of Geodesy and Geophysics (chmn. Tsunami commn. 1987-95), Am. Geophys. Union, Oceanography Soc. Office: Pacific Marine Environ Lab 7600 Sand Point Way NE Bldg 3 Seattle WA 98115-6349 E-mail: Eddie.N.Bernard@noaa.gov.

BERNARD, ESTRADA JEFFERSON, JR., neurosurgeon; b. Washington, Jan. 19, 1960; s. Estrada J. Sr. and Jennie Siata (Johnson) B.; m. Cora Ducette Spaulding, May 9, 1987; 1 child, Estrada Jefferson III. BS, Morehouse Coll., 1979; MD, Duke U., 1983. Diplomate Am. Bd. Neurol. Surgery. Asst. prof. divsn. neurosurgery U. N.C., Chapel Hill, 1990-96, dir. neurosurgery ICU divsn. neurosurgery, 1992—, assoc. prof. divsn. neurosurgery, 1996—, chief divsn. neurosurgery, 1997—. Fellow ACS; mem. AMA, Am. Assn. Neurol. Surgeons, Soc. Neurol. Surgeons., Congress Neurol. Surgeons. Office: CB # 7060 148 Burnett Womack Bldg Chapel Hill NC 27599-0001

BERNARD, H. RUSSELL, anthropologist, educator, scientific editor; b. N.Y.C., June 12, 1940; s. Herman Fink and Lillian (Rosenfeld) B.; m. Carole May Phillips, Jan. 28, 1962; children: Elyssa Lynn, Sharyn Kymm. BA, CUNY, 1961; MA, PhD, U. Ill., 1968. From asst. prof. to assoc. prof. Wash. State U., Pullman, 1966-72; rsch. assoc. Scripps Inst. Oceanography, La Jolla, Calif., 1972; from assoc. prof. to prof. W.Va. U., Morgantown, 1972-79; prof. anthropology U. Fla., Gainesville, 1979—. Prof. Nat. Mus. Ethnology, Osaka, Japan, 1991, U. Cologne, 1994-95. Editor (with B.P. Pelto): (books) Technology and Social Change, 1972; editor: (with J. Salinas) The Otomi, 1978; editor: Technology and Social Change, 1987, Handbook of Methods in Cultural Anthropology, 1998, (journal) Cultural Anthropology Methods Jour., 1989—98, (books) Native Ethnography, 1989, (journal) Field Methods, 1999—; author: (books) Research Methods in Cultural Anthropology, 1988, 1994, 2002, Social Research Methods: Qualitative and Quantitative Approaches, 2000; co-author (with W. Penn Handweker): Data Analysis with MYSTAT, 1994—; collaborator : (films) Aegean Sponger Divers (Chris Plaque award 1975), 1969—; contbr. articles. Recipient Alexander von Humboldt Rsch. award, 1994-95; Fulbright Rsch. scholar, 1969-70; grantee NSF, 1967—, NEH, 1976-85, Am. Philol. Soc., 1972. Mem. Soc. for Applied Anthropology (editor Human Orgn. 1976-81), Am. Anthrop. Assn. (editor-in-chief Am. Anthropologist 1981-89). Office: U Fla Dept Anthropology 1112 Turlington Hall Gainesville FL 32611

BERNARD, J. M., JR., manufacturing executive; V.p., gen. mgr. Sunland Svcs.; founder, pres., CEO The Shaw Group, Inc., Baton Rouge, 1987—, also bd. dirs., chmn., bd. dirs., 1990—. Office: 8545 United Plaza Blvd Baton Rouge LA 70809

BERNARD, JOHN MARLEY, lawyer, educator; b. Phila., Feb. 6, 1941; s. Edward and Opal (Marley) B.; children: John Marley Jr., Kendall M., Katherine M., James M.; m. Esther L. von Laue, May 31, 1986. BA, Swarthmore Coll., 1963; LLB, Harvard U., 1967. Bar: Pa. 1967. Assoc. Montgomery McCracken Walker & Rhoads, Phila., 1967-73, ptnr., 1973-86, Ballard Spahr Andrews & Ingersoll, LLP, Phila., 1986—. Lectr. Temple U. Law Sch., Phila., 1975-95; instr. Phila. Acad. for Employee Benefits Tng., 1996-99; guest instr. U.S. Dept. Labor, Washington, 1984-96; instr. U. Pa. Wharton Sch., Phila., 1989-90; bd. dirs. PENJERDEL Employee Benefits Assn., Phila. Contbg. author: Handbook of Employee Benefits, 1989. Mem. ABA, Pa. Bar Assn. Office: Ballard Spahr Andrews & Ingersoll LLP 1735 Market St Fl 51 Philadelphia PA 19103-7599 E-mail: bernard@ballardspahr.com.

BERNARD, LOUIS JOSEPH, surgeon, educator; b. Laplace, La., Aug. 19, 1925; s. Edward and Jeanne (Vinet) B.; m. Lois Jeannette McDonald, Feb. 1, 1976; children: Marie Antonia, Phyllis Elaine. BA magna cum laude, Dillard U., New Orleans, 1946; MD, Meharry Med. Coll., 1950. Diplomate: Am. Bd. Surgery. Instr. surgery Sch. Medicine, Meharry Med. Coll., Nashville, 1958-59, prof., 1973-90, chmn. dept. surgery, 1973-87, dean, 1987-90, v.p. for health svcs., 1988-90; practice medicine specializing in surgery, 1959-69; mem. clin. faculty U. Okla., 1959-69, assoc. prof., vice chmn. dept. surgery, 1969-73, chmn. dept. surgery, 1973-87, disting. prof. emeritus, 1990—. Dir. Drew-Meharry Morehouse Consortium Cancer Ctr., 1990-96. Contbr. articles in field to profl. jours. Mem. Okla. State Bd. Corrections, 1968-69. With M.C. U.S. Army, 1951-53. USPHS research fellow NCI, U. Rochester, 1953-54 Fellow ACS, Southeastern Surg. Congress; mem. Soc. Surg. Oncology, Internat. Surg. Soc., Am. Assn. Cancer Edn., Alpha Omega Alpha. Democrat. Roman Catholic. Home: 156 Queens Ln Nashville TN 37218-1826

BERNARD, MARCELLE THOMASINE, physician; b. N.Y.C., Aug. 11, 1920; d. Rene Jules and Antoinette (Byrnes) Bernard. AB Magna cum laude, Coll. of St. Elizabeth, 1941; MD, N.Y. Med. Coll., 1944. Diplomate Nat. Bd. Med. Examiners. Intern Flower and Fifth Ave. Hosps., 1944—45; gen. practice medicine N.Y.C., 1947—75; attending phys. St. Francis Hosp., Bronx, NY, 1950—57, Union Hosp., N.Y.C., 1957—75; attending staff Frances Schervier Home and Hosp., N.Y.C., 1952—75; pres. med. bd., 1959—60; sec., 1962; attending staff St. Patrick's Home, N.Y.C., 1954—75; pres. med. bd., 1962. Mem. exec. com. Bronx Tb and Health Assn., 1956—60; hon. surgeon Life Sav. Svc., N.Y.C., 1959—62; v.p. Bronxboro Commn. on Aging, 1961—62. Mem. Ladies of Charity. Lt. USMC, lt. Women's Res. USN, 1945—47. Fellow: Am. Geriatrics Soc., Am. Acad. Family Practice.

BERNARD, MICHAEL MARK, lawyer, city planning consultant; b. N.Y.C., Sept. 5, 1926; s. H.L. and Henryetta (Siegel) B.; m. Laura Jane Pincus, Aug. 28, 1958; 1 dau., Daphne Michelle. AB, U. Chgo., 1949; JD, Northwestern U., 1953; MCity Planning, Harvard U., 1959. Bar: Ill. 1952, U.S. Dist. Ct. (no. dist.) Ill. 1953, N.Y. 1955, U.S. Ct. Appeals (1st cir.) 1956. Pvt. practice law, Chgo. and N.Y.C., 1953-55; rsch. asst. Law Sch. Harvard U., 1955-56; city planning cons., atty.-adviser Puerto Rico, 1956-58; rsch. atty. Model Laws Project Am. Bar Found., 1959-60; city planner, legal adviser Chgo. Dept. City Planning, 1960-64; cons. planning and land regulation, 1964—; cons. Chgo. Area Transp. Study, 1964-65; mem. exec. faculty Boston Archtl. Ctr., 1967—. Adv. to Gov.'s Exec. Office on reorgn. Commonwealth Mass., 1968-72; chmn. 1st Nat. Transp. Needs Study Mass.; cons. A.I.A. Rsch. Corp., 1974; cons. Mass. Atty. Gen., 1981—; mem. com. urban devel. and housing World Peace Through Law Ctr., 1965—; mem. com. transp. law transp. research bd. NRC-NAS, 1966—; cons. White House Policy Adv. Com. to D.C., 1966; del. World Congress Housing and Planning, Paris, France, 1962, Tokyo, Japan, 1966; fellow Ctr. Advanced Visual Studies, M.I.T.; prin. investigator Northwestern U. Transp. Ctr.; lectr. in field; vis. prof. urban and regional planning U. Iowa, 1969-70; vis. lectr. Harvard U., MIT, U. Mich.; mem. faculty Am. Law Inst., 1978—. Author: Constitutions, Taxation and Land Policy, 2 vols., 1979-80, Airspace in Urban Development, 1963; co-editor: Policy Studies Jour.; editor, pub.: Reflections on Space; revision project mgr.: Constitutional Uniformity & Equality in State Taxation, 2 vols., 1984, Transformation of Property Rights in the "Space Age", 1993, (U.S. Govt. manual) Transportation Planning for Small Cities, 1973; spl. editor: Urban Law Ann. Washington U. Sch. Law; columnist: Jour. Real Estate Devel.; bd. editors: Real Estate Fin.; contbr. articles to profl. jours. Patron Hull House Assn., Chgo., 1965; v.p., trustee Cambridge Community Art Ctr., 1971-73; mem. standing com. Unitarian Ch.; mem. founding site com. Mus. Contemporary Art, Chgo. With USN, 1944-46. Recipient cert. of commendation for teaching Boston Archtl. Ctr., 1984; grantee NRC-NAS, 1964-66. Fellow Lincoln Inst. Land Policy; mem. ABA (land use, planning and zoning com., chmn. T.D.R. subcom. 1984-89, air and space com.), Internat. Fedn. Housing and Planning, Am. Arbitration Assn. (cert., bldg. and constrn. arbitrator),Am. Soc. Pub. Adminstrn., Policy Studies Orgn., Am. Planning Assn. (chmn. legis. com. Met. Chgo. sect. 1963-65, Mass. state reporter planning and law div. 1990—), Boston Soc. Architects (affiliate), Nat. Space Soc. (bd. dirs., space law com. Boston chpt.), Am. Underground Space Assn., Internat. Ctr. for Land Policy Studies, Urban Affairs Assn. (jour. rev. editor), Am. Crafts Coun., Mass. Assn. Craftsmen (v.p. 1975-78), Boston Visual Artists Union (hon., sec.-gen. 1971-72), New England Poetry Club (life), U. Chgo. Club Boston (bd. dirs.), Boston Athenaeum (life, dir. Poetry program). Home: 25 Stanton Ave Auburndale MA 02466-3005 *It seems to me that man's random, specialized intervention in the universe will prove to be the most constant cause for concern in the future. The problem might be seen not so much as how to keep the earth whole, but as how man may keep whole himself: this remains the role and strength of creative, intuitive endeavor, the source of everything I find of true value. Hopefully, ours will not become the "Age of the Idiot Savant".*

BERNARD, RICHARD LAWSON, geneticist, retired; b. Detroit, Aug. 12, 1926; s. Clarence Rolla and Ilda Gentry (Lawson) B.; m. Ruth V. Thorne, June 14, 1952 (div. 1975); children: Betty Ruth Marnell, Richard Thorne Bernard, Alice Jean Woodley, Daniel Lawson Bernard. Student, U. Mich., 1943—45, Okla. State U., 1947—48; BS, Ohio State U., 1949, MS, 1950; PhD, NC State U., 1960. Research geneticist USDA, Urbana, Ill., 1954-88; prof. plant genetics U. Ill., Champaign, 1966-92, prof. emeritus, 1992—. Served with USAF, 1945-47. Baptist.

BERNARD, RICHARD MONTGOMERY, retired physician; b. Long Beach, Calif., Feb. 21, 1925; s. Francis M. and Irma V. (Phillips) B.; m. Virginia Marie Thompson, Sept. 19, 1946 (div. Mar. 1971); children: Richard Jr., David, Mary, Danielle; m. Nancy Johnston, Nov. 18, 1971; stepchildren: Vivienne Kouba, N. Catherine Thompson. BS in Chemistry, U. Calif. Berkeley, 1945; MD, U. Chgo., 1950. Charter Diplomate Am. Bd. Family Practice. Pvt. practice Westslope, Portland, Oreg., 1954-60, Beaverton, Oreg., 1960-86; assoc. with Dr. D. Graham, Beaverton, 1986-90; family practitioner St. Vincent Tanesbourne Med. Plz., Beaverton, 1990-91; locum tenens Oreg., 1991-92; family practitioner Providence Health Sys., Wilsonville, Oreg., 1992-98. Prof. emeritus clin. medicine Family Practice dept. Oreg. Health Sci. U., Portland, 1984—. Transp. adv. commn. City of Wilsonville, 1994-96, long range planning commn., 1996-98; healthcare ombudsman Portland Metro Elders in Action, 2000—; v.p., bd. dirs. Oreg. Medications Edn. Program, 2001-03. vol. staff, mem. bd. dirs., Wilsonville Public Library Found., 2003—; Capt. USNR, WWII, 1942-46, Korea, 1950-53, ret., 1985. Recipient Meritorious Achievement award Oreg. Health Science U., 1988. Mem. Oreg. Med. Assn. (ho. of del. 1975—), Charbonneau Country Club (bd. dirs. 2000—). Republican. Avocations: fishing, golf, travel, photography, toy and model making. Home: 31530 SW Village Green Ct Wilsonville OR 97070-8426

BERNARD, RICHARD PHILLIP, lawyer; b. Chgo., May 29, 1950; s. Martin Joseph Jr. and Ruth (Hadka) B.; m. Svetlana Shoutova; children: Rachel, Benjamin, Alex. BA, Mich. State U., 1972; JD, NYU, 1976; M of Pub. Affairs, Princeton U., 1976; grad. Advanced Mgmt. Program, Harvard U., 1998. Bar: N.Y. 1977. Assoc. Milbank, Tweed, Hadley & McCloy, N.Y.C., 1976-84, ptnr., 1985-94; exec. v.p., gen. counsel New York Stock Exchange, N.Y.C., 1996—; exec. dir., resource sec. Russian Securities Commn., Moscow, 1995. Participating atty. Legal Aid Soc. Community Law Offices, N.Y.C., 1977-80; mem. internat. legal adv. com. Cairo Stock Exchange, 2001—. Mem. ABA (banking and bus. sects., com. on fed. regulation of securities). Democrat. Avocations: russia, carpentry. Office: New York Stock Exchange 11 Wall St New York NY 10005-1905

BERNARD, ROBERT WILLIAM, plastic surgeon; b. N.Y.C., Aug. 18, 1942; Student, U. Mich., 1959-60; BA in Zoology with honors, U. Vt., 1963, MD cum laude, 1967. Diplomate Am. Bd. Surgery, Am. Bd. Plastic Surgery. Intern U. Pa. Hosp., Phila., 1967-68; resident in gen. surgery NYU Hosp., N.Y.C., 1968-72, resident in plastic surgery, 1972-74; chief plastic surgery No. Westchester Hosp., Mt. Kisco, NY, 1982-87, 96—, White Plains (N.Y.) Hosp., 1979-86, United Hosp., Port Chester, NY, 1986-94. Author, ediotr: book Aesthetic Restoration of the Aging Face, 1997; editor: Aesthetic Surg. Jour., 1993—98; contbr. articles to profl. jours. Fellow: ACS; mem.: AMA (Recognition award 1983, 1984, 1986, 1988, 1990, 1992, 1995, 1998), Am. Cancer Soc., Westchester County Med. Soc., N.Y. Regional Soc. Plastic and Reconstructive Surgery (chair sci. program com. 1984—85, pres. 1986—87, mem. exec. com. 1987—88), N.Y. State Med. Soc. (pres. plastic surgery sect. 1983—84), Am. Soc. Aesthetic Plastic Surgery (pres. 2003—04), Am. Soc. Plastic Surgery. Office: 10 Chester Ave White Plains NY 10601-5112 also: 91 Smith Ave Mount Kisco NY 10549-2810

BERNARD, RONALD ALLAN, computer performance analyst; b. Dover, N.H., Sept. 28, 1953; s. Robert Ronald and Joyce (Bodwell) B.; children: Laura Jean, Jessica Diane. BS, U. Vt., 1975. Characterization engr. IBM, Essex Junction, Vt., 1979-83, diffusion engring. group leader, 1983-85, evaporation engring. group leader, 1985-87, VM performance analyst, 1987-89, performance group leader, 1989-91, AiX support, 1991—. Task force mem. IBM N.E. Region Info. and Telecom. Support Svcs. Consolidation, Endicott, N.Y., 1988-89; spkr. VM Internal Tech. Exch., 1988, SHARE, 1988-89, L.Am. Guide Group, 1989; task force mem. World Wide LAN Security Task Force, White Plains, N.Y., Essonnes, France, Dublin, Vinercode, Italy and Toronto, Ont., Can., 1992—. Bd. dirs. Royal Parke Assn., 1986—, v.p., 1987-91, pres., 1992—. Mem. Racquet Edge Club (Essex, Vt.), Amnesty Internat. (writer 1988—). Roman Catholic. Avocations: racquetball, nautilus, swimming. Home: 37 Northshore Dr Burlington VT 05401

BERNARD, THELMA RENE, property management professional; b. Phila. d. Michael John and Louise Thelma (Hoffman) Campione; m. Gene Bernard (div.). Sec. Penn. Mut. Life Ins. Co., Phila., Suffolk Franklin Savs. Bank, Boston, Holmes and Narver, Inc., Las Vegas; constrn. site office mgr. Miles R. Nay, Inc., Las Vegas; adminstrv. asst to pres. N.W.S. Constrn. Corp., Inc., Las Vegas, 1982-86, corp. sec., 1982-86; gen. mgr., corp. sec. property mgmt. com. D.A.P., Inc., Las Vegas, 1991-97, pres. property mgmt. com., 1991-99. Author: Blue Marsh, 1972, Winds of Wakefield, 1972, Moonshadow Mansion, 1973, 2d edit., 1976, Spanish transl., 1974, German transl., 1977; author, concept creator, prodr. (CD) Knight Flights, 1999; contbr. articles to Doll Reader, Internat. Doll World, other mags.; past editor Cactus Courier; editor, pub. The Hoyer Enthusiastic Ladies Mail Assn., 1980-90, 96—; Friendly Tymes, 1991-2001, Lady Charleen, 1995-2000; writer song lyrics. Mem. Keats-Shelley Assn. Am. Inc., Broadcast Music Inc., Nat. League Am. Pen Women (v.p. Red Rock Canyon br. 1986-88), Original Paper Doll Artists Guild, Heritage Rose Soc., Byron Soc. Am. Office: PO Box 14002 Las Vegas NV 89114-4002

BERNARD, TRACEY MARIE, ergonomics educator, industrial engineer; b. Indiana, Pa., Sept. 18, 1966; d. Edward Frank and Shirley Irene Bernard. BS in Indsl. Engring., Pa. State U., 1988, MS in Indsl. Engring. and Ops. Rsch., 1991; PhD in Indsl. Engring., Tex. Tech U., 1995. Registered profl. engr., Ky. Rsch./tchg. asst. Pa. State U., University Park, 1989-91, Tex. Tech U., Lubbock, 1991-94; indsl. engr. NIOSH, Cin., 1991; asst. prof. Murray State U., Ky., 1995—2002, assoc. prof., 2002—. Biomechs. rschr. US Army, Natick, Mass., 1997; ergonomics cons. Occupl. Safety and Health Tng. Ctr., Murray, 1996—; cons. Work Enhancement Ctr. Ky., Murray, 1995--96. Contbr. articles to profl. jours. Grantee Am. Soc. Safety Engr., 1998, Murray State U. CISR, 1999-2002. Mem. Human Factors and Ergonomics Soc., Am. Indsl. Hygiene Assn., Inst. Indsl. Engr., Soc. Women Engr., Am. Soc. Engring. Educators, Murray Woman's Club, Am. Soc. of Safety Engr. Office: Murray State U 157 Industry & Technology Murray KY 42071

BERNARDI, JOHN LAWRENCE, JR., economic historian, educator, consultant; b. Cambridge, Mass., Feb. 29, 1944; s. John Lawrence Sr. and Edith Louise (Rotti) B.; m. Victoria Mason Butler, Sept. 7, 1977 (div. Jan. 1991); 1 child, Sarah Louise. AB in Econs., Boston U., 1965; MA in Econs., Northeastern U., 1967; MA in Econ. History, U. Pa., 1969, PhD in Econ. History, 1971. Lectr. part-time Northeastern U., Boston, 1971-75; asst. prof. Stonehill Coll., North Easton, Mass., 1971-74, Frostburg (Md.) State Coll., 1975-76, St. John's U., N.Y.C., 1977-81, Western Conn. State U., Danbury, 1981-83; vis. asst. prof. U. Vt., Burlington, fall 1984; vis. lectr. U. Lowell, Mass., 1985-86, Northeastern U., Boston, 1988-89; substitute tchr. Local Pub. Schs., Boston area, 1987—. Cons. Mass. State Banking Commn., Boston, 1985; cons., mem. bd. advisors S.I. Hist. Assn., 1979-81. Northeastern U. teaching fellow, 1965-67. Mem. Am. Econ. Assn., Am. Hist. Assn., Econ. History Assn., AAUP (faculty rep. Frostburg State Coll. 1975-76), Friends Econ. and Bus. History. Avocations: travel, reading, swimming, walking. Home and Office: 27 Fairlawn Ln Lexington MA 02420-2714

BERNARDI, MARIO, conductor; b. Kirkland Lake, Ont., Can., Aug. 20, 1930; s. Leone and Rina (Onisto) B.; m. Mona Kelly, May 12, 1962; 1 d., Julia. Ed., Coll. Piox, Treviso, Italy, Benedetto Marcello Conservatory, Venice, Italy, Mozarteum, Salzburg, Austria, Royal Conservatory, Toronto. Began career as pianist, Italy; music dir. Sadler's Wells Opera Co., 1967-69; music dir., condr. Nat. Arts Centre, Ottawa, Ont., 1969-82; music dir. Calgary Philharm. Orch., 1984-93; prin. condr. CBC Vancouver Orch., 1982—. Guest condr. with San Francisco Opera, Royal Opera House at Covent Garden, Vancouver Opera, Canadian Opera Co., Met. Opera, Chgo. Symphony, Washington Opera, Houston Symphony Orch.; prin. condr. with CBC, Vancouver Orch. Decorated companion Order of Can. Office: Columbia Artists Mgmt ATT Judie Janowski 165 W 57th St New York NY 10019-2201

BERNARDINI, CHARLES, lawyer, former alderman; BS, U. Ill., 1968, JD, 1972; LLM, John Marshall Law Sch. Legis. asst. to Spkr. Ill. Ho. of Reps., 1972-73; sr. counsel Am. Hosp. Supply Corp., 1974-81; alternate del. Dem. Nat. Conv., 1980; spl. prosecutor for election fraud Cook County, Ill., 1981-83; commr., 1986-92; mem. Gov.'s Election Reform Commn., 1985; del. Dems. Abroad Dem. Conv., 1992; alderman City of Chgo., 1993-99; ptnr. Dykema Gossett Law Firm, Chgo., 1999—. Instr. internat. law Loyoa U. Chgo., Rome campus, 1981; counsel Allstate Ins. Co., 1983-91. Mem. Chgo.-Milan Sister City Com., 1988—. Mem. Am. C. of C. in Italy (mng. dir.). Office: Dykema Gossett Law Firm 55 E Monroe St Ste 3050 Chicago IL 60603-5709 E-mail: crb43@aol.com.

BERNARDINO, MICHAEL E. academic administrator, physician, educator; Grad., Case Western Res.U.; MD, Ohio State U., 1973; MBA, Emory U., 1996. Diplomate Am. Bd. Radiology. Resident in diagnostic radiology George Washington U. Hosp.; past positions with Sys. Cancer Ctr. U. Tex.; past mem. staff Anderson Hosp., Houston, Everett (Wash.) Gen. Hosp.; with Sch. Medicine Emory U., 1982—, prof. radiology Sch. Medicine; past dir. dept. MRI, dept. abdominal radiology Emory Univ. Hosp., past. prof. Winship Cancer Ctr.; past mem. staff Tumor Inst., Houston; assoc. clin. dir. managed care Emory Clin. Inc.; dir. managed care Emory Univ. Sys. Health Care, Atlanta; interim dean Sch. Medicine U. Buffalo, 1997—, v.p. health affairs, dean Sch. Medicine, 1998—. Editor: 2 books; contbr. chapters to books, articles to profl. jours. Mem.: Soc. Gastrointestinal Radiologists, Soc. Magnetic Resonance in Medicine, Soc. Computer Body Tomography (past pres.). Office: U Buffalo 155 Biomed Edn Bldg Buffalo NY 14214

BERNARDO, ALDO SISTO, retired foreign language educator; b. Molise, Italy, May 17, 1920; came to U.S., 1924; s. Ernesto Bernardo and Adele De Orchis; m. Claudia Louise Marcantonio, Oct. 25, 1942 (wid. May 1976); children: Donald, Joanne, Adele; m. Reta Anne Mohney, Nov. 6, 1976. BA, Brown U., 1942, MA, 1946; PhD, Harvard U., 1950. From instr. to Disting. Prof. SUNY, Binghamton, 1949-87, chair Humanities Div., 1959-67, emeritus, 1987—. Vis. prof. Johns Hopkins U., Balt., 1970, Folger Shakespeare Libr., Washington, 1974; pres. Verrazzano Coll., Saratoga Springs, N.Y., 1973-75. Author: (book) Petrarch, Scipio and The Africa, 1962, Petrarch, Laura and The Triumphs, 1974; translator: Petrarch, Familiares, 3 vols., 1975-84; editor: The Classics in the Middle Ages, 1990, Petrarch, Letters of Old Age, 2 vols., 1992, (with Reta Bernardo) A Concordance to Petrarch's Familiares, 2 vols., 1994. Chair Concerned Citizens for Rational Alternatives, Johnson City, N.Y., 1989-94; chair State Task Force for Excellence in Ednl. Methods, 1994—. Recipient Fulbright Rsch. grant U.S. Govt., Vatican Libr., Rome, 1955-56, Order of Merit, Italian Govt., 1966, Guggenheim fellowship Guggenheim Fund., Florence, Italy, 1964-65. Mem. MLA (life), Am. Assn. Tchrs. of Italian (Disting. Svc. award 1988), Am. Civic Assn. (pres. 1992-95), N.Y. Assn. of Scholars (v.p. 1990—, acting pres. 1995). Home: 25 3rd St Johnson City NY 13790-1816 E-mail: bernie@binghamton.edu.

BERNASCONI, STACEY CHRISTINE, project data manager; b. July 5, 1970; BA in Polit. Sci., Providence Coll., 1992; MPH, So. Conn. State U., 1994. Cert. sexual assault crisis counselor, community first aid and safety ARC, adult and child CPR ARC. Grad. tchg. asst. So. Conn. State U., New Haven, 1992-94; health and nutrition coord. Head Start program City of Meriden, Conn., 1994-95; rsch. asst. Addiction, Prevention, Treatment Found., New Haven, 1995-96; data mgr. Yale U., New Haven, 1996-98, Boehringer Ingelheim, Ridgefield, Conn., 1998—. Vol. Am. Heart Assn., New Haven, 1992—, Am. Lung Assn., New Haven, 1992—. Mem.: APHA, Conn. Pub. Health Assn., So. Conn. State Univ. Alumni Assn., Providence Coll. Alumni Admissions Assocs., Providence Coll. Alumni Assn. Home: 45 Farview Commons Southbury CT 06488-4423 Office: Boehringer Ingelheim 175 Briar Ridge Rd Danbury CT 06810 Business E-Mail: sbemasc@rdg.boehringer-ingelheim.com. E-mail: sbernasconi@snet.net.

BERNAT, JAMES LAWRENCE, neurologist, educator; b. Cin., May 23, 1947; s. Mitchell Joseph and Ruth Claire (Betagole) B.; m. Judith Elaine Lenzner, June 8, 1969; children: Deborah Eden, David Clare. BA, U. Mass., 1969; MD, Cornell U., N.Y.C., 1973. Diplomate Am. Bd. Psychiatry and Neurology. Resident in medicine Dartmouth-Hitchcock Med. Ctr., Hanover, N.H., 1973-74, resident in neurology, 1974-77, staff neurologist Lebanon, 1995—, assoc. chmn. neurology sect., 1999—2002; staff neurologist VA Med. Ctr., White River Junction, Vt., 1977-94; prof. medicine Dartmouth Med. Sch., Hanover, 1991—, asst. dean, 1995—99, dir. program in med. ethics, 1995—. Author: Neurology: Problems in Primary Care, 1987, 2d edit., 1993, Ethical Issues in Neurology, 1994, 2d edit., 2002; editor (editl. bd.): Neurocritical Care; co-editor: Palliative Care in Neurology, 2003. Bd. dirs. Vt. Ethics Network, Montpelier, 1995-2000, New Eng. Organ Bank, 1999—, Hospice V.N.H., 1999-2002. Fellow ACP, Am. Acad. Neurology (chair ethics, law & humanities com. 1993-03, exec. bd. 1993-97). Office: Neurology Sect Dartmouth-Hitchcock Med Ctr Lebanon NH 03756

BERNATOWICZ, FRANK ALLEN, management consultant, expert witness; b. Chgo., Nov. 3, 1954; s. Chester and Pauline (Maciula) B.; m. Kathleen Ann Carlson, Apr. 29, 1978; children: Amy Elizabeth, Laura Ann. BSEE, U. Ill., 1976; MBA in Fin., Loyola U., Chgo., 1981, postgrad. in acctg., 1982-84. Registered profl. engr., Ill.; CPA, Ill. Engr. Commonwealth Edison Co., Chgo., 1976—79, gen. engr., 1979—82, prin. engr., 1982—84; sr. cons. Brenner Group, Chgo., 1984—85; supr. Ernst & Young (formerly Ernst & Whinney), Chgo., 1985, mgr., 1985—86; sr. mgr. Ernst & Young, Chgo., 1986—88, ptnr., 1989—96; prin. J. Alix & Assoc., Chgo., 1996—99; ptnr. PricewaterhouseCoopers, Chgo., 1999—2001, BDO Seidman, Chgo., 2001—03; mng. prin. FAB Adv. Svcs., LLC, Chgo., 2003—. Spkr. in field. Mem. bd. regents Mercy Boys Home, 1990—. Mem. ABA (assoc.), AICPA, Am. Bankruptcy Inst., Ill. Soc. CPAs, Nat. Soc. Profl. Engrs., Turnaround Mgmt. Assn., Comml. Law League, Am. Bankruptcy Inst., Chgo. Soc. Clubs (Met.). Avocations: golf, racquetball, computers, investments. Home: 6543 Hillcrest Dr Hinsdale IL 60527 Office: FAB Adv Svcs 77 W Wacker Dr Ste 4800 Chicago IL 60601 E-mail: pwcfab@msn.com., fab@fabadvisory.com.

BERNAU, SIMON JOHN, mathematics educator; b. Wanganui, New Zealand, June 12, 1937; came to U.S., 1969; s. Earnest Lovell and Ella Mary (Mason) B.; m. Lynley Joyce Turner, Aug. 11, 1959; children: Nicola Ann, Sally Jane. B.Sc., U. Canterbury, Christchurch, New Zealand, 1958, M.Sc., 1959; BA, Cambridge (Eng.) U., 1961, PhD, 1964. Lectr. U. Canterbury, 1964-65, sr. lectr., 1965-66; prof. math. U. Otago, Dunedin, New Zealand, 1966-69; assoc. prof. U. Tex., Austin, 1969-76, prof., 1976-85; prof., head math. dept. Southwest Mo. State U., Springfield, 1986-88; prof., chmn. dept. math. scis. U. Tex., El Paso, 1988-95; dean Coll. Sci. Calif. State Poly., Pomona, 1995—2002, prof. dept. math., 2002—. Researcher numerous pubs. in field, 1964— ; referee profl. jours., 1965— . Gulbenkian jr. research fellow Churchill Coll., Cambridge U., 1963-64 Mem. Am. Math. Soc. (reviewer 1965—), Math. Assn. Am., London Math. Soc. Office: Calif State Poly U Coll of Sci 3801 W Temple Ave Pomona CA 91768-2557 Home: 1322 Crown Way Paso Robles CA 93446

BERNAUER, DAVID W. retail company executive; married; three children. Grad., N.D. State U., 1967. Pharmacist Walgreen Co., 1967-79, dist. mgr., 1979-87, regional v.p., 1987-90, v.p., treas., 1990-92, v.p. pres. purchasing, chief info. officer, 1992-94, sr. v.p., chief info. officer, 1996-99, pres., COO, 1999—2002, pres., CEO, 2002—. Office: Walgreen Co 200 Wilmot Rd Deerfield IL 60015

BERNAY, BETTI, artist; d. David Michael and Anna Gaynia (Bernay) Woolin; children: Manette Deitsch, Karen Lynn. Grad. costume design, Pratt Inst.; student, Nat. Acad. Design, N.Y.C., Art Students League. Exhibited one man shows at Galerie Raymond Duncan, Paris, France, Salas Municipales, San Sebastian, Spain, Circulo de Bellas Artes, Madrid, Spain, Bacardi Gallery, Miami, Fla., Columbia (S.C.) Mus., Columbus (Ga.) Mus., Galerie Andre Weil, Paris, Galerie Hermitage, Monte Carlo, Monaco, Casino de San Remo, Italy, Galerie de Arte de la Caja de Ahorros de Ronda, Malaga, Spain, Centro Artistico, Granada, Spain, Circulo de la Amistad, Cordoba, Spain, Studio H Gallery, N.Y.C., Walter Wallace Gallery, Palm Beach, Fla., Mus. Bellas Artes, Malaga, Harbor House Gallery, Crystal House Gallery, Internat. Gallery, Jordan Marsh, Fontainebleau Gallery, Miami Beach, Carriage House Gallery, Galerie 99, Pageant Gallery, Miami Beach, Rosenbaum Galleries, Palm Beach; exhibited group shows at Painters and Sculptors Soc., Jersey City Mus., Salon de Invierno, Mus. Malaga, Salon des Beaux Arts, Cannes, France, Guggenheim Gallery, Nat. Acad. Gallery, Salmagundi Club, Lever House, Lord & Taylor Art Gallery, Nat. Arts Gallery, Knickerbocker Artists, N.Y.C., Salon des Artistes Independants, Salon des Artistes Francais, Salon Populiste, Paris, Salon de Otono, Nat. Assn. Painters and Sculptors Spain, Madrid, Phipps Gallery, Palm Beach, Artists Equity, Hollywood (Fla.) Mus., Gault Gallery Cheltenham, Phila., Springfield (Mass.) Mus., Met. Mus. and Art Center, Miami, Fla., Planet Ocean Mus., Charter Club, Trade Fair Ams.; represented in permanent collections including Jockey Club Art Gallery, Miami, Mus. Malaga, Circulo de la Amistad, I.O.S. Found., Geneva, Switzerland, others. Bd. dirs. Men's Opera Guild, Project Newborn Neonatal unit Jackson Meml. Hosp.; mem. adv. bd. Jackson Meml. Hosp. Project Newborn; mem. women's com. Bascom Palmer Eye Inst., mem. adv. coun.; mem. working com. Greater Miami Heart Assn., Am. Heart Assn., Am. Cancer Soc., Alzheimer Grand Notable, 2d Generation Miami Heart Inst., Sunrisers Mentally Retarded, Orchid Ball Com., Newborn Neonatal Intensive Care Unit, U. Miami, Jackson Meml. Hosp.; founder Mt. Sinai Hosp., Miami; benefactor Miami Heart Rsch. Inst.; grand benefactor Neonatal Project Newborn, Jackson Meml. Hosp., Miami Opera, Am. Cancer Soc., Am. Heart Assn., Alzheimers Notable Care Unit, Greater Miami Opera Guild, March of Dimes, CancerLink, Sylvester Cancer Unit; adv. coun. Bascom Palmer Eye Inst.; founder Mt. Sinai Hosp. Recipient medal City N.Y., medal Sch. Art Leagues, N.Y.C., Prix de Paris Raymond Duncan, others. Mem. Nat. Assn. Painters and Sculptors Spain, Nat. Assn. Women Artists, Société des Artistes Français, Société des Artistes Independants, Fedn. Francais des Sociétés d'Art Graphique et Plastique, Artists Equity, Am. Artists Profl. League, Am. Fedn. Art, Nat. Soc. Lit. and Arts, Met. Mus. and Arts Center Miami, Pres.'s Club U. Miami, Palm Bay Club, Jockey Club, Turnberry Club, Club of Clubs Internat. Address: 10155 Collins Ave Apt 1705 Bal Harbour FL 33154-1629

BERNAYS, ANNE FLEISCHMAN, writer, educator; b. N.Y.C., 1930; m. Justin Kaplan; 3 children Student, Wellesley Coll., 1948-50; BA, Barnard Coll., 1952. Mng. editor Discovery Mag., N.Y.C., 1953-56; editorial asst. Houghton Mifflin Co., N.Y.C., 1954-56; tech. writer MIT, 1972; instr. fiction workshop Buckingham-Browne and Nichols Sch., Cambridge, Mass., 1972-73, Brookline High Sch., Mass., 1973-74, Commonwealth Sch., Boston, 1974-76; writer-in-residence Emerson Coll., Boston, 1976-77, 80-81; contbg. editor Harvard Mag., 1976-85; instr. fiction workshop Harvard U. Extension, 1977-92; vis. writer U. Mass., 1985. Vis. lectr. Coll. Holy Cross, Worcester, Mass., 1988, 89, Jenks prof. contemporary letters, 1992—95; vis. lectr. Boston Coll., 1991—92; lectr. Boston U. Coll. Comms., 1997—; writing instr. Nieman Found., Harvard, 1993—; cons. writing panel Mass. Coun. Arts and Humanities, 1972—74; resident Bellagio Study and Conf. Ctr., Italy, 1990; panelist Nat. Book Awards, 1991; mem. selection panel Nieman Fellowship, 1993, 2002; mem. adv. bd. Nat. Writers Union; lectr. in field. Author: (novels) Short Pleasures, 1962, 63, The New York Ride, 1966, Prudence, Indeed, 1967, The First To Know, 1975, Growing Up Rich, 1975 (Edward Lewis Wallant award 1975), The School Book, 1980, The Address Book, 1983, Professor Romeo, 1989, (with Pamela Painter) What If?, 1990, text edit., 1994, (with Justin Kaplan) The Language of Names, 1997, (with Justin Kaplan) Back Then, 2002; contbr. articles and book revs. to profl. jours., newspapers and mags. Bd. dirs. Vilna Ctr. Jewish Heritage, Boston Jewish Film Festival; chmn. bd. trustees Fine Arts Work Ctr., Provincetown, 1990-94. Recipient Matrix award, 1981 Mem. PEN (co-founder N.E. Chpt. 1978), Century Assn. Home: 16 Francis Ave Cambridge MA 02138-2010 E-mail: AFBernays@aol.com.

BERNBACH, JOHN LINCOLN, corporate strategies and investment executive; b. 1944; s. William Bernbach. Grad. polit. sci., Georgetown U. Trainee account mgmt., then v.p. account services Gilbert Advt., 1966-72; with DDB Needham Worldwide, Inc. (formerly Doyle Dane Bernbach), Paris, 1972-79, London, 1979-84, pres., chief exec. officer internat. div. N.Y.C., 1984-86, pres., 1986-93, vice chmn., 1993-94; chmn., CEO The Bernbach Group, Inc., N.Y.C., 1994—; gen. ptnr. Barnet-Bernbach-Carduner LLC, 2000—. Office: Barnet-Bernbach-Carduner LLC 800 3rd Ave Ste 2700 New York NY 10022-7604

BERND, CLIFFORD ALBRECHT, language educator; b. Bronxville, N.Y., May 14, 1929; s. Wilhelm Ludwig and Bertha Maria (Albrecht) Bernd; m. Eline Christa Schmidt-Nickels, Dec. 29, 1972; children: Matthias Albrecht, Christian Wilhelm. BA, N.Y. Univ., 1950; MA, Univ. Md., Coll. Pk., Md., 1952; PhD, Univ. Heidelberg, Heidelberg, Germany, 1958. Instr. in German Princeton Univ., Princeton, NJ, 1958—61, asst. prof. German, 1961—64; assoc. prof. of German Univ. Calif., Davis, Calif., 1964—68, prof. of German, 1968—. Vis. prof. German Univ. Leicester, England, 1977; chair Univ. Calif., Davis, Calif., 1965—76. Author: Theodor Storm's Craft of Fiction, 1963, 1966, German Poetic Realism, 1981, Poetic Realism in Scandinavia and Central Europe, 1995. Fellow, Fritz Thyssen Found., 1971; Fulbright Rsch. Scholar, Fulbright Assn. and Found., 1968. Mem.: MLA, Grillparzer Soc. (pres. 1992—), Am. Assn. of Tchrs. of German (pres NJ chpt. 1962—64), Theodor Storm Gesellschaft, Germany (corr.). Cath. Home: 1013 Plum Ln Davis CA 95616 Office: Dept of German Univ Calif 1 Shields Ave 622 Davis CA 95616

BERND, PAULETTE SALLY, anatomy and cell biology educator; b. N.Y.C., Jan. 21, 1953; d. Addie and Elizabeth (Drucker) B.; m. Steven Erde, Aug. 7, 1982; children: Alex, David, Rebecca. AB, Colgate Univ., 1975; PhD, Columbia U., 1980. Postdoctoral fellow NYU, 1980-82; asst. prof. Mount Sinai Sch. of Medicine, N.Y.C., 1982-87; assoc. prof. SUNY Health Sci. Ctr., N.Y.C., 1987-00; prof. SUNY HSC, N.Y.C., 2000—. Contbr. articles to profl. jours. including Developmental Biology, Jour. of Neurobiology, Internat. Jour. Devel. Neurosci. Grantee NSF, 1992-95, Dysautonomia Found., 1994-95, Am. Heart Assn. Office: SUNY Health Sci Ctr 450 Clarkson Ave Brooklyn NY 11203 E-mail: paulette.bernd@downstate.edu.

BERNDT, ERNST RUDOLF, economist, educator; b. Crespo, Entre Rios, Argentina, Apr. 13, 1946; came to U.S., 1949; s. Markus William and Charlotte Marie (Zimmerman) B.; m. Martha Ann Mirly, June 10, 1967 (div. 1982); children: Jeffery, Nathan; m. Joan Margaret Curran, May 15, 1994. BA with honors, Valparaiso U., 1968; MS., U. Wis., 1971, PhD, 1972; PhD (hon.), Uppsala U., 1991. Staff economist Exec. Office of the Pres. U.S. Govt., Washington, 1971-72; asst. prof. U. (Vancouver) B.C., Can., 1973-78, assoc. prof., 1978-80; prof. applied econs. MIT, Cambridge, Mass., 1980—. Dir. program on technol. progress and productivity measurement Nat. Bur. Econ. Rsch., Cambridge; rsch. assoc. Nat. Bur. Econ. Rsch., Cambridge, 1980—; acad. affiliate Analysis Group, Inc., Belmont, Mass., 1985—. Contbr. profl. articles. Most cited economist under age 40 in 1985. Mem. Am. Econ. Assn., Econometric Soc., Conf. Rsch. in Income and Wealth. Independent. Lutheran. Office: MIT Sloan Sch of Mgmt 50 Memorial Dr # E52 452 Cambridge MA 02142-1347 E-mail: ebermdt@mit.edu.

BERNDT, MARTIN R. career officer; Grad., West Chester U., 1969; student, Amphibious Warfare Sch., 1980, USMC Command and Staff Coll., 1984, U.S. Army War Coll., 1987. Commd. 2d lt. USMC, 1969, advanced through grades to maj. gen., 1998; weapons platoon commdr. 9th Marines, Okinawa, Japan, 1969; rifle platoon comdr., co. exec. officer 7th, 1st Marines, Vietnam; instr., platoon comdr. Officer Candidate Sch., 1971, The Basic Sch.; officer selection officer N.Y.; ops. officer 3d Reconnaissance Bn.; various assignments Marine Aircraft Group 26, 1980-84, 2d Marine Divsn., 1987-90, Stuttgart, Germany, 1990-94; polit.-mil. planner Office Joint Chiefs Staff, 1984-86; exec. officer Marine Forces Panama, 1988-89; comdr. MEU (SOC), 1994-95; dep. comdr. USMC Forces, Atlantic, 1995; dir Joint Tng, J-7 U.S. Atlantic Commd.; dep. commdg. gen. U.S. Marine Corps. Combat Devel. Command, Quantico, Va.; comdr. U.S. Marine Corps Forces, Atlantic, Europe, South, Northern Command, Strategic Command, 2002—, U.S. Fleet Marine Force, Atlantic, Europe, 2002—, U.S. Marine Corps Bases, Atlantic, 2002—. Office: US Marine Corp Forces Atlantic 1468 Ingram St Norfolk VA 23551-2596*

BERNE, BRUCE J. chemistry educator; BS, Bklyn. Coll., 1961; PhD (NASA fellow, NSF fellow), U. Chgo., 1964. NATO postdoctoral fellow U. Brussels, 1964-65; asst. prof. chemistry Columbia U., N.Y.C., 1966-69, assoc. prof., 1969-72, prof., 1972—98, Higgins prof. natural chemistry, 1998—, chmn. Dept. Natural Sci., 2002—. Vis. prof. U. Tel Aviv, 1972-73, Sackler Disting. lectr., 1985, Miller Inst. U. Calif., Berkeley, 1993-94; vis. scientist IBM Thomas J. Watson Rsch. Labs., Yorktown, N.Y., 1990-92; Reilly lectr. U. Notre Dame, 1998; Davidson lectr. U. Kans., 1998; Albert K. Moscowitz lectr. U. Minn., 2000; Moses Gomberg lectr. U. Mich., 2000. Mem. editl. bd. Jour. Statistical Physics, 1976-79, Advances in Chemical Physics, 1984—, Jour. Phys. Chemistry, 1985-88, Jour. Chem. Physics, 1985-88, Chemical Physics Letters, 2000—; Assoc. editor Phys. Rev. Letters, 2000—. Recipient Alexander von Humboldt Found. award 1998, award in theoretical chemistry Am. Chem. Soc., 1995, Joseph O. Hirschfelder prize in theoretical chemistry U. Wis., Joel Henry Hildebrand award in theoretical and exptl. chemistry of liquids Am .Chem. Soc., 2002; Alfred P. Sloan Found. fellow, 1968-71, John Simon Guggenheim Found. fellow, 1972-73. Fellow: AAAS, Am. Acad. Arts and Scis., Am. Phys. Soc.; mem.: Nat. Acad. Scis. Office: Dept Chemistry Columbia U MC 3103 3000 Broadway New York NY 10027-6941 E-mail: berne@chem.columbia.edu.

BERNE, STANLEY, author; b. Staten Island, New York, June 8, 1923; s. William and Irene (Daniels) B.; m. Arlene (Zekowski), May 17, 1952. BS, Rutgers Univ., 1951; MA, N.Y.Univ., 1952; post grad. fellow, La. State U., 1954-59. Cert. tchr., mentally retarded, N.Y. Tchg. fellow La. State U., Baton Rouge, 1954-59; assoc. prof. English Ea. N. Mex. U., Portales, 1960-80, rsch. assoc. prof. in English, 1980—. Chmn. of the bd. Am., Canadian Publishers, Inc., Santa Fe, N. Mex., 1980-97; bd. dir. New Arts Found., Inc., Santa Fe, N. Mex., 1990—; guest lectr. U. Ams., 1965, U. S.D., 1968; Styrian Hauptshulen Paedagogische Akademie, Graz, Austria, 1969; founder, developer first dept. for tchg. mentally retarded, Dallas Pub. Sch., 1952-53. Author: A First Book of the Neo-Narrative, 1954; Cardinals and Saints, 1958; The Dialogues, 1962; The Multiple Modern Gods and Other Stories, 1964; The Unconscious Victorious and Other Stories, 1969; The New Rubaiyat of Stanley Berne, 1973; Future Lang., 1976, The Great Am. Empire, 1981; Every Person's Little Book of P-L-U-T-O-N-I-U-M, 1992; Alphabet Soup, 1998; To Hell with Optimism!!, 1996; Gravity Drag, 1998; Swimming to Significance, 1999; At One With Birds, 2000; Empire Sweets-Or-How I Learned to Live and Love in the Greatest Empire on Earth, 2003; Legal Tender or It's All About Money!, 2003; You and Me or How to Survive in the Greatest Empire on Earth!, 2003; (inclusion in anthologies) Trace, 1965; First Person Intense, 1978; Breakthrough Fictioneers, 1979; American Writing Today, 1992; Dictionary of the Avant-Gardes, 1993; New World Writing II, 1957; The Living Underground, 1999; prodr. and co-host (with Arlene Zekowski) nine Part TV Series for PBS, Future Writing Today; The Am. Emprire, a trilogy. Served in USAF, 1942-46, PTO. Decorated Medal of Philippine Liberation; World War II Victory medal; recipient four Rsch. Awards, Ea. N. Mex. U.; recipient St. John Perse Award for internat. prose, 1998. Mem. PEN, com. of small mag., editors, poets, New Eng. Small Press Assn.; Rio Grande Writers Assn.; Santa Fe Writers Coop. Avocations: painting, design, collage. Home: PO Box 4595 Santa Fe NM 87502-4595 Address: Rising Tide Press N Mex PO Box 6136 Santa Fe NM 87502-6136

BERNENE, JAMES LOUIS, physician; b. Mt. Kiso, N.Y., July 31, 1940; s. James C. and Elizabeth B.; m. Diane N. Nicandri, June 17, 1943; children: J. Christopher, Melissa. BS, Middlebury Coll., 1963; MD, Albany Med. Coll. Diplomate Am. Bd. Internal Medicine. Resident, dir. Greenwich (Conn.) Hosp., 1976-81, Samaritan Health Svc., Phoenix, 1981-88; chmn. dept. medicine, assoc. chmn. New Britan Gen. Hosp. - U. Conn., 1988—; prof. medicine U. Conn., Farmington, 1988—. Contbr. articles to profl. jours. Fellow Am. Coll. Physicians (gov. elect 1995-97, gov. Conn. chpt. 1997-2001); mem. Conn. Endocrine Soc. (sec.). Avocations: skiing, scuba diving, reading. Office: New Britain Gen Hosp Dept Medicine 100 Grand St Dept Medicine New Britain CT 06052-2017

BERNER, ANDREW JAY, library director, writer; b. Bronx, NY, Apr. 5, 1952; s. Bernard and Phyllis (Stern) B. BA in History cum laude, Herbert H. Lehman Coll., 1974, MA in History, 1979; MS in Libr. and Info. Sci., Pratt Inst., 1982. Tchr. NYC Bd. Edn., NY, 1979-82; asst. libr. The Univ. Club Libr., NYC, 1982-84, assoc. libr., 1984-86, acting dir., 1986-87, dir., 1987-93, dir., curator of collections, 1993—. Co-founder, dir. OPL Resources, Ltd., 1984-99. Author: Time Management in the Small Library, 1987, (with Guy St. Clair) The Best of OPL, 1990, The Best of OPL II, 1997, Time Management in Libraries and Information Services, 1999, The University Club: An Architectural Celebration, 1999, Treasures of The University Club, 1999; author, editor The Illuminator, 1990—, The Univ. Club Libr. Quar., 1984-90; editor (newsletter) The One-Person Libr., 1984-98; contbr. articles to profl. jours. Fellow Spl. Librs. Assn. (chair, chair-elect mus., arts and humanities divsn. 1990-92, pres.-elect, pres. NY chpt. 1994-96, bylaws chair, pub. rels. chair, dir. awards); mem. Century Assn., Grolier Club. Office: The Univ Club Libr 1 W 54th St New York NY 10019-5404

BERNER, ARTHUR SAMUEL, lawyer; b. NYC, Nov. 12, 1943; s. Hyman and Sylvia Berner; children: Jocelyn, Evan, Christina, Sara. BA, CCNY, 1964; JD cum laude, NYU, 1967. Bar: N.Y. 1967, Tex. 1980. Assoc. Cahill & Gordon, N.Y.C., 1967-70; with Inexco Oil Co., Houston, 1970-85; v.p. legal, sec. United Fin. Group Inc., Houston, 1985-91; shareholder Winstead, Sechrest & Minick, 1991—99; ptnr. Haynes and Boone, LLP, Houston, 1999—. Bd. dirs. Ctr. Internat. Affairs. Bd. dirs. Soc. Performing Arts Search, Houston Grand Opera, Houston Symphony, Tex. Opera Theatre, Delia Stuart Dance Co., Jewish Fedn., Jewish Cmty. Ctr., Jewish Family Svc., Anti-Defamation League, Search; pres. Am. Jewish Com. Mem. ABA, Houston Bar Assn., City Bar Assn., Tex. Bar Assn., N.Y. State Bar Assn. Jewish. Office: Haynes and Boone LLP 1000 Louisiana St Ste 4300 Houston TX 77002 E-mail: bernera@haynesboone.com.

BERNER, FREDERIC GEORGE, JR., lawyer; b. Washington, May 7, 1943; s. Frederic George and Florence Grace (Carlton) B.; m. Lorraine Ann Ouellette, Sept. 28, 1968; children: Frederic George, III, Christina Lorraine, Jennifer Jane. BA, Middlebury Coll., 1965; MBA, Am. U., 1970; JD, George Washington U., 1973. Bar: D.C. 1973, U.S. Dist. Ct. (D.C. dist.) 1973, U.S. Ct. Appeals (D.C. cir.) 1974, U.S. Ct. Appeals (4th cir.) 1977, U.S. Ct. Appeals (11th cir.) 1984, U.S. Ct. Appeals (10th cir.) 1994, U.S. Ct. Appeals (7th cir.) 2001, U.S. Supreme Ct. 1980. Econ. intelligence officer CIA, Washington, 1965-67, 70; assoc. Sidley & Austin, Washington, 1973-80; ptnr. Sidley Austin Brown & Wood LLP, Washington, 1980—. Contbr. articles to legal publs.; bd. editl. advisors Pub. Utilities Fortnightly. Gen. counsel, bd. dirs. Washington chpt. Nat. Hemophilia Found., 1976-80; mem. Natural Gas Roundtable. Served to 1st lt. U.S. Army, 1967-70. Mem.: ABA, D.C. Bar, Energy Bar Assn. (v.p., bd. dirs. 2003—), Order of Coif. Republican. Presbyterian. Home: 7605 Glenbrook Rd Bethesda MD 20814-1319 Office: Sidley Austin Brown & Wood LLP 1501 K St NW Washington DC 20005 E-mail: fberner@sidley.com.

BERNER, JUDITH, mental health nurse; b. Tamaqua, Pa., June 19, 1938; d. Ralph Edgar and Ethel Mary (Williams) B. Diploma in nursing, Temple U. Hosp., 1959; AS, Coll. of Ganado, 1975, MS in Cmty. Health, D of Med. Adminstrn. (hon.), Coll. of Ganado; BA, Stephens Coll., 1977; MEd, U. Ariz., 1980; LD (hon.), U. Iceland. RN, Ariz., N.Mex., Pa. Nursing adminstr. Project HOPE Internat. Office & Hosp. Ship, Washington, 1970-72; assoc. adminstr. Navajo Nation Health Found., Ganado, Ariz., 1972-79; clin. instr. psychiat. nursing Mo. So. State Coll., Joplin, 1986; nurse/therapist Presbyn. Kaseman Hosp., Albuquerque, 1986-93; emergency svcs. clinician for mental health svcs. Presbyn. Healthcare Sys., 1994-95, Heights Psychiat. Hosp., 1994-95, Charter Heights Behavioral Health Sys., Albuquerque, 1995-2000; regional clin. coord. Mental Health Svcs., Inc., 1995-97; psychiat. cons.-liaison nurse U. N.Mex. Health Scis. Ctr., 1996—, Medication Monitoring, Pathways, Inc., 2000—. Mem. ANA (cert. in psychiat. and mental health nursing), AACD, Internat. Acad. Behavioral Medicine, Counseling and Psychotherapy, Inc.

BERNER, LEO DE WITTE, JR., retired oceanographer; b. Pasadena, Calif., Feb. 11, 1922; s. Leo De Witte and Maude Alena (Wright) B.; m. Arvetta Jo Hankins, June 28, 1947; children: Jo Anne Berner Thomas, Ernestine Elizabeth Berner Ice. BA, Pomona Coll., 1943; MS, UCLA-Scripps Instn. Oceanography, 1952, PhD, 1957. Fishery biologist U.S. Fish and Wildlife Service, La Jolla, Calif., 1957-58; asst. research biologist Scripps Instn. Oceanography, La Jolla, 1958-60, acting curator marine invertebrates, 1960-61; vis. asst. prof. U. Oreg., Oreg. Inst. Marine Sci., 1961; asso. program dir. NSF, Washington, 1961-65; adminstrv. scientist Tex. A&M U., College Station, 1965-66, asso. prof., 1966-72; asst. dean Tex. A&M U. (Grad. Coll.), 1967-71, assoc. dean, 1971-84, dean, 1984-87, prof. oceanography, 1972-87, prof. emeritus, dean emeritus, 1987—. Vol. George Bush Presdl. Libr. Archives, 1990-2002. Served with USNR, 1943-47. Fellow AAAS; mem. Am. Soc. Limnology and Oceanography, Oceanographic Soc., Assn. Tex. Grad. Schs. (1st v.p. 1981-82, pres. 1982-83), Sigma Xi. Home: 514 Helen Greathouse Cir Midland TX 79707-6116 Personal E-mail: bunsen@cox.net.

BERNER, ROBERT FRANK, managerial statistics educator, administrator; b. Cleve., Nov. 30, 1917; s. Frank Otto and Marie (Gideon) B.; m. Ruth Harriet Levis, Nov. 6, 1943; children: Robert Frank, Mary Elizabeth, John David, Jean Harriet (dec.). BS, U. Buffalo, 1939, MBA, 1948; PhD, U. Chgo., 1961. Tchr. Palmyra (N.Y.) H.S., 1939-41; instr. stats. U. Buffalo, 1946-48, acting chmn. dept., 1948-49; asst. dean U. Buffalo (Evening Coll.), 1949-52, asst. prof. stats., 1952-63; assoc. prof. dept. mgmt. sci. SUNY, Buffalo, 1963-65, prof. mgmt. sci. and ops. analysis, 1965-81, prof. emeritus, 1981—; pres. emeritus Ctr. of SUNY, Buffalo, 1983-85; chmn. MBA program com., 1976-81. Adj. prof. internat. exec. program, 1982-90, acting dean divsn. continuing edn., 1952-55, dean, 1955-76; Fulbright prof. Robert Coll., Istanbul, Turkey, 1968-69, U. Nairobi, Kenya, 1975-76 Chmn. adult edn. com. Cmty. Welfare Coun. Buffalo and Erie County, 1962-64; bd. dirs. Creative Edn. Found., 1969-89, emeritus trustee, 1990; bd. dirs. Ch. Mission Help Western N.Y., 1990-96, sec., 1992, treas., 1993-96, mem. Rep. Coun., Canterbury Woods, western N.Y., 1999-2003. Capt. F.A., 10th Mountain divsn. AUS, 1941-45. Decorated Bronze Star, Silver Star. Mem. AAUP, Assn. Univ. Profs., Assn Univ. Evening Colls. (past pres.), Nat. Univ. Extension Assn., Am. Coun. Edn., Assn. Continuing Higher Edn., Am. Assn. Univ. Adminstrs., Am. Soc. Tng. Dirs. (chpt. sec. 1952-56), Theta Chi, Beta Gamma Sigma, Alpha Sigma Lambda (past nat. pres.) Episcopalian (warden Calvary Ch. 1973-74, 76-77, 86-88, treas. 1996-2000, mem. commn. ministry Diocese Western N.Y. 1971, 95—, chmn. commn. on continuing edn. 1974-76, diocesan coun. 1988-91, diocese planning and vision com. 1989-92). Club: Equality (pres. 1986-87). Home: 735 Renaissance Dr Apt 301 Williamsville NY 14221-8043 E-mail: berner@acsu.buffalo.edu.

BERNER, ROBERT LEE, JR., lawyer; b. Chgo., Dec. 9, 1931; s. Robert Lee and Mary Louise (Kenney) B.; m. Sheila Marie Reynolds, Jan. 12, 1957; children: Mary, Louise, Robert, Sheila, John. AB, U. Notre Dame, 1953; LL.B., Harvard U., 1956. Bar: Ill. 1956, NY 1989. With Petit, Olin, Overmyer & Fazio, Chgo., 1957—63, Baker & McKenzie, Chgo., 1963—; ptnr., 1964—2000; sr. counsel, 2000—. Mem. vis. com. Northwestern U. Law Sch., 1981-85; mem. legal adv. com. N.Y. Stock Exch., 1995-98. Mem. vis. com. U. Chgo. Div. Sch., 1972—, chmn., 2001—; mem. legal aid com. Met. Family Svcs., Chgo., 1972—, chmn.; mem. adv. bd. Cath. Charities, Chgo., 1971—, Loyola U., 1972—; mem. coun. Coll. Arts and Letters, U. Notre Dame, 2001—; trustee Cath. Theol. Union, Chgo., 1999—; bd. dirs. Link Unltd., Chgo., 1969; pres., bd. dirs. World Trade Ctr. of Chgo., 1990—93. Mem. ABA (chmn. bus. law sect. 1987-88), Ill. State Bar Assn., Chgo. Bar Assn., Legal Club Chgo. (pres. 1974-75), Law Club Chgo. (pres. 1991-92). Home: 932 Euclid Ave Winnetka IL 60093-1418 Office: Baker & McKenzie One Prudential Plz 130 E Randolph St Ste 3500 Chicago IL 60601-6342 E-mail: robert.l.berner@bakernet.com.

BERNER HARRIS, CYNTHIA KAY, librarian; b. Concordia, Kans, Aug. 31, 1958; d. William Clifford and Donna Darlene (Brown) B.; m. Dwight Harris, May 1, 1999. AA, Cottey Coll., 1978; BA, U. Kans., 1980; MALS, U. Denver, 1981. System cons. Panhandle Libr. Network, Scottsbluff, Nebr., 1981-82; dir. Winfield (Kans.) Pub. Libr., 1982-84; from Westlink br. mgr. to coord. ext. svcs. Wichita (Kans.) Pub. Libr., 1984-95, coord. adminstrv. svcs., 1995—, dir. of librs., 2000—. Editor Propeller mag., 1995-96 (Jr. League Wichita); editor (newsletter) LWV, Wichita Met., 1993. Pres. PEO Sisterhood (chpt. IM), Wichita, 1989—90; active Jr. League Wichita; project chair STARBASE, 1997—98, dir. cmty. rels., 1998—99; trustee at large Bibliog. Ctr. for Rsch., 2001—; tech. adv. bd. City of Wichita, 2000—; exec. com. Bibliographic Ctr. for Rsch., 2002—. Mem.: ALA, Kans. Libr. Assn. (chair pub. libr. sect. 1988—89, mem. legis. com. 1997—2001, nominating com. 1998—99, mem. legis. com. 2002—), Mountain Plains Libr. Assn. (chair profl. devel. grants com. 1983—84, 1986—87, chair pub. libr. sect. 1988—89, chair intellectual freedom com. 1988—90, sec. 1996—97, mem. nominating com. 1998—2000), Pub. Libr. Assn. (dir. pub. libr. sys. sect. 1995—98, dir. pub. libr. sys. com. 1998—2001). Methodist. Home: 6418 Oneil St Wichita KS 67212-6327 Office: Wichita Pub Libr 223 Main St Wichita KS 67202 E-mail: cberner@wichita.lib.ks.us., cberner@iwichita.com.

BERNFELD, GERALD E. editor, writer, retired nursing educator; b. New Britain, Conn., Nov. 2, 1939; s. Edward Emil Bernfeld and Helene Betty Jenosky; m. Elizabeth Linda Jack, July 11, 1964; children: Edward Gerald, Michael Christopher, Maria Helena Flaherty. AB, Thomas Edison State Coll., Trenton, NJ, 1973; Diploma, 2076th USAR Sch., Wilmington, DE, 1981, Ind. U., Bloomington, IN, 1960—61. LPN, Del., 1981, N.J., 1981, N.Y., 1981. Intelligence rsch. analyst USAF Fgn. Tech. Divsn., Dayton, Ohio, 1965—67; transl. editor, mgr. Frank C. Farnham Co., Philadelphia, Pa., 1968—72; sr. clin. info. scientist Squibb Inst., Princeton, NJ, 1972—75; clin. data mgr. E.R. Squibb and Sons, Princeton, NJ, 1976—79; clin. svcs. mgr. Wyeth-Ayerst Rsch., Radnor, Pa., 1979—84, clin. compliance mgr., 1984—95; rsch. adminstrn. mgr. Wyeth-Ayerst, Radnor, Pa., 1995—97. Chief wardmaster, chief med. instr. USAR. Translator books, editor jour. articles. Master sgt. USAR. Mem.: Drug Info. Assn. (spkr.), Am. Translators Associtaion, Past Chpt. (vice-president), Am. Med. Writers Assn., Past Chpt. (vice-president). Roman Catholic. Achievements include Senior Editor, first computer-aided translation facility. Avocations: military enthusiast, cartoonist, writing, linguistics, travel. Home: 1503 Cliff Road Wynnewood PA 19096-3530

BERNFELD, PETER HARRY WILLIAM, retired biochemist; b. June 1, 1912; arrived in U.S., 1949, naturalized, 1955; s. Isidor and Elsa (Gutfreund) B.; m. Helen Cecily Kroch, Nov. 21, 1940; children: Michele Marion, Mark Raymond. MS, U. Leipzig, 1935; PhD, U. Geneva, Switzerland, 1937. Rsch. fellow U. Geneva, Geneva, 1937—39, chief chemist dept. chemistry, 1939—49, privat docent enzymology, faculty sci., 1947—49; asst. prof. Sch. Medicine Tufts U., 1949—51, assoc. prof. dept. biochemistry and nutrition, 1951—57, biochemist cancer rsch. unit, 1949—57; sr. v.p., dir. rsch. Bio-Rsch. Inst. and Bio-Rsch. Cons., Cambridge, Mass., 1957—88; ret., 1988. Editor, contbg. author: Biogenesis of Natural Compounds, 1963, 2d edit., 1967. Recipient Werner medal, Swiss Chem. Soc., 1948. Mem.: AAAS, Am. Coll. Toxicology, NY Acad. Scis., Am. Assn. Cancer Rsch., Am. Inst. Chemists, Am. Chem. Soc., Soc. Exptl. Biology and Medicine, Am. Soc. Biol. Chemistry and Molecular Biology, Sigma Xi.

BERNHAGEN, LILLIAN FLICKINGER, retired school health consultant; b. Cleve., Oct. 1, 1916; d. Norman Henry and Bertha May (Rogers) Flickinger; m. Ralph John Bernhagen, Sept. 2, 1940; children: Ralph, Janet Elizabeth Darling, Penelope Anne Braat. Student, Ohio Wesleyan U., 1934-37; BS, RN, Ohio State U., 1940, MA, 1958; postgrad., LaVerne Coll., 1972-73. Cert. health edn. specialist; cert. holistic coach Journeys of Wisdom. Asst. dir. Kiwanis Health Camp for Underprivileged Children, Steubenville, Ohio, summer 1940; asst. dir. nurses Jefferson Davis Hosp., Houston, 1940-41; ARC instr. Ohio State U., 1943, 63, elem. edn. lectr., 1970; dir. health services Worthington (Ohio) City Schs., 1951-76; health edn. instr. Ohio State U., 1976-77; spl. cons. venereal disease and sex edn. Ohio Dept. Health, 1976-82; sch. health cons., 1976-98; vice chmn. medicine/edn. com. on sch. and coll. health AMA, 1976-78, chmn., 1978-80. Author: Sex Education: Understanding Growth and Social Development, 1968, What A Miracle You Are-Boys, 1968, 3d rev. edit., 1986, What A Miracle You Are-Girls, 1968, 3d rev. edit., 1986, Toward a Reverence for Life, 1971, Personality, Sexuality and Stereotyping, 1974, (with others) Growth Patterns and Sex Education: A Suggested Curriculum Guide K-12, 1967; contbr. articles to profl. jours., mags. Bd. dirs. Hearing and Speech Ctr. of Columbus and Franklin County, 1954-57, sec., 1957; mem. nat. adv. com. Nat. Ctr. for Health Edn., 1978-82; sec.-tres. Ohio Wesleyan U. Class of 38, 1968-78, 83-88; bd. dirs. V.D. Hotline Columbus and Franklin County, 1974-87, bd. expansion chmn., 1978-85, pres., 1985-86; mem. profl. adv. com. Ptnrs. Home Health Inc., 1991-97; mem. Worthington Hist. Soc., Doll Docent, 1982—; mem King Ave. United Meth. Ch., 1938—, mem. marriage counseling com., 1997-98, mem. choir, 1950—, pres., 1961-63, pastor/parish rels. com., 1985-88, bd. trustees, 1989-92, adminstrv. coun., 1992-98, homosexual study com., 1998-99, edn. commn., 1982-85, nominations and pers., 1992-94; treas. Franklin County Women's Golf Tournament, 1992. Recipient Centennial award Ohio State U., 1970, Outstanding Alumna award Ohio State U. Sch. Nursing, 1964, Disting. Service award Mich. Sch. Nurses Assn., 1972, hon. mention La Sertoma Internat. Woman of Yr., 1972, Alumni award of hon. Ohio Wesleyan U., 1998. Fellow Am. Sch. Health Assn. (v.p. 1974, pres. 1976, governing coun. 1973-88, chmn. health guidance in sex edn. com. 1963-67, 71-77, chmn. sr. adv. coun. 1983-89, Disting. Svc. award 1969, Howe award 1979, cert. of merit, 1985, mem. awards com. 1986-89, mem. hist. com. 1989—, constn. and bylaws com. 1997-99), APHA (chmn. com. on urban health problems 1972); mem. NEA (life, ret.), Sex Edn. and Info. Coun. of U.S., Worthington Edn. Assn. (v.p. 1961-62, Tchr. of Year 1972-73), Ctrl. Ohio Tchrs. Assn. (chmn. sch. health svcs. sect. 1963), Ohio State U. Women's Golf Assn. (chmn. 1973, parliamentarian 1988—), Ohio Wesleyan U. Alumni Assn. (bd. dirs., chmn. alumni recognition com. 1994-95, chmn. bylaws revision com. 1991-96, mem. orgn. com. 1994-95), Columbus Women's Dist. Golf Assn. (treas. 1985, sec. 1987, v.p. 1989, pres. 1990, adv. bd. 1991-98, parliamentarian 1996-98), Chi Omega (pres. Columbus Alumnae chpt. 1947-49, fin. adv. Ohio Wesleyan U. 1964-76, Outstanding Alumna of Yr. State of Ohio 1986), Pi Lambda Theta (citation award 1971, mem. program com. 1986-89, chmn. by laws revision com. 1990-00, parliamentarian), Journeys of Wisdom, Monnett Club, Worthington Women's Club, Sigma Theta Tau, Phi Delta Kappa. Home and Office: 5916 Linworth Rd Worthington OH 43085-3357 E-mail: Lfbern@aol.com.

BERNHARD, ALEXANDER ALFRED, lawyer; b. New Orleans, Sept. 20, 1936; s. John Helenus and Dora (Solosko) B.; m. Martha Ruggles, Nov. 21, 1959 (div.); children: John, Jason, Frederic; m. Joyce Harrington, Dec. 30, 1976 (div.); m. Myra Mayman, Nov. 2, 1986. BS, MIT, 1957; LLB, Harvard U., 1964. Bar: Calif. 1964, Oreg. 1965, Mass. 1966, N.H. 1991. Law clk. to judge U.S. Ct. Appeals (9th cir.), 1964-65; assoc. Johnson, Johnson & Harrang, Eugene, Oreg., 1965-66, Bingham, Dana & Gould, Boston, 1966-71, Hale and Dorr, Boston, 1971-73, jr. ptnr., 1973-75, sr. ptnr., 1975—. Trustee, bd. dirs. Mass. Eye and Ear Infirmary, chmn., 1992-96, chmn. emeritus, 1996—. Lt. (submarines) USNR, 1957-61. Mem. ABA, Boston Bar Assn., Union Boat Club, Longwood Cricket Club. Democrat. Office: Hale and Dorr LLP 60 State St Boston MA 02109-1803 E-mail: alexander.bernhard@haledorr.com.

BERNHARD, HERBERT ASHLEY, lawyer; b. Jersey City, Sept. 24, 1927; s. Richard C. and Amalie (Lobl) B.; m. Nancy Ellen Hirschaut, Aug. 8. 1954; children: Linda, Alison, Jordan, Melissa. Student, Mexico City Coll., 1948; BEE, N.J. Inst. Tech., 1949; MA in Math., Columbia U., 1950; JD cum laude, U. Mich., 1957. Bar: Calif. 1958, U.S. Dist. Ct. (cen. dist.) Calif. 1958, U.S. Dist. Ct. (no., ea. and so. dists.) Calif. 1963, U.S. Ct. Claims 1966, U.S. Dist. Ct. (ea. dist.) Wis. 1982, U.S. Dist. Ct. (ea. and we. dists.) Ark. 1982, U.S. Dist. Ct. Nebr. 1982, U.S. Ct. Internat. Trade 1979, U.S. Tax Ct. 1969, U.S. Ct. Appeals (2d, 3d, 4th, 5th, 7th, 8th, 9th, 10th, 11th and D.C. cirs.) 1969, U.S. Supreme Ct. 1965. Research engr. Curtis-Wright Co., Caldwell, N.J., 1950-52, Boeing Aircraft Co., Cape Canaveral, Fla., 1952-55; assoc. O'Melveny & Myers, Los Angeles, 1957-62; ptnr. Greenberg, Bernhard, et al, Los Angeles, 1962-85, Jeffer, Mangels, Butler & Marmaro, Los Angeles, 1985—. Instr. math. U. Fla., Cape Canaveral, 1952-55; instr. elec. engrng. U. Mich., Ann Arbor, 1955-57; referee L.A. Superior Ct., 1985—, arbitrator, 1988—, judge pro tem, 1988—; judge pro tem L.A. Mcpl. Ct., 1985—, Beverly Hills Mcpl. Ct., 1989—, Malibu Mcpl. Ct., 1994—. Contbr. articles to profl. jours. Chmn. adv. com. Skirball Mus., 1976-98; bd. overseers Hebrew Union Coll., 1976-98. With USAF, 1946-47. Recipient Disting. Achievement award N.J. Inst. Tech., 1998. Mem. Jewish Publ. Soc. (trustee 1986-96). Office: Jeffer Mangels Butler & Marmaro 1900 Ave Of The Stars Fl 7 Los Angeles CA 90067-4308

BERNHARD, JAMES M., JR., engineering executive; m. Dana Bernhard. Grad., La. State U., 1976. Chmn., pres., CEO, founder The Shaw Group, Inc., Baton Rouge, 1987—. Mem. Com. of 100 for State of La.; chmn. Select Coun. for Revenues and Expenditures for La.'s Future; active La. State U. Alumni Assn., Tiger Athletic Found., La. Tech. U. Found., St. George Cath. Ch. and Sch., Ducks Unltd., Krewe of Endymion; supporter United Way, Baton Rouge Area Found., St. George Cath. Ch., St. George Cath. Sch., East La. Tech. U. Named Entrepreneur of Yr. in La., Marketer of Yr., Perpetual Founder of Cath. H.S.; named one of Top Ten CEOs, Greater Baton Rouge Bus. Report; recipient Ernst and Young Entrepreneru of Yr. award, 2001, Prevent Child Abuse La.'s

Corp. Champions for Children award, Ace award, La. State U. Golf Program, Tiger Athletic Found. Augie Cross Meml. Mem. of Yr. award. Avocations: golf, duck hunting, horseback riding, bill fishing, coaching Little League sports. Office: 4171 Essen Ln Baton Rouge LA 70809*

BERNHARD, JEFFREY DAVID, dermatologist, editor, educator; b. Buffalo, Oct. 31, 1951; AB, Harvard Coll., 1973; MD, Harvard Med. Sch., 1978. Diplomate Am. Bd. Dermatology. Knox fellow St. John's Coll. Cambridge U., England, 1973—74; chief resident dermatology Harvard Med. Sch., Boston, 1982; fellow photomedicine Mass. Gen. Hosp., 1983; mem. faculty Med. Sch. U. Mass., Worcester, 1983—, chief dermatology, assoc. prof. Sch. Medicine, 1986—, assoc. dean for admissions Med. Sch., 1989-95, prof. Med. Sch., 1992—. Author: Itch: Mechanisms and Management of Pruritus, 1994; asst. editor Jour. Am. Acad. Dermatology, 1993-98, editor, 1998—; mem. editl. bd. Jour. European Acad. Dermatology and Venereology, Yearbook of Cancer, 1981-88, Yearbook of Dermatology, 1988-97, Internat. Jour. Dermatology, Jour. Geriat. Dermatology, 1993-97. Named J. Graham Smith, Jr., hon. lectr., 2000, Narins Meml. Lectr., 2001, Novy lectr., U. Calif., Davis, 2002, Lorincz lectr., Chgo. Derm. Soc., 2002, Luscombe lectr., Jefferson Med. Coll., 2003; named an hon. mem., Czech. Soc. Dermatol, 2002. Mem.: Coun. Sci. Editors, European Soc. for History of Dermatology, History of Dermatology Soc., Quinsigamond Dermatol. Soc., New Eng. Dermatol. Soc. (pres. 1990—91), Assn. Profs. Dermatology, Sir James Saunders Soc., Royal Soc. Medicine, Am. Dermatol. Assn., European Acad. Dermatology and Venereology, Soc. for Investigative Dermatology (bd. dirs. 1981—83), Am. Acad. Dermatology (Presdl. citation 2000), Czech Soc. Dermatology (hon.), James C. White Club, Aesculapian Club Boston, Sigma Xi, Alpha Omega Alpha, Phi Beta Kappa. Office: U Mass Meml Med Ctr 55 Lake Ave N Worcester MA 01655-0002

BERNHARD, ROBERTA, research psychologist; b. Iwakuni, Japan; d. Harold Magness and Shigeko Hoernlein; m. Urs Bernhard. Cert., U. Fribourg, 1984; MA, San Francisco State U., 2001. Asst mgr. PaineWebber Internat., Geneva, 1986—87; acctg. supr. S.G. Warburg-Soditic S.A., Geneva, 1990, Capital Internat., Geneva, 1991—94; tax/ fin. analyst Franklin/ Templeton, San Mateo, Calif., 1994—96; sr. rsch. assoc. NASA Ames Rsch. Ctr./ SJSU, Moffett Field, Calif., 2001—. Contbr. articles to jour. Grantee Calif. State Scholarship, UC Regents. Mem.: Assn. Aviation Psychology, Am. Psychol. Soc. Office: NASA Ames Rsch Ctr SJSU Moffett Field CA 94035-1000

BERNHARD, WILLIAM FRANCIS, thoracic and cardiovascular surgeon; b. Bklyn., Dec. 11, 1924; s. William and Helen (Conroy) B.; m. June Horne, Sept. 17, 1948; children— Susan, William Francis, Christine, Margaret, Catherine, John, Ann, James, Robert, Peter. BA, Williams Coll., 1946; MD, Syracuse U., 1950; MS (hon.), Harvard U., 1990. Intern Syracuse U. Hosp., 1950-51; asst. resident Children's Hosp. Med. Center, Boston, 1951-52; dir. surg. research lab. Children's Hosp., Boston, 1960—, assoc. surgeon, 1962-66; sr. assoc. in cardiovascular surgery Children's Hosp. Med. Center; asst. resident, Peter Bent Brigham Hosp. 1952-57; attending staff cardiovascular surgery, 1973—; attending staff, 1974—; resident Bellevue Hosp., Columbia div., N.Y.C., 1957-58, Columbia-Presbyn. Hosp., N.Y.C., 1959; attending surgeon thoracic and cardiovascular surgery VA Hosp., West Roxbury, Mass., 1960—; clin. assoc. surgery Harvard Med. Sch., 1962-66, asst. clin. prof. surgery, 1966-68, assoc. clin. prof. surgery, 1968-71, prof. surgery, 1971—; sr. surgeon Brigham and Woman's Hosp., Boston, 1987; prof. surgery emeritus Harvard Med. Sch., 1994. Cons. in cardiothoracic surgery Beth Israel Hosp., Boston, 1986. Ensign USNR, 1944-46. Mem. A.C.S., New Eng. Surg. Soc. (sr.), Am. Heart Assn., Mass. Med. Soc., Am. Assn. Thoracic and Cardiovascular Surgery, Soc. Thoracic Surgery, Soc. Univ. Surgeons, Am. Acad. Pediatrics, New Eng. Cardiovascular Soc., Internat. Soc. Heart Transplantation, Soc. Vascular Surgery, Am. Soc. Artificial Internal Organs, Am. Surg. Assn. Home: 58 Singletary Ln Framingham MA 01702-6161 Office: Children's Hosp 300 Longwood Ave Boston MA 02115-5737

BERNHARDT, ARTHUR DIETER, building industry executive and consultant; b. Dresden, Germany; arrived in U.S., 1966; s. Rudolf B. and Charlotte (Apitz) B. Dipl. Ing., U. Tech., Munich, Fed. Republic Germany, 1965; postgrad., U. So. Calif., 1966-67; M. City Planning, MIT, 1969. Various positions constrn. cos., 1955-68; dir. Program in Industrialization of Housing Sector, MIT, Cambridge, Mass., 1969-76; pres. Program in Industrialization of Housing Sector, Cambridge, 1977-89; chief exec. officer, dir. Program in Industrialization of Housing Sector, Inc., Cambridge and N.Y.C., 1989—2001; pres. DBG Berlin, Germany and N.Y.C., 2001—. Internat. building industry cons., Cambridge, Mass., and N.Y.C., 1973—; asst. prof. MIT, 1970-76 Author books; contbr. articles to profl. jours. Mem. exec. com. Mass. Gov.'s Adv. Com. on Manufactured Housing, 1974-75; NRC del. 8th Gen. Assembly Internat. Council Bldg. Research, 1974. Fed. Republic Germany fellow, 1965, 66, 67, 68; MIT fellow, 1968, 69; MIT grantee, 1970; Fed. Republic Germany grantee, 1965; Alfred P. Sloan Found. grantee, 1970; Dept. Commerce grantee, 1972; HUD grantee, 1972, 74. Mem. Internat. Coun. Bldg. Rsch., Am. Acad. Polit. and Social Sci., Am. Planning Assn., Am. Judicature Soc. (assoc.)

BERNHARDT, BARBARA IZABELA, language educator, writer; arrived in U.S., 1989; d. Jerzy Bernhardt and Teresa Halina Balde; children: Aleksandra Gajer, Veronika Gajer. MA, Wroclaw U., Poland, 1988, SUNY Stony Brook, 1992. Adj. prof. Am. U., Washington, 1999—, Montgomery Coll., Rockville, Md., 2000—; lang. coach Washington Opera, 2002—; lectr. consular divsn. Polish Embassy, Washington, 2002—. Lit. dir, New Polish Theater of Metropolitan area, Va., 1999—; cons. rsch., lit. critic publications, Washington, 2000—03, Poland, 2000—03; freelance lang. translator, Washington, 2002—. Contbr. to literary jours.; prodr.: (video) Polish Lang. ednl. video/Foreign Svc. Inst., 2003. Grantee scholarship doctoral studies, SUNY Stonybrook, 1990—92. Avocations: painting, opera, tennis, Buddhism. Home: 7201 14th Ave Takoma Park MD 20912 Office: Language/Foreign Studies Dept The American University 4400 Massachussetts Ave NW Washington DC 20016-820

BERNHARDT, CAROL ANN, musician, educator; b. Shelby, Ohio, Nov. 25, 1942; d. Wayne Woodrow and Iscah Irene (Carnes) Hunter; m. Donald Raymond Bernhardt, June 18, 1961 (dec. Oct. 1996); children: Melanie Sue, Anne Olaloquee. Student, Oberlin Coll., 1960-61; BA in Music, Ashland U., 1996. Cert. oboe tchr., Ohio. Prin. oboe Mansfield (Ohio) Symphony, 1975-98, Ashland (Ohio) Symphony, 1980—2001, Tuscarawas Philharm., Dover, Ohio, 1984—; pvt. oboe and piano tchr. Mansfield, 1975—. Oboe instr., jr. high coord. Double Reed Camp, Holland, Mich., 1981-96. Coord. ensemble in nursing home programs Mansfield Symphony, 1985-98. Mem.: Ohio Music Tchrs. Assn. (sec.-treas. North Ctrl. dist. 1997—2001, vice chmn. North Ctrl. dist. 2001—03, sec. North Ctrl. Dist. 2003—), Am. Fedn. Musicians, Internat. Double Reed Soc., Bernhardt Music Club (counselor), Ashland Musical Club. Congregationalist. Avocations: sewing, knitting, chamber music. Home: 470 Marion Ave Mansfield OH 44903-2039 E-mail: Caroboe@aol.com.

BERNHARDT, JAY MICHAEL, health communications researcher, educator; b. Princeton, NJ, Mar. 1, 1969; s. Lewis Jules and Rochelle Bernhardt; m. Sheryl Lisa Ball; children: Lila, Nathan. BA, Rutgers U., 1992; MPH, U. Medicine and Dentistry N.J., 1994; PhD, U. N.C., 1999. Asst. prof. U. Ga. Sch. Health and Human Performance, Athens, 1999—2001, Emory U. Rollins Sch. Pub. Health, Atlanta, 2001—. Founder, pres. Pub. Health Student Caucus, 1994—97; dir. Health Comm. Tech. Lab., Atlanta, 2002—. Asst. editor: Health Edn. Rsch. Mem.: APHA (exec. bd. mem. 2002—, Jay S. Drotman Meml. award 1998, Early Career award pub. health edn. and health promotion sect. 2000), Ga. Pub. Health Assn. (exec. bd. mem. 2001—). Avocations: writing, cooking, personal computing. Office: Emory Univ Sch Pub Health 1518 Clifton Rd NE #524 Atlanta GA 30322 Business E-Mail: mail@jaybernhardt.com.

BERNHARDT, MARCIA BRENDA, mental health counselor; b. Jersey, N.J., Aug. 22, 1938; d. Jerome and Mitzie (Cohen) B. BA, Fairleigh Dickinson U., 1960; MA, Columbia U., 1960-63, postgrad., 1968-70, Hunter Coll., 1973-74. Nat. cert. counselor. Rsch. asst. Tchrs. Coll., Columbia U., N.Y.C., 1963-64; counselor JOIN, N.Y.C., 1965-66; project assoc. Bd. Higher Edn. N.Y., N.Y.C., 1966-68, Tchrs. Coll, Columbia U., N.Y.C., 1968-70; counselor Nassau Community Coll., Garden City, N.Y., 1970-72; rsch. scientist Div. for Youth, N.Y.C., 1972-73; rsch. assoc. Family Svc. Assn., N.Y.C., 1974-76; counselor Div. Blind Svcs., West Palm Beach, Fla., 1984-96. Sec., chairperson adv. bd. com. Lighthouse for the Blind, West Palm Beach, 1984-90. Mem. AAUW, Am. Mental Health Counselors Assn., Fla. Mental Health Counselors Assn., Mental Health Counselor Assn. Greater Palm Beach County, Am. Soc. for Handicapped Children in Israel, Hadassah. Democrat. Jewish. Avocations: theater, ballet, opera, art, swimming. Home: 40 Chatham B West Palm Beach FL 33417-1807 E-mail: mbbernhardt@hotmail.com.

BERNHARDT, RICHARD C. secondary school educator, band director; b. Evansville, Ind., June 5, 1944; s. Henry Carl and Mary Katherine Bernhardt; m. Mary Jane Mengon, Dec. 26, 1971; 1 child, Richard Henry. BME, U. Evansville, 1971; MA, Ind. State U., Terre Haute, 1974. Lic. tchr. Ind. Asst. band dir. Petersburg (Ind.) H.S.; h.s. band dir. Pike Ctrl. H.S., Petersburg. Pres. Pike County Tchrs. Assn., Petersburg, 1980—81. Vol. firefighter Elberfeld (Ind.) Fire Dept., 1980—; elder 1st Presbyn. Ch., Evansville, Ind. Airman 1st class USAF, 1966—70. Mem.: NEA, VFW, Ind. Music Educators Assn., Classroom Tchrs. Assn., Inst. State Tchrs. Assn., Ind. Band Masters Assn., Am. Legion. Republican. Avocations: boating, golf. Home: PO Box 116 Elberfeld IN 47613

BERNHARDT, ROBERT, music director, conductor; m. Jennifer Bernhardt; children: Alexander, Charlotte. Grad. summa cum laude, Union Coll.; MMus with honors, U. So. Calif. Assoc. condr. Louisville Orch., 1981-87; music dir. Amarillo Symphony, 1985-88; music dir., condr. Tucson Symphony Orch., 1988—; prin. condr. Ky. Opera; music dir. Chattanooga Symphony & Opera, 1993—; prin. condr., art dir. Rochester (N.Y.) Philharm. Guest condr. Pitts. Symphony, Phoenix Symphony, Chattanooga Symphony, Seattle Symphony, Rochester Philharm., L.A. Chamber Orch., Denver Chamber Orch., Jacksonville Symphony, Nashville Opera, Birmingham Civic Opera, Chattanooga Opera, Louisville Ballet, Lone Star Ballet, others; recs. include for Vanguard, First Edit. Records. Mem. Phi Beta Kappa. Office: Chattanooga Symphony & Opera Tivoli Theatre 630 Chestnut St Chattanooga TN 37402-1707

BERNHARDT-KABISCH, ERNEST KARL-HEINZ, English and comparative literature educator; b. Chemnitz, Germany, Nov. 15, 1934; came to U.S., 1955; s. Karl-Heinz and Brunhild Anna Bertha (Kabisch) Bernhardt; m. Eva Carolyn Dessau, Sept. 1, 1956; 1 child, Ethan Karl. BA, U. Calif., Berkeley, 1957, MA, 1959, PhD, 1962. Instr. Ind. U., Bloomington, 1962-64, asst. prof., 1964-68, assoc. prof., 1968-80, prof., 1980-99, prof. emeritus, 1999—. Dir. Living Learning Ctr., Ind. U., Bloomington, 1977-90, resident dir. Overseas Study Program, Hamburg, Germany, 1990-91, 94-95; translator. Author: Robert Southey, 1977, Begegnungen mit Erda, 1991; co-editor: Yearbook of Comparative and General Literature, 1980-90; contbr. articles and revs. to profl. jours.; translator (German) fiction radio plays, TV documentaries, essays. Mem. AAUP, Am. Comparative Lit. Assn., Modern Lang. Assn., Oesterreichischer Alpenverein, N.Am. Soc. for Study of Romanticism. Democrat. Avocations: mountain climbing, skiing, gardening, music, poetry. Home: 616 S Jordan Ave Bloomington IN 47401-5122 Office: Dept English Ind Univ Bloomington IN 47405 E-mail: bernhard@indiana.edu.

BERNHEIMER, ALAN WEYL, microbiologist; b. Phila., Dec. 9, 1913; s. Eugene Seligman and Helen (Weyl) B.; m. Harriet Poller, MAr. 29, 1942; 1 child, Alan Jr. BS, Temple U., 1935, MA, 1937; PhD, U. Pa., 1942. Biology asst. Temple U., Phila., 1935-37; instr. bacteriology Pa. State Coll. Optometry, Phila., 1937-39, N.Y. U. Coll. Medicine, N.Y.C., 1941-45, asst. prof., 1945-52; assoc. prof. N.Y. U. Sch. Medicine, N.Y.C., 1952-58, prof., 1958-84, chmn. basic sci., 1969-74, prof. emeritus, 1984—. Cons. in field; trustee Cold Spring Harbor Lab., 1963-68; mem. micro tng. com. NIH, 1960-62. Author: Reflectographs, 1965, Perspectives in Toxinology, 1977; editor: Mechanisms in Bacterial Toxinology, 1976. Fellow AAAS, N.Y. Acad. Sci.; mem. Am. Soc. Microbiology, Am. Acad. Microbiology, Am. Microscopical Soc., Mineralogical Soc. Am., Am. Assn. Immunologists. Avocations: photography, sculpture, cartoons, mineralogy, lepidoptera. Home: 51 5th Ave New York NY 10003-4320 Office: NYU Med Sch 550 1st Ave New York NY 10016-6402

BERNHEIMER, MARTIN, music critic; b. Munich, Sept. 28, 1936; came to U.S., 1940, naturalized, 1946; s. Paul Ernst and Louise (Nassauer) B.; m. Lucinda Pearson, Sept. 30, 1961 (div. Feb. 1989); children: Mark Richard, Nora Nicoll, Marina and Erika (twins); m. Linda Winer, Sept. 27, 1992. MusB with honors, Brown U., 1958; student, Munich Conservatory, 1958-59; MA in Musicology, NYU, 1961. Free-lance music critic, 1958—; contbg. critic N.Y. Herald Tribune, 1959-62; mem. music faculty NYU, 1959-62; contbg. editor Mus. Courier, 1961-64; temporary music critic N.Y. Post, 1961-65; N.Y. corr. Brit. Publ. Opera, 1962—65; L.A. corr., 1965—; corr. West Coast Brit. Opera Mag., 1965—; asst. to music editor Saturday Rev., 1962-65; mng. editor Philharmonic Hall Program, N.Y.C., 1962-65; music editor, chief critic L.A. Times, 1965-96; N.Y. corr. Brit. Publ. Opera, 1997—. Mem. faculty U. So. Calif., 1966-71, music faculty UCLA, 1969-75, Calif. Inst. Arts, 1975-82, Calif. State U., Northridge, 1978-81, Rockefeller Program for Tng. of Music Critics; mem. Pulitzer Prize Music Jury, 1984, 86, 90; L.A. corr. for Swiss publ. Opernwelt, 1984—. Contbg. author New Groves Dictionary; contbr. liner notes for recordings; appearances on radio and TV, Met. Opera Broadcasts; contbr. articles to Vanity Fair, Music Quar., The Critic, Opera News, Mus. Am., Fin. Times, London, Sidewalk N.Y. (internet), others; contributing feature writer Fin. Times, N.Y. Newsday; lectr., moderator, essayist on Met. Opera Broadcast. Recipient Deems Taylor award ASCAP, 1974, 78, Headliners award, 1979, Pulitzer Prize for disting. criticism, 1981, Lifetime Achievement award Svc. to Music, Calif. Assn. Profl. Music Tchrs., 1990. Mem. Nat. Opera Inst. (ind. selection com. 1980), Pi Kappa Lambda (hon.).

BERNHOFT, FRANKLIN OTTO, psychotherapist, psychologist; b. Fargo, N.D., Aug. 12, 1944; s. Otto and Irene Bernhoft; m. Dorothy Ann Larsen, Aug. 11, 1973; children: Kimberley, Brady, Heather. BA in English, N.D. State U., 1966; MA in Counseling Psychology, U. N.D., 1970; MA in English, Calif. State U., 1978; PhD in Counseling Psychology, Brigham Young U., 1985. Cert. therapist, hypnotherapist, counselor, secondary tchr.; lic. psychologist, marriage, family and child counselor, ednl. psychologist. Instr. Chapman Coll., Brigham Young U., U. N.D., U.S. I.U.; staff trainer Sacramento (Calif.) County Office Edn., 1977-82; therapist Lodi and Stockton, Calif., 1985—; therapist, family fitness trainer, master trainer systematic helping skills, devel. capable people trainer U. Pacific Behavioral Medicine Clinic. Co-founder prevention/intervention project, Sacto County, 1977; presenter in field. Contbr. articles to profl. jours. Lt. U.S. Army, 1967-69. H.H. Kirk R. Askanase scholar; cert. achievement Ft. Carson; decorated Bronze star, combat med. badge Nat. Def. Svc. Vietnam; named Support Person of Yr. Phi Delta Kappa, 2000-2001. Mem. ACA, Children with Attention Deficit Disorders, Nat. Assn. Sch. Psychologists, Assn. Mormon Counselors and Psychotherapists, Calif. Assn. Marriage and Family Therapists, Calif. Psychol. Assn., Sacramento Area Sch. Psychologists Assn., Calif. Continuation Edn. Assn. (past treas.), Calif. Assn. Lic. Edn. Psychologists, Mensa, Eye Movement Desensitization and Reprocessing Internat. Assn., Calif. Assn. Psychologists, Am. Assn. Christian Counselors, Internat. Critical Incident Stress Found. Office: Creative Therapy 2000 W Kettleman Ln Ste 103 Lodi CA 95242-4334

BERNHOLC, JERZY, physicist, educator; b. Szczecin, Poland, Feb. 12, 1952, came to U.S., 1978; s. David and Irene Bernholc; m. Alissa Seligman, Aug. 1, 1982; children: Stuart, Judith. BS in Physics and Math., U. Lund, Sweden, 1973, PhD in Physics, 1977. Postdoctoral IBM Watson Rsch. Ctr., Yorktown Heights, N.Y., 1978-80; sr. physicist Exxon Corp. Rsch. Labs., Clinton, N.J., 1980-86; assoc. prof. physics N.C. State U., Raleigh, 1986-90, prof., 1990-2000, Drexel prof., 2000—; sci. advisor comm. Ctr. for Nanophase Materials Scis. Oak Ridge Nat. Lab., 2002—. Chmn. Electronic Structure Algorithms, Raleigh, 1992, organizing com. ann. workshops, 1992—; co-chmn. Grid, Wavelet and Multigrid Methods, Lyon, France, 1996, NATO Workshop Multiscale Methods in Chemistry, Eilat, Israel, 2000; mem. ONR Panel on Fgn. Field Offices, 1992; joint peer rev. bd. NSF Supercomputing Ctrs., 1988—91; adv. coun. N.C. Supercomputing Ctr., Research Triangle Park, NC, 1990—92, Research Triangle Park, 1998—; chair N.C. Com. on Partnership for Advanced Computational Infrastructure, 1996—99; panel high performance computing NSF, Washington, 1992; exec. com. Nat. Computational Sci. Alliance, Urbana, Ill., 1998—2002, leader nanomaterials/electronic structure team, 1998—2002; com. of visitors NSF Supercomputing Ctrs. and Computational Infrastructure Program, 1999; program com. Internat. Conf. on Computational Physics, San Diego, 2003; chair Prog. Com. Divsn. Computational Physics of APS, 2002; mem. southeastern sect. prog. com. Prog. Com. Divsn. Comparative Physics of APS, 2003; sci. adv. com. Ctr. for Nanotechnology Materials Scis. Oak Ridge Nat. Lab., 2002—, disting. vis. scientist, 2002—; strategic planning workshop Dept. of Energy, 2003; Grand Challenges in Nanomaterials workshop NSF, 2003. Specialist editor materials sci. Computer Physics Comm., 1998-2002. Panel mem. AIChE, 2002. Recipient Outstanding Innovation award IBM Rsch. Divsn., Yorktown Heights, N.Y., 1979, Alumni Oustanding rsch. award N.C. State U., Raleigh, 1992, Creativity Ext. award NSF, Washington, 1996, finalist sci. category Computerworld Smithsonian, Washington, 1997. Fellow: Am. Phys. Soc. (divsn. computational physics vice chair 2001, chmn.-elect 2002, chmn. fellowship com. 2002, chmn. 2003); mem.: Materials Rsch. Soc., Sigma Xi. Home: 2309 Byrd St Raleigh NC 27608-1411 Office: NC State U Dept Physics PO Box 8202 Raleigh NC 27695-8202 E-mail: bernholc@ncsu.edu.

BERNI, ROSEMARIAN RAUCH, rehabilitation and oncology nurse; b. Portland, Oreg., Sept. 30, 1925; d. George Laverne and Mabel (Rose) Rauch; m. Albert Hawthorne Berni, Oct. 25, 1947; children: George, Michael, William, Albert. Student, Oreg. State Coll., 1943-44; BS in Nursing, Univ. Oreg., 1947; M in Nursing, U. Wash., 1973. RN Wash., Oreg. Clin. nursing instr. Univ. Oreg. Sch. of Nursing, Portland; spl. duty nurse Doernbecher Hosp., Portland, Oreg., 1948; night supr. Halcyon Psychiat. Hosp., Seattle, Wash., 1962; staff nurse psychiat. nursing unit U. Wash. Hosp., Seattle, 1963, head nurse phys. medicine and rehab. nursing unit, 1964-66, asst. dir. nursing, 1966-67; dir. rehab. med. intermittent catheter team U. Hosp. and Harborview Med. Ctr., Seattle, 1973-82; rehab. clin. nurse specialist U. Wash. Med. Ctr., Seattle, 1973—. Clin. instr. U. Wash. Sch. Nursing, 1967-76, instr. dept. rehab. medicine, 1967-73; dir. nursing svc. Rehab. Nursing Unit, Dept. Rehab. Medicine, U. Wash., Seattle, 1967—; asst. prof. dept. rehab. medicine, U. Wash., 1973-78, assoc. prof. emeritus, 1981, mem. grad. sch. faculty, 1975—; dir. Rehab. Nursing Pathways in Depth, 1967—; chmn. rehab. nursing ctr., ARN 1981; presenter World Rehab. Fund, Cyprus; active on numerous hosp. and univ. coms., presenter many seminars and workshops in Wash. and nationwide. Author: (with Fordyce, Wilbert E.) Behavior Modification and the Nursing Process, 1973, 2nd edit., 1977; contbr. articles to profl. jours. and chpts. to books; producer films, audio and video presentations and course curricula. Vol. RN, Whidbey Island, Wash., 1981-2000; tutor pub. schs. Recipient Svc. award, Wash. State Health Facilities Assn., 1974, Wash. State Heart Assn., 1976, Leadership award, Rehab. Nursing Inst., 1981. Mem. ANA (coun. clin. nurse specialists), Nat. League of Nursing, Assn. of Rehab. Nurses (founding pres. Wash. chpt., nat. pres. 1980, Leadership award 1980), Assn. Women in Sci., N.Y. Acad. Sci., N.W. Neurological Rehab., Nat. Stroke Assn., Wash. State Head Injury Found., Univ. Wash. Alumni Assn., Sigma Theta Tau, Alpha Lambda Delta, Alpha Tau Delta. Home: PO Box 868 Freeland WA 98249-0868 Office: Stroke Support Group Whidbey Gen Hosp Dept Rehab Medicine Seattle WA 98195-0001

BERNICK, ALAN E. lawyer, accountant; b. St. Paul, June 20, 1958; s. Herbert Jay and Marcia Bernick; m. Elisa Kim Neff, Aug. 24, 1986; children: Joshua Norton, Daniel Noah, Matthew David. BA, U. Minn., 1980, JD, 1983. Bar: Minn. 1983, U.S. Dist. Ct. Minn. 1983, U.S. Tax Ct. 1985; CPA, Minn. Ptnr. Oppenheimer Wolff & Donnelly LLP, St. Paul, 1983-2000; v.p., gen. counsel, corp. sec. Andersen Corp., Bayport, Minn., 2000—. Mem. exec. bd. Indianhead coun. Boy Scouts Am., 1993-2002. Mem. AICPA, Minn. State Bar Assn. (chair tax sect. 1995-97), Minn. Soc. CPAs (chair 1995-96). Avocations: family, outdoor activities, golf. Home: 621 Hampshire Dr Mendota Heights MN 55120-1935 Office: Andersen Corp 100 4th Ave N Bayport MN 55003-1096

BERNICK, CAROL LAVIN, corporate executive; m. Howard Bernick; three children. BA, Tulane U., 1974. Mem. mktg. staff Alberto-Culver Co., Melrose Park, Ill., 1974-79, dir. new products, 1979-81, dir. new bus. devel. group, 1981-84, v.p., 1984-88; co-dir., 1984; group v.p. Alberto-Culver Co., Melrose Park, Ill., 1988-90, exec. v.p. worldwide mktg., 1990-92, exec. v.p., 1992—94; pres. Alberto-Culver USA, Melrose Park, Ill., 1994—98; vice chmn., pres. N.Am. Alberto-Culver Co., Melrose Park, 1998—2002; pres. Alberto Culver Consumer Products Worldwide, Melrose Park, 2002—. Founder Friends of Prentice; mem. women's bd. Resurrection Home Health Svcs., Boys and Girls Clubs of Chgo.; regent Lincoln Acad. Ill.; mem. exec. com. of adv. bd. Kellogg Sch., Northwestern U.; bd. dirs. Northwestern Meml. Healthcare. Recipient Leadership in Bus. award YWCA Met. Chgo., 1992, award for philanthropy Harvard Club of Chgo. Mem. World Pres. Orgn., Econ. Club Chgo., Exec. Club Chgo., Com. 200 Chgo. Network. Office: Alberto-Culver Co 2525 Armitage Ave Melrose Park IL 60160-1163

BERNICK, DAVID M. lawyer; b. San Francisco, June 16, 1954; s. Herman Charles and Joan (Schutz) B.; m. Christine A. Clougherty, Aug. 13, 1983; 1 child, Evan Daniel. BA, U. Chgo., 1974, JD, 1978; MA, Yale U., 1975. Bar: Ill. 1978. Ptnr. Kirkland & Ellis, Chgo., 1984—. Mem. Univ. Club, Mid-Am. Club, Phi Beta Kappa. Office: Kirkland & Ellis 200 E Randolph St Fl 54 Chicago IL 60601-6636

BERNIER, GEORGE MATTHEW, JR., physician, medical educator, medical school dean; b. Portland, Maine, June 29, 1934; s. George Matthew and Lillian Theresa (Wallace) B.; m. Mary Jane Marron, June 29, 1963; children: George Matthew, III, Elizabeth Wallace. AB, Boston Coll., 1956; MD, Harvard U., 1960. Intern Univ. Hosps., Cleve., 1960-61, resident, 1961-62, 65-66, U. Fla. Hosps., Gainesville, 1964-65; fellow in biochemistry U. Fla., 1962-64; instr. Case Western Res. U., Cleve., 1966-67, asst. prof. medicine, 1967-72, assoc. prof., 1972-75, prof., 1975-78; dir. div. med. oncology Univ. Hosps., Cleve., 1974-78; prof., chmn. dept. medicine Dartmouth Med. Sch., Hanover, N.H., 1978-86, Joseph M. Huber prof. medicine, 1982-86; dean, prof. medicine U. Pitts. Sch. Medicine, U. Pitts., 1987-95; dean medicine, v.p. acad. affairs U. Tex. Med. Br., Galveston, 1995-99, v.p. edn., 1999—. Contbr. articles to profl. jours. Trustee Jackson Labs., Bar Harbor, Maine, 1973— . Served to lt. col. M.C. U.S. Army, 1967-70. Leukemia Soc. Am. scholar, 1970-75 Fellow A.C.P.; mem. Am. Soc. Hematology, Am. Soc. Clin. Oncology, Am. Soc. Clin. Investigation, Am. Assn. Immunologists., Assn. Am. Physicians, Am. Clin. and Climatological Assn., Nat Bd. Med. Examiners (mem.-at-large 2000—, mem. presdl. commn. policy for complementary and alter. medicine 2000-2002). Office: U Tex Med Br 301 University Blvd Galveston TX 77555-5302

BERNIERI, FRANK JOHN, social psychology educator; b. Bklyn., May 2, 1961; s. Gene J. and Rose (Autunnale) B.; divorced; 1 child, Jennifer. BA, U. Rochester, 1983; PhD, Harvard U., 1988. Asst. prof. social psychology Oreg. State U., Corvallis, 1988—93, assoc. prof., 1993—94, 2003—, chmn. psychology dept., 2003—; assoc. prof. U. Toledo, 1994—2003. Author: (with others) Coordinated Movement in Human Interaction, 1991, Interpersonal Sensitivity, 2001; mem. editorial bd. Jour. Nonverbal Behavior, 1990—; contbr. articles to profl. jours. Fellow Harvard U., 1987; grantee NIH, 1988, Oreg. State U. Coll. Liberal Arts, 1990; NSF Young Investigator awardee, 1992. Mem. AAAS, APA, Am. Psychol. Soc., Soc. for Personality and Social Psychology, Soc. for Exptl. Social Psychology. Democrat. Office: Oreg State Univ Dept Psychology Corvallis OR 97331

BERNING, LARRY D. lawyer; b. Kendallville, Ind., Oct. 21, 1940; s. Melvin and Dolores (Sorge) B.; m. Phyllis Low Cameron, Oct. 24, 1987; children: Emily Lyn, Scott Michael. AB, Ind. U., 1963, JD, 1968. Bar: Ill. 1968, Ind. 1968. Assoc. Sidley Austin Brown & Wood, Chgo., 1968-74, ptnr., 1974—. Trustee Old People's Home of Chgo., 1999—2001; pres. William H. Miner Found. With U.S. Army, 1963—65. Mem. ABA, Ill. Bar Assn., Chgo. Bar Assn., Ind. Bar Assn., Am. Coll. Trust and Estate Counsel, Chgo. Estate Planning Coun., Mid-Day Cub. Law Club, Legal Club, Skokie Country Club. Office: Sidley Austin Brown & Wood Apt 605 425 W Surf St Chicago IL 60657-6139 E-mail: lberning@sidley.com.

BERNING, RANDALL KARL, lawyer, consultant, educator, publisher; b. Highland Park, Ill., Apr. 13, 1950; s. Karl Ives and Alpha (Mikkelsen) B.; m. Carol Ann Bublitz, Oct. 22, 1983. BA, U. Ill., 1973; JD, Golden Gate U., 1977; LLM in Health Law, Loyola U., Chgo., 1989. Bar: Ill. 1977, D.C. 1980. Asst. atty. gen. State of Ill., Chgo., 1977-79, contractural hearing officer Ill. sec. of state, 1981-83; pvt. practice law Chgo., 1979—, Washington, 1986—; pvt. practice cons. Burlingame, Calif., 1979—, Naples, Fla., 1997—. Cons. to coun. on dental practice ADA, Chgo., 1987—; clin. asst. prof., Dept. Oral Health Care Delivery, U. Md., Balt., 1992—; mem. nat. adv. coun. for nursing rsch., dept. health and human svcs., Nat. Inst. Health, 1994-98; dir. practice adminstrn., adj. prof. dental jurisprudence U. Ill. at Chgo. Coll. of Dentistry, 1993-2000; clin. instr., dept. pub. health and hygiene U. Calif. at San Francisco Sch. of Dentistry,

1992—; also affiliated with Gardner, Carton & Douglas health law dept. and Arthur Andersen LLP, higher edn. cons. practice, 1998-2001. Editl. bd. Jour. Law and Ethics in Dentistry, 1987-92; pub. The Expert Series for Dentists, The Expert Series for Physicians; originator, sponsor Ann. Dentistry and the Law Conf., 1988-94. Active Rep. Com.; vol. various civic activities; bd. deacons United Ch. of Christ, 1990-93, 2002—; mem. Boy Scouts Am. Friends of Scouting Campaign, 2003. Mem. ABA, Ill. Bar Assn., D.C. Bar Assn., Am. Health Lawyers Assn., Am. Dental Edn. Assn., Nat. Spkrs. Assn. Home: 5850 Cloudstone Ct Naples FL 34119-4606 Office: 3400 Tamiami Trl N Ste 201 Naples FL 34103-3717 also: Ste 200 312 W Randolph St Chicago IL 60606-1758 also: Ste 700 1300 Pennsylvania Ave NW Washington DC 20004 also: Ste 200 1818 Gilbreth Rd Burlingame CA 94010 E-mail: rkberning@berning-affiliates.com.

BERNING, ROBERT WILLIAM, librarian; b. Carroll, Iowa, Dec. 2, 1949; s. Norbert John and Marjorie Lavine (Miller) B. BSE, N.W. Mo. State U., 1972; MLS, Emporia State U., 1974. Cert. pub. libr., Iowa. Sch. libr. Mount Ayr (Iowa) Cmty. Schs., 1974-76, Wall Lake (Iowa) Cmty. Schs., 1977-79, West Point (Nebr.) Pub. Schs., 1979-81; dir. Dubuque County Libr., Farley, Iowa, 1981-82; sch. libr. HLV Cmty. Schs., Victor, Iowa, 1982-84; dir. Carlisle (Iowa) Pub. Libr., 1985—. Mem. adv. bd. State Libr. Iowa, Des Moines, 1987, 89; mem. adv. com. Ctrl. Iowa Regional Libr., Clive, 1992-94, 98—. Libr. rep. Lanning Bequest com. City of Carlisle, 1995-97, Mng. Info. for Rural Am. (MIRA), 1998; mem. com., task force Iowans Can't Wait (Enrich Iowa), State Libr. Iowa, Des Moines, 1995-96; mem. Mayor's Select Com. on Property Taxes, Des. Moines, 1998-99. Mem. ALA, KC, Iowa Libr. Assn. (govtl. affairs com. 1988-91), Iowa Small Libr. Assn. (sec. 1985-87), Carlisle Lion's Club, Carlisle C. of C. (libr. rep. 1990—), Alpha Phi Omega (life). Roman Catholic. Avocations: collecting antiques, travel, gardening. Office: Carlisle Pub Libr 135 School St PO Box S Carlisle IA 50047

BERNS, KENNETH IRA, physician; b. Cleve., June 14, 1938; s. Charles and Delnet (Cohn) Berns; m. Laura Louise Lawless, June 26, 1964; children: Jonathan Charles, Deborah Louise. Student, Harvard U., 1956—59; AB, Johns Hopkins U., 1960, PhD, 1964, MD, 1966. Intern Johns Hopkins Hosp., 1966—67; asst. prof. microbiology Johns Hopkins U. Sch. Medicine, 1970—74, asst. prof. pediat. 1970—76, asso. prof. microbiology, 1974—76; dir. Johns Hopkins U. Sch. Medicine (Year I program), 1973—76; prof., chmn. dept. immunology and med. microbiology, prof. pediat. U. Fla. Coll. Medicine, Gainesville, 1976—84; R.A. Rees Pritchett prof., chmn. dept. microbiology Cornell U. Med. Coll., 1984—97; dean U. Fla. Coll. Medicine, 1997—2002, v.p. health affairs, 2000—02; pres. and COO Mt. Sinai Med. Ctr., N.Y.C., 2002—. Howard Hughes med. investigator, 1970—75; mem. microbiology test com. Nat. Bd. Med. Examiners, 1979—82, chmn., 1983—86, mem. exec. bd., 1986—95; mem. Recombinant DNA adv. com. NIH, 1980—83, chmn., 1982—83; mem. genetic biology panel NSF, 1981—84; Fogarty sr. internat. fellow virology dept. Weizmann Inst. Sci., Rehovot, Israel, 1982—83; ad hoc mem. Bd. Sci. Counselors Nat. Inst. Allergy and Infectious Diseases, 0198—1982, permanetn mem., 1992—96; del. U.S.-Japan Coop. Program on Recombinant DNA, 1981; mem. Internat. Com. Taxonomy of Viruses, 1981—98; mem. virology study sect. NIH, 1985—89; mem. virology and microbiology adv. com. Am. Cancer Soc., 1985—89, mem. liaison com. on med. edn., 1989—92; mem. composite com. U.S. Med. Licensing Exam., 1995—98; nat. adv. coun. Nat. Ctr. Rsch. Resources, 1999—. Served with USPHS, 1967—70. Recipient faculty rsch. award, Am. Cancer Soc., 1975—76; fellow Shell Oil, 1963—64; grantee NIH, 1970—76, 1980—, NSF, 1973—75, 1979—80, Am. Cancer Soc., 1970—72. Mem.: NAS, AAAS, Inst. Medicine NAS, Internat. Union Microbiol. Socs. (v.p. 1990—94), Soc. Pediatric Rsch., Soc. Gen. Microbiology, Am. Soc. Virology (pres. 1988—89), Assn. Med. Sch. Microbiology Chairmen (counselor 1980—83, chmn. com. pub. policy 1979, pres. 1985), Am. Soc. Microbiology, Am. Soc. Biol. Chemists, Am. Acad. Microbiology (bd. pub. and sci. affairs, chmn. 1990—96, pres. 1996—97), Alpha Omega Alpha, Sigma Xi, Phi Beta Kappa. Office: Univ Fla Miller Health Ctr PO Box 100014 Gainesville FL 32610-0014

BERNS, PHILIP ALLAN, lawyer; b. N.Y.C., Mar. 18, 1933; s. Milton Benjamin and Rose (Aberman) Bernstein; m. Jane Klaw, June 7, 1959; children: David, Peter, Jay. BS in Marine Transp., N.Y. State Maritime Coll., 1955; LLB, Bklyn. Law Sch., 1960. Bar: N.Y. 1960, Calif. 1990, U.S. Ct. Appeals (2d cir.) 1962, U.S. Ct. Appeals (9th cir.) 1982. Admiralty atty. admiralty sect. U.S. Dept. Justice, N.Y.C., 1960-71, asst. atty. in charge admiralty sect., 1971-77, atty. in charge torts br. San Francisco, 1977—, rep. to Supreme Ct. subcom. on admiralty rules, 1996—. Adj. prof. McGeorge Law Sch., Sacramento, 1978-88; bd. dirs. Pacific Admiralty Seminar, San Francisco. Assoc. editor Am. Maritime Cases, 1978—; mem. bd. editors Benedict's Maritime Bull., 2002—. Chmn. exec. com. S.I. (N.Y.) Community Bds., 1969-70, 1st vice chmn. no. 3 bd., 1975-77, treas. no. 3 bd., 1973-74; chmn. 122d Precinct, Community Counsel, S.I., 1968-71; pres. Walnut Creek (Calif.) Little League, 1984-85, v.p. 1978-83; pres. Chestnut Hill Civic Assn., S.I., 1968-74, Congregation B'nai Jeshurun, S.I., 1973-76, v.p., 1971-73; cub pack leader Boy Scouts Am., S.I., 1969-70; bd. dirs. Mid-Island Little League, S.I., 1972-77, Jewish Community Ctr., S.I., 1976, Little League Dist. 4, Contra Costa (Calif.) County, 1984-90. Lt. USN, 1955-57 Named United Jewish Appeal Man of Yr., Congregation B'Nai Jeshurun, 1976. Mem. ABA (admiralty and maritime law com. 1991-94), Maritime Law Assn. U.S. (exec. com. 1991-94, vice chmn. practice and rules com. 1976-91, chmn. govt. liaison com. 1994—, mem. sec. 2002—, no. dist. Calif. admiralty rules com. 1998—). Avocations: athletics, volunteer work. Home: 3506 Sugarberry Ln Walnut Creek CA 94598-1746 Office: US Dept Justice Torts Br PO Box 36028 450 Golden Gate Ave San Francisco CA 94102-3661

BERNSDORFF, OLIVER THOMAS, social sciences educator; b. Barranquilla, Colombia, Aug. 3, 1971; s. Basil Schkolnik and Jutta Bernsdorff; m. Jennifer R. Davis, Dec. 17, 1999. MEd, U. South Fla., 2001, postgrad., 2002—. Resource tchr. for ednl. tech. Pinellas County Schs., Largo, Fla., 1996—. Adj. instr. social foundations of edn. U. South Fla., 2003—. Mem.: NAACP, History of Edn. Soc., Tiger Bay, Phi Delta Kappa. Avocations: book collecting, scuba diving, travel. Home: 2068 Powderhorn Dr Clearwater FL 33755 Office: Pinellas County Pub Schs 1895 Gulf-to-Bay Blvd Clearwater FL 33765 Personal E-mail: otbernsdorff@yahoo.com.

BERNSEN, HAROLD JOHN, manufacturing executive; b. Boston, Nov. 25, 1936; s. Harold Arthur and Solveig Bachrud (Birkrem) B.; m. Doris Ann Champion, Mar. 5, 1960. BA, Dartmouth Coll., 1958. Commd. ensign USN, 1958, advanced through grades to rear adm., 1988, comdg. officer USS LaSalle, 1980-82, comdg. officer USS Lexington, 1983-84, dir. plans and policy, staff comdr. in chief U.S. Cen. Command Tampa, Fla., 1985-86, comdr. Mideast Force, 1986-88, dir. plans and policy staff comdr. in chief Atlantic Fleet, 1988-91; dep., chief of staff, comdr. in chief Atlantic Fleet, 1991; ret., 1991. Spkr. on Mid. East issues. Bd. dirs. Am. Bahraini Friendship Soc., Nat. Coun. on U.S.-Arab Rels., Nat. U.S. Arab C. of C., the Unicorn Group; pres. trustees Physicians for Peace. Decorated Disting. Svc. Medal, Def. Superior Svc. Medal, Legion of Merit; Royal Norwegian Order of Merit (Norway); Order 1st Class (Bahrain). Mem. U.S. Naval Inst., Assn. Naval Aviation, N.Y. Yacht Club, Army Navy Club Avocations: sailing, golf, cooking, gardening. E-mail: hbernsen@cox.net.

BERNSON, MARCELLA S. psychiatrist; b. N.Y.C., Aug. 24, 1952; d. Maxwell Isaac and Priscilla Edith (Zuckerman) Bernson; m. Robert A. Foster, Aug. 7, 2001. BA in Biology summa cum laude, Hofstra U., 1973; MD, Albert Einstein Coll. Medicine, 1976. Diplomate Am. Bd. Psychiatry and Neurology. Resident in psychiatry Bronx (N.Y.) Mcpl. Hosp. Ctr., 1976-79; assoc. dir. med. student edn. in psychiatry U. Medicine and Dentistry N.J.-N.J. Med. Sch., Newark, 1979-81; pvt. practice psychiatry Westfield, NJ, 1981-86; cons. psychiatrist Healthwise EAP, Elizabeth, NJ, 1985-86; staff psychiatrist Elizabeth Gen. Med. Ctr., 1985—88, 1992—95, med. chief adult ambulatory svcs. dept. psychiatry, 1986-87, asst. dir. dept. psychiatry, 1987-88; dir. tng. psychiat. svc. VA Med. Ctr., East Orange, NJ, 1988-89; med. dir. partial care Occupl. Ctr. Union County, Roselle, NJ, 1989-92; cons. psychiatrist Union County Ednl. Svcs. Commn., Westfield, 1992-95; med. dir. Richard Hall CMHC, Bridgewater, NJ, 1995—99, staff psychiatrist, 2003—; with devel. disabilities ctr. Morristown (N.J.) Meml. Hosp., 1999—2003. Instr. U. Medicine and Dentistry N.J.-N.J. Med. Sch., Newark, 1979—81, asst. prof. clin. psychiatry, 1988—89; mem. human rights com. Divsn. Devel. Disabilities, State of N.J. Mem.: N.J. Psychiat. Assn. (Union County rep. 1989—90, Morris County rep. 2000—02), Am. Psychiat. Assn. Avocation: short fiction. Office: Richard Hall CMHC 500 N Bridge St Bridgewater NJ 08807

BERNSTEIN, ALAN, research scientist, federal agency administrator; PhD in Med. Biophysics, U. Toronto, 1972. Post doc Imperial Cancer Rsch. Fund Lab., London, 1972—74; mem. staff Ontario Cancer Inst., Canada, 1974—85; from mem. staff to prof. U. Toronto, 1974—84, prof. molecular & med. genetics, 1984—; head molecular & develpmental biology Samuel Lunenfeld Rsch. Inst. Mount Sinai Hosp., 1985—88, assoc. dir., 1988—94, dir., 1994—2000; pres. Canadian Inst. Health Rsch., Ottawa, Canada, 2000—. Scientific leader Lunenfeld Inst., 1990—2000; cons. in field. Contbr. articles more than 180 to profl. jours; mem. editl. bd.: Science mag. Recipient Award of Excellence, Genetics Soc. Can., Robert L. Noble award, Nat. Cancer Inst. Can., McLaughlin medal, Royal Soc. Can., Henry Friesen award, Canadian Soc. Clin. Investigation, 2000, medal, Australian Soc. Med. Rsch., 2001, Order of Can., 2002. Office: Canadian Inst Health Rsch 410 Laurier Ave W 9th Fl 4209A Ottawa ON K1A 0W9 Canada

BERNSTEIN, ARTHUR HAROLD, venture capital executive; b. N.Y.C., June 8, 1925; s. Charles and Eva (Aronson) B.; m. Barbara R. Ettinger, June 24, 1951; children: Jeffrey R., Diane. B of Chem. Engrng., Cornell U., 1947, JD, 1950. Bar: N.Y. 1950, Fla. 1956, U.S. Supreme Ct. 1962, Calif. 1972. Staff atty. N.Y. Cen. R.R. Co., N.Y.C., 1950-55; gen. counsel Ryder System, Inc., Miami, 1955-58, v.p., treas., 1958-65; sr. assoc. Lazard Freres & Co., N.Y.C., 1966-68; v.p. Norton Simon, Inc., Los Angeles, 1968-70; sr. v.p. Max Factor & Co., Los Angeles, 1970-77; mgr. gen. ptnr. Calif. Capital Investors, Ltd., L.A., 1980-93; pres. Bancorp Capital Group Inc., Bancorp Venture Capital Inc., L.A., 1988—, also bd. dirs. Bd. dirs. WM Group of Funds, Seattle. Chair emeritus, bd. dirs. Phillips Grad. Inst., Encino, Calif. With USN, 1943-46, PTO. Mem. ABA, Fla. Bar Assn., State Bar Calif. Jewish. Office: 11661 San Vicente Blvd Ste 701 Los Angeles CA 90049-5115

BERNSTEIN, BARRY JOEL, lawyer; b. Charleston, S.C., Feb. 11, 1961; s. Charles Stanley Bernstein and Sara Blum Baumwald; m. Charlene Wilkins, May 29, 1998; children: Brandi Nichole, Alexander Nicholas. BA, U. S.C., 1983, JD, 1995; postgrad., U.S. Army Command & Gen. Staff Coll., 2001. Bar: S.C., U.S. Dist. Ct. S.C. Security mgr. Boeing, Wichita, Kans., 1986-88; pres. Security Cons., Inc., Charleston, S.C., 1988-92; law clk. Bernstein and Bernstein, P.A., Charleston, 1992-95; ptnr. Breland and Bernstein, Greenville, S.C., 1995-97; owner, pres. Bernstein Law Firm, Greenville, 1998-2000; gen. counsel Adjutant Gen. of S.C., 2000—. Dir. Homeless Animal Res. and Placement, Greenville, 1995-2000. 1st lt. U.S. Army, 1983-86, ltc. JAG S.C. N.G., 1978—. S.C. Nat. Guard scholar U. S.C., 1980, Helen Gullickson scholar U. S.C. Sch. of Law, 1994, Claude M. Sapp scholar; named Officer of Yr. ROA, Kans.. Mem. ABA, S.C. Trial Lawyers Assn., Comml. Law League Am., Scottish Rite, Masons (past master), Phi Delta Phi (magister 1994-95, province pres. 1996-98), Zeta Beta Tau. Jewish. Home: 304 Lost Creek Columbia SC 29212 Office: Adjutant General of SC 1 National Guard Rd Columbia SC 29201-4766 E-mail: bernsteinbj@sc-arng.ngb.army.mil.

BERNSTEIN, BARRY S. lawyer; b. N.Y.C., Sept. 18, 1946; s. Sidney I. and Anne (Ness) B.; m. Leslie Beth Prager, June 5, 1988; 1 child, Jared Douglas. BA, CUNY, 1967; JD, Bklyn. Law Sch., 1971. Bar: N.Y. 1972, U.S. Dist. Ct. (ea. and so. dists.) N.Y. 1974. Atty. Corp. Counsel's Office, N.Y.C., 1972-75; assoc. Schneider, Kleinick & Wietz, N.Y.C., 1975-76; asst. corp. counsel City of N.Y., 1976-77; ptnr. Judge, Livoti & Bernstein, N.Y.C., 1977-87, Livoti, Bernstein & Moraco, N.Y.C., 1987—. Arbitrator U.S. Dist. Ct. (ea. dist.) N.Y., 1988—. Mem. ATLA, N.Y. State Trial Lawyers, N.Y. State Bar Assn., Am. Arbitration Assn., K.P. Democrat. Jewish. Avocations: scuba diving, travel, reading, photography. Home: 2 Bay Club Dr Apt 14G Bayside NY 11360-2928 E-mail: bbernstein@nyc.rr.com.

BERNSTEIN, BRUCE S. chemist, consultant; b. Bklyn., May 19, 1931; s. Harry M. and Edithe A. Bernstein; m. Valerie Gail Gordon, Apr. 1, 1962; children: Neil, Mark. BS, CUNY, 1953; MS, Iowa State U., 1955. Sr. chemist RAI Rsch. Corp., Queens, NY, 1961—65, Reigel Paper Corp., Milford, NJ, 1966—69; mgr. chem. Radiation Tech. Inc., Rockaway, 1969—72; v.p. Phelps-Dodge Wire and Cable Corp., Yonkers, NY, 1972—75; tech. mgr. Sun Chem. Corp., Paterson, NJ, 1976—77; target leader, tech. advisor, project mgr. Elec. Power Rsch. Inst., Washington, 1977—2001; cons. Bruce S. Bernstein Cons., LLC, Rockville, Md., 2001—. Tchr. U. Wis., Madison, 1988—. Co-author: Electrical Power Cable Engineering, 1999, Expanding Monomers, 1992. With USN, 1955—56. Fellow: IEEE. E-mail: b.s.bernstein@ieee.org.

BERNSTEIN, CHARLES BERNARD, lawyer; b. Chgo., June 24, 1941; s. Norman and Adele (Shore) B.; m. Roberta Luba Lesner, Aug. 7, 1968; children: Edward Charles, Louis Charles, Henry Jacob. AB, U. Chgo., 1962; JD, DePaul U., 1965. Bar: Ill. 1965, U.S. Supreme Ct. 1972. Assoc. Axelrod, Goodman & Steiner, Chgo., 1966-67, Max & Herman Chill, Chgo., 1967-74, Bellows & Assocs., Chgo., 1974-81, Marvin Sacks Ltd., Chgo., 1981; sole practice, 1981—. Basketball press dir. U. Chgo., 1967-74. Author: (with Stuart L. Cohen) Torah and Technology: The History and Genealogy of the Anixter Family, 1986; (with Neil Rosenstein) From King David to Baron David: The Genealogical Connections Between Baron Guy de Rothschild and Baroness Alix de Rothschild, 1989; The Rothschilds of Nordstetten: Their History and Genealogy, 1989; contbr. articles to mags., profl. jours. Officer Congregation Rodfei Zedek, 1979—83, 2002—, bd. dirs., 1978—93, 2000—. Recipient Am. Jurisprudence award, 1963, My Brother's Keeper award Am. Jewish Congress, 1977, Kovod award Rodfei Zedek Men's Club, 1998; co-receipient 2d Century award Jewish Theol. Sem. Am., 1999. Mem. Chgo. Bar Assn., Ill. State Bar Assn., Chgo. Jewish Hist. Soc. (treas. 1977-79, v.p. 1979-82, dir. 1977—), Chgo. Pops Orch. Assn. (treas., exec. com. 1975-81), Am. Jewish Hist. Soc., Art Inst. of Chgo., Chgo. Hist. Soc., Jewish Geneal. Soc. (dir. 1977—), Nu Beta Epsilon, B'nai B'rith (citation meritorious svc. Dist. Grand Lodge 6 1969). Home: 5400 S Hyde Park Blvd Apt C10 Chicago IL 60615-5828 Office: 161 N Clark St Ste 1325 Chicago IL 60601-3295 E-mail: gmn540@ameritech.net.

BERNSTEIN, DANIEL LEWIS, lawyer; b. Durham, N.C., Aug. 19, 1937; s. Edward Morris and Edith (Lewis) B.; m. Ann Lust; children: Kenneth, Margaret. AB, Amherst Coll., 1959; LLB, Harvard U., 1962. Bar: N.Y. 1962, D.C. 1976. Assoc. Law Offices of A.L. Bienstock, N.Y.C., 1962-66, Hale Russell & Gray, N.Y.C., 1966-69, ptnr., 1970-84, Reid & Priest, N.Y.C., 1984-91, mng. ptnr., 1990-91; ptnr. Mannheimer Swartling, Stockholm, Sweden, N.Y.C., 1991-93, Law Office of Daniel L. Bernstein, N.Y.C., 1994—; sr. v.p., gen. counsel Lantis Eyewear Corp., N.Y.C., 1996—; ptnr. Sussman, Sollis, Ebin, Tweedy & Wood LLP, 2001—. Trustee Georges Lurcy Charitable and Ednl. Trust, N.Y.C., 1982—. Dir. The Arts and Scis. Found. U. N.C., Chapel Hill, 1994-2000; trustee The Colleen Giblin Found., Oradell, N.J., 1994—, Walnut Hill Sch., Natick, Mass., 1999—. Mem.: ABA, Bar Assn. of City of N.Y. Office: 461 Fifth Ave Rm 1700 New York NY 10017 E-mail: dan@bernsteinlex.com.

BERNSTEIN, DAVID, gastroenterologist; b. N.Y.C. BA, Johns Hopkins U., 1984; MD, SUNY, Stony Brook, 1988. Attending hepatology U. Miami (Fla.) Sch. Medicine, 1994-96; chief clin. gastroenterology Winthrop Univ. Hosp., Mineola, N.Y., 1996-99; dir. hepatology North Shore Univ. Hosp., Manhasset, N.Y., 1999—. Mem. sci. adv. bd. Am. Liver Found., N.Y.C., 1996—. Fellow ACP, Am. Coll. Gastroenterology; mem. Am. Assn. Study of Liver Disease, Am. Gastrointestinal Assn., Am. Soc. Gastrointestinal Endoscopy, NY Gastrointestinal Assn. (pres.). Office: North Shore Univ Hosp 300 Community Dr Manhasset NY 11030-3801 Fax: 516-562-2683.

BERNSTEIN, DAVID WILLIAM, lawyer; b. Bklyn., Feb. 13, 1938; s. Sidney Abraham B. and Carol Elsa Silverman; m. Carol Ellen Lamberg, June 16, 1959 (div. 1977); m. Melissa Lewis, Mar. 7, 1980; children: Andrew, Donna, Lauren. BA magna cum laude, Harvard U., 1959, LLB magna cum laude, 1962. Bar: N.Y. 1962. Assoc. atty. Rogers & Wells, N.Y.C., 1962-67; ptnr. Clifford Chance Rogers & Wells, N.Y.C., 1967—, chmn. corp. dept., 1989-97. Contbr. numerous articles to Internat. Fin. Law Rev., 1996—. Bd. dirs. Internat. Preschs., 1966—. Mem. Inwood Country Club (sec. 1982-91). Republican. Jewish. Avocation: golf. Office: Clifford Chance Rogers & Wells 200 Park Ave New York NY 10166-0005 Fax: 212-878-8375. E-mail: david.bernstein@cliffordchance.com.

BERNSTEIN, DONALD CHESTER, brokerage company executive, lawyer; b. St. Louis, July 29, 1942; s. Michael Charles and Laura (Schmidt) B.; m. Estelle Marla Cohen, Jan. 17, 1946; children: Kimberleigh, Chad, Aaron. BSBA, Washington U., 1964, JD, 1967; LLM, U. London, 1968. Bar: Mo. 1967. V.p., counsel A.G. Edwards & Sons, Inc., St. Louis, 1969—. Mem. Mo. Bar Assn., Bar Assn. Met. St. Louis. Republican. Jewish. Home: 22 Twin Springs Ln Saint Louis MO 63124-1138 Office: A G Edwards & Sons Inc 1 N Jefferson Ave Saint Louis MO 63103-2205

BERNSTEIN, DONALD SCOTT, lawyer; b. Bklyn., July 11, 1953; s. Emanuel and Shirley (Smithline) B.; m. Jo Ellen Finkel, May 31, 1987; children: Daniel Emanuel, Julia Clare. BA, Princeton U., 1975; JD, U. Chgo., 1978. Bar: N.Y. 1979, U.S. Dist. Ct. (ea. and so. dists.) N.Y. 1979. Assoc. Davis Polk & Wardwell, N.Y.C., 1978-86, ptnr., 1986—. Panelist Practicing Law Inst., N.Y.C., 1983—, Am. Law Inst., ABA, 1991—, Am. Bankruptcy Inst., 1991—; mem. vis. com. U. Chgo. Law Sch., 1995-98, chmn., 1997-98; mem. ofcl. U.S. del. Insolvency Working Group, UN Commn. on Internat. Trade Law. Contbg. author Collier on Bankruptcy, 1996—, bd. editors, 2000—. Bd. dirs. Altro Health and Rehab. Svcs., Bronx, N.Y., 1988-90, N.Y. chpt. Am. Diabetes Assn., 1992-96; mem. exec. com. bankruptcy lawyers div. United Jewish Appeal Fedn., 1985—. Mem. ABA (bus. bankruptcy com., com. on legal opinions), Am. Coll. Bankruptcy (bd. dirs., 2001—), New York County Lawyers Assn. (bd. dirs. 1992-94), Nat. Bankruptcy Conf. (exec. com. 1996-99), Am. Bankruptcy Inst., Assn. Bar City N.Y. (audit com. chmn., 2000—, com. on bankruptcy and corp. reorgn. 1979-83, 85-88, chmn. 1993-96, mem. tribar opinion com. 1988—, chmn. 1998—), Internat. Insolvency Inst. (bd. dirs.). Office: Davis Polk & Wardwell 450 Lexington Ave Fl 21 New York NY 10017-3982

BERNSTEIN, DOUGLAS LON, writer, composer, actor; b. N.Y.C., May 6, 1958; s. Robert Alan and Vicki (Kanner) B.; m. Ellen Foley, Apr. 29, 1990; children: Timothy, Henry. BA valedictorian, Amherst Coll., 1980. Condr., mus. dir. N.Y. Talent System, N.Y.C., 1981-83; cabaret dir. Weston (Vt.) Playhouse, 1991-96. Creative dir. Am. Express Tony Award Campaign, N.Y.C., 1982-84, Save the Theaters Gala, N.Y.C., 1983, Manhattan Theater Club, N.Y.C., 1984-86, Inner Circle Show, N.Y.C., 1991-93. Author, composer, actor (revues) Upstairs at O'Neal's, 1982, Everything the Traffic Will Allow, 1988, Showing Off, 1989 (Bistro award), Varieties, 1991; (mus.) A Backers' Audition, 1984, 92 (Drama Desk nomination), Gotham, 1996, 2000; contbg. author, composer: The No Frills Revue, 1987, Hello Muddah! Hello Fadduh!, 1991, A, My Name is Still Alice, 1992, Nicky Silver's Shrinks, 1995, Secrets Every Smart Traveller Should Know, 1998; appeared as actor in Mayor (mus.), 1985, Bingo Inferno (film), 1986, It Could Happen To You (film), 1994, Pete 'n Pete (TV), 1994; writer (TV pilot) More Than Nine Lives, 1990; writer (TV series) Silver Spoons, The Charmings, 1986-87, Wish You Were Here, 1990, Modern Marriage, 1991; contbg. writer, composer (TV series) Comedy Zone, 1984; contbg. writer (anthology) One on One: The Best Monologues for the 90's. Mem. SAG, Dramatists Guild, ASCAP, Actors Equity Assn., Writers Guild Am. Home and Office: 251 W 89th St New York NY 10024-1712

BERNSTEIN, EDWIN S. judge; b. Long Beach, N.Y., Aug. 15, 1930; s. Harry and Lena (Strizver) B.; children: Andrea, David. BA, U. Pa., 1952; LLB, Columbia U., 1955. Bar: N.Y. 1955, U.S. Ct. Appeals (2d cir.) 1962, U.S. Dist. Ct. (ea. and so. dists.) N.Y. 1962, U.S. Tax Ct. 1962, U.S. Supreme Ct. 1964, Md. 1981, D.C. 1982. Mem. bd. contract appeals Dept. Army, Heidelberg, Fed. Republic Germany, 1968-72; regional counsel U.S. Navy, Quincy, Mass., 1972-73; adminstrv. law judge U.S. Dept. Labor, Washington, 1973-79, Fed. Mine Safety and Health Rev. Commn., Washington, 1979-81, U.S. Postal Svc., Washington, 1981-87, USDA, Washington, 1987-2000. Liaison rep. Adminstrv. Conf. of U.S., Washington, 1983-84; guest lectr. SUNY-Albany, 1978, U. Md., 1982, George Washington U., 1984. Author: U.S. Army Procurement Handbook, 1971; Establishing Federal Administrative Law Judges as an Independent Corps, 1984, also articles Bd. dirs. Washington Hebrew Congregation, 1985-88. Recipient Meritorious Civilian Svc. award Dept. Army, 1972. Mem. ABA, Fed. Bar Assn., D.C. Bar Assn., Fed. Adminstr. Law Judges Conf. (pres. 1983-84), Papermill Assn. (pres. 1980-81). Lodges: Masons. Avocations: golf, bridge, sailing, wines, opera. Home and Office: 7642 Elmridge Dr Boca Raton FL 33433

BERNSTEIN, ELIZABETH ANN, retired executive secretary; b. London, Aug. 13, 1928; arrived in U.S., 1960; d. Eugene and Ethel (Housley) Horsfall-Ertz; m. Alvin Bernstein, Mar. 5, 1975. Sec. various firms, 1948—58, Icelandic Airlines, Reykjavik, Iceland, 1958—59; legal and med. sec. various firms, 1960—82, 1982—89; ret., 1989. Author (poetry): Tsunami, 1994, Pull of the Tides, 1998, Many Moons Rising, 2002, numerous poems. Mem.: Bay Area Poets Coalition, Calif. State Poetry Soc. (1st pl. poems 1999). Democrat. Avocations: reading, writing, music, gardening, travel. Mailing: PO Box 94 Paradise CA 95967-0094

BERNSTEIN, ELLIOT ROY, chemistry educator; b. N.Y.C., Apr. 14, 1941; s. Leonard H. Bernstein and Geraldine (Roman) Goldberg; m. Barbara Wyman, Dec. 19, 1965; children— Jephta, Rebecca. A.B., Princeton U., 1963; Ph.D., Calif. Inst. Tech., 1967. Postdoctoral fellow U. Chgo., 1967-69; asst. prof. Princeton U., N.J., 1969-75; assoc. prof. Colo. State U., Ft. Collins, 1975-80, prof. chemistry, 1980— ; vis. prof. Bilbao, Madrid, Saville, Spain, 2000; cons. Los Alamos Nat. Lab., 1975-83, Philip Morris, 1984-91, Du Pont Corp., 1985-92. Contbr. articles to profl. jours. NSF fellow, 1961-62; Woodrow Wilson fellow, 1963-64, JSPS fellow, 1996, Third Cycle in Chemistry lectr., Switzerland, 1998. Fellow AAAS, Am. Phys. Soc.; mem. Am. Chem. Soc., Sigma Xi. Office: Colo State U Dept Chemistry Condensed Matter Scis Lab Fort Collins CO 80523 0001 Business E-Mail: erb@lamar.colostate.edu.

BERNSTEIN, ERIC MARTIN, lawyer; b. Passaic, N.J., May 5, 1957; s. Abbot Alan and Jean Hausman (Schwartz) B. BA, Drew U., 1979; JD, U. Okla., 1982; MS in Indsl. and Labor Rels., Cornell U., 1985. Bar: N.J. 1982, U.S. Dist. Ct. N.J. 1982, D.C. 1985, U.S. Ct. Appeals (3d cir.) 1985, U.S. Supreme Ct. 1986. Assoc. Mandelbaum Salsburg Gold & Lazaris, East Orange, N.J., 1982-83; pvt. practice Clifton, N.J., 1983-84; sr. assoc. Gerald L. Dorf, P.A., Rahway, N.J., 1984-87; of counsel Vaida & Vaida, P.C., Flemington, N.J., 1987-88; pvt. practice Bridgewater, Clifton and Three Bridges, N.J., 1988-92; ptnr. Weiner Lesniak, Parsippany, N.J., 1992-97, Mauro Savo Camerino & Grant, Somerville, N.J., 1998-00, Eric M. Bernstein & Assocs., LLC, Warren, N.J., 2000—. Lectr. Bur. Govt. Rsch., Rutgers U., New Brunswick, N.J., 1983—; mem. adj. faculty Raritan Valley C.C., Somerville, N.J., 1988-90; city atty. City of Passaic, N.J., 1990-92; mcpl. atty. Washington Twp.-Warren County, 1991—, Hardwick Twp.-Warren County, 1992-2001, West Windsor-Mercer County, 1993-97, North Plainfield-Somerset County, 1997—, Bethlehem Twp.-Hunterdon County, 1998-2000, Stillwater Twp.-Sussex County, 1998-2000, Paramus Borough-Bergen County, 1999-2001, Franklin Township-Hunterdon County, 1999—, Union City-Hudson County, 1999-2000, Lebanon Twp.-Hunterdon County, 2001—, High Bridge Borough, Hunterdon County, 2003—; bd. atty. Englewood Bd. Edn.-Bergen County, 1996-99, Lincoln Park Bd. Edn.-Morris County, 1997-2000; planning bd. atty. Bethlehem Twp.-Hunterdon County, 2000-02, Hillsborough Twp.-Somerset County, 2001—. Asst. editor, co-author: Governing New Jersey Municipalities, 1984, co-editor, author, 6th edit., 1995; asst. editor N.J. Mcpl. Attys. Mag., 1984-92; editor N.J. State Bar Assn. Local Govt. Law Newsletter, 1995—. Vol. atty. Lawyers for the Arts, N.J., 1986—. Mem. ABA, Fed. Bar Assn., N.J. Bar Assn. (1st vice chair local govt. law sect. 1995—), D.C. Bar Assn., Passaic County Bar Assn., Somerset County Bar Assn., Nat. Arbitration Forum (arbitrator). Republican. Jewish. Avocations: tennis, golf, stamp collecting, classical and jazz music. Home: 10 Timberline Dr Bridgewater NJ 08807-1204 Office: 2 North Rd PO Box 4922 Warren NJ 07059-0922 E-mail: embernstein@embalaw.com.

BERNSTEIN, GEORGE L. lawyer, accountant; b. Phila., Feb. 22, 1932; s. Leon B. and Elizabeth (Seidman) B.; m. Phyllis Wagner, June 27, 1954; children: Harris, Lisa. BS in Econs., U. Pa., 1953, JD cum laude, 1956. Bar: Pa. 1957; CPA, Pa. Accountant Laventhol & Horwath, Phila., 1950-90, exec. ptnr., chief exec. officer, 1980-90; chief oper. officer Dilworth, Paxon, Attys., Phila., 1991-94; CFO, CAO HFA, Inc., Exec. Search Cons., Phila., 1994—2002. Nat.

chmn. profl. divsn. State of Israel Bonds, 1988-90; co-chmn. bd. trustees Am. Jewish Congress, Phila., 1988-90; bd. dirs. Mann Ctr. for Performing Arts, Phila.; trustee Einstein Health Care Network, Phila. Recipient Humanitarian award State of Israel Bonds, 1989. Mem. AICPA (coun. 1976-79, 81-87, strategic planning com. 1986-90, v.p. 1986-87, bd. dirs. 1981-84, com. small and medium sized firms 1978-80, MAS exec. com. 1971-75), Pa. Inst. CPAs (pres. 1976-77, com.m on past pres., chmn. MAS com., long-range objectives com., budget and fin. com.), Locust Club (pres. 1990-92, exec. com., bd. dirs.). Democrat. Avocations: golf, walking, music, theatre.

BERNSTEIN, GERALD WILLIAM, management consultant, researcher; b. Boston, Nov. 25, 1947; s. Alan Irwin and Anne (Fine) B.; m. Kathleen Ann Chaikin, Jan. 12, 1985. BS in Aero. Engring., Rensselaer Poly. Inst., 1969; MS in Engring., Stanford U., 1978. Transp. engr., dept. transp. State of N.Y., Albany, 1969-70; transp. planner Kennebec Regional Planning Com., Winslow, Me., 1974-77; dir. transp. dept. SRI Internat., Menlo Park, Calif., 1979-95; v.p. BACK Mgmt. Svcs., San Francisco, 1995-98; mng. dir. Stanford Transp. Group, San Francisco, 1998—. Session chmn. aviation workshop NSF, 1985, 91, 99, 2002; profl. conf. chmn.; bd. dirs. GlobTran Corp., 1993-98. Contbr. articles to profl. jours. Chmn. transp. com. Glenn Park Neighborhood Assn., San Francisco, 1982-85; dir. Balboa Terrace Neighborhood Assn., San Francisco, 1986-88; trustee Congregation Beth Israel-Judea, 1991-93. With U.S. Army, 1970-72. Recipient Cert. Appreciation City of Waterville, Maine, 1977. Mem. Am. Inst. Aeronautics and Astronautics (sr. mem.), Transp. Research Bd. of Nat. Research Council (chmn. econs. and forecasting com.). Clubs: Toastmasters (Menlo Park, pres. 1986). Democrat. Jewish. Avocations: flying, skiing. Office: Stanford Transp Group 236 W Portal Ave Ste 359 San Francisco CA 94127-1423

BERNSTEIN, GUY THOMAS, physician, urological surgeon; b. Newark, June 26, 1956; s. Aaron and Ruth Paula (Mendelsohn) B.; m. Nancy Lynn Golden, July 31, 1983; children: Jeffrey, Carly. AB magna cum laude, Brown U., 1978; MD, Columbia U., 1982. Diplomate Am. Bd. Urology. Intern, jr. resident in surgery N.Y. Hosp.-Cornell Med. Ctr., N.Y.C., 1982-84; resident in urology Brigham and Women's Hosp.-Harvard Med. Sch., Boston, 1984-85; clin. fellow dept. surgery Harvard Med. Sch., Boston, 1984-88; ptnr., v.p. James W. Thompson MD, Ltd., Bryn Mawr, Pa., 1988—; investigator SmithKline Beecham, 1996, Ortho-McNeil, 2000—, Denoreon, 2000—, Myriad, 2001—, Sanofi-Syntneld, 2002—. Instr. urology Jefferson Med. Coll., Phila., 1988-94, clin. asst. prof., 1995—; mem. attending staff Bryn Mawr Hosp., 1988—, Lankenau Hosp., 1997—, Paoli Meml. Hosp., 1997—; mem. cons. staff Bryn Mawr Rehab. Hosp., 1988—. Contbr. articles to profl. jours. Recipient prize in urology Coll. Phys. and Surg., 1982, J. Hartwell Harrison award Brigham and Women's Hosp., 1988. Fellow ACS; mem. AMA, Pa. Med. Soc., Montgomery County Med. Soc., Phila. Urologic Soc., Am. Urol. Assn., Am. Fertility Soc., Urol. Assn. Pa., Am. Assn. Clin. Urologists, Phi Beta Kappa, Alpha Omega Alpha. Avocations: tennis, skiing, photography. Office: Center for Urologic Care 245 S Bryn Mawr Ave Bryn Mawr PA 19010-2221

BERNSTEIN, HENRIETTA RUTH, publishing executive, writer; b. L.A., Feb. 9, 1926; d. Abraham and Anna Rosen; m. Norman Robert Bernstein, June 15, 1947; children: Alan, Bruce, Anna. BA, U. So. Calif., 1948; postgrad., Santa Monica (Calif.) Coll., 1968—69. Propr. Ryder Art Gallery, L.A., 1958—63, Beverly Palms Hosp., L.A., 1963—68; dir. Light Am. Wisdom, L.A., 2001—. Founder, chair Elec. Magnetic Energy and Elec. Magnetic Medicine confs., L.A., 1985; dir. Cabalah Rsch. Found., Bosque Farms, N.Mex., 1989—. Author: Cabalah Primer, 1984, The Crone Oracles, 1994, Ark of the Covenant-Holy Grail, 1998. Dir., chair Veritat Found. (affiliated with philosopher Manly P. Hall), L.A., 1985—96. Avocations: philosophy, American history, electromagnetic medicine.

BERNSTEIN, HERBERT JOSEPH, physicist, consultant, educator; b. Washington, Apr. 21, 1943; s. Harry S. and Edith Bernstein; m. Mary Marcia Mayers, Apr. 4, 1971; children: Carolyn Joy, Laila Jael. BA, Columbia U., 1963; MS, U. Calif., San Diego, 1965, PhD, 1967. Postdoctoral Inst. for Advanced Study, Princeton, NJ, 1967—69; rsch. physicist Cambridge (Mass.) Electron Accelerator, 1969-70; prof. physics Hampshire Coll., Amherst, Mass., 1971—, dir. sci. policy program, 1972-73. Pres. Inst. for Sci. and Interdisciplinary Studies, 1991—; vis. scientist MIT, Cambridge, 1981—, Brookhaven Nat. Lab., Upton, NY, 1968; guest scientist Stanford (Calif.) Linear Accelerator Ctr., 1974; vis. asst. prof. physics U. Leuven, Louvain, Belgium, 1970—71; asst. prof. physics U. Mass., North Dartmouth, Mass., 1969—70; summer staff physicist Advanced Computer Lab. Naval Air Devel. Ctr., Johnsville, Pa., 1961—63; cons. Gov. Am. Samoa, Pago Pago, 1971; tech. dir. Vols. in Tech. Assistance, Washington, 1977—78; sci. tech. cons. World Bank, 1976—79; sci. pol. cons. Pres.'s Sci. Adv., 1975—78. Co-author: New Ways of Knowing, 1987, Muddling Through: Pursuing Science & Truths for the 21st Century, 1998; contbr. articles to profl. jours. Active Havurat Ha-Emek, Amherst, Mass., 1979—; faculty trustee Hampshire Coll., 1972-74. Recipient Procter prize, Sigma Xi, 1984; fellow, Kellogg Found., 1985—88, NSF, 1965—67; scholar, Inst. for Theoretical Physics, U. Calif., Santa Barbara, 2000—03. Fellow Inst. for Advanced Studies in Humanities; mem. Am. Phys. Soc., Assn. Mems. Inst. for Advanced Study (trustee, nominating chair 1986—). Jewish. Avocations: cross country skiing, creative parenting, gardening. Office: Inst for Sci & Interdisciplinary Studies Hampshire Coll Amherst MA 01002

BERNSTEIN, HOWARD MARK, lawyer; b. Washington, May 3, 1952; s. Howard and Mary Delia (Sliney) B.; m. Alice Ruth Huneycutt, Nov. 28, 1981; children: Ashley Laughton, Laura Whitney. Bar: Fla. 1976, U.S. Dist. Ct. (so. dist.) Fla. 1976, U.S. Ct. Appeals (5th cir.) 1981, U.S. Ct. Appeals (11th cir.) 1981, U.S. Dist. Ct. (mid. dist.) Fla. 1982, U.S. Ct. Claims 1982, U.S. Supreme Ct. 1982, U.S. Ct. Appeals (fed. cir.) 1982, U.S. Tax Ct. 1982. Assoc. Bradford, Williams, McKay, Kimbrell, Hamman & Jennings, P.A., Miami, Fla., 1976-78, Lane, Mitchell & Harris, P.A., Miami, 1978-81, Jacobs, Robbins, Gaynor, Hampp, Burns, Cole & Shasteen, P.A., St. Petersburg, Fla., 1981-83, Schultz & Walsh, P.A., Brandenton, Fla., 1983-85; asst. county atty. Pinellas County, Clearwater, Fla., 1985-97, Fisher & Sauls, P.A., 1997—. Mem. ABA, Clearwater Bar Assn., St. Petersburg Bar Assn., Barristers Soc. (lord high chancellor 1975-76). Democrat. Roman Catholic. Office: Fisher & Sauls PA 100 2d Ave S Ste 701 Saint Petersburg FL 33701 Home: Apt 202 4948 Sentinel Dr Bethesda MD 20816-3555

BERNSTEIN, I. MELVIN, university official and dean, materials scientist; b. N.Y.C., N.Y., Oct. 14, 1938; s. Emanuel and Helen (Wolitzer) B.; m. Katherine Sarah Russo, June 7, 1964; 1 child, Elana BS, Columbia U., 1960, MS, 1962, PhD, 1965. Postdoctoral assoc. Central Electricity Generating Bd., Berkeley, Eng., 1966-67; scientist U.S. Steel Research Lab., Monroeville, Pa., 1967-72; from asst. prof. to prof. Carnegie-Mellon U., Pitts., 1972-87, assoc. dean engring., 1978-82, prof., head dept. metall. engring and materials sci., 1982-87; provost, acad. v.p. Ill. Inst. Tech., Chgo., 1987-90, chancellor, 1990-91; v.p. arts, scis. and engring., dean faculty Tufts U., Medford, Mass., 1991-2001; provost, sr. v.p. Brandeis U., 2001—03; dir. univ. programs Dept. of Homeland Security, Washington, 2003—. Chief cons. MCL, Monroeville, 1972-82; liaison scientist Office Naval Research, London, 1977-78; mem. Nat. Materials adv. bd., 1990-96. Co-editor: Handbook of Stainless Steel, 1977, Hydrogen Effects in Metals, 1973, 76, 1981; assoc. editor Metall. Trans., 1977-82. Mem. Pitts. Dem. Com., 1971-75; bd. govs. Ben Gurion U., Israel, 1993—. Jewish. E-mail: mel.bernstein4@verizon.net.

BERNSTEIN, JACOB, lawyer; b. Glen Cove, N.Y., Dec. 23, 1932; s. David and Ida (Miller) B.; m. Eva Belle Smolokoff, June 28, 1959; children: Diane Susan, Neal Robert. AB, U. Rochester, 1954; JD, U. Mich., 1957. Bar: N.Y. 1957, U.S. Supreme Ct. Mem. Ralph J. Marino, 1959-64, Marino & Bernstein, 1964-73, Marino, Bernstein & La Marca, Oyster Bay, N.Y., 1973-99, Marino & Bernstein, 2000—. Lectr. in field. Actor Sagamore Players, 1972—. Dir. Waterfront Ctr., 2002—; mem. EPTL-SCPA adv. com. N.Y. State Legis., 1990—; foundingmem., trustee Cmty. Found., 1962—; trustee Oyster Bay Jewish Ctr., 1962—, pres., 1965—67, 2000—02; sec. bd. dirs. Oyster Bay Youth and Family Counseling Agy., 1975—2002, Oyster Bay Main St. Assn.; pres. Oyster Bay E. Norwich Youth Coun., 1976—78; bd. dirs., counsel America's Sail, 1994—; divsn. chmn. United Jewish Appeal, 1965—74. With U.S. Army, 1958—59. Named Man of Yr., Oyster Bay Jewish Ctr., 1986, 2002; recipient Award of Honor, United Jewish Appeal, 1972. Mem. ABA, N.Y. Bar Assn., U.S. Dist. Ct. Bar Assn., Nassau County Bar Assn., Nassau Lawyers Assn., North Shore Lawyers Assn., Rotary (pres. 1967-68, dist. parliamentarian 1986-87, govs. aide 1999-2000), Sagamore Yacht Club (chief legal officer 1973-99, 2001—). Republican. Office: PO Box 180 Oyster Bay NY 11771-0180

BERNSTEIN, JAN LENORE, lawyer; b. N.Y.C., Apr. 24, 1957; d. James Hanley and Joan Mathilda (Wertheimer) B. BA magna cum laude, U. Pa., 1979, JD, Rutgers U., 1982. Bar: N.J. 1982, Pa.1983, N.Y. 1990. Law clk. to hon. Herbert S. Glickman, Newark, 1982-83; ptnr. Riker, Danzig, Scherer, Hyland and Perretti LLP, Morristown, N.J., 1983—. Mem. jud. performance com., jud. and prosecutorial appts. commn., econ. consequences of dissolution com., dis. X fee arbitration com. N.J. Supreme Ct.; mem. exec. com. family law sect.; past mem. family practice com.; presenter in field. Mem. editl. bd. N.J. Lawyer mag.; bd. dirs. N.J. Lawyer newspaper; contbr. articles to profl. jours. Dem. committeeperson; assoc. trustee U. Pa., chair woemn's atheltic bd., mem. trustee coun. Penn Women, bd. of athletic advisors. Mem. N.J. Bar Assn. (past chair women's rights sect.), Morris County (N.J.) Bar Assn. (family law com.). Office: Riker Danzig Scherer Hyland & Perreti LLP Headquarters Plaza Speedwell Ave Morristown NJ 07962 also: 50 W State St Ste 1010 Trenton NJ 08608-1220 Fax: 973-538-1984. E-mail: jbernstein@riker.com.

BERNSTEIN, JAY, pathologist, researcher, educator; b. NYC, May 14, 1927; s. Michael Kenneth and Frances (Kaufman) B.; m. Carol Irene Kritchman, Aug. 11, 1957; children: John Abel, Michael Kenneth. BA, Columbia U., 1948; MD, SUNY, Bklyn., 1952. Diplomate Am. Bd. Pathology. Asst. pathologist Children's Hosp. Mich., Detroit, 1956-58, assoc. pathologist, 1959, attending pathologist, 1960-62, cons. in lab. medicine, 1977—93, cons. emeritus, 1993 ; attending pathologist Bronx Mcpl. Hosp. Ctr., N.Y.C., 1962-68; asst. prof. pathology Albert Einstein Coll. Medicine, Bronx, N.Y., 1962-64, assoc. prof. pathology, 1964-68; chmn. dept. anatomic pathology William Beaumont Hosp., Royal Oak, Mich., 1969-90, dir. Rsch. Inst., 1983-98, assoc. med. dir., 1990-98, hon. consulting pathologist, 1999—; clin. prof. pathology Wayne State U. Sch. Medicine, Detroit, 1977—99. Chmn. sci. adv. bd. Nat. Kidney Found. Mich., 1986-88, nat. sci. adv. bd., 1976-82; sci. advisor Nat. Inst. Child Health, USPHS, 1976-81; profl. adv. bd. Nat. Tuberous Sclerosis Assn., 1990-93; clin. prof. health sci. Oakland U., Rochester, Mich., 1980-90; vis. prof. pathology Albert Einstein Coll. Medicine, Bronx, 1974-2001; com. on renal disease WHO; cons. pathologist Internat. Study of Kidney Diseases in Children, Lupus Study Group. Co-editor: Perspectives in Pediatric Pathology; past contbg. editor Jour. Pediatrics; past mem. editl. bd. Pediatric Nephrology; mem. editl. bd. Jour. Urologic Pathology; contbr. articles to profl. jours. With USN, 1945-46. Recipient Henry L. Barnett award Am. Acad. Pediats., 1997. Mem. AMA, Am. Soc. Investigative Pathology, Internat. Acad. Pathology (U.S.-Can. divsn.), Am. Soc. Clin. Pathologists, Soc. Pediatric Pathology (co-founder, past pres., Farber lectr. 1982, Spl. Disting. Colleague award 1987, 97), Am. Pediatric Soc., Am. Soc. Nephrology, Internat. Pediat. Nephrology Assn., Renal Pathology Soc. (past pres., Renal Pathology Founder award 1997), Am. Soc. Pediatric Nephrology (Founder's award 1999). Office: William Beaumont Rsch Inst 3601 W 13 Mile Rd Royal Oak MI 48073-6712 E-mail: jaybernstein@earthlink.net.

BERNSTEIN, JOSEPH, lawyer; b. New Orleans, Feb. 12, 1930; s. Eugene Julian and Lola (Schlemoff) Bernstein; m. Phyllis Maxine Askanase, Sept. 4, 1955; children: Jill, Barbara, Elizabeth R., Jonathan Joseph. BS, U. Ala., 1952; LLB, Tulane U., 1957. Bar: La. 1957. Clerk to Justice E. Howard McCaleb of La. Supreme Ct., 1957; assoc. Jones, Walker, Waechter, Poitevent, Carrere & Denegre, 1957—60, ptnr., 1960—65; pvt. practice New Orleans, 1965—. Former gen. counsel Alliance for Affordable Energy. Past pres. New Orleans chpt. March of Dimes, New Orleans Jewish Cmty. Ctr.; past nat. exec. com. Am. Jewish Com.; trustee New Orleans Symphony Soc.; past mem. adv. council New Orleans Mus. Art. 2d lt. AUS, 1952—54. Mem.: ABA, La. Bar Assn., Zeta Beta Tau, Phi Delta Phi. Republican. Jewish. Home: 708 Explanade Ave Bay Saint Louis MS 39520 E-mail: Joelou1@bellsouth.net.

BERNSTEIN, LARRY HOWARD, clinical pathologist; b. Highland Park, Mich., Dec. 28, 1941; s. David Mordecai and Lillian Cecilia (Schwartz) B.; m. Audrey Jean Mellen, Dec. 20, 1969; children: Rachel Laura, Naomi Beth. BS, Wayne State U., 1963, MS, 1966, MD, 1968. Intern pathology Kans. U. Med. Ctr., Kansas City, 1968-69; resident and fellow in pathology U. Calif.-San Diego, La Jolla, 1970-73; pathologist Armed Forces Inst. Pathology, Washington, 1973-75; asst. prof. pathology U. South Fla., Tampa, 1975-77; assoc. prof. pathology U. South Ala., Mobile, 1977-78; dir. chemistry Iowa Meth. Med. Ctr., Des Moines, 1979-80, United Health Svcs., Binghampton, N.Y., 1981-82; dir. chemistry and blood bank Bridgeport (Conn.) Hosp., 1983—. Cons. Beckman, Boehringer Mannheim, Eastman Kodak, Brea, Calif., Rochester, N.Y. and Indpls., 1985-95; Nat. Com. Clin. Lab. Scis. rev. com., Chgo., 1988-92. Contbr. articles to Nutrition, Clin. Chemistry, Cancer, Arch. Pathol. Lab. Medicine, Jour. Biol. Chemistry, Brit. Jour. Cancer, Jour. Molecular Cellular Cardiology. Fellow Am. Assn. Clin. Chemistry (lectr., program chmn. nat. mtgs. 1985—), Coll. Am. Pathologists, Am. Coll. Nutrition; mem. ASTM, Clin. Lab. Mgmt. Assn. (lectr., nat. mtgs. 1985), AHSR, others. Democrat. Jewish. Achievements include patents for lactate dehydrogenase method, malate dehydrogenase mthod; rsch. in effect of nutritional states; rsch. in determining decision values for laboratory tests using truth-table comprehension and quality management using data classification and analysis; rsch. in diagnosis of acute myocardial infarction (heart attack), and in cancer markers in serum and body fluids. Office: NY Meth Hosp Dept Pathology Bridgeport CT 06610-2870

BERNSTEIN, LEROY G. state legislator; m. Kathleen Bernstein; 4 children. Pres., owner Valley Movers, Inc.; mem. N.D. Ho. of Reps. from 45th dist., 1989—; speaker N.D. Ho. of Reps., 2001—. Vice chmn. Transp. Com. N.D. Ho. of Reps., mem. Indsl. Appropriations Com, Govt. Ops., Bus. and Labor Com. Mem. DAV, KC, U.S. C. of C., Am. Legion, Eagles. Republican. Address: 3949 N 10th St Fargo ND 58102-1048

BERNSTEIN, LESTER, editorial consultant; b. N.Y.C., July 18, 1920; s. Isidore and Rebecca (Axelrod) B.; m. Jacqueline Lipscomb, Feb. 6, 1946; children: Lynn, Nina, Paul, Daniel. AB, Columbia U., 1940. Reporter N.Y. Times, 1940-48; writer, fgn. corr., editor Time mag., 1948-58; dir. info. NBC, 1958-60, v.p. corp. affairs, 1960-62; nat. affairs editor Newsweek, 1963-65, exec. editor, 1965-69, mng. editor, 1969-72, editor, 1979-82; editorial cons., 1982-85; v.p. corporate communications RCA Corp., 1973-79. Cons. N.Y. Internat. Festival of the Arts, 1987-92. Recipient Nat. Mag. award for gen. excellence, 1981. Mem.: Century Assn. Home: 44 Buxton St Long Beach NY 11561-5009

BERNSTEIN, LIONEL M. gastroenterologist, educator; b. Chgo., Sept. 10, 1923; married, 1952; 3 children. BS, U. Ill., 1944, MD, 1945, MS, 1951, PhD in Physiology, 1954. Diplomate Am. Bd. Internal Medicine. Rsch. assoc. med. and clin. sci. U. Ill., 1952—53, instr. med. and physiology, 1953—54; chief metabolism rsch. divsn. Med. Nutrition Lab. Fitzsimmons Army Hosp., Denver, 1954—55; physician sr. grade VA Hosp., Sepulveda, Calif., 1955—56, chief gastroent. sect. Hines, Ill., 1956—57, assoc. chief of staff, 1957—62; chief med. svcs. VA West Side Hosp., Chgo., 1962—67; dir. rsch. svc. VA Ctr. Office, 1967—70; assoc. dir. extramural programs Nat. Inst. Arthritis and Metabolism Disorders, 1970—73; dir. office program ops. HEW, 1973—74; spl. asst. Office Asst. Sec. Health, 1975—77; asst. dep. dir. rsch. and edn. Lister Hill Nat. Ctr. Biomed. Nat. Libr. Medicine, 1977—78, dir., 1978—83; prof. health professions edn. Coll. Medicine, acting head U. Ill., 1985—88, 1988—90, prof. med. edn. Coll. Medicine, 1988—. VA mem. Gen. Med. Study Sect., NIH, 1962—67; clin. prof. medicine George Washington U., 1982—; pres. Knowledge Sys., Inc., 1983—. Fellow: ACP; mem.: Am. Coll. Med. Informatics, Am. Med. Informatics Assn., Am. Fedn. Clin. Rsch., Am. Gastroent. Assn., Inst. Medicine-NAS. Office: 1802 Kalorama Sq NW Washington DC 20008-4022

BERNSTEIN, LOUIS, civil engineer; b. Cumberland, Md., Aug. 10, 1954; s. Milton and Rosanne (Fichter) B. BSCE, MIT, 1977. Registered profl. engr. Civil engr. U.S. Army C.E., Mobile, Ala., 1977-79; hydraulics technician Ulster Poly., Newtonabbey, No. Ireland, 1978; civil engr. Raymond E. Lindahl, Inc., San Francisco, 1981-82; inspector O'Brien-Kreitzberg & Assocs., Inc., San Francisco, 1983-84; mgr. L. Bernstein Furniture Co., Inc., Cresaptown, Md., 1988-98; civil engr. WESTech Engring., Cresaptown, 1991—; English lang. tchr. LAPO Internat. Coll., Silver Spring, Md., 2000; project engr. Antietam Design, Hagerstown, Md., 2002—. Author: (Corps of Engrs. report) Sources of Information-Appendix E of Tennessee-Tombebee Corridor Plan of Study, 1979; co-author: (Corps of Engrs. report) An Investigation for Flood Control in the Chickasawhay River Basin Mississippi, 1979. Group chairperson We. Md. Group Sierra Club, 1995-96, vice chair, 1997-98; San Francisco rep. Internat. Yoga Fellowship, Bihar Sch. of Yoga, Satyananada Ashram, 1982-88; paleontology vol. Sonoma State U. Mammoth Expdn., Death Valley, Calif., 1983, Page Mus., Los Angeles, 1984-1987, Tyrell Mus. Paleontology, Dinosaur Provincial Park, Can., 1986, Paleoworld Rsch. Found./Hell Creek Dinosaur Mus., Mt., 2003. Recipient Award of Merit, City of San Francisco, 1984. Mem. ASCE, Soc. Am. Mil. Engrs., Globetrotters' Club London, Phi Mu Delta (social chmn. 1974-75). Mem. Green Party. Home: 10000 Country Club Rd SE Cumberland MD 21502-8338 E-mail: louisbernstein@alum.mit.edu.

BERNSTEIN, MARK R. retired lawyer; b. York, Pa., Apr. 7, 1930; s. Phillip G. Bernstein and Evelyn (Greenfield) Spielman; m. E. Louise Bernstein, May 10, 1955; children: Phillip, Cary, Adam, Andrew, Jonathan, Evan. BA, U. Pa., 1952; JD, Yale U., 1957. Bar: N.C., U.S. Dist. Ct. (we. dist.) N.C., U.S. Ct. Appeals, U.S. Custom Ct. Atty. Kennedy, Covington, Lobdell, & Hickman, Charlotte, N.C., 1957-60, Haynes, Graham, Bernstein & Baucom, Charlotte, N.C., 1960-67, Parker, Poe, Adams & Bernstein, Charlotte, N.C., 1968-98, chmn., 1992-97. Bd. dirs. Family Dollar Stores, Inc., Nat. Welders Supply Co., Inc. Bd. dirs. Wildacres Found., Wildacres Leadership Initiative, Found. for the Carolinas; bd. dirs., past chmn. The Found. of the Carolinas, Inc.; past pres. Charlotte Symphony Assn.; past chmn. mayor's com. for a Performing Arts Ctr., 1983-85, com. mem. Performing Arts Ctr. Task Force, 1987, past chmn. N.C. Econ. Devel. Bd.; past pres. Temple Beth El, Charlotte Jewish Cmty. Ctr., Charlotte Civitan Club, Am. Symphony Orch. League, Golden Circle Theatre, Found. of Shalom Park; past mem. exec. com. Yale Law Sch.; past mem. bd. N.C. Blumenthal Performing Arts Ctr.; co-chair Cultural Resources Master Plan. 1st lt. inf. U.S. Army, 1952—54. Recipient Disting. Svc. award Jaycees, 1961, State of Israel Humanitarian award, 1981, Charlotte Fedn. of Jewish Charities A Man of the Ages award, 1985, Silver Medallion award NCCJ, 1995, Israel Humanitarian award, The Vanguard award for personal svcs. Arts and Sci. Coun., 1998. Mem. Mecklenburg County Bar Assn. (past pres.), Charlotte City Club, The Tower Club (bd. dirs.), Olde Providence Racquet Club (past pres.). Democrat. Home: 5300 Hardison Rd Charlotte NC 28226-6426

BERNSTEIN, MELVIN, provost; BS, MS, PhD, Columbia U. Formerly with U.S. Steel Fundamental Rsch. Lab.; former mem. faculty, head dept. materials sci. and engring., assoc. dean engring. Carnegie-Mellon U., Pitts.; former provost, acad. v.p., chancellor, sr. v.p. Ill. Inst. Tech.; v.p. arts, scis. and engring., dean faculty arts, scis. and engring. Tufts U., Medford, Mass., 1991—2001; provost, sr. v.p. acad. affairs Brandeis U., Waltham, Mass., 2001—. Lectr., presenter in field; mem. Nat. Materials Adv. Bd.; tech. cons. in field. Contbr. articles to profl. jours. Bd. overseers Boston Mus. Sci.; bd. govs. Ben-Gurion U., Israel. Fellow: Am. Soc. Materials. Office: Brandeis U Office of Provost 415 South St MS 134 Waltham MA 02454

BERNSTEIN, MERTON CLAY, law educator, lawyer, arbitrator; b. N.Y.C., Mar. 26, 1923; s. Benjamin and Ruth (Frederica (Kleeblatt)) B.; m. Joan Barbara Brodshaug, Dec. 17, 1955; children: Johanna Karin, Inga Saterlie, Matthew Curtis, Rachel Libby. BA, Oberlin Coll., 1943; LL.B., Columbia U., 1948. Bar: N.Y. 1948, U.S. Supreme Ct. 1952. Assoc. Schlesinger & Schlesinger, 1948; atty. NLRB, 1949-50, 50-51, Office of Solicitor, U.S. Dept. Labor, 1950; counsel Nat. Enforcement Commn., 1951, U.S. Senate Subcom. on Labor, 1952; legis. asst. to U.S. Sen. Wayne L. Morse, 1953-56; counsel U.S. Senate Com. on R.R. Retirement, 1957-58; spl. counsel U.S. Senate Subcom. on Labor, 1958; assoc. prof. law U. Nebr., 1958-59; lectr., sr. fellow Yale U. Law Sch., 1960-65; prof. law Ohio State U., 1965-75; Walter D. Coles prof. law Washington U., St. Louis, 1975-96, Walter D. Coles prof. emeritus, 1997—; mem. adv. com. to Sec. of Treas. on Coordination of Social Security and pvt. pension plans, 1967-68. Prin. cons. Nat. Commn. on Social Security Reform, 1982-83; vis. prof. Columbia U. Law Sch., 1967-68, Leiden U., 1975-76; mem. adv. com. rsch. U.S. Social Security Adminstrn., 1967-68, chmn., 1969-70; cons. Adminstrv. Conf. of the U.S., 1989, Dept. Labor, 1966-67, Russell Sage Found., 1967-68, NSF, 1970-71, Ctr. for the Study of Contemporary Problems, 1968-71. Author: The Future of Private Pensions, 1964, Private Dispute Settlement, 1969, (with Joan B. Bernstein) Social Security: The System That Works, 1988; contbr. articles to profl. jours. Mem. Bethany (Conn.) Planning and Zoning Commn., 1962-65, Ohio Retirement Study Commn., 1967-68; co-chmn. transition team for St. Louis Mayor Freeman Bosley Jr., 1993; mem. Bd. of Health, City of St. Louis, 1993-2000; bd. dirs. St. Louis Theatre Project, 1981-84; pres. bd. Met. Sch. Columbus, Ohio, 1974-75; del. White House Conf. Aging, 1995; mem. Brewster (Mass.) Bd. Health, 2001-, chair, 2002—. With AUS, 1943-45. Fulbright fellow, 1975-76, Elizur Wright award, 1965. Mem. ABA (sec. sect. labor rels. law 1968-69), Internat. Assn. for Labor Law and Social Security (bd. dirs. U.S. chpt. 1973-83, 88-91), Fulbright Alumni Assn. (bd. dirs. 1976-78), Indsl. Rels. Rsch. Assn., Am. Arbitration Assn. (mem. adv. com. St. Louis region 1987—), Nat. Acad. Social Ins. (founding mem., bd. dirs. 1986-91). Democrat. Jewish. E-mail: bernstein@wulaw.wustl.edu.

BERNSTEIN, MITCHELL HARRIS, lawyer; b. N.Y.C., Sept. 19, 1949; s. Melvin and Gladys (Weissman) B.; m. Barbara Veitch, Oct. 8, 1978; children: Jonathan, Matthew, Emily. AB, U. Pa., 1970; JD, Yale U., 1973. Bar: N.Y. 1974, U.S. Ct. Appeals (2d cir.) 1974, U.S. Dist. Ct. (so. and ea. dists.) N.Y. 1974, U.S. Ct. Appeals (5th and D.C. cirs.) 1980, U.S. Supreme Ct. 1980, D.C. 1981, U.S. Ct. Appeals (4th cir.) 1981, U.S. Dist. Ct. D.C. 1982, U.S. Ct. Appeals (3d cir.) 1985. Assoc. Breed, Abbott & Morgan, N.Y.C., 1974-77; sr. atty. U.S. EPA, Washington, 1977-81; assoc. Skadden, Arps, Slate, Meagher & Flom, Washington, 1981-83, ptnr., 1983-93; mem. Van Ness Feldman, Washington, 1994—. Bd. advisors Chem. Waste Litigation Reporter, Washington, 1985—. Mem. ABA, D.C. Bar Assn. Office: Van Ness Feldman Ste 7 1050 Thomas Jefferson St NW Washington DC 20007-3837 E-mail: mhb@vnf.com.

BERNSTEIN, NADIA J. lawyer; b. Salford, Lancashire, Eng., Feb. 26, 1945; came to U.S., 1948; d. David Colin and Rose (Bolton) Cohen; m. David J. Adler, Mar. 1977 (div. 1992); m. Robert Bernstein, May, 1997. BA, CCNY, 1966; JD, NYU, 1973. Bar: N.Y. 1974, U.S. Dist. Ct. (so. and ea. dists.) N.Y. 1974, U.S. Ct. Appeals (2d cir.) 1975, U.S. Supreme Ct. 1983. Assoc. Rosenman Colin Freund Lewis & Cohen and predecessor firms, NYC, 1973-82; ptnr. Rosenman & Colin, NYC, 1983-87; v.p., gen. counsel Montefiore Med. Ctr., NYC, 1987-89, sr. v.p., gen. counsel, 1989-98; v.p., gen. counsel, corp. sec. C.R. Bard, Inc., Murray Hill, NJ, 1999—. Mem. legal affairs com. Greater N.Y. Hosp. Assn., N.Y.C., 1987-99; mem. bioethics task force, subcoms. on patient decision making, reproductive techs. and physician-assisted suicide, commn. women's equality Am. Jewish Congress, N.Y.C., 1989—; mem. bd. ethics Village Briarcliff Manor, N.Y., 1997—; conf. bd. Coun. Chief Legal Officers, 1999—; mem. N.J. Gen. Counsel's Group, 1999—. Bd. dirs. Berkeley-in-Scarsdale (N.Y.) Assn., 1989-91. Mem.: ABA (forum on health care, bus. law com., law practice mgmt. com.), NJ Gen. Counsels' Group, Coun. Chief Legal Officers (conf. bd. 1999—), Am. Soc. Corp. Secs., Am. Corp. Coun. Assn. (law mgmt. com. 2000—), Advanced Med. Tech. Assn. (legal com. 2002—), Women Bus. Leaders U.S. Health Care Industry, Exec. Women of NJ, NY State Bar Assn. (exec. com. health law sect. 1996—99, co-chair in-house counsel com. health law sect.), Am. Health Lawyers Assn., Assn. Bar of City of NY. Democrat. Office: C R Bard Inc 730 Central Ave New Providence NJ 07974-1199

BERNSTEIN, NEIL HOWARD, music educator; b. Freeport, Ny, July 30, 1953; s. Lester Ralph and Helen Harriet Bernstein; m. Wallis Beth Bernstein, Aug. 16, 1975; children: Bryn, Amie. BM, SUNY Fredonia, Fredonia, NY, 1971—75; ME, Nazareth Coll., Rochester, NY, 1979; PD, CW Post, Long Island, NY, 1988. Band dir. Newark H.S., Newark, NY, 1975—82, Syosset H.S., Syosset, NY, 1983—89; music chairperson Sayville H.S., Sayville, NY, 1989—. Composer (string orchestra) Super Strings March. Office: Sayville High School 99 Greeley Ave Sayville NY 11782-2300 Office Fax: 631-244-6679.

BERNSTEIN, PAUL, retired academic dean; b. Phila., Jan. 19, 1927; s. Abraham and Jennie (Geek) B.; m. Irma Shuster, Apr. 10, 1949; children: Jay Ira, Lisa Beth. BS, Temple U., 1949, MEd, 1950; PhD, U. Pa., 1955. Tchr. social scis. Phila. pub. schs., 1949-55; prof. European history, chmn. social scis. dept. Lock Haven (Pa.) State Coll., 1955-64, Plattsburg (N.Y.) State U. Coll., 1964-66; dean Coll. Gen. Studies, Rochester Inst. Tech., 1966-76, dean grad.

studies, 1976-92, ret., 1993. Tchr. Elderhostel, Bradenton, Fla., 1998-99. Author: (with R. Green) History of Civilization, 2d edit., 1962, Career Education and the Quality of Working Life, 1980, American Work Values, 1997; mng. editor Lock Haven Bull., 1959-64; author articles on Swedish labor mgmt. issues capitalism and consumerism; manuscript reviewer Polity Press, 1998. Co-chmn. Citizens for Humphrey, Monroe County, N.Y., 1968. Served with AUS, 1944-47; mem. adv. bd. Rochester Bus. Hall of Fame Selection Group, 2002—. Grantee Am. Philos. Soc., 1959; Grantee Swedish Bicentennial Com., 1980 Mem. Ind. Rel. Research Assn., Assn. Gen. and Liberal Studies (exec. bd., pres. 1978-79) Clubs: Elks. Republican. Jewish. Home: 1 Linden Cv Pittsford NY 14534-4614 E-mail: pxbbu@rit.edu.

BERNSTEIN, PAUL STEVEN, cardiologist; b. Schenectady, N.Y., July 22, 1950; s. Stanley and Meta B.; m. Susan, Dec. 30, 1973; children: Avi, Becky, Sari. BA, U. Chgo., 1972, MD, 1976, MA, 1996. Diplomate Am. Bd. Internal Medicine. Intern, resident Michael Reese Hosp. and Med. Ctr., Chgo., 1976-79; fellow Rush Presbyn. St. Lukes, Chgo., 1979-81; cardiologist Milw. Med. Clinic, Milw., 1981-90, Milw. Cardiology Assoc., 1990-92, Assocs. in Cardiology, Ltd., Elmhurst, Ill., 1992-94, Cardiovascular Assocs., Ltd., Milw., 1994—. Staff mem. St. Luke's Med. Ctr., Milw., 1983—, chief cardiology, 2001—; staff mem. St. Francis Hosp., St. Mary's Hosp., Columbia Hosp. Fellow Am. Coll. Cardiology; mem. ACP, Am. Heart Assn. Office: Cardiovascular Assocs Ltd 2801 W KK River Pkwy Ste 840 Milwaukee WI 53215-3668 E-mail: psabs@exec.pc.com.

BERNSTEIN, PENNY L. biologist, educator; b. Newark, Mar. 30, 1947; d. Arthur and Grace E. Bernstein; m. Lowell Thomas Lambert; 1 child, Christopher Lambert. BA, U. Pa., 1969, PhD, 1978. NIMH postdoctoral fellow Inst. of Animal Behavior, Rutgers U., Newark, 1978—80; rsch. assoc. Rutgers U., New Brunswick, NJ, 1984—85, Wetlands Inst., Stone Harbor, NJ, 1983—84; asst. prof. Kent State U., Canton, Ohio, 1994—2000, assoc. prof., 2000—; vis. rschr. Smithsonian Inst., Washington, 1981. Editl. bd. Anthrozoos, London, 2000—. Mem. Supt.'s Adv. Com., Canal Fulton, 1989—. Recipient Distinguished Teaching Award, 2000; grantee, NSF, 1995—98, Am. Philos. Soc., 1979, Edn. Conf. Grant, Martha Holden Jennings Found., 1998. Mem.: Internat. Soc. Anthrozoology (sec. 2001—), Internat. Soc. for Anthrozoos, Soc. for Integrative and Comparative Biology, Am. Ornithol. Union, AAAS, Internat. Soc. for Anthrozoos (editl. bd.), Animal Behavior Soc. (chair edn. com. 2000—). Office: Kent State U Stark 6000 Frank Ave Canton OH 44720 Office Fax: 330-494-6121.

BERNSTEIN, PHYLISS LOUISE, psychologist; b. Balt., Nov. 27, 1940; d. Samuel Wilfred and Helen Dorothy (Gerson) Wilke; m. Robert Bernstein, June 7, 1964; children: Steve, Susan, David. BA in Psychology summa cum laude, Avila Coll., 1980, MS in Psychology summa cum laude, 1981; PhD in Couseling Psychology with high honors, U. Mo., Kansas City, 1986. Lic. psychologist Mo. Psychotherapist Community Counseling Ctr., Kansas City, Mo., 1983-85; assoc. psychologist Counseling and Human Devel. Svcs., Kansas City, Mo., 1985-86; psychologist in pvt. practice Kansas City, Mo., 1996—. Staff privileges Bapt. Med. Ctr., Menorah Med. Ctr.; dir. Jewish Vocat. Svcs., Kansas City, 1988—91, U. Mo. Edn. Dept., Kansas City, Jewish Family and Children Svcs., Jewish Cmty. Found. Contbr. Life mem. Nat. Coun. Jewish Women, Kansas City; bd. dirs. Avila Coll.; adv. bd. mem. Friendship House, 2001—. Mem.: APA, Greater Kansas City Psychol. Assn., Psi Chi, Pi Lambda Theta, Phi Kappa Phi. Avocations: scuba diving, bungy jumping, skiing, horseback riding.

BERNSTEIN, PHYLLIS J. financial consultant; b. N.Y.C., Oct. 10, 1955; d. Stanley and Esther Bernstein; m. Robert Kuchner, Dec. 10, 1978. BBA, Hofstra U., 1977. CPA NY. Staff auditor promoted to sr. Pantasote, Greenwich, Conn., 1977—79; sr. promoted to mgr., corp. auditing RCA (now GE), N.Y.C., 1979—85; tech. mgr., personal fin. planning AICPA, N.Y.C., 1985—88, sr. tech. mgr., personal fin. planning, 1988—91, dir., personal fin. planning, 1991—2001; pres. Phyllis Bernstein Consulting, Inc, N.Y.C., 2001—. Editl. adv. bd. mem. Jour. of Accountancy, Jersey City, 2002—; editl. adv. bd. The Tax Advisor, Jersey City, 2002—; adv. bd. mem. Personal Fin. Planning Monthly, Denver, 2002—, Fee-only Client Newsletters, Jericho, NY, 1998—; founder AICPA Ctr. for Investment Adv. Services, 1998—2000; creator and dir. AICPA Personal Fin. Specialist Designation Program, New York, NY, 1985—2001, AICPA Personal Fin. Planning Membership Sect., New York, NY, 1985—2001. Author: (trade book) Financial Planning for CPAs, 2000, Investment Advisory Relationships: Managing Client Expectations in an Uncertain Market, 2002; contributor and editor: book Guide to Registering as an Investment Adviser, 1997; editor: (newsletter) The Planner, 1985—. Sec. and concours chair Jaguar Touring Club, Monclair, NJ, 1995—98; mem. Young Leadership Cabinet United Jewish Appeal, N.Y.C., 1994—2000; bd. dirs. Jewish Fedn. of Ctrl. NJ Endowment Found., Scotch Plains, 1998—2002; chair investment com. Jewish Fedn. Ctrl. N.J., 2002. Named Top 100 Most Influential Persons in Acctg., Acctg. Today, 1997—2001, Top 10 Names to Know in PFP, 1999—2002, One of four movers, shakers and decision makers, Fin. Planning mag. Mem.: AICPA (legis. and regulation task force pers. fin. planning sect. 2001—02), NY State Soc. of CPAs (fin. planning com. 2002), Fin. Planning Orgn., All-Star Fin. Group (v.p. 2002), Jaguar Touring Club (sec. and concours chair 2000). Democrat. Avocations: skiing, travel, shopping, dining, restoring Jaguars, gardening. Office: Phyllis Bernstein Consulting Inc 7 Penn Plaza Ste 1600 New York NY 10001 Office Fax: 212-643-1951. Personal E-mail: phyllis@pbconsults.com. E-mail: phyllis@pbconsults.com.

BERNSTEIN, RICHARD ALLEN, food products executive; b. N.Y.C., June 28, 1946; s. Sidney and Ethel Helen (Shankman) Bernstein; m. Amelia Fishman, Nov. 21, 1944; children: Bradley Ross, Jennifer Anne. BA in Econs., NYU, 1968. V.p. Pease & Ellman Inc., N.Y.C., 1968-70; pres. P&E Properties Inc., N.Y.C., 1970—; chmn. Western Pub. Co. Inc., N.Y.C., 1984-96; chmn., pres., CEO Western Pub. Group Inc., N.Y.C., 1984-96; chmn. Gen. Med. Corp., Richmond, Va., 1987-93, Harris Wholesale Co., Cleve., 1988-92; chmn., pres., CEO Rabco Health Svcs., Inc., N.Y.C., 1991-93; chmn. Millbrook Distbn. Svcs., Inc., Leicester, Mass., 1997—; chmn., CEO, Rabco Luxury Holdings LLC, 1997—, Breguet LLC, 1997—, B. Manischewitz Co., 1998—. Chmn., pres., CEO Penn Corp., 1986—96; mem. adv. bd. Chase Manhattan Bank, 1985—; chmn., CEO R.A.B. Holdings, Inc., 1996—, Millbrook Distbn. Svcs., Inc., 1997—, Brequet LLC, N.Y.C., 1997—2002, Rabco Luxury Holdings LLC, N.Y.C., 1997—. Trustee Police Athletic League, N.Y.C., 1982—, NYU, 1988—; bd. dirs. Big Apple Circus, Inc., 1992—98, Hosp. for Joint Diseases, N.Y.C., N.Y. State Employee Retirement Sys., N.Y.C.; mem. N.Y. State Commn. on Regulation of Lobbying, Albany, 1982—86; bd. overseers Stern Sch. Bus. NYU; candidate for comptr. City of N.Y., 1981. With U.S. Army, 1969. Fellow, Yeshiva U., 1986. Mem.: Econ. Club N.Y. Republican. Jewish. Office: RAB Holdings 444 Madison Ave Ste 601 New York NY 10022-6903

BERNSTEIN, ROBERT, retired physician, state official, former army officer; b. N.Y.C., Feb. 20, 1920; s. Morris and Rose (Gordich) B. BA, Vanderbilt U., 1942; MD, U. Louisville, 1946. Diplomate Nat. Bd. Med. Examiners, Am. Bd. Internal Medicine. Commd. 2nd lt. U.S. Army, 1942, advanced through grades to maj. gen., 1973; intern Grasslands Hosp., Valhalla, N.Y., 1946-47; resident Walter Reed Army Med. Ctr., Washington, 1952-55, dep. comdr., 1972-73, comdg. gen., 1973-78; surgeon U.S. Mil. Assistance Command, Vietnam, 1970-72; ret., 1978; commr. for spl. health svcs. Tex. Dept. Health, Austin, 1978-80, commr. of health, 1980-91. Adj. prof. U. Tex. Health Sci. Ctr., 1982—. Contbr. articles to mil. and med. jours. Decorated D.S.M. with oak leaf cluster, Legion of Merit with two oak leaf clusters, Bronze Star with oak leaf cluster, Purple Heart. Fellow ACP; mem. Soc. Med. Consultants to Armed Forces, Internat. Soc. Internal Medicine, Phi Delta Epsilon, Phi Kappa Phi, Alpha Epsilon Pi, Alpha Omega Alpha. Home: 3805 Greystone Dr Austin TX 78731-1505 E-mail: rakgen@aol.com.

BERNSTEIN, SAMUEL, insurance company executive; b. Bklyn., Dec. 4, 1940; s. David Solomon and Blanche Bernstein; m. Nina Lia Hersh, Jan. 5, 1973; 1 child, Jennifer Lori. BA, Adelphi U., 1962. Regional sales mgr. Union Underwear Co., N.Y.C., 1963-65; nat. sales mgr. Kayser-Roth Hosiery Co., N.Y.C., 1965-73, regional sales mgr. L.A., 1973-75; pres. Bernstein Ins. Svcs., L.A., 1975—. Officer Life Ins. Leaders Roundtable, L.A., 1980-83; pres. Agts. Adv. Coun., L.A., 1984-86. Author: (monthly newsletter) Life Ins. and Estate Planning, 1996—. Bd. trustees Temple Beth Hillel, 1990-94; bd. dirs., mem. Am. Jewish Com., planned giving com., 1996—, pres. coun. Peter Zippi Fund for Animals. Staff sgt. USAF, 1962-68. Named Agt. of Yr., Mfrs. Life/Penn Mut. Life, 1987-93. Mem. Life Underwriters Assn. of L.A. (com. mem. 1988-90), Nat. Wildlife Found., Braemar Country Club, Fraternity of Friends LA Music Ctr., U.S. Profl. Golfers Assn. PGA (capt. of marshals, Championship sr. open). Avocations: golf, reading, model building, traveling. Office: Bernstein Ins Svcs 3345 Wilshire Blvd Ste 715 Los Angeles CA 90010-1818 E-mail: bernsteinis@aol.com.

BERNSTEIN, SANFORD IRWIN, biology educator; b. Bklyn., June 10, 1953; s. Harold and Adele Dorothy (Kutner) B.; m. Laurel Spear, July 10, 1983. BS, SUNY, Stony Brook, 1974; PhD, Wesleyan U., 1979. Rsch. fellow U. Va., Charlottesville, 1979-82; asst. prof. biology San Diego State U., 1983-85, assoc. prof., 1985-88, prof., 1988—. Assoc. dir. Molecular Biology Inst., 1987-92, dir. 1992-95; co-dir. DNA cert. program, 1983—, chair biology dept., 1995-2000, coord. joint-doctoral program in cell and molecular biology with U. Calif. San Diego, 2000—; established investigatorship Am. Heart Assn., 1989-94; mem. grant rev. panels NIH, Am. Heart Assn. Mem. editl. bd. Devel. Biology, 1991-95; contbr. articles to profl. jours. Muscular Dystrophy Assn. fellow, 1979-82, grantee, 1984—; grantee NIH, 1983—, NSF, 1997-2000. Mem.: AAAS, Am. Physiol. Soc., Biophys. Soc., Am. Soc. Microbiology, Am. Soc. Biochemistry and Molecular Biology, Am. Soc. Cell Biology, Genetics Soc. Am., Sigma Xi. Achievements include research in developmental regulation of muscle gene expression in Drosophila, muscle protein isoform function, alternative RNA splicing. Office: San Diego State U Biology Dept and Molec Bio Inst San Diego CA 92182-4614 E-mail: sanford.bernstein@sdsu.edu.

BERNSTEIN, SOL, cardiologist, educator; b. West New York, N.J., Feb. 3, 1927; s. Morris Irving and Rose (Leibowitz) B.; m. Suzi Maris Sommer, Sept. 15, 1963; 1 son, Paul. AB in Bacteriology, U. Southern Calif., 1952, MD, 1956. Diplomate Am. Bd. Internal Medicine. Intern Los Angeles County Hosp., 1956-57, resident, 1957-60; practice medicine specializing in cardiology L.A., 1960—; staff physician dept. medicine Los Angeles County Hosp. U. So. Calif. Med. Center, L.A., 1960—, chief cardiology clinics, 1964, asst. dir. dept. medicine, 1965-72; chief profl. services Gen. Hosp., 1972-74; med. dir. Los Angeles County-U So. Calif. Med. Center, L.A., 1974-94; med. dir. central region Los Angeles County, 1974-78; dir. Dept. Health Services, Los Angeles County, 1978; assoc. dean Sch. Medicine, U. So. Calif., L.A., 1986-94, assoc. prof., 1968—; med. dir. Health Rsch. Assn., L.A., 1995—. Cons. Crippled Childrens Svc. Calif., 1965—. Contbr. articles on cardiac surgery, cardiology, diabetes and health care planning to med. jours. Served with AUS, 1946-47, 52-53. Fellow A.C.P., Am. Coll. Cardiology; mem. Am. Acad. Phys. Execs., Am. Fedn. Clin. Research, N.Y. Acad. Sci., Los Angeles, Am. heart assns., Los Angeles Soc. Internal Medicine, Los Angeles Acad. Medicine, Sigma Xi, Phi Beta Phi, Phi Eta Sigma, Alpha Omega Alpha. Home: 4966 Ambrose Ave Los Angeles CA 90027-1756 Office: 1640 Marengo St Los Angeles CA 90033-1036

BERNSTEIN, STAN, federal bankruptcy judge; b. L.A., 1941; m. Jane Ellen Hirschfield; 3 children. BA, Brandeis U., 1962; MA, U. Chgo., 1964; PhD, Harvard U., 1970; JD, Rutgers U., 1973. Bar: Mich. 1974, Ohio 1974, Calif. 1985, Ariz. 1989, Mass. 1991. Mem. faculty U. Calif., Davis, 1967-70, Rutgers U., 1970-73; assoc., ptnr. Honigman, Miller, Schwartz & Cohn, Detroit, 1974-82; bankruptcy judge for Ea. Dist. Mich., U.S. Bankruptcy Ct., Detroit, 1982-84; ptnr. Gendel, Raskoff, Shapiro & Quittner, L.A., 1984-85, Dickinson, Wright, Detroit, 1985-89; shareholder Brown & Bain, Phoenix, 1989-90; ptnr. Foley, Hoag & Eliot, Boston, 1991-96; bankruptcy judge for Ea. Dist. N.Y., U.S. Bankruptcy Ct., Central Islip, 1996—. Mem.: Nat. Conf. Bankruptcy Judges. Office: US Bankruptcy Ct 290 Federal Plz Central Islip NY 11722-4437 E-mail: Stan_Bernstein@nyeb.uscourts.gov.

BERNSTEIN, STANLEY JOSEPH, manufacturing executive; s. David William and Irene Mildred Bernstein; m. Cathy Ann Grey; children: Michael A., Geoffrey T. BA, Brown U., 1965; JD, U. Pa., 1968. Bar: Mass. 1968. Mgr. Am. Biltrite Inc., Chelsea, Mass., 1968-71, div. gen. mgr. Cambridge, Mass., 1971-78, v.p. corp. devel., 1978-82; exec. v.p. The Biltrite Corp., Waltham, Mass., 1983-85, chmn., chief exec. officer, 1986—, also bd. dirs. Bd. dirs. Shenzhen Biltrite-SPEC Soling Co., Ltd., Shenzhen, China, Atlanta. Life trustee Roxbury Latin Sch., West Roxbury, Mass.; trustee Brown U.; fellow Harvard Sch. Dental Medicine. Office: The Biltrite Corp PO Box 9045 51 Sawyer Rd Waltham MA 02454-9045 E-mail: stanley.bernstein@biltrite.com.

BERNSTEIN, STUART A. ambassador; b. Washington, D.C., 1938; Leader in real estate devel., investment and mgmt. Mid-Atlantic region, Washington; U.S. amb. to Denmark, 2001—. Apptd. commr. Internat. Cultural and Trade Ctr., 1991; apptd. trustee John F. Kennedy Ctr. for Performing Arts, 1992—2001. Former bd. trustees Am. Univ.; former bd. dirs. Weizman Inst. of Sci. Office: DOS Amb 5280 Copenhagen Pl Washington DC 20521*

BERNSTEIN, SUSAN See DVORA, SUSAN

BERNSTEIN, WILLIAM, film company executive; b. N.Y.C., Aug. 30, 1933; s. Philip and Sadie (Lazar) B.; m. Evelyn Pauline Schnur, Aug. 3, 1958; children: Marian Suzanne, Steven Laurence. BA, NYU, 1954; LLB, Yale U., 1959. Atty. United Artists Corp., N.Y.C., 1959-67, v.p. bus. affairs, 1967-72, sr. v.p. bus. affairs, 1972-78; exec. v.p. Orion Pictures Corp., N.Y.C., 1978-91, pres., chief exec. officer, dir., 1991-92; exec. v.p. Paramount Pictures Corp., L.A., 1992—. Mem. ABA, Acad. Motion Picture Arts and Scis. Home: 282 Bentley Cir Los Angeles CA 90049-2414 Office: Paramount Pictures Corp 5555 Melrose Ave Los Angeles CA 90038-3197

BERNSTEIN, WILLIAM ELLIOTT, lawyer; b. Worcester, Mass., Jan. 19, 1930; s. Max L. and Sophie (Kaplan) B.; m. Marjorie R. Burwick, Nov. 3, 1957; children— David, Laurie, Robert, Richard. B.B.A., Clark U., 1953; J.D., Boston U., 1956. Bar: Mass. 1956, Conn. 1956, U.S. Dist. Ct. Mass., U.S. Supreme Ct. 1969. Assoc. Dodge, Saunders & Hinkley, Worcester, 1956-57; assoc., then ptnr. Burwick & Burwick, Worcester, 1957-82; pres. Weinstein, Bernstein & Burwick, P.C., Worcester, 1982— ; trustee, dir., mem. fin. com. Consumers Savs. Bank, Worcester, 1983— ; mem. Mass. Bd. Bar Overseers, 1985—, Gov.'s Task Force on Liability Issues, 1986—; del. White Ho. Conf. on Small Bus., 1986—; trustee Mass. Continuing Legal Edn. Mem. adv. council U.S. SBA Mass., 1974-80, chmn., 1980-83, mem. nat. adv. council, 1984—, mem. exec. com., 1985 ; mem. New Eng. region civil rights com. Anti-Defamation League, B'nai B'rith, 1983— ; mem. Lawyers Alliance for Nuclear Arms Control, Inc.; trustee Anna Maria Coll., 1979— . Served with USAR, 1949-51. Named Atty. Advocate of Yr., U.S. SBA, 1984. Fellow Am. Bar Found., Mass. Bar Found. (life); mem. ABA (ho. of dels.), Mass. Bar Assn. (pres. 1983-84, bd. dels.), Am. Bd. Trial Advocates (trustee), New Eng. Bar Assn. (bd. dels.), Bar Assn. U.S. Supreme Ct. (bd. dirs.), Worcester C. of C. Club: Mount Pleasant Country (past pres.). Office: Weinstein Bernstein & Burwick PC 370 Main St Worcester MA 01608-1723

BERNSTEIN, WILLIAM JOSEPH, glass artist, educator; b. Newark, Dec. 3, 1945; s. Jacob and Rosalind (Merliss) B.; m. Katherine Schachter, July 21, 1968; children: Joshua, Alex. BFA, Phila. U. of Arts, 1968. Artist in residence Penland (N.C.) Sch. of Crafts, 1968-70; instr. Summervail Workshop, Vail, Colo., U. So. Calif., L.A., Pilchuck Glass Ctr., Stanwood, Wash., Naples (N.Y.) Mill Sch.; tchr. Bezalel Acad., Jerusalem, Israel, 1997—. One-man show Hodges Taylor Galley, Charlotte N.C., 1997; exhibited in group shows at Somerhill Gallery, Chapel Hill, N.C., Grohe Glass Gallery, Boston, Marx Gallery, Chgo., Am. Craft Mus., N.Y.C., John Michael Kohler Arts Ctr., Sheboygan, Wis., Spaso House, Moscow, U.S.S.R., The Denver Art Mus., Laguna Art Mus., Laguna Beach, Calif., Milwaukee Art Mus., J.B. Speed Art Mus., Louisville, Ky., Va. Mus. Fine Arts, Richmond, Ark. Arts Ctr. Decorative Arts Mus., Little Rock, Galerie Angela Hollings, Hameln, Germany, J&L Lobmeyr, Vienna, Austria, Galerie Rob van den Doel, The Hague, The Netherlands, Isetan Galleries, Japan; represented in permanent collections the Corning (N.Y.) Mus. of Glass, the Mint Mus. Art, Charlotte, N.C., Nat. Collection Fine Art, Washington, Greenville (S.C.) County Mus. Art, Australian Coun. for the Arts, Sidney, Morse Gallery Art, Winter Park, Fla., Ft. Lauderdale (Fla.) Mus. Arts, R.J. Reynolds Collection, Winston-Salem, N.C., Craft and Folk Mus., L.A., Glasmus., Frauenau, Germany, Ark. Art Ctr., Little Rock, Glasmus., Ebeltoft, Denmark, J&L Lobmeyr, Vienna, Austria, Asheville (N.C.) Mus. Art, Yamaha Corp., Japan, Chrysler Mus. Norfolk, Va., Newark (N.J.) Mus., Charles A. Wustan Mus. Arts, Racine, Wis. Louis Comfort Tiffany Found. grantee, 1975, NEA Master Craftsman Apprenticeship, 1976; NEA fellow, 1974, N.C. Arts Coun. fellow, 1983, masterworks fellow Creative Glass Ctr. Am., 1990. Office: 469 Hannah Branch Rd Burnsville NC 28714-7569 E-mail: wberns1141@aol.com.

BERNSTEIN, WILLIAM ROBERT, banker; b. Newark, Apr. 14, 1947; s. Leonard H. and Gwen (Burstein) B.; m. Roberta Ann Sipkin, June 25, 1972; children: Carrie, Elizabeth, Michael. BS, Rensselaer Poly. Inst., 1969, BArch, 1970; M of Urban Planning, U. Wash., 1972. Project planner Jersey City Redevel. Agy., 1972-74; v.p. Matthews & Wright Inc., N.Y.C., 1974-79, Thompson Mckinnon Securities, N.Y.C., 1979-81; mng. dir. Drexel Burnham Lambert, N.Y.C., 1981-89; sr. v.p. The Tokai Bank, Ltd., N.Y.C., 1990-99; mng. dir. Mesco Ltd., Ridgefield, Conn., 1999—; dir. Inceptor Ltd., Metro Mktg. Resources Inc., Hamden, Conn. Pres. Nat. Leased Housing Assn., Washington, 1987-88, chmn., 1988-89, chmn. emeritus, 1989—; bd. dirs. Pixel Devices Internat., Metromktg. Resources, Inc. Trustee Congregation B'nai Yisrael. Home: 29 Wampus Lake Dr Armonk NY 10504-1122 Office: Mesco Ltd 470 Main St Ridgefield CT 06877-4516 E-mail: bill@mesco-ltd.com.

BERNSTINE, DANIEL O'NEAL, law educator, university president; b. Berkeley, Calif., Sept. 7, 1947; s. Annias and Emma (Jones) B.; m. Nancy Jean Tyler, July 27, 1971 (div. Mar. 1986); children: Quincy Tyler, Justin Tyler. BA, U. Calif., Berkeley, 1969; JD, Northwestern U., Chgo., 1972; LLM, U. Wis., 1975; LLD (hon.), Hanyang U., Seoul, Korea, 1999, Waseda U., Tokyo, 2003. Bar: D.C. 1970, Wis. 1979. Prof. law Howard U. Law Sch., Washington, 1975-78, gen. counsel, interim dean, 1987-90; prof. law U. Wis. Law Sch., Madison, 1978-97, dean, 1990-97; pres. Portland (Ore.) State Univ., 1997—. Author: Wisconsin and Federal Civil Procedure, 1986. Bd. dirs. Madison Cmty. Found., 1990-94, Portland Urban League, Legacy Health Sys., Willamette United Way, 2001—; mem. Portland Multnomah Progress Bd., 1998—, Kellogg Commn. on the Future of State and Land-Grant Univs., 1997-2000. Mem. Am. Law Inst., Portland C. of C. (bd. dirs.). Office: Portland State Univ PO Box 751 Portland OR 97207-0751

BERNT, BENNO ANTHONY, business executive, entrepreneur and investor; b. Bielitz, Austria, Mar. 14, 1931; came to U.S., 1953, naturalized, 1961; s. Victor and Grete Bernt; m. Constance Smigel, June 22, 1957; children: Karin, Eric, Steve. BS in Engring. cum laude, Fed. Inst. Tech., Vienna, Austria, 1952; DCS in Bus. and Econs. cum laude, U. Econs. & Bus. Adminstrn., Vienna, 1953; MBA, Carnegie Mellon U., 1954. Fin. and mfg. exec. Chrysler Corp., 1954-59; mfg. and bus. planning exec., subs. gen. mgr. Whirlpool Corp., 1959-68; pres. Cissell Mfg. Co., Louisville, 1968-70; gen. mgr. Simonds Abrasive Co., Phila., 1970-73; v.p. fin. ESB Ray-O-Vac Corp., Phila., 1973-76, exec. v.p., dir., 1977-78; pres., CEO RAYOVAC, Madison, Wis., 1979-82; sr. v.p. fin. and planning, CFO Nat. Intergroup Inc., Pitts., 1983-87; chmn. The Griffin Group, Pitts., 1988—, Univ. Ptnrs., Inc., 1997—; interim CEO Carnegie Tech. Edn., Inc., 1998-99. Bd. dirs. Pitts. Tissue Engring. Initiative, Carnegie Sci. Ctr.; dir. tech. transfer Carnegie Mellon U., 1992—97. Bd. dirs. Pitts. Symphony; adv. bd. Sch. Computer Sci. chmn., and Sch. Music Carnegie Mellon U., 1993—. Mem. Duquesne Club, Fox Chapel Golf Club, Pitts. Golf Club. Office: Univ Partners Inc 308 Schenley Rd Pittsburgh PA 15217-1173 E-mail: bbernt@andrew.cmu.edu. *I believe the measure of one's true success lies in how well we are using our own potential, and how well we are serving others.*

BERNT, JOSEPH PHILIP, communications educator; b. Portland, Oreg., June 5, 1947; s. Philip Nicholas and Lavinia Catherine Bernt; m. Phyllis Ethel Weinroth, May 20, 1972. BA in English, Portland (Oreg.) State U., 1971; MA in English, U. of Nebr., 1972, PhD in English, 1980. Instr. English U. of Nebr., Lincoln, Nebr., 1973—80; info. specialist Nebr. Career Info. Sys., Lincoln, Nebr., 1980—82; asst. dir. of pubs. U. of Nebr., 1982—89; asst. prof. of journalism Ohio U., Athens, Ohio, 1989—94, assoc. prof. of journalism, 1995—2000, prof. of journalism, 2001—. Chmn. Ohio U. Grad. Coun., 2001—03. Author: Postsecondary School Information, 1981; editor: A Celebration of the Legacies of E. W. Scripps: His Life, Works and Heritage, 1993, The Big Chill: Investigative Reporting in the Current Media Environment, 2000 (Sigma Delta Chi award Soc. of Profession Journalists, 2001), Vanguard (All-American award Associated Collegiate Press, 1970), Portland Rev. (Nat. Third Pl. prize Coun. of Coll. Lit. Mags., 1971); assistant editor: Journalism History, 2001—; co-author: Corporate Magazines of the United States, 1992, Trade, Industrial, and Professional Periodicals of the United States, 1994, Cyberscribes.1: The New Journalists, 1997, History of the Mass Media in the United States, 1998, Encyclopedia of Advertising, 2003; contbr. articles to profl. jours. and mags. Nebr. press rep. Fred Harris for Pres., Lincoln, Ohio, 1975—76. Recipient Outstanding Tutor award, Ohio U. Honors Tutorial Coll., 2002; fellow, Woodrow Wilson Found., 1971—72, Nat. Def. Edn. fellow, U.S. Dept. of Edn., 1971—72, Maude Hammond Fling fellow, U. of Nebr., 1972—73; grantee, Ohio Bd. of Regents, 1996, 1997, NSF, 2001—; scholar KISN Comm. scholar, Portland State U., 1970—71, Newcomer's scholar, Coun. for Advancement and Support of Edn., 1983. Mem.: Rsch. Soc. for Am. Periodicals, Broadcast Edn. Assn., Popular Culture Assn., Am. Journalism Historians Assn. (mem. of dissertation award com. 2001—), Assn. for Edn. in Journalism and Mass Comms. (head of mag. divsn. 2002—03). Democrat. Roman Catholic. Avocations: book collecting, bird hunting, deep sea fishing, boat building, free-speech advocacy.

BERNTHAL, FREDERICK MICHAEL, association executive; b. Sheridan, Wyo., Jan. 10, 1943; s. Erwin and Erna Bernthal; m. Heather A. Lancaster; 1 child, Justin. BS, Valparaiso U., 1964; PhD, U. Calif.-Berkeley, 1969. Research staff Yale U., New Haven, 1969-70; prof. Mich. State U., East Lansing, 1970-80; legis. asst. Senator Howard Baker, Washington, 1978-80, chief legis. asst., 1980-83; mem. U.S. Nuclear Regulatory Commn., Washington, 1983-88; asst. sec. oceans, environment, and sci. Dept. of State, Washington, 1988-90; dep. dir. NSF, Washington, 1990-94; pres. Univs. Rsch. Assn., Washington, 1994—. Bd. dirs. PPL Corp., Challenger Ctr. Space Sci. Edn., Sci. Svc., Inc. Contbr. 45 articles to sci. jours. NATO Sr. Scientist fellow U. Copenhagen, 1977; Congl. Sci. fellow Am. Phys. Soc., 1978-79 Fellow Am. Phys Soc.; mem. AAAS, Am. Chem. Soc., Cosmos Club of Washington. Republican. Lutheran. Office: Univs Rsch Assn 1111 19th St NW Ste 400 Washington DC 20036-3627 E-mail: bernthal@ura.nw.dc.us.

BERNTHAL, HAROLD GEORGE, healthcare company executive; b. Frankenmuth, Mich., June 11, 1928; s. Wilfred Michael and Olga Bertha (Stern) B.; m. Margaret Hrebek, Jan. 25, 1958; children: Barbara Anne, Karen Elizabeth, James Willard. BS in Chemistry, Mich. State U., 1950. Pres. Am. Hosp. Supply Corp., Evanston, Ill., 1974-85; chmn. Cobern Inc., Lake Forest, Ill., 1986—. Life trustee Northwestern Meml. Hosp., Chgo.; hon. bd. dirs. Valparaiso (Ind.) U.; former chair Wheat Ridge Ministries; former governing mem. Chgo. Symphony Orch. Served with AUS, 1950-52. Recipient Lumen Christi medal Valparaiso U., 1988. Mem. Health Industries Assn. (past pres.), Health Industry Mfr.'s Assn. (past mem. exec. com.), Pharm. Mfrs. Assn. (past chmn. med. device com., Knollwood Club, Old Elm Club, The Reserve, Bigfoot Country Club.

BERNTSON, GARY GLEN, psychiatry, psychology and pediatrics educator; b. Mpls., June 16, 1945; s. Edward Mathias and Meryle (Nelson) B.; m. Susan Berntson, July 11, 2002. BA, U. Minn., 1968, PhD, 1971. Postdoctoral fellow Rockefeller U., N.Y.C., 1971-73; asst. prof. dept. psychology Ohio State U., Columbus, 1973-77, assoc. prof., 1977-81, prof., 1981—, prof. dept. pediatrics, 1983—, prof. of psychiatry, 1988—. Affiliate scientist Yerkes Regional Primate Rsch. Ctr., Emory U., Atlanta, 1984-95; mem. initial rev. group ADAMHA, Washington, 1989-91, NIMH, Washington, 1991-93; mem. fellowship rev. panel NSF, Washington, 1991-95. Contbr. over 150 articles to profl. jours., 20 chpts. to books. Fellow NSF, 1969, USPHS, 1972. Mem. Soc. for Neurosci., Soc. for Psychophysiol. Rsch.; fellow AAAS. Achievements include novel concepts of control of the autonomic nervous system and psychosomatic relations. Office: Ohio State U Dept Psychology 1885 Neil Ave Columbus OH 43210-1222

BERO, JOSEPH MARTIN, manufacturing engineer; b. Chgo., Apr. 27, 1965; s. Stephen and Doris May (Bausch) Bero; m. Dawn Maria Calvert; children: Maxwell Alexander, Nathanial Joseph, Quindlan Joseph, Kenten Joseph. BSChemE, U. Ill., 1987. Registered profl. engr., Calif., Md., Va., Ga. Design engr. Chevron, U.S.A., Richmond, Calif., 1987—88; staff mem. BDM Fed., Germantown, Md., 1992—93; project engr. Castol Heavy Duty Lubricants Inc., Balt., 1993—96, mgr. engring. and regulatory affairs, 1996—98, mfg. and engring. mgr., 1998—2001, key projects mgr., 2001—. Lt. USN, 1988-92. Mem. ASME, NSPE, Nat. Coun. Examiners for Engring. and Surveying. Avocations: woodworking, racquetball, basketball. Home: 4327 Federal Hill Rd Street MD 21154-1124 Office: Castrol Heavy Duty Lubricants Inc 9300 Pulaski Hwy Baltimore MD 21220-2418 E-mail: bero@illinoisalumni.org., bero.jdmn@worldnet.att.net.

BEROLZHEIMER, KARL, lawyer; b. Chgo., Mar. 31, 1932; s. Leon J. and Rae Gloss (Lowenthal) B.; m. Diane Glick, July 10, 1954; children: Alan, Eric, Paul, Lisa. BA, U. Ill., 1953; JD, Harvard U., 1958. Bar: Ill. 1958, U.S. Ct. Appeals (7th cir.) 1964, U.S. Ct. Appeals (9th cir.) 1969, U.S. Supreme Ct. 1976. Assoc. Ross & Hardies, Chgo., 1958-66, ptnr., 1966-76, of counsel, 1993—; v.p. legal Centel Corp., Chgo., 1976-77, v.p., gen. counsel, 1977-82, sr. v.p., gen. counsel, 1982-88, sr. v.p., gen. counsel, sec., 1988-93. Nat. adv. bd. Ctr. for Informatics Law, John Marshall Law Sch., Chgo., 1988-93; mem. Corp. Counsel Ctr., Northwestern U. Law Sch., 1987-93, mem. emeritus, 1993—; mem. adv. bd. Litigation Risk Mgmt. Inst., 1989-95; bd. dirs. Milton Industries, Chgo., Devon Bank, Chgo.; cons. Mt. Pulaski Tel. and Elec. Co., Lincoln, Ill., 1981-86; sec., gen. counsel Consol. Water Co., Chgo., 1968-72; mem. human rels. task force Chgo. Cmty. Trust, 1988-90. Bd. dirs. The Nat. Conf. Commn. and Justice, Chgo., presiding co-chmn., 1987-90, mem. nat. exec. bd. dirs., 1988-98, chair investment com., 1991-94, nat. co-chair, 1992-95, pres., 1993-94, chair, 1995-98; exec. bd. Internat. Coun. Christians and Jews, 1996-2000, v.p., 1998-2000; bd. dirs. Evanston (Ill.) Mental Health, 1975-82, chair, 1978-80; dir. Evanston Cmty. Found., 1996-2003, vice chair, chair grants com., 1996-98, chair, 1999-2001; bd. dirs. Beth Emet Found., 1997; trustee Northlight Theatre, Evanston, 1992—, vice-chair, 1993-99; mem. coun. The Communitarian Network, 1993-96; trustee Beth Emet Synagogue, Evanston, 1985-87, 89, sec., 1985-89; chair Capital Campaign Plan com., 1994-97; discrimination priority com. United Way, 1990-97, vice-chair, 1993; mem. assembly Parliament of the World's Religions, 1993; mem. Ill. atty. gen.'s ad hoc com. for creation of justice commn., 1994; adv. com. Ill. Justice Commn., 1995-96; adv. bd. Nat. Underground R.R. Freedom Ctr., 1997—. 1st lt. U.S. Army, 1953-55. Fellow Am. Bar Found.; mem. ABA (chair telcom. com. bus. law sect. 1982-86, dispute resolution com. 1986-90, office com. 1991-95, mem. Coalition for Justice 1993-97, bd. editors Bus. Law Today 1995-97, co-chair conflicts of interest com. 1997-2001, past chair 2001-03), Chgo. Bar Assn. (devel. of law com. 1963-77, chair 1971-73), Chgo. Coun. Lawyers. Democrat. Home: 414 Ashland Ave Evanston IL 60202-3208 Office: Ross & Hardies 150 N Michigan Ave Ste 2500 Chicago IL 60601-7567 E-mail: dkberolz@aol.com.

BERON, GAIL LASKEY, real estate analyst, appraiser, consultant; b. Detroit, Nov. 13, 1943; d. Charles Jack Laskey and Florence B. (Rosenthal) Eisenberg; divorced; children: Monty Charles, Bryan David. Cert. real estate analyst, Mich. Chief/staff appraiser Ft. Wayne Mortgage Co., Birmingham, Mich., 1973-75; pvt. practice fee appraiser S.C., Iowa, Mich., 1976-80; pres. The Beron Co., Southfield, Mich., 1980—. Cons. ptnr. Real Estate Counseling Group Conn., Storrs, 1983—, Real Estate Counseling Group Am., prin., 1984—; lectr. real estate confs. Recipient M. William Donnally award Mortgage Bankers Assn. Am., 1975. Mem. Appraisal Inst. (nat. faculty 1991-97), Soc. Real Estate Appraisers (bd. dirs. Detroit chpt. 1980-82, nat. faculty 1983-91), Am. Inst. Real Estate Appraisers (bd. dirs. Detroit chpt. 1982-86, nat. faculty 1984-91), Nat. Assn. Realtors, Detroit Bd. Realtors, Southfield Bd. Realtors, Women Brokers Assn. (treas. Southfield chpt. 1981-83), Young Mortgage Bankers (bd. dirs. 1974-75). Avocations: art, music, piano, reading. Home: 7008 Bridge Way West Bloomfield MI 48322-3527 Office: Beron Co Ste 28 33000 Covington Club Dr Apt 28 Farmington Hills MI 48334-1649

BERON, KURT JAMES, economics educator; b. N.Y.C., Sept. 12, 1956; s. Peter K. and Ilene (Israel) B.; m. Laurie L. LeFebvre, May 23, 1987; children: Jenna, Celia. BSBA, U. N.C., Greensboro, 1977; MSW, U. N.C., Chapel Hill, 1980, PhD in Econs., 1985. Assoc. prof. U. Tex., Richardson, 1985—; assoc. dean, dir. undergrad. studies, Sch. of Social Scis. Univ. Tex., Dallas, 1993—96, assoc. dir. Ctr. Edn. and Social Policy, 1994—98; faculty rep. Nat. Collegiate Athletic Assn., 2000—. Reviewer TCMP grants IRS, Washington, 1990—; coord. undergrad. econ. prog., 1992-94; chair, computing in the Social Scis. com., 1992-2001. Assoc. editor Structural Equation Modeling: A Multidisciplinary Jour., 1993-96, Evaluation Rev., 1989-92; contbr. articles to profl. jours. Rsch. grantee State of Tex., 1988-90. Mem. Am. Econ. Assn., So. Econ. Assn., Law and Soc. Assn. Avocations: soccer, computers, chess. Office: U Tex at Dallas PO Box 830688 Richardson TX 75083-0688

BERONA, DAVID A. computer systems librarian, educator; b. Dayton, Ohio, Mar. 19, 1950; s. Daniel Anthony Berona and Dorothy Janet Voltz; m. Rose E. O'Brien, Aug. 11, 1981. BSc, Wright State U., 1974; MSc, Simmons Coll., 1990; MA, U. of NH., 2001. Libr. Westbrook Coll., Portland, Maine, 1990—96; systems libr. U. of New Eng., Biddeford, Maine, 1996—99; head, libr. computer systems U. of NH., 1999—. Contbr. book of essays: language of comics; reviewer Internat. Jour. of Comic Art, 1992—; editor: Image & Narrative Online, 2001—; contbr. articles to jours. on woodcut novels and wordless comics. Grantee Bingham Foundaton Faculty Enrichment grant, Westbrook Coll., 1993—96; Faculty Devel. grant, U. of NH, 2002, Instrnl. Tech. grant, 2002, Parents Assn. grant, 2001, 2002. Mem.: AAUP, Comic Book Def. League, Popular Culture Assn., Soc. for the History of Authorship, Reading and Pub., New Eng. Libr. Assn., Libr. and Informational Tech. Assn., Assn. of Coll. and Rsch. Libraries, Am. Libr. Assn. Avocations: watercolors, swimming. Home: PO Box 448 Gilmanton NH 03237 Office: University of New Hampshire 18 Library Way Durham NH 03824 Office Fax: 603-862-0247. E-mail: david.berona@unh.edu.

BERQUIST, ANGELA SU, writer, philosopher; b. Portland, Oreg., Oct. 31, 1955; d. Herbert Carl and Helen Marie Berquist; m. Michael George Betts, Aug. 16, 1997. BA in Clin. Psychology, San Francisco State U.; PhD, Calif. Inst. Integral Studies, 2001. Ballet dancer Frankfurt (Germany) Ballet, 1975—76; mgr. classical music soloist Wolfgang Basch, Frankfurt, 1977—88. Author: Eyes Over Courtrai, A Thing of Value, Road to Armageddon, Walks in the Garden of All Possibilities, Spinning Wheels, Eighty Nights, Old New Path. Zen Buddhist. Achievements include development of Field Theory of Consciousness. Avocations: travel, food, theoretical science, classical music, humor. Personal E-mail: zadekim@comcast.net.

BERRA, P. BRUCE, computer educator; b. Smiths Creek, Mich., Apr. 14, 1935; s. Mike John and Dorothy (Nelson) B.; 1 son, Marshall R. BS, U. Mich., 1958, MS, 1962; PhD, Purdue U., 1968. Sr. engr. Hughes Aircraft Corp., Culver City, Calif., 1958-60; engr., tech. advisor Bendix Corp., Ann Arbor, Mich., 1960-63; instr. U. Mich. Dearborn, 1964-65; asst. prof. info. engring. Boston U., 1965-66; assoc. prof. Syracuse U. (N.Y.), 1968-74, 74—, prof., chmn. indsl. engring. and ops. research, 1978-82, prof. elec. and computer engring., 1982-96; dir. N.Y. State Ctr. for Advanced Tech./Software Engring., 1991-96; dir. Info. Tech. Rsch. Inst., disting. prof. info. tech. Wright State U., Dayton, Ohio, 1997-2000. Cons. IBM Corp., Bell No. Rsch., IITRI, PAR Tech., SCEEE, Singer Link, TRW, KAMAN, Opticomp. Gen. chmn., organizer Workshop on Database Machines, 1980-89. USAF Office of Sci. Research univ. resident research fellow, 1982-83 Fellow IEEE; mem. IEEE Computer Soc. (editor-in-chief CS Press 1981-83, vice chmn. publs. bd. 1984-85, governing bd. 1985-86, 89-91, disting. visitors program 1986-88, 89-91, gen. chmn. internat. conf. on data engring. 1986). E-mail: bberra@worldnet.att.net.

BERRA, ROBERT LOUIS, human resources consultant; b. St. Louis, June 24, 1924; s. Angelo John and Clara Catherine B.; m. Vivian Lorene Miles, Nov. 11, 1944; children— Kathleen Patricia Berra Schrage, Patricia Susan Berra Babcock. BS in Econs, St. Louis U., 1947; MBA, Harvard U., 1947. Faculty mem. St. Louis U., 1947-51; with Monsanto Co., 1951-70, 74-89, v.p. personnel, 1974-80; sr. v.p. adminstrn. St. Louis, 1980-89. V.p. pers. and pub. rels. Foremost-McKesson, Inc., San Francisco, 1970-74; adj. faculty Washington U., U. Ill., Urbana-Champaign. Bd. trustees St. John's Mercy Med. Center, St. Louis; trustee Maryville Coll. Recipient Alumni Merit award St. Louis, U., 1977, Tchr. Yr. award Washington U. Olin Sch. Business, 1994. Fellow Nat. Acad. Human Resources; mem. Soc. Human Resource Mgmt. (past chmn.), Indsl. Rels. Assn. St. Louis (past pres.), Bellerive Country Club, Isla Del Sol Country Club, Vinoy Renaissance Country Club. Roman Catholic.

BERRAN, LAWRENCE CHARLES, finance company executive; b. Rome, N.Y., June 23, 1971; s. Lawrence William and Theresa Antiunette Berran. BS, LaSalle U., Phila., 1993. CPA. Assoc. Coopers & Lybrand LLP, Phila., 1993—97; supervising sr. assoc., acctg. mgr. Safeguard Sci., Inc., Wayne, Pa., 1997—99, Internet Capital Group, Inc., Wayne, 1999—2002, v.p., 2002; pres. iPipeline, Exton, Pa., 2002—. Bd. dirs., treas. Childrens Advocacy Ctr., Phila., 1996-2001; gen. ptnr., pres. Liberty Bell Capital Assocs., Phila., 1998—. Mem. Phi Gamma Delta (sect. chief.) E-mail: lberran@yahoo.com.

BERRESFORD, GEOFFREY CASE, mathematics educator; b. N.Y.C., May 25, 1944; s. Richard Case Berresford and Katherine Marsters Hurd; m. Barbara Oppenheim; children: Lee, Christopher. BA, Lawrence U., 1967; MS, NYU, 1971, PhD, 1974. Lectr. in natural sci. SUNY, Purchase, 1973—74, asst. prof., 1974—75, L.I. U., Brookville, NY, 1975—79, assoc. prof., 1979—85, prof. math., 1985—. Cons. Charter N.Y. Leasing (Irving Trust Co.), N.Y.C., 1975—79. Author: Calculus with Applications to the Management, Social, Behavioral, and Biomedical Sciences, 1989, Calculus with Finite Mathematics, 1999, Applied Calculus, 2d edit., 2000, Brief Calculus, 3d edit., 2000, Finite Mathematics, 2001. Mem.: Bernoulli Soc., Soc. Indsl. and Applied Math., Am. Math. Soc., Math. Assn. Am. (chair N.Y. spkrs bur. 1985—96, Disting. Svc. award 2000). Avocations: woodworking, hiking. Home: 20 Waterside Plz New York NY 10010 Office: LI U Math Dept Brookville NY 11548 Office Fax: (516) 299-4049. E-mail: gberres@liu.edu.

BERRESFORD, SUSAN VAIL, philanthropic foundation executive; b. N.Y.C., Jan. 8, 1943; d. Richard Case and Katherine Vail (Marsters) Berresford Hurd; m. David F. Stein (div.); 1 son, Jeremy Vail Stein. Student, Vassar Coll., 1961-63; BA cum laude in Am. History, Radcliffe Coll., 1965. Vol. UN Vol. Services, N.Y.C., summer 1962; sec. to Theodore H. White, summer 1964; program officer Neighborhood Youth Corps, N.Y.C., 1965-67; program specialist Manpower Career Devel. Agy., N.Y.C., 1967, human resources adminstrn. specialist, 1968; free-lance cons., writer Europe and U.S., 1968-70; program officer nat. affairs div. Ford Found., N.Y.C., 1970-80, program officer in charge, 1980-81, v.p., 1981-95, exec. v.p., COO, 1995-96, pres., 1996—.

BERREY, ROBERT FORREST, lawyer; b. Oak Park, Ill., Dec. 7, 1939; s. Rhodes Clay and Regina (Kasprovich) B.; m. Rebecca L. Newell, Apr. 10, 1993; children from previous marriage: Adam Forrist, Ellen Catherine, Kevin Joseph. AB, Harvard U., 1962; JD, U. Chgo., 1968. Bar: Ill. 1969, Ohio 1986. Atty. Torshen, Fortes & Eiger, Chgo., 1970-75; atty. Jewel Cos., Inc., Chgo., 1975-76, sec., 1976-80, v.p., sec., gen. counsel, 1980-85; v.p., gen. counsel Tomkins (formerly Philips) Industries, Inc., 1986-91; ptnr. Chernesky, Heyman & Kress, Dayton, Ohio, 1991-98; formerly of counsel Bieser, Greer & Landis LLP, Dayton, Ohio; pvt. practice Chapel Hill, N.C. With AUS, 1962-65. Mem. ABA, Governors Club, Old Chatham Golf Club. E-mail: robert@berrey.org.

BERRI, MOHAMAD HUSSEIN, electrical and computer engineer, educator, researcher; b. Tebnine, South, Lebanon, Mar. 5, 1959; came to U.S., 1987; s. Hussein Ali and Zahra Taleb (Fawaz) Berri; m. Marine Adballah Berri, July 27, 1973; children: Ali, Dena, Danny, Reem. BSEE, Gar-Younis U., Bengazi, Lebia, 1985; MSEE, Wayne State U., 1991, PhD, 1996. Rsch. asst. Wayne State U., Detroit, 1989-96, adj. prof., 1996—; rsch. engr. Ford Motor Co., Dearborn, Mich., 1994-97; sr. project engr. TRW Automotive Electronics, Farmington Hills, Mich., 1996-99; design specialist Ford Motor Co.-Visteon, Dearborn, Mich., 1999—. Recipient achievement award City of Dearborn, 1994, Nat. Collegiate Engring. award. Mem.: N.Y. Acad. Sci. (Excellent Acad. Achievement award 1994), Internat. Conf. on Acoustics Speech and Signal Processing7, Advanced Speech Application and Tech., Am. Voice Input/Output Soc., Control Sys. Soc., SAE (recognition award 1995), NAS, IEEE (mem. exec. bd. South East Mich., dir. mem. South East Mich.), Wayne State Alumni Assn. Avocations: reading, swimming, social activity, traveling, music. Home: 6889 Fairwood Dr Dearborn Heights MI 48127 Office: Wayne State Univ 3100 Engineering Detroit MI 48202

BERRIDGE, GEORGE BRADFORD, retired lawyer; b. Detroit, June 9, 1928; s. William Lloyd and Marjorie (George) B.; m. Mary Lee Robinson, July 6, 1957; children: George Bradford, Elizabeth A., Mary L., Robert L. AB, U. Mich., 1950, MBA, 1953, JD, 1954. Bar: N.Y. 1954. Assoc. Chadbourne & Parke, N.Y.C., 1954-61; gen. atty., v.p. law Am. Airlines, Inc., N.Y.C., 1961-71; sr. v.p., gen. counsel Americana Hotels, Inc., N.Y.C., 1971-74, Nat. Westminster Bank U.S.A., N.Y.C., 1975-89, Nat. Westminster Bancorp, N.Y.C., 1989-93; ret., 1993. Contbr. articles to U. Mich. Law Rev. Served to lt. (j.g.) USN, 1951-53. Recipient Howard P. Coblentz prize U. Mich. Law Sch., 1954. Episcopalian. Home: 2 Circle Ave Larchmont NY 10538-4219 E-mail: gberr2@aol.com.

BERRIDGE, MARY LLOYD, photographer; BA in Arts and Ideas-Lit. & Photography, U. Mich., 1986; MFA in Photography, Yale U., 1991. Adj. instr. Concordia Coll., Bronxville, NY, 1992, Fairleigh Dickinson U., Rutherford, NJ, 1992—94, Nassau C.C., Garden City, NY, 1994—96, Sch. Visual Arts, N.Y.C., 1997; artist-in-residence, adj. instr. Coll. New Rochelle, NY, 1993; lectr. Princeton (N.J.) U., 1998—99. Exhibitions include The Ctr. for Photography, Woodstock, N.Y., 1991, Mus. Modern Art, N.Y.C., 1991, Berkshire Mus., Pittsfield, Mass., 1992, OPSIS Found., N.Y.C., 1992, Coll. New Rochelle, 1993, Midtown Y Photography Gallery, N.Y.C., 1993, Ind. Arts Gallery, Jamaica, N.Y., 1994, U. Rochester, N.Y., 1995, Blue Sky Gallery, Portland, Oreg., 1996, San Marino Mus. Photography, 1997, Robert Mann Gallery, N.Y.C., 1997, Soc. for Contemporary Photography, Kansas City, 1997—98, Mus. Fine Arts, Houston, 1997, M.H. de Young Meml. Mus., San Francisco, 1997, Cathedral of St. John the Divine, N.Y.C., 1997, Portland (Maine) Mus. Art, 1998, San Francisco Camerawork, 1998, U. Mich., Ann Arbor, 1999, Ctr. for Documentary Studies, Duke U., Durham, N.C., 1999, Pleasures and Terrors of Domestic Comfort, 1991, The Human Condition/Photography, 1995, 1996, Double Take, 1996—97, A Positive Life: Portraits of Women Living with HIV, 1997. Recipient The Ernst Haas award, Maine Photographic Workshops, 1996, The Dorothea Lange-Paul Taylor prize, Ctr. for Documentary Studies, Duke U., 1996, The Romeo Martinez Internat. award, Ministry of Culture of the Republic of San Marino, 1997; fellow Fellowship award, Soc. for Contemporary Photography, Kansas City, Mo., 1997, Artist's fellow, N.Y. Found. for the Art, 1996; John Simon Guggenheim Meml. fellow, 1997. E-mail: berridge@princeton.edu.

BERRIER, J. ALAN, transportation executive, entrepreneur; b. Lexington, N.C., Jan. 14, 1951; s. John Pitts and Etta Kaye (Hiatt) B. Student, Brevard (N.C.) Coll., 1969-70, High Point (N.C.) U., 1970-72. Shipping coord. Furnitureland South, Inc., Jamestown, N.C., 1992-96; over-the-road mgr. Royal Transp., Inc., Jamestown, 1996-98; commodity trader, 1998—, restaurateur, 2001—. Mem. Nat. Audubon Soc., Soc. Hist. Preservation, Libr. Congr., Smithsonian Inst. Avocations: photography, travel. Home and Office: 198 Old Thomasville Rd Winston Salem NC 27107-9278 E-mail: alanb_sl@yahoo.com.

BERRIGAN, DAVID, epidemiologist; m. Sarah Locke; children: Jacob, Samual. BA, Reed Coll., Portland, Oreg., 1983; MPh, U. of Calif., Berkeley, 2000; PhD, U. of Utah, 1993. Rschr., lectr. U. of Wash., Seattle, 1993—99; cancer prevention fellow Nat. Cancer Inst., Bethesda, Md., 1999—. Editl. bd. mem. Functional Ecology, United Kingdom, 2002—. Contbr. sci. articles to profl. jours. Mem. Montgomery County mid-County Recreation Adv. Bd., Rockville, Md., 2002—. Recipient Rsch. and Fellowship grants, NSF, USDA, NIH, 1991—2002. Office: Nat Cancer Inst 6130 Executive Blvd Bethesda MD 20892

BERRIGAN, PATRICK JOSEPH, lawyer; b. Niagara Falls, Ont., Can., Nov. 3, 1933; came to U.S., 1950; s. Thomas Joseph and Florence Cecilia (Glynn) B.; m. Shirley Mae Snyder, July 6, 1957; children: Carolyn, Deborah, Patrick Jr., Susan, Ann, Mary, James, Tara. BA in English, Holy Cross Coll., 1954; LLB, Notre Dame U., 1957. Bar: N.Y. 1958, U.S. Dist. Ct. (we. dist.) N.Y. 1960, U.S. Dist. Ct. (we. dist.) Pa. 1976, U.S. Ct. Appeals (2d cir.) 1962, U.S. Ct. Appeals (3rd cir.) 1977. Assoc. Runals, Broderick, Shoemaker, et al, Niagara Falls, N.Y., 1959-78; pvt. practice, Niagara Falls, 1978—. Spl. investigator City of Niagara Falls, 1972; spl. dist. atty. County of Niagara N.Y., Lockport, 1974-76; mem. Judicial Conf. of the State of N.Y., 1978-80; counsel N.Y. State Assembly Com. on mortgages, Albany, 1960-63; hearing officer Com. on Jud. Conduct, 1992—. Mem. Niagara U. Adv. Bd., Lewiston, N.Y., 1978-82; bd. dirs. Nat. Conf. of Christian and Jews, Niagara Falls, 1977; mem. Youth Bd., Niagara Falls, 1965-68. Sgt. U.S. Army, 1957-59; pres. Mount St. Mary's Adv. Bd., 1982—, bd. trustees, 1990-97; bd. dirs. Health System Niagara, 1997-99; trustee, v.p. Mount St. Mary's Hosp., 1999—. Mem. ABA (gen. practice sect. labor law 1991—), Niagara Falls Country Club (bd. govs.), Niagara Falls Bar Assn., Niagara County Bar Assn., N.Y. Bar Assn. Republican. Roman Catholic. Avocations: hockey player (old timers), golf. Home: 790 Thornwood Dr Lewiston NY 14092-1167 Office: PO Box 712 800 Main St Niagara Falls NY 14302-0712 E-mail: bpglawfirm@adelphia.net., pberrigan@adelphia.net.

BERRING, ROBERT CHARLES, JR., law educator, law librarian, former dean; b. Canton, Ohio, Nov. 20, 1949; s. Robert Charles and Rita Pauline (Franta) B.; m. Leslie Applegarth, May 20, 1998; children: Simon Robert, Daniel Fredrick. BA cum laude, Harvard U., 1971; JD, M.L.S., U. Calif.-Berkeley, 1974. Asst. prof. and reference librarian U. Ill. Law Sch., Champaign, 1974-76; assoc. librarian U. Tex. Law Sch., Austin, 1976-78; dep. librarian Harvard Law Sch., Cambridge, Mass., 1978-81; prof. law, law librarian U. Wash. Law Sch., Seattle, 1981-82, U. Calif., Boalt Hall Law Sch., Berkeley, 1982—, dean sch. library and info. scis., 1986-89, Walter Perry Johnson chair, 1998—, interim dean, 2003—. Mem. Westlaw Adv. Bd., St. Paul, 1984-91; cons. various law firms; mem. on Legal Exch. with China, 1983—, chmn., 1991-93.; vis. prof. U. Cologne, 1993. Author: How to Find the Law, 8th edit., 1984, 9th edit., 1989, Great American Law Revs., 1985, Finding the Law, 1999; co-author: Authors Guide, 1981; editor Legal Reference Svc. Quar., 1981—; author videotape series Commando Legal Rsch., 1989. Chmn. Com. Legal Ednl. Exch. with China, 1991—93. Robinson Cox fellow U. Western Australia, 1988; named West Publishing Co. Acad. Libr. of Yr., 1994. Mem. Am. Assn. Law Libraries (pres. 1985-86), Calif. Bar Assn., ABA, ALA, Am. Law Inst. Office: U Calif Law Sch Boalt Hl Rm 345 Berkeley CA 94720-0001

BERROA, REI, literature educator, poet; b. Santiago, Dominican Republic, Mar. 11, 1949; s. Mélida Méndez and Juan Berroa; m. Ana M. Alonso, Aug. 8, 2000; 1 child, Olivia. BA, Universidad Católica, Puerto Rico, 1966—70; MA, PhD, U. of Pitts., 1979—82. Prof. of spanish lit. Humboldt State U., 1982—83, Blackburn Coll., Carlinville, Ill., 1983—84; prof. of spanish lit. & lit. criticism George Mason U., Fairfax, Va., 1984—. Mem. of the editl. bd. Gradiva, Revista Literaria, Bogotá, Colombia, 1985—87; co-founder & co-editor Mundo: Problemas y Confrontaciones, Mex. City, Mexico, 1986—92; mem. of the bd. Códice: Revista de poéticas, Lima, Peru, 1987—97; chair Biennial Symposium on Internat. Cultural Perspectives in Poetics and Linguistics, Fairfax, Va., 1988—90; editor for creative writing Discurso Literario, Stillwater, Okla., 1988—98; lit. advisor Teatro de la Luna, Arlington, Va., 1991—; v.p. Woodburn Found., Fairfax Co., Va., 1993—95; faculty advisor Hispanic Culture Rev., Fairfax, Va., 1994—. Author: (poetry) Book of Fragments, (literary analysis) Lit. of the Americas; editor: (literary criticism) León Felipe: Homenaje; author: (essay) La memoria contra el olvido, Poetry and Painting: Garcia Lorca's Dual Manifestation, Formación y transformación del héroe hernandiano, Recordar para vivir: Historia, alegoría y dialéctica en la crónica de Pedro Mir, Iconos y representación en el Bestiario de Cortázar, Discurso poético y exilio interior en España (1939-1944), La crítica de Fuente como lectura conflictiva: De Fuentes, a España, a Cervantes; singer: (music & poetry recital) The Poetry & Music of Rei Berroa; author: (poetry) Libro de los fragmentos; musician: (recital) Words in Music/Music in Words; composer: Poems Set to Music by Rei Berroa; video, Rei Berroa en Tobogán; author: (essay) Sobre Muerte constante más allá del amor de García Márquez, Poesía y pintura: símbolo y metáfora en García Lorca, Al tercer día el poeta subió a los cielos: García Lorca cumple 100 años; contbr. poetry; author: (essay) Notas y viñetas de mis andanzas, (poetry) Los otros, En el reino de la ausencia, Retazos para un traje de tierra; translator: (essay) Desarrollo y dignidad: Bienestar de los pueblos y la Fundación Interamericana, (short story) El hombre con el pelo de habichuela colorá; editor: (collection of essays) La literatura Dominicana en el Siglo XX; author: (lit. criticism) Ideología y retórica: Las prosas de guerra de Miguel Hernández. V.p. Woodburn Ctr. for the Mentally Ill, Fairfax, Va., 1991—95; judge D.C. Coun. for the Arts, Wash., 1993—94; mem. at large Teatro de la Luna, Arlington, Va., 1991—2003; reviewer The Am. Biog. Inst., Raleigh, NC, 1994—2003; spanish programs Ctr. for Global Edn., Fairfax, Va., 1994—2003. Recipient Hispanic of the Yr., El Pregonero, the Hispanic Mag. of Wash., DC, 1987, Man of the Yr., Internat. Biog. Ctr., 1993; fellow Tchg. & Rsch. Fellowship, U. of Pitts., 1979-1982, Rsch. Fellowship at the Consejo Superior de Ciencias, Spain's Ministry of Edn., 1977-78; grantee Latino Writers in the U.S., Nat. Endowment for the Humanities, 2001, Latino Writers in the US, Am. Libraries Assn., 2001. Fellow: Phi Beta Delta (hon.); mem.: MLA (corr.). Avocations: travel, gardening. Office: George Mason U 4400 University Dr MS 3E5 Fairfax VA 22030 Home Fax: 703-993-1245; Office Fax: 703-993-1245. E-mail: rberroa@gmu.edu.

BERRY, BOYD MCCULLOCH, English educator; b. Chgo., May 29, 1939; s. Albert McCulloch and Carolyn Julia (Fischer) B.; m. Sally Virginia Dowd; children: Rachel Elizabeth, Jonathan Adebisi. BA, Harvard U., 1961; MA, U. Mich., 1962, PhD, 1966. Asst. prof. Ind. U., Bloomington, 1966-74; lectr. U. Ife, Nigeria, 1970-71, sr. lectr., 1978-79; assoc. prof. Dept. English Va. Commonwealth U., Richmond, 1974—. Author: Process of Speech, 1976. ACLS fellow, 1985-86; NEH grantee, 1991-92, 94-95, 95-96. Mem. MLA, Southeastern Renaissance Conf. Avocation: housebuilding. Office: Virginia Commonwealth Univ Dept English PO Box 842005 Richmond VA 23284-2005 Business E-Mail: bberry@vcu.edu.

BERRY, BRIAN JOE LOBLEY, geographer, political economist, urban planner; b. Sedgley, Stafford, Eng., Feb. 16, 1934; came to U.S., 1955, naturalized, 1965; s. Joe and Gwendoline Alice (Lobley) B.; m. Janet Elizabeth Shapley, Sept. 6, 1958; children: Duncan Jeffrey, Carol Anne (dec.), Diane Leigh, Karen. BSc with honors, Univ. Coll., London, 1955; MA, U. Wash., 1956, PhD, 1958; AM (hon.), Harvard U., 1976. Instr. geography, civil engring. U. Wash., Seattle, 1957-58; asst. prof. geography U. Chgo., 1958-62, assoc. prof., 1962-65, prof., 1965-72, Irving B. Harris prof. urban geography, 1972-76, dir. Ctr. Urban Studies, chmn. dept. geography, 1974-76; Frank Backus Williams prof. urban and regional planning Harvard U., 1976-81, chmn. Ph.D. Program in Urban Planning, dir. Lab. for Computer Graphics and Spatial Analysis, fellow Inst. Internat. Devel., 1976-81, prof. sociology, 1978-81; dean H. John Heinz III Sch. of Pub. Mgmt. Carnegie-Mellon U., 1981-86, Univ. prof. urban studies and pub. policy, 1981-86; founders prof. U. Tex., Dallas, 1986-91, prof. polit. econ., 1986—; Lloyd Viel Berkner Regental prof., 1991—; chmn. Bruton Ctr. for Devel. Studies U. Tex., Dallas, 1988-95. Author numerous books; contbr. articles to profl. jours. Fellow Univ. Coll., U. London, 1983; recipient Victoria medal Royal Geog. Soc., 1988, Rockefeller prize Dartmouth U., 1992; named Lord of Hastingleigh, County Kent, 2000. Fellow AAAS, Am. Acad. Arts and Scis., Urban Land Inst., Brit. Acad. (corr.), Weimer Inst. Real Estate and Land Econs., Royal Geog. Soc., So. Regional Sci. Assn.; mem. NAS (coun. 1999-2002), Assn. Am. Geographers (hon. award 1968, pres. 1978-79, Anderson medal 1987), Am. Inst. Cert. Planners, Regional Sci. Assn., Inst. Brit. Geographers, Sigma Xi. Office: U Tex-Dallas Sch Social Sci Richardson TX 75083-0688 E-mail: heja@utdallas.edu., bjlb@comcast.net.

BERRY, BUFORD PRESTON, lawyer; b. Nov. 20, 1935; Fellow Am. Coll. Tax Counsel, Am. Bar Found., Tex. Bar Found.; mem. ABA (chmn. natural resource com. tax sect. 1983-85), Tex. Bar Assn., Southwestern Legal Found. (chmn. tax sect. 1984-85), Dallas Club, Brook Hollow Golf Club. Methodist. Office: Thompson & Knight 3300 1st City Ctr Dallas TX 75201

BERRY, CHARLENE HELEN, librarian, musician; b. Highland Pk., Mich., Jan. 4, 1947; d. Harold Terry and Mattie Lou (Colvin) B. BSE, Wayne U., 1964-68, MA, 1969-70, MLS, 1971-74; postgrad., Howard Sch. Broadcast Arts, 1992, Irene's Myomassology Inst., 1997; DMin, U. Sem. Ch., 1997. Ordained music minister. Libr. asst. Wayne State U., Detroit, 1970-74; libr. serials cataloger SUNY, Stony Brook, 1975-79; cataloger Madonna U., Livonia, Mich., 1980—. Organist various area chs., Detroit, 1981—, 1st Ch. of Christ,

Wyandotte, Mich., 1986—; music min. Gospel Light House Ministries, Detroit, 1991—; scholar, performer, tchr. hammer dulcimer, 1986—; libr. cons. Superior Twp. (Mich.) Libr. Bd., 1989-91; host Charlene Berry's Dulcimer World, Sta. WCAR, Garden City, Mich., WALE, Providence, R.I., WLLZ 560 AM, Southfield, Mich., 1997—, Sta. WPON AM 1460, Southfield, Mich., 1997—. Composer: Dulcimer Delights, 1991, marches, waltzes, free compositions and solo symphony, 1993, Dulcimer Praise, 1993, Fruits of the Spirit, 1993; solo recs.: Traditional Dulcimer, 1989, Christmas Dulcimer, 1989, Sacred Dulcimer, 1990, Dulcimer Fun, 1991, Dulcimer Praise, 1993, Fruits of the Spirit, 1993, Dulcimer Americana, 1994; (video) Hammering the Hammer Dulcimer, 1994, Music of Light/Light and Life, 1995, Under der Linden, 1996, Joy, Peace, Healing, 1998, Hymns of Prayer and Praise, 1999. Pres. Libr. Staff Assn., SUNY, 1978-79; ch. libr. Ch. Bds. Coms., Long Island, Detroit, 1975—; bd. dirs. Livonia Symphony Soc.; performing artist Mich. Touring Arts Agy., 1994—. Recipient Performance award Silver Springs Dulciner Soc., 1988, 89, 90, Interat. Order of Merit, ASCAP; named Internat. Woman of Yr., 1992-93, Most Admired Woman of Decade. Fellow Internat. Biographical Assn. (life). Am. Biographical Inst. (Woman of Yr. 1993); mem. AAUW, ALA, NAFE, Am. Biographical Rsch. Assn. (hon. dep. gov.), Bus. and Profl. Women, Am. Soc. of Notaries, Am. Fedn. Musicians, Am. Guild Organists (bd. dirs. 1985-88), Plymouth C. of C., Luth. Ch. Musicians Guild, Order Ea. Star, Kappa Delta Pi. Home and Office: Dulcimer Evente 49614 Oak Dr Lot 67 Plymouth MI 48170-2353

BERRY, CHARLES RICHARD, lawyer; b. Louisville, Apr. 19, 1948; s. Charles Russell and Lillie Juanita (Crady) B.; m. Joan Phyllis Rosenberg, Aug. 29, 1970; children: Kevin Charles, Ryan Andrew. BA, Northwestern U., 1970, JD, 1973. Bar: Ariz. 1973, U.S. Dist. Ct. Ariz. 1973, U.S. Ct. Appeals (9th cir.) 1983. Assoc. Snell & Wilmer, Phoenix, 1973-77; ptnr. Tilker, Burke & Berry, Scottsdale, Ariz., 1978-80, Norton, Berry, French & Perkins, P.C. and predecessor firm Norton, Burke, Berry & French, P.C., Phoenix, 1980-86; dir. Fennemore Craig, Phoenix, 1986-90; ptnr. Titus, Brueckner & Berry, Scottsdale, 1991—. Mem. Ariz. Bar Assn. (chmn. securities regulation sect. 1996-97), Paradise Valley Rotary Club (pres. 1995-96). Mem. Unitarian Ch. Home: 6148 E Mountain View Rd Scottsdale AZ 85253-1807 Office: Titus Brueckner & Berry 7373 N Scottsdale Rd Ste B252 Scottsdale AZ 85253-3527 Fax: 480-483-3215. E-mail: cberry@tbb-law.com.

BERRY, CHRIS DAVID, artist, writer; b. Birmingham, Ala., Sept. 14, 1966; s. Jack Lee and Carolyn Sue Berry; 1 child, Christian Tyler. Cert., Cornell U., 1987; AA, Art Instrn. Sch., 1990. Regent U. Divinity Sch., 1992; cons. in field. Co-author: The Life of Rev. Rickels, 1991. Fundraiser World Vision, Ala., 2000, UNICEF, Ala., 2000; mentor, tchr. Pharaston Divinity Sch., 1998; curriculum writer Sunday Sch. Bd., Nashville, 1991—93. Recipient Merit award, Poetry Publ., 1994, Appreciation award, World Vision, 1996, Merit award, U. Ala., 1998; scholar McCain scholar, 1999. Republican. Avocations: music, tennis, photography, writing. Home: 810 Country Ln Hayden AL 35079

BERRY, CLARE GEBERT, real estate broker; b. Carlisle, Pa., Oct. 4, 1955; d. George Robert and Helen (Davis) Gebert; m. James Isaac Vance Berry Jr., June 16, 1977; 1 child, James Isaac Vance Berry III. BA, Auburn U., 1977. Advt. assoc., circulation mgr. The News-Gazette, Lexington, Va., 1977-79; sales and editorial asst. Ponte Vedra Recorder Newspaper, Fla., 1979-81; co-founder, bus. mgr. The Sun-Times Newspaper, Jacksonville Beach, Fla., 1981-82; mgr. Arvida-Clearview Cable TV, Ponte Vedra Beach, 1982-85; broker, agt. Watson Realty Corp., Ponte Vedra Beach, Fla., 1985-90, Marsh Landing Realty, Ponte Vedra Beach, 1990-93; founder, broker, owner Berry & Co. Real Estate, Ponte Vedra Beach, 1993—. Com. chmn. The Players Championship, Ponte Vedra Beach, 1982—; dir. Marsh Landing Homeowners Assn. Bd., Ponte Vedra Beach, 1989-90; dir. Ponte Vedra Pub. Edn. Found., 1994—, N.E. Fla. Regional Planning Coun., 2000—. Recipient Realtor of Yr., Realtors' Assn., 1992, Residential Mem. of Yr., 1998. Mem. Fla. Assn. Realtors, Nat. Assn. Realtors, N.E. Fla. Builders Assn. Sales and Mktg. Coun., N.E. Fla. Assn. of Realtors (bd. dirs. 1998-00, chmn. edn. com. 2000), Ponte Vedra Rotary. Avocations: writing, promotions, aviation, music, tennis. Home: 113 Linkside Cir Ponte Vedra Beach FL 32082-2032 Office: Berry & Co Real Estate 330 Hwy A1A Ste 200 Ponte Vedra Beach FL 32082-1824

BERRY, CYNTHIA JOAN, psychologist, consultant; b. Florissant, Mo., Sept. 27, 1976; d. William C. and Susan C. Gandolfo; m. Erik S. Berry, Dec. 1, 2001. BA, Lindenwood U., 1997; MA, So. Ill. U., Carbondale, 2001. Sr. rsch. assoc. Applied Rsch. Consultants, Carbondale, 1998—2001; cons. City of O'Fallon, Mo., 2001—02, asst. human resource dir., 2002—. Mem.: Alpha Sigma Tau, Pi Gamma Mu, Alpha Lambda Delta.

BERRY, DANIEL JOHN, orthopedist, surgeon; s. John R. and Elizabeth Berry; m. Camilla Guthrie, Aug. 30, 1993; children: Charlotte, John. BA, Dartmouth Coll., 1980; MD, Harvard U., 1984. Diplomate Am. Bd. Orthopaedic Surgery, 1993. Gen. surgery intern, jr. resident Harvard Fifth Surg. Svc., New England Deaconness Hosp., Boston, 1984—86; orthopedic surgery resident Brigham and Women's Hosp./Children's Hosp./Mass. Gen. Hosp., Boston, 1986—89; chief resident in orthopedic surgery Brigham and Women's Hosp., Boston, 1989; Maurice E. Müller fellow in hip surgery Switzerland, 1990; fellow in adult reconstructive surgery Mayo Clinic, Rochester, Minn., 1990—91; orthopaedic surgeon Mayo Found., Rochester, 1991—. Chmn. Maurice E. Muller Found. N.Am., Berne, Switzerland, 1999—. Author: Reconstructive Surgery of the Joints, 2nd Ed., 1996, The Adult Hip, 1997; contbr. articles to profl. jours.; editor (assoc. editor): Jour. Am. Acad. Orthopaedic Surgeons, 2001—, Jour. Bone & Joint Surgery, 2001—. Mem.: The Knee Soc., Internat. Hip Soc., The Hip Soc. Office: Mayo Clinic 200 First Street SW Rochester MN 55905

BERRY, DAWN BRADLEY, writer, lawyer, jeweler; b. Peoria, Ill., Mar. 11, 1957; d. Raymond Coke and Clarette (Williams) Bradley; m. William Lars Berry, July 12, 1980. BS, Ill. State U., 1979, MS, 1982; JD, U. Ill., 1988. Bar: N.Mex. 1988, U.S. Dist. Ct. N.Mex. 1988, U.S. Ct. Appeals (10th cir.) 1993. Assoc. Modrall, Sperling, Roehl, Harris and Sisk, Albuquerque, 1988-90; pvt. practice Tijeras and Albuquerque, 1990-2000; assoc. Hinkle Law Offices, Albuquerque, 1995-96. Author: Equal Compensation for Women, 1994, The Domestic Violence Sourcebook, 1995, The Divorce Sourcebook, 1995, The Fifty Most Influential Women in American Law, 1996, The Divorce Recovery Source Book, 1998, The Estate Planning Sourcebook, 1999. Pres., bd. dirs. Talking Talons Youth Leadership, Tijeras, 1993-98, v.p., 1998-2000. Recipient Outstanding Young Alumni award Ill. State U., 1996; Rickert scholar for pub. svc. U. Ill., 1988. Mem.: NAFE, Authors Guild, The Ocean Inst., Internat. Wenches Guild, F. Scott Fitzgerald Soc. Avocations: travel, dance, tall ship sailing, hiking, renaissance fairs. Home and Office: 450-G Liberty Dr San Marcos CA 92069 E-mail: dreamlizard@worldnet.att.net.

BERRY, DEAN LESTER, lawyer; b. Chgo., Ill., Jan. 20, 1935; s. Ruben W. and Leonore C. (Nelson) B.; m. Donna J. Zack, Nov. 16, 1962; children: Megan, Thomas. BA with distinction, DePauw U., 1955; JD with distinction, U. Mich., 1960. Bar: Ohio 1961, U.S. Dist. Ct. (no. dist.) Ohio 1962. Assoc. Squire, Sanders & Dempsey L.L.P., Cleve., 1960-70, ptnr., 1970—2002, counsel, 2002—03. Lectr. various programs, Order of Coif. Author: Local Government in Michigan, 1960; contbr. articles to profl. jours.; participant in Quiz Kids radio program, 1945-47. Mem. council City of Rocky River, Ohio, 1967-71; mem. cen. com. Cuyahoga County Rep. Orgn., Ohio, 1963-75, mem. exec. com., 1969-2001. Served to 1st lt. USAF, 1955-57. Mem. Ohio Bar Assn., Greater Cleve. Bar Assn. (com. chmn. 1978) Soc. Profl. Journalists, Sigma Delta Chi. Methodist. Avocations: traveling, crossword puzzles. Home: 478 Ravine Dr Aurora OH 44202-8236

BERRY, DONALD LEE, accountant; b. Ft. Dodge, Iowa, Nov. 8, 1940; s. John Donald and Margaret Ann (Lichter) B.; m. Barbara B. Beyer, Aug. 11, 1962; children: Patrick Curtis, Dawn Marie. AA, Edison Community Coll., 1965; BS in Acctg., Fla. Atlantic U., 1967. CPA, Fla. Sr. acct. Haskins & Sells, CPAs, Ft. Lauderdale, Fla., 1967-71; corp. controller King Motor Ctr., Ft. Lauderdale, 1971-73, Krehling Industries, Naples, Fla., 1973-74; stockholder Wentzel, Berry, et. al., Naples, 1974-89; mng. prin. Wentzel, Berry, Wentzel & Phillips, Naples, 1989—. Past activities Moorings Park, Inc., Mother of God, House of Prayer; bd. dirs. Guadalupe Ctr., 2000; treas. Ricky King Found., 1999—. Recipient Outstanding Citizen award Naples Daily News, 1990. Mem. AICPA, Fla. Inst. CPAs (exec. com. 1989-91, bd. govs. 1984, pres. S.W. Fla. chpt. 1978-79, pres. PAC 1993-94, Pub. Svc. award 1993), Naples Area C. of C. (former pres., bd. govs.), Fellowship of Christian Athletes (former pres.), Fla. Inst. CPAs Ednl. Found., Inc. (v.p., past pres.), KC (past pres.), Pelican Bay Bus. Assn. (past pres.), Leadership S.W. Fla., Naples H.S. Quarterback Club (former pres.), Pelican Bay Rotary (former pres.), Collier One Hundred Club (pres. 2001). Republican. Roman Catholic. Avocations: golf, fishing, bird watching. Office: Wentzel Berry Wentzel & Phillips 801 Laurel Oak Dr Ste 303 Naples FL 34108-2707 E-mail: berry@swflcpas.com.

BERRY, ESTER LORÉE, vocational nurse; b. St. Joseph, La., Sept. 19, 1945; d. Sim and Ruby Jordan; (div.); children: Roderick Bryant, Pamela Elaine. Assoc. degree in nursing and art, Calif. State U., 1996. Lic. vocat. nurse. Ward clk. Santa Fe Hosp., Compton, Calif., 1969-72; supr. J.C. Penney's, Carson, Calif., 1973-80; asst. mgr. Std. Comm., Carson, 1981-84; lic. vocat. nurse, nurse King Drew Med., L.A., 1984-94; medicine nurse Martin Luther Jr. Hosp., 1996-99. Contbr. poetry to Internat. Libr. Poetry; author Am. Poet Soc. Named hon. mem. Vets. Am., 1999-2001, Best Poet of Yr.; recipient Editors Choice award, 1999, 2000, 2001, Silver Internat. Poet of Merit, Bronze Comemortive Medallion, Best Poet award, 2002-03, Internat. Libr. of Poetry, Bronze Leader award, Disabled Am. Vets. Commanders Club, 2002-03. Avocations: fishing, sewing, photography, crocheting, outdoor camping. Home: Apt P230 27-700 Landau B Cathedral City CA 92234

BERRY, FRED CLIFTON, JR., author, magazine editor, book packager; b. Neponset, Ill., May 11, 1931; s. Fred C. and Dorothy (Benedict) B.; m. Irene Semcho, Nov. 10, 1958; children— Jeffrey, Thomas BS, George Washington U., 1961; MA, Stanford U., 1967. Commd. 2d. lt. U.S. Army, 1955, advanced through grades to col. (select), 1975; editor-in-chief Air Force Mag., Washington, 1980-83; chief U.S. editor, exec. v.p. Interavia Pub. Group, Washington, 1983-86; pres. FCB Assocs., Arlington, Va., 1986—; exec. v.p. Pathfinder Assocs., Fairfax, VA, 1978-79. Author: Sky Soldiers, 1987, Strike Aircraft, 1987, Chargers, 1988, Gadget Warfare, 1988, Air Cav, 1988, Inventing the Future, 1993, Inside the CIA, 1997; Milestones of the First Century of Flight, 2002, United State Army at War- 9/11 Through Iraq, 2003; co-author: CNN: War in the Golf, 1991, Flights, 1994; editor: Avon Books illustrated series on poor future warfare 1990, Air Traffic Control, 1990; editor Air Power History mag., 1989-91; contbr. articles to profl. jours. Trustee Air Force Hist. Found. Mem. Authors Guild Am., Nat. Press Club (Washington). Avocation: flying. Office: FCB Assocs PO Box 710654 Herndon VA 20171-0654

BERRY, GLENN, educator, artist; b. Feb. 27, 1929; s. B. Franklin and Heloise (Sloan) B. BA magna cum laude, Pomona Coll., 1951, BFA (Honnold fellow); MFA, Sch. Art Inst. Chgo., 1956. Faculty Humboldt State U., Arcata, Calif., 1956-69, prof. art, 1969-81, emeritus, 1981—. One-man shows include Ingomar Gallery, Eureka, Calif., 1968, Ankrum Gallery, L.A., 1970, Esther Bear Gallery, Santa Barbara, Calif., 1971, Coll. Redwoods, Eureka, 1989, Humboldt State U., Arcata, Calif., 1992, Morris Graves Mus. of Art, Eureka, Calif., 2000; exhibited in group shows at Palace of Legion of Honor, San Francisco, Pasadena (Calif.) Art Mus., Rockford (Ill.) Coll., Richmond (Calif.) Art Mus., Henry Gallery U. Wash., Seattle, Morris Graves Mus. Art, Eureka, 2000; represented in permanent collections Storm King Art Ctr., Mountainville, N.Y., Kaiser Aluminum & Chem. Corp., Oakland, Calif., Desert Mus., Hirshhorn Mus., Washington, others; mural Griffith Hall, Humboldt State U., 1978, Morris Graves Mus. Art, Eureka, Calif. Mem. Phi Beta Kappa. Home: PO Box 2241 Mckinleyville CA 95519

BERRY, GUY CURTIS, polymer science educator, researcher; b. Greene County, Ill., May 11, 1935; s. Charles Curtis and Wilma Francis (Wickes) B.; m. Marilyn Jane Montooth, Jan. 26, 1957; children: Susan Jane, Sandra Jean, Scott Curtis. BSCh.E., U. Mich., 1957, MS in Polymer Sci., 1958, PhD, 1960. Fellow Mellon Inst., Pitts., 1960-65, sr. fellow, 1965—90; assoc. prof. chemistry Carnegie-Mellon U., Pitts., 1966-73, prof., 1973—2002, acting dean, 1981-82, acting head dept. chemistry, 1983-84, head dept. chemistry, 1990-95, Univ. prof., 2002—. Vis. prof. U. Tokyo, 1973, Colo. State U., Ft. Collins, 1979, U. Kyoto, Japan, 1983 Editor Jour. Polymer Sci., 1988-93, Progress in Polymer Sci., 2002--; mem. editl. bd. Jour. Rheology, 1990—, Chemtracts-Macromolecular Chemistry, 1990-94; contbr. over 200 articles to sci. jour. Recipient Bingham medal Soc. of Rheology, 1990; Polymeric Materials: Sci. and Engring. fellow. Fellow Am. Phys. Soc., Polymeric Materials: Sci. and Engring.; mem. AAAS, Am. Chem. Soc. (Pitts. Chemistry prize 1994), Soc. Rheology. Office: Carnegie Mellon U Dept Chem 4400 5th Ave Pittsburgh PA 15213-2617 E-mail: gcberry@andrew.cmu.edu.

BERRY, HALLE, actress; b. Cleve., Aug. 14, 1966; d. Jerome and Judith (Hawkins) B.; m. David Christopher Justice, Jan. 1, 1993 (div.); m. Eric Benet, Feb. 7, 2001. BA, Cuyahoga C.C., Cleveland, 1986. Appeared in films Jungle Fever, 1991, The Last Boy Scout, 1991, Strictly Business, 1991, Boomerang, 1992 (Image award nominee 1992), Father Hood, 1993, The Program, 1993, The Flintstones, 1994, Losing Isaiah, 1995, The Rich Man's Wife, 1996, Executive Decision, 1996, Race The Sun, 1996, Girl 6, 1996, B*A*P*S, 1997, Bulworth, 1998, Why Do Fools Fall in Love, 1998, Victims of Fashion, 1999, Ringside, 1999, X-Men, 2000, Swordfish, 2001, Monsters Ball, 2002 (Best Actress Acad. Award 2002), Die Another Day, 2002, X2: X-Men United, 2003; TV mini-series Queen, 1992, Solomon & Sheba, 1995, The Wedding, 1998, Introducing Dorothy Dandridge, 1999 (Outstanding Lead Actress in Miniseries or Movie Emmy 2000, Best Performance by Actress in Miniseries or Motion Picture Made for TV Golden Globe 2000, Actor award, Spl. award, Image award, SAG award and three NAACP Image awards 2000); TV series include Living Dolls, 1989, Knots Landing, 1992; also appeared in episodes of Amen, A Different World, They Came From Outer Space, Frasier (voice). Named Miss Teen All-Am., 1985, Miss U.S.A., 1987. Office: William Morris Agy c/o Bill Butler 151 El Camino Dr Beverly Hills CA 90212*

BERRY, JACOB OBADIAH, not-for-profit developer, rancher; b. LA, Aug. 14, 1954; s. Francis Oscar and Harriet Leaf Beregi. BA, Denver U., 1976. Prin., owner 120 acre farm, Newell, SD, 1979—85; ranch hand cattle ranches in western S.Dak., SD, 1985—96; pres. Am. Cross Found., Amarillo, Tex., 1996—. Author: Horse Creek, 1999, (screenplays) Pagan Desire, 2002. Achievements include patents for Cross design; patents pending in field. Avocations: country western dance, horseback riding. Office: Am Cross Found PO Box 9492 Amarillo TX 79105 Business E-Mail: americancross@amcrfo.us.

BERRY, JAMES ALAN, plant pathologist, research scientist; b. Des Moines, July 6, 1948; s. James Richard and Dorothy Marie Berry; m. Catherine Ann Berry, Nov. 23, 1968; children: James P., Brian M., Amy L. BS, Iowa State U., 1970, MS, 1972. Plant pathologist Pioneer Hi-Bred Internat., Inc., Johnston, Iowa, 1972—. Chmn. working group Internat. Assn. Plant Breeders/Internat. Feed Trade Fedn., Nyon, Switzerland, 1999—; chair tech. panel Nat. Seed Health Sys., 2000—. Author, editor (CDs) The Art and Sci. of Plant Disease Diagnosis, Field Inspection: Corn; patentee in field. Recipient DuPont Sustainable Excellence in Environment award, 2000. Mem. Am. Phytopathology Soc., Mycol. Soc. Am., N.Y. Acad. Scis., Iowa Acad. Sci. Avocations: landscaping, gardening. Office: Pioneer Hi Bred Internat 7300 NW 62d Ave Johnston IA 50131 E-mail: jim.berry@pioneer.com.

BERRY, JAMES LEE, retired educator; b. Hollywood, Calif., May 19, 1939; s. Ralph (Red) Lee and Lillie Pauline (Pilkenton) B.; m. Sharon Joyce Hess, April 14, 1963; children: Jamie, Diana, Daniel. BS in Edn., Pitts. State U., 1961; MEd, Ga. Southern U., 1975; grad., Command and Gen. Staff Coll., 1978; MBA, Webster U., 1983. Advanced through grades to lt. col. U.S. Army, 1982, ret., 1982; spl. agent Dept. Defense, San Antonio, Tex., 1983-84; sr. army instr. Northeast Military Magnet, Kansas City, Mo., 1986-2000; ret., 2000. Coach shooting, weighlifting. Decorated Bronze Star, Meritorious Svc. medal with 3 oak leaf clusters, Army Commendation medal, 1 oak leaf cluster; Vietnam Cross of Gallantry. Avocations: shooting, weightlifting, painting. Home: PO Box 751 Lawrence KS 66044-0751

BERRY, JANIS MARIE, lawyer; b. Everett, Mass., Dec. 20, 1949; d. Joseph and Dorothy I. Sordillo; m. Richard G. Berry, Dec. 27, 1970; children: Alexis, Ashley, Lindsey. BA magna cum laude, Boston U., 1971, JD cum laude, 1974. Bar: Mass. 1974, U.S. Dist. Ct. Mass. 1975, U.S. Ct. Appeals (1st cir.), 1980, U.S. Supreme Ct. 1982. Law clk. Mass. Supreme Jud. Ct., Boston, 1974-75; assoc. Bingham, Dana & Gould, Boston, 1975-80; asst. U.S. atty. Boston, 1980-81; spl. atty. dept. justice N.E. Organized Crime Strike Force, Boston, 1981-84; chief atty. dept. justice N.E. Organized Crime Drug Task Force, Boston, 1984-86; ptnr. Ropes & Gray, Boston, 1986-94; pvt. practice, 1995; ptnr. Roche, Carens & DeGiacomo, 1996-97, Rubin & Rudman LLP, 1997-2001; justice Mass. Appeals Ct., 2001—. Vis. instr. Harvard Law Sch., 1983-86, Inst. Trial Advocacy, Boston, 1984-87; lectr. Dept. Justice Advocacy Inst., 1986; mem. Mass. Bd. of Bar Overseers, 1989-93; bd. mem. Mass. Housing Fin. Agy., 1995-2001, Franciscan Children's Hosp.; chmn. merit selection panel U.S. Magistrate, 1989, Mass. Jud. Nominating Coun., 1991-92; trustee Social Law Libr., 1999-2001. Author: Defending Corporations Public Contracts Jour., (with others) Federal Criminal Practice, 1987. Candidate Mass. Atty. Gen., 1994; mem. Mass. Com. for Pub. Counsel Svcs., Boston, 1986-91; v.p. Boston Inn of Ct., 1990-91; trustee Atlanticare Hosp., 1990-94; bd. dirs. Franciscan Children's Hosp. Spl. Commendation award Dept. of Justice, Washington, 1983. Mem. Mass. Bar Assn., Boston Bar Assn., Am. Law Inst., Phi Beta Kappa. Office: Mass Appeals Ct 1500 New Courthouse Boston MA 02108

BERRY, JAY ROBERT, JR., English educator; b. Cleve., Oct. 12, 1957; s. Jay Robert and Nettie Marie (Stanish) B.; m. Regenia Dee Bailey, Nov. 25, 1989. PhB, Miami U., 1979; MA, U. Iowa, 1983. Instr. U. Iowa, Iowa City, 1980-87, 88-93, Iowa State U., Ames, 1994-97, adj. asst. prof., 1997—2002; instr. Kirkwood Cmty Coll., 2002—. Vis. instr. Carleton Coll., Northfield, Minn., 1987-88, Mt. Mercy Coll., Cedar Rapids, Iowa, 1991-93. Mem.: Coll. Lang. Assn. Office: Kirkwood Cmty Coll Dept English Cedar Rapids IA 52406 E-mail: jrb@avalon.net.

BERRY, JEAN STANFIELD, artist, retired art educator; b. Sedalia, Mo., Feb. 15, 1929; d. Albert Pressley Stanfield and Bess Allison Merideth; m. Karl J. Berry, June 10, 1948 (dec. Feb. 1986); children: John S., Stephen P. AA, State Fair C.C., 1970; BS, Ctrl. Mo. State U., 1972, MS, 1974. Life cert. art grades K-12. Part-time art instr. State Fair C.C., Sedalia, 1972-80; art instr. Sedalia Pub. Sch., 1974-89. One-woman shows include Ctrl. Mo. State U., 1972, 74, Fine Arts Studio, Sedalia, 1975, Unity Village, Kansas City, Mo., 1977, State Fair C.C., 1978, 82, Ctrl. Stake Gallery, Independence, Mo., 1978, Mo. Coun. on the Arts, 1979; works exhibited at Mo. Coun. on the Arts, Springfield Art Mus. Annual Exhbn., Springfield, Ft. Smith (Ark.) Ctr. Annual Competition, Mo. State Fair, Sedalia, Sch. of the Ozarks, Point Lookout, Mo., Mo. State Fair. Recipient 1st pl. State Fair C.C., 1969, 2nd Purchase awards Art Show of the Ozarks, 1970, 3rd pl. Mo. State Fair, 1971, 4th pl. Ft. Smith Art Ctr., 1972, Best of Show Purchase award Ctrl. Mo. State U., 1972, Purchase award Ft. Smith Art Show, 1975, 76. Mem. Mo. Art Educators Assn., Mo. State Tchrs. Assn., Mo. Coun. for the Arts, Mid-Mo. Art Assn., Sedalia Art Assn., Citizens for the Arts, Phi Delta Kappa, Phi Kappa Phi. Avocations: golf, dancing, gardening. Home: 850 Brentwood Ave Sedalia MO 65301-8600

BERRY, JOHN CHARLES, clinical psychologist, educational administrator; b. Modesto, Calif., Nov. 29, 1938; s. John Wesley and Dorothy Evelyn (Harris) B.; A.B., Stanford, 1960; postgrad. Trinity Coll., Dublin, Ireland, 1960-61; Ph.D., Columbia, 1967; m. Arlene Ellen Sossin, Oct. 7, 1978; children— Elise, John Jordan, Kaitlyn. Research assoc. Judge Baker Guidance Center, Boston, 1965-66; psychology asso. Napa State Hosp., Imola, Calif., 1966-67, staff psychologist, 1967-75, program asst., 1975-76; program dir. Met. State Hosp., Norwalk, Calif., 1976-77; asst. supt. Empire Union Sch. Dist., Modesto, Calif., 1977-93, dep. supt., 1993—. Mem. Am. Psychol. Assn., Assn. Calif. Sch. Adminstrs., Sigma Xi. Contbg. author: Life History Research in Psychopathology, 1970. Home: 920 Eastridge Dr Modesto CA 95355-4672 Office: Empire Union Sch Dist 116 N Mcclure Rd Modesto CA 95357-1329

BERRY, JOHN NICHOLS, III, publishing executive, editor; b. Montclair, N.J., June 12, 1933; s. John Nichols and Marian Petrea (Chase) B.; m. Louise Parker, June 5, 1982; children: Elizabeth Ann, John Nichols IV, Thomas Parker. AB in History, Boston U., 1958; MS in L.S, Simmons Coll., Boston, 1960. Youth-reference librarian Reading (Mass.) Pub. Library, 1959-60; reference librarian Simmons Coll., 1960-62, asst. dir. library, 1962-64; lectr. Sch. Library Sci., 1961-64; asst. editor Library Jour., R. R. Bowker Co. (div. Xerox), N.Y.C., 1964-66; editor book editorial dept. R. R. Bowker Co. (div. Xerox), 1966-68, editor-in-chief Library Jour., 1969-89; v.p., editor-in-chief Libr. Jour. Reed Bus. Info., Inc., N.Y.C., 1989—; journalist in residence Sch. of Libr. and Info. Sci. La. State U., 1989. Vis. prof. Sch. Info. and Libr. Sci., Pratt Inst., Bklyn., 1994—, Dominican U., River Forest, Ill., 2000; adj. prof. Sch. Libr. Resources and Info. Studies, U. Ariz., Tucson, 2002—03; lectr. Sch. Libr. and Info. Sci., U. Pitts., 1972—73, Sch. Libr. and Info. Studies, U. Wash., Seattle, 1982; William Gillard lectr. dept. libr. and info. sci. St. John's U., 1986; Rudi Weiss lectr. N.Y. Libr. Assn., 1988. Contbg. author: Library Issues The Sixties, 1970; editor: Directory of Library Consultants, 1969, Bay State Libr., 1962-64 (ALA-H.W. Wilson Libr. periodical award 1962); contbr. articles to profl. jours. Served with AUS, 1955-57. Recipient First Annual Alumni Achievement award Sch. Library Sci. Simmons Coll., 1970, Joseph W. Lippincott award Am. Lib. Assn., 1992, Spl. Svc. award Assn. Lib. and Info. Sci. Edn., 1993. Mem. ALA, Am. Soc. for Info. Sci., Spl. Libr. Assn. (chmn. div. pub. 1969), Archons of Colophon, Beta Phi Mu. Democrat. Home: 41 Chester St Stamford CT 06905-3945 Office: Libr Jour 360 Park Ave S New York NY 10010 E-mail: jberry33@optonline.net., jberry@reedbusiness.com.

BERRY, JONI INGRAM, hospice pharmacist, educator; b. Charlotte, N.C., June 6, 1953; d. James Clifford and Patricia Ann (Ebener) Ingram; div.; children: Erin Blair, Rachel Anne, James Rosser. BS in Pharmacy, U. N.C., 1976, MS in Pharmacy, 1979, postgrad., 1999. Lic. pharmacist, N.C. Resident in pharmacy Sch. Pharmacy, U. N.C., Chapel Hill, 1977 79, adj. asst. prof., 1985—; pharmacist Durham County Gen. Hosp., Durham, N.C., 1977-79; coord. clin. pharm. Wake Med. Ctr., Raleigh, N.C., 1979-80; co-dir. pharmacy edn. Wake Area Health Edn. Ctr., Raleigh, 1980-85; pharmacist cons. Hospice of Wake County, Raleigh, 1980—; co-owner Integrated Pharm. Care Systems, Inc., 1995—. Mem. editorial adv. bd. Hospice Jour., 1985-91, 94—, Jour. Pharm. Care in Pain and Symptom Mgmt., 1992—; reviewer Am. Jour. Hospice Care, 1996-98; editor pharmacy sect. notes NHO Coun. Hospice Profls.; contbr. articles to profl. jours. Troop leader Girl Scouts U.S.A., Raleigh, 1987—, trainer, 1989-91, mgr. svc. unit, 1990-94; Sunday sch. tchr. St. Phillips Luth. Ch., Raleigh, 1990-92, 94-95, asst. min., 1995—, choir mem. 1998—. Recipient Silver Pinecone award Girl Scouts U.S., 1991, Golden Rule award J.C. Penney Co., 1991. Mem.: Wake County Pharm. Assn. (sec. 1982—85), N.C. Hosp. Pharmacists (bd. dirs. 1984—86, program com. 1988—91), N.C. Pharm. Assn. (mem. continuing edn. com. 1986—87, chair com. 1981—84, Don Blanton award 1985), Am. Pain Soc., Nat. Hospice Orgn., Am. Soc. Hosp. Pharmacists, Acad. Pharmacy Practice and Mgmt. (mem.-at-large 1996, chair specialized sect. 1999—2002), Am. Pharm. Assn. (hospice pharmacist steering com. 1990—), Nat. Coun. Hospice Profls. (pharmacy sect. leader 1998—), Rho Chi. Democrat. Avocations: gardening, weight lifting, aerobics. Office: Hospice Wake County 1300 Saint Marys St Raleigh NC 27605-1276 E-mail: momsberry@aol.com.

BERRY, KATHLEEN A. English language educator; b. L.A., Calif., June 22, 1958; d. Raymond Albert and Robin Lee Berry. BA in Linguistics, MA in Edn., U. Calif., Berkeley, 1981, credential in single subject tchg./English, 1982. Instr. English U. Calif. Ext., Berkeley, 1992—, tchr. trainer, 1992—; instr. English U. Calif., Berkeley, 1994, Contra Costa C.C., San Pablo, Calif., 1996—, Laney C.C., Oakland, Calif., 2001—. Cons. grammar Am. Med. Writers Assn., San Francisco, 1999—. H.s. program coord. Albany (Calif.) Adult Sch., 1984. Mem.: Tchrs. of English to Spkrs. of Other Langs. Avocations: yoga, quilting. Office: Laney C C 900 Fallon St Oakland CA 94607 E-mail: katy622@yahoo.com.

BERRY, KENNETH JAY, JR., aerospace engineer, consultant; b. Colfax, Wash., Aug. 12, 1952; s. Kenneth Jay Berry, Sr. and Nancy Louise Berry; m. Mary Beth Wintersteen, Oct. 3, 1952; children: Cristine Elizabeth, Laura Jayne, Brett Douglas. BSEE, Ariz. State U., 1977. Systems engring. mgr. Motorola, Scottsdale, Ariz., 1977—95, chief systems engr. aerospace systems payloads, 1995—2001; advanced programs systems engring., sr. mem. tech. staff Gen. Dynamics, Scottsdale, 2001—. Mem. sci. and tech. soc. Motorola, Scottsdale, 1979—2001. Communications system development, High Volume Data Forwarding System (Meritorious Achievement Award from US Govt., 1995).

Master: AIAA (sr. corp. mem.); mem.: Assn. Old Crows, Tau Beta Pi, Eta Kappa Nu. Achievements include invention of Complex Signal Conditioning Processor. Office: General Dynamics 8201 E McDowell Rd Scottsdale AZ 85251 E-mail: kenneth.j.berry.jr@gd-decisionsystems.com.

BERRY, KIM LAUREN, artist; b. Hollywood, Calif., June 5, 1962; d. Gary and Judith Debra (Epstein) B.; m. Stanley Mark Carroll, Dec. 2, 1990. Studied with Jon Serl, Lake Elsinore, Calif., 1983-90; cert. in biomed. art, BFA in Illustration, Calif. State U., Long Beach, 1985; MFA in Painting, Claremont (Calif.) Grad. Sch., 1990. Instr. visual art Bixby Sch., Long Beach, Calif., 1993-94. Cons. visual art, artist Fullerton (Calif.) Sch. Dist., 1990-91. Art dir.: (film) The Secret of Easter Island, 1991 (Cine Golden Eagle award 1991); one-man show West Gallery, Claremont Grad. Sch., 1990; represented in group shows Double Rocking G Gallery, L.A., 1983, Coll. Bd., Princeton, N.J., 1984, Gallery C Calif. State U., Long Beach, 1985, DA Gallery, Pomona, Calif., 1988, West and East Galleries Claremont Grad., 1989, Helen Lindhurst Gallery, U. So. Calif., L.A., 1990, Am. Film Inst. Warner Theatre,L.A., 1991, Out of Darkness Gallery, Long Beach, 1991, 92, IPSO FACTO Gallery, Fullerton, Calif., 1992, Found. Art Resources, L.A., 1993, The Caged Chameleon Gallery, Santa Ana, Calif., 1993, A.R.C. Gallery William Rainey Harper Coll., Palatine, Ill., 1993, Nat. Congress Art Design, Salt Lake City, 1995, Aids Resource Ctr., Milwaukee, 1995, Fairfield (Calif.) Cultural Ctr., 1995, Huntington Beach (Calif.) Cultural Ctr., 1996, Orange County Ctr. Contemporary Art, Santa Ana, 1997, Gallery by the Sea, San Pedro Art Assn., 1997; artist wildlife mural, Torrance, Calif., 2000; pub. art commn. City of Fullerton, Calif., 2001. Active benefit exhibit Art for AIDS, AIDS Resource Ctr. of Wis., Milw., 1995, Animal Assistance League Benefit Exhibit, Ipso Facto Gallery, Fullerton, 1992, Homeless Benefit Exhibit, The Caged Chameleon Gallery, Santa Ana, Calif., 1993, vol. Brit. Petroleum Bird Rescue, Long Beach, 1990, Hemopet Greyhound Rescue, Irvine, Calif.; bd. dirs., co-dir., curator spl. projects Gallery by the Sea, San Pedro, 1998-99; panelist Orange County Ctr. for Contemporary Art Roundtable Forum, 1998. Calif. State Grad. fellow in Humanities, 1990; Claremont Grad. Sch. Travel and Rsch. grantee, 1989. Home: 5891 Pinon Dr Huntington Beach CA 92649-4927

BERRY, L. CLYEL, lawyer; b. Twin Falls, Idaho, July 17, 1949; s. Clyel J. and Nellie B.; m. Jill Brunzell, July 17, 1970; children: Jacob Clyel, Matthew Robert. BABA, Wash. State U., 1973; JD, U. Idaho, 1975. Bar: Idaho 1976, U.S. Dist. Ct. (dis. Idaho) 1976, U.S. Ct. Appeals (ninth cir.) 1982. Assoc. Emil F. Pike, Twin Falls, 1976-78; ptnr. Pike and Berry, Twin Falls, 1978-83; prin. Twin Falls, 1983—. Mem. Idaho State Bar Assn., Idaho Trial Lawyer Assn. (regional dir. 1981-82), Assn. Trial Lawyers of Am., Fifth Jud. Dist. Bar Assn. (sec.-treas. 1977-78). Avocations: whitewater rafting, kayaking, lic. Alaska guide, skiing, fishing, travel. Office: PO Box 302 Twin Falls ID 83303-0302

BERRY, LEORA MARY, school nurse; b. Peoria, Ill. d. William Henry and Harrietta Estella (Booker) Wilson; div. ADN, Ill. Ctrl. Coll., 1971; BSN, Wright State U., 1984; MS, Ohio State U., 1990. Cert. sch. nurse, Ohio. Staff nurse U. Ill. Hosp., Chgo., 1971-72; burn unit head nurse Childrens Med. Ctr., Dayton, Ohio, 1973-80, recovery rm. nurse, 1980-86; grad. tchg. asst. Ohio State U., Columbus, 1987-88; staff nurse VA Med. Ctr., Dayton, 1988-89; clin. instr. Dayton Sch. Practical Nursing, 1990-91; sch. nurse Dayton Pub. Schs., 1991—. Mem. adv. bd. Horizons in Nursing, Wright State U., 1989-90. Vol. health screening Delta Sigma Theta, Health Fair, 1985; vol., mem.Miami Valley Dressage and Eventing Bd., U.S. Pony Club. Mem. Ohio Nurses Assn. (polit. action com. 1988-90, dist. 10 pres. 1992-94, dist. 10 bd. dirs. 1988-94, chmn. nominating com. dist. 10 2001-, Nurse of Yr. 1994), Dayton Black Nurses Assn., Sigma Theta Tau. Methodist. Avocations: horseback riding, traveling, camping.

BERRY, LOREN CURTIS, retired lawyer, consultant; b. N.Y.C., Apr. 30, 1912; s. Gordon Lockwood and Katharine Wolcott (Dwight) B.; m. Florence Hoyt Bateson, May 10, 1941; children: Rosina B. Dixon, Roger Wolcott, Lucinda B. AB cum laude, Yale U., 1934; LLB, Columbia U., 1938. Bar: Miss. 1937, N.Y. 1939. Assoc. Rogers & Wells and predecessor firms, N.Y.C., 1939-41, 45-53, ptnr., 1953-83, cons. on estates & trusts, 1983-90, sr. counsel, 1990-2000. Dir. Church & Dwight Co., Inc., 1961-84. Councilman Town of Huntington, N.Y., 1953-57; v.p. Assn. Towns State of N.Y., Albany, 1957-60; del. from 2d senatorial dist. to N.Y. State Constl. Conv., 1967; clerk of vestry St. John's Ch., Cold Spring Harbor, N.Y., 1982-88; mem. Suffolk County N.Y. Rep. Com., 1952-85. With USNR, 1941-45, lt. commdr. 1944-45, WWII Navy Scouting Squadron Assn., counsel, 1994—. Mem. N.Y. State Bar Assn., Suffolk County Bar Assn., Huntington C. of C. (dir. 1958-63), Elks, Union Club N.Y., Tahawus Club. (sec. 1975-95). Home: PO Box 23664/Fairfield Sta Hilton Head Island SC 29925-3664

BERRY, LYNN MARINA, healthcare researcher; b. Chgo., June 15, 1955; d. Frank William and Ruth Wyatt (Sieber) Latzel; m. James F. Berry, Aug. 2, 1997. AA, Coll. DuPage, 1986; BA, Elmhurst Coll., 1988; MLA, U. Chgo., 2001. Sr. rsch. assoc. Jt. Commn. on Accreditation of Healthcare Orgns., 1999—. Mem. German Am. Nat. Congress, Czech and Slovak Am. Genealogy Soc. Ill., Czechoslovak Geneal. Soc. Internat., Mensa, Psi Chi, Phi Theta Kappa. Avocations: reading, films, dining out, geneal. rsch., interior decorating. Office: Joint Commn on Accreditation Healthcare Orgns 1 Renaissance Blvd Oakbrook Terrace IL 60181-4294

BERRY, MARION, congressman; b. Aug. 27, 1942; m. Carolyn Berry; 2 children. BS, U. Ark., 1965. Ptnr., gen. mgr. family farm, Gillett, Ark.; commr. Ark. Soil and Water Conservation Commn., 1986-94, chmn., 1992; spl. asst. to Pres. Agrl. Trade and Food Assistance, 1993; mem. U.S. Congress from 1st Ark. dist., 1997—; mem. agr. com., transp. and infrastructure com. Democrat. Avocations: hunting, fishing. Office: 1113 Longworth Ho Office Bldg Washington DC 20515-0404*

BERRY, MARY FRANCES, federal agency administrator, history and law educator; b. Nashville, Feb. 17, 1938; d. George Ford and Frances Southall (Wiggins) B. BA, Howard U., 1961, MA, 1962; PhD, U. Mich., 1966, JD, 1970; hon. degree, Cen. Mich. U., Howard U., U. Akron, 1977, Benedict Coll., U. Md., Grambling State U., 1979, Bethune-Cookman Coll., Clark Coll., Del. State Coll., 1980, Oberlin Coll., Langston U., 1983, Marian Coll., Haverford Coll., 1984, Colby Coll., CUNY, 1986, DePaul U., 1987. Bar: D.C. 1972. Asst. prof. history Central Mich. U., Mt. Pleasant, 1966-68; asst. prof. Eastern Mich. U., Ypsilanti, 1968-69, assoc. prof., 1969-70, U. Md., College Park, 1969-76; acting dir. Afro-Am. studies, 1970-72, dir., 1972-74, acting chmn. div. behavioral and social scis., 1973-74, provost div. behavioral and social scis., 1973-76; prof. history, prof. law U Colo. at Boulder, 1976-80, chancellor, 1976-77; prof. history and law Howard U., Washington, 1980—; asst. sec. for edn. HEW, Washington, 1977-80; vice chair Civil Rights Commn., 1980—82; chmn U.S. Commn. on Civil Rights, 1993—. Adj. assoc. prof. U. Mich., 1970-71; mem. com. visitors U. Mich. Law Sch., 1976-80; mem. nat. adv. panel on minority concerns Coll. Bd., 1980-84; mem. adv. bd. Feminist Press, 1980— ; mem. research adv. com. Joint Ctr. for Polit. Studies, 1981— ; mem. editorial adv. com. Marcus Garvey Papers, 1981 ; mem. adv. bd. Inst. for Higher Edn. Law and Governance, U. Houston, 1983— ; Geraldine R. Segal prof. of Am. social thought U. Pa., 1987—. Author: Black Resistance/White Law, 1971, Military Necessity and Civil Rights Policy, 1977, Stability, Security and Continuity, Mr. Justice Burton and Decision-Making in the Supreme Court, 1945-58, 1978, (with John Blassingame) Long Memory: The Black Experience in America, 1982; Why ERA Failed, 1986; asso. editor Jour. Negro History, 1974-78; contbr. articles, revs. to profl. jours. Bd. dirs. ARC, Washington, 1980— ; trustee Tuskegee U., 1980— ; mem. adv. bd. Project '87, 1978— ; mem. council UN U., 1986— Recipient Athena (disting. alumni) award U. Mich., 1977, Roy Wilkins Civil Rights award NAACP, 1983, Image award, 1983, Allard Lowenstein award, 1984, President's award Congl. Black Caucus Found., 1985, Woman of Yr. award Nat. Capital Area YWCA, 1985, Hubert H. Humphrey Civil Rights award Leadership Conf. on Civil Rights, 1986, Rosa Parks award SCLC, Black Achievement award Ebony Mag., Woman of Yr. award Ms. Mag., 1986. Mem. ABA, Nat. Bar Assn., D.C. Bar Assn., Nat. Acad. Public Adminstrn., Orgn. Am. Historians (exec. bd. 1974-77), Assn. Study of Afro-Am. Life and History (exec. bd. 1973-76), Am. Hist. Assn. (v.p. for profession 1980-83), Am. Soc. Legal History, Coalition 100 Black Women (hon.), Delta Sigma Theta (hon.) Independent. Office: Commn on Civil Rights Office of Chmn 624 9th St NW Ste 553 Washington DC 20425-0002*

BERRY, MARY PAT, real estate developer, consultant; b. Norwalk, Ohio, Jan. 4, 1948; d. Robert Valentine Rice and Catherine Mary Hickey; m. Christopher S. Berry, Oct. 3, 1970; children: Ryan Patrick, Nolan David. BA, Dominican U., River Forest, Ill., 1970; MA, Cardinal Stritch U., 1980. Tchr. pvt. schs., Chgo./Milw., 1972—76; reading specialist Shorewood Pub. Sch., Milw., 1976—83; grants specialist Ronald McDonald House Charities, Madison, Wis., 1996—99. Cons. St. Thomas, Chgo., 1972—76; trainer Shorewood (Wis.) Sch. Sys., 1976—83; grants cons. Jr. League Madison, 1990. Founder, chair Foster Care Rev. Bd., Milw., 1980—84; vice chair Cmty. Needs Assessment on Children, 1990; active Dane County Youth Commn., Madison, 1992—2000; bd. and com. mem. Assn. Jr. Leagues Internat., N.Y.C., 1995—97, 1999—2000. Named Vol. of Distinction, Assn. Jr. Leagues Internat., 1996. Mem.: Women's Philanthropy Inst. (bd. mem. 2003—, com. chair 2003—), Jr. League Madison (founder, com. chair, v.p., pres. 1988—95). Roman Catholic.

BERRY, MICHAEL WAYNE, civil engineer; b. Kansas City, Mo., Jan. 8, 1959; s. Rex Wayne and Teresa Rae (Masur) B.; m. Nancy Jan Kady, Aug. 2, 1980; children: Grace Anne, April Florence. BSCE, Kans. State U., 1980, MSCE, 1981. Registered profl. engr., Kans., Mo., Nebr.; land surveyor, Kans. Grad. rsch. asst. Kans. State U., Manhattan, 1980-81; design engr. Profl. Engring. Cons., PA, Wichita, 1981-84, project engr., 1984-90, sr. assoc., 1990 92; mgr. land devel. div. Profl. Engring. Cons., P.A., Wichita, 1992-97, mgr. Topeka, 1997—, dir., 2001—. Mem. ASCE (pres. Wichita chpt. 1989-90), Nat. Soc. Profl. Engrs., Kans. Soc. Profl. Engrs. (Young Engr. award 1989). Office: Profl Engring Cons 1263 SW Topeka Blvd Topeka KS 66612-1852

BERRY, MICHELLE COURTNEY, communication executive, performance artist; b. N.Y.C., Feb. 17, 1967; d. Glenn Walter and Dorothy Williams Wright; m. Robert Wesley Lofthouse. BA, Binghamton (N.Y.) U., 1988; MPS, Cornell U., 1992. Pres. Courtney Cons., Binghamton, 1992—; dir. cmty. rels. City of Binghamton, 1993-96; cmty. coord. Gannett Found. and PEW Charitable Trusts, Binghamton, 1996-99; comms. and media rels. officer The Johnson Sch., Cornell U., 1999-2000; dir. comms. and media rels. Wells Coll., Aurora, N.Y., 2000—. Cons. Chase, IBM, Universal Instruments, Cornell U. Author: The Month of Not Speaking, 1997; opening poet for Dr. Maya Angelou, 1995; poet-in-residence N.Y. State Divsn. for Youth, 2001—, Ithaca Sch. Dist., 2001—. Vice chair pub. rels., bd. dirs. United Way of Broome City, Vestal, 1997-2000; bd. dirs. 21st & Wells, Aurora, N.Y., 1990-92; chair Partnership for Peace, Broome City, N.Y., 1995-96; fundraiser The United Way, Broome City, 1994-99; critical incidence stress debriefer CISD Nat., 1994—; bd. dirs. Discovery Ctr. Children's Mus., 1994-96; adv. mem. Historic Ithaca, 2001—, mktg. com. 2001—. Named Disting. Alumna Harpur Coll., 1999, Woman of Yr. Status of Women Coun., 1997; recipient Outstanding Pub. Rels. award United Way of Am., 1997, regional winner So. Tier Performance Poets; 2000 regional winner Grand Poetry Slam. Mem. Broome City Performing Arts (vets. arena 1998-2000). Democrat. Roman Catholic. Avocations: reading, traveling, skiing, writing, collecting antiques. Home: 525 W Buffalo St Ithaca NY 14850 Office: Courtney Consulting and Counseling PO Box 6832 Ithaca NY 14851-6832 E-mail: mcb45@cornell.edu.

BERRY, MORRELL JOHN, cultural organization administrator; BA summa cum laude, U. Md., 1980; MPA, Syracuse U., 1981. Asst. to chief Office of cable TV, Montgomery County, 1982-84; staff dir. Md. State Fin. Com., Annapolis, 1984-85; legis. asst. Rep. Steny H. Hoyer, 1985-86; assoc. staff House Appropriations Com., Washington, 1986-94; dep. asst. Sec. of Treasury, acting asst. sec. Dept. Treasury, Washington, 1994-95; dir. Office Govt. Rels., sr. policy advisor to under sec. Smithsonian Inst., Washington, 1995-97; asst. sec. for policy, mgmt. budget U.S. Dept. Interior, Washington, 1997—. Herbert H. Lehman fellow, 1981. Office: US Dept Interior Office Sec Policy Mgmt/Budget 1849 C St NW Washington DC 20240-0001

BERRY, OMEGA MAKEECE, nursing assistant; b. San Diego, Mar. 27, 1979; d. Greg and Brinetta Berry. Cert. nurse asst. Nurse asst. Cleveland County Nursing Home, Rison, Ark., 1998—2002.

BERRY, PATRICK LOWELL, chemical engineer; b. Hillsboro, Ohio, Mar. 24, 1951; s. Russell Luther and Phyllis Louise Berry; m. Verna Ann McMullen, Sept. 11, 1971; children: Sean Patrick, Brenna Kathleen. BSChemE, Ohio State U., 1973; MS in Ops. Rsch., George Washington U., 1986. Cert. Army Acquisition Corps - Level III U.S. Army, 1992. Chem. engr. U.S. Army Edgewood CB Ctr., Aberdeen Proving Ground, Md., 1978—86, supervisory chem. engr., 1986—. 1st lt. U.S. Army, 1974—78. Mem.: AIChE, Internat. Soc. for the Systems Scis., Am. Assn. for Aerosol Rsch., Inst. for Ops. Rsch. and the Mgmt. Scis., Hon. Order of the Dragon, Omega Rho. Democrat. Achievements include development and fielding of the first U.S. Army Biological Detection Systems, M31 and M31A1. Avocations: birding, hiking, travel. Home: 3138 Aldino Rd Churchville MD 21028 Office: US Army Edgewood Chem Biol Ctr 5183 Blackhawk Rd Aberdeen Proving Ground MD 21010-5424 Home Fax: 775-251-6125; Office Fax: 410-436-3236. Personal E-mail: bidsberry@aol.com. E-mail: patrick.berry@us.army.mil.

BERRY, REBECCA DIANE, artist, art educator; b. Mexico, Mo., June 23, 1952; d. Paul Gilmore and Joanna Clayton Sappington; m. Dennis Gale Berry, Dec. 1, 1973; children: Jessica Laraine, Ginger Renee. AA, Columbia Coll., 1972; BA, William Woods U., 1992, MA, 1996. With The Mexico (Mo.) Ledger, 1972-73; clk. Lacrosse Lumber, Mexico, 1973-79; tchr. Van-Far H.S., Vandalia, Mo., 1993—. Free-lance artist. V.p. PTA, 1989—90; leader 4-H, 1989—; team leader Jr. Team, 2000; active Drug & Violence Free Task Force; vol. Becky Erdel State Rep. campaign, 1998; Sunday sch. tchr. Mexico, 1986—; trustee United Meth. Ch., 2002—03. Named to Est. Leaders Honor Roll, U. Mo., 2002. Mem. Nat. Art Edn. Assn. (Cmty. 2000 mem.), Mo. Art Edn. Assn., Fulton Art Guild, Mex. Art Guild, Sigma Delta Phi. Methodist. Avocations: painting, horseback riding, drawing, volunteering. Home: 27360 ACR 808 Mexico MO 65265 Office: Van Far High Sch 2200 W Highway 54 Vandalia MO 63382-1199

BERRY, RICHARD LEWIS, writer, magazine editor, lecturer, programmer; b. Greenwich, Conn., Nov. 6, 1946; s. John William and Dorothy May (Buck) B.; m. Eleanor von Auw, June 7, 1968 BA, U. Va., 1968; MSc, York U., Can., 1972. Rsch. asst. MacMaster U., Hamilton, Ont., Can., 1973-74; project engr. Intraspace Internat., Toronto, Ont., 1974-75; tech. editor Astronomy mag., Milw., 1976-78, editor, 1978-82, editor-in-chief, 1982-91; editor Telescope Making Mag., Milw., 1978—91; editl. dir. Earth mag., 1990-91, cons., 1992; freelance writer, programmer, lectr., 1991—; editor Cookbook Camera Newsletter, 1994-99. Mem. adv. bd. Global Network of Automatic Telescopes; com. chair Internat. Space Sta. Amateur Telescope Project, Astron. League, 2002—. Author: Build Your Own Telescope, 1985, Discover the Stars, 1987, (with others) The Star Book, 1984, Introduction to Astronomical Image Processing, 1991, AIP Image Processing Software, 1991, BatchPIX Image Processing Software, 1992, Choosing and Using a CCD Camera, 1992, The CCD Camera Cookbook, 1994, The Dobsonian Telescope: A Practical Manual for Building Large Aperture Telescopes, 1997, Handbook of Astronomical Image Processing, 2000; contbg. author: Robotic Observatories, 1989, ST6PIX Image Processing Software, 1992, CB245 Image Processing Software, 1994, Multi245 Image Compositing Software, 1995, QColor Color Synthesis Software, 1997, Astronomical Image Processing for Windows, 2000; editor: Telescope Optics, Design and Evaluation, 1988. Mem. adv. bd. Global Network of Automatic Telescopes; mem. Internat. Space Station Amateur Telescope com. Astron. League. Recipient Clifford-Holmes award Astronomy for Am., 1981, Dorothea Klumpke-Roberts award Astron. Soc. Pacific, 1990, Omega Centauri award Tex. Star Party, Clyde W. Tombaugh award Riverside Telescope Makers Conf., 1995, G. Bruce Blair award Western Amateur Astronomers, 1998, Leslie C. Peltier award Astron. League, 2001, Astron. League award, 2002; Asteroid 3684 Berry named in his honor by Internat. Astron. Union, 1990. Mem. Internat. Amateur Profl. Photoelec. Photometry, Internat. Dark Sky Assn., Am. Astron. Soc. Avocation: photography.

BERRY, RICHARD MORGAN, lawyer; b. Newport, R.I., Jan. 29, 1945; s. George Morgan and Eleanor (Prior) B.; m. Jane D'Esti; 1 child, David Alric. BA, Pa. State U., 1967; MS in Mgmt. Scis., SUNY, Binghamton, 1973; JD, Bklyn. Law Sch., 1973. Bar: N.Y. 1974, Ill. 1982. Staff atty. med. soc. State of N.Y., Lake Success, 1973-77; mgr. profl. relations med. soc. County of N.Y., N.Y.C., 1977-78; sr. research atty. The Research Group, Inc., Charlottesville, Va., 1978-81; state legis. counsel ADA, Chgo., 1981-85, asst. gen. counsel, 1984-85, assoc. gen. counsel, 1985-93, dep. gen. counsel, 1993—. Lectr. various nat. health orgns., 1982—. Columnist legislation and litigation JADA, 1981-94. Mem. ABA. Roman Catholic. Avocations: golf, travel, writing, cartooning. Home: 1499 Shermer Rd Northbrook IL 60062-5367 Office: ADA 211 E Chicago Ave Chicago IL 60611-2637

BERRY, RICHARD STEPHEN, chemist; b. Denver, Apr. 9, 1931; s. Morris and Ethel (Alpert) B.; m. Carla Lamport Friedman, Sept. 4, 1955; children: Andrea, Denise, Eric. AB, Harvard U., 1952, AM, 1954, PhD, 1956. Instr. chemistry Harvard U., 1956-57, U. Mich., 1957-60; asst. prof. Yale U., 1960-64; assoc. prof. U. Chgo., 1964-67, prof., 1967—, James Franck Disting. Svc. prof., 1989—; Arthur D. Little prof. MIT, 1968; Phillips lectr. Haverford Coll., 1968. Cons. Avco-Everett Rsch. Labs., 1964—83, Argonne Nat. Lab., 1976—, Oak Ridge Nat. Labs., 1978—81, Los Alamos Sci. Lab., 1975—, mem. adv. com. theory; vis. prof. U. Copenhagen, 1967, 79; mem. adv. panel for chemistry NSF, 1971—73; mem. rev. com. radiol. and environ. rsch. divsn. Argonne Nat. Lab., 1970—76; mem. evaluation panel measures for air quality Nat. Bur. Standards; mem. numerical data adv. bd. NRC, 1978—86, chmn., 1981—86, mem. com. strengthening linkages between math. and scis., 1997—99, mem. steering com. panel on environ. monitoring, mem. com. on atomic and molecular sci., 1984—89; com. on chem. scis NAS-NRC, 1977—79; mem. adv. panel on health of sci. and tech. enterprise, mem. adv. panel on nat. labs. Office Tech. Assessment; mem. adv. bd. Environ. Health Resource Ctr., Chgo., Inst. for Theoretical Physics, Santa Barbara, 1989—91; mem. vis. com. divsn. applied physics Harvard U., 1977—81; Hinshelwood lectr. Oxford (Eng.) U., 1980; mem. adv. panel dept. chemistry Princeton U., 1978—81; prof. associé U. Paris-Sud, 1979—80; Newton Abraham prof. Oxford U., 1986—87, Phi Beta Kappa lectr., 1989—90, Welch Symposium lectr., 1995; pres. Telluride Summer Rsch. Ctr., 1989—93; chair com. transnat. exch. sci. data Nat. Rsch. Coun., 1994—97; Frederick Kaufman lectr. U. Pitts., 1996; Sackler lectr. Tel Aviv (Israel) U., 1999; F.C. Bartell lectr. U. Mich., 1999. Author: Understanding Energy, 1988; co-author: TOSCA, The Total Social Cost of Fossil and Nuclear Power, 1979, Physical Chemistry, 1980, 2d edit., 2000, Thermodynamic Optimization of Finite Time Processes, 2000; assoc. editor: Jour. Chem. Physics, 1971-74, Accounts Chem. Rsch., 1975-90, Revs. Modern Physics, 1983-95, Phys. Rev. A, 1986-92, Phys. Rev. E, 1992-94, Phys. Chemistry Chem. Physics, 1999-2002; bd. dirs. Bull. Atomic Scientists, 1974-83; adv. editor: Resources and Energy, 1978-92; contbr. articles to profl. jours. Recipient Heyrovsky medal Czech Acad. Sci., 1997; Alfred P. Sloan fellow, 1962-66; Guggenheim fellow, 1972-73, MacArthur prize fellow, 1983; Alexander von Humboldt Stiftung prize fellow, 1993. Fellow AAAS (chmn. chemistry sect. 1993-94), Am. Phys. Soc. (coun. 1993-95, publs. oversight com. 1996-2000, panel on pub. affairs, 2001—, chmn. few-body sys. topical group 1994-95), Am. Acad. Arts and Scis. (v.p. 1987-90, 95-98), Japan Soc. for Promotion of Sci.; mem. NAS (home sec. 1999-2003, chair regents rev. com. 2000--), Am. Chem. Soc., Royal Danish Acad. Arts and Letters (fgn.), Sigma Xi (nat. lectr. 1976-77). Office: Univ Chgo Dept Chemistry 5735 S Ellis Ave Chicago IL 60637-1403 E-mail: berry@uchicago.edu.

BERRY, ROBERT BASS, construction executive; b. Tulsa, Jan. 29, 1948; s. Guy Leonard and Barbara (Bass) B.; m. Catherine Cowles, Jan. 16, 1971; children: Matthew Knipe, Eli Banjamin. BA in Fin., Okla. U., 1970. Ops. mgr. D.C. Bass & Sons Constrn., Inc., Enid, Okla., 1971-73, CEO, exec. v.p., 1973-75, pres., 1975—; CEO, pres. Mosher Devel. Co., Enid, 1975—; pres. Bobsfarm, Inc., Enid, 1975—. Active Gov.'s Internat. Trade Team, 1986-88, Leadership Okla., Oklahoma City, 1991, Habitat for Humanity, Enid, 1984; trustee Okla. chpt. The Nature Conservancy; chmn. State Alcohol Beverage Law Enforcement Commn., Oklahoma City, 1984-88, State Tort and Liability Task Force, 1986-87; bd. dirs. Enid Wellness Ctr., 1985-87, Enid Joint Indsl. Found., 1984-2002. Capt. C.E. US Army, 1971-75. Named Exec. of Yr., Profl. Secs. Internat., 1981; recipient Pres.'s Coun. award Phillips U., 1984, Developer's award Heritage League Enid, 1985. Mem. Okla. State C. of C. (bd. dirs. 1986—, chmn. 1989), Enid C. of C. (bd. dirs. 1975-78, 81-84, Vol. of Yr.), Associated Gen. Contractors (bd. dirs. 2001—). Republican. Avocations: running, skiing, hunting, scuba, climbing. Office: DC Bass & Sons Constrn Co 205 E Maine Ave Enid OK 73701-5743

BERRY, ROBERT JOHN, architect; b. Concord, Mass., Nov. 10, 1947; A in Archtl. Engring., Wentworth Inst. Tech., 1967; BArch, U. Ariz., 1971. Registered architect, Mass. Asst. prof. Wentworth Inst. Tech., Boston, 1974-81, 90-94; prin. Robert J. Berry, Architect, Boxborough, Mass., 1974—. Mem. Am. Soc. Archtl. Perspectivists (exhibitor 1986). Avocations: photography, golf, oil painting. Home and Office: 171 Summer Rd Boxboro MA 01719-2001

BERRY, ROBERT VAUGHAN, retired electrical manufacturing company executive; b. Newark, Mar. 24, 1933; s. Harold Silver and Elizabeth Lippincott (Vaughan) B.; m. Victoria Shaw, Mar. 8, 1958; children— Patricia E., Michael V. BA, Dartmouth Coll., 1954. With Thomas & Betts Corp., Memphis, 1957-95, dir., 1972-85, v.p. fin., 1975-83, sr. v.p., 1983-95; ret., 1995; pres. Thomas & Betts Internat., Inc., 1975. Bd. dirs. Ames Rubber Corp., Hamburg, N.J. Trustee Carrier Found. Psychiat. Hosp., Belle Mead, N.J., 1984-92. 1st lt. Airborne Corps U.S. Army, 1954-57. Mem. Baltusrol Golf Club (Springfield, N.J.), Harbour Ridge Golf Club (Stuart, Fla.), Summerlea Golf and Country Club (Montreal, Que., Can.), Mid Ocean Club (Bermuda), Royal and Ancient Golf Club of St. Andrews (Scotland). Republican. *Have a little fun each day - if you wait until the end you might miss it.*

BERRY, ROBERT WORTH, lawyer, educator, retired army officer; b. Ryderwood, Wash., Mar. 2, 1926; s. John Franklin and Anita Louise (Worth) Berry. BA in Polit. Sci., Wash. State U., 1950; JD, Harvard U., 1955; MA, John Jay Coll. Criminal Justice, 1981. Bar: D.C. 1956, U.S. Dist. Ct. (D.C.) 1956, U.S. Ct. of Appeals (D.C. cir.) 1957, U.S. Ct. Mil. Appeals 1957, Pa. 1961, U.S. Dist. Ct. (ea. dist.) Pa. 1961, U.S. Dist. Ct. (ctrl. dist.) Calif. 1967, U.S. Supreme Ct. 1961, Calif. 1967, U.S. Ct. Claims 1975, Colo. 1997, U.S. Dist. Ct. Colo. 1997, U.S. Ct. Appeals (10th cir.) 1997, U.S. Tax Ct. 1959. Research assoc. Harvard U., 1955-56; atty. Office Gen. Counsel U.S. Dept. Def., Washington, 1956-60; staff counsel Philco Ford Co., Phila., 1960-63; dir. Washington office Litton Industries, 1967-71; gen. counsel U.S. Dept. Army, Washington, 1971-74, civilian aide to sec. army, 1975-77; col. U.S. Army, 1978-87; prof., head dept. law U.S. Mil. Acad., West Point, N.Y., 1978-86; ret. as brig. gen. U.S. Army, 1987; mil. asst. to asst. sec. of army, Manpower and Res. Affairs Dept. of Army, 1986-87; asst. gen. counsel pub. affairs Litton Industries, Beverly Hills, Calif., 1963-67; chair Coun. of Def. Space Industries Assns., 1968; resident ptnr. Quarles and Brady, Washington, 1971-74; dir., corp. sec., treas., gen. counsel G.A. Wright, Inc., Denver, 1987-92, dir., 1987-2000; pvt. practice law Fort Bragg, Calif., 1993-96; spl. counsel Messner & Reeves LLC, Denver, 1997—. Bd. dirs. G.A. Wright Mktg., Inc., v.p./gen. counsel, 2001-; bd. dirs. Denver Mgmt. Svcs. Inc., v.p., gen. counsel, 2001— ; foreman Mendocino County Grand Jury, 1995-96. Served with U.S. Army, 1944-46, 51-53, Korea. Decorated Bronze Star, Legion of Merit, Disting. Service Medal; recipient Disting. Civilian Service medal U.S. Dept. Army, 1973, 74, Outstanding Civilian Service medal, 1977. Mem. FBA, Bar Assn. D.C., Calif. Bar Assn., Pa. Bar Assn., Colo. State Bar Assn., Denver Bar Assn., Army-Navy Club, Army-Navy Country Club, Phi Beta Kappa, Phi Kappa Phi, Sigma Delta Chi, Lambda Chi Alpha. Protestant. E-mail: rberry@messner.reeves.com.

BERRY, RONALD GEORGE, marketing professional; b. New Haven, June 18, 1940; s. Roger Henry and Elsie Elizabeth (Yarucci) B.; m. Joan Ann Mariani, Apr. 18, 1969; children: Juliette, Keith. AS in Engring., U. Bridgeport, 1967, BS in Bus., 1971, MBA, 1972; PhD, Walden U., Mpls., 1984. Purchasing agt. Gen. Dynamics, Groton, Conn., 1963-65, Superior Industries, West Haven, Conn., 1965-67; mgr. materials Gen. Electric, Bridgeport, Conn., 1967-70; contracts adminstr. Avco Lycoming, Stratford, Conn., 1970-71; mgr. purchasing, materials Dean Whitter, N.Y.C., 1972-73; CFO, COO. West Haven (Conn.) Bd. Edn., 1973-75; v.p. mktg. Conn. Health Plan, Bridgeport, 1975-77; prof. mktg. and law U. Bridgeport, 1977-83; pres. The Media Works Inc., Bridgeport, 1976-93; cons., prin. RGB Assocs., 1994—. Realtor Munson Real Estate, 1998—; tax preparer H&R Block, Westport, Conn., 1999—; mgr., fin. advisor Am. Express, Norwalk, Conn., 2000-02; mgr., fin. advisor Metlife, 2002- Dir. Citizens for Easton (Conn.), 1981-83. Col. U.S. Army, 1963-96. Mem. Am. Mktg. Assn., Am. Soc. Tng. and Devel., Am. Mgmt. Assn., MIT Venture Capital

Assn., Conn. Venture Capital Assn., Sr. Army Res. Cmdrs. Assn., Res. Officers Assn., The Ret. Officers Assn., Easton Soccer Club (pres. 1986-88), Beta Gamma Sigma. Roman Catholic. Home: 165 Mile Common Rd Easton CT 06612-1507

BERRY, SHARON ELAINE, interior designer; b. Kansas City, Mo., May 27, 1945; d. Ralph Epping Hohmann and Ruth Justine (Sturm) Hohmann Gibson; m. Max Allen Berry, Apr. 8, 1984. Grad. high sch., Kansas City; grad, Pierce Sch. Interior Design, 1972. Designer Danie Dunn Interiors, Kansas City, 1972-76, 80-83; co-owner, operator Clift-Willard Interiors, Leawood, Kans., 1976-80; head decorating dept. Carpets by Johnson and Johnson, Overland Park, Kans., 1983-84; owner, operator Nouveau Interiors, Shawnee Mission, Kans., 1984-92; coord. Met. Orgn. To Counter Sexual Assault, Kansas City, 1994-96, mem. adv. bd. adult survivor program, 1996—; pres. Recovery Records, 1996-98; dir. funding and devel. Cypress Recovery, Inc., Olathe, Kans., 1999-2000, bd. dirs., 1998; dir. fund devel. Rick's Place Found., 2000—01; owner Wild Berry Interior Design, 2002—. Vol. Design Excellence Awards Com., Kansas City, 1982-88; designer Designers Showhouse, Kansas City, Mo., 1975-90; participant Design '81 Congress, Helsinki, 1981, Gourmet March of Dimes, 1988, 90; writer City Limits, entertainment mag., Family News mag. Editor newsletter Survivors United Reading Empowerment (S.U.R.E.); contbr. to anthology The Bridge Is Out But I Can Fly; co-writer, co-prodr. CD Who Will Save the Children; editor, writer, newsletter Cypress Recovery. Vol. exec. dir. Recovery Is For Everyone Found., Olathe, 1996; vol. dir. pub. rels. Women's Resource Network, Shawnee Mission, 2000-02; v.p. internat. tng. in comm. JoCo Club. Recipient 2 Telly awards, gold award Houston Internat. Film Festival, 2d place Kans. Film Festival, cert. of merit Internat. Film and Video competition for video Who Will Save the Children, 1995. Avocations: writing, painting, sewing, gardening. E-mail: wildberry@prodigy.net.

BERRY, STEPHEN JOSEPH, reporter; b. Ft. Jackson, S.C., May 2, 1948; s. Charles and Marjorie (Sheehan) Berry; m. Cheryl C. Berry, Nov. 24, 1973; 1 child, Stephen Richard. BA in Polit. Sci., U. Montevallo, 1970; MA, U. N.C. at Greensboro, 1984. Mem. staff Dothan (Ala.) Eagle, 1970—72, Greensboro (N.C.) News and Record, 1971—, Orlando (Fla.) Sentinel, 1989—96, The L.A. Times, 1996—. Recipient Pulitzer Prize, 1993, Pub. Svc. award, AP News Execs. Coun. Calif.-Nebr., 1998, 1st pl., Soc. Profl. Journalists Excellence award in sports reporting, 1994, Benjamin Fine award, 1985, N.C. Sch. Bell award, 1986. Mem.: Phi Alpha Theta. Home: 6527 Ellenview Ave West Hills CA 91307-2717 Office: LA Times Times Mirror Sq Los Angeles CA 90053

BERRY, WILLIAM LEE, business administration educator; b. Indpls., Dec. 24, 1935; s. George Lee and Anna Marie (Hansert) B.; children: Ann Kathleen, Lee Michael, Lynn Colleen. BS, Purdue U., 1957; MS, Va. Poly. Inst., 1964; DBA, Harvard U., 1969. Mfg. trainee GE, various locations, 1957-60, supr. mfg. Salem, Va., 1960-64; from asst. prof. to assoc. prof. indsl. mgmt. Purdue U., West Lafayette, Ind., 1968-76; prof. prodn. mgmt. Ind. U., Bloomington, 1976-82; C. Maxwell Stanley prof. prodn. mgmt. U. Iowa, Iowa City, 1982-87, sr. assoc. dean Coll. Bus. Adminstrn., 1983-87, dir. Mfg. and Productivity Ctr., 1986-87; Belk prof. bus. adminstrn., chmn. ops. mgmt. area U. N.C., Chapel Hill, 1988-92; prof. bus. adminstrn. Ohio State U., 1992—, Richard Ross chair in mgmt., dir. Ctr. Excellence in Mgmt., 1995—. Vis. prof. IMD, Lausanne, Switzerland, 1987-88; cons. in field. Co-author: Operations and Logistics Management, 1972, Production Planning, Scheduling and Inventory Control: Concepts, Techniques and Systems, 1974, Master Production Scheduling: Principles and Practice, 1979, Manufacturing Planning and Control Systems, 1984, 2d edit., 1988, 3rd edit., 1992, 4th edit., 1997, ITEC: Manufacturing Planning and Control/Manufacturing Strategy Simulation, 1992, Production and Inventory Control Integrated, 1992; contbr. articles to profl. jours. 1st Enterprise fellow Kenan Inst., 1988-90. Fellow Decision Scis. Inst. (v.p. 1983-84, sec. 1985-86, pres.-elect 1987, pres. 1988); mem. Inst. Indsl. Engrs. (v.p. 1979-81, dir., Disting. Service award 1979), Ops. Mgmt. Assn. (v.p. 1981-85, pres.-elect 1985-86, pres. 1986-87, dir., Disting. Leadership award 1987), Am. Prodn. and Inventory Control Soc., Inst. Mgmt. Sci., Ops. Research Soc. Office: Fisher Coll of Bus Ohio State U Columbus OH 43210

BERRY, WILLIAM MARTIN, financial consultant; b. Chgo., June 21, 1920; s. William John and Mary Frances (Martin) B.; m. Julia McIntire Vail, Dec. 19, 1972; children: William E., Mary P., Peter D. BS, St. Mary's Univ., 1941; MA, DePaul U., 1949. Divsn. contr. Hughes Aircraft Co., Culver City, Calif., 1950-55; div. contr. TRW, Redondo Beach, Calif., 1955-58; mgr. mgmt. cons. dept. Peat, Marwick, Mitchell and Co., L.A., 1958-61; v.p. Litton Industries Inc., Beverly Hills, Calif., 1961-74; chmn., CEO NN Corp., Milw., 1974-80; chmn. Northwestern Nat. Ins. Group, 1981-84. Bd. dirs. PK Tool & Die Mfg. Co., Chgo. Bd. dirs. Columbia Hosp., Milw., 1976—, Milw. Assn. Commerce, 1976-81, Milw. Symphony Orch., 1974-81, United Performing Arts Fund., Milw., 1977-81. With U.S. Army, 1941-46. Mem. Fin. Execs. Inst., Milw. Club, Milw. Country Club, Univ. Club. Avocations: woodworking, languages. Home and Office: 13800 N Birchwood Ln Mequon WI 53097-1702

BERRY, WILLIAM WILLIS, retired utility executive; b. Norfolk, Va., May 18, 1932; s. Joel Halbert and Julia Lee (Godwin) B.; m. Elizabeth Mangum, Aug. 23, 1958; children: Preston Blackburn, John Willis, William Godwin. BSEE, Va. Mil. Inst., 1954; MS in Commerce, U. Richmond, 1964. Registered profl. engr., Va. Engr. Gen. Electric Co., 1954-55; with Va. Power, Richmond, 1957-92, v.p. div. ops., then sr. v.p. comml. ops., 1976-78, exec. v.p., 1978-80, pres., chief oper. officer, 1980-83, pres. chief exec. officer, 1983-85, chmn., chief exec. officer, 1985-86, Dominion Resources Inc., 1986-90, chmn., 1990-92. Bd. dirs. Ethyl Corp., Richmond. Chair ISO New England, Holyoke, Mass. Mem. Commonwealth Club, Country Club of Va., Norfolk Yacht and Country Club. Republican.

BERRY, WINIFRED L. medical technologist; b. Monroe City, Ind., May 1, 1932; d. Paul G. and Annalee (McCoy) Wilson; m. Donald W. Berry, June 29, 1952; children: Krista J. (Berry) Meyer, Kimberly J. (Berry) Lane. AS, Vincennes (Ind.) U., 1952; BS, Ind. State U., 1964. Registered med. technologist Am. Soc. Clin. Pathologists. Med. technologist Good Samaritan Hosp., Vincennes, Ind., 1955—58; med. technologist, x-ray technologist Burows & McRoberts Clinic & Hosp., Killeen, Tex., 1953—55; instr. Vincennes U., 1960—66; med. technologist Daviess County Hosp., Washington, Ind., 1979—92. Pres. Grouseland Found., Inc., Vincennes, 1999—2002. Named Outstanding Alumnus, Monroe City High Sch. Alumni Assn., 2000. Mem.: Knox County C. of C., DAR (treas. Francis Vigo chpt. 1993—99), Hist. and Antiquarian Soc., Assn. Ind. Mus. Mem. Ch. Of God. Avocations: organ, choir.

BERRY BERTRAM, KATHRYN, editor in chief science publication; b. Binghamton, N.Y., July 9, 1958; d. William Earl Berry and Barbara (Ellis) Dickay; m. Mark Robert Bertram, Aug. 17, 1996. BA, Wittenberg U., 1980; M in Pub. Adminstrn., Ind. U., 1983. Assoc. instr. Ind. U., Bloomington, 1980-81; ranger, spokesperson U.S. Park Svc. Denali (Alaska) Nat. Park and Preserve, 1981-84 summers; sci. and investigative reporter Fairbanks (Alaska) Daily News Miner, 1984-88; publs. editor, br. mgr. Alaska Natural History Assn., Denali Park, 1988-89; free lance writer and editor Alaska Bus. Monthly, Anchorage Daily News, Alaska Geographic, Fairbanks, Alaska, 1989-91; supr. info. and edn. outreach Geophys. Inst. U. Alaska, Fairbanks, 1991—. Co-author, editor: (book) Black Tides: The Alaska Oil Spill, 1989; editor: (books) A Backcountry Companion, 1989, The Geology of Denali National Park, 1989; editor Geophys. Inst. Quarterly Newsletter, 1991— (1st pl. writing and editing Alaska Press Women, 1995, Nat. Press Women, 1995, Bronze award Coun. for Advancement and Support of Edn., 1994). Officer United Way, Fairbanks, Alaska, 1994—; bd. dirs. Presbn. Hospitality House, Fairbanks, 1995—. Recipient Alaska Legislature citation for publ. excellence, 1994, 95, 96, First Place Nat. award for editing and producing "Global Change and Polar Regions" Jour. of Govt. Info., 1995. Mem. Alaska Press Women, Nat. Press Women, Soc. Profl. Journalists. Democrat. Lutheran. Avocations: lead singer jazz and folk bands, dog musher, outdoor enthusiast. Office: Geophys Inst U Alaska 903 Koyukuk Dr Fairbanks AK 99775-7320 E-mail: info@gi.alaska.edu.

BERRYHILL, GEORGIA GENE, web designer, photographer, educator; b. Wlliamsport, Ind., Aug. 27, 1947; d. Detro Horace and Bliss Berniece Sells; m. Robert Earl Berryhill, Aug. 10, 1966; children: Deven Earl, Joel Eugene. BA in Biomed. Illustration, Calif. State U., Long Beach, 1979; MA in Graphic Design, Calif. State U., L.A., 1986; PhD, Walden U., Mpls., 1993. Graphic designer, art dir. Illustrated Sci., Seal Beach, Calif., 1976-86; bio-med. illustrator UCLA Med. Ctr., Torrance, Calif., 1979-80; design instr., curriculum developer Glendale (Calif.) C.C. Ext., 1984-88; creative dir. Berryhill Prodns., Laguna Beach, Calif., 1986—; art/design/photo instr. Biola U., La Mirada, Calif., 1987-89; art/design instr. Art Inst. of So. Calif., Laguna Beach, 1991-93; instr. computer graphics, digital arts U. Calif. Ext., Irvine, 1992—2000; assoc. prof. art Biola U., 1999-2000; instr. U. Nations, Kona, Hawaii, 2000—; assoc. prof. profl. studies Biola U., 2001—. Cons. Martin Luther King Hosp., L.A., 1980, U. So. Calif., L.A., 1980, UCLA Med. Ctr., 1980-86, Beckman Found., 1996; program adminstr. Beckman Found., 1997; hon. prof. arts Yunnan Arts Inst., Kunming, China, 1999; media photographer/Quest, Summer Olympics, Sydney, Australia, 2000. Author: The Social Impact of Graphic Symbolism, 1993, Designing Website Images: A Practical Guide, 2000; contbr. articles to profl. jours.; spkr. in field; juried exhbns. include Festival of Arts/Pageant of the Masters, Laguna Beach, Calif., 1998, 99, 2000, Internat. Festival Arts, Kunming, China, 1999; musician The Surfaris. Mem.: Women in Photography Internat. (profl.), Nat. Press Photographers' Assn. (profl.), Coll. Art Assn., Assn. for Advancement of Policy Rsch. Devel. in the 3d World, Soc. of Environ. Graphic Design, Am. Inst. of Graphic Arts, Internat. Soc. Electronic Arts, Kappa Pi. Republican. E-mail: gene.berryhill@biola.edu.

BERRYHILL, HENRY LEE, JR., geologist, researcher; b. Charlotte, N.C., Nov. 6, 1921; s. Henry Lee and Viola Estelle (Johnston) B.; m. Louise Randall Russell, Sept. 13, 1947; children: Stuart Randall, Keith Courtney. BS, U. N.C., 1947, MS in Geology, 1949. With U.S. Geol. Survey, 1948-86, chief publs. officer, 1963-65, research marine geologist, 1965-66, chief marine geology Gulf of Mexico-Caribbean region office, 1967-70; chief Office Marine Geology, Washington, 1970-73, sr. research marine geologist Corpus Christi, 1973-86; gen. cons., 1986-99; ret., 1999; Tech. adviser offshore prospecting com. ECAFE, 1972-73; Dept. Interior rep. Fed. Intragy. Com. on Marine Sci. and Engring., 1970-73; program mgr. integrated environ. assessment Outer Continental Shelf N.W. Gulf of Mexico, 1973-86; U.S. rep. marine geology panel U.S.-Japan Coop. Programs in Natural Resources, 1973-95. Cons. Nat. Center for Geoscis., India, 1981-87. Author: Geology and Coal Resources of Belmont County, Ohio, 1963, Geology of the Ciales Area, Puerto Rico, 1965, Coal-Bearing Upper Pennsylvanian and Lower Permian Rocks, Washington Area, Pennsylvania, 1971, The Worldwide Search for Petroleum Offshore-A Status Report for the Quarter Century, 1947-72, 1974, Seismic Models of Late Quaternary Facies and Structure, Northern Gulf of Mexico, 1986. Contbr. articles to sci. publs. Served with USAAF, 1942-45. Decorated DFC, Air medal with 3 oak leaf clusters; recipient Outstanding Performance award U.S. Geol. Survey, 1969, a seafloor feature of the Gulf of Mexico named Berryhill Basin in his honor, 1995. Fellow Geol. Soc. Am.; mem. Am. Assn. Petroleum Geologists (co-recipient Jules Braunstein meml. award 1987), Sierra Club (chmn. Coastal Bend group 1980-81, 86-89), Sigma Xi. Episcopalian. Home and Office: 922 Burnt Hickory Cir Marietta GA 30064 *Besides an innate enthusiasm for learning, the greatest single factor that has shaped my life has been the choice of a profession that I could pursue as if it were my hobby.True satisfaction comes from the heartfelt knowledge of work well done. No amount of praise can supplant that innermost feeling of achievement. Above all, never fear to try.*

BERRYHILL, MARY FINLEY, emergency nurse; b. Miami Beach, Fla., Dec. 11, 1944; d. Clyde A. and Alice J. (White) Finley; m. Michael W. Berryhill (div. Nov. 1977); children: Jennifer Ann, John Michael; m. Robert L. Snyder, July 18, 1996. BSN, U. Fla., 1967. RN; cert. emergency nurse, emergency nursing pediatric course instr., trauma nurse core course instr. Staff nurse, nurse clinician Shand's Teaching Hosp. U. Fla., Gainesville, 1967-68; rsch. assoc. Coll. Nursing U. Fla., Gainesville, 1968-70; childbirth educator Ocala, Fla., 1970-78; outpatient obstetrics nurse Heith H. Knorr, Ocala, 1970-72; state coord. Am. Soc. Psychoprophylaxis, Ocala, 1974-78; student health svc. nurse Berkshire Sch., Sheffield, Mass., 1978-90; nurse emergency dept. Fairview Hosp., Great Barrington, Mass., 1984—, shift dir., 1992—. Tchr. emergency childbirth, pediatric emergency care and child abuse recognition and care to EMTs. Emergency childbirth instr. South Berkshire Vol. Ambulance Squad, Great Barrington, Mass., 1983-93, mem., v.p., 1984-85. Recipient OGYN Nurse of Yr. Fla. NAACOG, 1977. Mem. Emergency Nurses Assn. (treas. Berkshire chpt. 1993, pres. 1998, 99, trauma nurse core curriculum instr. 1992—, emergency nurse pediat. curriculum instr. 1993—, Mass. state pediat. com. 1994—). Avocations: cross-country skiing, hiking, backpacking, white water canoeing, birding. Home: PO Box 587 Great Barrington MA 01230-0587 Office: Fairview Hosp 29 Lewis Ave Great Barrington MA 01230-1796

BERRYHILL, MAURICE JUDD, human services administrator; b. Livermore, Iowa, Mar. 23, 1943; s. Judd and Althea M. Berryhill; m. Luanne Collins, Apr. 1969 (div. 1972); 1 child, Meredith Ann; m. Susan Joann Jebron, Aug. 25, 1972; children: Timothy Judd, Lisa Jo-Marie. Student, Iowa Ctrl. C.C., 1970—71, U. Iowa, 1971—72; MA, Columbia Pacific U., 1983. Cert. clin. addictions specialist 1981, reality therapist 1983, employee assistance profl. 1994, lic. NC, 1998. With U.S. Army Alcohol and Drug Program, Ft. Bragg, NC, 1972—99; program dir. substance abuse Cumberland County Regional Juvenile Detention Ctr., Fayetteville, NC, 1991—95; clin. supr. N.C. Med. Bd. Impaired Physicians, 1984—86; substance abuse counselor N.C. Bar Assn. Impaired Attys., 1986—88, 1998—; ret., 1999. With U.S. Army, 1962—65. Office: Cumberland County Mental Health Ctr 111 Bradford Ave Fayetteville NC 28303

BERRYMAN, PATRICIA LORD, software engineer; b. Bklyn., Jan. 16, 1953; d. Pascoe and Louise (Lord) B.; m. Rober Hilton LeMoine, June 15, 1972 (div. 1977); m. Paul Walter Mortensen, Aug. 21, 1988; children: Ian Michael, Alison Louise. BS, L.I. U., 1975; postgrad. work in immunology, U. Pa., 1980. Rsch. technician Meml. Sloan Kettering Cancer Ctr., N.Y.C., 1975-76; rsch. assoc. in pathology Duke U., Durham, N.C., 1981-83; computer programmer U. N.C., Chapel Hill, 1983-85; quality assurance mgr. SAS Inst., Cary, NC, 1985—99, sr. software mgr., 1999—. Office: SAS Inst Sas Campus Dr Cary NC 27513

BERRYMAN, RICHARD BYRON, lawyer; b. Indpls., Aug. 16, 1932; s. Herbert Byron and Ruth Katherine (Mayerhoefer) B.; m. Virginia Marie Asti, June 9, 1957; children: Steven, Susan, Kenneth. BA, Carleton Coll., 1954; JD, U. Chgo., 1957. Bar: D.C. 1957. Atty. bur. of aeronautics U.S. Dept. Navy, Washington, 1957-59, atty. office gen. counsel, 1959-62; assoc. Cox, Langford & Brown, Washington, 1962-65, ptnr., 1965-68, Fried, Frank, Harris, Shriver & Jacobson, Washington, 1968-90; pvt. practice Washington, 1990—. Mem. vis. com. Law Sch. U. Chgo., 1978-82; trustee Carleton Coll., Northfield, Minn., 1982-86; dir. Pericles Inst., Washington, 1996-2000. Mem. ABA. Office: 6901 Old Gate Ln Rockville MD 20852 also: 1200 6 St NW Ste 800 Washington DC 20005

BERRYMAN, ROBERT GLEN, accounting educator, consultant; b. Freeport, Ill., Nov. 22, 1928; s. Loyd Vernon and Gladys Leone (Hicks) B.; m. Ruth Madelyn Bjorngjeld, Aug. 25, 1955; children: Peter, David, Kathryn. BSBA, Northwestern U., 1950, MBA, 1951; PhD, U. Ill., 1958. CPA, Ill., Minn. Staff auditor Deloitte & Touche, Chgo., 1951-54, mgr. Mpls., 1969-70; instr. U. Ill., Champaign, 1954-58; asst. prof. acctg. U. Minn., Mpls., 1958-61, assoc. prof., 1961-65, prof., 1965-95, dir. grad. studies in acctg., 1980-83, chmn. dept. acctg., 1963-65, 70-73, 1990-95; exec. dir. fin. Cedar Riverside Assocs., Mpls., 1974-75. Cons. in field. Mem. editl. bd. Issues in Acctg. Edn., 1995-98; contbr. articles to profl. publs. Adviser to audit com. Minn. State Colls. and Univs., 1997-2001 Recipient Horace T. Morse-Amoco All Univ. Tchg. award U. Minn., 1976, Outstanding Tchr. award Carlson Sch. Mgmt., U. Minn., Green Eyeshade award Minn. Acctg. Assn., Tchg. award U. Minn. Alumni Assn., Mpls., 1978, Leon Radde Outstanding Educator award Inst. Internal Auditors, 1988. Mem. AICPA (chmn. acctg. theory subcom. 1979-83, continuing profl. edn. exec. com. 1979-82, bd. examiners 1980-83, Disting. Achievement in Acctg. Edn. award 1999), Inst. Internal Auditors (bd. regents 1979-83, bd. govs. Twin City chpt. 1981-91, cert. internal auditor), Minn. Soc. CPA (bd. dirs. 1965-69, 78-83, first recipient and honoree R. Glen Berryman award 1976), Minn. Acctg. Aid Soc. (pres. and bd. dirs.), Am. Acctg. Assn. (Outstanding Acctg. Educator 1994, Auditing Educator 1992). Home: 1462 Brenner Ave Saint Paul MN 55113-1671 Office: Univ MN Carlson Sch of Mgmt 321 19th Ave S Minneapolis MN 55455-0438 E-mail: gberryman@csom.umn.edu.

BERRYMAN, WARREN, dean; b. Hastings, Nebr., Nov. 16, 1950; s. Warren and MaryAnne Berryman; m. Terryl Hodgskin, July 28, 1952; children: Jessica Johanna, Jeanna Berryman, Berryman Jefferson. BSEE, Wash. U., St. Louis, 1980; MS, Case Western Res. U., 1977; MBA, Kent State U., 1982; PhD, Mich. State U., 2002. Dean Cornerstone U., Grand Rapids, Mich., 1992—. Office: So Nazazrene Univ 6729 NW 39th Exwy Bethany OK 73008 Office Fax: 405-491-6302. E-mail: dberryma@snu.edu.

BERS, ABRAHAM, electrical engineering and physics educator; b. Cernauti, Bukovina, Romania, May 28, 1930; came to U.S., 1949; s. Isaias and Berta (Lechter) B.; m. Anita Alden Burrage, June 17, 1966; children: Rachel, Joshua. BS, U. Calif. with highest honors, Berkeley, 1953; SM, MIT, 1955, ScD, 1959. Rsch. asst. Rsch. Lab. Electronics MIT, Cambridge, Mass., 1953-58, instr. dept. elec. engring. and computer sci., 1958-59, asst. prof., 1959-63, assoc. prof., 1963-71, prof., 1971—. Dir. rsch. Ecole Polytechnique, Paris, 1979-80; vis. prof. U. Paris-Orsay, 1981-92; vis. scientist CEA-Euratom, Cadarache, France, 1995, Limeil-Valenton, France, 1995. Co-author: Waves in Anisotropic Plasmas, 1963, Physique des Plasmas, Vols. 1-2, 1994; contbr. chpts. to books, articles to profl. jours. Faculty Exch. fellow Ford Found., Tech. U. Berlin, 1966, fellow J.S. Guggenheim Meml. Found., U. Paris, 1968-69. Fellow: Am. Phys. Soc. (chmn. divsn. plasma physics 1991—92); mem.: AAAS, Univ. Fusion Assn. (pres. 1988—89), N.Y. Acad. Sci., St. Botolph Club Boston. Avocations: tennis, skiing.

BERS, DONALD MARTIN, physiology educator; b. N.Y.C., Dec. 13, 1953; s. Harold Theodore and Penny (Wall) B.; m. Kathryn Eileen Hammond, July 17, 1976; children: Brian Alexander, Rebecca Ann. BA, U. Colo., 1974; PhD, UCLA, 1978. Postdoctoral research fellow UCLA, 1978-79, asst. research physiologist, 1980-82, adj. asst. prof., 1981-87; postdoctoral research fellow Edinburgh (Scotland) U., 1979-80; asst. prof. U. Calif., Riverside, 1982-86, assoc. prof., 1986-89, prof., 1989-92, divisional dean, dir. biomed. scis. program, 1991-92; prof., chmn. dept. physiology Loyola U., Chgo., 1992—. Author: Excitation-Contraction Coupling and Cardiac Contractile Force, 1991, 2001; assoc. editor News in Physiol. Sci.; mem. editl. bd. Am. Jour. Physiology, Circulation Rsch., Jour. Pharm. and Exptl. Therapeutics, Jour. Molecular Cell Cardiology; contbr. articles to profl. jours. Bd. dirs. Am. Heart Assn., Riverside, 1985-92, pres., 1989-91. Fellow Am. Heart Assn., L.A., 1978-80, Brit.-Am., Am. Heart Assn., 1980-81; recipient New Investigator Rsch. award NIH, 1982-85, Rsch. Career Devel. award NIH, 1985-90. Fellow: Internat. Soc. Heart Rsch. (mem. coun.), Am. Heart Assn.; mem.: AAAS, Biophys. Soc. (mem. coun., mem. exec. bd.), Am. Physiol. Soc., Soc. Gen. Physiology.

BERS, ERIC LAWRENCE, civil engineer; b. Balt., Mar. 13, 1950; s. Harold and Bernice (Feldstein) B.; m. Jane Margaret Sneider, May 29, 1977; children: Rebecca Suzanne, Amy Lynne. BSCE, Washington U., St. Louis, 1972; MS, Ga. Inst. of Tech., 1975, MSCE, 1976. Engr. Met. Atlanta Rapid Transit Authority, 1975-77; staff engr. Sverdrup, Parcel & Assocs., Silver Spring, Md., 1977-78; gen. engr. ICC, Washington, 1978-79; transp. engr. U.S. Dept. Transp., Washington, 1979-90; pres., chief exec. officer Pacesetter Homes, Inc., Ellicott City, Md., 1990—. Bd. dirs. pres. Columbia Commuter Bus Corp., 1982-84. Reviewer profl. jours.; co-editor Managing Urban Transportation As a Bus, 1988; contbr. articles to profl. jours. Tech. advisor Fort Hill Community Assn., Ellicott City, 1979. Mem. ASCE (chmn. Urban Transp div., conf. chair), Am. Soc. Engring. Edn., Inst. Transp. Engrs., NAS (Transp. Rsch. Bd.), Wash. U. Alumni Assn. (Balt. coord.). Jewish. Home: PO Box 841 Ellicott City MD 21041-0841

BERSH, PHILIP JOSEPH, psychologist, educator; b. Phila., Sept. 9, 1921; s. Michael and Sophie (Faggen) B.; m. Jacqueline Edith Fratkin, June 8, 1952; children: Lauren Helene, Marilyn Ellen. AB, Temple U., 1944; AM, Columbia U., 1947, PhD, 1949. Lectr. Columbia U., 1948-54, research assoc., 1951-54; lectr. U. Wis., 1951; chief intelligence and electronic warfare br. Rome Air Devel. Ctr., N.Y., 1954-62; lectr. Utica Coll., Syracuse U., N.Y., 1958-60, Hamilton Coll., 1961-62; chief combat systems lab. U.S. Army Behavioral Sci. Rsch. Inst., Washington, 1962—67, assoc. dir. human performance experimentation, 1966—67; lectr. George Washington U., 1966-67; prof. psychology Temple U., Phila., 1967—. Vis. prof. dept. psychology Inst. Psychiatry U. London, 1979; cons. U.S. Army Research Inst. for Behavioral and Social Scis. Cons. editor: JSAS; Catalog Selected Documents in Psychology, 1976-79; mem. editorial bd. Jour. Exptl. Analysis of Behavior, 1980-83, 85-87; contbr. articles on psychology to profl. jours. Served with AUS, 1942-46, ETO. NRC postdoctoral fellow, 1950 Fellow APA, AAAS, Am. Psychol. Soc., Assn. Behavior Analysis; mem. Psychonomic Soc., Ctr. for Behavioral Studies, Ea. Psychol. Assn., Sigma Xi. Home: The Fairmont # 413 41 Conshohocken State Rd Bala Cynwyd PA 19004-2438 E-mail: pbersh@astro.temple.edu.

BERSHAD, JACK R. retired lawyer; b. Philadelphia, May 20, 1930; m. Helen Abby (Jay), Apr. 7, 1957; children: Thomas, Daniel, Robert. BS, Temple U., 1951; JD, Harvard U., 1954; LHD, Moore Coll. Art. Bar: D.C. 1954, Pa. 1955, U.S. Supreme Ct. 1985. Mem. firm Blank Rome, LLP, Phila., 1958—2002, chmn., 1991—99, chmn. emeritus, 2000—, ret., 2002. Bd. dirs. Commerce Bancorp, Inc., Commerce Bank, N.A. Former chmn. bd. mgr. and trustees Moore Coll. Art, Phila.; trustee Phila. Mus. Art, 1989—; bd. dirs. Opera Co., Phila., 1989—, v.p., 1990—; trustee Jewish Fedn. Greater Phila.; bd. dirs. Ben-Gurion U. of the Negev, Am. Assocs., 1998—, chair Mid. Atlantic Region; bd. govs. Mid. East Forum, 2000—, chmn., Phila. U.S. Army, 1954-56. Mem. ABA, Pa. Bar Assn., D.C. Bar Assn., Phila. Bar Assn. Office: Blank Rome LLP 1 Logan Sq Fl 3 Philadelphia PA 19103-6998

BERSHAD, NEIL JEREMY, electrical engineering educator; b. Bklyn., Oct. 20, 1937; BEE, Rensselaer Poly. Inst., 1958, PhD EE, 1962; MSEE, U. So. Calif., 1960. Mem. tech. staff Hughes Aircraft Co., Culver City, Calif., 1958-62, staff engr., 1964-69; prof. elec. engring. and computer sci. U. Calif., Irvine, 1966-94, prof. emeritus, 1994—. Contbr. more than 100 articles on communication theory, signal processing and adaptive filtering to profl. jours. 1st lt. USAF, 1962-65. Fellow IEEE (assoc. editor communications jour., acoustics, speech and signal processing jour.). E-mail: bershad@ece.uci.edu.

BERSHTEIN, HERMAN SAMMY, lawyer; b. New Haven, Sept. 2, 1925; s. William and Bessie (Burke) B.; children: Joy, Richard, Jan. BA, Yale U., 1950; LLB, U. S.C., 1954. Bar: Conn. 1954, S.C. 1954, U.S. Dist. Ct. Conn. 1955. Pvt. practice law, Hamden, Conn., 1954-69; pres. Bershtein Bershtein & Bershtein, Hamden, 1969—. Arbitrator Am. Arbitration Assn., Hamden, 1969—. Judge advocate for Jewish War Vets, Hamden, 1955-75. 2d lt. U.S. Army, 1943-46. Judge adv. Jewish War Vets., Hamden, 1955-75. Served U.S. Army, 1943—46. Office: Bershtein Bershtein & Bershtein 1188 Dixwell Ave Hamden CT 06514-4732 E-mail: blawfirm@aol.com.

BERSIN, ALAN DOUGLAS, lawyer, school system administrator; b. Bklyn., Oct. 15, 1946; s. Arthur and Mildred (Laikin) B.; m. Elisabeth Van Aggelen, Aug. 17, 1975 (div. Dec. 1983); 1 child, Alissa Ida; m. Lisa Foster, July 20, 1991; children, Madeleine Foster, Amalia Rose. AB magna cum laude, Harvard U., 1968; student, Oxford U., 1968-71; JD, Yale U., 1974; LLD (hon.), U. San Diego, 1994, Calif. Western Sch. Law, 1996, Thomas Jefferson Sch. Law, 2000. Bar: Calif. 1975, U.S. Dist. Ct. (ctrl. dist.) Calif. 1975, U.S. Ct. Appeals (9th cir.) 1977, Alaska 1983, U.S. Dist. Ct. Alaska 1983, U.S. Dist. Ct. Hawaii 1992, U.S. Dist. Ct. (so. dist.) Calif. 1992, U.S. Supreme Ct., 1996. Exec. asst. Bd. Police Commrs., L.A., 1974-75; assoc. Munger, Tolles & Olson, L.A., 1975-77, ptnr., 1978-92; spl. dep. dist. atty. Counties of Imperial and San Diego, Calif., 1993-98; supt. pub. edn. San Diego City Schs., 1998—. Adj. prof. of law U. So. Calif. Law Ctr.; vis. prof. Sch. Law U. San Diego, 1992-93; named spl. rep. for U.S. s.w. border by U.S. Atty. Gen., 1995-98; mem. Atty Gen.'s adv. com. of U.S. Attys., 1995-98; tech. adv. panel Nat. Inst. of Justice Law Enforcement, adv. com. FCC/NTIA Pub. Safety Wireless; founder U.S./Mex. Binat. Lab. Program; chmn. bd. dirs. U.S. Border Rsch. Tech. Ctr., S.W. Border Coun.; chmn. Calif. Commn. on Tchr. Credentialing, 2000-02; mem. Nat. Bd. Profl. Tchg. Stds. Recognition, 2002; coun. visitors Calif. We. Sch. Law, 2002--. Named Rhodes scholar 1968; recipient Resolution of Merit award Mayor and City Coun. L.A., 1991, Spl. Achievement award Hispanic Urban Ctr., 1992, Peacemaker's award San Diego Mediation Assn., 1997, Morgan award San Diego LEAD, 1998, Learned Hand award, AJC, 2001, Courageous Leadership

award, San Diego C. of C., 2003. Mem. Assn. Bus. Trial Lawyers (bd. govs. 1986-88), Inner City Law Ctr. (chmn. bd. dirs. 1987-90). Democrat. Jewish. Avocations: scuba diving, skiing, travel. Fax: 619-291-7182. E-mail: abersin@mail.sandi.net.

BERSIN, RICHARD LEWIS, physicist, plasma process technologist; b. NYC, July 4, 1929; s. Maxwell Hilary and Virginia (Greenfield) B.; m. Lillian Freda Braudy, Mar. 21, 1954 (div.); children: Joshua Morris, Adam Samuel; m. Ruth Ann Hargrave, July 25, 1976; children: Jacob David Antonio, Rebekah Adeline Juana. BS in Physics, MIT, 1950; MS in Maths. and Physics, Northeastern U., Boston, 1962. Physicist Tracerlab, Inc., Boston, 1950-58; divsn. mgr. Lab. for Electronics Corp., Waltham, Mass., 1958-69; pres., founder Internat. Plasma Corp., Berkeley, Calif., 1969-74; exec. v.p. Dionex Gas Plasma Sys., Hayward, Calif., 1974-79; dir. of dry processing Perkin Elmer Corp., Wilton, Conn., 1979-83, dir. tech. mktg., 1983-84; pres., cons. Emergent Techs. Corp., 1985—; engring. specialist Ulvac Japan, Ltd., Chigasaki, Japan, 1989-92; sr. tech. staff mem. Ulvac Techs., Inc., Methuen, Mass., 1992—2002. Patentee in field. Mem. IEEE, Am. Vacuum Soc., Semi Internat., Am. Chem. Soc. Democrat. Episcopalian. Fax: 978-887-1923. E-mail: dickbersin@mindspring.com.

BERSIN, RUTH HARGRAVE, priest, social services administrator; b. LaPorte, Ind., Sept. 16, 1939; d. Jacob Harold and Rowena Adeline (Hullett) Hargrave; m. Richard Lewis Bersin; children: Jacob David Antonio, Rebekah Bersin. BS in Edn., Ind. U., 1962; MA in Religion, Colgate Rochester Div. Sch., 1965; MDiv, Yale Div. Sch., 1982; D of Ministry, Grad. Theol. Found., 1993. Ordained priest, 1984. Dir. ednl. devel. ctr. Commodore, Japan, 1972-75; dir. spl. projects, refugees svcs. coord. Episcopal Social Svcs., Bridgeport, Conn., 1982-89; priest St. Peters, Cheshire, Conn., 1983-85, St. Lukes, Bridgeport, Conn., 1985-89; exec. dir. Tokyo English Lifeline, 1989-92; asst. dir. Interfaith Conf. Met. Washington, 1992-93; asst. priest Good Shepherd Episcopal Ch., Burke, Va., 1994; priest St. Monica's Capitol Hill, Washington, 1995-96; assoc. priest Grace Episcopal Ch., Lawrence, Mass., 1996-99; dir. Devel. Trauma Ctr., Brookline, Mass., 1996-99; pastoral psychotherapist Greater Lowell Pastoral Counseling Ctr., 1997—; exec. dir. Refugee Immigration Ministries, 1998—. Mem. Ecumenical commn. Diocese of Conn., 1984-89, Diocese of Washington, 1995, Diocese of Mass., 1996—; Episc. Congregation, U.S. Naval Base, Yokosuka, Japan, 1989-92; chaplain Washington Nat. Cathedral, 1995-96; chair task force on violence against women Diocese of Washington, 1995-96; nat. dir. Interfaith Spiritual Care Givers, 2002--. Leader NOVA Trauma Team, Oklahoma City, 1995, Refugee Adv. Coun., State of Conn., 1984-89, Refugee Welfare Com. Nat. Ch. World Svc., 1986; bd. dirs. Women's Crisis Ctr., Norwalk, Conn., 1980-83; mem. Nat. Coalition Against Sexual Assault; mem. Mass. Immigrant and Refugee Advocacy Coalition, Boston Theol. Inst. Working Group on Restorative Justice, Women's Crisis Com. Diocese of Mass., Task Force on Domestic Violence, Lowell, Mass., Mass. Coun. Chs. Strategy and Action Com.; mem. Wider Mission Commn. Diocese of Mass., 2001—; bd. dirs. Peace at Home, 2003—. Mem. Am. Assn. Pastoral Counseling, Assn. Trauma Stress Specialists, Internat. Soc. Traumatic Stress Studies, Nat. Soc. Fund Raising Execs. (cert. fund raising exec.), Assembly of Episcopal Hosps. and Chaplains. Democrat. Avocations: music, swimming, reading, gourmet cooking. E-mail: rimboston@mindspring.com.

BERSIN, SUSAN JOYCE-HEATHER (REIGNBEAUX JOYCE-HEATHER BERSIN), critical care nurse, police officer; b. Reservation, MD, July 11, 1945; d. Richard George Sr. and Ireene Rose (Brenner) Bersin; m. Robert Joseph Okragley, Dec. 23, 1972 (div. Apr. 1993); 1 child, MaryRose Reignbeaux. BS in Zoology, Kent State U., 1975, BSN, BS in Chemistry, Kent State U., 1976; MS in Med.-Surg Nursing, Case Western Res. U., 1979. RN, Ohio; cert. critical care nurse. Driver Waite Transport, Akron, Ohio, 1967-68, Cleve. Transit System, 1968-70; CEO, chief technician Corvair Repair & Mobile Svc., Berea, Ohio and Cleve., 1970—; critical care nurse Deaconess Hosp., Cleve., 1976-79, St. Luke's Hosp., Cleve., 1979-81, St. John Hosp., Cleve., 1981—; police officer Cleve. Police Dept., 1971—. Served with USN, 1963-67, Viet Nam. Mem. Sigma Theta Tau (charter mem. Delta Xi chpt.). Roman Catholic. Avocations: reading, ice figure skating, aeronautics and sky-diving. Home: 2250 Community College Ave 617 Cleveland OH 44115-3163

BERSOFF, DONALD NEIL, lawyer, psychologist; b. NYC, Mar. 1, 1939; s. Irving and Mina (Cohen) B.; children by previous marriage: David, Judith; m. Deborah Leavy, Oct. 16, 1988; 1 child, Benjamin. BS, NYU, 1958, MA, 1960, PhD, 1965; student, U. Va. Law Sch., 1973-74; JD, Yale U., 1976. Bar: Md. 1976, D.C. 1984, Pa. 1990. Asst. prof. Ohio State U.; assoc. prof. U. Ga., U. Md. Sch. Law; ptnr. Ennis, Friedman & Bersoff, Washington, 1982-88, Jenner & Block, Washington, 1988-89; coord. joint JD and PhD program in law and psychology U. Md. Sch. Law and Johns Hopkins U. Dept. Psychology., 1976-82; dir. law and psychology program Med. Coll. Pa.-Hahnemann U., Phila., 1990-2001, Villanova (Pa.) U. Law Sch., 1990-2001, prof. emeritus, 2001—. Adj. prof. Drexel U., Phila., 2001—; psycholegal cons., 2001—. Author: Learning to Teach: A Decision-Making System, 1976, Ethical Conflicts in Psychology, 1995, 3d edit., 2003, Law and Mental Health-Pennsylvania, 1999. With USAF, 1965-68. N.Y. State Regents coll. teaching fellow. Mem. ABA, APA (mem. coun. of reps. 1991-94, bd. dirs. 1994-97, chair policy and planning bd. 1999, coun. of reps. 1999-2001), Am. Psychology-Law Soc. (pres. 1980-81. Lifetime Achievement award 2002). Home: 780 College Ave Haverford PA 19041-1205 Office: Villanova Law Sch Villanova PA 19085 E-mail: bersoffd@law.villanova.edu.

BERSON, ELIOT LAWRENCE, ophthalmologist, medical educator; b. Boston, 1937; MD, Harvard U., 1962. Intern Calif. Hosp., San Francisco, 1962-63; resident in ophthalmology Barnes and McMillan Hosps., St. Louis, 1963-66; clin. assoc. ophthalmologist Nat. Inst. Neurol. Diseases and Blindness, Bethesda, Md., 1966-68; asst. Mass. Eye and Ear Infirmary, Boston, 1968-73, asst. surgeon, 1974-78, dir. Berman-Gund Lab. for Study of Retinal Degenerations, Harvard Med. Sch., 1974—, assoc. surgeon in ophthalmology, 1979-84, surgeon in ophthalmology, 1984—. Instr. Harvard U. Sch. Medicine, Boston, 1968-70, asst. prof., 1971-76, assoc. prof. ophthalmology, 1976-82, Chatlos prof. ophthalmology, 1982 . Surgeon USPHS, 1966-68. Mem. AMA, Assn. for Rsch. in Vision and Ophthalmology, Am. Acad. Ophthalmology, Am. Ophthal. Soc. Office: Berman-Gund Lab Mass Eye and Ear Infirmary 243 Charles St Boston MA 02114-3002

BERSON, JEROME ABRAHAM, chemistry educator; b. Sanford, Fla., May 10, 1924; s. Joseph and Rebecca (Bernicker) B.; m. Bella Zevitovsky, June 30, 1946; children: Ruth, David, Jonathan. BS cum laude, CCNY, 1944; MA, Columbia U., 1947; PhD, 1949. NRC postdoctoral fellow Harvard U., 1949-50; asst. chemist Hoffmann-LaRoche, Inc., Nutley, N.J., 1944; asst. prof. U. So. Calif., 1950-53, asso. prof., 1953-58, prof., 1958-63, U. Wis., 1963-69, Yale U., 1969-79, Irénée du Pont prof., 1979-92, Sterling prof., 1992-94; Sterling prof. emeritus, 1994—; dir. div. phys. sci. and engring. Yale U., 1983-90. Vis. prof. U. Calif., U. Cologne, U. Western Ont., U. Karlsruhe, U. Lausanne; Fairchild Disting. scholar Calif. Inst. Tech.; cons. Riker Labs., Goodyear Tire & Rubber Co., am. Cyanamid Co., IBM, Cord Labs., SMC Corp., B.F. Goodrich Corp., Lubrizol Corp.; mem. medicinal chemistry study sect. NIH, 1969-73; mem. adv. panel chemistry NSF, 1964-70. Author: Chemical Creativity, 1999, Chemical Discovery and the Logistician's Program, 2003; mem. editorial adv. bd.: Jour. Organic Chemistry, 1961-65, Accounts of Chemical Rsch., 1971-77, 94-96, Nouveau Journal de Chimie, 1977-85, Chem. Revs., 1980-83, Jour. Am. Chem. Soc., 1988-93; contbr. articles to profl. jours. Served with AUS, 1944-46, CBI. Recipient Alexander von Humboldt award, 1980, Townsend Harris medal Alumni Assn. CCNY, 1984, Merit award NIH, 1989, Lit. award German Chem. Industry Assn., 2000; John Simon Guggenheim fellow, 1980 Fellow Am. Acad. Arts and Scis.; mem. NAS, Am. Chem. Soc. (Calif. sect. award 1963, James Flack Norris award 1978, Nichols medal 1985, Roger Adams award 1987, Arthur C. Cope scholar 1992, Oesper award 1998, chmn. div. organic chemistry 1971), Chem. Soc. London, Phi Beta Kappa, Sigma Xi, Phi Lambda Upsilon. Home: 45 Bayberry Rd Hamden CT 06517-3401 Office: Yale U Dept Chemistry PO Box 208107 New Haven CT 06520-8107 E-mail: jerome.berson@yale.edu.

BERSOUX, HENRI ROBERT, management executive; b. Liege, Belgium, Oct. 20, 1959; came to US, 1975; s. Roger Victor and Julia May (Jones) B.; m. Susan Adele Fowler, Nov. 10, 1990; children: Sarah, Natalie, Allison, Paul, Nicholas, Daniel, Patrick. BA, Samford U., 1980. Trainee European Econ. Communities, Brussels, 1981; from jr. assoc. to acct. assoc. David Apter & Assoc., Washington, 1982-84; mng. ptnr. B2 Comm., Inc., Rockville, Md., 1985-88; comm. assoc. Am. Coun. Life Ins., Washington, 1989-91; sr. comm. assoc. Am. Coun. Life Insur., Washington, 1992-93; pub. rels. mgr. Ernst & Young, NYC, 1993-94, asst. dir. nat. sales and mktg., 1994-95, assoc. dir. nat. mktg., 1995-96, assoc. dir. nat. corp. mktg., dir. innovative methods, internet site mgr. Cleve., 1996-97, dir. nat. mktg., 1997-98, dir. client connectivity, 1998—99; v.p., gen. mgr. E-Bus. Computer Task Group, Inc., Buffalo, 2000—01; pres., CEO ACA-Assurance, Manchester, NH, 2002—. Republican. Roman Catholic. Avocations: genealogy, riflery, photography. Home: 8 Main St Bennington NH 03442 Office: ACA-Assurance 52 Concord St Manchester NH 03101

BERSTEIN, IRVING AARON, biotechnology and medical technology executive; b. Providence, Oct. 11, 1926; s. Robert Louis and Laura (Sperber) B.; m. Suzanne D'Amico, Apr. 16, 1972; children: Jonathan, Robert Laurance. ScB, Brown U., 1947; PhD, Cornell U., 1951. Assoc. tech. dir., sr. scientist Tracer Lab Inc., 1951-57; pres., tech. dir. Controls for Radiation, Inc., Cambridge, Mass., 1957-69, Controls for Radiation Inc. (acquired by Teledyne Inc.), Cambridge, Mass., 1969; v.p. Isotopes Inc. (subs. Teledyne Inc.), Cambridge, Mass., 1969-70; dir. med. div., v.p. AGA Corp., Secaucus, NJ, 1970-71; asst. dir. rsch. program devel. div. health sci. and tech. Harvard U.-MIT, 1972-86; founder and chmn. bd. Hygeia Sci. Inc., 1980-87; pres., CEO Hygeia Sci., Inc. (merged Hygeia Sci. Inc. into Tambrands, Inc.), 1985-87; sr. sci. advisor Hygeia Sci., Inc., 1988-90; chmn. bd. Endogen, Inc., Boston, 1990-95; bd. of advisors Rogers Foam Co., 1992 . Pres. Berstein Tech. Corp., 1980—; Bd. of Adv., J. Walter Co. Ltd., 2001-, cons. for Med. and Biotech., Corp. Devel. Francis Wayland scholar; Cornell U. fellow. Mem. Chief Exec. Orgn., Forty-Niners (pres. N.E. chpt. 1984, 96), Harvard Club Boston, Cornell Club Boston, Sigma Xi. Home and Office: 42 Buckman Dr Lexington MA 02421-6040 Fax: 781-862-3533. E-mail: sberstein@aol.com.

BERSUKER, ISAAC BORUKHOVICH, chemistry researcher, educator; b. Kishinev, Moldova, Feb. 12, 1928; came to U.S., 1993; s. Borukh Y. and Bella H. Bersuker; m. Liliya B. Kogan, Mar. 24, 1951; 1 child, Gennadi. PhD, Leningrad (Russia) U., 1957, DS, 1964. Cert. in theoretical physics, quantum chemistry, chem. physics. Lectr., divsn. chmn. Pedagogical Inst., Beltsy, Moldova, 1954-59; sr. rsch. scientist Inst. Chemistry, Acad. Scis., Kishinev, Moldova, 1959-64, head lab. quantum chemistry, 1964-93; sr. rsch. scientist, adj. prof. U. Tex., Austin, 1993—. Author: (monographs) Electronic Structure and Properties of Transition Metal Compounds, 1996, Vibronic Interactions in Molecules and Crystals, 1989, The Jahn-Teller Effect and Vibronic Interactions in Modern Chemistry, 1984, others; contbr. articles and maj. revs. to profl. jours. Recipient State Prize Laureat, 1978, USSR Registered Discovery N202, 1979. Mem. Acad. Scis. of USSR, Acad. Scis. Moldova (corr. and life mem., divsn. chmn. 1972-93), Am. Chem. Soc., Acad. Scis. of USSR (rsch. coun. on inorganic chemistry 1972-93, rsch. coun. on chem. physics 1972--). Office: U Tex-Austin Dept Chemistry/Biochemistry Austin TX 78712 Fax: 512 471 8696. E-mail: bersuker@mail.cm.utexas.edu.

BERT, CAROL LOIS, retired educational assistant; b. Bakersfield, Calif., Oct. 15, 1938; d. Edwin Vernon and Shirely Helen (Craig) Phelps; m. John Davison Bert, Sept. 26, 1964; children: Mary Ellen, John Edwin, Craig Eric, Douglas Ethan. BSN, U. Colo., 1960. Med. surg. nurse U.S. Army, Washington, 1960-62, Ascom City, Korea, 1962-63, San Antonio, 1963, Albuquerque, 1964-65; ednl. asst. Jefferson County Schs., Arvada, Colo., 1979-2000, ret. Sec. Parent Tchr. Student Assn. Arvada West H.S., 1987-88. Mem. Colo. Quilting Coun. (1st v.p. 1988, 89, Hall of Fame 1992). Avocations: quilting, reading, camping, fishing, tennis. Home: 5844 Oak St Arvada CO 80004-4739

BERT, CHARLES WESLEY, mechanical and aerospace engineer, educator; b. Chambersburg, Pa., Nov. 11, 1929; s. Charles Wesley and Gladys Adelle (Raff) B.; m. Charlotte Elizabeth Davis (June 29, 1957); children: Charles Wesley IV, David Raff. BSME, Pa. State U., 1951, MS, 1956; PhD in Engring. Mechanics, Ohio State U., 1961. Registered profl. engr., Pa., Okla. Jr. design engr. Am. Flexible Coupling Co., State Coll., Pa., 1951-52; aero. design engr. Fairchild Aircraft div. Fairchild Engine and Airplane Corp., Hagerstown, Md., 1954-56; prin. M.E. Battelle Inst., Columbus, Ohio, 1956-61; sr. research engr., 1961-62; program dir., solid and structural mechanics research, 1962-63; cons., 1964-65; assoc. prof. U. Okla., 1963-66, prof., 1966—; dir. Sch. Aerospace and Mech. Engring., 1972-77, 90-95, Benjamin H. Perkinson Chair prof. engring., 1978—. Instr. engring. mechanics Ohio State U., Columbus, 1959-61; vis. scholar U. Calif., San Diego, 1996; cons. in field; chmn. Midwestern Mechanics Conf., 1973-75; Honor lectr. Mid-Am. State Univs. Assn., 1983-84; seminar lectr. Midwest Mechanics, 1983-84; Plenary lectr. Internat. Conf. on Composite Structures, Paisley, Scotland, 1987. Mem. editl. bd. Composite Structures Jour., 1982—, Jour. Sound & Vibration, 1988—, Composites Engring., 1991-95, Mechanics of Composite Materials and Structures, 1993-2001, Applied Mechanics Revs., 1993—, Composites, 1996-98, Internat. Jour. Structural Stability and Dynamics, 2000—, Jour. of Sandwich Structures and Materials, 1997—, Mechanics of Advanced Materials and Structures, 2002-; assoc. editor: Exptl. Mechanics, 1982-87, Applied Mechanics Revs., 1984-87; contbr. chpts. to books and articles to profl. jours. 1st lt. USAF, 1952-54. Sr. Rsch. scholar U. Calif., San Diego, 1996; recipient Disting. Alumnus award Ohio State U. Coll. engring., 1985. Fellow AAAS, AIAA (nat. tech. com. structures 1969-72, chmn. Ctrl. Okla. sect. 1966-67), ASME (Cen. Okla. sect. exec. com. 1973-78, 90-95, 99-01, sec. 1990-91, region X mech. engring. dept. heads com. 1972-77, 90-95, chmn. 1975-77, 10-session symposium named in his honor 1999), Am. Soc. Composites (bd. dirs. 1996-98, Disting. Rsch. award 1999), Am. Acad. Mechs. (bd. dirs. 1978-82, pres.-elect 2001-02, pres. 2002-03), Soc. Exptl. Mechanics (monograph com. 1978-82, chmn. 1980-82, sec. Mid-Ohio sect. 1958-59, chmn. 1959-60, adv. bd. 1960-63), Soc. Engring. Sci. (bd. dirs. 1982-88); mem. NSPE, Okla. Acad. Sci., Okla. Soc. Profl. Engrs., Scabbard and Blade, Pa. State Alumni Assn. (Outstanding Engring. Alumnus award 1992), Sigma Xi, Sigma Tau, Pi Tau Sigma, Sigma Gamma Tau (Disting. Engr. award), Tau Beta Pi (Disting. Engr. award). Achievements include co-development of world's smallest pressure transducer capable of measuring both steady and fluctuating pressures; first general solution of cylindrically orthotropic plates of radially varying thickness under arbitrary body forces; origination of several minimum-weight optimal designs for multicell cylindrical pressure vessels, experimental techniques and associated data reduction equations for determining residual stresses in both flat-sheet and thick-walled cylindrical specimens of composite materials; first successful application of Kennedy-Pancu system identification method to shell structures, noninteger polynomial version of Rayleigh's method to heat conduction; first application of differential quadrature method to static structural problems, structural vibration problems and non-linear structural problems; first application of noninteger polynomial method to finite element analysis; first dynamic stability analysis of unicycles and monocycles; origination of concept of stress gages for composite materials; research on sandwich structures with bimodular facings, prediction of ply steer behavior of automobile tires, non-linear flutter of laminated composite panels; many others. Home: 2516 Butler Dr Norman OK 73069-5059 Office: U Okla Sch Aerospace and Mech Engring 865 Asp Ave Norman OK 73019-1052 *Set high yet realistic goals, put forth the extra effort to achieve them, and practice the Golden Rule.*

BERT, CLARA VIRGINIA, retired home economics educator, administrator; b. Quincy, Fla., Jan. 29, 1929; d. Harold C. and Ella J. (McDavid) B. BS, Fla. State U., 1950, MS, 1963, PhD, 1967. Cert. tchr., Fla.; cert. home economist; cert. pub. mgr. Tchr. Union County High Sch., Lake Butler, Fla., 1950-53, Havana High Sch., Fla., 1953-65; cons. rsch. and devel. Fla. Dept. Edn., Tallahassee, 1967-75, sect. dir. rsch. and devel., 1975-85, program dir. home econs. edn., 1985-92, program specialist resource devel., 1992-96, program specialist, spl. projects, 1996-99, program dir. grants mgmt., 1999-2000; ret., 2000. Cons. Nat. Ctr. Rsch. in Vocat. Edn., Ohio State U., 1978; field reader U.S. Dept. Edn., 1974-75. Author, editor booklets. Mem. devel. bd., mem. adv. bd. Fla. State U. Coll. Human Scis. Family Inst., 1994—; mem. nat. com. for the capital campaign Fla. State U. Found., 2002—. U.S. Office Edn. grantee, 1976, 77, 78; recipient Dean's award Coll. Human Scis., Fla. State U., 1995; named Disting Alumna Coll. Human Scis., Fla. State U., 1994. Mem. Am. Home Econs. Assn. (state treas. 1969-71), Am. Vocat. Assn., Fla. Vocat. Assn., Fla. Vocat. Home Econs. Assn., Am. Vocat. Edn. Rsch. Assn. (nat. treas. 1970-71), Nat. Coun. Family Rels., Am. Ednl. Rsch. Assn., Fla. State U. Alumni Assn. (bd. dirs. home econs. sect. 1976-81, pres.-elect 1978-79, 79-80), Havana Golf and Country Club, Fla. State U. Ctr. Club, Kappa Delta Pi, Kappa Omicron Nu (chpt. pres. 1965-66), Delta Kappa Gamma (pres. 1974-76), Sigma Kappa (pres. corp. bd. 1985-91), Phi Delta Kappa.

BERTANI, LILLIAN ELIZABETH TEEGARDEN, biologist, researcher, educator; b. July 9, 1931; BS, U. Mich., 1953, PhD, Calif. Inst. Tech., 1957. Rsch. assoc. U. So. Calif., L.A., 1957-60; postdoctoral fellow NIH/USPHS, 1960-61; asst. prof. U. Stockholm, 1965-66; Swedish Med. Rsch. Coun. fellow Karolinska Inst., Stockholm, 1966-75, rsch. assoc., 1961-65, asst. prof., 1975-85; vis. assoc. in biology Calif. Inst. Tech., Pasadena, 1981—95, 1995—2000, lectr. biology, 1993—98, mem. profl. staff, 2000—. Home: 975 Dale St Pasadena CA 91106-4018 Business E-Mail: lebert@its.caltech.edu.

BERTE, NEAL RICHARD, academic administrator; b. May 7, 1940; s. Edward H. and Wenonah Maureen (Stevens) B.; m. Anne; children: Becky, Julie, Mark, Scott. BS in Polit. Sci, U. Cin., 1962, MS (Ford Found. scholar), 1963, EdD, 1966; Rockefeller Found. fellow, Union Theol. Sem., N.Y.C., 1962-63; postgrad., Garrett Theol. Sem., Evanston, Ill., 1966-67, Harvard U., 1966; LHD (hon.), U. Cin., 1993. Asst. dir. Coll. Entrance Exam. Bd., Evanston, 1966-68; exec. asst. to pres., asst. prof. Ottawa (Kans.) U., 1968-70; dean New Coll.; assoc. prof. U. Ala., 1970-74; v.p. ednl. devel., dean New Coll., 1974-76; pres. Birmingham (Ala.)-So. Coll., 1976—. Project dir. NSF grants, 1972; chmn. session Internat. Council on Edn. for Teaching World Assembly, Nairobi, Kenya, 1973; faculty Danforth Found. sponsored C.C. Inst., Stephens Coll., 1973; steering com. Carnegie Found. funded project Coop. Assessment of Experiential Learning, 1974-77; mem. Commn. on Ednl. Credit, Am. Council Edn., 1975-81, Danforth Found. exec. com. for Danforth Fellows Program, 1974-75; nat. adv. council for career edn. HEW, Office Edn., 1976-79; sec.-treas. So. U. Conf., 1977-80, v.p., 1984-85, pres., 1985-86; vis. scholar Inst. for Ednl. Mgmt., Harvard Grad. Sch Edn., 1990-91; co-chmn. Region 2020, Ala., 1997—; bd. dirs. Ala. Ctr. for Law and Civic Edn. Contbr. articles to edn. jours. Mem. adminstrv. bd. Canterbury United Meth. Ch., Birmingham, 1977—, univ. senate United Meth. Ch., 1986-88; chmn. Univ. United Fund campaign, 1973; bd. dirs., mem. exec. com. United Fund, Tuscaloosa, Ala., 1974-75, chmn. edn. div., 1975; chmn. sect. for pvt. ednl. insts. Jefferson-Shelby-Walker Counties United Appeal, 1977; chmn. pub. employees div. United Way campaign, 1978; v.p. Coun. for Advancement Pvt. Colls. in Ala., 1977-82, pres., 1982-83; chmn. com. to select Man of Year in Birmingham, 1977; chmn. selection com. Rhodes Scholarships for Ala., 1976-81; bd. dirs. Jefferson-Shelby Counties Lung Assn., 1978-79, Ala. Partners for Progress with Guatemala Program, 1977—, Carraway Meth. Hosp., 1977-80, Brookwood Hosp., 1982-90, Neighborhood Housing Svc., Birmingham, 1977-78, Birmingham Symphony Assn., 1976-80, 82-87, Community Affairs Com., 1976-87, Operation New Birmingham, 1976-89; bd. govs. Relay House Club, Birmingham, 1983-87, Circle S Industries, Selma, Ala., 1983—, Parisian, Inc., Birmingham, 1983-88; bd. dirs. NCCJ, 1978—, Birmingham Summerfest, 1979—, March of Dimes, 1979-86, Am. Heart Assn., 1980-84, So. Rsch. Inst., 1982—, Leadership Birmingham, 1981—, Leadership Ala., 1990-93; bd. dirs., chmn. long range planning com., chmn. program for Scout Expn. Jefferson County council Boy Scouts Am., 1977—; exec. com. Men's Com., Birmingham Symphony Assn., 1977-84; bd. dirs. Jefferson Fed. Savs. and Loan Assn., Birmingham, 1978-91, Birmingham Festival Arts, 1982-89, bd. advisors, 1989, trustee, 1990, pres., 1981—; chmn. Birmingham Area United Way, 1983; trustee Advent Epic. Day Sch., 1977-87, Gorgas Scholarship Found., 1976-88, New Coll.-Sarasota, U. South Fla., 1977-79; founding mem., bd. dirs. Progressive Alliance, 1986—; bd. dirs. Met. Devel. Bd., 1987-88, Greater Birmingham Conv. and Visitors Bur., 1988; commn. pub. rels. Nat. Assn. Ind. Colls and Univs., 1992-94, bd. dirs., 1994; adv. bd. pub. Edn. Found. Jefferson County Bd. Edn., 1999—; bd. dirs. Civil Rights Inst., 2000. Recipient Outstanding Citizens award Lawson State C.C. Coll., 1977, Outstanding Citizen award in Birmingham Erskine Ramsay Award Com., 1978, Brotherhood award NCCJ, 1984, Outstanding Svc. award Black Student Union, 1986, Outstanding Cmty. Svc. award Mortar Bd., 1986, James M. Tingle award, 1986, Disting. Svc. award, Sigma Alpha Epsilon, 1991, Medal of Honor, DAR, 1995, Leadership award Birmingham Regional Planning Commn. promoting regional cooperation, 2000; elected to Ala. Acad. Honor, 1979; named one of 10 Outstanding Cmty. Leaders Birmingham Post-Herald, 1984, one of Top 10 Current Leaders in Birmingham, The Birmingham News, 1990, 99, one of 10 leaders Bus. First jour., 1990, Birmingham Citizen of Yr. award for outstanding civic and cmty. svc., 1986, Outstanding Ala. Civic Leader Nat. Soc. Fund-Raising Execs., 1991, Disting. Citizen City Coun. of Birmingham, 1992, one of top ten mems. of 1997 Class of Movers and Shakers, Birmingham Bus. Jour.; named to Sigma Alpha Epsilon Leadership Sch. Hall of Fame, 1994. Mem. Am. Assn. Univ. Adminstrs. (pres. Alpha chpt. 1978-79), Greater Birmingham Area C. of C. (bd. dirs., exec. com. 1978-80, v.p. for govtl. rels., policy com. 1986, pres. 1988, chmn. exec. com. 1989), Am. Assn. Colls. (pres.'s adv. coun. 1977-78), Am. Assn. for Higher Edn. (chmn. Southeastern Regional Coun. 1973, chmn. panel on three-year degree programs 1973, program chmn. 1974, adv. bd. NEXUS Project 1974-75), Assn. for Innovation in Higher Edn. (adv. bd. 1973), Kiwanis Internat. (Disting. Pres. award 1992-93, George F. Hixon fellow 1995), Phi Beta Kappa (pres. 1975), Phi Delta Kappa. Clubs: The Redstone Club, The Jefferson Club, Downtown Birmingham Kiwanis (chmn. Ministers Day 1977, chmn. Youth-of-the-Year selection com. 1978, pres. 1992-93). Office: Birmingham So Coll Box 549002 Birmingham AL 35254-0001

BERTELSEN, DALE ALAN, communications educator; b. Clifton Springs, N.Y., Nov. 22, 1949; s. Karl I. and Frances E. (Weston) B.. BS, Rider Coll., Trenton, N.J., 1972; MA, Pa. State U., 1985, PhD, 1989. Dir. forensics Pa. State U., State College, 1987-88, instr., 1987-88; asst. prof. comms. Bloomsburg (Pa.) U., 1988-93, assoc. prof., 1993-96, prof., 1996—. Author: Analyzing Media, 1996; editor: Comm. Quar., 2000—03; contbr. articles to profl. jours. Mem.: Pa. Comm. Assn. (Disting. Svc. award 1999), Kenneth Burke Soc. (editor publs. 1991—93), Speech Comm. Assn. Pa., Ea. Comm. Assn. (pres. 1995—96, Outstanding Scholar 1997, Disting. Tchg. fellow 1997, Disting.Svc. award 1998), Nat. Comm. Assn., Mach I Srs. Kayaking Team (v.p. 2000—01). Avocations: kayaking, hiking, swimming. Office: Bloomsburg U 400 E 2d St Bloomsburg PA 17815

BERTELSMAN, WILLIAM ODIS, federal judge; b. Cincinnati, Ohio, Jan. 31, 1936; s. Odis William and Dorothy B.; m. Margaret Ann Martin, June 13, 1959; children: Kathy, Terri, Nancy. BA, Xavier U., 1958; JD, U. Cin., 1961. Bar: Ky. 1961, Ohio 1962. Law clk. firm Taft, Stettinius & Hollister, Cin., 1960-61; mem. firm Bertelsman & Bertelsman, Newport, Ky., 1962-79; judge U.S. Dist. Ct. (ea. dist.) Ky., Covington, 1979—, chief judge, 1991-98; instr. Coll. Law U. Cin., 1965-72; city atty., prosecutor Highland Heights, Ky., 1962-69. Adj. prof. Chase Coll. of Law, 1989—. Contbr. articles to profl. jours. Served to capt. AUS, 1963-64. Mem.: U.S. Jud. Conf. (standing com. on practice and procedure 1989—95, liaison mem. adv. com. on civil rules 1989—95), Ky. Bar Assn. (bd. govs. 1978—79), ABA. Republican. Roman Catholic.

BERTENSHAW, WILLIAM HOWARD, III, radio and television producer, b. NYC, Nov. 28, 1930; s. William Howard Jr. and Grace Annette (Miller) B.; m. Betty J. Underriner, July 7, 1956 (dec. Nov. 1975); children: Jane Ann, Judith Ann, Jo Ann; m. Bobbi C. Slachofsky, Dec. 16, 1984 (div. Sept. 2002). BA in Communications, Ohio Wesleyan U., 1950. Asst. mktg. editor Bus. Week mag., N.Y.C., 1953-55; radio-TV dir. Hardy Burt Assocs., N.Y.C., 1955-57; radio-TV producer Empire Broadcasting Corp., N.Y.C., 1957-60, Nat. Episcopal Ch., N.Y.C., 1960-70; producer MBS, N.Y.C., 1970-75; dir. communications Council of Chs. City of N.Y., 1975-84; exec. producer, chief exec. officer Radio & TV Roundup Prodns., N.Y.C., 1984—; producer TKR Cable TV, N.Y.C., 1987—. Guest lectr. Upsala U., East Orange, N.J., 1970-75, So. Meth. U., Dallas, 1972, Seton Hall U., South Orange, N.J., 1974, Pace U., N.Y.C., 1980, Syracuse (N.Y.) U., 1982; vice chmn. dept. communications N.J. Coun. Chs., 1986—; host People Working for People, Sta. WWOR-TV, N.Y.C., 1988; programmer Cable TV Network of N.J., 1985-2000; producer The Jersey Cape TV series, 1990—. Host Inner-Dimension Community Concerns, Union Eyes and Perspective on the News Sta. WOR Radio, WOR Special Report, N.Y., 1970—. Pres. Rep. Club, West Cape May, N.J., 1986-87; vice chmn. communications N.J. Coun. Chs., 1986-89; committeman Cape May County N.J. Rep. Orgn., 1987-90, Essex Coun. N.J. Rep. Orgn., 1960-85. Sgt. U.S. Army, 1951-53. Recipient Gabriel award Washington Conf., 1966-67, Radio Program-

ming award Ohio State U., 1969, Columbus Film Festival award Ohio Coun. Chs., 1970, Radio-TV award N.J. Coun. Chs., 1983, Olive award, 1984, Cape award Cable TV Network NJ, 1987, Angel award Excellence in Media, Hollywood, Calif., 1999-2003. Mem. AFTRA, Delfon Recording Soc. (dir. comm. 2001—), Nat. Lima Bean Assn. (founder), Alpha Sigma Rho, South Jersey Bird Club. Clubs: Suburban Sports Car (N.J.) (v.p., co-founder 1956-61). Episcopalian. Home: 653 Sun Haven Dr Clayton NJ 08312-1955 E-mail: delfon@att.net., whb@att.net.

BERTHAUD, VLADIMIR, physician; b. Gonaives, Haiti, Oct. 18, 1953; came to U.S., 1983; s. Louis Rostand and Marie Antonine (Brutus) B.; m. Judith Collin, Mar. 19, 1983; children: Jimmy Vladimir, Jonathan Vladimir. Diploma of Statistician, Ctr. of Stats., Port-au-Prince, Haiti, 1979; BS, Sch. Internat. Affairs, Port-au-Prince, Haiti, 1980; MD, State U. Sch. Medicine, Port-au-Prince, Haiti, 1980; MPH in Biostats., Columbia U. Sch. Pub. Health, 1994. Diplomate Am. Bd. Internal Medicine, Infectious Dis., Tropical Medicine and Traveler's Health. Pulmonary and TB resident Sanatorium, Port-au-Prince, 1980-82; med. resident Kingsbrook Jewish Med. Ctr., Bklyn., 1986-89; house physician Cath. Med. Ctr., Queens, N.Y., 1984-85, attending physician emergency medicine, 1989-94; surg. house physician Maimonides Med. Ctr., Bklyn., 1985-86; fellow, infectious disease Columbia U. Coll. Physicians and Surgeons, N.Y.C., 1989-91, Cornell U. Med. Coll., N.Y.C., 1991-92; asst. attending physician Harlem Hosp. Ctr., N.Y.C., 1992—; asst. prof. clin. medicine Columbia U. Coll. of Physicians and Surgeons, N.Y.C., 1992-2001; assoc. prof. medicine Meharry Med. Coll., 2001—, dir. div. infectious diseases, 2001—; dir AIDS Ctr. Excellence McHarry-Nashville Gen. Hosp., Tenn., 2002; co-dir. ctr. for AIDS rsch. Vanderbilt-McHarry Med. Ctrs., 2003—. Adj. prof. medicine Vanderbilt U., 2001—; mem. quality assurance and utilization rev. com. Harlem Hosp. Ctr., NYC, 1992—; reviewer Clin. Infectious Diseases, 1995, 2000, 01, 02, Contemporary Topics in Internal Medicine, 1997, Internat. Cochrane Collaborative Rev. Group; mem. Chochrane Group on Infectious Diseases and HIV/AIDS; dir. antimicrobialformulary Harlem Hosp. Ctr., 1992—2001; mem. internat. steering com. Adult Aids Clin. Trial Group, 2002—; liason Vanderbilt, Cornell, Haiti AIDS Clin Trials Unit, 2002—; leadership faculty U.S. Mil. Acad/, West Point, NY, 2003—. Coord. editor Jour. Assn. Haitian Physicians Abroad, 1998—; contbr. articles to profl. jours. Major USAR, 2001—. Fellow ACP; mem. APHA, Am. Soc. Tropical Medicine and Hygiene, Am. Coll. Forensic Examiners (bd. cert.), Am. Soc. for Microbiology, N.Y. Acad. Scis., Infectious Diseases Soc.

BERTHELSDORF, SIEGFRIED, psychiatrist; b. Shannon County, Mo., June 16, 1911; s. Richard and Amalia (Morschenko) von Berthelsdorf; m. Mildred Friederich, May 13, 1945; children: Richard, Victor, Dianne. BA, U. Oreg., 1934, MA, MD, 1939. Lic. psychiatrist, psychoanalyst. Intern U.S. Marine Hosp., Staten Island, N.Y., 1939-40; psychiat. intern Bellevue Hosp., N.Y.C., 1940-41; psychiat. resident N.Y. State Psychiat. Hosp., N.Y.C., 1941-42; research assoc. Columbia U. Coll. Physicians and Surgeons, N.Y.C., 1942-43; asst. physician Presbyn. Hosp. and Vanderbilt Clinic, N.Y.C., 1942-51; supervising psychiatrist Manhattan (N.Y.) State Hosp., 1946-50; asst. adolescent psychiatrist Mt. Sinai Hosp., N.Y.C., 1950-52; psychiat. cons. MacLaren Sch. for Boys, Woodburn, Oreg., 1952-84, Portland (Oreg.) Pub. Schs., 1952-67. Clin. prof. U. Oreg. Health Scis. Ctr., 1956—; tng. and supervising analyst Seattle Psychoanalytic Inst., 1970—. Author: Treatment of Drug Addiction in Psychoanalytic Study of the Child, Vol. 31, 1976, Ambivalence Towards Women in Chinese Characters and Its Implication for Feminism, American Imago, 1988, (with others) Psychiatrists Look at Aging, 1992. Bd. dirs., v.p. Portland Opera Assn., 1960-64, Portland Musical Co., 1987-92; bd. dirs. Portland Chamber Orch., 1964-70, 92-94, 96-97, exec., 1997—. Maj. USAF, 1943-46. Recipient Henry Waldo Coe award U. Oreg. Med. Sch., Portland, 1939, citation Parry Ctr. for Children, Portland, 1970, Child Advocacy award ORAPT, 1998. Fellow Am. Psychiat. Assn. (life), Am. Geriatrics Soc. (founding fellow); mem. Am. Psychoanalytic Assn. (life), Portland Psychiatrists in Pvt. Practice (charter, pres. 1958), Mental Health Assn. (bd. dirs., chmn. med. adv. com. 1952-60), Multnomah County Med. Soc. (pres.'s citation 1979), Oreg. Psychoanalytic Found. (founding mem.), Am. Rhododendron Soc. (bd. dirs., v.p. Portland chpt. 1956-58, Bronze medal and citation 1974), Am. Rhododendron Species Found. (bd. dirs. 1960-75), Phi Beta Kappa, Sigma Xi, Phi Sigma, Phi Mu Alpha. Avocations: farming, music. Home: 1125 SW St Clair Ave Portland OR 97205-1127 E-mail: SiegfriedMD@aol.com. *Life's challenge is to close the hiatus between what we are and what we aspire to be: "Edel sei der Mensch, Hilfreich und gut! --".*

BERTHIAUME, WAYNE HENRY, electrical engineer; b. Worcester, Mass., Aug. 3, 1955; s. Henry Louis and Lorraine Anne (Beland) B. ASEE cum laude, Worcester Jr. Coll., 1982; BEE cum laude, Cen. New Eng. Coll., Worcester, 1987. cert. profl. ski. instr., snowboard inst. Draftsman Henry L. Berthiaume Design Svcs., Northboro, Mass., 1969-71; TV repair technician Color Visual Tech., Northboro, Mass., 1971-72; technician Data Gen. Corp., Southboro, Mass., 1972-76, lead technician, 1974-76, final acceptance technician, 1976-77, lead technician, 1977, engr., 1977-83, sr. engr., 1983-2000, EMC Corp., Hopkinton, 2000—. Marshal Boston Five Classic Golf Tournament, Danvers, Mass., Digital Sr. Golf Classic, Sudbury, Mass. Mem. NRA (life). Roman Catholic. Avocations: golf, skiing, windsurfing, woodworking. E-mail: berthiaume. Home: 38 Plain St Hopedale MA 01747 Office: 80 South St Hopkinton MA 01471 E-mail: wayne_berthiaume@hotmail.com.

BERTHOLD, JOHN WILLIAM, III, physicist; b. York, Pa., May 24, 1945; s. John William and M. Pauline (Decker) B.; m. Jacqueline Reed, Oct. 5, 1974; children: John William, Margaret H. BA, Gettysburg (Pa.) Coll., 1967; MS, U. Ariz., 1974, PhD, 1976. Sr. tech. aide Bell Telephone Labs., Inc., Murray Hill, N.J., 1967-69; rsch. asst., assoc. Optical Sci. Ctr. U. Ariz., Tucson, 1969-76; physicist U.S. Dept. Def., Ft. Meade, Md., 1976-79; sr. rsch. physicist Babcock & Wilcox Co./McDermott Technology, Inc., Alliance, Ohio, 1979-2001. Cons. Iota Engring., Inc., Tucson, 1973-76; jwbc.llc, Ohio, 2001—, lectr. in field; sr. acad. coun. Ohio Acad. Sci., 1993—. Contbr. articles to profl. jours., chpts. to books; patentee in field. Owens-Ill. fellow, 1972-73; NASA Tech. Brief awardee, 1977. Fellow Internat. Soc. Optical Engring.; mem. Optical Soc. Am., Instrument Soc. Am. (sr.), IEEE (affiliate), Salem Golf Club.

BERTHOLD, ROBERT VERNON, JR., lawyer; b. Charleston, W.Va., June 23, 1951; s. Robert V. and Betty Jeanne (Harkins) B.; m. Jacqueline G. Baisden, Aug. 9, 1976; children— Robert V., III, Matthew Chandler. B.S. cum laude, W.Va. U., 1973; J.D., 1976. Bar: W.Va. 1976, U.S. Dist. Cts. (no. and so. dists.) W.Va. 1976, U.S. Ct. Appeals (4th cir.) 1977. Assoc. Hoyer & Sergent, Charleston, W.Va., 1976-79; ptnr. Hoyer, Hoyer & Berthold, Charleston, 1979-87; pvt. practice, 1988— ; arbitrator Am. Arbitration Assn., 1978— . Mem. ABA, W.Va. Bar Assn., W.Va. Trial Lawyers Assn., (bd. dirs. 1984—), Assn. Trial Lawyers Am., Kanawha County Bar Assn. Democrat. Presbyterian. Avocation: sports. Home: 2 Monticello Pl Charleston WV 25314-2372 Office: 208 Capitol St Charleston WV 25301-2219

BERTHOT, JAKE, artist; b. Niagara Falls, N.Y., Mar. 30, 1939; Ed., New Sch. Social Rsch., 1960-61, Pratt Inst., 1960-62. Mem. faculty Cooper Union, 1960-62, Yale U., New Haven, 1982-90, Sch. Visual Arts, N.Y.C., 1992—. Artist in residence Dartmouth U., fall 1995. One-man shows include Portland Ctr. Visual Arts, Oreg., 1973, Galerie de Gestlo, Hamburg, Fed. Republic Germany, 1973, 77, O.K Harris Gallery, N.Y.C., 1970, 72, 75, David McKee Gallery, N.Y.C., 1976, 78, 82, 83, 86, 88, 89, 91, 95, 96, U. Calif. Berkeley, 1984, Nina Nielsen Gallery, Boston, 1979, 84, 92, 95, 96, 2000-02, Nat. Gallery, Washington, 1989, Nigel Greenwood Gallery, London, 1979, 91, Galleri Olsson, Stockholm, 1987, 90, 96, Cork Gallery Lincoln Ctr., N.Y.C., 1991, Jaffe-Friede and Strauss Gallery, Hanover, N.H., 1995, The Phillips Collection, Washington, 1996; group shows include Whitney Mus. Art, N.Y.C., 1969, 72, 74, 78, Art Inst. Chgo., 1971, Mus. Modern Art, N.Y.C., 1977, 81, 83, 84, 85, Meadows Art Gallery, Dallas, 1985, numerous others; represented in permanent collections Australian Nat. Gallery, Balt. Mus. Art, U. Calif. Berkeley Mus., Dallas Mus. Fine Arts, Fogg Art Mus. at Harvard U., Guggenheim Mus., Mus. Modern Art, Whitney Mus. Art., others. Guggenheim fellow, 1981; recipient Acad. Inst. award Am. Acad. Arts & Letters, 1994; named academician Nat. Acad. Design; grantee The Elizabeth Found., 1995-96. Address: David McKee 745 5th Ave New York NY 10151-0099

BERTHOUEX, PAUL MAC, civil and environmental engineer, educator; b. Oelwein, Iowa, Aug. 15, 1940; s. George Albert and LaVadia Fay (McBride) B.; m. Susan Jean Powell, Sept. 8, 1962; 1 child, Stephanie Fay. BSCE, U. Iowa, 1963, MSCE, 1964; PhD, U. Wis., 1969. Registered profl. engr., Iowa. Instr. U. Iowa, Iowa City, 1964-65; asst. prof. civil engring. U. Conn., Storrs, 1965-67; chief rsch. engr. GKW Cons., Mannheim, Fed. Republic of Germany, 1969-71; prof. civil engring. U. Wis., Madison, 1971-99, emeritus prof., 1999—. Author: Strategy of Pollution Control, 1978, Statistics for Environmental Engineers, 1994, 2d edit., 2002; contbr. numerous articles to profl. jours. Recipient Radebaugh Prize, CSWPCA, 1989, 91. Mem. ASCE (Rudolf Herring medal 1974, 92), Water Environment Fedn. (Eddy medal 1971), U. Iowa Disting. Engring. Alumni Acad. Office: U Wis 1415 Johnson Dr Madison WI 53706-1607

BERTI, PHYLLIS MAE, health information management specialist; b. Blue Island, Ill., Jan. 27, 1941; d. Louis J. and Helen Beatrice (Smola) Hankus; m. Jerome Leon Berti, May 27, 1967; children: James Louis, Jeffrey Jerome, Joseph Gregory, Cynthia Ann. AS in Health Info. Mgmt., Stark Tech. Coll., Canton, Ohio, 1992. Claims processor Mass. Mut. Ins. Co., Hazel Crest, Ill., 1981-84; physician billing rep. Ingalls Meml. Hosp., Harvey, Ill., 1984-87; coder, abstractor Timken Mercy Med. Ctr., Canton, Ohio, 1987-89, Wooster (Ohio) Cmty. Hosp., 1989-92; coord. clin. records Quest Recovery Svcs., Canton, 1992-93; health info. mgmt. specialist So. Health Care Ctr., Southaven, Miss., 1994-99, Bapt. Progressive Care Ctr., Southaven, 1999—2002, cons., 2002—03; health info. mgmt. mgr. Brookewood Nursing Ctr., De Queen, Ark., 2003—. Mem.: Ark. Health Info. Mgmt. Assn., Am. Health Info. Mgmt. Assn. (long term care sect., registered health info. technician). Avocations: crafts, gardening, fishing, swimming, boating. Home: 111 Country Club Estates De Queen AR 71832

BERTIN, JOHN JOSEPH, aeronautical engineer, educator, researcher; b. Milw., Oct. 13, 1938; s. Andrea and Yolanda G. (Pasquali) B.; m. Ruth Easterbrook; children: Thomas Alexander, Randolph Scott, Elizabeth Anne, Michael Robert. BA, Rice Inst., Houston, 1960; MS, Rice U., 1962, PhD, 1966. Aerospace technologist NASA Johnson Space Ctr., Houston, 1962-66; prof. U. Tex., Austin, 1966-89; program mgr. for space initiative MTS, Sandia Nat. Labs., Albuquerque, 1989-94; vis. prof. USAF Acad., Colorado Springs, Colo., 1988-89, prof. aero. engring., 1994—. Cons. McGinnis, Lochridge & Kilgore, Austin, 1978-83, Sandia Nat. Labs., Albuquerque, 1980-89, BPD Difesa e Spazio, Rome, 1980-82, NASA, 1994-96, Sci. Applications Internat. Corp., 1996; detailed to Office of Space, U.S. Dept. Energy Hdqs., 1991-92; dir. Ctr. Excellence for Hypersonic Tng. and Rsch., 1985-89; mem. sci. adv. bd. USAF, 1989-93, mem. adv. group Flight Dynamics Labs., 1989-93; tech. chmn. Space 2000 Conf., 1998-99; aerothermodynamics cons. Columbia Accident Investigation Bd., 2003. Author: Engineering Fluid Mechanics, 1987, Hypersonic Aerothermodynamics, 1994, Aerodynamics for Engineers, 2002; contbg. author Letterwinner, 1999—; editor: Hypersonics, 1989, Advances in Hypersonics, 1992; assoc. editor Jour. Spacecraft and Rockets, 2000-01. Pres. Western Hills Little League, Austin, 1975; mem. arts subcom. NASA, 1987-91; mem. Aerospace Engring. Bd. Panel NRC, 1996-97, USAF hypersonics program rev. com., 1997-98; mem. attendance com. Rice Athletic Dept., 2002--; mem. adv. bd. Rice Owl Club, 2002-. Recipient Gen. Dynamics tchg. award U. Tex. Coll. Engring., 1978, Tex. Exec. tchg. award Ex-Students Assn. U. Tex., 1982, faculty award Tau Beta Pi, 1986, award for meritorious civilian svc. Dept. Air Force, 1993, Gen. Daley award USAFA, 1996, Exemplary Civilian Svc. Award medal, 1996, F.J. Seiler Rsch. award, USAFA, 1997. Fellow AIAA (dir. region IV 1983-86, Disting. Lectr., Thermophysics award 1997, publs. bd. 1998-2000, aerothermodynamic cons. Columbia accident investigation bd. 2003).

BERTIN, LEONARD GERARD, graphics designer, artist; b. Detroit, July 28, 1952; s. Julian Leonard and Helen Leona (Mussche) Bertin; m. Roberta Jan Gabler, May 29, 1976; 1 child, Jacquelyn. AS, Macomb Cmty. Coll., Warren, Mich., 1973. Artist Ambrose Assocs., Detroit, 1973—77, MacNamara Assocs., Detroit, 1977, Geo. N. Sepetys & Assocs., Southfield, Mich., 1977—79; artist, mgr. Skidmore Sahratian, Inc., Troy, Mich., 1979—90, Coomes/Dudek, Troy, Mich., 1990—2002; sr. creative assoc. Fusion/Design Comm., Madison Heights, Mich., 2002—. Contbr. articles to profl. jours. Chair Adv. Com. for Persons With Disabilities, Troy, Mich., 1999—2003, Ability Expo, Troy, Mich., 2003; mem. Leadership Troy, Mich., 2003; mem., Detroit Advocacy Com. Nat. Multiple Sclerosis Soc., Mich. Chpt., Southfield, 2003. Home: 5353 Rochester Rd Troy MI 48085 Office: Fusion/Design Comm 1423 E 12 Mile Rd Madison Heights MI 48071

BERTINI, CATHERINE ANN, international organization official; b. Syracuse, N.Y., Mar. 30, 1950; d. Fulvio and Ann (Vino) B.; m. Thomas Haskell, 1988. BA, SUNY, 1971; DSc (hon.), McGill U., Montreal, Can., 1997; DHL (hon.), SUNY, Cortland, 1999; DSc, Pine Manor Coll., 2000; DHL (hon.), Am. U. Rome, 2001; D in Pub. Svc. (hon.), John Cabot U., Rome, 2001; PhD (hon.), Slovak Agrl. U., Nitra, Slovak Republic, 2001. Youth dir. N.Y. Rep. State Com., 1971-74; with Rep. Nat. Com., 1975-76; mgr. pub. policy Container Corp. Am., 1977-87; dir. Office Family Assistance, U.S. Dept. Health and Human Svcs., 1987-89; acting asst. sec. U.S. Dept. HHS., 1989; asst. sec. USDA, 1989-92; UN panel mem. sec. gen.'s High Level Personalities on African Devel., UN, 1992-95; exec. dir. UN World Food Programme, Rome, 1992—2002; personal humanitarian envoy UN Sec. Gen., 2002; policy maker in residence Gerald Ford Sch. Pub. Policy U. Mich., 2002; chmn. U.N. Sys. Standing Com. on Nutrition, 2002—; under-sec. gen. U.N., 2002—. Mem. Ill. State Scholarship Comm., 1979-84; mem. Ill. Human Rights Comm., 1985-87; spl. envoy of Sec. Gen. to the Horn of Africa, 2000. Recipient Leadership in Human Svcs. award Am. Pub. Welfare Assn., 1990, Pub. Svc. award Am. Acad. Pediatrics, 1991, Leadership award Nat. Assn. WIC Dirs., 1992, Quality of Life award Auburn U., 1994, Disting. Alumni award Nelson A. Rockefeller Coll. Pub. Affairs and Policy, 1997. Fellow Harvard U., 1986. Office: UN Plaza First Ave at 46th St New York NY 10017 Business E-Mail: bertini@un.org.

BERTINO, FRED, advertising executive; V.p., creative group head Della Femina McNamee WCRS; pres., co-creative dir. Anderson Veduccio Bertino Advt.; with Hill Holliday, Boston, 1990—, now pres., chief creative officer. Mem. staff Art inst. New Eng. Recipient award N.Y. Advt. Club, N.Y. Art Dir.'s Club, One Show, Hatch Awards, Andy Awards, New Eng. Best of Broadcasting, Commn. Arts mag., Conn. Art Dir.'s Club, Grand Effie award for Creative Effectiveness, Arhena Newspapers, Stephen Kelly Awards, Grand Clio award. Office: Hill Holiday Coners Cosmopoulos Inc John Hancock Tower 200 Clarendon St Fl 40 Boston MA 02116-5084

BERTINO, JOSEPH ROCCO, physician, educator; b. Port Chester, N.Y., Aug. 16, 1930; s. Joseph and Madaleine (Posillipo) B.; m. Mary Patricia Hagemeyer, Sept. 29, 1956; children: Frederick, Amy Marie, Thomas Allen, Paul Phillip. Student, Cornell U., 1947-50; MD, Downstate Med. Center N.Y., 1954. USPHS Research fellow U. Wash. Sch. Medicine, Seattle, 1958-61; mem. faculty Yale U. Sch. Medicine, 1961-87, assoc. prof. pharmacology and medicine, 1964-67, prof., 1967-87, Am. Cancer Soc. prof., 1975—; head program molecular pharmacology and therapeutics Sloan Kettering Ctr., 1987—; prof. medicine and pharmacology Cornell U. Sch. Medicine, N.Y.C., 1987—. State scholar for medicine, 1950—54; disting. prof. medicine and pharmacology UMDNJ, 2002—. Contbr. articles to profl. jours. Recipient Honor medal Am. Cancer Soc., 1992. Mem. Am. Soc. for Clin. Investigation, Am. Soc. Hematology, Biol. Chemists, Pharmacology and Therapeutics. Home: 117 Sunset Hill Rd Branford CT 06405-6419 Office: 195 Little Albany St New Brunswick NJ 08901-1914 E-mail: bertinoj@umdnj.edu.

BERTLES, JOHN FRANCIS, physician, educator; b. Spokane, Wash., June 8, 1925; s. John Francis and Henrita Swart (Brown) B.; m. Jeannette Winans, 1948 (div. 1978); children: Mark Dwight, Jacquelyn Eve, John Francis.; m. Lila De Paganne, 1981. BS, Yale U., 1945; MD, Harvard U., 1952. Diplomate Am. Bd. Internal Medicine. Intern Presbyterian Hosp., N.Y.C., 1952-53, asst. resident in medicine, 1953-55; research fellow in hematology U. Rochester and Strong Meml. Hosp., 1955-56; research fellow in immunohematology Harvard U. Med. Sch. and Mass. Gen. Hosp., Boston, 1956-58, research fellow in hematology, 1958-59; instr. in medicine Harvard U. Med. Sch. at Mass. Gen. Hosp., 1959-61; dir. hematology-oncology div. St. Luke's Hosp. Center, N.Y.C., 1962-95, asst. attending physician, 1962-64, assoc. attending physician, 1964-71, attending physician, 1971-95; dir. transfusion services St. Luke's Roosevelt Hosp. Ctr., 1981-95; sr. research asso. dept. biol. scis. Columbia U., 1970-71, asst. clin. prof. medicine, 1962-67, assoc. clin. prof., 1967-71, assoc. prof., 1971-74, prof., 1974-95, prof. emeritus of medicine, 1995—; attending physician Montefiore Med. Ctr., N.Y.C., 1995-97; clin. prof. medicine Albert Einstein Coll. Medicine, N.Y.C., 1995-97. Vis. prof. medicine Nuffield dept. clin. medicine Radcliffe Infirmary, U. Oxford, Eng., 1977-78; cons. to various govt. agys., including hematology study sect. NIH, 1972-76, 82-84, blood rsch. rev. group, 1978-82; mem. dirs. coun. N.Y. Heart Assn., 1974-90; mem. basic rsch. adv. com. Nat. Found. March of Dimes, 1977-80. Contbr. articles to profl. publs. Ensign USNR, 1945-46. Fellow ACP; mem. Am. Soc. Clin. Investigation, Am. Physiol. Soc., Am. Soc. Hematology, Am. Fedn. Clin. Rsch., Am. Chem. Soc., Alpha Omega Alpha. Office: 72 Pondfield Rd W Apt 3K Bronxville NY 10708

BERTOIA, VAL, artist; b. Santa Monica, Calif., June 27, 1949; s. Harry and Brigitta (Valentiner) B.; m. Kylene Lantzy, May 29, 1976 (div. Jan. 1997); 1 child, Kyndi M. (dec.). Student, Ind. Inst. Tech., 1967-71. Sculptor, mgr. Bertoia Studio, Bally, Pa., 1978—. Authenticator, appraisor Harry Bertoia Artworks; juror Greater Norristown (Pa.) Art League, 1994. One-man show at The Hill Sch., 1992, Calvary Ch., 1994; exhibited in group shows at Wyomissing Inst. Fine Arts, 1987, 89, Mulhenberg Coll., 1990, Freyberger Gallery Pa. State Berks, 1990, 91, 93, Moravian Coll., 1991, Hazleton Art League, 1991, Reading Art Mus., 1987, The Hill Sch., 1993;, Boyertown HS, Pa., 1994, Greater Norristown (Pa.) Art League, 1994, Perkiomen Valley Women's Club, Pa., 1994; sculptures commd. by Northwestern U., Reading Area C.C.; (playground) Palm Schwenkfelder Ch., Mayfair, Allentown, (model) Limerick Power Co.(2d pl. Berks Art Alliance 1995), Capital Ctr., Trenton, N.J., Lenox, Inc., Alpo Petfoods Co., 90 ft. long Gong-Snake, Mayfair, Pa., (eco-sculpture pathway and stairway) Vitra Design Mus., Boisbuchet, France, 1999, (dragon hammock) Springford (Pa.) HS, 2000, others; sound sculpture Advanta Mortgage, Horsham, Pa., 1997; performance sound sculpture Allentown Art Mus., 1998, 99; patentee wind-rotor neutralizer; developer Ecol. Sculpture Pathway, 1974; writer Sonambient play entitled Mother, Made in America. co-author: World of Bertoia, 2003. Scoutmaster Boy Scouts U.S., Palm, Pa., 1979-83; recycling initiator Hereford (Pa.) Twp., 1989-90; appearanced on TV talk programs, Wyomissing, Pa., 1988. Recipient 4th place award Cornerstone, 1994, 1st place award Hackettstown, N.J., 1992, award of excellence Pottstown Area Artists' Guild, 1993, 2d pl. St. James Ch., Hackettstown, 1994, 2d pl. Perkiomen Valley Art Co., 1991. Mem. Pottstown Area Artists' Guild (pres. 1993), Artzon (cons. liaison 1994-95). Avocations: travel, designing woodland pathways, environmental-energy usage. Office: Bertoia Studio 644 Main St Bally PA 19503-0383 Fax: 610-845-7128. E-mail: valway@aol.com.

BERTOLAMI, CHARLES, oral surgeon; AA, Lorain County C.C., Elyria, Ohio, 1969; DDS summa cum laude, Ohio State U., Columbus, 1974; DMS, Harvard U., 1979. Diplomate Am. Bd. of Oral and Maxillofacial Surgeons, 1982. Chair oral and maxillofacial surgery UCLA Sch. of Dentistry, 1979—95; resident Mass. Gen. Hosp., 1980; asst. prof. Harvard Sch. of Dental Medicine, Boston, 1983—89; dean Sch. Dentistry, U. Calif., San Francisco, 1995—; asst. prof. Sch. Dental Medicine, U. Conn., Farmington. Recipient Callahan Meml. award, Ohio Dental Bd., 1974, Percy T. Phillips Vis. professorship, Columbia U. Sch. of Dental and Oral Surgery, 2002; Rsch. grants, NIH, 1983-1995. Fellow: Am. Assn. of Oral and Maxillofacial Surgeons; mem.: ADA, Am. Assn. for Dental Rsch. (pres. 2002—03). Achievements include Contribution to understanding the origin of abnormal wound healing in conditions of excessive scar formation. Office: UCSF Sch Dentistry 415 Parnassus Ave San Francisco CA 94143-0430 Office Fax: 415-476-4226. E-mail: bertolamic@dentistry.ucsf.edu.

BERTOLET, RODNEY JAY, philosophy educator; b. Allentown, Pa., Mar. 22, 1949; s. Frank and Helen (Johnson) B. BA, Franklin & Marshall Coll., 1971; PhD, U. Wis., 1977. Asst. prof. philosophy Purdue U., West Lafayette, Ind., 1977-82, assoc. prof. philosophy, 1982-90, prof. philosophy, 1990—, dept. head, 1991—. Author: What Is Said, 1990. Mem. Am. Philos. Assn., Ind. Philos. Assn. (pres. 1983-84). Office: Purdue Univ Dept Philosophy 100 N University St West Lafayette IN 47907-2098 E-mail: bertolet@purdue.edu.

BERTOLINI, JOSEPH CLIFFORD, political scientist, educator; m. Martha Ann Yellen, Aug. 22, 1982. BA, St. Johns's U., N.Y., 1969; MA, NYU, 1972, PhD in Polit. Sci., 1983. Dept. chair history and politics Kew-Forest Sch., Forest Hills, NY, 1998—2003. Adj. asst. prof. politics St. John's U., Jamaica, NY, 1978—99, NYU, N.Y.C., 1996—2001; mem. editl. adv. bd. Collegiate Press, San Diego, 1994—98. Author: The Serpent Within: Politics, Literature and American Individualism; co-author: Women Leaders in Contemporary United States Politics, New Europe at the Crossroads II; contbr. articles to profl. jours. Recipient Outstanding H.S. Tchr. award, U. Chgo., 1995. Mem.: Internat. Movement Interdisciplinary Study of Estrangement, Internat. Soc. Study European Ideas, Northeastern Polit. Sci. Assn., Am. Polit. Sci. Assn. Office: Kew-Forest School 119-17 Union Turnpike Forest Hills NY 11375

BERTOLLI, EUGENE EMIL, sculptor, goldsmith, designer, consultant; b. Boston, Feb. 19, 1923; s. Adolph and Julia (Manetti) B.; m. Jean Helen Tamburine, Apr. 21, 1956; children— Eugene Robert, Lisa Marie AB (hons.) cum laude, Boston Coll., 1943; postgrad., Washington and Lee U., 1944. Dir. ednl. reconditioning Madigan Convalescent Hosp., Tacoma, 1945-47; sr. v.p. design Napier Co., Meriden, Conn., 1947-85; sculptor, goldsmith Bertolli Studio, Meriden, Conn., 1947—, also cons. design and jewelry techniques, 1947—. Dir. City Savs. Bank, Meriden, Napier Co.; sculpture awards juror Am. Artists Profl. League, N.Y.C., 1993, Hudson Valley Art Assn., Inc., N.Y.C., 1984, 94. Works include bronze portrait The Outdoorsman (Am. Artists Profl. League award 1983) Mem. and officer Meriden Bd. Edn., 1958-63; pres. Meriden Pub. Libr. Bd., 1964-86; trustee Meriden-Wallingford Hosp. Capt. AUS, World War II. Recipient internat. outstanding jewelry design award Swarowski Internat., 1968, 69, John Manship Meml. award Rockport Art Assn., 1985, Franz Denghauser Meml. award for sculpture, 1988, award for sculpture Acad. Artists Assn., 1992, 94, Paul Manship Meml. award for excellence in sculpture North Shore Arts Assn., 1992, 93, portrait sculpture award Am. Artists Profl. League, 1994, L.J. Meiselman meml. award for Artistic Excellence of Sculpture for Portrait Bust, Am. Artists Profl. League, 1996 Grand Nat. Exhbn.; inducted into Meriden Hall of Fame for achievement in field of art, 1995. Mem. Acad. Artists Assn. (gold medal for sculpture 1982-84, 88-92, Hon. award 2000), North Shore Arts Assn. (juror of awards and membership admission 1993, spl. portrait sculpture award 1980, Katharine Taylor Weems sculpture award 1989), Am. Artists Profl. League (juror of awards 1993), Hudson Valley Art Assn. (juror of awards 1994), Mfg. Jewelers and Silversmiths, Internat. Platform Assn., Meriden Art Assn. (pres. 1957-58), Guild Boston Artists, Salmagundi Club. Roman Catholic. Home: 73 Reynolds Dr Meriden CT 06450-2532 also: PO Box 1391 Madison CT 06443-1391

BERTON, PIERRE, journalist, author; b. Whitehorse, Yukon, Can., July 12, 1920; s. Francis George and Laura (Thompson) Berton; m. Janet Walker, 1946; children: Penny, Pamela, Patricia, Peter, Paul, Peggy Anne, Perri, Eric. BA, U. B.C., 1941, DLitt (hon.), 1985; LLD (hon.), U. P.E.I., 1973, Dalhousie U., 1978, U. Brock, 1981, York U., 1974, U. Windsor, 1981, U. Athabasca, 1982, U. Victoria, 1983, McMaster U., 1983, U. Alaska, 1984, Royal Mil. Inst., 1985, Waterloo U., 1988; LLD (hon.), Lakehead U., Thunder Bay, Ont., Can., 2002, U. Western Ont., London, Ont., 2002. City editor Vancouver (B.C.) News Herald, 1941-42; feature writer Vancouver Sun, 1946-47; successive positions to mng. editor Maclean's Mag., Toronto, Ont., 1947-58; host The Pierre Berton Show, 1963-73; contbg. editor Maclean's Mag., 1963; asso. editor, daily columnist Toronto Daily Star, 1958-62; columnist Toronto Star, 1991-94; TV panelist Front Page Challenge, CBC, 1957-95. Chancellor Yukon Coll., 1988-93. Author: 47 books including The Royal Family, 1953, Stampede for Gold, 1955, The Mysterious North, 1956, Klondike Fever, 1958, Just Add Water and Stir, 1959, Adventures of a Columnist, 1960, The New City, 1961, The Secret World of Og, 1961, Fast, Fast, Fast Relief, 1962, Big Sell, 1963, Comfortable Pew, 1965, The Cool, Crazy, Committed World of The Sixties, 1966, Smug Minority, 1968, The National Dream, 1970, The Last Spike, 1971, The Impossible Railway, 1972, Drifting Home, 1973, Hollywood's Canada, 1974, My Country, 1976, The Dionne Years, 1977, The Wild Frontier, 1978, The Invasion of Canada, 1812-1813, 1980, Flames across the Border, 1981, Why We Act Like Canadians, 1982, The Klondike Quest, 1983, The Promised Land, 1984, Masquerade, 1985, Vimy, 1986, Starting Out, 1987, The Arctic Grail, 1988 (Periodical Marketers Can. Book of Yr. award), The Great Depression

1929-39, 1990 (Periodical Marketers Can. Authors award), Niagara, 1992, A Picture Book of Niagara Falls, 1993, Winter, 1994, My Times: Living with History 1947-1995, 1995, Farewell To The Twentieth Century, 1996, The Great Lakes, 1996, 1967-The Last Good Year, 1997, Seacoasts 1998, A Literary Resurrection, 1948-94, 1998, Worth Repeating, Pierre Berton's Canada, 1999, Welcome to the 21st Century, 1999, Marching As To War, 2001, Cats I Have Known and Loved, 2002, The Joy of Writing, 2003; screenwriter; narrator City of Gold; contbr. to numerous mags.and newspapers. Past chmn. Heritage Can. Found. Capt. Can. Army, 1942-45. Decorated Companion Order Can.; recipient Gov. Gen.'s award for creative non-fiction, 1956, 58, 72; Stephen Leacock medal for humor, 1959; J.V. McAree award for columnist of year, 1959; Nat. Newspaper awards for feature writing and staff corresponding, 1960; Grand Prix film awards.; Beefeater Club prize for lit., 1982; Can. Booksellers award, 1982, Companion Order Can., 1986, Gabriele Leger Nat. Heritage award, 1989, Coles Book award, 1989, Great Trekker award U. B.C., 1990, Graeme Gibson award, 1992, Author's Leadership award Periodical Marketers Can., 1992, Pierre Berton award, 1994, Responsibilty in Journalism award Com. for Investigation of Paranormal, 1996, Biomed. Sci. Ambs. award, 1997, John Drainie award for significant contbn. to radio or TV, 1999; named to Can. Newspaper Hall of Fame, 1982, Order of Mariposa, 1990. Mem. Authors League Am., Heritage Can., Assn. Can. Radio and TV Artists (award for integrity in broadcasting 1972, award for pub. affairs 1977), Writers Union Can. Office: 3 Hillcrest Ave Toronto ON Canada M4X 1W1

BERTONE, THOMAS LEE, management consultant; b. Pittsburg, Kans., Nov. 15, 1938; s. Anthony and Gaye Kittle Bertone; m. Ellen Reville Kniffin, Sept. 6, 1969; children: Elizabeth Reville, Katherine Logan. AB cum laude, Harvard U., 1960; MA, Stanford U., 1963; D Pub. Adminstrn., George Washington U., 1971. Budget examiner on def. U.S. Bur. Budget, Washington, 1964-67; cons., assoc. Booz Allen & Hamilton, Washington, 1967-69, 78-80; dir. budget rev. Office Fiscal Affairs, N.J. Legislature, Trenton, 1973-75, exec. dir. Office Fiscal Affairs, 1975-78; regional dir. state and local govt. cons. Coopers & Lybrand, Phila., 1980-82; dir. internat. cons. Grant Thornton, Chgo., 1986-90; pres. Thomas L. Bertone & Assocs., Pennington, N.J., 1982-86, 90—. World Bank decentralization adviser to permanent sec. Sri Lanka Ministry Local Govt., 1985-89; ADB advisor to budget dir. Budget Office, Federated States Micronesia, 1993-95; IMF budget advisor to min. fin. Palestine Authority, Gaza and West Bank, 1995; U.S. AID intergovtl. fiscal rels. advisor to prime min. and min. fin. Fedn. Bosnia Herzegovina, 1997. Sr. advisor on state fin. amd mgmt. to gov. candidate State of W.Va., Charleston, 1970-72; pro bono cons. N.J. Office Mgmt. and Budget, Trenton, 1999. 2d lt. U.S. Army, 1964, Korea. Mem. ASPA, Inst. Mgmt. Cons. (cert.), Assn. Govt. Accts. (cert. govt. fin. mgr.). Democrat. Avocations: scuba diving, skiing, horseback riding, shooting and gun collecting, dogs. Home and Office: 153 E Delaware Ave Pennington NJ 08534-2304 E-mail: tom_bertone_ab60@post.harvard.edu.

BERTONI, HENRY L. electrical engineering educator; b. Nov. 15, 1938; s. Henry and Frances (Brisky) B.; m. Kathy Guthmuller, Aug. 10, 1963 (div. Dec. 1978); children: Elliot S., Rachel E.; m. Helen Ebenstein, Apr. 6, 1990. BSEE, Northwestern U., 1960; MSEE, Poly. U., Bklyn., 1962, PhD, 1967. Prof. elec. engring. Poly. U., Bklyn., 1967—, head dept. elec. engring., 1990-95, vice provost, 1995-96, head dept. elec. engring., 2001—. Recipient Marconi Meml. award Vet. Wireless Operator Assn., 1993. Fellow IEEE (Disting. lectr. 1998-2000); mem. Internat. Radio Sci. Union, Radio Club Am. Office: Poly U 6 Metrotech Ctr Brooklyn NY 11201-3840

BERTONI, MAE, artist; b. Dec. 17, 1929; Cert., Parsons Sch. of Design, 1951. Greeting card artist Horcross Inc., NYC, 1951-62; free-lance artist, 1966—. One-woman exhbns. include Fairleight Dickenson U., Rutherford, NJ, 1963, Grand Ctrl. Galleries, NYC, 1970, 1979, Peerman Gallery, Corpus Christi, Tex., 1969, 70, Gallery Madison 90, NYC, 1976; Cove Gallery, W EllFleet, Mass., 1989, 2000; group exhbns. at Am. Watercolor Soc., Nat. Acad. Design, Nat. Arts Club, Catherine Lorillard Wolfe Art Club, NYC, Hudson Valley Art Assn., White Plains, NY, Knickerbocker Artists Assn., Painters and Sculptors Soc., New Rochelle (NY) Art Assn., Bay Ridge Festival Arts, Bklyn., Westchester (NY) Art Soc.; represented in permanent collections Columbia Presbyn. Med. Ctr., NY Life Ins. co., Dewey, Ballantyne law firm, William Esty Advt. Co. (all NYC), Peerman Archtl. Offices. Recipient Gold medal honor Catherine Lorillard Wolfe Art Club, 1966, 68; Hors de Concours, Washington Sq. Outdoor Art Exhibit, N.Y.C., 1970. Mem.: Hudson Valley Art Assn. (landscape award 1966), Am. Watercolor Soc. (William Esty prize 1965). Home: 10524 63rd Dr Flushing NY 11375-1635

BERTONIERE, NOELIE RITA, research chemist; b. New Orleans, Oct. 17, 1936; BS, St. Mary's Dominican Coll., 1959; PhD in Organic Chemistry, U. New Orleans, 1971. Rsch. chemist textiles & food USDA So. Regional Rsch. Ctr., New Orleans, 1960—. Mem. AAAS, Am. Chem. Soc., Am. Assn. Textile Chemists and Colorists, Fiber Soc., Sigma Xi. Achievements include research in cellulose chemistry, durable press cotton fabric, pore size distribution, supramolecular structure of cellulose, photochemistry of small ring heterocycles and carbenes. Office: USDA So Regional Rsch Ctr ARS PO Box 19687 1100 Robert E Lee Blvd New Orleans LA 70179

BERTRAM, CHRISTINE G. artist, painter/graphic designer; b. New Bedford, Mass., Dec. 28, 1952; d. Samuel David Doran and Marjorie Ruth (Dore) B.; children: Christian Allan, Michael Doran. BFA in Painting, Swain Sch. Design, 1974; MFA, Bklyn. Coll., 1976; BFA in Design/Typography magna cum laude, U. Mass., Dartmouth, 1995. Freelance scrimshaw artist, Mattapoisett, Mass., 1980-87; graphic designer New Bedford Std. Times, 1997—2002. Designer visual prevention program State of Mass. Lead Paint Prevention Program, 1995; designer Beth Soll Dance Inc., Boston, 1994-95; project mgr., rschr. Office of Hist. Preservation, New Bedford, 1978-80. Author: Palmers Light House, 1978; co-author: History of North Bedford, 1979; designer numerous posters, books, invitations, pamphlets, logos; exhibited in various art exhbns., 1974—. Vol. Tchrs. Ctr. Sch., Mattapoisett, 1989—2001, Boy Scouts Am., Mattapoisett, 1986—; Sunday sch. tchr. Congl. Ch., Mattapoisett, 1984—2002. U.S. govt. grantee for rsch. involved in New Bedford becoming a Nat. Park. Avocations: antique restoration, braided and hooked rugs, sewing, painting, gardening. Home: 124 Acushnet Rd Mattapoisett MA 02739-1221 E-mail: christieb43@aol.com.

BERTRAM, JACK RENARD, information systems company executive; b. Lincoln, Nebr., Nov. 20, 1943; s. John Lewis and Emma Louise (Doerr) B.; m. Ingrid Frieda Reschke, Feb. 14, 1975; children: Deborah Geniene, Kenneth Brian. BS, Stanford U., 1966, MA, 1971; MS, Santa Clara U., 1988. Scientific programming specialist Lockheed Missles & Space Co., Sunnyvale, Calif., 1980-92; pres. Hansatech Internat., Redwood City, Calif., 1993—. Mem. AIAA, IEEE Computer Soc., Am. Assn. for Artificial Intelligence, Am. Astronautical Soc., Assn. for Computing Machinery, Computer Profls. for Social Responsibility, Inst. Cert. Profl. Mgrs. (cert. mgr.). Democrat. Home: 685 Woodland Ave Menlo Park CA 94025 Office: Hansatech Internat PO Box 554 Redwood City CA 94064-0554

BERTRAM, JEAN DESALES, writer; b. Burlington, Iowa, Sept. 28; d. Val Randall and Ruth Cecilia Bertram; 1 child, Larkin Bertram-Cox Montgomery . BA, U. N.C., Greensboro, 1942; MA, U. Minn., 1951; PhD, Stanford U., 1963. Reporter Greensboro News Record, 1942-43; founder dept. pub. rels. Burlington Industries, Greensboro, 1943-49; asst. to dean U. N.C., Greensboro, 1949-50; instr. U. Minn., Mpls., 1950-51; dir. radio performance Mpls. Vocat. High Sch., 1951-52; dir. Children's Theatre Touring Co., Jr. League Mpls., 1951-52; prof. theatre arts San Francisco State U., 1952-88. Cons. Wadsworth Pub. Co., Belmont, Calif., 1966; dir. Readers' Repertory, San Francisco State U., 1967-72; dir. Jean De Sales Bertram Players, San Francisco, 1971-74; founder, developer storytelling program San Francisco State U., 1971-88; cons. Scott-Foresman, Chgo., 1983; senator acad. senate San Francisco State U., 1983-84, dir. com. for lectures, arts and spl. programs, 1985-87; tax preparer, 1994. Author: (textbooks) The Oral Experience of Literature, 1967, The Actor Speaks, 4 edits., 1981-87, Tell Me a Story!, 5 edits., 1982-88; author, dir. Girl Scout Nat. Convention pageant Finding Your Own Adventure, 1955; prodr., dir., adapter, editor: (religious plays) A Symphonetic Easter Drama, 1954, The Awakening, 1954, The Vision of Isaiah, 1970, The Cherry Tree, 1971; author, dir.: (plays) American Cameos, 1976, Jeremiah The Prophet, 1999; author: (poem) Cosmorama, 1971; actress one-woman show numerous women from Shakespeare's plays, 1971-88; author: (short story) The Giraffe and the Canary, 1999; contbr. articles to profl. jours. Stanford-Wilson fellow Stanford U., 1962-63. Mem. Found. Bibl. Rsch., Acad. Am. Poets, Phi Beta Kappa (sec. Omicron of Calif. chpt. 1977-79, 83-88, pres. 1979-81, v.p. 1981-83, ofcl. del. Triennial coun. 1979, 82). Avocations: sculpturing in clay, poetry writing, photography.

BERTRAM, MANYA M. retired lawyer; b. Denver; d. Samuel and Ruby (Feiner) Boran; m. Barry Bertram, June 19, 1938; children: H. Neal, Carel. JD magna cum laude, Southwestern U., 1962. Ptnr. Most and Bertram, L.A., 1963-83; of counsel Levin, Ballin, Plotkin, Zimring & Goffin, North Hollywood, Calif., 1983-92; ret. Former trustee Southwestern U. Sch. Law, former pres. Southwestern U. Sch. Law Alumni Assn.; former bd. advisors Whittier Coll. of Law, L.A., Beverly Coll. Law; commr. Calif. Commn. on Aging, Sacramento, 1977-82; bd. dirs. Jewish Family Svc., L.A., 1963-2001. Mem. ABA, Calif. State Bar Assn., Federacion Internac. de Abagados, Iota Tau Tau, B'nai B'rith (life mem.), Hadassah (life mem.). Avocation: geneology. E-mail: manyamin@california.com.

BERTRAM, MELISSA C. agricultural research scientist; b. Albuquerque, N.Mex., July 27, 1971; d. Bobby E. and Marilyn S. Bertram. BS, U. N.Mex., Albuquerque, 1994; postgrad., U. Idaho, Idaho Falls, 1995—. Intern Argonne Nat. Lab., Ill., 1994; rsch. asst. Argonne Nat. Lab. - West, Idaho Falls, 1995; lab tech. U. Idaho, Idaho Falls, 1995—99, sr. scientific aide, 1999—. Author: (abstract) Am. Potato Jour., 2000; co-author: (article) Potato Grower Mag., 1996, Am. Jour. Potato Rsch., 2003. Mem.: Idaho Assn. Plant Pathology, Am. Inst. Biol. Scis. Republican. Methodist. Avocations: skiing, hiking, horseback riding.

BERTRAM, PAUL BENJAMIN, English language educator; b. Buffalo, N.Y., Jan. 26, 1928; s. Irving Louis and Leona (Reinman) B. AB, NYU, 1948; MA, Harvard U., 1952, PhD, 1960. Instr. English Mount Holyoke Coll., South Hadley, Mass., 1955-56; instr. Rutgers U., New Brunswick, 1956-61, asst. prof., 1961-65, assoc. prof., 1965-69, prof., 1969-97, prof. emeritus, 1998—, assoc. dean Grad. Sch., 1966-72. Author: Shakespeare And "The Two Noble Kinsmen", 1965, White Spaces in Shakespeare, 1981; editor: The Three-Text Hamlet, 1991; mem. editl. bd. Shakespeare Bulletin, 1989—2003. Mem. MLA, Renaissance Soc. Am., Columbia U. Shakespeare Seminar. Home: 30 W 60th St Apt 4D New York NY 10023-7908

BERTRAM, SUSAN, rehabilitation counselor; b. Darlington, S.C., July 7, 1945; d. Ernest and Leigh (Ogburn) Lowry; m. John David Bertram, Dec. 7, 1980. BFA, U. Ga., 1966; MS, Ga. State U., 1993. Cert. rehab. counselor, nat. cert. counselor, Ga.; lic. profl. counselor, Ga. Social work/counselor State of Ga., Atlanta, 1967—95, rehab. counselor, 1995—. Mem. ACA, Nat. Rehab. Counseling Assn., Ga. Rehab. Assn. Avocations: travel, reading, yoga.

BERTRAM, VICTORIA ELAINE, dancer; b. Toronto, Ont., Can., Feb. 26, 1946; d. Russell Arthur and Lois Marguerite (McBride) B.; m. Jacques Germain Gorrissen, Jan. 5, 1970; children: Adrian Alexander, Cybele Justine. Grad. with honors, Nat. Ballet Sch., Toronto, 1963. Mem. corps de ballet Nat. Ballet of Can., Toronto, 1963-70, soloist, 1970-80, prin. dancer, 1980—, prin. character artist. Dancer (ballets) Giselle, Romeo and Juliet, Manon, Swan Lake, The Four Seasons, The Nutcracker, Washington Square. Office: Nat Ballet Can 470 Queens Quay W Toronto ON Canada M5V 3K4 Office Fax: 416-345-8323.

BERTRAND, FREDERIC HOWARD, retired insurance company executive; b. Montpelier, Vt., Aug. 5, 1936; s. George Joseph and Dolores Gertrude (Mallory) B.; m. Elinor Maude Pierce, June 11, 1960; children: Kimberly Sue, Michael Scott, John Frederic (dec.). BSCE magna cum laude, Norwich U., 1958; postgrad., Georgetown U. Law Sch., 1961-63, Carnegie-Mellon U. Sch. Indsl. Adminstrn., 1967-68; JD, Coll. William and Mary, 1967; D in Bus. Mgmt. (hon.), Norwich U., 1991. Bar: Va. 1967, Vt. 1970; registered profl. engr., Vt. Engr.-adminstr. CIA, Washington, 1960-70; asst. counsel, assoc. counsel, v.p., sr. v.p., bd. dirs. Nat. Life Ins. Co., Montpelier, 1970-83, exec. v.p., chief oper. officer, 1983-85, pres., chief oper. officer, 1985-87, chmn., chief exec. officer, 1987-97, also bd. dirs. Bd. dirs. Chittenden Trust Co., Burlington, Union Mut. Fire Ins. Co., New Eng. Guaranty Ins. Co., Montpelier; bd. dirs. Cen. Vt. Pub. Svcs. Co., Rutland, 1985—, chair, 1997—, Vt. Elec. Transmission Co., 1998—, Catamount Energy Corp., bd. dirs., 1995—, chair, 1997-2002; The Home Svc. Store, Rutland, 2000—; civilian aide to Sec. of Army, Washington, 1981-93. Alderman City of Montpelier, 1974-76, pres. city coun., 1975-76, mayor, 1976-78; bd. dirs. Ctrl. Vt. Econ. Devel. Corp., 1985-98; chmn. Vt. Bus. Roundtable, 1995-97, bd. dirs., 1987-98; trustee Norwich U., Northfield, Vt., 1979-85. Recipient Outstanding Alumnus award Norwich U., 1980, Citizen of Yr. award Vt. C. of C., 1992, U.S. Army Disting. Civilian Svc. award, 1993. Mem. Am. Coun. Life Ins. (bd. dirs. 1989-94, chmn. 1993), Vt. Bar Assn., Washington County Bar Assn., Theta Chi, Epsilon Tau Sigma. Republican. Roman Catholic.

BERTRAND, ROBERT SIMEON, manufacturing engineer; b. Waterbury, Conn., Oct. 26, 1946; s. Emile J. and Leannette (Bouffard) B.; m. Lorraine J. Boisvert, May 31, 1969 (div. Mar. 1983); children: Marcus J., Audra L. ASAS, Waterbury State Tech. Coll., 1970; BSMT, Ctrl. Conn. U., 1982. Mfg. engr., tool room foreman Miford Products Corp., Branford, Conn., 1983-85; designer, owner Bert Design, Chesire, Conn., 1985; sr. tooling engr. U.S. Surg., Norwalk, Conn., 1985-88; engring. mgr. O'Hara Metal Products, Brisbane, Calif., 1988-91; sr. tool engr., buyer Ethicon, Inc., Blue Ash, Ohio, 1991-93; sr. mfg. engr. Thomas & Betts, Tulsa, 1994, tooling engring. mgr. AUGAT divsn. Clinton Twp, Mich., 1994-97; sr. procurement engr. avionics and lighting divsn. Allied Signal, Olathe, Kans., 1997—2003; supplier devel. lean mfg. electonics and avionics sys. divsn Allied Signal (name now Honeywell Internat., Inc.), Olathe, 1998—2001. Mem. Soc. Mfg. Engrs. (sr.), Am. Soc. Metals (sr.). Home: PO Box 602 Watertown CT 06795-0602

BERTSCH, FREDERICK CHARLES, III, business executive; b. Bklyn., Mar. 17, 1942; s. Frederick Charles and Norma Elizabeth (Hodgkins) B.; m. Ana Maria Carmen Natteri, Aug. 20, 1971; children— Frederick C., Ana Cecilia BA, Wesleyan U., Middletown, Conn., 1965; MBA, U. Pa., 1967. Supr. Ford Motor Co., Dearborn, Mich., 1967-69; cons. Cresap, McCormick & Paget Inc., N.Y.C., 1969-73; dir. corp. devel. IU Internat., Phila., 1973-76; v.p. corp. devel. Enterra Corp., Radnor, Pa., 1976-84, v.p. fin., chief fin. officer, 1985-86; founder F.C. Bertsch & Co., Inc., St. Davids, Pa., 1988—; v.p., CFO Gladwin Corp., Coraopolis, Pa., 1995. Pres. Radnor ABC (A Better Chance), Wayne, Pa., 1984-85, now bd. dirs Avocations: golf, fishing, gardening. Home and Office: 416 Round Hill Rd Saint Davids PA 19087-4728 E-mail: fcbertsch@fast.net.

BERTSCH, GARY KENNETH, political scientist, educator; b. Vallejo, Calif., June 8, 1944; s. Gideon and Freda (Hepper) B.; m. Joan Elizabeth Brubacher, Feb. 29, 1964; children: Dawn, Todd, Jason. BA, Idaho State U., 1966; MA, U. Oreg., 1968, PhD, 1970. Vis. prof. U. Zagreb, Yugoslavia, 1969-70; prof. polit. sci. U. Ga., Athens, 1970—. Vis. prof. nat. security affairs Air U., Dept. Def., Maxwell AFB, Ala., 1981-82; Fulbright prof. politics U. Lancaster, Eng., 1984-85; dir. Ctr. Internat. Trade and Security, 1987—. Author numerous books, including East-West Strategic Trade and the Atlantic Alliance, 1983; Reform and Revolution in Communist Systems, 1991; editor: Engaging India, 1999, Dangerous Weapons, Desperate States, 1999, Crossroads and Conflict, 2000, also numerous articles. Recipient numerous awards for tchg. U. Ga., 1970—, profl. chair for disting. tchg., 1982—, numerous rsch. grants, 1970—. Mem. Am. Polit. Sci. Assn., Internat. Studies Assn. Home: 228 Henderson Ave Athens GA 30605-1037 Office: U Ga Dept Internat Affairs Athens GA 30602 E-mail: gbertsch@uga.edu.

BERTSCHY, TIMOTHY L. lawyer; b. Pekin, Ill., Nov. 12, 1952; AB magna cum laude, U. Ill., 1974; JD, George Washington U., 1977. Bar: Ill. 1977, U.S. Dist. Ct. (cen. dist.) Ill., U.S. Ct. Appeals (7th cir.) 1982, U.S. Supreme Ct. Ptnr. Heyl, Royster, Voelker & Allen, Peoria, Ill., 1977—. Fellow Ill. State Bar Found., Am. Bar Found.; mem. ABA (ho. dels. 1995—, co-chair sect. litigation bus. torts com. 2003—), Ill. State Bar Assn. (pres. 1998-99), Peoria County Bar Assn. Office: Heyl Royster Voelker & Allen PC 124 SW Adams St Ste 600 Peoria IL 61602-1352 E-mail: tbertschy@hrva.com.

BERTUCELLI, ROBERT EDWARD, accountant, educator; b. Bklyn., Mar. 23, 1948; s. Leo and Gertrude Augusta (Roggenkamp) B.; m. Maryann Marchese, June 13, 1970; children: Nikole, Gina. AAS, Suffolk C.C., 1968; BS, C.W. Post Coll., 1970; MS, L.I. U., 1974. CPA, N.Y.; cert. fin. planner; chartered life underwriter. Acct. Arthur Young & Co., Westbury, N.Y., 1970-72; sr. tax. mgr. Peat Marwick Mitchell & Co., Jericho, N.Y., 1972-77; prof. acctg. and taxation C.W. Post Coll., 1977—; pvt. practice Smithtown, N.Y., 1977-83, Hauppauge, N.Y., 1989-94; ptnr. Bertucelli Barragato & Co., Smithtown, 1983-89, Bertucelli & Malaga L.L.P., Ronkonkoma, NY, 1994—. Lectr. Person Wolinsky Assocs., 1977—. Mem. St. Patrick's Sch. Bd., Smithtown, N.Y., 1982-92, pres., 1985-88, 90-92; bd. trustees, St. Charles Hosp. and Rehab. Ctr., Port Jefferson, NY, 2003—. Mem.: AICPA, Estate Planning Coun. (pres. 1996—97), Nat. Assn. Accts., N.Y. Soc. CPAs (author, lectr. 1989—, Haskins Silver medal 1972), Smithtown C. of C. (treas. 1988—90). Roman Catholic.

BÉRUBÉ, MICHAEL, literature educator; Asst. prof. U. Ill., Urbana, 1989—93, assoc. prof., 1993—96, prof., 1996—, dir. Ill. program for rsch. in humanities, 1997—. Author: Life As We Know It (One of the Notable Books of Yr., N.Y. Times, 1996). Fellow, U. Ill., 1993—94; grantee, U.S. Info. Agy., 1993; scholar, U. Ill. Office: Univ Ill Dept Eng 608 S Wright Urbana IL 61801 Office Fax: 217-333-4321. E-mail: m-berube@uiu.edu.

BERUBE, PAUL E. obstetrician-gynecologist; b. Cambridge, Mass., Oct. 7, 1941; MD, Chgo. Med. Sch., 1983. Diplomate Am. Bd. Ob-Gyn. Intern U. N. Mex. Hosp., Albuquerque, 1983-84, resident ob-gyn., 1983-85; resident Pitt County Meml. Hosp.-E. Carolina U., Greenville, N.C., 1985 86, 86-87; attending physician Meml. Hosp., Carbondale, Ill., 1987—, sec. med. staff, 1994-98, chair ob-gyn., 1996-98; attending physician Union County Hosp., Anna, Ill., 1987—; clin. assoc. prof. So. Ill. U., Carbondale, 1989—; with Fed. Chartered Rural Cmty. Health Ctr., 1987—. Mem.: Alpha Omega Alpha. Office: RHI 513 N Main St Anna IL 62906-1668

BERUBE, RICHARD HENRY, electrical engineering educator, consultant; b. Providence, Dec. 6, 1937; s. Henry Richard and Thelma Lilla (Seymour) B.; m. Patricia Ann Pastille, Oct. 20, 1962. BSEE, U. R.I., 1962, MSEE, 1968. Electronics engr. College Hill Industries, Warwick, R.I., 1962-64; instr. engring. and math. C.C. R.I., Warwick, 1965-68, asst. prof. engring., 1968-73, assoc. prof., 1973-80, prof., 1980—, chmn. dept., 1972-80. Cons. F.N. Zaino Assoc., Cranston, RI, 1976-84, Gulton Industries, East Greenwich, RI, 1991; mem. solar energy com. RI Pub. Utility Commn., Providence, 1975-76; RI planning rep. N.E. Solar Energy Cu., Boston, 1977. Author: Electronic Devices and Circuits Using MCAP II, 1992, Electronic Devices and Circuits Using MCAP III, 1993, Experiments for Electronic Devices Using Electronics Workbench, 1996, 2d edit., 2000, Experiments for Electric Circuits Using Electronics Workbench, 1997, 2d edit. 2000, 3rd edit. 2004, Experiments for Digital Electronics Using Electronics Workbench, 1999, Learning Electronics Communicators Using Electronics Workbench Multism, 2002. Tech. advisor James Taft for Gov. Campaign, Providence, 1976. NSF grantee Brown U., 1975-76, grantee R.I. Bd. Govs. for State Colls., 1988-89. Mem. IEEE, Am. Soc. for Engring. Edn., Metacomet Country Club, Tau Beta Pi. Office: CC RI East Ave Warwick RI 02886 E-mail: rberube@ccri.edu.

BERVEN, NORMAN LEE, counselor, psychologist, educator; b. Des Moines, May 14, 1945; s. Arthur N. and Ruth N. (Sharp) B.; m. Estella Stone, Oct. 11, 1969; 1 child, Jennifer. BS, U. Iowa, 1967, MA, 1969; PhD, U. Wis., 1973. Lic. psychologist; cert. rehab. counselor, lic. profl. counselor. Rehab. counselor San Mateo County Mental Health Svc., San Mateo, Calif., 1969-71; rsch. assoc. Internat. Ctr. for Disabled, N.Y.C., 1973-75; asst. prof. counseling and spl. svcs. Seton Hall U., South Orange, N.J., 1975-76; asst. prof. to prof. rehab. psychology, program chair U. Wis., Madison, 1976—. Cons. to univ., govt. and pvt. non-profit programs. Editor: Rehab. Counseling Bull., 1985-92, assoc. editor, 1982-85, editorial bd., 1980-82, 92—; editorial bd. Rehab. Psychology, 1981-99, Vocat. Evaluation and Work Adjustment Jour., 1980—, Assessment in Rehab. and Exceptionality, 1992-96; contbr. articles to profl. jours., chpts. to books. Recipient Varsity Disting. Alumni award rehab. psychology program U. Wis., 1994, Disting. Alumni award grad. programs in rehab. U. Iowa, 1997; grantee U.S. Dept. Edn., 1986—, Spencer Found., 1981-82, Wis. Alumni Rsch. Found., 1979-80. Fellow APA (rehab., counseling and evaluation, measurement and stats. divsn.); mem. ACA (rsch. award 1986), Am. Rehab. Counseling Assn. (disting. profl. award 1990, rsch. award 1981, 84, 86, 92, 93, 95, 2000, Disting. Career Rsch. award 1998), Nat. Rehab. Counseling Assn. (bd. dirs. N.J. chpt. 1975-76, bd. dirs. Wis. chpt. 1981-83, bd. dirs. Calif. chpt. 1971, Meritorious Svc. award Wis. chpt. 1992), Nat. Rehab. Assn. (Grad. Lit. award 1968, bd. dirs. S.W. Wis. chpt., 1980—, San Mateo chpt. 1969-71, Disting. Svc. award Wis. chpt. 1997), Assn. for Counselor Edn. and Supervision, Assn. for Assessment in Counseling, Assn. for Specialists in Group Work, Vocat. Evaluation and Work Adjustment Assn., Nat. Coun. on Rehab. Edn., Nat. Coun. Measurement Edn., NAMI Wis. Home: 10 Southwick Cir Madison WI 53717-1415 Office: U Wis Madison Rehab Psychology 432 N Murray St Madison WI 53706-1407 E-mail: nlberven@facstaff.wisc.edu.

BERWICK, ROBERT CREGAR, computer science educator; b. Phila., July 25, 1951; s. Leonard and Mary (Cregar) B.; m. Marilyn Matz, Sept. 7, 1984; children: Elissa Matz, Shana Alexandra. BA, Harvard U., 1976; MS, MIT, 1980, PhD, 1982. Asst. prof. computer sci. MIT, Cambridge, 1982-87, assoc. prof., 1987-89, prof., 1989—, co-dir. Ctr. for Biol. and Computational Learning, 1993—. Bd. dirs. Ctr. for Biological and Computational Learning. Author: The Grammatical Basis of Linguistic Performance, 1984, The Acquistion of Syntactic Knowledge, 1985, Computational Linguistics, 1986, Computational Complexity and Natural Language, 1987, Principle-based Parsing, 1992, Cartesian Computation, 1995, Principal-based Parsing: From Theory to Practice, 1998; editor: Computational Models of Discourse, 1982. Recipient Edgerton Faculty award MIT, 1985; Guggenheim fellow, 1987. Mem. AAAS, Assn. Computational Linguistics, Sigma Xi. Avocation: astronomy. Home: 19 Brenton Rd Weston MA 02493-1003

BERZ, DAVID RICHARD, lawyer; b. Chgo., May 21, 1948; m. Sherry Kirschner, Sept. 5, 1970; children: Douglas, Alexander. BA, George Washington U., 1970, JD with honors, 1973. Bar: D.C. 1973, U.S. Supreme Ct. 1977, N.Y. 1985. Mng. ptnr. Weil, Gotshal & Manges, Washington, 1985—. Author: Environmental Law in Real Estate and Business Transactions, 3 vols., 1992; mem. bd. editors Chem. Waste Litigation Reporter, 1986—; contbr. articles to profl. jours. Bd. dirs., pres. Washington Hebrew Congregation; exec. bd. mem. Am. Jewish Com.; mem. adv. bd. George Washington Univ. Nat. Law Ctr. Mem. ABA (mem. environ. controls com., corp. banking and bus. law sect., vice chmn. environ. quality control com. sect. adminstrv. law 1978-81), FBA, D.C. Bar Assn., Def. Rsch. Inst. (mem. environ. law com.), U.S. C. of C. (mem. environ. com.). Office: Weil Gotshal & Manges LLP 1501 K St NW Ste 100 Washington DC 20005-5608

BERZAS, ELIZABETH ANN, marketing professional, public relations executive; b. New Orleans, Jan. 29, 1964; d. John Darwin and Norene Elizabeth (Betbeze) B. BS, U. New Orleans, 1986; MHA, Tulane U., 1992. Cert. Novell Network Sys. mgr. Planning and marketing, dir. vol. svcs. St. Tammany Hosp., Covington, La., 1992—, sr. health ins. info. program counselor, 1994—2002; program dir. of health svcs. adminstr. Our Lady of the Lake Coll., Baton Rouge, La., 2002—. Sec. Deaf Action Ctr., Fla. Parishes, 1997—2002; pres. Area Agy. Aging St. Tammany Parish, 1995—99; adv. com. Children's Advocacy Ctr., Covington, 1996—2002; chairperson transp. and infrastructure Chamber W. St. Tammany, Covington, 1997—2002, bd. dirs., 1997—2002; Leadership grad. St. Tammany C. of C., bd. mem., 1999. Mem. Am. Coll. Healthcare Execs. (diplomate), W. St. Tammany Exch. Club (pres., Exchangite of the Yr. 1996 Ark.-La.-Tex. dist.), St, Tammany-West C. of C. (com. 1997, 99, Bd. Dir. of the Yr. 1999). Avocations: volleyball, boating, fishing.

BERZINSKI, PATRICK ANTHONY, media consultant; b. New Brunswick, N.J., Sept. 14, 1964; s. Clement Anthony Berzinski, Ann Theresa (Whaley) Berzinski; m. Barbara Ann Melchione, Apr. 25, 1987. Radio broadcaster WFMU-FM, East Orange, NJ, 1980—84; technician, writer Beaty & Assocs., Orange, NJ, 1984—86, John L. Randolph Co., Bklyn., 1986—91; technician James A. Konzelman Co., Hoboken, NJ, 1991—97; specialist media and editl. Stevens Inst. Tech., Hoboken, 2000—. Ptnr. Restoration Assocs., Bloomfield,

NJ, 1997—. Contbr. Mem.: Sci. Writers N.Y. Republican. Roman Catholic. Avocations: world literature, public policy journals, scriptwriting, pipe organ building. Office: Stevens Inst Tech Office of Development Castle Point on Hudson Hoboken NJ 07030

BERZON, MARSHA S. federal judge; BA, Radcliffe Coll., 1966; JD, Boalt Hall Sch. Law, 1973. Bar: Calif. 1973, D.C. 1975. Clerk Judge James Browning, 9th Cir., 1973—74, Justice William Brennan, 1974—75; atty. Woll & Mayer, Washington, 1975—77, Altshuler, Berzon, Nussbaum, Berzon & Rubin, San Francisco, 1978—2000; judge U.S. Ct. Appeals 9th Cir., 2000—. Office: US Ct Appeals 9th Cir PO Box 193939 San Francisco CA 94119-3939

BESADA, HANY GAMIL, international affairs administrator, researcher; b. Macordi, Nigeria, Dec. 25, 1978; s. Gamil Fawzy Besada and Samia Aziz Malak. BA, U.S. Internat. U., San Diego, Calif., 2000, MA, 2001. Cert. Fgn. Svc. Asst. web monitor Web Side Story, San Diego, 2000; office mgr. U.S. Senator Dianne Feinstein, San Diego, 2000; asst. office mgr. UN Assn., San Diego, 2000; program coord. Amnesty Internat., San Diego, 1999—. Scholar People to People Internat., 1997—2000, Acad. Polit. Sci., 1999—2000, Leadership Inst., Arlington, Va., 2000—. Participant U.S. Naval Inst., Arlington, Va., 1997, 1999; spkr. Model UN, L.A., 1998; observer Acad. Coun. on UN Systems, N.Y.C., 1999. Mem.: World Coptic Assn., Amnesty Internat., Rotoract Internat., Ctr. Internat. Studies, Alumni of U.S. Internat. U., Am. Red Cross. Avocations: travel, reading French/Arabic literature, chess, writing poetry. Office: PO Box 232443 San Diego CA 92193

BESANT, DEREK MICHAEL, artist, educator; b. Ft. MacLeod, Alta., Can., July 15, 1950; m. Alexandra Haeseker, Aug. 1, 1974. BFA, U. Calgary, 1973, postgrad., 1974. Exhbn. designer Glenbow-Alta. Inst. Art Gallery and Mus., 1973-77; instr. Alta. Coll. Art, 1977—. Guest lectr. S.W. Tex. State U., San Marcos, 1982. Exhbns. include Can. Rep. Brit. Internat. Biennale, 1979, Bronx Mus., N.Y., Calgary Arch. and Urban Studies Alliance, Cabo Fio Internat. Biennial, Brazil, Premio Internat. Biella per L'Incisione, Italy, Salon des Nations, Paris, Biennale Internat. de Gravure, Yugoslavia, 4th Internat. Seoul (Korea) Biennale, Brit. Drawing Biennale, Middlesborough, Eng., Internat. Print Exhibit, China, 1983, Norske Internat. Biennale, Norway, 1984, Fredrikstad Biennale, Norway, 1984, 7th Tokyo Video Festival, 1985, Ethiopia Exhbn., Akron (Ohio) Art Mus., 1985, Ibiza (Spain) Internat., 1985, Kyoto (Japan) City Mus., 1985, Queensland Coll. Art Australian Tour, 1985, Artists' Response to Arch., Victoria, Tex., 1986, Para Mus. Art, Poland, 1986, Mira Godard Gallery, Toronto, 1986, U. New Delhi, 1986, Glenbow Mus., Banff, Alta., 1986, The Dong-A-Ilbo, Korea, 1986, Premio Biella Internat., Italy, 1987, Galantal Artpool Mus. Fine Arts, Budapest, Hungary, 1987, 12th Internat. Biennale, Krakow, Poland, 1988, Met. Mus., Miami, Fla., 1988, Internat. Buchkunst, Leipzig, 1989, S.W. Tex. Artforum, 1989, Mira Godard, Toronto, 1989, Wolujen/Udell/Vancouver, 1989, Gütersloh, Germany, 1989, Premio Biella, Italy, 1990, Art Gallery Hamilton, 1990, 3rd Biennale Intenrat., Cuba, 1990, 11th Brit. Internat. Biennale, 1991, Kharkov Art Mus., USSR, 1991, 1st Internat. Congress, Brussels, 1991, 6th Internat. Bapha Varna Biennale, Mus. Art, Bulgaria Internat. Triennale, 1991, Krakow Poland/Nünberg, Germany, 1991, Museu d'Arte de Sabadell, Barcelona, 1992, Ctr. de la Gravure, Et De L'Image Imprimee, Belgium, 1992, MECC, Maastricht, Holland, 1993, 8th Internat. Lodz Biennale, Poland, 1994, Flash Art Project, Berlin, 1994, Can. Festival Sao Paulo, Brazil, 1994, Wingfield Arts and Music Festival, Eng., 1994, Curs Internat. de Arquitectura, Spain, 1994, Mus. de'Arte Contemporaneo, Ags, Mex., 1995, Centrum voor Kunsten Openluchtmus., Gent, Belgium, 1995, Invitational Internat. Biella per l'Incisione, Italy, 1996, Deutsche Internat. Triennale Kunstverien Frechen Stadtsaal, Germany, 1996, Mus. Art, Yugoslavia, 1996, Art Contemporain et Multificiplinarité Found. Derouin, Val-David, Que., 1997, City Mus. Art, Poland, 1997, Centro de Arte Moderno, Buenos Aires, 2000, Mus. fuer Moderne Kunst Weddel, Germany, 2000, Florean Mus, Maramures, Romania, 2000, Kunstverein Bad Salzdetfurth, Germany, 2000, Janus Mus., Denmark, 2001, Nickle Arts Mus., Canada, 2001, Shanghai Mus., China, 2002; recent works include Flatiron Mural W. wall Gooderham Flatiron Bldg., Toronto, 1980, video documentation Christo-Surrounded Islands, Miami; commns.: Cineplex Odeon, N.Y.C., 1989, Scotia Plz., Toronto, 1989, Mount Royal Coll., Calgary, Can., 1989, Daydream Glass Skywalk, Calgary, 1995, Songlines Fibre Optic outdoor drawing Olympic Park, Can., 2002. Recipient 2nd prize Miami Internat. Biennale, 1977, World Culture prize for Letters, Arts and Sci., 1984, Centro Studi e Ricerche delle Nazioni, Italy, disting. alumni award U. Calgary, 1999; Can. Coun. grantee, 1985. Home: Box 48081 Midlake RPO 40 Midlake Blvd SE Calgary AB Canada T2X 3C0 Office: 1407 14th Ave NW Calgary AB Canada T2N 4R3 E-mail: besantd@cadvision.com.

BESANT, LARRY XON, librarian, administrator, consultant; b. Centralia, Ill., Mar. 13, 1935; s. Ben Vern and Marjorie Loyce (Jarboe) B.; m. A. Jean Hofstetter, Dec. 31, 1953; children: Vicki, Lizabeth, Paul, Peter, Mary AA, Centralia Jr. Coll., Ill., 1959; BS in Chemistry, U. Ill., Urbana, 1961, MSL.S., 1962. Asst. librarian Chem. Abstract Assn., Columbus, Ohio, 1962-68; asst. dir. U. Houston Library, 1968-71, Ohio State U. Library, Columbus, 1972-82; dir. libraries Linda Hall Library, Kansas City, Mo., 1982-85; dir. libraries Camden-Carroll Library Morehead (Ky.) State U., Ky., 1985—. Library cons. in field; speaker in field Contbr. numerous articles, revs. to Library Mgmt. Bull., Am. Libraries, other profl. publs. Served with USAF, 1954-57. Mem. ALA, Spl. Libra. Assn. (pres. Ky. chpt. 1996-97, 2002-2003), Ky. Libr. Assn. Democrat. Baptist. Avocations: fishing, book collecting (jack london). Home: 428 N Wilson Ave Morehead KY 40351-1172 Office: Morehead State U Camden-Carroll Libr Morehead KY 40351 E-mail: l.besant@morehead-st.edu.

BESAW, JENNEA D. music educator, entrepreneur; b. Dallas, Tex., Aug. 10, 1974; d. Danny E and Belinda Lee Potter; m. James Michael Besaw, June 9, 2001. Legal asst. Law Offices of R.E. Luna, Dallas, 1996—97; strategic change knowledge mgmt. PriceWaterhouse Coopers, Dallas, 1997—2001; owner/pres. Little Musicmaker, Arlington, Tex., 2001—. Ednl. rep. Brook Mays Music, Ft. Worth, 2001—. Author: (web site development) littlemusicmaker.com. Mem.: Music Teacher's Nat. Assn., Am. Coll. of Musicians, Tex. Music Teacher's Assn., Nat. Guild of Piano Teachers. Achievements include development of music education program offered to preschools. Avocation: running. E-mail: jennead@attbi.com.

BESCH, EMERSON LOUIS, physiology educator, past academic administrator; b. Hammond, Ind., June 9, 1928; s. Ernest Henry and Carolyn (Dieckmann) B.; m. H. Jean Whitstine, May 28, 1955; children: Karen J., Kevin D., Kathleen L., Kristine A. BS in Biology/Chemistry, S.W. Tex. State U., 1952, MA in Biology/Chemistry, 1955; PhD in Physiology, U. Calif., Davis, 1964. Grad. instr. biology dept. S.W. Tex. State U., San Marcos, 1954-55; research asst., NIH trainee U. Calif., Davis, 1960-64, research physiologist, lectr., 1964-67; research assoc. Pacific Missile Range, USN, Point Mugu, Calif., 1960-64; from assoc. to full prof., head dept. physiology Kans. State U., Manhattan, 1967-74, from assoc. to full prof. mech. engring., 1967-74; prof. mech. engring. U. Fla., Gainesville, 1974-93; prof. physiology U. Fla. Coll. Vet. Medicine, Gainesville, 1974-93, assoc. dean, 1974-87, acting dean, 1980-81, exec. assoc. dean, 1987-88, prof. emeritus, 1993—. Served to capt. USNR. Fellow Aerospace Med. Assn. (exec. council 1985-88, profl. excellence award 1987); mem. Am. Physiology Soc., Soc. for Exptl. Biology & Medicine, Aerospace Physiologist Soc. (pres. 1984-86), Am. Soc. Heating, Refrigerating & Air Conditioning Engring. Achievements include research in environmental physiology and acceleration biology. Home: 15207 Rompel Trail Dr San Antonio TX 78232-4255 Office: U Fla Coll Vet Medicine PO Box 100144 Gainesville FL 32610-0144

BESCH, EVERETT DICKMAN, veterinarian, university dean and educator emeritus; b. Hammond, Ind., May 4, 1924; s. Ernst Henry and Carolyn (Dieckmann) B.; m. Mellie Darnell Brockman, Apr. 3, 1946; children: Carolyn Darnell, Ceryl Lynn, Cynthia Lee, Charlotte Ann, Everett Dickman. D.V.M., Tex. A&M Coll., 1954; M.P.H., U. Minn., 1956; PhD, Okla. State U., 1963. Instr. U. Minn., 1954-56; asst. prof. Okla. State U., 1956-64, prof., head dept. vet. parasitology and pub. health, 1964-68; dean Sch. Vet. Medicine, La. State U., 1968-88, prof., 1988-89. Sec.-treas. Assn. Am. Vet. Med. Colls., 1974-78, sec. coun. deans, 1976-80, chmn. coun. deans, 1980-81; mem. Nat. Adv. Coun. Health Professions Edn., 1982-86; treas. Am. Vet. Med. Found., 1991-93, v.p., 1993-94, pres., 1994-95, mem., 1995-97; bd. dirs. Coun. Agrl. Sci. and Tech., 1992-95. Contbr. articles to profl. publs., chpts. to books. Served with USN, 1942-48. Mem. AVMA (ho. of dels. 1988-91, exec. bd. 1991-97), Assn. Tchrs. Vet. Pub. Health and Preventive Medicine (pres. 1968), La. Vet. Med. Assn., Tex. Vet. Med. Assn., Conf. Pub. Health Veterinarians (pres. 1971-72), Am. Assn. Food Hygiene Veterinarians (pres. 1976-77), Am. Assn. Vet. Parasitologists (pres. 1964-65). Achievements include research in arthropod vectors of disease, internal parasites of ruminants. Home: 1453 Ashland Dr Baton Rouge LA 70806-7838

BESCH, HENRY ROLAND, JR., pharmacologist, educator; b. San Antonio, Sept. 12, 1942; s. Henry Roland and Monette Helen (Kasten) B.; m. Frankie R. Drejer; 1 child, Kurt Theodore. B.Sc. in Physiology, Ohio State U., 1964, PhD in Pharmacology (USPHS predoctoral trainee 1964-67), 1967; USPHS postdoctoral trainee, Baylor U. Coll. Medicine, Houston, 1968-70. Instr. ob-gyn. Ohio State U. Med. Sch., Columbus, 1967-68; asst. prof. Ind. U. Sch. Medicine, Indpls., 1971-73, assoc. prof., 1973-77, prof., 1977, chmn. pharmacology and toxicology, 1977—2002, Showalter prof., 1980—; dir. Ind. State Dept. Toxicology, Indpls., 1991-96, dir. emeritus, 1996—. Can. Med. Rsch. Coun. vis. prof., 1979, Swiss Fed. Tech. Inst. vis. prof., 1995; investigator fed. grants, mem. nat. panels and coms.; cons. in field. Contbr. numerous articles pharm. and med. jours.; mem. editorial bds. profl. jours. Fellow Brit. Med. Research Council, 1970-71; Grantee Showalter Trust, 1975— Fellow Am. Coll. Cardiology, Am. Coll. Forensic Examiners; mem. AAAS, Am. Assn. Clin. Chemistry, Am. Physiol. Soc., Am. Soc. Biochem. Molecular Biology, Am. Soc. Pharmacology and Exptl. Therpeutics, Assn. Med. Sch. Pharmacologists (exec. com. 1985-96, pres. 1994-96), Biochem. Soc., Cardiac Muscle Soc., Internat. Soc. Heart Rsch. (exec. com. Am. sect. 1986-92), Nat. Acad. Clin. Biochemistry, N.Y. Acad. Scis., Sigma Xi. Office: Ind U Sch Medicine 635 Barnhill Dr Indianapolis IN 46202-5126 E-mail: besch@indiana.edu.

BESCH, NANCY ADAMS, county official; b. Lancaster, Pa., Nov. 12, 1926; AB in Psychology, Wilson Coll., 1948, LHD, hon. doctor of humane letters, 1989. Commr., vice chair Cumberland County, 1992-95, commr., chair, 1995—. Bd. dirs., publ. info. tng. com. chair County Commrs.' Assn. of Pa.; Capital Region Chamber of Commerce "Envision" Task Force; v. chmn. So. Ctrl. Assembly for Effective Governance; Capital Region Econ. Devel. Corp. Bd. Coun. mem. Camp Hill Borough, 1984-91; bd. dirs. Camp Hill Sch., 1975-81; commr. liaison Cumberland County Libr. Sys. Bd.; mem. exec. bd. Cumberland-Perry Mental Health/Mental Retardation, comm. mem. cmty. adv. bd. Harrisburg Acad. 1998-2001; mem. Capital Region Funders Collaborative, Cmty. Connections, Keystone Area Coun. Boy Scouts (exec. com., mem. Bd. of NE Coun. Boy Scouts of Am.), Fund Devel. Com. Hemlock Girl Scout Coun., Inc. 1980-99, Cmty. Devel. Block Grant Adv. Com. of Pa. Dept. of Cmty. and Econ. Devel., Cumberland County Children and Youth Svcs. Adv. Com., DUI Task Force, Domestic Violence Svcs. Cumberland and Perry Counties; polity com. Presbytery of Carlisle; personnel sub-com. Synod of The Trinity Presbyn. Church, USA. Recipient Outstanding Publ. Ofcl. award, Pa. Assn. County Human Svcs., 1998, Pa.'s Mem. of Yr. award County Commr.'s Assn., 1997, Dist. Daughters of Pa. award, awarded by Govnr. Ridge, 1997, Catalyst award Capital Region Econ. Devel. Corp. for Leadership in Support of Devel. in Harrisburg Region, 1994, Elected Ofcls. award Pa. Libr. Assn., 1993, Trustee award Dist. Svc. Wilson Coll., 1988, Dist. Alum. award, Wilson Coll. 1989, Hemlock award for Svc. Hemlock Girl Scout Coun., Ketchum, Inc. award for Leadership in Am. Philanthropy, "Thanks" Badge Girl Scouts of Am., hon. membership prog. agy. Presbyn. Church U.S.A.; fellow Am. Assn. State Psychology Bds., 1991, Silver Beaver award Keystone Area Coun. Boy Scouts Am., 1999; named to "Movers and Shakers in Central Pa." List Ctrl. Pa. Bus. Jour., 1998. Mem. Susquehanna Alliance, West Shore Chamber of Commerce, Cumberland Cty. Hist. Soc., Cumberland Cty. Transp. Authority. Home: 209 Willow Ave Camp Hill PA 17011-3653

BESCHER, ERIC PASCAL, engineering educator, researcher; s. Mauryce Yves Bescher. Maitrise Chimie Physique des Matériaux, Unive. de Rennes, France, 1987; M.S. in Materials Sci. and Engring., Ph.D. in Materials Sci. and Engring., UCLA, 1997. Dir. rsch. CTS Cement, LA, 2000; adj. asst. prof. UCLA, 2002—. Contbr. articles to profl. jours. Mem.: Am. Chem. Soc.

BESDINE, RICHARD WILLIAM, medical educator, scientist; b. N.Y.C., Apr. 12, 1940; s. Alan Xerus and Betty (Bronstein) Besdine; m. Judith Anne Bailey, June 22, 1963 (div. May 1980); m. Fox Wetle, July 1, 1981; children: Molly Bailey Besdine, Sarah Besdine Freedman. BS cum laude, Haverford Coll., 1961; MD, U. Pa., 1965. Diplomate in internal medicine and in infectious diseases and geriatrics Am. Bd. Internal Medicine; diplomate Nat. Bd. Med. Examiners. Intern Beth Israel Hosp. Medicine, Boston, 1965-66, asst. resident in internal medicine, 1966-67, fellow in immunology and infectious diseases, 1969-72; rsch. fellow in medicine Harvard Med. Sch., Boston, 1969-72, instr. in medicine, 1972-75, asst. prof. medicine, 1975-86, lectr. in medicine, 1986-89; assoc. prof. medicine, cmty. medicine and healthcare U. Conn. Health Ctr. Sch. Medicine, 1986-89, dir. Travelers Ctr. on Aging, assoc. prof. family medicine, 1988-2000; prof. medicine, cmty. medicine and healthcare U. Conn. Sch. Medicine, 1990-2000; from asst. to assoc. in medicine Beth Israel Hosp., 1972-75, asst. physician in medicine, 1975-82; assoc. physician in medicine Brigham and Women's Hosp. and Beth Israel Hosps., 1982-88; prof. medicine, Greer prof. geriatric medicine, dir. Ctr. Gerontology and Health Care Rsch., dir. divsn. geriat. Brown Med. Sch., 2000—; interim dean medicine and biol. scis. Brown U., 2002—. Staff internist Hebrew Rehab. Ctr. for Aged, Roslindale, Mass., 1972-86, dir. geriatric med. edn., 1981-86; attending med. staff John Dempsey Hosp., 1986—, Hebrew Home and Hosp., 1987—, McLean Home and Village, 1987—; mem. cons. med. staff Inst. Living, Newington VA Med. Ctr.; cons., presenter in field; Noble Wiley Jones lectr. U. Oreg. Health Scis. Ctr., Portland, 1980; mem. Harvard-Hastings Project on Ethical Issues in Care of Elderly, 1982-86; vis. prof. U. Toronto Sch. Medicine, 1983, Montreal (Can.) Neurol. Inst., 1984, U. Geneva, 1990, U. Mich., 1991, U. Wis., 1991, Baylor U., 1991, U. Kans. Med. Ctr., 1992, Fallon Clinic and Health Plan, 1992; chair fed. task force on geriatric edn. NIH, 1986; mem. adv. bd. John A. Hartford Found. grant Johns Hopkins U. Sch. Medicine, 1994; chmn. western delegation Seminar on Aging, Singapore, Hong Kong, Taipei and Kuala Lumpur, 1987; mem. spl. adv. group White House Conf. on Aging, 1980-81; mem. task force on reversible dementia in the elderly Nat. Inst. on Aging, 1978-80; dir. health stds. and quality bur., chief med. officer Healthcare Fin. Adminstrn., 1995-97. Co-author: Handbook of Geriatric Care, 1982; editor: Health and Disease in Old Age, 1982, 2d edit., 1988; mem. editl. bd. Geriat. Rev. Syllabus, 1989, 93, 96, assoc. editor, 1991, 93, 96; contbr. chpts. to books and articles to profl. jours. Surgeon USPHS Nat. Ctrs. for Disease Control, 1967—69; bd. dirs. Inst. for Cmty. Rsch., Hartford, 1987—2000, New Britain Meml. Hosp., 1993, Am. Fedn. for Aging Rsch., 1993—, Am. Geriat. Soc., 1994—, Alzheimers Assn., 1998. Royal Soc. Medicine Found. travelling fellow U. Glasgow, 1972; grantee Geriatric Edn. Ctr., 1983-91, John A. Hartford Found., 1988-94, Charles A. Dana Found., 1988-90, Conn. State Dept. on Aging, 1989-91, Travelers Rsch. Inst. on Health Promotion and Aging, 1990, Howard and Bush Found., 1990, Robert Wood Johnson Found., 1991-93, Travelers Found., 1991, 92, 94, NIH Pepper Ctr., 1996. Fellow ACP, Am. Geriat. Soc. (pres.-elect 2002, Milo D. Leavitt award 1991), Gerontol. Soc. Am. (Joseph T. Freeman award 1995), Am. Soc. Aging (Pres. award 1997). Home: 33 Broadview Dr Barrington RI 02806 Office: Brown Med Sch Box G-B Providence RI 02912 E-mail: richard_besdine@brown.edu.

BESEN, JANE PHYLLIS TRIPTOW, retired civic worker; b. Chgo., Aug. 6, 1921; d. Richard Herman and Rose (Krips) Triptow; m. Irving Besen, Mar. 25, 1951 (dec. 1978); children: Glenn, Allen. Student, Northwestern U., 1946-47, East Los Angeles Coll., 1967-68; BA in English, Calif. State U., L.A., 1978; postgrad. in English. Exec. sec. Chgo. Ordnance Dist., War Dept., 1941-46, Aubrey, Moore & Wallace Advt. Agy., Chgo., 1946; exec. sec. sales office McGraw-Hill Pub. Co., Chgo., 1947-51; exec. sec. Security Pacific Nat. Bank, L.A., 1978-90. Pub. Happy Literary Mag. N.Y., issues 2, 9, 10, 11, 12, 13, 1995-99. Publicity chmn. Am. Field Svc., 1967-68; sec. Citizens Com. for Good Govt., 1961; capt. United Crusade, Monterey Park, Calif., 1967—; publicity chmn. Monterey Park Art Assn., 1966-67, corr. sec., 1968, dir., 1965—, past pres., dir. newsletter, 1970—; chmn. Monterey Park Arts and Culture Com.; dir. in charge Bruggemeyer Libr. Shows, 1973-74; dep. registrar voters Calif. State U., L.A., 1971-74; 3d v.p. in charge publicity Cmty. Concerts Monterey Park, 1988—, pres., 1995—. Named Democrat of Yr., L.A. Ctrl. Com., Calif. Dem. Party. Mem. LWV (sec. Alhambra chpt. 1971-73, pres. chpt. 1973-74, action chmn., publicity chmn. 1977-78, hospitality chmn. 1980—), Nat. League Am. Pen Women (rec. sec., treas. 1961-65), United Dem. Club Monterey Park (pres. 1997, 98, sec. 1999-2000), Residents Assn. Monterey Park, Northwestern U. Alumni So. Calif. (corr. sec. 1979-80). Home: 1540 S Arriba Dr Monterey Park CA 91754-2350

BESEN, STANLEY MARTIN, economist; b. Bklyn., Dec. 17, 1937; s. Moe and Sylvia (Forgang) B.; m. Marlene Dublirer, June 10, 1961; children: Roberta Ann, Elizabeth Rebecca. BBA, CCNY, 1958; MA, Yale U., 1960, PhD, 1964. Acting asst. prof. econs. U. Calif.-Santa Barbara, 1962-63; economist Inst. Def. Analyses, 1963-65; mem. faculty Rice U., Houston, 1965-80, prof. econs., 1974-79, Cline prof. econs. and fin., 1979-80; co-dir. network inquiry spl. staff FCC, 1978-80; sr. economist Rand Corp., Washington, 1980-92; v.p. Charles River Assocs., Washington, 1992—. Vis. Henley prof. law and bus. Columbia U., 1988—89; vis. prof. law and econs. Georgetown U. Law Ctr., 1990—91; mem. task force nat telecomms. policy making Aspen Inst. Program Comms. and Society, 1977; mem. adv. panel on intellectual property rights in an age of electronics and info. Office of Tech. Assessment, 1984—85, mem. adv. panel on comms. sys. for an info. age, 1986—88; mem. com. on internet searching and the domain name sys. The Nat. Acads. Computer Sci. and Telecomm. Bd., 2001—; mem. bd. on earth scis. and resources, com. on licensing geographic data and svcs. NRC, 2003—. Author: Misregulating Television: Network Dominance and the FCC, 1984, also articles; co-editor Rand Jour. Econs., 1985-88; mem. editorial bds. profl. jours. Fellow Brookings Instn., 1971-72, NSF, 1973-75 Home: 4918 Western Ave Bethesda MD 20816-1714 Office: Charles River Assocs 1201 F St NW Ste 700 Washington DC 20004-1204 E-mail: sbesen@crai.com.

BESHAR, PETER JUSTUS, lawyer; b. N.Y.C., Nov. 20, 1961; s. Robert Peter and Christine (Wedemeyer) B.; m. Sarah Jones, Jan. 5, 1991; children: Isabel Emma, Henry Frederick, Sophie Charlotte. BA, Yale U., 1984; JD, Harvard U., 1989. Bar: N.Y. 1989. Law clerk the Hon. Vincent L. Broderick, N.Y.C., 1989-90; spl. asst. to the Hon. Cyrus Vance, Internat. Conf. on the Former Yugoslavia, 1992-93; asst. atty. gen. Office of Atty. Gen., N.Y.C., 1994; ptnr. Gibson, Dunn & Crutcher, N.Y.C., 1995—. Trustee Rye Country Day Sch. Mem. Coun. on Fgn. Rels. Office: Gibson Dunn & Crutcher 200 Park Ave Fl 47 New York NY 10166-0193

BESHAR, ROBERT PETER, lawyer; b. N.Y.C., Mar. 3, 1928; m. Christine von Wedemeyer, Dec. 20, 1953; children: Cornelia, Jacqueline, Frederica, Peter. AB honors with exceptional distinction, Yale U., 1950, LLB, 1953. Bar: N.Y. 1954. Asst. gen. counsel Waterfront Commn. N.Y. Harbor, 1954-55; law sec. Hon. Charles D. Breitel, Appellate div. 1st dept. N.Y. Supreme Ct., N.Y.C., 1956-58; spl. hearing officer Justice Dept., 1967-68; dep. asst. sec. Commerce; dir. Bur. Internat. Commerce; nat. export expansion coordinator Commerce Dept., Washington, 1971-72; pvt. practice, N.Y.C., 1972-2000; pres. various family enterprises, 1993—. Bd. dirs. Nat. Semicondr. Corp. (audit and dir's. affairs coms., counsel to bd. dirs. 1972-98); mem. bus. adv. panel Nat. Commn. for Rev. of Antitrust Laws, 1978-79; mem. Mcpl. Securities Rulemaking Bd., 1982-85; bd. govs. Fgn. Policy Assn., 1991—. Author: Current Legal Aspects of Doing Business With Sino-Soviet Nations, 1973; editor: Manhattan Auto Study, 1973. Trustee Westchester Coll. Found., 1992—; mem. Planning Bd. of Somers, 1984-97. Scholar of the House, Yale U., 1950. Mem. ABA (chmn. corp. and antitrust law com. 1982-85), N.Y. State Bar Assn., Elizabethan and Gypsy Trail Clubs, Phi Beta Kappa. Home: 120 E End Ave New York NY 10028-7552 also: PO Box 533 Somers NY 10589-0533 E-mail: rpbeshar@netscape.net.

BESHEAR, STEVEN LYNN, lawyer; b. Dawson Springs, Ky., Sept. 21, 1944; AB, U. Ky., Lexington, 1966, JD, 1968. Bar: N.Y. 1969, Ky. 1971. Assoc. White and Case, N.Y.C., 1968-70; later ptnr. Beshear, Meng and Green, Lexington; mem. Ky. Ho. of Reps., 1974-79; atty. gen. State of Ky., Frankfort, 1979-83, lt. gov., 1983-87; ptnr. Stites & Harbison, Lexington, 1987—. Bd. editors, Ky. Law Jour., (1967-68.). Mem. Fayette County Bar Assn., Ky. Bar Assn., ABA, Order of Coif, Phi Beta Kappa, Phi Delta Phi, Omicron Delta Kappa. Office: Stites & Harbison Lexington Fin Ctr 250 W Main St Ste 2300 Lexington KY 40507-1758 E-mail: sbeshear@stites.com.

BESHEARS, CHARLES DANIEL, insurance executive; b. Vandalia, Mo., Sept. 6, 1917; s. Charles D. and Anabel (Baker) B.; m. Mildred Domreis, Nov. 1941 (deceased); m. Louise Davis Clarke, Sept. 1980; children: Jacqueline, Charles, Scott (dec.), Melanie; stepchildren: Crescente, Maria-Asuncion, Hernan Errazuriz. Grad. exec. program bus. mgmt., UCLA, 1968; advanced mgmt. program, Harvard U., 1971; diplomas in property and casualty ins. and mgmt., Ins. Inst. Am.; grad., Am. Coll. Life Underwriters, 1978. CLU. With Farmers Ins. Group, L.A., 1937—79, v.p. field ops., 1966—68, v.p. charge property and casualty ops., 1968—73; pres., dir. Farmers New World Life Ins. Co., Mercer Island, Wash., 1973—79; dir. Ohio State Life Ins. Co., 1973—79, Investors Guaranty Life Ins. Co., 1973—79; cons. Chilean Ins. Industry, 1980—95; pres. Reaseguros Britania, Chile, 1999—. Bd. govs., honors. com. Internat. Ins. Soc. Inc. With USAAF, ETO, 1942-45. Mem. DAV, VFW, Am. Legion, Non-Commd. Officers Assn., Chile Club. Address: Casilla 331 Correo 12 La Reina Santiago Chile *You can accomplish any goal you want to set for yourself, if the desire is strong enough. Are you willing to pay the price?.*

BESHEARS, ROBERT GENE, lawyer; b. Charleston, Ark., Aug. 24, 1931; s. Allen and Goldie (Stovall) B.; m. Doris M. Muchmore, Dec. 31, 1952 (div. Aug. 1978); children— John Robert, Michael Arthur, Charles Phillip; m. Ardys K. Frederick, Nov. 2, 1978; children— Jodi, Tami. B.S.B.A., U. Ariz., 1958, LL.B., 1959. Bar: Ariz. 1959, U.S. Dist. Ct. Ariz. 1959, U.S. Ct. Appeals (9th cir.) 1975. Assoc. Cavanagh & O'Connor, Phoenix, 1959-63; ptnr. O'Connor, Cavanagh, Anderson, Westover, Killingsworth & Beshears, Phoenix, 1963— . Bd. editors Ariz. Law Rev., 1958-59. Contbr. articles to profl. jours. Active various civic fund-raising activities. Served with USAF, 1951-55. Pima County Bar Aux. scholar U. Ariz., 1958. Mem. Am. Bd. Trial Advs. (adv.), Internat. Assn. Def. Counsel (exec. com.), Fedn. Ins. Counsel, Phoenix Assn. Def. Counsel, Assn. Trial Lawyers Am., Personal Injury Trial lawyers Assn., Beta Gamma Sigma, Phi Kappa Phi. Republican. Episcopalian. Clubs: Paradise Valley Country, University, Plaza (Phoenix); Pinetop Country (Ariz.). Office: O'Connor Cavanagh Anderson 1 E Camelback Rd Ste 1100 Phoenix AZ 85012-1691

BESING, RAY GILBERT, lawyer, writer, lecturer; b. Roswell, N.Mex., Sept. 14, 1934; s. Ray David and Maxine Mable (Jordan) B.; children: Christopher, Gilbert, Andrew, Paul. Student, Rice U., 1952-54; BA, Ripon Coll., 1957; post grad., Georgetown U., 1957; JD, So. Methodist U., 1960. Bar: Tex. 1960. Ptnr. Geary, Brice, Barron, & Stahl, Dallas, 1960-74; sr. ptnr. Besing, Baker & Glast, Dallas, 1974-77; prin. Law Offices of Ray G. Besing, P.C., Dallas, 1977—. Lectr. trial procedures So. Meth. Sch. of Law, 1966-68; guest lectr. comm. law and policy, univ. and industry conf., 1984—; lectr. Bologna Ctr. of Johns Hopkins U., Nitze Sch. Advanced Internat. Studies, 1999; sr. rsch. fellow faculty law U. Coll. London, 2002-. Author: Who Broke Up AT&T?: From Ma Bell to the Internet, 2000; mng. editor, So. Methodist U. Law Jour., 1959-60. Pres. Dallas Cerebral Palsy Found., 1970; trustee Ripon Coll., 1969—76; mem. Tex. Gov.'s Transition Team on Telecom, 1982; bd. dirs. Dallas Symphony, 1972, Dallas Theatre Ctr., 1971, Found. for Santa Fe C.C., 2001—03, Found. for Santa Fe Concert Assn., 2003—. Tex. Moot Ct. champion, 1958 Mem. Tex. Bar Assn., Dallas Bar Assn., Dallas Jr. C. of C. (v.p. 1964), Sigma Chi. Democrat. Episcopalian (mem. exec. council diocese Dallas, 1969-72).

BESLEY, MORRISH ALEXANDER (TIM BESLEY), civil engineer; b. New Plymouth, New Zealand, Mar. 14, 1927; arrived in Australia, 1950; s. Hugh Morrish and Isobel (Alexander) B.; m. Nancy Marguerite Cave, Feb. 15, 1952 (dissolved 2001); children: Trevor J., Grant A., Rodney G.; m. Sarah Harrington, Aug. 11, 2001; children: Hugh I., Hannah Alice. BE in Civil Engring., U. New Zealand, 1950; B Legal Studies, Macquarrie U., Sydney, Australia, 1984; Barrister at Law, Supreme Ct. NSW, 1985; DSc (hon.), Macquarrie U., 2002. Chartered profl. engr., Australia. Engr. Ministry of Works, New Zealand, 1950; with Snowy Mountains Hydro-Electric Authority, 1950-67; 1st asst. sec. Dept. External Territories, 1967-72; exec. mem. Fgn. Investment Review Bd., 1975-76; 1st asst. sec. Dept. of Treasury, 1973-76; sec. Commonwealth Dept. Bus. and Consumer Affairs, ACT, Australia, 1976-81; comptroller gen. Customs, 1976-81; mng. dir. Monier Ltd., Sydney, 1982-87, chmn., CEO, 1987; chmn. Monier Redland Ltd., 1988, Redland Australia, 1988-95; exec. chmn. Commonwealth Indsl. Gases Ltd., Sydney, 1988-90; chmn. The CIG

Group, 1988-93, Commonwealth Banking Corp., 1988-91, Commonwealth Bank Australia, Sydney, 1991-99. Pres. Metal Trades Industry Assn., Sydney, 1989-91, nat. pres. 1990-92; chmn. Leighton Holdings Ltd., Sydney, 1990-2001. Chmn. Royal Bot. Gardens, Sydney, 1989—92; dir. O'Connell St. Assocs. Pty. Ltd., 1990—; mem. Red Shield Appeal Com., Sydney, 1987—99, Sydney Adv. Bd. The Salvation Army, 1994—99, Legacy Appeal Com., Sydney, 1988—2003; mem. mgmt. bd. Australian Grad. Sch. Mgmt., 1983—92, Chancellor Macquarrie U., 1994—2001; chmn. Australian Rsch. Coun., Sydney, Australia, 2002—. Decorated mem., officer and companion, Order of Australia. Fellow Australian Acad. Tech. Sci. and Engring. (pres. 1998-2002); mem. Royal Sydney Yacht Squadron, Nat. Press Club, Union Club, Elanora Country Club, Australian Club Sydney. Home: Pvt Box 304 Cammeray NSW 2062 Australia

BESMAN, PASCAL MICHEL, diversified financial services company executive; b. New York, Ny, Apr. 9, 1960; s. Jean-Pierre Jules and Rosette Annie B.; m. Linda Fuller, May 31, 1986; children: Chris Scott, Lauren Shae, Nastasia Kayleigh, Oliver Samuel. BS in Econs., London Sch. Econs., London, England, 1981. Certified Financial Manager Merrill Lynch, 1985, branch mgr. NASD, 1988, portforlio mgr. UBS, 2002. Sr. v.p. Lehman Bros., London, 1985—97; mng. dir. Bear Stearns, N.Y.C., NY, 1997—2001; sr. v.p. UBS, N.Y.C., 2001—. Author: Dead Heat; editor: (newsletter) Pascal's Update; editor: (financial editor) (magazine) American In London; interviewee (interview article) How to balance your portffolio; contbr. articles. Named Winner Bus. Mag. Portfolio Competition, 1986. Avocations: gastronomy, travel, oenology. Office: UBS 1285 6th Ave New York NY 10019 Home Fax: 516-487-4621; Office Fax: 212-713-6152. E-mail: pascal.besman@ubs.com.

BESOZZI, PAUL CHARLES, lawyer; b. N.Y.C., Aug. 22, 1947; s. Alfio Joseph and Lucy Agnes (Ducibella) B.; m. Caroline Lisa Hesterberg, Oct. 7, 1978; 1 child, Christina Claire. BS cum laude in Int. Affairs, Georgetown U., 1969, JD, 1972; MBA in Bus./Govt. Rels., George Washington U., 1977. Bar: Va. 1972, D.C. 1973, U.S. Ct. Mil. Appeals 1972, U.S. Ct. Appeals (4th cir.) 1978, U.S. Ct Appeals (3d cir.) 1996, U.S. Supreme Ct. 1977. Assoc. Arnold & Porter, Washington, 1977-80; gen. counsel, minority counsel U.S. Senate Com. on Armed Svcs., Washington, 1980-84; ptnr. Hennesey, Stambler & Siebert, P.C., Washington, 1984-86, Besozzi & Gavin, Washington, 1987-93, Besozzi, Gavin & Craven, Washington, 1993-95, Besozzi, Gavin, Craven & Schmitz, Washington, 1995-96, Patton Boggs LLP, Washington, 1996—. Editor Georgetown Law Jour., 1971-72; contbr. articles and revs. to legal jours. Alumni interviewer Georgetown U. Alumni Assn., Washington, 1981—, dir. Procurement Roundtable, 1991—; mem. bd. visitors Georgetown U. Sch. Fgn. Svc. Capt. JAGC, U.S. Army, 1972-76. Mem. Fed. Comms. Bar Assn., Georgetown U. Alumni Assn. (bd. govs. 1993—), Phi Beta Kappa, Phi Alpha Theta, Pi Sigma Alpha. Office: Patton Boggs LLP 2550 M St NW Ste 400 Washington DC 20037-1301 E-mail: pbesozzi@pattonboggs.com.

BESPALEC, DALE ANTHONY, clinical psychologist; b. Waukegan, Ill., Sept. 21, 1951; s. Anthony Frank Bespalec and Mildred B. (Glogovsky) Etolen; m. Marylou B. Bartholomae, June 23, 1973; 1 child, Christine Marie. BS magna cum laude with honors, Loyola U., 1973, MA, 1975, PhD, 1978. Lic. psychologist, Wis. Staff cons. psychologist Behavior and Mgmt. Cons., Inc., Milw., 1977-79; instr. U. Wis.-Parkside, Racine, 1979; staff psychologist St. Michael Hosp. Mental Health Ctr., Milw., 1979-86, mgr. outpatient, 1986-90; pvt. practice Milw., 1979-88; clinical prof. Wis. Sch. Profl. Psychology, Milw., 1985—, dir. clin. tng., 1990-92; mgr. mental health program Community Meml. Hosp., Menomonee Falls, Wis., 1992-96; sr. staff psychologist Taycheeda Correctional Inst., Fond du Lac, Wis., 1996-97, chief psychologist, 1997-2001; chief psychologist, sex offender treatment Bur. Health Svs., 2001—. Clin. instr. Med. Coll. Wis., Milw., 1981—. Contbr. articles to profl. jours. Past v.p. internal devel. Grafton Jaycees; past mem. bd. dirs United Way Ozaukee County; past chair ARC disaster svcs.; active Riveredge Nature Ctr. Fellow NIMH, 1973—74, USPH, 1973—74. Fellow: Wis. Psychol. Assn. (mem. adminstrv. coun. 1994—97, mem. divsn. 4 adv. bd. 1999—2000); mem.: APA, Wis. Assn. Treatment of Sexual Abusers (bd. dirs. 2003—), Am. Correctional Assn., Milw. Area Psychologists Assn. (pres. 1994—96), Alpha Sigma Nu. Roman Catholic. Avocations: horseback riding, gardening, hunting, historical reenactments. Office: 3099 E Washington Ave Madison WI 53704-4338

BESS, ALAN L. pharmaceutical executive, physician; b. Phila., Oct. 14, 1954; s. Harold L. and Elaine Bess; m. Kathryn Victoria Karas, Feb. 1, 1989; 1 child, James Millon. BA, Susquehanna U., 1976; MD, Temple U., 1980. Resident Thomas Jefferson U. Hosp., Phila., 1980-82; dir. med. svcs. Abbott Labs., North Chicago, 1982-86; sect. head drug safety Hoffmann-La Roche, Nutley, N.J., 1986-94, dir. drug safety, 1994-95, v.p. pharma devel. safety, 1995-2000; v.p. clin. safety and epidemiology Novartis Pharms., East Hanover, N.J., 2000—. Mem. AMA, Am. Acad. Pharm. Physicians, Am. Coll. Clin. Pharmacology, Pharm. Rsch. and Mfrs. Assn., Drug. Info. Assn., Inst. Internat. Rsch. Avocations: martial arts, antiquities. Home: 50 Westview Rd Wayne NJ 07470-6233 Office: Novartis Pharms 59 Route 10 East Hanover NJ 07936

BESS, JUDITH GREWELL, retired computer services executive, educator; b. New Orleans, Aug. 27, 1945; d. Raymond Walter and Dorothy Marie (Reymann) Potratz; m. John Nolting Grewell, Aug. 28, 1964 (dec.); children: Patricia Lynn, Amy Elizabeth; m. David Allen Bess, Oct. 29, 1999. BA with honors, Wayne State U., 1972; MA with honors, Oakland U., 1976. Cert. prodn. and inventory mgmt. Am. Prodn. and Inventory Control Soc. Supr. mfg. Chevrolet-Pontiac-GM of Can. div., Pontiac, Mich., 1978-80, purchasing agt., 1980-82, trainer, organizational cons., 1982-84; supr. systems tng. Electronic Data Systems Div., Troy, Mich., 1985-86, supr. tech. tng. devel., 1986-88, supr. tng. and communications, 1988-89, prin. sr. cons. divsn., 1989-95, client server program dir., 1995-2000; ret., 2000; program mgmt. cons., 2000—02; univ. instr. Oakland U., 2000—. Co-author: Capacity Measurement and Improvement, 1996. Mem. Midwest Soc. Orgnl. Learning, Pi Lambda, Phi Upsilon Omicron. Republican. Baptist. Avocations: art, fitness, reading, investing. Home: 4645 Rue St Michelle West Bloomfield MI 48323-2243 E-mail: judybess@yahoo.com.

BESS, LLOYD GEORGE, radiologist; b. St. Louis, Apr. 5, 1941; s. George Calvin and Henrietta (Hodges) Bess; m. Elizabeth Carney Bess, Sept. 12, 1998; children from previous marriage: Erica Imrie, Barbara Rayfield. BA in Chemistry, U. N.C., 1963; MD, U. Miss., 1968. Diplomate Am. Bd. Radiology. Intern Maricopa County Gen. Hosp., Phoenix, 1968-69; resident in radiology U. Ark. Med. Sch., Little Rock, 1971-74; radiologist Delta Med. Ctr., Greenville, Miss., 1974-78, North Ark. Radiology Assocs., P.A., Batesville, 1978—. Lt. USN, 1969—71. Fellow: Am. Coll. Radiology; mem.: AMA, Internat. Arabian Horse Assn., Independence County Med. Soc., Soc. Nuc. Medicine, Ark. Med. Soc. (dist. coun. 1990—2001), Am. Inst. Ultrasound Medicine, So. Med. Assn. Episcopalian. Avocation: equestrian activities. Home: 918 Eagle Mountain Blvd Batesville AR 72501-4218 Office: North Ark Radiology Assocs 1490 Byers St Batesville AR 72501 5892 E-mail: igbess@yahoo.com.

BESS, OLEAN, educator, counselor; b. Florence, S.C., Feb. 23, 1934; d. Yankey and Mary Jane Baker; m. Willie Bess, Sept. 13, 1953 (dec. Sept. 1988); children: Barbara, Sandra. B in Liberal Arts, Coll. New Rochelle, 1988; MDiv, N.Y. Theol. Sem., 1992; DD, United Theol. Sem., 1995. Bookkeeper Paintset Fashions, N.Y.C., 1960-71; office mgr. Rug Hold Inc., N.Y.C., 1971-92; substitute tchr. Pub. Sch. #176, Laurlton, N.Y., 1992—. Part-time counselor N.Y. Hosp. Rickers Island Jail, N.Y.C. and Elmont, N.Y., 1992—, King Harbor Nursing Home, Bronx, 1992—. Author: Mixed Felling, 1972, Poems and Things, 1973, Our World Stopped Turning and I Stepped Off, 1999. Home: 191-14 113th Rd Saint Albans NY 11412

BESS, RONALD W. advertising executive; b. Bloomington, Ill., July 9, 1946; s. Bloice Monroe and Mary (Trussel) B.; m. Teresa N. Shute, July 22, 1970; children: Daniel, Laura. BS in Mktg., U. Ill., Champaign, 1968, M, 1972. Account exec. Foote, Cone and Belding, Chgo., 1972-75; v.p. account dir. Needham, Harper and Steers, Chgo., 1975-81; sr. v.p. group account dir. DDB Needham, Chgo., 1981-87; pres. Bayer Bess Vanderwarker, Chgo., Foote, Cone & Belding, Chgo.; chmn., CEO diversified group Young Rubicam Inc., N.Y.C. Office: Young Rubicam Inc 230 Park Ave S Ste 1300 New York NY 10003-1513

BESSE, RALPH MOORE, retired lawyer; b. Shadyside, Ohio, Nov. 23, 1905; s. Jesse Allman and Hope (Fish) B.; m. Augusta Woodward Mitchell, Apr. 28, 1934; children: Jean Elizabeth Besse Minehart, William Truman, Robert Allen. AB magna cum laude, Heidelberg Coll., 1926; JD, U. Mich., 1929; LL.D., Baldwin-Wallace Coll., 1957, Oberlin Coll., 1962, Case Inst. Tech., 1962, Western Res. U., 1963, Cleve. Marshall Law Sch., 1959; L.H.D., Wilberforce Coll., 1963, Ursuline Coll., 1970. Bar: Ohio 1930. Assoc. Squire, Sanders & Dempsey, 1929-40, ptnr., 1940-48, 70-85; with Cleve. Electric Illuminating Co., 1948-70, pres., 1960-67, chmn. bd., chief exec. officer, 1967-70; chmn. Nat. Machinery Co., 1962-90, bd. dirs., 1962-94. Author: Besse: What Can One Man Do. Contbr. articles to profl. jours. Mem. adv. bd. Ctr. for the Book, Libr. of Congress, 1979; chief U.S. Army Ordinance Cleve. Dist., 1951-62; trustee Nat. History Day, 1980, Ursuline Coll., 1963, 92, John Huntington Art and Poly. Trust, 1966-86, John Huntington Fund for Edn., 1966-86, Heidelberg Coll., 1949-80, Case Western Reserve U., 1970-76, chmn. bd. dirs., 1971-75. Recipient Cleve. medal for pub. service Cleve. C. of C., 1960, Ursula Laurus award Ursuline Coll., 1965, Eisenman award Jewish Community Fedn. Cleve., 1966, Human Relations award NCCJ, 1967, award Cleve. Bus. League, 1967, Univ. medal Case Western Res. U., 1976, Wisdom award of honor Wisdom Soc., 1979, Disting. Service award Ohio Coll. Assn., 1980, Disting. Alumni award U. Mich., 1981, James Dodman Nobel award Coun. Human Rels., 1982; named Father of Community Colls. in Ohio, 1961; elected to Ohio Found. of Ind. Colls. Hall of Fame, 2000, Ohio Found. Hall Excellence, 2000, Educator of Yr., Heidelberg Coll. Alumni, 2000; Ralph M. Besse chair in bus. established by Heidelberg Coll., 1979, Ralph M. Besse award for teaching excellence established by Cuyahoga Community Coll., 1980; numerous other awards Fellow Am. Bar Found.; mem. ABA, Ohio Bar Assn., Bar Assn. Greater Cleve. Home: Cleveland, Ohio. Died Oct. 25, 2002.

BESSE, RONALD DUNCAN, publishing company executive; b. Stayner, Ont., Can., Dec. 7, 1938; s. Josiah Reuben and Annie Mae (Buie) B.; m. Barbara Jane Low, Jan. 26, 1963; children: Christopher, Alison. Student, Ryerson Poly. Inst., 1957-60. From sales rep. to v.p. edn. div. McGraw-Hill Ryerson Ltd., Toronto, Ont., Can., 1960-70, pres., CEO, 1973-76; mng. dir., editorial dir. Latin Am. Libros McGraw-Hill Mex., 1970-73; pres. Consol. Graphics Ltd., Toronto, 1976-78; pres., CEO Gage Pub. Ltd., Toronto, 1978-84; chmn., pres., CEO Can. Pub. Corp., Scarborough, 1984—2001; chmn., CEO Gage Learning Corp., Toronto, Canada, 2001—. Chmn RDB Capital Corp.; bd. dirs. Rogers Comm. Inc., Rogers Media Inc., Toronto, Luxembourg Cambridge Holding Group, C.I. Mutual Funds (now C.I. Fund Mgmt. Inc.); pres. Granite Golf Inc., 2000-03. Past bd. govs. The Shaw Festival, Niagara-on-the-Lake; past chmn. Ont. Liberals, Heritage Dinner; active Bd. of Trade. Mem. Can. Publs. Coun., World Pres.' Orgn. (past chmn. Ont. chpt., past internat. dir., chmn.-emeritus Upper Can. chpt.), Internat. Chief Execs. Orgn., Granite Club (past pres.), Bd. Trade, 4872 Club (past chmn.), The National Club, Muskoka Lakes Golf and Country Club, Ocean Reef Club, Card Sound Golf Club. Home: 19 Farnham Ave Toronto ON Canada M4V 1H6 Office: Gage Learning Corp 164 Commander Blvd Toronto ON Canada M1S 3C7 E-mail: rbesse@gagelearning.com.

BESSELSEN, DAVID GUY, veterinary pathologist, researcher; b. Ft. Wayne, Ind., Apr. 12, 1963; s. Clarence "Dutch" and Nancy Marie Besselsen; m. Carol Ann Besselsen, June 16, 1990. DVM, U. Mo., Columbia, 1988, PhD, 1995. Assoc. vet. Snyder Animal Hosp., Jacksonville, Fla., 1988-90; rsch. assoc. U. Mo., Columbia, 1991, resident in lab. animal medicine, 1991-94, NIH postdoctoral fellow, 1991-95; chief univ. animal care pathology svcs. U. Ariz., Tucson, 1995—, vet. specialist, 1995—. Contbr. articles to profl. jours. including Jour. Clin. Microbiology, Comparative Medicine. Grantee ACLAM Found., 1998, NIH, 1999—. Mem. Am. Coll. Lab. Animal Medicine, Am. Assn. Lab. Animal Sci., Am. Soc. Lab. Animal Practitioners. Avocations: snowboarding, wind surfing, backpacking, bicycling. Office: U Ariz PO Box 210101 Tucson AZ 85721-0101 E-mail: besselsd@u.arizona.edu.

BESSER, ALBERT GORDON, lawyer; b. Newark, Nov. 19, 1924; BA with highest distinction, Yale U., 1946; LLB, Yale Law Sch., 1949. Bar: NY 1949, US Dist. Ct. (ea. and so. dist.) NY 1949, US Ct. Appeals (2nd cir.) NJ 1949, US Ct. Appeals (2nd cir.) NJ 1953, US Ct. Appeals (3rd cir.) 1953, US Supreme Ct. 1954. Lectr. in law Rutgers Law Sch., 1953—55, 1960—62; asst. US atty. Dist. NJ, 1953—56; ptnr. Hannoch & Weisman, Newark. Editor: (jour.) Yale Law Jour., 1947—49, NJ Law Jour., 1970; contbr. articles. Mem.: Order of Coif, Essex County Bar Assn., NJ Bar Assn., Assn of Bar of City of NY, ABA, Phi Beta Kappa. Office: Hannoch Weisman 4 Becker Farm Rd Ste 11 Roseland NJ 07068-1734

BESSER, AMY HELENE, lawyer; b. Reading, Pa., July 11, 1956; d. Wallace and Trina Mae (Daniels) Rudolph; m. Marcus Peter Besser, Dec. 15, 1985. BS in Econs., U. Pa., 1978; JD, Rutgers U., 1981. Bar: Pa. 1981, N.J. 1981, U.S. Dist. Ct. N.J. 1981, U.S. Dist. Ct. (ea. dist.) Pa. 1986. Assoc. Sauer, Boyle, Dwyer & Canellis, Westfield, N.J., 1982-83, Korn, Kline & Kutner, Phila., 1983-86; house counsel Am. Equity Devel. and Mgmt. Cos., Doylestown, Pa., 1986-91, 97—. Democrat. Jewish. Avocations: reading, sports. Home: 11 Maryland Ave Havertown PA 19083-3008 E-mail: ahb_esq@yahoo.com.

BESSER, GARY STEVEN, obstetrician, gynecologist, surgeon; m. Eileen Teresa Regino, June 19, 1982; children: Haley Elena, Harrison Anthony. Degree, Syracuse U., 1976; postgrad., MIT; MD, SUNY, Bklyn., 1982. Diplomate Am. Bd. Ob-Gyn. Physician, surgeon The Stamford (Conn.) Hosp., 1982—86, ob-gyn. assocs., 1986—. Asst. prof. medicine Columbia Presbyn., N.Y.C., 2000—. Bd. dirs. Stamford Health Found., 1999—. Named one of Top Drs. in N.Y. Met. Area, Castle Connolly, 1999, 2001, 2002, Best Drs. In N.Y., N.Y. Mag., 2002. Fellow: Am. Urogynecol. Soc., Am. Coll. Ob-Gyn.; mem.: Am. Assn. Gynecol. Laparoscopists. Office: Ob & Gyn Assocs 190 W Broad St Ste 401G Stamford CT 06902 Fax: 203-975-7515.

BESSER, GRETCHEN ROUS, writer, educator; b. Bklyn., Dec. 1, 1928; d. Ben and Sidonya (Menkes) Rous; m. Albert Gordon Besser, Dec. 28, 1952; children: James, Neal, Brian. BA in French with honors, Wellesley Coll., 1949, MA, Middlebury Coll., 1950; PhD, Columbia U., 1967. Instr. Fairleigh Dickinson U., Rutherford, N.J., 1955-57, Columbia U., N.Y.C., 1957-59, 63-67; asst. prof. Lehman Coll., CUNY, Bronx, 1967-70, Rutgers U., Newark, 1972-73; PhD examiner Monash U., Victoria, Australia, 1979; instr. in lit. N.J. Com. for The Humanities, New Brunswick, 1985-90; faculty mem. New Sch. U., N.Y.C., 1989—; ski columnist Recorder Pub. Co., Stirling, N.J., 1993—; instr. Distance Instrn. for Adult Learners program New Sch. U., N.Y.C., 1994—2000; instr. New Sch. Online U., 2000—. Author: Balzac's Concept of Genius, 1969, Nathalie Sarraute, 1979, The National Ski Patrol, 1983, Germaine de Staël, Revisited, 1994; contbr. World Lit. Today, 1978—, French Rev., 1973—. Instr. first aid ARC, 1971-82; internat. liaison Nat. Ski Patrol, 1980-85, nat. historian, 1980—; mem. selection com. U.S. Nat. Ski Hall of Fame, 1982—, bd. dirs., 1997—; bd. dirs. Internat. Skiing History Assn., 1997—. Vt. Coun. on the Humanities, 2001—. Fulbright Commn. grantee, 1949-50; Wellesley scholar, 1949; recipient Ullr award Internat. Skiing History Assn., 1997. Mem. Am. Assn. Tchrs. French, Ea. Ski Writers Assn., Nat. Assn. Snowsports Journalists Am. Jewish. Avocations: opera, skiing, hiking. Home and Office: 3679 Stagecoach Rd Morrisville VT 05661 E-mail: grbesser@together.net.

BESSERMAN, PERLE S. writer, educator; b. N.Y.C., Aug. 21, 1948; d. Jacob A. Besserman and Lillian Tobachnikov; m. Manfred B. Steger, Feb. 9, 1988. PhD, Columbia U. Asst. prof. U. Hawaii, Honolulu, Ill. State U., Normal. Mem. curriculum com. women's studies dept., chair feminist issues com. dept. English Ill. State U., Normal, 2002—. Author: (book) Kabbalah: The Way of the Jewish Mystic, 1988; author: (with Manfred Steger) Grassroots Zen, 2001. Mem.: MLA. Avocation: Zen. Office: Ill State U Campus Box 4240 English Normal IL 61790

BESSETTE, HEIDI DEE, adult nurse practitioner; b. Fall River, Mass., Jan. 20, 1968; d. James and Charlotte Bessette; 1 child, Nicholas Medeiros. BS, U. Mass., 1990, MS, 1999. RN Adult nurse practitioner cert. Staff nurse St. Ames Hosp., Fall River, 1990—98; adult nurse practitioner Prima Care PC, Fall River, 1999—. Preceptorship for nurse practitioners U. Mass. Dartmouth, 2002; preceptorship for physician assts. Mass. Coll. Pharmacy, Boston, 2001—. Mem.: Mass. Coalition Nurse Practitioners. Avocations: sports, cake decorating. Home: 764 Rock St Fall River MA 02720 Office: Prima Care PC 187 Plymouth Ave Fall River MA 02724

BESSEY, PALMER QUINTARD, surgeon; b. Glen Ridge, N.J., Aug. 14, 1944; MD, U. Vt., 1975. Diplomate Am. Bd. Surgeons, Am. Bd. Critical Care Surgery. Intern U. Ala. Hosp., Birmingham, 1975-76, resident in surgery, 1976-81; fellow metabolism and nutrition Brigham and Women's Hosp., Boston, 1981-83; assoc. dir. Burn Ctr. N.Y. Presbyterian Hosp., 2000—; prof. surgery Weill Med. Coll. Cornell U., 2000—. Mem. ACS (region chief), Assn. Acad. Surgery, Soc Univ. Surgeons, Am. Assn. Surgery Trauma, ASPEN, Soc. Critical Care Medicine, Ctrl. Surg. Assn., Am. Surg. Assn., Am. Bd. Surgery (bd. dirs.), Am. Burn Assn. (com. on trauma). Office: Dept Surgery Box 137 P-703 525 E 68th St New York NY 10021 E-mail: pqb2001@med.cornell.edu.

BESSIE, SIMON MICHAEL, publisher; b. N.Y.C., Jan. 23, 1916; s. Abraham and Ella (Brainin) B.; m. Constance Ernst, Sept. 12, 1945; children: Nicholas, Katherine; m. Cornelia Schaeffer, Dec. 21, 1968. BA magna cum laude, Harvard U., 1936. Reporter Newark Star Eagle, 1936; with rsch. dept. RKO-Radio Pictures, 1936-38; editor Market Rsch. Monthly, 1938; free-lance writer Europe, Africa, 1938-39; assoc. editor, war editor, war corr. Look mag., 1940-42; editor Harper & Bros., 1946-52, gen. editor, 1952-59; co-founder Atheneum Pubs., 1959, pres., 1963-75; sr. v.p. Harper & Row, N.Y.C., 1975-81, v.p., 1988-91, also bd. dirs., 1975-87; pres. Joshuatown Pub. Assocs., Lyme, Conn., 1981—; co-pub. Cornelia and Michael Bessie Books, 1981—. Cons. editor Counterpoint Press, 1995-2002, Perseus Books Group, 1999-2002; lectr. English, Columbia U., 1953-59; dir. novel workshop New Sch., 1959-63, dir. Franklin book programs, 1963-72; chmn. vis. com. Harvard U. Press, 1972-78, bd. dirs., 1980-91; bd. dirs. Am. Book Pubs. Coun., 1964-69, Ctr. for Comm., 1981—; chmn. trade book div. Assn. Am. Pubs., 1970-72, bd. dirs., 1972-76, chmn., 1974-75, chmn. freedom to read com., 1975-78, internat. freedom to pub. com., 1975—; mem. exec. com. Ctr. for the Book, Libr. of Congress, 1979—, chmn., 1983—. Author: Jazz Journalism, 1938; contbr. numerous articles to mags. Bd. overseers vis. com. dept. history Harvard U., 1964-77; chmn. lit. panel Nat. Arts Council, 1971-74, chmn. spl. projects panel, 1974-81; chmn. bd. advisors Sta. WNET, 1979-83, trustee, 1983-96, life trustee, 1997—; chmn. book com. Alfred P. Sloan Found., 1986-91, mem. tech. book com., 1992-2001. Served as chief news bur. psychol. warfare br., 1943-44, Algiers, Sicily, Italy; chief psychol. warfare combat team 1944, So. France; dep. dir. USIS, 1944-46, France. Recipient Presdl. Medal of Freedom, 1946, Curtis Benjamin award Assn. Am. Pubs., 1986. Mem. Council Fgn. Relations, Assn. Harvard Alumni (dir. 1974-77), Phi Beta Kappa. Clubs: Century Assn. (N.Y.C.), Harvard (N.Y.C.); Federal City (Washington). Home and Office: 296 Joshuatown Rd Lyme CT 06371-3035 E-mail: mbessie@snet.net.

BESSINGER, RAYMOND CARLTON, dietician, educator; b. Pickens, S.C., July 25, 1948; m. Renee P. Pritchett, May 18, 1991. BBA, Ga. So. U., 1970; MBA, Ga. State U., 1974, MS in Exercise Sci., 1986, MS in Nutrition, 1988; PhD, U. N.C., 1996. Dietitian Am. Dietetic Assn., 1988. Instr. Clemson U., SC, 1974—75; pers. analyst State Merit Sys., State of Ga., Atlanta, 1976—78, pers. analysis supr., 1978—80; adj. instr. Coll. St. Francis, Atlanta, 1984; asst. prof. Marywood U., Scranton, Pa., 1996—99, Winthrop U., Rock Hill, SC, 1999—2003, prof., 2003—. Author, editor: book Management and the Brain, 1983; contbr. chapters to books, articles. With U.S. Army, 1971—72, Vietnam. Grantee, U. Rsch. Coun., Winthrop U., 2001—04; Nutrition Rsch. fellow, Inst. Nutrition, U. N.C., 1994—95. Mem.: Nat. Osteoporosis Found., SC. Dietetic Assn. (treas. and mem. of bd. of directors 2002—03), Am. Dietetic Assn. Office: Winthrop Univ 314 Life Sci Bldg Rock Hill SC 29733 Office Fax: 803-323-2254. E-mail: bessingerr@winthrop.edu.

BESSMAN, SAMUEL PAUL, pediatrician, biochemist; b. Newark, Feb. 3, 1921; m. Alice Neuman, July 3, 1945; children: Joel David, Ellen. Student, Coll. William and Mary, 1938-41; MD, Washington U., St. Louis, 1944. Intern, asst. resident St. Louis Children's Hosp., 1944-45; asst. prof. pediatrics George Washington U., 1947-54; dir. research Children's Hosp., Washington, 1947-54; asso. prof. pediatrics U. Md., 1954-59, prof. pediatric research, 1959-68, prof. biochemistry, 1962-68; prof., chmn. dept. pharmacology and nutrition U. So. Calif., 1968-91, prof. pediatrics, 1969-91, prof. emeritus, 1991—. Dir. research Rosewood State Hosp., Md., 1962-68, Jewish Home for Retarded Children, Washington, 1962-68 Founding editor Biochem. Medicine; mem. editorial bd. Analytical Biochemistry. Pres. First Dist. Cmty. Coun., Balt., 1965; trustee Robert Lindner Found.; pres. Molly Towell Found., Alsam Found. Served with USPHS, 1945-47. Recipient Crawford Long award U. Ga., 1963, Creative Scholar award U. So. Calif., 1978, Maimonides award Technion, 1979, Disting. Sci. Achievement award Am. Heart Assn., 1984, Inst. for Advanced Studies award Louis Pasteur Libr. and Sci. Found., 1986, Alumni Achievement award Washington U. Med. Sch., 1994. Fellow AAAS, Am. Acad. Pediat.; mem. Am. Soc. Biol. Chemists, Soc. Pediat. Rsch., Am. Inst. Nutrition, Am. Soc. Pharmacology and Exptl. Therapeutics, Sigma Xi, Alpha Omega Alpha. Achievements include introduction of EDTA treatment of lead poisoning, theoretical basis of hepatic coma, mechanism of insulin action chemistry mental retardation, genetic basis of malnutrition, artificial implantable pancreas, creatine phosphate energy shuttle. Home: 7404 Woodrow Wilson Dr Los Angeles CA 90046-1323 E-mail: bessman@usc.edu.

BEST, FRANKLIN LUTHER, JR., lawyer; b. Lock Haven, Pa., Dec. 14, 1945; s. Franklin L. and Hazel M. (Yearick) B.; m. Kimberly R., May 1, 1982 BA, Yale U., 1967; JD, U. Pa., 1970; postgrad., Columbia U., 1994. Bar: Pa. 1970. Assoc. MacCoy, Evans & Lewis, Phila., 1970-74; asst. counsel Penn Mut. Life Ins. Co., Phila., 1974-77, asst. gen. counsel, 1978-84, assoc. gen. counsel, 1985-99, mng. corp. counsel, 1999—; counsel, asst. sec. Penn Ins. and Annuity Co., Phila., 1983-96, counsel, sec., 1996—. Lectr. Pa. Bar Inst., 1976-84. Author: Pennsylvania Insurance Law, 1991, 2d edit., 1998; contbr. articles to profl. jours. Bd. dirs. Ctr. City South Neighborhood Assn., 1979-80, pres., 1978-79; mem. Com. of Seventy, 1978-84; sec. Washington Sq. Assn., 1977-87; mem. 30th Ward Rep. Exec. Com., 1972-84, West Pikeland Twp. Open Spaces Com., 1987-99, chair, 1995-99, planning commn., 1994—, chair, 1996—. Mem.: ABA, Phila. Bar Assn., Internat. Claim Assn. (sec./treas. (sec. 1995—2000, exec. com. 1979—81, 1985—88, 1995—, pres. 2002—03), Yale Club Phila. Baptist. Office: Penn Mut Life Ins Co 600 Dresher Rd Horsham PA 19044-2204

BEST, FREDERICK NAPIER, artist, designer, educator; b. Macon, Ga., Jan. 17, 1943; s. John Frederick and Sara (Napier) B.; m. Rebecca Alice Freeman, Apr. 6, 1974; children: Eric Jonathan, Emily Anne. Student, Auburn U., 1961-64; BA, Birmingham So. Coll., 1969; MA, U. Ala., Birmingham, 1994. Artist Birmingham News, 1969; design dept. mgr. Dampier-Harris, Alabaster, Ala., 1976—78; model designer Rust Engring., Birmingham, 1978—81; owner, mgr. Best Finesse Studio, Trussville, Ala., 1981—94; design instr. Jefferson State Coll., Birmingham, 1981—98; instr. Erwin H.S., Birmingham, 1994—95; edn. supr. ITT Tech. Inst., Birmingham, 1996—97; freelance artist, educator, 1997—2001. Artist in residence Moody Mid. Sch., 1998; art tchr. Smiths Station H.S., 2001-2002; freelance artist educator, 2002—. Contbr. articles to profl. jours. Recipient award of honor Birmingham Advt. Club, 1982, Purchase award, 2000; Artist Fellowship grantee Ala. State Coun. on the Arts, 1993, 94. Home: 209 Wildwood Dr Trussville AL 35173-2391

BEST, GARY THORMAN, commercial real estate broker; b. San Diego, Mar. 11, 1944; s. Roland Elmer and Mildred Mae (Thorman) B.; m. Hollyce Susan Hill, Feb. 22, 1967 (div. Mar. 1973); 1 child, Melissa Anne; m. Georgia Anne Flaherty, May 22, 1973; children: Roland Bryant, Heather Anne. AAS, Pima Community Coll., 1979. CCIM Comml. Investment Real Estate Inst. Sales Mohawk Data Sci. Corp, Tulsa, Okla., 1968-69; exec. v.p. Mid-Am. Mgmt. Corp., Tulsa, 1969-73; real estate sales Cragin Lang Free and Smythe, Cleve., 1973-74; land sales Coldwell Banker Comml., Tucson, 1975-80, mgr. sales Cin., 1981, resident mgr. Nashville, 1982-83, investment sales Tucson, 1984—86; v.p. Del E. Webb Realty and Mgmt. Co., Tucson, 1986-87; pres. Best Comml. Real Estate, Tucson, 1987-93; sec./treas. Best Asset Mgmt. Svc., Phoenix, 1993-98, chmn. credit rev. com., 1991-94; with Coldwell Banker Success Realty, Tucson, 1994-97; assoc. broker comml. div. Realty Exec. of Tucson, Inc., 1997—. Regional v.p. Comml. Investment Real Estate Inst., 1992-94, cert. comml. investment mem.; pres. So. Ariz. chpt. Cert. Comml. Investment Mems., Tucson, 1990; mem. New Am. Network, Tucson, 1987-93,

mem. adv. bd., 1992-93. Mem. fin. com. Symington for Gov., Tucson, 1990, Kolbe for Congress, Tucson, 1988; adv. bd. Goodwill Industries of Tucson, Tucson Unified Sch. Dist.; dir. Family Counseling Agy., 1995-01, treas., 1996-98, 1st v.p., 1998-99, pres., 1999-2000; chmn. adv. bd. Casa de la Luz, Tucson, 2000-2002, found. 2003; dir. Comin' Home, 2002—. Recipient Pres. of Yr. award Civitan Internat., Ariz. dist., Tucson, 1979. Mem. Tucson Bd. Realtors (bd. dir. 1988-91, v.p. 1992, treas. 2003, v.p., 1992-2004, govt. affairs com. 1998-2000), Ariz. Assn. Realtors (bd. dir. 1989-91, 92-94, exec. com. 1992, reg. v.p., 2004-2005), Tucson Econ. Devel. Corp. (bd. dir., chmn. 1990), Greater Tucson Econ. Coun. (bd. dir., exec. com. 1990-93), Tucson Met. C. of C. (bd. dir., chmn. 1993-94, Small Bus. Leader of Yr. award 1989, chmn. 1993-94). Independent. Avocations: travel, reading, geneology, soccer parent. Office: 1745 E River Rd Ste 245 Tucson AZ 85718-7634 E-mail: gbest11@comcast.net.

BEST, HOLLIS GARBER, judge; b. Curry County, N.Mex., July 10, 1926; s. Ernest and Neely Civil (Stratton) B.; m. Kathryn Jean LaFollette, Aug. 4, 1947; children: David S., Daniel E., Laura J. Best Marks, Kathryn A. AB, Fresno State U., 1948; JD, Stanford U., 1951. Bar: Calif. 1951. Dep. dist. atty. County of Fresno, Fresno, Calif., 1951-53; ptnr. Manfredo, Best & Forbes, Fresno, 1953-63, McCormick, Barstow, Sheppard, Coyle & Best, Fresno, 1963-72; judge Calif. Superior Ct., Fresno, 1972-84; assoc. justice Calif. 5th dist. Ct. Appeals, Fresno, 1984—, presiding justice, 1990-94; magistrate judge Ea. Dist. Calif., 1994—. Mem. exec. com., Conf. State Bar Dels., Calif., 1969-71; adj. prof. law, San Joaquin Coll. Law, Fresno, 1974-84. Lt. (j.g.) USNR, 1944-46, PTO. Mem. Calif. Judges Assn. (sec.-treas. 1979-80), Calif. Judges Found. (bd. dirs. 1987-90), Fresno County Bar Assn. (pres. 1963), Rotary. Republican. Avocations: golf, reading. Office: US Dist Ct Ea Dist PO Box 575 Yosemite National Park CA 95389-0575 E-mail: hbest@caed.uscourts.gov.

BEST, JACOB HILMER, JR., (JERRY BEST JR.), retired hotel chain executive; b. Evanston, Ill., July 21, 1937; s. Jacob Hilmer and Clara (Cornell) B.; m. Janet Patricia Donnelly, June 20, 1959; children: Jacob Hilmer III, Peter B., Julie Donnelly Best. BS in Hotel Adminstrn., Mich. State U., 1959; postgrad, Stanford U., 1979. From sales rep. to dir. of sales Sheraton Hotels, Chgo., Wash., 1960-62; asst. to owner Camelback Inn, Scottsdale, Ariz., 1963-64, from sales mgr. to exec. v.p. Marriott Hotels, 1964-84; pres. Ramada Inns, Phoenix, 1984-85; pres., CEO, Wyndham Hotels, Dallas, 1985-87, Red Lion Hotels & Inns, Vancouver, Wash., 1987-91, Omni Hotels, Hampton, N.H., 1992-96; ind. cons., 1996-98; COO Tauck Tours, Westport, Conn., 1998-99. Named charter mem. Mich. State U. Sch. of Hospitality Hall of Fame, 1995. Mem. Am. Hotel and Motel Assn. Republican. Roman Catholic. Avocations: golf, reading, fishing. Home: PO Box 56 Rancho Santa Fe CA 92067-0056 E-mail: pops7217@aol.com.

BEST, JERRY LAVON, insurance consultant; b. Garrett, Ind, Feb. 1, 1952; s. William E. Best and Marie Trausch; m. Donna Smith Jean, Sept. 2, 1978 (div. July 1980); m. Susan Shelby Aboulla, Aug. 10, 1954; children: Chelsea A., Natalie P. A in Bible Studies, Grace Bible Coll., Carey, NC, 1994; B in Psychology, Nat. Christian Counseling, Sarasota, Fla., 2000. Ordained min. Lovesent Ministries, 2003. With WRG Enterprises, Sarasota, 1975-77; sales ins. George Washington Life, Pt. Charlotte, Fla., 1978-80; CEO, pres. Best & Assoc. Svc., Venice, Fla., 1980-90, Consumer Awareness Group, Sarasota, 1990—. Cons. pres. Nat. Christian Consulting Assn., Sarasot, 1994-2000; mem. adv. bd. Crown Life, Inc., Sarasota, 1999-2001, Individual Med. Accountant I.M.A. Flexiarie Healing & Accident (Bonus Flex Annuity). Mem. Lions. Republican. Achievements include patents for Lighted Basketball Hoop; invention of Lazer Hoop; Bonus Flex. Avocations: charismatic Jazz, songwriter, musician, & guitarist., tennis, basketball, boating, skiing. Home: 5667 Creekwood Dr Sarasota FL 34233-1510 E-mail: JBEST19764@aol.com.

BEST, JUDAH, lawyer; b. N.Y.C., Sept. 4, 1932; s. Sol and Ruth (Landau) B.; m. Sally Joan Dial, June 29, 1962; 1 child, Stephen Andrew AB, Cornell U., 1954; LLB, Columbia U., 1959. Bar: N.Y. 1959, D.C. 1961, U.S. Supreme Ct. 1963. Trial atty. Solicitor's Office, U.S. Dept. Labor, Washington, 1960-61; asst. U.S. atty. for D.C., 1961-64; assoc., then ptnr. Chapman, DiSalle & Friedman, Washington, 1964-70; ptnr. Dickstein, Shapiro & Morin, Washington, 1970-80, Steptoe & Johnson, Washington, 1980-87, Debevoise & Plimpton, Washington, 1987—2002, of counsel, 2003—. Participant trial advocacy program U. Va. Sch. Law, 1981—. Contbr. articles to profl. publs. Served with U.S. Army, 1954-56 Fellow Am. Coll. Trial Lawyers; mem. ABA (coun., litigation sect. 1977-81, chmn. subcom. on litigation 1982-84, mem. fed. regulation securities com., corp. bank and bus. law sect., pub. contracts sect., vice chmn. ABA Task Force Report on RICO 1983-85, chmn. litigation sect. 1988-89, sect. del. 1989—, mem. standing com. on fed. judiciary 1990-93, chmn. 1996-97, mem. spl. com. on governance 1993-95), Fed. Bar Assn., D.C. Bar Assn., Am. Bar Found., Am. Law Inst., Cosmos Club, Washington Golf and Country Club, City Club of Washington. Home: 2808 Woodland Dr NW Washington DC 20008-2742 Office: Debevoise & Plimpton 555 13th St NW Ste 1100E Washington DC 20004-1163 also: 875 3rd Ave New York NY 10022-6225 E-mail: jbest@debevoise.com.

BEST, MELVYN EDWARD, geophysicist; b. Victoria, B.C., Can., Mar. 8, 1941; s. Herbert Best and Irene Jessie (Kelly) MacKenzie; m. Virginia Marie Pignato, July 19, 1970; children: Lisette Anne, Aaron Michael. BSc in Math. and Physics with honors, U. B.C., Vancouver, 1965, MSc in Physics, 1966; PhD in Theoretical Physics, MIT, 1970. Geophysicist mineral exploration Shell Can. Resources Ltd., Calgary, Alta., Can., 1972-77, divsn. geophysicist minerals, 1980-82, mgr. petroleum engring. rsch., 1982-85; head non-seismic rsch. Royal Dutch Shell Exploration and Prodn. Labs., The Hague, The Netherlands, 1978-80; geophys. advisor Teknica Resource Devel. Ltd., Calgary, 1985-86; head basin analysis subdivision Atlantic Geoscience Ctr. Geol. Survey Can., Dartmouth, N.S., 1986-90, dir. Pacific Geosci. Ctr. Sidney, B.C., 1990-94, sr. rsch. scientist, 1994-97; geophys. cons. Bemex Consulting Internat., Victoria, B.C., 1997—; environ. geophys. Lockheed-Martin Corp., Edison, N.J., 2001—. Vis. lectr., rsch. assoc. dept. physics McGill U., Montreal, Que., 1970—72; mem. panel Jeanne d'Arc hydrocarbon resource assessment Can. Govt., 1987—90; mem. petroleum geology working group Office Energy R&D, 1987—92; mem. oil and gas com. Can. Nfld. Offshore Petroleum Bd., 1990—94, official Can. rep. coom. coordination joint prospecting for mineral resources in Asian offshore waters, 1992—94; sessional lectr. Sch. Earth and Ocean Scis. U. Victoria, 1995—, adj. prof. earth and ocean scis., 1998—; adj. prof. geology and geophysics U. Calgary, 1998—; part-time sr. geophysicist Lockheed Martin Corp., Edison, NJ, 2001—. Author: Resistivity Mapping and Electromagnetic Imaging, 1992; editor: (with J.B. Boniwell) A Geophysical Handbook for Geologists, 1989, (with T.P. Ng) Development and Exploitation Scale Geophysics, 1995. Vol. lectr. Can. Coll. Chinese Studies, Victoria, B.C., 1995-99; vol. Victoria chpt. Habitat for Humanity, 1996-97. Recipient meritorious svc. award Can. Soc. Exploration Geophysicists, Calgary, 1996. Mem. Can. Soc. Exploration Geophysicists (chmn. continuing edn. com. 1982-85, mem. tech. com. 1985 convention, assoc. editor jour. 1986-93, 95-2003, editor jour. 1993-95), Soc. Exploration Geophysicists (prodn. and devel. geophysics com. 1985-88, geophys. rsch. com. 1988—, organizer workshop 1989, instr. continuing edn. 1985-2000), Soc. Environ. and Engring. Geophysics (assoc. editor jour. 1995-97, 2000—, editor 1997-2000, v.p.-elect 2003-), Assn. Profl. Engrs., Geologists and Geophysicists Alta. (cert.), Assn. Profl. Engrs. and Geoscientists B.C. (cert.). Avocations: competitive badminton, squash, tennis, hiking, sailing. Office: Bemex Cons Internat 5288 Cordova Bay Rd Victoria BC Canada V8Y 2L4

BEST, ROBERT MULVANE, insurance company executive; b. Newcomerstown, Ohio, May 9, 1922; s. Chester R. and Beatrice (Mulvane) B.; m. Shirley Marie Smith, Nov. 25, 1994; children: Eric, Linda, Grant. BS, Ohio State U., 1947. Agt. Bus. Men's Assurance Co. Am., Columbus, Ohio, 1946-48; mgr. group sales Security Mut. Life Ins. Co., Binghamton, N.Y., 1948-49, asst. supt. agys., 1949-51, dir. sales, 1951-53; asst. mgr. Bus. Men's Assurance Co., Columbus, 1952-61; v.p. in charge agys. Security Mut. Life Ins. Co. N.Y., Binghamton, 1961-66, exec. v.p., 1966-69, pres., 1969—, chief exec. officer, 1972-87, chmn. bd., 1977-90; chmn., chief exec. officer Home Mut. Ins. Co., 1986-89. Mem. exec. com. Life Inst. Guaranty Corp., N.Y.C., 1980-89; mem. N.Y. Inst. bd., N.Y.; chmn. bd. trustees bus. coun. Inst. Trust. Trustee Bus. Coun. N.Y. State, Inc.; former dir. Valley Devel. Found., Binghamtom; mem. coun. SUNY; bd. govs. Internat. Ins. Seminars; bd. dirs. Twin Tier Home Health Care, Inc., Binghamton; former mem. N.Y. State Bd. Regents, Am. Coun. Life Ins.; chmn. Med. Index Bur., Inc., Boston, 1989; dir. Greater Broome Cmty. Found., Inc. Lt. (j.g.) USNR, 1942-46. Mem. Am. Soc. CLUs (regional v.p. 1967-70), Am. Council Life Ins. (bd. dir.), Life Ins. Council N.Y. (bd. dir.), Broome County C. of C. (bd. dir. 1970-75, pres. 1974), Empire State C. of C. (former pres., bd. dirs.). Clubs: Binghamton City (bd. dirs. 1969-73); Oteyokwa Lake (Hallstead, Pa.) (pres. 1970-71); Econ. (N.Y.C.). Home: 41A Crestmont Rd Binghamton NY 13905-4117 E-mail: sbest12@aol.com.

BEST, SHARON LOUISE PECKHAM, college administrator; b. Elmira, N.Y., Aug. 4, 1940; d. Paul Arthur and Beatrice L. (Hunter) Peckham; m. Willard C. Best, Sept. 3, 1961; children: Meryl Elizabeth, Kevin Hunter. BA cum laude, William Smith Coll., 1977. Acting dir. alumnae rels. William Smith Coll., Geneva, N.Y., 1976-77; from assoc. dir. devel. to v.p. devel. Hobart & William Smith Colls., Geneva, 1977-97, v.p. devel. and gift planning, 1997—2000; ret. Cons. Nazareth Coll., Rochester, N.Y., 1985. Active Ontario County (N.Y.) rep. com., 1968-78, Geneva Hist. Soc., 1975-80; active Geneva Concerts, Inc., 1965—, bd. dirs. 1974-82, pres., 1976-78; mem. planning bd. City of Geneva, 1999—; trustee Geneva Free Libr., 2002-. Recipient Coun. on Advancement and Support of Edn. award capital fundraising USX Found., 1988. Mem. Coun. for Advancement and Support Edn. (bd. trustees Mid-Atlantic Dist. II 1987-89, Gold Medal-Decade Improvement in Fund Raising 1987, Circle of Excellence in Ednl. Fund Raising award 1994), Nat. Soc. Fund Raising Execs., LWV (bd. dirs. 1993-97), Geneva Country Club, Phi Beta Kappa, Phi Sigma Iota. Presbyterian. Home: 859 S Main St Geneva NY 14456-3205

BEST, SUSAN MARIE, artist, educator; b. Peoria, Ill., July 4, 1949; d. Robert H. and Shirley (Critchlow) Coyle; m. David G. Best, Sept. 12, 1970 (div. May 1987); children: Timothy, Molly, Abby, George; m. Richard J. Gualandi, Dec. 20, 1996. BPhar, U. Ill., Chgo., 1972; MA in Fine Arts, Ill. State U., Normal, 1988, MFA, 1991. Grad. pharmacist S&C Drugs, Peoria, 1972, Indian Hosp., Pine Ridge, S.D., 1974-76; instr. art Ill. State U., Normal, 1988-91, Bradley U., Peoria, 1992-93, Ill. Ctrl. Coll., Peoria, 1991-93; artist, 1970—. Gallery artist Struve Gallery, Chgo., 1991-93; active Longue Vue Mus. Art Program. Exhbn. Contemporary Art Ctr., Oleczyn, Poland. Bd. dirs. St. Thomas Sch., Peoria, 1980-83, Amateur Mus. Club, Peoria, 1982-84, bd. dirs. Peoria Art Guild, 1994—. Recipient Percent for Art award City of New Orleans, 1997, also various awards for art including 2 grants from Ill. Arts Coun. Access Program, 1995; Ill. State U. fellow, 1988-91. Mem. AAUP, AAUW, NOW, Contemporary Arts Ctr. of New Orleans, New Orleans Mus. Art, Chgo. Artists Coalition, Lakeview Art Mus., Sun Found., Planned Parenthood Assn. Democrat. Avocations: skiing, jogging, piano. Studio: 811 1/2 Opelousas Ave New Orleans LA 70114-2429

BEST, THOMAS L. trainer, consultant; b. Houston, June 27, 1946; s. Earl L. and Beverly H. Best; m. Bobbi D. Counce, Aug. 8, 1988; 1 child, Aleta. BA, U. Colo., 1983. Cert. neuro-linguistic programming, neuro-linguistic compresensive. Dir. Neuro-Linguistic Programming Austin, Tex., 1987-90, Neuro-Linguistic Programming Ctr., Hana, Maui, Hawaii, 1990-94, Blue Heron Prodns., Prescott, Ariz., 1994-98, Best Resources, San Antonio, 1999—. Author: (videotape) Native Culture and NLP Maps, 1999. Named hon. mem. Q'ero Tribe, North Ctrl. Peru, 1995—. Fellow Nat. Assn. NLP. Avocation: travel. Home: 14014 Tree Crossing San Antonio TX 78247 Office: Best Resources 14014 Tree Crossing San Antonio TX 78247 Fax: 210-545-3676. E-mail: bestresources@satx.rr.com.

BEST, WILLIAM ROBERT, physician, educator, university official; b. Chgo., July 14, 1922; s. Gordon and Marian Burton (Shapland) B.; m. Ruth Joanna Stuchlik, Sept. 2, 1944; children: Barbara Ann Best Mulch, Patricia Marian Best Williams. BS, U. Ill., 1945; MD, U. Ill., Chgo., 1947, MS, 1951; postgrad. math. biology, U. Chgo., 1964-65. Diplomate Am. Bd. Internal Medicine, Am. Bd. Hematology. From intern to fellow in hematology then to resident U. Ill. Hosp., 1947-51; asst. prof., assoc. prof. medicine U. Ill. Coll. Medicine, Chgo., 1953-67, prof., assoc. dean, 1972-81; chief Midwest Rsch. Support Ctr., VA Hosp., Hines, Ill., 1967-72, chief staff, 1981-92, sr. health svcs. rschr., 1992—; prof. medicine, assoc. dean for VA affairs Loyola U. Stritch Sch. Medicine, Maywood, Ill., 1981-92; chief staff U. Ill. Hosp., Chgo., 1976-81. Contbr. numerous articles to sci. jours. 1st lt. U.S. Army, 1951—53. Named Alumnus of Yr., U. Ill. Med. Alumni Assn., 1980. Fellow ACP; mem. AMA (br. pres. 1985), Am. Statis. Assn., AAAS. Episcopalian. Avocations: sailing, computing, radio-controlled model airplanes. Home: 1712 Waverly Cir Saint Charles IL 60174-5869 Office: Midwest Ctr Health Svcs and Policy Rsch Edward Hines Jr VA Hosp Hines IL 60141 E-mail: best@research.hines.med.va.gov., wmrbest@aol.com.

BESTEHORN, UTE WILTRUD, retired librarian; b. Cologne, Germany, Nov. 6, 1930; came to U.S., 1930; d. Henry Hugo and Wiltrud Lucie (Vincentz) B. BA, U. Cin., 1954, BEd, 1955, MEd, 1958; MS in Library Sci., Western Res. U. (now Case-Western Res. U.), 1961. Tchr. Cutter Jr. High Sch., Cin., 1955-57; tchr., supr. libr. Felicity (Ohio) Franklin Sr. High Sch., 1959-60; with libr. sci. dept. Pub. Libr. Cin. and Hamilton County, 1961-78, with libr. info. desk, 1978-91; ret., 1991. Textbook selection com., Felicity-Franklin Sr. High Sch., 1959-60; supr. Health Alcove Sci. Dept. and annual health lectures, Cin. Pub. Library, 1972-77. Book reviewer Library Jour., 1972-77; author and inventor Rainbow 40 marble game, 1971, Condominium game, 1976; patentee indexed packaging and stacking device, 1973, mobile packaging and stacking device, 1974. Mem. Clifton Town Meeting, 1988—; mem. Bookfest 90 com. Pub. Libr. Cin. and Hamilton County. Recipient Cert. of Merit and Appreciation Pub. Library of Cin., 1986. Mem. Cin. Chpt. Spl. Libraries Assn. (archivist 1963-64, 65-70, editor Queen City Gazette bull. 1964-69), Pub. Library Staff Assn. (exec. bd., activities com. 1965, welfare com. 1966, recipient Golden Book 25 yr. service pin, 1986), Friends of the Library, Greater Cin. Calligraphers Guild (reviewer New Letters pub. 1986-88), Delta Phi Alpha (nat. German hon. 1951). Republican. Mem. United Ch. of Christ. Avocations: calligraphy, painting and sketching, writing, photography, violin. Home: 3330 Morrison Ave Cincinnati OH 45220-1440

BESTEN, JR. JOHN JOSEPH, music educator; b. Springfield, Mass., Jan. 15, 1953; s. John and Carmella Besten; m. Susan Marie O'Connor, Aug. 14, 1976; children: Richard John Besten, Karen Marie Besten. AAS, Onondaga CC, Syracuse, N.Y., 1973; MusB Edn., Syracuse U., 1975. Instrumental music dir. Lafayette (N.Y.) Ctrl. Schs., 1975—, jazz ensemble dir., 1987—, orch. dir., 1984—, curriculum leader for music dept. Mem.: NY State Sch. Music Assn., Onondaga County Music Edn. Assn., NY State Bd. Dirs. Assn. Avocations: boating, gardening, golf. Home: 336 Sunset Drive East Syracuse NY 13057 Home Fax: 315-677-5507.

BESTENI, BARBARA AMNERYS, video producer, editor, director; b. Havana, Cuba, June 11, 1958; came to U.S., 1961; d. Felipe and Frances (Castellanos) B. BA, Bklyn. Coll., 1980. Prodn. assoc. Eyewitness News Sta. WABC-TV, N.Y.C., 1980-84; video coordinator TV program Good Morning Am., N.Y.C., 1984-87; producer, dir. Barbest Prodns., Miami, Fla. and Bklyn., 1987-88; chief videotape editor, mgr. day prodn. Video Jukebox Network, Miami, 1988-89; pres. Spl. EFX Prodns., Miami, 1989-98, Besteni Communications, Miami, 1989-98, Besteni Pub. & Media, Miramar, 1999—; sta. broadband prodr. WTVJ/NBC Channel 6, Miramar, 2000—; mng. editor NBC6.net, Miami, 2002—. Instr. Career Insts. Am., Miami Beach, Fla., 1989-92. Pub., editor: The Video File, 1991— Mem. Assn. Prof. Videographers (bd. dirs.). Avocations: music, writing, sports. Office: 15155 SW 44th St Miramar FL 33027-3391 E-mail: besteni@earthlink.net.

BESTERMAN, DOUGLAS, composer, orchestrator; Office: Local 802 AFM 320 W 48th St New York NY 10036-1302

BESTGEN, WILLIAM HENRY, JR., financial planner; b. Quincy, Mass., June 23, 1947; s. William Henry and Ebba Violet (Fristam) B.; m. Ann Marie Mahoney, Apr. 12, 1975; children: Brad William, Lauren Ann. BA, Northeastern U., 1970. CLU; Chartered Fin. Cons.; Cert. Estate Planner. Fin. planner Bay Fin., Waltham, Mass., 1970—. Pres. Yankee Planners, Inc., Middleboro, Mass. Mem. exec. bd. Boston Estate and Bus. Planning Coun. Mem. Am. Soc. CLUs, Nat. Assn. Life Underwriters, Internat. Assn. Fin. Planners, Million Dollar Round Table (life). Republican. Lutheran. Avocations: skiing, boating. Home: 30 Clara Howard Way North Easton MA 02356 E-mail: bill@bestgenfinancial.com.

BESTON, ROSE MARIE, retired college president; b. South Portland, Maine, Sept. 27, 1937; d. George Louis and Edith Mae (Archibald) Beattie; m. John Bernard Beston, Feb. 1, 1970 BA, St. Joseph's Coll., 1961; MA, Boston Coll., 1963; PhD, U. Pitts., 1967; cert. of advanced study, Harvard U., 1978. Mem. faculty St. Joseph's Coll., Maine, 1967-68, SUNY, Oneonta, 1968-69, S.E. Mo. State Coll., 1969-70, U. Queensland and Western Australian Inst. Tech., 1970-76, U. Hawaii, Manoa, 1976-77; assoc. acad. dean Worcester State Coll., Mass., 1978-80; dean for acad. affairs Castleton State Coll., Vt., 1980-84; pres. Nazareth Coll. Rochester, NY, 1984-98; ret., 1998. Former mem. Neylan Commn., Assn. Cath. Colls. and Univs., Pres. Network of Campus Compact. Contbr. articles to profl. jour. Mem. AAUW.

BESTWICK, WARREN WILLIAM, retired construction company executive; b. Missoula, Mont., June 27, 1922; s. William Andrew and Beatrice Anna (Eddy) B.; m. Glenette Haas, Sept. 11, 1949; children: Sharon Kaye, Carol Eddy, Jan Marie. Student, Glendale Coll., 1941, U. Mont., 1942; BA, U. Wash., 1949, postgrad., 1950. Sr. acct. Frederick & Nelson, Seattle, 1950; contr., bus. mgr. Va. Mason Hosp., Seattle, 1958-64; contr. Bumstead Woolford Co., Seattle, 1964-68; contr., treas. Wash. Asphalt Co., Seattle, 1968-72; exec. v.p., sec., treas. Wilder Constrn. Co., Inc., Bellingham, Wash., 1972-77, pres., COO, CFO, 1977-89, vice-chmn., 1989-92; ret., 1992. Past bd. dirs. Consumers Choice, Bellingham; bd. govs. Va. Mason Med. Ctr., Seattle; past chmn. Area IV adv. bd. Wash. Dept. Commerce and Econ. Devel.; past dir., vice chmn. Mt. Baker Bank, Bellingham; past bd. dirs. adv. bd. Mt. Baker Coun. Boy Scouts Am. Col., pilot USMCR. Decorated DFC (3), Air medal (7). Mem. Assn. Wash. Bus. (past dir.), Whatcom County Devel. Coun. (past dir. and pres.), Bellingham C. of C. (past dir.), Shukson Found. (past dir., pres., bd. dirs.), Marine Res. Officers Assn. (past dir. Seattle), Res. Officers Assn., Marine Corps League, The Beavers (Constrn. hon., emeritus), United for Wash., U. Wash. Alumni Assn., Ret. Officers Assn., Marine Aviation Assn., World Affairs Coun., Wash. Athletic Club (Seattle), Bellingham Golf and Country Club, Rotary (past pres.). Address: PO Box 2661 Rancho Santa Fe CA 92067-2661

BETANCOURT, CONCHITA, music educator; b. Pinar del Rio, Cuba, Aug. 2, 1949; arrived in U.S., 1962; d. Humberto and Yolanda Betancourt; m. Jose C. Suarez, Sept. 8, 1967 (div. Sept. 1985); 1 child, Jose H. Suarez; m. Arcadio Cancio, Feb. 5, 1995. MusB, U Miami, 1976, MusM, 1992. Piano tchr. pvt. practice, Miami, Fla., 1969—2003; assistanship U Miami (Fla) Sch. of Music, 1987, 1991—92. Chairperson Nat. Guild of Piano, Miami, 1994—2003. Mem. Women Fighters for Democracy, Miami, 1997—2003, Cuban Women's Club, Miami, 1997—2003. Recipient Honor Scholarship, U Miami, Coral Gables-,Fla., 1978. Cath. Home: 8840 S W 4 Terrace Miami FL 33174

BETANCOURT, RALPH ERNEST, mayor; b. N.Y.C., May 17, 1924; s. Raoul and Jacinta (Fernandez) B.; m. Carol Jean Betancourt, Aug. 27, 1955; children: Jean Ellen, Ralph Andrew. BS, Wagner Coll., 1949; MA, NYU, 1953; PhD, U. Madrid, 1964. Cert. tchr. N.Y. Tchr. St. Luke's Sch., N.Y.C., 1951—53, Massapequa (N.Y.) Pub. Schs., 1953—83; ind. photographer Daytona Beach Shores, Fla., 1983—89. Songwriter, music pub., Daytona Beach Shores, 1984—. Composer: (song) We Salute the United Nations; author(songs): Fla. Great Survivors, others. Mayor Daytona Beach Shores, 1997-01; exec. bd., ednl. adv. bd. for sch. dist., Massapequa, 1970s; bd. dirs. UNA-USA Assn. of Valusia Co., Fla., 1999; deacon, elder, 1st Presbyn. Ch., Babylon, N.Y., Westminster By the Sea Presbyn. Ch., Daytona Beach. With U.S. Army Signal Corp, 1943-45. Decorated medal Battle of the Bulge, WWII. Mem. ASCAP, Massepequa Tchrs. Assn. (v.p. 1960s), Casements Songwriters (pres. 1980s), Fla. Motion Picture and TV Assn. Achievements include patents for multi-foreign language kit. Avocations: tennis, swimming, performing arts, travel. Home: 3051 S Atlantic Ave Apt 1904 Daytona Beach FL 32118-6143

BETCHEN, STEPHEN JAY, marital, family and sex therapist; b. Coral Gables, Fla., Oct. 5, 1954; s. Herbert and Millie B.; m. Maria J. Wells, July 12, 1982; children: Jennifer, Melanie. BA, Rutgers U., 1978; MSW/DSW, U. Pa., 1986. Staff therapist Drenk Guidance Ctr., Mt. Holly, N.J., 1981-85, Marriage & Family Therapy Assocs., Marlton, N.J., 1985-87; sr. therapist, supr. Marriage Coun. Phila., 1986-92; pvt. practice Cherry Hill, N.J., 1992—. Postdoctoral fellow N.Y. Hosp.-Cornell Med. Ctr., 1987-88; psychoanalytic fellow Inst. Phila. Assn. Psychoanalysis, 1998-00; clin. assoc. psychiatry U. Pa. Sch. Medicine, 1989-92. Columnist Courier-Post Newspaper, 1992-2001; contbr. articles to profl. jours., chpts. to books. Mem. Am. Assn. Marriage and Family Therapy (approved supr.), Am. Assn. Sex Educators, Counselors and Therapists (cert. supr.), Soc. Sex Therapy and Rsch., Am. Bd. Sexology. Office: 1930 Marlton Pike E Ste B-10 Cherry Hill NJ 08003-4214 E-mail: stephenjb5@comcast.net.

BETENBAUGH, HELEN RECKENZAUN, Episcopal priest, disabilities activist; b. Morristown, N.J., Feb. 10, 1943; d. Paul Frederick and Norma Kathryn (Held) Reckenzaun; m. Gordon Murray Betenbaugh, June 5, 1965 (div. Oct. 1987); children: Melanie, Jennifer. MusB, Westminster Choir Coll., Princeton, N.J., 1964; MusM, Peabody Conservatory, Balt., 1968; MDiv with honors, So. Meth. U., Dallas, 1993, DMin, 1997. Cert. church musician. Min. of music First United Methodist Ch., El Dorado, Ark., 1968-75; min. of music and fine arts Westminster Presbyn. Ch., Lincoln, 1975-82; mem. faculty Union Coll., Lincoln, Nebr., 1976-79; music critic Lincoln Jour., 1977-80; staff U. Nebr., Lincoln, 1982-85; organist, choirmaster St. Paul's Episcopal Ch., Orange, Tex., 1987-89; dir. Christian Edn. Ministries, Episcopal Ch. of the Transfiguration, Dallas, 1990-96; asst. to rector Episc. Ch. of the Good Shepherd, Dallas, 1996-97, Episc. Ch. of the Ascension, Dallas, 1998-99; rector St. Alban's Epis. Ch., Wichita, Kans., 1999—2002. Adj. faculty Perkins Sch. Theology, 1997; profl. accompanist, 1965-89; organ and harpsichord recitalist, 1964-85; faculty, clinician, conductor, keynote speaker, presenter, facilitator for conventions, workshops, confs., profl. assns. and festivals in field. Contbr. articles to profl. jours., chpts. to books. Sec. bd. dirs. League of Human Dignity, Lincoln, 1982-85; mem. steering com. A World of Difference, Beaumont, Tex., 1988-89; mem. pres's. adv. com. on the needs of disabled persons So. Methodist U., Dallas, 1990-93. Recipient Harold M. Kaufman Meml. Social Ethics award B'nai Brith, 1993. Mem.: AAUW, N.Am. Acad. Liturgy, Episcopal Women's Caucus, Assn. Anglican Musicians, Assn. Physically Challenged Mins. (charter 1990, sem. rels. officer 1990—93, program dir. 1993, nat. co-chair 1994—95, lic. labyrinth facilitator 2001), Am. Guild Organists (newsletter editor 1985—87, dir., editor nat. conv. book, preacher nat. conv. 1994), Mensa. Avocations: travel, reading, writing. Home: 426 S Brookside St Wichita KS 67218-1708 E-mail: HBWheels@aol.com.

BETHE, HANS ALBRECHT, physicist, educator; b. Strassburg, Alsace-Lorraine, Germany, July 2, 1906; arrived in U.S., 1935; s. Albrecht Theodore and Anna (Kuhn) Bethe; m. Rose Ewald, 1939; 1 child, Henry;1 child, Monica. Ed. Goethe Gymnasium, Frankfurt on Main, U. Frankfort; PhD, U. Munich, 1928; DSc (hon.), Bklyn. Poly. Inst., 1950, U. Denver, 1952, U. Chgo., 1953, U. Birmingham, 1956, Harvard U., 1958. Instr. in theoretical physics univs. of Frankfort, Stuttgart, Munich and Tubingen, 1928—33; lectr. univs. of Manchester and Bristol, England, 1933—35; asst. prof. Cornell U., 1935, prof., 1937—75, prof. emeritus, 1975—. Dir. theoretical physics divsn. Los Alamos Sci. Lab., 1943—46; mem. Presdl. Study Disarmament, 1958. Author: Mesons and Fields, 1953, Elementary Nuclear Theory, 1957, Quantum Mechanics of One- and Two-Electron Atoms, 1957, Intermediate Quantum Mechanics, 1964; contbr. Handbuch der Physik, 1933, Revs. Modern Physics, 1936—37, Phys. Rev., Astrophys. Jour. Recipient A. Cressy Morrison prize, N.Y. Acad. Scis., 1938—40, Presdl. medal of Merit, 1946, Max Planck medal, 1955, Benjamin Franklin medal, 1959, Enrico Fermi award, AEC, 1961, Eddington Medal, 1961, Rumford prize, 1963, Nobel prize in Physics, 1967, Nat. medal of Sci., 1976, Order Pour le Merite for Arts & Sciences, Govt. of Germany, 1984, Vannevar Bush award, NSF, 1985, Albert Einstein Peace Prize Found., 1993, Oersted prize, Am. Assn. Physics Tchrs., Los Alamos Nat. Lab. Medal, 2001, Bruce Medal, 2001. Mem.: NAS (Henry Draper medal 1947), Am. Astron. Soc., Am. Phys. Soc. (pres. 1954), Am. Philos. Soc., Royal Soc. London (fgn. mem.). Office: Cornell U 320 Newman Lab Ithaca NY 14853*

BETHEA, LOUISE HUFFMAN, allergist; b. Jackson, Miss., Mar. 27, 1947; d. Theodore G. and Frances (Allen) Huffman; m. Henry L. Bethea, Sept. 15, 1946; children: Mary, Samuel, Sarah. BS, Miss. Coll., Clinton, 1968; MD, U. Miss., 1972. Diplomate Am. Bd. Allergy and Immunology, Am. Bd. Pediatrics. Resident pediatrics U. Miss., Jackson, 1973-75; fellow allergy & immunology U. Fla., 1977-79; pvt. practice Houston, 1983—. Instr. pediatrics U. Miss., 1975-77, U. Fla., 1979-80; active Houston Northwest Med. Ctr., 1983—; cons. in field. Fellow Am. Acad. Allergy and Immunology, Am. Coll. Allergy, Am. Acad. Pediatrics. Republican. Episcopalian. Avocations: photography, travel, arts and crafts. Home: 92 Hollymead Dr The Woodlands TX 77381-5121 Office: 17070 Red Oak Dr Ste 107 Houston TX 77090-2615

BETHEL, JOANN D. computer programmer, analyst; b. Ardmore, Okla., Nov. 20, 1956; d. Dorvin and Marian (McKinney) B. Student, U. Okla., 1998—; AS in Computer Sci., AS in Math., Oklahoma City C.C., 1999. Computer operator Security Nat. Bank and Trust, Norman, Okla., 1978-84, programmer, 1984-87, programmer analyst, 1987-90, tech. svc. officer, 1990-95; programmer analyst C-TEQ, Oklahoma City, 1995-2000, v.p., 2000-2001; programmer InterCept, Inc., Oklahoma City, 2001—. Okla. Coun. Tchrs. of Math. scholar, 1996. Mem.: Golden Key Honor Soc., Tau Beta Pi, Phi Theta Kappa. Home: 3915 Bellwood Dr Norman OK 73072-3622 E-mail: JDBethel@ix.netcom.com.

BETHEL, MARILYN JOYCE, librarian; b. Detroit, Jan. 14, 1935; d. Thomas Agmey and Mary Helen (Lisek) Hepfner; m. Herschel Earl Bethel, June 20, 1960 (div. Mar. 1969); 1 child, Mary Joyce. BA in Edn., Fla. Atlantic U., 1974; MLS, La. State U., 1975, MEd, 1976; postgrad., Fla. Atlantic U., 1977-78. Cert. reading specialist, Fla. Cons. Fla. Diagnostic and Learning Resources, Ft. Lauderdale, 1979-80; libr. Cocnut Creek (Fla.) Elem. Sch., 1980-82; cons. Fla. Coll. Bus., Pompano, 1982-84; libr. Broward County Librs., Hallandale, Fla., 1983, cataloger Ft. Lauderdale, 1983-90, br. head Deerfield, 1990-92, libr. Pompano, 1992-95, Ft. Lauderdale, 1995-2000, ret., 2000. Cons. Fla. Diagnostic and Learning Resources, 1979-80; mem. behavioral objectives writing team Broward County Spl. Edn., 1981. Advisor to periodical Biography Today, 1992—; writer newsletter Exceptional Student, 1979-80. Vol. crisis counselor Sexual Assault Treatment Ctr., Broward County, Fla., 1977-78; lectr., instr. New Covenant Ch., Pompano, 1984-87. With USAF, 1954-55. Recipient Cert. of Appreciation, Bd. County Commrs., Ft. Lauderdale, 1978. Mem. ALA (com. for cataloging for children 1989-95, liaison Freedom to Read 1979-80), Fla. Libr. Assn., Broward County Libr. Assn., Nat. Alzheimers Assn. Republican. Presbyterian. Avocations: floral arranging, snorkeling, swimming, reading. Home: 272 NE 39th Ct Pompano Beach FL 33064-3545

BETHJE, ROBERT, retired general surgeon; b. Braunschweig, Germany, Nov. 15, 1922; came to U.S., 1923; s. Robert Paul and Elisabeth Augusta (Lieder) B.; m. Maria Vatral, June 11, 1955; children: Susan Leslie, Robert Eric, Alan Randolph. BS cum laude, CCNY, 1945; MD, N.Y. Med. Coll., 1949. Diplomate Nat. Bd., 1950, Am. Bd. Surgery, 1958. Instr. Biology CCNY, 1946-48; asst. treas. Broome County Med. Soc., Binghamton, N.Y., 1964, v.p., 1965, pres., 1966; pres. med. staff Ideal Hosp., Endicott, N.Y., 1973-76, chief of surgery, 1971-77, Wilson Meml. Hosp., Johnson City, N.Y., 1979-80. Bd. dirs. Broome-Tioga Assn. for Retarded Children, Binghamton, 1983—. Capt. U.S. Army Med. Corps, 1951-53. Fellow Am. Coll. Surgeons; mem. Rotary (Endicott v.p. 1980-81, dir. 1981-84, pres. 1985-86). Avocations: painting, photography, fishing, hunting, gardening. Home: 4 Ivanhoe Rd Binghamton NY 13903-1424

BETHKE, LOUISE VIRGINIA, music educator, writer; b. Neenah, Wis., Mar. 22, 1932; d. Herbert August and Sigrid Natalie Bethke. Diploma in Theology and Music, Patten U., 1957; student, U. Calif., Berkeley, 1958—60, Holy Names Coll., Oakland, Calif., 1978—81. Performer (piano/organ) Christian Cathedral, Oakland, 1954—82; music instr. Patten U., Oakland, 1955—81, Music Studio in Home, Oakland, 1982—. Composer: (complete Easter cantata (words & music) Behold, The Lamb of God, author poetry. Named Honoree For Exceptional Achievement, Leadership & Svc., Patten U. Alumni Walk of Honor, 1997; recipient Talent award for organ, Patten Conservatory Music, 1957, Achievement award trophy, 1960. Mem.: Internat. Soc. Poets (life), Music Tchrs.' Assn. Calif. (life), Alumni Assn. Patten U. (life). Avocations: reading, writing, piano, organ, harp.

BETHLEN, FRANCIS R. emeritus business and economics educator, food distribution engineering specialist; b. Budapest, Hungary, July 2, 1925; came to U.S., 1952; s. Paul and Gabriella (Serenyi) B.; m. Ilona R. Szentimrey, Oct. 7, 1948; children: Anna Maria, Mihaly Antal. BS, Polytechnic U., Budapest, 1947; MS, Cornell U., 1956; PhD, Purdue U., 1962. Teaching asst. dept. agrl. econs. Purdue U., Lafayette, Ind., 1959-61; assoc. prof. econs. SUNY, Plattsburgh, 1961-63, prof., chmn. dept. econs., 1963-69, prof. bus. and econs., 1971-78, prof. mktg., 1981-96, prof. emeritus, 1996—; sr. vis. Fulbright prof. dept. econs. Rosario U., Cordoba, Argentina, 1969-70; vis. sr. prof. econs. and mktg. U. Nicaragua, Managua, 1978-79, UN Mgmt. Inst., Arusha, Tanzania, 1979. Vis. lectr. Rosario, Argentina, 1987, Budapest, 1989, 90, Moscow, 1990, 91, UFA, Bashkiria, 1992; exec. tng. specialist, Hungary, 1989, 90, 91, 92; internat. mktg. cons., Costa Rica, 1994, 96-97, Argentina, 1995, Hungary, 1996, 97, 99; market extensionist Grange League Fedn., Batavia, N.Y., 1955-59; grad. rsch. asst. Cornell U., Ithaca, N.Y., 1953-56; livestock market specialist Est. San Antonio, Olavarria, Argentina, 1949-52; milling products specialist Aranka Flour Mills, Bicske, Hungary, 1945-48; cons. Market Economist, 2000-01. Contbr. articles to profl. jours. Fulbright scholar, 1969, 70, 78. Mem. Am. Mktg. Assn., Rakoczi Found. (bd. dirs. 1984—), Global Energy Soc., Internat. Econs. Soc., Latin Am. Project Evaluators, Rotary, Knight of St. John of Hospitallers. Office: SUNY Redcay Bldg Beekman St Plattsburgh NY 12901-2701

BETHOUX, FRANÇOIS ANDRE, physiatrist, researcher; b. Paris, May 31, 1964; arrived in U.S., 1997; s. Pierre Andre and Janine Gabrielle (Monin) Bethoux; m. Sandrine Christine Delclaud, Apr. 9, 1988; children: Nicolas, Ambre. MD, A. Carrel Med. Sch., Lyon, France, 1990; Bd. Phys. Med. and Rehab., J. Monnet U., St. Etienne, France, 1994; DEA Handicap and Rehab., Bourgogne U., Dijon, France, 1994. Diplomate specializing in physical med and rehab. Resident U. Hosps., St. Etienne, France, 1991-94, acad. physiatrist, 1995-97; rsch. fellow Case We. Res. U., Cleve., 1994-95; fellow in neuroimmunology Mellen Ctr. Multiple Sclerosis, Cleve., 1997-2000, clin. assoc., 2001—02, staff physician, dir. rehab. svcs., 2003—. Rschr. Jean Monnet U., St. Etienne, 1992—97, tchr., 1995—97, Sch. Phys. Therapy, St. Etienne, 1992—97, Inst. Social Scis., St. Etienne, 1996—97; assoc rschr. Page Ctr Outcomes Rsch. Cleve. Clin, 2000—. Contbr. chapters to books, articles to profl jours; co-editor: Guide of Evaluation and Measurement Tools in Physical Medicine and Rehabilitation, 2003. Grantee, French Assn. Paralyzed People, 1994, Nat. Multiple Sclerosis Soc., 2002. Mem.: Am Acad Neurology, Int Soc Quality Life, French Soc Physical Med and Rehab. Avocations: music, reading, cycling. Office: Cleve Clin Found 9500 Euclid Ave Cleveland OH 44195-0001 Fax: 216-445-6259. E-mail: BETHOUF@ccf.org.

BETHUNE, GORDON, airline executive; married; 3 children. BS, Abilene Christian U., Dallas; AMP, Harvard U., 1992. Lic. comml. pilot, lic. airframe and power plant mechanic. V.p. engring. and maintenance Braniff and Western Airlines; sr. v.p. ops. Piedmont Airlines; v.p., gen. mgr. Renton div. Boeing Comml. Airplane Group, 1988-94; chmn., CEO Continental Airlines, Inc., Houston, 1994—. Served with USN. Named Aerospace Laureate for comml. air transport Aviation Week & Space Technology, 1996. Office: Continental Airlines Inc 1600 Smith St Houston TX 77002-7362

BETINIS, EMANUEL JAMES, physics and mathematics educator; b. Oak Park, Ill., Oct. 31, 1927; s. James Emanuel and Ioanna Helen (Kallas) B.; children: Demetrios, Joanna, Markos. BS in Chemistry and Math., Northwestern U., 1950; MS in Applied Math., U. Ill., 1952; MS in Physics, U. Chgo., 1979. Aerodynamicist Northrop Aviation, Hawthorne, Calif., 1953-54; theoretical reactor physicist Atomics Internat., Canoga Park, Calif., 1954-57; applied sci. rep. IBM, Chgo., 1957-61; math. cons. Math. Cons. Svc., Chgo., 1961-81; adj. prof. math. and physics IIT, Roosevelt U., Chgo., 1981-88; mathematician Batelle Meml. Labs., Willowbrook, Ill., 1988-89; asst. prof. physics Elmhurst (Ill.) Coll., 1990—. Contbr. articles to Jour. Geophys. Rsch., Jour. Brit. Interplanetary Soc., Hadronic Jour., Matrix, Lensor Soc. Great Britain; composer, prodr. (CD) Candia Suite. Mem. PTO. With U.S. Army, 1946-47. Fellow Brit. Interplanetary Soc.; mem. Am. Nuclear Soc., Sigma Pi Sigma, Pi Mu Epsilon. Republican. Orthodox. Achievements include patent in golf ball trajectory with lift and drag; research in analytic solution of boundary-value problems in arbitrary geometry, special relativity, quantum mechanical proof of speed of light limitation, analytic solution of 3 dimensional heat conduction equation in arbitrary geometry, nuclear potential and prediction of 470MeV elementary particles, analytic solution of non-linear hydrodynamics equations; development and manufacture of devices for entropy and Biot-Savart physics experiments, calculation of velocity of nucleons in the deuteron, EM theory relativistic time dilation and removal of velocity of light speed limit, EM theory relativistic Schroedinger equations, scattering cross-section for superluminal particles, faster than light quantum mechanics; quantum field theory derivation of the superluminal Schroedinger equation. Office: Elmhurst Coll Dept Physics 190 Prospect Ave Elmhurst IL 60126-3271

BETLEY, LEONARD JOHN, lawyer; b. Fort Wayne, Ind., June 30, 1933; s. Leonard Paul Betley and G. Margaret (Koch) Busse; m. Kathryn Gloin, Nov. 19, 1968; children: James R., Thomas L. BA, Yale U., 1955; JD, U. Mich., 1960. Bar: Ind. 1960, U.S. Dist. Ct. (so. dist.) Ind. 1960, U.S. Tax. Ct. 1962, U.S. Ct. Appeals (7th cir.) 1962. Assoc. Ice Miller Donadio & Ryan, Indpls., 1960-68, ptnr., 1969—; dir., sec. Fairbanks Communications, Palm Beach, Fla., 1975—, Design and Mfg., Connorsville, Ind., 1979-90. Bd. dirs. Hist. New Harmony, Inc., 1977-83, Park Tudor Sch., Indpls., 1982 91, Indpls. Mus. Art, 1990—; pres. bd. dirs. Regenstrief Found., 1987—; chmn. Ind. Nature Conservancy, 1991-93, Wishard Meml. Found., 1993. Served with U.S. Army, 1955-57. Mem. Ind. Bar Assn., Indpls. Bar Assn., Indpls. C. of C. (bd. dirs. 1982-93), Skyline Club (Indpls.). Home: 860 Williams Cove Dr Indianapolis IN 46260-5343 Office: Ice Miller Donadio & Ryan PO Box 82001 1 Am Sq Indianapolis IN 46282

BETON, JOHN ALLEN, communications company executive; b. Chgo., Aug. 25, 1950; s. John Henry and Anne Marilyn (Joseph) B.; BS, U. Ill., 1972; MBA, DePaul U., 1975. Market analyst ITT Telecommunications, Des Plaines, Ill., 1972-73, mgr. mktg. svcs., 1973-75, mgr. market planning, Hartford, Conn., 1975-77, area mgr., Detroit, 1977-80, mgr. mktg. ops., Des Plaines, Ill., 1980-81; v.p. mktg. NEC Tele., Inc., Melville, N.Y., 1981-82; v.p. mktg. Summa Four, Inc., Manchester, N.H., 1982-85; pres. Alston div. Conrac Corp., 1985—, Daniel Radiator Corp., 1989—; sr. v.p. Go/Dan Industries, New Haven, Conn., 1990—; prin. Beton Assocs., Chgo, 1992—. Mem. Am. Mktg. Assn., Am. Philatelic Soc., Pitcairn Islands Study Group, Phi Eta Sigma, Phi Kappa Phi, Beta Gamma Sigma. Presbyterian (deacon). Office: 7850 N Harlem Ave Niles IL 60714-3202

BETSINGER, PEGGY ANN, retired oncological nurse; b. St. Charles, Mo., Dec. 11, 1939; d. Edward and Dorothy (Brockgreitens) Oelklaus; m. Richard Betsinger, Mar. 17, 1964 (div. Mar. 1986); children: Bryon, Alicia. grandmother to 5 children. Diploma, St. John's Hosp. Sch. Nursing, St. Louis U., St. Louis, 1960; student, U. Colo., Colorado Springs, 1973, St. Joseph Coll., 1985. RN, Ohio, Mo.; cert. oncology-chemotherapy nurse; cert. in telemetry, renal and seizure. Charge nurse oncology unit Grandview Hosp., Dayton, 1976-81; asst. dir. nurses Alta Nursing Home, Dayton, Ohio, 1982-86; telemetry, renal, seizure, oncology nurse De Paul Hosp., St. Louis, 1986-2001; ret. Vol. nurse ARC, 1971-74. Capt. Nurse Corps, USAF, 1961-64. Mem. Oncology Nursing Soc. Office: 1035 Bellevue Suite 412 St Louis MO 63130

BETTA, PAMELA ALBERS, community health nurse, administrator, educator; b. St. Joseph, Mo., Feb. 8, 1955; d. Byron Albert Albers and Phyllis Roberta (Grimes) Albers Euler; m. Giuseppe Antonio Betta, Feb. 16, 1980; stepchildren: Sean, Sheree. BSN cum laude, Wichita State U., 1978; MS in Health Care Adminstrn., Cen. Mich. U., 1984; PhD in Nursing, Adelphi U., 1993; grad. pub. health leadership, U. South Fla., 2000. RN Fla., Pa., cert. profl. healthcare quality. Coronary critical care nurse Bethany Med. Ctr., Kansas City, 1978-79; recovery room nurse Menorah Med. Ctr., Kansas City, 1979-80; clin. supr., asst. cıln. supr., referral nurse, staff nurse Allegheny Gen. Hosp. Home Care, Pitts., 1980-83; acting dir. clinic quality assurance, problem analyst Straub Clinic and Hosp., Honolulu, 1984-86; asst. dir. utilization mgmt. and quality assurance Georgetown U. Hosp., Washington, 1987; coord. med. svc. Network Health Care Plan, Fairfax, Va., 1988; teaching asst. dept. continuing edn. Adelphi U., Garden City, N.Y., 1990-91, mem. adj. faculty, 1991; ambulatory health care nurse Mitchel Complex Family Health Ctr., Garden City, 1989-92; asst. prof. cmty. health nursing Med. U. S.C., Charleston, 1993-94, Belmont U., Nashville, 1994-95; RN cons. Office of Performance Improvement, Fla. Dept. Health, 1996-99, exec. cmty. health nursing dir., 1999-2000; nursing prof. Fla. State U., Tallahassee, 2001—. Instr. nurse refresher course Adelphi U., Feb. 1992; spkr. in field, 1996—. Author: (book study guide) Intermediate Research Design and Statistical Analysis Course Manual, 1991; contbr. articles to profl. jours. Vol. Family Svc. Ctr.-Mitchel Field, East Meadow, N.Y., 1991. Recipient Doctorate traineeship Adelphi U., 1990. Mem. First Marine Corps' Wives Club (chair 1991-94), Officers' Wives Club (officer 1983-87, 90-94), Sigma Theta Tau, Omicron Delta Kappa, Alpha Xi Delta. Avocations: walking, cooking, gardening, swimming. Home: PO Box 4391 Hidden Valley PA 15502

BETTAC, ROBERT EDWARD, lawyer; b. Ashland, Ohio, Aug. 13, 1949; s. Donald Albert and Ruth Lavina (Foos) B.; m. Suzanne Lee Shepherd, June 30, 1979; children: Jacqueline Lee, Robert Mitchell. BA in Polit. Sci., Ashland U., 1972; JD, U. Cin., 1979. Bar: U.S. Dist. Ct. (we. and so. dists.) Tex. 1983, U.S. Dist. Ct. (no. dist.) Tex. 1989, U.S. Ct. Appeals (5th and 11th cirs.) 1981, U.S. Dist. Ct. (ea. dist.) Tex. 2001. Assoc. Foster & Assocs., Inc., San Antonio, 1979-84; ptnr. Foster, Bettac & Heller, P.C., San Antonio, 1984-89, Akin Gump Strauss Hauer & Feld, San Antonio, 1989—2003. Author: (with others) Texas Practice Guide, 2d ed., 1983. Mem. Witte Mus. Coun., San Antonio, 1984—, San Antonio Public Library Found. Bd., 2003—. Home: 126 Rosemary Ave San Antonio TX 78209-3841 Office: Ogletree Deakins Nash Smoak & Stewart 112 E Pecan St Ste 2600 San Antonio TX 78205 E-mail: bob.bettac@odnss.com.

BETTENHAUSEN, MATTHEW ROBERT, lawyer; b. Joliet, Ill., Aug. 6, 1960; s. Robert Theodore and E. Colleen Bettenhausen. BS summa cum laude in Acctg., U. Ill., 1982, JD cum laude, 1985. Bar: Ill. 1985. Assoc. Sonnenschein, Carlin, Nath & Rosenthal, Chgo., 1985; law clk. to judge Chgo., 1985-87; asst. U.S. atty. U.S. Dept. Justice, Chgo., 1987—; dep gov Criminal Justice and Pub. Safety, 2000—. Dep. chief Criminal Receiving and Gen. Crimes Sects. U.S. Attys. Office, dep. chief Organized Crime and Drug Enforcement Task Force, acting chief appeals, assoc. chief entire criminal divsn.; adj. prof. adv. trial advocacy and evidence John Marshall Law Sch., Chgo.; lectr. in field. Bd. dirs. Bicentennial of Constl. Commn., Tinley Park, Ill., 1985—. Recipient Civic award, C. of C. Tinley Park, 1985, scholarship, Nat. Inst. Trial Advocacy, 1987.

BETTERIDGE, FRANCES CARPENTER, retired lawyer, mediator; b. Aug. 25, 1921; d. James Dunton and Emily (Atkinson) Carpenter; m. Albert Edwin Betteridge, Feb. 5, 1949 (div. 1975); children: Anne, Albert Edwin, James, Peter. AB, Mt. Holyoke Coll., 1942; JD, N.Y. Law Sch., 1978. Bar: Conn. 1979, Ariz. 1982. Technician in charge blood banks Roosevelt Hosp. and Mountainside Hosp., N.Y.C., Montclair, N.J., 1943-49, sub. tchr. Greenwich (Conn.) H.S., 1978-79; intern and asst. to labor contracts office Town of Greenwich, 1979-80; vol. referee Pima County Juvenile Ct., Tucson, 1981-85; sole practice immigration law Tucson, 1982-87; judge Pro Tempore Pima County Justice Cts., 1988-91. Commr. Juvenile Ct., Pima County Superior Ct., Tucson, 1985-87; hearing officer Small Claims Ct., Pima County Justice Cts., Tucson, 1982; mediator Family Crisis Svc., Tucson, 1982-85. vol. referee Pima County Superior Ct., 1981-85; lectr. Tucson Mus. Art, 1994—. Pres. H.S. PTA, Greenwich, 1970, PTA Coun., 1971; mem. Greenwich Bd. Edn., 1971-76, sec. 1973-76; com. chmn. LWV Tucson, 1981, bd. dirs., 1984-85; bd. dirs., sec. Let The Sun Shine Inc., Tucson, 1981—. Mem. ABA, Conn. Bar Assn., Ariz. Bar Assn., Pima County Bar Assn., Tucson Sr. Acad., Point o'Woods Club. Republican. Avocations: imports folk art from oaxaca, mex. Home and Office: 7659 S Vivaldi Ct Tucson AZ 85747 E-mail: FMotz@aol.com.

BETTI, JOHN ANSO, federal official, former automobile manufacturing company executive; b. Ottawa, Ill., Jan. 6, 1931; s. Louis and Ida (Dallari) B.; m. Joan Doyle, Aug. 22, 1953; children: Diane, Denise, Donna (dec.), Joan. BSMechE, Ill. Inst. Tech., 1952; MS in Engring., Chrysler Inst. Engring., 1954. Registered profl. engr., Mich. Student engr. to asst. chief engr. Chrysler Corp., 1952-62; with Ford Motor Co., 1962-89, from exec. engr. body engring. to v.p., gen. mgr. truck ops., 1962-76; v.p. product devel. Ford of Europe, Inc., Warley, Essex, Eng., 1976-79, also dir.; with N.Am. Automotive Ops., Dearborn, Mich., 1979-84, v.p. powertrain and chassis ops., 1979-83, v.p. mfg. and bus. devel., 1983-84; exec. v.p. tech. affairs and operating staffs Ford Motor Co., Mich., 1985—89, bd. dirs. fin. and exec. coms., exec. v.p. diversified products ops., 1988-89; undersecretary of def., acquisition and nat. armaments dir. Dept. Def., Washington, 1989-91. Instr. Lawrence Inst. Engring., Wayne State U., Detroit, 1953 59; chmn. bd. Ford Motor Co., Caribbean Inc., 1979-84, Ensite Ltd. Can., 1979-84, Ford Aerospace corp., 1988-89, Ford Electronics and Refrigeration Corp., 1988-89; dir. collins & Aikman Corp., 1991-94; mem. dir. compensation com. Breed Tech., 1992-94, Kaysor-Roth Corp., 1993-94. Bd. dirs. Mich. Opera Theatre, 1984-87; trustee Detroit Inst. for Children, 1985-89; mem. nat. adv. com. U. Mich. Engring. Sch., 1985-89; chmn. bd. trustees GMI Engring. and Mgmt. Inst., 1985-89. Recipient Alumni Profl. Achievement award Ill. Inst. Tech., 1980; John Morse Meml. scholar. Mem. Lost Tree Club (North Palm Beach, Fla.), Jupiter Hills Club (Tequesta, Fla.), Bloomfield Hills C.C., Tau Beta Pi, Pi Tau Sigma, Alpha Sigma Phi, Beta Omega Nu. E-mail: jbetti@bellsouth.net.

BETTINGER, JUDITH PEDERSEN, soprano, voice educator; b. Omaha; d. Paul David and Lilly Pedersen; m. Wilmer Clark Bettinger; 1 child, Christine. Diploma, London Opera Centre, 1968, BA magna cum laude, St. Olaf Coll., 1970; MusM with honors, Ind. U., 1972; postgrad., Acad. Vocal Arts, Phila., 1984-85; diploma d'etudier de langue Francaise, Alliance Francaise, Phila., 1999. Artistic dir., founder Brandywine Opera Connection; artist in residence arts in edn. program Del. Divsn. of Arts, 1992-96. Mem. mgmt. Am. Performing Artists, Ltd. Prin. singer operas including A Masked Ball, 1972, Cosi fan Tutti, 1972, Myshkin, 1975 (Peabody award), Sleeping Beauty, 1977, Gallantry, 1979, Little Red Riding Hood, 1984, Albert Herring, 1985, La Boheme, 1985, The Telephone, 1990, Le Convenienze ed Inconvenienze Teatrali, 2000, Don Giovanni, 2000; operettas include The Mikado, 1974, HMS Pinafore, 1978, The Gondoliers, 1987, Pirates of Penzance, 1991, others; musicals include Oklahoma 1973, Fiddler on the Roof, 1974, South Pacific, 1974, Kismet, 1975, Kiss Me Kate, 1976, others; numerous art song recitals and recs. Winner Am. Opera Auditions, 1984. Mem. Alliance Française, Nat. Assn. Tchrs. of Singing. Democrat. Lutheran. Avocations: ballet, needlework, knitting, gardening. Home: 1007 Jeffrey Rd Wilmington DE 19810-3007 E-mail: wilbett1@prodigy.net.

BETTINGHAUS, ERWIN PAUL, research scientist; b. Peoria, Ill., Oct. 28, 1930; s. Erwin Paul and Paula (Bretscher) B.; m. Carole Irma Overmier, Apr. 5, 1952; children: Karen Lee, Joyce Anne, Bruce Alan. BA, U. Ill., 1952, PhD, 1959; MA, Bradley U., 1953. Instr. Mich. State U., East Lansing, 1958-60, asst. prof., 1960 64, assoc. prof., 1964-69, prof., 1969-97; prof. emeritus Mich. State U., East Lansing, 1997—; chmn. dept. communication Mich. State U., East Lansing, 1972-76; dean Coll. Communication Arts and Scis., 1976-96, dean emeritus, 1997—; dep. dir. AMC Cancer Rsch. Ctr., Denver, 1997—2002; sr. scientist Cooper Inst., 2002—, assoc. v.p., 2003—. Vis. prof. U. Okla., 1970-71 Author: The Nature of Proof, 1971, Persuasive Communication, 1994. Mem. Nat. Cancer Adv. Bd., 1988-94. With U.S. Army, 1953-56. Mem. AAAS, APA, Internat. Comm. Assn. (pres. 1982), Am. Comm. Assn., Assn. for Edn. in Journalism, Assn. Comm. Adminstrn. (pres. 1991). Home: 2170 S Parfet Dr Lakewood CO 80227-1900

BETTINSON, BRENDA, artist, educator; b. King's Lynn, Eng., Aug. 17, 1929; arrived in US, 1960, naturalized, 1966; d. Randall Cecil and Edith Ottaline (Mitchley) Bettinson. Nat. diploma in design, Ctrl. Sch. Arts & Crafts, London, 1950; Elève Titulaire, Ecole Pratique des Hautes Etudes, Sorbonne, 1952; student, Acad. de la Grande Chaumiere, Paris, 1951-52, U. Paris, Sorbonne, 1950-3. Art editor WRVR-FM/Ednl. Radio Network, N.Y.C., 1961-65; mem. art dept. Pace U., N.Y.C., Westchester, N.Y., 1963-90, chair dept. art & design Westchester, N.Y., 1978-83, prof. emeritus N.Y.C., 1990—; lectr. Katonah (N.Y.) Mus., 1972, 89; represented by Mathias Fine Art, Trevett, Maine. One-woman shows include, US and Europe, 1949—, Ogunquit Mus. Am. Art, 2002—. Home and Office: 10 Mathias Dr Trevett ME 04571-3131

BETTIS, JEROME ABRAM, professional football player; b. Detroit, Feb. 16, 1972; Student, U. Notre Dame. Running back L.A. Rams (moved to St. Louis 1995), 1993—94, St. Louis Rams, 1995, Pitts. Steelers, 1996—. Named NFL Rookie of Yr., Sporting News, 1993; named to Pro Bowl, 1993, 1994, 1996. Office: 3400 S Water St Pittsburgh PA 15203-2349 Mailing: PO Box 6763 Pittsburgh PA 15212

BETTISCH, JOHANN, linguist, researcher; b. Temeschburg, Rumania, July 29, 1932; arrived in Germany, 1990; s. Matthias and Maria (Kanyady) B.; m. Katharina Reitter, Oct. 21, 1959; 1 child, Edmond. Diploma in Russian langs., U. Bucharest, 1957; D in Philology, U. Timisaora, Rumania, 1988. Electrotechnician Electromontaj, Timisoara, 1952-55; fgn. lang. tchr. German and Hungarian schs. Resita, 1957-63; sch. inspector County Caras-Severin, Resita, 1963-67; dep. dir. German H.S., Resita, 1967-74; fgn. lang. lectr. Engring Inst. (now named Eftimie Murgu U.), Resita, 1974-82, pro-dean, 1982-89; owner Trans. Bur., Stuttgart, 1990. Hon. prof. Internat. Albert Schweitzer U., Geneva. Author: (book) Breviary of Chinese Literature, 1981, 2nd edit., 2001, Technical English, 1983, Russian Language for Engineers, 1986, Die Technik auf Deutsch, 1988; editor: Grimaces behind the Mirror, 2000; ; translator: E. Gherasim's Pocketphilosophy, 2000; editor: Lang., Lit. and Folklore, 1968—78, Kaffeepause, 2001, Das verbotene Grinsen, 2001, La mintea cocosului, 2002; : Philosophische Pillen, 2002, The Cultural Doctorate in Philosophy of Linguistics, 2002, Gedankensplitter, 2003, Kurze Erzählungen, 2003, Zwischen Sinn und Unsinn, 2003, Zu Zweit um die Welt, 2003, others; contbr. over 150 articles to profl. jours.; editor: Zwischen Siun und Unsinn, 2003. With Rumanian mil., 1955-57. Recipient award County Caras-Severin Nat. Inventions Saloon, 1987. Mem. N.Y. Acad. Scis., World Writers Assn. Avocations: etymology research, esperanto, science fiction. Home and Office: Weilimdorfer Strasse 157 70469 Stuttgart Germany E-mail: jbettisch@aol.com.

BETTMAN, GARY BRUCE, sports league official, lawyer; b. N.Y.C., June 2, 1952; s. Howard G. and Gretel J. (Pollack) B.; m. Michelle Weiner, Aug. 24, 1975; children: Lauren, Jordan, Brittany. BS, Cornell U., 1974; JD, NYU, 1977. Bar: N.Y. 1978, N.J. 1978, U.S. Dist. Ct. (so. and ea. dists.) N.Y. 1979. Assoc. Proskauer Rose, N.Y.C., 1977-80, Gutkin, Miller et al, Milburn, N.J., 1980-81; asst. gen. counsel NBA, N.Y.C., 1981-84, v.p., gen. counsel, 1984-89, sr. v.p., gen. counsel, 1989-93; commr. NHL, N.Y.C., 1993—. Mem. N.Y. State Bar Assn., Assn. of Bar of City of N.Y. (chmn. com. on sports law), N.J. Bar Assn., Sports Lawyers Assn. (bd. dirs. 1985-93, entertainment and sports law com. 1990-93), Phi Kappa Phi. Avocations: skiing, sailing, tennis. Office: NHL 47th Flr 1251 Ave of the Americas New York NY 10020

BETTMAN, JAMES ROSS, management educator; b. Laurinburg, N.C., Sept. 15, 1943; s. Roland David and Virginia Gertrude (Hare) B.; m. Joan Carol Scribner, Dec. 16, 1967; 1 child, David James. BA, Yale U., 1965, MPhil, PhD, Yale U., 1969. Prof. mgmt. Grad. Sch. Mgmt., UCLA, 1969-82; IBM rsch. prof. Fuqua Sch. Bus., Duke U., Durham, N.C., 1982-83, Burlington Industries prof., 1983—. Author: An Information Processing Theory of Consumer Choice, 1979, The Adaptive Decision Maker, 1993, Emotional Decisions: Tradeoff Difficulty and Coping in Consumer Choice, 2001; co-editor Jour. of Consumer Rsch., 1981-87, editor monographs, 2002--; contbr. chpts. to books, articles to profl. jours. Recipient Melamed prize for bus. rsch., 2000; named ISI HIghly Cited Rschr., Econs./Bus., 2003. Fellow APA, Am. Psychol. Soc.; mem. Assn. Consumer Rsch. (bd. dirs. 1976-79, pres. 1987, fellow in consumer behavior 1992), Inst. Ops. Rsch. and Mgmt. Sci., Am. Mktg. Assn. (Harold M. Maynard award 1979, Paul D. Converse award 1992, Irwin/McGraw-Hill Disting. Mktg. Educator award 2000). Democrat. Episcopalian. Home: 213 Huntington Dr Chapel Hill NC 27514-2419 Office: Duke U Fuqua Sch of Bus Durham NC 27708-0120 E-mail: jrb12@mail.duke.edu.

BETTS, BARBARA LANG, lawyer, rancher, realtor; b. Anaheim, Calif., Apr. 28, 1926; d. W. Harold and Helen (Thompson) Lang; m. Roby F. Hayes, July 22, 1948 (dec.); children: John Chauncey IV, Frederick Prescott, Roby Francis II; m. Bert A. Betts, July 11, 1962; 1 child, Bruce Harold; stepchildren: Bert Alan, Randy W., Sally Betts Joynt, Terry Betts Marsteller, Linda Betts Hansen, LeAnn Betts Wilson. BA magna cum laude, Stanford U., 1948; LLB, Balboa U., 1951. Bar: Calif. 1952, U.S. Supreme Ct. 1978. Pvt. practice, Oceanside, Calif., 1952-68, San Diego, 1960—, Sacramento, 1962—. Ptnr. Roby F. Hayes &

Barbara Lang Hayes, 1952-60; city atty. Carlsbad, Calif., 1959-63; v.p. Isle & Oceans Marinas, Inc., 1970-80, W.H. Lang Corp., 1964-69; sec. Internat. Prodn. Assocs., 1968—, Margaret M. McCabe, M.D., Inc., 1977-78. Co-author: (with Bert A. Betts) A Citizen Answers. Chmn. Traveler's Aid, 1952-53; pres. Oceanside-Carlsbad Jr. Chambrettes, 1955-56; vice chmn. Carlsbad Planning Commn., 1959; mem. San Diego Planning commn., 1959; v.p. Oceanside Diamond Jubilee Com., 1958; candidate Calif. State Legislature, 77th Dist., 1954; mem. Calif. Dem. State Ctrl. Com., 1958-66, co-chmn. 1960-62; co-chmn. 28th Congl. Dist.; alt. del. Dem. Nat. Conv., 1960; co-sponsor All Am. B-24 Liberator Collings Found. Named to Fullerton Union H.S. Wall of Fame, 1986; recipient Block S award Stanford U. Mem. ABA, AAUW (legis. com. 1958-59, local pres. 1959-60, asst. state legis. chmn. 1958-59), DAR (regent Oceanside chpt. 1960-61), DFC Soc. (assoc.), Am. Judicature Soc., Nat. Inst. Mcpl. Officers, Calif. Bar Assn., San Diego County Bar Assn., Oceanside C. of C. (sec. 1957, v.p. 1958, dir. 1953-54, 57-59), Heritage League (2d divsn. 8th Air Force), No. San Diego County Assn. Cs. of C. (sec.-treas.), Bus. and Profl. Women's Club (so. dist. legislation chmn. 1958-59), San Diego C. of C., San Diego Hist. Soc., Fullerton Jr. Assistance League, Calif. Scholarship Fedn. (life), Loyola Guild of Jesuit H.S., Soroptimist Internat. (pres. Oceanside-Carlsbad 1958-59, sec. pub. affairs San Diego and Imperial Counties 1954, pres. pres.'s coun. San Diego and Imperial Counties, Mex. 1958-59), Barristers (Stanford, Sacramento), Disting. Flying Cross Soc. (assoc.), Stanford Mothers, Phi Beta Kappa. Home: 441 Sandburg Dr Sacramento CA 95819-2559 Office: 1830 Avenida Del Mundo #1608 Coronado CA 92118-3018 E-mail: blbbabbetts@earthlink.net.

BETTS, BARBARA STOKE, artist, educator; b. Arlington, Mass., Apr. 19, 1924; d. Stuart and Barbara Lillian (Johnstone) Stoke; m. James William Betts, July 28, 1951; 1 child, Barbara Susan (dec.). BA, Mt. Holyoke Coll., 1946; MA, Columbia U., 1948. Cert. tchr., N.Y., Calif., Hawaii. Art tchr. Walton (N.Y.) Union Schs., 1947-48, Presidio Hill Sch., San Francisco, 1949-51; freelance artist San Francisco, 1951; art tchr. Honolulu Acad. Arts, summer 1952, 59, 63, 85, spring 61, 64; libr. aide art rm. Libr. of Hawaii, Honolulu, 1959; art tchr. Hanahauoli Sch., Honolulu, 1961-62, Hawaii State Dept. Edn., Honolulu, 1958-59, 64-84; owner Ho'olaule'a Designs, Honolulu, 1973—; art editor Portfolio Cons. of Hawaii, 1990—. Staff artist: The Arcadian newsletter, 2000—; illustrator: Cathedral Cooks, 1964, In Due Season, 1986, From Nowhere To Somewhere On A Round Trip Ticket, 2003, exhibited in Hawaii Pavilion Expo '90, Osaka, Japan, State Found. Culture and Arts, group shows since 1964, one woman shows 1991, 96, 99; represented in Arts of Paradise Gallery, Waikiki, 1990-2001, Hale Ku'ai, a Hawaiian Coop., 1998-2001; traveling exhbns. include Pacific Prints, 1991, Printmaking East/West, 1993-95, Hawaii/Wis. Watercolor Show, 1993-94. Mem. Hawaii Watercolor Soc. (newsletter editor 1986-90), Nat. League Am. Pen Women (art chmn. 1990-92, sec. 1992-94, 2000-02, nat. miniature art shows 1991, 92, 93, 95), Honolulu Printmakers (dir. 1986, 87), Assn. Hawaii Artists, scholarship aid programs, Mount Holyoke Coll., Mary Lyon Soc., Rutgers Univ., Col. Henry Rutgers Soc. Republican. Episcopalian. Avocations: art, travel, writing, photography. Home: 1434 Punahou St Apt 1028 Honolulu HI 96822-4740

BETTS, BERT A. former state treasurer, accountant; b. San Diego, Aug. 16, 1923; s. Bert A. and Alma (Jorgenson) B.; m. Barbara Lang; children: Terry Lou, Linda Sue, Sara Ellen, Bert Alan, Randy Wayne, LeAnn, John Chauncey, Frederick P., Roby F., Bruce H. BBA, Calif. Western U., 1950. CPA, Calif. Accountant John R. Gillette, 1946-48; ptnr. Gillette & Betts, 1949-50; pvt. accounting practice, 1951-54; ptnr. Betts & Munden, Lemon Grove, Calif., 1954-57; sr. ptnr. Bert A. Betts & Co., 1958-59; treas. State of Calif., 1959-67; prin. Bert A. Betts & Assos., 1967-77. Chief exec. officer Internat. Prodn. Assocs., 1970-87; dir. Lifetime Communities Inc.; gen. partner Sacramento Met. Airport Properties 4, Ltd., 1970-2002. Author (with Barbara Lang Betts): A Citizen Answers. Mem. Lemon Grove Sch. Bd., 1954-57; Calif. chmn. Max Baer Heart Fund; state employees chmn. Am. Cancer Sco., 1962-64, bd. dirs. county br., 1963-69, Sacramento County campaign chmn., mem. exec. com., 1965, pres. Sacramento chpt., 1967-68; sponsor All Am. B-24 Liberator Collings Found. Served as 1st lt. USAAF, 1942-45. Decorated D.F.C., Air medal with four clusters; recipient Louisville award Municipal Finance Officers Assn. U.S. and Can., 1963; honored by Calif. Mcpl. Treas.'s Assn., 1964; inductee Hoover H.S. Hall of Fame, San Diego, 1998, Grossmont Health Dist. Gallery of Honor, 2002. Mem. Nat. Assn. State Auditors, Comptrs. and Treas's Mcpl. Forum N.Y., Calif. Soc. CPAs, San Diego Squadron Air Force Assn. (past vice comdr.), Am. Legion, 2d Air Div. Assn., 8th Air Force Hist. Soc., VFW, Commemorative Air Force (col.), Native Sons. Golden West, Internat. B-24 Liberator Club, Foresters, Lemon Grove Masonic Lodge, Calif. Scholarship Fedn. (life), DFC Soc., Sigma Phi Epsilon, Beta Alpha Psi (hon.), Alpha Kappa Psi (hon.). Clubs: Eagles; Men's (Lemon Grove) (pres.), Lions (Lemon Grove) (treas.); Commonwealth. Presbyterian. Home: 441 Sandburg Dr Sacramento CA 95819-2559 also: 1830 Avenida Del Mundo Coronado CA 92118-3018 E-mail: blbbabbetts@earthlink.net.

BETTS, DIANNE CONNALLY, economist, educator; b. Tyler, Tex., Sept. 23, 1948; d. William Isaac and Martine (Underwood) Connally; m. Floyd Galloway Betts Jr., Feb. 14, 1973. BA in History, So. Meth. U., 1976, MA in History, 1980; MA in Econ., U. Chgo., 1986; PhD in Econ., U. Tex., 1991. Affiliated scholar Inst. for Rsch. on Women and Gender/Stanford U., 1993—; economist, tech. analyst, fin. cons. Smith Barney, Dallas, 1994—2000; economist, fin. cons. Morgan Keegan, Dallas, 2000—. Mem. women studies coun. So. Meth. U., 1993-94, Fulbright campus interviewing com. mem. 1992-93, pub. rels. and devel. liaison dept. econ., 1990-92, faculty mentor U. honors first year mentoring program, adj. asst. prof. dept. econ. and history, 1992—, vis. asst. prof. 1990-92; faculty, Oxford, summer 1991-93, adj. instr. dept. history, 1989-90, adj. instr. dept. econ., 1985-89, tchg. asst. dept. history, spring 1980; lectr. dept. polit. economy U. Tex., Dallas, summer 1988. Author: Crisis on the Rio Grande: Poverty, Unemployment, and Economic Development on the Texas-Mexico Border, 1994, Historical Perspectives on the American Economy: Selected Reading, 1995; contbr. articles to profl. jours. Rsch. Planning grant NSF, 1992; recipient Marguereta Deschner Teaching award, 1991; Humanities and Scis. Merit scholar, 1978. Mem. Am. Econ. Assn., Am. History Assn., Econ. History Assn., Cliometric Soc., Social Sci. History Assn., N.Am. Conf. on British Studies, Nat. Coun. for Rsch. on Women (affiliate), Omicron Delta Epsilon, Phi Alpha Theta. Home: 6267 Revere Pl Dallas TX 75214-3099 Office: Morgan Keegan 5956 Sherry Ln # 2002 Dallas TX 75225-6531 E-mail: dcbetts@airmail.net.

BETTS, DORIS JUNE WAUGH, writer, English language educator; b. Statesville, N.C., June 4, 1932; d. William Elmore and Mary Ellen (Freeze) Waugh; m. Lowry Matthews Betts, July 5, 1952; children: Doris LewEllyn, David Lowry, Erskine Moore II. Student, Woman's Coll., U. N.C., 1950-53, U. N.C., 1954; DLitt (hon.), Greensboro Coll., 1987; DLitt, U. N.C., Greensboro, 1990, Queens Coll., 1995; LHD, Erskine Coll., 1994; DHL, Pembroke U., 1995. Newspaperwoman Statesville Daily Record, 1950-51, Chapel Hill (N.C.) Weekly and News-Leader, 1953-54; editorial staff Sanford Daily Herald, 1956-57, N.C. Democrat, 1961-62; editor Sanford (N.C.) News Leader, 1962; lectr. creative writing English dept. U. N.C., Chapel Hill, 1966-74, dir. freshman-sophomore English, 1972-76, assoc. prof., 1974-78, dir. Fellows program, 1975-76, prof., 1978—, asst. dean Honors program, 1979-81, chmn. faculty, 1982-85, Alumni Disting. prof., 1983-2001, chair faculty, 1980-83, prof. emerita, 2001—. Vis. lectr. creative writing Duke U., 1971; staff Ind. U. Summer Writers Conf., 1972, 73; mem. bd. Assoc. Writing Programs, lit. panel Nat. Endowment for Arts, 1979-81, chmn., 1981. Author: (story collections) The Gentle Insurrection, 1954 (G.P. Putnam-U. N.C. Fiction award 1954), The Astronomer and Other Stories, 1966, Beasts of the Southern Wild and Other Stories, 1973 (National Book award nomination 1974); (novels) Tall Houses in Winter, 1957 (Sir Walter Raleigh award 1957), The Scarlet Thread, 1964 (Sir Walter Raleigh award 1965), The River to Pickle Beach, 1972, Heading West, 1981, Souls Raised from the Dead, 1994 (Southern Book Critics award, Southeastern Libr. Assn. award), The Sharp Teeth of Love, 1997, (musical) Violet, 1997; editor: Young Writers at Chapel Hill, 1968; contbr.: Three by Three: Masterworks of the Southern Gothic, 1985, others; appeared in dramatized version of The Ugliest Pilgrim as Violet (Academy award Tex. Film Festival); bibliography in The Home Truths of Doris Betts, 1992. Mem. N.C. Tercentenary Commn., 1961-62, Sanford City Sch. Bd., 1965-71; lit. com. NEA, 1979-82, chair, 1982; mem. ctrl. com. Morehead Found., 1978-93, chair 1992-93; bd. trustees Nat. Humanities Ctr., 1993-96, Union Theol. Seminary, Richmond, Va., 1993-97. Recipient Short Story prize Mademoiselle mag., 1953, N.C. medal for lit., 1975, John Dos Passos award, 1983, medal of merit in short story divsn. Am. Acad. Arts and Letters, 1989, Parker award for lit. achievement, 1982-85, John Caldwell award for svc. to humanities, 1992; Guggenheim fellow, 1958-59, Doctor of Letters (hon.) from Greensboro Coll., Queens Coll., UNC-Pembroke, UNC-Greensboro, Erskine Coll., U. of the South, Carolinian Awd., 1998; Thomas Jefferson Awd., 1999, Judge P.E.N. Hemingway Awds., 1999, Lifetime Achievement award Christianity and Literature, MLA, 2000; Betts Professorship in Creative Writing created in her honor, U. N.C., Chapel Hill, 2001. Mem. N.C. Writers Assn. Address: Dept English 795-B NC #902 Pittsboro NC 27312

BETTS, DOROTHY ANNE, elementary school educator; b. Washington, Nov. 3, 1946; d. Thomas Joseph and Elizabeth Anne (McGee) Salb; m. Jerold LeRoy Betts, July 14, 1975; 1 child, Ellen Marie. BS in Elem. Edn., U. N.Mex., 1968, MA in Edn., 1976. Cert. tchr. N.Mex. Tchr. Newman (Calif.)-Gustine Dist., 1968—69, Albuquerque Pub. Schs., 1969—79, 1980—84, 1999—, ednl. asst., 1993—99; co-owner Stork News N.Mex. Zuni Elem. Sch. coord. Pennies for Patients Leukemia and Lymphoma Soc., Albuquerque, 2001. Mem.: Delta Kappa Gamma (1st v.p. 1982—84, pres. 1984—86, 2d v.p. 2000—02). Roman Catholic. Avocations: travel, family outings, crafts. Home: 10118 4th St NW Albuquerque NM 87114

BETTS, HENRY BROGNARD, physician, health facility administrator, educator; b. New Rochelle, N.Y., May 25, 1928; s. Henry Brognard and Marguerite Meredith (Denise) B.; m. Monika Christine Paul, Apr. 25, 1970. AB, Princeton U., 1950; MD, U. Va., 1954; DSc (hon.), Hamilton Coll., 1992; D in Pub. Svc. (hon.), Ohio State U., 2001. Diplomate: Am. Bd. Phys. Medicine and Rehab. Intern Cin. Gen. Hosp., 1954-55; resident, teaching fellow NYU Med. Center Inst. Rehab. Medicine (Rusk Inst.), N.Y.C., 1958-63; practice medicine, specializing in phys. medicine and rehab. Chgo., 1963—; staff physiatrist Rehab. Inst. Chgo., 1963-64, assoc. med. dir., 1964-65, med. dir., 1965-86, med. dir., CEO, 1986-94, pres., CEO, 1994-97, past med. dir., pres., CEO, 1997—; chmn. Rehab. Inst. Found., 1997. Chmn. dept. phys. medicine and rehab. Northwestern U. Med. Sch., 1967-94, prof., 1967—, Magnuson prof., 1994-97, assoc. mem. Robert H. Lurie Cancer Ctr., 1993—; cons. Northwestern Meml. Hosp., Chgo.; mem. adv. bd. Commn. on Future Structure of Vets. Health Care, Dept. Vets. Affairs, 1990-92, Vets. Adv. Com. on Rehab., 1990-96; med. adv. com. Spl. Olympics Internat., 1991—. Contbr. articles to profl. jours. Bd. dirs. Very Spl. Arts, 1981—, The Hastings Ctr., Nat. Orgn. on Disabilities, Old Masters Soc., Art Inst. Chgo.; chmn. Physicians Against Land Mines, Access Living, Am. Assn. People with Disabilities, The Admiral, Chgo. Botanic Garden, Crossroads Ctr./Antigua, Legal Clinic for the Disabled, World Com. Disability, World Rehab. Fund, Pres. Com. Employment of People with Disabilities, VSArts, 2001. Recipient Disting. Svc. award Ill. Congress Orgns. Physically Handicapped, 1982, Disting. Svc. award Marine Scholarship Found., Chgo., 1993, Individual Leadership award Infinitec-United Cerebral Palsy, 1994, Disting. Pub. Svc. award Am. Acad. Phys. Medicine and Rehab., 1994, John W. Goldschmidt award Nat. Rehab. Hosp., Washington, 1996, James Brady award Ill. Head Injury Assn., 1989, Disting. Svc. award Nat. Orgn. on Disabilities, 1989, Milton Cohen Disting. Career award Nat. Assn. Rehab. Facilities, 1990, Henry H. Kessler Human Dignity award Kessler Inst. Rehab. Inc., 1992, The Scopus award Am. Friends of the Hebrew U., 1995, The August W. Christmann award City of Chgo. Mayor's Office for People with Disabilities and MOPD Adv. Council, 1995, Hon. diploma Archeworks, Chgo., 1997, Achievement award Rusk Inst., 1997, Disting. Mem. award Am. Acad. Phys. Medicine and Rehab., 1998, Disting. Svc. award Am. Hosp. Assn., 1998, Disting. Alumnus award Dept. Rehab. Medicine Rusk Inst., NYU Med. Sch., 1998, Paul J. Corcoran Disting. lectr. Harvard Med. Sch. PM&R Grad., 1999, 2002, Madonna Spirit award Madonna Rehab. Hosp., 1999, Order of Lincoln award Lincoln Acad. Ill., 2001, Henry Russe Citation Exemplary Compassion in Healthcare, 2001, Lifetime Achievement award Am. Spinal Injury Assn., 2001, Order of Lincoln award Lincoln Acad. Ill., 2001; named Physician of Yr., Ill. Gov.'s Com., 1964, Exec. of Yr., Ill. Assn. Rehab. Facilities, 1989—; commended by Ill. Gen. Assembly, 1967; cited for meritorious svc. Pres.'s Com. on Employment of Handicapped, 1965. Mem. Ill. Med. Soc., Assn. Acad. Physiatrists (pres. 1968-69, bd. dirs. 1990-95, Pub. Svc. award 1998), Am. Congress Rehab. Med. (med. adv. com., pres. 1976-77, Gold Key 1984), Mid-Am. Soc. Phys. Med. and Rehab. (pres. 1969), Brain Trauma Found. (bd. dirs. 1990-93). Home: 1727 N Orleans St Chicago IL 60614 Office: Rehabilitation Inst 345 E Superior St Chicago IL 60611-4805

BETTS, JAMES WILLIAM, JR., financial analyst, consultant; b. Oct. 11, 1923; s. James William and Cora Anna (Banta) B.; m. Barbara Stoke, July 28, 1951; 1 child, Barbara Susan (dec.). BA, Rutgers U., 1946; postgrad., New Sch. for Social Rsch., 1948-49; MA, U. Hawaii, 1957. With Dun & Bradstreet, Inc., 1946-86, svc. cons., 1963-64, reporting and svc. mgr., 1964-65, sr. fin. analyst, 1965-86; owner Portfolio Cons. of Hawaii, 1979—. Cons. Saybrook Point Investments, Old Saybrook, Conn., 1979—; owner James W. Betts and Co., 1996—. Scrapbook Press, 2002. Author: From Nowhere to Somewhere on a Round Trip Ticket, 2003; contbr. articles to mags. With AUS, 1943. Mem. Am. Econ. Assn., Nat. Assn. Bus. Economists, Western Econ. Assn., Atlantic Econ. Soc., Col. Henry Rutgers Soc., Internat. Inst. Forecasters, Transp. Rsch. Forum. Republican. Episcopalian. E-mail: kimorail@aol.com.

BETTS, KATHLEEN VANETTA, human resources executive; b. West Newton, Mass., July 15, 1955; d. John Rickards and Cecelia (Fitzpatrick) B.; m. Steven P. Lewis, May 14, 1988; stepchildren: Audra and Corbin Lewis. BA magna cum laude, Boston Coll., 1977, MSW, 1979. Lic. ind. clin. social worker, Mass. Sr. clin. counselor Family Health Ctr., Worcester, Mass., 1979-81, dir. social svcs., 1981-83; personnel rep. U. Hosp. Boston, U. Med. Ctr., 1984-86, compensation mgr., 1986-87; human resources mgr. Polyken Tech. div. Kendall Co., Westwood, Mass., 1987-90; mgr. of compensation Magee-Womens Hosp., Pitts., 1991-95; v.p., dir. human resources Peritus Software Svcs., Inc., 1995—99; v.p. human resources Lightbridge, Inc., Burlington, Mass., 1999—. Cons. Natick (Mass.) pub. sch. system, 1983-84, AAC Counseling Agy., Malden, Mass., 1983-84. Mem. Am. Compensation Assn., Soc. for Human Resources Mgmt. Democrat. Roman Catholic. Avocations: travel, reading, jogging, cycling. Address: 199 Follen Rd Lexington MA 02421-5943

BETTS, KIRK HOWARD, lawyer; b. Jersey City, Mar. 5, 1951; s. Fred Semour and Mary Elizabeth (Morrell) B.; m. Christine Marlene Sheridan, Mar. 19, 1976; 1 child, Abigail Sheridan. BA, George Washington U., 1973; JD, Am. U., 1979. Bar: D.C. 1980, U.S. Dist. Ct. (D.C. dist.) 1980, U.S. Ct. Appeals (D.C., 5th and 11th cirs.) 1980, U.S. Supreme Ct. 1984, Md. 1986, U.S. Ct. Appeals (6th cir.) 1989, U.S. Dist. Ct. Md. 1995. Assoc. Northcutt Ely, Washington, 1979-82; mng. ptnr. Ely, Ritts, Pietrowski & Brickfield, Washington, 1982-84, Ely, Ritts, Brickfield & Betts, Washington, 1984-86; counsel Dickinson, Wright, Moon, Van Dusen & Freeman, Washington, 1986-87, ptnr., 1987-96, ptnr. in charge Washington office, 1993-95; mng. ptnr. Betts & Holt, Washington, 1996—. Asst. counsel U.S. Senate subcom. on intergovtl. rels., Washington, 1974-76; legis. aide to Hon. Wiliam V. Roth, Washington, 1973-74; bd. dirs. Luth. Ctr. Corp. Chmn. bd. mgrs. for Hallowood Conf. Ctr., St. Luke Luth. Ch., Silver Spring, Md., 1985—, ch. coun., 1987-90, 2000-02, v.p., 1989, 2000; chmn. Carl E. and Nathalia B. Rantzow Endowment for Sem. Edn., 1989—; pres.'s cabinet Luth. Theol. Sem., Gettysburg, 1995—; bd. dirs. Luth. World Relief, 1998—, sec., 2000-01, vice-chmn. 2002—. Named to Hon. Order Ky. Cols., 1988; awarded key to City of Vanceburg, Ky., 1987. Mem. ABA (sects. on pub. utility law, law practice mgmt., trust and real property, Best Article in Series award 1980), D.C. Bar Assn., Md. State Bar Assn., Energy Bar Assn., Wash. Coll. Law/Am. U. (alumni rels. com. 1987-88, devel. coun. 1989—, chmn. 1993-95, deans adv. coun. 1995—), ELCA Attys. Assn., Podickory Yacht Club (Annapolis, Md. vice commodore 1975-76). Republican. Lutheran. Avocations: sailing, woodworking, collecting lit. about Chesapeake Bay. Home: 6412 Goldleaf Dr Bethesda MD 20817-5830 Office: Betts & Holt West Tower 10th Fl 1333 H St NW Washington DC 20005-4707 E-mail: kbetts@bettsandholt.com.

BETTS, RICHARD KEVIN, political science educator; b. Easton, Pa., Aug. 15, 1947; s. John Rickards and Cecelia Agnes (Fitzpatrick) B.; m. Adela Maria Bolet, July 25, 1987; children: Elena, Michael, Diego. BA, Harvard U., 1969, MA, 1971, PhD, 1975. Lectr. in government Harvard U., Cambridge, Mass., 1975-76, vis. prof., 1985-88; rsch. assoc. Brookings Instn., Washington, 1976-81, sr. fellow, 1981-90; dir. Inst. War and Peace Studies, Columbia U., N.Y.C., 1990—, Shifrin prof. polit. sci., 1998—2002, Saltzman prof., 2002—; dir. nat. securities studies Coun. on Fgn. Rels., 1996-2000. Mem. staff Senate Select Com. on Intelligence, Washington, 1975-76, NSC, Washington, 1977; adj. prof. Johns Hopkins U., Washington, 1978-85, 88-90; cons. CIA, 1980-91, 93-99, 2003—; dir. ctrl. intelligence Nat. Security Adv. Panel, 1993-99; mem. Nat. Commn. on Terrorism, 1999-2000; occasion lectr. Nat. War Coll., Fgn. Svcs. Inst., U.S. Mil. Acad. Author: Soldiers, Statesmen and Cold War Crises, 1977 (2d edit. 1991, Lasswell award 1979), Surprise Attack, 1982, Nuclear Blackmail and Nuclear Balance, 1987, Military Readiness, 1995; co-author: The Irony of Vietnam, 1979 (Woodrow Wilson award 1980), Nonproliferation and U.S. Foreign Policy, 1980; editor: Cruise Missiles, 1981, Conflict After the Cold War, 1994, 2d edit., 2001. Mem. foreign policy staff Mondale Presidential Campaign, Washington, 1984; mem. Assn. for Retarded Citizens, Bergen County, N.J., 1990—. Recipient Sumner prize Harvard U., 1976, Article award Nat. Intelligence Study Ctr., Washington, 1979, '81. Mem. Internat. Inst. for Strategic Studies, Am. Polit. Sci. Assn., Internat. Studies Assn., Soc. for Historians Am. Fgn. Rels., Consortium for Study Intelligence. Democrat. Avocation: cinema history. Home: 1199 The Strand Teaneck NJ 07666-2020 Office: Columbia U Saltzman Inst War & Peace Studies 420 W 118th St New York NY 10027-7213

BETTS, RICHARD RUSSELL, science educator; b. Harrogate, Yorkshire, Eng., May 21, 1947; s. John Richard Mills and Margaret Agnes Betts; m. Katherine Anne Puusti, Oct. 23, 1976; children: Nicholas Alfred John, Alison Sarah. BA, Oxford U., Eng., 1968, MA, 1984; MS, U. Pa., 1969, PhD, 1972. Post doctoral U. Pa., Phila., 1972—73, Niels Bohr Inst., Copenhagen, 1973—75; asst. prof. Yale U., New Haven, 1975—79; physicist Argonne (Ill.) Nat. Lab., 1979—88, sr. physicist, 1988—99; fellow and tutor in physics Lady Margaret Hall, Oxford, 1984—86; lectr. Oxford U., 1984—86; adj. prof. U. Ill., Chgo., 1993—94, physics prof., 1994—. Contbr. articles to more than 200 publs. Avocations: music, theater, golf. Office: UIC Physics Department (M/C 273) 845 West Taylor Street Chicago IL 60607 Office Fax: 312-996-9016. E-mail: betts@uic.edu.

BETTS, ROLAND W. real estate developer; b. May 25, 1946; m. Lois Betts; children: Margaret, Jessica. JD, Columbia Law Sch., 1978; B, Yale U., 1968. Tchr., I.S. 201 The Teachers Inc., Ctrl. Harlem, NY, 1968; from tchr. to asst. prin. N.Y.C. Schools, 1968—76; with Paul, Weiss, Rifkind, Wharton & Garrison, 1978; founder & pres. Silver Screen Mgmt., Inc., 1983; chmn. & founder Chelsea Piers, L.P., N.Y.C., 1994—. Lead owner Tex. Rangers Baseball Club, 1989—97. Author: (book) Acting Out: Coping with Big City Schools, 1978. Mem. U.S. Olympic Com.; trustee Am. Mus. of Natural Hist., Meml. Sloan-Kettering Cancer Ctr., N.Y.C., Columbia U. Law Sch., Georgia O'Keefe Mus.; fellow Yale Corp.; mem. bd. directors Lower Manhattan Devel. Corp. Office: Chelsea Piers LP Chelsea Piers 62 Ste 300 New York NY 10011*

BETTY, CHARLES GARRY, communications executive; BChemE, Ga. Inst. Tech., 1979. Various positions IBM; sr. v.p. sales, mktg. and internat. ops. Hayes Microcomputer Products, 1984-89; CEO N.Y. Stock Exchange; pres., CEO Digital Comm. Assocs., Inc.; CEO EarthLink Inc., Atlanta. Chmn. Ga.'s High Tech Month, 1993; bd. dirs. DBT OnLine, allAutoRepair.com.; mem. Ga. Tech Adv. Bd.; chmn. Physician's Data Corp. Named Top 40 Under 40 list in Atlanta's bus. cmty., Outstanding Young Person, Atlanta Bus. Chronicle. Office: EarthLink Inc 1430 W Peachtree St NW Ste 400 Atlanta GA 30309-2935

BETZ, A. LORRIS, dean, pediatrician, educator, consultant; b. LaCrosse, Wis., Feb. 9, 1947; s. Alert L. and Charlotte M. (Kopp) B.; m. Ann C. Doyle, Aug. 30, 1968; children: Jennifer A., Bryan L. BS, U. Wis., 1969, MD., PhD, 1975. Intern pediatrics U. Calif., San Francisco, 1975, resident in pediatrics, 1975-79; asst. prof. pediatrics and neurology U. Mich., Ann Arbor, 1979-83, assoc. prof. pediatrics and neurology, 1983-87, prof. pediatrics, surgery, neurology, 1987—99, dir. neurosurg. rsch., surgery, 1987—99, assoc. dean for faculty affairs, 1993-97, interim dean Med. Sch., 1997—99; dean, sr. v.p. health sci. U. Utah Med. Sch., Salt Lake City, 1999—. Cons. NIH, Bethesda, Md., 1985—. Editorial bd.: Jour. Neurochemistry, 1986-94; contbr. articles to Sci., Brain Rsch., Sci. Am., Stroke, Am. Jour. Physiology. Grantee, NIH, Univ. Mich., 1980—; named Established Investigator, Am. Heart Assn., Univ. Mich., 1981. Mem. Internat. Soc. Cerebral Blood Flow and Metabolism (bd. dirs. 1991—, sec. 1995—), Internat. Soc. Neurochemistry, Am. Physiol. Soc., Soc. for Pediatric Rsch., Am. Pediatric Soc., Phi Beta Kappa, Sigma Xi, Alpha Omega Alpha. Achievements include research in basic mechanisms that are responsible for moving nutrients and electrolytes between the blood and the brain of mammals, processes that produce brain injury following a stroke. Office: Health Sci Ctr Moran Eye Ctrs Fl 5 50 N Med Dr Salt Lake City UT 84132-0001

BETZ, EUGENE WILLIAM, architect; b. Dayton, Ohio, Jan. 12, 1921; s. Jesse Earl and Elizabeth Freda (Meyer) B.; m. Marjorie Lois Frank, Oct. 30, 1948; children: Douglas William, Gregory Vincent. BS, U. Cin., 1944. Pres. Eugene W. Betz, Architects, Inc., Dayton, 1956—; Chmn. Bd. Building Standards and Appeals, 1960-63, Kettering Planning Commn., 1957-61. Served with AUS. Recipient Honor award Architects Soc. Ohio, 1967, 71; Award of Merit, 1968, 77, 78; Nation's Sch. Month award Nat. Council Schoolhouse Constrn., 1967; Nat. Citation Am. Assn. Sch. Adminstrs., 1967, 71; Masonry award of excellence, 1976, 78; Outstanding Health Care Facility award UCLA/Columbia U./Archtl. Record, 1980 Mem. AIA (nat. com. architecture for health, 25 Yr. Bldg. award, Dayton Lifetime Excellence in Arch. award), Masons (32nd degree), Rotary. Home and Office: 820 Greenspire Ct Dayton OH 45459-1500 E-mail: betzarcht@aol.com., betzEbetz@aol.com.

BETZ, HANS DIETER, theology educator; b. Lemgo, Lippe, Germany, May 21, 1931; came to U.S., 1963, naturalized, 1973; s. Ludwig and Gertrude (Vietor) B.; m. Christel Hella Wagner, Nov. 10, 1958; children: Martin, Ludwig, Arnold. Student, Kirchliche Hochschule, Bethel, Fed. Republic Germany, 1951-52, U. Mainz, Fed. Republic Germany, 1952-55, 56-58, Westminster Coll, Cambridge, Eng., 1955-56; Doctor Theologiae, U. Mainz, Fed. Republic Germany, 1957; Habilitation, U. Mainz, 1966. Pastor Evangelical Ch., Rhineland, Fed. Republic Germany, 1961-63; from asst. prof. to prof. Sch. Theology, Claremont Grad. Sch., Calif., 1963-78; prof. N.T. and early Christian lit. U. Chgo., 1978-2000, Shailer Mathews prof., 1989—; prof. emeritus; chmn. dept. N.T. and early Christian lit. U. Chgo., 1985-94. Rsch. fellow Inst. Advanced Study, Hebrew U., Jerusalem, 1999. Author, editor numerous books and articles in German and English, 1959— Recipient Humboldt Rsch. prize, 1986; Lady Davis fellow Hebrew U., Jerusalem, Israel, 1990, Sackler scholar Tel Aviv U., 1995; NEH rsch. grantee, 1970-83, Am. Assn. Theol. Schs. grantee, 1977, 84. Mem. Soc. Bibl. Lit. (pres. 1997), Studiorum Novi Testamenti Societas (pres. 1999-2000), Chgo. Soc. Bibl. Rsch. (pres. 1983-84). Office: U Chgo 1025 E 58th St Chicago IL 60637-1509 E-mail: hansbetz@midway.uchicago.edu.

BETZ, RONALD PHILIP, pharmacist; b. Chgo., Nov. 26, 1933; s. David Robert and Olga Marie (Martinson) B.; m. Rose Marie Marella, May 18, 1963; children: David Christian, Christopher Peter. BS, U. Ill., 1955; MPA, Roosevelt U., 1987. Asst. dir. pharmacy U. Ill., Chgo., 1959-62; dir. pharmacy Mt. Sinai Hosp., Chgo., 1962-2001; pres. Pharmacy Systems, Inc., 1982-89; teaching assoc. Coll. Pharmacy, U. Ill., Chgo., 1977-88. Adj. clin. asst. prof. pharmacy, U. Ill., 1988-2001; pres. Pharmacy Svc. and Systems, 1972-81; dir. Ill. Coop. Health Data Systems, 1976-80. Contbr. articles to profl. jours. Bd. dirs. Howard/Paulina Redevel. Corp., 1983-92. With U.S. Army, 1956-58. Mem.: No. Ill. Soc. Hosp. Pharmacists (pres. 1966), Ill. Acad. Preceptors in Pharmacy (pres. 1972), Ill. Pharm. Assn. (pres. 1975), Am. Soc. Health Sys. Pharmacists, Kappa Psi. Democrat. Lutheran. Home: 1021 Sussex Dr Northbrook IL 60062-3328 E-mail: rbetz@aol.com.

BETZER, SUSAN ELIZABETH BEERS, family physician, geriatrician; b. Evanston, Ill., Aug. 24, 1943; d. Thomas Moulding and Mary Ella (Waidner) Beers; m. Peter Robin Betzer, June 18, 1965; children: Sarah Elizabeth, Katherine Hannah. AB in Biol. Scis. magna cum laude, Mount Holyoke Coll., 1965; PhD in Oceanography, U. R.I., 1972; MD, U. Miami, 1978. Diplomate Am. Bd. Family Practice, Am. Bd. Geriatrics. Rsch. assoc. dept. marine sci. U. South Fla., St. Petersburg, 1973-74, rsch. scholar, scientist, 1975-76; resident in family practice Bayfront Med. Ctr., St. Petersburg, 1978-81; pvt. practice St. Petersburg, 1982—; clin. asst. prof. dept. family medicine U. South Fla., Tampa, 1982—. Cons. physician Fed. Employee Health Clinic, Honolulu, 1981-82.

Contbr. articles to profl. jours. Adv. com. St. Petersburg H.S., 1996—; bd. dirs. Fla. Orch., Tampa, 1983-86, 88—, pres., 1985-86, mem. exec. com., 1988—, vice-chair bd. trustees 1996-2002, sec., 2002—, founder, chair audience devel. com., St. Petersburg, 1990-94; bd. dirs. Suncoast Ctr. Cmty. Mental Health, St. Petersburg, 1992-93; trustee Bayfront Health Found., 1996—, chmn., 2001-03; trustee Bayfront Med. Ctr.; trustee Bayfront Health Svcs., 1992-96, vice-chair, 1993-96; vol. physician St. Petersburg Free Clinic, 1979—. Named Woman of Distinction, Suncoast coun. Girl Scouts U.S., 1994; recipient Golden Baton award, St. Petersburg Fla. Orch. Guild, 1994, Chmns. award, Fla. Orch., 1997, Svc. award, Pinellas County Med. Soc., 1999. Mem.: Fla. Acad. Family Physicians (Dr. of the Day, Fla. Legislature 1995, 1996), Am. Med. Women's Assn., Am. Acad. Family Physicians (Mead Johnson award 1980), Mount Holyoke Alumnae Assn. (alumnae honor rsch. com. 1988—91, alumnae devel. com. 1996—2003, pres. 2003—, Alumnae medal of honor 2000), Phi Beta Kappa. Avocations: symphony, birding, cooking, reading. Home: 1830 7th St N Saint Petersburg FL 33704-3322 Office: 461 7th Ave S Saint Petersburg FL 33701-4818

BETZJITOMIR, SUSAN MARIE, financial consultant, lawyer, educator; b. Bangor, Maine, Apr. 7, 1961; d. Andrew Kurchey and Trudy Louise (Box) Runyan; m. Howard Steven Jitomir; children: Roxanne Jitomir, Jennifer Stergion, Jean Jitomir, Susan Jitomir, Ebony Jitomir. AS with honors and distinction, Corning C.C., 1994; BS, Cornell U., 1997, JD, 2000. Model Vogue Agy., N.Y.C., 1980-81; elder deacon Campbell (N.Y.) Presbyn. Ch., 1982-86; farmer Thurston, N.Y., 1985-93, Beaver Dams, N.Y., 1995—; supplemental instrn. leader Corming (N.Y.) C.C., 1991-94; fin. svcs. rep. 1st Investors, Elmira, N.Y., 1997. Chmn. faculty senate Alfred State Coll., 2001—02. Contbr. articles to newspaper and periodical. Lectr. Merchantville Grange, Thurston, 1986—91; councilman Twp. of Thurston, 1987—93, coord. CD, 1989—93. Fellow, Equal Justice Am., 1999. Mmem. AAAS, N.Y. State Bar Assn., N.Y. State Sheriffs Assn., N.Y. State Trial Lawyers Assn., Schuyler County Bar Assn. (v.p. 2001—). Avocations: farming, photography, writing, politics, research. Home: Fish Hill Rd Beaver Dams NY 14812 E-mail: lawyer@betzjitomir.com.

BEUC, RUDOLPH, JR., architect, real estate broker; b. St. Louis, Nov. 7, 1931; s. Rudolph M. and Lillian Ann (Rethemeyer) B.; m. Mildred Hild, Jan. 25, 1968; children: Rudolph III, Ralph M. Archtl. draftsman Bank Bldg. & Equipment Corp. Am., St. Louis, 1950, Hammond & Gorlock, archs., St. Louis, 1957-58; designer Schwarz & Van Hoefen, archs., St. Louis, 1958; arch. George E. Berg Archs., St. Louis, 1958-60, R. Beuc, Archs., Inc., St. Louis, 1960—, pres., also dir., 1960—; pres., dir. Hilterdevco, Inc., St. Louis, 1964—, dir. pub. works Peerless Park, 1967-98. Deacon Webster Groves Presbyn. Ch. With AUS, 1955-57. Mem. AIA, Soc. Am. Registered Archs., Mo. Coun. Archs., Mo. Assn. Bldg. Ofcls. and Insps., Coun. Am. Bldg. Ofcls. Code Adminstrs., Nat. Coun. Archtl. Registration Bds., Am. Legion (past comdr.), Internat. Order Odd Fellows (past grand), Masons (PM), Lions (past pres.), Order Ea. Star, DeMolay, High Twelve (past state pres.), Scottish Rite, Washington U., Westborough Country. Home: 138 W Glendale Rd Saint Louis MO 63119-4060 Office: 142 W Glendale Rd Saint Louis MO 63119-4060 E-mail: rudybeuc@compuserve.com.

BEUCHERT, EDWARD WILLIAM, lawyer; b. NYC, Feb. 13, 1937; s. August Vincent and Anna Beuchert; m. Elizabeth Sadowski, Aug. 5, 1961; children: Edward, Jon, Philip, Suzanne, Alexandra. BA cum laude, Fordham U., 1958; JD cum laude, Harvard U., 1961. Bar: N.Y. 1962. Assoc., then ptnr. and counsel Seward & Kissel, N.Y.C., 1963-99. Bd. dirs. Cotswold Assn., Inc., v.p., 1979-80, 98-99, pres., 1980-82. Contbr. articles to profl. jours. Bd. dirs. Edgemont Cmty. Coun., Inc., 1984-90, sec., 1984-86, v.p., 1987-90. 1st lt. U.S. Army, 1961-63. Recipient Silver Box award, Edgemont Cmty. Coun., 1998. Republican. Roman Catholic. Home: 53 Inverness Rd Scarsdale NY 10583-3525

BEUERLEIN, STEVE TAYLOR, professional football player; m. Kristen Beuerlein; children: Taylor, Jake, Kailey. Profl. football player Oakland (Calif.) Raiders, 1989-91, Dallas Cowboys, 1991-93, Cardinals, 1993-95, Jacksonville, 1995; quarterback Carolina Panthers, Charlotte, 1996—2000, Denver Broncos, 2001—. Participant Pro Bowl, 1999. Office: 1701 Bryant St, Suite 100 Denver CO 80204

BEUGEN, JOAN BETH, communications company executive; b. Mar. 9, 1943; d. Leslie and Janet (Glick) Caplan; m. Sheldon Howard Beugen, July 16, 1967. BS in Speech, Northwestern U., 1965. Founder, prin., pres. The Creative Establishment, Inc., Chgo., N.Y.C., San Francisco and L.A., 1969—87; founder, pres. Cresta Comms. Inc., Chgo., 1988—. Spkr. on entrepreneurship for women. Contbr. articles to profl. jours. Trustee Mt. Sinai Hosp. Med. Ctr.; del. White House Conf. on Small Bus., 1979; bd. dirs. Chgo. Network, Chgoland Enterprise Ctr., Girl Scouts Chgo. Named Entrepreneur of Yr., Women in Bus.; recipient YWCA Leadership award, 1985. Mem.: Overseas Edn. Fund Women in Bus. Com., Nat. Women's Forum, Com. of 200, Women in Film, Chgo. Film Coun., Chgo. Audio-Visual Producers Assn., Midwest Soc. Profl. Cons., Chgo. Assn. Commerce and Industry, Ill. Women's Agenda, Nat. Assn. Women Bus. Owners (pres. Chgo. bhpt. 1979), Econ. Club Chgo. Office: The Cresta Group 1050 N State St Chicago IL 60610-7829

BEUGNOT, BERNARD ANDRE HENRI, French literature educator; b. Paris, July 3, 1932; s. Raoul P.H. Beugnot; m. Brigitte L'Hermite, June 11, 1960; children: Marie-Christine, Nicolas, Sophie. Student, Ecole Normale Superieure, Paris, 1954; licence, U. Sorbonne, Paris, 1955, MA, 1956, PhD, 1969; agregation, U. France, Paris, 1958. Prof. Coll. Chartres, France, 1960-62; assoc. prof. French U. Montreal, Que., Can., 1962-69, prof. French lit., 1970—, chmn. French dept., 1965-69, 85-91, prof. emeritus French dept., 1997—. Mem. editing com. Can. Coun. Humanities, Ottawa, 1970-75, 78-81; editor: J.L.G. Balzac, Entretiens, 1972, F. Ponge, Oeuvres Completes, 2 vols., 1999-2002, 20 other books and over 120 articles on 17th-century and contemporary lit.; co-author (monograph) Boileau, 1973, Manuel Bibliographie, 1982. Lt. inf. French Army, 1958-60. Recipient Prix Halphen Acad. Francaise, 1974, Prize 2000 for Hunanities, ACFAS, Ordre Nat. du Merite, Govt. France, 1977, Palmes Academiques, 1988. Fellow Royal Soc. Can. Home: 4720 Grosvenor Montreal QC Canada H3W 2L8 Fax: (514) 481-1355. E-mail: beugnotmontreal@videotron.ca.

BEUGRE, CONSTANT D. management educator, researcher; b. Gomeneberi, Fresco, Cote D'Ivoire (Ivory Coast), May 13, 1956; 1 child, Jean-Christophe A. PhD, Rensselaer Poly. Inst., 1996. Asst. prof. indsl./orgnl. psychology U. Cocody/Ivory Coast, Abidjan, 1984—91; asst. prof. mgmt. and info. sys. Tuscarawas campus Kent State U., New Philadelphia, Ohio, 1998—2002; assoc. prof. mgmt. Del. State U., Sch. Mgmt., Dover, 2002—. Vis. fellow Harvard U., 1996. Author: (book) Managing Fairness in Organizations, 1998, Motivation of African Managers, 1998; contbr. Recipient Disting. Contributions to Slavic Studies award, Am. Assn. Advancement Slavic Studies, 1999; scholar Fulbright scholar, Inst. for Internat. Edn., 1991—96, Rensselaer Poly. Inst., 1993—96. Fellow: APA (internat. fellow 1988, mem. nominating com. 1984—85, ad. com. ea. divsn. program com. 1986—89, ea. divsn. exec. com. 1990—93, nat. com. internat. coop. 1984—87, 1992—95); mem.: Acad. Mgmt. Roman Catholic. Avocation: travel. Home: 74 ParHaven Dr H34 Dover DE 19904 Office: Del State Univ Sch Mgmt 1200 N Dupont Hwy Dover DE 19901 E-mail: cbeugre@dsu.edu.

BEUKEMA, JOHN FREDERICK, lawyer; b. Alpena, Mich., Jan. 30, 1947; s. Christian F. and Margaret Elizabeth (Robertson) B.; m. Cynthia Ann Parke, May 25, 1974; children: Frederick Parke, David Christian. BA, Carleton Coll., 1968; JD, U. Minn., 1971. Bar: Minn. 1971, U.S. Ct. Mil. Appeals 1974, U.S. Dist. Ct. Minn. 1975, U.S. Ct. Appeals (8th cir.) 1981, U.S. Ct. Appeals (fed. cir.) 1984, U.S. Supreme Ct. 1988, U.S. Dist. Ct. (we. dist.) Wis. 1997, U.S. Ct. Appeals (9th cir.) 1999. Assoc. Faegre & Benson, Mpls., 1971, 75-79, ptnr., 1980—. Vestryman Cathedral Ch. St. Mark, Mpls., 1983-86, 2002-; bd. dirs. Neighborhood Involvement Program, Mpls., 1986-90, pres., 1989-90; bd. dirs. Ronald McDonald House of Twin Cities, 1991-97, sec., 1995-97. Lt. JAGC, USNR, 1972-75. Mem. ABA, Minn. State Bar Assn., Hennepin County Bar Assn. Republican. Episcopalian. E-mail: jbeukema@faegre.com.

BEUMER, RICHARD EUGENE, engineer, architect, construction firm executive; b. St. Louis, Feb. 26, 1938; s. Eugene Henry and C. Florence (Braun) Beumer; m. Judith Louise Rockett, June 25, 1960; children: Kathryn, Karen, Mark. BSEE, Valparaiso U., 1959. Registered profl. engr., Mo., Ill., Ariz., Md., Okla., Ohio, Ga., Va., Mich., D.C., Mass., N.Y., N.C. With Sverdrup Corp. Cos., 1959—; v.p. Sverdrup & Parcel and Assocs., St. Louis, 1974—78; sr. v.p., exec. v.p., dir. Sverdrup & Parcel Assocs., St. Louis, 1979—81; pres. Sverdrup & Parcel Assos., St. Louis, 1982—85; sr. v.p. Sverdrup Corp., 1986—88, exec. v.p., 1989—92, pres., 1993; pres., CEO Sverdrup Corp., 1994—95; chmn., CEO Sverdrup Corp., 1996. Dir. Sverdrup Ltd., St. Louis, 1979; vice-chmn. Jacobs Engring. Group, Inc., 1999, Jacobs Engring. Co., 2002—, Aid Assn. for Luths., Valparaiso U. Chmn. St. Louis Regional Chamber and Growth Assn., 1998—99; divsn. chmn. United Way St. Louis, 1980; bd. dirs. Downtown St. Louis, Inc., 1982—91, Jr. Achievement, St. Louis Sci. Ctr.; past chmn. Luth. Med. Ctr., St. Louis; trustee, chmn. St. Louis Luth. High Schs. Recipient Disting. Alumni award, Valparaiso U., 1983. Mem.: NSPE, Mo. Soc. Profl. Engrs., Constrn. Industry Pres. Forum, Design Profls. Coalition, Cons. Engrs. Coun. Mo. (pres. 1980), Am. Cons. Engrs. Coun. (nat. bd. dirs. 1979—82), St. Louis Elec. Bd. (pres. 1983), The Bogey Club, Old Warson Club, The Moles. Lutheran.

BEUSCH, JOHN ULRICH, engineer, researcher; b. Erie, Pa., Apr. 22, 1938; s. Andrew and Ruth B. Beusch; m. Donna Marie Williams, Dec. 23, 1961; children: Cheryl Susan, Laura Kristine. BS, Rochester Inst. Tech., N.Y., 1956—61; MBA, Boston U., 1969—71; PhD, MIT, Cambridge, 1961—65. Staff, group leader, divsn. head MIT Lincoln Lab., Lexington, Mass., 1965—. Chair Stow Conservation Commn., Mass., 1974—80; trustee Randell Library Fund, Stow, Mass., 1980—86; pres., dir. Stow Conservation Trust, Mass., 1986—. Achievements include patents in field. Avocations: aerobics, fitness, carpentry. Home: 416 Taylor Rd Stow MA 01775 Office: MIT Lincoln Lab 244 Wood St Lexington MA 02420

BEUSSE, JACQUELINE A. writer, marketing company executive; b. Albany, N.Y. d. H. A. and Christina M. (Collins) B. Bus. degree, The Wood Sch., N.Y.C., 1956; student mgmt. program for women, Pa. State U.; BA magna cum laude, Caldwell Coll., 1974; MA magna cum laude, N.Y. Inst. Tech., 1978. Sr. ct. stenographer Middlesex County Prosecutors Office, New Brunswick, N.J., 1955-57; adminstrv. asst. to Sen. John A. Lynch New Brunswick, 1957-61; adminstrv. asst. to Judge John J. Rafferty, 1957-61; product mgr. Johnson & Johnson, New Brunswick, 1961-73; dir. devel. and pub. rels. Caldwell (N.J.) Coll., 1974-76; pres., writer Mktg. by Objectives, Inc., Caldwell, 1978—. Cons. Gucci, Inc., Fraunces Tavern, Constn. Hall, JFK Ctr., Washington, D.C., 6 Frank Sinatra concerts, Am. Ballet Co., St. Luke's-Roosevelt Hosp., Hosp. for Spl. Surgery, Navy League, USO; cons., pub. N.Y. Cornell Med. Ctr. Concert Series; cons., prodr., pub. Urban League, Lincoln Ctr. Concerts; lectr. in field. Prodr. Dramatic Reading of The Letters of John and Abigail Adams, N.Y.C., 1986; exec. prodr., prodr., dir. Carnegie Hall Concert--Carmel Quinn and Friends, 1987; journalist Irish Echo, N.Y. Times, Star Ledger, Metro Mag., Cath. Advocate, Omni Mag., Garden St. Woman, The Progress; contbr. articles to mags. and newspapers. Chmn. Theater on the Hill; bd. dirs. John F. Kennedy Trust, 1991; N.J. state commr. Motion Picture and TV, 1979-93; chmn. Grover Cleveland Sesquicentennial Celebration-Presdl. Tribute, 1987; media co-chair N.J. State Dem. Com.; publicity chair Garden State Arts Ctr.-Irish Festival and Found.; cons. Meml. Sloan Kettering Cancer Ctr., Expo 2000; cons. prodr. 4 Bob Hope concerts for charity; prodr., cons. Am. Cancer Soc.; v.p. Ellis Island Restoration Commn., 1975—, v.p., mem. exec. com. Recipient Journalistic Excellence award Irish Am. Unity Conf., 1985, 86, West of Ireland Devel. and Ednl. award, 1987, CAMA Video award for documentary A Summer to Savor, Disting. Am. award, 1990-91, ASTRA 1st prize award for TV documentary We Are the Music Makers, 1991, 92; named Honoree Ellis Island Ceremony, 2000. Mem. USO (bd. dirs.), AAUW (bd. dirs.), N.J. Soc. to Prevent Blindness (bd. dirs.), West Essex C. of C. (v.p., mem. exec. com.), Kappa Gamma Pi. Democrat. Roman Catholic. Avocations: art, music, literature, historical research, ice-skating. Office: Mktg by Objectives Inc PO Box 136 Caldwell NJ 07006-0136

BEUTEL, ERNEST WILLIAM, thoracic surgeon; b. Chgo., Feb. 14, 1946; s. Ernest and Hazel Augusta (Zachow) B.; m. Anita Paulie Harrison, June 11, 1976; children: Ernest Wiley, William Andrew Harrison. BS magna cum laude, Loyola U., Chgo., 1967; MD, Loyola U., 1971, JD, 1985. Diplomate Am. Bd. Surgery and Am. Bd. Thoracic Surgery. Intern St. Joseph Hosp., Chgo., 1971-72, resident in surgery, 1972-76; resident in thoracic surgery Cook County Hosp., 1976-78; staff thoracic surgeon Naval Regional Med. Ctr., Great Lakes, 1978-80; assoc. Langston, Barker, Leininger, Inc., Chgo., 1980-84, pvt. practice thoracic surgery, 1984—; attending thoracic surgeon Resurrection Hosp., Chgo.; asst. clin. prof. Loyola U. Med. Sch. Adv. bd. Loyola U. Health Law Inst. Fellow ACS, Am. Coll. Chest Physicians, Am. Coll. Cardiology (assoc.); mem. AMA, Chgo. Surg. Soc., Ill. Bar Assn., Am. Coll. Legal Medicine, Chgo. Bar Assn., Alpha Omega Alpha, Phi Sigma Tau, Alpha Sigma Nu. Office: Taxman & Hurst Ltd 100 W Monroe St Chicago IL 60603 Home: 1481 Lawrence Ave Lake Forest IL 60045

BEUTLER, ARTHUR JULIUS, manufacturing company executive; b. La-Crosse, Wis., Sept. 2, 1924; s. Arthur Julius and Augusta Henrietta (Dobe) B.; m. Carolee Yvonne Crawford, Dec. 28, 1952; 1 child, Karen Elizabeth. BSEE, U. Wis., 1948, Grad. in EE, 1968. Registered profl. engr., Wis. Trainee inventor program Gen. Electric Co., Schenectady, N.Y., 1948-51, devel. engr. Milw., 1951-59, project engr., 1959-61, sr. engr., 1961-64; chief engr. Dings Magnetic Separator Co., Milw., 1964-67; pres., owner Creative Engring. Assocs., Inc., Greendale, Wis., 1967-72, 88—; v.p. mfg. Gettys Mfg. Co., Racine, Wis., 1972-79, v.p. internat., 1979-81; v.p. tech. planning div. motion control div. Gould, Inc. (formerly Gettys Mfg. Co.), Racine, 1981-88. Cons. engr. mfg. control systems, robotics. Patentee elec. controls. Served with U.S. Army, 1943-46, PTO. Mem. IEEE (sr., chpt. chmn. 1969-72), NSPE, Soc. Mfg. Engrs. (cert.), Tau Beta Pi, Eta Kappa Nu.

BEUTLER, ERNEST, physician, research scientist; b. Berlin, Sept. 30, 1928; arrived in U.S., 1936, naturalized, 1943; s. Alfred David and Kaethe (Italiener) Beutler; m. Brondelle Fleisher, June 15, 1950; children: Steven Merrill, Earl Bryan, Bruce Alan, Deborah Ann. PhB, U. Chgo., 1946, BS, 1948, MD, 1950; PhD (hon.), Tel Aviv U., Israel, 1993. Intern U. Chgo. Clinics, 1950—51, resident in medicine, 1951—53; asst. prof. U. Chgo., 1956—59; chmn. div. medicine City of Hope Med. Ctr., L.A., 1959—78; chmn. dept. clin. rsch. The Scripps Rsch. Inst., La Jolla, Calif., 1978—82, chmn. dept. basic and clin. rsch., 1982—89, chmn. dept. molecular and exptl. medicine, 1989—. Clin. prof. medicine U. So. Calif., 1964—79, U. Calif., San Diego, 1979—; mem. hematology study sect. NIH, 1970—74, 1989—91, nat. heart, lung, and blood adv. coun. mem., 1994—97; Spinoza chair U. Amsterdam, 1991. Author: 8 books; contbr. ; mem. editl. bds. profl. jours.:, Adv. com. Blood Products FDA, 1984—88. Recipient Gairdner award, 1975, Blundell prize, 1985, Nat. Heart, Lung, and Blood Inst. Merit award, NIH, 1987, Nat. Acad. Clin. Biochemistry Lectureship award, Kodak Instruments, 1990, Mayo Soley award, Western Soc. Clin. Investigation, 1992, 5th ann. Excellence award, Gen. Clin. Rsch. Program, 1993, City of Medicine award, 1994, Outstanding Rsch. award, Am. Soc. Clin. Pathologists, 2000, Profl. Achievement citation, U. Chgo., 2003. Mem.: NAS, Am. Soc. Human Genetics (mem. exec. com. 1968—72), Am. Soc. Hematology (mem. exec. com. 1968—72, v.p. 1977, pres. 1979, E. Donnall Thomas Lecture and Prize 2003), Western Assn. Physicians (pres. 1989), Am. Soc. Clin. Investigation, Assn. Am. Physicians, Am. Acad. Arts and Scis. Jewish. Achievements include invention of screening tests for galactosemia and other genetic disorders; co-discovery of glucose-6-phosphate dehydrogenase deficiency; origination of X inactivation hypothesis; research in glycolipid disorders; hemochromatosis. Office: The Scripps Rsch Inst 10550 N Torrey Pines Rd La Jolla CA 92037-1000 E-mail: beutler@scripps.edu.

BEUTLER, FREDERICK JOSEPH, information scientist; b. Berlin, Oct. 3, 1926; came to U.S., 1936, naturalized, 1943; s. Alfred David and Kaethe (Italiener) B.; m. Suzanne Armstrong, Jan. 5, 1969; children— Arthur David, Kathryn Ruth, Michael Ernest. SB, MIT, 1949, SM, 1951; PhD, Calif. Inst. Tech., 1957. Faculty U. Mich., Ann Arbor, 1957—, prof. info. and control engring., 1963-90, prof. emeritus, 1990—, chmn. computer info. and control engring., 1970-71, 77-90, chmn. grad. elect. engring. systems program, 1985-90. Vis. prof. Calif. Inst. Tech., 1967-68; vis. scholar U. Calif. at Berkeley, 1964-65 Editorial cons. Math. Rev., 1965-67, 75-88; contbr. articles to profl. jours. and books. Bd. dirs. Ann Arbor Civic Theatre, 1976-78, 91-94. With AUS, 1945-46. NSF rsch. grantee, 1971-75, 76-81, 92-94, Air Force Office Sci. Rsch. grantee, 1970-74, 75-80; NASA grantee, 1959-69. Fellow IEEE (life); mem. Soc. Indsl. and Applied Math. (coun. 1969-74, mng. editor Jour. Applied Math. 1970-75, editor 1984-90, editor Rev. 1967-70), Am. Math. Soc., U. Mich. Retirees Assn. (bd. dirs., sec.-treas. 1994—), Barton Boat Club, Racquet Club of Ann Arbor, Rotary Club of Ann Arbor. Office: Elec Engr and Comp Sci Bldg Univ Michigan Ann Arbor MI 48109-2122 E-mail: fjb@umich.edu.

BEUTLER, LARRY EDWARD, psychology educator; b. Logan, Utah, Feb. 14, 1941; s. Edward and Beulah (Andrus) B.; children: Jana, Kelly, Ian David, Gail. BS, Utah State U., 1965, MS, 1966; PhD, U. Nebr., 1970. Diplomate Am. Bd. Clin. Psychology. Asst. prof. psychology Duke U., Ashville, N.C., 1970-71; asst. prof. Stephen F. Austin State U., Nacogdoches, Tex., 1971-73; assoc. prof. Baylor Coll. Medicine, Houston, 1973-79; prof. U. Ariz., Tucson, 1979-90, U. Calif., Santa Barbara, 1990—2002, Pacific Grad. Sch. Psychology, Palo Alto, Calif., 2002—. Author: Eclectic Psychotherapy, 1983; co-author: Systematic Treatment Selection, 1990, Guidelines for the Systematic Treatment of the Depressed Patient, 2000, Integrative Assessment of Adult Personality, 1995, others; editor Jour. Cons. Clin. Psychology, 1990-96; editor Jour. Clin. Psychology, 1997—. Fellow Am. Psychology Assn. (pres. divsn. psychotherapy, 1997, pres. divsn. clin. psychology, 2002), Am. Psychol. Soc.; mem. Soc. Psychotherapy Research (pres. 1986-88). Home: 2620 Piedra Verde Ct Placerville CA 95667- Office: Pacific Grad Sch Psychology 940 E Meadow Palo Alto CA 94303 E-mail: lbeutler@pgsp.edu.

BEUTLER, SUZANNE A. retired middle school educator, artist; b. Cin., Oct. 23, 1930; d. Robert and Marguerite (Pierson) Armstrong; m. Frederick J. Beutler, Jan. 5, 1969; children: Richard and Mark Ireland. BA, U. Wis., 1954; MA, U. Mich., 1966, PhD, 1974, BFA, 2000. Cert. tchr. Middle sch. tchr. Ann Arbor (Mich.) Pub. Schs. Vis. lectr. U. Mich., Ann Arbor; adj. lectr. Eastern Mich. U., Ypsilanti. Author 3 manuals with Lang. Art Projects; contbr. articles to profl. jours.; developed writing program using personal classroom experiences. Recipient Tchr. Recognition award, 1986; grantee in field. Mem. Phi Delta Kappa (Svc. Key award 1992). Home: 1717 Shadford Rd Ann Arbor MI 48104-4543

BEUTTENMULLER, RUDOLF WILLIAM, lawyer; b. St. Louis, Dec. 20, 1953; s. Paul A. and Doris R. (Henle) B.; m. Ragina Lee Winters, July 14, 1984. AB cum laude, Princeton U., 1976; JD with distinction, Duke U., 1980. Bar: Tex. 1980, U.S. Dist. Ct. (no. dist.) Tex. 1980. Assoc. Jenkens & Gilchrist, Dallas, 1980-83; ptnr. Gregory, Self & Beuttenmuller, Dallas, 1983-88, Bradley, Bradley & Beuttenmuller, Irving, Tex., 1988-93; dir. Thomas & Self, Dallas, 1994—. Articles editor Duke Law Jour., Durham, 1979-80. Mem. Rep. Nat. Com., Washington, 1984. Mem. ABA, Dallas Bar Assn., Duke Law Alumni Assn., Princeton Alumni Assn. Home: 4428 Irvin Simmons Dr Dallas TX 75229-4247 Office: 5339 Spring Valley Rd Dallas TX 75254-3009 E-mail: rudybeutt@thomasandself.com.

BEVAN, NORMAN EDWARD, religious organization executive; b. Buffalo, July 6, 1937; s. Edward Albert and Catherine Irene (Coughlin) B. BA, St. Mary's Sem., Norwalk, Conn., 1961, BD, 1964; lic. in sacred theology, Gregorian U., Rome, 1966; DST, Acad. Alfonsiana, Rome, 1970. Theology prof. Tanzanian Episcopal Conf., Kipalapala, Tanzania, 1971-73; dir. formation Congregation of the Holy Ghost, Chgo., 1973-80, asst. gen. Rome, 1980-86, provincial superior Pitts., 1985-94; pres. Cath. Theol. Union, Chgo., 1995-97; instr. Holy Ghost Prep. Sch., Bensalem, Pa., 1997-99; dir. Bethel Animation Ctr., Bethel Park, Pa., 1999—. Roman Catholic. Mailing: Bethel Animation Ctr 6230 Brushrun Rd Bethel Park PA 15102-2214

BEVAN, ROBERT LEWIS, lawyer; b. Springfield, Mo., Mar. 23, 1928; s. Gene Walter and Blanche Omega (Woods) B.; m. Ronice Diane Gartin, Jan 25, 1977; children: Matthew Gene, Lisa Ann. AB, U. Mo., 1950; LLB, U. Kansas City, 1957. Bar: Mo. 1957, D.C. 1969. Adminstrv. asst. U.S. Senator T. Hennings Jr., Washington, 1957-60; legis. asst. U.S. Senator E.V. Long, Washington, 1960-69; sr. govt. relations counsel Am. Bankers Assn., Washington, 1970-84; ptnr. Hopkins & Sutter, Washington, 1984-95; of counsel Stinson, Mag and Fizzell, Kansas City, Mo., 1995-2001. Ghost author: The Intruders, 1967; contbg. editor U.S. Banker, 1985-88. Fieldman Dem. Nat. Com., 1968. Served with U.S. Army, 1946-47, 1951-53. Mem. ABA (bus. law sect., chmn. banking law com. 1988-92, commn. on IOLTA 1997-2000, co-chmn. joint banking com. 1999-2000), Echequer Club. Avocation: art and antiques. Office: 4545 Wornall Rd Ste 805 Kansas City MO 64111

BEVAN, TIM, film producer; m. Joehy Richardson, 1992 (sep. 1997); 1 child, Daisy. Formed Working Title Films (with Eric Fellner) 1982-; Prodr. films (with Sarah Radclyffe) My Beautiful Laundrette, 1986, Sammy and Rosie Get Laid, 1987, Paperhouse, 1989; Personal Svcs., 1987, For Queen and Country, 1989, Dark Obsession, 1990, The Tall Guy, 1990, Chicago Joe and the Showgirl, 1990, London Kills Me, 1992, Rubin and Ed, 1992; (with Graham Bradstreet) A World Apart, 1988, Fools of Fortune, 1990; (with Carlos Davis and Anthony Fingleton) Drop Dead Fred, 1991, (with Paul Webster and Ronna B. Wallace) Bob Roberts, 1992; (with Eric fellner) French Kiss, 1995, Moonlight & Valentino, 1995, Bean, 1997, The Matchmaker, 1997, The Borrowers, 1997,The Hi-Lo Country, 1997, Elizabeth, 1998 (BAFTA Best British Film, ALFS awd., 1999), What Rats Won't Do, 1998, Plunkett & MacLeane, 1999; For TV Tales of the City, 1993, The Borrowers, 1993, More Tales of the City, 1998, High Fidelity, 2000, Bridget Jones Diary, 2001, Captain Corelli's Mandolin, 2001, 40 Days and 40 Nights, 2002, Ali G Indahouse, 2002, About A Boy, 2002, The Guru, 2002, Johnny English, 2003, Love Actually, 2003, The Calcium Kid, 2003; exec. prodr.: The Rachel Papers, 1989, Year of the Gun, 1991, A Kiss Before Dying, 1991, Posse, 1993, Romeo is Bleeding, 1993, The Hawk, 1993, Four Weddings and a Funeral, 1994, The Hudsucker Proxy, 1994, Panther, 1995, Dead Man Walking, 1995, Loch Ness, 1995, Fargo, 1996, The Big Lebowski, 1998, Notting Hill, 1999, O Brother, Where Art Thou?, 2000, The Man Who Cried, 2000, The Man Who Wasn't There, 2001, Long Time Dead, 2002, My Little Eye, 2002, Thirteen, 2003, The Shape of Things, 2003, Ned Kelly, 2003, The Italian Job, 2003; prodr. TV: Frankie's House, 1992, Underbelly (exec.), 1992. Recipient ShowEast's Kodak award for excellence in filmmaking (with Eric Fellner), 2003. Office: Working Title Films 8 Kensington Gardens London W11 3HO England*

BEVAN, WILLIAM, retired foundation executive; b. Plains, Pa., May 16, 1922; s. William and Elizabeth Merle (Jones) B.; m. Dorothy Louise Chorpening, Feb. 17, 1945; children: William III, Mark Filbert, Philip Ross. AB with honors, Franklin and Marshall Coll., 1942, ScD, 1979; MA, Duke U., 1943, PhD, 1948, LLD, 1972; ScD, Fla. Atlantic U., 1968, Emory U., 1974, U. Md., 1981, Kans. State U., 1987; DHL, So. Ill. U., 1989. Instr. psychology Duke U., 1947, William Preston Few prof. psychology, 1974-92, prof. emeritus, 1992—, provost, 1979-83; instr., then asst. prof. psychology Heidelberg Coll., Tiffin, Ohio, 1946-48; mem. faculty Emory U., 1948-59, prof. psychology, 1958-59; prof. psychology, chmn. dept. Kans. State U., 1959-62, dean arts and scis., 1962-63, v.p. acad. affairs, 1963-66; fellow Center for Advanced Study Behavioral Scis., Stanford, Calif., 1965-66; sr. postdoctoral fellow NSF, 1965-66; v.p., provost Johns Hopkins U., Balt., 1966-70, prof. psychology, 1966-74; exec. officer AAAS, 1970-74, pub. Science, 1970-74; mem. adv. bd. Univ. Coll., U. Md., 1978-86; bd. govts. Research Triangle Inst., 1979-82; v.p. John D. and Catherine T. MacArthur Found., Chgo., 1983-91, ret., 1991. Mem. adv. bd. Ctr. Advanced Study U. Va., 1976-89. Editorial adv. bd.: Am. Men and Women of Sci., 12th edit, 1972, Social Sci. Citations Index, 1972-77; contbr. articles to profl. jours. Trustee Human Resources Research Orgn., 1968-88, Franklin and Marshall Coll., 1971-76, Coll. Retirement Equity Fund, 1972-90, Ctr. for Creative Leadership, 1972-79, Biosis. Info. Svc., 1974-80, Am. Psychol. Found., 1970-77, 83-89, Assn. Advancement of Psychology, 1974-78, William T. Grant Found., 1977-90, HumRRO Internat. Inc., 1985-89, Jackson Meml. Lab., 1986-90. With USNR, 1944-70. Recipient Franklin & Marshall Coll. Disting. Alumni award, 1966, Duke U. Disting. Alumni award, 1997-98; Fulbright scholar U. Oslo (Norway), 1952-53. Fellow: AAAS, APA; mem.: Am. Psychol. Soc., Soc. Exptl. Psychologists, Am. Acad. Arts and Scis., History of Sci. Soc., So. Soc. Philosophy and Psychology, Psychonomic Soc., Inst. Medicine of Nat. Acad. Sci., Cosmos Club (Washington), Sigma Xi, Phi Beta Kappa. Home: Croasdaile Village 10 Boardman Ct Durham NC 27705

BEVAN, WILLIAM ARNOLD, JR., emergency physician; b. Sault St. Marie, Mich., June 23, 1943; s. William Arnold and Syneva Lois (Martin) B.; m. Martha Lynn Peterson, Dec. 29, 1973; children: Terry Eugene, Brian William, PAtrick Jon. BS, U. Minn., 1966, MD, 1970. Diplomate Am. Bd. Family Practice, Am. Bd. Emergency Medicine. Intern U. Utah, 1970-71; family practitioner Vail Mtn. Med. Profl. Corp., Vail, Colo., 1972-83; emergency physician Vail Valley Emergency Physicians, 1983—. Dir. Vail Valley Emergency Dept., 1992—; adviser Western Eagle County Ambulance Dist., 1983—. Trustee Shattuck St. Mary's Sch., Faribault, Minn., 1977—; football coach Battle Mountain H.S., Vail, 1978—; trustee, bd. dirs. Vail Christian H.S., 1998—. Named Man of Yr. Boy Scouts Am., 1966, 77. Fellow Am. Coll. Emergency Physicians; mem. AMA, Rocky Mountain Med. Soc., Colo. Med. Soc., U. Minn. Alumni Assn. (life). Republican. Lutheran. Home: 0025 Cottonwood Rd Eagle CO 81631 Office: Vail Valley Emergency Dept 181 W Meadow Dr Vail CO 81657-5058

BEVAN, WILLIAM CHARLES, systems analyst; b. Cheverly, MD, Mar. 26, 1957; s. William Charles and Jean Bevan. BA Polit. Sci., George Wash. U., 1979; MS Info. and Telecom., MS Systems Mgmt., Capitol Coll., 1997; MBA, George Mason U., 1998; PhD Candidate Info. Systems, U. of Md. Balt., 2000. Bus. mgr. McGraw-Hill Publications, Washington, 1987—88; dir. of fin. Club Managers Assn. of Am., Alexandria, Va., 1990—91; aviation, biometric and intelligent sys. analyst FBI, Washington, 1991—; CEO Aviation by Bevan & Browne, North Bethesda, 1995—. Cons. Ab3, North Bethesda, 1995—. Author: (book) Around the World Under the Sea, 2002 (Toastmasters Internat. Dist. 36 Disting. Svc., 2001). Pres. FBI toastmasters Toastmasters Internat., Washington, 1999—2001; pilot CAP, Frederick, 1999—2002; divsn. gov. Toastmasters Internat., Rockville, MD., 2001—02, area gov. Washington, 2000—01. Second lt. CAP USAF, 1999—2002, Maryland. Mem.: IEEE, Am. Assn. for Artificial Intelligence, Am. Radio Relay League. Avocations: golf, scuba diving, flying, tennis, rocketry. Office: Federal Bureau of Investigation 935 Penn Ave NW Washington MD 20535 Office Fax: 202-324-8826. Personal E-mail: wbevan@juno.com. Business E-Mail: wbevanjr@leo.gov.

BEVANS, STEPHEN BENNETT, priest, educator; b. Balt., July 14, 1944; s. Bert Bennett and Bernadette (O'Grady) Bevans. BA, Divine World Coll., 1967; lic. in sacred theology, Gregorian U., 1972, MA, U. Notre Dame, 1984, PhD, 1986. Ordained priest Roman Catholic Ch. 1971. Prof. theology Immaculate Conception Sch. of Theology, Vigan Ilocos Sur, Philippines, 1972—81, Cath. Theol. Union, Chgo., 1986—98, prof. mission & culture, 1998—. Bd. dir. Ctr. for Parish Devel., Chgo.; dir. Ctr. for Global Ministries, Chgo., 1995—2000. Author: John Oman & His Doctrine of God, 1992, Models of Contextual Theology, 1992, rev. edit., 2002; co-editor: Dictionary of Mission, 1997. Bd. dirs. Vol. Missionary Movement, Milw., 1996—2002, Ctr. for Mission Study and Rsch., Maryknoll, NY. Recipient Hon. Mention award, Cath. Press Assn., 1992, Best Article award, 1996. Mem.: Internat. Assn. Mission Studies, Cath. Theol. Soc. Am., Am. Soc. Missiology. Democrat. Roman Catholic. Office: Catholic Theol Union 5401 S Cornell Ave Chicago IL 60615

BEVC, CAROL-LYNN ANNE, accountant; b. Jam, N.Y., Oct. 6, 1952; d. Joseph F. and Dorothea Mae (Kirshe) Bova; m. Frank P. Bevc, May 11, 1974; children: Christine, Elizabeth. CFO Wordwise, Inc., Winter Park, Fla., 1989-2000; acct. exec. Inner/g, Winter Park, 2000—01. Leader Citrus coun. Girl Scouts U.S.A., 1986-96. Mem. AAUW (pres. Seminole County br. 1985-87, 95-97, bd. dirs., dir. comm. Fla. state 1998-2002), DAR. Avocations: reading, writing, swimming, learning. Home: 1511 Black Bear Ct Winter Springs FL 32708-3860 E-mail: bevc@bellsouth.net.

BEVC, FRANK PETER, electrical engineer; b. Johnstown, Pa., Mar. 5, 1952; s. Frank Henry and Mildred (Gallo) B.; m. Carol-Lynn Bova, May 11, 1974; children: Christine, Elizabeth. BSEE, U. Pitts., 1973, MBA, 1976. Design engr., program mgr. Westinghouse, Pitts., 1973-83, mgr. tech. projects Orlando, Fla., 1983-90, mgr. steam sys. engring., 1990-92, mgr. advanced programs, 1992-97; dir. emerging tech. Siemens Westinghouse, Orlando, 1998—; treas. Gasification Tech. Coun., 1998-2000. Treas. Energy Frontiers Internat., Arlington, Va., 1996-98; bd. dirs. Gasification Techs. Coun. Contbr. articles to profl. jours. Mem. IEEE (sr.), World Energy Congress (mem. tech. bd. 1995-98), Gas Turbine Assn. (v.p. 1992-2001, pres. 2002—), Am. Nat. Stds. Inst. (mem. stds. bd. 1974-80), U.S. Advanced Ceramics Assn. (bd. dirs.1995-2002, treas. 2002), Nat. Biomass Industries Assn. Home: 1511 Black Bear Ct Winter Springs FL 32708-3860 Office: Siemens Westinghouse 4400 N Alafaya Trl Orlando FL 32826-2398 E-mail: bevc@bellsouth.com., frank.bevc@siemens.com.

BEVELACQUA, JOSEPH JOHN, physicist, researcher; b. Waynesburg, Pa., Mar. 17, 1949; s. Frank and Lucy Ann B.; m. Terry Sanders, Sept. 4, 1971; children: Anthony, Jeffrey, Megan, Peter, Michael, Karen. BS in Physics, Calif. State Coll., 1970; postgrad., U. Maine, 1970-72; MS in Physics, Fla. State U., 1974, PhD, 1976. Diplomate Am. Bd. Health Physics; cert. radiol. shield survey engr.; cert. health physicist (comprehensive and power reactors), sr. reactor operator cert. Teaching/rsch. asst. U. Maine, 1970-72; tchg. and rsch. asst. Fla. State U., 1973-76; rsch. asst. NSF, 1975-76, rsch. assoc., 1976; nuclear engr. Bettis Atomic Power Lab., West Mifflin, Pa., 1973, sr. nuclear engr., 1976-78; ops. rsch. analyst U.S. Dept. Energy, Oak Ridge, 1978-80, chief physicist advanced laser isotope separation program, 1980-83; sr. radiol. engr. GPU Nuclear Corp. (Three Mile Island Sta.-Unit 2), Middletown, Pa., 1983-84; Three Mile Island emergency preparedness mgr. GPU Nuclear Corp., Middletown, 1984-86, mgr. TMI-2 safety rev. group, 1986-89, dir. radiol. controls TMI-2, 1989; supt. health physics Point Beach Nuclear Power Plant Wis. Electric Co., Two Rivers, 1989-95; prodn. planning mgr. Point Beach Nuclear Plant, 1996—; pres., CEO Bevelacqua Resources, Richland, Wash., 1993—; sr. radiol.controls tech. advisor USDOE-Office River Protection, Hanford, 1996—, acting dir. environ. divsn., 2000. Cons. U.S. Dept. Energey Process Evaluation Bd. of Isotope Separation, Washington, 1981-82; acting asst. mgr. environ., safety, health, and quality USDOE- Office River Protection, Hanford. Author: Contemporary Health Physics: Problems and Solutions, 1995, Basic Health Physics: Problems and Solutions, 1999, 20 health physics tng. manuals pub. by Bevelacqua Resources, 3 CD-ROMS for health physics tng.; contbr. articles to profl. jours. including Physical Rev. Letters. Mem. Rep. Presdl. Task Force, Nat. Rep. Senatorial Com. Recipient Outstanding Performance award, Dept. of Energy, 1982, Profl. Excellence award, U. Pa., 2000; Grantee, USAF, NSF, Von Humboldt fellow, U. Hamburg. Mem. Am. Nuclear Soc., Am. Phys. Soc., Am. Acad. Health Physics (profl. devel. com. 1992-94, chmn. 1994, nom. com. 1994-96), Susquehanna Valley Health Physics Soc. (mem. exec. com.), N.Y. Acad. Scis., Soc. Nuclear Medicine, Nuclear Utility Coordinating Group on Emergency Preparedness Implementation, Babcock and Wilcox Owners Group on Emergency Preparedness, Profl. Reactor Operators Soc., Health Physics Soc. (placement com. 1989-92, nominating com. 1994-97), Am. Bd. Health Physics (vice chmn. comprehensive panel of examiners 1990, chmn. 1991, nat. office mem.), Oak Ridge Sportsman's Club, Sigma Pi Sigma. Republican. Lutheran. Achievements include research on theoretical studies of light nuclei, few nucleon transfer reactions, radiation shielding, laser isotope separation, neutron nuclei, symmetry violations in nuclei, grand unification theories, quark models of nuclear forces, neutrino interactions, nuclear fuel cycle, laser fusion and gravitational collapse of stars, beta dosimetry, internal dosimetry, health effects of ionizing radiation; nuclear reactor safety, radon health effects and mitigation, radioactive and mixed waste management, applied health physics, internal and external dosimetry, dark matter, strange matter, symmetry violations in nuclei, cosmology, quantum field theory, astrophysics, genetic approaches for cancer research, quantum chromodynamics, standard model of particle physics and radiation induced immune system activation. Home and Office: Bevelacqua Resources 343 Adair Dr Richland WA 99352-8563 E-mail: bevelresou@aol.com.

BEVER, CHRISTOPHER THEODORE, JR., neurologist; b. Washington, Apr. 10, 1949; s. Christopher Theodore and Josephine Jordan (Morton) B.; m. Patricia Ann Thomas, Sept. 23, 1978; children: Erica Jane, Theodore Louis, Katherine Meryl. AB, Washington U., 1971; MD with Distinction in Rsch., U. Rochester, 1975. Intern U. Cin., 1975-76; resident in internal medicine Rutgers Coll. Medicine and Dentistry N.J., Piscataway, 1976-77; resident in neurology Columbia-Presbyn. Med. Ctr., N.Y.C., 1977-80; vis. fellow Coll. Physicians and Surgeons Columbia U., N.Y.C., 1979-80; rsch. assoc. NIH, Bethesda, Md., 1980-82, sr. staff fellow, 1982-84; asst. prof. dept. neurology U. Tenn. Ctr. for Health Scis., Memphis, 1984-87; asst. prof. U. Md., Balt., 1987-92, assoc. prof., 1992-98, prof., 1998—. Vis. cons. dept. neurology Nat. Naval Med. Ctr., Bethesda, 1981-84; staff neurologist VA Med. Ctr., Memphis, 1984-87, Univ. Hosp. U. Tenn., 1984-87; cons. neurologist Bapt. Meml. Hosp., Memphis, 1986-87; staff neurologist VA Med. Ctr., Balt., 1987—, U. Md. Hosp., 1987—; co-dir. Mid South Multiple Sclerosis Clinic, Memphis, 1986-87; chief neurology svc. Dept. Vets. Affairs Med. Ctr., Balt., 1990—. Contbr. articles to profl. jours. and chpts. to books; ad hoc reviewer for numerous scientific jours. Fellow U. Rochester Alumni Assn., 1972, 73, NIH, 1979-80, Scottish Rite Com. on Rsch. in Schizophrenia, 1974. Fellow Am. Acad. Neurology; mem. AAAS, Md. Acad. Neurology, Soc. for Neurosci., Internat. Soc. for Interferon Rsch., Soc. for Neurochemistry, Am. Neurol. Assn. Office: U Md Hosp Dept Neurology 22 S Greene St #N4W46 Baltimore MD 21201-1544 E-mail: christopher.bever@med.va.gov.

BEVERIDGE, JO-ANNE FAY, laboratory director; b. Toronto, Ont., Can., Aug. 19, 1955; d. Denis F. and Olga L. Hagon; m. Jan. E. Beveridge, Aug. 21, 1976 (div. May 1992); children: Rachel E., Peter I. BS in Med. Tech., Mich. Technol. U., 1977. Med. technologist All Saints Episcopal Hosp., Ft. Worth, Tex., 1980-83, Mansfield (Tex.) Cmty. Hosp., 1984-87; lab. mgr. Arlington (Tex.) Diagnostic and Imaging Ctr., 1987-89; asst. lab. mgr. Allied Clin. Lab., Hurst, Tex., 1989-94; med. technologist North Hills Hosp., North Richland Hills, Tex., 1992-97; quality assurance coord. Ft. Worth Health Dept., 1995-97; lab. dir. Plaza Med. Ctr. Ft. Worth, 1997—. Advisor diabetes adv. bd. Plz. Med. Ctr. Ft. Worth; adj. instr. Tarleton State U., Stephenville, Tex. Standing chairperson handbook Birdville PTSA, North Richland Hills, 1999, 2000; leader troop 1205 Girl Scouts Am., North Richland Hills, 1990-97. Mem. Am. Soc. Clin. Pathologists (assoc., cert.), Clin. Lab. Mgmt. Assn., South Cen. Assn. Blood Banks, Am. Assn. for Clin. Chemistry. Episcopalian. Avocations: scuba, sewing, gardening. Home: 6504 Parkway Ave North Richland Hills TX 76180-4309 Office: Plaza Med Ctr Ft Worth 900 8th Ave Fort Worth TX 76104-3901 Fax: 817-347-5764. E-mail: joanne.beveridge@lonestarhealth.com.

BEVERIDGE, NORWOOD PIERSON, law educator; b. Boston, Nov. 5, 1936; s. Norwood Pierson and Dorothy Winifred (Woodrow) B.; children: Norwood Pierson III, Richard W., Susan C. AB, Harvard U., 1958, LLB, 1962; LLM, NYU, 1986. Bar N.Y. 1963. Assoc. Kramer Marx Greenlee & Backus, N.Y.C., 1962—68, ptnr., 1968—71; asst. sec., asst. gen. counsel Amerace Corp., N.Y.C., 1971—73, sec., corp. counsel, 1973—84; asst. prof. Lubin Sch. Bus. Pace U., Pleasantville, NY, 1985—86; assoc. prof. We. State U. Coll. Law, Fullerton, Calif., 1986—89, Oklahoma City U. Law Sch., 1989—92, prof., 1992—, assoc. dean, 1999—2003. Fellow Am. Bar Found. (life); mem. ABA (com. corp. law depts. 1974-86, com. partnerships and unicorp. bus. orgns. 1990—, com. corp. gov. 1998—), Harvard Club. Office: Oklahoma City U Sch Law 2501 N Blackwelder Ave Oklahoma City OK 73106-1402 Home: 7400 NW 115th Street Oklahoma City OK 73162 E-mail: paladin@okcu.edu.

BEVERIDGE, STEPHEN D, freelance/self-employed artist; b. Glasgow, Scotland, Jan. 29, 1958; arrived in U.S., 1969; s. David and Elizabeth (King) Beveridge; m. Gail P Egelhofer; children: Scot Klugherz, Glenn Klugherz. Prin. works include painting Wee Hoose, 1998 (Manhattan Arts Internat. award of excellence, 1998), film, The Big One, 2001. Bd. dirs. Unity Ch. N.Y., N.Y.C., 1999—2001. Mem.: Upper Manhattan Artists Way (pres. 1998—2000), N.Y. Artists Equity, Nat. Acrylic Painters Assn. Gt. Britain (assoc.), Abstract Art Repository. Home and Office: Scot'Style 4395 Broadway 6e New York NY 10040 E-mail: sdb@scotstyle.com.

BEVERIDGE, TERRANCE JAMES, microbiology educator, researcher; b. Toronto, Ont., Can., Apr. 29, 1945; s. Fredrick Charles and Doris Elizabeth (Hooks) B.; m. Janice Elizabeth Barnett, Sept. 9, 1970; children: Braden Charles, Jennifer Bree. BS, U. Toronto, 1968, Diploma in Bacteriology, 1969, MS, 1970; PhD, U. Western Ont., 1974. Rsch. assoc. U. Western Ont., London, 1975-78; from asst. prof. to assoc. prof. U. Guelph, Ont., 1978-86, prof., 1986—, Killam prof., 1995-97, Can. rsch. chair, 2002—. Vis. prof. Zentrum für Ultrastruckturforschung, Vienna, Austria, 1984, Biozentrum, Universität der Basel, Switzerland, 1987; dir. Nat. Scis. and Engring. Rsch. Coun. of Can. (NSERC) Gueiph Regional STEM Facility, 1980—. Editor: Metal Ions and Bacteria, 1989, Advances in Bacterial Paracrystalline Surface Layers, 1993; editor Can. Jour. Microbiology, 1982-88, Jour. Bacteriology, 1988-97, Biorecovery, 1987—, Internat. Jour. of Resource and Environ. Biotech., 1994—, Microbiology, 1997—, Arch. Microbiology, 1998—. Recipient Steacie prize, Nat. Sci. and Engring. Rsch. Coun. of Can., 1984, Can. Soc. Microbiology award, 1994, Sigma Xi award, 1994, Culling medal, 2001. Fellow Royal Soc. Can. (dir. life scis. 1992-95), Am. Acad. Microbiology, Austrian Acad. Sci.; mem. Can. Soc. Microbiologists, Microscopical Soc. Can., Am. Soc. Microbiology (divsnl. award 1984), Electron Microscopic Soc. Am., Nat. Centre Excellence, Can. Bacterial Disease Network, Can. Inst. Advanced Rsch. (assoc. 1988—). Avocations: hiking, cross-country skiing. Office: U Guelph Coll Biol Scis Dept of Microbiology Guelph ON Canada N1G 2W1

BEVERLEY, CORDIA LUVONNE, gastroenterologist; b. Jamaica, W.I., Oct. 19, 1950; d. Hurdley Aston and Joyce Ruby (Baker) B.; B.A., Hunter Coll., 1971; M.D., N.Y. U., 1975. Diplomate Am. Bd. Gastroenterology, Am. Bd. Internal Medicine. Intern, Columbia U., Harlem Hosp. Center, N.Y.C., 1975-76, resident in medicine, 1976-78; clin. fellow div. gastroenterology N.Y. Hosp./Cornell U. Med. Coll., N.Y.C., 1979-82; asst. physician Rockefeller U. Hosp., N.Y.C., 1978-81. Nat. Inst. Alcohol Abuse and Alcoholism postdoctoral fellow, 1980-82. Mem. Women's Med. Assn. N.Y.C. Office: 1085 Park Ave New York NY 10128-1168

BEVERLY, LAURA ELIZABETH, special education educator; b. Glen Jean, W.Va., Nov. 26; d. Sidney and Alma Logan. BA in Elem. Edn., W.Va. State Coll., 1960; MS in Spl. Edn., Bklyn. Coll., 1969; postgrad., Oxford (Eng.) U., 1974, N.Y.U., 1982. Cert. elem./spl. edn. tchr., N.Y. Tchr. Bd. Coop. Ednl. Svcs., Westbury, N.Y., 1966—. Mem. adv. bd. Am. Biographical Inst. Inc., Raliegh, N.C., 1985—. Mem. ASCD, Am. Inst. of Parliamentarians, Royal Soc. Health, Phi Delta Kappa. Avocations: reading, traveling. Home: PO Box 346 Glen Jean WV 25846-0346

BEVERLY, ZYLPHIA MARIE, mental health services professional; b. San Antonio, May 23, 1956; d. Robert James Sr. and Mae Ruth (Douglas) Davis; married, Mar. 5, 1994. BS, Tex. Women's U., 1978; MA, St. Mary's U., 1982. Lic. profl. counselor Nat. Bd. Cert. Counselor, Tex., chem. dependency counselor. Tchr. crisis interventionist Contact Crisis Hotline; child care worker II Children Svc. Bur., San Antonio, psychol. evaluation technician; case mgr., mental health provider Colonial Hills Hosp., San Antonio; caseworker, unit supr. and svc coord. III Ctr. Health Care Svcs., San Antonio. Home: 315 Astoria Dr San Antonio TX 78220-1601

BEVERSDORF, DAVID QUENTIN, neurologist, researcher; b. Bloomington, Ind., May 28, 1965; s. Samuel Thomas and Norma (Beeson) B.; m. Sheri Anderson, Dec. 26, 1990. BS, Ind. U., 1987; MD, Ind. U., Indpls., 1992. Med. resident Meth. Hosp. Ind., Indpls., 1992-93; neurology resident Dartmouth-Hitchcock Med. Ctr., Lebanon, N.H., 1993-96; behavioral neurology fellow U. Fla. Coll. Medicine, Gainesville, 1996-98; asst. prof. neurology Ohio State U. Med. Ctr., Columbus, 1998—. Contbr. articles to profl. jours. including Procs. Nat. Acad. Scis., Lancet, Neurology, Psychiatry Rsch.-Neuroimaging, Jour. Neurology, Neurosurgery and Psychiatry, and Physiology and Behavior. Rsch. grant Stallone Fund, L.A., 1994, grantee Nat. Inst. on Drug Abuse, 2002, Nat. Inst. Neurol. Diseases and Stroke, 2002. Mem. Am. Acad. Neurology, Cognitive Sci. Soc., Soc. for Neurosci., Cognitive Neurosci. Soc., Phi Beta Kappa. Office: Ohio State U Med Ctr Dept Neurology 1654 Upham Dr Columbus OH 43210-1250 E-mail: beversdorf-1@medctr.osu.edu.

BE VIER, WILLIAM A. religious studies educator; b. Springfield, Mo., July 31, 1927; s. Charles and Erma G. (Ritter) Be V.; m Jo Ann King, Aug. 11, 1949; children: Cynthia, Shirley. BA, Drury Coll., 1950; ThM, Dallas Theol. Sem., 1955, ThD, 1958; MA, So. Meth. U., 1960; EdD, ABD, Wayne State U., 1968. With Frisco Rlwy., 1943-45, 46-51, John E. Mitchell Co., Dallas, 1952-60; instr. Dallas Theol. Sem., 1958-59; prof. Detroit Bible Coll., 1960-74, registrar, 1962-66, dean, 1964-73, exec. v.p., 1967-74, acting pres., 1967-68; prof., dean edn., v.p. for acad. affairs Northwestern Coll., Roseville, Minn., 1974-81, prof., 1981-95, prof. emeritus, 1995—. Editor The Discerner. Bd. dirs. Religion Analysis Svc., Mpls., 1979—, pres., 1989—. With USMC, 1945-46, 50-51; ret. col. Army Res. Mem. Res. Officers Assn., Ind. Fund Chs. of Am. (nat. exec. com. 1991-94, v.p. 1993-94), Huguenot Hist. Soc., Bevier-Elting Family Assn., Phi Alpha Theta. Office: Religion Analysis Svc 5693 Geneva Ave N Oakdale MN 55128-1018 E-mail: wabjab41@juno.com.

BEVILACQUA, ANTHONY JOSEPH CARDINAL, archbishop emeritus; b. Bklyn., June 17, 1923; s. Louis and Maria (Codella) Bevilacque. Student, Cathedral Coll., Bklyn., 1941—43, Sem. Immaculate Conception, Huntington, N.Y., 1943—49; JCD, Gregorian U., Rome, 1956; MA in Polit. Sci, Columbia U., 1962; JD, St. John's U., 1975. Bar: N.Y. 1976, Pa. 1988, U.S. Dist. Ct. (we. dist.) Pa. 1984, U.S. Dist. Ct. (ea. dist.) Pa. 1988, U.S. Supreme Ct. 1989; Ordained priest Roman Cath. Ch., 1949, bishop 1980. Asst. pastor Sacred Heart, St. Stephen's Ch., St. Mary's Ch., 1949—50; prof. history Cathedral Prep. Sem., Bklyn., 1950—53; prof. canon law Sem. of Immaculate Conception, Huntington, NY, 1968—80; adj. prof. St. John's U. Sch. Law, Queens, NY, 1976—80; from asst. chancellor to chancellor Diocese of Bklyn., 1965—83, dir. Cath. migration and refugee office, 1971—83; bishop Diocese of Pitts., 1983—88; archbishop Archdiocese of Phila., 1988—2003; elevated to cardinal Coll. of Cardinals, 1991. Com. pro-life activities, 1989—; mem. Pontifical Congregation for Causes of Saints, 1991—, Pontifical Coun. Cor Unum, 1991—. Contbr. articles to profl. jours. Bd. dirs. Mercy Home for Children. Mem.: Fellowship of Am. Cath. Scholars, Pa. Bar Assn., Canon Law Soc. Am. Roman Catholic.

BEVILACQUA, MAURIZIO, member of Canadian parliament; b. Sulmona, Italy, June 1, 1960; m. Elena Cesaroni; 2 children. BA, York U., Toronto. Exec. asst. Members of Provincial and Federal Parliaments, Toronto, Ottawa, Can., 1982-88; mem. parliament Ho. of Commons, Ottawa, 1988—, chmn. standing com. on fin., 1997—2002, sec. of state sci., rsch. and develop., 2002, sec. state internat. fin. instns., 2002—. Opposition critic for employment: youth and disabled, assoc.. opposition critic for energy, mines and resources, 1988-90; mem. standing coms. on Energy, Mines and Resources; Labour, Employment and Immigration and Human Rights and Status of Disabled Persons, 1988-90; parliamentary sec. to Minister of Human Resources Devel., 1995-97; chair of standing com. on Human Resources Devel., 1995-97; chair standing com. on Fin., 1997—. Co-founder Vaughn Comty. of Assns. to Restore Environ. Safety; past pres. Coun. York Student Fedn.; active on many local bds. and in local assns. Office: Can Ho of Commons Rm 540 N Ctr Block Ottawa ON Canada KIA0A6

BEVILL, TOM, retired congressman, lawyer; b. Townley, AL, Mar. 27, 1921; s. Herman and Fannie Lou (Fike) B.; m. Lou Betts, June 24, 1943; children: Susan B., Donald H., Patricia Lou. BS, U. Ala., 1943, LLB, 1948; LLD(hon.), U. Ala., Tuscaloosa, 1981, Livingston U., 1986; LLD (hon.), U. North Ala., 1991, Troy State U., 1992. Bar: Ala. 1949. Pvt. practice law, Jasper, 1948-67; mem. Ala. Ho. of Reps., 1958-66, 90th-104th Congresses from 4th Ala. dist., 1967-97, mem. appropriations com., ret., 1997. Mem. ABA, Ala. Bar Assn., Walker County Bar Assn. (past pres.), Am. Judicature Soc. Home: 411 Ridge Rd Jasper AL 35501-4844

BEVINGTON, DAVID MARTIN, English literature educator; b. N.Y.C., May 13, 1931; s. Merle Mowbray and Helen (Smith) B.; m. Margaret Bronson Brown, June 4, 1953; children: Stephen, Philip, Katharine, Sarah. BA, Harvard U., 1952, MA, 1957, PhD, 1959. Instr. English Harvard U., 1959-61; asst. prof. U. Va., 1961-65, asso. prof., 1965-66, prof., 1966-67; vis. prof. U. Chgo., 1967-68, prof., 1968—, Phyllis Fay Horton disting. svc. prof. in the humanities, 1985—. Vis. prof. N.Y. U. Summer Sch., 1963, Harvard U. Summer Sch., 1967, U. Hawaii Summer Sch., 1970, Northwestern U., 1974 Author: From Mankind to Marlowe, 1962, Tudor Drama and Politics, 1968, Action is Eloquence, Shakespeare's Language of Gesture, 1984, Shakespeare, 2002; editor: Medieval Drama, 1975, The Complete Works of Shakespeare, 5th edit., 2003, The Bantam Shakespeare, 1988, English Renaissance Drama: A Norton Anthology, 2002. Served with USN, 1952-55. Guggenheim fellow, 1964-65, 81-82; sr. fellow Southeastern Inst. Medieval and Renaissance Studies, summer 1975; sr. cons. and seminar leader Folger Inst. Renaissance and Eighteenth-Century Studies, 1976-77 Mem. MLA, AAUP, Renaissance Soc. Am., Shakespeare Assn. Am. (pres. 1976-77, 95-96), Am. Acad. Arts and Scis., Am. Philos. Soc. Home: 5747 S Blackstone Ave Chicago IL 60637-1823 Office: Univ Chgo English Dept 5801 S Ellis Ave Chicago IL 60637-5418

BEVINGTON, E(DMUND) MILTON, electrical machinery manufacturing company executive; b. Nashville, Oct. 31, 1928; s. John Laurence and Mary (Halloran) B.; m. Elizabeth Anne Rickey, Sept. 8, 1951 (dec. June 1962); children: Milton, Rickey, Peter; m. Paula Maureen Lawton, Apr. 24, 1965; children: George, Mary-Laurence, Christian, Charles, Justin. Grad., Canterbury Sch., 1945; S.B. in Chem. Enging, Mass. Inst. Tech., 1949; MBA, Harvard, 1951. Plant supr. Dewey & Almy Chem. Co. (name changed to W.R. Grace Co., 1954), Cambridge, Mass., 1951-54, marketing research mgr., 1954-56; merchandising mgr. Westinghouse Electric Co., Staunton, Va., 1956-58, So. zone sales mgr. Atlanta, 1958-59; with The Trane Co., Atlanta and LaCrosse, Wis., 1959—, v.p., gen. mgr. consumer products div., 1969-70, exec. v.p., 1970-73; chmn., pres. Servidyne Systems, Inc., Atlanta, 1974—2002, Bevington & Co., Atlanta, 2002—. Bd. dirs. AAA South. Mem. corp. devel. com. MIT, 1978—, bd. dirs. MIT Corp., 1985-91; chmn. Ga. Conservancy, 1989-92, bd. dirs.; bd. dirs. Atlanta coun. Boy Scouts Am., also v.p., 1989-90, pres., 1990-92; bd. dirs. So. region Boy Scouts Am.; pres. Metro Group, 1992-97; bd. dirs. Ga. Dept. Cmty. Affairs, 1988-92; bd. dirs. Am. Humanics, 1998—; chmn. Clayton Coll. and State U., 1998—. Mem. Pres.' Cir. of NAS, MIT Alumni Assn. (v.p. 1983-85, pres. 1985-86), Piedmont Driving Club (Atlanta), Tau Beta Pi, Sigma Alpha Epsilon. Clubs: Harvard (N.Y.C. and Boston); Piedmont Driving (Atlanta).

BEVINGTON, PAULA LAWTON, museum administrator; b. Cleve., Sept. 25, 1937; d. G(eorge) Albert and Mary Patricia (Walsh) Lawton; m. E(dmund) Milton Bevington, Apr. 24, 1965; children: Milton, Rickey, George, Mary-Laurence, Christian, Charles, Justin, Peter (dec.). BA magna cum laude, Saint Mary's Coll., Notre Dame, Ind., 1958; JD, Yale U., 1961. Bar: Ga. 1960. Assoc. Sutherland, Asbill & Brennan, Atlanta, 1961-63; vol. various non-profit agys., LaCrosse, Wis., 1971-73, Atlanta, 1965-71, 73—; chmn. Servidyne Sys., LLC, Atlanta, 1980—2002; v.p. devel. The Sci. and Tech. Mus. Ga. (SciTrek), Atlanta, 2002—. Bd. dirs. Lathem Time, Inc., Atlanta; mem. adv. bd. Ga. State U. Coll. Law, Atlanta, 1995—. Mem. Jr. League of Atlanta, 1967—, pres., 1980; bd. dirs. Justice Ctr. Atlanta, pres. 1999-2002; bd. dirs., vol. ARC, Atlanta, chair, 1985-86; bd. dirs. World Trade Ctr., Atlanta, 1991-2002; bd. dirs. So. Ctr. for Internat. Studies, 1990--, vice chair, 2002--; bd. dirs. UNICEF-Atlanta, 1991-99, chair, 1994-96; trustee Oglethorpe U., Atlanta, 1982-91, Saint Mary's Coll., 1985-91; mem. Ga. Human Rels. Commn., 1987-99, chmn., 1990-98; bd. councilors The Carter Ctr., Atlanta, 1997—, chair 2003—. Recipient Disting. Alumna award Saint Mary's Coll., 1976, Peace and Justice award Martin Luther King Jr. Ctr., Atlanta, 1987, Brotherhood/Sisterhood award NCCJ, 1994, Outstanding Svc. award Atlanta Legal Aid Soc., 1997; Fulbright scholar, 1963-64. Mem. Yale Club (pres. Ga. chpt. 1995-96), Rotary (bd. dirs., pres. Atlanta 1999-00). Roman Catholic. Avocations: reading, travel, family activities. Home: 2500 Peachtree Rd NW # 104 Atlanta GA 30305-3604 Office: SciTrek 395 Piedmont Ave NE Atlanta GA 30308

BEVINS, KARL ALTEN, retired engineer, musician, educator; b. Weilman, Iowa, May 30, 1915; s. Daniel J. and Jennie (Alten) B.; m. Blanche Albert, June 3, 1946; 1 child, Jean Marie. BEE, Ga. Inst. Tech., 1939; cert. traffic engr., Yale U. Registered profl. engr., Ga. Traffic engr. Ga. Power Co., Atlanta, 1941-49; city traffic engr. City of Atlanta, 1949-78; instr. clarinet Ga. State U., 1966—. Tchr. pvt. lessons, clinics in clarinet, 1933—; nat. dir. Automobile Assn. Am., 1973-75; chmn. traffic engring. sect. So. Safety Conf., 1935-36. Prin. clarinetist Atlanta Philharmonic Orch., 1945-2000, Atlanta Pops Orch., 1945-67, Atlanta Symphony Orch., 1945-66; first chair clarinetist Mcpl. Theatre of Stars, 1954—; solo clarinetist Band of Atlanta, 1958-74; performer solo and chamber group recitals, theater, radio and TV concerts and dance band groups. Named one of Atlanta's 100 Leaders of Tomorrow, Atlanta C. of C. and Time Mag., 1953; Karl A. Bevins award of Inst. Traffic Engrs. named in his honor, 1981. Mem. Inst. Trasnp. Engrs. (hon.), Ga. Soc. Profl. Engrs., Ga. Engring. Soc.,

AIEE, Atlanta Fedn. Musicians (exec. bd. 1954—, pres. 1967-86, pres. emeritus 1986—), Kappa Kappa Psi, Atlanta Music Club. Home: #411 3747 Peachtree Rd NE Apt 411 Atlanta GA 30319-1338

BEVIR, WILLIAM MARK, political science educator; b. London, Feb. 18, 1963; s. William Lawrence and Phebe (Belton Cobb); m. Laura Grant, Apr. 7, 1990; children: Lawrence Anthony, Harry John. BA, Exeter U., Eng., 1985; DPhil, Oxford U., Eng., 1989. Rsch. fellow Madras U., India, 1990—92; Sir James Knott fellow Newcastle U., England, 1992—98, reader in polit. theory, 1998—2000; asst. prof. U. Calif., Berkeley, 2000—02, assoc. prof., 2002—. Mem. Internat. Next Generations Leaders' Forum, Seoul, Republic of Korea, 1995; vis. fellow Harry Ransom Humanities Rsch. Ctr., U. Tex., Austin, 1999, CERVL, Bordeaux, France, 2003; affiliate Inst. Govt. Studies, U. Calif., Berkeley, 2000—. Author: The Logic of the History of Ideas, 1999; co-author: Interpreting British Governance, 2003; contbr. articles to profl. jours. Mem.: Soc. for the Philosophy of History (v.p. 2001—). Office: Dept Polit Sci U Calif Berkeley CA 94720-0001

BEVIS, ROBERT E. retired oil company executive; b. N.Y.C. Attended in Bus. Adminstrn., NYU, 1936—42. Various sales positions with S.O. Co. of NJ and NY, 1937—47; various positions with Esso Std. Oil Co. S.A., 1953—54; former pres. Esso Std. Oil Co., San Juan, 1955; v.p., dir. Esso West Africa, Lagos, Nigeria, 1957—59; mktg. coord. for Africa, Mid. East, Spain and Portugal Esso Std. Mediterranean Inc., Geneva, 1961; acting div. mgr. Esso Std. Mediterranean Inc. Libya Div. of Std. (Near East), Inc., 1963; mktg. mgr. Esso Std. Near East, Tripoli, Libya, 1968-91; mgr. Exxon Co. U.S.A., Balt.; ret. Exxon Corp., 1970. Cons. NASA. Lt. Commander (Naval Aviator) USN, 1942—45, positions/special assignments with USN, 1945—53, ret. USN, 1957. Address: 310 Five Farms Ln Lutherville Timonium MD 21093

BEWES, TIMOTHY RICHARD THOMAS, language educator; b. Barking, Essex, Eng., Oct. 8, 1966; arrived in U.S., 2002; s. Richard Thomas and Elisabeth Ingrid Bewes. BA in English Lit. Honors, U. North London, 1992; MA in English Lit., U. Sussex, 1993, PhD of English Lit., 1996. Vis. lectr. Coventry U., England, 1997—99; postdoctoral fellow Liverpool John Moores U., Liverpool, England, 1999—2002; vis. asst. prof. Brown U., Providence, 2002—03, rsch. fellow Pembroke Ctr., 2003—. Vis. lectr. U. North London, 1992—99, Roehampton Inst. Higher Edn., 1997—99. Author: Cynicism and Postmodernity, 1997, Reification, or the Anxiety of Late Capitalism, 2002; co-editor: Cultural Capitalism, 2000. Mem.: Modern Langs. Assn., Cumberland Lawn Tennis Club London. Office: Brown Univ English Dept 70 Brown St Providence RI 02912

BEWKES, EUGENE GARRETT, JR., investment company executive, consultant; b. Norwood, Mass., Sept. 28, 1926; s. Eugene Garrett and Helen (Van Vlaanderen) B.; m. Marjorie Louise Klenk, Aug. 20, 1949; children: Eugene Garrett III, Jeffrey Lawrence, Robert David. BA, Colgate U., 1948; JD, Yale U., 1951; LLD, Colgate U., 1991. Bar: N.Y. 1952. With firm Chapman, Bryson, Walsh & O'Connell, N.Y.C., 1951-55; atty.-adviser also asst. Office Sec. USAF, 1955-57; with Am. Mgmt. Assn., 1957-61, gen. mgmt. div., mgr., 1959-61; gen. counsel, sec., asst. v.p. Reuben H. Donnelley Corp, 1961-67; v.p. law and adminstrn., sec. Canada Dry Corp., 1967-68; v.p. Norton Simon, Inc., N.Y.C., 1968-72, sr. v.p., 1972-73, exec. v.p., 1973-77, vice chmn. bd., 1977-81; chmn., pres., chief exec. officer Am. Bakeries Co., 1982-88; cons. Paine Webber Group, Inc., N.Y.C., 1988—. Bd. dirs. Interstate Bakeries Corp., numerous Paine Webber mutual funds. Chmn. emeritus bd. trustees Colgate U., Hamilton, N.Y. With USNR, 1945-46. Mem. Yale Club (N.Y.C.), Blind Brook Club, Johns Island Club, Redstick Golf Club, Sankaty Club Nantucket, Phi Beta Kappa, Delta Kappa Epsilon, Phi Delta Phi. Home: PO Box 8307 Vero Beach FL 32963-8307 Office: Lightyear Capital 23d Fl 51 W 52d St New York NY 10019-6096

BEWKES, JEFF, television broadcasting company executive; BA, Yale U.; MBA, Stanford U. Exec. v.p., CFO Home Box Office, N.Y.C., 1987—91, pres., COO, 1991—95, chmn., CEO, 1995—2002; chmn. ent. & networks grp. AOL Time Warner Inc., N.Y.C., 2002—. Office: HBO Inc 1100 Avenue Of The Americas New York NY 10036-6740

BEWLEY, JOHN DEREK, botany researcher, educator; b. Preston, Lancashire, Eng., Dec. 11, 1943; s. Clifford and Marion (Garner) B.; m. Christine E. Nee Kite, Sept. 3, 1966; children: Alexander, Janette Louise. BSc, U. London, 1965, PhD, 1968, DSc, 1983. Asst. prof. U. Calgary, Alta., 1970-73, assoc. prof., 1973-77, prof. biology, 1977-85; prof., chmn. dept. botany U. Guelph, Ont., 1985-90, prof. botany, 1990—, dir. plant biol. program, 1993-94. E.W.R. Steacie Meml. fellow in natural scis. and engring. Rsch. Coun. Can., 1979-81; recipient Career Rsch. Excellence award Sigma Xi, 1993, Disting. Biologist award Can. Coun. Univ. Chairs, 1994; named Highly Cited Author, ISI, 2002. Fellow Royal Soc. Can. (rapporteur plant biology div. 1984-85, convenor 1985-87); mem. Can. Soc. Plant Physiologists (C.D. Nelson award 1978, Gold medal 1992, sec. 1983-85, v.p. 1987-88, pres. 1988-90), Natural Scis. and Engring. Rsch. Coun. Can. (chmn. plant biology grant selection com. 1988-90), Internat. Soc. Seed Sci. (pres. elect, 2002-2005). Home: 26 Waverley Dr Guelph ON Canada N1E 6C8 Office: U Guelph Dept Botany Guelph ON Canada N1G 2W1 E-mail: dbewley@uoguelph.ca.

BEWLEY, PETER DAVID, lawyer; b. Atlantic City, N.J., Aug. 4, 1946; s. Philip Bessor and Gladys Elizabeth Bewley; m. Barbara L. Sell, June 1, 1968 (dec. June 25, 1971); 1 child, Peter David Jr.; m. Lee D. Catanese, Aug. 12, 1972; 1 child, Stephen Philip. BA in Politics cum laude, Princeton U., 1968; JD, Stanford U., 1971. Bar: Calif. 1971, D.C. 1972, U.S. Ct. Appeals (D.C. cir.) 1972, U.S. Supreme Ct. 1976. Assoc. Wilmer, Cutler & Pickering, Washington, 1972-76; gen. atty., from asst. gen. counsel Johnson & Johnson, New Brunswick, N.J., 1977-94; sr. v.p., gen. counsel, sec. Nova Care, Inc., King of Prussia, Pa., 1994-98, The Clorox Co., Oakland, Calif., 1998—. Dir. Non Prescription Drug Mfrs. Assn., Washington, 1991-94, Access World Wide Comms., Boca Raton, Fla., 1998-2001. Mem. editl. bd. Food and Drug Law Jour., 1992-94. City councilman City of Gladstone, N.J., 1993-94. Capt. USAF, 1971-72. Mem. ABA, Am. Corp. Counsel Assn., Am. Soc. Corp. Secs., Order of Coif. Avocations: travel, skiing, reading. Home: 6066 Mazuela Dr Oakland CA 94611-2208 Office: The Clorox Co 1221 Broadway Fl 13 Oakland CA 94612-1888 E-mail: pbewley@alumni.princeton.edu.

BEX, BRIAN WILLIAM LOUIS, educational administrator; b. Chgo., Feb. 5, 1943; s. John and Jeanne Rowena Bex; children: Jay, Charles, Kristophor. Student, Ind. U.; LLB, U. Chgo., 1965, JD, 1967. Pres., founder Am. Comms. Network-Brian Bex Report, Inc., Hagerstown, Ind., 1966—; pres., treas., founder The Remnant Trust, Hagerstown. Spkr. and lectr. Author: The Individualist Declaration, 1968, Decline and Fall of the American Republic, 1974, The Road, Never the Inn, 1976, The Vanishing Dinosaur, 1985, Out of Bounds, 1992, The Teeter Totter Equation, 1998, others. Address: 100 N Woodpecker Rd Hagerstown IN 47346-1431

BEXFIELD, JAMES NELSON, military analyst; b. Gallup, N.Mex., July 18, 1943; s. Frank William and Mildred (Johnson) Bexfield; m. Judith Lee Hermann, July 2, 1965; children: David, Karen, Kathryn. B in Mgmt. Engring., Rensalear Polytech Inst., 1965; MBA, Wharton Coll., 1967. With mil. ops. USAF, 1968—89; rsch. analyst Inst. Def. Analyses, Alexandria, Va., 1989—2002; dir. planning and analytical support divsn. Office of Sec. of Def., Arlington, Va., 2002—. Fellow: Mil. Ops. Rsch. Soc. (pres. 1983—85, Wanner award 1994). Avocations: bridge, racquetball, travel. Home: 2405 Crest St Alexandria VA 22302

BEXLEY, JAMES BYRON, banker; b. Waco, Tex., Jan. 11, 1934; s. Joe Dan and Rubye (Porter) B.; m. Elsie Mae Murphy, Feb. 5, 1955; children— Byron K., Tammie Bexley Graf BBA, U. Tex.; LL.B., Blackstone Sch. Law; MBA, U. Houston. V.p. Bank of S.W., Houston, 1964-71; sr. v.p. River Oaks Bank & Trust, Houston, 1971-73; pres. Houston State Bank, 1973-75, 1st Bank, Houston, 1975-80, Tex. Commerce Bank, McAllen, 1980-81, chmn., chief exec. officer, 1981-87, Corpus Christi, 1987—. Chmn., lectr. Intermediate Banking Sch., Dallas, 1978— ; lectr. Southwestern Grad. Sch. of Banking, Dallas, 1979— Author: Oil and Gas Forms, 1966, Banking Management, 1978; The Bank Director, 1985 Mem. Gov.'s Pvt. Sector Initiatives Com., Tex.; bd. dirs. Tex. Taxpayers Assn., Pan Am. U. Found.; past chmn. bd., bd. dirs. Leadership McAllen; chmn. Valley 2000 Econ. Com.; bd. dirs. McAllen Fgn. Trade Zone, McAllen Indsl. Bd. Served to capt. U.S. Army, 1957-58 Recipient Silver Beaver award Boy Scouts of Am., 1973, Outstanding Teaching award Houston Community Coll., 1975; Adult Outstanding Service award Sharpstown High Sch., Houston, 1975. Mem. Valley Bankers Assn. (pres. 1982-84, dir.), Tex. Bankers Assn. (chmn. ops. com. 1970-72, mem. legis. com. 1977), Bank Adminstrn. Inst. (nat. trust com. 1968-72), McAllen C. of C. (bd. dirs., chmn. econ. devel. council and past chmn. downtown devel. com.), Valley C. of C. (past pres.) Clubs: McAllen Country (bd. dirs. 1984), Tower. Lodges: Masons,. Baptist. Avocations: golf, tennis. Home: 5218 Greenbriar Dr Corpus Christi TX 78413-2825 Office: Tex Commerce Bank PO Box 749 Corpus Christi TX 78403-0749 also: Tex Commerce Bank 1701 W Us Highway 83 Mcallen TX 78501-5160

BEXTERMILLER METZGER, THERESA MARIE, architect, computer engineer; b. St. Charles, Mo., Feb. 9, 1960; d. Charles Frederick and Loretta Joan (Unterreiner) Bextermiller; m. Paul James Metzger III, Nov. 29, 2000; stepchildren: Jennifer, Michael, Stephen, Andrew. BArch, Kans. State U., 1983; MFA in Computer Graphics and Interactive Media, Pratt Inst., 1990. Registered architect, N.Y., 1989, Mo., 1990; cert. Nat. Coun. Archtl. Regis., 1996; real estate salesperson, Mo., 1995-98, broker, 2000—. Grad. arch. Mackey/Mitchell Assocs., St. Louis, 1983-84, Fleming Corp., St. Louis, 1984-85; project arch., prototype mgr. Casco Corp., St. Louis, 1985-87; grad. arch. HBE Corp., St. Louis, 1987-88; with telecomm. Western Union, 1992-93, Lucent Techs. (formerly AT&T Network Sys.), 1993—94; contract arch. M.K. Ferguson Group, 1994-95, Fru-Con Engring. Inc. and other firms, various locations, 1995-98; prin. TMB Architecture/Computer Graphics, 1997—, Theresa Marie Bextermiller Metzger, RA, MFA, NCARB, Broker, 2000—, Le Pique and Orne Archs.-Inc., 1998—, Hellmuth, Obata & Kassabaum, Inc., St. Louis, 1998—, Mr. Thomas T. Whitaker, 1999—; planner Infante Assocs., LLC, 1999—. Cons. to various cos. regarding software, including Alias/Wavefront, Washington U., St. Louis, Madrid, L.A., 1991—97; substitute tchr. St. Louis Pub. Schs., 2001—02; freelance architect. Mem.: AIA. Roman Catholic. Avocation: real estate. Home: 1120 Blendon Pl Saint Louis MO 63117-1911

BEY, JOAN S. retired public information specialist, writer; b. Boston, Ind., Nov. 30, 1927; d. Frank J. Schoemaker and Lestra J. (Turner) Schoemaker/Kelly; m. John J. Bey, May 8, 1954 (dec. June 1968); children: Anna Marie Bey Witt, Joseph M., John C. Bachelors degree, St. Mary of the Woods Coll., 1949. Reporter, food editor Indpls. Times, 1950-58; freelance pub. rels. profl., cons. Indpls., 1971-90; with pub. info. dept. Ivy Tech. State Coll., Indpls., 1983-97, ret., 1997. Recipient Vesta award Am. Meat Inst., 1952. Mem. Nat. Fedn. Press Women (writing awards 1980s, 90s), Woman's Press Club Ind. (historian 1984—, pres. 1982-84, Kate Milner Rabb award 1986), Soc. Ind. Pioneers, Ind. Hist. Soc. Roman Catholic.

BEY, LEE, municipal official; b. Chgo., Oct. 20, 1965; s. Lee Johnson Bey, Lula Mae Bey; m. Valencia Faye Scott; children: Ernest Scott, Candace, Cassandra, Sara. BA, Columbia Coll., 1988. News reporter City News Bur. Chgo., 1988—90, Daily Southtown, 1990—92; gen. assignment reporter Chgo. Sun-Times, 1992—93, edn. reporter, 1993—94, spl. projects reporter, 1994—96, architecture writer, 1996—97, architecture critic, 1997—2001; dep. chief of staff for planning and design Office of Mayor, Chgo., 2001—. Contbr. book. Recipient, Nat. Edn. Writers Assn., 1992, Cardinal's Comm. award, Archdiocese of Chgo., 1992, 1993, Peter Lisagor award, Chgo. Headline Club, 1994, Sarah Brown Boyden award for Outstanding Journalism, Chgo. Press Vets. Assn., 1997, Preservation award, Richard Driehaus Found., 1997, Best Series award, Chgo. Press Vets. Assn., 1999, award, Am. Planning Assn., 1999, Studs Terkel award, Cmty. Media Workshop, 2000. Mem.: Nat. Orgn. Minority Architects (hon.). Conservative. Avocations: architectural photography, drawing. Office: City of Chicago 121 N LaSalle Chicago IL 60602 Home Fax: 312-744-2324. Personal E-mail: lbey@cityofchicago.org.

BEYDOUN, SAID R. physician, neurology educator; b. Askala, Lebanon, Oct. 15, 1954; came to U.S., 1980; s. Rashid S. and Houda (Jamil) B.; m. Farah Rola, Mar. 8, 1980; children: Rashid, Lana. BS in Biology-Chemistry with honors, Am. U., Beirut, 1975, MD, 1980. Diplomate in neurology and neurophysiology Am. Bd. Neurology, Am. Bd. Electrodiagnostic Medicine. Instr. U. So. Calif., L.A., 1983—84, asst. prof. neurology, 1984—87, assoc. prof. neurology, 1987—94, prof. neurology, 1994—. Dir. EMG Lab., U Soc. Calif. Univ. Hosp., 1991—, vice chief neurology svc., 1991-96, chief neurology svc., 1996—; CEO, med. dir. USC Neurologists Inc., L.A., 1996-2001, chmn. exec. com., 2001-2002, mem. exec. com., 2002—. Fellow Am. Assn. Electrodiagnostic Medicine, Am. Acad. Neurology; mem. Am. Pain Soc., Daniel Bliss Soc., Alpha Omega Alpha. Avocations: swimming, computers, travel. Office: USC Univ Hosp Neurophysiology Dept 1450 San Pablo St Los Angeles CA 90033 E-mail: sbeydoun@usc.edu.

BEYEA, JAN EDGAR, physicist; s. Harold Edgar Beyea and Muriel Shaffer; m. Patricia Downs, Jan. 2, 1965 (div.); children: Alison, Brigit. BA, U. Amherst, 1962; PhD, Columbia U., 1970. Rsch. assoc. Columbia U., N.Y.C., 1968—70; asst. prof. of physics Holy Cross Coll., Worcester, Mass., 1970—76; rsch. staff Princeton U., Princeton, NJ, 1976—80; sr. scientist Nat. Audubon Soc., N.Y.C., 1980—91, chief scientist and v.p., 1992—95; sr. scientist Consulting in the Pub. Interest, Lambertville, NJ, 1996—. Mem. of study panels NRC, Washington, 1990—2002, advisor to divsn. on engring. & phys. sciences, 2001—; mem. of study panels Office of Tech. Assessment, Washington, 1984—88; co-chmn. composting com. Coalition of Northeastern Governors, Washington, 1994—96; mem. bd. on energy & environ. sys. NRC, 1993—98. Contbr. articles to profl. jours. Mem.: Radiation Rsch. Soc., Health Physics Soc., Am. Chem. Soc., Am. Phys. Soc., Soc. for Risk Analysis, Internat. Soc. of Exposure Analysis. Office: Consulting in the Public Interest 53 Clinton St Lambertville NJ 08530 E-mail: jbeyea@cipi.com.

BEYER, BARBARA LYNN, aviation consultant; b. Miami, Fla., Feb. 16, 1947; d. Morten Sternoff and Jane (Hartman) B. BA, George Washington U., 1978. Supr. printing office Saudi Arabian Airlines, 1966-67; ops. coord. Modern Air Transport, Miami, Fla., 1968-70, acct. Berlin, 1970-72; rep. Johnson Internat. Airlines, Washington, 1974-75; v.p., bd. dirs. Avmark, Inc., Washington, 1975—, pres., 1989—; chmn., bd. dirs. Avmark Internat., London, 1985—; mng. dir. Avmark Asia Ltd., Singapore, 1988-89, also bd. dirs., chmn. bd. dirs. Hong Kong, 1989—; pub. Avmark Aviation Economist, London, 1986—. Mem. adv. bd. aviation bus. dept. Embry-Riddle Aero. U. Mem. Aviation Space Writers (award 1978, internat. bd. dirs. 1986-88), Nat. Bus. Aircraft Assn., Am. C. of C., Fgn. Corr. Club, Aero Club, Internat. Aviation Club, Nat. Press Club. Avocations: reading, horseback riding, home improvement. Office: Avmark Inc 1925 N Lynn St Ste 403 Arlington VA 22209-1707 E-mail: bbeyer@avmarkinc.com.

BEYER, DONALD STERNOFF, JR., state official; b. Trieste, Free Territory of Trieste, June 20, 1950; came to U.S., 1952; s. Donald Sternoff Sr. and Nancy Prew (McDonald) B.; m. Carolyn Ann McInerney, July 15, 1972 (div.); children: Donald III, Stephanie; m. Megan Carroll, Sept. 19, 1987; children: Clara, Grace. BA in Econs. magna cum laude, Williams Coll., 1972. Former pres., v.p. and other positions Don Beyer Volvo, Falls Church, Va., 1974—; lt. gov. Commonwealth of Va., Richmond, 1990-98. Urban at large mem. Commonwealth Transp. Bd., Va., 1987-90; chmn. Va. Econ. Bridge Initiative, Va., 1990—. Chmn. Baliles for Gov., No. Va., 1985, Paul Simon for Pres., Va., 1988, Bill Clinton for Pres., Va., 1992; mem. 11th Dist. Dem. Com., Vienna, Va., 1992; Dem. nominee Gov. of Va., 1998. Named Time Mag. Quality Dealer of Yr. for Va., 1991. Mem. Land Rover Alexandria (pres. 1997—). Democrat. Episcopalian. Avocations: golf, skiing, climbing. Office: Don Beyer Volvo 1231 W Broad St Falls Church VA 22046-2167*

BEYER, KAREN HAYNES, social worker; b. Cleve., Jan. 30, 1942; Karen Beyer, a licensed clinical social worker, defied a court order to divulge her client's therapy records. The refusal was appealed to the U.S Supreme Court (1996, Jaffee vs. Redmond and the Village of Hoffman Estates). The Supreme Court majority decision supported her protection of client privacy and resulted in stronger guarantees of confidentiality in therapy. BA, Ohio State U., 1965; MSW, Loyola U., Chgo., 1969; postgrad. Family Inst., Northwestern U., 1979; MPA, Roosevelt U., 1992; CBA, U. Ill., Chgo., 1995. Lic. clin. social worker, Ill. With Cuyahoga County Divsn. Child Welfare, Cleve., 1965, Dallas County Child Welfare Unit, Dallas, 1966, Luth. Social Svsc. Ill., Chgo., 1967-73; pvt. practice psychotherapy, family mediation Schaumburg, Ill., 1975-93; therapist Family Svcs. Assn. Greater Elgin (Ill.), 1973-77, dir. prof. svcs., 1977-83; dir. HHS Village of Hoffman Estates, Ill., 1983-93; exec. dir. Larkin Ctr., Elgin, Ill., 1993-2000, Ecker Ctr., Elgin, 2000—. Mem. NASW, Rotary. Unitarian Universalist. Office: Ecker Ctr for Mental Health 1845 Grandstand Pl Elgin IL 60123

BEYER, LA VONNE ANN, special education educator; b. Estherville, Iowa, Mar. 24, 1925; d. (George) Harold and Florence Catherine (Mulvey) Schafer; m. Gerald P. Beyer, June 7, 1943; children: Gregg Allan Beyer, Douglas Lee Beijer, Jodie Lu Beyer, Michael E. Beyer, Stefan A. Beyer. BA, Calif. State U., Northridge, 1959, MA, 1974; EdD, U. So. Calif., 1985. Cert. spl. edn. tchr., Calif. Tchr., regular and spl. edn. L.A. Unified Sch. Dist., 1959-88; cadre mem. Beginning Tchr. Assistance Program Calif. State U., Northridge, 1992—. Faculty U. So. Calif. reading clinic, 1974-75, Valley C.C., Burbank, 1974-75, L.A. C.C. (ESL), 1976-78. Contbr. articles to profl. jours. Literacy tutor Laubach Literacy Internat. (Van Nuys, Calif. chpt.), 1967—; mem. steering com. Roosevelt Commn., 1988. Recipient Mayor's Cert. of Appreciation, L.A., 1970, Dir. of Vols. in Agencies award, Van Nuys, 1989, Community award L.A. Times, 1990. Mem. DAR, Coun. for Exceptional Children,Laubach Literacy Internat., Pi Lambda Theta (v.p., pres. 1985-91), Phi Delta Kappa. Avocations: volunteering, gourmet cooking, travel, genealogy.

BEYER, MARTIN GOTTFRIED, geologist, consultant; b. Munich, Dec. 12, 1929; arrived in U.S., 1973; s. Walther Paul and Marianne (Fröhlich) Beyer; m. Malle Reintamm, July 3, 1955; children: Olof, Anders. Fil. lic., U. Stockholm, 1960. Chief geologist Liberian Am.-Swed. Min. Co., Nimba Mts., Liberia, 1956—62; cons. geologist Gränges AB, Stockholm, 1962—65; chief geologist Terratest AB, Bromma, Sweden, 1965—72; dep. regional dir. UNICEF, Santiago, Chile, 1972—73, sr. adv. water and sanitation N.Y.C., 1973—89; exec. sec. water conf. UN Devel. Program, N.Y.C., 1989—90; internat. cons. Worldwater Corp., Pennington, NJ, 1991—; also bd. dirs. Chmn. inter-agy. group on water UN, NY, 1987—88. Sr. ombudsman UNICEF, N.Y.C., 1987—88. Sgt. Swedish Army, 1951—52. Named Disting. visitor, Sec. Recursos Hidricos, Argentina, 1984. Fellow: Chartered Inst. Water and Environ. Mgmt. (hon.); mem.: Geologiska Föreningen. Avocations: history, painting. Home: 228 rang St-Jean-Baptiste Saint-Urbain-de-Charlevoix QC G0A 4K0 Canada Fax: 418-639-8924. E-mail: martin.beyer@sympatico.ca.

BEYER, NORMA WARREN, secondary education educator; b. Bklyn., Dec. 1, 1926; d. Norman Hayden and Catherine Mary Warren; m. Daniel Joseph Beyer, July 10, 1954; children: Catherine Norma, Daniel Joseph Jr., Peter Norman, Maureen Bernadette. BS, CUNY, Bklyn., 1949; MA in Edn., NYU, 1953. Tchr. home econs. N.Y.C. Bd. Edn., Bklyn., 1950—. Bd. dirs. Clearmeadow Civic Assn., East Meadow, 1985—; pres. St. Brigid's Rosary Soc., Westbury, N.Y., 1987-94, 99-02; vol. spl. edn. tchr. religious edn., St. Raphael's; del. U. Fedn. Tchrs., 1989-90. Recipient St. Pius award Diocese of Rockville Ctr., 1975, Leader's Gold medal Nassau County 4H, 1978, Outstanding Community Svc. award Salisbury Rep. Club, 1993, Sr. Elizabeth Ann Seton medal, 1997. Mem. NAFE, Am. Home Econs. Assn., N.Y.C. Home Econs. Assn. (historian 1978-79), Cath. Tchrs. Assn., Bklyn. Coll., NYU Alumni Assn., Salisbury Rep. Club. Republican. Roman Catholic. Avocations: quilting, clothing design and construction, gardening. Home: 251 Clearmeadow Dr East Meadow NY 11554-1211

BEYER, RICHARD J. priest, writer; b. Burlington, Iowa, Nov. 13, 1949; s. Catherine Elizabeth and Kenneth Harold Beyer. MA, St. Paul Sem., 1981. Chaplain Ctrl. Tex. Vets. Healthcare Sys., Temple, 1993. Author: (book) Medjugorje: Day by Day, 1991, Blessed Art Thou, 1996. Mem.: Nat. Assn. Vet. Affairs Chaplains. Roman Catholic. Home: 1315 Chapelwood Dr Waco TX 76712 Office: Dept Vet Affairs Hosp 1901 Veteran's Blvd Temple TX 76504 Office Fax: 254-771-4523. Personal E-mail: PadreBeyer@aol.com. Business E-Mail: Richard.Beyer@med.va.gov.

BEYER, SUZANNE, advertising agency executive; b. N.Y.C, d. Harry and Jennie Hillman; m. Isadore Beyer; children: Pamela Claire, Hillary Jay. Grad., Conservatory of Mus. Art, N.Y.C., 1947; student, Nassau C. C., N.Y.C., 1963-65. Singer, tchr. piano, N.Y.C., 1947-66; asst. to v.p. media dir. Robert E. Wilson, Advt., N.Y.C., 1967-72; media planner, media buyer frank J. Corbett div. BBDO Internat., N.Y.C., 1972-77, Lavey/Wolff/Swift divsn. BBDO Advt., N.Y.C., 1977-80; sr. media planner Lavey/Wolff/Swift (divn. BBDO Advt.), N.Y.C., 1980-83, media supr., 1983-94, Lyons, Lavey, Nichel, Swift, N.Y.C., 1995-96; pharm. advt. med. media cons., 1996—. Soprano Opera Assn., Nassau, N.Y., 1976-99; soprano United Choral Soc., Woodmere, L.I., 1970-99, soprano Armand Sodero Chorale, Baldwin, Long Is., 1980-86, soprano Rockville Ctr. Choral Soc., 1986—. Mem. Pharm. Advt. Coun., L.I. Advt. Club, Healthcare Bus. Women's Assn. Home: 66 Fonda Rd Rockville Centre NY 11570-2751

BEYER, WERNER WILLIAM, retired English educator; b. Laporte, Ind., Mar. 22, 1911; s. Franz E. W. and Martha L. Beyer; m. Ruth K. Bibos, Nov. 19, 1954; children: Tanya Elena, Mary Deirdre. AB with spl. honors, Columbia Coll., 1934; MA, Columbia U., 1936, PhD, 1945. English sr. master Englewood (N.J.) Sch. for Boys, 1936-41; instr. in English Drew U., Madison, N.J., 1943-45; asst. prof. Rutgers U., New Brunswick, N.J., 1945-48; vis. asst. prof. Columbia U., N.Y.C., 1948; prof. English Butler U., Indpls., 1948-83; vis. prof. Ind. U. Grad. Sch., Bloomington, 1964-65. Dept. head Butler U., 1965-81. Author: Keats and the Daemon King, 1947, 1969, Enchanted Forest, 1967, (short stories) Islands Beneath the Moon, 1995, The Food of Love and Other Stories, 2001; contbr. articles to profl. jours. Cutting fellow, then Lydig fellow, 1941-43, Ford fellow, 1951-52. Fellow Internat. Inst. Arts and Letters (life); MLA, Columbia U. Alumni Assn., Phi Kappa Phi. Avocations: golf, canoeing, theater, opera, travel. Home: 5388 Thicket Hill Ln Indianapolis IN 46226-1457

BEYERL, SCOTT ALAN, investment company executive; b. Ridgewood, N.J., Dec. 12, 1961; s. Stuart C. and Theresa M. Beyerl. BJ, U. Mo., 1984. Reporter/anchor/photographer WBBH-TV, Fort Myers, Fla., 1984-88; reporter/anchor WIXT-TV, Syracuse, N.Y., 1988-93; sr. writer Fidelity Investments, Boston, 1993-94, editor, 1994-95, mgr. media relations, 1995-97, dir. media relations, 1997-98, sr. dir. media relations, 1998-2001, v.p., 2001—. Mem. Syracuse Press Club (various broadcasting awards). Office: Fidelity Investments 82 Devonshire St R26D Boston MA 02109-3614 E-mail: scott.beyerl@fmr.com.

BEYERLEIN, ADOLPH LOUIS, retired chemist, educator; b. Phillipsburg, Kans., May 2, 1937; s. Fred Michael Beyerlein and Ernestine Kolb; m. Anne Mo-Yung Wong; 1 child, Irene. BS, Kans. State Coll., 1960; PhD, U. Kans., 1966. Postdoctoral fellow Rice U., Houston, 1966—67; asst. prof. Clemson U., SC, 1967—72, assoc. prof., 1972—77, prof., 1977—2001, chair chemistry dept., 1995—2001, prof. emeritus, 2001—, bldg. cons., 2002—, coord. nanotech. and health scis. rsch., 2003—. Mem. commn. grad. studies Clemson U., 1986—89, 1989—92, chmn. chemistry dept. tenure and promotion com., 1980—81, 1989—91; presentor at nat. and internat. sci. confs. Contbr. articles. Coun. Luth. Ch., Clemson, 1996—99. Fellow Postdoctoral fellow, Welch Found., 1966—67; grantee, NSF, 1977—79, Los Alamos Nat. Lab., 1979—80, 1980—81, NSF, 1981—83, IAEA, 1985—88, SC. Energy Rsch. Devel. Ctr., 1986, EPA and Electric Power Rsch. Inst., 1988—91, Electric Power Rsch. Inst., 1992—2000, NSF, 1997—2001, Greenville Hosp. Biomedical Corp., 1999—2001. Mem.: AAAS, AIChE, Am. Soc. for Heating and Refrigeration Engrs., Am. Chem. Soc. (examinations inst. com. 1992—93), Sigma Xi, Phi Kappa Phi. Office: Clemson Univ Dept Chemistry Clemson SC 29631 Office Fax: 864-656-6613. Business E-mail: albrl@clemson.edu.

BEYER-MEARS, ANNETTE, physiologist; b. Madison, Wis., May 26, 1941; d. Karl and Annette (Weiss) Beyer. BA, Vassar Coll., 1963; MS, Fairleigh Dickinson U., 1973; PhD, Coll. Medicine and Dentistry N.J., 1977. NIH fellow Cornell U. Med. Sch., 1963-65; instr. physiology Springside Sch., Phila., 1967-71; teaching asst. dept. physiology Coll. Medicine & Dentistry N.J., N.J. Med. Sch., 1974-77, NIH fellow dept. ophthalmology, 1978-80; asst. prof. dept. ophthalmology U. Medicine and Dentistry N.J., N.J. Med. Sch., Newark,

1979-85, asst. prof. dept. physiology, 1980-85, assoc. prof. dept. physiology, 1986—, assoc. prof. dept. ophthalmology, 1986—. Vis. assoc. prof. dept. ophthalmology and vision sci. U. Wis., Madison, 1995—; cons. Alcon Labs. Contbr. articles in field of diabetic lens and kidney therapy to profl. jours. Chmn. admissions No. N.J., Vassar Coll., 1974-79; mem. minister search com. St. Bartholomew Episcopal Ch., N.J., 1978, fund-raising chmn., 1978, 79; del. Episc. Diocesian Conv., 1977, 78; long range planning com. Christ Ch., Ridgewood, N.J., 1985-87, vestry, 1994-95. Recipient NIH Nat. Rsch. Svc. award, 1978-80, Found. CMDNJ Rsch. award, 1980; grantee Juvenile Diabetes Found., 1985-87, NIH, NEI grantee, 1980-95, Pfizer, Inc. grantee, 1985-89, 93—. Mem. Am. Physiol. Soc., N.Y. Acad. Scis., Soc. for Neurosci., Am. Soc. Pharmacology and Exptl. Therapeutics, Assn. for Rsch. Vision & Ophthalmology, Internat. Soc. for Eye Research, AAAS, The Royal Soc. Medicine, Internat. Diabetes Found., Am. Diabetes Assn., European Assn. Study of Diabetes, Aircraft Owners and Pilots Assn., Sigma Xi. Home: 120 Ely Pl Madison WI 53705-4015

BEYERS, WILLIAM BJORN, geography educator; b. Seattle, Mar. 24, 1940; s. William Abraham and Esther Jakobia (Svendsen) B.; m. Margaret Lyn Rice, July 28, 1968. BA, U. Wash., 1962, PhD, 1967. Asst. prof. geography U. Wash., Seattle, 1966-74, assoc. prof., 1974-82, prof., 1982—, chmn. dept. geography, 1991-95. Mem. Assn. Am. Geographers, Regional Sci. Assn., Am. Econs. Assn., Western Regional Sci. Assn. Home: 7159 Beach Dr SW Seattle WA 98136-2077 Office: U Wash Dept Geography PO Box 353550 Seattle WA 98195-3550 Fax: 206-543-3313. E-mail: beyers@u.washington.edu.

BEYERSDORF, MARGUERITE MULLOY, educator; b. Terry, Mont., Apr. 20, 1922; d. John William and Laura Agnes (Mahar) Mulloy; m. Curtis Alexander Beyersdorf, 1946; 1 child, Mary Jo Wright. Kindergarten-Primary Cert., Coll. St. Catherine, St. Paul, 1942; PhB, Marquette U., 1945; postgrad., Gonzaga U., Spokane, Wash., 1957-62, Ea. Wash. State U., 1977-79. Tchr. grade 3 Sacred Heart Sch., Oelwein, Iowa, 1942-43; tchr. grades 1 and 2 Jr. Mil. Acad., Chgo., 1943-44; tchr. history, English Fairfield (Wash.) High Sch., 1945-46; substitute tchr. Riverside High Sch., 1957; tchr. Mead (Wash.) Sch. Dist., 1958-75; owner/mgr. First Ave. Parking Lot, Spokane, Wash., 1977—. Vol. Spokane N.W. Communities Found., 1982—; active United Way Spokane, 1950—95, ARC, Am. Cancer Soc., Multiple Sclerosis Soc., others; vol. coord. Dominican Outreach Found. to Domicile Single Parent Families; canteen vol. Spokane Blood Bank, 1981—; vol. Miryam's House of Transition, 1989—. Recipient Vol. of Yr. Golden Rule award J.C. Penney Co., 1993; grantee NSF, Whitworth Coll., 1967. Mem. NEA, APGA, AAUW (bd. dirs. Spokane br., chmn. scholarship com.), Wash. Edn. Assn.-Retired (del. rep. assembly, mem. comm. com 1993—, chmn. comm. commn. 1993—), Mead Edn. Assn. (sec., exec. bd., former bldg. rep., mem. curriculum com.). Avocations: golf, travel, reading, needlepoint, walking, bridge, crossword puzzles.

BEYLE, THAD LEWIS, political science educator, consultant; b. Syracuse, N.Y., May 11, 1934; s. Herman Carey and Madelon (McCulloch) B.; m. Patricia Fae Cain, Nov. 14, 1934; children: Carey, Jeffrey Lewis, Jonathan West, Aimee Maurine. AB, Syracuse U., 1956, AM, 1960; PhD, U. Ill., 1963. Asst. prof. polit. sci. Denison U., Granville, Ohio, 1963-64; faculty fellow Office of the Gov. of N.C., Raleigh, 1964-65; rsch. assoc. Study of Am. States, Duke U., Durham, N.C., 1965-67; asst. prof. polit. sci. U. N.C., Chapel Hill, 1967-69, assoc. prof., 1969-76, prof., 1976—; dir. Ctr. for Policy Rsch. Nat. Gov.'s Assn., 1974-76, sr. rsch. fellow, 1978-84; chmn. bd. dirs. N.C. Ctr. for Publ Policy Rsch., 1980-89; chmn. bd. dirs. N.C. Inst. Polit. Leadership, 1995-97. Editor: Governors and Hard Times, 1992; co-editor: Planning and Politics, 1969, The American Governor in Behavioral Perspective, 1972, Politics and Policy in North Carolina, 1975, Being Governor, 1983; editor State Government, annually 1985—, Gubernatorial Transitions, 1985, 89, Gubernatorial Re-elections, 1985-86, Governors and Hard Times, 1992. Mem. Am. Polit. Sci. Assn., Midwest Polit. Sci. Assn., So. Polit. Sci. Assn., Am. Soc. for Pub. Adminstrn. Democrat.

BEYLKIN, GREGORY, mathematician; b. St. Petersburg, USSR, Mar. 16, 1953; came to U.S., 1980; naturalized citizen, 1985; s. Jacob and Raya (Pripshtein) B.; m. Helen Simontov, 1974; children: Michael, Daniel. Diploma in Math., U. St. Petersburg, Leningrad, 1975; PhD in Math., NYU, 1982. Assoc. rsch. sci. NYU, 1982-83; mem. profl. staff Schlumberger-Doll Research, Ridgefield, Conn., 1983-91; prof. dept. applied math. U. Colo., Boulder, 1991—. Contbr. articles to profl. jours. Mem. Am. Math. Soc., Soc. for Indsl. and Applied Math., Soc. Exptl. Geophysicists. Home: 3897 Promontory Ct Boulder CO 80304-1053 Office: U Colo Dept Applied Math 526 UCB Boulder CO 80309-0526 E-mail: beylkin@boulder.colorado.edu.

BEYMAN, JONATHAN ERIC, information officer; b. Newark, Dec. 31, 1955; s. Bernard B. and Miriam (Simon) B.; m. Susan Elizabeth Bleckman, Aug. 23, 1981; children: Michael, Daniel, Max. BS, U. Ct., 1976; MBA, Cornell U., 1981. CPA, Conn. Sr. acct. Arthur Young and Co., N.Y.C., 1976-79; asst. v.p. Chem. Bank, N.Y.C., 1981-84; sr. cons. Am. Mgmt. Systems, N.Y.C., 1985; v.p. Citibank North Am. Investment Bank, N.Y.C., 1985-86, Lehman Bros., N.Y.C., 1986-88, sr. v.p., 1988-91, mng. dir., 1991-94, 99-00, mng. dir., chief info. officer, 2000—02, global head ops./tech. divsn., 2002—; chief info. officer and sr. v.p. CUC Internat., Stamford, Conn., 1994-97; co-chief info. officer, exec. v.p. Cendant Corp., Stamford, 1997-98; pres. Cendant Interactive, 1998-99; dir. Depository Trust Clearing Corp., 2002. Mem. AICPA. Democrat. Jewish. Avocations: bicycling, reading, running, carpentry. E-mail: jbeyman@lehman.com.

BEYSTER, JOHN ROBERT, engineering company executive; b. Detroit, July 26, 1924; m. Betty Beyster; 3 children. BS in Engring., U. Mich., 1945, MS, 1948, PhD, 1950. Registered profl. engr., Calif. Mem. staff Los Alamos Sci. Lab., 1951—56; chmn. dept. accel. physics Gulf Gen. Atomic Co., San Diego, 1957—69; founder, pres., chmn. bd. Sci. Applications, Inc., La Jolla, Calif., 1969—, now chmn. bd., CEO, pres.; mem. Joint Strategic Target Planning Staff, Sci. Adv. Group, Omaha, 1978—; panel mem. Nat. Measurement Lab. Evaluation panel for Radiation Research, Washington, 1983—; dir. Scripps Bancorp, La Jolla, 1983. Founder Found. for Enterprise Devel., La Jolla, Calif., 1986. Co-author: Slow Neutron Scattering and Thermalization, 1970. With USN, 1943—46. Named to, Nat. Acad. Engring., 1989. Fellow: Am. Phys. Soc., Am. Nuclear Soc.; mem.: NAE. Republican. Roman Catholic. Office: Science Applications Inter Corp 10260 Campus Point Dr San Diego CA 92121*

BEYTAGH, FRANCIS XAVIER, JR., law educator; b. Savannah, Georgia, July 11, 1935; BA magna cum laude(hon.), U. Notre Dame, 1956; JD, U. Mich., 1963. Bar: Ohio, 1964, U.S. Supreme Ct., 1967, Ind., 1972. Clk. Fuller, Seney, Henry, and Hodge, Toledo, 1961; sr. law clk. to Chief Justice Earl Warren U.S. Supreme Ct., Washington, 1963-64; assoc. Jones, Day, Cockley, and Reavis, Cleve., 1964-66; asst. to solicitor gen. U.S. Dept. Justice, Washington, 1966-70; prof. law U. Notre Dame, 1970-74, 75-76; prof., dean U. Toledo, 1976-83; Cullen prof. law U. Houston, 1984-85; prof., dean Ohio State U. Coll. Law, 1985-93, prof., 1993-97; spl. counsel Jones, Day, Reavis, and Pogue, Columbus, Ohio, 1993-96; pres., prof. Fla. Coastal Sch. Law, Jacksonville, 1997-98, prof., 1998—, founders' chair, 2000—. Vis. prof. law, U. Va., Charlottesville, 1974-75; U. Mich., 1983-84; So. Meth. U., Dallas, 1997. Editor in chief Mich. Law Rev., 1962-63; author: Supplement to Kauper's Constitutional Law: Cases and Materials, 1977; Constitutional Law: Cases and Materials, 5th edit., 1980,; supplements, 1981, 82, 84; Constitutionalism in Contemporary Ireland, 1997; contbg. articles to profl. jour. Capt. USNR; ret. Fulbright Fellow, 1994. Fellow Am. Bar Found.; mem. ABA; Fla. Bar, Jacksonville Bar Assn., Order of Coif. Home: 49 Marsh Creek Rd Amelia Island FL 32034-6414 Office: Fla Coastal Sch Law 7555 Beach Blvd Jacksonville FL 32216-3000

BEZANSON, RANDALL PETER, law educator; b. Cedar Rapids, Iowa, Nov. 17, 1946; s. Peter Floyd and Larrayne (Bing) B.; m. Elaine Ruth Croyle, June 22, 1968; children: Peter, Melissa. BA, Northwestern U., 1968; JD summa cum laude, U. Iowa, 1971. Bar: Iowa 1971, Va. 1988. Law clk., presiding justice U.S. Ct. Appeals (D.C. cir.), 1971-72; law clk., Justice Harry Blackmun U.S. Supreme Ct., Washington, 1972-73; prof. law U. Iowa, Iowa City, 1973-88, 96-98, asst. to pres., 1976-77, v.p., 1979-84; dean of law Washington and Lee U., Lexington, Va., 1988-94, prof. law, 1994-96; Charles E. Floete Distinguished Prof. U. Iowa Coll. Law, Iowa City, 1998—. Commr. Nat. Conf. of Commrs. on Uniform State Laws, 1983-88; reporter Uniform Defamation Act, NCCUSL, 1988—; dir. City Nat. Bank, Cedar Rapids, 1977-88, 1st Nat. Bank, Iowa City, 1984-88. Author (with Cranberg and Soloski): Libel Law and the Press: Myth and Reality, 1987; author: (with Soliski) Reforming Libel Law, 1992; author: Taxes on Knowledge in America, 1994, Speech Stores: How Free Can Speech Be?, 1998; author: (with Cranberg and Soloski) Taking Stock: Journalism and the Publicly Traded Newspaper Company, 2001; contbr. articles to legal jours. Bd. dirs. Hawkeye Area Coun., Boy Scouts Am., Cedar Rapids, 1979-88; pres. Iowa City Pub. Libr. Bd. Trustees, 1978-80; mem. Iowa City Pub. Libr. Found. Bd. 1980. Murray scholar, U. Iowa, 1971. Mem. ABA, Iowa Bar Assn., Order of Coif, Beta Alpha Psi. Republican. Presbyterian. Avocations: nature, golf. Home: 12 Woodland Hts NE Iowa City IA 52240-9136 E-mail: Randy-Bezanson@uiowa.edu.

BEZANSON, THOMAS EDWARD, lawyer; b. Hartford, Conn., Aug. 1, 1945; s. Philip Thomas and Lillian (Carlson) Bezanson; m. Janie H. Bezanson, Aug. 10, 1969; children: Philip, Jeffrey. BA, Grinnell, 1967; MA, Rutgers U., 1971, JD, 1974. Bar: NY 1975, U.S. Dist. Ct. (ea. and so. dists.) 1975, U.S. Ct. Appeals (2d cir.) 1975, U.S. Ct. Appeals (6th cir.) 1980, U.S. Supreme Ct. 1991. Assoc. Chadbourne & Parke, N.Y.C., 1974—81, ptnr., 1981—. Author: 42 poems, 1993. Bd. dirs. Westchester Philharm., 1992—98, NY Lawyers Pub. Interest Inc., 1997—, Legal Aid Soc., 1999—2002. With U.S. Army, 1967—69. Mem.: ABA, Asn Bar City New York, NY State Bar Asn. Office: Chadbourne & Parke 30 Rockefeller Plz Fl 31 New York NY 10112-0129 Business E-Mail: tbezanson@chadbourne.com.

BEZAR, GILBERT EDWARD, retired aerospace company executive, volunteer; b. Phila., May 24, 1930; s. Abraham Bernard and Leah (Hymowitz) B.; m. Norma Jean Davis, Sept. 4, 1964 (dec. 1968); children: Eric David, Robyn Lisa; m. Elaine R. Spitzer, Jan. 6, 1989. BS in Acctg., Temple U., 1951; MBA in Fin. and Mgmt., UCLA, 1957. V.p. Armco-Hitco, Irvine, Calif., 1972-77; v.p. fin. Armco-Nat. Supply Co., Houston, 1977-81; v.p. fin. affairs, treas. Armco, Inc., Middletown, Ohio, 1983-84; v.p. adminstrn. ARMCO Aerospace and Strategic Materials Group, Irvine, 1981-83; v.p. fin. and adminstrn. OCF Aerospace and Strategic Materials Group, Newport Beach, Calif., 1984-88; cons. Exec. Svc. Corps., 1990—. Cons. AARP Work Force, 1993—; bd. dirs. Oreg. Metall. Corp., Albany, 1983-97; instr. extension program UCLA, 1957-62, U. Calif. - Irvine, 1963-72. Served to lt. USNR, 1952-55 UCLA teaching fellow, 1955-57 Mem. Fin. Execs. Inst. (v.p. 1982-83), World Affairs Coun., Beta Gamma Sigma. Jewish. Home: 4 Sagitta Way Coto De Caza CA 92679-5102 Personal E-mail: gebezar@aol.com.

BEZERRA, MARCIO, musician, educator; b. Recife, Pernambuco, Brazil, Sept. 22, 1968; s. Virgilio Augusto Bezerra and Gisela Salvador Bezerra; m. Estibaliz Gastesi, June 17, 1994; 1 child, Ainhoa Bezerra-Gastesi;1 child, Naiara Bezerra-Gastesi. D of Musical Arts, U. Ariz., 1998; B of Music, Faculdade de Musica, Carlos Gounes, Sao Paulo, Brazil, 1991; M of Music, Az. State U., 1995. Music specialist Sch. Dist. of Palm Beach County, West Palm Beach, Fla., 2000—01; adj. prof. piano Palm Beach Atlantic U., West Palm Beach, 2000—. Music critic Palm Beach Daily News, 2002—. Contbr. articles to profl. jours. Named Best performer of contemporary North Am. Music, Joseph Klatzkin Meml., 1995; recipient Bridging the World award, KLM, 1995; grantee, Grad. Coll., U. Ariz., 1997; scholar, Fulbright Commn., 1991. Mem.: Coll. Music Soc., Am. Musicol. Soc. Achievements include World premieres of works by prominent contemporary composers of Europe, Brazil, and the U.S. Active in piano duo with Estibaliz Gastesi for over a decade. Home: 1738 Pierside Circle Wellington FL 33414 Office: Palm Beach Atlantic Univ POBox 24708 901 South Flagler Dr West Palm Beach FL 33416 Home Fax: 561-803-2424; Office Fax: 561-803-2424. Personal E-mail: marciobezerra@netscape.net. E-mail: marciobezerra@netscape.net.

BEZKOROVAINY, ANATOLY, medical educator, biochemist; b. Riga, Latvia, Feb. 11, 1935; s. Ignatius and Olga (Solovey) Bezkorovainy; m. Marilyn Grib, June 14, 1964; children: Gregory, Alexander. BS, U. Chgo., 1956; PhD, U. Ill., 1960; JD, Ill. Inst. Tech., 1977. Bar: Ill. 1977. Rsch. assoc. Oak Ridge Nat. Lab., Tenn., 1960—61; chemist USDA, Ames, Iowa, 1961—62; mem. faculty Rush-Presbyn. St. Luke's Med. Ctr., Chgo., 1962—, asst. prof., 1962—67, assoc. prof., 1967—73, prof. biochemistry, 1973—, assoc. chmn., dir. ednl. programs biochemistry dept., 1980—2000. Author: Basic Protein Chemistry, 1970, Biochemistry of Nonheme Iron, 1980; co-author (with Rafelson and Hayashi): Basic Biochemistry, 1980; co-author: (with Miller-Catchpole) Biochemistry and Physiology of BifidoBacteria, 1989; co-author: (with Rafelson) Concise Biochemistry, 1995; contbr. Numerous grants, NSF, NIH, Am. Heart Assn., indsl. instns., 1962—90. Mem.: Inst. Food Technologists, Am. Chem. Soc., Am. Soc. Biol. Chemists, Am. Dairy Sci. Assn. Eastern Orthodox. Home: 4242 W Touhy Ave Lincolnwood IL 60712-1932 Office: Rush Presbyn St Luke's Med Ctr Dept Biochemistry 1653 W Congress Pkwy Chicago IL 60612-3833 Business E-Mail: shirley-moore@rush.edu.

BEZOLD, CLEMENT, think tank executive; b. Coral Gables, Fla., 1948; BS, Georgetown U., 1970; PhD, U. Fla., 1976. Asst. dir. Ctr. Govtl. Responsibility, Fla.; vis. scholar The Brookings Inst., 1974-77; pres. Inst. for Alternative Futures, Alexandria, Va., 1977—. Pres. Alternative Futures Assocs., 1982—; cons. to local, state, fed. govts. in U.S. and internat., WHO, major corps. including Disney, AT&T, pharm. and health care cos.; tchr. Am. U., U. Fla., Antioch U.; spkr. in field. Editor: Anticipatory Democracy (introduction by Alvin Toffler), 1978, others; co-author: (with R. Carlson and J. Peck) The Future of Work and Health, 1985 (Am. Health Mag. book award); co-editor: (with Erica Mayer) Future Care: Responding to the Demand for Change, 1996, The Future of Complementary and Alternative Approaches (CAAs) in US Healthcare, 1998, (with J. Frenk & S. McCarthy) 21st Century Health Care in Latin American and the Caribbean, 1998, Genomics and Society Project for UK-ESIC, 2002. Bd. dirs. World Future Soc., U.S. Pharmacopeia. Office: Inst Alternative Futures 100 N Pitt St Ste 235 Alexandria VA 22314-3134 E-mail: cbezold@altfutures.com.

BEZOLD, LOUIS IRVING, III, pediatrician, cardiologist; s. Louis Irving Bezold, Jr and Dorothy Ann Bezold; m. Marsha Louise Kyle, Jan. 14, 1984; children: Lauren, Alaina, Kyle. BS, Loyola Coll., Balt., 1984; MD, U. Md., Balt., 1989. Diplomate Nat. Bd. Med. Examiners, 1992, Am. Bd. Pediat., 1993, Cardiology Sub-bd. Am. Bd. Pediat., 1998. Intern in pediats. Baylor Coll. Medicine, Houston, 1989—90, resident in pediats., 1990—92, fellow in pediat. cardiology, 1992—95, advanced pediat. cardiac imaging fellow, 1995, asst. prof. pediat., 1996—; med. dir. echocardiography lab. Tex. Children's Hosp., Houston, 2001—; co-med. dir. diagnostic cardiovasc. sonography program Alvin (Tex.) C.C., Alvin, 2002—. Vol. Am. Heart Assn., Houston Divsn., 1997—2001. Fellow: Am. Coll. Cardiology (congenital heart disease and pediatric cardiology Com. 2002—), Am. Acad. Pediat.; mem.: Am. Heart Assn. Coun. Cardiovasc. Disease in the Young, Soc. Pediat. Echocardiography, Am. Soc. Echocardiography, Alpha Omega Alpha (v.p. 1988). Office: Texas Childrens Hosp 6621 Fannin St Houston TX 77030 E-mail: lbezold@bcm.tmc.edu.

BEZOS, JEFFREY P. multimedia executive; Degree in elec. engring. and computer sci. summa cum laude, Princeton U., 1986. With Bankers Trust Co., N.Y., 1988-90, v.p., 1990; with D.E. Shaw & Co., N.Y., 1990-94, sr. v.p., 1992-94; founder, CEO Amazon.com Inc., Seattle, 1995—. Mem. staff FITEL, N.Y., 1986-88. Mem. Phi Beta Kappa. Office: Amazon com Inc 1200 12th Ave S Seattle WA 98144*

BEZROD, NORMA R. artist; b. Phila., May 17, 1938; d. Samuel Bezrod and Bessie Roffman; m. Arthur J. Cooperman, Aug. 22, 1959 (div. Apr. 1977); 1 child, Seth Alan Cooperman; m. William D. P. Riley, July 1, 1983 (dec. Oct. 1998). BA, Queens Coll., 1960, MS, 1974; EdD, Columbia U., 1986. Lic. fine arts tchr., N.Y. Art tchr. N.Y.C. Pub. Schs., 1960-77; exec. dir. art Sr. Ctr., Human Resources Adminstrn., N.Y.C., 1977-78; instr. art edn. Queens (N.Y.) Coll., 1978-79; edn. evaluator, case mgr. N.Y.C. Bd. Edn., 1980-88. Cons. N.Y. State Coun. on the Arts, 1977-79. Author: Don't Be Afraid of the Dark, 1977, (series) Lion and Pretty Bird, 1983-85; art critic Good Times, L.I., N.Y., 1971-75; paintings in collections of St. John's Univ. Libr., Queen's Coll. Mus. Teaching fellow Queens Coll., 1978-79. Home: PO Box 660125 Flushing NY 11366-0125

BEZUCHA, ROBERT JOSEPH, history educator; b. Racine, Wis., June 6, 1940; s. Robert Donald and Helen Anne (Wacek) B.; m. Jenny L. Kallick, Dec. 14, 1985; children from previous marriage: Thomas Gordon, Margaret Jeanne. BA, Lawrence U., 1962; MA, U. Mich., 1963, PhD, 1968; MA (hon.), Amherst Coll., 1981. Instr. U. Mich., Ann Arbor, 1967-68; asst. prof. Northwestern U., Evanston, Ill., 1968-75; assoc. prof. Syracuse (N.Y.) U., 1975-77; assoc. prof. history Amherst (Mass.) Coll., 1977-81, prof., 1981—, Andrew W. Mellon prof. humanities, 1989-92, George Daniel Olds prof. econs. and social instns., 1996—. Cons. Social Sci. Rsch. Coun., N.Y.C., 1978-80, New Eng. Bd. Higher Edn., Boston, 1990—, Nat. Coun., Glimmerglass Opera, 1994—. Author: The Lyon Uprising of 1834, 1974; editor: Modern European Social History, 1972; contbr. articles, essays, revs. to profl. jours. Vice chmn. bd. trustees Westfield (Mass.) State Coll., 1987-92. NEH rsch. grantee, 1973-74; Guggenheim Found. fellow, 1987. Mem. Am. Hist. Assn., Phi Kappa Phi. Home: 147 Shutesbury Rd Amherst MA 01002-1264 Office: Amherst Coll AC 2225 Amherst MA 01002-5000

BHADURI, RANJAN, investment management executive; b. Hamilton, Ont., Can., July 26, 1969; s. Rajat Kumar and Manjushree Bhaduri. BSc(hon.), McMaster U., Hamilton, 1991; M in Math, U. of Waterloo, Ont., 1992; PhD, U. of Hawaii at Manoa, Honolulu, 1999; MBA (co-op), McMaster U. (Exch. Program at Norwegian Sch. of Mgmt.), Hamilton and Oslo, 2001. Math. instr., prof. U. of Hawaii, Honolulu, 1992—99; affiliate East-West Ctr., Honolulu, 1997—99; fin. analyst Bank of Montreal, Toronto, 2000—00; risk analyst Scotia Markets, Toronto, 2001—02; assoc. Northwater Capital Mgmt., Toronto, 2002—. Math. cons., 1991—2001. Recipient McMaster U. Travel scholarship, 2001, grad. scholarship, U. of Waterloo, 1992, Undergrad. award, Nat. Sci. and Engring. Rsch. Coun., 1988—90; scholar, U. of Hawaii at Manoa, 1992—99. Mem.: Math. Assn. of Am., Am. Math. Soc., Am. Contract Bridge League. Achievements include research in created Chelios Rings and a new spectrum from arbitrary rings; combinatorial number theory and in the financial sector (applied mathematical finance). Home: 88 Golfview Crescent Dundas ON Canada L9H 6T6 Office: Northwater Capital Mgmt Inc Ste 4700 BCD Pl 181 Bay St Toronto ON Canada M5J2T3 Office Fax: 416-360-0671. E-mail: rbhaduri@northwatercapital.com.

BHAGAT, PHIROZ MANECK, mechanical engineer; b. Oct. 28, 1948; came to U.S., 1970; s. Maneck Phirozshaw and Khorshed Eduljee (Batliwala) B.; m. Patricia Jane Steckler, Oct. 13, 1979; children: Kay, Sarah. BTech, Indian Inst. Tech.-Bombay, 1970; MS in Engring., U. Mich., 1971, PhD, 1975. Rsch. fellow in applied mechanics Harvard U., Cambridge, Mass., 1975-77; asst. prof. engring. Columbia U., N.Y.C., 1977-81; staff engr. Exxon Mobil Rsch. & Engring. Co., Florham Park, N.J., 1981-83, sr. staff engr., 1983-2001; sr. engring. assoc. Exxon Mobil Rsch. and Engring. Co., Annandale, NJ, 2001—. Adj. asst. prof. Columbia U., N.Y.C., 1981-84; head sci. computing group Exxon/Mobil Rsch. & Engring. Co., Florham Park, 1988-90; mng. dir. Janus Enterprise Internat., 1992-94. Contbr. articles to profl. jours. K.C., Mahindra scholar, 1970, J.N. Tata scholar, 1970; Horace Rackham predoctoral fellow, 1973-74, 74-75. Mem. AIChE, ASME, N.Y. Acad. Scis., Tau Beta Pi, Sigma Xi. Achievements include rsch. devel. of Neural Nets in tech. and bus. applications, pattern recognition and forecasting for business strategies; rsch. on application of thermal sciences to model for technical and business strategies, petrochemical processes, science computing, heat transfer, fluid mechanics, thermodynamics, computer modeling, business global computer simulation. Home: 519 Alden St Westfield NJ 07090-3040 Office: ExxonMobil Rsch & Engring Co 1545 Rte 22E Annandale NJ 08801

BHAGWAN, SUDHIR, computer industry and research executive, consultant; b. Lahore, West Pakistan, Aug. 9, 1942; came to U.S., 1963; s. Vishan and Lakshmi Devi (Arora) B.; m. Sarita Bahl, Oct. 25, 1969; children: Sonia, Sunil. BSEE, Punjab Engring. Coll., Chandigarh, India, 1963; MSEE, Stanford U., 1964; MBA with honors, Golden Gate U., 1977. Engr. Gaylor Products, North Hollywood, Calif., 1964-68, Burroughs Corp., Pasadena, Calif., 1968-70, engring. mgr. Santa Barbara, Calif., 1970-78, Intel Corp., Hillsboro, Oreg., 1978-81, chmn. strategic planning, 1981-82, gen. mgr., 1983-88; pres., exec. dir., bd. dirs. Oreg. Advanced Computing Inst., Beaverton, 1988-90; strategic bus. mgr. INTEL Corp., Hillsboro, Oreg., 1990-92, gen. mgr. bus. multimedia products, 1992-93, bus. area mgr., 1993-94, dir. internat. mktg., 1995-99; pres. Bhagwan Enterprises LLC, 2000—. Spkr. to high tech. industry, Oreg., 1988—; mem. organizing com. Distributed Memory Computing Conf., 1989—90, gen. chmn., 1990—91; bd. advisors NSF (SBIR); chmn. computer tech. adv. bd. Oreg. Mus. Sci. and Industry, 1991—93; bd. advisors NSF, Ironspire, Inc., CB Capital IV LLC, Preusch Capital; bd. dirs. SnapNames, Passport Online; mem. Portland Venture Group; mem. selection com. Portland Angel Network, 2002—. Cons. Oreg. Econ. Devel. Dept., 1988-91; bd. dirs. St. Mary's Acad., Portland, 1989-92. Mem. Am. Electronics Assn. (higher edn. com. Oreg. chpt. 1989-90, exec. com. 1990). Avocations: electronics, photography, tennis, art. Home: 13940 NW Harvest Ln Portland OR 97229-3653 E-mail: sbhagwan@att.net.

BHALLA, DEEPAK KUMAR, cell biologist, toxicologist, educator; b. Kasauli, India, Aug. 31, 1946; s. Khazan Chand and Shyama Bhalla; 1 child, Neel. BS, Punjab U., India, 1968, MS, 1969; PhD, Howard U., Washington, 1976. Postdoctoral fellow Harvard U., Boston, 1976-79; asst. rsch. cell biologist U. Calif., San Francisco, 1979-82, asst. prof. Irvine, 1982-86, assoc. prof., 1986-95, Wayne State U., Detroit, 1995-98, prof., 1998—. Cons. USEPA, NIH; spkr. in field. Guest editor, mem. editl. bds. profl. jours.; contbr. articles and revs. to profl. jours. NIH grantee, 1985-99, Calif. Air Resources Bd. grantee, 1990-95. Mem. AAAS, Am. Thoracic Soc., Am. Soc. Cell Biology, Soc. Toxicology. Office: OEHS 5134 Eugene Applebaum Coll Pharmacy & Health Sci Wayne State U Detroit MI 48202

BHALODKAR, NARENDRA CHANDRAKANT, cardiologist; MB, BS, Baroda Med. Coll., India, 1971. Diplomate Am. Bd. Internal Medicine, Am. Bd. Cardiovasc. Diseases. Rotating intern Luth. Med. Ctr., Cleve., 1973-74; resident in internal medicine Bronx Lebanon Hosp., 1974-76, cardiology fellow, 1976-78, asst. adj. dept. medicine, assoc. cardiologist, 1978-80, assoc. dept. medicine, 1980—; asst. prof. medicine Albert Einstein Coll. Medicine, Yeshiva U. Adj. asst. prof. dept. medicine Baylor Coll. of Medicine, Houston, 1992; acting dir. CCU Bronx Lebanon Hosp., 1992, assoc. dir. cardiac cath lab., 1992, dir. preventative cardiology, 1993, dir. CCU, 1993, dir. clin. study unit, 1994. Fellow ACP, ACCP, Am. Coll. Cardiology, N.Y. Cardiology Soc., Am. Heart Assn., Coun. Geriat. Cardiology; mem. N.Y. State Soc. Internal Medicine, Am. Soc. Nuclear Medicine, Am. Assn. Physicians from India, Am. Assn. Cardiologists of Indian Origin, L.I. Heart Coun., Assn. Profl. Businessmen of the Bronx, Bronx County Med. Soc. Hindu. Office: 1650 Grand Concourse Bronx NY 10457-7717

BHANOT, KARAN, education educator; s. Kanwal and Pratima Bhanot; m. Neeta Bhanot, Oct. 14, 1968. MBA, Indian Inst. of Mgmt., Ahmedabad, 1990; PhD, U. of Iowa, 1992—97. Mba Indian Inst. of Mgmt. at Ahmedabad, 1990. Asst. prof. of fin. U. of Tex., San Antonio, 1998—.

BHARADWAJ, PREM DATTA, physics educator; b. Gorakhpur, India, May 20, 1931; arrived in U.S., 1960; s. Ganga Dhar and Bhagwati Devi (Sharma) B.; m. Vidya Wati Sharma, Feb. 14, 1949; children: Rakesh Kumar, Rajnesh Kumar, Vidhu Rani Eranki, Sudha Kar. BS 1st class with merit, NREC Coll. Khurja, India, 1950; MS 1st class 1st, Agra (India) Univ., 1952; PhD, SUNY, Buffalo, 1964. Asst. prof. physics B.R. Coll. Agra, 1952-54; lectr. physics GPIC Tehri, Tehri Garhwal, India, 1954-56, Govt. Coll. Meerut, India, 1956-59; asst. prof. physics B.R. Coll. Agra, 1959-60; grad. asst. physics SUNY, Buffalo, 1960-62; from asst. prof. physics to assoc. prof. physics Niagara U., Niagara Falls, N.Y., 1962-66, prof. physics, 1966—, chmn. dept. physics, 1976-86. Cons. NSF, 1966-71; reviewer N.Y. State Regents Exams. in Medicine and Dentistry, 1976; co-founder India Assn. Buffalo, 1961, Hindi Samaj Greater Buffalo, 1986; summer rsch. participant NSF, La. State U., Baton Rouge, 1965; vis. prof. dept. crystallography Rosewell Park Cancer Inst., Buffalo, N.Y., 1970-71. Co-author: Intermediate Agriculture Physics and Climatology, 1954; contbr. articles to profl. jours. Pres. Sathya Sai Ctr. Buffalo, Amherst, N.Y., 1990-93, Hindi Samaj of Greater Buffalo, Amherst, 1996-97; mem. trust com. Hindu Cultural Soc. Western N.Y., 1999-2001. Recipient Rajiv Gandhi Nat. Unity award for excellence Govt. India, 1995, Hind Rattan (Jewel of India) award Govt. of India, 1995; named Internat. Man of Yr. Internat. Biog. Ctr., Cambridge, Eng., 1999. Mem. India Assn. of Buffalo (award for outstanding

work in edn. and cmty. 1997), Hindi Samaj of Greater Buffalo, Am. Phys. Soc. Democrat. Hindu. Home: 100 N Parrish Dr Amherst NY 14228-1477 Office: Niagara U Physics Dept Lewiston Rd Niagara Falls NY 14109 E-mail: pdb@niagara.edu.

BHARDWAJ, ANISH, neuroscientist, medical educator; b. June 3, 1960; Diplomate Am. Bd. Neurology and Psychiatry. Intern Univ. Coll. Hosp., Ibadan, Nigeria, 1984—85; med. officer Sokoto Clinic, Nigeria, 1985—86; rsch. fellow dept. neurology Mt. Sinai Sch. Medicine, N.Y.C., 1987—89, resident in neurology, 1990—92, chief resident in neurology, 1992—93; resident in internal medicine Elmhurst Hosp., Mt. Sinai Sch. Medicine, N.Y.C., 1989—90; neurosci. crit. care fellow Johns Hopkins U. Sch. Medicine, Balt., 1993—95, nat. stroke assn. fellow, 1994—96, instr. depts. neurology, neurol. surgery, anesthesiology and crit. care medicine, 1995—96, dir. neurosci. crit. care fellowship tng. program, asst. prof. depts. neurology, neurol. surgery, anesthesiology and crit. care medicine, 1996—; staff attending neurosci. crit. care unit Johns Hopkins Hosp., Balt., 1995—99, asst. prof. neurology, 1998—, co-dir. neuro-critical care, 2000—. Spkr. in field. Contbr. articles to profl. jours.; ad hoc reviewer: Jour. Cerebral Blood Flow and Metabolism, Crit. Care Medicine. Fellow: Am. Heart Assn. (stroke coun., hon. mention Robert G. Siekert Young Investigator award in stroke 1995, Clinician-Scientist award 1996); mem.: AMA, Nigeria Med. Coun., Soc. for Neurosci., Nat. Stroke Assn. (Fellowship Career Devel. award 1994), Am. Acad. Neurology. Office: Johns Hopkins U Sch Medicine Meyer Bldg 8-140 600 N Wolfe St Baltimore MD 21287-0005

BHARDWAJ, SUSHIL, medical educator; b. New Delhi, Dec. 2, 1950; came to U.S., 1974; s. Chaman Lall and Shanti (Rampal) B.; m. Rita Singh, Dec. 18, 1978; children: Anuj, Aarti Sonia, Meera Priya. Pre-med. cert., U. Delhi, India, 1968; MBBS, All India Inst. Medical Scis., New Delhi, 1973. Diplomate Am. Bd. Internal Medicine, Am. Bd. Med. Oncology. Intern All India Inst. Medical Scis., New Delhi, 1973, jr. resident in medicine, 1974; resident in medicine Jewish Hosp. and Medical Ctr. Bklyn., N.Y., 1974-77, chief resident in medicine, 1976-77; clinical fellow dept. neoplastic Mt. Sinai Hosp., N.Y.C., 1977-79, clinical asst., 1979-87; staff physician medical svcs. FDR VA Hosp., Montrose, N.Y., 1982-83; asst. attending physician Mt. Sinai Hosp., 1988-89, assoc. attending physician, 1989—; asst. attending physician Nyack (N.Y.) Hosp., 1992-98, assoc. attending physician, 1999—2003, attending physician, 2003—; asst. attending physician Good Samaritan Hosp., Suffern, N.Y., 1992-97; assoc. clin. prof. divsn. neoplastic diseases dept. medicine Mt. Sinai Sch. Medicine, N.Y.C., 1993—; assoc. attending physician Good Samaritan Hosp., Suffern, N.Y., 1997-98, attending physician, 1998—. Dir. Bobbi Lewis Cancer program Good Samaritan Hosp., Suffern, 1993—, chief subsect. hematology/oncology, 1995; staff physician med. svcs. FDR VA Hosp., Montrose, N.Y., 1982-83; instr. dept. neoplastic disease Mt. Sinai Sch. Medicine, 1979-82; clin. instr., 1982; asst. prof. clin. neoplastic disease, 1983-87, head clin. rsch. stds. sect., 1984-89, assoc. prof., 1987-92; dir. clin. shared resources, 1989, assoc. chmn., 1990-92, assoc. clin. prof., 1992— asst. clin. prof. 1983, asst. dir. quality assurance and date mgmt.,1987-88; mem. vis. faculty program on oncology Albert Einstein Coll. and Montefiore Med. Ctr., Bronx, 1992—. Author chpts. in textbooks; contbr. articles to profl. jours. Vol. speaker at ednl. confs. Am. Cancer Soc., 1991—; spl. asst. to chmn. Cancer and Leukemia, Scarsdale, N.Y., 1981-82. Merit scholar All India Inst. Medical Scis., 1970-72, Merit prize in Anatomy, 1970, Merit prize in Physiology, 1970, Merit prize in Biochemistry, 1970, Sardari Lal Kalra Gold medal in Microbiology, 1971, Merit prize in medicine, 1973, Vijay Rattna award Internat. Friendship Soc. India, 1991. Fellow ACP. Avocations: reading, music, travel. Office: Good Samaritan Hosp Med Ctr 255 Lafayette Ave Suffern NY 10901-4817 E-mail: sushbhard@aol.com.

BHARITKAR, SUNIL GANPAT, research scientist, technology specialist; b. Pune, India, Apr. 20, 1969; came to U.S., 1991; s. Ganpat Raoji and Saraswati Ganpat B. BE, U. Pune, India, 1990; MS, Case Western Res. U., 1995; PhD, U. So. Calif., 2001. Vis. rschr. Hitachi, Japan, 1994; mem. tech. staff Ford Motor Co., 1998-99; tech. specialist Oppenheimer, Wolff & Donnelly LLP, 2000—02, Greenberg Traurig LLP, 2002—. Pres., co-founder Audyssey Labs., Inc., 2002—. Contbr. articles to profl. jours.; patentee in field. Home: 2461 Coolidge Ave #1 Los Angeles CA 90064 Office: U So Calif Signal/Image Processing Ins 3740 McClintock Ave Los Angeles CA 90089-2564 Fax: 213-740-4651. E-mail: bharitka@sipi.usc.edu.

BHARTIA, PRAKASH, defense research management executive, researcher, educator; b. Calcutta, West Bengal, India, Jan. 6, 1944; arrived in Can., 1967; s. Benarshi Prasad and Bhagwati Devi (Chirimar) B.; m. Savitri Kanhai, Apr. 27, 1971; children: Sanjay Manish, Anil Manoj. B in Tech. with honors, Indian Inst. Tech., Bombay, 1966; MSc, U. Man., Winnipeg, Can., 1968, PhD, 1971. Assoc. prof. U. Regina, Sask., Can., 1976, asst. dean, 1975-77; def. scientist, chief R&D br. Nat. Defence, Ottawa, Ont., Can., 1977—; head navigation sect. Defence Rsch. Establishment Ottawa, 1981-85; dir. R&D air Defence Hdqrs., Govt. of Can., Ottawa, 1985-86; dir. R&D commnications and space Nat. Defence, Govt. of Can., 1986-89; dir. sonar div. Defence Rsch. Establishment Atlantic, Halifax, 1989-91; dir. radar div. Defence Rsch. Establishment Ottawa, 1991—; chief Defence Rsch. Establishment Atlantic, 1992-97; dir.-gen. Def. Rsch. Establishment, Ottawa, 1997—. Adj. prof. U. Ottawa, 1977-96, Daltech, 1997—; dir. Can. Microelectronics Centre, Kingston, 1986-88; mem. elec. engring. grant selection com. Natural Scis. and Engring. Rsch. Coun., Ottawa, 1990—, chmn. ind. chair evaluation com., Victoria, 1991; bd. dirs. Tradex Investment Funds, Ottawa, Canadian Ctr. Marine Communication. Author: Microstrip Antennas, 1980, Millimeter Wave Engineering and Applications, 1984, E Plane Integrated Circuits, 1987, Millimeter Wave Microstrip and Printed Circuit Antennas, 1990; author, editor: Microwave Solid State Circuit Design, 1988, Microstrip Lines and Slotlines, 1996, RF and Microwave Coupled Line Circuits, 1999, Microstrip Antenna Design Handbook, 2000; patentee in field. Mem. engring. adv. com. Queen's U., Kingston, 1989-92, chmn. bd., 1992. Decorated Order of Canada. Fellow: IEEE, Can. Acad. Engrs., Royal Soc. of Can., Instn. Elec. and Telecomm. Engrs.; mem.: India Soc. Engrs., Eng. Inst. Can. Hindu. Office: Def Rsch Establish Ottawa 3701 Carling Ave Ottawa ON Canada K1A OZ4 Home: 5760 Owensmouth Ave # 7 Woodland Hills CA 91367 E-mail: bhartiaprakash.bhartia@hotmail.com.

BHASIN, MADAN MOHAN, research scientist; b. Lahore, India, June 23, 1938; came to U.S., 1959; s. Late L. Mela Ram and Bahain Devi (Sahni) B.; m. Anand Kumari Chugha, Aug. 5, 1961; children: Madhu Lata, Anoop Kumar. BS with hon., Delhi U., New Delhi, India, 1958; postgrad., Indiana U., 1959-60; PhD, U. Notre Dame, 1964. Chemist Union Carbide Corp., South Charleston, W.V., 1963-69, project scientist, 1969-77, research scientist, 1977-81, group supr., 1981-82, sr. research scientist, group supr., 1982-88, corp. fellow., group supr., 1988—. Spkr., lectr. in field. Patentee in field; contbr. articles to profl. jours. Chmn. India Ctr., Charleston, W.V., 1986-96, co-chair, India Heritage Fair, 1996—; bd. dirs. United Way, 2000. Recipient Eugene J. Houdry Award in Applied Catalysis, Catalysis Soc. N. Amer., 1995, Scientific Achievement Awd., Kanawka Valley Section of ACS (Am. Chem. Soc.), 1995, Amer. Chem. Soc. Awd. in Indsl. Chem., 1999, AZKO Nobel. Mem. AIChE, Am. Chem. Soc. (chmn. summer symposium Indsl. and Engring. Chem. div. 1986-88, exec. com. mem. 1983-87, chmn. I & EC div. 1990), Catalysis Secretariat (chair 1997), India Assn. (pres. 1979-80). Avocations: photography, tennis, badminton, gardening. Office: Union Carbide Corp Indust Chem Divs PO Box 8361 Charleston WV 25303-0361 E-mail: bhasin2m@excelonline.com.

BHASKAR, SURINDAR NATH, pathologist, periodontist; b. Rasul, India, Jan. 7, 1923; came to U.S., 1944; s. Jagan Nath and Maya Devi (Davesar) B.; married Jan. 7, 1950; children: William, Philip, Thomas. DDS, Northwestern U., 1946; MS, U. Ill., 1948, PhD, 1951. Diplomate Am. Bd. Oral Pathology, Am. Bd. Oral Medicine. Advanced through grades to maj. gen. U.S. Army, 1955-78; chief Oral Tumors Br. Walter Reed Inst. Rsch., Washington, 1960-61, chief Div. Oral Pathology, 1960-61, chief Div. Oral Pathology, U.S. Army Inst. Dental Rsch., 1961-69, dir. U.S. Army Inst. Dental Rsch.; dir. personnel Med. Dept. U.S. Army; prof. Sch. Medicine and Dentistry Georgetown U., Washington; chief Dental Corps U.S. Army, Washington, asst. surgeon gen. for dental svcs., maj. gen. Dental Corps. Cons. in oral pathology Asst. Surgeon Gen. and Chief of Dental Corps. Author: Synopsis of Oral Histology, 1962, Synopsis of Oral Pathology, 7th edit., 1986, Radiographic Interpretation for the Dentist, 3d edit., 1979, Oral Histology and Embryology, 11th edit., 1990, (with others), Atlas of Clinical Pathology of the Oral Mucuous Membrane, 1951, Tumors of Oral Regions, 1957, Pediatric Dentristy, 1961, Mechanisms of Hard Tissue Destruction, 1963, Adhesions in Biological Systems, 1970, among others; contbr. over 200 articles to profl. jours. Decorated Disting. Svc. medal, Legion of Merit, Meritorius Svc. medal; recipient lectr. awards from numerous dental socs. in U.S., Henry Spenadel award, 1971, Army Sci. award, 1972, India-Am. League award, 1974, Alpha Omega Achievement award, 1974, Albert L. Borish Meml. award Acad. Gen. Dentistry, 1979. Fellow AAAS, Am. Acad. Oral Pathology; mem. ADA, Calif. Dental Assn., Internat. Assn. Dental Rsch., Am. Acad. Periodontics, Calif. Soc. Periodontics, Western Soc. Periodontology, Assn. Mil. Surgeons (Founders medal 1973), Acad. Oral Medicine, Delta Sigma Delta, Sigma Xi, Omicron Kappa Upsilon. Office: 333 El Dorado St Monterey CA 93940-4606 also: 750 E Romie Ln Ste D Salinas CA 93901-4208

BHAT, CHANDRA R. engineering educator, consultant; b. Madras, India, July 5, 1964; s. Ramalinga and Kamakshi Bhat; m. Shrimathi Bhat; children: Prerna, Aarti. B. Tech, Indian Inst. Tech., 1982—85; MS, Va. Poly. Inst. State U., 1985—87; PhD, Northwestern U., 1988—91. Lic. P.E., 2001. Traffic engr. Raymond Keyes Associates, White Plains, NY, 1987—88; asst. prof. (rsch.) & lectr. Northwestern U., Transp. Ctr., Chicago, Ill., 1991—93; asst. prof. U. Mass., Amherst, 1993—97; asst. prof., dept. civil engring. U. Tex., Austin, 1997—2001, assoc. prof. and assoc. chmn., dept. civil engring., 2001—02. Cons. Oahu Met. Planning Orgn., 1994—96, KPMG Peat Marwick, Inc., 1997—99, Puget Sound Regional Coun., 2000—01, Houston Galveston Area Coun., 2000—02. Recipient Oustanding Rsch. Innovation Honor, Tex. Dept of Transp., 2001, Milton Pikarsky Meml. Dissertation Award, Coun. U. Transp. Centers, 1992; fellow Fluor Centennial Tchg. Fellowship in Engring., U. Tex. at Austin, 2001, Univ. of Mass. Fauclty Rsch. Fellowship, U. Mass., 1994. Mem.: TxDOT RMC2 Tech. Adv. Panel, Transp. Rsch. Bd. Com. on Passenger Travel Demand Forecasting, Transp. Rsch. Bd. Com. on Telecom. and Travel Behavior, Transp. Rsch. Bd. Com. on Traveler Behavior and Values, TRB Com. on Passenger Travel Demand Forecasting (chmn. 2001—), Iatbr (internat. steering com. for 2003 iatbr meeting 2001—02), Transp. (editl. adv. bd. 1998—), Internat. Jour. of Ops. and Quantitative Mgmt. (editl. rev. bd. 1995—), Transp. Rsch., Part B (editl. adv. bd. 1993—), Iatbr (sec./treas. 2000—), Iatbr (bd. mem. 1995—). Office: U Tex Austin 1 University Sta C 1761 Dept Civil Engring Austin TX 78712-0278 Office Fax: 512-475-8744. Business E-Mail: bhat@mail.utexas.edu.

BHAT, RAM J. anesthesiologist; b. Muroor, India, Mar. 25, 1949; came to U.S., 1975; MD, Karnatak Med. Coll., Hubli, India, 1973. Diplomate Am. Bd. Anesthesiology. Intern KMC Hosp., Hubli, 1973-74; resident in anesthesiology KEM Hosp., Bombay, 1974-75, Toledo Hosp., 1975-78; anesthesiologist Cleve. Clinic, 1978; staff anesthesiologist Elyria (Ohio) Meml. Hosp., 1978-79; mem. staff St. Charles Hosp., Oregon, Ohio, 1979—; pvt. practice Elyria, 1978—; anesthesiologist St. Anne Mercy Hosp., Toledo, 2002—. Sect. chief anesthesiology St. Charles Hosp., Oregon, 1981-93, 96-97. Mem. Am. Soc. Anesthesiologists, Ohio Soc. Anesthesiologists, Ohio State Med. Assn., Toledo Acad. Medicine. E-mail: rjbhat1@aol.com.

BHATIA, ANEETA, cardiac anesthesiologist; arrived in U.S., 1994; d. Hari Singh and Joginder Bhatia; children: Neha, Nupur Kantanuni. MBBS, Osmania U., Hyderabad, India, 1979; MD, Postgrad. Inst. Med. Edn. Rsch., Chandigarh, India, 1983. Cert. bd. cert. Nat. Bd. of Echocardiography, 1999, 2000. Residency Med. Coll. Wis. Milw., 1998; assoc. prof. anesthesiology, dir. cardiac anesthesia U. Cin., 1999—. Assoc. prof. anesthesiology, dir. cardiac anesthesia U. Cin., 1999—. Fellow: Royal Coll. Anesthetists (Ireland and U.K.). Home: 6984 Lexington Park Blvd Mason OH 45040 Address: PO Box 210531 Cincinnati OH 45221-0531

BHATIA, PETER K. newspaper editor, journalist; b. Pullman, Wash., May 22, 1953; s. Vishnu N. and Ursula Jean (Dawson) B.; m. Elizabeth M. Dahl, Sept. 27, 1981; children: Megan Jean, Jay Peter. BA, Stanford U., 1975. Polit. reporter, asst. news editor Spokesman Rev., Spokane, Wash., 1975-77; news editor Dallas Times Herald, 1980-81; asst. news editor San Francisco Examiner, 1977-80, news editor, 1981-85, dep. mng. editor/news, 1985-87; mng. editor Dallas Times Herald, 1987-88; editor York Dispatch, York, Pa., 1988-89; mng. editor The Sacramento Bee, 1989-93; exec. editor The Fresno Bee, 1993; mng. editor The Oregonian, Portland, 1993-97, exec. editor, 1997—. Pulitzer Prize juror, 1992-93, 98-99; bd. dirs. Am. Press Inst. Mem. adv. bd. Knight Ctr. Specialized Journalism U. Md.; mem. adv. bd. Murrow Sch. Communication Wash. State U.; mem. new media adv. bd. Oreg. State U.; bd. chmn. Albertina Kerr Ctrs. for Children, 2001—02; chmn. bd. St. John Fisher Sch., 2000—. Mem.: Investigative Reporters and Editors, South Asian Journalists Assn., Nat. Assn. Minority Media Execs., Asian Am. Journalists Assn., AP Mng. Editors (bd. dirs. 1991—97), Am. Soc. Newspaper Editors (bd. dirs. 1997—, treas. 2000—, sec. 2001—02, v.p. 2002-2003, pres. 2003-), Stanford U. Alumni Assn. (bd. dirs. 1998—2001), Theta Delta Chi, Sigma Delta Chi. Office: The Oregonian 1320 SW Broadway Portland OR 97201-3499

BHATIA, RAJAN, engineer, physicist, researcher; arrived in U.S., 1985, permanent resident; s. Prem S. and Shakun Bhatia. Student, U. Mont., Butte, 1985—88; BS in Engring. Physics, U. Maine, Orono, 1991. Laser systems rsch. engr. Amoco Laser Co., Naperville, Ill., 1990—90, Amoco Corp. - Amoco Tech. Co., Naperville, 1990—92; laser systems tech. engr., non-linear acoustics physicist Johnson & Johnson, Claremont, Calif., 1992—95, sr. laser systems engr. Palo Alto, Calif., 1996—97; laser systems rsch. engr. Cygnus, Monroe, Wash., 1995—96; sr. rsch. scientist IRIS/IRIDEX, Sunnyvale, Calif., 1997—99, Qculight Inc., Bothell, Wash., 1999—2000; sr. mem. tech. staff Tyco Internat., Eatontown, NJ, 2001—01; prin. photonics staff engr. NIS, San Jose, Calif., 2001—. Electro-optical sys. engr. NASA, Greenbelt, Md., 1990; presenter in field. Contbr. articles to profl. jours. Scholar, U. Maine, 1988—91. Mem.: ASM Internat., Japanese Soc. Applied Physics, Internat. Soc. Optical Engring., Optical Soc. Am. Achievements include research in in various diverse areas of Laser Engineering, Photonics, Electro-Optics, Biomedical Lasers, High Power Lasers, Non-Linear Optics, Fiber-Optics, Biomedical Acoustics & Ultrasound, design of various in Biomedical Lasers, High Power Lasers, Non-Linear Optics, Fiber-Optics, Biomedical Acoustics & Ultrasound. E-mail: guma7736@yahoo.com.

BHATNAGAR, HEMENDRA NARAIN, otolaryngologist; b. Bikaner, India, 1930; MD, SMS Med. Coll. Rajasthan U., 1954. Cert. otolarnygology. Intern St. Johns Hosp., Cleve., 1957-58; resident in otolarnygology Boston City Hosp., 1958-61. Mem. AAAestRestS, Am. Acad. Cosmetic Surgery, Am. Acad. Otolaryngology-Head and Neck Surgery, IACS, N.E. Otolarnygology Soc., Pan-Am. Acad. Otolarngology. Office: 10 School St Waterville ME 04901-7518 E-mail: hnb001@midmaine.com.

BHATNAGAR, MARY ELIZABETH, lawyer; b. Nashville, July 8, 1943; d. Thomas A. and Elizabeth D. (Levine) Kelly; m. Rajendra S. Bhatnagar, Feb. 27, 1966; children: Ranjit, Rajiv. BA, Duke U., 1965; MA, Northwestern U., 1968; JD, San Mateo Law Sch., 1979. Bar: Calif. 1979, U.S. Dist. Ct. (no. dist.) Calif. 1979. Pvt. practice, San Mateo, Calif., 1979—. Prof. bus. law Coll. San Mateo, 1979—. Bd. dirs. LWV of Cen. San Mateo county, 1989—. Mem. ABA, Calif. State Bar, San Mateo County Bar Assn. Democrat. Office: Bovet Prof Ctr 177 Bovet Rd Ste 600 San Mateo CA 94402-3191

BHATTACHARJEE, DEB, engineering; b. Calcutta, India, June 30, 1966; arrived in USA, 1994, permanent resident, 2003; s. Himangshu Kumar Bhattacharjee and Anima Bhattcharjee; m. Kakali Bose Bhattacharjee, May 7, 1993; children: Kuchol, Kushagro. BE, BE Coll., Honrah, WB, India, 1988; PGCGM, Indian Inst. of Mgmt., Calcutta, India, 1992; MS, Asian Inst. of Tech., Bangkok, Thailand, 1994; PhD, Purdue U, IN, 1997. Grad. rsch. asst. Purdue U, Ind., 1994—97; application engr. i 2 Technologies, Dallas, 1997—98; mgr. Ernst & Young, Cupertino, Calif., 1998—2000; sr. mgr. Cap Gemini Ernst & Young, Cupertino, Calif., 2000—01; sr. dir. NLOrbit Inc., San Jose, Calif., 2002—. Recipient Barbara Jones and Hughes, Asian Inst. of Tech./Thailand, 1994, moder, Purdue U, 1997. Democrat. Hindu. Avocations: soccer, percussion- tabla. Home: 4093 Lakecrest Ct San Jose CA 95148 Office: Orbit 3031 Tisch Way San Jose CA 95128

BHATTACHARJYA, ASHOKE SANJOY, economist, researcher; b. Shillong, India, Jan. 17, 1965; s. Arunoday and Supriya Bhattacharjya; m. Shamoli Bhattacharjya. BA with honors, Delhi U., 1985; MA, Delhi (India) Sch. Economics, 1987; PhD, MPhil, Columbia U., 1993. Instr. NYU, N.Y.C., 1990—93; adj. asst. prof. Columbia U., N.Y.C., 1993—94; economist, corp. planning and policy Pfizer, N.Y.C., 1993—96; assoc. dir. health econs. Janssen Pharmaceutica, Titusville, NJ, 1996—97, dir.,outcomes rsch., 1997—2001; sr. dir. bus. intelligence and analytics Jannsen Pharmaceutica, Titusville, NJ, 2001—. Lectr., program for econ. policy mgmt. World Bank, Columbia U., N.Y.C., 1992—93; invited lectr. program on pharm. industry MIT, Cambridge, Mass., 1997—98; invited conf. chair/spkr. numerous profl. orgns.; jour. referee Econ. Theory, Jour. Econ. Dymamics and Control, Health Econs. Contbr. articles to profl. jours. Recipient All India Entrance Merit scholarship, Delhi U., 1982—85, Naqvi Meml. Merit scholarship, Delhi Sch. of Economics, 1986—87, President's fellowship, Columbia U., 1987—90, Standards of Leadership award, Johnson &Johnson, 1997—2002. Mem.: Ad Hoc Pharm. Industry Working Group, Nat. Assn. Bus. Economists, Am. Econ. Assn. Home: 1 Colebrook Ct Princeton NJ 08540 Office: Janssen Pharmaceutica (Johnson&Johnson) 1125 Trenton-Harbourton Road Titusville NJ 08560 Office Fax: 609-730-2330. Personal E-mail: bashoke@aol.com. E-mail: abhattac@janus.jnj.com.

BHATTACHARYA, DEBANSHU, metallurgical engineer; b. Calcutta, June 26, 1947; arrived in U.S., 1969; s. Sudhansu S. and Anila Bhattacharya; m. Kalpana Bhattacharya, Feb. 28, 1979; children: Leena, Neil. B of Engring., Regional Engring. Coll., Durgapur, India, 1969; MS Wash. State U., 1971; PhD, Wash. State U., 1975. Rsch. assoc., sr. rsch. engr. Pa. State U., University Park, 1975—76; rsch. engr. Inland Steel Co., East Chicago, Ind., 1976—85, sect. mgr., 1985—91; mgr. Ispat-Inland Inc., East Chicago, 1991—. Contbr. articles to profl. jours. Recipient Excellence in Oral Presentation award, Soc. Automotive Engrs., 1991, 3d pl. award internat. metallographic exhibit, ASM, 1978, TMS Extractive Metallurgy Gold medal, 1988. Mem.: Iron and Steel Soc. (John Chipman award 1987). Achievements include patents for semi-finished steel article and method for producing same; method and alloy for introducing machinability increasing ingredients to steel; free machining steel with bismuth; bismuth-containing steel; semi-finished steel article; method for preventing mold explosions during continuous casting of free machining steel; preventing undissolved alloying ingredient from entering continuous casting mold. Office: Ispat-Inland Rsch Labs 3001 E Columbus Dr East Chicago IN 46312

BHATTACHARYA, JOYDEEP, economics educator; b. New Delhi, Mar. 22, 1968; s. Avijit and Dipti Bhattacharya; m. Helle Bunzel. BS, St. Xavier's Coll., Calcutta, India, 1989; MA, Delhi Sch. Econs., New Delhi, 1991, Cornell U., 1994, PhD, 1996. Asst. prof. dept. econs. Iowa State U., Ames, 1999—, SUNY, Buffalo, 1997—99; vis. asst. prof. U. So. Calif., L.A., 1996—97. Vis. scholar U. So. Calif., L.A., 1996—97. Fellow doctoral dissertation fellow, Alfred P. Sloan Found., 1995—96. Mem.: Soc. for Econ. Dynamics, Econometric Soc., Am. Econ. Assn. Office: Iowa State U Dept Econs 260 Heady Hall Ames IA 50011 Office Fax: 515-294-0221. Business E-Mail: joydeep@econ.iastate.edu.

BHATTACHARYA, RINA, economist; b. Newcastle, England, Jan. 26, 1965; came to U.S., 1997; d. Nirmalendu and Meena B. BA in Econs. with 1st class hons., Cambridge U., England, 1985; MS in Devel. Econs., Oxford U., England, 1986; PhD in Econs., Yale U., 1992. Lectr. U. East Anglia, England, 1992, U. Sussex, England, 1992-93; economist U.K. Treasury, England, 1994-96, Bank of England, 1996-97, Internat. Monetary Fund, Washington, 1997—. Co-author: Investment Growth and Employment, 1999; contbr. articles to profl. jours. Home: 901 N Monroe St # 907 Arlington VA 22201-2357 Office: Internat Monetary Fund 700 19th St NW Washington DC 20431-0001

BHATTACHARYA, SATYAJIT, research scientist; came to U.S., 1993; s. Amal and Rekha B. BS, U. Poona, Pune, Maharashtra, India, 1985, MS, 1987; diploma in Computer Sci., Indian Inst. Computer Studies, Pune, 1988; MS, U. Toronto, 1993; PhD, Calcutta U., India, 2001. Rsch. assoc. Mt. Sinai Sch. Medicine Vets. Affairs Med. Ctr., N.Y.C., 1993-94, asst. rsch. scientist, 1994-95, NYU Med. Ctr., N.Y.C., 1994-95; rsch. assoc. Amgen Inc., Thousand Oaks, Calif., 1995-96; rsch. scientist Meml. Sloan-Kettering Cancer Ctr., N.Y.C., 1996—. Inventor in field; contbr. articles to profl. jours. Coun. Sci. and Indsl. Rsch. fellow, 1991. Fellow Royal Microscopic Soc.; mem. AAAS, Am. Chem. Soc., N.Y. Acad. Scis., Histochem. Soc. (Outstanding Young Investigator award 1999), Metastasis Rsch. Sic., European Soc. Analytical and Cell Pathology (Best Oral Presentation award 2002), Internat. Soc. Quality and Diagnostic Pathology, Am. Molecular Pathology Soc., Harlem Children Soc. (founder, CEO, pres. 2000—), Sigma Xi (pres. Rockefeller U. chpt. 2003). Avocations: reading, writing, swimming, sports, music. Home: 536 East 82 St # 5F New York NY 10028 Office: Meml Sloan-Kettering Cancer Ctr Dept Pathology Box 105 1275 York Ave New York NY 10021 E-mail: bhattacs@mskcc.org.

BHATTACHARYA, SYAMAL KANTI, biomedical scientist, educator; b. Calcutta, India, Feb. 13, 1949; arrived in U.S., 1974, naturalized, 1983; s. Sudhir Chandra Bhattacharya and Prabhabati Battacharya; m. Keka Karabi Ghoshal, Dec. 11, 1969; children: Sumoulindra Titu, Julie Keka, Syamal Dave. BS with honors, U. Calcutta, 1968; BA in English Lit., 1969; MS, Murray State U., 1976; AM, Washington U., St. Louis, 1978; PhD, Memphis State U., 1979. Diplomate Am. Bd. Bioanalysis; cert. profl. chemist Nat. Cert. Commn. Chemistry and Chem. Engring., lic. med. lab. dir. Tenn. Dept. Pub. Health. Instr. chemistry Netaji Shakshaytan, Calcutta, India, 1968—69; sr. instr. chemistry Bhabanath Instn., Calcutta, 1969—70; R&D chemist Swastik Household and Indsl. Products Pvt. Ltd., Bombay, 1970—74; sr. rsch. tech. Washington U. Med. Sch., St. Louis, 1976—77; rsch. assoc. U. Tenn. Med. Ctr., Memphis, 1979—80, instr. medicine, 1980—82, mem. surgery faculty, 1983—, dir. surg. rsch. labs., 1982—, founding dir. chemistry and nutrient data output lab., 1982—, instr. surgery, 1983—84, asst. prof. surgery, 1984—88, asst. prof. medicinal chemistry, 1985—91, assoc. prof. medicinal chemistry, 1991—99, prof. pharm. scis., 1999—, assoc. prof. surgery, 1988—98, prof. surgery, 1998—, assoc. prof. anatomy and neurobiology, 1988—95, prof. neurology, 1999—. Adj. prof. surgery NY Med. Coll., 1988—97; vis. prof. surgery Yale U. Sch. Med., 1985; vis. prof. pediats. U. Cin. Med. Ctr. and Cin. Children's Hosp., 1985; vis. prof. pediatric surgery Johns Hopkins U. Sch. Med., 1987; vis. prof. surgery Rush-Presbyn.-St. Luke's Med. Ctr., Chgo., 1987, NY Med. Coll., 1987—88; vis. prof. biochemistry George Washington U. Sch. Medicine, Washington, 1988, Howard U., 1989; vis. prof. surgery East Tenn. State U., 1989; vis. prof. microbiology Bose Inst., Calcutta, 1999, Calcutta, 2001; external examiner doctoral dissertation faculty scis. Jadavpur U., Calcutta, 2002—; commr. Nat. Cert. Comm. Chemistry & Chem. Engrg., Washington, 1987—; v.p. Nat. Registry in Clin. Chemistry, Washington, 1999—2000, pres., 2000—01; grant reviewer, mem. pathology-A study sect. NIH, 1993—95. Contbr. numerous publs. to biomed. and sci. jours., to nat. and internat. sci. confs.; ad hoc reviewer: for numerous sci. and profl. jours. Grantee Am. Heart Assn., 1986—87, NIH, 1988—95. Grantee Muscular Dystrophy Assn. Am., 1983—84; recipient Presdl. rsch. fellowship, Memphis State U., 1978—79, Indian Nat. scholarship, Govt. India, New Delhi, 1965—69, Govt. India scholarship, Bank of India, 1974—75, rsch. grant, U. Physician's Found., 1985—86, Varian Instrument Group of Am., 1986—99, U. Tenn. Med. Group, 1997—99, Nat. Rsch. Svc. award in medicine, NIH, 1979—81. Fellow: Am. Coll. Nutrition, Indian Chem. Soc., Am. Instn. Chemists (cert. profl. chemist 1980); mem.: ACS, AAAS, Am. Oil Chemists' Soc., Internat. Soc. Brain Rsch., Soc. Neurosci., NY Acad. Scis., Am. Soc. Molecular Biology and Biochemistry, Coll. Am. Pathologists, Am. Fedn. Clin. Rsch., Royal Soc. Chemistry (chartered chemist 1981), U. Tenn. Faculty Club (Memphis), Phi Kappa Phi, Sigma Xi. Office: U Tenn Med Ctr 956 Court Ave Ste B220 Memphis TN 38163-2814 Fax: 901-448-7306. E-mail: sbhattachary@utmem.edu.

BHATTACHARYYA, ASHIM KUMAR, pathology and physiology educator, researcher; b. Kanpur, Uttar Pradesh, India, July 9, 1936; came to U.S., 1966; s. Vishwa Nath and Ashalata (Bhattacharya) B.; m. Bani Chatterjee, July 10, 1966; children: Rupa, Gopa. BSc with honors, Calcutta U., 1957, MSc, 1959, PhD, 1965, DSc, 1989. Postdoctoral fellow U. Minn., Mpls., 1966-68, U. Iowa, Iowa City, 1969-70, assoc. rsch scientist, 1970-74, rsch. scientist, 1974-75; asst. prof. pathology and physiology La. State U. Med. Ctr., New Orleans, 1975-80, assoc. prof. pathology and physiology, 1980-89; prof. pathology and physiology La. State U., New Orleans, 1989—. Contbr. over 80 articles to profl. jours. Trustee India Assn. New Orleans, 1982-85, founder and pres. La. Bengali

Cultural Assn., 1985. Recipient Emery Goff Rsch. award, Am. Heart Assn.-La., New Orleans, 1977-78; sr. rsch. grantee, Am. Heart Assn.-La., 1976-77,1980-81. Fellow Coun. on Arteriosclerosis, Am. Heart Assn.; mem. Am. Physiol. Soc., Am. Inst. Nutrition, Am. Soc. for Clin. Nutrition, Sigma Xi. Hindu. Achievements include discovery of Beta-Sitosterolemia and Xanthomatosis, a genetic disease in humans involving plant sterols. Home: 1156 Elmeer Ave Metairie LA 70005-1616 Office: La State U Med Ctr Dept Pathology 1901 Perdido St New Orleans LA 70112-1328

BHATTACHARYYA, KALYAN KUMAR, scientist, biomedical engineer; b. Calcutta, Jan. 5, 1951; arrived in U.S., 1983; s. Nalin Kumar and Kamala Bhattacharyya; m. Malabika Bhattacharyya, Jan. 23, 1952; children: Bidisha, Arpita. BS in Chemistry with honors, St. Xaviers Coll., Calcutta, 1971; MS in Biochemistry, U. Calcutta, 1973, PhD in Biochemistry, 1982. Postdoctoral fellow U. Wis., Madison, 1983-92, scientist, 1992-97, Mayo Clinic, Rochester, Minn., 1997—. Contbr. articles to sci. and profl. jours. Mem.: Indian Cultural Assn. Rochester, Vedanta Soc. Madison (pres. 1993—95), Am. Soc. Biochemistry and Molecular Biology, Soc. Biol. Chemists India. Home: 1864 Evergreen Dr NW Rochester MN 55901 Office: Mayo Clinic 200 First St SW Rochester MN 55905 E-mail: bhattacharyya.kalyan@mayo.edu.

BHATTI, NEELOO, environmental scientist; b. New Delhi, Jan. 30, 1955; arrived in Can., 1958, came to U.S., 1982; d. Daljeet Singh and Abnash (Singh) B.; m. James Joseph McAndrew, Sept. 14, 1985. MES, Yale U., 1984, PhD, 1988. Rsch. asst. McGill U., Montreal, Que., Can., 1976-78; teaching asst. Yale U., New Haven, 1983; postdoctoral fellow Argonne (Ill.) Nat. Lab., 1989-90, environ. scientist, 1990-98; environ. effects specialist World Bank, Washington, 1989—, environ. cons., 1998—. Mem. Homer Glen Environ. Com., 2001—. Author: Dispelling the North American Acid Rain Clouds, 1988, Responding to Threat of Global Warming: Options for Asia and Pacific, 1989, Acid Rain in Asia, 1992; co-editor: Adapting to Climate Change: Assessments and Issues, 1997. F.C.A.C. scholar Govt. Que., 1983-87; Yale U. fellow, New Haven, 1984-88. Mem.: Am. Soc. Foresters, Sigma Xi. Achievements include identification of specific regions within Asia at highest risk from acid deposition; identified basis of pollution problems in Romania, Poland, China; compiled emissions inventory for mercury in Great Lakes region and for SO2 in Asia; assisted in development of climate change strategy for the People's Republic of China. Home: 15425 Purley Ct Homer Glen IL 60441-9492 E-mail: jim10100@attbi.com.

BHAUMIK, MANI LAL, physicist; b. Calcutta, India, Jan. 5, 1932; came to U.S., 1959, naturalized, 1968; s. Gunadhar and Lolita (Pramanik) B. BS, U. Calcutta, 1951, MS, 1953; PhD, Indian Inst. Tech., 1958, DSc (hon.), 1995. Fellow U. Calif. at Los Angeles, 1959-63; with Xerox Electro-Optical Systems, Pasadena, Calif., 1961-67, Northrop Corp. Labs., Hawthorne, Calif., 1968-71, research dir., 1971-75; mgr. Laser Tech. Lab., Northrop Research and Tech. Center, 1976-84, sr. staff scientist, 1984-86. Lectr. physics Calif. State U., Long Beach, 1967-69. Contbr. articles to profl. jours.; patentee in field. Fellow Am. Phys. Soc., IEEE. Office: Laser Tech Lab PO Box 24050 Los Angeles CA 90024-0050 *A strong and innate belief in basic human goodness has often pulled me out of hostile circumstances where one is likely to lose faith in humanity.*

BHAVSAR, NATVAR PRAHLADJI, artist; b. Gothava, India, Apr. 7, 1934; came to U.S., 1962; s. Prahladji V. and Babu P. B.; m. Janet Brosious, Jan. 15, 1978; children: Shashin, Ajay, Rajeev. AM, Bombay State Higher Art Exam., 1958, Govt. Diploma Art, 1959; BA in Liberal Arts and English Lit, Gujarat U., Ahmedabad, India, 1960; MFA, U. Pa., 1965. Instr. in art U. R.I., 1967, 68, 69. One-man shows include Obelisk Gallery, Boston, 1968, 69, Max Hutchinson Gallery, N.Y.C., 1970, 71, 72, 74, 77, 78, in Houston, 1978, Gallery A. Sydney, Australia, 1970, Gallery Chemould, Bombay, 1970, Kenmore Gallery, Phila., 1963, 74, Kingspitcher Gallery, Pitts., 1977, Gloria Luria Gallery, Bayharbor Fl., 1978, 98, Wichita (Kans.) Art Mus., 1979, 85, Pembroke Gallery, Houston, 1985, 87; Gettler/Pall/Saper, N.Y.C., 1984, Bose-Pacia Modern Gallery, N.Y.C., 1986, ACP Viviane Ehrli Gallery, Zurich, Switzerland, 1997, Art-Garage, Zug, Switzerland, 2000, Dialectica, NY, 2000, Sundaram Tagore Gallery, 2001, 02, World Economics Forum, Davos, Switzerland, 2000; group shows include Jewish Mus., N.Y.C., 1970, Whitney Mus. Am. Art, 1970 (2), Indpls. Mus. Art, 1970, 78, U. Sydney, 1970, Columbus (Ohio) Gallery Fine Arts, 1971, U. Rochester, 1971, Max Hutchinson Gallery, 1973, Am. Acad. Arts and Letters Art Gallery, N.Y.C., 1973, Ruth S. Schaffner Gallery, Los Angeles, 1974, Reed Coll., 1974, Rockland Ctr. for Arts, West Nyack, N.Y., 1979, Fifth Triennale, New Delhi, India, 1981, Il Sud del Mondo, L'Altra Arte Contemporanea Galleria Civica de Arte Contemporarea, Pizzo, Italy, 1991, Gloria Lurie Gallery, Bay Harbor, Fla., 1978, 92, IlSud del Mondo, L'Attra Contemporanca, Commune di Marsa, Pizzo, Italy, 1991, Angolazioni e Prospettive Della Visione, Nell'Arte Contemporanea, Centro Museografico, Palazzo S.Domenico, Taverna, Italy, 1991, Viviane Ehrli Gallery, Art Cologne (Germany) Internat., 1998, 99; represented in permanent collections Met. Mus. Art, N.Y.C., Boston Mus. Fine Arts, Guggenheim Mus., N.Y.C., Chase Manhattan Bank, N.Y.C., Wichita Art Mus. (Kans.), Herbert F. Johnson Mus. at Cornell U., Australian Nat. Gallery, Canberra, Library of Congress, M.I.T., Ulrich Mus. Art, Wichita, Lannan Found., Power Inst., Sydney, Rose Art Mus. at Brandeis U., U. Mass., Amherst, U. Del., Whitney Mus. Am. Art, N.Y.C., Worcester (Mass.) Mus., Am. express co., N.Y.C., N.B.C., N.Y.C., Olympia and York, Toronto, Readers Digest, N.Y., United Bank of Switzerland, N.Y.C.; monograph Natvar Bhavsar Painting and the Reality of Color (Irving Sandler), 1998. John D. Rockefeller III Fund fellow, 1965-66, Guggenheim Meml. Found. fellow, 1975-76. Achievements include being subject of profl. articles. Home: 131 Greene St New York NY 10012-3220

BHAYRO, SIAM, religious studies educator; b. Erith, Kent, United Kingdom, Sept. 26, 1973; s. Suzanne Virginia and Thunkoomar Bhayro; m. Lisa Anne Kemp, Aug. 5, 1995. BA with honors, U. Coll. London, 1993—97, PhD, 1997—2000. Coll. tchr. U. Coll. London, 2000—01; rsch. assoc. Dictionary of Classical Hebrew Project, Sheffield, England, 2000—02; lectr. in semitic languages Yale U., 2002—. Mem. Fabian Soc., United Kingdom. Mem.: Brit. Assn. for Jewish Studies (sec. 2000—02), Am. Oriental Soc., Soc. of Bibl. Lit. Labor. Christian. Office: NELC Yale University PO Box 208236 New Haven CT 06520-8236

BHIDAYASIRI, ROONGROJ, neurologist, researcher; s. Mitr and Nisaratana Bhidayasiri. MD, Chulalongkorn U., Bangkok, Thailand, 1993. Diploma in Geriatric Medicine Royal Coll. of Physicians and Surgeons of Glasgow, 1998. Physician Innsbruck U. Hosp., Austria, 1994—95, Royal London U. Hosp. and Southend Hosp., London, 1995—96, U. Hospitals of Wales, Cardiff, England, 1997, U. Coll. London Hosp., 1997, U. of Oxford Hosp. Radcliffe Infirmary, England, 1998, Guy's, St. Thomas' and King's Coll. Hosps., London, 1998—99, 1998—99, U. Hosp. of Cleve., Cleveland, Ohio, 1999—2000, UCLA Med. Ctr. and Sch. of Medicine, 2000—. Bd. mem. Chulalongkorn U. Alumni of Calif., LA, 2002—. Author: (book) Neurological Differential Diagnosis, Neuroradiology Casebook, (jour. article) Am. Jour. of Ophthalmology, Annals of N.Y. Acad. of Sci., Jour. of Vestibular Rsch., Jour. of Neurology Neurosurgery Psychiatry, Annals of Oncology. Bd. mem. Thai Assn. of So. Calif., LA, 2002—03; chairperson New Wave Group, LA, 2002—03. Recipient New Millennium Investigator award, Dystonia Med. Rsch. Found., 2001—02. Fellow: Royal Soc. of Medicine (assoc.); mem.: Royal Coll. of Physicians of Edinburgh (licentiate), Royal Coll. of Physicians of London (licentiate), LA Coun. of World Affairs (assoc.), Assn. of Brit. Neurologists (assoc.), Am. Acad. of Neurology (assoc.). Buddhist. Achievements include research in New treatment in dystonia using transcranial magnetic stimulation. Avocations: violin, piano, chess, squash. Office: UCLA Med Ctr and Sch of Medicine 710 Westwood Plz Los Angeles CA 90095 Personal E-mail: rbh@ucla.edu. E-mail: rbh@ucla.edu.

BHIDE, MANOHAR GOPAL, nuclear scientist, educator; b. Pune, Maharashtra, India, Nov. 9, 1935; arrived in U.S., 1994, naturalized, 2001; s. Gopal Ramachandra and Manorama Gopal Bhide; m. Meena Mohiniraj Joshi, Jan. 7, 1981; children: Unmesh, Amit, Sonia. BSc in Math., U. of Mumbai, 1954, MSc, 1956, PhD, 1971. Registered profl. engr., Argonne Nat. Lab., IL, USA, 1958, cert. Atomic Energy Rsch. Establishment, Harwell, U.K., 1960. Fellow Ramnarain Ruia Coll., Mumbai, India, 1954—56; sci. officer Bhabha Atomic Rsch. Ctr., Trombay, Mumbai, India, 1956—94; adj. faculty in physics No. Va. C.C., Annandale, Va., 1997; substitute tchr. Fairfax County Pub. Schs., Va., 1998—. Exch. scientist Atomic Energy Rsch. Establishment, Harwell, Didcot, Berkshire, United Kingdom, 1958—60; affiliate Internat. Inst. of Nuc. Sci. & Engring., Argonne, Ill., 1960—62; sec. disarmament study group Dept. Atomic Energy Govt. of India, Mumbai, 1962—67; sci. sec. XII Pugwash Conf. on Sci. & World Affairs, Udaipur, Rajasthan, India, 1964—64; Indian del. IAEA Seminar on Physics of Fast & Intermediate Reactors, Vienna, 1961—61, Second UN Conf. on Peaceful Uses of Atomic Energy, Geneva, 1958—58; adj. prof. Southeastern U., Washington, 1999—. Editor: Vidnyan Kutuhal, Marathi Mahasangh-Vidnyan; contbr., articles to profl. jours. Co-founder, treas. Marathi Vidnyan Mahasangh, Mumbai, 1980—81; founder, treas., sec. Madhyamumbai Marathi Vidnyan Sangh, Mumbai, India, 1971—93; co-founder, treas. Mumbai (India) Shubham Karoti Parivar, Mumbai, 1979—88; camp leader Student Voluntary Work Camps, Turbhe, Gorkamat & Kadav, India, 1953—54; active Bhabha Atomic Rsch. Ctr. Maharashtra Mandal, Mumbai, 1970—94, Kokannagar Yuvak Mandal (Youth Club), Mumbai, 1965—75. Recipient V. K. Bhagawat prize, Ramnarain Ruia Coll., Mumbai, India, 1954; scholar, U. of Mumbai, India, 1952—54. Fellow: Soc. for Advancement of Electrochem. Sci. and Tech. (life; internal auditor Mumbai chpt. 1988—93); mem.: Am. Nuc. Soc., Indian Nuc. Soc. (life), Nat. Assn. for Applications of Radiation and Radioactive Isotopes (life), Assn. of Med. Physicists of India (life), Indian Assn. for Radiation Protection (life; mem. organizing com. of ann. conf. 1990), Indian Physics Assn. (life). Avocations: photography, nature walks, music, museums. Home: 8156 Larkin Lane Vienna VA 22182-5232 Personal E-mail: mhbhide@hotmail.com.

BHIDE, RAJEEV S. medical researcher; b. Mumbai, India, Aug. 31, 1956; arrived in USA, 1980; PhD, Case Western Res., 1986. Rsch. investigator Bristol-Myers Squibb, Princeton, NJ, 1990—98, group leader, 1999—2003. Mem.: Am. Assn. of Advancement of Sci., Am. Assn. of Cancer Rsch., Am. Chem Soc. Office: Bristol-Myers Squibb P O Box 4000 Princeton NJ 08543

BHUSHAN, BHARAT, mechanical engineer; b. Jhinjhana, India, Sept. 30, 1949; came to U.S., 1970, naturalized, 1977; s. Narain Dass and Devi (Vati) B.; m. Sudha Bhushan, June 14, 1975; children: Ankur, Noopur. BE Mech. Engring. with honors, Birla Inst. Tech. and Sci., 1970; MSME, MIT, 1971; MS in Mechanics, PhD in Mech. Engring., U. Colo., 1976; MBA, Rensselaer Poly. Inst., 1980; DSc, U. Trondheim, Norway, 1990; D of Tech. Scis., Warsaw (Poland) U. Tech., 1996; D honoris causa, Metal Polymer Rsch. Inst., Nat. Acad. Scis. at Gomel, Belarus, 2000. Mem. rsch. staff dept. mech. engring. MIT, Cambridge, 1971-72; rsch. asst., instr. dept. mech. engring. U. Colo., Boulder, 1973-76; program mgr. R&D divsn. Mech. Tech. Inc., Latham, N.Y., 1976-80; rsch. scientist SKF Industries, Inc., King of Prussia, Pa., 1980-81; adv. engr. IBM, Tucson, 1981-85, devel. engr., mgr., 1985-86; sr. engr., mgr. head-disk interface Almaden Rsch. Ctr. IBM, San Jose, Calif., 1986-91; Ohio eminent scholar, Howard Winbigler prof. mech. engring. Ohio State U., Columbus, 1991—, dir. Computer Microtribology and Contamination Lab., 1991—. Expert investigator Automotive Specialists, Denver, 1973-76; vis. sr. scientist Royal Norwegian Coun. for Sci. and Indsl. Rsch., U. Trondheim, 1987, USSR Acad. Sci., Moscow, 1989; vis. scholar dept. mech. engring., chemistry and materials sci. and mineral engring. U. Calif., Berkeley, 1989; Sony sabbatical chair prof. Sony Corp. Rsch. Ctr., Fujitsuka, Japan, 1997; guest prof. dept. physics and engring. U. Cambridge, 1999; invited presenter worldwide; spkr. internat. confs. Author: Tribology and Mechanics of Magnetic Storage Devices, 1990, Handbook of Tribology, 1991, Mechanics and Reliability of Flexible Magnetic Media, 1992, Handbook of Micro/Natrotribiology, 1995, 2d edit., 1999, Principles and Applications of Tribology, 1999, Modern Tribology Handbook, Vol. 1 Principles of Tribology, 2001, Vol. 2 Materials, Coatings and Industrial Applications, 2001, Introduction to Tribology, 2002; editor 25 books; editor-in-chief, founding editor ASME series Advances in Info. Storage Sys., 1991—; editor-in-chief CRC Mechanics and Materials Sci. series; co-editor-in-chief Microsystem Technologies: Micro-& Nanosystems and Information Storage and Processing Systems, 2002; contbr. handbook chpts., tech. papers, over4005 articles to profl. jours. Recipient Alfred Noble prize ASCE, IEEE, ASME, AIME, Western Soc. Engrs., 1981, Tech. Excellence award Am. Soc. Engrs. India, 1989, Cert. Appreciation award NASA, 1987, Alexander von Humboldt Rsch. prize for sr. scientists U. Ulm, 1998-99, U. Karlsruhe, 1998-99, Fulbright Sr. Scholar award and guest prof. Tech. U. Vienna, 1999, RUN Sr. TOKTEN Expert award, 1999, rsch. award for Outstanding Fgn. Scientists Max Planck Inst. for Metals Rsch., Düsseldorf, Germany, 2002; Ford Found. fellow MIT, 1971; grantee USN, NASA, Dept. Energy, USAF, Franco-Am. Commn. for Ednl. Exch. Interfound. grantee Ecole Cen. Lyon, 1999. Fellow ASME (cert. of recognition Design Engring. Conf., Henry Hess award 1980, Burt L. Newkirk award 1983, Gustus L. Larson Meml. award 1986, tribology divsn. Best Paper award 1989, Melville medal for best current original paper 1992, Bd. Govs. award 1997, 98, Charles Russ Richards Meml. award 2000), N.Y. Acad. Scis.; mem. NSPE, IEEE (sr.), Soc. Tribologists and Lubrication Engrs., Am. Soc. Lubrication Engrs., Am. Acad. Mechanics, Internat. Humanists Soc., Tri-City India Assn., Internat. Acad. Engring. Russia (fgn.), Byelorussian Acad. of Engring. and Tech. (fgn.), Acad. of Triboengring. of Ukraine (fgn.), Soc. of Tribologists of Belarus (hon. mem.), Rotary, Sigma Xi, Tau Beta Pi. Hindu. Achievements include 8 patents in field; pioneer in tribology and mechanics of magnetic storage devices; leading researcher in field of micro/nanotribology using single probe microscopy. Home: 10235 Widdington Close Powell OH 43065-9059 Office: Ohio State U 206 W 18th Ave Columbus OH 43210-1107 E-mail: bhushan.2@osu.edu.

BI, HONGGANG, pharmaceutical executive, researcher; arrived in Can., 1988,arrived in U.S., 1992; s. Hengru Bi and JinMei Zhou; m. Ping Du, July 24, 1985; children: Cathay, Jennifer. PharmB, Zhejiang U., 1982; PhD, McGill U., 1992. From rschr. to asst. dir. SmithKline Beechum Pharm., King of Prussia, Pa., 1993—96, asst. dir., 1996—97; dir. Parke-Davis Pharm. Rsch., Ann Arbor, Mich., 1997—2000, Pfizer Global R&D, Ann Arbor, 2000—01, Groton, Conn., 2001—. Adj. prof. U. Mich., Ann Arbor, 2001—. Mem.: Am. Assn. Pharm. Scientists, Am. Soc. Mass Spectrometry, Am. Chem. Soc. Office: Pfizer Global R&D Eastern Point Rd Groton CT 06340

BI, QI, telecommunications industry executive; b. China; MS Shanghai Jiao Tong U., 1981; PhD, Pa. State U., 1986. Dir. Lucent Techs., Whippany, NJ, 1988—. Tech. chair Wireless Mobile ATM Conf., 1998—99; organizer Lucent IS-95 and UMTS Tech. Conf., 1999—2000; guest prof. Shanghai Jiao Tong U., 2000; fellow Bell Labs, 2001; tech. chair 3G Wireless Conf., 2000—03, Wireless Symposium of IEEE Globecom, 2000—02; tech. vice chair Wireless Comm. and Network Conf., 2003. Dir.: (design and testing) Wireless Mobile CDMA Sys. Design, 2000 (Advanced Tech. Lab award, 1995, 1996, Bell Labs Pres. Gold award, 2000); editor (features): IEEE Comm. mag., 2001; editor: Wireless Comm. and Mobile Computing, 2002. Recipient Pres. Gold award, Bell Labs, 2002. Achievements include development of first wireless mobile CDMA systems; patents for 25 wireless sys. designs. Office: Lucent Techs 67 Whippany Rd Whippany NJ 07981 Business E-Mail: qbi@lucent.com.

BIAFORA, FRANK A. sociologist, educator, dean; s. Frank and Phyllis Biafora. BA in Sociology, U. Fla., 1986, MA in Sociology, 1988; PhD in Sociology, U. Miami, 1991. Rsch. asst. prof. U. Miami, 1991—93; asst. prof. sociology St. John's U., N.Y.C., 1993—99, assoc. prof. sociology, 1999—, assoc. dean, 1999—. Dir. rsch. Samaritan Village, N.Y.C., 1995—99; presenter in field. Contbr. articles to profl. jours. Named to, Outstanding Young Ams., 1998. Mem.: Ronald E. McNair Scholars Dirs., Compact for Faculty Diversity, Assn. Grad. Schs. in Cath. Colls. and Univs., Am. Sociol. Assn., Am. Soc. Criminology, Acad. Criminal Justice Scis., N.E. Assn. Grad. Schs., Coun. Grad. Schs., Am. Assn. Higher Edn., Assn. for Equality and Excellence in Edn. (bd. mem. 2003—), Sigma Delta Pi, Alpha Kappa Delta. Avocations: scuba diving, motorcycling, music. Office: St Johns Univ Grad Divsn 8000 Utopia Pkwy Jamaica NY 11439

BIAGI, RICHARD CHARLES, retail executive, real estate consultant; b. Crockett, Calif., Aug. 29, 1925; s. Louis Joseph and Angelina Antonette (Gambaro) B.; m. Emily Annette Gino, Aug. 7, 1949 (dec.); children: Sharon A. Biagi Juhnke, Sandra A. Biagi Ogden; m. Alice C. Mulder, Nov. 26, 1995. BSBA, U. Calif., Berkeley, 1950, cert. in real estate, 1956. Real estate analyst Safeway Stores inc., Oakland, Calif., 1953-58; real estate negotiator Lucky Stores Inc., San Leandro, Calif., 1958-60, div. real estate mgr., 1960-62, mgr. corp. real estate, v.p. corp. real estate mgr. Dublin, Calif., 1963-86; cons. real estate Alamo, Calif., 1986—. Served with USNR, 1943-46, PTO. Mem. Internat. Council Shopping Ctrs. (trustee 1971-76), U. Calif. Bus. Adminstrn. Alumni Assn. (pres. 1970), Calif. Bus. Properties Assn. (bd. dirs. 1972-92), Toastmasters (pres. San Leandro club 1959). Avocations: photography, biking, golf. Home (Winter): 75-335 St Andrews Ct Indian Wells CA 92210-7656

BIAGIOLI, FRANCES EMILY, physician; b. Saint Louis, Mo., Feb. 10, 1968; d. Mary and Philip Roos(Stepfather); m. Craig Edward Santos; children: Erin Santos, Dean Santos. MD, Med. Coll. of Ohio, 1991—95. Assoc. engr. Gen. Motors, Inland Fisher Guide Divsn., Dayton, Ohio, 1989—91; physician Family Med. Group, Portland, 1998—2000; asst. prof. Oreg. Health & Sciences U., 2000—. Adv. com. ODOT Child Safety Seat Resource Ctr., Portland, 2002—. Contbr. articles to jours. Child seat technician Nat. Hwy. Traffic Safety Adminstrn., Portland, 2000—03. Recipient Merle Pennington, M.D., award, Dept. of Family Medicince OHSU, 1998. Mem.: Oreg. Med. Assn. (del. 1998—2003). Catholic. Avocations: photography, exercising, sewing, art. Office: Oregon Health & Sciences University 4411 SW Vermont St Portland OR 97219

BIAGIOLI, MARIO, history of science educator; b. Prato, Italy, Dec. 17, 1955; came to U.S., 1981; s. Arnolfo Biagioli and Marina Menichetti; m. Kristine Ravetto; children: Gabriel Biagioli-Salzer, Luka Mrsic Ravetto. MFA, Rochester Inst. Technology, N.Y., 1984; MA, U. Calif., Berkeley, 1986, PhD, 1989. From lectr. to assoc. prof. dept. history UCLA, 1988-92; prof. dept. history sci. Harvard U., Cambridge, Mass., 1995—. Vis. prof. Stanford (Calif.) U., 1992, Ecole des Hautes Etudes en Sciences Sociales, Paris, 1992, 99; fellow Dibner Inst. MIT, Cambridge, Mass., 1994-95. Author, editor: Galileo Courtier, 1993, Science Studies Reader, 1999, (with Peter GAlison) Scientific Authorship, 2002. John S. Guggenheim Found. fellow, 1997-98. Mem. AAAS, History of Sci. Soc. (Derek Price award 1991), Social Studies of Sci. Soc., Coun. Sci. Editors, Soc. Ct. Studies, Sci. and Lit. Soc. Office: Harvard U Dept Sci Science Ctr 457 Cambridge MA 02138

BIAL, RAYMOND STEVEN, author, photographer; b. Danville, Ill., Nov. 5, 1948; s. Marion John and Catherine Louise B.; m. Linda Marie Bial; children: Anna, Sarah, Luke. BS, U. Ill., 1970, MS, 1979. Author, photographer: Corn Best Harvest, 1991, County Fair, 1992, Amish Home, 1993, Frontier Home, 1993, Shaker Home, 1994, Portrait of a Farm Family, 1995, The Underground Railroad, 1995, Needle and Thread: A Book about Quilts, 1996, Mist Over the Mountains: Appalachia and Its Poeple, 1997, The Strength of these Arms: Life in the Slave Quarters, 1997, Where Lincoln Walked, 1997, Cajun Home, 1998, One-Room School, 1999, A Handful of Dirt, 2000, The Navajo, 1999, The Cherokee, 1999, The Iroquois, 1999, The Sioux, 1999, The Ojibwe, 2000, The Pueblo, 2000, The Seminole, 2000, The Comanche, 2000, The Apache, 2001, The Huron, 2001, The Haida, 2001, Cheyenne, 2001, Ghost Towns of the American West, 2001, Tenement: Immigrant Life on the Lower East Side, 2002, Building America Series, 2002, The Blackfeet, 2002, The Long Walk: The Story of Navajo Captivity, 2002, The Choctaw, 2002, The Mandan, 2002, The Tlingit, 2002, The Fresh Grave and Other Ghostly Stories, 1997, The Ghost of Honeymoon Creek, 1999, Ivesdale: A Photographic Essay, 1982, In All My Years: Portraits of Older Blacks in Champaign-Urbana, 1985, Upon a Quiet Landscape: The Photographs of Frank Sadous, 1983, There is a Season, 1984, (with Kathryn Kerr) First Frost, 1985, Common Ground: Photographs of Rural and Small Town Life, 1986, Stopping By: Portraits from Small Towns, 1988, (with Linda LaPuma Bial) The Carnegie Library in Illinois, 1988, From the Heart of the Country: Photographs of the Midwestern Kentucky, 1991, Looking Good: A Guide to Photographing Your Library, 1991, Champaign: A Pictorial History, 1993, Visit to Amish Country, 1995, Zoom Lens Photography, 1996. Recipient Best Publicity of 1984 Lib. Pub. Rels. Coun., 1984, Best Publicity of 1986, 1987, Award of Superior Achievement Ill. State Hist. Soc., 1985, Cert. of Commendation Am. Assn. for State and Local History, 1986, Writer's Choice Selection Nat. Endowment for the Arts and the Pushcart Found., 1986, Outstanding Sci. Trade Book for Children, 1991. Mem. Soc. of Children's Book Writers and Illustrators (mem. children's reading roundtable). Roman Catholic. Avocations: gardening, fishing, hiking, traveling. Home: 208 West Iowa St Urbana IL 61801 Office: PO Box 593 Urbana IL 61803-0593 E-mail: ray@raybial.com.

BIALASIEWICZ, JAN TADEUSZ, electrical engineering educator; b. Pruszkow, Poland, June 1, 1939; came to U.S., 1985; s. Piotr Pawel and Wanda Henryka Bialasiewicz; m. Ewa Teresa Wanasz, Sept. 30, 1967; children: Luiza, Seweryn. MS in Elec. Engring., Warsaw (Poland) Tech. U., 1962; PhD in Elec. Engring., Silesian Tech. U., Gliwice, Poland, 1966; DSc in Elec. Engring., Silesian Tech. U., 1972. Registered profl. engr., Colo. Head, computer control software dept. Indsl. Inst. Automation and Measurements, Warsaw, 1969-78; assoc. prof. elec. engring. Higher Inst. Electronics, Malta, 1979-80; head, computer control software dept. Nuc. Rsch. Inst., Warsaw, 1980-85; assoc. prof. elec. engring. U. Colo., Denver, 1985—. Vis. rsch. assoc., NASA Langley Rsch. Ctr., Hampton, Va., summers, 1990, 91, NASA/ASEE fellow, 1993; cons. Nat. Renewable Energy Lab., Golden, Colo., 1994—; vis. prof., Warsaw Tech. U., 1997. Author: Wavelets and Approximations, 2000; contbr. articles to profl. jours. Pres. Rocky Mountain chpt. Kosciuszko Found., Denver, 1993—. Named Prof. Tech. Scis., Pres. Republic of Poland, 2001. Mem. IEEE, AAUP, Polish Inst. Arts and Scis. in Am. Roman Catholic. Avocations: travel, skiing, classical music. Office: U Colo at Denver CB110 PO Box 173364 Denver CO 80217 E-mail: jtbialas@carbon.cudenver.edu.

BIALER, MARTIN GEORGE, geneticist; b. N.Y.C., June 10, 1952; s. Henry Bialer and Ethel (Raffel) Albert; m. Rachel Sydney Baron, May 5, 1991. BA, Cornell U., 1973; PhD, Med. U. S.C., 1980, MD, 1983. Diplomate Am. Bd. Pediatrics, Am. Bd. Med. Genetics. Intern and resident in pediatrics North Shore U. Hosp., Manhasset, N.Y., 1983-86, assoc. in genetics, 1989—; fellow in genetics U. Va., Charlottesville, 1986-89; asst. prof. pediatrics Cornell U., N.Y.C., 1989-97, NYU Sch. of Medicine, N.Y.C., 1997-99, assoc. prof. clin. pediats., 1999—, chief divsn. med. genetics, 1999—. Contbr. articles to Clin. Cardiology, Clin. Chemistry, Am. Jour. Med. Genetics, European Jour. Pediatrics. Muscular Dystrophy Assn. fellow, 1988-89. Fellow Am. Acad. Pediatrics; mem. AMA, Am. Soc. Human Genetics, Am. Coll. Med. Genetics, Nassau Pediatrics Soc., Alpha Omega Alpha. Democrat. Jewish. Office: North Shore U Hosp Dept Pediatrics 300 Community Dr Manhasset NY 11030-3801 E-mail: mbialer@lij.edu.

BIALKIN, KENNETH JULES, lawyer, director; b. N.Y.C., Sept. 9, 1929; s. Samuel and Lillian (Kastner) B.; m. Ann Eskind, Aug. 19, 1956; children: Lisa Beth, Johanna. AB, U. Mich., 1950; cert. of attendance, London Sch. Econ., 1952; JD, Harvard U., 1953. Bar: N.Y. 1953, U.S. Dist. Ct. (ea. dist.) N.Y. 1955, U.S. Supreme Ct. 1964, U.S. Dist. Ct. (so. dist.) N.Y. 1972, U.S. Ct. Appeals (2d cir.) 1976. Assoc. Willkie Farr & Gallagher, N.Y.C., 1953-60, ptnr., 1960-88, Skadden, Arps, Slate, Meagher & Flom, N.Y.C., 1988—. Adj. prof. law NYU, 1967-87; lectr., commentator legal and fin. symposia; mem. N.Y. Stock Exch. Legal Adv. Commn., 1983-92, 98—, chmn. internat. securities subcom., 1989-98; bd. dirs. Travelers Property and Casualty Co., 1986-2002, Mcpl. Assistance Corp. City of N.Y., Sapiens Internat., Ltd., Tecnomatix Techs., Ltd.; mem. Adminstrv. Conf. of U.S., 1987-92; chmn. Com. on Fin. Svcs.; vis. com. grad. faculty New Sch. for Social Rsch., 1992—. Editor: The Business Lawyer, 1980; bd. editors Corp. Governance Jour., 1992—; contbr. articles on corp., fin. investment law to profl. jours. Chmn. Conf. Pres. Major Am. Jewish Orgns., 1984-86; chmn. Am.-Israel Friendship League, 1995—; nat. chmn. Anti-Defamation League B'nai Brith, 1982-86; pres. Jewish Cmty. Rels. Coun. N.Y., 1989-92; vice-chmn., dir. Jerusalem Found., Inc., 1975—. Mem. ABA (chmn. fed. regulation securities com. 1974-79, chmn. com. to study fgn. investment in U.S. 1978-80, chmn. ad hoc com. on insider trading regulation 1988—, chmn. sect. corp. banking and bus. law 1981-82, 88), Am. Jewish Hist. Soc. (pres. 1997—), N.Y. County Lawyers Assn. (pres. 1986-88), Am. Bar Retirement Assn. (dir. 1981-84), Coun. Fgn. Rels., Harvard Club. Home: 211 Central Park W New York NY 10024-6020 Office: Skadden Arps Slate Meagher & Flom Fl 44 4 Times Sq New York NY 10036-6595 E-mail: kbialkin@skadden.com.

BIALLA, ROWLEY, lawyer; b. N.Y.C., Aug. 13, 1914; s. Edward and Amy (Rowley) B.; m. Marian L. Dunham, Mar. 23, 1945 (div. Mar. 1951); children: Margaret L., Jean B. Murphy; m. Mary S. Wilson, Aug. 21, 1954; 1 child, Nancy R. AB, Dartmouth Coll., 1937; LLB, Yale U., 1940. Bar: N.Y. 1940; U.S. Supreme Ct. 1945. Assoc. White & Case, N.Y.C., 1940-41, 46-51; house

counsel Guggenheim Interests, N.Y.C., 1952-79; pvt. practice, Northport, NY, 1979—2002. Sec. Daniel and Florence Guggenheim Found., N.Y.C., 1979-2002; sec., bd. dirs. Lavanburg Found., N.Y.C., 1981-2002. Capt. U.S. Army, 1941-45. Mem. ABA. Avocations: history, genealogy. Home and Office: Apt 7406 575 Osgood St North Andover MA 01845-1991 Fax: 978-794-8772.

BIALO, KENNETH MARC, lawyer; b. N.Y.C., Nov. 21, 1946; s. Walter and Mildred (Miller) B.; m. Katherine Ann Burghard; children: Darren Andrew, Caralyn Alyssa, Jacquelyn Anne, Matthew Joseph Geronimo, Kelsey Elizabeth Ariel. BS, U. Rochester, 1968; JD cum laude (Univ. scholar), NYU, 1971; LLM, London Sch. Econs., 1973. Bar: N.Y. 1972, U.S. Ct. Appeals (2d cir.) 1974, U.S. Ct. Appeals (fed. cir.) 1988, U.S. Supreme Ct. 1975. Law clk. Hon. L.W. Pierce U.S. Dist. Ct. (so. dist.) N.Y., 1971—72; assoc. Sullivan & Cromwell, N.Y.C., 1973—80; counsel, sr. counsel Exxon Corp., NYC, 1980—90; sr. counsel, chief litigation atty. Exxon Chem. Co., Darien, Conn., 1990—91; ptnr. Baker Botts, LLP, N.Y.C., 1992—. Lectr. Practicing Law Inst., N.Y.C., 1982, 88, N.Y. State Bar Assn., 1997; vice chmn. bd. State of N.Y. Mcpl. Bond Bank Agy., N.Y.C., 2000—. Contbg. editor: Family Legal Guide, 1974; contbr. articles to profl. jours.; note and comment editor: NYU Law Rev.; host The Larchmont Report, WVOX, Whitney Radio Group, New Rochelle, N.Y., 1995—, co-host Larchmont Today, LMC-TV, Mamaroneck, N.Y., 1995—, co-founder, prin. contbr.: Plugged In, Rep. Party Pub. Svc. Newsletter, 1996—. Trustee Village of Larchmont, N.Y., 1991-2002, mayor, 2002—; mem. PLI Adv. Com. on Litig., 1994—; bd. govs., Univ. Club Larchmont, 1995-1999, pres., 1998-1999; v.p., bd. dirs. Little League, Larchmont, 1985-94, mem. recreation com., 1987-89; treas., mem. exec. com. L.I. Sound Watershed Intermcpl. Coun., Westchester County, N.Y., 2000-2002; mem. Westchester County Legis. Stormwater Adv. Com., 2001—. Mem. ABA (litig. sect. task force on client concerns 1994-95, subcom. class action, litig. sect.), N.Y. State Bar (antitrust com., fed. and comml. litig. sect., former chmn. corp. counsel com. 1989-91), Assn. of Bar of City of N.Y. (arbitration com. 1983-85), Fed. Bar Coun. (com. 2d cir. cts. 1985-87), Am. Arbitration Assn. (mem. arbitrators panel), Order of Coif. Avocations: tennis, baseball, opera, symphony. Office: Baker Botts LLP 30 Rockefeller Plaza New York NY 10112-4498

BIANCHERIA, AMILCARE, environmental scientist, consultant; s. Annibale and Aggrepina Biancheria; m. Shirley Lynn Biancheria, Oct. 2, 1993; children: Damien(dec.), Christine. BA in Chemistry with Honors, Clark U, 1952, MA in Phys. Chemistry, 1954, PhD in Phys. Chemistry, 1957. Sr. engr. Westinghouse, Madison, Pa., 1960—67, mgr. fuel irradiation, 1967—80, mgr. fuel analysis, 1980—86; mgr. environ. restoration Westinghouse Material of Ohio, Cin., 1986—93; dir. mktg. AWK Cons. Engr.,Inc., Turtle Creek, Pa., 1994—96; cons. pvt. practice, Irwin, Pa., 1997—. Chmn. Plutonuim Lab. Safety Comm., Westinghouse, Cheswick, Pa., 1977—79; chair nat. team that devel. first of kind computer code for analyzing fast reactor fuel performance DOE, Gaithersurg, Md., 1979—82, chair nat. team for verifying safety properties of nuclear fuels, 1980—82. Contbr. scientific papers. Judge of elections East Adamsburg District, Hempfield, Pa., 1999—2003; mem. Greater Pitt Conv. & Vis. Ctr., Pitts., 2001—, Democratic Comm., Westmoreland County, Pa., 2002—06. Mem.: Am. Chemical Soc., N.Y. Acad. of Sci., Italian Sons & Daughters of Am. (Nat. Councilor 2000—), Toastmasters Internat. (Distinguished Toastmaster 1965). Achievements include patents for No.,477,222 Nuclear Fuel Elements; development of statistical method for establishing thermal limits of nuclear fuels; statistical method to predict fuel rod failure rates in fast reactor fuels. Avocations: chess, swimming, dancing, magic. Home and Office: 310 Arona Rd Irwin PA 15642

BIANCHI, CHARLES PAUL, technical and business executive, money manager, financial consultant; b. Texarkana, Tex., Sept. 3, 1945; s. Angelo Paul and Jewel Evelyn (LaFayette) B.; m. Stephanie Ellquist, Aug. 11, 1973; children: Charles Brandon LaFayette, Canaan Desiree Ellquist. BA, Dickinson Coll., 1967; M in Bus. Mgmt., Cen. Mich. U., 1976. Cert. fin. planner, registered investment adviser; cert. graphoanalyst. Vol. Peace Corps, 1969-71; employment orientation instr. Pa. Bur. Employment Security, Scranton, 1971-72; mgmt. analyst Defense Logistics Agy., Phila., 1972-75, program, sr. budget analyst Alexandria, Va., 1975-78; fed. budget specialist Exec. Office Pres., Office Mgmt. and Budget, Washington, 1978-83; owner, prin. Charles P. Bianchi Fin. Planning and Investment Adv. Services, Arlington, Va., 1984-89; internal cons. Inter-Am. Devel. Bank, Washington, 1983-89; pres. Wealth Conservancy Internat., Inc., Arlington, 1988—, pres./CEO Albany, Oreg., 1990-97. Rep. Office Mgmt. and Budget, Am. Assn. Budget and Prog. Analysts, Washington, 1976-77; reg. rep. affiliate Tucker Anthony, R.L. Day, 1987-89. Chair bd. dirs. Arlingtonians for a Clean Environment. Mem. Fin. Planning Assn., Washington Soc. Investment Analysts, Assn. Investment Mgmt. and Rsch., Capital Region Soc. Cert. Fin. Planners, Nat. Wildlife Fedn. (habitat steward), Kiwanis Club South Arlington (pres.), Theta Chi., The Red Cir., The World Affaris Coun. Avocations: military history, musician, military conflict simulation gaming, cross-country skiing graphoanalysis. Home and Office: 224 N Fillmore St Arlington VA 22201-1228 E-mail: wciicpb@earthlink.net.

BIANCHI, DAVID WAYNE, lawyer; b. Amsterdam, NY, June 12, 1950; s. Fred and Palma (Biasi) B.; m. Frances Shekter, Apr. 12, 1981; 1 child, Nicholas David. BS, Fla. State U., 1972; JD, San Fernando Valley Coll., 1979. Bar: Califr. 1979, U.S. Dist. Ct. (cen. dist.) Calif. 1981, U.S. Dist. Ct. (ea. dist.) Calif. 1992; cert. specialist in family law Calif. Bd. Legal Specialization. Dep. city atty. City of Lancaster, Calif., 1984-87; ptnr. Michelizzi, Schwabacher, Ward & Bianchi, Lancaster, 1980—. Past instr. bus. law Antelope Valley C.C., Lancaster; judge pro tem, referee LA County Superior Ct. Mem. adv. bd. Salvation Army, 1991—. Mem. Antelope Valley Bar Assn. (pres. 1988, chmn. fee arbitration com. 1994—), Kiwanis Club Antelope Valley (bd. dirs. 1984-2001, pres. 1998-99), Elks (exalted ruler 1986-87). Avocations: golf, fishing, sports, coaching soccer. Office: Michelizzi Schwabacher Ward & Bianchi 767 W Lancaster Blvd Lancaster CA 93534-3118

BIANCHI, HOLLIS DOLCE, writer, artist; b. Orange, NJ, June 25, 1952; d. Ovid Carlo Bianchi and Matilda Florence Dolce. AAS, Marymount U., Arlington, VA, 1978. Pvt. practice, Leonardo, NJ, 1992—. Mem.: Nat. Mus. Women Arts. Avocations: playing the harmonica, embroidery, reading classics. Home: 49 Florence Avenue Leonardo NJ 07737 Personal E-mail: dmapelli@aol.com.

BIANCHI, MARIA, critical care specialist, adult and acute care nurse practitioner, nursing administration; Grad., Catherine Laboure Sch. Nursing, 1979, Fitchburg (Mass.) State Coll., 1985; grad. clin. specialist in nursing adminstrn., Russell Sage Coll., Troy, N.Y. Cert. post-anesthesia care nurse; critical care clin. specialist. Recovery as mgmt. educator; mktg. and recruitment cons.; cons. in critical care nursing; adminstr. dept. spl. svcs., mgr. critical care Baystate Med. Ctr., Springfield, Mass., 1980-89; recruitment adminstrn. and sr. faculty St. Francis Med. Ctr. Sch. of Nursing, Hartford, Conn., 1989-92; grad. faculty U. Mass. Med. Ctr., Worcester, 1995-97; per diem nurse practitoner dept. surgery U. Mass. Sch. of Nursing, Worcester, 1995-97, 99—, faculty Amherst; clin. faculty Am. Internat. Coll., Springfield; asst. prof. Grad. Sch. U. Mass., Amherst, 1998-99. Rsch. in pain, burn trauma, stress reduction, holistic methods for high risk individuals in maximum security penitentiary and critical care patients; nat. cons. for critical care/post anesthesia issues, pres. TransInternat. Healthcare; nat. lectr. AHI, Balt.; expert witness, Mass. and Conn.; medicolegal cons.; laser med. provider; lectr. on critical care and post anesthesia issues, empowerment, acute pain, holistic techniques, medicological documentation, trauma. Invited ambassador del. People's for People's, Fed. Govt. Mem. AACN, Am. Soc. Post-Anesthesia Nursing (Boston chpt. editl. cons.), Soc. Critical Medicine, Mass. Gen. Hosp. Alumni Assn., Catherine Laboure Alumni Assn., Sigma Theta Tau. Office: PO Box 614 Suffield CT 06078-0614

BIANCO, ANTHONY, music educator; b. New Haven, Conn., Sept. 3, 1917; s. Giovanni and Immaculata Migliore Bianco; m. Angela Irene Boccella; children: Joseph, Marian, Celeste, Margaret, Louise, Anne, Lisa. Bassist New Haven Symphony, 1936—41, Hartford Symphony, Conn., 1938—41, N.Y. Opera Co., N.Y.C., 1941—44; prin. bass Pitts. Symphony, 1944—99, Chautauqua Symphony, NY, 1944—55; instr. Chatham Coll. Day Camp, Pitts., 1955—70; artist lectr. Carnegie Mellon U., Pitts., 1945—. Presenter internat. bass convs., 1984—2000; condr. summer bass workshops George Vance, Silver Spring, Md., 1995—; instr. master classes, 1984—; 1st performance Iadone Sonata - Hindemi Hi Class, 1944; 1st performance of Quincy Porter's Lyric Piece Yale U., 1949. With U.S. Army, 1942—43. Recipient 50 Yr. Tribute, Carnegie Mellon U., 1995, Golden Laureate award, Pitts. Symphony, 1999. Mem.: Pitts. Musicians Union. Roman Catholic. Avocations: walking, reading, travel. Home: 3833 Ridgeway Dr Allison Park PA 15101 Office: Carnegie Mellon Univ Sch of Music 5000 Forbes Ave Pittsburgh PA 15213

BIANCO, ANTHONY JOSEPH, III, newswriter; b. Oceanside, Calif., May 17, 1953; s. Anthony Joseph Jr. and JoAnn (Reavill) B.; 1 child, Marissa. BA, U. Minn., 1976. Reporter Mpls. Tribune, 1977; bus. editor Willamette Week newspaper, Portland, Oreg., 1978-80; corr. Bus. Week mag., San Francisco, 1980-82, dept. editor N.Y.C., 1982-84, assoc. editor, 1984-85, sr. writer, 1985-92, 1996—. Author: Rainmaker, 1991, The Reichmanns, 1997. Recipient media award for econ. understanding Amos Tuck Sch., Dartmouth Coll., 1979, award for feature writing Oreg. Newspaper Pubs., 1979, award for excellence in fin. writing N.Y. State Soc. CPA's, 1987, Disting. Editorial Achievement award McGraw-Hill, 1986, Nat. Bus. Book award, Can., 1997. Mem. Soc. Profl. Journalists, N.Y. Fin. Writers Assn. Home: 17 1st St Brooklyn NY 11231-5001

BIANCO, FERNANDO J. urologist, surgeon; b. Phila., Oct. 6, 1969; s. Fernando J. Bianco C. and Ylayaly Troconis-Berti. Student, Wayne State U., 1997—2003. Bd. cert. Am. Urol. Assn., 2003. With dept. urology Meml. Sloan-Kettering Cancer Ctr., N.Y.C. Contbr. articles to profl. jours. Achievements include research in field of urology. Office: Memorial Sloan-Kettering Cancer Ctr Dept Urology 1275 York Ave New York NY 10021 Personal E-mail: biancofj@mac.com. E-mail: biancofj@mac.com.

BIANCONI, MARCELO, education educator; b. Sao Paulo, Brazil, Apr. 28, 1956; m. Celia R.P. Bianconi, Feb. 11, 1955; 1 child, Giampaolo. MA, U. of Ill., 1985, PhD, 1988. Vis. asst. prof. U. of Wash., Seattle, 1989—89; assoc. prof. econs. Tufts U., Medford, Mass., 1989—. Cons. World Bank, 1987—88; exec. sec. Internat. Econs. and Fin. Soc., 2000—02. Author: (acad. jour. articles) Financial Economics. Mem.: Internat. Econs. and Fin. Soc. (life).

BIAS, DANA G. lawyer; b. Lexington, Ky., Mar. 12, 1959; d. Cyrus Dana and Betty Jo (Haddox) B. BA with highest honors, U. Louisville, 1981; JD magna cum laude, Boston U., 1984. Bar: Mass. 1985, N.Y. 1985, Ky. 1995, Tex. 2000, U.S. Dist. Ct. (so. and ea. dists.) N.Y. 1986, U.S. Dist. Ct. (ea. dist.) Tex. 2000. Counselor Mass. Half-Way Houses, Inc., Boston, 1982-83; sr. trial atty. Criminal Def. div. Legal Aid Soc., N.Y.C., 1984-89, mng. atty., 1989-94; sole practitioner Hauppauge, N.Y., 1995; sr. trial atty. Louisville-Jefferson County Pub. Defender Corp., 1995-97; asst. public advocate, capital trial atty. Dept. of Public Advocacy, 1997-2000; mng. atty. Lone Star Legal Aid, Nacogdoches, 2000—03, Beaumont, Tex., 2002—. Lectr. N.Y.C. Pub. Schs., 1989, AAUW, 2001. Contbr. articles to profl. jours. Mem. Nacogdoches Mayor's Com. on People with Disabilities. Mem. ABA, ACLU, N.Y. State Bar Assn., Nat. Assn. Criminal Def. Lawyers, Mass. Bar Assn., Ky. Bar Assn., Tex. Bar Assn., Jefferson County Bar Assn. (pro bono bd. dirs.), NLADA, N.Y. Civil Liberties Union, Woodcock Soc., Mortar Bd., Phi Kappa Phi, Phi Eta Sigma. Democrat. Office: Lone Star Legal Aid PO Box 2552 Beaumont TX 77704-2552 E-mail: dbias@lonestarlegal.org.

BIASINI, VIRGINIA, social worker; b. N.Y.C., July 5, 1939; d. Albert Eugene and Irene Veronica (Kuzmiak) B. BA, Coll. Mt. St. Vincent, Bronx, N.Y., 1977; MSW, Hunter Coll. CUNY, 1980. Cert. social worker, N.Y., sch. social worker, N.J., clin. hypnotherapist Wellness Inst., Seattle; diplomate Am. Bd. Examiners in Clin. Social Work; lic. clin. social worker, N.J. Office mgr. Wiltwyck Sch. for Boys, N.Y.C., 1963-66; adminstrv. asst. to law ptnr. Acme Quilting Co., Inc., N.Y.C., 1966-73; adminstrv. asst. to chmn. bd. Calvary Hosp., Bronx, 1973-77, oncology social worker, 1977-78, patient rep. program coord., 1978-81; med. social worker Westchester Sq. Med. Ctr., Bronx, 1981-84, sr. social worker, supr., 1984-86; asst. dir. social work dept. Cabrini Med. Ctr., N.Y.C., 1986; dir. social work discharge planning dept. Westchester Sq. Med. Ctr., Bronx, 1986-90; individual, family and group social worker, counselor Kimball-Manchester Ambulatory Care Ctr. div. Kimball Med. Ctr., Whiting, N.J., 1990-96; field work instr. Kean Coll., 1996—; Kimball field work instr. Georgian Ct. Coll., 1997—; with outpatient clinics bereavement program Kimball Med. Ctr. Lakewood Divsn., 1996—. Instr. field work Union Theol. Sem., 1978-79, Lehman Coll., CUNY, Bronx, 1988-90; mem. adj. faculty Coll. Mt. St. Vincent, 1981-82. Mem. NASW, Acad. Cert. Social Workers, Soc. Social Work Dirs., Nat. Soc. Social Work Dirs., Am. Hosp. Assn. Office: Kimball Med Ctr 600 River Ave Lakewood NJ 08701-5237

BIBAUD, RENE, artist, performer, consultant; b. Longbranch, N.J., Nov. 21, 1969; d. Richard Charles and Mildred Ellen Bibaud. Artist performer Cirque Du Soleil, Montreal, 1996—2001; artist performer/cons. self employed, Kirkland, Wash., 2001—02. Home: 10721 NE 138th Pl Kirkland WA 98034 Personal E-mail: renebibaud@compuserve.com.

BIBB, DANIEL ROLAND, antique painting restorer and conservator; b. Gadsden, Ala., June 10, 1951; s. Cassius Roland and Louise Selma B. Student, Jefferson State, 1969-70, DeKalb Coll., 1971-72. Sales cons. Macy's Antique Gallery, Atlanta, 1973; dir. Collector's Gallery, Atlanta, 1974-76, Connoisseur's Gallery, New Orleans, 1977-79; painting conservator Daniel R. Bibb Fine Painting Conservation & Restoration, Atlanta, 1980—; chief fund raiser Atlanta Rabbit Rescue. Researcher for pvt. collectors and museums, Atlanta, 1977-89; listed conservator, New Orleans Museum List of Restorers, New Orleans, 1988. Discovered a lost major painting of Philip IV of Spain; exhibited lost painting Atlanta High Mus. Art, 1980; publ.of discovered painting, High Mus. Monthly, 1980; conservator Anglo-Am. Art Mus., Baton Rouge, New Orleans Mus. Art.; owner Fabergè collection on loan to New Orleans Mus. Art, 1996; icon collection touring mus., La., Miss. and Ala., 1998—; contbr. articles on art and art rsch. to nat. mags. Fund raiser Am. Heart Assn., Atlanta, 1987, 88, March of Dimes, 1987, 88, Atlanta Rabbit Rescue, 1984—; mem. High Mus. of Art, Atlanta; vol. ARC Disaster Relief Team, Atlanta, 1992, Art Care Art Auction for fight against AIDS, 1992, 93, chmn. Live Auction, 1993. Recipient Design award, Most Authentic Design, Patio Planters of the Vieux Carre, New Orleans, 1977. Mem. Nat. Trust for Historic Preservation. Republican. Baptist. Achievements include raising funds and pub. awareness of animal cruelty. Home and Office: Bibb Painting Restoration 807 Summit North Dr NE Atlanta GA 30324-5641

BIBBO, CHRISTOPHER, physician; b. Teaneck, N.J., July 14, 1960; s. Anthony James Sr. Bibbo and Carolyn Elizabeth (Flaugher) Lynch; m. Lori K. Nilsen, June 28, 1986; children: Britta, Reid. BA, Rowan Coll. of N.J., 1983; DPM, Pa. Coll. Podiatric Medicine, 1988; DO, U. Medicine/Dentistry of N.J., 1994. Diplomate Am. Bd. Podiatric Orthopedics. Resident in podiatric medicine and surgery Med. Coll. Hosp., Warminster, Pa., 1989; intern U. Medicine and Dentistry N.J./Atlantic City Med. Ctr., 1994; resident in gen. surgery U. Medicine and Dentistry N.J./N.J. Med. Sch., 1995; resident in orthopedic surgery U. Medicine and Dentistry N.J., 1995-2000. Presenter in field. Contbr. articles to profl. jours. Fellow Am. Coll. of Foot Orthopedists; mem. AMA (student sect.), N.J. Med. Soc. (publs. com., student mem.), Am. Osteopathic Assn., N.J. Assn. of Osteopathic Physicians and Surgeons, Assn. of Mil. Osteo. Physicians and Surgeons, Student Osteopathic Surg. Assn. Avocations: outdoors, bicycling, gardening, lepidoptery, community activities. Home: 1000 Colonial St Marshfield WI 54449-1225 E-mail: bibboch@alltel.net.

BIBBO, MARLUCE, physician, educator; b. Sao Paulo, Brazil, July 14, 1939; d. Domingos and Yolanda (Ranciaro) B. M.D, U. Sao Paulo, 1963, Sc.D., 1968. Intern Hosps. das Clinicas, U. Sao Paulo, 1963; resident in morphology, 1964-66; instr. dept. morphology and ob-gyn U. Sao Paulo, 1966-68, asst. prof., 1968-69; fellow in cytology U. Chgo., 1969-70, asst. prof. sect. cytology dept. ob-gyn, 1971-73, assoc. prof., 1973-77, assoc. prof. pathology, 1974-77, prof. ob-gyn and pathology, 1978-92; assoc. dir. Cytology Lab., Approved Sch. Cytotech and Cytocybernetics, AMA-Am. Soc. Clin. Pathologists, 1970-91; dir. Cytology Lab., Phila., 1992; prof. pathology and cell biology Thomas Jefferson U., Phila., 1992—, Warren R. Lane prof. pathology & cell biology, 1993—. Mem. rsch. com. Ill. divsn. Am. Cancer Soc., 1976-91. Contbr. numerous articles to profl. jours. Fellow Internat. Acad. Cytology (pres.-elect, v.p. 1987, pres. 1992, dep. editor Acta Cytologica, editor 1995), Am. Soc. Clin. Pathologists (coun. on cytopathology); mem. Am. Soc. Cytology (exec. com., pres. 1982-83), U.S. Acad. Pathology, Can. Acad. Pathology, Soc. Analytical Cytology, Coun. Cytopathology. Home: 250 S 9th St Philadelphia PA 19107-5734 Office: Cytology Lab Rm 260 Main Bldg 132 S 10th St Philadelphia PA 19107-5244 E-mail: marluce.bibbo@mail.tju.edu.

BIBBY, JOHN FRANKLIN, political science educator, writer; b. LaCrosse, Wis., Aug. 26, 1934; s. Joseph Winder and Mildred May (Franklin) B.; m. Lucile Helen Hanson, Aug. 16, 1958; children: John F. Jr., Peter Mark. BS, U. Wis., LaCrosse, 1956; MA, U. Ill., 1957; PhD, U. Wis., 1963. Fellow in govt. Brookings Inst., Washington, 1961-62; asst. prof. U. Wis., Milw., 1962-63, assoc. prof., 1966-72, prof. polit. sci., 1972—; asst. prof. No. Ill. U., DeKalb, 1963-65; adminstrv. asst. to chmn. Rep. Nat. Com., Washington, 1965-66; exec. dir. Ho. Rep. Conf. U.S. Ho. Reps., Washington, 1969-70. Dir. congress study Am. Enterprise Inst., Washington, 1979-86; lectr. in field. Author: Party Organization in American Politics, 1984, Parties, Politics and Elections in America, 1987, 5th edit., 2003, Governing by Consent, 1st edit., 1992, 2d edit. 1995, Two Parties or More?, 1998, 2d edit., 2003; contbr. articles to profl. jours. Alt. del. Rep. Nat. Conv., Kansas City, 1976, Dallas, 1984, New Orleans, 1988; exec. dir. Platform Com. Rep. Nat. Conv., Kansas City, 1976; vice-chmn. Rep. Party Wis., Madison, 1977-85. Mem. Am. Polit. Sci. Assn. (trustee, devel. bd. 1994-99, chmn. polit. orgns. & parties field 1995-97, Best Pub. Paper, Eldsvold Lifetime Achievement award 2001), Pi Sigma Alpha (pres. 1996-98). Presbyterian. Avocations: golf, reading. Office: U Wis Dept Polit Sci PO Box 413 Milwaukee WI 53201-0413

BIBEAULT, DONALD BERTRAND, business executive, investor; b. Woonsocket, R.I., Nov. 14, 1941; s. George Bertrand and Renee (Herbert) B.; m. Gigi Loving, June 18, 1994 (div. June 2002); children: Zachary James, Jessica Renee, Dorothy Leigh. BSEE, U. R.I., 1963; MBA, Columbia U., 1965; PhD, Golden Gate U., 1979, JD (hon.), 2000. COO Pacific States Steel, Union City, Calif., 1975-78, PLM Internat., San Francisco, 1979-81; turnaround advisor Varity Corp., 1981-82; pres., CEO Best Pipe and Steel Co., San Francisco, 1983-86; workout advisor Bank of Am., 1987-89; chmn. Am. Nat. Petrol, Houston, 1990-91; chmn., CEO Tyler Dawson Supply Co., Tulsa, 1990-91, Iron Oak Supply Co., Sacramento, 1990-93; pres. Bibeault and Assocs., Inc., San Rafael, Calif., 1976—. Bd. trustees Golden Gate U., San Francisco, 1986-97; bd. advisors U. R.I. Bus., Kinston, 1993—; bd. overseers Columbia Grad. Sch. Bus., N.Y.C., 1994—; bd. visitors Golden Gate U. Law Sch., San Francisco, 2000—; CEO adviser underperforming cos., 1993—; chmn. bd. dirs. Biqune Corp., Seattle, 2003—. Author: Corporate Turnaround, 1982 (Fortune award 1982); contbr. articles to profl. jours. Adv. bd. on trade Dept. of Commerce, Washington, 1988-92. Lt. U.S. Army, 1963-65. Mem. Turnaround Mgmt. Assn. (founding dir. 1987-91), Bankers Club San Francisco. Home and Office: Bibeault Assocs 1 Dooley Ct Novato CA 94945 E-mail: bibeault@aol.com.

BIBERMAN, LUCIEN MORTON, physicist, researcher; b. Phila., May 31, 1919; s. Lewis and Eva (Kerns) Biberman; m. Anne H. Wilner, Mar. 8, 1941 (dec. 1997); children: Leslie Biberman Gordon, Judith Biberman Robinson, Candace Biberman Evans; m. Virgina L. Hewitt, May 25, 2002. BS, Rensselaer Poly. Inst., 1940; postgrad., Harvard U., 1940-41, Stevens Inst., 1941-42. Phys. chemist Nairn Rsch. Labs., 1942-43; physicist in charge Mayport Magnetic Survey Area, Navy Dept., 1943-44; various positions from physicist in charge phys. measurements group to cons. Aviation Ordnance Dept. and Weapons Devel. Dept. Naval Ordnance Test Sta., 1944-57; assoc. dir. Labs. for Applied Scis. U. Chgo., 1957-63; rsch. staff rsch. and engring. support div. Inst. for Def. Analysis, Alexandria, Va., 1963-71, rsch. staff sci. and tech. div., 1972-96; emeritus, 1996—. Vis. prof. dept. elec. engring. U. R.I., 1971-72; fellow Mil. Sensing Symposium, 1999. Decorated citation U.S. Army Ctr. for Night Vision and Electro Optics; recipient Andrew J. Goodpaster award, 1989. Fellow: Washington Acad. of Sci. (Disting. Career in Sci. award), Soc. Photo-optical Instrumentation Engrs. (emeritus), Soc. Info. Display (emeritus), Optical Soc. Am. (emeritus), IEEE (life), Military Sensors Symposium, Infrared Info. Symposia. Home: 5904 Lenox Rd Bethesda MD 20817-6050 Office: Inst for Def Analysis 4850 Mark Center Dr Alexandria VA 22311-1882

BIBILASHVILI, TAMAR, physicist, educator; b. Tbilisi, Georgia, Aug. 21, 1958; arrived in U.S., 2000; d. Nobar and Tina Bibilashvili; m. Shalva Taktakishvili, Dec. 20, 1980 (div. Sept. 1989); 1 child, David Taktakishvili; m. Merab Abdaladze. M, Georgian Tech. U., 1980; PhD of Physics and Math., Tbilisi State U., 1994. Sr. engr. Munition Rsch. Facility Mion, Tbilisi, 1980—86; rsch. officer Tbilisi State U., 1986—99, asst. prof., lectr. Physics Facility, 1999—. Mem. adv. bd. Oceanographic Rsch. Ctr. UNESCO, Tbilisi, 1999—; expert scientist Ministry Environment and Natural Resource Protection, Tbilisi, 1998—. Contbr. Recipient Award, U. Saarbrucken, 1999; grantee, Soros Found., 1998, Georgia Dept. Sci. and Tech., 1998. Mem.: N.Y. Acad. Scis., Am. Geophys. Union, European Geophys. Soc. Avocations: music, swimming, travel, philosophy. Office: Tbilisi State Univ Physics Facility 3 Chavchavedze Ave 380028 Tbilisi Georgia*

BIBLE, GEOFFREY CYRIL, former tobacco company executive; b. Canberra, Australia, Aug. 12, 1937; s. Cyril Edward Bible and Dorothea Elizabeth (O'Brien) McGrath; m. Sara Curtis Anderson-Emery, Sept. 10, 1965; children: Mary, Tom, Kim. Chartered Acct., Australia, cost and mgmt. acct., U.K. Fin. dir. UN, Lebanon and Jordan, 1959—64; budget mgr. ILO, Switzerland, 1965—66; fin. mgr. Esso Med., Switzerland, 1966—68; mgr. corp. planning Philip Morris Europe, Switzerland, 1968—70; mgr. R.W. king & Yuill, Stockbrokers, Switzerland, 1970—76; dir. corp. planning Phliip Morris, Switzerland, 1976—78; v.p. Philip Morris Internat., N.Y.C., 1976—81, exec. v.p., 1984—87, pres., CEO, 1987—90, 1994—95, CEO and chmn., 1995—2002. Mgr., dir. Philip Morris Australia, 1981—84, Benson Hedges Can., 1981—84; pres., chief adminstrv. officer Kraft Gen. Foods, Glenview, Ill., 1990—91. Chmn. Geneva English Sch., 1971—77. Roman Catholic.

BIBLE, PAUL ALFRED, lawyer; b. Reno, Oct. 3, 1940; s. Alan and Loucile Pauline (Jacks) B.; m. Judith Lynn Schmidt, Mar. 21, 1970; children— Chad Alan, Patrick Marshall. Student U. Colo., 1958-59; B.A. in Econs., U. Nev., 1962; J.D., Georgetown U., 1965. Bar: D.C. 1965, Nev. 1965. Assoc. McDonald, Carano, Wilson, Bergin, Bible, Frankovich & Hicks, Reno, 1969-72, ptnr., 1972-83; sole practice, Reno, 1983-84; ptnr. Bible, Santini, Hoy & Miller, 1984-85, Bible, Santini, Hoy, Miller & Trachok, 1985-87; Bible, Hoy, Miller, Trachok & Wadhams, 1987-91; Bible, Hoy, Trachok & Wadhams, 1991-92; instr. Old Coll. Sch. Law, Reno, 1983; chmn. Nev. Gaming Comm., Reno, 1983-87. Contbr. articles to law revs. and profl. jours. Pres. DETRAP, Reno, 1971-73; mem. Nev. State Apprenticeship Council, Reno, 1971-83, chmn., 1971-83; mem. Truckee Meadows Community Coll. Found., 1982—; adv. bd. Truckee Meadows Community Coll., 1980-91. Served to capt. JAGC, U.S. Army, 1966-68. Recipient Henry Albert Pub. Service award U. Nev., 1962. Decorated Bronze Star medal. Mem. ABA, State Bar Nev., Assn. Trial Lawyers Am., Calif. Trial Lawyers Assn., Nev. Trial Lawyers Assn., Am. Arbitration Assn., Washoe County Bar Assn., Ducks Unltd. Democrat. Methodist. Club: Greenhead Hunting. Avocations: hunting, fishing, running, hiking. Office: Bible Hoy Trachok Wadhams & Zive 201 W Liberty St Ste 300 Reno NV 89501-2017

BIBUS, THOMAS WILLIAM, lawyer; b. Cin., July 13, 1949; s. Howard Fred and Ernestine G. (Bross) B.; children: Thomas Bradley, William Jason, Rebecca Lynn, Barbara Ann. BA in Econs., U. Cin., 1971; JD, Chase Coll. of Law, 1976. Bar: Ohio 1976, U.S. Dist. Ct. (so. dist.) Ohio 1976. Expediter, dispatch inspector ILSCO Corp., Cin., 1971-72; mgmt. trainee trust dept. Provident Bank, Cin., 1972-73; purchasing agt. Cin. Butcher Supply Co., 1973-76; sole practice Cin., 1976—. Mem. membership adv. panel Choicecare, Cin., 1983-87, past vice chmn.; mem. Parents Without Ptnrs., Cin., 1984—, profl. adviser, 1998—, former membership dir.; founder, leader Coping with Separation; judge Concours d'Elegance, Arthritis Found., Jaguar Club N.Am. Mem. Ohio Bar Assn. (domestic rels. and probate com.), Butler County Bar Assn., Cheviot Westwood Bus. Assn. (v.p., bd. dirs. 1987-89), West Side Lawyers (founder), East Side Lawyers (founder), Sierra Club (Miami group, sub-chmn. family outings 1989-91), Jaguar Club of Greater Cin. (charter, registrar), West Coast Swing Soc. (charter), Westwood Civic Assn., Westwood Concern, Cin. Citizens Police Acad. Alumni Assn., Hope Cmty. Singles Group, St. Monica St. George Singles Group. Office: 2962 Harrison Ave Cincinnati OH 45211-6724

BICE, MICHAEL DAVID, retail and wholesale executive, marketing consultant, insurance consultant; b. Anderson, S.C., July 18, 1956; s. Johnnie Lee Richard and Virgie Ovaline (Martin) B.; m. Nancy Bice, 1993; children: Ansley

Deann Bice, Adam Michael Bice, Kristin Kennedy, Rebekah Kennedy, John WilliamKennedy. Student, U.S. Merchant Marine Acad., 1974, Tri-County Tech. Coll., 1981. Sales rep. Sav-A-Stop, Inc., Roanoke, Va., 1974-75, 76-77, 78-79; with mgmt. dept. Caper House Food Stores, Belton, S.C., 1975; material coord. Jeffrey Mfg., Belton, 1975-76; sales rep. Better Beer and Wine Co., Anderson, 1977-78; with mgmt. dept. Brown Shoe Stores, Anderson, 1979-81; ind. contractor Curtis Products Co., Anderson, 1981-85, sales rep., 1988-89, mgr. Ashland, Va., 1989-91, project coord. Alpharetta, Ga., 1992; CEO B & D Enterprises, Anderson, 1981-85; pres., COO Oriental Sources, Inc., Charlotte, N.C., 1985-87; CEO Jewelry Plus, Anderson, 1985-87; pres. Sales Plus, Anderson, SC, 1988-93, Richmond, Va., 1989-91, Ashland, Va., 1989-91, Greer, S.C., 1993—; gen. mgr. Bice & Assocs., LLC, 2002—. V.p. ops., Bice & Assocs., LLC, 2002—, v.p. ops. Maabe Possibilities, Inc., Anderson, 1992-97; comml. mktg. dir., comml. accts. coord. Atlantic Coast Candy, Inc., Anderson, Roswell, Ga., Ashland, Va., 1992-94; v.p. sales, state mgr. Pubrs. Guild of S.C., Taylors, 1994-95; cons. Alliance for Affordable Health Care, S.C., N.C., Ga., 1995-98; gen. mgr. Affordable Health Care Cons., N.C., S.C., Ga., 1996—; gen dir. Amcall, 1995-98; mgr. Bice & Assocs., 1996—; gen. mgr. Southeastern Future Diagnostics, Greer, S.C., 1998-99, sr. regional sales dir., 1999—; state referee U.S. Soccer Fedn., FIFA, 1998—; regional sales dir. AmeriPlan, USA, Greer, 1999—, regional sales rep. Hoist & Crane Svc. Grp., A Divsn. of Plant Mechanical Svcs., Inc., Metarie, Louisiana, 1999-2000; agy. mktg. dir. Am. Classics Agy., 2001-02, sr. mktg. dir. Am. Classics Agy., 2002—; mng. dir. Excel-Vartec, 2002—, tng. dir. Gxcel-Vartec, 2002—. Ofcl. referee U.S. Soccer Fedn., 1993—, assessor, 2000-03, assignor, 1999—, state assessor, 2003—. Mem. Nat. H.S. Ofcls. Assn., Nat. Intercollegiate Soccer Ofcls. Assn. (assessor 2001—, reg. assessor 2003—), S.C. Intercollegiate Soccer Ofcls. Assn. (treas. 2000—, assessor 2001—, chpt. contact 2000-04), S.C. Upstate Soccer Referee Soc. (sec. 1999-2000, chmn. 2000-02), Nat. Assn. Sports Ofcls., Masons. Avocations: water-skiing, snow-skiing, fishing, hunting, travel. E-mail: Bice8Associates@juno.com.

BICE, SCOTT HAAS, dean, lawyer, educator; b. Los Angeles, Mar. 19, 1943; s. Fred Haas and Virginia M. (Scott) B.; m. Barbara Franks, Dec. 21, 1968. BS, U. So. Calif., 1965, JD, 1968. Bar: Calif. bar 1971. Law clk. to Chief Justice Earl Warren, 1968-69; asst. prof., assoc. prof., prof. law U. So. Calif., Los Angeles, 1969 , assoc dean 1971-74 dean Law Sch., 1980-2000, Carl Mason Franklin prof., 1983-2000, Robert C. Packard prof. law, 2000—; CEO Five B Investment Co., 1995—. Vis. prof. polit. sci. Calif. Inst. Tech., 1977; vis. prof. U. Va., 1978-79; bd.dirs. Western Mut. Ins. Co., Residence Mut. Ins. Co., Imagine Films Entertainment Co., Jenny Craig, Inc. Mem. editl. adv. bd. Calif. Lawyer, 1989-93; contbr. articles to law jours. Bd. dirs. L.A. Family Housing Corp., 1989-93, Stone Soup Child Care Programs, 1988—, L.A. Child Guidance Clinic, 2003-; trustee Bice Passavant Found., 2000—. Affiliated scholar Am. Bar Found., 1972-74 Fellow Am. Bar Found. (life); mem. Am. Law Inst. (life), Calif. Bar, Los Angeles County Bar Assn., Am. Law Deans Assn. (pres. 1997-99), Am. Judicature Soc., Calif. Club, Chancery Club (treas. 2001-02, sec. 2002-03, v.p. 2003-), Long Beach Yacht Club, Catalina Island Yacht Club (judge adv. 2002—). Home: 787 S San Rafael Ave Pasadena CA 91105-2326 Office: U So Calif Sch Law Los Angeles CA 90089-0071 E-mail: sbice@law.usc.edu.

BICHEVIN, VICTOR VASILY, research scientist; b. Krasnojarsk, Russia, Mar. 25, 1935; s. Vasily Ivan and Hilda Henrik (Pelt) B.; m. Aleksandra Andrei Popov, July 18, 1960 (div. May 1976); children: Natalja, Pjotr. BS, Tartu U., Estonia, 1959, PhD, 1972. Jr. rsch. assoc. Inst. Physics, Tartu, 1960-63, 66-73, sr. rsch. assoc., 1973—. Contbr. over 50 articles to profl. jours. Mem. European Phys. Soc. Home: Aardla 144/49 EE2400 Tartu Estonia Office: Inst Physics Riia 142 EE2400 Tartu Estonia

BICHSEL, HANS, physicist, consultant, researcher; b. Basel, Switzerland, Sept. 2, 1924; came to U.S., 1951; s. Paul and Anna Maria Bichsel; m. Sue O. Greenwalt, Sept. 12, 1959; children: Elizabeth Christine, Joseph Oliver. MA, PhD, U. Basel, 1951. Rsch. asst. Princeton (N.J.) U., 1951-55; rsch. assoc. Rice U., Houston, 1955-57; asst. prof. physics U. Wash., Seattle, 1957-59; affiliate prof. physics U. Wash., Seattle, 1992—; assoc. prof., prof. radiology U. Wash., Seattle, 1969-80; asst. prof., assoc. prof. physics U. So. Calif., L.A., 1959-68; assoc. prof. U. Calif., Berkeley, 1968-69. Cons. Internat. Commn. on Radiation Units, Bethesda, Md., 1970—, Los Alamos (N.Mex.) Nat. Lab., 1978-83, IAEA, Vienna, Austria, 1990—; vis. scientist Nat. Inst. Radiol., Scis., Chiba, Japan, 1991-96, U. Sherbrooke Med. Sch., Que., Can.; rschr. Relativistic Heavy Ion Collider, Brookhaven Nat. Lab., 1999—; referee Phys. Rev., Nuclear Instruments and Methods, Physics in Medicine and Biology, also others. Contbr. articles to profl. jours. Fellow Am. Phys. Soc.; mem. Swiss Phys. Soc. Home and Office: 1211 22nd Ave E Seattle WA 98112-3534 E-mail: bichsel@sleepy.npl.washington.edu.

BICK, KATHERINE LIVINGSTONE, neurobiologist, international liaison, consultant; b. Charlottetown, Can., May 3, 1932; came to U.S., 1954; d. Spurgeon Arthur and Flora Hazel (Murray) Livingstone; m. James Harry Bick, Aug. 20, 1955 (div.); children: James A., Charles L. (dec.); m. Ernst Freese, 1986 (dec. 1990). BS with honors, Acadia U., Can., 1951, MS, 1952; PhD, Brown U., 1957; DSc (hon.), Acadia U., 1990. Rsch. pathologist UCLA Med. Sch., 1959-61; asst. prof. Calif. State U., Northridge, 1961-66; lab. instr. Georgetown U., Washington, 1970-72, asst. prof., 1972-76; dep. dir. neurol. disorder program Nat. Inst. Neurol. and Communicative Disorders and Stroke, NIH, Bethesda, Md., 1976-81, acting dep. dir., 1981-83, dep. dir., 1983-87; dep. dir. extramural rsch. Office of Dir. NIH, 1987-90; sci. liaison Centro Studio Multicentrico Internazionale Sulla Demenza, Washington, 1990-95. Cons. Nat. Rsch. Coun., Italy, 1991-97, The Charles A. Dana Found., N.Y.C., 1993-98, Edn. Commn. of the States, 1996-99. Editor: Alzheimer's Disease: Senile Dementia and Related Disorders, 1978, Neurosecretion and Brain Peptides, Implications for Brain Functions and Neurol. Disease, 1981, The Early Story of Alzheimer's Disease, 1987, Alzheimer Disease, 1994, 2d edit., 1999, Alzheimer Disease: The Changing View, 2000; contbr. articles to profl. jours. Pres. Woman's Club, McLean, Va., 1968-69; bd. dirs. Fairfax County (Va.) YWCA, 1969-70; pres. Avenel Homeowner's Assn., 1998; pres. Emerson Unitarian Ch., 1964-66; mem. Bethesda Pl. Cmty. Coun., 1992-95, pres., 1993-94; mem. Dana Alliance for Brain Initiatives, 1993—; bd. dirs. Wilmington N.C. Child Advocacy Commn., 1998-2002; mem. vol. guild St. John's Mus. Art, Wilmington; chair Vol. Guild Cameron Art Mus., Wilmington, 2002-2003, Cameron Art Mus. bd.,2003-. Recipient Can. NRC award Acadia U., 1951-52, NIH Dir.'s award, 1978, Spl. Achievement award NIH, 1981, 83, Superior Svc. award USPHS, 1986, Presdl. Rank award meritorious sr. exec., 1989; Universal Match Found. fellow Brown U., 1956-57, Fed. Exec. Inst. Leadership fellow, 1980. Fellow AAAS; mem. Am. Neurol. Assn., Am. Acad. Neurology, Assn. for Rsch. in Nervous and Mental Disease, Internat. Brain Rsch. Orgn., World Fedn. Neurology Rsch. Group on Dementias (exec. sec. Am. region 1984-86, chmn. 1986-93), Alzheimer's Disease Internat. (sci. and med. adv. bd.), Soc. for Neurosci., Acad. of Medicine Washington, Dana Alliance for Brain Initiatives.

BICK, RODGER LEE, hematologist, oncologist, researcher, educator; b. San Francisco, May 21, 1942; s. Jack Arthur and Pauline (Jensen) B.; m. Marcella Bick, Mar. 3, 1980 (dec. Feb. 1995); children: Shauna Nicole, Michelle Leanne; m. Marilyn Bick, Apr. 22, 2003. MD, U. Calif., Irvine, 1970; PhD, Acad. Medicine, Bialystok, Poland, 1995. Diplomate Am. Bd. Quality Assessment, Am. Bd. Forensic Medicine in Oncology, Hematology, Thrombosis, Hemostasis and Product Liability, Internat. Bd. Thrombosis, Hemostasis & Vascular Medicine, Am. Bd. Pain Mgmt. Med. intern Kern County Gen. Hosp., UCLA, Bakersfield, Calif., 1970-71, internal medicine resident, 1971-72; fellow in hematology-med. oncology Bay Area Hematology Oncology Med. Group, West Los Angeles, Calif., 1974-76; med. staff various hosps., Calif., 1974-77, med. staff, extensive adminstrv. and com. work, 1977-92; med. dir. oncology hematology Presbyn. Comprehensive Cancer Ctr., Presbyn. Hosp., Dallas, 1992-95. Staff hematologist/oncologist Bay Area Hematology Oncology Med. Group, Santa Monica, Calif., 1976-77, med. dir. Calif. Coagulation Labs., Inc., Bakersfield, 1977-92, San Joaquin Hematology Oncology Med. Group, 1977-92, Regional Cancer and Blood Disease Ctr. Kern, Bakersfield, 1986-92; asst. clin. prof. to clin. prof. medicine UCLA Ctr. Health Scis., 1976-94, assoc. prof. to prof. allied health profns. Calif. State U., Bakersfield, 1980-92, clin. prof. nursing and health scis., 1982-92; adj. assoc. prof. medicine/physiology, Wayne State U., Detroit; adj. clin. faculty Wesley Med. Ctr. and U. Kans. Med. Sch., Wichita, 1984-86; clin. prof. medicine U. Tex. Southwestern Med. Ctr., 1993—, clin. prof. pathology, 1993—; prof. haematology U. Tasmania Sch. Medicine, 1996; hematology cons. NASA; med. dir. UCLA/Kern Cancer Program, 1991-92, Ctrl. Calif. Heart Inst., 1990-92; invited spkr. and presenter in field, numerous internat. symposia and confs.; dir. numerous workshops in field. Author: Disseminated Intravascular Coagulation and Related Syndromes, 1983, Disorders of Hemostasis and Thrombosis: Principles of Clinical Practice, 1985, 2d. edit., 1992, 3d edit., 1997; guest editor, contbr.: Thrombohemorrhagic Disorders Perplexing to the Hematologist Oncologist, 1992; guest editor: Laboratory Diagnosis of Hemostasis Problems, I, 1994, II, 1995, (monograph) Seminars in Thrombosis and Hemostasis, 1994, Common Bleeding and Clotting Problems for the Internist, 1994; editor-in-chief: Hematology: Princples of Clinical and Laboratory Practice, 2 vols., 1993, Paraneoplastic Syndromes, Hematology Oncology Clinics of North America, 1996; editor: Current Concepts of Thrombosis, 1998; contbr. numerous chpts. to books; author monographs and lab. manuals; contbr. over 250 articles and papers and numerous revs. to profl. jours. and conf. procs.; patentee in field; editor-in-chief Jour. Clin. and Applied Thrombosis/Hemostasis & Vascular Medicine; mem. editl. bd. Am. Jour. Clin. Pathology, Internat. Jour. Haematology. Bd. dirs., exec. com. Bakersfield Symphony Orch., 1988-92. Fellow ACP, Am. Soc. Clin. Pathologists, Assn. Clin. Scientists, Am. Soc. Coagulationists, Internat. Soc. Hematology, Am. Coll. Angiology, Internat. Coll. Angiology, Nat. Acad. Clin. Biochemistry, Am. Heart Assn. (coun. on thrombosis, circulation and atherosclerosis; rsch. and grnat peer rev. com. 1980-86), Am. Geriat. Soc. (founding fellow); mem. AMA, AAAS, Am. Assn. Blood Banks, Am. Soc. Internal Medicine, Am. Soc. Hematology, Internat. Soc. Thrombosis and Haemostasis, Am. Assn. Study of Neoplastic Disease, Am. Assn. Clin. Rsch., Am. Cancer Soc., Internat. Assn. Study of Lung Cancer (founding mem.), Fedn. Am. Scientists, N.Y. Acad. Scis., Calif. Soc. Internal Medicine, Calif. Med. Assn., Calif. Thoracic Soc., Haematology Soc. Australia, Internat. Consensus Com. on Autithrombotic Therapy, numerous others. Lutheran. Avocations: ocean sailing, classical piano, brass musical instruments, photography, target archery, astronomy and astrophotography. Office: 10455 N Central Expy Ste 109 Dallas TX 75231-2215

BICKART, THEODORE ALBERT, university president emeritus; b. N.Y.C., Aug. 25, 1935; s. Theodore Roosevelt and Edna Catherine (Pink) B.; m. Carol Florence Nichols, June 14, 1958 (div. Dec. 1973); children: Karl Jeffrey, Lauren Spencer; m. Frani W. Rudolph, Aug. 14, 1982; 1 stepchild, Jennifer Anne Cumming. B Engring. Sci., Johns Hopkins U., 1957, MS, 1950, DEng., 1960, D Univ. (hon.), Dneprodzerzhinst State Tech. U, Ukraine, 1996. Asst. prof. elec. and computer engring. Syracuse (N.Y.) U., 1963-65, assoc. prof., 1965-70, prof., 1970-89, assoc. to vice chancellor for acad. affairs for computer resources devel., 1983-85, dean L.C. Smith Coll. Engring., 1984-89; prof. elec. engring., dean engring. Mich. State U., East Lansing, 1989-98; pres. Colo. Sch. Mines, Golden, 1998-2000. Vis. scholar U. Calif., Berkeley, 1977; Fulbright lectr. Kiev Poly Inst., USSR, 1981; vis. lectr. Nanjing Inst. Tech., China, 1981; hon. disting. prof. Taganrog Radio Engring. Inst., Russia, 1992—; mem. Accreditation Bd. for Engring. and Tch., Engring. Accreditation Commn., exec. com., 1998-2000; chmn. Engring. Workforce Commn., 1996-98; elected-mem. Johns Hopkins U. Soc. Scholars, 2001. Co-author: Electrical Network Theory, 1969, Linear Network Theory, 1981; contbr. numerous articles to profl. jours. Served to 1st lt. U.S. Army, 1961-63 Recipient numerous rsch. grants; Disting. Alumni award, Johns Hopkins U. Fellow IEEE (best paper awards Syracuse sect. 1969, 70, 73, 74, 77, chmn. com. on engring. accreditation activities 1996-98, chmn. accreditation policy coun. 2001—), Am. Soc. Engring. Edn. (v.p. 1997-99); mem. Am. Math. Soc., Assn. for Computing Machinery, Soc. for Indsl. and Applied Math., N.Y. Acad. Scis., Ukrainian Acad. Engring. Scis.), Internat. Higher Edn. Acad. Scis. (Russia), Internat. Acad. Informatics (Russia), Johns Hopkins U. Soc. Scholars., Johns Hopkins U. Alumni Assn. (Disting. Alumnus award). Avocations: bicycling, hiking, gardening. Home: 541 Wyoming Cir Golden CO 80403-0900 E-mail: tbickart@mines.edu.

BICKEL, FLOYD GILBERT, III, investment counselor; b. St. Louis, Jan. 10, 1944; s. Floyd Gilbert and Mary Mildred (Welch) B.; m. Martha Wohler, June 11, 1966; children: Christine Carleton, Susan Marie, Katherine Anne, Jennifer Anne, Laura Elizabeth, Andrew Barrett (dec.) BS in Bus. Adminstrn., Washington U., St. Louis, 1966; MS in Commerce, St. Louis U., 1968. Rschr. Yates, Woods & Co., St. Louis, 1966-67; asst. br. mgr. E.F. Hutton & Co., Inc., St. Louis, 1967-70, v.p. dir. consulting svcs., 1980-88; asst. v.p., resident mgr. Bache & Co., Inc., St. Louis, 1970-72; pres. Donelan-Phelps Investment Advisors, Inc., St. Louis, 1972-80; v.p. Merrill Lynch & Co., St. Louis, 1988—2003; sr. v.p. Morgan Stanley, St. Louis, 2003—. Bd. dirs. Summit Mktg. Group, Huntleigh Assocs., Eagle River LLC. Mem. City of Des Peres (Mo.), Planning and Zoning Commn., 1975-76; chm. St. Louis County Bd. Equalization, 1976-79; pub. safety commr. City of Des Peres, 1977-80, mem. audit and fin. com., 1980-86; mem. State of Mo. Gov.'s Crime Commn., 1981-92; bd. dirs. Villa Duchesne Sch., 1986-92; aldeman City of Huntleigh, 1998-2002, mayor, 2002—. Recipient Disting. Alumni awrd, Washington U., 2002. Mem.: John M. Olin Bus. Sch. Washington U. Alumni Assn. (pres. 1995—96, nat. coun. 2001—), St. Louis Soc. Fin. Analysts, Investment Mgmt. Cons. Assn., Internat. Soc. Cert. Employee Benefit Specialists, Eagle Springs Golf Club, Cordillera Golf Club, Beaver Creek Club, Bellerive Country Club. Republican. Roman Catholic. Home: 30 Huntleigh Woods Saint Louis MO 63131-4813 Office: Morgan Stanley 700 Corp Park Dr Saint Louis MO 63105

BICKEL, JOHN W., II, lawyer; b. Champaign, Ill., Sept. 9, 1948; s. John William and Virginia Bickel; children: Hannah, Molly, Sarah. BS, U.S. Mil. Acad., 1970; JD, So. Meth. U., 1976. Bar: N.Y. 1988, Tex. 1976, U.S. Ct. Appeals (5th and 11th cirs.) 1980, U.S. Supreme Ct. 1983. Assoc. Thompson & Knight, Dallas, 1980-83; ptnr. Brown, Thomas, Karger & Bickel, Dallas, 1983-84; co-mng., co-founder, ptnr. Bickel & Brewer, Dallas, 1984—; co-founding ptnr. Bickel & Brewer Storefront, PLLC, Dallas. Adv. mem. Tex. Supreme Ct. Jury Charge Task Force, 1992; mem. com. for qualified judiciary. Co-author: "Exhibits and other Evidence," Chpt. 13, Lawyers Cooperative Fed. Practice Guide. Mem. exec. bd. So. Meth. U. Sch. Law.; mem. Hiram A. Boaz Soc. So. Meth. U.; mem. Tex. Com.: A Time to Lead--The Campaign for So. Meth. U.; mem. adv. com. Southwestern Ball, 1997-2000, co-founder Future Leaders Program, Bickel & Brewer Nat. Pub. Policy Forum. Fellow Tex. Bar Found., Dallas Bar Found. (sustaining life); mem. ABA, State Bar Tex. (past chmn. litigation com. of environ. and natural resource law sect.), N.Y. Bar Assn., Dallas Bar Assn., Markey/Wigmore Inns of Ct. (Chgo. chpt.), West Point Assn. Grads. (trustee 1997-2000, strategic planning com. 1997—), West Point Soc. North Tex. (bd. dirs. 1992-). Office: Bickel & Brewer 4800 Bank One Ctr 1717 Main St Ste 4800 Dallas TX 75201-4651 E-mail: jwb@bickelbrewer.com.

BICKEL, MINNETTE DUFFY, artist; b. New Bern, N.C., June 24, 1921; d. Richard Nixon and Minnette (Chapman) Duffy; m. William Croft, Jan. 3, 1947; children: Minnette B. Boesel, Susan B. Scioli. One-woman shows include, N.C., statewide portrait exhbns., (two 1st place awards), regional juried shows, (winner three internat. awards); portraits include Gen. Claude Larkin, Tyrone Power, Thomas Graham, James Beckwith, Arthur Rolander, Frederick E. Fox, Senator Jesse Helms, Rachel Carson, R. Bud Dwyer, William Genge, Allison Williams, Dennis O'Connor, Frank Cahouet, Dr. Robert Edwards, Robert Wilburn, Henry L. Hillman. Mem. Am. Soc. Portrait Artists (affiliated), Stroke of Genius Gallery, Washington Soc. of Portrait Artists and Portrait Inst., Portrait Soc. Am. Republican. Home: 816 Saint James St Pittsburgh PA 15232-2113

BICKEL, PETER JOHN, statistician, educator; b. Bucharest, Romania, Sept. 21, 1940; arrived in U.S., 1957, naturalized, 1964; s. Eliezer and P. Madeleine (Moscovici) B.; m. Nancy Kramer, Mar. 2, 1964; children: Amanda, Stephen. AB, U. Calif., Berkeley, 1960, MA, 1961, PhD, 1963; PhD (hon.), Hebrew U. Jerusalem, 1988. Asst. prof. stats. U. Calif., Berkeley, 1964-67, assoc. prof., 1967-70, prof., 1970—, chmn. dept. stats., 1976-79, dean phys. scis., 1980-86, chmn. dept. stats., 1993-97. Vis. lectr. math. Imperial Coll., London, 1965-66; fellow J.S. Guggenheim Meml. Found., 1970-71, J.D. and Catherine T. MacArthur Found., 1984-89; NATO sr. sci. fellow, 1974; chmn.com. on applied and theoretical stats. NRC, 1998-2000, chmn. bd. on math. scis., 2000—; chmn. sci. adv. coun. Stats. and Applied Math. Inst., NSF. Author: (with K. Doksum) Mathematical Statistics, 1976, 2d edit., 2000, (with C. Klaassen, Y. Ritov and J. Wellner) Efficient and Adaptive Estimation in Semiparametric Models, 1993; assoc. editor Annals of Math. Stats., 1968-76, 86-93, PNAS, 1996—2000, Bernouilli, 1996—, Statistics Sinica, 1996—2003; contbr. articles to profl. jours. Fellow J.D. and Catherine T. MacArthur Found., 1984-89. Fellow AAAS (chair sect. U 1996-97), Inst. Math. Stats. (pres. 1980), Am. Statis. Assn.; mem. NAS, Royal Statis. Soc., Internat. Statis. Inst., Am. Acad. Arts and Scis., Royal Netherlands Acad. Arts and Scis., Bernoulli Soc. (pres. 1990). Office: U Calif Dept Stats Evans Hall Berkeley CA 94720 E-mail: bickel@stat.berkeley.edu.

BICKERS, DAVID RINSEY, physician, educator; b. Richmond, Va., Sept. 23, 1941; s. William McKenzie and Helen Virginia (Fitzpatrick) B.; m. Melinda-Lee Jaeger, May 30, 1970; 1 dau., McKenzie Winchester. AB, Georgetown U., 1963; MD, U. Va., 1967. Intern in medicine U. Iowa Hosps., Iowa City, 1967-68; resident in dermatology skin and cancer unit N.Y.U. Med. Center, 1970-73; NIH tng. fellow, guest investigator Rockefeller U., 1971-73, R.J. Reynolds scholar in clin. medicine, asst. prof., asso. physician, 1976-77; asst. prof. dermatology Columbia U. Coll. Physicians and Surgeons, 1973-76; asst. attending dermatologist Presbyn. Hosp., N.Y.C., 1973-76, med. dir., 1997—; prof. dermatology, chmn. dept. Case Western Res. U. Med. Sch., 1977-93, assoc. dean, 1990-93; med. dir. N.Y. Hosp., N.Y.C., 1997—. Dir. dermatology svc. U. Hosps., 1977-93, sr. v.p. med. program planning, 1977-89, chief staff, sr. v.p. med. affairs, 1990-93; dir. dermatology svc. Cleve. VA Hosp., 1977-89; mem. gen. medicine A study sect., NIH, 1980-84, chmn., 1982-84; mem. adv. coun. Nat. Inst. Arthritis, Musculoskeletal and Skin Diseases, NIH, 1988-92; Carl Truman Nelson prof. dermatology, chmn. Dept. Coll. Physicians and Surgeons, Columbia U., 1994—; dir. Dermatology Svc. the Presbyn. Hosp., N.Y., 1994—. Author: (with L.C. Harber) Photosensitivity Diseases: Principles of Diagnosis and Treatment, 1981, 2d. edit., 1989, (with Hazen and Lynch) Clinical Pharmacology of Skin Disease, 1984; mem. editorial bd. Jour. Am. Acad. Dermatology, 1979-85, Physicians Drug Alert, 1982—, Today's Therapeutic Trends, 1983—, Photodermatology, 1983-88; assoc. editor Jour. Investigative Dermatol., 1987-97. Served as officer M.C. USAF, 1968-70. Decorated Air Force Commendation medal. Mem. Assn. Am. Physicians, Am. Soc. Clin. Investigation, Am. Soc. Pharmacology and Exptl. Therapeutics, Am. Fedn. Clin. Rsch., Am. Soc. Photobiology, Am. Acad. Dermatology, Am. Dermatol. Assn., Soc. Investigative Dermatology (bd. dirs. 1985-89, sec.-treas. 1989—), Pasteur Club (Cleve.), Med. Strollers (N.Y., 1996), Skin Pharmacology Soc. (sec. 1985-87, pres. 1987-89), Dermatology Found. (sec.-treas. 1984, chmn. bd. 1987-88), Bicontinental Assn. Edn. and Rsch. in Dermatology (founding mem.), German Dermatol. Soc. (hon.), Am. Univ. Beirut (bd. trustees, 1996), Commanderie De Bordeaux, Expert Panel Rsch. Inst. for Fragrance Materials, Am. Bd. of Dermatology (dir. 1997—). Office: Columbia Presbyn Med Ctr AP 1410 161 Fort Washington Ave New York NY 10032-3713

BICKERSTAFF, MINA MARCH CLARK, university administrator; b. Crowley, Tex., Sept. 27, 1936; d. Winifred Perry and Clara Mae (Jarrett) Clark; m. Billy Frank Bickerstaff, June 12, 1954 (div. 1960); children: Billy Mark, Mina Gayle Bickerstaff Basaldu. AA, Tarrant County Jr. Coll., 1982; BBA, Dallas Bapt. U., 1991. Dir. pers. svcs. Southwestern Bapt. Theol. Sem., Ft. Worth, 1976—. Mem. Coll. and Univ. Pers. Assn., Seminary Woman's Club (past treas.), Alpha Chi. Baptist. Avocations: reading, music, genealogy. Office: Southwestern Bapt Theol Sem PO Box 22000 Fort Worth TX 76122-0001

BICKERSTAFF, PATSY ANNE, judge, writer, poet; b. Richmond, Va., Jan. 7, 1940; d. William and Doris Doeppe B.; m. G. Laurence Curley Jr., Oct. 17, 1959 (dec.); children: George L. III, William Geoffrey; m. Wilson Lee Seay, Jan. 7, 1988 (dec.). BA, U. Richmond, 1963, JD, 1978. Bar: Va. 1978. Atty.-at-law various orgns., Va., 1978-97; hearing officer Va. Employment Commn., Alexandria, 1997-99, appeals examiner Richmond, 1999—. Chair adv. bd. Mental Health Ctr., Shenandoah County, 1981-83; facilitator Richmond Poetry Workshop, 1994-97. Author: Alcohol-Free Entertaining, 1986, City Rain, 1989; author poems (numerous awards, including Robert Penn Warren award 1995). Organizing chair RESPONSE Domestic Violence Prevention, Shenandoah County, 1981-83; campaign asst. E.A. Plunket, Augusta County, Va., 1996. Mem. Poetry Soc. Va. (exec. bd., sec. 1978, v.p. 1998), Va. Writer's Club (pres. 1988-2000). Episcopal. Avocations: doll costuming and collecting, skiing, swimming, history, dancing. Home: 26 Skipwith Green Cir Richmond VA 23294

BICKFORD, DAVID LAWRENCE, librarian, educator; b. Bronxville, N.Y., Sept. 16, 1965; s. Lawrence Clark and Ann Elizabeth Bickford; m. Bonnie Mai Carr, June 14, 1998. BA, Brown U., 1987; MS in LS, U. N.C., 1989. Libr. Phoeniz Pub. Libr., 1989-93; mgr. acad. info. svcs. U. Phoenix, 1993-96, asst. to dir. for acad. devel., 1996-99, univ. libr., 1999—2003, instr., 1996—, dir. univ. libr., 2003—. Mem. ALA, Spl. Librs. Assn. (pres. Ariz. chpt. 1995-96), Assn. Coll. and Rsch. Librs. Office: U Phoenix 4615 E Elwood St MS 10-0068 Phoenix AZ 85040 Fax: 480-557-1436. E-mail: dlbickfo@email.uophx.edu.

BICKLEY, JOHN S. insurance association executive, educator, writer; b. Bethlehem, Pa., Dec. 30, 1917; m. Mary Louise Loftis; 1 child, Mary Carter. Student, Columbia U., Harvard U., U. Chgo.; BA, MBA, PhD, U. Wis. Life underwriter Coll. divsn. Mass. Mut. Life Ins. Co., 1939, Lincoln Nat. Life Ins. Co., 1940; dir. edn. State Auto Ins. Cos., 1957-85; Frank Parke Samford chair ins. emeritus U. Ala., 1975—; emeritus dir. Columbus Life Ins. Co., 1963—. Prof. ins. U. Ala., 1940-42, 47-48, 68-86, emeritus prof., 1986—, chmn. com. on internat. corp. rels., 1986—; prof. ins. U. Wash., 1948-50, Ohio State U., 1950-59, U. Tex., Austin, 1959-68; vis. prof. ins. Stanford U., 1953, U. Colo., 1957, U. Hawaii, 1962; chmn. dept. fin. U. Tex., Austin, 1965-68; spkr. in field in 30 nations. Author 3 books and monographs, numerous articles in profl. jours; founding editor Jour. of Risk and Ins., 1956-60. Trustee, founding bd. dirs. Griffith Found. for Ins. Edn., 1950—; founder, elector Ins. Hall of Fame, 1957—; bd. dirs. U. Ala. Cmty. Music Sch., 1999—; mem. internat. adv. bd. U. Ala., 1993—; bd. dirs. Tuscaloosa Symphony Orch., 1990—, chmn. pers. com., 1993—; bd. dirs. Tuscaloosa String Quartette Soc.; mem. bd. pensions Evang. Luth. Ch. in Am., 1966-78; founder, dir. Life Internat. Ins. Soc., 1989--; founding mem. chancellor's coun. U. Tex. System, founding chmn. com. on property-liability ins. terminology, 1959-69. 1st lt. USAAC, 1942-46. Decorated Order of Sacred Treasure with gold rays and neck ribbon (Japan); recipient decorations Min. of Fin., Republic of China, 1979, Min. of Fin., Republic of South Korea, 1986; Gold medal award named in his honor Ins. Hall of Fame (laureate 1988), Gold medal De La Salle U., The Philippines, Lifetime Achievement award Nat. Profl. Fraternity; recipient numerous awards and honors; rsch. fellow FTC, 1968-69, Fed. Home Loan Mortgage Corp., 1972. Mem. Am. Econ. Assn., Am. Fin. Assn. (exec. com.), Ins. Co. Edn. Dirs. Soc., Am. Meteorol. Soc., Am. Risk and Ins. Assn. (pres. 1958-59), Ala. Ins. Planning Commn. (pres.), Ala. Acad. Sci., Ohio State U. Ins. Soc. (founder, faculty sponsor), U. Tex. Austin inst. Soc. (founder, faculty sponsors), U. Ala. Ins. Soc. (founder, faculty sponsor), Newcomen Soc. (Ala. com.), Assn. Internat. Droit des Assurances, Corp. Ins. Agts. London (hon.), Internat. Assn. Accident and Health Underwriters (hon.), Am. Soc. for Ins. Mgmt. (hon.), Internat. Ins. Soc. (founder, chmn. emeritus, dir. for life), North River Yacht Club (Tuscaloosa, Ala., emeritus dir.), Univ. Club (Tuscaloosa), Jasons, Mortar Board, Sigma Phi, Alpha Kappa Psi, Gamma Iota Sigma, Phi Mu Alpha, Beta Gamma Sigma, Omicron Delta Kappa. Address: 1310 Indian Hills Tuscaloosa AL 35406

BICKMAN, MARTIN, literature educator, writer; b. Boston, Sept. 23, 1945; s. James and Sara Bickman; m. Louise Carol Danny, Oct. 21, 1968; children: Sarah Rachel, Jed Samuel. AB, Amherst Coll., 1967; MA in Tchg., Harvard U., 1969; PhD, U. Pa., 1974. Prof. U. Colo., Boulder, 1974—. Pres. tchg. scholar U. Colo., Boulder, 1988—. Author: (book) American Romantic Psychology, 1980; editor: Approaches to Teaching Herman Melville's Moby-Dick, 1985; author: Walden: Volatile Truths, 1992; editor: Uncommon Learning: Thoreau on Education, 1999; author: Minding American Education: Reclaiming the Tradition of Active Learning, 2003. Recipient Hoepner Prize for Best Writing, So. Humanities Rev., 1974. Mem.: MLA. Democrat. Avocations: running, travel. Office: Univ Colo English Dept Hellems 101 226 UCB Boulder CO 80309 Office Fax: 303-786-7144. E-mail: bickman@colorado.edu.

BICKNER, BRUCE, food products executive; b. 1943; BBA, De Pauw U., 1965; JD, U. Mich., 1968. Law clk. U.S. Dist. Ct., 1968-70; ptnr. Sidley & Austin, Chgo., 1970-75; with DeKalb (Ill.) Corp., 1975—, v.p., 1976, group v.p., 1980, exec. v.p., dir., 1980, pres., 1986-90, CEO, chmn. bd., 1988-98, DeKalb Energy Co., 1988-98, DeKalb Swine Breeders Inc.; co-pres. Monsanto Global Seed Group, Monsanto, Inc., DeKalb, 1998—, exec. v.p. agrl. sector. Office: Monsanto Global Seed Group 3100 Sycamore Rd Dekalb IL 60115-9600

BICKS, DAVID PETER, lawyer; b. N.Y.C., Mar. 16, 1933; s. Alexander and Henrietta (Isaacson) B.; m. Marian Ruef, Aug. 24, 1957; children— John Alexander, Jennifer Williams, Caroline Todd, Edward Thomas AB, Harvard U., 1955; LL.B., Yale U., 1958. Bar: N.Y. 1959, U.S. Ct. Appeals (2d cir.) 1960, U.S. Dist. Ct. (so. dist.) N.Y. 1961. Asst. U.S. atty. U.S. Dist. Ct. (so. dist.) N.Y., N.Y.C., 1959-61; spl. counsel SEC, N.Y.C., 1961-66; ptnr. LeBoeuf, Lamb, Greene & MacRae L.L.P., N.Y.C., 1966—2000, counsel, 2001— . Bd. editors Yale Law Jour., 1956-58 Served with U.S. Army, 1958-59 Mem. ABA, N.Y. State Bar Assn. Clubs: Castine Yacht (commodore 2000—), Castine Golf (gov. 2000—) (Maine); Harvard of N.Y. (N.Y.C.). Avocation: sailing. Home: 21 E 87th St New York NY 10128-0506 Office: LeBoeuf Lamb Greene & MacRae LLP 125 W 55th St New York NY 10019-5369

BICKSLER, DIANA GUIDO, lawyer; b. Berkeley, Calif., July 8, 1954; d. Salvador J. and Antonietta (D'Lessandro) G.; m. Gene Allen Bicksler, June 26, 1994. BA, U. Calif., Berkeley, 1976; MA, U. San Francisco, 1978; JD, U. Golden Gate, 1982. Bar: Calif. 1984, U.S. Dist. Ct. (no. dist.) Calif. 1984, U.S. Ct. Appeals (9th cir.) 1986. Assoc. Law Offices of James J. Duryea, San Francisco, 1982-85; assoc., mng. atty. Ericksen, Arbuthnot, Walsh, Paynter & Brown, San Jose, Calif., 1985-86; assoc. Tarkington, O'Connor & O'Neill, San Francisco, 1986-90; ptnr. Berding & Weil, Alamo, Calif., 1990-96; prin. Landmark Legal Profls., San Francisco, 1996-97, Cushing Bicksler Group, San Francisco, 1997—. Mem. ABA, San Francisco Bar Assn., Calif. Bus. Trial Lawyers Assn., Contra CostaBar Assn. Office: Cushing Bicksler Group Ste 290 2121 N California Blvd Walnut Creek CA 94596-7351 E-mail: dbicksler@cblawlink.com.

BICKWIT, LEONARD, JR., lawyer; b. Jan. 30, 1940; s. Leonard and Doris Bickwit. BA, Yale U, 1961, Oxford U, 1963; LLB, Harvard U, 1966. Bar: NY 1967, DC 1980. Counsel subcom. on environ., US Senate Commerce Com., Washington, 1969—74; chief legis. asst. Senator John Glenn, Washington, 1975—79; gen. counsel Nuc. Regulatory commn., Washington, 1979—83. Mem.: Miller & Chevalier. Office: Miller & Chevalier 655 15th St NW Ste 900 Washington DC 20005-5799

BICOY, BRET NALANI, think-tank executive; b. Honolulu, Hawaii; m. Carolyn Clare Bicoy. BA, Tufts U., Medford, Mass., 1992. Sr. found. officer Greater Green Bay (Wis.) Cmty. Found., 1998—2002; pres., CEO Marietta (Ohio) Cmty. Found., Inc., 2002—. Columnist Charity Matters. Adv. bd. Urban Hope, Green Bay, Wis., 1999—2002; alderman Green Bay (Wis.) City Coun., 2000—02; supr. Brown County Bd. of Suprs., Green Bay, Wis., 2000—02; dir. Multicultural Ctr. of Greater Green Bay (Wis.), 2002. Fellow Emerging Philanthropic Leader Fellowship, Coun. on Foundations in Wash., DC, 2003—. Mem.: Marietta Rotary Club. Office: Marietta Cmty Found Inc PO Box 77 Marietta OH 45750

BIDDINGTON, WILLIAM ROBERT, university administrator, dental educator; b. Piedmont, W.Va., Mar. 30, 1925; s. William M. and Sadie (Vogtman) B.; m. Dolores E. Berrett, June 14, 1947; 1 son, William Berrett. Student, Potomac State Coll., 1942-43, Hampden-Sydney Coll., 1943-44; D.D.S. cum laude, U. Md., 1948. Diplomate: Am. Bd. Endodontics. Gen. practice dentistry, Balt., 1949-59; instr. Balt. Coll. Dental Surgery, Dental Sch. U. Md., 1949-52, asst. prof., 1952-56, assoc. prof., 1956-59; prof., chmn. dept. endodontics Sch. Dentistry, W.Va. U., Morgantown, 1959-68, asst. dean, 1966-68, dean, 1968-91, interim v.p. academic affairs, 1979-80, interim v.p. health scis., 1981-82; v.p. Robert C. Byrd Health Scis Ctr. Morgantown, 1991-92, sr. assoc. v.p., 1992-93, assoc. v.p., 1993—; interim dir. Ctr. on Aging W.Va. U. Sch. Medicine, 1993-95. Mem. at large, sec., vice chmn., chmn. adminstrv. bd., v.p. council deans Am. Assn. Dental Schs., 1974-78, pres., 1983-84 Served with USNR, 1942-46, 48-49. Fellow Am. Coll. Dentists (regent 1983-87, v.p. 1988-89, pres.-elect 1989-90, pres. 1990-91, pres. ACD Found. 1991-92, William John Gies award 1998); mem. ADA (joint commn. on nat. dental exams. 1979-84, commn. on dental health of the coun. on sports medicine of the U.S. Olympic Com. 1980-88, chmn. commn. 1988—, mem. com. on accreditation, coun. on dental edn. 1986-90), W.Va. Dental Assn., Monongahela Valley Dental Soc., Monongahela County Dental Soc. (pres. 1966), Am. Assn. Dental Schs., Internat. Assn. Dental Rsch., Am. Assn. Endodontists, Gorgas Odontological Soc., Psi Omega, Omicron Kappa Upsilon (pres. Supreme chpt. 1965-67). Home: RR 7 Box 720 Morgantown WV 26505-9867 Office: 1157 HSCN PO Box 9001 Morgantown WV 26506-9001

BIDDLE, ALBERT GEORGE WILKINSON, III, (JACK BIDDLE), venture capitalist; b. Chgo., Jan. 24, 1961; s. A.G.W. and Leah Anne (Breen) B.; m. Forée Pendleton McCauley, Apr. 21, 1990; children: A.G.W. IV, Caldwell Knight, Brooks Christopher. BA in Econs., U. Va., 1983. Assoc. Bus. Devel. Ptnrs., Austin, Tex., 1983-85; exec. asst. to CEO, Gartner Group, Stamford, Conn., 1985-86; prin. Vanguard Atlantic, N.Y.C., 1986-90; pres., CEO, Intercap Systems, Annapolis, Md., 1990-95; gen. ptnr. Novak Biddle Venture Ptnrs., McLean, Va., 1996—. Bd. dirs. Object Video, Paratek Microwave, Matrics. Mem.: Computer and Comm. Industry Assn. (bd. dirs.), Annapolis Yacht Club, Chevy Chase Club. Office: Novak Biddle Venture Ptnrs Ste 1380 7501 Wisconsin Ave Bethesda MD 20814-6400 E-mail: jack@novakbiddle.com.

BIDDLE, BRUCE JESSE, social psychologist, educator; b. Ossining, N.Y., Dec. 30, 1928; s. William Wishart and Loureide Jeanette (Cobb) B.; m. Ellen Catherine Horgan; children: David Charles, William Jesse, Jennifer Loureide; m. Barbara Julianne Bank, June 19, 1976. AB in Math., Antioch Coll., Yellow Springs, Ohio, 1950; postgrad., U. N.C., 1950-51; PhD in Social Psychology, U. Mich., 1957. Asst. prof. sociology U. Ky., 1957-58; assoc. prof. edn. U. Kansas City, 1958-60; assoc. prof. psychology and sociology U. Mo., Columbia, 1960-66, prof., 1966-2000, prof. emeritus, 2000—, dir. Ctr. Rsch. in Social Behavior, 1966-96. Vis. assoc. prof. U. Queensland, Australia, 1965; vis. prof. Monash U., Australia, 1969, vis. fellow Australian Nat. U., 1977, 85, 93. Author: (with R.S. Adams) Realities of Teaching: Explorations with Videotape, 1970, (with M.J. Dunkin) The Study of Teaching, 1974, (with T.L. Good and J. Brophy) Teachers Make a Difference, 1975, Role Theory: Expectations, Identities and Behaviors, 1979, (with D.C. Berliner) The Manufactured Crisis: Myths, Fraud, and the Attack on America's Public Schools, 1995, (with L.J. Saha) The Untested Accusation: Principals, Research Knowledge, and Policy Making in Schools, 2002; editor: (with W.J. Ellena) contemporary Research on Teacher Effectiveness, 1964, (with E.J. Thomas) Role Theory: Concepts and Research, 1966, (with P.H. Rossi) The New Media: Their Impact on Education, 1966, (with D.S. Anderson) Knowledge for Policy: Improving Education Through Research, 1991, (with T.L. Good and I.F. Goodson) International Handbook of Teachers and Teaching, 1997, Social Class, Poverty, and Education, 2001. Served with U.S. Army, 1954-56. Fellow APA, Am. Psychol. Soc., Australian Psychol. Soc.; mem. Am. Ednl. Research Assn., Australian Assn. Rsch. Edn., Am. Sociol. Assn., Midwest Sociol. Soc. Home: 924 Yale Columbia MO 65203-1874 Office: U Mo Dept Psychology McAlester Hall Rm 210 Columbia MO 65211-0001 E-mail: BiddleB@missouri.edu.

BIDDLE, CATHARINA BAART, artist; b. The Netherlands; m. Livingston L. Biddle, 1973. MFA, George Washington U., Am. U., 1981. Art tchr. Am. Sch., Libya, 1964-66, Washington Pub. Sch. Sys., 1967-73; vol. NEA, 1973-81: Works in mus. and pvt. collections in New York and Wash. D.C. Home: 3050 P St NW Washington DC 20007-3052

BIDDLE, DANIEL R. editor, reporter; Grad., U. Mich. With Cleve. Plain Dealer, 1976-79; reporter Phila. Inquirer, from 1979, asst. city editor, 1991-92, dep. met. editor, 1996-97, Pa. editor, 1997-99, nat. editor, 1999. Co-recipient Pulitzer prize for investigative reporting, 1987; Nieman fellow Harvard U., 1989-90. Office: Phila Inquirer PO Box 8263 Philadelphia PA 19101-8263

BIDDLE, FLORA MILLER, writer; BA, Manhattanville Coll., 1978. Pres. Whitney Mus. Am. Art, N.Y.C., 1978-85, chmn., 1985—95, hon. trustee. Mem. N.Y.C. Art Commn., 1980-90. Author: The Whitney Women and the Museum They Made, 1999. Home and Office: 88 Kielwasser Rd New Preston Marble Dale CT 06777 E-mail: floramil@earthlink.net.

BIDDLE, TIMOTHY MAURICE, lawyer; b. San Jose, Calif., Dec. 1, 1940; s. Maurice Francis and Hazel Eda (Bold) B.; m. Florence Elizabeth Hickey, June 15, 1963; children: Elizabeth, Timothy Mark, Matthew, Rebecca. BA in History, Georgetown U., 1962; JD, Cath. U., 1971. Assoc. Jones, Day, Reavis & Pogue, Washington, 1971-77, ptnr., 1977-79, Crowell & Moring LLP, Washington, 1979—. Contbr. articles to profl. jours. Capt. USAF, 1962—67. Recipient Disting. Lawyer for 1991 Nat. Coal Assn., 1991. Mem.: ABA, Energy and Mineral Law Found. (trustee), Helicopter Assn. Internat. (bd. dirs., spl. advisor 1990—). Office: Crowell & Moring LLP 1001 Pennsylvania Ave NW Washington DC 20004-2595

BIDDULPH, DANA LEE, research scientist; b. Phoenix, Ariz., Nov. 18, 1964; s. David and Donna Biddulph; m. Nicole Baca, June 24, 1970; children: Taylor Anne, Gabrielle Margaret. MS, U of Ariz., Tucson, AZ, 1988—2002. Sr. rsch. specialist U of Ariz., Tucson, 1999—. M Sgt. E7 USAF, 2001—03, Luke AFB. Decorated Air Force Commendation Medal USAF. Home: 9160 E Deer Trail Tucson AZ 85710 Office: U Ariz PAS 81 1118 E 4th St Tucson AZ 85710 Personal E-mail: biddulph@physics.arizona.edu.

BIDELMAN, MARK, music educator; b. Watsonville, Calif., Dec. 4, 1952; s. Hal Edward Bidelman and Jerry Hanjer; m. Monica Meyer. BA, U. Calif. Santa Cruz, Santa Cruz, CA, 1975. Music educator Santa Cruz City Schools, Santa Cruz, Calif., 1975—, Cabrillo Coll., Apta, Calif., 1975—. Festival dir. Santa Cruz Jazz Festival, Santa Cruz, Calif. Contbr. articles profl. jour. Recipient Music Educator Of The Yr., Calif. Music Educators Assn., 1990, 2003. Home: PO Box 1015 Soquel CA 95073

BIDELMAN, WILLIAM PENDRY, astronomer, educator; b. L.A., Sept. 25, 1918; s. William Pendry and Dolores (De Remer) B.; m. Verna Pearl Shirk, June 19, 1940; children: Lana Louise Stone (dec. Mar. 2000), Linda Elizabeth McKinley, Billie Jean Little, Barbara Jo Talley. Student, U. N.D., 1936-37; SB, Harvard, 1940; PhD, U. Chgo., 1943. Physicist, Aberdeen Proving Ground, Md., 1943-45; instr., then asst. prof. astronomy Yerkes Obs., U. Chgo., 1945-53; asst. astronomer, then. assoc. astronomer Lick Obs., U. Calif., 1953-62; prof. U. Mich., 1962-69, U. Tex. at Austin, 1969-70, Case Western Res. U., Cleve., 1970-86, prof. emeritus, 1986—. Chmn. dept., dir. Warner and Swasey Obs., 1970-75; mem. adv. panel on astronomy NSF, 1959-62; mem. NRC adv. com. on astronomy Office Naval Rsch., 1964-67. Contbr. articles to profl. jours. Mem. Am. Astron. Soc. (councilor 1959-62, participant vis. prof. program 1961-65), Astron. Soc. Pacific (editor Publs. 1956-61), Internat. Astron. Union (commns. 29, 45, pres. 1964-67), Phi Beta Kappa. Presbyterian. Achievements include discovery of lines of mercury, krypton and xenon in stellar spectra; discovery of phosphorus stars; co-discovery of barium stars; research in spectral classification, astronomical data and observational astrophysics. Home: 3171 Chelsea Dr Cleveland Heights OH 44118-1256 Office: Case Western Res U Dept Astronomy 10900 Euclid Ave Cleveland OH 44106-7215 E-mail: wsobs@grendel.astr.cwru.edu.

BIDEN, JOSEPH ROBINETTE, JR., senator; b. Scranton, Pa., Nov. 20, 1942; m. Jill Tracy Jacobs, June 17, 1977; children: Ashley Blazer, Joseph Robinette, Robert Hunter. BA History and Polit. Sci., U. Del.; JD, Syracuse U., 1968. Bar: Del. 1968. Practice law, Wilmington, 1968-72; U.S. senator from Del., 1972—. Active New Castle (Del.) County Coun., 1970-72; chmn. jud. com., U.S. Senate, 1987-95, mem. 1995—, ranking minority mem., 1995-97; chmn. fgn. rels. com., 2001-02, chmn. subcom. on crime and drugs, ranking Dem. chmn. subcom. European affairs; chmn. Caucus Internat. Narcotics Control, 2001--. Democrat. Office: 221 Russell Senate Bldg Washington DC 20510-0001*

BIDERMAN, CHARLES ISRAEL, diversified financial services company executive; b. N.Y.C., Oct. 24, 1946; m. Brenda Carol Nicholson (div.); 1 child, John Patrick; m. Cheryl Marie Johnson, Sept. 8, 1985 (div.); 1 child, Christopher Isaac. BA, Bklyn. Coll., 1967; MBA, Harvard U., 1971. Assoc. editor Barron's Fin. Weekly, 1971-73; pres. Charles Biderman & Co., N.Y.C. and Nashville, 1980-89, Market St. Devel. Corp. (formerly Nashville Mgmt. Corp.), 1976-80; pres., CEO, Trimtabs Fin. Svcs., Inc., Santa Rosa, Calif., 1990—. Fin. editor Wall St. Final, N.Y.C.; editor Market Trim Tabs. (constructed over 200 home including) Gaslite Condominiums and Lafayette Townhouses, Seaside Park, N.J., Three Pence Brooke Townhomes, Jackson, N.J., N.J. Quail Farms, Jackson. Bd. dirs. Tenn. Dance Theater, 1977—80, Children & Family Cir., 1989. With USAF, 1966—67. Office: Trim Tabs Fin Svcs Inc 520 Mendocino Ave Ste 350 Santa Rosa CA 95401-5258

BIDLACK, JEAN MARIE, pharmacologist, educator, medical researcher; b. Rochester, N.Y., Dec. 4, 1953; d. William Henry and Mary Louise (Naughton) Bidlack. BA in Biology and Chemistry, Skidmore Coll., 1975; PhD in Biophysics, U. Rochester, 1979. Postdoctoral fellow U. Rochester, 1979-80, sr. instr. Ctr. Brain Rsch., 1980-81, asst. prof. brain rsch., 1981-87, assoc. prof. pharmacology, 1987-97, prof. pharmacology and physiology, 1997—, chair faculty senate, 2002—03. Cons. NSF, Washington, 1983—89, VA, Washington, 1986—88, Nat. Inst. Drug Abuse, Rockville, Md., 1987—, AIDS Study Sect., 1996—2002; secretariat Internat. Narcotics Rsch. Conf., 1999. Contbr. articles to profl. jours. Recipient Sr. Sci. award, KO5 NIH, 1998—; U. Rochester fellow, 1975—79. Mem.: Soc. Neurosci., Am. Soc. Pharmacology and Exptl. Therapeutics, Coll. on Problems of Drug Dependence Inc. Achievements include patents for immunossay of free kappa light chains for the detection of multiple sclerosis. Office: U Rochester/Sch Med and Dentistry Dept Pharm and Physiology 601 Elmwood Ave Rochester NY 14642-8711

BIDLACK, RUSSELL EUGENE, librarian, educator, former dean; b. Manilla, Iowa, May 25, 1920; s. Harold Stanley and Mabel (Thompson) B.; m. Melva Helen Sparks, June 13, 1942; children: Stanley Alden, Martha Sue, Christopher Joel, Harold Wilford. BA with honors, Simpson Coll., 1947, Litt.D. (hon.), 1976; AB in L.S. with honors, U. Mich., 1948, A.M. in L.S, 1949, A.M. in History, 1950, PhD (L.S.), 1954. Instr. library sci. U. Mich., 1951-56, asst. prof., 1956-60, assoc. prof., 1960-65, prof., 1965-85, dean Sch. Library Sci., 1969-85, prof. and dean emeritus, 1985—. Author: The City Library of Detroit, 1817-1837, 1955, Letters Home, the Story of Ann Arbor's Forty-Niners, 1960, John Allen and the Founding of Ann Arbor, 1962, The Yankee Meets the Frenchman, 1965, The ALA Accreditation Process, 1977, Ann Arbor's First Lady, Events in the Life of Ann I. Allen, 1998. Served to master sgt. AUS, 1941-46. Recipient Beta Phi Mu award for distinguished service to edn. for librarianship, 1977; Melvil Dewey medal creative profl. achievement, 1979; Joseph W. Lippincott award for disting. service to librarianship, 1983 Mem. ALA (chmn. subcom. to rewrite Standards accreditation 1969-72, chmn. com. 1974-76, chmn. Melvil Dewey award jury 1973-74, chmn. Am. Library History Roundtable 1973-74, mem. council 1972-76, chmn. nominating com. 1980-81), Mich. Library Assn. (pres. tech. services sect.), Assn. Library and Info. Sci. Edn. (chmn. deans and dirs. group 1978-79), Mich. Hist. Soc. Home: 1709 Cherokee Rd Ann Arbor MI 48104-4498

BIDLACK, WAYNE ROSS, nutritional biochemist, toxicologist, food scientist; b. Waverly, N.Y., Aug. 12, 1944; s. Andrew L. Bidlack and Vivian Pearl Cowles Williams; m. Wei Wang. BS, Pa. State U., 1966; MS, Iowa State U., 1968; PhD, U. Calif., Davis, 1972. Postdoctoral fellow dept. pharmacology U. So. Calif., L.A., 1972-74, asst prof. sch. medicine, 1974-80, assoc. prof., 1980-92, prof., 1992—, asst. dean student affairs, 1988-91, chmn. dept. pharmacology and nutrition, 1991-92; chmn. dept. food sci. and human nutrition Iowa State U., Ames, 1992-95; dean Coll. Agr. Calif. State Poly. U., Pomona, 1995—. Assoc. editor Biochem. Medicine and Metabolic Biology, 1986-87; mem. editl. bd. Jour. Am. Coll. Nutrition, 1995—; assoc. editor Environ. Nutritional Interactions, 1996-2000, Toxicology, 2000—. Chmn. Greater L.A. Nutrition Coun., 1982-83, So. Calif. Inst. Food Technologists, 1988-89, Toxicology and Safety Evaluation divsn. Inst. Food Technologists, 1989-90, food sci. communicator, 1986-90; chmn. Nat. Coun. Against Health Fraud, 1983-85; mem. expert panel on foods and nutrition, 1989-93. Recipient Outstanding Tchr. Award, U. So. Calif., Sch. Medicine, 1987-88, Meritorious Svc. award, Calif. Dietetic Assn., 1990, Disting. Achievement award, So. Calif. Inst. Food Technologists, 1990, Bautzer Faculty award, Calif. State U., 1998; fellow Inst. Food Technologists, 1998, Wang Family award of Excellence for Adminstrs., Calif. State U., 2002. Mem. Soc. Toxicology (chair awards com. food safety sect. 1993-94, chair 1994-95), Nat. Golden Key Soc. (hon.), Gamma Sigma Delta. Republican. Avocations: golf, book collecting. Office: Calif State Polytech U Coll of Agrl 3801 W Temple Ave Pomona CA 91768-2557 E-mail: wrbidlack@csupomona.edu.

BIDWELL, CHARLES EDWARD, sociologist, educator; b. Chgo., Jan. 24, 1932; s. Charles Leslie and Eugenia (Campbell) B.; m. Helen Claxton Lewis, Jan. 24, 1959; 1 son, Charles Lewis. AB, U. Chgo., 1950, AM, 1953, PhD, 1956. Lectr. on sociology Harvard U., 1959-61; asst. prof. edn. U. Chgo., 1961-65, assoc. prof., 1965-70, prof. edn. and sociology, 1970-85, Reavis prof. edn. and sociology, 1985-2001, Reavis prof. emeritus edn. and sociology, 2001—, chmn. dept. edn., 1978-88, chmn. dept. sociology, 1988-94, dir. Ogburn-Stouffer Ctr., 1988-94. Author books in field; contbr. numerous articles to profl. jours.; editor Sociology of Edn., 1969-72, Am. Jour. Sociology, 1973-78, Am. Jour. Edn., 1983-88. With U.S. Army, 1957-59. Guggenheim fellow, 1971-72 Fellow AAAS; mem. Sociol. Rsch. Assn., Nat. Acad. Edn. (sec.), Phi Beta Kappa. Office: Dept Sociology 5848 S University Ave Chicago IL 60637-1515 E-mail: cbidwell@uchicago.edu.

BIDWELL, JAMES TRUMAN, JR., lawyer; b. N.Y.C., Jan. 2, 1934; s. James Truman and Mary (Kane) B.; m. Gail S. Bidwell, Mar. 6, 1965 (div.); children: Hillary Day Bidwell Mackay, Kimberley Wade, Cortney E.; m. Katherine T. O'Neil, July 15, 1988. BA, Yale U., 1956; LLB, Harvard U., 1959. Bar: N.Y. 1959. Atty. USAF, Austin, Tex., 1959-62; assoc. Donovan, Leisure, Newton & Irvine, N.Y.C., 1962-68, ptnr., 1968-84, White & Case, N.Y.C., 1984-98; sr. counsel Linklaters, N.Y.C., 1998—2003; ptnr. Thelen, Reid, Pries LLP, 2003—. Pres. Youth Consultation Svc., 1973-78; trustee Berkeley Divinity Sch. Mem. ABA, Fed. Bar Assn., N.Y. State Bar Assn., N.Y. County Lawyers Assn. Episcopalian. Office: Thelen Reid & Priest LLP 875 Third Ave New York NY 10022-6225

BIDWELL, ROGER GRAFTON SHELFORD, biologist, educator; b. Halifax, N.S., Can., June 8, 1927; came to U.S., 1965; s. Roger Edward Shelford and Mary B.; m. Shirley Mae Rachael Mason, July 1, 1950; children— Barbara, Alison, Roger, Gillian. B.Sc., Dalhousie U., 1947; BA, Queen's U., 1950, MA, 1951, PhD, 1954. Tech. officer Canadian Def. Research Bd., Kingston, Ont., 1951-56; asst. research officer Nat. Research Council, Halifax, 1956-59; assoc. prof. biology U. Toronto, Ont., 1959-65; prof. biology Case Western Res. U., Cleve., 1965-69, chmn. dept., 1966-68; prof. biology Queen's U., Kingston, Ont., Can., 1969-79, prof. emeritus, 1979—; I.W. Killam research prof. Dalhousie U., Halifax, 1980-85; sr. ptnr. Atlantic Research Assocs. Ltd., Wallace, N.S., 1980-91; exec. dir. Atlantic Inst. Biotech., Halifax, 1985-88. Vis. prof. Cornell U., 1961-63; vis. scientist Atlantic Regional Lab., NRC, Halifax, summer 1966, 76; cons. Faculty Edn., Simon Fraser U., 1966; Can. Sci. Exch. visitor to People's Republic of China, 1975, 77. Author: Plant Physiology, 1974, 79; co-editor: Plant Physiology: A Treatise, 1978-90; contbr. over 150 articles to profl. jours., chpts. to textbooks on biochem. mechanisms in plants, protein metabolism, CO2 metabolism in leaves, photosynthesis and metabolism in marine algae, global climate change. Active Crime Stoppers, Cumberland region, 1993-97, chmn., 1994-97; mem. several coms. Anglican Diocese N.S.; pres., chmn. bd. Pugwash Coop. Ltd., 1995-2000; warden Parish of Pugwash/River John, 1998-2002; mem. diocesan coun. Diocese of Nova Scotia and Prince Edward Island, 1999-2001; mem. Pugwash and Area Cmty. Health Bd., 2001--. Recipient Queen Elizabeth II Silver Jubilee medal, 1977. Fellow AAAS, Royal Soc. Can.; mem. Canadian Soc. Plant Physiologists (founder, past sec.-treas., pres. 1972-73, Gold medal 1979), Biol. Council Can. (sec. 1973-76), Am. Soc. Plant Physiology. Avocations: bicycling, walking, skiing, bird watching, weaving.

BIDWILL, WILLIAM V. professional football executive; s. Charles W. and Violet Bidwill; m. Nancy Bidwill; children: William Jr., Michael, Patrick, Timothy, Nicole. Grad., Georgetown U. Co-owner St. Louis Cardinals Football Team (now Ariz. Cardinals), 1962-72, owner, 1972—, also chmn., 1972—, pres. Office: Ariz Cardinals PO Box 888 Phoenix AZ 85001-0888

BIEBEL, CURT FRED, JR., dentist; b. St. Louis, Dec. 7, 1947; s. Curt F. and Jewell (Frank) B.; children: Betheny Doreen, Brendon Matthew. AB in Psychology, U. Mo., Columbia, 1970; DDS, U. Mo., Kansas City, 1974. Assoc. dentist Louis R. Nolan, Inc., St. Louis, 1976-79; gen. practice dentistry Chesterfield, Mo., 1979—. Capt. USAF, 1974-76. Mem. ADA, Greater St. Louis Dental Soc., Chgo. Dental Soc., Country Club of St. Albans, Forest Park Handball Assn., St. Louis Hinder Club. Office: 14378 Wood Lake Dr Chesterfield MO 63017-5714

BIEBEL, PAUL PHILIP, JR., lawyer; b. Chgo., Mar. 24, 1942; s. Paul Philip Sr. and Eleanor Mary (Sweeney) B.; divorced; children: Christine M., Brian E., Jennifer A., Susan E. AB, Marquette U., 1964; JD, Georgetown U., 1967. Bar: Ill. 1967, U.S. Dist. Ct. (no. dist.) Ill. 1967, U.S. Ct. Appeals (6th cir.) 1985, U.S. Supreme Ct. 1972. Asst. dean of men Loyola U., Chgo., 1967-69; asst. state's atty. Cook County State's Atty., Chgo., 1969-75, dep. state's atty., 1975-81; 1st asst. atty. gen. Ill. Atty. Gen., Chgo., 1981-85; pub. defender Cook County Pub. Defender, Chgo., 1986-88; ptnr. Winston & Strawn, Chgo., 1985-86, 88-94, Altheimer & Gray, Chgo., 1994-96; judge Cir. Ct. Cook County, Ill., 1996—. Contbr. articles to profl. pubs. Mem. Fed. Bar Assn. (bd. dirs., pres. 1994-95), Cath. Lawyers Guild (bd. dirs., Cath. Lawyer of Yr. 1988), Ill. Judges Assn., Ill. Appellate Lawyers, 7th Cir. Bar Assn., Chgo. Bar Assn. (chmn. com. 1991-93), Georgetown Law Alumni Assn. (bd. dirs. 1991-96). Roman Catholic. Avocations: reading, golf. Home: 5415 N Forest Glen Ave Chicago IL 60630-1523 Office: Presiding Judge Criminal Divsn RM 101 2600 S California Ave Chicago IL 60608

BIEBER, KONRAD FERDINAND, retired language educator; b. Berlin, Mar. 24, 1916; arrived in U.S., 1947; s. Hugo and Lucy (Nathan) Bieber; m. Tamara Siew, Aug. 29, 1939; children: Thomas, Robert, Joel. Lic.-es-Lettres, U. Paris-Sorbonne, 1938; PhD in Comparative Lit., Yale U., 1953. Instr. in French Yale U., New Haven, 1948-53; from asst. prof. to prof., chmn. dept. Conn. Coll., New London, 1953-68; instr. in French Middlebury Coll. Summer Sch., 1949-51, 56; prof. French and Comparative Lit. SUNY, Stony Brook, 1968-86, prof. emeritus, 1986—. Vis. lectr. U. Colo., Boulder, 1952; adv. bd. Simone-de-Beauvoir Studies, 1996—. Author: (book) L'Allemagne vue par les Ecrivains de la Résistance Francaise, 1954, Simone de Beauvoir, 1979; contbr. ; translator: (hist. document) Outwitting the Gestapo, 1993, Historical Dictionary of World War II France, 1998, Vercors et son Oeuvre, 1999, Albert Camus The Rebel 50 Years Later, 2001; mem. editl. bd.: Press of SUNY, 1969—82, Novel of Brown U., 1966—; contbr. articles to profl. jours. Mem. NAACP, 1954—94; rep. French Assn. Against Racism and for Peace, 1966—86. Sgt. French Army and Resistance, 1940—44. Named Chevalier des Palmes Académiques, 1970; fellow Guggenheim, 1957—58. Mem.: MLA (sect. chmn. 1957—60), Internat. Comparative Lit. Assn., Simone-de-Beauvoir Soc. (co-founder, v.p. 1981—90). Democrat. Jewish. Avocations: tennis, ping pong. Home: 1211 Foulkeways Gwynedd PA 19436-1031

BIEBERICH, ERHARD, biologist; b. Cologne, Germany, Apr. 28, 1961; PhD, U. Cologne, 1991. Instr. Med. Coll. Va., Richmond, 1996—99, asst. prof., 1999—2000, Med. Coll. Ga., Augusta, 2000—. Contbr. scientific papers to profl. jours. Fellow, U. Bonn, Germany, 1991—96. Achievements include patents for Ceramide Analogs. Office: Med Coll Ga 1120 15th St Rm CB-2803 Augusta GA 30912

BIEBER-ROBERTS, PEGGY EILENE, communications educator, editor, journalist, researcher; b. Mobridge, S.D., Jan. 8, 1943; d. John J. and Lenora (Schlepp) Bieber; m. Phil Roberts. BS, No. State U., Aberdeen, S.D., 1966; MA, U. Wyo., 1984; PhD, U. Wash., 1990. Vol. Peace Corps, Turkey, 1966-68; tchr. secondary pub. schs., Idaho, 1968-69, Pine Ridge (S.D.) Reservation, 1969-71; co-founder Medicine Bow Post weekly newspaper, 1977; legis. reporter various weekly newspapers, Wyo., 1980-82; owner, pub. Capitol Times mag., Cheyenne, Wyo., 1982-84; pub. Skyline West Press, 1983—; lectr. pub. rels. and advt. U. Wash., Seattle, 1986-88; rsch. analyst Elway Rsch./Jay Rockey Co., Seattle, 1989-90; assoc. prof. mass media U. Wyo., Laramie, 1990-96; journalism faculty comm. tech. Higher Colls. of Tech., Dubai, United Arab Emirates, 1996-98; polit. campaign mgr. Phil Roberts gubernatorial campaign, Wyo., 1998; asst. prof. journalism and mass comms. Am. U. in Cairo, 1999—2001, assoc. prof., 2001—, chair dept. journalism and mass comm., 2000—02. Indexer McGraw/Hill, Bedford Books, also others, 1988—94. Author, editor: hist. almanacs for various states, 1984—87; contbr. articles to profl. jours., chapters to books. Publicity chmn. Laramie County Dem. Com., Cheyenne, 1982; publicity chmn., precinct committeewoman Albany County Dems., 1999—2000. Named Stout fellow, U. Wash., 1990; recipient 1st Place

award for feature writing, co-1st Place award for editorials, Wyo. Press Assn., 1982, Alumni Assn. Faculty Growth award, U. Wyo., 1994. Mem.: Mid East Studies Assn., Internat. Comm. Assn., Assn. Ednl. Journalism and Mass Comm., Internat. Assn. Mass Comm. Rsch., Turkish Studies Assn. Office: Am U Cairo 025 Social Sci Bldg Cairo Egypt

BIEBUYCK, JULIEN FRANCOIS, medical educator, administrator; b. South Africa, Feb. 2, 1935; came to U.S., 1971, naturalized, 1985; s. Lucien Jean and Drix J. B.; m. Jeanette A. Sumner, May 10, 1961; children: Gavin L., Richard M., Clare E. MB, U. Capetown, 1959; DPhil, Oxford U., Eng., 1971. Diplomat Am. Bd. Anesthesiology. Nuffield scholar Oxford U., Eng., 1969-71; asst. prof. anesthesiology Harvard Med. Sch., Mass. Gen. Hosp., Boston, 1971-76; Eric A. Walker prof., chmn. dept. anesthesia Pa. State U. Coll. Medicine, Hershey, 1977-97, assoc. dean, 1991-97, sr. assoc. dean for acad. affairs, 1997—2000; Robert G. Petersdorf scholar-in-residence Assn. Am. Med. Coll., Washington, 2001—02, sr. cons. acad. mgmt. programs, 2002—. Mem. anesthetic and life support drugs adv. com. FDA, 1995-97. Mem. editorial bd. Anesthesiology, 1985-93; co-editor Current Opinion in Anaesthesiology; contbr. chpts. to books, articles to med. jours. Med. Found. fellow, 1972-76. Fellow Royal Coll. Anaesthetists (hon., London), Australian and New Zealand Coll. Anaesthetists (hon.); mem. AMA, Assn. Univ. Anesthesiologists, Am. Soc. Anesthesiologists (com. on rsch. 1994-97), Am. Physiol. Soc., Soc. Acad. Anesthesia Chmn. (past pres.), Coun. Acad. Socs. of Assn., Am. Med. Colls., Biochem. Soc. (London), Soc. Parenteral Nutrition, Soc. Neurosci., Soc. Neurosurg. Anesthesia, Pa. Med. Soc., Trinity Coll. Soc., Harvard Club, Cosmos Club, Alpha Omega Alpha. Home: 405 Meadow Ln Hershey PA 17033 Office: Assn Am Med Colls 2450 N St NW Washington DC 20037-1127 Office Fax: 202-828-1125. Business E-Mail: jbiebuyck@aamc.org.

BIECK, ROBERT BARTON, JR., lawyer; b. Wiesbaden, Germany, Apr. 13, 1952; s. Robert Barton and Mary-Jean (Boeck) B.; m. Julia A. Dietz, Apr. 20, 1991. BA in Polit. Sci., U. Nebr., 1974; JD with high honors, Tex. Tech. U., 1977. Bar: Tex. 1977, La. 1977, D.C. 1992, U.S. Dist. Ct. (ea. dist.) La. 1977, U.S. Dist. Ct. (mid. dist.) La. 1978, U.S. Dist. Ct. (we. dist.) La. 1979, U.S. Dist. Ct. (no. and so. dists.) Tex. 1991, U.S. Dist. Ct. D.C. (1994, U.S. Ct. Appeals (D.C. cir.) 1992, U.S. Ct. Appeals (5th and 11th cirs.) 1981, U.S. Supreme Ct. 1980. Assoc. firm Jones, Walker, Waechter, Poitevent, Carrere & Denegre, New Orleans, 1977-82, ptnr., 1982—. Chmn. profl. liability practice group, Jones, Walker, et al. Recipient West Horn Book award West Pub. Co., 1976; Fulbright and Jaworski scholar, 1976. Mem. ABA (litigation sect., bus. law sect., federal regulation of securities com.), Securities Industry Assn., Nat. Soc. Compliance Profls., New Orleans Bar Assn., La. Bankers Assn., 5th Cir. Bar Assn., Order of Coif, Phi Kappa Phi, Phi Delta Phi. Home: 5708 Annunciation St New Orleans LA 70115 Office: Jones Walker Waechter Poitevent Carrere & Denegre 201 Saint Charles Ave Ste 5200 New Orleans LA 70170-5100 E-mail: rbieck@joneswalker.com.

BIEDERMAN, BARRON ZACHARY (BARRY BIEDERMAN), advertising agency executive; b. N.Y.C. s. William and Sophye (Groll) B.; m. Susan Howard, Apr. 1, 1967; children: Rachel, David. BA with distinction, Cornell U., 1952; MS in Journalism, Columbia U, 1953; postgrad., U. London, 1954. Copy group head Mogul, Williams & Saylor, N.Y.C., 1955-59; sr. writer Lennen & Newell, N.Y.C., 1960-62; v.p., assoc. creative svcs. dir. Cunningham & Walsh, N.Y.C., 1962-64; sr. v.p. Needham, Harper & Steers, N.Y.C., 1964-84, exec. creative dir., 1964-74, mgmt. rep., 1974-79, dir., 1981-84; mng. dir. NH&S Corp. Futures, 1979-80; chmn., chief exec. officer NH&S/Issues & Images, 1981-84; chmn. Biederman & Co., Inc. (name changed to Biederman, Kelly & Shaffer, Inc. 1989), 1984—; chmn. emeritus Biederman, Kelly, Krimstein Ptnrs., 1998—2001; ret., 2001. Lectr. in field. Bd. dirs. Liberty Club, N.Y., 1983-87, Alvin Ailey Dance Theatre, N.Y., 1974. Recipient various advt. awards; Ford Found. fellow Eng., India, 1953-55 Mem. Fin. Comms. Soc. (bd. dirs. 1982-89, pres. 1986-87), Internat. Advt. Assn., Bank Mktg. Assn., Copywriters Club N.Y. (bd. dirs. 1960-64). Avocations: reading, music, carpentry, gardening, travel. Home: 425 E 58th St Apt 17G New York NY 10022-2300

BIEDERMAN, EDWIN WILLIAMS, JR., retired petroleum geologist; b. Stamford, Conn., June 30, 1930; s. Edwin Williams and Thelma Frances (Morrow) B.; m. Margaret-Jane Bell White, Aug. 23, 1958; children: Robert, Mary, Jane, James. BA, Cornell U., 1952; PhD, Pa. State U., 1958. Cert. petroleum geologist. Project leader Cities Svc. Co., Tulsa, 1958-68, pres. staff Cranbury, N.J., 1968-72; asst. dir. Pa. Tech. Assistance program, University Park, Pa., 1972-77, sr. tech. specialist, 1980—2001; field ctr. dir. NSF Chautauqua Courses, University Park, 1977-80. Field ctr. dir. NSF Chautauqua Courses, University Park, 1977-80. Author: Atlas of Oil and Gas Reservoir Rocks From North America, 1986; contbr. articles to profl. jours.; holder 5 patents for geochem. exploration, in situ acidulation of phosphate rock, grate for vertical oil shale kiln, fire retardant foam, lightweight cement for oil wells. Petroleum officer USAF, 1952-54. Pa. State U. scholar 1956-58; am. Assn. Petroleum Geologists grantee 1957; recipient First Place award Project of Yr. Nat. Assn. Mgmt. and Tech. Assistance Ctrs., 1985. Mem. AAAS, Am. Assn. Petroleum Geologists, Soc. Econ. Paleontologists and Mineralogists, Geochem. Soc., Assn. Profl. Geol. Scientists.

BIEDRON, THEODORE JOHN, newspaper advertising executive; b. Evergreen Park, Ill., Nov. 30, 1946; s. Theodore John and Ione Margaret B.; m. Gloria Anne DeAngelo, Nov. 7, 1970; children: Jessica Ann, Lauren. BA in Polit. Sci., U. Ill., 1968. Recruitment advt. mgr. Chgo. Sun-Times, 1968-74; classified advt. mgr. Pioneer press, Wilmette, Ill., 1974-76, v.p. advt. and promotion, 1993-94, sr. v.p. sales and mktg., 1994-97, exec. v.p., 1997-2000. Pub. North Shore mag., 1997-2000; classified mgr., v.p. Lerner Newspapers, Chgo., 1976-79, assoc. pub., 1980-82, advt. dir., 1982-87; v.p., classified advt. mgr. Chgo. Sun-Times, 1987-92; pres. Chicagoland Pub. Co. divsn. Chgo. Tribune, 2000—. Pres. Northeastern Ill. U. Found., 1998-2002; trustee Northlight Theater, 1993-98. Home: 404 Jackson Ave Glencoe IL 60022- Office: Chicagoland Pub Co 2000 S York Rd Oak Brook IL 60523 E-mail: tbiedron@earthlink.net.

BIEGEL, DAVID ELI, social worker, educator; b. N.Y.C., July 3, 1946; s. Jack and Estelle (Lentin) B.; m. Margaret S. Smoot, Jan. 31, 1976 (div.); 1 child, Geoffrey S. BA, CCNY, 1967; MSW, U. Md., 1970, PhD, 1982. Field coord. United Farm Workers, AFL-CIO, Balt., 1971; exec. dir. Junction, Inc., Westminster, Md., 1971—72; dir. office planning and program devel. Cath. Charities, Balt., 1973—76; ctr. assoc., dir. neighborhood and family svcs. project U. So. Calif., Washington Pub. Affairs Ctr., 1976—80; asst. prof. social work U. Pitts., 1980—85, assoc. prof., 1985—86; Henry L. Zucker prof. social work practice Mandel Sch. Applied Social Scis., Case Western Res. U., 1987—, prof. psychiatry and sociology, 1987—, co-dir. Ctr. for Practice Innovations, 1991—97, chair doctoral program, 1998—2001. Co-dir. Cuyahoga County Cmty. Mental Health Rsch. Inst., 1994—2002; pres. Inst. for the Advancement of Social Work Rsch., 1999—2002; dir. rsch. and evaluation Ohio Substance Abuse and Mental Illness Coord. Ctr. of Excellence, 2000—; co-dir. Ctr. Substance Abuse & Mental Illness, 2002—. Co-editor: Innovations in Practice and Service Delivery with Vulnerable Populations Series, Family Caregiving Applications Series; editor Practice Concepts sect., The Gerontologist; contbr. articles to profl. jours., books; co-author: Neighborhood Networks for Humane Mental Health Care, 1982, Community Support Systems and Mental Health: Practice, Policy and Research, 1982, Building Support Networks for the Elderly: Theory and Applications, 1984, Social Networks and Mental Health: An Annotated Bibliography, 1985, Social Support Networks: A Bibliography 1983-1987, 1989, Aging and Caregiving: Theory, Research and Policy, 1990, Family Preservation Programs: Research and Evaluation, 1991, Family Caregiving in Chronic Illness: Alzheimer's Dsiease, Cancer, Heart Disease, Mental Illness, and Stroke, 1991, Family Caregiving: A Lifespan Perspective, 1994, The Jewish Aged in the U.S. and Israel: Diversity, Programs and Services, 1994, Innovations in Practice and Service Delivery with Vulnerable Populations Across the Lifespan, 1999. Cons. Vol. VISTA, Raton, N.Mex., and Balt., 1967-70; active Big Bros. Am., Balt., 1974-77. N.Y. State Incentive scholar, 1963-64; VISTA Fellows Program fellow, 1968-70. Fellow Gerontol. Soc. Am.; mem. NASW, Acad. Cert. Social Workers, Soc. Social Work Rsch. Democrat. Jewish. E-mail: deb@po.cwru.edu.

BIEGEL, EILEEN MAE, retired hospital executive; b. Eau Claire, Wis., Nov. 13, 1937; d. Ewald Frederic and Emma Antonia (Conrad) Weggen; m. James O. Biegel, Oct. 6, 1956; children: Jeffrey Allan, John William. Student, Dist. One Tech. Inst., 1974; corr. student, U. Wis., Madison; grad. mgmt. seminars; student, Upper Iowa U., 1984—. Cert. profl. sec. Exec. sec. to pres. Broadcaster Svcs., Inc., Eau Claire, Wis., 1969-74; exec. sec. to exec. v.p. Am. Nat. Bank, Eau Claire, 1975-77; exec. asst. to pres. Luther Hosp., Eau Claire, 1977—2000, asst. corp. sec., 1984—2000, mem. exec. staff, 1985—2000; asst. corp. sec. Luther Health Care Corp., 1984—2000; ret., 2000; sec. Dist. Atty. Offfic, 2002—. Mem. secretarial adv. council Dist. One Tech. Sch. 1975—; corp. sec. Northwest Health Ventures, 1988-92, bd. dirs. State pres. Future Homemakers Am., 1955; mem. governance com. Wis. Hosp. Assn.; sec. bd. dirs. Chestnut Properties; sec. Christ Ch. Cathedral, Eau Claire, 2001, dist. atty., Eau Claire, 2002. Mem. Eau Claire Womens Network (founder, mem. steering com.), Profl. Secs. Internat. (chmn. goals and priorities com., pres. Eau Claire chpt. 1982-83), Wis. Hosp. Assn. (gov. com.). Home: 4707 Tower Dr Eau Claire WI 54703-8717 E-mail: ebiegel23@aol.com.

BIEGEL, JEFFREY ROBERT, composer; b. Forest Hills, Ny, May 31, 1961; s. Eugene Biegel and Janet Needleman-Biegel; m. Sharon Leigh Susnow, July 1, 1990; children: Craig Andrew, Evan Scott. BM, Juilliard Sch., New York, NY, 1983, MM, 1984. Faculty Bklyn Coll., Brooklyn, NY, 1998—, Grad. Ctr., CUNY, New York, NY, 2000—. Composer: (choral music, pop music) Psalms for Choir; editor: (piano works) 25 Preludes by Cesar Cui, (music composition) Symphonie Concertante by Reicha; composer (with Craig Biegel): The World in Our Hands. Recipient first prize, Gina Bachauer Juilliard Competition, Juilliard Sch., NY, 1981, 1984, William Petschek Debut Award, 1986, First Prize, Long-Thibaud Competition, Paris, France, 1989, William Kapell Competition, 1985. Achievements include 5 World Premiere recordings, first live audio/video online piano recital in 1997. Personal E-mail: sharpnat@aol.com.

BIEGLER, DAVID W. energy executive; b. 1946; married. BS, St. Mary's U., 1968; postgrad., Harvard U., 1980. With Enserch Exploration Inc., 1966-78, petroleum engr., 1968-70, dist. petroleum engr., 1970-72, staff petroleum engr., then mgr. revenue control, 1972-74, chief engr., 1974-75, dir. engring. mktg. planning, then v.p. processing engring. mktg., 1975-77, v.p. land and mktg., 1977-78; exec. v.p. Pool Arabia, 1978-79; exec. v.p. eastern hemisphere Pool Intairdril, 1979-80; pres. Pool Well Servicing Co., 1980-84, pres. U.S. ops. Pool Co., 1984-85; pres., COO, CEO, chmn. Enserch Corp., Dallas, 1985—97; pres., COO, vice-chmn. TXU Corp. (formerly Tex. Utilities), Dallas, 1997—2001; mng. ptnr. Estrella Energy, Dallas, 2003—. Office: 1700 Pacific Ste 2920 Dallas TX 75201

BIEHL, KATHY ANNE, author, lawyer; b. Pitts., Jan. 27, 1956; d. Edward Robert and Julianne (Addis) B. BA with highest honors, So. Meth. U., 1976; JD with honors, U. Tex., 1979. Bar: Tex. 1979, U.S. Dist. Ct. (so. dist.) Tex. 1986, U.S. Ct. Appeals (5th cir.) 1986. Assoc. Schlanger, Cook, Cohn, Mills & Grossberg, Houston, 1979-82; sole practice Houston, 1982-98. Lectr. Rice U., Houston, 1982; adj prof. U. Houston, 1988; owner, mgr. Metaphysiques Tapes, Houston, 1988-99; co-owner, mgr. Mantic Door Music, Houston, 1992-97; co-owner Red Room Recs., Houston, 1999—. Co-author: The Lawyer's Guide to Internet Research, 2000; editor The Compedium of Urban Anthropology, 1988—; contbr. articles to profl. jours. Vol. Tex. Accts. and Lawyers for Arts, Houston, 1981-98, Orange Show Found., Houston, 1985-98. Mem. Tex. Bar Assn., Phi Beta Kappa. Democrat. E-mail: kbiehl@fortunaworks.com.

BIEHL, MICHAEL MELVIN, lawyer, author; b. Milw., Feb. 24, 1951; s. Michael Melvin Biehl and Frieda Margaret (Krieg) Davis. AB, Harvard U., 1973, JD, 1976. Bar: Wis. 1976, U.S. Dist. Ct. (ea. dist.) Wis. 1976. Assoc. Foley & Lardner, Milw., 1976-84, ptnr., 1984—. Adj. prof. law Marquette U. Law Sch., 2001—. Author: Medical Staff Legal Issues, 1990, Doctored Evidence, 2002, Lawyered to Death, 2003; editor: Physician Organizations and Medical Staff, 1996. Mem. Mt. Sinai Med. Ctr. Clin. Investigations Com., Hastings Ctr.; election monitor first multi-party elections in Rep. Ga., 1990; dir. Colorlines Found. for Arts and Culture, Inc., chmn., bd. dirs. Milw. Psychiat. Hosp. and Aurora Behavioral Health Svcs. Mem. ABA, Am. Health Lawyers Assn., Am. Coll. of Med. Quality, Am. Soc. Law and Medicine. Mem. Unitarian Ch. Home: 10315 N Versailles Ct Mequon WI 53092-5231 Office: Foley & Lardner 777 E Wisconsin Ave Ste 3800 Milwaukee WI 53202-5367

BIEHLE, KAREN JEAN, pharmacist; b. Festus, Mo., July 18, 1959; d. Warren Day and Wilma Georgenia (Hedrick) Hargus; m. Scott Joseph Biehle, Aug. 22, 1981; children: Lauren Rachel, Heather Michelle. Student of pre-pharmacy, U. Mo., Columbia, Mo., 1977-79; BS in Pharmacy, U. Mo., Kans. City, Mo., 1982. Reg. Pharmicist. Pharmacy res. U. Iowa Hosp. & Clinics, Iowa City, Iowa, 1982-83; pharmacist Jewish Hosp. of St. Louis, St. Louis, 1983-86; pharmacy mgr. Foster Infusion Care, St. Louis, 1986-88; staff pharmacist Cardinal Glennon Children's Hosp., St. Louis, 1988-90; pres. Lauren's Specialty Foods, Inc., St. Louis, 1988-89; pharmacy mgr. Curaflex Health Svcs., St. Louis, 1989-91; asst. dir. Cobb Hosp. and Med. Ctr., Austell, Ga., 1991-94; asst. dir. pharmacy Publix Supermarkets, Marietta, Ga., 1994-96; pharmacist Scottish Rite Children's Med. Ctr., Marietta, Ga., 1996—. Preceptor St. Louis Coll. Pharmacy, 1984-91, U. Ga. Sch. Pharmacy, 1992. Vol. March of Dimes Walk-a-thon, 1985-90. Recipient Roche Pharmacy Communications Award, Roche Pharmaceuticals, Kans. City, 1982, I Dare You Award, 4-H Club, Nevada, Mo., 1976. Mem. Am. Soc. Hosp. Pharmacists, Kappa Epsilon, Alpha Delta Pi (St. Louis Alumnae pres. 1989-90). Republican. Baptist. Avocations: tennis, horseback riding, swimming, cooking, golf. Home: 3200 Wicks Creek Trl Marietta GA 30062-4867

BIELEFELDT, CATHERINE C. sales executive; b. Bellwood, Ill. d. William Anton and Linda (Buchert) B. MusB in Piano Performance, Chgo. Conservatory Coll.; student, El Conservatorio de Mex., Mexico City; postgrad., Northwestern U., CBS Sch. Mgmt. Dept. mgr. Fair Store, Oak Park, Ill., 1950-62; piano sales cons. Lyon & Healy Co., Oak Park and Oak Brook, Ill., 1963-77; dir. Steinway Hall, dir. nat. sales tng. Steinway & Sons, Long Island City, NY, 1978—82; v.p. sales, pub. rels. and advt. Hendricks Music Co., Downers Grove, Ill., 1983—. Sales seminar instr. Jordan-Kitt's Music, Wells Music, Washington and Denver, 1983-85, Lauzon Music, Ottawa, Can., 1986—, Meridian Music, Indpls., 1989. Author: The Wonders of the Piano, The Anatomy of the Instrument, 1984, 3d edit., 2003; editor The Keynote Newsletter, 1983-91; contbr. articles to profl. mours. Mem. Evanston Music Club, Sigma Alpha Iota (past pres. alumnae chpt., recipient numerous awards). Home: 190 S Wood Dale Rd Apt 1101 Wood Dale IL 60191-2246 Office: Hendricks Music 421 Maple Ave Downers Grove IL 60515-3806 E-mail: ccbwonders@aol.com.

BIELENBERG, LEONARD HERMAN, lawyer; b. Genesee, Idaho, July 14, 1927; s. Herman Christian and Rosella Elizabeth (Roth) B.; m. Alta Fern Claney, Oct. 31, 1953; children: Terry, Anne, Paul, Mary. BS in Bus., U. Idaho, 1950, JD, 1952. Bar: Idaho 1952, U.S. Dist. Ct. Idaho 1952. Asst. atty. gen. State of Idaho, Boise, 1952-54; ptnr. Felton & Bielenberg, Moscow, Idaho, 1954-69; pros. atty. Latah County, Moscow, 1961-67; sr. ptnr. Felton, Bielenberg & Anderson, Moscow, 1969-73, Bielenberg & Anderson, Moscow, 1973-75, Bielenberg, Anderson & Walker, Moscow, 1975-97; ret., 1998. Lectr. U. Idaho Law Sch., Moscow, 1960-67; mem. Selective Svc. Civilian Rev. Bd. Pres. Moscow Jaycees, 1958-59; bd. dirs. Moscow Hosp. Assn., 1970-82. With USNR, 1945-46, PTO. Recipient Disting. Service award Moscow Jaycees, 1957. Mem. Idaho State Bar, Latah County Bar Assn. (exec. sec. 1964), Clearwater Bar Assn., Moscow C. of C. (bd. dirs. 1958-59), Lions (pres. Moscow 1971-72), K.C. (grand knight 1957-58), Elks, Moose. Republican. Roman Catholic. Avocations: skiing, fishing, motorcycling. Home: 1039 Virginia Ave Moscow ID 83843-9455

BIELEY, PEGGY M. economist; b. N.Y.C., June 5, 1934; d. Louis and Bella (Kenarik) Moses; m. Alfred D. Bieley, Dec. 25, 1953 (div. Aug. 1973): children: Harlan Clayton, Lily Beth Bieley McCausland. BS magna cum laude, NYU, 1950; MA, Stanford U., 1953. Rsch. economist Columbia U., N.Y.C., 1951-53; with Econ. Data Bank, Miami, Fla., 1955-73; econ. cons. Freedom Savs. and Loan, Tampa, Fla., 1973-77; sr. v.p., economist Am. Savs. and Loan, Miami, 1977-84; pres. Fin. Real Estate Cons., Miami, 1984—, Cert. Investors Svc., Miami, 1984—. Author and contbg. author various books on econs., 1950-53; contbr. articles to profl. jours. Trustee Pub. Health Trust Dade County, Miami, 1984-93. Home and Office: 5640 Collins Ave Apt 7C Miami FL 33140-2440

BIELIAUSKAS, VYTAUTAS JOSEPH, psychologist, educator; b. Plackojai, Lithuania, Nov. 1, 1920; came to U.S., 1949, naturalized, 1955; s. Antanas and Anele (Kasparaite) B.; m. Danute G. Sirvydaite, Mar. 12, 1947; children—Linas A., Diana B., Aldona O., Cornelius V. PhD in Psychology, U. Tuebingen, Germany, 1943. Diplomate Clin. Psychology, Marital Family Therapy, Am. Bd. Family Psychology, Am. Bd. Profl. Psychology. Asst. prof. U. Munich, Germany, 1944-48; instr. King's Coll., Wilkes-Barre, Pa., 1949-50; mem. faculty Sch. Clin. and Applied Psychology, Coll. William and Mary, 1950-58, prof. psychology, 1953-58, head dept. psychology, 1951-57; assoc. prof. Xavier U., Cin., 1958-60, chmn. dept. psychology, 1959-78, prof., 1960-78, Riley prof. psychology, 1978-88, disting. prof. psychology emeritus, 1988—. Author: zmogus siu dienu problematikoje, 1945, Community Relations Training for Police Supervisors, 1969; H-T-P Research Rev., 1980, CSSS for the H-T-P Drawings, 1981; contbr. articles to profl. jours. Pres., exec. officer Lithuanian World Cmty., 1988-92; exec. v.p. Lithuanian-Am. Cmty., Inc., 1994-2000; adviser on spl. programs Pres. of Republic of Lithuania, 1995-96. Lt. col. M.S.C., USAR, 1958-65. Recipient Ellis Island medal of honor, 1990. Fellow APA (pres. divsn. 13, 1986, Dist. Svc. award divsn. 36 1998); mem. Ohio Psychol. Assn. (pres. 1978-79, Disting. Svc. award 1980), Soc. Personality Assessment, Internat. Assn. for Study Med. Psychology and Religion (pres. 1972-75), Cin. Acad. Profl. Psychology, Psychologists Interested in Religious Issues (pres. 1971, exec. sec. 1973-75), Cath. Acad. Scis. in the U.S.A. (academician 1987—). Office: Xavier U Dept Psychology Cincinnati OH 45207 Business E-Mail: bieliaus@xu.edu.

BIELKE, PATRICIA ANN, psychologist; b. Bay Shore, N.Y., May 11, 1949; d. Lawrence Curtis and Marcella Elizabeth (Maize) Widdoes; m. Stephen Roy Bielke, July 10, 1971; children: Eric, Christine. BA, Carleton Coll., 1971; PhD, U. Minn., 1979. Lic. psychologist, Wis.; cert. marriage and family therapist. Rsch. asst. Nat. Inst. Mental Health, Washington, 1972-74; sch. psychologist Roseville Pub. Schs., St. Paul, 1978-79; psychologist Southeastern Wis. Med. and Social Svcs., Milw., 1979-93; staff psychologist Elmbrook Meml. Hosp., 1986-2000; pvt. practice Brookfield, Wis., 1991-2000; sch. psychologist Cedarburg (Wis.) Pub. Schs., 1999—2002, New Berlin (Wis.) Pub. Schs., 2000—. Bd. dirs. LWV, Brookfield, 1984-88, Elmbrook Sch. Bd., 1989-99. Mem. Nat. Sch. Psychologist Assn., Wis. Sch. Psychol. Assn. Home: 17455 Bedford Dr Brookfield WI 53045-1301 Office: New Berlin School Dist 18695 W Cleveland Ave New Berlin WI 53146 E-mail: bielke@execpc.com.

BIELORY, LEONARD, allergist, immunologist, medical school administrator; b. Neptune, N.J., Nov. 17, 1954; s. Max and Bessie (Spielberg) B.; m. Marilyn Miriam Gilan, July 5, 1981; children: Brett Phillip, Barry Mark, Amy Beth BS, MS, Lehigh U., 1976; MD, N.J. Med. Sch., 1980. Intern, resident U. Md. Hosp., Balt., 1980-82; clin. assoc. NIH, Bethesda, Md., 1982-85; dir. divsn. allergy and immunology N.J. Med. Sch., Newark, 1985—, co-dir. immuno-ophthalmology svcs., prof. medicine, pediats. and ophthalmology, 1992—; pres. med. staff Univ. Medicine and Dentistry N.J.-Univ. Hosp., 1993-95; pres., chmn. Univ. Physician Assocs., 1996-2000. Pres. med. staff ex-oficio mem. NIH Safety and Data Mgmt. Bd., 1993-98; bd. dirs Univ. Health Care Corp., acting med. dir., 1995-97; dir. Asthma & Allergy Rsch. Ctr., 1992—; prof. medicine, pediat. and ophthalmology, 2002—. Contbr. rsch. papers to profl. jours., chpt. to books. Bd. dirs. Congregation Israel, Springfield, N.J., 1988, pres., 1999-01; v.p. Kushner Yeshiva; bd. dirs. St.John's Cmty. Svc., 2002--. Recipient Young Investigator award Am. Acad. Allergy and Immunology, 1985; Schering Corp. Travel grantee, 1985. Fellow ACP, Am. Acad. Allergy and Immunology; mem. Med. Soc. N.J.; Nat. Inst. of Health Clin. Treatment Study Section (chmn. 1993). Jewish. Avocations: skiing, camping, rafting, bicycling. Office: NJ Med Sch Divsn Allergy & Immunology 90 Bergen St Ste 4700 Newark NJ 07103-2425 E-mail: bielory@umdnj.edu., bielory@mac.com.

BIELOWICZ, PAUL L. career officer; BA in Polit. Sci., Allegheny Coll., 1970; student, Chanute AFB, Ill., 1971, Squadron Officer Sch., 1975; MPA, U. Okla., 1978; student, Air Command and Staff Coll., 1981, Armed Forces Staff Coll., 1983, Indsl. Coll. Armed Forces, 1987, Def. Sys. Mgmt. Coll., 1993; MA in Procurement and Acquisitions Mgmt., Webster U., 1996. Commd. 2d lt. USAF, 1970, advanced through grades to brig. gen., 1996; flight line maintenance officer detachment 1 374th Tactical Airlift Wing, Ton Son Nhut Air Base, S. Vietnam, 1972; various positions 401st Tactical Fighter Wing, Torrejon Air Base, Spain, 1973-76; stationed at Cannon AFB, N.Mex., 1976-79; various positions Langley AFB, Va., 1979-86, Hdqs. USAF, Pentagon, Washington, 1987-91; stationed at Wright-Patterson AFB, Ohio, 1991-93; dir. tech. and indsl. support directorate San Antonio Air Logistics Ctr., Kelly AFB, Tex., 1993-95, comdr., 1997—; dir. logistics Hdqs. Air Edn. and Tng. Command, Randolph AFB, Tex., 1995-97; comdr. Def. Supply Ctr., Columbus, Ohio, 1997-98. Decorated Legion of Merit with oak leaf cluster, Bronze Star with V device, Small Arms Expert Marksmanship ribbon, Rep. Vietnam Gallantry Cross with Palm, Rep. Vietnam Campaign medal. Office: SAALC/CC 100 Moorman Kelly A F B TX 78241-5800

BIELSS, OTTO WILLIAM, JR., secondary school educator; b. Weatherford, Tex., Nov. 12, 1933; s. Otto William and Ada Susan (Thomas) B.; m. Patsy Lee Woolsey, Dec. 23, 1958; children: Otto William III, Paul Lee. BA, Hardin-Simmons U., 1954; MS, N. Tex. State U., 1971; postgrad., So. Meth. U., 1957-58, U. Tex., Arlington, 1965-67, U. Tex., Dallas, 1984-87. Engr. Tex. Hwy. Dept., Weatherford, 1954, Gen. Dynamics Corp., Fort Worth, 1956-59; tchr. Tarleton State Coll., Stephenville, Tex., 1959-65; math. tchr. Highland Park High Sch., Dallas, 1965-72, Skyline High Sch., Dallas, 1972-90; travel cons. Travelco, Irving, Tex., 1990-96; asst. prof. math. Paul Quinn Coll., Dallas, 1994—. Cluster coord. and dept. chairperson Skyline Math., 1983-90; instr. Dallas County C.C. Dist., various campuses, 1972—; grader coll. bd. advanced placement exams ETS. Author: Computer Mathematics, 1975; contbr. articles to profl. jours. Vol. various polit. campaigns, Stephenville, Tex., 1959-65, Irving, Tex., 1965—; bd. dirs. council airport noise, Irving, 1982—, Irving Community Concerts, 1991—. Served with U.S. Army, 1954-56, Korea. Grantee NSF, 1961, 67; recipient scholarship Hardin Simmon U., Abilene, Tex., 1951-54. Mem. AAUP, Math. Assn. Am., Greater Dallas Coun. Tchrs. (pres. 1974-76, bus. mgr. 1980-86, nat. rep. 1980-86), Tex. Coun. Tchrs. Math. (bus. mgr. 1980-86, pres. 1988-90), Nat. Coun. Tchrs. Math. (referee jour., rep.), Greater Dallas Tchrs. Math. (pres. 1988-90), Lions (bd. dirs. Irving 1985-87, treas. 1987-89, v.p. 1988-89, pres. 1989-91), Masons, Shriners (bd. dirs. 1988-89, 91, v.p. 1989-90, pres. 1990-91). Methodist. Avocations: photography, camping, gardening. Home: 2609 Trinity St Irving TX 75062-5257 E-mail: Bielss1@aol.com.

BIELUCH, WILLIAM CHARLES, judge; b. Nov. 12, 1918; AB magna cum laude, Brown U., 1939; JD, Yale U., 1942. Bar: Conn. 1942. Assoc. Covington, Burling, Rublee, Acheson & Shorb, Washington, 1942-43; ptnr. Bieluch, Barry & Ramenda and predecessors, Hartford, 1946-68; judge Cir. Ct. Conn., 1968-73, Ct. Common Pleas Conn., 1973-76, Superior Ct. Conn., 1976-85, Appellate Session, 1979-83, Appellate Ct. Conn., 1985-88; ret., 1988; judge trial referee, 1988—. Trustee emeritus S. S. Cyril and Methodius Roman Cath. Ch., Hartford; corporator St. Francis Hosp. and Med. Ctr., Hartford. Lt. (j.g.) USCG, WWII. Decorated Knight St. Gregory, Pope Paul VI; recipient Merit award Polish Legion Am. Vets., 1952, Man of Yr. award United Polish Socs., 1968, Archdiocesan medal of appreciation Archbishop John F. Whealon, 1970, Disting. Grad. award Nat. Cath. Elem. Sch., 1995. Mem. Conn. Bar Assn. (chmn. Jr. Bar Sect. 1948-49), Hartford County Bar Assn., KC, Phi Beta Kappa. Republican. Office: 95 Washington St Hartford CT 06106-4431

BIELUCKE, EDWARD ANTHONY, III, transportation executive, writer; b. Scranton, Pa., Feb. 6, 1955; s. Edward Anthony and Anne Lucille Bielucke; m. Irma Cristina Ruiz, Aug. 8, 1981 (div. Aug. 23, 1994); children: Briana Marie, Edward Anthony; m. Peggy Ann Downs, Nov. 9, 1996; 1 child, Steven Eugene. Cert. in indsl. electricity, Chaffey Coll., 2000; electrician diploma, Profl. Career Devel. Inst., 2001. Cert. electrician Chaffey Coll., Calif., 2000. Freelance writer, Calif., 1974—; sales rep., advisor Daewoo Motor Am., Inc., Ontario, Calif., 1998—99; asst. instr. elec. dept. Chaffey Coll., Rancho Cucamonga, Calif., 1999—2000; founder, editor, pub. Daewoo Driver Newsletter, Fontana, Calif., 1999—; founder, pres., CEO, chmn. bd. dirs. Daewoo Car Club Am., Riverside, Calif., 1999—. Author: (essays) New Millennium...and the Death & Birth of a Century, 2000; contbr. essays, articles, poems and advertisements. Named to Chaffey Coll. Ave. Excellence, Chaffey Coll. Found., 2001. Mem.: Jane Goodall Inst., Electric Auto Assn., Poetry Soc. Am., Acad. Am. Poets, Internat. Union Elevator Constructors, IEEE, Inc., Soc. Automotive Engrs., Le Cercle Concours

d'Elegance Car Club, Order Sons Italy in Am. Democrat. Roman Catholic. Avocations: collecting autographs, photography. Office: PO Box 3783 Riverside CA 92519-3783 E-mail: edbielucke@cs.com.

BIEMANN, KLAUS, chemistry educator; b. Innsbruck, Austria, Nov. 2, 1926; came to U.S., 1955, naturalized, 1965; PhD, U. Innsbruck, Austria, 1951. Postdoctoral fellow MIT, Cambridge, 1955-57, instr. in chemistry, 1957-59, asst. prof. chemistry, 1959-62, assoc. prof. chemistry, 1962-63, prof. chemistry, 1963-96, prof. emeritus, 1996—. Author: Mass Spectrometry, 1962; also rsch. publs. in mass spectrometry; assoc. editor Analytical Chemistry, 1985-89; mem. editl. bd. Organic Mass Spectrometry, 1967-75, Biomed. Mass Spectrometry, 1975-85, Fresenius Zeitschrift für Analytische Chemie, 1980-86, Mass Spectrometry Revs., 1981-98, Jour. Protein Chemistry, 1990-96, Jour. Am. Soc. Mass Spectrometry, 1990-96, Protein Sci., 1991-96. Trustee Drug Sci. Found., 1982-88. Recipient Tricentennial medal U. Innsbruck, 1970, Justin Powers award Am. Acad. Pharm. Scis., 1973, N.Y. sect. award Soc. Applied Spectroscopy, 1974, Exceptional Sci. Achievement award NASA, 1977, Fritz Pregl medal Austrian Microchem. Soc., 1977, Maurice F. Hasler award Spectroscopy Soc. Pitts., 1989, J.J. Thomson medal, 1991, P. Edman award, 1992, Assn. of Biomolecular Resource Facilities Beckman award, 1995. Fellow AAAS, Am. Acad. Arts and Scis.; mem. NAS, Am. Chem. Soc. (Field and Franklin award in mass spectrometry 1986, award in analytical chemistry 2001), Belgian Chem. Soc. (hon. mem., Gold medal 1962), Am. Soc. for Mass Spectrometry, The Protein Soc. Office: MIT Dept Chemistry Rm 18-587 Cambridge MA 02139-4307

BIEMULLER, MARTHA LYDIA, retired obstetrician-gynecologist; b. Phila., Feb. 10, 1926; BA, U. Pa., 1952; MD, Women's Med. Coll. Pa., Phila., 1956. Cert. Am. Bd. Obstets. and Gynecology. Intern Women's Med. Coll., Phila., 1956-57, resident in ob-gyn., 1957-61; resident in obstets. and gynecology Woman's Med. Coll. Pa. Hosp., 1957—61; clin. instr. dept. obstets. and gynecology Hosp. Woman's Med. Coll. Pa., 1961—64; pvt. practice in obstets. and gynecology, 1961—87; clin. asst. prof. dept. obstets. and gynecology Hosp. Woman's Med. Coll. Pa., 1965—88; pvt. practice in obstets. and gynecology, 1987—92; ret., 1992; dir. dept. obstets. and gynecology Roxborough Meml. Hosp., 1982—83, 1983—84, 1984—85, 1986—87, 1987—88, 1988—89, 1989—90, 1990—92. Fellow: Am. Coll. Obstets. and Gynecology; mem.: Am. Med. Assn. (Physician Recognition award 1995).

BIEN, AMOS, ecologist; b. N.Y.C., Feb. 12, 1951; s. Saul M. and Mina (Schneider) B.; m. Damaris Reyes; children: Natasha, Samantha, Pablo. BA in Biology, U. Chgo., 1973; MA in Ecology and Evolution, SUNY, Stony Brook, 1982. Systems programmer Met. Life Ins. Co., N.Y.C., 1973-74; software developer GTE Info. Systems (PMI), N.Y.C., 1975-77; rsch. asst. Dr.Barbara Bentley, Sarapiquí, Costa Rica, 1979-80; sta. mgr. La Selva Biol. Sta., Sarapiquí, 1980; prof. Sch. for Field Studies, Oriente, Ecuador, 1984-85; pres. Rara Avis S.A., Horquetas, Costa Rica, 1983—. Cons. ecotourism US-AID, Inst. Guat. Turismo, others, San José, Costa Rica, 1985—; lectr. rain forest conservation, 1983—. Author: Fallos y Aciertos en el Ecoturismo: Casos Concretos, 1999; contbr. articles to profl. jours. Pres. Costa Rican Youth Hostel Assn., San José, 1990-92; co-founder Hyde Park-Kenwood Recycling Ctr., Chgo., 1971-73; founder, pres. Costa Rican Pvt. Nature Res. Orgn., 1995-2000; founding mem. CONAGEBIO Nat. Commn. Regulation of Access to Biodiversity, 1999-2002; active Environment Liaison Ctr. Internat., 1999-2000; treas. Fedn. Costa Rican Environ. Orgns., 1998-2002. Mem. Internat. Soc. Tropical Foresters, Camara Nacional de Turismo, Assn. Tropical Biologists. Mailing: Apdo 8105 1000 San José Costa Rica E-mail: raraavis@racsa.co.cr, amosbien@racsa.co.cr.

BIEN, JOSEPH JULIUS, philosophy educator; b. Cin., May 22, 1936; s. Joseph Julius and Mary Elizabeth (Adams) B.; m. Françoise Neve, Apr. 8, 1965. BS, Xavier U., MA, 1958; DTC, U. Paris, 1968; postgrad., Laval Univ., 1958, Emory U., 1961-62, U. Edinburgh, 1962; D (hon.), Lucian Blaga U., 1999. Asst. prof. philosophy Univ. Tex., Austin, 1968-73; asso. prof. philosophy Univ. Mo., Columbia, 1973-79, prof. philosophy, 1979—, chmn. dept. philosophy, 1976-80, 81-83, 1993—99; vis. prof. Tex. A&M U., 1980, Dubrovnik Inst. Postgrad. Studies, Yugoslavia, 1983, 84, 85, 89, co-dir., 1990—; Mid-Am. States Univs. Assn. hon. lectr. in philosophy, 1985-86. Rsch. assoc. Russian and Slavic Rsch. Ctr., 1989-91; vis. prof. Lucian Blaga U., 1996, Hubei U., 1997, Wichita State U., 1998, U. Western Cape, 2000, Lille 3 U, 2002. Author: History, Revolution and Human Natue: Marx's Philosophical Anthropology, 1984; transl.: (M. Merleau-Ponty) Adventures of the Dialectic, 1973; editor: Phenomenology and the Social Sciences, A Dialogue, 1978, Political and Social Essays by Paul Ricoeur, 1974, Leviathan, 1986, Contemporary Social Thought, 1989, Ethics and Politics, 1992, Philosophical Issues and Problems, 1998. Am. Council Learned Socs. grantee, 1973; Dubrovnik Inst. Postgrad. Studies grantee, 1984; recipient U. Mo. faculty alumni award, 1998. Mem. Soc. Social and Polit. Philosophy (pres. 1979-80, 86-87, 93-94, 97-98), Ctrl. States Philos. Assn. (pres. 1978-79), Ctrl. Slavic Conf. (sec.-tres. 1977, 84), Southwestern Philosophy Soc. (pres. 1997-98). Democrat. Home: 100 W Brandon Rd Columbia MO 65203-3508 Office: Univ Mo Dept Philosophy Columbia MO 65211-0001

BIEN, PETER ADOLPH, English language educator, author; b. N.Y.C., May 28, 1930; s. Adolph F. and Harriet (Honigsberg) B.; m. Chrysanthi Yiannakou, July 17, 1955; children: Leander, Alec, Daphne. Student, Harvard U., 1948-50; BA, Haverford Coll., 1952; MA, Columbia U., 1957, PhD, 1961; postgrad., Bristol (Eng.) U., 1958-59, Woodbrooke Coll., Eng., 1970-71. Lectr. Columbia U., N.Y.C., 1957-58, 59-61; instr. dept. English Dartmouth Coll., Hanover, N.H., 1961-62, asst. prof., 1963-65, assoc. prof., 1965-68, prof., 1969-97, Geisel prof., 1974-79, Frederick Sessions Beebe '35 prof. in art of writing, 1989-97, prof. emeritus, 1997—; vis. prof. Harvard U., 1983, U. Melbourne, 1983, Woodbooke Coll., 1995, U. Thessaloniki, 1996, 2000, Princeton U., 2001. Author: L.P. Hartley, 1963, Constantine Cavafy, 1964, Kazantzakis and the Linguistic Revolution in Greek Literature, 1972, (with others) Demotic Greek I, 1972, Demotic Greek II, 1982, Nikos Kazantzakis, 1972, Antithesis and Synthesis in the Poetry of Yannis Ritsos, 1980, Three Generations of Greek Writers, 1983, Tempted by Happiness: Kazantzakis' Post-Christian Christ, 1984, Kazantzakis: Politics of the Spirit, Nikos Kazantzakis-Novelist, 1989, Words, Wordlessness, and the Word: Quaker Silence Reconsidered, 1992, (with Darren J.N. Middleton) God's Struggler: Religion in the Works of Nikos Kazantzakis, 1996, (with Chuck Fager) In Stillness There Is Fullness: A Peacemaker's Harvest, 2000, On Retiring to Kendal, 2003, Beyond: A Literary Excursion, 2003; translator: The Last Temptation, 1960, Saint Francis, 1962, Report to Greco, 1965 (all by Nikos Kazantzakis), Life in the Tomb (Stratis Myrivilis), 1977, 87, 2003; co-editor: Modern Greek Writers, 1972; assoc. editor Byzantine and Modern Greek Studies, 1975-82, Jour. Modern Greek Studies, 1983-89, editor, 1990-99. Trustee Kinhaven Music Sch., Weston, Vt., 1972-78, 81-84, 86-92, pres., 1988-90; trustee Pendle Hill, Wallingford, Pa., 1977-92, 94—, presiding clk., 1983-84, 86, Quaker in Residence, 1998; mem. corp. Haverford Coll., 1974-2001; pres. bd. trustees Hanover Monthly Meeting, Soc. of Friends, 1977-84; chair bd. overseers Kendal at Hanover, 1989-95, chair bd. dirs., 1995-96; trustee Am. Farm Sch., 1998—. Recipient E. Harris Harbison award for disting. teaching Danforth Found., 1968, Golden Cross St. Andrew Greek Orthodox Archdiocese Australia, 2000; Fulbright fellow, 1958, 83, 87. Mem. Modern Greek Studies Assn. (pres. 1982-84, 99-2002, mem. exec. com. 1968-85, 99—), Yale Club (N.Y.C.). Democrat. Home: 80 Lyme Rd # 171 Hanover NH 03755 Home (Summer): Terpni 207 Waddell Rd Riparius NY 12862 E-mail: peter.bien@dartmouth.edu.

BIENEN, HENRY SAMUEL, political science educator, university executive; b. N.Y.C., May 5, 1939; s. Mitchell Richard and Pearl (Witty) Bienen; m. Leigh Buchanan, Apr. 28, 1961; children: Laura, Claire, Leslie. BA with honors, Cornell U., 1960; MA, U. Chgo., 1961, PhD, 1966. Asst. prof. politics U. Chgo., 1965—66; asst. prof. politics & internat. affairs Princeton U., NJ, 1966—69, assoc. prof., 1969—72, prof., 1972—95, William Stewart Tod prof. politics and internat. affairs, 1981—85, James S. McDonnell Disting. Univ. prof., 1985, dir. Ctr. Internat. Studies, 1985—92, chair dept. politics, 1973—76, dir. African studies progrm, 1977—78, 1983—84, dir. rsch. Woodrow Wilson Sch. Pub. & Internat. Affairs, 1979—82, dean, 1992—94; pres. Northwestern U., Evanston, Ill., 1995—. Mem. exec. com. Inter-Univ. Seminar on Armed Forces and Soc., 1968—78; cons. U.S. State Dept., 1972—88, Nat. Security Coun., 1978—79, World Bank, 1981—89; mem. sr. review panel CIA, 1982—88; cons. Hambrecht & Quist Investment Co., Boeing Corp., Econ Corp., Enserch Corp., Ford Found., Rockefeller Found., John D. and Catherine T. MacArthur Found.; nat. co. dir. Movement for A New Congress, 1970—71; mem. Inst. Advanced Study, 1984—85, Ctr. Advanced Study in the Behavioral Scis., 1976—77; vis. prof. Makerere Coll., Kampala, Uganda, 1963—65, U. Coll., Nairobi, Kenya, 1968—69, U. Ibadan, 1972—73; bd. dirs. Univ. Corp. for Advanced Internet Devel.; mem. Coun. on Fgn. Rels., Matthews Internat. Capital Mgmt., LLC, Consortium on Financing Higher Edn., John G. Shedd Aquarium, Steppenwolf Theatre, Alain Locke Charter Sch., Com. on Roles of Acad. Health Ctrs. in the 21st Century at Nat. Acad.'s Inst. of Medicine; Acad. fellow Carnegie Corp. on Internat. Devel. Program. Editor: World Politics, 1970—74, 1978—, Vices of Power: World Leaders Speak, 1995—; author: Tanzania: Party Transformatin and Economic Development, 1967, The Military Intervenes: Case Studies in Political Change, 1968, Violence and Social Change, 1968, Tanzania: Party Transformatin and Economic Development, 1970, The Military and Modernization, 1970, Kenya: The Politics of Participation and Control, 1974, Armies and Parties in Africa, 1978, The Politcal Economy of Income Distribution in Nigeria, 1981, Political Conflict and Economic Change in Nigeria, 1985, Arms and the African Military Influence in Africa's International Relations, 1985, Of Time and Power: Leadership Duration in the Modern World, 1991, Power, Economics, and Security: The U.S.-Japanese Relationship, 1992. Grantee, Rockefeller Found., 1968—69, 1972—73, Seeger fellow, 1989. Mem.: Am. Acad., Coun. Fgn. Rels., Am. Polit. Sci. Assn. Office: Northwestern U z- 130 Crown, Evanston Campus Evanston IL 60208-0001*

BIENEN, LEIGH BUCHANAN, lawyer; b. Berkeley, Calif., Apr. 24, 1938; d. Norman Sharpe Buchanan and Janet Buchanan (Saniter) Arnold; m. Henry S Bienen, Apr. 28, 1961; children: Laura, Claire, Leslie. BA, Cornell U., 1960; MA, State U. Iowa, 1963; JD, Rutgers-Newark Sch. Law, 1975. Bar: NJ 1975, US Dist Ct NJ 1975, Pa 1977, NY 1982, US Supreme Ct 1982, DC 1983, Ill 1996. Rsch. atty. Ctr. for Rape Concern, Phila., 1975-76; law assoc. Boalt Hall, U. Calif., Berkeley, 1976-77; asst. dep. pub. defender Dept. Pub. Advocate, Trenton, N.J., 1977-91; adminstrv. dir. Princeton U. Woodrow Wilson Sch., 1991-94; sr. lectr. Northwestern U. Sch. Law, Evanston, Ill., 1995—; dir. Chgo. Hist. Homicide Project, 1998—. Lectr Univ Pa Sch Law, Philadelphia, Pa., 1981, Princeton Univ, Princeton, NJ, 1977, Princeton, 82, Princeton, 84, Princeton, 87, Princeton, 1991—94. Author: (book) Jurors and Rape, 1980, Learning from the Past, Living in the Present, 2000, (novels) The Left-Handed Marriage, 2001, Understanding Homicide in Chicagi, 1870-1930, 2003; author: (with G Geis) (book) Crimes of the Century; contbr. articles to profl jours. Dir Chgo. Hist. Homicide Project, 2000; bd. dirs. NJ ACLU, 1982—92, Womens Rights Law Reporter, 1977—; Rehab. Inst. Chgo., 2002—, Lookingglass Theatre, 2003—. Recipient Fiction prize, O'Henry Prize Stories, 1983; fellow, MacDowell Colony, 1979, 1982, YADDO, 1984, Blue Mountain Ctr, 1986—87; grantee Wallace Eljabar Fund, 1974, Am. Philos. Soc., 1981—82, Fiction, NJ Coun. Arts, 1986—87, Joyce Found, 1999, MacArthur Found., 2003—04, McCormick Tribune Found., 2003—; scholar Deans, Cornell Univ. Mem.: ABA (project on sex offender sentencing 1984—85). Office: Northwestern U Sch Law 357 E Chgo Ave Chicago IL 60611

BIENENFELD, DAVID GERALD, physician; b. Canton, Ohio, Mar. 9, 1953; s. Joseph and Freda (Weber) B.; children: Allison Rachel, Elliot Samuel. BA in Cellular and Molecular Biology, U. Pa., 1974; MD, U. Cin., 1978. Diplomate in psychiatry, geriatric and forensic psychiatry Am. Bd. Psychiatry and Neurology; diplomate Am. Bd. Med. Examiners. Resident in psychiatry U. Cin., 1978-81, fellow in geriatric psychiatry, 1981-82; physician P.W. Lewis Ctr., Cin., 1981-88. Asst. prof. psychiatry U. Cin., 1983-89, assoc. prof., 1989-90; assoc. prof. psychiatry Wright State U., 1990-97, prof., 1997—, vice-chair, dir. residency tng., 1990—; dir. Ctr. Adult Devel., U. Cin., 1984-90, dir. geriatric psychiatry, 1985-90. Editor Verwoerdt's Clinical Geropsychiatry, 3d edit.; contbr. articles to profl. jours. Exec. bd. Cin. Area Sr. Services, 1984-87. Recipient Maurice Levine Essay award U. Cin., 1982; NIMH grantee, 1985-89. Mem. Am. Psychiat. Assn., Am. Assn. Geriatric Psychiatry (bd. dirs. 1989-92), Assn. Acad. Psychiatry; Am. Assn. Dirs. Psychiatry Resident Tng. (exec. coun. 1991-99). Democrat. Jewish. Avocations: photography, cycling, cooking. Office: Wright State U Dept Psychiatry PO Box 927 Dayton OH 45401-0927 Home: Apt 1 2660 Vera Ave Cincinnati OH 45237-4526 E-mail: david.bienenfeld@wright.edu.

BIENENSTOCK, ARTHUR IRWIN, physicist, educator, federal official; b. N.Y.C., Mar. 20, 1935; s. Leo and Lena (Senator) Bienenstock; m. Roslyn Amy Goldberg, Apr. 14, 1957; children: Eric Lawrence, Amy Elizabeth(dec.), Adam Paul. BS, Poly. Inst. Bklyn., 1955, MS, 1957; PhD, Harvard U., 1962, Poly. U., 1998. Asst. prof. Harvard U., Cambridge, Mass., 1963—67; mem. faculty Stanford (Calif.) U., 1967—, prof. applied physics, 1972—, vice provost faculty affairs, 1972—77, dir. synchrotron radiation lab., 1978—97, dir. Lab. for Advanced Materials, 2002—03, vice provost, dean rsch. and grad. policy, 2003—; assoc. dir. sci. Office of Sci. and Tech. Policy, Washington, 1997—2001. Mem. U.S. Nat. Com. Crystallography, 1983—88; mem. sci. adv. com. European Synchrotron Radiation Facility, 1988—90, 1993—96; mem. com. condensed matter and materials physics NRC, 1996—97, mem. bd. chem. scis. and techs., 2001—03. Contbr. scientific papers to profl. jours. Bd. dirs. Calif. chpt. Cystic Fibrosis Rsch. Found., 1970—73, mem. pres.'s adv. coun., 1980—82; trustee Cystic Fibrosis Found., 1982—88. Recipient Sidhu award, Pitts. diffraction Soc., 1968, Disting. Alumnus award, Poly. Inst. N.Y., 1977; NSF fellow, 1962—63. Fellow: AAAS, Am. Phys. Soc. (gen. councilor 1993—96); mem.: Materials Rsch. Soc., Am. Crystallographic Assn. Jewish. Home: 967 Mears Ct Stanford CA 94305 Office: Geballe Lab Advanced Materials 476 Lomita Mall Stanford CA 94305 E-mail: a@slac.stanford.edu.

BIENENSTOCK, JOHN, physician, educator; b. Budapest, Hungary, Oct. 6, 1936; s. Maurice and Anne (Horn) Bienenstock; m. Dody Sanders, Nov. 24, 1961; children: Jimson Andrew, Adam Sebastian, Robin Anne. MB, BChir, Westminster Med. Sch., London, 1960; postgrad., Harvard Med. Sch., 1964—66, SUNY, Buffalo, 1966—68; MD (hon.), U. Göteborg, Sweden, 1998; CM, Order of Canada, 2002. Fellow Harvard U. Med. Sch., Boston, 1964-66; Buswell fellow SUNY, Buffalo, 1966-68, asst. rsch. prof. medicine, 1967-68; asst. prof. medicine McMaster U., Hamilton, Ont., Can., 1968-74, assoc. dean rsch., 1972-78, prof. medicine and pathology, 1974—, chmn. dept. pathology, 1978-89, v.p. health scis., 1989-97, dean health scis., 1992-97, univ. prof., 1997—; dir. brain-body inst. St. Joseph's Healthcare, 2001. Founder AB Biol. Supply, Inc., 1977, Agritech Rsch. Inc., 1980; D. W. Harrington lectr. SUNY, Buffalo, 1986; Rayne vis. prof. U. Western Australia, Perth, 1987; cons. WHO, Geneva, 1970—; chief sci. officer Oratol Inc., 1997—99; chmn. sci. adv. bd. Internat. Med. Innovations, 1999; bd. dirs. Prometic Life Sci. Inc.; cons. various pharm. cos.; dir. Brain-Body Inst. St. Joseph's Healthcare, Hamilton. Editor: (book) Immunology of Lung, 1984, Mast Cell Differentiation, 1986, Recent Advances in Mucosal Immunology, 1987, Handbook of Mucosal Immunology, 1994, Mucosal Immunology, 1998; contbr. articles to profl. jours. Chmn., bd. dirs. Can. Red Cross Soc.; chmn. bd. Dundas Valley Sch. Art., 1984—86; chmn. adv. com. nat. blood svcs., 1985—90. Recipient Prukynje medal, Assn. Czechoslovak Socs., Prague, 1989, Ross A. McIntyre Gold medal, U. Nebr., Omaha, 1989, Finkelstein prize, Crohn's and Colitis Found., Can., 1996. Fellow: RCP (London), RCP (Can.), Royal Soc. Can.; mem.: Coll. Internat. Allergologicum (pres. 1998—2002), Soc. Mucosal Immunology (pres. 1990—92), Internat. Union Immunological Socs. (mem. coun.), Am. Thoracic Soc., Swiss Soc. Allergy and Immunology (hon.), Am. Soc. Clin. Investigation, Assn. Am. Physicians, Can. Soc. Immunology (pres. 1985—87). Jewish. Avocation: painting. Home: 2-31 Dundonald St Toronto ON Canada M4Y 1K3 Office: McMaster U Fac Health Scis 1200 Main St W Rm 3N26H Hamilton ON Canada L8N 3Z5

BIENIAS, JULIA LOUISE, medical researcher, statistician; b. Chgo. d. Ignatius M. and Harriet L. (Huddy) B. BA in Psychology and History, MA in Psychology, Washington U., St. Louis, 1986; postgrad., U. Ill., 1986-88; ScD in Biostats., Harvard U., 1993. Rsch. asst. in gerontology and psychology Washington U., 1986; math. statistician U.S. Bur. Labor Statistics, Washington, 1987-88, U.S. Bur. Census, Washington, 1989-97; asst. prof. lectr. George Washington U., Washington, 1995-96; adj. asst. prof. U. Md., 1997—2003; asst. prof., sr. statistician Rush Coll Medicine, Chgo., 1997—2003, assoc. prof., 2003—, 2003—. Contbr. articles to profl. jours. Mem. Spl. Svc. Area Commn., City of Chgo., 2003—; bd. dirs. Park West Condo. Assn., 1999—, v.p., 1999—2001, pres., 2001—. NSF grad. fellow, 1987-92, Harvard tchg. fellow, 1992-93. Mem. Am. Statis. Assn. (various coms.), Internat. Biometric Soc. (regional adv. bd. 2000-02, various coms.), Caucus for Women in Stats. (rep.-at-large 1995-97)Pres. elect. 2004, Phi Beta Kappa, Pi Mu Epsilon, Psi Chi, Phi Alpha Theta. Unitarian Universalist. Avocations: piano, tennis, computer programming, jewelry design, interior decorating. Office: Rush Inst for Healthy Aging 1645 W Jackson Blvd Ste 675 Chicago IL 60612-3227 E-mail: jbienias@alum.wustl.edu.

BIENIAWSKI, ZDZISLAW TADEUSZ RICHARD, engineering educator emeritus, writer, consultant; b. Cracow, Poland, Oct. 1, 1936; came to U.S., 1978, naturalized; m. Elizabeth Hyslop, 1964; 3 children. Student, Gdansk (Poland) Tech. U., 1954-58; BS in Mech. Engring., U. Witwatersrand, Johannesburg, South Africa, 1961, MS in Engring. Mechanics, 1963; PhD in Rock Engring., U. Pretoria, South Africa, 1968; D in Engring. (hon.), U. Madrid, 2001. Prof. mineral engring. Pa. State U., Univ. Park, 1978-96, prof. sci., tech. & society, 1994-96, prof. emeritus, 1996—; pres. Bieniawski Design Enterprises, Prescott, Ariz., 1996—; Disting. prof. geol. engring. U. Madrid, Spain, 2001—. Vis. prof. U. Karlsruhe, Germany, 1972, Stanford U., 1985, Harvard U., 1990, Cambridge (Eng.) U., 1997; chmn. U.S. Nat. Com. on Tunneling Tech., 1984-85; U.S. rep. to Internat. Tunnel Assn., 1984-85. Author: Rock Mechanics Design in Mining and Tunneling, 1984, Strata Control in Mineral Engineering, 1987, Aiming High-A Collection of Essays, 1988, Engineering Rock Mass Classifications, 1989, A Tale of Three Continents, 1991, Design Methodology in Rock Engineering, 1992, Gaudeamus Igitur Poems, 1997, Alec's Journey, 1999; editor: Tunneling in Rock, 1974, Exploration for Rock Engineering, 1976, Milestones in Rock Engring., 1996; contbr. over 170 articles to profl. jours. Recipient Mayor's Proclamation of City of State College Bieniawski Day, 1983, Rock Mechanics Rsch. award, 1984, disting. toastmaster internat. award, 1974 Avocations: genealogy, cosmology, foreign policy, financial planning. Home: The Ranch 3023 Sunnybrae Cir Prescott AZ 86303-5770 Business E-Mail: z1b@psu.edu.

BIENVENU, JOHN CHARLES, lawyer; b. Modesto, Calif., Sept. 11, 1957; s. Robert Charles and Martha Louise (Beard) B.; m. Sarah Luciene Brick, May 10, 1983; children: Reed Charles, Loren John. Student, U. Calif., Berkeley, 1975-78; BA summa cum laude, U. N.Mex., 1985; JD with distinction, Stanford U., 1988. Bar: Calif., 1988, N.Mex., 1990; U.S. Ct. Appeals (9th cir.) 1988, U.S. Ct. Appeals (10th cir.) 1990; U.S. Ct. Fed. Claims, 1991. Assoc. Brobeck, Phleger & Harrison, San Francisco, 1988-90, Rothstein, Walther, Donatelli, Hughes, Dahlstrom & Cron, Santa Fe, N.Mex., 1990-93; prin. Santa Fe, 1993—. Mem. ACLU (cooperating atty. N.Mex.), N.Mex. State Bar. Democrat. Home: 1580 Cerro Gordo Rd Santa Fe NM 87501-6143 Office: PO Box 2455 1217 Paseo de Peralta Santa Fe NM 87501-1883

BIER, LOUIS HENRY GUSTAV, minister; b. Chgo., Jan. 12, 1933; s. Louis Wilfred and Ethel Lea (Laue) Bier; m. Helene Mueller, July 29, 1962; children: Richard Allen, Karen Elizabeth, Lisa Anne. BE, Chgo. Tchrs. Coll., 1954; B in Theology, Concordia Sem., 1959, MDiv in Theology, 1959; MEd, Boston State Coll., 1962; DRE, Smith Bapt. U., 1987, DD, 1986. Ordained to ministry Luth. Ch., 1959; lic. social worker. Vicar Redeemer Luth. Ch., Phila., 1957, 1st Lutheran Ch., Holyoke, Mass., 1957-58; pastor St. Paul's Luth. Ch., West Frankfort, Ill., 1959-61, Trinity Luth. Ch., Boston, 1961-98, emeritus, 1999—; chaplain VA New Eng. Health Care Sys., Boston, 1965—; instr. psychology Boston State Coll., 1967-81; mem. adj. faculty Holy Cross Greek Orthodox Sem., Brookline, Mass., 1998. Chaplain German Home for Elderly, Boston, 1962, also trustee, clk. of corp., 1971—; chaplain Arbour, Boston, 1969, West Roxbury VA Hosp., 1978—86; circuit counselor Luth. Ch. Mo. Synod; trustee Chapel of the Four Chaplains, Valley Forge, Pa., 2000; cons. Slavik Rsch. Inst.; mem. animal studies com. Beth Israel-Deaconess Hosp., Havard Med. Sch., 2000; bd. dirs. Interfaith Bible Readings, Inc. Mem. arboretum dist. Boston coun. Boy Scouts Am., 1976—79; mem. USO Coun. New Eng.; bd. mgrs. Sophia Snow Ho.; br. pres. A.A.L., 1982. Served to lt. col. CAP, 1975—, chaplain, col. Mass. State Def. Fort. Recipient Honored Citizen award, Kennedy VFW, 1973, Cmty. Svc. award, Greater Boston Assn. Retarded Citizens, 1974, Lamb award, Luth. Coun., 1975, George Meany Youth Svc. award, AFL-CIO, 1983, citation award of recognition, Slovik Rsch. Inst., 1999, Svc. award, Concordia Seminary, Ft. Wayne, Ind., 1999; fellow Emerson, Mil. Chaplains Assn. U.S.A., 1999, West, Boy Scouts Am., 1999. Mem.: Am. Assn. Mental Retardation (20 Year Citation 2002, Humanitarian Award 2002), Concordia Sem. (Servus Ecclesia Christi award), Mass. Chaplains Assn., German Aid Soc. Boston (trustee), Assn. Profl. Chaplains (life; cert., 25th Anniversary citation 2000), Mil. Chaplains Assn. (life; treas., v.p., pres.), Luth. Edn. Assn. (life), Vanderbilt Club. Avocations: swimming, golf, reading. Home: 169 Nahatan St Westwood MA 02090-3607

BIERBAUM, J. ARMIN, petroleum company executive, consultant; b. Oak Park, Ill., June 29, 1924; s. Armin Walter and Harriett Cornelia (Backmann) B.; m. Janith Turnbull, Apr. 17, 1948; children: Steve, Todd, Charles, Peter, Mark. BS, Northwestern U., 1945, MS, 1948. Project engr. Am. Oil Co., Ind., 1948-53; sales engr. Universal Oil Products Co., Des Plaines, Ill., 1953-56; tech. dir. Nat. Coop. Refinery Assn., McPherson, Kans., 1956-58; asst. plant mgr., treas., v.p., dir. Gen. Carbon & Chem. Corp., Robinson, Ill., 1958-61; cons. Williston, N.D., 1962-64; v.p. ops. Midland Coops., Inc., Mpls., 1964-72; sr. v.p. ops. Tosco Corp., Los Angeles, 1972-77; pres., chief exec. officer Gary Energy Co., Englewood, Colo., 1977-79, U.S. Ethanol Corp., Englewood, 1979-82; cons., 1983—. Served with USNR, 1942-45. Mem. Am. Inst. Chem. Engrs., Sigma Xi, Phi Epsilon Pi. Office: 1609 Ridgecrest Dr Loveland CO 80537-9073

BIERCE, WILLIAM B. lawyer; b. Englewood, N.J., Dec. 15, 1949; BA, Yale U., 1971; Licence en Droit with honors, U. Grenoble, France, 1972; JD, NYU, 1975. Bar: N.J. 1975, N.Y. 1976, U.S. Ct. Internat. Trade 1980, U.S. Ct. Appeals (D.C. and 9th cirs.) 1984. Assoc. Coudert Bros., N.Y.C., 1975-78, Pisar and Huhs, N.Y.C., 1978-80, Windels, Marx, Davies and Ives, N.Y.C., 1980-85, ptnr., 1985-90, Bierce & Kenerson, P.C., N.Y.C., 1990—. Adj. asst. prof. Pace U. Grad. Sch. Bus., N.Y.C., 1981-86; bd. advisors Expertises des Systemes d'Information, Paris, 1985-98; mgr. www.outsourcing-law.com. Editor articles NYU jour. Internat. Law Politics, 1974-75; contbr. articles to profl. jours. Trustee Dwight-Englewood Sch., 1982-84. Grad. fellowship Rotary Found., 1971-72; nominee PriceWaterhouse Coopers/Corbett Assocs. Outstanding Achievement of Yr. award, 1999. Mem. Computer Law Assn., Union Internat. des Avocats (mem. U.S. bd. govs. 1997—), Am. Fgn. Law Assn. E-mail: wbierce@biercekenerson.com.

BIERI, BARBARA NORMILE, systems analyst, consultant; b. Trenton, N.J., Jan. 4, 1951; d. William Donald and Beatrice Marie (Noon) Normile; m. Paul Daniel Bieri, Apr. 13, 1991. BS in Edn., St. Francis Coll., 1972; postgrad., Pa. State U., 1976, Mercer County C.C., 1983, 85-86. Cert. tchr. elem. and secondary math., N.J., Pa. Tchr. math. and sci. St. Anthony Sch., Trenton, N.J., 1972-77; tchr. math. Cumberland Regional H.S., Seabrook, N.J., 1977-82; programmer N.J. Dept. Human Svcs., Trenton, 1982-84; programmer, analyst Computer Svcs. Group, Trenton, 1984; sr. computer sys. designer Martin Marietta Data Sys., Princeton, N.J., 1984-86; sr. sys. mgr. Storey/Ross/Barker, Inc., Lambertville, N.J., 1987-90; cons. BPN Cons., Hamilton, N.J., 1990-93, MIACO Corp., Landover, Md., 1993-94; sr. sys. analyst Data Based Sys. Internat., Flemington, N.J., 1994—. Union rep., negotiating team Cumberland Regional Edn. Assn., Seabrook, N.J., 1980-81; computer tchr. adult edn. West Windsor (N.J.) Plainsboro Adult Edn. Program, 1983-86. Committeewoman Dem. Party, Bridgeton, N.J., 1980. Mem. NAFE, N.J. Novell Users Group, MDBS Users Group, Oracle Users Group, Gamma Sigma Sigma (v.p. 1971-72). Avocations: traveling, needlework, reading. Home: 249 Hobart Ave Hamilton NJ 08629-1622 Office: Data Based Sys 3949 Schelden Cir Bethlehem PA 18017 8936 E-mail: BPNB249@aol.com.

BIERIG, JACK R. lawyer, educator; b. Chgo., Apr. 10, 1947; s. Henry J. and Helga (Rothschild) B.; m. Barbara A. Winokur; children: Sarah. BA, Brandeis U., 1968; JD, Harvard U., 1972. Bar: Ill. 1972, U.S. Dist. Ct. (no. dist.) Ill. 1972, U.S. Ct. Appeals (1st-3d, 5th-11th and D.C. cirs.) 1974, U.S. Supreme Ct. 1980. Ptnr. Sidley Austin Brown & Wood, Chgo., 1972—; prof. Ill. Inst. Tech.-Chgo. Kent Coll. Law, 1974-95; lectr. U. Chgo. Law Sch. and Harris Sch. Pub. Policy, 2000—. Chmn. legal sect. Am. Soc. Assn. Execs., 1994-95. Contbr. articles to profl. jours. Pres. Neighborhood Justice Chgo., 1983-87; pres. Jewish Vocat. Svc., 1997-99. Mem. Ill. Assn. of Hosp. Attys. (pres. 1991), Chgo. Bar Assn. (bd. govs., 1982-84). Clubs: Standard (Chgo.). Jewish. Office: 1 Bank One Plz Chicago IL 60670-0001 E-mail: jbierig@sidley.com.

BIERLEY, PAUL EDMUND, aeronautical engineer, musician, author, publisher; b. Portsmouth, Ohio, Feb. 3, 1926; s. William Frederick and Minnie Genieve (Atkin) B.; m. Pauline Jeanette Allison, Sept. 17, 1948; children: Lois Elaine Bierley Walker, John Emerson. B of Aero. Engring., Ohio State U., 1953, DMusic (hon.), 2001. Aero. engr. N.Am. Aviation, Columbus, Ohio, 1953-73; engr., data mgr. Ellanef Mfg. Corp., Columbus, 1973-88; tubist Columbus Symphony Orch., 1965-81, Detroit Concert Band, 1973-92. Lectr. in field. Author: John Philip Sousa, A Descriptive Catalog of His Works, 1973, John Philip Sousa, American Phenomenon, 1973, rev. edit., 1986 (Deems Taylor award 1986), 2d rev. edit., 2000, Office Fun!, 1976, Hallelujah Trombone!, 1982, The Music of Henry Fillmore and Will Huff, 1982, The Works of John Philip Sousa, 1984, Sousa Band Fraternal Society News Index, 1997; co-author: (with K. Suzuki) All About Sousa Marches, 2001, also numerous articles, radio and TV copy, concert programs and record jackets; asst. condr., Rockwell Internat. Concert Band, 1961-76; tubist World Symphony Orch., N.Y.C., 1971, Brass Band of Columbus, 1984-97, Village Brass, 1983—; editor: Integrity Press, Columbus, 1982—, The Heritage Ency. of Band Music, 1991, supplement, 1996, El Capitan (John Philip Sousa), 1994, Marching Along (John Philip Sousa), 1994. Bd. trustees. Robert Hoe Found., Poughkeepsie, N.Y., 1984—, dir. rsch. Integrity Rsch. Found., 1999—. Recipient Deems Taylor award ASCAP, 1986, God and Country award Salvation Army, 1995, Ohioana Libr. Assn. Citation, 1996; inductee Wall of Fame, Portsmouth, Ohi, 1994, Columbus Sr. Musicians Hall of Fame, 1997. Fellow Acad. Wind and Percussion Arts; mem. Am. Bandmasters Assn. (hon., Edwin Franko Goldman citation 1974), Am. Sch. Band Dirs. Assn. (assoc., A. Austin Harding award 1990), Am. Fedn. Musicians, Sonneck Soc. for Am. Music, Nat. Band Assn., Assn. Concert Bands, Internat. Tuba-Euphonium Assn., Windjammers Unltd., John Philip Sousa Found. (Sudler medal 1986, Sudler Order of Merit 2001), Ohio Hist. Soc., Am. Aviation Hist. Soc., Westerville Hist. Soc., Masons, Phi Beta Mu (Outstanding Contbr. to Bands award 1983). Methodist.

BIERLY, SHIRLEY ADELAIDE, communications executive; b. Waterbury, Conn., Jan. 19, 1924; d. Samuel and Frances Ada (Bogorad) Brown; m. Leroy Elwood Bierly, Jan. 19, 1946 (div. 1951); children: Lee Jr., Dennis Ray, David Lincoln. Student, Orange Coast Coll., 1963—66, L.A. City Coll., 1967—69. Mgr. Pacific Telephone, San Francisco, Calif., 1953-82; exec. dir. Sr. Power Office, San Francisco, 1982—; Cmty. activist, 1982—. Editor: Sr. Power newsletter, 1990—. Pres. Calif. Legis. Coun. for Older Am., San Francisco, 1984—, treas. Calif. Assn. of Older Am., 1984—, bd. dirs. Sr. Action Network, San Francisco, 1991—, Congress of Calif. Sr., Sacramento, 1994—; bd. trustees Agape Found., 1994-2001; policy bd. Nat. Coun. Sr. Citizens, 1995-2001; commr. San Francisco Residential Arbitration and Stabilization Bd., 1997-2000, Calif. Commn. on Aging, 2000-03; bd. Planning for Elders in Central City, 2000-02; v.p. Yerba Buena Consortium, San Francisco, 1992—; mem. San Francisco Bd. Suprs. Pedestrian Safety Adv. Com., 2003—. Mem. Am. Civil Liberties Union, Older Women's League, Gray Panthers, Alliance Ret. Ams. (charter, exec. bd., cmty. rep. 2003—). Avocations: photography, theatre, reading, philately. Office: Calif Assn for Older Ams (aka Sr Power) 325 Clementina St San Francisco CA 94103-4104

BIERMACHER, KENNETH WAYNE, lawyer; b. Hartford, Conn., Oct. 15, 1953; s. Donald David and Ethel Pearl (Biermacher) Lawton; m. Joan; children: Carl Joseph II (dec.), Matthew Robert, Michelle Renee; 1 step child Brent Cohen. BS summa cum laude, U. New Haven, 1976; JD with honors, Drake U., 1979. Bar: Iowa 1980, Tex. 1985, U.S. Dist. Ct. (so. dist.) Iowa 1980, U.S. Dist. Ct. (no. dist.) Iowa, 1981, U.S. Ct. Appeals (8th cir.) 1981, U.S. Supreme Ct. 1983, U.S. Dist. Ct. (no. dist.) Tex. 1984, U.S. Dist. Ct. (so. and we. dists.) Tex. 1985, U.S. Dist. Ct. (ea. dist.) Tex. 1993, U.S. Ct. Appeals (5th cir.) 1985. Assoc. Whitfield, Musgrave, Selvy, Kelly, Eddy, Des Moines, 1980-84; shareholder Geary, Stahl & Spencer, P.C., Dallas, 1984-89, Leonard Marsh Hurt Terry & Blinn, Dallas, 1989-90; ptnr.-in-charge Dallas office Small, Craig & Werkenthin, P.C., Dallas, 1990-93; v.p., ptnr., dir. Kane, Russell, Coleman & Logan, P.C., Dallas, 1993—. Lectr. Iowa Defense Counsel Assn. Annual Meeting, 1982, Des Moines Area Community Coll. Legal Asst. Program, 1981-82, Human Resources Forum, Am. Electronics Assn., Dallas, 1986; legal research asst. Iowa State Bar Assn. Com. on Study Fed. Rules Evidence, 1982; chmn. spl. com. on Friends of Moot Ct. Drake Law Sch. Bd. Counsellors, 1983-84; founder shareholder, dir. Recruit TV, Inc., 2001—, Xlantic Records, Inc., Dallas, 2001—, Xlantic Music Pub., Inc., Dallas, 2001—, founder, pres., dir. Frontrunner Capital Corp., 1999—, CDRK, Inc., 2001—, others; bd. dirs. Retractable Techs., Inc.; bd. dirs., sec. MT Auctions.com, Inc., Dallas. Contbg. author: Understanding Iowa Law, 1984; editor: Energy and Nat. Resources Guide for Iowa, 1979; contbr. articles to law jours. Adv. U. New Haven Law Enforcement Explorers Post Boy Scouts Am., 1975; coach Johnston Sr. High Sch. Mock Trial Teams, Iowa, 1984; del. Polk County Rep. Conv., Des Moines, 1980, Iowa Rep. State Conv., 1980; deacon Canyon Creek Bapt. Ch., 1986-87; chmn. scholarship and fin. aid com. Canyon Creek Christian Acad., 1985-87; v.p., dir. Boys and Girls Clubs of Greater Dallas, Inc., 1997—, chmn. circus com., 1998—, chmn. resource devel. com., 1999—; bd. dirs. Henry C. Lee Inst. Forensic Sci., 1997, 2003--; adv. bd. Dallas Tower Club. Recipient Acad. Scholarship U. New Haven, 1973-76; semi-finalist Midwest Regional Moot Ct. Competition, 1979. Mem. ABA (subcom. on fraudulent and deceptive trade practices, sect. tort and ins. practice 1985-86, vol. atty. post-conviction death penalty representation project 1988-89), ATLA, FBA, Iowa State Bar Assn. (mem. Young Lawyer Sect. ethics com. 1981, law schs. panel com. 1982, law-related edn. com. 1983-84), Def. Rsch. Inst., Iowa Assn. Trial Lawyers (founding dir., chmn. Drake U. Law Sch. student bd. dirs. 1978-79, ex-officio mem. bd. dirs. 1978-79), Dallas Bar Assn. (mock trial com., law in changing soc. com. 1985, speech com. 1985-86, bus. litigation sect. ethic and courtesy com. 1988, qualified mediator 1989—, mem. cts. com. 1995, mem. fee dispute com. 1995), State Bar Tex. (legal assts. com. 1988-91), Dallas Assn. Young Lawyers (liaison with other profls., fed. opinions com. 1986), Order of Barristers, Atty.-Mediator Assn., Drake U. Law Sch. bd. counselors (regional v.p. for Tex. and Okla. 1986-89), Alpha Chi (vice chmn. Conn. chpt. 1975-76). Home: 4324 Hollow Oak Dr Dallas TX 75287-6847 Office: Kane Russell Coleman & Logan PC 1601 Elm St Ste 3700 Dallas TX 75201-7207 E-mail: kbiermacher@krcl.com.

BIERMAN, GEORGE WILLIAM, technical consulting executive, food technologist; b. Cleve., Mar. 2, 1925; s. George Henry and Esther Josephine (Johnson) B.; m. Nyo Jeanne Iserloth; children: Cynthia, Barbara, Marsha, Jill, Wendy, Mindy, G. Steven, Chris. BS, Rutgers U., 1951; PhD, MIT, 1956. Technician R & D Am. Can Co., Maywood, Ill., 1943-45, Schering Corp., Bloomfield, N.J., 1947-48; tech. dir. Friend Bros., Inc., Malden, Mass., 1951-58; v.p. Herbert V. Shuster, Inc., Boston, 1958-75, pres., Quincy, Mass., 1975-89, vice chmn. bd., 1989-95, sr. scientist, 1995-96; tech. cons. Shuster Labs. Inc., 1996—98, ret., 1998. Sgt. U.S. Army, 1945-47. Mem.: Nat. Fisheries Inst. (smoked fish com. 1968—98), Inst. Food Technologists, Assn. Smoked Fish Processors (tech. dir. 1968—98). Presbyterian. Avocations: gardening, motorcycling. Home: 19 Curwen Rd Peabody MA 01960-1205 Fax: (978) 535-4812.

BIERMAN, JAMES NORMAN, lawyer; b. St. Louis, Nov. 23, 1945; s. Norman and Margaret (Loeb) B.; m. Catherine Best, Apr. 10, 1983; 1 child, James Norman. AB magna cum laude, Washington U., 1967; JD, Harvard Law Sch., 1970. Bar: D.C. 1970, U.S. Supreme Ct. 1973. Assoc. Hogan & Hartson, Washington, 1970-72; asst. dean Harvard Law Sch., Cambridge, Mass., 1973-75; assoc. Foley & Lardner, Washington, 1975-79, ptnr., 1979—, ptnr. in charge, 1985-2001, mgmt. com., 1989—98. Mem. nat. coun. Washington U. Coll. Arts and Scis., 1999—. Mng. editor Harvard Jour. Legis., 1969-70. Mem. Civil Rights Reviewing Authority HEW, Washington, 1979-80. Mem. ABA, Fed. Bar Assn., Supreme Ct. Bar, Washington Lawyers Com. for Civil Rights and Urban Affairs (bd. dirs.), Phi Beta Kappa, Omicron Delta Kappa, Pi Sigma Alpha, Phi Eta Sigma, City Club (Washington). Home: 906 Peacock Station Rd Mc Lean VA 22102-1021 Office: Foley & Lardner 3000 K St NW Fl 5 Washington DC 20007-5143 E-mail: jbierman@foleylaw.com.

BIERMAN, LEONARD, management educator; b. Passaic, N.J., Feb. 24, 1954; s. Stuart Bertram Bierman, Barbara Levine Neufeld; m. Risa Jill Farber; children: David children: Joshua. BS, Cornell U., Ithaca, N.Y., 1971—75; MA in Econs., UCLA, 1978—80; JD, U. Pa., 1975—78. Bar: Wash. 1980, Fla. 1980, D.C. 1980. Spl. asst. to chmn. U.S. EEOC, Washington, 1986—87; counsel to the chmn. U.S. ITC, Washington, 1987—88; assoc. dep. undersec. of labor for internat. affairs U.S. Dept. of Labor, Washington, 1989—90; from asst. prof. to prof. mgmt. Tex. A&M U., College Station, 1982—. Mem. acad. steering com. N.Am. Commn. for Labor Coop., Washington, 1996—; coord. bus. and govt. track George Bush Sch. of Govt. and Pub. Svcs., Tex. A&M U., College Station, 1997—. Author: (numerous journal articles) in leading business, economic, and legal journals, 2001; contbr. articles. Jewish. Avocations: swimming, travel, reading biographies. Home: 2806 Brothers Blvd College Station TX 77845-5713 Office: Texas A&M Univ 4221 MS College Station TX 77843 Business E-Mail: Len-Bierman@Tamu.edu.

BIERMAN, SANDRA, artist; b. Bklyn., N.Y., 1938; d. John Charles Riesberg and Martha Lee Blair; m. Arthur Bierman, Oct. 1, 1983; children: Cheryl, Steven, James. Represented by Contemporary S.W. Gallery, Santa Fe, 1994—, David Haslam, Boulder, Colo., 1992—, Gallery East, Loveland, Colo., 1996—, Jack Meier Gallery, Houston, 1997—, Augustine Arts, Lake Tahoe, Nev., 1997—, Bakersfield (Calif.) Mus., 2001; instr. workshop Am. Acad. Women Artists, Wickenburg, Ariz., 1997, Oil Painting with Sandra Bierman, Kauai, Hawaii, 2000. One-person shows include Nat. Ctr. for Atmospheric Rsch., Boulder, 1992, David Haslam Gallery, 1993, 94, 95, Contemporary S.W. Galleries, 1996, Lincoln Ctr. for the Arts, Ft. Collins, Colo., 1998, Jack Meier Gallery, 1998, Bakersfield (Calif.) Mus. Art, 2001; group shows include C.S. Lewis Summer Inst. Show on Tour, 1994, Queens Coll. Art Gallery, Cambridge, Eng., 1994, 99th Nat. Exhbn. Nat. Arts Club, N.Y.C., 1995, 67th Grand Nat. Show, Salmagundi Club, N.Y.C., 1995, Artistes Americaines, Maison du Terroir, Genouilly, France, 1996, Colo. History Mus., 1996, Clymer Mus., Ellensburg, Wash., 1996, Desert Caballeros Mus., Wickenburg, Ariz., 1997, Colo. Gov.'s Invitational Show, Loveland (Colo.) Mus., 1997-2000, Art Expo, N.Y.C., 1998-99; works in permanent collections at City of Loveland, CSI Ltd., Cambridge, Eng., El Pomar Found., Colorado Springs, Colo., Gilford, Inc., N.Y.C., Herzog & Adams, N.Y.C., Harlow Club Hotel, Palm Springs, Calif., Loveland Mus., Telluride Gallery of Fine Art, Colo., Kaiser Permanente, Denver, Kohn Family Trust, Balt., Mfrs.-Hanover trust, N.Y.C., Mayo Women's Clinic, Scottsdale, Penrose Conf., Ctr., Colorado Springs, Philip Chamberlan Inc., Madison, Conn.; featured in Southwest Art Mag., Art Trends Mag., Mountain Living mag., Woman's Mag., Radiance mag., Sun Storm Fine Art Mag., US Art, Art World News, Art Bus. News, others. Recipient Colo. Gov.'s Purchase award, Loveland, 1988, Best of Show award Western Images, Boulder, 1993, medal of honor award Am. Artists Profl. League, N.Y.C., 1995. Mem. Am. Artists Profl. League, Nat. Mus. of Women in the Arts, Oil Painters Am., Am. Acad. Women Artists (nominating juror, exec. bd. dirs. 1997—).

BIERMANN, JANET SYBIL, orthopaedic surgeon, educator; b. Mar. 14, 1961; MD, Stanford U. Sch. Medicine, 1987. Diplomate Am. Bd. Orthopaedic Surgery. Intern U. Iowa, Iowa City, 1987-88, resident Orthopaedics, 1988-92; fellow Orthopaedic Oncology U. Chgo., 1992-93; staff surgeon VA Hosp., Ann Arbor, Mich., 1993-95, chief of Orthopaedic Surgery sect., 1995—; lectr. Orthpaedic Oncology U. Mich., Ann Arbor, 1993-95, asst. prof. Orthopaedics, 1995—2000, assoc. prof., 2002—. Mem. AAOS, Musculoskeletal tumor Soc., Correct Tissue Oncology Soc., Ruth Jackson Orthpaedic Soc. Office: U Mich 1500 E Med Ctr Dr Ann Arbor MI 48109-0946

BIERNAT, KATHY A. instructional designer; b. N.J. m. Timothy Biernat; children: Zachary S, Nicholas D, Luke H. Masters, U. of North Tex., 1987. Health educator Tarrant County Health Dept., Ft. Worth, 1989—90; sr. instrnl. designer Med. Coll. of Wis., Milw., 1990—. Author several jour. articles. Home: 3936 Dory Ct Franklin WI 53132 Office: Med Coll of Wis 8701 Watertown Plank Rd Milwaukee WI 53226

BIERON, LOUISE T. physician placement executive; b. Rochester, N.Y., Sept. 26, 1935; d. Samuel and Michelina Granata; m. Joseph Francis Bieron, July 4, 1959 (div. Mar. 1987); children: Paul, Belinda, Diane, Ramona, Elaine. BA in Philosophy and English, Canisius Coll., 1984, MS in Edn., 1988. Chair United Way Canisius Coll., Buffalo, N.Y., 1977-83, student recruiter, 1979-84, acad. advisor, 1984-88; phys. cons. Phys. Internat., Buffalo, N.Y., 1988-96; collection cons. NCO Fin. Sys., Getzville, N.Y., 1998—. Mem. Amherst (N.Y.) Taxpayers Assn., 2000; v.p. Condominium Assn., 1992—. Republican. Roman Catholic. Avocations: swimming, reading.

BIERS, MARTIN HENRY, physician; b. Bklyn., Oct. 10, 1931; s. Louis and Sarah (Naidich) Bierfass; m. Elizabeth Jaros Biers, Feb. 11, 1962; children: Eric, Carl, John. BA, NYU, 1951; MD, SUNY, Bklyn., 1955. Cert. in internal medicine and hematology. Intern Kings County Hosp., Bklyn., 1955-56; med. resident Bklyn. Vets. Hosp., 1956-57, Montefiore Hosp., Bronx, N.Y., 1957-58; hematology resident Mt. Sinai Hosp., N.Y.C., 1958-59; pvt. practice White Plains, N.Y., 1961—. Attending medicine and chief emeritus hematology dept. White Plains Hosp. Capt. USAF, 1959-61. Mem. Am., N.Y. Med. Soc., Westchester Med. Soc. Office: 170 Maple Ave White Plains NY 10601-5115

BIERSTEDT, PETER RICHARD, lawyer, entertainment industry consultant; b. Rhinebeck, N.Y., Jan. 2, 1943; s. Robert Henry and Betty Bierstedt; m. Carol Lynn Akiyama, Aug. 23, 1980 (div. Oct. 1995); m. Lieschen van Straaten, Aug. 11, 2000. AB, Columbia U., 1965, JD cum laude, 1969; cert., U. Sorbonne, Paris, 1966. Bar: N.Y. 1969, U.S. Supreme Ct. 1973, Calif. 1977. Atty. with firms in, N.Y.C., 1969-74; pvt. practice cons. legal and entertainment industry, 1971, 75-76, 88—; with Avco Embassy Pictures Corp., L.A., 1977-83, v.p., gen. counsel, 1978-80, sr. v.p., 1980-83, dir., 1981-83; gen. counsel New World Entertainment (formerly New World Pictures), L.A., 1984-87, exec. v.p., 1985-87, sr. exec. v.p. Office of Chmn., 1987-88, also bd. dirs.; pres. subs. New World Prodns. and New World Advt. New World Pictures, 1985-88. Guest lectr. U. Calif., Riverside, 1976-77, U. So. Calif., 1986, 91, UCLA, 1987, 95, 96; bd. dirs. New World Pictures (Australia) Ltd., FilmDallas Pictures, Inc., Cinedco, Inc. Exec. prodr. (home video series) The Comic Book Greats. Mem. Motion Picture Assn. Am. (dir. 1980-83), Acad. Motion Picture Arts and Scis. (exec. br.), LA Copyright Soc., ACLU. Democrat. Avocations: astronomy, literature, tennis, scuba diving. E-mail: peter@bierstedt.com.

BIERWIRTH, JOHN COCKS, retired aerospace manufacturing executive; b. Lawrence, N.Y., Jan. 21, 1924; s. John E. and Alice (Marguerite) B.; m. Marion Moise, June 14, 1946. BA, Yale U., 1947; JD, Columbia U., 1950. Bar: N.Y. 1951. Assoc. White & Case, N.Y.C., 1950-53; asst. v.p. N.Y. Trust Co. (now Chase Bank), 1953-57; asst. treas. Nat. Distillers & Chem. Corp., N.Y.C., 1957-58, v.p., 1958-69, head Internat. div., 1963-72, dir., 1966-72, exec. v.p., 1969-72; with Grumman Corp., Bethpage, N.Y., 1972-88, v.p. fin., 1972, pres., 1972, chief exec. officer, 1974-88, chmn. bd., 1976-88. Trustee Adelphi U. Named to L.I. Hall of Fame Mem. Cradle of Aviation Mus. (bd. dirs.), Yale-China Assn. (trustee), The Ocean Conservancy (trustee), Yale Club (N.Y.C.).

BIERY, EVELYN HUDSON, lawyer; b. Lawton, Okla., Oct. 12, 1946; d. William Ray and Nellie Iris (Nunley) Hudson. BA in English and Latin summa cum laude, Abilene (Tex.) Christian U., 1968; JD, So. Meth. U., 1973. Bar: Tex. 1973, U.S. Dist. Ct. (we. dist.) Tex. 1975, U.S. Dist. Ct. (so. dist.) Tex. 1977, U.S. Dist. Ct. (no. dist.) Tex. 1979, U.S. Ct. Appeals (5th cir.) 1979, U.S. Ct. Appeals (11th cir.) 1981, U.S. Supreme Ct. 1981. Atty. Law Offices of Bruce Waitz, San Antonio, 1973-76; mem. LeLaurin & Adams, PC, San Antonio, 1976-81; ptnr. Fulbright & Jaworski, San Antonio, 1981—, head bankruptcy, reorganization and creditors' rights sect., 1990—. Policy com. Fulbright & Jaworski, San Antonio, 1996-98; speaker on creditors' rights, bankruptcy and reorganization law; lectr. Southwestern Grad. Sch. Banking, Dallas, 1980, La. State U. Sch. Banking, 1994; presiding officer, U. Tex. Sch. of Law Bankruptcy Conf., 1976, 94, State Bar Tex. Creditors' Rights Inst., 1985, State Bar Tex. Advanced Bus. Bankruptcy Law Inst., 1985, State Bar Tex. Inst. on Advising Officers, Dirs. and Ptnrs. in Troubled Bus., 1987, State Bar Tex. Advanced Creditors Rights Inst., 1988; pres. San Antonio Young Lawyers Assn., 1979-80; mem. bankruptcy adv. com. fifth cir. jud. coun., 1979-80; vice-chmn. bankruptcy com. Comml. Law League Am., 1981-83; mem. exec. bd. So. Meth. U. Sch. Law, 1983-91. Editor: Texas Collections Manual, 1978, Creditor's Rights in Texas, 2d edit., 1981; author: (with others) Collier Bankruptcy Practice Guide, 1993. Del. to U.S./Republic of China joint session on trade, investment and econ. law, Beijing, 1987; designated mem. Bankruptcy Judge Merit Screening Com. State of Tex. by Tex. State Bar Pres., 1979-82; patron McNay Mus., San Antonio; rsch. ptnr. Mind Sci. Found., San Antonio; diplomat World Affairs Coun., San Antonio. Recipient Outstanding Young Lawyer award San Antonio Young Lawyers Assn., 1979. Fellow: Am. Coll. Bankruptcy Attys. (v.p.), Soc. Internat. Bus. Fellows (v.p.), Tex. Bar Found. (life), San Antonio Bar Found. (life); mem.: San Antonio Young Lawyers Assn. (pres. 1979—80), Tex. Assn. Bank Counsel (bd. dirs. 1988—90, 2001—02), Tex. Bar Assn. (chair bankruptcy com. 1982—83, chair corp., banking and bus. law sect. 1989—90), Zonta (Chair Z club com. 1989—90), Plaza Club San Antonio (bd. dirs. 1982—), Order of Coif. Office: Fulbright & Jaworski LLP 300 Convent St Ste 2200 San Antonio TX 78205-3720 also: 1301 Mckinney St Ste 5100 Houston TX 77010-3031

BIES, SUSAN SCHMIDT, federal agency administrator; b. Buffalo, May 5, 1947; d. Louis Howard and Gladys May (Metke) Schmidt; m. John David Bies, Aug. 29, 1970; children: John Matthew, Scott Louis. BS, State U. Coll.-Buffalo, 1967; MA, Northwestern U., 1968, PhD, 1972. Banking structure economist FRS, St. Louis, 1970-72; asst. prof. econs. Wayne State U., Detroit, 1972-77; assoc. prof. Rhodes Coll., Memphis, 1977-80; tactical planning mgr. First Tenn. Nat. Corp., Memphis, 1980-81, dir. corp. devel., 1982-83, treas., 1983-84, sr. v.p., chief fin. officer, 1984-85, exec. v.p., chief fin. officer, 1985—; gov. Fed. Reserve Sys., Washington, 2001—. Mem. fin. adv. com. City of Germantown, Tenn., 1978—, also budget com.; mem. investment adv. com. Tenn. Consol. Retirement System, Nashville, 1981-86; instr. MidSouth Sch. Banking, 1985-86; bd. dirs. Memphis Ptnrs. Pres., bd. dirs. North Germantown Homeowners Assn., 1978-83; treas. Germantown Area Soccer Assn., 1985-86; treas. Fury Soccer Club, 1988—; vice chmn. task force Com. on 21st Century, Rhodes Coll., Memphis, 1986-87; mem. exec. adv. bd. Sch. Accountancy Memphis State U.; bd. dirs. Memphis Youth Initiative, 1988; mem. BAI Acctg. and Fin. Commn., 1988—. Fellow Ctr. for Urban Affairs, 1968-69, Fed. Res. Bank Chgo., 1970. Mem. Am. Bankers Assn. (exec. com. 1986-88), Nat. Assn. Bus. Economists, Am. Econ. Assn., Planning Execs. Inst., Fin. Execs. Inst., (bd. dirs. Memphis chpt. 1988—), Planning Forum (Managerial Excellence award Memphis chpt. 1986), Memphis Area C. of C. (bd. dirs. 1988—, tax com. 1988—, chair 1989—), Econ. Club Memphis (bd. dirs. 1986—, vice chmn. 1987-88, chmn. 1988-89), Omicron Delta Epsilon, Lambda Alpha. Episcopalian. Avocations: gardening, golf, soccer. Office: Fed Reserve System Bd of Gov 20th & C Streets NW Washington DC 20551 Office Fax: 202-452-3819.

BIESEL, DAVID BARRIE, publishing executive; b. Chgo., Sept. 12, 1931; s. William James Trimble and Aileen Louise (Jacquith) B.; m. Donna Louise Scoggan, May 25, 1958 (div. 1975); children: Deborah Louise Biesel Brugger, William Warren; m. Diane Jane Stevens, Sept. 25, 1982. Student, U. Md., 1950-53. Supr. editl. dept. Fed. Electric Corp., Paramus, N.J., 1958-62; mgr. editl. dept. Am. Inst.Physics, N.Y.C., 1962-69; ref. book editor R. R. Bowker Co., N.Y.C., 1969-73; sr. editor Macmillan Pub. Co., N.Y.C., 1973-82, Elsevier Sci. Pubs., N.Y.C., 1983-84; v.p., editor-in-chief R. R. Bowker Co., N.Y.C., 1984-85; v.p., editorial dir. M. E. Sharpe, Armonk, N.Y., 1986-88; pres. St. Johann Press, Haworth, N.J., 1988—; dir. Assn. Publ. program Scarecrow Press, 1990-2000, editor Am. Sports History series. Author: Can You Name That Team, 1991 (named one of the best reference books 1991 Lib. Jour.); contbr. articles to profl. jours. Warden All Saints Episcopal Ch., Bergenfield, N.J., 1985-89, 94-2000, vestryman, 1982-85, treas. 2000—. With USMC, 1953-57. Mem. ALA, Soc. Am. Baseball Rsch., Profl. Football Rsch. Assn., N.Am. Soc. Sport History, Marine Meml. Assn., USMC Combat Correspondents Assn. (life), Soc. for Internat. Hockey Rsch., Marine Corps League. Home and Office: 315 Schraalenburgh Rd Haworth NJ 07641-1200 E-mail: d.biesel@worldnet.att.net.

BIESEL, DIANE JANE, editor, publishing executive; b. N.Y.C., Feb. 15, 1934; d. Douglas and Runa (Patterson) Stevens; m. Donald W. de Cordova, June 24, 1956 (div. July 1971); m. David Barrie Biesel, Sept. 25, 1982. BS, Trenton State Coll., 1956; MLS, Rutgers U., 1969; MA in Edn., Seton Hall U., 1974, cert. in supervision, 1976. Tchr., libr. Arlington (Va.) Bd. Edn., 1956-58; media specialist elem. schs., librs. River Edge (N.J.) Bd. Edn., 1958-91; lectr., instr. children's lit. Alphonsus Coll., Woodcliff Lake, NJ, 1969-72; series editor Scarecrow Press, Lanham, Md., 1992—; v.p., CFO St. Johann Press, 1994—. Field svc. cons. N.J. Dept. Edn., 1969—71; cons. new books preview Baker and Taylor Co., 1972—76; mem. com. academically gifted River Edge Bd. Edn., 1977—83, mem. study skills com., mem. affirmative action com., 1988—90; adj. prof. Seton Hall U., 1978—79; mem. award com. Rutgers U. Grad. Sch. Libr. Svc., 1978—79; mem. River Dell Librs. Coop., 1988—91; cons. Pro Libra Assocs., 1992—. Editor: School Library Media Series, School Librarianship Series. Mem. Child Devel. Ctr. Bd., 1999—; mem. choir All Saints Ch., Bergenfield, 1971—, lay reader, 1973—, del. Diocesan Conv., 1978—, vestrywoman, 1980—83; mem. ecumenical commn. Diocese of Newark, 1992. Mem.: Divsn. Sch. Media Specialists (nat. nominating com. 1978—79, coun. 1978—79, evaluation com. 1979, steering com. 1979—80, co-chmn. liaison com. with Am. Assn. Sch. Librs. 1979—83, nat. nominating com. 1980—82, mem. awards com. 1981—89, program com. 1982—84, bd. dirs. region II 1983—84, pres. 1986, co-author: Information Power 1988, mem. task force on librs. and info. sci., White House, writing com.), River Edge Tchrs. Assn. (pres. 1964—66), Bergen County Sch. Librs. Assn. (pres. 1966—68), Ednl. Media Assn. N.J. (state chmn. recruitment 1968—69, state chmn. hospitality 1972—73, state chmn. county liaison 1973—74, co-pres. 1977—78), Bergen Button Buffs (founding grandmother 1993), N.J. Button Soc. (v.p. 1999—2002), Nat. Button Soc. Home: 315 Schraalenburgh Rd Haworth NJ 07641-1200 E-mail: d.biesel@worldnet.att.net.

BIESELE, JOHN JULIUS, biologist, educator; b. Waco, Tex., Mar. 24, 1918; s. Rudolph Leopold and Anna Emma (Jahn) B.; m. Marguerite Calfee McAfee, July 29, 1943 (dec. 1991); children: Marguerite Anne, Diana Terry, Elizabeth Jane; m. Esther Aline Eakin, Mar. 9, 1992. BA with highest honors, U. Tex., 1939, PhD, 1942. Fellow Internat. Cancer Research Found., U. Tex., 1942-43, Barnard Skin and Cancer Hosp., St. Louis, also, U. Pa., 1943-44, instr. zoology, 1943-44; temporary research assoc. dept. genetics Carnegie Instn. of Washington, Cold Spring Harbor, 1944-46; research assoc. biology dept. Mass. Inst. Tech., 1946-47; asst. Sloan-Kettering Inst. Cancer Research, 1946-47, research fellow, 1947, assoc., 1947-55, head cell growth sect., div. exptl. chemotherapy, 1947-58, mem., 1955-58, assoc. scientist div., 1959-78; asst. prof. anatomy Cornell U. Med. Sch., 1950-52; assoc. prof. biology Sloan-Kettering div. Cornell U. Grad. Sch. Med. Scis., 1952-55, prof. biology, 1955-58; prof. zoology, mem. grad. faculty U. Tex., Austin, 1958-78; also mem. faculty U. Tex. (Coll. Pharmacy), 1969-71, prof. edn., 1973-78; prof. emeritus zoology U. Tex., Austin, 1978-99; prof. emeritus sect. molecular cell and developmental biol. U. Tex. Sch. Biol. Scis., Austin, 1999—. Cons. cell biology M.D. Anderson Hosp. and Tumor Inst., U. Tex., Houston, 1958-72; dir. Genetics Found., 1959-78; mem. cell biology study sect. NIH, 1958-63; Sigma Xi lectr. NYU Grad. Sch. Arts and Scis., 1957; Mendel lectr. St. Peter's Coll., Jersey City, 1958; featured spkr. on first Earth Day, Old Westbury Campus of N.Y. Inst. Tech., 1970; Mendel Club lectr. Canisius Coll., Buffalo, 1971; adv. com. rsch. etiology of cancer Am. Cancer Soc., 1961-64, pres. Travis County unit, 1966, adv. com. on personnel for rsch., 1969-73; counsellor Cancer Internat. Rsch. Coop., Inc., 1962-90; cancer rsch. tng. com. Nat. Cancer Inst., 1969-72; gen. chmn. Conf. Advancement Sci. and Math. Teaching, 1966. Author: Mitotic Poisons and the Cancer Problem, 1958; mem. editorial bd. Year Book Cancer, 1959-72; mem. editorial adv. bd. Cancer Rsch., 1960-64, assoc. editor, 1969-72; cons. editor: Am. Jour. Mental Deficiency, 1963-68; mem. editorial bd. The Jour. of Applied Nutrition, 1987-91; contbr. articles to profl. jours. Research Career award NIH, 1962, 67, 72, 77 Fellow N.Y., Tex. acads. scis., AAAS; mem. Am. Assn. Cancer Research (dir. 1960-63), Am. Soc. Cell Biology, Am. Inst. Biol. Scis., Phi Beta Kappa, Sigma Xi (pres. Tex. chpt. 1963-64), Phi Eta Sigma, Phi Kappa Phi. Achievements include rsch. in provision of early evidence for abnormal chromosome numbers in cancer cells, for occasional excessively multiple-stranded state of cancer chromosomes; demonstration of a direct relation of chromosomal size in mammalian tissues and organs to the local metabolic activity, as evidenced by the local content of B vitamins, of differential toxicity in certain antimetabolites to cancer cells in culture. Home: 2500 Great Oaks Pky Austin TX 78756-2908

BIFFLE, GREG, race car driver; b. Vancouver, Wash., Dec. 23, 1969; s. Jack and Sally Biffle. Race car driver Rousch Racing, 1998—. Named Cintas Rookie-of-the-Yr., Raybestos Rookie-of-the-Yr., 2001. Achievements include winner at Memphis Motorsports Park, Nashville Superspeedway, Nazareth Speedway, Milw. Mile, Lowe's Motor Speedway, Phoenix Internat. Raceway. Office: c/o Roush Racing 7020 Aviation Blvd Concord NC 28027-8196

BIGAJER, CHARLES, physician, educator; b. N.Y.C., Oct. 2, 1949; s. Henry and Maria (Halpern Ginsburg) B.; m. Dini Schick, Jan. 13, 1973; children: Rachel, Daniella, Elliott. BS in Chemistry, Bklyn. Coll., 1971; MD, Albert Einstein Coll. Medicine, 1974. Diplomate Am. Bd. Internal Medicine, Am. Bd. Gastroenterology, Am. Bd. Geriatrics. Intern, then resident Brookdale Hosp. Med. Ctr., Bklyn., 1974-78; fellow NYU Med. Ctr., 1978-80; clin. asst. prof. medicine Downstate Med. Ctr., Bklyn., 1980—; pvt. practice, Bklyn., 1980—. Mem. ACP, Am. Gastroenterol. Assn., Phi Beta Kappa. Office: 1 Brookdale Plz Brooklyn NY 11212-3139

BIGAL, MARCELO E, physician; b. Sao Paulo, Brazil, Oct. 13, 1969; s. Antonio C and Jamile I Bigal; m. Janaina M. Bigal, Nov. 18, 1995; children: Luisa, Hanna. MD, Sch. of Medicine at Ribeirao Preto, U. of Sao Paulo, 1989—94, MSc in Neurol. Scis., 2000, PhD in Neurol. Scis., 2001. Resident in neurology Sch. Medicine at Ribeirao Preto, U. Sao Paulo, 1995—99; neurology specialist Brazilian Bur. of Justice, 1999—2001, Brazilian Nat. Inst. Social Security, 1999—2001; prof. of neuro-psychology Barao de Maua U., 2000—01; chief of svc., dept. of neurology Santa Casa Hosp., 2000—01; rsch. assoc. The New Eng. Ctr. for Headache, Stamford, 2001—; asst. prof. of neurology Albert Einstein Coll. of Medicine, Bronx, 2002—. Co-investigator AstraZeneca (sponsor for rsch.), Glaxo SmithKline (sponsor for rsch.); rschr. Einstein Aging Study, Bronx; primary investigator UCB Pharma (sponsor for rsch.), 2002—; co-investigator Allergan (sponsor for rsch.), 2002—. Reviewer Cephalalgia, Headache, Clin. Therapeutics, Future Drugs, CNS Drugs, Arch Neuropsiquiatr, 2002, (jour.) Neurology, assoc. editor (website) Vertibrae; contbr. chapters to books, articles to profl. jours. Recipient Internat. Headache Soc. Ednl. award, 2001, Glaxosmithkline Ednl. award, 2001, Am. Headache Soc., Ortho-McNeil, 2002; Internat. Headache Soc. fellowship, 2001. Fellow: Internat. Headache Soc.; mem.: Brazilian Headache Soc., Internat. Headache Soc. (assoc.), Am. Headache Soc. Office: The Albert Einstein Coll of Medicine Rousso Building 1165 Morris Park Ave Bronx NY 10461 Office Fax: 718-430-3857. Personal E-mail: marcbigal@aol.com. E-mail: mbigal@aecom.yu.edu.

BIGATTI, SILVIA MARCELA, science educator; b. Buenos Aires, 1959; d. Osvaldo Omar Bigatti and Margarita Riba; m. Jose J. Alcala; children: Mariel Alcala, Alejandro Alcala, Joseph Louis Alcala. PhD in Clin. Psychology, San Diego State U. and U. of Calif. San Diego, 2000. Asst. prof. Ind. U. Purdue U., Indpls., 2000—. Rschr. Ind. U. Purdue U., Indpls., 2000—. Contbr. sci. reports to profl. publs. Recipient Minority Access to Rsch. Careers acholarship, NIH, 1982—95, Nat. Rsch. Svc. award, 1995—2000, Dissertation grant, Arthritis Found., 1998—2000, Burdette Kunkel grant, Walther Cancer Inst., 2001—02, Summer Rsch. fellowship, Ind. U. Purdue U., 2002, Rsch. grant, Walther Cancer Inst., 2002—03. Mem.: Soc. of Behavioral Medicine, Phi Chi, Phi Kappa Phi. Office: Ind U Purdue U LD 124 402 N Blackford St Fishers IN 46038

BIGDA, RUDOLPH A. business and financial consultant; b. Holyoke, Mass., Apr. 27, 1916; s. Alexander and Mary (Sakaske) B.; m. Josephine M. Baginski, June 22, 1946 (dec. July 1976); children: Donald R., Robert A.; m. Ann M. Willette, Dec. 9, 1981. BBA magna cum laude, Bryant Coll., 1935; postgrad., Dartmouth Coll., 1953. Vice pres. Parsons div. Am. Writing Paper Co., Holyoke, 1937-40; contr. F.W. Sickles div. Gen. Instrument Corp., Chicopee, Mass., 1946-54, Hano Bus. Forms Inc., Springfield, Mass., 1954-81; bus. and fin. cons. Palm Bay, Fla., 1981—. Instr. Western New Eng. Coll., Springfield, 1974-75; counselor SCORE, Springfield, 1983—; tax cons. AARP, West Mass Eldercare. Bd. dirs. Pulaski Heights Old Age Housing, Holyoke. Col. AUS, 1941-46, mem. Res. ret. Recipient alumni award Bryant Coll., 1967. Mem. Inst. of Mgmt. Accts. (pres. Pioneer Valley chpt. 1972-74), Fin. Execs. Inst., Ret. Officers Assn. (pres. Pioneer Valley chpt. 1978-80), Am. Legion, Elks. Republican. Roman Catholic. Avocations: computers, fishing, sports. Home and Office: 280 Berry Ct NE Palm Bay FL 32907-2163

BIGELEISEN, JACOB, chemist, educator; b. Paterson, N.J., May 2, 1919; s. Harry and Ida (Slomowitz) Bigeleisen; m. Grace Alice Simon, Oct. 21, 1945; children: David M., Ira S., Paul E. AB, NYU, 1939; MS, Wash. State U., 1941; PhD, U. Calif., Berkeley, 1943. Rsch. scientist Manhattan Dist., Columbia, 1943-45; rsch. assoc. Ohio State U., Columbus, 1945-46; fellow Enrico Fermi Inst., U. Chgo., 1946-48; sr. chemist Brookhaven Nat. Lab., Upton, N.Y., 1948-68; prof. chemistry U. Rochester, N.Y., 1968-78, chmn. dept., 1970-75; Tracy H. Harris prof. U. Rochester (Coll. Arts and Scis.), 1973-78; v.p. research, dean grad. studies SUNY, Stony Brook, 1978-80, Leading prof. chemistry, 1978-89, Disting. prof., 1989, Disting. prof. emeritus, 1989—. Vis. prof. Cornell U., 1953; NSF sr. fellow, vis. prof. Eidgen Techn. Hochschule, Switzerland, 1962—63; chmn. Assembly Math. and Phys. Scis. NRC-Nat. Acad. Scis., 1976—80. Mem. editl. bd.: Jour. Phys. Chemistry, Jour. Chem. Physics. Trustee Sayville Jewish Center, 1954—68. Recipient Gilbert N. Lewis lectr., 1963, E. O. Lawrence award, 1964, Disting. Alumnus award, Wash. State U., 1983; fellow John Simon Guggenheim, 1974—75. Fellow: AAAS, Am. Acad. Arts and Sci., Am. Chem. Soc., Am. Phys. Soc. (Nuc. award 1958); mem.: Nat. Acad. Scis. (councilor 1982—85), Phi Lambda Upsilon, Sigma Xi, Phi Beta Kappa. Achievements include research in photochemistry in rigid media, semiquinones, cryogenics, chemistry of isotopes, isotope separation, quantum statistics of gases, liquids and solids. Home: PO Box 217 Saint James NY 11780-0217 E-mail: jbigeleisen@notes.cc.sunysb.edu. *As a youth I became interested in a career in science because it offered the opportunity to test ideas and hypotheses objectively by experiment. This unique aspect of science, which differentiates it from all other branches of learning and knowledge, has been a guiding principle both in my professional and my personal life. My career has included research, teaching, administration and public service.*

BIGELIS, RAMUNAS, research scientist; b. Wunsiedel, West Germany, May 28, 1947; came to U.S., 1949, naturalized, 1958; s. Vincent and Liudvina (Raustis) B. BS, U. Ill.-Chgo., 1969; PhD, Purdue U., 1974. Rsch. asst. Purdue U., West Lafayette, Ind., 1970-74; postdoctoral fellow Cold Spring Harbor Lab. and Cornell U., Ithaca, N.Y., 1975-78; asst. prof. Wake Forest U., Winston-Salem, N.C., 1979-83; rsch. scientist Bayer (Miles, Inc.), Elkhart, Ind., 1983-85, sr. rsch. scientist, 1985-89; staff rsch. scientist Amoco Biotech. Co., Naperville, Ill., 1989-95; sr. rsch. scientist Wyeth Rsch., Pearl River, NY, 1996—. Contbr. chpts. to books, articles to profl. jours. Ill. State scholar, 1969. Mem. Am. Soc. Microbiology (newsletter ed. Ind. Br. 1983-87), AAAS, Inst. Food Technologists, Soc. Indsl. Microbiology, Sigma Xi. Office: Wyeth Rsch # 205/407 401 N Middletown Rd Pearl River NY 10965-1215 E-mail: bigelir@wyeth.com.

BIGELOW, CHARLES CROSS, retired biochemist, retired university administrator; b. Edmonton, Alta., Can., Apr. 25, 1928; s. Sherburne Tupper and Helen Beatrice (Cross) B.; m. Elizabeth Rosemary Sellick, Aug. 22, 1977; children: Ann K. Bigelow Siess, David C. BASc., U. Toronto, 1953; M.Sc., McMaster U., 1955, PhD, 1957. Postdoctoral fellow Carlsberg Lab., Copenhagen, 1957-59; assoc. Sloan-Kettering Inst. Cancer Research, N.Y.C., 1959-62; asst. prof. chemistry U. Alta., Can., 1962-64, assoc. prof., 1964-65; vis. prof. Fla. State U., Tallahassee, 1965; assoc. prof. biochemistry U. Western Ont., London, Ont., Can., 1965-69, prof., 1969-74; prof., head biochemistry Meml. U. Nfld., St. John's, Can., 1974-76; dean of sci., prof. chemistry St. Mary's U., Halifax, N.S., Can., 1977-79; dean of sci. U. Man., Winnipeg, Can., 1979-89, dean emeritus, 1990—, prof. chemistry, 1979-2000, ret., 2000. Fellow Univ. Coll., 1989, sr. adminstrv. fellow, 1993-94, Univ. Coll. provost 1995-97, sr. scholar, 1997-2000; vis. prof. U. Toronto, 1973-74; vis. scientist Nat. Inst. for Med. Rsch., London, 1984-85; chmn. Ont. Confedn. Univ. Faculty Assns., 1970-71; pres. Can. Assn. Univs. Tchrs., 1972-73. Contbr. articles on protein structure and denaturation to sci. jours. Bd. govs. U. Western Ont., 1972-73, U. Man., 1982-84, Man. Mus. of Man and Nature, 1986-91, bd. mgmt. TRIUMF, Vancouver, 1987-89; pres. N.S. New Democratic party, 1978-79; pres. Man. New Dem. party, 1982-84. Grantee NRC Can., Med. Research Council, Natural Scis. and Engring. Research Council Can. Fellow Chem. Inst. Can.; mem. Can. Biochem. Soc., Am. Chem. Soc., Am. Soc. Biol. Chemists, AAAS, Sigma Xi

BIGELOW, DANIEL JAMES, aerospace executive; b. Harrisville, Pa., Mar. 26, 1935; s. Raymond James and Hilda Irene (Graham) B.; m. Elizabeth Jane Allison, Sept. 10, 1955; 1 child, Allison Jane. BFA in Art Advt., Kent (Ohio) State U., 1957; MA in Edn., La. Tech. U., 1974; MS in Polit. Sci., Auburn U., 1986; MS, Air U., 1987; postgrad., Ohio State U., 1989—. Commd. 2d lt. USAF, 1957, advanced through grades to col., 1979, ret., 1987; command pilot 167 combat missions Vietnam; air attaché to Soviet Union, 1983-85; dir. Soviet program Air War Coll. Air U., Ala., 1985-87; gen. mgr. aerospace divsn. Modern Techs. Corp., Dayton, Ohio, 1988-98, dir. programs corp. hdqrs., 1998—2001, dir. bus. svcs. corp. hdqrs., 2002—03; dir. investor rels, corp. comm. MTC Tech., Inc., Ohio, 2003—. Contbr. articles to profl. jours.; author, editor: Soviet Studies, 1968—88. Decorated Legion of Merit with one oak leaf cluster, DFC, 14 Air medals, Def. Superior medal; recipient U.S. Am. Nat. award CIA Dir., William J. Casey, 1985; named to Nat. Aviation Hall of Fame, Blue Key Nat. Honor Soc., Kent State U. Chptr. Mem. Acad. Polit. Sci., Air Rescue Assn. (nat. bd. dirs., historian, chmn. reunion and symposium 2003), Air Force Assn. (v.p. state legis. affairs 2001-2002), Am. Def. Preparedness Assn., Discussion Club Dayton (v.p. 1999-2000), Internat. Platform Assn., F-86 Sabre Pilots' Assn., B-52 Stratofortress Assn., The Ret. Officers' Assn., Order Daedalians (flight capt., pres. 2001-02), Airlift/Tanker Assn., Dayton Area Def. Contractors Assn. (pres. 1999-2000, bd. dirs.), Armed Forces Comms. and Electronics Assn., Def. Planning and Analysis Soc., Miami Valley Mil. Affairs Assn., Inst. of Navigation, Pararescue Assn., Internat. Test & Evaluation Assn., Pedro Helicopter Assn., Royal Air Force Club, Electronic Engring. and Mfg. Group, Air Force Mus. Found., Nat. Def. Indsl. Assn., Mil. Officers Assn. Am., Nat. Mil. Intelligence Assn., Dayton Art Inst., Assn. Old Crows, Air Force Assn. Cmty. Ptnrs., Dayton Area C. of C. (vice-chmn. mil. and fed. affairs com. 2003—), DFC Soc., Mil. Officers Assn. Am., Nat Aviation Hall of Fame, Nat. Mil. Intelligence Assn., Nat. Investor Rels. Inst. Masons, Scottish Rite, Shriners, Blue Key. Presbyterian. Avocations: art, photography, jogging. Home: 2537 Indian Wells Trl Xenia OH 45385-9373 Business E-Mail: daniel.bigelow@mtctechnologies.com

BIGELOW, DONALD NEVIUS, educational administrator, historian, consultant; b. Danbury, Conn., Aug. 19, 1918; s. Harry R. and Bessie M. (Nevius) B.; m. Louise M. Fournel, Sept. 21, 1957; 1 son, Pierre Nevius. BA cum laude, Amherst Coll., 1939, MA, 1945; PhD, Columbia U., 1950. Spl. agt. Inland Marine Ins., North Brit. and Merc. Ins. Co., N.Y.C. and Detroit, 1939-43; with U.S. Engr. Dept., Fairbanks, Alaska, 1942; instr. history Amherst Coll., 1943-45; instr. Columbia U., 1947-50, asst. prof., 1951-55; assoc. prof. Brandeis U., 1955-60; chief lang. and area ctrs. program Office Edn., HEW, Washington, 1961-64; head task force NDEA Title XI Inst. Program, 1964-65, dir. divsn. ednl. pers. tng., 1965-67, dir. divsn. program adminstrn., 1967-68; dir. divsn. coll. programs Bur. Ednl. Pers. Devel., 1968-71; dir. Northeast divsn. Nat. Ctr. for Improvement Ednl. Sys., 1972-74; spl. asst., assoc. commr. for Instl. Devel. and Internat. Edn., 1974-76; chief grad. tng. Office of Postsecondary Edn., Dept. Edn., Washington, 1976-82; sr. adminstr. The Nat. Faculty, Atlanta, 1985-88; spl. asst. to dep. asst. sec. Office of Postsecondary Edn., U.S. Dept. Edn., Washington, 1988-93, sr. exec. Ctr. Internat. Edn., 1993, program mgr. Dwight D. Eisenhower Leadership Devel. Act of 1992, 1993-96. Exec. dir. Javits Fellowship Bd., 1996-2000, spl. asst. Office Internat. Edn. & Grad. Edn. Office Higher Edn., 1998—, sr. advisor, 2002; vis. Fulbright prof. Am. civilization U.S. Ednl. Fund, India, U. Baroda, U. Lucknow, 1954-55; prof. humanities N.Y. Sch. Music, 1949-56; vis. prof. U. So. Fla., 1969; postdoctoral rsch. fellow George Washington U., 1970-71; lectr. U. Va., 1973; adj. prof. Am. U., 1975; cons. Ford Found., 1957, Carnegie Corp., 1958, U.S. Office Edn., 1959-60; moderator ABC TV series Seminar, 1953-54, PBS WGBH TV series on ethnicity, 1956-57; assoc. dir. com. lang. and area ctrs. Am. Coun. Edn., 1960-61; book reviewer Nat. Pub. Radio series Options in Education, 1976-77. Author: William Conant Church and the Army and Navy Journal, 1952, (with Joseph Axelrod) Resources for Language and Area Studies, 1960, (with Lyman Legters) Language and Area Centers, 1964, (with others) Non-Western Studies in the Liberal Arts College, 1964; editor: (with Hiram Haydn) Makers of the American Tradition Series, 4 vols., 1953-55, The Annals (The Non-Western World in Higher Education), 1964, The Liberal Arts and Teacher Education: A Confrontation, 1971, Schoolworlds '76, New Directions for Educational Policy, 1976, Democracy at Risk: Leadership and Education, a Report on the Eisenhower Leadership Program, 1992-96, 1999. Home: 2901 Q St NW Washington DC 20007-3089 Office: US Dept Edn 1990 K St NW Washington DC 20006-8521 E-mail: don.bigelow@ed.gov.

BIGELOW, GEORGE E. psychology and pharmacology scientist; b. Washington, Aug. 31, 1943; Dir. behavioral pharmacology unit Johns Hopkins U., Balt., Md. Office: Johns Hopkins U Behavioral Pharma Unit 5510 Nathan Shock Dr Baltimore MD 21224-6823

BIGELOW, JONATHAN LEHR, editor, publishing executive; b. Mineola, N.Y., June 24, 1950; s. Benjamin and Anne (Lehr) B.; m. Mariann Cortissoz; 1 child, James Benjamin. AB, Brown U., 1972. Asst. production mgr. Miller and Fink Corp., Darien, Conn., 1972-73, staff editor Patient Care jour., 1973-75, mng. editor Patient Care jour., 1975-76; program editor Physicians Radio Network, N.Y.C., 1976-78; sr. editor Consultant jour. Cliggott Pub. Co., Darien, Conn., 1978-79, editor Jour. Respiratory Diseases, 1979-90, editor Jour. Musculoskeletal Medicine, 1983-88, editor Jour. Critical Illness, 1985-90, 97-98, v.p. group editl. dir., 1986-91, editl. dir., 1991-98, gen. mgr. projects divsn., 1991-94, editor Consultant jour., 1994-96, v.p., 1986-93, sr. v.p., 1993-97, exec. v.p., COO, 1997-98, pres., COO, 1998—. Contbr. numerous articles on clin. medicine and med. polit. issues to profl. jours. Counselor student alumni network Brown U., 1980—; ch. coun., bd. deacons 1st Congl. Ch. Darien, Conn., 1989—, moderator, 2002--. Mem. Nat. Assn. Sci. Writers, Assn. Med. Publs. (bd. dirs. 2002--, pres.-elect 2003), Lake Club, Landmark Club, Nature Conservancy, others. Home: 15 Marvin Ridge Pl Wilton CT 06897-2837 Office: Cliggott Pub Co 330 Boston Post Rd Darien CT 06820-3644

BIGELOW, KATHRYN, film director; b. San Carlos, Calif., Nov. 27, 1951; Student, San Francisco Art Inst., Whitney Mus. Ind. Study Program, Columbi U. Sch. Film. Former Gap model. Director: (films) The Loveless, 1982, Near Dark, 1987, Blue Steel, 1990, Point Break, 1991, Strange Days, 1995, The Set Up, 1998, The Weight of Water, 2003, (TV series) Homicide Life on the Street, 1993, (TV miniseries) Wild Palms, 1993; dir., prodr., K-19: The Widowmaker, 2002; script supr. Union City, 1980; author: (screenplays) (with Monty Montgomery) The Loveless, (with Eric Red) Near Dark, actor: Born in Flames, 1983 Office: First Light care Working title Films 9333 Wilshire Blvd Beverly Hills CA 90210-5408*

BIGELOW, MARGARET ELIZABETH BARR (M.E. BARR), mycology educator; b. Elkhorn, Man., Can., Apr. 16, 1923; d. David Hunter and Mary Irene (Parr) Barr; m. Howard Elson Bigelow, June 9, 1956 (dec.). BA with honors, U. B.C., Vancouver, Can., 1950, MA, 1952; PhD, U. Mich., 1956. Rsch. attaché U. Montreal, Que., Can., 1956-57; instr. U. Mass., Amherst, 1957-65, asst. prof., 1965-71, assoc. prof., 1971-76, prof., 1976-89, prof. emeritus, 1989—. Author: Diaporthales in N.A., 1978, Prodromus to Loculoascomycetes, 1987, Prodromus to Nonlichenized Members of Class Hymenoascomycetes, 1990; contbr. articles to profl. jours. With Can. Women's Army Corps, 1942-46. Mem. Mycol. Soc. Am. (v.p. to pres. 1980-82, editor 1975-80, Disting. Mycologist Award, 1993), Brit. Mycol. Soc., Am. Inst. Biol. Sci. (gen. chmn. ann. meeting 1986). Avocations: gardening, reading. Home and Office: 9475 Inverness Rd Sidney BC Canada V8L 5G8

BIGELOW, MARTHA MITCHELL, retired historian; b. Talladega Springs, Ala., Sept. 19, 1921; children: Martha Frances, Carolyn Letitia. BA, Montevallo U., 1943; MA, U. Chgo., 1944, PhD, 1946. Assoc. prof. history Miss. Coll., Clinton, 1946-48, Memphis State U., 1948-49; Assoc. prof. history U. Miss., 1949-50; assoc. curator manuscripts Mich. Hist. Collections, U. Mich., Ann Arbor, 1954-57; prof. history Miss. Coll., 1957-71, chmn. dept. history and polit. sci., 1964-71. Dir. Bur. of History, Mich. Dept. State, 1971-90; sec. Mich. Hist. Commn., Mich. Dept. State, state historic preservation officer, 1971-90; coord. for Mich., Nat. Hist. Publs. and Recs. Commn., 1974-90. Contbr. articles profl. publns. Fellow, Ency. Britannica, 1944—45; scholar Julius Rosenwald scholarship, 1943—44, Cleo Hearson scholarship, 1944. Mem. Am. Assn. State and Local History (v.p. 1979-80, pres. 1980-81, fellow summers 1958, 59), Orgn. Am. Historians, Nat. Assn. State Archives and Recs. Assn., So. Hist. Assn., Mich. Hist. Soc., Miss. Hist. Soc. Home: 201 Jefferson St Clinton MS 39056-4237

BIGELOW, NICHOLAS PIERRE, physicist, educator; b. Princeton, N.J., Dec. 26, 1958; s. Julian Himley and Mary Agnes (Milward) B.; m. Judith Anderson, July 26, 1981; children: Ian, Eric. BS in Elec. Engring. with high honors, Lehigh U., 1980, BS in Physics with high honors, 1981; MS, Cornell U., 1984, PhD, 1989. Lic. pilot. Mem. tech. staff AT&T Bell Labs., Holmdel, N.J., 1989-91; sr. rsch. assoc. dept. physics and astronomy U. Rochester, N.Y., 1991-92, asst. prof. physics, 1992-97, assoc. prof., 1997—, sr. staff scientist Lab. for Laser Energetics, 1992—, prof., 2000, Lee A. DuBridge prof. physics, prof. optics, 2001—. Rsch. assoc. Ecole Normale Supérieure, Paris, 1991-92, vis. prof., 1992-95. Mem. editl. bd. Laser Physics, Optics Letters; contbr. chpts. to books, numerous articles to profl. jours. and encys. Alfred P. Sloan Found. fellow, 1993-95; NSF grantee, 1994—; David and Lucile Packard Found. fellow, 1994—. Mem. Am. Phys. Soc., Optical Soc. Am., Tau Beta Pi. Achievements include theoretical and experimental investigations the fields of quantum optics and atomic physics. Office: U Rochester Dept Physics and Astronomy Rochester NY 14627

BIGELOW, PETER, electronics executive; b. Mineola, N.Y., Sept. 28, 1953; s. Benjamin and Anne (Lehr) B.; m. Margaret (Baldwin) B.; children: Emily Anne, Catherine Clare, David Ellis. BA in Bus., Ohio No. U., 1976. Supr. costing & pricing Burndy Corp., York, Pa., 1977-81; mgr. product mktg. & planning Champion Internat., Inc., Stamford, Conn., 1981-85; dir. mktg. Catty divsn. Rostra Holdings, Fairfield, Conn., 1985-86; dir. sales & mktg. M.H. Rhodes, Inc., Avon, Conn., 1986-90; ind. cons. Darien, Conn., 1990-92; v.p. sales & mktg. Beaver Brook Circuits, Inc., Bethel, Conn., 1992-94, pres., CEO, 1994—2001; prin. Conn. Coining, Inc., Bethel, 2001—02; pres., CEO IMI Inc., Haverhill, Mass., 2002—. Dir. Record-Jour. Pub. Co., Meriden, Conn., IPC, Northbrook, Ill.; dir., pres. Housitonic Edn. for Advanced Tech., 1999 . Chmn., pres. Darien Nature Ctr., Inc., 1996-99, dir., 1991-99; commr. Planning & Zoning Commn., Darien, 1999. Episcopalian. Home: 9 Clock Ave Darien CT 06820-5323 Office: IMI Inc 140 Hilldale Ave Haverhill MA 01832 E-mail: pbigelow@IMI.com.

BIGELOW, ROBERT P. lawyer, arbitrator, mediator, journalist; b. N.Y.C., Jan. 17, 1927; s. Robert R.L. and Doris W.S. (Bissell) B.; m. Katharine W. MacKenty Apr. 14, 1951; children: Katharine R., Robert S., Sanford W., Edward G. AB cum laude, Harvard U., 1950, JD, 1953. Bar: Mass. 1953, N.Y. 1980. Law clk. Supreme Ct. Mass., 1953-54; assoc. Bingham Dana & Gould, Boston, 1954-56; atty., asst. counsel John Hancock Mut. Life Ins. Co., Boston, 1956-66; pvt. practice Woburn and Boston, Mass., 1966-86; of counsel Hennessy Kilburn Killgoar & Ronan, Boston, 1973-84; ptnr. Bigelow & Saltzberg, Woburn, 1980-86; counsel Warner & Stockpole, Boston, 1986-87; sole practice, 1987-91, 95-97; counsel Bird & Bird, London, 1995-97; arbitrator, mediator, 1966—. Adj. prof. Dartmouth Coll., 1982-84, Suffolk Law Sch., 1986-92; acting dir. New Eng. Law Inst., 1974-75. Author: (with Susan Nycum) Your Computer and the Law, 1975, Contracting for Computer Hardware, Software and Services, 1984-95, Computer Contracts, 1987-92; editor Law Office Econs. and Mgmt., 1969-78, Computer Law Svc., 1973-81, Computer Law and Tax Report, 1974-84, Computer Law Newsletter, 1979-87; cons. editor, 1988-91; cons. editor Bull. Computer Law Assn., 1971-97, editor, 1997-98; contbg. editor Cyberspace Lawyer, 1998—, Lawyers Competitive Edge, 1999—; mem. adv. bd. Guide to Computer Law, 1998-2001; contbr. articles to profl. jours. With U.S. Army, 1945-46, 51-64. Fellow AAAS, Brit. Computer Soc. (life, qualified arbitrator), New Zealand Computer Soc., I.S.P. Can. Info. Processing Soc., Am. Bar Found. (life), Coll. Law Practice Mgmt. (hon.); mem. ABA (editor Computers and the Law 1966, 69, 81, Jurimetrics Jour. 1971-74, Bull. Law, Sci. and Tech. 1977-800, chmn. com. law relating to computers 1979-80, briefs editor Law Practice Mgmt. 1979-91, 93-96), Mass. Bar Assn. (chmn. econs. com. 1969-73, mem. com profl. ethics 1973-79, mem. coun. law practice 1981-84, chmn. bus. law sect. 1984-85), Computer Law Assn. (pres. 1977-79, dir. 1973-84, adv. bd. 1984—), Australian Computer Soc. Office: 10 Mount Vernon St # 252 Winchester MA 01890-2704

BIGELOW, ROBERT WILSON, trial lawyer; b. L.A., Oct. 22, 1964; s. William Phillips and Dona (Heath) B.; m. Madeline Garcia, Sept. 24, 1995; children: William, Emma. Student, UCLA, 1982-84; BA with distinction, U. N.Mex., 1990; JD, Georgetown U., 1993. Bar: N.Y. Intern FTC, Washington, 1992; mem. Georgetown Criminal Justice Clinic, Washington, 1992-93; sr. staff aty. Criminal Def. divsn. Legal Aid Soc., Bronx, N.Y., 1993-2001, supervising atty. N.Y.C., 2001—. Mentor John Jay Legal Svcs., Inc., White Plains, N.Y., 1997-2001. Mem. ABA (criminal justice sect. 1996—, def. function/svcs. com. 1996—), Assn. Legal Aid Attys. (rep. 1997-99, alt. v.p. 1999-2001). Democrat. Episcopalian. Avocation: baseball research. Home: 28 Cannon St West Orange NJ 07052 Office: Legal Aid Soc Criminal Def Divsn 49 Thomas St New York NY 10013

BIGG, DONALD MICHAEL, chemical engineer; b. Bayonne, N.J., July 15, 1945; s. Alfred and Marie (McGlynn) B.; m. Ellen Johanna McElligott, June 5, 1967; children: Margaret, Rosemary. BS in Chem. Engring., Cath. U., 1967; MS, U. Rochester, 1970; PhD, U. Mass., 1973. Engr. Eastman Kodak, Rochester, N.Y., 1967-70; rsch. leader Battelle Meml. Inst., Columbus, Ohio, 1973-94; mgr. rsch. and devel. R.G. Barry Corp., Pickerington, Ohio, 1994-99; sr. engr. Materials Engring. Tech. Sypport Svcs., Westerville, Ohio, 2000—. Adj. prof. Ohio State U., Columbus, 1981, 91-93, 2001; mem. adv. bd. Polymer Engring. and Sci., Brookfield, Conn., 1981-98. Contbr. articles to profl. jours. Mem. Soc. Plastics Engrs., Sigma Xi. Roman Catholic. Avocations: basketball, tennis, running, reading. Office: METSS 300 Westdale Ave Westerville OH 43082 E-mail: dbigg@metss.com.

BIGGERS, CORNELIA ANDERSON, musician; b. Iowa City, Iowa, Mar. 15, 1935; d. William Arthur Anderson and Ann Maria Riddell; m. James Wesley Biggers, Jr., May 31, 1958. BA summa cum laude, U. Iowa, 1957. 3rd bassoon and contra- bassoon Tampa Philharm., Fla., 1963—68; 3rd bassoon and contra-bassoon Fla. Gulf Coast Symphony, 1968—82; 3rd bassoon and contra-bassoon Fla. Symphony, Orlando, 1967—82, The Fla. Orch., Tampa, 1982—85; prin. bassoon The Richey Cmty. Orch., Hudson, 1991—, Hernando Symphony Orch., Spring Hill, 1996—97, 2000—; 3rd bassoon and contra -bassoon Imperial Symphony Orch., Lakeland, 1998—. Solo bassoon The Masonic Band, St. Petersburg, Fla., 1995—; substitute organist various chs.; bassoonist, mgr. Profl. Woodwind Ensembles, Clearwater. Author: The Contra-Bassoon: A Guide to Performance, 1977. Mem., officer Ind. Order Foresters Bounty Br., Clearwater; bldg. capt. Woodland Villas Condominium, Clearwater. Mem.: Internat. Double Reed Soc., Am. Fedn. Musicians (life), Mensa, Order Ea. Star, Phi Beta Kappa. Republican. Avocations: recorder, literature, Star Trek, ornithology.

BIGGERS, JONATHAN EDWARD, music educator, consultant; b. Oak Ridge, Tenn., Feb. 10, 1960; s. Robert Edward and Margaret Valentine Biggers. MusB, U. Ala., 1982, MusM, 1984; cert. perfectionnement, Conservatory of Music, Geneva, Switzerland, 1985, cert. virtuosity, 1986; DMA, Eastman Sch. Music, 1991. Dir. music 1st Meth. Ch., Fayette, Ala., 1982—84; organist Holy Trinity Anglican Ch., Geneva, 1984—87, 3d Presbyn. Ch., Rochester, NY, 1988—89, dir. music, organist, 1989—91; asst. prof. music, Link endowed chair U. Binghamton, NY, 1992—2001, assoc. prof. music, Link endowed chair, artist-in-residence, 2002—. Organ cons., organ projects in various chs. U.S., Switzerland. Performer: (CD recording) Sleepers Wake! A Reger Perspective, 1994, concerts on Pipedreams, Minn. Pub. Radio program, 1982—, numerous radio broadcasts;over 150 organ concerts and master classes, throughout U.S. and Europe, 1990—. (CD recording) Bach on the Fritts!, 1995. Recipient 1st prize (unanimous), Geneva Internat. Competition, 1985, Calgary (Can.) Organ Festival Concerto Competition, 1990. Mem.: Am. Guild Organists (bd. dirs. Binghamton chpt., 2d prize nat. playing competition 1982). Office: Binghamton U Dept Music PO Box 6000/Vestal Pkwy E Binghamton NY 13902-6000 E-mail: biggers@binghamton.edu.

BIGGERS, WILLIAM JOSEPH, retired manufacturing company executive; b. Great Bend, Kans., Mar. 16, 1928; s. William Henry and Frances (Jack) B.; m. Eathil Bonner, Nov. 17, 1956 (div. July 1981); children: Frances, Patricia; m. Diane McLaughlin, Feb. 14, 1983; 1 child, Michael C. BA, Duke U., 1949. C.P.A., Ga. Pub. acct., 1949-55; sec.-treas. Parker, Helms & Langston, Inc., Brunswick, Ga., 1955-59, Stuckey's, Inc., Eastman, Ga., 1959-60; sec.-treas., v.p. finance Curtis 1000 Inc., 1961-69; v.p. Am. Bus. Products, Inc., Atlanta, 1969-73, chief exec. officer, 1973-88, chmn. bd., 1983-94, chmn. exec. com., 1994-98. Bd dirs. Com. Publicly Owned Cos.; former trustee Ga. Coun. Econ. Edn., former mem. listed co. adv. com. N.Y. Stock Exch., Am. Stock Exch. Trustee Berry Coll.; bd. dirs. Atlanta Area coun. Boy Scouts Am. With USNR,

1946, with AUS, 1950-52. Mem. AICPA, NAM, Ga. Soc. CPAs, Fin. Execs. Inst., Am. Mgmt. Assn., Phoenix Soc. Atlanta, Capital City Club, Georgian Club, Marietta Country Club, Highlands Country Club, Rotary, Phi Kappa Psi.

BIGGERT, JUDITH BORG, congresswoman, lawyer; b. Aug. 15, 1937; d. Alvin Andrew and Marjorie Virginia (Mailler) Borg; m. Rody Patterson Biggert, Sept. 21, 1963; children: Courtney Ray, Alison Mailler, Rody Patterson, Adrienne Taylor. BA, Stanford U., 1959; JD, Northwestern U., 1963. Bar: Ill. 1963. Law clk. to presiding justice U.S. Ct. Appeals (7th cir.), Chgo., 1963-64; sole practice Hinsdale, Ill., 1964—. Rep. Ill. Gen. Assembly, 1993-98, asst. Rep. leader, 1995-98; mem. U.S. Congress from 13th Ill. dist., 1999—, mem. fin. svcs. com., edn. and workforce com. stds. ofcl. conduct, sci. com., mem. bipartisan working group on youth violence, co-chair womens caucus, speakers task force for drug free Am. Mem. bd. editors Law Rev., Northwestern U. Sch. Law, 1961-63. Pres. Hinsdale Twp. High Sch. Dist. 86 Bd. Edn., 1983-85; pres. Jr. League Chgo., 1976-78, treas., bd. mgrs., 1966—; chmn. Hinsdale Antiques Show, 1980; pres. Oak Sch. PTA, Hinsdale, 1976-78; pres.-treas. Chgo. jr. bd. Travelers Aid Soc., 1965-70; Sunday sch. tchr. Grace Episcopal Ch., Hinsdale, 1978-80, 82-85; chair, treas., 2d v.p. bd. dirs. Vis. Nurses Assn. Chgo., 1978; bd. dirs. Salt Creek Ballet, 1990—98. Recipient Servian award Jr. aux. U. Chgo. Cancer Rsch. Foun., Woman of Yr. in Govt., Politics, and Civic Affairs DuPage YWCA, 1995, Spirit of Enterprise award U.S. C. of C.; named on of 100 Women Making a Difference; inductee to Hinsdale Ctrl. H.S. Hall of Fame, 1997. Mem. ABA, Ill. Bar Assn., DuPage Bar Assn., Coalition Women Legislatures. Republican. Office: US Ho of Reps 1213 Longworth House Off Bl Washington DC 20515-1313 also: 13th Dist of Ill 115 W 55th St Ste 100 Clarendon Hills IL 60514-1593*

BIGGINS, ROBERT A. state legislator; b. Oak Park, Ill., Oct. 20, 1946; m. Judy Biggins; children: Jennifer, Kevin. BA, Northeastern Ill. U., 1969. Assessor Addison Twp., Ill., 1973-77; Ill. state rep. Dist. 78, 1992—. Mem. Gen. Svcs., Consumer Protection, Fin. Insts. and Revenue Coms.; tchr. Mannheim Jr. H.S., Northlake, Ill., 1969, Daniel Webster Elem. Sch., Chgo., 1970-73; property tax cons., Chgo., 1977-81; ptnr. Property Assessment Advisors, Inc., 1981—, exec. v.p. Bd. dirs. Suburban Bank Elmhurst, 1975—, chmn., 1983-84, chmn. Bank of Bellwood, 1981-85; mem. Elmhurst Gardens Homeowners Assn. (past pres.), Edison Sch. PTA (past pres.). Recipient award Internat. Assn. Assessing Officers, 1990. Mem. DuPage County Assessors Assn. (legis. liaison 1975-76, pres. 1976), Inst. Property Taxation (cert.). Address: 114 W Park Ave Elmhurst IL 60126-3399*

BIGGIO, CRAIG, professional baseball player; b. Smithtown, N.Y., Dec. 14, 1965; Grad. h.s., Houston. Second base player Houston Astros, 1988—. Named Catcher, The Sporting News Coll. All-Am. Team, 1987; named to Sporting News Silver Slugger Team, 1989, 94, The Sporting News Nat. League All-Star Team, 1994, named to Nat. League All-Star Team, 1991, 92, 94-98; recipient Gold Glove 2d base, 1994-96. Office: Houston Astros PO Box 288 Houston TX 77001-0288

BIGGOOSE, CHARLES, counselor; b. Pawnee, Okla., May 23, 1946; s. Leland Biggoose and Eva King; m. Vivian Dancingstar Biggoose, July 9, 1999. CEO Tribal Enterprises Found., Auburn, Calif., Inter-Tribal Cultural Found., Tulsa, Okla. Author: When The Whileman Smiles, 1993, I'll Send My Eyes, 1990. Avocations: chess, billiards. Home: 1210 S Cheyenn Ave Tulsa OK 74119 Office: Inter-Tribal Found 24128 Hwy 51 West Sand Springs OK

BIGGS, ALAN RICHARD, plant pathologist, educator; b. Lewisburg, Pa., June 22, 1953; s. Edgar Harold and Yvonne S. Biggs; m. Lise N. Sade, Oct. 3, 1981; children: Benjamin Jesse Biggs Sade, Skylar Rose Biggs Sade. BS, Pa. State U., 1976, MS, 1978, PhD, 1982. Rsch. scientist Can. Dept. Agr., Vineland, Ont., 1983-89; assoc. prof. W.Va. U., Kearneysville, 1989-95, prof., 1995—. Editor: Defense Mechanisms of Woody Plants Against Fungi, 1992, Cytology, Histology and Histochemistry of Fruit Tree Diseases, 1992; assoc. editor Jour. Phytopathology, 1986-88, Plant Disease, 1994-96; sr. editor Plant Disease, 1998-2000, editor-in-chief, 2001—. Recipient Lee M. Hutchins award, 1993, USDA Sec. Honor award, 2001, 2002. Mem. AAAS, Am. Phytopath. Soc. (Lee M. Hutchins award 1993). Avocations: photography, bicycling, jazz guitar. Office: WVa U Tree Fruit Rsch and Edn Ctr PO Box 609 Kearneysville WV 25430-0609

BIGGS, ARTHUR EDWARD, retired chemical manufacturing company executive; b. N.Y.C., Jan. 3, 1930; s. Arthur Edward and Pauline (Maier) B.; m. Charlotte Marion Elliott, Sept. 10, 1955; children— Arthur Edward III, William Elliott, Nancy Catherine, Andrew David BS in Acctg. and Fin. Magna cum laude, U. Md., 1951; MBA in Fin. and Prodn. with distinction, Harvard U., 1957. Mgmt. cons. McKinsey & Co., Inc., N.Y.C., 1957-62; asst. controller Mobil Oil Co., N.Y.C., 1963-66, controller, 1966-68; v.p., gen. mgr. plastics div. Mobil Chem. Co., Rochester, N.Y., 1969-73, exec. v.p. N.Y.C., 1974-82, pres., 1982-86. Chmn. bd. dirs. The Century Group, 1987-91. Vice pres. bd. dirs. Vis. Nurse Svc. N.Y., 1975-88; bd. advisers Pace U., N.Y.C., 1976-88; trustee Quinnipiac Coll., Hamden, Conn., 1982-92, chmn., 1986-90; bd. dirs. Ptnrs. in Care, N.Y.C., 1983-88, chmn., 1983-88; trustee Conn. Conf. Ind. Colls., chmn., 1987-89; trustee Harvard Sch. Bus. 1st lt., pilot USAF, 1951-55. Baker scholar Harvard U., 1957. Mem. Racquet Club Boca Raton, Woodfield Country Club (Boca Raton). Avocation: tennis.

BIGGS, EDMUND LOGAN, college administrator; b. Mattoon, Ill., Dec. 17, 1938; s. Lloyd William and Florence Violet (Fairbanks) B.; 1 child, Lloyd John. BS in Acctg., Kansas State U., 1965; MBA in Mgmt., U. New Haven, 1983; PhD, SUNY, Buffalo, 1991. Computer specialist Union Nat. Bank, Manhattan, Kans., 1963-65, mgmt. trainee, 1965-66; nuclear logistics officer USN, Kirtland AFB, N. Mex., 1967-68, computer programming officer, 1968-69; data automation officer Tan Son Knut, Vietnam, 1969-70; computer systems analyst Stuttgart, Fed. Republic Germany, 1970-72; supply officer USS Sellers, 1973-74; procurement officer def. gen. supply ctr. Richmond, Va., 1974-76; asst. supply/material officer, support force, 1976-78; planning and adminstrv. officer, aviation supply officer, 1978-79; comptr., commanding officer regional acctg. and disbursing ctr. Subase, New London, Conn., 1980-82; liaison officer def. logistics agy for maj. def. systems Syracuse, N.Y., 1982-83; instr. bus. Erie Community Coll., Buffalo, 1983-86, dept. head banking, ins., real estate, 1986—. Adminstr. Structurally Unemployed Retng. Program, Buffalo, 1985—. Mem. VFW, Am. Legion, Optimist Internat., Lions. Roman Catholic. Avocations: antiques, music, cooking, camping. Office: Erie Community Coll 4041 Southwestern Blvd Orchard Park NY 14127

BIGGS, JASON, actor; b. Pompano Plains, NJ, May 12, 1978; s. Gary and Angela Biggs. Student, NYU, Montclair State U. Actor: (films) Conversations With My Fahter, 1991, The Boy Who Cried Bitch, 1991, American Pie, 1999, Boys and Girls, 2000, Loser, 2000, Saving Silverman, 2001, American Pie 2, 2001, Prozac Nation, 2001, American Wedding, 2003; (TV series) Drexell's Class, 1991, As the World Turns, 1994—95; (Broadway plays) The Graduate, 2002. Office: c/o SFM 1122 S Robertson # 15 Los Angeles CA 90035*

BIGGS, JEFFREY ROBERT, educator; b. New Castle, Pa., May 2, 1941; s. Wallace R. and Janice E. Biggs; m. Janet Allen Mathews, May 24, 1969; children: Jennifer M., Jessica E. BA, Harvard U., 1963; MA, Victoria U., Wellington, New Zealand, 1965; PhD, George Washington U., 1975. With U.S. Consulate Gen., Rio de Janeiro, 1974-78; attache U.S. Embassy, Lisbon, Portugal, 1978-81; dir., pres. bur. inter-Am. affairs Dept of State, Washington, 1981-84; deputy chief of mission Am. Embassy, La Paz, Bolivia, 1985-87; press sec. spkr. of house U.S. Ho. Reps., Washington, 1987-94; sr. advisor Office Nat. Drug Control Policy, Washington, 1995; dir. congl. fellowship program Am. Polit. Sci. Assn., Washington, 1997—. Mem. adv. bd. sr. Fulbright enhancement program, Robert Wood Johnson Health Policy Fellowship Adv. Bd./Pub. Diplomacy Coun. Co-author: Honor in the House: Speaker Tom Foley, 1999; contbr. articles to profl. jours. Fulbright fellow, Wellington, New Zealand, 1964-65, Congl. fellow APSA, 1984-85. Mem. Am. Polit. Sci. Assn., Diplomatic-Consular Officers Ret. Assn., Pub. Diplomacy Coun. Avocations: fly fishing, hiking, writing. Home: 6406 Kenhowe Dr Bethesda MD 20817-5446 Office: Am Polit Sci Assn 1527 New Hampshire Ave NW Washington DC 20036-1203

BIGGS, JOHN HERRON, retired insurance company executive; b. St. Louis, July 19, 1936; s. Peter Willis and Lillian (Herron) B.; m. Penelope Frances Parkman, June 13, 1959; 1 child, Henry. AB magna cum laude, Harvard U., 1958; PhD in Econ., Wash. U., 1983. V.p., contr. Gen. Am. Ins. Co., 1970-77; vice chancellor for adminstrn. and fin. Washington U., St. Louis, 1977-85; chmn., pres., chief exec. officer Centerre Trust Co., 1985-89; pres., COO Tchrs. Ins. and Annuity Assn./Coll. Retirement Equities Fund, 1989-93, chmn., pres., CEO, 1993—2002. Bd. dirs. Boeing Co., JPMorganChase Co.; trustee Internat. Acctg. Stds. Com.; emeritus trustee, past pres. Mo. Bot. Garden. Trustee, past chmn. Nat. Bur. Econ. Affairs; trustee Washington U., Getty Trust, Fgn. Policy Assn., Danforth Found., Am. Sch. Classical Studies, Athens; bd. dirs., past chmn. United Way N.Y.C. Fellow: Soc. of Actuaries; mem.: Coun. Fgn. Rels., St. Louis Club, Harvard Club N.Y., Sky Club, Westchester Country Club. Home: 240 E 47th St Apt 23D New York NY 10017-2137 Office: TIAA/CREF 730 3rd Ave New York NY 10017-3206

BIGGS, ROBERT DALE, Near Eastern studies educator; b. Pasco, Wash., June 13, 1934; s. Robert Lee and Eleonora Christina (Jensen) B. BA in Edn, Eastern Wash. Coll. Edn., 1956; PhD, Johns Hopkins U., 1962. Research asso. Oriental Inst., Univ. Chgo., 1963-64; asst. prof. Assyriology, 1964-67, asso. prof., 1967-72, prof., 1972—. Author: ŠÀ.ZI.GA: Ancient Mesopotamian Potency Incantations, 1967, Inscriptions from Tell Abu Salabikh, 1974, Inscriptions from al-Hiba-Lagash: The First and Second Seasons, 1976; co-author: Cuneiform Texts from Nippur, 1969, Nippur II: The North Temple and Sounding E, 1978; editor: Discoveries from Kurdish Looms, 1983; assoc. editor: Assyrian Dictionary, 1964-87; editor Jour. Near Ea. Studies, 1972—; mem. editorial bd. Assyrian Dictionary, 1995—. Fulbright scholar Univ. Toulouse, France, 1956-57; fellow Baghdad Sch., Am. Schs. Oriental Rsch., 1962-63, Am. Rsch. Inst. in Turkey, 1972, Danforth fellow, 1956-62. Mem. Am. Oriental Soc. (pres. Mid. Western br. 1978-79), Archaeol. Inst. Am. (pres. Chgo. soc. 1985-92), Brit. Sch. Archaeology Iraq. Office: U Chgo 1155 E 58th St Chicago IL 60637-1540

BIGGS, WILLIAM CURTIS, endocrinologist; b. Merced, Calif., Nov. 16, 1956; s. Everett Eugene and Betty Louise (Allanach) B.; m. Grace Emily Asghar, June 25, 1983; children: Richard, William, Sarah Grace. BA, U. Calif. San Diego, 1978; MD, U. Tex. Southwestern, Dallas, 1982. Diplomate Am. Bd. Internal Medicine. Intern in medicine U. Calif., San Diego, 1982-83; resident in medicine New Eng. Deaconess Hosp./Harvard U., Boston, 1983-85; fellow in endocrinology Joslin Clinic/Harvard Med. Sch., Boston, 1985-86; pvt. practice Amarillo (Tex.) Med. Specialists, 1986—; mgr. CBLF Ptnrs., L.L.C., 1999—. Chmn. dept. internal medicine N.W. Tex. Hosp., Amarillo, 1989-93, pres. med. staff, 1994-96; bd. govs. N.W. Tex. Healthcare Sys., Amarillo, 1996—; asst. clin. prof. Tex. Tech U. Sch. Medicine, 1986—; mng. ptnr. Amarillo Med. Specialists, LLP. Bd. dirs. Amarillo affiliate Am. Diabetes Assn., 1992-93, hon. chmn. Walktoberfest, 1994; refugee camp vol. ARC, Camp Pendleton, Calif., 1975. Mem. AMA, ACP, Am. Diabetes Assn., Am. Assn. Clin. Endocrinologists, Tex. Med. Assn., Panhandle Amateur Radio Club, Potter Randall County Med. Soc. Home: 7807 Underwood Dr Amarillo TX 79121-1533 Office: Amarillo Med Specialists 1215 Coulter St Ste 400 Amarillo TX 79106-1784 E-mail: biggs@amarillomed.com.

BIGHAM, JAMES GEORGE, structural engineer; b. Berwyn, Ill., Aug. 27, 1937; s. James Dellard Bigham and Gladys Marie Zahn. BSCE, U. Notre Dame, 1959. Registered structural engr., Ill. Bridge engr. Ohio Hwy. Dept., Columbus, Ohio, 1959-62, Goodkind & Odea, Chgo., 1962-63; sales engr. Republic Steel Corp., Oak Park, Ill., 1963-65; structural engr. Army Corps. Engrs., Chgo., 1965-70, New Orleans, 1970-80, Rock Island, Ill., 1980-95; tutor, instr. Triton Coll., River Grove, Ill., 1998—. Chmn. Sheet Pile Structures-Corps. Engrs., Rock Island, 1980-95. With U.S. Army, 1961. Mem. Structural Engrs. Assn. Ill. Roman Catholic. Avocations: jogging, gardening. E-mail: jbigham@triton.cc.il.us.

BIGHAM, WANDA DURRETT, college president; b. Barlow, Ky., June 19, 1935; d. Herbert Martin and Ada Florene (Baker) Durrett; m. William M. Bigham, Jr., June 7, 1958; children: William M. III, Janet Kaye, Julia Lynn. BME, Murray State U., 1956; MM, Morehead State U., 1971, MHE, 1973; EdD, U. Ky., 1978; cert., Inst. For Ednl. Mgmt. -Harvard U., 1982; LittD (hon.), Loras Coll., 1989. Dir. TRIO programs Morehead (Ky.) State U., 1972-85, assoc. dean acad. affairs, dir. instructional sys., 1982-85, acting dean grad. and spl. acad. programs, 1984-85; exec. asst. to pres. Emerson Coll., Boston, 1985, v.p. for devel., 1986; pres. Marycrest Coll., Davenport, Iowa, 1986-92, Huntingdon Coll., Montgomery, Ala., 1993—. Bd. dirs. NAICU, 2002—, Asia-Pacific Fedn. Christian Schs., pres; bd. dirs. Internat. Assn. Meth.-Related Schs., Colls. and Univs., Montgomery, 1994—, Montgomery Symphony Orch., 1993—, Ala. Shakespeare Festival, 1996—, NASCUMC, 1996—; exec. com., pres. Univ. Senate United Meth. Ch., Ctrl. Ala. chpt. ARC, Montgomery, 1995; mem. Leadership Ala., 1994—; co-chair Quad Cities Vision for the Future, Davenport, 1987-92. Recipient Pres.'s award Davenport C. of C., 1988, Women of Spirit and Note award Cmty. Com. of Davenport, 1991, Hope for Humanity award Jewish Fedn. of QC, Rock Island, Ill., 1993; named to Alumni Hall of Fame, Morehead State U., 1988, Disting. Alumna, Murray State Coll., 1988, Woman of Discinction award Girl Scouts South Ctrl. Ala., 2001. Mem. Am. Coun. on Edn. (mem. coun. of fellows, bd. dirs. 1994-97, fellow in higher edn. adminstrn. 1983-84), Internat. Assn. Univ. Pres., Montgomery C. of C., Com. of 100, Sigma Alpha Iota (Sword of Honor 1956), Phi Kappa Phi, Kappa Delta Pi. Home: 1393 Woodley Rd Montgomery AL 36106-2435 Office: Huntingdon College 1500 E Fairview Ave Montgomery AL 36106-2148

BIGLARI, HAMID, investment banker; s. Manouchehr and Parvin Biglari; m. Laya Khadjavi, Apr. 1, 1994; children: Roxana Sahar, Mandana Yasmine. BA, BS, Cornell U., 1978—81; MS, Princeton U., 1981—84, PhD, 1984—87. Ptnr. McKinsey & Co., NYC, 1991—2000; head of corp. strategy Citigroup, NYC, 2000—. Bd. mem. Graham Windham, NYC, 2000—02. Home: 447 East 57th St Apt 11 New York NY 10022 Office: Citigroup 399 Park Ave 3rd floor New York NY 10043 Home Fax: 646-282-0191; Office Fax: 212-793-0408. E-mail: biglarih@citigroup.com.

BIGLER, GLADE S. lawyer; b. Brigham City, Utah, Apr. 21, 1928; s. Horace J. and Marie (Schow) Bigler; m. Lois A. Bigler, Sept. 4, 1951; children: Cathy, Nadine, Elaine, Thad, Pat. BS in Zoology, U. Utah, 1950, JD, 1956. Bar: Utah 1956, U.S. Dist. Ct. Utah 1956, U.S. Ct. Appeals (10th cir.) 1956, U.S. Supreme Ct. 1970. Ins. adjuster Travelers Ins. Co., 1956—58; gen. atty. VA, Salt Lake City, 1958—60, loan guaranty atty., 1960—68, dist. counsel, 1974—98, ret., 1998. Adminstrv. law judge, 1971—74; counsel, 1974—95; ret., 1995; lectr. in field; pres. Nat. Fedn. Fed. Employees Local 990, 1961—62. Served with USN, 1950—53, served with USNR, 1953—81. Fellow: Am. Coll. Legal Medicine; mem.: Fed. Bar Assn. (pres. 1964—65), Res. Officers Assn. (pres. Salt Lake chpt. 1978—79). Mem. Lds Ch. Home: 3003 Kenwood St Salt Lake City UT 84106-3704 E-mail: glade.bigler@juno.com.

BIGLER, HAROLD EDWIN, JR., retired investment company executive; b. N.Y.C., Apr. 27, 1931; s. Harold Edwin and Elizabeth Augusta (Cutler) B.; m. Lorinda Jennings Bailey, June 21, 1980; children by previous marriage: John Stephen, Diane Elizabeth Bigler Whatley, William Campbell. AB, Brown U., 1953; MBA, Babson Inst., 1957; postgrad., Harvard U. Bus. Sch., 1975. Investment analyst Conn. Gen. Life Ins. Co., 1957-64, asst. sec., 1964, sec., 1964, 2d v.p., 1966-68; v.p. Securities Group, Hartford, 1968-81; chmn. C.G. Investment Mgmt. Co., Inc., 1975-81; pres., dir. Conn. Gen. Fund, Income Fund, Mcpl. Bond Fund, Money Market Fund, Companion Fund, Companion Income Fund, 1975-81. Chmn. Bigler Investment Mgmt. Co.; chmn. bd. Bigler Ptnrs., Inc.; gen. ptnr. Crossroads Capital Fund, Crossroads Capital Fund; dir. Conn. Water Service, Inc., Vantage Computer Systems, Inc., various CIGNA mutual funds; chmn. investment adv. com., State of Conn., 1972-78; mem. investment com. Brown U., Providence, R.I., 1968-80; former chmn. Conn. Higher Edn. Student Loan Authority; bd. dirs. New Eng. Asset Mgmt. Co. Inc.; bd. dirs. New Eng. Monthly, Inc. Served as lt. (j.g.) USN, 1953-55. Mem. Am. Council Life Ins. (chmn. securities investment com. 1972-76), Fin. Analysts Fedn. (dir. 1974-76), N.Y. Soc. Security Analysts, Hartford Soc. Fin. Analysts (pres. 1966-67), The Hartford Club, Hartford Golf Club, The Moorings Club (Vero Beach, Fla.). Republican. Home: 14 Thicket Ln West Hartford CT 06107-1320

BIGLIN, KAREN EILEEN, library director; b. Hastings, Nebr., Apr. 23, 1954; d. James Eugene and Mary Ann (Truhlar) B.; m. Richard Jeffrey, Turnier, Aug. 4, 1979. BA, U. Ariz., 1976, MLS, 1978. Reference libr. No. Ariz. U., Flagstaff, 1978-80, sr. reference libr., 1980-84; reference libr. Tempe (Ariz.) Pub. Libr., 1984; circulation libr. Phoenix Coll., 1984-85; tech. svcs. libr. Scottsdale (Ariz.) C.C., 1985-93, libr. dir., 1993—, pres. faculty senate, 1994-95. Alice B. Good scholar U. Ariz., 1977. Mem. ALA, Ariz. Libr. Assn., Ariz. Online Users Group (pres. 1984-86), Phi Beta Kappa, Phi Kappa Phi, Beta Phi Mu. Avocation: scuba diving. Office: Scottsdale CC 9000 E Chaparral Rd Scottsdale AZ 85256-2625 E-mail: karen.biglin@sccmail.maricopa.edu.

BIGUM, RANDALL K. career officer; b. Lubbock, Tex., Dec. 11, 1949; BS in Bus., Ohio State U., 1973; student pilot tng., Williams AFB, Ariz., 1973-74; student F-4 pilot tng., 71st Tactical Fighter Squadron, MacDill AFB, Fla., 1974; student, USAF Fighter Weapons Sch., Nellis AFB, Nev., 1977; student F-15 pilot tng., 58th Tactical Tng. Wing, Luke AFB, Ariz., 1979; student, Squadron Officer Sch., 1980; M in Mil. Art and Sci., Army Command and Gen. Staff Coll., 1985; student, Nat. War Coll., 1993, Syracuse U., 1996. Commd. 2d lt. USAF, 1973, advanced through grades to brig. gen., 1998, various pilot assignments, 1974-77; weapons officer 59th Tactical Fighter Squadron, Eglin AFB, Fla., 1977-79, F-15 instr. pilot, 1979-80; various positions Nellis AFB, 1980-84; air ops. staff officer advanced program office Hdqs. Tactical Air Command, Langley AFB, Va., 1985-88, dep. chief. staff for requirements, 1985-88; ops. officer then comdr. 53rd Tactical Fighter Squadron, Bitburg Air Base, Germany, 1988-91; chief fighter devel. br. Office Undersec. Air Force Acquisition, Pentagon, Washington, 1991-92; comdr. 18th Ops. Group, Kadena Air Base, Japan, 1993-95; exec. officer to dep. comdr. in chief U.S. European Command, Stuttgart-Vaihingen City, Germany, 1995-97; comdr. 4th Fighter Wing, Seymour Johnson AFB, N.C., 1997-99; dep. dir. combat weapon sys. Hdqrs. Air Combat Command, Langley AFB, Va., 1999-2000, dir. combat weaon sys., 2000. Dir. requirements, Hdqrs. Air Combat Command, Langley AFB, Va., 2000—. Decorated D.F.C., Legion of Merit, Air medal with three oak leaf clusters, Small Arms Expert Marksmanship Ribbon. Office: ACC / DR 159 Sweeney Blvd # 200 Langley AFB VA 23665-2207

BIGWOOD, ROBERT WILLIAM, lawyer; b. Fergus Falls, Minn., June 30, 1956; s. Robert M. and Barbara I. (Barr) B.; m. Gretchen K. Brink, July 8, 1978; children: Maria, Daniel, Mark. BA cum laude, U. Minn., 1977; JD, 1980. Bar: Minn. 1980, U.S. Dist. Ct. Minn. 1983. Ptnr. Pemberton Sorlie and Rufer, Fergus Falls, 1980—. Pres., Campaign chmn. Fergus Falls United Fund, 1987-88; pres., Lakeland Hospice, Inc., Fergus Falls, 1985-87. Mem. Minn. State Bar Assn., Kiwanis, Phi Kappa Phi. Republican. Methodist. Home: 618 N Ann St Fergus Falls MN 56537-1717 Office: Perberton Sorlie and Rufer 110 N Mill St Fergus Falls MN 56537-2135

BIHLDORFF, JOHN PEARSON, hospital director; b. Boston, Aug. 3, 1945; s. Carl Birger and Martha Bowling (McCandless) B.; m. Jane Sargent Lyman, Mar. 30, 1968; children: Jennifer, Nathan, David. AB, Harvard U., 1969; MPH, Yale U., 1971. With McMaster U. Med. Ctr., Hamilton, Ont., Can., 1971-77, assoc. exec. dir., 1975-77; dir. program planning, asst. prof. divsn. med. adminstrn. Vanderbilt U. Med. Ctr. & Sch. Medicine, 1977-78; assoc. hosp. dir., COO U. Conn. Health Ctr.-John Dempsey Hosp., Farmington, 1978-81; asst. exec. dir. U. Conn. Health Ctr., 1981-82, hosp. dir., 1982-86; pres., CEO St. Luke's Health Found. and Hosp., New Bedford, Mass., 1986-91, Newton-Wellesey Hosp., Newton, Mass., 1991-2001. Chmn. bd. dirs. VHA of Mass., Inc., 1995-97; chmn. bd. dirs. VHA Healthfront, 1995-97; bd. dirs. Tufts Assocs. Health Plan, 1994-96. Home: 107 Elm St Canton MA 02021-1255

BIHORAC, AZRA, research scientist; d. Jusuf and Ferida Bihorac; m. Andrew Robert Maben, Aug. 25, 2000; children: Emir Salihovic, Emel. MD, U. Sarajevo, 1990. Bosnia and Herzegovina state exam. cert.; Turkish diploma of internal medicine specialty; Turkish diploma of nephrology subspecialty. Med. house officer Brcko (Bosnia-Herzegovina) County Hosp., Marmara U. Sch. Medicine, Istanbul, Turkey, 1994-98, instr. medicine, 1997-98, continuos ambulatory peritoneal dialysis instr. nephrology divsn., 1998-99; rsch. scientist divsn. nephrology U. Fla., Gainesville, 1999—. Mem. internal medicine curriculum com. Marmara Univ. Hosp., Istanbul, 1997-99, mem. ethical com. for med. rsch., 1997-99. Editor: Cultural Mag., Jour. Novi Vidik, 1990; author: (short stories) The Tailor and the Anesthesiologist; editor, invited reviewer articles; contbr. med. articles to profl. jours. Recipient Golden medal Youth Sci. of Yugoslavia, 1981, 82, 83; travel grantee for young investigators XV Internat. Soc. Nephrology Congress Buenos Aires, 1999, IX European Meeting on Hypertension, Milan, 1981. Mem. Internat. Soc. Nephrology (Internat. fellowship grantee 1999), Internat. Soc. for Peritoneal Dialysis, Turkish Soc. Nephrology, Am. Soc. Hypertension. Avocations: swimming, theater, art. Office: U Fla JHMHSC PO Box 100224 Gainesville FL 32610

BIJUR, PETER I. retired petroleum company executive; b. N.Y.C. m. Kjestine Anderson; children: Kristin Anne, Matthew Montgomery, David Barrett. BA in Polit. Sci., U. Pitts., 1964; MBA, Columbia U., 1966. Various dist. and regional sales positions Texaco, Inc., 1966—71, mgr. Buffalo sales dist., 1971—73, asst. to sr. v.p. for pub. affairs, 1973—75, staff coord. dept. strategic planning, 1975—77, asst. to exec. v.p. Buffalo sales dist., 1977—80; mgr. Rocky Mountain Refining & Mktg., 1980—81, asst. to chmn. bd., 1981—84; pres. Texaco Oil Trading and Supply Co., 1984, v.p. spl. projects, 1984—86; pres., chief exec. officer Texaco Can. Inc., Don Mills, Canada, 1987—89; chmn. Texaco Ltd., London, 1989—91; pres. Texaco Europe, 1990—92; sr. v.p. Texaco, Inc., White Plains, NY, 1992—96, vice chmn. bd., 1996, chmn. bd. dirs., CEO, 1996—2001. Adv. bd. ProudFoot Consulting Co., Gas Tech. Inst. Trustee Middlebury Coll., Mt. Sinai-NYU Med. Ctr. Office: 1055 Washington Blvd Stamford CT 06901

BIKALES, NORBERT M. chemist, science administrator; b. Berlin, Jan. 7, 1929; arrived in U.S., 1946; s. Salomon and Bertha (Bander) Bikales; m. Gerda V. Bierzonski, Apr. 28, 1951; children: Marguerite Sarlin, Edward A. BS in Chemistry, CCNY, 1951; MS in Chemistry, Polytech. U., 1956; PhD in Chemistry, Poly. U., 1961. Rsch. chemist Am. Cyanamid Co., Stamford, Conn., 1951-62; tech. dir. Gaylord Assocs., Newark, 1962-65; pres. N.M. Bikales & Co., Cons., Livingston, N.J., 1965-76; prof. chemistry, dir. continuing edn. in scis. Rutgers U., New Brunswick and Newark, N.J., 1973-79; dir. polymers program NSF, Washington, 1976-95, head Europe office Paris, 1995-98. Trustee Gordon Rsch. Conf., 1990—97, Fedn. Materials Soc., 1998—. Editor: Ency. Polymer Sci. and Tech., 1962—77; contbr. . Pres. Friends of Livingston Libr., NJ, 1968—72, Livingston Symphony Orch., 1970—76; judge internat. Tech. Film '89 Festival, Pardubice, Czech Republic, 1989; v.p., sec. OSE-USA, 2000—. Recipient Twp. of Livingston award, 1976, Great Medal, City of Paris, 1985, Disting. Alumnus award, Poly. U., Bklyn., 1986, Disting. lectr. award, Soc. Polymer Sci., Tokyo, 1986, Chevalier des Palmes Académiques award, French Govt., 1993, Polish Acad. Scis., 1997, Disting. Svc. award, NSF, 1999, Lifetime Achievement award, Queens Coll., 2001. Fellow: AAAS, Am. Phys. Soc., Internat. Union Pure and Applied Chemistry (titular, sec. 1979—87, 1993—97, chmn. commn. on recycling of polymers 1993—98), N.Y. Acad. Sci. (life); mem.: Groupe Français des Polymères (sci. counselor 1994—99), Soc. Plastics Engrs. (sr.; bd. dirs. 1979—82), Polish Chem. Soc. (hon.), Am. Chem. Soc. (councilor 1987—89, chmn. polymer divsn. 1983, emeritus 2000—). Achievements include patents for materials, chemicals and chemical processes. E-mail: nbikales@compuserve.com.

BIKEL, THEODORE, actor, singer; b. Vienna, May 2, 1924; came to U.S., 1954, naturalized, 1961; s. Josef and Miriam (Riegler) B.; m. Rita Weinberg, 1967. Student, U. London; grad., Royal Acad. Dramatic Art, London, 1948; DFA (hon.), U. Hartford, 1992; LHD, Steon Hall U., 2003. Apprentice with Habimah Theatre, Tel Aviv, 1942-44, a founder, Israel Cameri, 1944-46; theatrical prodns. include A Streetcar Named Desire, London, 1950, The Love of Four Colonels, London, 1950-52, Tonight in Samarkand, N.Y.C., 1954, The Lark, N.Y.C., 1955-56, Rope Dancers, N.Y.C., 1957-58, Sound of Music, N.Y.C., 1959-61, Fiddler on the Roof, various cities, 1968-72, 74, 77, 79, 80, 82-83, 85, 87-96, 98, 2000, 01, 02, The Rothschilds (nat. co.), 1972, Jacques Brel is Alive and Well and Living in Paris, various cities, 1974-75, The Good Doctor, various cities, 1975, Zorba, various cities, 1976, 78, Inspector Gen., N.Y.C., 1978, Threepenny Opera, Mpls., 1983, My Fair Lady, Phoenix, 1988-89, She Loves Me, various cities, 1989-90, Sholom Aleichem Lives, 1997, The Disputation, Miami, 1999, The Gathering, N.Y.C., Miami, 1999; opera

prodns. include La Gazza Ladra, Phila., 1990, Abduction from the Seraglio, Cleve., 1992, Ariadne auf Naxos, L.A. Opera, 1992; motion pictures include African Queen, 1951; The Little Kidnappers, 1951, The Enemy Below, 1957, I Want to Live, 1958, The Defiant Ones, 1958 (Academy award nomination), Blue Angel, 1959, My Fair Lady, 1964, Sands of the Kalahari, 1965, The Russians are Coming, 1966, Sweet November, 1967, My Side of the Mountain, 1969, Darker Than Amber, 1970, The Little Ark, 1971, See You in the Morning, 1989, Shattered, 1991, My Family Treasure, 1993, Crime and Punishment, 1993, Shadow Conspiracy, 1995, Second Chances, 1997; also numerous TV appearances, 1954—; star: TV prodns. The Eternal Light, 1958, Look Up and Live, 1958-60; host-editor: TV prodn. Directions 61, 1961; weekly radio program At Home with Theodore Bikel, 1958-63; concert folk singer, 1955—, rec. artist for, Elektra and Reprise; reader books on tape including The Hope (Herman Wouk), The Glory (Herman Wouk), The Name of the Rose (Umberto Eco); Author: Folksongs and Footnotes, 1960, (autobiography) Theo, 1994, rev. edit., 2002. Mem. Nat. Coun. for Arts, 1977-82; founder arts chpt. Am. Jewish Congress, 1961-63, nat. v.p., 1963-70, chmn. governing coun., 1970-80, sr. v.p., 1980-2002; del. Democratic Nat. Conv., 1968. Recipient Emmy award, 1988, Lifetime Achievement award Nat. Found. for Jewish Culture, 1997. Mem. AFTRA, SAG, AGMA, Acad. TV Arts and Scis. (gov. 1961-65), AEA (councillor 1961-64, 1st v.p. 1964-73, pres. 1973-82, pres. emeritus 1982—), Am. Coun. Arts (bd. dirs. 1970-80), Internat. Fedn. Actors (v.p. 1981-91), Associated Actors and Artists of Am. (pres. 1989—), Acad. Motion Picture Arts and Scis., Am. Fedn. Musicians. Address: Associated Actors & Artists of Am Fl 16 165 W 46th St New York NY 10036-2501 E-mail: theoLXX@aol.com. *If I am a universalist-and I believe myself to be one-I derive my general standard of humanity from a particularist experience. For, above all and before all else, I am a Jew. That, to me, means a heightened awareness of the human condition and the sad-sweet knowledge that where we stand someone has stood before. It means a mode of living and a method of survival. Spiritually and culturally to be a Jew is to be a man on the road from Jerusalem to Jerusalem. I am an American; this is my home and my daily solace. Jerusalem, however, is my hope and my inspiration.*

BIKLEN, PAUL, retired advertising executive; b. Burlington, Iowa, Apr. 2, 1915; s. Fred Ludwig and Lydia (Ruckenbrod) B.; m. Anne Chenoweth, Dec. 30, 1939; children: Stephen C., Douglas P; m. Eleanor Fladager, Mar. 18, 2000. Writer Gen. Electric Co., 1936-41; pub. relations dir. Kaiser Cargo Inc., Bristol, Pa., 1941-43; advt. exec. Fuller & Smith & Ross Inc., N.Y.C., 1947-52; v.p. N.W. Ayer & Son, N.Y.C., 1952-60; sr. v.p. Ogilvy & Mather, N.Y.C., 1960-72, mng. dir., Malaysia, 1973-75, dir. internat. tng., 1977-87. Author: (with Robert Breth) The Successful Employee Publication, 1946. Bd. dirs. Westport (Conn.) YMCA, 1953-56, Monadnock (N.H.) Hospice, 1993-96, Monadnock Family Svcs., 1997—; mem. Dublin (N.H.) Bd. Adjustment, 1978-86, Dublin Planning Bd., 1989-93. Lt. USN, 1943-45. Mem. Dublin Lake Club, Oriental Club (London). Home: 3515 Rosendale Rd Niskayuna NY 12309

BIKLEN, STEPHEN CLINTON, retired student loan company executive; b. Phila., Jan. 27, 1943; s. Paul Frederick and Anne (Chenoweth) Biklen; m. Britta Jorgensen Anderson, Oct. 21, 1989; children: Robert, Theodore. BA, Brown U., 1964; MBA, U. Pa., 1966. Auditor, acct. Coopers & Lybrand, N.Y.C., 1970-73; fin. analyst, contr. Citibank, N.Y.C., 1973-78; v.p. fin. Citibank N.Y. State, Rochester, 1978-80, bus. mgr. student loans, 1980-92, also bd. dirs.; pres., CEO, Student Loan Corp., Rochester, 1993-97, also bd. dirs.; ret., 1997. Mem. Nat. Adv. Com. Student Fin. Assistance, Washington, 1988—96; bd. dirs. Am. Student Assistance, Postsecondary Electronic Standards Coun., treas. Mem.: Consumer Bankers Assn. (chmn. edn. funding com. 1988—90, 1994—97). Avocations: golf, tennis. Personal E-mail: sbiklen@aol.com.

BILA, THOMAS A. not-for-profit fundraiser; b. Detroit, Mich., Sept. 2, 1947; s. Andrew V. and Loretta V. Bila. BA, U. of Detroit, 1969, MA, 1974, MEd, 1978; PhD, So. Ill. U., 1991. Tchr., dir. of student fundraising U. of Detroit SJ H.S. and Acad., 1969—83; external affairs dir. Cathedral Prep. Sch. for Boys, Erie, Pa., 1983—85; dir. ann. giving/spl. projects So. Ill. U., Carbondale, 1985—87; exec. dir. Rockford (Ill.) Meml. Health Sys. Found., Rockford, 1988—94; dir. of devel. Western New Eng. Coll., Springfield, Mass., 1995—96; pres. Coffey, Bila & Assocs., Mpls., 1997—98; exec. vi.p., found. affairs Benedictine Health Sys., Mpls., 1999—2001; pres. Bila, Graham & Assocs., Mpls., 2001—02; exec. dir. Minn. Friends of the Orphans, St. Paul, 2002—. Author various articles and books. Master: Assn. of Fundraising Profls. (treas., pres., bd. mem., treas. 1986, cert.fund raising exec.). Office: Minn Friends of the Orphans 70 County Rd C W Saint Paul MN 55117 Office Fax: 651-468-8088. E-mail: tbila@friendsmn.org.

BILANIUK, OLEKSA MYRON, physicist, educator; b. Ukraine, Dec. 15, 1926; came to U.S., 1951, naturalized, 1957; s. Petro and Maria B.; m. Larissa T. Zubal, Nov. 14, 1964; children: Larissa, Laada. Student, U. Louvain, 1947-51; MS, U. Mich., 1953, MA, 1954, PhD, 1957; Dr. honoris causa (hon.), Nat. Univ. Lviv, Ukraine, 2002. Postdoctoral fellow U. Mich., 1957-58; rsch. assoc., asst. prof. U. Rochester, 1958-64; assoc. prof. physics Swarthmore Coll., 1964-70, prof., 1970-82, Swarthmore Centennial prof., 1982—. Vis. scientist Argentine Atomic Energy Commn., Buenos Aires, 1961-62, Institut de Physique Nucléaire, Orsay, France, spring 1980, Laboratori Nazionali di Frascati, Italy, spring 1984, U. Munich, Germany, fall 1988; vis. prof., cons. Delhi U., summer 1966, Shivaji U., Kolhapur, India, summer 1969, Faculté des Scis., Rabat, Morocco, spring 1978, Kiev U. Ukraine, spring 1994, Inst. Med. Radiology, Kharkiv, Ukraine, summer 1996; Fulbright prof. Lima, Peru, summer 1971, Kinshasa, Zaïre, fall 1975. NSF fellow Max Planck Inst., Heidelberg, Germany, 1967-68, Inst. Physique Nucléaire, Orsay, 1972; NAS exch. scientist Kiev, Ukrainian SSR, 1976. Mem. Am. Phys. Soc., Nat. Acad. Scis. Ukraine, Ukrainian Acad. Arts and Scis. in U.S. (pres. 1998—), Schevchenko Sci. Soc. in U.S., European Phys. Soc., Société Française de Physique, Phi Beta Kappa, Sigma Xi. Achievements include research on nuclear structure; with Deshpande and Sudarshan challenged the view that Einstein's relativity precludes the possibility of existence of particles that travel faster than light, 1962. Office: Swarthmore Coll Dept Physics Swarthmore PA 19081 E-mail: obilani1@swarthmore.edu. *The most cherished possession of humanity is its spiritual and intellectual heritage. Contributing to the enrichment of this heritage I consider to be a human's loftiest goal.*

BILAS, RICHARD A. economist; b. Passaic, NJ, Feb. 3, 1935; s. Nestor Joseph and Helen Evelyn (Smith) B.; m. Janet Lianne Harris, June 23, 1956; children: Cathy, David, Ami. AB in Math., Duke U., 1956; PhD in Econs., U. Va., 1963. Asst., then assoc. prof. U. So. Calif., L.A., 1962-67; from assoc. prof. to prof. Ga. State U., Atlanta, 1967—70; E.C. Reid prof. econs. Calif. State U., Bakersfield, 1970-87, prof. emeritus, 2002—; commr. Calif. Energy Commn., Sacramento, 1987-95; Brock chair in energy econs. and policy Sarkeys Energy Ctr., Norman, Okla., 1995—96; commr. Calif. Pub. Utilities Commn., San Francisco, 1997—2002. Program on workable energy regulation bd. U. Calif., 1990—; pres. Calif. Pub. Utilities Commn., 1998—99. Author: Microeconomics, 1967, 71, Problems in Microeconomics, 1972, Macroeconomics, 1974; mem. editl. bd. Western Econ. Assn.'s Contemporary Econ. Policy, 1990—. Active Rep. Ctrl. Com., Kern County, Calif., 1978-82; pres. bd. dirs. Mendocino Art Ctr., 2000—; treas. Cmty. Found. Mendocino County, 2003. Nat. Def. fellow U. Va., 1959-62; recipient Honor cert. Freedoms Found., 1977, 79. Mem. Mont Pelerin Soc., Masons, Phi Beta Kappa. Republican. Episcopalian. Avocations: golf, model trains. Home: PO Box 2466 Mendocino CA 95460-2466 E-mail: rbilas@mcn.org.

BILBRAY, BRIAN P. former congressman; b. Coronado, Calif., Jan. 28, 1951; m. Karen; 5 children. Supr.ctrl. and so. coastal regions San Diego County, Calif.; mem. U.S. Congress from 49th Calif. dist., 1995-2001; mem. commerce com. Mem. commerce, fin. & hazardous materials, health & environment, oversight & investigations coms. Avocations: sailing, surfing, horseback riding.

BILBRAY, JAMES HUBERT, former congressman, lawyer, consultant; b. Las Vegas, May 19, 1938; s. James A. and Ann E. (Miller) B.; m. Michaelene Mercer, Jan. 1960; children: Bridget, Kevin, Erin, Shannon Student, Brigham Young U., 1957-58, U. Nev., Las Vegas, 1958-60; BA, Am. U., 1962; JD, Washington Coll. Law, 1964; D of Laws (hon.), U Nev. Las Vegas, 2001. Bar: Nev. 1965. Staff mem. Senator Howard Cannon U.S. Senate, 1960-64; dep. dist. atty. Clark County, Nev., 1965-68; mem. Lovell, Bilbray & Potter, Las Vegas, 1969-87, Nev. Senate, 1980-86, chmn. taxation com., 1983-86, chmn. interim com. on pub. broadcasting, 1983; mem. 100th-103rd Congresses from 1st Nev. dist., 1987-95; mem. fgn. affairs com., 1987-88; mem. house armed svs. com., mem. small bus. com., chmn. procurement, taxation and tourism subcom., 1989-95; ptnr. Alcalde & Fay, Arlington, Va., 1995—. Mem. subcoms. Africa, trade exports and tourism, select com. on intelligence, 1993-95; alt. mcpl. judge City of Las Vegas, 1987-89; del. North Atlantic Alliance, 1989-95; bd. visitors U.S. Mil. Acad., West Point, 1995-99, vice chmn., 1996-97; mem. adv. bd. Ex-Import Bank U.S., 1996-97; mem. adv. com. U.S. Nat. Security Policy, 2000-01. Bd. regents U. Nev. Sys., 1968—72; mem. Nat. Coun. State Govts. Commn. on Arts and Historic Preservation; mem. bd. visitors USAF Acad., 1991—93; mem. U.S. Nat. Security Policy Bd. Adv. Com., 2000—01, Dem. Nat. Com., 1996—. Named Outstanding Alumnus U. Nev., Las Vegas, 1979, Man of Yr. Am. Diabetes Assn., 1989, Man of Yr. Haddassah (Nev.), 1990 Mem. Nev. State Bar Assn., Clark county Bar Assn., U. Nev.-Las Vegas Alumni Assn. (pres. 1964-69, Humanitarian of Yr. 1984), Rotary, Phi Alpha Delta, Sigma Chi, KC Democrat. Roman Catholic.

BILDERBACK, GEORGE GARRISON, III, alcohol/drug abuse services professional; b. Portsmouth, Ohio, Jan. 11, 1964; s. George Garrison Jr. and Jane (Rhodes) B. BSBA in Mgmt. and Fin., Ohio No. U., 1986; BS in Employee Assistance, Franklin U., 1996; MS in Edn. and Allied Professions, U. Dayton, 1999. Cert. Chem. Dependency Coun., Ohio Dept.Alcohol and Drug Addiction Svcs. Customer svc. specialist Nationwide Life Ins. Co., Columbus, Ohio, 1986—87, licensing and commn. specialist, 1987—88; rsch. analyst Wausau Ins. Co., Columbus, 1988—89; sr. mktg. specialist Nationwide Life Ins. Co., Columbus, 1989—92, regional mktg. dir. Portsmouth, NH, 1992; registered rep. MML Investors Svcs., Inc., West Worthington, Ohio, 1993—94; jr. ptnr. Moyer Fin. Group, West Worthington, 1993—94; investment exec. Hamilton Investments Inc., Columbus, 1994—95; co-case mgr. Recovery Assistance, Inc., Westerville, Ohio, 1995—96; counselor Harding Hosp., Worthington, Ohio, 1996—97; intake coord. Stevens House, Columbus, 1996—97; case mgr. The Alliance of Children and Family Svcs., 1996—99, clin. coord., 1997—98; health info. specialist House of Hope, Inc., 1997—99; outreach counselor Directions for Youth, 1999—2000, team coord., 2000—01, family counselor, 2001—02; counselor Columbus Health Dept., 2002—. Dir. local club Civitan Internat., Columbus, 1989-91, 1st v.p. programs, 1991-92, pres., 1994-95, past pres., 1995—. Recipient Transfer Achievement award Franklin U., 1996. Mem. ACA, Employee Assistance Student Assn. (pres. 1996-97), Employee Assistance Profl. Assn. (newsletter editor 1996-98, sec. So. Ohio chpt. 1996-2000), Pa. R.R. Tech. and Hist. Soc. Republican. Avocations: railroad enthusiast, history, painting, reading. Home: 3168 Indianola Ave # C Columbus OH 43202-1352 Office: Columbus Health Dept Alcohol and Drug Abuse Program 240 Parsons Ave Columbus OH 43215

BILDERBACK, JAMES WILLIAM, II, lawyer; b. Fresno, Calif., Oct. 21, 1963; s. Dean Loy Bilderback and Florence Elizabeth (Gillmore) Ellsworth; m. Leslie Ann Reed, July 15, 1989; children: Emma Christine, Claire Elizabeth. BA, U. Calif., Berkeley, 1985; JD cum laude, U. San Francisco, 1992. Bar: Calif. 1992, U.S. Dist. Ct. (no. dist.) Calif. 1992, U.S. Dist. Ct. (ctrl. dist.) Calif. 1993, U.S. Ct. Appeals (9th cir.) 1993, U.S. Supreme Ct. 1998. Deputy atty. gen. Calif. Dept. Justice, L.A., 1992—. Mem. L.A. County Bar Assn., L.A. County Bar Assn. Barristers (pres. 1999-2000, sec. 1996-98). Office: Calif Dept Justice 300 S Spring St Fl 5 Los Angeles CA 90013-1230

BILDERSEE, ROBERT ALAN, lawyer; b. Albany, N.Y., Jan. 22, 1942; s. Max U. and Hannah (Marks) B.; m. Ellen Bernstein, June 9, 1963; 1 child, Jennifer M. BA, Columbia Coll., 1962, MA, 1964; LLB, Yale U., 1967. Assoc. Wolf Block Schorr & Solis Cohen, Phila., 1967-72; sole practice Phila., 1972-73; assoc., then ptnr. Fox Rothschild, O'Brien & Frankel, Phila., 1973-80; ptnr. Morgan Lewis & Bockius LLP, Phila., 1980-97; founding ptnr. Bildersee & Silbert, LLP, Phila., 1997—. Lectr. Temple U. Sch. Law, Phila., 1978-91; asst. in instrn. Yale U. Law Sch., New Haven, 1966. Author: Pension Regulation Manual, Pension Administrator's Forms and Checklists, 1987; contbg. author: Employee Benefits Handbook, 1982-98; editor: Beyond the Fringes; contbr. articles to profl. jours. Woodrow Wilson fellow, 1962. Mem. ABA, Pa. Bar Assn., Phila. Bar Assn. Avocation: wildlife photography. Office: Bildersee and Silbert LLP 1617 JFK Blvd Ste 1111 Philadelphia PA 19103-1826 E-mail: erisaplus@aol.com.

BILDHAUER, W. MATHIAS, philosophy educator, real estate broker; b. Sublette, Ill. s. Mathias F. and Rosemary Bildhauer; m. Edita Zelenik; 1 child, David;children: Rosemarie, Mathias, Catherine, Juliann. BA, DePaul U., 1960; MA, U. Notre Dame, 1961; PhD, U. Ariz., 1972. Mem. faculty U. Notre Dame, Ind., 1972—73; program coord., mem. faculty Yavapei Coll., Prescott, Ariz., 1973—77; dir. S.W. Ednl. Inst., Phoenix, 1977—88; adminstr. DePaul U., Chgo., 1988—92; adj. faculty Maricopa C.C., Phoenix, 1993—; assoc. broker John Hall & Assocs., Phoenix, 1995—. Edn. and tng. cons. USN Chief of Pers., Arlington, Va., 1971; cons. USN Chief of Naval Tng., Pensacola, Fla., 1972. Editor: (mag.) Diversions, 1983; contbr. articles to profl. publs. Bd. dirs. Ariz. Humanities Coun., Phoenix, 1977—81. Lt. comdr. USN, 1960—75. Fellow Karl Jaspers fellow, U. Ariz., 1970—71. Mem.: Am. Philos. Assn., Soc. Slovene Studies. Green Party. Avocation: hiking. Home: 8150 N Central Ave # 9 Phoenix AZ 85020 E-mail: mathias711@earthlink.net.

BILELLO, JOHN CHARLES, materials science and engineering educator; b. Bklyn., Oct. 15, 1938; s. Charles and Catherine (Buonadonna) B.; m. Mary Josephine Gloria, Aug. 1, 1959; children: Andrew Charles, Peter Angelo, Matthew Jonathan. B.E., NYU, 1960, MS, 1962; PhD, U. Ill., 1965. Sr. rsch. engr. Gen. Telephone & Electronics Lab., Bayside, N.Y., 1965-67; mem. faculty SUNY, Stony Brook, 1967-87, asst. prof., 1967-71, assoc. prof., 1971-75, prof. engring., 1975-87, dean, 1977-81; dean Sch. Engring and Computer Sci., prof. mech. engring. Calif. State U., Fullerton, 1986-89; prof. materials sci. and engring., prof. applied physics U. Mich., Ann Arbor, 1989—, dir. Ctr. for Nanomaterials Scis., 1995—. Vis. rsch. assoc., Calif. Inst. Tech., Pasadena, 2003, vis. prof. Poly. of Milan, 1973-74; vis. scholar King's Coll., London U., 1983; vis. fellow NATO exchange scholar Oxford U., 1986; project dir. synchroton topography project Univ. Consortium, 1981-86; NATO vis. fellow Oxford (Eng.) U., 1998—. NATO sr. faculty fellow Enrico Fermi Center, Milan, Italy, 1973 Fellow Am. Soc. for Metals; mem. AIME, Am. Phys. Soc., Materials Rsch. Soc. Office: U Mich Dept Material Sci Engring Ann Arbor MI 48109

BILES, GLORIA C. historian, educator; d. George Graham and Lillian Oriol Crevenstene; married, June 21, 1949. B in Bus. Adminstr., U. Houston, 1947, MEd, 1957, MA, 1972; PhD, Rice U., 1979. Tchrs. Cert. Tex. Tchr. mid. and HS Houston Ind. Sch. Dist., 1957—67; lectr. U. Houston, Clear Lake, 1979—81, U. Houston, West Houston, 1979—81; adj. prof. Houston Bapt. Univ., 1984—86, asst. prof., 1986—93, assoc. prof., 1993—2002; ret., 2002. Mem. Houston Grand Opera, 1952—, Gilbert and Sullivan Soc., 1999—, Heritage Soc., 1979—, PBS, 1999—, Am. Carousel Soc., 1989—, Houston Symphony Soc., 1999—, Bush Pres. Libr., Coll. Sta., Tex., 1999—, Nat. Trust for Hist. Preservation, Mus. of Printing History, 1999—. Mem.: Delta Kappa Gamma (com. chairs), AHA, Phi Alpha Theta, NEA, Phi Gamma Nu, AAUP. Avocation: collecting antique carousel horses, steuben glass and miniature animals.

BILES, JOHN ALEXANDER, pharmacology educator, chemistry educator; b. Del Norte, Colo., May 4, 1923; s. John Alexander and Lillie (Willis) Biles; m. Margaret Pauline Off, June 19, 1943; children: Paula M. Murphy, M. Suzanne. BS, U. Colo., 1944, PhD (AEC fellow), 1949. Prof. pharm. chemistry Midwestern U., 1949-50; asst. prof. pharm. chemistry Ohio State U., 1950-52, U. So. Calif., L.A., 1952-53, assoc. prof., 1953-57, prof., 1957-98, disting. emeritus prof., 1999—, dean, prof. pharm. scis., 1968-94, John Stauffer dean's chair in pharmacy, 1988-94, John Biles prof., 1994—, Disting. emeritus prof., 1998—. Bd. dirs. Marion Merrell Dow; cons. Allergan Pharms., 1953—68, Region IX Bur. health Manpoer Edn., Health Resources Adminstrn., 1973, Region X, 1974, Region VI, 1975, VA Ctrl. Office Pharmacy Svcs.; mem. Nat. Adv. Coun., Edn. Health Professions, 1970—71, nat. study commn. on pharmacy, 1972—75; mem. adv. panel on pharmacy for study costs of educating profls. Nat. Acad. Scis., Inst. Medicine, 1973; mem. interdisciplinary tng. in health scis. com. Bur. Health Manpower Edn., 1972, post contrn. evaluation com., 72, health facilities survey com., 71; mem. adv. coun. Howard U. Coll. Pharmacy, 1985—90; bd. grants Am. Found. for Pharm. Edn., 1996—. Reviewer: Jour. AMA1, 1982—90. Bd. grants Am. Found. Pharm. Edn., 1996—, bd. dirs., 1999—2001, chmn. bd. grants, 1998—; elder Presbyn. Ch., Pacific Palisades, Calif., 1997—. Recipient S.C. Assocs. award for excellence in tchg., 1962; scholar Lehn and Fink, 1945. Fellow: Am. Assn. Pharm. Scientists, Acad. Pharm. Scis.; mem.: Calif. Pharm. Assn., Nat. Adv. Health Svcs. Coun. (bur. heatlh svcs. rsch. 1974), Am. Assn. Colls. Pharmacy (study commn. on pharmacy 1973—75, pres. 1990—91), Am. Cancer Soc. (mem. sci. adv. com. Los Angeles County), Am. Pharm. Assn., Phi Kappa Phi. Office: 1985 Zonal Ave Los Angeles CA 90089-0105 E-mail: BilesJohn@aol.com.

BILFINGER, THOMAS VICTOR, surgeon, educator; b. Ridgewood, N.J., May 4, 1952; s. Victor Wilhelm and Heidi Erika (Muser) B.; m. Celia Betty Dameron; children: Elizabeth, Christine, Michael. MD, U. Zurich, Switzerland, 1978, ScD, 1979. Intern U. Chgo., 1980-81, rsch. fellow, 1981-82; resident in surgery U. Tex. Med. Br., Galveston, 1982-86, resident in cardiovascular surgery, 1986-88, instr. in surgery, 1988-89; asst. prof. surgery SUNY, Stony Brook, 1989-92, assoc. prof. surgery, 1992-99, prof. surgery, chief thoracic surgery, 1999—. Bd. dirs. cardiovascular intensive care unit SUNY, Stony Brook; rsch. assoc. Neurosci. Inst., SUNY, Old Westbury; sr. rsch. scientist Mind/Body Med. Inst., Harvard med. Sch., Mass.; mem. spl. populations rsch. dept. faculty NIDA, 1994—. Co-author: Evaluation of the Cardiac Surgical Candidate, 1992; mem. editl. bd. Advances in Neuroimmunology, Acta Pharmacologica Sinica, 1999—, Modern Aspects of Immunobiology, 2000—, Placebo, 2001—; guest editor: Internat. Jour. Cardiology, 1996, 98. Recipient Rsch. grant U. Chgo., 1981, Rsch. grant Eli Lilly, 1989, Rsch. grant NIH, 1991, Career Opportunity Rsch. Tng. award NIMH. Fellow ACS, Am. Coll. Cardiology, Am. Coll. Chest Physicians; mem. Am. Assn. Thoracic Surgery, Assn. for Acad. Surgery, Soc. Critical Care Medicine, Swiss Soc. Thoracic and Cardiovasc. Surgery, Soc. Thoracic Surgery. Office: SUNY Stony Brook Health Sc Ctr T19 Rm 080 Stony Brook NY 11794-0001 E-mail: thomas.bilfinger@sunysb.edu.

BILGER, BRUCE R. lawyer; b. Balt., Feb. 27, 1952; BA, Dartmouth Coll., 1973; MBA, JD, U. Va., 1977. Bar: Tex. 1977. Mem. Vinson & Elkins, L.L.P., Houston. Mem. Phi Beta Kappa. Office: Vinson & Elkins LLP 2300 First City Tower 1001 Fannin St Houston TX 77002-6760 E-mail: bbilger@velaw.com.

BILGER, DORINNE POTTER, musician, educator; b. Penn Yan, N.Y., Apr. 9, 1945; d. Lyndon Wainwright and Emma Anna Sarah (Salecker) Potter; m. David Victor Bilger, Dec. 30, 1966; 1 child, Daniel Victor. MusB, Ithaca Coll., 1967; postgrad., U. Hartford, 1970. Music specialist Haverling Schs., Bath, N.Y., 1967-68, Gov. Mifflin Schs., Shillington, Pa., 1968—70; piano instr. Bilger Music Studio, Shillington and Wyomissing Hills, 1968—; ptnr., pres. Bilger Products, Wyomissing Hills, 1980—. Piano performer Bilger and Bilger Duo, 1970-97, Duo Bilger-Gross, 2001-03; adjudicator for piano festivals and competitions, 1985—. Recorded several chamber music repertoires, 1977-94. Mem. Am. Coll. Musicians Piano Tchrs. Guild, Pa. Music Tchrs. Assn., Reading Music Tchrs. Assn., Music Tchrs. Nat. Assn., Oracle Soc., Sigma Alpha Iota, Pi Kappa Lambda. Home: 33 Park Rd Reading PA 19609-1723

BILGILI, ECEVIT ATALAY, chemical engineer, researcher; b. Istanbul, Turkey, Dec. 9, 1974; came to U.S., 1996; s. Mustafa and Mensure Bilgili; m. Melike Bilgili, May 23, 1997; 1 child, Melisa Ecem. BSChE with high honors, Bogazici U., Istanbul, 1996; PhD in Chem. Engring., Ill. Inst. Tech., 2001. Intern, engr. Bozkurt Textile Factory, Istanbul, summer 1993, Roche Pharms., Inc., Istanbul, summer 1994, Turkish Electric Inc., Istanbul, summer 1995; rsch. asst. Ill. Inst. Tech., Chgo., 1996-2001; post-doctoral rsch. fellow Engring. Rsch. Ctr. U. Fla., Gainesville, 2001—. Cons. McKinsey & Co., China, 2000. Referee Jour. Elastomers and Plastics, Particle and Particle Systems Characterization; contbr. articles to profl. jours.; patentee in field. Scholar Edn. Found. of Turkey, 1991-96; recipient Prof. Turgut Noyan award Bogazici U., 1996, Outstanding Acad. Achievement award Ill. Inst. Tech., 2001. Mem.: AIChE (session chair ann. meeting 2003), Am. Chem. Soc. (rubber divsn.). Avocations: reading social psychology and politics, environmental activism, teaching. Office: U Fla Engring Rsch Ctr Particle Sci & Tech PO Box 116135 Gainesville FL 32611-6135 E-mail: ebilgili@erc.ufl.edu.

BILIMORIA, KARL D. aerospace engineer; b. Bombay, 1960; arrived in U.S., 1982; s. Dhun K. and Najoo D. Bilimoria. BTech. in Aero. Engring., Indian Inst. of Tech., Kanpur, India, 1982; MS in Aerospace Engring., Va. Tech., 1984, PhD in Aerospace Engring., 1986. Asst. prof. Ariz. State U., Tempe, 1987—91, rsch. scientist, 1991—93, vis. asst. prof., 1993—94; rsch. specialist NASA-Ames divsn. Sterling Fed. Sys. Group, Moffett Field, Calif., 1994—96; rsch. aerospace engr. (GS-15) NASA Ames Rsch. Ctr., Moffett Field, Calif., 1996—. Guest editor (Air Traffic Control Quarterly spl. issue) Distributed Air/Ground Traffic Management, 2001; contbr. articles various profl. jours. Fellow: AIAA (assoc.; mem. atmospheric flight mechanics tech. com. 1995—98, mem. guidance, nav., and control tech. com. 2000—03, assoc. editor Jour. of Guidance, Control, and Dynamics 2001—, mem. air transp. sys. tech. com. 2003—); mem.: Internat. Fedn. of Automatic Control (mem. tech. com. on air traffic control automation 2000—01), Sigma Gamma Tau. Achievements include finalist NASA astronaut selection, 1996. Office: NASA Ames Rsch Ctr Mail Stop 210-10 Moffett Field CA 94035

BILINSKY, YAROSLAV, political scientist; b. Lutsk, Ukraine, Feb. 26, 1932; s. Peter Bilinsky and Natalia (Balabaj) Bilinska; m. Wira Rusaniwskyj, Feb. 18, 1962; children: Peter Yaroslav, Sophia Vera Yaroslava, Nadia Yaroslava, Mark Paul Yaroslav. AB magna cum laude, Harvard U., 1954, postgrad. in Soviet affairs, 1956-57; PhD, Princeton U., 1958. Asso. Harvard U. Russian Research Center, 1956-58; instr. polit. sci. Douglass Coll., Rutgers U., New Brunswick, N.J., 1958-61; asst. prof. U. Del., Newark, 1961-65, assoc. prof., 1965-69, prof., 1969—2002, prof. emeritus, 2002—. Vis. instr. U. Pa., 1961; vis. prof. Columbia U., 1976 Author: The Second Soviet Republic: The Ukraine after World War II, 1964, Endgame in NATO's Enlargement: The Baltic States and Ukraine, 1999. Corr. sec. Peter and Paul Ukrainian Orthodox Ch., Wilmington, Del., 1965-66, trustee, 1967-71. Mem. Am. Assn. Advancement Slavic Studies (pres. Mid-Atlantic Slavic Conf. 1992-93), Ukrainian Acad. Arts and Scis. in U.S. (pres. 1987-90). Home: 2 Mimosa Dr Newark DE 19711-7523 E-mail: yby@udcl.edu. *My favorite quotation is from Shakespeare: The readiness is all. I have tried to be always prepared to serve my country, my students, and my family. I am ready to live and, if it be God's will, ready to die.*

BILIRAKIS, MICHAEL, congressman, lawyer, business executive; b. Tarpon Springs, Fla., July 16, 1930; s. Emmanuel and Irene (Pikramenos) B.; m. Evelyn Miaoulis, Dec. 27, 1959; children: Emmanuel, Gus. BS in Engring., U. Pitts., 1959; student, George Washington U., 1959-60; JD, U. Fla., 1963; JD (hon.), Stetson U.; hon. degree, U. Tampa. Bar: Fla. 1964; cert. coll. tchr., Fla. Atty., small businessman, Pinellas and Pasco Counties, Fla., 1968—; mem. 98th-108th Congresses from 9th Dist. Fla., 1983—; mem. energy & commerce com., vice chair vets. affairs com., chair health subcom. Mem. Rep. Task Force on Social Security; co-chmn. Task Force on Infant Mortality; founder, charter pres. Tarpon Springs Vol. Ambulance Service; dir. Greek Studies program U. Fla.; dir. emeritus Juvenile Diabetes and Hospice; mem. Pres.' Coun. U. Fla. Sgt. USAF, 1951-55. Named Citizen of Yr. Greater Tarpon Springs, 1972-73, Man of Yr. United Way, 1989-90. Mem. Am. Legion (comdr. 1977-79), VFW, Amvets, USAF Sgts., NCOA, Air Force Assn., Greater Tarpon Springs C. of C. (past pres., dir.), Pinellas C. of C. (gov.), West Pasco Bar Assn., Am. Judicature Soc., Fla. Bar Assn., Gator Boosters, Fla. Blue Key (hon.), Mason (33 degree), Shriner, Jester, Moose, Elks, Rotary, Eastern Star, Phi Alpha Delta, Sigma Pi. Lodges: Masons; Shriners; Moose; Tarpon Springs Rotary; Elks; Eastern Star; White Shrine of Jerusalem. Republican. Greek Orthodox. Office: US Ho of Reps 2269 Rayburn House Ofc Bldg Washington DC 20515-0909*

BILKA, PAUL JOSEPH, retired physician; b. N.Y.C., Oct. 12, 1919; s. John and Josephine (Hlavaty) B.; m. Madge Ayres Mussey, Dec. 26, 1943. BS, Trinity Coll., Hartford, Conn., 1940; MD, Columbia U., 1943; MS in Medicine, U. Minn., 1950. Intern Hartford Hosp., 1944-45; fellow in internal medicine Mayo Found, Rochester, Minn., 1947-50; asst. in rheumatology Mayo Clinic, 1949-50; practice medicine specializing in rheumatology Mpls., 1950-91; ret. Clin. prof. medicine U. Minn. Med. Sch.; cons. Mpls. VA Hosp. Author numerous papers in field; also producer films on rheumatology. Served to capt. M.C. AUS, 1945-47. Mem. Am. Coll. Rheumatology (master designation 1992), Nat. Soc. Clin. Rheumatology (pres. 1985-87). Clubs: Lafayette (Minnetonka, Minn.). Home: 4384 Manitou Rd Excelsior MN 55331-9445

BILL, DANIEL JOSEPH, executive planning consultant; b. Ft. Wayne, Ind., Nov. 3, 1941; s. Calvin Ernest and Alice Neoma Bill; children: Ann Marie, Christopher Joseph. BA in Anthropology, Ind. U., 1966, MS in H.E. Student Pers. Svcs., 1967, EdD in H.E. Adminstrn., 1978. Dir. univ. divsn. Ind. U. and Purdue U., Ft. Wayne, 1970—72; clinics mgr., adminstrv. asst. for ambulatory care svcs. Riley Hosp. for Children Ind. U. Hosps., Ind. U. Sch. Medicine, Indpls., 1974—83; handicap access planning cons. Office of the V.p. Ind. U. and Purdue U., Indpls., 1983—84; adminstrv. officer Elkhart (Ind.) County Health Dept., 1984—86; exec. dir., CEO Northeastern Mental Health Ctr., Inc, Kendallville, Ind., 1986—89; asst. scientist dept. med. and molecular genetics Ind. U. Sch. Medicine, Indpls., 1989—95; exec. planning cons. Wright-Moore Internat. Corp., Ft. Wayne, 1995—96; grants devel. specialist and behavioral clinician Ind. Dept. Correction, Indpls., 1998—2000; vocat. rehab. counselor, visually impaired specialist Family and Social Services Adminstrn. - State of Ind., Indpls., 2002. Founder Tri County Spl. Svcs. Coalition, Inc., Noblesville, Ind., 1980—80; fed. resource cons. Tri-State Midwest Regional Resource Ctr., Ohio State U., Indpls., 1981—81; chmn. statewide com. to structure the regional devel. disability councils in Ind. State Dept. Mental Health, Indpls., 1983—83; Ind. state rep. Ea. U.S. Ambulatory Care Regional Conf., Chgo., 1985—85; v.p. N.E. Ind. mental health dist. State of Ind., Indpls., 1987—89; co-chair legis. subcom. to study the desirability and feasibility of estaglishing a devel. disabilites rsch. ctr. State Ind. Legis. Com., Indpls., 1993—93; chmn. long range plan com. Ind. Protection and Advocacy Svcs. Com., Indpls., 1995—95. Contbr. articles to profl. jours. Governor's appointee Long Term Needs of Persons with Mental Illness and Devel. Disabilities Study Com., Indpls., 1991—93; chmn. legis. affairs com. Janus Devel. Ctr., Inc, Noblesville, Ind., 1978—83; bd. mem. Elkhart County Urban League, 1984—86, Alfred Adler Inst., Ft. Wayne, 1986—2000, Ind. Protection and Advocacy Svcs. Commn., State of Ind., Indpls., 1989—2000. Recipient Ind. Cmty. Svc. award, Ind. Protection and Advocacy Svcs. Commn., 1984. Mem.: Nat. Rehab. Assn. (assoc.). Republican. Achievements include development of Huntington DiseaseGenetic Presymptomatic Test Service Grant. Avocations: golf, travel, writing. Home: 419 Lions Creek Cir Noblesville IN 46060 Personal E-mail: dbill10024@aol.com. E-mail: billdj@fssa.state.in.us.

BILL, TONY, producer, director; b. San Diego, Aug. 23, 1940; Student, Notre Dome U. Founder Bill/Phillips Prodns. (with Julia and Michael Phillips), 1971-73; ind. producer, 1973—. Bd. govs. Acad. Motion Picture Arts and Scis. Prodr.: Deadhead Miles, Steelyard Blues, 1973, The Sting, 1974, Going in Style, 1979, Hearts of the West, 1975, Harry and Walter Go to New York, 1976, Boulevard Nights, 1979; exec. producer: The Little Dragons, 1978; dir.: The Ransom of Red Chief, 1977, My Bodyguard, 1980, Six Weeks, 1982, Love Thy Neighbor, 1984, Five Corners, 1987, Crazy People, 1990, Untamed Heart, 1993, A Home of Our Own, 1993, Next Door, 1995, Beyond the Call, 1996, Oliver Twist, 1997, A Change of Snow, 1998, Harlan County War, 2000, In the Time of the Butterflies, 2001, Whitewash the Clarence Brandley Story, 2002, Last Call, 2002. Office: Barnstorm Films 73 Market St Venice CA 90291-3603

BILLAU, ROBIN LOUISE, engineering and consulting executive; b. Denver, Sept. 19, 1951; d. Emerson Roy and Catherine Louise (Brewster) Billau; m. Edward E. Adams. BA, Western State Coll., 1973; MS, Colo. State U., 1977. Cert. indsl. hygienist. Life sci., indsl. hygienist Mont. Energy Devel. & Rsch. Inst., Butte, 1977-79; indsl. hygiene supr. Mountain States Energy, Butte, 1979-81; asst. prof. Mont. Coll. Mineral Sci. Tech., Butte, 1981-83; indsl. hygiene supr. EG & G Idaho, Idaho Falls, 1983-85, unit mgr., 1985-87, group mgr., 1987-88, sr. tech. adv., 1988-90; cons. environ. mgmt., indsl. hygiene RLB Cons., Inc., Houghton, Mich., 1990-92; mgr. Jason Assocs. Corp., Idaho Falls, Idaho, 1992-94, Lockheed Martin Environ. Systems, Pocatello, Idaho, 1994-95; cons. environ. health and safety Indoor Air Quality $ Occupational Health, Bozeman, Mont., 1996—; owner Indoor Air Quality and Occupational Health, Bozeman, Mont., 2001—. Owner Ranch Goddess Brand, Inc., 2001, Indoor Air Quality & Occupant Health, 2000. Mem. Am. Bd. Indsl. Hygiene Democrat. Avocations: skiing, gardening, raising worms and poultry, mountain biking, reading. Home and Office: 174 Quinn Creek Rd Bozeman MT 59715-9635 E-mail: rlbillau@imt.net.

BILLAUER, BARBARA PFEFFER, lawyer, educator; b. Aug. 9, 1951; d. Harry George and Evelyn (Newman) Pfeffer. BS with honors, Cornell U., 1972; JD, Hofstra U., 1975; MA, NYU, 1982; cert. in risk scis. and pub. policy, Johns Hopkins U., 1999. Bar: N.Y. 1976, Fed. Dist. Ct. N.Y. 1977, U.S. Ct. Appeals (2d cir.) 1978, U.S. Supreme Ct. 1984. Assoc. Bower & Gardner, N.Y.C., 1974-78; sr. trial atty. Joseph W. Conklin, N.Y.C., 1978-80; assoc. dept. head Curtis, Mallet-Prevost, Colt & Mosle, N.Y.C., 1980-82; ptnr. Anderson, Russell, Kill & Olick, N.Y.C., 1982-86, Stroock & Stroock & Lavan, N.Y.C., 1986-90; ptnr., chair environ. and toxic tort practice Keck, Mahin, Cate & Koether, 1990-93; prin. Barbara P. Billauer & Assocs., Lido Beach, N.Y., 1993—. Vis. scholar Johns Hopkins U. Sch. Pub. Health, 1998-99; faculty SUNY Stony Brook Med. Sch.; adj. assoc. prof. NYU Grad. Sch., 1982-88; lectr. Rutger's U. Med. Sch.; jud. screening com. Coordinated Bar Assn., 1983-86; mem. spl panel Citywide Ct. Adminstrn. 1982-85; bd. dirs. Weizmann Inst., Am. Com. Co-author: The Lender's Guide to Environmental Law: Risk and Liability, 1993. Fellow Am. Bar Found.; mem. ABA (indoor air polution 1990-93), Met. Womens Bar Assn. (v.p. 1981-83, pres. 1983-85, chmn. bd. 1985-87), Nat. Conf. Womens Bar Assn. (bd. dirs., v.p. 1989-95), Internat. Coun. Shopping Ctrs. (environ. com.), Brit. Occupl. Hygiene Soc., Environment Toxic Torts. E-mail: omniscience@starpower.net.

BILLECI, ANDRE GEORGE, art educator, sculptor; b. N.Y.C., Dec. 2, 1933; s. Salvatore Daniel and Rosaria Grace (Turco) B.; m. Carol Loretta Farinola, Sept. 1, 1956; children: Andrew, John. BFA cum laude, SUNY, Alfred, 1960, MFA, 1961. Instr. SUNY Coll. Ceramics, Alfred, 1961-69, asst. prof., 1969-71, assoc. prof., 1971-82, prof. art, 1982-89, prof. emeritus, 1989—. Cons. Steuben Glass, N.Y., 1974, Royal Coll. Art, London, 1975, Mary McFadden Inc., N.Y.C., 1978; guest spkr. 1st Internat. Symposium on Glass Edn., La Granja, Segovia, Spain, 1990; guest lectr. Found. for Glass, Barcelona, Spain, 1990. One-man shows include Am. House Gallery, N.Y.C., 1971, Mus. Contemporary Crafts, N.Y.C., 1970, Corning Mus. Glass, N.Y., 1972, Pilkington Glass Mus., St. Helen's Lancashire, Eng., 1973; represented in permanent collections Nat. Galleries de Prague, Czechoslovakia, Australian Nat. Gallery, Canberra, Mus. Kunsthandwerk, Frankfurt, West Germany, Lannin Found., Palm Beach, Fla.; commissions include Penn Mutual Life, 1983, E.I. DuPont de Nemours Co., 1985. Cons. for India travel/rsch. Corning Mus., 1986, 87, 97, 99, Vitras s.a., Quetzaltenango, Guatemala, 1988, Argucia & Martinez Crafts, Tegucigalpa, Honduras, 1989, UNICEF, Herat, Afghanistan, 1993, Valley Forge Industries, Harare, Zimbabwe, 1996; award panelist N.Y. State Found. for Arts, 1989. NSF Travel grantee, India, 1986; rsch. grantee Inst. Glass Sci. and Engring., Greece, 1987. Mem. AAUP, Internat. Commn. on Glass (com. XVII 1985), Inst. Glass Sci. and Engring., Am. Ceramic Soc., Internat. Sculpture Ctr. Home: 4461 SW 8th Ln Vero Beach FL 32968

BILLER, GERALDINE POLLACK, art consultant, curator; b. Milw., Apr. 4, 1933; d. Sidney Samuel and Frieda (Eisenberg) Pollack; m. Joel Wilson Biller, May 1, 1955; children: Sydney Ellen, Andrew John, Charles Benjamin. BS, Northwestern U., 1955; MA, U. Wis., 1991. Tchr. art Va. Sch. System, 1955-56, Internat. Sch., The Hague, The Netherlands, 1959-62; adminstr. internat. rels. program Georgetown U., Washington, 1973-75; freelance graphic designer Washington, Milw., 1976-86; art historian, guest curator Milw. Art Mus., 1988-96; ind. art cons., Milw., 1996—. Pres. bd. dirs., Jewish Family Svcs., Milw., 1991-94, now life mem. bd. dirs.; bd. dirs. Alliance for Children and Families, 1998-2000; chair Jewish Family Svcs. Capital Campaign, 2000-01. Home and Office: 4716 N Wilshire Rd Milwaukee WI 53211-1262

BILLER, HENRY BURT, psychologist, educator; b. Providence, Oct. 30, 1940; s. David and Thelma (Rodin) B.; m. Margery Salter, Oct. 7, 1979 (div. July 1993); children: Jonathan, Kenneth, Cameron, Michael, Benjamin. AB magna cum laude, Brown U., 1962; PhD (USPHS fellow), Duke U., 1967. Asst. prof. psychology U. Mass., Amherst, 1967-69, George Peabody Coll., 1969-70; prof. U. R.I., Kingston, 1970—; cons. Northampton (Mass.) Welfare Dept., 1968-69, Protestant Youth Center, Baldwinville, Mass., 1969, Cape Cod (Mass.) Mental Health Center, 1970, Newport County (R.I.) Mental Health Center, 1970-71, VA Hosp., Providence, 1972-76, Emma Pendleton Bradley Hosp., Riverside, R.I., 1970-80, No. R.I. Mental Health Center, Woonsocket, 1980-82, No. R.I. Assn. for Retarded Citizens, Woonsocket, 1980-83, John E. Fogarty Ctr., North Providence, 1982—97, Elmwood Community Ctr., Providence, 1992-93, Newport County Regional Spl. Ednl. Program, 1993-94, St. Joseph's Ctr. for Family Clin. Svcs., Providence, 1993-94, Cmtys. for People, Providence, 1997—98; pvt. practice Warwick, R.I., 1970—. Author: Father, Child and Sex Role, 1971, Paternal Deprivation, 1974, Father Power, 1974, The Other Helpers, 1977, Parental Death and Psychological Development, 1982, Child Maltreatment and Paternal Deprivation, 1986, Stature and Stigma, 1987, Fathers and Families, 1993, (with Robert J. Trotter) The Father Factor, 1994, Creative Fitness, 2002; mem. editl. bd. Archives of Sexual Behavior, 1975-1997; mem. adv. bd., Men's Health Network, 1988—, cons. Editor Sex Roles, 1979-1997, Archives of Sexual Behavior, 1975-2000; assoc. editor Family Rels., 1980-81; contbr. chpts. to books, articles to profl. jours. Fellow Am. Psychol. Assn., Am. Psychol. Soc., Am. Assn. Applied and Preventive Psychology; mem. Phi Beta Kappa, Sigma Xi. Home: 4080 Post Rd Warwick RI 02886-9214 Office: U RI Dept Psychology Kingston RI 02881

BILLER, JOEL WILSON, lawyer, former foreign service officer; b. Milw., Jan. 17, 1929; s. Saul Earl and Mildred (Wilson) B.; m. Geraldine Pollack, May 1, 1955; children— Sydney, Andrew, Charles. BA, U. Wis., 1950; JD, U. Mich., 1953; MA, Northwestern U., 1959. Bar: Wis. 1953. Atty., Milw., 1953-55; vice consul Am. consulate, Le Havre, France, 1956-58; econ. officer Am. Embassy, The Hague, Netherlands, 1959-62; internat. relations officer State Dept., Washington, 1962-66; econ. officer, asst. dir. AID mission, Quito, Ecuador, 1966-69; econ. counselor Am. embassy, Buenos Aires, 1969-71; dir. AID mission, Santiago, Chile, 1971-73; spl. asst. to undersec. state for econ. affairs Washington, 1973-74; spl. asst. to dep. sec. state, 1974; dep. asst. sec. state for comml. and spl. bilateral affairs, 1974-76; dep. asst. sec. state for transp., telecommunications and comml. affairs, after, 1976; sr. v.p. Manpower Inc., Milw., 1979-97, sr. v.p., gen. counsel, 1997-98, sr. v.p. internat. corp. affairs, 1999—. Mem. Am. Fgn. Service Assn. Office: Manpower Inc 5301 N Ironwood Rd PO Box 2053 Milwaukee WI 53201-2053

BILLER, JOSE, neurologist; b. Montevideo, Uruguay, Jan. 18, 1948; B in Medicine, A.V. Acevedo Inst., Montevideo, Uruguay, 1965; MD, U. de la Republica, Montevideo, Uruguay, 1974. Diplomate Am. Bd. Psychiatry and Neurology (bd. dirs 1994—). Intern Columbus Hosp., Chgo., 1976-77; resident in neurology Henry Ford Hosp., Detroit, 1977-78, Loyola U. Hosp., Maywood, Ill., 1978-80; fellow cerebral vascular diseases Bowman Gray Sch. Med., Winston Salem, N.C., 1980-81; asst. prof. neurology Loyola U., Chgo., 1982-84, U. Iowa Coll. Medicine, Iowa City, 1984-87, assoc. prof. neurology, 1987-90, prof. neurology, 1990-91; prof. Northwestern Sch. Medicine, Chgo., 1991-94; dir. stroke program, dir. acute stroke care unit Northwestern Meml. Hosp., Chgo., 1991-94; prof., chmn. dept. neurology Ind. U., 1994—. Prof. ad-honorem U. of the Republic Sch. of Medicine, Uruguay, 1997—; mem. editl. bd. Stroke, Stroke-Clin. Update, Neurol. Rsch.; Internat. bd. editors: CNS Drugs; cons. physician neurology svc. VA Hosp., Iowa City, 1984-91, staff physician Northwestern Meml. Hosp., Chgo., 1991-94; neurology cons. Rehab. Inst. Chgo., 1991-94; active med. staff Ind. U. Hosps., 1994—, cons. Roudebush VA Med. Ctr., 1994—. Author, co-author of more than 430 articles, book chpts., abstracts; 6 edited books; editor Seminars in Cerebrovascular Diseases and Stroke, Jour. Stroke and Cerebrovascular Diseases. Fellow ACP, Am. Acad. Neurology, Stroke Coun. Am. Heart Assn.; mem. AMA, N.Y. Acad. Sci., Am. Soc. for Neurology Investigation, Internat. Stroke Soc., Inter-Am. Coll. Physicians and Surgeons, Am. Neurolog. Assn., Am. Heart Assn., Argentinian Neurol. Soc. (hon.), Uruguayan Neurol. Soc. (hon.). Office: Ind U Sch of Medicine Dept Neurology Emerson Hall 545 Barnhill Dr # 125 Indianapolis IN 46202-5124

BILLET, DONALD FRANKLIN, civil engineer, consultant; b. York, Pa., May 26, 1929; s. George Victor and Edna Mae (Daron) B.; m. Joe Ann Moore, May 25, 1955. B in Civil Engring., Syracuse (N.Y.) U., 1951; MS, U. Ill., 1953. Registered profl. engr., Pa., S.C., Ga. Mem. C.E. Corps, USN, 1953-79; civil engr., v.p. Sea Island Engring., Inc., Hilton Head Island, S.C., 1979-89; project design engr. for water and sewer sys. Hussey, Gay, Bell & De Young, Inc., Savannah, Ga., 1989—. Author: Genealogy of Jacob Dellinger, 1733 Immigrant to Pa., 1993, and Billet and Related Families of York, Lancaster and Dauphin Counties, Pa., 1751-97, 1998. Comdr. USN, 1953-79. Mem. SAR (Dr. Mosse chpt. Hilton Head Island 1992-2000). Office: Hussey Gay Bell & DeYoung Inc 329 Commercial Dr Savannah GA 31406-3630 E-mail: dbillet@hgbd.com.

BILLETER, ROBERT JAMES, newspaper publisher; b. Clarksburg, W.Va., Aug. 16, 1926; s. Arch and Mabel Edith (Westfall) B.; m. Eileen Billie Horvath, Apr. 14, 1972; 1 child, William Fletcher. BS, W.Va. U., 1951. Editor Pendleton Times, Franklin, W.Va., 1951-53; copy editor Herald-Dispatch, Huntington, W.Va., 1953-54; reporter The Post, Morgantown, W.Va., 1954-56; copy editor Sun-Telegraph, Pitts., 1956-60, Post-Gazette, Pitts., 1960-81, night city editor, 1981-85, makeup editor, 1985-91; pub. The Weston (W.Va.) Democrat, 1992—. With U.S. Army, 1945-47. Episcopalian. Avocations: wine tasting, sailing, hiking, skiing. Home: One E 4th St Weston WV 26452 Office: The Weston Democrat 306 Main Ave Weston WV 26452-2046

BILLETT, HENNY HEISLER, hematologist; b. Passaic, N.J., July 12, 1949; d. Michael and Freida Regina (Krieger) Heisler; m. Michael Edward Billett, July 6, 1973; children: Emily, Olivia. BA, U. Pa., 1970; MD, Mt. Sinai Sch. Medicine, 1974; MSc, London Sch. Hygiene, 1976. Diplomate Am. Bd. Internal Medicine, Am. Bd. Hematology. Sr. house officer St. Bartholomew's Hosp., London, 1976-77; med. resident Montefiore Hosp. Med. Ctr., N.Y.C., 1977-79, hematology fellow, 1979-81; instr. medicine SUNY, Stony Brook, 1981-83; physician-in-charge Coagulation Lab., asst. attending Queens Hosp. Ctr. affiliation L.I. Jewish-Hillside Med. Ctr., 1981-83; asst. attending physician Bronx Mcpl. Hosp. Ctr., 1983-91; asst. prof. medicine Albert Einstein Coll. Medicine, Bronx, 1983-91, assoc. prof. lab. medicine, 1992-96, prof. clin. medicine and pathology, 2002—; dir. clin. hematology Weiler Hosp./Albert Einstein Coll. Medicine, Bronx, 1983-91, 97—, dir. thrombosis prevention and treatment program, 2001—; dir. Heredity Clinic Albert Einstein Coll. Medicine, Bronx, 1985-91; dir. hematology tng. program Albert Einstein Coll. Medicine and Montefiore Hosp. Med. Ctr., Bronx, 1989-91; chief divsn. hematology dept. pathology L.I. Jewish Med. Ctr. affiliate Albert Einstein Coll. Medicine, Bronx, 1991-96. Cons. Nupraven Ltd., 1989—90, Boehringer Ingelheim, Ltd., 1990, Astra Zeneca, U.S. Govt., Washington, 1989, Pharmacia-Upjohn, 1999. Contbr. articles, abstracts to profl. publs. Grantee NIH, 1987-91, 88-92, L.I. Jewish-Hillside Med. Ctr., 1982-84, Tng. fellow, 1980-81, Divsn. Internat. Med. Edn. grantee Am. Med. Colls., 1973. Fellow ACP; mem. Royal Coll. Surgeons (U.K.), Am Soc. Hematology (hemophilia svcs. adv. com. region ((1983—), Soc. for Study Blood (sec./treas.), Am. Soc. Clin. Pathologists, Am. Assn. Blood Banks, Royal Coll. Physicians (U.K., lic.). Office: Albert Einstein Coll Medicine Weiler 960 Einstein Hosp Bronx NY 10461-1926

BILLIAS, GEORGE ATHAN, history educator; b. Lynn, Mass., June 26, 1919; s. Athan O. and Grace (Papadakis) B.; m. Joyce Baldwin, Dec. 28, 1948 (dec.); children: Stephen, Athan, Nancy; m. Margaret Neussendorfer, Aug. 17, 1986. BA magna cum laude, Bates Coll., 1948; MA, Columbia U., 1949, PhD, 1958. Nat. def. historian USAF, 1951-54; instr. U. Maine, 1954-57, asst. prof., 1957-59, assoc. prof., 1959-62, Clark U., Worcester, Mass., 1962-66, prof. Am. history, 1966—, Jacob and Frances Hiatt prof. history, 1983-89, Jacob and Frances Hiatt prof. emeritus, 1989—. Author: Massachusetts Land Bankers of 1740, 1959, General John Glover and His Marblehead Mariners, 1960, Elbridge Gerry: Founding Father and Republican Statesman, 1976; editor, contbr.: George Washington's Generals, 1964, Law and Authority in Colonial America: Selected Essays, 1965, The American Revolution: How Revolutionary Was It?, 1965, 4th edit., 1989, Interpretations of American History: Patterns and Perspectives, 2 vols., 1967, 7th edit., 2000, George Washington's Opponents, 1969, The Federalists: Realists or Ideologues?, 1970, American History: Retrospect and Prospect, 1971, Perspectives on Early American History, 1973, American Constitutionalism Abroad, 1990, The Republican Synthesis Revisited: Essays in Honor of George Athan Billias, 1992, George Washington's Generals and George Washington's Opponents, 1993; contbr. numerous articles to profl. jours. With M.C., U.S. Army, 1941-46, ETO. Decorated Bronze Star; Am. Philos. Soc. grantee, 1965; Guggenheim fellow, 1961-62; Am. Coun. Learned Socs. fellow, 1968-69, NEH fellow, 1970-71, 79, 86, Huntington Libr. fellow, 1989-90. Mem.: Am. Antiquarian Soc. (honoree symposium The Republican Synthesis Revisited 1989), Mass. Hist. Soc., Am. Hist. Assn., Inst. Early Am. History and Culture (coun. 1969—72), Columbia Seminar in Early Am. History, Phi Beta Kappa. Office: Clark U Dept History Worcester MA 01610

BILLICK, BRIAN, professional football coach; b. Fairborne, Ohio, Feb. 28, 1954; m. Kim Billick; children: Aubree, Keegan. Student, Brigham Young U. Mem. Dallas Cowboys, 1977; asst. coach U. Redlands, 1977-78; grad. asst. Brigham Young U., Provo, Utah, 1978; asst. dir. pub. rels. San Francisco 49ers, 1979-80; coach receivers, tight ends, quarterbacks San Diego State U., 1981-85; offensive coord. Utah State U., 1986-88; asst. coach Stanford (Calif.) U., 1989-91; offensive coord. Minn. Vikings, 1992-98; head coach Balt. Ravens, 1999—. Earned All Western Athletic Conf. honors and honorable mention All-America in 1976 as a tight end, Brigham YOung U. Achievements include being the architect of Minnesota Vikings offense that scored 556 points to break NFL record of 541 points. Office: c/o Baltimore Ravens 11001 Owings Mills Blvd Owings Mills MD 21117-2857

BILLIG, ETEL JEWEL, theater director, actress; b. N.Y.C., Dec. 16, 1932; d. Anthony and Martha Rebecca (Klebansky) Papa; m. Steven S. Billig, Dec. 23, 1956 (dec. Aug. 1996); children: Curt Adam, Jonathan Roark. BS, NYU, 1953, MA, 1955; student, Herbert Berghof Studio, N.Y.C., 1955-56. Cert. elem. and high sch. tchr. Actress Washington Square Players, N.Y.C., 1950-55, Dukes Oak Theatre, Cooperstown, N.Y., 1955, Triple Cities Playhouse, Binghampton, N.Y., 1956, Candlelight Dinner Playhouse, Summit, Ill., 1970, 73, 77, 79, 90; mng. dir. Theatre 31, Park Forest, Ill., 1971-73; asst. mgr. Westroads Dinner Theatre, Omaha, 1973-76; mng. dir., actress Forum Theatre, 1973, 94; mng. dir., actress, producing dir. Ill. Theatre Ctr., Park Forest, 1976—; mng. dir., actress Goodman Theatre, Chgo., 1987, 95, Ct. Theatre, 1990, Wisdom Bridge Theatre, 1991; dir. drama Rich Ctrl. H.S., Olympia Fields, Ill., 1978-86. Del. League of Chgo. Theatres Russian Exchange to Soviet Union, 1989; actress Drury Lane, Oak Brook, Ill., 1989; cons. and lectr. in field. Appeared in films including the Dollmaker, Running Scared, Straight Talk, Stolen Summer; (TV series) Hawaiian Heat, Missing Persons, Untouchables. V.p. Nat. Coun. Jewish Women, Park Forest, 1968-70; sec. Community Arts Coun., Park Forest, 1984-86; pres. Southland Regional Arts Coun., 1986-92. Recipient Risk Taking award NOW, 1982; grantee Nebr. Arts Coun., 1975, Ill. Arts Coun., 1993, 96, 2000, Athena award Matteson Area C. of C., 1997, Abby Found. award, 1997; named to Park Forest Hall of Fame, 2000. Mem. AFTRA, SAG, Actors' Equity Assn., League Chgo. Theatres, Ill. Arts Coun. Theatre Panel, Prodrs. Assn. Chgo. Area Theatre (sec. 1988-89), Bus. in the Arts Coun. of C. of C. (charter), Rotary (bd. dirs. Park Forest chpt. 1988-97, sec. 2000, hall of fame 2000). Avocations: travel, antiques. Office: Ill Theatre Ctr PO Box 397 Park Forest IL 60466-0397 E-mail: ilthctr@bigplanet.com.

BILLIG, FRANKLIN ANTHONY, chemist; b. L.A., Feb. 11, 1923; s. Frank Henry and Hazel (Rockwell) B.; m. Tetsuko Morinaga, Apr. 23, 1957; 1 child, Patricia Ann Kikuko Billig-Harvey. BS, U. So. Calif., L.A., 1954. CPC, CSS. Sr. rsch. chemist Am. Potash & Chem. Corp., Whittier, Calif., 1954-64; rsch. chemist/lab. mgr./safety officer, Dept. Chemistry U. So. Calif., L.A., 1964—. Cons. Flintridge Cons., Inc., Calif., 1980—, Hanson Lab. Furniture, Newberry Park, Calif., 1989; cons./staff assoc. Enterprise Environ. Svcs., L.A., 1981—. Author: Advances in Chemistry, 1959, 61, Organic Synthesis, 1959, Infra Red Spectra of Organic Sulfur Compounds, 1964, Infra Red Spectra of Sulfur Compounds, 1966; patentee in field. Master sgt. USAF, 1942-53, PTO, Korea. Fellow AAAS, L. Pasteur Inst. Advanced Med. Studies, Am. Inst. Chemists; mem. Sigma Xi. Republican. Roman Catholic. Avocations: quantum mechanics, egyptology, archaeology, geology, paleontology. Home: 12722 Spindlewood Dr La Mirada CA 90638-2735 Office: U So Calif Dept Chemistry University Park Los Angeles CA 90089-0001

BILLIG, ROBERT EMMANUEL, psychiatric social worker; b. N.Y.C., May 21, 1946; s. Benjamin and Pearl (Kwiat) B. BA, McKendree Coll., 1966; MS, Fort Hays (Kans.) State Coll., 1969; MSW, Marywood Coll., 1974. Diplomate Clin. Social Work Am. Bd. Examiners in Clin. Social Work; cert. hypnotherapist Nat. Bd. Hypnotherapist Examiners. Psychiat. social worker S.I. Devel. Ctr., 1974-76, Queens and Bklyn. Devel. Ctrs., 1976-79, Bellevue Psychiat. Hosp., N.Y.C., 1979-88; pvt. practice, 1988—. Adminstr. Bellevue Cmty. Support Sys., 1983-86. Mem. Acad. Cert. Social Workers, Nat. Assn. Social Workers, N.Y. State Soc. Clin. Social Work Psychotherapists, Am. Soc. Hypnotherapy, Am. Assn. Profl. Hypnotherapists, Am. Assn. Behavioral Therapists, Mensa. Jewish. Home: 10 Park Ter E New York NY 10034-1504

BILLIG, THOMAS CLIFFORD, publishing executive, marketing professional; b. Pitts., Aug. 20, 1930; s. Thomas Cliffor and Melba Helen S. Billig; m. Helen Page Hine, May 14, 1951; children: Thomas Clifford, James Frederick. BSBA summa cum laude, Northwestern U., 1956. Ins. mgr., asst. dir. pers., asst. to chmn. Butler Bros. (now City Products Corp.), Chgo., 1954-59; market rsch. mgr. R.R. Donnelley & Sons, Chgo., 1959-61; pres., dir. Indsl. Fiber Glass Products Corp., Scottville and Ludington, Mich., 1962-69; cons. mass mktg. mgr. Mpls., 1969-71; v.p. Mail Mktg. Systems and Services, St. Paul and Bloomington, Minn., 1971-74; pres., chmn., chief exec. officer Billig & Assocs., Mpls. and Duluth, Minn., 1974—; pres. NIARS Corp., Duluth, 1974-85, 95—, also bd. dirs.; pres. Fins and Feathers Pub. Co., Mpls., 1977-89; also bd. dirs. Fins. and Feathers Pub. Co., Mpls.; pres., dir. N. Coast Mktg. Corp., St. Paul, 1992—; chmn., CEO Sportsman's Mktg. Inc., Superior, Wis., Lake Elmo, Minn., 1998—, also bd. dirs. Author: Nat. Inc. Advt. Regulation Svc., 1972—; author, pub.: NAIC Model Laws, Regulations and Guidelines, 1976—83. With USNR, 1948—56. Recipient Samuel Dresner Plotkin award, Northwestern U., 1956. Mem.: Beta Gamma Sigma, Delta Mu Delta. Office: 1423 N 8th St Superior WI 54880-6664 also: 3394 Lake Elmo Ave N Box 852 Lake Elmo MN 55042-9799 E-mail: niarsi@aol.com.

BILLINGER, WAYNE MICHAEL, creative director; b. Hays, Kans., Feb. 12, 1955; s. Leo Robert and Rita Ester Billinger; m. Tammy Anne Billinger, June 28, 1986; children: Michael, Kelsey. Adminstr. Hays Bus. Improvement Dist., Hays, Kans.; regional sales mgr., promotion dir. Cable Network Advtg., Weatherford, Okla.; owner Advantage Advtg., Hays, Kans. Contbr. comedy scripts, songs to prof. publs. Commr. City of Hays, Kans., 1997—2001, mayor, 1998—99; bd. mem. Ellis County Extension, Hays, Kans., 2001—03. Recipient Recognition award, BID and City of Hays, 1991—2001; grantee ISTEA, State of Kans., 1992, 1994. Avocations: music, writing, golf. Home: 3707 JP Dr Hays KS 67601

BILLINGS, CHARLES EDGAR, physician; b. Boston, June 15, 1929; s. Charles Edgar and Elizabeth (Sanborn) B.; m. Lillian Elizabeth Wilson, Apr. 16, 1955; 1 dau., Lee Ellen Billings Kreinbihl. Student, Wesleyan U., 1947-49; MD, N.Y. U., 1953; M.Sc. (Link Found. fellow), Ohio State U., 1960. Diplomate: Am. Bd. Preventive Medicine. Instr. to prof. depts. preventive medicine and aviation Sch. Medicine Ohio State U., 1960-73, dir. div. environ. health Sch. Medicine, 1970-73, clin. prof. Sch. Medicine, 1973-83, prof. emeritus, 1983—; rsch. scientist indsl. and systems engring., 1992—. Med. officer NASA Ames Rsch. Ctr., Moffett Field, Calif., 1973-76; chief Aviation Safety Rsch. Office, 1976-80, asst. chief for rsch. Man-Vehicle Systems rsch. divsn., 1980-83, sr. scientist, 1983-91; chief scientist Ames Rsch. Ctr., 1991-92; cons. Beckett Aviation Corp., 1962-73; surgeon gen. U.S. Army, 1965-77, FAA, 1967-70, 75, 83; mem. NATO-AGARD Aerospace Med. Panel, 1980-86; assoc. advisor USAF Sci. Adv. Bd., 1978-90; mem. human factors adv. panel U.K. Civil Aviation Authority, 1999-2001; mem. aviation adv. bd. Ohio U., 2000-01. Contbr. chpts. to books, numerous articles in field to med. jours. Served to maj. USAF, 1955-57. Recipient Air Traffic Svc. award FAA, 1969, Walter M. Boothby rsch. award, 1972, PATCO Air Safety award, 1979, Disting. Svc. award Flight Safety Found., 1979, John A. Tamisea award, 1980, Laura Taber Barbour Air Safety medal, 1981, Outstanding Leadership medal NASA, 1981, 90, Jeffries Aerospace Med. Rsch. medal AIAA, 1986, Lovelace award NASA Soc. Flight Surgeons, 1996, Forrest and Pamela Bird award Civil Aviation Med. Assn., 2001, Henry L. Taylor Founders award Aerospace Human Factors Assn, 2002; Ames Rsch. Ctr. fellow, 1989. Fellow AIAA (assoc.), Royal Aero. Soc., Aerospace Med. Assn. (pres. 1979-80); mem. AMA, Internat. Acad. Aviation and Space Medicine. Home: 1372 Hickory Ridge Ln Columbus OH 43235-1131 Office: 265 Baker ISE Bldg 1971 Neil Ave Columbus OH 43210-1210

BILLINGS, FRANKLIN SWIFT, JR., federal judge; b. Woodstock, Vt., June 5, 1922; s. Franklin S. and Gertrude (Curtis) B.; m. Pauline Gillingham, Oct. 13, 1951; children: Franklin, III, Jireh Swift, Elizabeth, Ann. S.B., Harvard U., 1943; postgrad., Yale U. law Sch., 1945; JD, U. Va., 1947. Bar: Vt. 1948, U.S. Supreme Ct., 1958. With dept. electronics Gen. Electric Co., Schenectady, N.Y., 1943; bldg. dept. Vt. Marble Co., Proctor, 1945-46; pvt. practice law Woodstock, 1948-52; mem. firm Billings & Sherburne, Woodstock, 1952 66; asst. sec. Vt. Senate, 1949-55, sec., 1957-59; sec. civil and mil. affairs State of Vt., 1959-61; exec. clk. to gov., 1955-57; judge Hartford Mcpl. Ct., 1955-63; mem. Vt. Ho. of Reps., 1961-66, chmn. jud. com., 1961, speaker of ho., 1963-66; judge Vt. Superior Ct., 1966-75, assoc. justice, 1975-83, chief justice, 1983-84; judge U.S. Dist. Ct. Vt., 1984-94, chief judge, 1988-92, sr. ct. judge, 1994—. Active, Town of Woodstock, 1948-72. Served as warrant officer 1st class attached Brit. Army, 1944-45. Decorated Purple Heart; Brit. Empire medal. Mem. Vt. Bar Assn., Delta Theta Phi. Office: US Dist Ct PO Box 598 Woodstock VT 05091-0598

BILLINGS, HAROLD WAYNE, library director, editor; b. Cain City, Tex., Nov. 12, 1931; s. Harold Ross and Katie Mae (Price) B.; m. Bernice Schneider, Sept. 10, 1954; children: Brenda, Geoffrey, Carol. BA, Pan Am. Coll., 1953; MLS, U. Tex., 1957. Tchr. Pharr San Juan-Alamo (Tex.) High Sch., 1953-54, catalog librarian U. Tex., Austin, 1954-57, asst. chief catalog librarian, 1957-65, chief acquisitions librarian, 1965-67, asst. univ. librarian, 1967-72, asso. dir. gen. libraries, 1972-77, acting dir. gen. libraries, 1977-78, dir. gen. libraries, 1978—2003. Sec. Tex. Bd. Libr. Examiners; mem. adv. com. Tex. Higher Edn. Coordinating Bd. Libr. Formula, 1987-92, acad. support formula adv. com., 1993-94; mem. steering com. Tex-Share Project, 1993-94; trustee Amigos Bibliographic Coun., 1980-83; chmn. Coun. Acad. Rsch. Librs., 1979-81; chmn. rsch. libs. adv. com. Online Computer Libr. Ctr. (OCLC), 1980-82, 87-88, mem. OCLC Users Coun.; bd. dirs. Ctr. Rsch. Librs., Chgo., 1989-96, Assn. Rsch. Librs., 1989-92; mem. Tex. Coun. State Univ. Librs., Assn. Rsch. Librs. Preservation Com., Collection Devel. Com., Coun. on Libr. Resources Preservation and Access Com., Coun. on Libr. Resources/Assn. Am. Pubs. Joint Working Group on Electronic Info., 1993-94; mem. adv. bd. Project Muse-Johns Hopkins U. Press, Balt., 1995-98; mem. N.Am. adv. bd. Lit. Online, 1997—; assoc. Tex. Telecomms. Policy Inst., 1996-2003; mem. coun. on libr. and info. studies area studies materials task force ACLS, 1998-99; mem. adv. coun. for Stanford U. Librs., 1998—; steering com. Digital Libr. Fedn., 1999-2003; vis. coms. U. Tenn., U. Wyo.; project dir. numerous fed. grants. Author: Education of Librarians in Texas, 1956, Edward Dahlberg: American Ishmael of Letters, 1968, A Bibliography of Edward Dahlberg, 1972, The Shape of Shiel, 1865-1896, 1983, The Leafless American, 2d edit., 1986, Magic and Hypersystems: Constructing the Information-Sharing Library, 2002; editor books in field; contbr. to jours.; mem. editorial bd. Libr. Chronicle, 1970-97. Sec., trustee Littlefield Fund for So. History. Mem. ALA (Hugh C. Atkinson Meml. award 2002), Tex. Libr. Assn., Assn. Coll. Rsch. Librs. Democrat. Office: U Tex Librs PO Box P Austin TX 78713-8916

BILLINGS, RICHARD BRUCE, economics educator, consultant; b. Waukesha, Wis., Dec. 5, 1938; s. Floyd Henry and Edessa Mary (Burmeister) B.; m. Patricia Christy Barnum, Mar. 31, 1961 (dec. May 1999); children: Stephen Michael, David Christopher; m. Mary Judith TerMeer, Feb. 12, 2000. BA in Econs. and Math., U. Ariz., 1962, MA in Econs., 1963; PhD in Econs, Claremont (Calif.) Coll., 1969. Asst. prof. U. Ariz., Tucson, 1965-69, lectr. in econs., 1970-99, assoc. prof., 1999-2000; rsch. economist State of Ariz., Phoenix, 1969-70. Cons. State of Hawaii, Honolulu, 1984, Bur. Reclamation, Boulder, Colo., 1986, Tucson Water, 1988-89, State of Ariz., Phoenix, 1989. Author: Forecasting Urban Water Demand, 1996; contbr. articles to profl. jours. Pres. Campus Christian Ctr., Tucson, 1971, 75; pres., bd. dirs. 1st United Meth. Ch., Tucson, 1992-94, chair fin. com., 1989-93, 95-99; scoutmaster Boy Scouts Am., Tucson, 1981-86. Democrat. Avocations: hiking, camping, woodworking. Home: 1533 E Spring St Tucson AZ 85719 Office: U Ariz Dept Econs Mcclelland Hall 401 Tucson AZ 85721-0001

BILLINGS, THOMAS NEAL, computer and publishing executive, management consultant, entrepreneur, author, journalist, software designer and inventor; b. Milwaukee, Wis., Mar. 2, 1931; s. Neal and Gladys Victoria (Lockard) B.; m. Barta Hope Chipman, June 12, 1954 (div. 1967); children: Bridget Ann, Bruce Neal; m. Marie Louise Farrell, Mar. 27, 1982 (dec. Jan. 2003). AB with honors, Harvard U., 1952, MBA, 1954. V.p. fin. and adminstrn. and technol. innovation Copley Newspapers Inc., LaJolla, Calif., 1957-70; group v.p., dir. tech. Harte-Hanks Comm. Inc., San Antonio, 1970-73; exec. v.p. United Media Inc., Phoenix, 1973-75; asst. to pres., dir. corp. mgmt. systems Ramada Inns, Inc., Phoenix, 1975-76; exec. dir. NRA, Washington, 1976-77; pres. Strategic Ideation Inc., N.Y.C., 1977—; chmn. Bergen-Billings Inc., N.Y.C., 1977-80; pres. The Assn. Svc. Corp., San Francisco, 1978—, Recorder Printing and Pub. Co. Inc., San Francisco, 1980-82; v.p. adminstrn. Victor Techs. Inc., Scotts Valley, Calif., 1982-84; mng. dir. Saga-Wilcox Computers Ltd., Wrexham, Wales, 1984-85; chmn. Thomas Billings & Assocs., Inc., Reno, 1978—, Intercontinental Travel Svc. Inc., Reno, 1983-88, Oberon Optical Character Recognition Ltd., Hemel-Hemstead, Eng., 1985-86. Bd. dirs. 5M Corp., San Francisco, Intercontinental Rsch. Coun., London, Corp. Comm. Coun., Alameda, Digital Broadcasting Corp., Mountain View, Calif., Lenny's Restaurants, Inc., Wichita, Kans., Tymyndr Corp., Dover, Del., Zzyzzyx Corp., Reno, Harrod's Hotel & Casino Corp., Las Vegas, Pandemonium Pictures, Inc., San Moteo, Calif., Bonanza Enterprises, Inc., Virginia City, Nev., Quillmill Ltd., London, Better Betting Systems, Inc., Alameda, Calif., Video Stream, Inc., Cupertino, Calif., ResuMaster Corp., Walnut Creek, Calif., ProcessMaster Corp., Pleasanton, Calif., Enterprise House, Alameda, Chut! Cheri's Chic Chit Choppe, S.A., Laguna Beach, Calif., Waters Equipment Co., Inc., San Francisco, Goldstein Miller and Assocs. Inc., San Bruno, Calif., Silicon World Search Group, Inc., Alameda, Calif., Knicker's Ltd., Reno; dir., CEO Insignia Software Solution Group, High Wycombe, Eng., Cupertino, Calif., 1986-89; chmn. Intercontinental News Svc. Inc., London and Alameda, Calif., 1989—; v.p. Cromer Equipment Co., Oakland, Calif., 1991-94; chmn. Newton Group of Cos., Las Vegas, 1993—, Info. Integrity Internat., Inc., Las Vegas, London, 1994—, WordMaster Corp., Reno, 1995—, GolfDoctor!Inc., Las Vegas, 1998—, First Impact Inc., Alameda, Calif., 2000-; CEO Assurant Software, Inc., Palo Alto, Calif., 2002-; EDITOR, PUB., ceo tHE-vIEW-lESS-sEEN.COM, aLAMEDA, cALIF., 2001—; adj. prof. U. Phoenix, San Jose, Calif., 1999—, Coll. San Mateo, Calif., 2000-, Monterey (Calif.) Inst. Internat. Studies, 2001-, Deep Springs Calif. Coll., 2002-; spkr. and seminar leader; co-inventor StrokSavr Software, 1994. Author: Creative Controllership, 1978, Our Credibility Crisis, 1983, Non-Euclidean Theology, 1987, Ruminations on Meta Mentality, 1990, Fixing our Broken System, 1992, Our Dissembling Society, 1997, Our Co-Dependent World, 1998, A Christmas Carol-The Musical!, 1999, All Roads Lead to Ausfardt, 2000, The View Less Seen, 2002; (series) The Ethnic Epicure, 1995—, The View Less Seen, 2000—; editor: The Vice President's Letter, 1978-92; pub. The Microcomputer Letter, 1982-94, Synthetic Hardware Update, 1987-93, Windows on Tomorrow Magazine, 1994-99; editor: Intercontinental News Svc. London and Alamedia, Calif., 1985—; theatre critic, editl. columnist The Alameda Jour., 1998 . Bd. dirs. Nat. Allergy Found., 1973—, The Wilderness Fund, 1978—, San Diego Civic Light Opera Assn., 1965-69; chief exec. San Diego 200th Anniversary Expn., 1969; founder, exec. dir. Am. Majority Party, 1993—, The Millenium Three Found., 1996—, The Remembrance Soc., 1996—, People Finders' Inc., 1996—, Corp. Comm. Counsel Inc., 1996—, Alameda Cmty. Theatre Alliance, 1998—, Alameda Repretory Theatre, 1999—; voice talent Voice Wizardry, Alameda, Calif., 1999-; bass cantor and lector St. Joseph Basilica, Alameda, Calif., 1994-. With U.S. Army, 1955-57. Recipient Walter F. Carley Meml. award, 1966, 69. Fellow U.K. Inst. Dirs.; mem. Am. Newspaper Pubs. Assn., Inst. Execs. Inc. (dir.), Inst. Newspaper Fin. Officers, West Side Tennis Club, LaJolla Country Club, Washington Athletic Club, San Francisco Press Club, Harvard Club (N.Y.C.), Elks, Sigma Delta Chi. Office: PO Drawer I Alameda CA 94501-0262 also: Ste 104 1600 Hills of Red Dr Las Vegas NV 89128-8415 E-mail: himself@tnbillings.com.

BILLINGSLEY, DAVID STUART, chemical engineer, researcher, software developer; b. Chgo., June 6, 1929; s. Archibald Stuart and Helen Wilson (Murdoch) B. BSChemE, Tex. A&M U., 1950, BSME and BS in Indsl. Engring., 1956, MSChemE, 1958, PhD ChemE, 1961. System engr. IBM, Houston, 1961-63, with scientific staff, 1963-76, Palo Alto, Calif., 1976-82, internat. petroleum ctr. staff Houston, 1982-85; ind. software developer Houston, 1985—. Referee AIChE Jour., 1972-85, Canadian Jour. Chem. Engring., 1972. Author: Descendants of Richard Billingsley, 1992, The Billingsley Family of Canada, 2001; contbr. articles to profl. engineering jours. 1st lt. U.S. Army, 1951-53, Korea. Home: 4403 Bellaire Dr S Apt 222 Fort Worth TX 76109-5102

BILLINGSLEY, FRANK S. gynecologist, obstetrician, educator; b. Ark., July 16, 1923; s. Theodore N. and Irene Billingsley; m. Leslie A. Gaynor, Feb. 2, 1980; children: Becky Lee, Katherine Ann. BS, La. Poly. Inst., 1943; MD, U. Ark., 1958. Commd. ensign USN, 1944; commd. officer, subchaser USSC 677, 1944—45; psych. warfare officer U.S. Cinceur Headquarters, Germany; advanced through grades to capt. M.C., 1970; intern U.S. Naval Hosp., Charleston, SC, 1958; resident in ob-gyn. Nat. Naval Med. Ctr., Bethesda, Md., 1959—62; head gynecology svc. U.S. Naval Hosp., Bethesda, 1971—74; svc. in West Germany, Pacific and Thailand; ret., 1974; assoc. prof. ob-gyn., dir. ob-gyn. clinic Georgetown U. Med. Sch., 1974—82; assoc. dir. Washington Clin. Thermography, 1979—83; chmn. dept. ob-gyn. Sibley Meml. Hosp., 1984—. Cons. in gynecology Nat. Cancer Inst., NIH, 1976-90; cons. in field. Author papers in field, prodr.-dir. tng. films; patentee device for irradiating a body cavity. Decorated Navy Commendation medal; recipient various certs. merit and appreciation. Fellow ACOG, ACS, Royal Soc. Health; mem. AMA, Am. Soc. Breast Disease, So. Med. Assn., Congl. Country Club (Bethesda), Alpha Omega Alpha (hon.). Republican. Unitarian Universalist. Office: 5301 Westbard Cir Ste 5 Bethesda MD 20816-1429

BILLINGSLEY, JUDITH ANN SEAVEY, oncology nurse; b. Manchester, Conn., Aug. 4, 1947, d. John Frank and Carol Jean (Wood) Seavey; m. Michael Billingsley, June 7, 1969; children: Tamara Lynn, Tara Lynn. Diploma, Hartford Hosp. Sch. Nursing, 1968; student, Coll. of Albemarle, 1985-86, No. Va. C.C., 1990; grad. with honors, George Mason U., 1992. Cert. oncology nurse ANCC, 1995, 99. Staff nurse ICU Manchester Meml. Hosp., 1968—69; staff nurse recovery rm. Burlingame (Calif.) Hosp. and Med. Ctr., 1972—73; staff nurse St. Joseph's Hosp., Atlanta, 1987—89; clin. nurse Alexandria (Va.) Hosp., 1989—91; admissions nurse Hospice of No. Va., 1991—92; neuro-oncology clin. rsch. nurse Winship Cancer Ctr. Emory U. Sch. Medicine, Atlanta, 1992—98; clin. rsch. nurse Blood and Marrow Transplant Group Ga., Atlanta, 1998—2000, clin. program mgr., neuro-oncology, 2002—; sr. clin. project specialist Proxima Therapeutics, Inc., Alpharetta, Ga., 2000—02. Mem. Golden Key, Sigma Theta Tau, Alpha Chi. Home: 1273 Gray Squirrel Xing Marietta GA 30062-6275 E-mail: jbillingsley@proximatherapeutics.com.

BILLINGSLEY, LANCE W. lawyer; b. Buffalo, Apr. 18, 1940; m. Carolyn Gouza Billingsley, Aug. 25, 1962; children: Lance II, Brant, Ashlynn. BA, U. Md., 1961; JD, U. Buffalo, 1964; state and local, Harvard U., 1988. Pntr., assoc. Nylen & Gilmore, Riverdale, Md., 1964-75; ptnr. Meyers, Billingsley, Rodbell & Rosenbaum, P.A., Riverdale, 1975-2000, Rifken, Livingston, Levitan, Silver, Greenbelt, Md., 2000—. Bd. of regents Univ. Sys. of Md., 1995-2003, chmn. 1995-99; vice-chmn. U. of Md. Found., 1985-2000; bd. dirs. U. Md. Med. Sys.; asst. atty. gen. State of Md., 1967-68; city atty. Hyattsville, Md., 1976—; chmn. Nat. Wildlife Visitors Ctr., 1989-94; chmn. bd. Prince George's county Econ. Devel. Corp., Landover, Md., 1983-92. Contbr. articles to numerous law publs. Chmn. Dem. State Cen. Com., 1970-74, Dem. Com. Prince George's County, 1974-80. Named One of Outstanding Young Men Am., 1975-80. Mem.: Md. Bar Assn., ABA (young lawyers exec. com. 1972—74, editl. bd. Barrister mag. 1973—75), U. Md. Alumni Assn. (bd. govs.), M Club, Terrapin Club (bd. dirs. 1983—2001, pres. 1998—99), Columbia Country Club (Chevy Chase, Md.), Omicron Delta Kappa. Avocations: skiing, backpacking. Home: 7102 College Heights Dr Hyattsville MD 20782-1154 Office: Rifkin Livingston Levitan & Silver LLC 6305 Ivy Ln Ste 500 Greenbelt MD 20770-1405 Fax: (301) 345-1294. E-mail: billings@usmd.edu.

BILLINGSLEY, ROBERT THAINE, lawyer; b. Wichita, Kans., Jan. 9, 1954; s. Thaine Edward and Anita (Moore) B.; m. Anna Barron, Dec. 31, 1983; children: Carol Carothers, Leslie Hope. AB, Coll. of William and Mary, 1976; JD, U. Richmond, 1980. Bar: Va. 1980. Law clk. to presiding justice U.S. Dist. Ct., Roanoke, Va., 1980-81; assoc. McGuire, Woods & Battle, Richmond, Va., 1981-87, Hirschler, Fleischer, Weinberg, Cox & Allen, Richmond, Va., 1987-96; fin. advisr Kramnick & Assocs., Fredericksburg, Va., 1996—2001; rep. Northwestern Mutual Fin. Network, Fredericksburg, Va., 2001—. Bd. dirs. Make A Wish Found., Ctrl. and Western Va., 2000—. Bd. editors The Virginia Lawyer, 1984-86; mem. adv. bd. U. Richmond Law Rev., 1986-97; contbr. articles to profl. publs. Bd. dirs. Bethlehem Ctr., Richmond, 1985-89, United Meth. Found. of Va. Conf., Inc., 1993—, sec., 2000-02; bd. dirs. Hanover Indsl. Air Pk. Bus. Assn., 1994-96; mem. adminstrv. bd. Trinity United Meth. Ch., Richmond, 1986-89, trustee, 1988-96, chmn. bd. trustees, 1992-95, chmn. commitment campaign, 1995; team capt. United Way Greater Richmond, 1989, sect. chmn., 1991, divsn. chmn., 1993; team capt. Rappahannock Area United Way, 1998, divsn. chair, 1999; mem. Leadership Metro Richmond Class, 1992-93; bd. dirs. Arts Coun. of Richmond, Inc., 1994-96, exec. com., 1996; chmn. fin. com. Fredericksburg United Meth. Ch., 1999-2001; bd. dirs. College Heights Swimming Pool Assn. Mem.: ABA (litig. sect., state membership chmn., young lawyers divsn. 1985—89, state membership chmn. 1989—96), Fredericksburg Bar Assn., Richmond Bar Assn. (program com., vice chmn. 1990—91, chmn. 1991—92, adminstrn. of justice com. 1992—96), Va. State Bar Assn. (bd. govs. young lawyers conf. 1985—89, spl. com. on professionalism, legal edn., admission to bar), Va. Bar Assn. (com. on alternative dispute resolution), William and Mary Alumni Assn. (bd. dirs. Richmond chpt. 1993—95), Rotary (Rappahannock chpt. bd. dirs. 2000—, pres.-elect 2002—03, pres. 2003—), Richmond Jaycees (bd. dirs. 1984—86). Avocations: sports, travel, theatre. Home: 1604 College Ave Fredericksburg VA 22401-4637 Office: Northwestern Mutual Fin Network 725 Jackson St Ste 211 Fredericksburg VA 22401

BILLINGSLEY, SHIRLEY ANN, writer, poet; b. Center, Tex., Sept. 3, 1953; d. Leonard Waymon and Verna Mae (Moore) B.; m. Willie L. Skinner, Oct. 12, 1980; 1 child, Melinda Sue. Diploma, Coastal Coll., Bossier City, La., 1991. Author: articles, poems. Avocations: reading, writing, poetry. E-mail: bshirle2000@yahoo.com.

BILLINGSLEY, WILLIAM PATRICE, mathematician, educator; b. Chgo, June 6, 1961; s. William Brownlow Jr. and Willer Bell Billingsley. BSc in Math., Roosevelt U., 1987. Math. instr. Roosevelt U., Chgo., 1984—97; math. tutor Chgo. State U., Chgo., 1997—2001; math tchr. Bowen HS, Chgo., 2001—02; cadet Carver Mil. Acad., Chgo., 2002—03. Egungun priest Ifa (African religion); math. cons. Nabisco Foods, Inc., Chgo., 1988—89; math instr. Kennedy-King Coll., 1997—. Composer: (albums) America, 2002. Bd. dir. Feeding the Homeless for Christ Outreach Ministry, Chgo., 1996—2001, ednl. chmn., 1996—2001, treas., 1996—2001. Mem.: NRA (life), Nat. Coun. Tchr. of Math., Ill. State Rifle Assn. Democrat. Avocations: music, astronomy, african studies, chess, astrology, poetry. Home: 7800 S Throop St Chicago IL 60620-3757 Office: High Sch 2710 E 89th St Chicago IL 60614 E-mail: lonew6661@hotmail.com.

BILLINGTON, BARRY E. lawyer; b. Bruceton, Tenn., June 24, 1940; s. Charles Raymond and Edith Virginia (Bowles) B.; m. Bonnie Leslie Johnson; Oct. 16, 1971 (div. Mar. 23, 1990); children: Erin Alexis, Barry E., Jr. AB in Econs., Davidson Coll., 1964; JD, Emory U., 1968. Bar: Calif. 1969, Ga. 1971, U.S. Dist. Ct. (ctrl. dist.) Calif. 1969, U.S. Dist. Ct. (no. dist.) Ga. 1971. Assoc. Surr & Hellyer, San Bernardino, Calif., 1968-70; with Mfrs. Life Ins. Co., Atlanta, 1970-71; assoc. Carter, Ansley, Smith & McClendon, Atlanta, 1971-72; of counsel Raiford & Hills, Decatur, Ga., 1972-75; ptnr. Raiford, Hills, Billington & McKeithen, Atlanta, 1975-77; mem. Rich, Bass, Kidd, Witcher & Billington, Decatur, 1977-82; ptnr. Billington & Beasley, Decatur, 1982-83, Billington & Turner, Atlanta, 1983-85; owner Barry E. Billington & Assocs., Atlanta, 1985—. Editor: Ga. Rep. Party Newsletter, 1968. Rep. publicity dir. San Bernardino County Rep. Party, 1969-70, San Bernardino County for Ronald Reagan Com., 1970; alt. del. Rep. Ctrl. Com. of Calif., 1969-70; chmn. 4th dist. Conservative Caucus, 1977-79; candidate for Ga. Ho. Reps., 52nd dist., 1978, candidate for U.S. Congress, 4th dist., Ga., 1980. With U.S. Army Mil. Police Corps, 1958-60. Mem. Atlanta Bar Assn. (spkr.'s com., litigation, family law, criminal law sects. 1974-77), Decatur-DeKalb Bar Assn. (chmn. spkr.'s com. 1977-78), ABA (litigation sect. 1969-89), Ga. Trial Lawyers Assn., Assn. Trial Lawyers Am., Ga. Assn. Criminal Def. Lawyers, Nat. Assn. Criminal Def. Lawyers, Diplomat of Nat. Coll. of Advocacy Trial Advocacy Course. Home: 7208 Peachford Circle Atlanta GA 30338 Office: 3 Dunwoody Park Ste 103 Atlanta GA 30338-6709 E-mail: bebillesq@aol.com.

BILLINGTON, DAVID PERKINS, civil engineering educator; b. Bryn Mawr, Pa., June 1, 1927; s. Nelson and Jane Newkirk (Coolbaugh) B.; m. Phyllis Bergquist, Aug. 26, 1951; children: David Jr., Elizabeth Billington Fox, Jane Billington Flucker, Philip, Stephen, Sarah BS in Engring., Princeton U., 1950; postgrad. (Fulbright fellow), U. Louvain, Belgium, 1950-51, U. Ghent, 1951-52; DHL (hon.), Union Coll., 1990; DSc (hon.), Grinnell Coll., 1991; DEng (hon.), Notre Dame U., 1997. Registered profl. engr., N.J. Structural engr. Roberts & Schaefer Co., N.Y.C., 1952-60; assoc. prof. civil engring. Princeton U., N.J., 1960-64, prof. civil engring., 1964—, Gordon Y.S. Wu prof. engring., 1996—. A.D. White prof.-at-large Cornell U., 1987-93; cons. in field Author: Robert Maillart's Bridges, 1979 (Dexter award 1979), Thin Shell Concrete Structures, 1982, The Tower and the Bridge, 1983, Robert Maillart and the Art of Reinforced Concrete, 1990, The Innovators: The Engineering Pioneers Who Made America Modern, 1996, Robert Maillart: Builder, Designer, Artist, 1997, The Art of Structural Design: A Swiss Legacy, 2003. With USN, 1945-46. Recipient Dana award, Charles A. Dana Found., 1990, N.J. Prof. of Yr. award, Carnegie Found., 1995, Sarton medal, U. Ghent, Belgium, 1999, Sarton chair award, 1999—2000, Dir.'s award, NSF, 2003; grantee NSF, 1963—83, 1991—94, 2001—, NEH, 1969—89, NEA, 1977—79; vis. scholar, Phi Beta Kappa, 1984—85. Fellow Am. Acad. Arts and Scis., Am. Concrete Inst. (hon.); mem. NAE, ASCE (hon., 3 awards 1956-57, History and Heritage award 1986, George Winter award 1992), Internat. Assn. for Bridge and Structural Engring., Internat. Assn. Shell Structures, Soc. for History Tech. (Usher prize with J. Doig 1995). Republican. Episcopalian. Home: 45 Hodge Rd Princeton NJ 08540-3011 Office: Princeton U Dept Civil and Environ Engring Princeton NJ 08544-0001 E-mail: billington@princeton.edu.

BILLINGTON, GLENN EARLE, lawyer; b. Ithaca, N.Y., Nov. 8, 1943; s. Earle K. and Jean (Powell) B.; m. Anne Toth, Dec. 27, 1967; children: Peter J., Karen L., Steven J. AB, Cornell U., 1965; JD, Cleve. State U., 1970. Bar: Ohio 1970, U.S. Dist. Ct. (no. dist.) Ohio 1970, U.S. Ct. Appeals (6th cir.) 1972, U.S. Supreme Ct. 1975. Civil dir. Legal Aid Soc. Cleve., 1973-75; pvt. practice law Cleveland Heights, Ohio, 1975—. Chmn. Cuyahoga County Bd. Mental Retardation, Cleve., 1978-83; acting judge Cleveland Heights Mcpl. Ct., 1978-93; ctrl. committeeman Cuyahoga County Dems., Cleve., 1976—. Mem. Ohio Bar Assn. Methodist. Avocations: flying, political campaign management. Home: 2584 Exeter Rd Cleveland OH 44118-4244 Office: 1991 Lee Rd #102 Cleveland OH 44118-2571

BILLINGTON, JAMES HADLEY, historian, librarian; b. Bryn Mawr, Pa., June 1, 1929; s. Nelson and Jane (Coolbaugh) B.; m. Marjorie Anne Brennan, June 22, 1957; children: Susan Billington Harper, Anne Billington Fischer, James Hadley, Jr., Thomas Keator. BA, Princeton U., 1950; D Phil., Oxford (Eng.) U., 1953; LittD (hon.), Lafayette Coll., 1981, U. Pitts., 1988, Williams Coll., 1991, Duke U., 1995; LHD (hon.), LeMoyne Coll., 1982, Rhode Island Coll., 1982, Cath. U. Am., 1983, NYU, 1987, Va. Theol. Sem., 1990, Hood Coll., 1992, U. Scranton, 1992, SUNY, Albany, 1993, Georgetown U., 1993, Bates Coll., 1993, The Am. U., 1995, Mt. Holyoke Coll., 1995; HHD (hon.), Furman U., 1986, Ball State U., 1988; D Pub. Svc. (hon.), George Washington U., 1990; LLD (hon.), Dartmouth Coll., 1990, U. Notre Dame, 1995. Instr. history Harvard U., Cambridge, Mass., 1957-58, fellow Russian Research Ctr., 1958-59; asst. prof. history, 1958-61; assoc. prof. history Princeton (N.J.) U., 1962-64, prof., 1964-73; dir. Woodrow Wilson Internat. Ctr. for Scholars, Washington, 1973-87; librarian Libr. of Congress, Washington, 1987—. Chmn. Bd. Fgn. Scholarships (Fulbright program), 1971-73, mem. 1973-76; vice-chmn. Atlantic Council's Working Group on the Successor Generation, 1982-86; trustee St. Alban's Sch., 1979-82; dir. Am. Assn. for the Advancement of Slavic Studies, 1968-71; spl. cons. to Chase Manhattan Bank on East-West Matters, 1971-73; vis. rsch. prof. to Inst. History of Acad. Scis. of USSR in Moscow, 1966-67, U. Helsinki, 1960-61, École des Hautes Études en Sciences Sociales, Paris, 1985, 88; vis. lectr. to various univs. in Europe and Asia. Author: Mikhailovsky and Russian Populism, 1958, The Icon and the Axe: An Interpretive History of Russian Culture, 1966, (Serbian transl., 1988, Japanese transl, 2000, Russina transl., 2001), The Arts of Russia, 1970, Fire in the Minds of Men: Origins of the Revolutionary Faith, 1980, (Italian transl., 1986), Russia Transformed: Breakthrough to Hope, Moscow, August 1991, 1992, The Face of Russia, 1998 (Russian transl., 2001); writer, host: (3-part TV series) The Face of Russia, 1998; mem. adv. bd. Fgn. Affairs, 1974-92, Theology Today, 1974-84; script writer and host of Humanities Film Forum, 1973; contbr. chpts. to books, numerous articles to profl. jours. Trustee John F. Kennedy Ctr. for Performing Arts, Ctr. Theol. Inquiry, Nat. Bldg. Mus., Woodrow Wilson Internat. Ctr. for Scholars, Am. Folklife Ctr.; bd. regents Nat. Libr. Medicine. 1st lt. U.S. Army, 1953-56. McCosh faculty fellow Princeton U., Guggenheim fellow, 1960-61; Rhodes scholar, 1950-53; Fulbright rsch. professor U. Helsinki, 1960-61; decorated Chevalier 1985 and Comdr. 1991 Order of Arts and Letters of France; recipient Gwanghwa medal Republic of Korea, 1991, Woodrow Wilson award Princeton U., 1992, Knight Comdr.'s Cross of Order of Merit, Fed. Republic of Germany, 1995, Vologda Universal Sci. Lib. award, 1999, Pushkin medal, 1999, Russian Orthodox medal, 1994, UCLA medal, 2000. Mem. Am. Philos. Soc., Am. Acad. Arts and Scis., Russian Acad. Scis., Cosmos Club, Phi Beta Kappa. Office: The Library of Congress 101 Independence Ave SE Washington DC 20540-0002*

BILLINTON, ROY, engineering educator; b. Leeds, Eng., Sept. 14, 1935; s. Edwin and Nettie (Billinton); m. Alice Joyce McKenna, July 21, 1956; children— Leslie, Kevin, Michael, Christopher, Jeffrey. B.Sc.E.E., U. Man., 1960, M.Sc., 1963; PhD, U. Sask., 1967, D.Sc., 1975. Journeyman electrician McCaine Electric, Winnipeg, Man., Can., 1956; mem. system operation dept. and system planning dept. Man. Hydro, from 1960; asst. prof. to prof., head dept. elec. engring. U. Sask., Saskatoon, 1964—; now assoc. dean pres. PowerComp Assocs., cons. Author: Power System Reliability Evaluation, 1970, (with R. J. Ringlee and A. J. Wood) Power System Reliability Calculations, 1973, (with C. Singh) System Reliability Modelling and Evaluation, 1977; (with R.N. Allan) Reliability Evaluation of Engineering Systems, 1983, Reliability Evaluation of Power Systems, 1984, (with R.N. Allan) Reliability of Large Electric Power Systems, 1988, (with R.N. Allan, L. Salvaderi) Applied Reliability Assessment in Electric Power Systems, 1990, (with W Li) Reliability Assessment of Electric Power Systems Using Monte Carlo Methods, 1994; also articles. Recipient Sir George Nelson award Engring. Inst. Can., 1965-67, Ross medal, 1972, Centennial Disting. Svc. award Can. Elect Assn., 1991; Disting. Researcher award U. Saskatchewan. Fellow IEEE (Outstanding Power Engring. Educator award 1992, McNaughton medal 1994, Third Millenium medal 2000, Outstanding Engr. Educator award 2001), Royal Soc. Can., Engring. Inst. Can., U.K. Safety and Reliability Soc., Can. Acad. Engring. Home: 3 McLean Crescent Saskatoon SK Canada S7J 2R6 Office: U Sask Dept Elec Engring Saskatoon SK Canada S7N 0W0

BILLMAN, IRWIN EDWARD, publishing company executive; s. Herman Frank and Ruth (Dutchen) B. BS in Econs, Wharton Sch., U. Pa., 1962. Asst. controller Whelan Drug Co., 1965-66; v.p., treas. Curtis Circulation Co., Phila., 1966-71; exec. v.p., COO Penthouse Internat. Ltd. & Gen. Media Internat. Ltd., 1971—81; pres., publisher Oui Mag., N.Y.C., 1981-82; pres. Billman Media Group; ptnr. Mag. Communications Cons. Pres. Global Distribution Svcs., Inc. Mem. Periodical and Book Assn. Am. (pres. 1977-81), Am. Circulation Execs. Soc. (pres. 1998-2000), Assn. Circulation Execs. (U.K.). Home: PO Box 350 Westhampton NY 11977-0350 Office: PO Box 850 Remsenburg NY 11960-0850

BILLNITZER, BONNIE JEANNE, nurse, gerontology specialist; b. Mar. 7, 1935; d. George Gottfried and Sarah Edna Elizabeth (Park) Haffelder; m. Harold R. Billnitzer, Apr. 28, 1956; children: J. Stephen, David A., John Mark, Timothy P., Michael M. BA in Psychology, U. Mich., 1977; ADN, U. Toledo, Ohio, 1989; BSN, Med. Coll. Ohio, Ohio, 1992. RN, Ohio; cert. gerontol. nurse, cert. cardiovascular nurse. Adminstrv. mgr. Med. Coll. Ohio Ambulatory Care Ctr., Toledo, 1972-79; cardiovascular nurse St. Vincent Med. Ctr., Toledo, 1988-92; case mgr. The Vis. Nurse Svc., Toledo, 1992-97; pvt. practice RN case mgr. Perrysburg, Ohio. Mem. credentialing com. for RN St. Vincent Med. Ctr., Toledo, 1991-92. Recipient Logan award for Clin. and Theoretical Excellence in Nursing, U. Toledo, 1989. Mem. AAUW, ANA, Ohio Nurses Assn., Toledo

Dist. Nurses Assn. (1st v.p. 1995-96), Am. Holistic Nurses Assn., Am. Assn. Critical Care Nurses, Internat. Order St. Luke the Physician. Lutheran. Avocations: music, computer rsch., reading, quilting, antiquing. Home: 1084 Eastbrook Dr Perrysburg OH 43551-1646

BILLS, ROBERT E(DGAR), emeritus psychology educator; b. Nutley, N.J., Dec. 15, 1916; s. Willis Minard and Leah Catherine (Condit) B.; m. Annie Tarleton Carley, Dec. 22, 1944; children: Mary Ann Bills Niles, Leah Catherine Bills Hawkins. BS, Western Ky. U., 1938; MA, U. Ky., 1946; EdD, Columbia U., 1948. Tchr. sci. Breathitt County (Ky.) Bd. Edn., 1938-42; tchr. Anchorage Bd. Edn. (Ky.), 1943-44, prin., 1944-45; critic tchr. sci. U. Ky. Coll. Edn., 1945-46; faculty Coll. Arts and Scis., 1948-52, chmn. div. biol. scis., 1950-51, assoc. prof., 1952-56; prof. psychology, chmn. dept. Auburn U., 1956-61; prof. ednl. psychology U. Ala., 1961-69, rsch. prof. edn., 1969-70, rsch. prof. emeritus, 1979—, asst. dean rsch., 1961-63; interim dean Coll. Edn., 1963-65, dean, 1965-69, dean emeritus, 1979—. Mem. coun. psychol. resources of S. Regional Edn. Bd., 1953-56; chmn. Ky. Bd. Examiners Psychologists, 1954-56; vis. prof. U. Fla., 1953, 54, Mich. State U., 1956, U. Wash., 1963; lectr. in field. Author: Education for Intelligence or Failure?, 1982; contbr. chpts. to books, articles in field to profl. jours. Bd. dirs. Southeastern Ednl. Corp., 1966-67; sec. Ala. Coalition for Better Edn., 1969-70, pres., 1971-72. Served with U.S. Army, 1943-44; with USCG Aux., 1982-99. Recipient Ednl. Press Assn. award for distinguished contbn. to ednl. journalism, 1982. Fellow APA (sec.-treas. divsn. 1963-66), Mid-South Edn. Rsch. Assn. (v.p. 1978, pres. 1979), ASCD (dir. 1962-64), U.S. Coast Guard Aux. (mem. nat. staff 1989-98), Sigma Xi, Kappa Delta Pi, Psi Chi, Phi Delta Kappa. Home: 3448 Tall Pines Cir Tuscaloosa AL 35405-5401

BILLS, ROBERT HOWARD, political party executive; b. North Conway, N.H., Jan. 13, 1944; s. Howard William and Mary Catherine (Jackson) B.; m. Donna Gail Florian; children: Emily Ida, Katherine Mary. Staff writer Weekly People Newspaper, Bklyn., 1970-74, Palo Alto, Calif., 1974-76; nat. sec. Socialist Labor Party, Sunnyvale, 1980—, mem. nat. exec. subcom., 1976-79. Office: Socialist Labor Party of Am PO Box 218 Mountain View CA 94042-0218

BILLUPS, CHAUNCEY, professional basketball player; b. Sept. 25, 1976; Student, U. Colo., 1997. Guard Boston Celtics, 1996-97, Toronto Raptors, 1997-98, Denver Nuggets, 1998-00, Minnesota Timberwolves, Minneapolis, 2000—. Named Second Team All-Am. AP. Avocation: music. Office: Minn Timberwolves 600 1st Ave North Minneapolis MN 55403-9801

BILLUPS, NORMAN FREDRICK, college dean, pharmacist, educator; b. Portland, Oreg., Oct. 15, 1934; s. John Alexander and Myrtle I. (Morris) B.; m. Shirley Mae Brooks, July 7, 1956; children: Tamra Mae, Timothy Fredrick. Student, Portland State U., 1952-55; BS in Pharmacy, Oreg. State U., 1958, MS in Pharmacy, 1961, PhD (Am. Found. Pharm. Edn. fellow), 1963. Instr. Oreg. State U., 1958-60, grad. asst., 1960-63; asso. prof. pharmacy U. Ky., 1963-73, prof., 1974-77; dean, prof. pharmacy Coll. Pharmacy, U. Toledo, 1977-00; pharmacist Ohio, 1961—. Dir. internat. adv. com. Pharm@Sea. Author: American Drug Index, ann, 1977—. Lay leader, chmn. pastor-parish com. local Meth. Ch. Recipient Rsch. Achievement award Am. Soc. Hosp. Pharmacists, 1975, Outstanding Svc. award Ky. Pharm. Assn., 1977; NIH rsch. fellow, 1962-63; Dean Norman F. Billups Disting. Svc. award established by U. Toledo Pharmacy Alumni Assn., 1992. Mem. Am. Assn. Colls. Pharmacy (Lyman award 1971), Am. Pharm. Assn., Ohio Pharm. Assn. (bd.dirs., Beal award 2001), Ohio Soc. Health Care Pharmacists, Toledo Acad. Pharmacy (bd. dirs., Pharmacist of Yr. 1997), Coun. Ohio Colls. Pharmacy (chmn. bd. trustees, chmn. coun.), Ky. Col. Commn., Sigma Xi, Phi Kappa Phi (pres. U. Toledo chpt.), Rho Chi (chpt. advisor, nat. exec. com.). Phi Lambda Sigma (chpt. adv.), Kappa Psi (grand coun. dep., nat. officer, named Outstanding Alumnus), Lambda Kappa Sigma (hon. mem., nat. patron). Office: Univ Toledo Coll Pharmacy 2801 W Bancroft St Toledo OH 43606-3328 E-mail: snbillups@aol.com.

BILLY, BAHE, soil scientist, educator; b. Leupp, Ariz., Jan. 4, 1937; s. John and Ethel (Spencer) Billie; m. Florence Boyd, Dec. 17, 1965; children: Julie, Cristina, Brian, Tsosie, Aldean, Darryle, Jenny. BS in Agronomy, Utah State U., 1960; MS in Agrl. Chemistry and Soils, U. Ariz., 1964, PhD, 1970; student, Dallas Inst. Mortuary Sci., 1979. Asst. prof. Brigham Young U., Provo, Utah, 1970—72; soil scientist Navajo Agr. Product Industry, Farmington, N.Mex., 1973—78; dean of instrn. Navajo C.C., Shiprock, N.Mex., 1979—82; agronomist Navajo Tribe, Window Rock, Ariz., 1982—89; soil conservationist Bureau of Indian Affairs, Chinle, Ariz., 1989—96, soil scientist Gallup, N.Mex., 1997—98, soil conservationist Shiprock, N.Mex., 1999—. Math instr. Dine Coll., Tsaile, Ariz., 1996—97; instr. Rough Rock Cmty. Sch., Rough Rock, Ariz., 1998—99. Exhibited in group shows, 2000, 2001. Scholar, Standard Oil Co. Calif., 1955—56. Mem.: Am. Soc. Agronomy. Avocations: singing, songwriting, artist, poetry writer, interpreter. Home: 38 Rd 6405 Kirtland NM 87417 Office: Bureau of Indian Affairs PO Box 3538 Shiprock NM 87420 Fax: 505-368-3312. E-mail: bahebilly@bia.gov.

BILLY, DENNIS JOSEPH, priest; b. N.Y.C., Aug. 26, 1953; s. Michael and Lillian (Miano) B.. AB, Dartmouth Coll., 1975; MRE, 1979; MDiv, Mt. St. Alphonsus Sem., 1981; ThD, Harvard U., 1985; MA, U. Toronto, Ont., Can., 1987; MMRSc, U. Louvain, 1988; STD, The Pontifical U. St. Thomas, 1992; DMin, Grad. Theol. Found., Ind., 1999. Ordained priest Roman Cath. Ch., 1980. Adj. prof. Coll. Notre Dame, Balt., 1985-86, Loyola Coll., Balt., 1986; prof. Accademia Alfonsiana, Rome, 1988—. Author: 16 books; editor; contbr. articles to theol. publs. Mem.: Spiritual Dirs. Internat., Am. Acad. Religion, Cath. Theol. Soc. Am. Avocations: reading, music, jogging, sports. Home: Via Merulana 31 CP 2458 00100 Rome Italy Office: Acad Alfonsiana Via Merulana 31 CP 2458 00100 Rome Italy

BILLY, GEORGE JOHN, library director; b. Rahway, N.J., Apr. 10, 1940; s. George and Marie (Zeleznik) B.; m. Valerie Jean McGreevy, July 19, 1969; children: Margaret, Christine. BA in History, Rutgers U., 1962; MLS, Pratt Inst., 1968; MA in HIstory, Adelphi U., 1973; PhD in History, CUNY, 1982. Ref. libr. Buffalo and Erie County Pub. Libr., 1968-70; acquisitions and ref. libr. Queensborough Community Coll., Bayside, N.Y., 1970-76; reader svcs. libr. U.S. Mcht. Marine Acad. Libr., Kings Point, N.Y., 1977-84, chief libr., 1984—. Adj. prof. Palmer Sch. Libr. Info. Sci., C.W. Post/Long Island U., Greenvale, N.Y., 1983—. Author: Palmerston's Foreign Policy: 1848, 1993; compiler booklets in field. Mem. Selection com. Sch. Bd., Manhasset, 1992-94. Charles Freeman Meml. scholar, 1958-62, Buffalo and Erie County Pub. Libr. scholar, 1967-68. Mem. ALA, Assn. Coll. and Rsch. Librs., Spl. Librs. Assn. (transp. divsn.), L.I. Coun. Acad. Libr. Dirs., Nassau County Libr. Assn., Beta Phi Mu. Office: US Mcht Marine Acad 300 Steamboat Rd Kings Point NY 11024-1699

BILLY, GERRY DEE, sheriff, law enforcement instructor; b. Zanesville, Ohio, Feb. 6, 1951; s. Paul and Jean (Drake) B.; m. Mary Lynn Bibart, June 19, 1976; children: Angela Mishonne, Paul James. Assoc. Applied Sci. cum laude, Muskingum Area Tech. Coll., Zanesville, 1975; BA cum laude, Ohio Dominican Coll., 1980. Detective Muskingum Sheriff Dept., Zanesville, 1974-76; agent-in-charge Tri-County Anti-Crime Program, Newark, Ohio, 1976-78; investigator Porter, Wright Law Office, Columbus, Ohio, 1978-80; sheriff Licking County, Newark, 1981—; instr. criminal justice law enforcement Central Ohio Tech. Coll., Newark, 1978—; cons. Varasso & Assocs. Architects/Planners, Newark, 1981—. Asst. dir. Licking County Spl. Olympics, 1980—; chmn. Ohio Police Olympics, Columbus, 1976—; bd. dirs. Licking County chpt. ARC, 1983—; trustee Licking County Hist. Soc., 1982—; apptd. mem. Commn. on Prison Crowding, 1984. Served as mil. police investigator AUS, 1971-73. Named Outstanding Young Man of Am., U.S. Jaycees, 1981-83, Outstanding Young Man of Licking County, Newark Area Jaycees, 1982; recipient Disting. Service award Newark Area Jaycees, 1980-82, Appreciation award Ohio Spl. Olympics, 1983, cert. Accomodation, Am. Legion, 1983, Presidential award of Honor, Granville Jaycees, 1983, Disting. Service award U.S. Jaycees, 1982, Appreciation award Nat. Child Safety Council, 1981, Outstanding Instr. award Muskingum County Law Enforcement Acad., 1976. Mem. Narcotic Assn. of Regional Coordinating Officers of Ohio (pres. 1984—, Exec. Service award 1982), Buckeye State Sheriff's Assn. (tng. coordinator 1982—), Nat. Sheriff's Assn., Ohio Auto Theft Investigator's Assn., U.S. Dept. Justice Drug Trafficking Commn. (law enforcement coordinating com.), Am. Correctional Assn., Am. Jail Assn. (speaker nat. conf. 1985), VFW. Republican. Lutheran. Lodges: Masons, Honorable Order Ky. Colonels. Avocations: golfing, basketball, hunting, painting, design. Home: 14 Richards Rd Newark OH 43055-2159 Office: Licking County Sheriff's Dept 155 E Main St Newark OH 43055-5434 E-mail: sheriffbilly@alink.com.

BILOW, HOWARD L. health care company executive; b. Providence, R.I. BSBA, Boston U., 1973, MBA, 1975. V.p. corp. mktg. and managed care Fresenius Med. Care, Lexington, Mass., 1990-99; co-founder, exec. v.p. Am. Renal Assocs., Inc., Danvers, Mass., 1999—, also bd. dirs. Co-founder, bd. dirs. Renaissance Health Care, Inc., Westminster, Co., 1996-99; co-founder Optimal Renal Care, 1996. Office: American Renal Assocs Inc 5 Cherry Hill Dr Danvers MA 01923-2500 Fax: 508-650-1279. E-mail: hbilow@americanrenal.com.

BILSON, WESLEY, healthcare company executive; b. L.A., July 25, 1933; s. George and Hattie Bilson; m. Judith Wolfe, Sept. 17, 1995; children: Meredith, Amy, Jeffrey, David, Gregory, Jessica. BA, UCLA, 1955. Asst. film editor and writer Desilu Prodns., Hollywood, Calif., 1959-62; pres. W & W Hosp. Devel. Corp., Beverly Hills, Calif., 1962-65, Diversified Health Svcs., Inc., Beverly Hills, 1965-72, Druthers Agy., Inc., Marina Del Rey, 1972-78; chmn. Delano Regional Med. Ctr., Delano, Calif., 1978—92; pres. Delmed Corp., Pacific Palisades, 1992—, Cardiac Renewal Ctrs. Am., Pacific Palisades, 1999—. Health care bus. cons., 1965—; bd. dirs. Ecoly Internat., Inc., Chatsworth, Calif.; pres. United Hosp. Assn., L.A., 1986. Advisor to pres. of Soviet Union, 1988-92; bd. dirs. Kehelat Israel, Pacific Palisades, 1998—; founding mem. Bus. Execs. Move for Vietnam Peace, Washington, 1963-72. 1st lt. USAF, 1956-59. Mem. Riviera Country Club. Jewish. Avocations: political policy issues, skiing, tennis. Office: Demed Corp 881 Alma Real Dr Pacific Palisades CA 90272

BILTONEN, RODNEY LINCOLN, biochemistry and pharmacology educator; b. Ont., Can., Aug. 24, 1937; came to U.S., 1941; s. Frank Emil and Frances Cecilia (Castren) B.; m. Margaret Jane Kobel, Aug. 6, 1960; children— Michael Andrew, Eric Franklin AB, Harvard Coll., 1959; PhD, U. Minn., 1965. Asst. prof. Johns Hopkins U., Balt., 1966-72; assoc. prof. biochemistry and pharmacology U. Va., Charlottesville, 1972-77, prof., 1977-2003, prof. emeritus, 2003—, assoc. dean, 1979-81, assoc. provost, 1981-84. Vis. prof. Gulbenkian Inst., Portugal, 1970-71, U. Lund, Sweden, 1971, Cayetano, Lima, Peru, 1976, U. N.C., Chapel Hill, 1980, CNR, Genoa, Italy, 1993, The Technical U. Denmark, 1995; James Disting. prof. physics St. Francis Xavier U., Antigonish, N.S., 1984; cons. in field. Assoc. editor Biophys. Jour., 1991-95; mem. editl. bd. Chemistry and Physics of Lipids, 1995—; contbr. numerous articles to profl. jours. Recipient G.T. Walker award, Sigma Xi, 1965, Huffman Meml. award, Calorimetry Conf., 1989; fellow, NIH, 1965—66; grantee, NSF, 1968—99, NIH, 1970—. Fellow: Biophys. Soc. (councilor 1984—86); mem.: Am. Calorimetry Conf. (chmn. 1976—77), Am. Soc. Biol. Chemistry and Molecular Biology. Office: Univ Va Dept Pharmacology 1300 Jefferson Park Ave Charlottesville VA 22908-0735

BILYEU, GARY EDWARD, government official; b. Forest City, Iowa, Nov. 9, 1954; s. Roy Marcellus and Norma Jean (Hillesland) B.; m. Lonnie Jo Ann Bartel, Apr. 6, 1974; children: Rachel, Rebekah, Abraham, Deborah. AA, North Iowa Area Cmty. Coll., 1975. Cert. gen. real property appraiser, Iowa. Field appraiser Mason City (Iowa) Assesor, 1976-77, deputy assessor, 1977-80, Cerro Gordo County, Mason City, 1980-82; assessor Story County, Nevada, Iowa, 1982—; assessment adminstrn. specialist IAAO, 1998—. Author: Reference Handbook for Iowa's Property Tax System, 1999; contbr. articles to profl. jours. Apptd. pub. mem. Legis. Task Force to study Iowa's Sys. of State and Local Taxation, 1997. Mem. Internat. Assn. of Assessing Officers (assessment adminstrn. specialist designation 1998, sect. chair 1995-96). Mem. Assembly of God. Avocations: sports, basketball. Office: Story County 900 6th St Nevada IA 50201-2004

BILZ, LAURIE S. nursing educator; b. Hackensack, N.J., Nov. 27, 1951; d. Richard F. and Lila (Russell) B. AAS, Bergen Community Coll., Paramus, N.J., 1972; BSN, Dominican Coll., 1990; cert. British health care system, Wroxton Coll., Eng., 1990; MSN, Seton Hall U., 1992; MPA, L.I. U., 1994. RN, N.J.; cert. med.-surg. nurse; cert. clin. specialist in med.-surg. nursing. RN Pascack Valley Hosp., Westwood, N.J.; clin. nursing instr. Fairleigh Dickinson U., Teaneck, N.J., 1995—. Clin. nursing instr. Bergen C.C., 1993-97. Mem. ANA, N.J. Nurse's Assn., NLN. Home: 509 Bergen Ave Washington Township NJ 07676-5244

BIMSTEIN, PHILLIP KENT, composer; b. Chgo., Nov. 20, 1947; s. LeRoy Steele and Helen Agnes B.; m. Carol Ann Holmberg, Sept. 21, 1985 (div. Mar. 1990). MusB, Chgo. Conservatory, 1972. Composer in residence Am. Dance Festival, Durham, N.C., 1993; exec. dir. New Music Utah, Springdale, 1991-94; New Residencies composer in residence Meet the Composer, N.Y.C., 1997-99; mayor Town of Springdale (Utah), 1994—. Bd. dirs. Utah Humanities Coun., Salt Lake City, Utah League Cities and Towns, Am. Music Ctr. Composer (mandolin quartet) the Louie Louie Variations, 1989, (chamber ensemble) Garland Harschi's Cows, 1990, (wind quintet) The Bushy Wushy Rag, 2000, (string quartet/wind quintet) Dark Winds Rising, 1992, (wind quintet) Casino, 1996, (oboe solo) Half Moon at Checkerboard Mesa, 1997, (string quartet) Refuge, 1999, (voice and harmonica) Larkin Gifford's Harmonica, 2001. Pres. Zion Canyon Arts & Humanities, Springdale, 1990-94; governing bd. Family Now, Salt Lake City, 1995-2000; com. mem. Washington County Econ. Devel. Coun., St. George, Utah, 1998-2001; v.p. Am. Music Ctr., 2002—; chmn. Utah Humanities Coun., 2003—, The Mesa, 2003—. Mem. Am. Music Ctr. Avocations: hiking, meditation, yoga. Home: PO Box 301 Springdale UT 84767 Fax: 435-772-3830. E-mail: phillip@bimstein.com.

BINDENAGEL, JAMES DALE, foundation executive; b. Huron, S.D, June 30, 1949; s. Gordon Dean and Patricia Jean (Williams) B.; m. Jean Kathleen Lundfelt, Dec. 26, 1971; children: Annamarie, Carl Jakob. BA, U. Ill, 1971, MPA, 1977. Officer U.S. Embassy U.S. Dept. State, Seoul, Republic of Korea, 1975—77; with U.S. Consulate, Bremen, Germany, 1977-79; econ. officer Office Ctrl. European Affairs U.S. Dept. State, Washington, 1980-83; polit. officer Am. Embassy, Bonn, Germany, 1983-86; acting dir. Can. affairs U.S. Dept. State, 1988-89, 1988-89; dep. chief mission Am. Embassy, Berlin, 1989-90; divsn. chief developing countries and trade orgns. U.S. Dept. State Econ. and Bus. Affairs Bur., 1991; dir. Rockwell Internat., 1991-92; dir. Office Ctrl. European Affairs U.S. Dept. State, Washington, 1992-94; dep. chief mission Am. Embassy, Bonn, Germany, 1994-96, chargé d'affaires, acting amb., 1994-97; sr. coord. New Transatlantic Agenda German Marshall Fund, 1997-98; dir. Washington Conf. on Holocaust-era Assets; amb. spl. envoy for Holocaust issues, 1999—2002; spl. negotiator Conflict Diamonds, 2002—03; v.p. Chgo. Coun. on Fgn. Rels., 2003—. Bd. trustees Remembrance, Responsibility and Future Fund, 1999-2002. Capt. USAR, 1971-74. Recipient Disting. Honor award, U.S. State Dept., 2000, Commanders Cross of the Order of Merit, Germany, 2001. Mem.: Woodstock Bus. Conf., Coun. on Fgn. Rels., Am. Coun. on Germany, Am. Polit. Sci. Assn. (Congl. fellow 1987—88, Nat. Performance award 1998), Pi Sigma Alpha. Roman Catholic. Avocations: tennis, hiking. Office: 116 S Michigan Ave 10th Fl Chicago IL 60613 E-mail: JDBindenagel@ccfr.org.

BINDER, BETTYE B. author, lecturer; b. New Rochelle, N.Y., Feb. 12, 1939; d. Alex and Leah (Binder) B. BA, Barnard Coll., 1960; MA in Pub. Law and Govt., Columbia U., 1962. Spkr. Whole Life Expo, 1985-97; exec. prodr. Brain and Mind Symposium, L.A., 1992-94. Author: (books) Past Life Regression Guidebook, 1985, 3rd edit., 7th printing, 1999, Past Lives Present Karma Workbook, 1985, 92, Discovering Past Lives and Other Dimensions, 1994, (mini mag.) Who Were You in Past Lives?, 1992, (video) Meditative Techniques, Home Study Guide to Past Life Recall, 1998, The Transformation Workbook: Life Lessons as Challenges for Personal Growth, 2000, Meditations About Lemuna, 2002. Coord. Students for Kennedy-Johnson, N.Y. State, 1960; rschr., writer, Dem. Nat. Com., Washington, 1963-65; assoc. dir. Fight Inflation Together, L.A., 1973-76. Mem. Internat. Assn. Regression Rsch. and Therapies (bd. dirs. 1991-97, pres. 1993-97). Democrat. Jewish. Avocations: science fiction, ancient history, cats. Office: PO Box 4011 Culver City CA 90231-4011 E-mail: BettyeBinder@earthlink.net.

BINDER, DAVID FRANKLIN, lawyer, author; b. Beaver Falls, Pa., Aug. 1, 1935; s. Walter Carl and Jessie Maivis (Bliss) B.; m. Deana Jacqueline Pines, Dec. 25, 1971; children: April, Bret. BA, Geneva Coll., 1956; JD, Harvard U., 1959. Bar: Pa. 1960, U.S. Ct. Appeals (3rd cir.) 1963, U.S. Supreme Ct. 1967. Law clk. to chief justice Pa. Supreme Ct., 1959-61; counsel Fidelity Mut. Life Ins. Co., Phila., 1964-66; ptnr. Bennett, Bricklin & Saltzburg, Phila., 1967-68; mem. Richter, Syken, Ross, and Binder, Phila., 1969-72, Raynes, McCarty, Binder, Ross and Mundy, Phila., 1972—. Mem. faculty Pa. Coll. Judiciary; judge pro tempore Phila. Common Pleas Ct., 1991-97; lectr., course planner Pa. Bar Inst.; mem. civil procedural rules com., ad hoc. com. and permanent com. on evidence Supreme Ct. Pa. Author: Hearsay Handbook, 1975, ann. supplements, 4th edit., 2001, Binder on Pennsylvania Evidence, 1999, 3d edit., 2003. Recipient Disting. Alumnus award Geneva Coll., 1981. Mem. ABA, Pa. Bar Assn., Phila. Bar Assn., Assn. Trial Lawyers Am. (lectr.), Pa. Trial Lawyers Assn., Harvard Law Sch. Assn., Am. Bd. Trial Advs., Am. Coll. Trial Lawyers, Union League. Home: 1412 Flat Rock Rd Narberth PA 19072-1216 Office: Raynes McCarty Binder Ross and Mundy 1845 Walnut St Ste 2000 Philadelphia PA 19103-4767 E-mail: dfbinder@raynesmccarty.com.

BINDER, GORDON M. venture capitalist; b. St. Louis, 1935; Degree in elec. engring., Purdue U., 1957; MBA, Harvard U., 1962. With Litton Industries, 1962-64; fin. mgmt. Ford Motor Co., 1964-69; CFO Sys. Devel. Corp., 1971-81; v.p., CFO Amgen, Thousand Oaks, Calif., 1982-88, CEO, 1988-2000, chmn. bd., 1990-2000; mng. dir. Coastview Capital LLC, L.A., 2001—. Baker scholar Harvard U. Office: Coastview Capital LLC Ste 1850 11111 Santa Monica Blvd Los Angeles CA 90025

BINDER, L. JAMES, magazine editor, retired, journalist; b. Jackson, Mich., June 21, 1926; s. Leonard George and Ethel Cecile (Lilly) B.; m. Margery Elizabeth Rose, Sept. 6, 1950; children: Timothy James, Michael Paul, Douglas Harold. BS, Central Mich. U., 1952. Editor Wingfoot Clan, Goodyear Tire & Rubber Co., 1952-54, Wayne (Mich.) Eagle, 1954-55; news editor Pontiac (Mich.) Press, 1955-57; editor, newsman AP, 1957-60; state editor Detroit News, 1960-67; editor-in-chief Army mag., Washington, 1967-93; corr., book reviewer Nat. Observer, 1962-67; v.p publs. Assn. U.S. Army, 1992-94; ret., 1993. Author: Lemnitzer: A Soldier for His Time, 1997; editor: Front and Ctr., 1991; contbr. articles to various publs. Served with USN, 1944-46; with USAR, 1950-54. Recipient George Washington Honor medal Freedoms Found., 1975, George Washington award editorial, 1974, 76 Mem. VFW, Am. Soc. Mag. Editors, Soc. Profl. Journalists, Cosmos Club, Nat. Press Club, Detroit Press Club, Ends of Earth Club, Soc. of Midland Authors, Am. Legion, Tin Can Sailors. Methodist. Home: 681 N Golden Sands Dr Mears MI 49436-9655 also: 12728 Inverness Way Woodbridge VA 22192-5036 E-mail: ptsable@aol.com.

BINDER, MADELINE DOTTI, retail executive; b. Chgo., Oct. 7, 1942; d. Martin and Anne (Sweet) Binder; children: Mark Nathan, Marla Susan. BEd, Nat. Coll. Edn., 1964, MS, 1972, MS in Human Svcs-Counseling, 1993. Tchr. Rochester Schs. (Minn.), 1963-64, Orange County Schs., Orlando, Fla., 1967-68; reading cons. Palatine (Ill.) Schs., 1972-73; instr. Parent Effective Tng., Wilmette, Ill., 1974-76; tchr. Effectiveness Tng., 1974-76; pres. Profls. Diversified, Wilmette, 1976-89; remedial and enrichment reading tchr. Waukegan (Ill.) Pub. Schs., 1986; pres. Lifeline, 1989-90; mgmt. cons. World Wide Diamonds Assn., Schaumburg, Ill., 1979-89; Pearl direct distbr. Amway Corp., Ada, Mich., 1976-94; exec. distbr. NU Skin, 1992; distbr. Starlight Internat., 1994—. Psychotherapist, 1993-97. Author: Organic Gardening, 1975, The Go-Getters Planner, 1986, Singles Guide to Chicagoland, 1995, Divorce: Parent and Child, 2002. Leader, Camp Fire Girls, Evanston, Ill., 1963, 75. Ednl. scholar Nat. Coll. Edn., 1971. Mem. Phi Delta Kappa, Alpha Delta Omega. E-mail: weightloss1@earthlink.net., sunshineandlight@earthlink.net., livethegoodlifenow@earthlink.net.

BINDER, MILDRED KATHERINE, retired public welfare agency executive; b. York, Pa., Jan. 5, 1918; d. Jemie Irving and Emma Jane (Billet) B. BA in Sociology magna cum laude, Hood Coll., 1940. Sec., mgr. Stock's Appliances, York, 1940-42; from caseworker, supr. to exec. dir. York County Bd. Assistance/Pa. Dept. Public Welfare, 1942-83; ret., 1983. Past exec. com. York County Employment and Tng. Com.; past mem. dept. task forces state Social Service Delivery to Client Info. System, also mem. state ops. rev. bd.; co-chair Cmty. Dialogue Com., 1968-69; human svcs. planning coalition United Way, 1978-83, chair coun. agy. execs., 1967-71, 76-78; past mem. consumer adv. couns. Gen. Telephone, Met. Edison. Bd. dirs. Literacy Coun. York County, 1985-86; active York County Human Svcs. Adv. Com., 1983-87, York county Area Agy. on Aging Adv. Com., 1989-95. Recipient Commendation award Pa. gov., Pa. Ho. of Reps. Mem. AAUW (bd. dirs. York br. 1984-96), Am. Public Welfare Assn., York County Hist. Soc. (bd. dirs 1989-97), York Transp. Club (bd. dirs. 1987-91), Coll. Club York (bd. dirs. 1994—), Hood Coll. Club (pres. 1993-97). Home: 1611 W Market St York PA 17404-5416

BINDER, RICHARD ALLEN, hematologist, oncologist; b. Boston, Aug. 26, 1937; s. Harry Aron and Beatrice (Seltzer) B.; m. Elaine F. Kotell; children: Mark Stephen, Jonathan Stuart. BSChemE, Northeastern U., Boston, 1960; MD, Tufts U., Boston, 1964. Diplomate Am. Bd. Internal Medicine, also sub-bds. in Hematology and Med. Oncology. Intern in medicine/resident in medicine New Eng. Med. Ctr., Boston, 1964-66; resident in medicine Columbia Presbyn. Hosp., N.Y.C., 1966-67; fellow in hematology Mt. Sinai Hosp., N.Y.C., 1967-68; instr. Tufts U. Sch. Medicine, 1970-71; asst. prof. Georgetown U., Washington, 1971-75, assoc. clin. prof. medicine, 1975-78, clin. prof. medicine, 1978—; v.p. Inova Health Sys., 1994-95; med. dir. Inova Fairfax Cancer Ctr., 1998—2002, Washington Acad. Medicine, 2003—. Assoc. chmn. dept. medicine Inova Fairfax Hosp., 1978—, v.p. med. staff, 1989-91, pres. med. staff, 1992-94, v.p. physician affairs, 1995-96, chmn. cancer steering com., 1997-2000; bd. dirs. Inova Hosp., Inova Health Sys. Found. Bd., Hospice Palliative Care Metro. Washington; active Inova Hosps. Bd., 1988-95, Inova Health Sys. Bd., 1992-95, Hospice of No. Va. Bd., 1993-2001, vice-chmn., 1995-97, chmn. 1998-99; med. adv. bd. Lymphoma Found., 1999-. Editor Hematology Rev.-Family Practice, 1979; contbr. articles to profl. jours. Maj. U.S. Army, 1968-70. Recipient Golden Apple, Georgetown U., 1975, 76, Vicentennial medal Georgetown U., 1991, Excellence in Teaching award Fairfax Hosp., 1994—. Fellow ACP; mem. Am. Soc. Hematology, Am. Soc. Clin. Oncology, Fairfax Hosp. Assn. (bd. dirs. 1988-95), Alumni Assn. Tufts U. (bd. dirs. 1990—), Tufts U. Med. Sch. Alumni Assn. (bd. dirs. 1998—). Home: 6704 Bradley Blvd Bethesda MD 20817-3045 Office: Fairfax No Va Hematology Oncology 8503 Arlington Blvd Fairfax VA 22031

BINDER, SHELDON CARL, surgeon; b. Boston, Sept. 18, 1934; s. Abraham and Ida (Goldman) B.; m. Marilyn R. Taylor, June 2, 1962; children: Dawn N., Michael L. AB summa cum laude, Harvard U., Cambridge, Mass., 1956; MD cum laude, Harvard U., Boston, 1960. Diplomate Am. Bd. Surgery. Intern and resident in surgery Mass. Gen. Hosp., Boston, 1960-67; fellow in surg. oncology Mem. Sloan-Kettering Cancer Ctr., N.Y.C., 1967-68; attending surgeon Tufts-New Eng. Med. Ctr., Boston, 1968-76, Mt. Auburn Hosp., Cambridge, 1979-93; asst. prof. Tufts U. Sch. Medicine, Boston, 1968-76; chief surgery Youngstown (Ohio) Hosp. Assn., 1977-78, VA Med. Ctr., Ft. Meade, S.D., 1994; prof. Northeastern Ohio Univs. Coll. Medicine, Rootstown, 1977-78; instr. Harvard U. Med. Sch., 1978-93; assoc. prof. U. S.D. Sch. Medicine, Sioux Falls, 1994; part-time pvt. practice Belmont, Mass., 1994—. Contbr. articles and monographs to med. jours. Lt. comdr. USPHS, 1962-64. Fellow ACS; mem. Assn. for Acad. Surgery, Boston Surg. Soc., Am. Head and Neck Soc., Soc. for Surgery Alimentary Tract, Soc. Surg. Oncology, Am, Gastroent. Assn., New Eng. Cancer Soc., Am. Soc. Gen. Surgeons. Republican. Jewish. Avocations: ship model building, sailing, fishing. Home and Office: 41 Bow Rd Belmont MA 02478-3504

BINDER, STEVEN F. publishing executive; Assoc. pub. Golf Link; sr. acct. mgr. Golf Illsutrated; v.p., advt. dir. ELLE Mag.; v.p., exec. pub. Mirabella; v.p. corp. sales, regional sales dir. Hacjette Filipacchi, 1995; assoc. pub. Allure Mag., 1999—2001; sr. v.p., pub. Golf Digest Mag., 2001—. Office: The Golf Digest Cos 5520 Park Ave Trumbull CT 06611

BINDER, SUE, federal agency administrator; BS, McGill U.; MD, Tufts U. Med. Sch. Bd. certified in Internal Medicine. Commd. officer U.S. Pub. Health Svc.; officer, Epidemic Intelligence Svc. CDC, chief Childhood Lead Poisoning Prevention branch, assoc. dir. med. sci., Divsn. Parasitic Disease, Nat. Ctr.

Infectious Diseases, dir. Injury Ctr., 2000—. Contbr. articles to profl. jours. Recipient Arthur S. Fleming award for Excellence in Mgmt. Office: CDC Nat Ctr Injury Prevention and Control 4770 Buford Hwy NE K02 Atlanta GA 30340

BINDLEY, WILLIAM EDWARD, pharmaceutical executive; b. Terre Haute, Ind., Oct. 6, 1940; s. William F. and Gertrude (Lynch) B.; children: William Franklin, Blair Scott, Sally Ann. BS, Purdue U., 1961; grad. wholesale mgmt. program, Stanford U., 1966. Asst. treas. Controls Co. Am., Melrose Park, Ill., 1962-65; vice-chmn. E.H. Bindley & Co., Terre Haute, 1965-68; pres., chmn. bd., CEO Bindley Western Industries, Inc., Indpls., 1968—. Scholl scholarship guest lectr. Loyola U., Chgo., 1982; guest lectr. Young Pres. Orgn., Palm Springs, Calif. and Dallas, 1981, 82, 84, Ctr. for Entrepreneurs, Indpls., 1983, Purdue U., West Lafayette, Inc., De Pauw U., Greencastle, Ind., disting. lectr. Georgetown U., Washington, 1989—, mem. adv. bd.; bd. dirs. Key Bank NA, Cleve., Shoe Carnival, Inc.; former owner basketball team Ind. Pacers. State dir. Bus. for Reagan-Bush, Washington and Indpls., 1980; trustee Marian Coll., Indpls., Indpls. United Way, St. Vincent Hosp., Indpls.; bd. dirs. Indpls. Entrepreneurship Acad., Nat. Enterpreneurship Found., U.S. Ski Team, chmn. fin., exec. com. mem.; mem. adv. bd. Rose Hulman Inst. Tech.; mem. pres.'s coun. Purdue U., dean's adv. bd. Named Hon. Ky. Col., 1980, Sagamore of the Wabash, Gov. Orr, State of Ind., 1989, Entrepreneur of Yr., State of Ind., 1992. Mem. Young Pres. Orgn. (area dir., chmn. 1982, award 1983), Nat. Wholesale Druggists Assn. (dir. 1981-84, Svc. award 1984), Purdue U. Alumni Assn. (life), Woodstock Club, Meridian Hills Countryn Club. Republican. Roman Catholic. Avocations: skiing; tennis; golf; boating. Address: Bindley Western Ind 8909 Purdue Rd Indianapolis IN 46268-3146 Office: Bindley Western Industries Inc Ste 300 8909 Purdue Rd Indianapolis IN 46268-3146

BINDON, JAMES ROBERT, anthropology educator; b. San Francisco, Nov. 23, 1947; s. Richard Edward and Maxene Winifred Bindon; m. Kathleen Ranney, June 28, 1969; 1 child, Michael. AA in Anthropology, Coll. of San Mateo, 0191; AB in Anthropology with distinction, U. Calif., Berkeley, 1973; MA in Anthropology, Pa. State U., 1975, PhD in Anthropology, 1981. Asst. prof. of anthropology U. of Ala., Tuscaloosa, 1978—86, assoc. prof. of anthropology, 1986—92, prof. of anthropology, 1992—, chmn., dept. of anthropology, 1993—98, leadership bd. fellow Coll. Arts and Scis., 2002—. Contbr. articles to profl. jours. Cub/scoutmaster Boy Scouts of Am., Tusclaoosa, 1986—93. With USN, 1967—68. Recipient diabetes among the Miss. Choctaw, Nat. Inst. of Diabetes and Digestive and Kidney Diseases, 1991, Social Support and CHD Risk Factors: A Cmty. Study, Nat. Heart, Lung, and Blood Inst., 1993—96, Diabetes and modernization among Samoan Americans, Nat. Inst. of Diabetes and Digestive and Kidney Diseases, 1992, pPhysiol. stress and blood pressure among Filipino immigrants, NIH, 2000—. Fellow: Am. Assn. of Phys. Anthropologists (assoc. editor of the am. jour. of phys. anthropology 1993—97), Human Biology Assn. (program com. mem. 2002—); mem.: Am. Anthrop. Assn. (v.p. and editor of the communicator 1988—90, sec./treas. 1991—93, exec. program com. mem. 1993—94). Avocations: aerobic machines, blues guitar. Office: U Ala 16 ten Hoor Bldg Tuscaloosa AL 35487-0210 Personal E-mail: jbindon@tenhoor.as.ua.edu. E-mail: jbindon@tenhoor.as.ua.edu.

BINDSCHADLER, DAVID E. mathematician, department chairman, application developer; b. Pitts., Oct. 16, 1948; s. Ernest and Madora Bindschadler; m. Valerie Yvette Verreault, May 27, 1972; children: Michael David, Kevin Richard. BS in math., Ohio State U., Columbus, 1970; MA in math., Ind. U., Bloomington, 1973, PhD in math., 1976. Asst. to assoc. prof. Wayne State U., Detroit, 1976—85; sr. systems engr. Electronic Data Sys., Troy, Mich., 1985—97, Unigraphics Solutions, Troy, 1997—99; chair math. and computer sci. dept. Lawrence Tech. U., Southfield, Mich., 1999—. Presenter at profl. conf. Am. Math. Soc., 1977—, Soc. Indsl. and Applied Math., 1977—85; CAD/CAM trainer Electronic Data Sys.; judge Grand award Computer Sci. Internat. Sci. and Engring. Fair, Detroit, 2000. Contbr. articles to profl. jours. Coach Huntington Woods Pk. and Recreation, Mich., 1985, 1989; parent sponsor, Future Problem Solvers of Am. Berkley Pub. Sch., Mich., 1990, 1993; Sunday sch. tchr. First Presbyn. Ch., Royal Oak, Mich., 1993—94. Recipient cert. of appreciation, Berkley Pub. Sch., 1987. Mem.: Soc. for Indsl. and Applied Math., Am. Math. Soc. Achievements include development of condition for symmetries of area minimizing surfaces; invention of developable surface design tool. Avocations: chess, strategy games, racquetball. Office: Lawrence Tech U 21000 West Ten Mile Rd Southfield MI 48075

BINER, BULENT SULEYMAN, materials scientist, educator; b. Izmir, Turkey, Sept. 15, 1951; s. Lutfu and Mucella (Bayar) Biner; m. Zulal Kafali, Dec. 29, 1976. MSc, Istanbul Tech. U., TURKEY, 1973—73; PhD, Aston U., Birmingham, Eng., 1981; MBA, Iowa State U., Ames, 1996. Foundry rsch. metallurgist Turkish Iron and Steel Works, Karabuk, Turkey, 1973—76; postdoctoral rsch. fellow McMaster U., Hamilton, Canada, 1981—83; asst. prof. Bradley U., Peoria, Ill., 1984—88; assoc. rschr. Ames Nat. Lab. USDOE, Ames, Iowa, 1988—95; adj. asst. professsor Iowa State U., Ames, Iowa, 1989—95, adj. assoc. prof., 1995—2002; scientist Ames Nat. Lab. USDOE, Ames, Iowa, 1995—. Vis. scientist CAN-MET Nat. Sci. and Rsch. Coun., Ottawa, Ont., Canada, 1983—84. Contbr. articles in tech., profl., internat. jours. Mem.: Am. Ceramic Soc., Transactions of Metals Soc., Materials Rsch. Soc. Achievements include patents for Quasicrystal reinforced aluminum and aluminum alloy composites. Avocations: chess, jazz, classical, snorkeling. Home: 1783 NW 122ct Des Moines IA 50325 Office: Ames Lab USDOE Iowa State Univ Ames IA 50011 Office Fax: 515-294-8727. Personal E-mail: bulent@mchsi.com. Business E-Mail: sbbiner@iastate.edu.

BINES, HARVEY ERNEST, lawyer, educator, writer; b. Winthrop, Mass., Nov. 25, 1941; s. Carl and Lillian (Cooper) B.; m. Joan Carol Paller, Dec. 27, 1964; children: Jonathan W., Joel T., Susanne R., Benjamin E. BS, MIT, 1963; JD, U. Va., 1970. Bar: Mass 1971, Va. 1971, U.S. Dist. Ct. Mass., U.S. Dist. Ct. (ea. dist.) Va., U.S. Ct. Appeals (1st, 3d, 4th, 7th and D.C. cirs.), U.S. Supreme Ct. Law clk. to hon. John D. Butzner Jr. U.S. Ct. Appeals (4th cir.), Richmond, Va., 1970-71; asst. prof. Law Sch. U. Va., Charlottesville, 1971-74, assoc. prof. Law Sch., 1974-76; assoc. Sullivan & Worcester, Boston, 1976-79, ptnr., 1980—. Adj. prof. Boston Coll. Law Sch., Chestnut Hill, Mass., 1981-88, bd. dirs., treas. Schweitzer Fellowship, Boston. Author: Law of Investment Management, 1978. Lt. USNR, 1963-67. Mem.: Boston Bar Assn., Am. Law Inst. Home: 36 Clarke St Lexington MA 02421-4916 Office: Sullivan & Worcester 1 Post Office Sq Ste 2300 Boston MA 02109-2129 E-mail: hbines@sandw.com.

BINETTI, VINCENZO ANTONIO, Italian literature educator; b. Molfetta, Italy, Nov. 12, 1959; s. Lorenzo Binetti and Vincenza Balacco; m. Heidi Beatrice Busch, July 26, 1991; children: Soraya, Lorenzo, Delia. Laurea, U. Degli Studi, Firenze, Italy, 1984; MA, U. B.C., Vancouver, Canada, 1990; PhD, Harvard U., 1994. Tchg. fellow Harvard U., Cambridge, Mass., 1992—94; asst. prof. U. Chgo., 1994—98, U. Mich., Ann Arbor, 1998—2001, assoc. prof. modern and contemporary Italian lit. and culture, 2001—. Author: Cesare Pavese..., 1998; contbr. articles to profl. jours. Mem.: Am. Assoc. Italian Studies, Am. Assoc. Tchrs. of Italian, Modern Language Assoc. Office: U Mich 4108 MLB 812 E Washington St Ann Arbor MI 48109

BING, RICHARD MCPHAIL, lawyer; b. Lewes, Del., Aug. 23, 1950; s. Arden E. and Ellen Louise (Judd) B.; m. Valerie Lynn Wasson, Dec. 18, 1971; children: Jennifer Lynn, Kristin Tyler. BA, U. Richmond, 1972, JD, 1978. Bar: Va. 1979, U.S. Dist. Ct. (ea. and we. dists.) Va. 1979, U.S. Dist. Ct. (we. dist.) Pa. 1990, U.S. Dist. Ct. (no. dist.) N.Y. 1990, U.S. Dist. Ct. (ctrl. dist.) Ill. 1996, U.S. Ct. Appeals (4th cir.) 1979, U.S. Ct. appeals (2d cir.) 1990, U.S. Supreme Ct. 1994, U.S. Dist. Ct. (ctrl. dist.) Ill. 1996. Dir. ins. Bur. of Ins., Richmond, Va., 1978-79; resident gen counsel Va. Gasoline Retailers Assn., Richmond, 1979-83; ptnr. Pearce & Bing, Richmond, 1983-93, Bing & Assocs., P.C., Richmond, 1993—. Adj. prof. law J. Sargent Reynolds Community Coll., Richmond, 1984-85. Mem. Henrico County Rep. Com; bd. dirs. Three Chopt PTA, Richmond, 1984-85. Mem. ABA, Va. Bar Assn., Va. Bar, Richmond Bar Assn., Fed. bar Assn., Assn. Trial Lawyers Am., Va. Trial Lawyers Assn., Nat. Lawyers Club, Tuckahoe Jaycees (pres. 1981-82), Bull and Bear Club, Hermitage Country Club, Tobacco Co. Club, The Spider Club (bd. dirs.), Am. Assn. of Franchisees and Dealers, Svc. Sta. Dealers of Am., Inc., Affiliate Attys. Group. Avocations: golf, bicycling, photography. Home: 1701 Habwood Ln Richmond VA 23233-4451 Office: Bing & Assocs PC 300 Arboretum Pl Ste 140 Richmond VA 23236-3465

BINGAMAN, ANNE K. lawyer; b. Jerome, Ariz., July 3, 1943; d. William Emil and Anne Ellen (Baker) Kovacovich; m. Jeff F. Bingaman, Sept. 14, 1968; 1 child, John. BA in History, Stanford U., 1965; gen. course cert. with honors, London Sch. of Econs., England, 1964-65; LLB, Stanford U., 1968. Bar: Calif. 1969, N.Mex. 1969, Ariz. 1969, U.S. Dist. Ct. D.C. 1983. Atty. Brown & Bain, Phoenix, 1968-69, N.Mex. Bur. Revenue, Santa Fe, 1969-70, Modrall, Sperling, Roehl, Harris & Sisk, Albuquerque, 1970, N.Mex. Atty. Gen's. Office, Santa Fe, 1970-72; from asst. prof. to assoc. prof. U. N.Mex. Sch. Law, Santa Fe, 1972-76; founding ptnr. Bingaman & Davenport, Santa Fe, 1977-82; ptnr. Brown, Bain & Bingaman, Santa Fe and Washington, 1982-84, Onek, Klein & Farr, Washington, 1984-85, Powell, Goldstein, Frazer & Murphy, Washington, 1985-93; asst. atty. gen. anti-trust divsn. U.S. Dept. Justice, Washington, D.C., 1993-96; sr. v.p. LCI Internat., McLean, Va., 1997-98; chmn. bd. Valor Telecom, Irving, Tex., 1999—. Contbr. articles to profl. jours. Exec. com. Stanford Law Sch. Bd. Visitors, 1978-80, 88-90; mem. for N.Mex. of 10th Cir. Jud. Nominating Panel, 1977-80. Ford Found. fellow 1975; recipient Nat. Vol. award Stanford Assocs., 1989. Fellow Am. Bar Found.; mem. ABA, N.Mex. Bar (founder, vice-chair antitrust sect. 1982-85, chair com. to rewrite comm. property & other state laws to conform to ERA), Am. Law Inst. Democrat. Episcopalian. Office: Valor Telecom 1200 19th St SW 5th Fl Washington DC 20036-

BINGAMAN, JEFF, senator; b. El Paso, Tex., Oct. 3, 1943; s. Jesse and Beth (Ball) B.; m. Anne Kovacevich, Sept. 13, 1968. BA in Govt., Harvard U., 1965; JD, Stanford U., 1968. Bar: N.Mex. 1968. Asst. atty. gen., N.Mex., 1969; atty. Stephenson, Campbell & Olmsted, 1971-72; ptnr. Campbell, Bingaman & Black, Santa Fe, 1972-78; atty. gen. State of N.Mex., 1978; senator from N.Mex. U.S. Senate, 1982—, mem. armed svcs. com., mem. joint econ. com., mem. Senate Dem. steering and coordination com., mem. Senate Den. tech. and comm. com., ranking minority mem., mem. energy and natural resources subcom. of energy prodn. and regulation, mem. labor and human resources com. U.S. Army Reserves, 1968-74. Democrat. Methodist. Home: PO Box 5775 Santa Fe NM 87502-5775 Office: US Senate 703 Hart Senate Bldg Washington DC 20510-0001*

BINGER, WILSON VALENTINE, civil engineer; b. Greenwich, N.Y., Feb. 28, 1917; s. George and Blanche (Wilson) B.; m. Barbara Ridgway, May 19, 1947 (dec. 1984); children: Wilson Valentine, Mary Blanche, Julia Ridgway (Mrs. Nurettin Akgül); m. Jane E. Schwarz, Apr. 24, 1986. AB cum laude, Harvard, 1938, MS in Engring., 1939. Registered profl. engr., N.Y., Ohio. Soils engr. U.S. Army Engrs., Wilmington, Del., 1939-40; soils and found. engr. Gatun 3d Locks project, Panama Canal, 1940-43; soils engr., resident engr. Parsons Brinckerhoff, Hogan & MacDonald, Caracas, Venezuela, 1945-46, chief soils engr., 1948-49; chief soils and found. sect. Isthmian Canal Studies, Panama Canal, 1946-47; chief soils and geology br. Mo. River divsn. U.S. Army Engrs., Omaha, 1947-48; v.p. Porterfield-Binger Constrn. Co., Youngstown, Ohio, 1950-52; regional mgr. Tippetts-Abbett-McCarthy-Stratton, Bogota, Colombia, 1952-56; assoc. ptnr. Tippetts-Abbett-McCarthy-Stratton, N.Y.C., 1957-61, ptnr., 1962-84; chmn., 1975-84; cons. engr., 1985—. Author papers in field. Pres., trustee Chappaqua (N.Y.) Libr., 1967-69; trustee Robert Coll., Istanbul, Turkey, 1970—, vice chmn., 1974-78, sec., 1992—; bd. dirs. Regional Plan Assn., N.Y., 1983-88; chmn. bd. deacons Congl. Ch., 1959-62, trustee, 1985-88. Recipient Disting. Citizen award Warren (Ohio) Met. Area Assn., Steinmetz award Consulting Engr. Mag., Diamond Ann. Lifetime Achievement award N.Y. Assn. Cons. Engrs. Fellow ASCE, Inst. Civil Engrs. (U.K.), Am. Cons. Engrs. Coun. (v.p. 1973-75), N.Y. Acad. Scis.; mem. NAE, Royal Acad. Engring. U.K. (fgn. mem.), Am. Inst. Cons. Engrs. (councillor 1971-73, pres. 1973), NSPE, U.S. Com. Large Dams (mem. exec. com. 1964-69, sec. 1962-78), Internat. Com. Large Dams (v.p. 1978-81), N.Y. Assn. Cons. Engrs. (v.p., dir. 1964-65), Moles, Internat. Road Fedn. (dir. 1975-82, mem. exec. com. 1975-82), Fedn. Internat. des Ingenieurs Conseils (mem. exec. com. 1976-83, treas. 1976-79, v.p. 1980-81, pres. 1981-83), Century Club, Harvard Club (N.Y.C.), Univ. Club, East India Club (London), Phi Beta Kappa. Home: 1302 Meadow Ridge Redding CT 06896

BINGHAM, A. WALKER, III, lawyer, business executive; b. N.Y.C., Nov. 5, 1928; s. Arthur Walker and Mary D. Bingham; m. Nicolette Pathy, Oct. 28, 1967; children— Arthur Walker, IV, Alexander Dunwody, Nicole Pathy. B.A., Harvard U., 1951, LL.B., 1958. Bar: N.Y. 1959. Assoc. Milbank, Tweed Hadley & McCloy, N.Y.C., 1958-68; gen. atty. Abex Corp., N.Y.C., 1968-74, group counsel, Stamford, Conn., 1984—86; chmn. bd. Boorum & Pease Co., Elizabeth, N.J., 1974—85. Author: The Snake Oil Syndrome, 1994. Served to lt. USN, 1951-54. Mem. Assn. Bar City N.Y., Union Club, Harvard Club (N.Y.C.). Home: 19 E 72nd St New York NY 10021-4145

BINGHAM, CHRISTOPHER, statistics educator; b. N.Y.C., Apr. 16, 1937; s. Alfred Mitchell and Sylvia (Knox) B.; m. Carolyn Higinbotham, Sept. 23, 1967 AB, Yale U., 1958, MA, 1960, PhD, 1964. Research fellow Conn. Agrl. Expt. Sta., New Haven, 1958-64; research assoc. in math. and biology Princeton U., N.J., 1964-66; asst. prof. stats. U. Chgo., 1967-72; assoc. prof. applied stats. U. Minn., Mpls., 1972-79, prof., 1979—. Contbr. articles to profl. jours. Fellow Am. Statis. Assn., Inst. Math. Stats.; mem. Royal Statis. Soc., Biometric Soc., Soc. Indsl. and Applied Math. Unitarian Universalist. Home: 605 Winston Ct Mendota Heights MN 55118-1039 Office: U Minn Sch Stats 313 Ford Hall 224 Church St SE Minneapolis MN 55455-0493 E-mail: kb@umn.edu.

BINGHAM, ELIZABETH ELLIOTT, librarian; b. Butler, Ala., June 29, 1948; d. James Howard and Emogene (Shamburger) Elliott; m. Clifton O. Bingham, Jr., Apr. 16, 1965 (div. Mar. 1977); 1 child, Clifton O. BS, La. State U.-Baton Rouge, 1970, MS, 1971. Reference libr. East Baton Rouge Parish Libr., 1970-74, head mid-city br., 1974-75, head adult svcs., 1975—; sec. task force White House Conf. on Librs. and Info. Svcs., 1994-97, La. Endowment for Humanities, 1995-96, v.p. 1996-97. Contbr. articles to profl. jours. HEW fellow, 1975. Recipient YMCA Woman of Achievement, 1997. Mem. Libr. Adminstrn. and Mgmt. Assn. (sec. 1994-96), Intellectual Freedom Round Table (treas. 1995-97), Am. Library Assn. (pres. Jr. Mem. Round Table 1979-80, mem. coun. 1994—), La. Library Assn. (treas. 1979-80, recipient Mid-Career award 1983, 1st v.p./pres.-elect 1989-90, pres. 1990-91, Essae M. Culver Disting. Svc. award 1997), Southeastern Library Assn. Democrat. Presbyterian. Clubs: Altrusa Internat., Jr. League (Baton Rouge); Found. for Hist. La. E-mail: bbingham@ebr.lib.la.us. Home: 14215 Harwood Ave Baton Rouge LA 70816-2714 Office: E Baton Rouge Parish Library 7711 Goodwood Blvd Baton Rouge LA 70806-7625

BINGHAM, GEORGE WALTER CHANDLER, retired sales executive; b. Cambridge, Mass., Jan. 1, 1925; s. George Hutchins Jr. Bingham and Audrey Wellington (Wack) Bingham Suter; m. Carolyn Susan Webb, Nov. 25, 1967; 1 child, Susan Cordelia. Student, Dartmouth Coll., 1943-44, 46-48; BA, Gettysburg Coll., 1950; postgrad., Columbia U., 1950-51. With CBS TV, N.Y.C., 1951-55; account exec. Gill-Perna Sta. Reps., N.Y.C., 1955-56, Walker Representation Co., N.Y.C., 1956-57; v.p., mgr. New Eng. sales Walker-Rawalt, Inc., Boston, 1957-61; pres. New Eng. Spot Sales, Inc., Boston, 1961—95; mgr. New Eng. sales Stone Reps., 1960-70; mgr. New Eng. sales Jack Masla & Co., Boston, 1970-80, Weiss & Powell, Boston, 1983-86, Katz & Powell, Boston, 1987-95, New Eng. Spot Sales Inc., Belmont, Mass., 1995-2000; ret., 2000. Treas., co-owner So. Maine Broadcasting Corp., Sanford/York County, 1975-83, Essex Broadcasting Corp., Newburyport, Mass., 1977-83. Exec. com. Dartmouth Coll. Class of 1947; officer, dir. Camp Allen, Bedford, N.H., 1983—. With USNR, 1943-46. Mem. New Eng. Assn. Radio and TV Sta. Reps. (pres. 1963-64), Broadcasters Found., Mass. Soc. SAR, Mass. Soc. Mayflower Descs. (officer, dep. gov. 1976-87), Am. Legion (comdr. post 281 1974-76, 85-92), Boston's Advt. Post, Harvard Faculty Club, Boston Athenaeum, Kiwanis, Phi Alpha Theta, Kappa Kappa Kappa (hon.). Democrat. Episcopalian. Avocations: history, theater, cross-country skiing. Home: 208 Lewis Rd Belmont MA 02478-3833 Fax: 617-489-6749.

BINGHAM, H. RAYMOND, computer software company executive; b. Heber City, Utah, Oct. 18, 1945; s. Lyman Dunbar and Thora (Murdock) B.; m. Kristin Bernadine Allgood, Oct. 10, 1968; children: Ashley Dare, Derrick, Raymond, Erin Sloan, Adam Jay, Christopher Brian. BS, Weber State College, 1970; MBA, Harvard U., 1972. V.p. N_REN Internat., Peutie, Belgium, 1975-80; asst. treas. Marriott Corp., Bethesda, Md., 1980-81; mng. dir. Agrico Overseas Investment, Tulsa, Okla., 1981-85; exec. v.p., chief fin. officer Red Lion Hotels & Inns, Vancouver, Wash., 1985-93, Cadence Design Systems, Inc., San Jose, Calif., 1993-99, pres., CEO, 1999—. Bd. dirs. WTD Industries Inc., Portland. Bd. dirs. Oreg. Pub. Broadcasting Found., Portland, 1989—, Oreg. Symphony Assn., Portland, 1989—; mem. Harvard Bus. Sch. Assn. Oreg., Portland, 1985—. Mem. Urban Land Inst., Nat. Realty Inst., Fin. Execs. Inst. Republican. Mem. Lds Ch. Avocations: tennis, running, skiing. Home: 1 Bridal Ln Woodside CA 94062-2599 Office: Cadence Design Systems 2655 Seely Ave Bldg 5 San Jose CA 95134-1931

BINGHAM, J. PETER, electronics research executive; married; 2 children. BS in Physics cum laude, Polytechnic Inst., N.Y.; MS in Exptl. Physics, PhD in Elec. Engring., U. Md. With RCA Consumer Electronics, David Sarnoff Rsch. Ctr.; exec. v.p., tech. Thomson Consumer Electronics; v.p. engring. Philips Consumer Electronics Co., 1982-91; with Philips Rsch. Philips Electronics N.Am. Corp., 1991; pres. Philips Rsch., 1991—. Bd. dirs. Indsl. Rsch. Inst. Recipient David Sarnoff award, RCA Lab. Achievements award; Named in his honor Bingham Peak in Antarctica, Arctic Inst. of North Am. Office: 23 Brookwood Dr Briarcliff Manor NY 10510-2040

BINGHAM, JEFF, federal agency administrator; Chief of staff U.S. Sen. Jake Garn; cons. Synthesis Group; sr. policy analyst Sci. Applications Internat. Corp.; with Office Legis. Affairs NASA, Washington, dir. Space Sta. Info. Ctr., 1996—99, assoc. adminstr. legis. affairs, 2001—. Office: NASA Hdqrs Mail Code L 300 E St SW Washington DC 20546

BINGHAM, JINSIE SCOTT, broadcast company executive; b. Greencastle, Ind., Dec. 28, 1935; d. Roscoe Gibson and Alpha Edith (Robinson) Scott; m. Frank William Wokoun, Jr. (dec.); children: Douglas Scott, Richard Frank; m. Richard Innes Bingham, June 24, 1964. Student, DePauw U., Greencastle, 1952-53, Northwestern U., 1953, Coe Coll., 1953-54. Exec. sec. Ind. Young Dems., 1958-60; receptionist Ind. Ho. of Reps., Indpls., 1959; saleslady Avon Products, Greencastle, 1961-64; sales mgr. Sta. WJNZ (formerly WXTA), Greencastle, 1969-77, owner, pres., gen. mgr., 1977-94; owner Radio Greencastle, 1977—. Owner, pres. GM of WJNZ, 1977-94; former ptnr. Sta. WVTL, Monticello, Ill., Sta. KBIB, Monette, Ark.; speaker DePauw U. Comm. Seminar, 1981-85; vis. lectr., 1986—. Featured in Trainblazing Women of Ind., 1999—. Com. chair Legis. Awareness Seminar, 1978—86; co-chair Greencastle Gaelic Festival, 1983—84; charter mem. Greencastle 2001, 1985—, Greencastle Civic League, 1984—, Greencastle Merchant's Assn., 1983—97, Cmty. Resources Com., 1982—87; charter mem., corp. sec. Main St. Greencastle, 1983—87, v.p., 1987—88, pres., 1989—90, chmn., 1990—91; v.p. United Way, 1996—97, campaign chair, 1996—97, campaign advisor, 1998—99; announcer Putnam County Fair Parade, 1977—; co-chmn. centennial com. Putnam County Courthouse, 2001—; mem. Lilly Scholar Selection Com., 1998—, hon. bd. dirs., 2002—; v.p. Putnam County Mus., 2002, pres., 2003—; active Govs. Commn. for a Drug Free Ind., 1991—; tour guide Putnam County Conv. and Visitors Bur., 1998—; active Putnam County Coun. on Aging and Aged, 1999—; co-founder Greencastle H.S. Alumni Assn., 1995, founding chmn. scholarship fund, 1995—; v.p. West Ctrl. Econ. Devel. Coun., 2003—; vice chmn. Putnam County Dem. Ctrl. Com., 2001—; bd. dirs. Opportunity Housing, 1995—2002; charter mem., bd. dirs. Greencastle Vol. Fire Dept., 1986, Greencastle Devel. Ctr., 1988—89, Greencastle Cmty. Child Care Ctr., 1983—87; bd. dirs. Putnam County Comprehensive Ctr., 1994—2000; mem. Greencastle Zoning Bd. Appeals, 1984—, v.p., 1985—88, pres., 1988—. Sagamore of the Wabash, Ind. Gov. Evan Bayh, 1995; recipient Limestone State Seal, 1996, Seal of City, Greencastle, 1996; named Hoosier Know It All Champion, Sta. WTTV, Indpls., 1998; inducted into Ind. Broadcasters Hall of Fame, 1999; named one of 53 Trailblazing Women of Ind., 1999, Outstanding Citizen Greencastle Jaycees, 1981; name to Putnam County Agr. Hall of Fame Putnam County Farm Bur., 2002. Mem. AARP (Capital City task force 2000), NSDAR (Centennial chmn. Washburn chpt. 2002, chpt. regent 2003—), Broadcast Pioneers (life), Putnam County Bd. Realtors, Am. Women in Radio and TV (pres. Ind. chpt. 1979-82, Lifetime Achievement award 1996), Indpls. Network Women in Bus. (charter), Women in Comm., Inc. (bd. dirs. 1983-84, MATRIX co-chair 1984, Frances Wright award 1993), Am. Legion Aux., Nat. Assn. Broadcasters, Soc. Profl. Journalists, Ind. Broadcasters Assn. (v.p. FM 1982), Putnam County Extension Adv. Coun. (4H), Natural Resources Svc. Land Use Study Group, Greencastle Bus. and Profl. Women's Club (pres. 1976-77, 79-80, Woman of Yr. 1994), Indpls. Ad Club, Women's Press Club Ind., Indpls. Press Club, Nat. Fedn. Press Women, Ind. Dem. Editl. Assn. (sec. 1987, v.p. 1988, pres. 1990), Ind. C. of C., Greencastle C. of C. (bd. dirs. 1979-83, pres. 1982, amb. 2001—. Citizen of Yr. 1997), VFW (pres. ladies aux. 1966-68), Ind. Geneal. Soc., Milestone Care Soc., Packard Club Ind., Ind. Soc. Pioneers, Daus of 1812 (pres. Tippecanoe chpt. 1981, state v.p. 1982), DAR, Daughters of the Union, Internat. Order Job's Daus., Soc. Descendants of Valley Forge, Rotary (bd. dirs., pres. 1994-95, bull. editor 1995—, dist. conf. planner 1997, Paul Harris fellow 1998, del. world conf. 1998), Order Ea. Star, Women of Moose, Milestone Car Soc., Delta Theta Tau, Sigma Delta Chi. Mem. Christian Ch. (Disciples Of Christ).

BINGHAM, JUNE, writer, playwright; b. White Plains, N.Y., June 20, 1919; d. Max J.H. and Mabel (Limburg) Rossbach; m. Jonathan B. Bingham, Sept. 20, 1939 (dec. July 1986); children: Sherry B. Downes, Micki B. Esselstyn (dec. 1999), Timothy, Claudia B. Meyers; m. Robert B. Birge, Mar. 28, 1987; 1 stepchild, Robert R. Student, Vassar Coll., 1936-38; BA, Barnard Coll., 1940; LittD (hon.), Lehman Coll., 2002. Writer, editor U.S. Treasury, Washington, 1943-45; editorial asst. Washington Post, 1945-46; writer Tarrytown (N.Y.) Daily News, 1946. Author: Do Cows Have Neuroses?, Do Babies Have Worries?, Do Teenagers Have Wisdom?, Courage to Change: An Introduction to Life and Thought of Reinhold Niebuhr, 1961, Courage to Change: An Introduction to Life and Thought of Reinhold Niebuhr, paperback edit., 1992, U Thant: The Search for Peace, 1970, (plays) Triangles, 1986, Eleanor and Alice, 1996, You and the I.C.U., 1990; author: (with others) The Inside Story: Psychiatry and Everyday Life, 1953, The Pursuit of Health, 1985; author: (mus.) Squanto and Love, 1992, Young Roosevelts, 1993, The Other Lincoln, 1995, The Strange Case of Mary Lincoln, 2001; contbr. Bd. dirs. Riverdale Mental Health Assn., 1983—, Woodrow Wilson Found., Princeton, N.J., 1959-64, 83-89, Lehman Coll. Found., 1983-90, Ittleson Ctr. for Childhood Rsch., 1958-90, Franklin and Eleanor Roosevelt Inst., 1992-2002; founder T.L.C.; trained liaison comforter Vol. Program of Presbyn. Hosp., N.Y.C. Named Alumna of the Yr., Rosemary Hall, 1976. Mem. Authors Guild (nominating com. 1987-90), Dramatists Guild, PEN, Cosmopolitan Club. Democrat. Avocations: tennis, golf, theatre, movies, reading. Home: 5000 Independence Ave Bronx NY 10471-2804

BINGHAM, OUITA HYAMS, librarian; b. Shreveport, La., June 30, 1952; d. John Skipwith Hyams and Myrtis Juanita Temple; m. William Benjamin Bingham III, Apr. 10, 1982; children: Sarah S., Alexander H., Emily E. BS in Psychology, La. State U., 1975; MLIS, U. Tex., Austin, 1987. Cert. tchr. Tex. Libr. Austin Pub. Libr., Legis. Ref. Libr., Austin, 1998—2002; sch. libr. S.W. Tex. U., 2003—. Libr. Festival com., Austin, 1999; cons., youth story-times and puppet shows, Austin, 1990—; adv. bd. Austing Pub. Libr., 1990. Prodr., designer (slide shows) Closer Look at Looking, 1977, prodr., designer (various puppet shows). Chair nursery com. Dripping Springs (Tex.) Meth. Ch., 1996—99; fundraising chair First United Meth. Ch. Presch., Austin, 1998—2001. Mem.: ALA, Nat. Assn. Young Children, Tex. Libr. Assn. Methodist. Avocations: writing children's books, travel, puppets. Home: 755 Green Oak Dr Dripping Springs TX 78620 Office: Legis Ref Library State Capitol 1100 N Congress Ave Austin TX 78701 E-mail: ouitabingham@msn.com.

BINGHAM, RAYMOND JOSEPH, neonatal/perinatal nurse practitioner; b. Pensacola, Fla., Dec. 4, 1958; s. Joseph Lawson and Barbara June (Hansen) Bingham; m. Darcy Evelyn Pagones, May 14, 1982; children: John Joseph, Christopher Hansen, Robyn Brady. BA, U. Va., 1985; BSN, Cath. U., 1989; postgrad., George Mason U., 2002—. RN clinician, Va., cert. neonatal intensive care nurse. Staff nurse newborn ICU Georgetown U. Hosp., Washington, 1989-95; staff nurse Fairfax (Va.) Hosp., 1996—2000. Course reviewer Neonatal Network, Petaluma, Calif., 1993—96; tech. writer/editor Office of Sci. Policy, pub. liaison Nat. Inst. Nursing Rsch./NIH, 2001—. Contbg. editor: Jour. Nursing Jocularity, 1996—98; editl. cons., reviewer: Mother Baby Jour., 1998—2000, manuscript reviewer: Am. Jour. Nursing, 1999—. Treas. Stoddert PTA, Washington, 1994; mem. adv. bd. Acad. Neonatal Nursing, 2001—.

Mem.: Washington Met. Assn. Neonatal Nurses (comm. com. 1998—2000), Nat. Assn. Neonatal Nurses (comm. com. 1995—98). Avocations: running, hiking, writing. Home and Office: 19308 Meaderidge Pl Montgomery Village MD 20886-3929 E-mail: binghamr@mail.nih.gov.

BINGHAM, RICHARD DONNELLY, journal editor, director, educator; b. Orange, N.J., Oct. 27, 1937; s. Seymour Potter and Helen Barbara (Donnelly) B.; children from previous marriage: Connie Elizabeth, Paul Douglas; m. Claire L. Felbinger. BBA, Boston U., 1959; MAPA, U. Okla., 1971, PhD, 1973. Asst. prof. Marquette U., Milw., 1973-76, U. Wis., Milw., 1975-77, assoc. prof., 1977-84, dir. Urban Rsch. Ctr., 1982-86, prof., 1984-88; editor Econ. Devel. Quar., Cleve., 1985-94, founding editor, 1994—; dir. MS and PhD programs Cleve. State U., 1993-96. Mem. editl. bd. Urban Affairs Quar., 1978-80, 89-92, The Urban Interest, 1979-82, Rsch. in Urban Policy, 1982-92, State and Local Govt. Rev., 1984-87, 98—; program analyst HUD, Washington. Author: State and Local Government in an Urban Society, 1986, Evaluation in Practice, 1989, State and Local Government in a Changing Society, 1991, Managing Local Government, 1991, Beyond Edge Cities, 1997, Industrial Policy American Style, 1998, The Economics of Central City Neighborhoods, 2001, Evaluation in Practice, 2002; editor: Urban Economic Development, 1984, The Homeless Contemporary Society, 1987, Economic Restructuring of the American Midwest, 1990, Financing Economic Development, 1990, Theories of Local Economic Development, 1993, Dilemmas of Urban Economic Development, 1997, Global Perspectives on Economic Development, 1997, Financing Economic Development in the 21st Century, 2003; contbr. articles to profl. jours. With USAF, 1959-70. Recipient numerous grants from govt. orgns. and agencies. Mem. Am. Econ. Assn., Am. Polit. Sci. Assn. (past pres. Urban Politics sect.), Southwestern Social Sci. Assn., Am. Soc. Pub. Adminstrn., Policy Studies Assn. Avocations: fly fishing, reading. Office: Cleve State U Coll Urban Affairs Cleveland OH 44115 E-mail: dickb@urban.csuohio.edu.

BINGI, PRASAD, management and marketing educator, consultant; b. India; came to U.S., 1988; s. Krishnaiah Chetty and Narasamma Bingi; m. Revathi Bingi; 1 child, Harish. B of Tech., S.V. U., Tirupati, India, 1983; M of Tech., Indian Inst. Tech., 1985; PhD, Tex. Tech. U., 1995. Devel. engr. Bharat Earth Movers Ltd., Bangalore, India, 1985-88; rsch. asst. Tex. Tech U., Lubbock, 1988-90, tchg. asst., 1990-95; asst. prof. Ind.-Purdue U., Ft. Wayne, 1995-2001, assoc. prof., 2001—. Cons. Ind. Hunters and Jumpers, Ft. Wayne, 1999-2000; chmn. dept. mgmt. and mktg. Ind.-Purdue U., 2001-2003. Contbr. articles to profl. jours. Avocations: reading, movies. Office: Ind Purdue Univ Dept Mgmt and Mktg 2101 E Coliseum Blvd Fort Wayne IN 46805 E-mail: bingi@ipfw.edu.

BINGMAN, CHARLES FRANKLIN, public administration executive and educator; b. West Allis, Wis., Sept. 11, 1929; s. Clyde James and Bernice (Hengstler) B. BBA, U. Wis., 1952, MBA, 1956. Mgr. planning and control Nasa-Johnson Space Ctr., Houston, 1962-66; dep. dir. mgmt. programs Office Manned Space Flight Nat. Aero. and Space Adminstrn., Washington, 1967-71; dep. assoc. dir. orgn. mgmt. U.S. Office Mgmt. and Budget, Washington, 1971-76; dep. adminstr. Urban Mass Transp. Adminstrn. U.S. Dept. Transp., Washington, 1976-79, spl. asst. to dep. sec., 1982-83; exec. dir. Pres.'s mgmt. improvement coun. Exec. Office of The Pres., Washington, 1979-80, mgmt. advisor White House Office of Policy Devel., 1980-81; vis. prof. pub. adminstrn. dept. George Washington U., Washington, 1984-97; cons. U.S. and internat. govts., 1985—; fellow Ctr. for Study of Am. Govt., Johns Hopkins U., Washington, 1997—. Author: Japanese Government Leadership and Management, 1989, Serving Two Presidents: A History of the Bureau of the Budget, 1992, Revitalizing Federal Management, 1983; contbr. articles to profl. jours. Pres. Woodlake Towers Condo Assn., 1996—2002. Capt. U.S. Army, 1951—65. U.S. Info. Agy. grantee, 1992. Fellow Nat. Acad. Pub. Adminstrn.; mem. Sr. Execs. Assn. (pres. 1968-69, bd. dirs. 1982-85), Fed. Exec. Inst. Alumni Assn. (bd. dirs. 1983-86), William A. Jump Found. (bd. dirs. 1987—). Republican. Avocations: writing, jogging, hiking, reading. Home: 3100 S Manchester St Apt 815 Falls Church VA 22044-2716 E-mail: user7352@aol.com.

BINI, EDMUND J. gastroenterologist; b. Mar. 2, 1967; BA summa cum laude, Fordham U., 1988; MD, NYU, 1992. Diplomate Am. Bd. Internal Medicine with subspecialties in gastroenterology and internal medicine, Am. Bd. Med. Examiners. Intern and resident in internal medicine Mt. Sinai Med. Ctr., N.Y.C., 1992-95; fellow in gastroenterology NYU Med. Ctr./Bellevue Hosp. Ctr. and N.Y. VA Med. Ctr., N.Y.C., 1995-97; clin. tng. in liver diseases/transplant hepatology Mt. Sinai Med. Ctr., N.Y.C., 1997; dir. Liver Clinic N.Y. VA Med. Ctr., N.Y.C., 1998—; asst. attending in medicine Bellevue Hosp. Ctr., N.Y.C., 1998—, NYU Med. Ctr./Tisch Hosp., N.Y.C., 1998—. Attending physician in medicine, gastroenterology and hepatology N.Y. VA Med. Ctr., 1997—; instr. phys. diagnosis NYU Sch. Medicine, N.Y.C., 1995-97, tchg. asst. in medicine, 1995-97, instr. medicine, 1998-99, asst. prof. medicine, 1999—, lectr. gastrointestinal physiology course, 1998—; rsch. mentor for med. students, housestaff and GI fellows NYU Med. Ctr., Bellevue Hosp., VA Med. Ctr., 1998—; co-chmn. VA Hepatitis C Task Force, N.Y.C., 1999—; lectr. in field. Reviewer Italian Jou. Gastroenterology and Hepatology, 1999—, Am. Jour. Medicine, 1998—, Am. Jour. Gastroenterology, 1998—, New Eng. Jour. Medicine, 2000—; contbr. numerous articles to profl. jours. Bill Coughlin Acad. Excellence scholar, 1984-88, Fordham U. Acad. Dean's scholar, 1984-88, Local One ALA scholar, 1988-92, NYU Acad. scholar, 1988-92. Mem. ACP, AMA, Am. Soc. for Gastrointestinal Endoscopy, N.Y. Soc. for Gastrointestinal Endoscopy, Am. Coll. Gastroenterology, Am. Gastroenterol. Assn., N.Y. Gastroenterol. Assn., Am. Assn. for Study of Liver Diseases. Office: VA Med Ctr Dept Gastroenterol 111D 423 E 23d St New York NY 10010-5050 Fax: (212) 951-3481. E-mail: Edmund.Bini@med.va.gov.

BINIENDA, JOHN J. state legislator; b. Worcester, Mass., June 22, 1947; s. Thaddeus Andrew and Mary Gertrude (O'Coin) B.; children: Julie Ann, John Joseph Jr., Jamie Thaddeus. BA, Worcester State Coll., 1970, postgrad., 1970-74. State rep. Dist. 17 Mass. Ho. of Reps., 1987—, chmn. Com. on Energy. Mem. Ward 7 Dem. Com., 1987—; mem. South Worcester Neighbor Ctr. Mem. Worcester State Coll. Alumni Assn., Am. Legion (Main St. chpt.), Polish Naturalization Ind. Club, Polish Am. Vet. Club, K.C. (3d degree). E-mail: Rep.JohnBinenda@hou.state.ma.us.

BINKLEY, JOHN FREY, JR., financial consultant, writer; b. West Palm Beach, Fla., Jan. 22, 1932; s. John Frey Binkley and Adelaide Ghe Dodson; m. Noriko Kaneko Binkley, Dec. 3, 1952; children: Susan, Linda, John, Paul. BBA, U. Miami, 1956. Lic. life ins. broker Ind., lender Ind. Bus. trainee Internat. GE, N.Y.C., 1956—57; supr. material control ITT, Clifton, NJ, 1958—66; program mgr. Arvin Industries, Columbus, Ind., 1966—68; mfrs. rep., propr. Miltronics, Columbus, 1969—88; freelance author, artist Columbus, 1988—; fin. advisor, agt. Primerica divsn. Citicorp, Columbus, 2001—. Co-founder Machine Vision, Ann Arbor, Mich., 1984—86. Author: The Voice of the Cuckold, 2000 (Book of the Month slutwives.com website). Del. to gen. assembly Presbyn. Ch., Boston, 1966. With U.S. Army, 1951—54. Recipient So. Cross, Daus. of Am. Confederacy, 1975. Libertarian. Avocations: scuba diving, art. Home: 3809 Colonial Columbus IN 47203 E-mail: nefarious@iquest.net.

BINKLEY, LUTHER JOHN, philosophy educator; b. Wernersville, Pa., Oct. 7, 1925; s. Harry Garfield and Jennie Theresa (Yoder) B.; m. Betty Jane Bowman, June 5, 1964. AB, Franklin and Marshall Coll., 1945; BD, Lancaster (Pa.) Theol. Sem., 1947; PhD, Harvard U., 1950. Ordained to ministry United Ch. of Christ, 1949. Instr. philosophy Franklin and Marshall Coll., Lancaster, 1949-51, asst. prof., 1951-56, assoc. prof., 1956-62, prof., 1962-91, prof. emeritus, 1991—, chmn. dept., 1962-74, dir. humanities program, 1972-74. Vis. fellow Cambridge (Eng.) U., 1959-60, Princeton (N.J.) U., 1967, 69; adj. prof. Temple U., Phila., 1965-83, Pa. State U., Harrisburg, 1975-88. Author: The Mercersburg Theology, 1953, Contemporary Ethical Theories, 1961, Conflict of Ideals: Changing Values in Western Society, 1969. Mem. Pub. Coun. for Humanities in Pa., Phila., 1975-79; mem. instnl. ethics com. Lancaster Regional Med. Ctr., 1985—; mem. instnl. rev. bd. Lancaster Gen. Hosp., 1988—. Recipient Disting. Coll. Tchg. award Lindback Found., 1962. Mem. AAUP (pres. Franklin and Marshall chpt. 1962-63, 50 Yr. Svc. award 2000), Am. Philos. Assn., Philos. Soc. for Study Sport (pres. 1977-78), Hershey Golf Club, Lancaster Torch Club (pres. 1956-57, Silver award 1999), Phi Beta Kappa (pres. Theta chpt. Pa. 1970-71). Avocations: travel, golf, tennis, attending opera and symphony concerts, reading. Home: PO Box 473 Hershey PA 17033-0473 Office: Franklin and Marshall Coll PO Box 3003 Lancaster PA 17604-3003 E-mail: ljbinkley@aol.com.

BINKLEY, MARILYN ROTHMAN, educational research administrator; b. N.Y.C., Jan. 27, 1948; d. Edgar and Mollie (Rothenberg) Rothman. BA, Bklyn. Coll., 1968; MA, Columbia U., 1971; EdD, George Washington U., 1983. Tchr. N.Y.C. Pub. Schs., 1972-77; reading splst. Internat. Sch., Geneva, 1975-77; instr. Marymount Coll. Va., Arlington, 1978-80; edn. cons. Washington, 1980-85; sr. assoc. Office Ednl. Rsch. and Improvement U.S. Dept. Edn.; edn. policy fellow Inst. Ednl. Leadership, 1987-88; sr. assoc. Nat. Ctr. Edn. Statistics, 1988—. Nat. rsch. coord. Internat. Assn. for the Evaluation of Edn. Adv., reading literacy study, 1988—95; U.S. coord. Internat. Adult Literacy Study, 1994—99; cons. Severn Sch., 1980—83, Dept. Def. Dependent Schs., 1979, Dover Sch. Singapore, 1978; dep. dir. Internat. Life Skills Study, 1998—2001; nat. project dir. OECD Program for Indicators of Student Achievement, 1998—2001; internat. co-dir. Adult Literacy and Life Skills Survey, 1998—2000; dir. item devel. Nat. Assessment of Edn. Progress, 2001—. Mem. Am. Ednl. Rsch. Assn., Am. Statistical Assn., Nat. Assn. Ind. Schs., Nat. Coun. Tchrs. English, Nat. Assn. Measurement and Evaln., Nat. Reading Conf., Internat. Assn. Evaln. of Ednl. Achievement, Internat Reading Assn., Coll. Reading Assn., Orton Soc., Assn. Supervision and Curriculum Devel., Va. Reading Assn., Md. Reading Assn., Greater Washington Reading Assn., Delta Phi Epsilon, Phi Delta Kappa. Home: 12024 Gatewater Dr Potomac MD 20854-2875 Office: US Dept Edn 1990 K St NW Washington DC 20001-2029

BINKLEY, TIMOTHY, computer graphics educator; b. Balt., Sept. 14, 1943; s. Enos G. and Grace (Joy) Binkley; m. Sonya Shannon, 1993. BA in Math. with honors, U. Colo., 1965, MA in Math., 1966; PhD in Philosophy, U. Tex., 1970; postgrad. in computer sci., Courant Inst., NYU, 1979-82. Asst. prof. Notre Dame U., Ind., 1970-73; postdoctoral fellow Temple U., Phila., 1973-75; mem. faculty New Sch. for Social Rsch., N.Y.C., 1975-77; chair dept. humanities and scis. Sch. Visual Arts, N.Y.C., 1976-88, dir. computer edn., 1982—98, dir. Inst. for Computers in the Arts, 1986—98, chair MFA program in computer art, 1988—98; pres. Artware, 1996—. Author: Wittgenstein's Language, 1973; author (with others): Reason and Violence, 1974, Culture and Art, 1976, Philosophical Perspectives on Metaphor, 1981, Philosophy Looks at the Arts, 1987; author software: Paint Brush, 1983, Starmaker, 1988, Symmetry Studio, 1990, GMN Engine, 1999, Agent Wrangler, 2000; also numerous jour. articles, film revs., exhbn. catalogs; contbr. exhbns., films, videos, performances including interactive computer installations Face to Face and Drawn to the Light, in Computers and Art exhbn., IBM Gallery Sci. and Art, N.Y.C., 1988, Ctr. for Fine Arts, Miami, Fla., 1988, permanent installation at Franklin Inst., Phila, 1990, Autoform in Gretta Sarfaty's retrospective exhbn. Musea Da Imagem E Do Som, Sao Paulo, Brazil, 1988, collborative paintings with G. Sarfaty, Symmetrical Reincarnations I and II, 1988; computer art dir. videos A Price for Every Progress, 1987, Pink Slip Out of Nowhere, 1988; co-dir. telecommunications event Heinrich Hertz Centennial Celebration, Bronx and Bklyn., 1987; independent films Portrait of Sean, 1972, The Seasons, One Minute of Pure Chance, 1973, Existence, Synchrony, 1974 all shown at Artists Space and Whitney Mus., others; mem. editorial adv. bds. jours. Philosophy and Lit., 19876-85, Art & Academe, 1988—. NEH Younger Humanist fellow, 1973-74, Ford Found. fellow, 1974-75, Oldright fellow, NDEA fellow; O'Brien Rsch. grantee, 1971, NEH grantee, 1977. Mem. Assn. for Computing Machinery (bd. dirs. N.Y.C. 1987—, chair Spl. Interest Group on Computer Graphics 1988—), Am. Soc. for Aesthetics (trustee 1981-84), Phi Beta Kappa.

BINNEY, JAN JARRELL, publishing executive; b. Frankfort, Ind., Aug. 16, 1941; d. Robert and Susie (Meek) Jarrell; m. Joseph M. Binney, June 23, 1962; 1 child, Robert J. BS, Purdue U., 1962; MA, Coll. N.J., 1972. Speech-lang. pathologist pub. schs., various locations, 1962-84; pvt. practice speech pathology East Brunswick, N.J., 1982-85; v.p. sales and mktg. The Speech Bin, Inc. Pub., Vero Beach, Fla., 1984—. Editor profl. pubs. Deacon Presbyn. Ch., 1985-87, elder, 1987-90; bd. dirs., chpt. chmn. ARC, Indian River Country, Fla. Fellow Am. Speech, Lang. Hearing Assn. (legis. councilor 1981-89, bd. dirs. pub. info. exch. 1987-89, com. on equality 1988-90, bd. dirs. polit. action com.), N.J. Speech, Lang. Hearing Assn. (pres. 1981-82, hon. 1984), Exch. Club Indian River (charter, sec. 1998-99, bd. dirs. 2001-2002), Exch. Club Indian River Found. (sec. 2002—), Pi Beta Phi Alumnae Club (treas.). Office: The Speech Bin Inc 1965 25th Ave Vero Beach FL 32960-3000 E-mail: jan@speechbin.com.

BINNEY, ROBERT HARRY, bank executive; b. London, Oct. 21, 1945; s. Roy and Barbara (Poole) B.; m. Valerie Kay Greene, May 4, 1979; children: Alexandra, Christopher, Nicholas, Paul. MA in Mech. Scis., Cambridge (Eng.) U., 1967; MBA, Manchester (Eng.) Bus. Sch., 1971. Mktg. exec. Rank Xerox, Birmingham, Eng., 1967-69; with Chase Manhattan Bank, various locations, 1971-96; exec. Orion Bank, London, 1971-72; mgr. expansion and diversification Chase Manhattan Bank, N.Y.C., 1972-73, regional dir. expansion and diversification activities Hong Kong, 1973-74, 2nd v.p. London, 1975, exec. dir. Mid. East and Africa Chase Manhattan Ltd. subs., 1975-79, v.p., 1976, mng. dir. Chase Manhattan Asia Ltd. subs., 1980-83, country mgr., 1983-88, sr. v.p., 1985, sr. banker European fin. industries, 1988-90, bus. exec. Europe and Mid. East for global securities svc., 1991-96; mng. dir. Europe, Mid. East, Africa global securities svcs. Citibank, N.A., London, 1996—, mng. dir. global transaction svcs. in Europe, Mid. East, Africa. Mem. Surrey County Cricket Club. Anglican. Avocations: travel, tennis, bridge. Office: Citigroup Ctr Canada Sq Canary Wharf London E14 5LB England

BINNIE, NANCY CATHERINE, retired nurse, educator; b. Sioux Falls, S.D., Jan. 28, 1937; d. Edward Grant and Jessie May (Martini) Larkin; m. Charles H. Binnie. Diploma, St. Joseph's Hosp. Sch. Nursing, Phoenix, 1965; BS in Nursing, Ariz. State U., 1970, MA, 1974. Intensive care charge nurse Scottsdale (Ariz.) Meml. Hosp., 1968-70, coordinator critical care, 1970-71, John C. Lincoln Hosp., Phoenix, 1971-73; prof. nursing GateWay Community Coll., Phoenix, 1974-96. Coord. part-time evening nursing programs Gateway Community Coll., 1984-97, interim dir. nursing, 1989, 91. Mem. Orgn. Advancement of Assoc. Degree Nursing, Practical and Assoc. Coun. Nursing Educators, Ariz. Coun. Nurse Educators. Avocations: gardening, golf, sewing. Office: Gateway C C 104 N 40th St Phoenix AZ 85034-1704

BINNIG, GERD KARL, phycisist, educator; b. July 20, 1947; m. Lore Binnig, 1969; 2 children. BA in Physics, Goethe U., Frankfurt, Germany, 1973; PhD, Goethe U., Frankfurt, Fed. Republic Germany, 1978. Rsch. staff mem. IBM Zurich Rsch. Lab., 1978—, group leader, 1984—, fellow, 1987—; with Stanford U., 1985—86; hon. prof. physics U. Munich, 1987—. Mem. rsch. team IBM's Almaden Rsch. Ctr., San Jose, 1985—86; vis. prof. Stanford U., 1987—88; mem. tech. coun. IBM Acad., 1990—; mem. adv. bd. Bild der Wissenschaft, 1990—. Author: Aus dem Nichts, 1989; mem. editl. bd.: Rev. Sci. Instruments, 1990—92. Co-recipient Nobel prize in physics, 1986; named to Nat. Inventors Hall of Fame, 1994; recipient physics prize, German Phys. Soc., 1982, Otto Klung prize, 1984, Elliot Cresson medal, Franklin Inst., 1987, Grosses Verdienstkreuz mit Stern und Schulterband des Verdienstordens, 1987, Minnie Rosen award, Ross U., 1988. Fellow: Royal Microscopical Soc. (hon.), Acad. Scis. (assoc.). Avocations: music, tennis, soccer, golf. Office: IBM Zurich Rsch Lab Saumerstrasse 4 Postfach Rueschliken CH-8803 Zurich Switzerland*

BINNING, GENE BARTON, computer company executive; b. Denver, Feb. 7, 1953; s. Gene Hedgecock and Bette Finice (Ames) B. BA in Econs. and Bus. Adminstrn., Vanderbilt U., 1975; MBA, U. Okla., 1977; EdD, Okla. State U., 1996. Br. controller Trane Air Conditioning Dist. Office, Okla. City, 1977-86; cons. pvt. practice, Okla. City, 1986-99; instr. U. Cen. Okla., Edmond, Okla., 1988-99; tech. dir. Vectrix Corp., Oklahoma City, 1999—. Tech. editor On the Horizons, 1996-99. Vol. coord. Sooner State Games, Okla. City, 1985-87; state regents faculty adv. com., 1992-93. Mem. AAUP, Assn. Info. Tech. Profl., Assn. Info. Sys., Okla. Higher Edn. Faculty Assn. of U. Ctrl. Okla. (pres. 1992-93), Faculty Assn. U. Ctrl. Okla. (pres. 1991-92), Quail Creek Golf and Country Club. Republican. Home: 2933 Rolling Stone Rd Oklahoma City OK 73120-1921 Office: Ste 200 9636 N May Ave Oklahoma City OK 73120-2715

BINNING, WILLIAM CHARLES, political scientist, educator; b. Mar. 8, 1944; m. Maureen G. Fannon, Nov. 26, 1966; children: Patrick, Catherine. BA in Politics, St. Anselm's Coll., 1966; PhD in Govt. and Internat. Rels., U. Notre Dame, 1970. Asst. prof. polit. sci. Youngstown (Ohio) State U., 1970—77, assoc. prof., chmn. polit. sci., 1977—84, prof., 1984—. Project dir. NSF, 1978—79, grant evaluator, 1979; part-time staff mem. Office of Gov. G. Voinovich, Ohio, 1991—; arbitrator Am. Arbitration Assn., 2000—. Fellow, NDEA. Mem.: AAU, ASPA, Midwest Polit. Sci. Assn., Am. Polit. Sci. Assn. Office: Dept Polit Sci Youngstown State U 410 Wick Ave Youngstown OH 44555-0001 E-mail: wcbinning@ysu.edu.

BINNS, CATHLEEN ISABEL, retired secondary school educator; b. Fergus, Canada, Mar. 31, 1923; d. Andrew Bernard Schario and Eva Madeleine Lillian Gough; children: Geoffrey Maurice, Robert Bruce. BA, U. Of Calif., Riverside, 1968; MA, Claremont Grad. Sch., Calif., 1973. Cert. Tchr. Calif., 1969. Tchr., curriculum writer Chino (Calif.) Unified Sch. Dist., 1969—89, chair dept. English, 1975, ret., 1989. Vol. Ch. 9 Health Fair, Golden, Colo., 2001—, Jefferson County Rep. Party, Lakewood, 1999—; choir robe mistress, music libr. Trinity United Meth. Ch., 1991—98. Conservative. Avocations: skiing, writing, knitting, gardening. Home: 12210 West 26th Avenue Lakewood CO 80215 Personal E-mail: seabee13@att.worldnet.net.

BINNS, JAMES EDWARD, retired banker; b. Alameda, Calif., Oct. 5, 1931; s. Guy Vivian and Beatrice (Jury) B.; m. Marjean Friesen, Feb. 21, 1951; children: Cheryl Jean Binns Smith, Jana Lee Binns Gualco, Lori LeAnn Binns Mauer. Student, U. Nev., 1950-51; grad., Sch. Bank Audit and Control, U. Wis., 1963, Am. Inst. Banking, 1964. With Sierra Pacific Power Co., Reno, 1948-50; with First Interstate Bank of Nev., Reno, 1951-91, asst. cashier, 1957-63, asst. to cashier, 1963-65, auditor, 1965-84, asst. v.p., 1968-75, v.p., 1975-91; Cameo Jewelry and Loan, Reno, 1992-93; instr. Am. Inst. Banking. Past chmn. internal audit com. City of Reno. Mem. Sierra Nevada Cmty. Access TV, Reno Hot August Nights. Mem. AARP (past pres. Western Nev. chpt., treas., bd. dirs.), Am. Inst. Banking (past pres. Sierra-Nev. chpt., past nat. assoc. coun.), Bank Adminstrn. Inst. (cert. bank auditor, charter pres. chpt., past state dir.), Data Processing Mgmt. Assn. (charter mem. Sierra-Nev. chpt., past pres.), Inst. Internal Auditors (cert. internal auditor, past charter pres. chpt.), Western Indsl. Nev., Masons, Shriners, Elks, Lakeridge Tennis Club, Reno Toastmasters (past pres.), Reno H.S. Alumni Assn. (1st treas.), E. Clampus Vitus (Las Plumas Del Oro chpt.), Graeagle Tennis Club, Reno C. of C. (mem. spl. events coun., Vol. of Yr. award 2001). Home: 1720 Allen St Reno NV 89509-1252 *A true leader must accept all reasonable challenges being fully cognizant that his and the group's success can only be achieved through the combined efforts of all participants.*

BINNS, JANE CAMILLE, humanities educator; b. Ann Arbor, Mich., Aug. 4, 1967; d. Robert Caryl and Lenore Eloise Binns; m. Michael James Monkman, Aug. 11, 1990 (div. Apr. 4, 2002); 1 child, Cale August Monkman. BS, Ea. Mich. U., 1989; MEd, Syracuse U., 1995; MFA, Naropa U., Boulder, Colorado, 1999. Survey analyst, tech. writer Syracuse (N.Y.) U., 1993—97; coll. English instr. Met. State Coll. of Denver, 2000—. Author: (manual and audio tape) Talking to the Media: A How-to for New Readers; contbr. short stories to anthologies (Jack Kerouac fellowship for prose, 1998, Oakland C.C. Writer's at Work, 1999), articles to profl. publs. Process and procedures manual editor Women's Polit. Caucus, Ann Arbor, Mich., 1991—93; newsletter editor NOW, Ann Arbor, 1991—93. Avocations: swimming, playing piano, writing.

BINO, MARIAL DESOLYN, librarian, educator, psychologist; b. Hurley, Wis., May 11, 1916; d. John and Mary B. BE, U. Wis., 1939, cert. Aeronautics Instr., 1942; MS in Libr. Sci., Columbia U., 1958, MA in Devel. Psychology, 1966. Cert. tchr., Wis. Tchr. elem. schs., Wis., 1940-42, 50-52; aeronautic ground instr. U. Wis., Menomonie, 1942-43, aeronautic ground instr. civil air law Eau Claire, 1943-45; tchr. math., sooc. scis. Arbor Vitae-Woodruff (Wis.) H.S., 1945-46; social worker dept. social svcs. Iron County, Hurley, 1946-50; sch. dist. libr. Hurley Sch. Dist., 1952-91. Instr. children's lit. Gogebic C.C., Ironwood, Mich., 1963; vis. lectr. U. Wis., Platteville, summer 1963. Scout leader Girl Scouts Am., Hurley, 1946-50; youth leader ARC, Hurley, 1950-52; mem. City Coun., Hurley, 1982-84. Mem. AAUW, Charles F. Menniger Soc. Avocations: travel, lecturing, reading, writing, swimming.

BINSFELD, CONNIE BERUBE, former state official; b. Munising, Mich., Apr. 18, 1924; d. Omer J. and Elsie (Constance) Berube; m. John E. Binsfeld, July 19, 1947; children: John T., Gregory, Susan, Paul, Michael. BS, Siena Heights Coll., 1945, DHL (hon.), 1977; LLD (hon.), Mich. State U., 1998; DHL (hon.), Mich. State Univ., 1998, Thomas Cooley Sch. of Law, 1999; LLD (hon.), Grand Valley State U., 2000, Lake Superior State U., 2000; DHL (hon.), U. Notre Dame, 2000, Grand Valley State U., 2000. County commr. Leelanau County, Mich., 1970-74; mem. Mich. Ho. of Reps., 1974-82, asst. rep. leader, 1979-81; del. Nav. Conv., 1980, 88, 92; mem. Mich. Senate, 1982-90, asst. rep. leader, 1979, 81; lt. gov. State of Mich., 1990-98. Mem. adv. bd. Nat. Park Sys. Named Mich. Mother of Yr., Mich. Mothers Com., 1977; Northwestern Mich. Coll. fellow. Mem. Nat. Coun. State Legislators, LWV, Siena Heights Coll. Alumnae Assn. Republican. Roman Catholic.*

BINSTOCK, ROBERT HENRY, public policy educator, writer, lecturer; b. New Orleans, Dec. 6, 1935; s. Louis and Ruth (Atlas) B.; m. Martha Burns, July 27, 1979; 1 dau., Jennifer. AB, Harvard U., 1956, PhD, 1965. Lectr. Brandeis U., Waltham, Mass., 1963-65, asst. prof., 1965-69, assoc. prof., 1969-72, Stulberg Prof. law and politics, 1972-84, dir. Policy Ctr. Aging, 1979-84; prof. aging, health and soc. Case Western Res. U., Cleve., 1985—. Mem. com. on an Aging Soc. Nat. Acad. Scis., Washington, 1982-86. Author: America's Political System, 1972, 5th edit., 1991, America's Political System: Urban, State and Local, 1972, 3d edit., 1979, Feasible Planning for Social Change, 1966; editor: The Politics of the Powerless, 1971, Too Old for Health Care?, 1991, Dementia and Aging, 1992, International Perspectives on Aging: Population and Policy Changes, 1982, Handbook of Aging and the Social Sciences, 1976, 5th edit., 2001, The Future of Long Term Care, 1996, Home Care Advances: Essential Research and Policy Issues, 2000, The Lost Art of Caring: A Challenge to Health Professionals, Families, Communities and Society, 2001. Bd. dirs. White House Task Force on Older Ams., 1967-68; chmn. adv. panel Office Tech. Assessment, U.S. Congress, 1982-84 ; tech. adviser, del. White House Conf. on Aging, 1971, 81; trustee Boston Biomed. Research Inst., 1971-84; mem. gov.'s adv. com. Dept. of Elder Affairs Mass., 1974-84; chair, adv. bd. Nat. Acad. on Aging, 1991-95. Recipient Haak-Lilliefors award Mich. State U., 1979, Arthur S. Flemming award Nat. Assn. State Units on Aging, 1988, Key award APHA, 1992, Am. Soc. Aging award, 1994; fellow Ford Found., 1959-69; rsch. grantee NIH, 1968-73. Fellow Gerontol. Soc. Am. (pres. 1976, Donald P. Kent award 1981, Brookdale Prize award 1983), Assn. Gerontol. in Higher Edn.; mem. APHA (chair gerontol. health sect. 1996-97). Office: Case Western Res Univ 2040 Adelbert Rd Cleveland OH 44106-4901

BINTLIFF, BARBARA ANN, law librarian, educator; b. Houston, Jan. 14, 1953; d. Donald Richard and Frances Arlene (Appling) Hay; m. Byron A. Boville, Aug. 20, 1977 (div. 1992); children: Bradley, Bruce. BA, Cen. Wash. U., 1975; JD, U. Wash., 1978, MLL, 1979. Bar: Wash. 1979, U.S. Dist. Ct. (ea. dist.) Wash. 1980, Colo. 1983, U.S. Dist. Ct. Colo. 1983. Libr. Gaddis and Fox, Seattle, 1978-79; reference libr. U. Denver Law Sch., 1979-84; assoc. libr., sr. instr. Sch. Law U. Colo., Boulder, 1984-88, assoc. prof., libr. dir., 1989—2001, prof., 2001—, Nicholas Rosenbaum prof. law, 2002—. Legal cons. Nat. Ctr. Atmospheric Rsch., Environ. and Societal Impacts Group, Boulder, 1980; vis. prof. U. Wash., Seattle, 1996, chair U. Colo. Boulder, Faculty Assembly, 2003-; chmn. faculty assembly U. Colo., 2003—. Editor: A Representative Sample of Tenure Documents for Law Librarians, 1988, 2nd edit., 1994, Chapter Presidents' Handbook, 1989, Representatives Handbook, 1990; assoc. editor: Legal Reference Svcs. Quarterly, Perspectives: Teaching Legal Research and Writing; contbr. articles to profl. jours. Recipient Boulder Faculty Assembly Excellence Svc. award, 2001; named Disting. Alumnus, Ctrl. Wash. U., 2000. Mem. Am. Assn. Law Librs. (v.p./pres.-elect 2000-01, pres. 2001-02), Am. Law Inst. (elected), Colo. Bar Assn., Colo. Assn. Law Librs. (pres. 1982), Southwestern Assn. Law Librs. (pres. 1987-88, 91-92). Episcopalian. Office: U Colo Law Libr 2405 Kittredge Loop Dr Rm 190 Boulder CO 80309-0402

BINZEN, PETER HUSTED, columnist; b. Montclair, N.J., Sept. 24, 1922; s. Frederick William and Lucy Beckwith (Husted) B.; m. Elisabeth Virginia Flower, June 12, 1951; children: Lucy Binzen Wildrick, Jennifer Binzen Cardoso, Jonathan Peter, Katherine. BA in Polit. Sci, Yale U., 1947; postgrad. (Nieman fellow), Harvard U., 1962. Reporter UP, N.Y.C., 1947, Passaic (N.J.) Herald-News, 1947-50; reporter, editor Phila. Bull., 1951-82; reporter Phila. Inquirer, 1982-87; columnist Inquirer, 1987—. Author: Whitetown U.S.A, 1970, (with Joseph R. Daughen) The Wreck of the Penn Central, 1971, The Cop Who Would Be King, 1977; editor: Nearly Everybody Read It, 1998. Served with U.S. Army, 1943-45. Decorated Bronze Star. Office: Phila Inquirer 400 N Broad St Philadelphia PA 19130-4015

BIOLCHINI, ROBERT FREDRICK, lawyer; b. Detroit, Sept. 22, 1939; s. Alfred and Erma (Barbetti) Biolchini; m. Frances Lauinger, June 5, 1965; children: Robert F., Douglas C., Frances E., Tobin M., Thomas A., Christine M. BA, U. Notre Dame, 1962; LLB, George Washington U., 1965. Bar: Okla., Mich., 1965. Assoc. Doerner, Stuart, Saunders, Daniel, Anderson & Biolchini, Tulsa, Okla., 1968-71, ptnr., 1971-94, Stuart, Biolchini & Turner, Tulsa, 1994—. Pres., CEO Pennwell Corp.; chmn. bd. dirs., CEO, PennEnergy, Inc., Valley Nat. Bank, Ameritrust Holding Co., Old Faithful Underwriting Ltd.; mem. Lloyds of London, 1979—; bd. dirs. Lumen Energy Corp., Bank of The Lakes, Bank of Jackson Hole. Bd. dirs. Thomas Gilcrease Mus., past pres., chmn. bd., 1977-80, dir. emeritus, 1980—; bd. dirs., sec., legal clk. Tulsa Ballet Theatre, Inc., 1976-84; trustee Monte Cassino Endowment, 1978—; pres. Monte Cassino Sch. Bd., 1970-77; chmn. Christ the King Parish Coun., 1974-75; mem. adv. coun. U. Notre Dame Law Sch., 1982-2000, trustee U. Notre Dame, 2001—; chmn. Cath. Diocese Tulsa Fund for Future, 1998—; bd. dirs. legal counsel Tulsa Area United Way, 1986—; mem. pres.'s coun. Regis Coll., 1986—; Okla. chmn. Lawyers for Bush, 2000. Capt. U.S. Army, 1965-67. Mem. Okla. Bar Assn., Mich. Bar Assn., Met. Tulsa C. of C. (bd. dirs. 1992—), Summit Club, Southern Hills Country Club, Club Ltd., Knights of Malta, Knights of the Holy Sepulchre. Roman Catholic. Home: 1744 E 29th St Tulsa OK 74114-5402 Office: First Place Tower 15 E 5th St Ste 3300 Tulsa OK 74103-4340

BIONDI, ANTHONY, municipal official; b. Norristown, Pa., Apr. 10, 1962; s. Rober B. and Sylvia (Linfante) B.; m. Fran Biondi. BA, Villanova (Pa.) U., 1985. Fin. clk. Borough of Norristown, 1986-88, asst. dir. fin., 1988-91, dir. fin., 1991-94, borough administr., 1994—. Address: 235 E Airy St Norristown PA 19401-5003

BIONDI, FLORENCE, artist, cantor; b. N.Y.C., Sept. 25, 1924; d. Angelo and Frances Curreri; m. Albert Anthony Biondi, Apr. 15, 1951; children: Joseph, Albert, Thomas, Robert. Student, Bklyn. Mus. Art Sch., 1967-75, Art Student's League, New City, N.Y., 1976-79. Pen and ink illustrator Simplicity Patterns, N.Y.C., 1943-45, Reader Mail Inc., N.Y.C., 1948-86; draftsman W.L. Maxson & Co., N.Y.C., 1945-48; freelance artist, 1986—. Mem. chorus Conservatory of Music. Recipient Pen and Brush Club award, 2001. Fellow: Am. Artists Profl. League (various awards 1980—82, 1988, 2000); mem.: Catherine Lorillard Wolfe Art Club (Portrait Pastel award 1983, 1996, 2001), Pastel Soc. Am. (Kalkow award 1983), Nat. Assn. Women Artists, Audubon Artists. Roman Catholic. Avocations: music, gardening, sewing, reading, choral music. Home: 426 Mcdonald Ave Brooklyn NY 11218-2212

BIONDI, LAWRENCE, university administrator, priest; b. Chgo., Dec. 15, 1938; s. Hugo and Albertina (Marchetti) B. BA, Loyola U., Chgo., 1962, Ph.L., 1964, M.Div., S.T.L., Loyola U., Chgo., 1971; MS, Georgetown U., 1966, PhD in Sociolinguistics, 1975. Ordained priest Roman Cath. Ch., 1970. Joined Soc. Jesus; asst. prof. sociolinguistics Loyola U., Chgo., 1974-79, assoc. prof., 1979-81, prof., 1982-87, dean Coll. Arts and Scis., 1980-87; pres. St. Louis U., 1987—. Mem. Joint Commn. on Accreditation of Health Care Orgs., 1998—. Author: The Italian-American Child: His Sociolinguistic Acculturation, 1975, Poland's Solidarity Movement, 1984; editor: Poland's Church-State Relations in the 1980s, 1980, Spain's Church-State Relations, 1982. Trustee Xavier U., 1981-87, Loyola Coll., Balt., 1988-94, Santa Clara U., 1988-98, Kenrick-Glennon Sem., 1988-94, St. Louis U., 1982—, Loyola U., Chgo., 1988-97; bd. dirs. Epilepsy Found. Am., 1985-95, Civic Progress, St. Louis, 1987—, Regional Commerce and Growth Assn., 1987—, Mo. Bot. Gardens, 1987—, St. Louis Zoo, 1994, St. Louis Symphony, 1994, Harry S. Truman Inst. for Nat. and Internat. Affairs, 1987—, Tenet Health Care Sys., 1998—, St. Louis Sci. Ctr., 2000—, Boys Hope Girls Hope, 1996—, St. Louis Art Mus., 1997—, Grand Ctr., St. Louis, 1987—. Mellon grantee, 1974, 75, 76, 82 Mem. Linguistic Soc. Am., MLA, Am. Anthrop. Assn. Office: St Louis U 221 N Grand Blvd Saint Louis MO 63103-2006

BIONDI, MANFRED ANTHONY, physicist, educator; b. Carlstadt, N.J., Mar. 5, 1924; s. Manfred Anthony and Helen (Flaction) B.; m. Elaine Theresa Leitkam, May 12, 1952; children: David Mark, George Philip. BS in Physics, MIT, 1944, PhD, 1949. Research assoc. MIT, Cambridge, 1948-49; with Westinghouse Research Labs, Pitts., 1949-60, adv. physicist, 1952-57, mgr. physics dept., 1957-60; prof. physics U. Pitts., 1960-86, prof. emeritus, 1987—; also dir. Atomic Scis. Inst., 1968-79; exchange prof. U. Paris, 1976-86. Trustee Upper Atmosphere Rsch. Corp.; mem. adv. com. Army Rsch. Office, Durham, N.C., NAS, 1962-64; mem. exec. coun. Fedn. Am. Scientists, 1966-68; mem. adv. panel physics NSF, 1970-72; mem. Army basic rsch. steering com. NRC, 1985-88, chmn., 1987-88. Editorial bd.: Jour. Applied Physics, 1966-68. Served with USNR, 1943-46. Fellow AAAS, Am. Phys. Soc. (chmn. div. electron and atomic physics 1957, chmn. gaseous electronics conf. 1962-64, Davisson-Germer prize 1984); mem. Am. Geophys. Union, Earth and Sky (adv. bd. 1992-94). Home: 1375 Hillsdale Dr Monroeville PA 15146-4444 Office: U Pitts Dept Physics And Astro Pittsburgh PA 15260

BIONDI, MATT, Olympic athlete; b. San Diego, Oct. 8, 1965; Olympic swimmer, L.A., 1984, Seoul, 1988, Barcelona, 1992. Recipient 8 Olympic Gold medals, 2 Olympic Silver medals, 1 Olympic Bronze medal. Office: USA Swimming One Olympic Plz Colorado Springs CO 80909

BIONDI, O. FRANCIS, lawyer; b. Wilmington, Del., Jan. 1, 1933; s. Ferdinando and Mary C. (Masci) Biondi; m. Anita V. DiAngelo, June 30, 1962; children: O. Francis, Mary Catherine. BA magna cum laude, LaSalle Coll., 1954; MA in Econ., Boston Coll., 1955; LLB, U. Pa., 1958. Bar: Del. 1958, US Supreme Ct. 1965. City solicitor Wilmington, 1963—68; dep. atty. gen. Del., 1961—68; sr. ptnr. Biondi and Babiarz, PA and predecessor Biondi and Babiarz, 1967—72; pres., 1972—79; sr. ptnr. Morris, Nichols, Arsht & Tunnell, Wilmington, 1979—; mem. Long Range Ct. Planning Com. Del. Supreme Ct., 1972; vice chmn. Del. Agy. to Reduce Crime; titular chmn., 1973—74; chmn. Crime Reduction Task Force, 1973—74; chmn. bd. dir. Del. gov. Investigative Strike Force, 1973—74; chmn. Del. Franchise Tax Com., 1974, Del Supreme Ct. Bd. on Profl. Responsibility, 1980; chmn. Adv. Com. on Alt. Dispute Resolutions Del. Supreme Ct., 1982; Del. counsel Del. River and Bay Authority, 1973—; bd. dir. Del. Bar Found.; dir. First Nat. Bank Wilmington; mem. del. Dem. State Com., 1964—. Mem.: ABA, Assn. Trial Lawyers Am., Del. Trial Lawyers Assn., Del. Mem. Bel. Bar Assn. (chmn. com. gen. legis., pres. elect), Wesley Coll. (trustee), Del. region NCCJ, Del Council Banking (mem. 1970), Greater Wilmington Develop. Council, Grand Opera House (bd. dir.), Jefferson of Dem. Party (co-chmn. 1982—). Roman Catholic. Home: 132 Chatenay Ln Wilmington DE 19807-1429

BIONDI, PETER J. assemblyman; b. June 23, 1942; Dep. mayor Hillsborough Twp., 1985, mayor, 1986—93; assemblyman N.J. Gen. Assembly, 1998—; asst. rep. leader, 2002—. Mem. Hillsborough Twp. Com., 1983—84, Hillsborough Twp. Planning Bd., 1986—99, Somerset County Planning Bd., 1994—96, Somerset County Bd. Chosen Freeholders, 1994—97, dep. dir., 1995, dir., 96. Mem. Hillsborough Capital Planning Com., 1994—95; spl. commr. Joint Ins. Fund, 1996; mem. Somerset County Youth Svcs. Commn., 1996—, co-chair, 1997; mem. Indsl. Pollution Control Financing Authority, 1997. With USAR, 1961—67. Republican. Office: 1 E High St Somerville NJ 08876 E-mail: AsmBiondi@njleg.org.*

BIONDO, RAYMOND VITUS, retired dermatologist; b. N.Y.C., June 13, 1936; s. Joseph Pernice and Bena Biondo; m. Mary McKinnon, Dec. 24, 1976. BA in Biology, U. No. Colo., 1960; MS in Biochemistry, U. Ark., 1963, BS in Medicine, MD, U. Ark., 1967. Diplomate Am. Bd. Dermatology. Asst. mgmt. analyst 389th USAF Hosp., Francis E. Warren AFB, Wyo., 1954-58; rsch. trainee NIH at U. Ark., Little Rock, 1961-63; rsch. biochemist VA Hosp., Little Rock, 1963-65; intern U. Cin. Med. Ctr., 1967-68; resident in dermatology U. Ark., Little Rock, 1968-71, asst. clin. prof. dermatology, 1971-90; pres. North Little Rock (Ark.) Dermatology Clinic, 1971-90. Contbr. articles to profl. jours. Staff officer USCG Aux. Flotilla and Divsn., 1995; mem. nat. adv. com. on scouting for the handicapped Boy Scouts Am., 1976—81, nat. chmn. med. exploring com., 1981—84, nat. coun., 1977—, nat. exploring com., 1977—92, nat. scoutreach com., 1990—, nat. Jewish com. on scouting, 1981—84; mem. Ark. Kidney disease Commn., 1979—83; bd. dirs. Ctrl. Ark. Health Systems Agy., 1984, Ark. Health Care Access Found., 1998—2001, sec.-treas., 1998—99, 2000—01; founder, pres. Am. Red Magen David for Israel, Ark., 1987—92, 1994—2001; bd. dirs. Congregation B/nai Israel, Little Rock, 1982—84, Jewish Fedn. Ark., 1989—92. Recipient Outstanding Alumnus award, U. No. Colo., 1977, Shofar award, 1992, William H. Spurgeon and Whitney M. Young awards, Boy Scouts Am., 1981, Silver Antelope award, 1983, Silver Beaver award, 1977, Nat. Torch of Gold award, 1993, Spirit of Scouting award, 2000, cert. of achievement in cmty. health promotion, Ark. Dept. Health, 1993, Gov.'s Vol. Excellence award, 1983, 1998, 1999, Ark. cert. of appreciation for pub. svc., 1992, Father Joseph H. Biltz award, Ark. Coun. Nat. Conf. of Cmty. and Justice, 1990, numerous vol. awards, U.S. Dept. Vets. Affairs, 1991—2001, Vol. Svc. Leadership award, 1999, Nat. Disting. Svc. award, Jewish War Vets. of U.S., 1995, 1998, Golden Rule award finalist, JC Penney Co./United Way of Pulaski County, 1996, Golden Rule award, 1999, Spirit of Svc. award, Ark. Health Care Access Found., 1996, cert. appreciation, City of Little Rock, 1996, Adminstrn. award of Merit, USCG Aux., 1996, George Washington Honor medal, Freedoms Found., 1997, Man. of Vol. Achievement award, cert. of achievement for outstanding vol., Ret. and Sr. Vol. Program Ctrl. ARk., 1997, 1998, Pres.'s Svc. award nominee, 1997, 1998, 1999, Intergenerational Col. award, Ark. Aging Svc. Vol. Acad. Coun. Eldercare, 1998, Cmty. Svc. award, Sta. KARK-TV, Gov.'s Office and Ark. Divsn. of Vol. Dept. Human Svcs., 1999, Ark. Martin Luther King Jr. Comn. Cmty. Svc. award, 2000, Spl. Contbr. award, Congrl. Medal Hon. Soc., 1998, Silver Buffalo award, Boy Scouts Am., 2002, Sr. Leadership award, Ark. Gov.'s Coun. on Fitness, 2002. Fellow Am. Acad. Dermatology (adv. bd. nat. dermatology program 1973-75); mem. AMA (physicians recognition award 1971-90, cert of appreciation 1984), Ark. Med. Soc. (ho. of dels. 1971—), Ark Dermatol. Soc. (pres. 1977), Pulaski County Med. Soc., Jewish War Vets U.S. (founder, comdr. Ark. post 436, nat. surgeon 1993-98, 2000-2003, nat. vice Boy Scout officer 1993—, nat. White House liaison officer 1993-95, Judge Lawrence Gubow Meml. hon. mention 1989, Cert. of Appreciation Tex. dept. 1991, Cert. of Merit 1992, Chapel of Four Chaplains Legion of Honor 1994, Humanitarian award 1996, Bronze medallion 1997, Sr. Ark. Hall of Fame Cert. Recognition, 1997, inducted 1998), Sigma Xi, Alpha Omega Alpha, Golden Key (hon.). Jewish. Home: PO Box 6361 North Little Rock AR 72124-6361 E-mail: raybiondo@yahoo.com.

BIORDI, DIANA L. healthcare educator, dean; b. New Castle, Pennsylvania, Mar. 11, 1940; d. Dante and Mary Alice (Buzzelli) Biordi; m. Allan T. Luskin (div. Dec. 1980); 1 child from previous marriage, Joshua Dante Luskin. Diploma nursing, Fairviw Park Hosp. Sch.of Nursing, Cleve., OH., 1961; BA psychology, Baldwin-Wallace Coll., Berea, OH., 1965; MA med. sociology, U. Ill., Chgo., IL., 1971; PhD med. sociology, Northwestern U., Evanston, IL., 1984; MSN, Rush U., Chgo., IL., 1990; cert., in conflict mediation and family mediation, Acad. of Family Mediators, 1998. Staff and charge nurse Fairview Pk. Hosp., Cleve., 1961—62, instr., 1962—63; nurse, infirmary, and dispensary Baldwin-Wallace Coll., Berea, Ohio, 1962—65; rsch. assoc. IL. Inst. of Tech., Chgo., 1966—69; instr. Ind. U., Indpls., 1970—71; project dir. Butler U., Indpls., 1971—72; sr. cons. Medicus Sys. Inc., Chgo., 1972—76; rsch. asst. U. Ill., Chgo., 1978—80; asst. prof. U. Ill. Coll. of Nursing, Chgo., 1980—90, U. Ill. Coll. of Nursing, Chgo., 1990—92; assoc. prof. and asst. dean Kent St. U., Kent, Ohio, 1992—94, prof. and asst. dean rsch. and grad. affairs, 1995—, web ct. project mgr., 2002—. Recipient Assoc. Alumnae Award, NW. U., 1978, Comm. Svc. Award, Coleman Profl. Svc. Partial Hosp. Program, 1995; fellow, Am. Acad. of Nursing, 1995. Mem.: Midwest Nursing Rsch. Soc. (pres., treas. 1992—2000). Avocations: reading, needlecrafts, antiques, collecting, radio reader. Office: Kent State U Coll of Nursing Box 5190 Kent OH 44242-0001 Office Fax: 330-672-6387. E-mail: dbiordi@kent.edu.

BIPPUS, DAVID PAUL, manufacturing company executive; b. Evansville, Ind., Nov. 29, 1949; s. James Paul and Mary Louise (Elder) B.; m. Kohnne Susann Heikens, Aug. 28, 1971; 1 child, Laura. BS, Iowa State U., 1971; MBA with honors, Boston U., 1975. Cert. CPCU. Tech. mgr. Ill. Dept. Transp., Springfield, 1976; asst. dir. planning Horace Mann Ins. Co., Springfield, 1976-79; mgr. fin. planning Hydro-Transmission div. Sundstrand Corp., Ames, Iowa, 1979-82; controller Hydraulics div. Sundstrand Corp., Rockford, Ill., 1982-84; v.p. fin., sec., treas. Suntec Industries, Inc., Rockford, 1984-89, v.p. ops., sec., treas., 1989-94; corp. controller Reliant Industries, Inc., Rock Falls, Ill., 1994, CFO, 1995-99; v.p. fin. and info. tech. Haldex Barnes Hydraulics, Co., 1999—. Instr. Lincoln Land Community Coll., Springfield, 1976-78. Bd. dirs. New Am. Theater, Rockford, 1991-97, pres., 1993-95; bd. dirs. Parents for Gifted Edn., Rockford, 1989-91; bd. dirs. Rockford Civic New Comers, 1982-85; mem. Story County Planning and Zoning Commn.; mem. ch. coun. Zion Luth. Ch., 1998-2001, pres., 2000-2001. 1st lt. U.S. Army, 1972-76. Mem. Fin. Exec. Inst. (bd. dirs. local chpt. 1989—, pres. 1993-94), Soc. of CPCU's, Nat. Assn. Accts., Am. Legion. Republican. Avocations: photography, woodworking. Home: 9640 N Blaine Dr Byron IL 61010-9101 Office: Haldex Barnes Hydraulics Co 2222 15th St Rockford IL 61104-7313

BIRCH, ADOLPHO A., JR., state supreme court justice; b. Washington, Sept. 22, 1932; BA, JD, Howard U., 1956. Bar: Tenn. 1957. Pvt. practice, Nashville, 1958—66; asst. pub. defender, 1964—66; asst. dist. atty., 1966—69; judge Davidson County Gen. Sessions Ct., 1969—78, Tenn. Criminal Ct. (20th jud. dist.), 1978—87; former judge Tenn. Ct. Criminal Appeals; chief justice Tenn. Supreme Ct., Nashville, 1996—97, assoc. justice, 1994—. Assoc. prof. Nashville Sch. of Law. With USNR, 1956—58. Mem.: ABA, Napier Lobby Bar Assn. (past pres.), Nashville Bar Assn., Tenn. Bar Assn., Nat. Bar Assn. Office: 304 Supreme Court Bldg, 401 7th Ave N Nashville TN 37219-1407*

BIRCH, EUGENIE LADNER, urban planning educator; b. Montclair, N.J., June 30, 1943; d. George R. and Jeanette (Gross) Ladner; m. Robert S. Birch, Oct. 5, 1968; children: Foster, Rebecca, Victoria. AB, Bryn Mawr Coll., 1965; M in Urban Planning, Columbia U., 1969, PhD, 1975. Instr. urban planning Briarcliff (N.Y.) Coll., 1970-77; asst. prof. SUNY, Purchase, 1978-80; assoc. prof. Hunter Coll. CUNY, 1980-89, prof. Hunter Coll., 1989-98, chair dept. urban affairs Hunter Coll., 1993-94, 97—, assoc. provost, 1994-97; prof. U. Pa., 1998—, chair dept. city and regional planning, 1998—. Vis. lectr. Yale U., New Haven, Conn., 1977-78, Rutgers U., New Brunswick, N.J., 1977-78, Ohio State U., 1987-88. Editor: The Unsheltered Woman, 1986, Jour. Am. Planning Assn., 1988-93; contbr. articles to profl. jours. Mem. N.Y.C. Planning Commn., 1990-95. Fellow Am. Inst. Cert. Planners, 2000. Mem. Soc. for Am. City and Regional Planning (pres. 1987-92), Am. Planning Assn., Am. Inst. Cert. Planners, Assn. Collegiate Schs. of Planning (pres. 1995-97). Presbyterian. Office: Dept City and Reg Planning U Penn Philadelphia PA 19104-6311 E-mail: elbirch@pobox.upenn.edu.

BIRCH, PATRICIA, choreographer, director; b. Englewood, N.J. d. Abraham S. and Mary (Levinsohn) B.; m. A. William J. Becker III; children: Jonathan Heath, Alison Becker Hurt, Peter Heath. BA, Bennington Coll. Dancer Martha Graham Co., N.Y.C., West Side Story, 1960. Choreographer, dir. (Broadway and Off-Broadway prodns. music theater and opera stage work) You're A Good Man Charlie Brown, The Me Nobody Knows, A Little Night Music, Grease, Candide, Over Here, Diamond Studs, Pacific Overtures, The Mikado, Gilda Radner, Live From New York, Zoot Suit, They're Playing Our Song, The Cradle Will Rock, Street Scene, In the Time of the Comedian Harmonists, The Happy End, Lawyers, Lovers and Lunatics, Portraits in Jazz, Really Rosie, Raggedy Ann, A Walk on the Wild Side, Elvis, The Mass, The Jumping Frog of Calaveras County, The Gershwin Gala, Club 12, Fanny Hackabout Jones, What About Luv, American Enterprise, Band in Berlin, Parade, Exactly Like You, I Sent A Letter To My Love, The Snow Queen, King Island Christmas; dir., choreographer videos The Very Thought of You, NBC Olympic Video, Better Not Tell Her, True Colors, Money Changes Everything, Frankie, It's My Party, Beat Street Strut; choreographer videos Harlem Shuffle, She Bop, Jump, concert dance Ballet for The American Ballroom Theater, Mass. Opera Co. of Boston, N.Y.C. Opera, Abstract Opera U. Ark.; dir. TV programs Dance in America, Christmas With Flicka, Celebrating Gershwin, Natalie Cole, Unforgettable, 20th Anniversary, Dancing, Natalie Cole's Untraditional Xmas; musical staging/choreographer for TV programs Saturday Night Live, The Gary Shandling Show, Good Sports, The Orchestra, Robert Klein Special, The Oscars, American Music Awards, The Grammys, The Electric Co., The Muppets, Square One, Goldie Hawn Spl., This is the Moment TV Donny Osmond, films Grease, Big, Awakenings, Sleeping With the Enemy, Billy Bathgate, Cowboy Way, Used People, the Wild Party, Roseland, Grease II, First Wives Club, The Human Stain. Recipient 2 Emmy awards NATAS, 1988, 92, 5 Tony nominations, DGA nomination, Fred Astaire award. E-mail: patbirch@nycrr.com.

BIRCH, STANLEY FRANCIS, JR., federal judge; b. Langley Field, Va., Aug. 29, 1945; BA, U. Va., 1967; JD, Emory U., 1970, LLM in Taxation, 1976. Law clk. to Hon. Judge Sidney O. Smith Jr. U.S. Dist. Ct. (no. dist.) Ga., 1972—74; mem. firm Greer, Sartain & Carey, Gainesville, Ga., 1974—76, Deal, Birch, Jarrard & Link, Gainesville, 1976—83, Birch, Hartness & Link, Gainesville, 1983—85, Vaughan, Davis, Birch & Murphy, Atlanta, 1984—90, judge U.S. Ct. Appeals (11th cir.), Atlanta, 1990—. Lt. U.S. Army, 1970—72. Mem.: Lawyers Club Atlanta, 11th Cir. Hist. Soc., Gainesville Northeastern Bar Assn., Atlanta Bar Assn., Ga. Bar Found., State Bar Ga., Calvert Hall Alumni Assn., Emory U. Sch. Law Alumni Assn. (past pres.), U. Va. Alumni Assn., Ga. Legal History Found., Old Warhorse Lawyers Club, Theta Delta Chi. Office: US Ct Appeals 11th Cir 56 Forsyth St NW Atlanta GA 30303*

BIRCH, TOBEYLYNN, librarian; b. Los Angeles, Nov. 26, 1949; d. George Walter and Phyllis Jacqueline (Barnes) B.; m. Michael Frederick Cowan, May 17, 1975; children— Stephanie Gayle, Natalie Claire. B.A. in Psychology, U. Calif.-Santa Cruz, 1972; M.A. in Librarianship, U. Denver, 1976. Acquisitions asst. UCLA, 1976-79; asst. librarian Calif. Sch. Profl. Psychology, Los Angeles, 1980-81, dir. library, 1981—2001; univ. livr. Alliant Internat. U., 2001--. Mem. ALA (sec. Library Instrn. Round Table 1985-86, v.p. 1987-88, pres. 1988-89), AAHE, Calif. Acad. and Res. Libr., Assn. Mental Health Libra, Beta Phi Mu. Democrat. Home: 4510 W 231st St Torrance CA 90505-3417 Office: Alliant Internat U 1000 S Fremont Ave Unit 5 Alhambra CA 91803 Business E-Mail: tbirch@alliant.edu.

BIRCHARD, CATHERINE SUZANNE SIEH, artist; b. New Rochelle, NY, Jan. 20, 1964; d. Theodore and Eleanor Anne Becker Sieh; m. Richard Edward Birchard, Oct. 9, 1987; 1 child, Dylan. BA, Cornell U., Ithaca, N.Y., 1985. Monotype, Dissolution 3, 1996, painting, Munch (1938), 1997, exhibited in group shows at Westbeth Gallery, NYC, 1998, Gallery 402, 1998, Erector Sq. Gallery, New Haven, Conn., 1998, Silvermine Guild Galleries, New Canaan, Conn., 1998, The Macy Gallery, Valhalla, NY, 1999, The Art Club Gallery, NYC, 2000, NY Law Sch. Gallery of NYC, 2000, The Gallery on the Hudson, Irvington, NY, 2001, Pelham Arts Ctr. Gallery, Pelham, NY, 2002, The Arts Exch. Gallery, White Plains, NY, 2002—, Phoenix Gallery, NYC, 2002, The Macy Gallery, Valhalla, NY, 2003, Iona Coll. Arts Ctr., New Rochelle, NY, 2003. Recipient Juror's Selection Award, 1998, Cresson Pugh Award for Most Innovative, 1997; named Inaugural Westchester Biennial Artist, Castle Gallery, 1998. Mem. Mamaroneck Artists' Guild (bd. dir. 1998—, newsletter editor 1998-99, dir. programs 1998-2001, dir. publicity 2001-, membership juror 2001-), Orgn. Ind. Artists, Ctr. for Book Arts. Avocations: music, book collecting.

BIRCHENALL, JAVIER ARTURO, economist, researcher; b. Sogamoso, Colombia, May 5, 1974; arrived in U.S., 1999; s. Humberto Birchenall and Francisca Jimenez; m. Adriana Gonzalez, Apr. 24, 1999. BA in Econs., U. Javeriana, Bogota, Colombia, 1996; MSc in Econs., U. Los Andes, Bogota, Colombia, 1997; MA in Econs., U. Los Andes, 2001. Dir. internat. studies Dept Nat. de Planeacion, Bogota, 1997—99; lectr. in econs. U. Chgo., 2001—. Office: Dept Econs Univ Chicago 1126 E 59th St Chicago IL 60637

BIRCHER, ANDREA URSULA, psychiatric nurse practitioner; b. Bern, Switzerland, Mar. 6, 1928; arrived in U.S., 1947; d. Franklin E. Bircher and Hedy E. Bircher-Rey. Diploma, Knapp Coll. Nursing, Santa Barbara, Calif., 1957; BS, U. Calif., San Francisco, 1961, MS, 1962; PhD, U. Calif., Berkeley, 1966. RN. Staff nurse, head nurse Cottage Hosp., Santa Barbara, 1957—58; psychiat. nurse, jr., sr. Langley-Porter Neuropsychiatric Inst., San Francisco, 1958—66; asst. prof. U. Ill. Coll. Nursing, Chgo., 1966-72; prof. U. Okla. Coll. Nursing, Oklahoma City, 1972-93, prof. emeritus, 1993—. Contbr. articles to profl. jours. Mem.: NAFE, ANA, AAUP, Calif. Assn. Psychiat. Nurses in Advanced Practice, N.Am. Nursing Diagnosis Assn., Internat. Soc. Psychiat.-Mental Health Nursing, Am. Psychotherapy Assn. (diplomate), ANA Calif., Ventura County Writers Club, Phi Kappa Phi, Sigma Theta Tau. Republican. Avocations: indoor gardening, cooking, reading, yoga, writing. Home: 1161 Cypress Point Ln Apt 201 Ventura CA 93003-6074

BIRCHFIELD, JOHN KERMIT, JR., lawyer; b. Roanoke, Va., Jan. 8, 1940; s. John Kermit and Christine (Luke) B.; m. Glenys Garnell, Nov. 14, 1964; 1 child, Guthrie Kathryn BS in Econs., Roanoke Coll., 1968; JD, U. Va., 1971. Bar: N.Y., 1972, U.S. Dist Ct. (so. dist.) N.Y., 1972, U.S. Ct. Appeals (2d cir.), 1972. Assoc. Shearman & Sterling, N.Y.C., 1971-81; ptnr. Holtzmann, Wise & Shepard, N.Y.C., 1981-83; sr. v.p. legal and govtl. affairs, gen. counsel Ga. Pacific Corp., Atlanta, 1983-88; mng. dir. Century Ptnrs., Atlanta, Darien, Conn., 1988—; sr. v.p., gen. counsel, corp. sec. M/A-COM, Boston, 1990-95. Bd. dirs. Intermountain Industries, Inc., HPSC, Inc., Mass. Fin. Compass Group Mutual Funds, Displaytech, Inc., chmn., 1996—2001; former chmn. bd. dirs. Chas. P. Young Co.; chmn. bd. dirs. Dairy Mart Convenience Stores, Inc., 1999—2003. Author: How to Borrow on the Eurodollar Market, 1981, The Multinational Joint Venture, 1981. Chmn. adv. bd. Park Pride, 1986-90; bd. dirs., exec. com. Atlanta Ballet, 1984-88, chmn., 1987-88, vice chmn., 1986-87; bd. dirs. Atlanta Music Festival Assn., 1984-90, Friends Piedmont Hosp., 1985-90; bd. dirs., exec. com., treas. Assn. Am.-Indian Affairs, 1983-86; bd. dirs. High Mus. Art, 1986-91, exec. com., 1988-89; bd. visitors Emory U., 1985-88, bd. dirs. Emory U. Mus. Art and Archaeology, 1988-92; bd. dirs., chmn. collections com. Cape Ann Hist. Assn., 1993—; trustee Roanoke Coll., 1988—, Chatham Hall, 1988-94. Mem. ABA, Atlanta Bar Assn., Assn. Bar City N.Y., N.Y. State Bar Assn., Am. Law Inst., Am. Arbitration Assn., Racquet and Tennis Club, India House Club, Piedmont Driving Club, Farmington Country Club, Shendoah Club, Annisquam Yacht Club, Union Boat Club, Somerset Club. Home: Cranberry Hill 33 Way Rd Gloucester MA 01930-4315 E-mail: kermitb@displaytech.com.

BIRD, CAROLINE, author; b. N.Y.C., Apr. 15, 1915; d. Hobart Stanley and Ida (Brattrud) B.; m. Edward A. Menuez, June 8, 1934 (div. Dec. 1945); 1 dau., Carol (Mrs. John Paul Barach); m. John Thomas Mahoney, Jan. 5, 1957 (dec. 1981); 1 son, John Thomas. Student, Vassar Coll., 1931-34; BA, U. Toledo, 1938; MA, U. Wis., 1939; LHD (hon.), Keene State U., 1988. Desk editor N.Y. Jour. Commerce, 1943-44; edit. rschr. Newsweek mag., N.Y.C., 1942-43, Fortune mag., N.Y.C., 1944-46; with Dudley-Anderson-Yutzy, pub. relations, N.Y.C., 1947-68; Froman Disting. prof. Russell Sage Coll., 1972-73; Mather prof. Case Western Res. U., Cleve., 1977. Author: The Invisible Scar, 1966, Born Female, 1968, rev. edit., 1970, The Crowding Syndrome, 1972, Everything a Woman Needs to Know to Get Paid What She's Worth, 1973, rev., 1982, The Case Against College, 1975, Enterprising Women, 1976, What Women Want, 1979, The Two-Paycheck Marriage, 1979, The Good Years, 1983, Second Careers, 1992, Lives of Our Own, 1995; chief writer: The Spirit of Houston, 1978; also articles in nat. mags. Mem. review bd. Dept. State, 1974. Mem. Am. Soc. Journalists and Authors, Am. Sociol. Assn. Home: 4206 Stammer Pl Nashville TN 37215

BIRD, CHARLES ALBERT, lawyer; b. Stockton, Calif., July 1, 1947; s. Donald Gladstone and Elizabeth Clara (Jongeneel) B.; m. Charlotte Laura Soeters, June 28, 1969. BA, U. Calif., Davis, 1969, JD, 1973. Bar: Calif. 1973, U.S. Dist. Ct. (so. dist.) 1975, U.S. Dist. Ct. (cen. dist.) Calif. 1981, U.S. Ct. Appeals (9th cir.) 1975, U.S. Ct. Appeals (10th cir.) 1996, U.S. Ct. Appeals (6th cir.) 1999, U.S. Ct. Appeals (4th and fed. cirs.) 2002, U.S. Supreme Ct. 1980. Tchr. Woodland Unified Sch. Dist., Calif., 1969-70; law clk. justice Supreme Ct. Alaska, Juneau, 1973-74; assoc. Luce, Forward, Hamilton & Scripps, San

Diego, 1975-79, ptnr., 1980—. Contbr. articles to profl. jours. Bd. dirs. Defenders Orgn., San Diego, 1982—, pres., 1990-92; founding dir. San Diego Vol. Lawyer Program, 1982-86. Fellow Am. Acad. Appellate Lawyers; mem. Calif. Acad. Appellate Lawyers, San Diego County Bar Assn. (legis. chmn. 1980-81, bd. dirs. 1982-85, sec. 1984, v.p. 1985), State Bar Assn. Calif. (exec. com. real property sect. 1982-86, chmn. exec. com. 1985-86), Calif. Commn. Judicial Nominees Evaluation (chmn. 1999-2000). Democrat. Episcopalian. Home: 4182 Ingalls St San Diego CA 92103-1354 Office: Luce Forward Hamilton 600 W Broadway Ste 2600 San Diego CA 92101-3372 E-mail: cbird@luce.com.

BIRD, FORREST M. retired medical inventor; b. Stoughton, Mass., June 9, 1921; Technical air tng. officer Army Air Corps. Inventor Bird Universal Medical Respirator for acute or chronic cardiopulmonary care, 1958, "Baby-bird" respirator, 1970. Inductee Nat. Inventors Hall of Fame, 1995. Office: Nat Inventors Hall of Fame 221 S Broadway St Akron OH 44308-1505

BIRD, HENRY LONSDALE, biologist, priest; b. Wilmington, Del., May 29, 1927; s. Samuel Bancroft and Lonsdale (Miner) B.; m. Hildegarde deVermandois Brewster, June 14, 1955; children: William Brewster, Holloway Lonsdale, Thaddeus Bartholomew, Paul Barnabas, Anna Sara Love. BA in Biology, Princeton U., 1950; MDiv, Episc. Divinity Sch., 1956. Ordained deacon, June 16, 1956, priest, Dec. 16, 1956 Episc. Ch. Tchg. fellow in biology Bowdoin Coll., Brunswick, Maine, 1950-51; faculty mem. Middlesex Sch., Concord, Mass., 1952-54, 69-71; vicar St. Paul's Episc. Ch., Bedford, Mass., 1956-59; rector Episc. Parish, Vineyard Haven, Mass., 1959-66; biol. Gulf of Maine Biolog. Supply, Brunswick, 1966-68; priest trainer Navajoland, Farmington, N.Mex., 1972—79; vicar St. Paul's, Sacorro, N.Mex., 1979—85; Urban Indian Missioner Diocese of Rio Grande Albuquerque, 1985—87; vicar Downeast Episc. Cluster, Blue Hill, Maine, 1987-89; priest Episc. Ch., Richmond, Maine, 1989-95. Mem. com. on Indian Rels. Diocese of Maine, Portland, 1992—; water monitor Friends of Casco Bay, South Portland, Maine, 1990—; vol. Harpswell (Maine) Islands Sch., 1990—; tchr. Upward Bound, Bowdoin Coll., 167-72; dir. Upward Bound, U. Maine, Orono, 1968-1969; marine resources com. Harpswell, appeals bd. Mem. Alden Ocean Shell Assn. (bd. dirs.), Maine Rowing Assn., Sigma Xi. Democrat. Avocations: rowing, photography, gardening, cooking, reading. Home: Cundys Harbor 330 Bethel Point Rd Harpswell ME 04079 E-mail: hlbird@gwi.net.

BIRD, JOHN COMMONS, arbitrator, educator; b. Chgo., Nov. 16, 1922; s. Francis Henry and Harriet Mackay (Smith) B.; m. Irene Elizabeth Grogloth, June 12, 1948; children: Elizabeth Anne Bird Gellert, John Traill, Bruce Mackay. AB, Dartmouth Coll., 1943; JD, U. Cin., 1948. Bar: Ohio 1948, Pa. 1950, Ky. 1956, U.S. Dist. Ct. (we. dist.) Ky. 1957, U.S. Supreme Ct. 1971. Atty. U.S. Steel Corp., Pitts., 1948-52, 58-66, asst. sec. various locations, 1952-83, atty. homes div. New Albany, Ind., 1952-58, gen. atty. Birmingham, Ala., 1966-75, sr. gen. atty., 1975-83; sec. Birmingham Forest Products, Cordova, Ala., 1970-74; arbitrator Birmingham, 1983—. Adj. prof. Birmingham-So. Coll., 1987—; mem. roster of arbitrators Am. Arbitration Assn., 1983—, Fed. Mediation and Conciliation Svc., 1992—, Better Bus. Bur., 1983—. Precinct clk. Bd. Elections, Mountain Brook, Ala., 1980—. Lt. USNR, 1943-46, PTO. Ky. Col. Gov. of Ky., 1978. Mem. Birmingham Bar Assn., Kiwanis (bd. dirs. 1992-93), Delta Upsilon, Phi Delta Phi. Republican. Episcopalian. Avocations: fishing, walking, reading, writing, teaching. Home and Office: 3125 Guilford Rd Birmingham AL 35223-1216

BIRD, KAI, journalist, historian; b. Eugene, Oreg., Sept. 2, 1951; s. Eugene Hall and Jerine Newhouse Bird; m. Susan Gloria Goldmark, June 7, 1975; 1 child, Joshua Kodai Goldmark. BA in History, Carleton Coll., 1973; MS in Journalism, Northwestern U., 1975. Assoc. editor Newsweek Internat., N.Y.C., 1977, The Nation, N.Y.C., 1978-82, columnist, 1983-86, contbg. editor, 1987—. Author: The Chairman: John J. McCloy, The Making of the American Establishment, 1992, The Color of Truth: McGeorge Bundy & William Bundy, Brothers in Arms, 1998; co-editor: (anthology) Hiroshima's Shadow: Writings on the Denial of History and the Smithsonian Controversy, 1998. Fellow Thomas J. Watson Found., Providence, 1973-74, John Simon Guggenheim Found., N.Y.C., 1984, Alicia Patterson Journalism Found., Washington, 1984-85, German Marshall Fund, Washington, 1986-87, John D. and Catherine T. Macarthur Found., 1993-95; residency fellow Rockefeller Found. Study Ctr., Bellagio, Italy, 1997, Woodrow Wilson Internat. Ctr. for Scholars, 2001-02. Home: 1914 Biltmore St NW Washington DC 20009-1510 E-mail: Kai@Historians.org.

BIRD, L. RAYMOND, investor; b. Plainfield, N.J., Jan. 22, 1914; s. Lewis Raymond and Bessie (MacCallum) B.; student N.Y. U., 1946-47; m. May Ethel Siercks, June 5, 1949. With shipping dept. Horn & Hardart Co., 1936-46, control auditor, 1946-49, gen. supt. in commissary, 1949-51; asst. to treas. fin. and legal Lockheed Electronics Co. (formerly Stavid Engrng., Inc.), 1951-55, treas., 1955-60; pres., dir. State Bank of Plainfield (N.J.), 1960-62; investor, 1962—; treas. Route Twenty Two Corp. Plainfield area committeeman Young Life Campaign, Inc.; pres. Plainfield Camp of Gideons; mem. exec. com., treas. Christian Bus. Men's Com. of Cen. Jersey; bd. dirs. Child Evangelism Fellowship N.J., Sudan Interior Mission; chmn. bd. trustees, chmn. exec. com., chmn. fin. and investments com. Barrington Coll.; trustee Evangelistic Com. Newark and Vicinity; bd. dirs., treas. Friends in Christ. Served as gen. staff officer from pvt. to 1st lt. 6th Armored Div., AUS, 1941-45. Mem. Am. Mgmt. Assn., Internat. Christian Leadership, Plainfield Area C. of C. Baptist (deacon). Home and Office: 625 Robert Fulton Hwy Quarryville PA 17566-1400

BIRD, LARRY JOE, professional athletics manager, former professional basketball coach; b. West Baden, Ind., Dec. 7, 1956; s. Joe and Georgia B; m. Dinah Mattingly Oct. 1, 1989. Student, Ind. U., 1974, Northwood Inst., West Baden, Ind., 1974; BS, Ind. State U., 1979. Player Boston Celtics, 1979-92, spl. asst. to exec. v.p., 1992-97; head coach Ind. Pacers, Indianapolis, Ind., 1997—2000; pres., basketball ops. Ind. Pacers., 2003—. Mem. U.S. Olympic Basketball Team, 1992. Author: (with Bob Ryan) Drive, 1989; actor (film) Blue Chips, 1994. Mem. U.S. Gold Medal team World Univ. Games, Sophia, Bulgaria, 1977, Nat. Basketball Assn. championship team, 1981, 84, 86, Nat. Basketball Assn. All-Star Team, 1980-92; named Collegiate Player of Yr. AP, UPI and Nat. Assn. Coaches, 1978-79; Rookie of Yr. Nat. Basketball Assn., 1980; Most Valuable Player Nat. Basketball Assn. All-Star Game, 1982, Nat. Basketball Assn., 1984-86, Nat. Basketball Assn. Playoffs, 1984, 86. Office: Ind Pacers 300 E Market St Indianapolis IN 46204-2603

BIRD, MARK DOUGLAS, magnet designer, engineering researcher; b. Roanoke, Va., Apr. 5, 1966; s. Jennings Thrall and Marianne McKenzie Bird. BS in Mechanics, Mich. State U., 1988; MSME, Stanford U., 1989, PhD in Mech. Engrng., 1992. Mgr. resistive magnet program Nat. High Magnetic Field Lab., Tallahassee, 1992—, asst. scholar, scientist, 1992-96, assoc. scholar, scientist, 1996-2000, head engring. svcs., 1999—2001, scholar, scientist, 2000—. Contbr. articles to profl. jours.; inventor in field. Leadership donor United Way of the Big Bend, Tallahassee, 1999—. Grad. rsch. fellow NSF, 1988-91, Sage Grad. fellow Cornell U., Ithaca, N.Y., 1988, Andrew D. White fellow, 1988. Mem. ASME (assoc.). Methodist. Avocations: bicycling, volleyball. Home: 8750 Cabin Hill Rd Tallahassee FL 32311 Office: 1800 E Paul Dirac Dr Tallahassee FL 32310-3748 E-mail: bird@magnet.fsu.edu.

BIRD, MARY ALICE, fund raising consultant; b. Hershey, Pa., Mar. 31, 1938; d. George Wilbur and Rachel (Sutcliffe) Hocker; m. John Adams Bird, June 11, 1960; children: Edith Simonton, John Adams Jr., Sarah Hocker. BA in English, Wilson Coll., 1960; MA in Contemporary Letters, U. Tulsa, 1976. Various tchg. positions, 1960-77; dir. career devel. Lake Forest (Ill.) Coll., 1974-75; humanities faculty Tulsa (Okla.) Jr. Coll., 1977-85; program dir. Grace & Holy Trinity Cathedral, Kansas City, Mo., 1985-89; fund raising counsel Ketchum, Inc., Pitts., 1989-92; devel. dir. Farnsworth Art Mus., Rockland, Maine, 1992-95; fund raising counsel Demont & Assocs., Inc., Portland, Maine, 1995—; pvt. practice fund raising cons. Spruce Head, Maine, 1997—. Pres. S.W. Region Humanities Assn. of Cmty. and Jr. Colls., 1982-83. Contbr. articles, book revs. and poetry to profl. publs. Nat. bd. mem. Panel Am. Women, Kansas City, 1971-85, The Witness, 1990-95; cmty. grant writer Arts/Humanities Coun. of Tulsa, 1977-85; vol. grant writer various cmty. projects, Tulsa and Kansas City, 1977—; pres. Internat. Visitors Coun., Tulsa, 1984-85; vol. capital campaign cons. various clients, Maine, 1989—; vestry mem., sr. warden St. Peter's Episcopal Ch.; diocesan facilitator Episc. Diocese Maine; bd. mem., sec. Georges River Land Trust. Democrat. Avocations: gardening, kayaking, writing, meditation. Home: PO Box 345 Spruce Head ME 04859-0345

BIRD, MARY LYNNE MILLER, professional society administrator; b. Buffalo, Feb. 25, 1934; d. Joseph William and Mildred Dorothy (Wallette) Miller; m. Thomas Edward Bird, Aug. 23, 1958; children: Matthew David, Lisa Bronwen. AB magna cum laude, Syracuse U., 1956; postgrad., Columbia U., 1956-58. Mem. rsch. staff Ctr. for Rsch. in Personality, Harvard U., Cambridge, Mass., 1959-62, Ctr. Internat. Studies, Princeton (N.J.) U., 1962-66, Inst. Internat. Social Rsch., Princeton, 1965, Sch. Internat. Affairs, Columbia U., N.Y.C., 1966-67, Coun. Fgn. Rels., N.Y.C., 1967-69, Twentieth Century Fund, N.Y.C., 1969-72; asst. to pres. World Policy Inst., N.Y.C., 1972-74; dir. devel. Fund for Peace, N.Y.C., 1974-78; dir. fellows program Exec. Council Fgn. Diplomats, N.Y.C., 1978-79; dir. devel. Assn. Vol. Surgical Contraception, N.Y.C., 1979-83; exec. dir. Am. Geog. Soc., N.Y.C., 1983—. Cons. Fedn. Am. Scientists, Washington, 1974-75. Trustee Bel Canto Opera Co., N.Y.C., 1975-90; bd. dirs. Finding a Way Project. Maxwell Citizenship scholar Syracuse U., 1952-56. Fellow AAAS; mem. NAS (com. on geography, liaison mem. 1984-2000), Assn. Am. Geographers, Soc. Woman Geographers, Inst. for Current World Affairs (trustee), Nat. Coun. Geog. Edn., 100-Yr. Assn. N.Y., Conf. Latin Americanist Geographers, Planning Com. for Nat. Assessment on Ednl. Progress in Geography, St. David's Soc., Colonial Dames Am., Mid-Atlantic club N.Y.C. (bd. dirs.), Princeton Club, Am. Assn. of Assoc. Execs., Phi Beta Kappa, Phi Kappa Phi, Eta Pi Upsilon. Avocations: singing, sailing. Office: Am Geog Soc 121 Wall St Ste 100 New York NY 10005-3904 E-mail: MLBird@amergeog.org.

BIRD, PATRICIA COLEEN, business owner; b. Wolf Point, Mont., May 10, 1953; d. Harry Sidney and Pearl Rose (Firemoon) B. AA in Fine Arts, Haskell Indian JUCO, Lawrence, Kans., 1974; student, Kans. U., 1974-78; CDC Cert., Deaconess Hosp., Glasgow, Mont., 1990. Partnership bus. owner Blue Feather Indian Store, Wolf Point, Mont., 1980—2000. Indian arts steering com. mem. Mont. Arts Coun., Helena, 1991. Exhibitions include Beauty, Honor, and Tradition: The Legacy of Plains Indian Shirts Exhibit, George Gustav Heye Ctr., N.Y., 2001. First responder ambulance Trinity Hosp., Wolf Point, 1991-92; drug and alcohol facilitator Frazer (Mont.) Sch. Dist. 2-2B, 1990-91; acting sec. Frazer Community Coun., 1991-92; N.W. accrediting assn. mem. Poplar (Mont.) Sch., 1990-91; coord. "The Longest Walk", Davis, Calif., 1978, concert dir., 1978, Outstanding Young Women of Am., Ala, 1986, 87. Named Miss Nat. Congress of Am. Indians, 1975, The Modern Ms., 1975, Miss Haskell, 1974, Oil Discovery Celebration Pres., 1974, Oil Discovery Celebration Princess, 1973, 72, 71. Achievements include design of Smithsonian Inst., Nat. Museum of the Am. Indian, ribbon shirt made in 1981 was selected to become part of the Smithsonian's permanent plains Indian shirts collection from the 19th and 20th centuries. Avocations: indian art and crafts, sewing, reading, painting, drawing.

BIRD, RICHARD MILLER, economics educator; b. Fredericton, N.B., Can., Aug. 22, 1938; s. Robert Bruce and Annie Margaret (Miller) B.; m. Marcia Abbey, May 10, 1958; children— Paul, Marta, Abbey. BA, U. King's Coll., 1958; MA, Columbia U., 1959, PhD, 1961. Instr. economics Harvard U., 1961-63, lectr., 1966-68; sr. research asso. Columbia U., 1963-64; advisor Ministry of Fin., Colombia, 1964-66; assoc. prof. U. Toronto, 1968—70, prof., 1970—99, prof. emeritus, 1999—. Dir. Inst. Policy Analysis, 1980-85; chief tax policy div. dept. fiscal affairs Internat. Monetary Fund, Washington, 1972-74 Contbr. articles in field to profl. jours. Recipient Killam award Can. Council, 1969-70 Fellow Royal Soc. Can.; mem. Nat. Tax Assn. Tax Inst. Am. (dir. 1977-83, Internat. Inst. Public Fin., dir. 1973-81), Am. Econs. Assn., Canadian Econs. Assn., Can. Tax Found. Office: Rotman Sch Mgmt U Toronto 105 Saint George St Toronto ON Canada M5S 3E6

BIRD, ROBERT BYRON, chemical engineering educator, author; b. Bryan, Tex., Feb. 5, 1924; s. Byron and Ethel (Antrim) Bird. Student, U. Md., 1941—43; BS, U. Ill., 1947; PhD, U. Wis., 1950; postdoctoral fellow, U. Amsterdam, 1950—51; DEng (hon.), Lehigh U., 1972, Washington U., 1973, Tech. U. Delft, Holland, 1977, Colo. Sch. Mines, 1986; ScD (hon.), Clarkson U., 1980, The Technion U., Israel, 1993, Tex. A&M U., 1999; D in engring. sci. (hon.), Eidgenössische Tech. Hochschule, Zürich, Switzerland, 1994; DrEngring (hon.), Kyoto (Japan) U., 1996. Asst. prof. chemistry Cornell U., 1952—53, Debye lectr., 1973, Julian C. Smith lectr., 1988; rsch. chemist DuPont Exptl. Sta., 1953; mem. faculty U. Wis., 1951—52, 1953—57, prof. chem. engring., 1957—92, C.F. Burgess distinguished prof. chem. engring., 1968—72, John D. MacArthur prof., 1982—92, Vilas research prof., 1972—92, chmn. dept., 1964—68, emeritus prof., 1992—; Burgers prof. Technische Univ. Delft, The Netherlands, 1994. Vis. prof. U. Calif., Berkeley, Calif., 1977, Univ. Catholique de Louvain, Belgium, 1994; D. L. Katz lectr. U. Mich., 1971; W. N. Lacey lectr. Calif. Inst. Tech., 1974; K. Wohl Meml. lectr. U. Del., 1977; W. K. Lewis lectr. MIT, 1982; R. H. Wilhelm lectr. Princeton U., 1991; G. N. Lewis lectr. U. Calif., Berkeley, 1993; Ascher Shapiro lectr. MIT, 1997; lectr. Lectures in Sci. Humble Oil Co., 1959, 61, 64, 66; lecture tour Am. Chem. Soc., 1958, 75, Canadian Inst. Chemistry, 1961, 65; cons. to industry, 1965—90; mem. adv. panel engring. sci. divsn. NSF, 1961—64. Author (with others): Molecular Theory of Gases and Liquids, 2d printing, 1964; author: Transport Phenomena, 62d printing, 2001, Spanish edit., 1965, Czech edit., 1966, Italian edit., 1970, Russian edit., 1974, Chinese edit., 1990, 2d English edit., 2002, Een Goed Begin: A Contemporary Dutch Reader, 1963, 2d edit., 1971, Comprehending Technical Japanese, 1975, Chinese edit., 1985, Dynamics of Polymeric Liquids, Vol. 1, Fluid Mechanics, Vol. 2, Kinetic Theory, 1977, 2d edit., 1987, Japanese transl., 1999, Reading Dutch: Fifteen Annotated Stories from the Low Countries, 1985, Basic Technical Japanese, 1990, Technical Japanese Supplements: Polymer Science and Engineering, 1995, also numerous rsch. publs.; Am. editor (with others) Applied Sci. Rsch., 1969—86, 1989—98; mem. adv. bd. : Indsl. and Engring. Chemistry, 1970—72, mem. editl. bd.: Jour. Non-Newtonian Fluid Mechanics, 1975—; contbr. Served to 1st lt. AUS, 1943—46. Decorated Bronze Star; named Fulbright fellow, Holland, 1950, Guggenheim fellow, 1958, Fulbright lectr., 1958, Japan, 1962—63, Sarajevo, Yugoslavia, 1972; recipient Curtis McGraw award, Am. Assn. Engring. Edn., 1959, Westinghouse award, 1960, Corcoran award, 1987, Centennial Medallion, 1993, Nat. Medal Sci., 1987. Fellow: AIChE (William H. Walker award 1962, Profl. Progress award 1965, Warren K. Lewis award 1974, Founders award 1989, Inst. Lect. award 1992 1992), Am. Acad. Arts and Scis., Am. Phys. Soc.; mem.: NAE, NAS, Royal Flemish Acad. Belgium for Scis and Arts (fgn.), Royal Dutch Acad. Scis. (fgn.), Soc. Rheology, Soc. Chem. Engrs. Japan (hon.), Am. Chem. Soc. (chmn. Wis. sect. 1966, unrestricted rsch. grant Petroleum Rsch. Fund 1963), Am. Assn. Netherlandic Studies, Wis. Acad. Scis., Am. Acad. Mechanics, Arts and Letters, Sigma Tau, Omicron Delta Kappa, Phi Kappa Phi, Alpha Chi Sigma, Tau Beta Pi, Sigma Xi (v.p. Wis. sect. 1959—60), Phi Beta Kappa. Office: U Wis Dept Chem and Biol Engring 3004 Engring Hall 1415 Engineering Dr Madison WI 53706-1607 E-mail: bird@engr.wisc.edu.

BIRD, ROY KENNEDY, literature educator, director; b. Spanish Fork, Utah, Sept. 18, 1947; s. Roy Hall and Glenna Kennedy Bird; m. Corina Stan, Oct. 10, 1987; m. Penny Cherrington, May 28, 1970 (div. Aug. 24, 1985); children: Liviu Mihai, David Roy, Lora, Bryan Cherrington, Geoffrey Cherrington. BA, Brigham Young U., 1972; PhD, William Marsh Rice U., 1982. Editor, writer Brigham Young U. Press, Provo, Utah, 1974—76; instr. English Brigham Young U., Provo, 1976—81, asst. prof. English, 1981—84, U. Alaska Fairbanks, 1984—86, assoc. prof. English, 1986—91, prof. English, 1991—, dir. honors program, 1999—, chair dept. English, 2000—. Sr. Fulbright lectr. U. Cluj-Napoca, Romania, 1986—88, U. Galati, Romania, 1991—92, U. Timisoara, Romania, 1992—93. Author: Wright Morris: Memory and Imagination, 1984. Romanian Orthodox. Home: 130 Kelsan Way Fairbanks AK 99709 Office: Honors Program Univ Alaska Fairbanks Fairbanks AK 99775-6282 Personal E-mail: roy.bird@uaf.edu. E-mail: ffrkb@uaf.edu.

BIRD, SHARLENE, clinical psychologist; b. N.Y.C., Sept. 3, 1957; d. Rubin and Dina Bird. BA in Psychology & Hispanic Studies, Vassar Coll., 1979; MA in Applied Psychology, Adelphi U., 1986; MA in Human Resources Mgmt., New Sch. for Social Rsch., N.Y.C., 1987; PsyD in Clin. Psychology, Yeshiva U., 1992. Lic. psychologist, N.Y. Clin. extern St. Mary's Children and Family Svcs., Syosset, N.Y., 1980-81; behavior modifier Flower Hosp./Terence Cardinal Cooke, N.Y.C., 1981-82; clin. psychology extern Met. Ctr. for Mental Health, 1986-87; clin. psychology intern NYU Med. Ctr./Bellevue Hosp., N.Y.C., 1989-90; postdoctoral fellow in human sexuality N.Y. Hosp./Cornell Med. Ctr., 1990-92; family therapist Roberto Clemente Family Guidance Ctr., N.Y.C., 1991-93, 96-98; healthcare planning analyst Inst. for Family and Community Care, N.Y.C., 1993-96; pvt. practice N.Y.C., 1994—. Supr. NYU Med. Ctr./Bellevue Hosp., N.Y.C., 1992—; part-time clin. instr. dept. psychiatry NYU Med. Ctr., 1995—; tng. cons. Inst. for Family and Cmty. Care, N.Y.C., 1993; weekly permanent radio talk show co-host Siempre a Tu Lado, Sta. WADO 1280 AM, 1992—95. Chair bd. dirs. Mothers of Childrens with AIDS, N.Y.C., 1991-93. Mem.: APA, Assn. for Advancement of Behavior Therapy (chair pub. edn. and media dissemination com. 1996—99), Am. Group Psychotherapy Assn., Counselors and Therapists, Am. Assn. Sex Educators, Assn. Hispanic Mental Health Profls. (bd. dirs., mem.-at-large 1995—97, v.p. 1999—2001), Am. Orthopsychiat. Assn., N.Y. State Psychol. Assn., Sigma Delta Phi. Office: 112 W 56th St Rm C Ste 15 S New York NY 10019-3841

BIRD, SUE, professional basketball player; b. Oct. 16, 1980; Degree comm., U. Conn. Profl. basketball player Seattle Storm, 2002—. Named Two-time All.-Am., Player of Yr., Associated Press and Naismith, 2002; recipient Wade Trophy, 2002. Office: Seattle Sonics and Storm 351 Elliott Ave W Ste 500 Seattle WA 98119 Business E-Mail: StormFans@sonics-storm.com.

BIRD, THOMAS EDWARD, foreign language and literature educator; b. Rome, N.Y., Mar. 28, 1935; s. Harry J. and Paula W. (Boyce) B.; m. Mary Lynne Miller, Aug. 23, 1958; children: Matthew David, Lisa Bronwen. AB magna cum laude, Syracuse U., 1956; postgrad., Harvard U., 1958-59; MA, Middlebury Coll., 1960; AM, Princeton U., 1965; postgrad., Warsaw U., 1990—. Lectr., assoc. prof. Slavic langs. and lit. Queens Coll., CUNY, Flushing, 1965—; dir., co-dir. Ctr. Jewish Studies, 1996-98. Bd. dirs. Pax Romana, Benyumin Shekhter Found., Cymdeithas Madoc, St. David's Soc., St. Nicholas Soc., Soc. of Colonial Wars, chmn. Flag Svc. Com., 1997—. Gen. Soc. of the War of 1812 (pres. New York State Soc.), Soc. of Mayflower Descendants. Author: Patriarch Maximos IV, 1964; editor: Aspects of Religion in the Soviet Union, 1971, The Hard Life of Jura Odcesty, 1980, The 1863 Uprising in Byelorussia, 1980, Skovoroda: An Anthology, 1994; mem. editl. bd. Diakonia, Nationalities Papers, Polish Rev., Zapisy. Served with US Army (Military Intelligence) 1957-62. Recipient George Arents Library award, American Jewish Com. award for interreligious dialogue, Amer. Jewish Com., 1996, Maxwell Citizenship Scholar, 1952-56, NDFL fellow, 1962-65, Woodrow Wilson Fell., 1963, Presdl. Tchg. Awd., 1991. Fellow Soc. for Values in Higher Edn.; mem. AAUP, MLA, Amer. Assn. for Advancement of Slavic Studies, Amer Counc. of Tchrs. of Russ., Columbia U. Faculty Seminars, Belarusan Inst. Arts and Scis., Internatl. Assn. of Belarusan Studies (vice pres.), Polish Inst. Arts and Scis., Russian-American Scholars Assn., Shevchenko Scientific Soc., Ukrainian Acad. Arts and Scis., Hon. Soc. of Cymmrodorion, Dobro Slovo, Princeton Club of N.Y., Nassau Club of Princeton, Phi Beta Kappa, Phi Kappa Alpha. Office: Queens Coll CUNY Rufus King Hall 65-30 Kissena Blvd Flushing NY 11367-1597

BIRD, TOPANGA, artist, writer; d. Nora Gallagher and James Lott Ahern; m. Pierre deVise, Nov. 16, 1979 (div. June 30, 1983). BA in Comm. Arts, Columbia Coll., Chgo.; MA in Clin. Psychology, Pepperdine U., 1993—96. Exhibitions include As:If - Exploring the Intersection of Lang. and Form, Urban/Landscapes, Karen Finley/Memento Mori; editor: (newspaper) LA Bus. Jour. (Best Use of Photography, 1992, Best Spot News, 1993, 1st Pl. Editl. Writing, 1996). Dir. 46th ward city coun. office City Coun. of the City of Chgo., 1984—85, chief of staff/mcpl. code revision com., 1984—86. Mem.: Nat. Assn. of Broadcast Engineers and Technicians (hon.), Psy Chi (life). Office: Arena X7 P O Box 106 Hollywood CA 90068 E-mail: arenax7@yahoo.com.

BIRD, WENDELL RALEIGH, lawyer; s. Raleigh Milton and R. Jean B. BA summa cum laude, Vanderbilt U., 1975; JD, Yale U., 1978. Bar: Ga. 1978, Ala. 1980, Calif. 1981, Fla. 1982, U.S. Ct. Appeals (2d, 3d, 4th, 5th, 6th, 7th, 8th, 9th, 10th and 11th cirs.) 1979-83, U.S. Supreme Ct. 1983. Law clk. to judge U.S. Ct. Appeals (4th cir.), Durham, N.C., 1978-79, U.S. Ct. Appeals (5th cir.), Birmingham, Ala., 1979-80; pvt. practice San Diego, 1980-82; atty. Parker, Johnson, Cook & Dunlevie, Atlanta, 1982-86; sr. ptnr. Bird & Assocs., P.C., Atlanta, 1986—. Adj. prof. Emory U. Law Sch., Atlanta, 1985—90; lectr. Washington Non-Profit Tax Conf., 1982—. Author: The Origin of Species Revisited, 2 vols., 1987; contbg. author: Federal and State Taxation of Exempt Organizations, 1994, CCH Federal Tax Service, 1988—; mem. bd. editors Yale U. Law Jour., 1977-78, others; contbr. articles to profl. jours. Recipient Egger prize Yale U., 1978, Vanderbilt U. award, 1972. Mem. ABA (litigation sect., taxation sect., com. on exempt orgns., past chmn. subcom. on religious orgns., past chmn. subcom. on state and local taxes, chmn. subcom. on charitable contbns., sect. on real property probate and trust, com. charitable gifts), Am. Law Inst., Ga. Bar Assn., Fla. Bar Assn., Calif. Bar Assn., Ala. Bar Assn., Assn. Trial Lawyers Am., Phi Beta Kappa. Republican. Avocations: science, skiing, photography, genealogy, piano, architecture. Home: 92 Blackland Rd NW Atlanta GA 30342-4420 Office: Bird & Assocs PC 1150 Monarch Plz 3414 Peachtree Rd NE Atlanta GA 30326-1153

BIRDMAN, JEROME MOSELEY, drama educator, consultant; b. Phila., Dec. 4, 1930; s. Morris Schiowitz and Minerva B.; m. Evanira Pereira Mendes, July 1, 1959; children: Julia, Beatrice. BS, Temple U., 1956; A.M., U. Ill., 1957, PhD, 1970; mem. seminar for Arts Trustees, Harvard U., 1975. Mem. editorial staff Accent Quar. of New Lit., 1957-58; dir. cultural programming for Am. Forces, U.S. Info. Service, Northeast Italy, 1958-61; mem. faculty theatre dept. So. Ill. U., Edwardsville, 1961-71, acad. program officer, 1972-73; prof. dramatic arts, dean Coll. Fine Arts, U. Nebr., Omaha, 1973-78, Sch. Fine Arts, U. Conn., Storrs, 1978-92; dean emeritus, 1993; consultant, 1993—. Adv. bd. Nebr. Alliance for Arts Edn., 1976-78; lectr. USIS, Brazil, 1964; arts commr. Nat. Assn. State Univs. and Land Grant Colls., 1979-89, chmn., 1983-89; panelist NEH, 1976—. Nat. Endowment Arts, 1983—; adv. Conn. Dept. Edn., 1980— ; accreditor New Eng. Assn. Schs. and Colls.; cons. to various colls. and univs. in arts adminstrn. Contbr. articles on theatrical art to various profl. publs.; originator exhibit: Artists Who Teach, Washington, 1987; producer or director more than 40 plays, musicals and concerts at universities, 1963-76; translator Six Characters in Search of an Author, U. Mo., 1987-88. Mem. Mayor's Task Force on the Arts, Omaha, 1977-78; bd. dirs. Dance Concert Soc., St. Louis, 1970-73, New Music Circle, 1971-73, Prelude Civic Ballet, Ill., 1971-73, Omaha Opera Co., 1973-75, Omaha Symphony Assn., 1973-78, Stamford Ctr. for the Arts, 1984-89, Met. Arts Council, Omaha, 1976-78, Omaha Children's Mus., 1976-78. Served with U.S. Army, 1952-54. Recipient merit citation Provincia di Vicenza, 1961 Mem. Am. Theatre Assn., Internat. Council Fine Arts Deans, Soc. Theatre Research, Am. Soc. Theatre Research, Internat. Council Fine Arts Deans, Soc. Theatre Research Great Britain., Societé d'Histoire du Théâtre, Nat. Assn. State Universities and Land-Grant Colls., Am. Theatre Assn./Assn. for Theatre in Higher Edn. Address: 5430 E Gleneagles Dr Tucson AZ 85718-1806

BIRDSALL, ARTHUR ANTHONY, chemical executive; b. Oneonta, N.Y., Feb. 28, 1947; s. Charles Albert and Mary (Danzi) B.; m. Jane Elaine Fink, Jan. 28, 1967; children: Robert, Thomas, William. AAS in Chemistry, Erie County Tech. Inst., 1966; BS in Chemistry, Saginaw Valley Coll., 1969. Applications engr. Dow Corning Corp., Midland, Mich., 1966-70, product devel. chemist Elizabethtown, Ky., 1970-71, quality reliability engr., 1971-73, quality assurance supr. Chgo., 1973-75, product devel. specialist Midland, Mich., 1975-77, pilot plant mgr. Freeland, Mich., 1977-80; quality mgr., govt. rels. coord. Dow Corning Ophthalmics, Inc. divsn. Dow Corning Corp., Cosa Mesa, Calif., 1980, Midland, 1980-82, mgr. quality/regulatory affairs, 1982-85; corp. mgr. product stewardship Dow Corning Corp., Midland, Mich., 1985-88, program chmn. health environ. and safety bd., 1986-91, product liability issue mgmt. com., 1988-91, mgr. product stewardship, safety and regulatory compliance, 1988-91, European dir. health, environment and regulatory affairs, 1991-96, European dir. health, environ. and regulatory affairs; mem. Dow Corning Europe Environment, Health and Safety Coun., 1992-96, mgr. global product stewardship bus. program, 1996-97, Asia-Pacific environ., health and safety mgmt. advisor, 1996-98, dir. global environ., health and safety external affairs, 1998-2000, Sanilac county adminstr., 2002—. Cons. ophthalmic device regulations Dow Corning Corp., Midland, 1985; bd. dirs. Contact Lens Inst., also vice-chmn. bd. dirs., 1983-84, treas., 1984-85; chmn. pro-tem ophthalmic device com. Health Industry Mfrs. Assn., Washington, 1982-84, mem. Product Safety Mgmt. Forum; mem. Chem. Industry Dirs. Exch., Material Safety Data Sheet, Electronic Data Interchange Std. Coms., 1986-91; bd. dirs. Centre European des Silicones, 1991-96; environ, health and safety com. Am. C. of C.,

Belgium, 1991-96, China, 1998; mem. USCMA Fed. Regulator Roundtable, 1999-2000. Co-inventor silicone resins for optical devices, 1977; contbr. articles to profl. jours.; patentee in field. Chmn. Cub Scout Pack com., Midland, 1979; treas. local Parent Tchr. Orgn., Midland, 1977, v.p., 1978, pres., 1979; tchr. Cath. Youth Coun., Midland, 1985; mem. adv. bd. Midland County United Way Citizen, 1990—91; mem. panel Midland County United Way, 1999—2000; bd. dirs. Blessed Sacrament Sch., 1986—87, mem. edn. commn., 1986—88; bd. dirs. Sanilac County United Way, 2000—; adv. bd. Sanilac County Resource Recovery, 2001—; bd. dirs. Mid Thumb Habitat for Humanity, 2001—. Contbr. recipient I.R. 100 award silicone contact lens devel., 1982. Mem. Am. Soc. Quality Control, U.S. Chem. Mfrs. Assn. (fed. regulatory roundtable 1999-2000), Regulatory Affairs Profl. Soc., Ctr. European des Silicones (environ. com. 1991-94, mgmt. bd. 1991-96, bd. dirs. 1991-96). Independent. Roman Catholic. Avocations: reading, writing prose and poetry, gardening, collecting art. Home: 137 S Lake St Port Sanilac MI 48469-9620 E-mail: AABirdsall@aol.com.

BIRDSALL, CHARLES KENNEDY, electrical engineer; b. N.Y.C., Nov. 19, 1925; s. Charles and Irene Birdsall; m. Betty Jean Hansen, 1949 (div. 1977); children: Elizabeth(dec.), Anne(dec.), Barbara, Thomas, John; m. Virginia Anderson, Aug. 21, 1981. BS, U. Mich., 1946, MS, 1948; PhD, Stanford U., 1951. Various projects Hughes Aircraft Co., Culver City, Calif., 1951—55; leader electron physics group GE Microwave Lab., Palo Alto, Calif., 1955-59; prof. elec. engring. U. Calif., Berkeley, 1959-91, prof. Grad. Sch., 1994—. Founder Plasma Theory and Simulation Group, 1967; founder, 1st chmn. Energy and Resources Com., 1972—74; cons. to industry, Lawrence Livermore Lab. of U. Calif., 1960—86; prof. Miller Inst. Basic Rsch. in Sci., 1963—64; sr. vis. fellow U. Reading, England, 1976; rsch. assoc. Inst. Plasma Physics Nagoya (Japan) U., 1981, co-founder computational engring. sci. undergrad. program, 2000; Chevron vis. prof. energy Calif. Inst. Tech., 1982; area coord. phys. electronics/bioelectronics, 1984—86; lectr. Plasma Sch. Internat. Ctr. for Theoretical Physics, Trieste, Italy, 1985—99; joint U.S.-Japan Inst. Fusion Theory vis. prof. Inst. Plasma Physics, Nagoya U., fall 1988, spring 2002; vis. prof. Gunma U., Kirya, Japan, 2003; IPA Airforce Rsch. Lab., Albuquerque, 2002—. Author: (with W.B. Bridges) Electron Dynamics of Diode Regions, 1966, (with A.B. Langdon) Plasma Physics via Computer Simulation, 1985, 91, 93, 2002, (with S. Kuhn) Bounded Plasmas, 1994; patentee in field. Served with USNR, 1944-46. U.S.-Japan Coop. Sci. Program grantee, 1966-67; Fulbright grantee U. Innsbruck, 1991; recipient Berkeley Citation, 1991. Fellow IEEE (1st recipient Plasma Sci. and Applications award June 1988), AAAS, Am. Phys. Soc.; mem. Sigma Xi, Tau Beta Pi, Eta Kappa Nu. Achievements include being the co-originator many-particle plasma simulations in two and three dimensions using cloud-in-cell methods, 1966. Home: 4050 Valente Ct Lafayette CA 94549-3412 Office: U Calif EECS Dept Cory Hall Berkeley CA 94720-1770 E-mail: birdsall@eecs.berkeley.edu.

BIRDSALL, TIMOTHY CARROLL, naturopathic physician; b. Lake Geneva, Wis., July 4, 1951; s. Thomas Carroll and Mary Jane Birdsall; m. Kathryn June Williams, May 27, 1972 (div. June 13, 2003); children: Jeremy, Lisa, Aaron, Rebecca, James, John, Andrew, Addie. BA, Grace Coll., 1972; D of Naturopathic Medicine, Bastyr U., 1985. Clin. instr. Bastyr U., Kenmore, Wash., 1985—90; pvt. practice Kirkland, Wash., 1986—90; pres. Genesis Birth Ctr., Inc., Kirkland, 1987—89; tech. dir. Thorne Rsch., Inc., Sandpoint, Idaho, 1989—98; dir. naturopathic medicine Midwestern Regional Med. Ctr., Zion, Ill., 1998—2002; nat. dir. naturopathic medicine Cancer Treatment Ctrs. of Am., Zion, 1998—2002, v.p. integrative medicine, 2002—; clin. prof. grad. med. edn. Nat. Coll. Naturopathic Medicine, Portland, Oreg., 1999—. Author: How to Prevent and Treat Cancer with Natural Medicine; editor-in-chief Alternative Medicine Rev., 1996—98; contbr. Alternative Medicine Rev. Monographs, Vol. 1, articles to profl. jours. Recipient President's Award, Am. Association of Naturopathic Physicians, 2000. Mem.: AAUS, Idaho Assn. Naturopathic Physicians, Ill. Assn. Naturopathic Physicians (v.p. 1998—2000, pres. 2000—03, dir. 1993—98), Soc. Nutritional Oncology Adjuvant Therapy, Multinat. Assn. Supportive Care in Cancer, N.Y. Acad. Scis., Am. Assn. Naturopathic Physicians (life; spkr. ho. of dels. 1992—95, 2001—, dir. 1992—98, 2001—03, v.p. 1996—98, Pres.'s award 2000). Achievements include patents for quercetin chalcone and methods relating thereto. Office: Cancer Treatment Ctrs of Am 2520 Elisha Ave Zion IL 60099

BIRDSALL, WILLIAM FOREST, retired librarian; b. Farmington, Minn., Oct. 30, 1937; s. Herman Elden and Mae Elizabeth (Daugherty) B.; m. Ann Elizabeth Page, Dec. 20, 1965; children— Sarah, Stephanie, Thomas BA, U. Minn., 1955, MA, 1964; PhD, U. Wis., 1973. Reference libr. Iowa State U., Ames, 1961-63; head pub. svcs. Wis. State U., La Crosse, 1965-70; asst. dir. for pub. svcs. U. Man., Winnipeg, Canada, 1973-77, assoc. dir. for pub. svcs.er-vices, 1977-81; univ. libr. Dalhousie U., Halifax, Canada, 1981-97; exec. dir. Novanet, Inc., Halifax, 1998—2002; ret., 2002. Author: Myth of the Electronic Library, 1994, Understanding Telecommunications and Public Policy, 1998; contbr. articles to libr. periodicals. Mem. Atlantic Provinces Library Assn. (pres. 1984), Man. Library Assn. (pres. 1981), Can. Library Assn. (council 1981, 84) Home: 54 Village Crescent Bedford NS Canada B4A 1J2

BIRDSONG, ALTA MARIE, volunteer; b. Ft. Worth, July 18, 1934; d. Alton Roy and Artie Marguerite (Bentley) Flowers; m. Kenneth Layne Birdsong, Oct. 18, 1958; children: Suzanne Denise Huff, Jeffrey Layne Birdsong. BBA in Acctg. magna cum laude, U. North Tex., 1955. Cost engr. Tex. Instruments, Inc., Dallas, 1955-62; part-time acct. Atlanta, 1972—. Mem. DeKalb County Cmty. Rels. Com., 1981-93, chair, 1984-87; mem. Atlanta Regional Com. Adv. Group, 1981-88, Met. Atlanta United Way, 1985-98, resource investment vol. sch. age children; chair Sch. Age Child Care Com., 1987-90; mem. Dekalb County Task Force on Personal Care Homes, Dekalb County Task Force on Domestic Violence; mem. steering com. for bond referendum Dekalb B. Edn.; mem. Vision 2020 Governance Stakeholders ARC, 1994-95; mem. Camp Fire Boys and Girls. Recipient John H. Collier award for Camp Fire, 1991, Luther Halsey Gulick award for Camp Fire, 1993, Frederic E. Ruccius award for Camp Fire, 1993, Mortar Bd. Alumni Achievement award, 1991, Woman of Yr. award Atlanta Alumnae Panhellenic, 1983, Women Who Have Made a Difference award DeKalb YWCA, 1985, Ember award Camp Fire, 1998, Tom Murphy State Service Good Heart Vol. award, 2002. Mem.: AAUW (rec. sec. 1982—84, mem. v.p. 1984—86, pres. elect 1986—87, divsn. pres. 1987—89, assn. nominating com. 1993—97, chair 1995—97, Atlanta chpt. pres. 2001—03, co-chair Sister-to-Sister Summit 2002, chair Woman to Woman Summit 2002, Achievement award 1999), Nat. Women's Conf., Freedoms Found. at Valley Force (sec. 1983—85, treas. 1985—87, v.p. publicity 1988—89, v.p. 1990—91, Atlanta chpt. pres. 1991—92, ea.-so. region adv. 1994—97, treas. 1999—2000, Atlanta chpt. pres. 2000—01), Atlanta Coun. Camp Fire (region fin. officer 1989—90, v.p. 1990—92, pres. 1992—94), Atlanta Alumnae Panhellenic (v.p. 1977—78, pres. 1978—79), Delta Gamma Alumnae (treas. 1972—74, Atlanta chpt. 1st v.p. 1985—87, Oxford award 1992). Home: 5241 Manhasset Cv Atlanta GA 30338-3413

BIRDSONG, EMIL ARDELL, clinical psychologist; b. Detroit, Feb. 23, 1943; s. Emil Ardell and Ruby Carolyn (Weaks) B.; m. Beatrice Lee Johnson, Sept. 12, 1981. BA in Psychology, U. Mich., Dearborn, 1968; MA in Psychology, Merrill Palmer Inst., 1981; Psy. S Clin. Edn., Ctr. Humanistic Studies, Detroit, 1988; PhD of Clin. Psychology, Union Inst., Cin., 1994. Lic. psychologist, Mich. Spl. edn. educator Wolf Mid. Sch., Centerline, Mich., 1987-88; intern Ypsilanti (Mich.) Psychiat. Hosp., 1988-90; pvt. practice Detroit, 1994—; clin. supr. Boys & Girls Republic, Farmington Hills, MI, 1999—. Grant writer Law Enforcement Assist Act, Mich. With U.S. Army Med. Corps, 1968-70. Named Ky. Col. Gov. of Ky., 1993. Mem. APA, Am. Psychology Soc., Mich. Psychol. Assn., U. Mich. Alumni Assn. (bd. govs., bd. dirs. 1972-73). Democrat. Lutheran. Avocations: chess, genealogical research. Home: 21771 Dexter Ct Warren MI 48089-2826 Office: The Diagnostic Ctr Southfield Travelers Tower 26555 Evergreen Ste 800 Southfield MI 48076 Office Fax: 248-358-0352.

BIRDSONG, GEORGE YANCY, manufacturing company executive; b. Suffolk, Va., Nov. 8, 1939; s. William McLemore and Yancey (Brooking) B.; m. Sue Benton, June 10, 1961; children: Anne Cabell, David Jefferson, Charles Randolph. BA, Washington and Lee U., Lexington, Va., 1961; LLB, U. Va., 1964, diploma in basic advanced mgmt., 1968. Bar: Va. 1964. Mem. Godwin & Godwin, Suffolk, 1964-66; sec.-treas. Birdsong Peanuts divsn. Birdsong Corp., Suffolk, 1965—, exec. v.p., 1981-97, pres., 1997—99, CEO, 1999—. Bd. dirs. SunTrust Bank. Dir. Suffolk Redevel. and Housing Authority, 1966—85, chmn., 1966—83; pres. Louise Obici Meml. Hosp. Found., Suffolk, 1980—; chpt. pres. Tri-County Area Planned Parenthood, 1969—; mem. pres.'s adv. coun. Va. Wesleyan Coll., 1971—89, trustee, 1989—; mem. exec. com. Future of Hampton Roads, 1983—96; founding dir. Suffolk YMCA, 1987—91; mem adv. bd. Young Leaders Soc. of Hampton Roads, 2001—; bd. dirs. Hampton Roads United Way, 1980—84; sec., bd. dirs. Suffolk Cmty. Health Ctr., 1992—99; bd. dirs. Va. Found. Ind. Colls., 1994—. Recipient Disting. Svc. award Suffolk Jaycees, 1971, Order of the Red Triangle YMCA of South Hampton Rd., 1993, Humanitarian award Tidewater chpt. NCCJ, 1997; named 1st Citizen, Suffolk, 1997. Mem. Va. Bar Assn., Suffolk Bar Assn., Va. Mfrs. Assn. (bd. dirs. 1977-79, 87-89), Suffolk C. of C., Suffolk Sports Club, Suffolk Tennis Assn., Elks, Rotary. Methodist. Home: 608 Riverview Dr Suffolk VA 23434 Office: Birdsong Corp 612 Madison Ave Suffolk VA 23434

BIRDWELL, JAMES EDWIN, JR., retired banker; b. Chuckey, Tenn., Apr. 22, 1924; s. James Edwin and Mary Eleanor (Earnest) B.; m. Marilyn Margaretta Gibson, Dec. 20, 1949; children: James Edwin III, Amy Eleanor, Todd Gibson. AB, Tusculum Coll., 1949; MA, Vanderbilt U., 1951. Tchr., coach Doak H.S., 1948-50, field rep. 3d Nat. Bank, Nashville, 1951-52; trainee Va. Nat. Bank, 1957, v.p., from 1962; chmn., pres. 1st Am. Bank, Clinton, Tenn., 1973-84; vice chmn. 1st Am. Nat. Bank, Knoxville, Tenn., 1984-90. Bd. dirs., Coal Creek Mining & Mfg. Co., Areawide Devel. Corp. Commr. Bldgs. and Grounds Virginia Beach, Va., 1970-72; bd. dirs. Daniel Arthur Rehab. Ctr., Oak Ridge, Tenn., 1974-84, Oak Ridge Hosp., 1976-82, Meth. Med. Ctr. Found., Oak Ridge; v.p. Roane Anderson Econ. Coun., 1976-90; chmn. Clinton Port Authority, 1978—; mem. exec. com. Melton Hill Regional Indsl. Authority, Clinton, 1978-95; mem. Anderson County Tax Adv. Bd., 1978—, Indsl. Devel. Bd. Anderson County, 1978—. With USNR, 1942-46, 52-57. Decorated Air medal. Mem. Am. Bankers Assn., Tenn. Bankers Assn., Robert Morris Assocs., Bank Adminstrn. Inst., Bank Mkg. Assn., Oak Ridge Country Club, Civitans, LeConte Club. Republican. Methodist. Office: First Am Nat Bank 245 S Main St Clinton TN 37716-3603 E-mail: jjeb2jr@msn.com.

BIRELY, WILLIAM CRAMER, investment banker; b. Thurmont, Md., Nov. 13, 1919; s. Victor Morris and Dorothy Grace (Rouzer) B.; m. Luelle Avis Langness, July 21, 1943. Student, Strayer U., 1937-38, Am. U., 1941-42. With Folger, Nolan, Inc., Washington, 1947-52, v.p., 1950-52; gen. partner Rouse, Brewer & Becker (now Morgan Stanley), Washington, 1952-55; exec. v.p., treas. Birely & Co., Washington, 1955-62, pres., 1962-67; also dir.; v.p. Mason & Co. (now Legg, Mason, Wood, Walker, Inc.), 1967-70; investment banker Lang & Co., Washington, 1970-85, Chapin, Davis & Co., Balt., 1985-89, Lang Div. Moors & Cabot, Inc., Alexandria, Va., 1989—. V.p., dir. Thurmont (Md.) Bank (now Bank of Am.), 1962-73; adv. bd. Farmers & Mechanics Nat. Bank (now affilate of Mercantile Bankshares Corp, Balt.), Thurmont, 1975-76; mem. adv. council SBA, 1962-66 Mem. Bd. Appeals Montgomery County, 1965, Montgomery County Council, 1965-66; treas. Young Republican Club of Montgomery County, 1947, pres., 1948; del. Md. Rep. Conv., 1952, 56, 60; mem. gen. inaugural coms. Eisenhower and Nixon, 1953, 57, Nixon and Agnew, 1968, 72, Reagan and Bush, 1980, 84, Bush and Quayle, 1988. Served with F.A. AUS, 1943-44. Recipient Gov.'s citation for outstanding service to Md. Mem. Am. Legion (life), Huguenot Soc. Washington (life, former v.p.), S.A.R. (life, former nat. trustee), Soc. Mayflower Descs., Soc. Colonial Wars (life), Soc. War 1812, St. Andrews Soc., Frederick County Hist. Soc. (life), Carroll County Hist. Soc. (life), Washington Hist. Socs. (life), Montgomery County Hist. Soc. (life; mem. bd. mgmt.), Bond Club, Nat. Press Club, Army and Navy Club, Izaak Walton League Am. (nat. life). Home: PO Box 590 Olney MD 20830 Office: Lang Div Moors & Cabot Inc 1600 Prince St Ste 113 Alexandria VA 22314-2836

BIRENBAUM, LEO, retired engineering educator; b. N.Y.C., Dec. 1, 1927; s. Morris and Esther (Ditman) B.; m. Mary Giurato, Feb. 17, 1961; children: Eric, Nellie, Maija. BSEE, Cooper Union, 1946; MSEE, Poly. Inst. N.Y., 1958, MS in Physics, 1974. Electronics engr. N.Y. Naval Shipyard, Bklyn., 1948-51; from rsch. asst. to assoc. prof. Poly. U. N.Y., Bklyn., 1951-93, prof. emeritus, 1993—. Sec. C95.4 com. Am. Nat. Standards Inst., N.Y.C., 1969-79. *Leo Birenbaum performed research in the areas of biological effects of electromagnetic fields (1963-1985) and electric power (1974-1996).* Patentee microwave devices. Served with USN, 1946-47. Mem. IEEE (sr.), Bioelectromagnetics Soc., N.Y. Acad. Scis., Sigma Xi, Tau Beta Pi. Home: 44 Mohawk Rd Yonkers NY 10710-5010 Office: Polytech U 6 Metrotech Ctr Brooklyn NY 11201-3840 E-mail: lbirenba@duke.poly.edu.

BIRENBAUM, WILLIAM M. former university president; b. Macomb, Ill., July 18, 1923; s. Joseph and Rose (Whiteman) B.; m. Helen Bloch, Mar. 8, 1951; children: Susan, Lauren Amy, Charles. Dr. Law, U. Chgo., 1949; L.H.D., Columbia Coll., Chgo., 1970. Dean students Univ. Coll., 1955-57. Dir. research, conf. bd. Asso. Research Councils, Ford Found. project study post-doctoral internat. ednl. exchanges, 1954-55; asst. v.p. Wayne State U., 1957-61; dean New Sch. Social Research, N.Y.C., 1961-64; v.p., provost Bklyn. Center, L.I. U., 1964-67; pres. Edn. Affiliate, Bedford-Stuyvesant Devel. & Services Corp., Bklyn, 1967-68, S.I. Community Coll., 1968-76; pres. Antioch U., 1976-85. Author: Overlive: Power, Poverty and the University, 1968, Something for Everybody is Not Enough: An Educator's Search for His Education, 1971; Contbg. author: Student Personnel Work in Urban Colleges. Cons. Austrian Ministry Edn., Vienna, 1969; higher edn. adviser Republic of Zambia, 1972; cons. U. Zambia, 1972; faculty Salzburg Seminar in Am. Studies, 1976; founder Nat. Student Assn., 1946-48; chmn. Mich. Cultural Commn., 1960-61; founder, original dir. Detroit Adventure, vol. assn. cultural instns., 1958-61; bd. adv. Bklyn. Acad. Music, 1965—, Bklyn Inst. Arts and Scis; trustee Friends World Coll., Westbury, N.Y., Hasbro Childrens Found., 1985—, Lit. Vols. of N.Y.C., 1986—. Mem. Chgo. Bar Assn., Delta Sigma. Home: 108 Willow St Brooklyn NY 11201-2202

BIRES, DENNIS EUGENE, legal educator; b. Rochester, Pa., May 18, 1954; s. A.C. Jr. and Bernice L.B.; m. Marian J. Bires, June 14, 1987. BA, Allegheny Coll., 1976; JD, NYU, 1979, LLM in Taxation, 1984. Bar: Pa. 1979, U.S. Dist. Ct. (we. dist.) Pa. 1979. Assoc. Goehring, Rutter & Boehm, Pitts., 1979-81; tax analyst Chase Manhattan Bank, N.Y.C., 1981-84; asst. prof. Sch. of Law Oklahoma City U., 1984-87; assoc. prof. Coll. of Law, U. Tulsa, 1987—. Mem. ABA. Office: U Tulsa Coll Law 3120 E 4th Pl Tulsa OK 74104-2418 E-mail: dennis-bires@utulsa.edu.

BIRGE, JOHN ROBERTS, university administrator; b. Troy, N.Y., Aug. 13, 1956; m. Pierrette Gabrielle Birge, Aug. 23, 1980; children: Richard, Joelle. AB, Princeton (N.J.) U., 1977; MS, PhD, Stanford U., 1980. Asst. prof. U. Mich., Ann Arbor, 1980-86, assoc. prof., 1986-92, prof., 1992-99; dean McCormick Sch. Engring. and Applied Sci. Northwestern U., Evanston, Ill., 1999—, prof. indsl. engring. and mgmt. scis., 1999—. Pres. Inst. for Ops. Rsch. and the Mgmt. Scis., Linthicum, Md., 2000. Author: Introduction to Stochastic Programming, 1997; editor Math. Programming Series B., 1994-2000. Recipient Young Investigator awards Office of Naval Rsch., 1986. Mem. Inst. of Indsl. Engrs. (pres.-elect 2000), Math. Programming Soc. (sec., com. on stochastic programming 1994-99). Home: 51 Kenilworth Ave Kenilworth IL 60043 Office: McCormick Sch Northwestern U 2145 Sheridan Rd Evanston IL 60208 E-mail: jrbirge@northwestern.edu.

BIRGENEAU, ROBERT JOSEPH, physicist, educator; b. Toronto, Ont., Can., Mar. 25, 1942; came to U.S. 1963; s. Peter Duffus and Isobel Theresa (Meehan) B.; m. Mary Catherine Ware, June 20, 1964; children— Michael, Catherine, Patricia, Michelle. B.Sc., U. Toronto, 1963; PhD, Yale U., 1966. Vis. tchr. Benedict Coll., Columbia, S.C., summer 1965; instr. dept. engring. and applied sci. Yale U., New Haven, 1966-67; Nat. Research Council Can. postdoctoral fellow Oxford U., Eng., 1967-68; mem. tech. staff Bell Labs, Murray Hill, N.J., 1968-74, research head scattering and low energy physics dept., 1975; guest sr. physicist Brookhaven Nat. Lab., Upton, N.Y., 1968—; vis. scientist Riso, Roskilde, Denmark, 1971, 79; prof. physics MIT, Cambridge, 1975—2003, Cecil and Ida Green prof. physics, 1982—2001, assoc. dir. Research Lab. for Electronics, 1983-86, head condensed matter atomic and plasma physics, 1987-88, head dept. physics, 1988-91, dean sci., 1991-2000; pres. U. Toronto, 2000—. Cons. Bell Labs., 1977-80, IBM Rsch. Labs., Yorktown Heights, NY, 1980-83, Sandia Labs., 1985-92; mem. steering com. Panel on Neutron Scattering, NAS, 1977, mem. core com., major materials facilities com., 1984; co-chmn. Gordon Conf. on Quantum Solids and Fluids, 1979, Gordon Conf. on Condensed Matter Physics, 1986; mem. policy and adv. bd. Cornell High Energy Synchrotron Source, 1980-84, chmn., 1983-84; mem. rev. panel on neutron scattering Dept. Energy, 1980, 82, mem. basic energy sci. adv. com., 1991-95; mem. materials rsch. adv. com. NSF, 1989-90; mem. adv. coun. NEC, 1996-2000; chmn. DOE panel on rsch. reactor upgrades, 1996, DOE panel on synchrotron sources, 1997. Contbr. articles to profl. jours.; mem. editorial bd. Physical Review. Trustee Assoc. Univs., Inc., 1990-97, Mus. Sci., Boston, 1992-2001, Argonne Nat. Lab., 1992-2001, Brookhaven Sci. Assocs., 1998-2000. Recipient Yale Sci. and Engring. Alumni Achievement award, 1981, Wilbur Lucius Cross medal Yale U., 1986, Oliver E. Buckley Prize Am. Phys. Soc., 1987, B.E. Warren award Am. Crystal Assn., 1988, Magnetism award Internat. Union Pure and Applied Physics, 1997; 48th Richtmyer Meml. lectr. Am. Assn. Physics Tchrs., 1989, A.W. Scott lectr. Cambridge U., 2000. Fellow AAAS (exec. coun. 1992-94), Am. Phys. Soc. (Julius E. Lilienfeld award 2000), Am. Acad. Arts Sci., Royal Soc. London, Royal Soc. Can. Roman Catholic. Avocations: landscaping, squash, basketball. Home Fax: (416) 929-6844; Office Fax: (416) 971-1360. E-mail: president@utoronto.ca.

BIRIBAUER, RICHARD FRANK, lawyer; b. Cranford, N.J., May 30, 1950; s. Frank Anton and Mary M. (Valle) B.; m. Linda Carey, Aug. 26, 1972; children: James Richard, David Tyler, Tia Renee. AB, Rutgers U., 1972; JD, Washington and Lee U., 1975. Bar: Va. 1975, DC 1976. Assoc. Law Offices of Fulton Brylawski, Washington, 1975-77; trademark counsel Johnson & Johnson, New Brunswick, N.J., 1977-83, internat. trademark counsel, 1984-91, chief trademark counsel, 1991—. Contbr. articles to Washington and Lee U. Law Rev., Mng. Intellectual Property. Mem. ABA, DC Bar Assn., Va. State Bar Assn., Internat. Trademark Assn., Pharm. Trade Marks Group, Inter Am. Assn. Indsl. Property. Office: Johnson & Johnson One Johnson & Johnson Plz New Brunswick NJ 08933 Business E-Mail: rbiriba@corus.jnj.com.

BIRK, JOHN R. management consultant; b. Boston, Aug. 11, 1951; s. Harold F. and Jane Birk; m. Susan Arnold, Feb. 9, 1980; children: John R. Jr., Andrew A. BA in Econs. and English, Colgate U., 1974; Advanced Mgmt. Program, Harvard Bus. Sch., 1991. Sales rep. Procter & Gamble, N.Y.C., 1975-76, dist. field rep. White Plains, N.Y., 1976, unit mgr. Dallas, 1976-78; sales devel. mgr. Pepsi Cola Co., Purchase, N.Y., 1978-80, regional sales mgr. San Francisco, 1980-83; dir. sales and mktg. MCI Comm. Inc., Atlanta, 1983-84, v.p. sales and mktg., 1984-85; pres., bd. dirs. U.S. Telecomm Svcs. Co., Kansas City, 1985; pres. N.E. divsn. US Sprint, Purchase, 1986-87, pres. we. group San Francisco, 1987-88; exec. v.p., COO, dir. ADVO, Inc., 1988—89; pres., COO, dir. ADVO Inc., Windsor, 1989-92; pres., CEO, dir. Wright Express Corp., South Portland, Maine, 1992-94, chmn., 1994-95; pres. Ideon Group Inc. (formerly Safe Card Svcs., Inc.), Jacksonville, Fla., 1995; mgmt. cons. John R. Birk & Assocs., Ponte Vedra Beach, Fla., 1995—; operating exec. Evercore Ptnrs., 1996—. Bd. dirs. T.O. Richardson Mut. Funds, Splty. Products Insulation Inc., Security Assocs. Internat., Inc., Convergent Label Tech., Inc. Bd. dirs. Prevent Blindness, Atlanta, 1984-85, United Way, White Plains, 1986-87, Westchester County Assn., 1986-87, Bay Area Coun., 1987-88, United Way Greater Portland, 1993-95, Found. for Blood Rsch., Inc., 1993-95, Colgate U. Alumni Corp., 1995-99; chmn. Colgate U. Pres. Club, 1996-99. Republican. Roman Catholic. Avocations: tennis, golf, skiing. E-mail: jrbirk@aol.com.

BIRK, LEE (CARL LEE BIRK), psychiatrist, educator; b. New Albany, Ind., Feb. 8, 1935; s. Glover McMurtrey and Marie Clyde (Carpenter) B.; m. Emily Perkins Gantt, June 21, 1958 (div. Jan. 1970); children: Elizabeth Waring, Alexandria Lee; m. Ann Harrison Wegner, June 15, 1973 (div. June 1990); children: Lara Blakiston, Jeffrey Lee. Student, Speed Scientific Sch., 1952-53, U. Louisville, 1953-54; BA in Zoology & Chemistry, Valparaiso U., 1956; MD, Johns Hopkins U., 1960. Intern U. Va. Hosp., Charlottesville, 1960-61; resident Harvard Med. Sch., Mass. Mental Health Ctr., Boston, 1961-62, 63-66; instr. psychiatry Harvard Med. Sch., Cambridge, Mass., 1968-69, asst. prof. psychiatry, 1969-73, asst. clin. prof. psychiatry, 1973-76, assoc. clin. prof. psychiatry, 1976—; dir. Learning Therapies, Inc., Newton, Mass., 1971-89, Concord, Mass., 1989-98, Burlington, Mass., 1998—; atty. psych. McLean Hosp., Belmont, Mass., 2003—. Vis. prof. Inst. Living, Hartford, Conn., 1975; Rhoads lectr. Duke U. Sch. Medicine, 1994. Author/editor: Behavior Therapy in Psychiatry, 1972, Psychoanalysis and Behavior Therapy, 1973, Biofeedback: Behavioral Medicine, 1973; mem. editorial bd. Psychotherapy & Psychosomatics, 1974—, Family Process, 1975-78, 82-83, Jour. of Marital & Family Therapy, 1983-90, Jour. of Psychotherapy Integration, 1989—. Capt. USAF, 1962-63. Mem. Am. Family Therapy Assn., Am. Coll. Psychiatrists, Am. Soc. Clin. Psychopharmacology, Soc. Exploration of Psychotherapy Integration (co-founder). Independent. Avocations: helicopter skiing, whitewater rafting/kayaking. Mailing: 8 Hart St Burlington MA 01803-1525 Office: 22 Mill St St 405 Arlington MA 02476 E-mail: lbirkmd@comcast.net.

BIRK, ROBERT EUGENE, retired physician, educator; b. Buffalo, Jan. 7, 1926; s. Reginald H. and Florence (Diebolt) B.; m. Janet L. Davidson, June 24, 1950; children— David Eugene, James Michael, Patricia Jean, Thomas Spencer, Susan Margaret AB, Colgate U., 1948; MD, U. Rochester, 1952. Diplomate Am. Bd. Internal Medicine. Intern, resident Henry Ford Hosp., Detroit, 1952-57, chief 2d med. div., 1961-66, asst. to chmn. dept. medicine, 1965-66; practice medicine specializing in internal medicine Grosse Pointe, Mich., 1966-89; sr. active staff St. John Hosp., 1966-89, chief dept. medicine, 1967-70, dir. health edn., dir. grad. med. edn., 1975-86, exec. dir. continuing med. edn., 1975-86; dir. med. affairs St John Ambulatory Care Corp., St. John Home Care Svcs., 1980-89; v.p. clin. affairs St. John Health Corp., 1985-89. Assoc. prof. medicine Wayne State U., 1969-89 Contbr. articles to profl. jours. Mem. trustee's coun. U. Rochester, 1973-75, Med. Ctr. alumni coun., 1974-75; bd. trustees St. John Hosp., Macomb Ctr., 1986-89; corp. mem. bd. Boys Clubs Met. Detroit, 1973-89; trustee Mich. Cancer Found., 1980-89, bd. dirs., 1982-85. With U.S. Army, 1943-46. Fellow ACP, Detroit Acad. Medicine; mem. AMA, Assn. Hosp. Med. Edn. (trustee region IV 1986-87), Mich. Assn. Med. Edn. (trustee 1985-86), Am. Soc. Internal Medicine, Am. Acad. Med. Dirs., Alpha Tau Omega. Republican. Episcopalian. Home: 8 Eagle Claw Dr Hilton Head Island SC 29926-1853

BIRKBY, PAUL DONALD, library media specialist, consultant; b. Camden, N.J., Dec. 6, 1953; s. Fred Charles and Estella Kathryn (Senor) B.; children: Kathryn Elizabeth, Michael Thomas. BA, Hobart Coll., 1976; JD, Rutgers U., 1979; MLS, U. Buffalo, 1992. Bar: N.J. 1980; cert. sch. media specialist, N.Y., 1992. Jud. clk. Superior Ct. of N.J., Camden, 1980-81; pvt. practice Camden, 1981-88; spl. mcpl. pros. City of Camden, 1981-82; freelance legal writer, editor Rochester, N.Y., 1992-93; libr. media specialist Penfield (N.Y.) Ctrl. Schs., 1989—, mem. shared decision making team Scribner Rd. Sch., 1992-96, 2001—. Bd. trustees Penfield Pub. Libr., 1989—, pres., 1994-95. Mem. ASCD, N.Y. Libr. Assn., Rochester Area Sch. Librs. Office: Scribner Rd Elem Sch 1750 Scribner Rd Penfield NY 14526-9785 E-mail: Paul_Birkby@penfield.monroe.edu.

BIRKBY, WALTER HUDSON, forensic anthropologist, consultant; b. Gordon, Nebr., Feb. 28, 1931; s. Walter Levy and Margery Hazel (Moss) B.; m. Carmen Sue Gates, Aug. 18, 1955; children: Jeffrey Moss, Julianne. BA, U. Kans., 1961, MA, 1963; PhD, U. Ariz., 1973. Diplomate Am. Bd. Forensic Anthropology (pres. 1985-87, exec. com. 1980-87). Med. and X-ray technician Graham County (Kans.) Hosp., Hill City, 1955-58; phys. anthropologist Ariz. State Mus., Tucson, 1968-85; lectr. anthropology U. Ariz., Tucson, 1981-90, adj. rsch. prof. anthropology, 1990-96, emeritus prof., 1996—; curator phys. anthropology Ariz. State Mus., Tucson, 1985-96. Forensic anthropologist Pima County Med. Examiner's Office, Tucson, 1981—. Recovery of Victims of Alfred G. Packer party (1874), Lake City, Colo., 1989; dental cons. USAF Hosp., Davis Monthan AFB, Tucson, 1984-96; human osteologist U. Ariz.-Republic of Cyprus Archaeol. Expdn., 1985-87, Lugnano in Teverina (Italy) Expdn., 1990-91; dir. dept. anthropology masters program in forensic anthropology, 1983-96; cons. to Chief Armed Svcs. Graves Registration Office U.S. Army, 1987-93 97—, UN Internat. Criminal Tribunal for Yugoslavia, 1997-98; mem. disaster mortuary team Nat. Disaster Med. Sys., 1994-2000. Mem. editorial bd. (jour.) Cryptozoology, 1982—; bd. editors Am. Jour. Forensic Medicine and Pathology, 1992-97; co-author video tng. film Identification of Human Remains, 1980; contbr. articles to profl. jours. Served as sgt. USMCR, 1951-52, Korea. Recipient Achievement medal for meritorious svc. Pima

County Sheriff's Dept., 1992, Spl. Recognition award, 1995; NIH fellow U. Ariz., 1966-68. Fellow Am. Acad. Forensic Scis. (exec. com. 1978-81, T. Dale Stewart award in anthropology 1991); mem. Am. Assn. Phys. Anthropologists, Calif. Assn. Criminalists, Ariz. Homicide Investigators Assn., Sigma Xi (pres. local chpt. 1984-85). Republican. Avocations: photography, hunting, fishing. Home: 7349 E 18th St Tucson AZ 85710-4904 Office: Forensic Sci Ctr 2825 E District St Tucson AZ 85714-2081

BIRKELAND, BRYAN COLLIER, lawyer; b. Hibbing, Minn., May 29, 1951; s. Lionel Owen and Peggy Jean Birkeland; m. D.J. Loras, Jan. 5, 1974; children: Brett Holton, Blair Leigh, Blake Owen. Student, Washington and Jefferson Coll., 1969-70; BA with high honors, U. Tex., 1973, JD with honors, 1975. Bar: Tex. 1976. Ptnr. Jackson Walker, LLP, Dallas, 1982—. Pres., dir. Globalaw, Ltd. Grantee, Moody Found., 1971. Mem. ABA, State Bar Tex., Dallas Bar Assn., Order of Coif, Phi Beta Kappa, Phi Kappa Phi, Delta Sigma Rho, Tau Kappa Alpha. Presbyterian. Office: Jackson Walker LLP 901 Main St Ste 6000 Dallas TX 75202-3797 E-mail: bbirkeland@jw.com.

BIRKELBACH, ALBERT OTTMAR, retired oil company executive; b. Oak Park, Ill., Feb. 22, 1927; s. August and Ann B.; m. Shirley M. Spandet, Aug. 21, 1948; children: J.A., Lisa M., Grace L. Birkelbach Boland, Ann C. Birkelbach. BSCh.E., U. Ill., 1949. Various engring., supervisory and mgmt. positions Globe Oil & Refining Co., Lemont, Ill., 1949-53, Anderson Prichard Oil Corp., Cyril, Okla., 1953-58, Signal Oil & Gas Co., Los Angeles, 1958-64; mng. dir. Raffinerie Belge de Petroles, Antwerp, Belgium, 1964-74; v.p. Occidental Petroleum Corp., London, Eng., 1972-74; cons. in field, 1974-75; pres. ATC Petroleum Inc., N.Y.C., 1975-81, also dir.; pres. Amorient Petroleum Corp., Laguna Niguel, Calif., 1981-84; mgmt. cons., 1984-87. Served with USCG, 1945-47. Decorated knight Order Leopold Belgium). Home: 33957 N 66th Way Scottsdale AZ 85262 Address: 33957 N 66th Way Scottsdale AZ 85262-7231

BIRKELUND, JOHN PETER, investment banking executive; b. Chgo., June 23, 1930; s. George R. and Ruth (Olsen) B.; m. Constance I. Smiles, Oct. 25, 1958; children: Gwynne Tibbetts, Elizabeth Oberbeck, Constance Olivia, Diana. AB, Princeton U., 1952; doctorate (hon.), Brown U., 2002. Cons. Booz Allen & Hamilton, Chgo., 1956; v.p. Amsterdam Overseas Corp., N.Y.C., 1956-67; co-founder, chmn., dir. New Court Securities Corp., N.Y.C., 1967-81; pres. Dillon, Read & Co., Inc., N.Y.C., 1981-86, CEO, 1986-93; chmn. SBC Warburg Dillon Read Inc., N.Y.C., 1994-97; sr. advisor UBS Warburg LLC, N.Y.C., 1998—2002; gen. ptnr. Saratoga Ptnrs., N.Y.C., Darby Overseas Ptnrs., Washington. Chmn. Polish-Am. Enterprise Fund, N.Y.C., Polish.-Am. Freedom Found., Nat. Humanities Ctr., N.C., dir. Internat. Exec. Svc. Corp., Stamford Conn. Chair Thomas J. Watson Inst. for Internat. Studies, Providence; trustee N.Y. Pub. Libr., N.Y.C., 1990—. Lt. USNR, 1953—55. Mem. Coun. Fgn. Rels., Phi Beta Kappa, The Links Club, Univ. Club, The Blind Brook Club, Clove Valley Rod and Gun Club. Home: 510 Weed St New Canaan CT 06840-6127 Office: Saratoga Ptnrs 535 Madison Ave 4th Fl New York NY 10022

BIRKENHEAD, THOMAS BRUCE, theatrical producer and manager, educator; b. N.Y.C., Dec. 19, 1931; s. Thomas A. and Florence (Morison) B.; m. Susan Leslie Arkin, Dec. 3, 1954 (div. 1983); m. Maria Martins, May 26, 1999; children: Peter Lawrence, David Andrew, Richard James, Alison Jane, Leila Alessandra. BA, Bklyn. Coll. CUNY, 1954, MA, 1958; PhD, New Sch. Social Rsch., 1963. From lectr. to prof. econs. Bklyn. Coll. CUNY, 1957-72, prof., 1972-75; dean Sch. Social Scis., 1972-75; prof. emeritus Bklyn. Coll. CUNY, 1975—. Bus. mgr. Theatre II of Glen Cove, N.Y., 1970-74. Co-mgr. Do Black Patent Leather Shoes Really Reflect Up?, Present Laughter, Master Harold and the Boys, Children of a Lesser God, Ain't Misbehavin, Brighton Beach Memoirs, Biloxi Blues, Broadway Bound, Barbara Cook in Concert, Run For Your Wife, Rumors, Lost in Yonkers, Jake's Women, Goodbye Girl; gen. mgr.: Cape Cod Melody Tent, 1969—71, Twyla Tharp on Broadway, 1980; gen. mgr. Twyla Tharp on Broadway, 1981, Joe Egg, 1985, Social Security, 1986, Long Days Journey Into Night, London and Tel Aviv, 1986, Ain't Misbehavin, N.Y.C., 1988—89, Japan, 1990, Fresh Air Taxi, 1993, Honky Tonk Highway, 1994—96, Dream a Little Dream, 1994—95, Duke and the Dutchess, 2001—; co-prodr.: 1995 Tony Award Broadcast, N.H.K. Japan, —; prodr.: High Mountain Ghost, 1996—98; sec.-treas. : Highly Ent., 1995—; mgmt. cons. : Keystone Ctr. Performing Arts, 1999—. Founding mem., sponsor U.S. Shooting Team, U.S. Holocaust Meml. Mus., Am. Air Mus., Eng., U.S. Naval Meml. Found., WWII Meml., U.S. Olympic Com. T. Bruce Birkenhead scholarship in performing arts established by Performing Arts Mgmt. Program Bklyn. Coll. Mem. NRA, US Naval Inst., Habitat for Humanity, Amnesty Internat., Women in Mil. Svc. for Am., Groucho Club (Eng.), World Jewish Congress, Carter Ctr., Victorian Soc. Home and Office: 353 W 44th St Apt 1A New York NY 10036-5416

BIRKERTS, GUNNAR, architect; b. Riga, Latvia, Jan. 17, 1925; came to U.S., 1949, naturalized, 1954; s. Peter and Meria (Shop) B.; m. Sylvia Zvirbulis, July 29, 1950; children— Sven Peter, Andra Sylvia, Erik Gunnar. Diplomingeneur Architekt, Technische Hochschule, Stuttgart, Germany, 1949; D (hon.), Riga Tech. Univ., Latvia, 1990. Designer Perkins & Will, Chgo., 1950-51, Eero Saarinen & Assos., Bloomfield Hills, Mich., 1951-55; prin. chief designer Minoru Yamasaki & Assos., Birmingham, Mich., 1955-59; pres. Gunnar Birkerts & Assos., Inc., Birmingham, 1959; asst. prof. architecture U. Mich., 1961, asso. prof., 1963-69, prof., 1969-90; Graham fellow, 1970; architect in residence Am. Acad. in Rome, 1976; 1st Lawrence J. Plym. disting. prof. architecture U. Ill., 1982; Thomas S. Monaghan architect-in-residence prof. U. Mich., Ann Arbor, 1984; Bruce Alonzo Goff prof. of creative architecture U. Okla., 1990. Prin. works include Schwartz House, Northville, Mich. (First Honor award AIA 1962, Merit award Detroit chpt. AIA 1963, Archtl. Record award 1961), Univ. Reformed Ch., Ann Arbor Mich. (award Ch. Archtl. Guild Am. 1962), Peoples Fed. Savs. & Loan Bank, Royal Oak, Mich., 1963 (Merit award Detroit chpt. AIA 1963), Fisher Adminstrv. Ctr., Detroit (award of merit Mich. Soc. Architects 1967, Merit award Detroit chpt. AIA 1967), Detroit Inst. Arts addition (25 Yr. award AIA 2002), 1300 Lafayette Apts., Detroit, Tougaloo (Miss.) Coll. (award of honor Mich. Soc. Architects 1974), Vocat.-Tech. Campus, So. Ill. U., Glen Oaks Community Coll. Campus, Centreville, Mich., Lincoln Sch., Columbus, Ind. (AIA Detroit chpt. and nat. Honor awards 1968, 70, 25 yr. award Mich. AIA), Fed. Res. Bank, Mpls. (award excellence Am. Inst. Steel Constrn. 1974, design award Am. Iron and Steel Inst. 1975), IBM Corp. Computer Center, Sterling Forest, N.Y. (honor award Detroit chpt. AIA 1973), Contemporary Arts Mus., Houston (honor award Detroit chpt. AIA 1975), Dance Instructional Facility at Purchase (award honor Mich. Soc. Architects 1977, Honor award Detroit chpt. AIA 1978), Calvary Baptist Ch., Detroit (Honor award Mich. Soc. Architects 1979, award of excellence Am. Inst. Steel Constrn. 1979), IBM Office Bldg., Southfield, Mich. (Honor award Mich. Soc. Architects 1980, energy conservation award Owens Corning Fiberglas Corp. 1977), Duluth Public Libr. (Honor award Mich. Soc. Architects 1981), Fire Sta., Corning, N.Y. (honor award Mich. Soc. Architects 1977), Corning Mus. of Glass, Law Libr. Addition, U. Mich. (award of excellence AIA and ALA 1985), U.S. Embassy bldg., Helsinki, Finland, Coll. of Law bldg., U. Iowa (Award of Honor-Mich. Soc. Architects 1987), Uris Library addition, Cornell U. (honor award Mich. Soc. Architects 1984), Dist. Office Bldg., Green Bay, Wis., Ferguson Residence, Kalamazoo, Mich. (award of honor Mich. Soc. Architects 1986), Chapel & Ednl. Facility, Camp Wildflecken, Fed. Republic Germany (Silver Castle award U.S. Army Corps. Engrs., European div. 1986), St. Peter's Luth. Ch., Columbus, Ind. (award of honor Detroit chpt. AIA 1986, 90), Domino's world hdqrs., Ann Arbor, Mich. (bldg. recognition award Engring. Soc. Detroit 1987, M award for Excellence in Masonry Design Masonry Inst. Mich., 1989), Libr. Addition Conservatory Music Oberlin Coll., Ohio, Prototype Franchise Bldg. Domino's Pizza, Inc. (award of honor Mich. Soc. Architects 1989), Jackson, Mich., Cen. Libr. addition U. Calif., San Diego, Sports Svcs. Bldg. U. Mich., U.S. Embassy, Caracas, Venezuela, Libr. U. Mich., Flint (Design and Constrn. showcase '94 award), Coll. Law Ohio State U., (award of honor AIA Mich., 1995), Kemper Mus. Contemporary Art and Design, Kans. City Mo. (Lighting award, 1995), Ch. Servant, Kentwood, Mich.; exhbns. include Akron Inst. Art, 1954, Sao Paulo (Brazil) Bienniale, 1962, 40 under 40, USA-NY, Architects League, 1965, Mus. Modern Art, N.Y.C., 1971, Notre Dame U., 1973, N.Y. Mus. Modern Art, 1979, Neuberger Mus., Purchase, N.Y., 1981, Am. Acad. and Inst. Arts and Letters, N.Y.C., 1981, U. Ill., 1983, U. Md., College Park, 1985, Saginaw Art Mus., Mich., 1985, Notre Dame U., 1985, Pratt Inst., Bklyn., 1986, NYU, 1986, The Triennale, Milan, Italy, 1986, Judah L. Magnes Mus., Berkeley, Calif., 1986, Nat. Ctr. for Study of Frank Lloyd Wright, Ann Arbor, 1988, St. Peter's Cathedral, Riga, Latvia, 1989, Torino '90, Turin, Italy, 1990, The 3d Belgrade Triennial of World Architects, 1991, The Athenaeum Music and Art Libr., LaJolla, Calif., 1991, Kansas City Art Inst., 1992, Lawrence Tech. U., Southfield, Mich., 1993, Latvian Nat. Libr., 2000 (Am. Archtl. award Chgo. Atheanum), Venezia and Archtl. Bieniale, 2002. Named Young Designer of Year Akron Inst. Art, 1954, Mich. Artist of Yr. Mich. Artrain, 1993; recipient 1st prize Internat. Furniture competition, Cantu, Italy, 1955; 3d prize Internat. competition for Cultural Centre, Belgian Congo; Design award Progressive Architecture mag., 1957, 59, 61, 71; award of excellence Archtl. Record, 1968; Nat. Gold medal Tau Sigma Delta, 1971; Gold medal Detroit chpt. AIA, 1975; Gold medal Mich. Soc. Architects, 1980; Brunner Meml. prize Am. Acad. and Inst. Arts and Letters, 1981; Mich. Art award Arts Found. Mich., 1988, Disting. Prof. Assn. Collegiate Schs. Architecture, 1990; Order of Three Stars, Republic of Latvia. Fellow AIA, Graham Found., Latvian Architects Assn.; mem. Mich. Soc. Architects (Award of Honor 1989), Ch. Archtl. Guild, Hon. Order Ky. Cols. Office: 1830 Tahquamenon Bloomfield Hills MI 48302

BIRKETT, JAMES DAVIS, management consultant; b. Norwalk, Conn., Sept. 30, 1936; s. John George and Doris (Walker) B.; m. Sarah Page Burley, Dec. 17, 1960; children: Benjamin Thaddeus, John Hill, Lucy Belinda. BA, Bowdoin Coll., 1958; MS, Yale U., 1960, PhD, 1963. Sr. cons. Arthur D. Little, Inc., Cambridge, Mass., 1962-88; propr. West Neck Strategies, Nobleboro, Maine, 1988—. Mem. editorial bd. Desalination, 1985—. Chmn. Nobleboro Comprehensive Planning Com., 1990-93; mem. Lincoln (Mass.) Town Planning Bd., 1979-85; bd. dirs. Christmas Cove Improvement Assn., 1982-86; commodore Christmas Cove Fleet, 1986-88; trustee Lincoln Acad., Newcastle, Maine, 1991—. Mem. Internat. Desalination Assn. (bd. dirs., treas. 1981—, pres. 1985-87), Am. Desalting Assn. (bd. dirs. 1980-85). Avocations: skiing, sailing, tennis, history of technology. Home: 556 W Neck Rd Nobleboro ME 04555-8632 Office: West Neck Strategies PO Box 193 Nobleboro ME 04555-0193

BIRKHEAD, GUTHRIE SWEENEY, JR., political scientist, university dean; b. Holden, Mo., Oct. 28, 1920; s. Guthrie Sweeney and Yula Donna (Glass) B.; m. Louise Gartner, Aug. 16, 1952; children— Guthrie Sweeney III, Richard Gartner, Evan Clark. AA, Jefferson City (Mo.) Jr. Coll., 1940; AB, U. Mo., 1942, A.M., 1947; MA, Princeton, 1949, PhD in Politics, 1951. Mem. faculty Syracuse U., 1950—, prof. polit. sci., 1960—, chmn. dept., 1959-62, 66-67, dir. met. studies program, 1968-73; asso. dean Maxwell Sch., 1973-77, dean, 1977-88. Also dir. pub. adminstrn. programs, 1959-62; dir. research UN Inst. Pub. Adminstrn. for Turkey and Middle East, 1955-56; cons. Pakistan Adminstrv. Staff Coll., Lahore, 1962-64, Ford Found., Pakistan, 1967-68 Co-author: River Basin Administration and the Delaware, 1960, Science and State Government in New York, 1960, Decisions in Syracuse, 1962; Editor: Administrative Problems in Pakistan, 1966, A Look to the North: Canadian Regional Experience, 1974, Education for Public Service, 1980; Contbr. articles to profl. jours. Chmn. pub. finance com. Community Renewal Plan, Syracuse, N.Y., 1970-72; exec. dir. com. local govt. and home rule N.Y. State Constl. Conv., 1967, Syracuse Charter Commn., 1972-74; mem. Nat. Com. Water Quality Policy Nat. Acad. Scis.-NRC, 1974-76; com. to review the metropolitan Washington area water supply study Nat. Acad. Engring/Nat. Research Council, 1977-84. Served with inf. AUS, 1942-46. Fellow Nat. Mcpl. League, 1952-53. Fellow Nat. Acad. Pub. Adminstrn.; mem. AAAS, Am. Soc. Pub. Adminstrn., Phi Beta Kappa, Sigma Xi. Home: 220 Lockwood Rd Syracuse NY 13214-2035

BIRKHEAD, JOHN ANDREW, health services professional, mental health counselor; b. Anchorage, Jan. 10, 1954; s. Herbert Cecil and Eugenia Clarke (McChesney) B.; life ptnr. Matthew L. Cheney; children: Nathaniel Andrew, Colin Michael. BA, U. Colo., 1975; MA, U. Calif., Davis, 1984; PhD, Stanford U., 1994; MA in Counseling and Human Svcs., U. Colo., 2002. Commd. 2d lt. USAF, 1975, advanced through grades to maj., 1987, navigator, 1976-82; instr. polit. sci. USAF Acad., Colorado Springs, 1984-85; sr. navigator USAF, Okinawa, Japan, 1988-91; assoc. prof. USAF Acad., Colorado Springs, 1991-96; faculty dept. polit. sci. Pikes Peak C.C., Colo., 1994, 1999—2000, U. So. Colo., 1994—95, Colo. Coll., 1996; program dir. So. Colo. AIDS Project, 2002—. Mem. Pi Sigma Alpha, Chi Sigma Iota. Democrat. Avocations: running, reading, skiing, tennis. Home: 6145 Turret Dr Colorado Springs CO 80918-3216 E-mail: jbirkhead@s-cap.org.

BIRKHEAD, THOMAS LARRY, minister; b. Owensboro, Ky., Nov. 20, 1941; s. Thomas Butler and Ollie Mae (Brown) B.; m. Melva Jean Young, Oct. 18, 1968; 1 child, David. AB, Western Ky. U., 1963; MDiv, So. Bapt. Theol. Sem., 1968. Ordained to ministry So. Bapt. Conv., 1966. Pastor Mt. Vernon Bapt. Ch., Calhoun, Ky., 1966-69, Sorgho Bapt. Ch., Owensboro, 1969-73, Spottsville (Ky.) Bapt. Ch., 1973-82, Yelvington Bapt. Ch., Maceo, Ky., 1982-86, Ghent (Ky.) Bapt. Ch., 1986-93, Pond Run Bapt. Ch., Beaver Dam, Ky., 1993-98, New Barren Springs Bapt. Ch., Hopkinsville, Ky., 1998—2001, Robards (Ky.) Bapt. Ch., 2001—. Exec. bd. Ky. Bapt. Conv., Middletown, 1988-91. Co-author: Ghent Baptist Church History 1800-1990, 1990. Asst. moderator exec. bd. Ohio County Bapt. Assn., 1995-96, moderator exec. bd., 1996-97. Mem. Ohio County Ministerial Assn. (v.p. 1994-97, pres. 1997-98), Carroll County Mins. Assn. (treas. 1989-93). Home and Office: PO Box 236 Robards KY 42452-0236

BIRKHOLZ, RAYMOND JAMES, metal products manufacturing company executive; b. Chgo., Nov. 11, 1936; s. Raymond I. and Mary (Padian) B.; m. Judy Ann Richards, Apr. 23, 1966; children: Raymond J. Jr., Scott C., Matthew R. BSME, Purdue U., 1958; MBA, U. Chgo., 1963. Registered prof. engr., Ill. V.p. apparatus divsn. Gen. Cable Corp., Westminster, Colo., 1973-77; v.p. ops. metals divsn. Ogden Corp., Cleve., 1977-80, v.p. mfg. and engring. N.Y.C., 1980-81, pres. indsl. products, 1981-84, v.p., 1984-86; pres., COO Amcast Indsl. Corp., Dayton, Ohio, 1986-90; CEO Hollander Industries Corp., Dayton, Ohio, 1993-94; pres., CEO Republic Storage Systems Co., Inc., Canton, Ohio, 1994—. Home: 2268 Brookelake Dr Atlanta GA 30338-7015 Office: Republic Storage Systems Co 1038 Belden Ave NE Canton OH 44705-1454

BIRKINBINE, JOHN, II, philatelist; b. Chestnut Hill, Pa., Mar. 29, 1930; s. Olaf Weimer and Gertrude Marie (Tyson) B.; m. Ausencia Barrera Elen, Dec. 19, 1969; children: John III, Bayani Royd. Chmn., CEO Am. Philatelic Brokerages, Tucson, 1946—. Chmn. bd. dirs. Ariz. Philatelic Rangers, Tucson, 1987—; bd. dirs. Postal History Found. Chmn. bd. 1869 Pictorial Rsch. Assn., 1969, bd. dirs., 1970-76, chmn. Baha'i Faith Adminstrv. Body, Pima County, Ariz., 1977-81, 83-91; sheriff, chmn. Santa Catalina Corral of Westerners Internat., Tucson, 1986; bd. dirs. Tucson chpt. Nordmanns-Forburdet (Norse Fedn.), 2002—. Recipient Large Gold and Spl. award Spanish Soc. Internat., San Juan, P.R., 1982, New Zealand Soc. Internat., Auckland, 1990, Large Internat. Gold award Australian Soc. Internat., Melbourne, 1984, Swedish Soc. Internat., Stockholm, 1986, Singapore Soc. Internat., 1995, U.S. Soc. Internat., San Francisco, 1997, Internat. Gold award U.S. Soc. Internat., Chgo., 1986, Bulgarian Soc. Internat., Sofia, 1989. Mem. Am. Philatelic Soc. (U.S. Champion of Champions award 1985), U.S. Philatelic Classics Soc. (disting. philatelist award 1995), Am. Philatelic Congress (McCoy award 1969, 97), Scandinavian Collectors Club, Collectors Club N.Y., Western Cover Soc. Avocations: swimming, travel, music, West U.S. historical research, Japanese antiques. Office: Am Philatelic Brokerages PO Box 36657 Tucson AZ 85740-6657 E-mail: jbirkinbin@aol.com. *To look for and appreciate the good qualities in each individual, to have sympathy and empathy for their problems, and to provide exceptional service in an attempt to satisfy their needs and desires.*

BIRKMAYER, DONALD TEFFT, retired college official; b. Troy, N.Y., Mar. 15, 1925; s. Louis Albert and Helen Margaret (Tefft) B.; m. Virginia Abbott, June 19, 1949 (dec. Jan. 1984); children: Carolyn Cox, Richard A., Nancy Kane; m. Madonna Stahl, May 24, 1987. BS in Mgmt. Engring., Rensselaer Poly. Inst., Troy, 1949. Engr. N.Y. State Dept. Transp., Albany, 1949-85; ret., 1985; editor, pub. Intercollegiate Hockey Newsletter, Troy, 1954-94; ret., 1994; coll. hockey adminstr. and announcer Rensselaer Poly. Inst., Troy, 1949-2000, retired, 2000. Staff sgt. C.E., U.S.Army, 1944-46. Recipient cert. of appreciation Ea. Coll. Athletic Conf., 1985; Thomas J. Sheehan Meml. award Rensselaer Poly. Inst., 1985, Alumni Key award, 1986, named to Athletic Hall of Fame, 1995. Avocations: genealogy, local history, travel. E-mail: dtbrpi@yahoo.com.

BIRKY, JOHN EDWARD, banker, consultant, financial advisor; b. Minier, Ill., July 16, 1934; s. John G. and Gertrude K. (Nafziger) B.; m. Susan Becker, Dec. 13, 1937; children: John Brian, Kathleen Debera. BS in Indsl. Adminstrn., U. Ill., 1957; postgrad., Ohio State U., 1957; MBA, Case Western Res. U., 1975. Cert. data processor. Asst. to mgr. Caterpillar Tractor Co., Peoria, Ill., 1957-61; cons. Sutherland Co., Peoria, 1961-63; mgr. United Research Services, San Mateo, Calif., 1963-69; dir. Case Western Res. U., Cleve., 1969-72; v.p. Fed. Res. Bank, Cleve., 1972-79; exec. v.p. Banc Systems Assn., West Lake, Ohio, 1979-83, Citizens Banking Corp., Flint, Mich., 1983-92, also chmn. auto com., mem. corp. exec. com., 1986-92; fin. planner Bonita Springs, Fla., 1992-98; fin. adviser Amex Fin. Advisors, Inc.; ind. fin. cons. Hopedale, Ill. Bd. dirs. Citizens Bank, Flint, Comml. Nat. Bank, Berwyn, Ill., Citizens Leasing Corp., Grand Rapids, Mich., Flin Inst. Music; chmn. Magicline Inc., 1989-91; speaker various profl. confs. Contbr. articles to banking jours. Mem. Rep. precinct com., Sierra Vista, Ariz., 1964-65; life mem. Pres.'s Task Force, Washington, 1980; advisor automation commn. ARC, Flint, 1987; mem. exec. bd., treas. Flint Inst. Music, 1986-88, vice chmn.; mem. Am. Bank Adminstrn. Ins.; bd. dirs. Flint Inst. Music; elder, lay pastor 1st Presbyn. Ch., Flint, 1988-91; past mem. adv. com. U. Mich., Flint, Boys Club Cleve., Cuyahoga C.C., Ashland Coll. Capt. USAF, 1957-60. Mem.: Data Processing Mgmt. Assn., Am. Bankers Assn., Acacia, Am. Legion, U. Ill. Alumni Assn. (life), Tucson Alumni Club (v.p.), Saddlebrooke Country Club. Republican. Avocations: golf, tennis, barbershop singing. Address: 415 NE 2d St Hopedale IL 61747

BIRLE, JAMES ROBB, investor; b. Phila., Jan. 25, 1936; s. John George and Mildred C. (Donnelly) B.; m. Mary Margaret McDaniels, Jan. 28, 1961; children— James Robb, Jr., Anne Margaret, Alexandra Lea, John George II BSM.E., Villanova U., 1958. With Gen. Electric Co., San Jose, Calif., 1958, gen. mgr. nuclear energy bus., 1969-77, v.p., gen mgr. far east business div. N.Y.C., 1977-81, v.p., gen mgr. air condition div. Louisville, 1981-82, sr. v.p., group exec. constrn. and engring. svcs. group Westport, Conn, 1982-85, sr. v.p. corp. trading ops. N.Y.C., 1985-88; ptnr. The Blackstone Group, N.Y.C., 1988-94; co-chmn., CEO Collins & Aikman Group, N.Y.C., 1988-94; chmn., Resolute Ptnrs., LLC, Greenwich, Conn., 1994—. Bd. dirs. Mass. Mut. Fin. Svcs. Co., Drexel Industries LLC.; mem. Transparency Internat. Trustee Villanova U. Republican. Avocations: tennis; golf; reading; sailing. Office: Resolute Ptnrs LLC 2 Sound View Dr Greenwich CT 06830-6471

BIRMAN, ALEXANDER, physicist, researcher; b. Moscow, May 23, 1946; came to U.S., 1994; s. Yakov and Rozaliya (Krimerman) B.; m. Emily Freydman, Dec. 25, 1980; children: Igor, Eugene. MSc, Moscow Physico-Tech. Inst., 1970; PhD, Inst. Applied Physics, Moscow, 1975. Sr. rsch. scientist Inst. Applied Physics, Moscow, 1970-85; leading rsch. scientist Astrophysics Corp., Moscow, 1985-93; sr. optical scientist Dicon Fiberoptics, Inc., Richmond, Calif., 1995—. Lectr. Moscow Physico-Tech. Inst., 1987-92. Contbr. articles to profl. jours. Mem. IEEE, Optical Soc. Am., Internat. Soc. for Optical Engring., Am. Phys. Soc. Achievements include work on theory of ring lasers; contribution to design of laser and fiber-optic gyroscopes; development of optic components for advanced communication systems, including fiberoptic, thin-film, integrated optic and photonic crystal components. Home: 7585 Skyline Blvd Oakland CA 94611 Office: Dicon Fiberoptics 1689 Regatta Blvd Richmond CA 94804 E-mail: abirman@diconfiber.com.

BIRMAN, LINDA LEE, retired elementary school educator; b. Bellingham, Wash., Sept. 2, 1950; d. Ronald L. and Shirley Lee (Smith) Kindlund; m. Steven D. Birman, May 28, 1988; children: Stacy, Michele, Cameron, Colin. BA in Edn., We. Wash. State Coll., 1973; MA in Edn., We. Wash. U., 1978. Cert. elem. and secondary tchr., Wash. Tchr. 2d grade, Bellingham, Wash., 1973—2003; ret., 2003. Affiliated teaching faculty We. Wash. U., Bellingham, 1992; subject advisory com. Washington State Student Learning Commn. Author Stewart the Skyscraper Falcon, 1997. Mem. NEA.

BIRMAN, VICTOR MARK, mechanical and aerospace engineering educator, academic administrator; b. Leningrad, Russia, Jan. 13, 1950; came to U.S., 1984; s. Mark Samuel and Sima (Pesenson) B.; m. Anna Irene Rabkin, Apr. 9, 1977; children: Michael, Shirley. MS, Shipbuilding Inst., Leningrad, 1973; PhD, Technion, Haifa, Israel, 1983. Engr. Steel Structures Design Inst., Leningrad, 1973-78; grad. teaching asst. Technion, Haifa, 1979-82, rsch. fellow, 1983; engr. Israel Aircraft Industries, Lod, 1984; asst. prof. U. New Orleans, 1984-87, assoc. prof., 1987-89, U. Mo.-Rolla, St. Louis, 1989-96, prof., 1996—, dir. Engring. Edn. Ctr., 2000—. Mem. summer faculty Air Force Office of Sci. Rsch., Wright-Patterson AFB, 1992, 97, NASA Lewis Ctr., 1993-94; vis. scientist Air Force Inst. Tech., 1993, U. Natal (South Africa), 1993. Assoc. editor Composites Part B: Engring., 1991—, Applied Mechs. Revs., 2000—; translator; reviewer profl. jours., 1989—; contbr. rsch. papers to profl. jours., papers to profl confs. Recipient McDonnell Douglas Faculty Excellence award, 1993-94, 94-95, 95-96, 97-98, Award for Excellence in Rsch., U. New Orleans Alumni Assn., 1987; summer scholar U. New Orleans, 1986. Fellow AIAA (assoc.), ASME (composite materials com., structures and materials com.) Achievements include research in mechanics of composite and smart structures, sandwich structures, imperfection-sensitivity, thermoelasticity and buckling of stiffened composite shells, mechanics of ceramic matrix composites; research for Army Research Office, Office Naval Research, Air Force, Air Force Office of Sci. Rsch., NASA, and industry. Office: U Mo-Rolla Engring Edn Ctr 8001 Natural Bridge Rd Saint Louis MO 63121-4401

BIRMINGHAM, PATRICK MICHAEL, lawyer; b. St. Paul, Apr. 2, 1947; s. George Thomas and Nona Birmingham; m. Karen Ann Moir, Oct. 17, 1992. BS, Portland State U., 1970; JD, Western State U., 1975. Bar: Calif. 1975, U.S. Dist. Ct. (ctrl. dist.) Calif. 1975, U.S. Supreme Ct. 1978, Oreg. 1978, U.S. Dist. Ct. Oreg. 1978. With Riverside County (Calif.) Office of Pub. Defender, 1975-78; pvt. practice Portland, Oreg., 1978—. With U.S. Army N.G., 1970-75. Named in Best Lawyers in Am. and Nat. Directory Criminal Def. Lawyers. Mem. Oreg. Criminal Def. Lawyers (life), Calif. Attys. for Criminal Justice, Nat. Assn. Criminal Def. Lawyers, Multnomah Defenders Inc. (bd. dirs. 1990-92), Multnomah County Bar Assn. (mentor program 1994-99). Office: 1001 SW 5th Ave Ste 1625 Portland OR 97204-1132

BIRMINGHAM, RICHARD GREGORY, lawyer; b. Buffalo, Aug. 14, 1929; s. William Anthony and Laura Louise (Reimann) B.; m. Suzanne M. Cannon, May 20, 1961; children: Barbara A. McCarty, Maureen E., Gregory S. BA, U. Notre Dame, 1951; JD, SUNY, Buffalo, 1957. Bar: N.Y. 1957, Del. 1984, Pa. 1993. Law clk. to justices appellate div. N.Y. Supreme Ct. (4th dept.), Rochester, 1957-60; ptnr. Phillips, Lytle, Hitchcock, Blaine & Huber, Buffalo, 1960-84, 90-94, ret., 1994, ptnr. Wilmington, Del., 1984-90. Lt. comdr. USN, 1951-54, Korea. Mem. ABA, N.Y. State Bar Assn., Del. Bar Assn., Erie County Bar Assn., Rivermont Country Club. Republican. Roman Catholic. Office: 510 Shelli Ln Roswell GA 30075-2988 E-mail: rgsb510@hotmail.com.

BIRMINGHAM, RICHARD JOSEPH, lawyer; b. Seattle, Feb. 26, 1953; s. Joseph E. and Anita (Loomis) B. BA cum laude, Wash. State U., 1975; JD, Seattle U., 1978; LLM in Taxation, Boston U., 1980. Bar: Wash. 1978, Oreg. 1981, U.S. Dist. Ct. (we. dist.) Wash. 1978, U.S. Tax Ct. 1981. Ptnr. Davis Wright Tremaine, Seattle, 1982-93; shareholder Birmingham Thorson & Barnett, P.C., Seattle, 1993—. Mem. King County Bar Employee Benefit Com., Seattle, 1986, U.S. Treasury ad hoc com. employee benefits, 1988—. Contbg. editor: Compensation and Benefits Mgmt., 1985—; contbr. articles to profl. jours. Mem. ABA (employee benefits and exec. compensation com. 1982—), Wash. State Bar Assn. (speaker 1984-86, tax sect. 1982—), Oreg. State Bar Assn. (tax sect. 1982—), Western Pension Conf. (speaker 1986), Seattle Pension Round table. Democrat. Avocations: jogging, bicycling, photography. Home: 3820 49th Ave NE Seattle WA 98105-5234 Office: Birmingham Thorson & Barnett PC 3315 Two Union Square 601 Union St Seattle WA 98101-2341 Business E-Mail: RBirmingham@BTBPC.com.

BIRMINGHAM, STEPHEN, writer; b. Hartford, Conn., May 28, 1931; s. Thomas J. and Editha (Gardner) B.; m. Janet Tillson, Jan. 5, 1951 (div.); children: Mark, Harriet, Carey. BA cum laude, Williams Coll., 1950; postgrad., Univ. Coll., Oxford (Eng.) U., 1951. Advt. copywriter Needham, Harper & Steers, Inc., 1953-67. Author: Young Mr. Keefe, 1958, Barbara Greer, 1959, The Towers of Love, 1961, Those Harper Women, 1963, Fast Start, Fast Finish, 1966, Our Crowd: The Great Jewish Families of New York, 1967, The Right People, 1968, Heart Toubles, 1968, The Grandees, 1971, The Late John

Marquand, 1972, The Right Places, 1973, Real Lace, 1973, Certain People: America's Black Elite, 1977, The Golden Dream: Suburbia in the 1970's, 1978, Jacqueline Bouvier Kennedy Onassis, 1978, Life at the Dakota, 1979, California Rich, 1980, Duchess, 1981, The Grandes Dames, 1982, The Auerbach Will, 1983; The Rest of Us, 1984, The LeBaron Secret, 1986, Americas Secret Aristocracy, 1987, Shades of Fortune, 1989, The Rothman Scandal, 1991, Carriage Trade, 1993, The Wrong Kind of Money, 1997; contbr. numerous articles to numerous periodicals. Served with AUS, 1951-53. Mem. New Eng. Soc. of City of N.Y., Phi Beta Kappa. Democrat. Episcopalian. Address: 1247 Ida St Cincinnati OH 45202-1525

BIRMINGHAM, THOMAS F. lawyer, former state legislator; b. Aug. 4, 1949; married; two daughters. AB in Social Studies cum laude, Harvard Coll., 1972; Rhodes Scholar, Oxford Univ., 1972—75; JD cum laude, Harvard Coll., 1978. Bar: Mass.; U.S. Dist. Ct. Mass.; 1st Cir. Ct. of Appeals; U.S. State Supreme Ct. Asst. gen. counsel Internat. Union Electrical Workers, 1978-80; assoc. atty. Flamm, Kaplan, Paven & Feinberg, 1980-83; ptnr. Flamm & Birmingham, 1984-93; mem. Mass. Senate, Boston, 1991—2002, pres., 1996—2002; ptnr. Feinberg, Charnas & Birmingham, 1994—. Faculty mem. Boston Labor Guild Sch. Indsl. Rels., 1980-85; senate chair Edn. Arts and Humanities Com., 1991-92, Ways and Means Com. State Mass., 1993-2002; mem. Steering and Policy Com. State Mass., 1993-2002. Commr. Chelsea Redevelopment Authority, 1985-88; bd. dirs. New England Higher Edn., 1991—. Harvard Coll. Academic scholar, 1969-72, U. Coll. Galway scholar, 1970, Rhodes scholar, 1972-75; Teaching fellow Harvard Coll., 1971. Mem. Mass. Bar Assn. (labor law sec. coun. mem.). E-mail: Tbirming@sen.state.ma.us.*

BIRMINGHAM, WILLIAM JOSEPH, lawyer; b. Lynbrook, N.Y., Aug. 7, 1923; s. Daniel Joseph and Mary Elizabeth (Tighe) B.; m. Helen Elizabeth Roche, July 23, 1955; children: Deirdre, Patrick, Maureen, Kathleen, Brian. ME, Stevens Inst. Tech., 1944; MBA, Harvard U., 1948; JD, DePaul U., Chgo., 1953. Bar: Ill. 1953, U.S. Patent and Trademark Office, 1955, U.S. Dist. Ct. (no. dist.) Ill. 1960, U.S. Supreme Ct. 1961, U.S. Ct. Appeals (7th cir.) 1962, U.S. Ct. Appeals (3rd cir.) 1968, U.S. Ct. Mil. Appeals 1973, U.S. Ct. Appeals (Fed. cir.) 1982, U.S. Ct. Claims 1986; registered profl. engr., Ill., Ind. Chem. engr. Standard Oil Co. Ind., Chgo., 1948-53; patent atty., 1953-59; assoc. Neuman, Williams, Anderson & Olson, Chgo., 1959-60; ptnr., 1961-91, Leydig, Voit & Mayer, Ltd., Chgo., 1991-93; of counsel, 1994-96. Served to capt. USNR, 1942-75, ret. Mem. ABA, ASME, Fed. Cir. Bar Assn., Am. Intellectual Property Law Assn., Intellectual Property Law Assn. Chgo. Home: 233 Pine St Deerfield IL 60015-4853

BIRNBAUM, BERNARD A, radiology educator; b. Queens, NY, Oct. 2, 1957; m. Maj L Wickstrom, Aug. 30, 1998; 1 child, Sarah Bernice. BA magna cum laude, Brown U., 1975—79; MD, NY U. Sch. Of Medicine, 1979—83. Bd. Cert. Am. Bd. Of Radiology, 1988. Asst. prof. of radiology NYU Med. Ctr., 1988—93; assoc. prof. of radiology U. Of Pa., Med. Ctr., Phila., 1993—2001; prof. of radiology NYU Med. Ctr., 2001—. Sect. chief, computed tomography U. Of Pa., Med. Ctr., 1993—2001; vice chmn. of clin. affairs and ops. NYU Med. Ctr., 2001—; cons. to editor Radiology, 1998, assoc. editor, 1998—2002. Recipient Multiple Rsch. awards, Soc. Of Computed Body Tomography And Magnetic Resonance, 1991, Multiple rsch. awards, 1998, 1999, 2000, Radiology Editor's Recognition Award With Spl. Distinction, Radiology Jour., 1995, 1996, 1997. Fellow: Soc. Of Computed Body Tomography And Magnetic Resonance (chair, rrsch.-scientific com. 1999—2000); mem.: Soc. Of Gastrointestinal Radiologists (chmn., rsch. awards com. 2002—03), Alpha Omega Alpha, Xigma Xi, Phi Beta Kappa. Office: Dept Of Radiology 560 First Ave Irm-232 New York NY 10016

BIRNBAUM, CHARLES A. landscape architect; Pvt. practice; coord. landscape initiative Nat. Pk. Svc., 1992—. Loeb fellow Grad. Sch. Design Harvard U., 1998, instr. profl. devel. program Grad. Sch. Design; instr. Nat. Preservation Inst.; founder Cultural Landscape Found. Editor: Preserving Modern Landscape Architecture, Pioneers of American Landscape Design: An Encyclopedia for McGraw Hill. Fellow: Am. Soc. Landscape Archs. Office: Nat Park Svc 1201 Eye St Washington DC 20005*

BIRNBAUM, EDWARD LESTER, lawyer; b. Bklyn., Aug. 2, 1939; s. Edward Lester and Rita Birnbaum; m. Madeleine Birnbaum, Apr. 10, 1965; children: Amanda, Jordan. BA, CUNY, 1961; LLB, NYU, 1964. Bar: NY 64, U.S. Dist. Ct. (so. and ea. dists.) NY 67, U.S. Ct. Appeals (2d cir.) 70, U.S. Supreme Ct. 71, U.S. Dist. Ct. (we. dist.) NY 83. Assoc. Korkus & Korkus, N.Y.C., 1964—66, Herzfeld & Rubin, P.C., N.Y.C., 1967—. Lectr. in field; mem. faculty NYU Sch. Continuing Edn., Law and Taxation, 1987—; arbitrator small claims night ct. Contbr. articles to profl. jours. Coach Little League Baseball and Little League Basketball; pres., v.p. Village of Saddle Rock Civic Assn.; candidate trustee Village of Saddle Rock; town counsel North Hempstead, NY; del. to jud. conv. Liberal Party County Com. Mem.: ATLA, ABA, NY Bar Found., NY State Trial Lawyers Assn., Am. Arbitration Assn. (arbitrator), Nassau County Bar Assn., Queens County Bar Assn., NY County Bar Assn., NY State Bar Assn. (chmn. com. on Supreme Ct., ho. of dels.). Home: 70 Shelly Ln Great Neck NY 11023-1822 Office: Herzfeld & Rubin PC 40 Wall St New York NY 10005-2349 E-mail: ebirnbaum@herzfeld-rubin.com. *Life is to be lived with understanding and consideration for others and with understanding and consideration from others.*

BIRNBAUM, HOWARD KENT, materials science educator; b. N.Y.C., Oct. 18, 1932; s. Jack and Ida (Kornblau) B.; m. Freda Silber, Dec. 25, 1954; children: Elisa, Scott, Shari. BS, Columbia U., 1953, MS, 1955; PhD, U. Ill., 1958. Asst. prof. U. Chgo., 1958-61; assoc. prof. U. Ill., Urbana, 1961-64, prof., 1964-99, dir. Materials Rsch. lab., 1987—99, prof. emeritus, 2000. Contbr. numerous articles to profl. jours. Fellow AAAS, Am. Phys. soc., Am. Soc. Metals, Materials Soc., Japanese Inst. of Metals (hon.); mem. AIME (Inst. Metals lectr. 1984, Mehl Gold medal 1984, Materials Rsch. Soc. Von Hippel award, 2002), NAE, Am. Acad. Arts and Scis. Jewish. Office: U Ill Materials Rsch Lab 104 S Goodwin Ave Urbana IL 61801-2902

BIRNBAUM, IRWIN MORTON, lawyer; b. Bklyn., July 15, 1935; s. Sol N. and Rose (Cohen) B.; m. Arlene R. Burrows, June 8, 1957; children: Bruce J., Leslie R. Birnbaum Ventura, Amy G. Birnbaum Heath. BS in Acctg., Bklyn. Coll., 1956; JD, NYU, 1961. Bar: N.Y. 1962. Budget officer Montefiore Med. Ctr., Bronx, N.Y., 1962-70, v.p., chief fin. officer, 1970-86; counsel Proskauer & Rose LLP, N.Y.C., 1986-89, ptnr., 1989-97; COO Yale Univ. Sch. Medicine, New Haven, Conn., 1997—. Bd. dirs. N.Y. Regional Transplant Program, N.Y.C., treas., exec. com.; chmn. bd. dirs. FFH/N.E. Ins. Com.; mem. exec. com. and chair fin. com. MCIC Vt., Inc.; adj. prof. Robert Wagner Sch. Pub. Svc., NYU; lectr. pub. health, health policy, adminstrn. Sch. Medicine Yale U.; corporator South County Hosp., South Kingstown, R.I. Editor: Health Care Law Treatise, 1990. Trustee, treas., exec. com. Malmonides Med. Ctr., Bklyn., 1988—; sec./treas., exec. com. Hosp. Trustees N.Y. State, 1990-97; bd. dirs. Jewish Home for the Aged, New Haven. Fellow N.Y. Acad. Medicine; mem. Assn. of Bar of City of N.Y. (sec. com. on medicine and law 1989-90, sec. health law com. 1995-96), Am. Acad. Hosp. Attys. (spl. com. in health care systems). Avocations: sailing, tennis, reading, travel. Office: Yale Univ Sch Medicine 333 Cedar St I-209 SHM PO Box 208049 New Haven CT 06520-8049

BIRNBAUM, JEROME, pharmaceutical executive, consultant; married; 2 children. BS in Biology, CUNY, 1961, postgrad., 1961-63; MS in Microbiology, U. Cin., 1964, PhD, 1966. Sr. rsch. microbiologist dept. fermentation rsch. Merck Sharp and Dohme Rsch. Labs., 1966-69, assoc. dir., then dir. dept. fermentation rsch., 1969-74; sr. dir. basic microbiology Merck Inst. Therapeutic Rsch., 1974-75, exec. dir. basic biol. scis., 1975-80; v.p. microbiology and agrl. rsch. Merck Sharp and Dohme Rsch. Labs., Merck & Co., Inc., 1981-87; sr. v.p., therapeutic area dir. Bristol-Myers Co., Wallingford, Conn., 1987-89; exec. v.p. rsch. Bristol-Myers Squibb Co., Princeton, 1989-90, sr. v.p. pharm. devel., 1990—98, sr. v.p. strategic rsch. and devel. ops., 1998—2000; sr. v.p. rsch., co-founder Achillion Pharm., Inc., New Haven, 2000—, also bd. dirs. Bd. dirs. New Brunswic Sci. Corp.; adv. bd. biotech. program, Rutgers U., Newark, 1986-87, sci. adv. coun. Waksman Inst. Microbiology, Rutgers U., New Brunswick, 1983-88; mem. AIDS task force Pharm Mfrs. Assn., 1988-92; mem. adv. bd. internat. AIDS rsch. Inst. Medicine NAS, 1990-92; adv. bd. Nat. Inst. Cmty. Health Edn., 1990-96; mem. Provost's Sci Adv. Coun., Rutgers U., Newark, 1992-94; invited lectr. numerous confs., ednl. instns. Editorial bd. Jour. Antibiotics, 1982-90, Environ. and Applied Microbiology, 1976-79, Applied Microbiology, 1974-76; contbr. articles, abstracts to profl. publs. Bd. dirs. R.W. Johnson U. Hosp., New Brunswick, N.J., 1992-2000; trustee New Brunswick Cultural Ctr., 1992-2001, Robert Wood Johnson U. Hosp. Found., 2000—; bd. dirs. Robert Wood Johnson U. Hosp. Property Holding Co., Inc., 1994—, ASM Resources, Inc., Washington, 2000—; bd. assocs. Whitehead Inst., Cambridge, Mass., 1995-2001. NSF rsch. fellow U. Cin., 1963-66; recipient Award for Excellence, U. Cin., 1986, Daniel Drake award U. Cin. Coll. Medicine, 1987. Fellow Am. Acad. Microbiology; mem. AAAS, Infectious Disease Soc. Am., Am. Soc. Microbiology (vice-chmn. fermentation sect. 1971-72, chmn. 1972-73, exec. bd. 1972-78, chmn. nominations com. 1978), Theobald Smith Soc. N.J. (councilor 1974-77, program chmn. 1976, Waksmon award 1983), Am. Chem. Soc. (microbial tech. div.), Soc. Indsl. Microbiology, Internat. Soc. Antiviral Rsch. Achievements include 8 patents in microbial process development. Office: Achillion Pharms Inc 300 George St New Haven CT 06511

BIRNBAUM, JULIAN R. lawyer; b. Boise, Idaho, May 1, 1948; s. Milton and Audrey (Roossin) B.; m. Andrea Jean Pfeiffer, Jan. 5, 1980; children: Susan Adele, Molly Jean. AB, Harvard U., 1970; JD, U. Chgo., 1975. Bar: Ill. 1975, W.Va. 1981, N.Y. 1984, U.S. Dist. Ct. (no. dist.) Ill. 1975, U.S. Dist. Ct. (no. and so. dists.) W.Va. 1981, U.S. Dist. Ct. (so. dist.) N.Y. 1986, U.S. Dist. Ct. (ea. dist.) N.Y. 1987, U.S. Ct. Appeals (2d cir.) 1989, U.S. Ct. Appeals (3d cir.) 1995, U.S. Ct. Appeals (4th cir.) 2003. Staff atty. Legal Assistance Found. Chgo., 1975-80, Legal Aid Soc., Bklyn., 1983-86; civil rights atty. Appalachian Rsch. and Def. Fund, Charleston, W.Va., 1980-83; assoc. Vladeck, Waldman, Elias & Engelhard, P.C., N.Y.C., 1986-88, ptnr., 1988—. Contbr. articles to profl. jours. Mem. Nat. Lawyers Guild. Home: 468 E 16th St Brooklyn NY 11226-6501 Office: Vladeck Waldman Elias & Engelhard PC 1501 Broadway Ste 800 New York NY 10036-5560 E-mail: jbirnbaum@vladeck.com.

BIRNBAUM, NATHAN SIMCHA, dentist; b. Munich, Feb. 3, 1947; s. Jacob and Mira (Laudon) B.; m. Robin Wendy Lappe, Mar. 25, 1979; children: Daniel Ari, Heidi Sarah, Erica Ruth. AB, Harvard U., 1968; DDS, Northwestern U., 1972; cert. in prosthodontics, Boston U., 1974. Diplomate Am. Acad. Pain Mgmt. Clin. instr. fixed prosthodontics Boston U. Sch. Grad. Dentistry, 1974-76; asst. clin. prof. fixed prosthodontics Boston U. Grad. Dentistry, 1976-93; clin. instr. fixed prosthodontics Harvard U. Sch. Dental Medicine, Boston, 1982—; pvt. practice dentistry Newton, Mass., 1973-94, Wellesley, Mass., 1994—. Continuing edn. faculty Boston U. Sch. Grad. Dentistry, 1982-93. Bd. trustees Solomon Schechter Day Sch., Newton, 1987-93; chmn. dental divsn. Combined Jewish Philanthropies, Boston, 1986-90, bd. of overseers, 1992—; chmn. dental divsn. State of Israel Bonds of Greater Boston, 1978-79, 94-95, mem. campaign cabinet, 1993—, dept. chmn., 1996, chmn., 97-98; chmn. social action com. Congregation Beth-El-Atereth Israel, Newton, 1988-90. Fellow Internat. Coll. of Dentists, Am. Coll. of Prosthodontists, Am. Acad. Fixed Prosthodontics; mem. Internat. Coll. Prosthodontists, Am. Acad. Cosmetic Dentistry, Acad. Osseointegration, Alpha Omega Internat. Dental Frat. Avocations: computers, philately, golf, painting and drawing, art appreciation. Office: 1 Washington St Ste 306 Wellesley MA 02481-1706 E-mail: nate@birnbaum.org., bestdentist@rcn.com.

BIRNBAUM, NORMAN, author, humanities educator; b. N.Y.C., July 21, 1926; s. Silas Jacob and Jean (Bermen) B.; children: Anna, Antonia. BA, Williams Coll., 1947; MA, Harvard, 1951, PhD, 1958. Editor OWI, 1943-45; teaching fellow Harvard, 1948-52; tutor Adams House, 1949- 52; asst. lectr. London Sch. Econs. and Polit. Sci., U. London, 1953-55, lectr., 1955-59; fellow Nuffield Coll., Oxford (Eng.) U., 1959-66; vis. prof. faculty letters and human scis. U. Strasbourg, France, 1964-66; prof. grad. faculty New Sch. Social Research, 1966-68; prof. Amherst Coll., 1968—. Mem. Inst. Advanced Study, 1975-76; guest fellow Wissenschaftskolleg, Berlin, 1986; Mellon vis. prof. humanities Georgetown U. Law Ctr., 1979-81; prof. Georgetown U., 1981-2001, prof. emeritus, 2001—; cons. NSC, Exec. Office Pres., 1978; vis. prof. Ecole des Hautes Etudes en Scis. Sociales, Paris, 1991; chair scholarly adv. bd. Internat. Inst. Peace, Vienna, 1991—. Author: Sociological Study of Ideology (1940-60), 1962; (with others) Sociology and Religion, 1968, Crisis of Industrial Society, 1969, Towards a Critical Sociology, 1971, Beyond the Crisis, 1977, Social Structure and the German Reformation, 1980, The Radical Renewal, 1988, Searching for the Light, 1993, After Progress, 2001; contbg. editor Change mag. of Higher Edn., 1970-74; mem. editl. bd. Praxis, 1986-92, The Nation, 1978—; editl. cons. Patisan Rev., 1971-83. Cons. Giovanni Agnelli Found., 1972-75; mem. Wellfleet Psychohistory Conf., 1970— ; adviser United Automobile Workers, Congrl. Progressive Caucus, 1996—; mem. exec. com. New Democratic Coalition, 1978—, chmn. policy adv. council, 1980-82; mem. nat. exec. com. Dem. Socialist Organizing Com., 1973-77, nat. adv. bd., 1980-82; Mem. founding editorial bd. New Left Rev., London, 1959; sec. com. sociology religion Internat. Sociol. Assn., 1959—, chmn., 1970-74; adviser Democratic Nat. Campaign, 1976, Edward M. Kennedy campaign, 1979, Cranston campaign, 1980, Jackson campaigns, 1980, 1988; adviser, Euro. Socialist parties, 1979—; founding com. Campaign for Am. Future, 1996; Fulbright chair, Univ. Bologna, 1998; Visitor, London School of Economics, 1998; Nuffield College, 2001. Guggenheim fellow, 1971 Fellow: Inst. Policy Studies (sr.); mem.: Am. Sociol. Assn. (coun. 1979—82). Office: Georgetown U Law Ctr 600 New Jersey Ave NW Washington DC 20001-2075 E-mail: birnbaum@law.georgetown.edu. *I have always thought that one of the strongest ethical and biological forces propelling us is a concern for our children— for our own children and for the continuation of humanity. This elementary sense of care seems increasingly challenged, by doctrines of callousness and selfishness, poorly disguised as recognition of the sovereignty of the market. It is that sovereignty which threatens us as citizens, and which accounts for the outbursts of hatred and rage we know as the new ethnicity, the new fundamentalism, the new nationalism--all of them, alas,very old.*

BIRNBAUM, S. ELIZABETH, lawyer; b. Ft. Belvoir, Va., Jan. 20, 1958; d. Myron Lionel and Emma Jane (Steiner) Birnbaum. AB, Brown U., 1979; JD, Harvard U., 1984. Bar: Colo. 1984, D.C. 1985, U.S. Dist. Ct. D.C. 1987, U.S. Ct. Appeals (D.C. cir.) 1988, U.S. Ct. Appeals (10th cir.) 1988, U.S. Ct. Appeals (4th cir.) 1990, U.S. Supreme Ct. 1990. Clk. to Justice Dubofsky Supreme Ct. Colo., Denver, 1984-85; assoc. Dickstein, Shapiro & Morin, Washington, 1985-87; counsel to water resources program Nat. Wildlife Fedn., Washington, 1987-91; counsel com. resources U.S. Ho. Reps., Washington, 1991-99; spl. asst. to solicitor U.S. Dept. of Interior, Washington, 1999-2000, assoc. solicitor for mineral resources, 2000-2001; dir. govt. affairs American Rivers, Washington, 2001—. Editor-in-chief Harvard Environ. Law Rev., 1984. Bd. trustees Amphibian Conservation Alliance, 1997-99; mem. Arlington Co. Environ. and Energy Conservation Commn., 2002—. Mem. Am. Water Resources Assn. (v.p. nat. capital sect. 1999-2000), D.C. Bar (steering com. 1994-97, sect. environment, energy and natural resource law). Office: 1025 Vermont Ave NW Ste 720 Washington DC 20005

BIRNBAUM, SHEILA L. lawyer, educator; b. 1940; BA, Hunter Coll., 1960, MA, 1962; LL.B., NYU, 1965. Bar: N.Y. 1965. Legal asst. Superior Ct., N.Y.C., 1965; assoc. Berman & Frost, N.Y.C., 1965-70, ptnr., 1970-72; prof. Fordham U., N.Y.C., 1972-78, NYU, N.Y.C., 1978-86, assoc. dean, 1982-84; ptnr. Skadden, Arps, Slate, Meagher & Flom, N.Y.C., 1984—. Author: (with Rheingold) Products Liability, Law, Practice Science, 1974. Mem. N.Y.C. Bar Assn. (mem. exec. com. 1977—, jud. com. 1977), ABA (chmn. product gen. liability, consumer land coms.), Assn. of Bar of City of N.Y. (exec. com. 1978—, 2d century com. 1984-86), Phi Beta Kappa, Phi Alpha Theta, Alpha Chi Alpha. Office: Skadden Arps Slate Meagher & Flom 4 Times Sq Fl 24 New York NY 10036-6595 E-mail: sbirnbau@skadden.com.

BIRNBERG, JACK, financial executive; b. June 15, 1937; s. Max and Yetta (Halpern) B.; m. Louise Rothstein, June 7, 1959; children: Michael, Steven, John, Jeffrey. BS, Fairleigh Dickinson U., 1959. Acct. firm Scholtz, Simon & Miller, 1960-61; contr., officer Scott, Harvey Co., Inc., 1962-63; pres. M.A. Allan & Co., Inc., Clifton, N.J., 1963-71, dir., 1963-71; chmn. bd. Edios, Inc., 1969-77, Jack Birnberg & Assocs., Inc.; pres. NE Regional Assn. Small Bus. Investment Corp., N.Y., 1970—, Internat. Equities, Ltd., Clifton, 1970-71. Chmn. bd., dir. Tappan-Zee Capital Corp., 1973—, exec. com. NE Region; chmn. bd. BB Energy Corp., Waldorf Auto Leasing Corp., Waldorf Group, Inc.; dir., chmn. exec. com. Ferdon Equipment Corp.; chmn. bd. dirs. Tappan Zec Capitol Corp., 1973—, Met. Fin. Corp., 1968—, AIP Risk Group, 1968—, Ascot Solutions, Inc., 1980; mem. Midwest Stock Exch., 1968-76, Phila.-Balt.-Washington Stock Exch., 1968-76; guest lectr. Fla. Atlantic U., 2000-01. Co-host radio program Off The Record, Sta. WPBR, 2001-2001; radio talk show host Jack Birnberg Speaks Out, N.Y.C., 2001--. Pres. Passaic County Children's Shelter, 1967-68; bd. dirs. Birnberg Found., 1969—, Boys Club, Paterson, 1970 75, Barnert Hosp., 1971-91, Employee Retirement Benefit Assn., 1975—, Barnert Temple, 1976—; chmn. met. divsn. United Jewish Appeal, 1970; dir. greater Paterson YW-YMHA, 1970-75; pres. Daus. Miriam Home for Aged, 1971—, bd. dirs., 1995-97; chmn. Expo 200 Barnert Temple, 1976—; trustee various corps., U.S. Bankruptcy Ct. Mem. N.E. Regional Assn. Small Bus. Investment Corps. (pres. 1985-86), Nat. Assn. Small Bus. Investment Corps. (bd. govs. 1985-93), B'nai B'rith (trustee Greater Clifton chpt. 1962-64), Preakness Hills Country Club (bd. govs. 1992-96, treas. 1994-95), Polo Club Boca Raton. Home: 409 Carriage Ln Wyckoff NJ 07481-2306 Office: 201 Lower Notch Rd Little Falls NJ 07424-1802 E-mail: jackbirnberg@aol.com.

BIRNE, KENNETH ANDREW, lawyer; b. Englewood, N.J., Apr. 2, 1956; s. Alvin Aaron and Rita May (Gorsky) B.; m. Pamela Beth Ross; children: Jennafer Sara, Allison Francie, Jonathan Ross. BA in Polit. Sci., Ohio State U., 1978; JD, Case Western Res. U., 1981. Bar: Ohio 1981, U.S. Dist. Ct. (no. dist.) Ohio 1981. Sole practice, Cleve., 1981-85; ptnr. Peltz & Birne, Cleve., 1985—. Instr. Am. Inst. Paralegal Studies, Cleve., 1982-93, pers. dir. Cleve. area, 1984-93; cons. in field. Mem. Ohio Bar Assn., Cleve. Bar Assn. (chmn. practice and procedure clinic 1984-86, vol. Call for Action 1986, meritorious service award 1986), Cuyahoga County Bar Assn., Phi Eta Sigma, Zeta Beta Tau, Phi Delta Phi. Lodges: Masons. Office: Peltz & Birne Midland Bldg Ste 1880 Cleveland OH 44115-1093

BIRNEY, PHILIP RIPLEY, lawyer; b. Canton, Ohio, June 25, 1940; s. Forrest Earl and Jean Lois (Ripley) B.; m. Susanne Elaine St. John, July 11, 1964; children: Julie Michelle, Laurie Catherine, Nicole Susanne. BS in Bus. Adminstrn., Northwestern U., 1962; JD, U. Calif. Hastings Coll. Law, L.A., 1965. Bar: Calif. 1966, U.S. Dist. Ct. (all dists.) Calif., U.S. Ct. Appeals (9th and 11th cirs.), U.S. Supreme Ct. 1975; diplomate, cert. specialist med. profl. liability Am. Bd. Profl. Liability Attys. Dep. atty. gen. State of Calif., Sacramento, 1966-68; dep. dist. atty. Sacramento County, 1968-70; sr. ptnr., chief trial lawyer Wilke, Fleury, Hoffelt, Gould & Birney, Sacramento, 1970—. Fellow Am. Coll. Trial Lawyers; mem. ABA, Calif. State Bar Assn., Sacramento County Bar Assn. (judiciary com. 1991-94, jud. rev. com. 1992—, chmn. 1995—), Am. Bd. Trial Advs. (bd. dirs. Sacramento Valley chpt. 1994—, pres. Sacramento Valley chpt. 1998-99, Civility award 1995), Calif. Med.-Legal Com. (pres. elect 2003—), No. Calif. Assn. Def. Counsel (bd. dirs. 1986-88) Home: 832 Senior Way Sacramento CA 95831-2129 Office: Wilke Fleury Hoffelt Gould & Birney 400 Capitol Mall Fl 22 Sacramento CA 95814-4407 E-mail: sbi71164@aol.com., pbirney@wilkefleury.com.

BIRNEY, ROBERT CHARLES, retired academic administrator, psychologist; b. Westmont, N.J., May 2, 1925; s. Charles Alexander and Florence (Moore) B.; m. Margaret Ann Momerak, June 18, 1949; children: Reed Charles, Ruth Elizabeth, Barbara Ann, Robert Carl. BA, Wesleyan U., 1950; MA, U. Mich., 1951, PhD, 1955. Mem. faculty Amherst (Mass.) Coll., 1954-67, prof. psychology, 1965-67; dean Sch. Social Scis. Hampshire Coll., Amherst, 1968-70, v.p., 1971-78; dir. planning Colonial Williamsburg (Va.) Found., 1978, v.p. rsch., 1979-86, sr. v.p., 1986-90, ret., 1990. Vis. prof. Ruhr U., Fed. Republic Germany, 1966-67; spl. rsch. human motivation. Editor (with Richard Teevan) Van Nostrand Insight Series, 1961-70. Lt. USAAF, 1943-46. Decorated Air medal with 3 oak leaf clusters. Fellow Am. Psychol. Assn.; mem. AAUP, New Eng. Psychol. Assn. (pres. 1975), Cosmos Club, Phi Beta Kappa, Sigma Xi. Home: 3001 Willow Spring Ct Williamsburg VA 23185-3426 Office: Colonial Williamsburg Found S Henry St Williamsburg VA 23185

BIRNEY, WALTER LEROY, religious administrator; b. Garden City, Kans., Apr. 25, 1934; s. Claude David and Mildred Elizabeth (Ferris) B.; m. Iva Lou Mosher, June 18, 1954; children: Mickey, Scotty, Gary, Lorrie, Lindie. BA, Dallas Christian Coll., 1956. Min. First Christian Ch., Benjamin, Tex., 1954-57, Bellaire Christian Ch., San Antonio, 1957-58, Copeland (Kans.) Christian Ch., 1958-84; coord. Nat. Missionary Conv., Copeland, 1966—. Dean, promoter Ashland (Kans.) Christian Camp, 1961-84; promoter S.W. Sch. Missions, Copeland, 1973-84. Named Outstanding Alumnus Dallas Christian Coll., 1988. Mem. Christian Ch. Avocation: long distance running. Office: Nat Missionary Conv PO Box 11 Copeland KS 67837-0011 E-mail: wbirney11@aol.com.

BIRNKRANT, HENRY JOSEPH, lawyer; b. Phila., Jan. 24, 1955; s. Harry Philip and Myra Arlene (Hendler) B.; m. Lynn Rachel Goldin, Oct. 23, 1983; children: Aviva Michelle, Beth Elana. BA magna cum laude, U. Rochester, 1976; JD, Columbia U., 1979; LLM, NYU, 1983. Bar: D.C. 1979, U.S. Dist. Ct. D.C. 1980; U.S. Ct. Appeals (D.C. cir.) 1980, U.S. Tax Ct. 1984. Assoc. Bergson, Borkland, Margolis & Adler, Washington, 1979-82, Covington & Burling, Washington, 1983-88, Cole, Corette & Abrutyn, Washington, 1988-90, ptnr., 1991-96, Alston & Bird, Washington, 1997—. Author: (with others) Butterworth's International Taxation of Financial Instruments and Transactions, 1989; editor: Columbia Jour. Law and Social Problems, 1979; contbr. articles to profl. jours.; bd. advisors Jour. Internat. Taxation. Mem. ABA (tax section). Home: 5506 Durbin Rd Bethesda MD 20814-1012 Office: Alston & Bird North Bldg 11th Fl 601 Pennsylvania Ave NW Washington DC 20004-2601

BIRNKRANT, SHERWIN MAURICE, lawyer; b. Pontiac, Mich., Dec. 20, 1927; BBA, U. Mich., 1949, MBA, 1951; JD with distinction, Wayne State U., 1954. Bar: Mich. 1955, U.S. Dist. Ct. (ea. dist.) Mich. 1960, U.S. Supreme Ct. 1960, U.S. Ct. Appeals (6th cir.) 1966. Mem. Oakland County Bd. Suprs., 1967-68; asst. atty. City of Pontiac, Mich., 1956-67, city atty., 1967-83; of counsel Schlussel, Lifton, Simon, Rands, Galvin & Jackier, Southfield, Mich., 1983-90, Sommers, Schwartz, Silver & Schwartz, Southfield, 1990-95; shareholder Birnkrant & Birnkrant P.C., Bloomfield Hills, Mich., 1995—. Mem.: ABA (Mich. chmn. pub. contract law sect. 1979—97, chmn. urban, state and local govt. law sect. 1987—88, ho. dels. 1990—93, alt. del. to ho. dels. 1993—96, vice chmn. coordinating com. model procurement code state and local 1974—), Mich. Assn. Mcpl. Attys. (pres. 1975, coun. pres. 1992—), Am. Judicature Soc., Oakland County Bar Assn. (chmn. ethics and unauthorized practices com. 1961—62), State Bar Mich. (chmn. pub. corp. law sect. 1973—74, coun. adminstrv. law sect. 1975—76). Office: Birnkrant & Birnkrant PC 7 W Square Lake Rd Bloomfield Hills MI 48302

BIRNS, MARK THEODORE, physician; b. Bklyn., Sept. 24, 1949; s. Leon and Naomi B.; m. Ann Krieger, Aug. 15, 1976; children: Samantha Lynn, Michael Eric, Kevin Douglas. BA, Case Western Res. U., 1971; MD, Albert Einstein Coll. Medicine, 1974. Diplomate: Am. Bd. Internal Medicine, Am. Bd. Gastroenterology. Intern Bronx Mcpl. Hosp. Ctr. Albert Einstein Hosps., 1974-75, resident in medicine, 1975-77; fellow in gastroenterology U. Oreg. Health Scis. Ctr., 1977-79; asst. chief gastroenterology Walter Reed Army Med. Ctr., 1979-83; asst. prof. medicine U. Health Scis., 1980-83; emergency physician Shady Grove Adventist Hosp., part time, 1980-83, Frederick Meml. Hosp., Washington, 1980-83; practice medicine specializing in gastroenterology and endoscopic biliary surgery Rockville, Md., 1983—; active staff Shady Grove Adventist Hosp., sec. med. staff, 1986-87, chief gastroenterology sect., vice chmn. dept. medicine, 1988, 89, mem. exec. com., 1990-92, mem. laser com., 1992, 93, 94, 95, mem. OR com., 1996-97; assoc. clin. prof. medicine dept. gastroenterology Georgetown U., Washington, 1988—; active staff Suburban Hosp.; courtesy staff Montgomery Gen. Hosp. Vice chmn. Health Delivery Orgn., Mid Atlantic Med. Svcs. Health Plan, 1997—; treas., contract coord. Gastrointestinal Endoscopy Assocs., LLC, 1995—, Gastrointestinal Rsch. Assocs., LLC, 1999—. Major contbg. author: Radiology of the Liver, Biliary Tract, Pancreas and Spleen, 1987. Served to maj. USAR. Fellow ACP, Am. Coll. Gastroenterology; mem. AMA (Physician Recognition award 1978, 81, 84, 87, 90, 93), Am. Gastroent. Assn., Am. Soc. Gastrointestinal Endoscopy (postgrad. edn. com. 1991-92), Md. Soc. Gastrointestinal Endoscopy (exec. bd.), Montgomery County Med. Soc. Home: 11413 Twining Ln Rockville MD 20854-1860 Office: 9711 Medical Center Dr Ste 308 Rockville MD 20850-3388

BIRNS, NICHOLAS BOE, literature educator, editor; b. N.Y.C., May 30, 1965; s. Laurence Richard Birns and Margaret Ann Boe. AB, Columbia U., 1988; MA, NYU, 1990, PhD, 1992. Mem. faculty New Sch. U., N.Y.C., 1995—, Coll. New Rochelle, Bronx, N.Y., 1996—. Vis. asst. prof. Western Conn. State U., Danbury, 1992-93; invited lectr. U. Stockholm, 1997-98; vis. rsch. fellow U. Newcastle, Australia, 2001. Editor: Powys Notes, 1998—; book rev. editor: Antipodes, 1994-2001, editor, 2001—; contbr. articles to profl. jours. Devel. fellow NYU, 1988-89. Mem. Guild of Scholars of Episcopal Ch. Episcopalian. Avocations: baseball, music, following current events. Home: 205 E 10th St New York NY 10003-7634 Office: New Sch U 66 W 12th St New York NY 10011-8603 E-mail: nicbirns@aol.com.

BIRO, KATHY, advertising executive; BS in English Edn., NYU, 1973, MA in Ednl. Adminstrn., 1975; MBA in Mktg. and Fin., Columbia U., 1979. Product devel. mgr. Card Products Divsn. Citicorp, N.Y.C., 1979-81; v.p. Mktg. and Sales, Electronic Banking Chase Manhattan Bank1, N.Y.C., 1981-86; 1st v.p. Nat. Mktg.; dir. Credit Resources Shearson Lehman Hutton, N.Y.C., 1986-89; ptnr. Bank St. Consulting Group, N.Y.C., 1989-90; sr. v.p. Mktg. and Product Mgmt., Global Info. Bankers Trust, N.Y.C., 1990-91; sr. v.p. Mktg. Bronner Slosberg Humphrey, N.Y.C., 1991-99, also bd. dirs., 1991-99; founder, pres. and CEO Strategic Interactive Group, 1995-99; vice chmn., pres. Digitas, 1999—. Office: Digitas 800 Boylston St Prudential Tower Boston MA 02199

BIRO, LASZLO, dermatologist; b. Czechoslovakia, May 31, 1929; came to U.S., 1956; s. Sandor and Margaret (Klein) B.; m. Dolores Macchiaroli, July 9, 1961; children: David, Lisa, Deborah, Michele. MD, Univ. Med. Sch., Debrecen, Hungary, 1953. Diplomate Am. Bd. Dermatology. Intern Kings County Hosp., Bklyn., 1957-58; resident Bellevue Hosp., N.Y.C., 1958-60; pvt. practice medicine specializing in dermatology N.Y.C., 1960-61, Bklyn., 1960—; emeritus dept. dermatology Bklyn. Hosp., Luth. Med. Ctr.; clin. prof. dermatology SUNY, Downstate Med. Ctr., 1971—. Contbr. articles on skin tumors to profl. jours. Fellow ACP, Am. Acad. Dermatology, N.Y. Acad. Medicine; mem. AMA, Kings County Med. Assn., Bay Ridge Med. Soc. (pres. 1987-88), N.Y. State Dermatol. Soc., Bklyn Dermatol. Soc., Internat. Soc. Tropical Dermatology, N.Y. Acad. Scis., Am. Coll. Cryosurgery (v.p. 1996), Semmelweis Sci. Soc. (pres. 1985). Office: 9921 4th Ave Brooklyn NY 11209-8347

BIRON, CHRISTINE ANNE, medical science educator, researcher; b. Woonsocket, R.I., Aug. 8, 1951; d. R. Bernard and Theresa Priscilla (Sauvageau) B. BS, U. Mass., 1973; PhD, U. N.C., 1980. Rsch. technician U. Mass., Amherst, 1973-75; grad. researcher U. N.C., Chapel Hill, 1975-80; postdoctoral fellow Scripps Clinic and Rsch., La Jolla, Calif., 1980; fellow U. Mass. Med. Sch., Worcester, 1981-82, instr., 1983, asst. prof., 1984-87; vis. scientist Karolinska Inst., Stockholm, 1984; asst. prof. Sch. Medicine Brown U., Providence, 1988-90, assoc. prof., 1990-96, prof., 1996—, Esther Elizabeth Brintzenhoff prof., 1996—, chair Dept. Molecular Microbiology & Immunology, 1999—, dir. grad. program in pathobiology, 1995-99. Mem. AIDS and related rsch. study sect. 3 NIH, 1991-93; mem. exptl. immunology study sect. NIH, 1993-97, immunology working group sci. rev. Assoc. editor: Jour. Immunology, 1990—94, 2000, bd. editors: Procs. of Soc. for Exptl. Biology and Medicine, 1993—99, sect. editor: Jour. Immunology, 1995—99; editor: Jour. Nat. Immunity, 1994—98, Jour. Leukocyte Biology, 1999—2000; mem. editl. bd.: Virology, 2001—; contbr. articles, revs. to sci. jours.; mem. adv. bd. editors: Jour. Exptl. Medicine, 2002—. Leukemia Soc. Am. fellow, 1981, Spl. fellow, 1983, scholar, 1987; grantee NIH, 1985—; rsch. grantee MacArthur Found., 1991-96. Mem. AAAS (scholar 2002--), Am. Assn. Immunologists (co-chmn. symposium 1990, 94, 95, 96, 98, 99), Am. Soc. Virology, Am. Assn. Immunology (block co-chair nat. meetings 1996-99, program com. 1998-2000), Soc. Natural Immunity (co-chair program for 2001 meeting), Sigma Xi. Office: Brown U PO Box G-B618 Providence RI 02912-0001

BIROSIK, PJ, music company executive; b. N.Y.C., Sept. 2, 1956; BA, U. Redlands, 1977; MA, Columbia Coll., L.A., 1979. 3d class radiotelephone lic., FCC. Disc jockey, music dir. Sta. KUOR-FM, Redlands, Calif., 1973-76; music dir. Sta. KFXM-FM, San Bernadino, Calif., 1976-77; owner, mgr. Musik Internat. Corp., Hollywood, Calif., 1977-95, Boulder, Colo., 1995—. Author: How to Manage Talent, 1985, The New Age Music Guide, 1988, The Burrito Book, 1990, Salsa, 1992, Cilanto, 1994; editor, reviewer Body Mind Spirit, Billboard, L.A. Resources, New Frontier, BAM, Life Times, EarthStar, New Age Retailer, Nexus, Monthly Aspectarian, Conscious Connection, Healthy & Natural, Yoga Jour., Planetary Connections, Sedona Red Rock News, Boulder Weekly, New Tex., New Age Voice, AudioGliphix, Lotus, CDNOW, Crossroads, also others. Fundraiser Children of the Night, Hollywood, 1987. Recipient 2 Gold Record awards Mem. NARAS, Assn. for Ind. Music, Coalition Visionary Retailers, Los Angeles Women in Music (founder, v.p. 1986-88), Ind. Music Assn., Am. Booksellers Assn. Avocations: martial arts, music industry public speaking. Office: Musik Internat Corp 154 Betasso Rd Boulder CO 80302-9606 E-mail: info@musikinternational.com.

BIRREN, JAMES EMMETT, university research center executive; b. Chgo., Apr. 4, 1918; m. Elizabeth S., 1942; children: Barbara Ann, Jeffrey Emmett, Bruce William. Student, Wright Jr. Coll., 1938; BEd, Chgo. State U., 1941; MA, Northwestern U., 1942, PhD, 1947, ScD (hon.), 1985; postgrad., U. Chgo., 1950-51; PhD (hon.), U. Gothenberg, Sweden, 1983; LLD (hon.), St. Thomas U., Can., 1990. Tutorial fellow Northwestern U., 1941-42; research asst. project for study of fatigue Office Sci. Research and Devel., 1942; research fellow NIH, USPHS, 1946-47; research psychologist gerontology unit NIH, 1947-51; research psychologist NIMH, 1951-53, chief sect. on aging, 1953-64; dir. aging program Nat. Inst. Child Health and Human Devel., Bethesda, Md., 1964-65; dir. Gerontology Center; prof. psychology U. So. Calif., 1965-89, Disting. prof. emeritus, 1992—, dean Davis Sch. Gerontology, 1975-86, Brookdale Disting. scholar, 1986-90, dir. Inst. Advanced Study in Gerontology and Geriatrics, 1981-89; dir. Borun Ctr. Gerontol. Rsch. UCLA, 1989-93, assoc. dir. Ctr. on Aging, 1990—. Fellow Center for Advanced Study in Behavioral Scis., Stanford, Calif., 1978-79; Green vis. prof. U. B.C., 1979; vis. scientist Cambridge (Eng.) U., 1960-61; Harold E. Jones meml. lectr. U. Calif., Berkeley, 1965; mem. Los Angeles County Bd. Suprs.' Com. on Aging, 1967-69 ; sr. fellow U. So. Calif. Urban Ecology Inst., 1968-70; mem. Dean's Council, U. So. Calif., 1970-86 ; chmn. aging rev. com. Nat. Inst. Aging, 1974-75; program dir. Integration of Info. on Aging: Handbook Project, 1973-76; mem. steering com. Care of Elderly, Inst. of Medicine, 1976-77; bd. dirs. Sears Roebuck Found., 1977-80; chmn. life course prevention research rev. com. NIMH, 1985-87; cons. Roche Seminars on Aging Series, 1980-82. Author: Psychology of Aging, 1964; editor: Handbook of Aging and the Individual, 1959, (with K.W. Schaie) Handbook of the Psychology of Aging, 1996, Encyclopedia of Gerontology, 1996, (with R.B. Sloane) Handbook of Mental Health and Aging, 1992; contbr. articles to books, profl. publs.; bd. collaborators: Gerontologia, 1956-89; asst. editor: Jour. Gerontology, 1956-61, assoc. editor 1961-63, editor-in-chief 1968-74, chmn. publs. com., 1975-78, adv. editl. bd., 1956-69; bd. adv. editors: Devel. Psychobiology, 1967-69; adv. editor: Jour. Human Devel., 1957-58. Mem. adv. com. and del. White House Conf. on Aging, 1995. With USNR, 1943-46; to scientist dir. USPHS Scientist Corps, 1947-65. Recipient award for rsch. on problems of aging CIBA Found., 1956, Stratton award Am. Psychopathol. Assn., 1960, Sr. 65er award Dist. 65 Retail Workers and Dept. Store Union, Sr. 65er award AFL-CIO, 1962, medal for meritorious svc. USPHS, 1965, citation Am. Assn. Ret. Persons, 1970, Am. Pioneers in Aging award U. Mich., 1972, commendation for disting. contbns. to field of gerontology Mayor of L.A., 1968, 74, Merit award Northwestern U. Alumni Assn., 1976, Creative Scholarship and Rsch. award U. So. Calif., 1979, Disting. Educator award Assn. Gerontology in Higher Edn., 1983, Eminent Svc. award Stovall Found., 1984, award of Distinction Am. Fedn. for Aging Rsch., 1986, Sandoz prize for rsch. on aging, 1989, Can. Assn. Gerontology award, 1990, Disting. Emeritus award U. So. Calif., 1992, Pres.'s award Am. Soc. on Aging, 1996, Disting. Career Contbn. to Gerontology award Gerontol. Soc. Am., 2002; USPHS rsch. fellow, 1946-47. Fellow AAAS, Am. Geriatrics Soc. (founding fellow Western div.), Am. Psychol. Assn. (Disting. Sci. Contbn. award 1968, chmn. membership com. 1969, Disting. Contbn. award Div. Adult Devel. and Aging 1978, pres. div. 1955-56, editor newsletter 1951-55), Gerontol. Soc. (pres. 1961-62, chmn. publs. com. 1974-77, award for meritorious research 1966, Brookdale award 1980); mem. Am. Physiol. Soc., Internat. Assn. Gerontology (chmn. exec. com. 1966-69, chmn. program com. 1968-69), Psychonomic Soc., Western Gerontol. Soc. (dir. 1965—, pres. 1968-69), Golden Key Club, Skull and Dagger Club, Sigma Xi, Phi Kappa Phi. Office: UCLA Ctr on Aging 10945 Le Conte Ave Los Angeles CA 90024-2828

BIRSH, ARTHUR THOMAS, publishing executive; b. Englewood, N.J., Oct. 6, 1932; s. Abraham S. and Mary (Levinsohn) B.; m. Judith Rosenberg, June 29, 1955 (div. 1982); children: Andrew, Philip, Joanne.; m. Joan Alleman, 1983. Grad., Lawrenceville N.J. Sch., 1950; BA, Yale, 1954. Engaged in sales Western Pub. Co., Poughkeepsie, N.Y., 1956-58; founder Cross Road Press, Hyde Park, N.Y., 1958, pres., 1958-60; with Playbill mag., N.Y.C., 1961-92, publisher, 1965-94, chmn., 1993—. Group v.p. Metromedia, Inc., 1968-73 Served with AUS, 1954-56. Home: 18 Harbor Island Dr Key Largo FL 33037-5112 Office: Playbill 16505 NW 13th Ave Miami FL 33169 E-mail: abirsh@miami.playbill.com. *I have no philosophy, rather a hodge-podge of ideas and beliefs that keep me going; nature is a match for nurture; everybody's scared; love is a condition, not a contract; the stupid or silly things I have done usually seemed smart or important at the time; life is a series of moments—wallowing in the lows extends them— clutching the highs destroys them. Most enduring good things that have happened to me resulted from taking chances and making commitments. Luck beats brains!.*

BIRSTEIN, ANN, writer, educator; b. N.Y.C., May 27, 1927; d. Bernard and Clara (Gordon) B.; m. Alfred Kazin, June 26, 1952 (div. 1982); 1 child, Cathrael. BA, Queens Coll., 1948. Lectr. The New Sch. Queens Coll., N.Y.C., 1953-54; writer-in-residence CCNY, 1960; lectr. The Writers Workshop, Iowa City, 1966, 72; lectr. Sch. Gen. Studies Columbia U., N.Y.C., 1985-87; dir., founder Writers on Writing Barnard Coll., N.Y.C., 1988—. Adj. prof. English Hofstra U., L.I., 1980, Barnard Coll., N.Y.C., 1981-93; film critic Vogue mag. Author: Star of Glass, 1950, The Troublemaker, 1955, The Sweet Birds of Gorham, 1966, Summer Situations, 1972, Dickie's List, 1973, American Children, 1980, The Rabbi on Forty-Seventh Street, 1982, The Last of the True Believers, 1988, What I Saw at the Fair, 2003; co-editor: The Works of Anne Frank; contbr. articles to numerous mags. Nat. Endowment of Arts grantee, 1983; Fulbright fellow, 1951-52. Mem. PEN (former mem. exec. bd., former chair admissions com.), Authors Guild (former mem. coun.), Phi Beta Kappa (hon.). Democrat. Jewish. Home: 1623 3rd Ave # 27jw New York NY 10128-3638 E-mail: abirstein@aol.com

BIRSTEIN, SEYMOUR JOSEPH, aerospace company executive; b. N.Y.C., May 1, 1927; s. Harry D. and Golde (Lenoff) B.; divorced; 1 child, Diane. BA in Chemistry, NYU, 1947; MS in Phys. Chemistry, Mont. State U., 1948; postgrad., Bklyn. Poly. Inst., 1949-50, Cornell U., 1953. Rsch. chemist Airco, Murray Hill, N.J., 1949-50; br. chief Air Force Cambridge Rsch. Labs., Bedford, Mass., 1951-76; pres. SJB Assoc., Inc., Marlborough, Mass., 1977—. Contbr. articles to profl. jours.; patentee in field. Fellow Am. Inst. Chemists; mem. Am. Chem. Soc., Am. Meteorol. Soc., Sigma Xi. Home and Office: 24 Pippen Rd Marlborough MA 01752-1419 Fax: 508-624-7254. E-mail: sbirstein@aol.com.

BIRT, ROBERT EARL, philosophy educator, writer; b. Balt., Oct. 7, 1952; s. Oliver Lee and Hattie Mae Birt; m. Nancy Zapata, Feb. 17, 1972. BA, Morgan State U., W. Va., 1951; PhD in Philosophy, Vanderbilt U., 1984. Asst. prof. Tuskegee U., Ala., 1984—85, St. Joseph U., Phila., 1985—86, Tex. A&M U., College Sta., 1986—88, Prarie View A&M U., Tex., Morgan State U., Balt., 1991—. Author: (Anthology of Essays) Existence in Black, 1997, The Quest for Community and Identity, 2002; contbr. Essays. Fellow, Nat. Endowment for Humanities, 1997. Mem.: Am. Philos. Assn. (mem. staff of jour. 1990—95). Avocations: writing, poetry. Home: 1642C Waverly W Baltimore MD 21239 Office: Morgan State U Philosophy Dept 1700 E Cold Spring Ln Baltimore MD 21251 E-mail: rbirt@morgan.edu.

BIRTCHER, BARON R. writer, real estate broker; s. Ronald and Joanne Birtcher; m. Christina Birtcher. BA in fin., U. So. Calif., LA, 1981. Broker Birtcher Properties, Laguna, Calif.; owner Birtcher Sr. Properties, Laguna, Calif.; novelist Precis-Honu Holdings LLC, Kona, Hawaii. Author: (novels) Roadhouse Blues, 2000 (LA Times Bestseller, 2000), Ruby Tuesday, 2002 (Ind. Mystery Booksellers Assn. Bestseller, 2002), Run Like Hell, 2003. Mem.: Chains des Rotisseurs (chevelier 2002—), Hon. Order of Ky. Colonels. Office: Precis-Honu Holdings LLC C2 #22 77-6425 Kuakini Hwy Kailua Kona HI 96740 E-mail: BaronRBirtcher@aol.com.

BIRTEL, FRANK THOMAS, mathematician, philosopher, educator; b. New Orleans, Apr. 4, 1932; s. Frank N. and Virginia B.; m. Jane Ella C. Moriarty, Sept. 16, 1964 (dec. 1986); children: Rebecca Anne, Michael Teilhard; m. Margaret S. Bishop, July 28, 1990. BS, Loyola U. South, 1952; MS, U. Notre Dame, 1953, PhD in Math., 1960. Sr. mathematician USN Nuclear Power Schs., 1955-57; Instr. Conn. Coll. for Women, New London, 1956-57; lectr. Yale U., 1961-62; asst. prof. Ohio State U., 1960-62; asst. prof. math. Tulane U., 1962-64, assoc. prof., 1964-67, prof., 1967—, univ. prof., 1981—2002, spl. asst. to pres., 1975-76, dep. provost, 1976-78, acting dean Grad. Sch., 1978, acting provost, 1978, provost, dean, 1979-81, dir. program of Judeo-Christian Studies, 1982—; univ. prof. emeritus, 2002—. Vis. prof. U. Nijmegen, Netherlands, 1968-69; mem. Ochsner Found. Clin IRB, 2002—. Editl. adv. bd. Zygon: The Jour. of Sci. and Religion, 1995—. Trustee New Orleans Mus. Art, 1978-80, 83-86, St. Mary's Dominican Coll., New Orleans, 1977-86. Yale U. postdoctoral fellow, 1961-62; sr. Fulbright lectr. Eng., Scotland, Germany, Netherlands, 1968-69 Mem. Am. Math. Soc. (assoc. sec. 1977-88). Roman Catholic. Home: 1229 Cadiz St New Orleans LA 70115-3903 Office: Tulane U Dept Math New Orleans LA 70118

BIRTWHISTLE, TARA, dancer; b. Vancouver, Brit. Columbia; Student, Royal Winnipeg Ballet Profl. Div., 1986—91. Dancer (ballets) Dracula, Royal Winnipeg Ballet, Romeo and Juliet, The Sleeping Beauty, Giselle, Belong, (films) Dracula, Pages From a Virgin's Diary, (ballets) Giselle. Named one of 100 Young Canadians to Watch in the New Millennium, Maclean's, 2000. Office: Royal Winnipeg Ballet 380 Graham Ave Winnipeg MB Canada R3C 4K2

BISACCIA-HANSON, BETTY, marketing professional, public relations executive; b. Phila., Nov. 19, 1949; d. Albert James La Grotta and Carolyn Bernice Cifune-La Grotta; m. Nicholas Bisaccia, Nov. 20, 1971 (div. Apr. 2000); children: Melissa Nicole, Rachel Leigh, Valerie Renee; m. Daniel Hanson, June 28, 2002. BA in Comm., Temple U., 1983; MBA, Widener U., 1999. Dir. pub. rels. Martin Orgn., Phila., 1980—81; asst. dir. Rittenhouse Mktg., Phila., 1981—83; pub. rels. cons. Phila., 1983—86; advt. dir. Widener U., Chester, Pa., 1986—2000; mktg., internat. mgr. Delage Landen, Wayne, Pa., 2000—01; dir. mktg. and pub. rels. Thomas Jefferson U., Phila., 2001—. Mem.: Coll. & Uvvi. Pub. Rels. Assn. Pa. (bd. dirs. 1998—99), Pub. Rels. Soc. Am. Avocations: fashion design, dancing, films. Home: 535 Walnut Ln Swarthmore PA 19081 Office: Thomas Jefferson Univ Jefferson Coll Health Prof 130 S 9th St Ste 710 Philadelphia PA 19107 Fax: 215-503-9834. E-mail: betty.bisaccia@mail.tju.edu.

BISANZO, MARK THOMAS, sales executive; b. Port Chester, N.Y., Sept. 28, 1941; s. Dominic Daniel and Pauline Ann (Zak) B.; m. Mary Jane Ann Baldino, July 2, 1966; 1 child, Mark Christopher. AAS, Westchester C.C., 1963; BSME, N.Y. Inst. Tech., 1966; MBA, Fordham U., 1972. Instrument engr. Bechtel, N.Y.C., 1966-68, M.W. Kellogg, N.Y.C., 1968-70; sr. controls engr. Power Gas Corp., N.Y.C., 1970-71, Am. Electric Power, N.Y.C., 1971; sr. v.p. Control Assocs., Allendale, N.J., 1971—, 2000—. Mem. adv. bd. Fisher Controls Co., Marshalltown, Iowa, 1997—; bd. dirs. Control Assocs. Pres. Bergen Cath. H.S. Fathers' Club, Oradell, N.J., 1991-94; coach Park Ridge (N.J.) Athletic Assn., 1980-90; mem. Our Lady of Mercy Roman Cath. Ch. Noctornal Adoration Soc., Park Ridge, Middlebury Collegiate Alumni Coll. Parents Alumni Assn. Mem. Soc. Gas Operators, Instrument Soc. Am. (v.p. N.Y. chpt. 1984-85). Avocations: skiing, photography, travel. Home: 67 Degroff Pl Park Ridge NJ 07656-1406 Office: Control Assocs 20 Commerce Dr Allendale NJ 07401-1600

BISBEE, DAVID GEORGE, lawyer; b. Council Bluffs, Iowa, June 7, 1947; s. George Kimball and Margaret Ruth (McMurry) B.; m. J. Gail Bower, May 19, 1999; children: Michael, Christopher, Tyler. Student, Iowa State U., 1965-67; BA, Augusta Coll., 1973; JD, U. Ga., 1975. Bar: Ga. 1975, U.S. Dist. Ct. (no. dist.) Ga. 1976, U.S. Ct. Appeals (5th cir.) 1978, U.S. Ct. Appeals (11th cir.) 1981. Assoc. Troutman, Sanders, et al, Atlanta, 1975-81; ptnr. Bisbee, Rickertsen & Zerog, Atlanta, 1981-95; pvt. practice Atlanta, 1996-97; ptnr. McRae & Bisbee, LLP, 1997—. Served to capt. U.S. Army, 1968-72. Mem. ABA (bus. bankruptcy com.), Am. Bankruptcy Inst. (subcom. on internat. involvencies), Atlanta Bankruptcy Bar Assn. (bd. dirs. 1980-86), Order of Coif. Republican. Methodist. Home: 2929 Tall Pines Way NE Atlanta GA 30345-1404 E-mail: dbisbee@mcraebisbee.com.

BISBEE, GERALD ELFTMAN, JR., investment company executive; b. Waterloo, Iowa, July 12, 1942; s. Gerald Elftman Bisbee and Maxine Cole Prather; m. Linda Elaine Ude, Aug. 22, 1970; children: Gerald Elftman III, Katherine Elizabeth. BA, North Cen. Coll., Naperville, Ill., 1967; MBA, U. Pa., 1972; PhD, Yale U., 1975. Adminstr. Med. Ctr. Northwestern U., Chgo., 1966-70; asst. prof. Yale U., New Haven, 1974-78, assoc. dir. health svcs., 1975-78; pres. Hosp. Rsch. and Ednl. Trust, Chgo., 1978-84; v.p., shareholder Kidder, Peabody & Co., N.Y.C., 1984-88; chmn., chief exec. officer Sequel Corp., New Canaan, Conn., 1988-89, Apache Med. Systems, Inc., Washington, 1989-97; chmn., CEO The Health Mgmt. Acad., Alexandria, Va., 1998—; chmn., pres., CEO ReGen Biologics, Inc., Franklin Lakes, NJ, 1998—. Adj. prof. Northwestern U., Kellogg Sch. of Mgmt., Evanston, Ill., 1979-83; mem. visiting com. Harvard U. Health Svcs., Boston, 1986-92, exec. adv. com. Weatherhead Sch. of Mgmt. Health Systems Program, Case Western Res. U., Cleve., 1984-86; bd. dirs. Cerner Corp., HealthGate Data Corp., Aros Corp. ReGen Biologies Inc., The Health Mgmt. Acad. Author: (book) Multihospital Systems: Policy Issues for the Future, 1981, co-author: Managing the Finances of Health Institutions, 1980, Financing of Health Care, 1979, Musculo-skeletal Disorders: Their Frequency of Occurrence and Their Impact on the Population of the United States, 1978. Mem. adv. com. Waveney Care Ctr., New Canaan, 1987. Grantee USPHS, Washington, 1972-75. Mem. Yale Club (N.Y.). Home and Office: The Bisbee Group 110 Wellesley Dr New Canaan CT 06840-3530

BISBEE, JOYCE EVELYN, utility company manager; b. Portage, Wis., May 15, 1941; d. Orris Dean and Helen Paulina (Golz) B. BS, U. Wis., Stout, 1963; MEd, U. N.C., 1971. Cert. family and consumer sci. Ext. home economist U. Wis., Racine, 1964-68; tchr., dept. chair Oshkosh (Wis.) Pub. Schs., 1963-64, 68-74; mgr. ednl. rels. J.C. Penney, N.Y.C., 1974-78; v.p. Creamer Dickson Basford, PR, N.Y.C., 1978-81; consumer affairs rep. Bklyn. Union, Bklyn., 1983-85, consumer advocate, 1986-92, mgr. consumer outreach and edn., 1992-98; dir. consumer comm. and advocacy KeySpan Corporation, Bklyn., 1998—. Mem. consumer affairs com. Bar Assn. City N.Y., 1993-98. Mem. adv. com. N.Y.C. 4-H Youth Program, 1985-96; active East 60s Neighborhood Assn., N.Y.C., 1993—. Recipient Alumni Disting. Svc. award U. Wis.-Stout, 1978. Mem. Am. Gas Assn. (mem. consumer and cmty. affairs com. 1992-96), Am. Assn. Family and Consumer Sci. (v.p. 1977-79), Am. Coun. on Consumer Interests, Soc. Consumer Affairs Profls. in Bus., N.Y.C. Home Economists in Bus. (chair 1985-86, awrd 1993), N.Y. State Utility Consumer Affairs Profls. (chair 1991-92). Lutheran. Avocations: craft shows, cultural performances, cats, travel. Home: 245 E 63rd St New York NY 10021-7466 Office: KeySpan Corp One MetroTech Ctr Brooklyn NY 11201

BISCARDI, CHESTER, composer, educator; b. Kenosha, Wis., Oct. 19, 1948; s. Chester Frank and Anne Rose (Rizzo) B. Student, Università di Bologna (Italy) and Conservatorio di Musica G. B. Martini, Bologna, 1969-70; BA in English Lit. with honors, U. Wis., 1970, MA in Italian Lit. (Ford Found. fellow), 1972, MM in Composition, 1974; MMA, Yale U., 1976, DMA, 1980. Teaching asst. Italian U. Wis., Madison, 1970-73, ad hoc instr. Italian for reading knowledge, 1973-74, teaching asst. theory, 1973-74; teaching fellow Italian for singers Yale U., New Haven, 1975-76; seminar instr. Fed. Correctional Instn. at Oxford, Wis., summer 1978; faculty mem. music dept. Sarah Lawrence Coll., 1977—; seminar and program faculty Acad. Yr. in N.Y.C., 1984; chmn. dept. music Sarah Lawrence Coll., 1987—, William Schuman chmn. music, 1995—. Vis. prof. summer program in Florence at Villa Corsi-Salviati in Sesto Fiorentino with U. Mich., 1987, 94; composer-in-residence U. Wis., 1985, The Chamber Music Conf. and Composers' Forum of the East, Bennington, Vt., 1990. Composer: numerous compositions including Tartini, 1972, Turning, 1973, Chartres, 1973, Indovinello, 1974, orpha, 1974, Heabakès: Five Sapphic Lyrics, 1974, they had ceased to talk, 1975, Trusting Lightness, 1975, Tenzone, 1975, Music for the Duchess of Malfi, 1975, Trio, 1976, At the Still Point, 1977, Eurydice, 1978, Mestiere, 1979, Trasumanar, 1980, Di Vivere, 1981, Good-bye, My Fancy!, 1982, Music for Witch Dance, 1983, Chêz Vous, 1983, Piano Concerto, 1983, Incitation to Desire (tango), 1984, 1993, Tight-Rope, 1985, Piano Sonata, 1986, rev., 1987, Traverso, 1987, No Feeling is the Same as Before, 1988, Companion Piece (for Morton Feldman), 1989, 1991, Netori, 1990, Music for an Occasion, 1992, rev., 2003, The Gift of Life, 1990—93, Baby Song of the Four Winds, 1994, Guru, 1995, Resisting Stillness, 1996, What a Coincidence, 1997, I Wouldn't Know About That, 1997, Prayers of Steel, 1998, Now You See It, Now You Don't, 1998, The Child Comes Every Winter, 1999, Someone New, 1999, Music for NASDAQ Market Site TV, 1999, Recovering, 2000, In Time's Unfolding, 2000, At Any Given Moment, 2002, Modern Love Songs, 1997—2002. Recipient Prix de Rome, Am. Acad. in Rome, 1976-77, Aaron Copland award, 2001; Composer/Librettist grantee Nat. Endowment for Arts, 1977-78, 80-81; Composers' Conf. fellow, Johnson, Vt., 1974-75; Wis. Arts Bd. grantee, 1976; Nat. Acad. and Inst. Arts and Letters Charles E. Ives scholar, 1975-76; Guggenheim fellow, 1979-80; Mellon Found. grantee, 1979; Am. Music Ctr. grantee, 1980; McDowell Colony fellow, 1981, 84, 92, 94-95, 98, 2000; Martha Baird Rockefeller Fund grant, 1982, 2000; Creative Artists Pub. Svc. Program fellow in music, 1983; Japan Found. fellow, 1989-90; N.Y. Found. for Arts Artists fellow in music composition, 1990, 98; Rockefeller Found. Bellagio Study and Conf. Ctr. residency, Lago di Como, Villa Serbelloni, Italy, 1993; Humanities residency The Bogliasco Found., Villa Orbiana, Italy, 1999, Fromm Music Found. at Harvard Commn., 1999-2002, others. Mem. Am. Composers Alliance, Am. Acad. in Rome, Am. Music Ctr., Broadcast Music, MacDowell Colony, Century Assn., also others. Office: Sarah Lawrence Coll Music Dept Bronxville NY 10708 Home: 380 Riverside Dr 4C New York NY 10025-1819 E-mail: biscardi@mail.slc.edu.

BISCHEL, MARGARET DEMERITT, physician, managed care consultant; b. Moorhead, Minn., Nov. 8, 1933; d. Connie Magnus Nystrom and Harriett Grace (Petersen) Zorner; m. Raymon DeMeritt, 1953 (div. 1958); 1 child, Gregory Raymon; m. John Bischel, 1961 (div. 1964); m. Kenneth Dean Serkes, June 7, 1974. BS, U. Oreg., Eugene, 1962; MD, U. Oreg., Portland, 1965. Diplomate Am. Bd. Internal Medicine, Nat. Bd. Med. Examiners. Resident, straight med. intern Los Angeles County/U. So. Calif. Med. Ctr., 1965-68, NIH fellow nephrology, 1968-70, asst. prof. renal medicine, 1970-74; asst. prof., instr. medicine U. So. Calif., 1968-74; instr. nephrology East L.A. City Coll., 1971-74; dir. med. edn. Luth. Gen. Hosp., Park Ridge, Ill., 1974-78, dir. nephrology sect., 1977-80, pres. med. staff, 1974-88; founding mem., med. dir., dir. med. svcs. Luth. Health Plan, Park Ridge, 1983-87; clin. assoc. prof. medicine Abraham Lincoln Sch. Medicine U. Ill., 1975-80; sr. cons. Parkside Assocs., Inc., Park Ridge, 1986-88; pvt. practice Chgo., 1974-88; physician Buenaventura Med. Clinic, Ventura, Calif., 1989-94, med. dir., 1992-94; prin. Apollo Managed Care Cons., Inc., Santa Barbara, Calif., 1988—. Trustee Luth. Health Care System, Park Ridge, 1986-90, Unified Med. Group Assn., Seal Beach, Calif., 1993-94; hon. lifetime staff mem. Luth. Gen. Hosp., Park Ridge; mem. formulary com. HealthNet, 1992-94, med. adv. com. TakeCare, 1993-94, quality assurance com. PacifiCare, 1993-94; mem. doctor's adv. network AMA, 1994-96; JCAHO advisor for behavioral health care providers. Mem. editl. adv. bd. Capitation Mgmt. Report, author 35 texts including Medical Review Criteria Guidelines for Managed Care, 2002, Managing Behavioral Healthcare, 2001, The Credentialing and Privileges Manual, 2001; contbr. articles to profl. jours., chpts. to books; editor: Med. Mgmt. Manual, Managed Care Bull. Fellow: ACP (Calif. Gov.'s advisor 1993—95); mem.: Am. Coll. Physician Execs. Avocations: real estate, gardening. Office: Apollo Managed Care Consultants Inc 860 Ladera Ln Santa Barbara CA 93108-1626 E-mail: mbischel@apollomanagedcare.com.

BISCHOFF, DAVID CANBY, retired university dean; b. Bellefonte, Pa., May 27, 1930; s. Eugen Carl and Jean Stuart (Canby) B.; m. Patricia A. Halfacre, Aug. 15, 1954; children: Cynthia, Steven, Ingrid. BS, Pa. State U., 1952, PhD, 1958; MS, U. N.C., 1953. Asst. prof. dept. phys. edn. U. Mass., Amherst, 1957-60, asso. prof., 1960-63, prof., 1963—, asso. provost for profl. schs., 1972-79, dep. provost, 1982-84; assoc. chancellor, 1983-92; dean U. Mass. Sch.

Phys. Edn., 1973-92. Vis. prof. Wesleyan U., 1968-69; bd. dirs. Bay State Games. Past pres. Amherst Community Chest, Amherst Am. Field Service; mem. Amherst Planning Bd., 1958-62; trustee The Hotchkiss Sch., 1990-96; trustee Portland (Maine) Mus. Art. Capt. USAF, ret., 1953-55. Mem. AAHPER, Nat. Coll. Phys. Edn. Assn. (past pres.) Clubs: Algonquin, Hillsboro, Anglers (N.Y.C.). Home: 46 Burbank Farm PO Box 462 Yarmouth ME 04096-0462

BISCHOFF, FREDERICK CHRISTOPHER, III, retired accountant; b. Walhalla, S.C., Oct. 1, 1941; s. Frederick Christopher and Kathleen (Kay) B. Student, Ga. Inst. Tech., 1965; BBA, Ga. State U., 1966; BS (hon.), Ohio Christian U., 1968. Market devel. mgr. Grizzard Advt., Atlanta, 1966-71; v.p. Leedy Enterprises Inc., Atlanta, 1971-72; contract adminstr. APAC-GA Inc., Atlanta, 1973-92, APAC-Carolina, Inc., 1992—2003; ret., 2003. Active Fulton County Young Reps., Atlanta, 1964-68, High Mus. of Art; mem. Ga. Marine Safety Commn., 1959-62. Mem. Palmetto Trust for Hist. Preservation, Ga. Hist. Soc., Atlanta Hist. Soc., Am. Legion, S.C. Hist. Soc., Nat. Trust for Historic Preservation, Darlington C. of C. (bd. dirs.), Florence C. of C., Kiwanis, Darlington Pilot Club Found. (bd. dirs.), Ponte Vedra Club, Darlington Country Club. Methodist. Avocations: photography, travel. Home: 502 Cashua St Darlington SC 29532-2808 Office: APAC-Carolina Inc PO Box 521 Darlington SC 29540-0521

BISCHOFF, JOAN, English educator; b. Orange, N.J., Mar. 20, 1943; d. Herbert John and Jeannette Elizabeth (Thomas) B.; m. Egal Feldman, June 14, 1992; stepchildren: Tyla, Auora, Naomi. BS, East Stroudsburg State Coll., 1965; MA, Lehigh U., 1971, PhD, 1975. Cert. tchr., N.J., Pa. English tchr. various pub. schs., Pa., N.J., 1965-70; tchg. asst., fellow in English Lehigh U., Bethlehem, Pa., 1970-74; from instr. to assoc. prof. English Slippery Rock (Pa.) U., 1975-87; from assoc. prof. to prof. English U. Wis., Superior, 1988—2002, emeritus, 2002—. Contbr. articles to profl. jours. Rsch. grantee U. Wis., 1989-92. Mem. MLA. Home: 2019 Weeks Ave Superior WI 54880-6720 Office: Univ Wis Sundquist # 230 Superior WI 54880

BISCHOFF, KENNETH BRUCE, chemical engineer, educator; b. Chgo., Feb. 29, 1936; s. Arthur William and Evelyn Mary (Hansen) B.; m. Joyce Arlene Winterberg, June 6, 1959; children: Kathryn Ann, James Eric. BS, Ill. Inst. Tech., 1957, PhD, 1961. Asst. to assoc. prof. U. Tex., Austin, 1961-67; assoc. prof., then prof. U. Md., 1967-70; Walter R. Read prof. engring. Cornell U., 1970-76, dir. Sch. Chem. Engring., 1970-75; Unidel prof., biomed. and chem. engring. U. Del., 1976-98, emeritus, 1998—, chmn. dept. chem. engring., 1978-82. Mem. NRC Bd. on Chem. Scis. and Tech., 1984-86, various coms., 1984—; cons. Exxon Rsch. and Engring., NIH, Gen. Foods Corp., W.R. Grace Co., Koppers Co., DuPont Co. Author: (with D.M. Himmelblau) Process Analysis and Simulation, 1968, (with G.F. Froment) Chemical Reactor Analysis and Design, 1979, 2d edit., 1989; editor: (with R.L. Dedrick and E.F. Leonard) The Artificial Kidney, Proc. 1st. Internat. Symposium Chem. Reaction Engring., 1970, (with R.M. Koros and T.R. Keane) Proc. 9th Symposium, 1986; mem. editorial bd. Advances in Chemistry Series, 1973-76, 78-81, Jour. Bioengring., 1976-80, Jour. Pharmacokin, Biopharmaceutics, 1975-92, Biotech. Progress, 1987-2000, Advances in Chem. Engring., 1981-2000. Recipient Ebert prize Acad. Pharm. Scis., 1972, Founders award Chem. Indsl. Inst. Toxicology, 1992, Disting. Alumni award Ill. Inst. Tech., 1996, Profl. Achievement award, 1997; Shell Found. fellow, 1959, NSF fellow, 1960, U. Ghent fellow, 1960-61, NAE fellow. Fellow AAAS, AIChE (dir. 1972-74, chmn. food, pharm. and bioengring. divsn. 1985, chmn. nat. program com. 1978, Profl. Progress award 1976, Food Pharm. and Bioengring. divsn. award 1982, 34th Ann. Inst. lectr. 1982, R.H. Wilhelm award 1987); mem. Am. Inst. Chem. Engr., Am. Chem. Soc., Am. Soc. Artificial Internal Organs, Engrs. Coun. for Profl. Devel. (bd. dirs. 1972-78), Coun. Chem. Rsch. (governing bd. 1981-84, chmn. 1985), Catalysis Soc., AAUP, N.Y. Acad. Scis., Sigma XI, Tau Beta Pi, Phi Lambda Upsilon, Omega Chi Epsilon, Alpha Chi Sigma. Home: PO Box 467 Rehoboth Beach DE 19971-0467

BISCHOFF, MARILYN BRETT, clinical social worker, personal life coach; b. Mt. Vernon, N.Y., Apr. 16, 1930; d. Arthur Cushman and Mary Kathryn (Clark) Brett; m. Walter A. Bischoff, Mar. 25, 1961; children: Holly, Robert. BA magna cum laude, CCNY, 1959; MSSW, Columbia U., 1961; PhD in Social Work, Boston Coll., 1985; cert. in gerontology, U. Mass., Dartmouth, 2000. Diplomate in clin. social work Am. Bd. Examiners in Social Work. Clin. social worker Providence Child Guidance Clinic, 1961-65, 69-73; pvt. practice clin. social worker Attleboro, Mass., 1994—, Providence, 1965-94; instr. Providence Coll., 1988-89. Speaker in field. Active Attleboro (Mass.) Area Mental Health Assn., 1975-94. Columbia Univ. fellow, N.Y.C., 1959-60; Nat. Inst. Mental Health fellow, 1960-61. Mem. NASW (sec.-treas. S.E. Mass. chpt. 1967-68, mem. speaker's bur. R.I. chpt. 1987, diplomate clin. social work), Acad. Cert. Social Workers, R.I. Group Psychotherapy Soc. (chair membership com. 1985-96), Columbia U. Alumni Assn., Attleboro Ski Club, Phi Beta Kappa. Avocations: traveling, photography, sewing, bridge. Home and Office: 10 Norfolk Row Attleboro MA 02703-1629 E-mail: DRMARILYNB@aol.com.

BISCHOFF, SUSAN ANN, newspaper editor; b. Indpls, July 31, 1951; d. Thomas Anthony and Betty Jean (Coons) Bischoff; m. Jim B. Barlow, June 20, 1975; 1 child, Samantha Lynn Barlow Martinez. BA, Ind. U., 1973. Rschr., reporter Congl. Quar., Washington, 1973-74; city desk reporter Houston Chronicle, 1974-75, bus. reporter, 1975-79, asst. bus. editor, 1979-84, bus. editor, 1984-86, asst. mng. editor, 1986-2000, dep. mng. editor, 2000—03, assoc. editor, 2003—. Houston corr. Kiplinger, Tex. Letter, Washington, 1980-85. Mem. class policy Leadership Houston, 1992—94; mem. exec. com. Gulf Coast affiliate United Way, 1994—2002; bd. dirs. Houston Chronicle Employees Fed. Credit Union, 1980—87, San Jacinto Coun. Girl Scouts US, 1997—2003, Child Adv., US Olympic Festival VII, Houston, 1985—86, Gulf Coast Mar. of Dimes Birth Defects Found., 1989—2001, YES Coll. Prep. Sch., 1999—2002; founding bd. dir. Greater Houston Women's Found.; mem. bd. visitors Anderson Cancer Ctr. U. Tex. Named Outstanding Woman in Houston Journalism, YWCA, 1989, Fabulous Femme, Greater Houston Women's Found., 1994, Woman of Distinction, Crohn's & Colitis Found., 1996; recipient Outstanding Vol. Achievement award, Gulf Coast United Way, 1995, Outstanding Media award, Nat. Soc. Fund Raising Execs., 1997, Nat. Thanks award, San Jacinto Girl Scouts, 2001, Mayborn award, Cmty. Leadership Tex. Daily Newspaper Assn., 2001, honoree, Jewish Cmty. Ctr. of Houston Children's Scholarship Ball, 2002, Strong, Smart and Bold award, Houston Girls, Inc., 2003. Mem.: Am. Assn. Sunday and Feature Editors (named to Features Hall of Fame 2003), Am. Soc. Newspaper Editors (dir.), Press Club of Houston Ednl. Found. (founding bd. dir.). Home: 2929 Buffalo Speedway # 112 Houston TX 77098 Office: Houston Chronicle 801 Texas St Houston TX 77002-2996 E-mail: susan.bischoff@chron.com.

BISCONTI, ANN STOUFFER, public opinion research company executive; b. Chgo., Nov. 22, 1940; d. Samuel Andrew Stouffer and Ruth Rachel McBurney; m. Raffaele Ludovico Bisconti (dec. Oct. 19, 1999); children: Alessandra Ilus Wilkes, Giulia Rachel; m. Charles William Dyke, Oct. 13, 2002. Student, Harvard U., 1958 60; BA with honors, McGill U., 1962; PhD, The Union Inst., Cin., 1978. Assoc. study dir. Nat. Commn. on Allied Health Edn., Washington, 1977—79; dir. Washington office Higher Edn. Rsch. Inst., 1979—80; ptnr. Human Resources Policy Corp., Washington, 1980; dir. Nat. Ctr. for Allied Health Leadership, Washington, 1981—83; v.p. rsch. Nuc. Energy Inst., Washington, 1983—96; pres. Bisconti Rsch., Inc., Washington, 1996—. Mem. adv. com., risk comm. program EPA, Washington, 1988; advisor tech. cooperation program in Malaysia IAEA, Vienna, 1990; mem. adv. com., risk comm. Orgn. for Econ. Cooperation and Devel., Paris, 1991. Author: College and Other Stepping Stones, 1980; co-author: Higher Education and the Disadvantaged Student, 1972, The Power of Protest, 1975, College as a Training Ground for Jobs, 1977. Pres. Congl. Award Coun., 8th Congl. Dist., Md., 1990—93; advisor long-range planning com. Town of Somerset, Chevy Chase, Md., 2002; career advisor Harvard U., Cambridge, 1996; rsch. advisor NASA Alumni League, Washington, 1998. Recipient Disting. Svc. Award, Am. Soc. Allied Health Professions (now Assn. Schs. Allied Health Profls.), 1983. Mem.: World Assn. Pub. Opinion Rsch., Am. Nuc. Soc. (bd. dirs. 1993—96, Best Paper award 1989, Outstanding Session award 1990, 1992), Am. Assn. Pub. Opinion Rsch. Avocations: geography/travel, foreign languages, gardening.

BISER-ROHRBAUGH, ANN K. physician assistant; d. Geraldine C Biser; children: Caleb M. Rohrbaugh, Alexander E. Rohrbaugh. BS in Phys. and Life Sciences, Wilson Coll., 1989; A in Health Sciences, Physician Asst., Essex C.C., Balt., MD, 1996; MS in Neuroscience, Johns Hopkins U., 1996. Am. Acad. of Physician Assistants AAPA, 1998. Physician asst., Divsn. of Pediatric Orthopedics Johns Hopkins Hosp., 1998—2000; physician asst., Dept. of Emergency Medicine Penn State Milton S. Hershey Med. Ctr., 1999—, physician asst., Dept. of Neurosurgery, 2000—01; physician asst., divsn. of pediatric neurosurgery Johns Hopkins Hosp., 2001—. Contbr. articles various jours. Fellow: Am. Acad. of Physician Assistants; mem.: Md. Acad. of Physician Assistants. Office: Johns Hopkins Hospital Div of Neurosurg 600 N Wolfe St Harvey 811 Baltimore MD 21287-8811 E-mail: abiser@jhmi.edu.

BISGARD, EILEEN BERNICE REID, lawyer; b. Portland, Oreg., July 30, 1944; d. Elbert Hann and Bernice Elizabeth (Smythe) Reid; m. Stanley Howard Hargrove, Aug. 11, 1963 (div. 1973); children— Michael Dean, Kimberly Diane; m. William Harlow Bisgard, Nov. 27, 1974; children: Jeffery Beecher, Corrine Elizabeth, Alicia Naomi, Dawn Marie. B.S. with highest distinction, Colo. State U., 1966; J.D., U. Denver, 1977. Bar: Colo. 1977. Sole practice, Longmont, Colo., 1977-81; pres. Eileen B. Bisgard, P.C., Longmont, 1982-87 . Bd. dirs. Parents United, Boulder, Colo., 1983-85; founding pres., bd. dirs. Longmont Coalition Women in Crisis, 1979-82; bd. mgrs. St. Vrain Valley YMCA, Longmont, 1981-84; mem. youth ctr. adv. bd. City of Longmont, 1983-86; exec. dir. The Family Extension, Inc. (aka The Inn Between, Inc.), Longmont, 1986—. Mem. ABA, Colo. Bar Assn., Boulder County Bar Assn. (chmn. juvenile law com. 1984-85), Nat. Assn. Council Children, Child Welfare League Am. (steering com. western region, nat. standards com. for family foster care), Soroptimists. Office: 525 3rd Ave Longmont CO 80501-5906

BISGARD, GERALD EDWIN, biosciences educator, researcher; b. Denver, Aug. 4, 1937; s. Harry Herman and Lucille Margaret (Matson) B.; m. Sharon Kay Cummings, Sept. 9, 1961; children— Jennifer, Kristine, Bradley BS, Colo. State U., 1959, D.V.M., 1962; MS, Purdue U., 1967; PhD, U. Wis., 1971. Instr., then asst. prof. Purdue U., West Lafayette, Ind., 1962-69; asst. prof., then assoc. prof. bioscis. U. Wis., Madison, 1971-77, prof., 1977-2001, emeritus prof., 2001—, dept. chmn. bioscis., 1980-97. Vis. prof. U. Calif.-San Francisco, 1977-78; mem. respiratory and applied physiol. study sect. NIH, 1988-92. Recipient Merit award NIH, 1987; named NIH fellow, 1969-71, Fogarty NIH Sr. Internat. fellow Oxford U., 1993; grantee NIH, 1973—. Mem. Am. Soc. Vet. Physiologists and Pharmacologists (pres. 1982-84), Am. Physiol. Soc., AVMA, Wis. Assn. Biomed. Res. Edn. (pres. 1998-2000). Avocations: sailing; skiing; gardening; hiking. Office: U Wis Sch Vet Medicine 2015 Linden Dr W Madison WI 53706-1100

BISHARA, AMIN TAWADROS, management and consulting firm executive, technical services executive; b. Cairo, Oct. 22, 1944; came to U.S., 1973; s. Tawadros and Fakha (Boules) B.; m. Suzi Guirguis, Aug. 27, 1977; children: James A., Robert A. BSME, Ain Shams U., Cairo, 1968; MSME, Poly. U. N.Y., 1976. Registered profl. engr., N.Y., Tex., Ill., Ariz., Pa., Fla. Field engr. Gen. Engring. Co., Cairo, 1968-71; mech. engr. Engring. Co. for Indsl. Enterprises, Cairo, 1971-73; project engr. Cosentini Assocs., N.Y.C., 1973-76; sr. engr. Ebasco Svcs., Inc., N.Y.C., 1976-79, lead engr., 1979-84; chmn., chief exec. officer PTS Tech. Svcs., Inc., Hurst, Tex., 1985-96; v.p. Metzler & Assocs., 1997-98; sr. mgr. Ernst & Young LLP, 1999—. Mem. adv. bd. Entrepreuneurship Inst., Ft. Worth, 1990—. Lectr. in nuclear industry; strategic and bus. cons. Contbr. articles to profl. publs. Mem. NSPE, ASME Nuc. Air Treatment Sys. (main com.), Masons, Moslah Temple of Ft. Worth. Roman Catholic. Home: 2625 Brookridge Dr Hurst TX 76054-2761

BISHARA, SAMIR EDWARD, orthodontist; b. Cairo, Oct. 31, 1935; s. Edward Constantin and Georgette Ibrahim (Kelela) B.; children: Dina Marie, Dorine Gabrielle, Cherine Noelle. B. Dental Surgery, Alexandria U., Egypt, 1957; diploma in orthodontics, 1967; MS, cert. in orthodontics, U. Iowa, 1970, D.D.S., 1972. Diplomate Am. Bd. Orthodontics (pres. Coll. Diplomates 1992). Practice gen. dentistry, Alexandria, 1957-68; specializing in orthodontics Iowa City, Iowa, 1970—; fellow in clin. pedontics Guggenheim Dental Clinic, N.Y.C., 1959-60; resident in oral surgery Moassat Hosp., Alexandria, 1960-61, mem. staff, 1961-68; asst. prof. dentistry U. Iowa, 1970-73, asso. prof., 1973-76, prof., 1976—. Vis. prof. Alexandria U., 1974. Contbr. articles profl. jours., chpts. in books. Fellow Am. Coll. Dentists, Internat. Coll. Dentists; mem. ADA, AAAS, Am. Assn. Orthodontics, Internat. Dental Fedn., Internat. Assn. Dental Research, Am. Cleft Palate Assn., Assn. Egyptian Am. Scholars, Egyptian Orthodontic Soc. (hon.), Columbian Orthodontic Soc. (hon.), Greek Orthodontic Soc. (hon.), Mexican Bd. Orthodontists (hon.), Brit. Orthodontic Conf. (hon.), Omicron Kappa Upsilon, Sigma Xi. Home: 1014 Penkridge Dr Iowa City IA 52246-4930 Office: U Iowa Coll Dentistry Orthodontic Dept Iowa City IA 52242

BISHER, JAMES FURMAN, journalist, author; b. Denton, N.C., Nov. 4, 1918; s. Chisholm and Mamie (Morris) B.; m. Lynda Landon; children: Roger, James Furman Jr., Monte. Student, Furman U., 1934-36; AB in Journalism, U. N.C., 1938; Doctorate in Arts and Letters (hon.), Furman U., 1997. Editor Lumberton (N.C.) Voice, 1938-39; reporter High Point (N.C.) Enterprise, 1939-40; reporter, state editor Charlotte (N.C.) News, 1940-42, sports editor, 1946-50, Atlanta Constn., 1950-57, Atlanta Jour., 1957—; columnist The Sporting News, St. Louis; moderator weekly TV show, Football Rev., 1950-68. V.p. Bisher Hosiery Mill, Denton, N.C. Author: With A Southern Exposure, 1962, Miracle in Atlanta, 1966, Strange But True Baseball Stories, 1966, Arnold Palmer— The Golden Year, 1971, Aaron, 1974, The College Game, 1974, The Masters, 1976, The Furman Bisher Collection, 1989, Thankful, 1997, Atlanta Half-Century, 1997, also numerous articles; contbr. to: anthologies including Best Sports Stories of Year, 23 times. Chmn. Ga. Christmas Seal campaign, 1961; charter mem. Atlanta-Fulton County Stadium Authority.; mem. selection com. Pro Football Hall of Fame, Coll. Football Hall of Fame, Ga.; bd. dirs. Salvation Army Boys Club, mem. adv. bd. Sarazen World Open Golf Tournament; mem. Atlanta Sports Coun. Served to lt. USNR Air Corps, 1943-46. Recipient Ga. A.P. Sports Writing award, 18 times; UPI Sports Writing award, 4 times; Turf Writing award Fla. Throughbred Breeders Assn., 1972, 75; Jake Wade award Coll. Sports Info. Dirs. Am., 1979; Sigma Delta Chi awards for best sports commentary, 1982, 93, 90; Bert McGrane award for disting. svc. to coll. football, 1982; N.C. Gov.'s award, 1986; U. N.C. Journalism Hall of Fame, 1985; named Ky. col., 1958, Sportswriter of Yr. Ga. (18 times); hon. Tar Heel, 1961; Disting. Alumnus of Yr. Furman U., 1978; Red Smith award for disting. and meritorious contbn. to art of sportswriting, 1988, Bobby Jones Sportsman of Yr. award, 1994; named to Nat. Sportscasters and Sportswriters Hall of Fame, 1989, Internat. Golf Writers Hall of Fame, 1989, Ga. Sports Hall of Fame, 1990, N.C. Sports Hall of Fame, 1995, Lifetime Achievement in Journalism award PGA in Am., 1996, Ga. Soccer Hall of Fame, 1997, Meml. Golf Journalism award, 1997; sponsor Furman Bisher Acad.-Athletic scholarship Furman U., Roger C. Bisher Scholarship Ga. Tech.; Marvin Francis award for Svc., 2001, Nat. Conf. for Cmty. and Justice award, 2001, Lincoln Werden Meml. award, N.Y. Golf Assn., 2001. Mem. Nat. Sportscasters and Sportswriters Assn. (pres. 1974-76), Football Writers Assn. Am. (pres. 1959-60), Golf Writers Assn. Am. (pres. 1992-94), Assn. Golf Writers (Europe) (life), Canongate Golf Club, Legends at Chateau Elan, Capital City Club, The European Club, Sea Island Golf Club, Gridiron Club, Chi Psi. Presbyterian. Home: 431 Lester Rd Fayetteville GA 30215-4930 Office: 72 Marietta St NW PO Box 4689 Atlanta GA 30302-4689 *My good fortune in life is not to be confused with success, whose definition yet remains vague to me. Success is some mythical goal clamored and struggled for, and whose pursuit is never-ending. One level leads to a requirement to seek another. Success, in my mind, must be related to the status of that person who achieves happiness, and yet may never have been outside his county.*

BISHOP, ALAN DOUGLAS, music educator; b. Spartanburg, S.C., Apr. 27, 1962; s. William Jack and Gwendolyn Elaine Bishop; m. Lisa Lynn Haskell, Apr. 15, 1962; children: Abby Elizabeth, Michael Alan. MusM in Edn., Valdosta (Ga.) State U., 1987. Asst. band dir. Boiling Springs (S.C.) HS, 1984—86; grad. student asst. Valdosta (Ga.) State U., 1986—87; band dir. McBee (S.C.) HS, 1987—88, Ninety Six (S.C.) HS, 1988—97, Mid. Sch. of Pacolet, SC, 1997—2002; asst. band dir. Broome HS, Spartanburg, SC, 1997. Treas. Friends of Libr. Spartanburg County Pub. Library Cowpens Br., Cowpens, SC, 2002. Mem.: S.C. Band Dirs. Assn., S.C. Music Educator's Assn. (corr.), Music Educator's Nat. Conf. (corr.). Baptist. Avocation: music. Home: 108 Paula Court Cowpens SC 29330 Office: Cowpens Middle School 150 Foster Street Cowpens SC 29330 Personal E-mail: a-lbishop@juno.com. E-mail: abisho@spa3.k12.sc.us.

BISHOP, ALFRED CHILTON, JR., lawyer; b. Alexandria, Va., Oct. 3, 1942; s. Alfred Chilton and Margaret (Marshall) B.; divorced; 1 son, Alfred Chilton III; m. 2d Catherine Ann Keppel, May 17, 1980. B.A. with distinction, U. Va., 1965, LL.B., 1969; LL.M. in Taxation, Georgetown U., 1974. Bar: N.Y. 1970, U.S. Ct. Appeals (2d cir.), 1970, U.S. Tax Ct. 1971, U.S. Ct. Claims 1971, D.C. 1977. Assoc. Shearman and Sterling, N.Y.C., 1969-70; assoc. trial atty., Office of Chief Counsel IRS, Washington, 1970-74, sr. trial atty., 1974-80, sr. technician reviewer, 1980-81, br. chief, 1981— . Recipient Am. Jurisprudence award 1968, 1968. Mem. D.C. Bar Assn., Sr. Exec. Service Candidate Network (v.p. 1980-81, pres. 1981-82, dir. 1983), Sr. Exec. Assn., Phi Delta Phi. Episcopalian. Home: 7523 Thistledown Trl Fairfax Station VA 22039-2207

BISHOP, ANN SHOREY, oncological nurse; b. N.Y.C., Jan. 4, 1947; d. George Heaysman and Clara Bessie (Garrison) Shorey; m. Jeffrey Bishop; 1 child, George John. Diploma in nursing, Montgomery Hosp. Sch. Nursing, 1967; BSN, U. Pa., 1971; postgrad., Med. Coll. Va., 1976-77. RN Pa. Staff nurse med.-psychiatry Montgomery Hosp., Norristown, Pa., 1967-69; staff nurse psychiat. med.-surg. Capital Health Sys. (formerly Mercer Med. Ctr.), Trenton, NJ, 1972-76, Rancocas Valley Hosp., Rancocas, N.J., 1977-79; med., psychiat. mental health and chem. dependency staff nurse Capital Health Sys.-Fuld (formerly Helen Fuld Med. Ctr.), Trenton, 1980-2000; mentally and mutiply handicapped health nurse Woods Svcs., Langhorne, Pa., 2000—. Mem. Soc. Of Friends. Avocations: reading, rail fan, cooking, baking. Office: Woods Svcs Rt 413 & 213 Langhorne PA 19047

BISHOP, BARNEY TIPTON, III, political commentator, analyst, lobbyist, consultant; b. Panama City, Fla., Dec. 24, 1951; s. Barney and Margaret Lorraine (Rollo) B.; m. Shelby Lynn Stinson, Feb. 4, 1989. Student, Miami-Dade C.C., 1969-71; BS in Speech, postgrad. in Italy, Emerson Coll., 1973. Investigator Best & Sears, Attys. at Law, Orlando, Fla., 1975-76; chief investigator Alliance Investigative Agy., Winter Park, Fla., 1976-78; chmn., pres. TRAK Detective Agy., Inc., Orlando, 1978-83; regional ins. investigator Fla. Dept. Ins., Tallahassee, 1983, adminstrv. asst. to state ins. commr., 1983-84, state coord. consumer outreach program, 1984-87; regional coord. Acad. Fla. Trial Lawyers, Tallahassee, 1987-88, dir. legis. affairs, 1988, dir. fundraising, 1988-89, dir devel., 1990-91, Fla. Lawyers Action Group, Tallahassee, 1991; exec. dir. Fla. Dem. Party, Tallahassee, 1991-93; mng. dir. Fla. Dem. Party Trustees, Tallahassee, 1993-94; pres., CEO The Windsor Group, Tallahassee, 1993—. Co-founder, chmn. Fla. Investigative and Security Trust Polit. Action Com., Orlando, 1981-83, also lobbyist; bd. dirs. Fla. Consumer Action Network, 1988—; spkr. on consumer advocacy. Chmn. Orlando Solicitations Rev. Bd., 1981-84; sec. Orlando Leadership Coun., 1981-83; v.p. Fla. Young Dems., Tallahassee, 1982-83, pres., 1983-84; mem. Seminole County Dem. Exec. Com., 1980-83, Leon County Dem. Exec. Com., 1983-86; bus. cons.-tchr. Jr. Achievement, 1982; chmn. patient advocacy task force Fla. divsn. Am. Cancer Soc., 1989; bd. dirs. Fla. Dem. Leadership Coun., 1993-2002, exec. com., 1993, exec. v.p., 1993-2002; apptd. state ins. commr. Fla. Hurricane Catastrophe Fund Adv. Coun., 1995-2001; apptd. by gov. Fla. Commn. Cmty. Svc., 1997-2000, treas., mem. exec. com., 1998-2000, vice chair, 2000-01; apptd. to Tallahassee Regional Airport Adv. Com., 1999—, vice chair, 2000, chair, 2001-2002; bd. dirs. 21st Century Coun., sec., 2002; bd. dirs. Vol. Fla. Found., Inc., 1999—, chair, 2001—; apptd. to bd. trustees Fla. A&M U., 2003—, chmn. budget and fin. com., govt. affairs com., 2003—; bd. dirs. The Bill Rollo Found., Leon County Communities in Sch.; exec. bd. Suwanee River Area coun. Boy Scouts Am., 1997—; bd. dirs. Alliance for Fla.'s Economy; mem. bd. overseers Emerson Coll., 2002-; bd. dirs. Tallahassee (Fla.) Symphony Orch.; elected supr. com. S.C.O.R.E. Fed. Credit Union. Recipient Lighthouse award Acad. Fla. Trial Lawyers, 1990, award of excellence, 1990; Young Dem. of Yr. award Fla. Young Dems., 1983, 25th Anniversary award The Village, 1998, Am.'s Best Lobbyist award, 1998, Medal of Honor, Fla. Commn. on Cmty. Svc., 1999; scholar Rotary Internat. Found., South Africa, 1983. Mem. Am. Assn. Polit. Cons., Fla. Assn. Pvt. Investigators (v.p. 1978-79, pres. 1979-80, newsletter editor 1981-83), Nat. Soc. Fund Raising Execs., Emerson Coll. Alumni Assn., Nat. Eagle Scout Assn., Tallahassee C. of C., Tallahassee Soc. of Assn. Execs., Capital City Jaycees (bd. dirs. 1983-86), Seminole Boosters, Capital Tiger Bay Club (bd. dirs., 2d v.p. 1998, exec. dir. 1999, bd. dirs. 2000-01), Econ. Club of Fla., Gov.'s Club (mem. bd. govs.), Univ. Ctr. Club (founder), Rocky Ridge Hunt Club (ptnr.), Alpha Kappa, Alpha Phi Omega, Phi Rho Pi, Rho Delta Omega. Democrat. Methodist. Avocation: hunting. Home: 10976 Luna Point Rd Tallahassee FL 32312-9695 Office: 501 E Tennessee St Tallahassee FL 32308-4906 E-mail: barney@thewindsorsgroup.net., manager@thewindsorgroup.net.

BISHOP, BRUCE TAYLOR, lawyer; b. Hartford, Conn., Sept. 13, 1951; s. Robert Wright Sr. and Barbara (Taylor) B.; m. Sarah M. Bishop, Aug. 31, 1974; children: Elizabeth, Margaret. BA in Polit. Sci., Old Dominion U., 1973; JD, U. Va., Charlottesville, 1976. Bar: Va. 1977, U.S. Supreme Ct., Va. 1976, U.S. Dist. Ct. (ea. dist.) Va., U.S. Dist. Ct. (we. dist.) Va., U.S. Ct. Appeals (4th cir.); diplomate Am. Bd. Trial Advocates. Law clk. to chief judge U.S. Dist. Ct. (ea. dist.) Va., 1976-77; assoc. Willcox & Savage, P.C., Norfolk, Va., 1977-82, ptnr., 1983—. Bd. dirs. Nautical Adventures, Inc., Norfolk FestEvents, Ltd., 1981—, pres., 1982-85; pres. Va. OpSail 2000 Found.; mem. bd. visitors Old Dominion U., 1972-83, sec., 1979-81, chmn., mem. various coms.; speaker in field. Treas. Norfolk Reps., 1978-82, also mem. numerous coms.; bd. dirs., chmn. regional Key Club campaign United Way South Hampton Roads; chmn., co-chmn. United Negro Coll. Fund, 1981, Four Cities United Way Campaign; trustee Va. Stage Co., 1982; pres. Community Promotion Corp.; commr. Norfolk Redevel. and Housing Authority, chmn., 2000-02; pres. Ona Ednl. Found., 2003—; active numerous other community orgns. Named Outstanding Young Man, Norfolk Jaycees; recipient Disting. Alumni award Old Dominion U., Dominion Vol. of Yr. award, 1993. Mem. ABA (mem. various sects.), Fed. Bar Assn. (pres. Tidewater chpt. 1980-81), Am. Bd. Trial Advocates, Va. Assn. Def. Lawyers, Va. Bar Assn., Va. Trial Lawyers Assn., Norfolk-Portsmouth Bar Assn., Def. Rsch. Inst., Internat. Assn. Def. Counsel (nat. trial acad. faculty 1997), Assn. Def. Attys., Def. Rsch. Inst., Old Dominion U. Alumni Assn. (bd. dirs. 1978-83), Old Dominion U. Ednl. Found. (bd. dirs. 1987—, sec. 2000-02, pres. 2003—), Norfolk C. of C. (chmn. downtown devel. com. 1980-81), James Kent Am. Inn of Ct. (master). Avocations: basketball, tennis, gardening. Office: Willcox & Savage PC One Commercial Place Norfolk VA 23510 E-mail: bbishop@wilsav.com.

BISHOP, BUDD HARRIS, retired museum administrator, artist; b. Canton, Ga., Nov. 1, 1936; s. James M. and Mary E. (Ponder) B.; m. Julia Crowder, Nov. 30, 1968. AB, Shorter Coll., Rome, Ga., 1958; M.F.A., U. Ga., 1960; student, Arts Administrn. Inst. Harvard, 1970. Instr. art Ensworth Sch., Nashville, 1961-63; dir. creative services Transit Advt. Assn., N.Y.C., 1964-66; dir. Hunter Mus. of Art, Chattanooga, 1966-76, Columbus (Ohio) Mus. Art, 1976-87, Samuel P. Harn Mus. Art, U. Fla., Gainesville, 1987-98, dir. emeritus. Vis. lectr. Vanderbilt U., 1962; past pres. bd. Intermuseum Conservation Lab., Oberlin, Ohio Past trustee Fla. Arts Celebration, Gainesville; mem. Gainesville Art in Pub. Places Trust; mem. faculty Ctr. for Arts and Pub. Policy; bd. dirs. Fla. Assn. Mus. Found., Inc.; mem. nat. adv. bd. Philharm. Ctr. for Arts, Naples, Fla.; trustee Hist. Rugby, Inc., Tenn.; bd. dirs. Cordell Hull Mus. and Bhplace; pres.-elect Livingston-Overton County C. of C. Recipient gov.'s award Tenn. Art Commn., 1971, 73, Alumni Arts achievement award Shorter Coll., 1979, arts leadership award Columbus Day, 1986, Person of Yr. award in arts Gainesville Sun, 1995, Lifetime Achievement Mus. Svc. award Fla. Assn. Mus., 1997. Mem. Am. Assn. Museums, Assn. Art Mus. Dirs. (past trustee), Southeastern Museums Conf. (James R. Short award 1998), Fla. Art Mus. Dirs. Assn. (Lifetime Achievement award 1998).

BISHOP, C. DIANE, state agency administrator, educator; b. Elmhurst, Ill., Nov. 23, 1943; d. Louis William and Constance Oleta (Mears) B. BS in Maths., U. Ariz., 1965, MS in Maths., MEd in Secondary Edn., 1972. Lic. secondary educator. Tchr. math. Tucson Unified Sch. Dist., 1966-86, mem. curriculum council, 1985-86, mem. maths. curriculum task teams, 1983-86; state supt. of pub. instrn. State of Ariz., 1987-95, gov.'s policy advisor for edn., 1995-97, dir. gov.'s office workforce devel. policy, 1996-2000; asst. dep. dir. Ariz. Dept.

Commerce, 1997-2000; exec. dir. Gov.'s Strategic Partnership for Econ. Devel., 1997—2002; pres. The Vandegrift Inst., 2000—; exec. dir. Maricopa Health Found., 2002—. Mem. assoc. faculty Pima C.C., Tucson, 1974-84; adj. lectr. U. Ariz., 1983, 85; mem. math. scis. edn. bd. NRC, 1987-90, mem. new standards project governing bd., 1991; dir. adv. bd. sci. and engring. ednl. panel, NSF; mem. adv. bd. for arts edn. Nat. Endowment for Arts. Active Ariz. State Bd. Edn., 1984-95, chmn. quality edn. commn., 1986-87, chmn. tchr. crt. subcom., 1984-95, mem. outcomes based edn. adv. com., 1986-87, liaison bd. dirs. essential skills subcom., 1985-87, gifted edn. com. liaison, 1985-87; mem. Ariz. State Bd. Regents, 1987-95, mem. com. on preparing for U. Ariz., 1983, mem. high sch. task force, 1984-85; mem. bd. Ariz. State Community Coll., 1987-95; mem. Ariz. Joint Legis. Com. on Revenues and Expenditures, 1989, Ariz. Joint Legis. Com. on Goals for Ednl. Excellence, 1987-89, Gov.'s Task Force on Ednl. Reform, 1991, Ariz. Bd. Regents Commn. on Higher Edn., 1992. Woodrow Wilson fellow Princeton U., summer 1984; recipient Presdl. Award for Excellence in Teaching of Maths., 1983, Ariz. Citation of Merit, 1984, Maths. Teaching award Nat. Sci. Research Soc., 1984, Distinction in Edn. award Flinn Found., 1986; named Maths. Tchr. of Yr. Ariz. Council of Engring. and Sci. Assns., 1984, named One of Top Ten Most Influential Persons in Ariz. in Field of Tech., 1998. Mem. AAUW, NEA, Nat. Coun. Tchrs. Math., Coun. Chief State Sch. Officers, Women Execs. in State Govt. (bd. dirs. 1993), Ariz. Assn. Tchrs. Math., Women Maths. Edn., Math. Assn. Am., Ednl. Commn. of the States (steering com.), Nat. Endowment Arts (adv. bd. for arts edn.), Nat. Forum Excellence Edn., Nat. Honors Workshop, Phi Delta Kappa. Republican.

BISHOP, CALVIN THOMAS, landscape architect, educator; b. Alexander City, Ala., Oct. 11, 1929; s. Isaiah Washington and Flora Bernice (Carlton) B.; m. Lenna Graves, Aug. 28, 1950; children: Leigh Carlton, Beverly Lynn, Lane Amanda. B.Landscape Arch., Auburn U., 1951. Landscape architect John F. Highberger, Memphis, 1949-51; planner Auburn Planning Bd., 1951; landscape architect, designer Ralph Ellis Gunn, Houston, 1952-53; ptnr. Bishop & Walker, Houston, 1953-84; assoc. prof. landscape arch. La. State U., 1965-66; pres. Bishop Wholesale Greenhouses, Inc., Alexander City, Ala., 1982-88; assoc. prof. Miss. State U., Starkville, 1984-97, acting head dept. landscape architecture, 1986, 87-89, assoc. prof. emeritus, 1997—. Cons. landscape architecture, 1997—. Works include Am. Rose Center, Shreveport, La. Post adviser Boy Scouts Am., 1971-73; chmn. Gov.'s Houston-Gulf Coast Region-10 Year Goals for Tex. planning com., 1970, Houston Am. Bicentennial Commn., 1973-76; treas. Richmond Elementary PTO, 1975-76; mem. profl. adv. com. Sch. Environ. Design Tex. A.&M. U.; deacon Second Bap. Ch., Houston. Recipient Houston Mcpl. Arts Environ. Design Achievement awards, 1970-72 Mem. Am. Soc. Landscape Architects (pres. S.W. chpt. 1970-71, nat. v.p. 1973-74, 80, pres. 1981-82, coun. fellows 1978—, Nat. Honor award for design, del. to Internat. Fedn. Landscape Architects 1992-93), Houston C. of C., Houston-Auburn U. Alumni Assn. (pres. 1963-64), Pi Kappa Alpha. Lodges: Rotary (sgt. at arms 1978-79). Baptist. Home and Office: 9203 Bonhomme Rd Houston TX 77074-6613 *Man's relationship with gardens go back to the earliest beginnings as a standard for peace and quality of life. Preserving and designing our landscape is a great experience.*

BISHOP, CAROL, oil industry executive; b. Arlington, Mass., June 5, 1956; d. Francis Joseph and Mary Ruth (Robinson) Bishop; m. Lawrence A. Balboni, May 5, 1979 (div. 1982); m. Gary L. Renick, Jan. 31, 1986 (div. 1999). Grad., Harvard U., 1991. Mgr. Larson Ins., Arlington, Mass., 1979-85, v.p., 1987-88; mgr. Merrill Lynch Realty Ins. Svcs., Boca Raton, Fla., 1985-87; pres. Essex Ins. Planners, Haverhill, Mass., 1988-98; bus. devel. strategic planner Micro Power Electronics Inc., Hillsboro, Oreg., 1998—2001, Air Brit. Petroleum, Washington, 2001—. V.p. United Internat. Ins. Agy., Inc., Braintree, Mass., 1992-94. Vol. Mus. Sci., Boston, 1988, Mus. Sci., 1988—; vol.tutor Mass. Campaign for Literacy, 1988—. Democrat. Avocations: reading, travel, equestrian events.

BISHOP, CHARLES EDWIN, university president emeritus, economist; b. Campobello, S.C., June 8, 1921; s. Fred and Hattie Bess (Wall) B.; m. Lee N., June 1, 2002; children from a previous marriage: Susan Ann, Mary Catherine, Charles Edwin. BS, Berea Coll., 1946; MS, U. Ky., 1948; PhD (Farm Found. fellow 1948-49), U. Chgo., 1952. Research asst. agrl. econs. U. Ky., 1947-48; research assoc. econs. U. Chgo., 1949-50; mem. faculty N.C. State U., 1950-70, prof. agrl. econs., 1956-70, head dept. agrl. econs., 1957-65, head dept. econs., 1965-66, William N. Reynolds Disting. prof., 1957-70; v.p. U. N.C., Chapel Hill, 1966-70; exec. dir. Agrl. Policy Inst., 1960-66; chancellor U. Md., College Park, 1970-74; pres. U. Ark., Fayetteville, 1974-80, U. Houston System, 1980-86. Vis. prof. Grad. Sch. Bus., U. Va., 1961-63; cons. Universidad Agraria, Lima, Peru, 1961-65; mem. Nat. Com. Agrl. Policy, Nat. Planning Assn., 1958-70; agrl. bd. Nat. Acad. Scis., 1963-68; sci. adv. com. to sec. agr., 1962-68; mem. Nat. Manpower Adv. Com., 1962-68; exec. dir. Pres. Johnson's Nat. Adv. Com. on Rural Poverty, 1966-67; mem. food adv. com. Pres. Nixon's Cost of Living Council, 1972; mem. Pres. Carter's adv. com. White House Conf. on Balanced Nat. Growth and Econ. Devel., 1978 Co-author: Introduction to Agricultural Economic Analysis, 1958. Mem. com. on vet. med. edn. So. Regional Edn. Bd., 1974; trustee Farm Found., 1968-78; bd. dirs. Winthrop Rockefeller Found., 1975-78, Resources for the Future, 1976-90, chmn., 1987-90; co-chmn. bd. Nat. Rural Ctr., 1975-79; mem. N.C. Rural Econ. Devel. Ctr., 1986-96, chmn., 1991-96; mem. Pres. Carter's Commn. on Agenda for Eighties, 1980; bd. dirs. Houston Industries, 1984-92. Sr. fellow M.D.C., 1991-2000. Fellow Am. Econ. Assn.; mem. Am. Agr. Econs. Assn. (pres. 1967-68), Internat. Assn. Agrl. Econs., Commn. on Cen. European Econ. Devel., Alpha Zeta, Phi Kappa Phi, Gamma Sigma Delta.

BISHOP, CHARLES JOSEPH, manufacturing company executive; b. Gary, Ind., June 22, 1941; s. Charles K. and Angela (Marich) Yelusich; m. Yvonne M. Stazinski, June 8, 1963; children: Stephen, Scott. BS, Purdue U., 1963; PhD, U. Wash., 1969. Mgr. advanced energy systems Boeing Co., Seattle, 1969-77; mgr. systems devel. Solar Energy Research Inst., Denver, 1977-81; v.p. tech. A.O. Smith Corp., Milw., 1981—. Mem. adv. bd. S.W. Wis. Rsch. Ctr., Milw., 1987; bd. dirs. Indsl. Rsch. Inst., 1989-92, v.p., 1993, pres. 1995-96. Contbr. articles to profl. jours. Treas. Cedarburg Cmty. Scholarship Com., Wis., 1985-91; mem. indsl. liaison coun. U. Wis., Milw., 1985—, U. Wis. Coll. Engring., Madison, 1990-95; mem. Gov.'s Coun. on Sci. and Tech., 1992-94; mem. nat. coun. Alverno Coll. Recipient Cert. Recognition NASA, 1975. Mem.: Milw. Athletic Club. Republican. Roman Catholic. Avocations: fishing, travel, golf. Office: A O Smith Corp-Corp Tech 12100 W Park Pl Milwaukee WI 53224-3029

BISHOP, CLAIRE DEARMENT, small business owner, former librarian; b. Youngstown, Ohio, Oct. 12, 1937; d. Eugene Howard and Ruth (Bright) DeArment; m. Carl R. Meinstereifel, 1956 (div. 1964; children: Paul, Dawn; m. Olin Jerry Dewberry, Jr., 1974 (div. 1979); m. J. Bruce Bishop, May 6, 1992. BS, Clarion State U., 1967; MLS, Ga. State U., 1977. Cert. libr. media specialist, Ga. Libr. Henry County, Stockbridge, Ga., 1967-69; head libr. Russell H.S., East Point, Ga., 1969-84; engring. libr. Rockwell Internat., Duluth, Ga., 1984-88; rep. Govt. Industry Data Exch. Program, Corona, Calif., 1984-88; libr. Raytheon Co., 1990, Missile Sys. Divsn., Bristol, Tenn., 1988-90; owner, mgr. Claire's Collectibles, rubber stamp store, St. Augustine, Fla. Author newsletter Grin and Stamp It. Sec. San Marco Avenue Mchts. Assn. Mem. St. Augustine IBM Users Group (sec.), Six-Ninety-Six Investment Club (fin. officer), Mensa. Democrat. Avocations: computers, writing, information broker. Office: Claire's Collectibles 78 San Marco Ave Saint Augustine FL 32084-3258

BISHOP, DAVID FULTON, library administrator; b. N.Y.C., Nov. 23, 1937; s. Donald McLean and Clara (Zelley) B.; m. Nancy Driscoll, May 15, 1959; children: Karen McLean, Michael David. MusB, U. Rochester, 1959, postgrad., 1959-60; MS in Library Sci., Cath. U. Am., 1964; postgrad., U. Md., 1967-73. Head serials dept. U. Md. Libraries, College Park, 1967-69, coordinator tech. services, 1969-70, head systems, 1970-73; head cataloger U. Chgo. Libraries, 1973-75, asst. dir. tech. services, 1975-79; dir. libraries U. Ga., Athens, 1979-87; prof., univ. librarian U. Ill., Urbana, 1987-92; univ. libr. Northwestern U., Evanston, Ill., 1992—. Trustee Ednl. Comms. (EDUCOM), Washington, 1988-94; bd. dirs. Ctr. for Rsch. Librs., 1992-99; vice-chmn. bd. dirs. 1996-97, chmn. bd. dirs., 1997-98; bd. dirs. North Suburban Libr. System, 2000—. Mem. ALA, INFORMA (steering com. 1989-93), Assn. Coll. and Rsch. Librs., Coun. on Libr. Resources (proposal rev. com. 1991-95), Coalition for Networked Info. (steering com. 1992-98). Home: 2518 Indian Ridge Dr Glenview IL 60025-1032 Office: Northwestern U Librs Evanston IL 60201 E-mail: dbishop@northwestern.edu.

BISHOP, DAVID NOLAN, electrical engineer; b. Memphis, Jan. 14, 1940; s. Robert Allen Bishop and Sara Frances (Gammon) Bishop Marett; m. Lois Margaret Baudouin, Nov. 16, 1963; children: Julie Frances Bishop Malouse, Anne Marie Bishop Bryan. BSEE, Miss. State U., 1962, MSEE, 1965. Registered profl. engr., La., Miss., Fla. Constrn. engr. Chevron Oil Co., New Orleans, 1964-70, lead constrn. engr., 1970-72, sr. constrn. engr., 1972-78; staff elec. engr. Chevron U.S.A., Inc., New Orleans, 1978-82, sr. staff elec. engr., 1982-85, elec. engring. cons., 1985-92; facilities engring. elec. engring. cons. Chevron U.S.A. Prodn. Co., Houston, 1992-96, sr. elec. engring. cons., 1996-97; sr. cons. engr. Chevron Petroleum Tech. Co., 1998-99; cons., 1999—. Offshore safety and anti-pollution equipment rep. Am. Petroleum Inst., 1982-86, mem. various coms.; mem. Nat. Elec. Code Panel 14, 1989-99; instr. sch. elec. sys. oil and gas prodn. facilities Petroleum Ext. Svc., U. Tex., Austin, 1990—; mem. instrumentation craft com. New Orleans Regional Vocat. Tech. Inst., 1985-92; guest lectr. in field. Author: (book) Electrical Systems for Oil and Gas Production Facilities, 1988, 2d edit. 1992; contbr. articles to profl. jours. Asst. scoutmaster Boy Scouts Am., Metairie, La., 1964-69; adminstrv. bd. St. Matthew's United Meth. Ch., Metairie, 1974-76; adv. com. U. Tex., Austin, Petroleum Ext. Tex., 1980—; engring. adv. com. Miss. State U., 1982—, chmn. curriculum and rsch. subcom., 1986-89, sec., 1989-91, vice-chmn., 1992-93, chmn., 1993-94. With U.S. Army, Miss. N.G. Named Coll. Alumnus of Yr., Coll. Engring. Miss. State U., 1990, Disting. Engring. fellow, 1992, Chpt. Alumnus of Yr. Miss. State U. Alumni Assn., 1990. Fellow Instrument Soc. Am. (sect. pres. 1977-78, dist. v.p. 1983-85, chmn. coun. dist. v.p. 1984-85, v.p. stds. and practices 1988-90, host. com. chmn. ISA/90 1989-90, pres.-elect, sec. 1990-91, pres. 1991-92, chmn. honors and awards com. 1993-94, chmn. nominations com. 1994-95, New Orleans sect. Commendation award 1983-84, stds. and practices dept. Recognition Achievement award 1987-90, Stds. and Practices award 1995, Am. Nat. Standards Inst. meritorious svc. award 1995), Tau Beta Pi, Pi Eta Sigma, Eta Kappa Nu (student sect. pres. 1961-62), Omicron Delta Kappa. Republican. Avocations: hunting, gardening, genealogy, crossword puzzles. Home and Office: 112 Laura Ln Destrehan LA 70047-3022 E-mail: dnbishop@bellsouth.net.

BISHOP, DEBBIE, publishing executive, book designer, writer; b. Ingelwood, Calif., July 13, 1955; d. Gary Bishop and Judy Jueterbock; m. Rick Tiernen; 1 child, Tyler. Student, UCLA, L.A., 1977—. Actress, model, waitress various, L.A.; model JVC Cool Am., NJ; v.p. sales & mktg. Twin Tower Studios, Tarzana, Calif., A P Studios, Culver City, Calif.; v.p. sales Paerans, Sun Valley, Calif.; printing broker Left Field Prodn., Burbank, Calif.; bus. owner Left Field /Angel Gate, Burbank, Calif. Author: Martha's Got Nothing on Me-Pre Fat Cookbook, 2002, Black Tide Rising Enter the Game, 2003, (comic book series) Blacktide, 2001—. Avocations: martial arts, surfing, painting, gardening, cooking. Office: Left Field Ink/Angel Gate Press 3111 W Burbank Blvd #103 Burbank CA 91505

BISHOP, DELORES ANN, artist, educator; b. Balt., May 27, 1946; d. Edward James Boyle, Sr. and Norma Delores Boyle; m. John James Bishop, Jr.; children: Denise Anderson, Christine. Grad. h.s., Balt. Elite, one stroke cert. instr., cert. William Alexander instr. Fgn. lang. lab. asst. Baltimore County Md. Pub. Schs., Balt., 1964—71; asst. mgr. Ben Franklin Crafts, Cockeysville, Md., 1982—99; freelance decorative artist Balt., 1999—2001. Program mgr. Premises Providers, Inc (Arundel Mills Mall), Hanover, Md., 2000. Painted sculpture, The Shopper, 2000, Bushel of Crabs, 2000, Bass, 2000. Holiday vol. Cowenton Vol. Fire Dept. Sta. 200, Balt., 2000—01; Vol., asst. leader Girl Scouts Am., Balt., 1960—80. Mem.: Md. Art League, Inc., Balt. (Md.) Watercolor Soc., Decorative Painters Soc. Personal E-mail: dabishop@dabitup.com.

BISHOP, DONALD MICHAEL, foreign service officer; b. Nashville, Tenn., Oct. 2, 1945; s. Robert Milton and Anne Selene (Rowan) B.; m. Jemma Won-Ja Chong, Jul. 25, 1973; children: Jerome, John Patrick, Edward Austin. BA, Trinity Coll., 1967; MA, Ohio State Univ., 1974. Investment banking ops. Smith, Barney & Co., N.Y., 1968; adminstrv. officer U.S. Air Force, McGuire AFB, N.J., Phu Cat AB, Vietnam, 1968-70, info. officer Maxwell AFB, Ala., Kwang Ju, Korea, 1970-73; asst. prof. history U.S. Air Force Acad., Colorado Springs, Colo., 1974-79; fgn. svc. officer U.S. Info. Agy., 1979-99, with Dept. State, 1999—; vice consul Hong Kong, 1981-83; dir. USIS Am. Cultural Ctr., Taegu, Korea, 1985-87; info. officer and spokesman Am. Inst. in Taiwan, Taipei, 1988-91; fgn. affairs congressional fellow U.S. House Rep., Washington, 1991-92; course dir. fgn. svc. officer training U.S. Info. Agy., Washington, 1992-94; country pub. affairs officer Am. Embassy, Dhaka, Bangladesh, 1994-97, dep. pub. affairs officer Beijing, 1997-2000; country pub. affairs officer for Nigeria, Am. Consulate Gen., Lagos, Nigeria, 2000-01, Am. Embassy, Abuja, 2001—02, min.-counselor for press and cultural affairs Beijing, 2003—. Decorated Bronze Star medal, Meritorious Svc. medal, Air Force Commendation medal, Sustained Superior Performance award USIA, 1989, 94, 99. Mem. Am. Fgn. Svc. Assn., Air Force Assn., Vietnam Security Police Assn., The Hist. Soc. Roman Catholic. Avocation: history. Home and Office: American Embassy Beijing PSC 461 Box 50 Fpo AP 96521-0002 E-mail: donbishop99@yahoo.com.

BISHOP, ELIZABETH SHREVE, psychologist; b. Ann Arbor, Mich., Nov. 18, 1951; d. William Warner Jr. and Mary Fairfax (Shreve) B. AB, U. Mich., 1972; MA, Ohio State U., 1973, PhD, 1976. Lic. psychologist, Mich. Psychologist Franklin County Program for the Mentally Retarded, Columbus, Ohio, 1974, WC Mental Health, Willmar, Minn., 1977-83; chief psychologist Battle Creek (Mich.) Child Guidance Ctr., 1981; dir. psychometrics Meridian Profl. Psychol. Cons., East Lansing, Mich., 1983-92; pres. Arbor Psychol. Cons., Ann Arbor, 1991—. Trainer Girl Scouts U.S.A., 1993—, troop leader, 1968—69, 1973—74, 1980—82, 1984—86; deacon 1st Congl. Ch., 1996—2000, 2002—. Assoc. Univ. London Inst. Edn., 1976. Mem. APA, AAUW, LWV (Willmar v.p. 1979-81), Mich. Psychol. Assn., Mich. Women Psychologists (treas. 2002-), Coun. for Exceptional Children (local pres. 1977-78), Internat. Coun. Psychologists (bd. dirs. 1999-2002), Internat. Sch. Psychology Assn. Avocations: reading, traveling, birdwatching, photography, music. Home: 1612 Morton Ave Ann Arbor MI 48104-4441 Office: Arbor Psychol Cons 1565 Eastover Pl Ann Arbor MI 48104-6316 E-mail: arborpsych@att.net.

BISHOP, FRANCES BLACKBURN, civic worker; b. West Palm Beach, Fla., Mar. 3, 1925; d. Julius Magath and Adele Eleanor (Berg) Blackburn; B.Mus.Ed., Fla. State U., 1945; postgrad. Columbia, 1959-62; M.A. in Musicology, U. Mo., 1958; M.A. Teaching English as 2d Lang., Hunter Coll., 1986; m. Ben Bishop, May 20, 1946 (div. 1952); 1 dau., Jewel. Music tchr., Joiner, Ark., 1946-47, Franklin Square, N.Y., 1957-69; asst. placement dir. of internat. counselor exchange program. Assn. for World Travel Exchange, N.Y.C., 1970-74; exec. sec. Army Relief Soc., N.Y.C., 1975-76; adminstrv. sec. Am. Music Center, 1977-78; editorial asst. Sci. Digest, 1978-86; violinist Bloomingdale Chamber Orch.; tchr. English adult evening classes, N.Y.C., 1972-75; mem. Met. Greek Chorale. Vol. Internat. Center. Author reading textbook for English; collaborator on Japanese English dictionary of new words. Home: 36 W 84th St New York NY 10024-4739

BISHOP, GENE HERBERT, financial corporate executive; b. Forest, Miss., May 3, 1930; s. Herbert Eugene and Lavonne (Little) B.; m. Kathy S. Bishop, May 27, 1983. BBA, U. Miss., Oxford, 1952. With First Nat. Bank, Dallas, 1954-69, sr. v.p., chmn. sr. loan com., 1963-68, exec. v.p., 1968-69; pres., dir. SBIC subs. First Dallas Capital Corp.; pres. Lomas & Nettleton Fin. Corp., Dallas, 1969-75, Lomas & Nettleton Mortgage Investors, Dallas, 1969-75; chmn., CEO Merc. Nat. Bank, Dallas, 1975-81, MCorp., Dallas, 1975-90; vice-chmn., CFO Lomas Fin. Corp., 1990-91; pres., COO Lomas Mortgage USA, Dallas, 1990-91; chmn., CEO Life Ptnrs. Group, Inc., Dallas, 1991-94, also bd. dirs. Bd. dirs. Drew Industries, Inc., Liberté Investors. Bd. dirs. State Fair Tex., Dallas; trustee Children's Med. Ctr., Dallas Meth. Hosps. Found.; mem. Dallas Citizens Coun. 1st lt. USAF, 1952-54. Mem. Terpsichorean Club, Idlewild Club, Brook Hollow Golf Club, Eldorado Country Club, Vintage Club, Dallas Country Club. Methodist. Office: 5500 Preston Rd Ste 250 Dallas TX 75205-2699

BISHOP, GEORGE FRANKLIN, political scientist, educator; b. New Haven, July 26, 1942; s. George Elwood and Mary Bridget (Trant) B.; m. Pama Mitchell, July 15, 1995; 1 child, Kristina. BS in Psychology, Mich. State U., 1966, MA, 1969, PhD, 1973. Instr. multidisciplinary social sci. program Mich. State U., East Lansing, 1972-73; asst. prof. dept. sociology and anthropology U. Notre Dame, Ind., 1973-75; dir. Greater Cin. Survey, 1981-95; rsch. assoc. behavioral sci. lab U. Cin., 1975-77, sr. rsch. assoc. Inst. for Policy Rsch., 1981-93, dir. behavioral scis. lab., 1994-95, assoc. prof. polit. sci., 1982-87, prof., 1987—, dir. grad. cert. program in pub. opinion and survey rsch., 1999—; dir. Internet Pub. Opinion Lab. Univ. Cin., 2000—. Assoc. dir. Ohio Poll, 1981-95; guest prof. Zentrum für Umfragen, Methoden und Analysen, Mannheim, Germany, 1985, 90, 92; fellow Ctr. for Study of Dem. Citizenship, Dept. Polit. Sci., U. Cin., 1992-99, fellow Inst. for Data Scis., 1996-98; summer inst. faculty Survey Rsch. Ctr., Inst. for Social Rsch., U. Mich., summer 1993; sr. cons. Burke Mktg. Rsch., Inc., Cin., 1996-98. Sr. editor The Presdl. Debates: Media, Electoral and Policy Perspectives, 1978; sr. author various articles in profl. jours.; mem. editl. bd. Pub. Opinion Quar., 1987-90, Free Inquiry, 1999—; mem. editl. adv. bd. Public Perspective, 2000—. Served with U.S. Army N.G., 1960-63. NSF grantee, 1977-84. Mem. AAUP (Maita Levine Svc. award 2002), Midwest Assn. Pub. Opinion Rsch. (pres. 1977-78, Mapor fellow Disting. Scholarship in pub. opinion rsch. 1994), Am. Assn. Pub. Opinion Rsch., Am. Polit. Sci. Assn., World Assn. Pub. Opinion Rsch. (treas. 1983-85). Home: 825 Dunore Rd Cincinnati OH 45220-1416 Office: U Cin Cincinnati OH 45221-0001

BISHOP, GERALD IVESON, pharmaceutical executive; b. Madras, India, Apr. 19, 1935; came to U.S., 1961; s. James Alfred and Muriel Madeleine (Waller) B.; m. Bridget Carey, June 30, 1960; children: Elizabeth, James, Frances, Catherine. BSME, Durham U., Newcastle Upon Tyne, Eng., 1960; MS in Indsl. Engring., MBA, SUNY, Buffalo, 1971. Bus. cons. Associated Indsl. Cons., London, 1964-67; mgr. indsl. engring. Bell Aerospace, Buffalo, 1967-70; exec. asst. to CEO Ayerst Labs. Inc., Rouses Point, N.Y., 1971-76; mgr. I.E. E.R. Squibb & Sons, North Brunswick, N.J., 1977-78; mgr. internat. tech. ops. Johnson & Johnson, New Brunswick, N.J., 1978-92. Mayor Champlain (N.Y.) Cmty., 1975-77. Fellow IEE, Mech. Engrs. (U.K.); mem. Profl. Engrs. Ont., Freemasons (Barger lodge #325). Republican. Avocations: gourmet cooking, shooting, computer technology, travel, reading non-fiction. Home: 877 Penn Estates East Stroudsburg PA 18301-8614

BISHOP, GORDON BRUCE, journalist; b. Paterson, NJ, Jan. 1, 1938; s. Charles E. and Freda Mary (Romyns) B.; m. Jeanne Ann Reed, June 30, 1962; children: Jennifer, Elizabeth. Student, Am. Acad. Dramatic Arts, 1957; BA, Rutgers U., NJ, 1967. Reporter, columnist Herald-News, Passaic, NJ, 1959-67; spl. writer Star-Ledger, Newark, 1969-95; pres., TV prodr. Bishop Pub. Programs, Inc., Eatontown, NJ, 1969—. Lectr. Rutgers U., Princeton U.; pres. All Seasons Outdoor Beauty, Franklin, NJ, 2001—. Author: (with Frank Papps) The Purple Canary, 1963, Holding Onto Nothing, 1969, Gems of New Jersey, 1985, Greater Newark: A Microcosm of America, 1989, Gateway to America, 1988, The Greatest Century: 1901-2001 Upper Montclair Country Club, 2002, Quest for Survival, 2002; prodr. documentaries including It's My Home for PBS, 1980, Every Day Is Earth Day, 1990, The Baykeeper, 1993, Global War on Pollution, 1994, Gateway to America, 1995; prodr.-collaborator (mus.) Crispus, 1986; columnist N.J. Mayors mag., The Patriot N.J., The Courier; syndicated columnist Atlantic Highlands Herald, NJ, USA Daily.com, PatriotofNJ.com; politics NJ.com; host. N.J. Issues TV Program, 1988-96. Environ. commr. Eatontown, NJ, 1973-76; chmn. NJ Lit. Hall of Fame, 1988-96; dir. Battleship NJ Found., 1998-2001; pres. US Mil. Mus., Ft. Hancock, NJ, 2002—. Recipient Disting. Pub. Service award NJ Profl. Soc. Engrs., Nat. Environ. awards Scripps-Howard Found., 1971-75; Nat. Conservation awards Washington Journalism Ctr., 1971-72; Conservation award N.J. Audubon Soc., 1973; named Man of Yr. AABC Congregation, Irvington, NJ; NJ Press Assn. awards, 1971-88; NJ Pub. Health Assn. award, 1987; Mid-Atlantic States Air Pollution Control Assn. Disting. Service award, 1987; named NJ Journalist of Yr., 1986 (1st in NJ); Pub. Service award N.J. Profl. Journalism Soc., 1972, 73, 74, 76, 78, NJ, Conf. Mayors award, 1974; Nat. Recycling award Nat. Recycling Assn., 1973; Gold medal NJ Garden Club, 1980; award Ballew/McFarland Found., 1981, NJ Agrl. Soc., 1981; Nat. Wildlife Fedn.'s Nat. Conservation Achievement award, 1987, Good Journalism award Nat. Assn. Water Cos., 1992; Monmouth County Planning Award, 1989; Inst. Internat. Edn. scholar, U. Manchester, Eng., 1972; Environ. Edn. award NJ Edn. Assn., 1990, Environ. award Am. Soc. Landscape Architects, 1993, 94; inductee Literary Hall of Fame, 1990, chmn., 1988-96. Mem. Rutgers U. Alumni Assn. Office: 1715 Hwy 36 Middletown NJ 07748 E-mail: gjbishop@aol.com. *The will to live, to learn, and to inspire others flows from a genuine desire to want to work at your best and to share your love with those who seek it. This is our destiny: Work and Love. Without either, you can never realize your full potential as an individual.*

BISHOP, J. JOE, social studies educator; b. St. Petersburg, Fla., May 3, 1962; s. James Joseph and V. Joyce (Marigold) B.; m. Nola Marie Trapp, July 29, 1989; children: Kaia, Courtney, Jim, Katie. AA with Honors, Rainy River C.C., International Falls, Minn., 1984; BA cum laude Comms. Theory & Psychology, Winona State U., 1987; MA in Sociology, U. Iowa, Iowa City, 1989, MA in Anthropology, 1995, PhD in Edn., 1999. Tchr. sociology, rsch. asst. U. Iowa, Iowa City, 1987-89, tchg. asst. anthropology, 1991-93, tchg. asst. edn., 1996, project coord., 1996-99, rsch. asst. edn., 1996-97, test item devel., summer 1997, coll. supr., 1996-98; grad. tchg. fellow U. Oreg., Eugene, 1989-90; asst. prof. Coll. Edn., Dakota State U., Madison, SD, 1999—2002; asst. prof. social founds. of edn., dept. tchr. edn. Coll. Edn. Eastern Mich. U., Ypsilanti, 2002—. Adj. prof. Kirkwood C.C., Iowa City, 1990-2000; presenter in field. Contbr. articles to profl. jours. Mem. Am. Ednl. Studies Assn., Midwest Sociol. Assn., Nat. Coun. Social Studies, Comparative and Internat. Edn. Soc., Soc. Study Symbolic Interaction. Avocation, carpentry. Office: Eastern Mich U Coll Edn 314G Porter Bldg Ypsilanti MI 48197 E-mail: joe.bishop@emich.edu.

BISHOP, JAMES DODSON, lawyer, mediator; b. Washington, Sept. 28, 1957; s. James William and Jane Lillian (Dodson) B. BA magna cum laude in Polit. Sci., Lincoln (Pa.) U., 1979; JD, Howard U., Washington, 1982. Bar: Pa. 1985. Dir. Atty./Client Arbitration Bd. D.C. Bar, Washington, 1987-93; dir. Archdioscesan Legal Network of Cath. Charities, Washington, 1993—. Mediator, D.C. Superior Ct., Washington, 1987—; lay reader St. Georges Episcopal Ch., Washington, 1984—. Mem. ABA (vice chmn. State and Local Bar Dispute Resolution Com., 1993). Democrat. Episcopalian. Avocation: church activities. Home: 5157 33rd St NW Washington DC 20008-2011 Office: Catholic Charities 924 G St NW Washington DC 20001-4532

BISHOP, JAMES FRANCIS, executive search consulting company executive; b. Chgo., Mar. 14, 1937; s. Francis Joseph and Margaret Rose (Nagle) B.; m. Shirley Ann McNulty, Oct. 13, 1962; children: Michael Francis, Noreen Maura, James Francis Jr. BA, Marquette U., 1961, MA, 1965. Spl. agt. Office of Naval Intelligence, Chgo., 1962-65; sr. assoc. Burke & O'Brien Assoc., Inc., N.Y.C., 1965-67, v.p., 1967-74, sr. v.p., 1974-78, pres., 1978-83; pres., CEO Burke, O'Brien & Bishop Assoc., Inc., Princeton, N.J., 1983—. Trustee George St. Playhouse, 1988-93, N.J. Hosp. Assn., 1996-2002; trustee St. Francis Med. Ctr., Trenton, N.J., 1989—, chmn. bd., 1991-96; chmn., bd. trustees St. Francis Med. Ctr. Found., 1998—; councilman Piscataway, 1968-71; trustee N.J. Hosp. Assn., 1996-2002. With USMC, 1954-57. Mem. NJ Hosp. Assn., Marquette U. Alumni Assn. (v.p. 1985-87, pres. 87-88). Clubs: Marquette (N.Y.), Springdale Golf Club (Princeton). Republican. Roman Catholic. Home: 33 Richard Ct Princeton NJ 08540-3802 Office: Burke O'Brien & Bishop Assocs 301 N Harrison St Ste 111 Princeton NJ 08540-3512 E-mail: jmsbishop@aol.com.

BISHOP, JAMES FRANCIS, lawyer; b. Oak Park, Ill., Aug. 25, 1940; s. George H. and Helen E. (Newcomb) B.; m. Barbara Anderson; children: Christopher J., Pamela J., Jennifer Lynn. BS, St. Joseph's Coll., Rensselaer, Ind., 1963; JD, Chgo. Kent Coll., 1966. Bar: Ill. 1966, Nev. 1989; cert. food handling specialist, Ill. Trust officer Am. Nat. Bank & Trust Co., Chgo., 1964-67; assoc. Gould & Ratner, Chgo., 1967-73; ptnr. Bishop & Callas, Crystal Lake, Ill., 1973-98, Law Offices of James F. Bishop, Crystal Lake, Ill., 1998—. Mem. panel Am. Arbitration Assn. Dir. Adult and Child Rehab. Ctr., Woodstock, Ill., 1974—; vice chmn. McHenry County Sch. Dist. reorgn. com., Woodstock, 1985-87, McHenry County Ducks Unltd., Crystal Lake, 1976-89; bd. dirs. No. Ill. Med. Ctr., 1980-82; elected mem. Sch. Dist. 155, 1973-79,

pres., 1977-79; mem. Sch. Dist. 47, 1980-83. Mem. Nat. Solid Waste Assn. Mgmt. (mem. legis. com. 1988), Govt. Refuse Collection and Disposal Assn. (mem. legis. com. 1986-88), McHenry County Bar Assn., Ill. State Bar Assn., Clark County Bar Assn., State of Nev. Bar Assn., Ill. Restaurant Assn. Office: Law Offices of James F Bishop 550 W Woodstock St Crystal Lake IL 60014-3425

BISHOP, JOAN H. health facility administrator; b. Phila., Aug. 25, 1936; d. Thomas Dewitt and Marian Elsie (Wilson) Harvey; m. Arthur Howard Bishop, June 15, 1957 (div. 1985); children: Paul Harvey, Laura Melanie Bishop Fiveash. Student, Edinboro (Pa.) Coll., 1977-79, U. Va., 1980-83, George Mason U., Fairfax, Va., 1982-84. Adminstr. Leewood Nursing Home, Annandale, Va., 1974-83; dir. Inova Health Sys. Commonwealth Care Ctr., Springfield, Va., 1983-93; adminstr., cons. pvt. practice, Burke, Va., 1993-94; adminstr. Iliff Nursing and Rehab. Ctr., Dunn Loring, Va., 1994-98; cons. elderly svcs., 1998—. Cons. Am. Health Care Assn., Washington, 1981-83; Gubernatorial Apptee Va. State Bd. of Examiners, 1983-92, Va. State Bd. of Health, 1993-97; curriculum adv. com. Nova Nursing Sch., 1996-99. Books on tape reader for visually impaired sch. children, Hoover, Ala. Mem. Am. Coll. of Health Care Adminstrs. (treas. 1980-83, sec. nat. ethics. com. 1996-99). Protestant. Avocations: concerts, bridge. Home and Office: 5830 Willow Lake Dr Hoover AL 35244-4126 Fax: (205) 428-8870. E-mail: JOANBISHOP@worldnet.att.net.

BISHOP, JOHN MICHAEL, biomedical research scientist, educator; b. York, Pa., Feb. 22, 1936; married, 1959; 2 children. AB, Gettysburg Coll., 1957; MD, Harvard U., 1962; DSc (hon.), Gettysburg Coll., 1983. Intern in internal medicine Mass. Gen. Hosp., Boston, 1962—63, resident, 1963—64; rsch. assoc. virology NIH, Washington, 1964—66, sr. investigator, 1966—68; from asst. prof. to assoc. prof. U. Calif. Med. Ctr., San Francisco, 1968—72, prof. microbiology and immunology, 1972—, prof. biochemistry and biophysics, 1982—; dir. G.W. Hooper Rsch. Found., 1981—; Univ. prof. U. Calif. Med. Ctr., San Francisco, 1994—2000; chair. Nat. Cancer Adv. Bd., San Francisco. Chancellor U. Calif. Med. Ctr., San Francisco, 1998—. Recipient Nobel prize in physiology or medicine, 1989, Biomed. Rsch. award, Am. Assn. Med. Colls., 1981, Albert Lasker Basic Med. Rsch. award, 1981, Armand Hammer Cancer award, 1984, GM Found. Cancer Rsch. award, 1984, Gairdner Found. Internat. award, Can., 1984, Medal of Honor, Am. Cancer Soc., 1984; grantee, NIH, 1968—. Fellow: Salk Inst. (trustee 1991—); mem.: NAS, Nat. Cancer Adv. Bd., Inst. Medicine. Achievements include research in biochemistry of animal viruses; replication of nucleic acids; oncogenesis; control of cell growth; molecular genetics. Office: U Calif Hooper Rsch Found Dept Microbiology PO Box 552 San Francisco CA 94143-0001*

BISHOP, LEO KENNETH, clergyman, educator; b. Britton, Okla., Oct. 11, 1911; s. Luther and Edith (Scovill) B.; m. Pauline T. Shamburg, Sept. 15, 1935; 1 dau., Linda Paulette. AB, Phillips U., 1932; L.H.D., 1958; MA, Columbia U., 1944; MBA, U. Chgo., 1957; Litt.D., Kansas City Coll. Osteopathy and Surgery, 1964. Ordained to ministry Christian Ch., 1932; asso. minister Univ. Place Ch., Oklahoma City, 1932-35; minister First Ch., Paducah, Ky., 1935-41, Central Ch., Des Moines, 1941-45; dir. St. Louis office NCCJ, 1945-48, v.p., dir. central div., 1949-63; dir. pub. affairs People-to-People, Kansas City, Mo., 1963-66; v.p. Chgo. Coll. Osteopathy, 1966-72; pres. Bishop Enterprises, Colorado Springs, Colo., 1972—; also lectr. Contbr. religious and ednl. jours.; Developed: radio series Storm Warning; TV series The Other Guy, 1954. Cons. Community Social Planning Council, Mayor's Race Relations Com., YMCA, St. Louis; Am. del. Conf. World Brotherhood, Paris, 1950; bd. dirs. Am. Heritage Found. Recipient Paducah Jr. C. of C. Most Useful Citizen award, 1937, Distinguished Service award Dore Miller Found., 1958, Freedom Found. of Valley Forge award, 1961; named Chicagoan of Year, 1960 Mem.: Rotary, Union League, Winter Night. Home and Office: Montara Meadows A342 3150 E Tropicana Ave Las Vegas NV 89121

BISHOP, MARY OLTMAN, retired advertising executive; With Leo Burnett Co., Chgo., pres., chief mktg. officer. Office: 35 W Wacker Dr Chicago IL 60601-1614 E-mail: mary_bishop@chi.leoburnett.com.

BISHOP, MICHAEL, writer; Writer-in-residence LaGrange Coll., 1997—. Author: A Funeral for the Eyes of Fire, 1975, And Strange at Ecbatan the Trees, 1976, A Little Knowledge, 1977, Stolen Faces, 1977, Catacomb Years, 1979, Transfigurations, 1979, Eyes of Fire, 1980, No Enemy But Time, 1982 (Nebula award), Blooded Arachne, 1982, Who Made Stevie Crye?, 1984, One Winter in Eden, 1984, Ancient of Days, 1985, Close Encounters with the Deity, 1986, Philip K. Dick is Dead, Alas, 1987, The Secret Ascension, 1987, Unicorn Mountain, 1988, Emphatically Not SF, Almost, 1990, Count Geiger's Blues, 1992, Brittle Innings, 1994, At The City Limits of Fate, 1996, (novella) Blue Kansas Sky, 2000; author: (with Ian Watson) (novels) Under Heaven's Bridge, 1981, short stories; author: (under pen name Philip Lawson with Paul Di Filippo) Would It Kill You to Smile?, 1998; co-author: Muskrat Courage, 2000; editor: 3 Nebula award anthologies (Nebula awards 23, 1988, Nebula awards 24, 1990, Nebula awards 25, 1991), (anhtology) Light Years and Dark, 1984 (Locus award Best Anthology, 1984); co-editor (with Ian Watson): (anthology) Changes, 1983. Home and Office: PO Box 646 Pine Mountain GA 31822-0646 E-mail: mlbishop@juno.com.

BISHOP, OLIVER RICHARD, retired state official; b. El Dorado, Kans., Dec. 5, 1928; s. Oliver Harrison and Hazel May (Garabrandt) B.; m. Fuyo Oyake, Aug. 14, 1959; children: Lisa Naomi, Rachel Eri. BS in Pub. Adminstrn. magna cum laude, U. So. Calif., 1963; MS in Econs cum laude, U. S.D., 1971. Cert. planner, office automation profl., assisted housing mgr. Commd. 2d lt. USAF, 1956, advanced through grades to maj., 1966, ret., 1971; city mgr. City of Slater, Mo., 1971-73, City of Highland, Ill., 1973-76, City of Napoleon, Ohio, 1976-77; village mgr. Village of Westmont, Ill., 1977-85; revenue and fiscal advisor State of Ill., Chgo., 1985-99. Planning cons. Bishop's Cons. Services, Westmont, Ill., 1985—. Precinct committeeman Rep. Ctrl. com., Dupage County, Ill., 1987-88; candidate for County Bd. Dupage County Dist. 3, 1988; com. chmn. Westmont Planning Commn., 1986-95, 97—; bd. dirs. T.E.A.C.H., Inc., I-Care, Inc. Mem.: Inst. Cert Planners, Am. Planning Assn., Intertel, Mensa, Shriners, Masons, Elks, Omicron Delta Epsilon (pres. Lambda chpt.), Pi Sigma Alpha. Avocations: philately, photography.

BISHOP, PAUL LESLIE, civil and environmental engineering educator, environmental engineering consultant; b. Hyannis, Mass., Nov. 27, 1945; s. Paul Leslie and Victoria (Caisse) B.; m. Pamela Joan Neher, Mar. 30, 1949; children: Andrew Paul, Amanda Marie. BSCE, Northeastern U., 1968; MS in Environ. Engring., Purdue U., 1970, PhD, 1972. Registered profl. engr., N.H.; diplomate Am. Acad. Environ. Engrs. Environ. engr. Metcalf & Eddy, Inc., Boston, 1968; sanitarian Tippecanoe County, Ind., 1971-72; asst. prof. U. N.H., Durham, 1972-76, assoc. prof., chmn. dept. civil engring., 1976-82, prof. civil engring., 1982-87; environ. engring. cons. Durham, 1972-88; William Thomas prof., head dept. civil and environ. engring. U. Cin., 1988-93, Schneider prof. environ. engring., 1993—, assoc. dean engring. for rsch., 2000—. Vis. prof. Heriot-Watt U., Scotland, 1980, Tech. U. Denmark, Lyngby, 1986-87. Author: Marine Pollution and Its Control, 1983, Pollution Prevention: Fundamentals and Practice, 2000; co-author: Stabilization/Solidification, 1994; contbr. articles to profl. jours.; patentee in field. Bd. dirs. N.H. Solid Waste Mgmt. Bd., 1981-87, Lee Zoning Bd. Adjustment, N.H., 1981-86; chmn. Lee Planning Bd., 1975-80; mem. Durham/U. N.H. Sewer Policy Com., 1979-87, Gov.'s Task Force Waste Minimization, Ohio, 1989-92; mem. planning adv. com. Anderson Twp., Ohio, 1991-97, devel. adv. com., 1998-99. Faculty fellow ASTM, 1984; Grantee, NSF, EPA, NOAA, NIH, others. Mem. ASCE, Internat. Assn. Water Quality, Am. Acad. Environ. Engrs., Water Environ. Fedn., Assn. Environ. Engring. Profs. (pres. 1992-93), Sigma Xi. Democrat. Roman Catholic. Avocations: woodworking, reading, hiking. E-mail: Paul.Bishop@uc.edu.

BISHOP, RAND, retired humanities educator; b. Lansing, Mich., Feb. 3, 1933; s. David Rand and Myra Lu (Deacon) B.; 1 child, Andrew Nelson. BA, U. Mich., 1954, MA, 1961; cert., Fgn. Svc. Inst., 1964; PhD, Mich. State U., 1970. Cultural affairs officer USIA, Lomé, Togo, 1964-66, acting pub. affairs officer, 1965-66; asst. prof. Calif. State U., Sacramento, 1966-69, Mich. State U., East Lansing, 1970-71; prof. SUNY, Oswego, 1971-95; ret., 1995. Scholar-in-residence Fulbright program USIA, Washington, 1983-84; Fulbright prof. U. Nat. du Gabon, Libreville, 1974-75; vis. prof. McGill U., Montreal, Que., Can., 1974, U. Fla., Gainesville, 1979. Author: African Literature, African Critics: The Forming of Critical Standards, 1947-66, 88; contbr. articles to profl. jours., poems, short stories, to lit. mags. Fellow NEH, UCLA, 1978. Avocation: poetry. Mailing: SUNY Dept English Oswego NY 13126

BISHOP, ROB, congressman; b. Kaysville, UT, July 13, 1951; m. Jeralynn Hansen; 5 children. BA, U. Utah. Chmn. Utah State Rep. Party, 1997—2002; mem. U.S. Ho. Reps. from 1st Utah dist., 2003—. Office: 124 Cannon Ho Office Bldg Washington DC 20515-4401*

BISHOP, ROBERT, former political organization administrator, secondary school educator; Teacher Box Elder High School, Brigham City, Utah, 1974—; mem. Utah Ho. Reps, 1979-94, minority leader, 1990-92, spkr., 1992-94, contract lobbyist, 1995—; state chmn. Utah Rep. Party, 1997—2001. Mem. Utah Speech Arts Assn., 1975-87, chmn., 1981-84; mem. Utah State Ctrl. Com., 1992—; co-founder, mem. exec. bd. Western States Coalition, 1994—; chmn. Utah State Convention, 1990, chmn. Rules, Parliamentarian, 1996-97; mem. Rep. Nat. Com. Western State Chmn. Assn., 1997—. Mem. Brigham City Hist. Preservation Com., Brigham City Heritage Alliance Com.; chmn. Brigham City Cmty. Theater; Rep. candidate for Congress 1st Utah dist. Office: PO Box 2002 Brigham City UT 84302-1101

BISHOP, ROBERT CALVIN, pharmaceutical company executive; b. LA, Jan. 13, 1943; s. Harold Eames and Mary Frances (Allen) B.; m. Susan Elizabeth Ogden, Nov. 18, 1966; children: John Ogden, James Allen, Bryan Hutchings. AB in Psychology, U. So. Calif., 1966, PhD in Biochemistry, 1976; MBA, U. Miami, 1981. Rsch. assoc. Hyland Labs., Glendale, Calif., 1966-69; cons. L.A., 1970-75; program mgr. Am. Hosp. Supply Corp., Glendale, 1976-78, rsch. dir. Dade div. Miami, Fla., 1978-81, v.p. Evanston, Ill., 1981-85; pres. Allergan Med. Optics, Irvine, Calif., 1986-88; sr. v.p. Allergan Inc., Irvine, 1989; pres. Allergan Pharmaceuticals, Irvine, 1989-91, Allergan Therapeutics Group, 1991-92; pres., CEO, dir. AutoImmune, Inc., Lexington, Mass., 1992—. Bd. dirs. MFS/Sun Life Series Trust & Compass Accts., Caliper Tech. Corp., Optobionics Corp., Millipore Corp. Contbr. articles to profl. jours.; patentee in field. Bd. dirs. Eye Bank Assn. Am., Washington, 1988-90, Amyotropic Lateral Sclerosis Assn., LA, 1984-87. With USAR, 1963—69. Mem. Annandale Golf Club (Pasadena, Calif.). Republican. Presbyterian. Avocation: golf. Home: 1199 Madia St Pasadena CA 91103-1961 Office: AutoImmune Inc 1199 Madia St Pasadena CA 91103

BISHOP, ROBERT CHARLES, architect, metals and minerals company executive; b. Butte, Mont., June 6, 1929; s. Lester Farragut and Helen Katherine (Bauman) B.; m. B. Jean Rausch, June 29, 1957; children: Desta Fawn Bishop O'Connor, Valerie Dawn Magno. BS in Gen. Engring., Mont. State U., 1958, BArch., 1960. Assoc. architect various firms, Mont., 1960-64; owner, architect R.C. Bishop & Assocs., Butte, Great Falls and Missoula, Mont., 1965-69; owner, chief exec. officer Val-Desta 4M, Butte, 1980—, Val-Desta Mines and Minerals, Louisville, Ky., 1985—; prin. Archtl. Assocs., 1969—. Chief exec. officer, pres. Cove-Lock Log Home Mfrs., Inc., Butte, 1968-72, Busy Beaver Enterprises, Great Falls, 1968-72, New Horizon Homes, Missoula, 1968-72; asst. contracts adminstr. Davy-McKee Constrn. Engrs., Butte, 1982-83. Advisor, Kiwanis, Jaycees, Nat. Res., 1960-72, Am. Legion, 1976. With U.S. Army, 1953-55. Named One of 2,000 Men of Achievement Melrose Press, 1970, 73,. Mem. Internat. Platform Assn., Nat. Hist. Soc. (founding assoc. 1971), Elk Bow Hunting Club (bugle tchr. 1970-84), Butte Mulitlist Club (real estate tchr. 1978-84), Nat. Coun. Archtl. Registeration Bds. (registered architect seismic design 1965—). Presbyterian. Achievements include research in hydraulic trompe technology to retrofit existing hydroelectric generation in a Co-generation format to increase electrical production performance, to reduce fuel consumption and reduce particulate air emissions; research in contaminated waste-water remediation; development of radial dihedral stressed skin roof lens system; developed an additive to rejuvinate (acid-lead) terminally discharged batteries. Home and Office: 1008 W Galena St Butte MT 59701-1420 E-mail: montinfo@aol.com.

BISHOP, ROBERT LYLE, economist, educator; b. St. Louis, June 4, 1916; s. Lyle Austin and Helen (Craden) B.; m. Joan Frances Fiss, Sept. 12, 1942 (dec.). AB, Harvard, 1937, MA, 1942, PhD, 1949; postgrad., Princeton, 1938-39. Instr. econs. Harvard, 1939-42; mem. faculty Mass. Inst. Tech., 1942—, successively instr., asst. prof., asso. prof., 1942-57, prof. econs., 1957-86, prof. econs. emeritus, 1986—, head dept. econs. and social sci., 1958-65; dean Sch. Humanities and Social Scis., 1964-73. Vis. lectr. Harvard; vis. prof. Brandeis U. Mem. Am. Econ. Assn., Econometric Soc., Am. Acad. Arts and Scis., Phi Beta Kappa. Home: 27 Amherst Rd Wellesley MA 02482-6611

BISHOP, ROBERT MILTON, former stock exchange official; b. Elmira, N.Y., June 5, 1921; s. Milton W. and Florence E. (Crofutt) B.; m. Anne Selene Rowan, Oct. 30, 1943; children: Donald M., Anne Selene (Mrs. Donald R. Bennett), Elizabeth M. (Mrs. Thomas H. Speed), Robert Milton, Regina J.M. (Mrs. David P. Bergeland), Rowan J.S. AB, Union Coll., Schenectady, 1943; AM, Trinity Coll., Hartford, Conn., 1955. Asst. dir. pub. relations Union Coll., Schenectady, 1945-47; dir. pub. relations Trinity Coll., 1947-55; mem. staff N.Y. Stock Exchange, 1955-86. Dir. dept. mem. firms liaison, asst. dir. dept. mem. firms, 1961-63, v.p., assoc. dir. dept. mem. firms, 1963-65, v.p., dir. dept. mem. firms, 1965-73, sr. v.p. mem. firm regulation and surveillance group, 1973-81, sr. v.p. regulatory svcs. group, 1982-84, sr. v.p. regulatory quality rev. and long-range planning, 1984-86; cons. Lloyds of London, USAID, World Bank, Capital Markets Authorities and Stock Exchs. of Bulgaria, Dominican Republic, Egypt, Jamaica, Kazakhstan, Kenya, Hungary, Morocco, Pakistan, Serbia, Siberia, Singapore, Slovenia, Sri Lanka, Tunisia, Uganda. Author booklets, securities tng. manuals, and model basic rules for a stock exch. Trustee Cathedral Symphony at Cathedral Sacred Heart, Newark, 1984-92, Union Coll., 1989-93. With USAF, 1943-45. Mem.: India House, Stock Exchange Luncheon, Mohawk. Episcopalian. Home: 16 Heritage Ln Scotch Plains NJ 07076-2420

BISHOP, RUTH ANN, coloratura soprano, voice educator; b. Homewood, Ill., Feb. 21, 1942; d. George Bernard and Grace Mildred (Hoke) Riddle; m. John Allen Reinhardt, June 9, 1962 (div. 1975); children: Laura, Jonathon; m. Merrill Edward Bishop, Aug. 16, 1975; stepchildren: Mark, Lynn. BS in Music Edn., U. Ill., 1962; M of Music in Voice, Cath. U. Am., 1972; postgrad., U. Md., 1975. Music tchr. Prince Georges County (Md.) Schs., 1963-71, Yamaha Music Co., College Park, Md., 1971-73; voice tchr. Prince Georges Community Coll., Largo, Md., 1972-75, U. Md., College Park, 1975; profl. lectr. voice Chgo. Mus. Coll. Roosevelt U., 1977-82; tchr. voice McHenry County Coll., Crystal Lake, Ill., 1978-97; instr. voice Elgin (Ill.) C.C., 1981-97; pvt. voice tchr. Crystal Lake, 1975-97, Charlottesville, Va., 1997—; tchr. chorus, music and drama Burley Mid. Sch., Charlottesville, Va., 1997; asst. prof. music Piedmont Va. C.C., 1998—. Dir. music Epworth United Meth. Ch., Elgin, 1984-86, Cherub choir 1st Congl. Ch., Crystal Lake, 1986-88; mem. Camerata Singers, Lake Forest, 1988, Arts Chorale of Elgin Choral Union; performer, vocal dir. Woodstock (Ill.) Mus. Theatre Co., 1983-97; soprano soloist Internat. Band Festival, Besana Brianza, Italy, 1993; pvt. voice tchr., Charlottesville, Va., 1997—. Soprano soloist, Oratorio- The Psalms of David, 1986, opera, The Light of the Eye, 1985-86, Children's Day at the Opera, Washington, 1972, U.S. Navy Band, The White House, 1969; soloist with Crystal Lake Cmty. Choir and Band, 1987-97, 1st Congl. Ch., 1975-97, also others; performer Heritage Repertory Theatre, Charlottesville, Va., 1998, 99. Bd. mem. Opera Soc. Charlottesville, 1998-2000. Ill. State scholar, 1959. Mem. Nat. Assn. Tchrs. Singing (chpt. rec. sec. 1984-86, bd. mem. Chgo. chpt. 1995-97), Music Tchrs. Nat. Assn., Sigma Alpha Iota, Pi Kappa Lambda, Kappa Delta. Methodist. Avocations: travel, camping, hiking, bicycling, wildlife. Home: 1363 Wimbledon Way Charlottesville VA 22901-0635 E-mail: rambishop@aol.com.

BISHOP, SANFORD DIXON, JR., congressman; b. Mobile, Ala., Feb. 4, 1947; s. Sandford and Minne Dixon; m. Vivian Creighton. BA in Political Sci., Morehouse Coll., 1968; JD, Emory U., 1971. Ptnr. Bishop & Buckner, P.C., Columbus, Ga., 1972—96; mem. Ga. Ho. of Reps. from 94th Dist., 1977—90, Ga. State Senate, 1991—92, U.S. Congress from 2d Ga. Dist., 1993—; mem. agrl. com., intelligence com. Del. Dem. Nat. Conv. 1980, 84, 88; mem. Agrl. Com., Vets. Affairs Com.; chmn. Ga. legis. black caucus. Fellowship, 1971-72; named Man of the Yr. Men's Progressive Club Columbus, Ga., 1977, Black Georgian of the Yr., 1983, Most Influential Black Men in Ga.; recipient Outstanding Legis. award Ga. NOW, 1983-84, Legis. Svc. award, Ga. Mcpl. Assn., 1984, 86, Friend of the Children award Child Adv. Coalition. Mem. ABA, Nat. Bar Assn., Ga. Bar Assn., Ala. Bar Assn., Am. Judicature Soc., Shriners, Masons (32 degree), Phi Delta Phi, Pi Sigma Alpha, Kappa Alpha Psi. Democrat. Baptist. Office: US Ho of Reps 2429 Rayburn Ho Office Bldg Washington DC 20515-1002 also: Albany Towers 235 W Roosevelt Ave Ste 216 Albany GA 31701-2374 Fax: (202) 225-2203. E-mail: bishop.email@mail.house.gov.*

BISHOP, SID GLENWOOD, union official; b. Gladehill, Va., Nov. 11, 1923; s. Clarence Glenwood and Lillian Helen (Onks) B. Grad., U.S. Naval Trade Sch., 1942; cert. in labor rels., Concord Coll., Athens, W.Va., 1961. Telegraph operator Virginian R.R., 1946-47, C & O R.R., 1947-62; local chmn. Order R.R. Telegraphers, 1960-62; gen. chmn. C & O-Virginian R.R.'s, 1962-68; 2d v.p. Transp-Communication Employees Union, St. Louis, 1968-69; v.p. transp. com. divsn. Brotherhood Ry. and Airline Clks., Rockville, Md., 1969-73, asst. internat. v.p., 1973—. Mem. subcom. Labor Rsch. Adv. Coun., Dept. Labor, 1975, mem. com. on productivity, tech., growth Bur. Labor Statistics, 1975-77. With USN, 1941-46. Mem. AFL-CIO, Can. Labor Congress, Hunting Hills Homeowners Assn., VFW, Chantilly Nat. Golf and Country Club, Elks, Masons, K.T., Shriners. Home and Office: 676 NE 28th Ave Okeechobee FL 34972-3323 E-mail: bishlite@strato.net.

BISHOP, SIDNEY WILLARD, lawyer; b. Denver, Oct. 28, 1926; s. Sidney W. and Helen (Marihugh) B.; m. Betty Lou Dolan, May 10, 1947; children—Linda, Thomas, Nancy, Joan, Ann, Mary, Elizabeth, Sidney Willard III, Jane. BS, Regis U., Denver, 1949; JD, U. Denver, 1950. Bar: Colo. 1950, Calif. 1958. With January & Yegge, Denver, 1949-50; dep. dist. atty. Cheyenne County, Colo., 1951-56; pvt. practice Cheyenne Wells, Colo., 1950-56; with Prudential Ins. Co. Am., Los Angeles, 1956-61, 64-68; asst. counsel law dept., 1958-61; asst. gen. solicitor, 1964-66; dir. govt. relations, 1966-68; gen. counsel Am. Ins. Assn., N.Y.C., 1968-70; with firm Svenson & Garvin, Van Nuys, Calif., 1970-73; sr. v.p., gen. counsel Beneficial Standard Life Ins. Co., 1973-91; of counsel Adams, Duque, L.A., 1991-96, Beckman, Davis, Smith & Ruddy, L.A., 1996—. Confidential asst. to postmaster gen. U.S., 1961, asst. postmaster gen. bur. facilities, 1962-63, dep. postmaster gen., 1963-64 So. Calif. vice chmn. Statewide Water Devel. Com., 1959-60. Served with USNR, 1944-46. Office: 11355 W Olympic Blvd Ste 300 Los Angeles CA 90064-1614

BISHOP, SUE MARQUIS (INA SUE MARQUIS BISHOP), dean, psychiatric and mental health nurse educator, researcher; b. Charleston, W.Va., Sept. 30, 1939; d. Harold Edwin and Ina Mabel (Walkup) Marquis; m. Randal Young Bishop, Feb. 27, 1960; children: Jon Marquis, Heather Suzanne. RN, Norton Infirmary Sch. Nursing, 1960; BSN, Murray State U., 1963; MSN, Ind. U., 1967, PhD, 1983. RN, Ky., Ind., Fla., N.C. Ind. staff nurse psychiatry Norton Infirmary, Louisville, 1960-61; head nurse obstetrics, nursing supr. Murray (Ky.) Gen. Hosp., 1961-62; primary care nurse, crisis counselor infirmary Murray State U., 1962-63; staff nurse, clin. instr. Madison (Ind.) State Hosp., 1963-65; instr. through assoc. prof. Ind. U. Sch. Nursing, Indpls., 1967-89, developer child/adolescent psychiat., mental health nursing program, 1982-83, chairperson grad. dept., 1983-89; prof., asst. dean Coll. of Nursing U. South Fla., Tampa, 1989-91; dean Coll. Nursing U. N.C., Charlotte, 1992-95; dean U. N.C. Coll. of Nursing and Health Professions, Charlotte, 1995—, U. N.C. Coll. Health & Human Services, Charlotte, 2002—. Pvt. practice marital and family therapy, 1975-89; cons. in field. Founding editor-in-chief Jour. of Child and Adolescent Psychiatric and Mental Health Nursing, 1987-91; contbr. articles to profl. jours. Bd. dirs. Carolinas blood svcs. region ARC, 1997-2002, chmn. bd. dirs., 2000—. NIHM trainee Ind. U., 1965-67, USPHS profl. nurse trainee Ind. U., 1977-78; recipient Youth Advocacy award Ind. Advs. for Child Psychiat. Nursing, 1987, Disting. Svc. award Ind. U. Sch. Nursing Alumni Assn., 1989, Nat. Youth Advocacy award Advs. for Child Psychiat. Nursing, 1990, Disting. Alumni award Ind. U. sch. Edn., 2000. Fellow Am. Acad. Nursing; mem. ARC (bd. dirs. 1997—), ANA., Psychiat. Mental Health Nursing Coun., Soc. for Edn. and Rsch. in Psychiat. Mental Health Nursing (pres. 1988-90), Am. Assn. Marital and Family Therapy, So. Nursing Rsch. Soc., So. Piedmont Alzheimer's Assn. (bd. dirs. 1999-2000), New South Hospice of Charlotte and Lincoln County (bd. dirs. 1995—, chair 2002--), Sigma Theta Tau. E-mail: isbishop@email.uncc.edu.

BISHOP, SUSAN KATHARINE, executive search company executive; b. Palm Beach, Fla., Apr. 3, 1946; d. Warner Bader Bishop and Katharine Sue (White) McLennan; m. Robert Uchitel, Dec. 27, 1973 (div. 1979); 1 child, Rachel. BA, Briarcliff Coll., 1968; MBA, Fordham U., 1985. Actress, N.Y.C., 1968-72; producer, hostess Sta. KIMO-TV, Anchorage, 1972-74; dir. programming Visions Pay TV, 1974-79; recruiter Joe Sullivan & Assocs., N.Y.C., 1980-82; prin. Johnson, Smith & Knisely, 1982-88; ptnr. Schmitt Bishop Tolette, N.Y.C., 1989-91; pres. Bishop Ptnrs., Ltd., N.Y.C., 1991—. Mem. Cable TV Adminstrn. and Mktg. Soc., Women in Cable, Assn. Exec. Search Cons. (bd. dirs.). Office: Bishop Ptnrs 708 3rd Ave New York NY 10017-4201

BISHOP, THOMAS WALTER, French language and literature educator; b. Vienna, Feb. 21, 1929; came to U.S., 1940, naturalized, 1944; s. Martin M. and Katherine (Abeles) B.; m. Muriel Hausman, June 30, 1950 (div. 1967); children: Jeffrey Bishop (dec.), Katherine; m. Helen Gary, Dec. 15, 1967 (div. 1998). AB, NYU, 1950; AM, U. Md., 1951; postgrad., U. Paris, 1950-51; PhD, U. Calif., Berkeley, 1957. Asst. in French U. Calif., Berkeley, 1951-55; instr. NYU, 1956-59, asst. prof., 1959-61, assoc. prof., 1961-64, prof., 1964—, Florence Gould prof. French lit., 1975—, dir. La Maison Française, 1959-64, chmn. dept. French, 1966—2003. Chmn. Ctr. for French Civilization and Culture, 1978—; vis. prof. Ecole des Hautes Etudes en Scis. Sociales, Paris, 1980, 87, 94, 99, Harvard U., 1995. Author: Pirandello and the French Theater, 1960, rev. edit., 1970, L'Avant-Garde Théâtrale: French Theater Since 1950, 1970, rev. edit., 1975, Huis Clos de Jean-Paul Sartre, 1975, Beckett, 1976, 2d edit., 1985, Le Passeur d'Océan, 1989, From the Left Bank, 1997; co-editor: L'Amérique des Français, 1992; editor: Les Anti-Américanismes, 2001, Remembering Roland Barthes. Trustee French Inst.-Alliance Française NY, 1971-2001, Lycée Français, NYC, 1989-99; bd. dirs. French-Am. Found., 1976-86. Decorated chevalier Légion d'Honneur, commandeur Order Nat. du Mérite, officier Ordre des Arts et Lettres, officier Palmes Académiques; recipient Obie award, 1979, Grand Prix de l'Académie Française, 1993; Fulbright fellow, 1965. Fellow N.Y. Inst. Humanities; mem. MLA, PEN, Beckett Soc. (pres. 1986-88). Office: NYU 19 University Pl New York NY 10003-4556 E-mail: tom.bishop@nyu.edu.

BISHOP, TILMAN MALCOLM, retired state legislator, college administrator; b. Colorado Springs, Jan. 1, 1933; m. Pat Bishop, 1952; 1 son, Barry Alan. BA, MA, U. No. Colo. Adminstr., dir. student svcs. Mesa State Coll., Grand Junction, Colo., 1962-94; mem., pres. pro tem Colo. Senate, 1971-99, ret., 1999. Bd. dirs. Rocky Mountain Pub. Broadcasting TV, Colo. Duck Stamp Commn. World series com. Nat. Jr. Coll. Baseball; elected commr. Mesa County, 2002—. With U.S. Army. Mem. Elks, Lions. Republican. Methodist. Avocations: fishing, small game hunting. Home: 2255 Piazza Way Grand Junction CO 81506 E-mail: tilmanmb@bresnan.net.

BISHOP, TIMOTHY H. congressman; b. Southhampton, NY, June 1, 1950; m. Kathryn Bishop; children: Molly, Meghan. AB, Holy Cross Coll.; MPA, Long Island Univ., 1981. Provost L.I. U., Southampton, N.Y.; mem. U.S. Ho. Reps. from 1st N.Y. dist., 2003—. Office: 1133 Longworth Ho Office Bldg Washington DC 20515-3201*

BISHOP, VIRGINIA WAKEMAN, retired librarian and humanities educator, small business owner; b. Portland, Oreg., Dec. 28, 1927; d. Andrew Virgil and Letha Evangeline (Ward) Wakeman; m. Clarence Edmund Bishop, Aug. 23, 1953; children: Jean Marie Bishop Johnson, Marilyn Joyce. BA, Bapt. Missionary Tng. Sch., Chgo., 1949, Linfield Coll., McMinnville, Oreg., 1952, MEd, 1953; MA in Librarianship, U. Wash., 1968. Ch. worker Univ. Bapt. Ch., Seattle, 1954-56, 59-61, pre-sch. tchr. parent coop presch., 1965-66; libr. N.W. Coll., Kirkland, Wash., 1968-69; undergrad. libr. U. Wash., Seattle, 1970; libr., instr. Seattle Cen. Community Coll., 1970-91; co-owner small bus. Seaside, Oreg., 1972—. Leader Totem coun. Girl Scouts U.S., 1962-65; pres. Wedgwood Sch. PTA, Seattle, 1964-65; chair 46th Dist. Dem. Orgn., Seattle, 1972-73; precinct com. officer Dem. Party, 1968-88, 96-2000; candidate Wash. State Legislature, Seattle, 1974, 80; bd. dirs. Univ. Bapt. Children's Ctr., 1989-95, chair, 1990-95; vol. Ptnrs. in Pub. Edn., 1992-96. Recipient Golden Acorn

award Wedgwood Elem. Sch., 1966. Mem. AAUW of Seaside, LWV of Seattle (2d v.p. 1994-96), U. Wash. Grad. Sch. Libr. and Info. Sci. Alumni Assn. (1st v.p. 1986-87, pres. 1987-88). Baptist. Avocations: swimming, walking, reading. Home: 3032 NE 87th St Seattle WA 98115-3529 Office: 300 5th Ave Seaside OR 97138

BISHOP, WANDA CAROLINE, geriatrics nurse, medical/surgical nurse; b. Newark, July 18, 1937; d. Paul and Karolina (Werynska) Serafin; children: Carol Jean, Steven Michael; m. Eric J. Bishop, July 6, 1981. BSN, U. Cen. Okla., 1983, MEd in Gerontology, 1989. Cert. med. surg. nurse, gerontol. nurse. Med. office mgr. Henry J. Pearce, M.D., Edmond, Okla., 1969-81; staff nurse VA Med. Ctr., Oklahoma City, 1983-86; owner, adminstr. HomeCare Nursing Svcs., Inc., Edmond, 1985-89; dir. nursing Okla. Christian Home, Edmond, 1993-95, nurse educator, 1995—2000. Mem.: Okla. Gerontol. Nursing Assn., Ctrl. State U. Alumni Assn., Sigma Phi Omega, Alphi Chi. Avocations: square dancing, theatre. Home: 13317 Northview Dr Oklahoma City OK 73142-4308 E-mail: wandabishop@yahoo.com.

BISHOP, WILLIAM PETER, science administrator, management consultant; b. Lakewood, Ohio, Jan. 18, 1940; s. William Hall and Ethel Laverle (Evans) B.; m. Sarah Gilbert, Sept. 1, 1963. BA in Chemistry with honors (Nat. Merit scholar), Coll. Wooster, Ohio, 1962; PhD (NDEA fellow), Ohio State U., 1967. Resident research assoc. Ohio State U., 1967-69; mem. staff Sandia Labs., Albuquerque, 1969-75; head nuclear waste program NRC, Washington, 1975-78; dep. dir. environ. observation div. NASA, 1978-81, dep. dir. life scis. div., 1981-83; dep. asst. adminstr. satellites NOAA, 1983-85, acting asst. adminstr. satellites and info. services, 1985-87; v.p. SAIC, Washington, 1987-89; v.p. for rsch. Desert Rsch. Inst., Las Vegas, Nev., 1989-94; assigned to U.S. Dept. of Energy, 1995-99; pres. B-plus, Inc., Paonia, Colo., 1999—. Mem. Nat. Acad. Com. Earth Studies, 1989-91, Task Group on Priorities in Space Rsch., 1990-94; chair Adv. Commn. on Geoscis. NSF, 1994-97. Author articles in field. Trustee Keystone (Colo.) Ctr., 1986-95, Nev. Devel. Authority, 1989-95, Univ. Corp. for Atmospheric Rsch., 1991-97; bd. dirs. Opportunities Industrialization Ctrs., Albuquerque, 1974-75, Cave Rsch. Found., 1967-74; dir. Western Slope Environ. Resources Coun., 1999-. Recipient Meritorious Service award NRC, 1977; Spaceship Earth award NASA, 1981; Meritorious Service award U.S. Dept. Commerce, 1983, Spl. Act of Svc. award, U.S. Dept. Energy, 1999. Fellow Nat. Speleological Soc. (conservation editor bull. 1974-78), Am. Astron. Soc. (v.p. tech. 1987-88); mem. AAAS, Am. Geophys. Union, AIAA, Am. Meteorol. Soc., Am. Nuc. Soc., Sigma Xi, Phi Lambda Upsilon.

BISHOP, WILLIAM WADE, advertising executive; b. Mt. Vernon, N.Y., Apr. 17, 1939; s. Kenneth Farrington and Dorothea (Renz) B.; m. Jacqueline Kenton, May 21, 1966; children: William Jr., Christopher. BA, Ohio Wesleyan U., 1961. Account exec. Ogilvy & Mather, Grey, BBDO, N.Y.C., 1964-72; v.p. Ted Bates, N.Y.C., 1972-74; category mgr. Gen. Foods Corp., White Plains, N.Y., 1974-79; mng. dir. Mktg. Corp. Am., Westport, Conn., 1979-80; exec. v.p. MCA Advt., N.Y.C., 1980-84, pres., chief exec. officer, 1984-86, MCA Communications Group, 1986-89; pres. Ally & Gargano, N.Y.C., 1986-89; chmn., chief exec. officer CHC Advt., 1989-92; CEO CHC Advt. and M.E.D. Comms., 1992—; pres., CEO Ryan Direct, Westport, Conn., 1992-94; dir. South Beach Beverages, 1995—; chmn., CEO Sierra Comms. Group, 1995-2001; COO South Beach Beverage Co., 1999-2001. Owner LI Lizards, Lacrosse; ptnr. Blue Buffalo Co., 2002, B Group, 2001—. Served with USMC, 1962-68. Mem. Salem Golf Club. Republican. Congregationalist. Avocations: lacrosse, golf. Office: B Group 444 Danbury Rd Wilton CT 06897-4065

BISHOP, WILSIE SUE, dean, nursing educator; b. Lynchburg, Va., Sept. 9, 1948; d. William Curtis and Arye (Holmes) Paulette; m. Paul A. Bishop; 1 child, Joseph. BSN, Va. Commonwealth U., 1970; MS in Edn., U. So. Calif., 1976, MPA, 1987, DPA, 1989. RN, Tenn. Staff nurse in cardiac surgery ICU Med. Coll. Va., Richmond, 1970-71; assoc. instr. Western Ky. U., Bowling Green, 1971-74; clin. nurse 97th Army Gen. Hosp., Frankfurt, Germany, 1974-76; from asst. to assoc. prof. East Tenn. State U., Johnson City, 1978-83, asst. v.p. for acad. affairs, 1983-89, assoc. v.p. for health affairs, 1989-94, dean, prof., 1994—. Contbr. articles to profl. jours. including Pediat. Nursing, Am. Jour. Maternal-Child Nursing; prodr. (videotape) Factors which Promote Successful Breastfeeding, 1978. Bd. dirs. Tenn. Women's Econ. Coun., Nashville, 1998-2002; mem. Gateway Commn., Kingsport, 1996-2001; 2d v.p., fin. com. chair Appalachian Girl Scouts Coun., Johnson City, 1992-94; chairperson Appalachian chpt. Nat. Found. March of Dimes, Johnson City, 1991-92. Recipient Outstanding Nurse Alumna awrad Med. Coll. Va., 1980, Altrusa Hon. for Women and Industry Kingsport Altrusa Club, 1990, A.D. Williams scholarship award for Outstanding Grad. Student Med. Coll. Va., 1978. Mem. So. Assn. Colls. and Schs. (accreditation site vis. 1982—), Assn. Schs. Allied Health Professions (chair edn. com. 2000-01), So. Assn. Allied Health Deans Acad. Health Ctrs. (sec. 1998-2001, 2001-2004), Tenn. Pub. Health Assn., Rotary (Paul Harris fellow 1992). Presbyterian. Avocations: reading, tennis, travel, gardening. Home: 1421 Linville St Kingsport TN 37664 Office: East Tenn State U PO Bxo 70623 Johnson City TN 37614 Fax: (423) 439-5238. E-mail: bishopws@mail.etsu.edu.

BISHOP-GRAHAM, BARBARA, secondary school educator, journalist; b. Angwin, Calif., Apr. 22, 1941; d. Will Francis and Esther Clara (Blissérd) Bishop; children: Gregory Mark, Steven Bishop. BA in Journalism, BA in English, BA in Art History, BFA in Painting and Drawing, U. Hawaii, 1975; nat. cert. in journalism, Kans. State U., 1994; MA in Tech. Curriculum & Instrn., Calif. State U., Sacramento, 1999. Cert. tchr., Hawaii. Photography instr., art tchr. Hawaii Sch. for Girls, Honolulu, 1974-76; substitute tchr. English State Dept. Edn., Oahu, 1977-78; English and grammar instr. Hawaii Sch. for Bus., Honolulu, 1979-80; media dir., exec. asst., historian Oriental Treasures and Points West, Honolulu, 1981-82; legal asst. Goodsill, Anderson, Quinn, Honolulu, 1983-84; lang. arts and photography tchr. Lodi (Calif.) H.S., 1984-88, writing and lang. arts tchr., 1988-93, creative writing tchr., 1989-99, journalism adviser, 1993-95, lang. arts tchr., 1993—, Brit. lit. tchr., 1995—; tchr. rhetoric and European lit., 2001—. Mem. curriculum coun. Lodi Unified Sch. Dist., 1989-92, 97-2000; liaison to PTSA Lodi H.S., 1991-92, mentor tchr., 1991-94; student literary mag. advisor Lodi H.S., 1989—. Sportswriter Oakland Tribune, 1957-60, Author Three Poems, 1998; contbr. articles to profl. publs. Fundraiser chmn. Big Bros. of Am., San Francisco, 1967; media dir. Clements (Calif.) Cmty. Cares, 1985-89. Recipient Edn. Contbn. award Masons 1988-92, 20th Century Achievement award Am. Biographical Inst., 1999; grantee Nat. Endowment of Arts, rsch. Japanese Lit. 1989; social rschr. grantee Brazil, U. So. Calif. grantee, 1992; grantee S. Joaquin County Office Edn., 1996-97; champion Hawaii State barrel racing, 1980. Mem. NEA, Calif. Tchrs. Assn. (Calif. state tchrs. coun. rep. 1996-97), Lodi Edn. Assn. (conf. fund chair 1989-97). Republican. Seventh-Day Adventist. Avocations: writing, dressage riding, growing roses. Office: Lodi HS 3 S Pacific Ave Lodi CA 95242-3020

BISHOPRIC, KARL, investment banker, real estate executive, advertising executive; b. Greensboro, N.C., Jan. 5, 1925; s. James Robert Karl and Frances (Farrell) B.; m. Rose Anne Straub, Mar. 4, 1944 (div. Jan. 1972); children—Robert Lewis, James Nelson (dec.), Bruce Graham; m. Carmen Deruth Dunlop, May 26, 1973. BA, U. N.C., 1945. With Houck & Co., Roanoke, Miami, Va., Fla., 1946-54, pres., 1948-54, Bishopric-Green-Fielden, Inc., Miami, N.Y.C., 1954-68, chmn. bd., 1968-73, Lando-Bishopric, Inc., 1973-74; chmn., dir. Advt. & Marketing Internat. Network, Inc., 1972-74; pres. Miami Nat. Bank, 1974-75; assoc. Oscar E. Dooly Assos., Inc., 1974-76; prin. 1st Equity Corp. of Fla., 1976-2000; pres. 1st Equity Properties, Inc., 1976-2000; v.p., dir. Fundamental Mgmt. Corp., 1986-89; pres. Swiss Atlantic Corp., 1999-2000; prin. William R. Hough & Co., Miami, 2001—. Pres. United Fund Dade County, 1967-68, trustee, 1963— ; chmn. Port Action Com., 1969-71; bd. dirs. Community TV Found. S. Fla., 1965-67, v.p., 1969-72; mem. citizens bd. U. Miami, 1968—, pres. citizens bd., 1982-83, trustee, 1983-85; bd. dirs. Econ. Soc. S. Fla., 1969-73, Urban Coalition Greater Miami, 1968-72, Fla. Philharmonic Orchestra Found., 1992-98, Miami Lighthouse for the Blind, 1993—, chmn. fin. com., 1994-98; bd. dirs. Urban League Greater Miami, 1956-65, pres., 1956-60; chmn. budget leaders conf. United Funds and Community Councils Am., 1968; trustee Lowe Art Mus., 1973-86. Served to lt. (j.g.) USNR, 1944-46. Recipient Printer's Ink Silver medal. Mem. Greater Miami C. of C. (dir. 1971-74, trustee 1976—), Alpha Delta Sigma, Beta Theta Pi. Home: 600 Biltmore Way Coral Gables FL 33134-7541 Office: William R Hough & Co Ste 2520 80 SW 8th St Miami FL 33130 E-mail: rbishopric@hough.com.

BISHOPRIC, SUSAN EHRLICH, public relations executive; b. NYC; AAS, Fashion Inst. Tech., 1965. Exec.-in-tng. Bloomingdales, Abraham & Strauss; merchandise coord. Seventeen mag.; publicity dir. Germaine Monteil Cosmetiques; account exec. Rowland Co., 1968-69, account supr., 1969-73, v.p., 1973-75, sr. v.p., creative dir., 1975-78, exec. v.p., 1979-81; pub. rels. dir. Susan Gilbert & Co., 1984-86; head pub. rels. divsn. Beber Silverstein & Ptnrs., 1986-89; founder, pres. Bishopric Agy., Coral Gables, Fla., 1989-99, NYC, 1999—. Office: The Bishopric Agy 185 E 85th St #9M New York NY 10028 E-mail: sbishopric@nyc.rr.com.

BISORDI, JOSEPH EDMUND, nephrologist, medical center administrator; b. Mt. Vernon, N.Y., Sept. 18, 1949; s. Edmund P. and Winifred (Martin) B.; m. Carol Ann Keimig, May 18, 1975; children: John Edmund, Kathryn Elizabeth. BA, Manhattan Coll., 1971; MD, Georgetown U., 1975. Diplomate Am. Bd. Internal Medicine with subspecialty in nephrology. Resident internal medicine Geisinger Med. Ctr., Danville, Pa., 1975-77, chief resident, 1977-78, assoc. nephrology, 1980-93, v.p. clin. rsch., 1987-96, dir. dept. nephrology, 1993-99, med. dir., 2002—; sr. v.p. Med. Informatics, 1996-2001, assoc. chief med. officer, 2001—; fellow nephrology Albert Einstein Coll. Medicine, Bronx, 1978-80; prof. clin. medicine Pa. U. Coll. Medicine, 1998—. Clin. assoc. prof. medicine Thomas Jefferson Med. Coll., Phila., 1989—; mem. med. rev. bd. End Stage Renal Disease Network #24, King of Prussia, Pa., 1986-88, med. rev. chair Network #4, Pitts., 1988-97; mem. forum, 1995-97. Contbr. articles to profl. jours. Pres. Timberwood Homeowner's Assn., Danville, 1988-92. Rsch. fellow Nat. Kidney Found., 1978-79. Fellow ACP; mem. Am. Soc. Hypertension, Am. Soc. Nephrology, Am. Soc. Transplant Physicians, Internat. Soc. Nephrology, Hosp. Info. and Mgmt. Sys. Soc., Applied Rsch. Ethics Nat. Assn. (pres. 1989). Office: Geisinger Medical Center Dept Nephrology Academy Ave Danville PA 17822-0001

BISPING, BRUCE HENRY, photojournalist; b. St. Louis, Apr. 27, 1953; s. Harry and Marian B.; m. Joan M. Berg, Sept. 29, 1984; children: Erin Elizabeth Giovanna, Trevor Thomas. B.J., U. Mo., Columbia, 1975. Summer intern Cleve. Press, 1974, The Virginian/Pilot-Ledger Star, Norfolk, 1975; staff photojournalist Mpls. Tribune, 1975-82, Mpls. Star and Tribune, 1982—. Freelance photographer Black Star Pub. Co., N.Y.C., 1975—, Sporting News, St. Louis, Underwater USA, Business Week, Time, U.S. News World Report, Newsweek, Am. Illustrated, N.Y. Times, Los Angeles Times, other nat. and local publs.; past mem. faculty Mo. Photojournalism Workshop. Mem. Nat. Press Photographers Assn. (assoc. dir. Region 5 1981-82, dir. Region 5 1983-86, rep. to exec. com. 1984, Nat. Newspaper Photographer of Year award 1976, Regional Newspaper Photographer of Year award 1977, citation for dedication to profession 1985), Twin Cities News Photographers Assn. (pres. 1979-80), Profl. Assn. Diving Instrs. (open water instr. rating), Oldsmobile Club of Am. (bd. dirs. Minn. Club, news editor). Office: Mpls Tribune 6020 View Ln Edina MN 55436-1827 E-mail: bruceb65@citilink.com.

BISS, PAUL MARTIN, music educator; b. DeKalb, Ill., Sept. 2, 1944; s. Kurt and Raya Garbovsova Biss; m. Miriam Fried, June 29, 1969; children: Daniel, Jonathan. MusB, Ind. U., 1966; MusM, Juilliard Sch., 1968. Assoc. prof. Akron (Ohio) U., 1972—79; prof. music Ind. U., Bloomington, 1979—. Lectr. music Ind. U., Ft. Wayne, 1970—72; guest lectr. Rubin Acad. Music, Tel Aviv, 1977—78; mem. faculty Stearns Inst. Ravinia Festival, Chgo., 1994—. Vol. Big Bros. and Sisters, Bloomington, 2001—, abuse shelter, Bloomington, 1994. Office: Ind U Sch Music 300 N Jordan Ave #46 Bloomington IN 47405-1106 Office Fax: 812-332-7393. E-mail: biss@indiana.edu.

BISSADA, NABIL KADDIS, urologist, educator, researcher, author; b. Cairo, Sept. 2, 1938; s. Kaddis B. and Negma Bissada; m. Samia; children: Sally, Nancy, Mary, Amy, Andrew. MD, Cairo U., 1963. Diplomate Am. Bd. Urology. Intern Cairo Univ. Hosp., 1964-65; resident in urology Babelsharia Gen. Hosp., 1965-69; resident in urology U. N.C. Hosp., 1970-72, chief resident, 1972-73; asst. prof. urology U. Ark., 1973-77, assoc. prof., 1977-79; cons. urologist King Faisal Specialist Hosp. and Rsch. Ctr., Riyadh, Saudi Arabia, 1979-87; prof., chief urologic oncology Med. U. S.C., 1987—; chief urologic surgery Ralph H. Johnson Med. Ctr., 1987—2003; vice-chmn. dept. urology Med. U. S.C., 1999—2003; prof. urology U. Ark., Little Rock, 2003—, exec. vice chmn. Dept. Urology, 2003—; chief urology Ark. Children's Hosp., 2003—, dir. rsch., 2003—. Frequent spkr. to regional, nat. and internat. med. groups. Author: Lower Urinary Tract Function and Dysfunction: Diagnosis and Management, 1978; Pharmacology of the Urinary Tract and the Male Reproductive System, 1982; cons., guest editor several med. jours. and periodicals; sect. editor Archives of Andrology; bd. dirs. Internat. Edl. Bd., Arab J. Urol.; contbr. to hundreds of articles and book chpts.; pioneered several significant surgical and med. urologic treatment methods, developed the Charleston Pouch Technique for continent urinary diversion; conducted numerous local, nat., and internat. tchg. courses on urologic reconstructive techniques. Fellow ACS, Internat. Coll. Surgeons (co-chmn. divsn. urology U.S. sect. 1989-91, chmn. 1991-93); mem. Am. Urol. Assn.,, Egyptian-Am. Urol. Assn. (pres. 1990-92), Arab-Am. Urol. Assn. (pres. 1993-96), Carolina Urol. Assn. (pres. 1997-99), Soc. Internat. D'Urologie, Soc. Urologic Oncology, Urodynamic Soc., Soc. Urology and Engring., Sigma Xi. Office: Ark Children's Hosp Mail Slot 840 800 Marshall Street Little Rock AR 72202

BISSELL, BRENT JOHN, advertising and direct marketing executive; b. Dearborn, Mich., July 10, 1950; s. Ernest Ross and Virginia Jane (Pete) B.; m. Libby Schulak, Dec. 4, 1971; children: John, Sarah, Elizabeth, Daniel. BA, U. Toledo, 1971. Pres. Bissell Advt., Inc., Toledo, 1975—78; creative dir. Stark Bros. Nurseries & Orchards Co., Louisiana, Mo., 1979—80; divisional gen. mgr. Consumer Pub. Co., Canton, Ohio, 1980—82; mng. dir. D'Arcy Direct Mktg., Bloomfield Hills, Mich., 1982—85; v.p., mng. dir. Bozell Direct, Chgo., 1985—87; sr. v.p., gen. mgr. McCann-Erickson Direct, Troy, Mich., 1989—93; pres. Direct Target One, Minnetonka, Minn., 1993—. Lectr. in field; instr., bd. advisors Direct Mktg. Assn. Contbg. author: Direct Marketing Handbook, 2d edit., 1991, Next Step in Database Marketing: Consumer Guided Marketing, 1996. Mem. comms. bd. Nat. Assn. Congl. Chs., 1990-93; chair Folger Poetry Bd., 2002. Fellow Internat. Soc. of Strategic Mktg. (sr.); mem. SAR, Mayflower Descs., Masons.

BISSELL, GEORGE ARTHUR, architect; b. L.A., Jan. 31, 1927; s. George Arthur and Ruby Zoe (Moore) B.; m. Laurene Conlon, Nov. 21, 1947; children: Teresa Ann, Thomas Conlon, William George, Robert Anthony, Mary Catherine. BArch, U. So. Calif., 1953. Registered architect, Calif. Ptnr. Bissell Co., Covina, Calif., 1953-57, Bissell & Durquette, A.I.A., Pasadena, Calif., 1957-61; owner George Bissell, A.I.A., Laguna Beach, Calif., 1961-65; ptnr. Riley & Bissell, A.I.A., Newport Beach, Calif., 1965-72; pres. Bissell/August, Inc., Newport Beach, 1972-83, Bissell Architects, Inc., Newport Beach, 1983—. Bd. dirs. Newport Ctr. Assn., 1973-78, Lido Isle Community Assn., Newport Beach, 1985-87, Hamilton Cove Assn., 1991-92. With U.S. Mcht. Marine, 1944-46. Fellow AIA (pres. Orange County chpt. 1975, Calif. coun. 1978, nat. bd. dirs. 1980-83, Progressive Arch. award 1974, Nat. AIA Honor award 1978, 98, Merit award Calif. Coun. 1988, AIA Calif. Coun. Lifetime Achievement award 2000); mem. Newport Harbor Yacht Club, Lido Isle Yacht Club. Avocations: sailing, skiing, travel. Home: 108 Via Havre Newport Beach CA 92663-4905 also: Yacht Banshee Newport Beach CA 92663 Office: Bissell Architects 446 Old Newport Blvd Newport Beach CA 92663-4246 E-mail: Bisarch@aol.com.

BISSELL, JAMES DOUGAL, III, motion picture production designer; b. Charleston, SC, Aug. 6, 1951; s. James Dougal Sr. and Elizabeth McPherson (Jones) B.; m. Teresa Ann Atkinson, June 1, 1974 (div. Sept. 1987); m. Martha Wynne Snetsinger, Oct. 22, 1995; children: James Dougal, Alexander Wynne, Elizabeth Wynne. BFA in Theatre, U. N.C., 1973. Art dir. various TV movies, L.A., 1976-81; prodn. designer E.T. The Extra-Terrestrial, L.A., 1981, Twilight Zone-The Movie, L.A., 1982, The Falcon and The Snowman, Mexico City, 1983-84; prodn. designer, 2d unit dir. The Boy Who Could Fly, Vancouver, B.C., Can., 1985, Harry and the Hendersons, L.A., 1986; prodn. designer Someone to Watch Over Me, L.A. and N.Y.C., 1986-87, Twins, L.A. and Santa Fe, 1988—. Visual cons. St. Elmo's Fire, Hollywood, 1984; title co-designer Amazing Stories, Hollywood, 1985; art dir. The Last Starfighter, Hollywood, 1983; prodn. designer, 2nd unit dir. Always, L.A., Libby Mt., Epharata, Wash., 1989; prodn. designer Arachnophobia, Venezuela, Cambria, Calif., L.A. Prodn. designer Rocketeer, 1990, The Pickle, N.Y.C. and L.A., Dennis the Menace, Chgo., 1992, Blue Chips, L.A., Chgo., New Orleans, 1993, Jumanji, Vancouver, New Eng., 1994-95, Tin Cup, Tucson, Houston, 1995, My Fellow Americans, L.A., Asheville, N.C., The Sixth Day, 1999, Cats and Dogs, 2000, Confessions of a Dangerous Mind, 2002, Hollywood Homicide L.A., 2002; visual cons., 2d unit dir. 50 First Kisses, 2003, L.A. Mem.: Acad. Motion Picture Arts and Scis., Dir.'s Guild Am., Art Dir.'s Guild.

BISSELL, JOHN W. federal judge; b. Exeter, N.H., June 7, 1940; s. H. Hamilton and Sarah W. B.; m. Caroline M.; July 15, 1967; children— Megan L., Katharine W. AB, Princeton U., 1962; LLB, U. Va., 1965. Law clk. U.S. Dist. Ct., N.J., 1965-66; assoc. Pitney, Hardin & Kipp, Newark and Morristown, N.J., 1966-69, ptnr., 1972-78; asst. U.S. atty. N.J., 1969-71; judge Essex County, N.J., 1978-81, N.J. Superior Ct., 1981-82, U.S. Dist. Ct. N.J., Trenton and Newark, 1983—. Office: US Dist Ct Federal Square PO Box 999 Newark NJ 07101-0999*

BISSELL, MICHAEL GILBERT, pathologist; b. Ridgecrest, Calif., Mar. 5, 1947; s. Henry Robert and Margaret Alberta (Encell) Benefiel; m. Sherrie L. Lyons, Mar. 27, 1977 (div. June 1990); children: Cassandra, Grahame; m. Lita A. Hill, Nov. 29, 1991. BS in Chemistry, BS in Math., U. Ariz., 1969; MD, Stanford U., 1975, PhD in Neurobiol., 1977; MPH, U. Calif., Berkeley, 1978. Diplomate Am. Bd. Pathology. Resident Martinez VA Med. Ctr. U. Calif., Davis, 1978-81; rsch. fellow NIMH, Bethesda, Md., 1981-84; asst. prof. pathology U. Chgo. Med. Ctr., 1984-88; dir. clin. pathology City of Hope Nat. Med. Ctr., Duarte, Calif., 1988-91; v.p./med. dir. Nichols Inst. Reference Lab., San Juan Capistrano, Calif., 1991-93; dir. lab. medicine, assoc. prof. pathology U. Texas, 1993-97; dir. clin. pathology Allegheny Gen. Hosp., Pitts., 1998-2000; dir. lab. med., vice-chair pathology, assoc. dean app. rsch. Ohio State U., Columbus, 2000—. Speaker in field. Contbr. articles to profl. jours. Fellow Am. Soc. Clin. Pathologists, Coll. Am. Pathologists, mem. Nat. Com. Clin. Lab. Standards, Am. Assn. Clin. Chemistry, Clin. Lab. Mgmt. Assn. (treas.), Physicians for Nat. Health Program (activist, lectr.), Sierra Club, Sigma Xi. Democrat. Avocations: painting, philately, drawing, writing. Office: Ohio State U 410 W 10th Ave Columbus OH 43210 E-mail: bissell-1@medctr.osu.edu.

BISSELL, PHIL (CHARLES P. BISSELL), cartoonist; b. Worcester, Mass., Feb. 1, 1926; s. Ralph Kenneth and Dorothy Earle (Pennell) B.; m. Beverly Barrows, Sept. 17, 1948; children: Steven Barrows, Christopher William. Student, Sch. Practical Art, Boston, 1946-48; hon. degree, Art Instrn. Sch., Mpls., 1971. Theatrical and editl. sports cartoonist Christian Sci. Monitor, 1949-53; sports cartoonist Boston Globe, 1953-65; sports and editl. cartoonist Worcester Telegram and Evening Gazette, 1967-75; sports cartoonist Boston Herald, 1975-77; editl. cartoonist Lowell (Mass.) Sun, 1980-87; illustrator, cartoonist Cartoon Corner Syndicate, Forestdale, Mass., 2001. Cons. D.C. Graphics, Lexington, Mass., 1987—; originator football helmet logo New England Patriots, 1960; portrait artist City of Lowell Bridge Placque, 1982. Represented in permanent collections Basketball Hall Fame, Springfield, Mass., Football Hall of Fame, Canton, Ohio, Baseball Hall of Fame, Cooperstown, N.Y., Internat. Swimming Hall of Fame, Ft. Lauderdale, Fla., Dwight D. Eisenhower Meml. Libr., Abilene, Kans.; cartoonist: (book) Sportspot, 1978, World Ency. of Cartooning, 1980, Tall Tales from Tall Ships, 1992. Recipient N.Am. Racing Assn. award, 1958, Scarlet Quill award Boston U., 1976, Hockey award Mass. Bay Chiefs, 1981. Mem. Baseball Writers Assn. Am. Home: 4 Crosshill Cir Forestdale MA 02644-1630 Office: Cartoon Corner 4 Crosshill Circle Forestdale MA 02644-1630 E-mail: quikdraw@gis.net. *Humor and laughter can hold mankind together, and if you can share it with your fellow-man, I feel it's a successful day's work!.*

BISSELL, ROLIN PLUMB, lawyer; b. Yokosuka, Japan, Sept. 19, 1960; came to U.S., 1961; s. Elliston Perot III and Edith R. Bissell; m. Avery Boling, Sept. 12, 1987. BA in Philosophy and Econs., Columbia Coll., 1982; JD, U. Va., 1985. Law clk. to Chief Justice Richard Neely Supreme Ct. of W.Va., Charleston, 1985-86; assoc. Dewey Ballantine Bushby, Palmer & Wood, N.Y.C., 1986-88, Schnader Harrison Segal & Lewis LLP, Phila., 1988-93, ptnr., 1994—2003, Young Conaway Stargatt & Taylor, LLP, Wilmington, DC, 2003—. Contbr. articles to law jours. Dir. Chestnut Hill Hist. Soc., Phila., 1993-98, Landmarks Soc., Phila., 1998-2002; mem. Com. of Seventy, Phila., 1998-2002. Office: Young Conaway Stargatt & Taylor LLP 1000 West St 17th Fl Wilmington DE 19899-0391

BISSETTE, SAMUEL DELK, astronomer, artist, financial executive; b. Wilson, N.C., Aug. 10, 1921; s. Zachariah Coye and Annie Wright (Rice) B.; m. Ruby Graham Raynor, Sept. 8, 1943; children: Judy Sabra, David Coye, student pub. schs., various coll. courses. With Peoples Fed. Savs. and Loan Assn., Wilmington, N.C., 1939-89, pres., CEO, 1959-77, chmn. bd., 1973-89, dir., 1954-89; visual artist, 1972—. Exhibited in 65 one-man shows, 1972-2000; commd. by Wachovia Bank to execute 40 paintings Portrait of North Carolina, 1976; originated mosaic murals for Belk-Beery Co., Wilmington, 1979; originated exhbn. N.C. Circa 1900, 1983; traveling tour N.C. Mus., 1984-87; originated 35 piece exhbn. Images From the Microworld, 1991 (gift to U. N.C.-Wilmington 1999); created 60 painting exhbn. The Universe According to Earth, given to U.N.C., Wilmington, 1993; originator astromicroscopy, astrophotomicrography for astronomy, 1994. Author: A Guide to Astromicroscopy, 1994, An Astromicroscopy Study of the Southern Hemisphere Sky, 1995, Voices of the Cape Fear, 2001, From Inner Space to Outer Space, 2002. Trustee N.C. Mus. Art, Raleigh, 1980-85; chmn. N.C. Artists Exhbn., 1979. Served with USAAF, 1941-45. Mem. N.C. Watercolor Soc. (v.p. 1980), N.C. Art Soc. (dir. 1974-82), St. John's Mus. Art (pres. 1973-74), Cape Fear Club (pres. 1978), Carolina Yacht Club (Wilmington), Cape Fear Country Club (Wilmington). Republican. Baptist. Address: 1939 S Live Oak Pky Wilmington NC 28403-5321 E-mail: sambissette@isaac.net.

BISSETTE, WINSTON LOUIS, JR., lawyer, mayor; b. Statesville, N.C., Sept. 18, 1943; s. Winston Louis and Rubye (Goode) B.; m. Sara Oliver, Aug. 21, 1965; children: W. Louis III, Thomas Anderson. BA, Wake Forest U., 1965; JD, U. N.C., Chapel Hill, 1968; MBA, U. Va., 1970. Bar: N.C. 1968. Asst. v.p. Wachovia Bank & Trust Co., Winston-Salem, N.C., 1970-74; v.p., treas. Western Carolina Bank, Asheville, N.C., 1974-76; ptnr. McGuire, Wood & Bissette, P.A., Asheville, 1976—. Mayor City of Asheville, 1985-89, mem. city coun., 1983-89; co-chmn. I-26 corridor Assn., 1987—; chmn. West N.C. Devel. Assn., 1995-98; regional adv. coun. HUD, 1986-90; mem. Gov.'s Task Force on Urban Transp., 1986, Yr. of the Mtns. Commn., 1995-97; chmn. Asheville Sports Com., 1991-97, Buncombe County Econ. Devel. Commn., 1997-2003; vice chmn. Asheville Cmty. Betterment Found., 1992; bd. trustees Wake Forest U., 1996—, Western Carolina U., 1995-2003; chmn. Advantage Asheville, 1996—; chmn. Grove Arcade Pub. Mkt. Found., 1992—; bd. dirs. Mission-St. Joseph's Health Sys., Inc., 1996-99, Mercy Svcs. Corp., Blue Ridge Pkwy. Found., vice chmn. Mem. ABA, N.C. Bar Assn., Asheville Area C. of C. (pres. 1991-92), Wake Forest U. Alumni Assn. (pres. 1992-93), Country Club of Asheville, Biltmore Forest Country Club, Civitan Club. Republican. Presbyterian. Avocations: golf, running. Home: 321 Old Toll Rd Asheville NC 28804-3716 Office: McGuire Wood & Bissette PA 48 Patton Ave PO Box 3180 Asheville NC 28802-3180

BISSINGER, FREDERICK LEWIS, retired manufacturing executive, consultant; b. N.Y.C., Jan. 11, 1911; s. Jacob Frederick and Rosel (Ensslin) B.; m. Julia E. Stork, Aug. 4, 1935 (dec. Dec. 1989); children: Frederick Louis, Elizabeth Julia; m. Barbara S. Simmonds, Dec. 4, 1993. ME, Stevens Inst. Tech., 1933, MS in Chemistry, 1936, DEng (hon.), 1973; JD, Fordham U., 1938. Bar: D.C. 1937, N.Y. 1939, Ohio 1943, U.S. Supreme Ct. 1943. Instr. chemistry Stevens Inst. Tech., Hoboken, N.J., 1933-36; assoc. Pennie, Davis, Marvin & Edmonds, N.Y.C., 1936-42; counsel, bus. cons. Pennie, Davis, Marvin & Edmonds (name now Pennie & Edmonds), N.Y.C., 1976—; with Indsl. Rayon Corp., Cleve., 1942-61, v.p. charge rsch., 1948-57, group v.p. mktg. and rsch., 1957-59, v.p., gen. mgr., 1959-60, pres., chief exec. officer, 1960-61; group v.p. Midland-Ross Corp., Cleve., 1961-62; v.p., dir., mem. exec. com. Stauffer Chem. Co., N.Y.C., 1962-65; v.p. Allied Chem. Corp., N.Y.C., 1965-66, exec. v.p., 1966-69, pres., chief oper. officer, 1969-74, vice chmn., 1974-76, also bd. dirs. Bd. dirs. Selas Corp. Am. Chmn. emeritus bd. trustees Steven Inst. Tech.; trustee emeritus Fordham U.; mem. N.Y. State Econ. Devel. Bd., 1975. Mem. AAAS, Am. Chem. Soc., Soc. of Chem. Industry (Am. sect.), Societe de Chimie Industrielle, Chemists Club, Sky Club, Sakonnet Golf Club. Mem. Club. Home: 9 W Irving St Chevy Chase MD 20815-4218

BISSLER, RICHARD THOMAS, mortician; b. Ravenna, Ohio, Nov. 23, 1953; s. Richard Samuel and Ruth Marion (Cowan) B.; m. Jane H. Vair, Aug. 23, 1975; children: Stephanie Ann (Shawn) Arden, Carlie Jane. BS in Mortuary Sci., U. Minn., 1976; grad., Nat. Found. Funeral Svc. Mgmt., 1983. Lic. funeral dir. and embalmer Ohio; cert. crematory operator Cremation Assn. N.Am. Funeral svc. asst. Bissler & Sons Funeral Home, Kent, Ohio, 1970-74, mortician, 1976—, corp. sec., 1983-86, corp. sec.-treas., 1986-88, pres., 1988—. Bd. dirs. Home Savs. Bank, Kent, bd. dirs., treas. NSM Ins. Co. Ltd., 1997—2001. Trustee Kent Free Libr., 1986—, trustee St. Patrick's Sch. Endowment Fund, 1994—. Nat. Selected Morticians Ins. Trust, 1995-2001; bd. dirs. Selected Ind. Funderal Homes, 2003—; past bd. dirs., pres. Portage County A.C.S., Kent; past tres. NEO-SIDS Found., Akron, Ohio; mem. adult edn. adv. com. Kent City Schs.; steering com. Portage County Hospice; devel. com. United Christian Ministries, 1996-98; mem. Vision 2000 com. City of Kent; mem. Kent Bus. and Edn. adv. com.; bd. dirs. Portage Area Regional Transit Authority, 2002—. Recipient Disting. Svc. award Kent Jaycees, 1986. Mem. Nat. Funeral Dirs. Assn., Ohio Embalmers Assn., Ohio Funeral Dirs. Assn., Selected Ind. Funeral Homes (meeting chair 1989), Funeral Ethics Assn., Kent Area C. of C. (dir. 1985-89, Outstanding Bus. Person award 1992), Order of the Golden Rule, Kent Rotary (dir. 1991-93, pres. 1995-96), K.C. Republican. Roman Catholic. Avocations: golf, photography, travel. Office: Bissler & Sons Funeral Home 628 W Main St Kent OH 44240-2212

BISSON, CLAUDE, retired chief justice of Quebec; b. Three Rivers, Que., Can., May 9, 1931; s. Roger Bisson and Marcelle Morin; m. Louisette Lanneville, Oct. 12, 1957; children: Alain, Marie, Louis. BA, Laval U., 1950, Licentiate in Laws, 1953. Bar: Que. 1954. Pvt. practice, Three Rivers, 1954-69; judge Superior Ct. Dist. Montreal, Que., 1969-80, Ct. of Appeal, Province of Que., Montreal, 1980-96; also chief justice of Que., 1988-94; counsel McCarthy Tetrault, Montreal, 1996—. Decorated officer The Order of Canada, 1999. Mem. Can. Bar Assn., Que. Garrison Club, Quebec City. Home: 482 Chemin de la Cote Ste Catherine Montreal QC Canada H2V 2B4 Office: McCarthy Tetrault 1170 Peel St Montreal QC Canada H3B 4S8

BISSON, ROGER, middle school educator; b. Biddeford, Maine, Oct. 16, 1944; s. Napoleon and Simonne (Desrochers) B.; m. Janet Elizabeth Gerace, Aug. 9, 1969. BA in Biology, St. Michael's Coll., Winooski, Vt., 1969; MEd in Adminstrn. and Planning, U. Vt., 1991; tech. edn. cert., Lyndon State Coll., 1991. Cert. sci. tchr. grades 7-12, tech. edn. tchr. grades 7-12, prin. grades K-12, sci. and tech. edn. middle grades 5-8, mid. level endorsement Vt. Dept. Edn., 2001. 5th and 7th grade tchr. Sacred Heart Sch., Sharon, Mass., 1964-66; algebra I, French I and II and Latin I tchr. Notre Dame H.S., Fitchburg, Mass., 1966-68; 7th and 9th grade sci. tchr. Meml. Jr. and Sr. H.S., Bellingham, Mass., 1968-79; sci. and tech. edn. instr. grades 6, 7, 8 Folsom Sch., South Hero, Vt., 1979—2002, 8th grade sch.-to-work instr., 1992—2002; 8th grade sci. tchr. Albert D. Lawton Sch., Essex Junction, Vt., 2002—. Mem. info. tech. com. Grand Isle Supervisory Dist., North Hero, Vt., 1985-2002; tech. edn. cons. Alburg (Vt.) Elem. Sch., 1992-2002; sch.-to-work lead tchr. New Am. Sch.-Folsom, South Hero, 1992-2002, sci. lead tchr., 1994-2002; mem. tchr./bus. internship program Vt. Math. Coalition, Montpelier, summer 1994; initiator Electronic Portfolio Project 6, 7, 8, 1994-2002, Student/Bus. Internship Program, 1994—2002; tech. cons. Burlington Sch. Sys., 1996; presenter Nat. Ednl. Computing Conf., Boston, spring 1994, Vt. Fest '94, Fairlee, Vt., fall 1994, Sch.-to-Work Initiative Conf., Burlington, summer 1996, Regional Edn. Television Network Conf., Burlington, fall 1997, Vt. Fest '98 Info. Tech. Conf.; presenter in field. Contbr. articles to profl. jours. Initiator Grand Isle County Networking Initiative, Grand Isle County, Vt., 1991, Grand Isle County Peer Coaching Program, Grand Isle County, 1991. Recipient Sch.-to-Work Initiative Gov.'s Office, 1995, award Lake Champlain Regional C. of C., 1996, Vocat. Edn. award Grand Isle Rotary Club, 1998; co-recipient IBM Test Flight 1991 award, Essex Junction, Vt., 1992. Mem. ASCD, NEA, NSTA, Vt. Edn. Assn., Vt. Sci. Tchrs. Assn., Vt. Tech. Edn. Assn., Grand Isle Supervisory Union (bldg rep., negotiator, grievance com., past pres.), Vt. State Tech. Coun., Vt. Inst. Sci., Math. and Tech., Vt. Info. Tech. Assn. for Avancement of Learning. Roman Catholic. Avocations: woodworking, furniture refinishing, carpentry, computer technology, fine dining. Office: Folsom Sch 75 South St South Hero VT 05486-4913 E-mail: rbisson@ejhs.k12.vt.us.

BISSON, TERRY BALLANTINE, author, editor; b. Madisonville, Ky., Feb. 12, 1942; s. Max Willis and Martha (Ballantine) B.; m. Deirdre Holst (div. 1969); children: Nathaniel, Peter, Zöe; m. Judy Yost Jensen, 1971; children: Kristen, Gabriel, Welcome. Student, Grinnell Coll., 1960-62; BA, U. Louisville, 1964. Participant univ. and lit. confs.; keynote speaker ann. conf. So. Humanities Coun., Huntsville, Ala. Author: (novels) Wyrldmaker, 1981, Talking Man, 1987, Fire on the Mountain, 1988, Voyage to the Red Planet, 1990, Pirates of the Universe, 1996, The Pickup Artist, 2001; (novels pub. in Germany, Italy, Russia, Japan,and U.K.); (young adult biography) Nat Turner, Slave Revolt Leader, 1988, On a Move: The Story of Mumia Abu Jamal, 2001; Bears Discover Fire and Other Stories, 1993, In the Upper Room and Other Likely Stories, 2000; (novelizations of screenplays) Johnny Mnemonic, 1995, Virtuosity, 1995, The Fifth Element, 1997, Alien Resurrection, The X Files: Miracle Man, Galaxy Quest, 1999; creator No-Frills Books, 1981; co-author: Car Talk with Click and Clack, The Tappet Brothers, 1991, A Green River Girlhood, 1990; writer radio dramas: The Flat Edge of the Earth, 1998, Orson the Alien, 1998; co-editor: Hauling up the Morning, 1990; contbr. short fiction to Playboy, Omni, others. Recipient Hugo award World Sci. Fiction Conf., 1991, Mayor's award for excellence City of Owensboro, Ky., 1991, Phoenix award Deep South Conf., 1993, Theodore Sturgeon award U. Kans., 1991. Mem. Authors Guild, Sci. Fiction Writers Am. (Nebula award 1990). Office: care Susan Ann Protter Lit Agt 110 W 40th St Rm 1408 New York NY 10018-3640

BISSONNETTE, ANIK, dancer; b. Montreal, Can. First dancer Great Canadian Ballet, 1990—94, Les Grands Ballets Canadiens de Montréal, 1990—; co-founder Dance Theatre of Montreal, 1995. Dancer (ballets) Giselle, Great Canadian Ballets of Montreal, Romeo and Juliet, Cinderella, The Sylphids, The Nutcracker, dancer, creator Band at Share, Festival of Hiawatha Arts, 1994. Named Personality of the Week, The Press, 1985, Officer of Order of Can., 1995, Knight of Order of Quebec, 1996; recipient prize Best Individual Performance, Internat. Porsche of Can., 1985. Office: Les Grands Ballets Canadiens de Montréal 4816 rue Rivard Montreal QC Canada H2J 2N6

BISSONNETTE, VICTOR L. education educator; married. PhD, U. of Tex., 1992. Asst. prof. Southeastern La. U., Hammond, 1993—2000, Berry Coll., Mt. Berry, Ga., 2000—. Mem.: Am. Psychol. Soc. Office: Berry Coll PO Box 495019 Mount Berry GA 30149-5019 E-mail: vbissonnette@berry.edu.

BISTLINE, F. WALTER, JR., lawyer, photographer; b. Lakeland, Fla., Sept. 30, 1950; s. Frederick Walter and Mary Carolyn (Stansell) B.; m. Rabun Huff, Mar. 18, 1972. BA, Emory U., 1972; JD, Boston U., 1975. Bar: N.Y. 1976, Tex. 1979. Assoc. firm White & Case, N.Y.C., 1975-79; assoc. Johnson & Gibbs, P.C., Dallas, 1979-81, ptnr./shareholder, 1981-95; ptnr. Porter & Hedges, L.L.P., Houston, 1995—2001, of counsel, 2001—. Lectr. So. Meth. U. Sch. of Law, 1991; fellow Art Dept., U. Houston, 2002—. Contbr. articles to profl. jours.; contbr. articles to art history jours. Tchg. fellow, U. Houston, 2002—. Office: Porter & Hedges LLP 3500 Bank of America Ctr 700 Louisiana St Houston TX 77002-2700

BISTRIAN, BRUCE RYAN, internist, educator; b. Southampton, N.Y., Oct. 22, 1939; s. Peter and Mary Laura (Ryan) B.; m. Eleanor Alice Dix, Sept. 3, 1964; children: Tennille Ryan, Jordan Brooke, Britton Perry. BA, NYU, 1961; MD, Cornell U., 1965; MPH, Johns Hopkins U., 1971; PhD, MIT, 1975; AM (hon.), Harvard U., 1990. Diplomate Am. Bd. Internal Medicine; bd. cert. Critical Care Medicine. Intern Cornell U., N.Y.C., 1965-66; metabolism fellow U. Vt., Burlington, 1968-69, resident in medicine, 1969-70; from asst. clin. prof. to assoc. prof. Harvard U. Sch. Medicine, Boston, 1975-90, prof. medicine, 1990—. Clin. assoc. physician rsch. resources divsn. NIH, 1975-78; lectr. MIT, 1981-84. Mem. editl. bd. Jour. Parenteral and Enteral Nutrition, Harvard Health Letter, Women's Health Watch, Critical Care Medicine; contbr. more than 400 sci. articles to profl. publ. Capt. U.S. Army, 1966-68. Grantee Nat. Inst. Gen. Med. Scis., 1977-80, Nat. Inst. Arthritis, Metabolism and Digestive Disease, 1979-83, Nat. Inst. Arthritis, Diabetes, Digestive and Kidney Diseases, 1985-95, Nat. Cancer Inst., 1984-87. Fellow: ACP; mem.: Inst. Medicine (com. on military nutrition rsch. 2001—), Fedn. Am. Socs. for Exptl. Biologists (bd. dirs. 2001—), Mass. Med. Soc., Soc. Critical Care Medicine, Am. Soc. Parenteral and Enteral Nutrition (pres. 1989—90), Am. Soc. Clin. Nutrition (sec. 1993—96, v.p.-elect 1998, v.p. 1999, pres. 2000), Fedn. Am. Soc. Exptl. Biologists. Presbyterian. Achievements include more than 40 patents in field. Subspecialties: Nutrition (medicine); Biochemistry (medicine). Current work: protein calorie malnutrition; total parenteral nutrition; nutrition and infection. Home: Argilla Rd Ipswich MA 01938 Office: Beth Israel Deaconess Med Ctr 1 Deaconess Rd Boston MA 02215-5321 E-mail: bbistria@caregroup.harvard.edu.

BISWAS, BRIAN, writer; b. Columbus, Ohio, Mar. 7, 1957; s. Naren Biswas and Diane DiRosa; m. Elizabeth Phelan, Jan. 21, 1977; children: Mark, Eliza. BA, Antioch Coll., Yellow Springs, Ohio, 1980; MS, U. Ill., 1986. Author: (short stories) The Bridge, 1991, Solitary Confinement, 1992, The Museum of North African Treasures, 1992, The Nature of Love, 1993, Fare-Thee-Well, 1993, Others, 1993, The Vulture, 1997, A Betrayal, 1999 (Pushcart prize nominee, 2000), Apologia Du Amore, 2000, The Crystal, 2000, A Soldier's Lament, 2003. Home and Office: 412 Holly Ln Chapel Hill NC 27517

BISWAS, RUPAK, computer scientist; b. Calcutta, Feb. 21, 1960; s. Adhir Kumar Biswas and Dhira Das; m. Rina Banerjee, May 26, 1994; children: Monjira, Akash. BSc, U. Calcutta, 1982, BTech, 1985; MS, Rensselaer Polytech. Inst., 1988, PhD, 1991. Rsch. asst. Rensselaer Polytech. Inst., Troy, N.Y., 1985-91; rsch. scientist Rsch. Inst. Advanced Computer Sci., Moffett Field, Calif., 1991-96, sr. rsch. scientist Veridian/MRJ Tech. Solutions, Moffett Field, Calif., 1996-2000, Computer Scis. Corp., Moffett Field, Calif., 2000; computer scientist NASA Ames Rsch. Ctr., Moffett Field, Calif., 2000—, group lead Algorithms, Tools and Architectures Group, 2000—, task mgr. Advanced Computing Rsch. for CNIS project, 2002—. Editor: Parallel Computing Jour., 2000, Jour. Parallel and Distributed Computing, 1997, Applied Numerical Maths. Jour., 1996; contbr. articles to profl. jours. Recipient Nat. scholarship Govt. India, 1978-85; Best Paper award Supercomputing 99 Program Com., 1999, Best Student Paper award Supercomputing 2000 Program Com., 2000. Mem. IEEE, ACM. Avocations: travel, photography. Office: NASA Ames Rsch Ctr Mail Stop T27A-1 Moffett Field CA 94035

BITAR, SAAD R. internist; b. Tartous, Syria, Apr. 7, 1964; came to U.S., 1988; s. Riad Bitar and Hana Daya; m. Randa, May 4, 1966; children: Rami, Dalia. MD, Damascus U., 1987. Diplomate Am. Bd. Internal Medicine, Am. Bd. Cardiovascular Diseases, Am. Bd. Interventional Cardiology. Resident in neurology St. Louis U. Sch. Medicine, 1990-92, resident in internal medicine, 1992-94, resident in cardiology, 1994-97, resident in interventional cardiology, 1997-99, asst. prof. medicine, 1997—. Dir. coronary care unit St. Louis U., 1999—, med. rehab. of cardiac rehab., 1995-97. Contbr. articles to profl. jours. Office: St Louis Card Cons 11133 Dunn Rd Ste 2346 Saint Louis MO 63136 E-mail: srbitar@cs.com.

BITENSKY, SUSAN HELEN, law educator; b. N.Y.C., Jan. 3, 1948; d. Reuben Bitensky; m. Elliott Lee Meyrowitz, Apr. 17, 1982; 1 child, William N. BA magna cum laude, Case Western Res. U., 1971; JD, U. Chgo., 1974. Bar: Pa. 1974, U.S. Dist. Ct. (we. dist.) Pa. 1974, U.S. Ct. Appeals (3d cir.) 1975, U.S. Ct. Appeals (2d cir.) 1977, N.Y. 1979, U.S. Dist. Ct. (so. and ea. dists.) N.Y. 1979, Mich. 1988. Asst. gen. counsel United Steelworkers Am., Pitts., 1974-77; assoc. Cohen, Weiss and Simon, N.Y.C., 1977-81; assoc. counsel N.Y.C. Bd. Edn., Bklyn., 1981-87; assoc. prof. law Mich. State U.-Detroit Coll. Law, 1988-93, prof. law, 1993—. Contbg. author: Children's Rights in America: UN Convention on the Rights of the Child Compared with U.S. Law; contbr. articles to profl. jours. Mem. ABA, Phi Beta Kappa. Office: Mich State Univ Detroit Coll Law 447 Law College Bldg East Lansing MI 48824-1300 E-mail: bitensky@msu.edu.

BITHELL, THOMAS CHARLES, human resources and insurance consultant; b. Pocatello, Idaho, Oct. 21, 1946; s. Walter Charles and Nondus (Hoge) Bithell; m. Irene Lindsay, Nov. 12, 1947; children: Susan N., Thomas L., Steven H., Cathrin S., Lindsay A., Samuel H., U. Idaho, 1969; BS in Bus., Fairleigh Dickinson U., 1977. Owner Bithell Produce & Foods Co., Moscow, Idaho, 1965-67; dist. sales mgr. Produce Supply Co., Spokane, Wash., 1967-69; personnel dir. George A. Fuller div. Northrop Corp., N.Y.C., 1975-77, Taubman Co., Inc., Southfield, Mich., 1977-80, v.p., personnel Troy, Mich., 1980-84, sr. v.p. human resources and adminstrn. Bloomfield Hills, Mich., 1984-98; pres. Tb brand, LLC, Bloomfield Hills, 1998—, Human Asset Strategies, Bloomfield Hills, 1998—. Cons. in field. Bishop LDS Ch., Bloomfield Hills, 1986-90, pres. Bloomfield Hills stake, 1994—. Capt. AUS, 1969-75. Mem. Am. Compensation Assn., Detroit Area Personnel Mgmt. Assn., Am. Mgmt. Assn., Soc. Human Resource Mgmt., Beta Thea Pi., Elks. Republican. Avocation: scuba diving. Office: 5049 Mohr Valley Ln Bloomfield Hills MI 48304 E-mail: TBithell@HAssets.com.

BITNER, JERRI LYNNE, information technology professional, consultant; b. York, Pa., May 11, 1951; d. Ernest Maclellan and Gertrude Pauline (Beck) B. BS, Pa. State U., 1974. Procurement agt. Def. Indsl. Supply Ctr., Phila., 1975-77; contracts specialist Navy Ships Parts Control Ctr., Mechanicsburg, 1977-81; procurement analyst, then supr. Navy Fleet Material Support Office, Ctrl. Design Agy., 1981-87, dir. procurement systems div., 1987-94, dir. APADE/C2/Reengineering divsn., 1994-96, tandem rehost project mgr., 1996-98, dep. dir. tech. support dept., 1998-2001, dir. IT group e-bus. ops. office, 2001—03; dir. solution devel. dept. Navy Info. Sys. Support Activity, 2003—. Avocations: skiing, tennis, golf, camping, kayaking. Office: NAVSISA Mechanicsburg PA 17055 E-mail: jerri_l_bitner@fmso.navy.mil.

BITNER, JOHN HOWARD, lawyer; b. Indpls., Feb. 27, 1940; s. Harry M. Jr. and Jeanne B. (Eshelman) B.; m. Vicki Ann D'Ianni, 1961; children: Kerry, Holly, Robin. AB in English and History, Northwestern U., 1961; JD cum laude, Columbia U., 1964. Bar: Ill. 1964. Assoc. Bell, Boyd & Lloyd LLC, Chgo., 1964-71, ptnr., 1972-99, chair corp. and secs. dept., 1988-99, vice chmn. firm, 1992-99, mem., 2000—. Contbr. articles to profl. jours.; editor Columbia Law Rev. Mem. St. Gregory Episcopal Sch. Bd.; mem. bd. visitors Columbia Law Sch, tutor, GED students at Jobs for Youth Mem. ABA, Ill. Bar Assn., Chgo. Bar Assn., Union League, Mid-Day Club, Glen View Club, Lawyers Club, Delta Upsilon, Phi Delta Phi. Episcopalian. Avocations: tennis, reading, chess, golf. Home: 2329 Lincolnwood Dr Evanston IL 60201-2048 Office: Bell Boyd & Lloyd LLC 70 W Madison St Chicago IL 60602 Fax: (312) 827-8048. E-mail: jbitner@bellboyd.com.

BITNER, WILLIAM LAWRENCE, III, retired banker, educator; b. Harrisburg, Pa., Dec. 25, 1930; s. William Lawrence, Jr. and Anna (Horstick) B.; m. Wylla Mae Bowman, June 9, 1956; children: Lizabeth Anne, Lynne Ellen Bitner Ackner. BS in Edn., Pa. State U., Bloomsburg; MA, Rutgers U.; PhD in Adminstrn., NYU. Tchr. Scotch Plains High Sch., N.J., 1956-57; asst. supt. schs. Scotch Plains Sch. Dist., 1958-61, Plainview Sch. Dist., N.Y., 1961-63; supt. schs. Glen Falls Sch. Dist., N.Y., 1963-72; assoc. commr. edn. N.Y. State Edn. Dept., Albany, 1972-76; sr. v.p. 1st Nat. Bank Glen Falls, 1976, pres., CEO, 1977-93, Evergreen Bancorp, Inc., 1980-93; ret., 1993. Pres. Assoc. for Advancement of Internat. Edn., Dept. State, 1971-73; bd. dirs. Sandy Hill Corp., Hudson Falls, N.Y., N.Am. Med. Instrument Corp. Pres., chmn. bd. trustees, bd. dirs. Glens Falls Family YMCA, 1984-85; bd. trustees Hyde Collections, Glens Falls, 1963-88, chmn. bd., 1985-88; trustee Albany Med. Coll., 1977-85; bd. dirs. Glens Falls Hosp., 1988—, Lake Champlain Cancer Rsch. Orgn., Inc., Burlington, Vt., 1988—; chmn. Cmty. Lending Corp. N.Y., 1991-92; pres.-elect N.Y. State Coun. of Sch. Supts., 1971-72; dir. N.Y. State Health Care Trustees, 1998—. Recipient Dean John W. Withers Meml. award NYU Alumni Assn., 1964, Disting. Svc. award Bloomsburg U. Pa., 1972, Nat. PTA Life Membership, Adirondack coun. PTA, 1972, Outstanding Sch. Adminstr. award N.Y., 1976, Fgn. Lang. Tchrs. Assn., 1975, Spl. award Human Resources Sch., 1975, Disting. Svc. award Glens Falls YMCA, 1992; Charles F. Kettering Found. fellow Carleton Coll., 1966; named one of Outstanding Young Men in Am., N.Y. Jaycees, 1966. Mem. N.Y. State Coun. Sch. Dist. Adminstrs. (hon. life), N.Y. State Bankers Assn. (pres. 1989-90), Ind. Bankers Assn. N.Y. State (pres. 1984-85, Disting. Svc. award 1991), East Lake Woodland Country Club, Glens Falls Country Club, Univ. Club (N.Y.C.). Republican. Avocations: golf, squash. Home: 54 Wincrest Dr Queensbury NY 12804-1345 also: 4902 Turtle Creek Trl Oldsmar FL 34677-1969

BITONDO, DOMENIC, engineering executive; b. Welland, Ont., Can., June 7, 1925; came to U.S., 1950, naturalized, 1956; s. Vito Leonard and Vita Maria (Gallipoli) B.; m. Delphine May Dicola, June 11, 1949; children— Michael, Annamarie, David, Marisa. BS, U. Toronto, 1947, MS, 1948, PhD, 1950. Aerodynamist, Aerophysics div. N.Am. Aviation Co., Downey, Calif., 1950-51; project engr. to chief of aerodynamics Aerophysics Devel. Corp., Santa Barbara, 1951-59; staff engr. Northrup Corp., Hawthorne, Calif., 1959-60; head test planning and analysis TRW Systems, Inc., El Segundo, Calif., 1960-61; dept. head aeromechanics dept. Systems Research and Planning div., founder, dir. Advanced Ballistic Reentry Systems Program (ABRES) Aerospace Corp., El Segundo, 1961-63; dir. engring. Aerospace Systems div. Bendix Corp., Ann Arbor, Mich., 1963-69; engring. mgr. Apollo lunar sci. expts., 1966; dir., gen. mgr. Bendix Research Labs., Southfield, Mich., 1969-79; exec. dir. research and devel. Bendix Corp., Southfield, Mich., 1979-80; pres. Bitondo Assocs. Inc., Ann Arbor, 1980—. Gordon N. Patterson lectr. U. Toronto, 1976; trustee Central Solar Energy and Research Corp., Detroit, 1978-80; dir. Continental Controls Corp., San Diego.; Def. Research Bd. Can. asst., 1948, NRC asst., 1947 Contbr. tech. articles to profl. jours. Mem. AIAA, NRC (mem. com. on mgmt. tech.), NAS (mem. task force to Indonesia in methodology of tech. planning), Mich. Energy Resource Rsch. Assn. (trustee 1978), Nat. Mgmt. Assn. (Gold Knight award), Indsl. Rsch. Inst. (emeritus). Office: 5 Manchester Ct Ann Arbor MI 48104-6562 E-mail: deldom@mymailstation.com.

BITOY, MICHELE GARDNER, radio traffic director; b. Chgo., Nov. 10, 1966; d. Willie and Marie Allen Gardner(Stepmother); m. Eric Bitoy, June 1992; children: Eric, Erika. BA, So. Ill. U., 1988. Cert. child care mgmt. Ill. Programming and music dir. asst. Sta. WBMX/WVAZ-FM, Chgo., 1988—89; news dir., programming asst. Sta. WVAZ-FM, Chgo., 1989—90; traffic asst. Sta. WLS, Chgo., 1990—95; child care tchr. Beginnings, Westchester, Ill., 1995—98; traffic asst., afternoon exec. prodr. Sta. WGCI-FM, Chgo., 1999—2001, exec. prodr. Crazy Howard McGee morning show, 2001; traffic mgr. Sta. WGCI-AM, Chgo., 2003—; traffic reporter Sta. WVAZ-FM, Chgo., 2001; billing and traffic dir. Sta. WPWX-FM, Hammond, Ind., 2001—03. Camera operator Living Word Christian Ctr., Forest Park, Ill., 1997—. Mem.: Delta Sigma Theta. Avocations: cooking, exercising, reading. Personal E-mail: mbpsalm91@aol.com.

BITRAN, JACOB DAVID, internist; b. Thessaloniki, Greece, Sept. 23, 1947; came to U.S., 1952; s. David Jacob and Martha (Faratzi) B.; m. Linda Sue Androw, Dec. 26, 1970; children: Lauren, Dina. BS, U. Ill., Chgo., 1968, MD, 1971. Diplomate Am. Bd. Internal Medicine with subspecialties in med. oncology, hematology. Intern in medicine Michael Reese Med. Ctr., Chgo., 1971-72, resident in internal medicine, 1973-75, clin. asst. prof. medicine, 1977-81, clin. assoc. prof. medicine, 1981-84; resident in pathology Rush Presbyn. St. Luke's Med. Ctr., Chgo., 1972-73; fellow in hematology/oncology U. Chgo., 1975-77, assoc. prof. medicine, 1984-88, prof. medicine, 1988-91; dir. divsn. hematology/oncology Luth. Gen. Hosp., Park Ridge, Ill., 1991—; prof. medicine U. Ill., Chgo., 1996-98. Mem. sci. adv. bd. Lederle Labs., Wayne, N.J., 1986-89. Editor: Lung Cancer, 1988. Fellow ACP, Am. Coll. Chest Physicians; mem. Am. Assn. for Cancer Rsch. (program chmn. 1988-89), Am. Soc. Clin. Oncology (program chmn. 1990-91). Democrat. Achievements include development of usable chemotherapy regimen for non small cell lung cancer that has been in clinical use since 1976; rsch. in dose intensive chemotherapy in breast cancer. Office: Lutheran General Hospital 1700 Luther Ln Park Ridge IL 60068-1270 E-mail: jbitran@oncmed.net.

BITTEL, MURIEL ALBERS, managing editor; b. N.Y.C., Mar. 22; d. Ernest Henry and Helen Minnie (Seibel) Albers; m. Robert Gifford Walcutt, June 15, 1946; children— Lynn Lowell Walcutt, Mark James Walcutt, Judith Anne Walcutt; m. Lester Robert Bittel, May 8, 1973. B.A., Douglass Coll. Feature writer Daily Home News, New Brunswick, N.J.; editor Fawcett Pubs., N.Y.C., 1940-46; pub. relations dir. Electrovox/Walco Inc., East Orange, N.J., 1946-62; mng. editor Acad. Hall Pubs., Bridgewater, Va., 1974— . Mng. editor: Ency. Profl. Mgmt., 1978; Handbook Profl. Mgrs., 1985, A Surprise in Every Corner, 1994, Island Adventures, 1995. Home: 106 Breezewood Ter Bridgewater VA 22812-1433

BITTENBENDER, BRAD JAMES, safety and health engineer; b. Kalamazoo, Dec. 4, 1948; s. Don J. and Thelma Lu (Bacon) B.; m. Patricia Stahl Hubbell, June, 1992. BS, Western Mich. U., 1972; Cert. Hazardous Material Mgmt., U. Calif., Irvine, 1987; Cert. Environ. Auditing, Calif. State U., Long Beach, 1992. Cert. safety profl. of the Ams.; cert. hazardous materials mgr. Supr. mfg. Am. Cyanamid, Kalamazoo, 1973-77, Productol Chem. div. Ferro Corp., Santa Fe Springs, Calif., 1977-79, environ. adminstr., 1979-80; sr. environ. engr. Ferro Corp., Los Angeles, 1980-87; mgr. environ. safety and indsl. hygiene dept. Composites divsn. Ferro Corp., Los Angeles, 1988-91, Structural Polymer Systems, Inc., Montedison, Calif., 1991-95; dir. environ. safety and health dept. Culver City (Calif.) Composites Corp., 1996-98; mgr. safety, health and environ. dept. Cytec Fiberite-Calif. Divsn., L.A., 1998-99; safety specialist Gen. Electric Aircraft Engines/IDC, Lynn, Mass., 2000—. Bd. dirs., mem. adv. bd. safety and health extension program U. Calif. Irvine, 1985-91. Bd. dirs. adv. com. hazardous materials Community Right to Know, Culver City, Calif., 1987-91; mem. Calif. Mus. Found., L.A., 1985-90, Mus. Contemporary Art, L.A., 1985-2000; founding sponsor Challenger Ctr.; mem. R.I. Driving Club, 1999—. Mem. Am. Inst. Chem. Engrs., Nat. Assn. Environ. Mgmt., Acad. Cert. Hazardous Materials Mgrs., Suppliers of Advanced Composites Materials Assn. (mem. environ. health and safety com. 1989-92), Am. Indsl. Hygiene Assn., Am. Soc. Safety Engrs., Nat. Fire Protection Assn., Beta Beta Beta. Republican. Presbyterian. Avocations: breeding morgan horses, skiing, distance running, reading, equestrian carriage driving. Home: 215 Everett St Wrentham MA 02093-1105 E-mail: bradbittenbender@netscape.net.

BITTERMAN, MARY GAYLE FOLEY, foundation executive; b. San Jose, Calif, May 29, 1944; d. John Dennis and Zoe (Hames) Foley; m. Morton Edward Bitterman, June 26, 1967; 1 child Sarah Fleming. BA, Santa Clara U., 1966; MA, Bryn Mawr Coll., 1969, PhD, 1971. Exec. dir. Hawaii Pub. Broadcasting, Honolulu, 1974-79; dir. Voice of Am., Washington, 1980-81, Dept. Commerce, Honolulu, 1981-83, E.-W. Ctr. Inst. Culture and Comm., Honolulu, 1984-88; cons. pvt. practice, Honolulu, 1989-93; pres., CEO KQED, Inc., San Francisco, 1993—2002, The James Irvine Found., San Francisco, 2002—03; Dtr. Osher Lifelong Learning Inst., 2003. Bd. dir. Bank of Hawaii, Honolulu, 1984—, McKesson Corp., San Francisco, 1995-99; trustee Am.'s Pub. TV Stas., 1997-2002; vice chmn. TIDE 2000, Tokyo, 1984-93. Producer: (film) China Visit, 1978; contbr. numerous articles on internat. telecomms. to various pubs. Bd. dir. United Way, Honolulu, 1986-93; chmn. Kuakini Health System, Honolulu, 1991-94. Recipient Candle of Understanding award Bonneville (Utah) Internat. Corp., 1985; named hon. mem. Nat. Fedn. Press Women, 1986. Fellow Nat. Acad. Pub. Info.; mem. Pacific Forum, CSIS (bd. gov.), PBS (bd. dir.), Barclays Global Investors (bd. dir.), the Bernard OSHER Found. (bd. dir.), Commonwealth Club Calif. (bd. dir.) Office: 909 Montgomery St San Francisco CA 94133 Address: 229 Kaalawai Pl Honolulu HI 96816-4435

BITTERMAN, MORTON EDWARD, psychologist, educator; b. N.Y.C., Jan. 19, 1921; s. Harry Michael and Stella (Weiss) B.; m. Mary Gayle Foley, June 26, 1967; children— Sarah Fleming, Joan, Ann BA, NYU, 1941; MA, Columbia U., 1942; PhD, Cornell U., 1945. Asst. prof. Cornell U., Ithaca, N.Y., 1945-50; assoc. prof. U. Tex., Austin, 1950-55; mem. Inst. for Advanced Study, Princeton, N.J., 1955-57; prof. Bryn Mawr Coll., Pa., 1957-70, U. Hawaii, Honolulu, 1970—; dir. Békésy Lab. Neurobiology, Honolulu, 1991—2000. Author: (with others) Animal Learning, 1979; editor: Evolution of Brain and Behavior in Vertebrates, 1976; co-editor: Am. Jour. Psychology, 1955-73; cons. editor Jour. Animal Learning and Behavior, 1973-76, 85-88, Jour. Comparative Psychology, 1988-92. Recipient Humboldt prize Alexander von Humboldt Found., Bonn, W.Ger., 1981; Fulbright grantee; grantee NSF, Office Naval Research, NIMH, Air Force Office Sci. Research, Deutsche Forschungsgemeinschaft. Fellow Soc. Exptl. Psychologists (Warren medal 1997), Am. Psychol. Assn. (D. O. Hebb award 2001), AAAS; mem. Psychonomic Soc. Home: 229 Kaalawai Pl Honolulu HI 96816-4435 Office: Univ Hawaii Bekesy Lab of Neurobiology 1993 E West Rd Honolulu HI 96822-2321

BITTING, KEVIN NOEL, pediatric craniofacial orthotist, researcher; b. Kenmore, NY, Dec. 18, 1957; s. Harry Lincoln Jr. and Shirley Ann (Smith) B. BA, Villanova U., 1980; Degree in Prosthetics, Northwestern U., 1989. Cert.

orthotist, Md. Rsch. asst. Villanova (Pa.) U., 1979; orthotist-prosthetist S.W. Lab., Burbank, Calif., 1988-99; chief pediatric craniofacial orthotist Cranial Therapies, Inc., Burbank, 1991—. Avocations: alpine skiing, physical fitness/swimming, computers. Office: Cranial Therapies Inc 4444 Lankershim Blvd Ste 108 Toluca Lake CA 91602

BITTING, WILLIAM M. lawyer; b. Santa Monica, Calif., Apr. 17, 1939; AB, UCLA, 1962, JD, 1965. Exec. v.p., gen counsel Pabst Brewing Co., San Antonio, chmn., CEO, 1998—2000; former CEO, co-chmn., gen. counsel S&P Co., Mill Valley, Calif.; sr. ptnr Hill Farrer & Burrill LLP, Los Angeles, Calif. Office: Hill Farrer & Burrill LLP 300 S Grand Ave 37th Fl Los Angeles CA 90071*

BITTNER, RONALD JOSEPH, computer systems analyst, magician; b. Schenectady, N.Y., July 30, 1954; s. Richard John and Catherine (Stepnowski) B.; m. Elayne Louise Simpson, May 14, 1983; 1 child, Krysten Elayne. AS in Chemistry, Orange County C.C., Middletown, N.Y., 1978; BA in Bus. Mgmt., Herbert Lehman Coll., Bronx, N.Y., 1983. Internal cons. Internat. Paper Co., Tuxedo, N.Y., 1978-87; systems analyst McGraw-Hill News, N.Y.C., 1987-89; sr. systems analyst Orange County Info. Svcs., Goshen, N.Y., 1989-91, Columbia Tristar Home Video, N.Y.C., 1991-93; MIS mgr. Post Perfect, N.Y.C., 1993-94, Warner Bros., N.Y.C., 1994—. Cons. in magic Shawnee Playhouse, Poconos, Pa., 1985. Contbr. articles to newspapers and mags., 1980-88. Mem. Variety Club Internat., Soc. Am. Magicians (pres. 1985-87, assembly pres. 1993-2001, Magician of Yr. award 1995), Internat. Brotherhood of Magicians, Acad. Magical Arts, Microcomputer Mgrs. Assn. (program coord.). Avocations: scuba diving, underwater photography, cooking, bowling, chess. Home: 186 Forest Rd Wallkill NY 12589-2913

BITZEGAIO, HAROLD JAMES, retired lawyer; b. Coalmont, Ind., Jan. 29, 1921; s. Nicholas Gilbert and Dora Belle (Burns) B.; m. Betty Jean Law, Apr. 15, 1950; children: Judith L. Bitzegaio Wallin, Gail Ann Bitzegaio Wright, Susan R. Bitzegaio Denyer, James R., Jane E. Disney. BS, Ind. State U., 1948; JD, Ind. U., 1953; grad., Ind. Jud. Coll., 1980. Bar: Ind. 1953, U.S. Dist. Ct. (so. dist.) Ind. 1953, U.S. Ct. Appeals (7th cir.) 1956. Sole practice, Terre Haute, Ind., 1953-58, 81-97; judge Vigo Superior Ct., Terre Haute, 1959-80, of counsel Anderson & Nichols Law Office. Editor, contbr.: Indiana Pattern Jury Instructions, 1966. Mem. Ind. Adv. Com. Civil Rights, Indpls., 1961-70, Mayor's Com. Civil Rights, Terre Haute, 1967-68; bd. dirs. Wabash Valley Council Boy Scouts Am., Terre Haute, 1960-80. Served to lt. comdr. USN, 1941-46, PTO. Decorated D.F.C. with gold star, Air medal with two gold stars, Purple Heart; named Sagamore of the Wabash, Gov. of Ind., 1990. Mem. ABA, Ind. Bar Assn., Terre Haute Bar Assn., Ind. Judges Assn. (bd. mgrs. 1961-80, pres. 1977-78), Ind. U. Law Alumni Assn. (pres. 1973-74, recipient disting. service award 1974), VFW (life), Nat. Rifle Assn. (life), Ducks Unltd. (nat. trustee, emeritus). Clubs: Terre Haute Country (bd. dirs. 1974-76). Democrat. Home and Office: 2703 E Springhill Dr Terre Haute IN 47802-8406

BITZER, DONALD LESTER, electrical engineering educator, retired research laboratory administrator; b. East St. Louis, Ill., Jan. 1, 1934; s. Jess L. and Marjorie (Look) B.; m. Maryann Drost, July 2, 1955; 1 son, David. BS, U. Ill., 1955, MS, 1956, PhD, 1960; PhD (hon.), MacMurray Coll. Mem. faculty U. Ill.-Urbana, 1955—, asst. prof., 1960-63, assoc. prof., 1963-67, prof. elec. engring., 1967—, dir. Computer-Based Edn. Research Lab., 1967-89; disting. prof. rsch. N.C. State U., 1989—. Cons. in field. Contbr. articles to profl. jours.; pioneer PLATO-large computer-based edn. system; co-inventor plasma display panel. Recipient Indsl. Rsch. 100 award, 1966, Bobby Connelly Meml. award Miami Valley Computer Assn., 1973, Recognition award Soc. for Info. Display, 1979, Edn. award Am. Fedn. Info. Processing Socs., 1989, Elec. Engring. Disting. Alumni award U. Ill., 1992, Emmy award NATAS, 2002; named laureate Lincoln Acad of Ill., 1982; Internat. Engring. Consortium fellow, 1994. Fellow AAAS, IEEE, Assn. Devel. Computer-Based Instrnl. Sys., Internat. Engring. Consortium; mem. NAE (Vladimir K. Zworykin award), Data Processing Mgmt. Assn. (Computer Sci. Man of Yr. award), Am. Soc. Engring. Edn. (Chester Carlson award), Nat. Acad. Engring. Home: 104 Christofle Ln Cary NC 27511-6473 Office: NC State U Dept Computer Sci PO Box 8206 Raleigh NC 27695-0001

BIVENS, DONALD WAYNE, lawyer, judge; b. Ann Arbor, Mich., Feb. 5, 1952; s. Melvin Donley and Frances Lee (Speer) Bivens; children: Jody, Lisa, Andrew. BA magna cum laude, Yale U., 1974; JD, U. Tex., 1977. Bar: Ariz 1977, US Dist Ct Ariz 1977, US Ct Appeals (9th cir) 1977, US Ct Appeals (fed cir) 1984, US Supreme Ct 1982. Ptnr. Meyer, Hendricks & Bivens, P.A., Phoenix, 1977—. Judge pro tem Maricopa County Superior Ct, Ariz., 1987—, Ariz Ct Appeals, Phoenix, 1999—2000. Editor (note & comment ed): Tex Law Rev, 1976—77. Pres Scottsdale Men's League, 1980—82; vpres, bd dirs Phoenix Symphony Asn, 1980—86; mem adv bd Ariz Theater Co, 1987—88; pres Ariz Young Dems, 1980—82; bd dirs Scottsdale Arts Ctr Asn, 1981—84, Planned Parenthood Cent and Northern Ariz, 1989—92. Recipient Consul Award, Univ Tex Sch Law, 1977, 3 Outstanding Young Men Award, Phoenix Jaycees, 1981. Mem.: ABA (con litigation sect 1995—98, chmn computer litigation comt 1989—92, resource develop comt litigation sect 1992—, technical task force 1998—, state del House Dels 1999—), Thurgood Marshall Inn Ct (pres 1992—93), Maricopa County Bar Asn (bd dirs, pres 1991—92, chmn Trial Adv Inst 1986—87, Mem of the Yr 1998), Ariz Trial Lawyers Asn, State Bar Ariz (bd govs 1993—2000, pres 1998—99, peer rev comt 1992—), Ariz Bar Found, Am Bar Found. Democrat. Avocations: music, theater. Home: 6311 E Naumann Dr Paradise Valley AZ 85253-1044 Office: Meyer Hendricks & Bivens PA 3003 N Central Ave Ste 1200 Phoenix AZ 85012-2915

BIVENS, GORDON ELLSWORTH, economist, educator; b. Nevada, Iowa, Feb. 5, 1927; s. Clarence E. and Hazel Bivens; m. Muriel Katherine Collier, Feb. 14, 1953; children: Dale Mark, Carol Sue, Bruce Alan, Paul Wayne. BS, Iowa State U., 1950, MS, 1953, PhD, 1957. Instr., asst. prof., assoc. prof. Iowa State U., 1954-62; assoc. prof., prof. econs., founding dir. Center for Consumer Affairs, U. Wis.-Milw., 1962-68; consumption economist Consumer and Food Econs. Research div. Agrl. Research Service, Dept. Agr., 1967-68; prof. family econs. and agrl. econs. U. Mo. at Columbia, 1968-76; prof. dept. family environment Iowa State U., 1976-90, head dept., 1976-80, interim assoc. dean for rsch. and grad. edn. Coll. Family and Consumer Scis., 1989-90, Mary B. Welch disting. prof. home econs., 1983—, prof. emeritus, 1989—. Vis. scholar Inst. Behavioral Sci., U. Colo., Boulder, 1974-75; Mem. Consumer Task Force, White House Conf. on Food, Nutrition and Health, 1969; cons. Pres.'s Com. on Consumer Interests, Office Econ. Opportunity, Glick & Lorwin, John Wiley & Sons. Founding editor: Jour. Consumer Affairs, 1967-74. Trustee Am. Home Econs. Assn. Found.; chmn. bd. govs. Center for the Family. Served with USMCR, 1945-46. Mem. Am. Econ. Assn., Am. Family and Consumer Scis., Am. Agrl. Econ. Assn., Am. Assn. for Consumer Research, Am. Council on Consumer Interests (past pres.), Tau Kappa Epsilon, Phi Kappa Phi, Alpha Zeta, Gamma Sigma Delta, Omicron Nu., Soc. Friends. Home: 605 Southwoods Dr Nevada IA 50201-2560

BIVENS, KENNETH EDWARD, physician assistant; b. Washington, June 2, 1958; s. Edward Arthur and Nancy Elizabeth (Swarthing) B.; m. Julie Marie Thorne; children: Laura, Mary, Jennifer. AA, Charles County C.C., 1979; BS, grad. cert., George Washington U., 1983; M in Phys. Asst. Studies, U. Nebr., 2002. RN, Md., Washington, Va.; cert. physician asst., Md., Washington. Emergency room tech. Greater S.E. Cmty. Hosp., Washington, 1976-77, 77-78, So. Md. Hosp. Ctr., Clinton, 1978-79, RN, 1979-81, 81-83; physician asst. Charles County Jail, LaPlata, Md., 1983-84; physician asst. surgery Harbor Hosp., Balt., 1984-85; med. surg. house officer Greater S.E. Cmty. Hosp., Washington, 1985-88, physician asst. occup. health, 1988-92, supr. occupl. health, 1992—2003; physician asst. interventional radiology Civista Med. Ctr., La Plata, Md., 2003—. Emergency med. tech. Charles County Rescue Squad, LaPlata, 1977-88. With USN, 1975-76, lt. USCGR. Mem. Charles County Rescue Squad, La Plata, 1979-88, 96—. With USNR, 1975-81, lt. USCGR, 1985—. Mem. Am. Acad. Physician Assts., Md. Acad. Physician Assts., ANA, Md. Nursing Assn., Res. Officer Assn. Republican. Episcopalian. Avocations: hunting, indian artifact collecting, gun collecting, bowling, fishing. Home: 10500 Lofton Hill Pl La Plata MD 20646-3827 Office: Civista Med Ctr Dept Interventional Radiology La Plata MD 20646

BIVENS, LYNETTE KUPKA, director; b. Chgo., June 1, 1950; d. Walter Edward and Agnes (Berry) Kupka; m. William Joseph Bivens, Sept. 29, 1973; 1 child, Tia Lyn. BE, Govs. State U., 1990, MA in Math. Edn., 1994; grad., Nat. Staff Devel. Coun. Acad., 1998. Cert. elem. tchr., Ill. Tchr. math. Brooks Jr. High, Harvey, Ill., 1990-97; tchr. gifted OW Huth Mid. Sch., Matteson, Ill., 1997—2000; dir. tech. South Cook Intermediate Svc. Ctr., Chicago Hts., Ill., 2000—. Adj. prof. math edn., Governor's State U., 1998—. Mem.: ASCD, Nat. Staff Devel. Coun., Ill. Computing Educators (webmaster Ill. chpt.), Phi Delta Kappa. Democrat. Avocations: fine needlework, reading, photography, computers and technology. E-mail: lbivens@s-cook.org.

BIVINS, SUSAN STEINBACH, systems engineer; b. Chgo., June 5, 1941; d. Joseph Bernard and Eleanor Celeste (Mathes) S.; m. James Herbert Bivins, June 7, 1980. BS, Northwestern U., 1963; postgrad., U. Colo., 1964, U. Ill., 1965, UCLA, 1971. With IBM, 1967-94, supt mgr. East, 1977-78, sys. support mgr., western region L.A., 1978-81, br. market support mgr., 1981-84, mgr. IBM ops. and support L.A. Summer Olympics, 1984, mgr. IBM office supporting devel. FAA air traffic control sys. for 1990's, 1984-88, mgr. complex sys. mktg., 1988-89, acct. devel. mgr. aerospace engring. and mfg., 1989-91, mgr. cons. and outsourcing indsl. sector trading area, 1991-92, cons. orgn. task forces, 1992-93; project exec. IBM Integrated Sys. Solutions Corp., 1993-94; exec. dir. BDM Internat. Inc., 1995-98; sr. dir. Hitachi, 1998—2002; dir., project mgr. Habitat for Humanity Internat., 2003—. Pres. Jastech, 1986—. Developed program to retrieve data via terminal and direct it to any appropriate hardcopy device, 1973. Vol. tchr. computer sci. Calif. Mentally Gifted Minor Programs; vol. L.A. Youth Motivation Task Force; dir. pub. rels. Lake of the Ozarks Jazz Festival, 1993-95; bd. dirs. Greater Lake Area Arts Coun., 1993-95. Mem. Sys. Engring. Symposium, Project Mgmt. Inst. OPM3 and PPM Standards Teams, Cert. PMP, 2003, Pi Lambda Theta. Achievements include developed program to retrieve data via terminal and direct it to any appropriate hardcopy device, 1973, PMI cert. PMP, 2003; vol., PMI orgnl. project mgmt. maturity model, program/portfolio mgmt. std. Office: 216 Eagle Pt Four Seasons MO 65049-9024

BIVONA, JOHN VINCENT, lawyer; b. N.Y.C., July 14, 1941; s. Vincent James and Virginia Marie (Verno) B.; m. Anne Frances Carluccio, Jan. 13, 1968; children— Vincent John, Christopher John. B.A., Fordham U., 1963, J.D., 1966. Bar: N.Y. 1968, U.S. Dist. Ct. (so. and ea. dists.) N.Y. 1970. Law asst. N.Y. Supreme Ct., N.Y.C., 1969-71; assoc. firm Newman, Rich, Krinsly, Poses & Katz, N.Y.C., 1971-73; sr. ptng. Bivona & Cohen, N.Y.C., 1973— ; lectr. Def. Research Inst., Atlanta, 1982— . Contbr. articles to profl. jours. Bd. dirs. Neighborhood Council to Combat Poverty, N.Y.C., 1975—, Little Italy Restoration Soc., N.Y.C., 1977-80; pres. Heritage Theatre Nat. Arts Club, N.Y.C., 1974— ; co-pres. Tomorrow's Children's Fund, 1983— . Recipient Disting. Service award Heritage Theatre, N.Y.C., 1983. Mem. Def. Research Inst. (lectr. Atlanta 1982—), N.Y. State Trial Lawyers (lectr. 1983—), N.Y. County Lawyers Assn., Columbian Lawyers. Republican. Roman Catholic. Office: Bivona & Cohen Wall St Plz New York NY 10005 also: 4547 Cornhill London England Home: 235 Cambridge Oaks Park Ridge NJ 07656-2619

BIX, BRIAN, law educator; b. Mpls., Aug. 1, 1962; s. Harold Charles and Helen (Helman) B. BA, Washington U., St. Louis, 1983; JD, Harvard U., 1986; DPhil, Oxford (Eng.) U., 1991. Bar: Mass. 1994, Conn. 1995, Minn. 2002. Jud. clk. to Justice A. Handler N.J. Supreme Ct., Trenton, 1986-87; jud. clk. to Judge S. Reinhardt 9th Circuit Ct. of Appeals, L.A., 1987-88; lectr. in law Kings Coll., U. London, 1991-93; jud. clk. to Justice Benjamin Kaplan Mass. Appeals Ct., Boston, 1993-95; assoc. prof. law Quinnipiac Law Sch., Hamden, Conn., 1995-98, prof., 1998-2001; assoc. prof. law and philosophy U. Minn., 2001—02, prof., 2002—. Vis. prof. George Washington Law Sch., 1999, Georgetown U. Law Ctr., 2000. Author: Law, Language and Legal Determinacy, 1993, Jurisprudence: Theory and Context, 1996, 3d edit., 2003; editor: Analyzing Law, New Essays in Legal Theory, 1998, Contract Law, vols. I and II, 2000. Mem. Am. Law Inst. Office: U Minn Law Sch 229 19th Ave South Minneapolis MN 55455 E-mail: bixxx002@umn.edu.

BIXBY, FRANK LYMAN, lawyer; b. New Richmond, Wis., May 25, 1928; s. Frank H. and Esther (Otteson) B.; m. Katharine Spence, July 7, 1951; children— Paul, Thomas, Edward, Janet. AB, Harvard U., 1950; LLB, U. Wis., 1953. Bar: Ill. 1953, Wis. 1953, Fla. 1974. Ptnr. firm Sidley Austin Brown & Wood, Chgo., 1963—97, sr. counsel, 1998—. Editor-in-chief Wis. Law Rev, 1952-53; mem. editorial bd. Chgo. Reporter, 1973-89. Trustee MacMurray Coll., Jacksonville, Ill., 1973-85; bd. dirs. Chgo. Urban League, 1962—, v.p., 1972-86, gen. counsel, 1972—, chmn. 1986-89; bd. dirs. Community Renewal Soc., 1973-86, Voices for Ill. Children, 1987-90; chmn. trustees Unitarian Ch., Evanston, Ill., 1962-63; bd. dirs. Spencer Found., 1967-2001, chmn. 1975-90; mem. dist. 202 bd. edn. Evanston Twp. High Sch., 1975-81, pres., 1977-79. Recipient Man of Year award Chgo. Urban League, 1974 Mem. ABA, Ill. Bar Assn., Chgo. Bar Assn., Chgo. Coun. Lawyers, Chgo. Coun. Fgn. Rels., Order of Coif, Harvard Club (pres. 1964-65), Mid-Day Club., Phi Beta Kappa. Home: 505 N Lake Shore Dr Apt 4607 Chicago IL 60611-3409 Office: Sidley Austin Brown & Wood 10 S Dearborn St Chicago IL 60603-2000 E-mail: fbixby@sidley.com., kfbixby@yahoo.com.

BIXBY, HAROLD GLENN, manufacturing company executive; b. Lamotte, Mich., July 14, 1903; s. Charles Samuel and Laura (Schenk) B.; m. Pauline Elizabeth Summy, July 3, 1928; children: Mary Louise and Richard Glenn (twins). AB, U. Mich., 1927, LL.D. (hon.), 1972. Began in accounting dept. Ex-Cell-O Corp., Detroit, 1928, asst. sec., 1929, controller, 1933, sec., treas. and dir., 1937, became v.p., treas., dir., 1947, pres., gen. mgr., 1951-70, chmn. bd., chief exec. officer, 1970-72, chmn. bd., 1972—, chmn. exec. com., 1973-79. Bd. dirs., hon. trustee Kalamazoo Coll. Mem. Greater Detroit C. of C., Tau Kappa Epsilon. Clubs: Economic, Detroit Athletic, Detroit Golf. Home and Office: 16351 Rotunda Dr Ste 357 Dearborn MI 48120-1159

BIXBY, ROBERT EUGENE, computer, mathematics educator; b. Oakland, Calif., Sept. 14, 1945; m. 1966, 3 children. BA, U. Calif., Berkeley, 1968; MS, Cornell U., 1970, PhD in Opers. Rsch., 1972. Asst. prof. math. U. Ky., 1972-77; assoc. prof. Northwestern U., 1977-80, prof., 1980-84; prof. computer & appl. math. Rice U., 1984—; chmn. Cplex Optimization, Incline Village, Nev., 1984-97; chmn. tech. adv. bd. ILOG Inc., Incline Village, Nev. Mem. Nat. Acad. Engring., Math. Prog. Soc., Soc. Ind. Appl. Math. Home: 6020 Annapolis St Houston TX 77005-3112 Office: ILOG Inc Lake Tahoe Office 889 Alder Ave Incline Village NV 89451

BIXENSTINE, KIM FENTON, lawyer; b. Providence, Feb. 26, 1958; d. Barry Jay and Gail Louise (Traverse) Weinstein; m. Barton Aaron Bixenstine, June 25, 1983; children: Paul Jay, Nathan Alexis. BA, Middlebury Coll., 1979; JD, U. Chgo., 1982. Bar: Ohio 1982, U.S. Dist. Ct. (no. and so. dists.) Ohio 1983, U.S. Ct. Appeals (6th cir.) 1983. Law clk. to presiding judge U.S. Dist. Ct. (so. dist.) Ohio, Cin., 1982-83; assoc. Jones, Day, Reavis & Pogue, Cleve., 1983-90, ptnr., 1991-99; sr. counsel TRW Inc., Cleve., 1999—2001, v.p., chief litig. counsel, 2002—03; v.p., dep. gen. counsel Univ.. Hosp. Health Sys., Cleve., 2003—. Chair comml. adv. coun. N.E. Ohio chpt. Am. Arbitration Assn. Bd. dirs. Planned Parenthood Greater Cleve., 1991—99, sec., 1992—93, v.p., 1994—96, pres., 1996—98; chair corp. giving subcom. Cleve. Bar Found. Campaign, 2001—02; bd. dirs. Boys and Girls Club Cleve., 2001—03, chair pub. rels. com., 2002—03. Mem.: Cleve. Bar Assn. (commn. women in the law 1988—2001, bd. dirs. 1993—96, minority outreach com. 1993—99, chair standing com. lawyer professionalism 1994—96, bd. liaison to jud. selection com. 1996, nominating com. 1997—99, chair nominating com. 1998—99, long range planning com. 2002—03), Ohio Women's Bar Assn. (chair legis. com. 1994—95, trustee 1995—97). Avocations: jogging, reading. Office: Univ Hosps Health Sys WO Walker Ctr 10524 Euclid Ave STe 1100 Cleveland OH 44106

BIXLER, JOHN MOURER, lawyer; b. Washington, Oct. 14, 1927; s. John S. and Elsie (Mourer) B.; m. Miriam Calhoun, Aug. 16, 1952; children: Allyson Sue Switzer, Stephen J., Mary Lynn Frye. BS, U. Pa., 1949; LLB, Harvard U., 1954. Bar: D.C. 1954, Md. 1960. Staff mem. Charles S. Rockey & Co. CPAs, Phila., 1949-51; assoc. Miller & Chevalier, Washington, 1954-61; mem. Miller & Chevalier, Chartered, Washington, 1962-98; ptnr. Ross, Marsh & Foster, Washington, 1998—. Lectr. local estate planning couns. Am. Law Inst. ABA, NYU Inst. Fed. Taxation. Trustee D.C. Legal Aid Soc., Washington, 1975-92, U. Pa., Phila., 1975-80; trustee Concord-St. Andrew's United Meth. Ch., Bethesda, Md., chair 1975-90, treas., 1990-2001, 2003—; v.p. Meth. Home of D.C., 1982—; trustee Miller and Chevalier Charitable Found., Washington, 1969—, pres., 1969-94. Recipient Joseph Wharton award Wharton Sch. Club of Washington, 1982. Fellow Am. Bar Found.; mem. ABA (tax sect. coun. 1979-82), The Met. Club of City of Washington, Lawyers Club, The Barristers, Am. Coll. Trust and Estate Counsel (regent 1987-94, D.C. state chmn. 1983-87, Washington rep. 1987-2002), Am. Coll. Tax Coun., Confrerie des Chevaliers du Tastevin (grand chambellan hon., commanderie d'Amerique, v.p. dir. Tastevin Found., treas. sous-commanderie de Washington). Republican. Methodist. Avocations: gardening, travel. Home: 5304 Moorland Ln Bethesda MD 20814-1334 Office: Ross Marsh & Foster 2001 L St NW Ste 400 Washington DC 20036-4946 Business E-Mail: jbixler@rossmarshfoster.com.

BIXLER, THOMAS L. music educator; b. Wadsworth, Ohio, Apr. 30, 1959; s. Vernon Ned and Shirley Lavone Bixler; m. Kay Lynn Nicholson, Aug. 8, 1981 (div. Aug. 1, 2002); 1 child, Gregory Robert. BA Music Ed., Ohio State Univ., Columbus, OH, 1977—81. Cert. Teacher Ohio Dept. Edn. Dir. bands Ottoville Local Schools, Ottoville, Ohio, 1981—84, Port Clinton City Schools, Port Clinton, 1984—. Dist. ii pres. Ohio Music Educators Assn., Columbus, Ohio, 1997—99, music adjudicator, 1987—. Performer Port Clinton Cmty. Band, Port Clinton, Ohio, 1990. Mem.: Am. Fedn. of Teachers, Nat. Band Assn., Ohio Music Educator's Assn. (dist. pres. 1997—99). Avocations: travelling, golfing, golfing. Home: 226 1/2 Washington St Port Clinton OH 43452 Office: Port Clinton City Schools 821 South Jefferson St Port Clinton OH 43452 Office Fax: 419-734-4276. E-mail: tom_bixler@port-clinton.kiz.oh.us.

BIZIOU, PETER, cinematographer; Cinematographer: (films) Bugsy Malone, 1978, Monty Python's Life of Brian, 1979, Time Bandits, 1981, Pink Floyd-The Wall, 1982, Another Country, 1984 (Cannes award best artistic contbn.), 9 1/2 Weeks, 1986, A World Apart, 1988, Mississippi Burning, 1988 (Academy award best cinematography 1988, British Acad. award 1989, award British Soc. Cinematographers 1989), Rosencrantz and Guildenstern Are Dead, 1991, City of Joy, 1992, Damage, 1992, In the Name of the Father, 1993, Road to Wellville, 1994, Richard III, 1995, The Truman Show, 1998, Unfaithfull, 2001.

BIZUB, BARBARA L. elementary school educator; b. Newark, Jan. 14, 1947; d. Anthony Edward and Mary Travers Petti; m. William Joseph Bizub, Aug. 27, 1966; children: William Anthony, Melissa Catherine Bizub. BA in Elem. Edn., Kean Coll., 1975, MA in Early Childhood Edn., 1985. Cert. tchr. N-8. Tchr. grade one Roselle (N.J.) Bd. Edn., 1975-76, Title VII reading specialist, grades 1-4, 1976-78, tchr. second grade, 1978-79, kindergarten tchr., 1979—. Cons. whole lang. Roselle Bd. Edn., 1993—94; guest spkr. 31st Ann. Reading Conf./Kean Coll., Union, NJ, 1994; guest lectr. Kean Coll., 1996, 98, 99, 2000, 01; materials presenter 28th Ann. Reading Conf./Rutgers U., 1996; workshop presenter N.J. Assn. Edn. Young Children, 1997, 98, Nat. Coun. Tchrs. English, N.Y.C., 1998, N.J. Assn. Kindergarten Educators, 2003; presenter in field. Co-author: Family Life Curriculum, K-7, 1985-89; pilot tchr. Whole Lang. Initiative, Roselle, 1993. Recipient A-Plus for Kids Grant, A-Plus for Kids, 1994, 96. Mem. Nat. Coun. Tchrs. English (guest spkr. 1994), Internat. Reading Assn., Ctrl. Jersey Tchrs. of Whole Lang., N.J. Assn. Kindergarten Educators (workshop presenter 2003), Ctrl. Jersey Tchrs. Whole Lang., Phi Kappa Phi. Roman Catholic. Avocations: reading, fly fishing, aerobics, cooking, antiquing. Office: Roselle Bd Edn 710 Locust St Roselle NJ 07203-1919

BIZUB, JOHANNA CATHERINE, law librarian; b. Denville, N.J., Apr. 13, 1957; d. Stephen Bernard and Elizabeth Mary (Grizzle) B.; m. Scott Jeffrey Smith, 1992. BS in Criminal Justice, U. Dayton, 1979; MLS, Rutgers U., 1984. Law libr. Morris County Law Libr., 1981-83, Clapp & Eisenberg, Newark, 1984-86; dir. libr. Sills Cummis, 1986-94; libr. dir. Montville (N.J.) Twp. Pub. Libr., N.J., 1994-97; libr. dir. law dept. Prudential Ins. Co. Am., Newark, 1997—. Mem. ALA, N.J. Law Librs. Assn. (treas. 1987-89, v.p./pres.-elect 1989-90, 99-2000, pres. 1990-91, 2000-01, past pres. 1991-92, 2001-02), Am. Assn. Law Librs. (pvt. law librs. SIS, vice chair 1992-93, chair 1993-94, past chair 1994-95), N.J. Libr. Assn., Assoc. Libr. of Morris County (v.p. 1995, pres. 1996, treas. 1997-01), Spl. Libr. Assn. N.J. (treas. 1990-92), Am. Legion Aux. (treas. Rockden unit 175 1983-93). Democrat. Roman Catholic. Home: 11 Elm St Rockaway NJ 07866-3108 Office: Prudential Ins Co Am 22 Plz 751 Broad St Newark NJ 07102-3714

BIZZELL, MARY ANN, counselor; b. Cleve., Ohio, Aug. 2, 1958; d. Walter D. and Maudie Bizzell. BA, Wilberforce U., Wilberforce, Ohio, 1980. Cert. chemical dependency counselor, prevention specialist, alcohol & drug counselor. Substance abuse prevention specialist Ctr. Families and Children /RapArt, Cleve., 1994—. Roman Catholic.

BIZZELL YARBROUGH, CINDY LEE, school counselor; b. Griffin, Ga., June 20, 1951; d. William Emerson and Senora Elizabeth (Henderson) B.; m. Randy Yarbrough (dec. July 1999); m. Cary W. Martin, July 9, 2001; 1 child, Delana Michelle. Student, North Ga. Coll., 1969-70; BA in Elem. Edn., MS in Behavior Disorders, West Ga. Coll., 1993; MS in Learning Disabilities, MS in Counseling and Ednl. Psychology,, 1993. K-12 reading, math., sci. and elem. edn. tchr. Pike County Schs., Zebulon, Ga., 1972—; tchr., counselor of emotionally disturbed Pike County Elem. Sch., 1973—; tchr. of emotionally disturbed and behavior disorders Pike County H.S., 1993—; crisis counselor McIntosh Trail Mental Health Mental Retardation, 1994; counselor Pike County Primary Sch., 1999, Morningstar Family Svcs., 2001. Cons. Alcoholics Anonymous, Griffin, 1982—, Pike County Coun. on Child Abuse, 1990—; lectr., presenter in field. Author: Hippotherapy for the Emotionally Disturbed, 1988; contbr. articles to profl. publs. Leader, instr. Girl Scouts U.S., Meansville, Ga., 1969-90; co-coord. Ga. Spl. Olympics, Pike County, 1980—; pres. Internat. Reading Assn., Griffin, 1978; asst. leader 4H, 1992-93; substitute Sunday sch. tchr. local Meth. Ch. Recipient Sci. award Ford Found., 1966; named Res. Champion Open Jumper, Dixieland Show Cir., 1989. Mem. N.Am. Handicapped Riders Assn. (presenter), Profl. Assn. Ga. Educators. Democrat. Avocations: horseback riding, showing hunter jumpers. Home: 250 Silver Dollar Rd Barnesville GA 30204 Office: Pike County Schs Hwy 19 Zebulon GA 30295

BIZZI, EMILIO, neurophysiologist, educator; b. Rome, Feb. 22, 1933; arrived in U.S., 1963, naturalized, 1982; s. Vittorio and Anna (Galeazzi) Bizzi; m. Jane Stockton Shaw, Aug. 9, 1941. MD summa cum laude with highest honors, U. Rome, 1958. Postdoctoral trainee Inst. Med. Pathology, U. Siena, Italy, 1958-60; postdoctoral trainee Inst. Physiology, U. Pisa, Italy, 1960-63; rsch. assoc. neurophysiol. lab., dept. zoology Washington U., St. Louis, 1963-64; vis. assoc. sect. physiology, lab. clin. sci. NIMH, Bethesda, Md., 1964-66; rsch. assoc. dept. psychology MIT, Cambridge, 1966-67, lectr. dept. psychology, 1967-68, assoc. prof. neurophysiology, 1969-72, prof., 1972-80, Eugene McDermott prof. brain scis. and human behavior, 1980—2002, inst. prof., 2002—, dir. Whitaker Coll., 1983-88, chmn. dept. Brain and Cognitive Scis., 1986-97. Contbr. chapters to books, articles and abstracts to profl. jours.; mem. editl. bd.: Brain Theory Newsletter, 1980—, Jour. Motor Behavior, 1981—, Jour. Neurobiology, 1981—. Recipient Alden Spencer award, Columbia U. Coll. Physicians and Surgeons, 1978, Hermann von Hlmholtz award, 1992; fellow Found. Rsch. Psychiatry, 1978—. Mem.: NAS, Am. Acad. Clin. Neurophysiol., Acad. dei Lincei, Am. Acad. Arts and Scis., Internat. Brain Rsch. Orgn. Office: MIT Dept Brain & Cognitive Scis Cambridge MA 02139-4307

BIZZOCO, DREW FRANK, chiropractor; b. Bklyn., Feb. 5, 1961; s. Rose Josephine (Giglio) B. Student, Kingsboro Coll., 1978-79, Bklyn. Coll., 1980-81; D Chiropractic, N.Y. Chiropractic Coll., 1985; grad., Logan Chiropractic Coll., 1993. Diplomate in Chiropractic Neurology. Pvt. practice, Bklyn., 1987-93; chiropractor, owner, mgr. Spinecare, Bklyn., 1993—; owner, mgr. Colonie Chiropractic, Albany, 1997—2000. Quality assurance mgr. CHIRO, NJ, 1995—; sec., owner Uncle Louie G., Inc., 1999—; v.p., owner Uncle Louie G. Franchise, Inc., 2001—. Instr. T. Kang Tae Kwon Do, 1986—. Mem. Am. Chiropractic Assn., N.Y. State Chiropractic Assn. Republican. Avocations: martial arts, scuba diving, skiing, basketball, weight training. Office: Healthquest 3500 Nostrand Ave Brooklyn NY 11229-5107 E-mail: DrewBizz@aol.com.

BJERKAAS, CARLTON LEE, technology services company executive; b. Fergus Falls, Minn., Apr. 17, 1948; s. Jay Oscar and Anna Marie (Bangert) B.; children: Kristopher Scott, Eric Stefan, Todd Philip. BS, U. N.D., 1970; MS,

MIT, 1977; MPA, Auburn U., Montgomery, Ala., 1983. Commd. 2d lt. USAF, 1970, advanced through grades to col., 1992; weather forecaster Weather Detachment, Homestead AFB, Fla., 1971-73; flight examiner Weather Reconnaissance Squadron, Andersen AFB, Guam, 1973-75; radar rsch. meteorologist A.F. Geophysics Lab., Hanscom AFB, Mass., 1976-82; chief support br. operational requirements & testing Hdqrs. Mil. Airlift Command, Scott AFB, Ill., 1983-85; chief aerospace environ. requirements Hdqrs. A.F. Systems Command, Andrews AFB, Md., 1985-87; comdr. Weather Detachment, Lajes Field, Azores, Portugal, 1987-89; asst. chief of staff Hdqrs. Air Weather Svc., Scott AFB, 1989-91, dir. resource mgmt., 1991-92, dir. program mgmt., integration, 1992-94; dir. sys. and comm., 1994-95; dir. tech., plans and programs, 1995—; sr. scientist Hdqrs. Air Weather Svc., Scott AFB, Ill., 1995-96; divsn. mgr. Sci. Applications Internat. Corp., O'Fallon, Ill., 1996—2001, ops. mgr., 2001—. Contbr. articles to profl. jours. Com. chmn. Boy Scouts Am., O'Fallon, Ill., 1991-92; coach, referee youth sports, O'Fallon, 1989—; chmn. Sch. Bd., Lajes Field Azores, 1988-89; mem. Sch. Dist. Com., Lajes Field Azores, 1987. Fellow Am. Meteorol. Soc.; mem. AAAS, ASPA, N.Y. Acad. Scis., Acad. Polit. Sci., Air Weather Assn., Air Lift and Tanker Assn., Phi Beta Kappa, Sigma Xi, Phi Eta Sigma, Pi Alpha Alpha, Rotary. Methodist. Avocations: computers, soccer coaching, boy scouts. Office: Science Applications Intl Corp 731 Lakepointe Centre Dr O Fallon IL 62269-3073

BJERKE, H. SCOTT, surgeon; b. Mpls., Dec. 26, 1956; s. Robert Edward and Darline McMartin B.; m. Janet Anne Sikora, Sept. 25, 1995; 1 child, Duncan. BS with honors, U. Mich., 1979; MD, U. Hawaii, 1983. Resident New Eng. Med. Ctr., Boston, 1983-88; chief divsn. surg. critical care U. Nev., Las Vegas, 1991-99; med. dir. trauma svcs. Clarian Health, Indpls., 1999—. Bd. trustees Univ. Surgery Profls., Las Vegas, 1992-99. Co-author: (chpt.) Trauma, 4th edit., 1999. Med. dir. tactical medics Indpls. Police SWAT Team, 1999—; med. dir. Clark County Fire Dept., Las Vegas, 1992-99; IST physician FEMA Urban Search & Rescue, Oklahoma City, 1995; med. dir. Nye County Vol. Ambulance, Amargosa Spring, Nev., 1995-99. Recipient Congrl. Recognition Svc., Sen Bryan, 1995; Rsch. fellow UCLA Med. Ctr., L.A., 1988-90, Trauma fellow Cedars Sinai Med. Ctr., L.A., 1990-91. Fellow Am. Coll. Surgeons, Assn. Surgery Trauma, Ea. Assn. Surgery Trauma; mem. Internat. Assn. Police Surgeons (life). Avocations: sports cars, scuba diving. Office: 1701 N Senate Blvd Indianapolis IN 46202

BJERKNES, MICHAEL LEIF, dancer; b. Oak Park, Ill., Dec. 6, 1956; s. Christian Edward and Barbara Ann (Sirkin) B.; m. Pamela Booth Mitchell, July 15, 1979; children: Philip, Anna, Alexandra. Student, Rosary Coll., 1970-73; M in Internat. Mgmt., U. Md., 1997. Dancer Joffrey II, N.Y.C., 1973-74; soloist Chgo. Ballet, 1974-76, Houston Ballet, 1976-78, Joffrey Ballet, N.Y.C., 1978-79, 79-82, union rep., 1980-82, workshop tchr., 1982—, tchr. sch., 1983-85; repetiteur Washington Ballet, 1989-90. Guest ballet master Universal Ballet, 1994—; guest tchr. Md. Youth Ballet, 1997—; quality leader GE Info. Svcs., 1997-2001; pres., bd. dirs. Am. Dance Inst., 1999—, exec. dir., 2001—; arts panelist NEA, 1999. Prin. dancer Royal Winnipeg (Manitoba, Can.) Ballet, 1979, Milw. Ballet, 1984, Washington Ballet, 1985-90; guest artist No. Ballet Theatre, Manchester, Eng., 1981, Minn. Dance Theatre, 1982-85, Chamber Ballet, 1984, Ballet Chgo., 1990, Tulsa Ballet Sch., 1991, Universal Ballet, 1991; tchr. various ballet schs. U.S., 1972-79, Ruth Page Found., Chgo., 1982-84, Washington Sch. Ballet, 1986-93; ballet master Universal Ballet, Seoul, 1990-95, Washington Ballet, 1993-96; choreographer Universal Ballet, 1993; vol. project devel. mgr. Internat. Exec. Svc. Corps, 1997, Chgo. Dance Masters, 1997, 98; quality mgr. GE, 1997-99; v.p. Tech. Leaders, Inc., 1999. Mem. Am. Guild Musical Artists (bd. dirs. 1980-81), Can. Actor's Equity. E-mail: mbjerknes@americanance.org.

BJORCK, JEFFREY PAUL, psychology educator, clinical psychologist; b. Hackensack, N.J., Nov. 17, 1960; s. Walter Jr. and Irene Louise (Cubberley) B.; m. Sharon-Rose McConnell, Nov. 10, 1990. BA in Psychology summa cum laude, Colgate U., 1983; MA in Clin. Psychology, U. Del., 1987, PhD in Clin. Psychology, 1991. Lic. clin. psychologist, Calif. Adj. instr. psychology dept. U. Del., Newark, 1986-87; psychotherapist Cecil County Mental Health Ctr., Elkton, Md., 1987-88; psychol. assoc. Del. Guidance Svcs., Wilmington, Del., 1988-90; psychology assoc. Bayer & Langsdorf, PA, Elkton, 1989-90, A.D. Hart, PhD, Pasadena, Calif., 1990-93; asst. prof. Fuller Grad. Sch. Psychology, Pasadena, Calif., 1990-98, assoc. prof., 1998—; lic. clin. psychologist, 1993—; mem. affiliate staff Las Encinas Hosp., Pasadena, Calif., 1995-98; mem., bd. consulting editors Internat. Jour. for Psychology of Religion, 1998—. Owner Purepiano.com Author: Managing Managed Care Casebook: A Self-Study Guide, 2000; guest editl. reviewer jour. Rsch. in the Social Sci. Study of Religion, 1992—; composer, prodr., pianist Pure Piano Portraits CD, 1997, Pure Piano Panoramas CD, 2000; contbr. articles to profl. jours. Mem. APA, Calif. Psychol. Assn., Soc. for Sci. Study of Religion, Phi Beta Kappa. Evangelical Presbyterian. Office: Fuller Grad Sch Psychology 180 N Oakland Ave Pasadena CA 91101-1792 E-mail: jeffbjorck@purepiano.com.

BJORHOVDE, REIDAR, civil engineer, educator, researcher, consultant; b. Harstad, Norway, Nov. 6, 1941; s. Reidar Conradi and Rebekka Josefine (Gjertsen)) B.; m. Patricia Ellery Ordonez; Oct. 30, 1972; children: Ian Douglas, Heather Leah. MS, Tech. U. of Norway, 1964, Dr. of Engring., 1968; PhD, Lehigh U., 1972. Registered profl. engr., Mont., Can., Norway. Asst. prof. and govt. scholar Tech. U. of Norway, Trondheim, 1964-68; regional and research engr. Am. Inst. Steel Constrn., Boston and N.Y., 1972-76; prof. civil engring. U. Alta., Edmonton, Can., 1976-81, U. Ariz., Tucson, 1981-87; prof., chmn. civil engring. dept. U. Pitts., 1987-91, 95-96, prof. and dir., 1989-98; pres. The Bjorhovde Group, Internat. Engring. Consortium, Tucson, 1998—. Tech. sec. Structural Stability Rsch. Coun., Bethlehem, Pa., 1969-71; cons. to indsl. orgns., design firms, contractors, developers and rsch. labs. worldwide; disting. vis. prof. Ecole Normale Superieure, Paris, 1987, U. Witwatersrand, Johannesburg, South Africa, 1989, U. Tecnica Federico Santa Maria, Vina del Mar, Chile, 2002; mem. related faculty Ctr. Latin Am. Studies and Ctr. for West European Studies, U. Pitts., 1988-98; chmn. bd. Internat. Design Group, Louisville, 1989-99. Editor Jour. Constructional Steel Rsch., 1986—; contbr. over 200 articles to profl. jours. Trustee St. Luke's in the Desert, 1999—2003; bd. dirs. Humane Soc. So. Ariz., PRIME Sch. Music. Recipient Duggan medal Engring. Inst. Can., 1980, numerous others including NSF; rsch. fellow NATO, 1969-70, sci. fellow Royal Norwegian Coun. for Sci. and Indsl. Rsch., 1970-71, sr. guest scientist fellow NATO, 1987; Am. Inst. Steel Constrn. T.R. Higgins award, 1987; Japan Soc. for Promotion Sci. rsch. fellow, 1992. Fellow ASCE (coms., J. James R. Croes medal 1992, Shortridge Hardesty award 2000), Internat. Assn. for Bridge and Structural Engring.; mem. Structural Stability Rsch. Coun. (coun. vice chmn. 1995-98, coun. chmn. 1998-2002), Am. Inst. Steel Constrn. (numerous coms.), Am. Iron and Steel Inst. (numerous coms., Svc. award 1995), Mexican Soc. Structural Engrs., Assn. Bridge Constrn. and Design (bd. dirs.), Engrs. Soc. Western Pa. (numerous coms. including gen. chmn. Internat. Bridge Conf.), Steel Constrn. Inst. (U.K.), Norwegian Soc. for Steel Structures. Democrat. Office: The Bjorhovde Group PO Box 37168 Tucson AZ 85740-7168

BJORK, GORDON CARL, economist, educator; b. Seattle, Dec. 15, 1935; s. Gordon E. and Florence E. (Bloomberg) B.; m. Susan Jill Serman, Dec. 29, 1960; children: Katharine, Rebecca, Susannah, Anders. AB, Dartmouth Coll., 1957; BA (hon.), Oxford U., 1959, MA, 1963; PhD, U. Wash., 1963. Lectr. econs. U. B.C., Vancouver, Can., 1962-63; asst. prof. econs. Carleton U., Ottawa, Ont., 1963-64; assoc. prof. econs. Columbia U., N.Y.C., 1964-68; pres. Linfield Coll., McMinnville, Oreg., 1968-74; prof. econs. Oreg. State U., Corvallis, 1974-75; Lovelace prof. econs. Claremont McKenna Coll., Claremont Grad. Sch., Calif., 1975—. Henry Walker disting. vis. prof. bus. enterprise U. Hawaii, 1985-86; vis. prof. econs. Nottingham (Eng.) U., 1990; mem. nat. adv. com. on environ. policy and tech. EPA. Author: Private Enterprise and Public Interest: The Development of American Capitalism, 1969, Life, Liberty and Property: The Economics and Politics of Land Use Planning and Environmental Control, 1980, Stagnation and Growth in the American Economy, 1985, The Way It Worked and Why It Won't: Structural Change and the Slowdown of U.S. Economic Growth, 1999. Lt. USCGR, 1960-68. Rhodes scholar, 1957; Battelle Inst. fellow, 1975 Mem. Phi Beta Kappa Republican. United Ch. of Christ. Home: 4609 Vista Buena Rd Santa Barbara CA 93110-1945 Office: Claremont McKenna Coll Dept Econs Claremont CA 91711 E-mail: gbjork@mckenna.edu. *An educator teaches by what he is and what he does. My objective, as a teacher, is to mold the values and conceptual framework of the next generation.*

BJORK, ROBERT DAVID, JR., lawyer; b. Evanston, Ill., Sept. 29, 1946; s. Robert David and Lenore Evelyn (Loderhose) B.; m. Linda Louise Reese, Mar. 27, 1971; children: Heidi Lynne, Gretchen Anne. BBA, U. Wis., 1968; JD, Tulane U., 1974. Bar: La. 1974, U.S. Dist. Ct. (ea. dist.) La. 1974, U.S. Ct. Appeals (5th cir.) 1974, U.S. Dist. Ct. (mid. dist.) 1975, U.S. Supreme Ct. 1977, U.S. Dist. Ct. (we. dist.) 1978, U.S. Ct. Appeals (11th cir.) 1981, Calif. 1983, U.S. Dist. Ct. (no. dist.) Calif. 1983, U.S. Dist. Ct. (ea. dist.) Calif. 1984. Ptnr. Adams & Reese, New Orleans, 1974-83; assoc. Crosby, Heafey, Roach & May, Oakland, Calif., 1983-85; ptnr. Bjork Lawrence, Oakland, 1985—. Instr. paralegal studies Tulane U., New Orleans, 1979—82. Mem. Tulane U. Law Rev., 1973-74; editor Med. Malpractice newsletter, 1983-88. Bd. dirs. Piedmont (Calif.) Coun. Camp Fire, 1984-92, pres., 1987-89; treas. Couhig Congl. Com., New Orleans, 1980-82; bd. dirs. Camp Augusta Trust, 1990-2001. Lt. USNR, 1968-71. Mem. ABA, Internat. Assn. Def. Counsel, Calif. Bar Assn., La. Bar Assn. (chmn. young lawyers sect. 1982-83). Home: 1909 Oakland Ave Piedmont CA 94611-3706 Office: Bjork Lawrence 1901 Harrison St Ste 1630 Oakland CA 94612-3501 E-mail: rbjork@bjorklaw.com.

BJORK, ROBERT ERIC, language professional educator; b. Virginia, Minn., Feb. 19, 1949; s. George Emanual and Alice Celinda (Sandberg) B. BA, Pomona Coll., 1971; MA, UCLA, 1974, PhD, 1979, Adj. lectr. Writing Programs and Medicine UCLA, 1979-83; asst. prof., assoc. prof. English Ariz. State U., Tempe, 1983-89, prof., 1989—. Vis. scholar St. Catharine's Coll. Cambridge U., 1997; dir. Ariz. Ctr. Medieval Renaissance Studies, 1994—. Author: Old English Verse Saints' Lives, 1985; editor: Sources and Analogues of Old English Poetry II, 1983, Cynewulf: Basic Readings, 1996, A Beowulf Handbook, 1997; transl. Lars Hård Trilogy, 1983-85, Holme Trilogy, 1989-90, Only a Mother, 1991; co-editor Studies in Scandinavian Lit. and Culture, 1992-2001; gen. editor Modern Scandinavian Lit. in Translation, 1984-94; dir., gen. editor Medieval and Renaissance Texts and Studies, 1996—; editor: The Oxford Dictionary of the Middle Ages, 1999—. Recipient Tchg. award Burlington No. Found., 1988. Mem. Internat. Assn. U. Profs. English, Medieval Acad. Am. (dir. data project coun.), Renaissance Soc. Am. (coun.), Soc. Advancement of Scandinavian Study, Internat. Soc. of Anglo-Saxonistis (pres. 2002-4). Office: Ariz State Univ Ctr Medieval Renaissance Tempe AZ 85287 E-mail: robert.bjork@asu.edu.

BJORKHOLM, JOHN ERNST, retired physicist; b. Milw., Mar. 22, 1939; s. Jack W. and Marion B. (Anderson) B.; m. Mary J. Durbin, June 20, 1964; children— Kristin E., Laura J. BSE in Engring. Physics highest honors, Princeton U., 1961; MS, Stanford U., 1962, PhD in Applied Physics, 1966. Mem. tech. staff Electronics Rsch. Lab. AT&T Bell Labs., Holmdel, N.J., 1966-83, disting. mem. tech. staff, 1983-94, cons. in applied physics, 1994-96; prin. scientist Components Rsch., Intel Corp., Santa Clara, Calif., 1996—2002; ret., 2002. Contbr. numerous articles to profl. jours.; patentee in field Chmn. Gordon Rsch. Conf. on Nonlinear Optics and Lasers, 1977; comptr. Conf. on Lasers and Electro-Optics, 1989-91; trustee Princeton U., 1991-95. NSF fellow, 1961-62, Howard Hughes fellow, 1962-65 Fellow Am. Phys. Soc., Optical Soc. Am. (dir.-at-large 1988-90, fin. and investment com. 1988-91, exec. com. 1990, treas. 1992-96); mem. IEEE (sr.), NRC (com. on atomic, molecular and optical sci. 1988-91). Home: 408 Cabonia Ct Pleasanton CA 94566-5201

BJORKLUND, DIANE LOUISE, sociology educator; b. Rockford, Ill. d. Stanley Alexander and Alice Victoria Bjorklund; m. Paul M. Blumberg; children: David E. Shorter, Thomas N. Shorter. BA, U. Calif., Irvine; PhD, U. Calif., Davis, 1993. Asst. prof. dept. sociology and anthropology Ill. State U., Normal, 1998—. Author: Interpreting the Self: Two Hundred Years of American Autobiography, 1998. Recipient Herbert Blumer award Soc. for the Study Symbolic Interaction. Office: Ill State Univ Campus Box 4660 Normal IL 61790 E-mail: dlbjork@ilstu.edu.

BJORNCRANTZ, LESLIE BENTON, librarian; b. Jersey City, Mar. 1, 1945; d. David and Jeanne (Proctor) Benton; m. Carl Eduard Bjorncrantz, Aug. 31, 1968; 1 child, William. BA, Wellesley Coll., 1967; MLS, Columbia U., 1968. Rsch. libr. Alderman Libr. U. Va., Charlottesville, 1968-70; reference libr. Northwestern U. Libr., Evanston, Ill., 1974-78, curriculum libr., 1970—, edn. bibliographer, 1974—, psychology bibliographer, 1989—, core libr., 1989-97, mgmt. bibliographer, 1997—. Co-editor: (book) Curriculum Material Center Collection Policy, 1984, Guide for the Development & Management of Test Collections, 1985. Bd. dirs. Internat. Visitors Ctr., Chgo., 1973-76; class rep., fund raiser class of 1967, Wellesley (Mass.) Coll., 1987-92. Scholar Wellesley Coll., 1967. Mem. ALA, Assn. Coll. & Rsch. Librs. (sec. 1977-79, 85-87, chair curriculum materials com. 1984-85), Am. Ednl. Rsch. Assn., Spl. Libr. Assn., Phi Delta Kappa (historian NU chpt. 1982—). Avocations: reading, travel, food and wine. Home: 2146 Forestview Rd Evanston IL 60201-2057 Office: Northwestern U Libr 1970 Campus Dr Evanston IL 60208-0821 E-mail: l-bjorncrantz@northwestern.edu.

BJORNDAHL, DAVID LEE, electrical engineer; b. Rock Island, Ill., June 19, 1927; s. Richard Gideon and Olive Muriel (Winter) B.; m. Clara Mae Buck, Feb. 16, 1952; children: William, Jay, Jan, Jill. PhD in Elec. Engring., Purdue U., 1956. Sr. engr. Litton Guidance & Control Systems, Beverly Hills, Calif., 1956-58, project engr. Woodland Hills, Calif., 1958-62, dir. advanced programs, 1962-66; mgr. Martin-Marietta, Denver, 1966-67; dir. advanced programs Litton Aero Products, Woodland Hills, 1967-74, v.p. engring., 1974-86; chief scientist Litton Aero. Products, Moorpark, Calif., 1986-93; ret., 1993. Part-time cons., Chatsworth, Calif., 1993—. Contbr. articles to profl. jours. Mem. Sigma Chi, Eta Kappa Nu. Republican. Achievements include design of various electronic navigation systems for aircraft.

BJORNDAL, ARNE MAGNE, endodontist; b. Ulstein, Norway, Aug. 19, 1916; s. Martin I. and Anne Beito Bjorndal; m. Katharine G. Benson, Jan. 12, 1952; children: Katharine, Kari, Lee. BS, State Coll., Volda, 1939; DDS, U. Oslo, 1947, U. Iowa, 1954, MS, 1956. Diplomate Am. Bd. Endodontics, 1964. Instr. Coll. Dentistry U. Oslo, 1948-50, 51-53; intern Forsyth Dental Infirmary, Boston, 1950-51, NIDR, 1960; mem. faculty U. Iowa, Iowa City, 1954—, prof., 1964—, founder, head dept. endodontics, 1956-80. Vis. prof. U. Alexandria, Egypt, 1978, Tunisia, 1979. Author: Anatomy and Morphology of Human Teeth, 1983. Maj. USNG, 1963-70. Decorated King Haakon VII medal (Norway); Fulbright scholar, 1950-51. Fellow Am. Coll. Dentists; mem. ADA (Svc. Fgn. Countries award 1979), Iowa Dental Assn. (life), Am. Assn. Endodontics, N.Y. Acad. Sci., Optimists, Elks, Omicron Kappa Upsilon. Republican. Lutheran. Home: 2510 Bluffwood Cir Iowa City IA 52245-3543 E-mail: bjorndal@blue.weeg.uiowa.edu.

BJORNSON, CHRISTOPHER RAYMOND, lawyer; b. Washington, June 1, 1967; s. Neal Raymond and Patricia Marie Bjornson. B of Journalism, U. Tex., 1992, M of Pub. Affairs, 1996; JD, Cath. U. Am., 2000. Bar: (Va.) 2000, (D.C.) 2001. Law clk. FCC, Washington, 1998—99; atty. Mintz Levin Cohn Ferris Glovsky & Popeo, Washington, 2000—. Dir., treas. Travis County Credit Union, Austin, 1991—96. Vice-chmn., bd. dirs. Internat. Model UN Assn., Inc., N.Y.C., 1998—2000; pres. Washington Area LBJ Sch. Alumni Coun., Washington, 1998—99; scholarship Chair DC Texas Exes., Washington, 1997—99; bd. dirs. Hope for Kids. Named Super Texan, Texas Sec. of State, 1988; recipient State of Tex. Meritorious Svc. award, Tex. Sec. State, 1990, State of Tex. Outstanding Svc. award, Tex. Sec. of State, 1990. Mem.: D.C. Bar, State Bar of Va., Fed. Comms. Bar Assn. Lutheran. Home: #702 1201 Braddock Pl Alexandria VA 22314 Personal E-mail: cbjornson@aol.com. Business E-Mail: crbjornson@mintz.com.

BJORNSON, EDITH CAMERON, foundation executive, communications consultant; b. Orlando, Fla., Sept. 12, 1937; d. Hilliard Francis and Edith Muriel (McBride) Cameron; m. Carroll N. Bjornson, Jan. 11, 1963; children: Lisa Carol, Karl Cameron (dec.). BA, U. Fla., Gainesville, 1953, MA, 1956; profl. cert., Ecole de Cuisine LaVerenne, Paris, 1983. Copywriter Sta. WGGG, Gainesville, Fla., 1953-54; exec. asst. Actors' Studio, N.Y.C., 1956-58; prodn. asst. Omnibus, N.Y.C., 1958-59; assoc. prodr. Robert Saudek Assocs., N.Y.C., 1958-60, ABC News Adlai Stevenson Reports, N.Y.C., 1960; asst. gen. mgr. Sta. WNDT-TV, N.Y.C., 1960-63; co-prodr. The Open Mind, N.Y.C., 1963-69; dir. local programming Telepromter, Inc., N.Y.C., 1979-80; corporate v.p. programming Westinghouse Broadcasting and Cable, N.Y.C., 1980-83; cons. Sta. WNYC-TV, N.Y.C., 1984-86; v.p., sr. program officer The Markle Found., N.Y.C., 1986-98. Mem. working group Carter Commn. on Radio and TV, Atlanta, 1992—96; mem. strategic planning bd. Conn. Pub. TV; bd. dirs. N.Y. New Media Assn., N.Y.C., 1998—2002, chmn., 2002; bd. dirs. Conn. Pub. TV and Radio, 1999—, bd. advisors, 2003—; cons. in new media profit and non-profit orgns.; exec. dir. Fulfilling the Promise project on digital comm. Century Found. and Carnegie Corp., 1999—2001; sr. advisor, Morningside Ventures Columbia U., 1999—2001; website designer, editor Fulfilling the Promise The Century Found. Carnegie Corp., 1999—2001; website editor Digital Promise Project, 2002—03; project dir., website designer The Open Mind Digital Archive Project, Columbia Tchrs. Coll., 2002—; sr. advisor Fathom.com Columbia U., 1999—2001; sr. advisor video oral history project Healthcare Chaplaincy, 2002—; dir. oral history project The Healthcare Chaplainary, 2003—. Project advisor: (computer software) Voyager Co., 1993, SimHealth, 1994, (Internet software, multi-player online games) ReInventing America, 1995, President '96; contbr. articles to profl. jours. Vice chmn. bd. dirs. HealthCare Chaplaincy, N.Y.C., 1989-96; bd. dirs. Pro-Natura USA, N.Y.C., 1995-99; life trustee Health Care Chaplaincy, N.Y.C., 1997. Recipient Emmy award Acad. TV. Arts and Scis., 1960. Mem. Internat. Assn. Culinary Profls., Night Kitchen (computer software developers bd. dirs. 1996-98), Ocean Reef Club, Mortar Board, Delta Gamma. Republican. Avocation: cooking. Home: 34 E Lyon Farm Dr Greenwich CT 06831-4349

BLACHER, JOAN HELEN, psychotherapist, educator; b. LA, Calif, Aug. 10, 1928; d. Albert Scribner and Isabel (Marriott) Oakholt; m. Norman Blacher, July 27, 1973; stepchildren: Eric, Steven, Mark. BA, U. Calif., Berkeley, 1950; MEd, U. So. Calif., 1971, PhD, 1981. Lic. ednl. psychologist, Calif.; lic. marriage, family therapist, Calif. Elem. tchr. LA Unified Sch. Dist., 1962-71, sch. psychologist, 1971-72, 73-74, Pasadena Unified Sch. Dist., Calif., 1972-73, Ventura County Supt. Schs., Calif., 1974-79; prin. Ventura County Supt. Sch., Calif., 1979-86; assoc. prof. sch. edn., dir. counseling and guidance program Calif. Luth. U., Thousand Oaks, 1987-98, prof. emerita, 1998—; pvt. practice Ventura, Calif., 1984—. Co-author: Difficult Teens: A Parents Guide for Coping, 2002. Bd. dir. Coalition Against Household Violence, Ventura, 1984-85, Camarillo Hospice, 1994-2002, Interface Children Family Svc., 2000-02; mem Ventura County Mental Health Bd., 2002—. Mem. APA, Am. Counselors Assn., Am. Ednl. Rsch. Assn., Calif. Assn. Counselors, Educators, Suprs. (past pres.), Calif. Assn. Marriage and Family Therapists, Calif. Assn. Counseling Devel. Republican. Avocations: travel, writing.

BLACHER, RICHARD STANLEY, psychiatrist; b. N.Y.C., May 24, 1924; s. Charles and Bernardine (Zolotorofe) B.; m. Sara-Lee Rudolph, July 4, 1960 (dec. 1970); 1 child, Lisa; m. Marjory May Popky, Oct. 27, 1985. BA, Brown U., 1945; MD, U. Rochester, 1948; cert. in psychoanalysis, N.Y. Psychoanalytic Inst., 1963. Diplomate Am. Bd. Psychiatry and Neurology. Clin. asst. attending psychiatrist Mt. Sinai Hosp., N.Y.C., 1955-66, assoc. attending psychiatrist, 1966-74; assoc. clin. prof. Mt. Sinai Sch. Medicine, N.Y.C., 1967-74; clin. prof. Tufts U. Sch. Medicine, Boston, 1974-85, prof. psychiatry, 1985—, lectr. in surgery, 1977—. Psychiatry lectr. Boston U. Sch. Medicine, 1995—; bd. dirs. Internat. Consortium for Study of Neurol. and Psychol. Reactions to Cardiac Surgery, 1980—. Editor: The Psychological Experience of Surgery, 1987; editl. bd. Found. of Thanatology, N.Y.C., 1988—, Wiley Series in Psychiatry, N.Y.C., 1987—; contbr. over 50 articles to profl. jours. Pres. Tenafly (N.J.) Nature Ctr. Assn., 1972; mem. steering com. Greater Boston Physicians for Social Responsibility, Cambridge, Mass., 1983-92; trustee Boston Civic Symphony Orch., 1993—. Fellow Am. Psychiat. Assn. (life); mem. Am. Psychoanalytic Assn., Internat. Psychoanalytic Assn., Am. Psychosomatic Soc., Am. Coll. Psychoanalysts, N.Y. Psychoanalytic Soc., Boston Psychoanalytic Soc. Avocations: birding, natural history. Home and Office: 50 Plainfield St Newton MA 02468-1618 E-mail: RBLACHER@MASSMED.ORG.

BLACHLY, BEVERLY JEAN, vocational and insurance consultant; b. Portland, Oreg., Oct. 6, 1933; d. Arnold G. and Verna A. (Wilkenson) Manson; m. Paul H. Blachly, Oct. 16, 1956 (dec. July 1977); children: Kathryn, Cynthia, Brian, David, Jefery. Diploma in Nursing, Emanuel Hosp., Portland, 1954; Pub.Health Cert., Simmons Coll., 1960; BSN, Tex. Christian U., Ft. Worth, 1961; MS, U. Oreg., 1967; degree in parnish nursing, Concordia Coll., 2001. RN, Oreg.; CCM, Parish Nurse. Pediatric head nurse, maternal asst. USPHS, Ft. DeFiance, Ariz., 1955-56; rsch. asst. cardiovascular divsn. U. Oreg. Med. Sch. Hosps. and Clinics, Portland, 1962-65; pub. health nurse maternal-child care project Oreg. State Bd. Health, 1964-65; rsch. asst. dept. psychiatry U. Oreg. Med. Sch. Hosps. and Clinics, Portland, 1965-77; sr. nurse coord. Intracorp, Portland, 1977-95; Cigna dedicated supr. Intracorp/Cigna, Portland, 1991-95; ret., 1997; pvt. practice rehab. cons., 1997—2000; camp nurse Multnomah County Outdoor Sch. Program, 2001—03; asst. dir. nursing svc. Sr. Retirement Facility, 2002—. Patentee in field; contbr. articles to profl. jours. Recipient Achievement award N.W. Specialist award Intracorp, 1982-83, Recognition Disting. Med.-Vocat. Svc. Rehab., Nat. Disting. Svc. Registry, 1987. Mem. Assn. Rehab. Nurses (past pres., ednl. com. and program chair, legis. com.), Holistic Nursing Assn., City Club. Avocations: hiking, sewing, reading. Home: 3348 NW Skyline Blvd Portland OR 97229-3817

BLACHLY, JACK LEE, lawyer; b. Dallas, Mar. 8, 1942; s. Emery Lee and Thelma Jo (Budd) B.; m. Lucy Largent Rain, Jan. 15, 1972; 1 son, Michael Talbot. BBA, So. Meth. U., 1965, JD, 1968. Bar: Tex. 1968, U.S. Ct. Appeals (5th cir.) 1969, U.S. Supreme Ct. 1975, U.S. Tax Ct. 1977. Trust officer First Nat. Bank in Dallas, 1968-70; ptnr. firm Reese & Blachly, Dallas, 1970-71; assoc. firm Rain Harrell Emery Young & Doke, Dallas, 1971-76; staff atty. Sabine Corp., Dallas, 1976-77, mgr. legal dept., 1977-80, v.p., gen. counsel, 1980-89; asst. gen. counsel Pacific Enterprises Oil Co. USA (merger Sabine Corp. and Pacific Enterprise Oil Co. USA), Dallas, 1989-90; pvt. practice Dallas, 1990—. Mem.: Dallas Bar Assn., Tex. Bar Assn., Dallas Gun Club. Baptist. Office: 4409 Benton Elm Dr Plano TX 75024

BLACHMAN, MICHAEL JOEL, lawyer; b. Portsmouth, Va., Aug. 16, 1944; s. Zalmon I. and Rachel G. (Grossman) B.; m. Paula D. Levine, Nov. 23, 1969; children: Dara R., Erica Dale. BS, Am. U., 1966; JD, U. Tenn., 1969. Bar: Va. 1969, U.S. Dist. Ct. (ea. dist.) Va. 1971, U.S. Supreme Ct. 1974, U.S. Ct. Appeals (4th cir.) 1977. Asst. commonwealth's atty. Commonwealth of Va., Portsmouth, 1970-72; assoc. Bangel, Bangel & Bangel, Portsmouth, 1972-77, ptnr., 1977—. Chmn. Portsmouth Juvenile Adv. Com., 1975-78. Mem. Va. Dem. Steering Com. 1980-85; vice chmn. Indsl. Devel. Authority and Port and Indsl. Commn., Portsmouth, 1987-89, chmn. 1989-93; bd. dirs. United Jewish Fedn. Tidewater, 1980—, v.p. 1989—. With USCGR, 1966-72. Recipient Young Leadership award United Jewish Fedn. Tidewater, 1983. Mem. ABA, Assn. Trial Lawyers Am., Va. Bar Assn., Va. Trial Lawyers Assn. (v.p. 1985-88, pres. 1989-90), So. Trial Lawyers Assn. (bd. dirs. 1991—), Portsmouth Bar Assn., Portsmouth C. of C., Kiwanis (bd. dirs. Portsmouth club 1973-75), B'nai B'rith. Jewish. Avocations: tennis, travel, reading. Office: # B 116 82nd St Virginia Beach VA 23451-1802

BLACK, ALLEN DECATUR, lawyer; b. Pitts., July 27, 1942; s. Gerald Richard and Amy Elizabeth (Haymaker) B. AB, Princeton U., 1963; LLB magna cum laude, U. Pa., 1966. Bar: D.C. 1967, Pa. 1971, U.S. Supreme Ct. 1975. Law clk. to Hon. John Minor Wisdom, New Orleans, 1966-67; trial atty. Dept. Justice, 1967-68; asst. prof. law U. North Dakota, Grand Forks, 1971; practice comml. and antitrust litigation law Fine, Kaplan & Black, Phila., 1975—. Lectr. in law Rutgers U., 1972-77, Temple U., 1978, U. Pa., 1985. Served with JAGC USN, 1968-71. Fellow Am. Coll. Trial Lawyers; mem. Am. Law Inst. (mem. coun.), Pa. Bar Assn., Phila. Bar Assn., Phila. Art Alliance. Republican. Episcopalian. Office: 1845 Walnut St Philadelphia PA 19103-4708

BLACK, ALLIDA MAE, historian, educator, writer, consultant; b. Memphis, Feb. 27, 1952; d. Charles Gardner and Anna Lucado Black; life ptnr. Judy Anna Beck, May 1991. BA, Emory U., 1974; PhD, George Washington U., 1993. DePaul U., 2002. Asst. prof. history Pa. State U., Harrisburg, 1994—97; JMG postdoctoral fellow history George Mason U., Fairfax, Va., 1997—98; asst. prof. history Franklin and Marshall Coll., Lancaster, Pa., 1998—99, The George Washington U., Washington, 1999—2000, rsch. prof. history and internat.

affairs, 2000—, dir. and editor The Eleanor Roosevelt Papers, 2000—. Dir. The Eleanor Roosevelt Ctr. at Val-Kill, Hyde Park, NY, 1994—2000; v.p. Nat. Women's History Project, Calif., 1998—2002; cons. The Roosevelt Nat. Hist. Site, Hyde Park, 2000—, The Nat. Pk. Found., Washington, 2000—; dir. Franklin and Eleanor Roosevelt Inst., Hyde Park, 2001—; commr. Arlington County Human Rights Commn., Arlington, Va., 2002—. Author: (biography) Casting Her Own Shadow: Eleanor Roosevelt and the Shaping of Postwar Liberalism, (anthology) Courage In A Dangerous World: The Political Writings of Eleanor Roosevelt, What I Hope To Leave Behind: Selected Writings of Eleanor Roosevelt; curator (exhibit) Where Do Human Rights Begin: Eleanor Roosevelt and the Universal Declaration of Human Rights; contbr. articles to profl. jours. Sec. Gaea Found., Washington, 1998; commr. Arlington County Human Rights Commn., 2002; dir. The Eleanor Roosevelt Legacy, N.Y.C., 2002; mem. Cmty. Adv. Coun. WAMU-FM, Washington, 1996—2001. Recipient Person of Vision award, Arlington County Commn. on the Status of Women, 2001, Rsch. award, Leila and Henry Wallace Found., 2002; fellow, The George Washington U., 1984—88; Smithsonian Postdoctoral fellow, Smithsonian Instn., 1997, Schlesinger Postdoctoral fellow, Franklin and Eleanor Roosevelt Inst., 1999, Publ. grantee, The Nat. Hist. and Publications Commn., 2000—, Collaborative Rsch. grantee, NEH, 2002—. Mem.: Nat. Coun. on History Edn., Orgn. Am. Historians, Am. Hist. Assn., Assn. for Documentary Edit. (chair fundraising com. 2002). Democrat. Home: 2001 N Kenilworth St Arlington VA 22205 Office: The Eleanor Roosevelt Papers/GWU 2100 Foxhall Rd NW Washington DC 20007 Office Fax: 202-242-6730. Personal E-mail: amblack@gwu.edu. E-mail: amblack@gwu.edu.

BLACK, ALVIN M. application developer; b. Cleburne, Tex., June 13, 1943; s. Alvin M. Black and Jackie Virginia Lee; m. Betty Jo Masey, June 30, 1974; children: Elizabeth, Heather, Holli. BS, Tarleton State U, 1961—65; MS, U North Tex., 1965—69, EdM, 1975—80. Cert. tchr. cert. Tex. Aerosystems engr. Gen. Dynamics, Ft. Worth, 1957—72; software engr. Tex. Instr., Dallas, 1972—74; edn. dir. First Bapt. Ch., Haltom City, Tex., 1979—9809, Blvd. Bapt. Ch., Burleson, Tex., 1974—79; software engr. North RSP Grumman, Dallas, 1980—; adj. prof. Dallas (Tex.) Bapt. U, 1992—2002, Hill Coll., Hillsboro, Tex., 1991—2001. Mem. Gideons Internat., Johnson County, Tex., 1991—. Republican. Bapt. Avocation: Karate. Home: 205 Bellevue Dr Cleburne TX 76033

BLACK, ANDERSON DUANE, writer, business consultant; b. Jackson, Mich., May 15, 1928; s. Walter Ward and Mary Christmas (Anderson) B.; m. Sheila Eiko Ueda, Dec. 26, 1962. BS, Northwestern U., 1954; MA, U. Hawaii, 1959, MBA, 1979. Instr. U. Hawaii, Honolulu, 1959-62; mgr. Castle & Cooke, Inc., Honolulu, 1963-84; pres. A.D. Black Assocs., Lanai City, Hawaii, 1984—; adminstr. Lanai Cmty. Hosp., Lanai City, Hawaii, 1989-92. Author: (play) Tsunami!, 1960, (play) Year of the Great Poy Shortage, 1961, Golden Children of Hawaii, 1987, Lana'i, 2001. Bd. dirs. State Comprehensive Health Planning Coun., Honolulu, 1969-75; pres., bd. dirs. Pacific and Asian Affairs Coun., Honolulu, 1964-70; chair Hawaii Campaign Spending Commn., 1997—. Recipient Pacific House award Pacific and Asian Affairs Coun., 1969. Mem. Lanai City Lions Club (pres. 1963—), Lions Internat. (state sec. dist. 50 1983-84). Avocations: flying, travel. Home: 1634 Makiki St Apt 102 Honolulu HI 96822-4437 Office: AD Black Assocs PO Box 630765 Lanai City HI 96763-0765 E-mail: adblack@aloha.net.

BLACK, B. R. retired educational administrator, consultant; b. Tampa, Fla., Apr. 6, 1942; s. R.C. and Gladys (Gaines) B.; m. Katy Black, Apr. 2, 1987; children: Amy Christine, Dale Rainer. AA, Marion (Ala.) Inst., 1962; BA, Fla. State U., 1964; MEd, Rollins Coll., 1974; EdD, Nova U., Ft. Lauderdale, Fla., 1988. Tchr. biology, chmn. sci. dept., asst. prin. high sch., 1970-85; supr. MIS, Sch. Bd. Polk County, Bartow, Fla., 1985-86, supr. instrnl. computing, 1986-93, dir. instrnl. tech., 1993-97; ret., 1997; ednl. cons. Instrnl. Tech. Rsch., Crawfordville, Fla., 1997—. Presenter numerous workshops and confs. Author: Trouble Shooting Microcomputers; mem. nat. editl. adv. bd. Electronic Learning, 1989-92. Bd. dirs. Keep Wakulla County Beautiful, 2000—. Capt. U.S. Army, 1964-70. Mem.: ASCD (ednl. futurists network 1989—95), Internat. Soc. Tech. in Edn., Fla. Assn. Ednl. Data Systems, Fla. Assn. Computers in Edn., Fla. Instnl. Computing Suprs. (bd. dirs. 1988—90, state chmn. 1989), Fla. Coun. Instnl. Tech. Leaders (sec. 1995—97, newsletter editor 2000—03), Rotary (pres. 2003), Phi Delta Kappa. Home: 343 River Plantation Rd Crawfordville FL 32327-1517 Office: Instrnl Tech Rsch 343 River Plantation Rd Crawfordville FL 32327-1517 E-mail: blackbr@comcast.net.

BLACK, BARBARA ANN, publisher; b. Eureka, Calif., Dec. 11, 1928; d. William Marion and Letitia (Brunia) Black; m. Vinson Brown, June 18, 1950 (dec Dec. 1991); children: Tamara Pinn, Roxana Hodges, Keven Brown. BA, Western State Coll., Gunnison, Colo., 1950. Cert. tchr., Colo. Editor/proofreader Naturegraph Pubs., Los Altos, Calif., 1950-53, co-owner, mgr. San Martin, Calif., 1953-60, Healdsburg, Calif., 1960-76, owner/mgr. Happy Camp, Calif., 1976—. Author: Barns of Yesteryear, 1993; co-author: Sierra Nevada Wildlife, 1996, The Californian Wildlife Region, 1999; pub. over 100 titles on wildlife and Native Ams. Mem. Am. Booksellers Assn. Baha'i Faith. Avocations: gardening, backpacking, animal training. Home: PO Box 1045 3633 Indian Creek Rd Happy Camp CA 96039-9706 Office: Naturegraph Publishers Inc 3543 Indian Creek Rd Happy Camp CA 96039-9706

BLACK, BARBARA ARONSTEIN, legal history educator; b. Bklyn., May 6, 1933; d. Robert and Minnie (Polenberg) A.; m. Charles L. Black, Jr., Apr. 11, 1954; children— Gavin B., David A., Robin E. BA, Bklyn. Coll., 1953; LLB, Columbia U., 1955; MPhil, Yale U., 1970, PhD, 1975; LLD (hon.), N.Y. Law Sch., 1986, Marymount Manhattan Coll., 1986, Vt. Law Sch., 1987, Coll. of New Rochelle, 1987, Smith Coll., 1988, Bklyn. Coll., 1988, York U., Toronto, Can., 1990, Georgetown U., 1991. Assoc. in law Columbia U. Law Sch., N.Y.C., 1955-56; lectr. history Yale U., New Haven, 1974-76, asst. prof. history, 1976-79, assoc. prof. law, 1979-84; George Welwood Murray prof. legal history Columbia U. Law Sch., N.Y.C., 1984—, dean faculty of law, 1986-91. Editor Columbia Law Rev., 1953-55. Active N.Y. State Ethics Commn., 1992-95. Recipient Fed. Bar Assn. prize Columbia Law Sch., 1955 Mem. Am. Soc. Legal History (pres. 1986-90), Am. Acad. Arts and Scis., Am. Philos. Soc., Mass. Hist. Soc., Supreme Ct. Hist. Soc., Selden Soc., Century Assn. Office: Columbia U Sch Law 435 W 116th St New York NY 10027-7201

BLACK, BERT, state administrator, lawyer; b. NYC, Mar. 6, 1956; s. Thomas and Evelyn Gretel (Florio) B.; m. Cynthia H. Daggett; children: Sarah, Amy. BA in Biology, SUNY, Buffalo, 1976; JD, U. Minn., 1979. Bar: Minn. 1979, U.S. Dist. Ct. Minn. 1979. Reporter Adv. Task Force on Minn. Corp. Law, Mpls., 1979-81; dir. corp. divsn. State of Minn., St. Paul, 1981-99; legal analyst Office of Sec. of State of Minn., St. Paul, 1999—2002, planning dir., 2003—. Pres. Internat. Assn. Corp. Adminstrs., 1988-89; adj. prof. U. Minn. Law Sch., 1995, William Mitchell Coll. Law, 2002; observer Revision of Revised Uniform Ltd. Partnership Act, Nat. Conf. Commrs. on Uniform State Laws; lectr. in field. Editor: Minnesota Corporations Practice Manual, 1986. Chmn. Dem.-Farmer Labor Party, 59th Dist., 1982-84, chmn. Mpls. sect., 1983-85, assoc. chair, chair 5th congl. dist., 1986-94, mem. state exec. com., 1986-2000, mem. state ctrl. com. Minn., 1982—. Jewish. Home: 3932 Harriet Ave Minneapolis MN 55409-1439 Office: Sec of State of Minn Dept Bus and Legal Analyst 180 State Office Bldg Saint Paul MN 55155-1299 E-mail: Bert.Black@state.mn.us., Bert1956@aol.com.

BLACK, BOYD CARSON, small business owner; b. Spencer, Nebr., Mar. 31, 1926; s. Royal Mitchel and Gladys Emma (Carlson) B.; m. Margaret Ann Prchal, June 26, 1948; children: Barton, Cheryl, Brian, Roger, Eric. Student, Wayne State Coll. Boiler maker various firms, 1947-56; owner, operator Blacco Splicing and Rigging Loft, Newark, Ohio, 1956—. Seminar instr. Am. Recreational Equipment, Greenville, N.C., 1979-88; tng. insp. Ohio State Agrl. Insps., Columbus, 1980-82; instr. safety seminars on lift equipment, Ohio, 1980—. Patentee in field. Mem. Heath City (Ohio) Charter Commn., 1963-64; chmn. Heath Zoning Bd. Appeals, 1963-98; del. Ohio Leadership Initiative, Yugoslavia, USSR, Poland, Hungary, 1990. With USN, 1943-46, PTO. Named Small Bus. Person of Yr., 1985. Mem. Am. Subcontractors Assn., Newark C. of C., Moundbuilders Babe Ruth Assn. (bd. dirs.), Am. Legion, Masons, USN Armed Guard Vets. Methodist. Avocations: fishing, camping, antique collecting, history. Home: 140 Claren Dr Newark OH 43056-1276

BLACK, BRUCE D. judge; b. Detroit, July 27, 1947; BA, Albion Coll., 1969; JD, U. Mich., 1971. Judge N.Mex. Ct. Appeals, 1991-96, U.S. Dist. Ct. N.Mex., 1996—. Office: 333 Lomas Blvd NW Albuquerque NM 87102-2272

BLACK, CAROLYN MORRIS, microbiologist, educator, science administrator; b. L.A., July 23, 1957; d. Dock Felton Black and Diane Morris DeBlock; m. Efrain Maldonado Ribot; children: Elise Ribot, Denis Ribot. BS, Iowa State U., 1979; PhD, U. Calif., Davis, 1985. Rsch. assoc. NRC, Atlanta, 1988—90; rsch. microbiologist Immunology Lab. divsn. bacterial and mycotic diseases Nat. Ctr. Infectious Diseases, Ctrs. Disease Control and Prevention, Atlanta, 1989—93; chief Molecular Diagnostic Lab. Nat. Ctr. Infectious Diseases, Ctr. Disease Control and Prevention, Atlanta, 1992—93; chief chlamydia sect., divsn. AIDS/STDs and tuberculosis lab. rsch. Nat. Ctr. Infectious Diseases, Ctrs. Disease Control and Prevention, Atlanta, 1993—99, acting assoc. dir. minority and women's health, 1998—99, dir. sci. resources program, 1999—. Ad hoc mem. NIH subcom. vaccine devel. for chlamydial diseases Nat. Inst. Allergy and Infectious Diseases, NIH, Bethesda, Md.; advisor subcom. on immunologic testing for infectious diseases Nat. Com. Clin. Lab. Stds., Wayne, Pa., 1994—95; mem. organizing com. Internat. Conf. Emerging Infectious Diseases, Atlanta, 1999—; organizer, moderator Forum on STDs, U.S. Medicine Inst./Dept. of Def., Washington, 2001; adj. asst. prof. dept. medicine Emory U. Sch. Medicine, Atlanta, 1991—. Contbr. articles to numerous med. jours., also chpts. to books; reviewer: over 15 sci. jours. Fellow Regent's Grad. fellow, U. Calif., 1982, Earl C. Anthony fellow in microbiology, 1982, Dean's Postdoctoral fellow, Stanford U. Sch. Medicine, 1985—87. Mem.: AAAS, Am. Social Health Assn. (reviewer funding proposals 1997—), Assn. Pub. Health Labs. (mem. nat. chlamydia lab. com. 1998—2000), Am. STD Assn., Am. Soc. Microbiology (chair pub. health divsn. 2001—), Sigma Xi (pres. CDC chpt. 1996—97). Office: Centers for Disease Control and Preventi MS C17 1600 Clifton Rd NE Atlanta GA 30333 Office Fax: 404-639-3199. Business E-Mail: cblack@cdc.gov.

BLACK, CATHLEEN PRUNTY, publishing executive; b. Chgo., Apr. 26, 1944; d. James Hamilton and Margaret (Harrington) B. BA, Trinity Coll., 1966. Advt. sales rep. Holiday mag., N.Y.C., 1966-69, Travel & Leisure mag., N.Y.C., 1969-70, New York mag., 1970-72; advt. dir. Ms. mag., 1972-75, assoc. pub., 1975-77, New York mag., 1977-79, pub., 1979-83; pres. USA Today, 1983, pub., 1984-91; exec. v.p. mktg. Gannett Co., Inc., from 1985, also bd. dirs.; pres., CEO Newspaper Assn. Am., Reston, Va., 1992-95; pres. Hearst Mags., N.Y.C., NY, 1996—. Office: Hearst Mags 959 8th Ave New York NY 10019-3795

BLACK, CLANTON CANDLER, JR., biochemistry educator, researcher; b. Tampa, Fla., Nov. 27, 1931; s. Clanton Candler Black and Cora (Winfred) Eady B.; m. Betty Louise Dantzler, Apr. 10, 1952; children— Marjorie Kay, Clanton Candler III, Julia Renee BSA., U. Fla., 1953, MSA., 1957, PhD, 1960. NIH postdoctoral fellow Cornell U., Ithaca, N.Y., 1960-62; C. F. Kettering Found. fellow Kettering Research Lab., Antioch Coll., Yellow Springs, Ohio, 1962-63, staff scientist, asst. prof., 1963-67; prof. biochemistry U. Ga., Athens, 1967—, disting. rsch. prof. biochemistry/molecular biology, 1982—. Fulbright-Hays scholar to USSR, 1976; cons. plant biochemistry, physiology Internat. Atomic Energy Agy. Nat. Agr. U., Lima, Peru, 1981— Editor: CO2 Metabolism and Plant Productivity, 1976, Net Carbon Dioxide Assimilation in Higher Plants, 1972, Handbook of Biosolar Resources, Vol. IA, IB, 1982. Served to cpl. U.S. Army, 1953-55 Recipient Merit award Bot. Soc. Am., 1981, Alex Laurie award Am. Soc. Hort. Sci., 1984; Fulbright scholar, 1976, 98-99. Fellow AAAS; mem. Am. Soc. Plant Physiology (sec.-treas., v.p., pres. 1975-79), Am. Soc. Biol. Chemists, Russian Soc. Plant Physiology (hon.), Sigma Xi, Phi Kappa Phi, Phi Sigma, Gamma Sigma Delta. Baptist. Office: U Ga Dept Biochem and Molecular Bio Life Scis Bldg Athens GA 30602 E-mail: ccblack@bmb.uga.edu.

BLACK, CLIFFORD MERWYN, academic administrator, sociologist, educator; b. Lafayette, Ohio, Mar. 6, 1942; s. Richard Allen and Ivaloo Mae (Mosher) B.; m. Angelica Hernandez; children: Jonathan Andrew, Marisela, Jose Angel, Carlos Alberto. BA, Adrian Coll., 1963; MDiv, Meth. Theol. Sch., 1966; PhD, Northwestern U., 1972. Cert. clin. sociologist; lic. profl. counselor. Asst. prof. Wilberforce (Ohio) U., 1973-74, The Ohio State U., Mansfield, 1974-78; instr. U. North Tex., Denton, 1978-79, asst. prof., 1979-83, sociology program dir., 1982-83, assoc. prof., 1983-89, chair Ctr. for Pub. Svc., 1984-86, chair dept. sociology, 1986-87, assoc. dean Sch. Cmty. Svc., 1986-88, 91-92, acting dean Sch. Cmty. Svc., 1988-90, prof., 1989-92, Tex. A&M Internat. U., Laredo, 1989-92, dean Sch. Edn. and Arts and Scis., 1992-94, dean Coll. of Arts and Humanities, 1994-96, 96-2001, Webb Co. Tex. Planning Coun., 1996-2001, Webb Co. Tex. Drug Planning Com., 1996-2001, Webb Co. Tex. Jail Case Mgmt. Supervision, 1998-2001, Webb Co. Drug Ct. Supervising Com., 1998-2001; prin. investigator US Dept. Justice/Webb Co. Tex., Laredo, Tex., 1996—2001, 3d Party Payment Com.; dir. Internat. Justice Ctr., 1996—2002; pres. CJUS Rsch. and Program Cons. Internat. Inc., 2002—. Cons. Denton County Sheriff's Dept., Denton, 1984-89; mem. state coordinating bd. com. on Two Yr. Coll. Curriculum, 1986-89. Author: (book) Alternative Sentencing: Electronically Monitored Correction Supervision, 1992; contbg. editor for Clin. Sociology Newsletter, 1983-84; mem. editorial bd. Sociol. Practice, 1984-89; contbr. numerous articles to profl. jours. Pres. Sam Houston Elem. PTA, Denton, 1985-86; trustee Denton Ind. Sch. Dist., 1986-89; mem. United Way Bd., Laredo, 1994-95; active St. Martin de Porres Cath. Ch. Recipient U.S. Dept. Justice award for Rsch. Prgms. for Elimination of Illegal Drugs. Mem. Nat. Clin. Sociology Assn. (v.p. 1984-86, certification bd. mem. 1984-90, nat. certifier 1985-92, nat. program chair for ann. meeting 1984-85), Clin. Sociology Assn. Tex. (pres. 1982-84), Nat. Sociol. Practice Assn. (exec. bd. 1990-91), Nat. Sociol. Practice Assn. (certification bd. 1990-91), Am. Sociol. Assn. (sect bd. 1981-84, sociol. practice sect. sec./treas. 1981-84), Southwestern Sociol. Assn. (chair com. on professions 1983-86), Am. Criminology Soc., Acad. Criminal Justice Scis. Avocations: field archaeology, walking, reading, writing, drawing. Home and Office: 8506 Callow Ct Laredo TX 78045-1983

BLACK, COBEY, journalist, corporate executive; b. Washington, June 15; d. Elwood Alexander and Margaret (Beall) Cobey; m. Edwin F. Black; children: Star, Christopher, Noel, Nicholas, Brian, Bruce. BA, Wellesley Coll., 1944; postgrad., U. Hawaii. Exec. sec. to Irene, designer Metro-Goldwyn-Mayer, 1944; actress Fed. Republic Germany, 1945-46; women's editor Washington Daily News, 1947-50; columnist Honolulu Star Bull., 1954-65, Honolulu Advertiser, 1969-85. Cons. HEW, Peace Corps; bd. dirs. Pacific and Asian Affairs Coun., Honolulu Com. on Fgn. Rels., Soc. Asian Art of Hawaii, Honolulu Media Coun.; pres. Black & Black, Inc. Author: Birth of A Princess, 1962, Iolani Luahine, 1986, Hawaii Scandal, 2002; travel editor Bangkok World, 1968-69; publicist CBS-TV series Hawaii Five-O, 1978. Mem. Hawaii State Commn. on Status of Women, 1978-86. Mem. Nat. Press Club, Nat. Soc. Colonial Dames, Lady of Dumbarton, Royal Bangkok Sports Club, Outrigger Canoe Club, Waialae Country Club, Garden Club of Honolulu. Democrat. Episcopalian. Office: Black & Black Inc 3081 La Pietra Cir Honolulu HI 96815-4736

BLACK, CONRAD MOFFAT, publishing corporate executive; b. Montreal, Aug. 25, 1944; s. George Montegu and Jean Elizabeth (Riley) B.; m. Barbara J.E. Amiel. BA, Carleton U., 1965; LLL, Laval U., 1970; MA in History, McGill U., 1973; LLD (hon.), St. Francis Xavier U., 1979, McMaster U., 1979; LittD (hon.), U. Windsor, 1979; LLD (hon.), Carleton U., 1989. Chmn., co-owner Ea. Twps. Pub. Co., Ltd., Knowlton, Que., 1966—; pres., chmn. exec. com. Argus Corp. Ltd., 1978-79, chmn. bd., chmn. exec. com., 1979—, CEO, 1985; chmn. The Ravelston Corp. Ltd., 1978, Hollinger, Inc., 1985, CEO, 1987; chmn., CEO Telegraph Group Ltd., 1987; chmn. and CEO Hollinger Internat. Inc. Bd. dirs. Brascan Corp., Can. Imperial Bank of Commerce, Ltd., Spectator (1828) Ltd., Inc., Jerusalem Post Publs. Ltd., Sotheby's Holdings Inc., CanWest Global Comms. Corp.; chmn. bd. Nat. Interest, Washington, Coun. Fgn. Rels. Author: Duplessis, 1977, reprinted as Render Unto Caesar, 1998, A Life in Progress, 1993. Patron Malcolm Muggeridge Foun. Decorated officer Order of Can.; apptd. to Privy Coun. of Can., 1992, House of Lords, U.K., 2001. Mem. Hudson Inst., Ctr. Policy Studies (U.K.), Trilateral Commn. (UK), Americas Soc. (chmn.'s coun.), Internat. Inst. for Strategic Studies, Bilderberg Meetings (steering com.), Toronto Club, York Club, Toronto Golf Club, Granite Club, Univ. Club (Montreal), Mt. Royal Club (Montreal), Century Club (N.Y.C.), Everglades Club, Beach Club (Palm Beach), Athenaeum, Beefsteak, Whites (London), Garrick (London). Office: Hollinger Inc 10 Toronto St Toronto ON Canada M5C 2B7 also: Telegraph Group Ltd Canary Wharf, 1 Canada Sq London E14 5DT England also: Hollinger Internat 712 5th Ave New York NY 10019-4108

BLACK, CONSTANCE JANE, artist; b. Norwood, Mass., Oct. 15, 1929; d. William Arthur Broadley and Julia Abigail Eells; m. Carl Burton Black, Sept. 9, 1950; children: Melanie, Laura Black Simmons, Carl David. AA, Vesper Geroge Sch. Art, 1950. Author: (poetry) Litany of Days, 1998; one-woman shows include Collections Gallery, 1996, Charles Baltivik Gallery, 1997, Pen & Brush Inc., N.Y.C., 1998, Wellfleet Pub. Libr., 1999, Teichman Gallery, Brewster, Mass., 2002; group shows include Berta Walker Gallery, Provincetown, Mass., 1993, 95, Provincetown Art Assn. & Mus., 1957-99. Mem. Pen & Brush Inc. (Solo Show award 1998, 99), Provincetown Art Assn. and Mus. (bd. dirs. 1992-98). Mem. Baha'i Faith. Avocations: music, crafts, computers. Home: 6 Priscilla Alden Rd Provincetown MA 02657-1613 E-mail: connieart@attbi.com.

BLACK, CREED CARTER, newspaper executive; b. Harlan, Ky., July 15, 1925; s. Creed Carter and Mary (Cole) B.; m. Mary C. Davis, Dec. 28, 1947 (div. 1976); children: Creed Carter, Steven D., Douglas S.; m. Elsa Goss, Dec. 9, 1977; 1 child, Michelle. BS with highest distinction and honors in Polit. Sci., Northwestern U., 1949; MA, U. Chgo., 1952; LLD (hon.), Davidson Coll., 1991; LHD (hon.), Ctr. Coll., 1996. Reporter Paducah (Ky.) Sun-Democrat, 1942-43, 46; editor Daily Northwestern, 1947; copy editor Chgo. Sun-Times, 1949, Chgo. Herald-Am., 1950; editl. writer Nashville Tennessean, 1950-57, exec. editor, 1957-59; v.p., exec. editor Savannah (Ga.) Morning News and Savannah Evening Press, 1959-60, Wilmington (Del.) Morning News and Evening Jour., 1960-64; mng. editor Chgo. Daily News, 1964-68, exec. editor, 1968-69; asst. sec. for legislation HEW, 1969-70; editor Phila. Inquirer, 1970-77; chmn., pub. Lexington (Ky.) Herald-Leader, 1977-88; pres., trustee Knight Found., Miami, Fla., 1988-98. With 100th Inf. divsn. AUS, WWII, ETO. Decorated Bronze Star; recipient Northwestern U. Alumni medal, 1973 Mem. Newspaper Assn. of Am., So. Newspaper Pubs. Assn. (pres. 1987—), Am. Soc. Newspaper Editors (pres. 1983), Nat. Conf. Editl. Writers (pres. 1962), Riviera Country Club, Kappa Tau Alpha, Lambda Chi Alpha. Methodist. Home: 11044 SW 77th Court Cir Miami FL 33156-3766

BLACK, DAN A. economist; b. Emporia, Kans., Feb. 18, 1955; s. Lon L. and Jo Black(Stepmother); m. Susan Jane Black, Apr. 30, 1983; 1 child, James. PhD, Purdue U., 1979—83. Prof., economics Syracuse U., 1999—, U. of Ky., 1983—99; vis. prof., economics Carnegie-Mellon U., 1996—97, U. of Chgo., 1989—90; vis. scholar Australian Nat. U., Canberra, 2001—01. Author: (papers) Am. Econ. Rev., Jour. of the Am. Statis. Assn., Rev. of Economics and Statis., Jour. of Labor Economics, Jour. of Human Resources, Indsl. and Labor Rels. Rev. Grantee, NSF, 1984-1986, 1986-1992, 1999-2003, Dept. of Labor, 1988; 1994-1999; 2000-03, NIH, 1994-1996; 1998-1999; 1999-2003, EPA, 2001-3. Office: Center for Policy Research Syracuse U 426 Eggers Hall Syracuse NY 00130 Office Fax: 315-443-1081. E-mail: danblack@maxwell.syr.edu.

BLACK, DANIEL HUGH, retired secondary school educator; b. Arab, Ala., July 4, 1947; s. Lehmon Ray and Lillian Geneve (Divine) B. BS, U. Ala., Tuscaloosa, 1970; MEd, Ala. A&M U., 1976; PhD, Vanderbilt U., 1981; MA, St. John's Coll., Annapolis, Md., 1988. Social studies tchr., advanced placement govt. tchr. Grissom High Sch., Huntsville, Ala., 1970-98. Adj. instr. history Calhoun C.C., 1982—99, Ala. A&M U., 1989—94, Great Books in the Western World, U. Ala., Huntsville; essay reader advanced placement Am. govt. and politics exam. Ednl. Testing Svc., 1991—96; Internet store mgr. W.W.W. Blacks FurnitureCity.com. Mem. NEA, Ala. Edn. Assn., Huntsville Edn. Assn., Nat. Trust for Hist. Preservation (master class James Madison and Federalist Papers 1989), Phi Delta Kappa. Home: 1019 Old Monrovia Rd NW Apt 232 Huntsville AL 35806-3505 Office: Black's Furniture City 124 N Brindlee Mountain Pkwy Arab AL 35016-1316 E-mail: bfc@hiwaay.net.

BLACK, DAVID, writer, educator, producer; b. Boston, Apr. 21, 1945; s. Henry Arnold and Zelda Edith (Hodosh) B.; m. Deborah Hughes Keehn, June 22, 1968 (div. 1994); children: Susannah Haden, Tobiah Samuel McKee; m. Barbara Weisberg, June 20, 1996. BA cum laude, Amherst Coll., 1967; MFA, Columbia U., 1971. Free-lance writer, 1971—; writer-in-residence Mt. Holyoke Coll., South Hadley, Mass., 1982-86. Author: Like Father, 1978 (Notable Book of Yr. N.Y. Times, 1978, One of 7 Best Novels of Yr. Washington Post), Minds, 1982, Peep Show, 1986, An Impossible Life, 1998; (non-fiction) Ekstasy, 1975, The King of Fifth Avenue (Notable Book of Yr. N.Y. Times AP, N.Y. Mag. 1981), Murder at the Met, 1984, Medicine Man, 1985, The Plague Years, 1986 (Nat. Mag. award reporting, Nat. Assn. Sci. Writers award); (play) An Impossible Life, 1998; (screenplay) The Confession, 1999 (Winner Writers Guild Best TV Movie of Yr., Adaptation 1999), (teleplay) Final Jeopardy; contbr. articles and stories to Harper's, The Atlantic, N.Y. Times Mag., others; story editor Hill Street Blues; prodr. Miami Vice; supervising prodr. H.E.L.P., Gidgon Oliver, Law and Order (Golden Globe nominee 1992, Edgar nominee 1992, 99, Emmy nominee 1992, 98, ABA Certificate of Merit 1998); co-creator, supervising prodr.: The Nasty Boys; co-creator, exec. prodr.: Under Fire, The Good Policeman, The Cosby Mysteries, co-exec. prodr.: Sidney Lumet's 100 Centre Street, 1999-2002; exec. prodr.: CSI-Miami, 2003; cons. prodr. Richard Dreyfuss, The Education of Max Bickford, 2002, Monk, 2002; contbg. editor Rolling Stone, 1986-89. Recipient Atlantic Firsts award Atlantic Monthly, 1973, Playboy's Best Article of Yr. award Playboy Mag., 1979, Nat. Assn. Sci. Writers award, 1985, hon. mention for Best Essay of Yr., 1986, Giorgi award, Cert. Merit for excellence in writing, 1998; grantee Nat. Endowment Arts, 1979. Mem. SAG, Mystery Writers Am. (bd. dirs.), PEN, Internat. Assn. Mystery Writers, Authors Guild, Writers Guild East, Williams Club, Century Assn., Players, Explorer's Club, Columbia Club. Jewish/Unitarian.

BLACK, DAVID CHARLES, astrophysicist; b. Waterloo, Iowa, May 14, 1943; BS, U. Minn., 1965, MS, 1967, PhD in Physics, 1970. Fellow NAS, 1970-72; rsch. scientist theoretical astrophysics Ames Rsch. Ctr. NASA, Moffett Field, 1972—87, chief scientist space sta., 1985—87; dir. Lunar & Planetary Inst., Houston, 1988—2002; pres., CEO, Univcs. Space Rsch. Assn., Houston, 2000—. Mem. AAS, N.Y. Acad. Sci. Achievements include research in theoretical studies of the formation and evolution of stars and planetary systems, interpretation of rare gas isotopic data from meteorites and lunar samples. Office: Univs Space Rsch Assn Ctr for Advanced Space Studies 3600 Bay Area Blvd Houston TX 77058-1113

BLACK, DAVID DELAINE, retired investment consultant; b. Cin., Mar. 3, 1926; s. Robert L. Black and Anna (McNaughton) Smith; m. Maralyn Anderson (dec.); children: Robert, Dorothy, James; m. Polly P. Black, Oct. 7, 1967 (dec. Apr. 1996); children: Evelyn; m. Nancy Kohnen, Jan. 16, 2000. BS in Engring. with honors, Princeton U., 1949; MBA, Harvard U., 1951. Mgr. co. planning Cin. Millacron, Cin., 1952-77; owner Planning Counsel, Cin., 1977-84; sr. v.p. Gradison divsn. McDonald & Co., Cin., 1984—. Vice-chmn. bd. The Children's Hosp., Cin., 1985-97; chmn. bd. WCET-TV 48, Cin., 1980-83; pres. Cincinnatus Assn., 1966-67; chmn. Agnes and Murray Seasongord Good Govt. Found., 1993-95; chmn. Children's Hosp. Found., 1993-97; treas. Planned Parenthood Assn. Cin., 1986; vestry Indian Hill Ch., 1997-99; sec. bd. stewards, 2000—. Mem. Rotary (bd dirs. 1992-95, treas. Cin. Rotary Found. 1993-94).

BLACK, DAVID JOSEPH, physician; b. Detroit, Mich., Jan. 2, 1951; s. Bernard and Sarah Black; m. Barbara Buttram, Feb. 18, 1951; children: Leland, Tavenner. BS, Mich. State U., 1968—70, DVM, 1969—72; MS in physiology, U. of Fla., 1973—75, M.D, 1979—83. Diplomate Am. Coll. Lab. Animal Medicine, 1977, Am. Coll. Family Physicians, 1986. Sr. rsch. scientist Litton Industries, Rockville, Md., 1975—76; asst. prof. vet. medicine U. Tenn., Knoxville, 1976—78; asst. prof. U. Fla., Gainesville, 1978—79; pvt. practice, family practice Gainesville, 1986—2002. Zoo veterinarian Knoxville Zool. Pk., 1976—78; med. exec. com. Shands UF-AGH, Gainesville, FLA., 1997—2002; chief staff Shands at AGH, Gainesville, 1998—2000. Contbr. articles journ. Mem.: Am. Acad. Family Physicians. Avocation: triathlon. Office: David J Black MD 720 SW 2nd Ave Gainesville FL 32601

BLACK, DAVID LIONEL, computer scientist; b. Ithaca, NY, Jan. 24, 1961; s. Jonathan Black and Susan Starr (Williams) Collier; m. Kathryn D. Smith, July 15, 1989. BA, BSE, MA, U. Pa., 1983; MS, Carnegie Mellon U., 1985, PhD, 1990. Rsch. scientist The Open Group, Cambridge, Mass., 1990-98; sr. technologist EMC Corp., Hopkinton, Mass., 1998—. Cons. Hewlett Packard Labs., Palo Alto, Calif., 1988-89; program chair USENIX Mach Symposium, Santa Fe, N.Mex., 1993; co-chair IETF IP Storage WG, 2000—. Contbr. numerous articles to profl. jours. Mem. ACM, IEEE, Phi Beta Kappa, Tau Beta Pi. Achievements include being key member of design and implementation teams for Mach and other computer operating systems. Office: EMC Corp 176 South St Hopkinton MA 01748-2226 E-mail: black_david@emc.com.

BLACK, DEBORAH, information technology executive; BS in Computer Sci., MSE in Computer Engring., U. Mich. With Bell No. Rsch.; from program mgr. to corp. v.p. Microsoft, Redmond, Wash., 1992. Office: One Microsoft Way Redmond WA 98052-6399

BLACK, D(EWITT) CARL(ISLE), JR., lawyer; b. Clarksdale, Miss., Aug. 17, 1930; s. DeWitt Carlisle Sr. and Alice Lucille (Hammond) B.; m. Ruth Buck Wallace, June 6, 1970; children: Elizabeth B. Smithson, D. Carl Black III. BA, Miss. Coll., 1951, LLB, 1963, MPA, Princeton U., 1953; LLM in Taxation, NYU, 1965. Bar: Miss. 1963, U.S. Dist. Ct. (so. dist.) Miss. 1963, U.S. Ct. Appeals (5th cir.) 1965. Rsch. asst. Pub. Affairs Rsch. Coun., Baton Rouge, 1956-57; asst. mgr., dir. rsch. Miss. Econ. Coun., Jackson, 1957-64; ptnr. Butler, Snow, O'Mara, Stevens & Cannada, Jackson, 1965-98, of counsel, 1999—. Chair Miss. Tax Inst., Jackson, 1987. Treas. New Stage Theatre, Jackson, 1965-69; pres. Miss. Symphony Orch. Assn., Jackson, 1985-86, Miss. Symphony Found., Jackson, 1989-92. Cpl. U.S. Army, 1953-55. Fellow Am. Coll. Tax Counsel; mem. Miss. Bar Assn. (chair tax sect. 1989-90), Univ. Club, River Hills Club. Episcopalian. Avocations: fishing, reading. Home: 1704 Poplar Blvd Jackson MS 39202-2119 Office: 1700 Am South Plz Jackson MS 39201 E-mail: carl.black@butlersnow.com.

BLACK, DOROTHY MARY, librarian; b. Phila., June 4, 1936; d. Harry and Nellie Dixon Black. BS in Bible/Music, Phila. Bibl. U., 1965, M in Orgnl. Leadership, 2002; MS in Libr. Sci., Villanova U., 1969. Libr. pub. svcs. Phila. Bibl. U., Langhorne, Pa., 1965—. Author: (bibliography) Church Music Bibliography: Suggested Titles for the Bible College Library, 1996. Mem.: Music Libr. Assn., Assn. Acad. Libes. Office: Phila Bibl Univ 200 Manor Ave Langhorne PA 19047 Office Fax: 215-702-4374. Personal E-mail: dblack@pbu.edu. E-mail: dblack@pbu.edu.

BLACK, EILEEN MARY, retired elementary school educator; b. Bklyn., Sept. 20, 1944; d. Marvin Mize and Anne Joan (Salvia) B. Student, Grossmont Coll., El Cajon, Calif., 1964; BA, San Diego State U., 1967; postgrad., U. Calif., San Diego, Syracuse U. Cert. tchr., Calif. Tchr. La Mesa (Calif.)-Spring Valley Sch. Dist., 1967-2001, ret., 2001. NDEA grant Syracuse U., 1968. Mem.: AARP, Calif. Ret. Tchrs. Assn., Wilderness Soc., Greenpeace, San Diego Zool. Soc., Sierra Club. Roman Catholic. Avocations: reading, baseball, walking. Home: 9320 Earl St Apt 15 La Mesa CA 91942-3846 E-mail: eblack44@aol.com.

BLACK, FREDERICK A. b. July 2, 1949; s. John R. and Dorothy Black; m. Katie Black, Oct. 27, 1976; children: Shane, Shanthini, Sheena. BA, U. Calif., Berkeley, 1971; JD, Lewis and Clark Coll., 1975. Bar: Oreg. 1975, Guam 1976, U.S. Ct. Appeals (9th cir.) 1976. Dir. Office of Guam Pub. Defender, 1975-78; dep. dir. Office of Oreg. Fed. Defender, 1981-84; asst. U.S. atty. Dist. Guam and No. Mariana Islands, 1978-81, 84-89, 1st asst. U.S. atty., 1989-91; U.S. atty. Dept. Justice Dist. Agana, Guam and No. Mariana Islands, 1991—2003; sr. litigation counsel U.S. Attys Office, 2003—. Author: Oregon Search and Seizure Manual. Leader Boy Scouts Am. Recipient Spl. award Chief Postal Inspector, 1986, Drug Enforcement Adminstrn. award, 1986, 89. Mem. Guam Water Polo Team. Avocation: sailing. Office: US Atty's Office 108 Hernan Cortez Ave Ste 500 Hagatna GU 96910-5009

BLACK, GARY WILLIAM, industrial engineer; b. Altoona, Pa., Sept. 3, 1960; s. Thomas L. and Joanne M. Black; m. Elena S. Vengrzhinovskaya, Feb. 14, 1998. MS, U. Tenn., Knoxville, 1998; PhD, U. Ala., Huntsville, 2001; BS, Pa. State U., 1985. Indsl. engr. Raytheon Co., Andover, Mass., 1985—87, Bristol, Tenn., 1988—94, Siemens Energy & Automation, Johnson City, Tenn., 1995—2002; mfg. engr. def. divsn. Internat. Signal & Control, Lancaster, Pa., 1987—88; asst. prof. Tenn. Technol. U., Cookeville, 2002—. Mem.: Inst. Ops. Rsch. and Mgmt. Sci., Inst. Indsl. Engineers, Alpha Pi Mu. Home: 935 Franklin Ct Cookeville TN 38506 E-mail: GBlack@tntech.edu.

BLACK, HENRY RICHARD, physician; b. N.Y.C., June 1, 1942; s. David Robert and Beatrice (Morris) B.; children: Matthew, Dana; m. Benita L. Daniels, April 19, 2002. A.B., Columbia U., 1963; M.D., NYU, 1967. Diplomate Am. Bd. Internal Medicine; cert. hypertension specialist, Am. Soc. of Hypertension, 2001. Intern, Johns Hopkins Hosp., Balt., 1967-68, resident in internal medicine, 1970-71; resident Yale-New Haven Hosp., 1971-72, chief resident in internal medicine, 1974-75; fellow Yale U., 1972-74; practice medicine specializing in internal medicine and hypertension, New Haven, 1975-92; asst. prof. Yale U. Med. Sch., New Haven, 1975-79, assoc. prof. 1979-88, prof., 1988-92, dir. hypertension svcs., 1975-92; Charles J. and Margaret Roberts prof. and chmn. dept. preventive medicine, prof. internal medicine Rush-Presbyn.-St. Luke's Med. Ctr., Chgo., 1992—, assoc. v.p. rsch., assoc. dean rsch., 2000—. Bd. dirs. Am. Heart Assn. Conn., 1985—, fellow council on hypertension. Contbr. articles to profl. jours. Served with USPHS, 1968-70. Fellow ACP, Internat. Soc. Hypertension, Am. Heart Assn. (coun. epidemiology & prevention, fellow coun. on nutrition), Am. Soc. Hypertension (exec. com. 1991-96, exec. coun. 2002—); mem. Am. Fedn. Clin. Research, Columbia Coll. Alumni Assn. (bd. dirs. 1983-87, v.p. acad. affairs 1986-87), Am. Soc. Preventative Cardiology (pres.1994-95). Jewish. Office: Rush Presbyn St Lukes Med Ctr 1725 W Harrison St Chicago IL 60612-3828 Home: 1816 N Orleans St Chicago IL 60614-5304

BLACK, HILLEL MOSES, publisher; b. N.Y.C., Apr. 8, 1929; s. Isidore and Ida (Feldstein) B. BA, U. Chgo., 1949, M.English and Fgn. Langs., 1952. Copy boy N.Y. Times, N.Y.C., 1952-53; reporter AP, Pitts., Newark and Phila., 1954-58; freelance writer N.Y.C., 1959-65; editor Saturday Evening Post, N.Y.C., 1966-67; sr. editor William Morrow & Co., N.Y.C., 1967-77, editor-in-chief, 1977-82; pub. gen. books div. Macmillan Pub. Co., N.Y.C., 1983-87; pub. Richardson, Steirman & Black, N.Y.C., 1987-88; pres. Birch Lane Press, 1989-99; editorial dir. Carol Pub. Group, N.Y.C., 1989-99; exec. editor Sourcebooks, Naperville, Ill., 2000—. Author: The Watch Dogs of Wall Street, Buy Now, Pay Later, The American Schoolbook. Mem. Century Assn., Pubs. Club. Office: Sourcebooks 955 Connecticut Ave Ste 5303 Bridgeport CT 06607-1297

BLACK, J. COFER, government agency administrator; b. Stamford, Conn. B in internat. relations, U. So. Calif.; M in internat. relations, U. S. Calif. Coord. US Off. of Counter Terrorism, Washington, 2002—; dir. CIA Counter Terrorist Ctr., 1999—2001; task force chief Near East, South Asia Dvsn., 1995; deputy chief Latin Am. Dvsn., 1998—99. Recipient Distinguished Intelligence medal, George H. Bush medal for excellence, Exceptional Collector award, 1994. Office: 2201 C St NW Washington DC 20520*

BLACK, JACINTH BAUBLITZ, clinical social worker; b. Corpus Christi, Tex., Feb. 17, 1944; m. Donald James Baublitz, Oct. 26, 1968 (div. June 1979); children: Jessica Ruth, Stefanie Elizabeth; m. Robert Drummond Black, Mar. 14, 1987. BA, Sam Houston U., 1965; MSW, Boston Coll., 1972; postgrad., Am. Assn. Sex Educators, Counselors and Therapists, Washington, 1976-77; advanced studies with Maxie Maultsby Jr., U. Ky., 1980. Cert., Acad. Cert. Social Workers, 1976; lic. social worker and marriage and family therapist, Mich.; diplomate Acad. Social Workers, 1988; nat. bd. cert. clin. hypnotherapist, 1995. Tchr. English and Spanish Brazosport Schs., Freeport, Tex., 1965-67; caseworker Harris County Child Welfare Unit, Houston, 1967-69; vocat. counselor Mass. Employment Security, Lowell, 1969-70; family therapist Cath. Family Service, Saginaw, Mich., 1973-75; contractual clin. social worker Midland-Gladwin Community Mental Health Ctr., 1975-80; pvt. practice clin. social work Midland, Mich., 1975—. Adj. prof. psychology Northwood Inst., 1982-85; cons., lectr., speaker various profl. and lay orgns. Author: Relationshift, 1983, A Singles Guide to Tight Spots and Tricky Situations, 1986; newspaper advice columnist Bay Area Rev., 1985-89. Bd. dirs. Big Sisters Am., Inc., Midland, 1978-80; mem. bd. mgrs. Midland County Hist. Soc., 1996—. Mem. NASW. Episcopalian. Home: 4553 S Saginaw Rd Midland MI 48640-8554 Office: PO Box 2227 Midland MI 48641-2227

BLACK, SIR JAMES (SIR JAMES WHYTE BLACK), pharmacologist; b. June 14, 1924; MB, ChB, U. St. Andrews; MD (hon.), U. Edinburgh, 1989; DSc (hon.), U. Glasgow, 1989. Asst. lectr. physiology U. St. Andrews, 1946; lectr. physiology U. Malaya, 1947-50; sr. lectr. U. Glasgow Vet. Sch., 1950-58; with ICI Pharms. Ltd., 1958-64; head biol. rsch., dep. rsch. dir. Smith, Kline & French, Welwyn Garden City, 1964-73; prof., chmn. dept. pharmacology Univ. Coll., London, 1973-77; dir. therapeutic rsch. Wellcome Rsch. Labs., 1978-84; prof. analytical pharmacology King's Coll. Hosp. Med. Sch., U. London, 1984—93; chancellor Dundee (Scotland) U., 1992—. Decorated Knight, 1981; recipient Nobel prize for medicine, 1988, Order of Merit, 2000. Fellow Royal Coll. Physicians, Royal Soc. (Mullard award 1978); mem. Royal Coll. Vet. Surgeons (hon. assoc.). Office: U Dundee Chancellor's Office Dundee DD1 4HN Scotland*

BLACK, JAMES ISAAC, III, lawyer; b. Lakeland, Fla., Oct. 26, 1951; s. James Isaac Jr. and Juanita (Feemster) B.; m. Vikki Harrison, June 15, 1973; children: Jennifer Leigh, Katharine Ann, Stephanie Marie. BA, U. Fla., 1973; JD, Harvard U., 1976. Bar: Fla. 1976, N.Y. 1977, U.S. Tax Ct. 1984. Assoc. Sullivan & Cromwell, N.Y.C., 1976-84, ptnr., 1984—. Mem. ABA, N.Y. State Bar Assn. (persons under disability com. trusts and estates law sect. 1984-90), Assn. of Bar of City of N.Y. (sec. 1980-81, trusts estates and surrogates ct. com. 1980-83), Scarsdale Golf Club. Home: 23 Chesterfield Rd Scarsdale NY 10583-2205 Office: Sullivan & Cromwell LLP 125 Broad St Fl 28 New York NY 10004-2489

BLACK, JAMES M. state representative, optometrist; b. Charlotte, N.C., Mar. 25, 1935; m. Betty Black; 2 children. BS in optometry, So. Coll. Optometry, 1962; AB, Lenoir Rhyne Coll., 1958. Elected spkr. N.C. house of rep. State of N.C., 1999—2001, 2003—, house of rep., 1981—84, 1991—, majority whip, 1993—94, minority leader, 1995—98, Matthews town coun., 1987. Served with USN. Democrat. Methodist. Office: 2304 Legis Bldg Raleigh NC 27601-1096 Business E-Mail: jimb@ncleg.net.*

BLACK, JAMES ROBERT, industrial engineer; b. Davenort, Iowa, Feb. 17, 1948; s. Robert James and Anne Louise (Johnson) B.; m. Mary Ann O'Malley, June 5, 1971; 1 child, Robert Joseph. BS in Indsl. Engring., Iowa State U., 1970, MS, 1971; MBA, U. Chgo., 1976. Indsl. engr. Inland Steel Co., East Chicago, Ind., 1971-76, sr. indsl. engr., 1976-77; indsl. engring. supr. Clark Equipment Co., Jackson, Mich., 1977-78; indsl. engring. mgr. Harrison plant Graphic Sys. divsn. Rockwell Internat., Rockford, Ill., 1978-83; corp.supr. adminstrv. work mgmt. Kohler Co., Wis., 1983-87; mgr. mfg. svcs. Frigidaire Co.-Wet Products, Jefferson, Iowa, 1987—89, assembly ops. mgr., 1989—91, Kaizen facilitator Webster City, Iowa, 1991—93, paint process mgr., 1993, plant engring. mgr., 1993-95; sr. project mgr. Ctr. for Indsl. Rsch. and Svc., Iowa State U., 1995—; pres. James R. Black & Assocs., 1997—. Co-leader, guest lectr. Am. Mgmt. Assn., 1979-80; mem. adv. coun. Iowa State U. Ctr. Indsl. Rsch. and Svc., 1992-94; mem. planing com. Iowa conf. Mfg., 1991-93, chmn., 1993. Contbr. articles to profl. jours. Cons. project bus. divsn. Jr. Achievement, 1980; pack com. chmn. Boy Scouts Am., 1980—83, den leader, 1982—83, asst. scoutmaster, 1983—84, scoutmaster, 1984—88, dist. vice-chmn., 1984—86, dist. boy scouting chmn., 1986—88, unit commr., 2000—, dist. mem.-at-large, 2000—01, asst. dist. commr., 2001; dist. vice-chmn., 2000-2001, dist. commr., 2002-; asst. soccer coach, 1981—83; coach, 1984—85; mem. bd. dirs. Habitat for Humanity, exec. com., 2003—, chair pstnr. family rels. com., 2003—. Fisher Governor scholar, 1968-69, Maytag scholar, 1969-70; recipient Woodbadge Boy Scouts Am., 1986, Dist. award of Merit, 2003. Mem.: Kohler Engring. and Tech. Orgn. (program chmn. 1986, chmn. 1987), Mainstream Living and Story County Devel. Ctr. (phonathon co-chmn. 1993—95, bd. dirs. 1994—2001, treas. 1995—97, v.p. 1997—99, pres. 1999—2001), Assn. for Mfg. Excellence, Am. Soc. for Quality, Inst. Indsl. Engrs. (sr.; treas. 1979—80, pres. 1980—81, bd. dirs. 1989—91, v.p. 1991—92), Rotary Internat. (web page chmn. 2001—), K.C., Epsilon Sigma Phi, Alpha Phi Omega (univ. advisor 2000—02), Beta Gamma Sigma, Psi Chi, Gamma Epsilon Sigma, Tau Beta Pi, Phi Kappa Phi. Home: 3416 Valley View Rd Ames IA 50014-4613 Office: CIRAS/Iowa State U Coll Engring 2272 Howe Hl Ste 2620 Ames IA 50011-0001 E-mail: jimblack@ciras.iastate.edu.

BLACK, KENNETH, JR., retired insurance executive and educator, author; b. Norfolk, Va., Jan. 30, 1925; s. Kenneth and Margaret Virginia (Wolf) B.; m. Mabel Llewellyn Folger, Sept. 20, 1948; children— Kenneth III, Kathryn Anne Shoji. AB, U. N.C., 1948, MS, 1951; PhD, U. Pa., 1953. Ptnr. Colonial Ins. Agy., Chapel Hill, N.C., 1948-50; instr. U. Pa., 1952-53; chmn. ins. dept. Ga. State U., 1953-69, Regents' prof. ins., 1959-92, C.V. Starr prof. internat. ins., 1984-92, Regent's prof. emeritus, 1992—, dean Coll. Bus. Adminstrn., 1969-84, dean emeritus Coll. Bus. Adminstrn., 1992—; pres., CEO Internat. Ins. Soc., Inc., 1988-92, vice chmn., bd. dirs., 1992—2001. Author (with Russell): (books) Human Behavior and Life Insurance, 1963, 1993; author: Human Behavior and Property and Liability Insurance, 1964; author: (with Keir and Surrey) Cases in Life Insurance, 1965; author: (with Huebner and Webb) Property and Liability Insurance, 1968, 1996; author: (with Russell) Human Behavior in Business, 1972, Understanding and Influencing Human Behavior, 1981; author: (with Skipper) Life and Health Insurance, 2000; editor: (jour.) Jour. Fin. Svc. Profls., 1959—2001, (ins. series) Prentice Hall, Inc., 1959—. Vice chmn. Pres.'s Commn. R.R. Retirement, 1971-73; trustee Village of St. Joseph, 1969-80; exec. dir., trustee Ednl. Found., Inc., 1969-96. Served with USN, 1944-46. Recipient Solomon S. Huebner gold medal, Am. Coll., 1985, Laureate Ins. Hall Fame, 1993, Order of the Golden Fleece, UNC, 1948, John Newton Russell Meml. award, 1999, Round Table of N.Y. Lifetime Achievement award, 2001. Mem. Am. Risk and Ins. Assn. (pres. 1964), Phi Beta Kappa, Beta Gamma Sigma, Omicron Delta Kappa, Alpha Kappa Psi. Roman Catholic. Home: 1762 Nancy Creek Blf NW Atlanta GA 30327-1912

BLACK, KEVIN JOHN, psychiatrist; b. Provo, Utah, Nov. 15, 1962; s. John C. and Myrna J. (Murphy) B.; m. Winona Fay Pope, Dec. 19, 1985; children: Charissa, Ariana, Déia, William, Rose, Jonathan. BS with honors, Brigham Young U., 1986; MD, Duke U., 1990. Diplomate in psychiatry and geriatric psychiatry Am. Bd. Psychiatry and Neurology. Intern Barnes Hosp., St. Louis, 1990-91; resident in psychiatry Barnes Hosp./Washington U., St. Louis, 1990-94; fellow in PET and movement disorder Washington U., St. Louis, 1994-96; attending psychiatrist Barnes-Jewish Hosp., St. Louis, 1996—; asst. prof. psychiatry, radiology and neurology Washington U., St. Louis. Med. advisor Mo. Tourette Syndrome Assn., St. Louis, 1996—, Greater St. Louis chpt. Am. Parkinson's Disease Assn., St. Louis, 1996—; co-dir. med. student edn. in psychiatry Washington U. Sch. Medicine, 1997—. Active vol. Ch. of Jesus Christ of Latter-day Saints, 1980—; vol. Boy Scouts Am., St. Louis, 1994-. Mem. Am. Neuropsychiat. Assn., Movement Disorder Soc., Soc. Neurosci., Tourette Syndrome Assn. Office: 660 S Euclid Ave Campus Box 8134 Saint Louis MO 63110-1093 E-mail: kbmd@byu.net.

BLACK, KRISTINE MARY, physicist; b. St. Paul, July 11, 1953; d. Jaurd Oliver and Dorothy Helen (Amos) B. B in Physics, U. Minn., 1975, MS in Cell Biology, 1978, MS in Metallurgy and Materials Sci., 1981. Analytical physicist Cardiac Pacemakers, St. Paul, 1978, qualifications engr., 1978-81; biomaterials engr. St. Jude Med., Inc., St. Paul, 1981-83; mgr. quality assurance Unisys Semicondr. Ops., St. Paul, 1983-88; sys. assurance sect. mgr. Unisys, St. Paul, 1988-90; quality assurance mgr. SMPO divsn., San Diego, 1990-91; mgr. reliability and quality assurance Carborundum Co., Phoenix, 1991-93; supplier quality assoc. Hamilton Std. Comml. Aircraft Products, Mesa, Ariz., 1993-94; sr. mgr. materials QA Medtronic Ariz. Device Mfg., Tempe, Ariz., 1994—2003; sr. prin. wafer FAB process engr. Medtronic Microelectronics Ctr., Tempe, 2003—. Mem. Am. Soc. Quality, Am. Soc. Metals, U. Minn. Inst. Tech. Alumni Soc. (dir. 1980-87, v.p. 1986-87, pres. 1987-88). Office: Medtronic 2343 W Medtronic Way Tempe AZ 85281-5132

BLACK, LAWRENCE, librarian; b. Bronx, N.Y., May 28, 1940; s. Reuben and Florence (Kuhnberg) B.; m. Linda Perlis, Dec. 8, 1968; 1 child, David. BA, Long Island U., 1963; MLS, Pratt Inst., 1965; MA in Edn., NYU, 1973; cert. in Advanced Librarianship, Columbia U., 1981. Libr. U.S. VA Hosp., Northport, N.Y., 1965-66; libr. assoc. NYU Librs. Gen. U. Libr., N.Y.C., 1967-68; libr. N.Y. State Inst. for Basic Rsch. in Devel. Disabilities, Staten Island, N.Y., 1968—. Mem. adv. com. of librs. Med. Libr. Ctr. of N.Y., N.Y.C., 1969—; compiler of bibliographies, 1975-2003. Trustee Temple Emanu-El, Staten Island, N.Y., 1989—, founder, coord. book club 1999—. Scholarship N.Y. Libr. Club, N.Y.C., 1965; recipient Small award NYU Dept Hebrew Culture, 1969. Mem. Govt. Agy. Librs. N.Y. State, Med. Libr. Assn. N.Y., N.J. chpt., N.Y. Libr. Club., Spl. Librs. Assn., Medical Libr. Assn. (institutional rep.). Democrat. Jewish. Avocation: history. Office: NY St Inst Basic Rsch Devel Disabilities 1050 Forest Hill Rd Staten Island NY 10314-6356

BLACK, LEONARD JULIUS, retail store consultant; b. Bethlehem, Pa., Apr. 26, 1919; s. Morris and Reba I. (Perlman) B.; m. Betty Glosser, June 21, 1942; children: Susan Eiseman, Jodie Black. BS, U. Pa., 1941; LLD, St. Francis Coll. With Glosser Bros., Inc., Johnstown, Pa., 1946-86, mdse. mgr. ready to wear, 1954-59, exec. v.p. stores and supermarkets, 1959-69, pres., CEO, 1969-86, also bd. dirs. Cons. staff Coopers & Lybrand. Past bd. dirs. Conemaugh Valley Meml. Hosp., Greater Johnstown Com., Johnstown Econ. Devel. Com.; bd. dirs. Johnstown Area Regional Industries. Lt. comdr. USNR, 1942-46. Mem. Palm Beach Civic Assn., Citizens Assn. Palm Beach, Sunnehanna Country Club, High Ridge Country Club. Republican. Home and Office: 2780 S Ocean Blvd Palm Beach FL 33480-5581

BLACK, LISA, artist; b. Lansing, Mich., June 19, 1934; d. W. Eugene and Eugenia (Anikeeff) Hunter; m. Thomas Howard Black, June 6, 1959; children: Kelly Windsor, Leslie Cheney. Diploma, d'etudes de civilisation, Paris, 1955; BA, U. Mich., 1956. One-woman shows include Wildwood Studios, Lake Orion, Mich., Conn. Bank & Trust Co., New Canaan, Noroton Gallery, Darien, Conn., Gates Gallery, New Canaan, Easter Seal Rehab. Ctr., Stamford, Conn., Landmark Lobby Gallery, Stamford, Barnes & Noble Gallery, Norwalk, Darien, Town Hall Gallery, Fairbanks Shop Gallery, Darien, Borders, Wilton, Conn., Creative Framing Gallery, Greenwich, Conn., Barnes & Noble, 2003; group shows include Lionheart Gallery, Pound Ridge, N.Y., Terrain Gallery, N.Y.C., 1970, Stamford Mus., 1972, Williams Gallery, Darien, 1974, Greenwich Art Barn, Conn., 1976, New Haven Paint and Clay Ann. Juried Exhbn., Conn., 1983, Darien Sport Shop, Gallery Group, White Plains, N.Y., Landmark Tower, Stamford, Conn., Hospice of Branford, 1987, Eagle Tower, Stamford, 1987, Invited Artists of Westport Ctr., Bridgeport (Conn.) Hilton, 1988, Silvermine Guild, Art of N.E. 50th Juried Exhbn., 1999, Our World Gallery at the Stone Studio, Stamford, 2002, Ninth Life Fine Art Gallery, St. Thomas, V.I., 2003, Creative Framing Gallery, New Haven, 2003, Wilton Art Gallery, 2003, Ctr. for Contemporary Printmaking, 2003, Left of the Bank Gallery, Old Greenwich, Conn., 2003, others; represented in permanent collection Conn. Bank & Trust Co., Stamford (Conn.) Hosp. Vol. tchr. art, performance art, drawing Arts in Action program in local schs. Recipient 126 art show and art society awards including 1st prize Rowayton Arts Ctr., 1989, 91, 93, Fred Kraus award for painting Stamford Mus., 1992, 1st prize Rowayton Arts Ctr., 1996, Best in Show Rowayton Arts Ctr., 1997, 1st prize watercolors Greenwich Art Soc., 1999, Art Soc. of Old Greenwich, 1999, 2000, Randolph Chitwood award Greenwich Art Soc., 2002, Cmty. award 2d prize Rowayton Arts Ctr., 2002, many others. Mem. Greenwich Art Soc. (historian 1995-96), Art Soc. of Old Greenwich, Ctr. for Contemporary Printmaking,, New Caanan Soc. for the Arts, Rowayton Arts Ctr. (bd. dirs. 2000-01), N.Y. Inst. of Photography, Wilton Arts Ctr., Milford Arts Ctr., Darien Art Ctr., Rowayton Arts Ctr. (mem. exec. bd.), New Rochelle Art Assn., New Haven Paint and Clay Club. Republican. Avocations: handicrafts, family, antique shows, art history. Home: 17 Brushy Hill Rd Darien CT 06820-6008 E-mail: lisa@lisablack.com.

BLACK, LOUIS ENGLEMAN, lawyer; b. Washington, Aug. 5, 1943; s. Fischer Sheffey and Elizabeth (Zemp) B.; m. Cecelia Whidden, Sept. 5, 1966; 1 child, Kerrison Todd. BA, NYU, 1968, JD, 1971, LLM in Taxation, 1978. Bar: N.Y. 1972. Assoc. Carter, Ledyard & Milburn, N.Y.C., 1972-79; ptnr. Van Ginkel & Benjamin, N.Y.C., 1979-83; of counsel Zimet, Haines, Moss & Friedman, N.Y.C., 1983-84, DeForest & Duer, N.Y.C., 1984-86, ptnr., 1986—2001, Black & Assocs., 2002—. Vice-chmn. bd. dirs. MacMillan Ring-Free Oil Co., Inc., 1986-87; chmn. bd. Lee's Gourmet Farms, Inc., 1993-97, United Compressor, LLC, 2002—, Kingdom Techs., LLC, 2002—. Editor: NYU Jour. Internat. Law and Politics, 1970-71; author: Partnership Buy/Sell Agreements, 1977. Mem. ABA, N.Y. State Bar Assn. Home: 220 E 65th St Apt 24M New York NY 10021-6629 Office: Black & Assocs 20 E 46th St Ste 1401 New York NY 10017-2276 E-mail: lblack@blackesq.com.

BLACK, MARILYN HAMMER, non-profit organization executive; b. Sioux City, Iowa, Apr. 25, 1923; d. Franklin Wilfred and Ruth Marie (Gray) Hammer; m. Albert Scott Black; children: Barbara Black Miller, William Scott, Patricia Black Thompson. BA, U. Without Walls, 1975; MS, U. Houston-Clear Lake, 1980; PhD in Philosophy, Summit U., New Orleans, 1998. Dir. religious edn. St. Francis Episcopal Ch., Houston, 1968-72; program dir. NCCJ, Houston, 1972-80; exec. dir. Support Ctr. Houston, 1982-86; dir. C.G. Jung Edn. Ctr., Houston, 1987-91. Mem. mission coun. St. Francis Episcopal Ch., Houston, 1982. Mem. ASTD, Non-Profit Mgmt. Assn., Nat. Soc. Fund Raising Execs. (bd. dirs. 1982). Home: 2929 Post Oak Blvd Apt 602 Houston TX 77056-6117

BLACK, PAGE MORTON, civic worker; b. Chgo. d. Alexander and Rose Morton; m. William Black, Mar. 27, 1962. Student, Chgo. Mus. Coll. Singer, pianist Pierre Hotel, N.Y.C., Warwick Hotel, One Fifth Ave. Sherry Netherland Hotel; singer radio show and comml. Chock Full O'Nuts Corp.; rec. artist Atlantic Records, Den Records. Co-founder Page and William Black Post-Grad. Sch. Medicine, Mt. Sinai Med. Sch., 1965—; chmn. mem. exec. bd. Parkinsons' Disease Found., Columbia U. Med. Ctr.; mem. nat. vis. coun. Columbia U. Health Scis. Faculties; hon. chmn. Chock Full O' Nuts Corp., 1983—90; active Columbia Presbyn. Health Scis. Adv. Coun.; founding mem. ASPCA. Recipient Ann. award, Parkinsons' Disease Found., 1987, Police Athletic League, 1992, Manhattan Mag. award, 1992, Lifetime Achievement award, Parkinson's Disease Found., 1997, Dean's award for Disting. Svc., Columbia U. Coll. Physicians & Surgeons, 1998. Home: Premium Pt New Rochelle NY 10801

BLACK, PAUL HENRY, medical educator, researcher; b. Boston, Mar. 11, 1930; s. Samuel Louis and May (Goldberg) B.; m. Sandra Merkin, June 2, 1962; children: Scott, Marc, Jeffrey. AB, Dartmouth Coll., 1952; MD, Columbia U., 1956. Diplomate Am. Bd. Internal Medicine. Intern Mass. Gen. Hosp., Boston, 1956-57, asst. resident in medicine, 1957-58, clin. and rsch. fellow, 1958-60, resident in medicine, 1960-61; sr. asst. surgeon Lab. Infectious Diseases USPHS Nat. Inst. Allergy and Infectious Diseases, NIH, Bethesda, Md., 1961-63; sr. surgeon Lab. Infectious Diseases USPHS Nat. Inst. Allergy and Infectious Diseases, U. Glasgow Inst. Virology, Scotland, 1963-64; sr. surgeon, comdr. Lab. Infectious Diseases USPHS Nat. Inst. Allergy and Infectious Diseases, NIH, Bethesda, Md., 1964-67; asst. prof. medicine Harvard U. Med. Sch., Boston, 1967-70, assoc. prof. medicine, 1970-80; asst. physician Mass. Gen. Hosp., Boston, 1967-70, assoc. physician, 1970-80, hon. physician, 1980—; dir. Hubert H. Humphrey Cancer Rsch. Ctr. Boston U., 1979-83; chmn., prof. microbiology, research prof. surgery, prof. medicine Boston U. Sch. Medicine, 1979-96, prof. emeritus, 1996—. Cons. Roswell Park Meml. Inst., Buffalo, 1976-80, Monsanto Chem. Corp., St. Louis, 1976-82, Collaborative Rsch., Inc. (Genome Therapeutics Corp.), Waltham, Mass., 1984-90; mem. subcom. on evaluation cancer ctrs. Nat. Cancer Adv. Bd., Bethesda, 1975-80 ; sci. cons. U.S.-Israel Binat. Sci. Found., Jerusalem, Israel, 1974—; mem. NIH Study Sect. Virology, 1968-72, Tumor Virus Detection Segment, Spl. Virus Cancer Program, Bethesda, 1972-76; mem. subcom. on environ. carcinogens, Am. Cancer Soc. Task Force on Cancer Prevention, 1975-82, sci. adv. bd. Worcester Found. for Exptl. Biology, Mass., 1976-78, sci. adv. bd. Dartmouth-Hitchcock Med. Ctr., Hanover, N.H., 1976-80, Gov.'s Task Force on AIDS, Commonwealth of Mass., Boston, 1983-94; chmn. spl. virus cancer program contract rev. com., Nat. Cancer Inst., 1977-79 Author monograph; contbr. 226 articles to profl. jours., chpts. to books Nat. Cancer Inst. grantee, 1967-87. Fellow AAAS; mem. Am. Soc. Clin. Investigation, Infectious Diseases Soc., Am. Soc. Microbiology, Am. Soc. Virology, Am. Assn. Med. Sch. Microbiology

Chmn., Soc. Gen. Microbiology, Sigma Xi. Democrat. Jewish. Home: 21 Dawes Rd Lexington MA 02421-5926 Office: Boston U Sch Medicine 715 Albany St Boston MA 02118-2307 E-mail: pblack@bu.edu.

BLACK, PERCY, psychology educator; b. Montreal, Que., Can., Jan. 6, 1922; s. Ovido and Rose (Vasilevsky) B.; m. Virginia Arne, June 21, 1951; children—Deborah, David, Elizabeth, Jonathan BS, Sir George Williams Coll., Montreal, 1944; M.Sc., McGill U., 1946; PhD, Harvard U., 1954. Instr. in Social Scis. U. Ky., 1948-49; rsch. asst. in Race Rels. U. Chgo., 1950-51; rsch. assoc. in Child Psychology U. Minn., 1949-50; Asst. prof. psychology U. N.B., Fredericton, 1951-53; vis. scholar Univ. Coll., London, 1953-54; dir. research Social Attitude Survey, Yonkers, N.Y., 1955-67; prof. emeritus in Psychology Pace U., Pleasantville, N.Y., 1967—. Adj. prof. psychology U. Vt., 2000—. Contbr. author: Societies Around the World, 2 vols., 1953; author: The Mystique of Modern Monarcy, 1953; contbr. articles to profl. jours. Fellow AAAS; mem. APA, Am. Psychol. Soc., B'nai B'rith. Home: 2763 Lower Rd Barre VT 05641 E-mail: pblack@sover.net.

BLACK, PETE, retired state legislator, educator; b. Ansbach, Germany, Sept. 16, 1946; came to U.S., 1948; s. Howard and Kadi (Fietz) B.; m. Ronda Williams, July 12, 1970; 1 child, Darin. BS, Idaho State U., 1975, MEd, 1998. Cert. elem. tchr. Tchr. Pocatello (Idaho) Sch. Dist., 1975—; mem. Idaho Ho. Reps., Boise, 1983-96, asst. minority leader, 1987-96; tech. tng. specialist Sch. Dist. 25, 1996—. Mem. edn. tech. coun.; mem. adv. coun. chpt. II ESEA. Bd. dirs. Arts for Idaho; mem. State Libr. Bd. With USNR, 1964. Mem. NEA, Idaho Edn. Assn. (bd. dirs.), Idaho Libr. Assn., Idaho State U. Alumni Bd., Idaho Pers. Commn. Democrat. Home: 2249 Cassia St Pocatello ID 83201-2059 Office: Idaho House of Reps Statehouse Mail Boise ID 83720-0001 E-mail: blackcat1@cableone.net.

BLACK, PETER, surgeon, educator; b. Calgary, Alta., Can., Apr. 3, 1944; s. Thomas Herbert and Harriet Elizabeth (Peterson) B.; m. Katharine C. Black, June 15, 1967; children: Winifred, Libby, Katy, Peter Thomas, Christopher. AB, Harvard U., 1966; MD, CM, McGill U., 1970; PhD, Georgetown U., 1978. Diplomate Am. Bd. Neurosurgery. Staff neurosurgeon Mass. Gen. Hosp., Boston, 1980-87; neurosurgeon-in-chief Brigham and Women's Hosp., Boston, 1987—, Children's Hosp., Boston, 1987—; chief neurosurg. oncology Dana Farber Cancer Inst., Boston, 1991—; Franc D. Ingraham prof. neurosurgery Harvard Med. Sch., Boston, 1987—. Author 7 books, more than 350 articles. Office: Brigham and Women's Hosp 75 Francis St Boston MA 02115-6106

BLACK, REBECCA LEREE, special education educator; b. Pasadena, Calif., Sept. 15, 1954; d. James and Mary Black; m. Mario Isabella, Aug. 10, 1996. BA, San Diego State U., 1977, MA, 1987. Multiple subject tchg. credential Calif., cert. specialist credential-learning handicapped Calif., resource specialist. Substitute tchr. San Diego Unified Dist., 1978—80, Poway (Calif.) Unified Sch. Dist., 1978—79; resource specialist Coronado (Calif.) H.S., 1980—. Support provider Beginning Tchr. Support Assessment, Coronado, 2000—02; focus group leader Coronado H.S. Accreditation Com., Coronado, 2001—02. Club advisor Coronado H.S. Friday Night Live Club, Coronado, 1991—2001, Girls' Svc. Club, Coronado, 1980—83, Youth to Youth, Coronado, 1986—89. Scholar Anita Snow Meml., San Diego South County Selpa and Bonita Optimist Found., 2001. Mem.: Calif. Assn. Resource Specialists and Spl. Edn. Tchrs. Avocations: martial arts, golf, softball.

BLACK, RECCA MARCELE, educator; b. Marion, Ind., Feb. 4, 1964; d. Charles Lee and Jerry Ann Barbour. BA in Elem. Edn., Marion Coll., 1987, MEd; postgrad., Ind. Wesleyan U. Tchr. Marion (Ind.) Community Schs.; food svc. worker Marion Coll. Baldwin Food Svc.; casual clerk, cashier, sec. U.S. Post Office; audio-visual asst. VA Med. Ctr. Reporter Marion Newspaper. Contbr. numerous articles to profl. jours. Bd. dirs. YWCA. Recipient Freshman scholar, Shugar scholar. Mem.: NEA, AAUW (bd. dirs.).

BLACK, RICHARD BRUCE, business executive, consultant; b. Dallas, July 25, 1933; s. James Ernest and Minerva (Braden) B.; children: Kathryn Braden, Paula Anne (dec.), Erica Lynn. BS in Engring., Tex. A&M U., 1954; MBA, Harvard U., 1958; PhD (hon.), Beloit Coll., 1997. With Vulcan Materials Co., Birmingham, Ala., 1958-62; v.p. fin. Warner Electric Brake & Clutch Co., Beloit, Wis., 1962-67, dir., 1973-85; pres. automotive group, exec. v.p. corp. Maremont Corp., Chgo., 1967-72, pres. corp., COO, 1972-76, pres., chmn., CEO, 1976-79; pres., CEO, dir. Alusuisse of Am., Inc., N.Y.C., 1979-81; chmn., CEO, dir. AM Internat., Inc., Chgo., 1981-82; owner R. Black & Assocs., 1983—; chmn. ECRM, Boston, 1983—2002, pres., CEO, 2002—; gen. ptnr. KBA Ptnrs., LP, 1988-98, OpNet Ptnrs., LP, 2000—; pres. Oak Tech., Inc., Sunnyvale, Calif., 1998—99, vice chmn., 1999—. Bd. dirs. Gabelli Group Capital Ptnrs., Inc., GSI Lumonics, Inc., Oak Tech., Inc., ECRM, Inc., Applied Optoelectronics, Inc., Alliance Fiber Optics Products, Inc., Altigen Comms., Inc., Fortinet, Inc., CrossFiber, Inc., Benedetto Gartland, Inc., Trex Enterprises, Inc., Wave Precision, Inc.; lectr. econs. Beloit (Wis.) Coll., 1964-67. Author: (with Jack Pierson) Linear Polyethylene-Propylene: Problems and Opportunities, 1958. Trustee Beloit Coll., Am. Indian Coll. Fund., Denver, Teton Sci. Sch., Bard Coll. Ctr. for Curatorial Studies, Inst. for Advanced Study, Princeton, N.J., Snake River Conservancy Found.; trustee, nat. chmn. Inroads, Inc., 1973-77. 1st lt. USAF, 1954-56. Recipient Flame of Hope Lifetime Achievement award, Am. Indian Coll. Fund, 1998, Inroads Lifetime Achievement award, 1979. Mem. Am. Alpine Club, Harvard Club (N.Y.C.). Office: ECRM Inc 554 Clark Rd Tewksbury MA 01876

BLACK, RICHARD EUGENE, pediatric surgeon; b. Salt Lake City, Utah, Jan. 14, 1946; MD, U. Utah, 1974. Diplomate Am. Bd. Surgery, Am. Bd. Pediatric Surgery. Intern Duke U., Durham, N.C., 1974-75, resident in surgery, 1975-76, U. Utah, Salt Lake City, 1976-79; fellow in pediat. surgery U. Cin. Children's Hosp., 1979-81; assoc. prof. surgery U. Utah, Salt Lake City, 1989-99, prof. surgery, 1999—. Attending physician Primary Children's Med. Ctr., Salt Lake City, 1981—. Fellow ACS, Am. Acad. Pediatrics; mem. Am. Pediatric Surgeons Assn., Pacific Assn. Pediat. Surgeons. Office: Primary Childrens Med Ctr 100 N Medical Dr Ste 2600 Salt Lake City UT 84113-1103 E-mail: richard.black@hsc.utah.edu.

BLACK, ROBERT ALLEN, lawyer; b. Ocala, Fla., Aug. 15, 1954; s. Allen Harrison and Rose Marie (Dupree) B. BA, U. Tex., El Paso, 1977; JD summa cum laude, Tex. Tech U., 1980. Bar: Tex. 1980, U.S. Ct. Appeals (5th and 11th cirs.) 1980, U.S. Supreme Ct. 1985. Ptnr. Mehaffy & Weber, Beaumont, Tex., 1980—, mng. ptnr., 1998—. Adj. prof. law Lamar U., Beaumont, Tex., 1981-84. Case note editor Tex. Tech Law Rev., 1979-80; editor Jefferson County Bar Jour., 1991-93. Pres. Humane Soc. S.E. Tex., Beaumont, 1983-89; bd. dirs. YMCA, Beaumont, 1985-87, Beaumont Cmty. Players, 1989-91; host TV show Pets on Parade, Beaumont, 1986-87; mem. Beaumont City Planning and Zoning Commn., 1987-90; mem. Beaumont Hist. Landmark Commn., 1989-90. Named one of Outstanding Young Men of Am., Jaycees, 1982. Fellow: Tex. Bar Found. (chair Dist. 3 nominating com.); mem.: Am. Contract Bridge League (pres. unit 201 1991—93, bd. govs. 1992—96, pres. 1994—96), Tex. Bar Assn., Jefferson County Bar Assn. (treas. 1994—95, pres.-elect 1996—97, pres. 1997—98), ABA. Democrat. Avocations: book collecting, tennis, history. Home: 601 22nd St Beaumont TX 77706-4915 Office: Mehaffy & Weber 2615 Calder St Ste 800 Beaumont TX 77702-1993 E-mail: BobBlack@mehaffyweber.com.

BLACK, ROBERT CHARLES, author, lawyer; b. Detroit, Jan. 4, 1951; s. Robert Charles and Eileen Lois (Perry) B. BA, U. Mich., 1973; JD, Georgetown U., 1977; MA, U. Calif., Berkeley, 1984, SUNY, Albany, 1996. Bar: Calif. Rsch. atty. Mich. Ct. Appeals, Detroit, 1977-78, San Francisco, 1978-82; tchg. assoc. U. Calif., Berkeley, 1982-85; law intern ACLU, L.A., 1985; rsch. atty. SMH, Inc., Somerville, Mass., 1985-87; tchg. asst. SUNY, Albany, 1991-92. Adj. prof. Coll. St. Rose, Albany, 1994; cons. The Police Found. Author: The Abolition of Work and Other Essays, 1986, Friendly Fire, 1992, Beneath the Underground, 1994, Anarchy After Leftism, 1997. Regents fellow U. Calif., Berkeley, 1982, 83; Hindelaang fellow SUNY, 1989. Mem.: NY Civil Liberties Union (bd. dirs.), State Bar NY, State Bar Calif., Mensa, Phi Alpha Theta, Phi Beta Kappa, Phi Eta Sigma. Office: PO Box 3142 Albany NY 12203-0142 E-mail: abobob51@aol.com.

BLACK, ROBERT COLEMAN, judge, lawyer; b. Greenville, Ala., July 3, 1934; s. James Monroe and Mabel (Coleman) B.; m. Carolyn Musselwhite, Dec. 20, 1960; children: Elizabeth Anne, Robert C., Carolyn Jane. BS in Commerce and Bus. Adminstrn, U. Ala., 1960, LL.B., 1961. Bar: Ala. 1961. Law clk. to justice Ala. Supreme Ct., 1961-62; partner firm Hill, Hill, Carter, Flanco, Cole & Black, Montgomery, Ala., 1968—, spl. asst. atty. gen. Ala., 1969—; judge Circuit Ct., 1979—. Prof. law Jones Law Sch., Montgomery; instr. bus. law U. Ala. at Montgomery, Auburn U.; lectr. continuing legal edn. Ala. Bar Assn.; faculty Ala. Jud. Coll. City chmn. March of Dimes, 1966; bd. dirs. Montgomery YMCA, St. James Parrish Sch.; trustee Ala. Indsl. Sch. Served with USMCR, 1954-57. Mem. Ala. Bar Assn., Montgomery County Bar Assn. (chmn. exec. com. 1969-70, pres. 1971), Phi Delta Phi, Beta Gamma Sigma. Office: 425 S Perry St Montgomery AL 36104-4235

BLACK, ROBERT CORL, biology educator; b. Phila., June 16, 1941; s. Samuel Bogle and Alice Elizabeth (Corl) B.; m. Arleen Marie Bruno, Aug. 17, 1963; 1 child, Keith. BS, Pa. State U., 1963, MS, 1965, PhD, 1970. Food technologist Gen. Foods Corp., White Plains, N.Y., 1965-67; assoc. prof. biology Pa. State U., Media, 1970-97, prof., 1997—. Contbr. articles to profl. jours. Mem. AAAS, Am. Soc. Plant Physiologists. Home: 276 Rambling Way Springfield PA 19064-3536 Office: Pa State Univ 25 Yearsley Mill Rd Media PA 19063-5522 E-mail: rcb4@psu.edu.

BLACK, ROBERT DURWARD, ecumenical television producer; b. Flint, Mich., June 6, 1952; s. Joseph Perrin and Lois Jane (Hamilton) B. BA, Wheaton (Ill.) Coll., 1974; cert. bus. adminstrn., U. Ill., Chgo., 1991. Sr. account exec. NCR Corp., 1982-84; contr. Bob Horsley's, Inc., 1974-82, v.p., gen. mgr., 1984-87; pres., prodr. weekly ecumenical TV broadcast 30 Good Minutes, 1987—. Mem. bd. govs. Religion Comm. Coun., 2001—. Office: Chgo Sunday Evening Club 200 N Michigan Ave Chicago IL 60601-5909

BLACK, ROBERT FREDERICK, former oil company executive; b. Mansfield, Ohio, Jan. 9, 1920; s. Judson Ammi and Pauline (Remy) B.; m. Conita Fay McCoslin, June 25, 1944; children: Ronald Gregory, Peggy Lynn. Student, Miami U., Oxford, Ohio, 1946-47. Asst. mgr. Warner Bros. Theatres, Mansfield, 1935-42; asst. treas. Red Arrow Freight Lines, Inc., Houston, 1947-56; contr., sec. Cactus Petroleum Inc., Houston, 1956-62; project contr. Del E. Webb Corp., Clear Lake City, Tex., 1962-65; treas. Mitchell Energy & Devel. Corp., The Woodlands, Tex., 1965-82. With USAAC, 1942-46, CBI. Named to Honorable Order of Ky. Colonels. Mem. Fin. Execs. Inst. (life, past bd. dirs. Houston chpt.), CBI Vets Assn., DeMolay Alumni Assn., Burma Star Assn., Sun City West Hi 12 Club (past pres.), Masons (life, grand organist Grand Lodge of Ariz. 1997-98). Democrat. Home: 10628 W Saratoga Cir Sun City AZ 85351

BLACK, ROBERT L., JR., retired judge; b. Dec. 11, 1917; s. Robert L. and Anna M. (Smith) B.; m. Helen Chatfield, July 27, 1946; children: William C., Stephen L., Luther F. AB, Yale U., 1939; LLB, Harvard U., 1942. Bar: Ohio 1946, U.S. Ct. Appeals (6th cir.) 1947, U.S. Supreme Ct. 1955. Pvt. practice, Cin., 1946-53; ptnr. Graydon, Head & Ritchey, Cin., 1953-72; judge Ct. Common Pleas, Cin., 1973-77, Ct. Appeals, Cin., 1977-89, vis. and assigned judge, 1989-92. Mem. jury instrns. com. Ohio Jud. Conf. 1973—, chmn. 1986-92. Contbr. articles on law to profl. jours. Councilman Village Indian Hill (Ohio), 1953-65, mayor, 1959-65; mem. standing com. Diocese of So. Ohio, Episcopal Ch., 1958-64, lay del. to gen. assembly, 1966, 69; vestryman, warden Indian Hill Episcopal Ch.; chmn. Cin. Human Rels. Commn., 1967-70. Served to Capt. U.S. Army, 1942-45. Decorated Bronze Star. Mem. Cin. Bar Assn., Ohio Bar Assn., ABA, Am. Judicature Soc., Nat. Legal Aid and Defender Assn., Phi Beta Kappa, Queen City Club, Camargo Club, Commonwealth (Cin.) Club. Republican. Episcopalian. Home: 5900 Drake Rd Cincinnati OH 45243-3306 E-mail: bopblack@cinci.rr.com.

BLACK, ROBERT LINCOLN, pediatrician, educator; b. Los Angeles, Aug. 25, 1930; s. Harold Alfred and Kathryn (Stone) Black; m. Jean Wilmott McGuire, June 27, 1953; children: Donald J., Douglas L., Margaret S. AB, Stanford U., 1952, MD, 1955. Diplomate Am. Bd. Pediat. Intern Kings County Hosp., Bklyn., 1955—56; resident and fellow Stanford U. Hosp., 1958—62; practice medicine specializing in pediat. Monterey, Calif., 1962—. Clin. prof. Stanford U., 1962—; cons. Calif. Dept. Health, Sacramento, 1962—; mem. Calif. State Maternal, Child, Adolescent Health Bd., 1984—93. Author (with others): California Health Plan for Children, 1979. Mem. Monterey Peninsula Unified Sch. Bd., 1965—73, pres., 1968—70; mem. Mid-Coast Health Sys. Agy., Salinas, Calif., 1975—80, pres., 1979—80; bd. dirs. Lucile Packard Found. for Child Health, 2000—, Lyceum of Monterey Peninsula, 1963—, Carmel Bach Festival, Calif., 1972—81. With USAF, 1956—58. Fellow: Am. Acad. Pediat.; mem.: Monterey County Med. Soc., Calif. Med. Assn., Inst. Medicine NAS. Democrat. Home: 976 Mesa Rd Monterey CA 93940-4612 Office: 920 Cass St Monterey CA 93940-4507

BLACK, ROBERT PERRY, retired banker, executive; b. Hickman, Ky., Dec. 21, 1927; s. Burwell Perry and Veola (Moore) B.; m. Mary Rives Ogilvie, Oct. 27, 1951; children: Patty Rives, Robert Perry. BA, U. Va., 1950, MA, 1951, PhD, 1955. Research assoc. Fed. Res. Bank, Richmond, Va., 1954-55, assoc. economist, 1956-58, economist, 1958-60, asst. v.p., 1960-62, v.p., 1962-68, 1st v.p., 1968-73, pres., 1973-92. Part time instr. U. Va., 1953—54; asst. prof. U. Tenn., 1955—56; lectr. U. Va., 1956—57; J. Boone Aiken vis. prof. banking Francis Marion Coll., Florence, SC, 1991; mem. Gov.'s Adv. Bd. Revenue Estimates, 1976—92, Va. Econ. Recovery Commn., 1991—92; mem. adv. bd. Health Corp. Va., 1981—93; mem. bd. govs. Capital Area Assy., 1989—93, mem. exec. com., 1989—93; bd. dirs. Media Gen. Corp., 1993—2001, Winchester Evening Star, Inc., Rockingham Publ. Co., T. Rowe Price's Fixed Income Mutual Funds, 1993—98. Contbr. articles to profl. jours. Past dir. Ctrl. Richmond Assn.; former trustee Collegiate Schs., past chmn.; chmn. Main to the James Devel. Com., 1971-73; adv. coun. Robert E. Lee coun. Boy Scouts Am., 1977-78; bd. dirs. Retreat Hosp., 1988-98; past pres. United Way Greater Richmond, active Corp. Divsn., 1986; bd. dirs., mem. exec. com., treas., chmn. fin. com. Downtown Devel. Unltd., 1975-86; chmn. adv. com. Ctr. Banking Edn., Va. Union U., 1977-79; trustee E. Angus Powell Endowment for Am. Enterprise, 1980-88, Acad. for Econ. Edn., 1990-94; mem. adv. bd. Ctr. for Advanced Studies, U. Va., 1986-94; mem. Forum Club, 1987—; bd. dirs. Va. United Meth. Homes, Inc., 1990-94, v.p., 1991-92, chmn., 1992-94; mem. Gov.'s Com. on Def. Conv. and Econ. Adjustment, 1992-94; dir. Va. Biotech. Rsch. Park, 1992-94. With AUS, 1946-47. Recipient George Washington Honor medal award Freedoms Found., Valley Forge, 1978, Brotherhood citation NCCJ, 1991, J. Curtis Hall award for outstanding svc. Va. Coun. Econ. Edn., Outstanding Svc. award Ctrl. Richmond Assn., 1991, Silver Hope award Ctr. Va. chpt. Nat. Multiple Sclerosis Soc., 1992, Disting. Citizen award Robert E. Lee coun. Boy Scouts Am., 1993, Robert P. Black Rsch. Professorship in Econs. at U. Va. established by friends, 1993. Mem. Va. Inter-Govt. Inst. (bd. dirs. 1986-93), Country Club Va. (bd. dirs. 1980-85, 88, v.p. 1981-83, pres. 1983-85), The Commonwealth Club, Kinloch Golf Club, Raven Soc., Phi Beta Kappa (past pres. Richmond chpt.), Beta Gamma Sigma, Alpha Kappa Psi, Kappa Alpha. Methodist. Home: 10 Dahlgren Rd Richmond VA 23233-6104

BLACK, RONNIE DELANE, religious organization administrator, mayor; b. Poplar Bluff, Mo., Oct. 26, 1947; s. Clyde Olen and Leona Christine Black; m. Sandra Elaine Hulett, Aug. 27, 1966; 1 child, Stephanie. BA, Oakland City (Ind.) Coll., 1969; M Div, So. Bapt. Theol. Sem., 1972. Ordained to ministry Gen. Assn. of Gen. Bapts., 1967. Pastor Gen. Bapt. Ch., Fort Branch, Ind., 1972-78; stewardship dir. Gen. Bapt. Hdqrs., Poplar Bluff, Mo., 1978-97, exec. dir., 1997—; councilman City of Poplar Bluff, 1985-97, mayor, 1990-92, 95-96. Mem. Gen. Bapt. Ch. Office: Gen Bapts 100 Stinson Dr Poplar Bluff MO 63901-8736

BLACK, ROSS R., II, family physician; b. Cleve., June 7, 1948; s. Ross R. and Joyce Evelyn B.; m. Linda Rhoades, Aug. 1, 1970; children: Eric H., K. Edward. BA, Muskingum Coll., 1970; MD, Ohio State U., 1973. Diplomate Am. Bd. Family Practice. Asst. dir. edn. divsn. Am. Acad. Family Physicians Kansas City, Mo., 1978-81; assoc. dir., resident family practice Akron (Ohio) City Hosp., 1981-88; ptnr. Mill Pond Family Physicians, Cuyahoga Falls, Ohio, 1988—; clin. prof. family medicine North Eastern Ohio Coll. Medicine. Lt. comdr. USNR, 1976-78. Named Family Physician of Yr., Summa Health Sys., 2000; recipient Physician Recognition award, 2001, Outstanding Alumni award, Muskingum Coll., 2000. Fellow: Am. Acad. Family Physicians (bd. dirs. 1998—2001, Ohio Family Physician of Yr. 1998). Office: Mill Pond Family Physicians 3033 State Rd Cuyahoga Falls OH 44223-2545 E-mail: rrblack@aol.com.

BLACK, ROY, lawyer; b. N.Y.C., Feb. 17, 1945; s. Richard and Minna (Benett) B. BA, U. Miami, Fla., 1967, JD, 1970. Bar: Fla. 1970. Sr. asst. pub. defender Dade County, Miami, 1971-76; ptnr. Roy E. Black, P.A., Miami, 1976-79, Black and Furci, P.A., Miami, 1979-93, Black & Seiden, Miami, 1993-96, Black, Srebnick & Kornspan, Miami, 1996—2002, Black Srebnick Kornspan & Stumpf, Miami, 2002—. Author: Black's Law: A Criminal Lawyer Reveals his Strategies in Four Cliffhanger Cases, 1999. Recipient Nelson Potyner award ACLU, 1982, Criminal Justice award Dade County Bar Assn., 1991. Office: Black Srebnick Kornspan & Stumpf PA 201 S Biscayne Blvd Ste 1300 Miami FL 33131-4311 E-mail: RBlack@royblack.com.

BLACK, RUTH IDELLA, museum curator; b. Aug. 16, 1911; BA, Hastings Coll., 1933; MA, U. Nebr., 1952. Supt. of schs. Chester (Nebr.) Pub. Schs., 1948-54; head edn. dept. Fairbury (Nebr.) Jr. Coll., 1954-70; curator Fillmore County Hist. Soc. Mus., Fairmont, Nebr., 1987—, also bd. dirs. Mem. Ret. Tchr. Assn., Nebr. State Hist. Soc., Delta Kappa Gamma Rho (chpt. pres. 1965-67, state parlimentarian 1968), Pi Gamma Mu.

BLACK, SAMUEL HAROLD, microbiology and immunology educator; b. Lebanon, Pa., May 1, 1930; s. Harold William and Beatrice Irene (Steckbeck) B.; m. Elisabeth Martha Zandveld, Aug. 16, 1961 (dec. Aug. 1997); children: Vicki Ann, Alisa Jo. Student, Hershey Jr. Coll., 1948-50; BS, Lebanon Valley Coll., 1952; postgrad., U. Pa., 1952-54; MS, U. Mich., 1958, PhD, 1961. NSF fellow Tech. U. Delft, The Netherlands, 1960-61; instr. U. Mich., Ann Arbor, 1961-62; asst. prof. Baylor Coll. Medicine, Houston, 1962-67, assoc. prof., 1967-71, Mich. State U., East Lansing, 1971-73, prof., 1973-75; prof. microbiology and immunology Tex. A&M U., College Station, 1975—, head dept. med. microbiology and immunology, 1975-90, asst. dean for curriculum and undergrad. med. edn., 1985-87, interim dean Coll. Medicine, 1987-88, assoc. dean Coll. Medicine, 1988-91, prof. humanities in medicine, 1998—. Lectr. U. Houston, 1964-66; vis. prof. Swiss Fed. Inst. Tech., Zurich, 1969-70 Served with M.C., U.S. Army, 1954-56. Recipient citation Lebanon Valley Coll. Alumni Assn., 1981. Fellow Am. Acad. Microbiology; mem. Am. Soc. Microbiology, Am. Soc. Cell Biology, Soc. Gen. Microbiology, Electron Microscope Soc. Am., Soc. Invertebrate Pathology Home: 1205 King Arthur Cir College Station TX 77840-4827 Office: Tex A&M U Coll Medicine Dept Humanities In Medicine College Station TX 77843-1114 E-mail: shblack@tamu.edu.

BLACK, SARAH JOANNA BRYAN, secondary school educator; b. Port Arthur, Tex., Sept. 30, 1948; d. Foster Paul and Evelyn June (Whetsel) Bryan; m. David Lee Black, Nov. 26, 1971; children: Bryan Joseph, Kelley Allison, David Neal. BA, U. Tex., 1971. Tchr. math. Robert E. Lee H.S., Baytown, Tex., 1971-87, Lee Coll., Baytown, 1987—; tchr. math., chair dept. math. Ross S. Sterling H.S., Baytown, 1987—. Pres. Svc. League, Baytown, 1980; pres. Peter McKenney Soc. C.A.R., Baytown, 1984; treas. PTA of Stephen F. Austin Elem., Baytown, 1984; mem. John Lewis chpt. DAR, Baytown, 1980—, Colonial Dames, Tex., 1980—; treas. East League Little League, Baytown, 1986; treas. Grace Meth. Ch. Women, Baytown, 1985; mem. Cedar Bayou Meth. Ch., 1988-90; pres. Cedar Bayou PTO, 1988; historian Sterling PTSO, 1989. Named Secondary Tchr. of Yr., GCC Ind. Sch. Dist., 1991, 2003, Unsung Hero, Baytown Sun Newspaper, 2003, Ross. S. Sterling Tchr. of Yr., Southwest Bank, 2003; recipient Tex. Excellences award Outstanding H.S. Tchr., U. Tex. Ex-Student Assn., 1993, Seminole Pipeline Tchg. Achievement award, 1995, Unsung Hero award Baytown, 2003, Tchr. Achievement award Southwest Bank, 2003. Mem. Baytown Classroom Tchrs. (treas.), Baytown Edn. Assn., San Jacinto Coun. Math. Tchrs., Nat. Coun. Tchrs. of Math., Tex. Execs. (bd. dirs.), Welfare League, Bay Area Panhellenic (rush chmn.), Alpha Xi Delta (area rush chmn.), Alpha Delta Kappa, Delta Kappa Gamma. Republican. Methodist. Home: 3702 Autumn Ln Baytown TX 77521-2707 Office: 300 W Baker Rd Baytown TX 77521-2301

BLACK, STANLEY WARREN, III, economics educator; b. Charlotte, N.C., July 8, 1939; s. Stanley Warren Jr. and Julia Settle (Wilkes) B.; m. Roberta Burr Callison, June 26, 1965; children: Stanley Wilkes, Sarah Constance. AB in Econs. with honors, U. N.C., 1961; MA in Econs., Yale U., 1963, PhD, 1965. Acting instr. econs. Yale U., New Haven, 1964-65, vis. prof., 1980-81; mem. staff Pres.'s Coun. Econ. Advisers, Washington, 1965-66; asst. prof. Princeton (N.J.) U., 1966-71; vis. prof. Bd. Govs., Fed. Res. System, Washington, 1971-72; assoc. prof. Vanderbilt U., Nashville, 1972-76, prof., 1977-83; spl. asst. to undersec. econ. affairs U.S. Dept. State, Washington, 1977-78; Georges Lurcy prof. U. N.C., Chapel Hill, 1983—, chmn. dept. econs., 1985-90; dir. econ. studies Am. Inst. Contemporary German Studies, Washington, 1994-97. Cons. U.S. Agy. for Internat. Devel., Washington, 1974-75, Ulan Bator, 1998, U.S. Fgn. Svc. Inst., Arlington, Va., 1981-90; vis. scholar IMF, Washington, 1989, IMF Inst., 2000-01; guest scholar Brookings Inst., Washington, 1992; Bundesbank vis. prof. Free U., Berlin, 1997. Author: Floating Exchange Rates and National Economic Policy, 1977, A Levite Among the Priests: E.M. Bernstein and the Origins of the IMF, 1991; editor and contbr.: Europe's Economy Looks East, 1997; contbr. articles to profl. publs.; contbr. chpts. to econ. books. Fgn. Affairs fellow Coun. Fgn. Rels., N.Y.C., 1975-76; Fulbright Disting. lectr. Coun. Internat. Exch. of Scholars, U. Siena, Italy, 1988. Mem. Am. Econ. Assn., Econometric Soc., So. Econ. Assn. (v.p. 1983), Coun. on Fgn. Rels., Cosmos Club, Phi Beta Kappa. Democrat. Episcopalian. Avocations: golf, hiking. Office: Dept Econs U NC Cb 3305 Gardner Hl Chapel Hill NC 27599 Home: 100 Rhododendr Dr Chapel Hill NC 27517

BLACK, STEPHEN FRANKLIN, lawyer; b. N.Y.C., Nov. 28, 1944; s. Theodore Russel Black and Zelma Carmel Bernstein; m. Laurie N Bromberg, June 25, 1967 (div. Oct. 1988); children: Hilary F, Jane S, Katharine L; m. Anne M Richmond, Oct. 14, 1989. AB magna cum laude, Harvard U., 1965; JD magna cum laude, U. Mich., 1968; MLitt, Oxford (Eng.) U., 1970. Bar: DC 1969. Ptnr. Wilmer, Cutler & Pickering, Washington, 1970—2001; ret. Dir Am Soc for Legal Hist, 1979—82. Author: (book) Internal Corporate Investigations, 1985, Der Zivilprozess in Den Vereinigten Staaten, 1986, Complying with Foreign Corrupt Practices Act, 1997; contbr. articles to profl jours. Trustee Shakespeare Theatre, 2001—. Mem.: Cosmos Club Washington. Home: 1605 22nd St NW Washington DC 20008-1921

BLACK, STEPHEN L. lawyer; b. Cin., Ohio, Dec. 3, 1948; AB magna cum laude, Harvard U., 1971, JD, 1974. Bar: Ohio 1974, U.S. Ct. Appeals (6th cir.). Law clerk to Hon. George Edwards U.S. Ct. Appeals (6th cir.), 1974-75; mayor City of Indian Hill, Ohio, 1995-99; ptnr. Graydon, Head & Ritchey, Cin., 1980—. Mem. Ohio State Bar Assn., Cin. Bar Assn. Office: Graydon Head & Ritchey 1900 5th Third Ctr 511 Walnut St Cincinnati OH 45202-3157

BLACK, SUSAN HARRELL, judge; b. Valdosta, Ga., Oct. 20, 1943; d. William H. and Ruth Elizabeth (Phillips) Harrell; m. Louis Eckert Black, Dec. 28, 1966. BA, Fla. State U., 1965; JD, U. Fla., 1967; LLM, U. Va., 1984. Bar: Fla. 1967. Atty. U.S. Army Corps of Engrs., Jacksonville, Fla., 1968—69; asst. state atty. Gen. Counsel's Office, Jacksonville, 1969—72; judge County Ct. of Duval County, Fla., 1973—75; judge 4th Jud. Cir. Ct. of Fla., 1975—79; judge U.S. Dist. Ct. (mid. dist.) Fla., Jacksonville, 1979—90, chief judge, 1990—92; judge U.S. Ct. Appeals (11th cir.) Fla., Jacksonville, 1992—. Faculty Fed. Jud. Ctr.; mem. U.S. Jud. Conf. Com. on Jud. Improvements; trustee Am. Inns Ct. Found. Trustee emeritus Law Sch. U. Fla.; past pres. Chester Bedell Inn of Ct. Mem.: ABA, Jacksonville Bar Assn., Fla. Bar Assn. Episcopalian. Home: 4626 River Point Rd W Jacksonville FL 32207-1104*

BLACK, SYLVIA SLOAN, business educator; b. Phila., Pa., Oct. 24, 1946; d. Maceo A. and Charlotte Kennedy Sloan; m. Frederick Harold Black; children: Frederick Harold Black, Jr., Shana Sloan. BS, Howard U., Washington, 1968; MS, U. N.C., Chapel Hill, 1974; PhD, Columbia University, New York, NY, 1997; MBA, U. Kans., Lawrence, 1981. Instr. Fayetteville (N.C.) State U., 1973—74; opers. mgr. Pacific Trade Group, Waipahu, Hawaii, 1981—83; asst. mgr., fin. analyst Cadet Store, West Point, NY, 1984—93; asst. prof. U. N.C. Kenan-Flagler Bus. Sch., Chapel Hill, 1993—2001, N.C. A&T State U. Sch.

Bus. and Econs., Greensboro, 2001—. Faculty advanced leadership program U.S. Postal Svc., Potomac, Md., 1999—. Chair bd. advisors U.S. Army War Coll., Carlisle, Pa., 1997—2002. Mem.: Strategic Mgmt. Soc., Acad. Internat. Bus., Acad. Mgmt., Nat. Black MBA Assn. (life), Phi Beta Kappa, Beta Gamma Sigma, Delta Sigma Theta (life). Lutheran. Avocations: travel, reading. Office: NC A&T State U 1601 E Market St Greensboro NC 27411 Office Fax: 336-334-7093. Business E-Mail: ssblack@ncat.edu.

BLACK, THOMAS DONALD, retired religious organization administrator; b. Mercer, Pa., Feb. 7, 1920; s. Harry Alexander and Bessie (Gilkey) B.; m. Frances Anna Greenan, Mar. 1, 1923; children: David Alan, Donald Francis, Joseph Harry, Timothy John (dec.). BA, Grove City Coll., 1942, DD, 1955; MDiv, Pitts.-Xenia Theol. Sch., 1945; MST, Temple U., 1954. Ordained to ministry United Presbyn. Ch. N.Am., 1945. Founding pastor Creston Hills United Presbyn. Ch., Oklahoma City, 1945-50; pastor Blvd. United Presbyn. Ch., Phila., 1950-54, Am. Ch. in London, 1973-76; exec. sec. United Presbyn. Bd. Fgn. Mission, Phila., 1954-58; assoc. gen. sec. Commn. on Ecumenical Mission and Relations United Presbyn. Ch.-U.S.A., N.Y.C., 1958-70, gen. sec. Commn. on Ecumenical Mission and Relations, 1970-72, assoc. gen. dir. Program Agy., 1977-84; exec. dir. Gen. Assembly Council Presbyn. Ch. (USA), N.Y.C. and Atlanta, 1985-87; acting assoc. gen. sec. Nat. Coun. Chs. in U.S.A., 1989 90; interim dir. U.S. Office World Coun. Chs., N.Y.C., 1991-92. Chmn. bd. dirs. Christian Lit. Fund, Geneva, 1964-69, Ravemcco, Lit-Lit, N.Y.C., 1962-66. Author: Merging Mission and Unity, 1986; contbr. articles and pamphlets to mission and ch. publs. Interim assoc. Riverside Ch., 1992-93; pastoral assoc. Abington Presbyn. Ch., 1994-98. Presbyterian. Home: Rydal Park 617H 1515 The Fairway Rydal PA 19046-1435 *We want to be appreciated for what we are, but uncertain of being accepted, we try to justify our lives by what we have accomplished. God accepts us for what we are.*

BLACK, VICTORIA LYNN, writer, artist; b. Whittier, Calif., Nov. 23, 1943; d. Raymond Witty and Dorothy Ada (Burnett) Davenport; m. Bruce Robert Black, Aug. 30, 1997; m. Richard Dee Bandlow, Sept. 16, 1961 (dec. Dec. 2, 1972); children: Lisa Lynn Bandlow Dobbins, Lincoln Dee Bandlow. Student, Glendale Coll., 1986—2002. Model/actress Dale Garrick Agy., Beverly Hills, Calif., 1959—78, Bronson of Calif., L.A., 1968—79; prodn. asst./casting Pub. Svc. Co., Irvine, Calif., 1979—80; theatrical agt. William Carroll Agy., Burbank, Calif., 1980—83; office mgr. Greenline, L.A., 1984—86, Napier, L.A., 1986—88, Shah Safari, L.A., 1988—93; writer, artist L.A. Author poetry, short stories, articles; artist paintings and drawings, exhibited in group shows at Verdugo Hills Art Assn., Montrose, Calif., 1999—2003, Glendale (Calif.) Coll., 1998—2003, ERA Castle, La Canada, Calif., 2002, Pasadena (Calif.) Libr., 2002. Convalescent Hosp. L.A., 1997—99. Named Miss Palm Springs, 1960, Miss North Shore Beach, 1961, Miss Ma-Ha-Ya Lani, 1961, Miss Typical Teen, 1961. Mem.: Utah State Poetry Soc., W.Va. Poetry Soc., Poetry Soc. Okla., Mo. State Poetry Soc., Fla. State Poets Assn., Calif. State Poetry Soc., Ariz. State Poetry Soc., Verdugo Hills Art Assn., Alpha Gamma Sigma (life). Avocations: long walks, reading, collecting, gardening, museums and art shows. Home: PO Box 959 Sugarloaf CA 92386

BLACK, W. L. RIVERS, III, lawyer; b. Biloxi, Miss., Sept. 2, 1952; s. William L. Jr. and Virginia B.; m. Lisa A. Paige, Feb. 25, 1981 (div.); children: Jordanna, Caitlin; m. Elaine K., Apr. 25, 1993; children: Aristide, Hallie. BPA, U. Miss., 1974, JD, 1977; LLM in Marine Law, U. Wash., 1982; LLM in Internat. Law, U. Brussels, 1983. Bar: Miss. 1977, U.S. Ct. Mil. Appeals 1980, Wash. 1982, U.S. Ct. Appeals (9th cir.) 1983, U.S. Ct. of Internat. Trade, 1998. Instr. U. Md., Scotland and Italy, 1978-81; ptnr. Lane Powell Spears Lubersky, Seattle, 1983-99, Cozen and O'Connor, Seattle, 2000—. Mem. editl. bd. Maritime Law Reporter. Mem. assoc. bd. Corp. Coun. for the Arts; mem. bd., Pacific Marine Rsch. With USN, 1977-81, Morocco, Scotland. Capt. JAGC, USNR, 1983—. Mem. Seattle-King Bar Assn. (chair maritime sect. 1987-88), Inter-Pacific Bar Assn. (chair maritime law com. 1994-96), Asia-Pacific Lawyers Assn. (chair maritime com. 1986-89), Maritime Law Assn. of U.S. (Proctor), Washington Athletic Club, Naval Club (London). Methodist. Avocation: sailing. Office: Cozen O Connor 1201 3rd Ave Ste 5200 Seattle WA 98101-3071 E-mail: rblack@cozen.com.

BLACK, WALTER EVAN, JR., federal judge; b. Balt., July 7, 1926; s. Walter Evan and Margaret Luttrell (Rice) B.; m. Catharine Schall Foster, June 30, 1951; children: Walter Evan III, Charles Foster, James Rider. AB magna cum laude, Harvard U., 1947, LL.B., 1949. Bar: Md. 1949. Assoc. Hinkley & Singley, Balt., 1949-53, ptnr., 1957-67; asst. U.S. atty. Dist. Md., Balt., 1953-55, U.S. atty., 1956-57; ptnr. Clapp, Somerville, Black & Honemann, Balt., 1968-82; U.S. dist. judge Dist. Md., Balt., 1982—, chief judge, 1991-94; sr. status, 1994—. Sec.-treas. Parkwood Cemetery Co., Balt., 1967-82; also dir.; sec. So. Mech. Inc., Balt., 1971-82; also dir.; pres. Charles T. Brandt Inc., Balt., 1972-82; also dir. Chmn. Bd. Municipal and Zoning Appeals, Balt., 1963-67; mem. Jail Bd., Balt., 1971-73, Atty. Grievance Commn., 1978-82, Rev. Bd., 1975-78, chmn., 1975-76; mem. Gov.'s Commn. to Revise Annotated Code, 1975-82 Alt. Md. del. Republican Nat. Conv., 1960; chmn. Rep. City Com., Balt., 1962-66; Md. del. Rep. Nat. Conv., 1964; Bd. dirs. Balt. Urban League, 1963-69, 76-82; bd. dirs. Union Meml. Hosp.; dir. Hosp. for Consumptives of Md. Mem. Bar Assn. Balt. City, ABA, Md. Bar Assn., Rule Day Club, Lawyers' Round Table. Baptist. Office: US Dist Ct 101 W Lombard St Ste 710 Baltimore MD 21201-2605

BLACK, WILFORD REX, JR., former state senator; b. Salt Lake City, Jan. 31, 1920; s. Wilford Rex and Elsie Isabell (King) B.; m. Helen Shirley Frazer; children: Susan, Janet, Cindy, Joy, Peggy, Vanna, Gayle, Rex. Student pub. schs., Utah. Locomotive engr. Rio Grande R.R., 1941-81; mem. Utah Senate, Salt Lake City, 1972-96, spkr. 3d House, 1975-76, majority whip, 1977-78, minority leader, 1981-90. Sec. Utah State Legis. Bd., United Transp.; chmn. bd. Rail Operators Credit Union, 1958—87. Mission pres. Rose Park Stake Mormon Ch. Rose Park Stake Mormon Ch.; high priest group leader Rose Park 9th Ward, 1980—83, 10th Ward, 1996—99; mem. Rose Park Stake High Coun., 1957—63. Served with USAR, 1942—45. Recipient various awards r.r. and legis. activities . Democrat. Office: 826 N 1300 W Salt Lake City UT 84116-3877

BLACK, WILLIAM B. state legislator; b. Danville, Ill., Nov. 11, 1941; m. Sharon Black; 2 children. BA, William Jewel Coll.; MA, Ea. Ill. U.; postgrad., Ill. State U. Ill. state rep. Dist. 105, 1986—. Spokesman Econ. Devel. Com., mem. Edn. Com., Transp. and Motor Vehicles Com., Urban Redevel. Com., Elem. and Secondary Com., Human Svc. Com.; educator and adminstr. Address: 119 1/2 S Gilbert St Danville IL 61832-6229 Office: 634 State House Springfield IL 62706-0001*

BLACK, WILLIAM B., JR., government agency administrator; b. N.Mex. m. Iris Black; 3 children. BA in Polit. Sci., U. Md., 1971; postgrad., George Washington U., 1978—79, Nat. War Coll., Ft. McNair, Wash., 1979. Operational linguist/analyst NSA, Ft. George, Md., 1959—75, chief office of customer rels. and support to mil. ops., 1975—78, chief ops. maj. field installation, 1979—82, dep. chief, 1982—84, chief, 1984—86, chief office of collection mgmt., 1986—87, assoc. dep. dir. ops./mil. support, 1987—89, chief NSA/CSS rep. Europe office, 1989—92, chief of ops. analysis Group A, 1992—96, spl. asst. to dir. info. warfare, 1996—97, dep dir., 2000—; asst. v.p., dir. info. ops. Sci. Applications Internat. Corp./Info. Ops. Advanced Technologies and Solutions Group, 1997—2000. With U.S. Army, 1956—59. Recipient Exceptional Civilian Svc. award, U.S. Govt., 1986, 1997, Nat. Intelligence Disting. Svc. medal, 1996, Meritorious Civilian Svc. award, Sec. of Def., 1992, Sr. Exec. Svc. Presdl. Rank award, 1984, Meritorious Civilian Svc. award, Sec. of Def., 1974. Office: National Security Agency Central Security Svc 9800 Savage Rd Fort George G Meade MD 20755-6000

BLACK, WILLIAM REA, lawyer; b. N.Y.C., Nov. 4, 1952; s. Thomas Howard and Dorothy Chambers (Dailey) B.; m. Kathleen Jane Owen, June 24, 1978; children: William Ryan, Jonathan Wesley. BSBA, U. Denver, 1978, MBA, 1981; JD, Western State U., Fullerton, Calif., 1987. Bar: Calif., U.S. Ct. Appeals (fed. cir.), U.S. Dist. Ct.; lic. real estate broker; lic. pvt. investigator. Bus. mgr. Deere & Co., Moline, Ill., 1979-85; dir. Mgmt. Resource Svc. Co., Chgo., 1985-86; sr. v.p. Geneva Corp., Irvine, Calif., 1986-91; pvt. practice Newport Beach, Calif., 1991-92; gen. counsel Sunclipse, Inc., 1992—97; spl. counsel Amcor, Ltd., 1992—97; dir. gen. Amcor de Mex., S.A. de C.V., 1993—97; secretario KHL de Mex. S.A. de C.V., 1995—97; v.p., gen. counsel LL Knickerbocker Co., 1997-99; CEO Kuroi Kiku Corp., Kuroi Ryu Corp., First Reconnaissance Co., 1997—; v.p., gen. cousnel Thales Avionics, 1999—. Mng. editor Western State U. Law Rev., Fullerton, 1984-87. Instr. Pai Lum Kung Fu Karate, Hartford, Conn., 1970-75, U.S. Judo Assn., Denver, 1975-80, United Studios Kenpo, L.A., 1995—. Recipient Am. Jurisprudence award Bancroft-Whitney Co., 1984, 85, 86; Pres.'s scholar full acad. merit scholarship, 1983. Mem. ABA, Am. Soc. Appraisers, Inst. Bus. Appraisers, Assn. Productivity Specialists, Am. Employment Law Coun., Profls. in Human Resources Assn., Am. Mgmt. Assn., Orange County Bar Assn., L.A. County Bar Assn., Mu Kappa Tau. Avocations: karate (2d degree black belt), Judo, skiing, scuba, golf. Office: 17481 Red Hill Ave Irvine CA 92614-5630 E-mail: william.black@thales-ifs.com.

BLACKADAR, ALFRED KIMBALL, meteorologist, educator; b. Newburyport, Mass., July 6, 1920; s. Walter Lloyd and Harriett (White) B.; m. Beatrice J. Fenner, Mar. 23, 1946; children: Bruce Evan, Russell Lloyd, Thomas Alan. AB, Princeton U., 1942; PhD, NYU, 1950. From instr. to asso. prof. NYU, 1946-56; lectr. climatology Columbia U., 1953-55; mem. faculty Pa. State U., 1956—, prof. meteorology, 1961—, prof. emeritus, 1985—, head dept., 1967 81. Mem. exec. com. Univ. Corp. Atmospheric Rsch., 1965-68; mem. exec. com. divsn. earth scis. NRC, 1966-69; mem. Internat. Commn. on Dynamical Meteorology, 1978-94, chair working group A, 1978-85; vis. prof. Christian-Albrechts U., Kiel, Germany, 1985-95. Editor: Meteorological Research Revs., 1957; exec. editor: Weatherwise, 1981-95. Sec. Univ. Christian Assn., 1964-68. Served to maj. USAAF, 1942-46. Recipient Sr. Scientist award Alexander von Humboldt Found., 1973 Fellow AAAS, Am. Meteorol. Soc. (sec. 1965-69, pres. 1971-72, editor monographs, Charles F. Brooks award 1969, Cleveland Abbe award 1986, award for outstanding contbns. to the advance of applied meteorology 2002, chmn. publs. commn. 1978-84, chair com. on awards 1989-90), Am. Geophys. Union, Deutsche Meteorologische Gesellschaft (fgn. mem.), North Plainfield (N.J.) Hall of Fame. Baptist. Home: 805 W Foster Ave State College PA 16801-3938 Office: Pa State U 503 Walker Bldg University Park PA 16802-5013

BLACKBOURN, DAVID GORDON, history educator; b. Spilsby, England, Nov. 1, 1949; s. Harry and Pamela Jean (Youngman) B.; m. Deborah Frances Langton; 2 children. BA with honors, Cambridge U., England, 1970, PhD, 1976. Lectr. Queen Mary Coll., U. London, 1976-79, Birkbeck Coll., U. London, 1985-89, prof. history, 1989-92, Harvard U., Cambridge, Mass., 1992-97, Coolidge prof., 1997—. Vis. Kratter prof. history Stanford (Calif.) U., 1989-90, guest lectr. U.S., England, Italy, Yugoslavia, Germany, 1976—; ann. lectr. German Hist. Inst., London, 1998; Malcolm Wynn lectr. Stetson U., Fla., 2002; hist. cons. Channel 4 TV (U.K.), History Channel (U.S.). Author: Class, Religion and Local Politics in Wilhelmine Germany, 1980, (with G. Eley) The Peculiarities of German history, 1984, Populists and Patricians: Esssays in Modern German History, 1987; co-editor: (with R.J. Evans) The German Bourgeoisie, 1991, Marpingen: Apparitions of the Virgin Mary in Bismarckian Germany, 1993 (Am. Hist. Assn. prize best book), The Long Nineteenth Century: A History of Germany, 1780-1918, 1998, 2d edit., 2003; mem. editl. bd. Past and Present, 1988—; numerous appearances on Brit. Broadcasting Sys., 1977—; contbr. articles to profl. jours. Gov. Goodrich Sch., London, 1983—86. Rsch. fellow Jesus Coll., Cambridge, 1973-76, Inst. European History, Mainz, Germany, 1974-75, Alexander von Humboldt Found. fellow, 1984-85, John Simon Guggenheim Meml. Found. fellow, 1994-95; German Acad. Exch. grantee, 1977. Fellow: Royal Hist. Soc.; mem.: Am. Hist. Assn. (com. on honorary foreign membership 2001—, pres. conf. group on ctrl. European history 2003), German History Soc. (sec. 1979—81, com. 1981—86), Inst. European History Mainz (adv. bd. 1995—), German Hist. Inst. (acad. adv. bd. 1983—92). Avocations: writing, reading, jazz, politics, classical music. E-mail: dgblackb@fas.harvard.edu.

BLACKBURN, ALEXANDER LAMBERT, author, English literature educator; b. Durham, N.C., Sept. 6, 1929; s. William Maxwell and Elizabeth Cheney (Bayne) B.; m. Jane Allison, 1957 (div. 1974); children: David Alexander, Philip William Rhodes; m. Inés Dölz, Oct. 14, 1975. BA, Yale U., 1951; MA, U. N.C., 1956; PhD, Cambridge (Eng.) U., 1963. Instr. Hampden-Sydney (Va.) Coll., 1960-61, U. Pa., Phila., 1963-65; lectr. U. Md., RAF, Upper Heyford, England, 1967-73; prof. English U. Colo., Colorado Springs, 1973-95; prof. emeritus, 1996—. Author: The Cold War of Kitty Pentecost, 1979, The Myth of the Picaro, 1979, A Sunrise Brighter Still: The Visionary Novels of Frank Waters, 1991, Suddenly a Mortal Splendor, 1995, (essays) Creative Spirit: Toward a Better World, 2001, (memoir) The Long Habit of Living: A Family Narrative, 2004; editor: The Interior Country: Stories of the Modern West, 1987, Higher Elevations: Stories from the West, A Writers' Forum Anthology, 1993; editor-in-chief Writers' Forum, vols. 1-21, 1974—95. 1st lt. U.S. Army, 1951—53. Recipient Internat. PeaceWriting Award for Fiction, 2003, Chancellor's award U. Colo., 1994, Faculty Book award, 1993, Am. Acad. Poets award, 1959. Mem. Authors Guild, Colo. Authors League, Western Lit. Assn., Rocky Mountain MLA, PEN West, Assn. Lit. Scholars and Critics. Avocation: watercolor. Home: 6030 Twin Rock Ct Colorado Springs CO 80918-3239

BLACKBURN, BRYAN DAVID, title abstractor; b. Portsmouth, Ohio, Oct. 19, 1976; s. David Hassel and Deborah Ann Blackburn. Grad. H.S., Gahanna, Ohio, 1995. Stable worker, horse handler Willie's Last Resort, Canal Winchester, Ohio, 1995—97; underground utility locator Ctrl. Locating Svc., Columbus, Ohio, 1997, S.T.S., Brentwood, Tenn., 1997—98; line worker Pepsi Cola, Nashville, 1998; title abstractor Lawyer's Title, Nashville, 1998—99; pvt. practice title abstractor Pleasant Shade, Tenn., 2000—. Mem.: Tenn. Squire. Republican. Baptist. Avocations: painting, writing, music, horseback riding, reading. Home and Office: 227 Kemp Hollow Rd Pleasant Shade TN 37145-3533

BLACKBURN, ELIZABETH HELEN, molecular biologist; b. Hobart, Australia, Nov. 26, 1948; 1 child. BS, U. Melbourne, Australia, 1970, MS, 1971; PhD in Molecular Biology, Cambridge (Eng.) U., 1975; DSc (hon.), Yale U., 1991. Fellow in biology Yale U., New Haven, 1975-77; fellow in biochemistry U. Calif., San Francisco, 1977-78, from asst. prof. to assoc. prof. molecular biology Berkeley, 1978-86, prof. molecular biology, 1986-90; prof. U. Calif., San Francisco, 1990—, chair dept. microbiology and immunology, 1993-99. Recipient Eli Lilly award in microbiology, 1988, NAS award in molecular biology, 1990. Mem.: NAS (fgn. assoc. 1993), AAAS, Royal Soc. London (G.M. Sloan prize 2001), Am. Soc. Cell Biology (pres. 1998, Australian prize 1998, Gairdner prize 1998, Passano award 1999, Rosensteil award 1999, Keio prize 1999). Office: U Calif Biochem and Biophys Box 2200 San Francisco CA 94143-2200 E-mail: telomer@itsa.ucsf.edu.

BLACKBURN, HENRY WEBSTER, JR., retired physician; b. Miami, Fla., Mar. 22, 1925; s. Henry Webster and Mary Frances (Smith) B.; m. Nelly Paula Trocme, Jan. 10, 1951 (div. 1984); children: John Keith, Katherine Ann, Heidi Elizabeth; m. Stacy Richardson, Sept. 1, 1991. Student, Fla. So. Coll., Lakeland, 1942-43; BS, U. Miami, 1947; MD, Tulane U., 1948; MS, U. Minn., 1957; Dr honoris causa, U. Kuopio, Finland, 1988; DSc (hon.), Tulane U., 1999. Intern Chgo. Wesley Meml. Hosp., 1948-49; resident in medicine Am. Hosp. Paris, 1949-50; med. officer in charge USPHS, Austria, Fed. Republic Germany, 1950-53; med. fellow U. Minn., Mpls., 1953-56; retired Divsn. Epidemiology, 1996; med. dir. Mut. Svc. Ins. Co., St. Paul, 1956; asst. prof. physiol. hygiene U. Minn., 1958-61, assoc. prof., 1961-68, prof., 1968—, lectr. medicine, 1956—, dir. lab. physiol. hygiene Sch. Pub. Health, 1972—, prof. medicine, 1972—, chmn. div. epidemiology, 1983-90, Mayo prof. pub. health, 1990-96. Vis. prof. U. Geneva, 1970; mem. adv. coun. Nat. Heart, Lung and Blood Inst., 1989-93; mem. com. on diet and health NRC, 1986-89; Ancel Keys lectr., 1991; mem. food adv. com. FDA, 1995-2000. Author: Cardiovascular Survey Methods, 1968, On the Trail of Heart Attacks in Seven Countries, 1995, "P.K." Irreverent Memoirs of a Preacher's Kid, 1999, If It Isn't Fun...Memoir of a Different Sort of Medical Life, Vol. I, 2001; mem. editl. bd. numerous jours.; contbr. articles to profl. jours. Lt. (j.g.) USNR, 1942-50, capt. USPHS inactive res. Recipient Thomas Francis award in epidemiology, 1975, Naylor Dana award in preventive medicine, 1976, Louis Bishop award in cardiology, 1979, Gold Heart award Am. Heart Assn., 1990, Rsch. Achievement award Am. Heart Assn., 1992; Mayo chair in pub. health, 1988. Fellow APHA, Am. Coll. Cardiology, Am. Epidemiol. Soc.; mem. AAAS (chmn. med. sect.), Belgian Royal Acad. Medicine, Am. Heart Assn. (dir. 1971-74), Internat. Soc. Cardiology (coun. epidemiology 1971-74, chmn. 1986-91), Internat. Epidemiol. Soc., Alpha Omega Alpha, Phi Kappa Phi, Delta Omega. Home: 1525 Kaltern Ln Minneapolis MN 55416-3507 Office: U Minn Div Epidemiology 1300 S 2d St Minneapolis MN 55454-1075 E-mail: blackburn@epi.umn.edu.

BLACKBURN, JAMES B., III, lawyer; b. Pitts., Nov. 16, 1946; s. James B. Jr. and Ethel Louise (Herrod) B.; m. Cynthia Jan Coote, Aug. 10, 1974; children: Sarah Louise, James B. IV, Natalie Alice. BA, Princeton U., 1969; MPA, N.C. State U., 1974; JD, Duke U., 1980. Bar: N.C. 1980. Staff atty. Gen. Rsch. Divsn, N.C. Gen. Assembly, Raleigh, 1980-84; gen. counsel N.C. Assn. County Commrs., Raleigh, 1984—. Sgt. U.S. Army, 1970-72. Mem. Internat. Mcpl. Lawyers Assn., N.C. Bar Assn. Home: 1100 W Forest Hills Blvd Durham NC 27707-1626 Office: NC Assn County Commrs PO Box 1488 Raleigh NC 27602-1488

BLACKBURN, JOHN LESLIE, small business owner; b. Malta Bend, Mo., Dec. 21, 1924; s. Clarence Oliver and Vivian (Mitchener) B.; m. Gloria Bullington, June 10, 1950; 1 child, Holly. BS, Mo. Valley Coll., 1950; MEd, U. Colo., 1952; PhD, Fla. State U., 1969. Counselor to men Fla. State U., Tallahassee, 1952-56; from asst. dean of men to dean student devel. U. Ala., Tuscaloosa, 1956-69, v.p. devel., 1978-90; vice chancellor student affairs U. Denver, 1969-74, vice chancellor univ. resources, 1974-78; pres. Blackburn Ednl. Techs., Tuscaloosa, 1990—; gen. sec. Am. Assn. of U. Administrators, Tuscaloosa, Ala., 1993-97; interim dir. Challenge 21, Tuscaloosa, 1998-99. Mem. Model City Mayor's Adv., Denver, 1970-73, Nat. Adv. Coun. on Extension and Continuing Edn., Washington, 1976-78; cons. to sec. HEW, Washington, 1976; mem. Ala. Commn. on Aging, 2000—; mem. Gov.'s Task Force on Devel. of Economically Distressed Counties, 2000-01. Contbr.: Pieces of Eight, 1978. Sgt. AUS, 1943-46, CBI. The Blackburn Inst. was created in his honor by U. Ala., 1995, John L. Blackburn Exemplary award in his honor by AAUA, 1991. Mem. AAUA (pres. 1977-79), Am. Coun. on Edn. (acad. affairs commn. 1970-73), Nat. Assn. Student Pers. Adminstrn. (pres. 1973-74), Nat. Inst. Rsch. and Devel. (founder 1974). Home: 1601 St Andrews Dr Tuscaloosa AL 35406-2058 Office: Blackburn Ednl Techs PO Box 2615 Tuscaloosa AL 35403-2615 E-mail: johnblackburn1@hotmail.com.

BLACKBURN, JOHN OLIVER, economist, consultant; b. Miami, Fla., Sept. 13, 1929; s. Elmer E. and Proxie (Hughes) B.; m. Jeanne Elise Miles, Nov. 29, 1957; children: Katherine Elise, John Parkinson, David Laurence. AB, Duke U., 1951; postgrad., U. Miami, 1951-52; PhD, U. Fla., 1959. CPA, Fla. From asst. prof. econs. to prof. Duke U., 1959-81, provost, 1970-71, chancellor, 1971-76; asst. prof. bus. adminstrn. Am. U., Beirut, 1961-62. Vis. prof. Davidson Coll., 1983. Author: The Renewable Energy Alternative, 1987, Solar Florida: A Sustainable Energy Future, 1993. Bd. dirs. U.S. Found. of Univ. of the Valley of Guatemala, Orlando Philharm. Orch., Fla. With USNR, 1952—55. Mem. Archs., Designers and Planners for Social Responsibility, Phi Beta Kappa. Democrat. Mem. United Ch. of Christ. Home: 221 Shell Pt E Maitland FL 32751-5843 E-mail: Jblackburn3L751@aol.com.

BLACKBURN, JOY MARTIN, librarian; b. Marietta, Ohio, Oct. 28, 1925; d. Jonathan George and Helen Joy (Smith) Martin; m. Paul Edward Blackburn, Dec. 18, 1948 (dec. Dec. 20, 1996); children: Paul Conrow, Amy Joy. BA, Ohio Wesleyan U., 1947; MA, U. Minn, Mpls., 1948. Student counselor Ohio State U., Columbus, 1947—54; editor/libr. Jones & Laughlin Steel Co., Pitts., 1955—57; rsch. libr. Tech. Mktg. Assn., Concord, Mass., 1964—66; mgr. corp. libr. Washington Nat. Ins., Evanston, Ill., 1966—85; systems libr. Lutheran Gen. Hosp., Park Ridge, Ill., 1986—88; info. specialist C. Berger & Co., Carol Stream, Ill., 1989—93; retired. Rschr./editor U. Pitts. Med. Sch., 1959. Author: (Quarterly Tech. Bulletin for Non-tech. Readers) J&L Rsch. Bulletin, 1955—57. Vol. Chgo. Botanic Garden Libr., Glencoe, Ill., 1997—99. Mem.: U. Va. Libr. Assocs. (bd. dirs. 2001—03), Cook County Horticultural Soc. (hon.), Phi Beta Kappa. Avocations: history, photography, Arctic art, culture, travel.

BLACKBURN, MARSHA, congresswoman; b. Laurel, Miss., June 6, 1952; married; 2 children. BS, Miss. St. Univ., 1973. Retail mktg.; senator Tenn. State Senate, Nashville, 1998—2002; mem. U.S. Ho. of Reps. from 7th Tenn. dist., 2003—. Del. Am. Coun. Young Polit. Leaders, S.E. Asia, 1993; appointed by Gov. Don Sundquist exec. dir. Tenn. Film, Entertainment and Music Commn., 1995; chmn. Gov.'s Prayer Breakfast, 1996; bd. dirs. Benton Hall Sch., Nashville Symphony Guild, Arthritis Found., Nashville Zoo Friends; appointed Econ. Coun. on Women, 1999. Mem. Nat. Acad. Rec. Arts and Scis., Country Music Assn., Rotary, C. of C. Republican. Office: 509 Cannon Ho Office Bldg Washington DC 20515-4305 E-mail: sen.marsha.blackburn@legislature.state.tn.u.*

BLACKBURN, RICHARD WALLACE, lawyer; b. Detroit, Mich., Apr. 21, 1942; s. Wallace Manders and E. Jean (Beetham) B.; m. Dede Frances Reid, Aug. 29, 1964; children: David Thomas, Jeffrey Manders, Megan Louise. Student, Baldwin-Wallace Coll., 1960-62; AB, Mich. State U., 1964; JD, George Washington U., 1967; grad. advanced mgmt. program, Harvard Bus. Sch., 1988. Labor atty. Chesapeake & Potomac Tele. Co., Washington, 1967-70; gen. corp. atty. Chesapeake & Potomac Telephone Co., Richmond, Va., 1970-74; regulatory atty. AT&T, NYC, 1974-76; gen. atty. New Eng. Tele. Co., Boston, 1976-81, v.p., gen. counsel, 1981—91; exec. v.p., gen. counsel, sec. Duke Energy, Charlotte, NC, 1997; sr. positions NYNEX World Wide Svc. Group, 1991; pres. and group exec. NYNEX Worldwide Comm., 1995—96. Dir. New Eng. Legal Found., 1988; mem. Concord (Mass.) Zoning Bd. Appeals, chmn., 1984, 87; trustee Mass. Eye and Ear Infirmary. Mem. Fed. Communications Bar Assn., Am. Bar Assn., Newcomen Soc. N.Am., Boston Bar Assn. Republican. Episcopalian. Office: Duke Energy Corp 526 S Church St PO Box 1006 Charlotte NC 28202-1244

BLACKBURN, ROBERT PARKER, lawyer; b. Tacoma, Sept. 24, 1956; s. John Griffin and Dorothy Joan (Parker) B. BS with honors, Case Western Res. U., 1978; JD, Am. U., 1981. Bar: D.C. 1982, Calif. 1987. Atty. Banner, Birch, McKie and Beckett, Washington, 1981-84; asst. patent counsel Agrigenetics Research Corp., Boulder, Colo., 1984-86; atty. Ciotti and Murashige, Menlo Park, Calif., 1986-87; ptnr. Irell & Manella, Menlo Park, 1987-89; dir. intellectual property Chiron Corp., Emeryville, Cailf., 1989-91, v.p., chief patent counsel, 1991—. Disting. scholar Berkeley Ctr. for Law and Tech., U. Calif. Berkeley Sch. Law, 2001—. Mem. AAAS, ABA, Am. Chemical Soc., Am. Intellectual Property Law Assn. (biotech. task force mem., chem. practice com., biotechnology subcom. mem.). Office: Chiron Corp 4560 Horton St Emeryville CA 94608-2900

BLACKBURN, SADIE GWIN ALLEN, executive; b. San Angelo, Tex., Oct. 14, 1924; d. Harvey Hicks Allen and Helen (Harris) Weaver; m. Edward Albert Blackburn Jr., Feb. 25, 1946; children: Edward III, Catherine Ledyard Blackburn Helwick, Robert Allen. BA, Rice U., 1945, MA, 1975. Bookkeeper, trust dept. State Nat. Bank, Houston; tchr. elem. sch. Galveston, Tex.; mng. ptnr. Storey Creek Partnership, Houston, 1969—; spl. projects dir. San Jacinto State Park, San Jacin; dir. master plan State Historial Park. Lectr. in landscape design history; spkr. in field. Co-author: Houston's Forgotten Heritage, 1822-1914, 1991; contbr. articles to gardening publs. Newsheet chmn. Jr. League, Galveston, 1950-53, art chmn., Houston Jr. League, 1957-58, chmn. garden/design com., 1991-93, mental health study com., 1959-61, 2d v.p., 1962-63, provisional chmn., 1962-63, interview chmn., 1963-64; adv. bd. Bayou Bend Gardens chmn. Mus. Fine Arts, 1973-74, Bayou Bend adv. com., 1987-89; v.p. Mental HEalth Assn., 1957-62; asst. treas. Child Guidance Assn., 1962-65; mem. Rice U. Hist. Commn., 1974-75; pres. River Oaks Garden Club, Houston, 1975-76; mem. adv. com. Bayou Bend Gardens, 1991—; active Buffalo Bayou Partnership, Houston Nature Conservancy, 1993, Friends of Herman Park, 1994, Meml. Park Adv., 1995, Scenic Houston Bd., 1999. Recipient Sweet Briar Disting. Alumna award, 1991. Mem. Garden Club Am. (zone chmn. 1977-79, founders fund vice chmn. 1979-80, dir. 1980-82, rec. sec. 1982-84, v.p. 1984-86, archive co-chmn. 1986-87, 1st v.p. 1987-89, pres. 1989-91, Achievement medal 2002), Nat. Wildflower Rsch. Ctr. (bd. dirs.), Nat. Parks and Conservation Assn. Bd. (v.p. 1995-97, sec. 1997-99), San Jacinto Mus. History (pres. bd. 1975-77, bd. dirs.), Pi Beta Phi (Carolyn Herman Lichtenberg Crest award for disting. alumnae achievement 1998). Republican. Episcopalian. Avocations: gardening, fishing, hunting, bridge, golf. Home: 1030 Potomac Houston TX 77057-1916

BLACKBURN, SHARON LOVELACE, federal judge; b. Pensacola, Fla., May 7, 1950; BA, U. Ala., 1973; JD, Samford U., 1977. Law clk. to hon. Robert Varner U.S. Dist. Ct. Ala., 1977-78; staff atty. Birmingham Area Legal Svcs., 1979; asst. U.S. atty. U.S. Atty's. Office, 1979-91; judge U.S. Dist. Ct. (no. dist.) Ala., Birmingham, 1991—. Mem. Birmingham Bar Assn. Office: US Dist Ct 730 Hugo L Black US Cthouse 1729 5th Ave N Birmingham AL 35203-2000*

BLACKBURN, WILLIAM STANLEY, lawyer; b. Nashville, Nov. 7, 1951; s. William Hodge and Margaret Virginia (Ware) B.; m. Laura Ross Wilson, July 23, 1983; children: William, Margaret. BS in Economics, Auburn U., 1973; JD, U.Va., 1976. Assoc. Kilpatrick & Cody (now Kilpatrick Stockton, LLP), Atlanta, 1976—82, ptnr., 1982—. Co-chair Bus. Transactions Group, 1996—2001; mem. bus. law sect. State Bar Ga., sect. sec., 1998, sect. vice chair, 99, sect. chair, 2000, mem. legal opinions com., 1991—, chair, 1992—98, younger lawyers sect. long range planning com., 1979—80, pub. com., 1979—80, credit union com., 1980—81. Notes Editor Va. Law Review, 1975-76, mem. editorial bd., 1974-75. Sec. Boys and Girls Clubs of Metro Atlanta, Inc., 1984—, mng. bd. dirs., 1982—, mem. exec. com., 1984—; chmn. legal divsn. Fulton County, Am. Heart Assn., 1981; mem. Leadership Atlanta, 1983-84; sec. Young Men's Round Table, High Mus. Art, 1984-85, pres., 1985-86, mem., 1983-86; group chmn. United Way Atlanta, 1984, account exec.; bd. dirs. Japan-Am. Soc. Ga., 1986-90. Fellow: Am. Coll. Investment Counsel; mem.: ABA (young lawyers sect. banking law subcom. 1980—81, com. legal opinions 1992—, sect. bus. law), Cobb County C. of C. (internat. bus. coun. 1984—89), Can. Am. Soc. Atlanta (bd. dirs. 1998—2001), Atlanta Bar Assn. (cts. com. 1982—83, co-chmn. joint task force mcpl. ct. City of Atlanta 1982—83, law day com. 1984), Piedmont Diving Club, Lawyers Club Atlanta, Omicron Delta Epsilon, Phi Eta Sigma, Omicron Delta Kappa, Phi Kappa Phi, Order of Coif. Avocation: golf. Home: 2595 Habersham Rd NW Atlanta GA 30305-3557 Office: Kilpatrick Stockton LLP 1100 Peachtree St NE Ste 2800 Atlanta GA 30309-4530

BLACKBURN, WYATT DOUGLAS, insurance executive; b. July 6, 1954; s. Wyatt W. and Marjorie C. (Wyre) B.; m. Deborah L. Garland, Feb. 28, 1987; children: Wyatt Woodrow, Taylor Lynne. BBA, West Tex. State U., 1976. Staff acct. Harvey, Messenger & Co. CPAs, Amarillo, 1974-77; audit mgr. Martin W. Cohen & Co. CPAs, Dallas, 1977-78, sr. v.p. adminstrv. ops., 1978-88, sr. v.p., CFO, 1988-94, sr. v.p., COO, 1995-97; exec. v.p., COO State Nat. Cos., Ft. Worth, 1997—. Bd. dirs. State & County Mut. Fire Ins. Co., State Nat. Ins. Co., State Nat. Specialty Ins. Co., Tex. Mem. AICPA, Tex. Soc. CPAs, Omicron Delta Epsilon. Home: 1028 Diamond Blvd Southlake TX 76092-6208 Office: State Nat Cos 8200 Anderson Blvd Fort Worth TX 76120-3620

BLACKER, HARRIET, public relations executive; b. N.Y.C., July 23, 1940; d. Louis and Rebecca (Siegel) B.; m. Roland Algrant, Aug. 6, 1970 (div. Jan. 1981); m. Matthew E. Harlib, Aug. 25, 1988 (dec. 1994). BA, U. Mich., 1962. Exec. dir. publicity Random House, N.Y.C., 1974-79; East Coast v.p. Pickwick Maslansky Koenigsberg, N.Y.C., 1980-81; v.p. pub. relations Putnam Pub. Group, N.Y.C., 1981-85; pres. Harriet Blacker, Inc., N.Y.C., 1986-90; ptnr. Blacker Hunter Pub. Rels. Inc., N.Y.C., 1990—96; pres. Blacker Communications, N.Y.C., 1993—. Mem. Publishers Publicity Assn. (sec. 1973-75, treas. 1982-83, pres. 1983-85), Women's Media Group

BLACKFORD, ALAN RALPH, music educator; b. Camden, Nj, May 20, 1957; s. Ralph Kurtz and Jean Mabel Blackford. BMus Edn., Phila. Coll. of Performing Arts, Philadelphia, PA, 1980, MMus, 1982. Teacher of Music Grades K-12 NJ, Pa. Vocal tchr. Waterford Twp. Sch. Dist., Atco, NJ, 1985—. Accompanist, assoc dir., dir. Cinnaminson Cmty. Chorus, Cinnaminson, NJ, 1972—; organist, choir dir. Trinity Episcopal Ch., Delran, NJ, 1974—. Composer: (choral work) Sanctus. Recipient Phila. Coll. of Performing Arts Alumni Graduation Award, Phila. Coll. of Performing Arts Alumni Assn, 1980, Tchr. Recognition award, N.J. Gov., 1988; scholar Ezerman Piano Scholarship, Phila. Coll. of Performing Arts, 1977. Mem.: NJ Edn. Assn, Waterford Twp. Ednl. Assn, Music Educators Nat. Conf. Avocations: rare and unusual recordings, vintage wristwatches. Home: 2265 Gennessee Ave Atco NJ 08004

BLACKFORD, JASON COLLIER, lawyer; b. Findlay, Ohio, Oct. 30, 1938; s. Emerson Miller and Isabel (Collier) B.; ;m. Jane Edith Howells; children: Thomas, Melinda. BA, Denison U., 1960; LLB, Yale U., 1963. Bar: Ohio 1964, U.S. Dist. Ct. (no. dist.) Ohio 1966, U.S. Ct. Appeals (10th cir.) 1974, U.S. Ct. Appeals (6th cir.) 1985, U.S. Supreme Ct. 1985. Assoc. Weston, Hurd, Fallon, Paisley & Howley, Cleve., 1964-69, ptnr., 1969—. Adj. prof. Cleve. Marshall Sch. of Law. Author: Ohio Corporation Law and Practice, 2 vols., Organizing an Ohio Corporation, Business Organizations, 2 vols.; editor: Ohio Legal Form. Mem. Fairmount Presbyn. Ch. 1st lt. USAR, 1963-69. Mem. Ohio Bar Assn. (corp. law com. 1969—), Cleve. Bar Assn. (trustee 1978-81), Am. Arbitration Assn. (comml. and securities panel, chmn. regional adv. coun., nat. securities com.), Nat. Assn. Securities Dealers (panel of arbitrators). Avocations: writing, antique weapons. Office: Weston Hurd Fallon Paisley & Howley 2500 Terminal Towers Cleveland OH 44113

BLACKFORD, JOHN, magazine editor; b. Norfolk, Va., Feb. 8, 1944; s. Frank Robertson and Polly (Baldwin) Blackford; m. Anne Little; children: David, Jacob. BA, U. N.C., Chapel Hill, 1967; postgrad., Temple U., 1978. Book editor Rodale Press, Emmaus, Pa., 1978—82; editor Software Retailing, Dover, NJ, 1983—84, Computer Dealer, Dover, 1984—86; exec. editor Personal Computing, Hasbrouck Heights, NJ, 1986—91; editor Computer Shopper, 1991—95, editor-in-chief, 1995—. Co-author: Build Your Harvest Kitchen, 1982. Recipient Jesse H. Neal award for best feature article Computer Dealer mag., 1984. Mem.: Appalachian Train Conf., Nature Conservancy, Computer Press Assn. Avocations: landscape photography, hiking, old-time country music, science fiction, internet surfing. Office: Computer Shopper/Ziff Davis 28 E 28th St New York NY 10016-7930

BLACKFORD, ROBERT NEWTON, lawyer, director; b. Cin., Feb. 5, 1937; s. Robert Criley and Virginia Pendleton (Yowell) B.; m. Margaret Ann Williams, July 22, 1961; children: William Pendleton, John Whitner. BSBA, U. Fla., 1960; JD, Emory U., 1968. Bar: Fla. 1968, Ga. 1968. Mem., dir. Maguire, Voorhis & Wells, P.A., Orlando, Fla., 1972-98, sec., treas., 1972-95; ptnr. Holland & Knight LLP, Orlando, 1998—2001. Dir. Hughes Supply, Inc., Orlando, 1970—, sec., 1972-96, asst. sec., 1996-98; dir., sec. Princeton Fin. Corp., 1987-94. Mem. Orlando Mcpl. Planning Bd., 1969-75, Orlando Downtown Devel. Bd., 1972-77, chmn., 1975-77, bd. dirs. Crime Commn., Inc., 1985-88; mem. Orange County's Refuse Disposal Citizens Coordination Com., 1988-90, Orange County Solid Waste Adv. Bd., 1992-96; mem. neighborhood concerns com. Orlando Naval Tng. Ctr. Base Closing Commn., 1994-96; trustee Chelsey G. Magruder Found., Inc., 1981—, pres., 1982-85, 92-94, 2000-02, sec./treas., 1998-2000; trustee Orlando Mus. Art, 1980-82, 85-91, pres. 1985-86, chmn. bd., 1986-87, v.p. 1989-91; ruling elder First Presbyn. Ch., Orlando, 1989-2003, tchr., 1970-2000; bd. dirs. Univ. Club Orlando, 1994-97, sec., 1994-96. Mem. Fla. Bar Assn., Ga. Bar Assn., Orlando Area C. of C. (pres. 1980, chmn. bd. dirs. 1981), Orange County Hist. Soc. (bd. dirs. 1980-83), Country Club Orlando, Rotary Club Orlando (pres. 1991-92). Democrat. Home: 2931 Nela Ave Orlando FL 32809-6178 E-mail: rblackf398@aol.com.

BLACKHAM, ANN ROSEMARY (MRS. J. W. BLACKHAM), realtor; b. N.Y.C., June 16, 1927; d. Frederick Alfred and Letitia L. (Stolfe) DeCain; m. James W. Blackham Jr., Aug. 18, 1951; children: Ann C., James W. III. AB, St. Mary of the Springs Coll. (now Ohio Dominican U.), 1949; postgrad., Ohio State U., 1950. Mgr. br. store Filene & Sons, Winchester, Mass., 1950—52; broker Porter Co. Real Estate, Winchester, 1961—66; sales mgr. James T. Trefrey, Inc., Winchester, 1966—68; pres., founder Ann Blackham & Co. Inc. Realtors, Winchester, 1968—2001; v.p. Coldwell Banker, Winchester, 2001—. Bd. econ. advisors to Gov., 1969-74; participant White House Conf. on Internat. Cooperation, 1965; mem. Presdl. Task Force on Women's Rights and Responsibilities, 1969; exec. coun. Mass. Civil Def., 1965-69; chmn. Gov.'s Commn. on Status of Women, 1971-75; regional dir. Interstate Assn. Commn. on Status of Women, 1971-74; mem. Gov. Task Force on Mass. Economy, 1972; mem. Gov.'s Jud. Selection Com., 1972, Mass. Emergency Fin. Bd., 1974-75; bd. registration Real Estate Brokers and Salesman Commonwealth of Mass., 1991—, chmn. 1994—. Bd. visitors Ohio Dominican U., 1995—, nat. fund raising chair, 1998-99; corporator, trustee Charlestown Savs. Bank, 1974-84; corporator Winchester Hosp., 1983—, chair fund raising emergency room; bd. dirs. Winchester Hosp. Found., 1996—; mem. Winchester 350th Anniversary Commn.; design rev. commn. Town of Winchester; bd. dirs. Phoenix Found., 1980-90, Bay State Health Care, Mass. Taxpayers Found., Speech and Hearing Found., Baystate Health Mgmt., Realty Guild Inc., v.p. 1995-96, bd. dirs. 1996-99, pres. 1997-98; regional selection panel White House Fellows, 1973-74; com. on women in svc. U.S. Dept. Def., 1977-80; 2d v.p. Doric Dames, 1971-74, founding mem., 1969; dep. chmn. Mass. Rep. State Com., 1965-66; sec. Mass. Rep. State Conv., 1970, del., 1960, 62, 64, 66, 70, 72, 74, 78, 90, 98, 2002; state vice-chmn. Mass. Rep. Fin. Com., 1970; alt. del.-at-large Rep. Nat. Conv., 1968, 72, del., 1980, 84, 88, 92, 96; Rep. State Committeewoman, 1996—; pres. Mass. Fedn. Rep. Women, 1964-69; v.p. Nat. Fedn. Rep. Women, 1965-79; pres. Scholarship Found., 1976-78, Mass. Fedn. Women's Clubs; alumnae liaison The Beaumont Sch. for Girls; mem. Women for Romney, 2002; mem. Gov. Romney Inaugural Com. Recipient Pub. Svc. award Commonwealth of Mass., 1978, Merit award Rep. Party, 1969, Pub. Affairs award Mass. Fedn. Women's Clubs, 1975; named Civic Leader of Yr. Mass. Broadcasters, 1962, Banker and Tradesman Leader Making a Difference, 1999; recipient Bus. Owner of Yr. award New England Women Bus. Owners, 1995, Disting. Alumnae award Ohio Dominican Coll., 1999. Mem. Greater Boston Real Estate Bd. (hon., bd. dirs.), Eastern Middlesex Bd. Realtors (life mem. multi-million dollar club), Mass. Assn. Realtors (bd. dirs.), Nat. Assn. Realtors (women's coun.), Brokers Inst. (cert.), Coun. Realtors (cert., pres. 1983-84), Winchester C. of C. (bd. dirs.), Greater Boston C. of C., Nat. Assn. Women Bus. Owners, ENKA Soc. (treas. 2001—), Rotary Internat., Tequesta Fla. Country Club, Capitol Hill Club, Ponte Vedra Club, Winchester Boat Club, Winchester Country Club, Wychmere Harbor Club, Womens City Club, Winton Club (sec., bd. dirs.), Hyannis Yacht Club. Home: 60 Swan Rd Winchester MA 01890-3747 Office: Coldwell Banker 3 Church St Winchester MA 01890-2903 E-mail: ann.blackham@nemoves.com.

BLACKIE, SPENCER DAVID, physical therapist, administrator; b. Endicott, N.Y., Sept. 27, 1946; s. Norman and June (Spencer) B.; m. Bonnie Jean Randall Moulton, June 11, 1967 (div. Apr. 1985); children: Rhonda, Randy, Brenda; m. Sharon Joan Clingman, May 10, 1986; children: Kristen, Sean, Alex. BS, Loma Linda U., 1968; MA, U. So. Calif., 1973; MS, Boston U., 1980; NMD, So. Coll. Naturopathic Medicine, 2002. Cert. in manual therapy, clin. specialist in orthop. phys. therapy, quantum medicine, bd. cert. naturopathic physician, bd. cert in iridology. Clin. dir. Loma Linda (Calif.) U. Med. Ctr., 1972-74; dir. rehab. svcs. New Eng. Meml. Hosp., Stoneham, Mass., 1974-84, Mt. Carmel Hosp., Colville, Wash., 1984-92, Regina Med. Ctr., Hastings, Minn., 1992—. Mem. Pool Com., Hastings, 1994; chmn. Parks and Recreation Bd., Colville, 1991-92. Capt. U.S. Army, 1969-71. Cmty. Fitness grantee Perrier Mineral Waters, Stoneham, 1978; decorated U.S. Army commendation medal. Mem. Am. Naturopathic Med. Assn., Am. Phys. Therapy Assn., Am. Occupl. Therapy Assn., Am. Acad. Orthop. Manual Phys. Therapy, Am. Soc. Hand Therapists, Am. Acad. Quantum Medicine, Internat. Iridology Practitioners Assn., Minn. and Wis. Occupl. Therapy Assn., Rotary. Seventh-Day Adventist. Avocations: bicycling, classical guitar, Karate, hiking/backpacking. Office: Regina Med Ctr 1175 Nininger Rd Hastings MN 55033-1056 E-mail: blackied@reginamedical.com.

BLACKLEDGE, DAVID WILLIAM, retired academic administrator; b. Cin., Mar. 10, 1930; s. William Clinton and Helen Louise (Van Curen) B.; m. Diana Marjorie Wiley, June 5, 1953; children: David Noel, William Dean, Alan Keith, Naomi Karen. BS, Purdue U., 1953; MA, Rutgers U., 1965; grad., Nat. War Coll., 1975. Commd. 2d lt. U.S. Army, 1953, advanced through grades to col., 1974; asst. prof. mil. sci. Rutgers U., New Brunswick, N.J., 1961-64; instr. Am. history U. Md.-Far East Divsn., Bangkok, 1967-68; dir. nat. security studies U.S. Army War Coll., Carlisle, Pa., 1978-83; dir. fin. aid Pa. State U. Dickinson Sch. Law, Carlisle, 1983-94, dir. admissions and fin. aid, 1984-94, exec. asst. to the dean, 1994-2000; ret., 2000. Co-compiler: Blackledges in America: A Genealogy of Blackledge/Blacklidge Descendants with Roots in the USA, 2002. Bd. dirs. Carlisle area United Way, 1983-86, Sarah Todd Retirement Home, Carlisle, 1989-95. Decorated Legion of Merit with oak leaf cluster. Mem. Rotary. E-mail: dvb4@psu.edu.

BLACKLER, ANTONIE WILLIAM CHARLES, biologist; b. Portsmouth, Eng., Oct. 19, 1931; came to U.S., 1964; s. Leslie Guy and Florence (Harris) B.; m. Rochelle Lois Melkin, Mar. 12, 1970; children— Mia Samantha, Joshua Harris. BS in Zoology, U. Coll., London, 1953, PhD, 1956. Professeur extraordinaire U. Geneva, Switzerland, 1961-64; prof. zoology Cornell U., Ithaca, N.Y., 1964—. Achievements include research on origins of sex. Home: 14 Nottingham Dr Ithaca NY 14850-8704 Office: Cornell U Genetics Biotech Bldg Ithaca NY 14853

BLACKLEY, CHERYL ANN, freelance/self-employed music educator, musician; b. Woods Cross, Utah, June 8, 1960; d. LeGrande and Patricia Green Blackley. MusB in Secondary Edn., BS in Secondary Edn., Utah State U., 1988. Sole propr./owner and dir. S & D Music Studio, Woods Cross, 1988—; freelance musician on clarinets, saxophones, oboe/english horn & bassoon No. Utah area, 1988—. Prin. clarinet Utah State U. Alumni Band, Logan, 1984—; orch. mgr. Westminster Chamber Orch., Salt Lake City, 1992—94; founding exec. bd. mem., orch. mgr. Intermountain Chamber Orch., Salt Lake City, 1994—96; orch. mem.-reeds Utah Musical Theatre, Ogden, 1994—, orch. mgr., 1999—. Composer: (orch. composition) The Mist, (clarinet solo) 2257 (Utah Best of Category Instrumental Composer's Guild Composition Contest, 1999), (woodwind trio) Trio No. 1 for Flute, Oboe & Clarinet (1st Pl. Tchr. Composition Competition Utah Music Tchrs. Assn., 1997), Gently Raise the Sacred Strain, arr. for Mixed Woodwind Trio (award of merit instrumental divsn. LDS Ch. Music Competition, 1996), Trio No. 1 for Flute, Oboe & Clarinet (3rd Pl. music for children category Composer's Guild Composition Contest, 1995). Mem.: Utah Music Tchrs. Assn., Music Tchrs. Nat. Assn., Utah Music Educators Assn., Music Educators Nat. Conf., Golden Key, Phi Kappa Phi. Mem. Lds Ch. Avocations: reading, gardening, off-road desert racing, cooking, baking. Home: 1985 S 800 W Woods Cross UT 84087 Office: S & D Music Studio 796 W 2000 S Woods Cross UT 84087 E-mail: sdmusic@netzero.net.

BLACKLIDGE, RAYMOND MARK, lawyer; b. Ft. Belvoir, Va., May 17, 1960; s. Martin H. and Carol Ann (Fiarito) B.; m. Karen Marie Tennis, June 19, 1982; children: Robert Mark, Jonathon Michael, Sara Kathryn. BA, So. Ill. U., 1982; JD, John Marshall Law Sch., 1985. Bar: Ill. 1986, U.S. Dist. Ct. (no. dist.) Ill. 1986. Sole practice, West Chgo., Ill., 1986—87; ptnr., corp. sec. Grief, Bus & Blacklidge, P.C., Ill., 1987-92; sole practice West Chgo., 1992—2002, Tampa, Fla., 2002—. Bd. dirs., sr. v.p., gen. counsel, sec. The Jerger Co., Inc., Mobile Homeowners Ins. Agys., Inc., Jerger & Sons, Inc.; bd. dirs., gen. counsel, sec. Mobile USA Ins. Co., Inc., Mobile United Property & Casualty Ins. Co., Inc.; bd. dirs., sr. v.p., gen. counsel, sec., treas. MHIA Premium Fin. Co.; dir., sr. v.p., sec., treas. Mobile Adjustment Co., Inc.; arbitrator 18th Jud. Cir.; reg. lobbyist, Fla., 1994—; of counsel Edward J. Boltz, Christopher C. Benfante and David E. Caddigan, 1993-94; regional mgr. and counsel Alliance of Am. Insurers, 1992-96; title ins. agent Atty.'s Title Ins. Fund, 1994—; treas. USF Delta Chi Housing Corp., 2002—. Editor-in-chief Marshall Opinion, 1985. Pres., bd. dirs. West Chicago Clean and Proud, Inc.; bd. dirs. West Chicago R.R. Days, Inc., 1988-94; alderman City of West Chicago, 1989-94; Rep. precinct committeeman Winfield Twp. Precinct, DuPage County, 1991-94; Scoutmaster, BSA, Troop 148. St. Mark Parish, West Chgo., 1999—. Mem. Fla. Ins. Coun. (bd. dirs. 1996—), Alliance Am. Insurers (mem. govt. affairs com., alliance so. regional advisory com.), Gavel Soc., Columbian Club (v.p.), KC (trustee West Chicago 1985—, Knight of Yr. award 1987); Woodmen of the World (pres. Lodge 37, Tampa, 2001-02). Republican. Roman Catholic. Avocations: travel, religious studies, family, sports, roller blading. Office: Ste 300 8875 Hidden River Pkwy Tampa FL 33637 Fax: 813-975-7475. E-mail: rblackga@aol.com.

BLACKLOW, ROBERT STANLEY, internist, educator; b. Cambridge, Mass., June 24, 1934; s. Leo Alfred and Clara Edna (Cumenes) Blacklow; m. Winifred Young, Dec. 7, 1958; children: Stephen Charles, Kenneth Lawrence, David Alan. AB summa cum laude, Harvard U., 1955, MD cum laude, 1959; DSc (hon.), Kent State U., 1998; DMed. (hon.), U. Pecs, Hungary, 2001. Intern Peter Bent Brigham Hosp., Boston, 1959-60, resident, 1960-61, 63-64, 67-68; instr. Harvard U., 1967-70, asst. prof. medicine, 1970-76, assoc. prof., 1976-78, asst. to dean faculty of medicine, 1969-73, assoc. dean, 1973-78; prof. internal medicine Rush Med. Coll., 1978-85, dean, 1978-81; v.p. for med. affairs Rush-Presbyn.-St. Luke's Med. Center, Chgo., 1978-81; prof. medicine Jefferson Med. Coll., Phila., 1985-92, sr. assoc. dean, 1985-92; pres., dean Northeastern Ohio Univs. Coll. Medicine, 1992—2002, prof. cmty. medicine, prof. medicine, 1992—, pres., dean emeritus, 2002—; sr. fellow health policy Assn. Acad. Health Ctrs., Washington, 2002—. Mem. sci. adv. com. Nat. Fund Med. Edn., 1981—84, Nat. Cancer Inst., 1986—95; bd. dirs. Nat. Resident Matching Program, 1993—, pres.-elect, 1994—95, pres., 1995—96, treas., 1998—99, 2001—03, pres.-elect, 1999—2000, pres., 2000—01. Editor: (book) Signs and Symptoms, 1971, Signs and Symptoms, 6th edit., 1983; mem. editl. bd. Jour. Med. Humanities, 1997—. Trustee Chestnut Hill Sch., Newton, Mass., 1970—79, Belmont (Mass.) Hill Sch., 1973—79, Chgo. chpt. ARC, 1979, Greater Akron (Ohio) Musical Assn., 1993—2002, mem. exec. com., 1998—2002; dir. Akron Regional Devel. Bd., 1998—; mem. Ill. health svc. corps task force Ill. Dept. Pub. Health, 1980; corporator Belmont Hill Sch., 1978—. With USPHS, 1961—63. Sr. scholar, Assn. Acad. Health Ctrs., 2002—. Fellow: ACP, Chgo. Soc. Internal Medicine, Inst. medicine Chgo.; mem.: AAAS, Assn. Acad. Health Ctrs., Assn. Am. Med. Colls., NY Acad. Sci., Twin Lakes Country Club, Cliff Dwellers Club (Chgo.), Badminton & Tennis Club (Boston), Portage Country Club (Akron), Harvard Musical Assn., Longwood Cricket Club (Boston), Harvard Club (Boston, NYC, Chgo) (Chgo. bd. dir.), Literary Club (Chgo.), Franklin Inn (Phila.), Alpha Omega Alpha, Sigma Xi, Phi Beta Kappa. Office: Northeastern Ohio Univs Coll Medicine PO Box 95 Rootstown OH 44272-0095

BLACKMAN, ANDREW BART, accountant, personal financial specialist; b. N.Y.C., Apr. 8, 1953; s. Irving Paul and Babette Patricia B.; m. Lea, Jan. 1, 1981 (div. Oct. 1995); children: Max, Randy; m. Tatiana, Jan. 15, 2001. BS in Bus. Adminstrn., Boston U., 1975; M in Bus. Adminstrn., Fairleigh Dickinson U., Rutherford, N.J., 1979. Diplomate Am. Bd. Forensic Accts.; CFP; CPA. Staff acct. Touche, Ross & Co., N.Y.C., 1975-79; supervisory acct. Gelfand, Breslauer, Rennert & Feldman, L.A., Calif., 1979-80; mng. acct. Parks, Adams & Palmer, L.A., 1980-82; ptnr. Freedman & Blackman, L.A., 1983-90; mng. acct. Liebgold & Assocs., Hackensack, N.J., 1991-92; ptnr. Shapiro Lobel LLP, N.Y.C., 1992—. Mem. steering com. Media Entertainment Roundtable, N.Y.C., 1998—. Editor: (book) Tax Considerations for Professional Athletes & Entertainers, 1998; co-author: (book) Guide to Planning for Performing and Creative Artists, 1997. Named one of Best Fin. Advisers, Worth mag., 1996, 97, 98. Mem. AICPA (chmn. PFS com. 1995-99, exec. com. personal fin. planning com., 1992-95), N.Y. State Soc. CPAs (chmn. entertainment/sports com. 1998-2000, personal fin. planning com. 1995-97), N.J. Soc. CPAs (chmn. sports/entertainment com. 2000-02), Calif. Soc. CPAs. Avocations: theater, tennis, spectator sports, music, investments. Office: Shapiro Lobel LLP 111 W 40th St Fl 8 New York NY 10018-2506 E-mail: ablackman@shapirolobel.com.

BLACKMAN, DAVID LEE, research scientist; b. Chgo., Jan. 4, 1948; s. Sol and Carol Edith (Rothman) B. BS in Maths., U. Ariz., 1973; student, Laney Coll., Oakland, Calif., 1977-79; MS in Chemistry, San Francisco State U., 1983. Lic. technician. Rsch. cons. Detox Assn., San Bernadino, Calif., 1973-74; peer counselor Laney Coll., 1977-79; lectr. San Francisco State U., 1979-83; staff rsch. assoc. U. Calif., Berkeley, 1984—. Spkr. PEW Found., N.Y., 1989; hon. prof. Albert Schweitzer Internat. U.; presenter papers in field. Author: Flourescent Spectroscopy..., 1983; contbr. articles to profl. jours. Mem. adv. bd. P.P. Land Conservancy, Berkeley, 1984-86; bd. dirs. Cmty. Svcs. United, Berkeley, 1985-86; vol. No. Alameda ARES/RACES, Berkeley, 1992-95. NSF grantee, 1989, 1991. Mem. AAAS, Am. Assn. Physics Tchrs., Am. Radio Relay League, Co-op. Am., N.Y. Acad. Sci., Golden Gate Nat. Park Assn., Sierra Club, Mensa. Democrat. Jewish. Avocations: photography, computers, water coloring, swimming, non-linear dynamics. Home: 307 2nd St Phoenix OR 97535-7733 E-mail: GRIBEAR@mind.net.

BLACKMAN, DOROTHY F. library director; b. Lynn, Mass., Sept. 11, 1935; d. Harvey William and Marion Marie (Hooper) Loyte; m. John A. Blackman, June 11, 1955; children: David John, Deborah DeForest, Daren, Kathy Felker. Student, Gordon Coll., 1952—54. Data processing Gilson Brothers Wholesale Druggists, Boston, 1944—55; data processor CBS Hytton, Danvers, Mass., 1955—56, Bomac Labs, Beverly, Mass., 1956—58; dir., mgr. Edmeston (N.Y.) Free Libr., 1982—2003. Substitute tchr. Edmeston Ctrl. Sch., 1964—94. Author: The Long Sleep, 1992, Zeke, 1992; contbr. articles. Spkr., rep. Alcohol Edn. for Youth, NY, 1966—76. Recipient Cmty Svc. award, Wharton Valley Grange, Edmeston, N.Y. Baptist. Avocations: gardening, reading, cooking. Home: 60 High St Edmeston NY 13335 Office: Edmeston Free libr 6 West St Edmeston NY 13335

BLACKMAN, EDWIN JACKSON, software engineer; b. Pulaski, Tenn., Nov. 19, 1947; s. Alley J. and Martha (Williams) B.; m. Nancy Kamin, Mar. 11, 1982 (div. Mar., 1990); m. Michelle Fautz, May 25, 1990. AA, Martin Coll., Pulaski, Tenn., 1972; BS, Tenn. Tech. U., 1974. State auditor State of Tenn., Nashville, 1974-76; internal auditor Firestone Tire & Rubber Co., Akron, Ohio, 1976-79; mgr. internal audit Leewards Creative Crafts, Elgin, Ill., 1979-81; acct. mgr. Mgmt. Sci. Am., Oakbrook, Ill., 1981-85, sales cons., 1985-88, sr. mktg. rep., 1988-90; customer svc. mgr. Dun & Bradstreet Software, Columbus, Ohio, 1990-92, acct. exec., 1993-94; sr. application sales rep. Oracle Corp., Columbus, 1994-96; acct. exec. Microsoft Business Solutions, 1996—. With U.S. Navy, 1966-70, Vietnam. Mem. Moose, Young Ams. for Freedom, Elks, Exchange Club. Methodist. Avocations: sailing, golf. Home: 13824 Bainwick Dr Pickerington OH 43147-8722 Office: Microsoft 13824 Bainwick Dr NW Pickerington OH 43147-8722

BLACKMAN, JEANNE A. community program manager; b. Decatur, Ill., Sept. 23, 1943; d. Robert Russell and Elizabeth Irene (DeWolfe) Shulke; m. Gary L. Blackman, Apr. 16, 1963 (div. Aug. 1983); children: Jeffrey Lynn, Stephanie Sue; m. Bill Weitekamp, Nov. 21, 1995. BS Elem. Edn., Ind. U., 1965; MS in Edn. Adminstrn., Eastern Ill. U., 1979. Cert. tchr. and adminstr.; lic. real estate salesperson. Elem. tchr. Taylorville (Ill.) Community Sch. Dist., 1965-86; real estate salesperson Craggs-Adams Realtors, Taylorville, 1985-87; adminstrv. asst. to chief of staff Ill. Dept. of Aging, Springfield, 1986-87, consumer adv., 1987-89; lobbyist Ill. Guardianship and Advocacy Commn., Springfield, 1989-95; policy advisor Office of the Atty. Gen., Springfield, Ill., 1995-99; mgr. vol. program Ill. Commn. on Volunteerism and Cmty. Svc., Springfield, 1999—. Pres. Taylorville Edn. Assn., 1983-85; mem. adv. coun. Gov.'s Rehab., Springfield, 1987—; chmn. Springfield Civil Svc. Commn., 1995—. Co-founder, treas. Ill. Vol. Optometry Svcs. to Humanity, Taylorville, 1976—; pres. Capitol City Rep. Women's Club, 1988—; pres. Women in Mgmt., 1989—, pres.-elect, 1990; fundraiser, chairperson Ill. Women's Polit. Caucus, Springfield, 1985—; pres. Am. Field Svc. Student Exch. Program, Taylorville, 1985-87; bd. dirs. LWV Springfield chpt., 1984—; pres. bd. dirs. Mental Health Ctrs. Ctrl. Ill., 1994—; trustee Lincolnland C.C., 1989, vice chair 1992-93, chmn. 93-94, 96-97, bd. dirs.; pres. Ill. C.C. Trustees Assn., 1992; mem. Mayor's Commn. Internat. Visitors; chmn. Springfield (Ill.) Civil Svc. Commn., 1995-97; alderman City of Springfield, 1997-99; pres. Springfield Vol. Ctr., 2002--; bd. dirs. Lincolnland C.C. Found., 2001--; alumnae bd. Leadership Springfield, 2001--. Mem. AAUW (edn. chairperson Taylorville chpt. 1985—), DAR, Sister Cities Assn. Springfield, Ill. Women in Govt. (bd. dirs. 1988—, v.p. 1990—), Women's Legis. Network, Ill. Fedn. Rep. Women (v.p., bd. dirs. 1988—, ways and means com. 1987—, world affairs coun. 1990—), Greater Springfield C. of C., Rotary, Delta Delta Delta (pres. 2001). Presbyterian. Avocations: volunteer work, travel, reading. Home: 19 Washington Pl Springfield IL 62702-4634 Office: 535 W Jefferso Springfield IL 62702-1614

BLACKMAN, JEFFREY WILLIAM, lawyer; b. L.A., Oct. 24, 1948; s. Ralph Leonard and Judith Esther (Glantz) B. BA, U. Ariz., 1970, JD, 1976. Bar: Ariz. 1976, U.S. Dist. Ct. Ariz. 1977, U.S. Ct. Appeals (9th cir.) 1980, U.S. Supreme Ct. 1980, U.S. Dist. Ct. (no. dist.) Calif. 1988. Pvt. practice, Oracle, Ariz., 1977-85; assoc. various law firms, Phoenix, Tucson, 1986-87; pvt. practice Tucson, 1988—. Participant March for the Animals, Washington, 1990, 96. 2d lt. ROTC, U.S. Army. Recipient Cert. of Appreciation, Ctr. for Environ. Protecton of the Whale Protection Fund, 1984, UNICEF, Defenders of Wildlife, Nat. Humane Edn. Soc., ASPCA, Humane Soc. of U.S., Tiger Haven, Wine Diploma, San Francisco Wine Inst. Wine Adv. Bd., 1964, Cert. of Appreciation for Service in Israel during the Gulf War, Nation of Israel; named Ptnr. for Life, Cal Farley's Boy Ranch, Amarillo, Tex., 1982. Mem. State Bar Ariz., Pima

County Bar Assn., Mensa, Alliance Francaise, Animal Legal Def. Fund. Avocations: rock drummer, tennis, desert hiking, gardening, animal welfare. Office: PO Box 41624 Tucson AZ 85717-1624

BLACKMAN, JOHN CALHOUN, IV, lawyer; b. Monroe, La., Dec. 13, 1944; s. John Calhoun Blackman III and Marie (Collens) Bernstein; m. Judy Swayze, Apr. 19, 1986; children: Carrie Marie, Caroline Frances, Mary Winston. BA, La. State U., 1966, JD, 1969. Bar: La. 1969, U.S. Ct. Appeals (5th cir.) 1969, U.S. Tax Ct. 1972, U.S. Supreme Ct. 1976. Ptnr. Hudson, Potts & Bernstein, Monroe, 1969-79, Blackman, Arnold & Pettway, Monroe, 1979-88, Jones, Walker, Waechter, Poitevent, Carrere & Denegre, Baton Rouge, 1988—. Adj. prof. law La. State U., Baton Rouge, 1990-93; mem. com. of 100 econ. devel., 1993—; mem. trust code com. La. State Law Inst., 1982—. Mem. La. State U. Found.; mem. adv. commn. Estate Planning and Adminstrn. Cert., 1994—99, chmn., 1998—99. Fellow Am. Bar Found., Am. Coll. Trusts and Estates Counsel (bus. planning com.), Am. Coll. Tax Counsel; mem. ABA (litigation task force, employee benefits com., taxation sect.), La. Bar Assn. (cert. tax specialist, cert. estate planning and adminstrn. specialist, chmn. taxation sect. 1976-77, chmn. liaison com. with dist. dir. IRS 1981-82, liaison com. with regional commrs. office), Estate Planning Coun. N.E. La. (pres. 1975-76), NASD (arbitrator). Republican. Episcopalian. Office: Jones Walker et al 8555 United Plaza Blvd Fl 5 Baton Rouge LA 70809 E-mail: blackman@eatal.net., jblackman@joneswalker.com.

BLACKMAN, KENNETH ROBERT, lawyer; b. Providence, May 19, 1941; s. Edward and Beatrice (Wolf) B.; m. Meryl June Rosenthal, June 7, 1964; children: Michael, Susan, Kevin. AB, Brown U., 1962; LLB, MBA, Columbia U., 1965. Bar: N.Y. 1966. Law clk. to U.S. Dist. Judge, 1965-66; ptnr. Fried, Frank, Harris, Shriver & Jacobson, N.Y.C., 1966—. Mem. ABA, N.Y. Bar Assn., Assn. Bar City of N.Y., Phi Beta Kappa, Beta Gamma Sigma Office: Fried Frank Harris Shriver & Jacobson 1 New York Plz Fl 22 New York NY 10004-1980

BLACKMAN, LEE L. lawyer; b. Phila., Aug. 28, 1950; s. Harold H. and Mary Elizabeth Blackman; m. Kathryn M. Forte, Oct. 5, 1979; 1 child, Shane Forte. BA, U. So. Calif., 1973, JD, 1975. Bar: Calif. 1975, U.S. Dist. Ct. (ctrl. dist.) Calif. 1975, U.S. Ct. Appeals (9th cir) Calif. 1977, U.S. Supreme Ct. 1980, U.S. Dist. Ct. (ea. dist.) Calif. 1984, U.S. Dist. Ct. (no. dist.) Calif. 1988. Atty. Kadison, Pfaelzer, Woodard, Quinn & Rossi, L.A., 1975-81, assoc., ptnr., 1981-87; ptnr. McDermott, Will & Emery, L.A., 1987-2000. Arbitrator L.A. Superior Ct., 1986-90; judge pro tem Superior Ct. State of Calif., 1986-92; speaker in field. Mem. editl. adv. bd. Airport Noise Report, 1989-99; article editor ABA Health Litig. Reporter, 1996-97. Mem. State Bar of Calif., Legion Lex Inn of Ct. (master bencher 1989-2000). Office: 1562 Granvia Altamira Palos Verdes Estates CA 90274 E-mail: llblackman1@cox.net.

BLACKMAN, SUE ANNE BATEY, economics researcher; b. Hamilton AFB, Calif., June 21, 1948; d. Wayman C. and Lela M. (Fasgold) Batey; m. Martin R. Blackman, Apr. 7, 1977; 1 child, Emily Batey Blackman. BA in Polit. Sci., U. Colo., 1970. Econs. rsch. aide dept. econs. Princeton (N.J.) U., 1972-79, econs. rsch. asst. dept. econs., 1979-86, sr. rsch. asst. dept. econs., 1987—. Author: (with W.J. Baumol and E.N. Wolff) Productivity and American Leadership: The Long View, 1989, (with Baumol) Perfect Markets and Easy Virtue, 1991; contbr. articles to profl. jours. Office: Princeton U Dept Econs 101 Fisher Hall Princeton NJ 08544-1021

BLACKMAR, CHARLES BLAKEY, state supreme court justice; b. Kansas City, Mo., Apr. 19, 1922; s. Charles Maxwell and Eleanor (Blakey) B.; m. Ellen Day Bonnifield, July 18, 1943 (dec. 1983); children: Charles A. (dec.), Thomas J., Lucy E. Blackmar Alpaugh, Elizabeth S., George B.; m. Jeanne Stephens Lee, Oct. 5, 1984. AB summa cum laude, Princeton U., 1942; JD, U. Mich., 1948; LLD (hon.), St. Louis U., 1991. Bar: Mo. 1948. Pvt. practice law, Kansas City; ptnr. Swanson, Midgley and predecessors, 1952-66; profl. lectr. U. Mo. at Kansas City, 1949-58; prof. law St. Louis U., 1966-82, prof. emeritus; judge Supreme Ct. Mo., 1982—92, chief justice, 1989-91, sr. status, 1992; spl. asst. atty. gen. Mo., 1969-77; labor arbitrator, active sr. judge, 1992—. Chmn. Fair Pub. Accommodations Commn. Kansas City, 1964-66; mem. Commn. Human Rels. Kansas City, 1965-66. Author: (with Volz and others) Missouri Practice, 1953, West's Federal Practice Manual, 1957, 71, (with Devitt) Federal Jury Practice and Instructions, 1970, 3d edit., 1977, (with Devitt, Wolff and O'Malley) 4th edit., 1988-92; contbr. numerous articles on probate and corp. law to profl. publs. Mem. Jackson County Rep. Com., 1952-58; mem. Mo. Rep. Com., 1956-58. 1st lt., inf. AUS, 1943-46. Decorated Silver Star, Purple Heart. Mem. Am. Law Inst., Nat. Acad. Arbitrators, Mo. Bar (spl. lectr. insts.), Disciples Peace Fellowship, Scribes (pres. 1986-87), Order of Coif, Phi Beta Kappa. Mem. Christian Ch. (Disciples Of Christ). Home: 612 Hobbs Rd Jefferson City MO 65109-1075 Home (Winter): 2 Seaside Ln Apt 402 Belleair FL 33756-1989 E-mail: bcbb543@aol.com.

BLACKMER, DONALD LAURENCE MORTON, political scientist; b. Boston, July 6, 1929; s. Alan Rogers and Josephine (Bedford) B.; m. Joan Dexter, Aug. 25, 1951; children: Stephen, Alexander, Katherine. AB magna cum laude, Harvard U., 1952, AM, 1956, PhD, 1967. Sheldon traveling fellow Harvard U., 1952-53; exec. asst. to dir. Ctr. for Internat. Studies, MIT, Cambridge, 1956-61, asst. dir., 1961-68, lectr., 1960-61, asst. prof. polit. sci., 1961-67, assoc. prof., 1967-73, prof., 1973-95; prof. emeritus, 1995—; assoc. dean Sch. Humanities and Social Sci., 1973-81; dir. Program in Sci., Tech. and Soc., 1977-81, head dept. polit. sci., 1981-88. Research asso. West European studies Harvard U., 1973— Author: Unity in Diversity: Italian Communism and the Communist World, 1967, (with Annie Kriegel) The International Role of the Communist Parties of Italy and France, 1975; co-author, editor: (with Max F. Millikan) The Emerging Nations: Their Growth and United States Policy, 1961, (with Sidney Tarrow) Communism in Italy and France, 1975; The MIT Center for International Studies: The Founding Years 1951-1969, 2002. With U.S. Army, 1953-55. Home: 266 Main St Concord MA 01742-4942 Office: MIT E53-373 Cambridge MA 02139

BLACKMER, SALLY, secondary education educator; b. Canandaigua, N.Y., Dec. 12, 1933; d. Clifford Leslie Sr. and Sarah Olivia (Yerkes) Kuncs; m. Thomas Richmond Blackmer, Aug. 16, 1953 (dec. Dec. 1981); children: Cynthia, Mark. BS, SUNY, Geneseo, 1964; MEd, U. Rochester, 1970. Cert. tchr. grades K-6 and 7-12 secondary social studies. Tchr. Honeoye (N.Y.) Ctrl. Sch., 1964-67, 68—, Canandague, 1967-68. Guide, presenter Nat. Women's Hall of Fame, Seneca Falls, N.Y., 1992-99; edn. and cultural ctr. com. Women's Rights Nat. Hist. Pk., Seneca Falls, 1994-96; hist. rschr. Matilda J. Gage Found., Fayetteville, N.Y., 1999. Co-founder, grant writer, mem. United Neighborhood Involvement for Families and Youth, Honeoye, 1989-99; trustee Allens Hill Pub. Libr., Bloomfield, N.Y., 1992-99, pres., 1994, 95, 96. Mem. AAUW (mem.-at-large), NOW (mem.-at-large), Nat. Coun. for the Social Studies, Honeoye Tchrs. Assn. (grievance co-chairperson, grievance chairperson, negotiations co-chairperson, treas., v.p., Tchr. of the Yr. 1973, Roger Ward Meml. Essence of Success in Tchg. award 1999), Honeoye Assn. Hist. Soc., Amnesty Internat. (mem.-at-large), Delta Kappa Gamma (Alpha Tau chpt.). Avocations: traveling, cross-country skiing, researching, reading, birding. Home: 4718 Allens Hill Rd Honeoye NY 14471 E-mail: svblackmer@aol.com.

BLACKMON, WILLIE EDWARD BONEY, judge, military officer; b. Houston, Apr. 16, 1951; s. A. L. and Florence (Joseph) Blackmon. BBA in Mktg., Tex. A&M U., 1973; JD, Tex. Southern U., 1982. Bar: Nebr. 1984, U.S. Dist. Ct. (ea. dist.) Mich. 1984, U.S. Ct. Mil. Appeals 1984, Mich. 1985, U.S. Supreme Ct. 1987, Tex. 1989, U.S. Dist. Ct. (no. dist.) Tex. 1990, U.S. Dist. Ct. (so. dist.) Tex. 1993. Terr. sales mgr. Gillette Co., 1977-79; sales and mktg. coord. Drilco divsn. Smith Internat., 1973-77; legal intern Gulf Coast Legal Found., Houston, 1982; intern, ind. counsel City of Detroit, 1982-84; judge advocate USAF, Ellsworth AFB, Offutt AFB, S.D., 1984-89, USAFR, Reese AFB, Randolph AFB, Bergstrom AFB, Tex., 1989-94; staff judge advocate lt. col. Tex. Air N.G., Ellington Field, Tex., 1994—. Asst. criminal dist. atty. Lubbock County, Tex., 1990—91, Harris County, Tex., 1991—92; admissions liaison officer USAF Acad., 1990—; pvt. practice, Houston, 1992—97; assoc. mcpl. judge City of Houston, 1995—97, mcpl. judge, 1997—; adj. instr. Judge Adv. Gen.'s Sch. Air U., Maxwell AFB, Ala., 1996—; staff judge adv. 101st Air Refueling Wing, Pisa, Italy, 1996; internat. election supr. Orgn. Security and Coop. in Europe, Bosnia-Herzegovina, 1997; exec. dir. Assn. Minority Mil. Officers, 2000—01; lectr. in field. Bd. adv. Mickey Leland Libr. and Mus., 2003—. Decorated numerous mil. decorations; named to Tex. A&M U. Athletic Hall of Fame, 1994, Wheatley High Disting. Grad. Hall of Fame, 2002; recipient numerous awards. Mem.: NAACP (Alex award 1999), ABA, Coalition Ivorian Intellectuals Am. (adv. com.), Aggie Officers Assn., Houston Bar Assn., Mex.-Am. Bar Assn., Tex. Mcpl. Cts. Assn., Am. Judges Assn., Wolverine Bar Assn., Houston Lawyers Assn., Tex. Assn. African Am. Lawyers, Nat. Bar Assn. (Living Legend award 1990), State Bar Mich., Nebr. Bar Assn., State Bar Tex., Masons. Baptist. Avocations: scuba diving, skiing, hiking, bicycling, dancing. Home: 8766 Pattibob St Houston TX 77029-3334 Office: 1400 Lubbock St Ste 214 Houston TX 77002-1526

BLACKMORE, DENIS LOUIS, mathematics educator, researcher; b. Jamaica, N.Y., July 20, 1943; s. Louis John and Helma Paula (Hansen) B.; m. Diane McDonald, Jan. 22, 1967; 1 child, John. BS in Aerospace Engring., Polytech. U. of N.Y., 1965, MS in Maths., 1966, PhD in Maths., 1971. Rsch. asst. Polytech. U. of N.Y., Bklyn., 1964-65, instr. maths., 1968-71; with N.J. Inst. Tech., Newark, 1971—, assoc. chmn. maths. dept., 1986-88, prof. maths., 1982—. Assoc. dir. Ctr. for Applied Maths. and Stats., Newark, 1986-90. Author: (with others) Mathematics for Design, 1979, Integrable Dynamical Systems: Spectral and Differential Geometric Aspects, 2003. Mem. Newark Literacy Campaign, 1989—. Grantee NSF, 1971, 1991-93, 95-99, 2001-02, 2003-05, Office of Naval Rsch., 1992-95; recipient Harlan Perlis Rsch. award, 1993. Mem. SIAM, AAAS, N.Y. Acad. Scis., Am. Math. Soc., Gesellschaft fur Angewandte Mathematik und Mechanik, Sigma Xi, Omicron Delta Kappa, Sigma Gamma Tau, Pi Mu Epsilon. Democrat. Avocations: painting, poetry, sports. Home: 34 Baker St Maplewood NJ 07040-2619 Office: NJ Inst Tech Dept Math Sci Dr Martin Luther King Newark NJ 07102

BLACKSHEAR, A. T., JR., lawyer; b. Dallas, July 5, 1942; s. A. T. and Janie Louise (Florey) Blackshear; m. Stuart Davis Blackshear. BBA cum laude, Baylor U., 1964, JD cum laude, 1968. CPA Tex.; bar: Tex. 1968, U.S. Ct. Appeals (5th cir.) 1970, U.S. Tax Ct. 1970. Acct. Arthur Andersen & Co., Dallas, 1964-66; assoc. Fulbright & Jaworski, Houston, 1969-75, ptnr., 1975—, chmn. exec. com., 1992—2002. Bd. dirs. Tex. Med. Ctr., Inc. Trustee Baylor Coll. Medicine; chmn. bd. Meml./Hermann Healthcare Sys.; bd. dirs. Sam Houston area coun. Boy Scouts Am.; bd. dirs. Spiritual Leadership Inst. Mem.: ABA, Houston Bar Assn., State Bar Tex., Houston Country Club, Coronado Club, Houston Ctr. Club. Baptist. Office: Fulbright & Jaworski 1301 Mckinney St Fl 51 Houston TX 77010-3031

BLACKSON, BENJAMIN F(RANKLIN), clinical social worker; b. Newark, Del., Nov. 4, 1933; s. Benjamin Franklin and Lulu Etta (Taylor) B.; m. Sirletta Fordelma Belcher; children: Benita, Barbara. BS, Coll. N.J., 1972; MSW, MBA, Rutgers U., 1975; MSW advanced cert., U. Pa.; D of Human Service, The Fielding Inst., 1988. Bd. cert. diplomate in clin. social work; cert. social work. Commd. USAF, 1952, air traffic contr., D, multi engine pilot; clin. social worker USAFR, ret., 1993; with Blackson Enterprises, Bordentown, NJ, 1969-81; CEO B.E. Inc., Bordentown, 1975—. Vice-chmn. Bordentown Recreation Com., 1973. Fellow Am. Orthopsychiat. Assn.; mem. Acad. Cert. Clin. Social Worker, Nat. Assn. Social Workers (clin. chmn. N.J. 1978-80), Nat. Fedn. Socs. for Clin. Social Work, Am. Assn. Sex Edn. Counselors and Therapists. Fax: 609 298 1973. E-mail: blacs0n@cs.com.

BLACKSTAD, MILDRED MAE, retired music educator; b. Hillsview, SD, Apr. 25, 1938; d. Julius Fred Reiner and Helene Strobel; m. David Lloyd Blackstad. B Music Edn., Westmar Coll., 1959. Elem. music tchr., Windom, Minn., 1959—95; piano tchr., 1988—. Organist, pianist Bapt. Ch., Windom, 1973—. Mem.: Music Tchrs. Nat. Assn., Minn. Music Tchrs. Assn., Nat. Fedn. Music Clubs. Republican. Baptist. Avocations: biking, walking, water-skiing, snow skiing, scuba diving. Home: 2655 Cottonwood Lake Dr Windom MN 56101

BLACKSTOCK, JAMES FIELDING, lawyer; b. L.A., Sept. 19, 1947; s. James Carne and Justine Fielding (Gibson) B.; m. Kathleen Ann Weigand, Dec. 12, 1969; children: Kristin Marie, James Fielding. AB, U. So. Calif., 1969, JD, 1976. Bar: Calif. 1976, Tenn. 1994, U.S. Dist. Ct. (ctrl. dist.) Calif. 1977, U.S. Supreme Ct. 1980. Assoc. Hill Farrer Burrill, L.A., 1976-80, Zobrist, Garner, Garrett, L.A., 1980-83; ptnr. Zobrist & Vienna, L.A., 1983; v.p., gen. counsel Tatum Petroleum, La Habra, Calif., 1983; atty. Thorpe, Sullivan, Workman & Thorpe, L.A., 1984; ptnr. Sullivan, Workman & Dee, L.A., 1985-91; prin. James F. Blackstock, PLC, L.A., 1992-93; v.p., gen. counsel Nat. Auto/Truckstops, Inc., Nashville, 1993-97, Cracker Barrel Old Country Store, Inc., Lebanon, Tenn., 1997-98; sr. v.p., gen. counsel CBRL Group, Inc., Lebanon, Tenn., 1998—. Pres. Commerce Assocs., U. So. Calif., 1990-93. Mem. Town Hall, L.A., 1980-90; bd. dirs., Am. Red Cross (Tenn. Valley region). Served to lt., USN, 1969-73; capt. USNR (ret.). Mem. ABA, Tenn. Bar Assn., Nashville Bar Assn., U. So. Calif. Alumni Assn. (bd. govs. 1990-92), Pasadena Tournament of Roses Assn., Saddle and Sirloin Club, Rancheros Visitadores. Republican. Roman Catholic. Home: 533 Turtle Creek Dr Brentwood TN 37027-5632 Office: 305 Hartman Dr Lebanon TN 37087-2519 E-mail: jim.blackstock@cbrlgroup.com.

BLACKSTOCK, JERRY B. lawyer; b. Monticello, Ga., Mar. 9, 1945; s. J.B. and Eugenia (Jones) B.; m. Margaret Owen, June 10, 1967; children: Towner Anson, Michael Owen, Kendrick. BA, Davidson Coll., 1966; JD, U. Ga., 1969. Bar: Ga. 1969, U.S. Ct. Appeals (5th cir.) 1970, U.S. Supreme Ct. 1978, U.S. Ct. Appeals (11th cir.) 1981, U.S. Ct. Appeals (fed. cir.) 1984. With Powell, Goldstein, Frazer & Murphy, Atlanta, 1969—2002; chair Atlanta litigation team Hunton & Williams, LLP, 2002—. Adj. prof. law Emory U., Atlanta, 1975-81; mem. adv. bd. Jour. Intellectual Property Law, U. Ga. Sch. Law, 1992-2001; chair Ga. Jud. Qualifications Commn., 1994-2002. Author: Georgia Appellate Practice Handbook, 1977, Preparation of a Lawsuit for Trial, Pre-Trial Practice, Appellate Practice, 1980; (with others) Georgia Lawyers Basic Practice Handbook, 2d edit. Pres. parents coun. Trinity Sch. Inc., 1981-82; pres. parents club Woodward Acad. Lower Sch., 1986-88, bd. dirs., treas., Woodward Acad. Upper Sch., 1988-91, v.p., 1991-92, pres., 1992-94; chmn. Ga. Athlete Agt. Regulatory Commn., 1989-2000; chmn. bd. dirs. Pastoral Counseling Svc. Atlanta, mem. bd. visitors U. Ga. Sch. Law; bd. trustees Ga. Legal History Found.; mem. Leadership Ga., 1980; mem. Leadership Atlanta, 1990, exec. com., 1991-92; chair bd. trustees Riverside Mil. Acad., 1996—. Recipient Tradition of Excellence award for Def. Lawyer of Yr., State Bar Ga., 2002. Fellow Am. Bar Found., Am. Coll. Trial Lawyers, Internat. Acad. Trial Lawyers, Ga. Bar Assn. (editor-in-chief jour. 1984-85, bd. govs. 1982-98, exec. com. 1990-95, intellectual property law, tech. law and gen. practice and trial sects.), Ga. Bar Found.; mem. ATLA (intellectual property litig. com.), ABA (intellectual property, sci. and tech., tort and ins. practice and litig. sects.), So. Trial Lawyers Assn., Ga. Trial Lawyers Assn., Atlanta Bar Assn. (editor-in-chief Atlanta Lawyer 1972-73), Am. Law Inst., Atlanta Legal Aid Soc. (adv. bd. 1979-86), Atlanta Lawyers Club, Ga. Def. Lawyers Assn. (bd. dirs. 1989-91, dir. Trial Acad. 1987), Am. Bd. Trial Advs. (diplomate, bd. dirs. 1990—, state exec. com. 1985—), Am. Arbitration Assn. (arbitrator, comml. and constrn. panels, Ga.-Ala. adv. com. for large complex cases), Licensing Execs. Soc. Internat., Am. Intellectual Property Law Assn., Computer Law Assn., Davidson Coll. Atlanta Alumni Assn. (pres. 1982-83), Bleckley Am. Inn of Ct. (master of the bench), Commerce Club, Old War Horse Lawyers Club, Cherokee Town and Country Club, 191 Club. Methodist. Avocation: running. Home: 3364 Chatham Rd NW Atlanta GA 30305-1140 Office: Hunton & Williams 4100 Bank of Am Plz 600 Peachtree St Atlanta GA 30308 Fax: 404-888-4190. E-mail: jblackstock@hunton.com.

BLACKSTOCK, VIRGINIA HARRIETT, artist; b. St. Louis; d. Charles William Valentine and Ruth (Winn) Arnott; m. Ross Holcomb Blackstock, June 13, 1953; children: Susan, Kathleen, Julianne, Brian. BS, Mo. U., 1950; MA, U. Wis., 1952. Cert. tchr. Mo. Tchr. Ctrl. Mo. State U., U. of the South, Tenn., We. State Coll., Colo. Instr. watermedia painting and drawing workshops; judge, juror for art exhbns. Artist in watermedia; exhibited in 39 one person month-long gallery and mus. exhibits; group shows in Watercolor Soc. Exhbns. include Ala., Ariz., Colo., Kans., Ky., Mont., N.Mex., La., R.I., Okla., Pa., Utah, Wash., Wyo., Midwest, and San Diego Nat. Watercolor Soc., Rocky Mountain Nat. Exhbn., Nat. Watercolor Soc., Audubon Artists, Inc., N.Y., Allied Artists of Am., Adirondacks Nat., Red River Watercolor Soc., Springville Mus. of Art, C.M. Russell Mus. Auction; paintings in books include Creative Watercolor A Step by Step Guide, Beckwith, The Artistic Touch I and III, Unwin, Abstracts in Watercolor, Schlemm, Exploring Color (revised edit.), Leland. She was commissioned to do a painting for the cover of Ouray Summer Guide, '94, and a poster for the Ouray (Colo.) Chamber Music Festival; She created a 17' by 40' outdoor mural for the city of Delta, Colo. honoring the cattle industry. Quick draw artist at several fund raising auctions for non-profit orgns. painted a chair for ?Hospice Auction and donated many paintings to Partners and other worthy causes. Winner Am. Artist Mag. Preserving Our Nat. Resources Contest, 1990, hon. mention Artist's Mag. Mem. Colo. Watercolor Soc. (signature mem.), N. Mex. Watercolor Soc. (signature mem.), Pa. Watercolor Soc. (signature mem.), Mont. Watercolor Soc. (signature mem.), We. Colo. Watercolor Soc. (signature mem., exhbn. chair 1991, 92, 93, 98), La. Watercolor Soc. (signature mem.), Audubon Artists (signature mem.), Kans. Watercolor Soc. (signature mem.). Episcopalian. Avocations: skiing, biking, hiking, photography, gardening. Home: 3101 L Rd Hotchkiss CO 81419-9409 E-mail: ruthhb@dmea.net.

BLACKTON, CHARLES S(TUART), history educator; b. N.Y.C., Oct. 27, 1913; s. James Stuart and Paula Hunt (Hilburn) B.; m. Mary Jane Porri, Aug. 16, 1938 (dec. Aug. 1975); children: John Stuart, Susan Porri Blackton Tallman; m. Margaret Rosalind Hando (Baroness Delacourt-Smith), Dec. 21, 1978. BA, UCLA, 1936, MA, 1937, Ph.D, 1939. Teaching fellow UCLA, 1937-39; asst. prof. Adams State Coll., Colo., 1939-42; from instr. to assoc. prof. history Colgate U., Hamilton, N.Y., 1946-57, prof., 1957-74, Russell Colgate prof., 1974-82, Russell Colgate prof. emeritus, 1982—, dir. social scis. div., 1961-70. Mem. nat. selection com. Inst. Internat. Edn., 1954-56, chmn. India, Australia and Japan coms., 1956-58, mem. selection com. for Australia, 1983; cons., referee Nat. Endowment for the Humanities, 1975-81 Contbr. articles to profl. jours. Served as lt. USNR, 1943-46. Recipient award in Pacific History Am. Hist. Soc., 1940; grantee Social Sci. Research Council, 1951; Fulbright grantee, 1952-53; Fulbright lectr., 1963-64; vis. fellow U. Sri Lanka, 1971, 74, 78 Mem.: Army and Navy (Washington); Hamilton. Home: Hantana Farm PO Box 267 Hamilton NY 13346-0267

BLACKWELDER, BRENT FRANCIS, environmentalist; b. Buffalo, Jan. 4, 1943; s. Francis Winfield and Evelyn Hellen B.; m. Teresa Ann Stotzer, Apr. 5, 1975; children: Matthew, Laura. AB summa cum laude, Duke U., 1964; MA in Math., Yale U., 1966; PhD in Philosophy, U. Md., 1975. Chmn. math. dept. Philander Smith Coll., Little Rock, 1966-68; founder Environ. Policy Ctr., Washington, 1972; chmn., founder Am. Rivers, Washington, 1973-85; founder, staff mem. Environ. Policy Inst., Washington, 1974—; v.p. Friends of the Earth, Washington, 1989-94, pres., 1994—. Bd. mem. 20/20 Vision, Washington, 1990—, Am. Rivers, Washington, 1973-93. Author: Water Conservation, 1982, Bankrolling Successes I, 1988, II, 1995. Pres. Plan Takoma, Takoma Park, Washington, 1977-83; bd. mem. League Conservation Voters, 1980-97, chmn., 1981-91. Grad. fellow NSF, 1964, Woodrow Wilson fellow, 1964; recipient Disting. Alumni award U. Md., 2001. Episcopalian. Avocations: canoeing, golf, piano, magic, squash. Home: 3517 Rodman St NW Washington DC 20008-3118 Office: Friends of the Earth 1025 Vermont Ave NW Ste 300 Washington DC 20005-6303

BLACKWELL, BRUCE BEUFORD, lawyer; b. Gainesville, Fla., July 23, 1946; s. Benjamin B. and Doris Juanita (Beaty) B.; m. Julie McMillan, July 12, 1969; children: Blair Allison, Brooke McMillan. BA, Fla. State U., 1968, JD with honors, 1974. Bar: Fla. 1975, Ga. 1977, NY 1980, U.S. Supreme Ct. 1979. Atty. So. Bell Tel. & Telegraph Co., Charlotte, N.C., 1975-76, Atlanta, 1976-78; antitrust atty. AT&T, Orlando and N.Y.C., 1978-80; atty. Sun Banks, Inc., Orlando, Fla., 1980; assoc. Peed & King, P.A., Orlando, 1981-84; shareholder King & Blackwell, P.A., Orlando, 1984-97, King, Blackwell & Downs, P.A., 1997—. Counselor, master to First Ctrl. Fla. Inns of Ct., 1999—. Bd. dirs. Legal Aid Soc., Orlando, 1986-88; chmn. Winter Park (Fla.) Civil Svc. Bd., 1992-94; trustee Fla. State U. Found., 1985-86. Capt. USAF, 1968-72. Recipient award of excellence Legal Aid Soc., 1993, Judge J.C. Stone Pro Bono Disting. Svc. award, 1996, Annual Friend of FAWL award Fla. Assn. Women Lawyers, 1998. Mem. Fla. Bar (chmn. 9th cir. grievance com. 1985-87, chmn. mid-yr. meeting 1986, chmn. 9th cir. fee arbitration com. 1992-94, bd. govs. 1994-98, vice chair statewide disciplinary rev. com. 1995-96, co-chair 1997-98, vice-chmn. access to cts. com. 1995-97, chmn. annual meeting com. 1997, mem. supreme ct. spl. com. on pro bono svcs. 1996-97, mem. com. to determine need for a new DCA 1998, Fla. Bar Presidents' Pro Bono Svc. award 1997, chair spl. com. on solo/small firm practice 1997-98, mem. rules com. 1997-98, mem. edn. work force 1996-97), Fla. Bar Found. (life mem., bd. dirs. exec. com., chmn., adminstrn. justice com. 1998-2004), Orange County Bar Assn. (exec. coun. 1983-86, pres. 1987-88, co-chair fair campaign practices com. 1998-2001, William E. Trickel, Jr. Professionalism award 2003), Fla. State U. Alumni Assn. (nat. pres. 1985-86), Orlando Touchdown Club (pres. 1996-97), Gold Key, Order of Omega, Omicron Delta Kappa. Democrat. Presbyterian. Avocation: study of china. Home: 1624 Roundelay Ln Winter Park FL 32789-4042 Office: PO Box 1631 Orlando FL 32802-1631

BLACKWELL, DALE BASCOM, physicist; b. Toledo, Ohio, Nov. 1, 1930; s. Clyde Bascom and Minnie Velma (Myers) B.; m. Elizabeth Nell Dawson (div.); children: Marka Blackwell Barbour, Victoria Blackwell Bush; m. Nina Marie Gover, Sept. 10, 1967. BS, Ind. U., 1956. Acoustic engr. Electro-Voice, Inc., Buchanan, Mich., 1956-58; R&D engr. Kawneer, Co., Niles, Mich., 1958-61; acoustic engr. Empire Scientific, Garden City, N.Y., 1961-63; sr. engr. Fairchild Camera and Instrument Corp., Hauppage, N.Y., 1963-73; chief engr. Comml. Radio Sound Corp., N.Y.C., 1973-78, Dumont Instrumentation, Inc., Hauppage, N.Y., 1978-84; R&D engr. Northrop-Grumman Corp. assignment, Star Wars Sys. Los Alamos (N.Mex.) Nat. Lab., 1984—91; owner Design Group Ltd., Brazil, Ind., 1991—. Cons. Fairchild Graphics Corp., Plainview, N.Y., 1964-66, 3M Corp., Woodbury, Minn., 1995, Japan Electronics Mfg. Agy., Wilmette, Ill., 1996—, Protech Comms., Fort Pierce, Fla., 1993—. Contbr. articles to profl. jours. including Electrical Design News, Radio Electronics mag., Electronics Now mag. V.p. bd. dirs. Brazil Pub. Libr. With USAF, 1951-52. Mem.: Wabash Valley Amateur Radio Assn. Achievements include inventor Cockpit Voice Recorder (Black Box) used in all commercial airline planes, high speed, rotational magnetic detent with accuracy of 2 seconds of arc, transistorized version of the Color Film Analyzer that allows printing movie film with proper color balance, movie film projection system with an electronically driven mirror tracking film rather than a CAM-driven claw movement of film. Office: Design Group Ltd 1123 E Northwood Dr Brazil IN 47834-1232 E-mail: dbb_des_grp@juno.com.

BLACKWELL, DAVID C. foundation administrator; b. Donnelly, Idaho, Oct. 17, 1940; s. George W. Blackwell Jr. and Eilene Scott Evans; m. Sarah L. Patterson, May 1, 1969; children: Rebecca Fennell, Katherine. BA, Idaho State U., 1964. Staff asst. U.S. Senator Frank Church, Washington, 1964-65, 68-69; asst. dir. fin. aid Idaho State U., Pocatello, 1969-70, dir. fin. aid, 1970-72; adminstrv. asst. Idaho Atty. Gen., Boise, 1972-75; Idaho state coord. Family Tng. Ctr., Boise, 1975-80; exec. dir., pres. Family Tng. Ctr., Inc., Glasgow, Mont., 1980-81; exec. dir. Epilepsy Found. Idaho, Boise, 1982—. Mem. State Coun. on Developmental Disabilities, Boise, 1984-93; dir. Idaho Parent Unltd., Boise, 1986-98, Coalition Advs. for the Disabled, Boise, 1986-94; mem. exec. com. Epilepsy Exec. Leadership Coun., Landover, Md., 1988-90. Vol. Peace Corps, Bogota, Colombia, 1965-67; participant White House Conf. on Food, Nutrition and Health, Washington, 1969. Named Affiliate Exec. Dir. of Yr., Epilepsy Found. Am., 1994; named to Outstanding Young Men Am., 1973. Mem. Sigma Phi Epsilon. Roman Catholic. Avocations: genealogy, travel, reading, gardening. Office: Epilepsy Found Idaho 310 W Idaho St Boise ID 83702 Office Fax: 208-343-0093. E-mail: eedahow@velocitus.net., efid@epilepsyidaho.org.

BLACKWELL, F. ORIS, environmental scientist, educator; b. Feb. 27, 1925; s. Floyd Weaver and Mary Olive Blackwell; m. Eleanor Louise Edwards, May 5, 1951; children: Susan, Betsy, Mary Ruth, Stephen. BS in Bacteriology and Pub. Health, Wash. State U., Pullman, 1950; MS in Bacteriology and Pub. Health, U. Mass., 1954; MPH in Environ. Health Adminstrn., U. Calif., Berkeley, 1965, DPh in Health Adminstrn., 1967. Rsch. scientist Calif. Gen. sanitarian Benton-Franklin Dist. Health Dept., Pasco, Wash., 1950—53; health and sanitation advisor USAID Program, Peshawar, Pakistan, 1954—56, sr. sanitation advisor Dacca, 1957—59; asst. prof., acting chair dept. environ. health S.P.H. Am. U. Beirut, 1967—71; assoc. prof. environ. health Rutgers U., New Brunswick, NJ, 1967—71; assoc. prof. environ. health Sch. Medicine U.

Vt., 1971—74; prof. environ. health East Carolina U., Greenville, NC, 1974—82; prof., chair dept. environ. health sci. Ea. Ky. U., Richmond, 1982—90; ret., 1990. Mem. gov. coun. USPHA, Washington, 1984—88; mem. various site visits accreditation Nat. Coun. Environ. Curriculum, Ind. State U., Ferris State U., others, 1977—78; curriculum cons. dept. bacteriology Wash. State U., Pullman, 1977; cons. water supply devel. USAID-MetaMetrics Inc., Sri Lanka, 1980; leader pub. health del. People to People Program to People's Republic of China, 1987. Editor: (book revision) Health and Safety in the School Environment, 1978. Apptd. Citizen's Task Force on Chem. Weapons Disposal, Ky., 1984—90. With USNR, 1943—46. Named a Ky. Col., Gov. W. Wilkerson, 1988; recipient Walter Mangold award, Nat. Environ. Assn., 1989. Mem.: Am. Acad. Sanitarians (bd. dirs. 1972—77, bd. cert. diplomate, Laureate diplomate 1977), Nat. Enivron. Health Assn. (life; pres. 1975—77). Democrat. Quaker. Avocations: gardening, nature studies, conservation. Home: 305 Azalea Dr Washington NC 27889 E-mail: oris_eleanor@gotricounty.com.

BLACKWELL, JOHN, science educator; b. Oughtibridge, Sheffield, Eng., Jan. 15, 1942; came to U.S., 1967; s. Leonard and Vera (Brook) B.; m. Susan Margaret Crawshaw, Aug. 5, 1965; children: Martin Jonathan, Helen Elizabeth. BSc in Chemistry, U. Leeds, Eng., 1963, PhD in Biophysics, 1967. Postdoctoral fellow SUNY-Syracuse Coll. Forestry, 1967-69; vis. asst. prof. Case Western Res. U., Cleve., 1969-70, asst. prof., 1970-74, assoc. prof., 1974-77, prof. macromolecular sci., 1977—; chmn. dept., 1985-95; F. Alex Nason prof., 1991-2000; Leonard Case Jr. prof., 2001—. Vis. prof. Kennedy Inst. Rheumatology, London, 1975, Centre National de Recherche Scientifique, Grenoble, France, 1977, U. Frieburg, Fed. Republic Germany, 1982; chmn. Gordon Conf. on Liquid Crystalline Polymers, 1992; cons. in field. Author: (with A.G. Walton) Biopolymers, 1973; mem. editorial bd. Macromolecules, 1989-92; adv. bd. Jour. Macromolecular Sci.-Physics, 1986—; internat. adv. bd. Acta Polymerica, 1992—; contbr. articles to profl. jours. Recipient award for disting. achievement Fiber Soc., 1981, Sr. Scientist award Alexander von Humboldt Found., Max Planck Inst. for Polymer Rsch., Mainz, Fed. Republic Germany, 1991, Rsch. Career Devel. award, 1973-77. Fellow Am. Phys. Soc. (exec. com. divsn. high polymer physics 1986-90, vice chmn. 1987-88, chmn. 1988-89); mem. Am. Chem. Soc. (chmn. cellulose divsn. 1999, Anselm Payen award 1999, divsn. councillor 2000—), Am. Crystallography Soc. (chmn. fiber diffraction spl. interest group 1993-94), Biophys. Soc. (chmn. biopolymer subgroup 1975-76), Fiber Soc. Episcopalian. Home: 2951 Attleboro Rd Shaker Heights OH 44120-1815 Office: Case Western Res U Dept Macromolecular Sci Cleveland OH 44106-7202 E-mail: jxb6@po.cwru.edu.

BLACKWELL, JOHN ADRIAN, JR., computer company executive; b. Tulsa, Aug. 1, 1940; s. John Adrian and Daisy Edith (Webb) B. MusB, Westminster Choir Coll., 1962, MusM, 1963. Minister of music 1st Presbyn. Ch., Warren, Ohio, 1963-68, Oklahoma City, 1968-79; artistic dir. Okla. Choral Assn., Oklahoma City, 1980-82; pres. Okla. Digital Technologies Inc., Oklahoma City, 1987-92; ptnr. JJ Enterprises (now Megabyn Assocs., Inc.), pres., owner, 1992—; program mgr. S. Systems Corp., Oklahoma City, 1995-98. Cons. Union Oil Co. Calif., Oklahoma City, 1989-98; conductor Warren (Ohio) Symphony Orch., 1965-68; choral dir. NBC-TV Stars and Stripes Shows, Oklahoma City, 1975-76. Commd. ch. worker Presbyn. Ch. in the U.S.A., 1965. Recipient Paul Harris award Rotary Found., 1993. Mem. Rotary Internat. (pres. NW Oklahoma City chpt. 2001-02). Office: Megabyn Assocs 2413 NW 112th Ter Oklahoma City OK 73120-7202 E-mail: jblackwell@megabyn.com.

BLACKWELL, J(OHN) KENNETH, state official; b. Feb. 28, 1948; m. Rosa Blackwell; children: Kimberly, Rahshann, Kristin. BS, Xavier U., Cin., 1970, MEd, 1971. Cert. govt. fin. mgr. Treas. State of Ohio, Columbus, 1994-98, sec. of state, 1999—. Mem. city coun., City of Cin., 1977-89, vice mayor, 1977-78, 85-86, mayor, 1979-80; vice-chmn. Cin. Employees Retirement Sys. Fund., 1988; dep. undersec. U.S. Dept. HUD, 1989-90; mem. Nat. Commn. Econ. Growth and Tax Reform, 1995; participant Nat. Summit on Retirement Income Savings, 1998; ptnr. Bituminex Co., 1978-82; coord. urban affairs, Xavier U., 1971-74, asst. prof. edn., 1974-77, assoc. prof., 1977-91, dir. cmty. rels., 1975-79, assoc. v.p., 1979-91; assoc. prof. U. cin., 1993; chmn. bd. adv. trustees Govt. Investment Found., Inc., 1999; ambassador U.N. Human Rights Commn., 1992-93; adv. bd. John M. Ashbrook Ctr. Pub. Affairs Ashland U., 1997; Children's Ednl. Opportunity Am. Found., 1999; bd. dirs. Black Alliance for Edn. Options; pres. Nat. Electronic Commerce Coord. Coun., 2002; bd.dir. Nat. Coun. UN, Internat. League Human Rights, nat. Coun. Lawyer's Com. for Human Rights; mem. Fed. Election Commn. adv. panel, 1999; bd. trustees Am. Coun. Young Polit. Leaders, 1995' treas. State of Ohio, 1994-99; sec. State of Ohio, 1999-. Contbr. articles to profl. jours. Mem. The Jerusalem com., 1981, Harvard Policy Group on Network-Enabled Svcs. and Givt.; co-chmn. Hamilton County Reagan-Bush campaign, Ohi, 1984; mem. exec. com. Nat. Conf. Rep. Mayors; co-chmn. Blacks for Bush campaign, Ohio, 1988; mem. adv. coun. Ohio victims of Crime, 1989; bd. dirs. Internat. Rep. Inst., 1993, Campaign Finance Inst., Physicians for Human Rights, Congressional Human Rights Found.; nat. chmn. Steve Forbes for Pres. campaign, 1999; bd. dirs. Wilberforce U., 1989; chmn. Cin. Riverfront Classic and Jamboree, 2000-01; mem. exec. bd. Youth Voter Corps, 2001; mem. nat. bd. visitors Mazza Collection, U. Findlay, 1999; hon. co-chair Meml. to Our Lost Children, 1995; trustee Grant/Riverside Hosps., 1996, Wilmington Coll., 1996; v.p. Nat. Electronic Commerce Coordinating Coun., 2001, 02; mem. bd. advisors John M. Ashbrook Ctr. Pub. Affairs, Ashland U., 1997; exec. bd. Youth Voter Corps, 2001; fellow Nat. Acad. of Pub. Adminstrn.; mem. nat. adv. bd. Princeton Review, Youth for Christ, Jewish Inst. for NAt. Security Affairs; adv. coun. Employee Welfare and Pension Plan U.S. Dept. of Labor. Harvard U. fellow, 1987, The Aspen Inst., 1984, Salzburg Seminar, Austria, 1988, Heritage Found., 1992, The Ditchley Found., 1993; scholar-in-residence Urban Morgan Inst. Human Rights, 1993; recipient Disting. Alumnus award Xavier U., 1992, Superior Honor award U.S. Dept. State, 1993, Peace of City award Cin. Jewish Cmty. Rels. Coun., 1994, Family of Yr. award Nat. Coun. Negro Women, 1994, Advocacy award U.S. Small Bus. Adminstrn., 1995, Martin Luther King Dream Keeper award, 1996, Veritas award Albertus Magnus Coll., 1998, Thomas A. Van Meter scholar award Ashbrook Ctr., 1997, Pub. Svc. award NAACP, 1996, numerous others. Mem. Nat. Govt. Fin. Officers Assn. (excellence award 1999), Nat. Assn. State Treasurers, Nat. Assn. State Auditors, Comptrs. and Treasurers (exec. com. 1995-99, Pres. award, 1996), Nat. Taxpayers Union, Nat. Assn. of Secs. of State (v.p. midwest region 2001), Nat. Assn. Securities Profls., Internat. City Mgmt. Assn. (bd. dirs. 1999), Federalist Soc., Econ. club of Columbus. Republican. Office: State of Ohio Sec of State 180 E Broad St Fl 16 Columbus OH 43215 E-mail: blackwell@sos.state.oh.us.

BLACKWELL, JOHN WESLEY, securities industry executive, consultant; b. Evanston, Ill., Sept. 17, 1941; s. John Dakin Huggins and Mary Louise (Alger) Wells; m. Karen Alice Kralowetz, Dec. 19, 1964; children: Thomas Wesley, Julie Louise, Evan Stewart. BA, Mich. State U., 1964, MBA, 1965. V.p. A.G. Becker, N.Y.C., 1975-80, Drexel Burnham Lambert Inc., N.Y.C., 1980-82, 1st v.p., 1982-83, sr. v.p., 1983-89; cons., 1989—. Dist. leader United Way, Bronxville, N.Y., 1974, exec., Habitat for Humanity of Collier County. Mem. Island Country Club (Marco Island). Avocations: private investment, boating, tennis, scuba, riding, golf. Home: 870 S Collier Blvd Marco Island FL 34145-6164 E-mail: marcowes@mediaone.net.

BLACKWELL, MICHELLE S. media company executive; b. San Diego, June 22, 1971; d. Lizabeth and James; m. Ptah S. Shabaf; 1 child, Allahna. Prodn. assoc. DreamWorks SKG, Burbank, Calif., 1993—94; pub. rels. asst. Fox Broadcasting Co., L.A., 1994—98; CEO BDP Entertainment, L.A., 1998—. Program dir. SportZphere.com, Beverly Hills, Calif., 1999—2000. Prodr., writer: Good Sportz, 2000; author: Nubians - Special Agents, 2002. Youth activist Young People Against Violence, Long Beach, Calif., 1992—. Jewish. Office: BDP Entertainment/RadioSTR 468 N Camden Dr Ste 200 Beverly Hills CA 90210 E-mail: bdpentertain@aol.com.

BLACKWELL, PAUL EUGENE, SR., army officer; b. York, S.C., Aug. 19, 1941; s. Paul Webb and Ruby Mae (Hartness) B.; m. Janet Gail Glenn, June 23, 1963; 1 child, Paul Eugene Jr. BS, Clemson (S.C.) U., 1963, MS, 1965; postgrad., Clemson (S.C.) U., 1970-72; LLD, Clemson (S.C.) U., 1992. Commd. 1st lt. U.S. Army, 1963, advanced through grades to lt. gen., 1994, comdr. 1st Bn., 4th inf., 3d inf. divsn., 1980-82, ops. officer 9th Inf. Div. Ft. Lewis, Wash., 1983-85, chief staff 9th Inf. Div., 1985-86, comdr. 1st Brigade, 9th Inf. Div., 1986-88, dep. dir. ops. Nat. Mil. Command Ctr., Joint Staff Washington, 1988-89; asst. div. comdr. 3d Armored Div., Germany, 1989-91; comdg. gen. 2d Armored Div., Garlstedt, Germany, 1991-92; comdr. 24th Inf. Div., Ft. Stewart, Ga., 1992-94; dep. chief staff ops. Dept. Army, Washington, 1994-96; defense cons., 1996—2000; v.p. Integrated Command Ctrl. and Comm., Raythem Co., 2000—. Ruling elder Presbyn. Ch., Puyallup, Wash., 1985—88, Beth Shiloh Presbyn. Ch., 1998—2001, clerk of session, 1999—2001, supt., 1997—99. Decorated DSM with oak leaf cluster, Silver Star with oak leaf cluster, Legion of Merit with oak leaf cluster, Bronze Star with V device with eight oak leaf clusters, Purple Heart, Air medal, Army Commendation medal with V device and three oak leaf clusters, others. Mem. 82d Airborne Div. Assn., 9th Inf. Div. Assn. (pres. 1986-88), Marine Corps Assn., Assn. of U.S. Army, Tiger Brotherhood (hon.), Am. Ordnance Assn., Octofoil Assn., 3d Armored Div. Assn., 2d Armored Div. Assn., 24th Inf. Div. Assn., Assn. U.S. Army, DAV, Masons, Shriners, Ft. Stewart Skeet Club, Phi Kappa Phi, Gamma Sigma Delta, Alpha Zeta, Alpha Tau Alpha. Avocations: hunting, skeet shooting, running. Home: 650 N Shiloh Rd York SC 29745-8378

BLACKWELL, THOMAS FRANCIS, lawyer; b. Detroit, Nov. 25, 1942; m. Sandra L. Kroczek; children: Robert T., Katherine M. BA, U. Notre Dame, Ind., 1964; JD, U. Mich., 1967. Bar: Mich and U.S. Dist. Ct. (we. and ea. dists.) Mich. 1968, U.S. Ct. Appeals (6th cir.) 1969. Assoc. Smith, Haughey, Rice & Roegge, Grand Rapids, Mich., 1967-71, ptnr., 1971—, treas., 1979-85, 89—, exec. com., 1985-89. Spl. asst. atty. gen. State of Mich., 1972-82. Fellow Mich. State Bar Found.; mem. ABA, State Bar Mich., Grand Rapids Bar Assn., FBA, Products Liability Adv. Coun., Mich. Def. Trial Attys., Peninsular, Kent Country Club. Office: Smith Haughey Rice & Roegge 250 Monroe Ave NW Ste 200 Grand Rapids MI 49503-2251 E-mail: tblackwell@shrr.com.

BLACKWELL, THOMAS GEORGE, military police officer; b. Buffalo, N.Y., Aug. 7, 1960; s. Roger Inman Blackwell and Geneva Evelyn (Averett) Short; married. BA in Political Sci., English, Canisius Coll., 1982; MA in Russian & East European Studies, Univ. Kansas, 1992; postgrad., Defense Lang. Inst., Garmisch, Germany, 1990, U.S. Army Russian Inst., 1992-93; postgrad. Armed Forces Staff Coll., Nat. Def. U., Norfolk, Va., 1999. Commd. 2d lt. U.S. Army, 1982, advanced through grades to maj., 1994; exec. officer 523d Military Police Co., Aberdeen Proving Ground, Md., 1982-83, platoon leader, 1983-85; company commander U.S. MP Co., Johnston Island, 1986-87; adj. 759th Military Police Battalion, Ft. Carson, Colo., 1987-88, deputy ops. officer, 1988-89; mission comdr. U.S. On-Site Inspection Agy., Washington, 1993-95; chief force protection section HQ U.S. Army Europe, Provost Marshal's Office, Mannheim, Germany, 1996-97; chief staff actions divsn. HQ U.S. Army Europe, Office of the Chief of Staff, Heidelberg, Germany, 1997-99; sr. Balkans analyst Jt. Analysis Ctr., U.S. European Command, RAF, Molesworth, England, 1999—, sr. Eurasian analyst, 2000—02, chief Eurasia br., analysis divsn., 2001—02, sr. Eurasian analyst, 2000—01; chief Eurasia br. U.S. European Command, 2002—; chief policy sect. Def. Threat Reduction Agy., Darmstadt, Germany, 2002—03, dep. chief ops. br., 2003—. Decorated Def. Meritorious Svc. medal U.S. Dept. Def., 1995, Armed Forces Svc. medal, 1996, Army Commendation medal Dept. Army, 1985, 87, 89, 90, NATO medal, 1996, Meritorious Svc. medal Dept. Army, 1999, Armed Forces Expeditionary medal Dept. Def., 1999, Joint Svc. Commendation medal U.S. Dept. Def., 2000; Army ROTC scholarship U.S. Army, 1979. Mem. Am. Legion, Profl. Ski Instrs. Am. Avocations: snow skiing, racketball, running, golf. E-mail: thomas.blackwell@us.army.mil.

BLACKWELL, WILLIAM ERNEST, b. Rocky Mount, N.C., Apr. 1, 1932; s. Rosser I. and Ellen W. (Wilkinson) Blackwell; m. Elizabeth Levitan Blackwell, Mar. 22, 1972. BS, Davidson Coll., 1954; MBA, U. N.C., 1958. Security analyst Jefferson Standard Life Ins. Co., Greensboro, NC, 1958—66, asst. treas., 1966—69, 2d v.p., 1969—81; v.p. corp. devel. Jefferson-Pilot Corp., Greensboro, 1981—83, sr. v.p. corp. devel., 1983—85, exec. v.p., 1986; pres. Jefferson-Pilot Comm. Co., 1991—97, OmniVert Svcs., 1998—. Served in U.S. Army, 1954—56. Mem.: Nat. Assn. Life Underwriters, N.C. Soc. Fin. Analysts, Inst. Chartered Fin. Analysts. Office: OmniVest Svcs PO Box 3384 Greensboro NC 27402-3384

BLACKWILL, ROBERT D. ambassador; b. Aug. 1939; m. Wera Hildebrand; 5 children. Belfer lectr. internat. security Harvard U. John F. Kennedy Sch. Govt., assoc. dean; polit. counselor Am. Embassy in Tel Aviv Dept. State, dir. West European affairs Nat. Security Coun., prin. dep. asst. sec. of state for polit.-mil. affairs, prin. dep. asst. sec. of state for European affairs, U.S. amb. to India, 2001—. Editor: Arms Control and the US-Russian Relationship, 1996; co-editor: Conventional Arms Control and East-West Security, 1989, A Primer for the Nuclear Age, 1990; co-editor: (with Albert Carnesale) New Nuclear Nations, 1993; co-editor: (with Sergei Karaganov) Damage Limitation or Crisis? Russia and the Outside World, 1994; co-editor: (with Rodric Braithwaite and Akihiko Tananka) Engaging Russia, 1995; co-editor: (with Michael Sturmer) Allies Divided: Transatlantic Policies for the Greater Middle East, 1997; co-editor: (with Paul Dibb) America's Asian Alliances, 2000; contbr. articles to profl. jours. Recipient Comdrs. Cross of the Order of Merit, Fed. Republic of Germany. Office: DOS Amb 900 New Delhi Pl Washington DC 20521*

BLACKWOOD, EILEEN MORRIS, lawyer; b. West Chester, Pa., Sept. 4, 1958; d. Matthew Temple and Helen Stokes (Morris) B. AB, Dartmouth Coll., 1980; JD cum laude, Cornell U., 1986. Bar: Vt. 1987, U.S. Dist. Ct. Vt. 1987. Law clk. to Hon. Franklin S. Billings, Jr. U.S. Dist. Ct. for Vt., Rutland, 1986-87; assoc. Paul, Frank & Collins, Inc., Burlington, Vt., 1987-92; ptnr. Blackwood & Kraynak, Burlington, Vt., 1992-98; owner Blackwood Assocs., P.C., Burlington, Vt., 1998—. Contbr. articles to profl. jours. Bd. dirs. Childcare Resource and Referral Ctr., Williston, Vt., 1989-95, Vt. ACLU, Montpelier, 1989-92, v.p., 1991-92; bd. dirs. Samara Found. Vt., 1998-2003; active Williston Planning Commn., 1990-2002, chair, 1994-98; active Vt. Jud. Nominating Bd., 1997-2003; sec. no. Vt. chpt. Am. Inns of Ct. 1995-96. Mem.: ABA, Vt. Employment Lawyers Assn. (vice-chair 1994—95, chair 1996), Vt. Trial Lawyers Assn., Vt. Bar Assn. (chair women's sect. 1990—91, chair employment law com. 1996—99). Office: PO Box 875 90 Main St Burlington VT 05402 E-mail: blackwoodlaw@verizon.net.

BLACKWOOD, GEORGE DEAN, JR., lawyer; b. Buffalo, Kans., Aug. 10, 1939; s. George Dean and Tillie (Johnson) B.; m. Toni Adams, Dec. 30, 1978; children: Kendrick George, Joanna Lynn. B.A., Baker U., 1961; A.M. in Polit. Sci., Boston U., 1962; J.D., Kans. U., 1965. Bar: Mo. 1965. Ptnr. Blackwood, Langworthy & Schmelzer, Washington. Mem. com. steering, administrn., and intergovernmental rels. Nat. League of Cities, 1992—; bd. dirs. Natl. Mutiple Sclerosis Soc., 1989—, trustee, 1992—, area vice chmn., 1990—; mayor pro tem, 6th dist. councilman at large, vice chair fin. City of Kansas, Mo., 1991—. Mem. ABA, Kansas City Bar Ass., Lawyers Assn. Kansas City. Office: Blackwood Langworthy & Schmelzer PC 1220 Washington St Ste 300 Kansas City MO 64105-1439

BLACKWOOD, LOIS ANNE, elementary education educator; b. Denver, Sept. 18, 1949; d. Randolph William and Eloise Anne (Green) Burchett; m. Clark Burnett Blackwood, June 26, 1971; children: Anna Colleen, Courtney Brooke. BA, Pacific U., 1971; MA, U. Colo., 1997. Tchr. Forest Grove (Oreg.) Pub. Schs., 1971-72, Clarksville (Tenn.) Pub. Schs., 1972-73, Dept. of Defense Schs., Frankfurt, Germany, 1973-76, St. Vrain Valley Schs., Longmont, Colo., 1977—, presenter insvcs. and symposia, 1977-97, also tchr. of tchrs. Cons. Brush Pub. Schs., 1985; presenter U. No. Colo. Symposium, 1987, Greater San Diego Math. Conf., 1992-99, rural math. connections project U. Colo., 1992-94, So. sect. Calif. Coun. Math. Tchrs., 1992-98; cons. Brighton Pub. Schs., 2000-01. Recipient sustained superior svc. award U.S. Army, Frankfurt, 1975, outstanding performance award, 1976; Presdl. award for excellence in math. tchg. State of Colo., 1991, 94, Outstanding Elem. Math. Tchr. award Colo. Coun. Tchrs. Math., 1993; named Outstanding Tchr. of Yr., Longmont Area C. of C., 1992. Mem. NEA, Colo. Edn. Assn., St. Vrain Valley Tchrs. Assn., Phi Delta Kappa. Republican. Avocations: water and snow skiing, camping, tennis, family activities. Home: 1175 Winslow Cir Longmont CO 80501-5225 Office: Cen Elem Sch 1020 4th Ave Longmont CO 80501-5356 E-mail: clblackwood@hotmail.com.

BLADE, MELINDA KIM, archaeologist, educator, researcher; b. Jan. 12, 1952; d. George A. and Arline A. M. (MacLeod) B. BA, U. San Diego, 1974, MA in Tchg., MA, 1975, EdD, 1986. Cert. secondary tchr., Calif.; cert. C.C. instr., Calif.; registered profl. historian, Calif. Instr. Coronado Unified Sch. Dist., Calif., 1975-76; head coach women's basketball U. San Diego, 1976-78; instr. Acad. of Our Lady of Peace, San Diego, 1976—, chmn. social studies dept., 1983—, counselor, 1984-92, co-dir. student activities, 1984-87, coord. advanced placement program, 1986-95, dir. athletics, 1990. Mem. archaeol. excavation team U. San Diego, 1975—, hist. researcher, 1975—; lectr., 1981—. Author hist. reports and rsch. papers; editor U. San Diego publs. Vol. Am. Diabetes Assn., San Diego, 1975—; coord. McDonald's Diabetes Bike-a-thon, San Diego, 1977-78; bd. dirs. U. San Diego Sch. Edn. Mem. ASCD, Nat. Coun. Social Studies, Calif. Coun. Social Studies, Soc. Bibl. Archeology, Assn. Scientists and Scholars, Internat. for Shroud of Turin, Medieval Acad. Am., Medieval Assn. Pacific, Am. Hist. Assn., Register of Profl. Archaeologists, San Diego Hist. Soc., Phi Alpha Theta (sec.-treas. 1975-77), Phi Delta Kappa. Office: Acad Our Lady of Peace 4860 Oregon St San Diego CA 92116-1340

BLADEN, EDWIN MARK, lawyer, judge; b. Detroit, Feb. 2, 1939; s. Philip and Ruth Sara (Millstein) B.; m. Paula Dee Maskin, Sept. 2, 1962; children: Philip, Sara, Jeffrey. BA, Wayne State U., 1962, JD, 1965. Asst. atty. gen. State of Mich., Lansing, 1965-86; mng. atty. Moran & Bladen, Lansing, 1987-93; pvt. practice, East Lansing, Mich., 1994-97; adminstrv. law judge USCG, 1997—2003, Dept. Homeland Security, 2003—. Author: Consumer Law of Michigan, 1978. Mem. Dem. Polit. Reform Comm., Mich., 1968. With U.S. Army Security, 1957-60, Korea. Recipient Alexander Freeman scholarship Wayne State U., Detroit, 1962-65. Mem. State Bar Mich. (chmn. anti-trust sect., treas./sec. 1990-94), Nat. Assn. Fraud Units (pres. 1985-86). Office: 3448 Jackson Fed Bldg 915 2nd Ave Seattle WA 98174-1009

BLADES, G(ENE) GRANVILLE, accountant; b. Easton, Md., Nov. 17, 1967; s. Gene William and Jean (Wise) B. BA, Washington Coll., Chestertown, Md., 1986; PhD, Catholic U., Washington, 1990; JD, U. Md., 1994. CPA. Instr. Chesapeake Coll., Wye Mills, Md., 1990-93; ptnr. Kent & Blades, Denton, Md., 1994-95; pvt. practice Easton, 1995-98; pvt. practice, CPA Trappe, Md., 1998—. Legal counsel Trappe (Md.) Vol. Fire Dept., 1995-98; dir. Choptank-Talbot Agr. Corp. Easton, 1997—, cons. Blades Design, LLC, Trappe, 1991-98; v.p. Wise-Blades Farm Group, 1999—; pres. Trappe Acctg. Svcs., 2000—; v.p. Trappe Outreach Coun. Inc., 2000—; dep. to Gen. Conv. of Episc. Ch., 2000—. Author: Politics of Sectional Avoidance, 1990, Brief History of White Marsh Parish, 1997; editor The Epistle, 1995. Treas. Habitat for Humanity Talbot Co., Easton, 1997-99; dir. Talbot Co. Humane Soc., Easton, 1996-99, Cmty. of the Ascension, 2001; sec. Old White Marsh Cemetery Corp., Trappe, 1997—. Mem. ABA, AICPA, Am. Hist. Assn., Md. Assn. CPA's, Assn. Clin. Pastoral Edu., Md. Soc. Accts., Md. Hist. Soc., New Eng. Geneal. Soc. Republican. Episcopal. Avocations: photography, travel. Home: 2814 Ocean Gtwy Trappe MD 21673-1764

BLADES-ZELLER, ELIZABETH L. music educator, vocologist; b. Hornell, NY, May 25, 1951; d. Robert Uriah and Geraldine Anne (Frasure) Blades; m. Edmond Howard Zeller, June 24, 1978; children: Matthew Zeller, Andrew Zeller. Cert., U. Rennes, France, 1967; BA in geology, music, Skidmore Coll., 1973; MS in geology, U. Kansas, 1980; MusM, Eastman Sch. of Music, 1983, Mus D in music edn., 1993. Tchg. asst. U. Kans., Lawrence, 1973—76; instr. Pine Valley Cmty. Coll., Kans. City, Mo., 1975—76; music tchr., choral dir. St. Johns Sch., Spencerport, NY, 1986—87; music tchr. Indian Landing Elem. Sch., Penfield, NY, 1983—85; tchg. asst. Eastman Sch. of Music, Rochester, NY, 1988—92, asst. prof., 1993—94; voice faculty Hochstein Sch. of Music, Rochester, 1993—94. Author: A Spectrum of Voices: Prominent American Voice Teachers Discuss Teaching Singing, 2002, Singing With Your Whole Self: The Feldenkrais Method and Voice, 2002; co-author: The Singer's Edition; author: Vocal Pedagogy in the United States: Interviews With Exemplary Teachers of Applied Voice, 1993; contbr. articles various profl. jours.; composer: (films) The Adirondacks: The Land Nobody Knows, 1980, Adirondack Waters, 1997; dir, producer & performer (various Operas), 1997—2002. Mem.: NY State Music Tchrs. Assn., Ohio Music Educators Assn., Internat. Soc. for Music Edn., Music Educators Nat. Conf., Music Tchrs. Nat. Assn., Nat. Assn. of Tchrs. of Singing. Avocations: skiing, hiking, swimming, travel, equestrienne. Office: Nazareth Coll 4245 East Ave Rochester NY 14618

BLAGOJEVICH, ROD R. governor, former congressman; b. Chgo., Dec. 10, 1956; s. Rade and Millie (Govedarica) B.; m. Patti Blagojevich; 1 child, Amy. BA in History, Northwestern U., 1979; JD, Pepperdine U., 1983. Past pvt. practice law, Chgo.; past asst. state atty. Cook County, Ill.; mem. Ill. Ho. of Reps., 1992-96, U.S. Congress from 5th Ill. dist., 1997—2002; mem. govt. reform and armed svcs. coms.; gov. State of Ill., Springfield, 2003—. Pvt. practice atty. Democrat. Office: Office of the Governor 207 State House Springfield IL 62706 also: 4064 N Lincoln Ave Chicago IL 60618-3038 also: 11 W Conti Pkwy Fl 3 Elmwood Park IL 60707-4505*

BLAHA, VERLE DENNIS, golf course executive, electrical engineer; b. Detroit, Nov. 21, 1929; s. Maurice Lee and Clarice Annette Blaha; m. LuVeral Alma Blaha, Aug. 11, 1956; children: Bryan Jay, Lynn Renee Blaha Melchior. BS in Bus., U. Minn., 1966, MBA, 1969. Field supr. Aero. Radio Inc., Washington, 1952-56; mgr. quality assurance Gen. Mills Electronics, Mpls., 1956-63; sr. v.p. Litton Microwave Cooking, Mpls., 1963-82; v.p., gen. mgr. Holaday Industries Inc., Eden Prairie, Minn., 1982-86; pres. Celsion Corp., Columbia, Md., 1986-91, New Opportunities Ltd., North Oaks, Minn., 1984—, Thumper Pond Golf Course, Thumper Pond, Inc., Ottertail, Minn., 1998—. Lectr. on investments, U. St. Thomas, 1982-86. With USN, 1947-50, PTO. Fellow Internat. Microwave Power (chmn. bd. dirs. 1976-82). Republican. Lutheran. Avocations: hunting, fishing, building wildlife habitat. Office: New Opportunities Ltd 14 Sunset Ln North Oaks MN 55127-6454 E-mail: verle77@aol.com.

BLAHD, WILLIAM HENRY, physician, nuclear medicine physician; b. Cleve., May 11, 1921; s. Moses and Rae (Lichtenstader) B.; m. Miriam Weiss, Jan. 29, 1971; children— Andrea Margery, William Henry, Karen Ruth. Student, Western Res. U., 1939-40, U. Ariz., 1940-42; MD, Tulane U., 1945. Diplomate Am. Bd. Nuclear Medicine (chmn. 1982, v.p. 1986-97, exec. dir. 1998—), Am. Bd. Internal Medicine (bd. govs. 1981). Resident in pathology and internal medicine VA Wadsworth Med. Center, 1948-52, ward officer metabolic research ward, 1951-52, asst. chief radioisotope service, 1952-56, chief nuclear medicine dept., 1956-97, dir. nuclear medicine dept., 1997—; exec. dir. Am. Bd. Nuclear Medicine, L.A. Prof. dept. medicine U. Calif., Los Angeles; mem. ACGME residency rev. com. for nuclear medicine, 1979-97, chmn., 1991-97; mem. Joint Rev. Com. on Ednl. Programs in Nuclear Medicine Tech., 1986-93; mem. subcom. on naturally occurring and accelerator produced radioactive materials Com. on Interagency Radiation Rsch. and Policy Coordination, 1988-92; cons. nuclear medicine; mem. adv. com. on human uses radioisotopes Calif. Dept. Health Svcs.; mem. HEW Interagy. Task Force on Ionizing Radiation, 1978; dir. nuclear medicine Mt. Sinai Hosp., L.A., 1955-76, Valley Presbyn. Med. Ctr., Van Nuys, Calif., 1959-85, St. Joseph Hosp. Med. Ctr., Burbank, Calif., 1958-83. Author 3 textbooks on nuclear medicine. Contbr. numerous articles to med. jours. Served with U.S. Army, 1946-48. Grantee Muscular Dystrophy Assn. Am., 1965-69, Nat. Cancer Inst., 1973-76; recipient Lifetime Achievement award Wadsworth Physicians and Surgeons Alumni Assn., 2000, William H. Oldendorl Lifetime Achievement award West L.A. Med. Ctr., 2000. Fellow ACP, Am. Coll. Nuclear Physicians (bd. regents 1974-80); mem. AMA, Soc. Nuc. Medicine (trustee 1966-74, pres. 1977-78, Disting. Scientist award No./So. Calif. chpts. 1975, Disting. Sci. award We. Regional chpts. 1995, Disting. Pub. Svc. Career award Fed. Exec. Bd. L.A. 1998, Presdl. Disting. Svc. award 2000, 02), Health Physics Soc. (pres. So. Calif. chpt. 1964-66), Calif. Med. Assn. (sci. bd. 1975-81, chmn. adv. bd. nuclear medicine 1976-84), Am. Bd. Med. Spltys., COCERT, Soc. Exptl. Biology and Medicine, Los Angeles County, Calif. Med. Assns., We. Assn. Physicians, Am. Fedn. Clin. Rsch., Nat. Assn. VA Chiefs Nuclear Medicine (pres. 1985-87), We. Soc. Clin. Rsch., Alpha Omega Alpha. Office: Nuclear Med Dept VA Greater LA Healthcare 691/W115 11301 Wilshire Blvd Los Angeles CA 90073

BLAHUT, RICHARD EDWARD, electrical and computer engineering educator; b. Orange, N.J., June 9, 1937; s. Edward John and Julia Anna (Chamer) B.; m. Barbara Ann Krachenfels, Aug. 30, 1958; children: Gregory, Kenneth, Janice, Jeffrey. BS in Elec. Engring., MIT, 1960; MS in Physics, Stevens Inst. Tech., Hoboken, N.J., 1964; PhD in Elec. Engring., Cornell U., 1972. Engr. Kearfott (GPI), Little Falls, N.J., 1960-64, IBM, Owego, N.Y., 1964-94; courtesy prof. elec. engring. Cornell U., 1974-94; Henry Magnuski prof. and dept. head elec. and computer engring. U. Ill., Urbana, 1994-, adj. prof. elec. engring., 1986-94. Sys. cons. Ioptics Corp., Bellevue, Wash., 1994-99. Author: Theory and Practice of Error Control Codes, 1983, Fast Algorithms for Digital Signal Processing, 1985, Principles and Practice of Information Theory, 1987, Digital Transmission of Information, 1990, Algebrac codes for Data Transmission, 2003. IBM fellow, 1980. Fellow IEEE (pres. info. theory group 1982, editor Transactions on Info. theory, Alexander Graham Bell award 1998), NAE. Republican. Roman Catholic. Home: 1502 BridgePoint Ln Champaign IL 61822-9272 Office: U Ill Dept of Elect and Computer Engring Urbana IL 61801 E-mail: blahut@ribeye.csl.uiuc.edu.

BLAIH, SALAH MOUSTAFA, chemist, pharmacist, educator; b. Shabrakheet, Egypt, Oct. 24, 1950; came to U.S., 1994; s. Moustafa F. Blaih and Esmat A. El-Zemrany; m. Joan D. Paglialunga, Dec. 20, 1980; children: Yasmin, Hani. BS in Pharm. Scis., Alexandria (Egypt) U., 1971, MS in Pharm. Scis., 1976; PhD, Ohio State U., 1988. Vis. asst. prof. Denison U., Granville, Ohio, 1988; assoc. prof. Alexandria U., 1989—, Kent State U.—Trumbull, Warren, Ohio, 1997—. Cons. Resource Internat., Columbus, 1986, Amriya Rhone-Poulenc Pharm. Ind., Alexandria, 1989-95, WHO Egypt, Alexandria, 1991; adj. asst. prof. Ohio State U., Columbus, 1988, 89; adj. assoc. prof. Waynesburg (Pa.) Coll., 1995, U. Wis., Eau Claire, 1997; reviewer Alexandria Jour. Pharm. Sci., 1989-95. Contbr. articles on pharm. analysis, spectroscopy and chromatography to profl. jours. Soccer coach Morgantown (W.Va.) Youth Soccer Assn., 1994-95, youth basketball coach, Menomonie, Wis., 1997; vol. Boy Scouts Am., Warren, Ohio, 1997—. Recipient medal of Rsch. Excellence, Alexandria U., 1995. Mem. AAAS, ACS (Penn-Ohio Border Section chair 2001), Pharm. Soc. Egypt, Ohio Acad. Sci., Rho Chi. Avocations: raquetball, soccer, tennis. Office: Kent State U Trumbull 4314 Mahoning Ave NW Warren OH 44483-1931 E-mail: sblaih@kent.edu.

BLAIKIE, WILLIAM, government official; b. Transcona, Can., June 19, 1951; BA, U. Winnipeg, 1973; MDiv, U. Toronto, 1977. Ordained minister United Ch., 1978. Mem. parliament New Dem. Party of Can., Ottawa, Canada, 1979—, parliamentary leader; NDP critic nat. defense, vet. affairs, internat. trade & globalization. Office: House of Commons Rm 214 West Block Ottawa ON Canada K1A 0A6

BLAIKLOCK, PAUL MUSGRAVE, marketing consultant; b. London, Eng., Dec. 13, 1938; came to U.S., 1963; s. William Musgrave Blaiklock; m. Amaryllis Blaiklock, Aug. 1997 (div.); 1 child, Philip Musgrave; m. Patricia Allen, Oct. 10, 1997. BSc, Manchester U., 1960; ScD, MIT, 1967; MBA, U. Chgo., 1977. Registered profl. engr., Ohio. Rsch. engr. Foxboro (Mass.) Co.; cons. engr. Booz, Allen & Hamilton, Cleve.; product line mgr. Leeds & Northrup Co., North Wales, Pa.; market mgr. Tex. Instruments, Johnson City, Tenn.; sr. product mgr. Babcock & Wilcox, Lynchburg, Va.; pres. Blaiklock Cons. Inc., Roanoke, Va. Patentee in field. Recipient scholarship NATO, 1963. Mem. ASME, Inst. Mgmt. Cons., Instrument Soc. Am., Self-Realization Fellowship. Avocation: hiking. Office: Blaiklock Cons Inc 2409 Meml Ave Roanoke VA 24015

BLAIN, CHARLOTTE MARIE, internist, educator; b. Meadeville, Pa., July 18, 1941; d. Frank Andrew and Valerie Marie (Serafin) Blain; m. John G. Hamby, June 12, 1971 (dec. May 1976); 1 child, Charles J. Hamby. Student, Coll. of St. Francis, 1958-60, DePaul U., 1960-61; MD, U. Ill., Chgo., 1965. Diplomate Am. Bd. Family Practic, Am. Bd. Internal Medicine. Intern, resident U. Ill. Hosps., 1967-70; fellow in infectious diseases U. Ill., 1968-69; pvt. practice specializing in internal medicine and family practice Elmhurst, Ill., 1969—. Instr. U. Ill. Hosp., 1969—70; asst. prof. Loyola U., 1970—71; mem. staff Elmhurst Meml. Hosp., 1970—; clin. asst. prof. Chgo. Med. Sch., 1978—95, U. Ill. Med. Sch., 1995—, Rush Med. Coll., 1997—. Contbr. articles to profl. jours., chapters to books. Bd. dirs. Elmhurst Art Mus. Fellow: ACP, Am. Acad. Family Practice; mem.: AMA, DuPage Med. Soc., Am. Profl. Practice Assn., Am. Soc. Internal Medicine, Univ. Club (Chgo.). Roman Catholic. Avocations: Hapki Do (Black Belt), Tae-Kwan-Do (Black Belt), skiing. Home: 320 Cottage Hill Ave Elmhurst IL 60126-3302 Office: 135 Cottage Hill Ave Elmhurst IL 60126-3330

BLAIN, PETER CHARLES, lawyer; b. Milw., Nov. 15, 1949; s. Emile Octave and Mary Catherine (Usalis) B.; m. Katherine Stauber, June 12, 1971; children: Thomas Peter, Timothy Charles, Katherine Elizabeth, Peter James. BS, Wis. State U., Stevens Point, 1971; JD, Georgetown U., 1978. Bar: Wis. 1978. Budget analyst VA, Washington, D.C., 1974-78; atty. Reinhart, Boerner, Van Deuren S.C. and predecessor firms, Milw., 1978—. Chmn. Wis. State Bar Insolvency Sect., 1995-97; lectr. U. Wis., Milw., 1984—. Contbr. articles to profl. jours. 2d Lt. U.S. Army, 1972-74; mem. Ethics Com. Mequon, Wis. Listed Best Lawyers in Am., Woodward/White, 1987—. Mem. Milw. Bar Bankruptcy Sect. (prog. chmn. 1984-85, sect. chmn. 1986-87, co-chair bankruptcy sect. bench/bar com. 1998—), EDWI bankruptcy local rules com., 2002—. Democrat. Roman Catholic. Avocation: reading. Office: Reinhart Boerner Van Deuren 1000 N Water St Ste 1800 Milwaukee WI 53202-6650 E-mail: pblain@reinhartlaw.com.

BLAINE, DAVIS ROBERT, investment banker, valuation consultant executive; b. Gary, Ind., Oct. 30, 1943; s. Jack Davis and Virginia Sue (Mintzer) B.; m. Karen Ellen Levenson, Dec. 28, 1981; children: Davis Justin, Tristan D., Brittara K., Whitney K. BA, Dartmouth Coll., 1965; MBA, U. Mich., 1969. Founder, sr. v.p. Am. Valuation Cons., Chgo., 1971-78, chmn. bd., 1978; exec. v.p. Valuation Research, Chgo., 1978-80, pres. Los Angeles, 1980-83; sr. v.p. Arthur D. Little Valuation, Inc., Woodland Hills, Calif., 1983-87; owner, chmn. bd. Olesen, 1989-92; founder, mng. ptnr. Profls. Network Group, 1988—. Founder, chmn. bd. The Mentor Group Inc., Los Angeles, 1981— ; founder, pres. ICS Corp., Chgo., 1976-82, v.p. bd., 1982-87. Served to lt. (j.g.) USNR, 1966-68 Mem.: Beta Theta Pi. E-mail: dblaine@thementorgrp.com.

BLAINE, STEVEN ROBERT, lawyer; b. Tulsa, Aug. 24, 1969; s. Kent Robert and Barbara Ellen (Loftus) B.; m. Diana. BA, Bellarmine U., 1992; JD, U. Dayton, 1995. Bar: Ky. 1995. Staff atty. Frost Brown Todd LLC, Louisville, 1996—. Mng. editor Dayton Intellectual Property Law Jour., 1994-95. Ky. Gov.'s scholar. Mem. Ky. Bar Assn., Louisville Bar Assn. Avocations: tennis, yoga, celtic music, impressionist art, woody allen films, all things irish. Home: 747 Yorkwood Pl Louisville KY 40223-3555 E-mail: sblaine@fbtlaw.com.

BLAIR, ANDREW LANE, JR., lawyer, educator; b. Oct. 10, 1946; s. Andrew Lane and Catherine (Shaffer) B.; m. Catherine Lynn Kessler, June 21, 1969; children: Christopher Lane, Robert Brook. BA, Washington & Lee U., 1968; JD, U. Denver, 1972. Bar: Colo. 1972, U.S. Dist. Ct. Colo. 1972, U.S. Ct. Appeals (10th cir.) 1972. Assoc. Dawson, Nagel, Sherman & Howard, Denver, 1972-78; ptnr. Sherman & Howard, Denver, 1978—. Lectr. U. Denver Law Sch., 1980-83, U. Colo., Colorado Springs, 1984, U. Colo. Law Sch., Boulder, 1991. Author: Uniform Commercial Code sects. for Colorado Methods of Practice, 1982; contbr. articles to profl. jours. Mem. ABA, Colo. Bar Assn. Democrat. Methodist. Home: 1111 Humboldt St Denver CO 80218-3123 Office: Sherman & Howard 633 17th St Ste 2900 Denver CO 80202-3665 E-mail: ablair@sah.com.

BLAIR, ANN, historian; BA, Harvard U., 1984; MPhil, U. Cambridge, 1985; MA, Princeton U., 1987, PhD, 1990. Instr. U. Calif., Irvine, 1992—96; prof. history Harvard U., 1996—. Fellow Postdoc. fellow, NSF-NATO, 1990—91, NEH, 1996, MacArthur Found. fellow, 2002. Office: Harvard U Robinson 216 Cambridge MA 02138*

BLAIR, BONNIE, former professional speedskater, former Olympic athlete; b. Cornwall, N.Y., Mar. 18, 1964; d. Charlie and Eleanor Blair; m. David Cruikshank; 1 child, Grant B. Cruikshank Student, Mont. Tech. Univ. Mem. U.S. Olympic Team, Sarajevo, Yugoslavia, 1984; Gold medalist, 500m Speedskating, Bronze medalist 1,000m Calgary Olympic Games, 1988; Gold medalist, 500m Speedskating Albertville Olympic Games, 1992, Gold medalist, 1000m Speedskating, 1992; Gold medalist, 500m Speedskating Lillehammer Olympic Games, 1994, Gold medalist, 1000m Speedskating, 1994; pro tour speedskater, 1994-95; ret. from competitive speedskating, 1995. ABC sports commentator; motivational spkr.; founder Bonnie Blair Charitable Fund; active fundraiser Am. Brain Tumor Assn. Author: Bonnie Blair: A Winning Edge. Recipient James E. Sullivan award for Outstanding U.S. amateur athlete, 1993, Sportwoman of the Year, Sports Illustrated, 1994. Achievements include 1st American woman in any sport to win gold medals in consecutive Winter Olympics; 1st American speedskater to win a gold medal in more than one Olympics. Most decorated female Olympian of all time -- five gold medals, six total. Office: Advantage Internat Mgmt Inc 1751 Pinnacle Dr Ste 1500 Mc Lean VA 22102-3833

BLAIR, CAROL, social worker, therapist; b. South Ozone Park, N.Y., Apr. 27, 1946; d. Harold Arthur Mac Pherson and Muriel Dorothy Page; (div. Aug. 1985); children: Karen, Laura. BA in Psychology, SUNY, Old Westbury, 1978; MSW, Adelphi U., 1989. Cert. social worker; credentialed substance abuse counselor. Welfare examiner Dept. Social Svc., Nassau County, N.Y., 1980-90; staff social worker People Outpatient Clinic, Bethpage, N.Y., 1990-92, Care Ctr. Children's Alcohol Resource Edn., Freeport, N.Y., 1992-2000; pvt. practice specializing in addictions, co-dependency, generalized anxiety disorders, children's issues and personality disorders; dir. South Shore Child Guidance Care Ctr., 2000—01. Mem.: NASW, Soc. for Clin. Social Workers. Home: 92 E Lake Ave Massapequa Park NY 11762-2502

BLAIR, CHARLES LEE, physician, educator; b. Stamford, Conn., May 1, 1954; s. Charles Francis Jr. and Mae E. (Gallmoyer) B.; m. Ellen Jill Weiss; children: Eric Charles, Melanie Alison, Hayley Grace. BA, U. Vt., 1976; MD, U. Conn., 1981. Diplomate in psychiatry and geriatric psychiatry Am. Bd. Psychiatry and Neurology. Resident in psychiatry U. Conn. Sch. Medicine, Farmington, 1981-85, asst. clin. prof. psychiatry, 1985-93, assoc. clin. prof. psychiatry, 1993—; John C. Leonard fellow Hartford (Conn.) Hosp., 1985-86, dir. psychiat. edn., 1988-90; pvt. practice Hartford, 1985—. Mem. psychiatry residency tng. com. U. Conn. Sch. Medicine, Farmington, 1983-84, 88-90. Rock Sleyster Meml. scholar AMA, 1980-81. Mem. APA, Conn. Psychiat. Soc., Hartford County Med. Assn., Hartford Psychiat. Soc. (treas. 1991-92, sec. 1992-93, program chair 1993-94, pres. 1994-95), Phi Beta Kappa. Home: 149 Steele Rd West Hartford CT 06119-1047 Office: 100 Retreat Ave Ste 612 Hartford CT 06106-2528

BLAIR, CHARLIE LEWIS, elementary school educator; b. Troy, Ala., Dec. 22, 1940; s. James Horace and Dollie Rosa (Cannon) B.; m. Doshia Mae Anderson, mar. 31, 1962; children: Duane Alan, Mark Lewis. AAS, C.C. of Air Force, 1980; AS, U. S.C. Sumter, 1988; BA in Edn., Coastal Carolina Coll., 1989; MEd, U. So. Miss., 1995. Cert. elem. edn. educator, K-12 adminstr. Sgt. USAF, 1958-86; tchr. Lemira Elem. Sch., Sumter, S.C., 1989-90, High Hills Mid. Sch., Sumter, 1990-96; asst. prin. Lakewood H.S., Sumter, S.C., 1996-99; prin. Mayewood Mid. Sch., Sumter, 1999—2001, St. John Elem. Sch., Lynchburg, SC, 2001—02, Ebenezer Mid. Sch., Sumter, 2002. Mem. Disabled Am. Vets., 1989—, Am. Legion, Columbia, S.C., 1989—. Named Dean's Honor Student U. S.C. Sumter, 1988, Pres.'s Honor Student U. S.C. Sumter, 1989, to Nat. Dean's List U. S.C. Sumter, 1987-89. Mem. NEA, ASCD, Nat. Assn. of Secondary Sch. Prinicpals, Palmetto State Tchrs. Assn., S.C. Edn. Assn., U. S.C. Sumter Edn. Assn. (pres. 1988-89), Kappa Delta Pi, Phi Delta Kappa. Baptist. Avocations: woodworking, auto repair, upholstery, reading, music. Office: Ebenezer Mid Sch 3440 Ebenezer Rd Sumter SC 29153

BLAIR, DAN GREGORY, federal agency administrator, lawyer; b. Joplin, Mo., Feb. 23, 1959; s. Charles David and Conness (Johnston) B.; m. Michele Watts, Nov. 4, 1989. B in Journalism, U. Mo., 1981, JD, 1984. Bar: DC 1987, Mo. 1984. Gen. counsel minority staff com. Post Office and civil svc. US Ho. Reps., Washington, 1985-94, staff dir. postal svc. subcom., Govt. Reform & Oversight, 1995—98; dep. dir. OPM, Washington, 2002—; sr. Coun., US Senate Comm. on Gov. Affairs, 1998—2001; sr. Policy Adv. to the dir. US Office of Pers. Mgmt. Gen. counsel Taste of the South, Inc., Washington, 1985-90. Office: OPM Off of Dir Theodore Roosevelt Bldg 1900 E St NW Washington DC 20415-1000 Office Fax: 202-606-2183.

BLAIR, DAVID BELMONT, lawyer; b. Oslo, July 4, 1963; came to U.S., 1963; s. David William and Rosemary Blair; m. Bernice Blair, Aug. 5, 1989; children: David S., Edith C., John M. AB, Georgetown U., 1985; JD, Cornell U., 1989. Bar: Mass. 1990, D.C. 1996. Law clerk, Hon. Frank M. Johnson, Jr. U.S. Ct. Appeals 11th Cir., Montgomery, Ala., 1989-90; trial atty., tax div. U.S. Dept. Justice, Washington, 1990-95; assoc. Miller & Chevalier, Washington, 1995-98, mem., 1999—. Mem. ABA, Fed. Bar Assn. Office: Miller & Chevalier 655 15th St NW Ste 900 Washington DC 20005-5799 E-mail: dblair@milchev.com.

BLAIR, DAVID CHALMERS LESLIE, composer, writer; b. Long Beach, Calif., Apr. 8, 1951; s. David Chalmers Leslie and Eleanor LaVerne (Kramer) B. Student, Long Beach City Coll., 1976-78; BA in French, Calif. State U., Long Beach, 1979; postgrad., U. de Provence, Aix-en-Provence, France, 1979-80. Cert. tchr.ESL Calif. State U. Author: Death of an Artist, 1982, Vive la France, 1993, Death of America, 1994, Mother, 1998, Evening in Wisconsin, 2001, The Girls (and Women) I Have Known, 2001, A Small Snack Shop in Stockholm, Sweden, 2001; composer, writer and recorder of 101 albums including Her Garden of Earthly Delights, Sir Blair of Rothes, Europe, and St. Luke Passion. Leader Libertarian Party Chippewa Valley, Wis., 1994-97; candidate Wis. State Assembly-67th Dist., 1996. Avocations: the arts, marksmanship, travel. Home: 19331 105th Ave Cadott WI 54727-5529

BLAIR, DAVID WILLIAM, mechanical engineer; b. Santa Barbara, Calif., Oct. 5, 1929; s. David Sutherland and Norah Mildred (Higgins) B.; m. Rosemary Constance Miles, Jan. 30, 1954; children: Karen E., Barbara A., M. Maria, Amanda M., David B. O., Rachel P. BS, Oreg. State U., 1952; MS, Columbia U., 1954, PhD, 1961. From asst. to instr. mech. engring. Columbia U., N.Y.C., 1952-58; rsch. assoc. Princeton (N.J.) U., 1958-61; rsch. scientist AeroChem Rsch. Labs., Princeton, 1961-62; postdoctoral fellow Royal Norwegian Coun. Indsl. and Engring. Rsch., Kjeller, Norway, 1962-63; assoc. prof. Polytechnic Inst. Bklyn., 1963-69; engring. assoc. Corp. Rsch. Labs. Exxon Rsch. and Engring. Co., Linden, N.J., 1969-83; pres. Princeton Sci. Enterprises, Inc., 1985—. Contbr. articles to Handbook of the Engring. Scis., AIAA Jour., Jour. Quantitative Spectroscopy and Radiative Transfer, Environ. Sci. and Tech.; patentee for multi-stage process for combusting fuels containing fixed-nitrogen chemical species, efficient high temperature radiant furnace, conductive polymer ignitors. Mem. Princeton Twp. Com., 1975-82, Princeton Joint Commn. on Civil Rights, 1975-87, Princeton Consol. Commn., 1995-96. Mem. AIChE, Am. Phys. Soc., Combustion Inst., Tau Beta Pi, Sigma Tau, Phi Kappa Phi, Pi Mu Epsilon, Pi Tau Sigma. Democrat. Achievements include patent for multi-stage process for combusting fuels containing fixed-nitrogen chemical species, efficient high temperature radiant furnace, and conductive polymer ignitors. Home and Office: Princeton Sci Enterprises Inc 1108 Kingston Rd Princeton NJ 08540-4132

BLAIR, EDWARD MCCORMICK, investment banker; b. Chgo., July 18, 1915; s. William McCormick and Helen Haddock (Bowen) B.; m. Elizabeth Graham Iglehart, June 28, 1941; children: Edward McCormick, Francis Iglehart. Grad., Groton Sch., 1934; BA, Yale U., 1938; MBA, Harvard U., 1940. With William Blair & Co., Chgo., 1946—, ptnr., 1950-61, mng. ptnr., 1961-77, sr. ptnr., 1977—. Bd. dirs. George M. Pullman Ednl. Found.; life trustee Coll. of Atlantic, Bar Harbor, Maine; life trustee U. Chgo., Rush-Presbyn.-St. Luke's Med. Ctr., Chgo., Art Inst. Chgo. Lt. comdr. USNR, 1941-46. Home: PO Box 186 Sheridan Rd Lake Bluff IL 60044 Office: William Blair & Co 222 W Adams St Chicago IL 60606-5307

BLAIR, FRED EDWARD, social services administrator; b. Huntington, W.Va., Oct. 6, 1933; s. Fred E. and Pearl Amy (King) B.; m. Lois Ann Thomas, Aug. 16, 1958; children: Lesli Winifred, Annlyn Paige, Carter Thomas. BBA, Marshall U., 1955; MA, U. Iowa, 1965. Cert. healthcare exec. Adminstrv. asst. Jefferson Med. Coll. Hosp., Phila., 1964-66; asst. adminstr. Barberton (Ohio) Citizen Hosp., 1966-67; sr. asst. adminstrn. U. Ala. Hosp. and Clinics, 1967-68; exec. dir. Ohio Valley Med. Ctr., Wheeling, W.Va., 1969-83; pres. Ohio Valley Health Svcs. and Edn. Corp., 1983-86; pres., chief exec. officer United Care Inc. (formerly Peoples Community Hosp. Authority), Wayne, Mich., 1986-90; pres. Blair Ltd., Inc., 1991—. Instr. health services mgmt. U. Ala., Birmingham; dir. W.Va. Hosp. Service, Inc. (Blue Cross); preceptor health adminstrn. George Washington U., Med. Coll. Va. Bd. dirs. W.Va. Health Systems Agy., treas., 1978; bd. dirs. W.Va. Heart Assn., Wheeling Country Day Sch.; mem. exec. com. W.Va. Regional Med. Program; elder Vance Meml. Presbyn. Ch.; elder Mt. Pleasant (S.C.) Presbyn. Ch. Fellow Am. Coll. Healthcare Adminstrs.; mem. Am. Coll. Healthcare Execs., Am. Hosp. Assn., W.Va. Hosp. Assn., Nat. League Nursing, Am. Assn. Mental Health Adminstrs., Am. Pub. Health Assn., Mich. Hosp. Assn. (legis. and pub. policy com., svc. corp. com., HAPAC team, com. on govt. relations), S.E. Mich. Health Council (vice chair com. on health facilities planning, trustee), SAR, Rotary.

BLAIR, FREDERICK DAVID, interior designer; b. Denver, June 15, 1946; s. Frederick Edward and Margaret (Whitely) Blair. BA, U. Colo., 1969; postgrad., U. Denver, 1981—82. Interior designer The Denver, 1969-76, store mgr., 1976-80; v.p. Hartley Ho. Interiors, Ltd., Denver, 1980-83; pvt. practice Denver, 1983—. Com. mem. Ice Ho. Design Ctr., Denver, 1985—86, Design Directory Western Region, Denver, 1986; mem. edn. com. AIDS Nat. Conf., Denver, 1991; coord. Amb. Vol. Program Denver Internat. Airport, 2000—; mgr. concierge & visitors ctr. Cherry Creek Shopping Ctr., Denver, 2003. Designs shown in various mags. Bd. dirs. One Day, Very Spl. Arts, 1993, Supporters Children, 1996—, mem. steering com., 1994, pres.-elect, 1996—97, pres., bd. dirs., 1999—; mem. Rep. Nat. Com., Denver Art Mus., Nat. Trust Hist. Preservation, Hist. Denver. Recipient Aviation Ace Award, DIA, 2001. Mem.: Am. Soc. Interior Designers (co-chmn. com. profl. registration 1986, mem. edn. com. nat. conf. 1991, bd. dirs. Colo. chpt. 1990—, Humanist award 1997). Christian Scientist. Avocations: skiing, painting, tennis.

BLAIR, JAMES NEWELL, lawyer; b. Washington, July 29, 1940; s. Newell and Greta (Flinterman) B.; m. Wendy Ann Miller, Apr. 22, 1978; 1 child, Hilary Ann. AB, Dartmouth Coll., 1962; JD, Harvard U., 1970. Bar: N.Y. 1971, U.S. Dist. Ct. (so. dist.) N.Y. 1974, U.S. Ct. Appeals (2d cir.) 1975. Assoc. White & Coch, N.Y.C., 1970-71, Rogers Hoge & Hills, N.Y.C., 1972-80, ptnr., 1980-86; pvt. practice N.Y.C., 1987-88; ptnr. Teitler & Teitler, N.Y.C., 1988-91, Loselle, Greenawalt, Kaplan, Blair, N.Y.C., 1991-99, Wolman, Babitt & King, 1999—. Arbitrator small claims div. N.Y.C. Civil Ct., U.S. Dist. Ct. (ea. dist.) N.Y. Bd. dirs., treas. 600 West End Ave. Owner's Corp., N.Y.C., 1980—, mem. vestry Ch. of Christ the King, Stone Ridge, N.Y., 1991-96; mem. coun. Episcopal Diocese N.Y. Lt. USN, 1962-67. Mem. N.Y. State Bar Assn. (fed. cts. com. 1986-89, exec. com. comml. and fed. litigation sect. 1989—, chair civil practice law and rules com. 1991-95, 2000—, mem. adv. com. civil practice to chief adminstr. ctrs.), Assn. of Bar of City of N.Y. (com. on nuclear energy and the law 1989-92, others), Harvard Club of N.Y.C. Democrat. Episcopalian. Avocations: chamber music, cross-country skiing, rebuilding farmhouse. Home: 600 West End Ave Apt 10A New York NY 10024-1610 Office: 521 5th Ave New York NY 10175-0003 E-mail: jblair@wbklaw.net.

BLAIR, JAMES PEASE, retired freelance photographer; b. Phila., Apr. 14, 1931; s. Jacob Jackson and Dorothy Flagg (Pease) B.; m. Patricia Carol Wohlgemuth, Aug. 13, 1964 (dec. Nov. 2000); children: Matthew Ward, David Alexander; m. Elise de Vries-Ostroff, May 4, 2002. BS, Ill. Inst. Tech., 1954. Reporter, film photographer Sta. WIIC-TV, Pitts., 1958-59; freelance photojournalist, 1959-62, 94—; staff photographer Nat. Geog. Soc., Washington, 1962-94; ret., 1994. Instr. Rochester Inst. Tech., 1978, Internat. Ctr. of Photography, N.Y.C., 1992, Maine Photog. Workshops, 1988--, disting. vis. prof. U. Mo., 1992. Photographer: Listen With The Eye, 1964, As We Live And Breathe, 1971, Our Threatened Inheritance, 1984, Wooden Fences, 1997; one-man shows in, Pitts., 1962, New Haven, 1977, Teheran, 1975, St. Louis, 1990, Washington Cosmos Club, 2000. Lt. (j.g.) USN, 1954-56. Poynter fellow Yale U., 1977; recipient Overseas Press Club Best Photog. Reporting from Abroad award, 1977 Mem. White House News Photographers Assn., Am. Soc. Picture Profls., Nat. Press Photographers Assn., Cosmos Club. Home: 5116 Lowell Ln NW Washington DC 20016-2608 also: 27 Washington St Middlebury VT 05753

BLAIR, JIMMY, minister, educator; b. Bourbon, Miss., Aug. 2, 1947; s. Jimmy Blair, Sr. and Irma Lee Blair; m. Cathy Pigg, May 28, 1983; children: Britni Janique, J. Cedric, Brandon Jamal. AA, Coahoma Jr. Coll., 1972; BS in Bus. Adminstrn., Jackson State U., 1975; MA in Edn./Counseling, Golden Gate Sem., 1990. Lic. clergy So. Bapt. Ch., 1988, ordained min. So. Bapt. Ch., 1988, cert. home missionary So. Bapt. Ch., 1990. Foreman Desota/Gulf, Jackson, Miss., 1972—75; fin. ptnr. Fresh Start Enterprises, San Jose, 1975—87; contract negotiator Altus Corp., San Jose, Calif., 1979—85; founder, tchr., min. LifeBuilders, Modesto, Calif., 1990—. Guest lectr. Modesto Jr. Coll., 1994—; cons. Novell (S.C. Sys.), San Jose, 1986—87; seminar spkr. LifeBuilders, Marin, Calif., 1989, Modesto, 2001—; bus. dir. Nat. Inst. Sci., Tech. and Trade, 2003—. Mem. diversity team United Way, Modesto, 1995—97; pres. site coun. Martone Sch., Modesto, 1990—94; vol. counselor Juvenile Hall, Modesto, 1990—2000. SSG E-6 U.S. Army, 1975—79. Avocations: debating, walking, listening, softball. Office: LifeBuilders 16-B-212 2900 Standiford Ave Modesto CA 95350 E-mail: careblair5@aol.com.

BLAIR, JOHN, consultant; b. Budapest, Hungary, Dec. 5, 1929; came to U.S., 1950, naturalized, 1955; s. Eugene I. and Helen (Benedek) B.; m. Constance Smith Drown, Sept. 10, 1955; children: David E., Jennifer C. BS, MS, ScD, MIT. With Pacific Semiconductors/Ramo-Wooldridge, Culver City, Calif., 1955—57; elec. engring. faculty MIT, 1957-66; dir. corp. rsch. Raytheon Co., Lexington, Mass., 1966-94; prin. JBX Techs., Inc., Wayland, Mass., 1994—. Mem. energy R&D and nat. progress The White House, 1961; mem. Army Sci. Bd., Dept. Army, Washington, 1978-84, 86-90, 97—; rep. Indsl. Rsch. Inst., 1977-94, emeritus, 1994—; mem. adv. bd. Coll. Engring., U. Ill., Urbana, 1986—; mem. dean's adv. coun. Coll. Engring., U. Mass., Amherst, 1978-94; mem. vis. com. Sch. Elec. Engring and Computer Sci., Poly. U., Bklyn., 1991-98; mem. adv. bd. Ctr. for Intelligent Controls, MIT-Harvard U.-Brown U., 1987-94; mem. industry and univ. govt. com. U. Calif., Berkeley, 1970-74, chmn., 1974; mem. vis. com. on elec. engring. and computer sci. MIT, 1970-73, mem. vis. com. on ocean engring., 1991-95, lectr. ocean engring., 1995-98; external rev. com. Materials Sci., Los Alamos Nat. Lab., 1995-99, chmn., 1999; adv. com. Ctr. for Engring. Sci. Advanced Rsch., Oak Ridge Nat. Lab., 1996—; advisor Idaho Nat. Engring. and Environ. Lab., 1998-2001; mem. coun. on energy engring. rsch. Dept. Energy, 2000-01. State industry adv. coun. MIT Sea Grant Coll. Program, 1970—; mem. Nat. Sea Grant Rev. Panel, NOAA, Dept. Commerce, 1979-85. Recipient citations Sec. of Army, 1991, Sec. Def., 2001, Basic Energy Scis. Dept. Energy, 2001; Ford Found. fellow, 1960-61. Mem. Cosmos Club. Home: 25 Moore Rd Wayland MA 01778-1417

BLAIR, JOHN PAUL, academic administrator; b. Lebanon, Ky., Dec. 28, 1968; s. Robert Melvin and Doris Faye Blair; m. Stephanie Leslie Blair, July 11, 1992; 1 child, John Robert. BS, Western Ky. U., 1992; MEd, Vanderbilt U., 1997. Dir. devel. Campbellsville (Ky.) U., 1992-97; collegiate dir. devel. Western Ky. U., Bowling Green, 1997-98, dir. major gifts, 1998—2001, asst. v.p. instnl. advancement, 2001—. Active Campbellsville Bapt. Ch., 1993-97, drama participant, 1994, Ky. Bapt. Conv. del. 1995, 96, pub. rels. com. 1995-97; active Living Hope Bapt. Ch., 1997—. Named Outstanding Young Man of Am., 1996, 97, 98; Advancement Newcomers Leadership Devel. scholar, 1995; named to LaRue County H.S. Hall of Fame, 1987. Mem. Coun. for the Advancement and Support Edn. (awards judge 1997-98, session moderator 1998-2000, dist. III conf. com. 1999—, newcomers chair 2000, Award of Excellence 2000, Grand award 2001, Spl. Merit award 1998, 99, bd. dirs. 2001—), Coun. for the Advancement and Support Edn. Ky. (awards com. 1994-95, conf. com. 1995-2002, bd. dirs. 1996-2002, conf. chair 1998, 99, pres.-elect 1998-99, pres. 1999-2001, Grand awards 1994, 98, 2001, 2002, Merit award 2001), Nat. Com. on Planned Giving, Ky. Planned Giving Coun., Rotary Internat. (program com. 1995-97, co-chair club svc. com. 1996-97), Bowling Green/Warren County C. of C. (membership svcs. com. 1999). Democrat. Baptist. Avocations: recreational sports, travel, reading. Home: 1624 Crownridge Ct Bowling Green KY 42104 Office: We Ky Univ 1 Big Red Way Bowling Green KY 42101

BLAIR, JOHN RAYMOND, educational psychology educator; b. Brazil, Ind., Oct. 6, 1942; s. Raymond and Fama K. (Rissler) B.; m. Susan M. Blair, June 25, 1977; children: Jason, Alissa, Kelsey. BS, Ind. U., 1964, MS, 1966; PhD, U. Mich., 1970. Psychologist Muscatatuck State Hosp., Butlerville, Ind., 1966; asst. prof. Ea. Mich. U., Ypsilanti, 1970-76, assoc. prof., 1976-82, prof. ednl. psychology, 1982-99, prof. emeritus, 1999—; spiritual life dir. St. Peter's Parish Ctr., Douglas, Mich., 2000—01; cons., 1999—. Vis. scholar U. Mich., Ann Arbor, 1980, 1993—99, U. Notre Dame, Ind., 1992—96, 1998—2000, 2003—; vis. prof. Ind. U., Bloomington, 1995—96; mem. adv. bd. Ea. Mich. U. Alcohol and Other Drug Program, 1993, Inst. for Study of Children and Families, Ypsilanti, 1979—92; bd. dirs. Mich. Coun. on Family Rels., East Lansing, 1979—87. Assoc. editor Family Rels., 1979-86; contbr. articles to profl. jours. Trustee, treas. Saugatuck-Douglas (Mich.) Dist. Libr., 1995—. Mem. APA, Mich. Acad. Sci. Arts and Letters (chair psychology sect. 1985-86, instnl. rep. 1986-99, vice chair religion sect. 1995-96, co-chair edn. sect. 1996-99), Saugatuck-Douglas Ednl. Found. (trustee 2000—, v.p. 2002—), Spiritual Dirs. Internat. Benedictine Oblate. Avocations: service, advocacy. Home: 874 Campbell Rd Saugatuck MI 49453 E-mail: jrblair@umich.edu.

BLAIR, KATHIE LYNN, social services worker; b. Oakland, Calif., Sept. 29, 1951; d. Robert Leon Webb and Patricia Jean (Taylor) Peterson; m. Terry Wayne Blair, Dec. 29, 1970 (div. 1972); 1 child, Anthony Blair. Eligibility worker Dept. Social Services, San Jose, Calif., 1974-76; adult and family svcs. worker State of Oreg., Portland, 1977-90. Guest speaker welfare advocacy groups, Portland, 1987. Translator: Diary of Fannie Burkhart, 1991; contbr. articles to profl. jours.; developer word game for children. Mem. ACLU, AARP, Nat. Geog. Soc., A Brotherhood Against Totalitarian Enactments, Oreg. State Pub. Interest Rsch. Group, Nat. Headache Found., Clan Chattan Assn., Portland Highland Games Assn., Nature Conservancy, Nat. Wildlife Fedn., Harley Owners Group, Ladies of Harley, Sierra Club, Wilderness Soc., Defenders of Wildlife. Democrat. Avocations: history, women's studies, writing, photography, motorcycles. E-mail: good_foottoo@yahoo.com.

BLAIR, LOUIS HELION, foundation executive; b. Richmond, Va., Feb. 9, 1939; s. Jean Bichier and Jean Blair Helion; m. Suzanne Sessoms Lemon, June 1, 1982; 1 child, Robert. BEE, U. Va., 1961; MEE, MIT, 1962, degree elec. engrng. (hon.), 1960, LLD (hon.), William Jewell Coll., 1993; DSc (hon.), Baker U., 1994. Sr. rsch. staff Urban Inst., Washington, 1969-76; policy analyst Office of Sci. and Tech. Policy, Washington, 1976-79; staff mem. U.S. Radiation Policy Coun., Washington, 1979-81, U.S. Senate Commerce Com., Washington, 1981-83; cons. Washington and Paris, 1983-89; exec. sec. Truman Scholarship Fedn., Washington, 1989—. Mayor, coun. mem. City of Falls Ch., 1969-74; mem. Solid Waste Adv. Group, State of Va., 1971-72. Fellow Nat. Acad. of Pub. Adminstrn. Avocation: french cooking. Office: Truman Scholarship Found 712 Jackson Pl NW Washington DC 20006-4901 E-mail: Lblair@truman.gov.

BLAIR, LUDIE MAE RILEY, retired furniture company executive; b. Ashland, Ala., Feb. 7, 1918; d. David Love and Ludie Ann (Shores) Riley; m. George Elston Blair, July 21, 1943; children: George Stanley, Elder Thomas. BA, Jacksonville (Ala.) State U., 1937-40. Tchr. 4th grade New Site Sch., Alexander City, Ala., 1940-43; bookkeeper A.V. Riley's Furniture Co., Alexander City, Ala., 1944-45; co-owner AAA Furniture Co., Birmingham, Ala., 1947-90; ret. AAA Furniture Co. (presently Blair Furniture Inc.), Birmingham, Ala., 1990. Baptist. Avocation: creative modern art works. Home: PO Box 26703 Birmingham AL 35260-0703 Office: Blair Furniture Inc 2205 2nd Ave N # D Birmingham AL 35203-3805

BLAIR, M. WAYNE, lawyer; b. Spokane, Washington, Oct. 17, 1942; BS in Elec. Engr., U. Washington, 1965, JD, 1968. Bar: Wash. 1968. Mem. Wash. State Bd. for Jud. Adminstrn., 1995-2000. With USAF, 1968-72. Recipient Helen M. Geisness award, 1987, President's award, 1990. Mem. ABA (Ho. of Dels. 1988-91), Am. Judicature Soc., Washington State Bar Assn. (bd. govs. 1991-94, pres. 1998-99), Seattle-King County Bar Assn. (trustee 1981-83, pres. 1987-88). Office: 5800 Bank of America Twr 701 5th Ave Seattle WA 98104-7097

BLAIR, MARGARET MENDENHALL, research economist, consultant, law educator; b. Bartlesville, Okla., Nov. 8, 1950; d. Harold Leroy and Mary Winifred (Simmons) Mendenhall; m. Forrest Randall Blair, May 29, 1971 (div. Sept. 1979); m. Roger Lisle Conner, June 22, 1991; 1 child, Elizabeth LeeAnn Conner. BA, U. Okla., 1973; postgrad., Harvard U., 1982-83; MA, MPhil, PhD, Yale U., 1989. Reporter Houston Chronicle, 1973-75; reporter, bur. mgr. Fairchild Publ., Houston, 1975-77; corr. Bus. Week, Houston, 1977-79, bur. chief, 1979-82; economist Fed. Res. Bank N.Y., NYC, 1985; rsch. asst. Yale U., New Haven, 1985-86, lectr., 1986-87; rsch. assoc. Brookings Instn., Washington, 1987-94, sr. fellow, 1995-99; dir. Brookings Project on Corps. and Human Capital, 1996-99; co-dir. Brookings Project on Intangible Sources of Value, 1998-2001; rsch. dir., vis. prof. Sloan-GULC project bus. inst. Georgetown U. Law Ctr., 2000—. Mem. adj. faculty U. Md. Coll. Bus. and Mgmt., 1993—94; vis. prof. Georgetown U. Law Ctr., 1996—; mem. steering com., rapporteur Woodstock Seminar Series on Bus. Ethics, Washington, 1989—90; mem. subcoun. on capital allocation Competitiveness Policy Coun., 1993—96; rapporteur Salzburg (Austria) Seminar on Internat. Fin. Markets, 1989; mem. steering com. time horizons project Coun. on Competitiveness, Washington, 1990; mem. Task Force on Restructuring America's Labor Market Instns., MIT/Sloan Sch. Mgmt., 1997—2001; non-resident sr. fellow Brookings Instn., 2000—; bd. advisors George Washington U. Sloan Program on Bus. and Soc., 1998—; mem. World Econ. Forum Corp. Performance Coun., 1999—; bd. dirs. Sonic Corp., 2001—; trustee Woodstock Theol. Ctr., 2001—; mem. steering com. project on corp. responsibility Am. Acad. Arts and Sci., 2002—. Author: The Deal Decade Handbook, 1993, Ownership and Control: Rethinking Corporate Governance for the Twenty-first Century, 1995; co-author: Unseen Wealth: Report of the Brookings Task Force on Intangibles, 2001; editor: The Deal Decade: What Takeovers and Leveraged Buyouts Mean for Corporate Governance, 1993, Wealth Creation and Wealth Sharing: A Colloquium on Corporate Governance and Investments in Human Capital, 1996, Employees and Corporate Governance, 1999, The New Relationship Human Capital in the American Corporation, 2000; contbr. numerous articles to profl. and acad. jours. Vol. Big Sisters Washington Met. Area, 1989-92; organizer neighborhood watch group, Washington, 1990; mem. bd. advisors Ctr. for Cmty. Interest, 1993-98; mem. bd. dir. Christ Edn. Rock Spring United Ch. Christ, 2000-03; mem. Arlington County Adv. Coun. Instrn. Univ. fellow Yale U., 1983-86, Leo Model fellow Brookings Instn., 1987-88; rsch. grantee Boston U. Mfrs. Roundtable, 1990, Columbia U. Instnl. Investor Project, 1994, Alfred P. Sloan Found., 1995, 96, 98, 99. Mem. AAAS (mem. steering com. corp. responsibility project 2002—), Am. Econ. Assn., Am. Law Econs. Assn. Avocations: ballet, religious studies, cooking. Office: Georgetown U Law Ctr 600 New Jersey Ave NW Washington DC 20001-2075

BLAIR, MARIE LENORE, retired elementary school educator; b. Maramec, Okla., Jan. 9, 1931; d. Virgil Clement and Ella Catherine (Leen) Strode; m. Freeman Joe Blair, Aug. 26, 1950; children: Elizabeth Ann Blair Crump, Roger Joe. BS, Okla. A&M Coll., 1956; MS, Okla. State U., 1961, postgrad., 1965-68. Reading specialist Pub. Schs., Stillwater, Okla., 1966-88. Past bd. dirs. Okla. Reading Coun. Mem. Internat., Okla., Cimarron (past pres.) reading assns., NEA, Okla. Edn. Assn., Stillwater Edn. Assn., Demoley Mothers Club, Rainbow Mothers Club, Lahoma Club, White Shrine Jerusalem (past worthy high priestess), Order White Shrine Jerusalem (past supreme queen's attendent), Internat. Order of Rainbow for Girls (Okla. exec. com. emeritus), Order Ea. Star (past grand Martha, past grad rep. of Nebr. in Okla., grand rep. of Manitoba in Okla. Order), Order of Amaranth. Democrat. Home: 51200 E 55 Rd Maramec OK 74045-6124

BLAIR, PHYLLIS E. artist, sculptor, illustrator; b. N.Y.C., Oct. 5, 1922; d. Franz Joseph and Marian Jane (Burke) Emmerich; m. Thomas Slingluff Blair, Sept., 17, 1946; children: Joan Dix, George Dike, Hadden Slingluff. Student, Skidmore Coll., 1940-42, Art Students League, 1945, Westminster Coll., 1970-72, Bennington Coll., 1989. Asst. art dept. Skidmore Coll., Saratoga Springs, N.Y., 1940-42; art illustrator & engring. draftsman GE, Schenectady, N.Y., 1942-44, Bell Labs., N.Y.C., 1944-46; elem tchr. Clinton, Tenn., 1946-47. One-woman shows include Hoyt Inst. Fine Arts, New Castle, Pa., 1971, 93, Butler Inst. Am. Art, Youngstown, Ohio, 1982, Westminster Coll., New Wilmington, Pa., 1983, Butler Inst. Am. Art, Salem, Ohio, 1994. Art curator Human Svcs. Ctr., New Castle, 1968-89, Jameson Meml. Hosp., 1978-99, Jameson Care Ctr., Jameson Retirement Pl., 1978-99, Jameson Rehab Ctr., 1978-99, Almira Home, New Castle, 1990-99, Lawrence County Children and Youth Svcs., 2000, The Soup Kitchen, Boynton Beach, Fla., 2000; founding mem. Nat. Mus. of Women in the Arts, Washington, D.C. Recipient Benjamin Rush award Pa. Med. Soc., 1991. Mem. Hoyt Inst. Fine Arts (chair art com. & permanent collection 1967-99, trustee, 1967-99, Blair Sculpture Walkway named in her honor 1996), Am. Heart Assn. (Disting. Svc. award Lawrence County chpt. 1978). Avocations: golf, painting, sculpting. Home: 1611 Cold Spring Rd Williamstown MA 01267-2771

BLAIR, REBECCA SUE, English educator, lay minister; b. Terre Haute, Ind., Mar. 26, 1958; d. Albert Eldon and Genevieve Virginia (Smith) B.; m. Richard Volle Van Rheeden, May 27, 1989. BA in English magna cum laud, U. Indpls., 1980; MA in Medieval Lit. with honors, U. Ill., Springfield, 1982; MA, Ind. U., 1986, PhD, 1988. Grad. asst. U. Ill., Springfield, 1980—82; dir. English language tng. Ind. U., Bloomington, 1982-83, assoc. instr., 1982-88; assoc. prof., chmn. dept. English Westminster Coll., Fulton, Mo., 1989-99, dir. writing assessment, 1989-99; assoc. prof. U. Indpls., 1999—2003, Wartburg Coll., Waverly, Iowa, 2003—. Vis. prof. Webster U., St. Louis, Mo., 1988-89; writing assessment cons. Pepperdine U., Malibu, Calif., 1995, others; exec. com. of the faculty Westminster Coll.; mem. Assessment Com., College-Wide Budget Com., Profl. Stds. Com., Pers. Com., Dean's Cabinet Coun. of Chairs and Dirs., Edn. Task Force, Task Force to Reorganize the Acad. Area, Enrollment Svcs. Task Force; women's studies rep. Mid-Mo. Am. Coun. of Univs.; faculty sponsor Alpha Chi Scholastic Hon. Soc.; faculty organizer awareness of rape/domestic violence Take Back the Night Rally; presenter, spkr. in field. Author: The Other Woman: Women Authors and Cultural Stereotypes in American Literature, 1988; contbr. articles to profl. jours. Bd. dirs. Am. Cancer Soc., Callaway County, Mo., 1989-92; mem. pastor nominating com. First Presbyterian Ch., Fulton, Mo., 1990-91, elder, 1990—, session mem., elected mem., 1990-93, 97-2000, chmn. nominating com., 1993-94, chmn. music search com., 1994-95; pulpit supply Mo. Union Presbytery, 1995—, com. on ministry, 1997-2000, stated clk., 1997—; mem. Greater Mo. Focus on Leadership, 1992; vol. Habitat for Humanity, Fulton, 1993—; bd. dirs., founding mem. Coalition Against Rape and Domestic Violence, Fulton, 1995-97; bd. dirs. Friends of the Libr., Fulton, 1995-98, pres., 1997-98; sec. Fulton Art League, 1990—. Named Outstanding Faculty Mem., Westminster Coll., Fulton, 1991-92, Panhellenic Faculty Mem. of Year, Westminster Coll., 1996-97. Mem. Nat. Coun. for Rsch. on Women, Nat. Coun. Tchrs. of English, Am. Studies Assn., Midwest Modern Lang. Assn., Modern Lang. Assn., Writing Prog. Adminstrs., Coll. Composition and Comm., Fulton C. of C. (vol. 1992-96), Kiwanis (bd. dirs. 1990—, founder Circle K Club 1994, v.p. 1995-96, pres.-elect 1996-97, pres. 1997-98). Presbyterian. Avocations: gourmet cooking, reading, trains, writing. Home: 1916 Rainbow Dr Cedar Falls IA 50613 Office: Wartburg Coll 100 Wartburg Blvd Waverly IA 50677 Business E-Mail: rebecca.blair@wartburg.edu.

BLAIR, ROBERT ALLEN, business executive, lawyer; b. Suffolk, Va., June 25, 1946; s. Thomas Francis and Ossie Blair; m. Linda Britt, Dec. 27, 1970; children: Robert Allen II, Thomas Edward. BA in Math., Coll. William and Mary, 1968; JD, U. Va., 1973. Bar: Mass. 1974, U.S. Dist. Ct. Mass. 1974, U.S. Ct. Appeals (D.C. cir.) 1976, U.S. Dist. Ct. D.C. 1980. Assoc. Goodwin, Procter & Hoar, Boston, 1973-74, Surrey & Morse, Washington, 1974-78, ptnr., 1979-81; mng. ptnr. Anderson, Hibey & Blair, Washington, 1981-95; ptnr., chair govt. practice group Manatt, Phelps & Phillips, 1995-99; co-chmn., gen. counsel GlobalOptions, LLC, Washington, 1998-99; pres. The Blair Law Firm P.C., Washington, 1999—. Chmn. nat. adv. bd. IPG Photonics Corp., 1999—, vice chmn. bd. dirs., 2000—. Mem. editorial bd. Law Rev. U. Va., 1971-73. Chmn. bd. Inst. on Terrorism and Subnat. Conflict, Washington, 1982-95; co-counsel Citizens for Dem. Alternatives in 1980, Washington, 1979-81; mem. adv. panel on fgn. policy, def. and arms control Dem. Nat. Com., Washington, 1982-85; mem. drafting team for fgn. policy, def. and arms control issue workshop Dem. Nat. Conf., Phila., 1982, mem. bus. coun., 1988-90, 94—, mng. trustee, 1994-95; mem. Senate Dem. Roundtable, Washington, 1983—; mem. Senate Dem. Leadership Circle, Washington, 1983-2000; vice chmn. Potomac Group, Washington, 1983-84, chmn., 1984-85; mem. adv. council Dem. Platform Com., Washington, 1984; spl. counsel 1984 Dem. Nat. Conv., San Francisco, 1984; spl. counsel to nat. fin. chmn. Dem. Nat. Com., Washington, 1984-85, mem. fin. bd. dirs., 1983-85, 88; mem. Nat. Dem. Club, Senate Dem. Majority Trust, 1992-99; vice chmn. Washington Fgn. Affairs Soc., 1984-87; mem. Gov.'s Econ. Adv. Council, Va., 1986-94; commr. Va. Port Authority, Commonwealth Va., 1991-96, vice chmn. finance/planning com., 1992-94, chmn., 1994-96; chmn. S Corp. Assn., Washington 1996-2000, chmn. reform project, 1993-96; advisory bd. Thomas Jefferson Program Pub. Policy William and Mary, 1996—, chmn. devel. com., 1999—; bd. dirs. Everybody Wins, 1997-2000, Youth Leadership Inst., Washington, 1984-86. Named to Outstanding Young Men Am., U.S. Jaycees, 1976 Mem. ABA, Univ. Club (Washington). Home: 4936 Rodman St NW Washington DC 20016-3239

BLAIR, ROBERT CARY, insurance company executive; BS, Butler U., Indpls., 1961. From mgmt. chmn. and trainee to dir., CEO Westfield Cos., 1961—. Office: Westfield Cos 1 Park Cir Westfield Center OH 44251

BLAIR, ROBERT GROBERG, psychiatrist, educator; b. Bloomington, Ind., Nov. 7, 1958; s. Robert Wallace and Julia Blair; m. Christy Marie Anderson, Dec. 14, 1990; children: Justin Robert, Amanda, Elaina Marie. PhD, U of Utah, Salt Lake City, 1992—96. LMSW NASW/ NM, 2001. Asst. prof. N.Mex State U., Las Cruces, N.Mex., 2000—, Morehead State U., Morehead, Ky., 1997—2000. Clin. social worker FHP, Salt Lake City, 1989—92. Author: (publication) Risk factors in the mental health status of Cambodian refugees in UT. Bd. mem. The ARC, Las Cruces, N.Mex., 2000—03. Lds. Achievements include Paper presentation on resiliency. Avocations: swimming, tennis, travel. Office: New Mexico State University MSC 3SW PO Box 30001 Las Cruces NM Office Fax: 505-646-4116. E-mail: roblair@nmsu.edu.

BLAIR, ROSEMARY KASUL, social work educator; b. Chgo., Oct. 19, 1941; d. Vincent J. Therese (DeKreon) Kasul; m. Neal Edward McKinney, Nov. 11, 1962 (div. Jan. 1992); children: Michael, Kevin; m. Robert A. Blair, Dec. 17, 2002. B in Social Work, George Williams Coll., 1978, MSW, 1980. Lic. clin. social worker, Ill.; cert. sr. addiction counselor, eating disorders counselor, gerontol. counselor. Coord. inpatient program The Abbey, Winfield, Ill., 1980-82; counselor Parkside Med. Svcs., Winfield, 1982-83, coord. tng. Park Ridge, Ill., 1983-86; clin. social worker Pape & Assocs., Wheaton, Ill., 1986-88; prof. Coll. of Du Page, Glen Ellyn, Ill., 1988—2003, prof. emeritus, 2003—; counseling and cons. McKinney, Blair and Assocs., Wheaton, 1995—. Co-tchr. nat. symposium Internat. Assn. Eating Disorder Profls., 1994, 95, 96, 97; presenter Midwest NOHSE conf. 1995; presenter in field. Mem. NASW, Am. Soc. on Aging, Addiction Counselor Tng. Program Dirs. Home: 1240 Reading Ct Wheaton IL 60187-7710 E-mail: rmck1240@aol.com.

BLAIR, SANDRA JEAN, author, publisher; b. Denver, Apr. 14, 1938; d. Harold Eugene Blair and Elizabeth Mae (Alexander) Blair Dodd. Student, Phoenix Coll., 1969. Tchr. Arthur Murray Studio, Denver, 1956-57; supr. Dales Dance studio, Denver, 1958-60; with New Eng. Advt.-Dow, Denver, 1960-65; owner, mgr. Copper Penny Bar, Phoenix, 1965-71; tchr., salesperson Bobby Ball Agy., Phoenix, 1976-78; salesperson KMOG Radio, Payson, Ariz., 1982-84; owner Inspired Pub. Co., Payson, 1994—. Author: It Is Time to Try Paradise, 1995, "A Cosmic Journey", 2002. Mem. Payson Lightworker Assn., Payson Area Writers Soc. (sec.-treas. 1993-96), Ariz. Psychic Alliance, Payson Love Corp., Payson Tennis Club (pres. 1984-92). Avocations: golf, sailing, scuba diving, tennis, pool. E-mail: inspired@juno.com.

BLAIR, SYLVIA H. computer engineer, small business owner; BS in Physics, Lamar U., 1976. Computer resources project engr. on F-16 and F-22 fighter aircraft Ft. Worth divsn. Gen. Dynamics, 1979—89. Session chmn., tutorials chmn. AIAA/IEEE Digital Avionic Systems Conf., 1983—86; conf. chmn., tech. program chmn. AIAA Aerospace Engring. Conf. and Show, L.A., 1983—85; chmn. AIAA Digital Avionic Tech. Com., 1987—89. Min. Higher Way Ministries, Grapevine, Tex., 1995. Recipient Navy Superior Pub. Svc. medal, U.S. Sec. of the Navy, 1988. Avocations: writing, reading, fishing, travel. Office: Ambassador Consulting PO Box 3338 Grapevine TX 76099 E-mail: shblair@earthlink.net.

BLAIR, THOMAS DELANO, museum administrator; b. Plum Branch, S.C., Apr. 8, 1946; s. Richard and Evangeline B.; m. Frances V. Veney, 1973; children: Jayson T., Todd J. BS in Bus. Adminstrn., S.C. State Coll., 1967; MBA, U. Md., 1978. CPA, Md., Cert. Internal Auditor. Asst. bank examiner FDIC, Balt., 1967, 71; auditor U.S. Army Audit Agy., Linthicum Hghts., Md., 1971-72, Dept. Defense, Arlington, Va., 1973-74; supr. mgmt. analyst U.S. Gen. Acctg. Office, Washington, 1974-79; dir. office of inspector gen. Johnson Space Ctr. NASA Goddard Space Flight Ctr., Houston, Washington, Greenbelt, Md., 1979-84; regional mgr. Office of Inspector Gen., U.S. Dept. Vet. Affairs, Atlanta, 1984-90; inspector gen. Smithsonian Instn., Washington, 1990—. Mem.: AICPA, Inst. Internal Auditors, Assn. Govt. Accts. Office: Smithsonian Instn 750 9th St NW Washington DC 20560-0905 E-mail: tblair@oig.si.edu.

BLAIR, VIRGINIA ANN, public relations executive; b. Kansas City, Mo., Dec. 20, 1925; d. Paul Lowe and Lou Etta (Cooley) Smith; m. James Leon Grant, Sept. 3, 1943 (dec. July 1944); m. Warden Tannahill Blair, Jr., Nov. 7, 1947 (dec. Apr. 2002); children: Janet, Warden Tannahill III. BS in Speech, Northwestern U., 1948. Free-lance writer, Chgo., 1959-69; writer, editor Smith, Bucklin & Assocs., Inc., Chgo., 1969-72, account mgr., 1972-79, account supr., 1979-80, dir. pub. rels., 1980-85; pres. GB Pub. Rels., Chgo., 1985—. Judge U.S. Indsl. Film Festival, 1974, 75; instr. Writer's Workshop, Evanston, Ill., 1978; dir. Northwestern U. Libr. Coun., 1978-91, dir. alumnae bd., 1986—, John Evans Club bd., 1990-98. Author dramas (produced on CBS): Jeanne D'Arc: The Trial, 1961, Cordon of Fear, 1961, Reflection, 1961, If I Should Die, 1963; 3-act children's play: Children of Courage, 1967. Emmy nominee Nat. Acad. TV Arts and Scis., 1963; recipient Svc. award Northwestern U., 1978, Creative Excellence award U.S. Indsl. Film Festival, 1976, Gold Leaf merit cert. Family Cir. mag. and Food Coun. Am., 1977, cert. Excellence superior achievement in media rels. N.Am. Precis Syndicate, 1997, Ginny award Cremation Assn. N.Am., 2002. Mem. Pub. Rels. Soc. Am. (counselors acad.), Am. Advt. Fedn. (lt. gov. Ill. 6th dist.), Women's Advt. Club Chgo. (pres.), Publicity Club Chgo., Nat. Acad. TV Arts and Scis., John Evans Club (bd. dirs.), Woman's Club Evanston (pres.), Zeta Phi Eta (Svc. award 1978, 93), Alpha Gamma Delta, Philanthropic and Ednl. Orgn. (Ill. chpt. pres. dist. pres.). Home and Office: 2601 Central St Unit 206 Evanston IL 60201-1395

BLAIR, WARREN, artist, educator; b. Phila., Oct. 13, 1922; s. Mortimer Warren and Olive (Wilkinson) W.; m. Jane, Dec. 13, 1947; children: Heidi Beth Vassar. Cert., Phila. Mus. Sch. Indsl. Art, 1942, 47. Art mgr. to art dir. Smith, Kline & French Labs, Phila, 1950; design dir. SmithKline Corp., Phila., 1950-81; ret..., 1981. Design dir. World Corp., Phila., 1975-81. Design dir. The Fine Old House, 1980; Exhbns. include Am. Watercolor Soc., 1986, 88, 89, 90, 95, 99, Phila. Watercolor Club, 1984-96, 2002 (Hahn Gallery award 1992), John H. Geisel Watercolor Exhibit, 1987, 89, 90, 91, 92, Woodmere Art Mus., 1984-92 (Harrison Morris prize 1991), Reading Mus., 1992, 93, 98 (Merit award 1992), Mann Gallery, Reading, Pa., 1990, Phillip's Mill Annual, 1990, 91 (Cmty. Assn. award), Am. Coll. Life Underwriters, Bryn Mawr, Pa., 1991, 97, 98, Yellow Springs Annual, 1991, 92, 93, Reading Area C.C., 1994, 96. Sgt. U.S. Army, 1942-45, PTO. Decorated D.S.M. with two bronze stars; recipient Alumni award Univ. of the Arts, 1959, various other awards for advt. design. Mem. Art Dirs. Club Phila. (pres. 1959, 60, 61, Svc. award 1971, Man of Yr. award 1984, lifetime hon. mem.), Am. Watercolor Soc. (hon. mem.), Phila. Watercolor Soc. (life mem., Dana award 1981, Grumbacher award 1994, Winsor E.Newton Painting award 1995). Republican. Methodist. Avocations: golf, bridge, bowling.

BLAIR, WILLIAM GRANGER, retired newspaperman; b. Chgo., Nov. 17, 1925; s. William Mitchell and Martha (Granger) B.; m. Sue Cunningham, Apr. 19, 1952 (div.); children: Robert, Bruce (dec.), Laura; m. Ellen Lopin, Sept. 29, 1970. AB in English cum laude, Princeton U., 1950. Reporter Kansas City (Mo.) Star, 1950-52; mem. staff N.Y. Times, 1953-90. Fgn. corr., Paris, 1956-62, London, 1965-67, bur. chief, Jerusalem, 1962-65, mgr. employee communications, 1968, mgr. pub. relations, 1969-70, dir. pub. relations, 1970-73, broadcast corr., 1973-79, met. reporter, 1980-90. Served with USMCR, 1943-46, PTO. Mem. reporting team whose news coverage of regional flood helped to earn Pulitzer award for The Kansas City Star, 1952; corr. in France and Algeria when N.Y. Times won 1st Pulitzer prize awarded specifically to a fgn. news staff for internat. reporting, 1958. Mem. Ivy Club. Home: 320 E 52nd St New York NY 10022-6708 E-mail: wgbee@aol.com.

BLAIR, WILLIAM MCCORMICK, JR., lawyer; b. Chgo., Oct. 24, 1916; s. William McCormick and Helen (Bowen) B.; m. Catherine Gerlach, Sept. 9, 1961; 1 son, William McCormick III. AB, Stanford U., 1940; LL.B., U. Va., 1947. Bar: Ill. 1947, D.C. 1972. Assoc. firm Wilson & McIlvaine, Chgo., 1947-50; adminstrv. asst. to Gov. Adlai E. Stevenson of Ill., 1950-52; ptnr. firm Stevenson, Rifkind & Wirtz, Chgo., 1955-61, Paul, Weiss, Rifkind, Wharton & Garrison, N.Y.C., 1957-61; U.S. ambassador to Denmark, 1961-64, to Philippines, 1964-67; gen. dir. John F. Kennedy Ctr., 1968-72; ptnr. firm Surrey & Morse, Washington, 1978-84, of counsel, 1984-86. Bd. dirs. Am.-Scandinavian Found., N.Y.C.; v.p. bd. dirs. Albert and Mary Lasker Found., N.Y.C., 1968-98. Capt. USAAF, 1942-46. Decorated Bronze Star U.S.; officer Order of Crown, Belgium; Order of Sikatuna, Philippines; comdr. cross Order of Dannebrog 1st class, Denmark). Mem. Am. Coun. Ambs. (vice chmn., pres. 1985-89), Soc. Animal Protective Legis. (trustee), Phi Delta Phi. Office: 2510 Foxhall Rd NW Washington DC 20007-1123

BLAIS, BERNARD RAYMOND, ophthalmologist, occupational health physician, educator; b. Colchester, Vt., Sept. 19, 1931; s. Frederick Emille and Marguerite (Duffany) B.; m. Claire Aileen McCarthy, Sept. 5, 1955; children: Stephanie A. McMahon, Kristine Blais Miller. BS in Chemistry cum laude, St. Michael's Coll., Colchester, 1953; MD, U. Vt., Burlington, 1958. Diplomate Am. Bd. Ophthalmology, Nat. Bd. Med. Examiners, Am. Bd. Preventive Medicine; bd. qualified occupl. medicine. Med. intern Naval Hosp., Portsmouth, Va., 1958-59, resident in ophthalmology Phila., 1961-64; fellow in ophthalmic pathology Armed Forces Inst. Pathology, Washington, 1967-68; resident in occupl. medicine U. Cin. Sch. Medicine, 1980-83; assoc. ophthalmic pathologist Wills Eye Hosp., Phila., 1976—77; med. dir. Allied Health Sch., Naval Hosp., San Diego, 1968-72; chair ophthalmology dept. Naval Hosp., Phila., 1972-77; Nat. Naval Med. Ctr., Bethesda, Md., 1977-78; prof. surgery and ophthalmology USUHS, Bethesda, Md., 1977-87; dir. surface and sealift medicine USN Bur. Medicine and Surgery, 1978-82; force med. officer Mil. Sealift Command, Washington, 1978-87; regional med. dir. Lockheed-Martin Corp., Niskayuna, N.Y., 1988-96; clin. prof. ophthalmology Albany (N.Y.) Med. Coll., 1989—; cons., pres. Blais Consulting, Ltd., Clifton Park, N.Y., 1996—. Author: Basic Principles of Industrial Ophthalmology, 1999; contbr. articles to profl. jours. Decorated Navy Commendation medal, Nat. Def. medal with bronze star; recipient Gen. Chmn. award, Nat. Safety Coun., 1986, Maritime Health and Safety Outstanding Achievement award, 1986, Top Ophthalmologists 21st Century award for achievement, others. Fellow Am. Acad. Ophthalmology (liaison 1996—), ACS, Am. Coll. Occupl. and Environ. Medicine (chmn. eye and vision com. 1989—), Soc. Mil. Ophthalmologists (pres. 1975, sec.-treas. 1981-87, Dedicated Svc. award 1987). Republican. Roman Catholic. Avocations: skiing, photography, lecturing, volunteerism. Office: Blais Consulting Ltd 4 Innisbrook Dr Clifton Park NY 12065-2909 E-mail: bblais@nycap.rr.com.

BLAIS, ROGER NATHANIEL, physics educator; b. Duluth, Minn., Oct. 3, 1944; s. Eusebe Joseph and Edith Seldina (Anderson) B.; m. Mary Louise Leclerc, Aug. 2, 1971; children: Christopher Edward, Laura Louise. BA in Physics and French Lit., U. Minn., 1966; PhD in Physics, U. Okla., 1971; cert. in computer programming, Tulsa Jr. Coll., 1981; cert. in bus., UCLA, 1986. Registered profl. engr., Okla. Instr. physics Westark C.C., Ft. Smith, Ark., 1971-72; asst. prof. physics and geophys. scis Old Dominion U., Norfolk, Va., 1972-77; asst. prof. engring. physics U. Tulsa, 1977-81, assoc. prof., 1981-98, prof., 1998—; assoc. dir. Tulsa U. Artificial Lift Projects, 1983—98, chmn. physics, 1986-88, vice-provost, 1989-92, provost, v.p. acad. affairs, 1998—. Contbr. articles to profl. jours. Active Leadership Okla., 2002—03; mem. Leadership Pkla. XVI; bd. dirs. Light Opera Okla., 2003—, Hillcrest Splty. Hosps., 2003—. Recipient Great Leadership Okla. XVI, 2003. Fellow Instrumentation Sys. and Automation Soc. (dir. test measurement divsn. 1995-97, v.p. automation and tech. dept. 2003-), Leadership Okla. XVI; mem. AAAS, AAUP, NSPE, Am. Phys. Soc., Am. Geophys. Union, Soc. Petroleum Engrs., Am. Assn. Physics Tchrs., Am. Soc. Engring. Edn., N.Y. Acad. Scis., Iron

Wedge Soc., Phi Beta Kappa, Sigma Xi, Sigma Pi Sigma, Tau Beta Pi, Phi Kappa Phi. Home: 5348 E 30th Pl Tulsa OK 74114-6314 Office: U Tulsa Office of Provost 600 S College Ave Tulsa OK 74104-3139 E-mail: roger-blais@utulsa.edu., rblais71@cox.net.

BLAISDELL, CHARMARIE JENKINS, historian, educator; b. Phila., Jan. 23, 1934; d. Edward Cope Jenkins and June Franklin (Blaisdell) Jenkins; m. Robert Howard Webb, Sept 12, 1953 (div. Feb. 1974); children: Kristin Blaisdell Webb, Margaret Henderson Webb. BA, Boston U., 1955; MA, Tufts U., 1964, PhD, 1970. Asst. prof. Boston Coll., Chestnut Hill, Mass., 1970-71; asst. prof. history Northeastern U., Boston, 1971-72, assoc. prof., 1977—. Bd. dirs. History Making Prodns., Boston, 1987—, pres., 1997—; bd. dirs. Boston Oral History Ctr., 1996-2000, Coastal Sr. Coll., Maine, 2002--. Contbr. chpts. to books, articles to profl. jours. Cmty. mediator Marblehead (Mass.) Mediation Svcs., 1995—, Cmty. Mediation Svcs., Augusta, Maine; profl. facilitator Juvenile Restorative Justice Project, Augusta. Recipient award in Tchg. Excellence, Northeastern U., 1991, 99; sr. fellow 16th Century Studies, 1999. Mem. Am. Hist. Assn., Sixteenth Century Studies Assn. (pres. 1975), New Eng. Hist. Assn. (exec. com.), Am. Assn. State and Local History, Oral History Assn., Nat. Coun. on Pub. History, Hist. Perspectives (founder, prin.), Ednl. Perspectives (founder, prin.). Mem. Soc. Of Friends. Avocations: community theater, sailing, skiing. Home: PO Box 108 Tenants Harbor ME 04860 Office: Northeastern U Dept History ME 249 Boston MA 02115

BLAISING, CRAIG ALAN, religious studies educator; b. San Antonio, Sept. 28, 1949; s. Claude Lawrence and Mildred Helen (Craig) B.; m. Diane Sue Garrison, May 31, 1975; children: Emily Grace, Jonathan Craig. BS, U. Tex., 1971; ThM, Dallas Theol. Sem., 1976, ThD, 1979; PhD, U. Aberdeen, Scotland, 1988. Lic. to ministry Trinity Bapt. Ch., San Antonio, 1972. Adj. prof. dept. religion U. Tex., Arlington, 1978; asst. prof. systematic theology Dallas Theol. Sem., 1980-85, assoc. prof., 1985-89, acting dept. chmn., 1988-89, prof., 1989-95, Southwestern Bapt. Theol. Sem., 1995—96, dept. chmn., 1996—99, Joseph Emerson Brown prof. Christian theology, 1996—2000, assoc. v.p. acad. adminstrn., 1999—2001, exec. v.p., provost, dean, 2002—, prof. systematic theology, 2002—. Co-author: Progressive Dispensationalism, 1993, 2000; co-editor: Dispensationalism, Israel and the Church: The Search for Definition, 1992; contbr.: Bible Knowledge Commentary, 1985, Evangelical Dictionary of Theology, 1985, 2001, Handbook of Evangelical Theology, 1993, Encyclopedia of Early Chritianity, 1997, Three Views on the Millennium and Beyond, 1999; contbr. articles to religious jours. Rotary Found. fellow U. Aberdeen, 1978-79. Mem. Internat. Assn. Patristic Studies, Evang. Theol. Soc. (regional pres. 1986-87, nat. v.p. 2003), Dispensational Study Group (pres. 1988-90), Am. Acad. Religion, Soc. Bibl. Lit., N.Am. Patristic Soc., Tau Beta Pi. Office: Southwestern Bapt Theol Sem PO Box 22150 Fort Worth TX 76122-0001

BLAKE, BUD (JULIAN WATSON), cartoonist; b. Nutley, N.J., Feb. 13, 1918; s. George Wilbur and Hazel (Metcalfe) B.; m. Doris Gaskill, Jan. 4, 1941; children: Julian G., Mariana. Student, Nat. Acad. Design, 1935-36. Sketch artist, art dir., exec. art dir. Kudner Agy., N.Y.C., 1937-43, 46-54. Cartoonist: Ever Happen To You, syndicated by King Features; also free lance cartooning for various mags. and ads, 1954-65; cartoonist: syndicated comic strip Tiger, 1965— ; Paperback cartoon books include Tiger, Tiger Turns On; others. Served with inf. AUS, 1943-46. Mem. Nat. Cartoonists Soc. (Best Humor Strip award 1971, 78, 2000), Newspaper Features Coun. Home and Office: PO Box 146 Damariscotta ME 04543-0146

BLAKE, D. STEVEN, lawyer; b. Saginaw, Mich., June 2, 1940; BA, Mich. State U., 1963; JD, U. Calif., Davis, 1971. Bar: Calif. 1972. Sr. ptnr. Downey, Brand, Seymour & Rohwer, Sacramento, 1971—. Adj. prof. law U. Pacific, 1998-2000. Co-author: California Real Estate Finance and Construction Law, 1995. Mem. ABA (bus. law sect.), Am. Arbitration Assn. (arbitrator), State Bar Calif. (chair corp. com., sect., fin. instns. com., bus. law sect., panelist, presenter numerous seminars Calif. State Bar Continuing Edn. Bar 1981-91, co-chair corps. com. bus. law sect. 1997), Yolo County Bar Assn. Office: Downey Brand LLP 555 Capitol Mall Ste 1050 Sacramento CA 95814-4601

BLAKE, DARLENE EVELYN, political worker, consultant, educator, author; b. Rockford, Iowa, Feb. 26, 1947; d. Forest Kenneth and Violet Evelyn (Fisher) Kuhlemeier; m. Joel Franklin Blake, May 1, 1975 (dec. Jan. 1989); 1 child, Alexander Joel. AA, North Iowa Area Community Coll., Mason City, 1967; BS, Mankato (Minn.) State Coll., 1969; MS, Mankato (Minn.) State U., 1975. Cert. profl. tchr., Iowa; registered art therapist. Tchr. Bishop Whipple Sch., Faribault, Minn., 1970-72; art therapist C.B. Wilson Ctr., Faribault, 1972-76, Sedgwick County Dept. Mental Health, Wichita, Kans., 1976-79; cons. Batten, Batten, Hudson & Swab, Des Moines, 1979-81; pres. J.F. Blake Co., Inc., Des Moines, 1990—. Nat. adv. bd., polit. cons. to Alexander Haig for Pres., 1987-88; mgmt. tng. specialist Comms. Data Svcs., Inc., Des Moines, 1988-90, exec. mgr. customer svc. spl. interest fulfillment divsn., 1990-92; cert. cons. assoc. Drake, Beam, Morin, Inc., Mpls., 1993—; coord. staff devel. U. Iowa Hosps. and Clinics, Iowa City, 1998-01. Exhibited in one-woman show at local libr., 1970. Mem. U.S. Selective Svc. Bd. 26 and 27, Polk County, Iowa, 1981-98; sustaining mem. Rep. Nat. Com.; Rep. cand. Polk County Treas., Des Moines, 1982; chmn. Polk County Rep. Party, 1985-88; commr. Des Moines Commn. Human Rights and Job Discrimination, 1984-89; mem. Martin Luther King Scholarship Com., 1986-88; mem. Iowa State Bd. Psychology Examiners, 1983-90; active 5th Dist. Jud. Nominating Commn., 1990-96, Iowa Supreme Ct. Jud. Nominating Commn., 1996—, State Jud. Nominating Commn 1996—, Des Moines Sister Cities Commn., 1997-98, Am. in Bloom Judge, 2003—. Mem. Am. Art Therapy Assn., Iowa Art Therapy Assn. (pres. elect 1984-85, founder), Des Moines Garden Club (pres. 1984-85), Polk County Rep. Women (pres. elect 1983-85, Am. in bloom judge). Lutheran. Avocations: sewing, gardening, fine arts, music, reading. Home and Office: Unit 32 6001 Creston Ave Des Moines IA 50321-1255

BLAKE, DAVID GORDON, lawyer; b. Bryn Mawr, Pa., July 27, 1946; s. Alton David and Eleanore (Lavery) Gordon; m. Barbara Clemens Trimble, Aug. 7, 1976; children: Chad G., Scott B. BA, Tulane U., 1969; JD, Temple U., 1973. Bar: Pa. 1973, U.S. Supreme Ct. 1979. Ptnr. Cramp, D'Iorio, McConchie & Forbes, Media, Pa., 1973-96, Beatty, Cramp, Kauffman and Lincke, Media, 1996—2002, Beatty Lincke, Media, 2002—. Solicitor Radnor Twp., Pa., 2000—. Editor Del. County Legal Jour., 1980. Pres. Responsible Living Ltd., Media, 1980-81; bd. dirs. Fox Valley Community Assn., Glen Mills, Pa., 1984-86; mem. Rep. com., Radnor Twp., Pa., 1988-2000; v.p. Ithan PTO, 1989-90; pres. Radnor Soccer Club, 1989-96; treas. Radnor-Wayne Little League, 1989; mem. Nat. Rep. Presdl. Task Force. Named Man of Yr. Wayne area Jaycees, 1976. Mem. Del. County Bar Assn. (bd. dirs. 1986-88, 98-2000), Guy de Furia Am. Inns of Ct. Avocations: reading, coaching. Home: 906 Weatherstone Dr Paoli PA 19301-1923 Office: Beatty Lincke PO Box 901 Media PA 19063-0901 E-mail: DBlake@beattylincke.com.

BLAKE, GEORGE ROWLAND, soil science educator, water resources research administrator; b. Provo, Utah, Mar. 14, 1918; s. Samuel Henry and Annie Matilda (Bevan) B.; m. Kathryn M. Sumsion, Feb. 26, 1941; children: Carla Paul (dec.), Rowland, Lorraine Blake Phillips, Henry; m. Helen M. Patten, May 25, 1985. BA, Brigham Young U., 1943; PhD, Ohio State U., 1949. Missionary LDS Ch., Germany, 1937-39; with FBI, Washington, 1941-42; research fellow, teaching asst. Ohio State U., Columbus, 1946-49; asst. prof., asst. research specialist Rutgers U., New Brunswick, N.J., 1949-55; assoc. prof. dept. soil sci. U. Minn., St. Paul, 1955-60, prof., 1960-84, prof. emeritus, 1984—, dir. Water Resources Research Ctr., 1979-84. NSF sr. postdoctoral fellow, Braunschweig, Fed. Republic of Germany, 1962-63; Fulbright guest prof. U. Hohenheim, Fed. Republic of Germany, 1970-71; Ford Found. cons., Chile, 1967; guest prof. U. Kesthely, Hungary, 1974, U. Warsaw, Poland, 1981; USAID cons., Morocco, 1979-88; adj. prof. Institut Agronomique et Veterinaire Hassan II Rabat Morocco, 1982-88; guest prof. Humboldt U., Berlin, German Dem. Republic, 1986; Benson Inst. cons., Guatemala, 1990, 94. Contbr. articles to profl. jours. Pub. affairs vol. LDS Ch., Frankfurt, Germany, 1996-97. Recipient Georgicon award U. Kesthely, 1974, Müncheberg Plaque Acad. of Sci., German Dem. Republic., Spl. Emeritus Recognition award Brigham Young U. Emeritus Assn., 1996. Fellow Am. Soc. Agronomy, Soil Sci. Soc. Am.; mem. Internat. Soc. Soil Sci., Soil Sci. Soc. Am., Soil Conservation Soc. Am., Sigma Xi, Gamma Sigma Delta, Omicron Delta Kappa Home: 2215 N 1400 E Provo UT 84604-2103 E-mail: grblake@networld.com.

BLAKE, GERALD RUTHERFORD, banker; b. Knoxville, Tenn., Apr. 2, 1939; s. Roy Carl and Katherine Marie (Rutherford) B.; m. Jeanne Avonne Jones, May 11, 1962; children: Robert Alan, Douglas Mark. Student, U. Tenn., 1957-58, Sch. Bank Adminstrn., U. Wis., 1971-73. With Miller's. Inc., Knoxville, 1959-62, First Tenn. Bank, Knoxville, 1963—, eastern regional bldg. mgr., 1973—. Vice-chmn. planning com. Knoxville United Way, 1973— ; pres. Ramsey Community Club, 1966-67, Ramsey Elementary Sch. PTO, 1976-80; bd. dirs. Planned Parenthood Assn., 1976-77. Mem. Am. Inst. Banking, Bank Adminstrn. Inst. (pres., dir. Smoky Mountain chpt. 1976-77, state dir. 1977-79, 2d vice-chmn. Tenn. Title XX com.) Baptist. Home: 5233 Straw Plains Pike Knoxville TN 37914-6340 Office: 800 S Gay St Knoxville TN 37929-9729 *I always seem to be caught between the old and the new-in the middle of change from one accepted method or life-style to the new method or life-style, which has yet to be fully accepted. Perhaps everyone in every age is at the same situation. The time is upon us and the need is clear for a return to individualism and self-reliance, and a return to basic moral and religious principles. In doing so, one may just find the answers to most of life's problems.*

BLAKE, JOHN EDWARD, retired car rental company executive; b. Chgo., Aug. 9, 1933; s. Edward Aloysius and Laura (Schlichter) B.; m. Joan Patricia Kautz, Aug. 28, 1965; children: Kathryn, John, Amy. LLB, De Paul U., 1959. Bar: Ill. 1960. Supt. property U.S. Gypsum, Chgo., 1960-66; real estate rep. Ford Motor Co., Dearborn, Mich., 1966-68; mgr. real estate Roadway Express, Akron, Ohio, 1968-70; dir. properties Hertz Corp., N.Y.C., 1970-76, staff v.p., 1976-84, v.p., 1984-87, sr. v.p. Park Ridge, N.J., 1987-96; ret., 1996. Mem. bd. trustees Cath. Community Svcs., Archdiocese of Newark. Mem. Am. Assn. Airport Execs. (assoc.), Internat. Assn. Corp. Real Estate Execs. (chmn. bd. dirs. 1993-95, chmn. bd. trustees 1995 98, sr. advisor 1998-01). *With age hopefully comes wisdom and an ability to live within one's limitations while nurturing one's talents.*

BLAKE, JOHN FREEMAN, financial lawyer; b. Santa Clara, Calif., June 29, 1950; s. Freeman Dawes and Teresa (Seneker) B.; divorced; children: William, Braden. AB cum laude, U. Calif., Berkeley, 1972; postgrad., Tufts U., 1972-73; JD, U. San Francisco, 1979. Bar: Calif., D.C., N.Y. Asst. v.p., fin. counselor Bank Am., San Francisco, 1974-79; assoc. McCutchen, Doyle, Brown & Enersen, San Francisco, 1979-80, McCabe, Schwartz, Evans, Levy & Dawe, Concord, Calif., 1980-83, Silverstein & Mullens, Washington, 1983-87; sole practice Washington, 1987—. Mem. Joint Adv. Com. Calif. Continuing Edn. of Bar, 1981-83; adj. prof. estate planning Golden Gate U., San Francisco, 1982-83, George Washington U., Washington, 1984—; numerous seminars, lectures, forums. Author: Tax Management Financial Planning (4 vols.) 1985, also editor; author, editor: Financial Planning After the Tax Reform Act of 1986; author: The Role of Attorneys in Financial Planning, 1990; prepared numerous manuals, pamphlets on Calif. probate laws, estate planning; contbr. articles to profl. jours. Active Washington Estate Planning Council. Mem. ABA, State Bar of Calif., D.C. Bar Assn., N.Y. State Bar Assn., Internat. Assn. Fin. Planning (nat. bd. dirs. 1985-89), Registry Fin. Planning Practitioners, Cosmos Club, Phi Beta Kappa.

BLAKE, JONATHAN DEWEY, lawyer; b. Long Branch, N.J., June 14, 1938; s. Edgar Bond and Haven (Johnstone) B.; m. Prudence Anne Rowsell, Dec. 22, 1964 (div. June 1977); children: Juliet Haven, Deborah Anne, Susanna Rowsell; m. Elizabeth L. Shriver, Dec. 9, 1977; children: Jonathan Shriver-Blake, Molly Shriver-Blake. BA magna cum laude, Yale U., 1960, LLB cum laude, 1964; BA, MA, Oxford U., Eng., 1962. Bar: D.C. 1965, U.S. Supreme Ct. 1973, U.S. Dist. Ct. D.C. 1965, U.S. Dist. Ct. Md. 1985, U.S. Ct. Appeals (D.C. cir.) 1965, U.S. Ct. Appeals (2d cir.) 1973. Assoc. Covington & Burling, Washington, 1964-72, ptnr., 1972—, chmn. mgmt. com., 1996—2002. Tchr. Howard U., Washington, 1965-70, U. Va., Charlottesville, 1965-70. Contbr. articles to profl. jours. Pres. Great Falls Citizens Assn., Va., 1967-68; exec. com., bd. dirs. Deerfield Acad, Mass., 1980-85. Rhodes scholar, 1960; recipient Gordon Brown prize, 1959. Mem. ABA (chair internat. telecomm. com. 1993-2000), Fed. Comm. Bar Assn. (pres. 1980-85). Home: 4926 Hillbrook Ln NW Washington DC 20016-3208 Office: Covington & Burling 1201 Pennsylvania Ave NW Washington DC 20004-7566 E-mail: jblake@cov.com.

BLAKE, KENNETH WAYNE, III, principal, music educator; b. Milw., Wis., May 29, 1970; m. Deborah Marie Miskimen, July 18, 1992, children: Zachary Sean, Joshua David. M of Ch. Music, Concordia U., 2003. Prin. St. John's Luth. Sch., Beloit, Wis., 2001—; dir. music St. Peter's Luth. Ch., Reedsburg, Wis., 2000—01, Racine Luth. H.S., Racine, Wis., 1996—2000; chmn. performing arts Luther East H.S., Lansing, Ill., 1993—96. Mem. worship com. South Wis. Dist. - LCMS, Milw., 2000. Office: St John's Luth Ch and Sch 1000 Bluff St Beloit WI 53511 Office Fax: 608-361-0989.

BLAKE, LAURA, architect; b. Berkeley, Calif., Dec. 26, 1959; d. Igor Robert and Elizabeth (Denton) B. BA in Art History, Brown U., 1982; MArch, UCLA, 1985. Employee The Ratcliff Architects, Berkeley, 1986-90; architect IDG Architects, Oakland, Calif., 1990-92; assoc. ELS/Elbasani & Logan Architects, Berkeley, 1992-2000; architect Mark Cavagnero Assocs., San Francisco, 2000—. Organizer charity ball Spinsters San Francisco, 1988, sec., 1988-89, mem. adv. bd., 1989-92; mem. San Francisco Jr. League, 1991—. Recipient Alpha Rho Chi bronze medal, 1985. Mem. AIA, Soc. Calif. Pioneers. Republican. Episcopalian. Avocations: travel, photography, sport, the arts. Office: Mark Cavagnero Assocs 1045 Sansome St Ste 200 San Francisco CA 94111-1315

BLAKE, NORMAN, hotel executive; b. N.Y.C. m. Karen Blake; 3 children. MA, Purdue U., 1966, PhD (hon.), 1995. Various planning, mktg. and info. sys. positions GE, 1967-74, 76-79; exec. v.p. Top Inc., 1974, pres., 1975; v.p., gen. mgr. comml. and indsl. financing divsn. GE Credit Corp., 1979-81, exec. v.p. financing ops., 1981-84; chmn., CEO Heller Internat. Corp., Chgo., 1984-90; chmn., pres., CEO USF&G, Balt., 1991-97, Promus Hotel Corp., Memphis, 1999—. Bd. dirs. Enron Corp. Office: Promus Hotel Corp 755 Crossover Ln Memphis TN 38117-4900

BLAKE, PATRICIA, writer; d. Howard W. and Lucille (Page) Blake; m. Nicolas Nabokov, 1948 (div. 1955); m. Ronnie Dugger, 1983. BA, Smith Coll., Northampton, Mass., 1946. Reporter, corr. Life Mag., N.Y.C., 1953—62; assoc. editor Time Mag., N.Y.C., 1969—87; assoc. Davis Ctr. for Russian and Eurasian Studies, Harvard U., Cambridge, Mass., 1995—. Editor: Bedbug & Selected Poetry by Vladimir Mayakovsky, 1960, Halfway to the Moon: New Writing from Russia, 1964, Antiworlds: Poetry of Andrei Voznesensky, 1967, Dissonnant Voices in Soviet Literature, 1967, Writers in Russia by Max Hayward, 1980. Guggenheim Meml. fellow, 1980—81, St. Antony's Coll. fellow, 1981, Bunting Inst. fellow, Radcliffe Coll., 1998—99. Home: 115 Museum St Somerville MA 02143 Office: Davis Ctr for Russian/Eurasian Studies Harvard Univ 625 Massachusetts Ave Cambridge MA 02139

BLAKE, PETER JOST, architect; b. Berlin, Sept. 20, 1920; came to U.S., 1940, naturalized, 1944; Student, U. London, 1938; student in architecture, Regent St. Poly., London, 1939, U. Pa., 1941; BArch, Pratt Inst., 1949. Apprentice to Serge Chermayeff, Architect, London, 1938-39, George Howe, Oskar Stonorov and Louis Kahn, Architects, Phila., 1940-42; curator dept. architecture and indsl. design Mus. Modern Art, N.Y.C., 1948-50; assoc. editor Archtl. Forum, N.Y.C., 1950-61, mng. editor, 1961-64, editor-in-chief, 1965-72; ptnr. Peter Blake & Julian Neski, Architects, N.Y.C., 1956-60, James Baker & Peter Blake, Architects, N.Y.C., 1964-71; contbg. editor New York mag., N.Y.C., 1968-76; editor-in-chief Architecture Plus, N.Y.C., 1972-75; chmn. Sch. Architecture, Boston Archtl. Ctr., 1975-79; chmn. dept. architecture and planning Cath. U. Am., Washington, 1979-86, prof. architecture, 1986-91; prin. Peter Blake Architect, Washington, 1979-93; prof. emeritus Cath. U. Am., Washington, 1991—. Vis. critic, lectr. Harvard U., Cambridge, Mass., Yale U., New Haven, Cornell U., Ithaca, N.Y., Washington U., St. Louis, Tulane U., New Orleans, Pratt Inst., Cooper Union, New Sch. for Social Rsch., Bennington Coll., Columbia U., N.Y.C., Ill. Inst. Tech., U. Mich., Ann Arbor, also schs. of architecture in Hamburg, Aachen, Hanover, Braunschweig, and West Berlin, Fed. Republic of Germany, Vienna, Zurich, Halifax, N.S., Can., Maracaibo, Venezuela, Milan, and Hong Kong; chmn. Alcoa Conf. on Future of Housing, Boca Raton, Fla., 1957; chmn. Internat. Design Conf., Aspen, Colo., 1962, bd. dirs., 1965-73, advisor to bd., 1974-91; chmn. adv. panel on quality of Iranian housing, urban devel. and new town planning Shah of Iran, 1976; mem. U.S. del. Internat. Conf. on Theater Design, Berlin, 1960; participant Internat. Conf. on Urban Design, New Delhi, 1965, U.S./Yugoslav Conf. on Housing, Zagreb, 1974, Iran Internat. Congress on Architecture, Persepolis, 1974, U.S. del. Helsinki Cultural Forum, Budapest, Hungary, 1985; spkr. at seminar in Chandigarh, India, 1994. Author: The Master Builders, 1960, God's Own Junkyard, 1964, Form Follows Fiasco, 1977, No Place Like Utopia, 1993; contbr. articles to mags. and newspapers, important works include Hollis Unitarian Ch., Queens, N.Y., offices and warehouse, Queens, Temple Emanu-El, Livingston, N.J., Ford Found. Ideal Theater, Darrow Sch. Libr., New Lebanon, N.Y., Berlin-Tegel Airport Project, Manistee (Mich.) Town Planning Project, Max Planck Inst. Project, Berlin, Rehab. Ctr., Binghamton (N.Y.) State Hosp., Roundabout Theater, Stage One, N.Y.C., Neely Exptl. Theatre, Vanderbilt U., Nashville, P.R. Traveling Theatre, N.Y.C., Apt. Bldg., I.B.A., St. Lukas Ch., West Berlin; collaborator with Kevin Roche in Dept. State competition design new U.S. Embassy in Berlin, 1995. Served with AUS, 1943-47, ETO. Recipient Howard Myers award for archtl. journalism, 1960; Graham Found. Advanced Studies in Fine Arts fellow, 1962, several grants; Ford Found. grantee, 1960; disting. design fellow Nat. Endowment for Arts, 1984. Fellow AIA (Architecture Critics medal 1975). Home and Office: 80 Cedar St Apt 311 Branford CT 06405-3662

BLAKE, RICHARD E. sculptor, art educator; b. Phila., Feb. 24, 1943; s. Richard Blake and Marjorie Williams Blake; m. Nancy Rae Mata; children: Krystin Alexis, Brélan Kinzingér, Mia Mata. BFA, Temple U., 1967. Asst. prof. art West Chester (Pa.) U., 1975 98, prof. art, 1998—. Guest lectr. Phila. Coll. Art, 1971-74; drawing instr. Hussian Sch. Art, Phila., 1981-94; vis. lectr. Am. U., Washington, 1994. One-person shows include Fresno (Calif.) Mus. Art, 1999; exhibited in group shows Am. U., Watkins Gallery, Washington, 1995, Nat. Acad. Design, N.Y.C., 1996, Mid-Atlantic Art Exhbn., Norfolk, Va., 1997, Nat. Sculpture Soc., N.Y., 1997, 2000, Fine Arts Inst., Calif., 1997, Nat. Acad. Mus., N.Y., 1998. Recipient Meiselman award Nat. Acad. Mus., 1998, Merit award 10th Ann. Internat. Exhbn. Opus X, 1997, Profile award Manhattan Arts Internat., 1997, Bertelsen award Nat. Acad. Mus., 1996, Merit award Hoyt Nat. Exhbn., 1997, 1st prize 69th Ann. Juried Exhbn., 1996. Mem. Nat. Sculpture Soc. (Alex Ettl award 1996), N.Am. Sculpture Soc. (Cavanaugh award 1995). Home: 255 Harristown Rd Kinzer PA 17535

BLAKE, STANFORD, lawyer; b. Detroit, Sept. 13, 1948; s. Morris and Betty B.; m. Ellen Perkins, Mar. 5, 1978; children— Cary, Brandon, Stephanie. B.S., U. Fla. 1970; J.D., U. Miami, 1973. Bar: Fla. 1973, U.S. Dist. Ct. (so. dist.) Fla. 1973, U.S. Supreme Ct. 1980, U.S. Ct. Appeals (5th and 11th cirs.) 1981. Asst. pub. defender Dade County, Miami, Fla., 1973-78; ptnr. Todd, Rosinek & Blake, Miami, 1978-84, Rosinek & Blake, Miami, 1984-86; pvt. practice law, Miami, 1986-90; ptnr. Blake & Lida P.A., 1990—95; judge U.S. Dist. Ct. (11th cir.), Miami Dade, Fla., 1995—. Chmn. Jr. Maccabiah Games S. Fla., Miami, 1984—. Co-chmn. Dade County Outstanding Citizen award, 1986; v.p. congregation Bet Breira, 1987—. Mem. ABA, Fla. State Bar Assn. (chmn. grievance com. 1987), Fed. Bar Assn., Nat. Assn. Criminal Def. Lawyers, Fla. Criminal Def. Attys. Assn. (pres. 1982-83, chmn. 1985-90), So. Miami Kendall Bar Assn. (pres. 1984-85), B'nai B'rith (pres. 1980-81). Democrat. Jewish.

BLAKE, WILLIAM GEORGE, lawyer; b. Lamoni, Iowa, Dec. 10, 1949; s. George Charles and Mildred Lucille (Norman) B.; m. Barbara Kay Holseid, May 28, 1972; children: Jennifer Christine, Angela Sue. BA, Graceland Coll., Lamoni, 1972; JD, U. Nebr., 1975. Bar: Nebr. 1975, U.S. Dist. Ct. Nebr. 1975. Asst. city atty. City of Lincoln (Nebr.), 1975-79, chief asst. city atty., 1979-84; assoc. Pierson, Ackerman Fitchett, Akin & Hunzeker, Lincoln, 1984-85; ptnr. Pierson, Fitchett, Hunzeker, Blake & Loftis, Lincoln, 1986—. Judge Nebr. Commn. on Indsl. Rels., 2000—. Vice chmn. Lincoln Parks and Recreation Bd., 1987-88, chmn., 1989-91; mem. Lincoln Parks and Recreation Found., bd. dirs. 1992—, chmn. 1996-97, 2001—, vice chmn., 1998-2000; judge Nebr. Commn. Indsl. Rels., 2000—. Mem. ABA, Nebr. Bar Assn., Lincoln-Lancaster County Bar Assn. Republican. Mem. Comty. of Christ. Avocation: mountaineering. Office: Pierson Fitchett Hunzeker Blake & Loftis PO Box 95109 Lincoln NE 68509-5109 E-mail: wblake@pierson-law.com.

BLAKE, WILLIAM HENRY, credit and public relations consultant; b. Jasonville, Ind., Feb. 18, 1913; s. Straude and Cora (Pope) B.; m. Helen Elizabeth Platt, Jan. 2, 1937 (dec. Feb. 1990); children: William Henry, Allen Howard. Student, Knox Coll., 1932-35; BS, U. Ill., 1936, MS, 1941, postgrad., 1946; student, NYU, 1950-51, Am. U., 1955-56, 1958; grad., Columbia U. Grad. Sch. Consumer Credit, 1956, Northeastern Inst., Yale U., 1957. Cert. assn. exec. Tchr. Champaign (Ill.) Pub. Schs., 1936-41; exec. sec. Ill. Soc. CPAs, Chgo., 1941-44; dean men, assoc. prof. bus. adminstrn. Catawba Coll., 1947-51; dir. rsch. Nat. Consumer Fin. Assn., Washington, 1954-59; exec. v.p. Internat. Consumer Credit Assn., St. Louis, 1959-78; pres. Consumer Trends Inc., also Blake Enterprises, cons., 1978—. Cons. Decatur Consumer Credit Assn., 1979-88; adminstr. Soc. Cert. Consumer Credit Execs., 1961-78 Author: Good Things of Life on Credit, 1960, rev., 1975, How to Use Consumer Credit Wisely, 1963, rev., 1975, Home Study Courses in Credit and Collections, 1968, Human Relations, 1969, Communications, 1970, Retail Credit and Collections, rev., 1974, Adminstrative Office Management, 1972, Consumer Credit Management, 1974; pub.: Consumer Trends Newsletter, The Credit World mag. Mem. pres.'s adv. cabinet Southeastern U.; adviser Office Edn. Assn.; chmn. public relations com. Ill. Heart Assn., 1979-85; bd. dirs. Salvation Army, Decatur, 1979— ; mem. fund raising com. Sch. Edn., U. Ill., 1979-84; chmn. bd. trustees Alta Deana div. University City, 1970-73, congressional liaison, 1959-78; trustee Internat. Consumer Credit Assn. Ins. Trust and Retirement Program, 1960-78; mem. Session Westminster Presbyn. Ch., Decatur, 1971-84, fin. con., 1981-84, 89-92, trustee. 1981-84 ; apptd. by mayor to Decatur Aging Adv. Commn., 1991-94. Served to lt. USNR, 1944-47; lt. comdr. 1951-54, ret. Named Man of Yr., Mo. Consumer Credit Assn., 1977; recipient Knox Coll. Scroll of Honor, Knox-Lombard 50 Yr. Club, Galesburg, 1991, Alumni Achievement award Knox Coll., 1994, Class Agt. award, 1995. Mem. Credit Grantors Assn. Can. (bd. dirs. 1959-72), U.S. C. of C. (mem. banking and currency com. 1968-71, mem. trade assn. com. 1964-67), Am. Soc. Assn. Execs. (bd. dirs. 1965-66), Pub. Rels. Soc. Am. (chpt. sec.-treas. 1979-85), Internat. Platform Assn., Washington Trade Assn. Execs., Am. Pub. Rels. Assn. (nat. treas. 1960-61, chpt. pres. 1958-59), U. Ill. Alumni Assn., Press Club St. Louis, Capitol Hill Club (Washington), Exchequer Club (Washington), Rotary (pres. Decatur chpt. 1985-86, Paul Harris fellow 1984, Svc. Above Self award 1996), Phi Sigma Kappa. Republican. Home: 5 Edgewood Ct Decatur IL 62522-1860

BLAKE-INADA, LOUIS MICHAEL, cardiologist, researcher; b. Osaka, Japan, June 4, 1956; came to U.S., 1959; s. Edward Kneeland, Sr. and Setsuko (Inada) Blake. BA in Biochemistry and Molecular Biology, U. Calif., Santa Barbara, 1979; MD, Case Western Res. U., 1983. Diplomate in internal medicine and cardiovasc. diseases; Am. Bd. Internal Medicine; diplomate Am. Bd. Nuc. Medicine. Intern in gen. surgery Letterman Army Med. Ctr., San Francisco, 1983-84; resident in internal medicine Sch. Medicine Stanford U., Calif., 1988-90, resident in nuc. medicine, 1990-92, chief resident in nuc. medicine, 1991-92; fellow in cardiology Calif. Pacific Med. Ctr., San Francisco, 1992-93; fellow in cardiology, cardiac imaging U. Calif., San Francisco, 1993-95; fellow in invasive cardiology U. N.Mex. Health Sci. Ctr., 1997-98; asst. prof. medicine (cardiology), asst. prof. radiology U. Nev. Sch. of Medicine, Reno, 1998-2000; dir. echocardiography lab. Sierra Nevada VA Med. Ctr., Reno, 1999-2000; dir. nuclear cardiology Sierra Nevada Med. Ctr., Reno, 1999-2000; staff cardiologist Swedish Heart Inst., Seattle, 2000—. Contbr. articles to med. jours. including Am. Jour. Radiology, Jour. Nuc. Medicine, others; contbr. editor Jour. Am. Coll. Cardiology, 1993-95. Capt. U.S. Army, 1979-88. Recipient Evelyn Neizer srch. fellow, Stanford U., 1992. Fellow ACP, Am. Coll. Angiology, Am. Coll. Cardiology; mem. Am. Coll. Nuc. Physicians, Am. Heart Assn. (coun. on cardiovascular radiology), Am. Heart Assn. (coun. on vascular biology, coun. on cardiovascular and critical care medicine 1999—. coun. on vascular and molecular biology 1999—), Soc. Nuc. Medicine, Assn. Military Surgeons of the U.S., Stanford U. Alumni (life). Home: PO Box 1805 Edmonds WA 98020 Office: Swedish Med Ctr Seattle WA 98122

BLAKELEY, LINDA, psychologist, speaker; b. Bklyn., July 26, 1941; d. Charles and Blanche (Josephson) Berkow; m. Dec. 17, 1961 (div. 1983); children: Stacey, Scott. BA, UCLA, 1964; MA, Calif. State U., Northridge, 1977; PhD, Calif. Grad. Inst., 1985. Founder, dir. Parents Sharing Custody, Beverly Hills, Calif., 1984—87; pvt. practice self esteem, eating disorders,

leadership stress mgmt. Positive Self Images, Beverly Hills, 1984—95. Producer, host interview/talk show. Author: ABC's of Stress Management, 1989, Do It with Love-Positive Parenting After Divorce, 1988, (audio tape) Success Strategies, 1992; one-woman show The Magic Dress, 1998. Mem. adv. bd. Nat. Coun. Alcoholism and Drug Abuse, 1991-92. Mem.: Calif. Psychol. Assn. (state bd. dirs. media com. 1989—92, chair-elect media divsn.), Bulimia Assn. Disorders, Nat. Assn. Anorexia, Beverly Hills C. of C. (pres. women's network 1989—90, chmn. health care com. 1989). Avocations: writing, dancing, acting. Office: 420 S Beverly Dr Ste 100 Beverly Hills CA 90212-4410 Fax: (310) 578-2434. E-mail: Drlindablakeley@aol.com.

BLAKELEY-PEREZ, JOSE ALFREDO, software architect; b. Cd. Madero, Mexico, Dec. 17, 1956; s. Jose A. Blakeley-Arrieta and Josefina Pérez-Orozco; m. Lucinda Eva Ruiz-Gonzalez, Aug. 13, 1981; 1 child, Jose Alfredo Blakeley-Ruiz. Computer sys. engr., ITESM, Monterrey, Mexico, 1978; M in Math. (computer sci.), U. Waterloo, Canada, 1983; PhD in Computer Sci., U. Waterloo, 1987. Asst. prof. Ind. U., Bloomington, 1987-89; tech. staff Tex. Insts., Dallas, 1989-94; software design engr. Microsoft Corp., Redmond, Wash., 1994—. Assoc. editor Asssn. Computing Machinery, N.Y., 1993—. Contbg. author: (books) Modern Database Systems, Component Database Systems, Database Systems Concepts, 2001; contbr. articles to profl. jours.; 4 patents in field. Avocations: soccer, running. Office: Microsoft Corp One Microsoft Way Redmond WA 98052-6399 Fax: 425-706-7329. E-mail: joseb@microsoft.com.

BLAKELY, ALLISON, history educator; b. Clinton, Ala., Mar. 31, 1940; s. Ed Walton and Alice Blakely; m. Shirley Ann Reynolds, July 5, 1968; children: Shantel, Andrei. Student, Oreg. State Coll., Corvallis, 1958-60; BA, U. Oreg., 1962; MA, U. Calif., Berkeley, 1964, PhD, 1971. Instr. history Stanford (Calif.) U., 1970-71; asst. prof. history Howard U., Washington, 1971-77, assoc. prof. history, 1977-87, assoc. dean Coll. Liberal Arts, 1989-90, dir. honors program, Coll. Liberal Arts, 1990-93, prof. history, 1987-2001, Boston U., 2001—. Reader and test devel. cons., Ednl. Testing Svc., Princeton, N.J., 1974-2001; fellowship selection panelist, Am. Coun. Learned Socs., 2001, NEH, 1979-80, chair fellowship selection panel, Ford Found., N.Y.C., 1992-94; world history nat. stds. for panelist, Coun. Basic Edn., Washington, 1995-96. Author: Russia and the Negro: Blacks in Russian History and Thought, 1986 (Am. Book award, 1988), Blacks in the Dutch World: The Evolution of Racial Imagery in a Modern Society, 1994; contbr. articles to profl. jours., chpts. to books. Mem. Dem. Nat. Com., Washington, 1982—; pub. mem. Fgn. Svc. Selection Bd., U.S. State Dept., 1995. Mem. Am. Hist. Assn. (nom. com. 1999—, chmn. com. on minority historians 1993-97), World History Assn., Am. Assn. Advancement of Slavic Studies, U.S. Fgn. Svc. Pub. Mems. Assn. (bd. dirs.), Phi Beta Kappa Soc. (sen. at large 1993—). Democrat. Unitarian Universalist. Avocations: music, swimming, tai chi. Home: 1 Sunnyside Rd Silver Spring MD 20910 Office: Boston U 226 Bay State Rd Boston MA 02215 Fax: 617-353-0455; Office Fax: 617-358-1420. E-mail: ablakely@bu.edu.

BLAKELY, EDWARD JAMES, economics educator; b. San Bernardino, Calif., Apr. 21, 1938; s. Edward Blakely and Josephine Elizabeth (Carter) Proctor; m. Maaike C. Vander Sleesen, July 1, 1971; children: Pieta C., Brette D. BA, U. Calif., Riverside, 1960; MA, U. Calif., Berkeley, 1964; MBA, Pasadena Nazerene Coll., 1967; EdD in Edn. and Mgmt., UCLA, 1971. Mgr. Pacific Telephone Co., Pasadena, Calif., 1960-65; exec. dir. Western Community Action Tng., Los Angeles, 1965-69; spl. asst. U.S. Dept. State, Washington, 1969-71; asst. chancellor, assoc. prof. U. Pitts., 1971-74; assoc. dean and prof. applied econs. and behavioral scis. U. Calif., Davis, 1974-77, asst. v.p. Berkeley, 1977-85, prof., chmn. dept. city and regional planning, 1985—; dean Milano Sch. Mgmt. and Urban Policy New Sch. U., N.Y.C. Expert advisor Orgn. Econ. Cooperation and Devel., asst. to Mayor Elihu Harris, City of Oakland. Author: Rural Communities in Advanced Industrial Society, Community Development Research, Taking Local Development Initiative, Planning Local Economic Development SAGE, 1988, Separate Societies: Poverty and Inequality in U.S. Cities (Paul Davidoff award 1993), 1992, Fortress America: Gated Communities in the U.S., 1998. Chmn. fin. com. Pvt. Industry Council of Oakland (Calif.), 1978-85; vice chmn. Ecole Bilingue Sch., Berkeley, 1982-85, chmn., 1988—; chmn. bd. Royce Sch., Oakland, Calif., 1988—; sec., treas. Econ. Devel. Corp., Oakland, 1983; expert advisor Orgn. Econ. Corp. and Devel., Paris, 1986; apptd. to pres. trust Pres. Bill Clinton, 1997—; mayoral candidate City of Oakland, Calif., 1998. Served to 1st lt. USAF, 1961-63. Named 125th Anniversary Prof., U. Calif. at Riverside Berkeley Campus, 1992; named to, Athlete Hall of Fame, U. Calif. Riverside Alumni Press, 1992, Pres. Trust by Pres. Bill Clinton, 1997; recipient San Francisco Found. award, 1991, Paul Davidoff award, 1993, Rsch. award, Cmty. Devel. Soc., 2002; fellow, German Acad. Exch., 1984, Urban Studies Australian Inst. Urban St., 1985, John Simon Guggenheim fellow, 1995—96; scholar Fulbright St. scholar, Internat. Exch. Scholars, 1986. Fellow Nat. Acad. Pub. Adminstrn.; mem. Cmty. Devel. Soc. (bd. dirs. 1980-84, svc. award 1983, disting. svc. award 1990), Calif. Local Econ. Devel. (standing com. 1980-81), Am. Planning Assn. (accreditation com.), Am. Assn. Collegiate Schs. of Planning, Nat. Assn. State and Land Grant Colls. (exec. com. 1987), Phi Delta Kappa, Lambda Alpha. Clubs: Rueful Order. Office: New Sch U Sch Mgmt and Urban Policy New York NY 10011

BLAKELY, ROBERT GEORGE, lawyer; b. Beloit, Wis., Aug. 21, 1947; s. George Knowlton and Catherine Lucille (Mitchell) B.; m. Susan Bradford Amsler; children: Robert, Alison; m. Louise A. Delahoyde. BA, Denison U., 1969; JD, Marquette U., 1972. Bar: Wis. 1972, U.S. Dist. Ct. (ea. and we. dists.) Wis. 1972. Assoc. Blakely & Long, Beloit, Wis., 1972-74, Hansen Law Firm, Beloit, 1974-80; ptnr. Hansen, Eggers & Blakely, Beloit, 1980—. Instr. real estate law and continuing edn. Mem. Wis. State Bar (joint realtors com. 1997—), Beloit Jaycees (pres. 1972-84, Outstanding Young Man 1975). Republican. Congregationalist. Avocations: skiing, mountain biking. Address: 416 College St Ste A Beloit WI 53511-6310

BLAKEMAN, CAROL ANN, medical/surgical nursing educator; b. Jacksonville, Fla., Aug. 17, 1954; d. John Raymond and Marion Alice (Lasher) B.; m. Key Miller Sargent, Mar. 22, 1984. AA, Fla. Jr. Coll., Jacksonville, 1974; BSN, U. South Fla., 1976; MSN, U. Fla., 1989. RN advanced RN practitioner, Fla. Staff and head nurse Bapt. Med. Ctr., Jacksonville, Fla., 1976-84; staff nurse Winter Haven Hosp., Fla., 1984-88; instr., assoc. prof. Ctrl. Fla. C.C., Ocala, Fla., 1988—. On-call endoscopy nurse, Jacksonville, 1982—83; instr. Polk C.C., Winter Haven, Fla., 1987; cons. Student Nurses Assn. Ctrl. Fla. C.C., Ocala, 1989—. BCLS instr., 1988—91; judge competition Health Occupation Students Am., Orlando and Ocala, 1989—95; health examiner Nat. Youth Sports Program, Orlando, 1987; mem. C.C. Faculty Leaders Coalition Fla., 1997—2001, sec., 1999—2000. Mem. ANA, Fla. Nurses Assn., Dist. III Nurses Assn. (treas. 1993, 99—, pres. 1994-96), Fla. Nursing Students Assn. (hon. life mem.), Sigma Theta Tau, Phi Theta Kappa, Fla. Assoc. of Cmty. Coll. Democrat. Roman Catholic. Avocations: crafts, reading, bowling. Home: 206 SE 44th Terr Ocala FL 34471 E-mail: cblake3493@aol.com.

BLAKEMAN, JOHN CHARLES, political science educator; b. Middlesboro, Ky., June 1, 1966; s. Charles Coakley and Janet Rose Blakeman; m. Kathryn Hohman Hohman, June 10, 1965; children: Margaret Elizabeth, Angus Andrew. BA, Wake Forest U., 1988; MSc, London Sch. of Econs., 1989; PhD, U. of Va., 1996. Sec., treas. Blakeman Restaurant Svcs., Middleboro, Ky., 1988—94; v.p. Fodeskin, Inc., Middlesboro, 1991—95; instr. Sweet Briar (Va.) Coll., 1993, U. of Va., Charlottesville, 1994—96; asst. prof. Baylor U., Waco, Tex., 1996—2003, U. of Wis., Stevens Point, Wis., 2003—. Editor: (textbook) The American Constitutional Experience; author: (acad. monograph) The Bible in the Park, 2003; contbr. acad. ency. Polit. commentator Local ABC/CBS/NBC News affiliates, Waco, 1996—2003; vol. referee Tex. Soc. of Rugby Referees, Dallas, 2002; vol. coach Baylor U. Men's Rugby Football Club, Waco, 1996—2003, Maastricht U. Rugby Football Club, Netherlands, 2001; coach USA Rugby Collegiate Divsn. II Nat. Championship Team, Baylor U. Men's Rugby Club. Named Phi Beta Kappa Favorite Prof., Baylor U. Phi Beta Kappa, 1999, 1999; recipient Jr. fellowship, Soc. of Fellows, U. of Va., 1993. Mem.: Am. Polit. Sci. Assn., USA Rugby, Waco Geezers Rugby Football Club. Episcopalian. Avocations: fishing, travel, rugby. Office: U Wis 2100 Main St Stevens Point WI 54481-3897 E-mail: john.blakeman-alumni@lse.ac.uk.

BLAKEMAN, ROBYN L. advertising executive, educator; b. Omaha, Sept. 26, 1958; d. Harold Raymond and Gayle Marie Blakeman. BSc, U. Nebr., 1980; MLA, So. Meth. U., 1996. Art dir. Ad Agy., Dallas, 1984—88; instr. Art Sch., Dallas, 1987—88; asst. prof. advertising, graphic art So. Meth. U., Dallas, 1997—98; asst. prof. West Va. U., Morgantown, 1998—. Chair advt. program W. Va. U., Morgnatown, 1999—, coord. student affairs and curriculum, 1998—. Named Journalism Prof. of Yr., Perely Isaac Reed Sch. Journalism, 2000—01. Mem.: Kappa Tau Alpha. Office: West Va Univ PO Box 6010 Morgantown WV 26506

BLAKEMAN, ROYAL EDWIN, lawyer; b. N.Y.C., June 9, 1923; s. Jesse Herbert and Edythe Roslyn (Siegel) B.; m. Edith Hughes, Sept. 1, 1945; children: Carol, Elizabeth, Forrest. BA, Hofstra Coll., 1942; LLB cum laude, NYU, 1947. Bar: N.Y. 1947, U.S. Dist. Ct. (so. dist.) N.Y. 1956, U.S. Ct. Appeals (2d cir.) 1972, Calif. 1973, U.S. Supreme Ct. 1973. Pvt. practice, Lindenhurst, N.Y., 1947-51; assoc. Jack J. Katz, N.Y.C., 1951-53, Marshall Bratter, Greene & Klein, N.Y.C., 1953-55; ptnr. Marshall, Bratter, Greene, Allison & Tucker (specializing in theatrical law), N.Y.C., 1955-81; of counsel Pryor, Cashman, Sherman & Flynn, N.Y.C., 1981-91, Robert M. Blakeman & Assocs., Valley Stream, N.Y., 1991—; gen. counsel Nat. Acad. Rec. Arts and Scis. Officer, dir. Mark Goodson Prodns. Mem. editl. bd. TV Quar. Mem. TV com. Anti Defamation League, N.Y. Served to chief petty officer U.S. Maritime Service, 1942-46. Recipient George M. Esterbrook Disting. Svc. award Hofstra Alumni Assn., 1966. Mem. Nat. Acad. TV Arts and Scis. (pres., bd. govs. N.Y.C. chpt.; past nat. pres., trustee), Nat. Youth Coun., Nat. Acad. Rec. Arts and Scis. (gen. counsel 1977-2002, Trustees award 2003), Dads Club (Long Beach) (pres. 1955). Avocations: golf, bridge, music. Home: 750105B Lido Blvd Long Beach NY 11561-5236 Office: Robert M Blakeman & Assocs 108 S Franklin Ave Valley Stream NY 11580-6105 E-mail: rmbassoc98@aol.com.

BLAKEMORE, CLAUDE COULEHAN, banker; b. Los Angeles, Apr. 26, 1909; s. Claude Payne and Agnes C. (Coulehan) B.; m. Violet E. Alt, Aug. 27, 1937; children: Susan Blakemore Daniels, Bruce A. Student, UCLA, 1928-29, U. Iowa, 1929; grad., Stonier Sch. Banking, Rutgers U., 1951. With First Nat. Bank Santa Ana, Calif., 1930-41; comptroller of currency, asst. nat. bank examiner, 1941-42; bank examiner Fed. Res. Bank San Francisco, 1942-45; with First Nat. Bank San Diego, 1945-70, sr. v.p., 1962-64, pres., 1964-70, chief exec. officer, 1966-70; pres, chief exec. officer So. Calif. First Nat. Corp., 1969-71. Pres., trustee USF Investors; dir. Rice, Hall, James & Assos., Percy H. Goodwin Co., Western Bldg. Spltys. Bd. dirs. San Diego County Med. Rehab. Center Assn.; bd. dirs., pres. San Diego County council Boy Scouts Am.; bd. dirs., treas., chmn. bd. San Diego Hall of Sci.; bd. dirs. San Diego Symphony. Mem. Am. Bankers Assn. (exec. council), Calif. Bankers Assn. (pres., dir.), Sigma Pi. Home: 1822 Altamira Pl San Diego CA 92103-1202

BLAKEMORE, MICHAEL HOWELL, theatre and film director; b. Sydney, June 18, 1928; s. Conrad and Una Mary (Litchfield) B.; m. Shirley Bush, 1960 (div.); 1 child; m. Tanya McCallin, 1986, 2 children. Student, Kings Sch., Sydney U., Royal Acad. of Dramatic Art. Actor Birmingham Repertory Theatre, Shakespeare Meml. Theatre, 1952-66; co-dir. Glasgow Citizen's Theatre, 1966-68; assoc. artistic dir. Nat. Theatre, London, 1971-76; dir. Players, N.Y.C., 1978; resident dir. Lyric Theatre Hammersmith, London, 1980. Dir.: A Day in the Death of Joe Egg, 1967, Arturo Ui, 1969, The National Health, 1969, Long Day's Journey into Night, 1971, Forget Me Not Lane, 1971, The Front Page, 1972, Macbeth, 1972, The Cherry Orchard, 1973, Design for Living, 1973, Plunder, 1975, Knuckle, Deathtrap, Made in Bangkok, Separate Tables, 1976, Privates on Parade, 1977 (also film, 1982), Candida, 1977, Make and Break, 1980, Travelling North, 1980, The Wild Duck, 1980, All My Sons, 1981, Noises Off, 1982 (Drama Desk award 1983-84), Benefactors, 1984, Lettic and Lovage, 1987, Uncle Vanya, 1988, Tosca (Welsh Nat. Opera), 1992, The Sisters Rosenweig, 1994, City of Angels, 1989, Lettice and Lovage, 1990, After the Fall, 1990, The Ride Down Mount Morgan, 1991, Life, 1997, Copenhagen, 1998, Alarms and Excursions, 1998, Kiss Me Kate (Broadway, 1999) (Tony Award, Drama Desk award, TV 2003), Copenhagen Broadway, 2000 (Tony award, Drama Desk award), off-broadway: Death Defying Acts, 1995; writer, dir.: (film) A Personal History of the Australian Surf, 1981, also actor, (Std. Film award); actor, writer, dir. Country Life, 1994; author: Next Season, 1969, actor: (TV) Countdown to Woomera, 1961, Catch Us if You Can, 1965, The Last Bastion for chan. 10 TV in Australia, 1984. Named Best Dir. London Critics, 1972, Office of British Empire, 2002. Avocation: surfing. Home: 18 Upper Park Rd London NW3 2UP England Office: Lantz Office In 200 W 57th St #503 New York NY 10019*

BLAKENEY, ALLAN EMRYS, Canadian government official, lawyer; b. Bridgewater, N.S., Can., Sept. 7, 1925; s. John Cline and Bertha (Davies) B.; m. Mary Elizabeth Schwartz, 1950 (dec. 1957); m. Anne Louise Gorham, May 1959; children: Barbara, Hugh, David, Margaret. BA, Dalhousie U., 1945, LLB, 1947, LLD (hon.); BA (Rhodes scholar), Oxford U., 1949, MA, 1955; DCL (hon.), Mount Allison U.; LLD (hon.), York U., Toronto, U. Western Ont., London, 1991, U. Regina, 1993, U. Sask., 1995. Bar: N.S. 1950, Sask. 1951. Queen's counsel, 1961; sec. to govt. fin. office Govt. Sask., 1950-55; chmn. Sask. Securities Commn., 1955-58; ptnr. Davidson, Davidson & Blakeney, Regina, Sask., 1958-60, Griffin, Blakeney, Beke, Koskie & Lueck, Regina, 1964-70; premier of Sask., 1971-82; Mem. Sask. Legislature, 1960-88. Leader of the opposition Sask. Legislature, 1970-71, 82-87; prof. Osgoode Hall Law Sch., York U., 1988-90, U. Sask., 1990—; minister of edn., Sask., 1960-61, provincial treas., 1961-62, minister pub. health, 1962-64; mem. Royal Commn. on Aboriginal Peoples, 1991-93. Decorated officer Order of Can., Sask. Order of Merit. Fellow Royal Soc. Can. Home: 1752 Prince of Wales Ave Saskatoon SK Canada S7K 3E5 Office: U Saskatchewan Coll Law 15 Campus Dr Saskatoon SK Canada S7N 5A6

BLAKENEY, KAREN ELIZABETH, social service and community health program executive, consultant; b. Evanston, Ill., June 27, 1953; d. Elwood Francis and Irene Loretta (Filloon) Garlick; m. Lawrence Ray Blakeney, Sept. 6, 1975 (div.); life ptnr. Ydalia Granado; children: Jesse Alan, Aaron Paul. Cert. in Christian edn., Angeles Bible Coll., L.A., 1972; BA in Anthropology, Calif. State U., Long Beach, 1978; MS in Counseling Psychology, Mt. St. Mary's Coll., LA., 1992; cert. in non-profit mgmt., U. So. Calif., 1998. Commd. pastor Hosanna Ministries, 1994. Archaeologist VTM Corp., Vandenburg AFB, Calif., 1979-81; archaeologist, Arroyo Grande, Calif., 1981-82; acct. Airport Datsun/Volvo, Santa Maria, Calif., 1982-83; adminstrn. mgr. Concord Sys., Reseda, Calif., 1983-86; ins. broker Prudential Ins. Co., Torrance, Calif., 1986-87; mgr. legal compliance dept. G.J. Sullivan Cos., L.A., 1987-92; psychotherapy intern Hosanna Ministries, Santa Monica, Calif., 1990-95; children's social worker Dept. Children and Family Svcs., L.A., 1994-96; dir. social work Internat. Foster Family Agy., Carson, Calif., 1996-97; dir. youth svcs. L.A. Gay and Lesbian Ctr., Hollywood, Calif., 1997-99; dir. programs Chinatown Svc. Ctr., L.A., 1999—2002; exec. dir. Schutrum-Piteo Found., Burbank, Calif., 2002—03; CEO, pres. Blackwolf, LLC Consulting, 2001—; exec. dir. Grace Ctr., Pasadena, 2003—. Lectr. Calif. Poly. Inst. Archaeol. Field Sch., Mission San Antonio de Padua, 1978-81; co-founder, exec. dir. Inst. for trauma Intervention, L.A., 1993-96. Author: (poetry) Sacred Journey, 1995, Ydalia's Song, 1998. Bd. dirs. Art To Grow On, San Pedro, Calif., 1992-94, Desert Stream Ministries/AIDS Resource Ministry, L.A., 1985-91; mem. parent-tchr. adv. bd. Park Western Elem. Sch., San Pedro, 1993-94; dir. mem. Consortium for Homeless Youth Svcs., Hollywood, 1997-99; rep. L.A. County Svc. Planning Area Dist. 4 Coun., 1999-2002; mem. Asian-Pacific Islander police adv. com. L.A. Police Dept., 2000; mem. Nat. Network of Youth, 1997-2000; mem. Calif. Child, Youth and Family Coalition, 1998-2003; bd. dirs. Coalition Against Slave Trafficking, 1999-2002, Coalition for Cmty. Health, 2001-03, Schotrom-Pited Found., 2003-; mem. Dept. Pub. Social Svcs. long-term self sufficiency steering com. L.A. County, 2000-02, bd. dirs. Schutrum-Piteo Found., 2003-. Mem. Calif. Assn. Marriage and Family Therapists, Calif. Stat U.-Long Beach Anthropology Alumni Assn. (alumni bd. 1984-85). Avocations: artist, writing. Office: Blackwolf Cons LLC 3838 Brunswick Ave Los Angeles CA 90039- E-mail: kb0001@msn.com.

BLAKENEY, MARGARET ELIZABETH FLEMING, counselor, educator; b. McComb, Miss., Jan. 23, 1961; d. Hiram Lee Fleming and Lucy Joe Ann Fleming Curran; m. Ray Edward Blakeney, May 26, 1984; children: Matthew, Lacey. MEd, Miss. Coll., 1985, ednl. specialist degree in counseling, 2002. Tchr. Crystal Springs (Miss.) Elem., 1983—2002; acad. educator, counselor Miss. Job Ctr., Crystal Springs, 2002—. Southern Baptist. Avocations: travel, ocean, mountains, painting, reading. Home: 3055 Millsaps Rd Crystal Springs MS 39059 Office: Copiah County Schs 254 Gallatin St Hazlehurst MS 39083 E-mail: magsb47@hotmail.com.

BLAKE RAMOS, DEBRA BARBARA, writer; b. Bklyn., June 17, 1959; d. Rebecca Simmons and Jack Blake; m. Manuel Joseph Ramos, Apr. 2, 1957; children: Michael Young, Shameeka Shontele Ramos, Sarah Barbara Ramos, Abraham Joseph Ramos. Bus. degree, N.Y. Bus. Sch., 1981. Telephone technician, 1983; sec., 1984; writer, 1980—2003, 2003. Author (artist): (book) A New Birth Of Poetry (Editor's Choice award, 2001), Let Them Cry (Editor's Choice award, 2002), (CD) Serenity and Passion, 2000, Let Them Cry, 2002; songwriter Hill Top Record, 2001—03. Mem.: Internat. Soc. Of Poets (hon. Internat. Poet of Merit award 2001).

BLAKESLEE, DIANE PUSEY, financial planner; b. West Chester, Pa., Apr. 12, 1933; d. Norman S. and Leona (Ruth) Pusey; m. Earle B. Blakeslee, June 11, 1954; children: Samuel N., Barbara Blakeslee Porteous, David E., Ruth D. Blakeslee Overton. BA, Hood Coll., 1988. CLU; cert. fin. planner. Dist. mgr. Tchrs. Mgmt. and Investment Corp., Newport Beach, Calif., 1972-78, Walt Becker, Inc., Fresno, Calif., 1978-80; pres. Blakeslee & Blakeslee, San Luis Obispo, Calif., 1980—. Small firm adv. bd. NASD; statutory disqualification bd. Author: (column for Sr. Mag. and syndicated for radio) Dollars and Sense; co-editor: How to Survive on $50,000 to $150,000 a Year, 1984; host monthly TV program Welcome to The World of Financial Planning, 1984-87. Bd. dirs., treas. Pvt. Industry Coun., 1979-84; bd. dirs., treas. Child Devel. Ctr., 1980-83; bd. dirs. Cuesta Coll. Found., 1985—; bd. dirs., 1st v.p. San Luis Obispo Art Assn.; 1st v.p. San Luis Obispo Estate Planning Coun.; bd. dirs. Cert. Fin. Planners Bd. of Standards, Ethics and Profl. Rev., 1993-97; regent Coll. Fin. Planning, 1980-85; chmn. planned giving com. Cuesta Coll., 1984-86, pres. found. Named bd. mem. of Yr., Econ. Opportunity Coun., San Luis Obispo County, 1983, Woman of Achievement of Yr. cen. Calif. region Bus. and Profl. Women, 1985-86, Nat. Cert. Fin. Planner of Yr., 1986; recipient Disting. Alumni award George Sch., 1991. Mem.: NASD (dist. 2 com. 1999—2002, statutory disqualification com. 1999—, small firm adv. com. 2000—), Bur. Nat. Affairs Tax Mgmt. (bd. advisors 1986—), Nat. Life Underwriters Assn., Inst. Cert. Fin. Planners (chmn. pub. rels., bd. dirs. 1978—82), Internat. Assn. Fin. Planners, Womens' Network (San Luis Obispo). Republican. Mem. Soc. Of Friends. Avocations: hiking, gardening, sketching. Home: 88 Country Club Dr San Luis Obispo CA 93401-8908 Office: Blakeslee & Blakeslee 299 Madonna Rd San Luis Obispo CA 93405-5430

BLAKESLEE, EDWARD EATON, lawyer, insurance executive; b. N.Y.C., July 23, 1921; s. Edward Eaton and Ada Rainbow (Harris) B.; m. Janice Callaghan, Mar. 19, 1944; children— Edward, David. LLB cum laude, NYU, 1947, LLM in Taxation, 1957; grad. exec. program in bus. adminstrn., Columbia U., 1966. Bar: N.Y. 1947. Atty. Mut. Life Ins. Co. N.Y., 1947-69, 2d v.p., gen. solicitor, 1969-73, v.p., gen. solicitor, 1973, gen. counsel, 1974-85; gen. counsel, bd. dirs. Am. Life Ins. Co. of N.Y., 1986-88; mng. dir., chief exec. officer Sargasso Mut. Ins. Co., Ltd., Hamilton, Bermuda, 1986-93, also bd. dirs. Pres. Securities Investors Indemnification Co., Ltd., Hamilton, Bermuda, 1989-90; spl. counsel Rosenman & Colin, 1990-92; of counsel Shea & Gould, 1992-94, Werner & Kennedy, 1994-99; assessor Ins. Marketplace Stds. Assn., 1997—; cons. Nat. Exec. Svc. Corps, 2001—. With AC U.S. Army, 1943-46. Mem. ABA, N.Y. State Bar Assn., Assn. Bar City of N.Y., Assn. Life Ins. Counsel, NYU Alumni Fedn. (pres. 1981-83, dir. emeritus), Fellows Am. Bar Found. (life mem.), NYU Law Alumni Assn., Univ. Club. Home: 495 Birchtree Rd Oradell NJ 07649-1303

BLAKESLEE, WESLEY DANIEL, lawyer, consultant; b. Wilkes-Barre, Pa., May 28, 1947; s. Daniel Leo and Ann Blakeslee; m. Georgia Carroll Croft, July 28, 1973; children: Jaime Kiersten, Christopher Justin, Shaun Michael. BS, Pa. State U., 1969; JD, U. Md.-Balt., 1976. Bar: Md. 1976, U.S. Dist. Ct. Md. 1977, U.S. Tax Ct. 1984. Sys. analyst NASA, Greenbelt, Md., 1969-76; assoc. Semmes, Bowen & Semmes, Balt., 1976-78; pvt. practice Dulany & Davis, Westminster, Md., 1978-83; prin. Wesley D. Blakeslee, P.C., Westminster, 1984—2000; of counsel Blakeslee & Wallace PC, Westminster, 2000—. Assoc. Gen. Couns., Johns Hopkins Univ., 1999—, lectr., dir. computer devel. U. Md. Law Sch., Balt., 1984-89; dir. Union Nat. Bank, 1988-2000. Co-author, editor: Maryland District Court Practice, 1981, rev. 1983; author: Understanding Computers, 1984, 3d edit., 2003; co-author: Computers, 1984, UCITA, 2000. Bd. govs. Md. Law Sch. Fund, Balt., 1982—90. Mem. ABA, Fed. Bar Assn. (treas. Balt. chpt. 1984-90), Md. Bar Assn. (young lawyers sect. coun. 1982-84, outstanding svc. award 1984, litigation sect. coun. 1982—, chair 1995), Carroll County Bar Assn. (treas. 1984), Nat. Assn. Coll. and Univ. Attys. (co-chair intellectual property sect. 2000-01), Order of Coif, Delta Theta Phi. Roman Catholic. Home: 980 Hook Rd Westminster MD 21157-7335 Office: Johns Hopkins U 113 Garland Hall 3400 N Charles St Baltimore MD 21218 E-mail: blakesleew@jhu.edu.

BLAKESLEY, WAYNE LAVERE, JR., retired production engineer; b. Goshen, Ind., Mar. 26, 1926; s. Wayne L. Blakesley Sr. and Thelma (Brown) Cobb. Test engr. Bendix Missile Div., Mishawaka, Ind., 1952-53, engring. tech., 1955-59; field engr. RCA Service Co., Camden, N.J., 1953-55; design engr. Crown Internat., Elkhart, Ind., 1959-72, prodn. engr., 1978—95; pres. Blakesley Electronics, Syracuse, Ind., 1972-78; ret. Inventor, designer automated system for radio stas., printed circuit bd. prototyping system, printed circuit bd. multilayer overlay; designer multi-unit electronic learning lab. Mem. So. Mfg. Engrs. (sr. mem. Robotics Internat. div.), Mensa, Intertel. Avocation: public speaking. Home: PO Box 53 Syracuse IN 46567-0053

BLAKEY, MARION C. federal agency administrator; b. Gadsden, Ga; B Internatl Studies, Mary Washington Coll., U. Va.; postgead., Johns Hopkins U. With Dept. Commerce, Dept. Dept. Edn., NEH, Dept. Transp.; prin. Blakey & Assocs., Washington, 1993—2001; adminstr. Dept. Transp.'s Nat. Hwy. Traffic Safety Adminstrn., 1992—93; chmn. Nat. Transp. Safety Bd., 2001—02; adminstr. FAA, 2002—. Office: FAA 800 Independence Ave SW Washington DC 20591-0004

BLAKEY, SCOTT CHALONER, journalist, writer; b. Nashua, N.H., Nov. 19, 1936; s. Elmer F. and Mildred Livingstone (Chaloner) B.; m. Lone Erting, July 18, 1970 (div.); 1 child, Nicholas Scott; m. Caroline M. Scarborough, June 28, 1985 (div.); children: Alexandra Scarborough, Susannah Chaloner. BA, U. N.H., 1960. Reporter, photographer Nashua (N.H.) Telegraph, 1960-62, polit. reporter, 1963-64; legis. asst. Congressman James C. Cleveland, Washington, 1963; mng. editor Concord (N.H.) Monitor, 1964-68; urban affairs corr. San Francisco Chronicle, 1968-70, reporter, asst. city editor, 1979-84, TV corr., 1985-87; corr., asst. news dir. KQED-TV, San Francisco, 1970-74; free-lance writer San Francisco, 1974-79; news editor KRON-TV (NBC), San Francisco, 1987-89; nationally syndicated columnist KidVid L.A. Times Syndicate, 1990—; sr. news rep. div. corp. communications Pacific Gas & Electric Co., San Francisco, 1991—. Writer, field prodr. TV documentary 2251 Days, 1973 (2 Emmy awards 1974); author (books) San Francisco, 1976, Prisoner at War, 1978, Kid Vid, 1995; contbr. articles to profl. jours. Recipient Best Polit. Writing award New Eng. AP News Editors Assn., 1965, Dupont Columbia award, 1974. Mem. Nat. Soc. Newspaper Columnists, Authors Guild, Am. Air Mail Soc., Audubon Soc. Democrat. Avocations: philately, ornithology, photography, backpacking. Home: 1801 Turk St Apt 17 San Francisco CA 94115-4429 Office: Pacific Gas & Electric 77 Beale St Ste 2918 San Francisco CA 94105-2234

BLAKLEY, JOHN CLYDE, telecommunications consultant; b. Bogota, Colombia, Sept. 14, 1955; came to U.S., 1964; s. Arthur C. and Dorothy M. (Balcome) B.; m. Jean M. Padden, May 21, 1983. BS, U. Miami, 1977, MEd, 1979. Notary at large, Fla. Mgr., adminstrv. asst. U. Miami Student Union, Coral Gables, Fla., 1977-79; mgr. Aladdins Castle, Inc., South Miami, Fla., 1979-80; adminstrv. mgr., cons. Lexow Brackins, CPA's, Hollywood, Fla., 1981-84; firm adminstr., cons. Lexow, Brackins, Koffler, CPA's, Hollywood, 1985-89; firm adminstr., computer mgr. Dohan/Simon, CPA's, Miami, 1989-92; product mgr. Expert Software, Inc., 1992-93, IS mgr., 1993-96; sr. cons. Trien & Assocs., 1996—. Pres. Miami Apple Users Group, 1983; cons. YMCA, 1983. Chmn. Multiple Sclerosis Project Dance Marathon, Coral Gables, 1977-79; coord. United Way Miami, 1975-79. Recipient Whitten award Assn. Coll.

Unions, 1977, Outstanding Leadership award C. of C., 1973, Outstanding Vol., United Way, 1975, Outstanding Alumni award U. Miami, 1986, 92. Mem. Assn. Acctg. Adminstrs., Fla. Inst. CPA's, Assn. Coll. Unions Internat. (chmn. region 6, 1975-77), U. Miami Young Alumni Club (bd. dirs., pres.), U. Miami Alumni Assn. (bd. dirs.), Hurricane Club, Gold Coast Macintosh Computer Club (bd. dirs.). Home: 11501 SW 92nd Ct Miami FL 33176-4247 Office: Trien & Assocs 1591 Breakwater Terr Hollywood FL 33019 E-mail: John.Blakley@Trien.net.

BLALOCK, ANN BONAR, evaluation researcher; b. Parkersburg, W.Va., Apr. 16, 1928; E-mail: aglenski@earthlink.net. d. Harry and Fay (Conley) Bonar; m. Hubert Blalock, Jr., 1951 (dec. 1991); children: Susan Blalock Lyon, Kathleen Blalock McCarrell, James W.; m. Gerhard E. Lenski, 1996. AB, Oberlin Coll., 1950; MA, U. N.C., 1954; MSW, U. Wash., 1978. Pvt. cons. Admiralty Inlet Consulting, Hansville, Wash. Cons. OECD, Paris, 1990, European Commn., Brussels, 1995. Sr. author: Introduction to Social Research, 2d edit., 1982; editor, reviewer: Evaluation Forum, 1986-97, Evaluating Social Programs, 1990; co-editor: Methodology in Social Research, 1968; contbr. articles to profl. jours. Past pres. bd. dirs. Cmty. Mental Health Clin.; mem. Gov.'s Task Force on Accountability in Govt. Recipient Rsch. award Partnership for Employment and Tng. Careers. Mem. NASW (past pres. Wash. State chpt.), Am. Eval. Assn. (past com. chair), Assn. Pub. Policy Analysis and Mgmt. Home: PO Box 409 Hansville WA 98340-0409

BLALOCK, MARY WRIGHT, counselor; b. N.C. AAS with honors, Ctrl. Carolina C.C., Sanford, N.C., 1992; BAS, Campbell U., Buies Creek, N.C., 1994; MA, Campbell U., 1999. Dep. clk. of Ct. Adminstrv. Office of the Cts., Raleigh, N.C., 1978-83; computer lab. asst., news reporter Campbell U., 1992-94, asst. to curriculum materials coord., 1994-95; tutorial coord. Ctrl. Carolina C.C., 1995-96; data entry staff N.C. Dept. Environ. Health, Raleigh, 1997; counseling intern North Harnett Elem. Sch., Angier, N.C., 1997-98. Interviewer, counselor Employment Security Commn., 1998-2000; admissions counselor Campbell U., 2000—. Mem. Cape Fear Friends of the Fine Arts, Buies Creek, 1996—. Mem. Omicron Delta Kappa, Delta Kappa Pi. Democrat. Baptist. Avocations: reading, singing, horseback riding, photography, computers. Home: PO Box 234 Buies Creek NC 27506-0234

BLALOCK, SHERRILL, investment advisor; b. Newport News, Va., June 9, 1945; d. David Graham and Martha Lee (Bennett) B.; m. Jonathan L. Smith, Oct. 27, 1985; 1 child, Graham C.G. BA, Smith Coll., 1967. Chartered fin. analyst. Investment broker Legg Mason & Co., Washington, 1968-77, Blyth Eastman Dillon, Washington, 1977-80; portfolio mgr., mng. dir. Mitchell Hutchins, N.Y.C., 1980-88; gen. ptnr., portfolio mgr. Weiss Peck & Greer, N.Y.C., 1988-95; gen. ptnr. Delphi Asset Mgmt., N.Y.C., 1995-98; founder, mng. mem. Chesapeake Asset Mgmt., N.Y.C., 1998—. Chmn. univ. com. Chesapeake Asset Mgmt., N.Y.C., 2002—. Chair investment com., trustee Diocese of NY of Episcopal Ch., 2001—; trustee, vice chmn. bd. trustees, chair univ. com. Estate and Property of Diocese Conv. of N.Y., 1996—2002; trustee Cathedral of St. John the Divine, 1998—, chair investment com., 1999—. Mem. Washington Soc. Investment Analysts, Inst. Chartered Fin. Analysts. Office: Chesapeake Asset Mgmt 1 Rockefeller Plz Rm 1210 New York NY 10020-2002

BLAN, OLLIE LIONEL, JR., retired lawyer; b. Ft. Smith, Ark., May 22, 1931; s. Ollie Lionel and Eva Ocie (Cross) B.; m. Allen Conner Gillon, Aug. 19, 1960; children: Bradford Lionel, Elizabeth Ann, Cynthia Gillon. AA, Ft. Smith Jr. Coll., 1951; LL.B., U. Ark., 1954. Bar: Ark. 1954, Ala. 1959, U.S. Dist. Ct. (no. dist.) Ala. 1959, U.S. Dist.Ct. (mid. and so. dist.) Ala. 1960, U.S. Ct. Appeals (5th cir.) 1960, U.S. Ct. Appeals (11th cir.) 1982, U.S. Supreme Ct. 1991. Rsch. analyst Ark. Legis. Coun., 1954-55; law clk. to judge U.S. Dist. Ct. (no. dist.) Ala., Birmingham, 1959-60; assoc. Spain, Gillon & Young, Birmingham, Ala., 1960-64; ptnr. Spain & Gillon and predecessor firms, Birmingham, Ala., 1965-2001; tchr. Am. Inst. Banking, 1965-68; ret., 2001. Speaker Ala. Inst. Continuing Edn., 1978-2001. Contbr. articles to legal jours. Treas. Jefferson County Hist. Assn., 1972-81, vice chmn., 1981-86, chmn., 1986-93; mem. Jefferson County Rep. Exec. Com., 1973-76; mem. Briarwood Sch. Bd., Birmingham, 1982-86; chmn. Here's Life Birmingham, 1986-88. Capt. USMCR, 1955-58, ret. Mem. ABA, Am. Bd. Trial Advocates, Ark. Bar Assn., Ala. Bar Assn. (com. on admissions and legal edn. 1971-74, com. jud. office 1972-76, com. ins. programs, bd. bar commrs. 1987-92, chmn. task force on on disciplinary rules and enforcement 2001-03), Birmingham Bar Assn. (exec. com. 1986-89), Ala. Def. Lawyers Assn. (v.p. 1983-84, 91-93, bd. dirs. 1988-91, sec.-treas. 1993-94, pres. elect. 1994-95, pres. 1995-96), Am. Coun. Life Ins., Internat. Assn. Def. Counsel (chmn. accident, health and life ins. com. 1987-90, Ala. state rep. 1996-2000), Def. Rsch. Inst. (Ala. state rep. 1996-99, Louis B. Potter profl. svc. award 2000). Baptist. Home: 2100 English Village Ln Birmingham AL 35223-1729 *My desire has been to achieve the highest standard in whatever area of life I am thrust, guided by principles of ethics and Christianity.*

BLANAR, GEORGE J. business development executive; b. July 27, 1947; BS, U. Ill., 1970; MS, Northeastern U., Boston, 1973, PhD, 1976. Researcher Max Planck Inst., Munich, Ger., 1975-82, CERN, Geneva, 1975-82, DESY, Hamburg, Ger., 1979-80, Cornell U., Ithaca, N.Y., 1980-81; sales mgr. LeCroy S.A., Geneva, 1982-85; product mgr. LeCroy Corp., Spring Valley, N.Y., 1985-91, mktg. mgr., 1987-98, sr. scientist, 1991-93, dir. rsch. sys. products, 1994-98, dir. analog scope products, 1998; v.p. sales and mktg. Giga-tronics Inc., San Ramon, Calif., 1999—2000; pres. Blanar and Assocs., Bus. Devel. Cons., 1999—2000; v.p. for bus. devel. Carilion Biomed. Inst., Roanoke, Va., 2000—03; mng. bus. ptnr. Blanar and Assocs. Va. Evulations of Markets and Tech., 2003—. Cons., trainer Tuxedo, N.Y., 1990—; conf. chmn., procs. editor The Electronics for Future Collider Conf., 1991, 92, 93, 94, 95, 97, Conf. on Time of Flight Instrumentation, 1992; EMT, N.Y., Va. Contbr. over 150 sci. pubs. to profl. jours. Mem. Tuxedo Vol. Ambulance Corps, N.Y.; mem. Cave Spring Rescue Squad, Va.; mem. Back Creek Fire and Rescue, Va. Mem.: SPIE, IEEE, Nuc. and Plasma Soc. (adminstrv. coun.), Am. Phys. Soc., Nat. Ski Patrol, Phi Kappa Phi, Phi Eta Sigma. Achievements include landmark discoveries in elem. particle physics and product devel. of key electronic instrumentation. Office: Blanar & Assocs 7586 Autumn Pk Roanoke VA 24018 Home: 7586 Autumn Park Roanoke VA 24018-5729 E-mail: blanar@cox.net.

BLANC, PETER (WILLIAM PETERS BLANC), sculptor, painter; b. N.Y.C., June 29, 1912; s. Edward H. and Martha Elliott (King) B. BA, Harvard U.; LLB, St. Johns U.; postgrad., Corcoran Sch. Art.; MA, Am. U. Assoc. Pennie, Davis, Marvin & Edmonds, N.Y.C., 1935-44; instr. Am. U., Washington, 1950-53. One-man shows include Washington Pub. Libr., 1950, Passedoit Gallery, N.Y.C., N.Y., 1951, 53, 58, Albert Landry Galleries, N.Y., 1960, La Galeria Escondida, Taos, 1955, Hudson River Mus., 1961, 65, Associated Artists Gallery, Washington, 1962, Amel Gallery, N.Y.C., 1964, Ft. Worth Art Mus., 1966, Thomson Gallery, N.Y.C., 1969, Benson Gallery, Bridgehampton, N.Y., 1969, Southampton Coll., 1971, Avanti Galleries, N.Y.C., 1974, Elaine Benson Gallery, Bridgehampton, 1979, Goat Alley Gallery, Sag Harbor, N.Y., 1984, 86, 91, Benton Gallery, Southampton, N.Y., 1988, Art House Odeon, Sag Harbor, 1993, Clayton & Liberatore Gallery, Bridgehampton, 1995, 97; group shows include Corcoran Gallery, 1948, 51, Whitney Mus. Am. Art, 1952, City Art Mus., St. Louis, 1951, Washington Water Color Club, 1949, 51, 52, Riverside Mus., 1950, 54, 58, 64, New Sch. for Social Rsch., 1956, Springfield Mus. Art, 1952, Nat. Collection Fine Art, Washington, 1953, Balt. Mus. Art, 1953, Bklyn. Mus., 1955, Fogg Mus. Art, 1959, NYU, 1960, St. Paul Gallery, 1961, Internat. Gallery N.Y., 1961, Fort Worth Art Mus., 1963, Assoc. Art Gallery, Washington, 1961, Hudson River Mus., 1965, Parrish Art Mus., Southampton, 1965, Benson Gallery, Bridgehampton, 1966-67, 77, Daniels Gallery, N.Y.C., 1965, East Hampton Guild Hall, N.Y.C., 1966-67, 73, Southampton Coll., 1967-72, Iona Coll., N.Y., 1968, Mercy Coll., N.Y., 1970, Ashawagh Hall, Springs, N.Y., 1971-77, 80, 82-87, 89, 91, 92, 93, Artists Equity Assn., N.Y.C., 1975, N.Y. Artists-Union Carbide Gallery, N.Y.C., 1975, 77, Art Guild, N.Y.C., 1976, Abe Rattner Ctr. for Arts, Sag Harbor, 1979, Guild Hall Mus., East Hampton, 1980, 86, 87, 89, Rattner Meml. Studio, Sag Harbor, 1980, Jacob K. Javits Fed. Bldg., N.Y.C., 1983, Old Jail Art Ctr., Albany, Tex., 1984, Lever House, N.Y.C., 1985, Goat Alley Gallery, Sag Harbor, 1983-2003 Gallery Art 54, N.Y.C., 1986, Taos Arts Festival, N. Mex., 1986, Benton Gallery, Southampton, N.Y., 1987-90, Westbeth Galleries, N.Y.C., 1988-91, Lexington Ave. Armory, Artists of the Hamptons, N.Y.C., 1992, Art House Odeon, Sag Harbor, 1992, 93, Broome Street Gallery, N.Y.C., 1992, 93. Aaron Galleries, Chicago, 1994 Millenium Gallery, E. Hampton, 1995—, Clayton-Liberatore Gallery, Bridgehampton, N.Y., 1996-97. Lt. U.S. Army, 1944-46. Recipient awards Corcoran Gallery Art, 1949, awards Soc. Washington Artists, 1951, 53, awards Washington Water Color Club, 1949, 52 Mem. Spiral Group, N.Y. Artists Equity Assn. (dir. 1963-70), Artists Guild Washington (pres. 1951-53), Soc. Washington Artists, Proto-V Group, Am. Soc. Contemporary Artists, Artists' Alliance East Hampton. Home: PO Box 138 87 Jermain Ave Sag Harbor NY 11963-0003 Address: 161 W 75th St New York NY 10023-1801

BLANCATO, LOUIS SEBASTIAN, anesthesiologist; b. N.Y.C., 1920; MD, N.Y. Med. Coll., 1945. Cert. anesthesiology. Intern Grasslands Hosp., Valhalla, N.Y., 1945-46; resident in internal medicine Mt. Vernon Hosp., 1948-49; resident in anesthesiology Bellevue Hosp. Ctr.-NYU, N.Y.C., 1949-51; with St. Lukes-Roosevelt Hosp. Ctr., N.Y.C., 1951-87; ret., 1987. Prof. anesthesiology Colum Physicians and Surgeons. Fellow Am. Coll. Anesthesiologists; mem. AMA, Am. Soc. Anesthesiology.

BLANCHAERT, REMY HENRY, JR., oral and maxillofacial surgeon; b. Kansas City, Mo., July 3, 1965; s. Remy Henry and Alice Noretta Blanchaert. BA in Chemistry, William Jewell Coll., 1987; DDS, U. Mo., Kansas City, 1991; MD, U. Conn., 1994. Diplomate Am. Bd. Oral and Maxillofacial Surgery. Assoc. prof. oral and maxillofacial surgery Sch. of Medicine and Sch. of Dentistry U. Mo., Kansas City, 1996—. Editor: Oral Cancer, 1999; contbr. chpt. to book. Vol. Health Vols. Overseas, India, 1997. Fellow Am. Assn. Oral and Maxillofacial Surgery, Am. Coll. Oral and Maxillofacial Surgery; mem. AMA, ADA, Psi Omega, Omnicron Kappa Upsilon. Republican. Roman Catholic. Home: 318 W 7th St #203 Kansas City MO 64105 Office: Truman Med Ctr 2301 Holmes St Kansas City MO 64108 E-mail: remy.blanchaert@tmcmed.org.

BLANCHARD, BRIAN WHEATLEY, lawyer; b. State College, Pa., Nov. 7, 1958; s. Converse Herrick and Margaret (Wheatley) B.; m. Mary Willoughby; children: Will, Ben, Allison. BA, U. Mich., 1980; JD, Northwestern U., 1989. Bar: Ill. 1989, Wis. 1997, U.S. Dist. Ct. (we. dist.) Wis., U.S. Dist. Ct. (no. dist.) Ill., U.S. Ct. Appeals (7th cir.). Reporter Miami Herald, 1980-86; law clk. Hon. Walter J. Cummings U.S. Ct. Appeals (7th cir.), Chgo., 1989-90; asst. U.S. atty. Office of the U.S. Atty., Chgo., 1990-97; assoc. Quarles & Brady, Madison, Wis., 1997-2000; dist. atty. Dane County, Wis., 2000—. Editor-in-chief Northwestern U. Law Rev. Mem. Dane County Bar Assn., Chgo. Coun. Lawyers (bd. govs. 1994-96), Order of Coif. Office: Ste 523 210 Martin Luther King Blvd Madison WI 53703-3346 E-mail: blanchard.brian@mail.da.state.wi.us.

BLANCHARD, BRUCE, civil engineer, government official; b. Ft. Stotsenburg, Philippines, Dec. 26, 1932; s. Wendell and Marcella (Palmer) B.; m. Mary Josie Cain, July 31, 1992; children: Wendell, Laura, Renee. SB in Civil Engring., MIT, 1957, SM in Civil Engring., 1964; honor. grad., Commd. and Gen. Staff Course, Ft. Leavenworth, Kans., 1980. Tchg. and rsch. asst. MIT, 1957-59, asst. lacrosse coach, 1958-59, 64; hydraulic engr. Bur. Reclamation, Dept. Interior, Denver, 1959-60, 60-61; water resources planning engr. Phoenix, 1961-66; sr. staff specialist Water Resources Coun., Washington, 1966-69; environ. specialist Office of Sec. Dept. Interior, Washington, 1970-71; dir. Office Environ. Project Rev., Washington, 1971-89; dep. dir. U.S. Fish and Wildlife Svc., Dept. of Interior, Washington, 1989-97; spl. asst. for tribal self-governance Office of Sec. of Interior, 1997—. Editor: The Nation's Water Resources, 1968. With U.S. Army, 1951-53, 60; col. Md. N.G., 1967-85; lt. Ariz. N.G., 1961-66. Decorated Army Commendation medal, Army Meritorious Svc. medal, Army Achievement medal; recipient Commendation medal State of Md., 1976, 78, 79, Meritorious Svc. medal State of Md., 1983, Meritorious Svc. medal Dept. Interior, 1985, Disting. Svc. medal, 1999. Fellow: AAAS; mem.: ASCE, Sr. Execs. Assn., Am. Soc. Pub. Adminstrn., U.S. Armor Assn., Soc. Am. Mil. Engrs., N.G. Assn. U.S., Am. Water Resources Assn., Am. Geophys. Union, MIT Alumni Assn. (bd. dirs. 2001—), Explorers Club (Washington group treas. 1997—), MIT Club of Washington (bd. dirs. 1997—, v.p. 1998—99, pres. 1999—2000), Phi Gamma Delta (Disting. Fiji award). Home: 80 Observatory Cir NW Washington DC 20008-3611 Office: Interior Bldg Ms2548 Washington DC 20240-0001 E-mail: bruce_blanchard@alum.mit.edu.

BLANCHARD, BRUCE ROY, principal, minister; b. Bozeman, Mont., Feb. 12, 1954; s. Glen Lewis and Betty Jean Blanchard; m. Sherrie Louise Maurer, July 6, 1974; children: Justin, Joshua, Bruce, Rebecca. BA, N.W. Coll. Assemblies of God, 1976; MDiv, Assemblies of God Theol. Sem., 1991; BA cum laude, Evangel U., 1997. Ordained min. Ch. of God, 2001; cert. tchr. Mo. Pastor Mabton (Wash.) Assembly of God, 1976—77; constrn. worker Tri-Cities, Wash., 1977—88; lead custodian Evangel U., Springfield, Mo., 1988—97; tchr. Gainesville (Mo.) HS, 1997—2000; sch. adminstr., prin. Marrero (La.) Christian Acad. and HS, 2000—. Student coun. advisor Gainesville HS, 1997—2000; sec., v.p. S.W. Mo. Social Studies Tchrs. Orgn., Springfield, 1997—2000; mem. Soc. Pentecostal Studies, 1988—94. Treas. Ozark County Youth Fair Bd., Gainesville, 1997—2000; youth leader Royal Rangers, Tri-Cities, 1982—88; candidate City Coun., Gainesville, 1998, 2000. Mem.: Assn. for Supervision and Curriculum Devel., Assn. Christian Schs. Internat. (cert. secondary tchr., seminar presenter 2002), N.Am. Hunting Club (life). Republican. Avocations: reading, woodworking, hunting, fishing, writing. Office: Marrero Christian Acad & HS 2590 Barataria Blvd Marrero LA 70072 Office Fax: 504-340-1320. E-mail: mebrb2@netscape.net.

BLANCHARD, CHARLES ALAN, lawyer, former state senator; b. San Diego, Apr. 14, 1959; s. David Dean and Janet (Laxson) B.; m. Allison Major, 2001. BS, Lewis & Clark Coll., 1981; M of Pub. Policy, JD, Harvard U., 1985. Bar: Ariz. 1987, U.S. Dist. Ct. Ariz. 1988, U.S. Ct. Appeals (D.C. cir.) 1988, U.S. Ct. Appeals (9th cir.) 1988, U.S. Supreme Ct. 1994. Law clk. to hon. Harry T. Edwards, Washington, 1985-86; law clk. to hon. Sandra Day O'Connor U.S. Supreme Ct., Washington, 1986-87; assoc. ind. counsel Ind. Counsel James McKay, Washington, 1987-88; atty. Brown & Bain, P.A., Phoenix, 1988-97; state senator State of Ariz., Phoenix, 1991-95; dir. Office of Legal Counsel Office of Nat. Drug Control Policy, Washington, 1997-99; gen. counsel U.S. Army, 1999-2001; ptnr. Brown & Bain PA, Phoenix, 2001—. Adj. prof. Ariz. State U. Coll. Law, 1996, 2003—; chmn. Senate Judiciary Com., Phoenix, 1991-93; Dem. candidate U.S. Congress, 1994; dir. homeland security State of Ariz., 2003. Contbr. articles to profl. jours. Bd. dirs. Florence (Ariz.) Immigrant and Refugee Rights Project, 1990-97, 2001-, Homeless Legal Assistance Project, Phoenix, 1992-97, Tempe Comty. Action Agy., 1994-97, ABA Com. on Immigration Law, 1996-98, ABA Com. on Substance Abuse, 1998-02, Luth. Vol. Corps., Washington, 1986-88; state committeeman Ariz. Dem. Party, Phoenix, 1991-97; chmn. Ariz. Dem. Leadership Coun., Inc., 1992-97. Recipient Disting. Svc. award Ariz. Atty. Gen., 1992, Disting. Civilian Svc. award U.S. Army, 2001; Toll fellowship Coun. of State Govts., 1991; named Disting. Young Alumni Lewis and Clark Coll., 1987. Mem. ABA. Home: 1814 Palmcroft Dr NE Phoenix AZ 85007 Office: PO Box 400 Phoenix AZ 85001-0400

BLANCHARD, DANIEL G. cardiologist; b. Mnpls., Mar. 13, 1959; s. Robert and Jeannine Blanchard; m. Jennifer Neely, Apr. 20, 2002; 1 child, Rachel Jeanette. MD, U. Calif. San Diego Sch. of Medicine, 1985; BS, Calif. State U., 1980. Cert. Am. Bd. of Internal Medicine, 1988, Subspecialty in Cardiology Am. Bd. of Internal Medicine, 1991, Am. Bd. of Internal Medicine, 2002. Dir. cardiac noninvasive labs. U. Calif. San Diego Med. Ctr., 1994—; prof. of medicine U. Calif. San Diego Sch. of Medicine, 2003—; chief of cardiology Thornton Hosp, U. Calif. San Diego Med. Ctr., 2002—. Author: (sci. articles, book chpts.) Cardiologic Medical Literature. Fellowship, Am. Coll. of Cardiology, 1994, Am. Heart Assn., 2000. Achievements include research in Noninvasive cardiac imaging, Transesophageal echocardiography. Office: Univ Calif San Diego Cardiology 9350 Campus Point Dr #0975 La Jolla CA 92037

BLANCHARD, DAVID JOSEPH, research scientist; b. Vero Beach, Fla., May 6, 1974; s. Stephen Tracy and Mary Elizabeth Blair Blanchard; m. Keta Lea Montgomery Blanchard, May 31, 1997. BS, Va. Tech., 1997, MS, 2000. Asst. staff MIT Lincoln Lab., Lexington, Mass., 2000—. Contbr. articles to profl. jours. Grantee, Biol. Scis. Initiative Com., 1996—97, Sigma Xi, 1999, Grad. Rsch. Devel. Project, 1999. Mem.: Am. Soc. Plant Biologists, Alpha Psi, Phi Sigma. Avocations: mountain biking, hiking, canoeing. Home: 135 Summerwalk Dr Gaithersburg MD 20878 Office: US Patent and Trademark Office 1911 Jefferson Davis Hwy Arlington VA 22202 Home: 2541 Miranda Ct Woodbridge VA 22191

BLANCHARD, DAVID LAWRENCE, aerospace executive, real estate developer, management consultant; b. Taulbee, Ky., Feb. 13, 1931; s. Charles Lorraine and Gwyndolyn (Johnson) B.; m. Allene Irma Horne, June 28, 1958; children: Leslie Ruth, David Lawrence Jr. AB in Religion, Ind. Wesleyan U., 1953; MS in Physics, U. Louisville, 1959; PhD in Applied Physics, Cath. U. Am., 1971. Instr. U. Louisville, 1955-57, Ind. Wesleyan U., 1957-58; rschr. Naval Ordnance Lab., White Oak, Md., 1958-64; aerospace rschr., engr. NASA Goddard Space Flight Ctr., Greenbelt, Md., 1964-71, supr., mgr., 1971-79, sr. exec., 1979-81; staff cons., dir. rsch. Ford Aerospace Corp., Houston and Detroit, 1981-84; chief engr. Ford Aerospace, Houston, 1984-85, dir., exec. dir. space programs Seabrook, Md., 1985-90; pres. Loral AeroSys, Seabrook, Md., 1990-96, Lockheed Martin Space Mission Systems, 1996-97; founder, prin. COGENT-LLC., Kennewick, Wash., 1997—; prin., sec., treas. BBS Assocs. LLC, Kensington, Md., 1981—. NASA rsch. fellow Eidgenossische Technische Hochschule, Zurich, Switzerland, 1974-75; rsch. advisor NRC, Greenbelt, Md., 1979-80; mem. pres.'s adv. coun. Ind. Wesleyan U., 1998—; mentor for small start up businesses Dingman Sch. Entrepreneurship, 1997—; mem. ind. rev. team on space infrared telescope facility NASA, 1998—. Patentee fuze arming device. Chmn., charter mem. bus. and industry steering com. DuVal Aerospace Magnet Sch., Prince Georges County Schs. Seabrook, 1989-92, mem. bus. and industry adv. com. on sci. and tech., 1989-91; charter mem. bd. Opportunity Skyway, 1990-97; trustee, chmn. fin. com. Houghton Coll., N.Y., 1987-96, trustee, 1997—, gen. chmn. $45 million capital campaign, 1999—; charter mem., bd. trustees Md. Space Bus. Roundtable, 1989-97, pres., 1991-93; bd. visitors U. Md. Univ. Coll., 1994-2001, U. Md. Found., 1996-2001; charter mem., bd. trustees World Hope Internat., 1996—; bd. dirs. Willard J. Houghton Found., 1987—, chair bd., 1997—; bd. advisors Nanticoke Homes, 2000-02, Innovative Concepts, Inc., 1999—; chair pres. adv. coun. excellence Ind. Wesleyan U., 2000—. With U.S. Army and USAR, 1957-64. Recipient Exceptional Svc. award NASA, 1968, Exceptional Performance award, 1973. Fellow Washington Acad. Scis., AIAA (assoc.); mem. Sigma Xi, Sigma Pi Sigma. Lutheran. Achievements include research in gravity-gradient stabilization experiment on 1500 foot antenna array in low earth orbit.

BLANCHARD, GEORGE SAMUEL, retired army officer; b. Washington, Apr. 3, 1920; s. George S. and Elizabeth (Blanchard) B.; m. Beth Howard, June 9, 1944; children: Kate E. (Mrs. Ronald Hausner), Marylou C. (Mrs. John Hennessey), Deborah E. (Mrs. Eberhard Roell), Blythe H. (Mrs. Charles Watkins). Student, Am. U., 1938—40; BS, U.S. Mil. Acad., 1944; MS, Syracuse U., 1948; grad. Advanced Mgmt. Program, Harvard Bus. Sch., 1966. Commd. 2d lt. AUS, 1944, advanced through grades to gen., 1975; served as co. comdr. and staff officer Europe, 1944-47; adviser, 1955-57; with 82d Airborne Div., 1958-60, 1961-62, 1966-68; comdr. 82d Airborne div., 1970-72; mem. Pentagon staff, 1962-66, 68-70; comdg. gen. VII Corps U.S. Army Europe, 1973-75; comdr. in chief U.S. Army Europe, 1975—79; ret., 1979. Past pres. World USO, Gen. Analysis, Inc.; bd. dirs. Atlantic Coun. U.S. Contbr. to Ency. Brit. Vice chmn. Literacy Coun. Moore County. Decorated D.S.M. with 3 oak leaf clusters, Silver Star with oak leaf cluster, D.F.C., Bronze Star with oak leaf cluster. Mem. Assn. U.S. Army, Ret. Officers Assn. (past pres.), VFW, U.S. Soc. French Legion of Honor, Nat. Mil. Families Assn. Episcopalian.

BLANCHARD, JAMES ARTHUR, engineer, computer systems specialist, marketing professional; b. Evanston, Ill., Oct. 26, 1949; s. Arthur Knights and Verna Eloise (LeMann) B.; m. Debra Kathleen Smith, July 10, 1976; children: Andrew, Charles, Kenneth. BSCE, Northwestern U., 1972; MBA, U. Chgo., 1987. Registered profl. engr., Ill. Trainee DeLeuw, Cather and Co., Chgo., 1969-72, Chgo. Transit Authority, 1972-74, procedural analyst, 1974-78, supt. capital program support, 1978-90, dir. capital program support, 1990-92, mgr. capital investment support, 1992—. Mem. Chgo. Area Transp. Study Unified Work Program com., 1981; prin. Strategic Info. Solutions, 1997; v.p. mktg. Lincoln Fin. Advisors, 1998. Bd. dirs. Morton Grove (Ill.) Baseball Assn., 1991-97; active Park View Sch. Parents Assn. Mem. Mensa, Beta Gamma Sigma. Roman Catholic. Avocations: investment analysis, gardening, travel, baseball, fine dining. Home: 8517 Austin Ave Morton Grove IL 60053-2928 E-mail: jblanchard@lnc.com.

BLANCHARD, JULIA SMITH, secondary school educator; b. Richmond, Va., July 29, 1963; d. Richard Bryan and Elizabeth Jean (Dunn) Smith; m. David Wayne Blanchard, Jr., Feb. 23, 1965; children: Grace Bird, Mary Winters. BA in English, U. Ga., 1985. Profl. tchrs. cert. secondary English and libr. media specialist Va. Tchr. Caroline County Schs., Milford, Va., 1988—92, Highland County Schs., Monterey, Va., 1992—. Bd. mem. Highland County Pub. Libr., Monterey. Clk. of session Beulah Presbyn. Ch., Mill Gap, Va., 1999—; bd. mem. Highland County Arts Coun., Monterey, 1995—97, Highland County Pub. Libr., 2001—. Mem.: Highland County Edn. Assn. (pres. 2002—03). Home: PO Box 503 Monterey VA 24465 Office: Highland High Sch 430 Meyers Moon Rd Monterey VA 24465

BLANCHARD, LEONARD ALBERT, educator, consultant, writer; b. New Britain, Conn., July 30, 1947; s. Albert Edward and Sophie Marian (Lemanski) B.; children: Sarah Maddin Henniger, Henry Wyche Hunter. BA in English cum laude, Washington & Lee U., 1969; MA, Emory U., 1974, PhD, 1975. Instr. English, coach Oak Ridge (N.C.) Mil. Inst., 1969-71, St. Mark's Sch., Dallas, 1974-75; instr. English El Centro Coll., Dallas, 1975-79; writer, developer, liaison Southland Corp., Dallas, 1979-87; dir. devel. Franchise Group Internat., Little Rock, 1987-88; cons. Len Blanchard, Bradenton, Fla., 1988—. V.p. human resources Harken Internat., Bedford, Tex., 1989—90; mgmt. cons. Tropical Breeze Inn, Sarasota, 1996—99; instr. English Manatee C.C., Bradenton, Fla., 1999—. Author essays and poems, including An American Passion, 1999. Mem. Acad. Am. Poets, Musical Heritage Soc., Washington & Lee U. Alumni Assn. Democrat. Avocations: swimming, hiking, classical music. Office: Manatee CC Dept English 5840 26th St W Bradenton FL 34207-3522 E-mail: blanchl@mccfl.edu.

BLANCHARD, NORMAN HARRIS, retired pharmaceutical company executive; b. Pittsfield, Mass., Aug. 21, 1930; s. Norman Harris and Edna May (Perkins) B.; m. Margaret Eugenie Rahm, Apr. 10, 1954; children: Norman James, Michèle Blanchard Langstaff. BS in Geology, Tufts U., 1953; BS in Internat. Trade, Am. Grad. Sch. Internat. Mgmt., 1959. Geologist U.S. Geol. Survey, Harrisburg, Pa., 1957-58; internat. mgmt. trainee Upjohn Internat. Ops., Kalamazoo, 1959-60; adminstrv. dir. Sprout Waldron of France, Paris, 1961-66; european dir. Salsbury Labs., Charles City, Iowa, 1967-71, Smith Kline Animal Health, Phila., 1972-74, internat. dir., 1975-76, internat. v.p., 1977-81, pres., 1982-89, SmithKline Beecham Animal Health Products, London, 1989-92; corp. v.p. Smith Kline Beecham Corp., Phila., 1989-92; ret., 1992. Chmn. Animal Health Inst., Alexandria, Va., 1988-89; mem. president's council Am. Grad. Sch. Internat. Mgmt., Phoenix, 1985-89. Chmn. Jr. Achievement of Del. Valley, Newtown Sq., Pa., 1986, 87; trustee Internat. House, Phila., 1984, 85. With CIC, U.S. Army, 1953-56. Avocations: skiing, sailing, flying. Home: 5 Half Hill Rd Spring City PA 19475-9507

BLANCHARD, PAMELA SNYDER, special education educator; b. Winston-Salem, N.C., Feb. 5, 1951; d. Roger Alexander and Marie Gobble Snyder; m. George Winborne Blanchard, July 26, 1975; children: Andrew Micah, Justin Warren, Nathan Winborne. BA in Elem. Edn., St. Andrews Presbyn. Coll., 1973; Cert. in Spl. Edn., U. Tenn., 1990; MA in Ednl. Tech., Bible, Johnson Bible Coll., 2000. Cert. tchr. N.C., edn. and spl. edn., and Career Ladder I tchr. Tenn. Title I math. tchr. Durham (N.C.) City Schs., 1973—75; algebra tchr. Davidson County Schs., Welcome, NC, 1976; Chpt. I reading and math. tchr. Knoxville (Tenn.) City Schs., 1976—79, 1980—85; ednl. cons. Discovery Toys, Knoxville, 1989—90; spl. edn. extended resource tchr. Sevier County Schs., Sevierville, Tenn., 1990—91; spl. edn. resource specialist Knox County Schs., Strawberry Plains, Tenn., 1992—. Mem. leadership com., sch. improvement team, tech. com., webmistress Carter Elem. Sch., 1999—. Vol. counselor Sexual Assault Crisis Ctr., Knoxville, 1991—92; chairperson missions bd. Seymour (Tenn.) United Meth. Ch., 1988—90, chairperson assimilation com., 1990—92, sec. adminstrv. coun., 2000, 2001—02; missionary Charleston, SC, 2001—02, Damascus, Va., 2001—03, 2003. Grantee Multicultural Cooking Unit, Knoxville Jr. League, 1994, Accelerated Reader Books, East Tenn. Edn. Found., 1995. Mem.: ASCD, NEA, Internat. Reading Assn., Knox County Edn. Assn., Tenn. Edn. Assn., Children with Attention Deficit Disorder, Learning Disabilities Assn., Divsn. Learning Disabilities, Coun. for Exceptional Children, Nat.

Honor Soc. Democrat. Methodist. Avocations: reading, hiking, computers, travel. Home: 705 Forest View Ct Seymour TN 37865 Office: Carter Elem Sch 9304 College Ln Strawberry Plains TN 37871

BLANCHARD, PAUL, academic administrator, educator; b. Flint, Mich., Apr. 5, 1943; s. Floyd E. and Loretta G. Blanchard; m. Elizabeth L. Brandt, June 18, 1966 (div. Feb. 19, 2003); children: Jaclyn(dec.), Brian; m. Mary M. Donigan, Apr. 12, 2003; children: Geoffrey, Brian. BA in Social Sci., U. Mich., Flint, 1965; MA in Polit. Sci., So. Ill. U., Carbondale, 1968; PhD in Polit. Sci., U. Ky., Lexington, 1973. Social studies tchr. Beecher H.S., Flint, Mich., 1965—67; prof., polit. sci. Ea. Ky. U., Richmond, 1970—99, dir. Ctr. for Ky. History and Politics, 1999—; edn. program specialist S.C. Dept. Edn., Columbia, 1975—76; legis. liaison Ky. Atty. Gen.'s Office, Frankfort, 1985—86. Cons. Nat. Sch. Bds. Assn., Washington, 1976—78, Ky. Dept. Edn., Frankfort, 1985—86; state coord. Nat. Bicentennial Project, 1986—88. Contbr. chapters to books, articles to profl. jours.; talk show host Ea. Ky. U. Television, Richmond, 1982—92. Fellow, Nat. Def. Edn. Act, 1968—70. Democrat. Methodist. Avocations: walking, reading, tennis, golf. Office: Eastern Ky Univ 113 McCreay Hall 521 Lancaster Ave Richmond KY 40475-3102 Business E-Mail: paul.blanchard@eku.edu.

BLANCHARD, RICHARD FREDERICK, construction executive; b. Orange, N.J., Feb. 8, 1933; s. William F. and Dorothy Dew (Wright) B.; m. Jill Isles, Nov. 23, 1985. BA, Dartmouth Coll., 1955; MBA, Harvard U., 1957. Apprentice Wm. Blanchard Co., Newark, 1958-62, estimator, 1962-65, project mgr. Springfield, N.J., 1965-72, pres., 1972—. V.p. Newark Mus., 1986—. With U.S. Army, 1957-58. Mem. Bldg. Contractors Assn. N.J. (trustee 1986—), N.J. State C. of C. (bd. dirs. 1980-88). Presbyterian. Avocations: mountain climbing, skiing.

BLANCHARD, ROBERT J. neuroscientist; b. Waltham, MA, Apr. 12, 1937; s. Joseph Shein and Blanche La Fond Blanchard; m. D. Caroline Hutchens, June 7, 1962; 1 child, Matthew. PhD, U. Iowa, 1962. Prof. psychology and neuroscience U. Hawaii, Honolulu, 1964—2002. Nat. Acad. Scis. Exch. fellow Inst. Study Higher Nervous Activity, Moscow, 1969—70; Japan Sci. Found. prof. Tskuba U., Tokyo, 1991—92; German Sci. Found. prof. U. Gottingen, Germany, 1999—2000. Author: books, contbr. articles to profl. jours. 1st lt. U.S Army, 1962—64. Fellow: Internat. Behavioral Neuroscience Soc. (pres. 2003—), Internat. Soc. Rsch. Aggression (pres. 1996—98). Office: Pacific Biomedical Research Center, 1993 East West Road Honolulu HI 96822 Office Fax: 808 956 9612. Business E-Mail: blanchar@hawaii.edu.

BLANCHARD, RONALD JOSEPH, food service executive; b. Camden, N.Y., June 27, 1946; s. Earl Roland and Margaret Virginia (Platt) B. AS in Hotel and Restaurant Tech., SUNY, Canton, 1968; BA in Human Svcs., U. Mass., Boston, 1990. Gen. mgr. restaurant Howard Johnson Co., Miami, Fla., 1968-83, gen. mgr. hotel, 1983; mgr. tng. and devel. Marriott Family Restaurants, Quincy, Mass., 1984-87; sr. mgr. tng. and devel. Ground Round, Inc., Braintree, Mass., 1987-96; corp. dir. tng. Night Sky Restaurant Group, N.Y.C., 2001—, Windows on the World, 1996—2001. Bd. dirs. Worcester Sq. Area Neighborhood Assn., Boston, 1988-96, pres. 1992-95; block leader East Brookline St. Neighborhood, Boston, 1988—; mem. Boston Redevel. Authority Working Group for Master Plan, Boston, 1991-96. Mem. ASTD, Zeta Alpha Phi. Democrat. Roman Catholic. Avocations: electronics, music, computers, gardening, biking. Home: 66 Pearl St Apt 407 New York NY 10004-2444 Office: Nightsky LCC 1604 Broadway New York NY 10019 E-mail: work_center@msn.com, rblanchard@nightsky.com.

BLANCHARD, SHIRLEY LYNN, primary school educator, consultant; b. Medford, Oreg., Sept. 5, 1954; d. Richard L. Grigsby, Helen L. Grigsby; m. John T. Blanchard, Sept. 6, 1975; children: Andrew Blanchard children: Martin Blanchard, Richelle Blanchard. BA in Edn., So. Oreg. State Coll., 1975, BS, 1978; MA in Edn., So. Oreg. U., 1985. Nat. bd. cert. tchr. Nat. Bd. Profl. Tchg. Stds., 2000. Music tchr. Jackson County Sch. Dist. #6, Central Point, Oreg., 1975—81, kindergarten tchr. Eagle Point, Oreg., 1983—99; primary tchr. Jackson County Sch. Dist. #9, Eagle Point, Oreg., 1999—. Home schooling parent educator RIGGS Inst., So. Oreg., 1987—91, reading cons. for home schooling parents, 1987—91; continuing edn. presenter early childhood literacy So. Oreg. U./Medford Sch. Dist. 549C, Medford, 1995—96; site based mgmt. team chmn., mem. Glenn D. Hale Elem. Scho., Eagle Point, 1996—98; contract bargaining team mem. Eagle Point Edn. Assn., Eagle Point, 1997—98. Leader Wynema Girl Scout Counsel, Medford, 1972—75; 4H leader Oreg. State Ext. Svc., Central Point, Oreg., 1997—98. Recipient Slice of Life award, Williams Bread & McKenzie Farms Bakery and KOBI-TV, 2002. Fellow: Nat. Kindergarten Alliance Network; mem.: NEA, Oreg. Edn. Assn., Nat. Assn. Edn. Young Children. Avocations: internet mentoring, horses, technology, writing music, birds. Home: PO Box 1511 Eagle Point OR 97524 Office: Jackson County Sch Dist #9 PO Box 197 215 E Main Eagle Point OR 97524 Home Fax: (541) 826-3221; Office Fax: (541) 826-3221. Business E-Mail: blanchards@eaglepnt.k12.or.us. *I am a life long learner seeking to instill in young children the love of learning above all else. By modeling a continued quest to learn, grow, and be actively involved in a variety of pursuits I believe that their minds are opened to endless possibilities. This love for learning will broaden their world and open up opportunities in their futures of unimaginable proportions.*

BLANCHARD, TOWNSEND EUGENE, retired service companies executive; b. Du Quoin, Ill., Jan. 30, 1931; s. Townsend and Anna Belle (Jackson) B.; m. Norma Louise Barr, Dec. 18, 1960; children: John Barr, Susan Melody, Jayne Ann Blanchard Reishus, Stephen Eugene. BS, U. Ill., 1952; MBA, Harvard U., 1957. Cons. Ill. Sch. Bond Svc., Monticello, 1958-62; co-founder, treas., chief fin. officer Americana Nursing Ctrs., Monticello, 1962-75; v.p. fin., treas., CFO, chief of staff Cenco, Inc., Chgo., 1975-79; sr. v.p., CFO DynCorp., McLean, Va., 1979-97. DynCorp; chmn. Employee Stock Ownership Plan. Elder Presbyn. Ch.; bd. dirs. Combined Health Appeal, 1986-96; bd. advisors Cameron Glen Care Facility, 1989-92. Lt. USNR, 1952-55. Decorated Spl. Commendation letter. Mem. Fin. Execs. Inst. (chpt. pres. 1988-89, nat. v.p. and bd. dirs. 1991-94), U. Ill. Alumni Club, Harvard U. Bus. Sch. Club, Harvard Club Washington, Am. Legion, Delta Sigma Phi (trustee nat. found. 1982-89, pres. nat. found. 1988-89, Harvey W. Herbert award 1975, Mr. Delta Sig award 1988). Home and Office: 1222 Aldebaran Dr Mc Lean VA 22101-2305

BLANCHET, BERTRAND, archbishop; b. Montmagny, Que., Can., Sept. 19, 1932; s. Louis and Alberta (Nicole) B. BA, Coll. Ste-Anne-de-la Pocatiere, 1952; L.Th., Laval U., 1956, D.Sc., 1975. Ordained priest Roman Catholic Ch., 1956, consecrated bishop, 1973; tchr. biology Coll. and Coll. d'Enseignement Gen. et Profl., La Pocatiere, 1963-73; bishop of Gaspe Que., 1973-92; archbishop of Rimouski, 1992—. Mem. Chevaliers de Colomb, Rimouski. Roman Catholic. Address: CP 730 34 Eveche Ouest Rimouski QC Canada G5L 7C7

BLANCHET, JEANNE ELLENE MAXANT, artist, educator, performer; b. Chgo., Sept. 25, 1944; d. William H. and L. Barbara (Martin) Maxant; m. Yasuo Shimizu, Apr. 28, 1969 (div. 1973); m. William B. Blanchet, Aug. 21, 1981 (dec. May 1993). BA summa cum laude, Northwestern U., 1966; MFA, Tokyo U., 1971; MA, Ariz. State U., 1978; postgrad., Ill. State U., 1979-80; PhD, Greenwich U., 1991. Instr. Tsuda U., Kodaira, Japan, 1970-71; free-lance visual, performing artist various cities, U.S., 1973—; artist in residence YMCA of the Rockies, Estes Park, Colo., 1976-81 summers; prof. fine arts Rio Salado Coll., Surprise, Ariz., 1976-91. Lectr. Ariz. State U. West, Sun City, 1985-93; evaluator several arts couns. including Ariz. Humanities Coun., 1993, Ariz. Humanities Coun. Scholar's SPkrs. Bur., 1998—; Prescott Melodrama ragtime pianist, 1993, 94; artist with Performing Arts for Youth, 1994—. Selected for regional, state, nat. juried art shows, 1975—, mus. and gallery one-woman shows of computer art, 1988—; author: Original Songs and Verse of the Old (And New) West, 1987, A Song in My Heart, 1988, Reflections, 1989, The Mummy Story, 1990; contbr. articles to newspapers, profl. jours. Founding mem. Del Webb Hosp. Woodrow Wilson fellow, 1966; ADA B.C. Welsh scholar, 1980; recipient numerous art, music awards, 1970—, major computer art awards in regional, nat., and internat. shows, 1990—. Mem. Nat. League Am. Pen Women (sec. chpt. 1987, v.p. 1988, pres. 1990-92, pres. Colo. chpt. 1996-97), Ariz. Press Women (numerous awards in original graphics and writing 1980s, 90s), Nat. Fedn. Press Women, Northwestern U.'s John Evans Club, Henry W. Rogers Soc., P.E.O. (rec. sec. chpt. BV 1998—), Phi Beta Kappa. Avocations: computers, ragtime piano, hiking, parapsychology, duplicate bridge (life master). Home and Office: 10330 W Thunderbird Blvd # C-311 Sun City AZ 85351 *To live is to think, to create.*

BLANCHET-SADRI, FRANCINE, mathematician, educator; b. Trois-Rivieres, Quebec, Can., July 25, 1953; came to U.S., 1990; d. Jean and Rolande (Delage) B.; m. Fereidoon Sadri, July 28, 1979; children: Ahmad, Hamid, Mariamme. BSc in Math., U. Quebec a Trois-Rivieres, Can., 1976; MS, Princeton U., 1979; PhD, McGill U., 1989. Rsch., tchg. asst. U. Quebec, Trois-Rivieres, Quebec, Can., 1974-76, lectr., 1976; rsch. asst. Princeton (N.J.) U., 1978; lectr. U. Tech. Isfahan, Iran, 1982-84, McGill U., Montreal, Quebec, 1988-89; prof. U. N.C., Greensboro, 1990—. Contbr. articles to profl. jours. Recipient Rsch. Excellence award 1991; Natural Scis. and Engring. Coun. Can. postgrad. fellow, 1976-80, Fonds pour la Formation de Chercheurs et L'aide a la Rsch. fellow, 1985-87, Natural Scis. and Engring. Rsch. Coun. Can. fellow, 1990; New Faculty grantee U. N.C., Greensboro, 1990-91, NSF grantee, 1991—. Mem. Am. Math. Soc., Assn. for Computing Machinery. Achievements include discovery that the dot-depth of a generating class of aperiodic monoids is computable. Office: U NC Dept Math Scis PO Box 26170 Greensboro NC 27402-6170 E-mail: blanchet@uncg.edu.

BLANCHETTE, JAMES GRADY, JR., lawyer; b. Dallas, Apr. 29, 1922; s. James Grady and Thelma (Keys) B.; m. Bess Neblett, May 29, 1944; children: Linda Blanchette Ponti, Kay Blanchette Hill, Martha Blanchette Caschette. BBA, U. Tex., 1943, LLB, 1947; MBA, Harvard U., 1948. Bar: Tex. 1947. Chmn. exec. com. Chancellor's Coun. U. Tex. System, 1983; pres. Dads' Assn. U. Tex., 1972-73. Served to lt. USNR, 1943-45. Fellow: Tex. Bar Found.; mem.: ABA, Dallas Bar Assn., Tex. Bar Assn., Northwood Club (pres. 1971). Presbyterian. Address: 8600 Skyline Dr # 1212 Dallas TX 75243-4170 E-mail: blanchett@aol.com.

BLANCHETTE, OLIVA, philosophy educator; b. Berlin, N.H., May 6, 1929; s. Delphis and Odelia (Morneau) B.; m. Dorothy M. Kennedy, May 25, 1975; children: Nicole Elizabeth, Frances Kathleen. AB in Philosophy, Boston Coll., 1953, MA, 1958; Licentiate in Philosophy, Coll. St. Albert de Louvain, Belgium, 1954; Licentiate in Sacred Theology, Weston Coll., 1961; PhD in Philosophy, U. Laval, Que., Can., 1966. Prof. Latin, Greek and English Boston Coll. High Sch., 1954-57; instr. philosophy Boston Coll., 1964-65, asst. prof., 1965-67, asso. prof., 1967-74, prof., 1974—; dean Sch. of Philosophy, 1968-73. Dir. Inst. for Social Thought. Author: Initiative in History: A Christian-Marxist Exchange, 1967, For a Fundamental Social Ethic: A Philosophy of Social Change, 1973, The Perfection of the Universe According to Aquinas: A Teleological Cosmology, 1992, Philosophy of Being: A Reconstructive Esay in Metaphysics, 2003; contbr. articles on philosophy of history, metaphysics, philosophy of religion, and social ethics to scholarly jours. Mem. Hegel Soc. Am., Metaphys. Soc. Am., Internat. Soc. Metaphys. Home: 28 Florence St Natick MA 01760-2121 Office: Dept Philosophy Boston Coll Chestnut Hill MA 02467

BLANCHFLOWER, DAVID GRAHAM, economics educator; b. Brighton, Eng., Mar. 2, 1952; arrived in U.S., 1989; s. Dennis Roy and Mary Elisabeth (Abraham) B.; m. Sian Elizabeth Owen, May 21, 1983; children: Kathryn Sian, Jennie Greta Marie, Daniel John. BA, Leicester (Eng.) U., 1973; PGCE, Birmingham (Eng.) U., 1975; MSc, U. Wales, 1982; PhD, U. London, 1985. Tchr. Northicote High Sch., Wolverhampton, Eng., 1975-76; lectr. Kilburn Poly., London, 1976-77, Farnborough (Eng.) Coll. Tech., 1977-79; rsch. fellow U. Warwick, Eng., 1984-86; lectr. U. Surrey, Guildford, Eng., 1986-89; assoc. prof. econs. Dartmouth Coll., Hanover, N.H., 1989-93, prof. econs., 1993—. Rsch. assoc. Ctr. for Econ. Performance, London Sch. Econs., 1985—; rsch. assoc. Nat. Bur. Econ. Rsch., Cambridge, 1989—. Author: The Wage Curve, 1994; contbr. articles to econs. jours. Mem. Royal Econ. Soc., Am. Econ. Assn. Avocations: golf, skiing. Home: 27 Mulherrin Farm Rd Hanover NH 03755-4907 Office: Dartmouth Coll Dept Econs Hanover NH 03755

BLANCK, RONALD RAY, health science university administrator, internist, military officer; b. Lancaster, Pa., Oct. 8, 1941; s. Harvey Ray and Mildred Katherine (Smith) B.; m. Donna Rae Ault, Sept. 17, 1971; children: Jennifer, Susan. BS, Juniata Coll., 1963; DO, Phila. Coll. Osteo. Medicine, 1967; DSc in Osteopathy (hon.), New Eng. Coll. Osteo. Medicine, 1982; LLD (hon.), Phila. Coll. Osteo. Medicine, 1991. Diplomate Am. Bd. Internal Medicine. Intern Lancaster Osteo. Hosp., 1967-68; resident in internal medicine Walter Reed Army Gen. Med. Ctr., 1970-73; commd. capt. U.S. Army, 1968, advanced through grades to lt. gen., 1996, ret., 2000, gen. med. officer, 1968-69, 1969-70; asst. chief gen. med. svc. Walter Reed Army Med. Ctr., Washington, 1973-74, asst. chief dept. medicine, 1974-76; asst. dean student affairs Sch. Medicine Uniformed Svcs. U., Bethesda, Md., 1976-79; chief dept. medicine Brooke Army Med. Ctr., San Antonio, Tex., 1979-82; chief med. corps career activities office Army Med. Dept. Pers. Support Act, Washington, 1982-85; comdr. U.S. Army Hosp., Berlin, 1986-88, Army Regional Med. Ctr., Frankfurt, Germany, 1988-90; dir. prof. svcs., chief med. corps affairs Office of Surgeon Gen., Fall Church, Va., 1990-92; comdr. Walter Reed Army Med. Ctr., Washington, 1992-96; surgeon gen., comdr. MECOM U.S. Army, Falls Church, Va., 1996-2000; pres. U. North Tex. Health Sci. Ctr., Ft. Worth, 2000—. Asst. prof. clin. medicine Georgetown U., Washington, 1972—78; clin. instr. medicine Howard U., Washington, 1975—77; assoc. prof. medicine USUHS, Bethesda, 1976—; clin. prof. medicine U. Tex., San Antonio, 1979—80, San Antonio, 1980—82; disting. prof. mil. medicine USUHS, Bethesda, Md., 1998—. Guest editor Osteopathic Annals, 1981; mem. editorial adv. bd. History of Medicine in Vietnam, 1981. Advisor bd. regents Uniformed Svcs. U. Health Scis., Bethesda, 1992; bd. dirs. Nat. Med. Vets. Soc., Chgo., 1993; bd. regents Potomac Inst. for Policy Studies, 2000; bd. dirs. Annapolis Ctr., 2002. Decorated DSM, Bronze Star, Legion of Merit, Def. Superior Svc. medal; recipient Founder's award Tex. Coll. Osteo. Medicine, 1991. Master ACP (gov.); mem. AMA (alt. del.), Am. Osteo. Assn., Assn. Mil. Surgeons U.S. (John Shaw Billings award 1976), Berlin Internat. Med. Soc., Assn. Mil. Osteo. Physicians and Surgeons, Soc. Med. Cons. Armed Forces (assoc.), Nat. Bd. Med. Examiners. Episcopalian. Avocations: reading, jogging. Office: U North Tex Health Sci Ctr 3500 Camp Bowie Blvd Fort Worth TX 76107-2699

BLANCO, JANA M. assistant principal; b. Cin. d. Laura Webb. BA in Edn., U.New Mex., 1974; MA in Educational Adminstrn., U. San Francisco, 1986; postgrad. studies in edl. computing and tech., Barry U., Miami Shores, Fla., 1986. Bilingual multicultural resource tchr. Paramount Unified Sch. Dist, Calif., 1974—77; English as second lang. tchr. lang. arts gifted and talented Lynwood (Calif.) H.S., 1977—83; English as second lang. tchr. lang. arts Hacienda La Puenta Adult Sch., Hacienda Hghts., Calif., 1987—90; tchr. English as second lang. lang. arts gifted and talented Miami Northwestern H.S., 1990—93; middle sch. lang. arts tchr. Miami-Dade County Schs., Miami, 1993—98; CSI instr. North Miami Beach Sr. H.S., 2001—. English coord. Internat. Corr. Schs., Port-au-Prince, Haiti, 1983—87; adj. prof. Broward C.C. North, Coconut Creek, Fla., 1995—2000, Barry U., Miami Shores, Fla., 1998; lang. arts tchr. North Miami Beach Sr. H.S., 2000; chair title IX project Paramount (Calif.) Unified Sch. Dist., 1976—77; pres., owner E&J Tile, Inc., Pembroke Pines, Fla. Chair counseling program for underprivileged minorities Lynwood Unified Sch. Dist., Calif., 1977—78; Am. rep. to Haitian Com. for Combite Creole Am. Embassy, Port au Prince, Haiti, 1983—86. Mem.: Fla. Assn. Computer Educators, Dade County Tchrs. of English. Home: 7836 Ramona St Miramar FL 33023-2458 Office: E&J Tile Inc 6621 Pembroke Rd Pembroke Pines FL 33027

BLANCO, JOSEFA JOAN-JUANA (JOSSIE BLANCO), social services administrator; b. Havana, Cuba, Jan. 31, 1954; came to U.S., 1962; d. Oscar Manuel and Josefa (Rodriguez) B.; m. John Franklin Hurt III, Nov. 18, 1979 (div. June 1985); children: John Franklin IV, Jeaninne Bernadette; 1 child, Richard Manuel Tejeda. BA in Psychology and Religion, Fla. Internat. U., 1975, MA in Sch. Psychology, 1976, postgrad. in pub. adminstrn., from 1983; MS in Human Resource Adminstrn., Villanova U., 1979; PhD in Adminstrn., West Coast U. Lic. tchr., Fla.; tng. lic. clin. and child care svcs. Psychometrician Mailman Ctr. for Child Devel., U. Miami, 1975-76; supr. adoptions Health and Rehabilitative Svcs. Fla., Miami, 1972-75, 76-80; instr. psychology Draughons Jr. Coll., Memphis, 1980-81; spl. project dir. Children's Psychiat. Ctr., Miami, 1981-84; exec. dir. Community Habilitation Ctr., Miami, 1984-86; shelter dir. Miami Bridge, Inc., Miami, 1986-89; regional dir. Luth. Ministries Fla., Ft. Lauderdale, 1989-90; exec. dir. Residential Pla. at Blue Lagoon Inc., Miami, 1990; grant writer, researcher, speaker at confs., 1990—; instr. Dade County Pub. Sch. System, 1991—; health ctr. adminstr. Dade County Pub. Health Dept. State of Fla. Dept. Health and Rehab. Svcs., 1992-94; instr. Dade County Pub. System, 1994—; instr. psychology Fla. Nat. Coll., 1998—, acad. adv., 1999—. Facilitator nat. confs. Nat. Justice Dept.; bd. dirs. Internat. Biog. Inst. Bd. dirs. S.E. Region Com. To Study AIDS and AIDS Prevention; mem. Adult Congregate Living Facility. Recipient award for svc. to runaways Fla. Network, 1989, plaque for work with troubled youth Friends Fla. Network, 1989; named one of One Thousand Great Ams., Internat. Biog. Inst., 2001; Miami Herald scholar, 1969. Mem. Residential Child Car Assn. (bd. dirs., chmn. advocacy com.), Fla. Network Youth and Family Svcs. (quality assurance com., tng. com.), NAFE. Republican. Roman Catholic. Avocations: water sports, tennis. Address: 10521 SW 48th St Miami FL 33165-5649

BLANCO, KATHLEEN BABINEAUX, lieutenant governor; m. Raymond; 6 children. With La. State Legis. Dist. 45, 1984-88, mem. house edn. com., mem. house transp., hwys., and pub. works com., Pub. Svc. Commn., La., 1988-94, chair, 1993-95; lt. gov. State of La., 1995—. Democrat. Office: Office of the Lt Gov Pentagon Barracks 900 N 3rd St Baton Rouge LA 70802*

BLANCO, LUCIANO-NILO, physicist; b. Havana, Cuba, May 28, 1932; s. Luciano and Maria Teresa (Zayas) B.; m. Noemi de los A. Vitier, Dec. 16, 1956; 1 child, Marina Margarita. Student, U. Havana, 1949-54; fellow, Pa. State U., MIT, 1954-55; PhD in Physics, U Havana, Acad. Scis., 1962, 63. Inspector Chas. Martin Co. of Cuba, Havana, 1953-54; researcher Co. Rayonera Cubana, Matanzas, 1955-59; rsch. scientist Comision de Fomento Nacional, Havana, 1959-63; instr., physics prof. U. Havana, 1959-65; dir., rsch. physicist Acad. Scis., Havana, 1963-70; dir. phys. lab. and operation rsch. Avron, SA, Madrid, 1970-76; rsch scientist, mem. faculty physics U. Miami, Coral Gables, Fla., 1976-94; prof. physics, dir. Inst. Theoretical Rsch., Coral Gables, Fla., 1990—. Sci. advisor Internat. Yrs. of the Quiet Sun, Havana, 1964-65; cons. Clean Energy Rsch. Inst. U. Miami, Coral Gables, 1980—; cons. physicist, U.S.A., Spain, 1970—. Editor: Energias No-Convencionales, 1983; editor Boletin de Geofisica, 1965-67, EnergyNotes and EnergyLetters, 1990-94; contbr. articles to profl. jours. Fellow Fgn. Ops. Adminstrn. and U.S. Weather Bur., Washington, 1954, Clean Energy Rsch. Inst., Coral Gables, 1982. Mem. Am. Phys. Soc., Internat. Energy Soc. (pres. 1992-95), N.Y. Acad. Scis., Royal Instn. Gt. Britain, Sigma Xi. Achievements include research in solar-terrestrial relationships, neutrino physics and astrophysics, fundamental principles in energy, theoretical physics, biophysics. Office: Inst Theoretical Rsch PO Box 248514 Miami FL 33124-8514 E-mail: lnblanco@sigmaxi.org.

BLANCO MENDOZA, HERMINIO, Mexican government official; b. Chihuahua, Mex., July 25, 1950; married; 2 children. BA in Econs., Monterrey Inst. Tech., Mex., 1971; student, U. Colo., 1971-72; MA, PhD, U. Chgo., 1978. Analyst U. Chgo., 1975-78; asst. sec. treas. Govt. Mex., 1978-80; prof. economy Rice U., Houston, Tex., 1980-85; advisor to presidency Govt. Mex., 1985-88, undersec. for fgn. trade Secretariat of Trade and Industry, 1988-90, head negotiator Free Trade Treaty, 1990-93, undersec. for trade negotiations, 1993-94, sec. of trade and indsl. promotion, 1995—. Rschr. MIT, 1981. Office: Sec Trade & Indsl Promotion Alfonso Reyes 30 06170 Col Cordesa Mexico

BLAND, SIR CHRISTOPHER (FRANCIS BUCHAN BLAND), freight company executive; b. May 29, 1938; s. James Franklin MacMahon and Jess Buchan (Brodie) B.; m. Jennifer Mary May, 1981; 1 child; 4 stepchildren. Ed., Oxford (Eng.) U. Gov. Prendergast Girls Grammar Sch. and Woolwich Poly., 1968-70; chmn. Bow Group PLC, 1969-70; dir. Northern Ireland Fin. Corp., 1972-76; dep. chmn. Ind. Broadcast Authority, 1972-80; chmn. Sir Joseph Causton & Sons, 1977-85, London Weekend TV Holdings, 1984-94, Century Hutchinson Group, 1984-89, Life Scis. Internat. PLC (formerly Philcom PLC), 1987—, Nat. Freight Consortium PLC, London, 1994—, BBC, London. Mem. bd. govs. BBC, 1996—. Editor Crossbow, 1971-72. Mem. Greater London Coun., Lewisham, 1967-70, Burnham Com., 1970, Prime Min.'s Adv. Panel on Citizen's Charter, 1991-94; mem. Chancellor's Pvt. Fin. Panel, 1994—, chmn., 1995—; chmn. rev.group on nat. tng. coun. and nat. staff coms. Nat. Health Svc., 1982; chmn. Hammersmith and Queen Charlotte's Hosps., 1982-94, Hammersmith Hosps. Nat. Health Svc. Trust, 1994—; mem. coun. Royal Postgrad. Med. Sch., 1982—. St. Mary's Med. Sch., 1984-88; mem. Irish Olympic Fencing Team, 1960; capt. modern pentathlon team Oxford U., 1959-60, capt. fencing team, 1961. 2nd lt. 5th Royal Inniskilling Dragoon Guards, 1956-58; lt. North Irish Horse Territorial Arty., 1958-69. Mem. Beefsteak Club. Office: BBC Broadcasting House Portlands Pl London W1A 1AA England

BLAND, EVELINE MAE, real estate broker, musician, music instructor; b. Hughesville, Pa., Aug. 24, 1939; d. Burton Anthony and Mary Margaret (Mack) Morgan; m. Theodore D. Bland; 1 child, Susanna Elisabeth. BA, Mansfield (Pa.) U., 1961; Orff Schulwerk cert., Royal Conservatory, Toronto, Ont., Can., 1976; MBA, Century U., 1992. Tchr. Newburgh (N.Y.) Jr. High Sch., 1961-62, Cedar Grove (N.J.) Bd. Edn., 1962-66, West Caldwell (N.J.) Bd. Edn., 1973-76, Covenant Christian Sch., North Plainfield, N.J., 1976-77; salesperson Janett Realtors, Verona, N.J., 1977-79; sales mgr. Degnan Boyle Realtors, Caldwell, 1979-88, Schlott Realtors, Montclair, 1988-91; realtor Coldwell Banker, Sarasota, Fla., 1992; mortgage broker Sarasota, 1992—; tchr. Faith Christian Sch., Sarasota, 1992-95, Sarasota Music Ctr., 1993-98. Prin. Camp Shawnee, Waymart, Pa., 1961-71, Melody One Music Studios Club, 1993—, Music Studio, 1995-2003; instr. Sarasota Fine Arts Acad., 1992; music arranger Mouse Mountain Toy Co., 2002-2003. Music dir. Players, Sarasota Broadway Goes to Hollywood; prof. vocal soloist, N.J., Pa. Opera, Oratorios, Broadway-type shows, 1971-91; apprentice Paper Mill Playhouse, Millburn, N.J., 1962-66. Organist, choir dir. 1st Congl. Ch., Verona, 1978-87; organist Venice 1st Bapt. Ch., 1992-95; accompanist Sarasota Bapt. Ch., 1991; trustee Montclair Hist. Soc., 1970-87; bd. dirs. State Repertory Opera, Montclair Kiwanis, 1990-91; mem. Sarasota Opera Guild, 1992. Mem. Nat. Assn. Tchrs. of Singing, Nat. Realtors Assn. (cert.), N.J. Assn. Realtors (profl. stds. and edn. coms. 1987), West Essex Bd. Realtors (v.p., sec. 1985-86, pres. 1987, career trainer 1987, Realtor of Yr. 1987), Sarasota Bd. Realtors, Fla. Assn. Realtors, Music Tchrs. Nat. Assn., Fla. State Music Tchrs. Assn. (chmn. state conf. 2000, treas. 1999), Sarasota Music Tchrs. Assn., Christian Profl. and Bus. Women (project advisor 1992), Am. Guild of Organists, West Essex C. of C., Montclair C. of C., FIABCI-USA, SMTA (treas. 2002, 2003), Gideons Aux. (various offices 1982-87), Kiwanis, Lambda Mu. Republican. Baptist. Avocations: golfing, tennis, painting, reading, gardening.

BLAND, FREDERICK AVES, architect; b. Galveston, Tex., Dec. 21, 1945; s. David and Florence (Aves) B.; m. Morley Ann Thomson, Dec. 21, 1968; 1 child, Chloe Thomson. BA, Yale U., 1968, MArch, 1972. Registered architect, N.Y., Conn., Fla., Va., NJ, Md., Ky. Assoc. Beyer Blinder Belle, Architects & Planners, N.Y.C., 1974-77, dir. design, 1977-79, ptnr., 1979—. Chief architect Yale Archeol. project Royal Abbey St. Denis, Paris, 1970-80. V.p. Bklyn. Heights Assn., 1981-86, pres., 1992-94; panel mem. N.Y. State coun. on Arts, 1985-86; exec. com. Friends of Edn., Mus. of Modern Art; trustee Bklyn. Botanic Garden, 1993—, chmn. horticulture com., 1996—, exec. com., 1996—, vice-chmn., 1999—; bd. trustees Bklyn. Hist. Soc.; v.p. N.Y. Found. Architecture, 1998, pres., 1999; bd. trustees The Evergreens Cemetary, 1998—. Mem. AIA (nat. com. on design, coll. of fellows, jury of fellows 1995-97), Am. Inst. Cert. Planners, Mcpl. Art Soc. N.Y., Heights Casino Club (bd. govs. 1981-87, pres. 1987-90), Rembrandt Club (pres. 2001-03), Yale Club (N.Y.C.). Democrat. Episcopalian. Home: 26 Pierrepont St Brooklyn NY 11201-7209 also: Wallace Rd Stony Creek CT 06405 Office: Beyer Blinder Belle Architects 41 E 11th St New York NY 10003-4602

BLAND, JAMES THEODORE, JR., lawyer; b. Memphis, June 16, 1950; s. James Theodore and Martha Frances (Downen) B.; m. Pattie L. Martin, Apr. 12, 1974. BBA magna cum laude, Memphis State U., 1972, JD, 1974. Bar: Tenn. 1975, U.S. Dist. Ct. (we. dist.) Tenn. 1976, U.S. Tax Ct. 1976, U.S. Supreme Ct. 1983, U.S. Ct. Claims 1987; cert. Estate Planning specialist. Estate tax atty. IRS, Memphis, 1974-76; atty. Armstrong, Allen, Braden, Goodman, McBride & Prewitt, Memphis, 1976-91; prin. James T. Bland, Jr. and Assocs., Memphis, 1991—. Instr. in taxation, bus. law State Tchr.'s Inst., Memphis, 1975-83; bd. dirs. Thomas W. Briggs Found., Memphis. Fellow Am. Coll. Trust and Estate Counsel, Tenn. Bar Found., Memphis and Shelby County Bar Found. (pres.

1991-93); mem. ABA (legis. initiatives com., taxation sect., specialization in estate planning real property, probate and trust sect., Achievement award 1983, 85), Fed. Bar Assn. (pres. 1987-88, nat. coun. 1979—, bd. dirs. young lawyers divsn. 1979-84, pres. Memphis mid south chpt. 1979-80), Tenn. Bar Assn. (chmn. tax sect. 1984-85, bd. govs. 1984-85, 89-90, 90-91), Tenn. Young Lawyers Conf. (pres. 1985), Memphis Bar Assn. (bd. dirs. 1990-91), Tenn. Soc. CPA's. Republican. Methodist. Office: PO Box 770566 Memphis TN 38177-0566 E-mail: blandjr@worldnet.att.net.

BLAND, JANEESE MYRA, editor; b. Evanston, Ill., Feb. 20, 1960; d. James Milton and Jeanette Malisa (Bryant) B. BA, U. Ark., 1980. Cert. tchr., Ark., Ill. Tutor counselor U. Ark., Pine Bluff, 1979; tchr. Pine Bluff High Sch., 1980, Chgo. Bd. Edn., 1981-84; editor, author, columnist, creator Beautiful Images Hollywood (Calif.) Gazette Newspaper, 1985—. VIP organizer People's Choice Awards, Beverly Hills, 1984—; exec. prodr. stas. Chgo. Access Corp., Century Cable Comms., L.A., BH-TV, Beverly Hills; hostess The Janeese Bland Show. Proof editor: Nursing Rsch. Jour., 1989. Polit. vol. Rep. Party, Santa Monica, 1988—; vol. organizer Windfeather, Inc., Beverly Hills, 1983—, United Negro Coll. Fund, L.A., 1984—, Sickle Cell Disease Rsch. Found., L.A., 1985—; pres., founder June Maria Bland Scholarship Found, Recipient Image award Fred Hampton Scholarship Found., 1983, Wiley W. Manuel award State Bar Calif., Cert. Merit, Bet Tzedek Legal Svcs., Ill. Cmty. Leader of the Yr. award Nat. Coun. Negro Women and Quaker Oats, 1998. Mem. SBA (pres.). Republican. Baptist. Home and Office: 269 S Beverly Dr # 420 Beverly Hills CA 90212-3807 E-mail: landofbland@aol.com.

BLAND, JOHN LLOYD, lawyer; b. Wichita Falls, Tex., Sept. 20, 1944; Student, Vanderbilt U.; BA, U. Tex., 1967, JD with honors, 1969. Bar: Tex. 1969. Mem. Bracewell & Patterson, LLP, Houston, 1969—. Mem. State Bar Tex., Houston Bar Assn., Phi Delta Phi. Office: Bracewell & Patterson LLP 2900 S Tower Pennzoil Pl 711 Louisiana St Houston TX 77002-2781 E-mail: jbland@bracepatt.com.

BLAND, MARYBETH, volunteer, artist; b. Queens, N.Y., Aug. 24, 1956; d. John Domminck Bland and Lorraine E. Groser; m. Anthony Paul O'Leary, May 1, 1981. BA, L.I. U., 1978; alcohol studies cert., Seattle U., 1983. Cert. chem. dependency counselor, Wash. Resident counselor Resource Found., Stanwood, Wash., 1977-80; mental health worker Alderwood Inn, Mountlake Terrace, Wash., 1980; team leader Ruth Dykeman Ctr., Burien, Wash., 1980-84; counselor Pt. Job Around, Seattle, 1985-86; adolescent program coord. Intercept, Federal Way, Wash., 1986 90; harmonica tchr. Olympia (Wash.) Parks and Recreation, 2000—. Harmonica player and storyteller at sr. ctrs. and pre-schs., 1999—. Bicycle pedestrian adv. com. City of Olympia, 1995-98; advisor for bike pedestrian safety and edn. com., Olympia, 1997-2000; diversity panelist The Olympian, Olympia, 1998-2000; vol. Stream Team, Olympia, 1996—, Olympia Friends, 1998—. Recipient Cert. of Appreciation Alcohol Drug Helpline, 1991, Recognition award Olympia City Coun., 1998. Avocations: playing harmonica, swimming, reading, bird watching.

BLAND, TERESA P. policy analyst, consultant; b. N.Y.C., Oct. 19, 1957; d. Richard James and Janet (Mycrs) B. BA in Art History and Comparative Lit., Fordham U., 1989. Adminstrv. asst. Juilliard Sch., N.Y.C., 1988-90; bursar Grad. Sch. Figurative Art, N.Y.C., 1990-91; registrar Cunningham Dance Found., N.Y.C., 1993-94, fin. officer, 1994-95; contr. Stephen Gaynor Sch., N.Y.C., 1995-96; internal controls analyst Office of the Comptr., City of N.Y., 1998—. Archivist Found. for Dance Promotion, N.Y.C., 1996. Vol. Kids and the Power of Work. Charlotte W. Newcombe Found. scholar, 1988, 89. Mem. Film Soc. Lincoln Ctr., Mus. Modern Art, Fordham U. Alumni Fedn., Inst. Mgmt. Accts. (bd. dirs. N.Y. chpt. 2002–), Orgn. Staff Analysts (vice chair chpt.). Democrat. Avocations: opera, ballet, cinema, travel, museums. Home: 3900 Greystone Ave Bronx NY 10463-1944 Office: Comptr's Office Mcpl Bldg One Centre St New York NY 10007 E-mail: tbland@comptroller.nyc.gov., tpbland@yahoo.com.

BLANDA, SANDI, artist; b. N.Y., Jan. 30, 1949; m. Robert S. Blanda, Feb. 24, 1973; children: Jaime, Elyse. BA, Queens Coll., 1971. Folk artist, Great Neck, N.Y., 1983—. Instr. workshops including Cahoon Mus Am. Art, 2001—03. Designer sea shell mosaics in octagonal mahogany cases "Sailor's Valentine"; exhbns. include Sailor's Valentine Gallery, Nantucket, Mass., 1984-99, Quester Gallery, Greenwich and Stonington and Greenwich, Conn., 1994—, Bailey-Matthews Shell Mus., Sanibel, Fla., 1996—, The Christina Gallery, Martha's Vineyard, Mass., 1997—, Stephanie Hoppen Ltd., London, 1997—, Hoorn-Ashby Gallery, N.Y.C., Nantucket, Mass., 1999—, The Cahoon Mus. of Am. Art, 2000, Workshops Cahoon Mus., 2001-03, Featured spkr. The Atheneum, Nantucket, Mass., 2002, Newport (R.I.) Scrimshanders, 2002—. Recipient numerous 1st and 2nd prizes for folk art, Sanibel Shell Fair, 1990-2003. Home: 18 Oxford Blvd Great Neck NY 11023-2239 E-mail: sgblanda@aol.com.

BLANDER, MILTON, chemist; b. Bklyn., Nov. 1, 1927; s. Benjamin and Yetta (Schwartzman) B.; children: Benjamin, Alice, Kathryn, Daniel, Joshua. BS, CUNY, 1950; PhD, Yale U., 1953. Rsch. assoc. Cornell U., Ithaca, N.Y., 1953-55; chemist Oak Ridge (Tenn.) Nat. Lab., 1955-62; chemist, group leader Rockwell Internat. Sci. Ctr., Thousand Oaks, Calif., 1962-71; sr. chemist, group leader Argonne (Ill.) Nat. Lab., 1971-97; founder Quest Rsch., South Holland, Ill., 1995—. Recipient Materials Rsch. award U.S. Dept. Energy, 1984, Alexander von Humboldt award. Fellow AAAS, Meteoritical Soc.; mem. Metall. Soc., Am. Chem. Soc., Electrochem. Soc. (Max Bredig award 1987), Norwegian Acad. Tech. Scis. E-mail: mblander2@aol.com.

BLANDFORD, ROGER DAVID, astronomy educator; b. Grantham, Eng., Aug. 28, 1949; s. Jack George and Janet Margaret (Evans) B.; m. Elizabeth Kellett, Aug. 5, 1972; children: Jonathan, Edward. BA, Magdalene Coll., Cambridge U., 1970; MA, PhD, Cambridge U., 1974. Rsch. fellow St. John's Coll., Cambridge U., 1973-76; asst. prof. astronomy Calif. Inst. Tech., Pasadena, 1976-79, prof., 1979-89, Richard Chace Tolman prof. theoretical astrophysics, 1989—; mem. Inst. Advanced Study, Princeton, 1974-75. Contbr. articles to profl. publs. W.B.R. King scholar, 1967-70; Charles Kingsley Bye fellow, 1972-73; Alfred P. Sloan research fellow, 1980, Guggenheim fellow, 1988—. Fellow Royal Soc., Royal Astron. Soc. (Eddington medal 1999), Cambridge Philos. Soc.; mem. Am. Astron. Soc. (Warner prize 1982, Heineman prize 1998), Am. Acad. Arts and Scis. Office: Calif Inst Tech Dept Astrophysics Pasadena CA 91125-0001

BLANE, HOWARD THOMAS, research institute administrator; b. De Land, Fla., May 10, 1926; s. Chesley Thomas and Olive Henrietta (Van Heest) B.; children: Benjamin, Eva. BA cum laude, Harvard U., 1950; MA, Clark U., 1951, PhD, 1957. Instr. Harvard Med. Sch., Cambridge, Mass., 1957-66, asst. clin. prof., 1966-70; assoc. prof. U. Pitts., 1970-72, prof., 1972-86; rsch. prof. SUNY, Buffalo, 1986—; dir. Rsch. Inst. Addictions, Buffalo, 1986-96. Cons. Nat. Inst. on Alcohol Abuse and Alcoholism, Washington, 1970—; v.p. Health Edn. Found., Washington, 1975—; bd. dirs. Rsch. Found. for Mental Hygiene, Albany, N.Y., 1986-96; principal investigator numerous grants. Author: The Personality of the Alcoholic, 1968; editor: Frontiers of Alcoholism, 1970, Youth, Alcoholism and Social Policy, 1979, Psychological Theories of Drinking and Alcoholism, 1987, 2nd edit., 1999. Bd. dirs. Jellinek Meml. Fund, Toronto, 1995—. Clark U. scholar, Worcester, Mass., 1950-51. Fellow APA, Am. Psychol. Soc.; mem. APHA, AAAS, Rsch. Soc. on Alcoholism. Office: Rsch Inst on Addictions 1021 Main St Buffalo NY 14203-1014 E-mail: blaneonfind@msn.com.

BLANEY, DAVE, race car driver; b. Sharon, Pa. Race car driver Pennzoil World of Outlaws, NASCAR. Owner World of Outlaws Racing Team. Achievements include World of Outlaws champion, 1995; winner of Amoco Knoxville Nats., 1997, King's Royal, Eldora, Ohio, 1997. Office: Jasper Motorsports 110 Knob Hill Rd Mooresville NC 28117

BLANK, A(NDREW) RUSSELL, lawyer; b. Bklyn., June 13, 1945; s. Lawrence and Joan B.; children: Adam, Marisa. Student, U. N.C., 1963-64; BA, U. Fla., 1966; postgrad., Law Sch., 1966-68; JD, U. Miami, 1970. Bar: Ga. 1971, Fla. 1970; cert. civil trial advocate Nat. Bd. Trial Advocacy. Law asst. Dist. Ct. Judge, Atlanta, 1970-72; ptnr. A. Russell Blank & Assocs., PC, Atlanta, 1985—. Contbr. articles to profl. jours. Pub. adv. com. Atlanta Regional Commn., 1972-74. Recipient Merit award Ga. Bar Assn., 1981. Mem. ABA, ATLA, Atlanta Bar Assn., Ga. Bar Assn. (Merit award 1981), Ga. Trial Lawyers Assn. (officer), Lawyers Club Atlanta, Fla. Bar Assn., Am. Bd. Trial Advocates (advocate, bd. dirs. 2000—, pres. Ga. chpt.), Xenix Soc. (bd. dirs.). Office: 230 Peachtree St NW Ste 2600 Atlanta GA 30303-1516

BLANK, ARTHUR M. professional sports team executive, retired home and lumber retail chain executive; b. Queens, NY, 1942; Acct. Arthur Young & Co., N.Y.C., 1963-67; with Daylin Inc., Los Angeles, 1967-74; v.p., treas. Handy Dan Home Improvement Ctrs. Inc., Los Angeles, 1974-78; co-founder Home Depot Inc., Atlanta, 1978—, co-chmn., bd dirs, pres., CEO, 1997—2001; owner Atlanta Falcons Football Club, 2002—. Office: Atlanta Falcons 4400 Falcon Pkwy Flowery Branch GA 30542*

BLANK, EUGENE, pediatrician, radiologist, educator; b. Balt., May 8, 1924; s. Maurice Blank and Fannie Edith Jacob; m. Esther Honikberg, June 22, 1958; children: Lisa, Anne, Linda. BA, Johns Hopkins U., 1948, MD, 1954. Diplomate Am. Bd. Pediat., 1960, Am. Bd. Radiology, 65. Prof. emeritus in pediats. and radiology Oreg. Health Scis. U., Portland, 1991—. Author: Pediatric Images Casebook of Differential Diagnosis, 1997. 2d lt. USMC, 1942—45, South Pacific. Democrat. Avocation: writing. Home: 4940 SW Humphrey Park Rd Portland OR 97221

BLANK, FLORENCE WEISS, literacy educator, editor; b. Bridgeport, Conn. d. Maurice Herbert and Henrietta Helen (Shapiro) Weiss; m. Bernard Blank, Apr. 10, 1965 (dec. Aug., 1989). Student Journalism, English, Psychology, Richmond Profl. Inst.; student, U. Richmond, Northwestern U., Va. Union U., 1967, 73, 74, U. Wis., Milw., 1971, Va. Commonwealth U., 1973, D.C. Tchrs. Coll., 1975. Tchr. adult edn. dept. Richmond (Va.) Pub. Sch. System, 1952-77; project dir., tchr. tng. and edn. dir., tchr. Right to Read Fed. Grant, D.C., 1976-79; in-svc. tchr. tng. U. D.C., Washington, 1975-87; cons.-tchr. in-svc. tchr. tng. program Durham (N.C.) City Schs., 1983-87; tchr. adult edn. dept. Henrico County (Va.) Pub. Schs., 1987—. Dir., condr. numerous in-svc. tng. seminars, classes for elem. and secondary sch. and adult edn. tchrs. in Va., D.C., Md.; tchr. of ESL classes in evening sch.; tchr., spl. com. tng. program for Chesapeake and Ohio Ry., Richmond, 1955-59; tchr. spl. class for postal and fed. employees at Phyllis Wheatley YWCA, Richmond, 1968; dir., tchr. Weiss Reading Inst., Richmond, 1960-76. Co-author: (with Carolyn W. Guertin) Sound Skill Builder, 1976; editor-in-chief: Sure Steps to Reading and Spelling, 1976, The Science of Reading and Spelling. Mem. Am. Assn. for Adult and Continuing Edn., Learning Disabilities Assn., The Learning Disabilites Coun. of Richmond, Altrusa Internat. Inc. of Capital City of Va. Avocations: creative writing, English lang. rsch., composer, lyricist. Home: 5309 W Grace St Richmond VA 23226-1113

BLANK, LETA SONDRA, health and long term care insurance specialist; d. Newton B. and Molly Lerner Stenberg; m. Howard A. Blank. BA, CUNY; MBA, Marymount U.; Cert. of Design, Phila. Inst. Design. Fin. counselor U. Md. Corp. Extension Svc., Derwood, 1992-94; program dir. Sr. Health Ins. Asst. program U. Md., Derwood, 1994—. With Consortium Washington SHIP coords., 1996—. Contbr. (book) How to Retire Happy, 2000; contbr. Washington Post; featured and quoted in mags. Bd. assoc. Nat. Rehab. Hosp., Washington, 1994—; active Medicare beneficiary adv. bd., 1995—; program coord. Curb Abuse in Medicare/Medicaid, Md. Dept. Aging, 1996—. Mem. Delta Epsilon Sigma. Avocations: painting, golf, dance. Home: 8801 Mayberry Ct Potomac MD 20854 Office: U Md CES 18410 Muncaster Rd Derwood MD 20855 E-mail: lblank@erols.com.

BLANK, MARION SUE, psychologist, educator; b. N.Y.C., Dec. 20, 1933; d. Morris David and Tillie Jean (Sherman) Hersch; m. Martin Blank, July 3, 1955; children: Donna, Jonathan, Ari. BA, CCNY, 1955, MS in Edn, 1956; PhD, Cambridge (Eng.) U., 1961. Asst. prof. Albert Einstein Coll. Medicine, 1965-70, asso. prof., 1970-73; prof. dept. psychiatry Rutgers Med. Sch., Piscataway, N.J., 1973-83; mem. adj. faculty dept. psychiatry Columbia Coll. Physicians and Surgeons, N.Y.C., 1980-83; pres. PHAT Phonics, 2001—. Dir. reading disabilities rsch. inst., pvt. practice, cons., 1983—; Nat. Tour lectr. Speech Pathology Assn. Australia, 1996. Author: Teaching Learning in the Preschool - A Dialogue Approach, Preschool Language Assessment Instrument, 1978, (with Rose and Berlin) The Language of Learning, 1978, (with Marquis and Klimovitch) Directing School Discourse, 1994, Directing Early Discourse, 1995, Sentence Master, 1990-96, (with Berlin) A Parent's Guide to Educational Software, 1991, (with Marquis and Klimovitch) Directing School Discourse, 1994, Directing Early Discourse with Marquis and Klimovitch, 1995, Your Cure for the Reading Crisis: PHAT Phonics, 2003. Pinsent-Darwin fellow, 1960; recipient award of commendation N.J. Speech and Hearing Assn., 1979, Spl. Edn. award Software Pubs. Am., 1990, N.J., USPHS Career Devel. award, 1965-73; named N.J. nominee Kleffner Lifetime Svc. award Am. Speech Lang. Hearing Assn., 1994, 95. Fellow APA; mem. Assn. for Children with Learning Disabilities. Home: 157 Columbus Dr Tenafly NJ 07670-1635 E-mail: msb5@columbia.edu., msblank@optonline.net. *It is heartening, albeit at times difficult, to live in a period of revolutionary change for women.*

BLANK, MATTHEW C. broadcast company executive; m. Susan McGuirk; children: Meredith, Gordon. Degree, U. Pa.; MBA, Baruch Coll. Past sr. v.p. consumer mktg. Home Box Office; exec. v.p. mktg. Showtime Networks, Inc. (Showtime, The Movie Channel, Fliz, Showtime Extreme, Showtime en Español, Showtime Event TV), N.Y.C., 1981-91, pres., COO, 1991—, past CEO, also chmn. bd. dirs., bd. dirs., mem. exec. com. Sundance Ch. Bd. dirs. Comedy Central, Phoenix Pictures; chmn., CEO Showtime Network, Inc. Trustee Rheedlen Ctrs. Children and Families; bd. dirs. Walter Kaitz Found.; mem. exec. com. Cable Positive, active Nat. Minorities in Cable. Recipient Vanguard award for mktg., 1991, Chmn.'s award Cable TV and Mktg., 1991, Friends of Children award Rheedlen Ctrs. Children and Families, 1996, 1991, Chmn.'s award Cable TV and Mktg., 1991, Friends of Children award, Rheedlen Ctrs. Children and Families, 1996, Fairness award, Gay and Lesbian Alliance Against Defamation, 1997. Mem.: Pub. Edn. Needs Civic Involvement in Lng., Nat. Cable TV Assn. (bd. dirs.), Nat. Acad. Cable Programming (bd. govs.), NCCJ (mem. exec. bd. dirs). Office: care Showtime Networks 1633 Broadway New York NY 10019-6708

BLANK, MYRON NATHAN, theater executive; b. Des Moines, Aug. 30, 1911; s. Abraham Harry and Anna (Levy) B.; m. Jacqueline Navran, Oct. 22, 1935; children: Beverly, Alan, Steven. BA, U. Mich., 1933. With Ctrl. States Theatre Corp., Des Moines, 1933—, pres., 1950—. Founder A.H. & Theo Blank Performing Arts Ctr.; mem., chmn. trust com. Iowa Des Moines Nat. Bank, 1950-82. Salvage chmn. War Prodn. Bd. Polk County, 1940-42; past bd. dirs. Salvation Army, Child Guidance Ctr., YMCA; built Raymond Blank Lodge and Sick Bay, Camp Mitigwa Boy Scout Camp, Anna Blank Hosp. for Child Guidance Ctr., A.H. Blank Park Zoo; chmn. Des Moines United Way dr., 1976; endowed permanent chair for gifted and talented children U. Iowa, permanent scholarship, Weitzmann Inst., Israel; pres. Greater Des Moines Com., 1953, Theatre Owners of Amer., 1957-58; bd. dirs. Iowa Meth. Hosp., Des Moines C. of C., Simpson Coll., Des Moines Club, Wakonda Club; hon. chmn. Variety Club Telethon, 1999. Lt. comdr. USN, 1943-46. Recipient Brotherhood award NCCJ, 1976, Am. Humanitarian award Variety Club Am., 1980, The Iowa award Nat. Soc. for Fund Raising Execs., Disting. Alumni award U. Iowa, 1990, Jr. Achievement Laureate award, 1997; inducted into Midwest Nat. Assn. Theatre Owners Hall of Fame, 2000. Mem. Nat. Assn. Theatre Owners (bd. dirs.), Theatre Owners Am. (pres. 1955, chmn. bd. dirs. 1956-57). Jewish. Avocations: golf, hunting, fishing. Office: Ctrl States Theatre Corp 414 Insurance Exchange Des Moines IA 50309-2321 Office Fax: 515-243-2625.

BLANK, PHILIP BERNARDINI, lawyer, educator; b. N.Y.C., May 22, 1934; s. Arthur J. and Consuelo Inez (de Pasquale) B.; m. Mary Grace Marcello, Sept. 8, 1962; children— Arthur, Philip, Jr., Tricia Ann, Gregory. B.S., Fordham U., 1956, LL.B., 1959. Assoc. atty. Law Offices-S.W. Rowe, White Plains, N.Y., 1962-66, staff atty. Allstate Ins. Co., White Plains, 1960-62, County Trust Co., White Plains, 1966-68; law asst./referee Surrogate's Ct., White Plains, 1968-79; prof. law Pace Law Sch., White Plains, 1979—, assoc. dean external affairs, 1985— ; faculty mem. N.Y. State Bar Assn., Albany, 1974—, Practising Law Inst., N.Y.C., 1977, NYU Sch. Continuing Edn., N.Y.C., 1975, Manhattanville Coll. Continuing Legal Edn., 1976-77. Author: textbook Wills, Intestate Succession and Trusts, 1983; contbr. articles to journs. Mem. Zoning Bd. Appeals, Mount Pleasant, N.Y. 1972—, chmn., 1978— . Served to staff sgt. USAR, 1960-66. Mem. White Plains Bar Assn., Westchester County Bar Assn. (chmn. trusts and estate sect. 1984—), N.Y. Bar Assn., ABA. Republican. Roman Catholic. Club: Westwood Swimming and Tennis Assn. (Thornwood, N.Y.). Office: Pace U Sch Law 78 N Broadway White Plains NY 10603-3710

BLANK, REBECCA MARGARET, economist; b. Columbia, Mo., Sept. 19, 1955; d. Oscar Uel and Vernie (Backhaus) B.; m. Johannes Kuttner, 1994; 1 child, Emily. BS, U. Minn., 1976; PhD, MIT, 1983. Cons. Data Resources, Inc., Chgo., 1976-79; asst. prof. econs. Princeton U., 1983-89; assoc. prof. econs. Northwestern U., Chgo., 1989-94, prof. econs., 1994-99; sr. staff economist Coun. of Econ. Advisors, Washington, 1989-90, mem., 1998-99; dean, Henry Carter Adams prof. Gerald R. Ford Sch. Pub. Policy, U. Mich., Ann Arbor, 1999—; co-dir. Nat. Poverty Rsch. Ctr., U. Mich. Author: It Takes A Nation: A New Agenda for Fighting Poverty, 1997, other books; contbr. articles to profl. jours. Vis. Professorships for Women grantee, 1988-89; Sloan Found. fellow, 1982-83; recipient Jr. Faculty Teaching award Princeton U., 1985, David Kershaw award Assn. Pub. Policy Analysis and Mgmt., 1993, Richard Lester award for best book on labor econs., 1997. Mem. Nat. Bur. Econ. Rsch., Am. Econs. Assn., Assn. of Pub. Policy Analysis and Mgmt., Indsl. Rels. Rsch. Assn. United Ch. of Christ.

BLANK, ROBERT DANIEL, medical educator; b. Antwerp, Belgium, Oct. 25, 1956; s. Lester Earl and Victoria Elvire (Benyacar) Blank; m. Susan Nan Coppersmith, Dec. 21, 1981; 1 child, Deborah Louise. AB, Columbia U., 1978; BA, U. Cambridge, U.K., 1980; MD, PhD, NYU, 1988; postdoctoral fellow, Rockefeller U., 1990-95. Diplomate Am. Bd. Internal Medicine, Am. Bd. Endocrinology and Metabolism. Resident N.Y. Hosp., 1988-90; clin. fellow N.Y. Hosp. and Meml.-Sloan Kettering Cancer Ctr., N.Y.C., 1990-95; asst. scientist Hosp. for Spl. Surgery, N.Y.C., 1996-2000; asst. prof. medicine Cornell U., N.Y.C., 1998-2000, U. Wis., Madison, 2000—. Cons. Geo-Med Pharms., Fremont, Calif., 1998-99; scientific adv. bd. Gen. Clin. Rsch. Ctr., Cornell U. Med. Coll., 1998-2000, chief diabetes svc., Madison VA Hosp, 2001-, Geriatrics, Rsch., Edn. and Clin. Ctr. Contbr. articles to profl. jours. Fellow ACP; mem. Am. Soc. for Bone and Mineral Rsch., Ctrl. Soc. for Clin. Rsch., Endocrine Soc., Internat. Soc. for Clinical Densitometry Avocations: bridge, skiing. Office: U Wis Med Sch Endocrinology Sect Dept Med 600 Highland Ave Madison WI 53792

BLANK, STANLEY BRUCE, secondary school educator; s. Harold L. and Irene M. Blank(Stepmother), Robert B. (Stepfather) and Mary L. Kneemyer; m. Julie D. Kessler, Dec. 8, 1979; children: Kyle S., Kurtis L., Kory D. BS, U. Ill., 1977; MS, Ea. Ill. U., 1980; PhD, So. Ill. U., 1996. Educator Wayne City (Ill.) H.S., 1978—; instr. So. Ill. U., Carbondale, 2002—. Computer programmer Resampling Stats, Inc., Arlington, Va., 1998—. Author: Calculus for Calculators and Microcomputers, 1985. Mem.: Math. Assoc. of Am., Soc.Indsl. Applied Math., Nat. Speleological Soc. Home: 706 Brook St Wayne City IL 62895 Office: Wayne City High School Mill St Wayne City IL 62895

BLANK, WILLIAM RUSSELL, mathematics educator; b. Utica, N.Y., Aug. 7, 1916; s. William Nicholas and Marguerite Dorothy (Pugh) B.; m. Elizabeth Jeanette Roman, Sept. 12, 1942; children: William Keith, Marvin Darryl, Ronald Paul. BA, Union Coll., Nebr., 1939; postgrad., U. Mich., 1939-40, Syracuse U., 1952-56; MA, U. Nebr., 1953. Cert. tchr. math., phys. sci., N.Y. Tchr. math., sci. Staatsburg (N.Y.) Union Sch., 1941-42, Fresno (Calif.) Union Acad., 1946-48; instr. math. Union Coll., Lincoln, Nebr., 1948-50; tchr., dept. head Whitesboro (N.Y.) Cen. Sch., 1950-78. Adj. faculty Mohawk Valley C.C., Utica, 1956-2003; pvt. tutor in math., 1950—. Sgt. U.S. Army, 1942-45. Recipient awards NSF, 1957, 58, 59, 60. Mem. Ret. Tchrs. Assn., VFW, Am. Legion, IBM Magicians Club, SAM Magician Club, Pi Mu Epsilon, Phi Delta Kappa, Nat. Coun. Tchrs. Math. Avocations: travel, reading, music, church functions. Home: 34 Burr Ave New York Mills NY 13417-1305

BLANKART, CHARLES BEAT, economics educator; b. Lucerne, Switzerland, May 20, 1942; s. André and Gabrielle (Zelger) B.; children: Ludwig, Rudolf; m. Michaela Baier, Mar. 3, 1995. B Polit. Economy, U. Basel, Switzerland, 1967; D Econs., U. Basel, 1969. Lectr. U. Konstanz, Fed. Republic Germany, 1976-78; prof. econs. Free U. Berlin, 1978, U. German Armed Forces, Munich, 1978-85, Berlin Poly. U., 1985-92, Humboldt U. Berlin, 1992—. Mem. bd. acad. advisors Fed. Ministry Econs. and Tech.; mem. sci. adv. bd. Regulatory Commn. of Telecomms. and Posts. Author: Public Finance in Democracy, 4th edit., 2001; contbr. articles to sci. publs. Mem. European Pub. Choice Soc. (pres. 1984-85). Office: Humboldt U Berlin Econs Spandauerstr 1 10178 Berlin Germany E-mail: blankart@wiwi.hu-berlin.de.

BLANKE, RICHARD BRIAN, lawyer; b. St. Louis, Oct. 28, 1954; s. Robert H. and Phyllis I. (Kessler) Schaffler. BA, U. Pa., 1977; JD, U. Mo., 1980. Bar: Mo. 1980, U.S. Dist. Ct. (ea. and we. dists.) Mo. 1980. Ptnr. Blanke & Assocs., St. Louis County, Mo., 1980-90, Uthoff, Graeber, Bobinette & Blanke, St. Louis, 1991—. Mem. ABA, ATLA, Mo. Bar Assn., Mo. Assn. Trial Attys., St. Louis Met. Bar Assn. Office: Uthoff Graeber Bobinette & Blanke 906 Olive St Ste 300 Saint Louis MO 63101-1426 E-mail: rblanke@ugbblaw.com.

BLANKENBAKER, ZARINA, adult education educator, consultant; d. M Ali Din and Saira Bakash; m. John Ford Blankenbaker; children: Lauren Sarah, Ryan Ford. BSc in secondary edn., Ind. U., 1980—83, MA in applied linguistics, 1983—84; postgrad., Summer Inst. Intercultural Communication, Portland, Oreg., Nat. Inst. Leadership Devel., Dallas County C.C. Cert. tchg. State of Tex., 1989. Esol instr. Army Cmty. Svc., Lawton, Okla., 1985—86; fin. counselor Army Cmty. Services, Killeen, Tex., 1986—90; adj. instr. Ctrl. Tex. Coll., Killeen, 1989—90; adj. faculty/lab tutor/academic advisor Richland Coll., Dallas, 1993—97, faculty, 1997—. Bd. mem. Tex TESOL V, Dallas, 1997—99, newsletter editor, 1997—99; com. chair Tex TESOL State Conf., Dallas, 1998; sec. Richland Coll. Faculty Assn., Dallas, 2000—02. Mem.: Am. Assn. Women in Cmty. Colls., Assn. of Grad. Students in Higher Edn., Phi Kappa Phi. Office: Richland College 12800 Abrams Rd Dallas TX 75243-2199 Office Fax: 972-238-6166. E-mail: zblankenbaker@dcccd.edu.

BLANKENBURG, JULIE J. librarian; b. Madison, Wis., Dec. 22, 1956; d. Henry A. and Marjorie L. Blankenburg; m. Wayne I. Zimmerman, July 1991. BA in Theatre, U. Wis., 1979, MA in LS, 1980. Libr. svcs. asst. Law Libr., U. Wis., Madison, 1984—88; asst. libr. USDA Forest Products Lab. Libr., Madison, 1988-93, libr., 1994—. Mem. ALA, Spl. Librs. Assn., Wis. Libr. Assn., Theatre Libr. Assn. Office: USDA Forest Svc Forest Products Lab Libr One Gifford Pinchot Dr Madison WI 53726-2398

BLANKENHEIMER, BERNARD, economics consultant; b. N.Y.C., July 6, 1920; s. Benjamin and Anna (Barach) B.; m. Rosalind Drescher, Dec. 4, 1943, children— Alan Howard, Susan Leslie. BA, Bklyn. Coll., 1941; postgrad., N.Y. U., 1941-42; MA in Econs, George Washington U., 1950. With U.S. Dept. Commerce, 1942-76, jr. economist European div., 1942, asst. economist, 1945-47, internat. economist Africa sect. Brit. Commonwealth div., 1948-50, chief African sect. Africa-Near East div., 1950-61, dep. dir. Africa div., 1961, dir., 1962-68, dep. dir. Office Import Programs, 1970-72, dir. Office Import Programs, 1973-76; U.S. Fgn. Service sr. comml. officer Am. consulate gen. Johannesburg, Republic South Africa, 1968-70. Dir. U.S. Trade Mission to, Liberia, Ghana, Sierra Leone, Guinea, 1960, Mission to, Kenya, Uganda, Tanganyika, 1963; adviser U.S. del. 22d session GATT, Geneva, 1965; mem. U.S. observer del. UN Econ. Commn. for Africa Symposium on Industrialization, Cairo, 1966; mem. 9th Sr. Seminar in Fgn. Policy Dept. State, 1966-67; observer U.S. del. Unctad III, Santiago, Chile, 1972; mem. U.S. del UNESCO Meeting of Experts, Geneva, 1973, Internat. Rubber Study Group meetings, Geneva, 1973, 74, Djakarta, Indonesia, 1975; mem. U.S. del. to 5th Internat. Tin Conf. Negotiations, Geneva, 1975, Unctad Confs. on Tungsten and Copper, Geneva, 1976, Unctad Consultation on Copper, Geneva, 1976; asst. dir. econ. cons. services Wolf & Co., 1976-78; v.p. Econ. Cons. Services, Inc., Washington, 1978-79; lectr. African studies Johns Hopkins Sch. Advanced Internat. Studies, 1957-62, Am. U. Sch. Bus. Adminstrn., 1967, Howard U., 1962-68 Contbr. articles to govtl., profl. jours. Served with AUS, 1942-45. Recipient silver medal for distinguished authorship Dept. Commerce, 1960, spl. achieve-

ment award, 1972, 75 Fellow African Studies Assn., Royal Geog. Soc. Home and Office: 3210 N Leisure World Blvd Apt 811 Silver Spring MD 20906-5697 Personal E-mail: Bblank9443@aol.com.

BLANKENSHIP, DOLORES MOOREFIELD, principal, music educator, retired; b. Atlanta, June 4, 1929; d. Albert Talmadge and Willie Mae (Cole) Moorefield; divorced; 1 child, Diane Lee. BME, Northwestern U., 1951; MA, Ohio State U., Columbus, 1958. Cert. music tchr., secondary principal, Ohio. Vocal music tchr. Hoke Smith High Sch., Atlanta, 1951-52; vocal instr., tchr. Reynoldsburg (Ohio) Sch., 1952-53; substitute music tchr. various public schs., El Paso, Tex., 1953; vocal music tchr. Columbus (Ohio) Public Schs., 1956-73, asst. prin., 1973-86, prin., 1986-94. Adv. bd. Capital Area Humane Soc., Columbus, 1987-94; pres. Altrusa, Columbus, 1973, 87; mem. Columbus Mus. of Arts; docent Wexner Ctr. for Arts, 1994-2001; mem. planning com. Columbus Arts Festival, 1994-2001; vol. FACTLIVE Columbus Pub. Sch.; docent Columbus Symphony Orch., 1995; AARP coord. Capital City Task Force, 1997-2000. Mem. Nat. Middle Sch. Adminstr. Assn. (Ohio chpt., Columbus chpt. pres. 1990-91), Columbus Adminstr. Assn. (exec. bd. 1989-91), Ohio Assn. Deans, Adminstr., Counselors (treas. 1988-90). Avocations: reading, jazz music, movies, plays, travel. Home: 1291 Hanford Sq Columbus OH 43206-3668

BLANKENSHIP, EDWARD G. architect; b. Martin, Tenn., June 22, 1943; BArch, Columbia U., 1966, MSc in Arch., 1967; MLitt in Arch., Cambridge (Eng.) U., 1971. Sr. v.p. Landrum & Brown, Inc., Chgo. Home: 379 Woodland Rd Highland Park IL 60035 Office: 1021 W Adams St Chicago IL 60607-2911

BLANKENSHIP, J. RICHARD, ambassador; b. Troy, Ala. married. Diploma, Fla. State U. Former ptnr., dir. Capital South Group, Jacksonville, Fla.; former pres., CFO St. John's Capital; former mcpl. and govt. financing officer Raymond James and Assocs., St. Petersburg, Fla.; former acct. Peat, Marwick, and Mitchell, Jacksonville; former ptnr. J. Richard Blankenship & co.; U.S. amb. to The Bahamas, Bulgaria, 2001—; former acct. Price Waterhouse & Co., Tampa, Fla. Apptd. mem. State of Fla. Transp. Outreach Program; mem. Fla. Joint Task Force Evaluation Team. Office: DOS Amb 3370 Nassau Pl Washington DC 20521*

BLANKENSHIP, JENNY MARY, museum administrator; b. Mpls., Nov. 15, 1955; AA in bus., Weatherford Coll.; cert. paralegal, Southern Meth. U.; BBS in Mktg., BBA in Journalism, U. Tex.; PhD, So. Meth. U., 1998. Mktg. coord. Fingerhut Corp., Minnetonka, Minn.; pub. rels. coord. Family Svcs. Inc, Ft. Worth, Tex.; pres. Gloss Mgmt. Inc, Weatherford, Tex.; editor The Shorthorn, Arlington, Tex.; v.p., editor Randy Keck & Co., Boston; editor-in-chief Community Press, Hico, Tex.; dir. pub. affairs Hico Chiropractic; pub. Tex. Spotlight; promoter Dallas Cowboy Legends Event, 1997; mus. programs adminstr. Sci. Mus. Minn., 1999—. Dir. pub. rels. Hope Inc., Mineral Wells, Tex.; dir. Randy Keck & Co.; fundraising cons. WICI, Waco, Tex., instr. seminars Ctr. for Profl. & Exec. Devel. U. Tex; promoter Dallas Cowboy Legends, 1997. Author: Poetry of the Old Testament, 1987, The Business of Life, 1988, Do Over, 1994, The Brains, The Club and The Sneak, 1999, Shadows of Hate, 1999; pub. Tex. Spotlight. Vol. merit badge counselor, dist. officer, dist. tng. chair Boy Scouts Am. Recipient Best Layout, Column, Page award Columbia U., 1987, 90, Best Upstart Weekly in the State award Southwest Journalism Conf., 1994, Best Sports award South Tex. Press, 1995, Best Layout award South Tex. Press, 1995. Mem. Women In Communication, Inc. (Best Feature award, Best Advt. Campaign, 1991, Best Broadcast Feature award, 1990), MENSA, NAFE (com. mem), Soc. Profl. Journalists, United Meth. Women (pres.), Kiwanis. Methodist. Avocations: painting, singing, collecting headwear. Office: PO Box 96 Glen Rose TX 76043-0096

BLANKENSHIP, ROBERT EUGENE, biochemistry educator; b. Auburn, Nebr., Aug. 25, 1948; s. George Robert and Jane (Kehoe) Leech; m. Elizabeth Marie Dorland, June 26, 1971; children: Larissa Dorland, Samuel Robert. BS, Wesleyan U., Nebr., 1970; PhD, U. Calif., Berkeley, 1975. Postdoctoral fellow Lawrence Berkeley Lab., Berkeley, 1975-76, U. Washington, Seattle, 1976-79; asst. prof. Amherst (Mass.) Coll., 1979-85; assoc. prof. Ariz. State U., Tempe, 1985-88, prof., 1988—, chair, dept. chem. and biochem., 2002—, dir. Ctr. Study of Early Events in Photosynthesis, 1988-91. Author: Molecular Mechanisms of Photosynthesis, 2002; editor Anoxygenic Photosynthetic Bacteria, 1995; editor-in-chief Photosynthesis Rsch., 1988-99; cons. editor Advances in Photosynthesis, 1991-98; mem. editl. bd. Biophys. Jour., 2000-03, Biochemistry, 2001—, Internat. Jour. Astrobiology, 2001—; contbr. 190 articles to sci. jours. Recipient Alumni award Nebr. Wesleyan U., 1991, Disting. Rsch. award Ariz. State U., 1992, Mentoring award Ariz. State U., 1998. Mem. AAAS, Am. Chem. Soc., Biophys. Soc., Union of Concerned Scientists, Internat. Soc. of Photosynthesis Rsch. (pres. 2001-), Internat. Soc. for Study of Origin of Life. Democrat. Avocations: hiking, cooking, travel, fossil collecting. Home: 13824 S Canyon Dr Phoenix AZ 85048-9085 Office: Ariz State U Dept Chemistry And Bio Tempe AZ 85287-1604

BLANKENSHIP, ROY, conservator, artist, writer; b. Phila., Nov. 26, 1943; m. Lynn Ann Wilkers, Apr. 6, 1968 (div. May 1993); children: Troy Insley, Beth Lynn; m. Lois Showalter, Apr. 1, 2000. BAAS Arts and Sci., U Del., 1973. Art restoration apprentice/asst. Salter Studio, Arden, Del., 1966—72; art conservation student apprentice Winterthur (Del.) Mus., 1968—72; painting conservation asst. Ted Segal Studio Phila. Mus. Art, 1969—70; painting restoration asst./apprentice Twistback Conservation Ctr., Oxford, Pa., 1970—72; gen. mgr., layout design artist The Little Giant Shopper, Newark, Del., 1970—72; art tchr. Marbrook Elem., Wilmington, Del., 1971—72; part-time art tchr. Ursuline Acad., Wilmington, 1971—72; art history and studio art tchr. Brandywine H.S., Wilmington, 1972—73; curator, exhbn. coord. Morris Libr., U. Del., Newark, 1972—73; painting conservator-in residence Carspecken-Scott Gallery, Wilmington, 1972—78; founder Blankenship Painting and Conservation Studio, Wilmington, 1975—81; dir., owner Blankenship Conservation Ctr., Wilmington, 1981—; founder Blankenship's mail order bus., 1985—. Profl. fine art painting conservationist IIC, 1972; instr. art history U. Del., Newark, 1972; lectr., cons. in field, 1973—; curator, lectr. Albert Babb Insley retrospective exhbn. (traveling), 1984—85, Nardin Fine Arts, Ltd., Cross River, NY, 1988; organizer, guest curator, lectr. The McKissick Mus., U. S.C., Columbia, 1995; collections and chief painting conservator Boggs Fed. Bldg., Wilmington, Del., 1973—; curator Hastings Gallery, New Canaan, Conn., 1987; painting collections cons., restorer Del. Art Mus., Wilmington, Del., 1972—83; personal collections cons. to Ernest Dodge, dir. Peabody-Essex Mus., Salem, Mass., 1973—85; fellow, rsch. scientist AIC, Wash., DC, 1973—; conservators in pvt. practice Am. Inst. Cons., 1975—; chief painting conservator NEHGS, Boston, 1996—. Columnist Collecting (Gannett Papers), 1975—85; author, compiler, designer, pub.: The Delicate Palette of Albert Insley, 1982; editor: The Life and Times of Frank G. Speck (1881-1950), 1992; one-man shows include Atlas Chem. Emporium (photography), Wilmington, 1970, Swarthmore Coll., Pa., 1960, Bicentennial Retrospective exhbn., Wilmington Libr., Lou Polack Gallery, Rockport, Mass., 1978, 1983, Nancy Richardson Art and Antique Gallery, Essex, Conn., 1981, R.M. Worth Antiques and Fine Art, Chadds Ford, Pa., 2000, 2000, exhibited in group shows at Grand Opera Ho. and Del. Art Mus., Wilmington, Del., 1968, Del. Art Mus. Ceramics Retro., 1970, 1973, Chester County (Pa.) Art Assn., 2002, Hagley Mus., Wilmington, 2000, Rockport Contbg. Members Show, 2001, Main Hall, Kendal at Longwood, Pa., 2001, North Shore Ann. Exhbn., 1972—, Oil Painters of Am., 2002, one-man shows include R.M. Worth Antiques and Fine Art, Pa., 2000, exhbn. with wife, Main Hall, Kendal at Longwood, 2001, Wilmington Libr., Del., 2002, Sawyer Free Libr., Gloucester, Mass., 2002, Crosslands, Kennett Sq., Pa., 2003. Founder, organizer, head chairperson 1st Ann. Arden Ctr. Antiques Show and Sale, 1977; founder Blankenship Conservation Ctr., Wilmington, 1973—; organizer, co-chair 1st F.G. Speck Seminar, U. Pa., Phila., 1986. With USN, 1962—66, with USN, 1962—66. Mem.: NSAA, Am Artists Prof. League (Salmagundi Club), Am. Soc. Marine Artists, Soc. Del. Artists, Chester County Artist Assn. Address: PO Box 7221 Wilmington DE 19803

BLANKER, ALAN HARLOW, lawyer; b. Montague, Mass., Sept. 15, 1951; s. William Charles and Ann (Harlow) B. BA, Colby Coll., 1973; JD, Georgetown U., 1976. Bar: Mass. 1977, U.S. Dist. Ct. Mass. 1977. Ptnr. Levy, Winer, Greenfield, Mass., 1977—2002; dir., clk. Esleeck Mfg. Co., Inc., Montague, 1980—; sr. v.p., gen. counsel Greenfield Savs. Bank, 2002—. Incorporator Heritage Bank for Savs., Greenfield, 1980-86; incorporator, trustee Greenfield Savs. Bank, 1986—; trustee Greenriver Cemetery Co., 1997—. Editor Georgetown Law Jour., 1975-76. Mem. Greenfield Fin. Com., 1980-84; chmn. Greenfield Sch. Bldg. Com., 1977-81; mem. Greenfield Republican Town Com., 1976-85, Greenfield Town Coun., 1992-95, Greenfield Sch. Bldg. Com., 1996-99; incorporator Franklin Med. Ctr., 1979—, pres., treas.; bd. dirs., clk. Greenfield Area Devel. Corp.; dir. Greenfield Cmty. YMCA, 1995-2001. Mem. Franklin County C. of C. (chmn. tech. services com. 1982—), Phi Beta Kappa, Pi Sigma Alpha. Lodges: Kiwanis. Congregationalist. Home: 840 Colrain Rd Greenfield MA 01301-9763 Office: Greenfield Savs Bank PO Box 1537 Greenfield MA 01302-1537 E-mail: ablanker@greenfieldsavings.com.

BLANKFORT, LOWELL ARNOLD, newspaper publisher; b. N.Y.C., Apr. 29, 1926; s. Herbert and Gertrude (Butler) B.; m. April Pemberton; 1 child, Jonathan. BA in History and Polit. Sci., Rutgers U., 1946. Reporter, copy editor L.I. Star-Jour., NY, 1947—49; columnist London Daily Mail, Paris, 1949—50; copy editor The Stars & Stripes, Darmstadt, Germany, 1950—51, Wall St. Jour., N.Y.C., 1951; bus., labor editor Cowles Mags., N.Y.C., 1951—53; pub. Pacifica Tribune, Calif., 1954—59; free-lance writer Europe, Asia, 1959—61; co-pub., editor Chula Vista Star-News, Calif., 1961—78; co-owner Paradise Post, Calif., 1977—2003. Co-owner Monte Vista (Colo.) Jour., Ctr. (Colo.) Post-Dispatch, Del Norte (Colo.) Prospector, 1978-93, Plainview (Minn.) News, St. Charles (Minn.) Press, Lewiston (Minn.) Jour., 1980-98, Summit (Colo.) Sentinel, New Richmond (Wis.) News, 1981-87, Yuba City Valley Herald, Calif., 1982-85, TV Views, Monterey, Calif., 1982-87, Summit County Jour., Colo., 1982-87, Alpine (Calif.) Sun, 1987-93, Bassics Mag., 1998—, Fingerstyle Guitar Mag., 1999—. Columnist, contbr. articles on fgn. affairs to newspapers. Active Calif. Dem. Ctrl. Com., 1963; bd. dirs. Mus. Photographic Arts, San Diego, 2003—. Mem.: ACLU (pres. San Diego chpt. 1970—71), Soc. Profl. Journalists, Calif. Newspaper Pubs. Assn., East Meets West Found. (nat. v.p. 1992—98), World Federalist Assn. (pres. San Diego chpt. 1984—86, nat. bd. 1992—2000), UN Assn. (pres. San Diego chpt. 1991—93, nat. coun. 1992—97, nat. bd. 1997—2001, nat. coun. 2002—), Internat. Ctr. Devel. Policy (nat. bd. 1985—90), Ctr. Internat. Policy (bd. dirs. 1991—), World Affairs Coun. San Diego (pres. 1996—99, dir.), Inst. of the Ams. (assoc.; internat. coun. 1994—). Home: 4008 Old Orchard Ln Bonita CA 91902-2337 Office: Ste C25 310 3rd Ave Chula Vista CA 91910-3970

BLANKINSHIP, HENRY MASSIE, management consultant; b. Providence, Sept. 27, 1949; s. Ernest Randolph and Henrietta (Massie) B.; m. Linda Ferber, Jan. 17, 1981; children: John Byron, Kevin Mark, Sara Jane. Tech. mgr. Dept. of Navy, Washington, 1972-98; mgmt. cons., 1998-99; tech. dir. Brit. Aerospace, 2000—01, tech. cons., 2001—. Nat. corr. Karate Illustrated Mag., 1976-79. Head Karate instr. YMCA, Fairfax County, Va.; police spl. teams cons., Fairfax County. Recipient Outstanding Navy Civilian Svc. award, 1976-82, 84, 86, 88-95, Gold Wreath USN, 1977, Navy Spl. Acts award, 1983; named Ea. Region Karate Champion. Mem. Am. Mgmt. Assn., Nat. Assn. Combative Arts, Self Def. Sys. Internat. (Soke-Dai successor), Internat. Fedn. Jujutsuans, U.S. Kickboxing Assn., U.S. Karate Assn., Internat. Martial Arts Assn. (pres.), Taifung Martial Arts Assn. (chair bd. dirs., inductee Martial Arts Hall of Fame 1999). Republican. Avocations: jujitsu (black belt 8th degree), karate (black belt 8th degree). Office: Def Techs & Tactics PO Box A Dunn Loring VA 22027 E-mail: hmblan@aol.com.

BLANKSTEIN, MARY FREEMAN, violinist; b. Rutherfordton, N.C., Oct. 26, 1931; d. Spurgeon Lee and Dexter (Forney) Freeman; diploma (Scholar) Juilliard Sch. Music, 1955, BS, 1958; student (Fulbright fellow) Brussels Conservatoire, 1958-59; MusM, U. Maine, 1975; student Emmett Gore, Christine and Edouard Dethier, Arthur Grumiaux, Joseph Fuchs, Erica Morini, others; m. Joseph Blankstein, Mar. 6, 1958; children: Margot, Philip. pvt. tchr. violin, 1948—; violin soloist Juilliard Orch., 1955, Little Orch. Soc. in Town Hall, 1955; asst. concertmaster Am. Symphony, N.Y.C., 1964-68, concertmaster, 1968-72; tchr. violin, prep. div. Juilliard Sch. Music, N.Y.C., 1968-69; tchr. violin Manhattan Sch. Music, 1969-85; pvt. tchr. violin and chamber music, 1970—; head instrumental dept. Chapin Sch., N.Y.C., 1970-88; co-founder, mem. N.Y. Lyric Arts Trio, 1974-84; solo recitals, U.S. and Europe; co-founder Downeast Chamber Music Center, Castine, Maine, 1977; faculty Downeast Chamber Music Ctr.; mem. Masters Chamber Orch., Palm Harbor, Fla., 1990-93; rec. artist Musical Heritage Soc. Rec., also recs. with Am. Symphony under Leopold Stokowski. Mem. Am. Chamber Music Assn. Home: 126 26th Ave NE Saint Petersburg FL 33704-3464

BLANTON, EDWARD LEE, JR., lawyer; b. nr. Hope Mills, N.C., Oct. 31, 1931; s. Edward Lee and Margaret M. (Bullard) B.; m. Cathleen Estelle Edwards, Aug. 13, 1960; children: Edward Lee III, Cathleen Estelle, Margaret Ellyn. BS, Davidson Coll., 1953; MA, Vanderbilt U., 1954; LLB, U. Md., 1960. Bar: Md. 1960. Tchr. math. Balt. City schs., 1956-59; law clk. to judge Washington, 1960-62; assoc. Cross & Shriver, Balt., 1962—65; ptnr., mgr. Maxwell Hughes & Blanton, 1965—68; ptnr. Adelberg, Rudow & Blanton, 1969-72, Blanton & McCleary, 1973-93; asst. atty. gen. State Md., Balt., 1965-68. Chmn. subcom. drafting revision Md. election laws Md. Legis. Coun., 1966-67; chmn. subcom. drafting revision Md. income tax laws Hughes Commn., 1966-67. Bd. dirs. United Christian Citizens, 1971-92, pres., 1974-75; pres. Ctrl. Balt. Ecumenical Sch. Christian Edn., 1971-74, Hist. Long Green Valley, Inc., 1980-86, Long Green Valley Assn., 1979-89; dir. Ctr. for Prevention of Child Abuse, 1991-96; mem. State Rep. Ctrl. Com., 1982-86; mem. citizens adv. com. Charles H. Hickey Sch., 1983-91, chmn., 1987-91; mem. Ctrl. Towson Com. Christian Businessmen, Balt. Coun. Fgn. Affairs; v.p., dir. Long Green Valley Conservancy, Inc., 1995-98; trustee com. Presbyn. Ch., Balt., St. James Acad., Monkton, Md., 1989-95, Egenton Home, Balt.; Rep. nominee for Atty. Gen. of Md., 1990. 1st lt. AUS, 1954-56; capt. Md. N.G., 1957-62. Mem. Nat. Lawyers Assn., Bar Assn. Balt. County, Newcomen Soc. N.Am., Christian Legal Soc., Center Club, Masons, Delta Theta Phi. Presbyterian (elder). Home: Avondell Glen Arm MD 21057 Office: 305 W Chesapeake Ave Baltimore MD 21204-4255 E-mail: eblantonjr@msn.com.

BLANTON, HOOVER CLARENCE, lawyer; b. Green Sea, S.C., Oct. 13, 1925; s. Clarence Leo and Margaret (Hoover) B.; m. Cecilia Lopez, July 31, 1949; children: Lawson Hoover, Michael Lopez. JD, U. S.C., 1953. Bar: S.C. 1953. Ordained deacon, Bapt. Ch. Assoc. Whaley & McCutchen, Columbia, SC, 1953—66; ptnr. McCutchen, Blanton, Johnson and Barvette LLP, Columbia, 1967—. Dir. Legal Aid Service Agy., Columbia, chmn. bd., 1972-73. Gen. counsel S.C. Rep. Conv., 1962; del. Rep. State Conv., 1962, 64, 66, 68, 70, 74; bd. dirs. Midlands Cmty. Action Agy., Columbia, vice chmn., 1972-73; bd. dirs. Wildewood Sch., 1976-78; mem. Gov.'s Legal Svcs. Adv. Coun., 1976-77, Commn. on Continuing Legal Edn. for Judiciary, 1977-84, Commn. on Continuing Lawyer Competence, 1988-92, Commn. on Continuing Legal Edn. and Specialization, 1992-2000, sec. 1995, chmn., 1996-99. Mem. ABA. S.C. Bar (ho. of dels. 1975-76, chmn. fee disputes bd. 1977-81), Richland County Bar Assn. (pres. 1980), Def. Trial Attys. (state chmn. 1971-77, 80-95, exec. coun. 1977-80), Am. Bd. Trial Advs. (pres. S.C. chpts. 1989, Trial Lawyer of Yr. 2001), Toastmasters Club (pres. 1959), Palmetto Club, Phi Delta Phi. Home: 3655 Deerfield Dr Columbia SC 29204-3730 Office: 1414 Lady St Columbia SC 29201-3304

BLANTON, JACK SAWTELLE, oil company executive; b. Shreveport, La., Dec. 7, 1927; s. William Neal and Louise (Wynn) B.; m. Laura Lee Scurlock, Aug. 20, 1949; children: Elizabeth Louise Blanton Wareing, Jack Sawtelle Jr., Eddy Scurlock. BA, U. Tex., 1947, LLB, 1950. Bar: Tex. 1950. With Scurlock Oil Co., Houston, 1950-88, v.p., 1956-58, pres., 1958-83, chmn. bd., 1983-88; pres. Eddy Refining Co., Houston, 1988—. Chmn. bd. trustees Houston Endowment, Inc.; pres. Eddy Refining Co.; bd. dirs. Pogo Producing Co., Burlington No. Santa Fe, Inc. Past chmn. bd. trustees St. Luke's United Meth. Ch., Houston; past chmn. bd. regents U. Tex. System, 1985-89; past vice chmn., bd. dirs. Meth. Hosp., Houston. Mem. Nat. Petroleum Coun., Mid-Continent Oil and Gas Assn. (past pres.) Houston C. of C. (life), Sons Republic of Tex. (past pres. San Jacinto chpt.), Sam Houston Meml. Assn., Nat. Tennis Assn., U.S. Lawn Tennis Assn., Tex. Ind. Oil Producers and Refiners, Ex-Students Assn. U. Tex. (past pres.), Greater Houston Partnership (chmn. 1985-86), Delta Kappa Epsilon, Phi Delta Phi, Phi Alpha Delta. Clubs: Houston (Houston) (past pres.), River Oaks Country (Houston); El Dorado Country (Palm Springs, Calif.). Office: Eddy Refining Co 700 Louisiana St Ste 3920 Houston TX 77002-2731 also: Houston Endowment Inc 600 Travis St Ste 6400 Houston TX 77002-3000

BLANTON, JOHN ARTHUR, architect, writer; b. Houston, Jan. 1, 1928; s. Arthur Alva and Caroline (Jeter) Blanton; m. Marietta Louise Newton, Apr. 10, 1954 (dec. 1976); children: Jill Blanton Milne, Lynette Blanton Rowe(dec.), Elena Diane. BA, Rice U., 1948, BS in Architecture, 1949. With Richard J. Neutra, L.A., 1950-64; pvt. practice Manhattan Beach, Calif., 1964—. Lectr. UCLA Ext., 1967—76, 1985, Harbor Coll., L.A., 1970—72. Columnist: Easy Reader newspaper, 1994—96; contbr. articles to profl. jours. Mem. Capital Improvements Com., Manhattan Beach, 1966; city commr. Bd. Bldg. Code Appeals; chmn. Zoning Adjustment Bd., 1990, Planning Commn., 1993—99. With Signal Corps U.S. Army, 1951—53. Recipient Best Ho. of the Yr. award, C. of C., 1969—71, 1983, Preservation of Natural Site award, 1974, Design award, 1975, 1984. Mem.: AIA (contbr. book revs. to jour. 1972—76, Red Cedar Shingle/AIA Nat. Merit award 1979), Soc. Archtl. Historians. Office: John Blanton AIA Architect 1456 12th St # 4 Manhattan Beach CA 90266-6187

BLANTON, LAWTON WALTER, retired dean; b. Perry, Fla., Oct. 25, 1914; s. Lawton Walter and Minnie Florelle (Truesdale) B.; BS, U. Fla., 1936, MS, 1941; postgrad. U. Chgo., 1949, Columbia, 1951-53. Rsch. assoc. U. Fla., Gainesville, 1941-42, asst. prof. math., 1942-53; asst. dean students Coll. City N.Y., 1955-57; dir. admissions Montclair Coll., Upper Montclair, N.J., 1957-61, dean students, 1961-80, ret., 1980. Lawton W. Blanton Hall named in his honor Montclair State Coll., 1982. Mem. Am. Assn. Higher Edn., Nat. Assn. Student Pers. Adminstrs., Am., N.J. pers. and guidance assns., N.Y. Schoolmasters, Eastern Assn. Coll. Deans and Advisers of Students, N.J. State Coll. Chief Student Affairs Officers (pres. 1977-78), Nat. Collegiate Honors Council, Am. Hort. Soc., Am. Hemerocallis Soc., Am. Plant Life Soc., Am. Rhododendron Soc. Home: 1 Oak Cres Little Falls NJ 07424-2414

BLANTON, LEWIS M. federal judge; b. Cape Girardeau, Mo., Mar. 5, 1934; AB, St. Louis U., 1958, MA, 1962; JD, U. Mo., 1965. Bar: Mo. Atty. Thompson, Walther & Shewmaker, St. Louis, 1965-69, Blanton, Rice & Sickal, Sikeston, Mo., 1969-71, Robison & Blanton, Sikeston, 1971-78; assoc. judge Cir. Ct. of Scott County, Mo., 1979-91; magistrate judge U.S. Dist. Ct. (ea. dist.) Mo., Cape Girardeau, 1991—. Contbr. articles to profl. jours. Mem. ABA, Mo. Bar, Scott County Bar Assn., Cape Girardeau County Bar Assn., Bar Assn. Met. St. Louis, Fed. Magistrate Judges Assn. Office: 111 US Courthouse 339 Broadway St Cape Girardeau MO 63701-7330

BLANTON, LINDA GAYLE, counselor, former educator; b. Rockford, Ill., Mar. 15, 1940; d. Clyde Martin and Agatha (Happe) Christiansen; m. Paul Edward Blanton, Aug. 6, 1972; 1 child, Diane Renee Wren 1 stepchild, Linda Jean DeLawder. BS in Edn./Music Supervision, Wittenberg U., Springfield, Ohio, 1962; MEd, Wright State U., 1968, MS in Mental Health Counseling, 1990, Cert. in Gerontology, 1994. Lic. social worker, Ohio; lic. profl. counselor, Ohio; cert. tchr. elem. music, Ohio; cert. in reading supervision, Ohio; cert. elem. prin., Ohio; cert. counselor Nat. Bd. Cert. Counselors. Tchr. elem. music Northmont Schs., Englewood, Ohio, 1962—63; elem. tchr. New Carlisle (Ohio) Bethel Local Schs., 1963—69; instr. continuing edn. dept., music dept. Wittenberg U., 1968—80; instr. edn. dept. summer and Saturday programs Wright State U., Dayton, Ohio, 1968—80; supr. fed. edn., tchr. Ohio Vets. Children's Home, Xenia, 1969—86; ret, 1986; psychology asst., cognitive specialist Rehab Continuum, Cin., 1990—2002; ret., 2002. Developer elem. materials; editor Ohio Volkssport Assn. Jour. and News, 1996—. Youth leader, fin. sec. First Luth. Ch., Xenia, 1979-89; vol. Greene Meml. Hosp., Xenia, 1986—, Children's Med. Ctr., Dayton, 1990-92; Christian Relief Overseas Project for Hunger organizer Xenia Area Assn. Chs., 1990, 99, 2000; active Greater Xenia Habitat for Humanity, 1991-93. Recipient Outstanding Paper on Alzheimers Disease, Profl. and Sci. Ohio Conf. on Aging, Ohio Network Ednl. Cons. in the Field of Aging, Ohio Rsch. Coun. on Aging, 1995. Mem. ASCD, ACA, Ohio Mental Health Counselors Assn., Ohio Ret. Tchrs. Assn., Greene County Ret. Tchrs. Assn., Ohio Wander Freunde (v.p. 1997-2002), Wandering Wheels and Xenia Walking Club (corr. sec. 1989-92, membership chairperson 1991-99, v.p. 1992-96, pres. 1996-), Ohio Rsch. Coun. on Aging, Miami Valley Counseling Assn., Ohio Volkssport Assn. (treas. 2002-), Sigma Alpha Iota (v.p. 1966-67), Delta Kappa Gamma (v.p. 1976-78, pres. 1978-80, sec. 1988-90), Phi Delta Kappa. Lutheran. Avocations: walking, biking, crafts, reading, quilting. Home: 92 Kinsey Rd Xenia OH 45385-1537

BLANTON, MADGE BRANTLEY, family practice nurse practitioner; b. Candor, N.C., Oct. 19, 1934; d. Paul Adam Brantley and Donnie Mae Campbell; m. Robert G. Blanton, June 28, 1952; children: Robert N., John A., Angela B. Attended, Fla. State U., 1978. Cert. notary public SC, NC. Tech. rep. Herring RX Drugs, Myrtle Beach, SC, 1959—62; processor Western Union, Myrtle Beach, SC, 1959—62; asst. mgr. AAFES Svc. Sta., Myrtle Beach, SC, 1962—79; mgr. collections Fed. C.U., Myrtle Beach AFB, SC, 1972—93; nurse pvt. duty, Forest City, NC, 1998—. Cons. credit com. F.C.U., Myrtle Beach AFB, SC, 1979—82; nurse aid Shelby Hosp., NC, 1949—51. Author numerous poems. Mem.: VFW, Am. Legion. Home: 1007 Stonecutter St Spindale NC 28160-1736

BLANTON, MARY RUTHERFORD, lawyer, educator; b. Alexandria, Va., July 4, 1950; d. Arthur J. and Margaret (Cockrell) Rutherford; m. Theodore A. Blanton, May 27, 1972; children: William F., John A., Thomas Pennington, Mary Elizabeth. BA magna cum laude, Wake Forest U., 1972; postgrad., St. John's Grad. Inst., Santa Fe, 1973; JD cum laude, Georgetown U., 1981. Bar: Va. 1982, NC 1985; cert. specialist in family law, family fin. mediator, NC. Tchr., chmn. English dept. Martin Spalding High Sch., Severn, Md., 1972-75; Legis. aide Ho. of Reps., Washington, 1976-77; pvt. practice Springfield, Va., 1982-83; assoc. Ketner & Rankin, Salisbury, N.C., 1984-86; ptnr. Crowell, Porter, Blanton & Blanton, Salisbury, 1986-90, Blanton & Blanton, 1990-94; prin. Mary Blanton & Assoc., Salisbury, 1994—2002, Blanton Law Firm, PA, Salisbury, 2002—, Peace Seekers, Inc., 2002—. Vice-chair Nat. Assessment Ednl. Progress, 1990-98. Carswell scholar, 1969-71. Mem.: Va. State Bar Assn., NC State Bar Assn., Phi Beta Kappa. Episcopalian. Avocations: backpacking, skiing, reading. Home: 305 W Thomas St Salisbury NC 28144-5351 E-mail: mrb@blantonlawfirm.com.

BLANTON, PRISCILLA WHITE, social sciences educator, psychologist, researcher; b. Little rock, Ark., Aug. 13, 1947; d. Douglas Malcolm and Nell Chandler White; m. Horace Dewey Blanton, Aug. 4, 1984; children: Benjamin Douglas, Janelle Ruth. BS, Carson-Newman Coll., 1969; MS, U. Tenn., 1970, EdD, 1972. Lic. psychologist Tenn. Asst. prof. dept. child and famiy studies U. Tenn., Knoxville, 1972—77, assoc. prof., 1977—82, prof., 1982—. Dept. head U. Tenn., 1980—83, mem. faculty adv. com. Black Studies Program, 1972—76, mem. faculty adv. com. Women's Studies Program, 1979—91; program developer and leader Southea. Newspaper Pub.'s Assn. conf., Knoxville, 1979. Contbr. articles to profl. jours., chapters to books. Bd. dirs. East Tenn. Planned Parenthood, Oak Ridge, 1988—90. Grantee, Consortium for Clergy Families, 1993. Mem.: Nat. Coun. on Family Rels. (state treas. 1988—94). Avocations: gardening, golf, skiing. Home: 7324 Cresthill Dr Knoxville TN 37919 Office: U Tenn Dept Child & Family Studies JHB 115 Knoxville TN 37996

BLANTZ, THOMAS EDWARD, Roman Catholic priest, educator; b. Massillon, Ohio, June 18, 1934; s. Raymond Lawrence Blantz and Katherine Jeanette Chance. AB, U. Notre Dame, 1957; STL, Gregorian U., 1961; PhD, Columbia U., 1968. Ordained priest, Roman Cath. Ch., 1960. Asst. prof. U. Notre Dame, 1968-76, univ. archivist, 1969-78, v.p. student affairs, 1970-72, assoc. prof., 1976-94, prof., 1994—. Author: Priest in Public Service, 1982, George N. Shuster, 1993; contbr. articles to profl. jours. Trustee U. Notre Dame, 1970—. Mem. Am. Hist. Assn., Orgn. of Am. Historians, Am. Cath. Hist. Assn. Avocation: stamp collecting. Home: PO Box 927 Notre Dame IN 46556-0927 Office: U Notre Dame Dept of History Notre Dame IN 46556 E-mail: Thomas.E.Blantz.1@nd.edu.

BLASCH, ERIK PHILIP, research engineer, Air Force officer; b. McKeesport, Pa., Mar. 28, 1970; s. Bruce Bernard and Barbara Renk Blasch. BSME, MIT, 1992; MS in Indsl. Engring., MS in Mech. Eng., Ga. Inst. Tech., 1995; postgrad., U. Wis., 1996, PhD in Mech. Engring., 2001; MSEE, Wright State U., 1997; MBA, Wright State U., 1998, 1999; PhD in Elec. Engring., MS in Econs., Wright State U., 1999, MS in Psychology, 2001. Registered profl. engr. Design engr., cons. Ford Motor Co., Cambridge, Mass., 1989-92; design engr. Mobil Chem., Beaumont, Tex., 1991, Tex. Instruments, Attleboro, Mass., 1992, Ga. Inst. Tech., Atlanta, 1995-96; engr. Blasch Edn. and Rehab., Lilburn, Ga.,

1992—; program mgr. sensors dir. automatic target signatures br. Air Force Rsch. Lab., Wright-Patterson AFB, 2000—; asst. prof. Wright State U., 2000—. Contbr. numerous papers to profl. jours. (Best Paper award 1998, Sustained Profl. Soc. Devel. award); patent pending in field. Band mem. Epiphany Luth. Ch., Dayton, Ohio, 1997-2000; mem. Red Cross, Dayton, 1999-2001; Boy Scout coord.Wright State U. Sci. Fair, Dayton, 1996-2001. Capt. USAF, 1996-2000, Res., 2000. Winner Am. Tour de Sol, 1989, 90, 91, 92, Swiss Tour de Sol, 1991, 1st in World, Odyssey of the Mind, 1984, 85, 86, 88. Mem. Soc. Optical Engring. (conf. coord. 1998-2001), IEEE (conf. dir. 1999), Internat. Soc. Info. Fusion (bd. dirs. 1998-2003, treas. 1998-2003), Inst. Navigation. Lutheran. Avocations: marathons, travel, soccer, instrument pilot, scuba diving. Office: Air Force Rsch Lab Wright Patterson Afb OH 45433 E-mail: erik.blasch@wpafb.af.mil.

BLASCHAK, THOMAS R. lawyer; b. Johnstown, Pa., Mar. 16, 1967; m. Kimberli S. Goodall, June 18, 1994; children: Alexander T., Brittney S. BA in Fin., BA in Polit. Sci., U. Pitts., 1989; JD, U. Dayton, 1992. Bar: Ohio, 1992. Atty. Hyatt Legal Svc., Dayton, Ohio, 1993-95, mng. atty., 1995-97; pvt. practice Dayton, 1997—. Asst. text editor U. Dayton Law Rev., 1992. Office: 5568 Airway Rd Dayton OH 45431-1505

BLASCHKE, LAWRENCE RAYMOND, steel manufacturing executive, energy professional; b. Elgin, Ill., Feb. 24, 1950; s. Raymond Otto and Margaret Irma (Palm) B.; m. Diane Charlotte Hartwell, Apr. 12, 1974 (dec. 1986); children: Matthew Robert, Bryan Raymond; m. Karen Juliann Larson, Feb. 14, 1987 (dec. Aug. 1993); m. Terry Leigh, July 29, 1995. AS, William Rainey Harper Coll., 1973; student, Valparaiso U., 1974—; B of Scouting, U. Scouting, 1992, M of Scouting, 1993, D of Scouting, 1995. Cert. power engr., Ind.; registered elec. maintenance Am. Coun. on Edn. Audio visual technician multi-media systems William Rainey Harper Coll., Palatine, Ill., 1970-71; jr. engr., then assoc. engr. No. Ind. Pub. Svc. Co., Hobart, 1974-79, dist. engr., 1979-84, project engr., 1984-87, Gary, 1987-92, project engr. level III Merrillville, 1992-93, spl. projects engr. level III, 1994, project leader product strategic planning, 1994-96; dispatcher power sys. and utility svcs. dept. mgmt. supr. Bethlehem Steel Corp., Burns Harbor Divsn., Chesterton, Ind., 1996—2003. Co-owner, pres. TL Spectrum, Valparaiso, Ind., 2001—. Chmn. bd. social ministry Immanuel Luth. Ch., Valparaiso, 1983-84, sec. bd. evangelism, 1981-83, asst. Sunday sch. supt., 1984-85; cubmaster Boy Scouts Am., Valparaiso area, 1984-88, merit badge counselor, 1992—, asst. scoutmaster, 1992-95, com. mem., 1992-95, co-chmn. Dunes Moraine dist. advancement com. for Boy Scouts and adult leaders, 1996-97, chmn. advancement com. for scouts and adult leaders, 1996-97, mem. bd. rev., 1995-97; supervisory com. No. Ind. Fed. Credit Union, 1996-99, chmn., 1987-88, 90-96; treas. Montessori Sch. Porter County, 1981-83; bldgs. and grounds co-supt., 1983-84; sec., treas. Quality Devel., Inc., 1990-93; active Nat. Arbor Day Found., 1992-99; jr. varsity adult leader Awana Club, Christ Cmty. Ch., Hobart, Ind., mem. welcome team, usher, 1992-98; pres. Hobart Pub. Svc. Club, 1979-81; active mem. Project Teach, 1992-96; loaned exec. Lake Area United Way, 2003-04. Recipient Edward A. Filene award Ind. Credit Union League and Credit Union Nat. Assn., Inc., 1991, Man of Yr. award Am. Biog. Inst., 1995. Mem. IEEE (power soc. chmn. Calumet sect. 2002—), IEEE-Stds. Assn., Assn. Energy Engrs., Nat Parks and Conservation Assn., The Wilderness Soc., Consumers Union (life), Ind. Sheriffs Assn. (assoc.), Smithsonian Instn., Am. Biog. Inst. Rsch. Assn. (dep. gov.), Nat. Trust Hist. Preservation, Handyman Club Am. (life), Alpha Phi Omega (pres. 1973-74). Republican. Avocations: computers, stereo audio equipment and recording, woodworking, electronics. Home: 396 W Southfield Ln Valparaiso IN 46385-9633

BLASCHKE, TERRENCE FRANCIS, medicine and molecular pharmacology educator; b. Rochester, Minn., Oct. 4, 1942; s. Robert Elmer and Carmella Ann (Seeby) B.; m. Jeannette F. Martin, June 8, 1968; children: Anne, John. BS in Math. cum laude, U. Denver, 1964; MD, Columbia U., 1968. Diplomate Am. Bd. Internal Medicine, Nat. Bd. Med. Examiners. Intern in medicine UCLA Ctr. for Health Scis., 1968-69, asst. resident, 1969-70; clin. assoc. metabolism br. Nat. Cancer Inst., NIH, Bethesda, Md., 1970-72; clin. rsch fellow div. clin. pharmacology dept. medicine U. Calif. Med. Ctr., San Francisco, 1972-74; asst. prof. medicine (clin. pharmacology) Stanford (Calif.) U. Sch. Medicine, 1974-81, asst. prof. pharmacology, 1978-81, assoc. prof. medicine (clin. pharmacology) and pharmacology, 1981-91, prof. medicine (clin. pharmacology)-molecular pharmacology, 1991—, assoc. dean for med. student advising, 2002—; v.p. Pharsight Corp., Calif., 2000—02. Bd. govs. Am. Bd. Clin. Pharmacology, 1990-92; vis. worker div. molecular pharmacology Nat. Inst. for Med. Rsch., London, 1980-81, Ctr. for Biopharm. Scis., U. Leiden and dept. med. info. scis. Erasmus U., The Netherlands, 1990; mem. Medi-Cal drug use rev. bd. Calif. Dept. Health Svcs., 1993-96; chmn. generic drugs adv. com. FDA, 1990-94; mem. bd. sci. advisors Merck Sharp and Dohme Rsch. Labs., Rahway, N.J., 1986-90; mem. pharmacology study sect. NIH, 1979-83; faculty of medicine Moi U., El Doret, Kenya; vis. prof. Ctr. Drug Devel. Sci., Georgetown U., 1997-98; spl. govt. employee FDA, 1997—. Mem. editl. bd. Drug Therapeutics: Concepts for Physicians, 1978-81, Rational Drug Therapy, 1984-85, Clin. Pharmacology and Therapeutics, 1981—, Drug Interaction Facts, 1983-87, Drug Metabolism and Disposition, 1994-2000; assoc. editor Ann. Rev. Pharmacology and Toxicology, 1989—. Officer USPHS, 1970-72. Recipient faculty devel. award in clin. pharmacology Pharm. Mfrs. Assn. Found.; Burroughs-Wellcome scholar. Mem.: AAAS, ACP, Western Pharmacology Soc., Western Assn. Physicians, Western Soc. Clin. Investigation, Am. Fedn. Clin. Rsch., Am. Soc. Pharmacology and Exptl. Therapeutics (exec. com. clin. pharmacology divsn. 1986—89, chair clin. pharmacology divsn. 2002—03), Am. Soc. for Clin. Pharmacology and Therapeutics (chmn. liaison com. clin. pharmacology 1985—89, sci. program com. 1986—87, pres. 1988—89, assoc. sec.-treas. 1990—92, chmn. long range planning com. 1992—94, Rawls-Palmer award), Phi Beta Kappa, Alpha Omega Alpha. Office: Stanford U Med Ctr Div Clin Pharmacology S-009 300 Pasteur Dr Stanford CA 94305-5130 E-mail: blaschke@stanford.edu.

BLASE, ANTHONY IDOMENEUS, retired electronics executive, writer, poet; b. Chgo., July 30, 1929; s. Nicholas George and Tousa Marie Blase; m. Aspacia Mary Manos, Aug. 31, 1952; children: Mary Kadie Burgner, Nicolette Stephane Young. BSBA, Loyola U., Chgo., 1955. Lic. gen. ins. broker Ill.; real estate broker Ill. Contr. Universal Wire and Cable Co., Chgo., 1958—64; v.p., contr. Rockola Mfg. Corp., Chgo., 1964—78; exec. v.p., treas. Wells-Gardner Electronics, Chgo., 1978—88, also bd. dirs. Author: Contemplating Forms, 1989, In Search of Alexander, 1990, Thus the Gods Taught Man, 1991, On Moral Purpose, 1992, Byzantium, 1992, Religious Paradigm?, 1993, Vessels Without Dimension, 1994, The Ultimate Comprehension, 1995, The History of Western Philosophy, 1996, The Universal Will, 1997, Historical Essays, 1998, Embracing the Universe, 1998, But Grain of Sand, 1999, The Etaireia, 1999, Uncompromising Nature, 2000, As I Understand Aristotle, 2000, Hellenism in the Post Classical World, 2001, Idomenian Ethics, 2002. Cpl. U.S. Army, 1948—50. Avocation: world travel. Home: 3011 Applegate Ln Glenview IL 60025 E-mail: tekanis5@aol.com.

BLASE, NANCY GROSS, librarian; b. New Rochelle, N.Y. d. Albert Philip and Elsie Wise (May) Gross; m. Barrie Wayne Blase, June 19, 1966 (div.); m. Charles M. Goldstein, July 25, 1999; 1 child, Eric Wayne. BA in Biology, Marietta (Ohio) Coll., 1964; MLS, U. Ill., 1965. Info. scientist brain info. svc. Biomed. Libr., UCLA, 1965-66; libr. Health Sci. Libr., U. Wash., Seattle, 1966-68, Medlars search analyst, 1970-72, coord. Medline, 1972-79, head Natural Scis. Libr., 1979—. Mem. libr. adv. com. Elizabeth C. Miller Libr., Ctr. for Urban Horticulture, Seattle, 1986-90. Contbr. articles to profl. jours. NSF fellow interdept. tng. program for sci. info. specialists U. Ill., 1964-65. Mem. Am. Soc. for Info. Sci. (pres. personal computer spl. interest group 1993-94, chair constn. and bylaws com. 1994-97, chair Spl. Interest Group/Med. Informatics, 1998-99, rsch. grantee Pacific N.W. chpt. 1984-85), Internat. Tng. in Comm. (pres. Pacific N.W. region 1994-95), Phi Beta Kappa (pres. U. Wash. chpt. 1993-97, pres. Puget Sound Assn. 2001-2003), Bet Chaverim (pres. 1998-00). Avocations: walking, reading. Home: 10751 Durland Ave NE Seattle WA 98125-6945 Office: U Wash Natural Scis Libr Box 352900 Seattle WA 98195-2900 E-mail: nblase@u.washington.edu.

BLASER, ARTHUR WESTON, political science educator, writer; b. Seattle, July 1, 1953; s. Henry Weston and Jeanne (LeCrenier) B.; m. Barbara Ann James, Apr. 22, 1995; children: Christan Amalya, Marcus James. BA, U. Wash., 1974; MA, Ohio State U., 1977, PhD, 1979; JD, Southwestern U., L.A., 1990. Bar: Calif. Asst. prof. Augustana Coll., Sioux Falls, S.D., 1977-79; vis. assoc. prof. U. Notre Dame, Ind., 1987-89; from asst. prof. to prof. dept. polit. sci. Chapman U., Orange, Calif., 1981—. Cons. Augustana Rsch. Inst., Sioux Falls, 1981. Writer reference articles Salem Press, Pasadena, Calif., 1990-92, M.E. Sharp, Boston, 1995-97; contbr. articles to L.A. Times, Ragged Edge, The Futurist, Human Rights Quar., Disability Studies Quar., New Polit. Sci. Chair edn. task force So. Calif. Coalition Against the Death Penalty; area coord., sec. Unitarian Universalist Svc. Com. So. Calif.; bd. dirs. Dayle McIntosh Ctr. for Independent Living. Served with USCG, 1973-75. Recipient Human Rels. award Orange County Human Rels. Commn., 1999, Scudder Disting. Faculty award Chapman U., 1991. Mem. Soc. for Disability Studies, Internat. Studies Assn., Amnesty Internat., Calif. Bar Assn., Phi Beta Kappa. Mem. Christian Ch. (Disciples Of Christ, Elder). Avocations: cycling, disability-related civic activities, parenting. Home: 532 N Maplewood St Orange CA 92867-6917 Office: Chapman U Dept Polit Sci 1 University Dr Orange CA 92866-1005 E-mail: blaser@chapman.edu.

BLASGEN, SHARON WALTHER, lawyer; b. Bremerton, Wash., Apr. 12, 1942; d. William Edwin and Helen Walther; m. Michael William Blasgen, Sept. 10, 1965; children: Alexandra Helen, Nicholas William McKenna. BA, Scripps Coll., Claremont, Calif., 1964; JD, U. Calif., Berkeley, 1967. Bar: Calif. 1969, N.Y. 1970, D.C. 1983, U.S. Ct. Appeals (9th cir.), U.S. Dist. Ct. (no. and so. dists.) Calif., U.S. Dist. Ct. (so. dist.) N.Y. Law clk. Calif. Ct. Appeal, San Francisco, 1967-69; atty. IBM Corp., Armonk, N.Y., 1969-72; counsel, asst. sec. IBM World Trade Corp., N.Y.C., 1972-74; area counsel IBM Corp., San Jose, Calif., 1974-79, regional counsel Washington, 1979-83, div. counsel White Plains, N.Y., 1983-86, asst. group counsel, 1986-88, assoc. gen. counsel Somers, N.Y., 1988-93; gen. coun. SSD, San Jose, Calif., 1993-2000; gen. counsel, bd. dirs. iMimic Networking Inc., 2000—02. Bd. dirs. Zaxel Systems Inc. Bd. dirs. Opera San Jose, 1997—2001. Elected to YWCA Internat. Acad. Women Achievers, 1993. Mem. Silicon Valley Assn., Gen. Counsel's Assn. Home: 17418 Paseo Carmelo Los Gatos CA 95030-7559 E-mail: Sharon@Blasgen.com.

BLASI, ALBERTO, Romance languages educator, writer; b. Buenos Aires, Jan. 21, 1931; s. Alberto B. and Emma (Raffo) B. Diploma en Letras, U. Buenos Aires, 1957, Licenciado en Letras, 1965; D. Letras, U. La Plata, 1976; postgrad. (fellow), U. Iowa, 1975. Sr. lectr. U. Buenos Aires, 1965-69; prof. U. Rosario, Argentina, 1969-73; vis. writer U. Iowa, 1974-75; assoc. prof. Spanish Bklyn. Coll., CUNY, 1975-79, prof. modern langs, 1979—; prof. Spanish CUNY Grad. Sch., 1979—. Author: Los Fundadores, 1962, Introducción a Lucio López, 1965, La tarea del cuento en Fin de Siglo, 1968, Güiraldes y Larbaud: Una amistad creadora, 1970, Manuel Podestá, 1982, La luna del cazador, 2002; editor: La gran aldea, 1965, Fin de Siglo, 1968, Essays on Lucio Victorio Mansilla, 1981, Movimientos literarios del siglo XX en Iberoamérica: Teoría y práctica, 1982, Don Segundo Sombra, 1983, 2d edit., 1996; contbr. articles to profl. jours. Recipient French Govt. award, Bourse de Marque, 1972, Argentine Writers Soc. Book award, 1960, CUNY rsch. award, 1980—83, 1999—2000, Argentine Found. for the Arts award, 1966, 1969, Municipality of Buenos Aires Book award, 1967. Mem. PEN Club Internat., Internat. Assn. Hispanists, Internat. Comparative Lit. Assn. Office: Brooklyn Coll Dept Modern Languages Brooklyn NY 11210

BLASI, ANTHONY JOSEPH, sociology educator, writer; b. Dayton, Ohio, Apr. 3, 1946; s. Emmanuel Anthony and Mary Ella (Marshall) B. BA, St. Edward's Univ., 1968; MA, Notre Dame Univ., 1971, PhD, 1974; MA, U. St. Michael's Coll., 1985; ThD, Univ. of Toronto, 1986. Tchr. Notre Dame High Sch., Sherman Oaks, Calif., 1968-69, Holy Cross Sch., New Orleans, 1969-70; instr. St. Anselm Coll., Manchester, N.H., 1973-74; asst. prof. sociology DePauw Univ., Greencastle, Ind., 1974-75; vis. asst. prof. sociology U. Ala., Tuscaloosa, 1975-76; asst. prof. sociology U. Louisville, Ky., 1976-78; assoc. prof. sociology Daemen Coll., Amherst, N.H., 1978-80; asst. prof. sociology U. Hawaii, Hilo, 1986-90; assoc. prof. sociology Muskingum Coll., New Concord, Ohio, 1990-94; assoc. prof. Tenn. State U., 1994—99, prof., 1999—. Author 14 books; contbr. articles to profl. jours. Recipient William Rainey Harper Outstanding Scholar award Mustingim Coll., 1992. Mem. AAUP, Credo Internat. (bd. dirs.), Am. Sociol. Assn., Assn. Sociology of Religion (pres. 2000-01), So. Sociol. Soc., Soc. Sci. Study of Religion, Religious Rsch. Assn. Roman Catholic. Office: Tenn State U Dept Sociology 3500 John A Merritt Blvd Nashville TN 37209-1500

BLASI, GERALD J. humanities educator, lawyer; b. N.Y.C., July 28, 1945; s. Joseph B. and Lillian E. Blasi; m. Linda n.m.i. Manney, June 4, 1967; 1 child, Jennifer. BA, Boston U., 1967; JD, St. John's U., 1971; PhD, SUNY, Binghamton, 1996. Bar: (N.Y.) 1972. Pvt. practice, Binghamton, 1971—93; vis. asst. prof. SUNY, Brockport, 1996—97, SUNY, Binghamton, 1997—98; asst. prof. U. Mo., St. Louis, 1998—. Atty. for zoning bd., planning bd. and spl. counsel Village of Johnson City, NY, 1986—92; corp. counsel, of counsel City of Binghamton, 1990—93; Consultant to nonprofit organizations, St. Louis, 1999—2001. Ass. village judge Village of Johnson City, 1975—78; mem., pres., sec., bd. dirs. Endicott (N.Y.) Rotary Club, 1972—93; interim exec. dir. Broome County YMCA, Binghamton, 1990—91; interim chpt. mgr. Broome County Red Cross, Binghamton, 1991—92; chmn. Broome County Dem. Party, Binghamton, 1986—88; Dem. candidate for family ct. judge Binghamton, 1985—85; bd. dirs. various non-profit orgns., including YMCA, Red Cross, Broome County, NY. Mem.: Am. Soc. Pub. Adminstrn. Avocation: bicycle riding, travel, hiking, golf. Home: 915 Wood Ave Saint Louis MO 63122 Office: U Mo-St Louis SSB 490 8001 Natural Bridge Rd Saint Louis MO 63121-4499 Office Fax: 314-516-5210. Personal E-mail: blasi@umsl.edu. Business E-Mail: blasi@ums.edu.

BLASI, VINCENT A. lawyer, educator; b. 1943; BA, Northwestern U, 1964; JD, U Chgo., 1967. Bar: Tex. 1968. Asst. prof. U. Tex., Austin, Tex., 1967—69; vis. asst. prof. Stanford U, 1969—70; assoc. prof. U Mich., Ann Arbor, Mich., 1970—72, prof., 1972, Columbia U, NY, 2003; vis. prof. U Calif.-Berkeley, Berkeley, Calif., 1978—79. Author: (Press Subpoenas) An Empirical and Legal Analysis, 1972. Mem.; Order of Coif, Phi Beta Kappa. Office: Columbia Law Sch 435 W 116th St New York NY 10027-7297

BLASICK, JAMES DAVID, finance educator; b. Alton, Ill., May 8, 1958; s. Henry John and Mary Nelle Blasick; m. Patricia Diane Mills, July 11, 1999. BSc, Lambuth U., Jackson, TN, 1980; MBA, Sam Houston State U., 1990. Chair divsn. social sci. Bethel Coll., McKenzie, Tenn., 2002—, assoc. dean edn. outreach; instr. Sam Houston State U., Huntsville, Tex.; ops. mgr. Tex. Instruments. Contbr. articles to profl. jours. Home: 24 Fawnwood Cove Jackson TN 38305 Office: Bethel Coll 325 Cherry Ave Mc Kenzie TN 38201 E-mail: blasickj@bethel-college.edu.

BLASIER, COLE, political scientist, educator; b. Jackson, Mich., 1925; s. Stewart Parnell and Helen (Cole) B.; m. Martha Hiett, Sept. 20, 1947; children: Peter Cole, Martha Hamilton. AB, U. Ill., 1947; postgrad., U. Mex., 1947; AM, cert. Russian Inst., Columbia U., 1950, PhD in Polit. Sci., 1955. Career fgn. svc. officer U.S. Dept. State, Belgrade, Yugoslavia, 1951-54, Bonn, Federal Republic of Germany, 1954-57, Washington, 1957-60, Moscow, 1958; exec. asst. to pres., sec. bd. trustees Colgate U., Hamilton, NY, 1960—63; prof. polit. sci. U. Pitts., 1964-88; chief hispanic div. Libr. Congress, Washington, 1988-93; sr. rsch. assoc. North-South Ctr. U. Miami, Coral Gables, Fla., 1993-95. Dir. ctr. Latin Am. studies U. Pitts., 1964-74; adv. bd. Handbook Latin Am. Studies, 1972-88; exchange scholar Polish Inst. Internat. Affairs, Warsaw, Poland, 1978, Inst. Latin Am., Moscow, 1979; U.S. chmn. U.S./USSR Exchange in Latin Am. Studies, 1980-86; mgmt. cons. project to revive ancient libr., Alexandria, Egypt, 1993; Far Ea. State U., Vladivostok, Russia, 1999; adj. prof. Georgetown U., 1993-94; field work in Russia and Germany, 1996-2000; cons. in field. Author: The Hovering Giant, U.S. Responses to Revolutionary Change in Latin America, 1976, rev., 1985, The Giant's Rival, The USSR and Latin America, 1983, rev., 1987, Cuba in the World, 1979, The End of the Soviet-Cuban Partnership, Cuba After the Cold War, 1993, Russia's Institute of Europe, 1996, Electing Putin Po-Tartarski, 2000, Soviet Impact on Latin America, 2002; editor U. Pitts. Press Latin Am. series, 1968-91. Pres. UN Assn. Pitts., 1985. Lt. (j.g.) USNR, PTO, 1943-46. Fellow Rotary Santiago Chile 1947-48, Kennan Inst. Woodrow Wilson Ctr., 1978, Fulbright, Buenos Aires, Argentina, 1986, Heinz Endowment, 1988; Rockefeller Found. grantee, Cali, Colombia, 1963-64; decorated Knighthood of Isabel la Catolica (Spain), 1993. Mem. Lat. Am. Studies Assn. (pres. 1986-87), Am. Polit. Sci. Assn., Am. Fgn. Svc. Assn., Diplomatic and Consular Officers Retired, Washington Inst. for Fgn. Affairs, Cosmos Club. Home: 10450 Lottsford Rd #5009 Mitchellville MD 20721

BLASINGAME, BENJAMIN PAUL, electronics company executive; b. State College, Pa., Aug. 1, 1918; s. Ralph Upshaw and Sue Mae (Combs) B.; m. Ella Mae Perry, Aug. 29, 1942 (dec.); children— Nancy J. Blasingame Wambach, James P., Margaret A. Blasingame Kramer, John R.; m. Margaret A. Timmons, Mar. 21, 1992. BS in Mech. Engring., Pa. State U., 1940; Sc.D. in Aero. Engring., M.I.T., 1950. Commd. 2d lt. USAAF, 1941; advanced through grades to col. USAF, 1955; head astronautics dept. U.S. Air Force Acad., 1958-59; resigned, 1959; gen. mgr. electronics div. Gen. Motors Corp., 1959-70; mgr. Milw. operation Delco Electronics div., 1970-72, Santa Barbara operation, 1972-79. Author: Astronautics, 1964; patentee in field. Bd. dirs. Santa Barbara Cottage Hosp., 1977-87; chmn. Santa Barbara Metro, Nat. Alliance Bus., 1972-75; trustee Santa Barbara Found., 1982-93, pres., 1992-93; mem. adv. bd. Leonard Ctr. for Enhancement Engring. Edn., Pa. State U., 1993-97; dir. Santa Barbara Bank and Trust, 1984-94. Decorated Legion of Merit; recipient Public Service award NASA, 1969, Public Service medal, 1973 Mem. AIAA, Nat. Acad. Engring., N.Y. Acad. Scis., Internat. Acad. Astronautics, Santa Barbara C. of C. (bd. dirs. 1977-79) Clubs: La Cumbre Country. Unitarian Universalist. Home: 517 Carriage Hill Ct Santa Barbara CA 93110-2022 *Any list of the characteristics of a good manager must include knowledge of what is being managed. To think otherwise is to claim that an orchestra leader need not be a musician.*

BLASINGAME, DONALD RAY (DON BLASINGAME), banker; b. Wills Point, Tex., Mar. 2, 1925; s. Scott Vernon and Clora Hayden (Vance) B.; m. Christine E. Razz, May 19, 1949 (div. Nov. 1980); children: Kathryn Lynn, Alan Ray; m. Mildred Claudia McBay, Nov. 25, 1981. Student, Trinity Valley Coll., 1949-51. Loan officer Tyler (Tex.) Prodn. Credit Assn., 1947-52; mgr. Fed. Land Bank Assn., Sulphur Springs, Tex., 1952-58; regional mgr., asst. v.p. Fed. Land Bank of Houston, 1958, v.p., 1974; pres. Fed. Land Bank Assn. of Tyler, 1974-84, dir., 1990—, Citizens Nat. Bank, Wills Point, 1981-90, Farm Credit Bank of Tex., Austin, 1988-90. Fin. and legis. cons., Tyler. Advisor Tex. Farm and Ranch Fin. Program, Austin, 1985; chmn. bd. commrs. Smith County Fire Prevention Dist. 1, 1996-99. Named to Tex. Acad. of Honor in Agrl. Credit, 1994. Mem. East Tex. Fair Assn. (bd. dirs. 1980-90, pres. 1985-87), East Tex. Farm & Ranch Club (bd. dirs. 1977-81), Barb Wire Collector Soc., Masons (sec., jr. warden, sr. warden Wills Point lodge # 422 1984—). Methodist. Avocations: collecting barb wire, hunting, fishing. Home and Office: 12214 Jaysid St Tyler TX 75706-5609 E-mail: donblas@tyler.net.

BLASINGIM, CHARLOTTE OREN DESHAZOR, counselor, consultant; b. Port Lavaca, Tex., Nov. 13, 1943; d. Tom and Lois DeShazor; m. Roy Blasingim, June 19, 1976; children: Vernon Neal Reaser III, Ken Stierley. BS in Psychology and Sociology, Houston Bapt. U., 1993; MA in Counseling, Prairie View A & M U., 1997. Advt. salesperson Port Lavaca Wave Newspaper, 1975-76; advisor, censor media prodns. and ops. dept. Arabian Am. Oil Co., Dhahran, Saudi Arabia, 1981-85, sec. transp. dept., 1985-88; counselor clin. group therapy LifeGuide Cmty. Health Ctr., Houston, 1998; couselor Connections/STAR Program, Rockport, Tex., 2000—01. Lay Christian counselor on call Interdenominational Ch., Dhahran; vol. grief assistance program Houston Hospice; intern counselor St. Judes Personal Care Home, Silver Ridge Partial Hosp.; group counselor Life Guide, Cmty. Mental Health Ctr.; employee rels. cons., 2002. Supr. vols. Reaser campaign for Tex. State Rep., Victoria, 1998. Mem.: ACA, Tex. Assn. Marriage and Family Counselors, Tex. Assn. Multicultural Counseling and Devel., Tex. Counseling Assn., Am. Assn. Christian Counselors, Internat. Assn. Marriage and Family Counselors, Assn. Specialists Group Work, Assn. Spiritual, Ethical and Religious Values Counseling, Assn. Multicultural Counseling and Devel., Chi Sigma Iota. Democrat. Presbyterian. Home: 455 Elm Valley Dr Bulverde TX 78163 Office: RB Internat 2650 Fountain View Dr Ste 220 Houston TX 77057-7618

BLASINI-ALCIVAR, LYDIA M. health education specialist, consultant; b. Humacao, P.R., June 30, 1954; d. Gilberto L. B. and Lydia C. C.; m. Luis E. Alcivar, Sept. 7, 1997. BAE, U. P.R., 1976, M.P.H.E., 1980; PhD, Pa. State U., 1993. Cert. U.S. ARC HIV/AIDS instr. P.R.; health tchr.; health zone supr.; gen. health supr.; gen. adminstrv. supr. Sch. social worker sch. supt. office Dept. Edn., Humacao, P.R., 1976-79, health zone supr. sch. supt. office Juncos, P.R., 1980-88; HIV project coord. P.R. Dept. Edn., Hato Rey, 1988-90, health zone supr., dir. high sch. sch. supt. office Juncos, 1993-94, HIV project coord. Hato Rey, 1994; homebound bilingual tchr. York (Pa.) Suburban High Sch., 1993; asst. prof. So. Ill. U., Carbondale, 1994-96; health edn. splst. Ctr. Disease Control and Prevention, Atlanta, 1997—. Cons. WHO/Panam. Health Orgn., P.R. Health Dept. Mother and Child Health, Folic Acid Campaign, Rio Piedras, 1998—. Contgr. articles to profl. jours. Vis. scholar Julian Samora Rsch. Inst. Mich. State U., 1996; bilingual edn. fellow Coll. Edn. Dept. Curriculum and Instrn. Pa. State U., 1990-93. Mem. Am. Sch. Health Assn., Assn. Employees CDC/ATSDR (v.p. 1997—), Internat. Union Health Promotion and Edn., P.R. Assn. Health Educators (past pres.). Avocations: reading, dancing, collecting Native Am. pictures, travel. Home: 1175 La Vista Rd NE Apt 206 Atlanta GA 30324 Office: CDC/NCHSTP/DS Corp Sq Facility MS-E-27 1600 Clifton Rd Atlanta GA 30333

BLASINSKI, CLARE MARIE, librarian; b. Milw., Jan. 10, 1950; d. Henry Michael and Gertrude Julia (Bucholz) B. BS, U. Wis., Milw., 1974, MLS, 1979; MBA, Marquette U., 1990. Libr. Milw. Pub. Libr., 1983—. Recipient S.E. Asian Young Adult Literacy grant, LSCA, 1991—. Mem. Am. Libr. Assn., Am. Mktg. Assn., Am. Soc. Info. Sci., Shih Tzu Club of Southeastern Wis. (v.p. and webmaster), Beta Phi Mu. Roman Catholic. Avocations: hiking, breeding and exhibiting dogs. Home: 3162 S Brisbane Ave Milwaukee WI 53207-2606 Office: Milw Pub Libr 814 W Wisconsin Ave Milwaukee WI 53233-2309

BLASIOTTI, ROBERT VINCENT, accountant, consultant; b. Phila., Nov. 15, 1949; s. Vincent Mario Blasiotti and Hilda (Romani) Greer; m. Katheryn Phyllis Ombres, Dec. 15, 1973 (div. Apr. 1982); m. Gilda Maria Cipriani, June 17, 1988; children: Melissa, Gabriella, Robert Jr. BS, Pa. State U., 1971, MBA, 1973. CPA, Pa. Jr. acct. Goldenberg, Rosenthal & Co., Phila., 1971-73, sr. acct., 1973-75; mgr. acctg. Gross & Co., Jenkintown, Pa., 1975-77; owner Blasiotti & Co. CPAs, West Chester, Pa., 1977—. CPA, advisor Big Bros. Chester County, West Chester, 1985—; cons. Presdl. Adv. Coun., 1984; fin. advisor Exton Sq. Mall Merchants Assn., 1978-89; bd. advisors Med-Trans, Inc., 1982-84. Mem. Big Bros.-Big Sisters Chester County, 1978—; trustee Rep. Presdl. Task Force, 1982—; mem. coun. St. Maximilian Kolby Ch., 1994-97; bd. advisors Our Lady's Missionaries of Eucharist, 1999—; treas. Boy Scouts Am. Pack 153, 1999-2002; Pa. chmn. Congressional Bus. Adv. Coun., 2003—. Served from 2d lt. to capt. U.S. Army, 1971-79. Mem. C. of C., Jaycees (chmn. 1980-84), Italian Social Club (fin. sec. 1992-96), KC (treas. 1994, dep. grand knight 1995, grand knight 1996, trustee 1997-99), Lions (treas. 1980-81), Men of Malvern. Roman Catholic. Avocations: philately, numismatology, golf, horticulture, fishing. Office: Blasiotti & Co CPAs 106 W Marshall St West Chester PA 19380-2415

BLASS, ANDREAS RAPHAEL, mathematics educator; b. Nurnberg, Bavaria, Germany, Oct. 27, 1947; came to US, 1949; s. Gerhard Alois and Barbara Leonore (Siegert) B.; m. Mary Ellen Lloyd, May 26, 1978; children: Christina, Timothy, Philip. BS in Physics, U. Detroit, 1966; PhD in Math., Harvard U., 1970. Rsch. instr. U. Mich., Ann Arbor, 1970-72, asst. prof., 1972-76, assoc. prof., 1976-84, prof. of math., 1984—, assoc. chmn. math. dept., 1988-90, 1996—99. Vis. assoc. prof. U. Wis., Madison, 1978-79; vis. prof. Pa. State U., State Coll., 1985-86. Editor: Omega Bibliography of Mathematical Logic, 1989, 90; contbr. articles to profl. jour. Mem. Am. Math. Soc., Assn. Symbolic Logic (exec. com. 1989-91). Roman Catholic. Office: U Mich Dept Math Ann Arbor MI 48109-1109

BLASS, ELLIOTT M. psychologist, educator; b. N.Y.C., Sept. 10, 1940; s. Joseph Harry Blass and Edythe Horner; m. Lorraine B. Hirsch; children: David M., Joshua S.; m. Elizabeth S. Spelke; children: Bridget Mae Spelke, Joseph Alan. BS, Bklyn. Coll., 1963; MS, U. Conn., 1964; PhD, U. Va., 1967; postgrad., U. Pa., 1969. Cert. Bd. Cert. Psychologist Md. Asst. prof., assoc. prof., prof. Johns Hopkins U., Balt., 1969—90; prof. Cornell U., Ithaca, NY, 1990—96, U. Mass., Amherst, 1996—. Prof. Boston U. Sch. Medicine, Boston,

1996—. Editor: Handbook of Behavioral Neurology, 1988, rev. edit., 2001. Fellow, John S. Guggenheim Found., 1982, Fulbright Found., 1982; grantee Rsch. scientist, NIMH, 1988—2002. Green Party. Avocations: photography, reading, bicycling, cuisine. Office: Psychology Tobin Hall Univ Mass Amherst MA 01003

BLASS, JOHN PAUL, medical educator, physician; b. Vienna, Feb. 21, 1937; s. Gustaf and Jolan (Wirth) B.; m. Birgit Annelise Knudsen, Dec. 20, 1960; children: Charles, Lisa. AB summa cum laude, Harvard U., 1958; PhD, U. London, 1960; MD, Columbia U., 1965. Postdoctoral fellow Am. Cancer Soc., Columbia U., 1962-63; intern Mass. Gen. Hosp., Boston, 1965-66, resident in medicine, 1966-67; research assoc. Nat. Heart and Lung Inst., Bethesda, Md., 1967-70; asst. prof. psychiatry and biol. chemistry UCLA, 1970-76, assoc. prof., 1976-78; mem. staff UCLA Hosps. Clinics, 1970-78; Winifred Masterson Burke prof. neurology, prof. medicine Cornell U. Med. Center, 1978—. Attending neurologist N.Y. Hosp.; mem. NBS-1 rev. com. NIH, 1981-84; councilor Nat. Inst. Aging, 1986-89; chmn. Nat. Adv. Panel on Alzheimers's Disease U.S. Congress, 1987-91, mem., 1993-96. Jour. Neurochemistry, 1981—86, Neurochem. Rsch., 1984—86, Neurochem. Pathology, Neurobiol. Aging, Jour. Neurol. Sci., 1990—2000, Jour. Molecular Neurosci., 1999—, assoc. editor Jour. Am. Geriatric Soc., 1982—87, Age, 1993—95, Yearbook of Neurology and Neurosurgery, 1992—; co-editor: Caring for Alzheimer's Patients, 1990—, Familial Alzheimer's Disease, 1989—, Treatment of Alzheimer's Disease, 1989—, Principles of Geriatrics and Gerontology, 2d edit., 1990—, Principles of Geriatrics and Gerontology, 3d edit., 1994—, Principles of Geriatrics and Gerontology, 4th edit., 1998—; contbr. articles to profl. jours. Mem. sci. adv. bd. Will Rogers Inst., 1981-97, Allied Signal Aging Award Com., 1993-95. Served as asst. surgeon USPHS, 1967-70. Marshall scholar, 1958-60. Mem. Soc. Neurosci. (chmn. social issues com.), Biochem. Soc., Am. Soc. Biol. Chemists, Am. Soc. Neurochemistry (council, chmn. public policy com.), Internat. Soc. Neurochemistry (council, chmn. clin. com.), Am. Soc. Clin. Investigation, Am. Geriatrics Soc., Am. Fedn. Aging Rsch. (v.p., chmn. research com. 1982-87, pres. 1994-96), Assn. Alzheimers and Related Disease (sci. adv. bd. 1982-86), Am. Chem. Soc., Phi Beta Kappa, Sigma Xi, Alpha Omega Alpha. Jewish. Home: 1 Orchard Pl Bronxville NY 10708-2509 Office: Burke Med Rsch Inst 785 Mamaroneck Ave White Plains NY 10605-2523 E-mail: jpblass@mail.med.cornell.edu.

BLASS, WALTER PAUL, consultant, management educator; b. Dinslaken, Germany, Mar. 31, 1930; s. Richard B. and Malvi (Rosenblatt) B.; m. Janice L. Minott, Apr. 2, 1954; children: Kathryn, Christopher, Gregory. BA, Swarthmore Coll., 1951; postgrad., Princeton U., 1951-52; MA, Columbia U., 1953. Asst. Laos and Cambodia desk offoicer ICA, Wash., 1957-58; gen. mgr. R.B. Blass Co., Deal, NJ, 1958-61; economist AT&T, N.Y.C., 1961-65; country dir. Peace Corps., Afghanistan, 1966-68; asst. v.p. revenue requirement studies NY Telephone Co., N.Y.C., 1968-70; dir. corp. planning AT&T, 1970-82, dir. strategic planning, 1982-85; ret., 1985—. Pres., Strategic Plans, Unltd., Warren, N.J., 1985—. Exec. Fellow-in-Residence Martino Grad. Sch. Bus. Adminstrn., Fordham U., N.Y.C., 1986-90; cons. McKinsey & Co., Telecom. Authority Ireland, McDonnell Douglas, Heller Fin., Inc.; lectr. in field; vis. prof. U. Grenoble, France, 1988, Ecole Superieure de Commerce, Chambery and Grenoble, France, 1989—. Trustee Guilford Coll., 1975—, chmn. planning com., 1992-99, vice chmn. tchrs. and officers com., 1999—. Co-author: The Strategic Planning Handbook, 1982, Handbook of Strategic Planning, 1986. Lt., j.g., USNR, 1953-56. Woodrow Wilson Found., sr. fell., 1974-85. Mem., N.Y. Acad. Scis., Soc. Values in Higher Edn. (dir. 1983-86), Am. Econ.Assn., Nat. Assn. Bus. Economists, The Planning Forum (dir. 1972), Royal Econ. Soc. Home and Office: 6 Casale Dr Warren NJ 07059-6703

BLASSINGAME, RONALD JAY, social worker; b. NYC, Apr. 20, 1948; s. Samuel and Johnnie Mae Blassingame; m. Stephanie Moore, Oct. 21, 1981 (div. Sept. 1984); m. Hope Villanueva, Aug. 30, 1985; children; Aram, Nadirah, Willie, Samuel. BSW cum laude, SUNY, Buffalo, 1971; EdM in Adult Edn., Kans. State U., 1977; MS in Human Svcs., Boston U., 1983; PhD in Sociology, Columbia State U., 1997. Social worker Wis. Children's Treatment Ctr., Madison, 1972-73; asst. dir. youth svcs. Buffalo Urban League, 1973-75; social worker alcohol & drug prevention & control program Dept. of Army, Ft. Riley, Kans., 1975-76, 1976-78; adj. lectr. Ctrl. Tex. Coll./Overseas, Stuttgart, Germany, 1977-78; supr. group homes St. Barnabas Group Homes, N.Y.C., 1979-81; dir. spl. programs Inst. for Career and Life Planning Phelps-Stokes Sch., Bklyn., 1979-81; tchg. trainer Peace Corp., Monrovia, Liberia, 1981-83; instnl. supr. ESL and cultural orientation program Internat. Cath. Migration Commn., Morong, Philippines, 1984-90; project dir. Amerisian residential program Mohawk Valley Resource Ctr. for Refugees, Utica, n.Y., 1990-92; correction counselor Cape Vincent Correctional Facility N.Y. State Dept. Correctional Svcs., 1993-96, correction counselor Taconic Correctional Facility, 1996-98; alcohol and substance abuse treatment program coord. Watertown (NY) Correctional Facility, 1998—2003; asylum officer US Dept. Homeland Security INS, Miami, Fla., 2003—. Cons. Philippine Culture Commn. Svc. Corp., Manila, 1987-88, Voice of Am., Washington, 1980-81; mem. working group Non Govtl. Com. of UNICEF, N.Y.C., 1994-97; cons. in field. Mentor N.Y. State Mentoring Program, Thousand Island Ctrl. Sch. Dist., Cape Vincent, 1993-97; spl. asst. Family Ct. of State of N.Y., 1998—. With U.S. Army, 1975-78. Recipient Cert. of Appreciation from Pres. Ronald Reagan for dedicated Peace Corps svc., Cert. of Recognition from Sec. of Def. W.S. Cohen for mil. svc. during Cold War. Mem. Am. Sociol. Assn., World Futurist Soc., Nat. Peace Corps Assn., Am. Studies Assn. of the Philippines (v.p. Bataan chpt. 1986-90), Southern Poverty. Avocations: reading, cooking, sailing. Home: 7133 Bonita Dr Apt 4 Miami Beach FL 33141

BLASZCZYNSKI, ANDRE BOGUSLAW, economist, educator; b. Krakow, Poland, Feb. 12, 1952; came to U.S., 1962; s. Zdzislaw and Halina Blaszczynski; m. Elizabeth Blaszczynski, Sept. 21, 1974; 1 child, Christopher. BA in Econs., U. Conn., 1975, MA in Econs., 1983; MBA, Rensselaer Poly. Inst., 1980. Rsch. assoc. The Futures Group, Glastonbury, Conn., 1977-78; ops. mgmt. cons. Brook Internat. Corp., Montvale, N.J., 1978-79; instr. Morse Sch. of Bus., Hartford, Conn., 1980-81; asst. prof. Ctrl. Conn. State U., New Britain, Conn., 1981-86; instr. Tunxis C.C., Farmington, Conn., 1987-94, asst. prof., 1994-98, assoc. prof., chair dept. bus., 1998-2000; program dir., lectr. Polish Am. Bus. Sch., Krakow, 1990-91; cons. devel. program UN, Krakow, 1991; acting dean of learning Gateway C.C., New Haven, 2000—. Co-founder, moderator Conf. of Solidarity Support Orgns., 1983-90. Author: Slownik Pojec Ekonomicznych, 1993. Pres. Conn. divsn. Polish Am. Congress, Hartford, 1993-99; pres., founding mem. Polish Am. Found. Conn., New Britain, 1996—; pres. Fedn. Polish Ams., Washington, 2000—. Recipient Order of Merit Pres. of Republic of Poland, 1999. Republican. Roman Catholic. E-mail: AndreBB@home.com., gw_andre@commnet.edu.

BLATE, MICHAEL, author, lecturer; b. Queens, N.Y., June 24, 1938; s. Martin Stanley and Sylvia (Lax) B.; m. Bonnie Gloria Baker, Oct. 18, 1958 (div. 1962); children: Laurie Sue, Keith Martin; m. Barbara Gail Watson, June 21, 1998. Student, U. Miami, Oxford, Ohio, 1957, U. Miami, Coral Gables, Fla., 1959, U. Fla., 1962, Broward C.C., Davie, Fla., 1962. Registered principal, investment adviser. V.p. Western Water Co., Inc., Hollywood, Fla., 1959-65, Marina Products Mfg., Inc., Ft. Lauderdale, Fla., 1963-87; investment counsel pvt. practice, Davie, Fla., 1965-67; founder, reg. prin. officer M. Blate & Co., Davie, Fla., 1967-69; advisor Nova Convertible Inv. Fund, Ft. Lauderdale, Fla., 1969-88; founder, CEO Falkynor Communications, Davie, Fla., 1974-87; CEO Falkyn, Inc., Davie, Fla., 1987—; Author, radio-TV guest columnist The G-Jo Inst., Davie, Fla., 1975—. Spokesperson, columnist, journalist, The G-Jo Inst., Hollywood, Fla., 1975—. Author: The Natural Healer's Acupressure Handbook Vol. I, II, 1978, How to Heal Yourself Using Hand Acupressure, How to Heal Yourself Using Foot Acupressure, Acugenics: Beat Stress in Five Minutes, The Tao of Health: The Way of Total Well-Being, 1982, When the Market Makes a Bottom, Vendanta for the 21st Century, 1995, The Master of G-Jo Acupressure Home-Study Certification Program, 1995, The Instructor of G-Jo Acupressure Home-Study Certification Program, 1995, G-Jo Ear Acupressure, 1996, Sanjeevini ("Prayer-in-a-Bottle") Operator's Kit, 1996, Neti Yoga and the Seven Ultimate Secrets, 1997, A Yogi Explains the Bhagavad Gita: Enlightenment for the New Millennium, 1998, The Acugenics Longevity and Wellness Special Report, 1998, Better Sex with Acugenics, 1998, Better Sleep With Acugenics, 1998, Better Eyesight With Acugenics, 1998, Dynamic Nutrition! The Acugenics Way of Eating for Pleasure and Health, 1998, Lifelong Fitness With Acugenics, 1998, Lose Weight Easily With Acugenics, 1998, Stop Smoking (and Other Addictions) With Acugenics, 1998, How To Relieve Allergies With Acugenics, 1998, How To Relieve Arthritis With Acugenics, 1998, How To Relieve Back Pain With Acugenics, 1998, How To Relieve Colds and Influenza With Acugenics, 1998, How To Relieve Depression With Acugenics, 1998, How To Relieve Constipation With Acugenics, 1998, How To Relieve Diarrhea With Acugenics, 1998, How To Relieve Headaches and Migraines With Acugenics, 1998, How To Relieve Indigestion With Acugenics, 1998, How To Relieve Menopause With Acugenics, 1998, Better Vision With Acugenics, 1998, others; columnist: Healthy & Natural Mag., Wolfe's Digest of Alternative Medicine, Townsend Letter for Doctors and Patients, American Survival Guide. Dir. United Fund of Broward County, Ft. Lauderdale, Fla., 1961; officer, dir. Jaycees, Hollywood, Fla., 1959-60; mem. Rotary Internat., W. Hollywood, Fla., 1968-70; founder, Vegetarian Gourmet Soc., Davie, Fla., 1982-88, Sathya Prema Charitable Found. Recipient Jaycee Key Man of Qtr. and Yr. awards, Hollywood, Fla., 1961, Kinsa Nat. Photographer's awards, Eastman Kodak, Fla., N.Y.C., N.Y., 1973-75. Avocations: yachting, traveling, photography, organic fruit farming, oriental studies and philosophies. Office: The G Jo Institute PO Box 1460 Columbus NC 28722-1460

BLATT, HAROLD GELLER, lawyer; b. Detroit, Apr. 8, 1934; s. Henry H. and Berdye (Geller) B.; m. Elaine K. Greenberg, July 9, 1960; children— Lisa K., James G., Andrew N. BS, Washington U., St. Louis, 1955, LL.B., 1960; LL.M., NYU, 1961. Bar: Mo. 1960. Ptnr. Bryan Cave, St. Louis, 1961—. Dir. Artex Internat., Highland, Ill. Trustee Webster U., St. Louis, 1982-97, Washington U. Med. Ctr., St. Louis, 1983-96, Barnes-Jewish, Inc., 1993—; chmn. Jewish Hosp., St. Louis, 1983-88. 1st lt. U.S. Army, 1955-57. Mem. ABA, Mo. Bar Assn., Noonday Club (St. Louis), St. Louis Club.

BLATT, LAWRENCE M. pharmaceutical company executive; b. Chgo., Aug. 11, 1961; s. Harvey M. and Serane A. B.; m. Elyse Anne Salven, Apr. 20, 1990; children: Zachary, Zoe. BS in Microciology, Ind. u., 1983; MBA, Calif. State U., 1988; D of Pub. Health Adminstrn., U. LaVerne, 1996. Rsch. biologist Monsanto, St. Louis, 1983-84; dir. interferon rsch. Amgen, Thousand Oaks, Calif., 1984-96; v.p., devel. corp. officer Nat. Genetics Inst., L.A., 1996-98; v.p. rsch., corp. officer Ribozyme Pharms., Inc., Boulder, Colo., 1998—. Adj. prof. Scripps Clinic, La Jolla, 1998-2001; sr. rsch. scientist Huntington Hosp. Liver Ctr., Pasadens, Calif., 1996—. Contbr. articles to profl. jours. Rsch. grantee Norris Found., 1999. Mem. Internat. Soc. for Interferon and Cytolane Rsch., Am. Chem. Soc., Am. Soc. Microbiology. Fax: 303-449-6995. E-mail: blattl@rpi.com.

BLATT, RICHARD LEE, lawyer; b. Oak Park, Ill., May 24, 1940; s. B. Lee Gray and Madelyn Gertrude (Bentley) B.; m. Carol Milner Jenkinson, May 21, 1965 (div. Dec. 1984); children: Christopher Andrew Lee, Katherine Lee, Susannah Lee; m. Carolyn Elizabeth LeBlanc, Jan. 31, 1987; 1 child, Jennifer Lee DeNux Blatt. BA, U. Ill., 1962; JD, U. Mich., 1965. Bar: Ill. 1968, U.S. Dist. Ct. (no. dist.) Ill. 1968, U.S. Ct. Appeals (7th cir.) 1968, U.S. Supreme Ct. 1974, U.S. Dist. Ct. (so. dist.) Ill. 1977, U.S. Ct. Appeals (4th cir.) 1987, N.Y. 1989, U.S. Ct. Appeals (3rd cir.) 1990, U.S. Dist. Ct. (ea. and so. dists.) N.Y. 1998. Assoc. Peterson, Lowry, Rall, Barber & Ross, Chgo., 1968-75; ptnr. Peterson, Ross, Schloeb & Seidel, Chgo., 1975-91, Peterson & Ross, Chgo., 1991-94; sr. ptnr. Blatt, Hammesfahr & Eaton, Chgo., 1994-2000; sr. mem. Cozen & O'Connor, 2000—. Rep. Disting. Neutral Ctr. Pub. Resources Inst. for Dispute Resolution; regulation bd. arbitrators NASD. Author: (with Robert G. Schloerb, Robert W. Hammesfahr, Lori S. Nugent) Punitive Damages: A Guide to the Insurability of Punitive Damages in the United States and Its Territories, 1988; (with Robert W. Hammesfahr and Lori S. Nugent) Punitive Damges: A State-by-State Guide to Law and Practice, 1991, 2002, 2003 (in Japanese 1995); co-author: At Risk-Internet and E-Commerce Insurance and Reinsurance Legal Issues, 2000, At Risk-Version 2-The Definitive Guide to Legal Issues of Insurance and Reinsurance of Internet, E-commerce and Cyber Perils, 2002. Capt. USAR, 1965—67, Korea. Fellow Chartered Inst. Arbitrators; mem. ABA (litigation sect., dispute resolution sect.), NSSAR (Ft. Dearborn chpt.), Ill. State Bar Assn., Chgo. Internat. Dispute Resolution Assn. (planning com.), Soc. Mayflower Desc. State Ill., N.Y. State Bar Assn., Chgo. Bar Assn. (alternative dispute resolution com.), Chgo. Club, Pi Kappa Alpha Ednl. Found. (trustee), Phi Beta Kappa, Phi Kappa Phi. Home: 1415 N Dearborn Pkwy Chicago IL 60610-1559 Office: Cozen & O'Connor 222 S Riverside Plz Ste 1500 Chicago IL 60606-6000 Fax: 312-382-8910. E-mail: rblatt@earthlink.net., rblatt@cozen.com.

BLATT, SIDNEY JULES, psychology educator and investigator, psychoanalyst; b. Phila., Oct. 15, 1928; s. Harry and Fannie (Feld) Blatt; m. Ethel Shames, Feb. 1, 1951; children: Susan, Judith, David. BS, Pa. State U., 1950, MS, 1952; PhD, U. Chgo., 1957; postgrad., Western New Eng. Inst. for Psychoanalysis, 1972. Postdoctoral fellow Neuropsychiat. Inst. of U. Ill. Med. Ctr., Psychiat. and Psychosomatic Inst. of Michael Reese Hosp., 1957—59; instr. Univ. Coll. U. Chgo., 1959-60; mem. faculty Yale U., New Haven, 1960—, prof. psychology and psychiatry, 1974—; mem. faculty Western New Eng. Inst. for Psychoanalysis, 1975—. Sigmund Freud prof. psychoanalysis; Ayala and Sam Zacks prof. art history Hebrew U., 1988—89; Fulbright sr. rsch. fellow, 1988—89; mem. Rsch. Fellowship Rev. Panel NIMH, 1966—69, mem. Psychology Tng. Rev. Panel, 1969—74; vis. prof. Univ. Coll., London, 1999—2003, Cath. U. Leuven, 2003. Author: Experiences of Depression: Theoretical, Research and Clinical Perspectives, 2003; co-author (with J. Allison and C. Zimet): Interpretation of Psychological Tests, 1968, Interpretation of Psychological Tests, 2d edit., 1988; co-author: (with C.M. Wild) Schizophrenia: A Developmental Analysis, 1976; co-author: (with E.S. Blatt) Continuity and Change in Art: The Development of Modes of Representation, 1984; co-author: (with Z.V. Segal) The Self in Emotional Distress, 1993; co-author: (with R.Q. Ford) Therapeutic Change: An Object Relations Perspective, 1994; editor (with D. Diamond): Attachment Research and Psychoanalysis, vols. I-III, 1999—2003. Named Disting. Practitioner of Psychology, Nat. Acad. Practice, 1983; recipient Disting. Contbns. to Rsch. award, Assn. Med. Sch. Profs. Psychology and APA Divsn. Psychoanalysis, 2000, Founders' Disting. Tchg. prize, We. New Eng. Psychoanalytic Soc., 2001, Hans H. Strupp Disting. Contbns. to Psychoanalysis award, 2000, Bruno Klopfer and Marguerite R. Hertz awards for contbns. to psychol. assessment, Internat. Psychoanalytic Assn.; fellow Found. Fund Rsch. in Psychiatry, 1961—64. Mem.: AAUP, AAAS, APA, Soc. Personality Assessment (pres. 1984—86), Am. Psychoanalytic Assn. Office: Yale U 25 Park St New Haven CT 06519-1110 E-mail: sidney.blatt@yale.edu.

BLATTER, FRANK EDWARD, travel agency executive; b. Denver, Jan. 9, 1939; s. Anthony John and Irene Marie (Tobin) B.; m. Barbara E. Drieth, Sept. 6, 1959; children: Dean Robert, Lisa Kay Faircloth, Paul Kelly. BS, Regis U., Denver, 1961; grad., Colo. Sch. Banking, 1966, Sch. Bank Adminstrn., 1973. CPA, Colo. Acct. McMahon, Maddox & Rodriguez (C.P.A.s), Denver, 1960-63, United Bank Denver, 1963-65; with United Banks Colo., Inc., Denver, 1965-86; pres. Cath. Cmty. Svcs., Denver, 1987, Premiere Travel and Cruises, Denver, 1988—. Mem. nat. adv. coun. and devel. com., chmn. ann. funds coun. Regis U.; chmn. adv. coun. Camp Santa Maria; crusade chmn. Am. Cancer Soc., Denver. Mem. AICPA, Tax Execs. Inst. (past pres. Denver), Colo. Soc. CPAs, Fin. Execs. Inst. (dir.), Bank Adminstrn. Inst. (dir.), Arrowhead Golf Club. Roman Catholic. Office: 3900 S Wadsworth Blvd Ste 475 Denver CO 80235-2207

BLATTNER, FLORENCE ANNE, retired music educator; b. Rockford, Ill., Nov. 27, 1935; d. Keith F. and Grace L. (Turney) Perkins; m. Lewis Olof Blattner, Mar. 28, 1959; children: Gloria Grace Blattner Mundt, Gayle Mary Blattner Ludwig. BA, Carroll Coll., 1958; studied with, Vladimir Levitski, 1984—95, Weekly and Arganbright, U. Ind, 1993, 98, 2000, Joanne Tierney, 1995—2002. Elem. and jr. high sch. libr. Racine (Wis.) Pub. Schs., 1958—60, elem. substitute tchr., 1961—62, elem. and jr. high tchr., 1962; pvt. practice piano instr. Indpls., 1970—78; data processor OMS Internat., Greenwood, Ind., 1978; pvt. practice piano and theory instr. Des Moines, 1980—83; piano and theory instr. Prelude Piano Studio, Apple Valley, Minn., 1983—2003; ret., 2003. Duettist concerts duet lit., Racine, Wis., 1996, 1999, Apple Valley, Minn., 1996, 1998—2002, White Bear Lake, 1996, Dodge City, Kans., 2001, Bloomington, Minn., 1996—97, 2001, Godfrey, Ill., 1998, 2000, Alton, Ill., 1998, 2000. Ch. pianist, accompianist, 1970—; vol. Rep. Party-Minn., Apple Valley, 1992, 94, 96, 98. Mem. Music Tchrs. Nat. Assn., Minn. Music Tchrs. (assoc. cert., state ensemble festival chair 1994-97, cert. com. 1997-2001), South Suburban Music Tchrs. Assn. (1st v.p. 1995-97, pres. 1998-2000, newsletter editor 1995-2001, yearbook editor 2001-2002), Nat. Guild Piano Tchrs., Am. Fedn. Music Clubs. Avocations: canoeing, hiking, traveling, reading, piano. E-mail: flblattner@usfamily.net.

BLATTNER, MEERA MCCUAIG, computer science educator; b. Chgo., Aug. 14, 1930; d. William D. McCuaig and Nina (Spertus) Klevs; m. Minao Kamegai, June 22, 1985; children: Douglas, Robert, William. BA, U. Chgo., 1952; MS, U. So. Calif., 1966; PhD, UCLA, 1973. Rsch. fellow in computer sci. Harvard U., 1973-74; asst. prof. Rice U., 1974-80; assoc. prof. applied sci. U. Calif.-Davis, Livermore, 1980-91, prof. applied sci., 1991-99, prof. emeritus, 2000—; pres. Color Wheel Creations, 2001—. Adj. prof. U. Tex., Houston, 1977—99; vis. prof. U. Paris, 1980; program dir. theoretical computer sci. NSF, Washington, 1979—80. Co-editor: (with R. Dannenberg) Multimedia Interface Design, 1992; contbr. articles to profl. jours. NSF grantee, 1977-81, 93-99. Mem. Assn. Computing Machinery, Computer Soc. of IEEE. Office: Color Wheel Creations 850 S Durango Rd Ste 107 Las Vegas NV 89145 E-mail: meera.blattner@cvi.net.

BLATTNER, ROBERT A. lawyer; b. Lima, Ohio, July 9, 1934; s. Simon James and Estelle Leila (Aarons) B.; m. Judith Reinfeld, Feb. 5, 1964 (div. July 1980); children: Wendy Lynn, Lauren Jill; m. Eileen Savransky, Dec. 18, 1983 BA, Northwestern U., 1956; LLB, Case Western Reserve U., 1959. Bar: Ohio 1959, Ill. 1965, U.S. Supreme Ct. 1984. Assoc. Hribar & Conway, Euclid, Ohio, 1960-62, Ulmer & Berne, Cleve., 1962-65; exec. dir. Ohio State Legal Svcs., Columbus, Ohio, 1965-67; gen. counsel, dir. real estate Sawyer Bus. Colls., Evanston, 1967-72; assoc. Guren Merritt Feibel Sogg & Cohen, Cleve., 1972-75, ptnr., 1975-84, Benesch, Friedlander, Coplan & Aronoff, Cleve., 1984-93; shareholder Kaufman & Cumberland Co., LPA, Cleve., 1994—2000; pvt. practice Chagrin Falls, Ohio, 2001—. Author: Consumer Affairs, 1973, The Construction Loan Process, 1979, Real Estate Financing, 1978, Acquisition, Development and Financing of a Commercial Complex-A Case Study, 1982; contbr. articles to profl. jours. Pres. Am. Jewish Com., Cleve., 1980-82, officer, 1976-80, chmn. adv. com., 1998—; v.p. Criminal Justice Coord. Com., Cleve., 1980-84, Cleve. Play House, bd. dirs., 1978—, pres., 1992-94, chmn., 1994-96, [illegible] 1996— . Recipient Max Freedman Young Leadership award, Cleve., 1974. Mem. ABA, Ohio State Bar Assn., Cleve. Bar Assn. (chmn. real estate com. 1978-79, chmn. real estate law insts. 1979, 82, 87). Jewish. Avocations: tennis, golf, classical music, reading. Office: 25 S Franklin St Chagrin Falls OH 44022-3212

BLATZ, LINDA JEANNE, management professional; d. William Edmund and Jeanne Grace (Hyman) B. BS, U. Md., 1972. Mgr. sales Milliken & Co., N.Y.C., 1972-81; retail market mgr. Greenwood Mills Mktg. Co., N.Y.C., 1981-89; dist. mgr. Steelcase Inc., N.Y.C., 1989-94, tng. cons., 1994-95, tng. mgr., 1995-2000, tng. dir., 2000—03, sales tng. cons., 2003—. Contbr. articles to profl. jours. Mem. N.Y.C. Ballet Guild; corr. sec., pres. PEO; mem. jr. com. N.Y.C. Ballet; v.p. membership, bd. mgrs. exec. com. N.Y. Jr. League (Outstanding Vol. award 1991-92); nominating dir. Assn. Jr. Leagues Internat., 1997, centennial adv. bd., 1999—. Recipient Outstanding Vol. of the Yr. award N.Y. Jr. League, 1992. Mem.: ASTD, AAUW, Am. Woman's Econ. Devel. Corp., N.Y. Women's Agenda, U. Md. Alumni Assn., Women's City Club N.Y., East River Rowing Club, Alpha Gamma Delta. Congregationalist. Avocations: ballet, aerobic dancing, swimming, reading. E-mail: ljbeje@aol.com.

BLAU, BARRY, marketing executive, financial investor; b. N.Y.C., Oct. 4, 1927; s. Emanuel B. and Henrietta Marsha (Moses) B.; m. Eileen Diane Lefkowitz, Aug. 28, 1948; children: Shawn, Peter, Emily, Juliet. With Huber Hoge & Sons, N.Y.C., 1952-57, Sullivan, Stauffer, Caldwell & Bayles, 1958-67, O&M Direct Response, 1968-77; founder Blau Mktg. Techs. Group, 1978-98. Mem. Birchwood Country Club. Jewish. Office: MIII Assoc 9 Bayberry Rdg Westport CT 06880-1713

BLAU, HARVEY RONALD, lawyer; b. N.Y.C., Nov. 14, 1935; s. David and Rose (Kuchinsky) B.; m. Arlene Joan Garrett, Mar. 21, 1964; children: Stephanie Elizabeth, Melissa Karen, Victoria Gayle. AB, N.Y.U., 1957, LL.M., 1965; JD, Columbia U., 1961. Bar: N.Y. 1961. Practiced in N.Y., 1961—2002; sr. ptnr. Blau, Kramer, Wactlar & Lieberman, Jericho, NY, 1966—2002; law sec. to U.S. Dist. Judge Cooper So. Dist. N.Y., 1962-63; asst. U.S. atty. So. Dist. N.Y., 1963-66; CEO Griffon Corp., 1982—. Chmn. Griffon Corp., Aeroflex Corp.; bd. dirs. Nu Horizons Electronics Corp., Benjamin N. Cardozo Sch. Law; bd. trustees Mt. Sinai Hosp., N.Y. Mayor Village of Old Westbury. Served to capt. JAGC, AUS, 1958-66. Mem. Fed. Bar Assn., Assn. of Bar of City of N.Y., Bar Assn. of Nassau County. Home: 125 Wheatley Rd Old Westbury NY 11568-1210 Office: Griffon Corp 100 Jericho Quadrangle Jericho NY 11753-2708

BLAU, HELEN MARGARET, molecular pharmacology educator; b. London, May 8, 1948; (parents Am. citizens); d. George E. and Gertrude Blau; m. David Spiegel, July 25, 1976; children: Daniel Spiegel, Julia Spiegel. BA in Biology, U. York (Eng.), 1969; MA in Biology, Harvard U., 1970, PhD in Biology, 1975. Predoctoral fellow dept. biology Harvard U., Cambridge, Mass., 1969-75; postdoctoral fellow div. med. genetics, dept. biochemistry and biophysics U. Calif., San Francisco, 1975-78; asst. prof. dept. pharmacology Stanford (Calif.) U., 1978-86, assoc. prof. dept. pharmacology, 1986-91, prof. dept. molecular pharmacology, 1991—, prof. dept. microbiology and immunology, 2002—, chair dept. molecular pharmacology, 1997—2001, Donald E. and Delia B. Baxter prof., 1999—, dir. Baxter Lab. in Genetic Pharmacology, 2002—. Co-chmn. various profl. meetings. Mem. editorial bd. 14 jours. including Jour. Cell Biology, Somatic Cell Molecular Genetics and Exptl. Cell Rsch., Molecular and Cellular Biology, Genes to Cells, Molecular Therapy; contbr. articles to profl. jours. Mem. ad hoc molecular cytology study sect. NIH, 1987-88; mem. five-yr. planning com genetics and teratology br. NICHHD/NIH, 1989. Recipient Rsch. Career Devel. award NIH, 1984-89, SmithKline & Beecham award, 1989-91, Women in Cell Biology Career Recognition award, 1992, Excellence in Sci. award FASEB, 1999, McKnight Endowment Fund for Neurosci. award, 2001; Mellon Found. faculty fellow, 1979-80, William H. Hume faculty scholar, 1981-84; grantee NIH, NSF, Ellison Med. Found., Muscular Dystrophy Assn., March of Dimes, 1978—; Yvette Mayent-Rothschild fellow for vis. profs. Inst. Curie, Paris, 1995. Fellow AAAS; mem. NAS (del. to China 1991), Internat. Soc. Differentiation (pres. 2002—), Am. Soc. for Cell Biology (nominating com. 1985-86, program com. 1990), Soc. for Devel. Biology (pres. 1994-95). Avocations: skiing, swimming, hiking, music, theatre.

BLAU, JOHN, retired social worker; b. N.Y.C., Jan. 31, 1934; s. Alex Englander and Edith (Bachman) B. BBA, U. Ga., 1957; cert. of. supervision, Fordham U., 1971; MSW, Hunter Coll., 1974. Field supr. divsn. vol. and proprietary homes N.Y.C. Human Resource Adminstrn., 1962-95; ret. Former mem. N.Y.C. Interagy., Task Force on Mental Health; mem. N.Y. Found. for Sr. Citizens, N.Y. State Ombudsman Program; rschr. on adult and family home industry, homeless men and women, alternate levels of care. Former dist. leader Dem. Party 65th Assembly Dist. Part B, 1987-91; cmty. advisor N.Y. Found. for Sr. Citizens, ombudsman program long term care; co-chmn. NYCERS coalition of ret. N.Y.C. employees; chmn. Social Svc. ad-hoc com. Served with Intelligence Corps, U.S. Army, 1957-59, 61-62. Mem. Disabled Am. Vets. Assn., Acad. Cert. Social Workers, Nat. Assn. Social Workers, E 79th St. Block Assn., Nat. Alumni Assn. U. Ga., Alumni Assn. Fordham U., Alumni Assn. Hunter Coll. Home and Office: 440 E 77th St New York NY 10021-2316

BLAU, MONTE, retired radiology educator; b. N.Y.C., June 17, 1926; s. Samuel and Rose (Cohen) B.; m. Guitta Drimer, June 30, 1946; children: Saul, Hannah. BS in Chemistry, Poly. Inst. Bklyn., 1948; PhD in Phys. Chemistry, U. Wis., 1952. Rsch. chemist Geochronometric Lab., Yale U., 1952-53; with div. neoplastic diseases Montefiore Hosp., N.Y.C., 1953-54; cancer rsch. scientist Roswell Park Meml. Inst., Buffalo, 1954-75; prof., chmn. dept. nuclear medicine SUNY, Buffalo, 1975-83; vis. prof. radiology Harvard Med. Sch., Boston, 1983-90. Mem. USP adv. panel on radiopharms.; chmn. med. adv. com. N.Y. State bur. Radiol. Health; chmn. med. isotopes adv. com. Los Alamos Nat. Lab. Mem. editorial bd. Jour. Nuclear Medicine. With USN, 1944-46. Mem. Soc. Nuclear Medicine (v.p. 1964, pres. 1972), Am. Chem. Soc., Am. Assn. Physicists in Medicine. Home: PO Box 605 South Wellfleet MA 02663-0605

BLAU, RICHARD MILES (DICK BLAU), performing arts educator, photographer, film director; b. N.Y.C., Sept. 4, 1943; s. Albert Freedberg and Beatrice Mandell (Manley) Blau, Herbert Blau (Stepfather). BA, Harvard Coll., 1965; PhD, Yale U., 1973. From instr. to assoc. prof. Am. Studies SUNY, Buffalo, 1968-75; from assoc. to prof. dept. film U. Wis., Milw., 1975—, dept. chmn., 1979-99. Co-creator program Am. studies SUNY, Buffalo; co-founder dept. film U. Wis., Milw. Dir., editor : (films) Jidyll, 1990; co-author: (book) Plka Happiness, 1992, Bright Balkan Morning: Romani Lives and the Power of Music, 2002; co-dir.: (films) Oh, Rapunzel, 1996 (Dir.'s Choice Black Maria Film Festival, 1997); creative cons. (films) American Movie, 1998 (Grand Jury prize for documentary Sundance Film Festival, 1999), photographer (book) Living With His Camera, 2003; one-man shows include de Saisset Mus., Santa Clara, Calif., 1975, CEPA, Buffalo, 1975, Perihelion Gallery, Milw., Scala Galerie, Brno, Czech Republic, 1992, Paratiritis Gallery, Thessalonika, Greece, 1994, exhibited in group shows at Basquin Gallery, Milw., 1983, Nexus Gallery, Atlanta, 1985, W. A. Graham Gallery, Houston, 1986, Houston Internat. Foto Fest, 1988, Art Inst./Field Mus., Chgo., 1990, Milw. Art Mus., 1994, New Mus., 1999, Represented in permanent collections Art Inst. Chgo., Bklyn. Mus., Kosciuszko Found. Archive Polish-Am. Life, Macedonian Mus. Contemporary Art, Midwest Express Ctr., Milw., Mus. Modern Art, Wexner Ctr. Arts. Co-founder CEPA, Buffalo, 1973, Perihelion Art Gallery, Milw., 1978, Art Futures, Milw., 1987; founder Cmty. Media Project, Milw., 1986. Fulbright scholar, 1965, Woodrow Wilson fellow, 1966—67, Wis. Arts Bd. fellow for photography, 1978, 1980. Mem.: Phi Beta Kappa. Home: 2723 N Farwell Ave Milwaukee WI 53211-3759 Office: Univ Wis Dept Film PO Box 413 Milwaukee WI 53201-0413 E-mail: dickblau@uwm.edu.

BLAUER, A. CLYDE, microbiologist, educator, botanist; b. Burley, Idaho, Apr. 26, 1939; s. Henry William and Lucile Woodbury Blauer; m. Geaneen Whittle Blauer, Sept. 14, 1962; children: Alan C., Robert D., Lucile W., Anthony H., Elizabeth B., Amy G., Katie A. BS, Brigham Young U., 1964, MS, 1966; postgrad., Cornell U., 1965—66, U. Ala., 1973. Instr. Snow Coll., Ephraim, Utah, 1966—71; range rsch. technician Intermountain forest and range Experiment sta., Ogden, Utah, 1967—73; asst. prof. Snow Coll., Ephraim, Utah, 1971—78; botanist Intermountain forest and range Experiment sta., 1974—91, 1995—96; assoc. prof. Snow Coll., Ephraim, Utah, 1978—86, biology dept. head, 1978—96, prof., 1986—. Curator Herbarium Snow Coll., Ephraim, 1966—; pres. -elect, pres., past pres. Snow Coll. Faculty Assn., Ephraim, 1970—72; mem. People-To-People Internat. Bot. Sci. Del. to Republic South Africa. Contbr. articles to profl. jours. Scout master, unit com., M.B. councilor Boy Scouts Am., Ephraim; EMT Emergency Svcs., Ephraim, 1977—78; chmn. City Beautification Com., Ephraim, 1980—98. Recipient Dist. award of Merit, Boy Scouts Am., Ephraim, Jesse Madsen Brady Superior Tchg. award, Snow Coll., 1993. Republican. Mem. Lds Ch. Avocations: church service, choir singing, gardening. Office: Snow Coll 150 E College Ave Ephraim UT 84627 Office Fax: 435-283-6879.

BLAUFOX, MORTON DONALD, physician, educator, specialist in hypertension; b. N.Y.C., July 19, 1934; s. Emanuel and Elizabeth (Rosenblum) B.; m. Paulette Goldberg, Dec. 20, 1958; children: Laurie Beth, Ellen Ruth, Andrew David. Student, Harvard U., 1952-55; MD, SUNY, 1959; PhD, U. Minn., 1964. Diplomate Am. Bd. Internal Medicine, Am. Bd. Nuclear Medicine (bd. dirs. 1985-91). Intern Jewish Hosp. of Bklyn., N.Y.C., 1959-60; fellow in medicine Mayo Found. Med. Edn. and Research, Rochester, Minn., 1960-64; advanced research fellow Am. Heart Assn., 1964-66; research fellow in medicine Harvard Med. Sch., Boston, 1964-66; asst. in medicine and radiology Peter Bent Brigham Hosp., Boston, 1964-66; asst. prof. radiology, also assoc. in medicine Albert Einstein Coll. Medicine, Bronx, N.Y., 1966-71, dir. sect. nuclear medicine, 1966-76, dir. unified dept., 1976-82, chmn. unified dept., 1982—, assoc. dir. clin. research center, 1968-72, assoc. prof. radiology, 1971-76, prof. radiology, 1976—, assoc. prof. medicine, 1972-78, prof. medicine, 1978—; asst. attending physician Bronx Mcpl. Hosp. Center, 1966-71, assoc. attending, 1972, attending physician, 1972—; dir. div. nuclear medicine Montefiore Med. Center, 1976-82, chmn. dept. nuclear medicine, 1982—. Cons. kidney disease control program USPHS, 1967-72; me. adminstrv. coun. nuclear medicine VA, 1972-73; mem. panel on radiopharms. U.S. Pharmacopeia, 1970-76; mem. hypertension adv. com. N.Y.C. Dept. Health, 1975-76; mem. Am. Bd. Nuclear, 1984-90; treas. exec. com. Am. Bd. Nuclear Medicine, 1987-89, chmn., 1990; mem. clin. trials rev. com. Nat. Heart, Lung and Blood Inst., 1988-92, reviewer ready rsch., 1992—; mem. subcom. on non-pharmacologic therapy of Joint Nat. Com. on Detection Evaluation and Treatment of High Blood Pressure, 1991-92; mem. Brookhaven Linac Isotope Producer Users' adv. com. Brookhaven Nat. Lab., 1992-96; mem. internat. liaison com. World Fedn. Nuclear Medicine and Biology, 1992-94; active Coun. Cardiovascular Radiology; hon. prof. medicine Shanxi U. Med. Sch., China, 1997. Author: An Illustrated History of the Evolution of the Stethoscope, 2001; editor (with others): Seminars in Nuclear Medicine, 1970—; editor: Evaluation of Renal Function and Disease with Radionuclides, 1972—, 2d edit., 1989—, Procs. Internat. Symposium, 1972—, 1975—, 1980—, 1987—, 1990—, PDR for Nuclear Medicine and Radiology, 1971—80, Unilateral Renal Function Studies, 1978; editor: (with others) Secondary Hypertension: Current Diagnosis and Management, 1981; editor: Non-Pharmacologic Therapy of Hypertension, 1987, Newer Diagnostic Methods in Nephrology and Urology, 1986; mem. editl. bd.: Radionuclides in Nephrology, 1980, editl. bd.: Jour. Nuclear Medicine, 1973—81, Nephron, Uroradiology, 1978—, Jour. Nuclear Medicine and Allied Sci., 1982, Nuclear Medicine Comm., 1979—, Renal Failure, 1985—89, Am. Jour. Hypertension, 1987—, assoc. editor: Garnet's Pediatrics, 1972—, sect. editor for diagnostics and techniques: Current Opinions in Nephrology and Hypertension, 1992—96, contbr.: The Merck Manual, 14th, 15th and 16th edits., 1982—91, Merck Manual Medical Information Home Edit., 1997; co-author: Blood Pressure Measurement: An Illustrated History, 1998; contbr. ; author: An Ear to the Chest: An Illustrated History of the Evaluation of the Stethoscope, 2002. Recipient Edward Nobel Found. award, 1963, Albert Lasker pub. health service award, 1980, Lifetime Achievement award Internat. Soc. Radionuclides in NephroUrology, 2001. Fellow ACP, Am. Nephrology Soc., Am. Coll. Nuclear Physicians, Coun. on High Blood Pressure Rsch., Coun. Cardiovascular Radiology, N.Y. Acad. Medicine (libr. com. 1985—, chmn. sect. on nuclear medicine 1993-95, chmn. ad hoc com. artifact collection, chmn. history of medicine adv. com. 1995—); mem. AMA, Am. Heart Assn., Am. Physiol. Soc., Am. Fedn. Clin. Rsch., Am. Soc. Hypertension (membership com.), Soc. Nuclear Medicine (pres. Greater N.Y. chpt. 1975-76, chmn. acad. coun. 1976-77, exec. and sci. coms., chmn. publ. com. 1979-82, trustee, Berson-Yalow award 1989), Ind. Soc. Nuclear Medicine (Sarabhai Oration 1989), Internat. Soc. Nephrology, Internat. Hypertension Soc., Coun. on High Blood Pressure Rsch. (med. adv. bd.), N.Y. Med. Soc., Am. Nephrology Soc., Med. Collectors Assn. (pres. 1983—), Swiss Soc. Nuclear Medicine (hon., corr.), Sigma Xi. Achievements include research on hypertension, renal function and evaluation of renal function with radioisotopes, renal blood flow and renin secretion. Home: 101 Drake Smith Woods Ln Rye NY 10580-4316 Office: Montefiore Med Park 1695A Eastchester Rd Bronx NY 10461-2374 E-mail: blaufox@aecom.yu.edu. *My life has been directed toward the acquisition, clarification and dissemination of knowledge in the health sciences. The use of such goals to help train young people embarking on a career, with honesty and integrity, has been a particularly rewarding experience.*

BLAUNSTEIN, PHYLLIS REID, communications and marketing executive; b. N.Y.C., July 4, 1940; d. Alex and Elsie (Rothstein) Lepler; m. Robert Philip Blaunstein, June 17, 1962; children: Eric Reid, Marc Reid. BA in English, SUNY, Albany, 1962; MA in Speech Pathology and Audiology, U. Tenn., 1967. English tchr. Knox County Bd. Edn., East Cleveland Bd. Edn., Cleve., 1962-66; instr. speech pathology and audiology U. Tenn., Knoxville, 1968-73; dir. Hearing and Speech Clinic U. Tenn. Meml. Rsch. Hosp., Knoxville, 1972-73; program mgr., coord. for ethical practice affairs Am. Speech, Hearing and Lang. Assn., Washington, 1973-75; spl. asst. to dep. commr. Bur. Edn. for the Handicapped U.S. Dept. Edn., Washington, 1976-77; dir. spl. projects Nat. Assn. State Bds. Edn., Washington, 1977-78, assoc. exec. dir., 1978-79, dep. exec. dir., 1979-80, exec. dir., 1981-87; sr. counsel Widmeyer Comms., Washington, 1988—; pres. Phyllis Blaunstein and Assocs., Inc., Chevy Chase, Md., 1989—. Cons. Ford Found., U.S. Edn. Dept., USPHS, Md. State Dept. Edn., Ednl. Comm., Inc., Nat. Assn. State Dirs. Spl. Edn. Bd. dirs.nat. capital area NCCJ. Office: Phyllis Blaunstein and Assoc 2703 Daniel Rd Chevy Chase MD 20815-3150

BLAUVELT, BARBARA LOUISE, nutritionist; d. Starr Chester and Dorothy (Schofield) Blauvelt. PhD, U. Mass., 1969. Nutrition program supr. divsn. pub. health nutrition Va. Dept. Health, Roanoke, 1970-95. Pvt. cons., 2002—. Co-author: Kitchen Memories, 1998.

BLAVAT, JERRY (GERALD JOSEPH BLAVAT), radio and television personality, actor; b. Phila., July 3, 1940; s. Louis Blavat and Lucille Capuano; children: Kathi, Geraldine, Stacy, Deserie. Grad. high sch., Phila. Dancer Bandstand TV show, Phila., 1953-55; record promoter Cameo/Parkway Records, Phila., 1956-59; road mgr., mgr. various rock and roll groups including Danny and the Juniors, also Don Rickles, 1957-59; night club performer, live radio show host various clubs, radio stas., Phila., 1959-62; disc jockey radio stations including WCAU, WFIL, WCAM, WPGR, WSSJ, WTKU, WVLT, WPEN, WPAZ, Phila., Del. Valley, 1962—; program dir. Geator Gold Radio Network, Pa. Del., Md., N.J., 1989—. Owner night club Memories, Margate, N.J., 1970—; mem. nominating com. Rock & Roll Hall of Fame, Phila., 1988—; host live radio show on geatorgold.net, 1999—. TV appearances include The Monkees, Mod Squad, Joey Bishop Show, Tonight Show, Mike Douglas Show, Pat Boone Show, Merv Griffin Show; movie appearances include Baby, It's You, 1983, Desperately Seeking Susan, 1985, Cookie, 1989; producer, host TV shows Discophonic Scene, 1965-66, Jerry Blavat Show, 1966-70, On the Air with the Geator, 1991—, Backstage with Blavat, 1992—; co-prodr. Rock Rhythm and Doo Wop series PBS, 1999—; prodr. Legends of Rock, Legends of Soul, Legends of Harmony at Kimmel Regional Performing Arts Ctr., Phila.; prodr. over 30 record albums of collections/anthologies, rec. artist 5 pop singles; contbr. articles, biographies, liner notes to profl. jours., programs and record albums. Bd. dirs., performer Hero Scholarship Fund, Phila., 1963-70; bd. dirs. Police Athletic League, Phila., 1966-70; fundraiser numerous schs., chs., founds., and pub. TV. Recipient U.S. Congl. Horizon award, 2002; inductee Phila. Rock & Roll Hall of Fame, 1986, installed in permanent exhibit Rock and Roll Hall of Fame, Mus. of Radio and Records, 1998; inductee Phila. Music Alliance Walk of Fame, 1993. Mem. AFTRA, SAG, Am. Guild Variety Artists, Nat. Music Found. (adv. bd. 1989—), Broadcast Pioneers of Phila. Avocations: horseback riding, bicycling, reading, native american history. Office: Celebrity Showcase PO Box 25010 Philadelphia PA 19147-0210 E-mail: geatorgold@yahoo.com.

BLAWIE, JAMES LOUIS, law educator; b. Newark, Mar. 26, 1928; s. Louis Paul and Cecelia Ruth (Grish) B.; m. Marilyn June Beyerle, May 30, 1952; children: Elias J., Cecelia R., Christiana L. BA, U. Conn., 1950; AM, Boston U., 1951, PhD, 1959; JD, U. Chgo., 1955. Bar: Conn. 1956, Calif. 1965, U.S. Dist. Ct. (no. dist.) Calif. 1965, U.S. Ct. Appeals (9th cir.) 1967, U.S. Supreme Ct. 1968. Instr. polit. sci. Mich. State U., East Lansing, 1955; assoc. prof. U. Akron, Ohio, 1956-57, Kent State U., 1956-57; asst. prof. bus. law U. Calif., Berkeley, 1958-60; assoc. prof. law Santa Clara U., Calif., 1960-63, prof. law, 1963—; vis. prof. polit. sci. Calif. State U., Hayward, 1966-67; adminstrv. law judge U.S. Equal Employment Opportunity Commn., Washington, 1982-85. Complaints examiner U.S. Equal Employment Opportunity Agy., Office Equal Employment Opportunity; cons. in field. Author: (handbook) The Michigan Township Board, 1957; contbr. articles to profl. jours. Mem. Citizen's Adv. Com. on Capital Improvements, 1962-65; bd. dirs. Washington Hosp., 1964-68. Maj. U.S. Army, 1963-74. Boston U. Faculty fellow, 1951-53; U. Chgo. Law Sch. scholar, 1953-55; grantee Mich. State U. grantee, 1955-56, Helsinki Govt. Ministry Edn. grantee, 1980-81. Mem. ABA, Fairfield County Bar Assn., Mensa. Republican. Avocations: computers, photography, travel, rare diseases databases. Home: 41752 Marigold Dr Fremont CA 94539-4779 also: PO Box 1102 Fremont CA 94538-0110 Office: Santa Clara U Sch Law Santa Clara CA 95053-0001 E-mail: jimblawie@aol.com., macfig@aol.com.

BLAXALL, MARTHA OSSOFF, economist; b. Haverhill, Mass., Feb. 2, 1942; d. Michael M. and Eve Joan (Kladky) Ossoff; m. John Blaxall, May 15, 1970 (div. 1989); children: Jenifer, Johanna. BA, Wellesley Coll., 1963; PhD, Tufts U., 1971. Economist Abt Assocs. Inc., Cambridge, Mass., 1965-68; budget examiner Office Mgmt. and Budget, 1969-72; sr. profl. assoc. Inst. Medicine NAS, 1972-76; dir. rsch. Health Health Care Fin. Adminstrn., U.S. Dept. HHS, 1976-79; dir. Office Utilization and Devel., Nat. Marine Fisheries Svc., Dept. Commerce, 1979-82; assoc. prof. dept. cmty. and family medicine Georgeteown U. Med. Sch., 1982; pres. BBH Corp., 1982-87; prin. Chase, Brown & Blaxall, Inc., 1983-87; v.p. ICF Inc., Washington, 1987-89; economist Hill and Knowlton Econs. Group, Washington, 1990-91; dir. agribus. trade and investment group Devel. Alternatives Inc., Bethesda, Md., 1991-93, dir. mktg. devel. group, 1993-95, v.p., 1995—2001; dir. Ctrl. Asia and Caucasus Project Yale U. Ctr. for Study of Globalization, 2001—02; vis. scholar Nitze Sch. for Adv. Internat. Studies John Hopkins U., 2002—03. Vis. scholar Nitze Sch. for Advanced Internat. Studies Johns Hopkins U., 2002—; treas. Fedn. Ogrns. Profl. Woemn, 1974—76, 1983—84, exec. coun., 1982. Co-editor: Women in the Workplace: The Implications of Occupational Segregation, 1976. Trustee Sheridan Sch., Washington, 1978—86, Coun. for Excellence in Govt., 1991—; mem. Inst. Women's Policy Studies, 1993—2002, chair, 1998—2002; active Woolly Mammoth Theatre Co., 1997—, vice chair, 1999—; active Leadership Forum Internat., 2002—; bd. dirs. Washington-Moscow Exch., 1990—93, Children's Health and Environ. Ctr. NDEA fellow, 1964—65. Mem.: Nat. Economists Club (v.p. 1990—91), Am. Econ. Assn. Home: 1390 Birdsville Rd Davidsonville MD 21035 E-mail: moblaxall@aol.com.

BLAYDES, JUNE LOUISE, volunteer; b. Indpls., June 16, 1929; d. Charles Edwin Chalfin and Freda Viola Huls (Stinger) Comer; m. Louis Justus Schulz, Feb. 7, 1948 (dec. May 1974); children: Louis K., Judy A Schulz, Larry L.; m. Fred Blaydes, Apr. 9, 1976. Grad. H.S., Indpls. Realtor Louis Schulz Co., Indpls., 1961-71; pres., owner Floral Concepts Co., Indpls., 1981-90. Pres. Christian Mothers PTA, Christ the King Sch., Indpls., 1955-63; vol. St. Vincent's Hosp., Indpls., 1974-76, Indpls. Speech and Hearing Ctr., Indpls., 1979-84; choir mem. Christ the King Ch., Inpls., 1994-96; bd. dirs. Coburn Place Safe Haven, Indpls., 1996—. Named Vol. of the Month, WMYS (1430) Radio, Indpls., 1997. Mem. Riviera Club, Women of the Moose. Republican. Roman Catholic. Avocations: family activities, travel, mall walkers group, euchre club, bridge club. Home: 6727 Limerick Ct Indianapolis IN 46250-4415

BLAYDES, SOPHIA BOYATZIES, English language educator; b. Rochester, N.Y., Oct. 16, 1933; d. James George and Helene (Bougdanos) Boyatzies; m. David Fairchild Blaydes, June 4, 1961; children: Stephanie Anne, Jeffrey Glenn. BA, U. Rochester, 1955; MA, Ind. U., 1958, PhD, 1962. Teaching asst. English Ind. U., 1955-62; instr. to asst. prof. Am. Thought and Lang. dept. Mich. State U., 1962-65; instr. to prof. English W.Va. U., Morgantown, 1966-99, chair faculty senate, 1990-91, coord. program for sr. and retired faculty, 1994—; pres. Carolinas Symposium for British Studies, 1990-91. Co-dir. Lit. Discussion Group for Sr. Citizens, 1978—; mem. faculty Elderhostel, 1985, 87, 88, 90, 94; mem. ctrl. exec. com. Folger Inst., 1992-99; chair faculty senate, bd. advisors W.Va. U., 1990-91, rep. to adv. coun. to bd. trustees, 1993-99; state del. to the 1995 White House Conf. on Aging; bd. trustees Univ. Sys., 1998-99. Author: Christopher Smart as a Poet of His Time: A Re-Appraisal, 1966, (with others) Sir William Davenant, 1981, Sir William Davenant: An Annotated Bibliography, 1986; editor: (with others) Selected Papers from the W.Va. Shakespeare and Renaissance Association, 1976, The Literary Discussion Group, 1982, 85; contbr. chpts. to books, articles to profl. jours., encys., dictionaries, bibliographies. Mem. cen. exec. com. Folger Inst., 1992-99. Recipient Disting. Manuscript award Mich. State U., 1965, Gerontology Ctr. award, 1983; named Disting. West Virginian, W.Va. Gov., 1995; grantee W.Va. Found., 1973, W.Va. Humanities, 1980; W.Va. U. Senate rsch. grantee, 1984, 89; Folger fellow, 1981, Folger grantee, 1988, 91; recipient Sigma Tau Delta Outstanding Tchg. award, 1996. Mem. Am. Soc. 18th Century Studies, MLA, W.Va. Assn. Coll. English Tchrs. (pres. 1977), Shakespeare and Renaissance Soc. W.Va. (chmn. 1978, 84), Carolinas Symposium on Brit. Studies (chair program 1989, pres. 1990, conf. chair 1993). Home: 652 Bellaire Dr Morgantown WV 26505-2421 Office: W Va U PO Box 6296 Morgantown WV 26506-6296

BLAYLOCK, JAMES CARL, clergyman, librarian; b. Guntown, Miss., Jan. 27, 1938; s. Carl Houston and Katie Lee (Pugh) B.; m. Jo Ann Enlow, May 3, 1962; children: Jacquelyn Ann, John Thomas. AA, Southeastern Bapt. Coll., Laurel, Miss., 1962; BTh, N.Am. Theol. Sem., Jacksonville, Tex., 1964; BA, U. Tex., Tyler, 1976; MRE, Bapt. Missionary Sem., Jacksonville, 1977; MSLS, Tex A&M U., 1980. Ordained to ministry Bapt. Ch., 1962. Pastor Mt. Pleasant Ch., Bedias, Tex., 1962-64, Buena Vista Ch., Timpson, Tex., 1964-70, 1st Bapt. Ch., Maydelle, Tex., 1970-86, Corinth Ch., Jacksonville, Tex., 1986—; asst. dir. Bapt. News Svc., Jacksonville, 1969-88, dir., 1988-99; asst. editor Directory and Handbook of Bapt. Missionary Assn., Jacksonville, 1969-88, editor, 1988-99; libr. Bapt. Missionary Assn. Theol. Sem., Jacksonville, 1972—. Editor Mt. Olive Evangel, 1965-70; author: History of 1st Bapt. Ch. Maydelle, Tex., 1986, Buena Vista Bapt. Ch., 1986, Glimpses from the Past, 2003. Mem. Am. Theol. Libr. Assn., ALA, Tex. Libr. Assn. Baptist. Home: 625 W Kickapoo St Jacksonville TX 75766-4621 Office: Bapt Missionary Assn Theol Sem 1530 E Pine St Jacksonville TX 75766-5407 E-mail: jcblaylock@cox-internet.com.

BLAZEJOWSKI, CAROL, sports team executive, retired basketball player; Player N.J. Gems, 1980-81; v.p., gen. mgr. New York Liberty WNBA, 1997—. Named Kodak All-Am., Montclair State Coll., 1976—78, Converse Women's Player of Yr., 1977, Women's Basketball Player of Yr., 1978; named to Naismith Basketball Hall of Fame, 1994; recipient Wade Trophy, 1978. Achievements include All-Am. selection, 1976; All-Am. selection, 1977; All-Am. selection, 1978; single season and career women's basketball scoring records, 1976; mem. World Univ. Gold Medal team, Mexico City, 1979; Pan Am. Silver medal team, 1979; leading scorer Women's Basketball League, 1980-81. Office: New York Liberty 2 Penn Plz New York NY 10121-0101 also: c/o Basketball Hall of Fame PO Box 179 Springfield MA 01101-0179

BLAZEK-WHITE, DORIS, lawyer; b. Easton, Md., Nov. 17, 1943; d. George W. and Nola M. (Buterbaugh) Defibaugh; children: Christine T., Judson M.; m. Thacher W. White. BA, Goucher Coll., 1965; JD, Georgetown U., 1968. Bar: D.C. 1969, V.I. 1969, U.S. Ct. Appeals (3d cir. 1969), U.S. Ct. Appeals (D.C. cir.) 1971, Md. 1979. Gen. practice with Judge Warren H. Young, V.I., 1968-70; assoc. Covington & Burling, Washington, 1970-76, ptnr., 1976—. Mem. Am. Coll. Trust and Estate Counsel. Office: Covington & Burling 1201 Pennsylvania Ave NW Washington DC 20004 E-mail: dblazek-white@cov.com.

BLAZER, DAN GERMAN, II, psychiatrist, epidemiologist; b. Nashville, Tenn., Feb. 23, 1944; s. Dan German and Mary Elizabeth (Owsley) Blazer; m. Sherrill Walls, Aug. 19, 1966; children: Dan German III, Natasha Leigh. BA, Vanderbilt U., 1965; MD, U. Tenn., 1969; MPH, U. N.C., 1979, PhD, 1980. Diplomate Am. Bd. Psychiatry and Neurology. Fellow Montefiore Hosp. and Med. Ctr., N.Y.C., 1975—76; asst. prof., assoc. prof., then prof. psychiatry Duke U. Med. Ctr., Durham, NC, 1976—, J.P. Gibbons prof. psychiatry, 1990—, interim chair of psychiatry, 1990—93, prof. cmty. and family medicine, 1986—; dean of med. edn. Duke U., 1992—99. Chair, bd. dirs. Am. Geriat. Soc., NY, 1983; bd. dirs. ret. persons svcs. Am. Assn. Ret. Persons, Alexandria, Va., 1987—92; pres. Psychiat. Rsch. Soc., Salt Lake City, 1988; chmn. epidemiology and disease control study sect. NIH, Bethesda, Md., 1988—. Author: Life is Worth Living, 1987, Depression in Late Life, 1993, Freud vs. God, 1998, Introduction to Clinical Research in Psychiatry, 1998. Mem. Brooks Ave. Ch. of Christ, Raleigh, NC, 1982. Recipient Rsch. Career Devel. award, NIMH, 1977, Alex Haley award, East Tenn. Bapt. Hosp., Knoxville, 1986, Disting. Svc. award, U. N.C. Sch. Pub. Health, Chapel Hill, 1989, Milo Leavitt award, Am. Geriat. Soc., 1997, Rema LaPouse award, APHA, 2001. Fellow: Am. Psychopathol. Assn., Gerontol. Soc. Am., So. Psychiat. Assn., Am. Psychiat. Assn., Am. Coll. Psychiatrists; mem.: Inst. of Medicine NAS. Democrat. Avocations: hiking, reading. Office: Duke U Med Ctr PO Box 3003 Durham NC 27715-3003 E-mail: blaze001@mc.duke.edu.

BLAZEWICK, ROBERT B. lawyer, educator, military officer; s. Robert George and Jacqueline Rose B. BA, Marquette U., 1984, JD, 1987; MA, U.S. Naval War Coll., 1996. Bar: Wis. 1987, U.S. Dist. Ct. (ea. and we. dists.) Wis. 1987, U.S. Ct. Appeals (7th cir.) 1988, U.S. Supreme Ct. 1993, U.S. Armed Forces Ct. of Appeals 1998. Assoc. atty. Scanlan & Hartigan, Chgo., 1987; commd. ensign USN, 1986, advanced through grades to comdr., 1994; assoc. atty. Scanlan & Hartigan, Chgo., 1987; criminal def. U.S. Navy, Great Lakes, Ill., 1987-89, staff judge adv. USS Lincoln Norfolk, Va., 1989-91, Alameda, Calif., 1989-91, fed. tort atty. Washington, 1991-93, criminal def. Naples, Italy, 1993-95; law educator Naval Justice Sch. U.S. Navy Naval War Coll., Newport, R.I., 1995-99; staff judge adv. Cruiser Destroyer Group 3, Everett, Wash., 1999—2001; staff judge adv. Navy Region Europe, Naples, Italy, 2001—. Editor Naval Law Rev., 1998. Mem. ABA, FBA, Wis. Bar Assn. Roman Catholic. Avocations: theater, cars, fitness. Office: Staff Judge Advocate Navy Region Europe PSC 802 Box 20 Fpo AE 09499

BLAZEY, JUDITH LEISTON, school district administrator; b. Rochester, N.Y., Mar. 6, 1941; d. Emanuel R. and Julia (Nicoletti) Leiston; m. John T. Blazey, May 11, 1963; children: John T. II, James R., Jeffrey S. BS, SUNY, Brockport, 1962, MS, 1987, CAS, 1988. Cert. sch. dist. adminstr., sch. adminstr. and supr. English dept. coord. Palmyra (N.Y.)-Macedon High Sch., 1979-82, 84-88, 89-91, tchr., 1962-63, 64-66, 1972-95, ret., 1995; dist. English/lang. arts coord. Palmyra Macedon Cen. Sch., 1988-89. Adj. instr. SUNY Finger Lakes Cmty. Coll., Canandaigua, N.Y., 1982-86. Mem. Nat. Coun. Tchrs. English, N.Y. State English Coun., Delta Kappa Gamma.

BLAZEY, MARK LEE, management consultant; b. Canadaigua, N.Y., Nov. 14, 1948; s. Everett J. and Ann (Marrer) B.; m. Karen S. Davison, May 8, 1950; children: Elizabeth, Mark. BA, Syracuse U., 1970; MS in Edn., SUNY, Albany, 1976, MS in Psychology and Stats., EdD, SUNY, Albany, 1978; SMG cert., Harvard U., 1984. Cert. tchr., chief sch. officer and adminstr., N.Y. Tchr., cons. Syracuse City Schs., 1971-76; lectr. SUNY, Albany, 1976-78; higher edn. cons. N.Y. State Edn. Dept., Albany, 1976-78; policy analyst Office of Edn. HEW, Washington, 1978-80; sr. policy analyst Office Sec. U.S. Dept. Edn., Washington, 1980-81, dir. policy, 1981-83, dir. ops., 1983-85; prof. Rochester (N.Y.) Inst. Tech., 1985-86, dir., assoc. dean, 1986-88, dean, 1988-92. Bd. dirs. RIT Rsch. Corp.; pres. Quantum Performance Group, Inc.; sr. examiner Malcolm Balbrige Nat. Quality award, 1995-99; founding mem., lead judge Excelsior award, N.Y. Gov.'s exec. com., 1991-99, presiding judge Aruba Nat. Quality award, 1995-98; lead judge Vt. Quality Award, 1991-2000; judge Wis. Forward Quality Award, 2000—, Del. Quality award, 2002—. Author: Insights to Performance Excellence, 1996-2003. Bd. dirs. Horton Child Care Ctr., Rochester, 1985-89; mem. Geva Angels Repertory Theater, 1985—; bd. dirs. Finger Lakes Region Edn. Ctr. for Econ. Devel., 1990-92. Recipient Frandson award for Lit., 1993, Quality Champion award State Quality Award Network, 1995. Mem. Am. Soc. for Quality (cert. quality auditor), Phi Delta Kappa. Avocations: wood sculpture, skiing, golf, sailing. Office: 5050 Rushmore Rd Palmyra NY 14522-9414 E-mail: blazey@quantumperformance.com., QPG1@aol.com.

BLAZEY, MICHAEL ALAN, educator; b. Rochester, N.Y., Jan. 5, 1952; s. Charles Henry and Kathryn Blazey; m. Jennifer Anne Nestegard, July 6, 1991; children: Amanda Rose, Lauren Olivia. BA, U. Oreg., 1974; MS, S.D. State U., 1977; PhD, Pa. State U., 1984. Recreation supt. Brookings (S.D.) Parks and Recreation, 1974-77; instr. Kans. State U., Manhattan, 1977-79; recreation dir. Ketchikan (Alaska) Parks and Recreation, 1979-80; grad. asst. Pa. State U., University Park, 1980-83; instr. Western Carolina U., Cullowhee, 1983-84; assoc. prof. Wash. State U., Pullman, 1984-90; prof. Calif. State U., Long Beach, 1990—, interim chmn. Dept. Sociology, 1990—2003. Cons. Queen Mary, Long Beach, 1989-92, rsch. proposal cons. Am. Assn. Ret. Persons Andrus Found., Washington, 1993-96; cons. Calif. Parks and Recreation, Sacramento, 1993, Wash. Tourism Devel., Olympia, 1985-90, Landermann-Moore and Assocs., Anacortes, Wsh., 1995—, L.A. City Atty.'s Office. Contbr. articles to profl. jours. Bd. dirs. United Meth. Ch. Campus Ministry, Long Beach, 1991—; mem. Housing and Cmty. Devel. Citizen Participation Com., La Habra, Calif., 1995—98, La Habra Planning Commn., 1998—2003. Named Glenn E. Robinson lectr. S.D. State U., 1991; recipient Rsch. award Am. Assn. Ret. Persons/Andrus, 1988. Fellow: Am. Leisur Acad. (sr.); mem.: Am. Assn. Higher Edn., Soc. Park and Recreation Educators (comm. chmn. 1995—96, bd. dirs. 1999—, pres. 2003—), World Leisure and Recreation Assn., Calif. Parks and Recreation Soc., Nat. Recreation and Parks Assn. Avocations: gardening, bicycling, in-line skating, home improvement, travel. Office: Calif State U 1250 N Bellflower Blvd Long Beach CA 90840-4903 E-mail: mblazey@csulb.edu.

BLAZINA, JANICE FAY, transfusion medicine physician; b. Youngstown, Ohio, Apr. 20, 1953; d. Joseph and Cordelia Evelyn (Mitchell) B. BS, Youngstown State U., 1975; MD, Ohio State U., 1978. Diplomate Am. Bd. Pathology. Resident in anat. and clin. pathology U. Ala. Med. Ctr., Birmingham, 1978-82; assoc. pathologist various hosps., Bryan, Tex., 1982-83, High Plains Bapt. Hosp., Amarillo, Tex., 1983-84; fellow in blood banking Baylor U. Med.

Ctr., Dallas, 1984-85; asst. prof. dept. pathology Ohio State U., Columbus, 1985-93, asst. prof. Sch. Allied Med. Professions, 1987-93. Asst. dir. transfusion svc. Ohio State U. Hosp., 1985-89, assoc. dir., 1989-90, dir., 1990-93, med. dir. histocompatibility, paternity, apheresis and phlebotomy svcs., 1987-93, divsn. med. tech., 1987-93; asst. med. dir. Carter Blood Ctr., Ft. Worth, 1993-95, med. dir., 1995-96. Contbr. articles to profl. publs. Grantee: Bremer Found., 1987. Mem. AMA, Am. Soc. Apheresis, Am. Soc. Histocompatibility and Immunogenetics, Am. Assn. Blood Banks (insp. 1987—), Am. Med. Womens Assn., Ohio Assn. Blood Banks (trustee 1990-93, sec. 1992-93), Ohio Acad. Sci., Grad. Women Sci., Assn. Women Sci. Cen. Ohio (v.p. 1989-90, pres. 1990-91). Mem. Church of Christ. Avocations: gardening, cats, african violets.

BLAZKOWSKI, PHILLIP, community development and planning official; b. Tomahawk, Wis., Jan. 6, 1943; s. Ted Salvester and Phyllis (Egtvedt) B.; m. Roberta H. Schontag, July 24, 1971; 1 child, Sarah Louisa. BS cum laude, Northland Coll., 1971; MS, So. Ill. U., 1973; Cert. State and Local Govt., Harvard U., 1983. Mgr. Maine Supermarket, Wausau, Wis., 1968-69; planner S.E. N.H. Regional Planning Commn., Exeter, 1971-72, Ill. Dept. Local Affairs, Springfield, 1972-73; county planner Rock County Planning & Zoning Agy., Janesville, Wis., 1973-75; dir. planning Rock County Planning and Devel. Agy., Janesville, 1975-79; dir. Rock County Planning, Econ. and Cmty. Devel. Agy., Janesville, 1979—. Chair Rock County Econ. Devel. Tech. Com., Janesville, 1974—; mem. farmland preservation adminstrv. rules adv. com. Wis. Dept. Agr., 1995; mem. state hwy. plan adv. com. Wis. Dept. Transp. Editor: Illinois Planning Enabling Legislation, 1973; contbr. chpts. to books. Bd. dirs. Wis. River Rail Transit Commn., Pecatonica River Rail Transit Commn., Plattville, 1999—. Recipient Local Assistance Achievement award Nat. Assn. Counties, 1982. Mem. Am. Planning Assn. (chair Wis. chpt.), Nat. Assn. County Planning Dirs. (pres. Wisc.), Wis. Land Record Assn., Wis. Econ. Devel. Assn. (Outstanding Econ. Devel. Program award 1989), Am. Inst. Planners. Roman Catholic. Avocations: curling, hunting, fishing, golf, woodworking. Home: 1118 Grace St Janesville WI 53545-4154 Office: Rock County Planning Econs and Cmty Devel Agy 51 S Main-Courthouse Janesville WI 53545

BLAZZARD, NORSE NOVAR, lawyer; b. St. Johns, Ariz., July 8, 1937; s. Howard N. and Viola ([illegible]) B.; m. Mary Elizabeth [illegible], June 16, 1958; children: Howard Norse, Mary Catherine; m. Judith A. Hasenauer, July 2, 1977. AB, Stanford U., 1959; JD, U. Calif., Hastings, 1962. Bar: Calif. 1963, U.S. Dist. Ct. (no. dist.) Calif. 1966, Conn. 1974, U.S. Dist. Ct. Conn. 1975, U.S. Supreme Ct. 1975, U.S. Ct. Appeals (D.C. cir.) 1977, U.S. Ct. Appeals (2d cir.) 1978, Fla. 1993; CLU. Counsel Calif. Western Life Ins. Co., Sacramento, 1966-70; sr. v.p., gen. counsel NARE Life Svc. Co., Palo Alto, calif., 1970-74; pres. Blazzard, Grodd & Hasenauer, P.C., Westport, Conn., 1974—. Chmn. ins. products task force Fin. Products Stds. Bd., 1988-89; chmn. Nat. Assn. Variable Annuities, 1994. Bd. govs. Norwalk Symphony, 1979. Capt. JAGC, U.S. Army, 1962-66. Inductee Variable Annuity Hall of Fame, 1998. Mem. ABA, FBA, Calif. Bar Assn., Fla. Bar Assn., D.C. Bar Assn. Republican. Mem. Lds Ch. E-mail: norse.blazzard@bghpc.com.

BLEAKLEY, PETER KIMBERLEY, lawyer; b. Franklin, Pa., Aug. 19, 1936; s. Rollin R and Marion (St James) Bleakley; m. Mary B DeRosa; children: Jennifer A, Sarah A, Nicholas D. BA, U. Va., 1958, LL.B., 1962. Bar: Va 1962, DC 1966, US Ct Appeals (2d cir), US Ct Appeals (3d cir), US Ct Appeals (5th cir), US Ct Appeals (6th cir), US Ct Appeals (7th cir), US Ct Appeals (8th cir), US Ct Appeals (9th cir), US Ct Appeals (DC cir), US Supreme Ct, US Ct Appeals (fed cir). Trial atty. Fed. Trade Commn., Washington, 1962-66; trial atty. Dept. Justice, Washington, 1966; assoc. Arnold & Porter, Washington, 1966-70, ptnr., 1971—. Fellow: Am Col Trial Lawyers; mem.: ABA. Democrat. Avocations: tennis, skiing, bicycling, golf. Home: 3103 Hawthorne St NW Washington DC 20008-3540 Office: Arnold & Porter 555 12th St NW Washington DC 20004-1206 E-mail: peter_bleakley@aporter.com.

BLECHMAN, R. O. artist, filmmaker; b. Bklyn., Oct. 1, 1930; s. Samuel and Mae Blechman; m. Moisha Kubinyi, Mar. 3, 1960; children: Nicholas, Max. BA, Oberlin Coll., 1952. Freelance illustrator, N.Y.C., 1953—; freelance producer, designer animated films, 1975—; pres. R.O. Blechman, Inc., N.Y.C., 1978—, The Ink Tank, N.Y.C., 1979—. Author, illustrator: The Juggler of Our Lady, 1952, Onion Soup, 1963, Behind the Lines, an autobiography and anthology, 1980, The Life of Saint Nicholas, 1996, The Book of Jonah, 1997; exhibited one-man shows, Gallery Delpire, Paris, 1968, Graham Gallery, N.Y.C., 1978, ITC Gallery, 1981, Galerie Bartsch & Chariau, Munich, 1982, 92, 2000; represented in permanent collections, Mus. Modern Art, N.Y.C., Chase Manhattan Bank; executed murals, Mus. Natural History, U.S. Pavilion Expo '67, Folger Shakespeare Library.; films include The Juggler of Our Lady, 1958, Abraham and Isaac, 1971, Exercise, 1974, Simple Gifts, 1978, No Room at the Inn, 1978 (Clio award 1968, 69, 73), L'Histoire du Soldat, 1984 (Emmy award 1984); retrospective Mus. Modern Art, N.Y.C., N.Y., 2003. Trustee Swann found.; bd. dirs. The Olana Partnership. Mem. Alliance Graphique Internat., Am. Inst. Graphic Arts, Graphic Artists Guild. Office: The Ink Tank 2 W 47th St New York NY 10036-3319

BLECHNER, MARK JACOB, psychologist, educator; b. N.Y.C., Nov. 6, 1950; BA, U. Chgo., 1972; MS, Yale U., 1975, PhD, 1977; cert. in psychoanalysis, William Alanson White Inst., 1983. Trainee in clin. psychology NIMH, 1973-76; rsch. assoc. Haskins Lab., New Haven, 1974-77; pvt. practice clin. psychology, N.Y.C., 1977—. Asst. clin. prof. psychology dept. psychiatry Columbia Coll. Physicians and Surgeons, 1981-94; dir., HIV-Clini. Svcs., tng. analyst, supr. William Alanson White Inst., 1984—; dir. curriculum Manhattan Inst. for Psychoanalysis, 1985-90; asst. clin. prof. psychology postdoctoral program in psychoanalysis NYU, 1995—. Author: The Dream Frontier; editor Hope and Mortality; contbr. articles to profl. jours. Mem. AAAS, APA, N.Y. Acad. Scis., Sigma Xi. Address: 145 Central Park W New York NY 10023-2004 E-mail: mblechner@psychoanalysis.net.

BLECHSCHMIDT, EDWARD ALLAN, data processing executive; b. Harvey, Ill., Aug. 4, 1952; s. Edward and Virginia Blechschmidt; m. Kathleen Nash, Sept. 22, 1984; children: Jenica, Michael, Jeffrey. BS, Ariz. State U., 1973; MBA, San Diego State U., 1977. From contr. bus. info. systems group to v.p. fin. and adminstrn. Burroughs Corp., Detroit, 1983—86, pres. bus. forms divsn. Rochester, NY, 1986; pres. Memorex media products group Unisys Corp., Santa Clara, Calif., 1986—87, v.p. spl. projects office of pres. Blue Bell, Pa., 1987, v.p. Japan ops., pres. Unisys Japan Ltd., Tokyo, 1987—90; pres. Pacific Asia Ams. divsn. Unisys Corp., Blue Bell, 1990—95, corp. sr. v.p., 1994—96; pres. U.S./Can. divsn. Unisys Corp., Blue Bell, 1995—96, CFO, 1996; pres., CEO Siemens Nixdorf Americas, 1996—98; pres., COO Olsten Corp., Melville, 1998—99, pres., dir., CEO, 1999—. Bd. dirs. Nihon Unisys Ltd., Tokyo, Oki Unisys Kaisha, Tokyo, Tata Unisys Ltd., India, Aiesec U.S. Office: Olsten Corp 175 Broadhollow Rd Melville NY 11747-4902

BLECIC, DEBORAH DIANA, school librarian, educator; b. Berwyn, Ill., 1966; BA in Psychology, Northwestern U., 1988; MS in Libr. and Info. Sci., U. Ill., 1991. Resident libr. U. Ill., Chgo., 1991—93, acting bibliographer for life and health scis., 1993—94, bibliographer for life and health scis., 1994—. Assoc. prof. U. Ill., Chgo., 2000—. Contbr. articles; mem. editl. bd.: Sci. and Tech. Libr., 2001—. Mem.: ALA, Med. Libr. Assn. (Daniel T. Richards prize 2001), Acad. health Info. Profls. (sr.). Office: Univ Ill Chgo Libr Box 8198 Chicago IL 60680

BLECK, PHYLLIS CLAIRE, surgeon, musician; b. Oak Park, Ill., Mar. 10, 1936; d. William Fred and Mildred A. (Jones) B. BS, U. Ill., 1958; MM, Northwestern U., 1968; DMA, U. So. Calif., 1970; postgrad., Autonoma U., Guadalajara, Mex., 1973-76; MD, Rush Med. Coll., 1979; MS in Surgery, U. Ill., 1983. Diplomate Am. Bd. Surgery, Am. Bd. Thoracic Surgery. Prin. trumpet Fla. Symphony Orch., 1960-66, Orch. Sinfonica Nat. de Peru, 1965; instr. Thornton Jr. Coll., 1966-68; lectr. U. So. Calif., 1969-73; asst. prof. Whittier Coll., 1973; intern Rush Presbyn. St. Luke's Med. Ctr., Chgo., 1979-80, resident, asst. in gen. surgery, 1980-82, instr. gen. surgery, 1982-84; resident in cardiothoracic surgery U. Medicine and Dentistry N.J., 1984-87; pvt. practice medicine specializing in cardiothoracic surgery Aurora, Ill., 1987—; asst. prof. Rush U., 1996—. Editor: Mozart Divertimento for Winds; rsch. on vascular ischemia. Fellow ACS, Am. Coll. Chest Physicians, Ill. Thoracic Surg. Soc., Ill. Surg. Soc.; mem. AAAS, Soc. Thoracic Surgeons, Internat. Coll. Surgeons, Chgo. Surg. Soc., Kappa Delta Pi, Pi Kappa Lambda, Sigma Alpha Iota. Office: 120 Spalding Dr Ste 308 Naperville IL 60540 E-mail: pbleck@worldnet.att.net.

BLECKE, ARTHUR EDWARD, retired principal; b. Oak Park, Ill., Sept. 21, 1926; s. Paul Gerard and Mathilda (Ziebell); m. June Audrey Eckholm, Jan. 22, 1949; children: William, Robert, Carol. BS in Phys. Edn., U. Ill., 1950; M.Edn., Loyola U., 1967. Tchr., coach Buckley High Sch., Ill., 1951-52, Paxton High Sch., Ill., 1952-53; tchr., coach, dept. chmn. Luther High Sch. North, Chgo., Ill., 1953-65; asst. coach football and basketball Elmhurst Coll., Ill., 1965-66; dean, prin. Antioch Community High Sch., Ill., 1966-91. Cons. in field; lectr. Contbr. articles to profl. jours. Mem. sanitary dist. Village of Lindenhurst, Ill., 1968-92, chmn., 1972-92; planning commn., 1967-77; chmn. long range planning com. and bldg. com. Bella Vista Luth. Ch. Served with U.S. Army, 1945. Recipient Hon. Mention Those Who Excel, Ill. State Bd. Edn., 1980; named Prin. of Yr. for Ill. Nat. Assn. of Secondary Sch. Prins., The Coun. of Chief State Sch. Officer, and The Burger King Corp., 1987. Mem. Ill. Prins. Assn. (dir. 1980-81, 83-84, Herman Graves award, 1991), Nat. Assn. Secondary Sch. Prins. Lutheran. Avocations: golf, model building, model ralroading.

BLEDSOE, DREW, professional football player; b. Ellensburg, Wash., Feb. 14, 1972; Student, Wash. State U. Quarterback New Eng. Patriots, 1993—2002, Buffalo Bills, 2002—. Named to Pro Bowl, 1994. Achievements include holding NFL single season record for most passes attempted (691), 1994; single game record for most passes completed (45); most passed attempted without an interception (70), Nov. 13, 1994, vs. Minn. Vikings; led NFL in total passing yards (4,555), 1994. Office: c/o Buffalo Bills Ralph Wilson Stadium and Main Office 1 Bills Drive Orchard Park NY 14127

BLEDSOE, LAURITA, small business owner, publisher; b. Detroit, July 23, 1955; children: Miranda, Curtis, Kia. Assoc., Highland Park C.C., 1978. Clk. U.S. Postal Svc., Detroit, 1986—; owner Just For You Boutique, Detroit, 1995—; pres. Bledsoe Enterprises Inc., Detroit, 1998—. Author: Straight from the Heart, 2000; contbr. poems to anthologies (Merit award); author: Tomorrow Never Knows, 1995. Activist for juvenile causes, Detroit, 1998—; min. gospel Praise and Worship Leader. Inductee Black Inventors Mus., 2001, Detroit 300 Yr Almanac 2002, Charles H. Wright Mus. African Am. History, 2002. Mem. Internat. Soc. Poets, Detroit Writers Guild, Phi Theta Kappa. Achievements include invention of talking pottie training chair. Avocations: reading, art, design, liturgical dance. Office: 17660 W 12 Mile Rd Ste 5 Southfield MI 48076-1911

BLEDZKI, LESZEK ANDRZEJ, limnologist, researcher; b. Gdansk, Poland, Sept. 12, 1953; came to U.S., 1992; s. Jozef Roman and Helena (Chadzynska) B.; m. Maria Stanislawa Bedryj, Apr. 17, 1982; 1 child, Alicja. MS, N. Copernicus U., Torun, Poland, 1978, PhD, 1989. Scientist Exptl. Fish Culture Sta. Polish Acad. Sci., Golysz, Poland, 1978-79; asst. dept. marine ecology Rsch. Inst. on Environ. Devel., Gdansk, 1979-81; sr. asst. N. Copernicus U., Torun, 1981-89, asst. prof., 1989-93; rsch. asst. Mt. Holyoke Coll., South Hadley, Mass., 1995-96, rsch. assoc., 1997—. Mem. intergov. com. for marine environ. monitoring of Baltic Sea, Helsinki Conv., Gdansk, 1980-81; mem. Environ. Protection Com. for Local Govt., Torun, 1991-92. Recipient Congress award Soc. Internat. Limnologiae, 1989. Mem. Soc. Internat. Limnologiae-Internat. Assn. Theoretical and Applied Limnology (award 1989), Polish Hydrobiol. Soc. (sec. Torun chpt. 1982-93), Am. Soc. Limnology and Oceanography, Ecol. Soc. Am. Achievements include research in amount of phosphorous and nitrogen released by bdelloids rotifers. Home: 33 Old Chicope St Chicopee MA 01013-1700 Office: Mount Holyoke Coll 50 College St South Hadley MA 01075-1423 E-mail: lbledzki@mtholyoke.edu.

BLEE, FRANCIS J. state legislator, chiropractor; b. Absecon, N.J., May 29, 1958; m. Kathy; children: Samantha, Francesca. BA in Polit. Sci., Dickinson Coll., 1980; DC, Life Chiropractic Coll., Marietta, Ga., 1985. Jr. high sch. tchr. St. Nicholas Sch., 1980; chiropractor, Absecon, N.J., 1985—; mem. Absecon City Coun., N.J., 1991-95, pres., 1992-93; mem. N.J. Gen. Assembly, 1995—, mem. assembly appropriations com., assembly health com., 1996—, mem. commn. on capital budgeting and planning. Trustee Absecon Edn. Found.; past bd. trustees Atlantic Mental Health Orgn.; past varsity head coach Absecon Blue Devils Youth Football Team; past head coach St. Augustine Prep Cross Country and Track Teams; active 200 Club of Cape May and Atlantic County; vice chmn. Task Force on Regionalization, Capitol Commn. Assembly. Mem. Absecon Kiwanis (past bd. dirs.) Achievements include World Natural Powerlifting Fedn. Nat. and Internat. champion, 1994, 95, 98. Office: NJ Legis Offices 6814 Tilton Rd Unit H Egg Harbor Township NJ 08234-4490*

BLEECKER, EUGENE R. internist, educator; b. N.Y.C., Jan. 23, 1943; s. Eugene and Mary Bleecker; m. Margit Lukk; children: Karin A., E. Timothy. BA, NYU, 1964; MD cum laude, SUNY, Downstate, 1968. Diplomate Nat. Bd. Med. Examiners, Am. Bd. Internal Medicine, Am. Bd. Pulmonary Diseases. Intern in medicine Kings Hosp., Bklyn., 1968-69, resident in medicine, 1969-70; rsch. assoc. Gerontology Rsch. Ctr. NIH, 1970-72; sr. med. resident Johns Hopkins Hosp., Balt., 1972-73; pulmonary and critical care med. clin. trainee U. Calif., San Francisco, 1973-74, rsch. trainee, 1974-75, asst. rsch. physiologist, 1975-76; from asst. prof. to assoc. prof. medicine Johns Hopkins U., Balt., 1976-89; chief pulmonary sect. Balt. VA Med. Ctr., 1989-97; prof. U. Md., Balt., 1989-2000, prof. pediats., prof. epidemiology and preventive medicine, 1997-2000, dir. Ctr. Genetics Asthma and Complex Diseases, 1996-2000, adj. prof. medicine, 2000—; prof. medicine & pediat., co-dir. Ctr. Human Genomics Wake Forest Sch. Medicine, Winston-Salem, N.C., 2000—, dir. sec. pulmonary and critical care medicine. Guest scientist Gerontology Rsch. ctr. NIH, 1986-90; cons. Ministry Edn. and Sci., The Netherlands. Grantee Nat. Heart Lung and Blood Inst., 1975-76, 78-83, 84-92, Nat. Inst. Aging, 1983-88, 88-93, Health Effects Inst., 1984-87, Nat. Cancer Inst., 1985-88, Gen. Clin. Rsch. Ctr., 1985-89, NIH, 1986-89, 94—, 2000—, Ctr. Interdisciplinary Rsch., 1986-89, Geriatric Rsch. Edn. and Clin. Ctr., 1992-97, VA Med. Ctr., 1996-2000. Mem. Am. Thoracic Soc., Am. Fedn. Clin. Rsch., Am. Coll. Chest Physicians, Am. Acad. Allergy and Clin. Immunology, Am. Physiol. Soc., Am. Heart Assn., Am. Soc. Human Genetics, European Respiratory Soc. (cons.), Gerontol. Soc. Am. Office: Wake Forest U Sch Medicine Medical Center Blvd Winston Salem NC 27157 Fax: 336-713-7566. E-mail: ebleeck@wfubmc.edu.

BLEEZARDE, THOMAS WARREN, retired magazine editor; b. Bluffton, Ind., July 11, 1935; s. Warren VanBergen and Edith Burnette (Shoup) B.; m. Judith Kay Bacon, July 15, 1961; children: Philip Michael, Stephen Thomas. BA, Hamilton Coll., 1957. Bus. mgr. Berkshire Playhouse, Stockbridge, Mass., 1957; reporter, photographer, columnist Berkshire Eagle, Pittsfield, Mass., 1957-67; assoc. news editor Brattleboro (Vt.) Reformer, 1967-68; op-ed columnist Berkshire Eagle, 1971-75; editor alumni rev. Williams (Mass.) Coll., 1968-2000; ret. Bd. dirs. No. Berkshire Arts Coun., 1971-77; local dir. Miss Mass. Scholarship Pageant Inc., 1971-79; deacon White Oaks Congl. Ch., 1970-73; mem. troop 70 com. Boy Scouts Am., 1975—, chmn., 1981-84, treas., 1985—, chmn. com. Appalachian Trails dist., 1988-91, mem. nat. coun., 1992-95, v.p. Great Trials coun., 1991-99, mem. exec. com., 1981—; mem. parent adv. counc. Greylock Regional Sch., 1975-77; dir. Village Ambulance Svc., 1999—. With U.S. Army, 1958-60. New Eng. Soc. Newspaper Editor fellow U. Mass., 1963-65; recipient Dist. award of merit Boy Scouts Am., 1991, Silver Beaver award Boys Scouts Am., 1991, Eph Williams medal Soc. Alumni of Williams Coll., 2000. Mem. USGA, USSRA, USSPJ, Scouting Heritage Soc., NRA (cert. rifle, pistol, shotgun instr., instr. jr. rifle club 1977—), Mass. State Rifle and Pistol Assn., Hale Mountain Club, Taconic Golf Culb, Sigma Phi. Home: 187 Sand Springs Rd Williamstown MA 01267-2249 E-mail: thomas.w.bleezarde@williams.edu.

BLEIBERG, LAWRENCE RUSSELL, journalist; b. Alexandria, Va., July 28, 1962; s. Marvin Jay and Beulah Matt B.; m. Elizabeth Wideman, Apr. 1, 1990; 1 child, Michael Harrison. BS in Journalism, Northwestern U., Evanston, Ill., 1984. Staff writer Courier Jour. and Times, Louisville, 1984-90; editor Can. Press Wire Svc., Vancouver, 1990; copy editor Vancouver Sun, 1990-91; edn. writer Dallas Morning News, 1991-96, asst. travel editor, 1996-99, travel editor, 1999—. Team recipient Gen. New Coverage Pulizer prize, 1989, Pacific Asia Travel Assn. Gold award, 1998, Travel Journalist of the Yr. Lowell Thomas Awards, Hon. Mention, 2001. Mem. Soc. Am. Travel Writers (ctrl. states vice chmn. 1999-2001, Best Travel sect. in newspapers over 500,000 circulation 2002, Lowell Thomas award). Home: 1131 Timplemore Dr Dallas TX 75218 Office: Dallas Morning News PO Box 655237 Dallas TX 75265 Fax: 214-977-8321. E-mail: travelsection@dallasnews.com.

BLEIBERG, LEON WILLIAM, surgical podiatrist; b. Bklyn., June 9, 1932; s. Paul Pincus and Helen (Epstein) B.; m. Beth Daigle, June 7, 1970; children: Kristina Noel, Kelley Lynn, Kimberly Ann, Paul Joseph. Student, L.A. City Coll., 1950-51, U. So. Calif., 1951, Case Western Res. U., 1951-53; DSc with honors, Temple U., 1955; D in Podiatric Medicine, Pa. Sch. Podiatric Medicine, 1965; PhD, U. Beverly Hills, 1970. Served rotating internship various hosps., Phila., 1954-55; resident Bella Vista Hosp., Montebello, L.A., 1956-58; surg. podiatrist So. Calif. Podiatry Group, Westchester (Calif.), L.A., 1956-75; health care economist, researcher Drs. Home Health Care Svcs., 1976—; chmn. bd. Unltd. Healthcare, Metro Manila, Philippines; v.p. pub. rels. Bilbao Wellness Found., Upland, Calif.; CEO Med. Trianon, Newbury Park, Calif.; dir. biomechanics dept. Anti-Aging and Rejuvenation Clinic, Torrance, Calif. Podiatric cons. U. So. Calif. Athletic Dept., Morningside and Inglewood (Calif.) High Schs., Royal Navy Assn., Long Beach (Calif.) Naval Sta.; exec. cons. Thomas Med. Group, Pomona, Calif., 1995, Cardiotel, Van Nuys, Calif., 1995; lectr. in field; healthcare affiliate Internat. divsn. CARE/ASIA, 1987; pres. Medica, Totalcare, Cine-Medics Corp., Strategic World-Wide Health Care Svcs.; exec. dir. Internat. Health Trust; developer Health Banking Program; adminstr. Orthotic Concepts, 1993; prof. health care econs. and med. rehab. Global U., Ontario, Calif., chmn. dept. health care econs., chmn. dept. biomechanics and phys. rehab.; CEO Integrated Wellness Ctrs., The Med. Trianon Found.; exec. dir. The Med. Trianon; exec. dir. wellness divsn. Crown Golden Eagles; mem. nat. leadership Temple U., Phila.; bd. dirs. Power Search Unltd. Ministries, Quezon City, Manila, Philippines; coord. for U.S. Luntiang Pilipinas Found.; CEO Global Health Share 2000. Producer (films) The Gun Hawk, 1963, Terrified, Day of the Nightmare; contbr. articles to profl. jours. Hon. Sheriff Westchester 1962-64; commd. mem. Rep. Senatorial Inner Circle, 1984-86; co-chmn. health reform com. United We Stand Am., Thousand Oaks, Calif.; mem. exec. coun. State of Calif., United We Stand Am.; active 1st Security and Safety, Westlake Village, Calif., 1993—; lt. comdr. med. svcs. corps Brit.-Am. Sea Cadet Corps, 1984—; track coach Westlake High Sch., Westlake Village; exec. sec. Nat. Coalition Parents for Anti-Drug/Violence Corp., Inc. L.A. World Affairs Coun.; county inspector U.S. Election Com., Calif.; exec. sec. Nat. Coalition of Parents Against Drug Abuse and Violence, Exec. award, 1999; bd. dirs. Power Search Unltd. Ministries, Philippines and US; U.S. coord. Luntiang Pilipinas (Philippine Ecology Program). With USN, 1955-56. Recipient Medal of Merit, U.S. Presdl. Task Force, Grand award Top Personalities mag., 1999. Mem. Philippine Hosp. Assn. (Cert. of Appreciation 1964, trophy for Outstanding Svc. 1979), Calif. Podiatry Assn. (hon.), Am. Podiatric Med. Assn. (hon.), Acad. TV Arts and Scis., Royal Soc. Health (Eng.), Western Foot Surgery Assn., Am. Coll. Foot Surgeons, Am. Coll. Podiatric Sports Medicine, Internat. Coll. Preventive Medicine, Hollywood Comedy Club, Sts. and Sinners Club, Westchester C. of C., Hals Und Beinbruch Ski Club, Beach Cities Ski Club, Orange County Stamp Club, Las Virgenes Track Club, Masons, Shriners, Scottish Rite. Home and Office: 55 N Wendy Dr Newbury Park CA 91320-4351 Fax: 805-499-8877. E-mail: medicaltrianon@juno.com.

BLEICH, JEFFREY LAURENCE, lawyer, law educator; b. Neubreuke, Germany, May 17, 1961; came to U.S., 1964; s. Charles Allen Bleich and Linda Sue Caplan; m. Rebecca Lee Pratt, Aug. 12, 1984; children: Jacob, Matthew, Abigail. BA in Polit. Sci., Amherst Coll., 1983; MA in Pub. Policy, Harvard U., 1986; JD, U. Calif., Berkeley, 1989. Bar: Calif. 1989, D.C. 1990, U.S. Ct. Appeals (D.C. cir.) 1990, U.S. Dist. Ct. (no. dist.) Calif. 1992, U.S. Ct. Appeals (4th cir.) 1993, U.S. Supreme Ct. 1993, U.S. Ct. Appeals (9th cir.) 1994. Law clk. U.S. Ct. Appeals, Washington, 1989-90, U.S. Supreme Ct., Washington, 1990-91; legal asst. Iran-U.S. Claims Tribunal, The Hague, 1991-92; ptnr. Munger, Tolles & Olson LLP, San Francisco, 1992—. Adj. prof. U. Calif., Berkeley, 1993—. Editor-in-chief Calif. Law Rev., Nat. Debt; columnist San Francisco Atty. Mem. adv. bd. Coalition on Homelessness, San Francisco; dir. Nat. Youth Violence Initiative, 1999—. Recipient James Madison award Soc. Profl. Journalists, 1998. Mem. ABA (chair constnl. law com., award 1996, Pro Bono Publico award 1996), Bar Assn. San Francisco (pres.), Lawyers' Com. Civil Rights of San Francisco Bay Area (co-chair), Lawyers Com. Human Rights (bd. dirs. 1998—), Legal Aid Soc. (bd. dirs. 1998—), Barristers Club San Francisco (pres.). Democrat. Avocations: short story writer, tennis, kayaking, camping. Office: Munger Tolles & Olson 33 New Montgomery St Fl 19 San Francisco CA 94105-4506

BLEICHER, PAUL ALAN, health facility administrator; b. Bklyn., Dec. 31, 1954; s. Henry William and Annette Bleicher; m. Julia Lea Greenstein, June 19, 1977. BS, Rensselaer Poly. Inst., Troy, N.Y., 1976; MD, PhD, MS, U. Rochester, 1983. Med. diplomate Mass., 1984, cert. Am. Bd. Dermatology, 1988. Resident in medicine Beth Israel Hosp., Boston, 1983—85; resident in dermatology Harvard Med. Sch., Boston, 1985—87; rsch. fellow in molecular immunology Dana Farber Cancer Inst., Boston, 1987—88; asst. prof., instr. Mass. Gen. Hosp., Harvard Med. Sch., Boston, 1988—92; dir. PAREXEL Internat., Waltham, Mass., 1992—94; v.p. clin. affairs Alpha-Beta Tech., Worcester, Mass., 1994—97; founder and chmn. Phase Forward, Waltham, Mass., 1997—; CEO, pres. Phase Forward Inc., Waltham, Mass., 1997—98, 2002—. Named Entrepreneur of Yr., New Eng., Ernst and Young, 2002; recipient Robert Kates award, U. Rochester, 1983, Innovators award, Smaller Bus. Assn. of New Eng., 2002; Burroughs-Wellcome fellowship, Dermatology Found., 1989. Fellow: Am. Acad. of Dermatology; mem.: Drug Info. Assn. (chmn., steering com. N.Am., bd. dirs. 2001), Rensselaer Alumni Assn. (fellows award 2003). Achievements include first to Web-based Clinical Trials; patents for United States Patent #6,117,850. Patchen, M, and Bleicher, P. Mobilization of peripheral blood precursor cells by beta.(1,3)-glucan; patents pending for Web-based clinical trials; discovery of Role of CD1 as target for T cells. Avocations: technical rock climbing, tennis, bridge, skiing. Office: Phase Forward 1440 Main St Waltham MA 02465

BLEICHER, SAMUEL ABRAM, lawyer, government official; b. Omaha, June 21, 1942; s. David Bernard and Rachael (Faigin) Bleicher; m. Beatrice Koretsky, June 16, 1965 (dec. Nov. 12, 1995); children: Leo, Zena; m. Emily Blair Chewning, May 17, 1997 (div. 2002). BA, Northwestern U., 1963; JD, Harvard U., 1966. Bar: Nebr. 1966, Ohio 1972, D.C. 1979, Va. 1989, Md. 1991. Prof. law U. Toledo Coll. Law, 1966-76; dep. dir. for regulation and enforcement Ohio EPA, 1972-75; issues generalist Carter-Mondale Presdl. Campaign, Atlanta, 1976; policy analyst Carter-Mondale Transition Planning Group, Washington, 1976-77; spl. asst. to adminstr. NOAA Dept. Commerce, Washington, 1977, dir. Office Ocean Mgmt., 1977-78, dep. asst. adminstr., 1978-80, dep. gen. counsel, 1980-81; of counsel Blank, Rome, Comisky & McCauley, Washington, 1981-85; ptnr. Frank, Bernstein, Conaway & Goldman, Tysons Corner, Va., 1985-90; prin. Miles & Stockbridge P.C., Washington, 1990—2001. Contbr. articles to profl. publs. Democrat. Jewish. Office: Overseas Bldg Ops Dept State Washington DC 20520 E-mail: sambleicher@comcast.net.

BLEICHER, SHELDON JOSEPH, endocrinologist, medical educator; b. N.Y.C., Apr. 9, 1931; s. Max and Fannie (Klieger) B.; m. Diane D. Cole, Aug., 1990; children from previous marriages: Erick Max, Phillip Thaddeus Samuel, Deborah Ann Cote, Sandra Lynn Gable, Jodie Lisa Cole. AB, NYU, 1951; MS, Western Ill. U., 1952; MD, SUNY Downstate Med. Center, Bklyn., 1956. Intern L.I. Jewish Hosp. Ctr., New Hyde Park, N.Y., 1956-57; resident Boston City Hosp., 1959-60; chief rsch. fellow in medicine Harvard-Thorndike Meml. Lab., Boston, 1962-63; chief metabolic research unit Jewish Hosp. Med. Center, Bklyn., 1963-67, chief div. endocrinology and metabolism, 1967-77; pvt. practice specializing in endocrinology and diabetes Woodbury, N.Y., 1990—; prof. medicine SUNY Downstate Med. Center, 1975—; attending dept. internal medicine Bklyn.-Cumberland Med. Center, 1978-83, Bklyn.-Caledonian Med. Ctr., 1983-90. Cons. IAEA, Vienna, Austria, 1966—; mem. attending staff North Shore Univ. Hosp. at Syosset, North Shore Univ. Hosp. at Plainview, North Shore Univ. Hosp. at Manhasset. Mem. editorial bd. Diabetes in News, Practical Diabetes; contbr. articles to profl. jours. Vice pres. Locust Valley Central Sch. Bd., 1981-82, pres., 1982-85. Served to capt. M.C., USNR, 1957-92, ret. NIH fellow, 1960-63; NIH research career devel. award, 1970-75; recipient Torch of Liberty award Anti-Defamation League of B'nai Brith, 1982 . Fellow ACP, Am. Coll. Endocrinology; mem. AMA, N.Y. State Soc. Medicine,

Nassau County Med. Soc., Am. Soc. Internal Medicine, Am. Diabetes Assn. (bd. dirs. 1979-85, nat. com. quality care, Achievement award 1986, 90, Provider Recognition award), N.Y. Diabetes Assn. (bd. dirs. 1965-93), pres. 1976-78), L.I. Diabetes Assn. (pres. 1978-81), N.Y. State Soc. Internal Medicine (state bd. dirs., treas. Bklyn. chpt., chmn. continuing edn. com.), Bklyn. Soc. Internal Medicine (treas. 1983-85, sec. 1985-87, pres. 1987-89), Endocrine Soc., Am. Assn. Clin. Endocrinologists, Am. Coll. Endocrinologists, Internat. Diabetes Fedn., Juvenile Diabetes Found. Internat., Sagamore Yacht Club (L.I., fleet surgeon 1983-86). Jewish. Office: 165 Froehlich Farm Blvd Woodbury NY 11797-2906 E-mail: SJBleich@opton-line.net.

BLEIDT, BARRY ANTHONY, pharmacy educator; b. South Charleston, W.Va., Mar. 29, 1951; s. Robert Anthony and Mary Frances (Gash) B.; 1 child, Brittany Alice. B in Gen. Studies, BS in Pharmacy, U. Ky., 1974; PhD, U. Fla., 1982; PharmD, Xavier U., 1994. Registered pharmacist, Fla., La., Ga., W.Va., Va. Pres. Health Resources Cons., 1979—; asst. prof. pharmacy Northeastern U., Boston, 1983—86, U. Houston, 1986—89; assoc. prof. pharmacy adminstrn. Xavier U., 1989—94; med. info. scientist Astra/Merck Group, 1994—95; clin. coord., dir. postgrad. profl. edn. sch. pharmacy Hampton U., 1995—2002; asst. dean, prof., chair social and adminstrv. scis. dept. Loma Linda U. Sch. Pharmacy, 2002—. Faculty dir. Practicing Pharmacists Inst., Boston, 1983-86. Author, editor: Clinical Research in Pharmaceutical Development; contbr. articles to profl. jours.; guest editor Jour. Pharm. Mktg. and Mgmt., 1988; mem. editl. bd. Clin. Rsch. Reg. Affairs, 1983—, editor, 1999. Recipient Local Assn. Pres. of Yr., Va. Pharm. Assn., 2001. Mem.: APHA (leadership award 1999), Nat. Pharm. Assn. (James Tyson award 2001), Am. Soc. Health-Sys. Pharmacists, Am. Assn. Colls. Pharmacy (parliamentarian 1983—), Fla. Blue Key, Nat. Eagle Scout Assn., U. Fla. Hall of Fame, Phi Lambda Sigma, Omicron Delta Kappa, Rho Chi, Sigma Xi. Avocations: music, travel, ethnic restaurants, cinema. Home and Office: PO Box 578 Loma Linda CA 92354 E-mail: bbleidt@aol.com.

BLEIER, CAROL STEIN, writer, researcher; b. N.Y., Jan. 31, 1942; d. Shelley and Ruth (Brown) Stein; m. Michael Bleier, Oct. 9, 1966; children: Thomas, Lisa, Mark. BA in English Lit., Syracuse U., 1963; MLS, U. Pitts, 1986. Pub. info. specialist IRS, Washington, 1964-68; columnist Springfield (Va.) Ind., 1977-78; mktg. cons. Greater Pitts. Mus. Coun., 1986-88; pub. rels. dir. Greater Pitts. Literacy Coun., 1988-89; writer, 1985—. Author: (corp. history book) To Good Health and Life: L'Chaim A History of Montefiore Hospital of Pittsburgh, 1898-1990, 1997; co-author: (corp. history book) The Ketchum Spirit: A History of Ketchum Communications Inc., 1992; contbg. author: Encyclopedia of Library History, 1994; contbr. articles to periodicals. Mem. ALA, Beta Phi Mu. Democrat. Jewish. Avocations: reading, travel. Home: 214 Lynn Haven Dr Pittsburgh PA 15228-1821

BLEIER, MICHAEL E. lawyer; BA, U. Tulsa, 1962; JD, Georgetown U., 1965. Bar: Pa, D.C. Atty. Office of Gen. Counsel, Bd. Govs. Fed. Reserve System, 1971-78, sr. counsel, 1979-81, asst. gen. counsel, 1981-82; mng. counsel Mellon Bank Corp., Pitts., 1982-88; asst. gen. counsel Mellon Fin. Corp., Pitts., 1989-91, dep. gen. counsel, 1991-92, gen. counsel, exec. v.p., 1992—, sr. mgmt. com. Mem. Am. Bankers Assn. (vice chmn. bank counsel com. 1996-98), Lawyers Coun. Fin. Svcs. Roundtable (chmn. 1993-98). Office: Mellon Financial Corporation 1 Mellon Ctr Fl 19 Pittsburgh PA 15258-0001 E-mail: bleier.me@mellon.com.

BLEIFELD, STANLEY, sculptor; b. Bklyn., Aug. 28, 1924; s. Benjamin and Rose (Molshatsky) B.; m. Naomi Kaplan Ruby, Sept. 5, 1949; children: Becky Paula, Emily Harriet. BFA, Tyler Sch. Fine Arts, Phila., 1949; BSEd, Temple U., 1949, MFA, 1950; D of Fine Arts (hon.), Lyme Acad. Fine Arts, Conn., 1997. Fellow Tyler Sch. Fine Arts, Temple U., 1967—. One-person shows Peridot Gallery, N.Y.C., 1963, 65, 68, Fairfield (Conn.) U., 1967, FAR Gallery, N.Y.C., 1971, 73, 77, New Britain Mus. Art (Conn.), 1974, Kenmore Gallery, Phila., 1967, Franz Bader Gallery, Washington, 1987, 91; exhibited in group shows Internat. Art Festival, Newport, R.I., 1964, Am. Fedn. Arts, 1966, 67, Conn. Commn. on Arts, 1972, Parrish Art Mus., Southampton, N.Y., 1968, others; represented in permanent collections Mus. of City of N.Y., Fairfield (Conn.) U., New Britain Mus. Art, Tampa Bay Art Ctr., Fla., Temple U., Phila., Westmoreland Mus., Pa., Pa. State Mus., U. Edinburg (Scotland), L.B. Johnson Libr., Tex.; executed relief sculptures The Prophets, Vatican Pavilion, N.Y. Worlds Fair, 1964-65, Magic Carpet, Kokomo Pub. Libr., 1970, Family of Acrobats, Civic Ctr., Orlando, Fla., 1973, Alberta Family, Century Gardens, Calgary, Can., 1981, Father McGivney Meml. KC Internat. Hdqrs., New Haven, 1982, Christopher Columbus, 8'n KC Mus. of States, New Haven, 2000; sculptor U.S. Navy Meml., Washington, 1982—, Jacksonville, Fla., 1988, Great Lakes, Ill., 1997, San Diego, Calif., 1998, Henry C. Singleton, Sr. Monument, Key West, Fla., 1994, Marine Relief, Brookgreen Gardens, S.C., 1996, Life Size Pitcher and Catcher Besball Hall of Fame, Cooperstown, N.Y., 2000, Lone Sailor, Vista Point Golden Gate Bridge, San Francisco, 2000, Homecoming, Norfolk, Va., 2000; designer Medal of Liberty ACLU, 1984; dir. Bleifeld Sculpture Group, New Canaan, Conn., 1966—; instr. Silvermine Guild Art, New Canaan, Conn., 1963-66, asst. prof. art Western Conn. State Coll., New Haven, 1953-55. Served with USNR, 1944-46. Recipient Shikler award, Nat. Acad. Design, 1977, Agopoff prize for Classical Sculpture, 2001, Meiselman prize, 1997, 1998, Internat prize for sculpture, Pietrasanta Versilia in the World, XI edit., 2001; fellow Tiffany, 1967. Fellow: Nat. Sculpture Soc. (pres. 1991—93, chmn. editl. bd. Sculpture Rev., treas. 1994, John Gregory award 1964, Bronze medal 1970, Proskauer award 1977, Hexter award 1990, Henry Hering award 1990, Silver medal 1991, Bronze medal 1994, Chilmark award 1994, Hexter award 1998, Henry Hering award 2000); mem.: NAD (accademician coun. 2001—, corr. sec. 2001—), Century Assn., Fedn. Internationale de la Medialle, Portrait Soc. Am. (adv. bd. 2000—, Agopoff prize 2001). Jewish. Avocation: tennis. Home: 27 Spring Valley Rd Weston CT 06883-1546

BLEIGH, MILDRED ALLEN, genealogist; b. Danville, W.Va., Jan. 22, 1928; d. William Henry and Emma Cornelia (Stovall) Allen; m. Marvin Eugene Bleigh, July 12, 1952; children: Debbie Jean, Karen Sue, Peggy Jo. Student, Ohio U., 1945-46. Acct. Bank of Athens, Ohio, 1948-53. Author: Stovalls, 1985, It Happened in Athens County, 1989, Class of '45-'50 Year Reunion, 1995, Athens County Obituaries, 18 Vols., Our Allens, 1981, 2003. Leader Girls Scouts USA, Athens, 1961-65; v.p. Stovall 300 Yr. Reunion, Richmond, Va., 1984; sec. AAU Age Group Track, Athens, 1972-77. Mem. DAR, Daus. Confederacy, Colonial Dames, Boone County (W.Va.) Geneaol. Soc., Athens County (Ohio) Genealogy Soc. Avocation: doll collecting. Home: 7 Tulane Rd Athens OH 45701-1848

BLEILER, CHARLES ARTHUR, lawyer; b. Boston, Mar. 16, 1945; s. Charles Edward and Grace Rita Bleiler; m. Joyce Ann Kohlmyer, Oct. 6, 1972; children: Charles Edward. BS, Tufts U., 1967; JD, U. San Diego, 1973. BAr: Calif. 1973, U.S. Dist. Ct. (so. dist.) Calif. 1973. Commd. ensign U.S. Navy, 1967, advanced through grades to lt. comdr., resigned, 1978; ptnr. Williams, Clodig & Bleiler, San Diego, 1974-85, Bleiler & Reiter, San Diego, 1985-91, Malowney, Chialtas & Bleiler, San Diego, 1991-93; pres. Charles A. Bleiler A.P.C., San Diego, 1987—. Lectr. San Diego Trial Lawyers Assn., 1982. Bd. dirs. Rancho Santa Fe (Calif.) Cmty. Ctr., 1990-94, pres., 1993-94; mem. San Dieguito Soccer Bd., Encinitas, Calif., 1991-92; bd. dirs. Torrey Pines H.S. Found., Del Mar, Calif., 1996-98, pres., 1997-98; founding mem., lector Nativity Ch., Rancho Santa Fe; fundraiser for charitable orgns.; bd. dirs. Rancho Santa Fe Little League, 1989-92. Mem. ATLA, Calif. State Bar, San Diego County Bar Assn., Optimist Club (charter pres. Kearny Mesa club 1987-89). Republican. Roman Catholic. Avocations: sailing, horseback riding, skiing, coaching youth baseball and soccer. Home: PO Box 1653 Rancho Santa Fe CA 92067-1653 Office: 12770 High Bluff Dr Ste 380 San Diego CA 92130-2060 E-mail: bleiler@worldnet.att.net.

BLEILER, EVERETT FRANKLIN, writer, publishing company executive; b. Boston, Apr. 30, 1920; s. Joseph Eugene and Rose Caroline (Mayor) B.; m. Ellen Haas, May 12, 1956; children: Richard, John, Constance, Dorothy. AB cum laude, Harvard U., 1942; MA, U. Chgo., 1951; Diploma, U. Leiden, The Netherlands, 1952. Freelance writer, 1952-55; advt. mgr. Dover Publs., N.Y.C., 1955-60, mng. dir., 1960-65, exec. v.p., 1965-78; editorial cons. Charles Scribners Sons, N.Y.C., 1978-83. Author more than 60 books including The Checklist of Fantastic Literature, 1948, Essential Japanese Grammar, 1963, Best Tales of Hoffmann, 1967, Mother Goose's Melodies, 1970, Eight Dime Novels of the Victorian Period, 1974, Wagner, The Wehrwolf by G. W. M. Reynolds, 1975, Seventeenth Century Floral Engravings of Emanuel Sweerts, 1976, Richmond, Exploits of a Bow Street Runner, 1976, (under name Liberte E. LeVert) Prophecies and Enigmas of Nostradamus, 1979; A Treasury of Victorian Detective Stories, 1979, A Treasury of Victorian Ghost Stories, 1981, Science Fiction Writers, 1982, The Guide to Supernatural Fiction, 1983, Supernatural Fiction Writers, 1985, Science-Fiction: The Early Years, 1991, Science-Fiction: The Gernsback Years, 1998, Alice and the Snark, 2002, others; co-author: (with Wendell C. Bennett) Northwest Argentine Archeology, 1948, (with Guy Stern) Essential German Grammar, 1961. Sgt. U.S. Army, 1942-46. Recipient World Fantasy award World Fantasy Com., Providence, 1978, World Fantasy award (lifetime), London, 1988, Pilgrim award Sci. Fiction Rsch. Assn., 1984, Pres.'s award World Sci. Fiction Assn., 1986, Locus award for best non-fiction book, 1992; named to N.J. Literary Hall of Fame, 1979; Kt. Comdr., Order of Star, Realm of Redonda; Fulbright fellow, 1952. Democrat. Home: 4076 Interlaken Beach Rd Interlaken NY 14847-9632

BLENCOWE, PAUL SHERWOOD, lawyer, private investor; b. Amityville, N.Y., Feb. 10, 1953; s. Frederick Arthur and Dorothy Jeanne (Ballenger) Blencowe; m. Mary Frances Faulk, Apr. 11, 1992; children: Kristin Amanda, Alison Michelle, Caitlin Emily. BA with honors, U. Wis., 1975, MBA, U. Pa., 1976; JD, Stanford U., 1979. Bar: Tex. 1979, Calif. 1989. Assoc. Fulbright & Jaworski, Houston, 1979-86, London, 1986-87, ptnr., 1988-89, Fulbright & Jaworski L.L.P., L.A., 1989-2000, of counsel, 2000—. Editor: China's Quest for Independence: Policy Evolution in the 1970s, 1980; editor-in-chief Stanford Jour. of Internat. Law, 1978-79; contbr. articles on U.S. securities and corp. law to profl. jours. Mem. The Calif. Club, Phi Beta Kappa, Phi Kappa Phi, Beta Theta Pi. Office: Fulbright & Jaworski LLP 865 S Figueroa St Fl 29 Los Angeles CA 90017-2543 E-mail: pblencowe@fulbright.com.

BLENDON, ROBERT JAY, health policy educator; b. Dec. 19, 1942; s. Edward and Theresa Blendon; m. Marie C. McCormick, Dec. 31, 1977. BA, Marietta (Ohio) Coll., 1964; MBA, U. Chgo., 1966; MPH, Johns Hopkins U., 1967, DSc, 1969. Fellow Ind. U. Med. Ctr., Indpls., 1965—66; instr. dept. med. care and hosps. Johns Hopkins U. Sch. Hygiene and Pub. Health, Balt., 1969—70, asst. to assoc. dean for health care programs Sch. Medicine, 1969—70, asst. prof. dept. med. care and hosps., 1970—71; asst. dir. planning and devel. Office of Health Care Programs, Johns Hopkins Med. Instns., Balt., 1970—71; spl. asst. for health affairs to dep. undersec. for policy coordination HEW, Washington, 1971—72, spl. asst. for policy devel. to asst. sec. to health and sci. affairs, 1971—72; sr. v.p. Robert Wood Johnson Found., Princeton, NJ, 1987; prof. health policy and polit. analysis Harvard U. Sch. Pub. Health and Kennedy Sch. of Govt., Boston, 1987—; dep. dir. health policy Harvard U. Vis. lectr. Princeton U., 1972—87; sr. policy analyst com. on health svcs. industry Cost of Living Coun., Washington, 1971. Mem. editl. bd.: Jour. of Am. Med. Assn., 1992—. Mem.: Inst. Medicine NAS, Council Fgn. Rels. Home: 478 Quinobequin Rd Newton MA 02468-2127 Office: Harvard U Sch Pub Health 677 Huntington Ave Boston MA 02115-6028

BLENKARN, KENNETH ARDLEY, mechanical engineer, consultant; b. Amarillo, Tex., May 17, 1929; m. 1952. BA, Rice U., 1951, BS, 1952, MS, 1954, PhD in Mech. Engring., 1960. Instr. mechanical engring. Rice U., 1952-54; rsch. engr. Amoco Prod. Co., 1954-57, sr. rsch. engr., 1960-63, staff rsch. engr., 1963-68, rsch. assoc., 1968-72, rsch. supr., 1972-76, rsch. dir., 1976-86, cons., 1986—. Mem. Nat. Acad. Engring. Home: 9115 E 37th Ct Tulsa OK 74145-3414

BLENKO, WALTER JOHN, JR., lawyer; b. Pitts., June 15, 1926; s. Walter J. and Ardis Leah (Jones) B.; m. Joy Kinneman, Apr. 9, 1949; children: John W., Andrew W. BS, Carnegie-Mellon U., 1950; JD, U. Pitts., 1953. Bar: Pa. 1954. Pvt. practice law, Pitts., 1954—; ptnr. Eckert, Seamans, Cherin & Mellott, Pitts., 1984-93, of counsel, 1993—. Mem. adv. bd. dept. mech. engring. Carnegie-Mellon U., 1992—. Active Churchill Vol. Fire Co., 1970-82; charter and hon. mem. Wilkinsburg Emergency Med. Svc.; sec. Hampton Twp. Zoning Hearing Bd., 1991-92, vice-chmn., 1993; mem. Hampton Twp. Sch. Bd., 1993-97, pres. 1996; mem. Allegheny County Parks adv. bd., 2000-2002. With U.S. Army, 1944-46, ETO. Decorated Bronze Star, Combat Inf. badge; recipient Disting. Svc. award Carnegie-Mellon U. Alumni Assn., 1993, Recognition award Carnegie Mellon U. Andrew Carnegie Soc., 2002. Fellow Am. Coll. Trial Lawyers, Allegheny County Bar Found.; mem. ASME, Pa. Bar Assn., Allegheny County Bar Assn., Assn. Bar of City of N.Y., Pitts. Intellectual Property Law Assn. (pres. 1977-78), Engrs. Soc. Western Pa., Internat. Patent and Trademark Assn., Carnegie-Mellon U. Alumni Assn. (exec. bd. 1996-2001, exec. com. 1997-2001), Duquesne Club, Univ. Club, Princeton Club (N.Y.), Rolls-Royce Owners Club (bd. dirs. 1982-84, v.p. publs. 1984-87, treas. 1987-89). Avocation: old cars. Home: 4073 Middle Rd Allison Park PA 15101-1207 Office: Eckert Seamans Cherin & Mellott 600 Grant St Pittsburgh PA 15219-2702

BLERSCH, JEFFREY NEAL, music educator, composer; b. Cin., Aug. 3, 1967; s. Milton Kent and Fay Louise Blersch; m. Carla Sue Blersch; children: Aaron, Ryan. MusB in Organ Performance, M in Music Edn., Oberlin (Ohio) Coll. Conservatory of Music, 1990; D of Musical Arts, U. Mich., 1999. Prof. music Concordia Coll., Ann Arbor, Mich., 1992—2001; cantor Trinity Luth. Ch., Peoria, Ill., 2001—02; prof. music and univ. organist Concordia U., Seward, Nebr., 2002—. Composer numerous compositions for organ and choir. Organist St. John Luth. Ch., Seward, 2002. Recipient Liturgy Composition prize, The Luth. Ch., Mo. Synod, 2001. Mem.: Am. Choral Dirs. Assn., Assn. Luth. Ch. Musicians, Am. Guild Organists, Pi Kappa Lambda. Office: Concordia U 800 N Columbia Ave Seward NE 68434 Office Fax: 402-643-4073. E-mail: jeffrey.blersch@cune.edu.

BLESCH, K(ATHY) SUZANN, small business owner; b. Evansville, Ind., Dec. 14, 1951; d. Robert Lee McBride and E. Jean (Oliver) Schumacher; m. Larry J. Blesch, Aug. 17, 1974; children: Nicholas R., Spencer A., Clayton W. Grad. Grad. Realtors Inst., Ind. U., 1979; cert. residential specialist, Nat. Assn. Realtors, 1980. Waitress, hostess Skyway & Pete's, Evansville, Ind., 1971-73; operator, asst. mgr. Stecklers T.A.S., Evansville, 1969-71; salesperson, broker Midwest Realty, Evansville, 1973-78; broker, owner Blesch Realty, Evansville, 1978-80; broker, salesperson Brand Realty, Evansville, 1980-83; owner, operator Nick Nackery Pl., Evansville, 1985—. Bd. dirs. Hope of Evansville, 1976-79. Mem. Nat. Costumers Assn., Am. Taekwondo Assn. Avocations: family, reading. Home and Office: 201 E Virginia St Evansville IN 47711-5529

BLESER, KATHERINE ALICE, artist; b. Los Angeles, Apr. 3, 1942; BA, Northwestern U., 1973; MAT, Ga. State U., 1975. Three person shows include Carriage Barn Gallery, New Canaan, Conn., 1993; one-person show include Emory U., Atlanta, 1993, Chattahoochee Valley Art Mus., LaGrange, Ga., 1992, Atlanta Fin. Ctr., 1992, Capricorn Galleries, Bethesda, Md., 1991, Creative Arts Guild, Dalton, Ga., 1989, Ga. Tech. Student Art Gallery, Atlanta, 1988; exhibitions include Audubon Artists, N.Y.C., 1987, 88, 90, 91 (Mervin Honig Meml. award, 1993-2001, Renee Baczkier McNeely Meml. award 1993), Lake Worth (Fla.) Art League, (1st prize) 1987, (Delta/Shiva award) 1992, Parkersburg (W.Va.) Art Ctr., 1990, 93, 94, 97, (merit award) 1998, 2003 Artist's Mag., 1987, 91-94, 96-98 (second place), Fine Arts Inst. San Bernardino County Mus., Redlands, Calif., 1987, 92, 93, Manhattan Arts Mag. (Award of Excellence), 1992, 93, (Critic's Picks award) 1994, (award of excellence) 1995-97, (Artist Showcase award 1998, 99, 2000), Nat. Assn. Women Artists (Doris Kreindler Meml. award) 1988, 90, 91, (Grumbacher Gold Medal), 1992, Springfield (Mass.) Art League, 1988, (Merit award) 1990, (75th Anniversary award) 1994, 96, Am. Artists Profl. League, 1986, 87, 88, 90, Knickerbocker Artists, N.Y.C., 1987, John Pence Gallery, San Francisco, 2000, Columbia Coll., Mo., 1992, 94, 96, 98, 99 (Most Innovative Painting award 2000, Tara Materials Merit award 2002), many others; exhibited in Maralyn Wilson Gallery, Birmingham, Ala., Raleigh (N.C.) Contemporary Gallery, Steinway Gallery, Chapel Hill, NC, Little Gallery, Moneta, VA, Off the Wall, Savannah, ERL Originals, Winston-Salem, NC, Rutledge St. Gallery, Camden, S.C.; represented in permanent collections Chattahoochee Valley Art Mus., LaGrange, Ga., Springfield Art Museum, Springfield, MO, Zimmerli Art Museum, Rutgers U., New Brunswick, NJ, Telfair Museum of Art, Savannah, Fed. Res. Bank, Atlanta, State of Ga., Wachovia Bank, Atlanta, Arthur Andersen & Co., Atlanta, Price Waterhouse, Atlanta, O'Hare Hilton, Chgo., Drug Emporium, Worthington, Ohio, First Union Bank, Atlanta, Crescent Club, Memphis, Tenn., Encino (Calif.) Hosp., others. Mem. Audubon Artists, Catharine Lorillard Wolfe Art Club, Nat. Assn. Women Artists, Am. Artists Profl. League, Acad. Artists Assn., Oil Painters Am., Nat. League Am. Pen Women, Knickerbocker Artists Nat. Oil and Acrylic Painters' Soc. Avocations: gardening, reading. Office: PO Box 219 Decatur GA 30031-0219

BLESHMAN, MICHAEL HENRY, radiologist; b. Phila., June 28, 1946; MD, Hahnemann U., 1971. Intern Univ. Chgo., 1971-72; resident in radiology Temple Health Scis. Ctr., 1972-75; with Phoenixville Hosp., Pa.; vice-chair dept. radiology U. Pa., Phila. Mem.: Pa. Radiol. Soc., PCNM, Am. Inst. Ultrasound in Medicine, Radiol. Soc. N.Am., Am. Coll. Radiology. Office: Hosp of U Pa Dept Radiology 3400 Spruce St Philadelphia PA 19104-4283

BLESSEN, KAREN ALYCE, artist, writer; b. Columbus, Nebr. BFA, U. Nebr., 1973. Freelance illustrator, 1973-86; designer Dallas Morning News, 1986-89, freelance illustrator, designer, 1989—; owner, illustrator Karen Blessen Illustration, Dallas, 1989—. Illustrator Be An Angel, 1994, contbr. (art and articles) Dallas Morning News; commd. by Absolute to represent Tex. in Absolute Statehood series. Recipient Pulizer Prize for explanatory journalism, 1989, awards, N.Y. Art Dirs. Club, Soc. Newspaper Design, Dallas Press Club. Home and Office: Karen Blessen Illustration 6327 Vickery Blvd Dallas TX 75214-3348 E-mail: kblessen@aol.com.

BLESSING, TIM H. historian, educator; b. Huntington, Pa., Sept. 18, 1950; s. Minnick Guy and Martha (Harshbarger) Blessing. BA, U. Wyo., 1974; MPA, Pa. State U., 1976, MA in History, 1984, PhD in History, 1989. From instr. to asst. prof. history Pa. State U., University Park, 1981—93; assoc. prof. history Alvernia Coll., Reading, Pa., 1993—. Co-author: (book) Greatness in the White House, 1989; author: (poll) Murry-Blessing Presidential Ratings, 1983, 1991. Office: Alvernia College 400 Saint Bernardine St Reading PA 19607

BLESSINGER, TIMOTHY LOUIS, secondary school educator; b. Jasper, Ind., Feb. 7, 1953; B in Secondary Edn., St. Bernard Coll., 1975; M in Secondary Edn., Ind. State U., 1980. Lic. secondary sch. tchr., Ind. English tchr. Heritage Hills Mid./H.S., Lincoln City, Ind., 1975—. Coach Heritage Hills Mid./H.S., Lincoln City, 1975-86, advisor h.s. yearbook, 1982-99; mem. ISTEP and standards com. Ind. Dept. Edn., Indpls., 1996—; owner Blessinger Internat. Pub. House, LLC. Author: Lincoln: The Kentuckiana Years, 1997, Lincoln, Illinois Prairie Years, 1997, Lincoln: Washington, D.C., Years, 1997, The Seven Homes of Lincoln, 1999. Recipient Nat. Medal of Patriotism Am. Police Hall of Fame, Miami, Fla., 1996. Mem. NEA, North Spencer Reading Coun. (pres. 1977-78), Ind. State Reading Coun., Internat. Reading Assn., Ind. Coun. Tchrs. of English, Nat. Coun. Tchrs. of English, Nat. Mid. Sch. Assn. Avocations: art collecting, reading, writing, photography, sports. Home: RR 2 Box 303A Dale IN 47523-9545 Office: PO Box 1776 Lincoln City IN 47552-1776

BLETHEN, FRANK A. newspaper publisher; b. Seattle, Apr. 20, 1945; BS in Bus., Ariz. State U. Pub. Walla Walla Union-Bulletin, Wash., 1975-79; pub., ceo, circulation mgr. Seattle Times Newspaper Co., 1985—. Chmn. Walla Walla Union-Bull., Yakima (Wash.) Herald Republic, Blethen Maine Newspapers, Portland, Augusta, Waterville; pres. Blethen Corp. Mem. pres.' adv. bd. Wash. State U. and U. Wash.; campaign chair United Way King County, 1996, 97, bd. dirs., 1996; bd. dirs. Maynard Inst. for Minority Journalism Edn., 1994—. Recipient Pulitzer prize (3) for best newspaper reporting and investigative reporting, 1997, Nat. Reports, 1991, Ida B. Wells award for lifetime achievement in advancement of minority employment, 1997, Leadership Conf. on Civil Rights Chairperson's award for spl. merit, 1999, Edward R. Murrow award Wash. State U., 1998, Weldon B. Gibson Disting. Vol. award Wash. State U., 1998; named to Wash. State Hall of Journalistic Achievement, 1998. Mem. Nat. Assn. of Minority Media Execs., Am. Newspaper Pubs. Assn. (bd. dirs., chmn. telecomm. com.), Sigma Delta Chi. Office: Seattle Times PO Box 70 Seattle WA 98111-0070*

BLETHEN, SANDRA LEE, pediatric endocrinologist; b. San Mateo, Calif., May 16, 1942; d. Howard Albion and Laura Katherine (Wolf) B.; m. Fred I. Chasalow, Nov. 26, 1966. SB in Biochemistry, U. Chgo., 1961; PhD in Biochemistry, U. Calif., Berkeley, 1965; MD, Yeshiva U., 1975. Diplomate Am. Bd. Pediatrics. Fellow biochemistry Brandeis U., Waltham, Mass., 1965-68; instr. biochemistry U. Calif., San Diego, 1968-69; asst. prof. San Francisco State U., 1969-71; resident in pediatrics Columbia Presbyn. Med. Ctr., N.Y.C., 1975-77; fellow pediatric endocrinology U. N.C., Chapel Hill, 1977-79; asst. prof. pediatrics Washington U., St. Louis, 1979-84; assoc. prof. pediatrics SUNY, Stony Brook, 1985-96; assoc. attending pediatrician L.I. Jewish Med. Ctr., New Hyde Park, N.Y., 1984-90; attending pediatrician Univ. Hosp., Stony Brook, 1991-96; cons. Genentech, Inc., South San Francisco, Calif., 1985-96, sr. endocrinologist, 1996—, assoc. dir. product experience, 1997-2000, sr. clin. scientist, 1999—2002; v.p. med. affairs metabolic endocrinology Serono, Inc., Rockland, Md., 2002—. Cons. Diagnostic Systems Labs., Webster, Tex., 1989-96. Mem. editl. bd. Steroids, 1990—, Jour. of Endocrinology and Metabolism, 1995-98; contbr. more than 90 articles to profl. jours. Predoctoral fellow NSF, 1961-63, Postdoctoral fellow USPHS, 1965-67. Mem. Am. Pediatric Soc. (program com. 1994), Endocrine Soc., Lawson Wilkens Pediatric Endocrine Soc. (membership chair 1994-95), Soc. for Pediatric Rsch., Phi Beta Kappa, Alpha Omega Alpha. Avocation: sailing. Office: Serono Inc 1 Tech Pl Rockland MA 02370 E-mail: sandra.blethen@serono.com.

BLETTNER, JAMES DONALD, engineering company executive; b. Indpls., May 8, 1924; s. Joseph Anthony Blettner and Dorothea C. (Daum) Linville; m. Margaret P. Falkenroth, Aug. 22, 1948; 1 child, Dale Thomas. BEE, Purdue U., 1949. Registered profl. engr., Ind. Prodn. engr. Brown Rubber Co., Lafayette, Ind., 1949-52, tooling engr., 1952-55, head research div., 1955-58; supt. job shop Leaman Machines, Lafayette, 1958-60; pres. Blettner Engring. Co., Fairland, Ind., 1961—. Patentee in field. Elder St. James Luth. Ch., Lafayette, 1983-85. Served with USAF, 1943-46. Mem.: Power Squadron Stuart (Fla.). Republican. Avocations: sailing, fishing, swimming, golf. Home: 1600 NE Dixie Hwy B1-104 Jensen Beach FL 34958-3062 E-mail: donblet@aol.com.

BLEUSTEIN, JEFFREY L. automotive executive; b. 1939; B in Mech. Engring., Cornell U.; MS in Engring. Mechanics, PhD in Engring. Mechanics, Columbia U. Tchr. engring. and applied scis. Yale U.; with AMF, Inc., 1971; v.p. parts and accessories Harley-Davidson Motor Co., v.p. motor co., pres., COO, 1993—97, pres., CEO, 1997—, chmn., 1998—. Office: Harley Davidson Inc 3700 W Juneau Ave Milwaukee WI 53208*

BLEVEANS, JOHN, lawyer; b. Danville, Ill., Mar. 29, 1938; s. Edward Harold and Angelita (Robinson) B.; m. Luanna Harrison Burdick, Aug. 17, 1962; children: Lincoln Edward, Melanie Catherine. BA, Trinity U., 1960; LLB, U. Tex., 1965. Bar: Tex. 1965, D.C. 1967, U.S. Supreme Ct. 1969, Ill. 1971. Mem. gen. counsel's office Acacia Mut. Life Ins. Co., Washington, 1967-68; trial and appellate atty., civil rights div. U.S. Dept. Justice, Washington, 1966-67, 69-70; exec. dir. Washington Lawyers' Com., Civil Rights Under Law, 1970-71, chief counsel Lawyers' Com., Civil Rights Under Law, Cairo, Ill., 1971-72; assoc. Mayer, Brown & Platt, Chgo., 1972-74, ptnr., 1974-83, 91-92; sr. v.p., assoc., gen. counsel Continental Ill. Nat. Bank and Trust Co. of Chgo., 1983-89; dep. gen. counsel Continental Bank N.A., Chgo., 1989-91; ptnr. Mayer, Brown & Platt, Chgo., 1991-92; of counsel Arthur Andersen & Co., Chgo., 1992-95, Hong Kong, 1996-97, Sydney, Australia, 1995-96. Part-time bus driver Tri State Travel, Galena, Ill., 2002—; pres. Hanover Ambulance, Inc., 2000. Alderman City of Evanston, Ill., 1981-89; chmn. Evanston Zoning Bd. Appeals, 1991-92; vol. Hanover Ambulance, 1999—. Capt. USNR ret. Mem. Tex. Bar Assn., D.C. Bar Assn., Nat. Ski Patrol, Law Club Chgo.

BLEVINS, ADRIAN ELLEN, writer, educator; b. Abingdon, Va., June 21, 1964; d. Tedd Blevins and Phebe Fullerton Cress; m. Nathaniel Rudy; children: August children: Weston Church, Benjamin Church. BA, Va. Intermont Coll., 1986; MA, Hollins U., 1990; MFA, Warren Wilson Coll., 2002. Assoc. prof. English Hollins U., Roanoke, Va., 1991—99; writing instr. Roanoke Coll., Salem, Va., 2002—. Author: The Man Who Went Out for Cigarettes, 1996 (Bright Hill Press Poetry Chapbook award), The Brass Girl Brouhaha, 2003. Recipient Rona Jaffe Writers Found. award, 2002. Home: 2012 Berkley Ave SW Roanoke VA 24015 Personal E-mail: adrianb@cox.net.

BLEVINS, CHARLES RUSSELL, publishing executive; b. Kittaning, Pa., Apr. 6, 1942; s. Clarence Ray and Elizabeth Sarah (Warren) B.; m. Gale Watkins Crittenden, Dec. 16, 1967; children: Charles Jr., Rush. BS, Ind. U., 1964. Asst. prodn. exec. Wall St. Jour., Cleve., D.C. and Princeton, 1964-71, Gannett Co. Inc., El Paso Agy., El Paso, Tex., 1971-76; prodn. exec. Rockford Newspapers, Rockland, Ill., 1976-77; corp. prodn. dir. Gannett Corp. Hdqrs., Rochester, N.Y., 1977-79, v.p., prodn. Arlington, Va., 1979-89; CEO Blevins Harding Group, Vienna, Va., 1989-98; pres., CEO Chuck Blevins & Assocs., Vienna, 1998—. Speaker European Printing Conf., Newspaper Quality Meeting Conf.; chmn. Conf. Quality-Newspaper Assn., Conf. Research & Engring. Council, Chgo., Rsch. and Engring. Coun. Com. Graphic Arts Techs. Standards Unit Loading. Creator quality standards, operating procedures USA Today, 1981-86. Judge RIT/USA Today Quality Cup for Individuals and Teams, 1992—. Mem. Am. Newspaper Pub. Assn. (tech. com. 1985-89, officer internat. newspaper group 1989—), Rsch. and Engring. Coun. of Graphic Arts (v.p. 1985-94), Rochester Inst. Tech. Coun., W.Va. Inst. Tech. Adv. Coun., Inca Fiej Rsch. Assn. (press com.). Office: Chuck Blevins & Assocs 8396 Northhampton Naples FL 34120 E-mail: crblevins@aol.com.

BLEVINS, DALE GLENN, agronomy educator; b. Ozark, Mo., Aug. 29, 1943; s. Vernon Henry and Edna Gertrude Blevins; 1 child, Jeremy. BS in Chemistry, S.W. Mo. State U., 1965; MS in Soils, U. Mo., 1967; PhD in Plant Physiology, U. Ky., 1972. Postdoctoral fellow botany dept. Oreg. State U., Corvallis, Oreg., 1972-74; asst. prof. botany U. Md., College Park, 1974-78; assoc. prof. agronomy dept. U. Mo., Columbia, 1978-86, prof., 1986—. Mem. Am. Soc. Plant Physiology, Am. Soc. Agronomy, Crop Sci. Soc. Am. Office: Univ Mo Dept Agronomy 1-87 Agriculture Building Columbia MO 65211-7140

BLEVINS, JAMES RAY, lawyer, insurance company claims executive; b. Jefferson, N.C., Mar. 20, 1949; s. Oscar Ray and Helen Marie (Clark) B.; m. Patricia Fay Faltermann, Dec. 27, 1970; children: Jennifer Renee, James Ray Jr. BA, Wake Forest U., 1971, JD, 1978; MS in Edn., U. So. Calif., 1975. Bar: N.C. 1978, S.C. 1993; registered profl. adjuster. Claims atty. Integon Ins. Co., Winston-Salem, N.C., 1979-80, field claims mgr., asst. v.p., 1980-85; Mid-Atlantic regional claims mgr. Amerisure Ins. Co., Charlotte, 1985-90; v.p., claims mgr. Sedgwick James of the Carolinas, Columbia, S.C., 1990-92; pvt. practice claims cons. and lawyer Columbia, 1992-94; litigation mgr. Seibels Bruce Ins. Co., Columbia, S.C., 1994-98; dir. spl. claims Burlington (N.C.) Ins. Co., 1998—. Del. N.C. Dem. Conv., Raleigh, 1976, S.C. Dem. Conv., Columbia, 1996. 1st lt. U.S. Army, 1971-75, capt. N.C. Army Nat. Guard, 1975-87, lt. col. judge adv. USAR, 1987-97. Mem. ABA, N.C. Bar Assn., S.C. Bar Assn. Democrat. Presbyterian. Avocation: reading. Home: 9190 Hwy 194N Lansing NC 28643 Office: 238 International Rd Burlington NC 27215-5177

BLEVINS, JEFFREY ALEXANDER, lawyer; b. Forest Hills, N.Y., June 18, 1955; s. William E. and Mary J. Blevins; m. Pamela A. Manos, Nov. 26, 1983 (div. Mar. 1995); 1 child, Mary Alexandria; m. Diane L. Bannon, June 12, 1999; stepchildren: Meagan Elizabeth, Laura Leigh, Jeffrey Daniel. BA, Denison U., 1977; JD, DePaul U., 1981. Bar: Ill. 1981, U.S. Dist Ct. (no. dist.) Ill. 1981, U.S. Dist. Ct. (we. dist. Wis. 1984, U.S. Ct. Appeals (7th cir.) 1984, U.S. Supreme Ct. 1990. Personnel specialist Comerica Bank, Detroit, 1979-80; assoc. Bell, Boyd & Lloyd, Chgo., 1981-88, ptnr., mem., 1988—2001; mng. atty. The Law Office of Jeffrey A. Blevins LLC, Naperville, Ill., 2001—02; pub. interest atty. Prairie State Legal Svcs., 2002—. Lectr., author Ill. Inst. Continuing Legal Edn., others; chair employment sect. Ctr. for Disability and Elder Law, 1999—. Editor in chief DePaul Law Rev., 1980. Mem. Ill. State Bar Assn. (labor and employment coun. 1992-95), Chgo. Bar Assn., Mid-day Club, Omicron Delta Epsilon. Republican. Lutheran.

BLEVINS, STANLEY NANCE, minister, educator; b. Comanche, Tex., Oct. 2, 1938; s. A.J. and Ruby Blevins; m. Betty Jo Westfall, Apr. 17, 1960; children: Ronald, Kristi Dean. BA, Hardin-Simmons U., 1961; MDiv, Southwestern Bapt. Theol. Sem., 1964, D of Ministry, 1982. Sr. pastor First Bapt. Ch., Lueders, Tex., 1964—66, Jackson Ave. Bapt. Ch., Lovington, N.Mex., 1966—69, Oakwood Bapt. Ch., Lubbock, Tex., 1969—79, Ctrl. Bapt. Ch., Bryan, Tex., 1979—86, Highland Bapt. Ch., Lubbock, 1986—. Adj. prof. Wayland Bapt. U., Lubbock, 2000—; trustee Hardin-Simmons U., Abilene, Tex., 1988—97, bd. of devel., 1998—; exec. bd. Bapt. Gen. Conv. of Tex., Dallas, 1972—79, 1981—86. Contbr. articles to profl. jours. Recipient Disting. Alumnus award, Logsdon Sch. of Theology Hardin-Simmons U., 1999. Mem.: Aircraft Owners & Pilots Assn., Colo. RR Hist. Found., Rocky Mountain RR Club. Avocations: narrow gauge railroad history, photography, writing. Home: PO Box 93777 Lubbock TX 79493-3777 Office: Highland Baptist Church 4316 34th Street Lubbock TX 79410

BLEVINS, STEVEN W. chiropractor; b. Davenport, Iowa, Mar. 24, 1963; s. Dwayne Blevins and Nance D. Jakubowski; m. Amy L. Lorenzen, Oct. 5, 1985 (div. June 1994); children: Cara, Kurt; m. Meg Dolan, Sept. 27, 1997. BS, Regent's Coll., 1997; D of Chiropractic, Palmer Coll. Chiropractic, Davenport, 1988. Diplomate Am. Acad. Pain Mgmt. Clinic assoc. Westside Family Healthcare, Indpls., 1988-90; owner Lebanon (Ind.) Chiropractic Clinic, 1990-95; clinic assoc. Georgetown Family Chiropractic, Indpls., 1995-96; night shift ops. non-commd. officer in charge 21 Theater Area Army Command, Kaiserslautern, Germany, 1996-97; chiropractic physician Spinal Rehab. of Am., Naperville, Ill., 1997-98; owner Blevins Chiropractic Clinic, Cary, Ill., 1998—. Mem. med. staff World Gymnastics Championships, Indpls., 1991. 1st sgt. U.S. Army, 1996-97. Recipient 3 commendation medals, 2 achievement medals U.S. Army, 1987-97, Silver Marksmanship medal, 1996. Master Masons (pres. Lodge # 221 1987-88, Kaaba Temple Shrine, Davenport York Rite Bodies, Scottish Rite Bodies); fellow Internat. Acad. Med. Acupuncture; mem. Jaycees (treas. Cary Grove chpt. 1999-2000, pres. 2000-01, region dir. 2002, one of 10 Outstanding Young Persons, Ill. chpt. 2000), Christian Chiropractic Assn., Ill. Chiropractic Assn., Palmer Internat. Alumni Assn. (life), Am. Legion, AmVets (life), Cary-Grove C. of C., Chi Rho Theta (life). Avocations: bowling, shooting sports. Office: Blevins Chiropractic 652 NW Hwy Cary IL 60013 Fax: (847) 639-4473.

BLEVINS, THOMAS E. college administrator, educator; b. Welch, W.Va., Mar. 8, 1949; s. Casper Claude and Bessie Oliv (Shumate) B.; m. Brenda Louise Mabry Lamastus, Mar. 27, 1971 (div. Oct. 1980); children: Tracy, James, Matthew; m. Betty Ruth Rader, May 23, 1992. BS, Bluefield (W.Va.) State Coll., 1971; MA, Marshall U., 1973; CAGS, Va. Tech. U., 1980, EdD, 1986. Cert. tchr., W.Va. Tchr., asst. prin. Elkhorn Jr. H.S., Powhatan, W.Va., 1971-74; tchr., media ctr. dir. Northfork (W.Va.) H.S., 1974-77; coord. audiovisual svcs. Bluefield State Coll., 1977-84, dir. instrnl. tech., 1984—, dir. tchr. edn., 1990-96, prof. edn. and English, 1988—, dir. ctr. for extended learning and acad. computing, 1996—, chief tech. officer, interim pres., 2002—, dean Virtual Coll. and Tech., 2003. Mem. adv. panel W.Va. Humanities Found., Charleston, 1978—81; mem. tech. implementation planning team State Coll. and Univ. Sys. W.Va., Charleston, 1995—96, spl. asst. to the chancellors for tech.; sr. tech. officer Gov.'s Office of Tech., State of W.Va., 1999—; dir. W.Va. Satellite Network, 2000—; dir. W.Va. Virtual Learning Network W.Va. Higher Edn. Policy Commn., 2003. Recipient Edgar Dale award W.Va. Ednl. Media Assn./Assn. Ednl. Comms. and Tech., 1984. Mem. Assn. for Ednl. Comms. and Tech. (cert. com., accreditation com.), W.Va. Ednl. Media Assn. (pres. 1982-84), W.Va. C.C. Assn. (bd. dirs. 1995—), W.Va. Satellite Network, W.Va. Higher Edn. Instrnl. TV Consortium, Nat. Coun. for Accreditation of Tchr. Edn. (chmn. bd. examiners 1998—), Rotary of Bluefield (chair Rotoract and Rotary Info. 1995—), Elks. Democrat. Avocations: woodworking, reading, swimming. Home: 2339 Verdun Hts Bluefield WV 24701-4727 Office: Bluefield State Coll 219 Rock St Bluefield WV 24701-2100 E-mail: tblevins@bluefieldstate.edu.

BLEVINS, WILLARD AHART, electrical engineer; b. Jonben, W.Va., Nov. 20, 1949; s. Oakley Cameron and Peggy Jane (Agee) B.; m. Nancy Phyllis Bailey, June 26, 1971; children: Maria Dawn, Teresa Lynn. AA in Elec. Tech. with honors, N.D. State Sch. Sci., 1974; BSEE with honors, Ariz. State U., 1988. Technician Sperry Flight Systems, Phoenix, 1974-88; engr. Sperry/Honeywell, Phoenix, 1988—. Patentee out of lock detector. With USAF, 1968-72. Recipient Honeywell Tech. Achievement award, 1995; named Parent of Yr., Phoenix Children's Chorus, 1985. Avocation: playing bass guitar with pop group. Home: 15810 N 47th Ln Glendale AZ 85306-2602 Office: Honeywell PO Box 21111-w33C Phoenix AZ 85036

BLEVINS, WILLIAM EDWARD, management consultant; b. Boissevan, Va., Oct. 18, 1927; s. Howard Muncey and Elsie Jane (Wire) B.; m. Mary Hester Jenkins, Aug. 25, 1951; children— Jeffrey Alexander, Jennifer Lynn, Bradley Edward AB, Marshall Coll., 1951; MPA, CCNY, 1960. Personnel mgr. Equitable Life, N.Y.C., 1951-66; asst. v.p., dir. mgmt. devel. Nat. Bank Detroit, 1966-69, v.p., dir. personnel, 1969-74, sr. v.p., dir. personnel, 1974-91; exec. v.p., dir. human resources NBD Bancorp, Inc., Detroit, 1980-92; pres. WEB Communications Co., Detroit, 1993—. Bd. dirs. Blue Cross & Blue Shield Mich., Detroit, 1980—92, Human Resources Coun. AMA, 1979—84, 1987—92, Detroit Exec. Svc. Corps, 1996, Health Plan of Mich., 1997—2002. Trustee Bon Secour Hosp., Grosse Pointe, Mich., 1975-84, St. John Sr. Cmty., 1989—, chmn., 1995—, chmn. St. John Health Sr. Svcs., 2000—; bd. dirs. Oxford Inst., 1987-89, bd. dirs. Holy Cross Hosp., 1996-98; mem. corp. adv. bd. Am. Heart Assn., 1995-98; trustee Frances Rhodes, M.D. Meml. Found., 1999—; bd. dirs. Mich. Diabetes Assn., 1982-86, Mich. Soc. for Mental Health, 1984-87. Recipient Outstanding Alumnus award Marshall U., 1976, Hall of Fame award Lambda Chi Alpha, 1996. Mem. Am. Bankers Assn. (bd. dirs. 1974-75), Am. Inst. Banking (bd. dirs., bd. regents, chmn. 1983-90), Am. Soc. Employers (bd. dirs. 1970-94, treas. 1970-90, vice chmn. 1991-92, chmn. 1992-94), Alpha Bank Pers Group (founder, chmn. 1972-74, 86), Mich. Pers. Indsl. Rels. Group (chmn. 1980-92), Bank Adminstr. Inst. (human resources commn. 1983-88), Detroit Athletic Club, Country Club Detroit. Republican. Office: WEB Comms Co 551 Fisher Rd Grosse Pointe Park MI 48230-1214 E-mail: webmjb@comcast.net. *How lucky I am to live in the USA. It offers a fine education to those who want it; meaningful jobs to those who prepare and strive, a wonderful place for romance, an ideal place to raise a family. I have been truly blessed with lots of help along the way.*

BLEWETT, ALEXANDER, III, lawyer; b. May 2, 1945; s. Alexander and Fern Wynnett (Foerschler) B.; m. Andrea Ann Friedl, Aug. 18, 1975; children: Anders, Drew. BS in Math., Mont. State U., 1967; JD, U. Mont., 1971. Bar: Mont. 1971, U.S. Supreme Ct., U.S. Ct. of Appeals (6th and 9th cir.). Assoc. and ptnr. Jardine, Stephenson, Blewett & Weaver, Great Falls, Mont., 1971—85; ptnr. Hoyt & Blewett, 1985—2001, owner, 2001—. Recipient Cert. of Civil Trial Advocacy, Nat. Bd. Trial Advocacy, 1983—; Mont. Trial Lawyer of the Year, 1993-94. Mem. President's Club, Am. Trial Lawyers Assn., sustaining mem. Mont. Bar Assn., Mont. Trial Lawyers Assn., Fellow Am. Coll. Trial Lawyers, Internat. Acad. Trial Lawyers, Fellow Inner Circle of Advocates (Mont. Trial Lawyer of Yr. award 1993-94), Fellow Internat. Soc. Barristers, chapt. mem. Montana American Bd. of Trial Advocates (ABOTA). Democrat. Home: 1324 4th Ave N Great Falls MT 59401 Office: Hoyt & Blewett 501 2nd Ave N PO Box 2807 Great Falls MT 59403-2807 E-mail: zblewett@hoytandblewett.com.

BLEWETT, DAVID LAMBERT, English literature educator; b. Calgary, Alta., Can., Dec. 18, 1940; s. John and Sydnay Catherine (Cole) B. BA with honors, U. Man., Winnipeg, 1962, MA, 1963; PhD, U. Toronto, Ont., Can., 1971. Lectr. McMaster U., Hamilton, Ont., Can., 1969-71, asst. prof., 1971-77, assoc. prof., 1977-84, prof., 1984—2003, prof. emeritus, 2003—. Author: DeFoe's Art of Fiction, 1979, The Illustration of Robinson Crusoe: 1719-1920, 1995, Japanese trans., 1998; editor: Roxana, 1982, Amelia, 1987, Moll Flanders, 1989, Roderick Random, 1995, Passion and Virtue; Essays on the Novels of Samuel Richardson, 2001; editor Eighteenth-Century Fiction, 1988—2003. Grantee Social Scis. and Humanities Rsch. Coun. Can., 1989-90, 96-99. Mem. Am. Soc. for Eighteenth-Century Studies, Can. Assn. for Eighteenth-Century Studies, Can. Assn. Univ. Tchrs., Internat. Assn. U. Profs. of English, Royal Soc, Lit., Reform Club, McMaster U. Faculty Assn. (pres. 1992-93). Avocations: travel, music. Home: 390 Wellesley St E # 16 Toronto ON Canada M4X 1H6 E-mail: blewett@mcmaster.ca.

BLEWETT, ROBERT NOALL, lawyer; b. Stockton, Calif., July 12, 1915; s. Stephen Noall and Bess Errol (Simard) B.; m. Virginia Weston, Mar. 30, 1940; children: Richard Weston Blewett (dec.), Carolyn Blewett Lawrence. LLB, Stanford U., 1936, JD, 1939. Bar: Calif. 1939. Dep. dist. atty. San Joaquin County, 1942-46; practice law Stockton, 1946-98; ptnr., pres. Blewett & Allen-Garibaldi, Inc., Stockton, 1971-98. Chmn. San Joaquin County chpt. ARC, 1947-49; v.p. Goodwill Industries, 1967-68; vice chmn. Stockton Sister City Commn., 1969-70; adv. bd. bus. adminstrn. dept. U. Pacific; trustee San Joaquin Pioneer and Haggin Galleries. Fellow Am. Coll. Estate and Trust Counsel, Am. Bar Found.; mem. ABA, Am. Judicature Soc., Am. Law Inst., State Bar Calif. (mem. exec. com. on conf. of dels. 1969-72, vice chmn. 1971-72), Order of the Coif, Rotary (pres. 1987-88), Yosemite Club, San Francisco Banker's Club, Masons, Shriners, Delta Theta Phi, Theta Xi. Republican. Home: 3016 Dwight Way Stockton CA 95204

BLEWITT, GEORGE AUGUSTINE, physician, consultant; b. Pittston, Pa., May 8, 1937; s. George Augustus and Virginia (Wills) B.; m. Anne Katherine Mullahy, June 16, 1962; children: George, Mary Katherine, John, Patrick. BS, King's Coll., Wilkes-Barre, Pa., 1958; MD, Thomas Jefferson U., Phila., 1962. Diplomate Am. Bd. Internal Medicine. Intern Phila. Gen. Hosp., 1962-63; resident Phila. VA Hosp., 1963-66; fellow Thomas Jefferson U., Phila.; clin. instr. Stanford U. Sch. Medicine, Calif., 1967-75; staff physician Palo Alto VA Hosp., Calif., 1973-75; clin. prof. medicine Jefferson Med. Coll., 1977-80; assoc. dir. clin. services Smith, Kline & French, Phila., 1976-78; med. dir. Menley & James Labs., Phila., 1978, v.p. research devel., 1978-80; assoc. med. dir. Bristol-Myers Products, N.Y.C., 1980-81, v.p., med. dir., 1981-82, v.p., dir. research devel., 1982-91, v.p. sci. resources, 1991-93; pres. George A. Blewitt, M.D. & Assocs., Inc., Fayetteville, Pa., 1993—. Adj. prof. U. Calif., Santa Barbara, 1989-98, Jefferson Med. Coll., Phila., 1993-98. Served to maj. USAR, 1963-71 Fellow: ACP; mem.: AMA, Pa. Med. Assn., Am. Heart Assn. Home and Office: 6902 Saint Annes Dr Fayetteville PA 17222-9440

BLEWITT, THOMAS MICHAEL, federal magistrate judge; b. Pittston, Pa., Nov. 20, 1949; m. Evelyn Bubser; three children. BA, U. Scranton, 1972; MPA, Marywood Coll., 1979; JD, Temple U., 1983. Bar: Pa. 1983. Spl. investigator Pa. Bur. Consumer Protection, Harrisburg, 1972-80; assoc. Law Office Marshall E. Anders, Stroudsburg, Pa., 1983-84; asst. dist. atty. Lackawanna County, Scranton, 1984-86; asst. fed. pub. defender for mid. dist. Pa. Office Fed. Pub. Defender, Scranton, 1986-92; assoc. Lenahan & Dempsey, Scranton, 1988-89; magistrate judge for mid. dist. Pa., U.S. Magistrate Ct., Scranton, 1992—; chief magistrate judge Mid. Dist. Ct. Pa., 2002—. Office: US Magistrate Ct 217 Fed Bldg PO Box 443 235 N Washington Ave Scranton PA 18501-0443

BLEY, ANN, program analyst, business manager; b. N.Y.C., July 12, 1954; d. Albert Vincent and Autilia (Eliseo) Rizzo; m. Elmer Raymond Bley; 1 child, Shannon Kathryn Bley. BA cum laude, U. Mich., 1976; MBA cum laude, Boston U., 1978. Mgmt. analyst U.S. Army Tank-Auto. Command Force Devel. Div., Warren, Mich., 1979-85; Program, Budget analyst PM Abrams Tank Systems, Warren, Mich., 1985-91; program analyst PM Combat Mobility Sys., DSA, Tacom, Warren, Mich., 1991-99, acting bus. mgr., 1999; program analyst PM Brigade Combat Team, 2000-2001, sr. program analyst, bus. mgr., 2001—. Contbr. articles to profl. jours. Protegee to Dep. Asst. Sec. Plans, Programs, Policy, Dept. of Army, 1995-96; registration chair Mich. Women's Vote 96; mem. exec. bd. Common Cause of Mich., 1998—. Mem.: Am. Soc. Mil. Comptrs., Federally Employed Women (nat. tng. program chair 1985, chpt. pres. 1995—97, nat. awards chair 2000—02, nat. v.p. for Congress and govt. rels. 2002—, Nat. award for compliance activities 1993), Beta Gamma Sigma. Avocations: boating, travel. Home: 31080 Mckinney Dr Franklin MI 48025-1313 Office: US Army Tank Auto Command Pm Brigade Combat Team SFAE-GCS-BCT-P Warren MI 48397 E-mail: abley@prodigy.com.

BLEY, CARLA BORG, jazz composer; b. Oakland, Calif., May 11, 1938; d. Emil Carl and Arlene (Anderson) Borg; m. Paul Bley, Jan. 27, 1959 (div. Sept. 1967); m. Michael Mantler, Sept. 29, 1967 (div. 1992); 1 dau., Karen. Student public schs., Oakland. Mem. adv. bd. Jazz Composers Orch. Assn. Freelance jazz composer, 1956—, pianist, Jazz Composers Orch., N.Y.C., 1964—, European concert tours, Jazz Realities, 1965-66; founder, WATT, 1973—, toured Europe with Jack Bruce Band, 1975; leader, Carla Bley Band, touring, U.S. and Europe, 1977—; composed, recorded: A Genuine Tong Funeral, 1967, (with Charlie Haden) Liberation Music Orch., 1969; opera Escalator Over the Hill, 1970-71 (Oscar du Disque de Jazz 1973), Tropic Appetites, 1973; composed: chamber orch. 3/4, 1974-75; film score Mortelle Randonnèe, 1983; recorded: Dinner Music, 1976, The Carla Bley Band: European Tour, 1977, Musique Macanique, 1979, (with Nick Mason) Fictitious Sports, 1980, Social Studies, 1980, Carla Bley Live!, 1981, Heavy Heart, 1984, I Hate to Sing, 1985, Night Glo, 1985, Sexted, 1987, Duets, 1988, Fleur Carnivor, 1989, The Very Big Carla Bley Band, 1991, Go Together, 1993, Big Band Theory, 1993, Songs with Legs, 1995, Goes to Church, 1996, Fancy Chamber Music, 1998, Are We There Yet?, 1999, 4x4, 2000, Looking for America, 2003. Named winner internat. jazz critics poll Down Beat mag., 1966, 71, 72, 78, 79, 80, 83, 84; Best Composer of Yr., Down Beat Readers' Poll, 1984, composer/arranger of yr., 1985-92; Guggenheim fellow, 1972; Cultural Coun. Found. grantee, 1971, 79; Nat. Endowment for the Arts grantee, 1973, Oscar du Disque de Jazz (for Escalator Over the Hill) 1973; named Best in Field Jazz Times critics poll, 1990, Best Arranger, Downbeat Critics Poll, 1993, 94, Best Arranger, Downbeat Readers' Poll, 1994; recipient Prix Jazz Moderne from Academie du Jazz for The very Big Carla Bley Band album, 1992. Office: Watt Works PO Box 67 Willow NY 12495-0067 E-mail: watt@ulster.net.

BLEZNICK, DONALD WILLIAM, Romance languages educator; b. N.Y.C., Dec. 24, 1924; s. Louis and Gertrude (Kleinman) B.; m. Rozlyn Burakoff, June 15, 1952; children— Jordan, Susan BA, CCNY, 1946; MA, U. Nacional de Mex., 1948; PhD, Columbia U., 1954. Instr. romance langs. Ohio State U., 1949-55; prof. Pa. State U., 1955-67, U. Cin., 1967—, head dept., 1967-72; instr. Romance langs. Vis. prof. Hebrew U., Jerusalem, 1974. Bibliographer, MLA Internat. Bibliography, 1966-81; rev. editor Hispania, 1965-73, editor, 1974-83, editor's adv. coun., 1984—, El Ensayo Espanol del Siglo Veinte, 1964, Historia del Ensayo Espanol, 1964, Duelo en el Paraiso (Goytisolo), 1967, Madrugada (Buero Vallejo), 1969, (with W.T. Pattison) Representative Spanish Authors, 1971, Quevedo, 1972, Variaciones interpretativas en torno a la nueva narrativa hispanoamericana, 1972, Directions of Literary Criticism in the Seventies, 1972, Sourcebook for Hispanic Literature and Language, 1974, 3d expanded edit., 1995, Homenaje a Luis Leal, 1978, Studies on Don Quixote and other Cervantine Works, 1984, Critical Edition of La Diana (Jorge Montemayor), 1990, The Thought of Contemporary Spanish Essayists, 1993, Studies in Honor of Donald W. Bleznick, 1995; translator (from Spanish and Portuguese) Identity in Dispersion: Selected Memoirs from Latin American Jews, 2000; founder, exec. editor Cin. Romance Rev., 1982-88; field editor: Twayne Spanish Literature Series, 1981—; contbr. articles to profl. jours., Ency. Americana. With CIC, 1946-47. Decorated Knight's Cross Order Civil Merit (Spain); Am. Philos. Soc. rsch. grantee, 1964; Downer fellow CCNY, 1947-48; U. Cin. Taft rsch. and publ. grantee, 1972, 75, 78, 83, 88, 89, 92; named 1 of 15 outstanding scholars in Spanish lit. in Cuadernos Salmantinos de Filosofia, Salamanca, Spain, 1977; recipient Rieveschl award for excellence in rsch. U. Cin., 1980, award Hispania, U. So. Calif., 1983; fellow U. Cin. Grad. Sch., 1984. Mem. AAUP, Am. Assn. Tchrs. Spanish and Portuguese (exec. com. 1975—, award 1984, v.p. 1992, pres. 1993, Honored for Outstanding Career 1995, disting. svc. award 1997), MLA, Los Ensayistas (adv. bd. 1976—), Comediantes, Midwest Modern Lang. Assn., Conf. Editors of Learned Jours. (exec. com. 1978-79), Celestinesca, Cervantes Soc. Am., Phi Beta Kappa (pres. Delta chpt. of Ohio 1971-72, 86-87), Sigma Delta Pi (state dir. Ohio 1968-74, Order of Don Quijote 1970, v.p. Midwest 1975-83, Jose Martel award 1980, hon. pres. 1998), Phi Sigma Iota, Kappa Delta Pi. Home: 2444 Madison Rd Apt 1806 Cincinnati OH 45208-1255 Office: U Cin Dept Romance Langs Cincinnati OH 45221-0001 E-mail: donald.bleznick@uc.edu.

BLEZNICK, SUSAN RISA, writer, television producer, photographer; b. State College, Pa., Aug. 9, 1958; d. Donald W. and Rozlyn (Burakoff) Bleznick. Grad. cum laude, Walnut Hills H.S., Cin., 1976; BA, NYU, 1981; MS, Ohio U., 1988. Daily newspaper reporter Athens (Ohio) Messenger, 1988, Sandusky (Ohio) Register, 1988-89; news editor, editorial asst. McGraw-Hill Archtl. Record Mag., N.Y.C., 1989-91; writer WGTE Pub. TV, Toledo, 1991-93; exec. editor Montage Mag., Toledo, 1993; TV series project dir. Bowling Green (Ohio) State U./WBGU-TV, 1994-95; freelance writer/producer for TV stas., prodn. cos., mags., newspapers, corps., others, 1991—. Contbr. articles to nat. and regional mags., alumni mags., newspapers and newsletters; author: (monograph) Media Coverage of Jackson Pollock, Abstract Expressionist Painter, 1988. Vol. pub. TV stas. and art orgns. that work with children and families., 1993—. Recipient Crystal Award Women in Comms., 1993. Mem.: Am. Women in Radio and TV, Stanford U. Ballroom Dance Club, Kappa Tau Alpha. Avocations: music, hiking, photography, film, dancing. Home: Apt 2602 373 River Oaks Cir San Jose CA 95134-1964 E-mail: sbleznick@yahoo.com.

BLICK, KENNETH EDWARD, clincial chemist, educator; b. Bluefield, W.Va., June 1, 1944; s. Isham Trotter II and Elinor (Wells) B.; m. Helen Veida Worthington, Mar. 15, 1969; children: David, Sharon, Brian. BS, Western Ky. U., 1966; PhD, U. Ky., 1970. Diplomate Am. Bd. Clin. Chemistry, Nat. Acad. Clin. Biochemistry. Sr. rsch. assoc. dept. chemistry U. Ky., Lexington, 1971-75, chmn., asst. prof. phys. scis. Prestonsburg, 1971-75; asst. prof. allied health Midway Coll., Lexington, 1975-78; asst. prof. med. tech. Ind. State U., Evansville, 1978-82; asst. prof. pathology U. Okla., Okla. City, 1982-84, assoc. prof., 1984-99, prof., 1999—; chmn. radiation safety U. Okla. Health Sci. Ctr., Okla. City, 1991—. Adj. prof. dermatology U. Okla. Health Sci. Ctr., 1984—, med. tech., 1982—, prof. grad. program, 1984—; dir. Lab. Computer Systems Okla. Med. Ctr., 1982—, sci. dir. endocrinology, 1982—, dir. clin. chemistry; dir. State of Okla., State Bd. Tests, 1998—; adj. prof. chemistry U. Ctrl. Okla., 1999—2002. Co-author: Principles in Clinical Chemistry, 1985, 90. Regional dir. Metrication, Prestonburg, Ky., chmn. faculty senate U. Okla. Health Sci. Ctr., 1994-95. Mem.: Medlab Users Group, Assn. Clin. Scientists, Okla. State Assn. Pathologists, Am. Assn. Clin. Chemistry (chmn., founder lab. info. systems divsn. 1983—98, chmn. Tex. sect. 1991, lab. informatics, Outstanding Clin. Chemist, Tex. sect.), Phi Kappa Phi, Sigma Xi. Presbyterian. Avocations: music, sports. Home: 3001 Broken Bow Rd Edmond OK 73013-7866 Office: U Okla Health Scis Ctr PO Box 26307 Oklahoma City OK 73126-0307

BLICK, ROBERT HOWARD, economist, consultant; b. Petersburg, Va., Mar. 14, 1957; s. Howard Lee and Evelyn Virginia Blick. MS, Fla. State U., 1989, EdS, 1998, PhD, 2001. Statistician I Fla. Dept. Health and Rehabilitative Svcs., Tallahassee, 1980-81, statistician II, 1981-83, statistician III, 1983-86; engring. technician IV Fla. Dept. Transp., Tallahassee, 1986-87; revenue economist Fla. Dept. Revenue, Tallahassee, 1987-89, planning and rsch. economist, 1989-95, appraiser specialist, 1995-2001; tng. and rsch. cons. Tallahassee, 2001—. Respite caregiver Alzheimer's Project Tallahassee, 1994—98. Mem.: Phi Lambda Theta, Phi Kappa Phi. E-mail: robertblick@robertblick.com.

BLICKENSTAFF, DANNY JAY, retired civilian military employee; b. Hagerstown, Md., Mar. 2, 1946; s. Daniel Webster and Mildred Elmira (Greenwalt) B.; m. Jean Ann McSwain, Oct. 10, 1965 (div. 1977); children: Ramona Glynn, Andrea Mae, Camellia Kay; m. Sharon Elizabeth Ward, Aug. 26, 1978. BA, U. Md., 1975, MBA, 1979. Electronics technician U.S. Naval Ordnance Lab., White Oak, Md., 1964-71; R & D electronics lab. supr. U.S. Dept. Transp., McLean, Va., 1971-81; program analyst U.S. Army Hdqs. 7th Signal Command, Ft. Ritchie, Md., 1981-86, program/ops. rsch. analysis officer, 1986-93; program mgr. Def. Info. Svc. Agy., Ft. Ritchie, 1993-96, security specialist, 1996-99; ret., 1999. Active Totem Pole Playhouse, Fayettville, Pa., 1976, Washington County Assn. Retarded Citizens, Hagerstown, Md., 1986. Mem. NRA, Md. Christmas Tree Assn., Am. Paulownia Assn. Republican. Mem. Brethren Ch. Avocations: live theater, travel, gardening, raising christmas trees and llamas. Home: 16345 Mount Tabor Rd Hagerstown MD 21740-1030 E-mail: mcta@erols.com., palownia@erols.com.

BLICKLE, PETER, German language and literature educator, novelist; b. Ravensburg, Germany, Sept. 26, 1961; came to U.S., 1984; s. Ernst and Hedwig (Wetzel) B.; m. Jaimy Gordon, Dec. 23, 1988. BA in Classics and English, We. Mich. U., 1987; MA in Comparative Lit., U. Mich., 1989, PhD in German Lit., 1995. Tchg. asst. German U. Mich., Ann Arbor, 1988-89, 91-95, lectr. German, 1995-96; asst. prof. German Western Mich. U., Kalamazoo, 1996—2001, assoc. prof. German, 2001—. Author: Maria Beig und die Kunst der scheinbaren Kunstlosigkeit, 1997, Heimat: A Critical Theory of the German Idea of Homeland, 2002, Blaulicht im Nebel, 2002; translator from the German (with Jaimy Gordon) Lost Weddings, 1990, (German) Im Schatten der Drei Schwestern, 2002. Mem. MLA, Am. Assn. Tchrs. of German, German Studies Assn., Literarisches Forum Oberschwaben, Women in German, Gesellschaft Oberschwaben, Verband deutscher Schriftsteller. Home: 1803 Hazel Ave Kalamazoo MI 49008-2843 Office: Dept Fgn Langs and Lits Western Mich Univ Kalamazoo MI 49008-5091 E-mail: blickle@wmich.edu.

BLICKWEDE, DONALD JOHNSON, retired steel company executive; b. Detroit, July 20, 1920; s. Frederic H. and Laura L. (Johnson) B.; m. Meredith Lloyd, Aug. 23, 1943; children: Karen (Mrs. Kimball J. Knowlton), Jon Frederic. BS, Wayne U., 1943; postgrad., Stevens Inst. Tech., 1943-45; ScD, Mass. Inst. Tech., 1948; postgrad., Harvard, 1969. Metallurgist Curtiss Wright Corp., 1943-45; head high temperature alloys br. Naval Research Lab., 1948-50; rsch. engr. Bethlehem Steel Corp., Pa., 1950-52, div. head, 1952-63, v.p., 1964-82. Campbell Meml. lectr. Am. Metal Congress, 1968, William Park Woodside Meml. lectr., 1969, Zay Zeffries Meml. lectr., 1970; Andrews Meml. lectr. Porcelain Enamel Inst., 1972. Fellow Am. Soc. Metals (hon., pres. 1983); mem. AIME, Am. Acad. Engring., Am. Iron and Steel Inst. (chmn. gen. rsch. com. 1971-73), Indsl. Rsch. Inst. (pres. 1975), Iron and Steel Inst. Japan (hon., Yukawa Meml. lectr. 1984). Home: 3 Surrey Run Pl The Woodlands TX 77384

BLIESNER, JAMES DOUGLAS, municipal/county official, consultant; b. Milw., Mar. 19, 1945; s. Milton Carl and Dorothy (St. George) B.; m. Phyllis Jean Byrd, June 15, 1966 (div. 1985); children: Tris, Cara. BA in Philosophy, Ea. Nazarene Coll., 1968; MA in Social Ethics, Andover, Newton Theol. Sch., 1973; postgrad., Boston U., 1969-70; student, N.Y. Studio Sch./Decordoua, Mus. Sch., Milw. Tech. Art Sch. Exec. dir. San Diego Youth and Community Svcs., 1974-78, cons., analyst San Diego Housing Commn., 1979-84; dir. San Diego City-County Reinvestment Task Force, 1984—. Founder, interim CEO S.D. Capital Collaborative; bd. dirs. Calif. Cmty. Reinvestment Corp.; vice chmn. Calif. Reinvestment Com., 1989-91; founder, chmn. City Heights Cmty. Devel. Corp., San Diego, 1980-89; fin. com. chair Mid-City Revitalization Com., San Diego, 1988; founding bd. dirs. Neighborhood Nat. Bank; instr. San Diego State U. Author monographs, 1979; visual arts exhbns. include San Diego Arts Inst., Soc. Western Artists, Santa Barbara Contemporary Arts Forum, Calif. Coun. for Humanities; films exhibited in Centro Cultural, Tijuana, Mex.; exhibited in group shows in Venice, Paris, Jerusalem, Mex., Eng., China; internat. invitee Habana Bienale. Coun. appointee City of San Diego Com. on Reapportionment, 1990, Com. on Growth and Devel., San Diego, 1989; gov. appointee Gov.'s Office of Neighborhoods, Calif., 1987; mem. City Heights Redevel. Project Com., San Diego, 1992; pres. San Diego Housing Consortium; bd. dirs. Advocates for Social Justice; com. appointee S.D. Cmty. Found. U.S.-Mex. Fund for Culture grantee, 2000, 02; recipient Award of Honor, Am. Planning Assn., 1987, Spl. Project award, 1987, Merit award, 1989, Lifetime Achievement award Non-Profit Fedn. San Diego, Outstanding Achievement award Calif. Reinvestment Commn., 1999; named Citizen of Yr. Mid-City C. of C., 1986, award Calif. Coun. Humanities, Nat. Leadership award Nat. Cmty. Reinvestment Com., 2000. Mem.: S.D. Artists Guild. Methodist. Avocation: visual arts. Home: 4106 Manzanita Dr San Diego CA 92105-4508 Office: City County Reinvestment Task Force 3989 Ruffin Rdwy Rm A6 San Diego CA 92123

BLILEY, THOMAS JEROME, JR., former congressman; b. Chesterfield County, Va., Jan. 28, 1932; s. Thomas J. and Carolyn F. Bliley; m. Mary Virginia Kelley, June 22, 1957; children: Mary Vaughan, Thomas Jerome III. BA, Georgetown U., 1952. Pres. Joseph W. Bliley Funeral Home, 1972-80; mem. U.S. Congress from 7th Va. dist., Washington, 1981-2001; former ranking minority mem. D.C. com.; former chmn. House Commerce Com.; sr. adv. govt. rels. and pub. policy Collier Shannon & Scott, Washington, 2001—. Vice-mayor Richmond City Council, 1968-70, mayor, 1970-77; past bd. dirs. Nat. League Cities; past pres. Va. Mcpl. League Past bd. dirs. Crippled Children's Hosp.; past bd. dirs. St. Mary's Hosp.; bd. visitors Va. Commonwealth U.; bd. govs. Va. Home for Boys. Served with USN. Republican. Roman Catholic. Office: Collier Shannon & Scott Washington harbour, Ste 400 3050 K St NW Ste 400 Washington DC 20007-5108

BLIM, RICHARD DON, retired pediatrician; b. Kansas City, Mo., Nov. 8, 1927; s. Miles G. and Latha Mae (Daniels) Blim; m. Myrle Rae Blim, Apr. 12, 1952; children: Richard David, Carol Rae, John Miles. BA, U. Kans., 1949, MD, 1953. Diplomate Am. Bd. Pediat. Intern U. Kans., 1953—54, resident in pediat., 1954—56; practice medicine specializing in pediat.; pres. Pediatric Assocs., Kansas City, Mo., 1956—89; dir. med. affairs St. Lukes Hosp., Kansas City, 1989—99. Peter T. Bohan lectr. U. Kans., Kansas City, 1978; Max Seham lectr. U. Minn., Mpls., 1982; mem. editl. bd. Mo. Medicine, 1978—92, Pediatric Annals, 1982—92, Pediatric News, 1983—92, Health Care Mgmt. Rev.; mem. VHA Phys. Leadership Coun. Bd. dirs. Marillac Spl. Sch. for Children, 1976—79. Served to sgt. U.S. Army, 1946—48, PTO. Named Outstanding Med. Alumnus, U. Kans. Sch. Medicine, 1978; recipient Clifford G. Grulee award, 1984, Katherine Berry Richard MD award, Children Mercy Hosp., 1997. Fellow: Am. Acad. Pediat. (chmn. Mo. chpt. 1964—67, exec. bd. 1973—80, pres. 1980—81); mem.: AMA, Coun. Med. Spltys. Soc. (rep., exec. bd. 1974—80), Met. Med. Soc. (merit award 1996), Mo. Med. Assn., S.W. Pediatric Assn. (pres. Kansas City 1963), Jackson County Med. Soc. (pres. 1973), Inst. Medicine NAS, Kans. U. Med. Alumni (pres. 1973), Loch Lloyd Club, Alpha Omega Alpha. Republican. Presbyterian. Home: 100 W 172d St Belton MO 64012

BLIND, JOY BAILEY, women's health nurse; b. Greenwood, S.C., Feb. 20, 1963; d. Hiram Earl and Marlene Courtney Bailey; m. Stanley Thomas Blind, Dec. 22, 1984; children: Melanie, Jennifer, Kenneth Robert. AD, Lander Coll., 1984. Nat. cert. low risk neonatal nursing. Nursing asst. Med. Coll. of Ga., Augusta; ARC nurse Hahn AFB (Fed. Republic of Germany) Hosp.; ob-gyn. nurse Marian Med. Ctr., Santa Maria, Calif., Lompoc (Calif.) Community Hosp.; level II nurse Beaufort (S.C.) Meml. Hosp.; sch. nurse Dept. Health and Environ. Control, St. Matthews, SC; dir. nursing and patient care svcs. Allendale County Hosp., Fairfax. Home: 105 Coachman Dr Lexington SC 29072 E-mail: jblind@sc.rr.com., don@achospital.org.

BLINDER, ABE LIONEL, management consultant; b. Osage, Iowa, Nov. 7, 1909; s. Heimer and Fanny (Zellner) B.; children: Henry David, Jonathan. Ph.B., U. Chgo., 1931. Circulation mgr. Apparel Arts, Chgo., 1932-33, Esquire, Inc., Chgo., 1933-36, circulation dir., 1936-45, dir., 1945-84, v.p., 1945-51, exec. v.p., 1952-61, pres., 1961-77, chmn. bd., 1977-80, chmn. internat. ops., treas., 1984-2000, cons., 1984-89. Bd. dirs., vice chmn. Alliance for Resident Theatres, N.Y.C. Mem. Phi Beta Kappa. Clubs: Harmonie (N.Y.C.); Metropolis Country. Home: 5 Horseguard Ln Scarsdale NY 10583-2310

BLINDER, ALBERT ALLAN, judge; b. N.Y.C., Nov. 27, 1925; s. William and Sarah (Gold) B.; m. Meredith Zaretzki, Nov. 16, 1961 (dec.); 1 child, Adam Z.; m. Joan Goodman, Jan. 20, 1985 (dec.). AB, NYU, 1944, postgrad., 1944-45; JD, Harvard U., 1948. Bar: N.Y. 1949, U.S. Dist. Ct. (so. dist.) N.Y. 1953, U.S. Ct. Appeals (2d cir.) 1953, U.S. Supreme Ct. 1967. Asst. U.S. atty. for so. dist. N.Y., 1950-53; asst. counsel N.Y.C. Bd. High Edn., 1953-54; asst. dist. atty. County of Bronx, N.Y., 1954-60; ptnr. Saxe, Bacon & O'Shea, N.Y.C., 1960-64, Blinder, Steinhaus & Hochhauser, N.Y.C., 1965-73; judge N.Y. State Ct. Claims, 1973-96; jud. hearing officer N.Y. State Supreme Ct., 1996—. Rsch. counsel N.Y. Commn. on Law of Estates, 1965; assoc. counsel N.Y. Commn. Revision of Penal Law, 1966-70; asst. counsel N.Y. Commn. on Eminent Domain, 1970-73; rsch. asst. N.Y. Commn. State Ct. System, 1971-73. Assoc. editor Am. Criminal Law Quar., 1968-70, mem. adv. bd., 1969-70. Mem.: ABA, Am. Judges Assn., Am. Arbitration Assn. (nat. panel arbitrators 1965—73), N.Y. County Lawyers Assn., Assn. Bar City N.Y., N.Y. State Bar Assn., Internat. Bar Assn. Office: 115 Broadway Fl 15 New York NY 10006-1604 E-mail: ABLINDER@aol.com.

BLINDER, BARTON JEROME, physician, psychiatrist, psychoanalyst, educator; b. Phila., July 30, 1938; s. Jacob Herman Blinder ans Sarah Podolsky; m. Roberta Mildred Blinder, June 26, 1960; children: Madaline, David, Andrea. BA, U. Pa., 1960, MD, 1964; PhD, So. Calif. Psychoanalytic Inst, 1990. Diplomate Am. Bd. Psychiatry and Neurology, Am. Bd. Child Psychiatry. Resident in psychiatry U. Pa., Phila., 1965-69, resident in child psychiatry, 1965-69; clin. prof. dept. psychiatry Coll. of Medicine, U. Calif., Irvine, 1972—; pvt. practice in adult and child psychiatry/psychoanalysis Newport Beach, 1971—; dir. eating disorder rsch. dept. psychiatry U. Calif., Irvine, 1981—. Rschr. in field. Editor: Eating Disorders, 1988; editor: Child Psychiatric Research and Treatment, 1980, Emotional Disorder in Children and Adolescents, 1980; contbr. articles to profl. jours. Maj. USAF, 1969-71. Fellow Am. Psychiat. Assn. (life, assembly rep. com. 1985-2001), Am. Acad. Child and Adolescent Psychiatry (pres. local chpt. 1989—). Democrat. Jewish. Avocations: swimming, sports, historical scholarship, religious history. Office: 400 Newport Center Dr Ste 706 Newport Beach CA 92660-7661

BLINDER, JANET, art dealer; b. L.A., Sept. 21, 1953; d. Joseph and Margaret (Nadel) Weiss; m. Martin S. Blinder, Dec. 10, 1983. Founder Nationwide Baby Shops, Santa Monica, Calif., 1976-82; adminstr. Martin Lawrence Ltd. Editions, Van Nuys, Calif., 1982-90; art dealer L.A., 1990—. Mem. benefit com. AIDS Project L.A., 1988, prin. sponsor ann. fundraiser, 1990; mem. benefit com. Art Against AIDS, L.A., 1989; patron, sponsor Maryvale Orphanage, Rosemead, Calif., 1984—; patron Scottsdale Ctr. for the Arts. Recipient Commendation for Philanthropic Efforts City of L.A. Mayor Tom Bradley, 1988. Mem. Mus. Modern Art, Whitney Mus. Am. Art, Guggenheim Mus., Palm Springs (Calif.) Mus. Art, Mus. of Contemporary Art, Scottsdale (Ariz.) Ctr. for the Arts.

BLINDER, MARTIN S. business consultant, art dealer; b. Bklyn., Nov. 18, 1946; s. Meyer and Lillian (Stein) B.; m. Janet Weiss, Dec. 10, 1983. BBA, Adelphi U., 1968. Acct. exec. Bruns, Nordeman & Co., N.Y.C., 1968-69; v.p. Blinder, Robinson & Co., Westbury, NY, 1969-73; treas. BHB Prodns., L.A., 1973-76; pres. Martin Lawrence Ltd. Edits., Van Nuys, Calif., 1976-94, chmn., 1986-94, bd. dirs., 1994—; dir. AZ/NY Gallery, Scottsdale, Ariz., 2000—. Pres., dir. Corp. Art Inc., Visual Artists Mgmt. Corp., Art Consultants Inc.; pres., owner, founder MSB Fine Art, Phoenix, 1994—; lectr. bus. symposia. Contbr. articles to mags. and newspapers; appeared on TV and radio. Mem. Dem. Nat. Com., benefit com. AIDS project, L.A., 1988; bd. dirs. Very Spl. Arts, 1989—, chmn. visual arts Internat. Very Spl. Arts Festival, 1989; patron Guggenheim Mus., N.Y.C., Mus. Modern Art, N.Y.C., L.A. County Mus. Art, L.A. Mus. Contemporary Art (hon. founder), Whitney Mus. Am. Art, Palm Springs Mus. Art, Hirschorn Mus., Washington, Skirball Mus., L.A., Diabetes Found. of City of Hope, B'nai B'rith Anti-Defamation League, 1999, Very Spl. Arts, Scottsdale (Ariz.) Ctr. for the Arts, Scottsdale Mus. Contemporary Art (lectr. on Keith Haring); mem. Citizens for Common Sense; bd. dirs., pres. Rsch. Found. for Crohns Disease; mem. benefit com. Art Against AIDS, 1989; co-chair artists com. for Don't Bungle the Jungle Companions of Arts and Nature, 1989; prin. sponsor, ann. fundraiser AIDS Project, L.A., 1990. Recipient resolution of commendation L.A. City Coun., 1983, State of Calif. resolution for contbn. to arts in Calif., 1983, Merit award Republic Haiti for contbn. to arts, 1985, U.S. Senate commendations, 1983, County of L.A. Bd. Suprs. resolution for contbn. to arts in So. Calif., 1983, Gov. of R.I. resolution for contbns. to arts, 1985, commendation County of L.A.-Supr. Ed Edelman, 1991, commendation for contbns. to the arts and the healing arts City of L.A., 1991, commendation for contbns. to arts and philanthropy Mayor David Dinkins, N.Y.C., 1992; Nov. 18, 1985 declared Martin S. Blinder Day in L.A. in his honor by Mayor Tom Bradley, spl. award San Diego Youth and Cmty. Svcs., Bruin Bear award for establishing Blinder Rsch. Found., UCLA Sch. Medicine, 1994. Mem. Fine Art Pub.'s Assn. (bd. dirs. 1990-94), Med. Art Assn. at UCLA. Office: MSB Fine Art PO Box H82013 Scottsdale AZ 85251

BLINKEN, DONALD, ambassador, investment banker; b. N.Y.C., Nov. 11, 1925; s. Maurice Henry and Ethel (Horowitz) B.; m. Vera Evans, Oct. 15, 1975; 1 child, Antony John. BA magna cum laude, Harvard U., 1947. Cons. Marks & Spencer, Ltd., London, 1950-51; pres. Exchange Trading Corp., N.Y.C., 1952-53; v.p. Stein's Stores, Inc., N.Y.C., 1953-58, E.M. Warburg & Co., Inc., 1961-72; sr. v.p., chmn. exec. com. E.M. Warburg, Pincus & Co., Inc., N.Y.C., 1970-81, mng. dir., 1981-86, dir., 1987-94; U.S. amb. Budapest, Hungary, 1994-97; dir. Ion Track Instruments, Inc., 2000—02. Author: Wool Tariffs and American Policy, 1948; chmn. publ. com. Commentary, 1984-87. Pres. Bklyn. Acad. Music, 1971—76, Mark Rothko Found., 1976—88; mem. trustees' coun. Nat. Gallery Art, 1984—94; trustee SUNY, 1976—2000, chmn. bd., 1978—90; bd. dirs. N.Y. Philharmonic Soc., 1986—94, vice chmn., 1989—94; mem. U.S. 2d Circuit Nominating Panel, 1979; trustee Manville Personal Injury Settlement Trust, 1986—91, N.Y. Pub. Libr., 1990—94; dir. Inst. Internat. Edn., 1990—94, hon. trustee, 1999—; trustee Isamu Noguchi Found., 1987—94; bd. overseers Nelson Rockefeller Inst. Govt., 1985—94; chancellor Internat. Coun. Ctrl. European U., 1998—2001; trustee Ctrl. European U., 2001—; mem. adv. bd. Sch. Internat. and Pub. Affairs, Columbia U., 1998—; mem. exec. com. Citizens Democracy Corps, 1999—; hon. bd. dirs. N.Y. Philharm. Soc., 1999—; hon. trustee Inst. Internat. Edn., 1999—; sec.-gen. World Fedn. UN Assns., 2000—. With USAAF, 1944—45. Mem. Century Assn. Club, River Club (N.Y.C.), Coun. Fgn. Rels., Coun. Am. Ambs. Home: 435 E 52nd St New York NY 10022-6445 Office: 466 Lexington Ave New York NY 10017-3140

BLINKEN, ROBERT JAMES, manufacturing and communications company executive; b. N.Y.C., Apr. 18, 1929; s. Maurice Henry and Ethel (Horowitz) B.; m. Jeanne Pagnucco, Mar. 5, 1955 (div. Jan. 1967); children: Robert James, Rachel; m. Allison Matsner, Dec. 14, 1967; children: Anna, Ingrid. Grad., Horace Mann Sch., N.Y.C., 1946; BA cum laude, Harvard U., 1950. Pres. Teleprinter Corp., Paramus, N.J., 1953-61; v.p. Mite Corp., New Haven, 1961-63, pres., 1963-75, chmn., 1975-85, Comm. Network Enhancement, Mountainside, N.J., 1986—. Trustee Albright Inst. Archeol. Rsch., N.Y. Blood Ctr. Served to 1st lt. USAF, 1950-53. Office: 230 Park Ave Fl 26 New York NY 10169-2699

BLISH, RICHARD CLARK, II, reliability engineering manager; b. Chgo., Mar. 17, 1942; s. Richard Clark and June Frodin Blish; m. Susan Lindsay Spencer, Sept. 7, 1963; children: William Spencer, Catherine Anne. BS in Physics, Calif. Inst. Tech., 1963, MS in Materials Sci. and Econs., 1964, PhD in Materials Sci. and Econs., 1967. Mem. tech. staff Bell Labs., Murray Hill, N.J., 1967-69; from mem. tech. staff to sr. scientist Signetics, Inc., Sunnyvale, Calif., 1969-80; mgr. package reliability engring. Intel Corp., Santa Clara, Calif., 1980-84, mgr. package reliability fundamentals and failure analysis Chandler, Ariz., 1984-87, mgr. ASIC/C4 reliability Santa Clara, 1987-88, project mgr. microcomputer group and components rsch., 1988-93, project mgr. next generation TAB Chandler, 1993-94; sr. mem. tech. staff Advanced Micro Devices, Sunnyvale, Calif., 1995-98, AMD fellow reliability engring., 1998—. Chair SEMATECH Reliability Tech. Adv. Bd., Austin, Tex., 2000-2001. Editor: (jour.) IEEE-Tech. of Devices & Materials Rsch., 2000; patentee in field; contbr. tech. papers to profl. jours. and symposia. Precinct dir. Calif. Assembly candidate, San Jose, 1974; bd. advisors Adolescent Counseling Svcs., Palo Alto, Calif., 1998-2001. Mem. IEEE (sr., sec., vice chair Silicon Valley sect. CPMT), Internat. Reliability Physics Symposium (chair bd. dirs. 1994-95, chair product reliability session 2000-2001, mem. tech. program com. for packaging 1995—, Best Paper award 1983), IEDM (mem. tech. program), Caltech Alumni Assn. (dir.), Sigma Xi. Democrat. Achievements include patents in field. Avocations: bicycling, political action, abstract art, classical music. Office: Advanced Micro Devices PO Box 3453 1 AMD Pl MS 143 Sunnyvale CA 94088-3453 E-mail: richard.blish@amd.com.

BLISS, DONALD TIFFANY, JR., lawyer; b. Norwalk, Conn., Nov. 24, 1941; s. Donald Tiffany and Marina (Popova) B.; m. Nancy Arnold, Sept. 14, 1974; children: Evan Hale, Bion Northam. JD, Harvard U., 1966. Bar: N.Y. 1969, D.C. 1971, U.S. Dist. Ct. D.C. 1975, U.S. Ct. Appeals (D.C. cir.) 1971, 84, U.S. Supreme Ct. 1975. Atty. Peace Corps, 1966-67; legis. counsel Congress of Micronesia, 1968; cons. judiciary, American Samoa, 1968; assoc. firm LeBoeuf, Lamb, Leiby & McCrae, N.Y.C., 1969; asst. to sec. HEW, 1969-72; spl. asst. to adminstr. EPA, 1972-73; exec. sec. AID, 1973-74; dep. gen. counsel U.S. Dept. Transp., 1975-77, acting. gen. counsel, 1976-77; ptnr. and chair, transp. practice group firm O'Melveny & Myers, Washington, 1979—. Mem. Maritime Adv. Com., 1984-85; pres. Harvard Law Sch. Assn. D.C., 1985-86; chmn. transp. sect. FBA, 1987-90; mem. interior task force Grace Commn.; nat. pres. The Ripon Soc. Author: The Law of Airline Customer Relations: Stability, Security, Safety and Service, 2002, Drug Testing and Federal Employees: Lessons from the Transportation Experience, 1988, Economic Deregulation and Safety: Are The Compatible, 1989, A Challenge to the U.S. Aviation Leadership: Launching the New Era of Global Aviation, 1991, Supreme Court Preemption Analysis: Differentiating the Hamiltonians and Jeffersonians, 1993; play The Return of Halley's Comet, 2002. Trustee Studio Theatre; trustee, 1st v.p. Arts for the Aging; pres. Dara's Canine Found., Inc. Recipient spl. citation HEW, 1972, 73, Pres.'s Cert. Exec. Mgmt., 1973, Superior Achievement award Dept. Transp., 1976. Mem. ABA (chmn. air and space law forum 1997-99), D.C. Bar Assn. (co-chmn. sect. adminstrv. law and agy. practice 1988-90), City Club D.C., Chevy Chase Club. Home: 6732 Newbold Dr Bethesda MD 20817-2223 Office: O'Melveny & Myers 555 13th St NW Ste 500W Washington DC 20004-1159 E-mail: dbliss@omm.com.

BLISS, RICHARD JON, lawyer; b. Rice Lake, Wis., Apr. 27, 1951; s. Richard Burt and Lolly (Davis) B.; m. Susan Elizabeth Ramage, June 19, 1976; children: Jon, Steve, Brock. BA, Wheaton (Ill.) Coll., 1973; JD, U. Wis., 1976. Bar: Wis. 1976, U.S. Dist. Ct. (ea. dist.) Wis. 1976. Assoc. Godfrey & Kahn, S.C., Milw., 1976-82, shareholder, 1983—, mng. ptnr., pres., 1996—. Bd. dirs. Ward Adhesives, Inc., Runzheimer Internat., Inc. Note editor U. Wis. Law Rev., 1975-76. Bd. dirs. Vine and Brs. Found., Inc., Milw., 1996—, Milw. Ctr. for Independence, 1993-98, Neighborhood House, Inc., Serve Enterprises, Inc. Mem. Univ. Club of Milw., Town Club, Milw. Club. Avocations: aviation, tennis. Home: 706 E Lexington Blvd Whitefish Bay WI 53217-5338 Office: Godfrey & Kahn SC 780 N Water St Ste 1500 Milwaukee WI 53202-3590 E-mail: rbliss@gklaw.com.

BLISS, RICK WAYNE, engineer; b. Rupert, Idaho, Apr. 7, 1953; s. Delford Victor Bliss and Naomia Katherine Olenslager; m. Colleen Taggart, July 27, 1985; children: Richard Halley, Christopher Taggart. BS in Physics, U. Utah, 1975, MS in Mech. Engring., 1976. Registered profl. engr., Utah. Tech. specialist Hercules, Inc., Magna, Utah, 1976—95; sr. engr. ATK, Magna, 1995—. Contbr. articles to profl. jours. Chair Bluffdale City Parks Com., 1991—93; founding mem., chair South Valley Jordan River Pkwy., 1993—; chair, pres. Found. for the Provo/Jordan River Pkwy., Salt Lake City, 1996—2000. Recipient Svc. award, Lions, Bluffdale, 1993, Recognition award, Bluffdale City, 2000. Mem.: AIAA. Achievements include development of advanced constitutive model that has been incorporated in LLNL's Nikead; advanced micromechanics model for composite kimina; quater math. Home: 1945 Rock Hollow Rd Bluffdale UT 84065

BLISS, ROBERT HARMS, lawyer; b. Paris, Tex., Nov. 20, 1940; s. Jack Edward and Ruth Eugenia (Harms) B.; m. Juliee Dixie Fuselier, Dec. 29, 1964; 1 child, Katherine Elaine. BA, U. Colo., 1964; JD, U. Tex., 1967. Bar: Tex. 1967; cert. civil trial specialist, mediator-arbitrator, spl. master. Since practiced in, Dallas; assoc. Johnson, Bromberg, Leeds & Riggs, 1967-72; ptrn. Bliss, Danner & Bishop, 1972-74; individual practice, 1974; pres. Bliss & Hughes, P.C., Dallas, 1978-88; pvt. practice Robert Harms Bliss P.C., 1988-98; ptnr. Glast, Phillips & Murray, PC, 1998—2002; pvt. practice, 2002—. Mem. faculty advanced real estate law State Bar Tex., 1985, 92-93, 95, 97, 99, 2000, 02; mem. faculty CLE series So. Meth. U. Sch. Law, Dallas, 1989, 92, 94, 97, 98, 99, 2000; mem. faculty Mortgage Lending Inst., U. Tex. Sch. Law, 1994, 97, 98, 99, 2000, mem. faculty advanced real estate drafting course, 1995, 2000-02, course dir., 2002. Contbr. articles to profl. jours. Bd. dirs. Dallas Symphony Orch. Guild, Dallas Classic Guitar Soc.; mem. Gov.'s Task Force on Immigration, 1983-84, Tex. Real Estate Commn., 1983-87; adv. bd. Tex. Real Estate Rsch. Ctr., Tex. A&M U., 1985-87; ch. atty. Episcopal Diocese Dallas. Mem. Am. Coll. Real Estate Lawyers, State Bar Tex. (past chair real estate, probate and trust sect.), Dallas Bar Assn. (past chmn. real property sect.), Tex. Coll. Real Estate Attys., Assn. Atty.-Mediators (pres.), U. Tex. Tchg. Quiz-Masters Assn., Phi Delta Phi. Home: 29 Ashton Ct Dallas TX 75230-1977 Office: PO Box 12825 Dallas TX 75225

BLISS, RONALD GLENN, lawyer; b. Buckeye, Ariz., Mar. 22, 1943; s. Glenn Francis Bliss and Jessie Marie (Waymire) Harrington; m. Charlene Wallace, Sept. 18, 1965; children: Erik, Jason. BS, USAF Acad., 1964; JD, Baylor U., 1976. Bar: Tex. 1976, U.S. Dist. Ct. (so. dist.) Tex. 1977, (no. dist.) Tex. 1981, (we. dist.) Tex. 1985, U.S. Ct. Appeals (5th cir.) 1979, (11th cir.) 1982, (D.C. cir.) 1982, U.S. Supreme Ct. 1980. Capt., fighter pilot USAF, U.S., Vietnam, 1964-74; prisoner of war Vietnam, 1966-73; assoc. Fulbright & Jaworski, Houston, 1976-84, ptnr., 1984—. Mem. adv. com. So. Dist. Tex., 1992; chmn. Tex. Aerospace Commn., 1995-96. Contbr. to profl. jours. Pres. Norchester Club Inc., 1980; bd. dirs. Athletic Club Houston, 1984-85; bd. govs. Houston Center Club, 1987—, cert. mediator. Inductee Tex. Aviation Hall of Fame. Mem.: ABA, Houston Intellectual Property Law Assn., Am. Intellectual Property Law Assn., Tex. Bar Assn., 4th Allied POW Wing. Office: Fulbright & Jaworski LLP 1301 Mckinney St Ste 5100 Houston TX 77010-3031 E-mail: rbliss@fulbright.com.

BLISSETT, WILLIAM FRANK, English literature educator; b. East End, Sask., Can., Oct. 11, 1921; s. Ralph Richardson and Gladys (Jones) B. BA, U. B.C., 1943; MA, U. Toronto, 1946, PhD, 1950. Lectr dept. English U. Toronto, 1946-50, prof. English, 1965-87, prof. emeritus, 1987; assoc. prof. dept. English U. Sask., 1950-57, prof., 1957-60; prof., head dept. English Huron Coll., London, Ont., 1960-65. Author: The Long Conversation, 1981; editor: Editing Illustrated Books, 1980; editor U. Toronto Quar., 1965-76; adv. bd.: Ency. of Shakespeare and Music, 1991, Chesterton Rev., 1984—; co-editor: Spenser Ency., 1982-90; joint editor: A Celebration of Ben Jonson, 1974; subject of book: Craft and Tradition: Essays in Honour of William Blissett, 1990. Huron Coll. hon. fellow, 1966; Royal Soc. Can. fellow, 1979 Mem. Internat. Assn. Univ. Profs. English, David Jones Soc. Anglican.

BLISSITT, PATRICIA ANN, nurse; b. Knoxville, Tenn., Sept. 23, 1953; d. Dewitt Talmadge and Imogene (Bailey) B. BSN with high honors, U. Tenn., 1976, MSN, 1985; PhD in Nursing, U. Wash., 2002; postgrad., U. Pa., 2003—. RN; cert. in case mgmt., trauma nurse core course, ACLS. Staff nurse neurosci. unit City of Memphis Hosp., 1976-78, head nurse neurosci. unit, 1978-79; physician's asst. Dr. John D. Wilson, Columbus, Miss., 1979-81; staff nurse med.-surg.-trauma ICU U. Tenn. Meml. Hosp., Knoxville, 1982-83; staff nurse neurosci. ICU Bapt. Meml. Hosp., Memphis, 1985-86, clin. nurse specialist neurosci., 1986-94, trauma coord., 1991-93, neuro case mgr., 1993-94; staff nurse neurosurg. ICU Harborview Med. Ctr., Seattle, 1994—2000, 2001—02; NIH postdoctoral fellow neuro critical care U. Pa., Phila., 2003—; neurotrauma staff nurse surg. ICU Hosp. U. Pa., 2003—. Nurse cons. neurosci. VA Hosp., Memphis, 1986; adv. com. Tenn. Bd. Nursing Practice; mem. test devel. com. Am. Bd. Neurosci. Nursing, 1996-2001, trustee, 2000-03, treas., 2002-03, chair test devel. com., 2003—. Author: (with others) Critical Care Nursing in Clinics of North America, 1990, Jour. Neurosci. Nursing, 1986, 92, 96, 2001, 03, Guidelines for Critical Care Nursing, Care Management, 2001; abstractor: Nursing SCAN in Critical Care, 1995-99; contbr. articles to sci. jour., chpt. to book; mem. editl. cons. bd. Focus on Critical Care, 1990-92. Mem. rev. com. Neurosci. Nursing Found./AANN Scholarship com., 2001. Grantee biobehavioral nursing tng. grantee, NIH/NINR/U. Wash., 1999—2002; scholar scholarship, AANN Scholar Com., 2001, Wash. State Nurses Found., 1998, Am. Assn. Neurosci. Nurses, 1999. Mem.: ANA (mem. coun. med.-surg. nurses, cert. med.-surg. clin. nurse specialist), AACN (life; pres.-elect Greater Memphis area chpt. 1989—90, mem. CCRN corp. exam. devel. com. 1989—92, pres. 1990—91, editl. cons. bd. 1990—92, past pres., chair nat. critical care awareness week 1990—93, chpt. cons. Region II 1991—93, NTI spkr. 1992, chpt. of yr. com. chair 1992—94, NTI spkr. 1993, chair-elect Puget Sound chpt. program 1995—96, chair program com. 1996—97, editor elect newsletter Puget Sound chpt. 1997—98, mem. program com. 1997—2003, newsletter editor Puget Sound chpt. 1998—99, pres.-elect 1999—2001, pres. 2002—03, cert., lectr., edn. com. 2003—, newsletter com. 2003—), Neurocritical Care Soc. (charter), Tenn. Nursing Congress (pres. 1990—94), Western Inst. Nursing, Tenn. Nurses Assn. (mem. com. on practice 1992—93), Wash. Nurses Assn., Am. Assn. Spinal Cord Injury Nurses, Am. Assn. Neurosci. Nurses (pres. local chpt. 1989—90, program/seminar chair local chpt. 1990—93, program/seminar chair mid-South chpt. 1990—93, chair nat. resource devel. com. 1992—94, pres. Memphis chpt. 1995—98, editor newsletter 1998—2000, chair role delineation study task force 2000—01, editor newsletter 2001—02, cert. neursci. nurse, nat. lectr., mem., chmn. resource devel. com., nurse practice com., mem. contg. edn./ann. sci. program com.), Am. Assn. Neurol. Surgeons (assoc.), Sigma Theta Tau. Methodist. Avocation: music. Home: 2200 Benjamin Franklin Pkwy W 610 Philadelphia PA 19130 E-mail: blissitp@uphs.upenn.edu.

BLITMAN, HOWARD NORTON, construction company executive; b. N.Y.C., Dec. 9, 1926; s. Charles H. and Anna (Palestine) B.; m. Maureen Lefcort-Winter, 1975. CE, Rensselaer Poly. Inst., 1950; MA, New Sch. Social Research, 1973. Registered profl. engr., N.Y., N.J., Conn., Mass., S.C. Field engr. Drier Structural Steel Co., N.Y., 1950-51; design engr. Blitman & Tischler, N.Y.C., 1952-60; project engr. Blitman Constrn. Corp., N.Y.C., 1960-61, coordinator, 1961-62, exec. v.p., 1962-69, pres., 1969-81; pres., dir. Blitman

Bldg. Corp., 1981—. Mem. housing com. State Constnl. Conv., 1968; mem. N.Y.C. Commn. Investigation Water Main Breaks; chmn. adv. bd. to dept. civil engring. Rensselaer Poly. Inst., 1999—. Mem. sch. bd. Mt. Pleasant Cottage Sch., Union Free Sch. Dist., Pleasantville, N.Y.; pres., bd. dirs. Jewish Child Care Assn. N.Y.; v.p. bd. dirs. Beth Israel Med. Ctr.; mem. coun. Rensselaer Poly. Inst. ; chmn. archtl. rev. bd. Town of Scarsdale, N.Y., trustee 1989-93; trustee Village of Scarsdale, 1989, dep. mayor, 1992—; mem. Planning Bd. Scarsdale, 1994—, chmn., 1998—. 2d lt. Chem. Corps AUS, 1944-47; 1st lt., 1951-53. Recipient Norman Tishman Human Rels. award, 1967, Albert DeMers medal, Rensselaer Poly. Inst. Fellow: NSPE (chmn. profl. engrs. in constrn., pres. 1997, chmn. 1996—97, nat. treas. 1999—2001, pres.-elect 2001—02, pres. 2002—03); mem.: ASME, ASCE, N.Y. State Soc. Profl. Engrs. (pres. 1978, pres. N.Y. chpt. 1974—75), Harmonie Club (N.Y.C.), Masons (N.Y.C.). Home: 3 Elmdorf Dr Scarsdale NY 10583-4203

BLITT, RITA LEA, artist; b. Kansas City, Mo., Sept. 7, 1931; d. Herman Stanley and Dorothy Edith (Sofnas) Copaken; m. Irwin Joseph Blitt, Apr. 18, 1951; 1 child, Chela ne Connie. Student, U. Ill., 1948-50; BA, Kans. City U., 1952; postgrad., Kans. City Art Inst., 1951-55. Painter/sculptor, Aspen, Colo., Emeryville, Calif., Leawood, Kans. Author: Nessie the Sculpture, 1978; author: (video), 1993, (7-minute video) Flag: 1976, 1976; subject (audio interview) Goodnewsbroadcast, collaborations with dancers and musicians St. Joseph Ballet, Santa Ana, Calif., 1995, dancer/choreographer David Parsons, 1996, cellist Yehuda Hanani, 1986, creator words and paintings for internat. distributed poster "Kindness is Contagious, Catch It!", led to the founding of the Kindness Program sponsored by the Stop Violence Coalition; one-woman shows include Unitarian Gallery, Kansas City, Mo., 1965, Hall's, 1967, Spectrum Gallery, N.Y.C., 1969, Johnson County C.C., Overland Park, Kans., 1974, 1979, Angerer Gallery, Kansas City, Mo., 1974, Battle Creek (Mich.) Civic Art Ctr., 1975, Harkness Gallery, N.Y.C., 1977, Martin Schweig Gallery, St. Louis, 1977, Gargoyle Gallery, Aspen, Colo., 1978, Tumbling Waters Mus., Montgomery, Ala., 1978, St. Louis U., 1980, Rockhurst Coll., Kansas City, Mo., 1984, Jewish Cmty. Ctr., Omaha, Nebr., 1984, 2001, Ctrl. Exch., Kansas City, Mo., 1985, 1991, 1995, Leedy-Voulkos Gallery, 1987, Joy Horwich Gallery, Chgo., 1987, Goldman Gallery, Haifi, Israel, 1989, Bet Shmuel, Jerusalem, 1989, Mark Twain Bank, Kansas City, Mo., 1989, 1990, Goldman Kraft Gallery, Chgo., 1990, Singapore Nat. Mus., 1991, Albrecht-Kemper Mus., St. Joseph, Mo., 1991, Aspen (Colo.) Inst., 1992, Foothills Art Ctr., Golden, Colo., 1992, Mackey Gallery, Denver, 1992, Jewish Cmty. Campus, Overland Park, Kans., 1992, U. Ill., Urbana, 1994, Kennedy Mus., U. Ohio, Athens, 1994, Krasl Art Ctr., St. Joseph, Mich., 1994, La Quinta Sculpture Park, La Quinta, Calif., 1994, Baker U., Baldwin, Kans., 1995, Aatchison (Kans.) Muchnik Gallery, 1996, Marines Meml. Theater, San Francisco, 1997, Resourceful Women, 1997, City Ctr., N.Y., 1998, Brandeis U., Waltham, Mass., 2000, Leedy Voulkos Art Ctr., 2001, Aspen Dance Theater, 2001, Marion Meyer Contemporary Art, Laguna, Calif., 2001—, Walter Wickisen Gallery, N.Y.C., exhibited in group shows at Kansas City (Mo.) Mus., 1959, Ringling Mus., Sarasota, Fla., 1967, Springfield (Mo.) Mus., 1967, Joslyn Mus., Omaha, 1972, Doug Drake Gallery, Kansas City, 1975, Conry Gallery, Kansas City, Mo., 1976, Cyvia Gallery, New Haven, 1977, Gargoyle Gallery, Aspen, Colo., 1979, Putney Gallery, Aspen, 1979, Carrefour Gallery, N.Y.C., 1979, Elaine Benson Gallery, Bridgehampton, N.Y., 1980, Tall Grass Fine Arts Gallery, Kansas City, Mo., 1980, 1981, Art and Design Gallery, N.Y.C., 1982, Winter Manhattan (Kans.) Streker Gallery, 1983, Joanne Lyons Gallery, Aspen, 1984, Banaker Gallery, 1987, 1988, Andrea Ross Gallery, Santa Monica, Calif., 1990, LA 90, L.A., 1990, Eva Cohon, Chgo., 1995, Oberle Galerie, Berlin, 1995, Din Deutsches Inst., 1995, Nat. Mus. Women in Arts, Beijing, China, 1995, Dance Aspen, Colo., 1997, The Art Source, Indpls., 1998, Paula Vincenti Gallery, Marbella, Spain, 1999, Marion Meyer Contemporary Art, Laguna Beac, Calif.;; Represented in permanent collections Albrecht Kemper Mus., St. Joseph, Mo., Am. Embassy, Barbados, Ga. Inst. Tech., JFK Libr., Cambridge, Mass., Kennedy Mus. Ohio U., Athens, Nat. Mus. Singapore, Skirball Mus., L.A., Spencer Mus. Art. U. Kans., Lawrence, Spertus Mus., Chgo., Kansas City (Mo.) Children's Mus., Ga. Tech. Ctr. for the Arts, I-Lan Taiwan City Hall, other numerous pub. and pvt. collections, Conservatory of Music and Sci. Bldgs., U. Mo., Kansas City; sculptures in numerous pub. places including Australia, Calif., Ill., Kans., Mo., Md., N.Y., N.J., Japan, Singapore, Israel, print sent to every country in the UN and Palestinian Liberation Orgn. in honor of Norway helping Israel and the Palestinian Liberation Orgn.'s first steps toward peace, 1993; one-woman shows include Nev. Mus. Art, Reno, 2003, Penn Valley C.C., Kansas City, Mo., 2003, Michelson Mus., Marshall, Tex., 2003; author: Rita Blitt: The Passionate Gesture, 2000 (ltd. edit. includes 6⊒"x6⊒" wood sculpture, Omni Award). Mem. Soc. Fellow The Nelson Gallery Found., The Aspen Inst.; bd. dirs. Trio Found.; mem. The Stop Violence Coalition; rsch. assoc. The Internat. Rsch. on Jewish Women. Co-honoree Parsons Dance Co., 2000. Mem. Internat. Sculpture Ctr., Kansas City Artists Coalition. Avocations: music, dance, travel, walking. E-mail: rita@ritablitt.com.

BLITZ, BRIAN G. mathematician, educator; b. White Plains, N.Y., Nov. 22, 1968; s. Alan I. and Phebe A. Blitz; m. Catherine L. Tide, June 1, 2002. BS, U. of Chgo., 1990; MS, No. Ariz. U., 1994; PhD, Wash. State U., 2000. Asst. prof. of math. U. of Alaska S.E., Juneau, Alaska, 2000—. Adv. bd. Alaska Coun. of Tchrs. of Math., Alaska. Mem.: Math. Assn. Am. Office: University of Alaska Southeast 11120 Glacier Highway Juneau AK 99801 E-mail: brian.blitz@uas.alaska.edu.

BLITZ, CHARLES AKIN, lawyer; b. Honolulu, Sept. 2, 1949; s. Howard Samuel and Marjorie C. (Cooke) B.; m. Karen Lee Sherwood, May 6, 1976; children: C. Tyler, Derek A., Colby S. BA, Willamette U., 1972; JD, Lewis & Clark Coll., 1975; LLM in Labor and Employment, Georgetown U., 1979. Bar: Wash. Supreme Ct., 2002, Oreg. Supreme Ct., 1975, U.S. Dist. Ct. (Oreg.), 1975, U.S. Dist. Ct. (9th cir.), 1975, U.S. Mil. Ct. Appeals, 1976, U.S. Ct. Appeals (4th cir.), 1977, U.S. Ct. Appeals (DC cir.), 1978, U.S. Supreme Ct., 1979. Assoc. Cass Scott Woods & Smith, Eugene, Oreg., 1979-82; asst. atty. gen. Oreg. Dept. Justice, Salem, 1982-83; assoc. Spears Lubersky Law Firm, Portland, 1983-85; ptnr. Lane Powell Spears Lubersky, Portland, 1985-98; shareholder Bullard Smith Jernstedt Wilson, Portland, 1998—. Legal advisor Hillsboro Police Dept. Author: Model Policies and Procedures for Special Districts, Including Administrative Rules, 1994, 2nd edit., 1996, 3rd edit., 2002. Chmn. Civil Svc. Reform Task Force for the City of Portland, 1985-86, Enhanced Sheriff's Patrol Dist. Bd., Washington County Sheriff's Office, Hillsboro, Oreg., 1988-91; asst. scoutmaster, coun. v.p., chmn. risk mgmt. and Butte Creek Ranch com. Cascade Pacific Coun., Boy Scouts Am., Portland, 1988—; mem. Citizens Crime Commn., Portland, 1992-03; exec. bd. mem. Cascade Pacific Coun., Boy Scouts Am., Portland, 1993—; trustee Charitable Trust Rotary Club Portland, 1994-97; ski patroller Mount Hood Ski Patrol, Portland, 1996—; alpine ski racing ofcl. Capt. USMC, 1975-79, maj. USMCR, 1982. Recipient Vigil Honor, Boy Scouts Am.-Cascade Pacific Coun., Portland, 1996, Silver Beaver award Boy Scouts Am., Portland, 1998; James E. West fellow Boy Scouts Am., Portland, 1996, Paul Harris fellow Rotary Internat., Portland, 1994, 97. Mem. Oreg. State Bar (chmn. labor law sect. 1995-96), Oreg. Assn. Chiefs of Police and Oreg. State Sheriff's Assn. (legal counsel 1987—, Presdl. award of merit 1990, 91, 93), Rotary Club Portland (dir. 1995-98). Republican. Episcopalian. Avocations: skiing, western trail riding. Office: Bullard Smith Jernstedt Harnish 1000 SW Broadway Ste 1900 Portland OR 97205-3071 Fax: 503-224-8851. E-mail: ablitz@bullardlaw.com.

BLITZ, STEPHEN M. lawyer; b. N.Y.C., July 29, 1941; s. Leo and Dorothy B.; m. Ellen Sue Mintzer, Sept. 23, 1962; children: Catherine Denise, Thomas Joseph. BA, Columbia U., 1962, BS, 1963; LL.B., Stanford U., 1966; MS in Acctg., U. Colo., 2001. Bar: Calif. 1967, U.S. Dist. Ct. (cen. dist.) Calif. 1967, Colo. 1996. Law clk. to judge U.S. Dist. Ct. Central Dist. Calif., 1966-67; ptnr. Gibson, Dunn & Crutcher, L.A., 1967-96, Denver, 1996-2001; spl. counsel Fleishman & Shapiro, Denver, 2001—. Adj. prof. law U. West Los Angeles Sch. Law, 1978-80, dir. Pub. Counsel, 1981-83, 94-96. Bd. dirs. Colo. Preservation, Inc., 1999—. Mem. ABA, L.A. County Bar Assn. (exec. com. 1986-96, chmn. 1994-95, real property sect.), Colo. Bar Assn., Denver Bar Assn., Order of Coif, Beta Gamma Sigma. Office: Fleishman & Shapiro PC 1600 Broadway Ste 2600 Denver CO 80202-4926

BLITZER, ANDREW, otolaryngologist, educator; b. Pitts., Apr. 25, 1946; s. Martin Hollander and Lyrene Iris (Lave) B.; m. Patricia Volk, Dec. 21, 1969; children: Peter Morgen, Polly Volk. BA, Adelphi U., 1967; DDS, Columbia U., 1970; MD, Mt. Sinai Sch. Medicine, 1973. Diplomate Am. Bd. Otolaryngology. Resident in gen. surgery Beth Israel Hosp., N.Y.C., 1973-74; resident in otolaryngology Mt. Sinai Hosp., N.Y.C., 1974-77; asst. prof. otolaryngology Coll. Phys. & Surg., Columbia U., N.Y.C., 1977-82, assoc. prof. otolaryngology and oral surgery, 1982-84, prof. clin. otolaryngology and oral surgery, 1984—, prof. clin. otolaryngology in neurology, 1993-95, vice chmn. dept. otolaryngology, 1983-91; dir. divsn. head and neck surgery Columbia-Presbyn. Med. Ctr., N.Y.C., 1980-94, acting chmn. dept. otolaryngology, dir. otolaryngology svc., Columbia-Presbyn. Med. Ctr., 1991-94, dir. residency edn., 1978-94; lectr. dept. otolaryngology Mt. Sinai Sch. Medicine, N.Y.C., 1977—; sr. attending otolaryngologist and dir. N.Y. Ctr. for Voice and Swallowing Disorders St. Luke's/Roosevelt Med. Ctr., 1994—; dir. N.Y. Ctr. for Clin. Rsch.; mem. spl. senses and lang. study sect. NIH. Co-author several books; assoc. editor: Otolaryngology-Head and Neck Surgery; mem. editl. rev. bd. The Laryngoscope, Jour. Otolaryngology, Jour. Rhinology; contbr. chpts. to books, articles to profl. jours. Recipient award for excellence Am. Assn. Orthodontists, 1970, Tchr.-Investigator award Nat. Inst. Neurol. Communicative Disorders and Strokes, 1978-83, Maxwell Abramson Meml. award Excellence in Resident Teaching, 1993. Fellow ACS, N.Y. Acad. Medicine, Am. Soc. Head and Neck Surgery, Am. Acad. Facial Plastic and Reconstructive Surgery, Am. Laryngol. Assn. (James Newcomb award 1998), Am. Larynol., Rhinol. and Otol. Soc., Am. Acad. Otolaryngology-Head and Neck Surgery (bd. dirs. 2002--, Honor award, Disting. Svc. award 1996), Am. Broncho-esophagological Assn. Office: 425 W 59th St New York NY 10019-1104

BLITZER, JUDI RAPPOPORT, retired bank executive, consultant; b. N.Y.C., Feb. 24, 1949; d. Murray Benjamin and Jeannette (Srebnick) Rappoport; m. David Mayers Blitzer, June 8, 1973; children: Mark Rappoport Blitzer, Julie Rappoport Blitzer. BA in Polit. Sci., Brown U., 1970. Mng. dir., head corp. mergers and aquisitions The Chase Manhattan Corp. (now JP Morgan Chase), N.Y.C., 1970-99; prin. JRB Advisors LLC, N.Y.C., 2000—; dir. Citizens Union Found., 2000—, Threshold Dance Projects, Inc., 2002—. Mem. Paper Bag Players, N.Y.C., benefit com., 1988—, dir., 2003—, pres. bd., 2003—; mem. bus. adv. bd. Next Jump, Inc., 2001—. Home: 320 West End Ave New York NY 10023-8110 Office: JRB Advisors LLC 320 West End Ave Fl 7 New York NY 10023-8110 E-mail: jrblitzer@yahoo.com.

BLIZARD, SUSAN KENNEDY, biology educator; b. Omaha, Apr. 21, 1949; d. George L. and Bernice E.A. Kennedy; m. John S. Blizard, Mar. 8, 1980. BS in Zoology, U. Nebr., Lincoln, 1972, MS in Zoology, 1974; MBA in Mgmt., Golden Gate U., 1985; ArtsD in Biology, Idaho State U., 1994. Rsch. technician Eppley Cancer Inst., U. Nebr. Med. Ctr., Omaha, 1975-80; rsch. technician U. Calif., Davis, 1980-82; adj. prof. biology C.C. So. Nev., North Las Vegas, 1983-88, prof., 1990—, chmn. sci. dept., 1996—99, chmn. biology dept., 1999—2001, interim dean of sci. and math., 2002—03, prof. biology, 2003—. Fellow Idaho State U., 1988-90. Avocation: reading mystery novels. Office: CC So Nev Biol Scis Dept H3C 3200 E Cheyenne Ave North Las Vegas NV 89030-4228 E-mail: sue_blizard@ccsn.nevada.edu.

BLIZNAKOV, EMILE GEORGE, biomedical research scientist; b. Kamen, Bulgaria, July 28, 1926; came to U.S., 1961, naturalized, 1966; s. George P. and Paraskeva B. MD, Faculty of Medicine, Sofia, Bulgaria, 1953. Dir. Regional Sta. for Hygiene and Epidemiology, Ministry Health; chief dist. dept. health Pirdop, Bulgaria, 1953-55; staff scientist, microbiologist Rsch. Inst. for Epidemiology and Microbiology, Ministry Health, Sofia, 1955-59; vis. scientist Gamaleya Research Inst. Epidemiology and Microbiology, Acad. Med. Scis., Moscow, 1958-59; sr. staff scientist, prof. life scis. New Eng. Inst., Ridgefield, Conn., 1961-81, dir. personnel, 1968-74, v.p., 1974-76, pres., 1976-81; exec. dir. research and devel. Libra Research, Rockville, Md., 1981-83; pres., sci. dir. Lupus Rsch. Inst., Rockville, Md., 1981—; biomed. rsch. cons., 1988—. Cons. to indsl., pharm. pub., and pub. rels. firms in U.S., Europe and Japan; lectr. in fields. Author med. books; contbr. articles to profl. jours.; patentee in fields. Fannie E. Rippel Found. grantee, 1972-80; G.M. McDonald Found. grantee, 1972-81; Whitehall Found. grantee, 1971-75; Wallace Genetic Found. grantee, 1972-81 Fellow Royal Soc. Tropical Medicine and Hygiene (London); mem. AMA, AAUP, AAAS, Inflammation Rsch. Assn. (USA), Internat. Soc. for Infectious Diseases, Internat. Soc. Chronobiology, Interam. Soc. Chemotherapy, Am. Fedn. Clin. Rsch., Am. Soc. Microbiology, Am. Coll. Toxicology, Am. Soc. Neurochemistry, Internat. Assn. Biomed. Gerontology, Am. Aging Assn., Bioelectromagnetic Soc., Soc. for Leukocyte Biology, Internat. Coenzyme Q10 Assn., N.Y. Acad. Scis. Home and Office: 2821 N Course Dr Apt H-205 Pompano Beach FL 33069-3078

BLIZNAKOV, MILKA TCHERNEVA, architect, educator; b. Varna, Bulgaria, Sept. 20, 1927; came to U.S., 1961, naturalized, 1966; d. Ivan Dimitrov and Maria Kesarova (Khorozova) Tchernev; m. Emile G. Bliznakov, Oct. 23, 1954 (div. Apr., 1974). Architect-engr. diploma, State Tech. U., Sofia, 1951; PhD, Engring.-Structural Inst., Sofia, 1959; PhD in Architecture, Columbia U., 1971. Sr. researcher Ministry Heavy Industry, Sofia, 1950-53; pvt. practice architecture Sofia, 1954-59; assoc. architect Noel Combrisson, Paris, 1959-61; designer Perkins & Will Partnership, White Plains, N.Y., 1963-67; project architect Lathrop Douglass, N.Y.C., 1967-71; assoc. prof. architecture and planning Sch. Architecture, U. Tex., Austin, 1972-74; prof. Coll. Architecture, Va. Poly. Inst. and State U., Blacksburg, 1974-98, prof. emerita, 1998—; prin. Blacksburg, 1975—. Bd. dirs. founder Internat. Archives Women in Architecture, Va. Poly. Inst. and State U., The Parthena award, 1994. Prin. works include Speedwell Ave. Urban Renewal, Morristown, N.J., 1967—69, Wilmington (Del.) Urban Renewal, 1968—70, Springfield (Ill.) Ctrl. Area Devel., 1969—71, Arlington County (Va.) Redevel., 1975—77; author (with others): Utopia e Modernitá, 1989, Reshaping Russian Archtecture, 1990, Russian Housing in the Modern Age, 1993, Nietzsche and Soviet Culture, 1994, New Perspectives on Russian and Soviet Artistic Culture, 1994, The Eastern Dada Orbit: Russia, Georgia, Ukraine, Central Europe, 1996, Signs of Times, Culture and the Emblems of Apocalypse, 1998, Women Architects in Eastern Europe: The Contributions of the Bulgarians, 1997, International Archive of Women in Architecture, 1997, 1999, 2001, 2002, Encyclopedia of Eastern Europe, 2000, Centropa, 2001; author: (with others), 2003; author: (with others) Women Architects in Japan, 2002, Housing in Russia: 20th Century, 2002; author: (with others) Encyclopedia of Twentieth Century Architecture, 2003. William Kinne scholar, 1970, vis. scholar Inst. Advanced Russian Studies, The Wilson Ctr. of Smithsonian Instn., 1988; NEA grantee, 1973-74, Am. Beautiful Found. grantee, 1973, Internat. Rsch. and Exch. Bd. grantee, 1984-93; Fulbright Hays rsch. fellow, 1983-84, 91; recipient Parthena award, 1994. Mem. Internat. Archive Women in Architecture (founder, chair bd. dirs.), Am. Assn. Tchrs. Slavic and East European Langs., Soc. Archtl. Historians, Nat. Trust Hist. Preservation, Am. Assn. Advancement of Slavic Studies, Assn. Collegiate Schs. of Planning, Inst. Modern Russian Culture (chairperson architecture, co-founder, dir.), Bulgarian Studies Assn., Assn. Collegiate Schs. of Architecture. Home: 2813 Tall Oaks Dr Blacksburg VA 24060-8109 Office: Va Poly Inst and State U Coll Architecture Blacksburg VA 24061 E-mail: mbliznak@vt.edu.

BLIZZARD, ALAN, artist; b. Boston, Mar. 25, 1939; s. Thomas and Elizabeth B. BFA, Mass. Coll. Art; MA, U. Ariz.; MFA, U. Iowa, 1963. Instr. in art U. Iowa; vis. asst. prof. art Albion Coll., U. Okla.; assoc. prof. UCLA; now prof. painting Scripps Coll. and; Claremont Grad. Sch. Represented in permanent collections Bklyn. Mus., Met. Mus. Art, N.Y.C., Art Inst. Chgo., Denver Art Mus., La Jolla (Calif.) Mus. Art, Ashland U., Columbia U., McGeorge Sch. Law, Pomona Coll., Sacramento State U., Pitzer Coll., Fluor Corp., Kouri Capital Corp., N.Y.C. Office: Scripps Coll Art Dept Claremont CA 91711

BLOBEL, GÜNTER, cell biologist, educator; b. Waltersdorf, Silesia, Germany, May 21, 1936; MD, U. Tübingen, Germany, 1960; PhD in Oncology, U. Wis., 1967. Intern, Germany, 1960-62; fellow lab. cellular biology Rockefeller U., 1967-69, asst. prof. cell biology, 1969-73, assoc. prof., 1973-76, prof., 1976—; investigator Howard Hughes Med. Inst., 1986—. Founder, pres. Friends of Dresden, Inc. Contbr. articles to profl. jours. and chpts. to books. Recipient Gairdner Found. award, 1982, Warburg medal German Biochem. Soc., 1983, Wilson medal Am. Soc. Cell Biology, 1986, U.D. Mattia award Roche Inst. Molecular Biology, 1986, Louisa Gross Horwitz prize Columbia U., 1987, Waterford Biomedical Sci. award, 1989, Albert Lasker Basic Med. Rsch. award, 1993, King Faisal internat. prize for sci., 1996, Mayor's award for Excellence in Sci. and Tech., 1997, Massry Prize, 1999, Nobel Prize for Medicine, 1999, Ellis Island Medal of Honor, 2000. Mem. Nat. Acad. Scis. (U.S. Steel award in molecular biology 1978, Richard Lounsbery award 1983), Am. Acad. Arts and Scis., Japan Biochem. Soc. (hon.), Am. Soc. Cell Biology (pres. 1990), German Soc. Cell Biology (hon.), Am. Philos. Soc., European Molecular Biol. ORgn. (assoc.). Office: Rockefeller U Cell Biology Lab 66th and York Ave New York NY 10021-6339

BLOCH, BOBBIE ANN, nurse, educator; BSN, Wayne State U., 1969; MSN, U. Calif. San Francisco, 1976; PhD in Curriculum and Instrn., U. Toledo, 1992. Asst. prof. nursing U. Mich. Sch. Nursing, Ann Arbor, 1976-82; edn. specialist Community Health Nursing U. Mich. Hosps. Ambulatory Care, Ann Arbor, 1982-83; asst. prof. nursing Gerontol. Nursing Dept., Med. Coll. Ohio Sch. Nursing, Toledo, 1983-85; dir. edn. and tng. Calvert Meml. Hosp., Prince Frederick, Md., 1993-95; dir. edn. Lorien Nursing and Rehab. Ctr., Columbia, Md., 1995-97, Hebrew Home Greater Washington, Rockville, Md., 1997-99, AIMM for Health, Hyattsville, Md., 1999; DON Iliff Nursing and Rehab. Ctr., 1999-2000, The Washington Home, 2000—01, Survey Solutions, 2001—02, Eastpoint Nursing Facility, Balt., 2002. Nurse cons. Jo Anne Wilson Gerontol. Nurse Ventures, 2000-2001. Contbr. articles to profl. jours. Recipient Wash. State Nurses Assn. Cert. Recognition award for Outstanding Book, 1983, Am. Jour. Nursing Pub. Book of Yr. awards for Publication in 1983. Mem. ANA, Md. Nurses Assn., Internat. Soc. Performance and Instrn., Nat. Nursing Staff Devel. Orgn., Sigma Theta Tau. Home: 12209 Castle Pines Dr Beltsville MD 20705 E-mail: Bobbie.Bloch@verizon.net.

BLOCH, DONALD MARTIN, lawyer; b. Lynn, Mass., May 16, 1939; s. Meyer James and Bertha (Berman) B.; m. Ellen Ann Green, June 18, 1961; children: Andrew Louis, Linda Phyllis, David Michael. BA, Bowdoin Coll., 1960; LLB, Harvard U., 1963. Bar: Mass. 1963, U.S. Dist. Ct. Mass. 1974. Assoc. Lane, Altman & Owens LLP, Boston, 1966-71; ptnr. Lane, Altman & Owens LLP, Boston, 1972-2001; of counsel Posternak, Blankstein & Lund, LLP, Boston, 2001—. Mem. Framingham (Mass.) Town Meeting, 1970-95, Town Charter Commn., Framingham, 1978-79, Town Finance Com., 2002—; bd. dirs. South Middlesex Assn. for Retarded, Framingham, 1980-86, Metrowest Mental Health Assn., Framingham, 1983-95, Mary Morse Healthcare Inc., 1997—, vice chair, 2000-01, chair, 2001—; mem. Mass. Adv. Com. to U.S. Civil Rights Commn., 1991-93. Capt. U.S. Army, 1963-65. Named one of Outstanding Citizens, Greater Framingham Jewish Fedn., 1983. Mem. Harvard Club Boston, Bowdoin Club Boston (officer, bd. dirs.), Phi Beta Kappa. Republican. Office: Posternak Blankstein & Lund LLP 100 Charles River Plz Boston MA 02114 E-mail: donmbloch@aol.com., dbloch@pbl.com.

BLOCH, ERICH, retired electrical engineer, former science foundation administrator; b. Sulzburg, Germany, Jan. 9, 1925; arrived in U.S., 1948, naturalized, 1952; s. Joseph and Tony Bloch; m. Renee Stern, Mar. 4, 1948; 1 child, Rebecca Bloch Rosen. Student, Fed. Poly. Inst., Zurich, Switzerland, 1945—48; BSEE, U. Buffalo, 1952; hon. degrees, U. Mass., George Washington U., Colo. Sch. Mines, SUNY Buffalo, U. Rochester, Oberlin Coll., U. Notre Dame, Ohio State U.; hon. degree, Rensselaer Poly. Inst., 1989, Washington Coll., 1989, CUNY, N.Y.C., 1991, Poly. U., Bklyn., N.Y., 1993. With IBM, 1952—75, v.p. gen. mgr., 1975—80, v.p. tech. personnel devel. Armonk, NY, 1980—84; mem. com. computers in automated mfg. NRC, 1980—84; dir. NSF, Washington, 1984—90; fellow Coun. on Competitiveness, 1990—; prin. Washington Adv. Group, 1998—; mem. Pres.'s Coun. of Advisors for Sci. and Tech., 2001—. Past vis. disting. prof. George Mason U. Patentee in field. Recipient U.S. medal of tech., 1985, Computer World/Smithsonian award for innovation, 1991, Swedish Royal Order of the Polar Star, Robert Noyce award, Semiconductor Industry Assn., 1999, Eugene Merchant Mfg. medal, ASME and Soc. Mfg. Engrs., Vanevar Bush award, Nat. Sci. Bd., 2002. Fellow: AAAS, IEEE (Founder's award 1990, Computer Pioneer award 1993, 1994); mem.: NAE (Arthur M. Bueche award 1997), Japan Acad. Engring., Royal Swedish Acad. Engring. Scis., Am. Soc. Engring. Edn., Am. Soc. Mfg. Engrs. (hon.). E-mail: ebloch@theadvisorygroup.com.

BLOCH, FARRELL EDWARD, economist, writer; b. Phila., Apr. 16, 1948; s. Jules and Gertrude Bloch. BA, Swarthmore Coll., 1969; MS, Stanford U., 1970, MA, 1972, PhD, 1973. Asst. prof. econs. Princeton U., 1974—78; econ. policy fellow Brookings Instn., 1976—77; sr. economist Pres.'s Coun. Wage and Price Stability, 1978—79; co-founder, sr. ptnr. Econometric Rsch., Inc., Washington, 1979—82; sr. economist Econ. Policy Office, antitrust divsn. US Dept. Justice, Washington, 1982—87; pres. Farrell Bloch Assocs., 1987—. Presenter, cons. in field. Author: Statistics for Nonstatisticians, 1987, 3rd edit., 1997, Antidiscrimination Law and Minority Employment, 1994, Michael's Inheritance, 2003; editor: Evaluating Manpower Training Programs, 1979; mem. editl. bd. Jour. Labor Rsch., 1980—91. Office: 4813 41st St NW Washington DC 20016-1707 E-mail: fbloch@alum.swarthmore.edu.

BLOCH, FRANK SAMUEL, law educator; b. Jan. 16, 1945; s. Felix Jacob and Lore Clara (Misch) B.; m. Melissa Roth, Mar. 12, 1972; children: Julia Devi, Sara Shanti. BA, Brandeis U., 1966, MA, 1971, PhD, 1978; JD, Columbia U., 1969. Bar: Calif. 1970, Tenn. 1980, U.S. Dist. Ct. (no. dist.) Calif. 1971, U.S. Ct. Appeals (7th cir.) 1976, U.S. Dist. Ct. (mid. dist.) Tenn. 1980, U.S. Ct. Appeals (6th cir.) 1983. Assoc. atty. Calif. Rural Legal Assistance, Madera, Calif., 1971-72, directing atty., 1972-73; lectr. in law, clin. fellow U. Chgo., 1974-79; assoc. prof. law Vanderbilt U., Nashville, 1979-86, prof., 1986—, dir. clin. edn., 1979-2001. Pres. Legal Svcs. of Mid. Tenn., Inc., 1991-92, 95-96; cons. Internat. Social Security Assn., 1993-2000; cons. Adminstrv. Conf. of U.S., 1988-93. Author: Disability Determination, 1992, Bloch on Social Security Disability, 2003; editor: Who Returns to Work and Why?, 2001; contbr. articles to profl. jours. Rsch. fellow Internat. Social Security Assn., 1992-93; Fulbright grantee, 1986. Mem.: ABA, Nat. Acad. Social Ins. Democrat. Jewish. Home: 1119 Park Ridge Dr Nashville TN 37215-4515 Office: Vanderbilt Univ Law Sch 131 21st Ave S Nashville TN 37203-1181

BLOCH, HENRY WOLLMAN, tax preparation company executive; b. Kansas City, Mo., July 30, 1922; s. Leon Edwin and Hortense Bienenstok; m. Marion Ruth Helzberg, June 16, 1951; children: Robert, Thomas M., Mary Jo, Elizabeth Ann. BS, U. Mich., 1944; D of Bus. Adminstrn. (hon.), Avila Coll., Kansas City, Mo., 1977, U. Mo., Kansas City, 1989; LLD (hon.), N.H. Coll., 1983, William Jewell Coll., Liberty, Mo., 1990, Kansas City Art Inst., 1999. Ptnr. United Bus. Co., 1946-55; hon. chmn., past CEO H & R Block, Inc., Kansas City, 1955—, also dir. Bd. dirs. Commerce Bancshares, Inc., Kansas City, CompuServe, Inc., Valentine Radford Advt.; past chmn. Midwest Rsch. Inst. Past bd. dirs. Menorah Med. Ctr.; bd. dirs., past pres. Menorah Med. Ctr. Found.; former mem. pres.'s adv. coun. Kansas City Philharmonic Assn.; chmn., dir. H & R Block Found.; past pres. of trustees U. Kansas City, Nelson-Atkins Mus. Art, trustee, dir., past chmn. bus. coun.; past bd. dirs. Jewish Fedn. and Coun. Greater Kansas City; dir., past pres. Civic Coun. Greater Kansas City; gen. chmn. United Negro Colls. Fund, 1986; bd. dirs. St. Luke's Hosp. Found., Internat. Rels. Coun., Kansas City Cmty. Found.; former mem. bd. dirs. Coun. of Fellows of Nelson Gallery Found., Am. Jewish Com.; former mem. bd. govs. Kansas City Mus. History and Sci.; bd. dirs. Midwest Rsch. Inst., vice chmn.; bd. dirs. Kansas City Symphony, past dir.; bd. dirs. Greater Kansas City Community Found.; gen. chmn. Heart of Am. United Way Exec. Com., 1978; past met. chmn. Nat. Alliance Businessmen; former mem. bd. regents Rockhurst Coll.; former mem. bd. chancellor's assocs. U. Kans. at Lawrence; former mem. bd. dirs. Harry S. Truman Good Neighbor Award Found.; bd. dirs. Internat. Rels. Coun.; bd. dirs., v.p. Kansas City Area Health Planning Coun.; past pres. Found. for a Greater Kansas City; dir. Mid-Am. Coalition on Health Care, St. Luke's Found.; trustee Jr. Achievement of Mid-Am.; vice chmn. corp. fund Kennedy Ctr. 1st lt. USAAF, 1943-45. Decorated Air medal with 3 oak leaf clusters; named Mktg. Man of Yr. Sales and Mktg. Execs. Club, 1971, Chief Exec. Officer of Yr. for svc. industry Fin. World, 1976, Mainstreeter of Decade, 1988, Entrepreneur of Yr., 1986; recipient Disting. Exec. award Boy Scouts Am., 1977, Salesman of Yr. Kansas City Advt. Club, 1978, Civic Svc. award Hyman Brand Hebrew Acad., 1980, Golden Plate award Am. Acad. Achievement, 1980, Chancellor's medal U. Mo.-Kansas City, 1980, Pres.'s trophy Kansas City Jaycees, 1980, W.F. Yates medal for disting. svc. in civic affairs William Jewell Coll., 1981, bronze award for svc. industry Wall Street Transcript, 1981, Disting. Missourian award NCCJ, 1982, Lester A. Milgram Humanitarian award, 1983, Hall of Fame award Internat. Franchise Assn., 1983; named to Bus. Leader Hall of Fame Jr. Achievement, 1980; honoree Sales and Mktg. Execs. Internat. Acad. of Achievement, 1991. Mem. Greater Kansas City C. of C. (past pres.), C. of C. Greater Kansas City (Mr.

Kansas City award 1978), Acad. Squires, Golden Key Nat. Honor Soc. (hon.), Oakwood Country Club, River Club, Carriage Club, Kansas City Country Club. Jewish. Office: H&R Block Inc 4400 Main St Kansas City MO 64111-1812

BLOCH, HERBERT, classicist, medievalist, historian, educator; b. Berlin, Aug. 18, 1911; came to the U.S., 1939, naturalized, 1946; s. Ludwig and Alice (Gutmann) B.; m. Clarissa Coolidge Holland, Nov. 23, 1943 (dec. Aug. 1958); children: Anne Coolidge, Nini; m. Ellen Cohen, Aug. 25, 1960 (dec. May 1987). Dottore in Lettere, U. Rome, 1935, diploma di Perfezionamento, 1937; LLD, U. Cassino, Italy, 1989. Instr. Greek and Latin Harvard U., Cambridge, Mass., 1941, asst. prof. Greek and Latin, 1942-47, assoc. prof. Greek and Latin, 1947-53, prof. Greek and Latin, 1953-73, Pope prof. Latin lang. and lit., 1973-82, Pope prof. Latin lang. and lit. emeritus, 1982—; with excavation of Ostia Italy, 1938-39. Mem. Inst. for Advanced Study, Princeton, N.J., 1953-54; prof.-in-charge Sch. Classical Studies, Am. Acad. Rome, 1957-59; mem. bd. Syndics Harvard U. Press, Cambridge, 1961-65; trustee Loeb Classical Libr. Harvard U., Cambridge, 1964-73, sr. fellow Soc. of Fellows, 1964-79. Author: I bolli laterizi e la storia edilizia romana, 1948, 2d edit., 1968, Supplement to Volume XVI of the Corpus Inscriptionum Latinarum Including Complete Indices to the Roman Brick-Stamps, 1948, 2d edit., 1967, Monte Cassino in the Middle Ages, 3 vols., 1986 (Haskins medal The Medieval Acad. Am. 1988, Praemium Urbis, Rome, 1987), The Atina Dossier of Peter the Deacon of Monte Cassino. A Hagiographical Romance of the Twelfth Century, 1998. Recipient Fulbright award, Italy, 1950-51; Guggenheim fellow, 1950-51; fellow for ind. study and rsch. NEH, 1976-77. Fellow Am. Acad. Arts and Scis., Med. Acad. Am. (pres. of fellows 1990-93); mem. Am. Philological Assn. (dir. 1959-64, 66-70, v.p. 1966-68, pres. 1968-69), Am. Philos. Soc., Deutsches Archaeologisches Inst., Pontificia Accademia Romana di Archeologia (hon.), Zentraldirektion der Monumenta Germaniae Historica (corr.), Finnish Acad. Sci. and Letters, Premio Cultori di Roma, Rome, 1999. Home: Cadbury Commons 66 Sherman St Apt 316 Cambridge MA 02140-3529

BLOCH, JULIA CHANG, educator, former ambassador, former bank executive; b. Mar. 2, 1942; came to U.S., 1951, naturalized, 1962; d. Fu-yun and Eva (Yeh) Chang; m. Stuart Marshall Bloch, Dec. 21, 1968. BA, U. Calif., Berkley, 1964; MA, Harvard U., 1967; postgrad. in mgmt., 1987; DHL (hon.), Northeastern U., Boston, 1986. Vol. Peace Corps, Sabah, Malaysia, 1964-66; tng. officer East Asia and Pacific region, Washington, 1967-68, evaluation officer, 1968-70; mem. minority staff U.S. Senate Select Com. on Nutrition and Human Needs, Washington, 1971-76, chief minority counsel, 1976-77; dep. dir. Office of African Affairs U.S. Internat. Comm. Agy., Washington, 1977-80; fellow Inst. Politics Harvard U., Cambridge, Mass., 1980-81; asst. adminstr. Bur. for Food For Peace and Voluntary Assistance AID, Washington, 1981-87; asst. adminstr. Bur. for Asia and Near East, 1987-88; assoc. U.S.-Japan Rels. Program, Ctr. for Internat. Affairs Harvard U., Cambridge, Mass., 1988-89; amb. Kingdom of Nepal, 1989-93; group exec., v.p. Bank Am., San Francisco, 1993-96; pres. The U.S.-Japan Found., 1996-98; dir. Am. West Airlines, 1994-98, Penn Mutual Life Ins., 1997; prof. Am. studies Beida Univ., Beijing; amb. in residence U. Md., 2000—. Trustee Eisenhower Exchange Fellowship, 1995-97, Nat. Com. U.S. China Rels., 1998—; U.S. Senate rep. World Conf. on Internat. Women's Yr., Mex., 1975; advisor U.S. Del. to Food and Agr. orgn. Conf., Rome, 1975; rep. Am. Council Young Polit. Leaders, Peoples Republic China, 1977, charter mem. Sr. Exec. Svc., 1979; head U.S. del. Biennial Session World Food Programme, Rome, 1981-86, Devel. Assistance Com. Meeting on Non-Govtl. Orgns., Paris, 1985, Intergovtl. Group on Indonesia, The Hague, The Netherlands, 1987, World Bank Consultative Group Meeting, Paris, 1987, mem. exec. women in govt., 1988-93, mem. coun. fgn. rels., 1991—; vis. prof. internat. rels. Peking U., 1998—; Starr sr. fellow U.S. China Rels. Fudan U., Shanghai, adj. prof. Author: A U.S.-Japan Aid Alliance, 1991; co-author: Chinese Home Cooking, 1986. Exec. bd. mem. Internat. Ctr. for Rsch. on Women, 1974-81; mem. adv. bd. Women's Campaign Fund, 1976-78; mem. nat. adv. coun. Experiemtn in Internat. Living, 1981-83; mem. U.S. Nat. Com. for Pacific Econ. Cooperation, 1984—, Nat. Presdl. Debate Forum, 1987-92; mem. presdl. adv. couns. Peace Corps, 1988-89; mem. com. to visit art mus. Harvard U., 1989; founder Women Fgn. Policy Group; mem. Am. Refugee Com. Bd., 1993; mem. Am. Himalayna Found. Bd., 1994; commr. Asian Art Mus., San Francisco, 1994; trustee, bus. leadership circle, 1994—. Hon Fulbright fellow, 1996; recipient Hubert Humphrey award for internat. svc., 1979, Humanitarian Svc. award AID, 1987, Leader for Peace award Peace Corps, 1987, Asian Am. LEadership award, 1989, Brotherhood/Sisterhood award Nat. Conf. on Christians and Jews, 1996; named Outstanding Woman of Color, Nat. Inst. for Women of Color, 1982, Woman of Distinction, Nat. Conf. for Coll. Women Student Leaders and Women of Achievement, 1987, Disting. Pub. Svc. award Nat. Assn. Profl. Asian Pacific Am. Women, 1989; Ford Found. Study fellow for internat. devel. Harvard U., 1966, Paul Harris award Rotary, 1992, Award of Honor Narcotic Enforcement Assn., 1992. Mem. Orgn. Cinese Am. Women (founder, chair 1977—, bd. dirs., Woman of Yr. 1987), Asia Soc. (pres. coun. 1989, trustee, 1994), Am. Studies Ctr. (vice-chair), Prytannean Honor Soc., Coun. Fgn. Rels., Mortar Bd., Cosmos Club. Republican. Avocations: ceramics, gourmet cooking, collecting art. E-mail: jcbloch@aol.com.

BLOCH, KURT JULIUS, physician; b. Germany, Oct. 17, 1929; s. Max and Mathilde B.; m. Margot Bendit, June 25, 1953; children: Kenneth D., Donald B. BS, CCNY, 1951; MD, NYU, 1955. Diplomate Am. Bd. Internal Medicine, Am. Bd. Allergy and Immunology, subspecialties Rheumatology, Diagnostic Lab. Immunology. Intern, asst. resident Bellevue Hosp., N.Y.C., 1955-57; resident in medicine Mass. Gen. Hosp., Boston, 1960-61, physician, 1974—, chief clin. immunology and allergy units, 1976—2000, chief clin. immunology unit, dir. clin. immunology lab., 2000—02; instr. medicine Harvard Med. Sch., Boston, 1965-68, asst. prof., 1968-70, assoc. prof., 1970-74, prof., 1974—. Sr. investigator Arthritis Found., 1964-69 Contbr. articles to profl. jours. With USPHS, 1957-60. Mem. Am. Soc. Clin. Investigation, Am. Assn. Physicians. Achievements include research on the biologic functions of antibodies, mechanisms of inflammation of the intestine, the immunobiology of sensorineural hearing loss, and the clinical significance of antibodies to heat shock proteins. Office: Mass Gen Hosp Cardiovascular Rsch Ctr Boston MA 02114

BLOCH, MARC JOEL, lawyer; b. Cleve., Feb. 14, 1943; s. David R. and Sylvia C. (Levof) B.; m. Barbara Ann Bandler; children: Stephen, Robin. B.A., Miami U., 1965; J.D., Cleve. State Law Sch., 1969. Bar: Ohio 1969. Field atty NLRB, Cleve., 1969-72; assoc. Robert P. Duvin & Assocs., Cleve., 1973-79; prin. Duvin, Cahn & Hutton, Cleve., 1979— . Contbr. numerous articles to profl. jours. Pres. Pub. Sector Labor Relations Assn. Cleve. Mem. Greater Cleve. Bar Assn., ABA, Fed. Bar Assn., Beechmont Country Club (trustee), Phi Alpha Delta. Office: Erieview Tower 20th Fl 1301 E 9th St Cleveland OH 44114-1800

BLOCH, PETER, editor; Editor Penthouse Mag., N.Y.C. Office: Penthouse Mag General Media 11 Penn Plz Fl 12t5H New York NY 10001-2006

BLOCH, PETER CONRAD, economist, educator; b. N.Y.C., June 8, 1944; s. Konrad Emil and Lore (Teutsch) B.; m. Marianne Nieman; children: Benjamin, Emilie. AB, Harvard U., 1967; MA, Johns Hopkins U., 1969; PhD, U. Calif., Berkeley, 1974. Maitre asst. assoc. U. Dakar, Senegal, 1974-76; vis. assoc. prof. Fletcher Sch. of Law and Diplomacy, Tufts U., Medford, Mass., 1977-80; asst. prof. Grinnell (Iowa) Coll., 1980-83; sr. scientist Land Tenure Ctr., U. Wis., Madison, 1984—, vis. asst. prof. dept. econ., 1983-85, faculty assoc. dept. forest ecology, 1999—. Pres. Terra Inst., Ltd., Mt. Horeb, Wis., 1994-97; cons. Swedish Govt., Stockholm, 1989-98, U.S. Agy. Internat. Devel., Washington, 1975—, World Bank, Washington, 1985—. Contbr. articles to profl. publs. and chpts. to books. Grantee British Know How Fund, Lincoln Inst. Land Policy, U.S. Agy. Internat. Devel., World Bank. Mem. Assn. Recherches et Etudes sur le Foncier en Atrique. Avocations: gardening, travel. Home: 21 Foxboro Cir Madison WI 53717-1201 Office: U Wis Land Tenure Ctr 1357 University Ave Madison WI 53715-1054 E-mail: pcbloch@facstaff.wisc.edu.

BLOCH, RICHARD, physician; b. Hamburg, Germany, Aug. 5, 1948; s. Leon and Helena (Wozniak) B.; 1 child, Andrew R. BA, Ind. U., 1970, MD, 1973. Diplomate Am. Bd. Internal Medicine, Am. Bd. Internal Medicine Nephrology. Intern in internal medicine Indpls. U. Hosps., 1973-74, resident in internal medicine, 1974-76, clin. fellow in nephrology, 1976-77, rsch. fellow in nephrology, 1977-78; mem. Arnett Clin., Lafayette, Ind., 1978-87, Nephrology and Internal Medicine, Indpls., 1987-99. Med. dir. dialysis St. Elizabeth Hosp., Lafayette, 1979-87; med. dir. inpatient dialysis, Meth. Hosp., Indpls., 1994-2002. Patentee in field; contbr. articles to profl. jours. Mem. Am. Coll. Physicians, Am. Soc. Nephrology, Renal Physician Assn. Office: Nephrology and Internal Med #355 1801 Senate Blvd Ste 355 Indianapolis IN 46202-1296

BLOCH, RICHARD ISAAC, labor arbitrator; b. East Orange, N.J., June 15, 1943; s. Jacques Henry and Hannah (Levi) B.; m. Susan Low, July 11, 1966; children: Rebecca Low, Michael Low. AB, Dartmouth Coll., 1965; JD, U. Mich., 1968, MBA, 1974. Bar: Mich. 1969, D.C. bar 1975. Asso. firm Seyfarth, Shaw Fairweather & Geraldson, Chgo., 1968; lectr. U. Mich. Grad. Sch. Bus. Adminstrn., 1969-71; asst. prof. law U. Detroit, 1971-75; prin. Richard I. Bloch, P.C. (labor arbitrator), Washington, 1969—. Vis. prof. law Wayne State U., 1974, George Washington U., 1983; adj. prof. Am. U., 1978, Georgetown U. Law Ctr., 1989-90; chmn. fgn. svc. grievance bd. Dept. State, 1977-80; chief umpire United Mine Workers and Bituminous Coal Operators Assn., 1980-81; arbitrator Maj. League Baseball, 1983-85, Nat. Hockey League, Electric Boat Co., Metal Trades Coun., Nat. Football League; permanent arbitrator Alcoa and United Steelworkers Am. Author: Arbitration of Discipline Cases, 1979, Labor Agreement in Arbitration, 1983, Interest Arbitration, 1986; contbr. articles to profl. jours. Mem. Dartmouth Coll. Alumni Council, 1974-77. Mem. ABA, Mich. Bar Assn., D.C. Bar Assn., Indsl. Rels. Rsch. Assn., Nat. Acad. Arbitrators (bd. govs., pres.-elect 2001, pres. 2002-). Home and Office: 4335 Cathedral Ave NW Washington DC 20016-3560

BLOCH, SAUL K. obstetrician-gynecologist; b. Springfield, Mass., Mar. 18, 1927; MD, Tufts U., 1955. Diplomate Am. Bd. Ob-Gyn. Intern St. Vincents Hosp., Toledo, 1956-57; resident Kaiser Found. Hosp., San Francisco, 1957-60; pvt. practice L.A. Attending ob-gyn. St. John's Hosp., Santa Monica, 1993—; asst. clin. prof. dept. ob-gyn., UCLA, 1993—. Fellow ACOG. Office: 921 Westwood Blvd Los Angeles CA 90024-2942 E-mail: s.bloch@gte.net.

BLOCH, STUART MARSHALL, lawyer; b. Detroit, Nov. 5, 1942; s. A. Howard and Pauline Betty (Rappaport) B.; m. Julia Chang, Dec. 21, 1968. AB, U. Miami, 1964; LLB, Harvard U., 1967. Bar: Mich. 1968, D.C. 1968. Ptnr. Ingersoll and Bloch, Washington, 1972—; chmn. Real Estate Reporter, Ltd., Washington, 1978—. Author: A Periodical Guide to FIRREA, 1989, The Workout Game, 1987, 90, The Liability Game, 1988; editor State Digest of Land Sales, 1977—, D.C. Real Estate Reporter, 1979—; fellow Salzburg Seminar, 1988. Chmn. Land Devel. Inst., Washington, 1974—; trustee Arena Stage, 1983, Black Student Fund, Washington, 1983; major gifts chmn. Harvard U. Law Sch., 1983; 25th reunion chmn. U. Miami, 1989; pres. Internat. Found. for Timesharing, 1983; mem. corp. Northeastern U., Boston, 1983; mem. bd. individual vol. svc. Jewish Nat. Fund, 1994. Recipient spl. citation Am. Land Devel. Assn., 1980; citation D.C. City Coun., 1982, Jewish Nat. Fund Tree of Life award, 1991. Mem. ABA, D.C. Bar Assn., Mich. Bar Assn., Univ. Club (Washington). Office: Ingersoll & Bloch 1736 St NW Washington DC 20005-1910

BLOCHOWIAK, MARY ANN, cultural organization administrator, writer; b. Shawnee, Okla., Dec. 18, 1943; d. Casimir Joseph Blochowiak, Mary Roberta Blochowiak. BA in History, U. Ctrl. Okla., 1979, MA in History, 1984. RN. Staff nurse Mercy and Deaconess Hosps., Oklahoma City, 1964—90; asst. editor Okla. Hist. Soc., Oklahoma City, 1988—89, asoc. editor, 1990—99, pub. divsn. dir., 1993—, editor The Chronicles of Oklahoma, 2000—. Book awards judge Okla. Ctr. for the Book, Oklahoma City, 1998—. Contbr. articles. Mem.: Okla. Mus. Assn., Okla. Assn. Profl. Historians, Okla. Hist. Soc., Western History Assn. Avocations: history, reading, needlecrafts. Office: Okla Hist Soc 2100 N Lincoln Blvd Oklahoma City OK 73105-4997 Office Fax: 405-/521-2492. Business E-Mail: mablochowiak@ok-history.mus.ok.us.

BLOCK, ALLAN JAMES, communications executive; b. Oct. 1, 1954; s. Paul Jr. and Marjorie (McNab) B. BA, U. Pa., 1977. Coord. electronic tech. planning Toledo Blade Co., 1981-83, dir. electronic planning, 1984-85; dir. mktg. Buckeye Cablevision Inc., Toledo, 1985-87; v.p. cablevision and TV Blade Communications, Inc., Toledo, 1987-88, exec. v.p., 1989, mem., chief exec. com., co-CEO, 1989—; vice-chmn. bd. Block Comm. (formerly known as Blade Communications, Inc.), Toledo, 1990—2001; mng. dir., prin. exec. officer Block Comms. Inc., 2002—. Bd. dirs. Toledo Blade Co., P.G. Pub. Co., Buckeye Cablevision Inc. Bd. dirs. C-SPAN, Nat. Cable TV Coop., Inc., 2000-03, Am. Cable Assn.; trustee Med. Coll. Ohio, 1991-2000. Mem. Toledo Club, Met. Club (N.Y.C.), Penn Club (N.Y.C.), Downtown Assn. (N.Y.C.), Duquesne Club (Pitts.). Home: 235 14th St Toledo OH 43624-1401 Office: Block Communications Inc 541 N Superior St Toledo OH 43660-1000 E-mail: ABlock@blockcommunications.com.

BLOCK, ALVIN GILBERT, publishing executive; b. Moline, Ill., Sept. 15, 1946; s. Sylvan Emory Block and Pauline (Kutten) Salzman; m. Sarah Cannon Michael, June 17, 1977 (div. 1984); m. Ellen Marie Chapman, Jan. 19, 1992; children: Will Chapman, Thomas Chapman. BA, Bradley U., 1968. Editl. asst. Playboy mag., Chgo., 1970; exec. Salzman & Co., Davenport, Iowa, 1971-74; editor Ketchum (Idaho) Tomorrow, 1975-77; reporter Idaho Statesman, Ketchum, 1978-80; freelance writer, Sacramento, 1980-82; mng. editor Calif. Jour., Sacramento, 1983-94, editor, columnist, 1995-2000, editor-in-chief news and publs., 2000—03, pub., 2003—. Commentator Sta. KXPR-FM, Sacramento, 1985—88; co-editor Calif. Polit. Almanac; editor Calif. Govt. and Politics Annual, 1995—2000; v.p., editor-in-chief State Net, 1996—. Councilman City of Ketchum, 1979. With U.S. Army, 1969-74. Recipient award for column Idaho Newspaper Assn., 1975, Soc. Profl. Journalists, 1995. Avocations: baseball, military history, railroading, writing. Home: 1133 Marian Way Sacramento CA 95818-3718 Office: Calif Jour 2101 K St Sacramento CA 95816-4920 E-mail: agb@statenet.com., agb2@mindspring.com.

BLOCK, AMANDA ROTH, artist; b. Louisville, Feb. 20, 1912; d. Albert Solomon and Helen (Bernheim) Roth; m. Gordon J. Wolfe, June 16, 1931 (div. 1947); 1 child, Joseph G. Wolf; m. Maurice Block, Jr., July 15, 1949. Student, Smith Coll., 1930-31, U. Cin., 1933, Art Acad. Cin., 1933-40; BFA, Ind. U.-Purdue U., Indpls., 1960. Instr. Herron Sch. Art, Ind. U. Purdue U., Indpls., 1969-73; instr. lithography Indpls. Art Ctr., 1974. Adv. bd. Indpls. Art League Found., 1979-81. One-woman shows, 1444 Gallery, Indpls., 1962, Sheldon Swope Art Gallery, Terre Haute, Ind., 1963, 73, Park Avenue Gallery, Indpls., 1964, Harriet Crane Gallery, Cin., 1965, Talbot Gallery, Indpls., 1967, Merida Gallery, Louisville, 1967, Herron Mus. Art, Indpls., 1969, Editions Ltd. Gallery, Indpls., 1972, 79, Franklin (Ind.) Coll., 1973, Tucson Mus. Sch., 1977, Indpls. Art League, 1992; two-woman shows, Jason Gallery, N.Y.C., 1964, Orange County Coll., Middletown, N.Y., 1964, Washington Gallery, Frankfort, Ind., 1975, Edits. Ltd. Gallery, Indpls., 1983; exhibited in group shows, Cpo. Art Inst., 1941, Butler Inst. Am. Art, Youngstown, Ohio, Burr Gallery, N.Y.C., Hanover Coll., Wabash, Ind., De Pauw U., Soc. Am. Graphic Artists AAA Gallery, Purdue U., Istan Gallery, Tokyo, Phila. Print Club, Pa. Acad. Fine Arts, 1969, Imprint Gallery, San Francisco, 1972, Van Straaten Gallery, Chgo., 1973, McNay Inst., San Antonio, 1972, Pratt Graphics, N.Y.C., 1976, Ind. State Mus., 1976, Indpls. Mus. Art, 1977, Tucson Mus. Art, 1978, internat. traveling exhbn., Soc. Am. Graphic Artists, 1974-75, traveling exhbn., 1977, 78; represented in permanent collections, Continental Ill. Bank, Chgo., De Pauw U., Ind. State Coll., Terre Haute, Ind., Med. Soc., Indpls., Sheldon Swope Art Gallery, Stevens Coll., Boston Public Library, USIA, Lafayette (Ind.) Art Center, Lippman Assos., architects, Indpls., J.B. Speed Mus., Louisville, IBM Bldg., Indpls., Phila Mus. Art, Bklyn. Mus., Cin. Art Mus., N.Y. Public Library, Columbia U. Gallery, N.Y.C., Biodynamics Inc., Indpls., Fidelity Bank, Carmel, Ind., Tuscon Mus. Art, Indpsl. Mus. Art, Indianapolis Art Ctr. Retrospective Print and Drawing Exhib., 1992. Recipient award Ben and Beatrice Goldstein Found., N.Y.C., 1971. Mem. Soc. Am. Graphic Artists. Jewish. Home: Villa Valencia 24552 Paseo de Valencia A631 Laguna Hills CA 92653 E-mail: minblock@cs.com.

BLOCK, BILL, film company executive; Student, Columbia U. Talent agent, head West Coast ops. Internat. Creative Mgmt., 1980-97; pres. Artisan Entertainment, Santa Monica, Calif., 1997—. Founder InterTalent Agy., 1988 (merged with Internat. Creative Mgmt. 1992). Office: Artisan Entertainment 2700 Colorado Ave Fl 2 Santa Monica CA 90404-5502

BLOCK, DENNIS JEFFREY, lawyer; b. Bronx, N.Y., Sept. 1, 1942; s. Martin and Betty (Berger) B.; m. Lauren Elizabeth Troupin, Nov. 27, 1967; children: Robert, Tracy, Meredith. BA, U. Buffalo, 1964; LLB, Bklyn. Law Sch., 1967. Bar: N.Y. 1968, U.S. Dist. Ct. (ea. dist.) N.Y., U.S. Dist. Ct. (so. dist.) N.Y., U.S. Ct. Appeals (2d, 3d, 5th, 6th, 7th, 8th, 9th, 10th and 11th cirs.), U.S. Supreme Ct. Br. chief SEC, N.Y.C., 1967-72; assoc. Weil, Gotshal & Manges, L.L.P., N.Y.C., 1972-74, ptnr., 1974-98, Cadwalader, Wickersham & Taft, LLP, N.Y.C., 1998—. Co-author: The Business Judgment Rule: Fiduciary Duties of Corporate Directors and Officers, Law & Business, Inc., 1987, 5th edit., 1998; co-editor: The Corporate Counselor's Desk Book, 1982, 5th edit., 1999; contbr. articles to profl. jours. Chmn. major gifts lawyers div., United Jewish Appeal Fedn., 1987-89, chmn. lawyers div., 1989-91. Mem. ABA (coun. litigation sect., com. on corp. laws sect. bus. law), Assn. of Bar of City of N.Y., Am. Law Inst.

BLOCK, DENNIS WILLIAM, emergency physician; b. Dec. 20, 1952; BA in Biochemistry, Drake U., 1976, BS in Pharmacy, 1979; DO, U. Osteo. Med./Health Scis., 1983. Emergency medicine resident Highland Gen. Hosp., Oakland, Calif., 1984-87; emergency physician Physician's Emergency Svcs., Blue Springs, Mo., 1999—; dir. emergency svcs. Ft. Osage Fire Dist., Buckner, Mo., 1991—, Cen. Jackson County Fire Dist., Blue Springs, 1999—. Mem. Mayor's Adv. Com. for EMS, Independence, Mo., 1993-99 E-mail: dblockerdoc@comcast.net.

BLOCK, EMIL NATHANIEL, JR., retired air force officer; b. Newark, Ohio, Oct. 3, 1930; s. Emil Nathaniel and Louise Jeanette (Palmer) B.; m. Marian Lou Davis, June 9, 1956; children: Eric, Emil Darin. BS, U.S. Naval Acad., 1956; MSE in Instrumentation, MSE in Aero. and Astronautical Engring, U. Mich., 1961; MS in Bus. Adminstrn, George Washington U., 1966. Commd. 2d lt. U.S. Air Force, 1956, advanced through grades to maj. gen., 1979; spl. asst. for B-1 matters, dep. chief staff for research and devel. Hdqrs. USAF, Washington, 1976-78; chief of staff mil. airlift command, dir. Air Force C-X task force, Scott AFB, Ill., 1978-80; dir. plans Hdqrs. USAF, Pentagon, Washington, 1980-81; pres. Blime, Inc., 1981—. Decorated D.S.M. (2), Legion of Merit (3), D.F.C., Bronze Star, Meritorious Service medal (2), Air medal (5); Jimmy Doolittle fellow, 1978 Mem. Air Force Assn. E-mail: blime@his.com.

BLOCK, FRANCESCA LIA, writer; b. Hollywood, Calif., Dec. 3, 1962; d. Irving Alexander and Gilda Rona (Klein) B.; m. Chris Schuette; children: Jasmine Angelina Schuette, Samuel Alexander Schuette. BA in English Lit., U. Calif., Berkeley, 1986. Author: Weetzie Bat, 1989 (ALA Best Book award, 1989), Witch Baby, 1991 (Sch. Libr. Jour. Best Book award), Cherokee Bat and the Goat Guys, 1992 (ALA Best Book award, N.Y. Times Book Rev. Notable Book), Ecstasia, 1993, Missing Angel Juan, 1993 (ALA Best Book award, 1993), Primavera, 1994, The Hanged Man, 1994, Baby Be Bop, 1995 (Pub.'s Weekly Best Book award, 1995, ALA Best Book award, 1995), Girl Goddess # 9, 1996, Dangerous Angels, 1998 (L.A. Times Rev. Best Seller), I Was a Teenage Fairy, 1998; author: (with Hillary Carlip) Zine Scene, 1998, Violet and Claire, 1999 (L.A. Times Rev. Best Seller), The Rose and the Beast, 2000 (L.A. Times Rev. Best Seller, Pub.'s Weekly Best Book award, 2000), Nymph, 2000, Echo, 2002; author: Guarding the Moon, 2003, Wasteland, 2003, various translations into French, Italian, German, Japanese, Czech, Danish, Finnish and Norwegian. Mem. Phi Beta Kappa. Democrat. Jewish. Office: c/o Lydia Wills Writers and Artists Agy New York NY 10019-5206

BLOCK, ISAAC EDWARD, professional society administrator; b. Phila., Aug. 8, 1924; s. Louis Emanuel and Stella Florence (Goodman) B.; m. Marline Beryl Lewin, June 16, 1957; children: Nancy Anne, Kathie Sue, Stephen Edward BS in Physics, Haverford Coll., 1944; MA in Math., Harvard U., 1947, PhD in Math., 1952. Math. cons. Philco Corp., Phila., 1951-54; mgr. computer ctr. Burroughs Corp., Phila., 1954-59; mgr. engring. computer ctr. Univac div. Sperry Rand Corp., Phila., 1959-61, mgr. applied math. systems Blue Bell, Pa., 1961-64; tech. advisor Auerbach Corp., Phila., 1964-65; mgr. Auerbach Info. Inc., Phila., 1965-67, v.p., gen. mgr., 1967-72; v.p., dir. product planning and devel. Auerbach Pub. Inc., Phila., 1972-76; mng. dir. Soc. for Indsl. and Applied Math., Phila., 1976-94, cons., 1994—. Sec./founder, 1951-53, chmn. pubs. com., 1954-63, v.p., 1964-74, council, 1957-65, trustee, 1971-75, chmn. bd. trustees, 1974-75; lectr. Computation Lab, Wayne State U., summers 1954-55 Served with USNR, 1944-45 Fellow AAAS; mem. Assn. Computing Machinery, Am. Math. Soc., Phi Beta Kappa, Sigma Xi. Avocations: photography, music. Home: 7904 Cobden Rd Glenside PA 19038-7255

BLOCK, JAMES A. hospital administrator, pediatrician; b. Dayton, Ohio, 1940; Grad., Haverford Coll., 1962; MD, NYU, 1966. Chief ambulatory svcs. Surgeon General's Comprhensive Health Planning office; assoc. dir. Community Health Svc. Health Svcs. and Mental Health Adminstrn. USPHS; intern pediatrics Strong Meml. Hosp., Rochester, NY, 1966—67; resident pediatrics and ambulatory medicine Strong Meml. Hosp. U. Rochester, 1969—71; pediatrician, head ambulatory svcs. Genesee Hosp., 1971—79; pres. Rochester Area Hosps. Corp., NY, 1979—85; asst. to pres., then pres., CEO U. Hosps. Cleve., 1985—86; pres., CEO Johns Hopkins Hosp., Johns Hopkins Health System, Balt., 1992—97; asst. to pres., then pres., CEO U. Hosps. Cleve., 1986—92. Adj. prof. health policy Case Western Res. U., 1991; faculty Hosp. Fin. Mgmt. Assn., Am. Assn. Med. Colls.; chmn. bd. ops. com. RHN; mem. gov.'s commn. ambulatory care cost containment State of N.Y., 1977—; mem. HCFA Physician Discussion Group; adj. prof. pediats. Johns Hopkins U. Sch. Medicine; adj. prof. health policy Jhns Hopkins Sch. Hygiene and Pub. Health; cons. in field; spkr. in field; bd. dirs. MMI Cos., Inc., Greater Balt. Com.; del. Coun. Tchg. Hosps., Assn. Am. Med. Colls.; sr. cons. UN Found., N.Y.C., 1998—. Mem. editl. adv. bd. Jour. Ambulatory Care Mgmt.; contbr. articles. Campaign cabinet mem. United Way; mem. Lombardi Task Force; cmty. hosp. med. staff Primary Group Practice Program; corp. mem. United Way; bd. dirs. Robert Wood Johnson Found.; sr. program cons. Primary Group Practice Program, 1982; bd. dirs. Unicef Mercantile Bankshares, Inc., Omna Inc., Soc. Med. Adminstrs.; trustee Johns Hopkins U. Fellow Johns Hopkins Health Sys./Johns Hopkins Hosp. Health fellow, Nat. Urban Coalition, 1971—72. Mem.: AMA, APHA, Med. Adminstrs. Conf., Ambulatory Pediat. Assn. Home: 1207 Malvern Ave Baltimore MD 21204-6721

BLOCK, JOHN ROBINSON, newspaper publisher; b. Toledo, Oct. 1, 1954; s. Paul Jr. and Marjorie Jane (McNab) B. BA, Yale U., 1977. Reporter AP, Miami, Fla., 1977-78, N.Y.C., 1978-80; Washington corr. The Toledo Blade, 1980-82, European corr., 1982-83, Sunday editor, 1983-85, asst. mng. editor, 1985-87, exec. editor, 1987-89; co-pub., editor-in-chief The Blade, Toledo, 1989—; co-pub. Pitts. Post-Gazette, 1999—2001, editor-in-chief, 1993—, pub., 2001—; v.p., bd. dirs. P.G. Pub. Co., Pitts. Exec. v.p., bd. dirs. Block comms., Inc., Toledo. Chmn. City Mgr.'s Hist. Preservation Com., Toledo, 1983-85; chmn. airport com. Toledo-Lucas County Port Authority, 1994-97. Mem. Am. Soc. Newspaper Editors, Soc. Profl. Journalists, Internat. Press Inst. Clubs: Nat. Press (Washington), Yale (N.Y.C.), Belmont Country (Perrysburg, Ohio), Grolier (N.Y.C.), Duquesne (Pitts.), Athletic (Columbus, Ohio). Office: The Blade 541 N Superior St Toledo OH 43697-0921 also: Pitts Post-Gazette 34 Blvd Of The Allies Pittsburgh PA 15222-1204 E-mail: jrblock@theblade.com.*

BLOCK, JOHN RUSLING, former secretary of agriculture; b. Galesburg, Ill., Feb. 15, 1935; children: Hans, Cynthia, Christine, Savannah. BS, U.S. Mil. Acad., 1959. Farmer, Gilson, Ill., 1960-77; dir. Ill. Dept. Agr., Springfield, 1977-81; sec. agr. U.S. Dept. Agr., Washington, 1981-86; pres. Food Distbrs. Internat., Falls Church, Va., 1986—2002; exec. v.p., pres. wholesale divsn. Food Mktg. Inst., Washington, 2002—. Served to 2d lt. U.S. Army, 1958-60. Named Outstanding Young Farmer Am. Jaycees, 1969; inducted into Nat. 4-H Hall of Fame, 2003. Mem. Ill. Farm Bur., Knox County Farm Bur. Office: Food Mktg Inst 655 Fifteenth NW Ste 700 Washington DC 20005-5701

BLOCK, JON E. clinical trials consultant; b. Toledo, Ohio, Sept. 2, 1960; BA, Washington U., St. Louis, 1982; PhD, Inst. for Advanced Studies, Clayton, Mo., 1986. Rsch. specialist U. Calif., San Francisco, 1986-89; v.p. Advanced Biorsch. Assocs., Danville, Calif., 1990-93; pres. Jon E. Block, PhD, Inc., San Francisco, 1993—. Cons. FDA, Rockville, Md., 1997-98. Contbr. articles to profl. jours. Avocations: tennis, yachting. Home and Office: 2210 Jackson St # 401 San Francisco CA 94115 Fax: (415) 928-0765. E-mail: jonblock@sbcglobal.net.

BLOCK, JULES RICHARD, retired psychologist, educator, university official; b. N.Y.C., Nov. 23, 1930; s. Jules Irving and Elizabeth (Shinkle) B.; m. Elizabeth Ehrenstein, Dec. 21, 1952 (div. Nov. 1978); m. Patricia Clark, Feb. 29, 1980; children— Cheryl, Janet. BA, Hofstra Coll., 1952; PhD, N.Y. U., 1962. Lectr. Hofstra U., Hempstead, N.Y., 1956-60, instr., 1960-62, asst. prof., 1962-66, assoc. prof., 1966-70, prof., 1970-79, chmn. dept. psychology, 1968-78, exec. dir. research and resource devel., 1976-85, asst. to pres. for info. systems, 1985-87, v.p. planning and liaison, 1987—2001; ret., 2002. Rsch. asst. Human Resources Rsch. and Tng. Inst., Albertson, N.Y., 1957-59, rsch. assoc., 1959-61, dir. rsch., 1961-71; pres. Instrumental Psychol. Methods, Hempstead, Inst. for Rsch. and Evaluation, Hempstead; v.p. Y&B Assocs., Hempstead, 1983-98, pres., 1998—. Contbr. articles to profl. jours. Mem. Nassau County Youth Bd., 1968-70; Exec. dir. Initial Teaching Alphabet Found., 1965-72. Served with USNR, 1952-56. Recipient award for outstanding research in rehab. Nat. Rehab. Council, 1969 Mem. Am. Psychol. Assn. Home: 33 Primrose Ln Hempstead NY 11550-4633

BLOCK, LAWRENCE, author; b. Buffalo, June 24, 1938; s. Arthur Jerome and Lenore Harriet (Nathan) B.; m. Loretta Kallett, Mar. 10, 1960 (div. 1973); children: Amy Jo Block Reichel, Jill Diana, Alison Elspeth; m. Lynne Wood, Oct. 2, 1983. Student, Antioch Coll., 1955-59. Editor Scott Meredith Lit. Agy., N.Y.C., 1957-58; editor Whitman Pub. Co., Racine, Wis., 1964-66; free lance writer, 1957—. Pres., seminar leader Write for Your Life, N.Y.C. and Ft. Myers Beach, Fla., 1983-88; instr. Hofstra U., Hempstead, N.Y., 1981 Author: (novels) Mona, 1961, Death Pulls a Doublecross, 1962, The Girl With the Long Green Heart, 1965, The Thief Who Couldn't Sleep, 1966, The Cancelled Czech, 1966, Deadly Honeymoon, 1967, Tanner's Twelve Swingers, 1967, Two for Tanner, 1968, Tanner's Tiger, 1968, Here Comes A Hero, 1968, After the First Death, 1969, The Specialists, 1969, Such Men are Dangerous, 1969, Me Tanner, You Jane, 1970, No Score, 1970, Ronald Rabbit Is A Dirty Old Man, 1971, Chip Harrison Scores Again, 1971, Five Little Rich Girls, 1976, The Topless Tulip Caper, 1975, The Sins of the Fathers, 1976, In the Midst of Death, 1976, Time to Murder and Create, 1977, Burglars Can't be Choosers, 1977, The Burglar in the Closet, 1978, The Burglar Who Liked to Quote Kipling (Nero Wolfe award), 1979, Ariel, 1980, The Burglar Who Studied Spinoza, 1980, A Stab in the Dark, 1981, Eight Million Ways to Die, 1982, The Burglar Who Painted Like Mondrian, 1983, When the Sacred Ginmill Closes (Japanese Maltese Falcon award), 1986, Random Walk, 1988, Out on the Cutting Edge, 1989, A Ticket to the Boneyard, 1990, A Dance at the Slaughterhouse, 1991, A Walk Among the Tombstones, 1992, The Devil Knows You're Dead, 1993, The Burglar Who Traded Ted Williams, 1994 (German Marlowe award), A Long Line of Dead Men, 1994, The Burglar Who Thought He Was Bogart, 1995, Even the Wicket, 1997, The Burglar in the Library, 1997, Hit Man, 1998, Tanner on Ice, 1998, Everybody Dies, 1998, The Burglar in the Rye, 1999, Hit List, 2000, Hope to Die, 2001, Small Town, 2003; (nonfiction) Writing the Novel From Plot to Print, 1979, Telling Lies for Fun and Profit, 1981, Write forYour Life, 1985, Spider, Spin Me a Web, 1988; (with Delbert Ray Krause) Swiss Shooting Talers and Medals, 1965; (with Cheryl Morrison) Real Food Places, 1981; (with Harold King) Code of Arms, 1981, (with Ernie Bulow) After Hours, 1994; (short story collections) Sometimes They Bite (trophy 813 Societe of France), 1983, Like A Lamb to Slaughter, 1984, Some Days You Get The Bear, 1993, Ehrengraf for the Defense, 1994, One Night Stands, 1999, The Lost Cases of Ed London, 2001, Enough Rope, 2002, (anthologies) Death Cruise, 1999, Master's Choice, 1999, Opening Shots, 2000, Master's Choice 2, 2000, Speaking of Lust, 2000, Speaking of Greed, 2001, Opening Shots 2, 2002, Blood on Their Hands, 2003; contbg. editor Writer's Digest, 1976-90; contbr. stories to various mags. including Cosmopolitan, Playboy, GQ, Am. Heritage, mystery mags. Named Suspense Writer of Yr., Romantic Times, 1984, Grand Maitre du Roman Noir, Calibre 38, 1996. Fellow Flat Earth Soc. of Can. (U.S. plenipotentiary 1971—), Va. Ctr. for the Creative Arts; mem. The Players, Mystery Writers Am. (pres. 2000, Edgar Allan Poe award 1985, 92, 94, 98, Grand Master award 1994), Pvt. Eye Writers Am. (pres. 1984, Shamus award 1983, 85, 96, Life Achievement award 2002), Internat. Assn. Crime Writers, Internat. Narcotics Enforcement Officers Assn., Internat. Assn. for Study of Organized Crime, Crime Writers Can., Crime Writers Assn. (U.K.), Crime Writers of Norway. E-mail: LV@lawrenceblock.com.

BLOCK, LYNNE WOOD, accountant; b. New Orleans, July 13, 1943; d. John Sorber and Emilie Douglas (Poe) Wood: m. Lawrence Richard Block, Oct. 2, 1983. Student, Ursuline Acad., 1957-61, Hunter Coll., 1968-69, Pace U., 1978-79. Clk. Dunn & Bradstreet, New Orleans, 1961-64; fashion model Stewart Model's, N.Y.C., 1965-70; prin. The Real Tinsel Antiques, N.Y.C., 1970-75, Other World Furniture Imports, W. Hampton, N.Y., 1976, The Lynne Wood Co., N.Y.C., Ft. Myers Beach, Fla., 1976—; owner Lynne's Studded Jackets, 1988—. Seminar leader, Ft. Myers Beach, 1983-88; cons. Cross and Desire Corp., N.Y.C., 1980-85. Author: Evelyn the Raccoon, 1984, Photos in American Heritage Magazine, 1990; one-woman shows include VCCA, 1989, 90, Chuck Levitan Gallery, N.Y.C. of Port-A-Shrines, 1991-92, 94; group shows include Renee Fatoue Gallery, East Hampton, N.Y.; contbr. short story to mag. Vol. staff mem. Met. Mus. Art, N.Y.C., 1995—. Named Model of Yr., Photography Annual, 1968, Va. Ctr. for Creative Arts fellow, 1989, 90. Mem. Pilot Internat., Am. Bus. Women's Assn. (sec. 1986-88). Avocations: gardening, reading, antiques, travel, art.

BLOCK, MELVIN AUGUST, surgeon, educator; b. Evansville, Ind., July 2, 1921; s. August William and Alma (Klutey) B.; m. Marcia Jean Jacobs, May 28, 1955; children: Deborah Ann, Christopher Reed. BS, Ind. U., 1942, MD, 1944; PhD, U. Minn., 1953. Intern Ind. U. Med. Center, 1945; resident Mayo Clinic, Rochester, Minn., 1948-54; chmn. dept. surgery Henry Ford Hosp., Detroit, 1975-79, Scripps Clinic Med. Group, La Jolla, Calif., 1980-87; clin. prof. surgery U. Mich. Med. Sch., 1970-80, U. Calif., San Diego Med. Sch., 1980-93. Contbr. numerous articles to profl. jours. Served to capt. M.C. AUS, 1945-47. Fellow Royal Coll. Surgeons Can.; mem. ACS (past gov.), Am., Central, Western (past pres.) surg. assns., Am. Thyroid Assn., Am. Gastroenterology Assn., Soc. Surg. Alimentary Tract, Soc. Head and Neck Surgeons, Soc. Internationale de Chirurgie, AMA, Calif., San Diego County med. socs., Acad. Surg. Detroit (past pres.), Detroit Surg. Soc. (past pres.), Internat. Assn. Endocrine Surgeons, Am. Assn. Endocrine Surgeons, Sigma Xi, Alpha Omega Alpha. Home: 4575 Excalibur Way San Diego CA 92122-1513 Office: Scripps Clinic Med Group 10666 N Torrey Pines Rd La Jolla CA 92037-1027 *Time is our most valuable possession. It is limited qualitatively and quantitatively. This realization should be implied in most actions.*

BLOCK, NEAL JAY, lawyer; b. Chgo., Oct. 4, 1942; s. William Emanual and Dorothy (Harrison) B.; m. Frances Keer Block, Apr. 19, 1970; children: Jessica, Andrew. BS, U. Ill., 1964; JD, U. Chgo., 1967. Bar: Ill. 1967, U.S. dist. Ct. (no. dist.) Ill. 1967, U.S. Ct. Appeals (3d and 6th cirs.) 1968, U.S. Claims Ct. 1990, U.S. Ct. Appeals (Fed. cir.) 1991. Atty., advisor U.S. Tax Ct., Washington, 1967-69; assoc. Baker & McKenzie, Chgo., 1969-74, ptnr., 1974—, client credit dir., 1989—. Adj. prof. law Kent Law Sch., Ill. Inst. Tech., Chgo., 1986-90. Mem. ABA, Chgo. Bar Assn. (chmn. fed. tax com. 1983-84), Ill. State Bar Assn., AICPA (honorable mention award 1964), Ill. Soc. CPA's. (silver medal 1964, Leading Ill. Atty. 1997). Office: Baker & McKenzie 1 Prudential Pla 130 E Randolph St Ste 3500 Chicago IL 60601-6342

BLOCK, NED, philosopher, educator; b. Chgo., Aug. 22, 1942; s. Eli William and Blanche (Rabinowitz) Block; m. Susan Carey, May 17, 1970; 1 child, Eliza. SB in Physics and Philosophy, MIT, 1964; postgrad., Oxford (Eng.) U., 1964-66; PhD, Harvard U., 1971. Asst. prof. philosophy MIT, Cambridge, Mass., 1971-77, assoc. prof., 1977-83, prof., 1983-96, chair dept. philosophy, 1989-95, chair press cognitive rev. bd., 1992—95; prof. NYU, N.Y.C., 1996—. Mem. faculty NEH Inst., 1981, 93; grant reviewer NSF, Can. Coun.; vis. rschr. Ecole Poly., Paris, 1995—96; vis. prof. Harvard U., 2002—03. Adv. editor: Contemporary Psychology; mem. editl. bd. Cognition, Cognition and Brain Theory, Cognitive Sci., mem. adv. editl. bd. Lang. and Cognitive Processes, Mind and Lang. Philos. Studies, mem. bd. editl. advisors Behavioral and Brain Scis.; contbr. articles to profl. jours. Named one of 10 Best, Philosphers' Ann., 1983, 1990, 1995; fellow, Old Dominion Found., 1973—74, Sloan Found., 1980—81; grantee, U.S. Nat. Com. Internat. Union History and Philosophy Sci., 1979, 1983, NEH, 1979—82, NSF, 1985—86, 1988—90, Am. Coun. Learned Socs., 1988—89; Postdoctoral fellow, NIH, 1970—71, Sr. fellow, Ctr. Study Lang. and Info., Stanford U., 1984—85. Mem.: Assn. Sci. Study Consciousness (pres.-elect 2002—). Home: 37 Washington Sq W New York NY 10011-9181 Office: NYU Dept Philosophy Main Bldg 100 Washington Sq E New York NY 10003-6688 E-mail: ned.block@nyu.edu.

BLOCK, NELSON R(ICHARD), lawyer; b. San Antonio, Mar. 24, 1951; s. Norman and Ethel (Poliakoff) B. BA, Johns Hopkins U., 1973; JD, U. Tex., 1976. Bar: Tex. 1976. Law clk. 14th Ct. Appeals, Houston, 1976-77; assoc. Sheinfeld, Maley & Kay, P.C., Houston, 1977-83, shareholder, 1983-2001, Winstead Sechrest & Minick P.C., Houston, 2001—. Spkr. in field; founder Gilwell Fellow. Author: Commercial Law Manual: Ch. 40 Contractual Subordination, 1991, A Thing of the Spirit: The Life of E. Urner Goodman, 2000; pub. The Jour. of Scouting History. Mem. bd. dirs., legal counsel Sam Houston Area coun. Boy Scouts Am., 1984—, mng. trustee The Green Bar Bill Hillcourt Trust; mem. Baden-Powell World Fellowship. Mem. ABA, Tex. Bar Assn. (chmn. uniform comml. code com. 1982-84), Houston Bar Assn., Tex. Bar Found., Selden Soc. (state corr. 1978—), Houston Comml. Fin. Lawyers Forum (founder), Am. Coll. of Comml. Fin. Lawyers (regent). Avocations: camping, hiking, reading, history, sketching. Office: 910 Travis St Ste 2400 Houston TX 77002 E-mail: nblock@winstead.com.

BLOCK, NORMAN LOUIS, physician, medical educator; b. N.Y.C., Aug. 31, 1938; s. Abraham Harold and Rose (Bodatsky) B.; m. Carolyn Lee Peck, May 12, 1967; children: Joseph, David, Adam, Nathaniel, Jessica. BA, NYU, 1959, MD, 1963. Diplomate Am. Bd. Urology. Intern Baylor U. Med. Ctr., Dallas, 1963-64, resident in surgery, 1966—67; resident in urology NYU Med. Ctr., N.Y.C., 1967—71; fellow in urologic oncology Meml. Sloan Kettering Cancer Ctr., N.Y.C., NY, 1971-72; attending physician Miami VA Med. Ctr., 1972-96, Jackson Meml. Hosp., Fla., 1972—; chief urology VA Med. Ctr., 1975—85; assoc. prof. urology U. Miami, 1976-82, prof. urology, 1982—, prof. biomed. engring., 1982—, L. Austin Weeks prof., 1982—, prof. oncology, 1985—. Editl. reviewer 6 jours. Contbr. numerous articles to profl. jours., including Cancer Jour. Urology, Jour. Urology, Jour. Surg. Oncology. Capt. U.S. Army, 1964-66. Recipient numerous awards, fellowships, lectureships. Mem. AMA, ACS, AAAS, Internat. Urology Soc., Internat. Soc. for Artificial Organs, Am. Fertility Soc., Am. Urol. Assn. (Southeastern sect.), Am. Soc. for Artificial Internal Organs, Am. Assn. Lab. Animal Sci. (Fla. divsn.), Southeastern Cancer Rsch. Assn., Soc. Surg. Oncology, Soc. Univ. Urologists, Southeastern Coop. Oncology Group, Soc. Govt. Svc. Urologists, So. Med. Assn., Confedn. Am. Urologists, Soc. Urologic Oncology, Colombian Urol. Soc., Fla. Med. Assn., Fla. Urologic Assn., Greater Miami Urologic Soc., Dade County Med. Soc., Bellevue Urologic Alumni Assn. Republican. Jewish. Achievements include patents for five; research in new treatment for prostate cancer; development of new diagnostic test for bladder cancer; applied a new model for prostate cancer in animals; development of of an artificial bladder, ureter, urethra sphincter. Avocation: wildlife photography. Office: U Miami Sch Medicine Dept Urology M 814 PO Box 16960 Miami FL 33101-6960 E-mail: nblock@med.miami.edu.

BLOCK, PETER CARL, internist, cardiologist; b. Balt., Mar. 26, 1938; AB cum laude, Amherst Coll., 1959; MD cum laude, Harvard U., 1964. Diplomate Am. Bd. Internal Medicine, Am. Bd. Cardiovasc. Disease. Med. intern Mass. Gen. Hosp., Boston, 1964-65, asst. resident, internal medicine, 1965-66; biomed. investigator USN Med. Corps Naval Radiological Def. Lab., San Francisco, 1966-68; clin. and rsch. fellow in medicine Mass. Gen. Hosp., 1968-70; tchg. fellow in medicine Harvard Med. Sch., Boston, 1968-70; asst. in medicine Mass. Gen. Hosp., 1970-71, asst. physician, 1973-76, dir. cardiac catheterization lab., 1974-91, assoc. physician, 1977-83, physician, 1984-91; assoc. dir. The Heart Inst. St. Vincent Hosp. and Med. Ctr., Portland, Oreg., 1991-2000; dir. clin. rsch. dept. cardiology Emory U. Med. Sch., Atlanta, 2000—, prof. medicine, 2001—. Med. dir. coronary care unit, interventional cardiovasc. recovery unit, cardiac catheterization lab. St. Vincent Hosp., 1994—2000; instr. in medicine Harvard Med. Sch., 1970—72; asst. prof. medicine Mass. Gen. Hosp., 1972—81, assoc. prof. medicine, 1981—91; prof. biomed. sci. and engring. Oreg. Grad. Inst. of Sci. and Tech., 1993—2000; prof. medicine Oreg. Health Scis. U., Portland, 1996—2000; cons. in cardiology Chelsea (Mass.) Soldiers Home, 1970—91, VA Hosp., West Roxbury, Mass., 1983—91; prof. medicine Emory U. Med. Sch., 2000—, dir. interventional rsch. dept. cardiology, 2000—. Contbr. over 150 articles to profl. jours., as well as revs., editorials, and chpts. to books; editl. bd. The Am. Scholar, 1974-76, Catheterization & Cardiovasc. Diagnosis, 1988—, Am. Jour. Cardiology, 1990—, Internat. Jour. Cardiology, 1992—, Jour. Am. Coll. Cardiology, 1994—; program participant and med. cons. for script and prodn. of TV documentary The Frightening Feeling You Are Going to Die (Howard H. Blakeslee award Am. Heart Assn., 1977). Fellow Am. Coll. Cardiology, Am. Coll. Angiology, Am. Heart Assn. (coun. on clin. cardiology); mem. AMA (Physician's Recognition award in continuing med. edn. 1982, 85), Soc. for Cardiac Angiography and Interventions (gov. northwestern region 1995—), Western Assn. Vascular Tech., Oreg. Med. Assn., Mass. Heart Assn. Office: Emory U Hosp 1364 Clifton Rd NE Atlanta GA 30322 E-mail: peter-block@emory.org.

BLOCK, PHILIP DEE, III, investment counselor; b. Chgo., Feb. 14, 1937; married; 2 children. BS in Indsl. Adminstrn. with high honors, Yale U., 1958. Trainee and engr. Inland Steel Co., Chgo., 1958-60, raw materials coordinator, 1961-65, gen. mgr. purchases, 1966-72, gen. mgr. corp. planning, 1973-76; v.p. materials and services Inland Steel Container, Chgo., 1977-79, v.p. purchases, 1980-85; sr. v.p. Capital Guardian Trust Co., Chgo., 1986—. Bd. dirs. Children's Meml. Hosp.; trustee Chgo. Hist. Soc., Shedd Aquarium Soc. With USAFR, 1959-64. Home: 1430 N Lake Shore Dr Chicago IL 60610-6682 Office: Capital Guardian Trust Co 21 S Clark St Chicago IL 60603-2000

BLOCK, RICHARD L. sociologist, criminologist, educator; b. Cin., July 4, 1944; s. Mandell Jerold Block and Marian Abrams; m. Carolyn Rebecca Britt, June 30, 1966; children: Daniel, Devora. Prof. sociology and criminology Loyola U., Chgo., 1969—. Cons. Nat. Inst. Justice, Washington, 1980—, Chgo. Police Dept., 1985—, UN, Vienna, Austria, 1993-94. Fulbright Hayes fellow, 1978, 85-86. Mem.: Homicide Rsch. Working Group (founder), Phi Beta Kappa. Avocations: canoeing, photography. Office: Loyola U Chgo Dept Sociology 6525 N Sheridan Rd Chicago IL 60626 E-mail: rblock@luc.edu.

BLOCK, RICHARD RAPHAEL, lawyer, arbitrator; b. Phila., Nov. 9, 1938; s. Harry and Ida (Brandes) B.; m. Joanne Kramer, July 1, 1943 (div. Jan. 1973); 1 child, Jeffrey. AB, Dickinson Coll., 1959; LLB cum laude, U. Pa., 1962. Bar: Pa. 1963, N.J. 1980, D.C. 1982. Assoc. Folz & Bard, Phila., 1963-64; ptnr. Melzer & Schiffrin, Phila., 1964-75, Beitch & Block, Phila., 1975-90; dir. community rels. Dist. Atty. of Phila., 1991-96; chief tech. officer Phila. Dept. of Commerce, 1996—. Chmn. hearing com Disciplinary Bd. Supreme Ct. Pa., 1982-90. Contbg. author: Handbook of Pennsylvania Courts, 1970, Divorce Mediation, 1985, Prenuptial Agreements, 1989, Encyclopedia on Matrimonial Practice, 1991; assoc. editor U. Pa. Law Rev.; contbr. articles to profl. jours. Vice pres. Am. Jewish Congress, Phila., 1975; campaign mgr. Elect Joan Specter to City Coun., Phila., 1978, 82, 86. Mem. Pa. Bar Assn. (arbitrator Inter-Atty. Dispute Resolution 1987—, speaker 1988) Am. Arbitration Assn., Phila. Coll. Judiciary (lectr. 1984). Republican. Avocations: horse racing, computers, music.

BLOCK, ROBERT CHARLES, nuclear engineering and engineering physics educator; b. Newark, Feb. 11, 1929; s. George and Sue (Ehrenkranz) B.; m. Rita Adler, June 28, 1952; children: Keith, Robin. BSEE, Newark Coll. Engring., 1950; MA in Physics, Columbia U., 1953; PhD in Nuclear Physics, Duke U., 1956. Elec. engr. Nat. Union Radio Corp., W. Orange, N.J., 1950-51, Bendix Aviation Co., Teterboro, N.J., 1951; physicist Oak Ridge Nat. Lab., 1955-66; prof. nuclear engring. and sci. Rensselaer Poly. Inst., 1966-96, head dept. nuclear engring. and engring. physics, 1987-93, 1987-93, assoc. dean engring. for acad. & student affairs, 1993-96; prof. emeritus, 1997—; founder, v.p., treas. Becker, Block & Harris Inc., 1981-92. Vis. scientist Atomic Energy Rsch. Establishment, Harwell, Eng., 1962-63, Am. Inst. Physics, 1961-67; vis. prof. Kyoto (Japan) U., 1973-74; vis. physicist Brookhaven Nat. Lab., 1975, mem. vis. com. nuclear energy dept., 1982-86; cons. Gen. Electric Co., 1968-79; cons., mem. nuclear cross sect. adv. com. AEC, 1969-72; mem. U.S. Nuclear Data Com., 1972-74, NRC panel on low and medium energy neutrons, 1977; dir. Gaerttner Linac Lab., 1974—; vis. faculty Sandia Nat. Lab., 1986. Co-author chpt. in books. Recipient Glenn Murphy award Am. Soc. Engring. Edn., 1991, William H. Wiley Disting. Faculty award Rensselaer Poly. Inst., 1995; Japanese Ministry Edn. rsch. grantee, 1973-74. Fellow Am. Nuclear Soc.; mem. AAAS, AAUP, IEEE, Am. Phys. Soc., Sigma Xi, Sigma Pi Sigma, Phi Beta Tau, Tau Beta Pi. Achievements include research on neutron physics, radiation effects in electronics, and radiation applications. Home: 114 3rd St Troy NY 12180 Office: Rensselaer Poly Inst Gaerttner LINAC Lab 110 8th St Troy NY 12180-3590 E-mail: blockr@rpi.edu.

BLOCK, ROBERT I. psychologist, researcher, educator; b. Newark, N.J., Jan. 30, 1951; s. Milton and Harriet (Safier) B. BA with honors, Shimer Coll., 1969; MS, Harvard U., 1972, Rutgers U., 1977, PhD, 1981. Teaching asst. psychology dept. Rutgers U., New Brunswick, N.J., 1975-76; psychologist Lafayette Clinic, Detroit, 1982-84; rsch. assoc. psychiatry dept. Wayne State U., Detroit, 1982, instr., 1982-84; assoc. rsch. scientist dept. anesthesia U. Iowa, Iowa City, 1984-88, asst. prof. dept. anesthesia, 1988-94, assoc. prof. dept. anesthesia, 1994—. Cons. State of Mich., Lafayette Clinic, Detroit, Hoffmann La-Roche, Inc.; reviewer Psychopharmacology and Anesthesiology, NIH; mem. faculty senate Sch. of Medicine, Wayne State U., Detroit, 1982-84. Contbr. articles to Anesthesiology, Brit. Jour. Anaesthesia, Psychopharmacology, Pharmacol. Biochem. Behavior, Neuro Report. Fellow Rutgers U.; grantee Nat. Inst. on Drug Abuse, 1987-91, 93-2000. Mem. AAAS, Collegium Internat. Neuro-Psychopharmacologicum, Am. Psychol. Assn., Soc. Neurosci. Achievements include research on effects of nitrous oxide, benzodiazepines, marijuana, and other drugs on human associative processes, memory, cognition, brain structure and function. Home: 2029 Waterford Dr Coralville IA 52241-2734 Office: U Iowa Dept Anesthesia Westlawn Bldg Iowa City IA 52242

BLOCK, ROBERT MICHAEL, endodontist, educator, researcher; b. Ann Arbor, Mich., Oct. 15, 1947; s. Walter David and Thelma Violet (Levine) B.; m. Anne Powell Marshall, Sept. 4, 1977. BA, DePauw U., 1969; DDS, U. Mich.-Ann Arbor, 1974; cert. in endodontics, Va. Commonwealth U., 1977; MS in Pathology, Va. Commonwealth U., 1978. Diplomate Am. Bd. Endodontics. Clin. instr. Va. Commonwealth U., 1975-77, instr. pathology, 1977-78; rsch. assoc. endodontics U. Conn.-Farmington, 1975—; vis. sr. scientist Nat. Med. Rsch. Inst., Bethesda, Md., 1976-78; rsch. assoc. McGuire Vets. Hosp., Richmond, Va., 1975-78; vis. rsch. scientist U. Conn.-Farmington, 1978—; lectr. endodontics Flint Community Schs.; bd. dirs. Republic Bancorp, S.E., Republic Bank-S.E. div. Republic Bancorp. Contbr. articles profl. jours., chpt. in book. Exec. mem. campaign com. candidate for U. Mich. Bd. Regents, 1980; candidate for Mich. State Bd. Edn., 1982. HEW and NIH summer research fellow, 1970-71; research grantee McGuire Vets. Hosp., 1976-78. Fellow Am. Coll. of Endodontics; mem. Internat. Assn. Dental Rsch. (Edward P. Hatton award 1977), Am. Assn. Dental Rsch., Am. Assn. Endodontists (Meml. Research award 1977), Va. Dental Assn. (VAPAC com., state com. on infection control), Lapeer Dental Study Club (treas. 1978-82), ADA (Preventive Dentistry award 1973), Loudoun Dental Soc. (v.p.). Office: Loudoun Tech Ctr 21525 Ridgetop Cir # 220 Sterling VA 20166-6510 E-mail: Blcokendo@aol.com.

BLOCK, RUTH, retired insurance company executive; b. N.Y.C., Nov. 7, 1930; d. Albert and Celia (Shapiro) Smolensky; m. Norman Block, April 5, 1952. BA, Adelphi U., 1952. With Equitable Life Assurance Soc. of U.S., 1952-87, v.p., planning officer, 1973-77; sr. v.p. in charge individual life ins. bus., 1977-80; exec. v.p. individual ins. bus.'s; group life and health chief ins. officer, 1980—87; chmn., CEO Equitable Variable Life Ins. Co., 1980-84. Bd. dirs. of 55 ACM Mut. Funds; trustee Life Underwriter Tng. Coun., 1983-85; vis. exec. Mobil Co. U. Iowa, 1978. Bd. dirs. Stamford (Conn.) YWCA, 1977-80, Donaldson, Lufkin & Jenrette, 1983-86, Avon Products, 1985-91, BP Amoco, 1985-2001, ECOLAB Inc., 1985-2001, St. Lukes Cmty. Svcs., 1991-94; nat. chmn. Equitable United Way, 1978. Recipient Disting. Alumni award Adelphi U. Sch. of Bus., 1979, Catalyst award 1983, WEAL award, 1983, N.Y.C. YMCA award. Mem. Nat. Assn. Securities Dealers (gov. at large 1982-84), Com. of 200, Womens Econ. Round Table, Rsch. Bd. (emeritus), Bus. Execs. for Nat. Security, Women's Forum N.Y. and Conn. Office: PO Box 4653 Stamford CT 06907-0653

BLOCK, STEVEN D. music educator, composer; b. New York City, Nov. 5, 1952; s. Charles and Gloria Block; m. Stephanie A. Baker; children: Isaac A., Phillip Z., Sarah R.E., Jessica C., Rebecca M., Nathanael Z., Benjamin M. BA, Antioch Coll., Yellow Springs, Ohio, 1973; MA, U. Iowa, 1975; PhD, U. Pitts., 1981. Asst. prof. Northeastern Ill. U., Chgo., 1987—89; ptog., chmn. dept. of music U. N.Mex, Albuquerque, 1989—. Mediator, Albuquerque, 2001—03. Composer numerous musical compositions; contbr. articles to profl. publs. Dir. of liturgy Our Lady of Perpetual Help Byzantine Cath. Ch., Albuquerque, 2000—03; past pres., mem. John Donald Robb Trust, Albuquerque, 1991—2003; mem. Albuquerque Youth Symphony, 1999—2003. Recipient Andrew Mellon Predoctoral fellowship, U. Pitts., 1980—81, Leonard Bernstein fellowship, Berkshire Music Ctr., Tanglewood, 1983; grantee Composer grant, Paa Coun. for the Arts, 1983, Monroe Berger-Benny Carter Jazz Rsch., Inst. for Jazz Studies, 1996, Meet the Composer, 1983—84, 1987, 1991. Mem.: Coll. Music Soc., Soc. for Music Theory. Home: 325 Ellen St NW Los Lunas NM 87031 Office: U NMex Dept Music Albuquerque NM 87131 Home Fax: 505-866-0977; Office Fax: 505-277-0708. Personal E-mail: sblock@unm.edu. E-mail: sblock@unm.edu.

BLOCK, THOMAS ALAN, artist, educator; b. Washington, May 3, 1963; s. Victor Irving Block and Barbara Fern Block Gilbert; m. Deborah Spielberg, Oct. 9, 1998; 1 child, Dalya Spielberg. AB In English, Vassar Coll., 1987. Freelance journalist, 1984—88; artist-in-residence Longview Sch., Gaithersburg, Md., 1995—97; tchr. Summit Art Group, Gaithersburg, 1996—2000, Jewish Study Ctr., Washington, 2000—01; assoc. Gallery 10, 1996—2001. Exhibitions include Galena Riva Sinistra, Florence, Italy, 1999, Phoenix Gallery, N.Y.C., 2000, Art Without Walls, 2000, Palm Springs (Calif.) Internat. Art Fair, 2000, Kresge Mus., East Lansing, Mich., 2001, ARC Gallery, Chgo., 2001, Gallery 10, Washington, 2001. Recipient award, 5th Ann. Young Painters Competition, Sala El Brocense, Spain, 1995, Critics Residency award, Md. Art Pl., Balt., 2000; grantee, Arts Coun. of Montgomery County, Md., 1996—97, Montgomery County Art Assn., 1998.

BLOCK, WILLIAM, newspaper publisher; b. N.Y.C., Sept. 20, 1915; s. Paul and Dina (Wallach) B.; m. Maxine Horton, Mar. 23, 1944; children: William Jr., Karen Block Johnese, Barbara Block Burney, Donald G. AB, Yale U., 1936. With circulation, other depts. Toledo Blade, 1937-39, asst. to gen. mgr., 1939-41; co-pub. Pitts. Post-Gazette and Toledo Blade, 1941-87, pub., 1987-89; chmn. PG Pub. Co., Pitts., 1989—2001. Chmn. Blade Comm., Inc., 1987-2001; bd. dirs. Block Comms., Inc., Pitts. Post-Gazette, The Blade, Gateway to the Arts, Pitts. Glass Ctr., chmn. emeritus, 2001—; trustee emeritus Am. Assembly; sponsor Allegheny Conf. on Cmty. Devel.; bd. dirs. Hist. Soc. We. Pa.; chmn. emeritus Woodlands Found. Capt. AUS, 1941-46; served in mil. govt., Korea, 1945-46. Mem. Internat. Press Inst., Am. Soc. Newspaper Editors, Soc. Profl. Journalists.

BLOCK, WILLIAM K., JR., newspaper executive; b. New Haven, Nov. 28, 1944; s. William and Maxine (Horton) B.; m. Carol Pauline Zurheide, Aug. 1, 1970; children: Diana, Nancy, Katherine. BA, Trinity Coll., Hartford, Conn., 1967; JD, Washington and Lee U., 1972. Bar: Pa., U.S. Supreme Ct. Staff mem. Red Bank (N.J.) Register and Toledo Blade, 1972-77; advtg. mgr. Red Bank (N.J.) Register, Shrewsbury, NJ, 1977-79, sales mgr., 1979-80, pub., 1980-82; dir. ops. Toledo Blade Co., 1983-84, v.p. ops., 1984-86, v.p., gen. mgr., 1986-87, pres., 1987—, co-pub., 1990—, Pitts. Post Gazette, 1990—; v.p. Block Com., Inc., Toledo, 1987-88, pres., 1989—2001, chmn., 2002—. V.p. Toledo Sesquicentennial Commn., 1986-87; pres. Inland Press Assn., 1998-99; bd. dirs. Toledo Symphony; pres. Read for Literacy, Inc., 1989-2001, Newspaper Assn. Am., St. Luke's Hosp. With U.S. Army, Vietnam, 1968-70. Mem. Toledo Country Club, Toledo Club. Avocations: reading, tennis, travel, fishing. Office: Block Communications Inc 541 N Superior St Toledo OH 43660-0001*

BLOCK, WILLIAM KENNETH, lawyer; b. N.Y.C., Oct. 23, 1950; s. Louis and Catherine Veronica (Kerr) B. BA, Colgate U., 1973; JD, Union U., Albany, N.Y., 1976. Bar: N.Y. 1977. Gen. counsel N.Y.C. Tax Commn., 1978-81; asst. commn. fin. N.Y.C. Dept. Fin., 1981-84, dep. commr. fin., 1984-89; assoc. Schwartz, Weiss, Steckler & Hoffman, P.C., N.Y.C., 1989-91; pvt. practice, William K. Block, P.C., N.Y.C., 1992—. Adj. lectr. real estate NYU, 1992—. Contbr. articles to profl. jours. Mem. ABA, Internat. Assn. Assessing Officers

(chmn. met. jurisdiction coun. 1987-88, presdl. citation 1986, McCareen award 1988), N.Y. State Assessors Assn., N.Y. State Bar Assn., New York County Bar Assn. (com. on City of N.Y., real property com., govt. counsel com.), Real Estate Tax Rev. Bar Assn. (dir. 1995—), Assn. Bar City of N.Y. (com. on tax certiorari), Real Estate Tax Bd. N.Y. (com. on taxation). Democrat. Roman Catholic. Home: 115 E 34th St Apt 20K New York NY 10016-4631 Office: 295 Madison Ave Fl 38 New York NY 10017-6304 E-mail: Williamkblock@aol.com.

BLOCK, ZENAS, management consultant, educator; b. N.Y.C., Dec. 7, 1916; s. Joshua and Celia (Kaplow) B.; m. Lillian Bialek, June 12, 1938 (dec. 1985); children: Richard, Karen Block Chase Graubard, Margaret Block Walker; m. Janet Andre, Aug. 13, 1988. BS, CCNY, 1938; postgrad., Bklyn. Poly. Inst., 1939-41. Chemist Clairol Inc., N.Y.C., 1938-39; chief chemist Am. Dietaids Co., Yonkers, N.Y., 1938-48; dir. labs. DCA Food Industries, N.Y.C., 1948-55, v.p. rsch., 1955-60, pres. bakery divsn., 1960-64, group v.p., 1964-71, exec. v.p., 1971-77, vice chmn. bd., 1977-79, also bd. dirs. Chmn. bd. dirs. Nisshin DCA Foods Inc., Tokyo, 1975-79, DCA Industries Ltd., Eng., 1976-79; founder, pres. Haystack Cable Vision Inc., Lakeville, Conn., 1978-80, v.p. and treas., 1980-82; adj. prof. Grad. Sch. Bus. Adminstrn., U. Conn., 1979-81; clin. prof. NYU, 1984-94, adj. prof. entrepreneurship grad. divsn. Stern Schs. Bus., NYU, 1995-2001, entrepreneur-in-residence Stern Sch. Bus., 1999-2000, founder, assoc. dir. Ctr. for Entrepreneurial Studies, 1984-89; adj. prof. mgmt. Lally Sch. Mgmt., Rensselaer Poly. Inst., 1991-92, 97-98, vis. prof., 1996-97, curriculum cons., 1997-99. Author: It's All on the Label, 1981; (with I.C. MacMillan) Corporate Venturing: Creating New Businesses Within the Firm, 1993; mem. edit. bd. Jour. Bus. Venturing; contbr. articles to acad. and profl. jours.; patentee food processing field. Bd. dirs. N.Y.C. Mission Soc., 1983-87, Salisbury Family Svcs., 1983-87; trustee Salisbury Assoc., 1992-95; mem. bd. fin. Town of Salisbury, 1996—; mem. bd. govs. Sharon Hosp., 2002—. Home and Office: PO Box 530 Salisbury CT 06068-0530

BLOCKER-BURNETTE, MAXINE PETERSON, social worker; b. Long Island, NY, Jan. 8, 1948; d. Yancy Billy Peterson and Priscilla Mae (Garrett) Smith; m. William Jerome Blocker, Feb. 8, 1964 (div. July 1975); m. Kenneth Tyrone Burnette, Nov. 8, 1980; children: Roslyn Michelle, William Jerome Jr. BA in Social Welfare, U. D.C., 1977; BS in Criminal Justice, Trinity Coll., 1977. Cert. prevention profl.; lic. profl. counselor. Social worker DC Superior Ct., Washington, 1975-78; specialist mental health Alcohol and Drug Abuse Services, Washington, 1978-86, acting div. chief, 1986-90; equal employment counselor Addiction Prevention and Recovery Adminstrn., Washington, 1990—, chief personnel, 1990—. Chmn. community awareness, Operation PUSH, Washington 1974-76. Mem. Nat. Assn. Social Workers, Nat. Assn. Black Social Workers, Nat. Pol. Cong. Black Women. Democrat. Baptist. Home: 3114 Westover Dr SE Washington DC 20020-3720 Office: Addiction Prevention and Recovery Adminstrn 1300 1st St NE Washington DC 20002-3335

BLODGETT, DAVID WILLIAM, preventive medicine physician; s. Terry Marvin and Cheryl Ann Blodgett; m. Lisa Lynn Pearce, Aug. 5, 1995. BS (with hons.), So. Utah U., 1993; MD, U. Utah, 1999; MPH, Johns Hopkins U., 2001. Diplomate Am. Bd. Preventive Medicine. Congl. intern U.S. Congress, Washington, 1994; adminstr. Iron County Water Conservancy Dist. Com., Cedar City, Utah, 1995; intern Bassett Hosp., Cooperstown, NY, 1999—2000; resident Johns Hopkins Sch. Pub. Health, Balt., 2000—02, chief resident, 2002—. Med. officer Anne Arundel County Dept. of Health, Annapolis, Md., 2002—03; assoc. faculty Johns Hopkins Bloomberg Sch. Pub. Health, Balt., 2002—. Leader Boy Scouts of Am., Glen Burnie, Md., 1995—2003; campaign worker Campaign to Re-elect James V Hansen, Farmington, Utah, 1994; bishopric LDS Ch., Glen Burnie, Md., 2000—03. Scholar, Barry M. Goldwater Found., 1992—94, Med. scholar, Columbia HCA, 1995—96. Mem.: Am. Tchrs. Preventive Medicine, Am. Coll. Preventive Medicine, Delta Omega. Achievements include research in fatalities due to unintentional exposure to HydroFluoric Acid. Avocations: literature, travel, golf. Personal E-mail: dblodget@jhsph.edu. E-mail: dblodget@jhsph.edu.

BLODGETT, DEAN SCOTT, product development executive; b. Chgo., Feb. 16, 1966; BS, Rochester Inst. Tech., N.Y., 1984—89, MS, 1989—90; MBA, McCallum (Bentley) Grad. Sch. Bus., Waltham, Mass., 1993—95. Dir., product devel. CMGi, Andover, Mass., 1996—2000; dir., global product mgmt. One-Source Info. Svcs., Concord, Mass., 2001—. Maj. USAR, 1989—. Personal E-mail: scott_blodgett@yahoo.com.

BLODGETT, ELSIE GRACE, retired association executive; b. Eldorado Springs, Mo., Aug. 2, 1921; d. Charles Ishmal and Naoma Florence (Worthington) Robison; m. Charles Davis Blodgett, Nov. 8, 1940; children: Carolyn Doyel, Charleen Bier, Lyndon Blodgett, Daryl (dec.). Student Warrensburg (Mo.) State Tchrs. Coll., 1939-40; BA, Fresno (Calif.) State Coll., 1953. Tchr. schs. in Mo. and Calif., 1940-42, 47-72; owner, mgr. rental units, 1965—; exec. dir. San Joaquin County (Calif.) Rental Property Assn., Stockton, 1970-81; prin. Delta Rental Property Owners and Assocs., 1981-82; propr. Crystal Springs Health World, Inc., Stockton, 1980-86; bd. dirs. Stockton Better Bus. Bur., ret. Active local PTA, Girl Scouts U.S., Boy Scouts Am.; bd. dirs. Stockton Goodwill Industries; active Vols. in Police Svc., 1993-; capt. Delaware Alpine Neighborhood Watch, 1994—. Named (with husband) Mr. and Mrs. Apt. Owner of San Joaquin County, 1977. Mem. Nat. Apt. Assn. (state treas. women's div. 1977-79), Calif. Ret. Tchrs. Assn. Republican. Methodist. Lodge: Stockton Zonta. Home and Office: 4350 St Andrews Dr Stockton CA 95219-

BLODGETT, FORREST CLINTON, economics educator; b. Oregon City, Oreg., Oct. 6, 1927; s. Clinton Alexander and Mabel (Wells) B.; m. Beverley Janice Buchholz, Dec. 21, 1946 (dec. Dec. 2000); children: Cherine Eiline Klein, Candis Melis, Clinton George; m. Ilene E. Jensen Anderson, Jan. 12, 2002. BS, U. Omaha, 1961; MA, U. Mo., 1969; PhD, Portland State U., 1979. Joined C.E. U.S. Army, 1946, commd. 2d lt., 1946, advanced through grades to lt. col., 1965, ret., 1968, engrng. assignments, 1947-49, 1950-53, 1955-56, 1958 60, 1963, staff engr. 2d Army Air Def. Region, 1964-66; base engr. Def. Atomic Support Agy., Sandia Base, N.Mex., 1966-68; bus. mgr., trustee, asst. prof. econs. Linfield Coll., McMinnville, Oreg., 1968-73, assoc. prof., 1973-83, prof., 1983-90, emeritus prof. econs., 1990—; pres. Blodgett Enterprises, Inc., 1983-85; founder, dir. Valley Community Bank, 1980-86, vice chmn. bd. dirs., 1985-86. Commr., Housing Authority of Yamhill County (Oreg.), chmn., 1980-83; mem. Yamhill County Econ. Devel. Com., 1978-83; bd. dirs. Yamhill County Found., 1983-91, Oreg. Internat. Coun., 1995—. Decorated Army Commendation medal with oak leaf cluster; recipient Joint Service Commendation medal Dept. of Def. Mem. Soc. Am. Mil. Engrs. (pres. Albuquerque post 1968), Am. Econ. Assn., Western Econ. Assn. Internat., Nat. Ret. Officers Assn., Res. Officers Assn. (pres. Marion chpt. 1976), SAR (pres. Oreg. soc. 1985-86, v.p. gen. Nat. Soc. 1991-93), Urban Affairs Assn., Soc. for The History of Tech., Am. Law and Econs. Assn., Pi Sigma Epsilon, Pi Gamma Mu, Omicron Delta Epsilon (Pacific NW regional dir. 1978-88), Rotary (pres. McMinnville 1983-84). Republican. Episcopalian. Office: 1153 NE Multnomah Drive Fairview OR 97024-3783

BLODGETT, FRANK CALEB, retired food company executive; b. Janesville, Wis., Apr. 22, 1927; s. Frank Caleb Pickard and Dorothy (Korst) B.; m. Jean Ellen Fountain, June 23, 1951; children: Caleb J., Barbara F., David K. Grad., Beloit Coll., 1950; postgrad., Advanced Mgmt. Program, Harvard U., 1969. 1st v.p., dir. Frank H. Blodgett Inc., Janesville, 1947-61, pres., dir., 1961-62; with Gen. Mills Inc., Mpls., 1961-92, v.p., dir. mktg., 1967-69, gen. mgr., v.p., 1969-73, group v.p., 1973-76, exec. v.p., 1976-80, vice chmn., 1981-92, chief fin. and adminstrv. officer, 1985-92, dir., 1980-92; ret., 1992. Bd. dirs. Medtronic, Inc., Reliastar Fin. Corp. and subs., Northwestern Nat. Life Ins. Co., HealthSpan Health Sys. Corp.; dir. Waldorf Corp., 1993—. Trustee Gen. Mills Found., 1980-92, Washburn Child Guidance Ctr., 1972-75, Beloit Coll., 1976—, Nutrition Found., 1980-84; bd. dirs. Cereal Inst., 1970-76, chmn., 1973-74; bd. dirs. Abbott Northwestern Hosp. With USN, 1944-46, PTO. Recipient Disting. Svc. citation Beloit Coll., 1990. Mem. Millers Nat. Fedn., Young Millers Orgn. (past pres.), U.S. C. of C. (bd. dirs. 1982-88), Greater Mpls. C. of C. (bd. dirs. 1975-76), Phi Kappa Psi (trustee alumni bd. Beloit 1961-62), Phi Eta Sigma. Home: 688 Hillside Dr Wayzata MN 55391-9643

BLODGETT, OMER WILLIAM, electric company design consultant; b. Duluth, Minn., Nov. 27, 1917; s. Myron O. and Minnie (Foster) B.; m. Dorothy B. Sjostrom, June 11, 1949; 1 child, Robert W. B.Metall.Engrng. with distinction, U. Minn., 1941, M.E., 1976; DrSc, Le Tourneau U., 1995. Registered profl. engr., Ohio. Welding supt. Globe Shipbldg. Co., Superior, Wis., 1941-45; sales engr. Lincoln Electric Co., Cleve., 1945-54, design cons., then sr. design cons., 1954—. Condr. seminars Australian Inst. Steel Constrn., Australia, 1971, 75, 78, New Zealand, 1975, South African Inst. Steel Constrn., 1981, Republic of China, 1985, London, 1986, 88, Brazil, 1988, Tokyo, 1992, Istanbul, Turkey, 1993, Bahrain, 1998. Author: Design Weldments, 1963, Design of Welded Structures, 1966, also papers. Recipient Engrng. Luminary award Am. Inst. Steel Constrn., 1997, Lifetime Achievement award Am. Inst. Steel Constrn., 1999; Chair of Welding and Materials Joining Edn. established in his name LeTourneau, 1998; named one of 125 people for oustanding contbn. to constrn. industry Engrng. News-Record. Fellow ASME, Am. Welding Soc. (lectr. 1968, A.F. Davis silver medal 1962, 73, 80, 83, Higgins award 1983); mem. ASCE (hon.), Sigma Xi, Tau Beta Pi.

BLODGETT, PETER JOHN, curator; b. Lancaster, N.H., May 16, 1954; s. Benjamin Howard and Lyla Mary Blodgett; m. Sara Suzanne Hodson, Mar. 26, 1988. BA, Bowdoin Coll., 1976; MA, Yale U., 1978, MPh, 1979. Tchg. asst. Yale U., 1979-84; H. Russell Smith Found. curator Western Am. history Huntington Libr., San Marino, Calif., 1985—. Faculty mem. Western Archives Inst., 1994-96, 2000-02; mem. adv. bd. rsch. collection Ctr. for the Study of L.A., Loyola Marymount U., 1996—; mem. editl. bd. Western Hist. Quar., 2003—. Author: Land of Golden Dreams: California in the Gold Rush Decade 1848-1858, 1999; contbr. essays and articles to publs. Recipient award for meritorious performance Calif. Coun. for the Promotion of History, 2000. Mem. Soc. Am. Archivists (manuscripts repositories sect. steering com. 1997-99, vice-chair/chair 2000-2002, mem. awards com. 2001-2003), Soc. Calif. Archivists (chair publs. com. 1987-94, Sustained Svc. award 1999), Western History Assn. (membership chair 1995-98), Orgn. Am. Historians, Mining History Assn., Mormon History Assn., Calif. Hist. Soc. Democrat. Office: Huntington Libr 1151 Oxford Rd San Marino CA 91108

BLODGETT, TODD ALAN, publisher, marketing executive; b. Iowa City, Sept. 10, 1960; s. Gary Burl and Sandy Jean (Hodgson) B.; m. Linda Marie Reuber. BA in Journalism, Drake U., 1983. Fin. dir. Senator Roger W. Jepsen Re-election Com., Des Moines, 1983-84; staff asst. Reagan-Bush Inaugural Com., Inc., Washington, 1984-85; editorial asst. White House Staff News Summary, Washington, 1985-86; acct. exec. J.L. Whitehead & Assoc., Washington, 1986-87; domestic policy advisor Bush-Quayle '88 Com., Washington, 1987-88; sr. policy advisor analyst Rep. Nat. Com., Washington, 1989-90. Campaign advisor Blodgett for Iowa Legislature campaign, Mason City, Iowa, 1992-98, also re-election advisor; CEO Donor List Inc. Contbr. editor American Conservative, 1991—; assoc. pub. Slick Times Mag., 1993-96; exec. editor Firearms & Preparedness Mag., 1996-98; contbr. articles to popular mags.; regularly nterviewed on Am. politics on BBC. Mem. The Conservative Network, Washington, 1985—; sustaining mem. Rep. Ctrl. Com. of Iowa, Des Moines, 1983; mem. Lincoln Club of Iowa, Des Moines, 1988—. Mem. NRA (life), Ducks Unltd., Reagan Appointees Alumni Assn. (mem.), Kennedy-Warren Residents Assn. (pres. 1989-92), Univ. Club of Washington, D.C., Sigma Alpha Epsilon. Republican. Presbyterian. Avocations: hunting, snow and water skiing, numismatics, gun collecting, skeet shooting. Home: 8239 The Midway Annandale VA 22003-3716 Office: 8239 The Midway Annandale VA 22003-3716 Fax: (202) 319-9867.

BLODGETT, WARREN TERRELL, public affairs educator; b. Ranger, Tex., Sept. 15, 1923; s. William Serle Sr. and Alice Louise (Furman) B.; m. Dorothy Jean Chapin, Mar. 7, 1946; children: Robert Harold, William Arthur, Katherine Ann. BA, Baylor U., 1943; MS Pub. Adminstrn., Syracuse U., 1947. Research assoc. U. Tex., Austin, 1947-50, assoc. dir. policy rsch inst., 1982-90, Mike Hogg prof. urban mgmt., 1982-95, Mike Hogg prof. emeritus in urban mgmt., 1995—; personnel dir. City of Austin, 1950-52, adminstrv. asst. to city mgr., 1952-55, asst. city mgr., 1955-60; city mgr. City of Waco, Tex., 1960-63, City of Garland, Tex., 1963-64; adminstrv. asst. to gov. State of Tex., Austin, 1964-69; prin. in charge govt. cons. Peat, Marwick and Mitchell, Austin, 1969-82. Cons. Tex. Dept. Water Resources, Austin, 1984-86, Legis. Audit Com., Austin, 1984-85; Tex. Com. Economy and Efficiency in Govt., Austin, 1985-87, Tex. Office of Speaker, Austin, 1985-87. Chmn. bd. Tex. Mcpl. Retirement System, 1961-62. Served to 1st lt. U.S. Army, 1943-46. Mem. Nat. Acad. Pub. Adminstrn., Internat. City Mgmt. Assn. (fund for profession 1986-89, chmn. Found. 1980-84), Internat. City-County Mgmt. Assn. ((Disting. Svc. award 1993), Nat. Civic League (hon. life dir. 1989, chmn. 1986-87, vice chmn. 1987-88), Austin Area Urban League (treas. 1985-87). Democrat. Mem. Christian Ch. Avocation: tennis. Home and Office: 1801 Lavaca St Austin TX 78701-1341 E-mail: blodgett@mail.utexas.edu.

BLOEDE, VICTOR CARL, lawyer, academic executive; b. Woodwardville, Md., July 17, 1917; s. Carl Schon and Eleanor (Eck) B.; m. Ellen Louise Miller, May 9, 1947; children— Karl Abbott, Pamela Elena AB, Dartmouth Coll., 1940; JD cum laude, U. Md., Balt., 1950; LLM in Pub. Law, Georgetown U., 1967. Bar: Md. 1950, Fed. Hawaii 1958, U.S. Supreme Ct. 1971. Pvt. practice, Balt., 1950-64; mem. Goldman & Bloede, Balt., 1959-64; counsel Seven-Up Bottling Co., Balt., 1958-64; dep. atty. gen. Pacific Trust Ter., Honolulu, 1952-53; asst. solicitor for ters. Office of Solicitor, U.S. Dept. Interior, Washington, 1953-54; atty. U.S. Justice, Honolulu, 1955-58; assoc. gen. counsel Dept. Navy, Washington, 1960-61, 63-64; spl. legal cons. Md. Legislature, Legis. Council, 1963-64, 66-67; assoc. prof. U. Hawaii, 1961-63, dir. property mgmt., 1964-67; house counsel, dir. contracts and grants U. Hawaii System, 1967-82; house counsel U. Hawaii Research Corp., 1970-82; legal counsel Law of Sea Inst., 1978-82; legal cons. Rsch. Corp. and grad. rsch. divsn. U. Hawaii, 1982-92. Spl. counsel to Holifield Congl. Commn. on Govt. Procurement, 1970-73. Author: Hawaii Legislative Manual, 1962, Maori Affairs, New Zealand, 1964, Oceanographic Research Vessel Operations, and Liabilities, 1972, Hawaiian Archipelago, Legal Effects of a 200 Mile Territorial Sea, 1973, Copyright-Guidelines to the 1976 Act, 1977, Forms Manual, Inventions: Policy, Law and Procedure, 1982; writer, contbr. Coll. Law Digest and other publs. on legislation and pub. law. Mem. Gov.'s Task Force Hawaii and The Sea, 1969, Citizens Housing Com. Balt., 1952-64; bd. govs. Balt. Cmty. YMCA, 1954-64; bd. dirs. U. Hawaii Press, 1964-66, Coll. Housing Found., 1968-80; appointed to internat. rev. commn. Canada-France Hawaii Telescope Corp., 1973-82, chmn., 1973, 82; co-founder, incorporator First Unitarian Ch. Honolulu. Served to lt. comdr. USNR, 1942-45, PTO. Grantee ocean law studies NSF and NOAA, 1970-80. Mem. ABA, Balt. Bar Assn., Fed. Bar Assn., Am. Soc. Internat. Law, Nat. Assn. Univ. Attys. (founder & 1st chmn. patents & copyrights sect. 1974-76). Home: 635 Onaha St Honolulu HI 96816-4918

BLOEM, JAMES H. managed health care executive; JD, Vanderbilt U. Sch. Law; M in Bus. Adminstrn., Harvard. cert. CPA. CFO Herman Miller, Inc.; pres. personal care divsn. Perrigo Co.; pvt. fin. cons.; founder, principal Growth Strategies Cons./LatinWorks Mktg., Los Angeles; sr. v.p., CMO Humana, Louisville, Ky., 2001—. Office: Humana Inc 500 W Main St Louisville KY 40202

BLOEMBERGEN, NICOLAAS, physicist, educator; b. Dordrecht, The Netherlands, Mar. 11, 1920; arrived in U.S., 1952, naturalized, 1958; s. Auke and Sophia M. (Quint) Bloembergen; m. Huberta D. Brink, June 26, 1950; children: Antonia, Brink, Juliana. BA, Utrecht U., 1941, MA, 1943; PhD, Leiden U., 1948; MA (hon.), Harvard U., 1951; DSc (hon.), Laval U., 1987, U. Conn., 1988, U. Hartford, 1991, Moscow State U., 1997; LHD (hon.), U. Mass., Lowell, 1994, U. Ctrl. Fla., 1996, N.C. State U., 1998, Harvard U., 2000. Teaching asst. Utrecht U., 1942—45; research fellow Leiden U., 1948; mem. Soc. Fellows Harvard U., 1949—51, assoc. prof., 1951—57, Gordon McKay prof. applied physics, 1957—, Rumford prof. physics, 1974, Gerhard Gade univ. prof., 1980, prof. emeritus, 1990; prof. optics U. Ariz., 2001—. Vis. prof. U. Paris, 1957, U. Calif., 1965, College de France, Paris, 1980, U. Ariz., 2001—; Lorentz guest prof. U. Leiden, 1973; Raman vis. prof., Bangalore, India, 79; Fairchild Disting. scholar Calif. Inst. Tech., 1984; hon. prof. Fudan U., Shanghai; Disting. Vis. Prof. CREOL, U. Ctrl. Fla., 1995. Author: Nuclear Magnetic Relaxation, 1948, Nonlinear Optics, 1965, Enconters in Magnetic Resonance, 1996, Encounters in Nonlinear Optics, 1996; contbr. articles to profl. jours. Recipient Buckley prize for solid state physics, Am. Phys. Soc., 1958, Dirac medal, U. NSW, Australia, 1983, Stuart Ballantine medal, Franklin Inst., 1961, Half Moon trophy, Netherlands Club N.Y., 1972, Nat. med. of Sci., 1975, Lorentz medal, Royal Dutch ACad., 1978, Frederic Ives medal, Optical Soc. Am., 1979, von Humboldt sr. scientist award, Munich, 1980, von Humboldt medal, 1989, Nobel prize in Physics, 1981, Byvoet medal, U. Utrecht, 2001; fellow Guggenheim, 1957. Fellow: IEEE (Morris Liebmann award 1959), Am. Phys. Soc., Am. Phys. Soc.; mem.: Norwegian Soc. Scis. and Letters (fgn.), Paris Acad. Scis. (fgn. assoc.), Deutsche Akademie der Naturforscher Leopoldina, Optical Soc. Am. (hon.), Indian Acad. Scis. (hon.), Koninklyke Nederlandse Akademie von Wetenschappen (corr.), Am. Philos. Soc., Nat. Acad. Engring., Nat. Royal Dutch Acads. Scis. Office: Optical Scis Ctr Univ Ariz 1630 E Univ Blvd Tucson AZ 85721 E-mail: nbloembergen@optics.arizona.edu.

BLOEMER, GARY FRED, orthopedic surgeon, educator; b. Cin., Aug. 18, 1954; s. Raymond Charles and Mildred (Hudephol) B.; children: David Edward, Klye Raymond, Elizabeth Rose. BS, U. Louisville, 1976, MD, 1982. Diplomate Am. Bd. Orthopedic Surgeons. Intern gen. surgery U. Louisville, 1982-83, asst. clin. prof. orthopedics, 1988—; orthopedic surgery resident Med. Coll. of Ga., Augusta, 1984-87; sports medicine fellow Hughston Sports Medicine Clinic, Columbus, Ga., 1987; pvt. practice, Louisville, 1988—. Med. advisor St. Anthony Sports Medicine Ctr., Louisville, 1989-95; orthopedic cons. Campbellsville (Ky.) Coll., 1990—; exec. com. Frazier Rehab. Ctr., Louisville, 1992; vice chmn. emergency rm. com. Jewish Hosp., Louisville, 1994-96. Contbr. articles to profl. jours. Med. cons. Ky. Commn. for Handicapped Children, Louisville, 1988—; team physician Moore H.S., Louisville, 1988—. Fellow Am. Acad. of Orthopedic Surgeons; mem. AMA, Ky. Orthopedic Assn., Hughston Soc., Floyd E. Bliven Soc., Nat. Athletic Trainers Assn., Alpha Omega Alpha. Roman Catholic. Avocations: snow skiing, bicycling, boating, racquetball. Office: 3 Audubon Plaza Dr Ste 220 Louisville KY 40217-1319

BLOESCH, DONALD GEORGE, theologian, writer, educator; b. Bremen, Ind., May 3, 1928; s. Herbert Paul and Adele Josephine (Silberman) B.; m. Brenda Mary Jackson, Nov. 23, 1962. BA, Elmhurst coll., 1950; BD, Chgo. Theol. Sem., 1953; PhD, U. Chgo., 1956; DDiv, Doane Coll., 1983. Ordained to ministry Evang. & Reformed Ch., 1953. Prof. theology U. Dubuque Theol. Sem., 1957-93, emeritus prof. theology, 1993—. Vis. prof. religion U. Iowa, Iowa City, 1982, Ont. Theol. Sem., Toronto, Can., 1984, 92. Author: Essentials of Evangelical Theology, 2 Vols., 1978, 79, The Ground of Certainty, 1971, Freedom for Obedience, 1987, A Theology of Word and Spirit, 1992, Holy Scripture, 1994, God the Almighty, 1995, The Church, 2002, others; contbr. numerous articles to profl. jours. Fellow Am. Assn. Theol. Schs., 1963-64, 90, World Coun. Chs., 1956-57, Inst. for Advanced Christian Studies, 1978. Mem. Am. Theol. Soc. (pres. Midwest divsn. 1974-75), Karl Barth Soc. N.Am. Republican. United Ch. of Christ. Avocations: gospel and country music, swimming, piano playing. Home: 2185 St John Dr Dubuque IA 52002-2751 Office: U Dubuque 2000 University Ave Dubuque IA 52001-5050

BLOM, DANIEL CHARLES, lawyer, investor; b. Portland, Oreg., Dec. 13, 1919; s. Charles D. and Anna (Reiner) B.; m. Ellen Lavon Stewart, June 28, 1952; children: Daniel Stewart (dec.), Nicole Jan Heath. BA magna cum laude, U. Wash., 1941, postgrad., 1941-42; JD, Harvard U., 1948; postgrad., U. Paris, 1954-55. Bar: Wash. 1949, U.S. Supreme Ct. 1970. Tchg. fellow speech U. Wash., 1941—42; law clk. to justice Supreme Ct. Wash., 1948—49; since practiced in Seattle; assoc. Graves, Kizer & Graves, 1949—51; gen. counsel Northwestern Life Ins. Co., 1952—54; ptnr. Case & Blom, 1952—54; assoc., ptnr., of counsel Ryan, Swanson & Cleveland, 1956—; exec. v.p., gen. counsel Family Life Ins. Co., 1964—85, spl. counsel, 1985—91. Vice chmn. Wash. Bd. Bar Examiners, 1970-72, chmn., 1972-75; mem. industry adv. com. Nat. Assn. Ins. Commrs., 1966-68; pres. Wash. Ins. Coun., 1971-73, gen. counsel, 1975-78; mediator Arbitration Forums, Inc. Editor Wash. State Bar Jour., 1951-52; assoc. editor The Brief, 1975-76; author: Life Insurance Law of the State of Washington, 1980, Banking and Insurance, Deregulatory Cross-Currents, 1985, Hostile Insurance Company Takeovers: New Frontier of the Law, 1990, Administrative Finality Under the Washington Insurance Code, 1991, Business and Professionalism, 1994, The Civility Problem, 1995, Technics and the Civilization of Law Practice, 1997, Varieties of Regulatory Experience, 1998, Legislative Review of Administrative Rules in the State of Washington; A Light that Failed?, 2003. Chmn. jury selection Wash. Gov.'s Writer's Day Awards, 1976; bd. dirs. Crisis Clinic; trustee Bush Sch., 1971-79, v.p., 1976-77; trustee, v.p. Frye Mus., Seattle, 1976-82, World Affairs Coun. Seattle, 1972-94, Friends of Seattle Pub. Libr., 1982-87; bd. visitors U. Wash. Libr., 88-92, Friends of U. Wash. Librs., bd. dirs., 1991-95, pres., 1991-92. 2d lt. AUS, 1942-45, PTO. Decorated Bronze Star; Rhodes scholarship finalist, 1949. Fellow: Am. Bar Found.; mem.: ABA (vice chmn. com. on life ins. law, sect. tort and ins. pratice 1971—76, chmn. 1976—78, sect. program chmn. 1978—79, mem. coun. 1979—83, chmn. pub. rels. com. 1981—83, chmn. com. on profl. independence of the lawyer 1984—85, chmn. com. on scope and correlation 1985—86, chmn. com. on handbook and bylaws 1987—88, chmn. hist. com. 1991—94, del. ABA to Union Internat. des Avocats 1986—91, policy coord. tort and ins. practice sect. 1986—90), Fedn. Regulatory Counsel (dir. 1995—97, 2002—03), Found. UIA (coun. 1990—97), Am. Arbitration Assn., Am. Coun. Life Ins. (legis. com. 1982—85), Assn. Life Ins. Counsel, Am. Judicature Soc., N.Am. Found. for Internat. Legal Practice (dir. 1987—95, pres. 1987—89, chmn. 1990—95), Union Internat. des Avocats (v.p. 1987—92), Seattle Bar Assn., Wash. Bar Assn. (chmn. legal edn. liaison com. 1977—78, award of merit 1975), Harvard Assn. Seattle and Western Wash. (trustee 1976—77), Harvard Law Sch. Assn., Rainier Club, Tau Kappa Alpha, Phi Beta Kappa. Home: 100 Ward St # 602-3 Seattle WA 98109-5613 Office: Ryan Swanson & Cleveland 1201 3rd Ave Ste 3400 Seattle WA 98101-3034 E-mail: blomdc@msn.com.

BLOM, DAVE, healthcare industry executive; married; 3 children. BS, Ohio State U.; MS in healthcare adminstrn., The George Wash. U. Asst. adminstr. Holden (Mass.) Hosp.; adminstr. Joel Pomerene Meml. Hosp., Millersburg, Ohio; pres. and CEO Grant Med. Ctr.; exec. v.p. and COO OhioHealth; pres. Columbus OhioHealth, 1998—, OhioHealth, 1999—, CEO, 2002—. Office: Ohio Health 1087 Dennison Ave 3rd fl Columbus OH 43201

BLOM, FRANS LEENDERT, quality assurance professional; b. Leerdam, Zuid-Holland, Netherlands, Feb. 10, 1974; s. Teunis Arie Blom and Johanna Elizabeth Blom-van Hoogdalem. BBA, Hogeschool van Utrecht, 1993—98. Sales asst. AmEuro Metals B.V., Leerdam, Netherlands, 1997—99, quality assurance officer, 1999—. Event mgr. Oranjevereniging Leerdam, Leerdam, Netherlands, 1999—2001. Conservative. Protestant. Avocations: running, travel, reading, movies. Office: AmEuro Metals BV Techniekweg 14 Zuid-Holland Leerdam 4143 HV Netherlands Home Fax: +31 345 632060; Office Fax: +31 345 632060. Personal E-mail: franslblom@planet.nl. E-mail: fblom.ameuro@planet.nl.

BLOME, DOROTHY CARTER, pediatrics nurse; b. Dallas, Aug. 16, 1943; d. Paul Gilbert and Dorothy Mae (Lamb) Carter; div.; children: Craig A., Glenn C. BS, Tex. Woman's U., 1965, MN, Emory U., 1968; postgrad. pediatric nurse practitioner, U. Tex., Arlington, 1994. RN, CPNP, advanced nurse practitioner, Tex. Staff nurse pediatrics Parkland Meml. Hosp., Dallas, 1965, Bapt. Hosp., Pensacola, Fla., 1965; staff nurse Egleston Children's Hosp., Atlanta, 1966-67; staff nurse neonatal ICU Baylor Med. Ctr., Dallas, 1977; staff nurse, then head nurse pediatrics Richardson (Tex.) Med. Ctr., 1977-82; mem. faculty pediatric nursing Tex. Woman's U., Denton, 1982-88; clin. nurse specialist Children's Med. Ctr., Dallas, 1988-95; CPNP Devel. Pediatric Svcs., 1995—. Contbg. author: Nursing Care of Infants and Children, 1991. Mem. ANA, Tex. Nurses Assn. (Gt. 100 Nurse award 1992), Sigma Theta Tau. Avocations: reading, bridge, tennis. Office: Devel Pediatric Svcs 12655 North Central Expy Ste 300 Dallas TX 75243 E-mail: dblome@attglobal.net.

BLOMGREN, BRUCE HOLMES, real estate developer, marina developer, consultant; b. Evanston, Ill., Dec. 27, 1945; s. Charles Edwin and Jane Rebecca (Holmes) B.; m. Dawn Lewis, July, 1988; children: Tracy, Kirk, Chad, Rainey. BA in Speech, Monmouth Coll., 1969. V.p., program dir. Prairieland Broadcasters, Monmouth, 1966-70; asst. press sec. Gov. of Ill. Richard Ogilvie, Springfield, 1970-73; press sec. Gov. of Mo. Christopher Bond, 1973-77; advance staff Pres. Gerald Ford, Washington, 1976; dir. mktg. Arvida Corp., Boca Raton, Fla., 1977-79; pres., CEO Brandy Group, Inc., Boca Raton,

1979-92; pres. Nat. Marina's, Inc., 1988-90; exec. v.p. Brandy Group Assocs., Inc., 1989-93; pres. LCP/Brandy Marinas, Inc., 1989-91, Brandy Marinas, Inc., West Palm Beach, Fla., 1990-93; mktg. exec. for new product nat. campaign Liggett Tobacco Co., 1993; dir. mktg. programs El Cid Mega Resort, Mazatlan, Mexico, 1993-94; motivational speaker, affil. W. Edwards Deming Inst. of Miami, Boone, N.C., 1994-95; pres. Manistee (Mich.) Village Ptnrs., Harbor Village Properties, Inc., Manistee, 1995-97; mng. dir. Gynn Assocs., Tampa, Fla., 1997-98; pres., CEO Brandy Marine, Inc., 1998—. Mem. Recreational Devel. Coun. of Urban Land Inst., moderator Washington, 1985, Miami, 1984, St. Thomas, V.I., 1985; exec. v.p. Northstar Fin., Inc., 1988-90; lead moderator customer svc. program S.E. Build Co., 1997—; marina acquisitions and mgmt. cons. JMB Realty, Ptnrs., Walton St. Capital, L.L.C. Chgo., Marine Transp. Strategy Club Resorts, Dallas, Marina Devel. Acquisitions St. Joe Corp., Jacksonville, Fla.; lectr. in field; spkr. in field. Author: (with others) Developing with Recreational Amentites Golf, Tennis, Skiing, Marinas. Pres. Fla. Homebuilders Polit. Action Com., Boca Raton, 1978; mem. pub. affairs com. to Gov. Bob Graham, Fla., 1982-86; organizer charity boat race Handicapped Children's Fund, Sarasota, Fla., 1985-87; bd. advisors West Shore C.C. Capt. USCG, 1979—. Mem. Nat. Spkrs. Assn., West Mich. Tourist Assn. (bd. dirs. 1995-98), Manistee Area C. of C. (bd. dirs. 1996-97), Profl. Assn. Diving Instrs., Bird Key Yacht Club (Sarasota, Fla., dir. youth sailing), Sarasota Radio Controlled Squadron (chmn. edn. com.). Republican. Presbyterian. Office: PO Box 2016 Sarasota FL 34230-2016 Fax: 941-360-1105. E-mail: bblomgren@brandymarine.com.

BLOMQUIST, DAVID WELS, journalist; b. Detroit, June 16, 1956; s. August Wels and Sally Lou (Ball) B. AB, U. Mich., 1976; AM, Harvard U., 1978. Tchg. fellow Harvard U., Cambridge, 1978-82, asst. sr. tutor, 1981-82; supervising sect. editor CBS Inc., N.Y.C., 1982-84; staff writer The Record of Hackensack, N.J., 1984-86, state polit. corr., 1986-89, chief polit. writer, 1990-92, chief Trenton bur., 1992-94; dir. The Record Poll, Hackensack, 1992-99, dir. online devel., 1998-99; dir. new media Detroit Free Press, 1999—2001, sr. editor tech. and rsch., 2002—. Author: Elections and the Mass Media, 1982; contbr. articles to profl. jours. Mem. Am. Polit. Sci. Assn. (edn. com. 1984-86), N.J. Legis. Corrs. Club (pres. 1992), Harvard Club of N.Y., Nat. Press Club Washington. Avocations: music, ballet. Office: Detroit Free Press 600 W Fort St Detroit MI 48220-2700 E-mail: blomquist@freepress.com

BLOMQUIST, PRESTON HOWARD, ophthalmologist; b. Austin, Tex., Aug. 13, 1960; s. Gilbert Victor and Betty Jean Blomquist; m. Mary Denise Dobias, Mar. 31, 1960; children: Brooke Amanda, Kara Elyse. BSc in Engring., U. of Tex., 1982; MD, U. of Tex. Southwestern Med. Sch., Dallas, 1986. Lic. Am. Bd. of Ophthalmology, 1991. Chief of eye svcs. Permanent Med. Assn. of Tex., Dallas, 1993—94, assoc. med. dir. quality resource mgmt., 1996—97, physician dir. orgnl. performance and improvement, 1995—96; asst. prof. U. of Tex. Southwestern Med. Ctr., Dallas, 1998—. Ophthalmology residency program dir. U. of Tex. Southwestern Med. Ctr., Dallas, 2002—. Recipient Ho Din, Southwestern Med. Found., 1986. Fellow: ACS, Am. Acad. of Ophthalmology; mem.: Assn. for Rsch. in Vision and Ophthalmology, Assn. of Univ. Prof. of Ophthalmology (assoc.), Am. Soc. of Cataract and Refractive Surgeons. Office: Univ of Tex Southwestern Med 5323 Harry Hines Blvd Dallas TX 75390-9057

BLOMQUIST, ROBERT OSCAR, retired insurance company executive; b. Passaic, N.J., Aug. 19, 1930; s. Oscar and Adeline Louise (Hotaling) B.; m. Audrey M. Korn, Apr. 4, 1954; children: Dana C., Carin E. BA, Allegheny Coll., Meadville, Pa., 1952; MS, Columbia, 1953; PhD (hon.), Thiel Coll., 1999. With Chase Manhattan Bank, N.Y.C., 1957-76, gen. mgr., 1970, regional exec., 1971, sr. v.p., group exec., 1971-74, Nat. Banking Group, 1975-76; pres., dir. Chase Manhattan Leasing Corp., Chase Nat. Svcs. Corp., Chase Manhattan Realty Leasing Corp., 1974-76; chmn. Chase Banks-Internat., Chgo., L.A. and Houston, 1974-76; pres., dir. Franklin State Bank, Somerset, N.J., 1976-80; vice chmn., dir. Mercantile Bank, N.A., St.Louis, 1980-87; exec. v.p., chief credit officer Integra Fin. Corp., Pitts., 1988-93; chmn. bd. dirs. Luth. Brotherhood Life Ins. Co., Mpls., 1993-99; ret. Bd. dirs. Robert Morris Assocs., 1987-88. Contbr. articles to profl. jours. Bd. dirs. Luther N.W. Sem., St. Paul, 1982-85; trustee Thiel Coll., Greenville, Pa., 1988—. Lt. USNR, 1954-59. Mem. Kelly Greens Country Club (Ft. Myers, Fla.), Duquesne Club (Pitts.). Home: 16060 Kelly Cove Dr Fort Myers FL 33908-3114

BLOMQVIST, CARL GUNNAR, cardiologist; b. Båraryd, Sweden, Dec. 31, 1931; came to U.S., 1965, naturalized; s. Arvid Elias and Karin Johanna (Hullman) B.; m. Joan Barre Bakula, 1961; children: Mary Jennifer, Peter Carl. BM, U. Lund, Sweden, 1954, MD, 1960; PhD, Karolinska Inst., Stockholm, 1967. Rsch. fellow in cardiovasc. epidemiology U. Minn. Med. Ctr., Mpls., 1960-61; resident Karolinska Inst., 1962-65; mem. faculty U. Tex. Med. Ctr., Southwestern Med. Sch., Dallas, 1966—, prof. medicine and physiology, 1976—, prof. cardiology, 1998—. Mem. rsch. study com. Am. Heart Assn., 1970-73; mem. applied physiology study sect. NIH, 1974-78; mem. space biology and medicine com. NAS, 1986-90. Author articles in field; mem. editl. bd. profl. jours. Grantee NIH; Grantee NASA; established investigator Am. Heart Assn. Fellow Am. Coll. Cardiology, Am. Coll. Sports Medicine; mem. Internat. Acad. Astronautics, Am. Heart Assn. (fellow coun. epidemiolo), Aerospace Med. Assn. (Luis H. Bauer Founders award 1995), Am. Physiol. Soc. Home: 4229 Willow Grove Rd Dallas TX 75220-1935 Office: Southwestern Med Sch Div Cardiology Dallas TX 75235 Business E-Mail: cblomq@mednet.swmed.edu.

BLOMSTRAND, DOREEN KATHRYN, retired physician assistant; b. Superior, Wis., Sept. 25, 1929; d. Wesley Lawrence and Ann Kathryn (Okerstrom) Wright; m. Fritz Joseph Blomstrand, 1948 (dec. Dec. 26, 1982); children: Cynthia Dawn Reynolds, Heidi Jo Thomas, Jace Wright(dec.). Physician Asst. Program, U. of Wash., Seattle; Cmty. Health Adv. Program, Yakima Valley C.C., Wash. Physician Assistant MEDEX NW, U. of WA, 1985, Pa. Bd. Cert. Nat. Commn. on Cert. of Physician Assistants Bd., 1986, cert. EMT Ctrl. Wash. U., 1978; Tng. the trainer-qualified to teach others Ministry Tng. Ctrs., Oreg., 1997; Community Health Advocate Yakima Valley C.C., Wash., 1983, Cambodian Lang. study SE Asian Summer Study Intst. of Lang., U. of Hawaii, 1988. Full-time faculty MEDEX NW, U. of Wash., Seattle, 1990—2000; ret., still part-time faculty MEDEX NW, Sch. of Medicine, U. of Wash., Seattle, 2000—. Physician asst., health edn. coord. CAMA Svcs., United Nations Border Relief Ops., Thailand, 1986—90. Contbr. articles (Awarded second pl. in nonfiction articles, 2002). Ministry team, small group leader, mentor Eastside Foursquare Ch., Bothell, Wash., 1992—2003; vol. supplies and time with orphans Chang Mai, Thailand, 1998; vol. at distbn. ctr. for Russian immigrants Christian Friend's of Israel, Jerusalem, 1999; short-term vol. work with the poor IMPACT, Ensenada, 1999; short term med. mission Project Mercy, Yetebon, Ethiopia, 2000; vol. Northshore Sr. Ctr., Bothell, Wash., 2000—03, Kirkland Sr. Ctr., Wash., 2001—03; short term vol. team Eastside Foursquare Ch., Metro Manila, Philippines, 2002. Recipient Humanitarian Svc. award, MEDEX NW Alumni Assn., 2003. Mem.: Fellowship of Christian Physician Assts., U. of Wash. Retirement Assn., Wash. Acad. of Physician Assts. (past bd. mem., student affairs chair 1995—2000), MEDEX NW Alumni Assn. (life; bd. mem. 1996—2003), Writer's Info. Network, NW Christian Writers Assn. Avocations: short-term international missions, writing, teaching, reading, tap dancing. Office: MEDEXNorthwest U of Wash 4311 11th Aven NE Ste 200 Seattle WA 98105 Personal E-mail: dblomstrand@earthlink.net. E-mail: doreenb@u.washington.edu.

BLOMSTRÖM, MAGNUS CONRAD, economics educator; b. Sävsjö, Sweden, May 3, 1952; s. Stig Gustaf Konrad and Inga Tora (Holmberg) B.; m. Christina Ulrika Bergman, Dec. 20, 1988; children: Erik Gustaf Konrad, Emma Ulrika Eleonora. BA in Econs., U. Gothenburg (Sweden), 1975, PhD in Econs., 1983. Asst. prof. U. Stockholm, 1983-84; vis. fellow Columbia U., N.Y.C., 1984-85; rsch. economist Nat. Bur. Econ. Rsch., N.Y.C., 1985-89, rsch. assoc., 1989—; assoc. prof. Stockholm Sch. Econs., 1987-90, prof. econs., 1991—. Author: Development Theory in Transition, 1984, Foreign Investment and Spillovers, 1989, TNCs and Exports From LDCs, 1990, Diverging Paths, 1991, Economic Crisis in Africa, 1993, Transnational Technology, 1994, Scandinavia and the EU, 1994, Foreign Direct Investment: Firm and Host Country Strategies, 2000, Topics in Empirical International Economics, 2001, Japan's New Economy, 2001, Impediments to Growth in Japan, 2003. Office: Stockholm Sch Econs PO Box 6501 113 83 Stockholm Sweden E-mail: magnus.blomstrom@hhs.se.

BLOND, STUART RICHARD, newsletter editor; b. L.A., Sept. 1, 1953; s. Elmer George and Anne G. Blond; m. Stella Pyrtek, July 28, 1986. BA in Art, Calif. State U., 1977. V.p. advt. Packard Automobile Classics, Fords, N.J., 1988-97; sales Packard Industries, Boonton, N.J., 1989—. Editor (newsletter) The Cormorant News Bulletin, 1988—. Home and Office: 84 Hoy Ave Fords NJ 08863-1938 E-mail: stuartrblond@earthlink.net.

BLONDIN-ANDREW, ETHEL, Canadian government official; b. Tulita, N.W.T., Can., Mar. 25, 1951; d. Cecilia Modeste, adopted d. Joseph and Marie Therese Blondin; children: Troy, Tanya, Timothy. BEd, U. Alta., 1974, LLD, 2001. Tchr. Tuktoyaktuk, Ft. Franklin, Ft. Providence, 1974-81; tchr. lang. spl. dept. edn. Yellowknife, 1981-84; tchr. U. Calgary & Arctic Coll., 1983; mgr., then acting dir. Pub. Svc. Commn., Canada, 1984-86; sec. state tng. and youth Can., 1993-97, sec. state children and youth, 1997—. Mem. bd. dirs. Arctic Inst. N.Am., Nat. Steering Ctr., Aboriginal Lang. Policy Dvel.; chair Indigenous Lang. Devel. Rev. Ctr. Recipient Culture and Heritage Preservation award MLA, 1987, Hilroy Scholar award R.C. Hill Char. Found., 1982. Office: Human Resources Devel Canada Pl du Portage 2 Phase IV 140 Promenade du Portage12fl Hull QC Canada K1A 0J9 also: Ste # 102 51 02-50 Ave Yellowknife NT Canada X1A 3S8 also: House of Commons Ottawa K1A 0A6 Canada

BLONKVIST, TIM, architectural firm executive; Dual degrees architecture-(hon.), Univ. of Tex., Austin, Tex., 1979; grad., Sch. of Architecture, 1981. Registered designer State of Tex. Sr. designer Bank of China, Hong Kong, China, 1981, Luvre Museum, Paris, 1981; project planner Urban Assoc. of Austin, Kuwait; sr. designer I.M. Pei & Partners, New York City, NY, 1982—86. Prin. in charge/ designer Bd. of Overland Partners, So. Tex. Blood and Tissue Ctr. project, San Antonio, Bd. of Overland Partners, Clear Channel Comm. Corp. Hdqs. project, San Antonio, Bd. of Overland Partners, Riverbend Ch. project, San Antonio, Bd. of Overland Partners, Nelson A. Rockefeller Ctr. for Latin Am. Art project, San Antonio, Bd. of Overland Partners, Lady Bird Johnson Wildflower Rsch. Ctr. project, San Antonio, Bd. of Overland Partners, the adaptive reuse of the Aztec Theater in San Antonio, Tex. project, San Antonio, Bd. of Overland Partners, the Wildlife Experience Ctr. in Denver, Colo. project, San Antonio, Bd. of Overland Partners, the expansion of the Hockaday Girls' Sch. in Dallas, Tex. project, San Antonio; undergraduate study (late)O'Neill Ford, FAIA and Frank Welch, FAIA. One-man shows include permant displays, New York, Los Angeles, Zurich, and San Antonio, 1981—. Grantee Urban planning study, Royal Danish Acad./ Copenhagen. Mem.: Sch. of Architecture (pres. 1977), AIA (fellow 2003), Tex. Soc. of Architects, Nat. Trust for Hist. Pres., Am. Inst. of Architects. Office: Overland Partners 5101 Broadway San Antonio TX 78209 also: Overland Partners 612 E Main St Bozeman MT 59715*

BLONSHINE, SHEENA KAY, medical, surgical nurse; b. Traverse City, Mich., Oct. 15, 1945; d. LeRoy H. and Arta M. (Terry) Blonshine. Diploma, Orange Meml. Sch. Nursing, 1966; BSN cum laude, Boise State U., 1994. RN, Idaho, Fla. Staff nurse Tampa (Fla.) Gen. Hosp., 1966-72; pvt. scrub nurse Blank, Pupello, Bessone, M.D., Tampa, 1972-82; staff nurse St. Luke's Regional Med. Ctr., Boise, 1982-84, asst. head nurse, 1984-86, dir. cardiovasc. surgery, 1986—. Mem. nursing adv. bd. St. Jude Med., 1998-2000. Nagel scholar Boise State U. Mem.: Assn. Oper. Rm. Nurses (CNOR nat. cert. bd., ednl. lectr. nat. meeting 1988, bd. dirs. Treasure Valley chpt. 1990, 1994, pres.-elect 1997, pres. 1998, bd. dirs. 2000—02), Sigma Theta Tau (Mu Gamma chpt.). Office: Saint Luke's Regional Med Ctr 190 E Bannock St Boise ID 83712-6261 Home: 6205 N Heathrow Way Boise ID 83713-0991

BLOOD, ARCHER KENT, retired foreign service officer; b. Chgo., Mar. 20, 1923; s. Francis Earle and Hazel Mary (Brown) B.; m. Margaret Lloyd Millward, May 14, 1948; children: Shirley, Barbara, Peter, Archer. BA, U. Va., 1943; postgrad., Army War Coll., 1962-63; MA, George Wash. U., 1963. Commd. fgn. service officer Dept. State; vice consul Thessaloniki, Greece, 1947-48, Munich, Germany, 1949-50; 2d sec. Athens, Greece, 1950-52; vice consul Algiers, 1953; 2d sec. Bonn, Germany, 1953-55; consul Dacca, 1960-62; pers. officer Dept. State, 1963-65; dep. chief of mission Kabul, 1965-68; polit. counselor Athens, 1968-70; consul gen. Dacca, 1970-71; dep. dir. personnel Dept. State, Washington, 1972-74; dep. comdt. Army War Coll., 1974-77; dep. chief of mission Am. embassy, New Delhi, India, 1977-80, chargé d'affaires, 1980-81; vis. prof., diplomat-in-residence Allegheny Coll., 1982-90, prof. emeritus, 1990—. Author: The Cruel Birth of Bangladesh, 2001. Served with USNR, 1944-46. Recipient Christian A. Herter award, award for disting. civilian service Sec. Army. Mem. Phi Beta Kappa. Presbyterian.

BLOOD, MILTON RAY, association executive; b. Meadville, Pa., Aug. 3, 1938; s. Lawrence Ordell and Mary Elizabeth Blood; m. Barbara Diane Cheak, Mar. 31, 1991. BS, Ind. State U., 1960; BA, Centre Coll. Ky., 1964; MA, U. Ill., 1966, PhD, 1968. Asst. prof. psychology U. Calif., Berkeley, 1968-74; prof., assoc. dean Ga. Inst. Tech., Atlanta, 1974-83; mng. dir. AACSB-Internat. Assn. to Advance Collegiate Schs. of Bus., St. Louis, 1983—. Author: (chpt.) Role of Organizational Behavior in Business School Curriculum, 1994. Fellow APA (coun. 1978-81), Am. Psychol. Soc.; mem. Assn. Specialized and Profl. Accreditors (chair 1993-96). Lutheran. Avocation: songwriting. Office: AACSB Internat Assn Mgmt Edn 600 Emerson Rd Ste 300 Saint Louis MO 63141 Office Fax: 314-872-8495. E-mail: milton@aacsb.edu.

BLOOD, PEGGY A. college administrator; b. Pine Bluff, Ark., Feb. 8, 1947; m. Lawrence A. Davis, May 31, 1975; children: Lauren A., Pawnee A., Zelana P. BS, U. Ark., Pine Bluff, 1969; MFA, U. Ark., 1971; PhD, Union Inst., Cin., 1986; MA, Holy Names Coll., 1987. Art dir. Office Econ. Opportunity, Altheimer, Ark., 1969; acting. dept. chair, asst. prof. art Univ. Ark., Pine Bluff, 1971-74; activity coord. Good Samaritan Home, Oakland, Calif., 1978-80; art instr. Chabot Community Coll., Hayward, Calif., 1980-81, Solano Community Coll., Suisun, Calif., 1980-90; prin. Palma Ceia Christian Elem. Sch., Hayward, Calif., 1983-84; curriculum chmn., instr. Calif. IMPACT, Oakland, 1985-87; ctr. dir. Chapman U., Fairfield, Calif., 1988-97; head fine arts divsn. Savannah (Ga.) State U., 1998—. Cons. in field;; presenter workshop Savannah (Ga.) Art Assn., The SCAGA Comparative Design Study, Augusta, Ga.; presenter workshop (oils) Savannah Art Assn.; presenter paper Holy Names Coll. The Impact of Cuts in Aid to Calif., Oakland, 1975, Holy Names Coll. The Elementary School Teacher, Oakland, Coll. Assn. Inc. Transformation Vision from H.S. to Coll.; cons. universal web based courses, South Africa, St. Petersburg, Russia; presenter, cons. on curriculum devel., web-based courses on art and culture. One-woman shows include Chapman Unvi, Fairfield, Calif., AAUW, Oakland, Calif., Fort Mason, San Francisco, Calif., Hospic Savannah, Ga., CinQue Gallery, N.Y.C., and otherss, exhibitions include Univ. of Mobile, Ala., Horizon Art Festival, Martinex, Ga. (Selected Best of Show and First Prize), 2001—02, No. Calif. Women Art Festival, exhibitions include Seattle Ann. State Exhbn., Univ. Wash. Festival Show, Seattle, and many more; contbr. articles to profl. jour.; author: Apples are Blue, Fostering Creativity in the Challenged Student, Color Transformation, Knowledge Based Curriculum. Sch. bd. trustee Benicia (Calif.) Unified Sch. Dist., 1989-93; bd. mem. Nat. Inst. Art & Disabilities, Richmond, Calif., 1988-90, Girl Scouts Am., Solano County, Calif., 1995-96; legis. dist. action com. mem. Omega Boys and Girls Club, Oakland, Calif. Recipient Ledalle Morehead scholarship, U. Ark., Pine Bluff, 1968; scholar Fulbright Sr. Splt. Candidate award, 2002—; named first Afro-Am. grad. MFA in Art, U. Ark., Fayetteville, 1971, Outstanding Bay Area Artist, Oakland (Calif.) Arts, 1985; numerous grants Mem.: LWV (bd. dirs. 1980—82), AAUW, Willie B. Adkins Coll. Bound Program, Southeastern Art Assn., Nat. Art Edn. Assn., Coll. Arts Assn. Am., Artist Alliance of Assorted Black Colls. and Univs., Ga. Art Assn., Rotary, Alpha Kappa Alpha (1st Prize art award 1982—83). Roman Catholic. Achievements include traveled extensively thoughout Europe, Asia, and Africa.

BLOODGOOD-ABRAMS, JANE MARIE, artist; b. Queens, NY, Jan. 7, 1963; d. Clarence and Sheila Getty Bloodgood; m. Paul H. Abrams, June 13, 1992; children: Erica, Fiona. BS in Studio Art, Coll. of St. Rose, Albany, NY, 1985; MFA, SUNY, New Paltz, 1985. Exhibitions include Biennial, NY State Mus., Albany, 1999, Sacred Visions, Payerbach, Austria, 2000, Florence Biennale, Italy, 2001. Bd. mem. U.U. Congregation of the Catskills, Kingston, NY, 1999—2002. Recipient Mem. of the Year, Ulster County Arts Coun., 2000; grantee spl. opportunity stipend, NYS Found. Arts, 1998, Lewis Vogelstein Foundn., 2002. Mem.: Pastel Soc. Am. (signature mem. 1999—), Nat. Assn. of Women Artists (juried mem. 2002—), Catharine Lorillard Wolfe Art Club (juried mem. 2002—). Democrat. Unitarian Universalist.

BLOODWORTH, A(LBERT) W(ILLIAM) FRANKLIN, lawyer; b. Atlanta, Sept. 23, 1935; s. James Morgan Bartow and Elizabeth Westfield (Dimmock) B.; m. Elizabeth Howell, Nov. 24, 1967; 1 child, Elizabeth Howell. AB in History and French, Davidson Coll., 1957; JD magna cum laude with 1st honors, U. Ga., 1963. Bar: Ga. 1962, U.S. Supreme Ct. 1971. Asst. dir. alumni and pub. relations Davidson Coll., N.C., 1959-60; assoc. Hansell & Post, Atlanta, 1963-68, ptnr., 1969-84, Bloodworth & Nix, Atlanta, 1984-95, Bloodworth & McSwain, Atlanta, 1996—. Counsel organized crime com. Met. Atlanta Commn. on Crime, 1965-67; asst. sec., counsel Met. Found. Atlanta, 1968-76. Bd. dirs. Atlanta Presbytery, 1974-78; trustee Synod of S.E., Presbyn. Ch. in U.S.A., Augusta, Ga., 1982-87; trustee Big Canoe Chapel, Ga., 1983-86, 88-91, chmn. bd. trustees, 1985-86, 90-91; mem. pres.'s adv. coun. Presbyn. Homes, 1989—; mem. president's adv. coun. Thornwell Home and Sch. for Children, 1998—. elder North Ave Presbyn. Ch., Atlanta. 1st lt. Intelligence Corps, USAR, 1957-59. Recipient Jessie Dan MacDougal Scholarship award U. Ga. Found., 1963, Outstanding Student Leadership award Student Bar Assn., U. Ga., 1963. Fellow Am. Coll. Trust and Estate Counsel; mem. ABA, State Bar Ga., Atlanta Bar Assn., Atlanta Estate Planning Coun., North Atlanta Estate Planning Coun., Capital City Club, Lawyers Club, Sphinx Club, Gridiron Club, Phi Beta Kappa, Phi Kappa Phi, Omicron Delta Kappa, Alpha Tau Omega (pres. chpt. 1957), Phi Delta Phi (grad. of yr. 1963, pres. chpt. 1963). Republican. Presbyterian. Home: 3784 Club Dr NE Atlanta GA 30319-1108 Office: 706 Monarch Plz 3414 Peachtree Rd NE Atlanta GA 30326-1153 Fax: 404 231-9330. E-mail: bandm706@bellsouth.net.

BLOODWORTH, GLADYS LEON, educator; b. Natchitoches, La., July 9, 1946; d. Rudolph and Mary (LeRoy) Leon; m. John Edward Bloodworth, Aug. 14, 1971; children: John, Jeremy. BA, Southern U., Baton Rouge, 1968; MA, Calif. State U., Dominguez Hills, 1989. Nat. bd. cert. tchr. mid. childhood generalist NBCT/MC, 2001. Lang. arts tchr. grades 6-10 Natchitoches Parish Schs.; categorical program adviser L.A. Unified Schs., mentor tchr., 1999—, coord. gifted coord., 1988. Named Outstanding Math Tchr., 1987-88. Mem. NEA, United Tchrs. L.A., Calif. Tchrs. Assn., Women in Ednl. Leadership, Kappa Kappa Iota. Methodist.

BLOODWORTH, SANDRA GAIL, artist, arts administrator; b. Charleston, Miss., Nov. 22, 1950; d. Deward Dupree and Eva Pauline (Early) B. BSEd, Miss. Coll., 1972; MA, U. Miss., 1973; MFA, Fla. State U., 1980. Devel. assoc. Studio in a Sch., N.Y.C., 1987-88; mgr., Arts For Transit Met. Transp. Authority, N.Y.C., 1988-92, dep. dir., Arts For Transit, 1992-96, dir., Arts For Transit, 1996—. Mem. adv. bd. N.Y. Transit Mus., Bklyn., Fine Art Dept./FIT, N.Y.C.; vis. artist Berkshire Sch. of Contemporary Art, North Adams, Mass. Author: (catalogue) Art en Route: MTA Arts for Transit, 1994. Office: Arts for Transit Met Transp Authority 347 Madison Ave New York NY 10017-3706

BLOODWORTH, WILLIAM ANDREW, JR., academic administrator; b. San Antonio, Sept. 9, 1942; s. William Andrew Sr. and Ellan Oma (Gatliff) B.; m. Julia Ann Rankin, Nov. 27, 1964; children: Nicole, Paul William. BS, Tex. Luth. Coll., 1964; MA, Lamar U., 1967; PhD, U. Tex., 1972; grad., Harvard Inst. Ednl. Mgmt., 1989. Tchr. Boerne (Tex.) and Port Neches (Tex.) pub. schs., 1964-67; asst. instr. U. Tex., Austin, 1969-72; asst. prof. English E. Carolina U., Greenville, N.C., 1972-77, assoc. prof., 1977-82, prof., 1982-90, chmn. English dept., 1982-88, acting vice chancellor for acad. affairs, 1987-89; provost, v.p. for acad. affairs Cen. Mo. State U., Warrensburg, 1990-93; pres. Augusta (Ga.) State U., 1993—. Author: Upton Sinclair, 1977, Max Brand, 1993; contbr. articles to profl. publs., chpts. to books. Mem. Am. Assn. Higher Edn., Rotary, Phi Kappa Phi (chpt. pres. 1989-90), Phi Delta Kappa. Avocations: running, writing. Home: 819 Kamel Cir Augusta GA 30909-2709 Office: Augusta State U Office of the Pres Augusta GA 30904-2200

BLOOM, ADAM I. psychologist; b. Bklyn., May 18, 1964; s. Jeffrey and Eileen (Tannenbaum) B.; m. Michelle Longo, Mar. 23, 1991; 1 child, Matthew. BA in Psychology, SUNY, Oneonta, 1986; MS in Ednl. and Sch. Psychology, CUNY, Bklyn., 1988; D in Psychology, Yeshiva U., 1993. Lic. psychologist, N.Y.; cert. sch. psychologist, N.J., N.Y. Psychology extern Jewish Bd. Child and Family Svcs., Bklyn., 1986-87; psychologist in tng. N.Y.C. Bd. Edn., S.I., 1987-88, sch. psychologist, 1988-92, 93-94; clin. psychology intern Montefiore Med. Ctr., Albert Einstein Coll. Medicine, Bronx, N.Y., 1992-93; psychologist Mental Health Assn. Westchester (N.Y.), Inc., 1994-97; assoc. clinic dir. Mental Health Svcs./Family Ct., N.Y.C., 1997—. Tchg. asst. SUNY, Oneonta, 1986; leader Support Group for Parents of Children with Tourette's Syndrome, 1995—; pvt. practice forensic/clin. psychology, White Plains, N.Y., 1995—; consulting psychologist Spectrum Behavioral Health, Poughkeepsie, N.Y., 1996—; spkr. in field. Mem. APA, Nat. Assn. Sch. Psychologists (cert.), Nat. Register Health Svc. Providers in Psychology, N.Y. Assn. Sch. Psychologists, Westchester County Psychologists Assn., Westchester Tourette's Syndrome Assn. (v.p. 1994—), Kappa Delta Pi. Avocations: lifeguard instructing, tennis, swimming. Office: 62 Waller Ave White Plains NY 10605-1408

BLOOM, ALFRED HOWARD, academic administrator, educator; b. N.Y.C., Feb. 27, 1946; s. Alfred H, and Martha (Berrol) Bloom; m. Margaret Hennigan, Aug. 22, 1971. BA, Princeton U., 1967; PhD, Harvard U., 1974. Asst., assoc. prof. Swarthmore Coll., Pa., 1974—86, assoc. provost, 1985—86, pres., 1991—; dean of faculty, v.p. acad. affairs Pitzer Coll., Claremont, Calif., 1986—90, exec. v.p., 1990—91. Author: The Linguistic Shaping of Thought, 1981; contbr. articles to profl. jours. Fellow, Fulbright-Hays, 1968; grantee, SSRC, 1978, 1981, NEH, 1975, 1986. Mem.: Assn. Asian Studies. Avocations: study of languages and cultures, intercultural gastronomy. Office: Swarthmore Coll Office of Pres 500 College Ave Swarthmore PA 19081-1306 E-mail: abloom1@swarthmore.edu.*

BLOOM, BARRY MALCOLM, pharmaceutical consultant; b. Roxbury, Mass., Aug. 12, 1928; s. Morris and Ann (Levine) B.; m. Joan Martha Ensign, June 27, 1956; children: Catherine, Brian, Joanna. SB, MIT, 1948, PhD, 1951, postgrad., 1967; D of Humane Letters (hon.), Conn. Coll., 1992. Rsch. chemist Pfizer, Inc., Groton, Conn., 1952-63, dir. medicinal chems. and rsch., 1963-71, pres. cen. rsch. div., 1971-90, v.p. rsch., 1971-90, corp. mgmt. com., 1984-93, sr. v.p. R&D, 1990-92, exec. v.p. R & D, 1992-93; cons. pvt. practice, 1993—. Bd. dirs. Neurogen Corp., Congl. Commn. on Fed. Drug Approval Process, PMA Commn. on Drugs for Rare Diseases; cons. U.S. Congress Office Tech. Assessment, 1976-77; mem. Conn. Tech. Adv. Bd., 1985-90. Mem. editorial bd. Ann. Reports in Medicinal Chemistry, 1968-70; patentee in field. NRC postdoctoral fellow U. Wis., 1952; Poly. Inst. Tech. fellow N.Y.C., 1980; recipient Spl. Achievement award CT Innovations, Inc., 1997. Mem. Am. Chem. Soc. (chmn. div. medicinal chemistry 1967), Conn. Acad. Sci. and Engring., Pharm. Mfrs. Assn. (chmn. R&D sect. 1976). Home and Office: Mackintosh Rd Lyme CT 06371

BLOOM, CHARLES JOSEPH, lawyer; b. Pitts., July 7, 1946; s. Israel C. and Ida (Lample) B.; m. Susan Halsey Potts, May 14, 1971; children: Zachary B., Amanda H., Theodore L. BA, Princeton U., 1967; JD magna cum laude, U. Pa., Phila., 1971. Bar: Pa. 1971, U.S. Dist. Ct. (ea. dist.) Pa. 1971, U.S. Ct. Appeals (3d cir.) 1972, U.S. Supreme Ct. 1978. Law clk. U.S. Ct. Appeals (3d cir.), Phila., 1971-72; assoc. Pepper, Hamilton & Scheetz, Phila., 1972-78, ptnr., 1978-80, Hunt, Kerr, Bloom & Hitchner, Phila., 1980-85, Kleinbard, Bell & Brecker, Phila., 1985-92, Stevens & Lee, P.C., Wayne, Pa., 1992—. Bd. dir. Main Line Art Ctr., 1997-2003, Cloister Inn Princeton, 1980-89, chmn., 1983-85; commr. Lower Merion Twp., 1998—; v.p. Haverford (Pa.) Civic Assn., 1989—, pres., 1998. Mem. Phila. Bar Assn. (fed. cts. com. 1975—, chmn. unauthorized practice law com. 1985, bench-bar conf. com. 1985-90), Order of Coif. Avocations: numismatics, collecting antique toy trains. E-mail: cjb@stevenslee.com.

BLOOM, CHRISTOPHER ARTHUR, lawyer; b. Chgo., May 25, 1951; s. Charles G. and Lyra Anne (Eells) B.; m. Jo Anne Gazarek, Apr. 21, 1979; children: Anna Victoria, Mary Olivia. B.A. cum laude, Kenyon Coll., 1973; J.D., Ind. U., 1975. Bar: Ind. 1975, Pa. 1976, Ill. 1976, U.S. Dist. Ct. (so. dist.) Ind., 1975, U.S. Dist. Ct. (no. dist.) Ill. 1976, U.S. Dist. Ct. (no. dist.) Ind. 1980,

U.S. Ct. Appeals (7th cir.) 1975, U.S. Ct. Appeals (2d cir.) 1976, U.S. Supreme Ct. 1979. Assoc. Green & Brandwein, Chgo., 1976-78; assoc. Fox & Grove, Chartered, Chgo., 1978-82, ptnr., 1982-84; ptnr. Alexander, Unikel, Bloom, Zalewa & Tenenbaum, Ltd., Chgo., 1984-86, ptnr. Keck, Mahin & Cate, 1986—; instr. Loyola U., Chgo., 1976-79; gen. counsel Orch. of Ill., Chgo., 1976—, Grant Park Concerts Soc., Chgo., 1977— . Mem. ABA, Ill. Bar Assn., Chgo. Bar Assn. (fed. tax commn.). Home: 5490 S South Shore Dr Chicago IL 60615-5984

BLOOM, CLAIRE, actress; b. London, Feb. 15, 1931; d. Edward Max and Elizabeth (Grew) B.; m. Rod Steiger, Sept. 19, 1959 (div. Jan. 1969); 1 child, Anna Justine; m. Philip Roth, Apr. 29, 1990 (div. Mar. 1995). Student, Badminton Sch., Bristol, Eng., Fern Hill Manor, New Milton, Eng., Guildhall Sch. Music and Drama, London. Disting. vis. prof. Hunter Coll., N.Y.C., 1989-90. Appeared as Ophelia, Stratford-Upon-Avon, 1948; plays include Ring Around the Moon, London, 1949-51, Romeo and Juliet, also as Juliet in Old Vic tour of U.S.; film roles in Limelight, Richard III, 1956, Alexander the Great, 1956, The Brothers Karamazov, 1958, Look Back in Anger, 1958, The Brothers Grimm, 1962, The Chapman Report, 1962, The Haunting, 1963, 80,000 Suspects, 1963, Alta Infidelita, 1963, Il Maestro di Vigeuono, 1963, The Outrage, 1964, The Spy Who Came in from the Cold, 1965, The Illustrated Man, 1969, Three into Two Won't Go, 1969, A Severed Head, 1971, A Doll's House, 1973, Islands in the Stream, 1976, Clash of the Titans, 1981, Always, 1984, Sammy and Rosie, 1987, Crimes and Misdemeanors, 1989, Mad Dogs and Englishmen, 1994, Daylight, 1995, The Book Eve, 2002, Imagining Argentina, 2002; Broadway prodns. include Rashomon, 1959; other theatre appearances include Duel of Angels, London, 1958, Altona, Royal Court Theatre, London, 1960, Ivanov, London, 1964, A Doll's House, Hedda Gabler, 1971, Vivat! Vivat Regina!, 1972; N.Y. appearance The Innocents, 1976; London appearances A Doll's House, 1973, A Streetcar Named Desire, 1974, Rosmersholm, 1977, The Cherry Orchard, 1981, These are Women, 1982-83, When We Dead Awaken, 1990, Daughters, Wives and Mothers, 1991, Silenced Voices, 1992, Women in Love, 1993, The Cherry Orchard, 1994, Long Days Journey into Night, 1996, Electra, 1998, Conversations After a Burial, 2000, A Little Night Music, 2001, A Little Night Music NYCO, 2003; many roles Brit. and U.S. TV including In Praise of Love, 1975, A Legacy, 1975, Henry VIII, 1979, Hamlet, 1979, The Ghost Writer, 1983, Cymbeline, 1983, King John, 1983, Brideshead Revisited, 1981, Shadowlands, 1984, Time and the Conways, 1985, miniseries Queenie, 1987, Anastasia, 1987, Shadow in the Sun, 1988, The Camomile Lawn, 1991, The Mirror Crack'd, 1992, Remember, 1993, Village Affairs, 1994, Family Money, 1996, When the Dead Man Heard, 1997, The Lady in Question, 1999; author: Limelight and After, 1982, Leaving A Doll's House, 1996. Recipient Evening Standard award, London, 1974, Brit. Film and TV award, London, 1984; nominee Tony award, 1998, 99. Office: Marion Rosenberg Agy 8428 Melrose Pl West Hollywood CA 90069-5308

BLOOM, DAVID ALAN, pediatric urology educator; b. Buffalo, July 26, 1945; m. Martha Lichty, June 8, 1980. BS, Rensselaer Poly. Inst., 1967; MD, SUNY, Buffalo, 1971. Diplomate Am. Bd. Surgery, Am. Bd. Urology (exam. com. 1992-1996, Trustee, 2003), Nat. Bd. Med. Examiners. Intern UCLA, 1971-72, resident in surgery, 1972-75, chief resident, 1975-76, resident in urology, 1976-77, sr. resident, 1978-79, chief resident, lectr., 1979-80; vis. fellow, registrar Inst. Urology and St. Peter's Hosp., U. London, 1977-78; asst. prof. surgery U. Mich., Ann Arbor, 1984-86, assoc. prof., 1986-93, prof., 1993—, chief pediatric urology, 1984—, assoc. dean faculty affairs Sch. Medicine, 2000—. Cons. urology surgery br. Nat. Cancer Inst., NIH, Bethesda, Md., 1982, Naval Regional Med. Ctr., Portsmouth, Va., 1983, Walter Reed Army Med. Ctr., Washington, 1985, VA Hosp., Ann Arbor, 1985; locum in urology Gt. Ormond Street Hosp. for Sick Children and Inst. Urology, Shaftesbury Hosp., London, 1986; asst. prof. surgery, then assoc. prof. Uniformed Svcs. U. Health Scis. Sch. Medicine, Bethesda, 1980-84, clin. assoc. prof., 1985, assoc. prof. pediat., 1984; mem. exam com. Am. Bd. Urology, 1992-96, trustee, 2003—; presenter and cons. in field. Author: (with McGuire, Catalona and Lipshultz) Advances in Urology, 1995-97; mem. editl. bd. Urology, 1992—, Jour. Endourology, 1997-2003, Contemporary Urology, 1997—, British Jour. Urology, 1999-2002. Lt. col. M.C., U.S. Army, 1980-84. Mem. USAR 1984-1986, Fellow ACS (motion picture com. 1996-2002); mem. AMA, Am. Acad. Pediat. (exec. com. sect. on urology 1989-93, historian 1993-2000, chmn. 2001-02); Am. Assn. Clin. Urologists, Halsted Soc. (photographer, dir. 1999-2001), Longmire Surg. Soc., Reed M. Nesbit Soc., Soc. for Pediatric Urology, Soc. Genitourinary Reconstructive Surgeons, Soc. Univ. Urologists, Am. Assn. Genito-uniary Surgeons, Uniformed Svcs. U. Surg. Assocs., Nat. Urologic Forum (sec.-treas. 1995-2002), European Assn. Urology, Soc. Internat. Urology. Office: U Mich 1500 E Medical Center Dr Ann Arbor MI 48109-0330

BLOOM, DAVID LEWIS, radiologist; b. Boston, May 18, 1930; s. Morris and Sara (Galner) Bloom; m. Phyllis Schneider, Jan. 9, 1955; children: Deborah Faye, Gordon Merrill, Adrienne Janet. AB, Harvard U., 1951; MD, Tufts U., 1955. Med. intern N.E. Med. Ctr., Boston, 1955-56; resident in radiology Beth Israel Hosp., Brookline, Mass., 1956-57, 59-61; fellow neuroradiology Nat. Hosp., London, 1961-62; instr. radiology Yale Med. Ctr., New Haven, 1962-63, asst. prof. radiology, 1963-66; chmn. dept. radiology Morristown (N.J.) Meml. Hosp., 1966-83; CEO NMR of Am., 1983-87, med. dir., 1990-95, Med. Diagnostic, Inc., 1987-97, Alliance Imaging, 1997—, Med. Resources Inc., Bloomfield, NJ, 1995—, Medical Online, Lexington, Mass., 1999—2002. Contbr. articles to profl. jours. Capt. USAF, 1957-59. Fellow Am. Coll. Radiology; mem. Radiology Soc. N.Am., Am. Soc. Neuroradiology, Internat. Soc. Magnetic Resonance in Medicine. Jewish. Avocations: tennis, theatre, symphony, travel. Home: 388 Beacon St # 1 Boston MA 02116-1002 Office: Alliance Imaging 600 Federal St Andover MA 01810

BLOOM, EDWIN JOHN, JR., retired human resources consultant; b. Yonkers, N.Y., Nov. 12, 1931; s. Edwin John Sr. and Marion (Baude) B.; m. Mary C. Caciola, June 9, 1956; children: Mary Catherine, Edward Joseph, Theresa Ann, Donna Marie. Student, Columbia U., 1950-51, 54; BS, Cornell U., 1957. Supr. employment and employee services GAF Corp., Binghamton, N.Y., 1957-65; mgr. indsl. relations Philco-Ford Corp., Phila., 1965-70; dir. employee relations Zenith Radio Corp., Chgo., 1970-72; v.p. personnel Lechmere div. Dayton Hudson, Cambridge, Mass., 1973-77; pres. Employee Relations Assocs., Inc., Concord, Mass., 1977-98. Cons. Small Bus. Adminstrn., Boston, 1978-83; asst. prof. Lasell Jr. Coll., Newton, Mass., 1977-86; instr. Bunker Hill Community Coll., Boston, 1977-97; corporator Middlesex Savs. Bank, Concord, 1980—. Corporator Mus. of Transp., Boston, 1984-86; pres. bd. dirs. Minute Man Assn. for Retarded Citizens, Concord, 1973-78, Eliot Community Mental Health Ctr., 1979-81; area bd. dirs. Mass. Dept. Mental Health Concord Area, 1975-79, 82-88; mem. Ctrl. Middlesex Adv. Com. Mass. Dept. Mental Retardation, 1988—, regional tng. coun., 1993-96, citizens monitoring team, 1993-95; mem. Ayer Coun. on Aging, 2000—. Sgt. U.S. Army, 1951-54. Recipient Cert. of Merit, United Way, Mass., 1974, Merit cert. Mass. Dept. Mental Health, 1978, Recognition plaque Eliot comty. Mental Health Ctr., Mass., 1981, Leadership award United Way Acton, Mass., 1993, citations from Mass. state senate and Mass. ho. of reps. in recognition of commitment and accomplishments for mentally retarded, 1995. Mem. Indsl. Rels. Rsch. Assn., Am. Cons. League (chartered cons., accredited profl. cons.), Mass. Businessmen's Assn., Am. Legion. Roman Catholic. Avocations: reading, woodworking, coin collecting. Home: 19 Pingry Way Ayer MA 01432-1775

BLOOM, EUGENE CHARLES, gastroenterologist, educator; b. Tupelo, Miss., June 3, 1933; s. Robert Harold and Anna Esther (Kronick) B.; m. Joan Ellen Margolis, July 22, 1956; children: Marjorie Wynne Bloom Albert, Stacey Bloom Schlafstein, Robin Bloom Wolf. Student, Emory U., 1951-55, U. Fla., 1955-56; MD, U. Miami, 1960. Diplomate Am. Bd. Internal Medicine. Intern Cook County Hosp., Chgo., 1960-61; resident in internal medicine Jackson Meml. Hosp., Miami, 1961-63; resident in gastroent. Coral Gables VA Hosp., 1963-64; rsch. fellow dept. medicine, divsn. gastroent. U. Miami (Fla.) Sch. Medicine, 1964-65, rsch. scientist, 1964-66, instr. medicine, 1964-74, clin. asst. prof. medicine, 1974—; gen. practice medicine Miami, 1966—96. Mem. staff Bapt. Hosp. Miami, sec.-treas. med. staff, 1979-80, chief of staff, 1980-82; acting chief of staff Oakland Park VA Med. Ctr., 1998-99; med. cons. Social Security Adminstrn., 1996—. Contbr. articles to profl. jours. Bd. dirs. Jewish Vocat. Svc.; active Greater Miami Jewish Fedn., chmn. physicians divsn., 1979-80. Capt. M.C., U.S. Army, 1963-67, Vietnam. Recipient Disting. Alumnus award, U. Miami Sch. Medicine, 1998, Cmty. Tchr. award, Fla. chpt. ACP, 1999. Mem. AMA, AAAS, Am. Acad. Sci., Am. Coll. Gastroenterology, Am. Soc. Gastroent. Endoscopy, U. Miami Med. Alumni Assn. (chmn. Dade County chpt. 1972-75, nat. pres. 1975-77, v.p. pub. rels. 1987-89, v.p. 1987-90), Gen. Alumni U. Miami (bd. dirs. 1973-77, v.p. 1988-95, bd. overseers 1988—, sec. 1990, v.p. 1991), Fla. Gastroent. Soc., Greater Miami Jewish Fedn., Woodfield Country Club, Alpha Omega Alpha, Omicron Delta Kappa. Democrat.

BLOOM, FLOYD ELLIOTT, physician, research scientist; b. Mpls., Oct. 8, 1936; s. Jack Aaron and Frieda (Shochman) B.; m. D'Nell Bingham, Aug. 30, 1956 (dec. May 1973); children: Fl'Nell, Evan Russell; m. Jody Patricia Corey, Aug. 9, 1980. AB cum laude, So. Meth. U., 1956; MD cum laude, Washington U., St. Louis, 1960; DSc (hon.), So. Meth. U., 1983, Hahnemann U., 1985, U. Rochester, 1985, Mt. Sinai U. Med. Sch., 1996, Thomas Jefferson U., 1997, Washington U., 1998. Intern Barnes Hosp., St. Louis, 1960-61, resident internal medicine, 1961-62; research asso. NIMH, Washington, 1962-64; fellow depts. pharmacology, psychiatry and anatomy Yale Sch. Medicine, 1964-66, asst. prof., 1966-67, asso. prof., 1968; chief lab. neuropharmacology NIMH, Washington, 1968-75, acting dir. div. spl. mental health, 1973-75; commd. officer USPHS, 1974-75; dir. Arthur Vining Davis Center for Behavorial Neurobiology; prof. Salk Inst., La Jolla, Calif., 1975-83; dir. div. preclin. neurosci. and endocrinology Scripps Rsch. Inst., La Jolla, 1983-89, chmn. dept. neuropharmacology, 1989—; editor in chief Science Magazine, 1995-2000; chief exec. officer Neurome, Inc., 2000—02, chmn. bd., 2000—. Mem. Comm. on Alcoholism, 1980—81, Nat. Adv. Mental Health Coun., 1976—80; chmn. scientific adv. bd. Neurome, Inc., 1994—98; bd. dirs. Alkermes, Inc.; chmn. sci. adv. bd. Advancis Corp. Author: (with others) Biochemical Basis of Neuropharmacology, 1971, 8th edit., 2002, (with Lazerson and Hofstadter) Brain, Mind and Behavior, 1984, (with Lazerson) 2d edit., 1988, (with C.A. Nelson) 3d edit., 2000, (with W. Young and Y. Kim) Brain browser, 1989; editor: Peptides: Integrators of Cell and Tissue Function, 1980, Progress in Brain Research, vol. 199, 1994, vol. 100, 1997, (with D.J. Kupfer) Neuro-Psychopharmacology: The Fourth Generation of Progress, 1994, Handbook of Chemical Neruoanatomy, 1997, The Primate Nervous System, 1997, vol. II, 1998, vol. III, 1999, (with Beal and Kupfer) The Dana Guide to Brain Health, 2003; co-editor: Regulatory Peptides, 1979-90, (with M. Randolph) Funding Health Sciences Research, 1990; assoc. editor: Biological Psychiatry, 1993-95; editor-in-chief Science, 1995-2000. Trustee Washington U., St. Louis, 1998—, chmn. nat. med. coun., 2000—. Recipient A. Cressy Morrison award N.Y. Acad. Scis., 1971, A.E. Bennett award for basic rsch. Soc. Biol. Psychiatry, 1971, Arthur A. Fleming award Science mag., 1973, Mathilde Solowey award, 1973, Biol. Sci. award Washington Acad. Scis., 1975, Alumni Achievement citation Washington U., 1980, McAlpin Rsch. Achievement award Mental Health Assn., 1980, Lectr.'s medal College de France, 1979, Steven Beering medal, 1985, Janssen award World Psychiat. Assn., 1989, Passerow Found. award, 1990, Herman von Helmholtz award, 1991, Pythagora award, 1994, Presdl. award Soc. for Neurosci., 1995, Golgi prize U. Brescia, 1996, Meritorious Achievement award Coun. Biology Editors, 1999, Gold medal Soc. Biol. Psychiatry, 1997, Disting. Svc. award Am. Psychiat. Assn., 2000; Disting. fellow Am. Psychiat. Assn., 1986; named scientist of the yr. Achievement Rewards for Coll. Scientists, 1996. Fellow AAAS (bd. dirs. 1986-90, pres.-elect 2001, pres. 2002), Am. Coll. Neuropsychopharmacology (mem. coun. 1976-78, chmn. program com. 1987, pres. 1988-89, Hoch award 1998); mem. NAS (chmn. sect. neurobiology 1979-83), Inst. Medicine (mem. coun. 1986-89, 93-95), Am. Philos. Soc., Am. Acad. Arts and Scis., Soc. Neurosci. (sec. 1973-74, pres. 1976, chmn. publs. com. 1999—), Am. Soc. Pharmacology and Exptl. Therapeutics, Am. Soc. Cell Biology, Am. Physiol. Soc., Am. Assn. Anatomists, Rsch. Soc. Alcoholism (chmn. program com. 1985-87, pres.-elect 1989-91, pres. 1991-93), Swedish Acad. Sci. (fgn. assoc. 1989). Home: 628 Pacific View Dr San Diego CA 92109-1768 Office: The Scripps Rsch Inst 10550 N Torrey Pines Rd La Jolla CA 92037-1000 E-mail: fbloom@scripps.edu.

BLOOM, FRANCES VIRGINIA, retired music educator; b. Chgo., Oct. 31, 1911; d. Joseph and Bertha (Walker) Bloom. Student, coll. night sch. With ins. co.; stenographer, sec. L.A. County; newspaper columnist Glendale News Press, others; music tchr. violin, piano, guitar. Author: Grace Notes mag. Grantee grantee, Hilton Hotel, others. Mem.: Calif. Music Tchrs.' Assn.

BLOOM, HAROLD, humanities educator, writer; b. NYC, July 11, 1930; s. William and Paula (Lev) B.; m. Jeanne Gould, May 8, 1958; children: Daniel Jacob, David Moses. BA, Cornell U., 1951; PhD, Yale U., 1955; LHD, Boston Coll., 1973, Yeshiva U., 1976, U. Bologna, 1997, St. Michael's Coll., 1998, U. Rome, 1999, U. Coimbra, 2001, V. Mass at Dartmouth, 2002. Mem. faculty Yale U., 1955—, prof. English, 1965-77, DeVane prof. humanities, 1974-77, prof. humanities, 1977—, sterling prof. humanities, 1983—. Vis. prof. Hebrew U., Jerusalem, 1959, Breadloaf Summer Sch., 1965-66, Soc. for Humanities, Cornell U., 1968-69; vis. Univ. prof. New Sch. Social Rsch., NYC, 1982-84; Charles Eliot Norton prof. of poetry Harvard U., 1987-88; Berg prof. Eng., NYU, 1988—. Author: Shelley's Mythmaking, 1959, The Visionary Company, 1961, Blake's Apocalypse, 1963, Commentary on Blake, 1965, Yeats, 1970, The Ringers in the Tower, 1971, The Anxiety of Influence, 1973, Wallace Stevens: The Poems of Our Climate, 1977, A Map of Misreading, 1975, Kabbalah and Criticism, 1975, Poetry and Repression, 1976, Figures of Capable Imagination, 1976, The Flight to Lucifer: A Gnostic Fantasy, 1979, Agon: Towards a Theory of Revisionism, 1981, The Breaking of the Vessels, 1981, The Strong Light of the Canonical, 1987, Freud: Transference and Authority, 1988, Poetics of Influence: New and Selected Criticism, 1988, Ruin the Sacred Truths, 1988, The Book of J, 1990, The Am. Religion, 1992, The Western Canon, 1994, Omens of Millennium, 1996, Shakespeare: The Invention of the Human, 1998, How to Read and Why, 1999, Stories and Poems for Extremely Intelligent Children of all Ages, 2000, Genius, 2002, Hamlet: Poem Unlimited, 2003; editor Chelsea House Modern Critical Views and Interpretations, 1984—. Recipient John Addison Porter prize Yale U., 1955; Newton Arvin award, 1967; Melville Cane award Poetry Soc. Am., 1970; Zabel prize Am. Inst. Arts and Letters, 1982, Christian Gauss prize Phi Beta Kappa, 1989, Internat. prize Catalonia, 2002; Reyes Internat. Prize, Mexico, 2003; Guggenheim fellow, 1962; Fulbright fellow, 1955; MacArthur prize fellowship, 1985. Mem. Am. Acad. Arts and Letters (Gold medal 1999), Am. Philos. Soc. Home: 179 Linden St New Haven CT 06511-2407 *Most instances of religion are mere manifestations of religiosity, which is endemic in our nation, where nine of ten say that God loves them. Spinoza observed that we should love God without expecting that God would love us in return.*

BLOOM, HEATHER LYNN, physician; b. Long Beach, Calif., June 26, 1969; d. Thomas Kirby and Barbara Lee Bloom; m. O. Austin Collins, Apr. 7, 2002. MD, U. Vt., Burlington, 1991. Diplomate U. Vt. Coll. of Medicine, 1991. Cardiology fellow U. Calif. Davis Med. Ctr., 2000—03; electrophysiology fellow Emory U., Atlanta, 2003—. Med. rsch. U. Calif. Davis Med. Ctr., 2000—03. Fellow: Am. Coll. of Cardiology; mem.: U. Calif. Davis Ice Hockey Team. Office: Univ Calif Davis Med Ctr Deptf Cardiology 4860 Y St Suite 2820 Davis CA 95616 Office Fax: 916-734-0409.

BLOOM, HOWARD KENNETH, paleopsychologist, writer; b. Buffalo, June 25, 1943; s. Irving and Ann (Shalwitz) B.; m. Linda Jean Rider (div.); 1 child, Noelle Maria Pollet; m. Diane Starr Petryk; 1 child, Walter Petryk. BA magna cum laude, NYU, 1968. Lab. asst. in biochemistry Roswell Pk. Meml. Cancer Rsch. Inst., Buffalo, 1958; writer, editor Middlesex County Mental Health Clinic, New Brunswick, N.J., 1963-64; co-founder Cloud Studio, N.Y.C., 1968-71; editor Circus Mag., N.Y.C., 1971-73; nat. dir. artist and pub. rels. ABC Records, N.Y.C., 1974-75; prin. Howard Bloom Orgn., Ltd., N.Y.C., 1976-88; founder, dir. Internat. Paleopsychology Project, 1997—; founder, mng. dir. Sci. of the Soul Initiative, 2002. Guest lectr. CUNY, 1975, Ga. State U., Atlanta, 1978-83, NYU, 1980-89, Wesleyan U., Middletown, Conn., 1989; exec. editor (mag.) If I'd Known It Was Harmless, I'd Have Killed It Myself, (supported by Danish Ministry of Culture) 2002; founding bd. mem. Epic of Evolution Soc.'s Founding Coun. Mem., Darwin Project; founder Big Bang Tango Media Lab., 2003. Author: The Lucifer Principle: A Scientific Exploration into the Forces of History, 1995, Global Brain: The Evolution of Mass Mind from the Big Bang to the 21st Century, 2000, Eine Geschichte des globalen Gehirns, 1998; exec. editor New Paradigm Book Series, 1998—; contbr., author intro.: You Are Being Lied To: The Disinformation Guide to Media Distortion; contbg. author: Everything You Know Is Wrong, Abuse Your Illusions; contbr. articles to profl. jours.; video lectr.: Rising Tide Summit, N.Y.C., 1999, Spiral Dynamics Summit, 1999, 2001, 2002, Rsch. Librs. Group Ann. Mtg., Amsterdam, 2002, 03, QuantumViz, Exploratorium, San Francisco, 2002; subject of TV spl.s Het Kvaad demens, VPRO-TV, The Netherlands, 1996, Global Brain, Het Gevael Van der Poel, PRO-TV, The Netherlands, 2002, Disinfo Nation, Channel 4, Eng., 2001. Writer Max McCarthy for Congress, 1964, Ted Weiss for Congress, 1965. Named Publicist of Yr., Performance Mag., 1983, 84, 85, 86. Mem.Am. Psychol. Soc., N.Y. Acad. Scis., Acad. Polit. Sci., Nat. Com. Ind. Scholars, Internat. Paleopsychology Project (founder, dir. 1996—), Epic of Evolution Soc. (bd. dirs. 1998—), youthactivism.org (mem. bd. advs.), Phi Beta Kappa. Democrat. Jewish. Home and Office: 705 President St Brooklyn NY 11215-1260 E-mail: howard@howardbloom.net., howard@paleopsych.org.

BLOOM, HOWARD MARTIN, lawyer; b. Brookline, Mass., Oct. 7, 1951; m. Cheryl Denise Goldstein, May 14, 1978. BA cum laude, U. Mass., 1973; JD cum laude, Suffolk U., 1977. Bar: Mass. 1977, U.S. Dist. Ct. Mass. 1978, U.S. Ct. Appeals (1st cir.) 1978, U.S. Dist. Ct. R.I. 1981, U.S. Dist. Ct. Conn. 1981, U.S. Supreme Ct. 1982. Sole practice, Boston, 1977-79; assoc. firm Siegel, O'Connor & Kainen, P.C., Boston, 1979-85, ptnr., 1985-86; of counsel, Jackson, Lewis, Schnitzler & Krupman, 1986-87, ptnr., 1988—. Co-author: Employer's Guide to Employment Law, 1984; contbr. articles to profl. jours. Mem. ABA, Mass. Bar Assn. (labor law sect. council 1983-86), Newton-Needham C. of C. (bd. dirs. 1983—). Office: Jackson Lewis Schnitzler & Krupman One Beacon St Ste 3300 Boston MA 02108

BLOOM, JAMES EDWARD, commodity trading and financial executive; b. Milw., Aug. 24, 1941; s. Edward Harry and Clarina Louise (Hoppe) B. Cert. in radiology tech., Columbia Hosp., 1963; AA in Edn. with honors, Milw. Area Tech. Coll., 1964; BBA in Sales Mktg. with honors, BBA in Bus. Mgmt. with honors, Concordia U., 1968; postgrad., Marquette U., 1969-72. Radiologic technologist Columbia Hosp., Milw., 1963-69; asst. adminstr. Bel Air Convalescent Ctr., Inc., Milw., 1969-70; asst. mktg. mgr. Champion Internat. Inc., Milw., 1970-72, human resources mgr., safety and tng. dir., 1972-75; corp. dir. indsl. rels. Weyenburg Shoe Mfg. Co., Milw., 1975; gen. mgr. Aqua Spray, Inc., Milw., 1976; mgmt. cons. Bloom & Assocs., Milw., 1976—; pres. M.F.C., Milw., 1985—; internat. agt. Superior Coffee and Foods divsn. Sara Lee Corp., Milw., 1991—; internat. and U.S. rep. Al-Sabah Internat., Safat, Kuwait, 1992—; internat. and U.S. rep. shipping and trading and contracting svc. W.L.L., Kuwait, Switerland, U.S.A., 1992—; internat. agt. Moti Enterprises Internat., 1992—, Protea Diamond Corp. (site holders: DeBeers Cons. Mines), 1992—. Guest lectr. mgmt. Milw. Area Tech. Coll., 1974-75, Marquette U., Milw., 1975, U. Milw.-Wis., 1975; advisor bus. devel. State Wis., 1978—; internat. disting. agt. Al-Ewan Med. Establishment, 1993—, Kingdom Saudi Arabia, 1993—, Hovercraft Am., 1993—, Mico Farms, Malaysia, 1993—, Steenberg Homes, 1994—, Lemke Seed Farms, Inc., 1994—, Xiangtan Fgn. Econ. Rels. and Trade Corp., China, 1994—, Greg Orchards and Produce, Inc., 1994—, Miller Brewing Co., 1994—, Holsum Foods, 1994—, Manipal Printers and Pubs. Ltd., India, 1994—; Protea site holder DeBeers Mines Ltd., Alpha Remarketing Corp.; internat. distbn. agt. Polfa Tarchomin, S.A., Poland, B.B.M. Internat. S.A., De C.V., Mex., 1995—, Valezzi, S.A., De C.V., Mex., 1996, DIMSA, Mex., Intercon Internat., Bulk Connection, Inc., 1997; brand mgmt. and mktg. ptnr. Wis. gold Harvest, 1998; mktg. ptnr. Cuming County Cattle Co., Sioux-Preme Packing Co., Intermountain Pork; Harker's Distbn. Inc., 1999, Right Time Foods, Inc., 1999, Great Plains Pork, 1999; commodity agt. Archer Daniels Midland Co., 1998; mktg. agt. DuQuoin Processing Co., Inc./DuQuoin Specialty Meats, 2000, E.H. Wolf & Sons, Inc., 2001; mktg. ptnr. Farm Connect, U. Minn., 2001, Roode Packing Co./Roode Feedlots, 2001, North Platte Feeders, 2001. Mem. ASTD, Am. Mgmt. Assn., Indsl. Rels. Rsch. Assn., Am. Soc. for Human Resource Mgmt., Am. Soc. Safety Engrs., Assn. for Corp. Growth, Am. Soc. Radiologic Technologists, Nat. Assn. Purchasing Mgmt., Mfr.'s Agts. Nat. Assn., Wis. Agri-Svc. Assn., Inc. Home: 8060 N Navajo Rd Fox Point WI 53217-2726 Office: 1009 W Glen Oaks Ln Ste 204 Mequon WI 53092-3383

BLOOM, JANE MAGINNIS, emergency physician; b. Ithaca, N.Y., June 22, 1924; d. Ernest Victor and Miriam Rebecca (Mansfield) M.; m. William Lee Bloom, Mar. 31, 1944; children: David Lee, Jan Christopher, Carolyn Wells, Eric Paul, Joseph William, Robert Carl, Mary Catherine, Thomas Mark, Patrick Martin (dec.), Arthur Emerson. BS, U. Mich., 1968, MD, 1974. Bd. cert. Am. Bd. Internal Medicine, Am. Bd. Emergency Medicine. Rotating intern Wayne County Gen. Hosp., Eloise, Mich., 1974-75; resident in internal medicine St. Mary's Hosp., Rochester, NY, 1975-77; emergency physician Emergency Physicians Med. Group, Ann Arbor, 1986—. Fellow Am. Coll. Emergency Physicians (life); mem. AMA, Mich. State Med. Soc., Am. Coll. Physicians, Am. Med. Womens Assn., Am. Assn. Women Emergency Physicians, Washtenaw County Med. Soc., Am. Coll. Emergency Physicians. Avocations: bird watching, planting trees, classical music, walking. Home and Office: 537 Elm St Ann Arbor MI 48104-2515

BLOOM, JILL ELIZABETH, physician assistant; b. Drexel Hill, Pa., Apr. 12, 1969; d. Fred E. and Gloria J. Bloom; m. Russell C. Hendershot, Sept. 3, 1994; children: Leah Elizabeth, Erin Nicole. BS, Temple U., 1991, Hahnemann U., 1994; M Physician Asst. Studies, U. Nebr., 2002. Cert. physicians asst. Physician asst. Planned Parenthood, West Chester, Pa., 1995, St. Joseph's Cmty. Health Ctr., Reading, Pa., 1995-97, Bornemann Internal Medicine, Reading, 1996-97, Keystone Health Ctr., Chambersburg, Pa., 1998-2000, Kanouse Med. Group, Berwick, Pa., 2000—01, Planned Parenthood N.E. Pa., 2002—. Vol. med. staff Pa. State Keystone Games; former mem. Pa. Dept. Pub. Welfare HIV/AIDS Clin. Guidelines Workgroup. Mem. Am. Acad. of Physician Assts., Pa. Soc. of Physician Assts. Avocations: hiking, biking. E-mail: rjle@sunlink.net.

BLOOM, JOHN PORTER, historian, editor, administrator, archivist; b. Albuquerque, Dec. 30, 1924; s. Lansing Bartlett and Maude Elizabeth (McFie) B.; m. Eva Louise Platt, 1954 (div.); children: Katherine Elizabeth Bloom Jassen, John Lansing, Susan Marie; m. Nancy Jo Tice, July 30, 1968. AB, U. N.Mex., 1947; AM, George Washington U., 1949; PhD, Emory U., 1956; cert. in pre-meteorology, Reed Coll., 1944. Mem. faculty No. Ga. Coll., 1950-51, Brenau Coll., 1952-56, U. Tex., El Paso, 1956-60; historian, mus. planner, editor Nat. Park Service, Washington, 1960-64; editor Territorial Papers of the U.S., 1964-80; sr. specialist western history Nat. Archives, Washington, 1964-80; dir. Holt-Atherton Pacific Ctr. Western Studies, Stockton, Calif., 1981-84; editor Pacific Historian, U. Pacific, Stockton, 1981-84. Program com. chmn. Conf. History Am. West, Santa Fe, 1961, 71; cons. NEH div. pub. programs Nat. Hist. Publs. and Records Commn., Va. History and Mus. Fedn., 1976-79; mem. adv. bd. Capitol Studies, U.S. Capitol Hist. Soc., 1971-73 Editor: monograph The American Territorial System, 1973, Territorial Papers of the U.S., 1969, 71, Treaty of Guadalupe Hidalgo, 1848-1998, 1999, Papers of the Sesquicentennial Symposium, 1999; editor, co-editor: monograph Soldier and Brave and other vols., 1963; book reviewer, contbr. articles to profl. jours. Chmn. Fairfax County Hist. Commn., 1972-73; active Cultural Heritage Bd., Stockton, Calif., 1982-85 ; bd. dirs. Gateway Inc., Alexandria, Va., 1971-75; sheriff Potomac Corral of the Westerners Internat., 1974; bd. dirs. Joseph Priestley Chapel Assocs. Inc., 1978-81. Served with USAAF, 1943-45. So. Fellowships Fund fellow, 1955-56 Mem. Western History Assn. (hon., life, pres. 1974, v.p. 1973, mem. Ray Allen Billington award com. 1979-82, Spl. Svc. award), Westerners Internat. (pres. 1981-83, bd. dirs. 1988-95), Westerners Soc. (Golden Spike award 1969), Coun. Am.'s Mil. Past (bd. dirs. 1982-96), Orgn. Am. Historians, Ea. Nat. Pks. and Monuments Assn., So. Hist. Assn., Pioneer Am. Soc., Rio Grande Hist. Found., Mus. N.Mex. Assn., Hist. Soc. N.Mex. (bd. dirs., 1st v.p. 1999-2000, sec. 2000—, mem. editl. adv. bd. N.Mex. Hist. Rev. 1998—). Home: 5620 Real Del Norte Las Cruces NM 88012-7268 E-mail: jbloom@zianet.com.

BLOOM, JONATHAN M. humanities educator, writer; b. NYC, N.Y., Apr. 7, 1950; s. Robert D. Bloom and Yetta Herman; m. Sheila S. Blair, Sept. 6, 1980; children: Felicity R., Oliver D. AB, Harvard Coll., 1972; AM, U. of Mich., 1975; PhD, Harvard U., 1980. Asst. prof. Dept. of Fine Arts Harvard U., Cambridge, Mass., 1981—87; area editor Islam and Ctrl. Asia The Dictionary of Art, London, 1987—94; prof. of Islamic and Asian art Fine Arts Dept. Boston (Mass.) Coll., Chestnut Hill, Mass., 1994—. Prin. cons. for Islam: Empire of Faith Gardner Films, Balt., 1998—2001. Author: Paper Before Print: The History and Impact of Paper in the Islamic World; editor: Early Islamic Art and Architecture; author: Minaret: Symbol of Islam; co-author: Islam: A Thousand

Years of Faith and Power, Islamic Arts, The Art and Architecture of Islam: 1250-1800. Incorporator Monadnock Cmty. Found., Keene, NH, 2001; trustee Richmond (N.H.) Pub. Libr., 1996. Fellow, NEH, 1989—92, Andrew Mellon Sr. fellow, Met. Mus. of Art, 1990—91, Max van Berchem Found., Geneva, 1995—2001, NEH, 1998; grantee, J. Paul Getty Trust, 1990—91. Office: Fine Arts Department Boston College 140 Commonwealth Ave Chestnut Hill MA 02467 Office Fax: 617-552-0134. E-mail: jonathan.bloom@bc.edu.

BLOOM, JULIAN, artist, editor; b. Cleve., May 6, 1933; s. John Bernard and Lillian Judith (Finkel) B.; m. Shirley Ann Harper, Nov. 29, 1954; children: Sandra Layne Walker, Andrea Sue Wells. AA, Cypress Coll., 1972; student, U. LaVerne (Calif.), 1983-86. Lab tech. Harvey Aluminum, Torrance, Calif., 1956-64, foreman, 1964-66; sr. draftsman Northrop Corp., Anaheim, Calif., 1966-67; designer Northrop Aircraft, Anaheim, Calif., 1967-69, facilities engr., 1969-81, design to corp. cost designer, 1982-84, mfg. engring. mgr., 1984-85, mfg. mgr., 1985-92; artist, owner Realistic Watercolors, Cypress, 1992—. Instr. watercolor Huntington Beach Art Ctr., 1997—, City of Cypress, 1998—. Featured in The Best of Watercolor, 1995; columnist Event Newspapers, 1998—. Co-chmn. Cypress (Calif.) Cultural Arts Planning Com., 1993-95; pres. Cypress Art Art League, 1993-96; commr. Cypress Cultural Arts, 1999-2002. Served with U.S. Army, 1954-56. Fellow Am. Artists Profl. League (Signature award 1993); mem. Nat. Watercolor Soc. (assoc. mem. 1989—, editor newsletter 1994-97, bd. dirs. 2002), Watercolor West (bd. dirs. 1999—, v.p. 2003—, newsletter editor 2003—), Am. Soc. Marine Artists (artist mem., Signature award 2000). Republican. Jewish. Avocations: travel, computers, photography. Home and Office: 4522 Cathy Ave Cypress CA 90630-4212 E-mail: h2optr@hotmail.com.

BLOOM, KATHRYN RUTH, public relations executive; d. Morris and Frances Sondra (Siegel) B. BA, Douglass Coll.; MA, U. Toronto, Can. Dir. spl. projects United Jewish Appeal, N.Y.C., 1973-78; mgr. pub. affairs Bristol-Myers-Squibb Co., N.Y.C., 1978-86; mgr. pub. rels. pharm. and nutritional Bristol-Myers Squibb Co., N.Y.C., 1986-90, dir. pharm. and rsch. comms., 1990-91; dir. comms. Biogen, Inc., 1992—2001, sr. dir. pub. affairs, 2001—. Overseer Beth Israel Deaconess Med. Ctr., 2000—; v.p., bd. dirs. N.Am. Conf. on Ethiopian Jewry, N.Y.C., 1985-93; overseer Boston Lyric Opera, 1995-2000. Mem.: Am. Technion Soc. (N.E. region bd. dirs. 2000—), The Boston Club, Phi Beta Kappa. Office: Biogen Inc 14 Cambridge Ctr Cambridge MA 02142-1481

BLOOM, LAWRENCE STEPHEN, retired clothing company executive; b. New Rochelle, N.Y., Apr. 30, 1930; s. Hyman and Eleanor (Bursch) B.; m. Mary Ann Hendricks, Aug. 15, 1959; children: Mark, Julie. BS in Commerce and Fin, Bucknell U., Lewisburg, Pa., 1952. Trainee Gimbels, N.Y.C., to 1954; with Warnaco Inc., 1954-90; former chmn. Warnaco Men's Knitwear (Puritan, Thane and Hathaway Knitwear), Altoona, Pa. Bd. dirs. Woolknit Assocs., Nat. Sportwear and Outerwear Assocs.; chpt. chair Svc. Corps of Retired Execs. Served with AUS, 1952-54. Home: 340 Deer Run Rd Hollidaysburg PA 16648-3110 E-mail: blooml@msn.com.

BLOOM, LEE HURLEY, lawyer, public affairs consultant, retired household products manufacturing executive; b. N.Y.C., June 21, 1919; s. Harry and Harriet (Bresel) B.; m. Mary Louise Tolan, Dec. 15, 1945; children: Daniel, Louise, Douglas. BS, MIT, 1940; LL.B., Harvard U., 1943. Bar: Mass. 1947, N.Y. 1951. Atty. legal div. Lever Bros. Co., N.Y.C., 1947-67, v.p., sec., gen. counsel, 1968-70, adminstrv. v.p., dir., 1970-82; pres. Unilever U.S., Inc., 1978-82, vice chmn., 1982-83. Donald L. Wilson prof., Grinnell Coll., Iowa, 1986. Chmn. bd. Larchmont (N.Y.) chpt. ARC, 1961—63; mem. Mamaroneck Planning Bd., 1959—69, Mamaroneck Town Bd., 1969—85, dep. supr., 1982—83; coord. N.Y. State Sch. and Bus. Alliance for Yonkers Pub. Schs., 1987—93; chmn. Ctr. for Performing Arts Lehman Coll., 1987—93, Sheldrake Environ. Ctr., 1995—; mem. Town of Mamaroneck (N.Y.) Rep. Com., 1957—69. Served to lt. comdr. USNR, 1941—46. Mem. Soap and Detergent Assn. (dir. 1971-83, vice chmn. 1978-79, chmn. 1980-82), Assn. Pvt. Enterprise Edn. (exec. com. 1985-93), Internat. C. of C. (trustee U.S. coun. 1978-86, exec. com. 1980-86, vice chmn. 1982-85, sr. trustee 1987—), UN Assn. U.S.A. (pres. so. N.Y. state divsn. 1989-93). Home and Office: 22 Myrtle Blvd Larchmont NY 10538-1823

BLOOM, MAX ROBERT, economics educator, consultant; b. N.Y.C., Dec. 4, 1916; s. Borice and Dora (Rosenbloom) B.; m. Pearl Brook, May 25, 1941; children: Diane, Amy Bloom Connolly. BS, CCNY, 1939; cert., New Sch. for Social Rsch., 1940; PhD, Am. U., 1959. Prof. Sch. of Mgmt. Syracuse (N.Y.) U., 1956-83, prof. emeritus Sch. of Mgmt., 1983—; asst. prof. Sch. of Bus. Adminstrn. U. Calif., Berkeley, 1955-56; Fulbright prof. Israel Inst. Tech., Haifa, 1960-61. Tech. expert, del. UN-Econ. Commn. for Europe confs. on housing, planning and econ. devel., 1974-85; vis. prof. N.Y. State Coll. of Human Ecology, Cornell U., Ithaca, N.Y., 1976; cons. Joint Legis. Com. on Housing and Urban Devel., Albany, N.Y., 1969-73, Senate Select Com. on Housing and Urban Devel., 1973-75, Master Plan Nicosia, Cyprus, 1982, others; mem. adv. bd. Study Inst. in Urban Planning and Devel. Hebrew U., Jerusalem, Chinese Acad. Social Scis., 1989; spkr. in field. Contbr. numerous articles to profl. jours. Rsch. dir., cons. joint legis. com. on met. areas study N.Y. State, 1963-65; bd. dirs. Syracuse Friends Chamber Music, 1975-2003. 1st lt. AUS, 1943-45, CBI. Mem. Am. Econ. Assn., Am. Real Estate and Urban Econs. Assn. (bd. dirs. 1968), Regional Sci. Assn. (chmn. panel of 21st European Cong. 1981), Soc. Govt. Economists, Beta Gamma Sigma. Home: 319 Hillsboro Pky Syracuse NY 13214-2026 Office: Syracuse U Sch Mgmt Fin Dept 900 S Crouse Ave Syracuse NY 13244-0001

BLOOM, MYER, physicist, educator; b. Montreal, Que., Can., Dec. 7, 1928; s. Israel and Leah (Ram) B.; m. Margaret Holmes, May 29, 1954; children—David, Margot. B.Sc., McGill U., 1949, M.Sc., 1950; PhD, U. Ill., 1954; D (hon.), Tech. U. Denmark, 1994; DSc (hon.), U. B.C., 2000. Research fellow U. Leiden, 1954-56; faculty U. B.C., Vancouver, 1956—, assoc. prof., 1960-63, prof. physics, 1963-93; D (hon.) Concordia U., 1995. Recipient Steacie prize, 1967, Jacob Biely prize, 1968, Gold medal Can. Assn. Physicists, 1973, Sci. Coun. of B.C. Chmn.'s award for career achievement, 1992, Izaak Walton Killam Meml. prize in natural sci., 1995; Alfred P. Sloan fellow, 1961-65; John Simon Guggenheim fellow, 1964-65; Izaak Walton Killam Meml. scholar, 1978-79. Fellow Royal Soc. Can., Am. Phys. Soc., Can. Inst. for Advanced Rsch. Achievements include research in structure and molecular motion in biological and model membranes, nuclear magnetic resonance. Home: 5669 King's Rd Vancouver BC Canada V6T 1K9

BLOOM, ROBERT, language professional educator; b. N.Y.C., May 28, 1930; s. Michael and Fannie (Hecker) B.; m. Gloria Loebenson, Aug. 29, 1953; children: Claudia, Madeline, Jonathan. BA, NYU, 1951; MA, Columbia U., 1952; PhD, U. Mich., 1960. Asst. prof., assoc. prof. English U. Calif. Berkeley, 1960-72, prof. English, 1972—. Author: The Indeterminate World: A Study of the Novels of Joyce Cary, 1962, Anatomies of Egotism: A Reading of the Last Novels of H.G. Wells, 1977; contbr. articles to profl. jours. Lt. j.g. U.S. Coast Guard, 1952-54. Bruern fellow in Am. Civilization U. Leeds, 1963. Mem. Modern Lang. Assn., Phi Beta Kappa. Avocations: playing piano, cycling, music, reading. Office: Univ Calif Dept English Berkeley CA 94720-0001

BLOOM, SHERMAN, retired pathologist, educator; b. Bklyn., Jan. 26, 1934; s. Philip and Sadie (Kaplan) B.; m. Miriam Fishman, Feb. 11, 1960; children: Naomi, Stephanie. BA, NYU, 1955, MD, 1960. Diplomate Am. Bd. Anat. Pathology. Intern in medicine Kings County Hosp., Bklyn., 1960-61; fellow in exptl. pathology, resident in anatomic and clin. pathology NYU Med. Ctr. and Bellevue Hosp., N.Y.C., 1961-65; instr. pathology NYU Sch. Medicine, 1965-66; asst. prof. U. Utah Coll. Medicine, Salt Lake City, 1966-70, assoc. prof., 1970-72, U. South Fla. Coll. Medicine, Tampa, 1973-76, prof. pathology, 1976-77, George Washington U. Coll. Medicine, Washington, 1977-88; prof., chmn. dept. pathology U. Miss. Med. Ctr., Jackson, 1988-2000, prof. emeritus, 2000—, ret., 2000; nature photographer Photozon, 2001. Cons. Sci. Rev., NIH; mem. cardiovascular study sect. NSF, FDA; dir. coun. on cardiovascular and geriatric health Amer Coll. Nutrition, 1998-01; bd. dirs. Scientists Ctr. Animal Welfare, pres. elect, 1987, pres., 1988. Mem. editorial bd. Jour. Am. Coll. Nutrition, 1982, Am. Jour. Cardiovascular Pathology, 1985; assoc. editor Cardiovascular Pathology, 1990; contbr. numerous articles to profl. publs. Del. Utah State Dem. Party, 1968. NIH fellow, 1962; Dilthey Found. fellow, 1982. Fellow Am. Coll. Nutrition; mem. Internat. Acad. Pathologists, Am. Physiol. Soc., Am. Assn. Pathologists, Internat. Soc. Heart Research, Soc. Cardiovascular Pathology (pres. 1986-87). Jewish. Home: 4433 Wedgewood St Jackson MS 39211-6219

BLOOM, WILLIAM MILLARD, furnace design engineer; b. New Kensington, Pa., Aug. 10, 1925; s. William Lewis and Natalie Tillbrook (McMillan) B.; m. Judith Ann Callen, May 23, 1953; children: Kimberly Ann, Stacey Ellen. BA, Geneva Coll., 1951; BSME, Carnegie Inst. Tech., 1951. Registered profl. engr., Pa. Fuel engr. maintenance dept. Brackenridge (Pa.) Plant, Allegheny Ludlum Steel, 1951-56; fuel engr. gen. engring. divsn. Allegheny Ludlum Steel Corp., Brackenridge, 1956-59, sr. engr. furnaces and fuels, gen. engring. divsn., 1959-61; chief engr. furnaces and fuels gen. engring. divsn. Allegheny Ludlum Industries, Pitts., 1961-71; asst. to v.p. engring. spl. assignments Allegheny Ludlum Steel Corp., Brackenridge, 1971-81, mgr. furnace design engring., mfg. engring. Pitts., 1981-92; pvt. practice cons. indsl. furnaces Pitts., 1992—. Cons. Alloy Rods Corp., Hanover, Pa., 1989, Timet Corp., Henderson, Nev., Toronto, Ohio, IPM Corp., Ridgeway, Pa., Columbus, Ohio, Tube Turn Corp., Louisville, True Temper, Geneva, Ohio, Arnold Engring., Chgo., Altech, Dunkirk, N.Y., Posco, Korea, Kuhlman Electric, Lexington, Ky., 1961-92. With U.S. Army, 1944-46, ETO. Mem. NSPE, Assn. Iron and Steel Engrs. (life, bd. dirs., chm. combustion com., AISE-KELLY award 1st pl. 1979), 70th Divsn. Assn. (life), Theta Xi (life). Republican. Methodist. Achievements include patents for Bar Furnace Seals, Annealing Apparatus, Coil Quench, Conveyor Roll, Tunnel Furnace, Annealing Furnace, Steel Scrap Preheater, Apparatus Scrap Preheater, Roll Turner/Remover, Jet Heat Reucperator, Replaceable Ladle Heater Seals, High Temp Fan Plug, Hot Strip Mill Cover Heat Retention; developed high temperature hydrogen anneal tunnel furnace for grain oriented silicon steels that significantly lowered watt losses/pound to develop class of steel, jet heat recuperators that reduce continous anneal furnaces fuel input by 50% and increases production 50%. Home: 1522 King John Dr Pittsburgh PA 15237-1590

BLOOMBERG, JUDITH, stockbroker; b. Johannesburg, Transvaal, South Africa, Sept. 27, 1935; came to U.S., 1997; d. Simon and Freda Joffe; m. Barnet Bloomberg, Aug. 7, 1955; children: Gavin Lloyd, Howard Vaughan. Grad., Tech. Coll. Bookkeeper Levison's, Johannesburg, Hubby's Cars, Johannesburg; acct. asst. Urban Real Estate, Johannesburg; fin. mgr. Kuper's Properties, Johannesburg; fin. dir. Lew Geffen's Estates, Johannesburg; stockbroker A.G. Edwards, Boca Raton, Fla., 1997—. Jewish. Avocations: tennis, bridge, swimming, bird watching. Home: 550 S Ocean Blvd Apt 1505 Boca Raton FL 33432-6282

BLOOMBERG, LAWRENCE S. securities executive, art collector; b. Montreal, Que., Can., May 28, 1942; s. Sol and Sylvia Bloomberg; m. Frances Bloomberg; children: Debra, Bonnie, Jonathon. B of Commerce, Sir George Williams U., 1963; MBA, McGill U., 1965; LLD (hon.), Concordia U., 1996. Chartered fin analyst. Various mgmt. positions including head of rsch., v.p., dir. Instnl. Equity Sales, Nesbitt Thomson and Co., 1965-76, v.p., dir., 1975-79; founding mem. 1st Marathon Securities, Ltd., 1979; pres., CEO, dir. 1st Marathon Inc., 1984-99; adv. Nat. Bank Fin., Inc., 1999—. Past mem. Young Pres.'s Orgn.; past mem. bd. govs. Toronto Stock Exch.; founding mem. Concordia's Faculty of Commerce and Admininstrn. Bus. Adv. Com.; bd. dirs. Cinram Ltd., Nat. Bank Can.; founding dir., bd. dirs. MARS. Chmn. Mt. Sinai Hosp.; mem. budget and fin. com., Baycrest Ctr. for Geriatric Care; trustee Simon Wiesenthal Ctr., Inc.; co-chmn. toronto's 1994 United Jewish Appeal/Operation Exodus Campaign; active United Way campaigns; past gov. Jr. Achievement of Can.; mem. Rector's Cir., Concordia U., founding mem. Faculty of Commerce and Adminstrn. Bus. Adv. Com.; bd. dirs. Toronto Internat. Film Festival Group, Royal Ont. Mus. Found.; mem. Can. Inst. Internat. Affairs; former bd. dirs. Toronto Stock Exch. Recipient Human Rels. award Can. Coun. Christians and Jews. Mem. XPO, World Pres.'s Orgn., Bus. Coun. on Nat. Issues, C.D. Howe Inst., Rector's Cir. of Concordia U., Investment Dealers Assn. of Can. (bd. dirs., exec. com.). former mem. CDN Coun. of Chief Exec. Avocations: running, golf. Office: Nat Bank Financial 130 King St W Toronto ON Canada M5X 1J9

BLOOMBERG, MICHAEL RUBENS, mayor; b. Medford, Mass., Feb. 14, 1942; divorced; 2 children. Graduate, Johns Hopkins U., 1964; MBA, Harvard U., 1966. Processing clerk Salomon Brothers, 1966, gen. ptnr. sys. devel.; pres. founder Bloomberg L.P., N.Y.C., 1981—, pres., CEO; pub. Bloomberg Business News, N.Y.C.; gen. mgr. Bloomberg Television, Bloomberg Radio, Sta. WBBR-AM 1130, N.Y.C.; pub. Bloomberg Mag./Bloomberg Personal Mag., Princeton, N.J., Bloomberg Personal, Skillman, N.J.; mayor N.Y.C., 2002—. Author: (autobiography) Bloomberg by Bloomberg, 1997. Chmn. bd. trustees Johns Hopkins U.; trustee Big Apple Circus, Ctrl. Park Conservancy, Met. Mus. Art, H.S. Econs. And Fin., Inst. Advanced Study, Lincoln Ctr. Performing Arts, Jewish Mus., N.Y. Police and Fire Widows' and Childrens' Fund, Spence Sch., Prep for Prep, S.L.E. Found., U.S. Ski Team Ednl. Found., Serpentine Gallery, London. Mem. U.S. C. of C. (trustee). Office: City Hall 52 Chambers St New York NY 10007-1222*

BLOOMBERG, SANFORD, psychiatrist; b. Burlington, Vt., Dec. 12, 1924; s. Hyman and Esther (Pocher) B.; m. Louise Bloomberg, June 29, 1952; children: Paul, Jonathan, David, Rebecca. BA, U. Vt., 1950, MD, 1957; MA in English Lit., Columbia U., 1951. Diplomate Am. Bd. Psychiatry and Neurology. Intern Degoesbriand Meml. Hosp., Burlington, Vt., 1957-58; resident Northville (Mich.) State Hosp., 1958-61, dir. children's svc., 1961-62; sch. psychiatrist Birmingham (Mich.) Pub. Schs., 1966-69; assoc. physician psychiatry Amherst (Mass.) Coll., 1969-92; med. dir. Beacon Detoxification Ctr., Greenfield, Mass., 1979-90; sch. psychiatrist Amherst (Mass.) Pub. Schs., 1969-82; continuing edn. faculty Smith Coll. Sch. Social Work, Northampton, Mass., 1972-84, clin. asst.prof., 1986-90; assoc. prof. psychiatry U. Mass. Med. Sch., Worcester, 1973-87; med. dir. psychiatry programs Franklin Med. Ctr., Greenfield, Mass., 1969-88; pvt. practice psychiatry Northampton, Mass., 1969—. Instr. Sch. Nursing Wayne State U., Detroit, 1963-64; med. dir. Beacon Alcohol and Drug Programs, Greenfield, 1970-91; staff psychiatrist Clin. and Support Options, Greenfield, 1991-2000, med. dir., 1995-98; psychiat. cons. Hilltown Cmty. Health Ctrs., Worthington, Mass., 2000—. Cpl. U.S. Army, 1943-46. Fellow Am. Psychiat. Assn. (dist. life); mem. Mass. Psychiat. Assn., Western Mass. Psychiat. Soc. ADA Dist. Life Fellow, 2003. Home: 112 Washington Ave Northampton MA 01060-2825 Office: 16 Center St Rm 226 Northampton MA 01060-3031

BLOOMBERG, STU, broadcast executive; Chmn. ABC Entertainment, co-chmn. Office: ABC Inc Exec Ste 2040 Avenue Of The Stars Los Angeles CA 90067-4785

BLOOMER, HAROLD FRANKLIN, JR., retired lawyer; b. N.Y.C., Nov. 4, 1933; s. Harold Franklin and Allene (Cress) B.; m. Mary Jane Lloyd, July 16, 1955 (div. June 1976); children: Sarah Allene, Margaret Gail, Leslie Lloyd; m. Freya Donald, Nov. 30, 1985; children: Katharine Roma, Alice Donald. AB, Amherst Coll., 1956; LLB, Columbia U., 1967. Bar: Conn. 1967, N.Y. 1968, U.S. Dist. Ct. Conn. 1968, U.S. Dist. Ct. (so. and ea. dists.) N.Y. 1974, U.S. Ct. Appeals (2d cir.) 1974. Assoc. Debevoise, Plimpton, Lyons & Gates, N.Y.C., 1967-77; counsel Burlington, Underwood & Lord, Jeddah, Saudi Arabia, 1977-78; chief internat. counsel Saudi Rsch. & Devel. Corp., London, 1978-80; counsel Morgan, Lewis & Bockius LLP, London and N.Y.C., 1980-81, ptnr., 1981-2000; ret., 2000. Adj. prof. Pepperdine U. Sch. Law, London, 1985. Trustee San. Products Trust, Riverside, Conn., 1965—74; trip leader Adventure Cycling Assn., Missoula, Mont., 2000; mem. Conn. com. East Coast Greenway, 2001—; co-chmn. bd. Coastal Corridor Transp. Investment Area, State of Conn., 2001—; mem. Rep. Town Meeting, Greenwich, Conn., 1964—74, 1992—, chmn. pub. works com., 1971—74, chmn. land use com., 1998—; mem. Rep. Town Com., Greenwich, Conn., 1973—74. Lt. j.g. USNR, 1957—60. Kent scholar Columbia U., 1965-66, Stone scholar Columbia U., 1966-67. Mem. Am. Arbitration Assn. (panel of arbitrators 1990—), Riverside Yacht Club. Republican. Episcopalian. Avocations: sailing, canoeing, skiing, biking, running.

BLOOMER, LISA A. mathematician, educator; d. John G. Bloomer and Janet L. Tillotson. PhD, Ga. Inst. Tech., 2000. Scientist Naval Surface Warfare Ctr., Dahlgren, Va., 2000—01; asst. prof. Mid. Tenn. State U., Murfreesboro, 2001—. Office: Mid Tenn State U Box 34 Murfreesboro TN 37130

BLOOMER, WILLIAM DAVID, radiation oncologist, educator; b. Aug. 19, 1944; s. Ward LaVern and Vera Catherine (Rochefort) B.; m. Lauren S. Taslitz, Aug. 10, 1986; children: Whitney Dana, Brian Andrew, Gregory Stewart. AB, U. Pa., 1966; MD, Jefferson Med. Coll., Phila., 1970. Diplomate Am. Bd. Radiology, Am. Bd. Nuclear Medicine. Intern Univ. Hosps., Cleve., 1970-71; clin. fellow in radiation therapy Harvard U. Med. Sch., Boston, 1971-74, instr., 1974-76, asst. prof., 1976-80, assoc. prof., 1980-83; rsch. mem. Harvard MIT Divsn. Health Scis. and Tech., Boston, 1978-83; mem. sr. common room Lowell House Harvard Coll., Boston, 1983-87; dir. radiotherapy, radiotherapist-in-chief Mt. Sinai Hosp., N.Y.C., 1983-87; prof., chmn. dept. radiation oncology U. Pitts. Sch. Medicine, 1987-92; dir. Joint Radiation Oncology Ctr., 1987-92; dir. radiation oncology Presbyn. U. Hosp., Magee-Women's Hosp., Shadyside Hosp., 1987-92; assoc. dir. Pitts. Cancer Inst., 1987-92; pres. U. Radiotherapy Assocs., Inc., 1989-92; sr. lectr. engring. in medicine Carnegie Mellon U., 1989-92; chmn. radiation medicine Evanston Northwestern Healthcare, 1992—. Prof. radiology Northwestern U. Med. Sch., 1992—, pres. Radiation Medicine Inst., 1992—; dir. radiation oncology svcs. Swedish Covenant Hosp., 1993—. Contbr. articles to profl. jours. Mem. AAAS, Am. Coll. Radiology, Am. Soc. Therapeutic Radiologists, Soc. Nuclear Medicine, Radiation Rsch. Soc., Am. Assn. Cancer Rsch., Am. Soc. Clin. Oncology, Am. Coll. Radiation Oncology (Gold medal 1998). Office: Evanston Northwestern Healthcare 2650 Ridge Ave Evanston IL 60201-1718 Fax: 847-570-1878. E-mail: wbloomer@enh.org.

BLOOMER, WILLIAM JOHN, lawyer; b. Rutland, Vt., Apr. 22, 1952; s. Robert Asa and Mary Elizabeth Bloomer; m. Margery Elizabeth Pierce, June 9, 1973; children: Matthew A., Mary Katelin, Aaron P., Geoffrey E. BA, U. Vt., 1973; JD, Boston U., 1976. Bar: Vt. 1976, U.S. Dist. Ct. Vt. 1977. Attorney, officer Bloomer & Bloomer, P.C., Rutland, 1976—. City atty. City of Rutland, 1981-83; justice of peace, Rutland. Alderman City of Rutland, 1979-81, pres. bd. aldermen, 1980-81; freshman baseball coach Rutland H.S., 1994-99. Roman Catholic. Office: 22 Cottage St Rutland VT 05701-3404

BLOOMFIELD, CLARA DERBER, oncologist, medical institute administrator; b. Flushing, L.I., N.Y., May 15, 1942; d. Milton and Zelda (Trenner) Derber; m. Victor A. Bloomfield, June 11, 1962 (div. 1983); m. Albert de la Chapelle, Jan. 1, 1984. Student, U. Wis., 1959-62; BA, San Diego State U., 1963; MD, U. Chgo., 1968. Diplomate Am. Bd. Internal Medicine, Nat. Bd. Med. Examiners. Intern in medicine U. Chgo. Hosps. and Clinics, 1968-69, resident internal medicine, 1969-70, U. Minn., Mpls., 1970-71, med. oncology fellow, 1971-73, chief resident in medicine, Jan.-June, 1972, instr., 1972-73, asst. prof. medicine, 1973-76, assoc. prof., 1976-80, prof. medicine div. oncology, 1980-89, dir. fellowship program med. concology, 1987—89, mem. univ. senate, 1986-89, mem. all univ. Commn. on Women, 1988-89; prof. medicine, chief div. oncology SUNY, Buffalo, 1989—97; head dept. medicine Roswell Pk. Cancer Inst., Buffalo, 1989—97; William G. Pace III prof. cancer research Ohio State U. Coll. Med. & Pub. Health, 1997—, dir., div. hematology & oncology, dept. Internal Medicine, 1997—. Mem. Kettering selection com. GM Cancer Rsch. Found., 1986-87; cons. Office Tech. Assessment, U.S. Congress, 1988; participant, chair various coms. Internat. Human Gene Mapping Workshops, Helsinki, Finland, 1985, France, 1987, Internat. Workshops Chromosomes in Leukemia, Lund, Sweden, 1980, Chgo., 1982, Tokyo, 1984, London, 1987, Buffalo, 1991; mem. nat. and sci. adv. bds. NIH, 1977—, mem. bd. sci. counselors divsn. cancer treatment, 1991—, organizer Internat. Hodgkins Disease Symposium, 1981; bd. dirs. cancer and leukemia group B, 1982—, mem. other coms., 1973— sponsored clin. trial groups, Nat. Cancer Inst., cons. S.W. oncology group; mem. nat. and sci. adv. bd. Don and Sybil Harrington Cancer Ctr., Amarillo, Tex., 1979—, Med. Coll. Pa., 1988—; bd. trustees Berlex Oncology Found., 1992—; vis. prof. dept. medicine W.Va. U., 1973, U. Ariz., Tucson, 1979, U. Fla., Gainesville, 1979, Emory U., Atlanta, 1980, U. Chgo., 1982, George Washington U., Washington, 1982, U. Tex., San Antonio, 1982, Brown U., Providence, 1982, Mayo Clinic, Rochester, Minn., 1982, U. Zurich, Switzerland, 1983, U. P.R., 1984, U. Witwatersand, S. Africa, 1984, Nihon U., Tokyo, 1984, Leukemia Soc. Mass., 1991; frequent invited speaker, guest lectr. symposia, workshops, continuing edn. courses, seminars, med. congresses, univs. in U.S., Europe, S. Am., Scandinavia, Eng., Japan, Republic of South Africa, New Zealand. Author: (with others) Recent Advances in Bone Marrow Transplantation, Vol. VII, 1983, New Prospectives in Human Lymphoma, 1984, Neoplastic Diseases of the Blood, 1985, Current Therapy in Hematology/Oncology 1984-85, 1985, Medical Genetics: Past, Present, Future, 1985, Directions in Oncology, Vol. 1, 1985, Medical Oncology, Basic Principles and Clinical Management of Cancer, 1985, Tumor Aneuploidy, 1985, Malignant Lymphomas and Hodgkins Disease: Experimental and Therapeutic Advances, 1985, Current Therapy in Internal Medicine, 1987, Genetic Maps, Vol. 4, 1987; contbr. over 250 articles, abstracts to profl. jours.; editor ann. Adult Leukemia series in Cancer Treatment and Rsch., 1979-85; cons. editor Leukemia and Lymphoma Yearbook of Cancer, 1980—; assoc. editor Cancer Rsch., 1981-88, editor, 91, Leukemia Rsch., 1984-87, Leukemia, 1987-89; mem. editorial bd. Jour. Clin. Oncology, 1983-88, Cancer Genetics and Cytogenetics, 1983-87, Directions in Oncology, 1984-86, Cancer Rsch. Bull., 1984-85, Med. and Pediatric Oncology, 1987—, Blood, 1988—, Annals of Medicine, 1989—, Seminars in Oncology, 1989—; editorial bd. Am. Jour. Hematology, 1985, assoc. editor, 1988—; reviewer 23 med. jours. Recipient Nat. Bd. award Med. Coll. Pa., 1981, Past State Pres.' Bus. and Profl. Women award U. Tex. System Cancer Ctr., M.D. Anderson Hosp. and Tumor Clinic, Houston, 1987; prin. or co-prin. investigator 8 grants, NIH, 1975—, also ACS, 1980-84, Minn. State Spl. Coleman Leukemia Rsch. Fund, 1981-89, Coleman Leukemia Rsch. Fund Endowment, 1981—, Baltzar W.A. von Platen Found., 1984-85, Genentech/Hoffman -LaRoche, 1988—. Mem. ACP, AAAS, Am. Assn. Cancer Rsch., Am. Soc. Hematology, Am. Soc. Clin. Oncology (bd. dirs. 1991—), Am. Fedn. Clin. Rsch., Cen. Soc. Clin. Rsch., N.Y. Acad. Scis., Inst. Medicine, Internat. Assn. Comparative Rsch. Leukemia and Related Diseases, Med. Soc. Finland (external mem.), Phi Beta Kappa, Alpha Omega Alpha, Sigma Delta Epsilon. Office: Comprehensive Cancer Ctr 320 W 10th Ave Columbus OH 43210

BLOOMFIELD, DAVID CHARLES, lawyer, educator, public and not-for-profit executive; b. N.Y.C., Feb. 19, 1952; BA, Brandeis U., 1975; JD, Columbia U., 1984; MPA, Princeton U., 1984. Bar: N.Y. 1984, D.C. 1985; cert. primary and elem. tchr., Mass.; cert. prin./supr., N.J.; cert. supt. N.Y. Tchr. New Lincoln Sch., N.Y.C., 1975-79; analyst Advocates for Children of N.Y., Queens, N.Y., 1979-80; law clk. to Judge Robert L. Carter U.S. Dist. Ct. (so. dist. N.Y.), N.Y.C., 1984-85; assoc. Hogan & Hartson, Washington, 1985-86; atty. N.Y.C. Law Dept., 1986-89; adminstr. N.Y.C. Bd. Edn., Bklyn., 1989-90, gen. counsel, 1990-91; gen. counsel, sr. edn. advisor Manhattan Borough Pres., N.Y.C., 1991-94; exec. dir. Partnership for Effective Edn. Mgmt., N.Y.C., 1994-96; adj. asst. prof. Tchrs. Coll. Columbia U., N.Y.C., 1996—98; assoc. prof. Bklyn. Coll., CUNY, 1999—. Head edn. adminstrn. program Bklyn. Coll., 2001. Author: No Child Left Behind, 2003, Technology Based Peer Education, 1999, Attendance Improvement Programs in N.Y.C. Schools, 1979, African Ethnicity, 1976, Children First: N.Y.C. School Governance Legislation, 1993, Strategic Management of N.Y.C. Schools, 1997, 2d edit., 2003, Technology-Based Peer Education, 1999, Church/State Separation, 2001, No Child Left Behind Act, 2003, others. Recipient Paul Robeson prize Columbia U., N.Y.C., 1982, Harlan Fiske Stone scholar, 1982, Princeton (N.J.) U. fellow, 1982, African-Am. Inst. fellow, N.Y.C., 1976. E-mail: david11201@nyct.net.

BLOOMFIELD, DAVID SOLOMON, lawyer, educator; b. Dec. 13, 1944; s. Jerome P. and Anne M. (Knoll) Bloomfield; m. Sally Ward, June 4, 1969; children: David S., Paul W. BS, Ohio State U., 1966, JD, 1969; postgrad. in Law, NYU, 1969—71. Bar: Ohio 1969, U.S. Dist. Ct. (so. dist.) Ohio 1970, U.S. Dist. Ct. (no. dist.) Ohioi 1972, U.S. Ct. Appeals (6th cir.) 1973, U.S. Tax Ct. 1970, U.S. Supreme Ct. 1973. Mem. staff Lybrand Ross Bros. & Montgomery, N.Y.C., NY, 1969—70; chief tax sect. Atty. Gen. Ohio, Columbus, 1970—71; assoc., then ptnr. Ward Kaps Bainbridge Maurer Bloomfield & Melvin, and predecessor, Columbus, Ohio, 1971—92; ptnr. Bloomfield & Kempf, 1992—. Lectr. Capital U., 1972—78, Ohio Paralegal Inst., 1979; adj. prof. Capital U. Coll. Law, Columbus, 1980—, The Ohio State U., 1996—. Contbr. articles to profl. jours. Active Columbus United Way, 1979—; campaign chmn. Price for

Judge, Columbus, 1980; bd. dir. N.W. Mental Health Assn., 1979—82. Recipient Merit award, Ohio Law Inst., 1975, Pub. Svc. award, U.S. Dept. Justice, 1996. Fellow: Ohio State Bar Assn.; mem.: ABA, Columbus Bar Assn. (chair coms., bd. commrs. on grievance and discipline of Supreme Ct. Ohio, client security fund Supreme Ct. Ohio), Ohio Bar Assn. (coms.), Ohio State U. Pres.'s Club (Columbus chpt.), Athletic Club. Democrat. Jewish. Avocation: woodworking. Home: 3741 Romnay Rd Columbus OH 43220-4877 Office: Bloomfield & Kempf 199 S 5th St Columbus OH 43215-5234 E-mail: dbloo@msn.com.

BLOOMFIELD, JOHN V. musician, educator; s. Clarence V. and Mary S. Bloomfield. BA, Furman U., 1975; MusM, Manhattan Sch. Music, 1982. Instr. Adelphi U., Garden City, NY, 1982—88; instr. prep. divsn. Manhattan Sch. Music, N.Y.C., 1984—94. Faculty chmn. Taubman Inst. Piano, 1992—2002; cons., tchr., lectr., clinician festivals, symposia, workshops on Taubman Approach. Named State winner, Nat. Soc. Arts and Letters Piano Competition, 1982, State and dist. winner, Nat. Fedn. Music Clubs biennial auditions, 1979; Performing Pianist scholar, Internat. Inst. for Chamber Music, Munich, 1982. Mem.: Music Tchrs. Nat. Assn. Democrat. Achievements include expertise in Taubman Approach, a ground-breaking analysis of the motions that function underneath a virtuoso piano technique, which can help pianists overcome limitations and playing-related injury. Avocations: travel, cultural activities, fitness.

BLOOMFIELD, LINCOLN PALMER, federal agency administrator; b. Boston, July 7, 1920; m. Irirangi Pamela Coates, 1948; children: Pamela, Lincoln, Diana. SB, Harvard U., 1941, MPA, 1952, PhD, 1956. With Dept. State, Washington, 1946-57, spl. asst. to asst. sec., 1952-57; sr. staff ctr. for internat. studies MIT, Cambridge, 1957—, prof. polit. sci., 1963-91, prof. emeritus, 1991—; dir. global issues Nat. Security Council, Washington, 1979-80; asst. sec. for polit. mil. affairs U.S. Dept. State, Washington, 2001—. Mem. Presdl. Commn. on 25th Anniversary of UN, 1970-71; vis. prof. Grad. Inst. Advanced Internat. Studies, Geneva, 1965, 72, 77, 79, Salzburg Seminar faculty, 1982, 86, 92, 95, moderator State Dept. seminar on fgn. policy and global issues, 1992-99; disting. vis. lectr. State Dept. Fgn. Svc. Inst., 1995. Host Christian Sci. Monitor TV program Fifty Years Ago Today, 1989—92, moderator EcoForum TV series, 1997—99; author: Evolution or Revolution?, 1957, The UN and U.S. Foreign Policy, rev. edit., 1967, In Search of American Foreign Policy, 1974, The Foreign Policy Process: A Modern Primer, 1982, co-author; editor: International Military Forces, 1964, Kruschchev and the Arms Race, 1966, Outer Space: Prospects for Man and Society, rev. edit., 1968, Controlling Small Wars, 1969, The Management of Global Disorder, 1987, Prospects for Peacemaking, 1987, Managing International Conflict, 1997. Bd. dirs. Unitarian-Universalist Assn., 1958-64, World Affairs Council of Boston, World Peace Found., Nat. Def. U., 1984-89, Can. Inst. Internat. Peace and Security, 1989-92. Lt. USNR, 1942-46. Recipient Chase prize Harvard U., 1956, EDUCOM prize Disting. Software, 1988, New Eng. Emmy award, 1992; Littauer fellow, 1952; Rockefeller fellow, 1954, 75. Fellow World Acad. Art and Sci. (elected); mem. Coun. on Fgn. Rels. Achievements include research on foreign policy, international organizations, political gaming, conflict-minimizing and policy planning strategies and systems. Office: US Dept State Political- Military Affairs 2201 C St NW Washington DC 20520

BLOOMFIELD, LOUIS AUB, physicist, educator; b. Boston, Oct. 11, 1956; s. Daniel Kermit and Frances (Aub) B.; m. Karen Shatkin, Aug. 28, 1983; children: Elana, Aaron. BA in Physics, Amherst Coll., 1979; PhD in Physics, Stanford U., 1983. Postdoctoral physicist AT&T Bell Labs., Murray Hill, NJ, 1983-85; asst. prof. U. Va., Charlottesville, Va., 1985-91, assoc. prof., 1991-96, prof, 1996—. Author: (Book) How Things Work: The Physics of Everyday Life. Recipient Alumni Tchr. award U. Va., 1992, Pres.'s Rsch. prize, 1994; named Presdl. Young Investigator NSF, 1986, Young Investigator Office of Naval Rsch., 1988, Va. Outstanding Faculty award, 1998; Alfred P. Sloan fellow, 1989. Fellow Am. Phys. Soc. (Apker award 1980, Pegram medal 2001). Jewish. Office: Univ of Va Dept Physics PO Box 400714 Charlottesville VA 22904-4714 E-mail: bloomfield@virginia.edu.

BLOOMFIELD, MAXWELL HERRON, III, history and law educator; b. Galveston, Tex., Aug. 17, 1931; s. Maxwell Herron and Violet Clemons (Turner) B.; m. Helen Lorraine Anderson, Sept. 11, 1965. BA, Rice U., 1952; LLB, Harvard U., 1957; PhD in History, Tulane U., 1962. Bar: Tex. 1957. Lectr. Tulane U., 1961-62; instr. Ohio State U., 1962-66; asst. prof. history Cath. U. Am., Washington, 1966-68, assoc. prof., 1968-74, prof., 1974—98, chmn. dept. history, 1977-80, prof. law, 1985-98, prof. emeritus, 1998—. Vis. prof. U. Va., 1973. Author: Alarms and Diversions: The American Mind Through American Magazines, 1967, American Lawyers in a Changing Society, 1776-1876, 1976, (with John McWilliams and Carl Smith) Law and American Literature, 1983, Peaceful Revolution: Constitutional Change and American Culture from Progressivism to the New Deal, 2000; mem. editl. bd. Md. Hist. Mag., 1974-75, Capitol Studies, 1979-80, Legal Studies Forum, 1985-96. With U.S. Army, 1952-54. Am. Bar Found. fellow, 1968-69, Project '87 fellow, 1981; ABA grantee, 1979-80. Mem. State Bar Tex., Am. Soc. Legal History, Am. Hist. Assn., Am. Cath. Hist. Assn., Orgn. Am. Historians, Phi Beta Kappa. Democrat. Roman Catholic. Home: 1913 Saratoga Dr Hyattsville MD 20783-2102

BLOOMFIELD, MICHAEL J. astronaut; b. Flint, Mich., Mar. 16, 1959; s. Rodger and Maxine Bloomfield; m. Lori Miller; 2 children. BSc in Engring. Mechanics, USAF Acad., 1981; MSc in Engring. Mgmt., Old Dominion U., 1993. Commd. 2d lt. USAF, 1981, advanced through grades to lt. col., various assignments, 1981—83; assigned to Holloman AFB, N.Mex., 1983—85, Bitgurg Air Base, Germany, 1987—89, Langley AFB, Va., 1989—92, Edwards AFB, Calif., 1992—95; astronaut NASA, Houston, 1995—. Astronaut Space Shuttle Atlantis, 1997, Space Shuttle Endeavour, 2000. Capt. USAF Acad. Football Team, 1980. Decorated Meritorious Svc. medal USAF, Commendation medal, Aerial Achievement medal. Mem.: Air Force Assn., USAF Acad. Assn. Graduates. Avocations: reading, gardening, all sports, family. Office: Astronaut Office CB NASA Johnson Space Center Houston TX 77058

BLOOMFIELD, PAMELA, state agency manager; b. Washington, Dec. 25, 1950; d. Lincoln Palmer and Irirangi (Coates) B.; m. Alexander Culver, Aug. 28, 1982; children: Nicholas Bloomfield Culver, Adrian Bloomfield Culver. BA in Sociology cum laude, Smith Coll., Northampton, Mass., 1972; MPA, Harvard U., 1976. cert. inspecter gen.; cert. govt. fin. mgr. Ind. cons., San Francisco, Washington, 1975-77; mgmt. cons. Crain & Assocs., Inc., Menlo Park, Calif., 1977-81; sr. mgmt. analyst Dept. Fin. and Adminstrn., Washington County, Oreg., 1981-82, asst. dir., 1982-83; sr. mgmt. analyst Mass. Office of Inspector Gen., Boston, 1983-86, prin. mgmt. analyst, 1986-92, dep. fin. investigations unit, 1992, chief, program monitoring unit, 1992-93, dep. inspector gen. for mgmt., 1993—2003, sr. asst. inspector gen., 2003—. Author short fiction; contbr. articles to profl. jours. Home: 20 Sagamore Dr Andover MA 01810-5106 Office: Mass Office Inspector Gen 1 Ashburton Pl Rm 1311 Boston MA 02108-1518 E-mail: pbsaga@aol.com.

BLOOMFIELD, SARA J. museum director; BA in English Lit., Northwestern Univ.; MA in Education. V.P. Cleveland Financial Group; dir. U.S. Holocaust Memorial Museum, Washington, 1998—. Established the first Learning Disability Program for the Shaker Heights City School System. Recipient of the Young Leadership award from the American Jewish Com., 1986, Jan Karski award from the Anti-Defamation League, Washington Chap. Bd. mem, Women's Political Caucus, the Cleveland City Club and the American Jewish Com. Office: US Holocaust Meml Mus 100 Raoul Wallenberg Pl SW Washington DC 20024-2126

BLOOMFIELD, STEVEN B. think-tank executive; AB in History magna cum laude, Harvard Coll., 1977, EdM in Internat. Edn., 1982. Vol. U.S. Peace Corps, Ecuador, 1978-80; program dir. Latin Am. scholarship program Am. Univs., Harvard U., Cambridge, Mass., 1986-93, dir. Fellows Program, Weatherhead Ctr. for Internat. Affairs. Office: Weatherhead Ctr for Internat Affairs 1737 Cambridge St Rm 622 Cambridge MA 02138-3016

BLOOMGARDEN, KARENNE JO, elementary special education educator, company president; b. N.Y.C., July 5, 1951; d. Kermit and Carol (Lane) B. BS, Bradley U., 1973; M Secondary Edn., Mercy Coll., 2000. Health and phys. edn. tchr. N.J. Bd. Edn., Plainfield, 1973-76, phys. edn. tchr. Orange, 1976-79; camp dir. Orange YWCA, 1977-85; health and phys. edn. tchr. Newark Bd. Edn., 1980-83; exec. dir. Am. Camping Assn., N.Y.C., 1984-87; tchr., trainer N.Y.C. Bd. Edn., 1988-90, adaptive phys. edn. tchr., 1990—; pres. KB Camp Svc., Inc., 1985—. Camp dir. Balt. Cancer Soc., 1977-85, 86-91; dir. The Summer Camp, N.Y.C., 1985-92; stds. accreditation vis. Am. Camping Assn., N.Y.C., 1980—; spokesperson Children and Adults with Attention Deficit Disorder, N.Y.C., 1993—; pres. KB Camp Svc., Inc., 1985—. Contbr. articles to mags. Vol. Starlight Found., N.Y.C., 1989—, Ronald McDonald House, N.Y.C., 1990-92, Coalition for the Homeless, N.Y.C., 1990—, Yorkville Pantry Shelter, N.Y.C., 1993—; founder Girl Club of Am., Peoria, Ill., 1973. Named Tchr. of Yr., P.U.S.H., N.J., 1975; featured in Time Mag., 1986, N.Y. Times,1994, LA Times, 2001. Mem. Am. Camping Assn. (cert. camp dir.). Home and Office: 351 E 84th St New York NY 10028-4423 E-mail: kbcamp@rcn.com.

BLOOMGARDEN, KATHY FINN, public relations executive; b. N.Y.C., June 9, 1949; d. David and Laura (Zeisler) Finn; m. Zachary Bloomgarden; children: Rachel, Keith, Matthew. BA, Brown U., 1970; MA, PhD, Columbia U. Pres. Rsch. & Forecasts, N.Y.C.; pres., dir. Ruder-Finn, Inc., N.Y.C., 1988—98, pres., 1998—, CEO, 2001—. Mem. comms. com. Brown U., Providence. Mem.: Coun. Fgn. Rels., Am. Mgmt. Assn. (bd. dirs.), Pub. Rels. Soc. Am. Jewish. Office: Ruder Finn 301 E 57th St New York NY 10022-2900

BLOOMQUIST, KENNETH GENE, music educator, university bands director; b. Boone, Iowa, Dec. 29, 1931; s. Carl Arvid and Alma Florence (Lindahl) B.; m. Carole Ann Murphy, Feb. 14, 1954; children: Leslie Ann, Laurie Kathleen, Daniel John. BS in Music Edn., U. Ill., 1953, MusM, 1957. Band dir. Urbana (Ill.) Pub. Schs., 1956-57; band dir., supr. music Taylorville (Ill.) Pub. Schs., 1957-58; asst. band dir., trumpet tchr. U. Kans., Lawrence, 1958-68, dir. bands, 1968-70, Mich. State U., East Lansing, 1970-78, 88-93, dir. Sch. Music, 1978-88; dir. bands, 1988-93; dir. bands emeritus Mich. State U., East Lansing, 1993. Guest band condr., U.S., Europe, Asia, 1968—; condr. fgn. tours, 1964, 75, 76, 78, 85, 92, 95, 98, 2001; cons. adjudicator of music, U.S., Europe, Mex., Taiwan, Indonesia, Japan, Thailand, Korea, Czech Republic. Contbr. articles to profl. jours., others. Pres. Music Boosters Okemos (Mich.) Pub. Schs., 1970—72, Northport (Mich.) Cmty. Arts Ctr., 2001—03; bd. dirs. Lansing Symphony Orch., 1978—84, Okemos Cmty. Ch., 1984—87, Traverse Symphony Orch., 2003—. Sgt. U.S. Army, 1953—55. Recipient Alumni award U. Ill., 1966. Em. Nat. Band Assn. (nat. pres. 1980-82), Am. Band Masters Assn. (nat. pres. 1995-96), Coll. Band Dirs. Assn., Music Educators Nat. Conf., Nat. Bd. Assn. Acad. Winds and Percussion Arts (Hall of Fame for Disting. Band Condrs., NBA Hall of Fame), Phi Mu Alpha. Avocations: golf, bridge, tennis, travel, reading. E-mail: bloomqui@traverse.com.

BLOOMQUIST, RODNEY GORDON, geologist; b. Aberdeen, Wash., Feb. 3, 1943; s. Verner A. and Margaret E. (Olson) B.; m. Linda L. Lee, Dec. 19, 1964 (div. July 1968); m. Bente Brisson Jørgensen, Aug. 4, 1977; 1 child, Kira Brisson. BS in Geology, Portland State U., 1966; MS in Geology, U. Stockholm, 1970, PhD in Geochemistry, 1977. Rschr. U. Stockholm, 1974-77; asst. prof. Oreg. Inst. Tech., Klamath Falls, 1978-80; geologist Wash. State Energy Office, Olympia, 1980-96; chief scientist Wash. State U., Olympia, 1996—2003, dir. CHP Application Ctr., 2003—. Author: Regulatory Guide to Geothermics, 1991; mem. editl. bd. Geothermics, 1985-88; also numerous books and articles. Smitts fellow, Sweden, 1974, Royal Rsch. fellow, Sweden, 1975-77; rsch. grantee U. Stockholm, 1975-77. Mem.: N.Am. Dist. Heating and Cooling Inst. (bd. dirs. 1988—92), Internat. Geothermal Assn. (chmn. edn. com. 1988—, bd. dirs. 1990—2001), Internat. Dist. Energy Assn. (western sect. bd. dirs. 1990—, bd. dirs. 1994—97, chmn. com. govt. rels. 1997—2002, bd. dirs. 2001—), Geothermal Resources Coun. (pres. Pacific N.W. sect. 1982—85, bd. dirs. 1985—92, pres. 1989, bd. dirs. 2001—), Am. Blade Smith Soc. (bd. dirs. 1989—2002). Democrat. Lutheran. Avocations: skiing, backpacking, fishing, hunting. Office: Wash State Univ 925 Plum St SE Olympia WA 98501-1529

BLOOMSTER, BRENT NOEL, psychologist, counselor; b. Erie, Pa., Dec. 22, 1960; s. Donald Everett and Shirley June Bloomster; m. Carmen Ruth Knull, July 7, 1960; children: Heather, Kyle, Jordan. BA in Psychology, Taylor U., 1982; MEd in Counselor Edn., Temple U., 1986; PhD in Counselor Edn., Ohio State U., 1997. Lic. psychologist, clin. counselor, Ohio. Psychologist, cons., sch. intervention program coord. Moundbuilders Guidance Ctr., Newark, Ohio, 1987—, asst., interim dir. Project Discovery, 1998-99. Course instr. Licking-Muskingum Cmty. Correction Ctr., Newark, 1997— Recipient Nat. Model of Creative Svc. Delivery award APA, 1998. Mem. ACA, Am. Sch. Counselor Assn., Phi Kappa Phi. United Methodist. Avocations: travel, singing, camping, canoeing, bicycling. Home: 2923 Grand Haven Dr Pickerington OH 43147 Office: Moundbuilders Guidance Ctr 65 Messimer Dr Newark OH 43055 E-mail: drbloomster@toast.net.

BLOOR, W(ILLIAM) SPENCER, electrical engineer, consultant; b. Trenton, N.J., Oct. 16, 1918; s. W. Harry and Eva (Averre) B.; m. Barbara P. Walters, Jan. 19, 1952; children: William G., Robert S. BS in Elec. Engring, Lafayette Coll., 1940, D.Eng. (hon.), 1981. With Leeds & Northrup Co., 1940-81, product market devel. mgr., 1966-68, engring. coordination mgr. North Wales, Pa., 1968-69, mgr. steam and nuclear power systems, 1969-81; cons. in pvt. practice, 1981—. Cons. staff Beacon Rsch. Found., Arcadia U., Franklin Inst., past chmn. com. on sci. and arts. Served to lt. USN, 1943-46. Named Engr. of Yr. Delaware Valley, 1980 Fellow IEEE, Instrument Soc. Am. (v.p. publs. 1968-70, pres. 1974, chmn. history com., mem. IEEE Lamme medal com. 1989-91); mem. NAE, Phi Beta Kappa, Tau Beta Pi, Eta Kappa Nu. Presbyterian. Achievements include design and application of control and monitoring systems for electric power generating stations. Died Dec. 8, 2002.

BLOOSTON, ROSELEE, cultural organization administrator, writer; b. Washington, Sept. 29, 1952; d. Arthur and Leone Isaacs Blooston; m. Jerry Michael Mosier, Sept. 9, 1983; 1 child, Oliver Blooston Mosier. BA in Drama, Vassar Coll., 1973; MFA in Theater, Trinity U., 1975. Drama instr. Smithsonian Instn., Washington, 1976; acting instr. U. Tex., Austin, 1976—79; faculty New Sch. for Social Rsch., N.Y.C., 1982—83; master tchr., dir. Paper Mill Playhouse, Millburn, NJ, 1991—96; dir., tchg. artist N.J. Performing Arts Ctr., Newark, 1997; adj. faculty Montclair (N.J.) State U., 1992—2000; founder, dir. Tunnel Vision Writers' Project, Inc., Montclair, 1998—. Cons. Job Performance Seminars, Bklyn., 1984—89; dir., playwriting coord. The Gathering/Whole Theater, Montclair, 1988—89; head speech dept. Action Theater Conservatory, Clifton, NJ, 1995—97. Author short stories; prodr.: 5 plays. Mem. edn. com. Montclair Editors and Writers, 2001—; mem. spoken arts com. Montclair Art Mus., 2001—. Recipient Greer Garson Theater Arts award, Dallas Theater Ctr., 1974. Mem.: Internat. Womens Writers Guild, Dramatists Guild, Actors Equity Assn., Phi Beta Kappa. Office: Tunnel Vision Writers' Project PO Box 43323 Upper Montclair NJ 07043

BLOSKAS, JOHN D. financial executive; b. Waco, Tex., July 13, 1928; s. George and Alvina (Schrader) B.; m. Anna Louise Nelson, Feb. 7, 1955; children: Suzzanne (dec.), John D., Kenneth Douglas. Exec. sec. Waco Jr. C. of C., 1953-55; assoc. editor Mexia (Tex.) Daily News, 1955-56; dir. publicity Valley C. of C., Weslaco, Tex., 1956-57; religion editor Houston Chronicle, 1957-58; v.p. pub. rels. annuity bd. So. Bapt. Conv., Dallas, 1984-90, v.p., endowment officer annuity bd., 1984-90; v.p. Lady Love Cosmetics, Dallas, 1981-83; ret., 1990; fin. mgmt. cons., conf. spkr., 1990—. Chmn. Greenville (Tex.) Airport adv. bd. Author: Staying in the Black, Financially, Living Within Your Means; editor: THe Years Ahead. Chmn. adv. bd. Greenville (Tex.) Airport. Served with USNR, 1945-49, 50-51. Mem. Southern Bapt. (past pres.), Tex. Bapt. Assn. (past pres.), Pub. Rels. Assn., Pub. Rels. Soc. Am. (accredited), Religious Pub. Rels. Coun., Sales and Mktg. Execs., Bapt. Devel. Officer's Assn., Assn. Bapt. Found. Execs., Dallas Estate Planning Coun., Fellowship Christians in Arts, Media and Entertainment. Home: 7508 Blossom Ln Frisco TX 75034-5470 Office: PO Box 1192 Frisco TX 75034-1192 E-mail: jbloskas@sbcglobal.net., anjoblossom@hotmail.com.

BLOSSER, HENRY GABRIEL, physicist; b. Harrisonburg, Va., Mar. 16, 1928; s. Emanuel and Leona (Branum) B.; m. Priscilla May Beard, June 30, 1951 (div. Oct. 1972); children: William Henry, Stephan Emanuel, Gabe Fawley, Mary Margaret; m. Mary Margaret Gray, Mar. 16, 1973 (dec. Jan. 1995); m. Amy June Conley, May 11, 1995 (div. Feb. 1997); m. Lois Pearlena Lynch, Oct. 17, 1998. BS, U. Va., 1951, MS, 1952, PhD, 1954. Physicist Oak Ridge (Tenn.) Nat. Lab., 1954-56, group leader, 1956-68; assoc. prof. physics Mich. State U., East Lansing, 1958-61, prof., 1961-90, Univ. Disting. prof., 1990—, dir. Cyclotron Lab., 1961-89. Cons. Harper Hosp., Detroit, 1983—, Ion Beam Applications, Belgium, 1996—, others; adj. prof. radiation oncology Wayne State U., Detroit, 1996—. Bd. dirs. Midwest Univs. Rsch. Assocs., 1960-63. With USNR, 1946-48. Predoctoral fellow NSF, 1953-54, sr. postdoctoral fellow, 1966-67; Guggenheim fellow, 1973-74. Fellow Am. Phys. Soc. (Bonner prize 1992); mem. Sigma Xi, Phi Beta Kappa, Kappa Alpha. Home: 2350 Emerald Forest Cir East Lansing MI 48823-7200 Office: Mich State U Nat Cyclotron East Lansing MI 48824-1321 Business E-Mail: blosser@nscl.msu.edu.

BLOSSER, PAMELA ELIZABETH, metaphysics educator, counselor, minister; b. Norman, Okla., Dec. 12, 1946; d. William Bernard and Emma Elizabeth (Ambrister) Carpenter; m. William Richard Stewart, June 10, 1969 (div. Apr. 1979); m. Paul Gerald Blosser Jr., Sept. 24, 1994. BA, Tex. Christian U., 1969; DDiv, Interfaith Ch. Metaphysics, Windyville, Mo., 1992; DMetaphysics, Sch. Metaphysics, Windyville, 1994; degree with honors, Maria Montessori Tng. Divsn., London, 1977. Ordained to ministry Interfaith Ch. of Metaphysics, 1992; cert. in counseling. Dir. metaphysics ctrs. Sch. Metaphysics, various locations, 1979-89; directress Golden Moments Montessori, Columbia, Mo., 1987-89; instr. metaphysics Sch. Metaphysics, various locations, 1977-89, readings coord. Windyville, 1989—98, dir. printing, 1989—, instr. metaphysics, 1991—; min. of music Interfaith Ch. Metaphysics, Windyville, 1990-96, min., 1995—. Dir. Camp Renaissance for Young People, Sch. Metaphysics, Windyville, 1990—; ordination bd. Interfaith Ch. of Metaphysics, 1993—; bd. govs. Sch. Metaphysics, 1997—, pres., 2002—. Author: Power of Structure, 1988, Total Recall, 1993, Motivation: From Existence to Fulfillment, 1997, The 7 Steps to Deepen Meditation, 2001, Essay in Interpreting Dreams for Self-Discovery, 2001; contbr. articles to profl. jours. Mem. Dallas County Homemakers (sec.-treas. 1995-96, sec. 2000-01, pres. 2001-03), Homemaker Club Windyville (v.p. 1995, 98, pres. 1996, 99-2001, sec. 2002). Republican. Avocations: reading, playing celtic harp. Home and Office: Sch of Metaphysics 163 Moon Valley Rd Windyville MO 65783-9703

BLOSSMAN, ALFRED RHODY, JR., banker; b. Madisonville, La., Oct. 21, 1931; s. Alfred Rhody and Mabel (Perrin) B.; m. Royanne Elaire Hurd, Dec. 28, 1957; children: Alfred Rhody III, Roy Edward, Gary Bennett, Christopher Hurd, David Quintin, John Eric. AB in Gen. Bus., La. State U., 1955. Pres. Blossman Hydratane Gas, Inc., Covington, La., 1963-67; chmn. First Nat. Corp., First Nat. Bank, Covington, 1968-84; pres., CEO, First Nat. Bank, 1980-84; pres., CEO Parish Nat. Bank, Covington, 1986—2002, chmn. bd., 1992—2002, 2002—. Capt. USAF, 1956—58. Mem. Phi Delta Theta. Republican. Roman Catholic. Home: 10 Blossman Ln Covington LA 70433-4707 E-mail: fredb@parishnational.com. *My formula for life is shaped by the moral and ethical guidelines of my religious faith and my own personal code of ethics. Thank God, strong self discipline has made that possible, as well as channelling my enthusiasm for whatever role I have played; being it business, or hobby; educational, military service, parent or grandparent, in a positive direction.*

BLOSSOM, BEVERLY, choreographer, dance educator; b. Chgo., Aug. 28, 1926; d. Theodore and Florence (Pfeiffer) Schmidt; m. Roberts Blossom, 1966 (div.); 1 child, Michael. BA, Roosevelt U., 1950; MA, Sarah Lawrence, 1953. Dancer Alwin Nikolais Co., N.Y.C., 1952-62; instr. Adelphi U., L.I., N.Y., 1964-66; prof. dance dept. U. Ill., Urbana, 1967-90. Choreographer Festival Theatre, Krannert Ctr., Urbana, Radio Show, 1985, Quick-Step, 1985, Heartbeat, 1985, Interlude from Veranda, 1985; choreographer: Rehearsal for a Class Act, 1983, You Are Still With Me, Fred, 1983, Dad's Ties, 1983, Ordinary Heartbreak, 1984, Egg, 1984, Weatherwatch, 1986, Potpourri, 1986, Eye of the Beholder, 1986, Russian Tea Room, 1986, Entitled, 1987, Grass Widow, 1987, Inch, 1987, Castles in Spain, 1988, Swansong, 1989, ...Exit, 1990, The Cloak, 1990, Onward, 1991, Shards, 1993, Dead Monkey, 1996, Cynicism, 1996, more. Choreography grantee Nat. Endowment for the Arts, 1986, 87, 88, 89, 90, 92, 93, 94, 95, Ill. Arts Coun. Choreography grantee, 1980, 81, 82; recipient Bessie award, 1993. Mem. Am. Guild of Musical Artists (cert.), Screen Actors Guild (cert.), Union of Profl. Employees (cert.).

BLOSTEIN, MICHAEL DAVID, music educator; b. Troy, NY, Dec. 16, 1973; s. David Frank and Robin June Blostein; m. Alyssa Danielle Wagner, June 29, 2002. MusM in Composition, U. Ariz., 1999; MusB in Music Edn., SUNY, Potsdam, 1996. Ptnr. Stop 13 Music, Troy, 2001—; music instr. Averill Pk. H.S., Averill Park, NY, 2000—. Composer: (classical music) Impression #1, Impression #2, Seven, Nebulous. Master: Masons; mem.: ASCAP (composer, pub. 2000—02), Music Educators Nat. Conf., Am. Music Ctr. (composer 2000—02). Avocations: woodworking, art. Home: 28 25th Street Troy NY 12180 Office: Averill Park High School 146 Gettle Road Averill Park NY 12018 Personal E-mail: mblostein@hotmail.com.

BLOTNER, NORMAN DAVID, lawyer, real estate broker, corporate executive; b. Boston, Dec. 6, 1918; s. Leon and Sarah B.; m. Helen I. Whitman (dec.), Aug. 13, 1954; 1 son, James B. McClain (dec.). AB, Harvard U., 1940, JD, 1947. Bar: N.Y. 1948. Mem. firm Spiro, Felstiner, Prager & Treeger, N.Y.C., 1947-52; with Lane Bryant Inc., N.Y.C., 1953-82, sr. v.p., gen. counsel, sec., dir., 1968-82, ret., 1982. Bd. dirs. Better Bus. Bur. Met. N.Y., until 1982. Lt. comdr. USNR, 1941—46. Named Lacrosse All-am., 1940. Mem. Assn. of Bar of City of N.Y., Harvard Varsity Club, New Rochelle Tennis Club. Republican. Home: 140 Overlook Rd New Rochelle NY 10804-4139

BLOUCH, TIMOTHY CRAIG, food company executive; b. Lebanon, Pa., June 26, 1954; s. Charles and Elaine (Krick) B.; m. Donna Joyce Walmer, June 18, 1977. AA, Harrisburg Area Community Coll., 1974; BBA, Pa. State U., 1977, MBA, 1991. Prodn. supr. Kraft, Inc., Allentown, Pa., 1977-78, Hershey (Pa.) Chocolate USA, 1978-82, mgr. inbound and fleet ops., 1982-83, mgr. inbound ops., 1983-84, mgr. transp. rates, 1984-86, mgr. traffic services, 1986-90, transp. planning mgr., 1990-93, mgr. transp. planning and rates, 1993—2001, mgr. tranps. financials and analysis, 2002—. Republican. Avocations: tennis, fine arts. Office: Hershey Foods Corp 19 E Chocolate Ave Hershey PA 17033-1314

BLOUIN, FRANCIS XAVIER, JR., history educator; b. Belmont, Mass., July 29, 1946; s. Francis X. and Margaret (Cronin) B.; m. Joy Alexander; children: Benjamin, Tiffany. AB, U. Notre Dame, 1967; MA, U. Minn., 1969, PhD, 1978. Asst. dir. Bentley Library U. Mich., Ann Arbor, 1974-75, assoc. archivist Bentley Library, 1975-81, dir. Bentley Library, 1981—, asst. prof. history and library sci., 1979-83, assoc. prof., 1983-89, prof., 1989—. Author: The Boston Region..., 1980, Vatican Archives: An Inventory and Guide to Historical Documentation of the Holy See, 1998; editor Intellectual Life on Michigan Frontier, 1985, Archival Implications Machine..., 1980. Trustee Much. Student Found., 1986-91; dir. Am. Friends of Vatican Libr., 1981—, Coun. on Libr. and Info. Resources, 2001—. Fellow Soc. Am. Archivist (mem. governing council 1985-88); mem. Am. Hist. Assn., Hist. Soc. Mich. (trustee 1982-88, pres. 1987-88), Assn. Records Mgrs. and Adminstrs., Internat. Council on Archives. Office: U Mich Bentley Hist Libr 1150 Beal Ave Ann Arbor MI 48109-2113

BLOUNT, BENROE WAYNE, physician; b. Augusta, Ga., Feb. 8, 1950; s. Benroe and Loreen Moellering B.; m. Merry Teresa Van Dam, Feb. 14, 1974 (div. May 8, 1974); m. Young Hui Cho, Nov. 23, 1976; children: Teresa Jana, Daniel Paul. BS, U.S. Mil. Acad., 1972; MA, U. Calif., Berkeley, 1975; MD, U. Miami, 1983; MPH, U. Wash., 1990. Commd. 2d lt. U.S. Army, 1972, advanced through grades to lt. col., 1990, ret., 1994; intern, resident DeWitt Army Hosp., Alexandria, Va., 1983-86; divsn. chief, dept. vice-chair Emory Sch. Medicine, Atlanta, 1994-99; chair dept. family medicine U. Tenn., Memphis, 1999—2002; prof. Emory U., 2002—; chief family practice Kaiser, S.E., 2002—. Contbr. articles to profl. jours., chpts. to books. Named one of Outstanding Young Men of Am., Nat. Jaycees; recipient Chmn. of Joint Chief of Staff award for Excellence in Mil. Medicine, 1993, Best Dr. in Am., 2000, 2001, 2002. Independent. Avocation: church.

BLOUNT, CHARLES WILLIAM, III, lawyer; b. Independence, Mo., Nov. 14, 1946; s. Charles William and Mary Marguerite (Van Trump) B.; m. Susan Penny Smith Turner, Dec. 20, 1969 (div. Nov., 1987); children: Charles William IV, Chaille Elizabeth; m. Bonnie M. Harp., Jan. 1, 1991. BS in Journalism, U.

Kans., 1968; JD cum laude, U. Toledo, 1981. Bar: Mo. 1981, U.S. Dist. Ct. (we. dist.) Mo. 1981, Tex. 1985, U.S. Dist. Ct. (no. dist.) Tex. 1988, U.S. Ct. Appeals (5th cir.) 1995, U.S. Supreme Ct. 1997; cert. in civil appellate law Tex. Bd. Legal Specialization. Litigation assoc. Shugart, Thomson & Kilroy, Kansas City, Mo., 1981-84, Hughes & Luce, Dallas, 1984-87, Simpson & Dowd L.L.P., Dallas, 1987-91, ptnr., 1991-94; mem. Dowd & Blount, Dallas, 1994-99; ptnr. Perry-Miller & Blount, L.L.P., Dallas, 1999—2002; sr. counsel Smith, Underwood & Perkins, P.C., Dallas, 2002—. Mem. West Group Tex. Editl. Bd., 1999. Bd. govs. U. Toledo Coll. Law, 1980-81; trustee Episcopal Diocese We. Mo., Kansas City, 1983-84; mem., chmn. com. Boy Scouts of Am., Kansas City, 1983-84, Richardson, Tex., 1984-92. 1st lt. U.S. Army, 1968-72. Mem. Phi Kappa Phi, Phi Kappa Tau (pledge pres., social chmn., activities chmn., 1965—). Avocations: music, reading. Office: Smith Underwood & Perkins PC 5420 LBJ Frwy Ste 600 Dallas TX 75240 E-mail: cblount@suplaw.com.

BLOUNT, DARLENE, small business owner, consultant; b. Houston, July 30, 1949; d. Cecil Troy and Margaret Mary Prater; m. Clyde Gilmore, Apr. 21, 1970 (div. Dec. 1982); children: Shawn Corey Gilmore, Shane Howard Gilmore. Student, San Jacinto Jr. Coll., Houston, 1983—85; A in Bus. Mgmt., North Harris C.C., Houston, 1987. Divsn. sec. to capt. Harris County Sheriff's Dept., Houston, 1983—87; part-time office asst. Marriott Facilities Mgmt., 1988—91, maintenance sec., 1991—93; pub. rels./billing specialist SOGA Clinic, Houston, 1995—99; owner, cons. Spl. Techniques Office Procedures, Houston, 1983—. Author: The Adventures of Jerusalem Forest, 2001. Mem.: South Tex. Women's Ministries. Avocations: writing, crafts, computer games, travel. Office: Spl Techniques Office Procedures PO Box 41655 Houston TX 77241-1655

BLOUNT, JAMES ROBERT, military career officer; b. Columbus, Ohio, Dec. 13, 1958; s. Robert and Beatrice Louise Blount; m. Kelle Ann Bush, Jan. 2, 1978; children: Daniel O., Natalie M. AA in Criminal Justice, Rollins Coll., 1980; BA in Bus. Adminstrn. and Acctg., Nat. U., 1984; student, USN-Office Candidate Sch., 1984-85, USN-Surface Warfare Sch., 1985, 92; ministerial cert. studies, Berean Coll., 1988; MA in Nat. Security Affairs, Naval Postgrad. Sch., 1991. Commd. ensign USN, 1985, advanced through grades to lt. comdr., 1995—, mine countermeasures officer USS Leader, 1985-87, exec. asst., navigator, legal officer USS Pensacola Little Creek, Va. 1987-89, combat cargo officer, weapons officer USS Racine Long Beach, Calif., 1992-93, 1st lt. USS Durham San Diego, 1993, ops. officer, comdr. mine countermeasure squadron one Ingleside, Tex., 1994-95; instr., co. officer, tng. officer, facilities mgr. U.S. Naval Acad., Annapolis, Md., 1995-98; comdg. officer Mil. Entrance Processing Sta., Oklahoma City, 1999—; CO Mil. Entrance Procesing Sta., 1999—2001, ret., 2001. Youth leader various chs., Seaside, Calif., Rockport, Tex., Annapolis; martial arts instr. various recreation ctrs., Charleston, Monterey, Calif., Long Beach. Cpl. USMC, 1977-78, sgt. USMC, 1981-84; with USN, 1979-81. Mem. Fed. Exec. Bd. Avocations: martial arts, weight lifting, running, scuba diving. Home: 1340 SW 108th Pl Oklahoma City OK 73170-4219 E-mail: soaringeagle@mail.com., okccdr@mepcom.army.mil.

BLOUNT, MICHAEL EUGENE, lawyer; b. Camden, N.J., July 9, 1949; s. Floyd Eugene and Dorothy Alice (Geyer) Durham; m. Janice Lynn Brown, Aug. 22, 1969; children: Kirsten Marie, Gretchen Elizabeth. BA, U. Tex., 1971; JD, U. Houston, 1974. Bar: Tex. 1974, Ill. 1980, D.C. 1981, U.S. Ct. Appeals (D.C. cir.) 1978, U.S. Ct. Mil. Appeals 1975, U.S. Supreme Ct. 1977. Atty. advisor Office of Gen. Counsel SEC, Washington, 1977-78, legal asst. to chmn., 1978-79; assoc. Gardner, Carton & Douglas, Chgo., 1980-84; ptnr. Arnstein, Gluck, Lehr, Barron & Milligan, Chgo., 1984-86, Seyfarth Shaw, Chgo., 1987—. Lt. JAGC USN, 1974—77. Mem.: ABA (fed. regulation of securities com.), Chgo. Bar Assn., Order of Barons, Assn. SEC Alumni, Univ. Club (Chgo.), Phi Alpha Delta (chpt. treas. 1973). Home: 1711 Galloway Dr Barrington IL 60010-5737 Office: Seyfarth Shaw 55 E Monroe St Ste 4200 Chicago IL 60603-5863 E-mail: mblount@seyfarth.com.

BLOUNT, ROBERT HADDOCK, corporate executive, retired naval officer; b. Miami, Fla., Dec. 8, 1922; s. Uriel and Aleve Sadie (Haddock) B.; m. Jeannette Mae Barclay, May 13, 1951 (dec. 1998); children: Barbara Mae, Jennifer. B.E.E., MIT, 1947; MS in Systems Engring, George Washington U., 1970; student, Naval War Coll., 1958-59. Commd. ensign USNR, 1946; transferred to U.S. Navy, 1947, advanced through grades to rear adm., 1973; comdr. submarines, service in MTO, PTO, Scotland, Panama; chief staff, aide to comdr. Submarine Flotilla 6, 1970-72; comdr. Naval Sta., Naval Base, 1972-73; comdr. U.S. Naval Forces, So. Command; also comdt. 15th Naval Dist., 1973-75; dir. undersea and strategic warfare div. Office Chief Naval Ops. Washington, 1975-77; dep. dir. research, devel., test and evaluation OPNAV, 1977-78; comdr. Operational Test and Evaluation Force, 1978-82, ret., 1982; pvt. industry cons., 1986-90; ret. Va. Ops. div. EDO Corp., 1990. Pres. C.Z. council Boy Scouts Am., 1974. Decorated D.S.M., Meritorious Service medal with star, Navy Expeditionary medal; recipient Scroll of Honor Navy League, 1974 Mem. Naval Submarine League, U.S. Naval Inst., Norfolk Yacht and Country Club, Rotary. Address: 1516 Blanford Cir Norfolk VA 23505-1706 E-mail: rhblount@aol.com.

BLOUNT, STANLEY FREEMAN, marketing educator; b. Detroit, June 12, 1929; s. Harry Alfred and Thelma (Freeman) B.; m. Constance Parker, Aug. 30, 1957; children— Jeffrey Parker, Lori Maria. BA, Wayne State U., 1952, MA, 1959; PhD, Northwestern U., 1962. Account exec. Jam Handy Corp., Detroit, 1952-54; marketing mgr. Chrysler Corp., Detroit, 1954-58; instr. Northwestern U., 1961-62; asst. prof. U. Ill., 1962-63; assoc. prof. Kent State U., 1963-67; prof., dept. chmn. State U. N.Y. at Albany, 1967—, chmn. ednl. policies council, 1970—. Disting. vis. prof. U. of Americas, Mexico, 1966; dir. Femtec Inc.; exec. dir. U. Albany Found. Chmn. sub-com. legis. affairs N.Y. State affiliate Am. Heart Assn., 1974-99 . Served with AUS, 1946-48. Named Outstanding Faculty Mem. Kent State U., 1964 Mem. Sigma Xi, Gamma Theta Upsilon. Clubs: Essayons, Audubon, Phalanx. Achievements include research on environment analysis and preception, digitized land use mapping, land use and resource mgmt. Home: 11 Pheasant Ln Delmar NY 12054-4109 Office: SUNY at Albany Sch Business Albany NY 12222-0001

BLOUNT, WINTON MALCOLM, III, investment executive; b. Albany, Ga., Dec. 14, 1943; s. Winton Malcolm Jr. and Mary Katherine (Archibald) B.; m. Riley Sikes; children: Winton Malcolm IV, K. Stuart, William, Judkins. Student, U. Ala., 1962-63; BA, U. South, 1966; MBA, U. Pa., 1968. With Blount Bros. Corp., Montgomery, Ala., 1968-73, project mgr., 1972-73; with Mercury Constrn. Corp., Montgomery, 1973-77, pres., 1975-77; chief exec. officer, chmn. bd. Benjamin F. Shaw Co., Wilmington, Del., 1977-80; pres., chief operating officer Blount Internat., Ltd., Montgomery, 1980-83, pres., chief exec. officer, 1983-85, chmn., chief exec. officer, 1985-87; sr. v.p. Blount Inc., 1985-87, vice chmn., 1987-89; chmn., chief exec. officer Winton Blount III & Assocs., 1989—. Chmn., chief exec. officer Wright Plastics Co., 1989—, Cobb Pontiac-Cadillac & Royal Motor Co., 1990-2000, Blount-Strange Ford, Lincoln, Mercury, 1991-2000; bd. dirs. Dunn Constrn. Co., Birmingham, Ala., 1977-99. Mem. fin. com. Ala. Rep. Com., 1980-82, chmn., 1999-01; bd. dirs. So. Rsch. Inst., 1995-99, Montgomery YMCA, Episcopal High Sch., 1988-89, 95—, Ala. Pub. Affairs Rsch. Coun., 1979-83, Bus. Coun. Ala.; active Tukabatchee Area coun. Boy Scouts Am., 1980-83; bd. visitors U. Ala. Coll. Commerce and Bus. Adminstrn., 1983-88; mem. bd. control Com. of 100; mem. bd. Leadership Ala., 1989-93, 95-98, chmn. bd., 1997-98, Ala. Coun. Econ. Edn. Mem. Chief Execs. Orgn., World Pres.'s Orgn.), Montgomery C. of C. (dir. 1981-88), Del. C. of C. (dir. 1979-80), NAM (dir. 1982-85). Episcopalian. Office: 1919 South Hull Street, PO Box 230039 Montgomery AL 36123-0039

BLOUT, ELKAN ROGERS, biological chemistry educator, university dean; b. N.Y.C., July 2, 1919; s. Eugene and Lillian B. Blout; m. Joan E. Dreyfus, Aug. 27, 1939; children: James E., Susan, William L.; m. Gail A. Ferris, Mar. 29, 1985; 1 child, Darya L.M. AB, Princeton U., 1939; PhD, Columbia U., 1942; A.M. (hon.), Harvard U., 1962; D.Sc. (hon.), Loyola U., 1976. With Polaroid Corp., Cambridge, Mass., 1943—62, successively rsch. chemist, assoc. dir. rsch., 1948—58, v.p., gen. mgr. rsch., 1958—62; rsch. assoc. Harvard U., 1950—52, 1958—60, lectr. on biophysics, 1960—62, prof. biol. chemistry, 1962—90, Edward S. Harkness prof. biol. chemistry, 1964—90, Edward S. Harkness prof. emeritus, 1990—, head dept. biol. chemistry, 1965—69; dean for acad. affairs Harvard Sch. Pub. Health, 1978—89, chmn. dep. environ. sci. and physiology, 1986—88, dir. div. biol. scis., prof., 1987—91; prof. emeritus Harvard Sch. of Pub. Health, 1991—. Rsch. assoc. Children's Hosp. Med. Ctr., Boston, 1950—52, cons. chemistry, 1952—; mem. conseil de surveillance Compagnie Financière du Scribe, 1975—81; trustee Bay Biochem. Rsch., Inc., 1973—83; mem. exec. com. divsn. chemistry and chem. tech. NRC, 1972—74, mem. assembly of math. and phys. scis., 1979—82; mem. sci. adv. com. Ctr. for Blood Rsch., Inc., 1972—92, emeritus trustee, 1992—, also mem. bd. dirs.; mem. rsch. adv. com. Children's Hosp. Med. Ctr., 1976—80, 1984—90, chmn., 1987—90; mem. vis. com. dept. chemistry Carnegie-Mellon U., 1968—72; bd. visitors Faculty Health Scis. SUNY, Buffalo, 1968—70; overseer Boston Mus. Sci. ; trustee Boston Biomed. Rsch. Inst., 1990—, v.p., 1990—94; bd. govs. Weizmann Inst. Sci., Rehovot, Israel, 1978—90, gov. emeritus, Israel, 1990—; bd. dirs. Nat. Health Rsch. Found., ESA, Inc. ; bd. dirs., sec.-treas. Nat. Acads. Corp. ; gen. ptnr. Gosnold Investment Fund Ltd. Partnership, 1985—95; bd. dirs., investment mgr Auburn Investment Mgmt. Corp., 1985—; sci. advisor Affymax Rsch. Inst., 1988—92; sr. adviser sci. FDA, 1991—99; mem. sr. adv. bd. The Ency. of Molecular Biol., 1991; mem. coun. visitors Marine Biol. Lab., 1992—; pres., trustee Inst. for Internat. Vaccine Devel., 1997—. Mem. adv. bd.: Jour. Polymer Sci, 1956—62, mem. editl. bd.: Biopolymers, 1963—85, hon. founding editor:, 1985—, mem. editorial bd. : Am. Chem. Soc. Monograph Series, 1965—72, Internat. Jour. Peptide and Protein Rsch., 1978—89, mem. editl. adv. bd. : Macromolecules, 1967—70, Jour. Am. Chem. Soc., 1978—82; contbr. Recipient Princeton Class of 1939 Achievement award, 1970, Nat. Med. Sci. award, 1990, John Phillips award, Phillips Exeter Acad., 1998; fellow NRC, 1942—43. Fellow: AAAS (fin. com. 1977—84, com. on investments 1984—2001, chmn. budget com. 1988—92, treas. 1992—98), Optical Soc. Am., N.Y. Acad. Arts and Scis. (past pres. New Eng. sect.); mem.: NAS (adv. com. USSR and Eastern Europe 1979—84, treas. 1980—92, mem. com. sci. engring. and pub. policy 1992—95, treas. emeritus 1992—, audit com. 1994—2000), Fedn. Am. Socs. Exptl. Biology (investments adv. com. 1981—85), Internat. Orgn. Chem. Scis. in Devel. (coun. 1981—, chmn. fin. com. 1982—, treas. 1985—, bd. dirs. 1985—, v.p.), Commn. on Phys. Scis., Math., and Resources of NRC, Biophys. Soc., Am. Soc. Biol. Chemists (fin. com. 1973—82), Am. Chem. Soc. (nat. councillor 1958—61, Ralph F. Hirschmann award 1991), Russian Acad. Scis. (fgn.), Inst. Medicine. Achievements include patents in field. Home: 1010 Memorial Dr Cambridge MA 02138-4859 Office: Harvard U Med Sch Dept Biol Chemistry and Molecular Pharma 1010 Memorial Dr Cambridge MA 02138-4859

BLOW, GEORGE, lawyer; b. Chgo., Oct. 4, 1928; s. George Waller and Katharine Rowland (Cooke) B.; m. Sarah Wendel Kuhn, Nov. 4, 1957; children: Mary Allmand Blow Prevost, George Rowland, Wendel Matthiessen. AB cum laude, Harvard U., 1950; JD, U. Va., 1953. Bar: Va. 1953, D.C. 1954, U.S. Ct. Appeals (D.C. cir.) 1954, U.S. Ct. Mil. Appeals, 1955, U.S. Supreme Ct. 1956, U.S. Ct. Appeals (4th cir.) 1961, U.S. Ct. Appeals (fed. cir.) 1982. Assoc. Covington & Burling, Washington, 1953-63; ptnr. Patton, Boggs & Blow, Washington, 1963-93. Mem. adv. coun. Internat. Human Rights Law Group, Washington, 1988-98. Mem. Com. of 100 on Fed. City, Washington, 1984—, trustee, 1985-87; mem. Washington Inst. Fgn. Affairs, 1976—, bd. dirs., 1976-98; bd. dirs. Sheridan-Kalorama Hist. Assn., Washington, 1987-89. Mem. D.C. Bar, Va. State Bar, Soc. of Cincinnati in State of Va., Soc. Colonial Wars, Met. Club Washington, Order of Coif, Phi Delta Phi.

BLOWER, JOHN GREGORY, special education educator; b. Orange, Calif., Mar. 18, 1952; s. James Girard and Juanita Mae (Pierce) B.; 1 child, Becky Renee. BS in Psychology, Pacific Christian, 1975; MEd in Spl. Edn., Idaho State U., 2002. Assoc. minister edn. 1st Christian Ch., Santa Ana, Calif., 1972-75; spl. edn. tchr. Fremont County Schs., St. Anthony, Idaho, 1977—. Vice chmn., con. People for Spl. People, St. Anthony, 1986—. Program coord. Idaho Spl. Olympics, St. Anthony, 1978—, bd. dirs., Boise, 1982-88, chmn. bd. dirs., Boise, 1987-88. Mem. Coun. for Exceptional Children, Nat. Edn. Assn. Office: South Fremont High Sch 855 S Bridge St Saint Anthony ID 83445-2034

BLOYD, STEPHEN ROY, environmental manager, educator, consultant; b. Alameda, Calif., Aug. 17, 1953; s. William Allen and Alice Louella (Scott) B. Grad. high sch., Reedley, Calif., 1971. Cert. environ. mgr., Nev.; registered hazardous substances specialist. Reagent tech. Tenneco Corp., Gold Hill, Nev., 1982; environ. tech. Pierson Environ. Drilling, Modesto, Calif., 1982-84; pres. Bloyd and Assocs., Dayton, Nev., 1986—. Author: Hazardous Waste Site Operations for General Site Workers, 1992; editor: (newsletter) Pumper, 1991. Firefighter Dayton Vol. Fire Dept., 1975, capt., 1976-78, chief, 1978-83, tng. officer, 1984-96; mem. Silver City (Nev.) Fire Dept., 1996—; coord. Ctrl. Lyon County Hazardous Materials, 1997—; asst. prof. Dodd/Beals Fire Protection Tng. Acad. U. Nev., Reno, 1990-96; instr. chemistry hazardous materials Nat. Fire Acad., Emmitsburg, Md., 1989—, instr. hazardous materials incident mgmt., 1996—; mem. bylaw com. Dayton Regional Adv. Coun., 1989; instr. Emergency Response to Terrorism, 1998—; tech. assistance team mem. Fed. Emergency Mgmt. Agy. Comprehensive Hazardous Materials Emergency Response Capability Assessment Project, 2000—. Named Firefighter of Yr., City of Dayton, 1992. Mem. NRA, Nat. Environ. Tng. Assn., Nat. Environ. Health Assn., Nev. State Firemen's Assn. (1st v.p. 1992-93, 2d v.p. 1991-92, pres. 1993-94, chmn. hazardous materials com. 1987-93, legis. com. 1991, bylaws com. 1986), Nev. Fire Chief's Assn., Internat. Platform Assn., Soc. Nat. Fire Acad. Instrs. Libertarian. Avocations: fishing, motorcycles, firearms, camping, reading. Office: PO Box 113 Silver City NV 89428-0113 E-mail: hazmatpro@hotmail.com.

BLUE, BETH-ANNE, psychologist, writer; b. Columbus, Ohio, Apr. 27, 1968; d. Jason Almon Blue and Marjorie Irene Yoder. BA, Denison U., Granville, Ohio, 1990; MS, Pacific Grad. Sch. Psychology, Palo Alto, Calif., 1994; PhD, Pacific Grad. Sch. Psychology, 1995. Lic. psychologist Ohio. Asst. Palo Alto VA Med. Ctr., 1992—93; clinic mgr. Pacific Grad. Sch. Psychology, Palo Alto, 1993—94; psychology intern U. Wyo., Laramie, 1994—95; psychology resident Scioto Paint Valley Mental Health Ctr., Washington, Ohio, 1996—98; cons. psychologist Bur. of Disability Determination, Columbus, 1999—2002; psychologist Comprehensive Svcs., Inc., Columbus, 1999—2002; specialist, Ctr. for Sexual Assault/Abuse Recovery and Edn. coord. U. Fla., Gainesville, 2002—. Mem. subcom. on alcohol policy U. Fla., Gainesville, 2002—, judge law sch. competition, 1995; instr. Peace Officer Tng. Coun., Fayette County, Ohio, 1997. Author: (novels) Face of an Angel, 2001 (Top 10 in category, 2002), Beside the Water, 2002, (screenplays) Mute Swan, 2002. Judge Knox County Teen Pageant, Mt. Vernon, Ohio, 2000; spkr. Knox County Big Bros./Big Sisters, Mt. Vernon, 2000—01. Fellow Psychology fellow, Denison U., 1989—90; grantee Sci. Rsch. grantee, 1989. Mem.: Nat. Assn. Cognitive Behavioral Therapists, Am. Coll. Forensic Examiners. Avocations: walking, writing, tennis, rollerblading. Home: 4830 NW 43d St Apt H-123 Gainesville FL 32606 Office: SHCC/Univ of Florida PO Box 117500 Gainesville OH 32611-7500

BLUE, CHINA, artist; b. Berkeley, Calif., May 24, 1962; d. Gordon Patrick Wong and Mary Joyce Wartenweiler. BFA, Calif. Coll. Arts & Crafts, 1992; MFA, CUNY, 1994. Guest panelist Yale U., 1997. Exhbns. include Koa Gallery, Honolulu, 1995, Reed Coll., Portland, Oreg., 1995, Art in General, N.Y.C., 1995, Bronx Mus., 1995, Side St. Project, Santa Monica, Calif., 1995, Asian Am. Writers Workshop, N.Y.C., 1996, Bronx Mus. Arts, 1996, Williamsburg Art & Hist. Soc., Bklyn., 1997, Galapagos, Bklyn., N.Y., 1999, New Mus. Contemporary Art, N.Y.C., 1999, TIAA CREF, N.Y.C., 1999, 107 Rivington, N.Y.C., 1999, Refusalon, San Francisco, 1999, Kuenstlerhausen Bremen, Bassum Germany, 1999, Greikist Kulturcentrum, Stockholm, 1999, Sculpture Ctr., N.Y.C., 1999, Snug Harbor Cultural Ctr., S.I., N.Y., 2000, Bklyn. Mus., 2000, Gallery Benjamin, Sweden, 2000, Lance Fung Gallery, N.Y.C., 2000, State of Art Bklyn., 2001, Hopper House, N.Y., 2001, Queens Coll. Art Ctr., N.Y., 2002, Sonoma Mus. Visual Art, Santa Rosa, Calif., 2002, Front Room, Williamsburg, N.Y., 2002, Bronx River Mus., 2002, Dumbo Arts Ctr., Bklyn., 2002, 03, Lance Fung Gallery, N.Y.C., 2003, Interface, France, 2004, Atheneum, France, 2004. Bd. dirs. Godzilla, N.Y.C., 1995-96; head symposium Queens (N.Y.) Mus., 1996, Coll. Arts Assn., N.Y.C., 1997.

BLUE, JAMES MONROE, lawyer; b. St. Petersburg, Fla., Oct. 5, 1941; s. James Monroe and Mildred (Hobbs) B.; m. Barbara Ann Alderson, Jan. 3, 1981; children: Tammy Marlene, Kelli Christine, Shannon Kathlene. BA, Fla. State U., 1963; JD with honors, Stetson Coll., 1967. Bar: Fla. 1967, U.S. Dist. Ct. (mid. dist.) Fla. 1968, U.S. Ct. Appeals (11th cir.) 1968, U.S. Supreme Ct. 1978. Assoc. Carlton, Fields, Ward, Emmanuel, Smith & Cuttler, Tampa, Fla., 1967-69; ptnr. Alley, Alley & Blue, Miami, Fla., 1969-75, Smith, Young & Blue, Tallahassee, 1975-79, Allen, Norton & Blue, Tampa, 1979—. Mem. ABA, Fla. Bar Assn., Fla. Bar (chmn. labor law sect. 1978-79, Fla. C. of C. (human resources com. 1989—), Tampa C. of C. (com. of 100, 1987—). Republican. Presbyterian. Avocations: golf, boating, reading. Office: 324 S Hyde Park Ave Ste 350 Tampa FL 33606-4110 E-mail: jmb@anblaw.com.

BLUE, J(OHN) RONALD, evangelical mission executive; b. Milw., Sept. 4, 1935; s. Earl R. and Wretha J. (Teater) B.; m. Elizabeth F. Wood, Sept. 7, 1962; children: Elisa, Laurie, David. BA, U. Nebr., 1957; cert. contact lens fitter, Ohio State U., 1960; ThM, Dallas Theol. Sem., 1965; PhD, U. Tex., Arlington, 1983. Contact lens fitter Ohio State U., Columbus, 1960-61; field dir. C.Am. Mission, Guatemala, Salvador, Guatemala, Salvador and Spain, 1965-75; dept. chmn. Dallas Theol. Sem., 1975-92; pres. CAM Internat., Dallas, 1992-2000; coord. Spanish-lang. Doctor Minsitries program Dallas Theol. Seminary, 2001—. Mem. adv. bd. Proclamation, Inc., Dallas, 1992—, Art Yohner Mission Ministries Info., Bradenton, Fla., 1998—, Christar, Reading, Pa., 1999—; mem. edit. bd. Evang. Missions Quar. Contbg. author: Walvoord: A Tribute, 1982, Bible Knowledge Commentary, 1983, 85, Essays in Honor of J.D. Pentecost, 1986, Devotions for Kindred Spirits, 1995, Basic Theology Applied, 1996; author: Evangelism and Missions, 2001. Lt. USN, 1957-59. Mem. Pi Epsilon Pi, Theta Xi. Republican. Avocation: travel. Home: 3504 Halifax Dr Arlington TX 76013-1909 Office: Dallas Theol Seminary 3909 Swiss Ave Dallas TX 75204

BLUE, JOSEPH EDWARD, physicist; b. Quitman, Miss., Sept. 29, 1936; s. Edward Lee and Allie Belle (Corley) B.; m. Neva Rosetta Deal, Apr. 14, 1962; children: Tracy Marie, Gina Lynn. BS in Physics, Miss. State U., 1961; MS in Engring. Sci., Fla. State U., 1966; PhD in Mech. Engring., U. Tex., 1971. Physicist Navy Mine Def. Lab., Panama City, Fla., 1961-68; rsch. sci. engr. U. Tex., Austin, 1968-71; rsch. physicist Naval Rsch. Lab., Orlando, Fla., 1971-73, Meas br. head, 1973-81, supt., 1981-96; pres. Leviathan Legacy Inc., Orlando, Fla., 1996—. Author: (with others) Benchmark Papers in U/W Acoust, 1975; contbr. articles to Jour. Acoustical Soc. Am. Fellow Acoustical Soc. Am. Democrat. Methodist. Achievements include patents for low frequency acoustic source, color sonar display, time internal to pulse height converter, device for alerting manatees to danger from boats, method of alerting sea cows of the danger of approaching motor vessels; research in resonant scattering, parametric depth sounder using water's nonlinearity, substantial sound pressure from tow-powered sources, and manatee hearing, collision of whales and ships. Office: Leviathan Legacy Inc 3313 Northglen Dr Orlando FL 32806-6338 E-mail: joeblue@earthlink.net.

BLUE, MONTE LYNN, college president; b. Ft. Worth, Feb. 25, 1945; s. Bert Leonard and Mary Lee (Cooper) B.; m. Sheryl Doris O'Connor, July 1, 1966; children: Michelle Denea, Laura Lynn. BA, North Tex. State U., 1967, MA, 1972; EdD, U. Houston, 1979. Illustrator Gen. Dynamics, Ft. Worth, 1967-71; instr. advt. art, Cen. Campus San Jacinto Jr. Coll., Pasadena, Tex., 1971-74, dist. dir., instr. media, 1975-79, dean student services, South Campus, 1979-81, dean student services, Cen. Campus, 1981-83, pres., 1983—. Bd. dirs. Deer Park Ednl. Found., 1996—; bd. dirs. Southeast Econ. Devel. Coun., 1995—, chmn. bd., 1997-98; moderator Bd. of Southmore Med. Ctr.; consumer credit counselor svc. bd. dirs., 1999-2000; spkr. numerous presentations to various comty., civic and profl. groups. Contbr. articles to profl. jours.; speaker numerous presentations to various community, civic and profl. groups. Vice chmn. bd. dirs. San Jacinto YMCA, Pasadena, 1986-87, chmn., 1987-88. Named Outstanding Alumni, Ft. Worth Ind. Sch. Dist., 1984. Mem.: Tex. Pub. Cmty. Jr. Coll. Assn., Assn. Tex. Colls. and Univs., Nat. Orgn. on Legal Problems in Edn., Am. Assn. Higher Edn., Am. Assn. Cmty. Jr. Colls., LaPorte/Bayshore C. of C. (bd. dirs. 1987—89, pres. 1989), Rotary (local pres. 1986—87), Phi Theta Kappa (hon. mem. Mu Omicron Chpt., Hall of Honor 1985). Republican. Baptist. Avocation: painting. Office: San Jacinto Coll Cen 8060 Spencer Hwy Pasadena TX 77501-2007

BLUE, MYRNA KAY, retired music educator; b. Joliet, Ill., Feb. 18, 1937; d. John Quincy and Katherine Margaret Adams; m. Edward Alfred Blue, Aug. 12, 1961; children: Kimberly Kay Blue, Brian Lance Blue. B in Music Edn., St. Louis Inst. of Music, 1959. Vocal music tchr. Lansdowne Jr. H.S., East St. Louis, 1959-61, Longfellow Elem. Sch., East St. Louis, 1961-67; gen. music and band choir, grades 1-8 Holy Childhood of Jesus, Mascoutah, Ill., 1977-85; conductor Belleville Philharm. Youth Orch., 1983-85; string orch. tchr. Shaw Visual and Performing Arts Ctr., St. Louis Pub. Schs., St. Louis, 1986-99; asst. dir. string orch. camp South East Mo. State, Cape Girardeau, 1983-84; fed. aviation adminstrn. FAA Test Ctr., Cahokia, Ill., 1988-93. Adj. faculty So. Ill. U., 1968. Cellist Belleville (Ill.) Phil. Orch., 1966—; with St. Louis Pub. Sch. Music Faculty Wind Ensemble, 1986-2000. Bd. dirs. Belleville Philharm., 1983-85; group leader St. Louis Christmas Carol Assn., 1987-2000; organizer many children's, music groups, Ill., Mo.; leader Daisy scout Troop 836, Girl Scouts USA, 1998-99. Mem. Mo. Music Educators Assn. (orch. v.p. 1988-89), Mo. State Tchrs. Assn. (resolutions com.), Nat. Sch. Orch. Assn., Women Band Dirs. Internat. Avocations: computers, writing, handwork, charcoals, pastels. Home: 8 Tulip Dr New Baden IL 62265-0047

BLUE, ROSE, writer, educator; b. N.Y.C., 1931; d. Irving and Frieda (Rosenberg) Bluestone. BA, Bklyn. Coll., 1953; postgrad., Bank St. Coll. Edn., 1967. Tchr. N.Y.C. Pub. Schs., 1967—. Writing cons. Bklyn. Coll. Sch. Edn., 1981-83. Author: A Quiet Place, 1969, Black, Black Beautiful Black, 1969, How Many Blocks Is The World, 1970, Bed-Stuy Beat, 1970, I Am Here (Yo Estoy Aqui), 1971, A Month of Sundays, 1972, Grandma Didn't Wave Back, 1972 (teleplay 1983), Nikki 108, 1973, We are Chicano, 1973, The Preacher's Kid, 1975, Seven Years from Home, 1976, The Yo Yo Kid, 1976, The Thirteenth Year, 1977, Cold Rain on the Water, 1979, My Mother The Witch, 1981 (teleplay 1984), Everybody's Evy, 1985, Heart to Heart, 1986, Goodbye Forever Tree, 1987, The Secret Papers of Camp Get Around, 1988, Barbara Bush First Lady, 1990, Colin Powell Straight to the Top, 1991, Barbara Jordan-Politician, 1992, defending Our Country, 1993, Working Together Against Hate Groups, 1993, People of Peace, 1994, The White House Kids, 1995, whoopi Goldberg Entertainer, 1995, Bring Me A Memory, 1996, Good Yontif, 1997, Who's That In the White House?, 1998, Staying Out of Trouble in a Troubled Family, 1998, Madeline Albright U.S. Secretary of State, 1999, You're the Boss: Positive Attitude and Work Ethic, 1999, Who Lived In The House Divided, 2000, Chris Rock, 2001, Benjamin Banneker--Mathematician and Stargazer, 2001, Monica Seles, 2002; lyricist: Drama of Love, 1964, Let's Face It, 1961, Give Me a Break, 1962, My Heartstrings Keep Me Tied To You, 1963, Homecoming Party, 1966; contbg. editor: Tchr. mag., Day Care mag. Mem. PEN, Authors Guild Am., Authors League Am., Mensa, Profl. Womens Caucus, Broadcast Music, Inc. Home and Office: 1320 51st St Brooklyn NY 11219-3552

BLUESTEIN, BARBARA ANN, librarian; b. Pitts., Feb. 3, 1952; d. Griffith and Mary Jane (Thompson) Ray; m. Michael Richard Bluestein, Aug. 26, 1973; children: Matthew Alan, Jeremy Micah. BS in Edn., Miami U., Oxford, Ohio, 1974; MEd, Xavier U., 1977. Permanent tchg. cert. ednl. media grades 7-12, Ohio. Libr. Princeton H.S., Cin., 1974-89, head libr., 1989—. Mem. adv. bd. InfOhio Oh! Teach, 2000-01. Den leader pack 72 Boy Scouts Am., Cin., 1990-95, merit badge counselor, 1992—2003, sch. night coord., 1994-97. Named Key Leader Boy Scouts Am.-Dan Beard Coun., Cin., 1994; recipient Meritorious Svc. award Boy Scouts Am.-Dan Beard Coun., Cin., 1995, Dist. Award of Merit, 1997; Jennings scholar, 1986-87. Mem. DAR, Cin. Area Sch. Librs. Assn., Reviewers Young Adult Lit. (v.p. 1997-99, pres. 1999-2001). Avocations: reading, swimming, waterskiing. Home: 3249 Braewood Dr Cincinnati OH 45241-3184 Office: Princeton HS 11080 Chester Rd Cincinnati OH 45246-3802

BLUESTEIN, EDWIN A., JR., lawyer; b. Hearne, Tex., Oct. 16, 1930; s. Edwin A. and Frances Grace (Ely) B.; m. Marsha Kay Meredith, Dec. 21, 1957; children: Boyd, Leslie. BBA, U. Tex., 1952, JD, 1958. Bar: Tex. 1957, U.S. Ct. Appeals (5th cir.) 1960, U.S. Dist. Ct. (so. dist.)Tex. 1959, U.S. Dist. Ct. (ea. dist.)Tex. 1965, U.S. Supreme Ct. 1967, U.S. Ct. Appeals (11th cir.) 1982. Law clk. U.S. Dist. Ct., Houston, 1958-59; assoc. Fulbright & Jaworski, Houston, 1959-65, participating atty., 1965-71, ptnr., 1971-97, head admiralty dept., 1984-93, sr. ptnr., 1990-97, of counsel, 1998—. Mem. permanent adv. bd. Tulane Admiralty Law Inst., New Orleans, 1983-2001; mem. planning com. Houston Marine Ins. Seminar, 1970-76; lectr. profl. seminars Assoc. editor:

American Maritime Cases; contbr. articles to profl. jours. Mem. Tex. Coastal Mgmt. Adv. Com., Austin, 1975-78; bd. dirs. Barbour's Cut Seafarers Ctr., 1992—, Houston Internat. Seafarers Ctr., 1993—; chair Morgan's Point Beach Preservation Restoration Assn., 2001-. Served with U.S. Army, 1952-54. Recipient Yachtsman of Yr. award Houston Yacht Club, 1978; Eagle Scout, Boy Scouts Am., 1944. Mem. Tex. Bar Found., Maritime Law Assn. U.S. (mem. exec. com. 1980-83), Houston Maritime Arbitrators Assn. (sec.-treas. 1999—), Houston Mariners Club (pres. 1970), Southeastern Admiralty Law Inst. (dir. 1983-85, Houston C. of C. (chmn. ports and waterways com. 1978-79), Propeller Club U.S., Theta Xi (chpt. pres. 1952). Clubs: Houston Yacht (commodore 1979-80). Methodist. Home: 603 Bayridge Rd La Porte TX 77571-3512 Office: Fulbright & Jaworski 1301 Mckinney St Houston TX 77010-3031

BLUESTEIN, HOWARD BRUCE, meteorology educator; b. Chelsea, Mass., Oct. 8, 1948; BSEE, MIT, 1971, MSEE, MS in Meteorology, MIT, 1972, PhD in Meteorology, 1976. Asst. prof. meteorology U. Okla., Norman, 1979-83, assoc. prof., 1983-90, prof., 1990—, Samuel Roberts Noble Presdl. prof. meteorology, 2000—. Vis. asst. prof. meteorology U. Okla., Norman, 1976-79. Author: Synoptic-Dynamic Meteorology in Midlatitudes, Vol. I, 1992, Vol. II, 1993, Tornado Alley, 1999. Named Okla. Prof. of Yr., Coun. Advancement and Support of Edn., 1989. Fellow Am. Meteorol. Soc. (chair severe local storms com 1993-95, recipient Louis J. Battan Author's award, 2001). Avocations: photography, folkdancing. Office: U Okla Sch Meteorology 100 E Boyd St Rm 1310 Norman OK 73019-1015 E-mail: hblue@ou.edu.

BLUESTEIN, PAUL HAROLD, management engineer; b. Cin., June 14, 1923; s. Norman and Eunice D. (Schullman) B.; m. Joan Ruth Straus, May 17, 1943; children: Alice Sue Bluestein Greenbaum, Judith Ann. BS, B.Engring. in Mgmt. Engring., Carnegie Inst. Tech., 1946; MBA, Xavier U., 1973, MA in Humanities, 1992. Registered profl. engr., Ohio. Time study engr. Lodge & Shipley Co., 1946-47; adminstrv. engr. Randall Co., 1947-52; partner Paul H. Bluestein & Co. (mgmt. cons.), 1952—, Seinsheimer-Bluestein Mgmt. Services, 1964-70; gen. mgr. Baker Refrigeration Co., 1953-56; pres., dir. Tabor Mfg. Co., 1953-54, Bluejay Corp., 1954—, Blatt & Ludwig Corp., 1954-57, Jason Industries, Inc., 1954-57, Hamilton-York Corp., 1954-57, Earle Hardware Mfg. Co., 1955-57, Hermas Machine Co., 1956—, Panel Machine Co., Ermet Products Corp., 1957-86, Tyco Labs., Inc., 1968-69, All-Tech Industries, 1968. Gen. mgr. Hafleigh & Co., 1959-60; sr. v.p., gen. mgr. McCauley Ind. Corp., 1959-60; gen. mgr. Am. Art Works div. Rapid-Am. Corp., 1960-63; sec.-treas., dir. Liberty Baking Co., 1964-65; pres. Duguesne Baking Co., 1964-65, Goddard Bakers, Inc., 1964-65; pub. Merger and Acquisition Digest, 1962-69; partner Companhia Engenheiros Indsl. Bluestein Do Brasil, 1970-84; v.p., gen. mgr. Famco Machine div. Worden-Allen Co., 1974-75; exec. v.p., gen. mgr. Peck, Stow & Wilcox Co., Inc., 1976-77, mem. Joint Engring. Mgmt. Conf. Com., 1971-78 Com. mem. Cin. Art Mus. With AUS, 1943-46. Mem. ASME, Internat. Inst. Indsl. Engrs., Am. Soc. Engring. Mgmt., C.I.O.S.-World Council Mgmt. (dir., 1982-87). Home and Office: 3420 Section Rd Amberley Village Cincinnati OH 45237

BLUESTEIN, SANFURD G. radiologist; b. Paterson, N.J., Jan. 2, 1921; s. Abram Isaac and Esther (Altholz) Bluestein; m. Iris Weiner, June 12, 1948 (dec. Dec. 22, 1969); children: Abbey Reisman, Joel; m. Fela Weissman, Sept. 3, 1974 (dec. Dec. 19, 1998). BA, Lafayette Coll., 1942; MD, Yale U., 1946. Intern Mt. Sinai Hosp., N.Y.C., 1946-47, resident in radiology, 1950-52, fellow, 1950-51; resident and instr. in pathology Yale Med. Sch., 1947-48. Bd dirs. Pharmac Corp., Allentown, Pa.; bd dirs. emeritus Chilton Hosp, Pompton Plains, NJ, Barnert Hosp, Paterson, NJ. Bd. dirs. N.Y.C. Opera. Mem. Am. Coll. Radiology, AMA, Am. Soc. Nuclear Medicine. Office: 309 Upper Mountain Ave Upper Montclair NJ 07043 Office Fax: 973-746-3546.

BLUESTEIN, VENUS WELLER, retired psychologist, educator; b. Milw., July 16, 1933; d. Richard T. and Hazel (Beard) Weller; m. Marvin Bluestein, Mar. 7, 1954. BS, U. Cin., 1956, MEd, 1959, EdD, 1966. Diplomate Am. Bd. Profl. Psychology. Psychologist-in-tng. Longview State Hosp., Cin., 1956-58; sch. psychologist Cin. Pub. Schs., 1958-65; asst. prof. psychology U. Cin., 1965-70, assoc. prof., 1970-79, prof., 1979-93, prof. emerita, 1993—, dir. sch. psychology program, 1965-70, co-dir. sch. psychology program, 1970-75, dir. undergrad. studies, 1976-91, dir. undergrad. advising, 1991-93. Cons. child psychologist. Sec., U.S. exec. com. rsch. Children's Internat. Summer Villages, 1964-68; chmn. Ohio Interuniv. Coun. Sch. Psychology, 1967-68. Editor Ohio Psychologist, 1961-68, co-editor, 1972-79; contbr. articles to profl. publs. Vol. Hmilton County Parks, 1982—, vol. naturalist, 1995—; vol. educator Cin. Zoo, 1983—. Recipient George B. Barbour award, 1985, 20 Yrs. of Svc. award Cin. Zoo, 2002, Hamilton County Parks Dist., 2002. Mem. AAUP, APA, Nat. Assn. School Psychologists, Ohio Psychol. Assn. (citation 1972, Disting. Svc. award 1968), Southwestern Ohio Sch. Psychol. Assn., Cin. Psychol. Assn. (sec. 1961-62), Sch. Psychologists Ohio, Forum for Death Edn. and Counseling, Kappa Delta Pi, Sigma Delta Pi, Psi Chi (award for outstanding mentor 1985, award for outstanding contbns. to undergrad. psychology students 1994). Avocations: horseback riding, wildlife photography. Office: U Cin Dept Psychology Ml 376 Cincinnati OH 45221-0001

BLUESTONE, ANDREW LAVOOTT, lawyer; b. N.Y.C., Feb. 16, 1951; s. Henry Robert and Joan (Lavoott) B.; m. Janet Francesca Whelehan, May 1987; 1 child, Gabrielle. BA, Alfred U., 1973; MA, SUNY, Oswego, 1975; JD, Syracuse U., 1978. Bar: N.Y. 1979, U.S. Dist. Ct. (so. and ea. dists.) N.Y. 1979. Sr. trial asst. dist. atty. Kings County Dist. Atty., Bklyn., 1978-84; sr. assoc. Davis & Hoffman, N.Y.C., 1984-86, Donald Ayers, N.Y.C., 1986, Alexander, Ash, Schwartz & Cohen, N.Y.C., 1986-88, Trolman & Glaser, N.Y.C., 1988-89; pvt. practice, N.Y.C., 1989—. Arbitrator Small Claims Civil Ct. City of N.Y.; lectr. Practice Law Inst., N.Y. State Trial Lawyers Assn. Bd. dirs. Scandia Symphony, N.Y.C., St. Luke's AME Ch., N.Y.C. Mem. ABA, N.Y.C. Trial Lawyers Assn., Def. Assn. N.Y., Assn. Trial Lawyers Am. (lectr.), N.Y. State Trial Lawyers Assn., Bklyn. Bar Assn. Office: 233 Broadway Fl 51 New York NY 10279-5199

BLUESTONE, BARRY ALAN, economics educator; b. Bklyn., Dec. 27, 1944; s. Irving Julius and Zelda B.; m. Mary Ellen Colten, Jun 14, 1987; 1 child, Joshua. BA in Econs., U. Mich., 1966, MA in Econs., 1968, PhD in Econs., 1974. Prof. econs. Boston Coll., Chestnut Hill, Mass., 1971-86; dir. pub. policy PhD program U. Mass., Boston, 1987-98; Russell B. and Andrée B. Stearns trustee/prof. polit. economy Northeastern U., Boston, 1999—, also founding dir. Ctr. for Urban and Regional Policy. Dir. Nommos Cons. Group, Salem, Mass., 1990—. Author: (books) The Deindustrialization of America, 1982, The Great U-Turn, 1988, Negotiating the Future, 1992, Growing Prosperity, 2000, The Boston Renaissance: Race, Space, and Economic Change in an American Metropolis, 2000. Sr. advisor House Dem. leader Washington, 1995; founding dir. Econ. Policy Inst., Washington, 1985—. Recipient Outstanding Merit award U. Mass., Boston, 1995. Mem. Gorbachev Found. (sr. fellow), Internat. Ctr. for Social Studies (scientific com. 1997—), Urban Outreach Coun./Northeastern U. (com. chair 1999—). Democrat. Avocations: bicycle riding, tennis. E-mail: b.bluestone@neu.edu.

BLUFORD, GUION STEWART, JR., engineering company executive; b. Phila., Nov. 22, 1942; s. Guion Stewart and Harriet Lolita (Brice) B.; m. Linda M. Tull, Apr. 7, 1964; children: Guion Stewart, James Trevor. BS in Aerospace Engring., Pa. State U., 1964; grad., Squadron Officers Sch., 1971; MS in Aerospace Engring., Air Force Inst. Tech., 1974, PhD in Aerospace Engring., 1978; D.Sc. hon., Fla. A&M U., 1983; MBA, U. Houston, 1987; DSc (hon.), Tex. So. U., Va. State U., Morgan State U., Stevens Inst. Tech., Tuskegee U., Bowie (Md.) State Coll., Thomas Jefferson U., Chgo. State U., Georgian Ct. Coll., Drexel U., Kent State U., Ctrl State U. Commd. 2d lt. U.S. Air Force, 1965, advanced through grades to col., 1993, F-4C fighter pilot 12 Tactical Fighter Wing, 1966-67, T-38 instr. pilot 3630 Flying Tng. Wing Sheppard AFB, Wichita Falls, Tex., 1967-72; chief aerodynamics and airframe br. Air Force Flight Dynamics Lab., Wright-Patterson AFB, Dayton, Ohio, 1975-78; NASA astronaut Johnson Space Ctr., Houston, 1978-93; ret., 1993; v.p., gen. mgr. div. engring. svcs. NYMA Inc., Greenbelt, Md., 1993-97; v.p., gen. mgr. aerospace sector Fed. Data Corp., Bethesda, Md., 1997—2000; v.p. microgravity R&D ops. Northrup Grumman Info. Tech., Herndon, Va., 2000—02; pres. The Aerospace Tech. Group, 2002—. Decorated Air medal with 9 oak leaf clusters, Def. Superior Svc. medal, Legion of Merit; named Black Engr. of Yr., 1991; named to Internat. Space Hall of Fame, 1997; recipient Mervin E. Gross award Air Force Inst. Tech., 1974, Disting. Nat. Scientist award Nat. Soc. Black Engrs., 1979, Group Achievement award NASA, 1980, Group Achievement award, NASA, 1980, 1981, 1989, Nat. Intelligence medal of achievement, 1993, Space Flight medal, 1983, 1985, 1991, Def. Meritorious Svc. medal, 1989, 1992, 1993, Space Flight medal, 1992, Exceptional Svc. medal, 1992, Disting. Svc. medal, 1994, Disting. Alumni award, Pa. State U. Alumni Assn., 1983, 1985, 1985, 1991, 1992. Fellow: AIAA (bd. dirs.); mem.: U.S. Space Found. (bd. dirs.), Aerospace Corp. (trustee), Nat. Rsch. Coun. Aeronautics and Space Engring. Bd., Tau Beta Pi. Christian Scientist. Office: The Aerospace Tech Group PO Box 549 North Olmsted OH 44070-0549 E-mail: gsbluford@adelphia.net.

BLUH, BONNIE, writer, playwright, performer; b. N.Y.C., Mar. 29; d. Morris and Mary (Steinberg) B.; children: Craig, Kenn, Brian. Cons. Lincoln Repertory Theater, N.Y.C., 1962; dir. improvisational theater East Brunswick (N.J.) Jr. H.S., 1965; creative drama tchr., Phila., 1968-71; Emmy judge, 1989—; mentor Young Writers Inst., West Hartford, Conn., 1995—; lectr. in field. Author: Woman to Woman, 1974, Banana, 1976, The Old Speak Out, 1979, The Eleanor Roosevelt Girls, 1999, (plays) N, My Name is Nicki, 1962, Light a Candle for Charlie, 1964, Lifetime Policy, 1975, The Day God Died, 1992; co editor: Broadway's Fabulous Fifties, 2002; actor: Many Wonder, 1989, Jesus Christ is Alive, 1990, One Woman Show, 1991, and assorted TV roles. Recipient Best Actor award Festival Short Films, N.Y., 1990. Mem. AFTRA, Authors Guild, New Dramatists (alumna exec. com.), Dramatists Guild. Jewish. Home: 55 Bethune St New York NY 10014-2010 E-mail: bbluh@aol.com.

BLUHER, GREGORY, computer scientist, mathematician; b. Odessa, Ukraine, May 9, 1960; arrived in U.S., 1979; s. Froim and Alla (Shvetz) Blyukher; m. Antonia Rose Wilson, May 25, 1986; children: Andrew Emmanuel, Julia Elizabeth, Sarah Elena. MA in Math. with honors, Johns Hopkins U., 1983; PhD in Math., Princeton U., 1988; MS in Computer Sci., UCLA, 1992. Cert. software devel. profl. Asst. prof. The Coll. of N.J., Trenton, 1987-88, Whittier (Calif.) Coll., 1988-89; programmer The Software Toolworks, L.A., 1989-90; rschr. computer sci. dept. UCLA, 1990-92; staff programmer IBM, San Jose, 1992-93; project leader ORACLE, Redwood City, Calif., 1993-95; computer specialist Social Security Adminstrn., Balt., 1995-96; sr. computer scientist Dept. of Def., Washington, 1996-2001; IT Apps. team leader EPA, Washington, 2001—. Translator: Introduction to the Classical Theory of Abelian Functions, 1990. Interviewer alumni coun. Johns Hopkins U., Balt., 1985-89. IBM scholar, 1983. Mem. IEEE-Computer Soc., Assn. Computing Machinery, Project Mgmt. Inst., Phi Beta Kappa. Home: PO Box 252 Simpsonville MD 21150-0252 E-mail: gbluher@3dinet.com.

BLUHM, BARBARA JEAN, communications agency executive; b. Chgo., Mar. 5, 1925; d. Maurice L. and Clara (Miller) B. Student Coll. William and Mary, 1943-45; BS, U. Wis., 1947. Exec. tng. program Carson Pirie Scott & Co., Chgo., 1947-52; home economist Lever Bros. Co., Chgo., 1952-57; field rep. The Merchandising Group, Chgo., 1957-62, v.p. N.Y.C., 1962-82, pres., 1982-87, chmn., 1987-90. Publicity chmn. James Lenox House Assn., N.Y.C., 1980—90; vol. Venice Hosp., Venice Little Theatre; mem. Coll. Club of Venice, Venice Art League, Venice Symphony. Mem. Venice Yacht Club, Venice Golf and Country Club, Venice Hist. Preservation League. Republican. Presbyterian. Home: 1470 Colony Pl Venice FL 34292-1550 E-mail: bbluhm@iopener.net.

BLUHM, WILLIAM THEODORE, political scientist, educator; b. Newark, Oct. 13, 1923; s. Frederick Theodore and Charlotte Catherine (Walz) B.; m. Eleanor Elizabeth Kearns, Apr. 22, 1950; children: Catherine Elizabeth, Susanna Marie, Andrew Edward Frederick. BA, Brown U., 1948; MA, Tufts U., 1949; PhD, U. Chgo., 1957. Instr. polit. sci. U. Rochester, 1952-53, asst. prof., 1957-63, assoc. prof., 1963-67, prof., 1967-92, prof. emeritus, 1993—; instr. polit. sci. Brown U., 1953-57. Cons. C.H. Beck Verlag, Munich, 1966-70 Author: Theories of the Political System, 1965, Building an Austrian Nation: The Political Integration of a Western State, 1973, Ideologies and Attitudes, 1974, Force or Freedom?: The Paradox in Modern Political Thought, 1984; co-author: The World of the Policy Analyst, 1990, 3d edit. 2002; editor: The Paradigm Problem in Political Science, 1982; contbr. articles profl. jours. Served with Signal Corps AUS, 1943-46. Decorated Bronze Star Medal; U. Rochester research grantee, 1963-64, 68-69; Fulbright research fellow to Austria, 1965-66; NSF summer grantee, 1967, 68; U. Rochester Bridging fellow, 1980-81; Nat. Endowment for Humanities grantee, 1976 Mem. Am. Polit. Sci. Assn., Sigma Nu. Democrat. Roman Catholic. Office: U Rochester Dept Polit Sci Rochester NY 14627

BLUITT, KAREN, information technology executive; b. N.Y.C., Oct. 25, 1957; d. James Bertrand and Beatrice (Kaufman) B.; m. Kenneth Mark Curry, Nov. 24, 1979 (div. Dec. 1991). BS, Fordham U., 1979; MBA, Calif. State Poly. U., 1982; postgrad., George Mason U., 1994-98; PhD, Kennedy Western U., 2000. Software engr. Hughes Aircraft Co., Fullerton, Calif., 1979-81; microprocessor engr. Beckman Instruments Co., Fullerton, 1981-82, Singer Co., Glendale, Calif., 1982-83; sr. software engr. Sanders Assoc., Nashua, N.H., 1983-85; software project mgr. GTE Corp., Billerica, Mass., 1985-86; sr. software engr. Wang Labs., Lowell, Mass., 1986-87; project task leader Vanguard Rsch., Lexington, Mass., 1987-88; program mgr. Applied Rsch. & Engring., Bedford, Mass., 1989-91, Sparta, McLean, Va., 1992-93; prin. software engr. Sci. Applications Internat., Arlington, Va., 1993-94; tech. mgr. CACI, Arlington, 1994, Booz-Allen & Hamilton, Vienna, Va., 1995, MRJ Tech. Solutions, Inc., Fairfax, Va., 1996-97, Softek Systems, Inc., Fairfax, 1998—2001; pres. QSCI, Ashburn, Va., 2001—. 1st lt. U.S. Army, 1979-88. Scholar Gov. N.Y. Scholarship Com., 1975-79, Beta Gamma Sigma, 1978—. Mem. IEEE, AAUW, Am. Women in Sci., Am. Brokers Network, Assn. Computing Machinery, Soc. Women Engrs., Wash. Soc. of Engrs.

BLUM, ARTHUR, social work educator; b. Cleve., May 25, 1926; s. Rebecca (Pivowar) Blum; m. Lenore Sharrie Secord, Dec. 26, 1954; children: Alex, Joel. AB, Western Res. U., 1950, MS in Social Adminstrn., 1952, DSW, 1960. Group worker Cleve. Jewish Community Ctr., 1952, Cleve. Child Guidance Ctr., 1954-58; project dir. Case Western Res. U., Cleve., 1958-60, prof. social work, 1960—, Grace Longwell Coyle chair, 1987—; prof. Smith Coll., Northampton, Mass., 1961-63. Cons. Bellefaire Regional Treatment Ctr., Cleve., 1962-85, City of East Cleve., 1967-70, Jewish Welfare Fedn., Cleve., 1968-72, Fedn. Community Planning, Cleve., 1976-78, 20 other human svcs. agys., 1960—; vis. prof. Tel Aviv U., 1971-72, 79-80. Editor: Healing Through Living, 1971, Aging and Care Giving, 1990, Innovations in Practice and Service Delivery, 1999; contbr. numerous articles to profl. jours. Sgt. U.S. Army, 1945-46, with Med. Svcs. Corp, 1952-54. Recipient Outstanding Alumnus award Case Western Res. U., 1968. Mem. AAUP, Nat. Assn. Social Workers, Coun. Social Work Edn., Assn. Group Workers. Democrat. Jewish. Avocations: camping, sailing, racquetball, gardening. Office: Case Western Res U Sch Applied Social Scis Univ Circle Cleveland OH 44106

BLUM, BARBARA DAVIS, investor; b. Hutchinson, Kans. d. Roy C. and Jo (McKinnon) Davis; children: Devin, Hunter, Ragan, Davis. BA, Fla. State U., 1960, MSW, 1961. Founder, ptnr. Mid-Suffolk Ctr. for Psychotherapy, Hauppage, L.I., N.Y., 1965-67; v.p. Restaurant Assocs. Ga., Inc., Atlanta, 1967-75; dep. adminstr. U.S. EPA, Washington, 1977-81; mem. Pres.'s Interagy. Coordinating Coun.; chair, pres., CEO Abigail Adams Nat. Bancorp and Adams Nat. Bank, Washington, 1983-98; CEO BDB Investment Partnership, 1998—. Chair U.S./Japan Environ. Agreement, 1977—81; head 1st U.S. Environ. Del. to China, 1978; chmn. Environ. Policy Inst., 1981—84; sr. advisor UN Environ. Program, 1981—84; pres. UN Univ. Peace, 1986—89; chair emeritus Ctr. for Policy Alternatives; trustee Fed. City Coun., 1988—99; nat. adv. bd. U.S. SBA, 1993—2001; chmn. D.C. Econ. Devel. Fin. Corp., 1986—2002. Del. UN Mid Decade Conf. on Women, 1980; Presdl. appointee trustee and treas. Inst. for Am. Indian Art; founder, chmn. Leadership Washington, 1989; trustee, treas. Southeastern U.; trustee, chmn. investment com. D.C. Retirement Bd.; dep. dir. Carter-Mondale U.S. Presdl. campaign, 1976; dir. Carter-Mondale Transition Team, Washington, 1976—77; panelist Clinton-Gore Econ. Conf., Little Rock and Atlanta; bd. dirs. Kaiser Health Plan of Mid Atlantic, 1989—; bd. dirs., chair exec. com. Kaiser Health Plan, Inc., 2001—, Kaiser Found. Hosp., 2001—; bd. dirs. Stimpson Ctr. Decorated comdr.'s cross Order of Merit W. Ger.; recipient Disting. Svc. award Federally Employed Women, Spl. Conservation award Nat. Wildlife Fedn., Orgn. of Yr. award Ga. Wildlife Fedn., 1974, Disting. Svc. award Americans for Indian Opportunity; named Bus. Woman of Yr. Nat. Assn. Bus. Women, Leukemia Soc., Assn. Women Contractors. Mem. Washington Women's Forum, Internat. Women's Forum, Cosmos Club. Democrat.

BLUM, BARBARA MEDDOCK, retired association executive; b. Oil City, Pa., Nov. 8, 1938; m. Stuart Hollander Blum, Sept. 21, 1963. BA in Psychology, Allegheny Coll., 1960. Psychometrist, researcher Hofstra U., Hempstead, N.Y., 1960-62; adminstrv. asst., editor The Asia Soc., N.Y.C., 1962-66, exec. asst., 1966-72, adminstrv. officer, 1972-85, dir. adminstrn., 1985-88, ret. 1988.

BLUM, BETTY ANN, footwear company executive; Student, Vanderbilt U. Various positions Zayre Dept. Store, Framingham, Mass., 1970-75; divsn. pres. Mootsie Tootsies, pres. Jones N.Y., exec. v.p. Maxwell Shoe Co., Hyde Park, Mass., 1976-88, exec. v.p., 1988—. Mem. bd. women's study group Brandeis U., 1998. Trustee Dana Farber Cancer Inst., 1998; dir. 210 Internat. Found., 1991.

BLUM, BRADLEY D. food service executive; BA, Denison U., Ohio, 1976; MA, Northwestern U., 1978. Mktg. asst. Betty Crocker General Mills, 1978, v.p. mktg. Cereal Ptnrs. Worldwide; sr. v.p. mktg. then pres. Olive Garden N.Am., 1994—96; exec. v.p., mem. bd. of dirs., vice chmn. Darden Restaurants Inc., 1997—2002; CEO Burger King, Corp., 2003—. Chmn. Economic Devel. Bd., City of Winter Park, Fla. Bd. trustees Atlantic Ctr. for Arts, Fla.; adv. bd. Sun Trust Bank. Recipient Operator of the Year, Multi-Unit Foodservice, 2000. Avocations: skiing, tennis, race car driving. Office: Burger King Corp 5505 Blue Lagoon Dr Miami FL 33126*

BLUM, GERALD HENRY, department store executive; b. San Francisco, 1926; s. Abe and Mildred (Loewenthal) B.; children: Shelley, Todd, Ryan, Derek. AB, Stanford U., 1950. Mdse. trainee Emporium, San Francisco, 1950-51; with Gottschalks Inc. (formerly E. Gottschalk & Co., Inc.), Fresno, Calif., 1951-98, v.p., 1954-63, exec. v.p., 1963-82, pres. and vice chmn., 1982-94, ret., 1995, bd. dirs. Bd. dirs. Fresno Conv. Bur., 1954—, pres., 1985-87; bd. dirs. Better Bus. Bur., Fresno, 1954-77, Blue Cross, Calif. 1972-85; chmn. C.A.R.E., Fresno County, 1957—, Eagle Scout Awards Banquet, 1993, Calif. State U. Bus. Coun., Fresno, 1997-98; mem. adv. com. Fresno County Arts Ctr., 1982-85, bd. dirs., 1958-66, v.p. 1961, 88-94; mem. Area VII Calif. Vocat. Edn. Com., 1972-75, Mayor's Bi-Racial Com., 1968-69; founding v.p. Jr. Achievement, Fresno County, 1957-63; bd. dirs. Fresno Boys Club, 1958-62, Central Calif. Employers Coun., 1956-62, treas. 1958; bd. dirs. Fresno Philharm. Orch., 1954-58, Salvation Army, Fresno, 1956-67, Youth Edn. Svc., 1956-57, Fresno County Taxpayers Assn., 1954, San Joaquin Valley Econ. Edn. Project, 1953; bd. dirs., bus. adv. coun. Fresno City Coll., 1955-57; trustee Valley Children's Hosp., 1955-57, United Crusade, Fresno, 1952-62; mem. adv. bd. Liberty Mut. Ins. Co., 1990-2001. Recipient Disting. Svc. award Fresno Jaycees, 1959; winner World's Championship Domino Tournament, 1969, 86, 88. Mem. Nat. Retail Fedn. (dir. 1978-94), Calif. Retailers Assn. (dir. 1964-94), Fresno C. of C. (dir. county, city 1955-57, Boss of Yr., Jr. C. of C. 1980), Retail Mmgt. Inst., U. Santa Clara (dir. 1986-98), Nat. Secs. Assn. (Boss of Yr. 1978), Fresno County Stanford U. Alumni Assn. (pres. 1952), Pres. Club of Calif. State U., Rotary (v.p. Fresno club 1962). Clubs: Univ. Sequoia Sunnyside, San Joaquin Country, Downtown Club (Fresno) (pres. 1978). E-mail: gblum2020@aol.com.

BLUM, GERALD MYRON, psychiatrist; b. N.Y.C., Aug. 11, 1932; s. Theodore and Anne (Kasmer) B.; m. Marilyn Greisman, June 9, 1957 (dec. Dec. 1987); children: Susan, Howard; m. Isolde Sommer, Apr. 9, 1989. BA, NYU, 1953, MD, 1957. Diplomate Am. Bd. Psychiatry and Neurology. Intern in Pediatrics Bronx Mcpl. Hosp. Ctr., 1957-58; resident in Psychiatry Bklyn. State Hosp., 1958-61; child psychiatrist Canarsie Clinic, Bklyn. Juvenile Guidance Ctr., N.Y.C., 1960-61; chief psychiatry and neurology USAF Hosp. Loring AFB, Limestone, Maine, 1961-62; clinic med. dir. Canarsie Clinic Bklyn. Psychiat. Ctr., N.Y.C., 1962-67; chief divsn. pediatric psychiatry Jewish Hosp. and Med. Ctr. Bklyn., N.Y.C., 1967-81, chief psychiat. clinic, 1976-81; med. dir. Interboro Consultation Ctr., N.Y.C., 1985-88; child psychiatrist Hudson Guild Mental Health Clinic, N.Y.C., 1988-95, N.Y. Founding Hosp., N.Y.C., 1990-99; pvt. practice N.Y.C., 1962—. Capt. USAF, 1961-62. Mem. AMA, Am. Psychiat. Assn., Am. Acad. Child and Adolescent Psychiatry, N.Y. Coun. on Child Adolescent Psychiatry, Bklyn. Psychiat. Soc., Kings County Med. Soc. (sub-com. on mental health), Phi Beta Kappa. Jewish. Avocations: antique clocks, gardening, reading, foreign travel. Office: 156 5th Ave New York NY 10010-7002

BLUM, IRVING RONALD, lawyer; b. Phila., Mar. 3, 1935; s. William and Dorothy (Gaskin) B.; m. Rochelle S. Klempner, June 17, 1956; children—Loren, Karen, Jill, Jason. BA, Wayne State U., 1956; JD, Detroit Coll. Law, 1959. Bar: Mich. 1959, U.S. Dist. Ct. (ea. dist.) Mich. 1959. Detroit. Ptnr., Akerman, Kaplan & Blum, Detroit, 1959-62, Blum, Brady & Rosenberg, Detroit, 1962-82, Blum, Kobheim, Elkin & Blum, Southfield, 1982—. Mem. Trial Lawyers Am., Mich. Trial Lawyers, 300 Club (bd. dirs.). Democrat. Jewish. Home: 132 Vintageisle Ln Palm Beach Gardens FL 33418-4603

BLUM, JACOB JOSEPH, physiologist, educator; b. Bklyn., Oct. 3, 1926; s. Paul and Anna (Brown) B.; m. Ruth Marsey, June 3, 1960; children: Mark, Douglas, Lisa, Laura. BA, NYU, 1947; MS, U. Chgo., 1950, PhD, 1952. Mem. staff Naval Med. Rsch. Inst., Bethesda, Md., 1953-56; chief biophysics sect. gerontology br. NIH, Balt., 1958-62; prof. physiology Duke U., Durham, N.C., 1962—, James B. Duke prof., 1980-97, James B. Duke prof. emeritus, 1997—. With AUS, 1945-46. Merck postdoctoral fellow, 1952, Guggenheim fellow, 1969, Fogarty sr. internat. fellow, 1992. Mem. Am. Physiol. Soc., Soc. Protozoologists (pres. 1991). Home: 2525 Perkins Rd Durham NC 27705-1018 E-mail: j.blum@cellbio.duke.edu.

BLUM, JOAN KURLEY, fundraising executive; b. Palm Beach, Fla., July 27, 1926; d. Nenad Daniel and Eva (Milos) Kurley; m. Robert C. Blum, Apr. 15, 1967 (dec. Apr. 2001); children: Christopher Alexander, Martha Jane, Louisa Joan. BA, U. Wash., 1948. Cert. fund raising exec. U.S. dir. Inst. Mediterranean Studies, Berkeley, Calif., 1962-65; devel. officer U. Calif., Berkeley, 1965-67; pres. Blum Assocs., Fund-Raising Cons., San Anselmo, Calif., 1967-92; ptnr. Philmark Australia, 1980—2001; pres. The Blums of San Francisco, 1992-2001, ret., 2001. Mem. faculty U. Calif. Extension, Inst. Fund Raising, S.W. Inst. Fund-Raising U. Tex., U. San Francisco, U.K. Vol. Movement Group, London, Australasian Inst. Fund Raising. Contbr. numerous articles to profl. jours. Recipient Golden Addy award Am. Advt. Fedn., Silver Mailbox award Direct Mail Mktg. Assn., Best Ann. Giving Time-Life award, others; decorated commdr. Sovereign Order St. Stanislas. Mem. Nat. Soc. Fund-Raising Execs. (dir.), Nat. Assn. of Hosp. Devel., Women Emerging, Rotary (San Francisco), Fund Raising Inst. (Australia), Tahoe Yacht Club. Office: 202 Evergreen Dr Kentfield CA 94904-2708

BLUM, JOHN CURTIS, agricultural economist; b. Terryville, Conn., July 5, 1915; s. John A. and Marion D. (Curtis) B.; m. Mable L. Brooks, Oct. 21, 1939; children— Joanne M. Blum Kraft, John Curtis, Nancy J. BS, U. Conn., 1937, MS, 1939; postgrad., U. Wis., 1941, Dept. Agr. Grad. Sch., 1946; student, Indsl. Coll. Armed Forces, 1965-66. With Dept. Agr., 1939-75; asst. dir. dairy div. Agrl. Marketing Service, 1960-61, dir. div., 1961-63; economist Office of Adminstr., 1963-64, asst. dept. adminstr., 1964-67, dep. adminstr., 1967-74, asso. adminstr., 1974-75; economist E.A. Jaenke & Assos., Inc., Washington, 1975-83. Violinist Fairfax County (Va.) Symphony Orch., 1957-95, bd. dirs., 1957-70, pres., 1959-61, treas., 1965-67; violinist McLean (Va.) Symphony, 1995—, Reston (Va.) Chamber Orch., 1998—; dist. dir. North Va. dist. PTA, 1961-63; treas. Va. Congress Parents and Tchrs., 1963-65, regional v.p., 1965-67, chmn. extension com. 1967-69, budget chmn., 1969-71, bd. mgrs., 1961-71. Lt. (j.g.) USNR, 1944-46, PTO. Mem. Am. Agr. Econ. Assn., Grange. Home: Apt 1310 20510 Falcons Landing Cir Sterling VA 20165-7596

BLUM, JOHN MORTON, historian, educator; b. N.Y.C., Apr. 29, 1921; s. Morton Gustave and Edna (LeVino) B.; m. Pamela Louise Zink, June 28, 1944; children: Pamela, Ann, Thomas Tyler. AB, Harvard U., 1943, MA, 1947, PhD, 1950, LLD (hon.), 1980; MA, Cambridge (Eng.) U., 1963; DHL (hon.), Trinity Coll., 1970; LLD (hon.), Colgate U., 1978. Research assoc., then asst. prof.

history, assoc. prof. M.I.T., 1948-57; prof. history Yale U., 1957-91, ret., 1991; Pitt prof. Cambridge U., 1963-64; Harmsworth prof. Oxford U., 1976-77. Author: Joe Tumulty and the Wilson Era, 1951, The Republican Roosevelt, 1954, Woodrow Wilson and the Politics of Morality, 1956, From the Morgenthau Diaries, Vol. I, 1959, Vol. II, 1965, Vol. III, 1967, Yesterday's Children, 1959, The Promise of America, 1966, Roosevelt and Morgenthau, 1970, V Was for Victory, 1976, The Progressive Presidents, 1980, Years of Discord, 1991, Liberty Justice Order, 1993; assoc. editor: (with Elting E. Morison) Letters of Theodore Roosevelt (8 vols.), 1951-54; editor: The National Experience, 1963, The Price of Vision, 1973; Public Philosopher, 1985. Trustee Buckingham Sch., 1954-56, Hotchkiss Sch., 1964-70; mem. Andover Alumni Council, 1957-60. Served from ensign to lt. USNR, 1943-46. Harvard U. fellow, 1970-79. Mem. Am. Acad. Arts and Scis., Mass. Hist. Soc., Century Assn., Phi Beta Kappa. Home: 313 St Ronan St New Haven CT 06511-2327

BLUM, JOSEPH R. secondary school educator, emergency nurse practitioner; b. Buryrus, Ohio, Aug. 12, 1949; s. Raymond A. and Alice C. Blum; m. Sandrea A. Piernik, Nov. 27, 1971; children: Amy C. Blum Schnipke, Joseph F. BS in Edn., U. Dayton, 1971; LPN, William Beaumont Army Hosp., 1972; MA in Edn., Ashland Coll., 1988. Lic. practical nurse, Ohio. Tchr. Buckeye Ctrl. Schs., New Washington, Ohio, 1973—; emergency rm. nurse St. Elizabeth Hosp., Dayton, Ohio, 1973; med. surg. nurse Willard (Ohio) Hosp., 1974; emergency rm. nurse Galion (Ohio) Cmty. Hosp., 1975—. Co-author: Dutch Town, Your Days in History, 1974. Councilman New Washington Village Coun., 1975—; mem. ctrl. com. Dem. Party, Bucyrus, Ohio, 1982—. With U.S. Army, 1971—77. Named Ohio Educator of Yr., Ohio Am. Legion, 1996; recipient Individual Achievement award, Ohio Assn. Hist. Socs., 1990, Outstanding Tchr. Am. History award, Ohio DAR, 1994. Mem.: KC, New Washington Hist. Soc. (pres.), Am. Legion. Roman Catholic. Avocations: collecting antique bottles, collecting old bricks. Home: 217 N Center St New Washington OH 44854 Office: Buckeye Ctrl HS 306 Kibler St New Washington OH 44854

BLUM, JUNE, artist, curator; b. N.Y.C., Dec. 10, 1929; d. Henry Charles and Elsie Druiett; m. Maurice C. Blum (dec.). MA, Bklyn. Coll., 1959; attended, Bklyn. Mus. Art Sch., Pratt Graphic Art Ctr., New Sch. Social Rsch. Curator contemporary art Suffolk Mus., Stony Brook, N.Y., 1971-75; curator at large Cocoa Beach, 1975—, dir. Women for Art, Cocoa Beach, Fla., 1976—; dir. mus. Individual Mus., Cocoa Beach, Fla., 1980—. One-person shows include Bronx Mus., 1975, NN Gallery, Seattle, 1977, Nassau County Mus. Fine Arts, Roslyn, N.Y., 1980, Brevard C.C., Melbourne, Fla., Cocoa, Fla., 1984, King Performing Art Ctr. Gallery, Melbourne, 1990, SOHO 20 Artists, N.Y.C., 1998, Mus. Art and Sci., Melbourne, 1998; exhibited in group shows including Bklyn. Mus., 1975, Queens Mus., Flushing, N.Y., 1976, Nassau County Mus. Fine Art, Bklyn., 1980, Brevard Mus., Cocoa, 1995, Mus. at Stony Brook, 1996; author: Metamorphosis of June Blum, 1976, Betty Friedan Series, 1976, Female Connection, 1978, A Woman's Space, 1980. Art chairperson, v.p. Cocoa Beach Libr., 1992—, mem. time capsule com., 1998; art chairperson Brevard Commn. Women, 1985; art chairperson holiday decorating com. City of Cocoa Beach, 2001-2002. Recipient Anne Eisner Putnam Meml. prize Nat. Acad. Nat. Assn. Women Artists, N.Y.C., 1968, honorable mention White Mountain Festival Arts, Jefferson, N.H., 1977. Mem. Womens Caucus Art, Coll. Art Assn., East Ctrl. Fla. Women Caucus Art (pres. 1980—). Home: 120 Boca Ciega Rd Cocoa Beach FL 32931-2602

BLUM, LESTER, educator; b. June 25, 1919; s. Morris and Rae (Altman) Blum; m. Harriet Schlesinger, Apr. 11, 1943; children: Dilys Ellen, Sydney Laura, Galen Elizabeth. BS cum laude, Mich. State U., 1942; MS, Iowa State U., 1944, PhD, 1949. Economist OPA, 1942—43; instr.. rsch. and extension assoc. Iowa State U., 1943—47; mem. faculty Colgate U., Hamilton, NY, prof. econs., 1959—84, chmn. dept., 1962—70, prof. emeritus, 1984—, dir. econs. study groups in Norway, Eng., Israel. Cons. OPS, 1951—52; pub. mem. NY State Minimum Wage Bd. for Cleaning and Dyeing Industry, 1956—57. Recipient Creative Tchg. in Econs. Nat. award, Joint Coun. on Econs. Edn., 1982; fellow, Fund for Advancement Edn., Stanford, 1950—51, Asian Study Israel, 1967—68. Mem.: AAUP (pres. Colgate chpt. 1952—53), Am. Econ. Assn. Home: 2353 Brookview Dr Hamilton NY 13346-0057

BLUM, MELVIN, chemical company executive, researcher; b. N.Y.C., Jan. 8, 1936; s. Paul Henry and Dora (Schneiderman) B.; m. Paula Linda Weiss, July 11, 1969; 1 child, Lara Joyce. BS, Columbia U., 1957, MA, 1959; PhD, Duke U., 1964, Burlington Inst., 1970. Sales mgr. Nuclear Corp. Am., Burbank, Calif., 1960-62; pres. Atomergic Chemetals Corp., Farmingdale, N.Y., 1963—, Burlington Sci. Corp., Farmingdale, 1974—; v.p. Am. Roland Chem. Co., S.I., N.Y., 1984—. Author: Handbook of Rare Elements, Encyclopedia of Chemical Technology, Strategic Metal Investments, (mag.) DMSO Reporter. Capt. USAFR, 1959-65. Mem. Am. Chem. Soc., Am. Soc. Metals, Am. Nuclear Soc., Am. Inst. Physics, N.Y. Acad. Scis., Chemists Club. Home: 1385 Lyon Pl Wantagh NY 11793-2919 Office: Atomergic Chemetals Corp 71 Carolyn Blvd Farmingdale NY 11735-1527 E-mail: mblum@optonline.net.

BLUM, RICHARD ARTHUR, writer, media educator; b. Bklyn., July 28, 1943; w. Albert Elias and Eve (Griboff) B.; m. Barbara Fierstein, Sept. 16, 1967 (div. 1986); children: Jason Robert, Jennifer Rebecca; m. Ilene Shatoff, Sept. 2, 1995. BA, Fairleigh Dickinson U., 1965; MS, Boston U., 1968; PhD, U. So. Calif., 1977. Producer, dir., fellow Sta. WGBH-TV, Boston, 1965-67; program exec., writer, assoc. exec. producer Columbia Pictures-TV, L.A., 1968-74; instr. to asst. prof. U. Tex., Austin, 1974-78; sr. program officer NEH, Washington, 1978-82; sr. exec. producer Rainbow Programming Svc., N.Y.C., 1982; vis. faculty Harvard U., Cambridge, Mass., 1984-86; asst. prof. U. Md., College Park, 1984-88, assoc. prof., dir. RTUF Writing Program, dir. undergrad. studies, 1989-92; dir. TV and Film Writing Inst., U. Md., College Park, 1991-92; prof., dir. motion picture divsn. U. Ctrl. Fla., Orlando, 1993-95, prof. film dept., 1996—. Mem. faculty Am. Film Inst. Workshops, 1982-86, The Writers Ctr., Bethesda, 1982-92. Author: Television Writing: From Concept to Contract, 1980, rev. edit., 1984, American Film Acting: The Stanislavski Heritage, 1984, Working Actors: The Craft of TV, Film and Stage Performance, 1989, (with Richard Lindheim) Primetime: Network TV Programming, 1987, (with Richard Lindheim) Inside Television Producing, 1991, Television and Screenwriting, 1995, 4th edit., 2001; screenwriter (with Frank Tavares) The Elton Project, 1992, Desert Fire, 1987, (with A. Gerson) Sonja's Men, 1991; screenwriter MODE VIII, 1999; screenwriter TAL, 1999, Key Hole, 2003. Judge Nicholl Screenwriting fellowships Acad. Motion Picture Arts and Scis., 1986-89, Corp. Pub. Broadcasting awards, 1988-90; bd. mem. Ctrl. Fla. Film Coun., 1992-95, Fla. Inst. for Film Edn., 1992-95, Ind. Prodrs. Project, Enzian Theatre-Fla. Film Festival Grants, 1995. Recipient Creative and Performing Arts award U. Md., 1986, Arts and Humanities award, 1987, Ford Found. award, 1988. Mem.: Univ. Film and Video Assn., Broadcast Edn. Assn. Home: 3338 Hadleigh Crest Orlando FL 32817-2051 Office: U Ctrl Fla Film Dept PO Box 163120 Orlando FL 32816-3120

BLUM, RICHARD H. obstetrician-gynecologist, educator; b. Jersey City, Mar. 17, 1945; MD, U. Medicine Dentistry N.J., 1970. Cert. in ob-gyn. Intern Newark Beth Israel Med. Ctr., 1970-71; resident in ob-gyn. Columbia-Presbyn. Med. Ctr., N.Y.C., 1971-75; with Overlook Hosp., Summit, N.J. Clin. asst. prof. Robert Wood Johnson Med. Sch.; clin. instr. Coll. Medicine and Dentistry N.J. Office: 226 Saint Paul St Westfield NJ 07090-2100

BLUM, RICHARD HOSMER ADAMS, educator, writer; b. Ft. Wayne, Ind., Oct. 7, 1927; s. Hosmer and Imogene (Heino) B. AB with honors magna cum laude, San Jose State Coll., 1948; PhD, Stanford U., 1951. Research dir. Calif. Med. Assn., San Francisco, 1956-58, San Mateo County (Calif.) Mental Health Service, San Mateo, 1958-60; lectr. Sch. Criminology, U. Calif., Berkeley, 1960-62; mem. faculty Stanford (Calif.) U., 1962-78, prof. dept. psychology, 1970-75, prof. dept. gynecology and obstetrics, 1982-97; mem. faculty Stanford (Calif.) U. Law Sch., 1975-78; chmn. bd. Am. Lives Endowment, Portola Valley, Calif., 1979—. Chmn. Intern. Rsch. Group on Drug Legis. and Programs, Geneva, 1969-78; pres. Bio-Behavioral Rsch. Group, Inc., Palo Alto, 1964-87; owner/operator Shingle Mill Ranch, 1964—; vis. fellow Wolfson Coll. U. Cambridge, 1984; vis. prof. social and polit. sci. U. Cambridge, 1997-98; dir. ethics program World Jurist Assn./World Peace Through Law Ctr., Washington, 2000—. Author 22 books in field of health, criminology, public policy, psychology; author 9 books of fiction. Served in U.S. Army, 1951-53, Korea. Fellow APHA, AAAS, APA, Am. Psychol. Soc., Am. Sociol. Assn., Soc. Advanced Legal Studies (hon., life); mem. Archaeol. Inst. Am., Sigma Xi, Cosmos Club, Athenaeum Club, San Francisco Univ. Club. Unitarian Universalist. Home and Office: PO Box 620482 Woodside CA 94062-0482

BLUM, ROBERT ALLAN, psychiatrist; b. Phila., May 16, 1938; s. Frank Abraham and Sara (James) B.; m. Irene Harriet Segal, Aug. 2, 1959; children: Marc Daniel, Lisa Michelle, Lora Danielle, Amy Lynne. BS, MIT, 1959, MS, 1960; MD, U. Pa., 1964. Diplomate Nat. Bd. Med. Examiners, Am. Bd. Psychiatry and Neurology, Am. Bd. Psychoanalytic. Engr. Burroughs Corp., Paoli, Pa., 1956-57, Gen. Atronics Corp., Wyndmoor, Pa., 1958-61; rotating intern Meml. Hosp., Long Beach, Calif., 1964-65; teaching fellow Harvard U., Boston, 1965-67; staff assoc. NIMH, Washington, 1967-69, rsch. psychiatrist, 1969-71, NIAAA, Washington, 1971-74; pvt. practice Washington, 1968—. Cons. U.S. Govt., Washington, 1974—; regional med. officer/psychiatry Am. Embassy, Singapore, 1995-97, regional med. officer/psychiatry, London, 1997-99; instr. Johns Hopkins U., Balt., 1969—; asst. prof. Georgetown U., Washington, 1972-92; assoc. prof. Uniformed Svcs. U. Health Scis., Bethesda, Md., 1987—; tchg. analyst Balt.-Washington Inst. Psychoanalysis, Laurel, Md., 1978—. Contbr. articles to profl. publs., sect. to book. Lt. comdr. USPHS, 1967-69. C. Mahlon Kline scholar, 1960-63, Mosby scholar, 1964; NSF fellow, 1959, 60. Fellow Am. Psychiat. Assn., Royal Soc. Medicine; mem. Am. Psychoanalytic Assn., Am. Soc. Indsl. Security, Internat. Psychoanalytic Assn., Internat. Soc. Hypnosis, Soc. Clin. and Exptl. Hypnosis. Home: 112 Corwin St San Francisco CA 94114-2342 Office: 9819 Hill St Kensington MD 20895-3136 E-mail: rabmd@tetrex.com.

BLUM, SAMUEL, retired research scientist; b. Aug. 1920; BS, PhD Phys. Chemistry, Rutgers U.; cert. meterology, weather forecasting, UCLA. Ret. rsch. scientist IBM Watson Rsch. Ctr., 2002. Active alumni work Rutgers U. Recipient Nat. Inventors Hall of Fame. Avocations: travel, gardening.

BLUM, SARAH LEAH, nurse psychotherapist; b. Atlantic City, N.J., Dec. 5, 1939; d. David and Diana (Fedner) B.; m. Joseph J. McGoran, Aug. 24, 1970 (div. 1986); children: Lorna Hope Marie, Sean-David Justin. BSN, Seattle U., 1971; M in Nursing, U. Wash., 1976. Cert. clin. specialist. Nurse Atlantic City Hosp., 1960-62, Kaiser Found. Hosp., L.A., 1963-66; instr. nursing North Idaho Coll., Coeur D'Alene, 1972-74; pvt. practice Federal Way, Wash., 1977-85, Auburn, Wash., 1985—; Nurse psychotherapist Christian Counselling Svc., Tacoma, 1977-83; founder The Found. for Planetary Healing; creator Drums, Dreams & Re-Membering; cons. in field; presenter workshops. Contbr. articles to profl. jours. Creator Healing Day, 1985. Capt. Nurse Corps, U.S. Army, 1966-71, Vietnam. Fellow Am. Orthopsychiatric Assn.; mem. ANA, Nat. Nursing Hon. Soc., Internat. Transactional Analysis Assn., Inst. Developmental Edn. and Psychotherapy (bd. dirs. 1989-93, chair profl. membership com. 1991-94), Vietnam Veterans of Am. (bd. dirs. 1983-85, 1st woman mem.). Avocations: music, cross country skiing, sailing, Djembe and Japanese Taiko drumming. Home and Office: 303 O St NE Auburn WA 98002-4645 E-mail: sarahbarnp@earthlink.net.

BLUMBERG, ADELE ROSENBERG, volunteer; b. Harrisburg, Pa., Jan. 19, 1916; d. Robert and Mary (Katzman) Rosenberg; m. Leonard Blumberg, June 16, 1940; children: Joyce Kozloff, Bruce, Allen. AB, Dickinson Coll., Carlisle, Pa., 1937; grad. cum laude, Froelich Sch. Music, Harrisburg, 1932. Tchr. piano, various cities, 1933-47; with Pa. Dept. Pub. Assistance, Harrisburg, 1937—40; assoc. pubr. Somerset Star, Somerville, NJ, 1951-55; sec. Raritan Valley Pub. Co., Manville, NJ, 1951—55. Pres. coun. Girl Scouts U.S., 1954—55, pres. Rolling Hill coun., 1966—72; pres., sec., bd. dirs. Bridgewater (N.J.) Local Assistance Bd., 1957—94; bd. dirs. Somerset County Jewish Family Svc., 1980—89, Inst. Arts and Humanities Edn., NJ, 1983—94, People Care Ctr., Finderne, NJ, 1985—91, Arts Found. N.J., New Brunswick, 1986—93, St. George Playhouse, Bridgewater Com. Creative Arts, 1995—, Brook Art Ctr., 2001—, Somerset County Cmty. Concerts, Opera Theater N.J., Jewish Home for Aged, Somerset County, 1995—99; chmn. Printmakers Coun. N.J., 1975—79; pres. Somerset chpt. Hadassah, 1950—52, Jewish Fedn. Somerset County, 1974—76. Named Adele Blumberg Day in her honor, Mayor of Bridgewater, 1983; recipient Hannah G. Solomon award, Nat. Coun. Jewish Women, 1969, Cmty. Patriot, Bridgewater Edn. Assn., 1976, Tercentenary award, Bd. Freeholders and Cultural and Heritage Commn. Somerset County, 1988, Good Scout award, Boy Scouts Am., 1993, Raritan award, Leonard and Adele Blumberg Edn. Found. Bridgewater, Citizen of the Yr. award, Somerset C. of C., 1995, Hon. award, Dickinsooon Law Sch., 1998. Mem.: AAUW, Zonta (v.p. 1970—71). Democrat. Jewish. Avocations: music, piano, needlecrafts, travel, photography. Address: 1820 Woodland Ter Bound Brook NJ 08805-1449

BLUMBERG, AVROM AARON, physical chemistry educator; b. Albany, N.Y., Mar. 3, 1928; s. Samuel and Lillian Ann (Smith) B.; m. Eleanor Leah Simon, Aug. 5, 1955 (dec. Sept. 1967); 1 child, David Martin; m. Judith Anne Kohlhagen, Mar. 9, 1969; children: Susan Margaret, Jonathan Samuel. BS in Chemistry, Rensselaer Poly. Inst., 1949; PhD in Phys. Chemistry, Yale U., 1953. Fellow glass sci. Mellon Inst., Pitts., 1953-59, fellow polymer sci., 1959-63; from asst. to assoc. prof. phys. chemistry DePaul U., Chgo., 1963-75, prof., 1975—, head div. natural scis. and math., 1966-82, chmn. dept. chemistry, 1986-92. Vis. lectr. chemistry dept. U. Pitts., 1957-58; cons. in field. Author: Form and Function, 1972; contbr. articles to profl. jours. Participant scientists and speakers program Mus. Sci. and Industry, Chgo., 1985—; Dem. precinct capt., Evanston, Ill., 1970-78. Mem. Am. Chem. Soc. (speakers program Chgo. sect. 1983—), Royal Soc. Chem. London, Arms Control Assn., Sigma Xi. Jewish. Avocations: music, reading, art, travel, cooking. Home: 1240 S State St Chicago IL 60605-2405 Office: DePaul U Dept Chemistry 2320 N Kenmore Ave Chicago IL 60614-3210

BLUMBERG, BARBARA SALMANSON (MRS. ARNOLD G. BLUMBERG), retired state housing official, housing consultant; b. Bklyn., Oct. 2, 1927; d. Sam and Mollie (Greenberg) Salmanson; m. Arnold G. Blumberg, June 19, 1949 (dec. June 1989); children: Florence Ellen Schwartz, Martin Jay, Emily Anne. BA, De Pauw U., 1948; postgrad., New Sch. for Social Rsch., N.Y.C. Mem. pub. rels. dept. Nate Fein & Co., N.Y.C., 1948-51; freelance pub. rels. cons., 1960—; councilwoman North Hempstead, N.Y., 1975-82; adviser to energy com. N.Y. State Assembly, N.Y.C., 1982-84; dir. spl. needs housing Divsn. Housing and Cmty. Renewal, State of N.Y., 1984-89, ret., 1989. Mem. bd. visitors Pilgrim State Hosp. Pres. UN Assn. Great Neck, N.Y., 1967-69, chmn. China Study Workshop, 1966-67; pres. Shalom chpt. Hadassah, 1955-57; exec. v.p. Lakeville PTA, Great Neck, 1963-65, Great Neck South Jr. H.S., 1965-66; co-chair UNICEF, Great Neck, 1968-70, spkrs. bur., 1971—; v.p. Herricks Cmty. Life Ctr., 1976-77, B'nai B'rith, Lake Success, N.Y.; coord. 6th Congl. Dist., N.Y. McGovern for Pres.; bd. dirs. New Dem. Coalition Nassau, Am. Jewish Congress, Day Care Coun. Nassau County, Citizens Sch. Com., Great Neck; active Reform Dem. Assn. Great Neck; platform com. Nassau Dem. Com.; del. Dem. Nat. Conv., 1992; adv. com. to spkr. N.Y. State Assembly; resource coun., housing devel. com. Cmty. Advocates; chair North Hempstead Housing Authority; trustee L.I. Power Authority, 1994-96. Recipient award Anti-Defamation League, New Hyde Park, N.Y., 1975, Alumni award DePauw U., 1977, Hadassah New Life award, 1980, Women's Pole of Honor, North Hempstead, 1994. Mem. North Shore Archeol. Assn. (chmn. study group), Women in Comm., Internat. Platform Assn., L.I. Womens Network (co-convenor), Interfaith Nutrition Network (v.p.), Cmty. Advocates (bd. dirs.), Mental Health Assn. Nassau County (bd. dirs.), North Shore NAACP, N.Y. Alumni Club DePauw U. (trustee), Alpha Lambda Delta. Home: 12 Birch Hill Rd Great Neck NY 11020-1309

BLUMBERG, BARUCH SAMUEL, academic research scientist; b. N.Y.C., July 28, 1925; s. Meyer and Ida (Simonoff) B.; m. Jean Liebesman, Apr. 4, 1954; children: Anne, George, Jane, Noah. BS, Union Coll., Schenectady, 1946; MD, Columbia U., 1951; PhD, Oxford (Eng.) U., 1957; 20 hon. doctoral degrees. Intern, then resident Columbia div. Bellevue Hosp., N.Y.C., 1951—53; fellow in medicine Columbia-Presbyn. Med. Ctr., N.Y.C., 1953—55; chief geog. medicine and genetics sect. NIH, Bethesda, Md., 1957—64; assoc. dir. clin. rsch. Fox Chase Cancer Ctr., Phila., 1964—86, v.p. population oncology, 1986—89, Fox Chase disting. scientist, 1989—, sr. advisor to pres., 1989—; univ. prof. medicine and anthropology U. Pa., 1977—; dir. NASA Astrobiology Inst., Moffett Field, Calif., 1999—2002; sr. adv. to the adminstr. NASA Hdqtrs., Washington, 2000—01. George Eastman vis. prof. Oxford U., 1983—84; Raman vis. prof. Indian Inst. Scis., Bangalore, India, 1986; Ashland vis. prof. U. Ky., Lexington, 1986—87; master Balliol Coll., Oxford, England, 1989—94; disting. vis. Nat. U. Singapore, 1992; vis. prof. U. Otago, Dunedin, New Zealand, 1994; James W. McLauglin vis. prof. U. Tex.; vis. prof. dept. medicine Stanford U. Med. Ctr.; sr. advisor to pres. Fox Chase Cancer Ctr., 1989—; fellow Ctr. Advanced Study Behavioral Scis. Stanford U., Larry Lokey disting. vis. prof. human biology. Contbr. articles to profl. jours. Lt. USNR, 1943—46. Recipient Albion O. Berstein, M.D. award Med. Soc. State of N.Y., 1969, Grand Sci. award Phi Lambda Kappa, 1972, Ann. award Eastern Pa. br. Am. Soc. Microbiology, 1972, Passano award Williams & Wilkens Co., 1974, Modern Medicine Disting. Achievement award, 1975, Internat. award Gairdner Found., 1975, Karl Landsteiner Meml. award Am. Assn. Blood Banks, 1975, Nobel prize in physiology or medicine, 1976, Scopus award Am. Friends of Hebrew U., 1977, Strittmatter award Philadelphia County Med. Soc., 1980, Disting. Service award Pa. Med. Soc., 1982, Zubrow award Pa. Hosp., 1986, Achievement award Sammy Davis Jr. Nat. Liver Inst., 1987, John P. McGovern award Am. Med. Writers Assn., 1988, Gov.'s Award in the Scis. Commonwealth of Pa., 1989, John Blundell award Brit. Blood Transfusion Soc., 1989, Gold Medal award Can. Liver Found. and Can. Assn. Study of Liver, 1990, Showa Emperor Meml. award Japan, 1994, Outstanding Leadership medal NASA, 2002; elected to Nat. Inventor Hall of Fame, 1993. Fellow ACP, Royal Coll. Physicians; mem. NAS, AAAS, Inst. Medicine of NAS, Am. Acad. Arts and Scis. (inst. medicine), Assn. Am. Physicians, Am. Soc. Clin. Investigation, Am. Soc. Human Genetics, Explorers Club N.Y., Athenaeum (London). Office: Fox Chase Cancer Ctr 7701 Burholme Ave Philadelphia PA 19111-2497 E-mail: bs_blumberg@fccc.edu.

BLUMBERG, DONALD FREED, management consultant; b. Phila., Jan. 30, 1935; s. Harry and Sara (Freed) Blumberg; m. Judith Blumberg, June 16, 1960; children: Michael, Susan. BA, U. Pa., 1952, BEE, 1957, MBA, 1958, postgrad., 1963. Sr. planner IBM Corp., 1960—61; dir. planning and rsch. svc. Pa. Rsch. Assocs., 1962—65; dir. ops. rsch. and long range planning Philco Ford Corp., 1965—68; mgr. mgmt. sci. div. Sci. Mgmt. Corp., 1968; v.p. Computer Scis. Corp., 1969; pres., CEO D.F. Blumberg & Assocs., Inc., Ft. Washington, Pa., 1969; sole practice, 1973; chmn. Blumberg Shaw Cons., Ltd., London, London, 1988. Instr. U. Pa.; lectr. Am. Mgmt. Assn., Temple U., 1993—94; mem. Upper Dublin Twp. Govt. Study Commn., 1974—75; acting prin. dep. asst. sec. def. U.S. Dept. Def., 1975. Author: Managing Service As A Strategic Profit Center, Managing Service Using CRM Technology (award McGraw Hill); contbr. articles over 450 on field to profl. jours. Mem. bd. dirs. U. Pa. Engring. Sch.; pres. Enclave High Rise Condominium. Served to 1st lt. U.S. Army, 1959—60. Mem.: IEEE, Ops. Rsch. Soc. Am., Inst. Mgmt. Scis., Assn. Field Service Mgrs (Del. Valley chpt. chair), Inst. Dirs. Democrat. Jewish. Home: 1922 Audubon Dr Dresher PA 19025-1902 Office: D F Blumberg & Assoc Inc 1300 Virginia Dr Ste 110 Fort Washington PA 19034-3223 E-mail: dfba@dfba.com.

BLUMBERG, EDWARD ROBERT, lawyer; b. Phila., Feb. 15, 1951; BA in Psychology, U. Ga., 1972; JD, Coll. William and Mary, 1975. Bar: Fla., 1975, U.S. Dist. Ct. Fla. 1975, U.S. Ct. Appeals, 1975, U.S. Supreme Ct. 1979. Assoc. Knight, Peters, Hoeveler & Pickle, Miami, Fla., 1976-77; ptnr. Deutsch & Blumberg, P.A., Miami, 1978—. Adj. prof. U. Miami Sch. Paralegal Studies. Author: Proof of Negligence, Mathew Bender Florida Torts, 1988. Mem. ABA (ho. of dels. 1996-2002), ATLA, Dade County Bar Assn., Fla. State Bar (bd. govs., pres. elect 1996-97, pres. 1997-98), Acad. Fla. Trial Lawyers, Nat. Bd. Trial Advocacy (cert. civil trial adv.), Fla. Bar Found. (bd. dirs. 1996-99, bd. govs. 1996-99), Bankers Club (chmn. bd. govs. 2003-). Office: Deutsch & Blumberg PA 100 Biscayne Blvd Fl 28 Miami FL 33132-2304

BLUMBERG, GERALD, lawyer; b. N.Y.C., July 25, 1911; s. Saul and Amelia (Abramowitz) B.; m. Rhoda Shapiro, Jan. 7, 1945; children: Lawrence, Rena, Alice, Leda. AB cum laude, Cornell U., 1931; JD cum laude, Harvard, 1934. Bar: Mass. 1934, N.Y. 1934. Pvt. practice, N.Y. 1934—; mem. firm Gerald & Lawrence Blumberg LLP. Instr. econs. Cornell U., 1931; mem. Harvard Legal Aid Bur., 1934. Bd. dirs., v.p., exec. com. Am. Com. Weizmann Inst. Sci.; internat. bd. govs. Weizmann Inst. Sci., 1982— . Mem. ABA, N.Y. State, Westchester, Yorktown bar assns., Phi Beta Kappa, Phi Kappa Phi. Home: 1305 Baptist Church Rd Yorktown Heights NY 10598-5810 Office: Gerald & Lawrence Blumberg LLP 521 5th Ave New York NY 10175-0003

BLUMBERG, GRACE GANZ, law educator, lawyer; b. N.Y.C., Feb. 16, 1940; d. Samuel and Beatrice (Finkelstein) Ganz; m. Donald R. Blumberg, Sept. 9, 1959; 1 child, Rachel. BA cum laude, U. Colo., 1960; JD summa cum laude, SUNY, 1971; LL.M., Harvard U., 1974. Bar: N.Y. 1971, Calif. 1989. Confidential law clk. Appellate Divsn., Supreme Ct., 4th Dept., Rochester, NY, 1971-72; tchg. fellow Harvard Law Sch., Cambridge, Mass., 1972-74; prof. law SUNY, Buffalo, 1974-81, UCLA, 1981—. Reporter Am. Law Inst., Prins. of the Law of Family Dissoulution, 2002. Author: Community Property in California, 1987, 1999, 2003, Blumberg's California Family Code Annotated; contbr. articles to profl. jours. Office: UCLA Sch Law Box 951476 Los Angeles CA 90095-1476

BLUMBERG, JOEL MYRON, cardiologist; b. N.Y.C., Oct. 17, 1940; s. Howard Godfrey and Lily Ruth (Goldberg) B.; B.A., DePauw U., 1962; M.D., N.Y. U., 1966; m. Judith Ellen Green, Aug. 23, 1964; children: Amy, Hillary, Michelle. Intern, N.Y. U.-Bellevue Med. Center, N.Y.C., 1966-67, resident in internal medicine, 1969-71; fellow in cardiology Cornell U.-N.Y. Hosp., 1971-73; pvt. practice internal medicine and cardiology, Greenwich, Conn., 1973—; attending staff Greenwich Hosp., 1973—, coronary care cons., 1973—; physician to out-patients N.Y. Hosp., 1973-77; clin. instr. Cornell U. Med. Coll., 1971-77; clin. asst. prof. Yale Sch. Medicine, 1975—; lectr. in preventive cardiology to civic groups; bd. visitors DePauw U., bd. incorporators Greenwich Hosp. Diplomate Am. Bd. Internal Medicine. Fellow A.C.P., Am. Coll. Cardiology, Am. Coll. Chest Physicians, Am. Heart Assn. (council on clin. cardiology)selected best doctors in Am., 2002, best doctors in N.Y., 2002, best doctors in Conn., 2002, Excellence in teaching award, 2002; mem. Am. Soc. Internal Medicine, N.Y. Heart Assn., Greenwich, Fairfield County, Conn. State med. socs. Club: B'nai B'rith (Stamford, Conn.). Contbr. articles to profl. jours. Home: 59 Old Stone Bridge Rd Cos Cob CT 06807-1511 Office: 2 1/2 Deerfield Dr Greenwich CT 06831-5335

BLUMBERG, JUNE BETH, artist; b. Abington, Pa., May 14, 1959; d. Frederick Blumberg and Elin (Brunswick) Binder. A of Gen. Studies, Montgomery Community Coll., 1985; BFA, Moore Coll. of Art, Phila., 1991; AAS, C.C. of Phila., 2000. Stats. clk. Crime Prevention Assn., Phila., 1980-81; workshop tchr. Jefferson Hosp. Evening Program, Phila., 1986-87; art asst. Mildred Greenberg, Phila., 1988-89; vis. artist Moore Coll. of Art & Design, Phila., 1990; admission rep. Franklin Inst., Phila., 1990-92; rsch. scientist, artist Phila., 1979—. Sec. fellowship Pa. Acad. Fine Art, 1995, 96. Shows include Nexus Art Gallery, Phila., 1979, Moore Coll. Art & Design, Phila, 1985-90, upper Saddle Cultural Ctr., N.J., 1986, Art Ctr. N.J., Milford, 1986, Ky. Highlands Mus., Ashland, 1988, Studio Arts Ctr. Internat., Florence, Italy, 1989, Palette and Chisel Acad. Fine Arts, Chgo., 1990, West Bend Gallery, Wis., 1990, Rittenhouse Fine Arts Ann., Phila., 1985-87, 90, Pen and Brush Club, N.Y.C., 1987, 89, 90, Clinton St. Gallery, Schenectady, N.Y., 1990, Pa. Acad. Fine Arts, Phila., 1991, 93, Phila. Print Club, 1991-97, Reno Gazette Jour. Bldg., Nev., 1991, Woodmere Art Mus., Phila., 1991, 92, 98, 99, Axis Gallery, Phila., 1992, Artcetera, Auburn, Calif., 1992, Dellora Norris Cultural Ctr., St. Charles, Ill., 1992, Gallery Cedar Hollow, Malvern, Pa., 1993, 479 Gallery, Phila., 1993, City Hall, Phila., 1993, Art Initiatives, N.Y.C., 1993, 94, Border Book Store, Phila., 1994, 95, 98, 99, Mills Pond House, St. James, N.Y., 1994, Nat. Arts Club, N.Y.C., 1994, Highwire Gallery, Phila., 1993, 94, The Police Bldg. Gallery, N.Y.C., 1995, Internat. Platform Assn., Washington, 1995, Riverbank Arts, Stockton, N.J., 1997, The Bear and Koala Tea Co., Bordentown, N.J., 1998, Main Line Art Ctr., Haverford, Pa., 1998, Phila. Sketch Club, 1998, N.Y. Law Sch., N.Y.C., 1998, 99, Cmty. Arts Ctr., Wallingford, Pa., 1999, Cumberland County Coll., Vineland, N.J., 1999, Wilmington Pub. Libr., 1999, Gallery One, Auburn, Calif., 1999, La. State U. Sch. Vet. Med., Baton Rouge, 1999, Gallery 402, N.Y.C., 1999, Salon des Amis, Malvern, Pa., 1999, Walter Greer Gallery, Hilton Head, S.C., 1999, Gallery One, Auburn, Calif., 1999, Salon des Amis, Malvern, Penn., 1999, 2000, Mayer, Brown Platt, N.Y.C., 2000, The Ethical Soc., 2000, Calif. State U. Long Beach, 2000, Zaren/Golde Ort Inst., Chgo., 2000, The Smithtown Cultural Ctr., 2001, Gallery EGG, Chgo., 2001, Chester County Art Assn., 2001, others. Tutor Homeless Shelter, 1986. Recipient scholarship, 1983-85, Spl. Merit award Pen and Brush Club, 1990, cert. of merit Manhatt Art Internat. Mag., 1999, cert. of excellence Manhatt Art Internat.

mag., 1999. Mem. NAFE, APHA, World Affairs Coun., Pastel Soc. West Coast, The Internat. Platform Assn. (Best of Show 1995), Toastmasters, Phi Theta Kappa. Democrat. Avocations: politics, reading, swimming, philosophy. Address: PO Box 148 Bala Cynwyd PA 19004-0148

BLUMBERG, MARK STUART, health services researcher; b. N.Y.C., Nov. 16, 1924; s. Sydney N. and Mollie (Leshrowitz) B.; m. Luba Monasevitch, 1952; children: Bart David, Eve Luise; m. 2d Elizabeth R. Conner, 1974. Student, Johns Hopkins U., 1942-43, Harvard U., 1943-44, D.MD, 1948, MD, 1950, student Sch. Public Health, 1955. Intern, children's med. service Bellevue Hosp., N.Y.C., 1950-51; ops. analyst Johns Hopkins U. Ops. Research Office, Chevy Chase, Md., 1951-54; exchange analyst Army Ops. Research Group (U.K.), West Byfleet, Eng., 1953-54; staff Occupational Health Program, USPHS, Washington, 1954-56; asso. ops. analyst to dir. health econs. program Stanford (Calif.) Research Inst., 1956-66; asst. to v.p. adminstrn. to dir. health planning, office of the pres. U. Calif., Berkeley, 1966-70; corp. planning advisor to dir. spl. studies Kaiser Found. Health Plan, Inc., Oakland, Calif., 1970-94; dir. Kaiser Found. Health Plan of Conn., Hartford, 1982-94, Kaiser Found. Health Plan Mass., 1987-94; cons. risk adjusted measures Oakland, 1994—; co-founder, v.p. R&D TruRisk LLC, 1998—. Various times cons. Pan Am. Health Orgn., Calif. State Dept. Mental Hygiene, Carnegie Commn. on Higher Edn., various agys. HHS. Contbr. writings to profl. publs. Vol. Grenfell Med. Mission, Harrington Harbour, Que., Can., summer 1948; mem. tech. adv. com. AB 524 State of Calif., 1992—. Served with USNR, 1943-45; with USPHS, 1954-56. Mem. Ops. Research Soc. Am. (past mem. council, Health Applications sect.), Hosp. Mgmt. Systems Soc. (charter), Inst. of Medicine of Nat. Acad. Scis.

BLUMBERG, MICHAEL ZANGWILL, allergist; b. Phila., July 29, 1945; s. Jerome Blumberg and Vivian Rose (Liebman) Steiger; m. Barbara Sue Gurman, June 9, 1973; children: Jessica Lynn, Jason Mark. AB, Brandeis U., 1967; MD, Jefferson Med. Coll., 1971; MSHA., Va. Commonwealty U., 1998. Diplomate Am Bd Pediatrics, Am Bd Allergy and Immunology. Intern, resident N.Y. Hosp., Cornell U. Med. Ctr., 1971-73; fellow in allergy and immunology Nat. Jewish Hosp.-U. Colo. Med. Ctr., 1973-75; chief allergy sect. major Scott Air Force Base, Ill., 1975-77; physician-ptnr. Va. Adult and Pediat. Allergy and Asthma, Richmond, 1977—, mng. ptnr., 1998—; asst. clin. prof. pediatrics Med. Coll. Va., Richmond, 1977—2002, assoc. clin. prof. pediatrics, 2000—; chief of allergy Children's Hosp. of Richmond, 1987-2000; ptnr. Clin. Rsch., Richmond, 1998—. Med advisor Aventis, Astra Zeneca, Glaxo SmithKline, Merck. Contbr. articles and abstracts to profl jours; contbg. editor: Review in Allergy, 1978; mem ed bd: Jour Asthma, 1996—. Mem exec comt, pres, bd dirs, chmn Beth Shalom Home Va, Richmond, 1987—95; bd dirs Jewish Community Ctr, Richmond, 1984—87; bd dirs endowment fund, mem budget comt Jewish Fedn; v.p. Richmond Jewish Found., 2002. Fellow: Am Acad Pediatrics, Col Chest Physicians, Am Col Allergy, Asthma and Immunology (pub. rels.com.); mem.: Allergy and Asthma Soc. Va. (pres. 2002—), Am Thoracic Soc, Am Acad Allergy, Asthma and Immunology (managed care com.), Am Col Allergy Sports Med (practice standards com. 1994—95), Friends of Brandeis Athletics, Masons, Phi Kappa Phi. Jewish. Avocations: American history, aerobic exercise. Home: 1602 Swansbury Dr Richmond VA 23233-4628 Office: Va Adult & Pediat Allergy and Asthma 7605 Forest Ave Ste 103 Richmond VA 23229-4936 E-mail: mshadoc@cavtel.net., mblumberg@vaallergy.com.

BLUMBERG, PETER STEVEN, manufacturing company executive; b. Bklyn., Feb. 18, 1944; s. Howard G. and Lily G. (Goldberg) B.; m. Judith E. Pauly, Apr. 22, 1967; children: Anne Pauly, Matthew Edward, Heather Rebecca, Emily Jessica. BS, U. Va., 1967. Salesman Coll. House, Inc., Westbury, N.Y., 1967-71, sales mgr., 1971-76, gen. mgr., 1977-78; sec.-treas. Sch. Tchrs. Supply Corp., Westbury, N.Y., 1979-2000; pres., CEO College House, Richmond, Va., 1979—. Rsch. assoc. Fred Hutchinson Cancer Rsch. Ctr., Seattle, Sloan-Kettering Meml. Cancer Ctr.; active Nat. Right-to-work Legal Def. Found., United Jewish Appeal, World Jewish Congress, Leukemia Soc. Am., Coalition to Stop Gun Violence, Handgun Control, Inc., Leadership Coun. So. Poverty Law Ctr., Simon Wiesenthal Ctr. Holocaust Studies, Ams. Against Union Control of Govt., Jewish Chautaququa Soc., Hebrew Immigrant Aid Soc.; charter supporter U.S. Holocaust Meml. Coun.; Jewish Cmty. Ctr. of Richmond. Mem. Nat. Assn. Coll. Stores, Screenprinting and Graphic Imaging Assn. Internat., U. Va. Alumni Assn. (life), Richmond Symphony, Hurrycanes Running Club, Richmond Road Runners. Jewish. Home: 817 Colony Bluff Pl Richmond VA 23233-5561 Office: 1400 Chamberlayne Ave Richmond VA 23222-5204

BLUMBERG, PHILLIP IRVIN, law educator; b. Balt., Sept. 6, 1919; s. Hyman and Bess (Simons) B.; m. Janet Helen Mitchell, Nov. 17, 1945 (dec. 1976); children: William A.M., Peter M., Elizabeth B., Bruce M.; m. Ellen Ash Peters, Sept. 16, 1979. AB, Harvard U., 1939, JD, 1942; LLD (hon.), U. Conn., 1994. Bar: N.Y. 1942, Mass. 1970. Assoc. Willkie, Owen, Otis, Farr & Gallagher, N.Y.C., 1942-43, Szold, Brandwen, Meyers and Blumberg, N.Y.C., 1946-66; pres., CEO United Ventures Inc., 1962-67; pres., CEO, trustee Federated Devel. Co., N.Y.C., 1966-68, chmn. fin. com., 1968-73; prof. law Boston U., 1966-74; dean U. Conn. Sch. Law, Hartford, 1974-84, prof. law, 1984-89, dean, prof. law emeritus, 1989—. Bd. dirs. Verde Exploration Ltd.; mem. legal adv. com. to bd. dirs. N.Y. Stock Exch., 1989-93; mem. adv. com. on transnat. corps. U.S. Dept. State, 1976-79; advisor corp. governance project, restatement of suretyship and restatement of agy. Am. Law Inst.; vis. lectr. U. Brabant, Tilburg, Netherlands, 1985, U. Internat. Bus. and Econs., Beijing, 1989, U. Sydney, 1992, Jagiellonian U., Cracow, Poland, 1992. Author: Corporate Responsibility in a Changing Society, 1972, The Megacorporation in American Society, 1975, The Law of Corporate Groups: Procedure, 1983, The Law of Corporate Groups: Bankruptcy, 1985, The Law of Corporate Groups: Substantive Common Law, 1987, The Law of Corporate Groups: General Statutory Law, 1989, The Law of Corporate Groups: Specific Statutory Law, 1992, The Multinational Challenge to Corporation Law, 1993, The Law of Corporate Groups: State Statutory Law, 1995, The Law of Corporate Groups: Enterprise Liability, 1998; mem. editl. bd. Harvard Law Rev., 1940-42, treas., 1941-42; contbr. articles to profl. jours. Trustee Black Rock Forest Preserve, Inc.; trustee emeritus Conn. Bar Found. Capt. USAAF, 1943-46, ETO, maj. Res. 1946-55. Decorated Bronze Star Mem. ABA, Conn. Bar Assn., Am. Law Inst., Hartford Club, Harvard Club (Boston), Army & Navy Club (Washington), Phi Beta Kappa, Delta Upsilon. Home: 791 Prospect Ave Apt B-5 Hartford CT 06105-4224 Office: U Conn Sch Law 65 Elizabeth St Hartford CT 06105-2290 E-mail: pblumber@law.uconn.edu.

BLUMBERG, SHERRY HELENE, Jewish education educator; b. Mar. 7, 1947; BA in Drama Edn., U. Ariz., 1969; MA in Librarianship, San Jose State U., 1973; MA in Jewish Edn., Hebrew Union Coll., L.A., 1976, PhD in Jewish Edn., 1991. Cert. Reform Jewish educator. Sr. reference specialist Stanford (Calif.) U. Libr., 1969-73; dir. edn. B'nai Israel, Sacramento, 1976-79, Temple Israel, Long Beach, Calif., 1979-85; assoc. prof. Jewish edn. Hebrew Union Coll.-Jewish Inst. Religion, N.Y.C., 1985-99; vis. assoc. prof. Jewish edn. Gratz Coll., York, Pa., 1999; dir. edn. Congregation Shalom, Milw., 1999—; adj. prof. St. Francis Sem., Milw., 2002—, lectr., 2002—. Participant 1st internat. sem. on interreligious dialogue, Beijing, 1998. Author: God: The Eternal Challenge, 1980, A Teacher's Guide To Rooftop Secrets and Other Stories of Anti-semitism, 1987; co-author: Death, Burial and Mourning in the Jewish Tradition, 1978, Divorce in the Jewish Tradition, 1979, Teaching About God and Spirituality: A Resource for Jewish Settings, 2002. Mem. exec. bd. Coalition for Jewish Learning, Milw., 2001—; mem. editl. and adv. bd. for women's Torah commentary project Women of Reform Judaism. Mem. Internat. Seminar on Religion, Edn. and Values, Assn. Profs. and Rschrs. in Religious Edn. (mem. nat. bd. 1993-96), Religious Edn. Assn. (exec. bd. 1991—, acting pres. 1995-96, pres. 1999-2000), Union Am. Hebrew Congregations (exec. bd. com. Jewish edn. 1997-2000), ASCD, Nat. Assn. Temple Educators, Coalition on Alternatives in Jewish Edn. Office: Congregation Shalom 7630 N Santa Monica Blvd Milwaukee WI 53217-3299 E-mail: blumberg@teacher.com., sherry@cong-shalom.org.

BLUME, ARTHUR WALTER, IV, addictive behaviors researcher, therapist; b. Port Hueneme, Calif., May 23, 1959; s. Arthur Walter Blume III and Mary Kathleen Edwards; m. Karen B. Schmaling, May 14, 1994; children: Amanda Kathleen, Rachel Frances. MDiv, McCormick Sem., Chgo., 1985; MS in Psychology, U. Wash., 1999, PhD in Clin. Psychology, 2001. Substance abuse therapist St. John's Med. Ctr., Springfield, Mo., 1986-91; pvt. practice Springfield, 1991-94; psychometrist, dual diagnosis therapist U. Wash., Seattle, 1994-97, addictive behaviors rschr., 1997—, rsch. therapist, 1999-2000; therapist Tulalip Tribes, Marysville, Wash., 1999-2000. Substance abuse cons. St. John's Med. Ctr., Springfield, 1991-94. Co-author: Harm Reduction, 1998; contbr. articles to profl. jours. Summer youth mission worker Presbyn. Ch., 1973-82; civil rights activist People's Ch., Chgo., 1982-85; instr. ESL Doremus Cmty. Ctr., Chgo., 1983-84; bd. dirs. Met. Coun. Chs., Springfield, 1991-93, vol. homeless shelter Jewish League, Seattle, 1995-97. Rsch. grantee, NIH, Tex. and Alcohol and Drug Abuse Inst., Seattle, 1997, Tex. Higher Edn. Bd., El Paso, 2001, NIH, 2003; pre-doctoral rsch. fellow NIH, Rockville, Md., 1998-99; recipient Stanley Found. award Nat. Alliance of Mentally Ill, 2000. Mem. APA, Assn. for Advancement of Behavior Therapy (Early Career Contbn. in Addications Rsch. award 2003), Assn. Profl. Psychometrists (bd. dirs. 1995-97). Avocations: poetry, backpacking, softball, snorkeling, travel.

BLUME, CRAIG LEE, music educator; b. Logansport, Ind., Mar. 19, 1954; s. Ronald Keith and Doris Jeanette Blume; m. Andra Joy Fuerstenberg, Feb. 2, 1953; children: Nathan Joel, Matthew Ryan, Brian Christopher. MusM, Butler U., 1983; MusB Edn., Valparaiso U., 1976. Band dir. Logansport (Ind.) Cmty. Sch. Corp., Logansport, 1976—81, Pioneer Regional Sch. Corp., Royal Center, Ind., 1981—. Bus. owner Custom Glass Images, Inc., Logansport, 1991—. Mem. choir Calvary Presbyn. Ch., Logansport, 1983—2002. Mem.: Music Educators Nat. Conf., Internat. Trumpet Guild, Pioneer Classroom Tchrs. Assn. (pres., v.p. 1984—2002), Ind. State Tchrs. Assn., NEA, Phi Beta Mu (hon.). Presbyn. Avocations: running, hunting, gardening. Home: 1486 West Sadler Hill Road Logansport IN 46947 Office: Pioneer Regional School Corporation 317 South Chicago Street PO Box 547 Royal Center IN 46978 Home Fax: 574-732-9258; Office Fax: 574-643-2020. Personal E-mail: cgi@cqc.com. E-mail: blumec@pioneer.k12.in.us.

BLUME, GINGER (ELAINE BLUME), psychologist; b. Lock Haven, Pa., Apr. 8, 1948; d. Martin Luther and Virginia Ruth (Rudy) B. BA, U. Fla., 1970, MA, 1975, PhD, 1979. Predoctoral intern in psychology VA Hosp., West Haven, Conn., 1976-77; postdoctoral intern in psychology Elmcrest Psychiat. Inst., Portland, Conn., 1977-78; pvt. practice clin. psychology Dr. Ginger E. Blume and Assocs., Middletown, Conn., 1978—. Assoc. Harrison Assocs., Inc., Cons., Berkeley, Calif.; co-owner, program dir. PMT Assocs. Inc.; co-owner/trainer TeamMasters; mem. affiliated faculty New Eng. Type Inst.; mem. adj. psychology faculty Middlesex C.C., Antioch Grad. Sch., Keene, N.H.; bd. dirs. Gilead House, halfway facility, SAFE, sexual assault clinic, Family Resource Ctr.; developer Doc-U-Chart; cons. in field. Host daily AM radio talk show, 1996 2000; monthly columnist on psychology Middletown Press, 1996—; co-author 3 workbooks on managing violence. Recipient 1st prize adults, Patton Writing Contest, 2002. Mem. APA (bus. of practice network, rep. for state of Conn. 1997-2003), ASTD, Conn. Psychol. Assn. (chmn. mktg., Disting. Contbn. in Media award 1996), Orthopsychiatry Assn., Internat. Imagery Assn., AAUW (chmn. edn. found. program), Soroptimists, Exch. Club, Phi Kappa Phi, Kappa Delta. Achievements include being world's youngest twin engine female pilot at age 17. Home: 77 Oak Ridge Dr Haddam CT 06438-1053 Office: 300 Plz Middlesex 2d Fl Middletown CT 06457-5153 E-mail: gblumeasso@aol.com.

BLUME, JAMES BERYL, financial advisor; b. N.Y.C., Apr. 9, 1941; s. Philip Franklin Blume and Mary Kirschman Asch; m. Kathryn Weil Frank, Jan. 20, 1984; 1 child, Zachary Thomas Philip. BA, Williams Coll., Williamstown, Mass., 1963; MBA, Harvard U., Boston, 1966; M. Psychology, The Wright Inst., Berkeley, Calif., 1983, PhD in Psychology, 1986. Security analyst Faulkner, Dawkins & Sullivan, N.Y.C., 1966-68; sr. v.p. Faulkner, Dawkins & Sullivan Securities, Inc., N.Y.C., 1968-73; ptnr. Omega Properties, N.Y.C., 1973-74; exec.v.p. Arthur M. Fischer, Inc., N.Y.C., 1974-77; psychotherapist in pvt. practice Berkeley, 1985-91; fin. cons., 1987—; pres. James B. Blume, Inc., fin. counsel and mgmt., Berkeley, 1993-94. Bd. dirs. Ploughshares Fund. Bd. dirs. ACLU No. Calif., San Francisco, 1988-94, treas., 1993-94; bd. dirs. East Bay Clinic for Psychotherapy, Oakland, Calif., 1981-85, Marin Psychotherapy Inst., Mill Valley, Calif., 1986-87; trustee The Wright Inst., 1981-85. Mem. Berkeley Tennis Club, Williams Club (bd. govs. 1968-72). Democrat. Jewish. Avocations: tennis, piano, political science. Office: 1708 Shattuck Ave Berkeley CA 94709-1700 E-mail: jbbinc41@pacbell.net.

BLUME, JEFFREY DAVID, adult education educator, researcher; PhD in Biostats., Johns Hopkins Sch. of Pub. Health, Balt., 1999. Office: Brown Univ Box G-H 167 Angell St 2nd Fl Providence RI 02912

BLUME, JUDY, author; b. Elizabeth, N.J., Feb. 12, 1938; d. Rudolph and Esther (Rosenfeld) Sussman; m. John M. Blume, Aug. 15, 1959 (div. Jan. 1975); children: Randy Lee, Lawrence Andrew; m. George Cooper, June 6, 1987; 1 stepchild, Amanda. BA in Edn., NYU, 1960; LHD (hon.), Kean Coll., 1987, Endicott Coll., 1995. Author: (fiction) including The One in the Middle is the Green Kangaroo, 1969, Iggie's House, 1970, Are You There God? It's Me, Margaret (selected as outstanding children's book 1970), Freckle Juice, 1971, Then Again, Maybe I Won't, 1971, It's Not the End of the World, 1972, Tales of a 4th Grade Nothing, 1972, Otherwise Known as Sheila the Great, 1972, Deenie, 1973, Blubber, 1974, Forever, 1975, Starring Sally J. Freedman as Herself, 1977, Superfudge, 1980, Tiger Eyes, 1981, The Pain and the Great One, 1984, Just As Long As We're Together, 1987, Fudge-A-Mania, 1990, Here's to You, Rachel Robinson, 1993, others; (adult novels) Wifey, 1977, Smart Women, 1984, Summer Sisters, 1998, Double Fudge, 2000; (other writings) Letters to Judy: What Kids Wish They Could Tell You, 1986,; exec. producer (25 min. film) Otherwise Known As Sheila The Great, Barr Films, 1988. Founder, trustee The Kids Fund, 1981. Recipient Carl Sandburg Freedom to Read award Chgo. Pub. Libr., 1984, The Civil Liberties award ACLU, 1986, John Rock award Ctr. for Population Options, 1986, Margaret A. Edwards for lifetime achievement ALA, 1996, numerous Children's Choice award, U.S.A., Europe, Australia. Mem. Authors Guild (bd. dirs.), Nat. Coalition Against Censorship (adv. bd.), Soc. Children's Book Writers (bd. dirs.). Jewish. Office: care William Morris Agy 1325 Ave of Ams New York NY 10019*

BLUME, LAWRENCE DAYTON, lawyer; b. Kansas City, Mo., July 7, 1948; s. Dayton G. and Meredith L. B. BA, U. Ariz., 1970; JD, U. Mo., 1974. Bar: Mo. 1974, D.C. 1989, U.S. Dist. Ct. (we. dist.) Mo. 1974, U.S. Ct. Appeals (fed. cir.) 1984, U.S. Supreme Ct. 1978, U.S. Tax Ct. 1980, U.S. Ct. Internat. Trade 1981, N.Y. 1996. Ptnr. Swanson, Midgley, Gangwere, Clarke & Kitchin, Kansas City, 1974-80; prin. Miller & Blume, P.C., Washington, 1980-89; ptnr. Graham & James, Washington, 1989-2000, D.C. mng. ptnr., 1992-94; N.Y. mng. ptnr. Graham & James LLP, N.Y.C., 1994-98, firm chmn., 1998-2000; prin. Greenberg Traurig LLP, N.Y.C., 2000—. Lectr. Nat. Assn. Fgn. Trade Zones, Washington, 1981—, Am. Assn. Exporters and Importers, N.Y.C., 1984—, various colls., univs. and trade groups, 1980—; prin. instr. Seminar on Internat. Bus. Transactions and Litigation Techniques. Mem.: ABA, Order of Barristers, Customs and Internat. Bar Assn., Licensing Execs. Soc. Internat., Am.-Intellectual Property Law Assn., Am. Assn. Exporters and Importers, Internat. Trade Bar Assn., Inter Am. Bar Assn. (sr.), Nat. Dem. Club. Democrat. Office: Greenberg Traurig 885 Third Ave Ste 2100 New York NY 10022 E-mail: blumel@gtlaw.com.

BLUME, MARSHALL EDWARD, finance educator; b. Chgo., Mar. 31, 1941; s. Marshall Edward Blume and Helen Corliss (Frank) Gilbert; m. Loretta Ryan, June 25, 1966; children: Christopher, Caroline, Catherine. SB, Trinity Coll., Hartford, Conn., 1963; MBA, U. Chgo., 1965, PhD, 1968; MA (hon.), U. Pa., 1970. Lectr. applied math. Grad. Sch. Bus., U. Chgo., 1966, instr. bus. fin. and applied math., 1967; lectr. fin. U. Pa., Phila., 1967, asst. prof., 1968-70, assoc. prof., 1970-74, prof., 1974-78, Howard Butcher prof., 1978—, chmn. dept., 1982-86, assoc. dir. Rodney White Ctr., 1978-86; prin. Prudent Mgmt. Assocs., 1982—; dir. Rodney White Ctr., 1986—. Mem. U.S. Compt. Gen. adv. bd. on Oct. 1987 stock market crash, 1987-88; prof. fin. European Inst., Brussels, 1975-76, New U. Lisbon, Portugal, 1982; vis. prof. Stockholm Sch., spring 1976, U. Brussels, 1975. Author: Mutual Funds and Other Institutional Investors, 1970, The Changing Role of the Individual Investor, 1978, The Structure and Reform of the U.S. Tax System, 1985, Revolution on Wall Street: The Rise and Fall of the New York Stock Exchange, 1993; editor: Encyclopedia of Investments, 1982, The Complete Guide to Investment Opportunities, 1984; assoc. editor Jour. Fin. and Quantitative Analysis, 1967-76, Jour. Fin. Econs., 1976-81, Jour. of Portfolio Mgmt., 1985—; mng. editor Jour. Fin., 1977-80, assoc. editor, 1985-88, Jour. of Fin. Income, 1990—. Contbr. articles to profl. publs. Trustee Trinity Coll., Hartford, Conn., 1980-86, Rosemont (Pa.) Sch., 1991—; commr. Bi-Partisan Commn. on Pa. Pension Fund Investments, 1989-93. Mem. Am. Fin. Assn. (officer 1977-80), Am. Econs. Assn., Fin. Economist Roundtable, Corinthian Yacht Club Phila., New Castle (Del.) Sailing Club, NASD (chmn. econ. adv. bd. 1998), NASDAQ Ednl. Found. (dir. 2000-2001), Measey Found. (mgr. 1997—), Shadow Regulatory Commn. Home: 204 Woodstock Rd Villanova PA 19085-1419 Office: U Penn Rodney L White Ctr Fin Rsch 3250 Steinberg Hall Philadelphia PA 19104

BLUME, MARTIN, physicist; b. Bklyn., Jan. 13, 1932; s. Julius and Frances (Cohen) B.; m. Sheila Bierman, June 12, 1955; children— Frederick, Janet. AB, Princeton U., 1954; A.M., Harvard U., 1956, PhD, 1960. Fulbright rsch. fellow Tokyo U., 1959-60; rsch. assoc. Atomic Energy Rsch. Establishment, Harwell, Eng., 1960-62; with Brookhaven Nat. Lab., Upton, N.Y., 1962—, sr. physicist, 1970—, head solid state physics, dep. chmn. physics dept., 1975-79, assoc. dir., 1981-84, dep. dir., 1984-96; editor-in-chief Am. Phys. Soc., Ridge, N.Y., 1997—. NSF grantee, 1973-78; E.O. Lawrence award Dept. of Energy, 1981; A.H. Compton award, 2003. Fellow Am. Acad. Arts and Scis., Am. Phys. Soc., AAAS, N.Y. Acad. Scis.; mem. Phi Beta Kappa, Sigma Xi. Home: 284 Greene Ave Sayville NY 11782-3003 Office: Am Phys Soc 1 Rsch Rd Ridge NY 11961 also: Brookhaven Nat Lab Physics Dept Bldg 510 Upton NY 11973 E-mail: blume@aps.org.

BLUME, PAUL CHIAPPE, lawyer; b. Omaha, Oct. 11, 1929; s. Herman Alexander and Marie (Simoni) B.; m. Mary Lou Higgins, June 28, 1958; children: Nancy, Julie, Paul II, William. BS in Commerce, Loyola U., Chgo.; JD. Bar: Ill. 1957. Legal sect. mgr. Aldens Inc., 1957-58; assoc. Lord, Bissell & Brook, 1959-63, of counsel, 1983—; v.p., gen. counsel Nat. Assn. Ind. Insurers, Des Plaines, Ill., 1963-83, Ill. Ins. Info. Svc., 1987-96; pres. Ins. Briefs, Inc., 1984—. Capt. U.S. Army, 1951-53. Mem. Chgo. Bar Assn., Fedn. Ins. Counsel. Office: 115 S La Salle St Chicago IL 60603-3801

BLUME, SHANE L. music educator; b. Richmond, Tex., Aug. 5, 1971; s. James Lawrence and Helen Jane Blume; m. Katrina Ann Davis Blume, June 7, 1997; children: Andrew Thomas, Jacob Alexander. MusB, Sam Houston State U., Huntsville, tx, 1998; MusM, Sam houston state U., Huntsville, TX, 2002. Choir dir./music Conroe Isd, Conroe, Tex. Author: (sound recording) Chasin' Dreams (European top 100). Roman Catholic. Avocations: singing, composing music, writing songs, fishing, hunting. Home: 12000 Sawmill Road Apt 1107 The Woodlands TX 77380

BLUMEL, JOSEPH CARLTON, university president; b. Kansas City, Mo., Mar. 3, 1928; s. Joseph F. and Lillian M. (Spinner) B.; m. Priscilla Bryant, June 16, 1961; children— Christina, Carolyn. BS, U. Nebr., 1950, MA, 1956; PhD, U. Oreg., 1965; LL.D. (hon.), U. Hokkaido, Japan, 1976. Prof. econs. Portland (Oreg.) State U., 1968, dean undergrad. studies, assoc. dean faculty, 1968-70, v.p. acad. affairs, 1970-74, pres., 1974-86, pres. emeritus, disting. sr. prof., 1986—. Served with U.S. Army, 1951-53. Mem. Phi Kappa Phi, Alpha Kappa Psi, Beta Gamma Sigma. Home: 9580 SW Melnore St Portland OR 97225-4137

BLUMENAUER, EARL, congressman; b. Portland, Oreg., Aug. 16, 1948; m. Janice Babcock; 2 children. BA, Lewis and Clark Coll., 1970, JD, 1976. Asst. to pres. Portland State U., 1971-73; mem. Oreg. Ho. of Reps., 1973-79, Multnomah County Bd. Commrs., Portland, 1979-87; commr. Portland City Coun., 1987-96; mem. U.S. Congress from 3d Oreg. dist., 1996—; mem. transp. and infrastructure com., internat. rels. com. Recipient Nat. Bldg. Mus. Apgar Award, 2000, Am. Planning Assn. Legislator of the Year ; fellow German Marshall, 1995. Democrat. Avocations: bicycling, running. Office: US House of Reps 2446 Rayburn HOB Washington DC 20515-3703 also: 729 NE Oregon St Ste 115 Portland OR 97232*

BLUMENCRANZ, PETER WILLIAM, surgeon; b. N.Y.C., Mar. 8, 1946; s. Bernard and Evelyn (Guttman) B.; m. Ann Frances Garfes, June 6, 1970; children: Brett, Lisa, Jennifer, Deborah, Todd. BA, U. Pa., 1966; MD, Cornell U., 1970. Diplomate Am. Bd. Surgery. Resident in surgery N.Y. Hosp.-Cornell U. Med. Ctr., N.Y.C., 1970-76; fellow in surg. oncology Meml. Hosp.-Sloan Kettering Cancer Ctr., N.Y.C., 1976-77; surgeon Diagnostic Clinic, Largo, Fla., 1977-79, Fla. Surg. Assocs., Clearwater, Fla., 1980-95; pres. Surg. Assocs. West Fla., Clearwater, 1995—. Bd. dirs. Morton Plant Mease Health Care, Dunedin, Fla., 1992—98, Fla. Surg. Soc., 1998—; trustee Morton Plant Hosp., Clearwater, Fla., 1992—98; med. dir. Moffitt Morton Plant Cancer Care, Tampa, Fla., 2001—. Trustee Shorecrest Prep. Sch., St. Petersburg, Fla., 1982-88. Lt. comdr. USN, 1972-74. Fellow Soc. Surg. Oncology, Am. Coll. Surgeons, Southeastern Surg. Congress; mem. AMA, Am. Soc. Breast Diseases, Fla. Soc. Clinical Oncology, Fla. Med. Assn., Am. Soc. Breast Surgeons. Avocations: tennis, running. Office: Surg Assocs West Fla 455 Pinellas St Clearwater FL 33756-3354

BLUMENFELD, ANITA, community relations director; b. London; came to U.S. d. Samuel and Eva (Lehrman) Leigh; m. George Blumenfeld; children: Michael Russell, Vincent Joseph. Student, City of London Coll. Adminstrv. asst. Jewish Nat. Fund & Mogen David Adom (Israeli Red Cross), London, 1951-55; field cons. AMIT Women, L.A., 1978-81; pub. rels. rep. Mercury Savs. & Loan, Long Beach, Calif., 1981-84; cmty. rels. dir. Ams. AMIT Women for Torah & Israel, L.A., 1986-90; freelance cmty. rels. cons., 1990—. Editor, collator: British Evacuees during World War II, 1977-79; compiler: Social Action Conference Reports, 1977, 79, 85. Social action chmn. Temple Menorah, 1970-79; co-pres. Vols. for Israel, 1988-89; del. to Soviet Union, Refusniks, 1990—; active various other civic orgns. Recipient Humanitarian award, Temple Menorah, L.A., 1994. Mem. Amnesty Internat., Ams. for Safe Israel, Hadassah. Jewish. Avocations: reading, travel, interpretive dance. Home: 2743 W 233rd St Torrance CA 90505-3111

BLUMENFELD, CHARLES RABAN, lawyer; b. Seattle, May 24, 1944; s. Irwin S. and Freda I. (Raban) B.; m. Karla Axell; children: David, Lisa. BA, U. Wash., JD, 1969. Bar: Wash. 1969, U.S. Dist. Ct. (wc. dist.) Wash. 1969, U.S. Ct. Appeals (9th cir.) 1975, U.S. Supreme Ct. 1979, U.S. Dist. Ct. D.C. 1981, U.S. Ct. Appeals (D.C. cir.) 1981. Legis. counsel U.S. Senator Henry M. Jackson, Washington, 1969-72; ptnr. Bogle & Gates, Seattle, 1973-99, Perkin-sCoie, Seattle, 1999—. Mem. ABA (sect. natural resources, energy and environment). Office: PerkinsCoie 1201 3rd Ave Fl 48 Seattle WA 98101-3029

BLUMENFELD, HARRY, retired social worker; s. Jack and Helen (Krakower) Blumenfeld; life ptnr.. MSW, Forham U., 1956. Cert. social worker N.Y. Asst. exec. dir. Jewish Bd. Family and Childrens Svcs., N.Y.C., 1956—93; ret., 1993. Adj. prof. Smith Coll. Sch. Social Work, Northampton, Mass., 1965—93, NYU Sch. Social Work, N.Y.C., 1965—93, Columbia U. Sch. Social Work, N.Y.C., 1973—93, Hunter Coll. Sch. Social Work, N.Y.C., 1980—93. Fellow: Am. Assn. Psychiatric Svcs. for Children; mem.: NASW (life; bd. dirs. NYC chpt. 1987—90). Home: 1901 N Ocean Blvd Fort Lauderdale FL 33305 Personal E-mail: harryehfl@aol.com.

BLUMENFELD, JEFFREY, lawyer, educator; b. N.Y.C., May 13, 1948; s. Martin and Helen Kay (Smith) B.; m. Laura Madeline Ross, June 11, 1970; children: Jennifer Ross Blumenfeld, Joshua Ross Blumenfeld. AB in Religious Thought cum laude, Brown U., 1969; JD, U. Pa., 1973. Bar: D.C. 1973. Asst. U.S. atty. U.S. Atty. for D.C., Washington, 1975-79; trial atty. Antitrust div. U.S. Dept. of Justice, Washington, 1973-75, sr. trial atty. U.S. versus AT&T staff, 1979-82, asst. chief spl. regulated industries, 1982-84, chief U.S. versus AT&T staff, 1984, spl. counsel, 1995-97; ptnr. Blumenfeld & Cohen, Washington, 1984—2002; sr. trial counsel, antitrust divsn. U.S. Dept. Justice, 1996-97; gen. counsel, chief legal officer Rhythms Net Connections, 1997-2001; ptnr. Gray, Cary, Ware & Freidenrich, LLP, Washington, 2002—. Adj. prof. Georgetown U. Law Ctr., Washington, 1983—; spl. counsel antitrust divsn. U.S. Dept. Justice, 1995-97. Bd. dirs. Charles E. Smith Jewish Day Sch., Washington, 1991-93. Democrat. Jewish. Office: Gray Cary Ware & Freidenrich LLP Ste 300 1625 Massachusetts Ave NW Washington DC 20036-2247

BLUMENFELD, ROCHELLE S. REZNIK, artist; b. Pitts., June 19, 1936; d. Lawrence S. and Rose (Fairman) Reznik; m. Irving L. Blumenfeld, Dec. 3, 1955; children: Harold E., Beth A., Louis C. Student, Carnegie Mellon U.;

student of, Samuel Rosenberg. Exhibited in one and two person shows at Regent House, Pitts., 1962, Arts and Crafts Ctr., Pitts., 1966, Pitts. Plan for Art, 1973, 75, 80, 83, Wellsboro Artmobile, 1967, Carnegie Mus. of Art, Pitts., 1971, Gallery G., Pitts., 1987, Jewish Cmty. Ctr., Pitts., 1997, Pitts. Theol. Sem., 1999, others; group exhbns. include Regent House, Carnegie Mus. of Art, Three Rivers Arts Festival, Pitts., Pitts. Plan for Art, Assoc. Artists of Pitts., Associated Artist Exhbn., Dunferline, Scotland, Copley Soc., Boston, Westmoreland Mus. Art, Greensburg, Pa., Americans in Paris (France), Abstraction, Lambertville, N.J., 2000; represented in collections at U. Pitts., Nat. Steel Co., Carneie Mus. of Art, Mellon Bank, Pitts., Humble Oil Co., Enjay, N.J., Blue Cross of Western Pa., Pitts., Beth Israel Synagogue, Greenville, S.C., Allegheny Steel Co., Pitts., Blount Inc., Montgomery, Ala., Ballet Lovers Guide, 2001, others; subject of articles including full color photo's of dance series Revelations. Recipient numerous awards for art works. Mem. Assoc. Artists of Pitts., Pitts. Ctr. for the Arts, Am. Guild Judaic Art.

BLUMENREICH, GENE ARNOLD, lawyer; b. Washington, Apr. 1, 1943; s. Sidney M. and Dorothy N. Blumenreich; m. Margaret Jacobs, Sept. 4, 1966; children: Megan, Stephen, Kate. BA, U. Va., 1964; JD, Harvard U., 1967. Bar: Mass. 1969. Assoc. Surrey, Karasik, Gould & Greene, Washington, 1967-68, Fine & Ambrogne, Boston, 1968-73, ptnr., 1973-90; dir. Powers & Hall, Boston, 1990-95; ptnr. Nutter, McClennen & Fish, LLP, Boston, 1995—. Pres. League Sch. of Boston, Newton, 1979-81; chmn. Newton Ambulance Com., 1973-76; bd. dirs. Friends of Longfellow House, Cambridge, 1996—; trustee New Eng. Bapt. Hosp. Office: Nutter McClennen & Fish LLP World Trade Ctr W 155 Seaport Blvd Boston MA 02210

BLUMENSHINE, MAHLON, banker; b. Washington, Ill., May 11, 1928; s. Mahlon and Mabel Mae (Schick) B.; m. Carolyn Sue Longden, June 26, 1960; children: J. Wesley, Bradley Ward, Blake Alan. Standard Banking degree, So. Ill. U., 1967; Grad. Banking degree, U. Wis., 1974. V.p. Community Bank, East Peoria, Ill., 1956-75; pres., trust officer Sunnyland Bank, Washington, Ill., 1975-2001, also bd. dirs. Bd. dirs. Morton Cmty. Bank. Alderman City of Washington, Ill., 1979-83; treas. Dist. 50 Schs., Washington, 1983-87; past chmn. Easter Seal Drive, Heart Fund Drive, Cancer Fund Drive. Served as cpl. U.S. Army, 1950-52. Mem. Am. Inst. Banking (pres. cen. Ill. chpt. 1957-58), Washington C. of C., Am. Legion, VFW. Lodges: Kiwanis. Republican. Methodist. Avocations: stamp and coin collecting, gardening, golf. Home: 910 Hampton Rd Washington IL 61571-1258 Office: 2301 Washington Rd Washington IL 61571-1859 E-mail: cblumen@aol.com.

BLUMENTHAL, ANNA CATHERINE, English educator; b. Providence, R.I., Feb. 7, 1952; d. Andrew J. and Marion Sabol; m. Robert A. Blumenthal, Aug. 22, 1973 (div. Mar. 2000); 1 child, Rachel A. BA, Univ. Rochester, 1974; M in Eng., Washington Univ., 1976, PhD, 1986. Asst. prof. Eng. Morris Brown Coll., Atlanta, 1989-93, Morehouse Coll., Atlanta, 1993-97, assoc. prof. Eng., 1997—. Invited spkr. confs., 1992, 93, 97, 98; referee for articles, 94; Faculty Resource Scholar (summer participant at NYU), 1999—2002. Contbr. articles to profl. jours. Named Activity Dir. (with Joan Hildenbrand), U.S. Dept. Edn., 1991-93. Mem. MLA, South Atlantic MLA. Office: Morehouse Coll Dept Eng 830 Westview Dr SW Atlanta GA 30314-3773

BLUMENTHAL, CARLENE MARGARET, vocational-technical school and language arts educator; d. Carl and Helen (Chervenak). BA, U. Ill., 1959; MA, Chgo. State U., 1969; student, No. Ill. U., Oxford, Eng., Nat. Louis U. Cert. in secondary lang. arts, social studies. Tutor Triton Coll., River Grove, Ill.; tchr. bus. English Robert Morris Coll., Chgo.; developer vocat. and bus. English curriculum Chgo. Pub. Schs. Participant Nat. Louis U. Right-o-Soar Project, YMCA Coll., 1990; curriculum cons. Pyramid Tech., Rassias Inst.; columnist Substance newspaper, 1999—; student tchr. supr. DePaul U., 2003—; presenter in field. Contbr. articles to profl. jours. Del. Dem. Nat. Conv., 1996; vol. Field Mus., 1999-2000. Tchr.-Sponsor of Yr., VFW, Ill., 1993; grantee U. Chgo., 1990, 91, 93; Mellon fellow, 1992-94, Annenberg fellow, 1995. Mem. NAFE, ACTE (VIM-secretary 2001-02, AIM sec. 2002-03), Nat. Coun. Tchrs. English (panel chair conv. 1996), Ill. Assn. Tchrs. English (workshop presenter 1995, 99), IACTE (affiliate mem. bd. dirs. 1997, del. Nat. Women's Rights Conv., workshop presenter 1999, 2000-01), Ill. Fedn. Tchrs., Chgo. Tchrs. Union (3 coms., workshop presenter 1994, 30 yr. award 2003), Coalition Labor Union Women (chair membership com. 2003—), Phi Delta Kappa (tchr. task force 1996). Home: 5649 W Leland Ave Chicago IL 60630-3221

BLUMENTHAL, DEBORAH T. neuro-oncologist; b. Flint, Mich., Sept. 17, 1964; d. Warner and Caroline Blumenthal; m. Yaron Meshulam; children: Gabriel, Shani, Etai. MD, Med. Coll. Ga., 1990. Ass.t prof. neurology, neurosurgery, and oncology U. Utah/Huntsman Cancer Inst., Salt Lake City, 1998—. Chair brain com. SW Oncology Group. Mem.: Am. Soc. Clin. Oncology, Soc. Neurooncology, Am. Acad. Neurology. Office: Huntsman Cancer Inst/Univ Utah 2000 Circle of Hope Salt Lake City UT 84112 Office Fax: 801-585-0159. E-mail: deborah.blumenthal@hsc.utah.edu.

BLUMENTHAL, HERMAN THEODORE, physician, educator; b. N.Y.C., Apr. 8, 1913; s. Samuel and Jennie (Price) B.; m. Eleonore Gottlieb, Aug. 18, 1940 (dec. 1972); children: Daniels S., Frederic A.; m. Margaret B. Phillips, May 29, 1974; children: Edward P., Shana P. BS, Rutgers U., 1934; MS, U. Pa., 1936; PhD, Washington U., St. Louis, 1938, MD, 1942. Resident in pathology Jewish Hosp., St. Louis, 1942-43; dir. labs of various hosps., 1945-65; asso. prof. pathology St. Louis U., 1947-52, adj. prof. community medicine, 1975—; mem. faculty Washington U., 1965—, research prof. gerontology, 1965—; dir. Midwest Med. Lab., 1965-82. Author: (with J.G. Probstein) Pancreatitis— A Clinical-Pathological Correlation, 1954; Editor: Cowdry's Arteriosclerosis— A Survey of the Problem, 2d edit, 1967, Medical Aspects of Gerontology, 1962, Interdisciplinary Topics in Gerontology, Vols. 1-8, 1968-71, Handbook of Diseases of Aging, 1981, Dilman's Elevational Hypothalmic Mechanisms in Aging and Disease, 1981; Contbr. articles on aging, transplanation, endocrinology, cancer, pathology to profl. jours.; editor Handbook of Diseases of Aging, 1983. Served to maj. M.C. AUS, 1942-45. Mem. Soc. Exptl. Biology and Medicine, Am. Heart Assn., Am. Diabetes Assn., Am. Assn. Cancer Research, Soc. Pathologists and Bacteriologists, Am. Soc. Exptl. Pathology, Gerontol. Soc., AAUP, Sigma Xi. Home: 6203 Washington Ave Saint Louis MO 63130-4847

BLUMENTHAL, JOAN H. executive recruiter; b. Burbank, Calif., Nov. 26, 1944; d. Joseph I. and Ruth E. Hartstein; m. D. Jeffrey Blumenthal, Aug. 21, 1966; children: Andrew, Marianne. AA, Long Beach (Calif.) City Coll., 1964; BA, San Jose State U., 1967; MBA, Lake Forest Grad. Sch. Mgmt., 1990. Owner Just for Kits, Deerfield, Ill., 1976-82; supr. corp. employee benefits Underwriters Labs., Inc., Northbrook, Ill., 1982-89; cons. Jeffrey Corp., Deerfield, 1989-90; dir. ann. fund, alumni rels. Roosevelt U., Chgo., 1990-92; dir. devel. St. Francis Hosp., Evanston, Ill., 1992-93; assoc. v.p. Lauer, Sbarbaro Assocs., Chgo., 1994-98; prin. Blumenthal-Hart, Chgo., 1999—. Dir. Deerfield Area Hist. Soc., 1974-77; dir., chair long range fin. com. Deerfield Pk. Found., 1991-95; chair Deerfield 1992 Care-A-Thon, 1992-93; newsletter editor, advisor Career Renewal, Deerfield, 1995-97; mem. devel. com. Make-A-Wish Found. No. Ill., Chgo., 1996-98; trustee, mem. pers. com. Union League Boys and Girls Clubs, 1999—. Mem.: Human Resources Mgmt. Assn. Chgo., Coun. Advancement and Support Edn., Assn. Forum Chicagoland, Assn. Fundraising Profls. (chair found. rels. 1992—93), Internat. Assn. Corp. and Profl. Recruitment (chair program Chgo. chpt. 2000—01), Union League Club Chgo. (mem. pub. affairs com., chmn. River Walk 1999—2000, bd. dirs. 2000—, chair long range planning com., mem. pers. and adminstrn. com.). Office: Blumenthal-Hart LLC 53 W Jackson Blvd Ste 1307 Chicago IL 60604 Fax: 312-663-0405. E-mail: admin@blumenthal-hart.com.

BLUMENTHAL, RICHARD, state attorney general; m. Cynthia Blumenthal; 4 children. BA, Harvard Coll.; JD, Yale U., 1973. Law clk. Justice Harry A. Blackmun, 1974—75; U.S. atty. State of Conn., 1977—81, former rep., 1984—87, senator, 1987—90, state atty. gen., 1990—. Sgt. USMC, Res. Democrat. Office: Atty Gen Office 55 Elm St Hartford CT 06106-1746

BLUMENTHAL, RONNIE, lawyer; b. Passaic, N.J., Nov. 27, 1944; d. Paul and Marga (Stern) B. BA, George Washington U., 1966, JD, 1969. Bar: D.C. 1969. Gen. atty. EEOC, Washington, 1969-71, spl. asst. to commr., acting chmn., 1971-78, sr. atty., 1978-82, dir. spl. svcs. staff, 1982-85, dir. compliance programs, 1985-91, acting dir. Office of Communications-Legis. Affairs, 1991-92; spl. asst. U.S. atty. Dept. Justice, Washington, 1992, dir. Office Fed. Ops., 1992-99, mediator, 1999—. Legis. fellow U.S. Senate, 1982; chmn. Performance Review Bd., Exec. Resources Bd; lectr., cons. in field. Mem. ABA, D.C. Bar Assn., Fed. Bar Assn., Exec. Women in Govt., Womens Bar Assn., Soc. Profls. in Dispute Resolution. Home: 853 Vanderbilt Beach Rd # 327 Naples FL 34108-8746

BLUMENTHAL, SUSAN J. physician; BA, Reed Coll., Portland, Oreg., 1971; MD, U. Tenn., Memphis, 1976; MPA, Harvard U., 1982; PhD (hon.), Trinity Coll., Washington, 1998; DSc (hon.), Pine Manor Coll., Newton, Mass., 1998. Head suicide rsch. unit NIMH, Rockville, Md., 1982-85, chief behavioral medicine rsch br., 1986-94; dep. asst. sec. for women's health HHS, Washington, 1993—98, U.S. asst. surg. gen., rear adm., sr. med. sci. and e-health adv., 1995—; clin. prof. psychaitry Georgetown Sch. Med., Washington, Tufts U. Med. Ctr., Boston. Distging. vis. prof. women's studies Brandeis U., 2000—; chmn. Fed. Coord. Coms. on Women's Health, OPHS Consumer Info. Svcs. Task Force, NIH Health and Behavior Coord. Com.; chmn., organized Mind/Body Conf. NIH-Body Conf.; co-chmn. Nat. Action Plan for Breast Cancer; dir. major nat. rsch. programs at NIH; TV host and med. dir. for award winning 13-part TV series on women's health; sr. advisor for pub. health White House Coun. on Youth Violence, 2000—01; sr. advisor for pub. health and sci. to sec. USDA, 2000—01. Editor: Suicide over the Life Cycle; sci. editor: Surgeon General's Call To Action To Prevent Suicide; columnist Elle mag., U.S. News and World Report; contbr. articles to profl. jours. Recipient Meritorious Svc. medal, USPHS, Outstanding Svc. medal, Commendation medal. Office: HHS Pub Health & Sci US Asst Surgeon Gen 200 Independence Ave SW Rm 727H Washington DC 20201

BLUMENTHAL, SUSAN JANE, psychiatrist, educator, public health agent; b. N.Y.C., June 29, 1952; d. Stanley and Eloyse Blumenthal; m. Edward John Markey. BA, Reed Coll., 1971; MD, U. Tenn., 1976; MPA, Harvard U., 1982; PhD (hon.), Trinity Coll., 1996; DSc (hon.), Pine Manor Coll., 1998. Diplomate Am. Bd. Psychiatry and Neurology. Intern. Stanford U. Sch. Medicine, 1976-77, residency and fellowship, 1977-80; fellow NIMH, 1980-81, assoc. dir. Psychiatry Tng. Rev., head suicide rsch. unit and coord. of project depression, 1982-85, chief behavioral medicine program, 1985-93, chief behavioral rsch. branch, 1991-93; clin. asst. prof. Tufts Med. Ctr., 1981-82; clin. asst. prof. psychiatry George Washington Sch. Medicine, 1982-86; clin. assoc. prof. psychiatry Georgetown Sch. Med., 1986-91; clin. prof. psychiatry Georgetown Sch. Medicine, Washington, 1991—; dep. asst. sec. health (women's health) HHS, Washington, 1993—97, asst. surgeon e-health, 1998—, sr. med. advisor Office GLobal Health; sr. health adv., 2002—; clin. prof. psychiatry Tufts Sch. Medicine, 1995—; assoc. v.p. for health affairs George Washington U. Med. Ctr., 1998. Vis. prof. ob-gyn. George Washington U. Med. Ctr., 1998-99; disting. vis. prof. women's studies Brandeis U., 1999—; chair NIH Coord. Com. on Health and Behavior, 1991-94; co-chair NIH Reunion Task Force, 1992-94; chair fed. coord. com. breast cancer, fed. coord. com. women's health and the environ., co-chair nat. breast cancer action plan, coord. com. women's health issues USPHS, 1994-98; mem. Pres.'s Interagy. Coun. on Women; sr. advisor for pub. health White House Coun. on Youth Violence, 2000-02, sr. advisor on sec. pub. health and sci. to the sec., USDA, 2000-02. Editor: Suicide Over the Life Cycle, 1989, Premenstrual Syndrome, 1985; mem. editl. bds.: Jour. Women's Health, Depression, health columnist : Elle Mag., Ladies Home Jour., U.S. News and World Report; contbr. articles to sci. jours. Mem. Nat. Commn. on Sleep Disorders Rsch., workgroup on mental health Pres. Task Force on Health Care Reform; U.S. rep. global commn. on Women's Health WHO. Capt. USPHS, 1992-94, rear adm., 1994—. Recipient Outstanding Svc. medal, 1989, Commendation medal, 1990, Meritorious Svc. medal, USPHS, 1992, Surgeon Gen.'s Exemplary Svc. medal, 1997, Spl. Assignment Svc. medal, 1998, 2002, Achievement medal, 2002, Sec.'s Honor award for Domestic Violence, 1996, Asst. Sec. for Health's award for Breast Cancer, 1996, Am. Med. Writers award, 1996, Gretchen Poston award, The Nat. Race for the Cure, 1996, Founder's award, 1996, Pub. Svc. award, Nat. Alliance for the Mentally Ill, 1996, Gracie award, Assn. Women Radio and TV Profls., 1997, Inspiration Leader award, Pa. Diabetes Assn., 1997, Women of Distinction award, Nat. Assn. Women in Higher Edn., 1998, Woman of Valor award, United Jewish Fedn., 1999, Mosaic award, Komen Found., 2000, Founder's award, 2000, Feminist First award for Health, Feminist Majority, 2000, Congl. award, 2001, Women's Ctr. Leadership award, 2003. Mem. AMA, Am. Psychiat. Assn. (cons. Joint Coun. on Pub. Affairs, Francis Braceland award for pub. svc. 1998), Am. Coll. Psychiatrists, Am. Med. Women's Assn. (past chair com. on publicity and pub. rels., Pres.'s citation, 1996), Congl. Club, Nat. Assn. Bus. and Profl. Women (Magnificent Seven award 1996), Internat. Club, Internat. Women's Forum, Am. Suicide Found. (past bd. dirs. Washington divsn., pres.), Starlight Found. (past chmn. sci. adv. bd.). Office: HHS Rm 727H 200 Independence Ave SW Washington DC 20201

BLUMENTHAL, WILLIAM, lawyer; b. White Plains, N.Y., Nov. 4, 1955; s. Louis and Mary (Meyer) B.; m. Marjory Susan Spodick, Dec. 30, 1979; 1 child, Deborah Louise. AB, MA, Brown U., 1977; JD, Harvard U., 1980. Bar: D.C. 1980, U.S. Dist. Ct. D.C. 1986. Cons. Policy & Mgmt. Assocs., Inc., Boston, 1977-80; teaching fellow Harvard U., Cambridge, Mass., 1978-80; assoc. Jones, Day, Reavis & Pogue, Washington, 1980-83, Sutherland, Asbill & Brennan, Washington, 1983-87, ptnr., 1988-93, Kelley Drye & Warren, Washington, 1993-95, King & Spalding, Washington, 1995—. Editor Horizontal Mergers: Law and Policy, 1986; contbr. to book: The Merger Review Process, 1995, Mergers & Acquisitions Handbook, 1986. Harvey A. Baker fellow Brown U., 1977. Mem. ABA (chmn. Clayton Act com. 1992-94, chmn. monograph com. 1989-92, vice chmn. antitrust sect. 1997-98). E-mail: wblumenthal@kslaw.com.

BLUMER, DENNIS HULL, lawyer, academic administrator; b. Dayton, Ohio, Sept. 23, 1940; s. Robert Howard and Mary Eleanor (Hull) Blumer; m. Alice Painter Howard, Oct. 30, 1965; children: Mackenzie Hughes, Alexandra Paige. BA, Yale Coll., 1962, JD, 1965. Asst. to pres. Ctrl. State U., Wilberforce, Ohio, 1965-66; asst. to v.p. for adminstrn. U. Wis. Sys., Madison, 1966-68, spl. asst. to pres., 1968-71; exec. asst. to pres. U. Md., College Park, 1971-95; v.p., gen. counsel George Washington U., Washington, 1995—. Home: 2801 Davenport St NW Washington DC 20008-1014 Office: George Washington U 2100 Pennsylvania Ave NW Washington DC 20052-0001 E-mail: dblumer@gwu.edu.

BLUMER, FREDERICK ELWIN, retired philosophy educator; b. Glencoe, Okla., Sept. 16, 1933; s. Edward H. and Eva Marie (Forbes) B.; m. Ann Louise Anderson, June 9, 1956; children— Frederick Edward, William Robert. BA, Millsaps Coll., 1955; BD, Emory U., 1958, PhD, 1962; postgrad., Georg August U., Goettingen, Germany, 1960-61. Ordained to ministry United Meth. Ch., 1962; chaplain, instr. philosophy and religion Nebr. Wesleyan U., Lincoln, 1962-63, asst. prof., 1963-65, assoc. prof., 1965-67, prof., 1967-76, v.p. acad. affairs, 1967-70, provost, v.p. acad. affairs, 1970-76; pres. Lycoming Coll., Williamsport, Pa., 1976-89; Moll prof. faith and life Baldwin-Wallace Coll., Berea, Ohio, 1989-99, prof. emeritus, 1999—. Dean, dir. Graz (Austria) Ctr., 1972-73; mem. univ. senate United Meth. Ch., 1980-88, 93-97, pres., 1980-88, chmn. Commn. on Theol. Edn.; exec. com. Commn. Ind. Colls. and Univs. Pa., 1978-81, treas., 1988-89. Editor: Nebr. Wesleyan Univ. Press, 1967-76; Contbr. articles to profl. jours. Dir. edn. Lincoln United Way, 1971; bd. dirs. N.E. Lincoln YMCA, 1968-71, Lincoln Symphony Orch., 1971-76, Williamsport/Lycoming United Way, 1976-83; bd. mgrs. Williamsport Hosp., 1982-89; chmn. Found. Ind. Colls. Pa., 1987-88; bd. dirs. Pine Street Found., 1982-86, Lycoming Found., 1985-89. Recipient Pres.'s award Nebr. Wesleyan U., 1966; Cokesbury fellow, Dempster fellow, Rockefeller doctoral fellow Emory U. Mem. Nat. Assn. Schs., Colls., Univs. of United Meth. Ch. (pres. 1987-89), Williamsport-Lycoming C. of C. (dir., exec. com. 1976-85), Phi Kappa Phi, Pi Gamma Mu, Theta Phi, Omicron Delta Kappa. Republican. Home: 20798 Burgandy Dr Strongsville OH 44149-5602

BLUMKIN, LINDA RUTH, lawyer; b. Aug. 25, 1944; d. Louis and Edith (Fortus) Blumkin. AB cum laude, Barnard Coll., 1964; LLB cum laude, Harvard U., 1967, LLM, 1973. Bar: N.Y. 1968, U.S. Dist. Ct. (so. dist.) N.Y. 1969, U.S. Ct. Appeals (2nd cir.) 1969, U.S. Supreme Ct. 1982. Assoc. Fried, Frank, Harris, Shriver & Jacobson, N.Y.C., 1967—71, ptnr., 1979—. Lectr. Boston U., 1971, asst. prof. mgmt., 1972—73; assoc. Breed, Abbott & Morgan, N.Y.C., 1973—77; asst. dir. Bur. Competition, Fed. Trade Commn., 1977—79. Mem.: ABA, N.Y.C. Bar Assn. Office: Fried Frank Harris Shriver & Jacobson 1 New York Plz Fl 24 New York NY 10004-1901

BLUMMER, KATHLEEN ANN, counselor; b. Iowa Falls, Iowa, Apr. 17, 1945; d. Arthur G. and Julia C. (Ericson) Thorsbakken; m. Terry L. Blummer, Feb. 13, 1971 (dec. 1980); 1 child, Emily Erica. AA, Ellsworth Coll., Iowa Falls, 1965; BA, U. Iowa, 1967; postgrad., Northeastern Ill. U., 1969-70, U. N.Mex., 1980—; MA, Western N.Mex. U., 1973. Asst. buyer Marshall Field & Co., Chgo., 1967-68; social worker Cook County Dept. Pub. Aid, Chgo., 1968-69; tchr. Chgo. Pub. Schs., 1968-69; student fin. aid counselor Western N.Mex. U., Silver City, 1971-72; family social worker, counselor Southwestern N.Mex. Svcs. to Handicapped Children and Adults, Silver City, 1972-74; career edn. program specialist Galluo McKinley County (N.Mex.) Schs., 1974-76; dir. summer sch. Loving (N.Mex.) Mcpl. Schs., 1977; counselor, dept. chmn. Carlsbad (N.Mex.) Pub. Schs., 1977-82; counselor Albuquerque Pub. Schs., 1982—. Mem. AAUW (topic chmn. Carlsbad chpt., v.p. Albuquerque chpt.), N.Mex. Personnel and Guidance Assn., Theos Club, Highpoint Swim and Racquet Club (Albuquerque), Elks. Democrat. Lutheran.

BLUMREICH, KATHLEEN MARIE, language educator; d. William Raymond and Mary Helen (Kirkland) Blumreich; life ptnr. Diana Graham Pace. PhD, Mich. State U. Prof. English Grand Valley State U., Allendale, Mich., 2003—. Author, editor (book) The Middle English 'Mirror': An Edition Based on Bodleian Library. Sponsor Childreach. Dorothy Collins Brown fellow, Huntington Libr., San Marino, Calif., 1994. Mem.: Medieval Feminist Soc., Internat. Courtly Lit. Soc., Internat. Arthurian Soc., Internat. Critical Incident Stress Found., Inc., Phi Beta Kappa. Democrat. Office: Grand Valley State U Department of English Lake Huron Hall Allendale MI 49401 Personal E-mail: blumreik@gvsu.edu. E-mail: blumreik@gvsu.edu.

BLUMSTEIN, ALFRED, urban and public affairs educator; b. N.Y.C., June 3, 1930; m. Dolores Reguera, Jan. 26, 1958; children: Lisa, Ellen, Diane. BS in Engring. Physics, Cornell U., 1951, PhD in Ops. Rsch., 1960; MS in Stats., U. Buffalo, 1954; JD (hon.), John Jay Coll., 1996. Prin. ops. analyst Cornell Aeronautical Lab., Buffalo, 1951-61; rsch. staff Inst. Def. Analyses, Arlington, Va., 1961-69; dir. sci. and tech. task force Pres.'s Commn. Law Enforcement and Adminstrn. Justice, Washington, 1966-67; J. Erik Jonsson Univ. prof. urban sys. and ops. rsch. H. John Heinz III Sch. Pub. Policy and Mgmt. Carnegie-Mellon U., Pitts., 1969—, dean, 1986-93, dir. Nat. Consortium on Violence Rsch., 1996—. Overseas fellow Churchill Coll. Cambridge U., 1983—; chmn. various panels NRC Com. Rsch. Law Enforcement and Adminstrn. Justice, 1982-86, chmn. com., 1980-83; mem. NRC Commn. Behavioral and Social Scis. and Edn., 1994-2000. Mem. editl. bd. Ops. Rsch. Letters, Jour. Rsch. in Crime and Delinquency, Evaluation Rev., Jour. Criminal Justice, Sci. Commn. of Internat. Soc. of Criminology, 1985-91, others; co-editor Cambridge Criminology Series; contbr. articles to profl. jours. Chmn. Pa. Commn. Crime and Delinquency, Harrisburg, 1979-90; mem. Pa. Commn. on Sentencing, 1986-96; bd. dirs. Police Found., 1990-96; nat. adv. com. Inst. Rsch. on Poverty at U. Wis., 1989-94; trustee Jewish Healthcare Found., 2001--. Fellow AAAS, Am. Soc. Criminology (pres. 1991-92, Sutherland award 1987); mem. Ops. Rsch. Soc. Am. (pres. 1977-78, Kimball medal 1985, Pres.'s award 1993), Am. Statis. Assn., Inst. Ops. Rsch. and Mgmt. Scis. (pres. 1996), Law and Society Assn., The inst. Mgmt. Scis. (pres. 1987-88), Internat. Fedn. Operational Rsch. Socs. (v.p. N.Am. 1992-94), Consortium of Social Sci. Assns. (pres. 1999—), Cosmos Club, Omega Rho (hon.). Mem. NAE, 1998—. Home: 1455 Wightman St Pittsburgh PA 15217-1260 Office: Carnegie-Mellon U H John Heinz III Sch Pub Policy Mgmt Pittsburgh PA 15213 E-mail: ab0q@andrew.cmu.edu.

BLUMSTEIN, EDWARD, lawyer; b. Phila., Aug. 24, 1933; s. Isaac and Mollye (Rodofsky) B.; m. Susan Perloff, Aug. 13, 1983; 1 child, Daniel Blumstein. BS in Econs., U. Pa., 1955; JD, Temple U., 1958. Bar: U.S. Dist. Ct. (ea. dist.) Pa. 1959, U.S. Ct. Appeals (3rd cir.) 1959. Pvt. practice, Phila., 1959-85; ptnr. Blumstein, Block & Pease, Phila., 1985—2002, Edward Blumstein, PC, Phila., 2002—. Adj. prof. Sch. Law Temple U., 1994—. Gen. Counsel to North American Ski Journalists Assn. With U.S. Army, 1958-64. Mem. ABA, Pa. Bar Assn., Phila. Bar Assn. (bd. govs. 1984-85, past chmn. family law sect. 1984), Assn. Conflict Resolution, Family Mediation Assn. Del. Valley (pres. 1990-91), B'nai B'rith. Republican. Jewish. Avocations: skiing, reading, photography. Office: 1500 Walnut St Ste 1600 Philadelphia PA 19102 Fax: 215-790-1988.

BLUMSTEIN, JAMES FRANKLIN, law educator, lawyer, consultant; b. Bklyn., Apr. 24, 1945; s. David and Rita (Sondheim) B.; m. Andree Kahn, June 25, 1971 BA in Econs., Yale U., 1966, MA in Econs., LLB, 1970. Bar: Tenn. 1970, U.S. Ct. Appeals (6th cir.) 1970, U.S. Dist. Ct. (mid. dist.) Tenn. 1971, U.S. Supreme Ct. 1974, N.Y. 1985. Instr. econs. New Haven Coll., 1967-68; pre-law adviser office of dean Yale U., New Haven, 1968-69, sr. pre-law adviser office of dean, 1969-70, asst. in instrn. law shc., 1969-70; asst. prof. law Vanderbilt U., Nashville, 1970-73, assoc. prof., 1973-76, prof., 1976-99, spl. advisor to chancellor for acad. affairs, 1984-85, Centennial prof., 1999—, Univ. prof. law and medicine, 2003—, chair faculty senate, 2001—02, univ. prof., 2003—. Assoc. dir. Vanderbilt Urban and Regional Devel. Ctr., 1970-72, dir. ctr., 1972-74; sr. rsch. assoc. Vanderbilt Inst. for Pub. Policy Studies, 1976-85, sr. fellow, 1985—, dir. health policy ctr., 1995—; Commonwealth Fund fellow, vis. assoc. prof. law and policy scis. law sch. Duke U. and Inst. of Policy Scis. and Pub. Affairs, 1974-75; adj. prof. health law med. sch. Dartmouth U., scholar-in-residence intermittently, 1976-78; John M. Olin vis. prof. Sch. Law, U. Pa., 1989; elected mem. Inst. Medicine NAS, 1990—; cons. law, health policy, civil and voting rights, land use, state taxation, torts; lectr. in field. Editor: (with Eddie J. Martin) The Urban Scene in the Seventies, 1974, (with Benjamin Walter) Growing Metropolis: Aspects of Development in Nashville, 1975, (with Lester Salamon) Growth Policy in the Eighties (Law and Contemporary Problems Symposium), 1979; (with Frank A. Sloan and James M. Perrin) Uncompensated Hospital Care: Rights and Responsibilities, 1986, (with Frank A. Sloan and James M. Perrin) Cost, Quality, and Access in Health Care: New Roles for Health Planning in a Competitive Environment, 1988; (with Frank A. Sloan) Organ Transplantation Policy: Issues and Prospects, 1989, (with Frank A. Sloan) Antitrust and Health Care Policy (Law and Contemporary Problems Symposium), 1989, (with Clark C. Havighurst and Troyen A. Brennan) Health Care Law and Policy, 1998, bd. Jour. Health Politics, Policy and Law, 1981-01; mem. adv. bd. NF IB Legal Found., 2003-; mem. pub.'s adv. bd. Nashville Banner, 1982-98; contbr. articles to profl. jours., op-ed articles to newspapers. Mem. Health Econs. Task Force, Middle Tenn. Health Sys. Agy., 1979; mem. adv. bd. LWV, 1979-80; mem. Nashville Mayor's Commn. on Crime, 1981; cons. Leadership Nashville, 1977—. Tenn. Motor Vehicle Commn., 1986-87, Leadership Music, 1989-02; panelist Am. Arbitration Assn., 1977-02; chmn. Tenn. adv. com. U.S. Commn. on Civil Rights, 1985-91, mem., 1991-97; sec. Martin Luther King Jr. Holiday Com., State of Tenn., 1985-87; bd. dirs. Jewish Fedn. Nashville and Middle Tenn., 1981-90, mem. exec. com., 1988-90, chmn. cmty. rels. com., 1980-82, chmn. campus com., 1987-89; chmn. Yale Alumni Schs. Com. Middle Tenn., 1983—; mem Tenn. Gov.'s Task Force Medicaid, 1992-94; mem. adv. panel Office Tech. Assessment study of defensive medicine and use of med. tech., 1991-94; chmn. task force cost containment and med. malpractice Rand Corp., 1991-92; active Inst. Medicine Com. on Adequacy of Nursing Staffing, 1994-96; mem. adv. com. on The Records of Congress, 1997-99. Bates Jr. fellow, 1968-69; grantee Ford Found./Rockefeller Found. Population Program, 1970-73, Health Policy grantee HCA Found., 1986-90; grantee State Justice Inst., 1991—, Robert Wood Johnson Found., 1994—; nominated Adminstr., Office Info. and Regulatory Affairs, Office Mgmt. and Budget, 1990; named One of Outstanding Young Men in Am. U.S. Jaycees, 1971; recipient award Univ. Rsch. Coun., 1971-72, 73-74, 79-80, 94-95, Earl Sutherland prize achievement in rsch. Vanderbilt U., 1992, Paul J. Hartman award Outstanding Prof., 1982. Mem. ABA (sec. sect. legal edn. and admissions to bar 1982-83, chmn. subcom. on state and local taxation com. on corp. law and taxation sect. on corp., banking and bus. law 1983—, mem. accreditation com. sect. legal edn. and admissions to bar 1983-89, mem. com. on state and local taxation sect. on taxation 1983—), NAS (inst. of medicine), Assn. Am. Law Schs. (chmn. law, medicine and health care sect. 1987-88, mem. exec. com. 1988-92, 2d vice chmn. sect. local govt. law 1976-78, mem. sect. coun. 1980-86), Tenn. Bar Assn., N.Y. State Bar Assn., Nashville Bar Assn. (Liberty Bell award 1987), Hastings Ctr., Assn. for Pub.

Policy Analysis and Mgmt., Assn. Yale Alumni (del.), Yale U. Law Sch. Alumni Assn. (exec. com. 1985-88), Univ. Club (Nashville). Home: 2113 Hampton Ave Nashville TN 37215-1401 Office: Vanderbilt U Sch Law 21st Ave S Nashville TN 37240-0001

BLUMSTEIN, RENEÉ J. research and statistical consultant; b. Bklyn., Apr. 1, 1957; d. Robert and Rosalie (Burak) B.; m. Vic DiVenere, May 12, 1996; children: Robert Victor DiVenere, Joseph Dante DiVenere. BA, Queens Coll., N.Y., 1978; MA, Columbia U., 1980, MEd, 1982, MPhil, 1984, PhD, 1986. Rsch. psychologist CCNY, 1980-85; rsch. cons. AT&T, N.Y.C., 1986; rsch. analyst Citibank, N.Y.C., 1986-87, rsch. and statis. cons., 1987—, Informed Decision Svcs., Inc., L.I.; adj. prof. rsch. methods CUNY, 1990—. Scholar Columbia U., 1981. Mem. Am. Psychol. Assn., Nat. Assn. Women Bus. Owners, Am. Edn. Rsch. Assn. Avocations: travel, biking, swimming. Home and Office: 14 Ingold Dr Dix Hills NY 11746-7804 E-mail: rjb@researchforeducation.com.

BLUMSTEIN, SHEILA ELLEN, former academic administrator, linguistics educator; b. N.Y.C., Mar. 10, 1944; d. Edgar and Bernice Marjorie (Heineman) B. BA, U. Rochester, 1965; PhD, Harvard U., 1970. Asst. prof. linguistics Brown U., Providence, 1970—76, assoc. prof., 1976—81, prof., 1981—91, Albert D. Mead prof. cognitive and linguistic scis., 1991—, dean of coll., 1987—95, interim pres., 2000—01, interim provost, 1998; research assoc. Aphasia Research Ctr., VA Med. Ctr., Boston, 1970—. Vis. scientist MIT, Cambridge, 1974, 77-78; mem. study sect. NIH, 1976-80, exec. com. Com. on Hearing, Bioacoustics, Biomechanics, NRC, 1980-82, sci. program adv. com. Nat. Inst. Neurol. and Comm. Diseases and Strokes, 1982-84; Henry R. Luce vis. prof. Wellesley Coll., Mass., 1982-83; mem. adv. coun. Nat. Inst. Deafness and Other Comm. Disorders, 1989-93; mem. sci. adv. bd. McDonnell-Pew Program in Neuroscis., 1989-2000. Author: A Phonological Investigation of Aphasic Speech, 1973, (with P. Lieberman) Speech Physiology Acoustics and Speech Perception, 1987; editor: (with H. Goodglass) Psycholinguistics and Aphasia, 1973; mem. editorial bd. Brain and Lang., 1978-83, Cognition, 1982-90, Applied Psycholinguistics, 1984-89; adv. editor Contemporary Psychology, 1981-83; contbr. articles to profl. jours., chpts. to books Recipient Javits neurosci. investigator award, 1985-92; Guggenheim fellow, 1977-78, Radcliffe Inst. fellow, 1977-78 Fellow Acoustical Soc. Am., Am. Acad. Arts and Scis.; mem. Linguistics Soc. Am., Acad. Aphasia, Am. Philos. Soc., Phi Beta Kappa, Phi Sigma Iota. Jewish. Avocations: tennis, piano, music, gardening. Home: 14 Broadview Dr Barrington RI 02806-4012 Office: Brown Univ PO Box 1978 Providence RI 02912-1978*

BLUMSTEIN, SUSAN BENDER, fundraiser; b. Phila., Dec. 20, 1943; d. Israel Boris and Lillian (Zebooker) B.; children: Eve, Zachary. BA, U. Pa., 1965. Exec. v.p. Am. Friends Israel Philharmonic Orch., N.Y.C., 1981-89; asst. v.p. devel. Jewish Theol. Sem., N.Y.C., 1989-94; rep. World ORT Union, 1994-96; v.p. external affairs Manhattan Sch. Music, N.Y.C., 1997—. Cons. Nat. Found. Jewish Culture, N.Y.C., 1989, Israel Bonds, N.Y.C., 1990, Internat. Mendelsshon-Stiftung, Leipzig, Germany, 1993, JCCA, N.Y.C., 1994, Ecole Americaine Fontainebleau. Chair U.S.A. Women's Lecture Series, N.Y., 1990-92; cons. St. Petersburg Philharm., 1997-99, Oesterfestspiele, 1999. E-mail: sblumstein@msmnyc.edu.

BLUNCK, KLAIRE DARLENE, nurse; b. Oconomowoc, Wis., May 3, 1954; d. Wynn F. and Frances Lavern (Bartlein) Kemnitz; m. William Randel Blunck, Aug. 11, 1973; children: Jacob William, Joseph Randel. AD, Milw. Area Tech. Coll., 1974; BSN, Carroll Coll., 1992. Cert. CPR, neonatal resuscitation and pitocin adminstrn., lactation educator, lactation counselor, pediat. emergency care nurse; cert. inpatient obstet. nurse. Mem. ob-gyn/pediatrics staff Oconomowoc Meml. Hosp., 1974-76, head quality improvement ob-gyn. unit, 1976—; trainee high risk perinatal clinic Waukesha Meml. Hosp., 1999. Part-time mgr. high risk perinatal clinic Oconomowoc Meml. Hosp.; part-time staff nurse ob-gyn/pediatrics Oconomowoc Meml. Hosp. Profl. Office Bldg., 1999—; part-time instr. breast-feeding classes. Pres. ch. women Dr. Martin Luth. Ch., Oconomowoc, 1994, 95, 96, guitarist, vocalist contemporary svcs., 2001. Laureate Group scholar. Mem. Order Ea. Star (conductress Oconomowoc/Hartland chpt. 1997, worthy matron 1999-2000).

BLUNDELL, RICHARD WILLIAM, economics educator; b. Shoreham, Sussex, Eng., May 1, 1952; s. Lionel and Marjorie (Davies) B.; m. Anne Aberdeen; children: Katie, Jack. BS in Econs., U. Bristol, Eng., 1973; MS in Econometrics, London Sch. Econs., 1975, D (hon.), U. St. Gullen, 2003. Lectr. U. Manchester, Eng., 1975-84; prof. econs. Univ. Coll. London, 1984—, dir. rsch. Inst. for Fiscal Studies, 1986—, dir. ESRC Ctr. for Micro-Econ. Analysis of Fiscal Policy, 1991—, head dept., 1988-92, Leverhulme Personal Rsch. prof., 1999. Vis. assoc. prof. U. B.C., Vancouver, 1980-81, MIT, Cambridge, 1993, U. Calif., Berkeley, 1994-99. Author: The Measurement of Household Welfare, 1994; editor Jour. Econometrics, 1993-97, Econometrica, 1997—2001; contbr. articles to profl. jours. Recipient Yrjo Jahnsson prize Jahnsson Found., 1995, Frisch prize, 2000. Fellow Econometrics Soc., British Acad., Coun. of Econometric Soc., Inst. Actuaries (hon.); mem. European Econ. Assn. (coun. 1997—), Am. Econ. Assn. (hon.), Fgn. Mem. Am. Acad. Arts and Sciences, European Econ. Assn. (v.P. 2002-) Avocations: music, theatre, cycling, travel. Office: Univ Coll London Dept Econs Gower St London WC1E 6BT England E-mail: r.blundell@ucl.ac.uk.

BLUNDELL, WILLIAM RICHARD CHARLES, retired electric company executive; b. Montreal, Apr. 13, 1927; s. Richard C. and Did Aileen (Payne) B.; m. Monique Audet, Mar. 20, 1959; children: Richard, Emily, Michelle, Louise. BSc, U. Toronto, 1949. Registered profl. engr., Ont. Sales engr. Can. Gen. Electric Co., Toronto, 1949-51, travelling auditor, 1951, various fin. positions, 1951-66, treas., 1966-68, v.p.-fin., 1968-70, v.p., exec. consumer div., 1970-72, v.p., exec. apparatus div. Lachine, Que., 1972-79; pres., CEO, Camco Inc., Weston, Ont., 1979-83; pres., COO, Can. Gen. Electric Co. Ltd., Toronto, 1983-84; chmn., CEO Gen. Electric Can. Inc., Toronto, 1985-90; ret., 1991. Chmn. Mfrs. Life Ins. Co., 1994—98, chmn. pub. sector pension investment bd., 2000—03; vice chair Can. Inst. for Advanced Rsch., 1998—; bd. dirs. CableServ, Inc., Metallic Ventures Inc. Decorated officer Order of Can.; recipient Engring. Alumni medal U. Toronto, 1990. Home: 29 Rothmere Dr North York ON Canada M4N IV3 E-mail: bill_blundell@rogers.com.

BLUNK, JOYCE ELAINE, artist, educator; b. Moorland, Iowa, May 13, 1939; d. George Daniel and Burnice Margaret (Taylor) Blunk. BA, U. Iowa, 1963, MA, 1970, MFA, 1971. Cert. tchr., Iowa. Grad. tchg. asst. U. Iowa, Iowa City, 1970-71; instr. Western Carolina U., Cullowhee, N.C., 1978-82; adj. instr. U. N.C., Asheville, 1992; artist, tchr. Vt. Coll. of Norwich U., Montpelier, 1997-98 99-2000; artist Joyce Blunk Studio, Asheville, N.C., 1975—. Mem. exhbn. com. Asheville Area Arts Coun., 1999—. Exhibited in solo shows at Mint Mus. Art, Charlotte, N.C., 1991, U. Alaska, Anchorage, 1999, Cecilia Coker Bell Gallery, Coker Coll., Hartsville, S.C., 2002, Black Mountain (N.C.) Ctr. for the Arts, 2002; group shows include Künstlerhaus, Schwandorf, Germany, 1990, Chateau de la Napoule, France, 1994, Hunter Mus. Am. Art, Chattanooga, 2002, Tryon Ctr. for Visual Arts, Charlotte, N.C., 2002. Poll clk. local and nat. elections Buncombe County, N.C., 1999—; campaign worker Mayoral Election, Asheville, 1997. Fellow, Va. Ctr. for Creative Arts, Salzburg, Austria, 1999, Cill Rialaig Internat. Artists' Retreat, Ballinskelligs, County Kerry, Ireland, 2003; grantee, Pollock-Krasner Found., 1991—92; visual artist fellow, N.C. Arts Coun., 1996—97, material on file, Archives on Women Artists, The Libr. and Rsch. Ctr. of the Nat. Mus. of Women in the Arts. Mem. Asheville Art Mus., Internat. Sculpture Ctr., Nat. Assn. Women Artists Inc. Democrat. Avocations: reading, attending classical music concerts, hiking, travel. Home: 31 Samayoa Pl Asheville NC 28806-2913 E-mail: joyceblunk@yahoo.com.

BLUNT, MATT, secretary of state; b. Missouri; m. Melanie Blunt, Mar. 1997. BA in history, Naval Acad., Annapolis, Md. Elected sec. state State of Mo., 2000. Served USNR, 2001, Ops. Enduring Freedom, engineering officer USNR, USS Jack Williams, navigator, adminstrv. officer USS USNR. Decorated Navy, achievement award Marine Corps, Humanitarian Svc. Medal. Mem.: Mo. Farm Bureau, Am. Legion, State Historical Soc. Mo. Baptist. Office: Sec State Mo State Capitol Rm 208 Jefferson City MO 65101

BLUNT, ROY D. congressman; b. Niangua, Mo., Jan. 10, 1950; s. Leroy and Neva (Letterman) B.; children: Matthew Roy, Amy Roseann, Andrew Benjamin BA, S.W. Bapt. U., 1970; MA, S.W. Mo. State U., 1972. Tchr. Marshfield (Mo.) High Sch., 1970-73; instr. Drury Coll., Springfield, Mo., 1973-82; clk. Greene County, Springfield, 1973-85; sec. of state State of Mo., Jefferson City, 1985-93; pres. Southwest Bapt. U., 1993-96; mem. 105th-108th Congresses from 7th Mo. dist., 1997—; apptd. chief dep. majority whip 106th-107th Congress; elected Ho. majority whip 108th Congress. Mem. Fed. Election Commn. Adv. Panel; del. Atlantic Treaty Assn. Conf., 1987; mem. Congressional Com. on Commerce, 1999—, Internat. Rels., 1997-98, Ho. Reps. Steering Com., 1997—; del. Nat. Hist. Publs. and Records Commn., 1997—; mem. ho. appropriations com., 1999. Author: (with others) Missouri Election Procedures: A Layman's Guide, 1977; Voting Rights Guide for the Handicapped Bd. dirs. Ctr. for Democracy; mem. Mo. Mental Health Advocacy Coun., 1998-99; mem. exec. bd. Am. Coun. of Young Polit. Leaders, 1998-99; chmn. Mo. Housing Devel. Commn., Kansas City, 1981, Rep. State Conv., Springfield, 1980; chmn. Gov.'s Adv. Coun. on Literacy; co-chmn. Mo. Opportunity 2000 Commn., 1985-87; Rep. candidate for lt. gov. of Mo., 1980; active local ARC, Muscular Dystrophy Assn., others. Named One of 10 Outstanding Young Americans U.S. Jaycees, 1986, Springfield's Outstanding Young Man Jaycees, 1980, Mo.'s Outstanding Young Civic Leader, 1981 Mem. Nat. Assn. Secs. of State (chmn. voter registration and edn. com., sec., v.p. 1990). Am. Coun. Young Polit. Leaders. Lodges: Kiwanis, Masons. Republican. Baptist. Office: US Ho of Reps 217 Cannon Ho Office Bldg Washington DC 20515-0001 also: Whip's Office H-329 The Capitol Washington DC 20515 E-mail: blunt@mail.house.gov.*

BLUST, STEVEN R. commissioner; BA, US Merchant Marine Acad., 1971; MBA, Tulane U., 1979. Commr. US Fed. Maritime Comm., Washington, 2002—; ceo Tampa Bay Int. Terminals, Inc., 1997—2001; exec. Lykes Brothers Steamship Co., Inc.; mgr. Jacksonville Port Authority, Crowley Delta Lines. Office: 800 N Capital St NW Washington DC 20573*

BLUTH, B. J. (ELIZABETH JEAN CATHERINE BLUTH), sociologist, aerospace technologist; b. Phila., Dec. 5, 1934; d. Robert Thomas and Catherine Cecelia (Boxman) Gowland; m. Thomas Del Bluth, Aug. 20, 1960 (dec. Aug. 6, 1980); children: Robert Thomas, Richard Del. BA in Sociology (Washington semster fellow), Bucknell U., 1953; MA, Fordham U., 1960; PhD, UCLA, 1970. Teaching fellow in methods of social research Fordham U., 1957-58; reading instr. St. Margaret's High Sch., Tappahannock, Va., 1958-59; instr. history, civics and English, Rosary High Sch., San Diego, 1959-60; successively instr., asst. prof. sociology Immaculate Heart Coll., Los Angeles, 1960-65; prof. sociology Calif. State U., Northridge, 1965-87; grantee NASA Ames Research Ctr., Moffett Field, Calif., 1982-83; grantee space sta. program NASA, Washington, 1983-87, aerospace technologist system engring. div. space sta. program office Reston, Va., 1987-90, spl. asst. to dep. program dir. space sta. freedom program and ops., 1990-94, spl. tech. asst. to dir. edn. divsn., mgr. edn. evaluation Washington, 1994—2003, program mgr. on-line edn. evaluation program, 1994—. Cons. Immaculate Heart Cmty., L.A., 1967-69; engring. rsch. NASA Space Sta. design Boeing Aerospace Co., 1982-83; mem. Presdl. Citizens Adv. com. on Space, Coun. Nat. Space Policy, Nat. Tech. Com. on Soc. & Tech., UN team on relevance of space activities to econ. and social devel.; professor emeritus Calif. State U., 1987—; computational scis. and informatics inst. dir.'s search com. George Mason U., 1992-93. Editor: (with others) Search for Identity Reader, vol. I and II, 1973, (with S.R. McNeal) Update on Space, vol. I, 1961, Parson's General Theory of Action, 1982, Space Station Habitability Report, 1983, Soviet Space Station Analog, 1983, Space Station Human Productivity Study NASA, 1986, Russian Mir Space Station Analog, 1993, Marching with Sharpe, 2001; contbr. articles to profl. jours. Recipient Alpha Omega faculty awards, 1966, 1974. Fellow Am. Astronautical Soc.; mem. AIAA (chpt. award for outstanding program 1980), Am. Sociol. Assn., L5 Soc., Brit. Interplanetary Soc., Inst. Social Sci. Study of Space (acad. adv. bd.), Space Studies Inst., Internat. Acad. Astronautics (com. on space econs. and benefits), Phi Beta Kappa. Republican. Office: NASA Code Office of Edn 300 E St SW Washington DC 20546-0005 *To seed the universe with intelligence you must: never give up, no matter how little progress you see day-to-day for it's the "big picture" where the changes show up; always concentrate on the practical, no matter how enticing theories appear; never forget that ideas and systems and institutions are nothing more than ideas, and ideas can change— that is the true vehicle to freedom. Always reach beyond the horizon, knowing that horizons have no limit save that of our imagination.*

BLY, CARL ANTHONY, retired music educator; b. Carbondale, Pa., Mar. 20, 1946; s. Musin Jackson and Jeanette Rose Bly; m. Randi Jean Shoremount, June 15, 1974; children: Gretchen Elizabeth, Heidi Marie. MusB in Edn., Shenandoah Conservatory of Music, 1967; MA in Conducting, George Mason U., 1987. Collegiate Professional License State Bd. of Edn., 1971. Band dir. John Randolph Tucker HS, Richmond, Va., 1971—76, Lake Braddock Secondary Sch., Fairfax County, Va., 1976—88; band dir. and dept. chair Centreville (Va.) HS, 1988—2001. Com. mem. Nat. Fedn. of HS's, Indpls., 1984—88. Musician and conductor: concert Mid-West Band and Orchestra Clinic, Bands of America's Nat. Concert Band Festival; dir.: (marching band performance) Marching Bands of America's Grand National Championship. With U.S. Army, 1966—68, Viet Nam. Recipient Presdl. Citation, Va. Governor's Sch., 1994, 1996, 1997, Citation of Excellence, Nat. Band Assn., 1998, 1999, Presdl. Citation, Va. Governor's Sch., 2001, Citation of Excellence, Nat. Band Assn., 2001; fellow Conducting fellow, Am. Symphony Orch. League, 1975—77. Mem.: Va. Band & Orch. Dirs. Assn. (pres. 1984—86, bd. dirs. 1982—), Va. Music Educators Assn., Music Educators Nat. Conf., Circus Fans Am., Circus Model Builders Assn., Circus Hist. Soc., Phi Beta Mu (pres. 1993—98). Home: 6008 Rockton Ct Centreville VA 20121-3080 Office: Same Personal E-mail: carl.bly@verizon.net.

BLY, CAROL MCLEAN, writer, educator; b. Duluth, Minn., Apr. 16, 1930; d. Charles Russell and Mildred Barr (Washburn) McLean; m. June 24, 1955 (div. 1979); children: Mary, Bridget, Noah, Micah. BA in English, Wellesley Coll., 1951; DHL, Northland Coll., 1985. Instr. writing U. Minn., Mpls., 1981—. Vis. disting. Benedict prof. Carleton Coll., U. Minn., 1990, Edelstein-Keller disting. author, 1998-99; bd. dirs. The Loft, Mpls.; co-founder Collaborative of Tchrs. & Sch. Social Workers, St. Paul, 1993. Author: Letters from the Country, 1981, 1999, My Lord Bag of Rice, 2000, Beyond the Writers' Workshop, 2001, others. Bd. dirs. Episc. Cmty. Svcs., Mpls., 1980. Democrat. Avocation: tree planting. Home: 1668 Juno Ave Saint Paul MN 55116-1415 E-mail: carolbly@visi.com.

BLY, CHARLES ALBERT, nuclear engineer, research scientist; b. Winchester, Va., Jan. 11, 1952; s. Theodore and Nancy Irma (Fisher) B.; m. April Marie Monnen, July 24, 1976. BS in Nuclear Engring., U. Va., 1978, MS in Nuclear Engring., 1983; student, Nat. Acad. Nuclear Tng., 1992-93; postgrad. in nuclear engring., U. Va., 1994—, cardiovasc. rsch. tng., 1999—. Nuclear reactor operator Nuclear Reactor Facility of the U. Va., Charlottesville, 1977-80, sr. reactor operator, 1980-83, rsch. engr., 1981-83; vis. engr. Brit. Nuclear Fuel Ltd. Springfields Works, Preston Lancashire, England, 1983; nuclear engr. Comml. Nuclear Fuel div. Westinghouse Electric, Pitts., 1983-92, Beaver Valley Power Sta. Duquesne Light Co., Shippingport, Pa., 1992-94; lead prof. Oak Ridge (Tenn.) Nat. Lab. Am. Tech. Inst., 1994-95; nuclear reactor staff Nuclear Reactor Facility of U. Va., Charlottesville, 1995-99; staff U. Va. Health Svcs. Cardiovasc. Gene Therapy Lab., Charlottesville, 1999—. Contbr. numerous articles to profl. jours. Candidate Shenandoah County (Va.) Bd. of Supervisor, 1975; mem. Ad Hoc Com. to Prevent Extension of I-66 Hwy. Through George Washington Nat. Forest, Strasburg, Va., 1979, Ad Hoc Com. to Preserve the Pitts. Aviary, 1991. Mem. ASME, IEEE, ASTM, AAAS, Am. Nuc. Soc., Am. Phys. Soc., ASM Internat., Assn. Energy Engrs., The Engring. Soc., Profl. Engr.'s Soc., Fedn. Am. Scientists, Engr.'s Soc. Western Pa., N.Y. Acad. Scis., Internat. Platform Assn. Democrat. Lutheran. Achievements include invention of fusion and hybrid fission/fusion nuclear fuel rod, combined cycle steam turbine, gas turbine nuclear power plants, neutron flux driven cold fusion in palladium; discovery of neutrino-driven nuclear fission chain reactions/nucleon decay chain reactions; discovery of graviton-driven fermion fission chain reactions; development of Bohr model of nucleons; development of Bohr model of gravitation; development of a generalized Bode's Law; development of a fundamental subatomic particle rest mass correlation. Home: 777 Mountainwood Rd Apt D Charlottesville VA 22903-6507 Office: U Va Nuclear Reactor Facility Charlottesville VA 22903-2442 E-mail: cab7t@virginia.edu., charles.bly@technicolor.com.

BLY, JAMES CHARLES, JR., financial services executive; b. Kane, Pa., Jan. 24, 1952; s. James Charles Bly Sr. and Dorothy Hau Bly Smith; m. Laurie Ann Ramadon, June 6, 1987; children: Alana W., Bridget R., James C. III, Chase N. BA, St. Bonaventure U., 1973. CLU, cert. mergers and acquisitions Alliance of Mergers and Acquisitions Advisors. Mgmt. trainee Conn. Gen. Life, Washington, 1974-76; rep. CIGNA Fin. Svcs., McLean, Va., 1976-79; mng. exec. Integrated Resources Equity Corp., N.Y.C., 1980-82; pres. Source Capital, Ltd., Pitts., 1982—; chmn., CEO Source Cos., LLC, 1998—. Mem. adv. bd. John J. Kirlin, Inc., Rockville, Md., 1980—, Royal Bank of Can., Global Fin. Svcs. Network, 1991—97; bd. dirs. Holgate Toy Co., Draper Holdings Bus. Trust, Liberty-Pitts. Sys., Inc. Mem.: Alliance of Merger and Acquisition Advisors, Nat. Assn. Securities Dealers, Assn. Corp. Growth, Soc. Fin. Svcs. Profls., Allegheny Country Club, Edgeworth Club, The Stonedale Guns, Duquesne Club. Republican. Avocations: music, automobiles, history, travel, golf. Home: Spanish Tract Rd Sewickley PA 15143 Office: Source Cos LLC 1 Gateway Ctr # 1850 Pittsburgh PA 15222-1435

BLY, MARK JOHN, playwright, educator; b. Sioux Falls, S.D., Feb. 1, 1949; s. Myrle S. and Lois L. Bly. BA, U. Minn., 1974; MA, Boston Coll., 1977; MFA, Yale U., 1980. Script reader Yale Repertory Theater, New Haven, 1977-80, assoc. artistic dir., 1992—; assoc. literary mgr. Arena Stage, Washington, 1980-81; dramaturg, literary mgr. The Guthrie Theater, Mpls., 1981-89; artistic assoc., dramaturg Seattle Repertory Theatre, 1989-92; co-chair dramaturgy and dramatic criticism dept. Yale Sch. Drama, New Haven, 1992-97, chair playwriting dept., 1992—. Editor: The Production Notebooks, 1996, Vol. 2, 2001; contbg. editor Yale's Theater Mag., 1985-93, 98—, advisory editor, 1993-98; contbr. articles to profl. jours. and books. Mem. Literary Mgrs. and Dramaturgs Am. (regional v.p. 1989-90, v.p. for comm. 1991-92). Avocation: paleontology. Office: Yale Univ Sch Drama PO Box 208244 New Haven CT 06520-8244

BLY, ROBERT MAURICE, lawyer; b. Connersville, Ind., Oct. 31, 1944; s. Karl H. and Faye Virginia (DeHoff) B.; m. Ann Patrice Gleason, Aug. 24, 1968; 1 child, Thomas Robert. BS, Ball State U., 1966; JD, U. Tenn., 1973. Bar: Ill. 1973, Ind. 1974, U.S. Dist. Ct. (so. dist.) Ind. 1974, U.S. Dist. Ct. (no. dist.) Ind. 1978, U.S. Supreme Ct. 1981, Tenn. 1991, U.S. Dist. Ct. (ea. dist.) Tenn. 1992. Pub. sch. tchr. pub. schs., Ind., 1966-71; regional counsel's staff Chgo. (Ill.) Title & Trust Co., 1973-75; dep. prosecutor Porter County Ind., Valparaiso, 1975-76; pvt. practice law Valparaiso and Kokomo, Ind., 1976-91, Knoxville, Tenn., 1992—. Adj. instr. Ind. U., Kokomo, 1987-91; del. Ho. of Dels., Ind. Bar Assn., Indpls., 1988; founder Southeast Estate Planning Inst.; chmn. bd. trustees Thomas Bly Found.; prin. Regents Adv. Group, LLC; guest lectr. in field. Columnist Fairfield Glade Sun, 1993-94; contb. author: Generations Planning Your Legacy, 1999. Pres. Vols. in Cmty. Svc., Kokomo, 1980-85. Fellow: Mid South Estate Planning Forum (chmn. 1997—2001, founding mem.), Offshore Inst.; mem.: Tenn. Bar Assn. (tax, probate and trusts sect.), Am.'s Assn. Asset Protection (gen. coun.), Nat. Network Estate Planning Attys. Episcopalian. Avocations: collecting and restoring classic automobiles, traveling. Office: 9111 Cross Park Dr Ste D200 Knoxville TN 37923-4521

BLYAKHMAN, YEFIM MOISEI, chemist, researcher; b. Leningrad, Russia, Dec. 11, 1937; came to U.S., 1986; s. Moisei Isaak Blyakhman and Anna S. (Itzkov) Lohs; m. Irina A. Teverovskaya, Mar. 25, 1958; 1 child, Alexander. M in Chem. Engring., Leningrad Inst. Tech., 1960, PhD in Polymer Chemistry, 1965. Chem. engr. R&D Prodn., Leningrad, 1960-64; group leader Assn. Plast-Polymer, Leningrad, 1965-71, lab. dir., 1972-84; staff scientist Ciba-Geigy, Ardsley, N.Y., 1987-92; sr. staff scientist Ciba Specialty Chemicals, Brewster, N.Y., 1993—. Adv. bd. Org. Sci. Tech. Advancement, Leningrad, 1965-81; scientific technological counsel Plast-polymer R&D and Prodn., Leningrad, 1972-78. Contbr. 154 articles to books and profl. jours.; contbr. article to Polymer Encyclopedia, 1977. Recipient 3 Gold medals Govt. Russia, Moscow, 1968, 72, 73. Mem. Am. Chem. Soc., Soc. Advancement Materials Process Engrs. Achievements include 197 patents in the area of thermoset polymers chemistry and tech. New routes to materials having high thermal stability, mechanical strength, and corrosion resistance for structural composites, adhesives coatings, electrical and electronic. Designer of numerous inventions from 1961-98 with 3 gold medals awarded in 1965, 67, 71. Home: Apt 2L 4705 Henry Hudson Pkwy Bronx NY 10471-3231 Office: Ciba Specialty Chemicals 281 Fields Ln Brewster NY 10509-2624

BLY-MONNEN, APRIL M. quality assurance professional; b. Akron, Ohio, Apr. 15, 1949; d. Chester Thomas Monnen and Rita M. Cassinelli; m. Charles A. Bly. BS in Edn., Miami U., 1970; PhD in Instrnl. Tech., U. Va., 1983. Cert. ISO internal quality auditor. Sr. instrnl. designer Applied Sci. Assocs., Butler, Pa., 1986-92; tech. info. mgr., quality assurance mgr. INOVA Corp., Charlottesville, Va., 1995—. Mem. ASTD, Am. Soc. for Quality chmn. sect. 1108 Blue Ridge 2002--), Acad. Am. Poets, N.Y. Acad. Sci. Avocations: handcrafts, amateur botany. Home: 777-D Mountainwood Rd Charlottesville VA 22903 Office: INOVA Corp 11 Avon St Charlottesville VA 22902 Fax: 804-817-8004.

BLYNN, GUY MARC, lawyer; b. Bklyn., May 26, 1945; s. S. Jerry and Viola T. Vogel Blynn; children: Daniel Scott, Harlan Sterling, Aaron Seth. BS in Econs. cum laude, U. Pa., Wharton Sch. of Fin. Commerce, 1967; JD cum laude, Harvard U., 1970. Bar: N.C., N.Y., U.S. Ct. of Appeals for Fed. Cir., U.S. Ct. of Appeals for the 2d Cir., U.S. Dist. Cts. for the Middle Dist. of N.C., Southern and Eastern Dist. N.Y. Assoc. Kaye, Scholer, Fierman, Hays & Handler, N.Y.C., 1970-78; assoc. counsel R.J. Reynolds Industries Inc., Winston Salem, N.C., 1978-79; sr. counsel RJR Nabisco Inc., Winston Salem, N.C., 1979-86; dep. gen. counsel R.J. Reynolds Tobacco Co., Winston Salem, N.C., 1986-1989, v.p., dep. gen. counsel, sec., 1989—. Lectr. Wake Forest U. Sch. of Law, 1980-93; cons. Dept. Commerce, 1987-90. Contbr. articles to profl. jours. Chmn. Brand Names Edn. Found., 1988-94; bd. dirs. N.C. Vol. Lawyers for the Arts, 1985-91, pres., 1987-91; bd. dirs. Urban League Winston-Salem. Mem. ABA, Am. Arbitration Assn. (panel of arbitrators 1975-95), Carolina Patent Trademark & Copyright Law Assn. (v.p. 1979-80, pres. 1980-81), Am. Intellectul Property Law Assn. (chmn. taxation and fin. matters com. 1991-92), Am. Bar Assn. Forum Com. on Entertainment And Sports Industries, Assn. of Bar of City Of N.Y. (chmn. com. on trademarks and unfair competition 1975-78, subcommittee on patent and trademark office practice 1976-77), Anti-Defamation League (N.C. regional adv. bd. 1987—, chmn. elect 1991-93, chmn. 1993—, vice chmn. 1990-91), U.S. Trademark Assn. (bd. dirs. 1982-90, v.p. 1984-85, exec. v.p. 1985-86, pres., chmn. 1986-87). Home: PO Box 20383 Winston Salem NC 27120-0383 Office: R J Reynolds Tobacco Co 401 N Main St Winston Salem NC 27101-3804

BLYSTONE, JOHN B. manufacturing executive; Degree in Math and Econs., U. Pitts., car. With GE, 1978, with aircraft engine divsn.; v.p. J.I. Case divsn Tenneco, Inc., 1988-91; v.p., gen. mgr. GE superabrasives GE, 1991; pres., CEO Nuovo Pignone, Florence, Italy, 1994, Europe Pole of GE Power Sys., 1995; chmn., pres., CEO SPX, 1995—. Office: SPX Corp 700 Terrance Point Dr Muskegon MI 49440

BLYTH, ANN MARIE, secondary education educator; b. Sharon, Pa., June 18, 1949; d. Chester Stanley and Mary Clara (Romian) Kacerski; m. Lynn Allan Blyth, June 26, 1976 (dec. June 1983); 1 stepchild, Breton Alan Blyth; 1 child, Amanda Lynn. BS in Edn., Kent (Ohio) State U., 1971; postgrad., Loyola U., New Orleans, 1973-74; MS in Teaching, John Carroll U., 1978. Cert. comprehensive sci., maths. and physics tchr., Ohio. Jr. high math. tchr. New Philadelphia (Ohio) Bd. of Edn., 1971-72; high sch. sci. and math. tchr. Hubbard (Ohio) Exempted Village Bd. of Edn., 1972-76, Painesville (Ohio) City Local Bd. Edn., 1976—; head dept. sci. Harvey H.S., 2001—. Instr. math. Morton Salt, Painesville, 1979-80; part-time faculty Lake Erie Coll., 1992. Mem. Adv. Bd. Western Res. br. Am. Lung Assn. of Ohio, Painesville, 1986-89, sec, 1988-89, Northeastern br., Youngstown, Ohio, 1989-99; judge state level Nat. Pre-teen and Pre-Teen Petite Pageants, 1990. Martha Holden Jennings Found. scholar, 1984-85; named Tchr. of the Yr., Harvey High Sch. Key Club, 1981-82. Mem. NEA, Ohio Edn. Assn., Northeastern Ohio Edn. Assn., Painesville City Tchrs. Assn., Am. Assn. Physics Tchrs. (Ohio sect.), Nat. Sci.

Tchrs. Assn., Cleve. Regional Coun. of Sci. Tchrs. Democrat. Episcopalian. Avocations: travel, gourmet cooking, baking, gardening, music. Home: 7243 Scottsdale Cir Mentor OH 44060-6408 Office: Thomas W Harvey High Sch 167 W Washington St Painesville OH 44077-3328

BLYTH, JEFFREY, journalist; b. Chester-Le-Street, Durham, Eng., Mar. 20, 1926; came to U.S., 1957; m. Myrna Blyth, Nov. 1962; children: Jonathan, Graham. Fgn. corr. London Daily Mail, 1951-71; radio journalist BBC/SABC, N.Y.C., 1971-95; editor-in-chief Interpress, N.Y.C., 1972—. Pres. Fgn. Press Assn., N.Y.C., 1969-71. Mem. Overseas Press Club, London Press Club. Office: Interpress 90 Riverside Dr Apt 15B New York NY 10024-5322

BLYTH, JOHN E. lawyer, educator; b. Rochester, NY, Oct. 19, 1931; s. Ray G. and Ruby Luella (Spaulding) B.; m. Joanna E. Jennings, Aug. 24, 1963; children: Geoffrey E., Jennifer E. Blyth-Schmandt, Jane Blyth Warren, James E. AB, Colgate U., 1953; LLB, NYU, 1960; JD, Goethe U., 1962. Bar: NY 1961. Ptnr. Harter, Secrest & Emery, Rochester, 1961-93, Hiscock & Barclay, Rochester, 1994-95, Blyth & Lamb, Rochester, 1995-2000, Fix Spindelman Brovitz & Goldman, Rochester, NY, 2000—02; lawyer Blyth Law Offices, 2002—. Speaker in field; adj. prof. Cornell U. Law Sch., Ithaca, NY, 1990—; former trustee Keuka Coll., Keuka Pk., NY, 1986—. Contbr. articles to profl. jour. Pres. Palmyra (NY) Macedon Sch. Bd., 1969-72, Citizen's Tax League, Rochester, 1984-86. Sgt. US Army, 1954-57, ETO. Named Internat. Exec. of Yr., Rochester C. of C., 1994. Mem. NY State Bar Assn. (chair real property law sect. 1990-91), Am. Coll. Real Estate Lawyers. Avocation: organist. Home: 1428 Hidden Pond Ln Walworth NY 14568-9538 Office: 1115 Midtown Tower Rochester NY 14604 E-mail: 2@frontiernet.net.

BLYTH, MYRNA GREENSTEIN, publishing executive, editor, author; b. N.Y.C., Mar. 22, 1939; d. Benjamin and Betty (Austin) Greenstein; m. Jeffrey Blyth, Nov. 25, 1962; children: Jonathan, Graham. BA, Bennington (Vt.) Coll., 1960. Sr. editor Datebook mag., N.Y.C., 1960-62, Ingenue mag., N.Y.C., 1963-68; book editor Family Health mag., 1968-71; book and fiction editor, then assoc. editor Family Circle mag., N.Y.C., 1972-78, exec. editor, 1978-81; editor-in-chief Ladies' Home Jour., 1981—2002, pub. dir., sr. v.p., 1987—2002, editor-in-chief, pub. dir., More Mag., 1998—2002, v.p., editl. dir., 2002—03; with new product devel. Meredith Corp., 2002—03, freelance writer. Author: (novels) Cousin Suzanne, 1975, For Better and For Worse, 1978; contbr. articles to New Yorker mag., New York mag. Mem. nat. adv. bd. Susan G. Komen Breast Cancer Found.; active The Communitarians; Nat. Commn. on Am. Jewish Women.; bd. dirs. Child Care Action Campaign, N.Y.C., 1989. Recipient Headliner award Women in Comms., Inc., 1992, Human Rels. award, Am. Jewish Com.'s Pub. Divsn., 1992. Mem.: Women's Media Group, N.Y. Women in Comm., Inc. (past pres., Amb. of Excellence, Matrix award 1988), Am. Soc. Mag. Editors (exec. com. 1989—), Overseas Press Club (bd. govs.), Authors League.*

BLYTHE, JAMES DAVID, II, lawyer; b. Indpls., Oct. 20, 1940; s. James David and Marjorie M. (Horne) B.; m. Sara S. Frantz, Nov. 21, 1974; 1 child; Amanda Renee. BS, Butler U., 1962; JD, Ind. U., 1966. Bar: Ind. 1966, U.S. Supreme Ct. (so. dist.) Ind., 1966, U. S. Supreme Ct. 1980, U.S. Ct. Appeals (7th cir.), 1993. Diplomate, U.S. congl. staff asst. Ct. Practice Inst., 1965-69; majority atty. Ind. Ho. of Reps., 1967, 69; dep. prosecutor Marion County Prosecutor's Office, 1966, 68; pvt. practice Indpls., 1966—; sr. ptnr. Blythe & Ost, 1994—. Mem. com. on character and fitness Ind. Supreme Ct., 1974-94; host TV show Ask a Lawyer, 1977-79. Bd. dirs. Marion County chpt. Am.Cncer Soc., 1971-76 (pres. 1975-76), Cen. Ind. coun. Boy Scouts Am., 1969-72, exec. com., 1969-71, Crossroads of Am. Coun., 1972-87, executive com. 1976-84, pres., 1979-81, life mem 1987, Salvation Army, 1975—, vice chmn., 1986, chmn., 1987, 88, life mem., 2003; Ind. chmn. W.I. Amb. Exch., Jaycees, 1972-73; pres. North Ctrl. H.S. Alumni Assn., 1996-98, life mem., 2002; mem. lawyers fund raising com. Indpls. Mus. Art., 1973-74; co-membership chmn, Friends of Channel 20, 1975; hon. chmn. ann. dinner Muscular Dystrophy Family Found., 2001. Named Man of Yr., Am. Cancer Soc., 1974, Sagamore of the Wabash, 1981; named to North Ctrl. H.S. Hall of Fame, 1999; recipient cert. of merit, Am. Cancer Soc., 1971, 1974—75, Outstanding Svc. award, Indpls. br. Am. Cancer Soc., 1972—73, Richard E. Rowland award, Jaycees, 1971—72, Stanley K. Lacy Meml. award, 1974, Dist. Svc. award, Ind. Jaycees, 1974, Silver Beaver award, Boy Scouts Am., 1981, Life Mem. award, Nat. Eagle Scout Assn., 1996, commendation, Gov. State of Ind., 1973, Day named in his honor, Mayor of Indpls., 1976. Mem. Ind. Bar Assn. (legal ethics com. 1995—), Indpls. Bar Assn. (bd. mgrs. 1978-81, 89-90, chmn. grievance com. 1980-88), Kiwanis (v.p. Indpls 1986-87, pres. 1987-88, found pres. 1988-89, Indpls. Kiwanis found. 1989-99, pres. Ind. Dist. Found. 1995-98, civic award, 1991, Abe Lincoln Fellow, 1993, named Kiwanis Man of the Year, 1997), Gyro Club of Indpls. (bd. dirs. 2000-01, 03—), Kappa Sigma, Phi Delta Phi. Republican. Presbyterian. Home: 11028 E Lakeshore Dr Carmel IN 46033-4402 Office: 10585 N Meridian St Ste 200 Indianapolis IN 46290-1067 E-mail: jdb2@iquest.net.

BOACKLE, K F. lawyer, writer, real estate broker; b. Jackson, Miss., Mar. 13, 1944; s. Abraham Milton and Clara Josephine Boackle; m. Sheila Marie Ashker; children: David, Paul, Mark. BBA, Loyola U., 1966; JD, Jackson Sch. Law, 1972. Real estate broker, Jackson, 1972—; pvt. law practice, 1979—. Author: Mississippi Real Estate Contracts and Closings, 1991, 2d edit., 2000, Mississippi Real Estate Foreclosure Law, 1994, 2d edit., 2001, Real Estate Closing Deskbook, 1997, 2d edit., 2003. Mem. ABA, Miss. Bar Assn., Tri-County Real Estate Attys. Assn. (pres. 1989-90), Hinds County Bar Assn, Madison County Bar Assn. Office: Boackle Law Firm PLLC 1020 Northpark Dr Ste B Ridgeland MS 39157-5299

BOAL, BERNARD HARVEY, cardiologist, educator, author; b. Winnipeg, Man., Can., May 14, 1937; came to U.S., 1964; s. Charles and Bessie (Carr) B.; m. Pamela Sures Brownstone, Oct. 28, 1962; children: Steven, Jeremy, Hilary. BS in Medicine, MD, U. Man., 1962. Licentiate Med. Coun. Can.; diplomate Nat. Bd. Med. Examiners, Am. Bd. Internal Medicine in medicine and cardiology. Intern Winnipeg Gen. Hosp., 1962-63, resident in medicine, 1963-64, U. Utah Hosps., Salt Lake City, 1964-66; USPHS trainee in cardiology NYU Med. Ctr., N.Y.C., 1966-68; practice medicine specializing in cardiology Queens, N.Y., 1969—; chief sect. cardiology Booth Meml. Med. Ctr., 1969-87; chief cardiology Cath. Med. Ctr. Bklyn. and Queens, 1987-2000; cons. L.I. Jewish Hosp.; mem. staff NYU Hosp., Bellevue Hosp., 1968-81; clin. assoc. prof. medicine N.Y. Med. Coll., 1981-89, Cornell U. Med. Coll., 1989-95; assoc. prof. medicine Albert Einstein Coll. Medicine, 1995-2000, N.Y. Med. Coll., 2000—; chief cardiology Bklyn.-Queens region St. Vincents Cath. Med. Ctrs. N.Y., Jamaica, 2000—02; physician, electrophysiology sect. North Shore Univ. Hosp., Manhasset, NY, 2003—. Lectr. worldwide on cardiac pacing. Guest editor several major cardiology jours.; asst. editor: HeartNet; contbr. chpts. to books, articles to med. jours. Co-inventor Kolker-Boal Cardiac Pacemaker Electrode. Chmn. physicians divsn. Queens County Cabinet United Jewish Appeals of Greater N.Y., 1978-80; charter mem., founding treas. B'nai B'rith UN unit, 1984—; U.S. physician rep. pacemaker working group of the Internat. Standards Orgn., Geneva, 1988—, chmn., 1990—. Capt. M.C., USAR, 1970-73. Fellow N.Y. Cardiol. Soc., Am. Coll. Cardiology (chmn. med. devices com. Heart House campaign 1976-78, chmn. bequests and endowments com. 1980-85, pacemaker com. 1987-95, trustee 1985-90, mem. electrocardiology com. 1995-2001, mem. budget/fin./investment com. 1996-2002, devel. com. 1997-2003), ACP (treas. Queens chpt. 1976-78, sec. 1978-79, v.p. 1979-81, pres. 1981-85; govs. adv. coun. N.Y. State 1982-85); mem. AMA, Assn. Advancement of Med. Instrumentation (pacemaker com. 1976—, chmn. pacemaker com. 1988—, bd. dirs. 1983-86, co-chmn. strategic planning com. 1983-85), Am. Heart Assn. (fellow coun. clin. cardiology), N.Y. Heart Assn., Am. Soc. Internal Medicine, Queens Soc. Internal Medicine, N.Am. Soc. Pacing and Electrophysiology (founding mem., mem. nat. adv. coun. 1984-85, mem. exec. com. 1985-88, chmn. fin. com. 1985-88, trustee 1987-91), U.S. divsn. Israeli Med. Assn. (founding mem.). Office: North Shore Univ HOsp Manhasset NY E-mail: bboal@aol.com.

BOAL, DANIELLE K. radiologist, educator; b. Berkeley, Calif., Feb. 19, 1947; d. Barnard Taylor and Dorothy (Calvin) Bird; m. Richard John Boal; children: Brian, Andrew, Jonathan. BA, Trinity U., 1968; MD, Temple U., 1972. Diplomate Am. Bd. Radiology, Am. Bd. Pediat. and Pediat. Radiology. Intern Presbyn. Med. Ctr., Denver, 1972—73; pediat. intern St. Christopher's Hosp., Phila., 1973—75; resident Radiology Temple U., Phila., 1975—77, Children's Hosp., Boston, 1977—78; asst. prof., assoc. prof. Milton S. Hershey Med. Ctr., Hershey, Pa., 1979—95, prof. Radiology, 1995—. Chief Pediat. Radiology Milton S. Hershey Med. Ctr., Hershey, 1979—; dir. Radiology Elizabethtown Hosp. Children, Elizabethtown, Pa., 1979—91. Contbr. . Mem. Med. Legal Adv. Bd. Atty. Gen. Office Pa., 1984—. Fellow: Am. Coll. Radiology; mem.: Pa. Radiol. Soc., Radiol. Soc. N.Am., Soc. Pediat. Radiology (Bd. dirs., treas. 1997—2000, Presdl. award 2003). Avocations: horseback riding, skiing, reading, flying.

BOAL, DEAN, retired arts center administrator, educator; b. Longmont, Colo., Oct. 20, 1931; s. Elmer C. and L. Mildred (Snodgrass) B.; m. Ellen Christine TeSelle, Aug. 23, 1957; children: Brett, Jed. B.Music, B.Music Edn., U. Colo., 1953; M.Music, Ind. U., 1956; D. Musical Arts, U. Colo., 1959. Mem. faculty Hastings (Nebr.) Coll., 1958-60; head piano dept. Bradley U., Peoria, Ill., 1960-66; dean, pianist Peabody Conservatory, Balt., 1966-70; prof. piano, chair music SUNY, Fredonia, 1970-73; pres. St. Louis Conservatory, 1973-76; dir. radio sta. KWMU, St. Louis, 1976-78; v.p., gen. mgr. Sta. WETA-FM, Washington, 1978-83; dir. arts and performance programs Nat. Pub. Radio, Washington, 1982-89; pres. Interlochen (Mich.) Ctr. for the Arts, 1989-95; pres. emeritus, 1995—. Author: Concepts and Skills for the Piano, Book I, 1969, Book II, 1970, Interlochen: A Home for The Arts, 1998; contbr. articles to profl. jours. Mem. adv. bd U. Colo. Coll. Music, 1987-2000; trustee Alma Coll., 1992-95; bd. dirs., chmn. Peak Assn. of the Arts, 1998-2000. Served with U.S. Army, 1953-55. Woodrow Wilson teaching fellow, 1983-89; recipient Disting. Alumnus award in Profl. Music Univ. Colo., 1987. Mem. Eastern Public Radio Network (chmn. 1979-82), Coll. Music Soc., Pi Kappa Lambda, Mu Phi Epsilon, Phi Mu Alpha. Presbyterian.

BOAL, LYNDALL ELIZABETH, social worker; b. London, Feb. 19, 1936; came to U.S., 1953; d. George Woodall and Mary Barbara (Pearce) Cadbury; m. R. Bradlee Boal Aug. 29, 1959 (div. Sept. 1983); children: Jennifer, Peter. BA with honors, Swarthmore (Pa.) Coll., 1957; MS, Simmons Coll. Sch. Social Work, Boston, 1959. Cert. sch. social worker, N.Y.; lic. social worker, Mass. Social worker Beth Israel Hosp., Boston, 1959-60, Mt. Sinai Hosp., N.Y.C., 1960-61, Meml. Sloan-Kettering Hosp, N.Y.C., 1961-63; cons. Dist. Nursing Svc., Mt. Kisco, N.Y., 1964-65; exec. dir. Planned Parenthood, Mt. Kisco, N.Y., 1965-68; dir. social worker No. Westchester Hosp., Mt. Kisco, N.Y., 1968-78; social worker Fox lane High Sch., Bedford Schs, 1978-81; chmn. com. on handicapped Bedford (N.Y.) Schs., 1981-86; social worker Chappaqua (N.Y.) Sch., 1988—; instr. Fordham U. Sch. Social Svcs., 1994—. Bd. dirs. No. Westchester Guidance Ctr., Mt. Kisco; pres. Soc. Hosp. Social Work Dirs., Westchester, N.Y., 1976-78; mem. adv. bd. Mercy Coll. Social Work Program, 1997—, Concordia Coll. Social Work Program, 2001—; v.p. Westchester Children's Assn., 1999—. Chmn. Narcotics Guidance Coun., Bedford, 1972-75; No. Westchester Coun. Equality pres., Bedford, 1984-86; bd. dirs. Sherrill House, Boston, 1986-88; Dem. committeeman, Bedford, 1983-86. Mem. NASW (sec. N.Y. state chpt. 1993-95, pres. N.Y. State chpt. 1996-98, chair state pers. com. 1993-94, pres. Westchester divsn. 1969-71, 91-92, Merit Svc. award Westchester divsn. 1993, sch. social work sect. steering com. 1994-96), Am. Orthopsychiat. Assn., N.Y. State Sch. Social Workers Assn., Kappa Delta Pi. Democrat. Mem. Soc. Of Friends. Avocations: skiing, travel, spending time with family. Home: 508 Millwood Rd Mount Kisco NY 10549-3700 Office: Chappaqua Schs Off of Sch Social Worker Chappaqua NY 10514

BOAL, MARCIA ANNE RILEY, clinical social worker, administrator; b. Carthage, Mo., Sept. 29, 1944; d. William Joseph and Thelma P. (Simpson) Riley; m. David W. Boal, Aug. 12, 1967; children: Adam J. W., Aaron D. Boal. BA, U. Kans., 1966, MSW, 1981. Lic. clin. social worker. Child therapist Gillis Home for Children, Kansas City, Mo., 1981; social worker Leavenworth (Kans.) County Spl. Edn. Cooperative, 1981-84; sch. social worker, dir. health and social svcs. Kans. State Sch. for the Blind, Kansas City, Kans., 1984—. Pvt. practice adoption counseling and workshops, 1981—; field instr. Sch. of Social Welfare, Kans. U., 1986—. Author: Surviving Kids, 1983, Teaching Social Skills to Blind and Visually Impaired Children, 1987. Nat. networking chmn. Jr. League Kansas City, 1977-81; bd. dirs. Wyandotte House Inc., 1973-81, Kans. Action For Children, Topeka, 1981, Gov.'s Commn. on Parent Edn., Topeka, 1984—, Lake of the Forest, 1994— (sec.). Named Kans. Sch. Social Worker of Yr., 1989. Mem. Council Exceptional Children, Nat. Assn. Social Workers, Kans. Assn. Sch. Social Workers, Am. Orthopsychiat. Assn., Kans. Conf. Social Welfare, R.P. Found., Phi Kappa Phi. Home: Lake Of The Forest Bonner Springs KS 66012 Office: Kans St Sch for Blind 1100 State Ave Kansas City KS 66102-4411 E-mail: mboal@kssb.net.

BOARD, JOSEPH BRECKINRIDGE, JR., political scientist, educator; b. Princeton, Ind., Mar. 5, 1931; s. Joseph Breckinridge and Rachel Eleanor (Unthank) B.; children from previous marriage: Ian Robert, Annika Caroline, Amanda Anne; m. Mary Squire, Jan. 1, 1998. AB with highest honors, Ind. U., 1953, JD, 1958, PhD, 1962; BA (Rhodes scholar 1953-55), Oxford (Eng.) U., 1955, MA, 1961; PhD (hon.), Umea U., Sweden, 1973. Tchg. fellow govt. Ind. U., 1955-58, lectr. govt., 1958; asst. prof. polit. sci. Elmira Coll., 1959-61; assoc. prof. polit. sci., chmn. dept. Cornell Coll., 1961-64; prof. polit. sci., chmn. dept. Union Coll., Schenectady, 1964—, Robert Porter Patterson prof. govt., 1973—, chmn. faculty, 1983-85; pres. Paralegals-Plus Assocs., Inc., 1986—. Acad. visitor London Sch. Econs. and Polit. Sci., 1972-73; adj. prof. Albany Law Sch., 1974—; lectr. Green Mountain Acd. Lifelong Learning; scholar-in-residence Sch. Law Ind. U., 1999—; acting prof., chmn. dept. polit. sci. U. Umea, 1979; vis. prof. U. Paris (Sorbonne), 1987; mem. Rhodes Scholarship Selection Com. Nebr., 1961-62, Iowa, 1963-64, N.Y., 1991, 92; mem. regional selection com. for Woodrow Wilson Fellowships, 1966—; mem. exec. coun. Iowa Conf. Polit. Scientists, 1963-65; spl. adv. coll. and univ. affairs Young Citizens for Johnson, 1964; cons. Nat. Endowment Humanities, 1968, N.Y. State Dept. Edn., 1968; mem. polit. sci. adv. com. Fulbright-Hays Program, 1969-73; assoc., adv. com. for Western Europe Coun. for Internat. Exchange of Scholars; chmn. Scandinavian peer rev. com. Linkages Project; mem. U.S. Com. on NATO Fellowships; cons., co-host Nobel Prize broadcast Nat. Pub. Radio, 1976; vis. fellow Oriel Coll., Oxford, 1994—; acad. assoc. The Atlantic Coun.; chair bd. advisors Transnat. Rsch. Project on Effects of European Unification. Author: The Government and Politics of Sweden, 1970. Bd. adv. Schenectady Salvation Army; trustee, treas. Schnectady County CC; trustee Oriel Coll. (Oxford U.), Devel. Trust, 1991—; pres. bd. trustees Martha Canfield Libr., Arlington, Vt.; vestry mem. Zion Episcopal Ch., Manchester, Vt. Fulbright lectr. Sweden, 1968-69; Ctrl. Am. fellow Assoc. Colls. Midwest, 1962, NDEA fellow, Portuguese, 1963, Acad. Law Sch. Alumni fellow Ind. U.; recipient Disting. Svc. award SUNY Bd. Trustees Cmty. Colls., 1997. Mem. AAUP, Am. Assn. Rhodes Scholars, Am. Polit. Sci. Assn., Ind. Bar, Am. Arbitration Assn., Am-Scandinavian Found. (com. on fellowships 1981—), Northeastern Polit. Sci. Assn. (exec. Coun. 1972), Soc. for Advancement Scandinavian Studies (exec. coun. 1972), United Oxford and Cambridge U. Club (London), Soc. Letters (Lund U.), Acacia, Phi Beta Kappa. Democrat. Episcopalian. Home: 3319 River Rd Arlington VT 05250-8998 Office: Union Coll Political Sci Dept Schenectady NY 12308

BOARD, RHONDA M. pediatrics nurse, researcher; d. Constantine John and Jennifer D. Meeker; m. Thomas E. Board; children: Alexis N., Samantha T. BS, SUNY, Binghamton, 1988; MS, Ohio State U., 1994, PhD, 1999. RN N.Y., 1986, CCRN in pediat., AACN, 1992. Staff nurse United Health Svcs., Binghamton, NY, 1986—88; staff nurse pediatric icu Albany Med. Ctr., Albany, NY, 1988—91; staff nurse pediatric ICU Columbus Children's Hosp., Columbus, Ohio, 1991—98; grad. assoc. Ohio State U., Columbus, Ohio, 1992—97; asst. prof. nursing Northeastern U., Boston, 1999—. Rsch. coun. Boston Children's Hosp., Boston, 2000—; manuscript reviewer Pediat. (jour.), 2002, Heart and Lung (jour.), 2000; textbook reviewer Lippincott, 2001. Recipient rsch. tng. award, Nat. Inst. Nursing Rsch., NIH, 2000, Grad. Student Alumni Rsch. Award, The Ohio State U., 1996, Vertus Tchg. Award, Northeastern U. Sch. of Nursing Class of 2001, 2001, Grad. Student of the Yr., Sigma Theta Tau, Epsilon Chpt., 1995; fellow Nat. Rsch. Svc. award, Nat. Inst. of Nursing Rsch. at NIH, 1997-1999. Mem.: AACN (Am. Nurses Found. grant 2000—02), Ea. Nursing Rsch. Soc., Phi Kappa Phi, Sigma Theta Tau Internat. (acad. counselor Gamma Epsilon chpt., Boston 2002—). Achievements include research in pediatric critical care. Avocation: swimming. Office: Northeastern U Sch Nursing Huntington Ave Boston MA 02115 Office Fax: 617-373-8675.

BOARDMAN, DAVID, newspaper editor; m. Barbara Winslow; children: Emily, Madeline. BS in Journalism, Northwestern U., 1979; M in Comm., U. Wash., 1983. Copy editor Football Weekly, Chgo., 1977-79; reporter Anacortes (Wash.) American, 1979-80, Skagit Valley Herald, Mt. Vernon, Wash., 1980-81; reporter, copy editor The News Tribune, Tacoma, 1981-83; copy editor The Seattle Times, 1983, editor, reporter, 1984, nat. editor, 1984-86, local news editor, 1986-87, asst. city editor, 1987-90, regional editor, 1990-96, metro. editor, 1997—, asst. mng. editor, 1997—2003, mgn. editor, 2003—. Vis. faculty Poynter Inst. Media Studies, St. Petersburg, Fla. Recipient Goldsmith Prize in Investigative Reporting JFK Sch. Govt. Harvard U., 1993, Worth Bingham prize, 1993, Investigative Reporters and Editors award, 1993, AP Mng. Editors Pub. Svc. award, 1992, 1st place nat. reporting Pulitzer Prize, 1990, lead editor Pulitzer Prize in investigative reporting, 1997; finalist Pulitzer Prize, 1993, 98, 99, 2002, 03; juror Pulitzer Prizes, 1999-2000; fellow Japan-IBCC fellowship Ctr. Fgn. Journalists, 1995. Office: The Seattle Times PO Box 70 1120 John St Seattle WA 98109-5321 E-mail: dboardman@seattletimes.com.

BOARDMAN, ELIZABETH DRAKE, naval reserve officer; b. Columbus, Ohio, Oct. 14, 1955; d. Jack Martin and Marilyn Hawk Boardman; children: Melissa Grimsley, Stephanie Grimsley. BS Bus. Adminstrn., Ohio State U., 1977; BS in Computer Sci. summa cum laude, W. Ill. U., 2003; MS in Info. Assurance Program, Iowa State U., 2003—. Officer (lt., unrestricted line) U.S. Navy, Various, 1977—85; sr. computer software analyst Analysis & Tech., North Stonington, Conn., 1985—88; database adminstr. We. Ill. U., Macomb, Ill., 2000—02; tchg. asst. computer sci. Iowa State U., Ames, 2003. Mem., bd. of dirs. Girl Scouts Shining Trail Coun., Burlington, Iowa, 1995—99; fin. com. Trinity United Meth. Ch., Keokuk, Iowa, 2000—02; blue & gold officer U.S. Naval Acad., Annapolis, Md., 1992—94; vol. Girl Scouts of Am., various, 1990—99; life mem. Girl Scouts. Lt. NAVY, 1977—85, various, CDR (Intelligence) USNR, 1985—. Named Iowa Cmty. Hero Olympic Torch Bearer, Iowa Com. for Olympic Torch Run, 1996. Mem.: AAUW, Western Ill. Alumni Assn., Mil. Officers Assn. Am., The Ohio State U. Alumni Assn., Naval Res. Assn., Phi Kappa Phi, Upsilon Pi Epsilon, Chi Omega. Protestant. Avocations: volunteer work, computers, travel.

BOARDMAN, EUNICE, retired music educator; b. Cordova, Ill., Jan. 27, 1926; d. George Hollister and Anna Bryson (Feaster) Boardman. B. Mus. Edn., Cornell Coll., 1947; M. Mus. Edn., Columbia U., 1951; Ed.D., U. Ill., 1963; DFA (hon.), Cornell Coll., 1995. Tchr. music pub. schs., Iowa, 1947-53, prof. music edn. Wichita State U., Kans., 1955-72; vis. prof. mus. edn. Normal State U., Ill., 1972-74, Roosevelt U., Chgo., 1974-75; prof. mus. edn. U. Wis., Madison, 1975-89, dir. Sch. Music, 1980-89; prof. music, dir. grad. program in music edn. U. Ill., Urbana, 1989-98; ret. Author: Musical Growth in Elementary School, 1963, 6th rev. edit., 1996, Exploring Music, 1966, 3d rev. edit., 1975, The Music Book, 1980, 2d rev. edit., 1984, Holt Music, 1987; editor: Dimensions of Musical Thinking, 1989, Dimensions of Musical Thinking: A Different Kind of Music, 2002, Up the Mississippi: A Journey of the Blues, 2002. Mem. Soc. Music Tchr. Edn. (chmn. 1984-86), Music Educators Nat. Conf. Avocations: reading, antiques. E-mail: EunBoardman@aol.com.

BOARDMAN, GREGORY DALE, environmental engineer, educator; b. Montpelier, Vt., Dec. 12, 1950; s. Theodore Robert and June Irene B.; m. Gail Cynthia Bedell, June 6, 1970 (div. Dec. 1986); children: Heather Eve, Kristina Marie, Jessica Anne; m. Shelley Ann Mitchell, Aug. 28, 1987; 1 child, Courtney Dale. MS, U. N.H., 1973; PhD, U. Maine, 1976. Registered profl. engr., Va.; diplomate of environ. engring. Asst. prof. civil engring. Va. Poly. Inst. and State U., Blacksburg, 1976-83, assoc. prof., 1983-98, prof., 1998—, dir. Ctr. for Orgnl. and Technol. Advancement, 1997—2002. Mem. bd. Dept. Commerce, Richmond, Va., 1987-94; cons. to numerous cos., 1976—. Author 2 manuals; contbr. numerous articles to profl. jours., chpts. to books. Mem. Montgomery County Cmty. Shelter, Va., 1986-91, chmn. of program, 1990-91; mem. planning commn. Town of Blackburg, 1989-93. Rsch. grantee EPA, NIH, NOAA, Water Rsch., numerous others, 1976—. Mem. ASCE (coms.), Soc. Environ. Toxicology and Chemistry, Water Environ. Fedn., Internat. Assn. on Water Quality, Assn. Environ. Engring. Profs., Am. Water Works Assn., Sigma Xi, Tau Beta Pi, Phi Kappa Phi. Achievements include research on industrial waste treatment and development of short-term toxicity tests. Office: Va Poly Inst and State U Dept Civil/Environ Engring 417 Durham Hall Blacksburg VA 24061 E-mail: gboard@vt.edu.

BOARDMAN, HAROLD FREDERICK, JR., lawyer, retired corporate executive; b. Darby, Pa., Nov. 23, 1939; s. Harold Frederick and Juanita (Sorzano) B.; m. Martha Eltie, May 23, 1987; children: Kimberly, Leslie. BS, Trinity Coll., Hartford, Conn., 1961; JD with honors, George Washington U., 1964; grad. advanced mgmt. program, Duke U., 1988. Bar: D.C. 1964, Hawaii 1971, N.J. 1974, U.S. Dist. Ct. D.C. 1965, U.S. Ct. Appeals (D.C. cir.) 1965, U.S. Ct. Mil. Appeals 1965, U.S. Supreme Ct. 1969. Gen. atty. Fed. Home Loan Bank Bd., Washington, 1964-66; atty. Hoffmann-LaRoche, Inc., Nutley, N.J., 1966, with, 1973-94, sec., 1979-94, assoc. gen. counsel, 1981-88, v.p., gen. counsel, bd. dirs., exec. com., 1988-94, mem. pharms. mgmt. com., ret., 1995; of counsel Crummy, Del Deo, Dolan, Griffinger & Vecchione, Newark, 1995-96; exec. v.p., gen. counsel, bd. dirs. Rhone-Poulenc Inc., Princeton, N.J., 1996-98; sr. v.p., gen. counsel, bd. dirs., exec. com Rhone Poulenc Rorer, Collegeville, Pa., 1998-99; sr. v.p.-legal Aventis Pharms., 1999-2000, retired, 2000; of counsel Gibbons, Del Deo, Dolan, Griffinger & Vecchione, Newark, 2001—. Capt. JAGC USAF, 1966—73. Mem.: ABA, Pharm. Mfrs. Assn. (exec. com. law sect. 1991—94), D.C. Bar Assn., Hawaii Bar Assn., N.J. Bar Assn. Episcopalian. Avocations: golf, boating. Address: 25 Walnut Rd Ocean City NJ 08226 Home: 680 Waterside Dr Marco Island FL 34145

BOARDMAN, JOHN MICHAEL, mathematician, educator; b. Manchester, Eng., Feb. 13, 1938; came to U.S., 1969, naturalized, 1973; s. William Edgar and Carrie (Brown) B.; m. Jacqueline O'Brien Schulman, 1967 (div. 1977); children: Susan, Andrew. BA, Trinity Coll., Cambridge U., 1961, PhD, 1965. Vis. lectr. U. Chgo., 1966-67; asst. lectr. U. Warwick, Eng., 1967-68; assoc. prof. Johns Hopkins U., Balt., 1969-72, prof., 1972—. Author: Singularities of Differentiable Maps, 1967, (with R.M. Vogt) Homotopy Invariant Algebraic Structures on Topological Spaces, 1973, Modular Representations on the Homology of Powers of Real Projective Space, 1993; (with D.C. Johnson and W.S. Wilson) Unstable Operations on Generalized Cohomology, 1995, Conditionally Convergent Spectral Sequences, 1999. Served with RAF, 1956-58. Sci. Rsch. Coun. fellow, 1964-66; NSF grantee, 1970-88. Mem. Am. Math. Soc. Mem. Soc. Of Friends. Home: 6217 Northwood Dr Baltimore MD 21212-2802 Office: Johns Hopkins U Dept Math 3400 N Charles St Baltimore MD 21218-2680

BOARDMAN, MARK SEYMOUR, lawyer; b. Birmingham, Ala., Mar. 16, 1958; s. Frank Seymour and Flora (Sarinopoulos) B.; m. Cathryn Dunkin, 1983; children:Wilson Paul, Joanna Christina. BA cum laude, U. Ala., 1979, JD, 1982. Bar: Ala. 1982, U.S. Dist. Ct. (no., so. and mid. dists.) Ala. 1982, U.S. Ct. Appeals (11th cir.) 1983, U.S. Supreme Ct. 1987. Assoc. Spain, Gillon, Riley, Tate & Etheredge, Birmingham, 1982-84; ptnr. Porterfield, Scholl, Bainbridge, Mims and Harper, P.A., Birmingham, 1984-93, Boardman Carr Weed & Hutcheson PC, Birmingham, 1993—. Pres. Holy Trinity Holy Cross Greek Orthodox Cathedral, 1991, 92, sec., 1987, asst. treas., 1986, treas., 1988, 89, v.p., 1990, 96-2003, bd. auditors, 1994; mem. coun. Greek Orthodox Diocese of Atlanta, 1992-95; mem. Shelby County (Ala.) Work Release Commn., sec., 1996; mem. ednl. adv. com. Homewood Bd. Edn., 1999-2002, strategic planning com., 2000-02; pres. Beta Theta Pi House Corp., U. Ala., 2003; bd. dirs. Ala. Coun. Sch. Sch. Bd. Attys., 2001-2003. Mem. ABA, Ala. State Bar, Ala. Workers Compensation Claims Assn., Shelby County Bar Assn. (treas. 1992-93, sec. 1994, v.p. 1995, pres. 1996), Birmingham Bar Assn. (co-chmn. econs. of law com. 1997, local bar liaison com. 1997), Ala. Def. Lawyers Assn., Def. Rsch. Inst., Ala. Claims Assn., Order of Barristers, Phi Beta Kappa, Delta Sigma Rho-Tau Kappa Alpha, Pi Sigma Alpha. Greek Orthodox. Home: 1915 Wellington Rd Birmingham AL 35209-4026 Office: Boardman Carr Weed & Hutcheson PC PO Box 382886 Birmingham AL 35238-2886 also: 400 Boardman Dr Chelsea AL 35043-8211

BOARDMAN, MAUREEN BELL, community health nurse, educator; b. Hartford, Conn., June 11, 1966; d. Jack Russell and Mary Elizabeth (Brumm) Bell; m. Byron Earl Boardman, June 4, 1988; 1 child, Meghan Elizabeth. BSN, U. Maine, Orono, 1988; MSN, U. Tenn., 1991. RN, Tenn.; ACLS; cert. family

nurse practitioner. Charge nurse med.- surg. divsn. Scott County Hosp., Oneida, Tenn., 1988-89, employee health nurse, 1989-92; nurse team leader Oneida Home Health, 1989, Quality Home Health, Oneida, 1989-90; FNP, Straightfork Family Care Clinic, Pioneer, Tenn., 1992-96, Huntsville (Tenn.) Family Care Clinic, 1996-98, Oak Grove Primary Care Clin., 1998-2001, Cmty. Health Ctr., Hanover, N.H., 2001—; instr. cmty. and family medicine Dartmouth Med. Sch., Hanover, 2001—. Mem. child abuse rev. team Dept. Human Svcs., Huntsville, Tenn., 1993-2001; adj. prof. Coll. Nursing U. Tenn., 1997-2001. Med. advisor, liaison Scott County (Tenn.) Sch. Systems Sci. Fair Com., 1992-2001; bd. dirs., editor newsletter Appalachian Arts Coun., Oneida, 1993-2001, v.p., 1996-98, del., 1997; com. on health policy TNA, 1998-2000. Mem. Sigma Theta Tau (sec. Gamma Chi chpt. 1996—). Roman Catholic. Avocations: reading, biking, swimming, dancing. Home: 72 Anderson Hill Rd Enfield NH 03748-3152 Office: Cmty Health Ctr 1 Medical Center Dr Lebanon NH 03756 Personal E-mail: maureen.b.boardman@hitchcock.org. Business E-Mail: maureen.b.boardman@dartmouth.edu.

BOARDMAN, MICHAEL, mathematician, educator; b. Huntsville, Ala. BS, MS, Western Wash. U., 1981—87; PhD, U. Oreg., 1987—92. Asst. prof. Pacific U., Forest Grove, Oreg., 1995—98, chair, dept. math. and computer sci., 1998—2003. Chair, pacific nw sect. Math. Assn. Am. Chair Pacific NW Sect., MAA; mem. Oreg. Math. Edn. Coun., Oreg. Office: Pacific University 2043 College Way Forest Grove OR 97116

BOARDMAN, SEYMOUR, artist; b. Bklyn., Dec. 29, 1921; s. Joseph and Bessie (Warren) B. BSS, CCNY, 1942; postgrad., Ecole des Beaux-Arts, Paris, 1946-47, Atelier Fernand Leger, 1948, Art Students League, N.Y.C., 1949-50, Ecole de la Grande Chaumiere, 1950-51. One-man shows, Galerie Mai, Paris, 1951, Martha Jackson Gallery, N.Y.C., 1955, 56, Stephen Radich Gallery, N.Y.C., 1960-61, 62, A.M. Sachs Gallery, N.Y.C., 1965, 67, 68, Dorsky Gallery, N.Y.C., 1972, Aaron Berman Gallery, N.Y.C., 1978, Anita Shapolsky Gallery, N.Y.C., 1987, 91, Anderson Gallery, Buffalo, 1994; group shows include, Carnegie Internat., Pitts., 1955, Whitney Mus. Am. Art, 1955, 61, 67, Nebr. Art Assn., 1956, Kunsthalle, Basel, Switzerland, 1964, Santa Barbara Art Mus., 1964, Albright-Knox Gallery, Buffalo, 1967, Cornell U., 1971, Anita Shapolsky Gallery, N.Y.C., 1986, David Anderson Gallery, Buffalo, 1991-92; represented in permanent collections, Whitney Mus. Am. Art, Guggenheim Mus., Walker Art Ctr., Mpls., Santa Barbara Mus. Art, NYU. Served with USAAF, 1942-46. Longview Found. grantee, 1963; Guggenheim Found. fellow, 1972-73; Adolph and Esther Gottlieb Found. grantee, 1979, 83; Pollock-Krasner Found. grantee, 1985-86, 91, 98, 2001, 2003. Address: 234 W 27th St New York NY 10001-5901

BOARDMAN-FITE, LINDA IRENE, speaker, management consultant; b. Hereford, Tex., May 11, 1948; d. Herbert Daniel and Irene Teresa (Anderson) B.; 1 child, Nathan Daniel Gunn; m. Paul Boston Fite, III, Jan. 10, 1998. BA, Tex. Tech U., 1970. Cert. in neuro linguistic programming; cert. profl. mediator Resolution Group, Dallas. Psychologist assoc. R.G. Jones, Ph.D. & Assocs., Lubbock, Tex., 1970-76; vice prin. Calif. Acad. Integral Studies, San Rafael, 1977-80; mgr. biofeedback svcs. Psychol. Svcs., Houston, 1980-81; sr. cons., ptnr. Connector Mgmt. Group, Copenhagen, 1981-86; sr. cons. ActionSystems, Inc., Dallas, 1986-87, mgr. orgnl. leadership devel., 1987-90, master cons., 1988-90; dir. tng. & devel., sr. cons. Pritchett & Assocs., Dallas, 1990-94; prin. Boardman Assocs., Inc.: Focus Your Energy on Results, Springfield, Mo., 1994—. Spkr. Nat. Assn. Bank Women, Boston, 1988, Internat. TV Assn., New Orleans, 1990, Internat. Conf. ASTD, 1992, 94; adj. faculty S.W. Mo. State U., 2002—. Sec. LWV, Houston, 1972-73; bd. dirs. Youth Advocacy Coun., Carrollton, Tex., 1987-89. Mem. ASTD (spkr. 1992, 94), Internat. Customer Svc. Assn. (bd. dirs. 1987-88, spkr. 1986-91), Nat. Soc. Performance and Instrn., European Women's Mgmt. Devel. Assn., Internat. Soc. Poets. Avocations: amateur magic, t'ai chi, sailing, piano, reading. Office: 2539 S Forrest Heights Ave Springfield MO 65809-3524 Fax: 888-418-9608. E-mail: OrdrInKaos@aol.com.

BOARMAN, MARJORIE RUTH, prevention specialist, manufacturing company executive; b. Lakeland, Fla., Apr. 14, 1953; d. Hugh Francis and Nancy Addair (McCracken) Roberts; m. Edward F. Moore, June 28, 1975 (div. 1986); children: Kulani Anne, Brittany Elizabeth; m. James Louis Boarman, Feb. 5, 1987 (div. June 2003); 1 child, Joshua. BS in Edn., Fla. State U., 1975; MEd, U. Hawaii/Manoa, 1978. Cert. tchr., Fla., Mo. Substitute tchr. KCCA Preschs., Honolulu, 1975; tchr. Hickam Day Care Ctr., Hickam AFB, Hawaii, 1975-77; tchr., sales rep. Grolier Interstate Inc., Honolulu, 1977; tchr. Kiddie Kollege Presch., Hickam AFB, 1977-79, Our Lady of Sorrows Schs., St. Louis, 1979-80; program dir. Clayton (Mo.) YWCA, 1981-82; cons. Parent Talk Svcs., Phoenix, 1983-85; tchr. Polk County Schs., Polk City, Fla., 1986-89; co-owner Boarman Built Inc., Windsor, Mo., 1989—; dir. prevention and edn. Pathways Behavioral Cmty. Healthcare Inc., Clinton, Mo., 2000—. Co-creator: Bon Voyage board game, 1992. Leader, coord. Camp Fire Boys and Girls, Lakeland, 1988—; bd. dirs. Boswell PTA, Auburndale, 1991—92, Henry County R-1 Sch. Bd., 1999—, Mo. Womens Coun., 1998—2000; v.p. Green Ridge 2000 Team, 1995—; founder, exec. dir. Youth & Family Resource Ctr., 1999—2003. Mem.: NAFE, Sedalia Bus. and Profl. Women (2nd v.p. membership chmn. 1994—95, 1st v.p. issues mgmt. chmn. 1995—96, pres.-elect 1996—97, pres. 1997—98, dir. 1998—, State Individual Devel. award), Green Ridge C. of C. (bd. dirs. 1994—96), Auburndale C. of C. (bd. dirs. 1991—92), Windsor C. of C. (1st v.p. 1999—2001, bd. dirs.), Kappa Delta Pi. Republican. Pentecostal. Avocations: swimming, raquetball, camping, travel, sewing, gardening. Office: Pathways Cmty Behavioral Healthcare Inc 1800 Community Dr Clinton MO 64735 E-mail: mboarman@pbhc.org.

BOAS, FRANK, retired lawyer; b. Amsterdam, North Holland, The Netherlands, July 22, 1930; came to U.S., 1940; s. Maurits Coenraad and Sophie (Brandel) B.; m. Edith Louise Bruce, June 30, 1981 (dec. July 1992); m. Jean Scripps, Aug. 6, 1993 (div. Dec. 2000). AB cum laude, Harvard U., 1951, JD, 1954. Bar: U.S. Dist. Ct. D.C. 1955, U.S. Ct. Appeals (D.C. cir.) 1955; U.S. Supreme Ct. 1958. Atty. Office of the Legal Adviser U.S. State Dept., Washington, 1957-59; pvt. practice Brussels and London, 1959-79; of counsel Patton, Boggs & Blow, Washington, 1975-80; pres. Frank Boas Found., Inc., Cambridge, Mass., 1980—. Mem. U.S. delegation to UN confs. on law of sea, Geneva, 1958, 60; vice chmn. Commn. for Ednl. Exch., Brussels, 1980-87; mem. vis. com. Harvard Law Sch., 1987-91, Ctr. for Internat. Affairs, 1988—; dir. Found. European Orgn. for Research and Treatment of Cancer, Brussels, 1978-87, Paul-Henri Spaak Found., Brussels, 1981—, East-West Ctr. Found., Honolulu, 1990-01, Law of the Sea Inst., Honolulu, 1992-97, Pacific Forum CSIS, Honolulu, 1996—, Honolulu Acad. Arts, 1997—, U. Hawaii Found., 2000—; hon. sec. Am. C. of C. in Belgium, 1966-78. With U.S. Army, 1955-57. Decorated Officer of the Order of Leopold II, comdr. Order of the Crown (Belgium), comdr. Order of Merit (Luxembourg); recipient Tribute of Appreciation award U.S. State Dept., 1981, Harvard Alumni Assn. award, 1996. Mem. ABA, Fed. D.C. Bar Assn., Pacific and Asian Affairs Coun. (pres.), Honolulu Com. Fgn. Relations, Pacific, Outrigger Canoe (Honolulu), Travellers (London), Am. and Common Market (Brussels pres. 1981-85), Honolulu Social Sci. Assn. Home: 4463 Aukai Ave Honolulu HI 96816-4858

BOAT, THOMAS FREDERICK, physician, educator, researcher; b. Pella, Iowa, Sept. 7, 1939; s. Bert Reuben and Anne Marie (Schoenbohm) B.; m. Barbara Mary Walling, June. 9, 1962; children: Sarah Elizabeth, Mary Barbara, Anne Christine. BA, Cen. Coll., Pella, 1961; MS, U. Iowa, 1965, MD, 1966. Diplomate Am. Bd. Pediat., Am. Bd. Pediat. Pulmonology. Resident in pediat. U. Minn., Mpls., 1966-68; clin. assoc. NIH, Bethesda, Md., 1968-70; fellow in pediat. pulmonology Case Western Res. U., Cleve., 1970-72, instr. pediat., 1972-73, asst. prof., 1973-76, assoc. prof., 1976-81, prof., 1981-82; prof., chmn. dept. pediat. U. N.C., Chapel Hill, 1982-93; chmn. dept. pediat. U. Cin. Sch. Medicine, 1993—; dir. Cin. Children's Hosp. Rsch. Found., 1993—. Prin. investigator Pediat. Pulmonary Specialized Ctr. Rsch., NIH, 1991-93; chmn. Am. Bd. Pediat., 1994. Editor Current Opinions in Pediat., 1990-93; mem. editl. bd. Lung Rsch. jour. Bd. dirs. Ronald McDonald House, Chapel Hill, 1985-88, Cystic Fibrosis Found., chmn. rsch. devel. program, 1983—. Lt. comdr. USPHS, 1968-70. Fellow: Am. Acad. Pediat.; mem.: Inst. of Medicine, Assn. Med. Sch. Dept. Chairs (pres.-elect 1994—97, pres. 1997—99), Am. Thoracic Soc. (chmn. pediat. assembly 1983—84), Am. Pediat. Soc. (pres. 2000—01). Office: Children's Hosp Med Ctr 3333 Burnet Ave SEC D6 Cincinnati OH 45229-3039

BOATNER, JERRA, legal assistant; b. Meridian, Miss., June 11; d. Jerry Wayne and Marsha Jo (Shanks) B.; m. James Adrian Runnels, June 11, 1997. BA in Criminal Justice, U. So. Miss., 1995, MS in Criminal Justice, 1997. Dep. Metro Task Force, Hattiesburg, Miss., 1996; grad. asst. U. So. Miss., Hattiesburg, 1995-96, instr., 1996—; legal asst. Forrest Co. Dist. Atty., Hattiesburg, 1997—. Rschr.: (handbook) Mississippi Youth Court Handbook, 1995. Vol. Sexual Assault Crisis Ctr., Hattiesburg, Miss., 1995-96; campaign vol. Mayor John Robert Smith, Meridian, Miss., 1993. Recipient Alma B. Walters award Dept. Criminal Justice, U. So. Miss., 1995, Miss./Tenn. Lawman's Assn. scholarship, 1994. Mem. Phi Kappa Phi, Gamma Beta Phi. Democrat. Lutheran. Avocations: reading and rsch., walking, travel. Office: Forrest County Dist Atty PO Box 166 Hattiesburg MS 39403-0166

BOATRIGHT, ANN LONG, dancer, pianist, music educator, choreographer; b. Louisville, Jan. 11, 1947; d. William Frazier and Mary Madolin (Hagan) Long; m. Ned Collins Boatright Jr., June 15, 1968; 1 child, Elizabeth. Student, Jordan Coll. Music, 1960-65, Butler U., 1965-68; BA, SUNY, Plattsburgh, 1970; MusM, Ithaca Coll., 1974; MA in Dance/Composition, Ohio State U., 1993, postgrad., 1994—. Cert. tchr., N.Y., Ohio, mgmt. analyst CMA. Movement analyst pub. schs., Plattsburgh, Ithaca, and Rochester, N.Y., 1970-76, head dance program Columbus (Ohio) Sch. for Girls, 1977-82; instr. Suzuki piano Capital U., 1982-85, instr. eurythmics, 1982—, developer tchr. tng. for music and movement, 1985-88. Past tchr. eurythmics, music, movement Lake Forest Coll., Capital U., Wittenberg U., Ohio State U., Eastern Mich. U., Denison U., Utah State U.; tchr. Suzuki and traditional piano, Columbus, 1985—; instr. Suzuki Summer Music Insts. Capital U., clinician 1982 88; clinician classical dance Wittenberg U., 1989; ballet soloist with Jordan Coll. Music Co., Butler U., Ithaca Ballet Co.; dancer with Indpls. Civic Ballet Co., Columbus Theatre Ballet Co.; pianist with Butler U. String Trio; adj. faculty Santa Rosa Jr. Coll, district coord. Calif. Assn. Prof. Music Tchrs. Choreographer: (ballets, mus. comedies) Odds 'n Ends, 1980, Little Match Girl, 1979, Crusades, 1982, Ballet of Unhatched Chicks, 1982, Wheels, 1979, Marathon, 1981. Mem. Arts for Peace-Unify Ohio, 1986; mem. women's svc. bd. Grant Med. Ctr.; mem. Franklin Park Conservatory; mem. jr. coun. Columbus Mus. Art, Zephyrus League. Mem. Music Tchrs. Nat. Assn. (nat. cert.), Ohio Music Tchrs. Assn. (condr. various workshops, clinician 1986-87, 89, faculty summer camp 1988-91, instr. conv. at Kent State U. 1994), Nat. Guild Piano Tchrs., Am. Coll. Musicians (faculty), Suzuki Assn. Am., Suzuki Assn. Ohio, Sigma Alpha Iota, Alpha Chi Omega. Republican. Avocations: downhill skiing, bicycling, travel, gardening, art. Home: 12100 Elliot Ln Sebastopol CA 95472

BOATWRIGHT, CHARLOTTE JEANNE, marketing professional, public relations executive; b. Chattanooga, Dec. 12, 1937; d. Clifton Jerry and Veltina Novella (Braden) Blevins; m. Robert W. Boatwright; children: Lynn Kay, Janis Ann, Karen Jean, Mary Ruth, Melody Susan, April Celeste. Diploma, Erlanger Sch. Nursing, Chattanooga, 1963; BS, U. Tenn., Chattanooga, 1976, MEd, 1981; PhD, Columbia Pacific U., San Rafael, Calif., 1987. Diplomate Nat. Assn. Forensic Counselors, Nat. Bd. Addiction Examiners; cert. domestic violence counselor Nat. Assn. Forensic Counselors; mediator Mediation Assn. Surgeon's asst. William Robert Fowler, M.D., Chattanooga, 1963-64; instr. med.-surg. nursing Baroness Erlanger Hosp. Sch. Nursing, 1964-67, instr. fundamentals nursing, 1971-74, chmn. dept. mental health-psychiat. nursing, 1977-81; staff nurse Meml. Hosp., Chattanooga, 1967—68, nursing supr., 1968—70; dir. inservice edn. Hutcheson Med. Ctr., Ft. Oglethorpe, Ga., 1970-71; youth work cons. Sewanee Dist. Episcopal Chs., Chattanooga, 1975-76; dir. spl. projects N. Pk. Hosp., Chattanooga, 1984-87, dir. mktg. and pub. rels., 1987—. Pres. CBB Comm.; freelance writer. Founder, chairperson Domestic Violence Coalition Greater Chattanooga, 1994; bd. dirs. Family Violence Shelter Com., Sexual Abuse Resource Ctr., Coalition Against Family Violence Greater Chattanooga, Tenn. Dept. Children's Svcs. Child Abuse Prevention Coun.; mem. adv. bd. Opportunity Home, Chattanooga; mem. Cmty. Ptnrs. Neighborhood Change-Crime and Neighborhood Safety; mem. dept. youth work Episcopal Diocese Tenn., 1975—77, mem. violence in soc. resource team, pres. diaconate formation com., 2002; condr. adult ch. sch. groups St. Martin's Episcopal Ch., Chattanooga; vice chmn. Brynewood Park Cmty. Assn., 1985, 1986. Recipient Liberty Bell award, Chattanooga Bar Assn., 1997, Advocacy for Children award, S.E. Tenn. Coun. Children and Youth, 2000. Mem.: Chattanooga C. of C., Chattanooga Press Assn., Tenn. Soc. Hosp. Mktg. and Pub. Rels., Tenn. Hosp. Assn., Am. Coll. Healthcare Execs. (nominee), U. Tenn. Alumnae Assn. Republican. Avocations: music, reading, gardening, travel.

BOAZ, DAVID DOUGLAS, foundation executive; b. Mayfield, Ky., Aug. 29, 1953; s. Seth Thomas Jr. and Martha Elizabeth (Pruitt) B. BA, Vanderbilt U., 1975. Exec. dir. Young Am.'s Found., Sterling, Va., 1975-76; editor New Guard Mag., Sterling, Va., 1976-78; exec. dir. Coun. for a Competitive Economy, Washington, 1978-80; research dir. Clark for Pres. Com., Washington, 1980; v.p. Cato Inst., Washington, 1981-89, exec. v.p., 1989—. Bd. dirs. Ctr. for Ind. Thought, NYC, Women's Freedom Network; bd. regents Congl. Schs. Va., 1991—. Author: Libertarianism: A Primer, 1997; co-editor: Beyond the Status Quo, 1985, An American Vision, 1989, Market Liberalism: A Paradigm for the 21st Century, 1993, Cato Handbook for Congress, 2001; editor: Left, Right and Babyboom, 1986, Assessing the Reagan Years, 1988, The Crisis in Drug Prohibition, 1990, Liberating Schools: Education in the Inner City, 1991, The Libertarian Reader, 1997, Toward Liberty, 2002; contbr. to books and newspapers. Office: Cato Inst 1000 Massachusetts Ave NW Washington DC 20001-5400

BOBB, HAROLD DANIEL, chiropractor, consultant; b. Moline, Ill., Nov. 22, 1952; s. Harold Daniel and Clarice (Engholm) B.; m. Elizabeth Jean Lackey, Feb. 14, 1971 (div. Mar. 1974); m. Elzita Lemaster, Nov. 30, 1979; 1 child, Andrea; stepchildren: Kevin, Christopher. As, Black Hawk Coll., Moline, 1972; D Chiropractic, Palmer Coll., Davenport, Iowa, 1976; postgrad., Upper Iowa U., 1976-78. Diplomate chiropractic. Clinic dir. Bobb Chiropractic Ctr. P.C., Silvis, Ill., 1977—. Cons. Health Data Devel., Los Angeles, 1983—. Author: The Case Formula, 1987; contbr. articles to profl. jours. Bd. dirs. Silvis Sch. Dist. 34, 1982-86; alumni bd. dirs. Black Hawk Coll, 1987—. Mem. Ill. Prairie State Chiropractic Assn. (treas. 1980-82), Am. Chiropractic Assn., Nat. Acad. Sci., Optimist. Avocations: computers, camping, photography. Office: Bobb Chiropractic Ctr PC 813 1st Ave Silvis IL 61282-1079

BOBBA, KUMAR MANOJ, engineer, researcher; s. Yugandhar and Jamuna Rani Bobba; m. Lakshmi Priya Yalavarthy. BTech, Indian Inst. Tech., Madras, 1998; MS, Calif. Inst. Tech., 1999, PhD, 2003. Project assoc. Nat. Inst. Ocean Tech., Chennai, India, 1997; project asst. Indian Inst. Sci., Bangalore, 1997—98; tchg. asst. Calif. Inst. Tech., Pasadena, 1999—2001, rsch. asst., 1999—, tchg. asst., 2002—. Organizer confs. Indian Inst. Tech., Chennai, 1997, Indian Inst. Sci., Bangalore, 1997—98, Calif. Inst. Tech., 2000—, invited guest lectr., 2000—02. Contbr. articles to profl. jours.; reviewer jours. in field. Nominee Young Scientist Fellowship, US Nat. Congress on Computational Mechanics, 2003; recipient cert. of merit, Andhra Pradesh Assn. Math. Tchrs., 1994, Young Scientist award, Indian Sci. Congress Assn., 1997, Gold medal, NSF-KDI-IGPP Workshop, 2002; summer rsch. fellow, Jawaharla Nehru Ctr. for Advanced Sci. Rsch., 1997, Rajiv Gandhi Sci. Rsch. scholar, 1998. Mem.: ASME, ASA, APS, IEEE, SIAM. Office: MS 205-45 Galcit Caltech 1200 E California Blvd Pasadena CA 91125 Office Fax: 626-395-2677. E-mail: bobba@galcit.caltech.edu.

BOBBITT, JUANITA CRAWFORD, international organization executive; b. N.Y.C., Sept. 4, 1938; d. Philip Theodore and Lillian Beatrice (Nelson) Crawford; 1 child, Edmund Michael. BA in Romance Lang., CUNY, Bklyn., 1959; MA in Econ., NYU, 1982; MPA, Harvard U., 1984. Pub. adminstrn. officer UN, N.Y.C., 1974-84, econ. affairs officer, 1984-92, sr. pub. adminstrn. officer, 1992-97, head gender adv. svcs. unit, 1998, internat. devel. cons., 1999—. Contbr. articles to profl. jours. Exec. com. St. George's Cmty. Devel. Corp., Bklyn., 1994-99; rep. provincial coun. Episcopal Ch., 1993-96. Mem.: ASPA (exec. com., sect. internat. comparative adminstrn.), Tri-State J.F. Kennedy Alumni Assn. (exec. com. 1987—), Harvard Club (N.Y.C. chpt., program com. 1991—99, admissions com. 2001—03, 2001—03, program com. 2002—03, 2002—03), Delta Sigma Theta (pres. Bklyn. chpt. 1966—68, nat. projects com. 1973—74, chair internat. com. 1993—99, social action commn. 2002—03). Episcopalian. Avocations: reading, walking, dancing, arts.

BOBBITT, PHILIP CHASE, writer, educator, public official; b. Temple, Tex., July 22, 1948; s. Oscar Price and Rebekah Luruth (Johnson) B.; m. Selden Anne Wallace (div. 1990). AB, Princeton U., 1971; JD, Yale U., 1975; PhD, Oxford U., 1983, MA, 1984. Bar: Tex. 1977, U.S. Supreme Ct. 1989. Law clk. to Judge Henry Friendly U.S. Ct. Appeals (2d cir.), 1975-76; asst. prof. law U. Tex., Austin, 1976-79, prof., 1979—, A.W. Walker chair in law, 1996—. Assoc. counsel to Pres. U.S. for intelligence and internat. security, 1980-81; legal counsel U.S. Senate Select Com. on Secret Mil. Assistance to Iran and Nicaraguan Opposition, 1987-88; counselor on internat. law U.S. Dept. of State, 1990-93; dir. for intelligence NSC, 1997-98, sr. dir. critical infrastructure, 1998-99, sr. dir. strategic planning, 1999; mem. faculty Salzburg Seminar, 1987; vis. fellow Internat. Inst. Strategic Studies, 1981-82; jr. rsch. fellow Nuffield Coll., Oxford U., 1982-84, rsch. fellow, 1984-85, Anderson sr. rsch. fellow, 1985-91, mem. modern history faculty, 1984-91; guest scholar Woodrow Wilson Ctr. for Internat. Scholars, 1994; sr. rsch. fellow war studies King's Coll./U. London, 1994-97. Author: Democracy and Deterrence, 1988; (with Guido Calabresi) Tragic Choices, 1979, Constitutional Fate, 1982; (with Lawrence Freedman and Gregory Treverton) Nuclear Strategy, 1988, Constitutional Interpretation., 1991, The Shield of Achilles: War, Peace and the Course of History, 2002. Trustee Princeton U. Mem. Am. Law Inst., Internat. Inst. Strategic Studies (London), Austin Coun. Fgn. Affairs (pres. 1983—), Coun. Fgn. Rels. (N.Y.C.), Adminstrv. Conf. U.S. (spl. com. on ethics in govt.), Pacific Coun. on Internat. Policy, Nat. Infrastructure Assurance Coun., State Infrastructure Protection Adv. Com. (editl. bd. biosecurity and bioterrorism), Tex. Philos. Soc., Met. Club (Washington), Yale Club, Century Assn., The Brook, Knickerbocker Club (NYC). Democrat. Baptist. Office: U Tex Law Sch 727 E 26th St Austin TX 78705-3224

BOBBITT, RONALD ALBERT, lawyer; b. Chgo., Dec. 23, 1953; s. Booker T. and Clara M. Bobbitt; married; 2 children. BS, U. Ill., 1976; JD, Antioch U., 1979. Bar: Ill. 1979, U.S. Dist. Ct. (no. dist.) Ill. 1979, U.S. Ct. Appeals (7th cir.) 1979. Clk. to adminstrv. asst. to chief justice, 1978; sr. ptnr. Bobbitt & Assocs., Chgo., 1979—. Mem. NAACP, Chgo., 1990; mentor Adopt-a-Sch. program, Merrillac House. Recipient Key to City Mayor's Office, Birmingham, 1980, Goodwill Community Svc. award Chgo. Heights, Ill., 1981. Mem. ABA, Nat. Bar Assn., Nat. Bus. Execs., Nat. Urban League, Chgo. Bar Assn., Cook County Bar Assn., Psi Chi, Phi Eta Sigma. Avocation: horseback riding. Office: Bobbitt & Assocs 155 N Michigan Ave Chicago IL 60601-7511

BOBBITT, WARREN LESLIE, SR., director; b. Drakes Branch, Va., Aug. 26, 1921; s. Fred Anthony Bobbitt and Emma Jessie Lassiter; m. Jane Neal Herndon, June 7, 1952; children: Warren Leslie Jr., Margaret Neal Laney. BS, Northwestern U., 1947; MA in Edn., U. Va., 1951; EdD, U. Calif., Berkeley, 1959. H.S. tchr. Page County Bd. Edn., Shenandoah, Va., 1948—49, Newport News (Va.) Bd. Edn., Va., 1951—52; counselor Child Guidance Clinic, Bedford, NY, 1954—55; dir. student svcs. Fox Ln. Jr.-Sr. High, Bedford, 1956—58; dir., asst. supt. student svcs. Charlotte (N.C.)-Meck. County Sch. Bd., 1959—83. Prof. psychol. testing N.C. State U., Raleigh, 1960—65; cons. in field. Editor: (jour.) Am. Sch. Counselor Assn. Founder Planned Parenthood Greater Charlotte, 1981; pres. Charlotte Speech and Hearing Ctr., 1983—84; mem. precinct com. Dem. Party. Sgt. Army Air Force, 1942—45, ETO. Episcopalian. Home: 2138 Princeton Ave Charlotte NC 28207-2432

BOBCO, WILLIAM DAVID, JR., consulting engineering company executive; b. Chgo., Aug. 11, 1946; s. William David and Eleanor Josephine (Dvojack) B.; m. Donna Domenica DiFrancesca, Sept. 13, 1969; 1 child, Christina Marie. BS in Engring., U. Ill., Chgo., 1969; MBA in Prodn. Mgmt., U. Chgo., 1983. Prodn. mgr. Am. Can Co., Maywood, Ill., 1972-73; with Footlik & Assocs., Evanston, Ill., 1973—, exec. v.p., 1986—. Mem. indsl. adv. bd. U. Ill. Coll. Engring., Chgo., 1992—, chmn. alumni devel. com., 1991-95, mem. dean selection com., 1994. Vol. Art Inst. Chgo., 1983—84, Animal Care League, Oak Park, Ill., 2000—02; facilities and grounds com. St. Giles Parish, 1995—, co-chair, 1997—2001, chair, 2001—, treas. golf com., 2000—, chmn. golf com., 2002, chmn. golf scholarship com., 1999—, lions leap com., 1998—2001, steering com. capitol campaign, 2002; Eucharistic Minister St. Giles Ch., 2000—, chmn., treas. golf com., 2002—. Capt. Ordnance Corp. U.S. Army, 1969—72, W. Germany, Vietnam. Mem. ASME (bd. dirs. Chgo. sect. 1984-2001, newsletter editor 1987-98, vice chmn. 1991, chmn. Chgo. sect. 1992-94, region VI rep. to A World in Motion K-12 tng. program, SAE (co-sponsor 1993), Engring. Alumni Assn. U. Ill. Chgo. (pres. 1984-88, bd. dirs. 1975-99), U. Ill. Alumni Assn. (bd. dirs. 1985-91, nominating com. 1991, Loyalty award 1988, Constituent Leadership award 1991, Disting. Svc. award 1994). Roman Catholic. Avocations: travel, art, music. Office: Footlik & Assocs 2521 Gross Point Rd Evanston IL 60201-4993

BOBENHOUSE, NELLIE YATES, insurance company executive; b. Spickard, Mo., May 3, 1936; d. Joseph Howard and Nellie Elizabeth (Tuttle) Yates; m. Lewis L. Griffin, Apr. 22, 1956 (div. Jan. 1964); 1 child, Elizabeth Anne Griffin Van Blarcom; m. Robert A. Bobenhouse, Aug. 28, 1965 (dec. Apr. 29, 1999). Student, St. Joseph (Mo.) Jr. Coll., 1955, Grandview Coll., 1980. Sec. News-Press & Gazette, St. Joseph, 1954-56; sec., bookkeeper Wilson's Locker & Ins., Spickard, Mo., 1956-60, Oyler's Locker, Spickard, 1960-64; sec. Equitable of Iowa Agy., Des Moines, 1964-68, agy. office supr., 1968-94. City clk. City of Spickard, 1959-60; mem. Des Moines Women's Club, 1994—. Fellow Life Mgmt. Inst.; mem. Ins. Women Des Moines (com. chmn. 1975), P. Buckley Moss Soc., Beta Sigma Phi (sec.-treas. 1958-60, Woman of Yr. 1959), PEO (G.Y. chpt.), 1998—. Republican. Disciple of Christ. Avocations: gardening, antique cars, quilting, bridge. Home: 2801 E P True Pky Unit 602 West Des Moines IA 50265

BOBER, LAWRENCE HAROLD, retired banker; b. N.Y.C., Mar. 29, 1924; s. Michael N. and Julia (Verschleiser) B.; m. Natalie S. Birnbaum, Aug. 27, 1950; children: Stephen, Marc, Elizabeth. BS, NYU, 1949; postgrad., Grad. Sch. Bus. Adminstrn., 1949-50. With Hanover Bank (now Chase Bank), 1941-87, asst. sec., 1950-52, asst. treas., 1953-55, asst. v.p., 1955-60, v.p., 1960-71, sr. v.p. (North Am. div.-II), 1971-87, Bd. dirs. Fab Industries, Inc. Dir., past chm. The Reeneselaerville Inst., past vice chmn., bd. fellows Brandeis U.; past pres. Congregation Emanuel of Westchester; dir. emeritus Cobblefield Homeowners Assn. White Plains, N.Y. 1st lt. USAAF, 1942-45. Decorated D.F.C. with two oak leaf clusters, Air medal with three oak leaf clusters; recipient Human Relations award Am. Jewish Com., 1968, Community Service award Nat. Jewish Hosp. and Research Center, 1980, Community Service award Am. Jewish Congress, 1988. Home: 7 Westfield Ln White Plains NY 10605-5459 E-mail: lawrencebober@aol.com.

BOBIC, MICHAEL P. political scientist, educator; b. Binghampton, N.Y., Mar. 22, 1963; s. Robert J. and Jane P. Bobic; m. Jennifer L. Bobic. A, Appalachian Bible Coll., 1982; BA, Berea Coll., 1985; MA, U. Tenn., 1992, PhD, 1996. Tchg. asst. U. Tenn., Knoxville, 1990—93; adj. faculty Roane (Tenn.) State C.C., 1993—94, So. Ill. U., Carbondale, 1995—96; asst. prof. Emmnuel Coll., Franklin Springs, Ga., 1998—. Adj. faculty E. Tenn. State, Johnson City, 1991—93; typist Galbreath Chem. Labs., Knoxville, 1992—93. Contbr. articles. Mem.: KC, Phi Kappa Phi, Pi Sigma Alpha. Avocations: fencing, magic. Office: Emmnuel Coll 129 Springs St Franklin Springs GA 30639

BOBINSKI, GEORGE SYLVAN, librarian, educator; b. Cleve., Oct. 24, 1929; s. Sylvan and Eugenia (Sarbiewski) B.; m. Mary Lillian Form, Feb. 20, 1953; children-George Sylvan, Mary Anne. BA, Case Western Res. U., 1951, MS in Libr. Sci., 1952; MA, U. Mich., 1961, PhD, 1966. Rsch. asst. Bus Info. Bur., Cleve. Pub. Libr., 1954-55; asst. dir. Royal Oak (Mich.) Pub. Libr., 1955-59; dir. librs. State U. Coll. at Cortland, N.Y., 1960-67; prof., asst. dean Sch. Libr. Sci. U. Ky., 1967-70; prof. SUNY, Buffalo, 1970—2001, dean Sch. Info. and Libr. Studies, 1970-99, prof. emeritus, 2002—. Fulbright-Hays lectr. in libr. sci. U. Warsaw, Poland, 1977; trustee Western N.Y. Libr. Rsch. Coun., 1971-87, pres., 1972, 82; vis. scholar Jagiellonian U., Krakow, Poland, 1992, 97. Author: A Brief History of the Libraries of Western Reserve University, 1826-1952, 1955, Carnegie Libraries, Their History and Impact on American Public Library Development, 1969, Dictionary of American Library Biography, 1978, also articles. Mem. N.Y. Gov.'s Comm. on Librs., 1990—. With AUS, 1952-54. Recipient Meritorious Svc. medal Jagellonian U., Krakow, Poland, 1997. Mem. ALA (mem. pub. com., mem. coun.), N.Y. Libr. Assn., Assn. Am. Libr. Schs.

(chmn. coun. of deans 1985-86) Home: 69 Little Robin Rd Buffalo NY 14228-1125 Office: SUNY Buffalo Sch Informatics Baldy Hall Buffalo NY 14260 E-mail: bobinski@acsu.buffalo.edu.

BOBINSKI, MARY FORM, library director; b. Rochester, N.Y., Aug. 29, 1928; d. George H. and Lydia Mendenhall (Richards) Form; m. George S. Bobinski, Feb. 20, 1953; children: George S. Jr., Mary Anne. BA, U. Rochester, 1951; MS, Case Western Res. U., 1952. Children's work dir. Royal Oak (Mich.) Pub. Libr., 1952-53, 55-59; supr. sch. librs. Ft. Bragg, N.C., 1953-54; lectr. Coll. Libr. Sci. U. Ky., 1968-70; dir. Amherst (N.Y) Pub. Librs., 1973—. Producer, host weekly TV show Library Limelight. Mem. governing bd. Musicalfare Theatre, 2000—. Mem. N.Y. Libr. Assn. (pres. pub. libr. sect. 1978-79). Pub. Libr. Dirs. Assn. N.Y. State (pres. 1985-86), Beta Phi Mu. Home: 69 Little Robin Rd Amherst NY 14228-1125 Office: Amherst Pub Libr 350 John James Audubon Pky Amherst NY 14228-1142 E-mail: bobinskim@buffalolib.org.

BOBIS, DANIEL HAROLD, lawyer; b. N.Y.C., May 1, 1918; s. Morris N. and Sarah C. Bobis; m. Selma Linder, May 15, 1960; children: Jodee E. Bobis Verbow, Stacee M. Bobis Miccio. LLB, St. Lawrence U., 1939; BS, Columbia U., 1947. Bar: N.Y. 1949, U.S. Patent and Trademark Office 1950, U.S. Supreme Ct. 1961, U.S. Ct. Appeals (3d cir.) 1963, N.J. 1964, U.S. Dist. Ct. N.J. 1964, U.S. Ct. Appeals (fed. cir.) 1982. Patent atty. Worthington Corp. (now Studebaker-Worthington Corp.), Harrison, N.J., 1946-1952, patent counsel, until 1969; mem. firm Popper, Bain, Bobis, Gilfillan & Rhoades, Newark, N.J., 1969-74, Popper & Bobis, Newark, N.J., 1974-79, Popper, Bobis & Jackson, Newark, N.J., 1979-88; of counsel Lerner, David, Littenberg, Krumholz & Mentlik, Westfield, N.J., 1988—. Founder Ann. Outstanding Patent Award, N.J. Coun. for R & D, 1966; former instr. on intellectual property matters and causes Horizon Sch. for Parlegal Tng., Linden, N.J. Capt. pilot AC, AUS, 1943-46; ETO. Decorated Air medal with one silver and 3 bronze oak leaf clusters, Purple Heart. Mem. ABA (chmn., mem. intellectual property coms.), N.J. Bar Assn. (chmn., mem. intellectual property coms.), N.J. Patent Law Assn. (pres. 1966, chmn., mem. intellectual property coms.), various N.J. county bar assns. (chmn., mem. intellectual property coms.). Home: 30 Burnham Ct Scotch Plains NJ 07076-3129 Office: Lerner David Littenberg Krumholz & Mentlik 600 South Ave W Ste 300 Westfield NJ 07090-1497 E-mail: dbobis@ldlkm.com.

BOBLETT, MARK ANTHONY, civil engineering technician; b. Beckley, W.Va., Jan. 21, 1959; s. Murriel Garner and Meredith Genevieve (Sheppard) B.; m. Susan Renee Walker, June 26, 1982; children: Miranda Lauren, Adrienne Lisbeth. AS in Civil Engring. Tech., AS in Bldg. Constrn. Tech., W.Va. Inst. Tech., 1983. Quality control technician Pittsburgh Testing Lab., Houston, 1984, Elmo Greer & Sons, Beckley, 1984-86; quality control coord. Green Constrn. Co., Beckley, 1986-88; assoc. agt. Nationwide Ins., Beckley, 1987-88; lab. mgr. Law Engring. Inc., Raleigh, N.C., 1988-96; founder Tech IV Corp., Raleigh, 1997—. Baptist. Home: 111 Triple Crown Run Louisburg NC 27549-9010 Office: PO Box 150 Bunn NC 27508-0150

BOBO, GENELLE TANT (NELL BOBO), retired office administrator; b. Paulding County, Ga., Oct. 31, 1927; d. Richard Adolph and Mary Etta (Prance) Tant; m. William Ralph Bobo, May 1, 1948; children: William Richard, Thomas David (dec.). Student, Berry Coll., Mt. Berry, Ga., 1947. Exec. sec. Macon (Ga.) Kraft Co., 1951-54; med. sec. Drs. Loveman & Fleigleman, Louisville, 1954-55; tchr. Fulton County Schs., Palmetto, Ga., 1960-68; exec. sec. Rayloc, Atlanta, 1968-70; adminstrv. coord. U. Ga., Athens, 1970-77; assoc. to dir. Mission Svc. Corps, Home Mission Bd. So. Bapt. Conv., Atlanta, 1977-94. Rschr., writer Sta. 11-TV, Atlanta, 1989. Author: Driven by a Dream, 1992. Philanthropy chmn. Exec. Women, Inc., Atlanta, 1968-69; mem. adv. coun. Baylor U., Waco, Tex., 1993-99. Mem. NAFE. Baptist. Avocations: public speaking, teaching, music, sewing, reading. Home: 87 Vickers Rd Fairburn GA 30213-1139

BOBO, LEN DAVIS, musician, educator; b. Vicksburg, Miss., Feb. 1, 1949; s. Samuel Redus and Eugenia (Causey) Bobo; m. Pamela Jeannine Moore, Apr. 13, 1974; children: Celeste Nichole, Brittany Noelle. AA, Hinds Jr. Coll., 1969; MusB, Miss. Coll., 1971; MusM, U. Tenn., 1975. Cert. consecrated diaconal min. Meth. Ch. Dir. music Lakewood United Meth. Ch., No. Little Rock, Ark., 1976-79; music instr. U. Ark., Little Rock, 1975-90; ch. organist/ assoc. music dir. Pulaski Heights United Meth. Ch., Little Rock, 1979-93; music instr., coll. organist Hendrix Coll., 1983-98; minister of music First United Meth. Ch., Maumelle, Ark., 1993-94; instr. computer sci. The Anthony Sch., Little Rock, 1994-96; assoc. dir. music, organist, dir. Music and Arts Inst. First Presbyn. Ch., Pine Bluff, Ark., 1996—. Vis. instr. music. U. Ctrl. Ark., Conway, 1998—99; dir. music Covenant Presbyn. Ch., Jackson, Miss., 1999—; instr. music Millsaps Coll., 2001—, East Ctrl. C.C., Decatur, Miss., 2003—. Composer (organ solo): Psalm 23, 1973, Praise to the Lord, 1977, Enchamatics, 1987, Fantasie pour le Trompette en chamade, 1990; composer: (choral piece) The Lord's Prayer, 1979; composer: (vocal solo) The Magnificat and Nunc Dimitis, 1979. Organist Ark. Celebration of 150 Yrs. Statehood, 1986. Sgt. Ark. Air N.G., 1974—76. Recipient Disting. Alumnus Music Dept., Miss. Coll., 1997. Mem.: Nat. Fedn. Music Clubs (pres. Hot Springs chpt. 1981-82) (Ark. Chpt. Musician of Yr. award 1986), Presbyn. Assn. Musicians, Fellowship Meth. Musicians (pres. 1978-79), Am. Guild Organists, USCG Aux., Lions. Avocation: Avocations: boating, fishing, photography, biking. Home: 335 Stonecastle Dr Brandon MS 39047-8073 Office: Covenant Presbyn Ch 4000 Ridgewood Rd Jackson MS 39211-6425

BOBOWICK, A. ROGER, neurologist; b. Bridgeport, Conn., Oct. 31, 1940; s. Alphonse John and Stella (Ochman) B.; m. Barbara Alyce Rowins, Aug. 22, 1964; children: Scott Roger, Todd Daren. AB, U. Pa., 1962; MD, Tufts U., 1966. Diplomate in neurology Am. Bd. Psychiatry and Neurology. Intern Yale New Haven Hosp., 1966-67, resident in neurology, 1967-70; staff assoc. NIH, Bethesda, Md., 1970-72; cons. neurologist Fairfield Hills Hosp., Newtown, Conn., 1985-95, Southbury (Conn.) Tng. Sch., 1996-97. Contbr. chpt. to book, articles to profl. jours. Chmn. bd. trustees Southbury Tng. Sch., 1980-85. Fellow Am. Acad. Neurology; mem. Am. Epilepsy Soc., Am. Clin. Neurophysiol. Soc., Alpha Omega Alpha. Roman Catholic. Avocation: gardening. Office: 134 Grandview Ave Waterbury CT 06708-2507

BOBRICK, STEVEN AARON, transportation executive; b. Denver, Apr. 11, 1950; s. Samuel Michael and Selma Gertrude (Birnbaum) B.; m. Maria Diane Boltz, Oct. 5, 1980. Attended, U. Colo., 1968-72. Registered apt. mgr. Owner Bobrick Constrn., Denver, 1969-72; with Bell Mtn. Sports, Aspen, Colo., 1972-75; mgr. Compass Imports, Denver, 1975-80, Aurora (Colo.) Bullion Exch., 1980-81; contr. Bobrick Constrn., Aurora, 1981-85; appraiser Aurora, 1985—; property mgr. Aurora (Colo) Cmty. Mental Health, 1989-98, active real estate and constrn., facilities mgr., 1989-98; exec. mgmt. asst. E-470 Pub. Hwy. Authority, 1998, mktg./pub. rels. web master, 1998-99; bus. mgr. Northwest Pkwy Pub. Hwy. Authority, 1999—. Co-author: Are You Paying Too Much in Property Taxes, 1990. Coun. mem. City of Aurora, 1981-89; chmn. Explore Commercial Opportunities, Aurora, 1986-89, bd. dirs.; bd. dirs. Adam County Econ. Devel. Commn., Northglenn, Colo., 1985-89; vice chair Aurora Urban Renewal Authority, 1982-89; chmn. Aurora Enterprise Zone Found., 1991-94; bd. dirs. Aurora Community Med. Clinic, 1987-88, Aurora Cmty. Mental Health Ctr., 2001. Avocations: sking, mountain biking, exercise. Office: 555 Eldorado Blvd 130 Broomfield CO 80021

BOBROW, DAVIS BERNARD, public policy educator; b. Boston, Sept. 2, 1936; s. Robert and Elizabeth (Gelf) B. BA in Gen. Edn., U. Chgo., 1955, BA in Comm., 1956; BA in Philosophy-Politics-Econs., Queen's Coll., Oxford U., 1958; PhD., MIT, 1962. Lectr. dept. politics Princeton, 1961-62, asst. prof., 1962-64; sr. social scientist dir.'s div. Oak Ridge Nat. Lab., 1964-68; acting dir. Behavioral Scis. Office, Advanced Research Projects Agy., 1969-70; spl. asst. behavioral and social scis. Office of Dir. Def. Research and Engring., 1968-70; prof. dept. polit. sci. Sch. Pub. Affairs, U. Minn., Mpls., 1970-74; dir. Quigley Center Internat. Studies, 1970-74; prof., chmn. dept. govt. and politics U. Md., College Park, 1974-77, prof., 1977-88; dean Grad. Sch. Pub. and Internat. Affairs U. Pitts., 1988-95, prof., 1988—. Vis. Fulbright prof. Tel Aviv U., 1979-80; vis. rsch. prof. Inst. Policy Sci., Saitama U., 1982-83; vis. prof. Internat. U. Japan, 1983, Peking U., 1986; vis. Fulbright rsch. prof. Grad. Sch. Policy Sci., Saitama U., 1989-90; vis. fellow Rsch. Sch. Pacific Studies, Australian Nat. U., 1992, U. Warwick, 1998, European U. Inst., 2001; Fulbright sr. scholar, Germany, 2001-2002; mem. sr. cons., cons. Def. Sci. Bd., 1972-93; mem. polit. sci. panel NSF, 1976-78; mem. USAF Sci. Adv. Bd., 1971-76; mem. com. energy and environ. NAS and NRC, 1975-77; pres. Assn. of Profl. Schs. of Internat. Affairs, 1993; pres. Nat. Assn. Schs. Pub. Affairs and Adminstrn., 1994-95, Internat. Studies Assn., 1996-97. Author: International Relations: New Approaches, 1972; co-author: Understanding Foreign Policy Decisions: The Chinese Case, 1979, Policy Analysis by Design, 1987; Editor, co-author: Components of Defense Policy, 1965, Weapons System Decisions: Political and Psychological Perspectives on Continental Defense, 1969; co-editor, co-author: Computers and the Policy-Making Community: Applications to International Relations, 1968, National and International Security in the Late Twentieth Century, 1997, Prospects for Internatinal Relations: Conjectures about the Next Millennium, 1999; assoc. editor Policy Sciences, 1969-80; editl. assoc. Public Opinion Quar., 1963-64; mem. editl. bd. Jour. Conflict Resolution, 1972-84, Pacific Focus, 1987—, Internat. Studies Quar., 1999—, Internat. Rels. Asia-Pacific. Ford Found. scholar, 1954-56; Rhodes scholar, 1958; Social Sci. Rsch. Coun. fellow, 1960-62. Home: 2 Dunmoyle Pl Pittsburgh PA 15217-1029 Office: U Pitts Sch Pub and Internat Affairs Pittsburgh PA 15260 E-mail: bobrow@birch.gspia.pitt.edu.

BOBROW, HENRY BERNARD, lawyer; b. N.Y.C., Mar. 31, 1924; s. Jacob and Sadye (Smollen) B.; m. Phyllis-Fein, July 6, 1952; children: Joanne Schoelkopf, Richard S. BA, Johns Hopkins U., 1947; JD, Cornell U., 1952; LLM, N.Y.U. Law Sch., 1956. Bar: N.Y. 1952, U.S. Dist. Ct. (so. and ea. dists.) N.Y. 1954. Assoc. to ptnr. Carroad & Carroad, N.Y.C., 1953-58; ptnr. Bobrow, Handman & Katz, N.Y.C., 1958-69, Cutler & Cutler, N.Y.C., 1968-72, Candee, Solomon, Bobrow, Burton, Davidowitz & Distler, N.Y.C., 1972-75, Bobrow, Greenapple, Skolnik & Shakarchy (and predecessors), N.Y.C., 1975-95; of counsel Cox, Buchanan, Padmore and Shakarchy, N.Y.C., 1995-97, Roosevelt & Arfa, LLP, White Plains, N.Y., 1997-99, Bobrow & Sosis, White Plains, N.Y., 2000—. Pres. U.S. Patent Model Found., Washington, 1985-90; mem. Real Estate Bd. N.Y.C., 1987-91. Mem. Bd. Appeals, Scarsdale, N.Y., 1988-91; trustee Jewish Child Care Assn., N.Y.C., 1978—. Cpl. AUS, 1943-45, ETO. Named Outstanding Alumnus, Johns Hopkins U., 1978. Mem. ABA, Johns Hopkins Club (pres. 1966-68), Cornell Club of N.Y., B'nai B'rith (pres. 1964-66). Republican. Jewish. Avocation: tennis and swimming. Office: 150 Southfield Ave Ste 2444 Stamford CT 06902 E-mail: hbbobrow@aol.com.

BOBROW, RICHARD S. diversified financial services company executive; BSBA, MSBA, U. Kans. With Ernst & Young LLP, N.Y.C., 1976—, ptnr., 1984—, tech. specialist nat. tax on real estate and partnership matters, 1985—88, dir. West Region, real estate adv. svcs. L.A., 1988—91, dir. tax Indpls., 1991—93, nat. dir. tax, 1993—96, vice chair tax practice initiatives N.Y.C., 1996—98, sr. vice chair assurance and adv. bus. svcs., 1998—2000, Americas CEO, 2002—02, Global CEO, 2002—. Office: Ernst & Young LLP 5 Times Sq New York NY 10036-6530*

BOBROW, SUSAN LUKIN, lawyer; b. Cleve., Jan. 18, 1941; d. Adolph and Yetta (Babkow) Lukin; m. Martin J. Bolhower, Nov. 28, 1986 (div. Dec. 1988); children from previous marriage: Elizabeth Bobrow Pressler, Erica, David. Student, Antioch Coll., Yellow Springs, Ohio, 1958-61; BA, Antioch Coll., L.A., 1975; JD, Southwestern U., L.A., 1979. Bar: Calif. 1980. Pvt. practice, Beverly Hills, Calif., 1983-88; assoc. Schulman & Miller, Beverly Hills, 1988-89; staff counsel Fair Polit. Practices Commn., Sacramento, Calif., 1990-96; sr. counsel Calif. State Lottery, Sacramento, 1996-98; asst. gen. counsel Employment Tng. Panel, Sacramento, 1998-99, 1999—. Panel for paternity defense L.A. Superior Ct., 1984. Exhibited paintings at Death and Trasnfiguration Show, Phantom Galleries, Sacramento, 1994; exhibited photography U. Calif.-Davis Women's Art Collaborative, Phantom Galleries, Sacramento, 1997, Camera Arts, Sacramento, 1998, Viewpoint Gallery Exhibit, Sacramento, 1998. Bd. dirs. San Fernando Valley Friends of Homeless Women and Children, North Hollywood, Calif., 1985-88, Jewish Family Svcs., 1997; mem. adv. bd. Project Home, Sacramento Interfaith Svc. Coun., 1990-91; v.p. cmty. affairs B'nai Israel Sisterhood, Sacramento, 1991-93; bd. dirs. Sacramento Jewish Family Svcs., 1997-98. Recipient commendation Bd. Govs. State Bar of Calif., 1984. Mem. Inst. Noetic Scis., Sacramento Inst. Noetic Scis. (steering coun. 1994), Los Angeles County Bar Assn. (Barristers com. on adminstrn. of justice 1985), Sacramento County Bar Assn. (com. on profl. responsibility 1993-94, alt. del. to state bar conv. 1991), Sacramento Valley Photog. Arts Ctr. Democrat. Office: Employment Tng Panel 1100 J St Sacramento CA 95814-2827

BOBRUFF, CAROLE MARKS, radio producer, radio personality; b. N.Y.C., Nov. 11, 1935; d. Morris Frank and Harriet (Lehman) Marks; m. Jerome Bobruff, June 20, 1954 (div. 1986). Student, Quinnipac Coll., 1954-55, U. N.C., 1955-56; AS, U. New Haven, 1981; BS in Human Services, N.H. Coll., 1982. Founder, dir. Tyndall Air Force Daycare Ctr., Panama City, Fla., 1957-60; med. asst. Digestive Disease Assocs., New London, Conn., 1974-82; program coord. Pre-Trial Release Program, Norwich, New London, Conn., 1982-84; case mgr., counselor residential criminal justice program Cochegan House, Montville, Conn., 1984-85; exec. dir. Ret. Sr. Vol. Program So. New London County, 1984-91; producer, host nat. radio program A Touch of Grey, Groton, Conn., 1990-97; prodr., host Senior Focus Talk Am. Radio Network, Groton, Conn., 1997—; CEO Focus Commn. Treas. Dir. Vols. in Agys., New London, 1986—, Conn. RSVP Dirs., 1987; bd. dirs. Cochegan House, Widowed Persons Service, Waterford, Conn. Editor: Senior Citizens Guide to Discounts and Services, 1988; editor, author: RSVP Newsletter, 1984—; columnist: The Day, 1987. Pres. women's aux. New London County Med. Assn., 1986-87; bd. dirs. League Women Voters, New London, HOSPICE, New London, Am. Cancer Soc. New London County. Recipient Proclamation Community award Town of Waterford, 1989, Community Service award The Connection, Inc., 1987. Mem. Women's Network New London County, Children and Family Services, Pub. Relations Network, Nat. Assn. Female Execs., Brandeis U. Jewish. Home: 3 Pondside Ct Mystic CT 06355-3124 Office: 3 Pondside Ct Mystic CT 06355 Fax: 860-572-8239. E-mail: carole@atouchofgrey.com.

BOBRUFF, JEROME, physician; b. Hartford, Conn., June 18, 1930; s. Nathan and Mildred (Dobin) B.; m. Bernice S. Gendron, July 22, 1990; m. Carole Marks, June 20, 1954 (div. 1986); children: Ellen, Neal, Paul, Mark; stepchildren: Jeffrey Reynolds, Michael Reynolds. BA, Wesleyan U., 1952; MD, Yale U., 1955. Diplomate Am. Bd. Internal Medicine. Instr. Seton Hall Coll. Medicine, Jersey City, N.J., 1961-62; physician Lawrence Meml. Hosp., New London, Conn., 1962-95, chief gastroenterology, 1975-80. Pres. Digestive Disease Assocs., New London, 1969—95; cons. med. dir. MD Health Plan, New Haven, 1995—97; med. dir. Americares Free Clinic, 1999—2002; bd. dirs. Colonial IPA, New London. Contbr. articles to profl. jours. Mem. Gov.'s Commn. on Reading, Conn., 1968, Charter Rev. Com., New London, 1970, Zoning Bd. Appeals, New London, 1986-91, 2002-. Capt. USAF, 1957-59. Fellow: Am. Soc. Gastrointestinal Endoscopy; mem.: AMA (ho. of dels. 1989—2000), New London County Med. Assn. (pres. 1979—80, Disting. Physician award 1993), Conn. Med. Soc. (councillor 1979—88), Lions, Phi Beta Kappa. Democrat. Jewish. Avocations: skiing, sailing, golfing, bowling. Home and Office: 765 Pequot Ave New London CT 06320-4214

BOBYSHEV, DMITRY V. poet, education educator; b. Mariupol, Ukraine, Apr. 11, 1936; s. Zinaida Ivanovna Bobysheva and Vasily Konstantinovich Bobyshev(Stepfather); m. Galina Roubinchtein, Oct. 29, 1992. Attestate, H.S. # 157, Leningrad, 1944—53; B, Leningrad Inst. of Tech., 1957, M, 1959. Author: (literary memoirs) Mantext (Chelovekotekst), (books of poetry) Angels and Powers (Angely i Sily); author: (poet) Russian Terza Rima (Russkie Tertciny); author: Acquaintance of Words, Fire-Bush. Recipient The Fifth Rose (poem-)dedicated in his honor, Anna Akhmatova, 1963. Mem.: Union of St. Petersburg Writers (life), Am. Assn. of Teachers of Slavic and East European Languages. Home: 612 West Church Str Apt # 44 Champaign IL 61820 Office: University of Illinois 707 South Mathews Ave Urbana IL 61801 Home Fax: 217-333-7310; Office Fax: 217-333-7310. Personal E-mail: dbobyshe@staff.uiuc.edu. E-mail: dbobyshe@staff.uiuc.edu.

BOCAYA, RENATO BISO, pharmaceutical sales and marketing executive, entrepreneur; b. Tabaco, Albay, Philippines, Feb. 14, 1959; came to U.S., 1983; s. Santos B. and Benita B. (Biso) Bocaya. BA in Polit. Sci., Lyceum of the Philippines, Manila, 1978, BS in Fgn. Svc., 1979; MBA, U. Philippines, 1980; MS, L.I. U., 1990; postgrad., Northwestern U., 1992, Duke U., 1996. Territory mgr. Mead Johnson Philippines, Manila, 1978-83; sales mgr. GeneAsia Biopharmaceuticals Inc., N.Y.C., 1983-86; coagulation product mgr. Rhone-Poulenc Rorer/Armour, Collegeville, Pa., 1986-96; mgr. strategic bus. market devel.: Asia Centeon LLC, 1996-98; regional dir. North Am. Speywood Pharms. Inc., Milford, Mass., 1998-2000; pres. GenAsia Biotech LLC, N.Y.C., 2000—. Founder Renboc Internat. Corp., N.Y.C., 1997—. Bd. dirs. Jaycee Philippines, Davao City, 1980-81; vol. Internat. Exec. Svc. Corp.; v.p. Ako Ay Pilipino Movement, N.Y.C., 1999—. Recipient Leadership award Jaycee Philippines, Davao City, 1980. Mem. Am. Coll. Internat. Physicians (dir., cons. 1986-90, Humanitarian award 1989), N.Y. State Coun. Health Sys. Pharmacists. Lions Internat. (bd. dirs. 1990-91, Humanitarian award 1990). E-mail: genasia@surfshop.net.ph.

BOCCAGNA, DAVID LOUIS, finance company executive; b. Stamford, Conn., Mar. 16, 1933; s. Louis Salvatore and Emily Antoinette (Gallace) B.; div.; children: Kai Louis, Kim Marie. BA, U. Hartford, 1956, MA, 1958; PhD, U. Conn., Walden, 1973. Lectr. philosophy, aesthetics, logic, mgmt. U. Conn., 1959-72, U. Bridgeport, 1959-72, U. Hartford, 1959-72, U. Windham, 1959-72; adv., negotiator Aramco Oil Co., Dhahran, Saudi Arabia, 1972-78; assoc., ptnr. Prince Mohammad Mashari Abdulaziz Al Saud, 1978-86; v.p. First Republic Mgmt. Svc. Co. Ltd., Nassau, Bahamas, 1987-89; sr. v.p., CFO First Republic Fin. Svcs. Co. Ltd., Nassau, 1987-89; chmn. bd. dirs. First Republic Bank Ltd., Rarotanga, Cook Islands, 1989-96; pres. Investment Evaluative Svcs. Corp., Miami, Fla., 1996—. Chmn. bd. dirs. First Republic Bank Ltd., 1988—; mem. staff U. Santa Clara ext., 1974-78. Author: A Compendium of Agogic Terms, 1997, Inside the World of Investment, Frauds, Scams and Deceptive Practices, 1998, Mastering the World of Investment Fraud, Scams and Deceptive Practices, 1999, 120 Improvisational Etudes: II, V, I, 2000, The Progression of Improvisation, 2000, ...And So What Is Money, 2000, Manipulation of the ICC 400, 2000, Understanding of Letters of Credit, 2000, A Study of Bank Instruments in Legitimate and Fraudulent Applications, 2000, Understanding Bank Guarantees, 2000, Debunking Fraudsters Portfolios, 2001, The Many Faces of Ponzi, 2001, Somewhere Along the Line, 2001, The Deception of Perception, 2001, A Select Collection of Quotes, Aphorisms, Bon Mots and Humor, 2002. Mem. Stamford Conn. Bd. Edn. Recipient Outstanding Expatriate Businessman award Al Khobar C. of C., 1980, Industrialist Merit award Renbaxy-Murti Conglomerate, 1981. Office: Investment Evaluative Svc Corp PO Box 832647 Miami FL 33283-2647

BOCCARA, NINO, physicist; b. Tunis, Tunisia, May 30, 1931; s. Roger and Marcelle (Smadja) B.; m. Francoise Martin; children: Eliane, Bruno. Ingenieur, ESPCI, 1956; Lic.Scis., U. Paris, 1957, D.Scis., 1961. Mem. staff Nat. Ctr. Sci. Research, Paris, 1956-97, dir. Lab. Magnetism, 1975-80, rsch. dir., 1976-97; prof. math. Ecole Superieure de Physique et de Chimie, 1977—. Dir. Centre de Physique des Houches, 1983-93; vis. prof. U. Ill., Chgo., 1981, prof., 1985—. Author: Principes de La Thermodynamique Classique, 1968, Physique des Transitions, 1970, Symetries Brisees, 1976, Symmetries and Broken Symmetries in Condensed Matter Physics, 1981, Analyse Fonctionnelle, 1984, Functional Analysis, 1990, Probabilite, 1995, Integration, 1995, Fonctions Analytiques, 1996, Distributions, 1997. Home: 70 W Burton Pl Chicago IL 60610-1444 Office: 10 Vauquelin Paris 75005 France also: U Ill Physics Dept 845 W Taylor St Chicago IL 60607-7056 E-mail: boccara@uic.edu.

BOCCARDI, LOUIS DONALD, retired news agency executive; b. Bronx, N.Y., Aug. 26, 1937; s. Louis and Delphine Boccardi; m. Joan M. Quinlan, Jan. 18, 1964; children— Susan, Lynn, Paul, Mark, Lauren. BA, Fordham Coll., 1958; MS, Columbia U. Grad. Sch. Journalism, 1959. Reporter/desk editor N.Y. World Telegram & Sun, 1959-64; asst. mng. editor N.Y. World Jour. Tribune, 1966-67; asst. gen. news editor AP, N.Y.C., 1967-69, mng. editor, 1969-73, v.p., exec. editor, 1973-85, pres., 1985—2003, retired pres., CEO. Mem. Pulitzer Prize bd.; bd. visitors Columbia U. Sch. Journalism, Northwestern U. Medill Sch. Mem. nat. adv. bd. Media Studies Ctr. Recipient Alumni Achievement award Fordham Coll., 1967, Outstanding Alumnus award Fordham U., 1968 Mem. Am. Soc. Newspaper Editors (Disting. Svc. mem.).*

BOCCHINO, ANTHONY J. law educator, consultant; b. Meriden, Conn., July 31, 1947; s. Anthony and Kathryn (Wadilewski) B.; m. Linda L. Shafer, July 13, 1984. B.A., Bucknell U., 1969; J.D., U. Conn., 1972. Bar: Conn. 1972, N.C. 1973. Asst. prof. law Duke U. Law Sch., Durham, N.C., 1974-77, assoc. prof., 1977-79; sr. trial atty. Office of Insp.-Gen., GSA, Washington, 1979; assoc. prof. law Temple U. Law Sch., Phila., 1979-82, prof., 1982—; vis. George E. Allen prof. law U. Richmond Law Sch., Va., 1984; regional dir. Nat. Inst. Trial Advocacy, Phila., 1983, team leader, 1975; cons. on profl. tng. Steptoe & Johnson, Washington, 1982—. Author: North Carolina Trial Evidence Manual, 1976; Pennsylvania Evidence: Objections and Responses, 1983; Cases and Problems in Trial Advocacy, 1983, 84, 85. Bd. dirs. North Central Legal Services, Durham, 1977-79; guest lectr. Pa. Jud. Conf., Phila., John S. Bradway fellow Duke Law Sch., 1973-74; recipient award Mordecai Soc. Award, 1978, Williams Outstanding Teaching award Temple Law Sch., 1984. Mem. N.C. Bar Assn., ABA, Phila. Bar Assn., Conn. Bar Assn. Democrat. Roman Catholic. Home: 115 Edgewood Rd Ardmore PA 19003-2507

BOCCIA ROSADO, ANN MARIE, paralegal, legal association administrator; b. San Pedro, Calif., Apr. 23, 1958; d. Franklin S. and Julia (Mattera) Boccia; m. Robert Daniel Rosado. AA, Harbor Coll., 1983; paralegal cert., Continental Tech. Inst., L.A., 1986. Invoicing/sales rep. Bronson of Calif., Gardena, 1976-78; traffic mgr. GSC Athletic Equipment, San Pedro, 1978-81; exec. legal sec. Stein, Shostak, Shostak & O'Hara, L.A., 1981; office adminstr., paralegal Stolpman, Krissman, Elber & Silver LLP, Long Beach, Calif., 1981—. Cons. San Pedro Chiropractic Ctr., 1989-96; instr. Michaels Stores, Inc., 1997-2000. Recipient Presdl. award Calif. Trial Lawyers Assn., 1988; named Legal Sec. of the Yr., 1998. Mem. Nat. Paralegal Assn., Assn. Trial Lawyers Am., Consumer Attys. L.A.(formerly L.A. Trial Lawyers Assn.) (speaker 1989-92, moderator 1991, voter registration com. 1988-89, Ann. Law Day participant 1991-92, benefits 1995-2002, 2003—, pres. 2000-02, gov. 2003-), L.A. Paralegal Assn., Long Beach Legal Secs. Assn. (chmn. benefits 1995-2002, chmn. day-in-ct. 1998-2000, treas. 1998, v.p. 1999, pres. 2000-02). Democrat. Roman Catholic. Avocations: cruising, walking, reading, boating, motorcycling. Office: Stolpman Krissman Elber & Silver LLP 111 W Ocean Blvd Fl 19 Long Beach CA 90802-4632 E-mail: arosado@stolpman.com.

BOCEA, MARIAN, mathematician; arrived in U.S., 1999; s. Firu and Elena Bocea; m. Cristina Mariana Popovici, Sept. 21, 2000. MSc, U. Craiova, Romania, 1997, PhD, 2000; MSc, Carnegie Mellon U., 2000. Rsch. asst. U. Craiova, 1996—99; tchg. asst. Carnegie Mellon U., Pitts., 1999—. Contbr. articles to profl. jours. Grantee Math. Challenges of the 21st. Century, UCLA, Am. Math. Soc., 2000, Progress in Partial Differential Equations, ICMS, Edinburgh, European Commn. (FrameworkV), 2001; Doctoral fellow, Ministry Nat. Edn., Romania, 1996—99, TEMPUS fellow, European Commn., 1997, World Bank fellow, Nat. Coun. Sci. Rsch., Romania, 1999. Mem.: Soc. for Indsl. and Applied Math. (Student Travel award 2002), Am. Math. Soc. Achievements include research in Partial Differential Equations, Calculus of Variations, Continuum Mechanics. Office: Carnegie Mellon Univ Dept Math Pittsburgh PA 15213 E-mail: mbocea@andrew.cmu.edu.

BOCHERT, LINDA H. lawyer; b. East Orange, N.J., May 13, 1949; BA, U. Wis., 1971, MS, 1973, JD, 1974. Bar: Wis. 1974. Dir. environ. protection unit Wis. Atty. Gen. Office, 1978-80; exec. asst. to the secy. Wis. Dept. Natural Resources, 1980-91; ptnr. Michael, Best & Friedrich, Madison, Wis., 1991—. Mem. ABA, Wis. State Bar Assn. Office: Michael Best & Friedrich PO Box 1806 First Plaza 1 S Pinckney St Madison WI 53701-1806 E-mail: lhbochert@mbf-law.com.

BOCHNER, HART, actor, director; b. Toronto, Ont., Can., Oct. 3, 1956; BA in English, U. Calif. San Diego, La Jolla, 1978. Actor: (films) Islands in the Stream, 1975, Breaking Away, 1978, Rich and Famous, 1980, The Wild Life, 1984, Making Mr. Right, 1986, Die Hard, 1988, Apartment Zero, 1998, Fellow Traveller, 1989, Mr. Destiny, 1990, Mad at the Moon, 1991, The Innocent, 1992, The Breakup, 1997, Anywhere But Here, 1998, UL2, 1999, Speaking of Sex, 2000, Liberty Stands Still, 2001, Say Nothing, 2001; (TV miniseries) Haywire, 1979, East of Eden, 1980, Having It All, 1982, Sun Also Rises, 1984, War and Remembrance, 1986—87 (Emmy award, 1989), And the Sea Will Tell, 1990, Complex of Fear, 1992, Children of the Dust, 1994; dir.: (films) The Buzzz, 1992, PCU, 1993, 1994, High School High, 1995—96.

BOCHNOVICH, JOHN ANDREW, small business owner; b. Carbondale, Pa., Oct. 21, 1941; s. John and Pauline (Kelachava) B. Student, MIT, 1959-62, Columbia U., 1963-64; BA, Binghamton U., 1968. Lic. mgmt. cons., Fla., 1980. Entrepreneur, Johnson City, 1989—2002; businessman I.A.B., Binghamton, NY, 2003—. Author: Thoughts From a Friend, 1991, Best Octal Digits in the Whole Universe, 1995, A Revolutionary View of Mental Illness, 1996. Avocations: crossword puzzles, walking, astronautics. Home: 425 Robinson St Binghamton NY 13904

BOCHY, BRUCE, professional sports team manager, coach; b. Landes de Boussac, France, Apr. 16, 1955; m. Kim B.; children: Greg, Brett. Coach San Diego Padres, 1993-94, mgr., 1994—. Office: San Diego Padres PO Box 2000 San Diego CA 92112-2000

BOCK, BROOKS FREDERICK, emergency physician; b. Orange, N.J., Sept. 19, 1943; MD, Wayne State U., 1969. Intern Detroit Gen. Hosp., 1969-70; resident in surgery Wayne State U., 1970-71, resident in urology, 1971-73, prof., chmn. dpet. emergency medicine, 1985—; pvt. practice; pres. Am. Bd. Emergency Medicine, 2002—. Mem. AMA, Am. Coll. Emergency Physicians, Mich. State Med. Soc., Wayne County Med. Soc. Home: 5764 Bloomfield Glens West Bloomfield MI 48322-2501 Office: 4201 St Antoine Detroit MI 48201

BOCK, CAROLYN A. writer, interviewer, small business owner; b. Jan. 25, 1942; d. Wilfred Ignatius and Marcella Mary (Birkemeier) Gerschutz; m. Donald Charles Bock, Sept. 7, 1974 (dec. Nov. 1997); 1 child, Jonathon Edward. Student, Notre Dame Coll., 1960-62, John Carroll U., 1962-66. With sales and purchasing depts. Schaffer Diversified Corp. and other cos., Cleve., 1962-74; columnist, writer, 1979—; owner Dynmic Living Assocs., 1986—. Author: Authors, Artists and Auras, 1988, Gerschutz family history, 1989. Co-founder, trustee Cmty. Action Team, Westlake, 1980-85; trustee, co-founder Westlake Arts Coun., 1983-84, pres., 1984-85; chmn. Morning Sem., Rocky River, Ohio, 1981-85; pres. Westlake PTA Coun., 1980-82, Parkside Jr. High PTA, Westlake, 1983-84; active Boy Scouts, Clague Playhouse, Westlake Hist. Soc., 1985-98. Recipient Outstanding Svc. award Boy Scouts Am., 1980; named hon. life mem. Ohio PTA, 1982. Mem.: Soc. Profl. Journalists, Word Works, Westfield Ctr. Hist. Soc. Unitarian-Universalist. Avocations: travel, reading, history, gardening. Home: 9183 S Leroy Rd Westfield Center OH 44251 also: PO Box 240 Lodi OH 44254-0240

BOCK, EDWARD JOHN, retired chemical manufacturing company executive; b. Ft. Dodge, Iowa, Sept. 1, 1916; s. Edward J. and Maude (Juday) B.; m. Ruth Kunerth, Aug. 9, 1941; children: Barbara, Edward, Nancy, Roger. MS in Mech. Engring. Iowa State U., 1940. With Monsanto Co., St. Louis, 1941—, asst. gen. mgr. inorganic chems. div., 1958-60, v.p., gen. mgr., 1960-65, v.p. adminstrn., mem. exec. com., dir., 1965-68, pres., CEO, chmn. corp. mgmt. and exec. coms., dir., 1968-72; chmn. bd., CEO, Cupples Co., St. Louis, 1975-85; cons. Bd. dirs. Harbour Group Ltd. Past chmn. bd. trustees Deaconess Hosp.; past trustee Ladue Chapel; past bd. govs. Iowa State U. Found.; past bd. dir. YMCA. Recipient Silver Anniversary All-Am. Football award Sports Illustrated, 1963; Anston Marston award Iowa State U., 1972; Significant Sig award, 1971; named to All Am. Football Team, 1938; elected to Nat. Football Found. Hall of Fame, 1970, 1st elected to Iowa State U. Athletic Hall of Fame, 1997. Mem. ASME, Sigma Chi, Tau Beta Pi. Clubs: St. Louis, Old Warson Country (pres. 1972), Bogey, Arnold Palmer's Bay Hill. Avocation: ham radio. Home and Office: 2232 Clifton Forge Dr Saint Louis MO 63131-3107

BOCK, JERRY (JERROLD LEWIS), composer; b. New Haven, Nov. 23, 1928; s. George Joseph and Rebecca (Alpert) B.; m. Patricia Faggen, May 28, 1950; children: George Albert, Portia Fane. Student, U. Wis., 1945-49, L.H.D. (hon.), 1985. Writer: score for high sch. mus. comedy My Dream, 1945; score for original coll. musical Big as Life, 1948; wrote: songs for TV show Admiral Broadway Revue, also Show of Shows, 1949-51; composer songs, Camp Tamiment, summers 1950, 51, 53; writer: continuity sketches Mel Torme show, CBS, 1951, 52; writing staff: Kate Smith Hour, 1953-54; writer: original songs for night club performers, including night club revue Confetti; wrote: songs for Wonders of Manhattan (hon. mention Cannes Film Festival 1956); composer: music for Broadway show Catch a Star, 1955, Mr. Wonderful, 1956, (collaborated with Sheldon Harnick on) The Body Beautiful, 1958, Fiorello, 1959 (Pulitzer prize, Drama Critics award, Antoinette Perry award), Tenderloin, 1960, She Loves Me, 1963, revival, 1990, Fiddler on the Roof, 1964, Silver Anniversary prodn. nat. tour, 1989-90, revival, 1990-91, 93, The Apple Tree, 1966, The Rothschilds, 1972, revival, 1990-91; London prodn. of She Loves Me, 1964, off-Broadway, 1982, Jerome Robbins Broadway, 1989; London prodn. of Fiddler on the Roof, 1964 (Tony award), Warsaw prodn., 1985, Fiorello, Goodspeed Opera House, summer 1985, (film) A Stranger Among Us, 1992; wrote series of children's songs now pub. under title Sing Something Special; also recorded album, N.Y. Bd. Edn., radio broadcasts, 1961—; wrote music and lyrics for musicals, Children's Theatre Festival, U. Houston, 2000-03. Recipient 9 Tony awards Best Musical of Yr. Fiddler on the Roof, 1964, Johnny Mercer award Songwriters Hall of Fame, 1990, Olivier award Best Musical Revival for She Loves Me, 1994; named to Theatre Hall of Fame, 1990. Mem. Broadcast Music Inc. (adv. panel), Nat. Found. Advancement in Arts (endowment group).

BOCK, PHILIP KARL, retired humanities educator, playwright; b. N.Y.C., Aug. 26, 1934; s. Eugene Bock and Clara Fleishmann; m. Layeh Aronson (div.); children: Marian, Deborah, Kaaren; m. Barbara L. Ziem, July 30, 1976. BA, Fresno (Calif.) State Coll., 1955; MA, U. Chgo., 1956; PhD, Harvard U., 1963. Prof. anthropology U. N.Mex., Albuquerque, 1962—94. Presdl. prof. U. N.Mex., 1986—90; vis. prof. Columbia U., N.Y.C., 1967, U. Ibero Americana, Mexico City, 1970, Stanford U., Palo Alto, Calif., 1971—72. Author: Modern Cultural Anthropology, 1969, 2d edit., 1974, Shakespeare & Elizabethan Culture, 1984, Rethinking Psychological Anthropology, 1988, 2d edit., 1999; editor: Handbook of Psychological Anthropology, 1994; contbr. articles to profl. jours.; editor-in-chief: Jour. of Anthropol. Rsch., 1982—94; prodr.: (musicals) Not My Department, Cat on a Streetcar Named Iguana, Who Took My Honey?, Ms. Muffet, the Spider, and Dr. Rice. Bd. dirs. Adobe Theater, Albuquerque, 1998—2002; bd. pres. Musica Antigua, Albuquerque, 2001—02; pres. Soc. for Psychol. Anthropology, 1997—99. Capt. USAFR, 1955—66. Fellow: Am. Anthropol. Assn. Avocations: writing for theater, playing piano and composing. Home: 8301 4th St NW # 3 Albuquerque NM 87114 E-mail: pbock@unm.edu.

BOCK, ROBERT LEROY, law educator; b. Macksville, Kans., Sept. 5, 1925; s. Albert Jacob Bock and Alice May Doran; m. Susan Lyons Myers, Feb. 2, 1960 (div.); children: Billy George, Albert Timothy, Edward Jacob, David Frank. AB, U. Kans., 1948, MA, 1953; LLB, Washburn U., 1953; PhD, Am. U., Washington, 1960. Bar: Kans. 1953, D.C. 1953. Asst. prof. So. Ark. U., Magnolia, 1960—62, Ball State U., Muncie, Ind., 1962—63; assoc. prof. Patsons Coll., Fairfield, Iowa, 1963—65; prof. SUNY, Oswego, 1965—67; assoc. prof. Old Dominon U., Norfolk, Va., 1967—68; prof. Western New England Coll., Springfield, Mass., 1968. Kans. state rep., 1946—50. With USAF, 1944—45, With USAF, 1950—51. Avocations: chess, horseshoes. Home: 66 Holly St Springfield MA 01151-1420 E-mail: tbock1@mindspring.com., tbock@iopenet.net.

BOCK, RUSSELL SAMUEL, writer; b. Spokane, Wash., Nov. 24, 1905; s. Alva and Elizabeth (Mellinger) B.; m. Suzanne Ray, Feb. 26, 1970; children: Beverly A. Bock Wunderlich, James Russell. BBA, U. Wash., 1929. Part time instr. U. So. Calif., UCLA, 1942-50; with Ernst & Ernst, CPAs, Los Angeles, 1938, ptnr., 1951-69; cons. Ernst & Young, 1969—. Author: Guidebook to California Taxes, annually, 1950—, Taxes of Hawaii, annually, 1964— ; also numerous articles. Dir., treas. Cmty. TV So. Calif., 1964-74; dir., v.p. treas., So. Calif. Symphony-Hollywood Bowl Assn., 1964-70; bd. dirs. Claremont McKenna Coll., 1964-70, Cmty. Arts Music Assn., 1974-76, 78-84, Santa Barbara Symphony Assn., 1976-78, Santa Barbara Boys and Girls Club, 1980-93, UCSB Affiliates, 1983-85, Santa Barbara Civic Light Opera, 1995-97. Mem. Am. Inst. C.P.A.s (council 1953-57, trial bd. 1955-58, v.p. 1959-60), Calif. Soc. C.P.A.s (past pres.), Los Angeles C. of C. (dir. 1957-65, v.p. 1963), Sigma Phi Epsilon, Beta Alpha Psi, Beta Gamma Sigma. Clubs: Birnam Wood Golf, Santa Barbara Yacht. Office: 300 Hot Springs Rd Apt 190 Santa Barbara CA 93108-2069

BOCK, WALTER JOSEPH, zoology educator; b. N.Y.C., Nov. 20, 1933; s. Paul and Anne (Kalsch) B.; m. Katharine Lippitt, June 29, 1957; children: Katharine Rose, Susan Ruth, Walter David. BS, Cornell U., 1955; MA, Harvard U., 1957, PhD, 1959. NSF postdoctoral fellow Universität Frankfurt Main, 1959-61; asst. prof. dept. zoology U. Ill., 1961-64, assoc. prof., 1964-65; asst. prof. dept. biol. scis. Columbia U., 1965-66, assoc. prof., 1966-73, prof., 1973—. Research asso. Am. Mus Natural History, 1965— Author: (with J.J. Morony and J. Farrand) Reference List of the Birds of the World, 1975; Contbr. articles to profl. jours. Pres. Tenafly (N.J.) Nature Center, 1977-80; permanent sec. Internat. Ornithol. Com., 1986-98; pres. 23rd Internat. Ornithological Congress, 2002. NSF grantee, 1962-79 Mem. Am. Ornithologists Union (Coues award 1975), Am. Soc. Zoologists, Am. Soc. Naturalists (treas. 1978-80), Soc. Study Evolution, Soc. Systematic Biology, AAAS, Brit. Ornithologists Union (corres. mem.), Deutschen Ornithologen-Gesellschaft (hon.) Home: 114 Hudson Ave Tenafly NJ 07670-1004 Office: Columbia U Dept Biological Scis New York NY 10027 E-mail: wb4@columbia.edu. *Humans are not independent of the earth's environment in which they live and of their evolutionary history. As a scholar, I hope to learn about evolutionary and ecological mechanisms; as a teacher I hope to pass this knowledge on to others; and as a person I hope to preserve and enjoy the beauty of nature that exists about us.*

BOCKELMAN, MELVIN F. retired computer scientist, writer; b. Great Bend, Kans., Dec. 9, 1927; s. Louis J. Bockelman and Hulda D. Uppendahl; m. Harriet Bockelman; children: Melvin E., Ronald, Diane. Commd. USAF, 1946, advanced through grades to chief master sgt.; ret., 1966; mgr. computer systems Kansas City Police Dept., Kansas City, Mo., 1966 78. Author: (book) Concordia Veterans Who Served in WWII; contbr. Mem., flag to the next of kin of the deceased Concordia Honor Guard; mcpl. ct. Mo., Concordia, 1989—96; bd. dirs. House of Hope, Lexington, Mo., 1995—2001, Whiteman AFB Cmty. Coun., 2000—, Concordia Area C. of C., 1998—2001; mem. Nat. Crime Info. System, Washington, L.A. Command and Control System, 1975, Whiteman AFB Korean War Commemorative Com., 2001—02; organizer Ann. Concert in the Park, 1995—. With U.S. Merchant Marine, 1944—45. Decorated Philippine Liberation medal U.S. Merchant Marine, Air Force Commendation medal; recipient WW II medal, State of Mo., 2001. Mem.: Lions. Home: 1208 West St Concordia MO 64020

BOCKHOP, CLARENCE WILLIAM, retired agricultural engineer; b. Paullina, Iowa, Mar. 28, 1921; s. Fred Henry and Sophie Dorothea (Laue) B.; m. Virginia Buhman, July 9, 1949; children: Barbara Lucille, Nancy Jeanne, Bryan William, Karl David. BS in Agrl. Engring, Iowa State U., 1943, MS in Agrl. Engring, 1955, PhD in Agr. Engring. and Theoretical and Applied Mechanics, 1957. Mgr. service and edn. Stewart Co., Dallas, 1948-53; mem. faculty Iowa State U., Ames, 1953-57, 60-80, prof. agrl. engring., 1960-80, head dept. agrl. engring., 1962-80; prof., head dept. agrl. engring. U. Tenn., 1957-60; head dept. agrl. engring. Internat. Rice Research Inst., Los Banos, The Philippines, 1980-86. Vis. prof. U. Ghana, 1969-70 Gen. reporter, VIth Internat. Congress Agrl. Engring., Lausanne, Switzerland, 1964; Author articles in field. Served to capt. AUS, 1943-48. Fellow Am. Soc. Agrl. Engrs. (chmn. Tenn. sect. 1958-59, chmn. mid-central sect. 1960-61, chmn. Iowa sect. 1963-64, chmn. edn. and research div. 1966-67, dir. 1973-75); mem. Am. Soc. Engring. Edn. (chmn. agrl. engring. div. 1966-67), Sigma Xi, Gamma Sigma Delta, Phi Kappa Phi, Phi Mu Alpha, Tau Beta Pi. Lutheran. Address: Apt 1508 101 N Upper Broadway St Corpus Christi TX 78401-2752

BOCKIAN, JAMES BERNARD, computer systems executive, writer; b. Jersey City, Sept. 16, 1941; s. Abraham and Evelyn (Skner) B.; m. Donna M. Hastings; children: Vivian Shifra, Adrian Adena, Lillian Tova. BA, Columbia U., 1963; MPA, U. Mich., 1965; MA, Yale U., 1967. Vice-consul, fgn. svc. officer Dept. State, Washington, 1957-61; sr. systems analyst J.C. Penney Co., N.Y.C., 1961-67; mgr. systems svcs., head dept. systems projects McDonnell Douglas Automation Co., Florham Park, N.J., 1967-76; prin. JBBA (formerly James B. Bockian & Assocs., Inc.), Morristown, N.J., 1976—. V.p. MIS Thomas Cook, Inc., 1980-83, exec. cons. to Thomas Cook Group; cons. AT&T, major banks and brokerages in project mgmt. systems design and devel., 1997-2001; lectr. in field; cons. in sys. validation to the pharm. industry. Author: Management Manual for Systems Development Projects, 1979, Project Management for Systems Development, 1981, AT&T User Guide to Information Systems Development, 1980; contbr. articles to profl. jours. Mem. AAAS, N.Y. Acad. Scis., Internat. Assn. Cybernetics, Yale Club (N.Y.C.). Home: 280 James St Morristown NJ 07960 Office: 280 James St Morristown NJ 07960-6410

BOCKIUS, RUTH BEAR, nursing educator; b. Groffdale, Pa., Dec. 19, 1925; d. Weidler Romaine and Ruth Mary (Jacoby) Bear; m. Thomas B. Bockius Jr., Dec. 15 1945; children: Donna Ruth, Dawn Eileen. AA, Phoenix Coll., 1970; BSN, Ariz. State U., 1973, MEd, 1978. Instr. nursing Glendale (Ariz.) Community Coll.; coord. health edn. Samaritan Health Svcs., Phoenix; dir. patient/community edn. Maryvale Samaritan Hosp., Phoenix, edn. dir., ret., 1994. Grantee Fed. Nursing; AMA scholar, 1st Nat. Bank scholar. Mem. Am. Soc. Hosp. Edn. and Tng., Am. Hosp. Assn., Phi Theta Kappa, Phi Kappa Phi.

BOCKSERMAN, ROBERT JULIAN, chemist; b. St. Louis, Dec. 20, 1929; s. Max Louis and Bertha Anna (Kremen) B.; m. Clarice K. Kreisman, June 9, 1957; children: Michael Jay, Joyce Ellen, Carol Beth. BSc, U. Mo., 1952; postgrad., Far East Intelligence Sch, Tokyo, 1954; MSc, U. Mo., 1955. Chemist Sealtest Corp., Peoria, Ill., 1955-56; prodn. mgr. Allan Drug Co., St. Louis, 1957-59; rsch. chemist Monsanto Co., St. Louis, 1960-65, purchasing agt. Sauget, Ill., 1966-67; founder, pres. Pharma-Tech Industries, Inc., Union, Mo., 1967-84; tech. dir. Overlock-Howe Consulting Group, St. Louis, 1984-85; founder, pres. Conatech Consulting Group, Creve Coeur, Mo., 1985—. Sec., mem. industry packaging adv. com. Sch. of Engring. U. Mo., Rolla, 1979—, adj. prof. dept. food sci./nutrition, Columbia, adj. prof. dept. engring. mgmt., Rolla, vis. lectr., Clayton, Northwestern U., Evanston, Ill.; vol. tutor Ladue Sch. Dist.; tutor Parkway Sch. Dist., St. Louis, Clayton (Mo.) Sch. Dist.; tech. cons. Creve Coeur Fire Protection Dist. Tech. reviewer Jour. Inst. of Packaging Profls., Jour. Packaging Tech., Mo. Waste Control Scholarship Grants and Research, Medical Device and Diagnostic Industry Jour., Medical Plastics and Biomaterials Publication.; mem. editl. adv. bd. The Forensic Examiner; panelist (Help Desk column) Medical Device and Diagnostic Industry mag., The Forensic Examiner; contbg. author: Packaging Forensics - Package Failure in the Courts. Mem. Mo. Waste Control Coalition; mem. stormwater engring. com. City of Creve Coeur, Mo., also mem. recycling and environ. com.; nat. mem. Libr. Congress, Mo. Hist. Soc. With U.S. Army, 1952-54, Korea. Small Bus. Innovation rsch. grantee. Mem. ASTM, Am. Coll. Forensic Examiners, Cons. Packaging Engring. Coun., Inst. Packaging Profls. (cert. packaging profl.), Am. Technion Soc., Inst. Food Technologists Arrangements (St. Louis), Nat. Forensic Ctr., Teltech Resource Network, Am. Chem. Soc., Am. Plastics Coun., Mo. Acad. Scis., N.Y. Acad. Sci., Acad. Sci. St. Louis, Assn. Cons. Chemists and Chem. Engrs., Am. Nutraceutical Assn., Nat. Dir. Expert Witnessess, Rotary Internat. (Clayton, Mo.), Sigma Xi. Achievements include research on toxicological effects of additives from packaging materials upon foodstuffs, on biological and photo degradation of polymers, on technology of form/fill/seal packaging engineering, new sterilization technologies for medical devices and pharmaceuticals, barrier properties of polymer films, toxicology of chemical dusts and fumes, and food irradiation effects on humans. Home: 54 Morwood Ln Creve Coeur MO 63141-7621 Office: Conatech Cons Group 287 N Lindbergh Blvd Creve Coeur MO 63141-7849 E-mail: rjbockserman@conatech.com.

BOCKSTEIN, HERBERT, lawyer; b. NYC, Jan. 27, 1943; s. Stanley Joseph and Sylvia (Tannenbaum) B.; m. Bonnie Sue Ritt, Sept. 2, 1967 (div.); children: Andrew, Jana; m. Nadine Bernstein, June 27, 1988. BA, NYU, 1963, JD cum laude, 1971; MBA, Cornell U., Ithaca, N.Y., 1966. Bar: NY 1972, Mo. 1979. Assoc. Stroock & Stroock & Lavan, N.Y.C., 1971-78, Stolar, Heitzmann & Eder, St. Louis, 1978-80, Finley, Kumble, Wagner, Heine, Underberg, Manley & Casey, N.Y.C., 1980-83; ptnr. Finley, Kumble, N.Y.C., 1983-87, Myerson & Kuhn, N.Y.C., 1988-89, Ashinoff, Ross & Korff, N.Y.C., 1989-90, Newman Tannenbaum, N.Y.C., 1990—96, Blank Rome LLP, N.Y.C., 1996—. Mem. ABA, N.Y. State Bar Assn., Estate Planning Coun. N.Y.C., Order of Coif. Avocations: tennis, golf. Home: One Scarsdale Rd Apt 412 Tuckahoe NY 10707 Office: Blank Rome LLP 405 Lexington Ave New York NY 10174-0002 E-mail: hbockstein@blankrome.com.

BOCKSTRUCK, LLOYD DEWITT, librarian; b. Vandalia, Ill., May 26, 1945; s. Harry Earl and Olive Elsie (Blankenship) B. AB cum laude, Greenville (Ill.) Coll., 1967; MA, So. Ill. U., 1969; MS, U. Ill., 1973; student, Samford U., 1973. Teaching asst. So. Ill. U., Carbondale, 1967—69; tchr. Mombasa (Kenya) Bapt. High Sch., 1969—71; teaching asst. U. Ill., Urbana, 1972—73; libr. Dallas Pub. Libr., 1973—. Instr. Inst. Genealogy and Hist. Rsch., Samford U., Birmingham, Ala., 1973—; instr. Sch. Continuing Edn., So. Meth. U., Dallas, 1974-91; instr. Geneal. Inst. of Mid-Am., U. Ill., Springfield, 1994—; columnist Dallas Morning News, 1991—. Author: Virginia's Colonial Soldiers, 1988, Genealogical Research in Texas, 1992, Revolutionary War Bounty Land Grants Awarded by State Governments, 1996, Family Tree Weekly Newspaper Columns from the Dallas Morning News, 1991-96, 99, Naval Pensioners of the United States, 1800-1851, 2002; contbr. articles to profl. jours. Recipient Scholarship Key award Phi Alpha Theta, 1967, History award DAR, 1989, Profl. award for hist. preservation Dallas County Hist. Commn., 1992, Filby prize for Genealogical Librarianship, 1999, Lifetime Achievement award N.E. Tex. Libr. Sys., 2003; Nat. Geneal. Soc. fellow, 1992. Mem. ALA (life), SAR (libr. gen. 1981-83), SCW (dep. gov. gen. 2000), Soc. of the Cincinnati, Jamestowne Soc., Order of Ams. of Armorial Ancestry (genealogist gen. 1993-99), Order of Founders and Patriots of Am. (genealogist gen. 1986-2000), Dallas Geneal. Soc. (dir. 1979—). Republican. Christian. Avocation: genealogy. Home: 3955 Buena Vista St Apt C Dallas TX 75204-1667 Office: Dallas Pub Libr 1515 Young St Dallas TX 75201-5499

BOCKUS, HERMAN WILLIAM, JR., artist, educator, writer; b. Frazee, Minn., Feb. 21, 1915; s. Herman William and Emma (Kimmerle) B.; m. Janet Davidson Fisher, Jan. 15, 1944; children: Genevieve, Kim, William, Heidi, Jill. BBA, U. Minn., 1937, BS, 1948, MEd, 1949, PhD, 2000. Salesman Food Warehouse, New Ulm, Minn., 1937-39; interpreter U.S. Govt., Colon, Canal Zone, 1939-42; art tchr. Highlands U., Las Vegas, N.Mex., 1948; art prof. Pasadena City Coll., 1950-75, head dept. art, 1965-66; tech. writer Calif. Inst. Tech., Pasadena, 1960-64. Author: Advertising Graphics, 1969, 4th edit. 1986, Checklist for Better Tennis, 1973, Designers Notebook, 1977, Life Science Careers, 1991, Boys, 1995, The Universe, 1999, Double or Nuthin, 2003. Capt. USMC, 1942-45. Recipient Cert. of Merit, L.A. Art Dirs. Show, 1965, Writer's Digest, 2001. Avocation: tennis. Home: 1943 Coolidge Ave Altadena CA 91001-3505

BOCKUS, KIMMERLE, photographer, consultant; d. Herman W. and Janet F. Bockus. BFA cum laude, UCLA, Westwood, Calif. Organizer CalTech Food Co-op, Pasadena, Calif., 1970—71; mgr., graphic artist Erewhon Natural Foods, L.A., 1972—75; graphic artist Sunwheel Natural Foods, London, 1976—80; mgr. Neal's Yard Wholefoods, London, 1980—83; sr. cons. East West Ctr., London, 1981—84; editl. photographer L.A. Weekly, 1988—93. Photographer (photography exhibitions) Camden Arts Ctr., London, 1987, Whitechapel Gallery, London, 1988, La Luz Gallery, L.A., 1994, Eaton Canyon Nature Ctr., Pasadena, Calif., 2002, portraits pub. artists and musicians, 1995, fine art photography, 2002—. Avocations: Japanese cooking, architecture, opera.

BOCKWITZ, CYNTHIA LEE, psychologist, psychology and women's studies educator; b. Hallock, Minn., Apr. 11, 1954; d. Rodney Lee and Jeanette Yvonne (Vilen) B. AA in Arts and Scis., Richland Coll., 1983; BA in Devel. Psychology, U. Tex., Dallas, 1985; MA in Counseling Psychology, Tex. Woman's U., 1992. Lic. profl. counselor, Ga.; registered play therapist and supr. Pers. adminstr. Automatic Data Processing, Miami, Fla., 1974-77; office mgr. G.A. Dexter Co., Atlanta, 1977-79; regional human resources mgr. No. Telecom, Atlanta and Dallas, 1979-84; mental health asst. Timberlawn Psychiat. Hosp., Dallas, 1984-85; acct. NEC Am., Dallas, 1986-87; asst. program dir. Arbor Creek Hosp., Sherman, Tex., 1989; lic. profl. counselor Trinity Counseling Ctr., Carrollton, Tex., 1989-93; pvt. practice Atlanta, 1993—. Adj. instr. psychology Tex. Woman's U., Denton, 1988—92, Ga. Perimeter Coll., Atlanta, 1993—; adj. faculty Argosy U., Atlanta; cons. The Resource Ctr., Atlanta, 1993—94; clin. team leader Laurel Hts. Hosp., 1994—2000; mem. exec. com. Women Clinicians Network, Atlanta, 1994—95; psychiat. assessments Emory Pkwy. Med. Ctr., 2001. Mem.: Lic. Profl. Counselors Assn., Ga. Assn. for Play Therapy (bd. dirs. 2000—), Internat. Assn. for Play Therapy, Ga. Marriage and Family Therapy Assn. (legis. com. 1993—94, mem. metro Atlanta chpt. bd. officers 1999—2000), Am. Assn. for Marriage and Family Therapy (affiliate), Am. Psychotherapy Assn. (diplomate). Democrat. Avocations: wilderness camping, photography. Home: 711 Tuxworth Cir Decatur GA 30033-5620 E-mail: clbockwitz@aol.com.

BOCOBO-BALUNSAT, DALISAY, librarian, journalist; b. Manila, Philippines, Jan. 22, 1926; d. Jorge Bocobo; m. Anthony Anton Balunsat. PhB, U. Philippines, 1950. Faculty mem. Adamson U., Manila, 1950—53; corr., columnist Philippine-Am. press, 1953—; ref. libr. San Francisco Pub. Libr., 1958—84. Founder, dir. Philippine-Am. Cultural Celebration, San Francisco, 1973—2003, Filipino Artists, Writers and Performers, 1973—. Recipient Woman Warrior award, Pacific Asian Am. Women, John Cotton Dana Nat. Libr. award, ALA, 1976, U.S. Bicentennial award, Filipino Arts Fiesta, 1976. Mem.: Phillipino Am. Press Correspondants, Filipino Artists, Wrtiers and Performors, ALA (Dana Nat. Libr. award 1975). Avocation: reading, writing, travel, movies, TV. Office: Filipino Artists Writers and Performers 1437 19th Ave San Francisco CA 94122

BOCOCK, MACLIN, writer; b. Baton Rouge, Dec. 21, 1920; d. James Branch and June Lyndon Bocock; m. Albert J. Guerard, July 11, 1941 (dec. Nov. 2000); children: Collot Guerard, Nini Guerard, Lundie Guerard. BA, Radcliffe Coll., 1942. Reader Harvard U. Press, Cambridge, Mass., 1942—58; lectr. Stanford (Calif.) U., 1970-71, NEH, Washington, 1972. Author: Heaven Lies About, 1993, A Citizen of the World, 1999; co-author: The Personal Voice, 1964; contbr. short stories for periodicals. Recipient PEN syndicated Fiction award. Died Dec. 13, 2002.

BOCOCK, SCOTT GREGORY, historian; b. Hammond, Ind., Sept. 26, 1967; s. Carman Robert and Mary Ann Bocock. B in Gen. Studies, Ind. U. N.W., Gary, 1993. Hist. interpreter, groundskeeper Buckley Homestead Lake County Pk., Lowell, Ind., 1990; pres. Cedar Lake (Ind.) Hist. Assn., 1993—95; historian Town of Cedar Lake, 1994—2001; Ind. rm. page Gary (Ind.) Pub. Libr., 1999—2000. Historian City of Westminster, Colo., 2001—; vol. Cedar Lake Hist. Assn., 1989—2001, Adams County Hist. Soc., Brighton, Colo., 2002. Recipient cert. for contbn., Cedar Lake Hist. Assn., Lake of Red Cedars Mus., Ind., 1992, plaque, Cedar Lake Town Coun., 2001; scholar Cornelius O'Brien Confs. on Historic Preservation, Ind U., 1990—91. Mem.: Nat. Trust for Historic Preservation, Orgn. Am. Historians, Am. Assn. State and Local History. Achievements include helping in development of Lake of Red Cedars Museum; listing Old Monon Park Dancing Pavilion in Cedar Lake on the National Register of Historic Places. Avocations: reading, writing, antiques, preserving artifacts, genealogy. Home: 1698 W 115th Cir Westminster CO 80234 2608

BOCTOR, FOUAD NASSIF, pathologist, researcher; b. Cairo, June 21, 1943; arrived in U.S., 1986, naturalized, 1993; s. Nassif Boctor and Zakia Boules; m. Aziza Aziz Younan, Jan. 27, 1971; children: Peter F., Dina F., Christine F. BSc, Cairo U., 1965, MS, 1970; PhD, Mansoura U., Egypt, 1975; MD, Cairo U., 1984. Lic. Am. Bd. of Pathology. Rsch. asst. Nat. Rsch. Ctr., Dokki, Egypt, 1966—67, U.S. Naval Med. Rsch. Unit #3, Cairo, 1967—70, rsch. assoc., 1970—75, med. rsch. investigator, 1976—79; postdoctoral fellow Nat. Cancer Inst., NIH, Bethesda, 1976—77; rsch. assoc. Nat. Inst. of Allergy and Infectious Diseases, Bethesda, Md., 1977—79; rsch. investigator U.S. Naval Med. Rsch. Unit #3, Cairo, 1979—86; R&D rsch. dir. Splty. Lab. Inc, Santa Monical, Calif., 1986—89; resident in pathology U. of Conn. Med. Ctr., Farmington, 1989—92; med. resident NYU Med. Ctr., N.Y.C., 1992—94; pathology fellow Hartford Hosp./ U. Conn Med. Ctr., Hartford, 1994—95; pathologist, blood bank dir. Bronx Lebanon Hosp. Ctr., Albert Einstein Coll. Of Medicine, 1995—2000; asst. prof. Albert Einstein Coll. Of Medicine, Bronx, 1998—; pathologist, dir. of blood bank and transfusion medicine Montefiore Med. Ctr., Albert Einstein Coll. Of Medicine, Bronx, 2000—. Bd. dirs. Arabic Baptist Ch., Yonkers, NY, 1990. Mem.: Am. Assn. of Immunologists. Independent. Avocations: reading, walking. Office: Montefiore Med Ctr 1825 Eastchester Rd Bronx NY 10461-2373

BOCZEK, BOLESLAW ADAM, retired law educator; b. Bielsko, Poland, Mar. 29, 1922; arrived in U.S., 1958; s. Ludwik and Aniela Boczek; m. Annerose J. Mirsberger, June 6, 1963; children: Matthew, Andrew, Barbara. LLM, Jagiellonian U., Cracow, 1947, JD, MA, Jagiellonian U., Cracow, 1949; PhD, Harvard U., 1960. Rsch. asst. Harvard Law Sch., Cambridge, Mass., 1959—60, rsch. assoc., 1961—66; advisor UN, N.Y.C., 1960—61; prof. internat. rels. and law Kent (Ohio) State U., 1966—92; ret. Author: Flags of Convenience, 1962, Taxation in Switzerland, 1976, Dictionary of International Law, 1986, International Tribunals, 1994, International Law Dictionary, 2003. Fellow, Ford Found., NATO, 1988; Fulbright fellow, Mexico, 1970—71, Germany, 1979—80. Mem.: Am. Soc. Internat. Law. Home: 708 Allerton St Kent OH 44240

BODACK, MARK PETER, physician, medical educator; b. Rockville Center, Oct. 24, 1960; s. Walter R.F. and Patricia M. Bodack; m. Mary Ellen Monteiro. BS, Spring Hill Coll., 1984; MD, Royal Coll. Surgeons, Dublin, Ireland, 1990. Diplomate Am. Bd. Electrodiagnostic Medicine, Am. Bd. of Phys. Medicine and Rehab. Intern U. Conn. Health Ctr., Farmington, 1990-91; resident The N.Y. Hosp., Cornell Med. Ctr., N.Y.C., 1991-94; asst. attending physician N.Y. Hosp.-Cornell Med., N.Y.C., 1994-98; med. dir. rehab. St. Francis Hosp., Poughkeepsie, N.Y., 1998—; asst. prof. rehab. Cornell U. Med. Coll., N.Y.C., 1994-98, clin. asst. prof. rehab., 1998—. Residency dir., dept. rehab. medicine N.Y. Hosp., 1996-98. Contbr. articles articles and abstracts to profl. jours. Fellow Am. Bd. of Phys. Medicine and Rehab., Am. Bd. of Electrodiagnostic Medicine; mem. AMA, Assn. of Acad. Physiatrist, Dutchess County Med. Assn. Office: The Atrium St Francis Hosp 1 Webster Ave Ste 402 Poughkeepsie NY 12601

BODANSKY, ROBERT LEE, lawyer; b. N.Y.C. BA cum laude, Syracuse U., 1974; JD with honors, George Washington U., 1977; cert. postgrad. studies, Ctr. Internat. Legal Studies, Salzburg, Austria, 1978. Bar: Md. 1978, D.C. 1978, Va. 2000, U.S. Dist. Ct. Md. 1978, U.S. Ct. Appeals (D.C. cir.) 1980, U.S. Dist. Ct. D.C. 1980, U.S. Dist. Ct. (ea. dist.) Va. 2001, U.S. Ct. Appeals (4th cir.) 1981, U.S. Supreme Ct. 1982. First assoc., then ptnr. Feldman, Krieger, Goldman & Tish, Washington, 1978-83; ptnr. Feldman, Bodansky & Rubin, Washington, 1984-95; prin. Freer, McGarry, Bodansky & Rubin, P.C., Washington, 1995-97; ptnr. Nixon, Hargrave, Devans & Doyle, LLP (now Nixon Peabody LLP), Washington, 1997—. Advisor internat. bus. law and taxation programs McGeorge Sch. Law, Sacramento, Calif., 1985—. Author: Special Problems of Subcontractors and Suppliers, 1987. Legal advisor Parkwood Resident's Assn., Kensington, Md., 1984; bd. dirs. Ridgeleigh Residents' Assn., 1987-2001, Congregation Har Shalom, 1989-91, pres. 2003-; tchr. Adas Israel Congregation, Washington, 1975-91. Mem. ABA (chmn. subcom. internat. and foreign bus. law young lawyers div. 1978-80), Md. State Bar Assn., D.C. Bar Assn., Va. Bar Assn. Office: Nixon Peabody LLP 401 9th St NW Ste 900 Washington DC 20004-2134 E-mail: rbodansky@nixonpeabody.com.

BODANSZKY, MIKLOS, chemist, educator; b. Budapest, Hungary, May 21, 1915; came to U.S., 1957, naturalized, 1964; s. Lajos and Maria (Friedner) B.; m. Agnes A. Vadasz, Apr. 21, 1950; 1 child, Eva. Diploma in chem. engring, Tech. U. Budapest, 1939, DSc, 1949. Sr. lectr. Tech. U. Budapest, 1950-56; research assoc. Cornell U. Med. Coll., 1957-59; sr. research assoc. Squibb Inst. Med. Research, New Brunswick, N.J., 1959-66; prof. chemistry and biochemistry Case Western Res. U., Cleve., 1966-83, Charles Frederic Mabery prof. research in chemistry, 1978-83, prof. emeritus, 1983—. Author: Peptide Synthesis, 1966, 2d edit., 1976, Principles of Peptide Syntheses, 1984, 2d edit, 1993, The Practice of Peptide Synthesis, 1984, 2d edit., 1994, Greek transl., 1984, Indonesian transl., 1998, Peptide Chemistry, 1988, 2d edit., 1993, The World of Peptides, 1991; editorial bd. Jour. Antibiotics, 1971-87, Internat. Jour. Peptide Protein Rsch., 1978-89. Recipient Pierce award, 1977; Morley medal, 1978; A. von Humboldt award, 1979 Mem. Am. Chem. Soc., Am. Soc. Biol. Chemistry, Hungarian Acad. Scis. (fgn.). Achievements include research in Nitrophenyl ester method of peptide synthesis, 1954; first synthesis gastrointestinal hormone secretin, 1966; synthesis vasoactive intestinal peptide, 1973.

BODAS, MARGIE RUTH, lawyer; b. Virginia, Minn., Mar. 15, 1954; d. William Elmer and Delia Bodas. BA in Comms., U. Minn., Duluth, 1976; JD, William Mitchell Coll. Law, St. Paul, 1986. Bar: Minn. 1986, U.S. Dist. Ct. Minn. 1986. News editor Mesabi Dailey News, Virginia, 1976-80; exec. dir. Quad Cities Drug Commn., Virginia, 1980-82; with customer svc. West Pub., St. Paul, 1982-84; law clk. Hon. Hyam Segell, Ramsey County, St. Paul, 1984-86; assoc. Hanft, Friede, Swelbar & Burns, P.A., Duluth, Minn., 1986-87; lawyer, shareholder, practice mgmt. Lommen Nelson Cole & Stageberg, P.A., Mpls., 1988—. Mem. steering com. Leadership Mpls., 1997-2000, co-chair steering com., 1999-2000. Mem. ABA, Minn. Bar Assn. (chair publs. com. 1990-92), Hennepin County Bar Assn. (chair workers compensation sect. 1998-99), C. of C. Mpls. Lutheran. Avocations: photography, writing, gardening. Office: Lommen Nelson Cole & Stageberg PA 1800 IDS Ctr 80 S 8th St Minneapolis MN 55402-2100 E-mail: margie@lommen.com.

BODDEN, JANE ELLEN, retired airline reservations manager; b. Dec. 7, 1948; came to U.S., 1969; d. Clarence Vernon and Dorothy (Gressman) Thompson; m. Ashby A. Bodden, Sept. 10, 1969. BS in Profl. Aeros. magna cum laude, Embry Riddle Aero U., 1989. Receptionist Coral Caymanian Hotel, Seven Mile Beach, Grand Cayman, 1965-66; teller Royal Bank Can., Georgetown, 1966-69, Pan Am. Bank, N. Miami Beach, Fla., 1970-73; reservations Mackey Internat. Airlines, Ft. Lauderdale, Fla., 1973-78; reservations mgr. Cayman Airways Ltd., Miami, 1978-93, retired, 1993. Mem. South by Southeast, Miami, 1983—, pres., 1991-92; elder Faith Presbyn. Ch., Pembroke Pines, Fla., 1984-85, 93-96; chmn. Women of Ch. Ruth Circle, 1982-84. E-mail: janebodden@prodigy.net.

BODDIE, ARTHUR WALKER, JR., surgeon, cancer researcher; b. Detroit, Dec. 21, 1941; s. Arthur Walker Sr. and Ellena Louise B.; m. Joy Marie Marchbanks, Aug. 20, 1966; children: Elise Catherine, Ellena Lois. BA, Yale U., 1963, MD, 1967. Diplomate Am. Bd. Surgery. Commd. capt. USAF, 1968, advanced through grades to lt. col., 1976, ret., 1980; assoc. prof. surgery M.D. Anderson Hosp., Houston, 1980-90, U. Ill., Chgo., 1990-93, prof. surgery, 1993—, vice-chair dept. surg. oncology, 1997—. Patentee in field; contbr. articles to profl. jours. Recipient Med. Instrumentation award Am. Assn. for Advancement Med. Instrumentation, 1984. Fellow Internat. Coll. Surgery (mem. Japanese sect., hon.); mem. Am. Mensa Soc., Chgo. Surg. Soc. (pres. 1997-98), Sixteen Prof. Socs., VA (mem. oncology subcom. merit rev. bd. 1996—), Sigma Pi Phi. Avocations: golfing, sailing. Office: Dept Surg Oncology U Ill (m/c 820) 840 S Wood St Chicago IL 60612 E-mail: awboddiejr@aol.com., midway@webmail.uic.edu.

BODDIE, DON O'MAR, recording company executive, producer, recording artist; b. St. Louis, Mo., Nov. 22, 1944; s. George Palmer and Lucille (Owens) Johnson-Boddie; m. Martha Lee Brown, Oct. 11, 1970 (div. Dec. 1979); children: Don O'Mar, Anthony, Shawn, Shellie; m. Paula R. Smith, 1991; children: Courtney, George, Kyle. BS in Bus. Mgmt., BS in Mgmt., Tarkio Coll., 1988, St. Louis Music Inst., 1968; MA in Tchg., Webster U., 2002. Cert. cross categorical K-12, Mo. Rec. artist Bamboo Records, St. Louis, 1966-70; producer, writer Puzzletown Prodns., St. Louis, 1970-77, James Earl World Prodns., East St. Louis, Ill. and, Memphis, 1975-79, Hi Records, Memphis, 1975-79, Motown Records, Los Angeles, 1976-78; owner, prodr., writer, artist Chrome Records, St. Louis, 1978—. Cons. Archway Studios, St. Louis, 1970-85, Music Assocs. in Mo. Corp, Jefferson City, Mo., 1978—, JD Mgmt., St. Louis, 1978—; v.p. Scorpio Prodns., Pine Lawn, Mo., 1980-82, music prodr., 1980-84. Producer: Lets Be Lovers, 1985 (Heritage award), The Legend, 1986 (Heritage award); rec. artist Can't Stop the Fire, 1987 (Heritage award), New Thing Between Us (charted Top 5 on Midwest Survey 1990, 91), True Love (charted Top 5 on Midwest Survey, 1990, 91); host, presenter Gateway Music Awards Ceremony, 1991; headliner for Cigarettes/Salem Spirit Festival, 1985; featured performer Shock Wave Music TV Show, Friends of the Black Music Soc. Gateway Awards Lacledes Landing, 1991. Mem. entertainment com. to elect Irene Smith, St. Louis, 1982, Music Assocs. Mo. (pres. 1986—), St. Louis Bd. Edn. State Mo., 1991, Chpt. 1 reading tchr. (basic skills), 1995, secondary edn. gen. edn. devel. (ABE), sr. master tchr., Adult Basic Edn., 1997, 98, music dir., Clay Cmty. Edn. Ctr.; chpt. 1 reading tchr. St. Louis Pub. Sch. Dist., 1991—, vocal music tchr., 1996—, instrumental music tchr., 1996—, spl. edn. cross categorical tchr., 1998—. Recipient Named New R&B Rec. Artist of Yr. Gateway Music award, 1990, 91, citation for exceptional performance in edn. of children with spl. needs St. Louis Pub. Sch. Dist., 2002 Democrat. Roman Catholic. Avocations: basketball, martial arts. Office: Office Toussaint L'Ouverture Accelerated Mid Sch 3021 Hickory St Saint Louis MO 63118 E-mail: player112244@yahoo.com.

BODDIE, LEWIS FRANKLIN, retired medical educator; b. Forsyth, Ga., Apr. 4, 1913; s. William F. and Luetta T. (Sams) Boddie; m. Marian Bernice Claytor, Dec. 27, 1941; children: Roberta Boddie Miles, Lewis Jr., Bernice B. Jackson, Pamela, Kenneth, Fredda, Margaret Boddie Lewis. BA, Morehouse Coll., 1933; MD, Meharry Med. Sch., 1938. Diplomate Am. Bd. Ob-Gyn. (proctor parti exam L.A. area 1955-63). Intern Homer-Phillips Hosp., St. Louis, 1938-39, resident in ob-gyn, 1939-42; mem. attending staff Grace Hosp., Detroit, 1944-48, Parkside Hosp., Detroit, 1944-48; sr. mem. attending staff Queen Angels Hosp., L.A., 1949—, chmn. dept. ob-gyn, 1968—70; mem. attending staff L.A. County Gen. Hosp., 1952-79; asst. clin. prof. U. So. Calif. Sch. Medicine, L.A., 1953-79, asst. clin. prof. emeritus, 1979—; assoc. clin. prof. U. Calif., Irvine, 1956-81. Sec. Verndro Med. Corp., 1952—90. Steward African Meth. Episc. Ch., L.A., 1949—; vice chmn. bd. mgrs. 28th St YMCA, L.A., 1960—75. Fellow: ACOG (life), ACS (life), L.A. Ob-Gyn. Soc. (life); mem.: Child Welfare League Am. (bd. dirs. 1969—76), Children's Home Soc. (bd. dirs. 1952—89, trustee 1989—, v.p. 1963—68, pres. 1968—70), L.A. United Way (priorities and allocations coms. 1989—95, stds. com. 1987—95, new admission com. 1988—95). Republican.

BODDIE, REGINALD ALONZO, lawyer; b. New Haven, June 14, 1959; s. Gladys Geraldine (Harrell) B. BA, Brown U., 1981; JD, Northeastern U., 1984. Bar: N.Y., U.S. Dist. Ct. (ea. and so. dists.) N.Y. 1986, D.C. 1987, U.S. Ct. Appeals (2d cir.) 1989, U.S. Supreme Ct. 1990. Staff atty. Legal Aid Soc., N.Y.C., 1984-86, Harlem Legal Svcs., N.Y.C., 1986-88; asst. counsel Ctr. for Law and Social Justice Medgar Evers Coll. CUNY, 1988-95; pvt. practice Law Offices of Reginald A. Boddie, N.Y.C., 1995—. Arbitrator Lemon Law, N.Y. Atty. Gen. and Am. Arbitration Assn., N.Y.C., 1986-94. Founder, pres., exec. dir. United Youth Enterprises, Inc., New Haven, 1976—; founder, dir. Coll. Prep. program Ctrl. H.S., Providence, 1980-81; bd.dirs. Claremont Neighborhood Ctrs., Inc., Bronx, N.Y., 1994-96; vol. instr. ARC, New Haven, 1975-90; bd. dirs. Boys and Girls' Clubs of Union County, Union, N.J., 1996-97; vol. law edn. instr. N.Y.C. Pub. Schs., 1992—. Recipient Good Citizenship award Civitan Internat. Club, New Haven, 1977, 2 commendations Brown U., 1981, Outstanding Cmty. Svc. award New Haven Police Dept., 1984, Cmty. Svc. award Pub. Sch. 21, Bklyn., 1993, Trailblazer award for Cmty. Svc. Nat. Coun. of Negro Women, 2000, Cmty. Svc. award for Law Related Edn., Sch. Dist. 16, N.Y.C., 2000, others; named Vol. Lawyer of the Yr., N.Y.C. Civil Ct., 2000. Mem. Bklyn. Bar Assn., Optimist Internat. Club. Office: 19 Fulton St Ste 408 New York NY 10038-2100

BODDIGER, GEORGE CYRUS, insurance corporate executive, consultant; b. Polo, Ill., July 5, 1917; s. George E. and Bertha Belle (Billig) B.; m. Wilma Helen Ray, May 23, 1943; children: Nancy Boddiger Estrada, Jean Boddiger Johnstone, Kathryn Boddiger Jones. BS, U. Ill., 1939; MBA with distinction, Harvard U., 1943. Various positions Mut. of Omaha, Omaha, 1952-59; pres., dir. Pacific Fidelity Life Ins. Co., Los Angeles, 1959-71, Equitable Life Ins. Co., Washington, 1971-82; vice chmn., dir. Gulf United Corp., Jacksonville, Fla., 1982-84. Bd. dirs. Premier Parking Corp., Asbury Meth. Village; mem. adv. bd. DCG Corp. Author: Getting People To Work Together Effectively (A Practical Guide to First Line Supervision), 2000. Mem. U. Ill. Found., Pres.'s Coun.; trustee, sec. Nat. Capital chpt. Nat. Multiple Sclerosis Soc.; pres. Multiple Sclerosis Internat. Fedn., 1983-85, now pres. emeritus; elder Potomac Presbyn. Ch. With AUS, 1943-46. Recipient Norman Cohn Hope award Nat. Multiple Sclerosis Soc., Bess Goodman Humanitarian award, Lifetime Achievement award Internat. Fedn. Multiple Sclerosis Socs. Fellow Life Mgmt. Inst.; mem. Am. Coll. Life Underwriters (chartered), Harvard Bus. Sch. Club Washington (chmn., dir.), Sigma Alpha Epsilon. Clubs: Congressional Country (Bethesda, Md.); Met. (Washington). Office: 415 Russell Ave Apt 908 Gaithersburg MD 20877-2842 Fax: 301 216-5163.

BODE, BARBARA, Internet entrepreneur, foundation executive, freelance/self-employed writer; b. Evanston, Ill. d. Carl and Margaret Emilie (Lutze) B. BA magna cum laude, MA, U. Md.; scholar, Ludwig-Maximillians-Universitat, Munich; English Speaking Union scholar, U. London; Bundesrepublik scholar, Goethe Institut, Lubeck, W. Ger.; postgrad. NDEA fellow, UCLA. Woodrow Wilson teaching intern N.C. Central U., Durham; pres. Children's Found., Washington, 1970-86, Council on Founds., 1986-89; v.p. Coun. Better Bus. Bur., 1990-95; exec. dir. Coun. Bettter Bus. Bur. Found., 1990-95; founder Campaigns Online, Washington, 1998-2000; bd. mem. Children's Found., Washington, 1986—; founder CashCares.com, 2000—03. Bd. dirs. Children's Found., Rainbow TV Works, Disability Rights, 1974-99, Edn. and Def. Fund Partnership, 1993-2001, Women's Campaign Fund, 1984-88; founding mem. Women of Washington, 1992—, Leadership Washington, class of 1994, 94—; trustee The Richmond Found., 1978-99. Woodrow Wilson Nat. Found. fellow, 1963-64. Episcopalian. Office: BodeCorp 2400 Sixteenth St NW Ste 504 Washington DC 20009 E-mail: bb@cashcares.com.

BODE, RICHARD ALBERT, retired financial executive; b. Oak Park, Ill., July 26, 1931; s. Charles John and Esther (Burgert) B.; m. Marjorie Ann Lane, July 28, 1962; children— Anne, Julie, John, Ellen, Mary Elizabeth. Student, Loras Coll., 1949-51; BSC, DePaul U., 1953; MBA, U. Detroit, 1960. CPA, Ill. With Baumann, Finney & Co. (pub. accountants), Chgo., 1953-56; staff accountant Nat. Tea Co., Chgo., 1956- 58, divisional controller Detroit, 1958-62; asst. controller Eagle Food Centers, Rock Island, Ill., 1962-63; comptroller Brinks, Inc., Chgo., 1963-68, treas., 1968-69, v.p., treas., 1970-78; v.p. fin. DLM, Inc., Allen, Tex., 1978-89. Mem. Govt. Acctg. Stds. Adv. Coun., 1996-99. Mem. Village Hinsdale Plan Commn., 1969-75, Plano Bd. Adjustments, 1988-90; mem. Plano City Coun., 1990-2000, dep. mayor pro tem, 1995-96, mayor pro tem, 1996-97, 99-2000; sec.-treas. Allen Indsl. Found., 1983-88; bd. dirs. Plano Homeowners Coun., 1984-90, pres., 1987-88; mem. Regional Transp. Coun., 1993-2000; mem. adv. coun. Tex. Mcpl. Retirement Sys., 1996-2000; mem. Plano Econ. Devel. Bd., 1999-2000, Plano Sister City, Inc., 1994—, treas., 2000-02, Plano Heritage Commn., 2000-02; mem. leadership com. John Paul II H.S., 2000—; bd. dirs. Hope's Door, 2000—, treas. 2001—. Mem. Ill. C.P.A. Soc. (dir. 1976-78) Home: 2032 Switzerland Ave Plano TX 75025-3153 E-mail: dickb@plano.net.

BODEN, GUENTHER, endocrinologist; b. Ludwigshafen, Germany, Jan. 8, 1935; came to U.S., 1965; s. Alwin and Irma (Godelman) B.; m. Irene Ulrike Dingeldein, Dec. 12, 1970; children: Karin, Stephanie, Eric, Dirk. MS, Heidelberg U., Germany, 1956; MD, Munich U., 1959. Intern City Hosp. Hamburg, Germany, 1960-62; rsch. fellow in biochemistry U. Tübingen, Germany, 1963-65; rsch. fellow in medicine P.B. Brigham Hosp., Boston, 1965-67; resident physician Rochester (N.Y.) Gen. Hosp., 1967-70; rsch. prof. biochemistry Temple U. Sch. Medicine, Phila., 1986—, prof. medicine, 1977—2000, Laura H. Carnell prof. of medicine, 2000—. Chief div. endocrinology/metab. Temple U. Sch. Medicine, Phila., 1987—, dir. gen. clin. rsch. ctr., 1989—. Mem. editl. bd. Jour. Clin. Endocrine Metabolism, 1985-88, Clin. Diabetes, 1995—, Am. Jour. Physiology, 1998—; assoc. editor, Diabetes, 2001—; contbr. articles to profl. jours. Rsch. grantee NIH, 1973—, Am. Diabetes Assn., 1985—; recipient Rochester N.Y. Diabetes award Rochester Acad. Medicine, 1970. Fellow ACP; mem. Am. Diabetes Assn., Am. Soc. Clin. Investigation, Am. Endocrin Soc. Office: Temple Univ Hosp 3401 N Broad St Philadelphia PA 19140-5189 E-mail: bodengh@tuhs.temple.edu.

BODENHAMER, DAVID JACKSON, historian, educator; b. Macon, Ga., May 4, 1947; s. David Jackson and Mary Elizabeth (Cox) B.; m. Penny Jo McClelland, Dec. 27, 1988. BA, Carson-Newman Coll., 1969; MA, U. Ala., 1970; PhD, Ind. U., 1976. Asst. prof., then assoc. prof. U. So. Miss., Hattiesburg, 1976-84, prof., asst. v.p. acad. affairs, 1985-88; dir. Polis Ctr. Ind. U., Indpls., 1989—. Head N.Am. team, exec. com. Electronic Cultural Atlas Initiative, 1997—. Author: Pursuit of Justice, 1986, Fair Trial, 1991; editor: Encyclopedia of Indianapolis, 1994; co-editor: Ambivalent Legacy, 1984, Bill of Rights in Modern America, 1992; editor-in-chief Indiana Online: An Electronic Encyclopedia. Chmn. bd. dirs. South Miss. Community Action Agy., Hattiesburg, 1978-82; bd. dirs. Pine Belt Family YMCA, Hattiesburg, 1982-86; steering com. Regional Ctr. Plan, Indpls, 1989-92; mem. steering com. New Ind. State Mus. Task Force, 1998—, regional ctr. plan, 2002. With U.S. Army, 1970-72. Mem. Am. Soc. Legal History, Orgn. Am. Historians. Office: Polis Ctr Ste 100 1200 Waterway Blvd Indianapolis IN 46202-5140 E-mail: intu100@iupui.edu.

BODENHEIMER, GEORGE, broadcast executive; Pres. ESPN Inc., Bristol, CT, 1998—. Office: ESPN Inc Espn Plz Bristol CT 06010-1099

BODENSIECK, ERNEST JUSTUS, mechanical engineer; b. Dubuque, Iowa, June 1, 1923; s. Julius Henry and Elma (Sommer) B.; m. Margery Elenore Sande, Sept. 9, 1943; children: Elizabeth Bodensieck Eley, Stephen. BSME, Iowa State U., 1943. Registered profl. engr., Ariz. Project engr. TRW Inc., Cleve., 1943-57; supr. rocket turbomachinery Rocketdyne divsn. Rockwell Internat., Canoga Park, Calif., 1967-60, supr. nuclear turbomachinery, 1964-70; advance gear engr. Gen. Electric Co., Lynn, 1960-64; asst. mgr. engine components Aerojet Nuclear Systems Co., Sacto., 1970-71; gear and bearing cons. AIResearch divsn. Garrett Corp., Phoenix, 1971-81; transmission cons. Bodensieck Engring. Co., Scottsdale, Ariz., 1981—2001. Patentee in field. Mem. ASME, AIAA, Soc. Automotive Engrs. (various coms.), Aircraft Industries Assn. (various coms.), Am. Gear Mfrs. Assn. (mem. aerospace, gear rating and enclosed epicyclic coms.), Nat. Soc. Profl. Engrs., Pi Tau Sigma. Lutheran.

BODENSTEIN, IRA, lawyer; b. Atlantic City, Nov. 9, 1954; s. William and Beverly (Grossman) B.; m. Julia Elizabeth Smith, Mar. 9, 1991; children: Sarah Rose, George William, Jennie Kathryn. Student, Tel Aviv U., 1974-75; BA in Govt., Franklin & Marshall Coll., 1977; JD in Econs., U. Miami, 1980. Bar: Ill. 1980, U.S. Dist Ct. (no. dist.) Ill. 1980, U.S. Ct. Appeals (7th cir.) 1982, Fla. 1983. Assoc. James S. Gordon Ltd., Chgo., 1980-85, mem., 1985-89, Portes, Sharp, Herbst & Fox, Ltd., Chgo., 1990-91; shareholder Towbin & Zazove, Ltd., Chgo., 1991-93; ptnr. D'Ancona & Pflaum, Chgo., 1993-98; U.S. Trustee Region 11, Chgo., 1998—, Region 9, Cleve., 2001—02. Pres., bd. dirs., benefit chmn. Gus Giordano Jazz Dance, Chgo., 1990—; treas. Chgo. Pub. Art Group, 1995-99. Mem. ABA (bus. law sect., rep. young lawyers divsn. dist. 15, 1986-87, ann. meeting adv. com. 1990, spkr. spring meeting 1996, 97), Chgo. Bar Assn. (bd. dirs. young lawyers sect. 1985-87, chmn.-elect 1987-88, chmn. 1988-89, antitrust com., chmn. athletics com. 1984-85, bd. mgrs. 1990-92, chmn. pub. affairs and media rels. com., chmn. assn. meetings com., membership com. 1996, cert. of appreciation 1984-93, 96-97). Democrat. Jewish. Home: 2848 W Wilson Ave Chicago IL 60625-3743 Office: Office US Trustee 227 W Monroe St Ste 3350 Chicago IL 60606-5099 E-mail: ira.bodenstein@usdoj.gov.

BODENSTEINER, JOHN BURTON, neurologist; b. Decorah, Iowa, Sept. 27, 1944; s. Leonard Joseph and Helen Adams Bodensteiner; m. Donna Berge, Aug. 26, 1967; children: Peter Hans, Beth Adria. BA, Luther Coll., 1966; MD, U. Iowa, 1971. Cert. Am. Bd. Pediat., Am. Bd. Psychiatry and Neurology with spl. qualification in pediat. neurology. Intern Pediatrics Children's Hosp. L.A., 1971-73; resident neurology and pediatric neurology U. Iowa, 1973-76; clin. neuromuscular fellow Mayo Clinic, 1976-77; asst. prof. U. Tex. Med. Br., Galveston, 1977, 80; assoc. prof. U. Okla. Sch. of Medicine, Oklahoma City, 1980, 87; prof. neurology W.Va. U. Sch. of Medicine, Morgantown, 1987, 99; prof. neurologist Ind. U. Sch. of Medicine, Indpls., 1999—2002; chief pediat. neurology Children's Health Ctr. St. Joseph's Hosp., and Barrow Neurol. Inst., Phoenix, 2002—. XXII Preston Robb lectr. Montreal Neurol. Inst., 1997. Sr. assoc. editor Jour. of Child Neurology, 1987—; editor Seminars in Pediatric Neurology; editl. bd. Clin. Pediatrics, Neurology Revs.; contbr. over 300 articles to profl. publs. Adv. bd. Sturge-Weber Found., N.J., 1992—; clin. dir. Muscular Dystrophy Clinic, 1979—. Fellow Am. Acad. Neurology; mem. Am. Neurol. Assn., Child Neurol. Soc. (councilor 1994-96), So. Pediat. Neurol. Soc. (pres. 1988-90, 98-2000), Profs. of Child Neurology (pres. 1998-2000). Avocations: music, reading, golf, hiking. Office: 500 W Thomas Rd Phoenix AZ 85013- E-mail: Jbodens@chw.edu.

BODEY, BELA, immunologist, pathologist, oncologist; b. Sofia, Bulgaria, Jan. 18, 1949; came to U.S., 1985, naturalized, 1994; s. Joseph and Rossitza (Derebeeva) B.; m. Victoria Psenko, Aug. 29, 1979; children; Bela Jr., Vivian. MD, Med. Acad., Sofia, 1973; PhD in Immuno-Biology, Inst. Morphology, Bulgarian Acad. Sci., Sofia, 1977. Lic. physician, exptl. pathologist, embryologist, immuno-morphologist, thymologist, exptl. oncologist. Asst. prof. Semmelweis Med. U., Budapest, 1977-80; prof. Inst. Hematology, Budapest, 1980-83; rsch. assoc. Tufts U., Boston, 1985; rsch. fellow immuno-pathology Mass. Gen. Hosp./Harvard U., Boston, 1986; rsch. fellow Childrens Hosp. L.A., 1987-90, rsch. scientist, 1991-92; asst. prof. rsch. pathology, Sch. of Medicine Univ. Southern Calif., 1992—, prof. pathology Sch. Medicine, 1995—. Vis. prof. Alexander von Humboldt Found., Ulm, Fed. Republic Germany, 1984. Mem. Am. Assn. Cancer Rsch., Am. and Can. Acad. Pathology, French Soc. Cell Biology, French Soc. Electronmicroscopy, Internat. Soc. Exptl. Hematology, Internat. Soc. Comparative Oncology, N.Y. Acad. Scis., Free Masons. Roman Catholic. Avocations: travel, swimming, dancing. Home: 8000 Canby Ave Reseda CA 91335-1378 Office: Childrens Hosp Los Angeles 4650 W Sunset Blvd Los Angeles CA 90027-6062 E-mail: Bodey18@aol.com.

BODEY, GERALD PAUL, medical educator, physician; b. Hazelton, Pa, May 22, 1934; s. Allen Zartman and Marie Frances (Smith) B.; m. Nancy Louise Wiegner, Aug. 25, 1956; children: Robin Gayle Sparwasser, Gerald Paul Jr., Sharon Dawn Brantley. AB magna cum laude, Lafayette Coll., 1956; MD, Johns Hopkins U., 1960. Diplomate Nat. Bd. Med. Examiners, Am. Bd. Internal Medicine, Am. Bd. Infectious Diseases, Am. Bd. Oncology. Intern Johns Hopkins U., Balt., 1960-61, resident, 1961-62; clin. assoc. Nat. Cancer Inst., Bethesda, Md., 1962-65; resident U. Wash., Seattle, 1965-66; internist, prof. U. Tex./M.D. Anderson Cancer Ctr., Houston, 1975-95, chmn. dept. med. specialities, 1987-95, chief sect. infectious diseases, 1981-95, chief chemotherapy, 1975-83, med. dir. Cancer Clin. Rsch. Ctr., 1977-81, emeritus prof. medicine, 1995—2001, prof. medicine, 2001—. Prof. internal medicine & pharm. Univ. Tex. Health Sci. Ctr. Med. Sch., 1976—; clin. prof. Univ. Tex. Health Sci. Ctr. Dental Sch., 1979—95; adj. prof. microbiology immunology & medicine Baylor Coll. of Medicine, Houston, 1975—99; mem. lunar quartine ops. team Apollo 11-14, Manned Spacecraft Ctr., NASA, joint commn. accreditation healthcare orgns. Hospitalwide Indicators Task Force, 1987—89. Mem. editl. bd. Acad. Internat. Jour. of Oncology; contbr. over 1000 articles to profl. jour. Dir. Korean Collaborative Program, 1985-95; past trustee Med. Benevolence Found. Nat. AIDS Prevention Inst.; past bd. dir. Christian Coalition Reconciliation; scholar Leukemia Soc. of Am., 1969-74. Recipient Am. Chem. Soc. prize, 1956, Merck award, 1956, Robert B. Youngman Greek prize Lafayette Coll., 1956, Eugene Yourassowsky award U. Libre de Bruxelles, Belgium, 1995; Henry Strong Denison fellow Johns Hopkins Sch. Medicine, Balt., 1958-60; Leukemia Soc. Am. scholar, 1969-74. Fellow ACP, Am. Coll. Chest Physicians, Am. Coll. Clin. Pharmacology, Royal Coll. Medicine, Royal Soc. Promotion Health; mem. AMA, Am. Soc. Clin. Oncology, Infectious Diseases Soc. Am., Am. Soc. Clin. Pharmacology and Therapeutics, Am. Soc. Hematology, Am. Soc. Microbiol., Am. Sci. Affiliation, Internat. Soc. Complexity, Info. and Design, Christian Med. Soc., Tex. Med. Assn., Houston Acad. Medicine, Academia Peruana de Cirugia (hon.), Mediterranean Med. Soc. (hon.), Le Soc. Peruana Cancerologia (hon.), La Costarricensa Oncologie (hon.), Soc. Brasileira Cancerologia (hon.), Phi Beta Kappa, Sigma Xi. Methodist. Office: U Tex MDACC Box 402 1515 Holcombe Blvd Houston TX 77030-4009 E-mail: gbodey@mdanderson.org.

BODEY, RICHARD ALLEN, minister, educator; b. Hazelton, Pa., Nov. 27, 1930; s. Allen Zartman and Marie (Smith) B.; m. Ruth Lois Price, 1955; children: Bronnlyn Beth Spindler, Richard Allen Jr. Student, Muhlenberg Coll., 1948-49; AB, Lafayette Coll, 1952; MDiv, Princeton Theol. Sem., 1955; postgrad., U. Toronto, 1961, Gannon Coll., 1963-64, Winona Lake Sch. Theology, 1963; ThM, Westminster Theol Sem., 1972; D Ministry, Trinity Evang. Div. Sch., 1984, Seabury-Western Theol. Sem., 1985. Ordained to ministry Presbyn. Ch. U.S.A., 1955. Student pastor Zion Welsh Presbyn. Ch., Wind Gap, Pa., 1951; student supply pastor Italian Presbyn. Ch., Roseto, Pa., 1951; student pastor Westminster Presbyn. Ch., Allentown, Pa., 1952-55; pastor Marshall Meml. Presbyn. Ch., Lebanon, Ill., 1955-56; instr. Bible McKendree Coll., Lebanon, Ill., 1956; pastor 3d Presbyn. Ch., North Tonawanda, N.Y., 1956-62; instr. Buffalo Bible Inst., N.Y., 1961; stated supply pastor 1st Presbyn. Ch., Corry, Pa., 1962-64; pastor Dales Meml. United Presbyn. Ch., Phila., 1964-66; founding prof. preaching, chmn. Practical Theol. Dept. Reformed

Theol. Sem., Jackson, Miss., 1966-73; interim pastor 1st Presbyn. Ch., Hazlehurst, Miss., 1967-68; stated supply pastor Presbyn. Ch., Union Church, Miss., 1970-73; head of staff 1st Assoc. Reformed Presby. Ch., Gastonia, N.C., 1973-79; chaplain Civitan, 1975; founder, dir. Gastonia Sch. Bibl. Studies, NC, 1978-79; assoc. prof. practical theol. Trinity Evang. Divinity Sch., Deerfield, Ill., 1979-87, prof., 1987-95. Dir. continuing edn. Trinity Evang. Divinity Sch., 1982-87, DMin coord. and examiner, 1989-96; instr. preaching Moody Bible Inst. Corr. Sch., Chgo., 1982-86; vis. instr. Westminster Theol. Sem., Phila., 1987-88, lectr., 1990, cons. in continuing edn., 1990-91, DMin examiner, 1994-96; instr. North Chgo. Theol. Inst., 1991-94; vis. faculty Columbia (S.C.) Internat. U. and Seminary, 1991; seminar leader Nat. Conf. on Preaching, 1990-94; Bible conf. and retreat spkr. Author: You Can Live Without Fear of Death, 1980; editor, contbr. Good News for All Seasons: 26 Sermons for Special Days, 1987, (Korean edit., 1990), Inside the Sermon: Thirteen Preachers Discuss Their Methods of Preparing Messages, 1990, The Voice from the Cross: Seven Sermons on the Last Words of Our Lord, 1990, 2d edit., 2000, If I Had Only One Sermon to Preach, 1994; editor: Voices, 1980-88, Trinity Book Bull., 1989-94, The Lamb of God, 1994; co-editor: Come to the Banquet, 1998; contbr. to Ency. of Christianity, 1962-72, Ministers Manual, 1974, 82, Zondervan Pictorial Bible Ency., 1975, Baker Ency. of Bible, 1988, Handbook of Contemporary Preaching, 1993, The Complete Library of Christian Worship, 1996; co-editor, contbr.: Revelation Revealed Day by Day, 2001; contbr. articles to profl. jours. Chmn. Here's Life Metrolina, Gastonia Area, 1976; founding bd. chmn. Gaston Evang. Assn., 1978-79; bd. dirs. Gaston Christian Sch., 1978-79; chmn. planning com. Evang. Affirmations, 1989; chaplain Civitan, 1974. Recipient Porter Bible prize Lafayette Coll., 1950, David Fowler Atkins Jr. prize, 1952, Gastonia Evang. Assn. award, 1979. Mem. Am. Acad. Ministry (charter, adv. bd. mem.). Avocations: travel, collecting miniature cathedral models and cottages, collecting christian art and artifacts, music. *To me life's highest meaning and deepest satisfaction lie in a personal relationship with Jesus Christ as divine Saviour and Lord. My supreme aim and motive are to honor Him in everything I do. I can think of no worthier pursuit, no more challenging goal, for anyone in any age.*

BODGER, CAROLE, writer; b. Bklyn. d. Melvin M. Bodger and Shirley R. Garber; m. Edwin Bon, 1998. BA, NYU, 1980. Mng. editor New York Torch, N.Y.C., 1980-81; asst. editor Glamour Mag., N.Y.C., 1982-84; editor M.I. Mag., N.Y.C., 1984, South Fla. Newspaper Network, Deerfield Beach, Fla., 1992-94; assoc. editor Life & Leisure Weekly, Fort Lauderdale, 1994, Changes, Profl. Counselor and Adolescence Mags., Deerfield Beach, 1994-95, Boca Raton Mag., Fla., 1995-97; freelance writer Atlanta, 1997—. Author: Smart Guide to Getting Strong and Fit, 1998, Smart Guide to Relieving Stress, 1998, Smart Guide to Healing Back Pain, 1999, Little Book of Dirty Diet Tricks, 2002. Recipient Charlie award Fla. Mag. Assn., 1996, 97, FPA award Fla. Press Assn., 1994, Mag. Article Writer of Yr. award Fla. Dental Assn., 1993, Editor of Yr. award N.Y. Torch, 1981. Mem. Soc. Profl. Journalists.

BODI, SONIA ELLEN, library director, educator; b. Chgo., June 24, 1940; d. Franz Frithiof and Elsa (Noren) Bergquist; m. Peter Phillip Bodi, July 30, 1966; 1 child, Eric Christopher; stepchildren: Glenn Peter, John Jeffrey. Student, U. Edinburgh (Scotland), 1960-61; BA, Augustana Coll., Rock Island, Ill., 1962; MA Libr. Sci., Rosary Coll., 1977; MA, Northwestern U., 1986. Tchr. English and history Gemini Jr. H.S., Niles, Ill., 1962-64, Nagoya (Japan) Internat. Sch., 1964-65; tchr. English, Old Orchard Jr. H.S., Skokie, Ill., 1965-67; reference libr. Wilmette (Ill.) Pub. Libr., 1977-79, Kendall Coll., Evanston, Ill., 1979-81; head reference and instructional libr. North Park U., Chgo., 1981—, asst. prof. bibliography, 1985-87, assoc. prof., 1988-92, prof., 1992—, chmn. divsn. humanities, 1988-99, interim libr. dir., 1996-98, libr. dir., 1998—. Contbr. articles to profl. jours. Pres. PTA, Lincolnwood, Ill., 1977—79; mem. Bd. Edn., Lincolnwood, 1980—91, sec., 1981—84, pres., 1984—87, LIBRAS, 2001—02; chair Ill. Coop. Collection Mgmt. Program, 2002—03; elder First Presbyn. Ch. of Evanston, 1989—, Stephen ministry leader, 1992—98; bd. dirs. Chgo. Libr. Sys., 1999—, ILCSO, 2003—. Mem. Ill. Libr. Assn., ALA, Am. Assn. Coll. and Rsch. Librs., Beta Phi Mu. Democrat. Avocations: reading, bicycling, opera, music, piano. Home: 6710 N Trumbull Ave Lincolnwood IL 60712-3740 Office: North Park U 3225 W Foster Ave Chicago IL 60625-4895 E-mail: sbodi@northpark.edu.

BODINE, BRETT, race car driver; b. Chemung, N.Y., Jan. 11, 1959; m. Diane Bodine; 1 child, Heidi. Profl. race car driver NASCAR Winston Cup Races, 1986—. Named winner, First Union 400, 1990. Office: c/o NASCAR 1801 W Internat Speedway Daytona Beach FL 32114 also: Brett Bodine Racing 304 Performance Rd Mooresville NC 28115-9592

BODINE, FRANCIS L. state legislator; b. Jan. 10, 1936; married; children: Stewart, Kristin. BS, LaSalle U., 1960. City councilman, Moorestown, N.J., 1977-88; mayor, 1981-88; state assemblyman dist. 8, 1994—. Mem. judiciary, law and pub. safety, ind. authorities, labor, bus. and indsl. coms. N.J. State Assembly, mem. criminal justice subcom.; with Martin Manco & Co. Inc., 1987-89, South Jersey Port Corp., 1989-92. Commr. Delaware River Port Authority, 1983-90, former mem. exec. com., former vice chmn. operation and maintenance; active Am. Heart Assn., Alliance for Action, United Way, Boy Scouts Am. Office: Larchmont Commons Shopping Ctr 3111 Route 38 Mount Laurel NJ 08054-9754*

BODINE, GEOFF, race car driver; b. Chemung, N.Y., Apr. 18, 1949; children: Matthew, Barry. Profl. race car driver NASCAR, 1979—; owner, driver, 1993—. Named Rookie of Yr., NASCAR, 1982, winner, Daytona 500, 1986, Internat. Race of Champions, 1987, Holly Farms 400, 1989; Hanes 500, 1990, AC Spark Plug 500, 1990, Goody's 500, 1990, 1992, Mello Yello 500, 1991, Tyson/Holly Farms 400, 1992, Save art 300, 1993, Miller 500, 1994, Goodwrench 400, 1994, Tyson 400, 1994, Winston Select, 1994, The Bud at the Glen, 1996; recipient Busch Pole award, 1996. Office: c/o NASCAR PO Box 2875 Daytona Beach FL 32120-2875 also: Ste B 10420 Harris Oak Blvd Charlotte NC 28269-7518

BODINE, JAMES FORNEY, retired civic leader; b. Villanova, Pa., June 16, 1921; s. William Warden and Angela (Forney) B.; m. Jean G. Guthrie, June 25, 1949; children: Jane G., Margaret F., Murray G., Tracy W. BA, Yale U., 1944; MBA, Harvard U., 1948. With First Pa. Bank, Phila., 1948-78, v.p., 1958-63, sr. v.p., 1963-65, exec. v.p., 1965-68, sr. exec. v.p., dir., 1968-72, pres., 1972-77, First Pa. Corp., 1974-78; sec. of commerce Commonwealth of Pa., 1979-80; mng. partner Urban Affairs Partnership, 1980-87; co-chair United Bank Phila., 2000—03. Home: 401 Cypress St Philadelphia PA 19106-4206 Office: 1207 Chestnut St Philadelphia PA 19107-4102

BODINE, JOHN JERMAIN, pastor; b. Jamestown, N.Y., Jan. 21, 1941; s. Henry B. Lathrop and Josephine (Waring Bodine) Ward; Wilhelmina Thea Bijlefeld, Sept. 15, 1984; children: Melissa Heather, Courtney Joy. BA, St. John's Coll., 1963; BD, Hartford Sem. Found., 1967, PhD, 1973. Ordained to ministry United Ch. Christ, 1970. Asst. dean Hartford Sem. Found., Hartford, Conn., 1971-74; asst. dir. Macdonald Ctr. Study Islam, Hartford, 1974-77; pastor, tchr. Congl. Ch. Henniker (N.H.), 1979-83, Newent Congl. Ch., Lisbon, Conn., 1983-87, Stratham (N.H.) Cmty. Ch., 1987—2001, United Ch. of Warner (NH), 2001—. Scribe Rockingham Assn., United Ch. Christ, N.H., 1990-2000; chmn. HIV/AIDS Working Group, United Ch. Christ, N.H., 1990-93; mem. Task Force Homosexuality, Conn., 1985-87, Conn. Ch. Soc., United Ch. Christ, N.H., 1980-83, trustee N.H. conf., 1992-98, mem. exec. com. N.H. conf., 1994—, mem. nominating com., 1998—, mem. budget and fin. com., 1998—, pres., 1999-2001. Contbr. articles to profl. jours. Chmn. safety programs, Conn. Red Cross, Hartford, 1972-79; mem. Child Abuse Task Force, Concord, N.H., 1981-83; mem., bd. dirs. N.H. SPCA, 1996; bd. dirs. Pastoral Counseling Ctr., Durham, N.H., 1993—; signator Portsmouth N.H. Covenant of Conscience; trustee Wiggin Meml. Libr., Stratham, 1999-2001, chair, 2001. Campus Ministry fellow, Danforth Found., 1964-65, traveling fellow Hartford Sem. Found., 1966; recipient Thompson prize Hartford Sem. Found., 1966, Tyler prize, 1966. Office: United Ch of Warner Main St Warner NH 03278 E-mail: drjay58@hotmail.com.

BODINE, LARRY, marketing consultant; b. Kissimmee, Fla., Nov. 4, 1950; s. Cornelius and Tatiana (Krupenin) B.; 1 child, Theodore Laurence. Student, Universitat Munchen, Munich, Germany, 1970-71; BA, Amherst Coll., 1972; JD, Seton Hall U., 1981. Bar: Wis. 1981, U.S. Dist. Ct. (we. dist.) Wis. 1981. Reporter The Star-Ledger, Newark, 1973-76, N.Y. Daily News, N.Y.C., 1976-78; reporter, asst. editor Nat. Law Jour., N.Y.C., 1978-81; assoc. Stafford, Rieser, Rosenbaum & Hansen, Madison, Wis., 1982; assoc. editor ABA Jour., Chgo., 1982-85, editor, pub., 1986-89; pub. Lawyers Alert, 1989-91; dir. comm. Sidley Austin Brown & Wood, Chgo., 1991—2001; webmaster LawMarketing Portal, www.LawMarketing.com, 2001—, Legal Mktg. Assn., www.legalmarketing.org; founder, cmty. leader LawMarketing Listserv, www. lawmarketing-.BIZ, 1996—. Mktg. columnist: Law Practice Mgmt. Mag.; editor: LawMktg. Newsletter. Mem.: ABA, Legal Mktg. Assn. (bd. dirs. Chgo. chpt. 1995, 1997—98, 2000—02).

BODINSON, HOLT, conservationist; b. East Orange, N.J., Nov. 14, 1941; s. Earl Herdien and Hermoine (Holt) B.; m. Ilse Marie Maier, Feb. 29, 1970. BA, Harvard U., 1963. Sr. assoc. Am. Conservation Assn., Inc., N.Y.C., 1966-70; dir. Office of Policy Analysis N.Y. State Dept. Environ. Conservation, Albany, 1970-71, dir. divsn. ednl. svcs., 1971-77; dir. Ariz.-Sonora Desert Mus., 1977-78; exec. dir. Safari Club Internat./Safari Club Internat. Conservation Fund, Tucson, 1980-89; conservation dir. Safari Club Internat., Tucson, 1991-94, dir. wildlife and govtl. affairs, 1994-96; committeeman Montgomery Twp. Conservation Commn., 1967-70; sec. N.Am. Del. Conseil Internat. de la Chasse et de la Conservation du Gibier, 1988—2003. Gen. sec. World Hunting and Conservation Congress, 1988; dir. Internat. Wildlife Mus., 1991-96; nat. sec. United Conservation Alliance, 1994-96. Author: (with Clepper and others) Leaders in American Conservation, 1971; contbg. editor Jour. Environ. Edn., 1968-94; dir. Conservationist mag., 1971-77, N.Y. State Environment newspaper, 1971-77. Served with arty. AUS, 1964-66. Mem. Stony Brook-Millstone Watershed Assn. (dir.), Safari Club Internat. (dir. Ariz. chpt.), N.Y. Outdoor Edn. Assn. (dir.), Outdoor Writers Assn. Am., N.Y. State Rifle and Pistol Assn. (dir.), Harvard Club (So. Ariz.) (pres.). Episcopalian. Home: 4525 N Hacienda Del Sol Tucson AZ 85718-6619 Office: 5683 N Swan Rd Tucson AZ 85718-4565

BODKIN, HENRY GRATTAN, JR., lawyer; b. L.A., Dec. 8, 1921; s. Henry Grattan and Ruth May (Wallis) B.; m. Mary Louise Davis, June 28, 1943; children: Maureen L. Dixon, Sheila L. McCarthy, Timothy Grattan. BS cum laude, Loyola U., Los Angeles, 1943, JD, 1948. Bar: Calif. 1948. Pvt. practice, Los Angeles, 1948-51, 53-95; ptnr. Bodkin, McCarthy, Sargent & Smith (predecessor firms), L.A.; of counsel Sullivan, Workman & Dee, L.A., 1995—. Mem. L.A. Bd. Water and Power Commrs., 1972-74, pres., 1973-74; regent Marymount Coll., 1962-67; trustee Loyola-Marymount U., 1973-91, vice chmn., 1985-86. With USNR, 1943-45, 51-53. Fellow Am. Coll. Trial Lawyers; mem. Calif. State Bar (mem. exec. com. conf. of dels. 1968-70, vice chmn. 1969-70), California Club, Riviera Tennis Club, Tuna Club, Chancery Club (pres. 1990-91), Phi Delta Phi. Republican. Roman Catholic. Home: 956 Linda Flora Dr Los Angeles CA 90049-1631 Office: Sullivan Workman & Dee 800 S Figueroa St Fl 12 Los Angeles CA 90017-2521

BODKIN, LAWRENCE EDWARD, research development company executive, gemologist, inventor, writer; b. Sapulpa, Okla., May 17, 1927; s. Clarence Elsworth and Lillie (Moore) B.; m. Ruby Emma Pate, Jan. 15, 1949; children: Karen Bodkin Snead, Cinda, Lawrence Jr. Student, Fla. State U., 1947-50, grad., Gemological Inst., 1969. Chief announcer, program dir., mgr. various radio stations, Winter Haven, Fla., Tallahassee and Jacksonville, Fla., 1947-60; ind. jewelry salesman and appraiser Underwood Jewelers, 1961-87; pres. Bodkin Jewelers and Appraisers, Jacksonville, 1984—, Telanon, Jacksonville, 1981—, Bodkin Co., Jacksonville, 1974—; chmn., chief exec. officer Bodkin Corp., Jacksonville, 1975—; dir. elec. safety R&D in U.S. and Orient Innovative Designer Products Div. Brooke Shields Beauty Care, Kendall Park, N.J., 1989-92. Cons. gem and mineral groups, Jacksonville, 1960—, numerous corps. and industries (on inventions); lectr. in field. Author: Dual Imagery of Ultra Speed Bodies, 1971, Miniatures, 1976, Bodkin's Revised Law of Buoyancy, 2000; contbr. articles to sci. publs.; inventor Universal-Fault Circuit-Interrupter (Bodkin Circuit), TIP (tested immersion protection), Auto Test and Reset GFCI (ground fault cir. interrupter), Bodkin Jewelry Clasp, Height Measure, others. Mem. Jacksonville Mus. Sci. and Hist., 1981—, Jacksonville Symphony Assn., 1985—, Cummer Gallery Art, Jacksonville, 1985—, Ye Mystic Revellers, 1997—. Served with U.S. Army, 1945-47, ETO. Mem. Fla. State U. Alumni Assn., Mensa Internat., San Jose Country Club. Avocations: fossil collecting, beach combing, philosophy, writing, theoretical physics. Home: 1149 Molokai Rd Jacksonville FL 32216-3273 Office: 1043 Park St Jacksonville FL 32204 E-mail: larubodkin@aol.com.

BODKIN, ROBERT THOMAS, lawyer; b. Anderson, Ind., Jan. 26, 1945; s. Robert G. and Maggie Jean (Whelchel) B.; m. Penny Ann Nichols, June 17, 1967; children: Beth Ann, Bryan Thomas. BS, Ind. U., Bloomington, 1967; JD, Ind. U., Indpls., 1973. Bar: Ind. 1973, U.S. Dist. Ct. (so. dist.) Ind. 1973, U.S. Dist. Ct. (no. dist.) Ind. 1975, U.S. Ct. Appeals (7th cir.) 1974, U.S. Supreme Ct. 1977. Law clk. U.S. Dist. Ct., Indpls., 1973-75; assoc. Bamberger Foreman Oswald & Hahn LLP, Evansville, Ind., 1975-80, ptnr., 1980—. Town atty., Newburgh, Ind., 1984—; city atty. City of Boonville, Ind., 1988-91. Bd. dirs. Evansville Dance Theatre, 1983, Evansville Philharm. Orch., 1983-85; trustee Evansville Day Sch., 1983-86; chmn. bd. St. Mary's Warrick Hosp. Found; citizens adv. coun., IU Sch. Med. Fellow Ind. Bar Found., 1983. Fellow Am. Coll. Trial Lawyers; mem. ABA, Internat. Assn. Def. Counsel, Assn. Def. Trial Attys., Def. Rsch. Inst., Ind. Bar Assn., Evansville Bar Assn., Bar Assn. of 7th Fed. Cir., Ind. Mcpl. Lawyers Assn. (bd. dirs. 1986—), Def. Trial Counsel Ind. (dir. 1999-2002, treas. 2003—), Ind. Def. Trial Counsel (diplomat), Internat. Right-of-Way Assn. Democrat. Home: # 3 100 W Water St Newburgh IN 47630-1174 Office: Bamberger Foreman Oswald & Hahn 708 Hulman Bldg Evansville IN 47708 E-mail: tbodkin@bamberger.com.

BODKIN, RUBY PATE, corporate executive, real estate broker, educator; b. Frostproof, Fla., Mar. 11, 1926; d. James Henry and Lucy Beatrice (Latham) P.; m. Lawrence Edward Bodkin Sr., Jan. 15, 1949; children: Karen Bodkin Snead, Cinda, Lawrence Jr. BA, Fla. State U., 1948; MA, U. Fla., 1972. Lic. real estate broker Fla. Banker Barnett Bank, Avon Park, Fla., 1943-44, Lewis State Bank, Tallahassee, 1944-49; ins. underwriter Hunt Ins. Agy., Tallahassee, 1949-51; tchr. Duval County Sch. Bd., Jacksonville, Fla., 1957-77; pvt. practice realty Jacksonville, 1976—; tchr. Nassau County Sch. Bd., Jacksonville, 1978-83; sec., treas., v.p. Bodkin Corp., R&D/Inventions, Jacksonville, 1983—; assoc. Brooke Shields Innovative Designer Products, Inc., Kendall Park, N.J., 1988-92. Author: 100 Teacher Chosen Recipes, 1976, Bodkin Bridge Course for Beginners, 1996, Class Conscious, 1999, (autobiography) Grandma Bodkin, 2000, Essay on Death, 2003; author numerous poems. Mem. Jacksonville Symphony Guild, 1985—; mem. Southside Bapt. Ch. Recipient 25 Yr. Svc. award Duval County Sch. Bd., 1976, Tchr. of Yr. award Bryceville Sch., 1981. Mem. Am. Contract Bridge League, Nat. Realtors Assn., Southside Jr. Woman's Club, Garden Club Sweetbriar (bd. dirs.), Riverside Woman's Club Jacksonville (fin. dir. 1991-92, 3rd v.p. social dir. WCOJ, 1992-99), UDC (Martha Reid chpt. #19), Fla. Edn. Assn. (pers. problems com. 1958), Duval County Classrooms Tchrs. (v.p. membership 1957), Woman's Club Jacksonville Bridge Group, Fla. Ret. Tchrs. Assn., Fla. Realtors Assn., N.E. Fla. Realtors Assn., Jacksonville Geneal. Soc. (practicing genealogist, family historian 1986—), Friday Musicale of Jacksonville, San Jose Golf Country Club, Jacksonville Sch. Bridge. Baptist. Avocations: reading, writing, genealogy, photography, club bridge. Home: 1149 Molokai Rd Jacksonville FL 32216-3273 Office: Bodkin Jewelers & Appraisers PO Box 16482 Jacksonville FL 32245-6482 Fax: 904-725-6692. *Ruby Pate Bodkin, genealogist and honored teacher (1955-83) has traced her Pate and Bodkin ancestors backed to England and Ireland. Son Lawrence (Larry) Bodkin, Jr., 39, MEd, Fla. State U., Tallahasse, is currently a prosperous owner and CEO of his own founded company, Bodkin Management and Consulting (New Directions for Associations). Daughter Karen, 53, wed C.T. Snead III in 1976, grandson (by adoption) of U.S. congressman, senator Carl Vinson of Milledgeville, Ga. Ruby's husband of 54 years, Larry Bodkin, Sr. has more than 25 US patents on his own inventions.*

BODLEY, HARLEY RYAN, JR., editor, writer, broadcaster; b. Dover, Del., Nov. 24, 1936; s. Harley Ryan and Mildred Olivia (Carver) B.; m. Patricia Jean Hall, Dec. 4, 1981 BA, U. Del., 1959; postgrad., Am. U., 1960. Sports editor Del. State News, Dover, 1959-60; sports dir. Radio WDOV, Dover, 1958-62; sports writer News-Jour. Papers, Wilmington, Del., 1960-63, night sports editor, 1963-67, asst. sports editor, 1967-71, sports editor, 1971-82; baseball editor USA Today, Washington, 1982—. Discussion leader Am. Press Inst., Reston, Va., 1967—76; TV host Sta. WHYY-TV, Wilmington, 1967—74; columnist The Sporting News, St. Louis, 1978—83; commentator NBC-TV Baseball: An Inside Look, 1987, USA Today Radio Report, 1987—89, USA Today: The TV Show, 1988—89; commentator and host Baseball Sunday, Uniteed Syndications Radio Network, 1988—90; baseball analyst CNN, 1989—91; commentator CBS Radio Network baseball pre-game, 1990—97, Comcast Sports Net, 2000—. Author: I Learned To Fly, So Can You, 1967; The Team That Wouldn't Die, 1981, Countdown to Cobb, 1985; writer Best Sports Stories, 1967-71, 1977-79, 1982, 1985 Flight safety counselor FAA, Phila., 1968-72. Served as sgt. U.S. Army N.G. 1956-64. Named Sportswriter of Yr., Nat. Sportscasters and Sportswriters Assn., 1961, 63, 65, 67-70, 73-75, 78-79; recipient Best of Gannett award Gannett Co., Inc., 1981, Mark Twain award AP, 1980, 25th Year award Baseball Commr., 1983, USA Today All-Star award, 2000, 01. Mem. AP Sports Editors (pres. 1981-82, Best Sports Story award 1981, 1st place award 1982), Baseball Writers Assn. Am. (Phila. chpt. chmn. 1977-78), Wilmington Sportswriters and Broadcasters (pres. 1963 sec-treas. 1965-83), Sigma Delta Chi (Top Sports award 1982) Clubs: Wilmington Country; Northeast Yacht. Episcopalian. Avocations: golf, pilot, boating. Address: care Athletes & Artists 421 7th Ave New York NY 10001-2002 E-mail: hbodley@usatoday.com.

BODMAN, SAMUEL WRIGHT, III, specialty chemicals and materials company executive; b. Chgo., Nov. 26, 1938; s. Samuel W. Jr. and Lina (Lindsay) B.; m. M. Diane Barber, July 31, 1997; children: Elizabeth L., Andrew M., Sarah H. BSChemE, Cornell U., 1961; ScD, MIT, 1964. Tech. dir. Am. R & D, Boston, 1964-70; prof. MIT, Cambridge, Mass., 1964-70; v.p. Fidelity Venture Assn., Boston, 1970-74; pres. Fidelity Venture Assocs., 1974-77; chmn. Fidelity Venture Assn., 1977; pres. Fidelity Mgmt. & Rsch. Co., Boston, 1976-86; pres., COO FMR Corp., 1982-86; exec. v.p., dir. Fidelity Group Mut. Funds, 1980-86; pres., COO Cabot Corp., Boston, 1987-88, chmn., CEO, also bd. dirs., 1988—, now chmn., CEO. Bd. dirs. Westvaco, Inc., N.Y.C., John Hancock Fin. Svcs., Thermo Electron Corp., Houston, Security Capital Group Inc. Trustee, mem. exec. com. MIT, Cambridge; trustee Isabella Stewart Gardner Mus., Boston, New England Aquarium, Boston. Episcopalian. Office: Cabot Corp 2 Seaport Ln Ste 1300 Boston MA 02210-2019

BODMER, PAUL HERBERT, professional society administrator; b. Kenmare, N.D., May 26, 1943; s. Herbert Allen and Olive Agnetha Bodmer; m. Judith Ann Rice, June 12, 1966; children: Ethan, Jordana. BS, N.D. State U., 1965, MA, 1969. English tchr. Park River (N.D.) H.S., 1965—66, Wishek (N.D.) Pub. H.S., 1966—68; grad. tchg. asst. N.D. State U., Fargo, 1968—69; asst. prof. Bismarck (N.D.) State Coll., 1969—83, assoc. prof., 1983—99; assoc. exec. dir. Nat. Coun. Tchrs. English, Urbana, Ill., 2000—. Recipient Nell Ann Pickett award, Two-Yr. Coll. and English Assn., 1997. Mem.: Nat. Coun. Tchrs. English. Office: Nat Coun Tchrs English 1111 W Kenyan Rd Urbana IL 61801

BODNAR, PETER O. lawyer; b. Queens, N.Y., Mar. 19, 1945; s. John and Edith (Schultz) B. BA in Govt., NYU, 1966; JD, Fordham U., 1970. Bar: N.Y. 1971, U.S. Dist. Ct. (so. dist.) N.Y. 1973. Confidential law sec. to Hon. Evans V. Brewster Family Ct. and County Ct. Westchester County, N.Y., 1970-73; pvt. practice White Plains, N.Y., 1973-77; ptnr. Bodnar & Greene, P.C., White Plains, N.Y., 1977-80, Bender & Bodnar, White Plains, N.Y., 1980-98; prin. Law Offices of Peter O. Bodnar, White Plains, N.Y., 1998-99, Bodnar & Milone LLP, White Plains, N.Y., 1999—. Pres., CEO P.A.J. Am. Ltd./The Olo Corp., 1990—97; CEO Organica, USA, Inc., 1998—; lectr. Pace U. Sch. Law Women's Justice Ctr., 2001—, Appellate Divsn. 2d Dept. Law Guardian Program, 2003—; chair Com. for Children's Right to Counsel, 2003—. Trustee Village of Ossining, N.Y., 1975-77. Fellow: Am. Acad. Matrimonial Lawyers; mem.: ABA (family law sect.), Westchester County Bar Assn. (family law sect., exec. com. 1992—, chair 2000—02), N.Y. State Bar Assn. (family law sect., exec. com. 2000—, lectr. custody and visitation 2003—). Office: 140 Grand St White Plains NY 10601-4831 E-mail: usorganica@aol.com.

BODNER, BRUCE IRA, ophthalmologist; b. Norfolk, Va., Nov. 5, 1945; s. Herman Bodner and Freda Glazier; m. Joanne Berson. BA in Biology, Va. Mil. Inst., 1967; MD, U. Va., 1971. Diplomate Am. Bd. Ophthalmology. Intern U. Mich. Hosp., Ann Arbor, 1971-72; resident in ophthalmology Emory U. Sch. of Medicine, Grady Meml. Hosp., others, Atlanta, 1975-78; chief resident in ophthalmology Emory U. Sch. of Medicine, Grady Meml. Hosp., Atlanta, 1977-78; various ednl. and staff positions to dir. Cornea and Contact Lens Clinic Sentara Hosps., 1980-97; asst. to assoc. prof. dept. ophthalmology Ea. Va. Med. Sch., 1980—; founder, med. dir. Lions Med. Eye Bank and Rsch. Ctr. of Ea. Va., 1979—. Founder, med. dir. Lions Med. Eye Bank & Rsch. Ctr. Ea. Va., Inc., 1979—; commr. Joint Commn. Allied Health Pers. Ophthalmology, 1990—97; adv. bd. Contact Lens Coun., Washington, 1992—98; bd. councillors Am. Acad. Ophthalmology, 1993—95; med. dir. Laser Optic Ctr. Norfolk, Va., 1996—2002; presenter in field. Named in Best Doctors in Am., S.E. region, 1996—97, nat. listing, 1998—2003; fellow Cornea & External Disease, Emory U. Sch. Medicine, Atlanta, 1978—79, Melvin Jones, Lions Internat., 1989; scholar Norfolk Found., U. Va., 1967—71; Florence Smith scholar. Fellow: Am. Acad. Ophthalmology; mem.: AMA (Physicians Recognition awards 1978, 1990, 1991, 1993), Va. Ophthalmology and Otolaryngology Soc., Norfolk Acad. Medicine, Va. Soc. Medicine, Tidewater Ophthalmology and Otolaryngology Soc., Am. Soc. Cataract and Refractive Surgery, Ocular Immunology and Microbiology Study Group, Internat. Soc. Keratorefractive Surgery, Eye Bank Assn. Am. Castroviejo Soc., Contact Lens Assn. Ophthalmologists (dir. 1992—97), Am. Assn. Ophthalmology, Alpha Omega Alpha. Avocations: computer, astronomy. E-mail: vaeye@aol.com.

BODNER, DONALD ROGER, urologist, medical educator; b. Indpls., Aug. 31, 1953; s. Robert Stewart and Elizabeth (Wolf) B.; m. Linda Joy Abrams, Oct. 5, 1985; children: Robert, Daniel, Richard. BS, Trinity Coll., Hartford, Conn., 1975; MD, Ind. U., Indpls., 1979. Resident in urology Case Western Res. U., Cleve., 1979-84, instr. urology, 1984-85, asst. prof., 1985-92, assoc. prof., 1992—99, prof., 1999—. Section editor (urology) Jour. Spinal Cord Medicine, 1994—; guest editor: Urologic Clinical Procedures - Spinal Cord Injury, 1993. Mem. Am. Urologic Soc., Internat. Med. Soc. Paraplegia, Am. Paraplegia Soc. (pres. 1993-95). Office: Case Western Res Univ Dept Urology 11100 Euclid Ave Cleveland OH 44106-1736

BODNER, JOHN, JR., lawyer; b. Dover, N.J., May 4, 1927; s. John and Anna (Kushman) B.; m. Anne Potter; children: John Edward, Brit-Marie, Anne Kristin, Peter Andrew. Student, Cornell U., 1946-50; JD, Northwestern U., 1953; MLA, Johns Hopkins U., 1969. Bar: D.C. 1954. Bigelow teaching fellow U. Chgo. Law Sch., 1953-54; atty. Dept. Justice, Washington, 1954-56; assoc. Howrey & Simon, Washington, 1956-64; ptnr. Howrey Simon Arnold & White and predecessor, Washington, 1964—. Law lectr. various univs. With U.S. Army, 1945-46. Mem. ABA, FBA, D.C. Bar Assn., Met. Club. Roman Catholic. Home: 4707 Reservoir Rd NW Washington DC 20007-1906 Office: Howrey Simon Arnold & White 1299 Pennsylvania Ave NW Washington DC 20004-2420 E-mail: bodnerj@howrey.com.

BODNER, SUSAN RACHEL, marketing and communications executive; b. N.Y.C., Apr. 20, 1949; d. Milton Meyer and Muriel Ruby (Walash) Swersky; m. Lawrence Bodner, Oct. 25, 1970 (div. June 1975); children: Jennifer Lynn Bodner, Jason Ross Bodner. BA in Edn., U. Md., 1970; BA in English, 1971; paralegal cert., Barry Coll., 1980; MBA, Ga. State U., 1980. Tchr. devel. curriculum Solomon Shecter Hillel Community Day Sch., North Miami Beach, Fla., 1974-77; English tchr. Hebrew Acad. Atlanta, 1977-78; life underwriter, estate planner Life Va. Ins., Atlanta, 1978-79; paralegal, probate and estate mgmt. Abrams, Anton Robbins, Resnick, Schneider & Mager, Hollywood, Fla., 1980-81; svc. cons. mktg. dept. Southern Bell, Ft. Lauderdale, Fla., 1981-83; dir. community rels. The Jewish Home, Atlanta, 1984-87; dir. mktg. and comm. svcs. The United Jewish Fedn. Metrowest, Whippany, N.J., 1988-95; exec. dir. mktg. and comm. Jewish Fedn. Greater Phila., 1995—; pub.'s rep. The Jewish Pub. Group-The Jewish Exponent, 1995—. Pubs. rep., adminstr. The Metrowest Jewish News, Whippany, 1988-95; cons. strategic mktg., comms. and pub. rels. for philanthropic orgn. and beneficiary agys., Whippany, 1988-95; pub. Metrosource, community resource book, 1990—, Inside Quar., lifestyle mag., 1994. Life mem. Nat. Coun. Jewish Women, Millburn-Shorthills, 1984—; mem. Nat. United Jewish Cmtys.; adv. bd. Nat. Direct Mktg. Ctr., Nat. Mktg. Planning

Adv. Group. Mem. NAFE, N.J. Press Women (state and nat. comm. award 1990, 91, 92, 93, 94), N.J. Exec. Women, Pub. Rels. Soc. Am., Am. Mktg. Assn. Office: Jewish Fedn Greater Phila 2100 Arch St Philadelphia PA 19103-1300

BODNEY, DAVID JEREMY, lawyer; b. Kansas City, Mo., July 15, 1954; s. Daniel F. and Retha (Silby) B.; m. Sarah Hughes; children: Christian Steven, Anna Claire, Daniel Martin. BA cum laude, Yale U., 1976; MA in Fgn. Affairs, JD, U. Va., 1979. Bar: Ariz. 1979, U.S. Dist Ct. Ariz. 1980, U.S. Ct. Appeals (9th cir.) 1980, U.S. Supreme Ct. 1983. Legis. asst., speechwriter U.S. Senator John V. Tunney, Washington, 1975-76; sr. editor Va. Jour. of Internat. Law, 1978-79; assoc. Brown and Bain PA, Phoenix, 1979-85, ptnr., 1985-90; gen. counsel New Times, Inc., Phoenix, 1990-92; ptnr. Steptoe & Johnson, LLP, Phoenix, 1992—, mng. ptnr., 2002—. Vis. prof. Ariz. State U., Tempe, 1985, 94—. Co-author: Libel Defense Resource Center: 50-State Survey, 1982—. Bd. dirs. Ariz. Ctr. for Law in the Pub. Interest, Phoenix, 1983-90, pres., 1989-90; chmn. Yale Alumni Schs. Com., Phoenix, 1984-87; vice chmn. City of Phoenix Solicitation Bd., 1986-88, chmn., 1988-89; bd. dirs. Children's Action Alliance, 1995—, v.p., 1998—; mem. adv. panel on Civil Liberties to White House Commn. on Aviation Safety and Security, 1997. Mem. ABA (forum com. on communication law 1984—, concerned correspondents network com. 1979—), Ariz. Bar Assn. Clubs: Yale (bd. dirs. Phoenix club 1979—), Ariz. Acad. Democrat. Office: Steptoe & Johnson 201 E Washington St 16th Fl0 Phoenix AZ 85021

BODOFF, JOSEPH SAMUEL UBERMAN, lawyer; b. Bryn Mawr, Nov. 2, 1952; s. Bernard David and Ruth Irma (Uberman) B. BS, Pa. State U., 1974; JD, Villanova U., 1977. Bar: Pa. 1977, U.S. Dist. Ct. (ea. dist.) Pa. 1979, U.S. Ct. Appeals (3d cir.) 1980, U.S. Supreme Ct. 1988, Mass. 1987, U.S. Dist. Ct. Mass. 1988, U.S. Ct. Appeals (1st cir.) 1988, R.I. 1998, U.S. Dist. Ct. R.I. 1999. Jud. law clk. Phila. County Ct. of Common Pleas, 1977-79; assoc. Pincus, Verlin, Hahn & Reich, Phila., 1979-86; ptnr. Kaye, Fialkow, Richmond & Rothstein, Boston, 1986-91, Gaston & Snow, Boston, 1991, Warner & Stackpole, Boston, 1991-94, Hinckley, Allen & Snyder, Boston, 1994-98, Shechtman & Halperin, Boston, 1998-2000, Bodoff & Assocs., Boston, 2000—03, Bodoff & Slavitt LLP, Boston, 2003—. Dir. Am. Bankruptcy Inst., Alexandria, Va., 1995—2003, mem. exec. com., 2000—03; dir. Am. Bd. Certification, Alexandria; co-chair ABI Unsecured Trade Creditors Com., Alexandria, 1993—98, ABI Creditors' Com. Manual Task Force, 1993—94; chair ABI Task Force on Preferences, 1995—97; exec. editor ABI World, 2002—; chair NACM Bankruptcy and Insolvency Group, Portland, 1998—. Author: Cramdown: The Ultimate Chapter 11 Threat, 1992, (with others) Bankruptcy Business Acquisitions, 1998; contbr. articles to profl. publs. Mem. Mus. Coun. of Mus. of Fine Arts, Boston, 1997-99. Mem. ABA, Am. Bankruptcy Inst. (dir. 1995-2003, mem. exec. com. 2000-2003), Am. Bd. of Certification (dir. 1996-2000), Boston Bar Assn., Nat. Assn of Credit Mgmt. Avocations: skiing, tennis, wine collecting, piano. Home: 64 Forest St Chestnut Hill MA 02467-2930 Office: Bodoff & Slavitt LLP 77 N Washington St Boston MA 02114 E-mail: jbodoff@bodoffslavitt.com.

BODOH, WILLIAM T. federal judge; b. Newark, Ohio, Sept. 5, 1938; m. Janet Beth Neibusch; three children. BS, Ohio U., 1961; JD, Ohio State U., 1964. Bar: Ohio 1964, U.S. Supreme Ct. 1970, U.S. Dist. Ct. (no. dist.) Ohio 1972, U.S. Dist. Ct. (6th cir.) 1980. Asst. atty. gen. U.S. Atty. Gen.'s office, Columbus, 1964-65, 66-67; atty. Capital Fin. Corp., Columbus, 1965-66, East Ohio Gas Co., Cleve., 1967-72; assoc. Manchester, Bennett, Powers & Ullman, Youngstown, Ohio, 1972-85; bankruptcy judge U.S. Dist. Ct. (no. dist.) Ohio, Youngstown, 1985—, chief judge, 2001—. Author: A Local Rules Guide for Ohio Northern District Bankruptcy Court, 1988, A Few Useful Provisions — The Adoption of the Bill of Rights, 1991, The Parameters of the Non-Plan Liquidating Chapter 11: Refining the "Lionel" Standard, 1992, On Judging Judges, 1994, Inequality Among Creditors: The Unconstitutional Use of Successor Liability to Create a New Class of Priority Claimants, 1996, Protective Orders in the Bankruptcy Court: The Congressional Mandate of Bankruptcy Code Section 107 and Its Constitutional Implications, 1996; contbr. articles to legal jours. Recipient Steel Baton award Youngstown Symphony Soc., 1975. Fellow Am. Coll. Bankruptcy; mem. Nat. Conf. Bankruptcy Judges, Am. Bankruptcy Inst., John H. Clarke Am. Inn of Ct., Phi Delta Phi, Pi Kappa Alpha. Office: US Bankruptcy Ct No Dist Ohio 125 Market St Rm 218 Youngstown OH 44503-1780 Fax: 330-746-0480.

BODOVITZ, JAMES PHILIP, lawyer; b. Evanston, Ill., Aug. 20, 1958; s. Philip Edward and Dosha (Laurman) B. BS, U. So. Calif., 1980, JD, 1984. Bar: N.Y. 1985, D.C. 1989, Calif. 1990. Assoc. Shearman & Sterling, N.Y.C., 1984-89, San Francisco, 1989-92; br. chief divsn. broker-dealer enforcement U.S. Securities Exch. Commn., N.Y.C., 1992-96; v.p., assoc. gen. counsel law dept. The Equitable Life Assurance Soc. of U.S., N.Y.C., 1996—; sr. v.p., gen. counsel AXA Advisors, LLC, 1999—. Mem. ABA, Assn. Bar City N.Y. (Thurgood Marshall award 1998). Democrat. Office: AXA Financial Inc 12th Fl 1290 Ave of Americas New York NY 10104 E-mail: James.Bodovitz@axa-financial.com.

BODOW, WAYNE R. lawyer; b. Bklyn., Apr. 25, 1943; s. Charles G. and Rosalind L. B.; m. Alice Turski, Aug. 29, 1971 (div. Dec. 1977); 1 child, Amy Ellen; m. Linda S. Taylor, Dec. 16, 1988 (div. Oct. 1994); 1 child, Elana Sara; m. Lillian Stienmann, June 7, 1998. BA, Rockford Coll., 1965. Bar: N.Y. 1975; U.S. Dist. Ct. (no. and we. dists.) N.Y. 1975; cert. in consumer bankruptcy law Am. Bankruptcy Bd. Cert. Pvt. practice. Mem. alternate dispute resolution panel U.S. Bankruptcy Ct. No. Dist N.Y., 1999—, lectr. in field. Contbr. articles to profl. jours. Mem. Nat. Coun. Exchangors, Nat. Assn. Consumer Bankruptcy Attys. (founder, lobbyist), Nat. Assn. Chpt. 13 Trustees (assoc.), Nat. Assn. Consumer Advocates, Am. Bankruptcy Inst., Onondaga County Bar Assn. (chmn. consumer law sect., lectr.), Ctrl. N.Y. Bankruptcy Bar Assn., Coalition Medicaid Advs. We. N.Y., Turnaround Mgmt. Assn. Office: 1925 Park St Ste 1 Syracuse NY 13208-1080 Fax: 315-422-9113. E-mail: wbodow@choiceonemail.com.

BODSWORTH, FRED, author, naturalist; b. Port Burwell, Ont., Can., Oct. 11, 1918; s. Arthur John and Viola (Williams) B.; m. Margaret Neville Banner, July 8, 1944; children: Barbara (Mrs. Edward Welch), Nancy (Mrs. Richard Hannah), Neville. Student pub. schs., Port Burwell. Reporter St. Thomas (Ont.) Times-Jour., 1940-43; reporter, editor Toronto (Ont.) Daily Star, 1943-46; staff writer, editor Maclean's Mag., Toronto, 1947-56; novelist, 1956—. Organizer, leader numerous natural history tours Author: Last of the Curlews, 1954, 2d edit., 1995, The Strange One, 1960, The Mating Call, 1961, The Atonement of Ashley Morden, 1964, The Sparrow's Fall, 1967 (also pub. in Eng., fgn. translations), The Pacific Coast, Illustrated Natural History of Canada series, 1970; (with others) Wilderness Canada, 1970; editor: Illustrated Natural History of Canada series, 1980-81. Bd. dirs. Natural Sci. of Can., 1980-88; hon. bd. dirs. Long Point Bird Obs., 1970—; chmn. bd. trustees James L. Baillie Meml. Fund for ornithol. field research, 1975-88. Mem. Fedn. Ont. Naturalists (hon. life, pres. 1964-66), Internat. PEN, Writers Union of Can. Clubs: Ornithological, Field Naturalists (past pres.), Brodie (Toronto).

BODVARSSON, ORN BODVAR, economist, educator; b. Reykjavik, Iceland, Sept. 8, 1958; arrived in U.S., 1964; s. Gunnar and Tove Bodvarsson; m. Mary Christina Bodvarsson, June 26, 1999; children: Gunnar John, Hans Peter. BS, Oreg. State U., 1979, MS, 1981; PhD, Simon Fraser U., Vancouver, B.C., Can., 1986. Vis. instr. econs. We. Wash. U., Bellingham, 1983—84, Whitman Coll., Walla Walla, Wash., 1984—85; vis. asst. prof. U. Mont., Missoula, 1986—87, Ball State U., Muncie, Ind., 1987—88; from asst. prof. to assoc. prof. St. Cloud (Minn.) U., 1988—97, prof., 1997—. Cons. economist, St. Cloud, 1995—2000; vis. prof. U. Nebr., Lincoln, 2001—. Contbr. articles to profl. jours. Democrat. Avocations: classical piano, bicycling, cooking, outdoor activities, stock investments. Home: 4931 S 66th St Lincoln NE 68516 Office: U Nebr Dept Econs CBA 340 Box 880489 Lincoln NE 68588 E-mail: obodvarsson2@unl.edu.

BOE, DAVID STEPHEN, musician, educator, dean; b. Duluth, Minn., Mar. 11, 1936; s. Egbert Thomas and Beatrice Ella (Steen) Boe; m. Sigrid North, July 23, 1961; children: Stephen, Eric. BA, St. Olaf Coll., Northfield, Minn., 1958; M.Mus., Syracuse U., 1960. Asst. prof. music U. Ga., 1961-62; mem. faculty Oberlin (Ohio) Coll. Conservatory Music, 1962—2003, prof. organ and harpsichord, 1976—, dean, 1976-90; organ recitalist U.S. and Europe, 1962—. Mem. advanced placement music com. Coll. Entrance Exam. Bd., 1980—83; vis. prof. Fla. State U., 1991, U. Notre Dame, 1991—92. Trustee Westfield Ctr., 2000—; chmn. scholarship com. Presser Found., 2002—; dir. music, organist First Luth. Ch., Lorain, Ohio, 1962—2002. Scholar Fulbright, Germany, 1960—61. Mem.: Nat. Assn. Schs. Music (trustee, sec. 1981—87), Phi Beta Kappa, Pi Kappa Lambda (nat. pres. 1986—90). E-mail: david.boe@oberlin.edu.

BOE, GERARD PATRICK, health science association administrator, educator; b. Washington, Jan. 20, 1936; s. Harold David and Bernice Virginia (Lemon) Boe; m. Irene Margaret Dazevedo, Oct. 24, 1959 (div. Jan. 1988); children: Steven Alan, Christine Ann; m. Charlotte Greene Hudson, Dec. 30, 1989. BS in Biology, W.Va. Wesleyan Coll., 1958; MS in Clin. Pathology, Ohio State U., 1969; PhD in Edn. and Mgmt., Tex. A&M U., 1976. Commd. 2d lt. U.S. Army, 1963, advanced through grades to lt. col.; health care adminstr., 1963—81; ret., 1981; adminstrv. dir. Ga. Radiation Therapy Ctr., Augusta, 1981—83; pres. Profl. Mgmt. Cons., Augusta, 1983—89; exec. dir. Am. Med. Technologists, Park Ridge, Ill., 1989—. Faculty Webster U., So. Ill. U., 1980—. Contbr. articles to profl. jours. Recipient cert. of appreciation, ARC, 1976, Pres.'s award, Augusta chpt. Internat. Mgmt. Coun., 1989. Mem.: Am. Soc. Clin. Pathologists (cert.), Inst. Cert. Profl. Mgrs. (bd. regents 1990—), Clin. Lab. Mgmt. Assn., Nat. Clearing House for Licensure, Enforcement and Regulation, Soc. Armed Forces Med. Lab. Scientists (Pres.'s award 1982). Republican. Methodist. Avocations: coins, stamps, racquetball, sports. Office: Am Med Technologists 710 Higgins Rd Park Ridge IL 60068-5737

BOECKMAN, ROBERT KENNETH, JR., chemistry educator, organic chemistry researcher; b. Pasadena, Calif., Aug. 26, 1944; s. Robert Kenneth Sr. and Orletta Christine (Brinck) B.; m. Mary Helen Delton, June 19, 1976 BS, Carnegie Inst. Tech., 1966; PhD, Brandeis U., 1971. NIH fellow Columbia U., N.Y.C., 1970-72; from asst. prof. to prof. chemistry Wayne State U., Detroit, 1972-79; prof. chemistry U. Rochester, NY, 1980—2002, Marshall D. Gates. Jr. prof. chemistry, 2002—. Cons. Eastman Kodak, 1986—, Ricerca Inc., Painesville, Ohio, 1983-2001, Novartis Pharma AG, Basel, Switzerland, 1982—, Procter & Gamble Pharm., Cin., 1990—, Aventis, SA, 1992-99, 2001—, Emisphere Technologies, Hawthorne, N.Y., 1999—; bd. dirs. Organic Syntheses, Pet Pride of N.Y., Inc.; v.p. Organic Syntheses, Inc., 2002—. Mem. editl. bd. Organic Syntheses, 1988-96, mem. editl. adv. bd. Can. Jour. Chemistry, 2000—; assoc. editor Jour. Organic Chemistry, 1997—; contbr. articles to profl. jours. Recipient career devel. award NIH, 1976-81, award for acad. achievement Probus Club, 1979; fellow A.P. Sloan Found., 1976-80 Fellow Japanese Soc. for Promotion Sci. (Von Humboldt Rsch. Prize for Sr. Scientists 1992-93, Marshal Gates scholar 1996—); mem. Am. Chem. Soc. (chmn. organic chemistry divsn. 2001, past chair 2002), Royal Soc. Chemistry, Deutscher Chemiker Gesellschaft, Oakhill Country Club Rochester, Sigma Xi. Republican. Roman Catholic. Avocations: golf, basketball. Office: U Rochester Hutchinson Hall Dept of Chemistry Rochester NY 14627 E-mail: rkb@rkbmac.chem.rochester.edu.

BOECKMANN, ALAN L. engineering company executive; BS in elec. engrng., U. Ariz. Engr. Fluor Corp.; pres., CEO Fluor Daniel; pres. Fluor Daniel's Energy & Chem. group; chmn. bd., CEO Fluor Corp., 2002—. Dir. Burlington Northern Santa Fe, Am. Petroleum Inst., Bus. Coun. Internat. Understanding, Nat. Petroleum Coun. Office: One Enterprise Dr Aliso Viejo CA 92656

BOECKMANN, HERBERT F., II, automotive executive; b. Aug. 21, 1930; Bd. of police commr., L.A., 1984—91, 1993—2003; CEO, owner, and pres. Galpin Motors, North Hills, Calif. Office: Galpin Motors, Inc. 15505 Roscoe Blvd. North Hills CA 91343-6598*

BOEDER, THOMAS L. lawyer; b. St. Cloud, Minn., Jan. 10, 1944; s. Oscar Morris and Eleanor (Gile) B.; m. Carol-Leigh Coombs, Apr. 6, 1968. BA, Yale U., 1965, LLB, 1968. Bar: Wash. 1970, U.S. Dist. Ct. (we. dist.) Wash. 1970, U.S. Dist. Ct. (ea. dist.) Wash. 1972, U.S. Ct. Appeals (9th cir.) 1970, U.S. Supreme Ct. 1974, U.S. Ct. Appeals (D.C. cir.) 1975, U.S. Ct. Appeals (10th cir.) 1993. Litigation atty. Wash. State Atty. Gen., Seattle, 1970-72, antitrust div. head, 1972-76, chief, consumer protection and antitrust, 1976-78, also sr. asst. atty. gen. and criminal enforcement, 1979-81; ptnr. Perkins Coie, Seattle, 1981—. Served with U.S. Army, 1968-70, Vietnam. Mem. ABA (antitrust sect.), Wash. State Bar Assn. (antitrust sect.). Lutheran. Office: Perkins Coie 1201 3rd Ave Fl 40 Seattle WA 98101-3029

BOEDIGHEIMER, ROBERT DAVID, lawyer; b. Mpls., Nov. 13, 1962; s. David Eugene and Phyllis Kay (Bylander) B.; m. Wendi Suzanne Lusk. BA in Philosophy, Polit. Sci. and Speech Comm. with distinction, U. Minn., 1985, JD, 1988. Bar: Minn. 1990, U.S. Dist. Ct. Minn. 1990. Law clk. to Hon. Lynn C. Olson, Anoka, Minn., 1989-90; assoc. Adams & Cesario, P.A., Bloomington, Minn., 1990-95; ptnr. McCloud & Boedigheimer, Bloomington, Minn., 1995—. Mem. ABA (litig. sect.), Minn. State Bar Assn., Minn. Trial Lawyers Assn., Nat. Employers Lawyers Assn., Wash. County Bar Assn., Dakota County Bar Assn., Nat. Bd. Trial Advocacy (cert. civil trial specialist). Republican. Roman Catholic. Avocations: racquetball, golf, weight training, skiing, watercolor painting. Office: McCloud & Boedigheimer 5001 W 80th St Ste 201 Bloomington MN 55437-1110 E-mail: RDB@Boedigheimerlaw.com.

BOEDO, STEPHEN, mechanical engineer, consultant; b. Buffalo, Apr. 10, 1960; s. Gordon Eugene and Florence Frances (DeGeorge) B.; m. Sharon Lee Lindahl, Aug. 16, 1986; children: Stephen Matthew, Emily Frances. BA summa cum laude, SUNY, Buffalo, 1983; MS, Cornell U., 1986, PhD, 1995. Sr. engr. Borg-Warner Automotive, Ithaca, N.Y., 1986-92, staff engr., 1996-2000; sr. tech. analyst Fed.-Mogul Corp., Ann Arbor, Mich., 1992-96; gen. ptnr. Tribology Assocs., Ithaca, 1999—; asst. prof. dept. mech. engring. Rochester (N.Y.) Inst. of Tech., 2000—. Adj. instr. Tompkins-Cortland C.C., Dryden, N.Y., 1988-92; self-employed cons., Ithaca, 1986—; guest lectr. on mech. design various univs. Reviewer various jours., 1986—; contbr. articles to profl. jours.; patentee in field. Mem. ASME, Am. Soc. Engring. Edn., Soc. Automotive Engrs., Cornell Soc. Engrs., Phi Beta Kappa. Avocations: soccer, chess, astronomy. E-mail: sxbeme@rit.edu.

BOEDTKER, OLAF A. physicist; b. Colombo, Sri Lanka, Feb. 10, 1924; s. Egon and Rosy Boedtker; m. Dora Marguerite Wilhelm, June 16, 1952; children: Christina K., Beatrice A., Markus S. Dipl. Physics, Swiss Fed. Inst. of Technol., Zurich, Switzerland, 1951; MS, Engring. Sci., Cal Tech, Pasadena, CA, 1958, PhD, Eng. & Phys., 1961. Res. fellow MIT, Cambridge, Mass., 1952—54; res. fellow/grad. student Cal Tech, Pasadena, 1954—62; asst. prof. UC Berkeley, Berkeley, 1962—63; assoc. prof. Oreg. State Univ., Corvallis, 1963—86, prof. emeritus, 1987—. Cons. Bur. of Mines, Albany, Oreg., 1966—69. Office: Oregon State Univ Dept Physics 2760 NW Johnson Ave Corvallis OR 97330-5320

BOEGEHOLD, ALAN LINDLEY, classics educator; b. Detroit, Mar. 21, 1927; s. Alfred Lindley and Katherine Eleanore (Yager) B.; m. Julie Elizabeth Marshall, Apr. 3, 1954; children: Lindley, Alan M. Jones, David, Alison. AB in Latin, U. Mich., 1950; AM in Classical Philology, Harvard U., 1954; student, Am. Sch. Classical Studies, Athens, Greece, 1955-57; PhD in Classical Philology, Harvard U., 1958. From instr. to asst. prof. dept. classics U. Ill., Champaign-Urbana, 1957-60; from asst. prof. to prof. dept. classics Brown U., Providence, R.I., 1960-2001. Dir. summer session Am. Sch. Classical Studies, Athens, 1963-64, 74, 80, vis. prof., 1968-69; dir. Ancient studies program Brown U., 1985-91, chmn. dept. classics, 1966-71, acting chmn., 1973-74; vis. lectr. history Harvard U., 1967; vis. prof. classics Yale U., 1971, U. Calif., Berkeley, 1978; disting. vis. prof. Amherst Coll., 2001-03; mem. com. to evaluate dept. classics Swarthmore Coll., 1972, U. Va., 1982, 88, coms. humanities and history Yale U. Coun., 1982-87; interim pres., v.p. and sec. Naragansett Soc. Archaeol. Inst. Am.; vice-chmn. mng. com. Am. Sch. Classical Studies, 1985-90, chmn., 1990-98; invited lectr., spkr. in field. Editor: (with A.C. Scafuro) Athenian Identity and Civic Ideology, 1993; author, editor: Agora XXVIII, Law Courts at Athens, 1995; author: When A Gesture was Expected. A Selection of Examples from Archaic and Classical Greek Literature, Princeton, 1999; translator: In Simple Clothes (by Constantine Cavafy), 1992; mem. bd. advisors Am. Jour. Archaeology, 1981-85; interim referee papers and books to numerous assns. and presses; contbr. articles to profl. jours. Active ACLU, Amnesty Internat., Providence Athenaeum, Mass. Audubon Soc., Common Cause; trustee Gennadius Libr., Am. Sch. Classical Studies, Athens. Cpl. U.S. Army. Thomas Day Seymour fellow Am. Sch. Classical Studies Athens, 1955-56, Rsch. fellow, 1974-75, Rsch. fellow Agora Excavations, 1980-81, Charles Eliot Norton fellow Am. Sch. Classical Studies Athens (Harvard U.), 1956-57, Howard fellow Brown U., 1964-65, Sr. fellow NEH, 1980-81; grantee Am. Coun. Learned Socs., 1964-65. Fellow Explorers Club; mem. Am. Assn. Ancient Historians, Am. Philol. Assn., Archaeol. Inst. Am. (various coms.), Classical Assn. New Eng. (exec. com. 1968-70), Aegean Inst. (bd. advisors 1976-95), Inst. Nautical Archaeology (bd. dirs. 1973-82). Office: Brown Univ 48 College St Providence RI 02912-9021

BOEGEL, NICK NORBERT, accountant, lawyer; b. West Bend, Wis., Mar. 14, 1972; s. Kenneth and Portia (Steahl) B. BSBA, Boston U., 1994; MBA, Ind. U., 1997, JD, 1998. CPA Ind., Wis.; bar: Ind. 1998, Wis. 2001. Sr. assoc., tax cons. Deloitte & Touche LLP, Milw., 2002—. Mem.: AICPA, ABA, Wis. Bar Assn., Ind. Bar Assn. Avocations: golf, fishing, hunting, billiards, darts. Home: N105 W14676 Wilson Dr Germantown WI 53022

BOEHLER, GABRIEL D. aerospace company executive, educator; b. Paris, Aug. 6, 1926; s. Pierre Boehler and Noelle Ravier; m. Ingrid Onsager, June 29, 1957 (dec. Jan. 30, 1997); children: Pierre, Edith, Paul, Anne-Marie, Elisabeth. Licence-ès-Sciences, U. Paris, 1945—49; M in aero. engring., Cornell U., 1951—53; PhD, Cath. U. Am., 1951—53. Registered profl. engr., Wash. D.C., 1956. Rsch. asst. Cornell U., Ithaca, NY, 1949—51; chief aerodynamics Thieblot Aircraft Co., Bethesda, Md., 1951—56; pres. & chmn. bd. Aerophysics Co., Washington, 1956—; from asst prof. to assoc prof. Cath. U. Am., Washington, 1955—62, ordinary prof., 1962—99, prof. emeritus, 1999—. Cons. US Dept. Def., Washington, 1959—, six maj. aerospace companies, various locations in US, 1958—. Author 100 technical reports. Hon. co-chair Bus. Adv. Coun. Nat. Rep. Congl. Com., Washington, 2002. Pvt. French Resistance and French/US Army, 1942—45, France. Recipient Sigma Xi award, Soc. Sigma Xi, 1956, Tau Beta Pi award, Soc. Tau Beta Pi, 1957, DC 2003 Businessman Yr., Bus. Adv. Coun. (Congressman Reynolds Chmn.), 2003. Mem.: Nat. Def. Indsl. Assn., Am. Helicopter Soc., Soc. Mfg. Engineers, Soc. Automotive Engineers (past chmn., Wash. sect. 1966—67), Am. Soc. Heating, Refrigeration & Air Conditioning Engrs., Am. Inst. Aeronautics & Astronautics. Roman Catholic. Achievements include first to US independent co-inventor ground-effect machine; unmanned aerial vehicles (the only inherently-stable hovering platform); patents for author of five. Home: 2933 Ordway St NW Washington DC 20008 Office: Aerophysics Co 3010 Ordway St NW Washington DC 20008 Office Fax: 202-244-7501. E-mail: gboehler@netzero.net.

BOEHLERT, CARL JOSEPH, materials scientist, educator; b. Vestal, N.Y., Feb. 10, 1969; s. James Thomas and Rose Marie Boehlert; m. Paula Maria Somohano, Feb. 5, 1995; children: Victoria Rose, Nicolas Joseph, Lucas Samuel. BS in Agr. and Biol. Engring., Cornell U., 1991; MS in Materials Sci. and Enring., U. Dayton, 1993, PhD in Materials Sci. and Engring., 1997. Rsch. assoc. U. Dayton, Ohio, 1991-93; materials scientist UES Inc., Dayton, 1993-97; postdoctoral fellow Johns Hopkins U., Balt., 1998-99; postdoctoral rsch. assoc. Los Alamos Nat. Lab., 2000-01; asst. prof. Alfred (N.Y.) U., 2001—. Contbr. numerous articles to profl. jours. Recipient Career award, NSF, 2002. Mem.: The Materials Soc. (young leader 1999), Am. Soc. Materials Internat. Roman Catholic. Office: Alfred U 2 Pine St Alfred NY 14802

BOEHLERT, SHERWOOD LOUIS, congressman; b. Utica, N.Y., Sept. 28, 1936; s. Sherwood John and Elizabeth Monica (Champoux) B.; divorced; children: Mark C. Brooks, Tracy Boehlert Suk, Leslie; m. Marianne Willey Phillips, July 10, 1976; 1 stepchild, Laura Brooke Drahzal. BS in Pub. Relation, Utica Coll., Syracuse U., 1961. Mgr. pub. relations Wyandotte Chems. Corp., Mich., 1961-64; chief of staff Rep. Alexander Pirnie, Washington, 1964-73, Rep. Donald J. Mitchell, 1973-79; exec. Oneida County, 1979-82; mem. U.S. Congress from 24th N.Y. dist. (formerly 23rd), Washington, 1983—; mem. permanent select com. on intelligence, transp. and infrastructure com., homeland sec. com.; chmn. sci. com. Del. NATO parliamentary assembly; mem. N.E.-Midwest Congl. Coalition; co-chmn. N.E. Agr.; chmn. Fire Svcs. Caucus, Minor League Baseball Caucus. Author: Telling the Congressman's Story The Voice of Government, 1968. Bd. dirs. Utica Coll. Found. Served with U.S. Army, 1956-58. Mem.: Rotary. Republican. Office: Ho of Reps 2246 Rayburn Ho Office Bldg Washington DC 20515 also: Alexander Pirnie Fed Bldg Rm 200 10 Broad St Utica NY 13501-1233*

BOEHLKE, WILLIAM FREDRICK, public relations executive, consultant; b. Chgo., Dec. 16, 1946; s. William Fredrick and Cynthia Charlotte (Blackmore) B.; m. Christine Ann Chervenak, July 19, 1969. Student, Wharton Sch. Bus., Phila., 1965-69. Pres. and CEO Data Solve Corp., Chgo., 1981-84, Lati Corp. Inc., San Francisco, 1985-89; CEO Phase Two Strategies Inc., San Francisco, 1989—. Mem. Santa Rosa Golf & Country Club, Home House (London), Penn Club N.Y. Office: Phase Two Strategies Inc 111 Pine St 8th Fl San Francisco CA 94111 E-mail: william_boehlke@p2pr.com.

BOEHM, BARRY WILLIAM, computer science educator; b. Santa Monica, Calif., May 16, 1935; s. Edward G. and Kathryn G. (Kane) B.; m. Sharla Perrine, July 1, 1961; children: Romney Ann, Tenley Lynn. BA, Harvard U., 1957; PhD, UCLA, 1964; ScD (hon.), U. Mass., 2000. Programmer, analyst Gen. Dynamics, San Diego, 1955-59; head infosci. dept. Rand Corp., Santa Monica, 1959-73; chief scientist TRW Def. Sys. Group, Redondo Beach, Calif., 1973-89; dir. infosci. and tech. office Def. Advanced Rsch. Agy. Dept. Def., Arlington, Va., 1989-92, dir. software and computer tech. office, dir. def. rsch. and engring., 1992; TRW prof. software engring., dir. Ctr. for Software Engring. U. So. Calif., L.A., 1992—. Co-chmn. Fed. Coordinating Coun. Sci., Engring. and Tech. High Performance Computing WG, Washington, 1989-91; chmn. DOD Software Tech. Plan WG, Arlington, 1990-92, NASA G & C/Infosystems Adv. Com., Washington, 1973-76; guest lectr. USSR Acad. Sci., 1970; chmn. bd. visitors Carnegie Mellon U. Software Engring. Inst., 1997—; chmn. USAF-Sci. Adv. Bd. Info. Tech. Panel, 1994-97. Author: ROCKET, 1964, Software Engineering Economics, 1981; co-author: Characteristics of Software Quality, 1978, Software Risk Management, 1989, Software Cost Estimation with COCOMO II, 2000; co-editor: Planning Community Information Utilities, 1972. Recipient Warnier prize Soc. Software Analysts, 1984, Freiman award Internat. Soc. Parametric Analysts, 1988, Award for Excellence Office of Sec. of Def., 1992. Fellow Internat. Coun. on Sys. Engring., Assn. for Computing Machinery (Disting. Rsch. award in Software Engring. 1997), NAE, AIAA (chair TC computers 1968-70, Info. Sys. award 1979), IEEE (gov. bd. computer sci. 1981-82, 86-87, H.D. Mills award 2000). Office: U So Calif Computer Sci Dept Los Angeles CA 90089-0781 E-mail: boehm@sunset.usc.edu.

BOEHM, EDWARD GORDON, JR., college administrator, educator; b. Washington, Jan. 30, 1942; s. Edward and Catherine (Murray) B.; m. Regina Ellen Evans, June 25, 1966; children: Evan Arnold, Andrew Edward. BS in Edn., Frostburg State U., 1964; MEd, The Am. U., 1970, D of Higher Edn., 1977. Dir. univ. devel., dean for student devel., assoc. dean/dir. admissions, instr. Coll. Arts & Scis. The Am. U., Washington, 1968-79; assoc. vice chancellor acad. affairs, asst. prof. edn., dean admissions Tex. Christian U., Ft. Worth, 1979-89; sr. v.p., asst. prof. Coll. Edn., exec. dir. Found. Marshall U., Huntington, W.Va., 1989-95; pres. Keystone Coll., La Plume, Pa., 1995—. Mem. adv. coun. Tandy Tech. Scholars, Ft. Worth, 1989-99; trustee, mem. com. The Coll. Bd., N.Y.C., 1987-91. Contbr. book chpt.: Student Services and the Law, 1988; contbr. articles to profl. jours. Bd. dirs., v.p. Boys & Girls Club, Huntington, 1989-95, Tri-State coun. Boy Scouts Am., Huntington, 1989-95; bd. dirs., pres. United Way River Cities, Huntington, 1989-95; bd. dirs. Leadership W. Va., Charleston, 1992-95, Leadership Tri-State, Ironton, Ohio, 1991-95; mem. scholastic evaluation panel Am.'s Jr. Miss, 1995—; bd. dirs. Tyler Hosp., 1995-2001, Waverly Cmty. House, 1996-2000; mem. Leadership Wilkes-Barre Exec. Program, Class of '96, Leadership Lackawanna Exec. Program, Class of '96, N.E. Regional Cancer Inst. Adv. Bd.; pres. bd. dirs. Pa. Assn. of Nonprofit Orgns., 1998; mem. nonprofit adv. bd. Nonprofit Resource Ctr., U. Scranton, 1998—; bd. mem. Tyler Meml. Hosp. Cmty. Health Care Vision Task Force, 1999—; mem. Pa. Soc., 1997—, Team Pa. Amb., 1999—; life mem. Lackawanna Indsl. Fund Enterprises, 1999—; mem. task force Healthy N.E. Pa. Initiative, 1999-2001; bd. govs. Scranton Area Found., 2002--. Named W.Va. Outstanding Fundraising Exec., Nat. Soc. Fundraising Execs., 1993, Citizen of Yr., Herald Dispatch, 1993, Disting. West Virginian, 1995;

recipient Cir. of Excellence in Fundraising award Coun. for Advancement and Support of Edn., 1993, Nat. Tchr.'s award Radio Shack Adv. Coun., 2000; John Deaver Drinko Acad. fellow Marshall U. Mem. Huntington C. of C., Lawrence County C. of C., Greenup County C. of C., Engrs. Club Huntington, Huntington Rotary Club (bd. dirs. 1989-95). Avocations: tennis, soccer, history, golf, hiking. Home: 29 College Ave La Plume PA 18440 Office: Keystone Coll One College Green La Plume PA 18440-0200 E-mail: edward.boehm@keystone.edu.

BOEHM, ERIC HARTZELL, information management executive; b. Hof, Germany, July 15, 1918; came to U.S., 1934, naturalized, 1940; s. Karl and Bertha (Oppenheimer) Boehm; m. Inge Pauli, June 5, 1948 (dec.); children: Beatrice(dec.), Ronald James, Evelyn(dec.), Steven David. BA, Wooster (Ohio) Coll., 1940, Litt.D. (hon.), 1973; MA, Fletcher Sch. Law and Diplomacy, 1942; PhD, Yale U., 1951. With Dept. Air Force, 1951-58; bd. dirs. ABC-CLIO, Santa Barbara, Calif., 1960—; pres. Internat. Sch. of Info. Mgmt., 1987-94. Chmn. bd. dirs. Internat. Acad. at Santa Barbara, 1970—80; pub. Environ. Studies Inst., 1971—, Info. Inst., 1980—; cons. on bibliography, info. sys. Author: We Survived, 1949; microfilm Policy-making of the Nazi Government, 1969; editor Historical Abstracts, 1955-83, cons., 1983— ; editor America: History and Life, 1964-83, cons., 1983— ; editor Bibliographies on International Relations and World Affairs, an Annotated Directory, 1965, Blueprint for Bibliography, a System for Social Sciences and Humanities, 1965, Clio Bibliography Series, 1973— ; co-editor Historical Periodicals, 1961, 2d edit., 1983-85; pub. Advanced Bibliography of Contents: Political Science, 1969—, ART Bibliographies: Modern, 1972—, Environ. Periodicals Bibliography, 1972— ; bd. advisors Info. Strategy, The Exec.'s Jour., 1984— ; contbr. articles to profl. jours. Bd. dirs. UN Assn., Santa Barbara, 1973-77, Santa Barbara's Adv. Bd. Internat. Relationships (Sister Cities), 1974, Friends of Public Library, Friends of U. Calif. at Santa Barbara Library; mem. affiliates bd. U. Calif.-Santa Barbara; vice chmn. New Directions Found., 1984-88; adv. bd. Nuclear Age Peace Found., 1985— . With USAAF, 1942-46. Recipient Disting. Alumnus award Wooster Coll., 1990. Mem. AAAS, Am. Soc. Info. Sci., Assn. Bibliography in History (v.p. 1986, pres. 1987), Calif. Library Soc., Nat. Trust Historic Preservation, Santa Barbara Com. Fgn. Rels., Am. Friends of Wilton Park, Santa Barbara C. of C. (dir. 1980-84), Univ. Club, Rotary, Phi Beta Kappa. Home and Office: 800 E Micheltorena St Santa Barbara CA 93103-2220 E-mail: eboehm@silcom.com.

BOEHM, FELIX HANS, physicist, educator; b. Basel, Switzerland, June 9, 1924; came to U.S., 1952, naturalized, 1964; s. Hans G. and Marquerite (Philippi) B.; m. Ruth Sommerhalder, Nov. 26, 1956; children: Marcus F., Claude N. MS, Inst. Tech., Zurich, 1948, PhD, 1951. Research assoc. Inst. Tech., Zurich, Switzerland, 1949-52; Boese fellow Columbia U., 1952-53; faculty Calif. Inst. Tech., Pasadena, 1953—, prof. physics, 1961—, William L. Valentine prof., 1985-94, William L. Valentine prof. emeritus, 1995—; Sloan fellow, 1962-64; NSF sr. fellow Niels Bohr Inst., Copenhagen, 1965-66, CERN, Geneva, 1971-72, Laue-Langevin Inst., 1980. Recipient Humboldt award, 1980, 84. Fellow Am. Phys. Soc. (Tom W. Bonner prize 1995); mem. Nat. Acad. Scis. Achievements include research on nuclear physics, nuclear beta decay, neutrino physics, atomic physics, muonic and pionic atoms, parity and time-reversal. Home: 2510 N Altadena Dr Altadena CA 91001-2836 Office: Calif Inst Tech Mail Code 161 33 Pasadena CA 91125-0001 E-mail: boehm@caltech.edu.

BOEHM, JOHN CHARLES, music educator; b. Tampa, Fla, Oct. 13, 1948; s. T.S. Boehm and Mamie Boehm (Ausband) Mitchell; m. Nancy Perry, July 3, 1988; 1 child, Alison Boehm; stepchildren: Jason Cox, David Cox. AA, Gordon Mil. Coll., 1968; MusB, Carson-Newman Coll., 1971; MusM, Ga. State U., 1973. Choral dir. Richmond County Sch., Augusta, Ga., 1970-71, Fulton County Sch., Atlanta, 1971-72; instr. music Kennesaw Coll. (formerly Kennesaw Jr. Coll.), Ga., 1973-74; asst. prof., dir. music Atlanta Met. Coll. (formerly Atlanta Jr. Coll.), 1974-98; ret., 1998; owner The Tumlin House Bed and Breakfast, 1998—. Contbg. writer, project staff mem. Atlanta jr. coll. humanities curriculum devel. pilot project and 3 yr. grant NEH, 1976, 78. Performing mem. Atlanta Symphony Orch. Chorus and Chamber Chorus, 1977-90. Mem. NARAS (voting mem., bd. gov. 1987-91, chmn. edn. com. 1987-89), Am. Choral Dirs. Assn. (life, state chair 2 yr. coll. 1983-85, state chair ethnic/minority concerns 1985-87, 89-91, so. divsn. chair 2 yr. coll. 1992-1996), Music Ed. Nat. Conf., Ga. Music Educators Assn. (adjudicator 1982—, guest condr. 1982), Phi Mu Alpha (life). Home: PO Box 40 Cave Spring GA 30124-0040

BOEHM, PETER MICHAEL, ambassador, diplomat; b. Kitchener, Can., Apr. 26, 1954; s. Michael and Anna (Markus) B.; m. Julia Wayand, Dec. 19, 1981; children: Andreas, Alexander, Nikolas. Ba (hons.) in History, Eng. Lit., Wilfrid Laurier U., Can., 1977; Ma in Internat. Affairs, Carleton U., Can., 1978; PhD in History, U. Edinburgh, Scotland, 1983. From desk officer to dir. Dept. Foreign Affairs, Ottawa, Can., 1981-1995, dir.; 2d sec., vice consul Canadian Embassy, Havana, Cuba, 1983-86, counsellor and consul San Jose, Costa Rica, 1988-92; amb., permanent rep. Permanent Mission of Can. to OAS, Washington, 1997—2001; min. polit. and pub. affairs Can. Embassy, Washington, 2001—. Contbr. articles to profl. jours. Mem. Profl. Assn. Foreign Svc. Officers, Canadian Inst. Internat. Affairs, Inter-Am. Dialogue, Transylvania Club. Avocations: travel, reading, outdoor sports, alternative music. Office: Embassy of Canada 501 Pennsylvania Ave NW Washington DC 20001-2114 E-mail: peter.boehm@dfait-maeci.gc.ca.

BOEHM, RICHARD GLENNON, geography educator, writer; b. St. Louis, Aug. 29, 1937; s. Frank A. and Ivy M. Boehm; m. R. Denise Blanchard; children: Brian, Lori, Mike, Laura, Mitch, Nick. BS in Edn., U. Mo., 1960, MA in Geography, 1962; PhD in Geography, U. Tex., 1975. From instr. to asst. prof. dept. geography U. Mo., Columbia, 1971-76, chmn. dept. geography, 1976-77; from instr. to asst. prof. dept. geography and planning S.W. Tex. State U., San Marcos, 1963-71, dir. Inst. for Corridor Studies, 1983—, prof., chmn. dept. geography, 1977-94, Jesse H. Jones disting. chair in geog. edn., 1998—, dir. Grosvenor Ctr. for Geographic Edn., 1998—. Geography edn. cons. U.S. Dept. Edn., U.S. Dept. Def., AT&T Nat. Coun. on Crime and Delinquency, Ednl. Testing Svc., Nat. Geog. Soc., The Nat. Faculty, Nat. Coun. of Chief State Sch. Officers; assoc. fellow Nat. Ctr. for Juvenile Justice, Pitts., 1974-80; steering com. Geog. Edn. Nat. Implementation Project, 1984-87; writing team joint nat. curriculum guidelines project Assn. Am. Geographers/Nat. Coun. Geog. Edn.; organized Summit I in Geog. Edn., 1993 and Summit II in Geog. Edn., 1995; organizer The First Assessment : Rsch. in Geog. Edn. Conf., San Marcos, Tex. Grosvener Ctr. for Geog. Edn., 1997; dir. Scope and Sequence Project, Nat. Geographic Soc. Edn. Found., 2000. Author: Exporting Cotton in Texas: Relationships of Ports and Inland Supply Points, 1975, Careers in Geography, 1990, Missouri's Transportation System: Condition, Capacity and Impediments to Efficiency, 1976, Principal Interaction Fields of Missouri Regional Centers, 1976, Transport Regulation in Missouri, 1978, (with others) Guidelines for Geographic Education: Elementary and Secondary Schools, 1984, World Geography: A Physical and Cultural Approach, 1989, 5th edit., 2000, Geography: The World and Its People, 1996, 3d edit., 2002, Glencoe World Geography, 2003, (with others) Our World Today, 2003; co-author: Geography for Life: National Standards in Geography, 1994; (with others) Stories in Time, 7 vols., 1997, The First Assessment: Research in Geography Education, 1997, (with others) Harcourt Social Studies, 7 vols., 1999, (with others) Macmillan/McGraw-Hill Social Studies, 7 vols., 2003, Geography of the United States, 1999, (with others) Path Toward a World Literacy: A Scope and Sequence in Geographic Education, K-12, 2000; co-editor: Research in Geographic Education; contbr. articles to profl. jours. 2d lt. U.S. Army, 1960. Recipient Best Article award Jour. Geography, 1980, 87, Disting. Alumnus award U. Mo. Coll. Arts and Sci., 1996, Gilbert M. Grosvenor honors in geographic edn. Assn. Am. Geographers, 2002; grantee Nat. Geog. Soc. Edn. Fnd., 2000. Mem. Nat. Coun. Geog. Edn (treas. 1977, local arrangements chmn. 1979, 2d v.p. 1980, 1st v.p. 1981, pres. 1983, editor Media Materials 1972-77, gen. editor slide libr. 1974-77, George J. Miller award 1991, Disting. Tchg. Achievement award 1985), Nat. Geog. Soc. (co-coord. Tex. Alliance for Geog. Edn. 1986—, Disting. Geog. Educator 1990). Home: 733 Willow Ridge Dr San Marcos TX 78666-4919 Office: S W Tex State U Dept Geography San Marcos TX 78666 E-mail: rb03@swt.edu.

BOEHM, STEVEN BRUCE, lawyer; b. N.Y.C., May 22, 1954; s. Henry and Irene (Jonas) B. BA, Rutgers U., New Brunswick, N.J., 1975; JD, Rutgers U., Newark, 1978. Bar: N.J., 1978, D.C., 1982, U.S. Dist. Ct. N.J., U.S. Dist. Ct., D.C. Enforcement atty. SEC, Washington, 1978-81, atty. office gen. counsel, 1982, counsel to the commr., 1982-83; assoc. Sutherland Asbill & Brennan, LLP, Washington, 1983-87, ptnr., 1988—. Philip J. Levin scholar Rutgers U., 1975-78. Mem. ABA (corp., banking and bus. law com.), D.C. Bar Assn., Phi Beta Kappa, Pi Sigma Alpha. Office: Sutherland Asbill & Brennan LLP 1275 Pennsylvania Ave NW Washington DC 20004-2415 E-mail: sboehm@sablaw.com.

BOEHM, THEODORE REED, judge; b. Evanston, Ill., Sept. 12, 1938; s. Hans George and Frances (Reed) B.; children from previous marriage: Elisabeth, Jennifer, Sarah, Macy; m. Margaret Stitt Harris, Jan. 27, 1985. AB summa cum laude, Brown U., 1960; JD magna cum laude, Harvard U., 1963. Bar: D.C. 1964, Ind. 1964, U.S. Supreme Ct. 1975. Law clk. to Chief Justices Warren, Reed and Burton, U.S. Supreme Ct., Washington, 1963-64; assoc. Baker & Daniels, Indpls., 1965-70, ptnr., 1970-88, 95-96, mng. ptnr., 1980-87; gen. counsel major appliances GE, Louisville, 1988-89; v.p., gen. counsel GE Aircraft Engines, Cin., 1989-91; dep. gen. counsel Eli Lilly & Co., 1991-95; justice Ind. Supreme Ct., Indpls., 1996—. Pres. Ind. Sports Corp., 1980-88; chmn. organizing com. 1987 Pan Am. Games, Indpls.; chmn. Indpls. Culture Devel. Commn., 2001-. Mem. ABA, Am. Law Inst., Ind. Bar Assn., Indpls. Bar Assn. Office: Ind Supreme Ct State House Rm 324 Indianapolis IN 46204-2728 E-mail: tboehm@courts.state.in.us.

BOEHM, TONI GEORGENE, seminary dean, nurse; b. New Kensington, Pa., Dec. 28, 1946; d. Sylvio Chipoletti and Eula Gene (Smittle) Fox; m. Raymond Stawinski, Dec. 11, 1965 (div. Sept. 1978); 1 child, Michelle Stawinski Ivy; m. Jay Thomas Boehm, Apr. 28, 1983; children: Jonathon, Kimberly, Allison Cole, Amanda. Diploma, Allegheny Valley Sch. Nursing, Natrona Heights, Pa., 1967; family nurse practitioner cert., U. Kans., 1976; BA in Edn., Ottawa (Kans.) U., 1978; MSN, U. Mo., Kansas City, 1981; grad., Unity Sch. of Christianity, Unity Village, Mo., 1989; PhD in Religious Studies, Am. World U., 1997. Ordained to ministry Assn. of Unity Chs.; cert. occupl. health nurse. Nurse Allegheny Valley Hosp., Natrona Heights, 1967-74; head nurse, dir. nursing Truman Med. Ctr., Kansas City, Mo., 1974-78; mgr. med. Hallmark Card Inc., Kansas City, Mo., 1978-85; sr. staff specialist ANA, Kansas City, Mo., 1985-87; dean of adminstrn. Unity Sch. Christianity, 1987—2001, dir. strategic initiatives, 2001—02, dir. retreats and outreach and spl. events, 2003, interim dir. ministerial sch., 2003—, dir. retreats, 2004. Nat. spkr. and freelance writer for ministry and self-unfoldment. Author: The Spiritual Entrepreneur, 2003, One Day My Mouth Just Opened: Reverie, Reflections and Rapturous Musings on the Cycles of a Woman's Life, 2001, Embracing the Feminine Nature of the Divine, 2002. Mem. nat. steering com. for fundraising Unity Sch. of Christianity; mem. women's coun. U. Mo. Recipient scholarships. Mem.: NCCJ, ANA, Assn. Unity Chs. (urban curriculum com. 1987—2001, ministerial edn. com. 1987—2001, field licensing com. 1990—2001), Mo. Nurses Assn. (bd. dirs. 1975—85), U. Mo. Sch. Nursing Alumni Assn. Republican. Avocations: travel, reading, music, writing. Home: 430 N Winnebago Dr Greenwood MO 64034-9321 Office: Unity Sch Christianity Unity Village MO 64065-0001

BOEHMER, RICHARD A. lawyer; b. St. Louis, June 26, 1951; BA, Harvey Mudd Coll. and U. So. Calif., 1973; JD, Loyola U., L.A., 1976. Bar: Calif. 1976. With O'Melveny & Myers, L.A. Recipient Acad. scholarship Loyola U. Sch. Law, 1974, 75. Mem. ABA, L.A. County Bar Assn., Phi Beta Kappa, Phi Kappa Phi. Office: O'Melveny & Myers 400 S Hope St Los Angeles CA 90071-2899

BOEHMER, ROBERT G. academic administrator, educator; s. George Robert and Gabrielle Hortense Boehmer; m. Joyce Adele Kline, June 9, 1973; children: Megan Kline, Elizabeth Lynn. BS in Bus. Adminstrn., U. Oreg., Eugene, 1974, JD, 1977. Bar: Oreg. 1977. Ptnr. Hershner, Hunter, Miller, Moulton and Andrews, Eugene, Oreg., 1979—89; assoc. prof., legal studies U. Ga., Athens, 1989—, co-dir., Lilly Tchg. Fellows Program, 1996—, dir., self-study, 1999—2000, assoc. provost for instl. effectiveness, 2001—. Contbr. articles to profl. jours. Chair, ann. campaign United Way of Lane County, Eugene, Oreg., 1988, pres., 1989. Staff sgt. USAR, 1968—74, Ft. Vancouver, Wash. Mem.: Acad. Legal Studies in Bus., Oreg. State Bar. Avocation: running. Home: 161 Colonial Dr Athens GA 30606-4015 Office: Univ Ga 203 Adminstrn Bldg Athens GA 30602

BOEHNE, EDWARD GEORGE, banker; b. Evansville, Ind., May 15, 1940; s. Edward John and Lucy Naomi (Strieter) Boehne; m. Patricia Graffis, Jan. 24, 1960; 1 child, Lisa Elena. BS, Ind. U., 1962, MBA, 1963, MA, 1967, PhD in Econs, 1968; LLD (hon.), Widener U., 1989, U. Del., 2001, U. So. Ind., 2002. Economist Fed. Res. Bank, Phila., 1968—70, rsch. officer, economist, 1970—71, v.p., dir. rsch., 1971—73, sr. v.p., 1973—81, pres., 1981—2000. Tchr. Bradley U., 1963—65, Ind. U., 1965—67, Temple U., 1969—70; bd. dirs. Haverford Trust, 2000—, AAA Mid-Atlantic Co., 2000—, Beneficial Savs. Bank, 2000—, Toll Bros., 2000—, PennMut. Life Ins. Co., 2001—. Chmn. Pa. Hosp., 1993-97; chmn. University City Sci. Ctr., 1998-99. Recipient Lieber award Ind. U., 1967, Gov.'s citation for outstanding svc. to Pa., 1978, Whitney Young Leadership award 1986, Stephen Girard award, 1987. Office: 313 Devon State Rd Devon PA 19333-1411 Fax: 610-687-4748. E-mail: egboehne@msn.com.

BOEHNEN, DANIEL A. lawyer; b. Mitchell, S.D., Aug. 5, 1950; s. Lloyd and Mary Elizabeth (Buche) B.; m. Joan Bensing, May 22, 1976; children: Christopher, Lindsey. BS in Chem. Engring. cum laude, Notre Dame U., 1973; JD, Cornell U., 1976. Bar: Ill, U.S. Dist. Ct. (no. dist.) Ill., U.S. Ct. Appeals (7th and fed. cirs.), U.S. Supreme Ct. Atty. Allegretti, Newitt, Witcoff & McAndrews Ltd., Chgo., 1976—, assoc., 1982—; ptnr., exec. officer Allegretti & Witcoff, Ltd., Chgo., 1986—, bd. dirs., 1993—95; founder, mng. ptnr. McDonnell Boehnen Hulbert & Berghoff, Chgo., 1996—. Bd. dirs. Mitchell (S.D.) Prehist. Indian Village Soc., 1983—; commr. Northbrook Planning Commn., 1993—. Mem. ABA, AIPLA, Cornell Law Assn. Chg. (chmn.), Fed. Cir. Bar Assn. (bd dirs.), Assn. Patent Law Firms (pres., bd. dirs.). Avocations: skiing, photography, scuba diving. Office: McDonnell Boehnen Hulbert & Berghoff 300 S Wacker Dr Chicago IL 60606-6709 Office Fax: 312-913-0002.

BOEHNEN, DAVID LEO, lawyer; b. Mitchell, S.D., Dec. 3, 1946; s. Lloyd L. Boehnen and Mary Elizabeth (Buche) Roby; m. Shari A. Bauhs, Sept. 9, 1969; children: Lesley, Michelle, Heather. AB, U. Notre Dame, 1968; JD with honors, Cornell U., 1971. Bar: Minn. 1971. Assoc. Dorsey & Whitney, Mpls., 1971—76, ptnr., 1977—89; sr. v.p. law and external rels. Supervalu Inc., Mpls., 1991—97, exec. v.p., 1997—. Vis. prof. law Cornell U. Law Sch., Ithaca, NY, 1982. Bd. dirs. ATM Med. Inc.; mem. adv. coun. on arts and letters U. Notre Dame, 1993—; mem. adv. coun. Cornell U. Law Sch., 1983—92, chmn. coun., 1986—90. Mem.: Greater Mpls. C. of C. (bd. dirs. 1988—90), Minn. Bar Assn. (chmn. bus. law sect. 1986), Spring Hill Golf Club, Minikahda Club (Mpls.). Roman Cath. Home: 71 Otis Ln Saint Paul MN 55104-5645 E-mail: david.boehnen@supervalu.com.

BOEHNER, JOHN A. congressman; b. Reading, Ohio, Nov. 17, 1949; m. Deborah Gunlack, 1973; children: Lindsay M., Tricia A. BS, Xavier U., 1977. Pres. Nucite Sales, Inc.; mem. Ohio Ho. of Reps., 1984-90, U.S. Congress from 8th Ohio dist., Washington, 1991—; chmn. edn. and workforce com., mem. agr. com., oversight com. Exec. mem. Nat. Rep. Congl. Com.; chmn. Ho. Rep. Conf. Com. Active Ohio Farm Bur. Mem. KC, Cin., Dayton, Middletown C. of C. Roman Catholic. Republican. Office: US Ho of Reps 1011 Longworth Bldg Washington DC 20515-3508 also: District Office 8200 Beckett Park Drive, #202 Hamilton OH 45011*

BOEHNER, LEONARD BRUCE, lawyer; b. Council Bluffs, Iowa, Apr. 19, 1930; s. Bruce and Flora (Kruse) B. AB, Harvard U., 1952, JD, 1955. Bar: N.Y. 1956, U.S. Dist. Ct. (so. dist.) N.Y. 1963, U.S. Ct. Appeals (2d cir.) 1963, U.S. Supreme Ct. 1964. Assoc. Dewey, Ballantine, Bushby, Palmer & Wood, N.Y.C., 1959-66; ptnr. Clare & Whitehead, N.Y.C., 1966-73, Morris & McVeigh LLP, N.Y.C. 1973—. Served to lt. USN, 1955-59. Mem. Assn. Bar City N.Y. Club: Union (N.Y.C.). Office: Morris & McVeigh 767 3rd Ave New York NY 10017-2023

BOEKHOUDT-CANNON, GLORIA LYDIA, business education educator; b. Portsmouth, Va., Jan. 18, 1939; d. William and Clara (Virgil) Boekhoudt; m. George Edward Cannon, Dec. 27, 1959. AB in Sociology/Psychology, Calif. State U., San Diego, 1977; MA in Spl. Edn./Learning Disabilities, Calif. State U., Sacramento, 1981; EdD in Orgn. and Leadership of Higher Edn. and Curriculum and Instrn., U. San Francisco, 1989. Instr. bus. edn. Midway Adult Sch. extension San Diego City Coll., San Diego, 1974-78, San Diego City Coll., 1974-78; prof. bus. edn. Sacramento City Coll., 1979—. Author: Fundamentals of Business English, 1986. Mem. Women in Community Colls., Phi Delta Kappa. Democrat. Jewish. Avocations: golf, needlepoint. Office: Sacramento City Coll Dept Bus 3835 Freeport Blvd Sacramento CA 95822-1318

BOELTER, PHILIP FLOYD, real estate company officer, mortgage company executive; b. Independence, Iowa, Mar. 25, 1943; s. Floyd Joseph and Eileen R. (Wilson) B.; m. Linda Lee Franck, June 7, 1964; children: Carrie Lynn, John Philip. BS in Indsl. Engring., Iowa State U., 1965; JD, U. Iowa, 1968. Ptnr. Dorsey & Whitney, Mpls., 1968—2002; exec. v.p., chief oper. officer Kraus-Anderson Cos., Inc., Mpls., 2002—. Trustee Gustavus Adolphus Coll., 1996—; bd. dir. Jr. Achievement of the Upper Midwest, 2003—. Mem. Mpls. Athletic Club (treas. 1992, sec. 1993, v.p. 1994, pres. 1995). Lutheran. Avocations: landscape gardening, skiing, golfing, reading, volleyball. Office: Kraus-Anderson 525 S 8th St Minneapolis MN 55404 E-mail: pboelter.phil@k-a-c.com.

BOENNING, HENRY DORR, JR., investment banker; b. Phila., Oct. 16, 1914; s. Henry Dorr and Clara Virginia (Smith) B.; m. Clare Huston Miller, Feb. 18, 1946; m. Sara Ann Perkins, Aug. 19, 1964. BS, U. Pa., 1935; postgrad., Harvard Bus. Sch., 1935-37. Partner Boenning & Co., Phila., 1946-70; v.p. Boenning & Scattergood, Inc., 1970—. Served from 2d lt. to maj. AUS, 1939-46. Mem. Phi Gamma Delta. Home: 936 Rock Creek Rd Bryn Mawr PA 19010-1923 Office: 4 Tower Bridge 200 Barr Harbor Dr Fl 3D West Conshohocken PA 19428-2977

BOER, F. PETER, chemical company executive; b. 1940; AB, Princeton U., 1961; PhD, Harvard U., 1965. With Tex Div. Lab. Dow Chem. Co., 1965-78, dir; v.p., mgr. R & D Am. Can Co., 1978-83; v.p., pres. rsch. div., corp. tech. group W.R. Grace & Co., from 1983, sr. v.p., until 1989, exec. v.p., until 1995; pres., CEO, Tiger Scientific Inc., 1995—. Bd dirs. Nova Corp., ENSCO, Inc., Rhodes Techs. Inc., Laureate Pharma, Inc.; adj. prof. Sch. Mgmt. and chem. engring. Yale U.; mem. evaluation com. for nat. medals of tech. Dept. Commerce, 1990-97. Author: Valuation of Technology, 1999, The Real Options Solution, 2002. Mem. Nat. Acad. Engring. Office: Tiger Scientific Inc 47 Country Rd S Village Of Golf FL 33436-5615 E-mail: fpboer@concentric.net.

BÖER, KARL WOLFGANG, physicist, educator; b. Berlin, Mar. 23, 1926; arrived in US, 1961, naturalized, 1972; s. Karl and Charlotte (Gruhlke) B.; m. Renate Schröder, May 18, 1967; children: Ralf Reinhard, Katarina Karlotta. Dipl. physics summa cum laude, Humboldt U., 1949, dr. rer. nat., 1952, dr. rer. nat. habil., 1955. Founder, dir. divsn. diel. breakdown German Acad. Sci., Berlin, 1955-61; docent Humboldt U., Berlin, 1955-58, prof., chair IVth physics dept., 1958-61; prof. physics U. Del., Newark, 1962-71, prof. physics and engring., 1971-92, disting. prof. physics and solar energy, 1993-94, disting. U. rsch. prof., 1995—, dir. inst. energy conversion, 1972-75; chmn. bd. SES, Inc., Newark, 1972-81, chief scientist, 1975-85. Vis. prof. NYU, 1961-62, Stanford (Calif.) U., 1965, Tech. U., Berlin, 1966, U. NSW (Australia), 1977, Max Planck Inst., Stuttgart, Germany, 1979, 86, Paul Drude Inst., Berlin, 1993; U.S. rep. WISTA, Berlin, 1995-99; cons. in field. Author: Survey of Semiconductor Physics, Vol. I, 1990, 2d edit., 2002, Vol. II, 1992, 2d edit., 2002; founder, editor Phys. Status. Solidi, 1960—; editor-in-chief Advances of Solar Energy, Vols. I-VII, IX-XII, 1980-92, 94-99; editor Energy Conversion and Mgmt., 1995—; contb r. over 300 articles to profl. jours. Recipient first Böer award of U. Del., Pres. Jimmy Carter, Univ. Del. medal of distinction, 1998. Fellow IEEE, AAAS, Am. Phys. Soc., Am. Solar Energy Soc. (pres. 1976-77, Abbott award 1981); mem. Internat. Solar Energy Soc. (Farrington Daniels award 2003), Cosmos Club (Washington), Sigma Pi Sigma, Sigma Chi. Achievements include patents for solid state devices and solar cells; first to measure Franz-Keldysh effect; discovered moving high-field domains in semiconductor, first proposed Bose-Einstein condensation of excitons; designed Solar One house (first house to convert solar into heat and electricity). Home: 239 Buck Toe Hills Rd Kennett Square PA 19348-2719 Office: U Del Material Sci Newark DE 19716 E-mail: solpax@aol.com.

BOERINGER, JAMES LESLIE, music educator; b. Pitts., Pa., Mar. 4, 1930; s. Clyde Joseph and Mildred Elizabeth Boeringer; m. Grace Nocera Boeringer, Aug. 27, 1955; children: Lisa, Margaret Jane, Daniel Wilharm. Cert. AAGO Am. Guild of Organist 1953. Univ. organist U of SD, Vermillion, 1959—62, Okla. Bapt. U, Shawnee, 1962—64, Susquehanna U, Selinsgrove, Pa., 1964—80; dir. Moravian Music Found., Winston-Salem, NC, 1980—84; music dir. Ch. of the Pilgrims, Washington, 1985—2001, Messiah Luth. Ch., Germantown, Md., 2001—. Editor (music): Complete Flute Solos, 1973; author: Morning Star, 1986; author: (editor) Organa Britannica, 1988. Recipient Philips Disting. Vis. Award, Haverford Coll., 1970. Avocations: architectural restorations, gardening, acting. Home: 1311 Noyes Dr Silver Spring MD 20910

BOERNER, SHEILA GERTRUDE, secondary education educator; b. St. Paul, Dec. 10, 1946; d. William Thomas and Ardis Gwendolyn (Rice)Fahey; m. Ronald Ralph Boerner, June 5, 1971; children: James, Kevin, Brian, Sharleen, Anne, Cyndi. BS, U. Minn., 1968; MA, U. Nebr., 1973. Cert. tchr., Nebr. English tchr. North Platte (Nebr.) Sr. H.S., 1968-74, St. Patrick's Jr.-Sr. H.S., North Platte, 1994—. Mem. Nat. Coun. Tchrs. English. Roman Catholic. Avocations: reading, writing poetry, walking. Home: 1802 Birchwood Rd North Platte NE 69101-5910 Office: St Patrick's Jr-Sr HS PO Box 970 North Platte NE 69103-0970 E-mail: sboerner@esu16.org.

BOERSEMA, DAVID BRIAN, philosopher, educator; b. Ft. Monroe, Va., Dec. 23, 1951; s. Munroe Eskel and Waneeta Diana (Wren) B. BA, Hope Coll., Holland, Mich., 1973; MA, Mich. State U., 1978, PhD, 1985. Instr. Jackson (Mich.) C.C., 1977-78, Mich. State U., East Lansing, 1979-82, Delta Coll., Midland, Mich., 1982-84; asst. prof. Pacific U., Forest Grove, Oreg., 1985-91, assoc. prof., 1991-97, prof. philosophy, 1997—, Douglas C. Strain prof. of natural philosophy, chair, 1990—, Disting. U. prof., 2003—. Contbr. articles to profl. jours. Recipient S.S. Johnson award for tchg. Pacific U., 1994, Arthur and Lois Graves award Pomona Coll., 1994; J.J. Malone Faculty fellow Nat. Coun. on U.S.-Arab Relations, 1992, Hewlett fellow Pacific U., 2000; George F. Baker scholar, 1972. Mem. AAAS, History of Sci. Soc., Philosophy of Sci. Soc., Sigma Xi. Office: Pacific Univ 2043 College Way Forest Grove OR 97116-1797 E-mail: boersema@pacificu.edu.

BOERSMA, JUNE ELAINE (JALMA BARRETT), writer, photographer; b. NYC, Apr. 27, 1926; d. Arthur Oscar and Gertrude Ann (Connolly) Schiefer; m. Kenneth Thomas McKim, June 8. 1946 (div. 1957); children: Kenneth Thomas Jr., Mark Rennie; m. Lawrence Allan Boersma, Nov. 22, 1962; children: Juliana Jaye, Dirk John. Student, Edgewood Park Jr. Coll., 1944-46. Writer non-fiction; co-owner, photographer Allan/The Animal Photographers, San Diego, 1980—; co-owner Animal Art, San Diego, NY, 1999—. Author: (series) Wildcats of North America-Bobcat, Cougar, Feral Cat, Lynx, 1998, The Dove Family Tale, A True Story, 1998, Wild Canines of North America--Coyote, Foxes, Wolf, 2000, El Lince, 2002, El Lince Rojo, 2002, El Puma, 2002, El Coyote, 2002, El Lobo, 2002, Los Zorros, 2002; co-author: One Day in the Life of a Little Couger, 2001, One Day in the Life of a Coyote Pup, 2001; contbr. articles to Ladies' Home Jour., Horse Illus., Cat Fancy, Dog Fancy, Popular Photography, Studio Photography, Petersen's Photographic, Dog World, others. Mem.: Doris Day Animal League, The Wilderness Society. Home: 3503 Argonne St San Diego CA 92117-1009

BOERSMA, LAWRENCE ALLAN (LARRY ALLAN), animal welfare administrator, photographer; b. London, Ont, Canada, Apr. 24, 1932; s. Harry Albert and Valerie Kathryn (DeCordova) B.; m. Nancy Noble Jones, Aug. 16, 1952 (div. 1962) children: Juliana Jaye, Dirk John; m. June Elaine Schiefer McKim, Nov. 22, 1962; children: Kenneth Thomas McKim, Mark Rennie McKim. BA, U. Nebr., Omaha, 1953, MS, 1955; PhD, Sussex U., 1972; postgrad., U. Oxford, Eng., 1996. Journalism tchr. Tech. HS, Omaha, 1953-55;

dir. pub. rels., chair journalism dept. Adams State Coll., Alamosa, Colo., 1955-59; advt. sales analyst, advt. salesman Better Homes and Gardens, Des Moines, N.Y.C., 1959-63; advt. account exec. This Week Mag., NYC, 1963-66; eastern sales dir., mktg. dir. Ladies' Home Jour., NYC, 1966-75; v.p. assoc. pub., v.p. pub. Saturday Evening Post and The Country Gentleman, NYC, 1975; v.p., dir. mktg. and advt. sales Photo World Mag., NYC, 1975-77; advt. mgr. LaJolla Light, Calif., 1977-80; owner, photographer Allan/The Animal Photographers, San Diego, 1980—; pres., CEO The Photographic Inst. Internat., 1982-86; dir. comty. rels. San Diego Humane Soc./Soc. for Prevention Cruelty to Animals, 1985-94; assoc. exec. dir. The Ctr. for Humane Edn. for So. Calif., 1994-98; owner Animal Art, San Diego, 1999—. Adj. asst. prof. Grad. Sch. Bus., Pace U., NYC, 1964-65; adj. instr. NY Inst. Advt., 1974-77, others; adj. prof. Sch. Bus. Mesa Coll., San Diego, 1981-84, City Coll., San Diego, 1982-86, Winona Internat. Sch. Profl. Photography, Des Plaines, Ill., 1984-87, U. Calif., San Diego, 1985; adj. prof. Coll. Bus. Adminstrn. U. LaVerne, San Diego, 1985; tchr. Winona Internat. Sch. Profl. Photography, Photog. Inst. Internat., San Diego Natural History Mus., U. Calif. San Diego, Adams State Coll. of Colo.; pres., CEO United Animal Welfare Found., San Diego, 1992-94; chmn., CEO Internat. Dolphin Project, 1995; spkr. in field. Author: Strange Events at the House on Pk. Avenue: A Jack and Jimmy Mystery, 1996; (as Larry Allan) Creative Canine Photography, 2003; co-author: One Day in the Life of a Little Cougar, 2001, One Day in the Life of a Coyote Pup, 2001; photographer: (as Larry Allan) Wildcats of North Am. book series, 1998, Wild Canines of North America book series, 2000, Show Biz Tricks for Birds, 2001, El Lince, El Lince Rojo, El Puma El Coyote, El Lobo, Los Zorros, 2002; contbr. photography and articles to mags.; photographer calendars, books, and greeting cards; photographer: (motion picture) The Truth About Cats and Dogs; exhbn.: Art Photo Expo, LA, 1999, others. Spokesperson Coalition for Pet Population Control, San Diego, 1990, 93, Com. Against Proposition C-Pound Animals for Med. Rsch., San Diego, 1990; spokesperson Spay-Neuter Action Project, 1991, steering com., 1991, bd. dir., 1992-93; evaluation subcom. County San Diego Dept. Animal Control Adv. Com.; founder, chair Feral Cat Coalition San Diego County, 1992-93, clinic vol., 2001—, bd. dir. 2003-; Calif. State Humane Officer; vol. in pub. info. San Diego/Imperial Counties chpt. ARC, 1993-2002, chpt. centennial com., 1996-97; pub. info. officers San Diego County Emergency Svc. Orgn. 1993-95; vol. photographer Calif. Wolf Ctr., 1999-2002; others; bd. dir. Escondido Humane Soc. Found., 1994-99. Recipient Gold award, Communicating Arts Group San Diego, 1986, Belding award, Advt. Club LA, 1986, 1988, Excellence award, Communication Arts Mag., 1987, Gold award, One Show, 1989, 1st Pl. Mobius Advt. award, US Festivals Assn., 1991, Gold Mercury award, Internat. Acad. Comm. Arts & Sci., 1991, Merit award, PR Club San Diego, 1994, Commendation for disting. humanitarian pub. svc., San Diego County Bd. Supr., 1994, Spl. Commendation for love and concern for all animals, San Diego City Coun., 1994, Third Pl., Outdoor Photo. of the Yr., Calif., 2002. Fellow Royal Photog. Soc. Gt. Britain, Profl. Photographers Am. (Master of Photography award 1985, Photog. Craftsman award 1986), Profl. Photographers of Calif.; mem. PRSA (chmn. So. Tier NY chpt. 1971-72), Soc. Animal Welfare Adminstr., Nat. Soc. Fund Raising Exec. (cert., bd. dir. 1988-89, treas. San Diego chpt. 1990-91, mem. nat. faculty 1992-93), Shriners (pres. Al Bahr chpt., Businessmen's Club), Masons, Sierra Club, The Wilderness Society, Doris Day Animal League. Republican. Presbyterian. Home: 3503 Argonne St San Diego CA 92117-1009

BOERSMA, P. DEE, marine biologist, educator; b. Mt. Pleasant, Mich., Nov. 1, 1946; d. Henry W. and Vivian (Anspach) B. BS, Ctrl. Mich. U., 1969; PhD, Ohio State U., 1974; DSc (hon.), Ctrl. Mich. U., 2003. Asst. prof. Inst. Environ. Studies U. Wash., Seattle, 1974-80, assoc. prof., 1980-88, prof. environ. studies, 1988-93, prof. zoology, 1988—, adj. prof. women's studies, 1993—2003, assoc. dir., 1987-93, acting dir., 1990-91, prof. biology, prof. womens studies, 2003—; mem. sci. adv. com. for outer continental shelf Environ. Studies Program, Dept. Interior, 1980-83; prin. investigator Magellanic Penguin Project Wildlife Cons. Soc., 1982—. Evans vis. fellow U. Otago, New Zealand, 1995, Pew fellow in marine conservation, 1997-2000. Assoc. editor Ecological Applications, 1998-2001; exec. editor Conservation in Practice, 2000—; contbr. articles to profl. jours. Mem. adv. U.S. del. to UN Status Women Commn., N.Y.C., 1973, UN World Status Women Commn., N.Y.C., 1973, UN World Population Conf., Romania, 1974; mem. Gov. Lowry's Task Force on Wildlife, 1993; sci. adv. EcoBios, 1985-95; bd. dirs. Zero Population Growth, 1975-82, Washington Nature Conservancy, 1995-98; adv. bd. Walt Disney World Animal Kingdom, 1993—, Island press, 1999—, Compass, 2000—, ; bd. dirs. Peregrine Fund, 1995—, Bullitt Found., 1996-2000, Islandwood, 2001—; mem. scholar diplomatic program Dept. State, 1977. Recipient Outstanding Alumni award Ctrl. Mich. U., 1978, Matrix award Women in Comm., 1983; named to Kellogg Nat. Leadership Program, 1982-85; recipient Top 100 Outsiders of Yr. award Outside Mag., 1987, Outstanding Centennial Alumni award Ctrl. Mich. U., 1993; sci. fellow The Wildlife Conservation Soc., 1982—, Aldo Leopold Leadership fellow, 2000-01. Fellow AAAS, Am Ornithol. Union (regional rep. Pacific seabird group 1981-85); mem. AAAS, Ecol. Soc. Am., Wilson Ornithol. Soc., Cooper Ornithol. Soc., Soc. Am. Naturalists, Soc. for Conservation Biology (bd. govs. 1991-94, pres-elect 1995-97, pres. 1997-99, past pres. 1999-2001), Gopher Brokers Club (pres. Seattle chpt. 1982-83). Office: U Wash Dept Biology PO Box 351800 Seattle WA 98195-1800 E-mail: boersma@u.washington.edu.

BOES, LAWRENCE WILLIAM, lawyer; b. Bklyn., Aug. 3, 1935; s. Lawrence and Lissi (Schaefer) B.; m. Joan Mary Elward, Oct. 2, 1965; children: Lawrence, Siobhan, Thomas. AB, Columbia Coll., 1961; JD, Columbia U., 1964. Bar: N.Y. 1965, U.S. Dist. Ct. (ea. dist.) N.Y. 1968, U.S. Dist. Ct. (so. dist.) N.Y. 1968, U.S. Ct. Appeals (2d cir.) 1971, U.S. Ct. Appeals (8th cir.) 1974, U.S. Supreme Ct. 1974, U.S. Ct. Appeals (9th cir.) 1982, U.S. Ct. Appeals (3d cir.) 1988. Law clk. to judge U.S. Ct. Appeals (2d cir.), 1964-65; assoc. Reavis & McGrath, N.Y.C., 1965-70, ptnr., 1970-88, Fulbright & Jaworski L.L.P., N.Y.C., 1989-00, ret. ptnr., 2001—; atty. Law Office of Lawrence W. Boes, 2001—. Revs. editor Columbia Law Rev., 1963-64. Mem. code rev. commn. Village of Westbury, N.Y., 1983—, chmn., 1991—; trustee Westbury (N.Y.) Meml. Pub. Libr., 2002—. Cpl. U.S. Army, 1958—60. Pulitzer scholar N.Y.C. Bd. Edn., 1954; nat. scholar Columbia U., 1962. Mem. ABA, N.Y. State Bar Assn. (com. on stds. of atty. conduct 1999-2002), Bar Assn. Nassau County (chair 1998-00, profl. ethics com.), Univ. Glee Club N.Y.C. (sec. 1998—). Avocations: gardening, baseball, glee club singing. Office: Law Office Lawrence W Boes 256 Asbury Ave E Westbury NY 11590-2023 Fax: 516-997-2996. E-mail: larrywboes@aol.com.

BOESCH, DIANE HARRIET, retired elementary education educator; b. Erie, Pa., July 3, 1942; d. William Jacob and Dorothy Gertrude (Call) B. BS, Edinboro (Pa.) State U., 1964; MA, Kent (Ohio) State U., 1968; postgrad., So. Ill. U., Carbondale, 1969, CUNY, 1972, Norwalk State Tech. Coll., 1979, Northeastern U., Boston, 1982, Fla. State U., 1988. Tchr. math. Iroquois Area Sch. Dist., Erie, 1964-67; grad. asst. Kent State U., 1967-68; tchr., writer Comprehensive Sch. Math. Project, Carbondale, Ill., 1968-70; tchr. math. Weston (Conn.) Pub. Schs., 1970-2000, dept. chmn. math., 1989-2000; math edn. cons., 2000—. Dir. Weston Tchr. Ctr., 1983-84; condr. workshops on math. and writing, Conn., 1970—. Contbr. articles to profl. publs. Vol. nat. elections, Erie, 1960, West Haven, Conn., 1972. Recipient Celebration of Excellence award Conn. State Dept. Edn., 1988, Presdl. award NSF, 1990. Fellow Conn. Acad. for Edn. in Math. and Sci.; mem. NEA, Nat. Coun. Tchrs. Math., Conn. Educator Talent Pool, Conn. Edn. Assn., Weston Tchr. Assn., Coun. Presdl. Awardees in Math., Pi Mu Epsilon, Kappa Delta Pi. Republican. Lutheran. Avocations: genealogy, writing, music, reading, atlanta braves baseball. E-mail: dhb703@aol.com.

BOESCH, FRANCIS THEODORE, electrical engineer, educator; b. N.Y.C., Sept. 28, 1936; s. Victor and Margaret (Wright) B. BS, Poly. Inst. N.Y., 1957, MS, 1960, PhD, 1963. Instr., then asst. prof. elec. engring. Poly. Inst. N.Y., 1957-63; mem. mil. research staff Bell Telephone Labs., 1963-68, mem. research staff, 1969-79; prof. elec. engring. and computer sci., dept. head Stevens Inst. Tech., Hoboken, N.J., 1979-88, dean of faculty, 1988-93, prof. elec. engring., 1993—. McKay prof. elec. engring. and computer sci. U. Calif., Berkeley, 1968-69. Author: Large-Scale Networks, 1976; editor-in-chief: Networks, 1970-81; editor: Graph Theory, 1978-81; contbr. articles to profl. jours. Vice pres. Fair Haven (N.J.) Little League, 1974; scoutmaster Fair Haven council Boy Scouts Am., 1973-78, dist. commnr. Monmouth council, 1978-80. Fellow IEEE, N.Y. Acad. Scis.; mem. Assn. Computing Machinery, Am. Math. Soc., Sigma Xi, Eta Kappa Nu. Home: 16-02 Everett Ter Fair Lawn NJ 07410-2410 Office: Stevens Inst Tech Castle Point Sta Hoboken NJ 07030 E-mail: fboesch@stevens-tech.edu.

BOESE, GIL KARYLE, cultural organization executive; b. Chgo., June 24, 1937; s. Carl H. and Winifred A. Boese; m. Lillian R. Boese; children: Ann Carroll, Peter Austin, Sara Elisabeth. BA, Carthage (Ill.) Coll., 1959; MS, No. Ill. U., 1965; PhD; NIMH trainee 1970, Johns Hopkins U., 1973. Instr. biology Thornton Community Coll., Harvey, Ill., 1965-67; asst. prof. biology Elmhurst (Ill.) Coll., 1967-69; dep. dir. Chgo. Zool. Park, Brookfield, Ill., 1971-80; dir. Milw. County Zool. Gardens, Milw., 1980-89; pres. Zool. Soc. Milw. County, Milw., 1989—, Found. for Wildlife Conservation, 1993—. Tech. cons. Belize Zoo and Tropical Edn. Ctr. ; founder Birds without Borders Aves Sin Frontera internat. program; dir. Miller Brewery Friends of the Field. Bd. dirs. Dian Fossey Gorilla Found., chmn. 1998-99, internat. coordinating com., pres., 1997—; bd. dirs. Lewa Conservancy Kenya; improvement assn. bd. dirs. Pewaukee Lake, Wis. Fellow Royal Geog. Soc., Am. Assn. Zool. Parks and Aquariums (bd. dirs.); mem. Hemmingway Soc., Adventurers Club. Office: Zool Soc Milw County 10005 W Bluemound Rd Milwaukee WI 53226-4346 E-mail: boese@zoosociety.org.

BOESE, H. LAMAR, surgeon; b. Ardmore, Okla., June 28, 1924; MD, Tulane U., 1947. Diplomate Am. Bd. Surgery. Intern Toledo (Ohio) Hosp., 1947-48; resident in surgery Broward Gen. Hosp., Ft. Lauderdale, Fla., 1948-49; fellow in surgery Ochsner Found. Hosp., New Orleans, 1953-57; pvt. practice; active staff St. Francis Cabrini Hosp., Alexandria, La.; clin. assoc. prof. surgery Tulane U., New Orleans. Fellow ACS, Am. Soc. Colon & Rectal Surgeons, Ochsner Surg. Soc., SSC.

BOESEL, MILTON CHARLES, JR., lawyer, business executive; b. Toledo, July 12, 1928; s. Milton Charles and Florence (Fitzgerald) B.; m. Lucy Laughlin Mather, Mar. 25, 1961; children: Elizabeth Boesel Sagges, Charles Mather, Andrew Fitzgerald. BA, Yale U., 1950; LLB, Harvard U., 1953. Bar: Ohio 1953, Mich. 1953. Lt. USNR, 1953—56. Mem.: Toledo Country; Leland Country (Mich.). Sawgrass Country (Fla.). Episcopalian.

BOESHE, BARBARA LOUISE, real estate executive; b. Phila. d. Raymond Gerard and Gilda (Nicotera) Lepone; children: Diedrich R., Alison Dru, Tyson Phillip. BS, Temple U., 1963. Lic. real estate broker, N.J. Sales person Sofroney Real Estate, Sea Isle City, N.J., 1978-88; office mgr. Hoey Real Estate, Sea Isle City, 1988-93; pres. Farina & Boeshe Real Estate Co., Sea Isle City, 1994—. Ptnr., developer BB&D, Sea Isle City, 1986-90. Vice chmn. bd. adjustment, Sea Isle City, 1982-86, active Mayor's Adv. Com., 1985-86, Parking Authority, 1984-85; committeewoman Rep. County Com., Sea Isle City, 1982-85, 89-90, alt. Rep. city leader, 1991-92, 1992—; v.p. Cape May County Planning Bd., 1992-94, chairperson, 1994—. Recipient, 10 Million Dollar Gold award, Greater Wildwood Cape May County Bd. Realtors, 1998-2001, 15 Million Dollar award, 2002. Mem. Sea Isle City C. of C. (bd. dirs., sec. 1986-89, treas. 1989-90, v.p. 1991-92, pres. 1992-95), Greater Wildwood/Cape May County Bd. Realtors (million dollar award 1982-88, 92-95, 2-1/2 million dollar award 1989-91, 2-1/2 million dollar award 1996, 97). Roman Catholic.

BOETTCHER, ARMIN SCHLICK, lawyer, banker; b. East Bernard, Tex., Apr. 12, 1941; s. Clem C. and Frances Helene (Schlick) B.; m. Virginia Nan Barkley, Apr. 13, 1963; children: Lynn Frances, Laura Anne. BBA, U. Tex., Austin, 1963, JD, 1967. Various positions personal trust dept. Republic Bank Houston, 1967-75, sr. v.p., trust officer, head trust dept., 1975-82; exec. v.p., dir. Union State Bank, East Bernard, 1988-98; exec. v.p. Prosperity Bank, East Bernard, 1998—. Bd. dirs. Whispering Oaks Civic Club, 1980-85, pres., 1981. Mem. Houston Bus. and Estate Planning Coun., U. Tex. Ex-Students Assn. (life), Meml. Forest Club (dir. 1981-83), Clubs of Lakeway, Sigma Chi. Methodist. Office: Prosperity Bank Bldg PO Box 40 East Bernard TX 77435-0040

BOETTCHER, ROBERT WALTER, civil engineer; b. Gooding, Idaho, Apr. 3, 1931; s. Walter Alfred and Katherine Benedicta (Hansen) B.; m. Marguerite Patricia Warner, Oct. 1, 1960; children: Eric, Edwin, Vanessa. BSCE, Wash. State U., Pullman, 1953. Civil engr. U.S. Bur. of Reclamation, Bismarck, N.D., 1955-56; materials engr. Joseph K. Knoerle & Assocs., Chgo., 1956-59; project engr. Knoerle, Bender, Stone & Assocs., Chgo., 1959-62, project mgr., 1962-73, assoc., 1973-76; sr. assoc. Envirodyne Engrs. Inc., Chgo., 1976—; chief civil engr. O'Hare Assocs., Chgo., 1981-92, MESA Joint Venture, 1992-93; sr. assoc. AOR Joint Venture, Chgo., 1993, Consoer Townsend Envirodyne Engrs., Inc., Chgo., 1994—. With U.S. Army, 1953-55. Mem. ASCE, NSPE, Ill. Soc. Profl. Engrs. Home: 1047 Dell Rd Northbrook IL 60062-3911

BOETTGER, ROY DENNIS, barrister, solicitor; b. Nelson, B.C., Can., Sept. 5, 1948; s. Robert Harold and Jean Velora (Lewis) B.; m. Lynn Irene Carroll, June 2, 1973; children: Kristin Jennie, Jill Rebecca. BA, U. Calgary, 1970; LLB, U. Alta., 1973. Bar: Alta. Student-at-law Atkinson McMahon, Calgary, Alta., 1973-74, assoc., 1974-77, ptnr., 1977—. Bio-ethics com. Rockyview Hosp., 1987-97. Dir., chmn. The Calgary Found. Fellow Am. Coll. Trust and Estate Counsel; mem. Soc. Trust and Estate Practitioners, Calgary Bar Assn., Can. Bar Assn. (coun. mem. Alta. br. nat. exec. wills. and trust sect. Ottawa br. 1979-85), Law Soc. Alta., Estate Planning Coun. Calgary (exec. mem. 1983-89), Rotary. Office: Field LLP 1900 350 7th Ave SW Calgary AB Canada T2P 3N9 E-mail: rboettger@fieldlaw.com.

BOETTNER, DAISIE DAWSON, military officer, mechanical engineering educator; b. St. Louis, Mo., Jan. 16, 1959; d. Raymond Turner and Isabel Crichlow Wheeler; m. Brian Lee Boettner, Sept. 10, 1982 (div. Dec. 6, 2001); children: Sarah Leigh, Elizabeth Ann. BS, U.S. Mil. Acad., West Point, N.Y., 1981; MSE in Mech. Engring., U. of Mich., 1991; PhD, The Ohio State U., 2001. With U.S. Army, 1981—, advanced through grades to lt. col.; comdr. 89th Ordnance Co., Bremerhaven, Germany, 1983—85; logistics officer 24th Inf. Divsn. (Mech.), Ft. Stewart, Ga., 1986—89; instr., asst. prof. U.S. Mil. Acad., West Point, NY, 1991—94, assoc. prof., 2001—; support ops. officer 524th Corps. Support Bn., Schofield Barracks, Hawaii, 1995—96; chief, ammunition plans U.S. Army Pacific, Ft. Shafter, Hawaii, 1996—98. Dir., aero-thermo group U.S. Mil. Acad., West Point, NY, 2001—03, dir., mech. engring. program, 2003—. Author: (jour. articles) ASME Jour. for Energy Resources Tech., (chpt. in edited volume) Artificial Intelligence in Engring. Design Vol. I: Design Representation and Models of Routine Design. Decorated Army Commendation medal U.S. Army, Army Achievement medal, Meritorious Svc. medal. Mem.: Soc. of Women Engrs., Am. Soc. of Mech. Engrs., Delta Kappa Gamma, Phi Kappa Phi. Avocations: running, sewing, cooking. Office: Dept of Civil & Mech Engring US Mi Acad West Point NY 10996

BOEWE, CHARLES ERNST, historian, educator; b. West Salem, Ill., Mar. 11, 1924; s. Fred E. and Susie E. (Wolters) Boewe; m. Mary Scurrah, June 17, 1950; children: Abigail Burnett, Emily Oliver. AB, Syracuse U., 1947, MA, 1949; PhD, U. Wis., 1955. Instr. Syracuse (N.Y.) U., Syracuse, 1949—51, Lehigh U., Bethlehem, Pa., 1955—56; asst. prof. U. Pa., Phila., 1958—64; dir. US Edntl. Found., Karachi, Pakistan, 1964—67, US Commn. for Cultural Exch., Tehran, Iran, 1967—70, Am. Studies Rsch. Ctr., Hyderabad, India, 1970—71, US Ednl. Found., New Delhi, 1971—73, Islamabad, Pakistan, 1973—80; adj. rsch. prof. Transylvania U., Lexington, Ky., 1980—85; rsch. assoc. Filson Club History Soc., Louisville, 1985—92; editor Papers of C.S. Rafinesque, Fearrington village, NC, 1992—. Adv. com. Am. Studies Rsch. Ctr., Hyderabad, India, 1980—89; treas. Am. Inst. Pakistan Studies, 1981—85; cons. in field. Contbr. articles to profl. jours.; author: Prairie Albion: An English Settlement in Pioneer Illinois, 1962, 2d edit., 1999, Profiles of Rafinesque, 2003; editor: The World or Instability, 1956, Fitzpatrick's Rafinesque, 1982, John D. Clifford's Indian Antiquities, 2000. Rsch. assoc. Am. Philos. Soc., Phila., 1958—64; exec. sec. Am. Studies Assn., Phila., 1962—64; hist. manuscripts com. Acad. Natural Scis., Phila., 1963—64. With U.S. Army, 1943—46. Fellow, U. Pa., 1956—58; grantee, Am. Philos. Soc., Sicily, 1959, US Info. Agy., Egypt, 1980, Nat. Hist. Publ. and Records Commn., 1980—88. Mem.: Assn. for Documentary Editing. Achievements include discovery of letters and manuscripts of C.S. Rafinesque. Home: 320 Fearrington Post Fearrington Village NC 27312-8560

BOFF, KENNETH RICHARD, engineering research psychologist; b. N.Y.C., Aug. 17, 1947; s. Victor and Ann (Yunko) B.; m. Judith Marion Schoer, Aug. 2, 1969 (dec. Apr. 1997); children: Cory Asher, Kelissa Melissa; m. Jacque Aelanda Coppler, Aug. 20, 1999. BA, CUNY, 1969, MA, 1972; MPhil, Columbia U., 1975, PhD, 1978. Research scientist Human Resources Lab., Wright Patterson AFB, Ohio, 1977-80; sr. scientist Armstrong Aerospace Med. Rsch. Lab. (now Airforce Rsch. Lab.), Wright Patterson AFB, Ohio, 1980—, dir. design tech., 1980-91, dir. human engring. div., 1991-97; chief scientist, human effectiveness directorate Air Force Rsch. Lab., 1997—; Edenfield Exec.-in-Residence Sch. Ind. & Sys. Engrg. Georgia Inst. Tech., 2002—03. Project custodian Internat. Air. Standard Coordination Com., Washington, 1984; chmn. com. Tri-Service Human Factors Tech. Adv. Group, Washington, 1984—; chair human factors com. NATO Adv. Group Aerospace R&D, Paris, 1992—; chair human sys. tech. panel Dept. Def., 1994-97; U.S. coord. NATO Rsch. and Tech. Orgn. Human Factors, 1997—. Editor: Handbook of Perception and Human Performance, 1986, Human Engineering Data Compendium, 1988, System Design: Behavioral Perspectives on designers, Tools and Organizations, 1987; contbr. articles to profl. jours. Travel grantee Rank Prize Found., Cambridge, Eng., 1984; named Air Force Scientist of the Quarter, 1989; recipient Patent award for rap-com display tech., 1989, Human Factors Soc. award for best publ., 1989. Mem. IEEE, Human Factors Soc., Am. Psychol. Assn. (div. 21 engring. psychology). Avocations: computers, photography. Home: 6510 Shadow Wynd Cir Dayton OH 45459 Office: Armstrong Lab Human Engring Divsn Wright Patterson Afb OH 45433

BOFFA, LISA SAUNDERS See **BAUGH, LISA**

BOGAARD, WILLIAM JOSEPH, mayor, lawyer, educator; b. Sioux City, Iowa, Jan. 18, 1938; s. Joseph and Irene Marie (Hensing) B.; m. Claire Marie Whalen, Jan. 28, 1961; children: Michele, Jeannine, Joseph, Matthew. BS, Loyola Marymount U., L.A., 1959; JD with honors, U. Mich., 1965. Bar: Calif. 1966, U.S. Dist. Ct. (ctrl. dist.) Calif. 1966. Ptnr. Agnew, Miller & Carlson, L.A., 1970-82; exec. v.p., gen. counsel 1st Interstate Bancorp, L.A., 1982-96; vis. prof. securities regulation and banking Mich. Law Sch., Ann Arbor, 1996-97; lectr. securities regulation and corps. U. So. Calif. Law Sch., L.A., 1997—; mayor Pasadena, Calif., 1999—. Mem. Calif. Commn. on Jud. Nominees Evaluation, 1997-99. Mem. city coun., mayor City of Pasadena, Calif. 1978-86. Capt. USAF, 1959-62. Mem. Calif. State Bar, Los Angeles County Bar Assn. (Corp. Counsel of Yr. award 1988). Avocations: jogging, french and spanish languages, hiking. Office: 100 N Garfield Ave Pasadena CA 91101-1726 E-mail: bbogaard@ci.pasadena.ca.us.

BOGAN, ELIZABETH CHAPIN, economist, educator; b. Morristown, N.J., Aug. 22, 1944; d. Daryl Muscott and Tirzah (Walker) Chapin; m. Thomas Rockwood Bogan, June 5, 1965; children: Nathaniel Rockwood, Andrew Allerton. AB, Wellesley Coll., 1966; MA, U. N.H., 1967; PhD, Columbia U., 1971. Mem. faculty Fairleigh Dickinson U., Madison, N.J., 1971-92, prof. econs., 1982-92, chmn. merit scholarship com., 1981-82; reviewer univ. press Farleigh Dickinson U., Madison, N.J.; mem. faculty Princeton (N.J.) U., sr. lectr. in econs., 1992—. Vis. prof. Princeton U., 1991. Author articles and macroecons. text Recipient Outstanding Tchr. award Fairleigh Dickinson U., 1979, 86, 87, Richard Quandt award for tchg. econs. Princeton U., 1997; NSF fellow, Pres'. fellow, Earhart fellow Columbia U., 1968-71. Mem. AAUP, Am. Econ. Assn., Ea. Econ. Assn., Atlantic Econ. Soc. Clubs: Wellesley, Beacon Hill. Congregationalist. Home: 41 Windemere Ter Short Hills NJ 07078-2254 Office: Princeton U 109 Fisher Pl Princeton NJ 08540

BOGARD, CAROLE CHRISTINE, lyric soprano; b. Cin. d. Harold and Helen Christina (Whittlesey) Geistweit; m. Charles Paine Fisher, Dec. 30, 1966; children: Christine, Pamela. Student, San Francisco State U. Debuts include: Despina in Cosi fan Tutte (Mozart), San Francisco, 1965, Poppea in Coronation of Poppea (Monteverdi), Netherlands Opera, 1971; other appearances include, Boston Opera, N.E.T., orchs. Boston, Madrid, Minn., Phila., Pitts., San Francisco, summer festivals, Mostly Mozart, N.Y., Tanglewood, Carmel, Aston Magna, Gt. Barrington, Mass., appeared in concerts throughout Europe and with Smithsonian Chamber Players, 1976-; recorded numerous albums including 1st rec. of songs of John Duke for his 80th birthday, 1979, recital of Groupe des Six; premiered songs of Dominic Argento in, Holland, 1978, songs of Richard Cumming (in collaboration with Donald Gramm); regular participant rec. and scholarly projects, Smithsonian Instn.; judge regional auditions, Boston; tchr., with emphasis on technique as taught in last Century; recs. have been re-issued on CDs during the 1990s including Baroque Cantatas and Arias, Mozart C minor Mass, Mozart Coronation Mass., 2 CD collection American Songs, 2000; female lead 3 CD Handel opera Tamerlano, 2002. Mem. Sigma Alpha Iota Home: 161 Belknap Rd Framingham MA 01701-3886 *In my career, I've stuck to old-fashioned principles - trying to use my talent according to the standards which place singing technique on a level with the most taxing instruments. I sing for sincere acclaim and demand for my talent and my music, avoiding repertoire which would abuse my voice. I have refrained from pushing myself through "arranged" magazine articles about my hobbies and insipid appearances on TV talk shows. I have done my best rather than my most - by choice.*

BOGARD, LAWRENCE JOSEPH, lawyer; b. Champaign, Ill., July 12, 1952; s. Morris Ray and Norma Jean (Shingleton) B.; m. Rebecca Lynn Jackson, May 6, 1978; children: Caitlyn Elizabeth, Peter Jackson. AB, Vassar Coll., Poughkeepsie, N.Y., 1974; JD, Georgetown U., 1977. Bar: D.C. 1977. Atty. U.S. Customs Svc., Washington, 1977-80; assoc. Cladouhos & Brashares, Washington, 1980-84; atty. U.S. Dept. Commerce, Washington, 1984; ptnr. Rose, Schmidt, Hasley & Disalle, Washington, 1984-88, McKenna & Cuneo, Washington, 1988-98, Neville Peterson LLP, Washington, 1998—. Faculty Practicing Law Inst., 1984, 92; mem. U.S.-Can. Free Trade Agreement Ch. 19 Dispute Resolution Roster, 1991-94, panelist, 1992, panel chair 1993; mem. NAFTA Dispute Resolution Roster, 1994—, panel chair, 2001. Author: (with others) Commerce Speaks on Antidumping, 1984, Treatment of Non-Market Economies Under U.S. Antidumping and Countervailing Duty Law: A Petitioner's Perspective, 1992, (with others) Transnational Contracts, 2000—; supervisory editor Customs Law and Administration, 1998—. Mem. ABA, D.C. Bar Assn., Ct. Internat. Trade Bar Assn. Democrat. Presbyterian. Office: Neville Peterson LLP 1900 M St NW Ste 850 Washington DC 20036 E-mail: lbogard@npwdc.com.

BOGARDUS, CARL ROBERT, JR., radiologist, educator; b. Hyden, Ky., June 26, 1933; s. Carl Robert and Jeannette Wanda (Eversole) B.; m. Norma Gail Shields, June 24, 1956; children— Carl Robert III, Cynthia Gail. BA, Hanover Coll., 1955; MD, U. Louisville, 1959. Diplomate: Am. Bd. Radiology, Am. Bd. Nuclear Medicine. Intern Penrose Cancer Hosp., Colorado Springs, Colo., 1959-60, resident, 1960-63; mem. staff U. Okla. Med. Center, 1963-95, prof. emeritus dept. radiation therapy; dir. Okla. Cancer Treatment Ctr., Midwest City. Cons. Okla. hosps.; pres. Cancer Care Network, Inc.; pres. Bogardus Med. Sys. Inc. Author: Practical Applied Physics of Radiology and Nuclear Medicine, 1969; contbg. author: Benign and Malignant Tumors of the Bladder, 1971, Radiation Biology for the Physician, 1973; Contbr. profl. jours. Fellow Am. Coll. Radiology (bd. chancellors, sec.-treas. 1987-91, pres. 1991-92); mem. Okla. Soc. Nuclear Medicine (charter pres. 1966), Am. Soc. Therapeutic Radiology (nat. sec. 1968-70, treas. 1987-88, pres. 1989-90), S.W. Regions Soc. Nuclear Medicine, Okla. Radiol. Soc. (treas. 1970, pres. 1974-75, counselor to Am. Coll. Radiology 1976-85), Okla. County Radiol. Soc. (pres. 1974) Home: 3224 Lamp Post Ln Oklahoma City OK 73120-5621 Office: 230 N Midwest Blvd Midwest City OK 73110 E-mail: drcrb@cancercare.net.

BOGART, CAROL LYNN, columnist, journalist, writer; b. Lakewood, Ohio, Mar. 9, 1949; d. Lloyd William and Evelyn Mary (Overmyer) Bogart; 1 child, Michael Lloyd. BLS, Bowling Green State U., 1973; postgrad., Nat. Theater Conservatory, Denver, 1992. Reporter, anchor Sta. WNEP-TV, Scranton, Pa., 1975-76; reporter Sta. WXIA-TV, Atlanta, 1976-79; reporter, fill-in morning anchor Sta. WLS-TV, Chgo., 1979-82; anchor, reporter Sta. KMGH-TV, Denver, 1982-89; reporter, field prodr., writer Stas. WOIO-WUAB-TV, Cleve., 1995-96; radio host Sta. WTTF, Tiffin, Ohio, 1996; lifestyle editor, columnist, photographer Advertiser-Tribune, Tiffin, 1998—; talk show host TV 21, Fremont, Ohio, 1996-97; N.W. Ohio stringer AP, 1996—98; corr. Toledo Blade, 1998—; owner freelance writing, video prodn., voiceover, speech writing copywriting/editing and media cons. co. Bogart, Inc., 1989—. Guest spkr.

various schs. and univs., Denver, 1982—83, Cleve., 1994—96, Ohio, 1997—. Vol. pet therapy, grief counseling, adv. children with AD(H)D. Nominee Emmy award; recipient 3d Pl. medal, Internat. Film and TV Festival N.Y., 1st pl. in feature writing, AP, 1999, 2d pl. in enterprise reporting, 2001. Mem.: SAG, AFTRA, Ohio Farm Bur., Ohio Arts Coun. Avocations: gardening, investing, photography. E-mail: bogart@bright.net.

BOGART, KEITH CHARLES, retired neurologist; b. Lorain, Ohio, Apr. 12, 1936; s. Lloyd William and Evelyn (Overmyer) B.; m. Peggy Kumler, June 9, 1957 (div.); m. B. Diane Seigel, June 8, 1967; children: Keith Charles Jr., Catherine Michelle; m. Alice Craib, July 21, 1976; 1 child, Matthew William. BA, Ohio State U., 1958, MD, 1961. Diplomate Am. Bd. Psychiatry and Neurology, Am. Bd. Clin. Neurophysiology, Am. Bd. Neurorehabilitation. Asst. prof. neurology U. Wis., Madison, 1968-69, Creighton U., Omaha, Nebr., 1975-78; chmn. neurology Gunderson Clinic, Lacrosse, Wis., 1969-75; clin. neurologist Mansfield (Ohio) Neurology, Inc., 1978-99; med. dir. rehab. unit Mansfield Gen. Hosp., 1988-91; med. dir. SCCI Hosp., Mansfield, 1998; ret. Cons. neurology VA Hosp., Omaha, 1977-78. Bd. dirs. Boy Scouts Am., Mansfield, 1986, Hilton Head Alzheimer's Respite and Resource, 1999-2003; mem. curriculum com. Univ. S.C. Creative Retirement Ctr., 2001-02. Served to lt. comdr. USPHS, 1963-65. Fellow, Am. EEG Soc. (mem. lab. accreditation bd. 1984—87), Am. Acad. Neurology; mem.: AMA (Physicians Recognition awards), Richland County Med. Soc. (sec.-treas. 1986—87, pres. 1988), Wis. Neurol. Soc. (pres. 1973), Wis. Med. Soc. (chmn. neurology sect. 1975), Nebr. Epilepsy League (pres. 1976—78), Ctrl. Assn. EEGers (pres. 1977—78), Soc. Low Country Magicians (founder 2001, pres. 2002—03), Inner Magic Circle, Internat. Brotherhood of Magicians (v.p. ter. 1986—91, hon. mem. Ring 2, Ring 349, Presdl. citation 1988, 2002), Knights of Magic (pres. 1986—87, Magician of Yr. 1984, 1985, 1986, S.C. Magician of Yr. 2003), Psychic Entertainers Assn., Rotary (Hilton Head bd. dirs. 2001—03). Avocations: professional magician, travel, golf, reading. Home: 3 Sprunt Pond Rd Hilton Head Island SC 29928-5608 E-mail: bogie@adelphia.net.

BOGART, LEO, sociologist; b. Sept. 23, 1921; s. Jacob and Rachel (Blum) B.; m. Agnes Cohen, Aug. 9, 1948. children: Michele, Gregory. BA, Bklyn. Coll., 1941; MA, U. Chgo., 1948, PhD in Sociology, 1950. Instr. English Ill. Inst. Tech., Chgo., 1946-48; pub. opinion rsch. analyst Standard Oil Co., N.J., 1948-51; lectr. in Sociology NYU, 1949-50; dir. account rsch. svc. McCann-Erickson, Inc., N.Y.C., 1952-58; lectr. in sociology Columbia U., N.Y.C., 1953-57; dir. mktg. rsch. Revlon, Inc., N.Y.C., 1958-60; exec. v.p., gen. mgr. Newspaper Advt. Bur., N.Y.C., 1960 89; bus. cons., columnist Presstime mag.; adj. prof. Mktg. NYU, 1990-92. Bd. dirs. Innovation Internat. Media Cons. Group. Author: The Age of Television, 1956, Strategy in Advertising, 1967, Social Research and the Desegregation of the U.S. Army, 1969, Silent Politics, 1971, Premises for Propaganda, 1976, Press and Public, 1981, Polls and the Awareness of Public Opinion, 1985, Project Clear, 1991, Preserving the Press, 1991, Commercial Culture, 1995, Cool Words, Cold War, 1995, Finding Out, 2003, How I Earned the Ruptured Duck, 2004; contbr. numerous articles to profl. jours. Past mem. N.Y. adv. bd. City Innovation; past dir. Ctr. for Applied Linguistics, Nat. Safety Coun., Obor Found., Advt. Rsch. Found., Am. Advt. Fedn., Am. Mktg. Assn.; past pres. Soc. for Consumer Psychology. Served with U.S. Army, 1942-46. Decorated 4 Battle Stars; sr. fellow Gannett Ctr. for Media Studies, Columbia U., 1989-90; Fulbright fellow Inst. Nat. d'Etudes Demographiques, Paris, 1951-52; recipient awards from Am. Mktg. Assn., Am. Soc. Newspaper Editors, Internat. Circulation Mgrs. Assn., Internat. Newspaper Promotion Assn., Newspaper Rsch. Coun. Fellow APA, Am. Psychol. Soc., Soc. for Consumer Psychology; mem. Am. Sociol. Assn., Am. Assn. for Pub. Opinion Rsch. (past pres., award), World Assn. for Pub. Opinion Rsch. (past pres.), Market Rsch. Coun. (past pres., award), Radio and Television Rsch. Coun. (past pres.), Overseas Press Club Am., City Club N.Y., Dutch Treat Club. Address: 150 W 56th St Apt 4707 New York NY 10019-3838 E-mail: leobogart@att.net.

BOGART, LOUISE BERRY, education educator; b. N.Y.C., July 15, 1942; d. Herbert George and Flora Louise (Porcelli) Berry; m. Burton Stanley Bogart, Aug. 29, 1965; children: Samuel Isaac, Jonathan Douglas. BA, Kans. State U., 1964; MEd, Coll. Notre Dame, Belmont, Calif., 1973; PhD, U. Hawaii-Manoa, 2000. Cert. Montessori tchr.; cert. pvt. tchr., Hawaii; cert. tchr., prin., Ohio; cert. neurolinguistic profl., neurolinguistic master. Field advisor, sr. program dir., day camp dir. Kaw Valley Girl Scout Coun., Topeka, 1964-65; field advisor Seal of Ohio Girl Scout Coun., Columbus, 1966-67; elem. tchr. St. Joseph Montessori Sch., Columbus, 1970-78; pre-kindergarten tchr. Maryknoll Grade Sch., Honolulu, 1978-80; head tchr. elem. classes Montessori Cmty. Sch., Honolulu, 1980-83; asst. prof. edn. Chaminade U. of Honolulu, 1982-92, assoc. prof. edn., 1993—, acting chair dept. edn., 1988-90, dept. chair, 1994-96, Montessori Program dir., 1986-92. Active Girl Scouts U.S., Honolulu, 1978—. Eisenhower grantee U.S. Dept. Edn., 1989-90, 90-91, 91-92, 93-94, 95-96, others. Mem. ASCD, Am. Montessori Soc. (vice chair 1987-91; mem. tchr. edn. com.), Montessori Assn. Hawaii (v.p. 1980-81), Nat. Assn. Edn. of Young children, Hawaii Coun. Tchrs. Math., Internat. Inst. Peace Educators, World Coun. for Curriculum and Instrn., Am. Assn. of Univ. Women, Am. Edn. Rsch. Assn., Pi Lambda Theta. Home: 1035A Alewa Dr Honolulu HI 96817-1506 Office: Chaminade U Honolulu 3140 Waialae Ave Honolulu HI 96816-1510 E-mail: lbogart@chaminade.edu.

BOGART, WILLIAM HARRY, lawyer; b. Sayre, Pa., Mar. 5, 1931; s. Harry M. and Luella C. Bogart; m. Karin Rudolph, Dec. 12, 1962 (div. Dec. 1987); children: Barbara, Silke. AB, Duke U., 1953; AAA, The Hague Acad. Internat. Law, 1962; JD, Syracuse U., 1963. Bar: N.Y. 1964. Mem. Ali, Gerber, Parr & Bogart, Syracuse, N.Y., 1966-67, Bogart & Andrews, Syracuse, 1967-77, Bogart & Assocs., P.C., Syracuse, 1977—. Cons. in field to various govts, fin. instns., ednl. instns.; lectr. in field; active with Acad. Scis. and Russian Govt. drawing comml., ins. and banking laws. Contbr. articles to profl. jours.; drafted civil rights laws for Czechoslovak constn. Mem. missionary com. Presbyn. Ch., 1974-77. With USMC, 1951-52. Mem. ABA, Am. Arbitration Assn., N.Y. State Bar Assn., N.Y. State Trial Lawyers Assn., Onandaga County Bar Assn., Assn. Attenders and Alumni, Lawyers Intergroups, World Ct., Assn. Atty. and Advocates, UN Assn., Witte Soc., Univ. Club, Army and Navy Club, The Hague Club, Masons (32d degree). Democrat. Home: 110 E Lake Rd - 9 Day Ln Skaneateles NY 13152-9110 Office: 1600 State Tower Bldg 109 S Warren St Syracuse NY 13202-1798 E-mail: bogart@dreamscape.com.

BOGATY, LEWIS, writer, publisher, lawyer, educator; b. Bklyn., May 30, 1946; s. Harry and Helene Bogaty; m. Lissa Runyon Bogaty, Dec. 4, 1992; 1 child, Michael R. BA with distinction, George Washington U., 1968; MA, Ohio State U., 1974, PhD, 1976; JD, Columbia U., 1979. Bar: N.Y. (so. and ea. dists) 1980. Instr., lectr. Ohio State U., Columbus, 1974—76; atty. Kaye Scholer Fierman Hays & Handler, NY, 1980—82; sr. exec. editor Matthew Bender Co., NY, 1984—94; pub. Wislew Pubs., Ardsley, NY, 1995—. Adj. instr. N.Y. Law Sch., NY, 1987—93; editor Americans with Disability Act, Workplace Report, 1998—. Author: (essays) Columbia Law Rev., 1978, Va. Quarterly Rev., 2002; pub. (short stories) Descant, 1983, Sou' Wester, 1984, Miss. Rev., 1985, 1990, Kans. Quarterly, 1992 (Kans. Arts Commn. award), Sou' Wester, 1992, Another Chicago Mag., 1992, Confrontation, 1992, Wind Mag., 1993, Black River Rev., 1994, Callipe, 1994, Va. Quarterly Rev., 1995, Fan Mag., 1997; mem. editl bd.: Columbia Law Rev., 1978. Recipient Bronx Coun. Arts Fiction award, Bronx, N.Y., 1993. Mem.: Phi Beta Kappa. Office: Wislew Pubs PMB 254 923 Saw Mill River Rd Ardsley NY 10502 E-mail: LBogaty@Wislew.com.

BOGDAN, CAROLYN LOUETTA, financial specialist; b. Wilkes-Barre, Pa., Apr. 15, 1941; d. Walter Cecil and Ethna Louetta (Kendig) Carpenter; m. James Thomas Bogdan, May 5, 1961; 1 child, Thomas James. Grad. high sch., Kingston, Pa. Head bookkeeper Forty Ft. (Pa.) State Bank, 1959-63, U.S. Nat. Bank, Long Beach, Calif., 1963-65; office mgr. United Parts Exch., Long Beach, 1976-81; contract adminstr. Johnson Controls, Inc., Rancho Dominguez, Calif., 1981-88, credit coord., 1989-98; co-owner, acct. Bogdan Elec. R & D, Lakewood, Calif., 1981—. Mem. Radio Amateur Civil Emergency Svc., L.A. County Sheriff Dept., 1974—, records keeper, 1988—93, radio comm. officer, 1994—2002. Mem. Tournament of Roses Radio Amateurs (pin chmn. 1975—), Calif. State Sheriffs Assn. (assoc.), Calif. State Office Emergency Svcs. Republican. Avocations: crochet, gardening, electronics, advanced amateur radio lic. (HAM). Home: 3713 Capetown St Lakewood CA 90712-1437

BOGDAN, JAMES THOMAS, secondary education educator, electronics researcher and developer; b. Kingston, Pa., Aug. 14, 1938; s. Fabian and Edna A. (Spray) B.; m. Carolyn Louetta Carpenter, May 5, 1961; 1 child, Thomas James. BS in Edn., Wilkes U., Wilkes-Barre, Pa., 1960. Cert. chemistry and physics tchr., Calif. Tchr. Forty Fort (Pa.) Sch. Dist., 1960-63; tchr., chmn. sci. dept. L.A. Unified Sch. Dist., 1963-96; owner, mgr. Bogdan Electronic Rsch. & Devel., Lakewood, Calif., 1978—. Cons. Lunar Electronics, San Diego, 1978—83, T.E. Systems, L.A., 1988—89. Author, pub. The VHF Reporter newsletter, 1967-76. Tng. officer Los Angeles County Disaster Com., 1968—91, UHF and microwave sys. staff officer, 1991—94, dep. chief comm. officer, 1994—98, chief comm. officer, 1998—2001; pin chmn. Tournament of Roses Comm. Group, Pasadena, Calif., 1985—98, tournament liaison, 1998—; mem. Calif. State Office Emergency Svcs., 2002—. Republican. Achievements include development and manufacturing of specialized electronic test equipment for automotive and marine magneto ignition systems, of electronic bomb disposal equipment, of portable military satellite communication antenna, design and manufacture of aircraft/commercial direction finding antenna. Office: PO Box 62 Lakewood CA 90714-0062

BOGDAN, WOJCIECH, military officer; b. Oswiecim, Poland, Oct. 13, 1977; s. Jan Jozef and Bogumila Dorota Bogdan; m. Marta Malgorzata Dabrowska, June 28, 1980. BS in Computer Sci., Hawaii Pacific U., 2000. Cert. airframe and powerplant technician FAA, 1997, primary marksmanship instr. USMC, 2002, pistol/rifle range coach USMC, 2002. FAA airframe and powerplant technician Tower Airlines Inc., Jamaica, NY, 1996—97. Aircraft restoration cons. Hawaii Mus. Naval Aviation, Barbers Point Naval Air Sta., Hawaii, 1999—. Aircraft restoration cons./vol. Hawaii Mus. Naval Aviation, Barbers Point Naval Air Sta., 1999. Sgt. USMC, 1997—. Decorated Navy/Marine Corps Achievement medal 1st MARINE AIRCRAFT WING, Cert. of Commendation 1st Marine Aircraft Wing. Mem.: Pegasus Soc. (hon. Gold Wings award for profl. achievement in aero. studies 1997, Silver Wings award for profl. achievement in aero. studies 1996). Achievements include research in armored vehicle identification. Avocations: computer sciences, aircraft restoration, flying, competitive marksmanship. Home: 2551-D Manning St Kailua HI 96734 Office: Mag-24 Mals-24 400 Divsn Marine Corps Base Kaneohe Bay HI 96863 Personal E-mail: bogdanw001@hawaii.rr.com. E-mail: bogdanw@mag24.1maw.usmc.mil.

BOGDANOVICH, ALEXANDER, manufacturing executive; b. Riga, Latvia, June 28, 1950; arrived in U.S., 1991; s. Eugene and Valentina Bogdanovich; m. Elena Goryunova, Sept. 21, 1989 (div. May 28, 1991) MS, Latvian State U., 1972; candidate of sci., Latvian Acad. Sci., 1975, D of Engring., 1998; DSc, Kazan State U., 1987. Sr. rsch. fellow Inst. Polymer Mechanics, Riga, 1978—86, dep. dir., 1986—89, acting dir., 1988; rsch. dep. dir. Engring. and Tech. Ctr., Riga, 1990—91; vis. rsch. prof. N.C. State U., Raleigh, 1991—95; sr. rsch. scientist Ad Tech Systems Rsch., Inc., Dayton, Ohio, 1995—98; v.p. R&D 3Tex, Inc., Cary, NC, 1998—. Presenter in field. Author: Nonlinear Dynamic Problems of Composite Cylindrical Shells, 1993, Mechanics of Textile and Laminated Composites, 1996; contbr. articles to profl. jours.; mem. editl. bd. Composites Part B jour., 1992—. Mechanics of Composite Materials jour., 1988—, patentee in field. Recipient Friedrich Tsander award, Latvian Acad. Scis., 1987. Mem.: ASME, AIAA (sr.). Avocations: tennis, track and field, classical music, Russian literature. Home: 605 Knightsborough Way Apex NC 27502 Office: 3Tex Inc 109 MacKenan Dr Cary NC 27511 Business E-Mail: bogdanovicha@3tex.com.

BOGDANOVICH, PETER, film director, writer, producer, actor; b. Kingston, N.Y., July 30, 1939; s. Borislav and Herma (Robinson) B.; m. Polly Platt, 1962 (div. 1970); children: Antonia, Alexandra; m. L.B. Straten, 1988. Owner The Holly Moon Co., Inc., L.A., 1992—. Actor Am. Shakespeare Festival, Stratford, Conn., 1956, N.Y. Shakespeare Festival, 1958, (TV episode) Northern Exposure, 1993, Cybill, 1995, The Sopranos, 1999, (films) Mr. Jealousy, 1997, Highball, 1997, Fifty-Four, 1998, Coming Soon, 1999, The Shoe Store, 1999, Claire Makes It Big, 1999, Rated X, 2000, The Independent, 2000, (TV miniseries) Bella Mafia, 1997; dir., producer off-Broadway plays: The Big Knife, 1959, Camino Real, Ten Little Indians, Rocket to the Moon, 1961, Once in a Lifetime, 1964; film feature-writer for Esquire, N.Y. Times, Village Voice, Cahiers du Cinema, L.A. Times, N.Y. Mag., Vogue, Variety, others, 1961—; films: The Wild Angels (2d unit dir., co-writer, actor), 1966; Targets (dir., co-writer, producer, actor), 1968, The Last Picture Show (dir., co-writer, N.Y. Film Critics award, Brit. Acad. award 1971), 1971, Directed by John Ford (dir., writer, interviewer), 1971, What's Up, Doc? (dir., co-writer, producer, Writer's Guild Am. award 1972), 1972, Paper Moon (dir., producer, Silver Shell, Mar del Plata, Spain), 1973, Daisy Miller (dir., producer, Best Dir. Brussels Festival 1974), 1974, At Long Last Love (dir., writer, producer), 1975, Nickelodeon (dir., co-writer), 1976, Saint Jack (dir., co-writer, actor, Pasinetti award, Critics prize Venice Festival 1979), 1979, They All Laughed (dir., writer), 1981, Mask (dir.), 1985, Illegally Yours (dir., producer), 1988, Texasville (dir., producer, writer), 1990, Noises Off (dir., exec. producer), 1992, The Thing Called Love (dir.), 1993; dir. (TV films) Blessed Assurance, 1997, Rescuers: Stories of Courage: Two Women, 1997, Naked City: A Killer Christmas, 1998, A Saintly Switch, 1999; author: The Cinema of Orson Welles, 1961, The Cinema of Howard Hawks, 1962, The Cinema of Alfred Hitchcock, 1963, John Ford, 1968, Fritz Lang in America, 1969, Allen Dwan: The Last Pioneer, 1971, Pieces of Time: Peter Bogdanovich on the Movies, 1973, enlarged, 1985, The Killing of the Unicorn: Dorothy Stratten: 1960-80, 1984, (with Orson Welles) This Is Orson Welles, 1992; editor: A Year and a Day Engagement Calendar, 1991—; co-dir., writer, interviewer: The Great Professional: Howard Hawks, 1967; weekly network commentator CBS This Morning, 1987-89; dir. (TV series episode) Fallen Angels, 1995, Painted Word, 1995. Mem. Dirs. Guild of Am., Writers Guild of Am., Acad. Motion Picture Arts and Scis. Address: care Martin Baum and Rick Nicita CAA 9830 Wilshire Blvd Beverly Hills CA 90212-1804

BOGDANOWICZ, LORETTA MAE, artist, educator; b. West Palm Beach, Fla., Aug. 11, 1940; d. James Paul and Bessie Margaret (Smith) Cone; m. Lawrence Robert Bogdanowicz, July 18, 1959; children: Laura June Ford, Michael David, Denise Ann Pharris. AA, Ocean County Coll., 1982; BFA, U. Ariz., 1996. Cert. art tchr., Ariz. Art instr. Ariz. Theatre Co., Tucson, 1997-98, Catalina Foothills Cmty. Sch., Tucson, 1997-98, Tucson Mus. Art Edn., 1997—; incorporator Floorcloths and More, Inc., 2001; art instr. Pima CC, Vail, Ariz., 2002—. Exhibited in group shows. Vis. artist Devon Gables Health Care Ctr., Tucson, 1997-2001; instr. neighborhood classes; artist in residence Acacia Elem. Sch., Vail. Recipient Liquitex Paint Exch. award, 1996. Mem.: Tucson/Pima Arts Coun., Western States Art Fedn., Contemporary Art Soc. Tucson, Tucson Mus. Art, Nat. Assn. Artists Orgn., Phi Kappa Phi. Avocations: hiking, photography, gardening, reading, travel. E-mail: lbogdanowicz@msn.com.

BOGDON, GLENDON JOSEPH, retired orthodontist; b. Green Bay, Wis., Sept. 23, 1935; s. Joseph Frank and Anne Marie (Jacklin) B.; m. Susanne Ellen Daley, Aug. 8, 1959; 1 child, Amy Sue. BS, St. Norbert Coll., DePere, Wis., 1957; DDS, Marquette U., 1971, MS in Clin. Dentistry, 1973. Officer IRS, Chgo., 1958; social worker Cath. Welfare Bur., Milw., 1958 59; tchr. secondary sch. Door County Schs., Brussels, Wis., 1959-67; practice dentistry specializing in orthodontics Milw., 1973—2000; ret. Co-facilitator Alzheimer's support group Clement Manor Health Ctr. Writer fitness column Cath. Herald, Wis. Dental Assn. Bulletin; contbr. articles to profl. jours.; patentee in field. Vol. Clement Manor Health Care Ctr.; Vol. dentist Greater Milw. Dental Assn.; mem. family adv. coun. Clement Manor Health Care Ctr. Served with U.S. Army, 1957—58, served with U.S. Army, 1961—62. Mem. Greater Milw. Dental Assn. (Continuing Edn. award 1971-73), Wis. Dental Assn. (Continuing Edn. award 1971-74, 79-81, ADA (Continuing Edn. award 1976-78), Royal Soc. Health, Wis. Soc. Orthodontists, Midwestern Soc. Orthodontists, Am. Assn. Orthodontists, World Fedn. Orthodontists, Spitfire Soc., Am. Running and Fitness Assn., Orthodontic Ctrs. of Am. Democrat. Roman Catholic. Avocations: bread baking, jogging.

BOGDONOFF, MAURICE LAMBERT, physician; b. Chgo., May 11, 1926; s. Harry A. and Mary Ivy (Grogan) B.; m. Diana Edith Rauschkolb, June 29, 1956; children: Vivian, Gregory, Audrey. BS, Tufts U., 1948; MD, Yale U., 1952. Intern U. Ill. Rsch. and Edn. Hosp., Chgo., 1952-53; resident in internal medicine Boston City Hosp., 1953-54; resident in radiology Columbia-Presbyn. Med. Ctr., N.Y., 1955-57; asst. prof. to assoc. prof. radiology to prof. U. Ill., Chgo., 1958-69; attending radiologist Rush-Presbyn.-St. Luke's Med. Ctr., Chgo., pres. med. staff, 1975-77; prof. radiology and medicine Rush Med. Coll., Chgo., 1970-78, 1969-88, prof. emeritus, 1988—. Cons. Argonne (Ill.) Nat. Lab., 1963-88; cons., health dir. Canal Zone Panama, 1973-80; vis. lectr. nuclear power engring. Maine Maritime Acad., 1989. Contbr. articles to profl. jours. Pres. Wheaton (Ill.) Dist. 36 Sch. Bd.,1964-67; bd. visitors Coll. of DuPage Radio and TV Sys., Glen Ellyn, Ill., 1987-94. With USN, 1944-46. Fellow Am. Coll. Radiology, Inst. Medicine, also others; mem. Chgo. Lit. Club. Republican. Avocations: boating, astronomy, classics. Home: 203 W Willow Ave Wheaton IL 60187-5238

BOGDONOFF, MORTON DAVID, physician, educator; b. N.Y.C., Dec. 8, 1925; s. M. Myron and Minnie (Alpher) B.; m. Jano Segal, July 1, 1951 (div. 1971); children— Reid, Ladd, Jesse, Drue; m. Mary Patton Welt, May 9, 1975. MD, Cornell U., 1948. Diplomate: Nat. Bd. Med. Examiners, Am. Bd. Internal Medicine. Intern, jr. asst. resident, sr. asst. resident dept. medicine N.Y. Hosp., N.Y.C., 1948-50; sr. asst. surgeon USPHS, Nat. Heart Inst., Johns Hopkins U., Balt., 1950-52; sr. asst. resident dept. medicine Duke Hosp., 1952-53, Eli Lilly Research fellow div. endocrinology and metabolism, 1953-54, chief resident dept. medicine, 1954-55; attending physician, chief metabolic div. Durham VA Hosp., 1955-56, cons., 1959-62; asso. prof. clin. medicine Med. Sch. U. Miami, 1956-57; assoc. dept. medicine Duke U., 1955-56, asst. prof. medicine, 1957-59, asso. prof., 1959-62, prof. med., 1962-69, asst. dean grad. med. edn., 1967-69; prof., chmn. dept. internal medicine U. Ill., Chgo., 1970-75; prof. medicine to prof. emeritus Med. Coll. Cornell U., 1975-95, 95—. Cons. Ft. Bragg Hosp., 1959-62, VA Hosps., Fayetteville, Durham, West-Side, Chgo.; mem. study sect. health svcs. rsch. NIH, 1966-70, Commonwealth Fund, 1985-94, Cath. Med. Ctr., 1990-94, Nat. Med. Fellowships, 1987-2002. Editor: Clin. Rsch., 1959—64; chief editor Archives of Internal Medicine, 1967—77, New Developments in Medicine, 1986—90; sci. editor: Drug Therapy, 1978—94; contbr. articles to profl. jours. Fellow Center Advanced Study Behavioral Scis., Stanford, 1977-78 Fellow A.C.P.; mem. Am. Fedn. Clin. Research (past pres.), Am., So., Central socs. clin. investigation, Assn. Am. Physicians, AAAS (chmn. Sect. N 1981-82), Endocrine Soc., Psychosomatic Soc. (past nat. councillor), Soc. Exptl. Biology and Medicine, AMA, Harvey Soc., Alpha Omega Alpha. Office: NY Hosp/Cornell Med Ctr 525 E 68th St New York NY 10021-4885

BOGE, ARNOLD JOSEPH, construction executive, contractor; b. North Buena Vista, Iowa, Oct. 19, 1949; s. Norbert William and Loretta Marie (Dean) B.; m. Susan Diane Shultz, May 10, 1969 (div. 1978); children: Diane, Matthew, Laura; m. Carol Marie Urbain, June 28, 1980; children: Renae, Kayln. AS, North Iowa Area C.C., Mason City, 1981. Crane operator White Farm Equipment Co., Charles City, Iowa, 1972-73; constrn. foreman Merrill Masonry Inc., Brevard, NC, 1973-77; owner Boge Constrn., Ionia, Iowa, 1977—; supr. Chickasaw County, New Hampton, Iowa, 1987—. Bd. dirs. Golden Grain Energy LLC. Dir. 1st Jud. Dist. Corrections, Waterloo, Iowa, 1987—; mem. Chickasaw County Rep. Ctrl. Com., 1986-. With U.S. Army, 1969—71. Recipient State of Iowa Gov.'s Vol. award, 1989. Mem. VFW (comdr. 1989-91), Iowa County Suprs. Assn. (pres. dist. 2, 2003), Lions. Republican. Roman Catholic. Avocations: hunting, fishing, travel. Home: 2160 Amherst Pl Ionia IA 50645-9439 Office: Chickasaw County PO Box 311 New Hampton IA 50659-0311 E-mail: ajb@rconnect.com.

BOGEN, DAVID SKILLEN, law educator; b. L.A., Aug. 24, 1941; s. Emil and Jane (Skillen) Bogen; m. Patricia Yolande Ciricillo; children: Robert, Joshua, Jocelyn. BA, Harvard U., 1962, LLB, 1965; LLM, NYU, 1967. Bar: Mass. 1965, N.Y. 1967. Law clk. Mass. Supreme Jud. Ct., Boston, 1965-66; assoc. Debevoise, Plimpton, N.Y.C., 1967-69; asst. prof. Md. Law Sch., Balt., 1969-71, assoc. prof., 1971-74, prof. law, 1974—, assoc. dean, 1992-94, 97-99. Author: Bulwark of Liberty, 1984, Privileges and Immunities, 2003. Home: 4742 Rams Horn Row Ellicott City MD 21042-5979 Office: U Md Law Sch 500 W Baltimore St Baltimore MD 21201-1701

BOGEN, MARK ALAN, accountant; b. Bklyn., May 23, 1956; s. Jacob and Saundra (Lapidus) B.; m. Maria Angela Dipippo, Nov. 25, 1995; children: Angela, Sarah, Laura. BS in Mgmt., SUNY, Buffalo, 1977. CPA. Staff acct. SUNY Downstate, Bklyn., 1977-81, Brookdale Med. Ctr., Bklyn., 1981; sr. mgr. Pannell Kerr Forster, N.Y.C., 1981-89, DeLoitte & Touche, N.Y.C., 1989-91; v.p., CFO Preferred Health Network, Bklyn., 1991-96; prin. Nat. Capital Group, Lake Success, NY, 1996—97; pres. Bogen Cons. Group, Mineola, N.Y., 1997—. Mem. AICPA, Healthcare Financial Mgmt. Assn. (Follmer award 1994, Reeves award 2001), Am. Assn. Bakruptcy Inst., N.Y. State Soc. CPAs, Empire State Assn. PAs, Assn. Cert. Frand Auditors (assoc.) Republican. Jewish. Avocations: golf, music. Home: 2 Elkland Rd Melville NY 11747 Office: 33 Willis Ave Ste 100 Mineola NY 11501 E-mail: Bogengroup@aol.com.

BOGENSCHUTZ, J. DAVID, lawyer; b. Covington, Ky., May 15, 1944; s. John Francis and Virginia Margaret (Dugan) B.; m. Mary H. McCleary, Oct. 24, 1981; children: Kathleen, Emily. BA, Miami U., Oxford, Ohio, 1966; JD, U. Cin., 1969. Bar: Ohio 1969, U.S. Dist. Ct. (so. dist.) Ohio 1970, U.S. Ct. Appeals (6th cir.) 1971, Fla. 1971, U.S. Dist. Ct. (so. dist.) Fla. 1972, U.S. Ct. Appeals (5th cir.) 1980, U.S. Dist. Ct. (mid. dist.) Fla. 1981, U.S. Ct. Appeals (4th and 11th cirs.) 1981, U.S. Dist. Ct. (ea. dist.) Wis. 1989, U.S. Ct. Appeals (3d cir.) 1999. Instr. Criminal Justice Inst. Nova U., 1977; instr. Broward County Criminal Justice Inst., 1972; asst. solicitor County of Broward, 1971, chief asst. state's atty., 1974-77; ptnr. Bogenschutz & Dutko, P.A., Ft. Lauderdale, Fla. Mem. Gov.'s Com. on Criminal Justice Standards and Goals, 1975-76; mem. bench bar liaison com. U.S. Dist. Ct. (so. dist.) Fla., 1985—. Mem. ATLA, NACDL, Broward County Bar Assn. (criminal law sect. chmn. 1980-81, exec. com. 1981-86, sec., treas. 1985-86), Ohio Bar Assn., Fla. Bar Assn. (criminal law sect., grievance com. 17th jud. cir. 1982-84), Fed. Bar Assn., Greene County Bar Assn., Fla. Pros. Atty.'s Assn., Nat. Dist. Atty.'s Assn., Nat. Assn. Criminal Def. Attys. Democrat. Roman Catholic. Office: Bogenschutz & Dutko PA 600 S Andrews Ave Ste 500 Fort Lauderdale FL 33301-2851

BOGER, DALE L. chemistry educator; b. Hutchinson, Kans., Aug. 22, 1953; s. Lester W. and Elizabeth (Korkish) B. BS in Chemistry, U. Kans., 1975; PhD in Chemistry, Harvard U., 1980. Asst. prof. U. Kans., Lawrence, 1979-83, assoc. prof., 1983-85, Purdue U., West Lafayette, Ind., 1985-87, prof., 1987-91; Richard and Alice Cramer chair chemistry Scripps Rsch. Inst., La Jolla, Calif., 1991—. Recipient Career Devel. award NIH, 1983-88, Janssen award for creativity in organic synthesis, 2002; NSF fellow, 1975-78, Alfred P. Sloan fellow, 1985-89; Searle scholar, 1981-84. Mem. Am. Chem. Soc. (A.C. Cope scholar 1989, Aldrich creative work in organic synthesis 1999), Internat. Soc. Het. Chemistry (Katritky award 1997, Janssen Prize, 2002). Home: 2819 Via Posada La Jolla CA 92037-2205 Office: Scripps Rsch Inst 10550 N Torrey Pines Rd La Jolla CA 92037-1000

BOGER, DAN CALVIN, statistical and economic consultant, educator; b. Salisbury, N.C., July 9, 1946; s. Brady Cashwell and Gertrude Virginia (Hamilton) B.; m. Gail Lorraine Zivna, June 23, 1973; children: Gretchen Zivna, Gregory Zivna. BS in Mgmt. Sci., U. Rochester, 1968; MS in Mgmt. Sci., Naval Postgrad. Sch., Monterey, Calif., 1969; MA in Stats., U. Calif., Berkeley, 1977, PhD in Econs., 1979. Cert. cost analyst, profl. estimator. Rsch. asst. U. Calif., Berkeley, 1975-79; asst. prof. econs. Naval Postgrad. Sch., Monterey, 1979-85, assoc. prof., 1985-92, prof., 1992—, chmn. dept. command, control and comm., 1995—2001, chmn. dept. computer sci., 1997—2001, chmn. dept. info. warfare, 1997—2001, dean divsn. computer and info. scis. and ops., 1997—2001, founding chmn. dept. info. scis., 2002—. Bd. dirs. Evan-Moor Corp.; cons. econs. and statis. legal matters CSX Corp, others, 1977—. Assoc. editor The Logistics and Transp. Rev., 1981-85, Jour. Cost Analysis, 1989-92; mem. editl. rev. bd. Jour. Transp. Rsch. Forum, 1987-91; contbr. articles to profl. jours. Lt. USN, 1968-75. Flood fellow Dept. Econs. U. Calif., Berkeley, 1975-76; dissertation rsch. grantee A.P. Sloan Found., 1978-79. Mem.: IEEE, Inst. for Ops. Rsch. and Mgmt. Sci. (sec.-treas. mil. aplications soc. 1987—91), Econometric Soc., Am. Statis. Assn., Am. Econ. Assn., Internat. Coun. on Sys. Engring., Sigma Xi. Home: 27 Cramden Dr Monterey CA 93940-4145 Office: Naval Postgrad Sch Code IS Monterey CA 93943

BOGER, GAIL LORRAINE ZIVNA, reading specialist; b. Portland, Oreg., Sept. 15, 1946; d. Stephen Edward and Harriet Lucille (Laws) Zivna; m. Dan Calvin Boger, June 23, 1973; children: Gretchen, Gregory. BS in Edn., Oreg. State U., 1968; MA in Edn., Stanford U., 1973; MA in Reading, U. LaVerne, 1982. Cert. reading and lang. arts specialist, Calif. Elem. tchr. Monterey (Calif.) Peninsula Unified Sch. Dist., 1968-72, 73-75, lang. arts tchr., 1979-81; elem. tchr. San Ramon (Calif.) Unified Sch. Dist., 1976-79; Miller-Unruh reading specialist Monterey (Calif.) Peninsula Unified Sch. Dist., 1983—. Mem.: Reading is Fundamental Program, Monterey County Reading Assn., Calif. Reading Assn., Internat. Reading Assn., Delta Kappa Gamma (rec. sec. 1992—94, 2002—). Avocations: ballet, music, piano, reading, golf. Home: 27 Cramden Dr Monterey CA 93940-4145 E-mail: bogers@mbay.net.

BOGER, GENA CECILE, school psychologist; b. Highland, Ill., Mar. 27, 1953; d. Alvis Gene and Mary Thelma (Willeford) Zeller; m. Thomas Gene Boger, Aug. 11, 1973; children: Janna Lynn Pitchford, Emily Michelle Boger. BA, So. Ill. U., Edwardsville, 1975, MS, 1977. Cert. sch. svc. pers., Ill. Sch. psychologist Belleville (Ill.) Area Spl. Edn. Dist., 1978-91, East Alton (Ill.) Elem. Schs., 1991—. Village trustee Village of South Roxana, Ill., 1975-78; co-leader Brownie troop Girl Scouts U.S., South Roxana, 1986-87; coach Youth Baseball League, Roxana, Ill., 1995-97. Recipient Those Who Excel award Ill. State Bd. Edn., 1996. Mem. NEA, Ill. Edn. Assn., Nat. Assn. Sch. Psychologists, Ill. Sch. Psychologists Assn. (Sch. Psychology Practitioner of Yr. 1989), So. Ill. Psychol. Assn. Free Methodist. Avocations: volunteer school booster clubs, sports, music, reading, gardening. Home: 4816 Oak Ridge Dr East Alton IL 62024-2808 Office: East Alton Elem Sch Dist 13 210 E St Louis Ave East Alton IL 62024 E-mail: gboger@madison.k12.il.us.

BOGER, KENNETH SNEAD, lawyer; b. Concord, N.C., Sept. 8, 1946; s. Charles E. Jr. and Mary (Snead) B.; m. Robin Zaverl, Oct. 10, 1969; children: Adam S., Hallie S., Fiona G. AB, Duke U., 1968; MBA, U. Chgo., 1973; JD, Boston Coll., 1976. Bar: Mass. 1977. Assoc. Warner & Stackpole, Boston, 1976-82, ptnr., 1983-99, Kirkpatrick & Lockhart LLP, Boston, 1999—2001; sr. v.p., gen. counsel Vertex Pharms. Inc., Cambridge, Mass., 2001—. 1st lt. inf. U.S. Army, 1968-71, Vietnam. Home: 200 Church St Rear Newton MA 02458-1300 Office: Vertex Pharms Inc 130 Waverly St Cambridge MA 02139-4242 E-mail: ken_boger@vrtx.com.

BOGER, RICHARD EDWIN, JR., minister; b. Atlanta, May 13, 1952; s. Richard Edwin and Marie Yoder (Leonard) B.; m. Jill Roberta Howard, Apr. 26, 1980; 1 child, John Michael Howard. AB, Lenoir-Rhyne Coll., 1973, Hamma Sch. Theology, 1975; MDiv, Pacific Luth. Theol. Sem., 1978. Ordained to ministry Evang. Luth. Ch. Am., 1980. Vesper intern Vesper Soc., San Leandro, Calif., 1975-76; coord. vols. Care Network, San Leandro, 1978; intern Christ Our Shepherd, Peachtree City, Ga., 1979-80; pastor Luth. Ch. of Our Savior, Jacksonville, N.C., 1980-90, Nazareth Luth. Ch., Rural Hall, N.C., 1990-98; pastor, webmaster St. Thomas Net Ministry, www.stnm.org, Winston-Salem, N.C., 1999—; pastor St. Michael Luth. Ch., Highpoint, N.C., 2001—. Counselor Neighborhood Ch. Clinic, Springfield, Ohio, 1974; pastoral counselor Eden Hayward (Calif.) Pastoral Counseling Svc., 1975-76; mem. Jacksonville Ministerial Assn., 1980-81, Onslow County Ministerial Fellowship, 1984; mem. worship com., music com. N.C. Synod Luth. Ch. in Am., 1982, 84-86, 94, 97-99; assoc. N.C. Chaplains Assn., 1984; pres. Forsyth Luth. Coun., 1992. Pub. Nazareth Luth. Ch. Home Page, 1995. Bd. dirs. ARC, Jacksonville, 1981-89. Mem. Soc. of the Holy Trinity (founding mem.), Alban Inst., Forsyth Luth. Area Pastors (coord. 1996-98, 2000-2002), Forsyth Luth. Coun., Rural Hall-Stanleyville Mins. Assn. (pres. 1995-97), United Ministry Rural Hall (bd. dirs. 1994-98, sec. 1997). Office: St Michael Lutheran Church 100 Skeet Club Rd High Point NC 27265 E-mail: RichardBoger@stnm.org.

BOGER, WILLIAM HANNA, lawyer; b. Columbus, Ohio, Oct. 18, 1956; s. Frederic J. and Patricia B. Boger; m. Dorothy S. Boger, Apr. 8, 1990; children: William Hanna IV, Wolfgang Frederic. BA, Ohio State U., 1979; JD, U. Toledo, 1982; LLM in Internat. Law, Georgetown U., 1984. Bar: D.C. 1999. Legis. asst. U.S. Ho. of Reps., 1984, assoc. staff ho. appropriations com., 1985-89; assoc. Wilkinson, Barker, Knauer & Quinn, 1989-91, ptnr., 1992-99, Bingham Dana LLP, 1999—2001, Perkins, Smith, Cohen & Crowe, 2002—. Contbr. articles to profl. jours. Phila. Action Team profl. vol. 2000 Rep. Nat. Conv.; precinct chmn. Waynewood Precinct, Mount Vernon Dist., Fairfax County Rep. Party, 2000; mem. Fairfax REp. Com. Mem. ABA. Republican. Methodist. Avocations: music, sporting clays, golf. Office: Perkins Smith Cohen & Crowe Ste 810 1401 New York Ave NW Washington DC 20036 Fax: 202-393-5512. E-mail: wboger@psccdc.com.

BOGER, WILLIAM PIERCE, III, ophthalmologist; b. Phila., Oct. 16, 1945; s. William Pierce Jr. and Mae Elizabeth (Shelton) B.; m. Barbara Crawford, Aug. 10, 1968; children: Matthew, Andrew, John. AB in Biophysics magna cum laude honors, Amherst Coll., 1967; MD, Harvard U., 1971. Diplomate Am. Bd. Ophthalmology. Intern in medicine and pediat. U. Va. Hosp., Charlottesville, 1971-72; resident in ophthalmology Mass. Eye and Ear Infirmary, Boston, 1972-75; clin. fellow in ophthalmology Harvard U., Boston, 1975—76; fellow in pediatric ophthalmology and strabismus Children's Hosp. Med. Ctr., Boston, 1976, assoc. in ophthalmology, mem. full-time staff, 1976-80; pvt. practice specializing in pediatric ophthalmology, Concord, Mass., 1980—. Mem. staff Boston Children's Hosp. Med. Ctr., Boston, Emerson Hosp., Concord, Mass., Winchester Hosp., Mass., Mt. Auburn Hosp., Cambridge, Mass.; instr. Harvard U., 1976—; lectr. in field. Contbr. articles to med. jours., chpts. to book. Capt. M.C., USAR, 1971-81. Pathology grantee Mass. Gen. Hosp., Boston, 1969. Mem. AAAS, Am. Acad. Ophthalmology, Mass. Soc. Eye Physicians and Surgeons, New Eng. Ophthalmol. Soc., Am. Assn. for Pediatric Ophthalmology and Strabismus, Mass. Med. Soc., N.Y. Acad. Scis., Rsch. To Prevent Blindness, Phi Beta Kappa, Sigma Xi. Home: 357 Nashawtuc Rd Concord MA 01742-1616 Office: Lexington Eye Assocs John Cuming Bldg 3d Fl Concord MA 01742

BOGG, RICHARD ALLAN, sociologist, educator; b. Grosse Pointe, Mich., May 31, 1934; s. Sydney Elmer and Dorothy Marie B. BBA, U. Mich., 1956, PhD, 1971; postgrad., U. Exeter (Eng.), 1957-58; MHA, Washington U., St. Louis, 1960. Asst. adminstr. Port Huron (Mich.) Hosp., 1960-62; rsch. assoc. U. Mich. Sch. Pub. Health, 1965-69; asst. prof. dept. cmty. medicine Faculty Medicine U. Alta., Edmonton, Can., 1969-72; asst. prof. dept. sociology Ball State U., Muncie, Ind., 1972-77, assoc. prof., 1977—; assoc. editor Deviant Behavior, 1992—. Contbr. papers to profl. confs., encys. and jours. USPHS trainee, 1962-65; vol. Planned Parenthood of Delaware County. Mich. Ho. of Reps. spl. rsch. grantee, 1968. Mem. Am. Sociol. Assn., ACLU. Office: Dept Sociology Ball State U Muncie IN 47306-0001 E-mail: RBogg@gw.bsu.edu.

BOGGAN, JEFFREY SCOTT, college administrator; b. Asheville, N.C., May 30, 1960; s. Robert Edmond Jr. and Patricia Ann (Kirkpatrick) B. BA in Govt., Wofford Coll., Spartanburg, S.C., 1982; MA in Higher Edn. Adminstrn., Appalachian State U., Boone, N.C., 2000. Acct. rep. Quaker Oats Co., Greensboro, N.C., 1985-86; adminstrv. officer City of Charlotte, N.C., 1986-88; dir. alumni and parents programs Wofford Coll., 1988-95; dir. devel. and alumni programs Montgomery Acad., 1995-96; dir. advancement, COO Pi Kappa Phi Found., 1996-97; agt. coll. fund divsn. Universal Insurance Co. Inc., Charlotte, 1997-98; sr. dir. devel. Lees-McRae Coll., Banner Elk, N.C., 1998-2001; dir. devel., found. dir. North Ga. Coll. & State U., Dahlonega, 2001—. Author quar. alumni article Wofford Today, 1988-91. Dir. Spartanburg Youth Theater, 1990; bus. cons. Jr. Achievement, Spartanburg, 1991; campaign exec. United Way of the Piedmont, Spartanburg, 1991, loaned exec., 1993; class mem. Leadership Spartanburg, 1991-92, grad., 1992, mem. bd. regents; mem. Spartanburg 2000 Task Force Literacy and Lifetime Learning; v.p. Spartanburg AWARE, Inc., 1993-94, pres., 1994-95, Founding Bd. Mem., United Way of Lumpkin County, 2003-; 1st lt. US Army, 1982-85. Decorated Army Commendation medal (2). Mem. Assn. Fund Raising Profls., Nat. Coun. on Planned Giving, Ga. Planned Giving Coun., Coun. for Advancement and Support of Edn., S.C. Assn. Alumni Dirs. (sec. treas. 1993-94, pres. 1994-95), Assn. U.S. Army (life), Am. Legion, Rotary (com. chmn. 1991-92, chmn. Cmty. Literacy Project, Gov.'s award 1991), Pi Kappa Phi (Alumnus of Yr. 1989, 90, 97, chpt. advisor 1989-91). Republican. Methodist. Avocations: music, sports, reading, community service. Home: 20G Hawkins St Dahlonega GA 30533 Office: Alumni Ctr 70 Alumni Dr Dahlonega GA 30533 E-mail: jboggan@ngcsu.edu.

BOGGIA, EUGENE STEPHEN, lawyer; b. Glen Cove, N.Y., Nov. 12, 1946; s. Eugene and Elena Ebbie (Albertelli) B.; m. Suzanne McDonough, Sept. 18, 1982; children: Thomas, Catherine. AB, Georgetown U., 1968; JD, NYU, 1973. Asst. dist. atty. Office of the Dist. Atty., Phila., 1973-88; ptnr. Taylor and Taylor, Phila., 1988-92; claims adminstr., asst. gen. counsel Sch. Dist. of Phila., 1992—. Settlement master, judge pro tem Ct. of Common Pleas, Phila., 1992—. With USN, 1969-71; Vietnam. Mem. Serra Internat. (dist. 28 gov. 1985-86, Phila. chpt. pres. 1980-81, 98-2000, Serran of the Yr. 1989). Democrat. Roman Catholic. Avocations: history, playing piano, golf. Office: Sch Dist of Phila 2130 Arch St Philadelphia PA 19103-1315 E-mail: eboggia@phila.k12.pa.us.

BOGGIANO, MICHAEL HUMBERTO, geneticist, small business owner; b. Chiclayo, Peru, Feb. 14, 1967; s. Humberto and Michelle Boggiano; m. Danielle Dee Ann Crawford, June 5, 1993; children: Bonnie Michelle, Michael Tyler. MS in Molecular Genetics, U. Tex., El Paso, 1994. Cert. Am. Coll. Sports Medicine, 2003; molecular lab. specialist Lab. Testing Assn., 1998, Am. Coun. on Exercise, 1990, Internat. Dance and Exercise Assn., 1992. Genetecist Applied Genetics and The U. Tex. at El Paso, Austin/El Paso, 1992—97; faculty N.Mex State U., Las Cruces, 1994—97; pres., owner Powerhouse Gym Austin, Austin, 1999—. Author: (nutrition planning book) The PlaniT System. Sponsor United Youth Sports, Austin, 1999—2003. Achievements include research in cloning and sequencing of cDNA clones for casein kinase type I and II. Office: Powrhouse Gym Austin LLC Ste 201 907 West 5th St Austin TX 78703

BOGGIO, MIRIAM ALTAGRACIA, lawyer; b. NYC, July 28, 1952; d. Marco Antonio and Estella (Tejeda) B.; children: Andrew P. Boggio-Dandry, Edward M. Boggio-Dandry, Gregory A. Boggio-Dandry. BA in Polit. Sci. with honors, CUNY, 1973; JD, St. Johns U., 1976; AA in Fashion Design, Fashion Inst. Tech., 1984. Bar: N.Y. 1977, Fla. 1977, U.S. Dist. Ct. (ea. and so. dists.) N.Y. 1978, U.S. Tax Ct. 1982, U.S. Supreme Ct. 1982. Assoc. Schwartzman, Weinstock, Garelik & Mann PC, N.Y.C., 1977-84; counsel N.Y. Assembly Judiciary Com., Albany, 1977-84; dep. supt. N.Y. State Ins. Dept., N.Y.C., 1984-97; counsel govt. affairs, asst. corp. sec. Group Health Inc., N.Y.C., 1997-99; prin. ct. atty. N.Y. State Supreme Ct., N.Y.C., 2000—. SEEK scholar, 1973; recipient SEEK honors, 1973. Mem. Fla. Bar Assn., NY Co. Lawyers' Bar Assn., Phi Beta Kappa. Democrat. Roman Catholic. Office: NY State Supreme Ct 60 Centre St New York NY 10007

BOGGS, BETH CLEMENS, lawyer; b. Dubuque, Iowa, July 28, 1967; d. Theodore Alan and Mary Ann (Fleckenstein) Clemens; m. T. Darin Boggs, Mar. 9, 1991. BA, Govs. State U., 1987; JD, So. Ill. U., 1991. Bar: Ill. 1991, Mo. 1992, U.S. Dist. Ct. (so. dist.) Ill. 1991, U.S. Dist. Ct. (ea. dist.) Mo. 1992, U.S. Dist. Ct. (we. dist.) Mo. 2002, U.S. Dist. Ct. (cen. dist.) Ill. 1997. Clk. R. Courtney Hughes & Assocs., Carbondale, Ill., 1990-91; lawyer Sandberg Phoenix & von Gontard, St. Louis, 1991-93; assoc. LaTourette, Schlueter & Byrne, St. Louis, 1993-95; mng. ptnr. Landau, Omahana & Kopka, P.C., St. Louis, 1995-99; mng. and founding ptnr. Boggs, Backer & Bates, LLC, St. Louis, 1999—. Adj. faculty Webster U., 1995—. Editor student articles So. Ill. U. Law Jour., 1991; contbr. articles to profl. jours. Mem. Young Lawyers divsn. of ABA (vice chair corp. counsel com. 1991-92, editor Corp. Counsel Newsletter 1991-92), Bus. Women St. Louis, Women Lawyers Assn., Lawyers Assn. St. Louis, Def. Rsch. inst., Mo. Orgn. Def. Lawyers. Avocations: tennis, softball, golf. Office: BBB 7912 Bonhomme Ave Ste 400 Saint Louis MO 63105-3512 E-mail: bbblawyers@aol.com.

BOGGS, CHARLES HARMON, JR., retired surgeon; b. Washington, July 4, 1923; MD, Northwestern U., 1950. Diplomate Am. Bd. Surgery. Intern Emergency Hosp., Washington, 1951, resident, 1952-53; intern Passavant Meml., Chgo., 1952; resident Northwestern U., Chgo., 1953-56; with VA Hosp., Roanoke, Va., 1956-57; pvt. practice Morgantown, W.Va., 1957-58, VAMC, Salem, Va., 1958-91; clin. instr. U. Va. Sch. Medicine, 1971-79, asst. prof. surgery, 1979-91; ret., 1991.

BOGGS, DANNY JULIAN, judge; b. Havana, Cuba, Oct. 23, 1944; s. Robert Lilburn and Yolanda (Pereda) Boggs; m. Judith Susan Solow, Dec. 23, 1967; children: Rebecca, David, Jonathan. AB cum laude, Harvard Coll., Cambridge, Mass., 1965; JD, U. Chgo., 1968; LLD (hon.), U. Detroit Mercy, 1994. Dep. commr. Ky. Dept. Econ. Security, 1969—70; legal counsel, adminstrv. asst. Gov. Ky., 1970—71; legis. counsel to Rep. legislators Ky. Gen. Assembly, 1972; asst. to solicitor gen. U.S. Dept. Justice, Washington, 1973—75; asst. to chmn. FPC, Washington, 1975—77; dep. minority counsel Senate Energy Com., Washington, 1977—79; of counsel Bushnell, Gage, et al., Washington, 1979—80; spl. asst. to Pres. White House, Washington, 1981—83; dep. sec. U.S. Dept. Energy, Washington, 1983—86; judge U.S. Ct. Appeals (6th cir.), Cin., 1986—. Mem. adv. com. on appellate rules Jud. Conf. U.S., 1991—94, com. on automation and tech., 1994—2000. Mem. vis. com. U. Chgo. Law Sch., 1984—87, 1999—2002; trustee Lexington Sch., 1999—; del. Rep. Nat. Conv., 1972; staff dir. energy subcom. Rep. Platform Com., 1980. Mem.: ABA (chair appellate judges conf. 2001—02), Mont Pelerin Soc., Ky. Bar Assn., Phila. Soc., Phi Delta Phi, Order of Coif. Office: US Ct Appeals US Courthouse 601 W Broadway Ste 220 Louisville KY 40202-2227

BOGGS, GEORGE ROBERT, academic administrator; b. Conneaut, Ohio, Sept. 4, 1944; s. George Robert and Mary (Mullen) B.; m. Ann Holladay, Aug. 8, 1969; children: Kevin Dale, Ian Asher, Micah Benjamin. BS in Chemistry, Ohio State U., 1966; MA in Chemistry, U. Calif., Santa Barbara, 1968; postgrad. in ednl. adminstrn., natural scis., and edn., Calif. State U., 1969-72; PhD in Ednl. Adminstrn., U. Tex., 1984. Cert. std. tchg. specialization in jr. coll., C.C. supr., C.C. chief adminstrv. officer. Instr. chemistry Butte Coll., Oroville, Calif., 1968-85, divsn. chmn. nat. sci. and allied health, 1972-81, assoc. dean of instrn., 1981-85; pres., supt. Palomar C.C. Dist., San Marcos, Calif., 1985-2000; pres. Am. Assn. C.C.s, Washington, 2000—. Spkr. SCC-CIRA, Calif., 1985; adj. instr. Austin (Tex.) C.C., 1982; guest lectr. Calif. State U., Chico, 1970, 83, 84, panelist, 1975; tchg. asst. U. Calif., Santa Barbara, 1966-68, Ohio State U., 1965-66; mem. numerous coms. for colls. and univs., Calif., 1968—; cons. U. Calif., Berkeley, 1995-2000, U. Wis., Madison, 1997-2000, Pellissippi State Tech. Coll., 1995, El Camino Coll., 1994, U. Hawaii C.C., 1994, Dept. Nat. Edn., Rep. South Africa, 1993, San Joaquin Delta C.C. Dist., 1986, Marin C.C. Dist., 1985. Contbr. articles to profl. jours.; cons. editl. adv. bd. Jour. Applied Rsch. in the C.C., 1993-2000; mem. editl. bd. C.C. Rev., 1997-2000. Presenter Nat. Conf. Teaching Excellence and Conf. of Pres.'s, 1983, 93, 95, presenter, mem. coordinating com., 1984, chmn. steering com., 1985; presenter Profl. and Orgl. Devel. Network, 1984; ad hoc com. CPEC/FIPSE/Chancellor's Office, 1984; mem. steering com. Learning Assessment Retention Com., 1983-85, pres.-elect 1985-86; mem. instl. research design team No. Calif. Higher Edn. Council, 1984, mission charrette writing team, 1985. Named a scholar Gen., Ohio State U., 1963; named hon. elder, Nat. Coun. on Black Am. Affairs, 1993; named to Stadium Dormitory, 1962—65, San Diego Hall of Success, 1988; recipient Scholastic R, 1962, Nat. Honor Soc., 1962, Stanley A. Mahr Cmty. Svc. award, San Marcos Coun. C. of C., 1994, Cert. Achievement, Leadership Excellence and Cmty. Svc., Congress of U.S. Ho. Reps., 1994, Pacific Region CEO award, Assn. C.C. Trustees, Victoria, B.C., Can., 1993, Recognition award, Nat. Coun. for Rsch. and Planning Mgmt., 1997, Harry Buttimer Disting. Adminstr. award, Assn. Calif. C.C. Trustees, 1994, Dr. George R. Boggs Day proclaimed Jan. 14, in Vista, Calif., 1994, PBS O'Banion prize for tchg. and learning, 2001; fellow Richardson fellow, 1982—83. Mem. NSF (adv. com. to directorate for edn. and human resources 1995-97, evaluator 1992, 93, 98), Nat. Rsch. Coun. (undergrad. sci. edn. com. 1993-95, chmn. subcom. tchg. and learning 1993-95), Assn. Calif. Coll. Tutorial and Learning Assistance (presenter 1984), Calif. Assn. C.C. (conf. presenter 1984, com. on rsch. 1985—), Assn. Calif. C.C. Adminstrs. (commn. membership devel. 1985), C.C. League Calif. (bd. dirs. 1990-92, presenter confs. 1990-98), Faculty Assn. Calif. C.C., Calif. C.C. Chief Exec. Officers' Assn, San Diego and Imperial Counties C.C. Assn., Am. Assn. Cmty. and Jr. Colls. (presenter 1989, 90, 91, 94, 95, bd. dirs. 1990-95, fed. rels. com. 1990-91, 94-95, chair elect 1993—, chair bd. dirs. 1993-94, exec. com. 1993-95, chair bd. nominating com. 1994-95), So. Calif. C.C. Chief Exec. Officers Assn. (sec., treas. 1990-2000), Phi Kappa Phi, Upsilon Pi Upsilon (pres. 1965-66), Phi Rho Pi, Rotary (pres. Durham club 1980-81, dist. sec. Calif., 1983-84, various other offices and com. positions held locally and nationally). Home: 2301 N St NW Apt 616 Washington DC 20037-1138 Office: Am Assn CCs 1 Dupont Cir NW Ste 410 Washington DC 20036 E-mail: gboggs@aacc.nche.edu.

BOGGS, GEORGE TRENHOLM, lawyer; b. Charleston, SC, Apr. 17, 1947; s. Edwin and Laura (Blair) Boggs; m. Emilie Louise von Thelen, Sept. 6, 1975; children: George T. Jr., Blair M. AB, Princeton U., 1969; JD, U. Va., 1974. Bar: Va. 1974, D.C. 1975. Tchr. Taft Sch., Watertown, Conn., 1969—71; mem. Dickstein Shapiro Morin and Oshinsky LLP, Washington, 1974—, ptnr., 1980—. Editor (with John M. Paxman): The United Nations: A Reassessment, 1973. Mem.: ABA, Va. Bar Assn., Internat. Bar Assn. Republican. Episcopalian. Office: Dickstein Shapiro Morin & Oshinsky LLP 2101 L St NW Washington DC 20037-1526

BOGGS, JACK AARON, banker, publisher, municipal government official; b. Easley, S.C., July 4, 1935; s. Walter Benston and Bessie Mae (Jones) B.; m. Isabel Thomas Brown, July 7, 1965; children— James Benston, Renee Chaplin, Edward Cunningham, Donn Lester. BS in Bus. Econs, U. S.C., 1964; grad., Sch. Banking, U. Wis., 1974. Chartered bank auditor certified internal auditor. Sec.-treas. Cedarpoint Farms Corp., Columbia, S.C., 1963-67; auditor S.C. Nat. Bank, Columbia, 1967-76; pres. S.C. Automated Clearing House Assn., 1976—; sec., treas. Arcadia Publs., 2002—. Mem. 5th dist. ops. adv. com. Fed. Res. Bank of Richmond, 1997-99; instr. S.C. Bankers Sch., 1972-80; sec., treas. Five Star Pubs., 1986-88; bd. dirs. NACHA, Inc., 1989-2000; vice chmn. ACH Exec. Dirs. Group, 1989-90, chmn., 1991-93. Mem. town coun., Town of Arcadia Lakes, S.C., 1977-85, mayor, 1985-89, chief of police, 1990-91; treas. S.C. Fedn. Older Ams., 1982-84. With USNR, 1952-60, Air N.G., 1960-63. Mem. Nat. Assn. Accts., Inst. Internal Auditors (bd. govs. 1971-74, pres. 1973-74, internat. rsch. com. 1972-75, internat. membership com. 1976), Data Processing Mgmt. Assn., Bank Adminstrn. Inst. (1st award 1972), S.C. Ducks Unltd. (treas. 1984-92, 98-2002, state chmn. 1992-94), Sigma Delta Pi, Chi Psi. Democrat. Unitarian Universalist. Home: 804 Arcadia Lakes Dr Columbia SC 29206-1321 Office: SC Automated Clearing House Assn PO Box 1787 Columbia SC 29202-1787 *It's not who you are; it's what you do that counts.*

BOGGS, JAMES DOTSON, lawyer; b. Kansas City, Mo., Aug. 31, 1949; s. William C. and Helen C. (Harbison) B.; m. Vickie R. Boggs, May 27, 1972; children: William Christian, Meghan Raye. BA, U. Mo., Columbia, 1971; JD, U. Mo., Kansas City, 1975. Bar: Mo. 1975, U.S. Dist. Ct. (we. dist.) Mo., U.S. Ct. Appeals (8th cir.), U.S. Supreme Ct. Assoc. Witt and Shafer, Platte City, Mo., 1975-78; ptnr. Witt and Boggs, Platte City, Mo., 1979-81, Witt, Boggs & Shaw Platte City, Mo., 1982-85, Witt, Boggs, Shaw & Van Amburg, Platte City, Mo., 1985-87; pvt. practice Kansas City, Mo., 1987—. Chmn. Platte County Dem. PArty, 1985-86; commr. Platte County Jud. Commn., 1987-93, 93—. Mem. Mo. Bar Assn. (gov. 1992-97), Mo. Assn. Trial Attys. (govs., 1985—, exec. com. 1994—, v.p. 2000, pres. 2002), Reach Out Am. (dir. 1994—). Office: 6406 N Cosby Ave Kansas City MO 64151-2377

BOGGS, JAMES ERNEST, chemistry educator; b. Cleve., June 9, 1921; s. Ernest Beckett and Emily (Reid) B.; m. Ruth Ann Rogers, June 22, 1948 (dec. 2002); children: Carol, Ann, Lynne. AB, Oberlin Coll., 1943; MS in Chemistry, U. Mich., 1944, PhD, 1953. Rsch. chemist Manhattan Dist. Project, Linde Air Products, Tonawanda, N.Y., 1944-46; asst. prof. dept. chemistry Eastern Mich. U., Ypsilanti, 1949-52; instr. U. Mich. at Ann Arbor, 1952-53; mem. faculty dept. chemistry U. Tex., Austin, 1953—, assoc. prof., 1958-66, prof., 1966-98; emeritus prof., 1998—; asst. dean Grad. Sch. U. Tex., Austin, 1958-67, dir. Center for Structural Studies, 1969-79, acting dir. Inst. Theoretical Chemistry, 1979-81. Program officer for theoretical and computational chemistry NSF, 1991-94; founder, organizer series Austin Symposia on Molecular Structure, 1966—; chmn. subcom. on theoretical chemistry Internat. Union Pure and Applied Chemistry, 1995-01; internat. lectr. in field. Mem. editl. bd. Jour. Molecular Structure; contbr. over 280 articles to profl. jours. Mem. Am. Chem. Soc., Am. Phys. Soc., Nat. Acad. Scis. (India), Phi Beta Kappa, Sigma Xi, Phi Lambda Upsilon, Gamma Alpha. Achievements include research in structural chemistry, microwave spectroscopy, quantum chemistry. Office: U Tex Dept Chemistry Austin TX 78712 E-mail: james.boggs@mail.utexas.edu.

BOGGS, JOSEPH DODRIDGE, pediatric pathologist, educator; b. Bellefontaine, Ohio, Dec. 31, 1921; s. Walter C. and Birdella Z. (Coons) B.; m. Donna Lee Shoemaker, June 12, 1964; 1 son, Joseph Dodridge. AB, Ohio U., 1941, Litt.D., 1966; MD, Jefferson Med. Coll., 1945. Intern Jefferson Med. Coll. Hosp., Phila., 1945-46; resident Peter Bent Brigham Hosp., Boston, 1946-48, asso. pathologist, 1947-51; instr. pathology Harvard Med. Sch., Boston, 1948-51; with Children's Meml. Hosp., Chgo., 1951—, dir. labs., 1951—; prof. pathology Northwestern U., Chgo., 1952-92, prof. emeritus, 1992—; dir. BSP Ins. Co., Phoenix. Contbr. articles to profl. jours. Mem. med. adv. bd. Ill. Dept. Corrections, Springfield, 1971-77; bd. dirs. Blood Systems Inc., Phoenix, 1972-94, Community Hosp., Evanston, Ill., 1958-61, Lorretto Hosp., Chgo., 1971-72; chmn. Chgo. Regional Blood Program, 1978-80; bd. dirs. Ben Venue Labs., 1985—. Capt. M.C., U.S. Army, 1948-51. Mem. Am. Soc. Study of Liver Disease, N.Y. Acad. Scis., Midwest Soc. Pediatric Research, Inst. Medicine, Ill. Soc. Pathologists (pres. 1965), Ill. Assn. Blood Banks (pres. 1969-70) Office: 1448 N Lake Shore Dr Chicago IL 60610-6655

BOGGS, JUDITH SUSAN, lawyer, health policy expert; b. Bklyn., Feb. 11, 1946; d. Robert Henry and Ethel (Shapiro) Solow; m. Danny Julian Boggs; children: Rebecca, David, Jonathan. BA cum laude, Bklyn. Coll., 1966; JD, U. Chgo., 1969. Bar: Ky. 1970. Human rights rep. Ky. Human Rights Commn., Frankfort, Ky., 1969; legal counsel Ky. Dept. Mental Health, Frankfort, 1970-73; sr. legal advisor Social and Rehabilitation Service, Washington, 1973-77; dir., health systems div. Health Care Fin. Adminstrn., Washington, 1978-82, special asst. to assoc. adminstr. for policy, 1982-86, spl. asst. to adminstr., 1986-87; sr. policy analyst The White House, Washington, 1987-89; of counsel Alagia, Day, Trautwein & Smith, Louisville, 1989-93; sr. v.p., gen. counsel Ky. Hosp. Assn., 1993-94; pvt. practice, 1994—2002; mem. (judge) Adminstrv. Rev. Bd. U.S. Dept. Labor, 2002—. Apptd. mem. Ky. Registry Election Fin., 2001—02. Mem. ABA, Ky. Bar Assn., Am. Health Lawyers Assn., Louisville Bar Assn. Office: 200 Constitution Ave NW Washington DC

BOGGS, RALPH STUART, retired lawyer; b. Toledo, June 6, 1917; s. Nolan and Sarah (MacPhie) B.; m. Mary Frances Sharp Wiggins, Sept. 7, 1940; children: Sally Ann Boggs Bashore, William S., Robert A. AB, Denison U., 1939; LL.B., U. Mich., 1942. Bar: Ohio 1942, U.S. Supreme Ct. 1960. Spl. agt. FBI, 1942-45; practiced in Toledo, 1946-99; ptnr. Boggs, Boggs & Boggs (P.A.), 1946-87; of counsel Eastman and Smith, 1987-98; ret. Mem. Maumee Bd. Edn., 1953-69, Maumee Recreation Com., 1954-69; life mem. Toledo adv. com. Salvation Army, pres., 1981-83; pres. Maumee Men's Rep. Club, 1947-48; former chmn. bd. trustees Presbytery of Maumee, Inc.; trustee, sec. Masonic Toledo Trust, 1986-97; trustee Stranahan Theatre Trust, 1997—, sec., 1997-98; asst. sec. Otis Avery Browning Masonic Meml. Fund, 1987-97. Named to Toledo H.S. Athletes Hall of Fame, 1995. Mem. ABA, Ex-FBI Agts. Soc., Ohio Bar Assn., Lucas County Bar Assn., Toledo Bar Assn., Masons (33 degree), Shriners, Heather Downs Country Club (Toledo) (past pres., dir.), Sigma Chi (life). Presbyterian (elder). Home: 5916 Cresthaven Ln Apt B416 Toledo OH 43614-1200 *Education, preparation and perseverance are essential to attaining success.*

BOGGS, ROBERT WAYNE, human services administrator, consultant; b. St. Helena, Calif., Sept. 17, 1941; s. Wayne Cress Boggs and Ann Isham Stevenson; m. Donna J. Ferguson, Nov. 24, 1967; children: Jacquelin, Ryan. BS, Fresno State U., 1964; PhD, U. Calif., Davis, 1970. Bd. cert. nutritionist. Staff mem. Procter & Gamble, Cin., 1970-73, sect. head, 1973-76, assoc. dir., 1976-83, dir., 1983-99; cons. RWB Mgmt. Sys., Cin., 1999—. Author: (book) Transforming Clinical Development Performance Through Benchmarking and Metrics, 2001. Exec. sec. Procter Found., 1982—; mem. pharm. sci. bd. U. Cin., 1987—, mem. adv. bd., 1991—94; pres. Glendale Youth Sports, 1989; mem. athletic bd. St. Xavier H.S., 1991—93; mem. adv. bd. Cin. Classics, 1995; CFO Village of Glendale, 2001—; sr. warden Christ Ch. Glendale, 1988; bd. dirs. Cin. Riverhawks, 1997—. Mem.: Drug Info. Assn., Nutrition Today Soc., Am. Inst. Nutrition (mem. adv. bd. 1988—91). Avocations: soccer, equestrian events, John Deere tractor restoration.

BOGGS, SCOTT, information technology executive; BA in Acct., U. Wash., 1977. Mgr. in emerging bus. svc. Deloitte, Haskins & Sells, 1985—93; from mgr. to corp. v.p. Microsoft, Redmond, Wash., 1993—2000, corp. v.p., 2000—. Mem.: Fin. Exec. Inst. (v.chmn. com. on fin. & info. tech.). Office: One Microsoft Way Redmond WA 98052-6399

BOGGS, STEVEN A, electrical engineer; b. Miami, Fla., Mar. 15, 1946; MBA in Physics, U. of Toronto, 1968, PhD in Physics, 1972. Dir., engring. & rsch. Underground Systems, Inc., Armonk, NY, 1987—93; prof., elec. engring., physics & material sci. U. of Conn., Storrs, 1993—. V.p. Chgo. Condenser Corp., United States, 1987—93. Author numerous papers in area of high voltage engring. and dielect. Recipient 3rd Millenium Medal, Inst. of Elec. and Electronic Engineers, 2000. Fellow: IEEE. Home: 109 Hnath Rd Ashford CT 06278 Office: U Conn 97 North Eagleville Rd Storrs CT 06269-3131 E-mail: steven.boggs@ieee.org.

BOGGS, STEVEN EUGENE, real estate broker, lawyer; b. Santa Monica, Calif., Apr. 28, 1947; s. Eugene W. and Annie (Happe) B. BA in Econ., U. Calif., Santa Barbara, 1969; D of Chiropractic summa cum laude, Cleveland Chiropractic, L.A., 1974; PhD in Fin. Planning, Columbia Pacific U., 1986; JD in Law, U. So. Calif., 1990. Bar: Calif. 1990, U.S. Dist. Ct. (cen. dist.) Calif. 1990, Hawaii 1991, U.S. Ct. Appeals (9th cir.), Colo. 1999; CFP; lic. chiropractor Hawaii, Calif.; lic. radiography X-ray supr. and operator; real estate broker, Colo. Faculty mem. Cleveland Chiropractic Coll., 1972-74; pres. clinic dir. Hawaii Chiropratic Clinic, Inc., Aiea, 1974-87; pvt. practice Honolulu, 1991-99; mem. faculty Hawaii Pacific U., 1997-99; broker, dir. REO/asset mgmt. team (bank foreclosures) Coldwell Banker Walker & Co., 2000—02, RE/MAX Properties, Inc., 2002—. Cons. in field; seminar presenter 1990—. Contbr. articles to profl. jours. Recipient Cert. Appreciation State of Hawaii, 1981-84. Fellow Internat. Coll. of Chiropractic; mem. ABA, Am. Trial Lawyers Assn., Consumer Lawyers of Hawaii, Am. Chiropractic Assn., Hawaii State Chiropractic Assn. (pres. 1978, 85, 86, v.p. 1977, sec. 1979-84, treas. 1976, other coms., Valuable Svc. award 1984, Cert. Appreciation 1986, Cert. Achievement 1986, Chiropractor of Yr. 1986, Outstanding Achievement award 1991), Consumer Lawyers of Hawaii (bd. dirs.). Republican. Avocations: bicycling, car racing. Office: 19050 Archers Dr Monument CO 80132-2807 E-mail: steve@steveboggs.com., boggs@iglide.net.

BOGGS, THOMAS HALE, JR., lawyer, director; b. New Orleans, Sept. 18, 1940; s. Thomas Hale and Corinne (Claiborne) B.; m. Mary Barbara Denechaud, Dec. 27, 1960; children— Hale, Elizabeth, Douglas. AB, Georgetown U., 1961, LL.B., 1965. Bar: D.C. 1965, U.S. Ct. Appeals 1966, U.S. Supreme Ct. 1971. Economist Joint Econ. Com., U.S. Congress, 1961-65; spl. asst. to dir. Office Emergency Planning, 1965-66; practice in Washington, 1966—; mem. firm Patton Boggs, L.L.P., 1966—. Presdl. Commn. on Exec. Exch., 1979-81; Presdl. del. Independence of Solomon Islands, 1978, Trade Mission to People's Republic of China, 1979. Co-author: Private Trade Barriers in the Atlantic Community, 1964, Corporate Political Activity, 1984 Dem. candidate for U.S. Ho. of Reps. 8th Dist. Md., 1970; mem. Charter Commn., Dem. Nat. Com., 1973; trustee Fed. City Coun., Chesapeake Bay Trust, The Keystone Ctr. Mem. Am. Judicature Soc., ABA (com. chmn.), Martime, Fed. Bar Assns., Delta Theta Phi. Home: 6 E Kirke St Chevy Chase MD 20815-4217 Office: Patton Boggs LLP 2550 M St NW Ste 500 Washington DC 20037-1350 E-mail: tboggs@pattonboggs.com.

BOGGS, WILLIAM S. lawyer; b. Toledo, Ohio, May 17, 1946; AB summa cum laude, Wittenberg U., 1968; JD cum laude, Harvard U., 1972. Bar: Calif. Ptnr. Gray, Cary, Ware & Freidenrich, San Diego, 1979—. Mem. ABA, San Diego County Bar Assn., Internat. Assn. Defense Counsel, Assn. So. Calif. Defense Counsel, San Diego Defense Lawyers, Lincoln's Inn. Office: Gray Cary Ware & Freidenrich 401 B St Ste 1700 San Diego CA 92101-4297

BOGH, RUSSELL, state official; b. San Bernardino; m. Sheri Bogh; 2 children. BA in Bus. Econs., Calif. State U., San Bernardino. Mgr. bus. devel. Bogh Constrn.; candidate Dist. 65 Calif. State Assembly, 2000, state assembly mem. Dist. 65, 2001—. Mem. arts, entertainment, sports, tourism and Internet media com.; vice-chair banking and fin. com.; mem. higher edn. com.; mem. ins. com.; mem. jobs, econ. devel. and economy com. Republican. Mailing: Rm 3098 PO Box 942849 Sacramento CA 94249-0001 Office: 34932 Yucaipa Blvd Yucaipa CA 92399

BOGHAIRI, ANOUSHIRAVAN, cardiologist; b. Tehran, Iran, Aug. 5, 1944; arrived in US, 1973; s. Mahmood and Aghdass Boghairi; m. Azam Rashid, May 5, 1978; children: Salina, Cyrus. Grad. Tehran U., 1970. Diplomate Am. Bd. Internal Medicine, Am. Bd. Cardiovasc. Disease. Rotating intern Emam Khomeini Hosp., Tehran, 1968—70, St. John's Riverside Hosp., Yonkers, NY, 1973—74; resident in internal medicine Mt. Sinai Hosp., Hartford, Conn., 1974—75, Jersey City (N.J.) Med. Ctr., 1975—76; fellow in cardiology Jersey City Med. Ctr., 1976—77, Cleve. Clinic, 1977—78, Creighton U. Cardiac Ctr., Omaha, 1978—79, instr. medicine, 1978—79; attending cardiologist Alvarado Hosp. Med. Ctr., San Diego, 1979—80; pvt. practice La Mesa, Calif., 1980—. Former tchr. SHARP Family Physicians Residency Program; bd. govs. Grossmont Hosp. Found., La Mesa, 2002; asst. prof. medicine U. Calif., San Diego. Lt. med. corps. Iranian Army, 1971—73. Fellow: Am. Coll. Cardiology. Avocations: piano, fitness, santoor. Office: Bldg 1 Ste 115 5565 Grossmont Ctr Dr La Mesa CA 91942

BOGHANI, ASHOK BALVANTRAI, entrepreneur; b. Bombay, Aug. 8, 1949; came to U.S., 1970; s. Balvantrai Pranlal and Charusheela (Kapadia) B.; m. Meera Kapadia, May 30, 1977; children: Ami, Amar. B of Tech., Indian Inst. Tech., Bombay, 1970; MS, MIT, 1971, M in Mech. Engring., 1973, ScD, 1974. Staff engr. Foster-Miller, Waltham, Mass., 1974-77, project mgr., 1977-79; sr. cons. Arthur D. Little, Inc., Cambridge, Mass., 1979-90, dir., 1990-2000, v.p., 1994-2000, leader N.Am. transp. and automotive practice, 1998-2000; founder, v.p. bus. devel. IntellectExchange.com, 2000—. Mem. transp. hazmat com. Transp. Rsch. Bd., Washington, 1987-94; mem. Benefits, Evaluation and Assessment com., Intelligent Vehicle Hwy. Systems Am., Washington, 1992-96. Contbr. articles to profl. jours. Recipient cert. of recognition NASA, 1976, 78. Mem. ASME, Soc. Automotive Engrs., Indus Entrepreneurs-Atlantic (charter mem.), Democrat. Avocations: photography, travel, hiking, music. Home: 3 Sawmill Rd Acton MA 01720-5835 Office: IntellectExchange dot com 54 Middlesex Tpke Bedford MA 01730-1417 E-mail: ABoghani@alum.mit.edu.

BOGHOSIAN, PAULA DER, computer business consultant; b. Watervliet, N.Y., Nov. 19, 1933; d. Harry and Osgi (Piligian) der B. BS magna cum laude, Syracuse U., 1964, MS, 1967; postgrad., SUNY, Oswego, 1972, SUNY, Albany, 1974. Cert. profl. sec. Asst. prof. Cazenovia (N.Y.) Coll., 1964-73; instr. Bd. of Coop., Syracuse, N.Y., 1973-76, dir. bus. careers, 1976-92; cons. computer bus., prin. Syracuse, 1984—. Zonta scholar, 1964; Jessie Smith Noyes grantee Syracuse U., 1965. Mem. Assn. Info. Systems Profl. (com. chmn.), Bus. Tchrs. Assn. of N.Y. State, Adminstrv. Mgmt. Soc., Eastern Bus. Tchrs. Assn., Assn. for Supervision and Curriculum Devel., Assn. of Am. Jr. Colls., Assn. of Am. U. Profs., Nat. Assn. for Armenian Studies and Rsch. Harvard U., Internat. Tng. Communications (v.p. 1985-86), Delta Pi Epsilon, Beta Gamma Sigma, Phi Kappa Phi, Pi Lambda Theta, Sigma Lambda Delta. Republican. Mem. Armenian Apostolic. Avocations: music, golf, water colors, designer, travel. Home and Office: 3181 Bellevue Ave Apt B6 Syracuse NY 13219-3156

BOGHOSIAN, VARUJAN YEGAN, sculptor, educator; b. New Britain, Conn., June 26, 1926; s. Mesrop and Baidzar (Saylandzian) B.; m. Marilyn Cummins, Sept. 1, 1953; 1 dau., Heidi. Student, Conn. Tchrs. Coll., 1946-48, Vesper George Sch. Art, 1948-50; B.F.A., Yale U., 19—, M.F.A., 1959; MA (hon.), Brown U., 1965, Dartmouth Coll., 1969. Instr. art U. Fla., 1958-59, Pratt Inst., 1961, Yale U., 1962-64; asst. prof. art Cooper Union Coll., 1959-64; asso. prof. Brown U., 1964-68; artist-in-residence Dartmouth Coll., 1968, prof. art, 1968—, George Frederick Jewett prof. art, 1983—; sculptor in residence Am. Acad. in Rome, 1966-67, 75. Artist woodcut portfolios Orpheus, 1951, The River Styx, 1971; numerous one-man shows including Stable Gallery, N.Y.C., 1963, 64, 65, 66, Cordier and Ekstrom, N.Y.C., 1969, 71, 73, 75, 77-80, 82, 84, 87-89, Berry Hill Galleries, 1997, 99, Arts Club of Chgo., 1970, Claude Bernard Gallery, N.Y.C., 1991, Norton Gallery Art, Palm Beach, Fla., 1993; group shows include Obelisk Gallery, Rome, 1953, Mus. Modern Art, N.Y.C., 1956, Hanover Gallery, London, 1966, retrospective Hood Mus., Hanover, N.H., 1989; represented in numerous permanent collections including, Mus. Modern Art, N.Y.C., Whitney Mus. Am. Art, N.Y.C., Met. Mus. N.Y.C., Addison Gallery Am. Art, Andover, Mass., Worcester Art Mus., Phoenix Art Mus. Chmn. bd. MacDowell Colony. With USN, 1944-46. Recipient award Nat. Inst. Arts and Letters, 1972; Fulbright grantee, Italy, 1953; U.S. Dept. State specialists grantee, 1961; fellow Howard Found., 1966, John Simon Guggenheim Found. fellow, 1985 Mem. NAD, Am. Acad. Arts and Letters (St. Botolph award 1991), Century Assn. (N.Y.C.), St. Botolph Club (Boston). Clubs: Century (N.Y.C.). Office: Darmouth Coll HB 6081 Visual Studies Office Hanover NH 03755

BOGHOSSIAN, JOAN THOMPSON, artist; b. Newport, R.I., Mar. 6, 1932; d. Joseph and Hope (Bliss) Thompson; m. Paul O. Boghossian Jr., 1952 (dec. July 1995); children: Carol Boghossian Spencer, Paul O. III, David M., Nancy Boghossian Staples. BS, U. R.I., 1953. One person shows at Attletoro Mus., Newton Libr. Gallery, Charlestown Gallery; two-person shows at Providence Art Club (J. Banigan Sullivan prize 1984), Dodge House Gallery; group exhbn. at RI Watercolor Soc. (1st in watercolor 1988, 91, Block Artists Merchandise award 1989, Grumbacher Gold Medallion 1990, 93, 94, Dr. Edwin Dunlop award 1997), Mystic Art Assn. (1st in watercolor 1990, 92, 93, 95, Mystic Manor spl. award for aquatint 1992), Wickford Art Assn. (1st in watercolor 1986, 1st in all-media 1993, 2d in oil 1995), South County Art Assn. (award 1987, Florence B. Kane award 1989, Herbert Richard Cross award 1992, C. Gordon Harris award 1993, 1st prize award 1997), Peel Gallery-Danby, Vt., New Eng. South Shore Artists (Best in Show 1986), Cape Cod Art Assn. (1st in watercolor 1987, 90, 1st in graphics 1987, 2d in watercolor 1988, 92, Juror's award of merit 1994), Warwick Arts Found. (1st in watercolor 1985), RI Watercolor Soc. David Marsland Meml. Award, Providence Art Club, Wm. S. Brigham Award and Juror's Choice Award, Warwick Mus.Open, Am. Frame Award, 2002; others. Mem.: others, New Eng. Watercolor Soc. (James W. Duffy award 1998), South County Art Assn. (1st prize Open Annual South County award 1997, Kinney award Best Floral Painting 1996, C. Gordon Harris award 1993, Herbert Richard Cross award 1992, Best Marine Painting Loring award 1990, Florence B. Kane award 1989, Art Assn. award 1987), Wickford Art Assn. (1st pl. in show 1996, 2nd pl. in oil 1994, 1st pl. all-medal 1993), Mystic Art Assn. (1st pl. watercolor Annual Regional Exhbn. 1990, 1992, 1993, 1995, Mystic Manor Spl. award for Aquatint 1992), R.I. Watercolor Soc. (Dr. Edwin Dunlop Meml. award 1997, Grumbacher gold medallion 1990, 1993, 1994, 1st pl. Watercolor Soc. Open 1987, 1988, 1991), Providence Art Club (Frederick Sisson award 1988), Copley Soc. Boston, Catherine Lorillard Wolfe Art Club (Anna Hyatt Huntington medal 1996, Mary Hill Meml. award 1998). Home: 640 East Ave Pawtucket RI 02860-6158 Studio: 7 Thomas St Providence RI 02903-1314

BOGIN, MARC B. internist, cardiologist; b. Chgo., Feb. 24, 1958; s. Sydney and Ellen (Rieger) B.; m. Marianne Smith, June 5, 1987; children: Stephanie, Andrew. BA, U. South Fla., 1981; MD, U. Del Noreste, Tompico, Mex., 1985, postgrad., Mt. Sinai Sch. Medicine, N.Y.C., 1985-86. Diplomate Am. Bd. Internal Medicine with subspecialty in cardiovascular disease. Intern New York Hosp.-Queens, Flushing, 1986-87, resident in internal medicine, 1987-89, chief resident, 1989-90; fellow in cardiology St. Vincent's Med. Ctr., S.I., N.Y., 1990-93; ptnr., physician Vazzana & Bogin Cardiology Assocs., S.I., N.Y., 1993—. Clin. asst. prof. medicine N.Y. Med. Coll., 1998—. Contbr. articles to profl. jours. Fellow Am. Coll. Cardiology; mem. ACP, Richmond County Med. Soc. Jewish. Office: Vazzana & Bogin Cardiology Assocs 11 Ralph Pl Staten Island NY 10304-4419 E-mail: heartman3@aol.com.

BOGLE, JOHN CLIFTON, investment company executive; b. Montclair, NJ, May 8, 1929; s. William Yates, Jr. and Josephine (Hipkins) B.; m. Eve Sherrerd, Sept. 22, 1956; children: Barbara, Jean, John Clifton, Nancy, Sandra, Andrew. AB magna cum laude, Princeton U., 1951; LHD (hon.), Widener U., 1997; HHD (hon.), Albright Coll.; LLD (hon.), U. Del.; LHD (hon.), U. Rochester, 2000; LLD, Susquehanna U., 2001, New School U., 2001. With Wellington Mgmt. Co., Phila., 1951-74, asst. to pres., 1954-62, sec., adminstrv. v.p., 1962-66, exec. v.p., 1966-67, pres., CEO, 1967-74; founder, CEO, chmn. Vanguard Group Investment Cos., Valley Forge, Pa., 1974-96; sr. chmn. Vanguard Group, Valley Forge, 1996-99; pres. Bogle Fin. Makerts Rsch. Ctr., Valley Forge, 2000—. Kaufman vis. prof. NYU, 1999-2000; exec. com. CGU; chmn. corp. objectives com. Mead Corp.; bd. dirs. Instinet Corp. Author: Bogle on Mutual Funds: New Perspectives for the Intelligent Investor, 1993, Common Sense on Mutual Funds: New Imperatives for the Intelligent Investor, 1999, John Bogle on Investing: The First 50 Years, 2000, Character Counts, 2002; subject of biography: John Bogle and the Vanguard Experiment: One Man's Quest to Transform the Mutual Fund Industry, by Robert Slater, 1996; numerous articles to profl. jours., chpts. to books. Former chmn. bd. trustees Blair Acad.; chmn. bd. dirs. Nat. Constn. Ctr.; past adv. coun. econs. dept. Princeton U.; past bd. dirs. Independence Standards Bd., Am. Indian Coll. Fund. Recipient Woodrow Wilson medal Princeton U., 1999; named One of Four Investment Giants of the 20th Century Fortune mag., 1999. Mem. Nat. Assn. Securities Dealers (investment cos. com. 1967-74, long-range planning com. 1973-74), Investment Co. Inst. (gov. 1969-81, chmn. 1969-70), Securities and Exch. Commn. (market oversight and fin. svcs. adv. com.), Merion Cricket Club (Haverford), Merion Golf (Ardmore). Office: Vanguard Group PO Box 2600 Valley Forge PA 19482-2600

BOGNAR, JOSEPH ANDREW, music educator, musician; b. Hammond, Ind., June 26, 1972; s. John Alan Bognar and Cynthia Sue Blackmun; m. Jennifer Kavanagh, Aug. 5, 1994; 1 child, Alexander Joseph. MusB, Valparaiso U., 1994; Mus D, U. of Ill. at Urbana-Champaign, 2000. Asst. prof. of music Valparaiso U., Ind., 1997—. Artist, faculty The Maud Powell Music Festival, Peru, Ill., 2002; faculty mem. Luth. Music Program, Minneapolis, 1999—2000; pianist Castillon Piano Trio. Author: (jour. articles in) Music Research Forum, 1999. Fellowship, U. of Ill. at Urbana-Champaign, 1994, 1996. Mem.: Coll. Music Soc., Am. Musicological Soc., Pi Kappa Lambda, Phi Mu Alpha Sinfonia. Home: 306 Calumet Valparaiso IN 46383 Office: Valparaiso University 1709 Chapel Drive-VUCA Valparaiso IN 46383 Office Fax: 219-464-5244. Personal E-mail: joseph.bognar@valpo.edu.

BOGNER, DARLENE RUTH, retired social worker; b. Elgin, Ill., Nov. 19, 1932; d. Carroll Benjamin and Ruth Clara (Bruns) Bennorth; m. Dennis Dean Bogner, June 15, 1963; children: Sharon Marie, Barbara Jean. BS, Hamline U., 1955; MSW, U. Louisville, 1959. Cert. clin. social worker, S.D. Social worker Yankton (S.D.) State Hosp., 1955-57, 58, psychiat. social worker, 1963-72, Butler Count Mental Health Ctr., Hamilton, Ohio, 1959-63, Lewis & Clark Mental Health Ctr., Yankton, 1972-99; ret., 1999. Mem. Drug Prevention Coun. S.E. S.D., Drug Prevention Coun. Crofton, Nebr., 1991; sec. Sr. Citizens, Crofton, 1990—92; vol. Crofton Sr. Citizens, 1997—, Yankton (S.D.) Hospice Program, 1999—2000; mem. vol. corps Discovery Welcome Ctr., Crofton, 2001—. Democrat. Avocations: walking, sewing, knitting, music, reading. Home: 1208 W 4th St Crofton NE 68730

BOGNER, FRED KARL, civil engineering educator; b. Mansfield, Ohio, July 7, 1939; s. Fred William and Esther Viola (Swartz) B.; m. Mary Louise Reynolds, July 11, 1959; children: Fred Charles, Sharon Louise. BSCE, Case Inst. Tech., 1961, MS in Engring. Mech., 1964, PhD in Engring. Mech., 1967. Mem. tech. staff Bell Telephone Labs., Whippany, NJ, 1967-69; rsch. engr. Rsch. Inst. U. Dayton, Ohio, 1969-84, chmn. dept. civil engring., 1984-96, prof. civil engring. and engring. mechanics, 1986—; cons. Dayton, 1969—. Contbr. articles to profl. jours.; referee Jour. Engring. Mechs., 1990—, Jour. Composite Tech. and Rsch., 1987—. Mem. AIAA (jour. referee), ASCE, Am. Acad. Mechs., Soc. Engring. Sci. Achievements include rsch. in finite element analysis, structural damping, composite materials. Home: 9516 Bridlewood Trl Dayton OH 45458-9627 Office: U Dayton Dept Civil Engring Dayton OH 45469-0243

BOGOMILOV, BORIS, medical educator; b. Krasnodarskyi District, Russia, June 30, 1967; s. Edda Davidovna Korsunskaya and Vasil Bogomilov Stoilov; m. Cathy Chunlian; children: Michelle Qiu, Eva Bogomilova. MD(hon.), Med. U. Varna, Bulgaria, 1991; degree in computer programming, IZOT Engring-.Silistra, Bulgaria, 1988. Diplomate Am. Bd. Internal Medicine, Am. Bd. Cardiology, Clin. Cardiac Electrophysiology. Fgn. med. divsn. Nat. Health, London, 1993—94; clin. asst. instr. internal medicine SUNY, Bklyn., 1995—98; cardiology fellow Grad. Hosp., Med. Coll. Pa., Phila., 1998—2001; clin. asst. instr. cardiac electrophysiology SUNY, Bklyn., 2001—02; dir. dept. electrophysiology Cardiology of Tulsa, 2002—. Rsch. assoc. VA Med. Ctr., Bklyn., 1996—. Mem.: AMA, N.Am. Soc. for Pacing and Electrophysiology, Am. Coll. Cardiology. Office: Cardiology of Tulsa Dept Electrophysiology St Francis Hosp 6151 S Yale Ste 400 Tulsa OK 74136-1902

BOGORAD, BARBARA ELLEN, psychologist; b. N.Y.C. d. Albert Lyon and Miriam Ida (Serlin) B. BA, CUNY, 1969; MS, Rutgers U., 1972, Yeshiva U., 1981, PsyD, 1983. Lic. psychologist, N.Y.; diplomate Am. Bd. Profl. Psychol., 1992, Am. Bd. Forensic examiners, Am. Bd. Psychol. Specialities, Am. Bd. Disabilities; cert. psychopathologist; master addictions counselor. Psychotherapist South Shore Ctr. Psychotherapy, Merrick, N.Y., 1978 82; psychology intern Birch Ctr. Exceptional Children, Queens, N.Y., 1980-81; clinical intern Long Island Jewish Hosp., Glen Oaks, N.Y., 1981-82; clin. intern South Oaks Hosp., Amityville, N.Y., 1982-83; staff psychologist St. John's Episc. Hosp., Far Rockaway, N.Y., 1984-86, St. Charles Hosp., Port Jefferson, NY, 1987-88; pvt. practice Amityville, 1985-94; staff psychologist South Oaks Hosp., Amityville, 1988-94, dir. sexual abuse recovery program, 1991-94; pvt. practice Massapequa, N.Y., 1994—. Speaker in field; radio and TV appearances 1990—; adjunct staff Schneider's Children's Hosp., Long Island, Jewish Hosp., New Hyde Park, N.Y., 2000—. Fellow Am. Acad. Sch. Psychology; mem. APA, Am. Acad. Experts Traumatic Stress, Ea. Psychol. Assn., N.Y. State Psychol. Assn., Nassau County Psychol. Assn., Suffolk County Psychol. Assn., Am. Assn. Psychiat. Svcs. Children., Psychologists in Hosp. Practice, Am. Profl. Soc. Abuse of Children, Nat. Assn. Childcare Resource and Referral Agys. (aux.). Avocations: photography, gardening, travel, choral singing. Office: 627 Broadway Ste 201 Massapequa NY 11758-5031

BOGORAD, LAWRENCE, biologist, educator; b. Tashkent, USSR, Aug. 29, 1921; came to U.S., 1922; s. Boris and Florence (Bernard) B.; m. Rosalyn G. Sagen, June 29, 1943; children— Leonard Paul, Kiki M. Lee. BS, U. Chgo., 1942, PhD, 1949. Instr. botany U. Chgo., 1948-51, asst. prof. dept. botany, 1953-57, assoc. prof., 1957-61, prof., 1961-67; prof. biology Harvard U., Cambridge, Mass., 1967-92, chmn. dept. biology, 1974-76, dir. Maria Moors Cabot Found., 1976-87, Maria Moors Cabot prof. biology, 1980-92, prof. emeritus, 1992—. Vis. investigator Rockefeller Inst., N.Y.C., 1951-53; com. on sci. and pub. policy NAS, 1977-81; com. on sci. engring. and pub. policy NAS-NAE-IOM1990-92; mem. Assembly of Life Scis., NRC, Space Studies Bd., 1995-98; joint coun. on food and agrl. scis. Dept. Agr., 1978-82. Assoc. editor Bot. Gazette, 1958; mem. editl. com. Ann. Rev. Plant Physiology, 1963-67, Ann. Rev. Cell Biology, 1984-88; mem. editl. bd. Plant Physiology, 1965-66, Biochimica Biophysica Acta, 1967-69, Jour. Cell Biology, 1967-70, Jour. Applied and Molecular Genetics, 1981-85, Plant Molecular Biology, 1981-85, Plant Cell Reports, 1981-85; editor, chmn. editl. bd. Proc. Nat. Acad. Scis., 1991-95. Served with AUS, 1943-46. Merck fellow, 1951-53; Fulbright fellow, 1960; recipient Career Rsch. award NIH, 1963 Fellow Am. Acad. Arts and Scis.; mem. NAS (chmn. botany sect. 1974-77, mem. coun. 1989-92, editor procs., chmn. editl. bd. Procs. 1991-95), AAAS (bd. dirs. 1982-86, pres. 1986-87, chmn. bd. 1987), Am. Philos. Soc., Am. Soc. Biol. Chemistry, Am. Soc. Cell Biology, Am. Soc. Plant Physiologists (pres. 1968-69, Stephen Hales award 1982), Royal Danish Acad. Scis. and Letters (fgn.), Soc. Devel. Biology (pres. 1984). Office: Harvard U Dept Molecular/Cellular Bio 16 Divinity Ave Cambridge MA 02138-2020 E-mail: bogorad@mcb.harvard.edu.

BOGREN, HUGO GUNNAR, radiology educator; b. Jönköping, Sweden, Jan. 9, 1933; came to U.S., 1970; s. Gunnar Hugo and Signe Victoria (Holmström) B.; m. Elisabeth Faxén, Nov. 1, 1956 (div. 1976); children: Cecilia, Niclas, Joakim; m. Gunilla Lady Whitmore, July 2, 1988. MD, U. Göteborg, Sweden, 1958, PhD, 1964. Diplomate Swedish Bd. Radiology. Resident, fellow U. Göteborg, 1958-64, asst. to assoc. prof. radiology, 1964-69; from assoc. prof. to prof. radiology and internal medicine U. Calif. Davis, Sacramento, 1972—. Vis. assoc. prof. U. San Francisco, 1970-71; vis. prof. U. Kiel, Fed. Republic Germany, 1980, cardiac magnetic resonance unit Royal Brompton Hosp. and Imperial Coll., London, 1986-87, 93-94, 2002-03; participant in med. aid fact finding mission, Bangladesh, 1992. Contbr. numerous articles to profl. jours., chpts. to books. Sr. Internat. Fogarty fellow NIH, London, 1986-87. Fellow Am. Heart Assn., Radiol. Soc., N.Am. Soc. Cardiac Imaging, Assn. Univ. Radiologists, Soc. Thoracic Radiology, Internat. Soc. Magnetic Resonance, Soc. Cardiovasc. Magnetic Resonance, Swedish Assn. Med. Radiology; mem. Royal Gothenburg Sailing Club Sweden (hon.), Swedish Cruising Club, Rotary (del.). Lutheran. Avocations: ocean sailing, skiing, classical music. Office: U Calif Davis Med Ctr Div Diagnostic Radiology 4860 Y St Ste 3100 Sacramento CA 95817-2307 E-mail: hugo.bogren@ucdmc.ucdavis.edu.

BOGUCKI, PETER IGNATIUS, archaeologist; b. Phila., Mar. 11, 1954; s. Alfred and Jadwiga (Kulpinska) B.; m. Virginia Creeden, Dec. 10, 1978; children: Caroline, Marianna. BA, U. Pa., 1974; MA, Harvard U., 1977, PhD, 1981. Lectr. in anthropology U. Mass., Boston, 1982-83; dir. studies Forbes Coll. Princeton (N.J.) U., 1983-94, asst. dean sch. engring. and applied sci., 1994-2000, assoc. dean. sch. engring. & applied sci., 2000—. Lectr. Archaeol. Inst. Am., 1990-91. Author: Early Neolithic Subsistence and Settlement in the Polish Lowlands, 1982, Forest Farmers and Stockherders: Early Agriculture and its Consequences in North-Central Europe, 1988, The Origins of Human Society, 1999; editor: Case Studies in European Prehistory, 1993; mem. editl. adv. bd. Environ. Archaeology Jour., Jour. of Field Archaeology; ; co-editor Ancient Europe 8000 B.C. to A.D. 1000: An Encyclopedia of the Barbarian World, 2003; contbr. articles to profl. jours. Grantee Nat. Geographic Soc., 1989, 90. Mem. Am. Soc. Engring. Edn., European Assn. Archaeologists, Assn. for Environ. Archaeology, Sigma Xi. Office: Princeton U Sch Engring Applied Sci Princeton NJ 08544-5263

BOGUE, ALLAN GEORGE, history educator; b. London, Ont., Can., May 12, 1921; married; 3 children. BA, U. Western Ont., 1943, MA, 1946; PhD, Cornell U., 1951; LL.D., U. Western Ont., 1973; D.Fil (hon.), U. Uppsala, 1977. Lectr. econs. and history, asst. librarian U. Western Ont., 1949-52; from asst. prof. to prof. history U. Iowa, 1952-64, chmn. dept., 1959-63; prof. history U. Wis.-Madison, 1964-68, chmn. dept., 1972-73, Frederick Jackson Turner prof. history, 1968-91. Mem. hist. adv. com. Math. Soc. Sci. Bd., 1965-71; Scandinavian-Am. Found. Thord-Gray lectr., 1968; mem. Council Inter-Univ. Consortium Polit. Research, 1971-73, 89-91; vis. prof. history Harvard U., 1972; dir. Social Sci. Research Council, 1973-76 Author: Money at Interest, 1955, From Prairie to Corn Belt, 1963; co-author, editor: The West of the American People, 1970; co-author, contbr.: The Dimensions of Quantitative Research in History, 1972; co-editor, contbr.: American Political Behavior: Historical Essays and Readings, 1974; co-editor: The University of Wisconsin: One Hundred and Twenty Five Years, 1975; author: The Earnest Men, 1981, Clio and the Bitch Goddess, Quantification in American Political History, 1983, The Congressman's Civil War, 1989; co-editor: The Jeffersonian Dream: Studies in the History of American Law Land Policy and Development, 1996, Frederick Jackson Turner: Strange Roads Going Down, 1998, The Farm on the North Talbot Road, 2001. Lt. Can. Army, 1943-45. Social Sci. Rsch. Coun. fellow, 1955, 66, Guggenheim fellow, 1970, H.E. Huntington Libr. fellow, 1991, 93, Sherman Fairchild Disting. fellow Calif. Inst. Tech., 1975, Ctr. for Advanced Study in the Behavioral Scis. fellow, 1985, NEH fellow, 1985. Fellow Agr. Hist. Soc. (pres. 1963-64); mem. Orgn. Am. Historians (pres. 1982-83), Am. Hist. Assn., Econ. Hist. Assn. (pres. 1981-82), Social Sci. Hist. Assn. (pres. 1977-78), Nat. Acad. Scis., Western Hist. Assn. (hon. life). Office: 1914 Vilas Ave Madison WI 53711 E-mail: bogueag@mhub.history.wisc.edu.

BOGUE, ERNEST GRADY, academic administrator, educator; b. Memphis, Dec. 9, 1935; s. Emery Grady and Ardell (Wiseman) B.; m. Linda Young; children: Karin, Michele, Barrett, Sara, Michael. B.S., Memphis State U., 1957, M.A., 1965, Ed.D., 1968. Asst. v.p. acad. affairs Memphis State U., 1971-74; fellow in acad. adminstrn. Am. Council on Edn., Washington, 1974-75; assoc. dir. acad. affairs Tenn. Higher Edn. Com., Nashville, 1975-80; chancellor La. State U., Shreveport, 1980-90. Author: The Enemies of Leadership, 1985. Contbr. articles to profl. jours. Bd. dirs. Norwela council Boy Scouts Am., Shreveport, 1980—, Shreveport Opera Bd., 1981-84, United Way, Shreveport, 1983— . Served to capt. USAF, 1958-61. Mem. Shreveport C. of C. (dir. 1980-83), Am. Assn. State Coll. and Univs., So. Assn. Colls. and Schs. (chmn. personnel tng. com.), Phi Delta Kappa, Omicron Delta Kappa. Mem. Church of Christ. Avocations: racquetball; tennis; playing French Horn. Office: La State U One University Pl Shreveport LA 71115

BOGUS, CARL THOMAS, law educator; b. Fall River, Mass., May 14, 1948; s. Isidore E. and Carolyn (Dashoff) B.; m. Dale Shepard, Sept. 5, 1970 (div. 1987); children: Elizabeth Carol, Ian Troy; m. Cynthia J. Giles, Nov. 5, 1988; 1 child, Zoe Churchill. AB, Syracuse U., 1970, JD, 1972. Bar: Pa. 1973, U.S. Dist. Ct. (ea. dist.) Pa. 1973, U.S. Dist. Ct. Appeals (3d cir.) 1976, U.S. Supreme

Ct. 1977. Assoc. Steinberg, Greenstein, Gorelick & Price, Phila., 1973-79, ptnr., 1979-83; assoc. Mesirov, Gelman, Jaffe, Cramer & Jamieson, Phila., 1983-84, ptnr., 1985-91; assoc. prof. Roger Williams U. Sch. Law, Bristol, RI, 1996—2002, prof., 2002—. Vis. prof. Rutgers U. Sch. Law, Camden, 1992—96; mem. bd. visitors Coll. Law, Syracuse (N.Y.) U., 1976—2001; mem. Nat. adv. panel Violence Policy Ctr., 1993—. Author: Why Lawsuits Are Good for America: Disciplined Democracy, Big Business and the Common Law, 2001; editor: The Second Amendment in Law and History, 2001; contbr. articles to profl. jours. Bd. dirs. Handgun Control, Inc., 1987-89, bd. govs., 1992-93; bd. dirs. Ctr. to Prevent Handgun Violence, 1989-92, Lawyers Alliance for Nuclear Arms Control, 1987-89; mem. state governing bd. Common Cause R.I., 1999-2001. Recipient Common Cause Pub. Svc. award, RI, 2002. Mem. ABA (Ross Essay award 1991), Syracuse Law Coll. Assn. (exec. sec. 1979-83, 2d v.p. 1983-85). Democrat. Mem. Soc. Of Friends. Office: Roger William U Sch Law 10 Metacom Ave Bristol RI 02809-5103 E-mail: cbogus@law.rwu.edu.

BOGUSLAVSKY, GEORGE WILLIAM, psychologist, educator; b. Razdolnoye, Maritime, Russia, Oct. 17, 1911; came to U.S., 1930. s. Vasilii P. and Anna (Lysenko) B.; m. Geneva K. Bowers, Jan. 8, 1943. BA, U. Wash., 1939, MS, 1941; PhD, Cornell U., 1953. Lic. psychologist, N.Y. Instr. U. Conn., Storrs, 1947-51; asst. prof. Cornell U., Ithaca, N.Y., 1953-57; prof., chmn. dept. psychology Rensselaer Poly. Inst., Troy, N.Y., 1957-77. Cons. Am. Inst. Rsch., Pitts., 1952-77, Pergamon Inst., London, 1959-62; adv. N.Y. State Edn. Dept., Albany, 1957-59, Rensselaer Family Court, Troy, 1958-60. Contbg. author: Group Processes, 1957, Physiological Bases Psychiatry, 1958; also articles. Capt. Adjutant Gen.'s Dept., 1942-46, PTO. Rsch. grantee HEW, 1962-65. Mem. AAAS, APA, Assn. N.Y. Acad. Scis., Pavlovian Soc., Archives of History of Am. Psychology, Sigma Xi. Home: 71 Forest At Duke Dr Durham NC 27705-5639

BOGUSLAWSKI, ALEXANDER PRUS, Russian studies educator, artist, Internet designer; b. Warsaw, Apr. 3, 1951; came to U.S., 1977; s. Andrzej Prus and Noemi (Bialer) B.; children: Martin, Julia Laura, Antonia Christina; m. Kathryn Davidson-Bond, May 7, 1994. MA, U. Warsaw, 1975; PhD, U. Kans, 1982. Teaching asst. U. Kans., Lawrence, 1978-82; vis. lectr. Ohio State U., Columbus, 1982-83; asst. prof. Russian studies Rollins Coll., Winter Park, Fla., 1983-86, assoc. prof., 1987-91, prof., 1992—, chair Dept. Fgn. Langs., 1999—. Lectr. and presenter in field. Translator: Poetics of Old Russian Literature (Dmitri Likhachev), 1981, A School for Fools (Sasha Sokolov), 1984, Hotel Million Monkeys and Other Stories (Victor Brook), 2000, Between Dog and Wolf (Sasha Sokolov), 2001; contbr. articles to profl. jours.; exhibited at Olin Libr., Rollins Coll., 1986, Jewish Cmty. Ctr., 1986, 1994, Ormond Meml. Art Mus., 2000, Valencia C.C., 2001, Cornell Fine Art Mus., 2002. Fgn. Lang. and Area Studies fellow, 1979-81, U. Kans. fellow, 1980, 81-82; Jack B. Critchfield grantee Rollins Coll., 1984-86, 91, 99, NEH grantee, 1987, 2001. Mem. Am. Assn. Tchrs. Slavic and East European Langs., Am. Assn. for Advancement of Slavic Studies. Democrat. Avocations: music, photography. Home: 1925 Falmouth Rd Maitland FL 32751 Office: Rollins Coll Dept Fgn Langs Winter Park FL 32789

BOGUTZ, JEROME EDWIN, lawyer, educator; b. Bridgeton, N.J., June 7, 1935; s. Charles and Gertrude (Lahn) B.; m. Helene Carole Ross, Nov. 20, 1960; children: Marc Lahn, Tami Lynne BS in Fin., Pa. State U., 1957; JD, Villanova U., 1962. Bar: Pa., U.S. Dist. Ct. (ea. dist.) Pa., U.S. Ct. Appeals (3d cir.), U.S. Supreme Ct. Assoc. Dash & Levy, Phila., 1962—63, Abrahams & Loewenstein, Phila., 1963—64; dep. dir., chief of litigation Community Legal Svcs., Phila., 1964—68, dir., 1968—78; emeritus, 1978—; pvt. practice law, 1968—71; ptnr. Bogutz & Mazer, Phila., 1971—81, Fox Rothschild O'Brien & Frankel, Phila., 1981—98; judge Pro Tem Phila. Ct. Common Pleas, 1992—; ptnr. Christie, Pabarue, Mortensen & Young, P.C., Phila., 1998—. Adj. clin. prof. law Villanova (Pa.) U., 1969-72, lectr., 1987—, bd. consultors Law Sch., 1983—; pres. Internat. Mobile Machines, Phila., 1980-81, Interdigital Comm., 1980-81, also bd. dirs. ABA-JAD Lawyers Conf., 1987-92, mem. exec. coun., 1986-92, vice chmn., 1987-88, chmn., 1989-90, chmn. nominating com., 1989-90, mem. long range planning com., 1989-90; mem. adv. bd. Pa. Med. Profl. Liability Catastrophe Loss Fund, 2000—; bd. dirs. Jefferson Park Hosp., Phila. Bd. dirs. Am. Friends of Hebrew U., 1988-93, chmn. exec. com., 1991-93, pres., 1993-95, chmn. bd. 1995-98, chair steering com., pres. Pa. Futures Commn. on Justice in the 21st Century, 1993—, chmn. of bd., 1993-97. With USAR, 1956-60. Fellow Am. Bar Found. (life), Pa. Bar Found. (life, pres. 1986-88, bd. dirs. 1983—, lifetime dir. 1991—), Am. Judicature Soc. (life, bd. dirs. 1990—); mem. ABA (ho. of dels. 1980-84, 86-96, credentials and admissions com. 1987-88, nominating com. 1992, 93, chair ABA/JAD bench bar com., vice chmn. lawyer's conf. 1987-89, chair 1988-90, co-chair mid-yr. meeting com. 1987-88, planning com., conf. sect. officers, 1988-90, bd. mem. consortium on legal svcs. and pub. 1987-91, mem. disaster relief task force, bd. dirs., commr., chmn. ABA Commn. on Advt. 1988-91, adv. coun. ABA Commn. Responsibility 1999—), Pa. Bar Assn. (pres. 1985-86, bd. dirs. 1983-90, chair Governance Com., 1996-98), Phila. Bar Found. (pres. 1981), Phila. Bar Assn. (v.p. 1978, pres.-elect 1979, chancellor 1980, sec. 1975-78, trustee 1979—), Pa. Bar Trust (life mem., chmn. 1993-2001, chmn. emeritus 2001—), Pa. House of Dels. (life; chair governance com. 1996-98), Nat. Met. Bar Leaders (founder, pres. 1979-82, pres. emeritus 1983—), Nat. Conf. Bar Pres. (exec. coun. 1981-84), Phila. C. of C. (bd. dirs. 1980-83). Republican. Jewish. Avocations: golf, sailing. Home: Apt 6B 1901 Walnut St Philadelphia PA 19103 Office: Christie Pabarue Mortensen & Young 1880 JFK Blvd Fl 10 Philadelphia PA 19103-7424

BOGY, DAVID B(EAUREGARD), mechanical engineering educator; b. Wabbaseka, Ark., June 4, 1936; s. Jesse C. and Dorothy (Duff) B.; m. Patricia Lynn Pizzitola, Mar. 28, 1961; children: Susan, Rebecca. BS, Rice U., 1959, MS, 1961; PhD, Brown U., 1966. Mech. engr. Shell Devel. Co., Houston, 1961-63; asst. prof. mech. engring. U. Calif., Berkeley, 1967-70, assoc. prof., 1970-75, prof., 1975—, chmn. dept. mech. engring., 1991-99, founder, dir. computer mechanics lab., William S. Floyd, Jr. Disting. prof., 1993—. Cons. IBM Rsch., 1972-83; mem. nat. com. on theoretical and applied mechanics NRC. Contbr. more than 270 articles to profl. jours. Served with C.E. U.S. Army, 1961-62. Fellow ASME, IEEE; mem. NAE. Achievements include research in static and dynamic elasticity, fluid jets and mechanics of computer disk files and printers. Home: 8531 Buckingham Dr El Cerrito CA 94530-2533 Office: U Calif 6103 Etcheverry Hall Berkeley CA 94720-1740

BOH, ROBERT HENRY, civil engineer, construction company executive; b. New Orleans, Sept. 15, 1930; BS in Civil Engring., Tulane U., 1951, MS in Civil Engring., 1953. Civil engr. Boh Bros. Constrn. Co., New Orleans, 1951; mem. faculty dept. civil engring. Tulane U., 1952-53, civil engr., 1953-55, Boh Bros. Constrn. Co., 1955—, bd. dirs., v.p., treas., 1960—, pres., CEO, 1967-93, chmn. bd. dirs., 1986—. Vis. lectr. civil engring., 1959-68; mem. adv. bd. The Times-Picayune. Mem. New Orleans Bus. Coun., Metrovision Econ. Devel. Coun., Com. of 100 for Econ. Devel. of State of La.; immediate past chmn. bd. adminstrs. Tulane U. Edn. Fund, 1988-93; chmn. bd. dirs. Chamber/New Orleans and the River Region, 1985. Mem. ASCE, NSPE, La. Engring. Soc., Associated Gen. Contractors Am. (life dir.New Orleans dist. past pres.), Associated Gen. Contractors La. (dir., past pres.). Office: Boh Bros Construction Co PO Box 53266 New Orleans LA 70153-3266

BOHACHEF, JANET MAE, medical educator; b. Glendale, Calif., Aug. 24, 1957; d. William George and Lois Elizabeth Bohachef; 1 child, Andrew William Sauer. BA, Calif. State U., 1982; AAS, Shoreline Coll., 1985; student, Wayland Baptist U., 1999—. Cert. Clin. Lab. Tech., Med Lab. Tech. Nat. Certification Agy. Med. Lab. Pathologists, Med. Technologist Am. Soc. Clin. Pathologists. Med. technologist VA Med. Ctr., Seattle, Va., 1985—86, Amarillo, Tex., 1987—90, High Plains Baptist Hosp., Amarillo, 1990—93; med. lab. instr. Amarillo Coll., Amarillo, 1993—94, med. lab. program dir., 1994—. Mem. adv. bd. Amarillo Coll., 1994—, faculty senator, 1994—96; paper rev. Nat. Accrediting Agy. Clin. Lab. Sci., Chgo., 1995—, med. lab. accred. site visitor, 1995, 2000—02. Author: (poetry) www.Poetry.com, 2001. With USN, 1975—79. Grantee, Tech. Prep. Sch. to Careers, 2000. Mem.: Tex. C.C. Tchrs. Assn., Tex. Soc. Clin. Lab. Sci., Am. Soc. Clin. Lab. Sci., Am. Soc. Clin. Pathologists. Avocation: web design. Office: Amarillo College PO Box 447 Amarillo TX 79178 Home: 8101 Prosper Dr Amarillo TX 79119

BOHAN, THOMAS LYNCH, physicist, lawyer; b. Terre Haute, Ind., Feb. 12, 1938; s. Richard Timothy and Anna Elizabeth (Lynch) B.; m. Linda Ann Sian, Nov. 26, 1960 (div. Dec. 1981); children: Richard Michael, Cecilia Anne, John Charles; m. Rhonda Beth Berg, July 4, 1987. BS in Physics, U. Chgo., 1960; MS in Physics, U. Ill., 1964, PhD in Physics, 1968; JD, Franklin Pierce Law Ctr., 1980. Bar: Maine 1980, Mass. 1980, U.S. Dist. Ct. Maine 1980, U.S. Patent Office 1980, U.S. Ct. Appeals (1st cir.) 1992, U.S. Ct. Appeals (2nd cir.) 1994, U.S. Supreme Ct., 1996. Rsch. assoc. U. Ill., Urbana, 1968—69; asst. prof. physics Bowdoin Coll., Brunswick, Maine, 1969—76; assoc. Sunenblick, Fontaine and Reben, Portland, Maine, 1980—82; ptnr. Med. and Tech. Cons. (now MTC Forensics), Portland, 1982—86, sole propr., 1986—; propr. Thomas L. Bohan & Assoc., Portland, 1985—2001, Bohan Mathers & Assocs., Portland, 2002, of counsel, 2003—. Editor (with A. Damask) Forensic Accident Investigation: Motor Vehicles-1, 1995; editor Forensic Accident Investigation: Motor Vehicles-2, 1997; contbr. articles to profl. jours. Chmn. Community Devel. Com., Brunswick, 1976-78; organizer, treas., pres. Peaks Island Land Preserve, Inc., 1994-97. Research grantee Am. Heart Assn., 1970-76, The Research Corp., 1972-74, NSF/NATO, 1967; fellow Tex. Instruments, 1965; Fulbright scholar, Peru, 1972-73. Fellow: Am. Acad. Forensic Sci. (chair engring. sci. sect. 1997—98, bd. dirs. 1999—, exec. com. bd. dirs. 2000—); mem.: AASN, Nat. Assn. Patent Practitioners, Maine Patent Practitioners Group, Maine Trial Lawyers Assn., Cumberland County Bar Assn., Am. Phys. Soc., Sigma Xi. Home: 54 Pleasant Ave Peaks Island ME 04108-1188 Office: MTC-Forensics and Bohan Mathers & Assoc 371 Fore St Portland ME 04101-5010 E-mail: tbohan2@maine.rr.com., tlb@bohanlaw.com., tlb@mtcforensics.com.

BOHANAN, DAVID JOHN, management consultant; b. Utica, N.Y., Dec. 13, 1946; s. Clifton Ralph and Florence Susan Bohanan; m. Judith Ann Petrocci, July 31, 1977; children: Luke, Jacob. BFA in Ceramics and Painting, Alfred U., 1968; BS in Commerce, U. Md., 1979; MBA in Mgmt., Boston U., 1981. Pub. R&R in the Med Mediterranean Pubs. Srl., Vicenza, Italy, 1974-81; pvt. practice fin. cons. Jersey City, 1981-86; bus. cons. S&B Practice Mgmt. Assocs., Greenbrook, N.J., 1986—; fin. planner Fin. Found., Inc., Greenbrook, N.J., 1986-98. Rep. Nathan & Lewis Securities, Inc., N.Y.C., 1982-93, Cadaret, Grant & Co., Syracuse, N.Y., 1994-2000, Nat. Planning Corp., 2001—. Capt. F.A., U.S. Army, 1968-74. Decorated Bronze Star with oak leaf cluster. Republican. Home: 10 Saw Mill Rd Lebanon NJ 08833-4618 Office: S&B Practice Mgmt Assocs 314 Us Highway 22 Green Brook NJ 08812-1700 E-mail: dave@bohanan.com.

BOHANNAN, JAY KIRBY, artist; b. N.Y.C., Jan. 30, 1950; s. Jules Kirby and Lucyann Bohannan. BFA, Va. Commonwealth U., Richmond, 1973; cert., L'Alliance Francais, Paris, 1985. Free lance artist Assn. Preservation Va. Antiquities, 1976, Lancaster Pub., Gadsden, Ala., 1986, Retail Merchants Greater Richmond, 1988, City of Hopewell, Va., 1989, Hirschler Fleischer Weinberg Cox & Allen, 1993, Atlantic Monthly, Boston, 1995, Abbeville Press, N.Y.C., 1996, Richmond Mag., Philip Morris U.S.A., 1995-2003, Assoc. Gen. Contractors Va., 1999; exhibited in group shows at Chrysler Mus., Norfolk, Va., 1992, Addison-Rippley, Washington, 1999; represented in collections at IBM, Manassas, Va., Sallie Mae, Washington, Med. Coll. Va., Richmond, U. Va., Charlottesville, Valentine Mus., Richmond, others. Avocation: american scene painting. Home and Office: 3 N Colonial Ave Richmond VA 23221-3033

BOHANNAN, PAUL JAMES, anthropologist, writer, former university administrator; b. Lincoln, Nebr., Mar. 5, 1920; s. Hillory and Hazel (Truex) B.; m. Laura Marie Smith, May 15, 1943 (div. 1975); 1 child, Denis Michael; m. Adelyse D'Arcy, Feb. 28, 1981. BA, U. Ariz., 1947; B.Sc., Oxford U., Eng., 1949, DPhil, 1951. Lectr. social anthropology Oxford (Eng.) U., 1951-56; asst. prof. anthropology Princeton (N.J.) U., 1956-59; prof. Northwestern U., Evanston, Ill., 1959-75, U. Calif., Santa Barbara, 1976-82; prof., dean social scis. and communications U. So. Calif., Los Angeles, 1982-87, prof. emeritus, 1987—. Author: Justice and Judgement, 1957, Africa and Africans, 1964, 4th edit., 1995, Divorce and After, 1970, We, the Alien, 1991, How Culture Works, 1995. Served to capt. U.S. Army, 1941-45. Decorated Legion of Merit Mem. Am. Anthrop. Assn. (pres. 1979-80), Am. Ethnol. Soc. (dir. 1963-66), African Studies Assn. (pres. 1963-64), Social Sci. Research Council (dir. 1962-64) E-mail: paulboh@aol.com.

BOHANNON, CAMILLE, news anchor; b. Las Vegas, N.Mex., May 30, 1946; d. George W. Skora and Lillian Marie Guffey; m. James E. Bohannon, Sept. 26, 1970 (div. July 1987). BA, N.Mex. Highlands U., 1968. News anchor, asst. program dir. Clear Sight Cable TV, Las Vegas, 1967-68; classical music announcer Sta. WETA Radio, Washington, 1970-72; news anchor Sta. WTOP Radio, Washington, 1975-77, Sta. WRC Radio, Washington, 1977-80, WCFL Radio Chgo., 1980-83, UPI Radio Network, N.Y.C., 1983-84, Sta. WRC Radio, Washington, 1984-87, NBC/Mut. Radio Nets, Washington, 1987-92, AP Radio Network, Washington, 1992—. Ch. and choir mem. Covenant United Meth. Ch., Gaithersburg, Md., 1984—; mem. Gaithersburg Cmty. Chorus, 2000—. Recipient Best Newscast award Ill. AP Broadcasters, 1983, Outstanding Pub. Svc. Program award Chesapeake AP Broadcasters, 1987, Outstanding Spot News Reporting award, 1977. Mem. Soc. Profl. Journalists (bd. dirs. 1982), Am. Women in Radio and TV (established multicoll. chpt. coll. students in broadcasting 1978-80). Methodist. Avocations: biking, sports viewing, reading, dogs. Office: AP Radio Network 1825 K St NW Washington DC 20006

BOHANNON, CHARLES TAD, lawyer; b. Dallas, June 25, 1964; s. Charles Spencer and Donna Pauline (Smith) B.; m. Gayle Renee Alston, July 26, 1986. BA, Hendrix Coll., 1986; JD, U. Ark., Little Rock, 1992; LLM, Washington U., St. Louis, 1993. Bar: Ark. 1992, Tex. 1993, U.S. Dist. Ct. (ea. and we. dists.) Ark. 1992, U.S. Dist. Ct. (no. dist.) Tex. 1994, U.S. Ct. Appeals (5th and 8th cirs.) 1994, U.S. Tax Ct. 1994. Staff atty. U.S. Ct. Appeals (8th cir.), St. Louis, 1992-94; assoc. Gill Law Firm, Little Rock, 1994-98; ptnr. Wright, Lindsey & Jennings, LLP, Little Rock, 1998—. Contbr. articles to profl. jours. Mem. ABA, Ark. Bar Assn., Pulaski County Bar Assn., Nat. Transp. Safety Bd., Bar Assn. State Bar of Tex., Nat. Assn. Bond Lawyers, Aircraft Owners and Pilots Assn. Avocations: soccer (player, referee, coach), flying, fly fishing, home renovation. Office: Wright Lindsey & Jennings 200 W Capitol Ave Ste 2300 Little Rock AR 72201-3699 E-mail: ctbohannon@wlj.com.

BOHANNON, SARAH VIRGINIA, personnel professional; b. Roanoke, Va., Mar. 1, 1947; AA in Bus. Adminstrn. Mgmt., Nat. Bus. Coll., 1983. Pers. appointment clk. IRS, Richmond, Va., 1983—84; pers. technician Commonwealth of Va., Richmond, Va., 1985—97, pers. asst., 1997—98, pers. technician, 1999—2000, pers. adminstrv. specialist dept. human resource mgmt., 2001—02. Mem. Am. Biog. Inst. (life, dep. gov. 1991, mem. women's inner circle of achievement 1991). Home: 2220 Clarke St Richmond VA 23228-6049

BOHANNON-KAPLAN, MARGARET ANNE, publisher, lawyer; b. Oakland, Calif., July 6, 1937; d. Thomas Morris and Ruth Frances (Davenport) Bohannon; m. Melvin Jordan Kaplan, Feb. 2, 1961; children: Mark Geoffrey Kaplan, Craig Andrew Kaplan, Stephen Joseph Kaplan, David Benjamin Kaplan, Jonathan Michael Kaplan. Student, Smith Coll., 1955-56, U. Cin., 1956; BA in Philosophy, U. Calif.-Berkeley, 1960; LL.B., LaSalle Extension U., 1982, Coll. Fin. Planning, 1985. Bar: Calif. 1982; cert. CFP. Engaged in property mgmt., real estate investment Kaplan Real Estate, Berkeley and San Francisco, 1961-77; investment exec. Wellington Fin. Group, San Francisco, 1977—; cons. fin. planning and law San Francisco and Carmel, Calif., 1982—; pres. Wellington Publs., Carmel, 1983—, Exec. Advt., Carmel, 1983—. Talk show host Sta. KNRY, KIEZ, 1999. Author (pseudonym Helen P. Rogers): Everyone's Guide to Financial Planning, 1984; author: Social Security: An Idea Whose Time Has Passed, 1985, The American Deficit: Fulfillment of a Prophecy, 1988, The Election Process, 1988, The Deficit: 12 Steps to Ease the Crisis, 1988, (11 book series) Taking a Stand On, 1991, Alternatives, 1992, Another Way, 1997; editor: What Role if Any, Should Government's Role be Regarding Child Care in the United States?, 1991, What if Any, Should Government's Role be Regarding Health Care in the Untied States?, 1992, What Role Does, And What Role Should Media Play in Choosing Our Candidates for National Office?, 1993, 1997, Doesn't Anyone Care About the Children?, 1994, Responsibility: Who Has It and Who Doesn't and What That Means to the Nation, 1994, 1996—98, White Hats: People Who Try to Make a Difference, 1994, Governments Struggling with Limited Resources, 1995—97, Should Government Intervene to Help Children and Teens in Trouble, If So How?, 1995, Kids R Us, 2000, Social Security in the Twenty-First Century, 1996, Excerpts from Three 1997 Harry Singer Foundation National High School Essay Contests, 1997, The Budget Process and the National Debt, 1998, The Role of Personal Responsibility in Balancing Individual Liberty and the Common Good, 1999, others. Mem.: ABA, Ind. Sector, Fin. Planning Assn., Calif. Bar Assn., Philanthropy Round Table, Commonwealth Club (San Francisco). Office: PO Box 223159 Carmel CA 93922-3159

BOHANON, LUTHER L. federal judge; b. Ft. Smith, Ark., Aug. 9, 1901; s. William Joseph and Artelia (Campbell) B.; m. Marie Swatek, July 17, 1933; 1 son, Richard L. LLB, U. Okla., 1927; LLD (hon.), Oklahoma City U., 1991. Bar: Okla. 1927, U.S. Supreme Ct. 1937. Gen. practice law, Seminole, Okla. and Oklahoma City, 1927-61; judge U.S. Dist. Ct. Okla. (no., ea., and we. dists.), 1961-74, sr. judge, 1974—. Mem. platform com. Democratic Nat. Conv., 1940. Served to maj. USAAF, 1942-45. Recipient citations and awards including citation from Okla. Senate and Ho. of Reps., 1979, Okla. County Bar Assn. and Jour. Record award, 1987, Humanitarian award NCCJ, 1991; Luther Bohanon Am. Inn of Ct. named in his honor Am. Inn of Ct. XXIII/U. Okla., 1991. Mem. U.S. Dist. Judges Assn. (10th cir.), Fed. Judges Assn., Okla. Bar Assn., Oklahoma County Bar Assn., Oklahoma City C. of C., Sigma Nu, Phi Alpha Delta. Clubs: Mason (Shriner, 32 deg.), K.T, Jester, Kiwanis, Com.of 100, Men's Dinner Club. Methodist. Office: US Dist Ct PO Box 1514 Oklahoma City OK 73102-3028

BOHATA, EMIL ANTON, rancher; b. Sept. 10, 1918; s. Frank and Mary Frances (Vodraska) B.; m. Ruth Joan Fletcher, July 14, 1963; children: Ruth Marie, Robert Anton. Student, S.W. Tex. State U., 1942-43. Lifelong rancher, Brookville, Kans., 1935-42, 1945—. Trustee United Meth. Ch., Carneiro, Kans., 1970-88, chmn. bd., 1988-96; treas. Carneiro Twp., 1975-2003. With U.S. Army, 1944-46. Recipient Fred Astaire Bronze, Silver and Gold Dance trophies Fred Astaire Dance Studio, Salina, Kans., 1960-62, Bankers' Award for Soil Conservation, 1996. Mem. Ellsworth County Farm Bur., Kans. Livestock Assn., Polled Hereford Assn., Friends Marymount Coll., Arts Series Soc., Salina Art Ctr., Am. Legion, Gideon Internat. Republican. Methodist. Avocations: dancing, reading, listening to music. Home and Office: 765 27th Rd Brookville KS 67425-9208

BOHEN, DOLORES BOYLSTON, retired school administrator; b. N.Y.C., Nov. 2, 1929; d. Adrian F. Boylston and Louise Montanez; m. John McGee Bohen (dec. Apr. 1979); children: Christina, Pamela, Kerry, Sean, Michele, Patricia. BA in English, Adelphi U., 1951; MEd, Tulane U., 1968; PhD, George Mason U., 2000. Elem. tchr., Leavenworth, Kans., 1966-67; tchr. mid. sch. New Orleans, 1967-68; tchr., chmn. dept. English Fairfax (Va.) H.S., 1968-75, resource tchr., 1975-76; lang. arts specialist K-12 Fairfax County Pub. Schs., 1976-80, instrnl. coord., 1981-82, spl. asst. to dep. supt., 1982-84, asst. supt. comm., 1984-98. Author textbook series McDougal, Littell Spelling Grades 1-8, 1982, 85, 90, 94; contbr. articles to profl. jours. Bd. dirs. Arts Coun. of Fairfax County, Va. Mem. ASCD, Assn. Ednl. Pubs., Phi Delta Kappa, Kappa Delta Pi Home and Office: 4505 Tempest Pl Annandale VA 22003-3968

BOHI, LYNN, state legislator; b. Cleve., Feb. 20, 1947; m. Charles W. Bohi. BA, Olivet Coll., 1970; postgrad., Plymouth State U. State rep. Vt. Ho. of Reps., 1989—90, 1993—98, 2001—; chair local govt. com., 1997—98; vice chair local govt. com., 2003. Active Conn. River Joint Commn. Upper Valley River Subcom., Human Svcs. Coun., 1987-89, United Way Upper Valley, 1981-88, Hartford Recycles, Workforce Investment Bd., Adult Edn. Coun., Cmty. Partnership of Orange and Windsor Counties; trustee EarthRight, 1991-94. Mem. No. Light Quilting Guild, Hartford Garden Friends. Address: 156 Manning Dr White River Junction VT 05001-8075 E-mail: lbohi@leg.state.vt.us.

BOHLAND, EUGENE R., JR., music educator; b. Toledo, Jan. 9, 1956; s. Eugene R. and Marian L. Bohland; m. Carol A. Christoph, Apr. 6, 1989; children: Kathryn L., Lindsey M. EdB, U. Toledo, 1978, EdM, 1986. Asst. band dir. Napoleon (Ohio) H.S., 1978—86, Sylvania (Ohio) Northview H.S., 1986—89, dir. bands, 1989—. Mem.: NEA, Toledo Jazz Soc. (bd. mem. 1999—), Music Educators Nat. Conf., Phi Beta Mu. Avocations: music, golf.

BOHLE, ROBERT HENRY, journalism educator; b. Oak Park, Ill., June 24, 1947; s. William Henry and Vivian Grace (Frasier) B.; m. Suzanne Egan, Mar. 12, 1994; children: Cameron Jay, Christopher Robert. BA in English cum laude, Calif. State U., Long Beach, 1970, MA in English lit., 1972; PhD in Comm., U. Tenn., 1984. Sports reporter and copy desk, copy clk., news copy clk. Long Beach Ind., 1968-72; tchr. English and journalism Monache High Sch., Porterville, Calif., 1972-74; instr., acting chmn. Orange Coast Coll., Costa Mesa, Calif., 1974-76; instr. Palomar Coll., San Marcos, Calif., 1976, Coll. of the Sequoias, Visalia, Calif., 1976-83; assoc. prof. Sch. of Mass Comm., Va. Commonwealth U., Richmond, 1983-95; prof. dept. Comms. and Visual Arts U. North Fla., Jacksonville, 1995—. Spkr. and presenter workshops and seminars; publ. and internet cons. Author: From News to Newsprint, 2d edit., 1992, Publication Design for Editors, 1990, (with others) Color in American Newspapers, 1986; contbr. numerous articles to profl. jours. Recipient Presdl. Citation Coll. Media Advisers, Inc., 1983, Outstanding Young Man in Am. award U.S. Jaycees, 1982, Gannett Found. Graduation scholarship, 1982; Freedom Forum Prof.'s Publ. grantee, 1992. Mem. Assn. for Edn. in Journalism and Mass Comm. (editl. adv. bd. Journalism and Mass Comm. Educator 1988-2001), Soc. News Design (mem. edn. com. 1985—, contbg. editor Design jour. 1993-95), Kappa Tau Alpha, Phi Kappa Phi. Avocations: soccer, hiking, canoeing, golf, bicycling, fishing. E-mail: rbohle@unf.edu.

BOHLE, SUE, public relations executive; b. Austin, Minn., June 23, 1943; d. Harold Raymond and Mary Theresa (Swanson) Hastings; m. John Bernard Bohle, June 22, 1974; children: Jason John, Christine K. BS in Journalism, Northwestern U., 1965, MS in Journalism, 1969. Tchr. pub. high schs, Englewood, Colo., 1965-68; account exec. Burson-Marsteller Pub. Relations, Los Angeles, 1969-73; v.p., mgr. pub. relations J. Walter Thompson Co., Los Angeles, 1973-79; founder, pres. The Bohle Company, L.A., 1979—; pres., CEO The Bohle Co., L.A.; former exec. v.p. Ketchum Pub. Rels., L.A. Free-lance writer, instr. communications Calif. State U. at Fullerton, 1972-73; instr. writing Los Angeles City Coll., 1975-76; lectr. U. So. Calif., 1979—. Contbr. articles to profl. jours. Dir. pub. rels. L.A. Jr. Ballet, 1971-72; pres. Panhellenic Advisers Coun., UCLA, 1972-73; mem. adv. bd. L.A. Valley Coll., 1974-75, Coll. Communications Pepperdine U., 1981-85, Sch. Journalism U. So. Calif., 1987-95, Calif. State U., Long Beach, 1988-93; bd. visitors Medill Sch. Journalism Northwestern U., 1984—. Recipient Alumni Svc. award Northwestern U., 1995; Univ. scholar, 1961-64, Panhellenic scholar, 1964-65; named to Hall of Achievement, Medill Sch. Journalism, 1997, charter mem. Hall of Fame; named to 50 Top Women in PR, PR Week, mag., 2001. Fellow Pub. Rels. Soc. Am. (bd. dirs. L.A. chpt. 1981-90, v.p. 1983, pres. 1989, del. nat. assembly 1980, 94, 95, 96, co-chmn. long-range strategic com. 1990, pres.'s adv. coun. 1991, exec. com. Counselors Acad. 1984-86, sec.-treas. 1990, chmn. 1992, sec. Coll. Fellows 1993, vice chair 1994, chmn. 1995, Silver Anvil award 1994); mem. Worldcom PR Network (bd. dirs. 2002—), World Com., Women in Comm., Shi-ai, Delta Zeta (editor The Lamp 1966-68, Woman of Yr. award 1993), Kappa Alpha Tau. Office: 1900 Avenue of the Stars # 200 Los Angeles CA 90067-4301

BOHLEN, PATRICK JOSEPH, ecologist, researcher; b. Cin., Mar. 9, 1961; s. Frederick Robert and Mary Virginia B.; m. Julie Ann Mitchell, June 13, 1992; children: Paul, Madeleine. BS, U. Mich., 1983; MS, Miami U., 1989; PhD, Ohio State U., 1994. Postdoct. rsch. assoc. Inst. Ecosys. Studies, Millbrook, N.Y., 1994-98; rsch. biologist Archbold Biol. Sta., Lake Placid, Fla., 1998—. Author: Biology and Ecology of Earthworms, 1996. Fed. grantee NSF, 1998—, Mem. Ecol. Soc. Am. Home: 550 Buck Island Ranch Rd Lake Placid FL 33852 Office: MacArthur Agro-Ecology Rsch Ctr 300 Buck Island Ranch Rd Lake Placid FL 33852 Fax: (863) 699-2217. E-mail: pbohlen@archbold-station.org.

BOHLENDER, HUGH DARROW, lawyer; b. Sacramento, Oct. 27, 1951; s. Hugh S. and Dorothy Elrene (Darrow) B.; m. Eliese Susanna Wagenseil, June 9, 1973 (div. Feb. 1982); children: Philip Edward, Karen Leslie; m. Ingrid Elizabeth Rieck, Dec. 27, 1997. BS, U.S. Mil. Acad., 1973; MA, Northwestern U., 1982, JD, 1986, postgrad. Bar: Ill. 1986, U.S. Dist. Ct. (no. dist.) Ill. 1986. Commd. 2nd lt. U.S. Army, 1975, advanced through grades to capt., 1977,

resigned, 1981; lectr. Northwestern U., Evanston, Ill., 1984-85; assoc. Lord Bissell & Brook, Chgo., 1986-90; of counsel Allstate Ins. Co., 1990—. Dir. Ala. Ins. Guaranty Assn., 1992-93. Vice chmn. Northbrook (Ill.) Evang. Covenant Ch., 1988-91. Maj. USAR, 1986-93; ret. Mem. ABA, Ill. Bar Assn. Republican. Avocations: running, cycling, camping, photography, computers. Office: Allstate Ins Co Allstate Plz N Northbrook IL 60062

BOHLINGER, LEWIS HALL, state government official; b. Little Rock, July 8, 1942; s. Lewis Hall Bohlinger and Helen Elisa (Reid) Bragg; m. Kathleen Ann Klein, Jan. 30, 1967; children: Lewis Hall, Reid Watson. BS, Southeastern La. U., 1965; MS, Tulane U., 1970, ScD, 1975. Rsch. asst. Delta Primate Rsch. Ctr., Covington, La., 1965-69; health physicist La. Bd. Nuclear Energy, Baton Rouge, 1971-80; asst. adminstr. La. Nuclear Energy Divsn., Baton Rouge, 1980-87; dep. asst. sec. La. Office of Environ. Affairs, Baton Rouge, 1983-89; asst. sec. La. Office of Air Quality, Baton Rouge, 1984-86; dep. sec. La. DEQ, Baton Rouge, 1987-88; adminstr. La. Radiation Protection Divsn., Baton Rouge, 1989-94, La. Hazardous Waste Divsn., Baton Rouge, 1994-96; dep. sec. La. Dept. Environ. Quality, Baton Rouge, 1996—2002, sec., 2002—. Adj. asst. prof. Tulane U., New Orleans, 1988—; chair Ctrl. Interstate Low Level Radioactive Waste Compact Commn., 1983—89, 1991; chmn., mem. various state and fed. tech. coms. USPHS grant, 1969—71. Mem.: La. Air and Waste Mgmt. Assn., Health Physics Soc., La. Environ. Health Assn., Am. Nuc. Soc., Delta Omega Soc. Home: 11930 Parkbrook Ave Baton Rouge LA 70816-4672 Office: LA Dept Environ Quality PO Box 82263 Baton Rouge LA 70884-2263

BOHM, HENRY VICTOR, physicist; b. Vienna, July 16, 1929; came to U.S., 1941, naturalized, 1946; s. Victor Charles and Gertrude (Rie) B.; m. Lucy Margaret Coons, Sept. 2, 1950; children: Victoria Rie, Jeffrey Ernst Thompson. AB, Harvard U., 1950; MS, U. Ill., 1951; PhD, Brown U., 1958. Jr. physicist GE, 1951, 53-54; teaching, research asst. Brown U., 1954-58, research assoc., summer 1958; staff mem. Arthur D. Little, Inc., Cambridge, Mass., 1958-59; asso. prof. physics dept. Wayne State U., Detroit, 1959-64, acting chmn. physics dept., 1962-63, prof., 1964-93, prof. emeritus, 1993—, v.p. for grad. studies and research, 1968-71, v.p. for spl. projects, 1971-72, provost, 1972-75, on leave, 1978-83, interim dean Coll. Liberal Arts, 1984-86; pres. Argonne Univs. Assn., 1978-83. Vis. prof. Cornell U., 1966-67, U. Lancaster, Eng., summer 1967, Purdue U., winter, 1977, Rensselaer Poly. Inst., winter 1992; cons.-examiner commn. on instns. higher edn. N. Central Assn. Colls. and Schs., 1971-80, mem. commn., 1974-78 Bd. dirs. Center for Research Libraries, Chgo, 1970-75, chmn., 1973; bd. overseers Lewis Coll., Ill. Inst. Tech., 1980-83. Lt. USN, 1951-53. Fellow Am. Phys. Soc. Home: 39732 Eagle Trace Dr Northville MI 48167

BOHM, JACK NELSON, retired lawyer; b. Sharon, Pa., July 5, 1924; s. Joseph and Irene (Bohm) B.; m. Elizabeth Viscofsky, Sept. 27, 1947; children: Robert Mark, Richard Darrell, Lorie Joyce Klumb. Student, U. Pa., 1942-43, U. Ga., 1943-44; JD, Washington U., St. Louis, 1948. Bar: Mo. 1948, U.S Dist. Ct. (we. dist.) Mo. 1948, U.S. Ct. of Mil. Appeals 1955, U.S. Supreme Ct. 1955, U.S. Ct. of Appeals (8th Cir.) 1960, Kans. 1985, U.S. Dist. Ct. Kans. 1985. Assoc. Hall Bresler & Cohn, Kansas City, Mo., 1948—61; ptnr. Glass Bohm & Hirschman, Kansas City, Mo., 1961—71, Stoup & Bohm, Kansas City, Mo., 1971—81; chmn. bd. Buck Bohm & Stein, P.C., Kansas City/Leawood, Kans., 1981—97; sr. counsel Morrison & Hecker LLP, Overland Park, Kans., 1997—99, ret., 1999. Chief judge U.S. Army Ct. of Mil. Appeals, 1977-80, Mobilization Designation. Editor: State Variations of Commercial Law, 1985. Pres. Dist. 2 B'nai B'rith, 1964; co-chmn., NCCJ, Kansas City, 1968-71. With U.S. Army 1943-46, USAR, 1948-84, brigadier gen. AUS, ret. 1977-84. Legion of Merit U.S. Army, 1984. Mem. ABA, Mo. Bar Assn. (chmn. commr. law com. 1977-79), Kans. Bar Assn., Meadowbrook Country Club, Phi Alpha Delta. Home: 11300 Fontana St Leawood KS 66211-1751 E-mail: brgen@aol.com.

BOHM, JOEL LAWRENCE, lawyer, securities industry executive; b. N.Y.C., Dec. 27, 1942; s. Ernest Jonas and Laura (Ullman) B.; m. Karen Rea Brandt, July 3, 1966; children: Michelle Elizabeth, Lori Allison. BA in Polit. Sci., Bklyn. Coll., 1965; JD, Bklyn. Law Sch., 1970. Bar: N.Y. 1971, U.S. Ct. Appeals (2d cir.) 1972, U.S. Dist. Ct. (so. and ea. dists.) N.Y. 1975, U.S. Supreme Ct. 1976. Staff atty. Mohawk Data Scis. Corp., N.Y.C., 1971-72; asst. gen. counsel Gen. Cable Corp., N.Y.C., 1972-73; v.p., gen. counsel Securities Industry Automation Corp., N.Y.C., 1973— ; referee, arbitrator small claims N.Y.C. Civil Ct., 1984—, arbitrator Better Bus. Bur. of Greater N.Y., Inc., 1986-89. Trustee Temple Shaari Emeth, Englishtown, N.J., 1981; mem. Manalapan Twp. Juvenile Conf. Com., 1987—. With USN, 1961. Mem. ABA, Assn. Arbitrators, N.Y. State Bar Assn., N.Y. County Lawyers Assn., Assn. of Bar of City of N.Y. Office: Securities Industry Automation Corp 2 Metrotech Ctr Brooklyn NY 11201-3838

BOHMAN, RAYNARD FREDERICK, JR., transportation consultant, professional association administrator; b. Boston, July 31, 1933; s. Raynard Frederick Bohman Sr. and Theresa Dorothea Conlon; m. Douglas Ann Watson Boutin, Sept. 24, 1955; children: David John, Jack Duncan, Andrew Mackenzie. BS in Econs., U. Pa., 1955. Pres. Nat. Furniture Traffic Conf., Gardner, 1962-95, Bohman Indsl. Traffic Consultants, Gardner, Mass., 1965—; mng. dir. Internat. Furniture Transp. and Logistics Coun., Gardner, 2000—. Transp. cons. Toy Industry Am., N.Y.C., 1955—, Nat. Sch. Supply and Equipment Assn., Silver Spring, Md., 1968—, Outdoor Power Equipment Inst., Alexandria, Va., 1970—, Hobby Industry Assn., Elmwood Park, N.J., 1970—, others. Author: Guide to Freight Classification, 1968; editor: (manual) Furniture Packaging, 1955—, Bohman Traffic News Summary newsletter, 1972—, other newsletters; columnist Reed's Logistics Mgmt. mag., 1987—. 1st lt. U.S. Army, 1955-63. Recipient award Nat. Def. Transp. Assn., Washington, 1955; named Transp. Columnist of Yr., Transp. Claim Prevention Coun., Northport, N.Y., 1995, Transp. Cons. of Yr., Transp. Consumer Protection Coun., Huntington, N.Y., 1999. Mem.: Eastward Ho! Country Club (bd. govs. 1968—74). Republican. Episcopalian. Avocations: travel, golf, philately. Home and Office: 27 Bay Ln Chatham MA 02633

BOHME, DIETHARD KURT, chemistry educator; b. Boston, June 20, 1941; s. Kurt F. and Maria (Kiesel) B. B.Sc., McGill U., 1962, PhD, 1965. Asst. prof. dept. chemistry York U., Toronto, 1970-74, assoc. prof., 1974-77, prof. chemistry, 1977—, disting. rsch. prof. chemistry, 1994—, dir. grad. program in chemistry, 1979-85, chmn. dept. chemistry, 1985—90, 2000—03, Can. rsch. chair in phys. chemistry tier 1, 2001; mem. chemistry grant selection com. Nat. Scis. and Engring. Rsch. Coun. of Can., Ottawa, 1983-86. Contbr. articles to profl. jours. NAS-NRC postdoctoral rsch. assoc., 1965-67, A.P. Sloan fellow, 1974, sr. scientist vis. fellow U. Warwick, Eng., 1978, Killam rsch. fellow, 1991-93; recipient Rutherford Meml. medal in chemistry Royal Soc. Can., 1981, A.v. Humboldt rsch. award, 1990, 99, John C. Polanyi award in Phys. and Theoretical Chemistry, 1998, Fred P. Lossing award in mass spectrometry Can. Soc. for Mass Spectrometry, 2002. Fellow Royal Soc. Can., Chem. Inst. Can. (phys. chemistry divsn. exec. 1980-83, Noranda lectr. in phys. chemistry 1983); mem. Am. Soc. Mass Spectrometry, Am. Chem. Soc. Home: 38 Alberta Dr Concord ON Canada L4K 4X5 Office: York U Dept Chemistry 4700 Keele St Toronto ON Canada M3J 1P3 E-mail: dkbohme@yorku.ca.

BOHMONT, DALE WENDELL, agricultural consultant; b. Wheatland, Wyo., June 7, 1922; s. J.E. and Mary (Armann) B.; m. Marilyn J. Horn, Mar. 7, 1969; children: Dennis E., Craig W. BS, U. Wyo., 1948, MS, 1950; PhD, U. Nebr., 1952; M.P.A., Harvard U., 1959. Registered investment adv., SEC. Pub. sch. tchr., Rock River, Wyo., 1941-42; from research asst. to head plant scis. U. Wyo., 1946-60; assoc. dir. expt. sta. Colo. State U., 1961-63; dean, dir. agr. U. Nev., Reno, 1963-82, dean, dir. emeritus, 1982—; pres. Bohmont Cons. Inc., 1982—; mem. Brucheum Group, Waynesboro, Va., 1984; chief cons. Zygro Corp., 1999. Cons. Devel. & Resources Corp., N.Y.C., 1968—, Fredriksen, Kamine & Assocs., Sacramento, 1976, Nev. Agrl. Found., 1986—; pres. Enide Corp., Reno, 1974-80, Thermal Dynamics Internat., 1983-87, Cryabis, Inc., Reno, 1993-95; co-chmn. rsch. planning West Divsn. Agr. Expt. Stas., 1975; mem. exec. com., coun. adminstrv. heads agr. Nat. Assn. State Univ. Land Grant Colls., 1975. Author: Golden Years of Agriculture in Nevada, 1989; contbr. articles to profl. jours.; mem. editorial bd.: Crops and Soils, 1962— . Pres. Dale W. and Marilyn Horn Found., 1998—. Served with USAAF, 1942-45. Fellow AAAS, Agronomy Soc.; mem. Western Soc. Weed Scis. (hon.), Western Crop Sci. Soc. (pres. 1962-63), Nat. Expt. Sta. Dirs. Assn. (chmn. 1967-68), Am. Range Mgmt. Soc., Farm House (dir. 1962—), Weed Soc. Am. (hon.), Sigma Xi, Gamma Sigma Delta (pres. 1964-66), Alpha Zeta, Alpha Tau Alpha, Phi Kappa Phi. Lodges: Lions (v.p. 1985-86, pres. 1986-87 bd. dirs. 1985—). Home: 525 Court St Reno NV 89501 E-mail: bohconslt@aol.com. *There is nothing that has been done that could not have been done better; therefore, there is always room for improvement and always room at the top.*

BOHN, BARBARA ANN, retired laboratory director; b. St. Louis, Nov. 24, 1943; d. Arthur John Joseph and Eleanor Caroline (Kinsman) B. BS in Med. Tech., Loyola U., New Orleans, 1965; MBA, Old Dominion U., 1984. Med. technologist Broward Gen. Med. Ctr., Ft. Lauderdale, Fla., 1965-66; microbiologist Duke U. Hosp., Durham, N.C., 1966-71; tech. lab. coord. Harvard Cmty. Health Plan, Cambridge, Mass., 1971-77; tech. lab. dir. Louise Obici Meml. Hosp., Suffolk, Va., 1977-89; lab. mgr. Orlando (Fla.) Health Care Group, 1989-91; tech. lab. dir. Metpath of Fla., Deerfield Beach, 1992-93; ret., 1993. Tech. cons. ASCP; planning analyst, chmn. Diagnosis Related Group task force, 1983-85; dir. adv. bd. Western Tidewater Area Health Edn. Com., 1983-87; bd. dirs., sec. Edmarc, Inc., Suffolk, 1985-86, pres., bd. dirs., dir. 1986-87. Author: children's book, poems. Vol. ARC. Mem. Am. Soc. Clin. Pathologists (assoc., program chmn. workshops Boston 1977), Clin. Lab. Mgmt. Assn. (fin. chmn. 1983), Hosp. Purchasing Svc. (pres. lab. com. 1983), Am. Hosp. Assn. (adv. bd.), Soc. for Hosp. Planning and Mktg. (adv. bd.), Beta Beta Beta. Avocations: piano, tennis, published poet. Address: 3635 Whitehall Dr Bldg 1-404 West Palm Beach FL 33401-1088

BOHN, CHARLOTTE GALITZ, retired real estate executive; b. Chgo, Ill, Aug. 7, 1930; d. Chester Charles and Sarah Madelyn (McCarthy) B; m. Robert Allan Galitz, Nov. 25, 1955; children: Charles Robert, Thomas Allan, Madelyn Clare, (div. Sept. 1965). Student, Northwestern U., 1955, City Coll., Chgo., 1989. Lic. real estate salesperson, N.C. Lab. tech. Kraft Foods Rsch. Lab., Glenview, Ill., 1950-56; researcher data processing control Kemper Ins. Co., Chgo., 1967-70; jr. acct. Tractor Supply Co., Chgo., 1970-75; real estate salesman MGM Realty Co., Chgo., 1975-81, 85-88, Prime Realty, 1989-98; broker Bohn Real Estate Agy, Raleigh, NC, 1981-85; founder, pres. Pvt. Rsch., Chgo., 1985; ret., 1998. Researcher zoning map City of Raleigh, 1980-81; bd. dir. Off-Campus Writers Workshop. Contbr. various rsch. projects and sci. proposals. Vol. Chgo. Boys' Club; treas. churchwomen of St. Mary's, Crystal Lake, Ill.; vol. lifeguard Easter Seal Soc.-Multiple Sclerosis, Raleigh, 1983-84, PTA, 1967-77; bd. dir. Off-Campus Writer's Workshop; chair grammar sch. 50th reunion, 1994; scholarship judge Mensa, Chgo., 1995, 96, 99; nominating com., Chgo. Cath. U. Club, 2003. Recipient Adviser Emblem of Merit award Jr. Achievement, 1955. Mem. AAAS, Smithsonian Inst. (assoc.), Nat. Trust Hist. Preservation, Raleigh C. of C., Jaycee Aux. (restaurant mgr.), Chgo. N. Side Realty Bd., Nat. Geog. Soc., Wilson Ctr. Assn., Mensa (nominating), Am. Assn. Ret. Persons, Irish Am. Heritage Ctr., Libr. Congress (assoc. charter), Chgo. Cath. U. Club, Nominated, 2003-2004. Roman Catholic. Avocations: textiles, sports, antiques, music, poetry. Home and Office: Private Rsch 6126 W Roscoe St Chicago IL 60634-4145

BOHN, CYNTHIA JANE, lawyer; b. Portsmouth, Ohio, June 3, 1963; d. Jerry Ray and Joy (Roberts) B. BS in Arts and Scis., Vanderbilt U., 1985; JD, Nashville Sch. Law, 1994. Bar: Tenn. 1994. Owner Laurells Raw Bar, Nashville, 1993; assoc. Law Office of Charlotte Fleming, Nashville, 1994-97; pvt. practice Nashville, 1997—. Campaign mgr. Com. to Elect Andrei Lee, Nashville, 1997-98. Mem. TLAW, TTLA, Tenn. Bar Assn., Nashville Bar Assn., Lawyers Assn. for Women. Avocations: gardening, auctions, antiques. Office: 501 Union St Ste 502 Nashville TN 37219-1777

BOHN, DENNIS ALLEN, electrical engineer, executive; b. San Fernando, Calif., Oct. 5, 1942; s. Raymond Virgil and Iris Elouise (Johnson) B.; 1 child, Kira Michelle; m. Patricia Tolle, Aug. 12, 1986. BSEE with honors, U. Calif., Berkeley, 1972, MSEE with honors, 1974. Engring. technician GE Co., San Leandro, Calif., 1964-72; research and devel. engr. Hewlett-Packard Co., Santa Clara, Calif., 1973; application engr. Nat. Semicondr. Corp., Santa Clara, 1974-76; engring. mgr. Phase Linear Corp., Lynnwood, Wash., 1976-82; v.p. rsch. and devel., ptnr. Rane Corp., Mukilteo, Wash., 1982—; founder Toleco Systems, Kingston, Wash., 1980. Suicide and crisis ctr. vol., Berkeley, 1972-74, Santa Clara, 1974-76. Served with USAF, 1960-64. Recipient Am. Spirit Honor medal USAF, 1961; Math. Achievement award Chem. Rubber Co., 1962-63. Editor: We Are Not Just Daffodils, 1975; contbr. poetry to Reason mag.; tech. editor Audio Handbook, 1976; contbr. articles to tech. jours.; columnist Polyphony mag., 1981-83; 2 patents in field. Fellow Audio Engring. Soc.; mem. IEEE, Tau Beta Pi. Office: Rane Corp 10802 47th Ave W Mukilteo WA 98275-5098 E-mail: dennisb@rane.com.

BOHN, DONNA MAY, music educator; b. Kans. City, Mo., June 22, 1965; d. Martin Lewis and Barbara Lee Bohn. BS, U.of Ala., 1983—87; MusM, Wichita State U., 1987—89; Mus D, U. of Ala., 1991—94. Percussionist/timpanist freelance, Kans. City, Mo., 1989—91; grad. tchg. asst. U. of Ala., 1991—94; adj. percussion instr. U. of Montevallo, Ala., 1991—94; asst. prof. of music Quincy U., Quincy, Ill., 1994—2000; percussion faculty Interlochen Arts Camp, Interlochen, Mich., 1993—; assoc. prof. of music Quincy U., Ill., 2000—. Timpanist Muddy River Opera Co., Quincy, Ill., 1995—, Quincy Symphony Orch., Ill., 1994—; percussionist Interlochen Festival Orch., Interlochen, Mich., 1993—, Tuscaloosa Symphony Orch., Tuscaloosa, Ala., 1991—94, Ala. Symphony Orch., Birmingham, Ala., 1991—93, Am. Heartland Theatre, Kans. City, Mo., 1989—91. Musician: (solo percussion performance) Quincy U. Faculty Recitals. Newsletter and program editor Muddy River Opera Co., Quincy, Ill., 1995—2000; chair, artistic adv. com. Quincy Symphony Orch., Ill., 1996—97. Mem.: Nat. Assn. of Coll. Wind and Percussion Instructors, Music Educators Nat. Conf., Coll. Music Soc., Percussive Arts Soc. (Ill. chpt. pres. 1999—2001). Avocation: tennis. Office: Quincy University 1800 College Ave Quincy IL 62301

BOHN, HENNING, economist, educator; b. Frankfurt, Germany, Aug. 10, 1960; came to the U.S., 1982; s. Lothar and Marianne Bohn; m. Oda Bittel, Aug. 20, 1983; children: Timon, Samantha, Christopher, Angelina, Eliana. PhD, Stanford U., 1986. Asst. prof. fin. U. Pa., Phila., 1986-92; assoc. prof. econs. U. Calif., Santa Barbara, 1992-96, prof. econs., 1996—. Contbr. articles to profl. jours. Mem. Am. Econs. Assn., Econometrics Soc. Avocation: travel. Office: U Calif Dept Econs Santa Barbara CA 93106 E-mail: bohn@econ.ucsb.edu.

BOHN, JASON, golfer; b. Lewisburg, Pa., Apr. 24, 1973; m. Alicia Bohn. Degree in fin., U. Ala. Profl. golfer, 1995—; mem. Can. Profl. Golf Tour, 1997—. Named winner, Shell Payless Open, 2001, Bayer Champaionship, 2001. Mem.: Cartersville Country Club. Avocations: music, camping. Office: Canadian Tour 212 King St W Ste 203 Toronto ON Canada M5H 1K5

BOHN, MARSHA J. anthropologist, researcher; d. David M. and Evelyn H. Kipley; m. Fred Bohn, Feb. 7, 1970; children: Jeffrey, Marcus, Rochelle. AA, Saddleback Coll., Mission Viejo, Calif., 1993; student, Oxford (England) U., 1993; BS in Social Anthropology, London Sch. Econs. and Polit. Sci., 1996; MA in Med. Anthropology, Sch. Oriental and African Studies, London, 1998; postgrad., Ariz. State U., 2002—. Exec. asst. Nichols Inst. Diagnostics, San Juan Capistrano, Calif., 1989—92, Airparks Internat., San Juan Capistrano; rsch. cons. Capital Oil & Gas Ltd., London. Fellow: Am. Anthrop. Assn., Royal Anthrop. Soc.; mem.: Wellcome Inst., Med. Anthropology Assn., Alumni Assn. Sch. Oriental and African Studies, Alumni Assn. London Sch. Econs. and Polit. Sci., Alumni Assn. Saddleback Coll., Mus. Mankind, London, Honor Soc. Saddleback Coll., Alpha Gamma Sigma. Personal E-mail: marshabohn-alumni@lse.ac.uk.

BOHN, MONICA J. multi-media specialist, educator; b. Sheboygan, Wis., Feb. 2, 1957; d. Eugene J. Bohn, Marilyn J. Bohn. BS, U. Wis., Oshkosh, 1980. Cert. edn. libr. Substitute tchr. Kewaskum (Wis.) Pub. Schs., 1980—81; elem. & mid. sch. media dir. Horicon Pub. Schs., 1981—. Bd. dirs. Horicon Pub. Libr., 1981—99. Recipient Mem. of the Yr., Winnebagoland Uniserv, 1998, Svc. award, Horicon Pub. Libr., 1999. Mem.: Wis. Ednl. Media Assn., Kiwanis (pres. elect 1999—2001). Lutheran. Avocations: travel, precious moments collector, football, basketball. Home: 721 Minerva St Horicon WI 53032 Office: Van Brunt Elem/Mid Sch 611 Mill St Horicon WI 53032 Business E-Mail: mbohn@horicon.k12.wi.us.

BOHN, PAUL BRADLEY, psychiatrist, psychoanalyst; b. Santa Monica, Calif., Apr. 11, 1957; m. Pamela Summit, Nov. 17, 1990. BA in Pharmacology, U. Calif., Santa Barbara, 1980; MD, U. Calif., Irvine, 1984; postgrad. in Psychoanalysis, L.A. Psychoanalytic Inst., 1988-93; PsyD, Grad. Inst. Contemporary Psychoanalysis, 1995. Diplomate Am. Bd. Psychiatry and Neurology, added qualifications in addiction psychiatry. Psychiat. resident UCLA, 1984-88, assoc. dir. anxiety disorders clinic, 1989-95, assoc. clin. prof. psychiatry, 1989—, dir. social anxiety clinic, 1993-95; fellow U. So. Calif., L.A., 1988-89; v.p. Pacific Psychopharmacology Rsch. Inst., Santa Monica, 1990—; pvt. practice psychiatry Santa Monica, 1988—. Expert reviewer, Med. Bd. Calif. Grantee Ciba-Geigy, Santa Monica, 1992, 92, Novartis, 1998. Fellow Am. Psychiat. Assn.; mem. So. Calif. Psychiat. Assn. (past pres.), Anxiety Disorders Assn. of Am., Obsessive Compulsive Found. Office: 2730 Wilshire Blvd Ste 325 Santa Monica CA 90403-4747

BOHN, RALPH CARL, educational consultant, retired educator; b. Detroit, Feb. 19, 1930; s. Carl and Bertha (Abrams) B.; m. Adella Stanul, Sept. 2, 1950 (dec.); children: Cheryl Ann, Jeffrey Ralph; m. JoAnn Olvera Butler, Feb. 19, 1977 (div. 1990); stepchildren: Kathryn J., Kimberly J., Gregory E.; m. Mariko Tajima, Jan. 27, 1991; 1 child, Thomas Carl; 1 stepchild, Daichi Tajima. BS, Wayne State U., 1951, EdM, 1954, EdD, 1957. Instr. part-time Wayne State U., 1954-55, summer 1956; faculty San Jose (Calif.) State U., 1955-92, prof. div. tech., 1961-92, chmn. dept. indsl. studies, 1960-69, assoc. dean ednl. svc., 1968-70, dean continuing edn., 1970-92, prof. emeritus, 1992—; cons. Calif. State U. Sys., 1992—; cons. quality edn. sys. USAF, 1992-2000; dir. nat. program on non-collegiate sponsored instrn. Calif. State Univ. Sys., 1995—2000, Calif. State U. Inst., 1997—99; pres. Univ. Cons., 1994—. Guest faculty Colo. State Coll., 1963, Ariz. State U., 1966, U. P.R., 1967, 74, So. Ill. U., 1970, Oreg. State U., 1971, Utah State U., 1973, Va. Poly. Inst. & State U., 1973, U. Idaho, 1978; cons. U.S. Office Edn., 1965-70, Calif. Pub. Schs., 1960, Nat. Assessment Ednl. Progress, 1968-79, ednl. div. Philco-Ford Corp., 1970-73, Am. Inst. Rsch., 1969-83, Far West Labs for Ednl. Rsch. Devel., 1971-86; adv. bd. Ctr. for Vocat. and Tech. Edn., Ohio State U., 1968-74; dir. project Vocat. Edn. Act, 1965-67, NDEA, 1967, 68; co-dir. Project Edn. Profession Devel. Act, 1969, 70; mem. commn. coll. and univ. contracts Western Assn. Schs. and Colls, 1976-78, chmn. spl. com. on off-campus instrn. and continuing edn., 1978-88; chmn. continuing edn. accreditation visit U. Santa Clara, 1976; chmn. accreditation team Nellis AFB, Nev., 1992, 2002, U. Nev., Las Vegas, 2000, Nat. U., 2000, Oreg. State U., 2001, Golden Gate U., 2001; chmn. accreditation team to Yokusaka Naval Sta., Japan, 2000, Atsugi Naval Air Facility, Japan, 2000, Yokota Air Base, Japan, 2000, Camp Pendleton Marine Corps Base, 2001, Naval Air Sta., Lamoore, 2002, Dyess AFB, 2003, Twentynine Palms Marine Corps. Base, Calif., 2003, eArmyU web-based degree programs U.S. Army, Washington; sr. cons. Global Partnership Devel. Calif. State U. Sys., 2000-03. Author: (with G.H. Silvius) Organizing Course Materials for Industrial Education, 1961, Planning and Organizing Instruction, 1976; (with A. MacDonald) Power-Mechanics of Energy Control, 1970, 2d edit., 1983, The McKnight Power Experimenter, 1970, Power and Energy Technology, 1989, Energy Technology: Power and Transportation, 1992; (with others) Basic Industrial Arts and Power Mechanics, 1978, Technology and Society: Interfaces with Industrial Arts, 1980, Fundamentals of Safety Education, 3d edit., 1981, Energy, Power and Transportation Technology, 1986; (with A. MacDonald) Energy Technology, Power and Transportation, 1991; editor (with Ralph Norman) Graduate Study in Industrial Arts, 1961; indsl. arts editor Am. Vocat. Jour., 1963-66; editor Jour. Indsl. Tchr. Edn., 1962-64. Lt. (j.g.) USCGR, 1951-53, capt. Res. ret. Recipient award Am. Legion, 1945; Wayne State U. scholar, 1953. Mem. NEA, Nat. Assn. Indsl. Tech. (bd. accreditation), Am. Indsl. Arts. Assn. (pres. 1967-68, Ship's citation 1971), Am. Coun. Indsl. Art Tchrs. Edn. (pres. 1964-66, Man of Yr. award 1967), Nat. Univ. Continuing Edn. Assn. (chair accreditation com. 1988-91), Nat. Assn. Indsl. Tchr. Educators (past v.p.), Calif. Indsl. Edn. Assn. (State Ship's citation 1971), Am. Drive Edn. Assn., Nat. Fluid Power Soc., Am. Vocat. Assn. (svc. awards 1966, 67), N.Am. Assn. for Summer Sessions (v.p. western region 1976-78), Luth. Acad. Scholarship, Calif. Employees Assn. (pres. San Jose State Coll. chpt. 1966-67), Western Assn. Summer Session Adminstrs. (newsletter editor 1970-73, pres. 1974-75), Calif. C. of C. (edn. com 1969-77), Industry-Edn. Coun. Calif. (bd. dirs. 1974-80), Sci. and Human Values, Inc. (bd. dirs. 1974-2003, chmn. bd. 1976-2002), Tahoe Tavern (bd. dirs. 1987-91, chmn. bd. 1988-90), Seascape Lagoon Homeowners Assn. (bd. dirs. 1988-95, chmn. 1989-95), Nat. Gold Key Honors Soc. (hon. life). Home and Office: 713 Clubhouse Dr Aptos CA 95003-5431 E-mail: rmbohn@cruzio.com.

BOHN, ROBERT HERBERT, lawyer; b. Austin, Tex., Sept. 2, 1935; s. Herbert and Alice B.; m. Gay P. Maloy, June 4, 1957; children: Rebecca Shoemaker, Katherine Bernat, Robert H., Jr.. BBA, U. Tex., 1957, LLB, 1963. Bar: Tex. 1963, Calif. 1965. Ptnr. Boccardo Law Firm, San Jose, Calif., 1965-87, Alexander & Bohn, San Jose, 1987-91; Bohn, Bennion & Niland, 1992-97; Bohn & Bohn, 1998—. Spkr. Calif. Continuing Edn. of Bar; judge pro tem Superior Ct. of Calif., San Jose, 1975-96. Mem. ATLA, Am. Coll. Barristers, Consumer Attys. Calif., Am. Bd. Trial Advocates, Santa Clara County Bar Assn., Calif. State Bar Assn., Santa Clara County Trial Lawyers Assn. (pres. 1999, Trial Lawyer of Yr. 2000), Trial Lawyers Pub. Justice, Roscoe Pound Found., Million Dollar Advocates Forum, Silicon Valley Capital Club, Texas Cowboys Assn., Phi Gamma Delta. Office: 152 N 3rd St Ste 200 San Jose CA 95112-5515 E-mail: rbohn@bohnlaw.com.

BOHNEN, MICHAEL J. lawyer; b. Buffalo, 1947; m. Joyce B. Oppenheim, 1969; children: Sharon, Deborah. BA, Harvard U., 1968, JD, 1972. Bar: Mass. 1972. Assoc. Nutter, McClennen & Fish, LLP, Boston, 1972-80, ptnr., 1980—. Lectr. Boston U. Law Sch., 1981—2001. Co-author: Mass. Corporate Forms, 1990-2002. Pres. Solomon Schechter Day Sch., Newton, 1980—82; chmn. Jewish Coun. for Pub. Affairs, 2002—; trustee United Jewish Cmtys., 1999—; pres. Jewish Cmty. Rels. Coun., Boston, 1991—93; chmn. Combined Jewish Philanthropies, 1993—95, Gann Acad., 1995—. Mem. Boston Bar Assn. (chmn. corp. law com. 1997-99). Home: 60 Nathan Rd Newton MA 02459-1105 Office: Nutter McClennen & Fish LLP World Trade Center West Boston MA 02210

BOHNEN, ROBERT FRANK, hematologist, oncologist, educator; b. Huntington, N.Y., Jan. 3, 1941; s. Oscar and Sarah Leah (Piel) B.; m. Mollyn Villareal, June 20, 1965; children: Sharon Kay, Scott Owen David, Paul Alan. BS in Zoology, Syracuse U., 1961; MD, Columbia U., 1965. Diplomate Am. Bd. Internal Medicine, Am. Bd. Med. Oncology, Am. Bd. Hematology. Intern Buffalo (N.Y.) Gen. Hosp., 1965-66; resident in medicine SUNY, Buffalo, 1968-69, U. Utah, Salt Lake City, 1969-70, clin. hematology fellow, 1970-71, med. oncology fellow, 1971-72; physician hematology and med. oncology Cons. Med. Group, Carmichael and Roseville, Calif., 1972-91, Cancer Treatment Ctr. Merle West Med. Ctr., Klamath Falls, Oreg., 1991—. Instr. medicine and hematology/oncology U. Calif., Davis, Sacramento, 1973-77, asst. clin. prof. medicine and hematology/oncology, 1977-83; clin. instr. dept. family medicine Oreg. Health Scis. U., Portland, 1994—; sr. staff Mercy Am. River Hosp., Carmichael, Calif., Mercy San Juan Hosp., Carmichael, Roseville (Calif.) Cmty. Hosp.; courtesy staff Sutter Cmty. Hosp. Sacramento; active staff Merle West Med. Ctr., Klamath Falls; med. dir. Hospice Roseville, Calif.; prin. investigator No. Calif. Oncology Group Clin. Trials; med. adv. bd. Vis. Nurses Assn.; lectr. and presenter in field. Contbr. articles to profl. jours. Chmn. Greater Sacramento Cancer Coun. Clin. Trials Com./No. Calif. Oncology Group Outreach Com.; bd. dirs., sec. Greater Sacramento Cancer Coun.; chmn. prof. edn. com., bd. dirs. Tri-County chpt. Am. Cancer Soc.; soloist Sacramento Valley Concert Choir, Klamath Chorale; active Masterworks Chorus; cast member Linkville Players and Ross Ragland Theater Prodns., Klamath Falls, 1991—; choir dir. Sacred Heart Ch., Klamath Falls, 1992—. Med. Oncology fellow Am. Cancer Soc., U. Utah Med. Ctr., 1971-72. Mem. Am. Soc. Clin. Oncology, Phi Beta Kappa. Democrat. Roman Catholic. Avocations: musical theater, photography, choral singing and directing. Office: Cancer Treatment Ctr Merle West Med Ctr 2610 Uhrmann Rd Klamath Falls OR 97601-1123 E-mail: rbohnen@mwmc.org.

BOHO, DAN L. lawyer; b. Chgo., Sept. 18, 1952; s. Lawrence M. and Genevieve A. (Zurek) Boho; m. Sheri L. Krisco, Sept. 10, 1977; children: Courtney, Ashley. BA, Loyola U., Chgo., 1974, JD, 1977. Bar: Ill. 1977, Fed. Trial Bar 1977. Sr. ptnr., group leader litigation group Hinshaw & Culbertson, Chgo., 1977—. Mem. Fedn. Ins. and Corp. Counsel (chmn. bus. torts and comml. law sect.), Ill. Soc. Trial Lawyers (past bd. dirs.), Def. Rsch. Inst., Assn.

Def. Trial Attys., Ill. Def. Coun., Advs. Soc., Ill. Bar Assn. (past del. assembly), Polish Am. Assn. (past chmn. bd. dirs.), Japan Am. Soc. (bd. dirs.), Heartland Alliance (bd. dirs.), Chgo. Trial Lawyers Club (past pres.), Phi Alpha Delta (past pres. Webster chpt.). Avocations: travel, tennis, skiing.

BOHR, VILHELM ALFRED, laboratory chief; b. Copenhagen, Dec. 3, 1950; arrived in U.S., 1982; s. Aage Niels and Marietta Bettina Bohr; m. Diane S. Okumoto, July 17, 1987; children: Christina, Eliot, Kenneth. MD, U. Copenhagen, 1978, PhD, DSc, 1987. Resident in medicine U. Copenhagen, 1978-80, postdoctoral fellow, 1980-82; rsch. scholar Stanford (Calif.) U., 1982-86; sr. staff fellow Nat. Cancer Inst., Bethesda, Md., 1986-88, med. officer, 1988-92; chief lab. molecular genetics Nat. Insts. Aging., NIH, Balt., 1992—. Office: NIH Nat Insts Aging Lab Molecular Gerontology 5600 Nathan Shock Dr Baltimore MD 21224-6825 E-mail: vbohr@nih.gov.

BOHREN, MICHAEL OSCAR, lawyer; b. Appleton, Wis., Feb. 27, 1947; s. Oscar Robert and Martha (Anderson) B.; m. Mary Joset Morse, Nov. 26, 1977; children: Juliana Rose, Katherine Elizabeth. AB, Ripon Coll., 1969; JD, Marquette U., 1975. Bar: Wis. 1978, U.S. Dist. Ct. (ea. and we. dists.) Wis. 1975, U.S. Ct. Appeals (5th and 7th cirs.) 1976, U.S. Supreme Ct. 1978. Atty. USDA, Washington, 1975; gen. counsel Aries Ltd., Milw., 1975—78; atty. Marola & Bohren, Milw., 1978—2000; cir. ct. judge br. I Waukesha County, 2000—; presiding judge Criminal Traffic divsn. Waukesha County, 2002—. Bd. dirs. Kettle Moraine Sch. Dist., Wales, Wis., 1982-2000, pres., 1986-94, 96-99; bd. dirs. Waukesha (Wis.) Symphony, 1997—; v.p. Greenfield (Wis.) Sch. Dist., 1977-81. Mem. Wis. Bar Assn., Wis. Trial Lawyers Assn., Masons, Kiwanis (mem. exec. bd.). Avocations: geology, politics, reading. Home: W315 W496 Christopher Way Delafield WI 53018 Office: Waukesha County Courthouse Waukesha WI 53187 E-mail: moblawgo@execpc.com.

BOHRNSTEDT, GEORGE WILLIAM, educational researcher; b. Arcadia, Wis., Sept. 28, 1938; s. Russell Gail and Agnes (Brecht) B.; m. Josephine Orlanda, Aug. 11, 1962 (div. 1973); children— Elizabeth (dec.), Brian, Matthew; m. Jennifer Lou Cain, Sept. 28, 1980; 1 child, Kassandra Student, Winona State Coll., 1956-58; BS, U. Wis., 1960, MA, 1963, PhD, 1966. Research assoc. U. Wis., Madison, 1966-69; assoc. prof. Mpls., 1969-73, chmn. dept. sociology, 1970-72; prof. Ind. U., Bloomington, 1972-88, chmn. dept sociology, 1982-86, dir. Inst. Social Research, 1974-79; sr. v.p., dir. Am. Inst. for Rsch., Palo Alto, Calif., 1988-96, sr. v.p. for rsch., 1996—. Author: (with others) Statistics for Social Data Analysis, 3d edit., 1994; Basic Social Statistics, 1991; editor: Sociological Methodology, 1970; editor Sociol. Methods and Rsch., 1971-79, 84-87, Social Psychology Quar., 1980-82. Served to U.S. Army, 1962 Fellow NSF, 1963, NIMH, 1964-66, Ctr. for Advanced Studies in Behavioral Scis., 1986-87; Found. for Child Devel. Belding scholar, 1976-77 Mem. Am. Sociol. Assn., Psychometric Soc., Soc. Exptl. Social Psychologists Avocation: jazz. Office: Am Insts Rsch Behavioral Scis John C Flanagan Rsch Ctr 1791 Arastradero Rd Palo Alto CA 94304-1337 Home: 94 Clavel Ct Palm Desert CA 92260

BOHY, RIC, magazine editor, consultant, broadcast commentator; b. Detroit, Sept. 8, 1951; s. Raymond Robert Bohy, Patty Jean Bohy; m. JoAnn DiMaggio; children: Nathan, Jordan. BA, U. Mich., 1973. Editor Hour Detroit mag., Royal Oak, Mich., 1997—2003; editl. dir. Hour Media L.L.C., Royal Oak, 2000—. Commentator, editl. writer WDIV-TV, Detroit, 1994—. Home: 1614 Fairview Apt A Royal Oak MI 48073 Office: Hour Detroit 117 W Third St Royal Oak MI 48067 Home Fax: 248-655-0009; Office Fax: 248-691-4531. Personal E-mail: wordsdeeds@earthlink.net. Business E-Mail: rbohy@hourdetroit.com.

BOICE, CRAIG KENDALL, management consultant; b. Portland, Oreg., June 25, 1952; s. Charles A. and Audrey (Larson) B.; m. Jacinta E. Remedios, Nov. 21, 1979. BA summa cum laude, Beloit Coll., 1973; MA, Yale U., 1974, M.Phil., 1976, M in Pub. and Pvt. Mgmt., 1979. Instr. fellow philosophy Yale U., New Haven, 1978-79; economist Overseas Pvt. Investment Corp., Washington, 1978; sr. cons. Coopers and Lybrand, Washington and London, 1979-81; v.p. ops. Internat. Licensing Network, N.Y.C., 1981-82; pres., chmn., chief exec. officer Boice Dunham Group, N.Y.C., 1983—. Adj. asst. prof. NYU, 1984-99. Cons. Lake Placid Olympic Organizing Com., (N.Y.), 1979, New Haven Homesteading Program, 1979. Mem. Am. Mktg. Assn., Assn. Energy Engrs., Automated Meter Reading Assn., Computer and Automated Sys. Assn., Soc. Mfg. Engrs., Internat. Assn. Energy Econ., World Future Soc. Democrat. Office: Boice Dunham Group 30 W 13th St Apt 3C New York NY 10011-7988

BOICE, JUDITH LYNETTE, physician, writer, educator; b. Toledo, Mar. 20, 1962; d. William Vincent and Martha Hibbert Boice; children: Vincent Boice-Washburn, Sebastian Boice-Washburn. BA, Oberlin Coll., 1984; D in Naturopathic Medicine, Nat. Coll. Naturopathic Medicine, 1994; M in Acupuncture and Oriental Medicine, Oreg. Coll. Oriental Medicine, 1996. Cert. naturopathic physician Oreg. Bd. Naturopathic Examiners, lic. acupuncturist Oreg. State Med. Bd., acupuncturist Colo. Staff physician Portland (Oreg.) Addictions Acupuncture Ctr., 1995—96; staff physician, lectr. Transitions for Health, Portland, 1996—98; pvt. practice Columbia River Wellness Ctr., Portland, Oreg., 1996—97, Portland, 1998—2000, Ancient Arts Healing Therapies, Montrose, Colo., 2001—02, Seven Winds Inst., Montrose, 2002—. Spkr., trainer U.S. Forest Svc., Portland, 1995; spkr. Nat. Wellness Inst., Stevens Point, WIS., 1997—2000, Ind. Pharmacy Alliance of Am., Inc, N.Y.C., 1998. Author: (book) At One With All Life: A Personal Journey in Gaian Communities, 1990, The Art of Daily Activism, 1992, The Pocket Guide to Naturopathic Medicine, 1996, "But My Doctor Never Told Me That!": Secrets for creating lifelong health, 1999; editor: Mother Earth: Through the Eyes of Women Photographers and Writers, 1992, Mother Earth Postcard Book, 1993, Mother Earth: Through the Eyes of Women Photographers and Writers, revised edition, 2002. Grantee, Mellon Found., 1984; scholar Vorheiss, U. Cin., 1980-81. Mem.: Nat. Coun. Cert. Acupuncture and Oriental Medicine (cert. acupuncture), Nat. Writers Union, Am. Assn. Naturopathic Physicians, Phi Beta Kappa. Avocations: gardening, photography, hiking, swimming, qigong. Home: 1008 W Oak Grove Rd Montrose CO 81401 Office: 1008 W Oak Grove Rd Montrose CO 81401 Home Fax: 970-252-0967. Personal E-mail: drjudith@drjudithboice.com.

BOIES, WILBER H. lawyer; b. Bloomington, Ill., Mar. 15, 1944; s. W. H. and Martha Jane (Hutchison) B.; m. Victoria Joan Steinitz, Sept. 17, 1966; children: Andrew Charles, Carolyn Ursula. AB, Brown U., 1965; JD, U. Chgo., 1968. Bar: Ill. 1968, U.S. Dist. Ct. (no. dist.) Ill. 1968, U.S. Dist. Ct. (ea. dist.) Wis. 1973, U.S. Ct. Appeals (7th cir.) 1974, U.S. Ct. Appeals (5th cir.) 1975, U.S. Ct. Appeals (3d cir.) 1977, U.S. Supreme Ct. 1978, U.S. Ct. Appeals (8th cir.) 1994, U.S. Ct. Appeals (9th cir.) 1995. Assoc. Altheimer & Gray, Chgo., 1968-71; ptnr. McDermott, Will & Emery, Chgo., 1971—. Contbr. articles to profl. jours. Active CPR Inst. for Dispute Resolution. Mem. ABA, Bar Assn. 7th Fed. Cir., Chgo. Bar Assn. (chmn. class litigation com. 1991-92), Chgo. Coun. Lawyers, Lawyers Club Chgo., Met. Club, Chgo. Bar Found.(dir.). Office: McDermott Will & Emery 227 W Monroe St Ste 4400 Chicago IL 60606-5096 E-mail: bboies@mwe.com.

BOIMAN, DONNA RAE, artist, art academy executive; b. Columbus, Ohio, Jan. 13, 1946; d. George Brandle and Donna Rae (Rockwell) Hall; m. David Charles Boiman, Dec. 8, 1973 (div. Aug. 1990). BS in Pharmacy, Ohio State U., 1969; student, Columbus Coll. Art & Design, 1979-83. Registered pharmacist, Ohio. Pharmacist, mgr. various retail stores, Cleve., 1970-73, Columbus, 1973-77; owner L'Artiste, Reynoldsburg, Ohio, 1977-81; pres. Cen. Ohio Art Acad., Reynoldsburg, 1981—2002, Art Acad. Ctrl. Ohio, Reynoldsburg, 1990—; owner Big Red Designs, Reynoldsburg, 1989—; pub. rels. mgr. Freedom Farm Equestrian Ctr., Pataskala, Ohio, 1991—; design dir., v.p. Sterling Automotive Mgmt., Inc; owner www.AllTheWildHorses.com, 2001, www.AllTheWildCats.com, 2001. Cons. to Mayor City of Reynoldsburg, 1986-87, webmaster, 1999—; owner Ctrl. Ohio Art Graphics/Design/Website Design; jewelry designer Zarah Co. Calif., 2001. Represented in permanent collections including Collector's Gallery Columbus Mus. Art, Gallery 200, Columbus Art Exch., The Huntington Collection, Dean Witter Reynolds Collection, Zanesville Art Ctr., Mt. Carmel East Hosp., Columbus, Corp. 2005, Radisson Hotels, Mich. and Ohio, Fifth 3d Bank, Bexley, Ohio, On Line Computer Libr., Dublin, Ohio, Columbus Torah Acad.; author: Anatomy Made Easy: Draw, Color and Learn, Anatomy and Structure: A Guide for Young Artists, 1988, Shadow of the Queen; creator Warriors line of cat jewelry and Shadow of the Queen children's book series. Mem. Columbus Better Bus. Bur.; founder Forest Warrior Project, 2002. Recipient John Lennon Meml. Award for the Arts, Internat. Art Challenge com., 1987. Mem. Pa. Soc. Watercolorists, Nat. Soc. Layerists in Multimedia, Allied Artists of Am. (assoc.), Nat. Wildlife Fedn., Ohio State U. Alumni Assn., Ohio State U. Pharmacy Alumni Assn. (charter), U.S. Dressage Fedn., Internat. Arabian Horse Assn., Soc. Concerned Scientists. Avocations: showing horses, skiing, white water river running, judging figure skating. Office: Cen Ohio Art & Graphics PO Box 209 7347 E Main St Reynoldsburg OH 43068-2105

BOIME, ALBERT ISAAC, art history educator; b. St. Louis, Mar. 17, 1933; s. Max and Dorothy (Rubin) B.; m. Myra Block, June 23, 1964; children: Robert, Eric. AB, UCLA, 1961; MA, Columbia U., 1963, PhD, 1968. Instr. social history of art Columbia U., 1966-67; assoc. prof. SUNY, Stony Brook, 1967-72, prof., chmn. dept. Binghamton, 1972-74, prof., 1974-78; prof. social history of art UCLA, 1978—. Art historian in residence Coll. Creative Studies, U. Calif.-Santa Barbara, 1973; judge NEH, Washington, 1975; mem. adv. council N.Y. Acad. Art, N.Y.C., 1981— Author: The Academy and French Painting in the 19th Century, 1971, Thomas Couture and the Eclectic Vision, 1981, the Social History of Modern Art: Vol. 1: Art in an Age of Revolution, 1987, Hollow Icons: The Politics of Sculpture in Nineteenth Century France, 1987, Vincent Van Gogh: Sternennacht, 1989, The Art of Exclusion: Representing Blacks in the Nineteenth Century, 1990, The Social History of Modern Art Vol. 2: Art in an Age of Bonapartism, 1990, The Magisterial Gaze: Manifest Destiny and American Landscape Painting (ca. 1830-1865), 1991, The Art of the Macchia and the Risorgimento, 1993, The Odyssey of Jan Stussey in Black and White, 1995, Art and the French Commune, 1995, Violence and Utopia: The Work of Jerome Boime, 1996, The Unveiling of the National Icons: A Plea for Patriotic Iconoclasm in a Nationalist Era, 1998 (Gustavus Myers Outstanding Book award 1999). Served with AUS, 1955-58. Am. Council Learned Socs. fellow, 1970-71; Guggenheim fellow, 1974-75, 84-85; Regents fellow Smithsonian Institution, 1989-90. Mem. Coll. Art Assn., Soc. Fellows Am. Acad. at Rome Office: UCLA Dept Art 405 Hilgard Ave Los Angeles CA 90095-9000 *I am grateful for this opportunity to join with my listing the memory of my dear brother, Jerome Philip Boime, whose rare, provocative mind inspired me with the sheer joy of intellectual pursuit. Whatever present success I may have, I owe to my capacity to thoroughly enjoy my work, to exult in ideas and the unboundedness of scholarly activity, and to commit this love to my developing engagement with political, philosophical and social issues.*

BOINPALLY, RAMESH RAO, research scientist, pharmacist, educator; b. Karimnagar, India, June 6, 1964; s. Rama Rao and Subadhra Devi Boinpally; m. Sandhya Devi Jakkaraju, May 11, 1996; 1 child, Niharika. BPharm, Kakatiya U., India, 1985, MPharm, 1987, PhD, 1991. Registered pharmacist Pharmacy Coun. of India, 1985. Lectr. pharmacy Kakatiya U., Warangal, India, 1991—94; daad fellow Inst. Clin. Pharmacology, Tech. U., Dresden, Germany, 1994—95; asst. prof. pharmacy Kakatiya U., Warangal, 1995—2000; Boyscast fellow Karmanos Cancer Inst., Wayne State U., Detroit, 2000—01, rsch. scientist, 2001—. Insp. Pharmacy Coun. of India, New Delhi, 1998—. Contbr. articles. Nat. svc. scheme programme officer Kakatiya U., Warangal, 1995—99. Recipient Career award, All India Coun. for Tech. Edn., 1998—2000; grantee UO1 (Co-investigator), Nat. Cancer Inst., Nat. Inst. Health, 2002—08; Jr. Rsch. fellow, U. Grants Commn., New Delhi, 1985—87, Rsch. grant, 1998, Sr. Rsch. fellow, Coun. of Sci. and Indsl. Rsch., New Delhi, 1988—91. Mem.: AAAS., Am. Coll. Clin. Pharmacology, Am. Assn. Pharm. Scientists, Indian Pharm. Assn. (life), Siddartha Ednl. Soc. (hon.; pres. 1999). Hindu. Achievements include development of formulations for anticancer and other drugs, pharmacokinetic modeling of investigational anticancer agents in animals and patients; demonstrated the feasibility of transdermal delivery of peptide/protein drugs; first to demonstrate that circadian rhythms influence drug-drug interactions; demonstrated that salivary secretion of water insoluble drugs is dependent on circadian rhythms an important aspect in therapy monitoring through saliva. Avocations: reading, gardening. Home: Apt 806 3737 Beaubien Blvd Detroit MI 48201 Office: Karmanos Cancer Inst 532 HWCRC 110 E Warren Detroit MI 48201 Office Fax: 313-966-7322. Personal E-mail: ramesh_boinpally@yahoo.com. E-mail: boinpall@karmanos.org.

BOISE, AUDREY LORRAINE, retired special education educator; b. Hackensack, N.J., Feb. 12, 1933; d. Paul George and Lillian Rose (Goedecker) B. BA, Wellesley (Mass.) Coll., 1955; MA, Fairleigh Dickinson U., 1977. Cert. tchr. K-8, learning disabilities, supervision. Tchr. Township of Berkeley Heights, N.J., 1958-67; learning cons. Borough of New Providence, N.J., 1978-82, 86-00, ret., 2000; learning cons. Scotch Plains/Fanwood, N.J., 1984-86; instr. Fairleigh Dickinson U., Madison, N.J., 1975-78. Several other short-term teaching positions; supr. student tchrs., 1968, 1975-78, 2000-02; lectr. on fgn. countries in areas of U.S.; travel agt. (part-time). Mem. Rep. Nat. Com.(life)(pres. club 2003), Nat. Rep. Senatorial Com., Washington, Rep. Presdl. Task Force, Washington, Rep. Congl. Com., Washington, N.J. State Rep. Com., Trenton, Nat. Fedn. Rep. Women, Washington. Recipient Rep. of Yr. Gold medal, Nat. Rep. Congress, 2002, 2003. Mem. NEA, AAUW, N.J. Assn. Learning Cons., Assn. for Children with Learning Disabilities, N.J. Edn. Assn., Internat. Platform Assn., Fortnightly Club, Hist. Soc. Summit, Canoe Brook Country Club. Methodist. Avocations: travel, photography.

BOISJOLY, RUSSELL PAUL, international consultant; b. Lowell, Mass., Sept. 3, 1950; s. Antonio Joseph and Isabelle Boisjoly; m. Diana Blanchard, Aug. 1973 (div. Sept. 1980); m. Carol Somers, Aug. 15, 1987. BS in Indsl. Mgmt. with honors, U. Mass., Lowell, 1972; MBA in Fin. with high honors, Boston U., 1973; DBA in Fin., Ind. U., 1978. Asst. prof. fin. U. Md., College Park, 1976-77, 78-82; assoc. prof., chair dept. mgmt. Simmons Coll., Boston, 1982-85; assoc. prof., chair fin. dept. U. Mass., Lowell, 1985-89; prof. fin. Fairfield (Conn.) U., 1989-99, assoc. dean Sch. Bus., 1989-93, dean Sch. Bus., 1993-97; dean Sch. Bus., prof. fin. Adelphi U., Garden City, N.Y., 1999-2000; CEO RB Cons., 2000—. Vis. asst. prof. Ind. U., Bloomington, 1977-78; sr. staff analyst OAO Corp., Beltsville, Md., 1980-81; mem. bus. edn. com. Charter Oak Coll., 1992-97, mem. accreditation com. New Eng. Assn. of Schs. and Colls. accreditation com., 1995, mem. accreditation visitation team Am. Assembly of Collegiate Schs. of Bus.; with Barry U., 1998-2000, St. Joseph's U., 1998-99, Fairleigh Dickinson U., 1999, Winthrop U., 1999-2000; internat. cons. in field; presenter in field. Exec. editor Jour. Bus. and Econ. Studies, 1990-96; manuscript reviewer Jour. Econs. and Bus., Jour. Fin. Rsch., Jour. Acctg. and Pub. Policy, Fin. Rev., N.E. Jour. Econs. and Bus., Rev. Quantitative Fin. and Acctg.; contbr. articles to profl. jours. Trustee 1580 House Trust, 1984-94, 2001-03, pres., 1985, co-treas., 1986-94; fin. svcs. planning com. Mass. Photovoltaic Ctr., 1987-88; bd. dirs. N.E. Bus. and Econs. Assn., 1990-96; ops. evaluation planning com. Town of Stratford, Conn., 1991-92; planning bd. Town of Sturbridge, Mass., 1994-97, chair Rte. 15 study com., 1996-97; edn. com. Conn. Tech. Coun., 1995-97; steering com. for consortium MBA in China, Assn. Jesuit Bus. Sch. Deans, 1995-97, bd. dirs., at-large rep., 1996-97; design com. Magnet H.S. for Bus. Computer Sci. and Enterpreneurship, Cambria Heights, NY Jacob Ziskind Meml. scholar U. Mass., Lowell, 1971, MBA scholar Boston U., 1972, Boston U. scholar, 1972; Ind. U. fellow, 1975-76, Bur. Bus. and Econ. rsch. fellow U. Md., 1979, Wilson Elkins rsch. fellow U. Md., 1981; instrnl. aid grantee U. Md., 1978; grantee Bay State Skills Corp., 1985, Mass. Photovoltaic Ctr., 1987, 1988, Am. Pub. Power Assn., 1987, U.S. Dept. Edn., 1992-94, GE Found., 1994-98, PepsiCo Found., 1994-99. Mem. Am. Fin. Assn., Acad. Internat. Bus., Fin. Execs. Inst., Fin. Mgmt. Assn., Western Fin. Assn., Tech.-Lowell Alumni Assn. (bd. dirs. 2000–), Beta Gamma Sigma, Tau Epsilon Sigma. Roman Catholic. Avocations: golf, birdwatching. Address: 58 Sagamore Ave Medford MA 02155-2143 E-mail: rboisjuly@comcast.net.

BOISSEAU, JERRY PHILIP, financial services company executive; b. Plattsburgh, N.Y., June 5, 1939; s. Augustine Arthur and Genevieve Francis (Poland) B.; m. Linda Gael Cummings Aug. 18, 1961; children: Gregory Philip, Lisa Michele. B of Gen. Studies, U. Nebr., 1970; MEd in Adminstrn., Fitchburg State Coll., 1978; MBA, Western New Eng. Coll., 1981. Cert. fin. planner; lic. registered prin.; registered investment advisor. Enlisted U.S. Army, 1961, commd. 2d lt., 1963, advanced through grades to lt. col., 1979, ret., 1981; account exec. Prudential-Bache Securities, Springfield, Mass., 1981-87; pres. Arlington Beach Co., Seaside Park, N.J., 1987-91, resigned, 1991; lectr. Ocean County Coll., 1991—99; adj. faculty mem. Coll. For Fin. Planning, Denver, 1992-99. Instr., lectr. U. Mass., Amherst, 1982-87, Greenfield (Mass.) C.C., 1983-86; owner, mgr. Amherst Fin. Svcs., Toms River, N.J., 1987—; mem. bd. trustees Cmty. Med. Ctr. Found., sec., 2001—; bd. dirs. Ocean Harbor House, treas., 1998-2000, v.p. 2000-2002, pres. 2002—; bd. dirs. Ocean County YMCA, sec., 1998-2000; bd. dirs., organizer Shore Cmty. Bank, 1996—. Past pres. parish coun. St. Catharines of Siena Ch., Seaside Park; ocean devel. adv. com. Children's Specialized Hosp., 1994-97. Mem. Fin. Planning Assn., KC (4th degree), Fin. Planning Assn. N.J. (bd. dirs. 2000-2002), Toms River C. of C., Toms River County Club, Seaside Park Yacht Club (treas. 1995-96), Rotary (pres. Amherst 1986-87, Paul Harris fellow; bd. dirs. Ctrl. Ocean Club, pres. 1997-98). Republican. Roman Catholic. Home: PO Box 591 Seaside Park NJ 08752-0591 Office: PO Box 1959 Toms River NJ 08754-1959

BOISSON, JACQUES LOUIS, diplomat, ambassador; Permanent rep. to UN Govt. Monaco, N.Y.C., 1993—. Office: Monaco's Perm Mission UN 866 United Nations Plz Rm 520 New York NY 10017-1822 E-mail: monaco@un.int.

BOISVERT, LAURIER JOSEPH, communications executive; b. Legal, Alta., Can. married with three children. Honors Degree in Commerce, Carleton U., Ottawa, 1981. Tech. tng. supr. Bell Can., 1964-72, Telesat, Gloucester, Ont., Can., 1972-73, mgr., 1973-75, dir. Earth Sta. Ops., 1982-84, dir. network svcs. ops. Ottawa, 1984-88, v.p. network svcs. ops., 1988-93, pres., COO, 1993, CEO, pres., 1993—; vice chmn. Mobile Satellite Ventures LP. Bd. dirs. Comm. Rsch. Coun., Infosat Comms. Inc., Wildblue Comms. Inc., Hellas Sat Consortium Ltd., Mobile Satellite Ventures (Can.) Inc., Mobile Satellite Ventures Holdings (Can.). Office: Telesat Canada 1601 Telesat Ct Gloucester ON Canada K1B 5P4

BOISVERT, MARC EDWARD, surgeon, researcher; b. New Bedford, Mass., Oct. 19, 1955; s. Roger Gerald and Eveline Bertha (Bertrand) B.; m. Elena Sallitto, June 23, 1979; children: Jacqueline Nicole, Alexander Joseph. BS, Georgetown U., 1977, MD, 1981. Diplomate Am. Bd. Surgery. Intern Hosp. St. Raphael, New Haven, Conn., 1981-82, resident, 1982-86; pvt. practice Washington, 1986—; clin. asst. prof. surgery Georgetown U., Washington, 1994—; dir. Breast Care Ctr. Washington Cancer Inst., Washington Hosp. Ctr., 1995—. Vol. surgeon Archdiocesan Health Network, Washington, 1995—. Recipient Edward Cornwell Teaching award Dept. Surgery, Washington Hosp. Ctr. Fellow ACS, Southeastern Surg. Congress; mem. Soc. Am. Gastrointestinal Endoscopic Surgeons, Am. Soc. Clin. Oncology, Washington Acad. Surgery, Am. Soc. Breast Disease. Office: 110 Irving St NW Ste CG 185 Washington DC 20010-2976 E-mail: marc.e.boisvert@medstar.net.

BOISVERT, RONALD FERNAND, computer scientist; b. Manchester, N.H., July 26, 1951; s. Fernand Lucien and Irene Dorothy (Demers) B.; m. Rita Linda Lefebvre, Dec. 30, 1972; 1 child, Linette. BS, Keene (N.H.) State Coll., 1973; MS, Coll. William and Mary, Williamsburg, Va., 1975, Purdue U., 1977, PhD, 1979. Programmer Coll. William and Mary, Williamsburg, Va., 1973-74; programmer Inst. for Computer Applications in Sci. & Engring ICASE, NASA Langley Rsch. Ctr., Hampton, Va., 1974-75; teaching asst. Purdue U., West Lafayette, 1975-76, rsch. asst., 1976-79; computer scientist Nat. Inst. Standards and Tech., Gaithersburg, Md., 1979-92, leader math. software group, 1992-98, chief math. and computational scis. divsn., 1998—. Co-author: Solving Elliptic Problems Using Ellpack, 1985, Guide to Available Mathematical Software, 1984, 90; editor: The Quality of Numerical Software: Assessment and Enhancement, 1997, The Architecture of Scientific Software, 2001, Computational Science, Mathematics and Software, 2002. Recipient Bronze medal U.S. Dept. Commerce, 1984, 2001, Silver medal 1992, Alumni Achievement award Keene State Coll., 2002. Mem. Soc. for Indsl. and Applied Math., Assn. Computing Machinery (assoc. editor Transactions on Math. Software 1987-92, editor-in-chief 1993—, publs. bd. 1995—, Outstanding Contbn. award 2000), Internat. Fedn. for Info. Processing Working Group 2.5 (chair 2001—). Home: 9631 Shadow Oak Dr Gaithersburg MD 20886-1125

BOITANO, BRIAN, Olympic athlete; b. Mountain View, Calif., Oct. 22, 1963; Competitive in amateur ice-skating events, 1978—88; Bronze medallist World Figure Skating Championships, 1985; Gold medallist U.S. Nat. Figure Skating Championships, 1985, World Figure Skating Championships, 1986, Silver medallist, 1987; Gold medallist U.S. Nat. Figure Skating Championships, 1988, World Figure Skating Championships, 1988; Silver medallist U.S. Nat. Figure Skating Championships, 1994; U.S. Olympics 6th place, 1994; U.S. Olympic Figure Skating Gold medallist, 1988. Owner White Canvas Prodns. Author (with Suzanne Harper): Boitano's Edge: Inside the Real World of Figure Skating, 1997; performer : (TV films) Carmen on Ice, 1990 (Emmy award, 1990); featured on cover: Sports Illustrated. Named Role Model of the Yr., Profl. Skaters' Cooperative, 1998; named to U.S. Figure Skating Hall of Fame, 1996, World Figure Skating Hall of Fame, 1996; recipient Gustav Lussi award, Profl. Skaters Assn., 1999.*

BOIVIN, MICHAEL J. psychologist, educator, psychologist, researcher; b. Detroit, July 28, 1955; s. Joseph R. Boivin and Huguette M. Maclean; m. Grace R. Abell, Apr. 19, 1953; children: Monique D., Daniel R., Marjorie J., Matthew I. BA, Spring Arbor Coll., 1976; MPH, U. Mich., 1993; MA, PhD, Western Mich. U., 1980. Prof. psychology Spring Arbor (Mich.) Coll., 1978—96, Ind. Wesleyan U., Marion, 1996—. Adj. rsch. investigator psychiatry U. Mich., Ann Arbor, 1991—. Contbr. articles to profl. jours. Sch. bd. The King's Acad., Marion, 2001—02; head ofcl. Marion InLine Hockey Assn., 1998—2003. Recipient Outstanding Paper in Humility Theology award, John Templeton Found., 1993; fellow Fulbright Rsch. award, U.S. State Dept., 1990—91, 1993—94; scholar Kellogg Found. Leaders in Pub. Health, Kellogg Found., 1991—93; Summer Rsch. fellow, West African Rsch. Assn., 1997, Rsch. fellow, 1997, Templeton/Oxford fellow, John Templeton Found., Coun. Christian Colls. and Univs., 1999—2001. Mem.: Nat. Acad. Neuropsychology, Am. Psychol. Soc. Achievements include first to neuropsychological effects of early cerebral malaria; neuropsychology of pediatric HIV, cognitive effects of intestinal parasite treatment; research in health interventions and neuropsychological development of children in the tropics. Home: 1455 Sylvan Dr Marion IN 46953 Office: Indiana Wesleyan Univ 4201 S Washington St Marion IN 46953 Office Fax: 765-677-2487. Personal E-mail: mjboivin1@hotmail.com. E-mail: michael.boivin@indwes.edu.

BOJAR, ROBERT MICHAEL, cardiothoracic surgeon; b. Boston, June 14, 1951; s. Samuel and Leah Sonia B.; m. Mercedes Von Deck, June 9, 1996. BA, Brown U., 1973, MD, 1976. Diplomate Am. Bd. Surgery, Am. Bd. Thoracic Surgery. Resident in surgery Mass. Gen. Hosp., Boston, 1976-81; fellow in cardiovascular-thoracic surgery Rush-Presbyn. St. Luke's Med. Ctr., Chgo., 1981-84; cardiothorac surgeon New Eng. Med. Ctr., Boston, 1984-89, sr. cardiothoracic surgeon, 1989—, acting chief cardiothoracic surgery, 1999-2000; asst. prof. surgery Tufts U., Boston, 1984-89, assoc. prof. surgery, 1989—; chief cardiothoracic surgery St. Vincent's Hosp. at Worcester Med. Ctr., 2002—. Author: Manual of Perioperative Care in Cardiac Surgery, 1989, 3rd edit., 1999, Adult Cardiac Surgery, 1991. Fellow ACS, Am. Coll. Cardiology, Am. Coll. Chest Physicians; mem. Soc. Thoracic Surgeons, Internat. Soc. for Heart and Lung Transplantation. Jewish. Avocations: music, gardening, competitive ballroom dancing. Office: New Eng Med Ctr 20 Worcester Center Blvd Worcester MA 01608 E-mail: robert.bojar@tenethealth.com.

BOK, DEAN, cell biologist, educator; b. Douglas County, S.D., Nov. 1, 1939; s. Kryn Arie and Rena (Van Zee) B.; m. Audrey Ann Van Diest, Aug. 21, 1964; children: Jonathan, Jeremy, James. BA, Calvin Coll., 1960; MA, Calif. State U., Long Beach, 1965; PhD, UCLA, 1968. Sci. instr. Valley Christian High Sch., Cerritos, Calif.; prof. neurobiology and Dolly Green prof. ophthalmology UCLA; assoc. dir. Jules Stein Eye Inst., 1972—78. Wellcome vis. prof. biomed. scis., 1994; mem. Nat. Adv. Eye Coun., 1998—. Mem. nat. adv. bd. Eye Coun., 1999—. Recipient disting. teaching awards UCLA, sr. sci. investigator award Rsch. To Prevent Blindness Inc., 1986, 95, Disting. Alumnus award Calif. State U., 1986, Calvin Coll., 1990; grantee Nat. Eye Inst., Nat. Retinitis Pigmentosa Soc.; William and Mary Greve internat. rsch. scholar Rsch. To Prevent Blindness Inc., 1982. Fellow AAAS; mem. Nat. Eye Inst. (bd. sci. counselors 1980-82, MERIT award 1987-96), Assn. Research in Vision and Ophthalmology (trustee 1978-82, Friedenwald award 1985, Alcon award 1985), Am. Soc. Cell Biology. Home: 2135 Kelton Ave Los Angeles CA 90025-5705

BOK, DEREK, law educator, former university president; b. Bryn Mawr, Pa., Mar. 22, 1930; s. Curtis and Margaret (Plummer) B.; m. Sissela Ann Myrdal, May 7, 1955; children: Hilary Margaret, Victoria, Tomas Jeremy. BA, Stanford U., 1951; JD, Harvard U., 1954; MA, George Washington U., 1958. Fulbright scholar, Paris, 1954-55; faculty Harvard U. Law Sch., Cambridge, Mass., 1958—, prof., 1961—, dean, 1968-71; pres. Harvard U., Cambridge, 1971-91, 300th anniversary univ. prof., 1991—. Editor: (with Archibald Cox) Cases and Materials on Labor Law, 1962; author: (with John T. Dunlop) Labor and the American Community, 1970, Beyond the Ivory Tower: Social Responsibilities of the Modern University, 1982, Higher Learning, 1986, Universities and the Future of America, 1990, The Cost of Talent, 1993, (with William G. Bowen) The Shape of the River, 1998, The Trouble with Government, 2001; contbr.: In the Public Interest, 1980, The State of the Nation, 1997. Bd. dirs., nat. chmn. Common Cause, 1999—; chmn. bd. overseers Cts. Inst. Music, 1997-2002; chmn. bd. Spencer Found., 2002-; facility chmn. Haupen Ctr. for Non-Profit Orgs., 2002-. Fellow Ctr. for Advanced Studies in the Behavioral Scis., 1991-92. Fellow Am. Acad. Arts and Scis., mem. Nat. Acad. Edn., Phi Beta Kappa. Office: Harvard U JFK Sch of Govt Cambridge MA 02138

BOK, JOAN TOLAND, utility executive; b. Grand Rapids, Mich., Dec. 31, 1929; d. Don Prentiss Weaver and Mary Emily Toland; m. John Fairfield Bok, July 15, 1955; children: Alexander Toland, Geoffrey Robbins. AB, Radcliffe Coll., 1951; JD, Harvard U., 1955. Bar: Mass. 1955. Assoc. Ropes & Gray, Boston, 1955-61; pvt. practice Boston, 1961-68; atty. New England Electric Sys., Westborough, Mass., 1968-73, asst. to pres., 1973-77, v.p., sec., 1977-79, vice-chair, 1979-84, pres., CEO, 1988-89, chair, 1984-98, chair emeritus, 1998—. Bd. dirs. ALTIComm., Inc. Past pres. bd. overseers Harvard U.; bd. dirs. Boston Adult Literacy Fund, Nat. Osteoporosis Found., Vt. Hist. Soc., Worcester Found. for Biomed. Rsch., Woods Hole (Mass.) Oceanog. Inst. Fellow Am. Bar Found.; mem. Boston Bar Assn., Am. Acad. Arts and Scis., Phi Beta Kappa. Unitarian Universalist. Home: 53 Pinckney St Boston MA 02114-4801 Office: 25 Research Dr Westborough MA 01582-0001

BOK, JOHN FAIRFIELD, lawyer; b. Boston, Aug. 30, 1930; AB magna cum laude, Harvard U., 1952, LLB magna cum laude, 1955. Bar: Mass. 1955, N.Y. 1982, Pa. 1984. Assoc. firm Ropes & Gray, Boston, 1957-62, 64-69; counsel to devel. adminstr. Boston Redevel. Authority, 1962-64; ptnr. firm Csaplar & Bok, Boston, 1969-90, Gaston & Snow, Boston, 1990-91; of counsel Foley, Hoag & Eliot, Boston, 1991-2000. Instr. law Boston Coll. Law Sch., part-time 1974-75; lectr. Practicing Law Inst., 1974, New Eng. Law Inst., 1973 Editor Harvard Law Rev., 1954-55. Pres. Cambridge St. Comty. Devel. Corp., 1972-75, Citizens Housing and Planning Assn., 1968-70, Met. Cultural Alliance, 1973-75, Beacon Hill Civic Assn., 1959-61, Beacon Hill Nursery Sch., 1964-65, Peddock's Island Trust, 1982-85, Mus. Wharf, 1989-94, Boston Ballet, 1991-94, Peter Faneuil Devel. Group, Inc., 1992—, Mass. Hort. Soc., 1995-98; v.p. The Cmty. Builders, Inc., 1969-97, pres. or chmn., 1998—; chmn. Boston Children's Mus., 1976-78, Mass. Housing Partnership, 1985-92, Social Policy Rsch. Group Inc., 1985-92, Boston Mcpl. Rsch. Bur., 1979-81, bd. dirs. and/or officer Boston Neighborhood Housing Svcs., 1974-76, Boston Waterfront Devel. Corp., 1970-85, Archti. Conservation Trust for Mass., 1978-92, Wheelock Coll., 1980-95, Strawberry Banke, Inc., 1981-86, Met. Boston Housing Partnership, Inc., 1984-95, Cambridge Coll., 1984-95, Boston Housing Authority monitoring com., 1984-90, The Boston Harbor Assn., 1984-92, Back Bay Assn., 1988-92, Hist. Mass., 1989—, African Am. Meeting House, 1993—; mem. Boston Archives and Records Advt. Commn., 1988-95, Cmty. Music Ctr., 1995—, Island Alliance, 1995—, Light Boston!, 1995—. Fulbright-Hays scholar, 1976 Mem. ABA, Mass. Bar Assn., Boston Bar Assn. (chmn. land use com. 1971-74), Phi Beta Kappa. Home: 53 Pinckney St Boston MA 02114-4801

BOK, SISSELA, philosopher, writer; b. Stockholm, Dec. 2, 1934; d. Gunnar and Alva (Reimer) Myrdal; m. Derek Bok, May 7, 1955; children— Hilary, Victoria, Tomas BA, George Washington U., 1957, MA, 1958, LHD (hon.), 1986; PhD, Harvard U., 1970; LLD (hon.), Mt. Holyoke Coll., 1985; LHD (hon.), Clark U., 1988, U. Mass., 1991, Georgetown U., 1992. Lectr. Simmons Coll., Boston, 1971-72; lectr. Harvard-MIT Div. Health Scis. and Tech., Cambridge, 1975-82, Harvard U., Cambridge, 1982-84; assoc. prof. philosophy Brandeis U., Waltham, Mass., 1985-89, prof. philosophy, 1989-92; fellow Ctr. for Advanced Study, Stanford, Calif., 1991-92; Disting. fellow Harvard Ctr. Population and Devel. Studies, Cambridge, Mass., 1993—. Mem. ethics adv. bd. HEW, 1977-80; bd. dirs. Population Coun., 1971-77; mem. Pulitzer Prize Bd., 1988-97, chmn., 1996-97. Author: Lying: Moral Choice in Public and Private Life, 1978 (Melcher award, George Orwell award), Secrets: On the Ethics of Concealment and Revelation, 1982, Alva: Ett kvinnoliv, 1987, A Strategy for Peace, 1989, Alva Myrdal: A Daughter's Memoir, 1991 (Melcher award), Common Values, 1996, Mayhem: Violence as Public Entertainment, 1998; mem. editl. bd. Ethics, 1980-85, Criminal Justice Ethics, 1980—, Contention, 1990-96, Common Knowledge, 1991—, (with others) Euthanasia and Physician-Assisted Suicide, 1998. Bd. dirs. Inst. for Philosophy and Religion, Boston U.; mem. Pulitzer Prize Bd., 1989-97. Recipient Abram L. Sachar Silver medallion Brandeis U., 1985, Radcliffe Coll. Grad. Soc. medal, 1993, Barnard Coll. medal of distinction, 1995, centennial medal Harvard Grad. Sch. Arts & Scis., 1998. Fellow Hastings Ctr. (dir. 1976-84, 94-97); mem. Am. Philos. Assn.

BOKHARI, SABAHAT, cardiologist; Clin. instr. Robert Wood Johnson U. Hosp., New Brunswick, NJ, 1996—98, N.Y. Presbyn. Hosp./Columbia U., N.Y.C., 1998—. Contbr. articles to profl. jours. Home: 67 Ridge Rd Green Brook NJ 08812 Home Fax: 908-868-8659. Personal E-mail: bokharis@aol.com.

BOKUNIEWICZ, HENRY JOSEPH, oceanography educator; b. Chgo., July 29, 1949; s. Henry Joseph and Alice Rose (Weber) B.; m. Linda Joan Sedey, Aug. 14, 1971; 1 child, Roxanna. BA, U. Ill., 1971; MPhil, Yale U., 1973, PhD, 1976. Assoc. prof. SUNY, Stony Brook, 1982-87, assoc. dean edn., 1992-98; dir. L.I. Groundwater Resource Inst., Stony Brook, 1993—; prof. oceanography SUNY, Stony Brook, 1991—. Environ. cons. Great Lakes Dock and Dredge/Amboy Aggregates, Oakbrook, Ill. and Amboy, N.J., 1985-99, Port Authority N.Y., N.Y.C., 1998-99, U.S. Army CE, N.Y.C., 1998-99. Rsch. grantee Suffolk County Water Authority, 1993-94, N.Y. State, 1997-99, U.S. Army C.E., 1997-99, NRC, 1996-98. Mem. Internat. Coun. Sci. Unions (mem. working group 1998-99), Internat. Geosphere Biosphere Program (mem. working group 1998-99), Internat. Coun. for Exploration of Seas (mem. working group 1986-99). Roman Catholic. Home: 14 Keats Pl Greenlawn NY 11740-2606 Office: Marine Scis Rsch Ctr Suny Stony Brook NY 11794-0001 E-mail: hbokuniewicz@notes.cc.sunysb.edu.

BOLAN, RICHARD STUART, urban planner, educator, researcher; b. Salem, Mass., Dec. 11, 1927; s. Robert Stuart and Mildred Elizabeth (Fay) B.; m. Elizabeth Ann Murphy, Sept. 4, 1954 (dec. 1977); 1 child, Geoffrey Stuart; m. Margaret Mary Altschul, Mar. 30, 1978 (div. May 1983); m. Nancy Jane Johnston, Dec. 19, 1987. B of Engring., Yale U., 1954; M of City and Regional Planning, MIT, 1956; PhD, NYU, 1974. Planner Providence Redevel. Authority, 1956-57, Planning and Renewal Assocs., Cambridge, Mass., 1957-58; prin. planner Boston City Planning Bd., 1958-60, dir. renewal planning Boston Redevel. Authority, 1960-62; dir. planning Boston Regional Transp. Study, 1962-64; asst. to dir. Joint Ctr. for Urban Studies of MIT and Harvard, Cambridge, 1964-67; prof. Boston Coll., Chestnut Hill, Mass., 1967-85; prof. urban planning U. Minn., Mpls., 1985-98, prof. emeritus, 1998—. Editor: Planning Metropolitan Boston, 1967; co-author: Urban Planning and Politics, 1975, Poland's Path to Sustainable Development: 1989-93, 1994; co-editor workshop procs., 1991; contbr. articles to profl. jours. Vol. United Way, Mpls., 1986-98, bd. dirs. Minn. Jobs with Peace, Mpls., 1989-96. Sgt. USAF, 1945-47, 50-51. Mem. Am. Planning Assn., Am. Inst. Cert. Planners, Assn. Collegiate Schs. of Planning (sec.-treas. 1989-93). Democrat. Unitarian Universalist. Home: 2833 E Lake Of The Isles Pky Minneapolis MN 55408-1055 Office: U Minn Humphrey Inst Pub Affairs Minneapolis MN 55455 E-mail: dbolan@hhh.umn.edu.

BOLAND, BEVERLY JOYCE, music educator; b. Decatur, Ill., Apr. 1, 1939; d. Orville Clarence and Dorothy Gladys (Brubaker) Merritt; m. Richard Brian Boland; children: Camilla Durbin, David Boland. BS in Edn., Ea. Ill. U., 1961, MS in Edn., 1964. Cert. tchr., Mo. Prof. Bapt. Bible Coll., Springfield, Mo., 1973—. Organist Cherry St. Bapt. Ch., Springfield, Mo., 1975—, dir. children's choir, 1986-96; adjudicator local piano contests, Springfield & Bolivor, 1990s, pub. spkr. Christian Women's Retreats, various locations, 1990s. Mem. Nat. Musics Tchrs. Assn., Am. Guild Organists, Piano Guild, Springfield Music Tchrs. Assn. (v.p. 1990-95). Baptist. Avocations: music, reading, camping. Home: 1906 E Sayer Cir Springfield MO 65803-4720 Office: Bapt Bible Coll 628 E Kearney St Springfield MO 65803-3426

BOLAND, CHRISTOPHER THOMAS, II, lawyer; b. Scranton, Pa., June 10, 1915; s. Patrick J. and Sarah (Jennings) B.; m. Nora Cusick, Jan. 23, 1943; m. Cornelia Bingham, Mar. 1, 1980. BSS cum laude, Georgetown U., 1937; LL.B., Harvard, 1940. Staff dir. Spl. Senate Com. on Atomic Energy, 1945—47; staff dir., counsel Joint Senate-House Com. on Atomic Energy, 1947; pvt. practice Washington, 1947—; sr. ptnr. Gallagher Boland & Meiburger, Washington, 1955—93, sr. counsel, 1994—. Utility specialist Dept. Energy. Served to lt. col., intelligence USAAF, 1941-45. Mem. ABA, D.C. Bar Assn., Fed. Energy Bar Assn. (pres. 1970), Congressional Country Club (pres. 1974), Harvard Club (Washington), Burning Tree Club (Bethesda, Md.), Rehoboth Beach (Del.) Country Club. Home: 5309 Cardinal Ct Spring Hill Bethesda MD 20816 Office: 1023 15th St NW Ste 900 Washington DC 20005-2627 E-mail: cboland@gbmdc.com.

BOLAND, ELIZABETH, social services company financial executive; BBS, U. Notre Dame, 1981. From mem. audit staff to sr. audit mgr. Price Waterhouse LLP, Boston, 1981-90; v.p. fin. The Olsten Corp., home-health care-temporary staffing svcs., Boston; CFO, The Visionaries Inc., ind. TV prodn. co., Boston, 1994-97, Bright Horizons Family Solutions, Inc., Watertown, Mass., 1997—. Office: Bright Horizons Family Solutions 200 Talcott Ave Watertown MA 02472-5705

BOLAND, GERALD LEE, health facility financial executive; b. Harrisburg, Pa., Apr. 2, 1946; s. Vincent Harry and Alice Jane (Geiste) B.; 1 child, Peter Alexander. BS, Lebanon Valley Coll., 1968. Acctg. trainee Armstrong Cork Co., Millville, NJ, 1968; payroll supr, plant ops. acct. Armstron Cork Co., Millville, N.J., 1969-70; sr. fin. acct. Lancaster 9Pa.) Gen. Hosp., 1970-71, mgr. gen. acctg., 1972; corp. acctg. mgr. HMW Industries Inc., Lancaster, 1972; corp. contr. Fleck-Marshall Co. subs. Gable Industries, Lancaster, 1973-74, sec.-treas., 1974-75; contr. Dominion Psychiat. Treatment Ctr., Falls Church, Va., 1975-76; contr., dir. fin. Miller & Byrne Inc., Rockville, Md., 1976-79; v.p. internal auditing Medlantic Healthcare Group, 1979-88; v.p. ops. Kapner, Wolfbreg Y Assocs., Van Nuys, Calif., 1988-89; dir. acctg. Providence Hosp., 1989-95, asst. contr., 1995-2001, contr., 2001—. Mem. Am. Acctg. Assn., Inst. of Mgmt. Accts., Healthcare Fin. Mgmt. Assn., Eastern Fin. Assn., Am. Hosp. Assn., Am. Mgmt. Assn., Fin. Mgmt. Assn., Inst. Internal Auditors. Home: 1142 Cranston Ct Crofton MD 21114 E-mail: jboland@provhosp.org.

BOLAND, JAMES PIUS, surgeon, educator; b. Phila., Mar. 6, 1931; s. John Patrick and Beatrice Christine (Murphy) B.; m. Kathryn Ann Watts, May 18, 1963; children: Beatrice, James, Kathryn, Sara, Angela, Genevieve. BS, St. Joseph's Coll., Phila., 1948-52; MD, Jefferson Med. Coll., Phila., 1952-56; MPH, U. South Fla., 1998. Diplomate Am. Bd. Surgery, Am. Bd. Thoracic Surgery, Am. Bd. Surg. Critical Care. Asst. prof. to prof. Med. Coll. Pa., Phila., 1964-76; prof. surgery W.Va. U., Charleston, 1976—, chmn. dept. surgery, 1976—. Capt. USNR, ret. Decorated Navy Commendation medal. Fellow ACS. Roman Catholic. Home: 1939 Parkwood Rd Charleston WV 25314-2241 Office: W Va U/CAMC 3110 Maccorkle Ave SE Charleston WV 25304-1210

BOLAND, JANET LANG, judge; b. Kitchener, Ont., Can., Dec. 6, 1924; d. George William and Miriam Janet (Geraghty) Lang; m. John Brown Boland, Oct. 1, 1949; children: Michael, Christopher, Nicholas; m. Taylor Stallen, Oct. 27, 2001. BA, Waterloo Coll., 1946; law degree, Osgoode Hall, 1950; hon. doctorate of law, Sir Wilfred Laurier U. Bar: Ont. 1976, named Queen's counsel 1965. Mem. firm White, Bristol, Beck & Phipps, Toronto, Ont., 1959-69; partner firm Lang Michener, Toronto, 1969-72; county ct. judge Toronto, 1972-76; judge Supreme Ct. of Ont., Toronto, 1976—. Co-chmn. Penal Reform for Women Joint Com., 1956-58 Mem. Jr. League Toronto (hon. pres.), Can. Women's Sr. Golf Assn. Roman Catholic. Office: 1605 - 33 Harbour Sq Toronto ON Canada M5J 2G2

BOLAND, JOHN KEVIN, bishop; b. Apr. 25, 1935; Ordained priest Roman Cath. Ch. 1959. Appointed Bishop Savannah Diocese, 1995—. Office: Catholic Pastoral Center 601 E Liberty St Savannah GA 31401-5196*

BOLAND, MICHAEL JOSEPH, state legislator; b. Davenport, Iowa, Aug. 20, 1942; s. Francis Charles and Opal (Waites) B.; m. Mary Rose Lavorato, 1967; children: Susan, Barbara Ann. BA, Upper Iowa U., Fayette, 1967; MSE, Henderson State U., Arkadelphia, 1972. Del. County and Iowa State Conv., 1970; East Moline chmn. and 36th legis. dist. chmn. Polit. Action Coms. for Edn., 1974-75; mem. Bicentennial Com.; del. Ill. State Dem. Conv., 1978; alt. del. Dem. Nat. Mid-Term Conf., 1978; del. Dem. Nat. Conv., 1980; mem. from dist. 71 Ill. Ho. of Reps., 1994—. Coord. West Ill. Coalition for Polit. Honesty's Legis. Cutback Amendment; mem. United Twp. H.S. Bd. Edn., 1984-85; v.p. Citizens Utility Bd., Ill.civ Nat. bd. dirs. UN Reform Campaign Com.; libr. bd. trustees, East Moline, Ill., 1975-79. Named one of 11 Who Made a Difference in Ill., Chgo. Tribune Sunday Mag. Mem. LWV (mem. govt. com. 1980-81), Ill. Coalition Polit. Honesty (bd. dirs. 1987), Consumers and Taxpayers Together (founding mem.). Address: 2041-J Stratton Bldg Springfield IL 62706-0001 also: 4416 River Dr Moline IL 61265-1734*

BOLANOS, MICHAEL TEMPLETON, new media executive; b. Denville, N.J., Jan. 29, 1965; s. Henry and Jean Mary (Chardi) B. Mng. dir. Bell and Barter Theater/Arts Ctr., Rockaway, N.J., 1981-83; pres. The Musicom Corp., N.Y.C., 1981—, U.S./Soviet Exch. Initiative, 1985-86; ptnr. Hart-Bolanos and Assocs., N.Y.C., 1987-88; pres. Global Programming Inc., N.Y.C., Tokyo, 1990-93; pres., CEO Entertainment Drive, N.Y.C., 1995—. Artistic coord. U.S./Soviet Exch. Initiative; mem. bd. Friends of Am. Theatre Wing, 1991—92; cons. NHK-TV, Tokyo, Fujisankei Group, Osaka, Japan, 1989—91, Compuserve, Columbus, Ohio, 1993—94; lectr. Yale U.; exec. prodn. advisor Eisenhower Inst., 2001—; exec. prodr. Ofcl. Cindy Crawford website, Ofcl. Britney Spears website, NewYorkPix.com. Creator/reporter (Kidcast) KAMR-TV, Amarillo, Tex., 1975—76, co-creator/patentee (eDrive) Movie Viewer, 1994, creator Entertainment Drive on Compuserve, 1994, eDrive Japan on NiftyServe, 1997, (official website) www.cindy.com, 1998, www.britneyspears.com, (websites) StarClubs.com, NewYorkPix.com, 2001. Artist coord. Rally for Soviet Jewry, Coalition to Free Soviet Jews, 1987; exec. prodr. on-line coverage of telethon Muscular Dystrophy Assn., 1994-95, exec. prodr. on-line chat Artists' Rights Found., 1995; bd. dirs. U. Metaphys. Studies. Recipient Cyber 60 award N.Y. Mag., 1995, CyberStar award Virtual City Mag., 1996. Mem. The Japan Soc. (concert prodr. 1987), Am. Acad. Children's Entertainment (bd. outside advisors), Actor's Fund Am. (Inner Cir.), Internet Content Coalition, Young Entrepreneurs Assn., N.Y. New Media Assn., Sales and Mktg. Execs. N.Y., Assn. for Interactive Media, U. Metaphysical Studies. Avocations: acting, singing, travel, japanese language and art. Office: Entertainment Drive 2545 East Sunrise Blvd #207 Fort Lauderdale FL 33304

BOLAS, GERALD DOUGLAS, art museum administrator, art history educator; b. Los Angeles, Nov. 1, 1949; s. Norman Theodore and Elizabeth Louise (Douglas) B.; m. Deborah Jean Wohletz, Nov. 25, 1978; children: Ellen Claire, John David. BA, U. Calif., Santa Barbara, 1972, MA, 1975; PhD, CUNY, 1998. Tchg. asst. U. Calif., Santa Barbara, 1973-74; NEH mus. intern Yale U. Art Gallery, New Haven, 1975-76, asst. to dir., 1976-77; dir. Washington U. Gallery of Art, St. Louis, 1977-88, Portland (Oreg.) Art Mus., 1988-92, Ackland Art Mus. at U. N.C., Chapel Hill, 1994—. Adj. prof. art history Washington U., 1982-88, U. N.C., Chapel Hill, 1994—; advisor Mo. Arts Coun., St. Louis, 1981-82; field reviewer Inst. Mus. Svcs., Washington, 1980-83; panelist NEA, 1989, NEH, 1990, 95, N.C. Arts Coun., 1995; bd. dirs. Asian Art Soc. of Washington U., 1983-88; mem. No. Calif. adv. com. Archives of Am. Art; active Lake Oswego Arts Commn., 1993-94. Author: Illustrated Checklist of Washington University Collection, 1981; contbr. to books: Ketav: Flesh and Word in Israeli Art, 1996, Paris in Japan: The Japanese Encounter with European Painting, 1987; also contbr. articles to other publs.; numerous catalog forewords. Organizer numerous exhbns. Fellow Winterthur Mus., 1993, Smithsonian Instn., 1993. Mem. Coll. Art Assn., Assn. Art Mus. Dirs. Office: U NC Ackland Art Mus PO Box 3400 Chapel Hill NC 27599-0001 E-mail: gdbolas@unc.edu.

BOLCH, CARL EDWARD, JR., petroleum company executive, lawyer; b. St. Louis, Feb. 28, 1943; s. Carl Edward and Juanita (Newton) Bolch; m. Susan Bass; children: Carl, Allison, Natalie, Melanie, Jordan. BS in Econs, U. Pa., 1964; JD, Duke U., 1967. Cert. Fla., 1967. CEO, chmn. bd. dirs. RaceTrac Petroleum,Inc., Atlanta, 1967—. Edition editor Close Corporations, 1967. Mem.: Nat. Assn. Convenience Stores (bd. dirs. 1994—), Soc. Ind. Gasoline Marketers (pres. 1987—89), Fla. Bar Assn., ABA. Office: RaceTrac Petroleum Inc PO Box 105035 Atlanta GA 30348-5035 also: RaceTrac Petroleum Inc 300 Technology Ct Smyrna GA 30082*

BOLCOM, WILLIAM ELDEN, musician, composer, educator, pianist; b. Seattle, May 26, 1938; s. Robert Samuel and Virginia (Lauermann) B.; m. Fay Levine, Dec. 23, 1963 (div. 1967); m. Katherine Agee Ling, June 8, 1968 (div. 1969); m. Joan Clair Morris, Nov. 28, 1975. BA, U. Wash., 1958; MA, Mills Coll., 1961; postgrad., Paris Conservatoire de Musique, 1959-61, 64-65; D of Mus. Art, Stanford U., 1964; D of Music (hon.), San Francisco Conservatory, 1994, Albion Coll., 1995; studied with, Berthe Poncy Jacobson, 1949-58, John Verrall, 1951-58, Leland Smith, 1961-64, Darius Milhaud, 1957-61; George Rochberg, 1966. Acting asst. prof. music dept. U. Wash., Seattle, 1965-66; lectr., asst. prof. music Queens Coll., CUNY, Flushing, 1966-68; vis. critic music theater Drama Sch., Yale U., 1968-69; composer in residence Theater Arts Program, NYU, N.Y.C., 1969-71; asst. prof. U. Mich. Sch. Music, Ann Arbor, 1973-77, assoc. prof., 1973-83, prof., 1983-94, Ross Lee Finney disting. prof. composition, 1994—. Mem. jury Nat. Endowment for Arts, 1976-77, 84, 85. Composer: 6 symphonies, 1957, 64, 79, 86, 89, 97, String Quartets 1-8, 1950-65, String Quartet #9 (Novella), 1972, String Quartet #10, 1988, Décalage for cello and piano, 1961-62, Fantasy-Sonata for piano, 1960-62, Concertante for Flute, Oboe, Violin, and Orch, 1960, cabaret opera Dynamite Tonite, 1960-63, rev., 1966, Octet, 1962, Concerto-Serenade for Violin and Strings, 1964, 12 Etudes for Piano, 1959-66, Fives, Double Concerto for Violin, Piano and Strings, 1966, Morning and Evening Poems (Cantata), 1966, Session I for Chamber Ensemble, 1965, Session II for violin and viola, 1966, Session III for clarinet, violin, cello, piano, percussion, 1966, Session IV for chamber ensemble, 1967, Black Host for organ, percussion and taped sounds, 1967, Piano Rags, 1967-74, cabaret opera Greatshot, 1967 69, Praeludium for vibraphone and organ, 1969, Dark Music for timpani and cello, 1970, Duets for Quintet, 1970, Unpopular Songs, 1969-71, Hydraulis for organ, 1971, Commedia for chamber orch, 1971, Whisper Moon (chamber ensemble), 1971, Frescoes for two pianists, 1971, Seasons for solo guitar, 1974, Open House, song cycle on poems by Roethke, 1975, Piano Concerto, 1975-76, Piano Quartet, 1976, Revelation Studies for Carillon, 1976, Mysteries for Organ, 1976, score for stage works Puntila (Brecht), 1976, Man is Man (Brecht), 1977, Beggar's Opera (posthumous collaboration with Darius Milhaud), 1978, Violin Sonatas, 1956, 78, 92, 94, 12 Gospel Preludes for Organ, 1979, 81, 84, Humoresk for organ and orch., 1969, Brass Quintet, 1979, 24 Cabaret Songs, 1963-96, Aubade for Oboe and Piano, 1982, Songs of Innocence and of Experience (Blake), 1956-82, Violin Concerto in D, 1983, Lilith (saxophone, piano), 1984, Abendmusik, 1977, Little Suite of Dances in E flat for clarinet and piano, 1984, Orphée-Sérénade, 1984, Fantasia Concertante for viola, cello and orch., 1985, Capriccio for Violoncello and Piano, 1985, orchestral dance suite Seattle Slew, 1986, 12 New Etudes for Piano, 1977-86 (recipient Pulitzer Prize, 1988), Spring Concertino for Oboe and Chamber Orch., 1986-87, Five Fold Five for woodwind quintet and piano, 1985-87, Clarinet Concerto, 1990, (musical) Casino Paradise (libretto Arnold Weinstein), 1986-90, Fairy Tales for viola, cello, bass, 1987-88, Sonata for Violoncello and Piano, 1989, (song cycle on Am. women poets) I Will Breathe a Mountain, 1989-90, The Mask (chorus and piano), 1990, Recuerdos for two pianos, 1991, opera McTeague (libretto A. Weinstein and R. Altman), 1990-92, Lyric Concerto for flute and orch., 1993, Trio for clarinet, violin and piano, 1993, Sonata for 2 pianos in one movement, 1993, Suite for play Broken Glass by Arthur Miller, 1994, Let Evening Come (soprano, viola, piano), 1994, A Whitman Triptych, (mezzo-soprano and orchestra), 1995, GAEA Concertos 1-3 for Left Hand and Orch., 1996, Second Piano Quartet, 1995, Briefly It Enters, 1996 (voice and piano), Fanfare for the Detroit Opera House, 1996 (brass), Cabaret Songs, Vol. 3&4 (voice and piano), 1996, Nine Bagatelles, 1996 (piano), Spring Trio, 1996 (piano trio), Turbulence-A Romance, 1996 (2 voices and piano), Sixth Sym., 1997, Collusions (piano written with Curtis Curtis-Smith), 1998, Illuminata (film score written with Arnold Black), 1998, A View From the Bridge (opera), 1998, The Digital Wonder Watch (voice and piano), 1999, The Miracle (male chorus, woodwind quintet, percussion), 1999, Bird Spirits (piano), 2000, Concerto Grosso for Saxophone Quartet and Orch., 1999-2000, From the Diary of Sally Hemings (medium voice and piano), 2000, Piano Quintet (string quartet and piano), 2000, Song (for band), 2001, Naumburg Cycle (baritone and piano), 2001, Borborygm (organ), 2001; pianist in recs: (with Gerard Schwarz) Cornet Favorites, (with Clifford Jackson, baritone) An Evening with Henry Russell, (with mezzo-soprano Joan Morris) Other Songs of Leiber and Stoller, (with Joan Morris and Max Morath) These Charming People, (with Joan Morris) The Girl on the Magazine Cover, (with Joan Morris) Songs of Ira and George Gershwin, (with Joan Morris and Lucy Simon) The Rodgers and Hart Album, (with Joan Morris and Max Morath) More Rodgers and Hart, (with Joan Morris) Silver Linings (anthology of Jerome Kern), (with Joan Morris) Blue Skies (anthology of Irving Berlin), (with Joan Morris) Black Max (Bolcom cabaret songs with A. Weinstein poetry), (with Joan Morris) Lime Jello: An American Cabaret, (with Joan Morris) Night & Day (anthology of Cole Porter), (with Joan Morris) Let's Do It, (with Sergiu Luca) Works for Violin and Piano (by Bolcom), (with Joan Morris) After the Ball, Vaudeville, Songs of the Great Ladies of the Musical Stage, Wild About Eubie, (with Joan Morris and Clifford Jackson and chorus) Who Shall Rule This American Nation: Songs of Henry Clay Work, (with Joan Morris and Robert White) Orchids in the Moonlight and The Carioca (songs of Vincent Youmans), (with Joan Morris) Moonlight Bay-Songs As Is and Songs As Was; recs. Bolcom's 4th Symphony (Grammy nominee 1987), Violin Concerto, 5th Symphony, Fantasia Concertante (Am. Composers Orch.), 10th String Quartet (Stanford String Quartet), 1st and 3rd Symphonies, Seattle Slew Suite (Louisville Orch.), Orphée-Sérénade (Grammy nominee 1994), others; solo recordings include Heliotrope Bouquet, Pastimes and Piano Rags, Bolcom Plays His Own Rags, Piano Music of George Gershwin, Piano Music of Darius Milhaud, Bolcom: 12 Etudes, Euphonic Sounds (Scott Joplin anthology); author: (with Robert Kimball) Reminiscing with Sissle and Blake, 1973, Trouble in the Music World, 1988; editor book of essays: The Aesthetics of Survival by George Rochberg, 1982; contbr. to Grove's Dictionary, 6th edit; contbg. editor: Annals of Scholarship. Recipient Kurt Weill award, 1963, William and Noma Copley award, 1960, Marc Blitzstein Award for Excellence Am. Acad. Arts and Letters, 1965, N.Y. State Coun. award, 1971, Nat. Endowment for Arts award, 1974, 79, 82-84, Koussevitzky Found. award, 1974, 93, Henry Russel award, U. Mich., 1977, Mich. Arts Coun. award, 1986, Gov.'s Arts award, 1987, Pulitzer Prize in Music, 1988, Citation of Merit U. Mich. Sch. Music Alumni Assn., 1989, Disting. Achievement award U. Wash., 1993, Alfred I. Du Pont award Del. Symphony Assn., 1994, Henry Russel lectr., U. Mich., 1997; named composer of yr. Am. Guild Organists, 1998; Guggenheim Found. fellow, 1964, 68; Rockefeller Found. grantee, 1965, 69, 72. Mem. Am. Acad. Arts and Letters, Am. Music Ctr., Am. Composer Alliance, Am. Repertory Theatre (bd. dirs.), Charles Ives Soc. (bd. dirs.), Delta Omicron (nat. patron), Azazels. Home: 3080 Whitmore Lake Rd Ann Arbor MI 48105-9649 Office: U Mich Sch Music 2243 Moore Bldg Ann Arbor MI 48109 E-mail: wbolcom@umich.edu.

BOLDEN, MELVIN WILBERFORCE, JR., lawyer; b. N.Y.C., Sept. 11, 1941; s. Melvin Wilberforce and Eloise (Thomas) B.; children: Danielle Lillian, Melvin Wilberforce, III. BA, Morgan State Coll., Balt., 1964; JD, Howard U., 1970. Bar: D.C. 1971, U.S. Dist. Ct. D.C. 1976, U.S. Ct. Appeals (D.C. cir.) 1976, U.S. Supreme Ct. 1987. Asst. gen. counsel NAACP, N.Y.C., 1970-72; atty. Commn. Human Rights City of N.Y., 1973-76; mng. atty. Neighborhood Legal Svcs., Washington, 1977-79; asst. chief Office of Corp. Counsel, Washington, 1980-82, chief, 1982—; mem. mental health rules com. D.C. Superior Ct., jud. conf. of D.C., 1982-91. Co-author The Search for Military Justice, Illinois Products Liability. Mem. ABA, Washington Bar Assn., D.C. Bar Assn., NAACP, Alpha Phi Alpha, Sigma Delta Tau. Democrat. Mem. African Methodist Episcopal Ch. Office: 4975 Bryantown Rd Waldorf MD 20601

BOLDEN, THEODORE EDWARD, dentist, consultant, dental educator; b. Middleburg, Va., Apr. 19, 1920; s. Theodore D. and Mary E. (Jackson) Bolden. AB, Lincoln U., 1941, LLD (hon.), 1981; DDS, Meharry Med. Coll., 1947, MS (John Hay Whitney Found. opportunity fellow), 1951, PhD (USPHS fellow), 1958. Diplomate Am. Bd. Oral Medicine, Am. Bd. Oral Pathology. Instr. operative dentistry, pedodontics and periodontics Meharry Med. Coll., 1948-49, chmn. oral pathology Sch. Dentistry, 1962-77, dir. rsch., 1962-75, assoc. dean, 1965-70; asst. prof. gen. and oral pathology Seton Hall Coll. Medicine and Dentistry, 1957-60, assoc. prof., 1960-62; prof. gen. and oral pathology, dean coll. U. Medicine and Dentistry N.J.-N.J. Dental Sch., Newark, 1977—78, acting chmn. gen. and oral pathology, 1979-80, prof. dept. oral pathology, biology and diagnostic scis., 1988-90, prof. emeritus, 1991—. Cons. dental rsch. Colgate-Palmolive Co., 1991—; trustee Am. Fund Dental Health. Author (with John Manhold Jr.): (book) Outline of Pathology, 1960; author: (with E. Mobley and E. Chandler) Detnal Hygiene Examination Review Book, 4th edit., 1982; author: 1 and 1 = 1 It Really Do!!, 1987, My Po Son dongon and Broke His Neck...and Mama Too!, 1990, The Tiger is Loose, 1992, Memories and Thanks, 1995, Big Mama, 1996, Angie Thre/Throws a Partie, 1997, Jovita's F.P.L., 1997, 55 Years Ain't So Baaaaaaaaad, 1997, Celebration Time, 1997, Louise Epperson---Lady Extraordinaire---We Salute You, 1998, Inflammation IS, 1999, Aftermath, 2002, Sweethearts & Lovers, 2003. Chmn. adv. health com. Montclair (N.J.) Health Dept., 1959—60; commr. urban redevelopment Town of Montclair, 1960—62; trustee Neighborhood Coun., 1987—. Served to sgt. U.S. Army, 1942—43, 1st lt. U.S. Army, 1951—52. Fellow: Am. Acad. Oral Medicine, Am. Acad. Oral Pathology; mem.: Internat. Assn. Dental Rsch., Ewell Neil Dental Soc., Capital City Dental Soc., Pan-Tenn. Dental Assn. (statistician 1977—91, historian 1983—91), Nat. Dental Assn. (editor quar. 1974—82), Sigma Xi, Kappa Sigma Pi, Omicron Kappa Upsilon. Baptist. Home: 29 Montague Pl Montclair NJ 07042-2808

BOLDOSSER, RANDY RICHARD, communications company executive; b. Pottstown, Pa., July 5, 1957; s. Randall Kermit and Regina Eleanor (Stofko) B.; m. Nancy June Shilay, June 13, 1981; children: Katherine Ann, Christina Dawn. BSEE, Lehigh U., 1979, MS in Computer Sci., 1983, MS in Mfg. Sys. Engring., 1986; MBA, Columbia U., 1992. Engr. Western Electric, Allentown, Pa., 1979-82; mem. tech. staff AT&T Bell Labs., N.J. & Pa., 1983-86, project mgr., 1987-91; product mgr. AT&T Network Systems, Warren, 1992-93; mgr. strategic planning AT&T, Bridgewater, N.J., 1993-96; dir. info. tech. Shilay Assocs. Inc., Wantagh, N.Y., 1993-99; mgr. bus. mgmt., wireless design Lucent Techs. Inc., Whippany, N.J., 1996-99; dist. mgr. govt. markets AT&T, Bridgewater, 1999—2003, mgr. divsn. govt. solutions, 2003—. Contbg. author: Prentice-Hall Handbook of Advanced Manufacturing Methods, 1986. Mem. IEEE (chair comm. soc. tech. com. 1995-96), Armed Forces Comms. and Electronics Assn., Am. Philat. Soc. Republican. Episcopalian. E-mail: boldosser@att.com.

BOLDREY, EDWIN EASTLAND, retinal surgeon, educator; b. San Francisco, Dec. 8, 1941; s. Edwin Barkley and Helen Burns (Eastland) B.; m. Catherine Rose Oliphant, Oct. 20, 1973; children: Jennifer Elizabeth, Melissa Jeanne. BA with honors, De Pauw U., 1963; MD, Northwestern U., Chgo., 1967. Diplomate Am. Bd. Ophthalmology. Rotating intern U. Wash., Seattle, 1967-68; resident in gen. surgery U. Minn., Mpls., 1968-69; resident in ophthalmology U. Calif., San Francisco, 1971-74; Heed Found. fellow in retinal and vitreous surgery Washington U., St. Louis, 1974-75; mem. staff dept. ophthalmology Palo Alto (Calif.) Med. Clinic, 1975-91; dept. chmn., 1989-91; pvt. practice, 1991—. Clin. instr. Stanford (Calif.) U. Med. Sch., 1975-79, asst. clin. prof., 1979-87, assoc. clin. prof., 1987—; cons. VA Hosp., Palo Alto, Calif., 1976—; vice chmn. dept. ophthalmology Good Samaritan Hosp., San Jose, 1993-95, chmn., 1995-97. Contbr. articles to med. jours., chpt. to book. Lt. comdr. M.C., USNR, 1969-71. Recipient Asbury award dept. ophthalmology U. Calif., San Francisco, 1973. Fellow: ACS, Am. Acad. Ophthalmology (honor award 1989); mem.: AMA, Cordes Eye Soc. (pres. 1995—96), Western Retina Study Club (charter, exec. sec.-treas. 1983—95), Peninsula Eye Soc. (pres. 1987—88), Am. Soc. Retinal Surgeons (charter), Retina Soc., also others. Avocations: skiing, hiking, travel. Office: No Calif Retina Vitreous Assocs Inc 2512 Samaritan Ct Ste A San Jose CA 95124-4002

BOLDT, HEINZ, aerospace engineer; b. July 12, 1923; s. August and Marie (Hamann) B.; m. Christa Friebel, Mar. 25, 1965; children: Pierre, Manon. Diploma in engring., Technische Universität, Berlin, 1951; student, Wirtschaftsakademie, Berlin, 1953-57. Tech. dir. Borsig AG, Berlin, 1951-66; mem. exec. bd. dor prodn., dir. Messerschmitt-Werke Flugzeug-Union Sud, München-Augsburg, Fed. Rep. Germany, 1967-70; exec. bd. prodn., gen. proxi Klöckner_Humboldt-Deutz, Köln, Fed. Rep. Germany, 1970-72; mem. exec. bd. for devel., constrn. and prodn. FAHR AG, Gottmadingen, Fed. Rep. Germany, 1970-72; pres. VDI-Bodenseebezirksverein, Friedrichshafen, Germany, 1971-76; mem. exec. bd. Dornier GmbH, Munich, 1972-77; pres. Deutsche Indistrieanlagen Gesellschaft mbH, Berlin, 1978-82; rep. Machinoexport. Holder over 100 patents in field. Served with German Army Air Force, 1942-45. Recipient Ring for Honour VDI-Ehrenring, 1962. Mem. Am. C. of C. Club: Club der Luftfahrt. Home: Golfclub The Oaks 280 Saratoga Ct Osprey FL 34229-9386 also: Pullach 6a 83059 Kolbermoor Germany

BOLDT, MICHAEL HERBERT, lawyer; b. Detroit, Oct. 11, 1950; s. Herbert M. and Mary Therese (Fitzgerald) B.; m. Margaret E. Clarke, May 25, 1974; children: Timothy (dec.), Matthew. Student, U. Detroit, 1968-70; BA, Wayne State U., 1972; JD, U. Mich., 1975. Bar: Ind. 1975, U.S. Dist. Ct. (so. dist.) Ind. 1975, U.S. Ct. Appeals (7th cir.) 1979, U.S. Supreme Ct. 1980, U.S. Ct. Appeals (D.C. cir.) 1983. Assoc. Ice Miller, Indpls., 1975-81, ptnr., 1982—. Bd. dirs. Brooke's Place for Grieving Young People, Inc. Contbr. articles to profl. jours. Mem. Ind. State Bar Assn., Indpls. Bar Assn., Highland Golf and Country Club (bd. dirs.). Office: Ice Miller Box 82001 1 American Sq Indianapolis IN 46282-0002 E-mail: Michael.Boldt@icemiller.com.

BOLDT, OSCAR CHARLES, construction company executive; b. Appleton, Wis., Apr. 20, 1924; s. Oscar John and Dorothy A. (Bartmann) B.; m. Patricia Hamar, July 9, 1949; children: Charles, Thomas, Margaret. BSCE, U. Wis., 1948; hon. degree, Ripon Coll., 2001, Lawrence U., 2003. Pres. O.J. Boldt Constrn. Co., Appleton, 1950-79, CEO, chmn. bd. dirs., 1979-84; chmn. bd. dirs. The Boldt Group Inc., Appleton, 1984—; sec. W.S. Patterson Co., 1963-89. Trustee Lawrence U., 1981—; emeritus bd. dirs. M&I Bank, L.A., 2002 Chmn. bd. dirs. Cmty. Found. for Fox Valley Region, 1991-93; pres. Appleton YMCA, 1955-57, Appleton Meml. Hosp., 1975-76; bd. dirs. United Health Wis., 1990-99; co-chmn. fund drive Fox Cities United Way, 1994. 2d lt. USAAF, 1943-45. Named to Paper Industry Internat. Hall of Fame, 2000, Wis. Bus. Hall of Fame, 2003, Jr. Achievement Hall of Fame, 2003, Appleton H.S. Hall of Fame, 1999; recipient Disting. Svc. award, Appleton Jaycees, 1960, Disting. Engr. award, U. Wis., 1985, Walter Rugland Cmty. Svc. award, 1988, Master Entrepreneur award, Ernst and Young, 1991, Renaissance award, 1991, Regent's award, St. Olaf's Coll., 1993, Exec. of Yr. award, N.E. Wis.'s Sales and Mktg. Mag., 1994, Disting. Alumni award, U. Wis. Alumni Assn., 1999, Disting. Contractor award, ASCE, 2000; Paul Harris fellow, 1979. Mem. Appleton Area C. of C. (pres. 1967), Appleton Rotary (pres. 1975-76, Vocat. Svc. award 1977, Paul Harris fellow), Riverview Country Club (pres. 1968-69). Republican. Presbyterian. Home: 1715 Reid Dr Appleton WI 54914-5175 Office: The Boldt Group Inc PO Box 373 2525 N Roemer Rd Appleton WI 54911-8623 Office Fax: 920-739-5329. Business E-Mail: oscar.boldt@boldt.com.

BOLDT, PATRICIA C. social worker; b. Jersey City, July 16, 1955; d. Edward J. and Agnes Brajczewski; m. Harry Boldt, Nov. 5, 1978. MSW, NYU, 1982. Lic. clin. social worker, social worker, N.J., N.Y.; cert. supr. in edn. Social worker Div. Youth and Family, Jersey City, 1983-86; sch. social worker Montville (N.J.) Bd. Edn., 1986-87, Barnegat Bd. of Edn., 1987—. Mem. Acad. Cert. Social Workers. Avocations: boating, stained glass.

BOLDT, SUSAN LUQUES, not-for-profit developer; d. John Stewart and Linda Heer Luques; m. Michael Robert Boldt, Aug. 31, 1985; children: Elise Marie, Geoffrey Michael. M in Applied Psychology, Mental Health Counseling, So. Oreg. U., 1998—2001. Exec. dir./v.p. Mobility Unlimited, Inc., Medford, Oreg., 2001—; counselor, 2001—; sch. counselor Eagle Point M.S., 2000—03. Vol. White City Cmty. Accountability Bd., 2001—. Grantee, Meyer Meml. Trust, 2002. Mem.: ACA. Avocations: gardening, sewing, reading. Office: Mobility Unlimited Inc 700 E Main St Suite 106B Medford OR 97504 Office Fax: 541-770-6640. E-mail: susan@mobilityunlimited.org.

BOLDUC, DIANE EILEEN MARY BUCHHOLZ, psychotherapist; b. Elizabeth, N.J., May 1, 1953; d. Howard Robert and Barbara Ann (Bowen) Buchholz; m. David Vianny Bucholz, May 21, 1977; children: Elizabeth, Katharine. BA cum laude in Psychology, U. N.H., 1975, MEd Counseling, 1976. Lic. clin. mental health counselor. Counselor, asst. supr., social worker III Divsn. Children & Youth Svcs., Manchester/Salem, NH, 1978—88; supr. Child Health Svcs., Manchester, NH, 1987—88; program coord. N.H. Task Force on Child Abuse & Neglect, Concord, 1988—91; dir. youth & family svcs. Luth. Social Svcs. New England, Concord, NH, 1992—94; home/sch. coord. Raymond Schs., NH, 1994—96; counselor Pelham H.S., NH, 1996—. Mem.: ACA, Am. Mental Health Counselors Assn., N.H. Sch. Counselors Assn., N.H. Mental Health Counselors Assn. (treas. 2001—), Women*Spirit*Song. Home: 189 Ray St Manchester NH 03104

BOLDUC, ERNEST JOSEPH, association management consultant, not-for-profit developer, consultant; b. Lawrence, Mass., June 11, 1924; s. Ernest Joseph and Ernestine (Mercier) B.; m. Grace Gaydis, June 23, 1945; children: Philip, Richard, Stephen. BS in M.E, Northeastern U., 1948. Cert. Assn. Exec. Market devel. rep. Kawneer Co., Boston and N.Y.C., 1950-55; market devel. rep. Kaiser Aluminum, N.Y.C., 1955-58; exec. sec. Com. Tool Steel Producers Am. Iron and Steel Inst., N.Y.C., 1958-66; exec. dir. Nat. Council Paper Industry for Air and Stream Improvement, N.Y.C., 1966-83; prin. EJB Assocs., Armonk, N.Y., 1983—. Lectr. in assn. mgmt., meeting planning; coord. program USAID for Mongolian C. of C. trade devel. delegation touring U.S., 1993; cons. to U.S. Dept. Commerce in Albania on assn. mgmt. project, 1995; cons. to World Environment Ctr. projects, Slovakia, Rumania, Bulgaria, Ukraine; cons. USAID-PEM Project, Haiti, 1998. Author: Curtain Wall Do's and Don'ts, 1955, Planning the Successful Meeting, 1959, The Art of Budgeting For Associations, 1980, The Three P's of Running Meetings, 1990; editor Tool Steel Trends, 1961-66. Vol. exec. Internat. Exec. Svc. Corps in Botswana, 1990, in Bulgaria, 1992; trustee No. Castle Hist. Soc., 1990-92; cons. to USAID Mission in Ghana, Africa on assn. mgmt. project, 1992; vol. advisor on assn. mgmt. related projects in Bulgaria for Citizens Democracy Corp in Bulgaria, 1995, Tbilisi, Georgia, 1999; vol. speaker Am. Cancer Soc. on prostate cancer, 1998—; vol. advisor ACDI, VOCA and Ctr. for Internat. Pvt. Enterprise, 2001, Romania. Decorated Air medal with 3 oak leaf clusters; recipient Man of Yr. award N.Y. Producers Coun., 1955, W. Erwin Story citation Northeastern U., 1991, Vol. Recognition award Am. Cancer Soc., 1998. Mem. Am. Soc. Assn. Execs. (life; awards com. 1978-80, internat. com. 1992), N.Y. Soc. Assn. Execs. (life; dir. 1979-80, chmn. govt. rels. com. 1979-81, presdl. citation 1987, Disting. Svc. award 1993), Meeting Planners Internat. (bd. dirs. N.Y. chpt. 1979-80), Am. Arbitration Assn. (panel arbitrators). Office: 2 Sunrise Pl Armonk NY 10504-1444 E-mail: ejbolduc@aol.com.

BOLDUC, J. EMILIEN, bank executive; b. Roberval, Que., Can., Mar. 10, 1939; s. François N. and Georgette N. (Neron) B.; m. Gisèle d. Benoit Pigeon, Dec. 11, 1976; children: Chantal, Eric. BS, Laval U., Can., MS, 1967. Joined Roberval (Can.) br. Royal Bank, 1957, various positions, credit officer Montreal main br., 1967-68, asst. mgr. St. James (Can.) br., 1968-69, credit officer Canadian loans head office, 1969-73, mgr. mgmt. devel., personnel, 1973-76, sr. asst. mgr. Montreal main br., 1976-78, dep. mgr., 1978-79, v.p. ea. U.S.A., 1979-82; mng. dir. Banque Belge pour l'Industrie (formerly Royal Bank), Belgium, 1982-85; sr. v.p. World Corp. Banking, Eng., 1985-86, sr. v.p., chief inspector, 1986-88, exec. v.p. fin., 1988-90, v.p., CFO, 1990-94; vice chmn., CFO Royal Bank Can., Montreal, 1994-97, vice chmn., 1997-99. Roman Catholic. Avocations: fishing, tennis. Home: 350 Chemin Pinacle Est Sutton QC Canada J0E2K03

BOLDUC, JEAN PLUMLEY, journalist, education activist; b. Hartford, Conn., Aug. 13, 1958; d. Peter Winslow and Elizabeth Josephine (Hamann) Plumley; m. Richard Allen Bolduc, Jan. 25, 1978; children: Brian Richard, Robert Allen. BA, U. N.C., 1994. Mktg. analyst Ctrl. Carolina Bank, Durham, N.C., 1984-87; computer trainer/cons. On Site Svcs., Chapel Hill, N.C., 1987-91; pres. Pub. Edn. Press, Inc., Hillsborough, N.C., 1994—; coord. safe schs. program Orange County Sheriff's Dept., Hillsborough, N.C., 1995-96; exec. dir. The Odyssey Project, Hillsborough, 1996-97; owner Pen & Inc. New Media Pub. and Editl. Svcs., Hillsborough, 1997—; reporter Chapel Hill (N.C.) Herald, 1999—; new media editor Aero Connections Mag., 2002—03; mng. editor, pub. Flying Life Mag., 2003—. Mem. adv. bd. Project Graduation, Hillsborough, 1995-96; lit. jour. advisor Orange County Schs., Hillsborough, 1995-96; asst. editor Aero Connections Mag., 2002-2003. Author: Zero to Zen in 60 Seconds, 2000; writer The Triangle LifeStyle mag. Chair Orange County Human Rels. Commn., 1989-91, Orange County Safe Schs. Task Force, 1993-95; chair sub-com. Blue Ribbon Task Force on African-Am. Student Achievement, Chapel Hill Schs., 1991; pres. AIDS Svc. Agy., Inc., Chapel Hill, 1990-91, Sycamore Presch., Inc., Chapel Hill, 1993-94; charter dir. Alliance of AIDS Svcs.-Carolina, 1999—; dir. AIDS Svc. Agy. Orange County, 1999—. Recipient Key to Chapel Hill for cmty. svc. Chapel Hill Town Coun., 1991. Home: 5519 Hideaway Dr Chapel Hill NC 27516-9517 Office: Pen & Inc PO Box 1561 Hillsborough NC 27278-1561 E-mail: jean@penandinc.com.

BOLEK, CATHERINE, university research director; b. Pitts., Feb. 14, 1945; d. Paul and Catherine Schwabedissen; m. Frank Bolek, Nov. 26, 1985; children: John Errico, Katrina, Sarah. BA, U. North Fla., 1978, MS, 1979. Project officer Nat. Cancer Inst., Bethesda, Md., 1980-83; dir. spl. populations rsch. and tng. Nat. Insts. on Drug Abuse, Rockville, Md., 1983-91; dir. office of sponsored rsch. and programs U. Md. Ea. Shore, Princess Anne, 1991—. Author: Substance Abuse Among Ethnic Minorities in America, 1992; editor: Ethnic and Multicultural Drug Abuse, 1992. Biomed. capacity bldg. grant USPHS, 1992-95; grantee EPA, 1995—, U.S. Dept. Def., 1998—.

BOLEN, DAVID BENJAMIN, ambassador, former corporation executive; b. Dec. 23, 1923; m. Betty Gayden; children: Cynthia, Myra, David B. BS, MS, U. Colo., 1950; MPA, Harvard U., 1960; student, Nat. War Coll. Joined Fgn. Service, 1950; adminstrv. asst. Monrovia, Liberia, 1950-52; econ. asst. Karachi, Pakistan, 1952-55; detailed internat. economist Dept. Commerce, Washington, 1955-56, State Dept., 1957-58; desk officer for Afghanistan, 1958-59; detailed advanced econ. studies Harvard, 1959-60; econ. officer Accra, Ghana, 1960-62; staff asst. Washington, 1962-64; officer-in-charge Nigerian affairs, 1964-66; detailed Nat. War Coll., 1966-67; econ. and comml. officer, econ. counselor, 1967-72; econ.-comml. counselor Belgrade, 1972-74; ambassador to Botswana, Lesotho, Swaziland, 1974-76; dep. asst. sec. state for African affairs U.S. Dept. State, Washington, 1976-77; ambassador to German Democratic Republic, 1977-80; assoc. dir. internat. affairs E.I. duPont de Nemours & Co., Inc., Wilmington, Del., 1981-89, cons., 1989-94. Author (collection): Bolen Papers Repository, Hoover Archives, Stanford U.; contbg. editor: World Economic Problems and Policies, 1965. Mem. preliminary investigation com. Del. Ct. on the Judiciary, 1990-92; mem. polit. sci. vis. com. MIT, 1983-88; trustee U. Del., 1983-92; bd. dirs. Med. Ctr. Del., Del. Coun. Econ. Edn., U.S. Coun. on Internat. Bus., 1981-89, Internat. Mgmt. Devel. Inst., 1981-89, Pacific Basin Trade and Econ. Coun., 1981-89, U.S.-USSR Trade and Econ. Coun., 1981-89, U.S.-German Dem. Republic Trade and Econ. Coun., 1981-89, Coun. Fgn. Rels., U.S.-Yugoslav Econ. Coun., 1986-90, U. Colo. Found., Inc., 1990-96; mem. U. Colo. Bus. Dean's Adv. Coun., 1992-98; dir. Denver Com. on Fgn. Rels., 1994-99; mem. U.S. Olympic track and field team, 1948; advisor Berlin Sculpture Fund, 1997—. Recipient Robert Russell Meml. award, 1948; Norlin Disting. Alumni award U. Colo., 1969; named to Hall of Honor, 1969, Alumni of Century, 1976; recipient Disting. Service award U. Colo., 1983; inducted U. Colo. Athletic Hall of Fame, 2000. Mem. Am. Coun. on Germany (chmn. Denver chpt. 1995-99), Nat. War Coll. Alumni Assn., Fgn. Serv. Assn., Wilmington World Affairs Coun. (dir. 1981-92), Internat. Amateur Athletic Assn., Wilmington Club, U. Colo. Alumni Assn., Harvard Alumni Assn.

BOLEN, ERIC GEORGE, biology educator; b. Plainfield, N.J., Nov. 24, 1937; s. Wilbur Fraser and Doris (Wicks) B.; m. Rebecca Ann Woodhull, Aug. 20, 1967 (div. Jan. 1981); children: Brent F., Staci L.; m. Elizabeth Ann Danek, May 27, 1986. BS, U. Maine, Orono, 1959; MS, Utah State U., 1962, PhD, 1967. Instr. biology Tex. A&M U., Kingsville, 1965-66; asst. prof. dept. range & wildlife mgmt. Tex. Tech U., Lubbock, 1966-73, assoc. dean grad. sch., 1978-88; dean grad. sch. U. N.C., Wilmington, 1988-94, prof. biology, 1988—2002, prof. emeritus, 2003. Asst. dir. Welder Wildlife Found., 1973-78. Co-author: (coll. textbooks) Wildlife Ecology and Management, 1984, 5th edit., 2003, Waterfowl Ecology and Management, 1994, Ecology of North America, 1998; contbr. over 180 articles to profl. jours., ency. Named Disting. Alumnus, U. Maine, 1991; recipient Achievement award Utah State U., 1997. Mem. Am. Ornithol. Union., Wilson Ornithol. Soc., Cooper Ornithol. Soc., Southwestern Assn. Naturalists, Wildlife Soc. Office: Univ NC Dept Biol Scis 601 S College Rd Wilmington NC 28403-5915

BOLENDER, TODD, choreographer; b. Canton, Ohio, 1914; Student, Hanya Holm, N.Y.C.; enrolled, Sch. American Ballet, N.Y.C., 1936. Joined Lincoln Kirstein's Ballet Caravan, 1937; formed Am. Concert Ballet; choreographed 1st ballet, 1943; also danced with Ballet Theatre, 1944 and Ballet Russe de Monte Carlo, 1945, joined Ballet Soc., 1946; prin. dancer N.Y.C. Ballet, 1948-61; dir. ballet cos. of opera houses of Cologne and Frankfurt; numerous nat. and internat. freelance choreography assignments, 1952-80; artistic dir. State Ballet of Mo., Kansas City, 1981-96, artistic dir. emeritus, 1996. Recipient Mo. Arts Coun. awrd, 1987, W.F. Yates for disting. svc. William Jewell Coll., 1995. Office: Kansas City Ballet 1601 Broadway Kansas City MO 64108-1207

BOLENE, ROSALIE STEELE (MARGARET BOLENE), bacteriologist, civic worker; b. Kingfisher, Okla., July 11, 1923; d. Clarence R. and Harriet (White) Steele; m. Robert V. Bolene, Feb. 6, 1948; children: Judith Kay, John Eric, Sally Sue, Janice Lynn, Daniel William. BS, U. Okla., 1946. Technican bacteriology dept. Okla. Dept. Health, Oklahoma City, 1946-48; asst. bacteriologist Henry Ford Hosp., Detroit, 1948-49; bacteriol. cons., also asst. bus. mgr. Ponca Gynecology and Obstetrics, Inc., 1956-92, ret. Organizing dir. Bi-Racial Coun., 1963; lay adviser Home Nursing Svc., 1967-68; mem. exec. bd. PTA, 1956-71; active various cmty. drives; sponsor Am. Field Svc.; patron Ponca Playhouse; bloodmobile vol. ARC; vol. Helpline; Rep. precint organizer, 1960. Mem. AAUW (treas. 1964-66), DAR (life, sec.-treas. 1961-67, 1st vice regent 1972-73, chpt. treas. 1974-84, chpt. chaplain 1991-2000, state schs. chmn. 1990-94), Kay-Noble County Med. Aux. (treas. 1957-58, 66-67), Ponca City Art Assn., Pioneer Hist. Soc., Okla. Heritage Assn., Okla. Hist. Soc., Friends Cultural Ctr., Mus. Found., Inc. (publicity chmn. 2000), Friends Md. Mansion, Daus. Founders and Patriots (life, state pres. 1980-84, registrar 1993-2001), Nat. Huguenot Soc. (corr. sec.), Hereditary Order First Families Mass. Daus. Am. Colonists (chpt. regent 1982-84, state flag chmn. 1990-92), Magna Charta Dames (treas. Okla. chpt. 1984, life), Plantagenet Soc., Order Colonial Physicians and Chirurgiens (life), Ancient and Honorable Arty. Co. Women Descs. Okla. Ct. (life, treas. 1983-84, registrar 1986-2001), Dames of Ct. of Honor, Colonial Dames of 17th Century, Daus. of Colonial Wrs (registrar 1998—), Colonial Daus. 17th Century, U. Okla. Assn. (life), Ponca City Music Club, Red Rose Garden Club (pres. 1983-84, treas. 1993-95), Twentieth Century Club (rec. sec. 1992-94), Wall St. Ladies Investment Club, Lambda Tau, Phi Sigma, Alpha Lambda Delta. Presbyterian (elder 1983-86, trustee 1998-2001). Home: 8722 NW 49th Dr Coral Springs FL 33067-1841 E-mail: rsbolene@bellsouth.net.

BOLER, JOHN M. manufacturing executive; b. 1934; Founder, pres. & chmn. Boler Co., Itasca, Ill., 1978—. Office: Boler Co 500 Park Blvd Ste 1010 Itasca IL 60143-1285*

BOLES, DAVID LAVELLE, lawyer; b. Tulia, Tex., May 22, 1937; s. Jerry Hoytt and Irma Ruth (Walker) B.; m. Kerstin Gunilla Stenrudh, May 25, 1959 (div. 1984); children— David LaVelle Jr., Kerstin Regina Boles Davenport, William Gail-Holger. Student North Tex. U., 1955-57; B.S., Trinity U., 1959; J.D., U. Tex., 1963. Bar: Tex. 1963. Asst. atty. gen. Tex., Austin, 1963-67; sole practice, Denton, Tex., 1967-69; house counsel, corp. officer Sam P. Wallace Co., Inc., Dallas, 1969-73, adminstrv. mgr. contracts, labor, indsl. rels., ins., 1973-85, house counsel, corp. officer MMR/Wallace Group, Inc. and subs., 1985-90; pvt. practice, 1990-2002. Deacon Presbyn. Ch., Austin, Denton, 1963-74, elder, Taos, N.Mex., 1999—. Mem. Tex. Bar Assn., Denton County Bar Assn., Trinity Alumni Assn. (pres. 1965), Denton C. of C. Home and Office: HC 71 Box 100A Taos NM 87571-9501

BOLES, DONALD MICHAEL, lawyer; b. N.Y.C., Nov. 30, 1951; s. Oreste George and Rosina Constance (D'Angelo) B.; m. Patricia G. Stachnick, Dec. 28, 1973; children: Jennifer Anne, Christopher Michael. Student, Fairleigh-Dickinson U., 1972-73; BEE, JD, U. Dayton, 1976. Bar: Pa. 1979, U.S. Patent and Trademark Office 1980, N.Y. 1986, N.J. 1987, U.S. Dist. Ct. N.J. 1987, U.S. Dist. Ct. (ea. dist.) N.Y. 1987, U.S. Dist. Ct. (so. dist.) N.Y. 1988. Patent atty. Westinghouse Electric Co., Pitts., 1980-82, AMP, Inc., Harrisburg, Pa., 1982-85, Ostrolenk, Faber et al, N.Y.C., 1985-86, Weingram & Zall, Maywood, N.J., 1987-89; atty. IBM, East Fishkill, N.Y., 1989-92; sr. atty. Siemens Corp., 1992-97; v.p. intellectual property Interdigital Comm. Corp., King of Prussia, Pa., 1997—. Adj. instr. L.I. U., West Point, Sparkill, N.Y., 1987-95. With USMC, 1970-71 Mem. Pa. Bar Assn., N.J. Bar Assn., Am. Intellectual Property Law Assn. Office: InterDigital Patents Corp 781 Third Ave King Of Prussia PA 19406-1409 E-mail: donald.boles@interdigital.com., donald_boles@yahoo.com.

BOLES, JOHN, professional baseball coach, manager; b. Chgo., Aug. 19, 1948; m. Rosemary Boles; children: Blake, Kevin. Head baseball coach St. Xavier Coll., Chgo., 1973-79, U. Louisville, 1980-81; mgr. Gulf Coast League White Sox, 1981-85; dir. player devel. Kansas City Royals, 1986-89; field coord. Montreal (Can.) Expos, 1989-90, dir. player devel., 1990-91, Fla. Marlins, Miami, 1991-95, v.p. player devel., 1995-98, mgr., 1998—2001.*

BOLES, JOHN P. bishop; b. Boston, Jan. 21, 1930; Student, Boston Coll. Ordained priest Roman Cath. Ch. 1955. Titular bishop Nova Sparsa and aux. bishop, Boston, 1992—. Office: 307 Bowdoin St Dorchester MA 02122-1834*

BOLES, LENORE UTAL, nurse psychotherapist, educator; b. N.Y.C., July 3, 1929; d. Joseph Leo and Dorothy (Grosby) Utal; m. Morton Schloss, Dec. 17, 1955 (div. May 1961); 1 child, Howard Alan Schloss; m. Sam Boles, May 24, 1962; children: Anne Leslie, Laurence Utal; stepchildren: Harlan Arnold, Robert Gerald. Diploma in nursing, Beth Israel Hosp. Sch. Nursing, 1951; BSN, Columbia U., 1964; MSN, U. Conn., 1977. Lic. clin. specialist in adult psychiatry/ mental health nursing, advanced practice registered nurse. Staff nurse Beth Israel Hosp., N.Y.C., 1951, Kingsbridge VA Hosp., Bronx, N.Y., 1951-55; night supr. Gracie Square Hosp., N.Y.C., 1959-60; head nurse Elmhurst City Hosp., Queens, N.Y., 1960-62; nursing instr. Norwalk (Conn.) Hosp., 1966-74; asst. prof. U. Bridgeport, Conn., 1976-78; nurse psychotherapist Nurse Counseling Group, Ltd., Norwalk, 1979—; nursing faculty Western Conn. State U., Danbury, 1978-80. Adj. asst. prof. Sacred Heart U., Bridgeport, Conn., 1983-89; adj. faculty Western Conn. State U., Danbury, 1994, 96-2000; lectr.• Yale U. Sch. Nursing, 2000-02; nurse cons. Bradley Meml. Hosp., Southington, Conn., 1982, Lea Manor Nursing Home, Norwalk, 1982, St. Vincent's Hosp., Bridgeport, 1982-92; staff devel. nurse Silver Hill Hosp., New Canaan, Conn., 1980-86, 94; cons. in field, 1980—. Author: (book chpt.) Nursing Diagnoses for Psychiatric Nursing Practice, 1994. V.p. Sisterhood Beth El, Norwalk, 1969-71; bd. dirs. religious sch. Congregation Beth El, Norwalk, 1971-75, 79-80, rec. sec. bd. trustees, 1975-77, v.p. congregation, 1977-80, bd. trustees, 1980-83. Named Speaker of Yr., So. Fairfield County chpt. Am. Cancer Soc., 1976. Mem. ANA, Northeastern Nursing Diagnosis Assn. (chair N.E. region conf. 1985, chair planning com. 1984-85, chair nominating com. 1989-91), N.Am. Nursing Diagnosis Assn., Coun. Psychiat./Mental Health Clin. Specialists, Conn. Nurses Assn. (Del. to convs. 1975-2000, legis. com. dist. 3 1984-86, nominating com. 1988-90, Florence Wald award 1984, Conn. Nursing Diagnosis Conf. Group 1980-87), Conn. Soc. Nurse Psychotherapists (founding mem.). Democrat. Jewish. Avocations: travel, reading, gardening, spending time with grandchildren. Home: 173 E Rocks Rd Norwalk CT 06851-1715 Office: Nurse Counseling Group Ltd 71 East Ave Ste F Norwalk CT 06851-4903 E-mail: ncgshrinks@aol.com.

BOLES, ROGER, otolaryngologist; b. Oakland, Calif., Jan. 13, 1928; s. Albert and Julia Boles; m. Marianna Reeves, June 16, 1956; children: Martin Reeves, Melissa. AB, Stanford U., 1949; postgrad., Denver U., 1950-52; MD with distinction, George Washington U., 1956. Diplomate Am. Bd. Otolaryngology, Am. Bd. Med. Specialties. Intern Fitzsimmons Army Hosp., Denver, 1956-57;

asst. resident through sr. clin. instr. Mich. U. Hosp., Ann Arbor, 1959-63, faculty dept. otorhinoloaryngology, 1963-74, prof., 1973-74; prof., chmn. otolaryngology U. Calif. San Francisco Sch. Medicine, 1974-89; pres. med. staff U. Calif., San Francisco, 1982-83, prof. otolaryngology, 1989-98, prof. emeritus otolargyngology, 1998—, ret., 1998. Cons. for otolaryngology to Surgeon Gen., USAF, 1975-85; mem. staff San Francisco Gen. Hosp., 1984—, Childrens Hosp. San Francisco (bd. dirs. 1987-91); cons. in otolaryngology Va. Hosp., Ann Arbor, Wayne County Hosp., Eloise, Mich., So. Mich. Prison, Jackson, Fed. Penitentiary, Milan, Mich., 1963-74, Letterman Gen. Hosp., Presidio of San Francisco, U.S. Naval Hosp., Oakland, Calif., 1974-93, Kaiser Hosp., Oakland, 1975, Va. Hosp., San Francisco; bd. dirs. Council Med. Splty. Socs., 1981-82, sec., 1982-83; bd. dirs. Am. Acad. Otolaryngology-Head and Neck Surgery, 1981-88, coord. for continuing med. edn., 1980-83, pres., 1987; mem. Accreditation Coun. for Continuing Med. Edn., 1986-92, chmn., 1990; chmn. PEPP com., 1988-89, 90, vice chmn., 1989, residency rev. com. for otolaryngology; Marshall-Hale Hosp., San Francisco, 1975-83, bd. dirs., 1983-87; mem. Am. Bd. Med. Specialties, 1984-89, exec. com., 1988-89; vis. prof. various univs.; participant in confs., convs., workshops, seminars, insts. Contbr. chpts. to books, numerous revs., articles and abstracts to profl. lit. Served with M.C., AUS, 1956-59. Fellow ACS (chmn. adv. coun. for otolaryngology 1977-80, adv. com. for continuing med. edn. 1982-83), Am. Laryngol. Soc.; mem. AMA (ho. dels. 1975-82, bd. editors archives otolaryngology 1975-85, mem. reference com. on ins. and med. svc. 1978, adv. com. for continuing med. edn. 1981-87), AOA Hon. Med. Soc., Am. Acad. Opthalmology and Otolaryngology (assoc. sec. com. on continuing edn. 1974-80, chmn. manuals editorial com. 1977-80, mem. at large exec. com. div. otolaryngology 1977-78, mem. interspecialty cooperation com. med. specialty socs. 1978-88), Am. Acad. Facial Plastic and Reconstructive Surgery (co-chmn. standards com. 1977-80, med. edn. com. 1979-81—), Soc. Univ. Otolaryngologists (sec.-treas. 1973-80, chmn. com. on undergrad. curriculum 1969-74, mem. exec. council 1968-79, pres. 1978), Council Acad. Socs.-Assn. Am. Med. Colls., Assn. Acad. Depts. Otolaryngology (vice chmn. subcom. Nat. Cancer Inst. liaison com. 1977-81, chmn. edn. nominating coms. 1978-79), Am. Bronco-Esophagological Assn. (mem. council 1981-82), Am. Bd. Otolaryngology(bd. dirs. 1974-91, exec. com. 1981-88, mem. various coms. 1974-91, chmn. ad hoc com. for nomination process for membership on bd. dirs. 1976-77, pres. 1986-88), Am. Council Otolaryngology (mem. subcom. on hearing 1976-80, research adv. com. 1977-81, pres. 1978-79), Am. Laryngol., Rhinological and Otolaryn. Soc. (mem. editl. bds. transactions 1978-88, mem. council 1982-88, pres. 1986-87, historian 1994—), Am. Soc. for Neck and Head Surgery, Otosclerosis Study Group, Am. Tinnitus Assn. (sci. adv. bd. 1978-81), Pacific Coast Oto-Opthal. Soc., Soc. Med. Cons. to Armed Forces, Calif. Med. Assn. (program co-chmn. sects. on allergy and otolaryngology, neurology and otolaryngology 1977-78, chmn. adv. council of otolaryngology 1979-80), Calif. Otolaryn. Soc. (pres. 1978-80), U. Calif. San Francisco Sch. Medicine Alumni-Faculty Assn. (pres. 1978-79), Am. Otological Soc., Am. Laryngol. Assn. (coun. 1983-84), San Francisco Med. Soc. (bd. dirs. 1983-90, treas. 1989-90), Royal Coll. Surgeons in Ireland (hon.), U. Mich. Med. Ctr. Alumni Assn. (bd. govs. 1983), Gold Headed Cane Soc. (hon.), U. Calif. San Francisco Sch. Medicine. Office: Univ Calif San Francisco Dept Otolaryngology 400 Parnassus Ave # A-717 San Francisco CA 94122-2721 Home: PO Box 620203 Woodside CA 94062-0203

BOLESTA, MICHAEL JOSEPH, orthopedic surgeon; b. St. Louis, Sept. 28, 1954; s. Edward Joseph and Mary Frances Bolesta; m. Sharon Farris, June 6, 1981; 1 child, Michael J. II. BSEE, U. Mo., 1977, MD, 1981. Diplomate Am. Bd. Orthopedic Surgery. Instr. orthopedic surgery Case Western Res. U., Cleve., 1988-89, asst. prof. orthopedic surgery, 1989-93; orthopedic surgeon Columbia (Mo.) Orthopedic Group, 1993-94; asst. prof. orthopedic surgery U. Tex. Southwestern Med. Ctr., Dallas, 1994—2001, assoc. prof. orthopedic surgery, 2001—. Adj. asst. prof. biomed. engring. U. Tex. Southwestern Med. Ctr., 1998—; mem. spine edn. com. AO N.Am. Spine, Paoli, Pa., 1999—; orthopedist Minimally Invasive Spine Ctr. U. Tex. Southwestern Med. Ctr., Dallas, 1997—. Contbr. articles to profl. jours. Lector, CCD tchr. St. Rita Cath. Cmty., Dallas, 1998—, adult tchr., 1999—; troop com. Boy Scouts Am., Dallas, 1995-2001. N.Am. Travelling fellow Am. Orthopedic Assn., 1988, Piedmont Orthopedic fellow Duke U., 1985. Fellow ACS, Am. Acad. Orthop. Surgeons, Cervical Spine Rsch. Soc., Scoliosis Rsch. Soc.; mem. N.Am. Spine Soc., Am. Orthop. Assn. Roman Catholic. Office: UT Southwestern Med Ctr 5323 Harry Hines Blvd Dallas TX 75390-8883

BOLEY, ANDREA GAIL, secondary school educator; b. Lewistown, Pa., July 27, 1956; d. Robert Banks and Marjorie Katheryn (Shearer) Henry; m. Richard C. Shiley, m. May 13, 1978 (dec. June 1996); 1 child, Evan Andrew; m. Daniel M. Boley, Feb. 6, 1999. BS in Music Edn., Indiana U. of Pa., 1978; Jr. High Sci. Cert., Brevard Community Coll., Melbourne, Fla. Choral dir./tchr. S.W. Jr. High Sch., Brevard County Sch. Dist., Palm Bay, Fla., 1988—. Contbr. articles to profl. jours. Named Stone Middle Sch. tchr. of the Yr., 1984-85. Mem. ASCD, AAUW, Music Educators Nat. Conf., Fla. Music Educators Assn. (bd. dirs.), Fla. Vocal Assn., Brevard Fedn. Tchrs., Am. Fedn. Tchrs., Tri-M (Fla. chmn.), Nat. Tri-M Adv. Com. Home: 1255 Sapulpa Rd SW Palm Bay FL 32908-6802

BOLEY, BRUNO ADRIAN, engineering educator; b. Gorizia, Italy, May 13, 1924; came to U.S., 1939, naturalized, 1945; s. Orville F. and Rita (Luzzatto) Bolaffio; m. Sara R. Kaufman, May 12, 1949 (dec. Sept. 1983); children: Jacqueline Boley Acquaviva, Daniel L. B.C.E., CCNY, 1943, D.Sc. hon., 1982; M. in Aero. Engring., Poly. Inst. Bklyn., 1945, D.Sc. in Aero. Engring., 1946. Asst. dir. structural research, aero. engring. dept. Poly. Inst. Bklyn., 1943-48; engring. specialist Goodyear Aircraft Corp., 1948-50; assoc. prof. aero. engring. Ohio State U., 1950-52; assoc. prof. civil engring. Columbia U., 1952-58, prof., 1958-68, dir. postdoctoral preceptor program, 1962-68; Joseph P. Ripley prof. engring., chmn. theoretical and applied mechanics Cornell U., Ithaca, N.Y., 1968-72; dean Technol. Inst., Walter P. Murphy prof. Northwestern U., Evanston, Ill., 1973-86, dean, prof. emeritus, 1986—; prof. civil engring. and engring. mechanics Columbia U., N.Y.C., 1987—. Mem. adv. com. George Washington U., Princeton U., Yale U., Cornell U., FAMU/FSU Inst. Engring., Duke U., Lehigh U., Nat. Cheng Kung U., Republic of China, Istanbul Tech. U., Rowan Coll. N.J.; mem. sci. adv. coun. Internat. Ctr. for Mech. Sics., Udine, Italy, 1980—, Istanbul Tech. U.; chmn. Midwest Program for Minorities in Engring., 1975-82; bd. govs. Argonne Nat. Lab., 1983-86; bd. advisors Who's Who in Sci. and Engring. Author: Theory of Thermal Stresses, 1960, High Temperature Structures and Materials, 1964, Thermoinelasticity, 1970, Crossfire in Professional Education, 1976; also articles, numerous tech. papers; editor-in-chief: Mechanics Research Communications; bd. editors Jour. Thermal Stresses, Bull. Mech. Engring. Edn., Internat. Jour. Computers and Structures, Internat. Jour. Engring. Sci., Internat. Jour. Fracture Mechanics, Internat. Jour. Mechs. and Control, Internat. Jour. Mech. Engring. Scis., Internat. Jour. Solids and Structures, Jour. Applied Mechanics, Jour. Structural Mechanics Software, Letters in Applied and Engring. Sci., Nuclear Engring. and Design. Recipient Disting. Alumnus award Poly. Inst. N.Y., 1974, Townsend Harris medal, 1981, commendation Ill. Ho. of Reps., 1986, Theodore von Karman medal ASCE, 1991, Outstanding Scholar award Sigma Xi, 1996, Lagrange Lectr. award Accademia Nazionale dei Lincei, Rome, 1996; NATO fellow, 1964-65, NSF fellow, 1965, Japan Soc. Promotion of Sci. Rsch. fellow, 1987. Fellow AIAA, AAAS, Am. Acad. Mechanics (pres. 1974, Disting. Svc. medal 1987), Am. Soc. Engring. Edn.; mem. ASME (hon., exec. com., pres. applied mechanics divsn. 1975, bd. govs. 1984-86, Worcester Reed Warner medal 1991, Daniel C. Drucker medal 2001), NAE (life, chmn. task force engring. edn. 1979-80, edn. adv. bd. 1982-86, editl. bd. The Bridge 1986-90, membership com. 1984-88, awards com. 1993-95, chair 1996), Soc. Engring. Scis. (pres. 1975, Disting. Svc. medal 1987, life), Assn. Chairmen Depts. Mechanics (founder, pres. 1970-72), Internat. Assn. Structural Mechanics in Reactor Tech. (chmn. 1977, adv.-gen. 1979—), Thermal Stress Congress (advisor-gen. 1997), Internat. Union Theoretical and Applied Mechanics (sec. Congress com. 1976-96, bur. 1988-96, treas. 1992-96, personal mem. Gen. Assembly 1980—, treas. 1992—), Am. Soc. Engring. Edn. (project bd. 1987, Centennial award 1993), N.Y. Acad. Scis. (Outstanding Educator of Am. 1971), U.S. Nat. Com. Theoretical and Applied Mechanics (chmn. 1975-79, personal mem. Gen. Assembly 1980—), Ill. Coun. Energy Rsch. and Devel. (chmn. 1979-84), Engring. Found. (conf. com. 1986-88). Home: 310 W 106th St New York NY 10025-3429

BOLEY, DENNIS LYNN, construction company executive; b. Lima, Ohio, Aug. 27, 1951; s. James Cloyral and Joan Marie (Bevington) B.; m. Marjorie Ann Ribic, Dec. 13, 1975; children: Lisa Marie, Amanda Michelle. BSCE, Tri State Coll., 1974; MSCE, Ga. Inst. Tech., 1977. Registered profl. engr., Pa., Ohio; registered profl. land surveyor, Pa. Staff engr. D'Appolonia Cons. Engrs., Inc., Pitts., 1974-77, asst. project engr., 1977-78, project engr., 1978-82, mgr. civil group, 1982-83; dir. engring. research and devel. Nicholson Constrn. Co., Pitts., 1983-87, v.p., 1987-89; pres. Nicholson Constrn. Inc., Atlanta, 1989-92; mgr. Bauer-Nicholson Joint Venture, Atlanta, 1992-96; pres., gen. mgr. Denver Grouting Svcs., Inc., 1996-98; v.p. Gibson's Pressure Grouting Svcs., Inc., Smyrna, Ga., 1998—. Contbr. more than 25 articles to profl. jours. Lay speaker, councilman Alpha Luth. Ch., Turtle Creek, Pa., 1986-87; coun. pres. St. Thomas Luth. Ch., Roswell, Ga., 1991-93. Mem. ASCE (sec. Pitts. sect. 1980-83, bd. dirs. 1984-85, v.p. 1985-86, pres. 1986-87, past pres. 1987—, Outstanding Young Civil Engr. of Yr. 1987). Republican. Avocations: reading, carpentry, swimming, fishing, weight lifting. Home: 1800 Belshire Ct Roswell GA 30075-5252 E-mail: dboley@bright.net.

BOLGER, DAVID P. insurance company executive; b. Aug. 23, 1957; BS in Acctg./Fin., Marquette U., 1979; MM in Fin., Northwestern U., 1980. Credit analyst Am. Nat. Bank & Trust Co., Chgo., 1980-82, comml. banking officer, 1982-89, sr. v.p., CFO, 1989-92, exec. v.p., 1992-93, exec. v.p., treas., 1993-94, pres., 1996 98; exec. dir. Banc One, Chgo., 1998—2001; exec. v.p., CFO Aon Corp., Chgo., 2003—. Bd. dirs. Mercy Hosp. & Med. Ctr., Impulse Theatre Co., Fist Non-Profit Ins. Co.; active United Way/Crusade of Mercy. Mem. Chgo. Hist. Soc., Execs. Club Chgo., Robert Morris Asscos. Office: Aon Ctr 200 E Randolph St Chicago IL 60601*

BOLGER, DOREEN, museum director; BA, Bucknell U., 1971; MA, U. Del., 1973; PhD, CUNY, 1983. Mem. curatorial staff Am. Wing Met. Mus. Art, N.Y.C., curator Am. painting and sculpture; curator painting and sculpture Amon Ctr. Mus., Ft. Worth, 1989-94; dir. RISD Mus., Providence, 1994-98, Balt. Mus. Art, 1998—. Panelist NEA, NEH; field reviewer Inst. Mus. Libr. Sci.; jury 1998 Biennial Exhibn. Howard County Arts Coun.; curator woemn artists exhibn. for Govt. House, Annapolis, Md.; Ailsa Mellon Bruce vis. sr. fellow Ctr. for Advanced Study in the Visual Arts Nat. Gallery of Art; lectr. in field. Bd. dirs. several orgns. Chester Dale fellow Met. Mus. Art; grantee NEH, Met. Mus. Art Office: Balt Mus Art 10 Art Museum Dr Baltimore MD 21218-3898

BOLGER, MARY PHYLLIS JUDGE, special education educator; b. Newark, Aug. 19, 1926; d. Michael Francis and Loretta Margaret (Reinhardt) Judge; m. William Patrick Bolger, Nov. 27, 1948 (dec. May 1973); children: Loretta, Francis, Christopher, Michael. BA, Montclair State U., 1946; MA, Reading Specialist, Seton Hall U., 1973. Cert. reading specialist, tchr. English, social studies, Spanish, and reading, learning disabilities tchr., cons. Tchr. English Bd. Edn., Irvington, NJ, 1946-49; tchr. West Side HS, Newark, 1963-69; reading specialist Roosevelt Jr. HS, West Orange, NJ, 1969-77; learning disability tchr., cons. West Orange HS and Hazel Ave., 1977-91. Tchr. ESL South Orange (N.J.) Maplewood Adult Schs., 1949—64; adj. prof. edn. Seton Hall U., South Orange, 1974—96; cons. dept. curriculum and spl. svcs. West Orange Bd. Edn., 1987—2002, cons., workshop presenter, 2000—01; mem. adv. bd. Prospect Ho., East Orange, NJ, 1994—97; cons. to therapeutic friendship groups for retarded adults, 1999—; cons., workshop presenter Lifelong Learning Inst., Caldwell (N.J.) Coll., 2000—01; freelance lectr., workshop presenter. Editor: (book) Beyond Common Sense: The Art of Intelligent Living, 1992, doctoral dissertations Seton Hall U., 1993—97. Eucharistic min. St. Barnabas Hosp., Livingston, NJ, 1991—2001, Ward Homestead, Maplewood, NJ, 1992—2000; coord. eucharistic ministry to the homebound Our Lady of Sorrows, South Orange, NJ, 1989—2000, Homebound Ministry, 1989—2002. Mem.: Seton-Essex Reading Coun. (pres., v.p.), N.J. Reading Assn. (co-chairperson Reading/Learning Disabilities com.), South Orange Sr. Circle (rec. sec. 2001—), Rosary Altar Soc. Roman Catholic. Avocations: writing, travel, reading, watercolors. Home and Office: 34 Mitchell Ave Roseland NJ 07068-1306 E-mail: ga-ga@prodigy.com.

BOLGER, ROBERT JOSEPH, retired trade association executive; b. Phila., Aug. 9, 1922; s. Harold Stephen and Edna (Adams) B.; m. Helen Siegfried, May 22, 1954; children: Robert, Mary T., Cynthia A., Ann M., Catherine B., David A. BS, Villanova U., 1943; postgrad., Northwestern U., 1945-46, U. Pa., 1946-47, U. Geneva, 1948-49; DS in Pharmacy (hon.), Mass. Coll. Pharmacy, 1983. Salesman Container Corp., Phila., 1947; supr. sales Kraft Food Co., Phila., 1949-52; overseas mgr., dir. retail rels. Smith, Kline Beckman Corp., Phila., 1952-62; asst. to exec. v.p. Nat. Assn. Chain Drug Stores, Inc., Arlington, Va., 1962-67, pres., 1967-87; ret., 1987. Founder, developer Robert J. Bolger Assocs., 1988—; bd. dirs. Barr Labs., Pomona, NY, Am. Pharm. Inst., Washington, Am. Found. Pharm. Edn., Nat. Drug Trade Conf., pres., 1974—82. Co-author: Chain Drug Retailing, 1980. Bd. dirs. Nat. Coun. on Patient Info. and Edn.; hon. bd. dirs. Nat. Assn. Chain Drug Stores Inc.; Nacos Edn. Fedn. Lt. comdr. USNR, 1943—46, PTO. Decorated Air medal; named Man of Yr. Cosmetic and Toiletry sect. United Jewish Appeal, 1972, Chain Exec. of Yr., Chain Drug Rev., 1979; recipient Torch of Learning award Am. Friends of Hebrew U., 1987, Chain Drug Rev. Bd. Lifetime Achievement award, 1988, Robert B. Begley award for contbns. to chain drug industry, 1988. Mem. Am. Pharm. Assn., Com. of 100, U.S. C. of C., Cen. Coun. Nat. Retail Assns. (chmn.), Am. Retail Fedn. (bd. dirs.), Nat. Assn. Cmty. Pharmacists, Joint Commn. Pharmacy Practitioners, Pharmacists Against Drug Abuse (bd. dirs. 1986—), Am. Soc. Assn. Execs. (life), Nat. Assn. Execs. Club (bd. dirs.), Am. Druggist Bd. Advisers, Key Exec. Industry Coun., Alexandria Chief Execs., Belle Haven Country Club. Home and Office: 7705 Maid Marian Ct Alexandria VA 22306-2718 Fax: 703-660-8473. E-mail: helenbolger@iopener.net.

BOLGER, STEPHEN GARRETT, English and American studies educator; b. Phila., Apr. 27, 1927; s. Stephen Joseph and Marjorie Louise (Carroll) B.; m. Mary Patricia Whalen, Sept. 3, 1951; children: Christine, Patricia, Elizabeth, Garrett, Cecilia, Madeleine. BA, U. Notre Dame, 1950; MA, U. Pa., 1951, PhD, 1971. Instr. English Georgetown U., Washington, 1953-58; prof. emeritus English and Am. studies Rosemont (Pa.) Coll., 1958—. Author: Irish Character in American Fiction 1830 1860, 1976; editor: Bulletin of the Hist. Soc. of Montgomery County. Served with USNR, 1944-46. Recipient Disting. Teaching award Lindbach Found., 1983, Teaching Excellence award Sears-Roebuck Found., 1990. Mem. Am. Conf. for Irish Studies, Soc. for the Study of Nineteenth Century Ireland, Friendly Sons of St. Patrick. Democrat. Roman Catholic. Avocations: music, birdwatching. Home: 42 Airdale Rd Bryn Mawr PA 19010-1601 Office: Rosemont Coll Bryn Mawr PA 19010 E-mail: gbolger@bee.net.

BOLGER, T(HOMAS) MICHAEL, lawyer; b. Minocqua, Wis., Dec. 23, 1939; s. Patrick Edward and Mary Frances (McConville) B.; B.A., Marquette U., 1961; M.A., St. Louis U., 1966, Ph.L., 1966; J.D., Northwestern U., 1971; m. Virginia Kay Empey, Aug. 24, 1968; children— John, Jennifer. Admitted to Wis. bar, 1971; mem. firm Quarles & Brady, Milw., 1971—, partner, 1978— ; instr. philosophy Marquette U., Milw., 1967-68. Vice chmn. United Performing Arts Fund drive, 1976 77; bd. dirs. Kearney Negro Welfare Found., 1974—, Milw. Repertory Theatre, 1977—, Milw. Ballet Found., Inc., 1981—, Permanent Diaconate Program of Milw. Archdiocese, 1977—, chmn. ednl. found., 1987—; pres. Artreach, Inc., 1979—, Milw. Repertory Theater, 1980— ; pres. bd. trustees Highland Community Sch., 1976—, Milwaukee Ballet, 1987—; trustee, sec.). U. Wis.-Milw. Found., 1976— ; pres. bd. dirs. Hickory Hollow, 1978— . Named Alumnus of the yr. Marquette U., 1986; recipient Spirit of Milwaukee award, 1986. Mem. Am. Bar Assn., Milw. Bar Assn., Wis. Bar Assn., Fed. Bar Assn., Marquette U Alumni Assn. (pres. 1982-84), Alpha Sigma Nu, Phi Sigma Tau. Clubs: Univ., The Town. Contbr. articles in field to profl. jours.; editor Northwestern Jour. of Criminal Law, 1970-71. Home: 137 E White Oak Way Thiensville WI 53092-6266 Office: 8701 Watertown Plank Rd Milwaukee WI 53226 E-mail: tbolger@mcw.edu.

BOLIEK, ROBERT GERALD, JR., writer, lawyer; b. Greensboro, N.C., Feb. 13, 1958; s. Robert Gerald and Doris (Westbrook) B.; m. Virginia Shipp, May 24, 1986; 1 child, Kathryn. BA, Auburn U., 1980; JD, U. Ala., Tuscaloosa, 1986, MFA, 1999. Bar: Ala. 1986. Law clk. Ala. Supreme Ct., Montgomery, 1986-88; adj. prof. legal reasoning and law Cumberland Sch. Law Samford U., Birmingham, 2000—. Contbr. poems to lib. publs. Mem. Ala. State Bar, Ala. Writers' Forum. Office: PO Box 660099 Birmingham AL 35266-0099

BOLIN, BERT RICHARD JOHANNES, atmospheric physicist, research meteorologist; b. Nyköping, Sweden, May 15, 1925; s. Richard and Karin Lovisa (Johansson) B.; m. Ulla Karin Frykstrand, June 7, 1952 (div. 1979); children: Dan, Karina, Göran. BS, U. Uppsala, 1946; MS, U. Stockholm, 1949, PhD in Meteorology, 1956. Assoc. prof. U. Stockholm, 1956-61, prof., 1961-90; scientific dir. European Space Rsch. Orgn., Paris, 1965-67; dir. Internat. Meteorol. Inst., 1961-91; scientific advisor to Swedish Prime min./vice prime min. Stockholm, 1986-91. Chmn. joint orgn. com. GARP WMO, Geneva, 1967-71; vice chmn. Swedish Natural Sci. Rsch. Coun., 1977-80; chmn. intergovtl. panel on climate change WMO/UNEP, Geneva, 1988-97. Contbr. articles to profl. jours. Recipient OMI prize World Met. Orgn., 1981, Tyler prize U. So. Calif., 1988, Grüne Rosette Köber Stiftung, 1990, Milkankovic medal European Geophys. Soc., 1993, Blue Planet prize Asahi Glass Found., 1995, Environ. prize U. Lund, 1995, Swedish Royal medal, size 12, 1997, award for sci. co-op AAAS, 1998, Climate Protection award EPA US, 1998, Global Environ. Leadership award GEF, World Bank, 1999. Mem.: Italian Acad. Scis., Indian Acad. Sci., Norwegian Acad. Sci., Academia Nazionale delle Scienze Italy), U.S. Nat. Acad. Scis., Russian Acad. Scis., Swedish Acad. Engring. Scis., Royal Swedish Acad. Scis. (Arrhenius gold medal 2000). Mem. Social Dem. Party. Avocations: choir singing, outdoor life. Home: S Åsvägen 51 18452 Österskär Sweden E-mail: bolin.bert@telia.com.

BOLIN, DANIEL PAUL, music educator; b. Indpls., Apr. 11, 1948; s. Gillespie Green and Myrtle Genell (Runner) B.; m. Marilyn Jo McBride Rader, Aug. 8, 1970 (div. Mar. 1984); children: John William, Douglas Patrick; m. Jane Ann Crecelius, Oct. 29, 1987. BM, Butler U., 1970, MM, 1975, secondary adminstrn. cert., 1981; postgrad., U. Mich., summer 1976; EdD, Ind. U., 1988. Cert. music tchr., secondary sch. adminstr., supt., Ind. Band dir., gen. music orch. dir., asst. band dir. Wood H.S., Indpls., 1970-72; orch. dir., asst. band dir. Manual H.S., Indpls., 1972-73, band dir., 1973-74; band dir., chmn. fine arts dept. Lebanon (Ind.) H.S., 1974-77; band and choir dir., chmn. music dept. Southport H.S., Indpls., 1977-83, asst. prin., 1983-87; dir. secondary edn. Met. Sch. Dist. Perry Twp., Indpls., 1987-89, dir. pers. and student svcs., 1989-91, interim supt., 1992-93, asst. supt., 1991-95; prof., chair music dept. Butler U., Indpls., 1995—2001, assoc. prof. of music, 2001—. Facilitator I.U. Project LEAD, 1988-89; chmn. ISSMA Contest Manual Revision Com., 1982; sec. ISMA-NISBOVA Merger Com., 1978-81; bd. dirs. ISSMA, 1981-84; dir. BallState U. Mid-Am. Music Clinic, 1982, 83; mem. staff Ind. U. Music Clinic, 1974; chmn. Indpls. All-City H.S. Band, 1974; music dir. Eli Lilly Co., 1974; guest condr. Anthaneum Orch., 1974, Ctrl. Ind. Youth Wind Ensemble, 1980, Ind. All Region Jr. High Band, 1981; marching band com. ISMA, 1975, mem. music selection com., 1978; mem. camp staff Purdue U. Band Camp, 1981; co-founder, co-dir. Gt. Lake Music Camps, Inc., 1981—; coord. Ind. State Band, Orch. and Choir Finals, 1985-88; guest condr., host U.S. Army Field Band, 1986, 88, 89, 93, 95, 97, U.S. Marine Band, 1989, 94; guest condr. USAF Band of the Rockies. Conferee White House Conf. for Drug-Free Am., 1987-88; mem. program bd. Young Audiences of Ind., 1992—, bd. dirs., 1994—, chmn. bd., 1996—; coord. awards ceremonies X Pan-Am. Games, 1987; v.p. bd. dirs. Indpls. Chamber Orch., 1997. Performance scholar Butler U. Mem. Am. Sch. Band Dirs. Assn. (Stanbury award 1979), Am. Assn. Sch. Adminstrs., Music Educators Nat. Conf., Ind. Music Educators Assn., Ind. Assn. for Supervision and Curriculum Devel., Ind. Assn. Pub. Sch. Supts. (charter), Ind. All-State Music Festivals Assn. (bd. dirs. 1978-81, facilities coord. 1979-80, sec. 1980-81), Ind. State Sch. Music Assn., Ind. Sch. Music Assn., Northern Ind. Sch. Band, Orchestra, & Vocal Assn., Phi Delta Kappa, Pi Lambda Theta, Phi Kappa Lambda, Phi Mu Alpha, Kappa Kappa Psi. Avocations: music, travel, historical readings. Office: Butler U Coll Fine Arts 4600 Sunset Ave Indianapolis IN 46208-3487

BOLIN, EDMUND MIKE, electrical engineer, franchise engineering consultant; b. Bowman, S.C., Sept. 16, 1944; s. Wells Connor and Rebecca May (Dukes) B.; m. Patricia Elmira McGowan, Sept. 1, 1979 (div. Jan. 1990); 1 child, Theresa Michele Lufkin. AA, Brevard (N.C.) Jr. Coll., 1965; BSEE, Clemson U., 1968. Registered profl. engr., S.C. Engr., dir., videographer Communications Ctr., Clemson (S.C.) U., 1965-68; supervisory nuclear engr. Charleston (S.C.) Naval Shipyard, 1968-87; video, comm. and multimedia prodr. Space & Naval Warfare Sys. Ctr., Charleston, 1987—2002, ret., 2002; CEO Carolina Bus. & Commerce, Charleston, 2002—. Quality and tech. cons. Support Systems Internat., Charleston, 1977-79, Exposure 60 Corp., Charleston, 1992—; producer, scriptwriter Trident Prodns., Charleston, 1989—; staff writer, photographer Santee (S.C.) Scene and Scene Newspaper Group, 1990-92, North Charleston News, 1992—; editor/pub. Carolina Bus. & Commerce, 1994—; lectr. Gibbs Art Mus., Charelston, 1990—. Weekly columnist What's Happening in and Around S.C., 1990—, From the White House, 1991—; editor, pub. Carolina Business and Commerce; inventor automated R-meter, improved satellite receiver, laser alignment sys.; free lance artist and fashion designer; editor, webmaster www.carolina-news-line.com. Mem. Charles County Rep. Com., Rep. Nat. Com. for S.C.; tech. adv. Edn. Svc. Corp. Action 2,000, S.C., 1991—; photographer and technical adv. S.C. Christian Coalition, 1991—. Recipient Cert. of Spl Congl. Recognition, 1997; Elks Club scholar, 1963. Mem. S.C. Registered Profl. Engrs. Assn., Advt. Fedn. Charleston, Trident C. of C., Charleston Tall Club (media rep. 1990—), Trident Amateur Radio Club. Avocations: computers, inventing, innovative consulting, writing, photography. Home: 7650 Ovaldale Dr Charleston SC 29418-3241 Office: Carolina Bus & Commerce 1133 Hillside Dr Ste 2B Charleston SC 29407 E-mail: editor@carolina-news-line.com.

BOLIN, HENRY ROBERT, retired engineer; b. N.Y.C., Nov. 24, 1926; s. Henry Otto John and Bertha (Cserkits) B.; m. Hermina Mildred Franck, Nov. 6, 1954; children: Nancy Jeanne, Robert Henry. BS in Physics, Columbia U., 1965. Jr. engr. IBM, Burlington, Vt., 1965-66, assoc. engr., 1966-68, sr. assoc. engr., 1968-72, staff engr., 1972-87, adv. engr. East Fishkill, N.Y., 1987-91; ret., 1991. Radiol. monitor Def. Preparedness Agy./FEMA St. of Vt., 1977-83. Sgt. USAF, 1948. Mem. IEEE, Am. Vacuum Soc., Soc. for Indsl. Archaelogy, Steamship Hist. Soc., Nat. Railway Hist. Soc., Pa. R.R. Tech. and Hist. Soc., Nat. Model RR Soc. Home: 13 Old Farm Rd Jericho VT 05465-2502 E-mail: hrbolin@worldnet.att.net.

BOLIN, RICHARD LUDDINGTON, industrial development consultant; b. Burlington, Vt., May 13, 1923; s. Axel Birger and Eva Madora (Luddington) B.; m. Jeanne Marie Brown, Dec. 18, 1948; children: Richard Luddington, Jr., Douglas, Judith, Barbara, Elizabeth. BSChemE, Tex. A&M U., 1947; MSChemE, MIT, 1950; Diploma Advanced Mgmt. Program, Harvard U., 1969. Jr. rsch. engr. Humble Oil & Refining Co., Baytown, Tex., 1947-49; staff mem. Arthur D. Little, Inc., Cambridge, Mass., 1950-56, Caribbean office mgr. San Juan, 1957-61; gen. mgr. Arthur D. Little de Mex., Mexico City, 1961-72; pres. Internat. Parks, Inc., Flagstaff, Ariz., 1973-94, chmn., 1995—. Bd. dirs. Parque Indsl. de Nogales, Nogales, Sonora, Mex.; dir. The Flagstaff Inst., 1976—, Secretariat World Econ. Processing Zones Assn., 1985—; mem. adv. bd. Lowell Obs., Flagstaff, 1993-94, Astrogeology Mus., Flagstaff, 1998-02. With U.S. Army, 1942-46. Mem. Univ. Club of Mex. Office: PO Box 986 Flagstaff AZ 86002-0986

BOLIN, VERNON SPENCER, microbiologist, consultant; b. Parma, Idaho, July 9, 1913; s. Thadeus Howard Bolin and Jennie Bell Harm; m. Helen Epling, Jan. 5, 1948 (div. 1964); children: Rex, Janet, Mark; m. Barbara Sue Chase, Aug. 1965; children: Vladimir, Erik. BS, U. Wash., 1942; MS, U. Minn., 1949. Tchg. asst. U. Minn., Mpls., 1943-45; rsch. assoc. U. Utah, Salt Lake City, 1945-50, fellow in surgery, 1950-52; rsch. virologist Jensen-Salsbery Labs., Inc., Kansas City, Mo., 1952-57; rsch. assoc. Wistar Inst., U. Pa., 1957-58; rsch. virologist USPHS, 1958-61; founder Bolin Labs., Phoenix, 1959—, also bd. dirs. Contbr. articles to profl. jours. Served with U.S. Army, 1931-33. Mem. N.Y. Acad. Scis., Phi Mu Chi. Home: 36629 N 19th Ave Phoenix AZ 85086-9143

BOLING, EDWARD JOSEPH, university president emeritus, educator; b. Sevier County, Tenn., Feb. 19, 1922; s. Sam R. and Nerissa (Clark) B.; m. Carolyn Pierce, Aug. 8, 1950; children: Mark Edward, Brian Marshall, Steven Clark. BS in Accounting, U. Tenn., 1948, MS in Stats., 1950; EdD in Ednl. Adminstrn, Vanderbilt U., 1961; LLD (hon.), U. Richmond, 1984. With Wilby-Kinsy Theatre Corp., Knoxville, Tenn., 1940-41, Aluminum Co. Am., 1941-42; instr. statistics U. Tenn., 1948-50; research statistician Carbide & Carbon Chem. Corp., Oak Ridge, 1950; supr. source and fissionable materials

accounting Carbide & Carbon Chem. Corp. (K-25 plant), 1951-54; budget dir. Tenn., 1955-59; commr. finance and adminstrn., 1959-61; v.p. U. Tenn., 1961-70, pres., 1970-88, pres. emeritus, 1988—, univ. prof., 1988-92. Mem. So. Regional Edn. Bd., 1957-61, 70-81, 83-90, 92-96, mem. exec. com., 1974-75, 79-81, vice chmn., 1986-88; mem. Edn. Commn. of States, 1970-82; trustee, chmn. Am. Coll. Testing Program, 1983-85; dir. emeritus Allied Signal Corp., CSX, N.A. Philips, United Foods, Home Fed. Bank. Author: (with D. A. Gardiner) Forecasting University Enrollment, 1952, Methods of Objectifying The Allocation of Tax Funds to Tennessee State Colleges, 1961. Mem. Nat. Govs. Conf. Good Will Tour to Brazil and Argentina, 1960; Mem. com. on taxation Am. Council on Edn. Served with AUS, 1943-46, ETO. Mem. Am. Statis. Assn., Assn. Higher Edn., Nat. Assn. Land-Grant Colls. (com. on financing higher edn.), Am. Coll. Pub. Rels. Assn. (trustee chmn. com. taxation and philanthropy), Am. Coun. on Edn., Knoxville C. of C. (bd. dirs., chmn. bd. 1989-91), Tenn. Resource Valley (dir., chmn. bd. 1991-92, chmn. supr. com. 1992-02, chmn. 21st century jobs initiative), Am. Legion, Phi Kappa Phi (Scholarship award 1947), Beta Gamma Sigma (charter pres. Alpha chpt. 1948), Phi Delta Kappa, Omicron Delta Kappa, Beta Alpha Psi. Democrat. Office: U Tenn System Andy Holt Towers Ste 731 Knoxville TN 37996-0001

BOLING, ELDON AVERY, physician; b. Elma, Wash, Aug. 29, 1925; s. Dawson and Nellie (Beam) B.; m. Lenore Altschule, Feb. 13, 1948; children: Peter, Alice, Lucy, Sarah, Deborah, Eli. BA, Whitman Coll., Walla Walla, Wash., 1946; MD, U. Calif., San Francisco, 1950. Intern San Francisco Gen. Hosp., 1950-51; rsch. fellow Peter Bent Brigham Hosp., Boston, 1952-54; resident in medicine Boston VA Hosp., 1954-57; staff physician Boston VA Med. Ctr., 1959-95, cons. physician, 1995—98. Patentee in field. Lt. comdr. USNR, 1957-59. Avocation: music.

BOLING, JOSEPH EDWARD, numismatist, retired military officer; b. San Antonio, Oct. 17, 1942; s. Jack Leroy and Judy Alice B.; m. Helen-Louise Phelps, June 11, 1964 (div. 1984); children: L. Margaret, David A., Evan J. BS in Metallurgy, MIT, 1964; MBA, U. Wash., 1973; grad., Japanese Nat. Def. Coll., 1984. Commd. 2d lt. U.S. Army, 1964, advanced through grades to col., 1987; dep. chief staff computer architecture U.S. Army, Europe, 1989-92; asst. dep. dir. Worldwide Mil. Command Control System Def. Communications Agy., Reston, Va., 1983-89, retired U.S. Army, 1992. Author: (with others) WWII Military Currency, 1978, WWII Remembered History in Your Hands, A Numismatic Study, 1995, (also editor) Paper Money of the 20th Century: Japan Vol. 1 1979, Japan Vol. 2, 1988. Fellow Am. Numismatic Soc. (life, East Asian coinage com. 1985—), Royal Numismatic Soc.; mem. Internat. Bank Note Soc. (life, pres. 1986-90, treas. 1993—, Gold medal for svc. 2001), Am. Numismatic Assn. (life, chief judge 1991-93, 95—, dir. judges' familiarization-cert. seminar 1986—, summer seminar instr. 1999—, medal of merit 1991, Howland Wood award 1995, Glenn Smedley award 2000), Pacific N.W. Numismatic Assn. (life, sec. 1994-96, sec.-treas. 1996—), Numismatic Lit. Guild, Assn. U.S. Army. Republican. Avocation: research and publishing on Japanese numismatics. Address: PO Box 4718 Federal Way WA 98063-4718 E-mail: joeboling@aol.com.

BOLING, JUDY ATWOOD, civic worker; b. June 19, 1921; d. Carroll Eugene and Marion Frances (Ayrer) Atwood; m. Jack Leroy Boling, Apr. 8, 1941 (dec. July 1988); children: Joseph Edward, Jean Ann, James Michael, John Charles. AA, San Antonio Jr. Coll., 1940; student, Rogue C.C., Grants Pass, Oreg., 1978-79, So. Oreg. State Coll. First aid instr. ARC, various locations, 1940-65. Contbr. articles to profl. jours. Chmn. vols. Calif., 1961-62, Eng., 1964-65; den mother cub scouts Boy Scouts Am., Monterey, Calif., 1951-52; active Girl Scouts U.S., 1952—, coun. pres., Winema (Oreg.) Coun., 1971-73, 79-82, historian, 1990—, del. to nat. coun., 1966, 72, 81, cons. for nat. publs., 1971, 70; Sun. sch. tchr. Base Chapel, Pyote, Tex., 1949-51, choir dir., 1951; Sun. sch. adminstr. Base Chapel, Morocco, 1954-55; Sun. sch. tchr. Hermon Free Meth. Ch., L.A. 1956-57; active United Way Campaign, 1967-84, Childrens Festival, 1974-88; former liaison with local people in Japanese-Am., Franco-Am., Anglo-Am. orgns.; mem., patron Rogue Craftsmen Bd., Grants Pass, 1972-85, sec., 1972-78, v.p., 1978-85; bd. dirs. Rogue Valley Opera Assn., 1978-85, sponsor/mem., 1978—; bd. dirs. Cmty. Concert, 1979-88, 92-97; mem. Grants Pass Friends of symphony, 1989—, bd. dirs., 1989-2002; vol. RSVP, 1982—; historian Josephine County Rep. Women, 1982-86, treas., 1986-94, 98, sec., 1994-96; elected Rep. precinct committeeperson, 1991—; sustaining mem. Sta. KSYS Pub. TV; mem. Sta. KSOR Pub. Radio; frequent pub. spkr. Recipient Thanks Badge Girl Scouts U.S., 1957, 60, 73, Thanks II Badge, 2000, Thanks Badge Girl Scouts Japan, 1959, U.K. Girl Guides, 1982, cert. of appreciation USAF, 1959, City of Hagi, City of Fukuoka (Japan), Gov. of Fukuoka Prefecture, 2 citations Internat. Book Project; Oreg. Vol. award Sen. Packwood, 1983, Cmty. Woman of Yr. award Bus. and Profl. Women, 1984, Nat. award Juliette Gordon Low World Friendship medal Girl Scouts U.S., 1995. Mem. P.E.O. (DC, Oreg. chpt.), Josephine County Hist. Soc. (bd. dirs. 1992—), So. Oreg. Resources Alliance, Am. Host Found., Knife and Fork Club (bd. dirs. 1994-97), Phi Theta Kappa. Address: 710 NW Midland Ave Grants Pass OR 97526

BOLINO, AUGUST CONSTANTINO, economics educator; b. Boston, Sept. 30, 1922; s. Nicholas and Rose (Capozzi) B.; m. Thora Johnson, Sept. 15, 1951; children: Bradlee, Douglas, Jacquelyn, Gregory. BBA, U. Mich., 1948, MBA, 1949; postgrad., U. Wash., 1950-52; PhD in Economics, St. Louis U., 1957. Instr. Statistics U. Wash., Seattle, 1950-51; instr. Bus. and Econ. Idaho State U., Pocatello, 1952-55; from asst. to assoc. prof. Econs. St. Louis U., 1955-62; chief div. econ. analysis of automation, Office Manpower Automation and Tng. U.S. Dept. Labor, Washington, 1962-66; assoc. prof. Cath. U., Washington, 1966-69, prof., 1970—. Lectr. U. Md., College Park, 1963, 70-76; adj. prof. econs. Am. U., Washington, 1964-66; dir. evaluation of manpower devel. and utilization of programs br., U.S. Dept. Health, Edn., and Welfare, 1964-66; asst. to U.S. Commr. of Edn., 1964-66; cons. in field. Author: The Development of the American Economy, 1961, Manpower and the City, 1969, Career Education: Contributions to Economic Growth, 1973, The Ellis Island Source Book, 1985, The Watchmakers of Massachusetts, 1987, A Century of Human Capital by Education and Training, 1989, Thomas Angel, American, 2001, Brother Brigham's Trial, 2002; contbr. articles to profl. jours. V.p. rsch. Ellis Island Restoration Commn., 1978—. Lt. USAF, 1942-45, ETO. Rsch. fellow U. Mich., 1949; Ford Found. grant U. Minn., 1957, Rsch. grantee Am. Philosophical Soc., 1969, US Manpower Adminstrn., 1971-72, DC Cmty. Humanities Coun., 1983. Mem. Alpha Kappa Psi (disting. service award 1949, 60). Democrat. Roman Catholic. Avocation: coin and watch collecting. Home: 8515 2nd Ave Silver Spring MD 20910-3465 Office: 309 McMahon Hall Cardinal Sta Washington DC 20064

BOLIVAR ZAPATA, FRANCISCO, biochemist; b. Mexico City, Mar. 7, 1948; s. Jose and Carmen (Zapata) B.; children: Francisco, Paulina, Jose. Degree in chemistry, Nat. Autonomous U. Mex., Mexico City, 1971, M Biochemistry, 1973, PhD in Biochemistry, 1975; D Honoris Causa, U. Lieje, Belgium, 1994. Assoc. rschr. Nat. Autonomous U. Mex., 1973—, full rschr. level I, 1977-83, full rschr. level III, 1983—, chmn. molecular biology dept., 1980—, dir. genetic engring. ctr., 1982—, dir. biotech. inst., 191-99, chief investigator biotech inst. Cuernavaca, Mex., 1999—. Editor jour. Gene, 1982—; contbr. more than 120 articles to profl. jours. Recipient Manuel Noriega prize in Sci. OAS, 1988, Nat. U Prize, 1990, Prince of Asturias prize in sci. Govt. of Spain, 1991, Nat. Prize in Sci. Pres. of Mex., 1992, TWAS prize in Biology, 1997. Mem. Am. Soc. Microbiology, Academia Investigacion Cientifica, Mex. Colegio Nacional, Academia Mexicana de Ciencias (pres. 1998—). Office: UNAM Inst Biotech PO Box 510-3 Cuernavaca 62271 Mexico also: Academia Maxicana de Ciencias Ave San Jeronimo 260 Jardines del Pedregal DF 04500 Mexico

BOLKER, HENRY IRVING, retired chemist, research institute director, educator; b. Montreal, Que., Can., Feb. 19, 1926; s. Abraham Isaac and Mary (Ballon) B.; m. Estelle Ruth Samuels, Nov. 22, 1953; 1 dau., Louise Ellen. BA, Queen's U., Kingston, Ont., Can., 1948; MA, Queen's U., 1950; PhD, Yale U., 1952. Rsch. chemist DuPont of Can., Ltd., Kingston, Ont., 1954-60, Pulp and Paper Rsch. Inst. Can., Pointe Claire, Que., 1960-67, sect. head, 1967-77, div. dir., 1977-80, asst. dir. rsch., 1980-81, assoc. dir. rsch., 1981-83, dir. rsch., 1984-86, dir. acad. affairs, 1987-90; exec. dir. Nat. Network of Ctrs. of Excellence on Mech. Pulps, 1990-93. Rsch. assoc. McGill U., Montreal, 1962-91. Author: Natural and Synthetic Polymers, 1974; contbr. articles to profl. jours.; patentee in field. Pres. Youth Sci. Found., Ottawa, 1965-66; sec. Lakeshore Chamber Music Soc. Ste. Anne de Bellevue, Que., 1973-74; pres. Lakeshore Dog Tng. Assn., Pointe Claire, 1975-77; chmn. Pointe Claire Cultural Centre, 1978-80. Fellow Internat. Acad. Wood Sci. (sec.-treas. 1989-92), Chem. Inst. Can. (chmn. 1979-81, v.p. 1986-87, pres. 1987-88, Montreal medal 1984), Sigma Xi; mem. Am. Chem. Soc., Can. Pulp and Paper Assn. Home: 110 Spartan Cres Pointe Claire QC Canada H9R 3R5

BOLLA, WILLIAM JOSEPH, lawyer; b. Chester, Pa., Aug. 2, 1947; s. William Andrew and Margaret Mary (Campbell) B.; divorced; children: Christopher Campbell, Gregory Gibson. BS in Psychology, Pa. State U., 1969; JD, Dickinson Sch. Law, 1972. Bar: Pa. 1972, U.S. Supreme Ct. 1986. Assoc. McGavin DeSantis & Koch, Reading, Pa., 1973; asst. dist. atty. Bucks County, Doylestown, Pa., 1973-76; ptnr. Heckler & Bolla, Doylestown, 1976-85, McNamara, Heckler & Bolla, Doylestown, 1986-98, McNamara, Bolla. Williams & Panzer, Doylestown, 1998—. Bd. dirs. Bucks County chpt. Am. Cancer Soc., Doylestown, v.p., 1991—92, pres., 1993—95; bd. dirs. Bucks County Symphony Soc., 1995—96, Doylestown Twp. Pks. and Recreation Bd., 1992—95, Bucks County Writers' Rm., 2003—; founder, pres. Bucks County Challenger Baseball Program for Handicapped Children, 1994—99; mem. adv. bd. Big Bros./Big Sisters Bucks County, Doylestown, 1987—93; chair Ctrl. Bucks Teen Ctr. Bldg. Com., 2000—01; mem. Doylestown Borough Revitalization Com., 2000—; minority counsel state govt. com. Pa. Senate, Harrisburg, 1976—77, mem. fin. com., 1978—81. Mem. Pa. Bar Assn. (ho. dels. 1997-98), Bucks County Bar Assn. (bd. dirs., chmn. young lawyers com. 1976-77, chmn. real estate sect. 1987-88, chmn. merit selection of judges 1984-85, chmn. bench and bar com. 1992-95, chmn. realtor legal com. 1991—, v.p./pres.-elect 1995-96, pres. 1996-97). Republican. Avocations: Civil war, travel. Office: McNamara Bolla Williams & Panzer 122 E Court St Doylestown PA 18901-4321 E-mail: wjbolla@mbwplaw.com.

BOLLAG, JEAN-MARC, soil biochemistry educator, consultant; b. Basel, Switzerland, Feb. 19, 1935; came to U.S., 1965; naturalized, 1975; s. Marcel and Renee (Levy) B.; m. Brigitte Gertrud Baumgartner, Apr. 26, 1960; children: Daniel, Gideon, Roni, Judith. PhD, U. Basel, 1959. Grad. rsch. asst. Bot. Inst. U. Basel, 1956-59; postdoctoral rsch. assoc. Weizmann Inst. Sci., Rehovot, Israel, 1963-65, Cornell U., Ithaca, NY, 1965-67; asst. prof. soil microbiology Pa. State U., University Park, 1967-71, assoc. prof., 1971-77, prof., 1977—2002, prof. emeritus, 2002—. Vis. sci. CIBA-Geigy, Basel, 1975-76; dir. Ctr. for Bioremediation and Detoxification; cons. to fed. agys., chem. cos. Co-editor Soil Biochemistry Series; contbr. numerous articles in environ. microbiology and microbial control of soil pollution to profl. publs. Recipient badge of merit Polish Min. Agr., 1977, rsch. award Gamma Sigma Delta, 1982; Julius Baer fellow Weizmann Inst. Sci., 1963-65. Fellow Soil Sci. Soc., Am. Soc. Agronomy (environ. quality rsch. award 1995), Am. Acad. Microbiology; mem. AAAS, Internat. Soc. Soil Sci., Internat. Humic Substances Soc. Democrat. Home: 368 Bradley Ave State College PA 16801-6322 Office: Penn State Ctr for Bioremediation & Detox 129 Land Water Research University Park PA 16802-4900 E-mail: jmbollag@psu.edu.

BOLLE, DONALD MARTIN, retired engineering educator; b. Amsterdam, The Netherlands, Mar. 30, 1933; came to U.S., 1955, naturalized, 1961; s. Maarten C. and Petronella (Kramer) B.; m. Barbara June Girton, Nov. 29, 1957; children— Alan Martin, Thomas Raymond, John Kenneth, Cornelis Adrianus. BS, Durham U., Eng., 1954; PhD, Purdue U., 1961; MA (hon.), Brown U., 1966. Asst. prof. elec. engring. Purdue U., 1961-62; NSF postdoctoral fellow dept. applied math. and theoretical physics Cambridge (Eng.) U., 1962-63; asst. prof. engring. Brown U., 1963-66, asso. prof., 1966-70, prof., 1970-80; Chandler-Weaver chair elec. engring. Lehigh U., Bethlehem, Pa., 1980-81; dean Lehigh U. (Coll. Engring. and Applied Sci.), 1981-88; interim vice provost info. resources Lehigh U., 1999-2000; sr. v.p. acad. affairs Poly. U., Bklyn., 1988-91, prof., 1991-99, v.p. adminstrn., 1995-96. Richard Merton vis. prof. Technische Hochschule, Braunschweig, Germany, 1967; cons. in field. Fellow IEEE, AAAS, IEE (U.K.). Home: 6448 Eichler Cir Coopersburg PA 18036-1382

BOLLEN, SHARON KESTERSON, artist, educator; b. Cin., Apr. 27, 1946; d. Marc J. and Regina (Rolfs) Kesterson; m. Jerry H. Bollen, June 22, 1968; children: Heather, Christopher. BA in Art, Coll. of Mt. St. Joseph, Cin., 1968; MA in Art Edn., U. Cin., 1970, EdD in Art Edn., 1980. Tchr. art Marian H.S., Cin., 1968-77; prof. art Coll. of Mount St. Joseph, Cin., 1977—. Fabric surface design art works in juried and invitational regional and nat. exhbns.; book reviewer Nat. Art Edn. Assn. Women's Caucus newsletter, 1985—. Recipient Alumni Appreciation award Coll. of Mount St. Joseph, 1993, Disting. Teaching award, 1981. Mem. Nat. Art Edn. Assn. (Student Chpt. Sponsor award 1994, Outstanding Ohio Art Educator of Yr. 1990, Western Region Higher Edn. Art Educator of Yr. 2001), Ohio Art Edn. Assn. (Outstanding Art Educator 1988, Higher Edn. Art Educator of Yr. 2000), Nat. Surface Design Assn., Am. Crafts Coun., Nat. Mus. for Women in the Arts (charter), Georgia O'Keeffe Mus. Roman Catholic. Home: 1138 Cryer Ave Cincinnati OH 45208-2803 Office: Coll of Mount St Joseph Art Dept 5701 Delhi Rd Cincinnati OH 45233-1670

BOLLENBACH, STEPHEN FRASIER, hotel executive; b. Los Angeles, July 14, 1942; s. Walter and Betty (Mason) B.; m. Suzanne Weimer, Apr. 13, 1963 (div. Dec. 1969); m. Barbara May Christeson, Dec. 31, 1970; children: Christopher, Keat. BS in Fin., UCLA, 1965; MBA, Calif. State U., 1968. CFO D.K. Ludwig Group, N.Y.C., 1977-80; chmn., CEO S.W. Savs. & Loan, Phoenix, 1980-82; sr. v.p. fin., treas. Marriott Corp., Washington, 1982-86; sr. v.p., CFO, dir. Holiday Corp., Memphis, 1986-90, Promus Cos., Memphis, 1990; exec. v.p., CFO Marriott Corp., Washington, 1992-93; pres., CEO Host Marriott Corp., Washington, 1993-95; sr. exec. v.p., CFO Walt Disney Co., Burbank, Calif., 1995-96; pres., CEO Hilton Hotels Corp., Beverly Hills, Calif., 1996—. Bd. dirs. Carr Realty Corp., Washington, Mid-Am. Apt. Cmtys., Inc., Memphis, Am. West Airlines, Phoenix; mem. adv. bd. CFO Mag., Boston. Office: Hilton Hotels Corporation PO Box 5567 Beverly Hills CA 90209-5567

BOLLENBACHER, HERBERT KENNETH, steel company official; b. Wilkinsburg, Pa., Apr. 16, 1933; s. Curtis W. and Ebba M. (Frendberg) B.; m. Nancy Jane Cercena, June 29, 1957; children: Mary E., Kenneth E. AB, U. Pitts., 1960, MEd, 1963. Cert. safety profl. Staff asst. tng. J & L Steel Co., Pitts., 1963-66; mgr. tng., devel. and accident prevention Textron Corp., Pitts., 1966-72; supr. safety Copperweld Steel Co., Warren, Ohio, 1972-75, mgr. safety, security, 1975-78, mgr. human resources conservation, 1978-94; exec. v.p. Charles Mgmt., Inc., 1994—; mem. adj. faculty Pa. State U. mem. Eastminster Presbytery Com. on Ministry; bd. dirs. Trumbull County Prison Ministry. Served with U.S. Army, 1954-56. Mem. Am. Soc. Safety Engrs. (past pres. Ohio-Pa. chpt., Ohio Safety Profl. of Yr. 1983-84, 92-93), Ohio Soc. Safety Engrs. (state chaplain), Am. Iron and Steel Inst. (chmn. safety task force), Mfrs. Assn. Eastern Ohio and Western Pa. (safety chmn. 12 yrs.; safety profl. of yr. award 1984, coordinator Ohio seat belt coalition 1986, Gov.'s spl. recognition award), Gov.'s Traffic Safety Coun., 1989, Tinkham Camp Gideons Internat. (past pres.), Ohio Gideons (area coordinator, membership cabinet), Rotary (Paul Harris fellow, pres., benefactor, Ideal of Svc. in Workplace award), Boy Scouts Am. (western reserve coun., loss prevention com.). Presbyterian (elder). Author suprs. monthly discussion guide, article for tech. publ. Avocations: softball; volleyball; reading. *Personal philosophy: The chief end of man is to glorify God and be a blessing to your fellow men.*

BOLLER, PAUL FRANKLIN, JR., retired American history educator, writer; b. Spring Lake, N.Y., Dec. 31, 1916; s. Paul Franklin and Grace (Hall) B. BA, Yale U., 1939, PhD, 1947; DLitt, Tex. Wesleyan U., 1993. From asst. to full prof. So. Meth. U., Dallas, 1948-66; prof. U. Mass., Boston, 1966-76; Lyndon Johnson prof. history Tex. Christian U., Ft. Worth, 1976-83, prof. emeritus, 1983—. Vis. prof. U. Tex., Austin, 1963-64. Author: (with J. Tilford) This Is Our Nation, 1961, George Washington and Religion, 1963, Quotemanship, 1967, American Thought in Transition, 1865-1900, 1967, American Transcendentalism, 1830-1860, 1974, Freedom and Fate in American Thought, 1978, Presidential Anecdotes, 1981, Presidential Campaigns, 1984, (with R. Story) A More Perfect Union, 1984, (with R.L. Davis) Hollywood Anecdotes, 1987, Presidential Wives, 1988, (with J. George) They Never Said It, 1989, Congressional Anecdotes, 1991, Memoirs of an Obscure Professor, 1992, Not So!, 1995, Presidential Inaugurations, 2001. Lt. (j.g.) USN, 1942-46. Mem. Tex. Inst. Letters, Authors Guild, Phi Alpha Theta, Phi Beta Kappa. Democrat. Avocations: music, films, hiking, jogging, swimming. Office: Tex Christian Univ PO Box 297260 Fort Worth TX 76129-0001

BOLLERSLEV, TIM PETER, economics educator; b. Copenhagen, May 11, 1958; m. Marian Staer; children: Tasha, Nico, Adrian. MS in Econs. and Math., U. Aarhus, Denmark, 1983; PhD in Econs., U. Calif., San Diego, 1986. Assoc. prof. econs. Northwestern U., Evanston, Ill., 1986-88, asst. prof. fin. J.L. Kellogg Grad. Sch., 1988-91, assoc. prof. fin., 1991-95, Nathan S. and Mary P. Sharpe prof. fin., 1995; Commonwealth prof. econs. U. Va., Charlottesville, 1996-98; Juanita and Clifton Kreps prof. econs., prof. fin. Duke U., Durham, N.C., 1998—. Rsch. assoc. Nat. Bur. Econ. Rsch. Contbr. articles to profl. jours. including Am. Econ. Rev., Econometrica, Jour. Econometrics, Jour. Fin., Jour. Polit. Economy, Rev. Econ. and Stats., Rev. Econ. Studies; mem. editl. bd. Econ. Policy Rev., 1997—, European Fin. Rev., 1996—, Jour. Applied Econometrics, 1990—, Jour. Bus. and Econ. Statistics, 1992-2002, Jour. Empirical Fin., 1991-2002, Jour. Marcoecons. Dynamics, 1996-2000, Jour. Internat. Fin. Markets, Instns., and Money, 1996-2002, Rev. Fin. Studies, 1994-98, Studies in Nonlinear Dynamics and Econometrics, 1995-2002. Grantee, NSF. Fellow Econometric Soc.; mem. Am. Fin. Assn., Am. Statis. Assn. Office: Duke U Dept Econs Durham NC 27708-0097

BOLLES, CHARLES AVERY, librarian; b. Pine Island, Minn., Aug. 10, 1940; s. Arthur Marston and Clarice Ione (Figy) B.; m. Marjorie Elaine Hancock, May 17, 1964; children: Jason Brice, Justin Brian. BA, U. Minn., 1962, MA in Libr. Sci., 1963, PhD in Libr. Sci., 1975. Catalog and serials librarian U. Iowa, Iowa City, 1964-67; asst. prof. Emporia (Kans.) State U., 1970-76, dir. Sch. Libr. Sci., 1978-80; dir. libr. devel. divsn. Kans. State Libr., 1976-78; state librarian State of Idaho, Boise, 1980—. Mem. ALA, Chief Officers State Libr. Agys., Western Coun. State Librs. (chmn. 1985-86, 98-99), Pacific N.W. Libr. Assn. (pres. 1990-91), Idaho Libr. Assn. Office: Idaho State Libr 325 W State St Boise ID 83702-6014

BOLLES, DONALD SCOTT, lawyer; b. Buffalo, Dec. 17, 1936; s. Theodore H. and Marie (Heth) B.; m. Jean Waytulonis Oct. 12, 1963 (dec. May 1983); children: Scott Matthew; m. Geraldine Novinger, Feb. 14, 1988. BA, Alfred U., 1960; JD cum laude, U. San Diego Sch. Law, 1970. Bar: Calif. 1971, U.S. Dist. Ct. (so. and no. dists.) Calif. 1971. Ptnr. Hutton, Foley, Anderson & Bolles, Inc., King City, Calif., 1971-95, Anderson & Bolles, Inc., King City, Calif., 1995-99. Editor lead articles San Diego Law Rev., 1969-70. Chmn. King City Recreation Commn., 1974—77; candidate mcpl. judge primary and gen. election Monterey County, Calif., 1986; trustee Mee Meml. Hosp., King City, 1974—78, chmn., 1978—80; sec., founding mem. bd. dirs. Project Teen Ctr. Inc., 1986—90; bd. dirs. Sun St. Ctrs., 1991—99, Monterey Coll. Law, 1995—2002, pres., 2000—01; pres. Corral de Tierra Homeowners Assn., 1996—98, pres., 2001—; mem. Camerata Singers, 2000—. Decorated Combat Infantryman's badge, Army Commendation medal. Mem. Monterey County Bar Assn. (exec. com. 1985-86). Clubs: Toastmasters (King City) (pres. 1972-74). Lodges: Lions (pres. 1975-76, sec. 1984-86 King City club). Republican. Avocations: application of computer science to practice of law, tennis, golf, bridge, choir. Home: 23799-18 Monterey Salinas Hwy Salinas CA 93908-9328 E-mail: dsbolles@aol.com.

BOLLEY, ANDREA, artist; d. Hildo and Laura Pia (Maurino) B. BFA, U. Windsor, 1975. Tchr. Activity Ctr. Art Gallery Ont., 1979, 80, Arts Sake, Toronto, 1982. One-woman shows include IDA Gallery York U., 1976, Art Gallery Brant, 1977, Pollock Gallery, Toronto, 1977, 78, 80, Agnes Etherington Art Ctr., Kingston, 1981, Gallery One, Toronto, 1984, 85, 86, Klonaridis Gallery, Toronto, 1989, 90, 91, Upper Can. Brewing Co., 1993, Studio Show, 1994, 95, 96, 97, 98, 99, 2000, 2002, Masterworks Found., Bermuda, 2003; group exhbns. include Grapestake Gallery, San Francisco, 1980, Alta. Coll. Art, Calgary, 1980, Art Gallery Ont., 1981, Art Gallery Hamilton, 1981, Gallery One, 1984, 85, 86, Triangle N.Y., 1985, 91, Klonaridis Gallery, 1988, John Schweitzer Gallery, Montreal, 1989, Mississauga Civic Ctr. Art Gallery, 1990, Magnum Books, Ottawa, 1991, Bennington Coll., Vt., 1991, Upper Can. Brewing Co., 1992, Robert Kidd Gallery, Birmingham, Mich., 1999, Group of Ten Corkin-Shopland, Toronto, Can., 2003, McGill U., Montreal, 2003others; represented in permanent collections Can. Coun. Art Bank, Art Gallery Windsor, Labatt's Can. Ltd., Citicorp Ltd., Can., Can. Imperial Bank Commerce, Max Factor Ltd., Chatelaine Mag., J.E. Seagram Ltd., McGill Club, Imperial Oil, Citibank Can., Toronto-Dominion Bank, Casey House, Am. Express, Guaranty Trust, Abitibi Paper, Triangle, Toronto Sund, Arthur Gelgoot and Assoc., Premiere Mag., Bells & Whistles, and various pvt. collections. Grantee Ont. Arts Coun., 1975, 76, 78, 79, 84, 85, Can. Coun., 1976, 80; recipient Ont. Soc. Artists Purchase award J.E. Seagram and Son Ltd., 1980. Office: 132 Jarvis St Toronto ON Canada M5B 2B5 E-mail: andreabolley@hotmail.com.

BOLLICH, ELRIDGE NICHOLAS, brokerage house executive; b. Eunice, La., Sept. 10, 1941; s. Nicholas Joseph and Caroline (Manuel) Bollich; m. Shirley Anne Yackel, July 14, 1973; children: Jennifer, Brian, Sandra. BBA in Fin., Tex. A&M U., 1963. Registered rep. N.Y. Stock Exch. Assoc. Rotan Mosle, Houston, 1966—69, asst. v.p., 1966—74, v.p., 1975-86; 1st v.p. Rotan Mosle Paine Webber, Houston, 1986-88, Smith Barney, Houston, 1988-97; sr. v.p. UBS Paine Webber, Houston, 1997—. Dir. devel. bd. Nat. Commerce Bank, Houston, 1987—88; mem. devel. bd. Tex. A&M U. Sch. Liberal Arts. Cubmaster Boy Scouts Am., Houston, 1987—91, mem. troop com. Troop 642, 1992—97. 1st lt. U.S. Army, 1963—65, Vietnam, capt. USAR, 1967—69. Mem.: VFW, N.Y. Athletic Club, Stock and Bond Club, Houston Securities Dealers, Houston Racquet Club, KC. Roman Catholic. Avocations: hunting, tennis, theater, coaching boys and girls basketball, Boy Scouts. Office: UBS Paine Webber Inc Ste 900 4400 Post Oak Pkwy Houston TX 77027-3414

BOLLIGER, EUGENE FREDERICK, former surgeon; b. Detroit, Sept. 19, 1923; s. Eugene Hans and Julia Frederick (Larson) B.; m. Lois Ann Doan, Dec. 16, 1946; children: Mark, Glen, Cynthia. MD, U. Mich., 1946. Diplomate Am. Bd. Surgery. Intern, then surg. resident Grace Hosp., Detroit, 1947-52; ward surgeon Madigan Army Hosp., Ft. Lewis, Wash., 1952-54; asst. chief surgery 2d Gen. Hosp., Munchweiler, Germany, 1954-55; chief surgery U.S. Army Hosp., Pirmasson, then Wurzburg, Germany, 1955-57; attending surgeon Northwestern Hosp., Mpls., 1957-58; chief of surgery Dickey County Meml. Hosp., Ellendale, N.D., 1958-82; surgeon SHARE HMO, Mpls., 1982-87; chief of surgery Mid-Dakota Hosp., Chamberlain, S.D., 1988-91, Gregory (S.D.) Community Hosp., 1991-94; retired, 1994. Surg. cons. West Holt Hosp., Atkinson, Nebr., 1992-94, St. Anthony's Hosp., O.Neill, Nebr., 1992-94; real estate cons. Westin-Reid, Mpls., 1987-88. Major U.S. Army, M.C., 1949-57. Fellow ACS; mem. AMA. Republican. Lutheran. Avocations: piano, singing, woodworking, former pilot. E-mail: EugeneB868@aol.com.

BOLLINGER, LEE CARROLL, academic administrator, law educator; b. 1946; BS, U. Oreg., 1968; JD, Columbia U., 1971. Law clk. to Judge Wilfred Feinberg U.S. Ct. Appeals (2nd cir.), 1971—72; law clk. to Chief Justice Warren Burger U.S. Supreme Ct., 1972—73; asst. prof. law U. Mich., 1973—76, assoc. prof., 1976—78, prof., 1978—94, dean, 1987—94, pres., prof. law, 1997—; provost, prof. govt. Dartmouth Coll., 1994—96; pres. Columbia Univ., 2002—. Rsch. assoc. Clare Hall, Cambridge U., 1983. Co-author (with Jackson): (novels) Contract Law in Modern Society, 1980, The Tolerant Soc., 1986, Images of a Free Press, 1991. Bd. dirs. Gerald R. Ford Found., Royal Shakespeare Co. Fellow Am. Rockefeller Humanities. Fellow: Am. Acad. Arts and Scis. Office: Columbia University 2960 Broadway New York NY 10027-6902 also: 535 W 116th St 202 Low Library Mail Code 4309 New York NY 10027

BOLLINGER, MARK W. school system administrator; b. Elwood, Ind., Jan. 6, 1955; s. Donald Gene and Patsy Marlene Bollinger; m. Ginger JoAnne Whittaker, Oct. 12, 1974; children: Anthony Travis, Adam Paul. BSBA, Ind. Wesleyan U., Marion, 1999. Pres., CEO Bollinger Electric, Inc., 1977—; maintenance supr. Elwood (Ind.) Cmty. Sch. Corp., 1990—94; dir. bldgs, grounds, transp. and projects Greenfield-Ctrl. Cmty. Sch. Corp., Ind., 1994—2001, bus. mgr., 2002—. City coun. City of Elwood, Ind., 1987—94; exec. bd. C. of C., Elwood, Ind., 1987—94. Staff sgt. USAF, 1975—77.

Scholarship, State of Ind., 1973. Home: 1338 Greenhills Rd Greenfield IN 46140 Office: Greenfield-Ctrl Cmty Sch Corp 110 W North St Greenfield IN 46140 Office Fax: 317-467-4227. Personal E-mail: mbollinger@insightbb.com. E-mail: mbollinger@gcsc.k12.in.us.

BOLLINGER, MICHAEL, artistic director; b. St. Louis, July 1, 1954; s. Rollie Bollinger and Blanche (Bush) Easley; m. Stephanie McClain Bollinger; children: Tanner Michael, Allison Jeanette. Student, Webster U., 1972-73, U. Mo., 1973-74, U. Mo., St. Louis, 1974-75; BFA, Webster U., 1978. Producing dir., founder Mainstage Theatre, Lake of the Ozarks, Mo., 1978-84; artistic producing dir. Arrow Rock (Mo.) Lyceum Theatre, 1980—. Dir. Lyceum Airwaves Theatre, 1985-88; guest instr. acting Mo. Baptist Coll., St. Louis, Stephens Coll., Columbia, Mo. Valley Coll., Marshall, mem. theatre adv. panel Mo. Arts Coun., St. Louis, 1987-90; co-prodr. Mo. State Theatre Conf., St. Louis; mem. citizens adv. bd. KBIA-PBS Radio; adv. com. InterAct; Teen to Teen Theatre, Columbia, 1992-93; adjudicator Am. Coll. Theatre Fest. Ruston, La., 1992, Tenn. Arts Commn. Artist Fellowship, Nashville, 1994, Am. Coll. Theatre, 1997. Prodr., dir., actor : nearly 200 plays and musicals, including 6 world premieres and numerous Mo. premieres. Facilities chmn. cultural planning com. Columbia Com. on the Arts, 1993—95; adjudicator Prelude Awards, Indpls., 1993, 1996, Am. Assn. Cmty. Theatre Festival Adjudication, Ill., 1997; judge Mo. State Show Choir Festival, 2003. Recipient Mo. Arts award Mo. Arts Coun., 1983, 94, Outstanding Young Men of Am. award U.S. Jaycees, 1983. Mem. Actors Equity Assn. Liberal. Baptist. Avocations: raising children, photography, outdoor activities, feminine appreciation, history. Office: Arrow Rock Lyceum Theatre High St Arrow Rock MO 65320 E-mail: Director@LyceumTheatre.org.

BOLLINGER, RALPH RANDAL, surgeon, researcher; b. Dearborn, Mich., Oct. 3, 1944; s. Ralph Perry and Edith Delores (Algren) B.; m. Monika Irmgard Koch, May 1, 1965; children: Christine Laura, Mark Randal. BS in Biology, Tulane U., 1966, MD, MS in Biochemistry, Tulane U., 1970; PhD in Immunology, Duke U., 1977, MBA with Cert. in Health Svc. Mgmt., 1997. Diplomate Am. Bd. Surgery. Stress physiology rsch. physician USAF Sch. of Aerospace Medicine, Brooks AFB, Tex., 1972-74; postdoctoral fellow, instr. in surgery, dept. immunology Duke U., Durham, N.C., 1974-76; resident in surgery Duke U. Med. Ctr., Durham, 1970-72, chief resident in surgery, 1979-80, asst. prof. surgery, 1980-86, asst. prof. immunology, 1981-86, assoc. prof. immunology, 1986—95, assoc. prof. surgery, 1986-91, prof. surgery, 1991—, prof. immunology, 1995—, chief of surg. transplantation, 1983—99, chief gen. surgery, 1994—. Vice councillor United Network for Organ Sharing, Richmond, Va., 1986-88, councillor, 1989 91, v.p., 1991-92, pres., 1992-93; sec. Southeastern Organ Procurement Found., Richmond, 1988-89, v.p., 1989-90, pres., 1990-91; v.p. Carolina Organ Procurement Agy., Greenville, N.C., 1985-87, pres., 1987-89; trustee N.C. Kidney Found., Chapel Hill, 1983-90. Contbr. numerous articles to profl. jours.; editor: Transplant Management, 1988; mem. editl. bd. Am. Surgeon, 1988, Jour. Surg. Rsch., 1993—, Jour. ACS, 1996, Graft, 1998, Jour. Investigative Surgery, 2001. Com. chmn. Troop 408, Boy Scouts Am., Durham, N.C., 1982-89; mem. staff/parish rels. com. Duke Meml. Meth. Ch., Durham, 1985-87, chmn., 2003—, coun. on ministries, 1983-85. Maj. USAF MC, 1972-74. Recipient La. Pathology Soc. award Tulane U., 1979, Golden Apple award Duke U., 1984, 89. Fellow ACS; mem. Aerospace Med. Assn. (environ. sci. award 1978), Am. Soc. Transplant Surgeons (membership com. 1988, councillor 1989-93), Soc. Univ. Surgeons, Transplantation Soc., Am. Surg. Assn., N.C. Assn. Biomed. Rsch. (sec. 1992—). Republican. Avocations: scuba diving, gardening, white water canoeing. Home: 1120 Infinity Rd Durham NC 27712-9765 Office: Duke U Med Ctr PO Box 2910 Durham NC 27710-2910 E-mail: bolli001#@mc.duke.edu.

BOLLMAN, MARK BROOKS, JR., communications executive; b. Meriden, Conn., Aug. 24, 1925; s. Mark B. and Esther (Stevens) B.; m. Barbara Ann Smith, July 8, 1928; children— Mark Brooks, III, Richard N., Steven A. AB, Princeton U., 1949; MBA, Harvard U., 1951. Sr. v.p. Benton & Bowles Inc., N.Y.C., 1968-70; exec. v.p. Diners Club Inc., N.Y.C., 1970-72; corp. v.p. Magnavox Co., N.Y.C., 1972-75; pres. McDonald & Little Inc., Atlanta, 1975-77; sr. v.p., sr. ptnr., dir. N.W. Ayer and Ptnrs., N.Y.C., 1977-95; pres. M & B Communications, 1978—. Served with AUS, 1944-46. Decorated Purple Heart. Mem.: Clinton (Conn.); Stanwich (Greenwich, Conn.). Republican. Episcopalian. Home: 20 Rockwood Ln Greenwich CT 06830-3815

BOLLWAGE, J. CHRISTIAN, mayor; b. Elizabeth, N.J., Dec. 7, 1954; s. Frank and Jeanne (Hasson) B.; m. Nancy; 1 child. BA in Econs., Kean Coll., 1981, M in Pub. Adminstrn., 1989. Cert. in local planning and zoning continuing edn., Rutgers U. Sr. inward documentation clk. Sea-Land Svc. Inc., 1978-79; revenue receivables clk. Puerto Rico Marine Mgmt. Inc., 1979-80; traffic coord. Kerr Steamship Inc., 1980-85; sales & mktg. A&J Trading Corp., 1985-92; adj. prof. pub. adminstrn. Kean Coll., Union, N.J., 1989-92; mem. planning bd. Elizabeth, N.J., 1983-87; mem. city coun., 1983-92; mem. Urban Enterprise Zone Commn., Elizabeth, 1984-92; mayor City of Elizabeth, 1993—. Pres. exec. bd. N.J. State League of Municipalities, 2003—. Recipient N.J. Assn. Advancement of Mentally Handicapped award. Mem. U.S. Conf. of Mayors, Knights of Columbus, Ancient Order of Hibernians, Pi Alpha Alpha. Democrat. Roman Catholic. Home: 1113 Coolidge Rd Elizabeth NJ 07208-1005 Office: City Hall 50 Winfield Scott Plz Elizabeth NJ 07201-2462*

BOLOGNINI, DOROTHY BARBER, not-for-profit developer; b. Chgo., Aug. 5, 1923; d. George Michael and Helen Stephens Barber; m. Ennio Bolognini, Jan. 17, 1961 (dec. July 1979). Student, Roosevelt Coll., Chgo., 1941—42, Northwestern U., Evanston, Ill., 1943—44. Pvt. music tchr., Chgo., 1940—88; copywriter Trailer Travel Mag., Chgo., 1945—47; editor preview news Continental Casualty, Chgo., 1947—56, head sales promotion, 1947—56; asst. founder, libr. Las Vegas Phil. Orch., Nev., 1963—68; original mem., trustee Las Vegas Performing Arts Ctr., 1991—. Solo performer piano Thorne Hall-Northwestern U., Evanston, Ill., 1945. Active Rep. Women, 1980; mem. Rep. Nat. Com., 1980—; dir. Meadows Preservation Soc., Las Vegas, 1998—. Republican. Greek Orthodox. Avocations: golf, tennis, classical music, travel, photography. Home: 328 Bedford Rd Las Vegas NV 89107

BOLOKER, ROSE L. school psychologist; b. Bklyn., Mar. 18, 1951; d. Charles and Frances (Frey) B. BS in Psychology with honors, Bklyn. Coll., 1984; MS in Edn., Bklyn. Coll., CUNY, 1986. Cert. sch. psychologist. Sch. psychologist N.Y.C. Bd. Edn., Bklyn., 1986—, field trainer, 1990—. Co-dir. Biofeedback Tng. Inst., Bklyn., 1987-88. Bd. dirs., crew chief, tng. officer Flatlands Vol. Ambulance Corps, Bklyn., 1975-82. Mem. Nat. Assn. Sch. Psychologists, N.Y. Assn. Sch. Psychologists, Assn. Applied Psychophysiology and Biofeedback, Kappa Delta Pi. Home: 2163 E 23rd St Brooklyn NY 11229-3645 Office: NYC Bd Edn CSE Dist 19 301 Vermont St Brooklyn NY 11207-3511

BOLOMEY, ROGER HENRY, sculptor; b. Torrington, Conn., Oct. 19, 1918; s. Henry Albert and Ida (Vurlod) B.; m. Alice Susanne Ryser, June 11, 1948; children: Florence Susanne, Yvonne Marguerite. Student, Acad. Fine Arts, Florence, Italy, 1947, U. Lausanne, Switzerland, 1947-48, Calif. Coll. Arts and Crafts, Oakland, 1948-50, Prof. Herbert H. Lehman Coll., CUNY, 1968-75; prof., chmn. dept. art Calif. State U. at Fresno, 1975-83; painter, 1948-60; sculptor, 1960—. Mem. adv. bd. Mus. No. Ariz. Art Inst., Flagstaff, 1976-78, Nat. Sculpture Conf., U. Kans., Lawrence, 1971-80 Chosen to execute 2 large sculptures for state office bldg., Albany, N.Y., 1967, sculpture for, new Nassau County Supreme Ct. Bldg., 1968, Lehman High Sch., Bronx, N.Y., 1969, Eastridge Mall, San Jose, Cal., 1970, N.Y. State Office Bldg., Hauppauge, N.Y., 1973, others.; one-man shows including, Bolles Gallery, San Francisco, 1960, Royal Marks Gallery, N.Y.C., 1964, 65, numerous group exhbns., 1960—, including, 66th Arm. Exhbn., Chgo. Art Inst., 1962, Salon de Mai, Paris (France) Mus. Art, 1963, 64, Whitney Mus., 1964, Larry Aldrich Mus., Ridgefield, Conn., 1964, Carnegie Inst. Internat. Exhbn., 1964, Whitney Mus., 1964, 66, Highlights, 1964-65, Larry Aldrich Mus., 1965, Quatrieme Expn. Suisse de Sculpture, Bienne, Switzerland, 1966, Amerikanische Kunst aus Schweizer Besitz, St. Gallen, Switzerland, 1966, Contemporary Am. Painting and Sculpture, U. Ill. at Urbana, 1967; represented permanent collections, Mus. Modern Art, San Francisco Mus. Modern Art, Whitney Mus., Städlische Kunsthalle, Mannheim, W.Ger., Larry Aldrich Mus., Bundy Art Gallery, Waitsfield, Vt., San Francisco Art Inst., Oakland Mus., Los Angeles County Mus., U. Calif. Mus. Art, Berkeley, Chase Manhattan Bank, N.Y.C., also numerous pvt. collections; curator: Forgotten Dimension. Recipient 1st prize, commn. for large mural San Jose (Calif.) State Coll. competition, 1962, 1st prize, purchase award Bundy Art Gallery competition, 1963, Sculpture prize 84th Ann. competition San Francisco Art Inst., 1965 Hon. fellow Royal Acad. Fine Arts (Hague, Netherlands); mem. San Francisco Art Inst., Am. Fedn. Arts. Achievements include being the first to use polyurethane from its fluid form as a medium of art. Address: 6968 Sweetwater Ct Boulder CO 80301-3836 E-mail: bolomey3@attbi.com. *My ultimate goal is to live a fully creative life with the hope that what I do and the way I live will stimulate others to do the same.*

BOLOOKI, HOOSHANG, cardiac surgeon; b. Langeh, Iran, Mar. 28, 1937; came to U.S., 1960, naturalized, 1976; s. Hossein and Fatima (Arjomand) B.; m. C. Joanne McDonald, Aug. 30, 1975; children: Hooshang Michael, Cyrus William, Andrew John. BS cum laude, Alborz Coll., Tehran, 1954; MD, Tehran U., 1960. Intern, resident in surgery Kings County Hosp.; asst. instr. SUNY Med. Center, Bklyn., 1961-67; resident in thoracic and cardiovascular surgery Jackson Meml. Hosp. and U. Miami Sch. Medicine, 1967-69; faculty U. Miami (Fla.) Med. Sch., 1969-77, prof. surgery, 1977—; attending surgeon, dir. adult cardiac surgery Jackson Meml. Hosp., 1969—; dir. cardiopulmonary transplant program U. Miami Jackson Meml. Hosp., 1986-98, Cons. VA Hosp., Miami, 1977-90; mem. adv. panel cardiovascular surgery Ethicon Inc., Davis & Geck Co., Inc., 1974-1995; hon. prof. U. Marón Sch. Medicine, Argentina. Author: Clinical Application of Intra-Aortic Balloon Pump, 1976, 3d edit., 1998, Medical Examination Review, Thoracic Surgery, 2d edit., 1972, 3d edit. Vol. 18, 1981, Cardiovascular Surgery, Vol. 38, 1981; contbr. articles to profl. jours. Recipient Rsch. Career Devel. award NIH, 1972-77, grantee, 1972-75; recipient Grand award U. Tex. Med. Br., 1968, Masterpiece award Transplant Found. South Fla., 1996, Achievement award Iranian-Am. Med. Assn., 1999, award for outstanding svc. 2000, award for contbn. to cardiovasc. surgery Onassis Cardiac Surgery Ctr., 2000, Achievement award Onassis Surg. Found., 2000. Fellow ACS, Royal Coll. Surgeons Can., Am. Coll. Cardiology, Am. Coll. Chest Physicians; mem. AMA (cert. merit), Am. Surg. Assn., Am. Assn. Thoracic Surgery, Soc. Univ. Surgeons, Am. Heart Assn., Fla. Heart Assn. (cert. of merit), Fla. Thoracic Soc., Soc. for Thoracic Surgeons, So. Thoracic Surg. Assn. (membership com. 1985-87, chmn. 1989, v.p. 1991), Soc. Internat. de Chirugie, Internat. Cardiovascular Soc., Soc. Vascular Surgery, Internat. Soc. Heart & Lung Transplantation, Soc. Acad. Surgeons, David Park Racquet Club, Ski Club. Republican. Moslem. Office: U Miami Sch Med Thoracic Cardio Surgery R-114 Miami FL 33101 E-mail: hbolooki@med.miami.edu.

BOLOTOWSKY, ANDREW ILYITCH, flutist, composer; b. NYC, Aug. 20, 1949; s. Ilya Yulevitch and Meta (Cohen) B.; 1 child, Anastasia Elena. Studied with William Kincaid, Phila., 1963-67; studied with Elaine Schaffer, N.Y.C., 1967; studied with Jean-Pierre Rampal, France, 1967; BA, New Sch. Social Rsch., 1971. 1st flute Pan Am. Orch., 1982—; flutist Am. Festival of Microtonal Music, N.Y.C., 1983-99, Downtown Music Ensemble, NYC, 1983—84, 1992—94, 2003, Downtown Music Prodns., 1983-96, 2000—; 1st flute Philharm. Symphony Westchester, 1987-90; baroque flutist Muse, 1987—, Am. Landmark Festival Concerts, 1973—, New Amsterdam Baroque, 1998—, Wood Hill Players, 1999—; founding mem. Brooklyn Baroque, 2000. Performer over 2500 concerts, 1967—; vis. artist Beloit (Wis.) Coll., 1970-73; mime and flute in concert, 1974-84; Delbarton Baroque Ensemble, 1978-81; Criterion Concerts Guggenheim Mus., NYC, 1979; artist N.Y. Com. for Young Audiences, NYC, 1980-87; artist in residence summer mus. theater workshop NYU, 1981; pres. SoHo Baroque Opera Co., NYC, 1983—, Laurel Arts Festival, Jim Thorpe, Pa., 1991-94. Rec. artist (Orion master recording) 6 Serenades by Fernando Carulli, 1978, (Orion master recording) 20th Century Music for Flute and Guitar, 1978, Music for Flute and Mime, 1982, Behavioral Drift by Franz Kamin, 1980, What The Wind Told, 1979, Scribble Music Sampler by Franz Kamin, 1983, Poetry Music Quilts by Beth Anderson, 1982, Mark Steven Brooks: Compositions 1973-87, 1987; recs. include Pitch, Vol. I No. 3, 1988-89, Indian Summer by Tui St. George Tucker, Opus 1 records No. 107, Timepieces by Rita Falbel, 1991, Between the Keys, Newport Classic CD, 1992, Open Secrets (by Jackson Maclow), 1993 XICD, The Music of Frank Wigglesworth, CRI CD 733, Raj Kapoor's CD Kathmandu Embrace, 1997, Crayon (Jackson Maclow issue), 1997, Melody Sumner Carnahan The Time IS Now, Frog Peak Music CD, 1998, Johnny Reinhard's Raven, Stereo Soc. CD, 1999, Judith St. Croix's Vision of Light and Mystery, Sonic Muse CD, 1999, (4tayCD) Elodie Lauten's The Deus Ex Machina Cycle, 1999, Lenore Von Stein's I Haven't Been Able to Lie and Tell the Truth (CD), 2002, Daniel Goode's Eight Thrushes in New York Frole Peak Music CD, 2003, others; editor Flute Charts for "Pitch", vol. I number 4, 1990; performances on radio and tv including Stas. WBAI, WQXR, WNYC New Sounds, WKCR, WFUV, NBC, CBS, NYC-TV; extra (films) Eyewitness, 1980, Godfather III, 1990. Grantee Carnegie Recital Hall, Tully Hall Criterion Found., 1976-79, Meet the Composer, 1978, 80. Avocations: study of earlier flute systems, walking tours, Russian literature. Office: PO Box 492 New York NY 10276

BOLSTER, ARCHIE MILBURN, retired foreign service officer; b. Ames, Iowa, Apr. 9, 1933; s. Horace Goodwin and Ella Schimpf B.; m. Ann Dorcas Matthews, Mar. 22, 1959; children: Christopher, Matthew, Amy. BA in Internat. Relations, U. Va., 1955; MA in Pub. Policy and Adminstrn., U. Wis., 1972. Commd. fgn. service officer Dept. State, 1958; assigned Phnom Penh, Cambodia, 1959-60, Tabriz, Iran, 1961-63, Tehran, Iran, 1964-66, 74-76, Bur. Intelligence and Research, 1966-68, Office Fuels and Energy, 1969-71; consul gen. Antwerp, Belgium, 1978-81; dep. dir. Div. Office Security Assistance and Sales, 1981-83; dep. chief Aviation Negotiations Div., 1983-84; spl. projects officer Bur. Refugee Programs, 1984-86. Freedom of Info. Act reviewer, 1984-94, 97—; mem. White House Counsel's Iran-Contra Task Force, 1987-90; mem. staff U.S.-Iran Claims Tribunal, The Hague, Netherlands, 1994-96. Chmn. editl. bd. Fgn. Svc. Jour., 1971. Pres. Williamsburg Civic Assn., Arlington, Va., 1969-70. Served with USNR, 1955-58. Mem. Am. Fgn. Svc. Assn., Assn. Part-Time Profls. (bd. dirs., v.p. 1989-91). Home: 2738 N Lexington St Arlington VA 22207-1437

BOLSTER, ARTHUR STANLEY, JR., history educator; b. Bismarck, N.D., Jan. 30, 1922; s. Arthur S. and Gertrude (Pierce) B.; m. Elizabeth Barker Winkfield, Oct. 8, 1949; children: Stephen Clark, Gregory Pierce. AB, Dartmouth, 1943, MA, Harvard, 1947, PhD, 1954. Tchr. history Grosse Pointe (Mich.) High Sch., 1952-57, Pelham (N.Y.) High Sch., 1957-59; mem. faculty Harvard U., Cambridge, Mass., 1959—, prof. edn., 1967-82, prof. emeritus, 1982—. Author: James Freeman Clarke, Disciple to Advancing Truth, 1954. Served to lt. USNR, 1943-46. Mem. New Eng. History Tchrs. Assn. (pres. 1968-69, Kidger award 1970), Phi Beta Kappa. Mem. United Ch. of Christ (deacon). Home: 587 Laconia Cir Lake Worth FL 33467-2662 Office: Harvard U Grad Sch Edn Longfellow Hall Cambridge MA 02138

BOLSTER, JACQUELINE NEBEN (MRS. JOHN A. BOLSTER), communications consultant; b. Woodhaven, N.Y.; d. Ernest William Benedict and Emily Claire (Guck) Neben; student Pratt Inst., Columbia U.; m. John A. Bolster, May 8, 1954. Promotion mgr. Photoplay mag., 1949-53; merchandising mgr. McCall's, N.Y.C., 1953-64; dir. promotion and merchandising Harper's Bazaar, N.Y.C., 1964-71; dir. advt. and promotion Elizabeth Arden Salons, N.Y.C., 1971-76; dir. creative services Elizabeth Arden, Inc., 1976-78, dir. communications Elizabeth Arden Salons, 1978-87, communication cons., 1987—. Recipient Art Director's award 1961, 66. Mem. Fashion Group, Fashion Execs. Roundtable, Advt. Women N.Y. (life), Women's Nat. Rep. Club (life). Episcopalian. Home and Office: 8531 88th St Woodhaven NY 11421-1308 also: Halsey Neck Ln Southampton NY 11968

BOLSTER, WILLIAM LAWRENCE, broadcast executive; b. Waterloo, Iowa, Nov. 28, 1943; s. William and Mildred Bolster; m. Eileen Bolster; children: Bilil, Brian, Barry; m. Eileen Madigan. BA, Loras Coll. On-air announcer, salesman KDTH, Dubuque, Iowa, 1965; with Am. Blackhawk Broadcasting Co., Waterloo, 1967—73, v.p., 1973—83; v.p., gen. mgr. Sta. KWWL-TV div. Am. Blackhawk Broadcasting Co., Waterloo, 1977—83, Sta. KSDK-TV, St. Louis, 1983—89; former pres. Multimedia Broadcasting Co.; pres., CEO, chmn. CNBC, Fort Lee, NJ, 2001—; pres. NBC4-TV, N.Y.C., 1991—96. Pres. NBC Latin Am. Bd. regents Briar Cliff Coll.; trustee St. Louis U., NBC-TV Affiliate; bd. dirs. Regional Plan Assn.; mem. adv. bd. TV Bur.; mem. TV Operators Caucus Bd. Named Man of Yr., Variety Club, 1983, King of TV Fin. News, N.Y. Times, One of 30 Most Powerful People in Investing, Smart Money mag., 2000, Cable Broadcasting Exec. of Yr., Delaney Report newsletter, 2000, One of Most Influential People, Fin. Svc. Ticker mag.s Power 50 List; recipient 1st Media award for outstanding coverage and fin. assistance to black cmty., NAACP, St. Louis, Ellis Island Gold medal of achievement. Mem.: NATAS (pres., bd. dirs. St. Louis chpt. 1987), Nat. Assn. Broadcasters (children's TV com.), Waterloo C. of C. (bd. dirs.). Office: 2200 Fletcher Ave Fort Lee NJ 07024-5005

BOLSTERLI, MARGARET JONES, English educator, farmer; b. Watson, Ark., May 10, 1931; d. Grover Clevel and Zena (Cason) Jones; m. Mark Bolsterli, Dec. 30, 1953 (div. Dec. 1964); children: Eric, David. BA with honors, U. Ark., 1952; MA, Washington U., St. Louis, 1953; PhD, U. Minn., 1967. Asst. prof. Augsburg Coll., Mpls., 1967-68; prof. English, U. Ark., Fayetteville, 1968-93, prof. emeritus, 1993—, dir. Ctr. for Ark. and Regional Studies, 1984-87. Fulbright lectr., Portugal, 1986; vis. rsch. fellow Yale U., 1997-98; bd. dirs. Ark. Humanities Coun., 1992-94. Author: The Early Community at Bedford Park, 1977, Vinegar Pie and Chicken Bread, 1982, Born in the Delta, 1991, A Remembrance of Eden, 1993; contbr. articles and stories to Jour. Modern Lit., So. Quar., others. NEH Younger Humanist grantee, 1970-71; Ark. Endowment for Humanities grantee, 1980, 81 Mem. MLA (pres. women's caucus), South Cen. MLA. Democrat. E-mail: mbolster@alltel.net

BOLSTRIDGE, ALICE M. writer, educator; b. Portage Lake, Maine, May 7, 1938; d. Albert Stanley Bolstridge and Mildred (Hathaway) Fullerton; m. Charles S. Mountain, Dec. 6, 1955 (div. Mar. 1971); children: Alan Roy, David Charles, Shelly Ann. BS in Edn., U. Maine, Presque Isle, 1970; MA in English, U. Maine, Orono, 1982; PhD in English Lit., Okla. State U., 1987. Tchr. grade 3 Sch. Adminstrv. Dist. # 32, Ashland, Maine, 1970-71; tchr. grades 3, 4 Millinocket (Maine) Sch. Dept., 1971-80; teaching asst. English U. Maine, Orono, 1980-82; teaching assoc. English Okla. State U., Stillwater, 1983-87; instr. English U. Cin., 1987-94; tchr. English Maine Sch. Sci. & Math, Limestone, 1995-2000; ret. Asst. dir. composition Okla. State U., Stillwater, 1985-86. Poetry editor Midland Rev., 1986; consulting editor To Make A Poem, 1993-94; contbr. poetry, essays and short stories to various publs. Host spl. events com. U. Cin., 1987-92, The Workshop, Cin., 1989-93; active Holy Fools, Cin., 1990-93; vol. Long Branch Teaching Farm, Cin., 1992. Clinton D. Keeler fellow Okla. State U., 1985; Taft Meml. grantee U. Cin., 1988, 91, 93; recipient Passager Poet award, 1995. Mem. Maine Alliance Pubs. and Writers, Alliance for the Mentally Ill (Maine), Phi Kappa Phi. Avocations: cross country skiing, swimming, camping, nature observing.

BOLT, BRUCE ALAN, seismologist; b. Largs, Australia, Feb. 15, 1930; came to U.S., 1963; naturalized, 1972; s. Donald Frederick and Arlene (Stitt) B.; m. Beverley Bentley, Feb. 11, 1956; children: Gillian, Robert, Helen, Margaret. BS with honors, New Eng. U. Coll., 1952; MS, U. Sydney, Australia, 1954, PhD, 1959, DSc (hon.), 1972. Math. master Sydney (Australia) Boys' High Sch., 1953; lectr. U. Sydney, 1954-61, sr. lectr., 1961-62; research seismologist Columbia U., 1960; dir. seismographic stas. U. Calif., Berkeley, 1963-89, prof. seismology, 1963-93, prof. emeritus, 1993—, chmn. acad. senate Berkeley divsn., 1993-94. Mem. com. on seismology NAS, 1966-72, chmn. nat. earthquake obs. com., 1979-81; earthquake and wind forces com. VA, 1971-75; mem. Calif. Seismic Safety Commn., 1978-93, chmn., 1984-86; earthquake studies adv. panel U.S. Geol. Survey, 1979-83, U.S. Geodynamics Com., Am. Geophys. Union, 1979-84; seismic adv. bd. Calif. Dept. Transp., 1994—; pres. Consortium Strong Motion Sys. Inc., 1999-2002. Author, editor textbooks on applied math., earthquakes, geol. hazards and detection of underground nuclear explosions. Recipient H.O. Wood award in seismology, 1967-72, Alquist Silver medal Calif. Earthquake Safety Found., 1995, Housner medal Earthquake Engrng. Rsch. Inst., 2000; Fulbright scholar, 1960; Churchill Coll. Cambridge overseas fellow, 1980, 91. Fellow Am. Geophys. Union (mem. geophys. monograph bd. 1971-78, chmn. 1976-78), Geol. Soc. Am., Calif. Acad. Scis. (trustee 1981-92, 1998—, pres. 1982-85, Fellows medal 1989), Royal Astron. Soc. (Jeffreys lectr. 1991, assoc.); mem. Nat. Acad. Engrng. (IDNDR com. 1992-94), Seismol. Soc. Am. (editor bull. 1965-70, bd. dir. 1965-71, 73-76, pres. 1974-75), Internat. Assn. Seismology and Physics Earth's Interior (exec. com. 1964-67, v.p. 1975-79, pres. 1980-83), Earthquake Engrng. Rsch. Inst. (Dist. Lectr. 1998), Calif. Univs. Rsch. Earthquake Engrng. (sec. 1988-91), Australian Math. Soc., Chit Chat Club, Bohemian Club, U. Calif. Berkeley Faculty Club (pres. 1996—). Achievements include research on dynamics, elastic waves, earthquakes, statistics geophys. observations; inferences on structure of earth's interior; cons. on seismic hazards. Home: 1491 Greenwood Ter Berkeley CA 94708-1935 E-mail: boltuc@socrates.berkeley.edu.

BOLT, DAWN MARIA, financial coach; b. Bklyn., June 12, 1949; d. Gulick Arthur B. and Georgette Helen (Werner) Bolt-Wiggs; widowed; children: Robert B. Williams, Wesley A. Williams. BA, Bklyn. Coll., 1971. Cert. fin. planner; chartered fin. analyst. Fin. analyst Blyth Eastman Dillon, N.Y.C., 1971-77; rating agy. analyst Fitch Investors Svc., N.Y.C., 1977-78; bank analyst Merrill Lynch, N.Y.C., 1978-80; fin. analyst Moodys Investors Svc., N.Y.C., 1980-86; real estate sales agt. J.R. Silvers Realty, N.Y.C., 1987-95, Coldwell Banker Hunt Kennedy, N.Y.C., 1995-98; pvt. practice fin. planning and coaching, 1998—. Avocations: bowling, tennis, skiing, reading, coaching. E-mail: jodiedawn49@hotmail.com.

BOLT, EUNICE MILDRED DEVRIES, artist; b. Clifton, N.J., Oct. 31, 1926; d. Lambert H. and Cora DeVries; m. Maurice L. Bolt (dec. Nov. 1989); children: Macyn Bolt, Tamsen Bolt, Valerie Bolt Wegner. Grad., Pratt Inst. Art & Design, Bklyn., 1949; BA, Calvin Coll., 1952; MA, Western Mich. U., 1973. Book illustrator Fideler Pubs., Grand Rapids, Mich., 1952-53, Zondervan Pub. Co., Grand Rapids, Mich., 1953-56; prof. Calvin Coll., Grand Rapids, Mich., 1962-67, Grand Rapids C.C., 1968-91; represented by Corporate Portfolios and Bergsma Gallery, Grand Rapids, Pineland Sta. Gallery, Hilton Head, S.C., Synchronicity Gallery, Glen Arbor, Mich. Internat. art study tours coord. and guide, 1978—; fine art exhbn. juror, 1987—; lectr. art history, 1991—, presenter watercolor workshops, 1991—; artist-in-residence, 1995—. Exhibited in group shows at Grand Rapids Art Mus., Kalamazoo Inst. Art, U. Mich. Schlusser Gallery, Pitts. Ctr. for the Arts, Westmoreland Mus. Art, Detroit Inst. Art. Home and Studio: 2481 Autumn Ash Dr Grand Rapids MI 49512 Studio: 110 Arango Ct Bluffton SC 29910-4580 E-mail: eunbolstudio@aol.com

BOLT, NANCY MARIE, library director; Dep. state libr., asst. commr. Colo. Dept Edn., Colo. State Libr., 1987—. Office: 201 E Colfax Ave Denver CO 80203

BOLT, THOMAS ALVIN WALDREP, lawyer; b. Anderson, S.C., Dec. 1, 1956; s. Thomas Alvin Waldrep Jr. and Jane Gray Sullivan; m. Jenifer Smith, Sept. 2, 1989; 1 stepchild, Royce Stevenson Ward. BA in Govt. and English, Wofford Coll., 1978; postgrad., U. S.C., 1980-81, JD, 1982. Bar: V.I., 1983. Asst. to Gov. Exec. Office of Gov., Columbia, S.C., 1979; exec. asst. S.C. Senate, Columbia, 1979-80; legal clk. S.C. Pub. Svc. Commn., Columbia, 1981; legis. asst. S.C. Ho. of Reps., Columbia, 1981-82; asst. to atty. gen. Office of Atty. Gen., Columbia, 1982; legis. counsel Legis. of V.I., St. Thomas, V.I., 1983-87, counsel to pres., 1987, counsel to the majority, 1987-88; exec. dir., counsel to the commn. V.I. Law Revision Commn., St. Thomas, 1988-91; pvt. practice Tom Bolt & Assocs. P.C., St. Thomas, V.I., 1991—. Intern UN, N.Y.C., 1976; commr. Nat. Conf. Commrs. on Uniform State Laws, Chgo., 1988—, chmn. drafting com. on Uniform Money Svcs. Act, 1996—; prof. law U. V.I., St. Thomas; tchr. history All Saints Cathedral Sch., 1983; mem. bd. advisors V.I. Bus. Jour., 1994-98; mem. V.I. Law Revision Commn., 2001—. Editor: Revised United States Virgin Islands Criminal Code, 1988-91. Mem. Friends of Denmark LWV, St. Thomas Arts Coun., V.I. Youth Multi-Svc. Ctr.; treas. Coun. on Alcoholism, St. Thomas-St. John, 1992—93; sec. St. Thomas Hist. Trust, 1987—88; pres. Blackbeard's Hill Neighborhood Assn., 1988—95; state committeeman S.C. Dem. Com., Columbia, 1980—83, vice chmn., 1980—82; territorial committeeman V.I. Dem. Com., St. Thomas, 1988—92; bd. dirs. Friends of Baa Pub. Libr., 1994—2001, pres., 1995—2002. Frank Hoke Leadership scholar Delta Sigma Phi, 1976, Am. Legion scholar, 1978-82. Mem.: ABA (ho. of dels. 1989—, membership com. 1989—, vice chmn. state adminstrv. law com. 1990—, sect. on internat. law and practice Caribbean law com. 1990—, drafting com. 1992—96, ho. com. state and local bar assns. 1996—98, select com. 1998—2000, Am. Law Inst.-ABA com. on continuing profl. edn. 1999—, sect. on gen. practice, solo and small firm, real estate interest group sect. on law practice mgmt., sect. on state and local govt., young lawyers divsn., exec. subcom., govt. lawyers com., vice chmn. cmty. law week com.,

govt. ops. com., sect. gen. practice, sect. on adminstrv. law and regulatory practice, chmn. liaison com. 2003—), Am. Law Inst., V.I. Bar Assn. (chmn. com. legis. and law reform 1987—93, bd. govs. 1988, 1990—, pres. 2002—03, Pres.'s award 2000), Am. Law Network (bd. dirs. 1992—95, 1999—), Attys. Liability Protection Soc. (bd. dirs. 1995—), Am. Law Inst.-ABA In-House, St. Thomas-St. John C. of C., Rotary (bd. dirs. St. Thomas II chpt. 1987—89, 1990—92, sgt. arms 1991—92, clk. consistory bd. dirs. 1991—93, bd. dirs. St. Thomas II chpt. 1998—, sgt. arms 1999—2000, pres. 2002—03). Mem. Reformed Ch. Am. Avocations: travel, sailing, hist. preservation. Home: Morning Star Beach St Thomas VI 00802 Office: Corporate Pl Royal Dane Mall Charlotte Amalie VI 00802-6410 E-mail: tbolt@vilaw.com.

BOLTEN, JOSHUA BREWSTER, federal official; b. Aug. 16, 1954; BA with distinction, Princeton Univ. Woodrow Wilsonn Sch. of Pub. and Internat. Affairs, 1976; JD, Stanford Law Sch., 1980. Editor Stanford Law Review, 1980; law clk. US Dist. Ct., San Francisco, 1980—93; pvt. practice Bolten, O'Melveny & Myers, 1980—85; Internat. Trade Counsel US Senate Fin. Com., 1985—89; Gen. Coun. US Trade Rep., 1989—92; Dep. Asst. to the Pres. for Legis. affairs White House, Washington, 1992—93; tchr., internat. trade Yale Law Sch., 1993; exec. dir., legal and govt. affairs Goldman Sachs Internat., London, 1994—99; Policy dir. Bush-Cheny pres. campaign, 1999—2000; asst. to pres. and Dep. Chief of Staff for policy Bush Adminstrn., Washington, 2001—03; dir. Office of Mgmt. and Budget, Washington, 2003—. Office: Executive Office of the Pres Office of Mgmt and Budget 725 17th St NW Washington DC 20503 Office Fax: 202-395-3888.*

BOLTON, CALVIN, music educator; s. Donald and Modenia Bolton; m. Ann Peeling; children: Daniel, David. D of Musical Arts, U. N.C. at Greensboro, 1991; MA, MusM, Ohio State U., 1984; BA, Limestone Coll., 1988. Cert. Instrumental Music K-12. Assoc. prof. music North Greenville Coll., Tigerville, SC, 1999—; dir. band Dist. 7 Schs., Spartanburg, SC, 1993—99; vis. asst. prof. U. Mont., Missoula, Mont., 1991—92; grad. tchg. assoc. U. N.C., Greensboro, 1988—91; dir. bands Rutherford County Schs., Forest City, NC, 1984—88; grad. tchg. assoc. Ohio State U., Columbus, 1981—84; music assoc., orch. dir. First Bapt. N Spartanburg, Spartanburg, SC, 1999—2003. Interim dir. orch. First Bapt. North, Spartanburg, SC, 2002; timpanist Charlotte Philharm. Orch., Charlotte, NC. Author: The Ludwig Drummer Vol. 1, 1999 (Who's Who Among America's Teachers, 2002), The Ludwig Drummer,Vol.2, 2002. Mem.: Music Educators Nat. Conf., Nat. Assn. Coll. Wind and Percussion Instrs., Percussive Arts Soc. Baptist. Avocation: fishing. Home: 117 Harvest Ln Boiling Springs SC 29316 Office: First Bapt North Spartanburg 8740 Asheville Hwy Spartanburg SC 29316-4999

BOLTON, CLAUDE M., JR., federal agency administrator, retired military officer; BEE, U. Nebr., 1969; MA in Mgmt., Troy State U., 1978; MA in Nat. Security and Strategic Study, Naval War Coll., 1991. Commd. 2d. lt. USAF, 1969, advanced through grades to major gen., 1998; pilot McConnell AFB, Ariz., 1971, Ubon Royal Thai AFB, Thailand, 1971-72; various assignments Cannon AFB, N. Mex., 1972-74; pilot, instr. Royal Air Force, Upper Heyford, England, 1974-76; test pilot Eglin AFB, Fla., 1978-82; various assignments Wright-Patterson AFB, Ohio, 1982-85, 88-93, 1996-98, The Pentagon, Washington, 1986-88, 96, program exec. officer fighter and bomber programs, 1998—2000; commandant Defense Sys. Mgmt. Coll., Fort Belvoir, Va., 1993-96; asst. secy. and army acquisitions exec. for acquisition, logistics and tech. U.S. Dept. Defense, Washington, 2001—. Decorated Defense D.S.M., DFC with oak leaf cluster, Legion of Merit, Meritorious Svc. medal with two oak leaf clusters, Air medal with 16 oak leaf clusters, Vietnam Svc. medal with three svc. stars, Rep. Vietnam Gallantry Cross. Office: US Dept Defense Acquisition Logistics and Tech 103 Army Pentagon Washington DC 20310-0103 Office Fax: 703-697-4003.

BOLTON, DAVID, lawyer, educator; b. N.Y.C., Nov. 12, 1912; s. Samuel Bolton, Annie (Danziger) Bolton; m. Ruth Davega (div.); children: Mickey, David Becker, Bert Gunn; m. Roxcy O'Neal; children: Bonnie, David, Baron. BS, Columbia U., 1933, LLB, 1936. Bar: N.Y., S.C., Tex., Fla., U.S. Supreme Ct. Counsel Com. on Interstate Commerce U.S. Senate, Washington, 1936—38; counsel Bd. Econ. Def., Washington, 1941—42, USN, 1942—64; spl. asst. atty. gen. State of Fla., Tallahassee, 1965—66; dir. legal clinic So. Meth. U., Dallas, 1966—. Chief prosecutor WWII USN War Crimes, 1947—49; vis. prof. law So. Meth U., Dallas, U. Miami, Fla. Author: Manuel for Legal Clinics, 1967, Manuel for Criminal trial Advocacy, 1967, Commentary on Handling Divorce, 1967. Spl. rep. Amb. to Japan, 1960—63. Comdr. USN, 1942—64. Recipient Letter of Commendation, USN, 1964, Outstanding Social Work award, Japanese Govt., 1963; grantee Dallas Legal Svcs. Project, Fed. Govt., 1966. Mem.: ABA, Am. Trial Lawyers Assn., Delta Theta Phi (life). Democrat. Jewish. Achievements include Inaugerated Seagoville Project by Fed. Bur. Prisons. Avocation: writing. Home: 124 Cadima Ave Coral Gables FL 33134

BOLTON, JOHN ROBERT, lawyer, government official; b. Balt., Nov. 20, 1948; s. Edward Jackson and Virginia (Godfrey) B.; m. Gretchen Brainerd, Jan. 1986; 1 child, Jennifer Sarah. BA summa cum laude, Yale U., 1970, JD, 1974. Bar: D.C. 1975, U.S. Dist. Ct. D.C. 1975, U.S. Ct. Appeals (D.C. cir.) 1975, U.S. Ct. Appeals (4th cir.) 1977, U.S. Ct. Appeals (3d cir.) 1978, U.S. Supreme Ct. 1978, U.S. Ct. Appeals (5th and 11th cirs.) 1981, U.S. Ct. Appeals (10th cir.) 1983, U.S. Ct. Appeals (1st, 6th, 7th, 8th and 9th cirs.) 1988, U.S. Ct. Appeals (2d cir.) 1989. Assoc. Covington & Burling, Washington, 1974-81, ptnr., 1983-85; legal cons. The White House, Washington, 1981; gen. counsel Agy. for Internat. Devel., Washington, 1981-82, asst. adminstr., 1982-83; exec. dir. com. on resolutions Rep. Nat. Com., Washington, 1983-84; asst. atty. gen. legis. affairs U.S. Dept. Justice, Washington, 1985-88, asst. atty. gen. civil div., 1988-89; asst. sec. internat. orgn. affairs bur. U.S. Dept. State, Washington, 1989-93; ptnr. Lerner, Reed, Bolton & McManus (and predecessor firms), Washington, 1993-99; of counsel Kutak Rock, 1999-2001; under sec. state for arms control and internat. security U.S. Dept. State, Washington, 2001—. Adj. prof. George Mason U. Law Sch., 1994-2001; pres. Nat. Policy Forum, Washington, 1995-96; sr. v.p. Am. Enterprise Inst., Washington, 1997-2001. Contbr. articles to profl. jours. Mem. Phi Beta Kappa, Pi Sigma Alpha. Republican. Lutheran. Office: US Dept State 21st & C Sts NW Washington DC 20520 E-mail: boltonjr@state.gov.

BOLTON, JULIA GOODEN, human services administrator; b. Wilmington, Del., Nov. 11, 1940; d. Merrill Harvey and Mary Rose (Amoroso) Gooden; m. Roger Edwin Bolton, June 27, 1964; children: Christopher Andrew, Jonathan Hughes. RN with honors, Johns Hopkins Hosp., Balt., 1961; BSN with honors, Case Western Res. U., Cleve., 1964; postgrad., Boston U., 1964-65; MS with honors, Russell Sage Coll., 1986. Lic. nurse, Vt. Staff nurse oper. rm., clin. instr. Johns Hopkins Hosp., Balt., 1961-62; instr. practical nursing, acting coord. med. programs Charles H. McCann Vocat. Sch., North Adams, Mass., 1966, clin. instr. manpower devel. tng. act program, 1968, clin. instr. med., surg. and pediatric nursing, 1972-73; staff orientation and tour program children North Adams Regional Hosp., 1973-74, clin. cons. patient care stds. project, 1985-86; health edn. cons. Williamstown (Mass.) Pub. Schs., 1978-81, Pine Cobble Sch., 1978-81; dir. staff edn. and quality assurance Southwestern Vt. Med. Ctr., Bennington, 1986-87, asst. v.p. nursing, 1988, v.p. nursing, 1988-92, interim pres., 1991, sr. v.p., 1992-99; v.p. ops., clin. svcs. Southwestern Vt. Sys., 1999—2001; co-founder, cons. Highpointe Bus. Solution, Inc., Troy, NY, 2001—. Dir. Vt. Ethics Network, 1995—98; mem. nurse exec. del. to Cuba, 2001. Mem. Williamstown Betterment Study Com., 1985; mem. adv. com. to plan declining enrollment Mt. Greylock Reg. HS, 1985; dir. Vt. divsn. Bennington County unit Am. Cancer Soc., 1986—88, United Way Bennington County, 1995—97; mem. profl. adv. com. Bennington Home Health Agy., 1988; bd. dirs., exec. com. Vt. Nursing Initiative Implementation Grant, Pew Charitable Trust Grant, 1992; active many other civic and charitable orgns.; alt. del. Diocesan Conv. No. Berkshire Deanery, Episc. Ch., 1987; vestry St. John's Episc. Ch., Williamstown, 1992; mem. adv. com. Putnam Meml. Sch. Practical Nursing, 1989—94. Mem.: New Eng. Healthcare Assembly (evaluation com.), Vt. Orgn. Nurse Leaders (pres. 1995), Nat. Forum Women Health Care Leaders, Am. Orgn. Nurse Execs., Am. Coll. Healthcare Execs., Sigma Theta Tau. E-mail: julia.bolton@highpointesolutions.com.

BOLTON, KENNETH ALBERT, management consultant; b. Mar. 6, 1941; s. Albert and Myrtle (Nelting) B.; m. Maryanne Lavelle; 1 child, Katharine. BS in Indsl. Engring., Pa. State U., 1978. Registered profl. engr., Calif. With GE, Allentown, Pa., 1961-63, system mgr. Phila., 1963-72; mgr. MCS Mgmt. Internat., Washington, 1972-80, Coopers & Lybrand, Phila., 1980-82; dir. cons. Worden & Risberg, Phila., 1982-83; v.p. mktg. Laminated, Inc., Hatfield, Pa., 1983-86; pres. Mgmt. Internat., Phila., 1986-90, Wm. P. Bolton, Inc., Phila., 1990—. Contbr. articles to profl. jours. Advisor Jr. Achievement, Media, Pa., 1970; mem. adv. bd. Salvation Army. Mem. NSPE, Am. Arbitration Assn. (panel of arbitrators), Phila. C. of C. (bd. dirs. 1975, lobbyist small bus. coun. 1978), Union League Phila., St. George's Club Bermuda. Republican. Avocations: golf, computers, antiques. Home: 5900 Atlantic Ave Ventnor City NJ 08406-2862 Office: Mgmt Internat 100 S Dorset Ave Ventnor City NJ 08406-2834

BOLTON, LAURA LEE, health/medical products executive; b. Royal Oak, Mich., Oct. 13, 1944; d. Thomas Ralph and Leona Gertrude (Somes) Specht; m. Russell Bolton, Feb. 21, 1968; children: Kenneth, Diane, William. BA in Psychology, U. Ill., 1966; MS, Stanford U., 1968; PhD in Psychobiology, Rutgers U., 1975. Rsch. asst. Child Welfare League Am., N.Y.C., 1969-70; asst. scientist Johnson & Johnson, New Brunswick, N.J., 1973-74, scientist, 1974-76, sr. scientist, 1976-82, prin. scientist, 1982-87; mgr. wound care R&D ConvaTec-Bristol-Myers Squibb, Skillman, NJ, 1987-91; dir. scientific affairs R&D ConvaTec-Bristol-Myers Squibb, Skillman, N.J., 1992—. Instr. Rutgers U., New Brunswick, 1972-73; adj. asst. prof. dept. surgery U. Med. Dentistry, New Brunswick, 1981-88, adj. assoc. prof., 1988-2000; mem. Nat. Pressure Ulcer Adv. Corp. Coun., 1994-2004; bd. dirs. Assn. Advances Would Care. Mem. editl. review bd. Advances in Wound Care, Wounds. Contbr. chpts. to books, 1981—; contbr. articles to profl. jours., 1967—; patentee in field, 1986, 88, 89. Fulbright Found. scholar, 1966; Woodrow Wilson fellow (declined), 1966; recipient Sharan Boranoski Founders award Clin. Symposium Advances Wound and Skin Care, 2001. Mem. Am. Acad. Dermatology, Am. Diabetes Assn., Wound Healing Soc., Sigma Xi (chpt. pres. 1985-86). Avocations: camping, skiing, hiking, guitar. Home: 15 Franklin Pl Metuchen NJ 08840-2307 Office: ConvaTec-Bristol-Myers Squibb 200 Headquarters Park Dr Skillman NJ 08558-2624

BOLTON, MARIE, elementary school educator, minister; b. July 26; d. Clarence Thompson and Katherine Washington; m. Lonnie D. Hughes (div.); children: Lakecia D. Hughes, Joquella M. Hughes; m. William Bolton (div.); 1 child, Kimberlyn C. Culinary arts, Gary, Ind., 1980—; wedding coord., 1995—; presch. tchr. King's Kids Daycare, Gary, 1998—. Min. Old Path Cogic Ch., Gary, 1999—, v.p. nurses guild, v.p. Genesis com. Avocation: crafts.

BOLTON, ROBERT HARVEY, banker; b. Alexandria, La., June 19, 1908; s. James Wade and Mary (Calderwood) B.; m. Elsie Elizabeth McLundie (dec. Mar. 1987); children: Robert Harvey Jr., Elizabeth McLundie (Mrs. Robert Conery Hassinger), Mary Calderwood (Mrs. James Kelly Jennings Jr.); m. Abigail Crow Goodwin. BS, U. Pa., 1930. With credit dept. Guaranty Trust Co., N.Y.C., 1930-32; asst. cashier Rapides Bank & Trust Co., Alexandria, 1932-36, cashier, 1936-43, v.p., 1943-47, exec. v.p., 1947-56, pres., 1956-86, chmn., 1986-90, sr. chmn., 1990—, also bd. dirs. Bd. dirs. New Orleans br. Fed. Res. Bank Atlanta., 1979-81, First Commerce Corp., New Orleans; nat. bd. dirs. Robert Morris Assocs., 1943-45; La. rep. to Conf. State Bank Suprs., 1964-71. Mem. La. State U. Found., Pineville, devel. bd., Pres.'s club, bd. dirs. James C. Bolton Libr., Alexandria; fin. steering com. Attakapas coun. Boy Scouts Am., 1971-84; chmn. Rapides Parish chpt. ARC, 1943, Alexandria Little Theatre, 1942; hon. chmn. La. Coll. Quality Edge Dr. '95; bd. dirs. Rapides United Givers, Indsl. Devel. Bd. Ctrl. La.; mem. exec. com. Ctrl. Cities Devel. Com., Coun. for Better La., 1970—, Bus. and Indsl. Devel. Corp. La., 1971-73; mem. La. Bapt. Conv. Fedn. Bd., 1994-95; deacon Emmanuel Bapt. Ch., chmn. fin. com., chmn. Every Mem. Canvass, 1937-74; mem. citizen's adv. com. La. Spl. Edn. Ctr., La. Pub. Broadcasting; chmn., mem. St. Francis Cabrini Hosp. Found. Bd.; mem. Pub. Affairs Rsch. Coun. Recipient Disting. Svc. award Jr. C. of C., 1943, Humanitarian of Yr. award Arthritis Found., 1990, Disting. Svc. award La. N.G., Disting. Citizen award Boy Scouts Am., 1991, Outstanding Citizen award YWCA, 1992, Disting. Svc. award Trustees La. Coll., 1993, Rapides Arts and Humanities Cultural Advocate award, 1994. Mem. VFW, Am. Bankers Assn. (pres. state bank divsn. 1955), Mortgage Bankers Assn. (mem. Washington com. 1962-74), La. Bankers Assn. (pres. 1980, mem. legis. study com. 1950—, fed. affairs com. 1971—, Lifetime Achievement award 2000). Home: 3200 Parkway Dr Alexandria LA 71301-4757 Office: Rapides Bank & Trust Co 400 Murray St PO Box 31 Alexandria LA 71309-0031

BOLTON, ROBIN JEAN, artist, painter; b. Americus, Ga., Sept. 13, 1943; d. Charles Robert and Sara Maude (Sumerford) Ricketson; m. Robert Emory Bolton III, Aug. 20, 1966; 1 child, Robin Jean. BFA, U. Ga., 1965. Graphic artist Shea/Rustin Pub., Atlanta, 1966-67, Davison's Dept. Store, Atlanta, 1967, Stein Printing Co., Atlanta, 1968, Naylor Assocs., East Point, Ga., 1968, Tucker Wayne & Co., Atlanta, 1968-70, Graphique Ltd., Chgo., 1970-72, Nan Miller Gallery, Rochester, N.Y., 1985—. Instr. Comml. Art Supply, Syracuse, N.Y., pvt. studio Bridgport, N.Y., Liverpool, N.Y.; label designer Persimmon Creek Vineyards, Ga. One-woman shows include The Frog & Peach Gallery, Clayton, Ga., 1997-2000, 2002, Nan Miller Gallery Rochester, N.Y., 2002, Gallery One, San Francisco; exhibited in group shows at Everson Mus. Art, Syracuse, 1976, The Jacob K. Javits Fed. Bldg., N.Y.C., 1986, Islip (N.Y.) Art Mus., 1989, Kirkpatrick Art Ctr., Oklahoma City, 1989, Nat. Assn. Women Artists Centennial Exhbn., 1989, Wyoming Sem. Juried Regional Exhibit, Kingston, Pa., 1996; permanent collections include the IBM Collection, State of Ga., State Capitol of Ga., Ga. Commn. on Women/Dept. of Labor Bldg. Atlanta, Talullah Falls Sch., Federated Hall, Talullah Falls, Ga.. Recipient Cooperstown Nat. 1st prize Cooperstown (N.Y.) Art Assn., 1975, Henry Mallory Meml. award, 1978, Arena '76 1st prize, Binghamton, N.Y., 1976, Grand prize Best of Show, Liverpool State Open, 1976, Liquitex-Binney & Smith award for outstanding achievement in field of art, Moravia Coll., Bethlehem, Pa., 1996; named Hon. Youth Art Month Artist, State of Ga., 2001. Mem. Nat. Assn. Women Artists, Liverpool Arts and Crafts Guild, DAR, UDC. Methodist. Avocations: golf, gardening, reading. Home: 4720 Sharron Point Ct Alpharetta GA 30004-3908

BOLTON, ROGER EDWIN, economist, educator; b. Dover, Pa., Nov. 23, 1938; s. Oscar Jacob and Edna Irene (Hughes) B.; m. Julia Carolyn Gooden, June 27, 1964; children: Christopher, Jonathan. AB, Franklin and Marshall Coll., 1959; PhD, Harvard U., 1964. Instr. Harvard U., Cambridge, Mass., 1964-66; asst. prof. econs. Williams Coll., Williamstown, Mass., 1966-69, assoc. prof., 1969-74, prof., 1974—2003, William R. Kenan Jr. prof., 1992-93, Edward Dorr Griffin prof., 1986-92, chmn. dept., 1975-76, 79-81, dir. Ctr. Humanities and Social Scis., 1985-87, chair faculty steering com., 1991-92, William Brough prof., 1994—2003, prof. emeritus, 2003—; rsch. assoc. Ctr. for Environ. Studies, 2003—. Vis. prof. Wellesley Coll., 1977, U. Pa., 1981-82; George A. Miller vis. prof. U. Ill., 1988; disting. vis. prof. U. Wis., Madison, 1989; vis. prof. Clark U., 1993; mem. assoc. staff Brookings Instn., 1965-68; sr. economist Curran Assocs., 1973-75; rsch. assoc. Joint Ctr. for Urban Studies, 1979-81; mem. com. on place-based decisionmaking NRC, 2000-02. Author: Defense Purchases and Regional Growth, 1966; co-author: Regional Diversity, 1981; editor: Defense and Disarmament, 1966; co-editor Internat. Regional Sci. Rev., 1985-89 (mem. editl. bd.); mem. editl. bd. Annals Regional Sci., Can. Jour. Regional Sci., Growth and Change; mem. editorial bd., book rev. editor Jour. Regional Sci.; also numerous articles. Mem. Berkshire County Regional Planning Commn., Mass., 1980-81, 82-88, clk., 1983-85, vice-chmn., 1985-87; mem. Williamstown Planning Bd., 1983-86, chmn., 1985-86; bd. dirs. No. Berkshire Indsl. Park and Devel. Corp., chmn., 1986-88. Recipient Outstanding Contbn. to Planning award Berkshire County Regional Planning Commn., 1989; Woodrow Wilson fellow, 1959-60, Danforth fellow, 1959-64. Mem. Am. Econ. Assn., Regional Sci. Assn. (councillor 1988-91), Regional Studies Assn., Assn. Am. Geographers, mem. bd. dir., Western Regional Sci. Assn., 2003-. Home: 30 Grandview Dr Williamstown MA 01267-2528 Office: Williams Coll Dept Econs Fernald House Williamstown MA 01267 E-mail: roger.e.bolton@williams.edu.

BOLTON-HOLIFIELD, ALICE RUTH, basketball player; b. Lucedale, Miss., May 25, 1967; d. Linwood and Leola Bolton; m. Mark Holifield. B of Exercise Physiology, Auburn U., 1989. Basketball player C.A. Faenza, Italy, 1993, Erreti Faenza, Italy, 1994—95, Sacramento Monarchs, 1997—; mem. 1996 & 2000 US Olympic Team (Gold Medal Winner). Mem. U.S.A. Women's Nat. Basketball Team; launched clothing line Runwear. Lead singer: Antidum Tarantula. 1st lt. USAR. Named USA Basketball's Female Athlete of Yr., 1991, 1st Am. woman to play profl. basketball in Hungary and Sweden, 1990—91; named to, NCAA 1989 Mideast Region All-Tournament Team, 1988, 1989, NCAA Final Four All Tournament Team honors, 1988, SEC-All Academic Team, 1988, 1989, All-SEC second team, 1989; recipient gold medal, U.S. Olympic Festival, 1986, World Univ. Games, 1991, World Championship Qualifying Team FIBA World Championship, 1993, 1994 Goodwill Games, 1994, Bronze medal, World Championship, 1994; earned SEC All-Tournament Team honors, 1988, All-WNBA 1st team, 1997, named first ever WNBA player of week, 1997, mem. gold medal winning Olympic team, Atlanta, 1996, mem., U.S. Basketball Women's Nat. Team, 1995—96. Office: Sacramento Monarchs Arco Arena Sacramento CA 95834

BOLTZ, GERALD EDMUND, lawyer; b. Dennison, Ohio, June 1, 1931; s. Harold E. and Margaret Eve (Hecky) B.; m. Janet Ruth Scott, Sept. 19, 1959; children: Gretchen Boltz Fields, Eric Scott, Jill Marie. BA, Ohio No. U., 1953, JD, 1955. Bar: Ohio 1955, U.S. Supreme Ct. 1964, Calif. 1978, U.S. Dist. Ct. (cen. dist.) Calif. 1978. Asst. atty. gen. State of Ohio, 1958; atty. spl. investigations unit SEC, 1959-60, legal asst. to commr., 1960-61, sr. trial and spl. counsel, 1961-66, regional adminstr. Ft. Worth, 1967-71, regional adminstr. and mng. ptnr. L.A., 1972-78; ptnr. Fine, Perzik& Friedman, L.A., 1979-83; mng. ptnr. Rogers & Wells, L.A., 1983-92; ptnr. Bryan Cave, L.A., 1992—. Co-author: Securities Law Techniques. Served with U.S. Army, 1955-57. Mem. ABA, Fed. Bar Assn., L.A. Bar Assn., Ohio Bar Assn., Calif. Bar Assn., Bel Air Bay Club. Republican. Presbyn. (elder). Avocations: sailing, piano. Home: 1105 Centinela Ave Santa Monica CA 90403-2316 Office: Bryan Cave 120 Broadway Ste 300 Santa Monica CA 90401-2386 E-mail: geboltz@bryancave.com.

BOLTZ, JAMES DONALD, retired human resources specialist, photographer; b. Portland, N.Y., Feb. 20, 1939; s. Edward Donald and Maggie Mae (Davis) B.; m. Margaret Louise Born, Sept. 3, 1966 (div. Dec. 1978); 1 child, David James Boltz; m. Carol Rae Barrett Hofmann, Jan. 10, 1981; children: Paul Barrett Hofmann, Lynn Marie Hofmann Ottney Waterfield. Regents diploma, Brocton (N.Y.) Ctrl. Sch., 1957. Prodn. coord. Gt. Lakes Color Printing, Dunkirk, N.Y., 1957-78, personnel mgr., 1978-81; corp. mgr. tng. Gtr. Buffalo Press, 1981-87, customer svc. rep., 1987-89; assoc. Wm. L. Holcomb Assocs., Buffalo, 1989-94; ret., 1994. Cons.; cons., trainer Chautauqua Pvt. Industry Coun., Jamestown, N.Y., 1988—. Chief Portland (N.Y.) Fire Dept., 1960-62; pres. Brocton Portland Jaycees, 1960-62; dir., sec. 1891 Fredonia (N.Y.) Opera House, 1994—; scoutmaster troop 60 Boy Scouts Am., Portland, N.Y., 1965-68; mem. bd., sec. Adams Art Gallery, Dunkirk, N.Y., 1990-94; sec. dir. North Chautauqua United Way, Dunkirk, 1984-88; mem. bd. Chautauqua ARC, Jamestown, N.Y., 1986-89; interim exec. dir. Fredonia Opera House, 2000; mem. grants com. No. Chautauqua Cmty. Found., 1998—. Sgt. US Army, 1962-64. Paul Harris fellow Fredonia (N.Y.) Rotary Club, 1995; recipient Spirit of Fredonia award Fredonia C. of C., Cmty. Svc. award Chautauqua County C. of C., 2000; named Fredonia Bus. Person of Yr., 1996. Mem. Fredonia (N.Y.) Preservation Soc. (pres. 1989-92, trustee 1978—), Buffalo Indsl. Photographers. Home: 37 Birchwood Dr Fredonia NY 14063-1203

BOLY, JEFFREY ELWYN, retired lawyer; b. Portland, Oreg., Mar. 16, 1942; s. Elwyn and Frances Rolland (Hulse) Boly; m. Mary Ione Van Beckum, Sept. 4, 1965; children: Jeffrey Elwyn, Justin; m. Linda Diehl, Sept. 4, 1993; 1 child, Brian. BA, Georgetown U., 1964; JD, U. Calif., San Francisco, 1967. Bar: US Dist. Ct. (no. dist.)/Calif. 1967, US Ct. Appeals (9th cir.) 1967, US Tax Ct. 1968, Oreg. 1971, US Dist. Ct. Oreg. 1971; US Supreme Ct. 1971. Trial atty. Office of Chief Counsel to Commr. IRS, San Francisco, 1967—71; ptnr. Wood Tatum Mosser brooke & Landis, Portland, Oreg., 1971—87, Hanna, Urbigkeit, Jensen, Goyak & O'Connell, Portland, 1987—88, Hanna, Murphy, Jensen & Holloway, 1988—89, Gravey, Schubert & Barer, Portland, 1989—. Mem.: Georgetown U. Alumni Assn. (pres. Portland chpt. 1977), Oreg. Dept. Revenue (liaison subcom. 1987—, sec. 1989—90, chair-elect 1990—91, chair 1991—92), IRS, Oreg. State Bar Assn. (mem. estate planning sect., mem. exec. com. 1983—87, chair 1985—86, newsletter editor 1985—86, mem. taxation sect., mem. exec. com. 1981—83, 1987—94), Multnomah County Bar Assn., Western Region Bar Assn. (Oreg. rep., IRS liaison 1987, chair 1991—92), Calif. Bar Assn., ABA (mem. tax sect.), Am. Lung Assn. of Oreg. (mem. planned giving com. 1991—), City of Portland (mem. estate planning coun., chmn. seminar com. 1988), Jesuit HS (mem. parents' bd. 1985—88, pres. parents' bd. 1988, mem. alumni bd. 1986—, chmn. planned giving com. 1993—), Portland Ctr. Stage (bd. dir. 1994—, sec. 1995—), Oreg. Shakespeare Festival (mem. adv. coun. 1991—94), Ballet Oreg. (bd. dir. 1983—88, chmn. 1984—85), Oreg. Advocates for Arts (bd. dir. 1980—87, pres. bd. dir. 1981—82). Democrat. Roman Catholic. Home: 2879 SW Champlain Dr Portland OR 97201-1833 Office: Garvey Schubert & Barer 121 SW Morrison St Fl 11 Portland OR 97204-3117

BOMAN, MARC ALLEN, lawyer; b. Cleve., Sept. 4, 1948; s. David S. and Shirley T. (Freier) B.; m. Leah Eilenberg, June 10, 1984; children: Autumn, Heidi, Jane, David. Student, Purdue U., 1966-68; BA, Case Western Res. U., 1971, JD, 1974. Bar: Ohio 1974, Wash. 1978, D.C. 1978, U.S. Dist. Ct. (we. dist.) Wash. 1980, U.S. Ct. Appeals (9th cir.), U.S. Dist. Ct. (ea. dist.) Wash. 1985, U.S. Ct. Appeals (fed. cir.) 1986. Atty.-advisor Office of Gen. Counsel U.S. Gen. Acctg. Office, Washington, 1974-78; dep. prosecuting atty. Office of Prosecuting Atty., King County, Wash., 1978-81; assoc. Perkins Coie, Seattle, 1981-86, ptnr., 1986—. Spl. ind. dep. prosecutor ethics investigation of county execs., 1994; mem. Seattle Ethics and Elections Commn., 1995-98; spkr. in field, spl. ind. prosecutor to Met. King Cty. State v. Ridgway capital murder case, 2002. Bd. dirs. Perkins Coie Cmty. Svcs. Fellowship, 1987-97, co-chmn., 1994-97; former bd. dirs. Totem coun. Girl Scouts U.S., Seattle Day Ctr. for Adults, Madrona Neighborhood Coun.; trustee Herzl-Ner Tamid Congregation, 1987-98, pres., 1994-96; mem. Leadership Tomorrow, United Way King County-Seattle C. of C., 1987-88; trustee King County Bar Found., 1995-2000, v.p., 1997-98, pres., 1998-99. Recipient Pres.'s award King County Bar Assn., 1999; Mayoral proclamation declaring Marc Boman Day named in honor of contbn. to citizens of Seattle, 1998. Mem. Seattle King Bar Assn. (trustee 1986-89, chmn. divsn. young lawyers 1984-85), Wash. State Bar Assn. (co-chair Blue Ribbon Panel on Criminal Def. 2003). Office: Perkins Coie 1201 3rd Ave Fl 40 Seattle WA 98101-3029

BOMAR, ROBERT LINTON, assistant principal; b. Americus, Ga., July 5, 1959; s. John Eugene and Blanche Alvenia (Shehee) B.; m. Laura Beth Elliott, June 27, 1987; 1 child, Sarah Beth. AA, Clayton Jr. Coll., Morrow, Ga., 1979; BA, U. Ga., 1981; MEd, Ga. State U., 1983, PhD, 1992. Tchr. social studies Henry County High Sch., McDonough, Ga., 1983-90; asst. prin. Locust Grove (Ga.) Elem. Sch., 1990-96, Wesley Lakes (Ga.) Elem. Sch., 1996-2000, McDonough (Ga.) Elem. Sch., 2000—02, Unity Grove Elem. Sch., Locust Grove, Ga., 2002—. Author: A Briefing Book for Hearings on Mexican Oil Imports and the Implications of Illegal Mexican Immigration, 1980 (William Jennings Bryan prize). Site coord. ann. campaign United Way, Locust Grove, 1990-96, Wesley Lakes, 1996-2000, McDonough Elem., 2000-02, Unity Grove Elem., 2002—. Mem. ASCD, Prof. Assn. Ga. Educators, Foxfire Tchrs. Network, Kappa Delta Pi, Phi Kappa Phi, Phi Beta Kappa, Phi Delta Kappa. Presbyterian. Avocations: hiking, cycling, ch. activities, so. Appalachian folklore. Home: 578 Walter Moore Rd Jackson GA 30233-4565 Office: Unity Grove Elem Sch 1180 Leguin Mill Rd Locust Grove GA 30248

BOMBACI, NANCY MARGARET, literature educator; b. Hartford, Conn., Mar. 25, 1963; d. Lucian and Anna Ferro Bombaci. BA, Trinity Coll., Hartford, Conn., 1985, MA, 1990; PhD, Fordham U., 1999. Vis. instr. Fordham U., Bronx, NY, 1998—99, vis. asst. prof., 2000—01, St. Joseph Coll., West Hartford, Conn., 1999—2000; adj. lectr. Capital Cmty. and Tech. Coll., Hartford, 2001—. Contbr. article in mag. Presdl. scholar, Fordham U., 1993—97, Sr. Tchg. fellow, 1996—97. Mem.: MLA. Personal E-mail: n.bomba@prodigy.net.

BOMBARDELLI, FABIAN ALEJANDRO, hydraulic engineer, researcher; b. La Plata, Buenos Aires, Argentina, May 12, 1966; s. Reynaldo Julio Bombardelli and Nidia Ethel Michelini. Bachiller, Colegio Nacional Rafael Hernández of La Plata, La Plata, Buenos Aires, Argentina, 1983; Master in Numerical Simulation and Control, U. Buenos Aires, 1999; PhD in Civil and Environ. Engring., U. Ill., 2003. Undergrad. asst. Bur. of Pub. Rds., Buenos Aires Province, La Plata, Argentina, 1989—91; rsch. engr. Nat. Inst. for Water, Ezeiza, Argentina, 1991—98; rsch. asst. dept. civil and environ. engring. U. Ill.,

Urbana, Ill., 1999—. Cons., Buenos Aires, 1997—98; v.p. and coord. Environ. Inst., Ctr. of Engrs. of Buenos Aires Province, La Plata, Buenos Aires, Argentina, 1994—98. Contbr. Counselor Argentine Cmty. at Urbana-Champaign, Urbana, Ill., 2002—03. Named Outstanding Rschr., Nat. Inst. for Water, Argentina, 1994; recipient Glenn and Helen Stout award, Dept. of Civil and Environ. Engring., U. of Ill. at Urbana-Champaign, 2001. Mem.: Internat. Assn. Hydraulic Rsch., Internat. Water Resources Assn., Phi Kappa Phi. Office: University of Illinois Urbana-Champaign Ven Te Chow Hydrosystems Lab 205 North Mathews Avenue Urbana IL 61801 Office Fax: 217-333-0687. E-mail: bombarde@uiuc.edu.

BOMBARDIR, BRAD, hockey player; b. British Columbia, Can., May 5, 1972; Hockey player Minn. Wild, 2000—. Named All Star, Am. Hockey League, 1996; named to 56th selection, Entry Draft, 1990. Office: Minn Wild 317 Washington St Saint Paul MN 55102

BOMBERGER, AUDREY SHELLEY, health facility administrator; b. June 12, 1942; Diploma in nursing, Reading Med. Ctr., 1963; BS in Edn., Millersville U., 1975; MS in Edn., Temple U., 1979; PhD in Health Adminstrn., Columbia-Pacific U., 1983. Enlisted U.S. Army, 1977, with Nurse Corps, 1977—99, ret. Col., 1999; dir. hosp. edn. and rsch. McKay-Dee Hosp., Ogden, Utah, 1984-87; dir. hosp. edn. Salinas (Calif.) Valley Meml. Hosp., 1987-91; owner Creative Health Svcs., Salinas, 1991-94; adminstr. profl. svcs. Al Hada Hosp., Tiaf, Saudi Arabia, 1994-95; dir. nursing Casa Serena Nursing Home, 1995-96; dir. quality mgmt., dir. profl. svcs. LifeCare Mgmt. Svcs., Dallas, 1996—99, clin. v.p. corp. offices, 1999—. Author: Radiation and Health: Disaster Planning, 1984; co-author: Disaster Planning, 1986, Medical/Surgical Nursing, 1982. Address: 7005 Chateau Dr Frisco TX 75035-6193

BOMBERGER, RUSSELL BRANSON, lawyer, writer; b. Lebanon, Pa., May 1, 1934; s. John Mark and Viola (Aurentz) B.; divorced; children— Ann Elizabeth, Jane Carmel. BS, Temple U., 1955; MA, U. Iowa, 1956, MA, 1961, PhD, 1962; MS, U. So. Calif., 1960; LLB, JD, LaSalle U.; grad., U.S. Marine Corps Command and Staff Coll., 1987, U.S. Naval War Coll., 1991. Bar: Calif. 1970, U.S. Supreme Ct. 1975. Mem. editorial staff Phila. Inquirer, 1952-54; lectr. U. Iowa, 1955-57, U. So. Calif., 1957-58; asst. prof. U.S. Naval Postgrad. Sch., Monterey, Calif., 1958-62, assoc. prof., 1963-75, prof., 1975-89, prof. emeritus, 1989—; practice law, 1970—. Free lance writer, 1952—, communications cons., 1963— ; safety cons. internat. program U. So. Calif. Inst. Safety and Systems Mgmt., 1983— ; cons. Internat. Ctr. for Aviation Safety, Lisbon, 1984— Author: (novel) The Alternate Candidate, (broadcast series) The World of Ideas, (motion picture) Strokes and Stamps, (stage play) Closely Held; abstracter-editor: Internat. Transactional Analysis Assn. Capt. USNR, 1966-94. Decorated Meritorious Civilian Svc. medal, 1989; Am. Psychol. Found. fellow Columbia U., 1954-55, CBS fellow U. So. Calif., 1957-58. Office: PO Box 8741 Monterey CA 93943-8741 E-mail: rbbomber@excite.com.

BOMBOY, JOHN DAVID, mathematics educator; b. Somerset, Pa., May 22, 1953; s. David E. and Betty (Smith) B.; m. Nancy L. Dutrow, Apr. 22, 1978; children: Amanda Joy (dec.), Amy Lynn (dec.). BS, Clarion State Coll., 1975, MS, 1980. Cert. secondary tchr., Ohio, Pa.; registered athletic dir., Pa. Math. tchr. East Palestine (Ohio) City Schs., 1975-77, Marion Center (Pa.) Area Schs., 1977—, dir. athletics, 1982—, dir. cmty. svcs., 1998-99. Mem. Pa. State Athletic Dir.'s Assn. (mem. exec. coun., chmn. awards com.), Nat. Interscholastic Athletic Adminstrs. Assn. (cert. master athletic adminstr.), Pa. Interscholastic Athletic Assn., Wrestling Ofcls., Am. Sport Edn. Program Instrs., Dist. 6 Athletic Dirs. Assn. (treas. 1994—), Appalachian Conf. (sec.-treas. 1987-2000), Heritage Conf. (sec.-treas. 2000—), Therapy Dog Internat. (assoc. vol. cert. handler). Republican. Lutheran. Avocations: jogging, collecting license plates, wrestling referee. Home: 306 Highland Dr Home PA 15747-9608 Office: Marion Ctr Area High Sch 22800 Rte 403 Hwy N PO Box 209 Marion Center PA 15759 E-mail: jbomboy@mcasd.net.

BOMER, ELTON, former state official; b. July 30, 1935; m. Ginny Bomer; 2 children. BBA in Bus. Mgmt., U. Houston, 1959. Computer sales and mktg. mgr. IBM Corp., 1965-74; mem. Tex. Ho. Reps., Austin, 1981-85; mem. bd. dirs. Sprint/United Telephone Midwest Corp., 1985-95; sr. v.p. East Tex. Nat. Bank, Palestine, Tex., 1990-95; mem. Tex. Ho. of Reps., Austin, 1991-95; commr. ins. Tex. Dept. Ins., Austin, 1995-99; sec. of state State of Tex., 1999—2001; consultant, 2001—. Named to Tex. Monthly 10 Best Legislators List, 1993. Democrat.

BOMES, STEPHEN D. lawyer; b. Providence, Jan. 15, 1948; s. Edward and Lillian L. (Dick) B.; m. Barbara Jean Thomas, Feb. 4, 1989; 1 child, Laura Alexandra. BS, Boston U., 1968; JD, U. Calif., Hastings, 1971; postgrad., Columbia U., 1974; LLM, NYU, 1975. Bar: Calif. 1972, N.Y. 1975, Fla. 1975, D.C. 1975, U.S. Dist. Ct. (no. and cen. dists.) Calif. 1972, U.S. Ct. Appeals (2d and 9th cirs.). Assoc. Milbank, Tweed, Hadley & McCoy, N.Y.C., 1975-79, London, 1979-81; ptnr. Brobeck, Phleger & Harrison, San Francisco, 1981-93, Loeb and Loeb, L.A., 1994-96, Heller Ehrman White & McAuliffe, L.A., 1997—. Instr. NYU 1973-75; adj. asst. prof. CUNY, 1974; mem. Brazil Soc. No. Calif., Pan. Am. Soc. Author: The Dead Hand: The Last Grasp, 1976, (with W.F. Johnson) Real Estate Transfer, Development and Finance, Cases and Materials, 1975; co-editor: Commercial Agency and Distributions in Europe, 1992; contbr. chpts. to books. Trustee 1066 Found. NYU fellow, 1973-75; included in Euromoney's Guide to the World's Leading Banking Lawyers. Mem. L.A., Assn. of Bar of City of N.Y., Internat. Bar Assn., Jonathan Club. Office: White & McAuliffe 601 S Figueroa St Fl 40 Los Angeles CA 90017-5704 E-mail: sdbomes@aol.com., sbomes@hewm.com.

BOMGARDEN, STANLEY RALPH, minister; b. Freeport, Ill., Nov. 4, 1946; s. Ralph George and Dorothy Lorraine (Heeren) B.; m. Theresa Jane McCarten, June 7, 1969 (div. 1976); children: Peter, Elizabeth; m. Sylvia Ann Stone Maurer, June 27, 1986; stepchildren: Timothy Maurer, Jane Parks, Sarah DeHahn. BA, Cen. Coll., Pella, Iowa, 1969; MDiv, Western Theol. Sem., Holland, Mich., 1972; postgrad., U. Iowa, 1975-78; DMin, Grad. Theol. Found., 2002. Ordained to ministry Ref. Ch. Am., 1975, Presbyn. Ch. (U.S.A.), 1988. Pastor 1st Ref. Ch., Rotterdam Jct., N.Y., 1973-75; assoc. pastor 1st Bapt. Ch., Iowa City, 1977-78; pastor 1st Presbyn. Ch., Beebe, Ark., 1988-91, Meml. Presbyn. Ch., Dayton, Ind., 1991—2002; counselor Highland Community Coll., Freeport, 1979-81; dir. Christian edn. 2d Presbyn. Ch., Freeport, 1983-87; pastor Fulton (Ill.) Presbyn. Ch., Ill., 2002—. Guest lectr. Ark. State U., Beebe, 1989-91; program coord. Freeport Area Ch. Coop., 1984-87; moderator witness com. Presbytery of Ark., 1990-91; moderator com. on ministry Presbytery of Wabash Valley, 1996-98, mem. peace/justice action com., 2000-2001; curriculum writer Presby. Ch.; moderator Com. on Prep. for Ministry, 2002. Illustrator: Young Server's Book of the Mass, 1987; contbg. editor Festivals mag.; mem. editorial bd. newsletter Body and Soul; contbr. stories and articles to profl. jours. Mem. Lions (pres. Beebe club 1990-91). Democrat. Home: 713 11th Ave Fulton IL 61252 Office: Fulton Presbyn Ch 311 N 9th St Fulton IL 61252-1897 E-mail: stanley.bomgarden@mchsi.com.

BOMHAN, RUTH WALKER, social studies educator; b. Wilmington, N.C, Dec. 17, 1955; d. Robert Henry and Edna (Barritt) Walker; m. Kenneth Earl Bomhan (div.); 1 child, Kenneth Earl Jr. BA, U. N.C., Wilmington, 1984. Cert. tchr. social studies. Tchr. New Hanover H.S., Wilmington, 1984-85, Hoggard Night Sch., Wilmington, 1985-88, Lakeside H.S., Wilmington, 1988-2000, Roland-Grise Mid. Sch., Wilmington, 2000—. Mem. Smithsonian Instn., Civil War Trust, Nat. Geog. Soc., Mus. of Confederacy, World War II Meml., N.C. Coun. Social Studies, Libr. Congress, Nat. Trust Historic Preservation, Friends of Nat. Park Gettysburg, N.C. Assn. Educators, Nat. Honor soc. Polit. Sci., Colonial Williamsburg Found. Avocations: bowling, lapidary, reading, travel, martial arts. Office: Roland-Grise Mid Sch 4412 Lake Ave Wilmington NC 28403

BOMHOF, ROBYN, artist, educator; b. Chgo., June 19, 1952; d. Emmett Earl and Ruth Carolyn Miller; m. James Alan Bomhof, Dec. 27, 1974; children: Russell, Allyson, Jessica. BFA with honors, Kendall Coll. Art and Design, Grand Rapids, Mich., 1997; MFA, Western Mich. U., 2001. Youth program dir. West YMCA, Grand Rapids, 1968-72; program dir. Vic Tanny, Inc., Detroit, 1974-76; creative dir., artist Genesis Advt., Grand Rapids, 1977-79; artist self employed, Grand Rapids, 1970—; tchr. Western Mich. U., Kalamazoo, 1998—2001, asst. dir. exhbns., 1999—2001. Mem. exec. bd. Westside Christian Sch., Grand Rapids, 1988-91; charter mem. Rivertown Artists Guild, Grand Rapids, 1990—; dir. word fellowship Sunshine Ministries, Grand Rapids, 1988-89. One-woman shows include Kendall Coll. Art and Design, 1997, Riley Galleries/Rapture, 1999, Western Mich. U., 2000, Newago Coun. for Arts 2002, exhibited in group shows at Fine Arts Gallery, 1998, Great Lakes Regional Competition, 1997, 1998, 1999, 2000, Lowell Coun. for the Arts Regional Show, 1997, Ferris State U., 1996, Muskegon Mus. Art, 1998 (Curator's award), Festival Regional, Grand Rapids, 1999, ARC Gallery, Chgo., 1999, Battle Creek Ctr. for the Arts, 1999, Carnegie Ctr. for Arts, 1999 (Best of Show), Kalamazoo Inst. of Art, 2000, works in various pub. and pvt. collections. Recipient awards for art and design; Vt. Studio Ctr. grantee, 1999; Western Mich. U. grantee, 1999; travel grantee Dietre Heineke. Mem. Coll. Art Assn., Grand Rapids Kennel Club (bd. dirs. 1976-85), Friesian Horse Assn. of N.Am. Avocations: reading, dogs, cats, Friesian horses (dressage and driving), driving. Home: Black Oak Farm 1701 14 Mile Rd Sparta MI 49345

BOMKE, LARRY K. state legislator; b. Springfield, Ill., June 6, 1950; m. Sally Jo; 2 children. Student, Lincoln Land C.C. Ptnr. Ins. Agy.; mem. Ill. Senate, Springfield, 1995—, mem. exec. appts. com., local govt. & elections com. Republican. Office: State Capitol 111 Capitol Bldg Springfield IL 62706-0001*

BOMMANNA, VASUDEVA M. allergist, immunologist; b. India, Oct. 3, 1959; MBBS, 1983. Diplomate Am. Bd. Pediats., Am. Bd. Allergy and Immunology. Rotating intern Jawaharlal Nehru Med. Coll., Belgaum, India, 1982-83; resident in pediatrics St. Luke's Roosevelt Med. Ctr., N.Y.C., 1993-95, fellow in allergy and immunology State U. - Children's Hosp., Buffalo, N.Y., 1995-97; asst. clin. instr. pediatrics SUNY, Buffalo, 1995-97; pvt. practice, 1997—. Mem.: AMA, Am. Coll. Allercy and Immunology, Am. Acad. Allergy and Immunology, Am. Acad. Pediatrics. Office: 607 Russell Blvd Nacogdoches TX 75965-1247

BOMPAS, DONALD GEORGE, charitable organization executive, consultant; b. Southgate, Eng., Nov. 20, 1920; s. Edward Anstie and Sissie Mary (Fraser) B.; m. Freda Vice Smithyman, Aug. 31, 1946; children: Catherine, Anthony George. MA, Oxford (Eng.) U., 1947. With Overseas Audit Svc., Singapore and Malaya, Malaysia, 1942—47, 1947-66, dep. auditor-gen., 1956—60, auditor-gen., 1960—66; dep. sec., then sec. Guy's Hosp. Med. Sch., London, 1966-82; dep. sec. United Med. and Dental Schs. Guys's and St. Thomas Hosps., London, 1982-84, sec., 1984-86, hon. fellow, 1996; mng. exec. Philip and Pauline Harris Charitable Trust, 1986—. Decorated companion Order St. Michael and St. George; hon. Johan Mangku Negara (Malaysia); hon. fellow King's Coll., London, 1998. Home: 8 Birchwood Rd Petts Wood BR5 1NY England

BONA, FREDERICK EMIL, public relations executive; b. Union City, N.J., Mar. 3, 1939; s. Henry C. and Clementina A. Bona; m. Doris L. Hurlbert, May 27, 1961; children: Lauri Paporello, Dawn Rizzo, Christine Cabana, F.A. (Rick). BS in Mktg., Fairleigh Dickinson U., 1962. Press rels. rep. W.R. Grace & Co., N.Y.C., 1962, mgr. press rels., 1970, dir. press rels., 1980, v.p. corp. communications div., 1983, dep. group exec., 1985, v.p., 1987-94; prin. The Dilenschneider Group, Inc., N.Y.C., 1994-95, LS Comms., Inc., N.Y.C., 1995—. Dep. communications mgr. Pvt. Sector Survey on Cost Control (Grace Commn.), Washington, 1982-85. Mem. Overseas Press Club (bd. govs. 1988-91, 94-97), Pub. Rels. Soc. N.Y. Roman Catholic. Office: LS Communications Inc 17 Devon Rd Boonton NJ 07005-9305 E-mail: bona888nj@aol.com.

BONA, JERRY LLOYD, mathematician, educator; b. Little Rock, Feb. 5, 1945; s. Louis Eugene and Mary Eva (Kane) B.; m. Pamela Anne Ross, Dec. 23, 1966; children: Rachael Elizabeth, Jennifer Dani'el. BS in Applied Math. and Computer Sci., Washington U., St. Louis, 1966; PhD in Math., Harvard U., 1971. Rsch. fellow U. Essex, Colchester, Eng., 1970-72; L. E. Dickson instr. U. Chgo., 1972-73, from asst. prof. to assoc. prof. to prof., 1973-86; prof. Pa. State U., University Park, 1986-90, Raymond Shibley prof., 1990-95, acting chmn., 1990-91, chmn., 1991-95; CAM prof. math. and physics U. Tex., Austin, 1995—2002; prof., chmn. U. Ill., Chgo., 2002—. Rsch. fellow Harvard U. dept. math., 1970, 73; U.K. Sci. and Engring. Rsch. Coun. sr. vis. fellow Fluid Mechanics Rsch. Inst., U. Essex, 1973, 74, 75, 77, 78; vis. rsch. assoc. Brookhaven Nat. Lab., 1976, 77; NAS exch. visitor to Poland, 1977; vis. prof. Centro Brasileiro Pesquisas Fisicas, Rio de Janeiro, 1980, Math. Rsch. Ctr., 1980-81, U. Brasilia, 1982, Lab. Anvendt Matematisk Fysik, Danish Tech. Sch., 1982, Inst. Math. and its Applications, U. Minn., 1985, 88, 90, 91, 2001; rsch. prof. Applied Rsch. Lab., Pa. State U., 1986-95; prof. invité U. Paris-Sud, Ctr. d'Orsay, 1982, 86-87, 88, 89, 92, 2001, 03, l'Inst. Nat. Sci. Rsch.-Oceanology, U. Que., 1982-87, Ecole Normale Superieure de Cachan, 1990-91, dir. rsch. CNRS, 1995, U. Bordeaux, 1995, 2001, 03; invited prof. Inst. Pure and Applied Math., Rio de Janeiro, 1991, 92, 93, 99, 2000, 02, Acad. Sinica, Beijing, 1991, 96, 99, Math. Scis. Rsch. Inst., Berkeley, Calif., 1994, U. de Paris Nord, Math. Lab. Villetaneuse, 1993, 95, 99, U. Oxford, 1995, TATA Inst., Bangalore, 1999, 2001, 03, Inst. Sci. de la Mer, U. Que., 1999—; invited spkr. ann. meeting Am. Phys. Soc., Notre Dame, 1979; invited spkr. Am. Math. Soc. meeting, Mpls., 1984, San Francisco, 1995; invited spkr. Internat. Biennial Fluid Mechanics Meeting, Blazjewko, Poland, 1979, Internat. Congress of Mathematicians, Helsinki, 1978; Britton lectr., McMaster U., 1986, SIAM ann. meeting, San Diego, 1989, Porcelli lectr. LSU, 1993, Taft lectr. U. Cin., 1996, Industl. Math Inst. Disting. Lctr., Univ. S. C., 2002; chmn. Com. Applied Math. U. Chgo., 1981-86; mem. coll. coun.U. Chgo., 1981-84; mem. Pa. State U. task force on undergrad. edn., 1989-91, hon. degree recipient recommendation com., 1994-95 ; mem. sci. adv. com. basic rsch. math. scis. U.S. Army Rsch. Office, 1979-82, review com. divsn. math. and computer sci. Argonne Nat. Lab., 1984-90, chmn., 1985-89; mem. rev. panel, site visit team NSF Sci. and Tech. Ctrs., 1988; mem. NATO postdoctoral fellowships rev. panel, 1991; mem. ABET evaluating team, 1992; chmn. proposal rev. panel Dept. Energy, 1993; co-dir. Math. Edn. Reform Network, 1993—; mem. vis. com. dept. math. U. Ill., Chgo., 1993, MIT, 1993-97, CUNY Bklyn. Coll., 1994, U. N.C., 1996, Howard U., 1999; mem. forum post secondary edn. Math. Scis. Edn. Bd., 1994—; chmn. nat. vis. com. N.Y. Collab. for Excellence in Tchr. Prep. in Math., Sci., Tech., 1996-2000. Mem. editl. bd. SIAM J. Math. Anal., 1979 , editor-in-chief, 1987-92; mem. editl. bd. 25 profl. jours.; contbr. more than 150 papers to profl. jours. Grantee W. M. Keck Found., 1989, NSF, 1972—; NSF grad. fellow Harvard U., 1966-70; Woodrow Wilson fellow Harvard U., 1966-67. Fellow AAAS (nat. com. chair 1994-97, nat. elected office 2001—); mem. Soc. for Indsl. and Applied Math. (com. mng. editors 1987-92, com. on coms. and appts. 1988-95, vis. lectr. 1992—, rep. to AAAS sect. com. on math. 1994-97, nat. com. chair 1987-92, Am. Math. Soc. (nat. com. chair 1989-96, 99—, mem. com. to select Steele prize winner 1984-87, adv. com. on newsletter on collegiate math. edn. 1987-88, bd. judges for Nat. Sci. and Engring. Fair 1990, 1991, chmn. liaison com. AAAS 1990-92, com. on edn. 1992-96, chmn. subcom. grad. and postdoctoral edn. 1993-95, univ. lectr. series com. 1994—, chmn., 1999—, nomination com. 1995-97, chmn. nomination com. 1995-96, com. on coms. 1998-2002, chmn. 1998-2002), Math. Assn. Am. (com. on undergrad. program in math. 1987-91, subcom. on major in math. scis. 1989-90, subcom. on calculus reform and 1st 2 yrs. 1989-91, rep. to AAAS sect. com. on math. 1993-96, program of cons. 1994—), Tau Beta Pi. Achievements include setting up a fluid mechanics lab in math. depts.; helping to organize interdisciplinary programs in science, engineering, economics, finance, computer science and mathematics. Home: 360 E Randolph St Apt 3903 Chicago IL 60601 Office: U Ill Chgo Math, Stat and Computer Sci Dept Chicago IL 60607

BONA, MIKLOS, mathematician, educator; b. Szekesfehervar, Fejer megye, Hungary, Oct. 6, 1967; s. Miklos Bona and Katalin Szegvari; m. Linda Grace Sciacca, July 8, 2000; children: Miklos Joseph, Benjamin Peter. MS, Eotvos U., Budapest, 1992, Paris 7 U., 1992; PhD, MIT, 1997. Asst. prof. U. of Fla., Gainesville, 1999—; mem. Inst. for Advanced Study, Princeton, NJ, 1998—99. Postdoctoral fellow U. of Que. at Montreal, Montreal, Quebec, Canada, 1997—98. Author: (textbook) A Walk Through Combinatorics. Recipient Young Investigator award, Nat. Security Agy., 2003—04, rsch. fellowship at Inst. for Advanced Study, Arcana Found., 1998—99, rsch. fellowship, UQAM Found., 1997—98, Ladislaus von Hoffman Rsch. fellowship at Inst. for Advanced Study, Arcana Found., 1998—99. Mem.: Am. Math. Soc. Roman Catholic. Home: 5141 NW 29th Ln Gainesville FL 32606 Office: U Fla Dept of Math 1300 W University Ave Gainesville FL 32606 Home Fax: 352-392-8357. Personal E-mail: lindamiki@aol.com. E-mail: bona@math.ufl.edu.

BONACORSI, GREGORY JAMES, mechanical engineer; b. Lawrence, Mass., Dec. 16, 1955; s. Dominic and Elaine Mary (Maloney) B.; m. Jody Michele St. Germain, Aug. 16, 1980 (div.); children: Jaime Michele, Jacquelyn Arlyne. BSME, U. N.H., 1978; MSME, Northeastern U., 1984. Registered profl. engr., Mass., N.H. Pvt. practice carpenter, Salem, N.H., 1972-78; with engring. devel. program Aircraft Engine Bus. Group, Gen. Electric Co., Lynn, Mass., 1978-80, evaluation engr., 1981-89; program mgr. GE, Lynn, Mass., 1989-94; prin. cons. Gas Turbine Svcs., Salem, 1994—. Ind. bldg. cons., Methuen, Mass., 1983—. Bd. dirs. Colonial Village Condo Assn., Methuen, 1986-88. Recipient Sanford A. Moss award, 1987, Managerial award Gen. Electric Co., 1987. Republican. Roman Catholic. Avocations: carpentry, computers, fishing, family activities, gardening. Home: 7 Dana Rd Salem NH 03079-3481

BONACQUIST, HAROLD FRANK, JR., lawyer; b. Schenectady, N.Y., June 14, 1948; s. Harold F. Sr. and Janice (Piper) B.; m. Lucy Carol Walters, Jan. 14, 1984; 1 child, Lucy Piper. BA, Cornell U., 1971; JD cum laude, Albany (N.Y.) Law Sch., 1974. Bar: N.Y., 1975. Litigation assoc. Weil, Gotshal & Manges, N.Y.C., 1976-81; legal rsch. clerk appellate divsn. 3d dept. Albany, 1975-76; counsel Traub, Bonacquist & Fox, N.Y.C., 1995-99, mem., 1982—95, ABA liaison to Romania, 1999—2001, ABA liaison to Slovakia, 2002; econ. officer U.S. Fgn. Svc., Vienna, Va., 2002—. Lectr. N.Y. State Commn. Corrections, Albany, 1973-74; legal writing instr. Albany Law Sch., 1973-74; mediator U.S. Bankruptcy Ct. So. Dist., N.Y.C., 1994—. Comments editor Albany Law Rev., 1973-74; contbr. articles to profl. jours. V.p., nat. legal advisor The Holiday Project, San Francisco, 1984-87; com. mem. The Presbyn. Ch., Mt. Kisco, N.Y., 1994-95. Mem. ABA, Justinian Soc. Republican. Home: 2763 Manhattan Pl Vienna VA 22180 E-mail: bonacquist@compuserve.com.

BONADONNA, RICCARDO C. endocrinologist; b. Palermo, Italy, Apr. 17, 1957; s. Giuseppe and Carmela (Scaletta) B.; m. Marina Marzani, Sept. 2, 1990; children: Ester, Marco. MD, Sch. Medicine, Genova, Italy, 1981. Resident in internal medicine Genova City Hosp., 1981-84; postdoctoral fellow CNR, Pisa, Italy, 1984-85, Yale U., New Haven, Conn., 1985-88; JDF fellow U. Tex., San Antonio, 1988-90; rsch. scientist CNR, 1990-93; clin. asst. prof. U. Tex., 1993—. Sr. cons. Verona (Italy) City Hosp., 1994-99; asst. prof. U. Verona, 1999—. Author: Obesity, 1992, International Textbook of Diabetes Mellitus, 1997; editor: Bioingegneria Dei Sistemi Metabolici, 1998. Mem. European Assn. Study of Diabetes, Am. Diabetes Assn., Italian Soc. Diabetes. Avocations: soccer, philosophy, painting. Office: Ospedale Civile Maggiore Piazzale Stefani 1 I37126 Verona Italy E-mail: rcbonado@tin.it.

BONAGURA, DIANE SUSAN, global study manager; b. Suffern, N.Y., Nov. 25, 1967; d. Anthony and Albina Bonagura. BS in Cmty. Health Edn., William Paterson U., 1989; MS in Biomed. Informatics, U. Medicine and Dentistry N.J., 2003. Global clin. sci. assoc. Hoffmann-LaRoche/Roche Labs., Nutley, NJ, 1998—99, global clin. ops. assoc., 1999—2001, global study mgr., 2001—. Clin. ops. coord. Hoffmann-La Roche/Roche Labs., Nutley, 1997-98. Mem. Drug Info. Soc. Office: Hoffmann-La Roche Inc Bldg 1/3 340 Kingsland St Nutley NJ 07110 Office Fax: 973-562-3220. E-mail: diane.bonagura@roche.com.

BONAGURA, VINCENT R. pediatrician, educator, researcher; b. N.Y.C., Mar. 30, 1949; s. Vincent P. and Vivian M. Bonagura; m. Barbara Ann Liskin, June 3, 1982 (dec. Apr. 1994); children: Elizabeth, Rebecca Amy. BA, Columbia U., 1971, MD, 1975. Diplomate Am. Bd. Pediatrics, Am. Bd. Allergy and Immunology (bd. dirs. 1999—), Bd. Diagnostic Lab. Immunology. Intern Babies Hosp.-Columbia-Presbyn. Med. Ctr., N.Y.C., 1975-76, resident in pediat., 1976-78; asst. prof. pediatrics Columbia U., N.Y.C., 1981-82, asst. prof. pediatrics and microbiology, 1982-85; chief divsn. allergy, immunology, rheumatology Schneider Children's Hosp./L.I. Jewish Med. Ctr., 1985-99; assoc. prof. pediatrics Albert Einstein Coll. Medicine, Bronx, N.Y., 1989-94, assoc. prof. pediatrics, microbiology and immunology, 1991-94, prof., 1994—; dir. divsn. allergy/immunology North Shore/L.I. Jewish Health Care Sys., 1999—. Adj. asst. prof. microbiology Columbia U.; dir. Am. Bd. Allergy and Immunology, 2000—; appointee allergy and immunology rrc ACGME, 2001—. Contbr. articles to profl. jours. Fellow Am. Acad. Allergy and Immunology (tng. dirs. exec. com.); mem. Am. Assn. Immunology, Soc. for Pediatric Rsch., Am. Coll. Rheumatology, Am. Acad. Pediatrics, Alpha Omega Alpha. Avocations: tennis, music, gardening. Office: LI Jewish Med Ctr Dept Pediatrics Schneider Children's Hosp New Hyde Park NY 11040 E-mail: bonagura@lij.edu.

BONANNI, VICTORIA, writer, small business owner; b. Jersey City, N.J., Dec. 13, 1952; d. Joseph Salvatore and Dolores DiMaria (Aidala) B. BA in English/Secondary Edn., SUNY, Stony Brook, 1974. Cert. ESL tutor, electronics technician. Sec., retail newsletter editor Zayre, Inc., Framingham, Mass., 1974; temporary sec., adminstrv. asst. Manpower, Inc., Salem, Mass., 1975; reporter/photographer The Beverly (Mass.) Times, 1976; mktg. comm. coord. United Shoe Machinery Corp., Middleton, Mass., 1977-79; adminstrv. writer HBH Co., Rosslyn, Va., 1979-80; technical writer Teradyne, Inc., Boston, 1981-89; sr. technical writer Panametrics, Inc., Waltham, Mass., 1989, EMC Corp., Hopkinton, Mass., 1991; owner, prin. writer VB Documentation Enterprises, Natick, Mass., 1991—; part-time customer svc. rep. May Dept. Stores Co. (Filene's), Natick, 1998—. Author, editor: A Blue Perfume, 1993; editor: Dolorata: Looking To The Future (Dolores Fiore), 1995, Burning Heads (Lawrence Carradini), 1996, A Bowl of Cherries: Just Spit The Pits (Mark Willman), 1996, I Wish That My Room Had a Floor Living With An Emotional Disorder (Rafael Woolf), 1996, A Pen Is Like A Piece (Gary Hicks), 1997, Hot Moon Night (Ann Murphy Fletcher), 1998, Of Rare Design (William J. Barnum), 1999; author: Ad Vivum, 2001. Direct mail fund raiser-coord. Kennedy Sr. Ctr., Natick, 1997. Recipient honorable mention "Writer's Digest", Cin., 1993, 2001, 80 Hrs. Cmty. Svc. award Natick Vis. Nurse Assn., 1996; recipient Cambridge Poetry Award, 2d prize, Mass., 2001. Mem. NAFE, Soc. Am. Poets, Natick Ctr. Assocs. Roman Catholic. Avocations: original greeting cards, miniatures, historical perspectives, theology, songwriting.

BONAPART, ALAN DAVID, lawyer; b. San Francisco, Aug. 4, 1930; s. Benjamin and Rose B.; m. Helen Sennett, Aug. 20, 1955; children— Paul S., Andrew D. AB with honors, U. Calif., Berkeley, 1951, JD, 1954. Bar: Calif. 1955, U.S. Tax Ct. 1965, U.S. Supreme Ct. 1971. Assoc. Bancroft & McAlister (formerly Bancroft, Avery & McAlister), San Francisco, 1959-62; ptnr. Bancroft & McAlister, San Francisco, 1962-93, Bancroft & McAlister, A Profl. Corp., 1993-99, Bancroft & McAlister LLP, 1999—. Past trustee Bancroft and McAlister Found.; mem. adv. com. Heckerling Estate Planning Inst., U. Miami, Fla., 1974-87, 92—, mem. faculty, 1974, 91-2000; past dir. Myrtle V. Fitchen Charitable Trust. Mem. ABA, Am. Coll. Trust and Estate Counsel, Bar Assn. San Francisco, State Bar Calif. (cert. in estate planning, probate and trust law Bd. Legal Specialization 1991). Office: Bancroft & McAlister LLP Ste 120 300 Drake's Landing Rd Greenbrae CA 94904-3123 E-mail: abonapart@bamlaw.com.

BONAR, DANIEL DONALD, mathematics educator; b. Murraysville, W.Va., July 7, 1938; s. Nelson Edward and Ada Polk Bonar; m. Martha Dolores Baker, Aug. 8, 1966; 1 child, Mary Martha. BSChemE, W.Va. U., 1960, MS in Math., 1961; PhD in Math., Ohio State U., 1968. Instr. Denison U., Granville, Ohio, 1965-66, asst. prof., 1966-68, 69-71, assoc. prof., 1971-77, prof., 1977—, George R. Stibitz disting. prof. math. and computer sci., 1995, chair dept. math and computer sci., 1971-77, 96-97; asst. prof. Wayne State U., Detroit, 1968-69. Vis. asst. prof. Ohio State U., Columbus, 1968. Author: On Annular Functions, 1971; contbr. articles to profl. jours. Active Granville Sch. Bd., 1973-79, pres., 1979; active Licking County Joint Vocat. Sch. Bd., Newark, Ohio, 1974-79, Granville Devel. Bd., 1974-79, Granville Found., 1996—. Inducted into W.Va. U. Chem. Engring. Dist. Alumni Acad., 1999. Mem. Nat. Coun. Tchrs. Math., Math. Assn. Am. Democrat. Methodist. Avocations: checkers, puzzles, local history buff, farming, traveling. Home: 237 W Elm St Granville OH 43023-1106 Office: Dept Math and Computer Sci Denison Univ Granville OH 43023 E-mail: bonar@denison.edu.

BONASSI, JODI, artist, marketing consultant; b. L.A., Aug. 22, 1953; d. Julian and Sara (DeNorber) Feldman; m. Raymond Gene Bonassi, June 7, 1986; 1 child, Spencer. Student, Otis Art Inst., L.A., 1972, Calif. State U., 1983-85, Calif. State U., Northridge, 1985-86. Participating artist Concern Found. and World Cup Soccer Gala Event for Cancer Rsch., Beverly Hills, Calif., 1994;

lectr., guest spkr. L.A. Pub. Libr., Canoga Park, 1999, Pierce Coll., 2003; mem. adv. bd. Park LaBrea Art Coun.; guest spkr. Pierce Coll., 2003. Artist, Creative With Words Publs., 1987, greeting cards, 1994—; one-woman shows include Pt. Adesa Gallery, Rancho Mirage, Calif., 1996, Orlando Gallery, 1999, Performing Arts Gallery, Calif. State U., Northridge, 2002; exhibited in group shows at Bowles-Sorokko Gallery, Beverly Hills, 1994, ChaChaCha, Encino, Calif., 1994—, Lyn/Bassett Gallery, L.A., 1994, Topanga (Calif.) Canyon Gallery, 1994, Hartog Fine Art Gallery, L.A., 1995, Charles Hecht Gallery, Tarzana, Calif., 1995, New Canyon Gallery, Topanga, 1995, Made With Kare, West Hills, Calif., 1995, Gail Michael Collection, Northridge, 1995, Mythos Gallery, Burbank, 1995-96, Nicole Brown Simpson Found., 1996, Orlando Gallery, Sherman Oaks, Calif., 1998, West Gallery, U. Calif., Fullerton, 1998, The Century Gallery at Mission Coll., 1998, Orlando Gallery, 1998-99, Christie's Beverly Hills Silent Auction, 1999, Palos Verdes Art Ctr. Gallery, 1999, White Meadows Gallery, 2000, St. Louis Artist Guild Gallery, 2000, Bank of Am., Laguna Beach, 2000, Almost Paradise Gallery, Laguna Beach, 2d City Gallery, Long Beach, 2002, Cambridge Nat. Prize Show, 2002, 03, 2d City Coun. Gallery Exhibit, 2003, Beckstrand Gallery, Palos Verdes, 2003, Pierce Art Gallery, 2003, Pierce Art Gallery, 2003, Lankershim Art Gallery, 2003, Beckstrand Gallery, Palos Verdes, Calif., 2003, others; represented in pvt. collections; commd. works include Von's Corp., Alhambra Bus. Assn., North Hollywood Revitalization Program; illustrator All About Us, 1996; featured in books, including Living Artists, 13th edit., 2003, New Art International, 4th edit., 2003, Community of Angels Book, 2001; featured in various articles and art revs. including Pasadena Star News and Pasadena Weekly, The Chronicle Rev., L.A. Daily News, Harpers Mag., Boston Globe, 2003, also Showtime Cable-TV Film: Trust Me, 1997, Chandler Outdoor Gallery Documentary, 2002, other exhbns.; featured artist in Living Artist, 2003; pub. art commn. MTA of N. Hollywood Fence Panel Project, 2003. Art tchr. K-12 West Valley Christian Ch. Schs., 1997—. Recipient Best Banner 2d prize L.A. County Mus. Art, Park LaBrea Arts Couns. for PLB/LACMA Family Art Fund, 1997, World Peace Tour, 1997, Spl. Judges Art award Park LaBrea Art Coun., 1998, nat. prize Cambridge Art Assn., 2002, Outstanding Painting award Nat. Portrait Gallery, Washington, 2003, Smithsonian Nat. Portrait Gallery. Mem. Calif. Women Bus. Owners, L.A. Mcpl. Art Gallery Registry, So. Calif. Women's Caucus for Art, Soc. Children's Bookwriters and Illustrators. Avocations: hiking, reading, swimming. E-mail: jbonassi@aol.com.

BONATO, PAOLO, electrical engineer, educator; arrived in U.S., 1996; Degree in elec. engring., Politecnico di Torino, Italy, MSEE, 1989; PhD, U. di Roma La Sapienza, 1995. Registered profl. engr., Italy, 1990. Rsch. asst. prof. Boston U., Boston, 1996—2002; asst. prof. PM&R Harvard Med. Sch., Boston, 2002—. Recipient Antonio Venerando award, Italian Soc. of Cardiology, 1995. Mem.: IEEE.

BONAVENTURA, LEO MARK, gynecologist, educator; b. East Chicago, Ill., Aug. 1, 1945; s. Angelo Peter and Wanda D. (Kelleher) B.; student Marquette U., 1963-66; M.D., Ind. U., 1970; married; children— Leo Mark, Dena Anne, Angela Lorena, Nicole Palmira, Leah Michelle, Adam Xavier. Intern in surgery, Cook County Hosp., Chgo., 1970-71; resident in ob-gyn., Ind. U. Hosps., 1973-76, fellow in reproductive endocrinology and infertility, 1976-78; asst. prof. ob-gyn., Ind. U., 1976—, asst. head sect. reproductive endocrinology and infertility, 1978-80, head sect., 1980-81. Served with USN attached to USMC, 1971-73. Named Intern of Yr., Cook County Hosp., 1971. Diplomate Am. Bd. Obstetrics and Gynecology, Am. Bd. Reproductive Endocrinology and Infertility. Mem. Central Assn. Ob-Gyn., Am. Coll. Obstetricians and Gynecologists, Am. Fertility Soc., Can. Fertility Soc., Soc. Reproductive Endocrinologists, Soc. Reproductive Surgeons. Roman Catholic. Contbr. articles to profl. jours. Office: 8091 Township Line Rd Indianapolis IN 46260-2494

BONAVITA, DENNIS JOSEPH, newspaper publisher; b. Warren, Pa., Dec. 7, 1942; s. Joseph L. and Ann R. (Critelli) B.; children: Christopher, Michael, Matthew, Theresa, Gregory, Natalie. Student, Gannon U., Erie, Pa., 1960-65. Sportswriter Erie Times-News, 1963-67; claims adjuster Erie Ins. Group, 1966-68; pharm. sales Ayerst Labs., Canton, Ohio, 1968-71; sports editor Warren Times Observer, 1968-71, news editor, 1971-72, city editor, 1972-89, mng. editor, 1989-90, The Courier-Express, DuBois, Pa., 1990—2000, publ., 2000—. Recipient Best Column Writing award Pa. Newspaper Pubs. Assn., 1979, 86, 89, 91, 94, 98, 2000. Mem. Nat. Conf. Editorial Writers, Pa. Soc. Newspaper Editors, AP Mng. Editors of Pa. (bd. dirs. 1993, pres. 2001-02, Best Editorial Writing award 1984, 85, 92). Roman Catholic. Avocations: teaching religious education, gardening, hunting. Home: 121 Barnett St Brookville PA 15825 Office: The Courier-Express PO Box 407 Du Bois PA 15801-0407 E-mail: dubedit@penn.com.

BONAZZI, ELAINE CLAIRE, mezzo-soprano; b. Endicott, N.Y. d. John Dante and Zina (Rossi) B.; m. Jerome Ashe Carrington, Sept. 21, 1963; 1 child, Christopher. BM (George Eastman scholar), Eastman Sch. Music. Currently artist-in-residence SUNY, Stonybrook; pvt. voice studio N.Y.C. Past faculty Peabody Conservatory; vis. prof. Eastman Sch. Music, Rochester, N.Y., 1979; judge nat. and internat. competitions. Debuts, Santa Fe Opera, 1958, Opera Soc. Washington, 1960, N.Y.C. Opera, 1965, Opera Internacional, Mexico City, Mexico, 1966, Metropolitan Opera at the Forum, 1973, Europe, West Berlin Festival opera, 1961, Spoleto (Italy) Festival, 1974, Castel Franco Festival Venetian Music, Venice, Italy, 1975, Berlin Bach Festival, 1976, Pks. Radio TV Difusion, 1980—; Netherlands Opera, 1978, Minn. Opera, 1985, Artpark Festival, 1987, Opera Theater of St. Louis, 1988, New Orleans Opera, 1988, Paris, 1979, Spoleto-Charleston Festival, 1981, Edmonton Opera Can., 1990, New Orleans Opera, 1990, Winnipeg Opera, 1993, Edmonton Opera, 1992; frequent Libr. of Congress concerts; title role in Pique Dame, Washington Opera, 1989, in Vanessa, Opera Theatre of St. Louis, 1988, Carlson's Midnight Angel, Opera Theatre of St. Louis, 1993, Glimmerglass Opera La Calisto, 1995; lead N.Y.C. Opera; soloist N.Y. Philharmonic, Phila. Orch., Boston Symphony, Cleve. Orch., Canadian Broadcasting Corp., PBS NET Opera Theatre, NBC, ABC, CBS TV networks, recs. on, Candide, Columbia, Vanguard, CRI, Folkways, Vox, Grenadilla, Pro Arte and Nonesuch Records; over 40 world premiers of major works by leading composers with major orchs. and opera cos. Named 1 of 6 honored alumni 50th Anniversary Year, Eastman Sch. Music, 1971, Trustees Council U. Rochester, 1976, Recital in honor of 75th Anniversary of Eastman Sch. of Music, 1996; formerly William Matheus Sullivan grantee; recipient Concert Artists Guild award, 1960; more operatic premiers than any other living Am. singer. Mem. Mu Phi Epsilon. Achievements include being chosen by Stravinsky, Hindemith, Menotti, Chavez, Rorem, Thomson, Argento, Pasatieri, Diamond, Elliott Carter for premieres of their works, master classes Europe and U.S. Office: care Trawick Artists 250 W 57th St New York NY 10107-6915 *In performing great music one tries to be honest as well as inventive-in communicating emotion. And one tries to remain true to the intentions of the composer. It can be a frustrating task requiring infinite patience and infinite care, but what joy for the performer when at last he can touch the heart of the listener.*

BONCHER, AUSTIN J. music educator, director; b. De Pere, Wis., Apr. 2, 1941; m. Judith A. Boncher, Aug. 20, 1941; children: Michael, Amy. MusM, Ind. U. Music tchr. Menaska Pub. Schs., Appleton (Wis.) Pub. Schs., dir. Music Dept., dir. Fine Arts, ret. Founder Appleton (Wis.) Boys Choir, White Heron Chorale; dir. Trinity Luth. Ch. Music. Recipient Renaissance award, Thrivant Fin., 1992, Paul Harris award, Rotary, 1998. Avocations: camping, hiking, travel, reading. Home: 803 S Pierce Ave Appleton WI 54914-5418

BONCHEV, DANAIL GEORGIEV, chemist, educator; b. Burgas, Bulgaria, Feb. 20, 1937;, naturalized, 2001; s. Georgi Nikolov and Penka Danailova Bonchev; m. Pravdolyuba Vladimirova, Oct. 31, 1960 (div. 1983); 1 child, Adelina Boncheva; m. Dimitrina Kostova, June 10, 1984; 1 child, Elina. MSChemE, High Inst. Chem. Tech., Sofia, Bulgaria, 1960; PhD in Quantum Chemistry, Acad. Scis., Sofia, Bulgaria, 1970; DSc in Math. Chemistry, State U., Moscow, 1984. Process engr. Chem. Kombinat, Dimitrovgrad, Bulgaria, 1960-63; asst. prof. chemistry High Inst. Chem. Tech. (name now Assen Zlatarov U.), Burgas, Bulgaria, 1963-72, assoc. prof., head dept phys. chemistry, 1973-91, prof. chemistry, 1987—, dean inorganic chemistry faculty, 1987-91. Head lab. math. chemistry Bulgarian Acad. Scis., Sofia, 1986-91; rector, founder Free Univ., Burgas, Bulgaria, 1991-94; rsch. cons., Houston, 1995—; adj. prof. Tex. A&M U., Galveston, 1999—; referee internat. jours. in theoretical chemistry; vis. scientist U. Tex., Houston, 1992-94; tchr. chemistry and physics Texas A&M U., 1994-96. Author: Information-Theoretical Characterization of Chemical Structures, 1983, (textbook) Structure of Matter, 1979, Physical Chemistry, 1994, Chemical Reaction Networks, 1996; editor: (series) Mathematical Chemistry, Graph Theoretical Approach to Chemical Reactivity; mem. editl. bd. Jour. Math. Chemistry, 1987-93, MATCH, 1989—, SAR and QSAR in Environ. Rsch., 1994—, Asian Jour. Spectroscopy, 1997—, ARKIVOC, 2000—, Chemistry and Biodiversity, 2003—; contbr. over 190 articles to internat. sci. jours., 2 monographs, 3 textbooks. Decorated Cyril and Methodius order II, State Coun. Bulgaria, Sofia, 1987. Mem. AAAS, . Soc. Math. Chemistry (officer), Am. Chem. Soc., N.Y. Acad. Scis., Bulgarian Acad. Scis. (corr.). Achievements include contbns. to characterization of molecular topology, molecular branching, cyclicity, centrality; in deriving the properties of chem. elements (transactinids), compounds, polymers and crystals from their structure; in the classification, coding, and complexity of chemical compounds and mechanisms of chemical reactions, in developing chemical information theory in quantifying biocomplexity, in characterising biological and ecological networks, etc. Office: Tex A&M U 5007 Ave U Galveston TX 77551 also: Assen Zlatarov U 8010 Burgas Bulgaria E-mail: bonchevd@tamug.tamu.edu., bonchevd@sbcglobal.net.

BONCI, ANDREW S. chiropractor; b. Yonkers, N.Y., Apr. 27, 1963; BA, U. Denver, 1986; D Chiropractic, Cleveland Chiropractic Coll., Kansas City, Mo., 1989. Diplomate Am. Acad. Pain Mgmt., Am. Acad. Experts in Traumatic Stress. Pvt. practice, N.Y.C., 1990-95; assoc. prof. Cleveland Chiropractic Coll., Kansas City, Mo., 1995—2002, chmn. dept. diagnosis, 1998—2002; dir. Radiant Heart Found., 1999—; founder Galilee Project, 2002—. Address: 5734 Russell St Mission KS 66202 Personal E-mail: andrew@galileeproject.net.

BONCI, ANTONELLO, neurologist; b. Pesaro, Italy; s. Bruno Bonci and Maria Lea Burioni; m. Maria Chiara Mar Sciani, July 24, 1994. MD, Cath. U. Rome, 1991; degree in Neurology, U. Rome, 1995. Diplomate Italy. Rsch. asst. prof. Hosp. S. Lucia, Rome, 1996—98; asst. prof. Ernest Gallo Clin. and Rsch. Ctr. U. Calif., San Francisco, 1999. Contbr. articles to profl. jours. Mem.: Rsch. Soc. Alcoholism, Soc. Neuroscience, Alzheimer's Assn. (founder 1994). Avocations: art, music, sailing, tennis, reading. Home: 1302 Baker San Francisco CA 94115 Office: Ernest Gallo Clinic and Rsch Center Ste 200 5858 Horton St Emeryville CA 94608-2007

BOND, ALMA HALBERT, psychoanalyst, author; b. Phila., Feb. 6, 1923; BA in Psychology (with honors), Temple U., 1944; MA in Psychology, NYU, 1951; PhD in Devel. Psychology, Columbia U., 1961. Diplomate Am. Bd. Psychotherapy. Pvt. practice psychoanalysis pvt. practice, N.Y.C., 1953-91; tng. analyst Inst. Psychoanalytic Tng. and Rsch., N.Y.C., 1963—. Author: Who Killed Virginia Woolf, A Psychobiography, 1989, 2000, (with Lucy Freeman) America's First Woman Warrior: The Courage of Deborah Sampson, 1992, Dream Portrait, 1992, Is There Life After Analysis?, 1993, On Becoming a Grandparent, 1994, Profiles of Key West, 1996, the Autobiography of Maria Callas, a Novel, 1998, 2000, I Married Dr. Jekyll and Woke Up Mrs. Hyde, or What Happens to Love, 2000, Tales of Psychology: Short Stories to Make You Wise, 2002; sr. writer CAYO mag.; contbr. Key West Citizen, Solaris Hill, Tropic Keys, Time Out, Remember. Lt. USN, 1944—46. Recipient Honors in Psychology Temple U., 1944, Winner Am. Literary Press Contest, 1993, Runner up First Novel Contest, 1995, Hemingway award, Fla. State awards for fine writing. Mem.: Inst. for Psychoanalytic Tng. and Rsch., Internat. Psychoanalytic Assn., APA. Home and Office: Harbor House Apt 1135S 10275 Collins Ave Bal Harbour FL 33154 E-mail: almahb@cs.com.

BOND, BEVERLY GREENE, education educator, writer; b. Memphis, Apr. 16, 1946; d. Julius B.L. and Freda Franklin Greene; m. Geraldus Bond, June 1, 1970; 1 child, Julia Bond Ellingboe. BS, Memphis State U., 1963, MA, 1968; MEd, Teachers Coll. Columbia U., 1976; PhD, U. Memphis, 1991. Tchr. Teaneck (N.J.) HS, 1971—85, Germantown (Tenn.) HS, 1985—96; asst. prof. U. Memphis, 1996—2002, assoc. prof., 2002—. Dir. African and African Am. studies U. Memphis, 2003—. Author: (book chpt.) Negotiating the Boundaries of Southern Womanhood, 2000, Trial and Triumph, 2002. Adv. com. Nat. Heritage Area for Civil War in Tenn., 1999—; mem., treas. Shelby County Hist. Commn., Memphis, 1997—; mem. West Tenn. Hist. Soc. Grantee Fulbright-Hays Travel Grant, U.S. Office Edn., 1977. Mem.: Orgn. of Am. Historians, So. Assn. of Women Historians, So. Hist. Assn. (com. of minority historians 2003—). Office: Univ of Memphis 3706 Alumni St Memphis TN 38152 Fax: 901-678-2720. E-mail: bgbond@memphis.edu.

BOND, CHRISTOPHER SAMUEL (KIT BOND), senator, lawyer; b. St. Louis, Mar. 6, 1939; s. Arthur D. and Elizabeth (Green) B.; 1 child, Samuel Reid. BA with honors, Princeton U., 1960; LLB, U. Va., 1963. Bar: Mo. 1963, U.S. Supreme Ct. 1967. Law clk. to presiding chief justice U.S. Ct. of Appeals (5th cir.), Atlanta, 1963-64; assoc. Covington & Burling, Washington, 1965-67; pvt. practice law Mexico, Mo., 1968; asst. atty. gen., chief counsel consumer protection div. State of Mo., 1969-70, gov., 1973-77, 81-85; auditor, 1971-73; ptnr. Gage & Tucker, Kansas City, 1985-87; U.S. senator from Mo., 1987—; chmn. small bus. com. 104th Congress. Mem. appropriations com., 1991—, chmn. subcom. on VA, HUD and ind. appropriations agys., 1991—, subcom. on def., 1993—, subcom. on fgn. ops., 1999—, subcom. on transp., 1995—; budget com., 1989—, environment and pub. works com., 1995—, subcom. on drinking water, fisheries and wildlife, 1995—; chmn. small bus. com., senate Rep. policy com.; pres. Gt. Plains Legal Found., Kansas City, Mo., 1977-80; chmn. Rep. Gov.'s Assn., Midwestern Gov.'s Conf., chmn. con. on econ. and community devel., 1981-83, chmn. con. on energy and environment, 1983-84. Republican. Presbyterian. Office: US Senate 274 Russell Senate Bldg Washington DC 20510-0001*

BOND, CLAYTON ALAN, foreign affairs fellow; b. Detroit, Mich., July 21, 1976; s. Alan D. and Claudette Robena (Davis) B. BA, Hampton U., 1998; M of Pub. Policy, Harvard U., 2000; MSc in Environ. Change and Mgmt., Oxon, 2001. Intern U.S. E.P.A., Washington, 1997, Louise Ellman, M.P., Ho. of Commons, London, 1998. Grad. fgn. affairs fellow Woodrow Wilson Nat. Fellowship Found., 1998-2000; Hampton U. Presdl. scholar, 1994-98. Mem. NAACP, Am. Fgn. Svc. Assn., Fulbright Assn., Rotary. Avocations: travel, reading, theater. Office: US Embassy Bogotá Unit 5108 Apo AA 34038 E-mail: clayton_bond@hotmail.com.

BOND, DENNIS EARL, auditor; b. Kansas City, Kans., Dec. 12, 1950; s. Earl Lloyd and Carrie Irene (Law) B.; m. Karla Jo Kennamer, July 28, 1979; children: Holly, Ryan, Blake. BS, Abilene Christian U., 1972. Sr. auditor Laventhol & Horwath, CPA, Dallas, 1972-73; sr. acct. Kruchten & Magnuson, CPA, Ft. Collins, Colo., 1973-74; advanced sr. auditor Blue Cross Blue Shield Kansas City, Mo., 1974-81; audit supr. Blue Cross Blue Shield Mo., Kansas City, Mo., 1981-84, br. mgr., 1984-90, unit mgr. St. Louis, Mo., 1990-92; mgr. Blue Cross Blue Shield Miss., St. Louis, 1992—. Mem. Healthcare Fin. Mgmt. Assn. (advanced). Republican. Mem. Ch. of Christ. Avocations: golf, boating, water skiing. Home: 430 Lantana Ln Saint Peters MO 63376-5309 Office: Blue Cross Blue Shield Miss Ste 350 13545 Barrett Parkway Dr Ballwin MO 63021-5896

BOND, FRANCES CURTIS, retired editor; b. Chgo., Feb. 9, 1909; d. Vine Harlan Sr. and Frances Lay (Watson) Curtis; m. Bradford Austin Bond, Mar. 8, 1940 (dec. Nov. 1991); 1 child, David Bradford (dec. Oct. 1997). B Journalism, U. Mo., 1932. Editor Nutrilite News Mytinger & Casselberry, Inc., Long Beach, Calif., 1948-58; dir. pub. info. and cmty. rels. Long Beach Commn. on Econ. Opportunities, 1967-77; cmty. editor Long Beach Rev. mag., 1978-90; ret., 1990. Bd. dirs., historian Ch. Women United, Long Beach, 1996; mission coord. United Meth. Women, Long Beach, 1996; mem. adminstrv. bd. Grace United Meth. Ch., Long Beach, 1996; former bd. dirs., exec. com. Pacific Coast Press Club; former adv. coun. com. on aging United Way; former mem. Calif. Atty. Gen.'s Adv. Com. on Consumer Info. and Crime Prevention for Sr. Citizens; former bd. dirs., sec. Calif. Dirs. Aging Programs; former mem. adv. bd. Sr. Opportunities and Svcs. Elderly Nutrition Program; former mem. adv. bd. Long Beach Children's Mus.; former bd. dirs. Internat. Cmty. Coun. of Calif. State U., Long Beach, Long Beach Ballet; former bd. dirs., exec. com. South Bay Indian Svcs., NAACP, Long Beach, Pacific Coast Press Club; docent, vol. Long Beach Aquarium of the Pacific, 1998—. Recipient 4 1st Pl. and 3 2d Pl. awards Internat. Indsl. Publs. Contest, 1951, Blue Pencil award for Outstanding Govt. Publs., Fed. Editors Assn., 1974, 75, 1st and 2d Pl. award Calif. Cmty. Action Exec. Dirs. Assn., 1976, Merit award Pacific Coast Press Club, 1988, Mission Recognition award United Meth. Ch., 1990; named Safe Driver of Yr. Long Beach, Nat. Safety Coun., 1963, Vol. of Mo., Long Beach Sr. Ctr., 1991, Lay Person of Yr., Grace United Meth. Ch., 1996. Mem. DAR (life, bd. dirs. Susan B. Anthony chpt. 1989-90), NAACP (life), Fulton County Ind. Hist. Soc. (life), Ind. Hist. Soc., Soroptimist Internat. (life, Soroptomist of Long Beach Hall of Fame 1997), Soc. Mayflower Descendants. Democrat. Avocations: photography, geneology, volunteering, writing. Home: 1625 E Appleton St Apt 3-J Long Beach CA 90802-4026

BOND, JOAN, retired elementary school educator; b. Americus, Ga., Dec. 24, 1945; d. Doyle Holden and Frances (Brown) B. BS in Elem. Edn., U. Ga., 1975, MEd, 1979, EdS, 1982. Clk. emergency room St. Mary's Hosp., Athens, Ga., 1963-64; receptionist, asst. Office Dr. Shu-Yun T. Tsao, Athens, 1964-66; tchr. remedial reading Danielsville (Ga.) Elem. Sch., 1975-76, primary tchr., 1975-2000; substitute tchr. Madison County Bd. Edn., Danielsville, 2000—. Tchr., dir. presch. Hull (Ga.) Bapt. Ch., 1970-84, asst. tchr. adult class, 1985—; mem. honor roll com. Danielsville Elem. Sch. PTO, 1990-92. Mem. Madison County Ret. Educators Assn., Ga. Ret. Educators Assn. Democrat. Avocations: beach activities, U. Ga. football, basketball and gymnastics fan. Home: 999 Glenn Carrie Rd Hull GA 30646-4210 Office: Danielsville Elem Sch PO Box 67 Danielsville GA 30633-0067

BOND, JOHN RICHARD, astrophysicist; b. Toronto, Ont., Can., May 15, 1950; s. Jack Parry and Margaret (Sandham) B. MS, Calif. Inst. Tech., 1975, PhD, 1979. Rsch. scientist Kellogg Radiation Lab., Calif. Inst. Tech., Pasadena, 1977-78; postdoctoral fellow U. Calif., Berkeley, 1978-81; rsch. fellow Inst. Astronomy, Cambridge, Eng., 1982-83; asst. prof. Stanford (Calif.) U., 1981-85; assoc. prof. Stanford U./CITA, Stanford, Toronto, 1985-87; prof. Canadian Inst. Theoretical Astrophysics (CITA), Toronto, 1987—, acting dir., 1990-91, 94-95, dir., 1996—. Assoc., fellow Can. Inst. for Adv. Rsch., Toronto, 1985-86, 86—. Contbr. over 150 articles to profl. jours. Richard P. Feynman fellow, 1974-75; Sloan Found. Rsch. fellow, 1985-89; E.W.R. Steacie fellow, 1989-91, Steacie prize, NRC, 1989, others; recipient C.S. Beals award Can. Astron. Soc., 1996, CAP/CRM prize in Theoretical Math. and Physics, 1998. Fellow: Am. Phys. Soc., Royal Soc. London, Royal Soc. Can.; mem.: Am. Acad. Arts and Scis. (hon. fgn.), Inst. Physics, Can. Astron. Soc., Internat. Astron. Union, Am. Astron. Soc. (Heineman prize 2002). Achievements include cosmological research on the nature of the dark matter that accounts for over 90% of the mass of the universe and on the origin and evolution of galaxies and other cosmic structures. Office: Can Inst Theoretical Astro 60 George St Toronto ON Canada M5S 3H8 E-mail: bond@cita.utoronto.ca.

BOND, JOHN WALTER, historian; b. Orlando, Ky., May 17, 1933; s. John Y. and Mary A. (McCracken) B.; m. Betty P. Cloyd, Aug. 17, 1957; children: Beverly, Tammy, Jonna. BA in History, Berea Coll., 1956; MA in History, Ind. U., 1959; postgrad., Am. U., 1967-68. Historian Petersburg (Va.) Nat. Mil. Park, 1959-60, Pea Ridge (Ark.) Nat. Mil. Park, 1960-62; rsch. historian Jefferson Nat. Expansion Meml., St. Louis, 1962-63; historian Home of Franklin D. Roosevelt and Vanderbilt Mansion, Hyde Park, N.Y., 1963-66; rsch. historian Nat. Park Svc., Washington, 1966-69; historian Statue of Liberty, Ellis Island Fed. Hall Theodore Roosevelt, N.Y.C., 1969-72; regional historian Mid-Atlantic Region U.S. Nat. Park Svc., Phila., 1972-77, chief history, archeology, architecture, 1977-79, assoc. regional dir., 1979-86, chief, park historic pres., 1986-92; hist. cons. Cherry Hill, N.J., 1992—. Author: Home of Andrew Johnson, 1967, Augustus Saint-Gaudens: The Man and His Art, 1968, ASPET (Home of Saint-Gaudens), 1969, East Saint Louis, Illinois, 1969; contbr. articles to profl. jours. Chmn. bd. dirs. Bethel Bapt. Ch., Cherry Hill, N.J., 1983-84, bd. deacons, 1979-85, 89-92, pres. Berean Class, 1976-79, 92—. With U.S. Army, 1953-55. Mem. Pi Gamma Mu, Pi Alpha Theta. Republican. Avocations: travel, conducting historical tours, gardening, furniture restoration. Home and Office: 309 Old Orchard Rd Cherry Hill NJ 08003-1216

BOND, JON ROY, political science educator; b. Chickasha, Okla., Dec. 30, 1946; s. Henry Lee and Othelle (Payne) B.; m. Patricia Anne Garner (div. Apr. 1989); 1 child, Lynn Elizabeth Bond; m. Wanda Karon Martin Frazier, July 11, 1992; children: Mika Karon Frazier, Monika Kara Frazier. BA, Okla. State U., 1969, MA, 1973; PhD, U. Ill., 1978. Prof. polit. sci. Tex. A&M U., 1976—. Co-author: President in the Legislative Arena, 1990, Promise and Performance of American Democracy, 2001; co-editor: Jour. Politics, 1993-97, Polarized Politics: Congress and the President in a Partisan Era, 2000; contbr. articles to profl. jours. Precinct chair Brazos County Democratic Party, College Station, 1984-87. Mem. Am. Polit. Sci. Assn., Midwest Polit. Sci. Assn. (exec. coun. 1992-95), Southern Polit. Sci. Assn. (mem. exec. coun. 2000-2001, v.p.-elect 2002. v.p. 2003—), Pi Sigma Alpha (exec. coun. 1994-98). Democrat. Methodist. Home: 1412 Frost St College Station TX 77845-5630 Office: Tex A&M U Dept Polit Sci 4348 TAMU College Station TX 77843-4348 E-mail: jonbond@polisci.tamu.edu.

BOND, JULIAN, civil rights leader; b. Nashville, Jan. 14, 1940; s. Horace Mann and Julia Agnes (Washington) B.; m. Pamela S. Horowitz, Mar. 17, 1990; children by previous marriage: Phyllis Jane, Horace Mann, Michael, Jeffrey, Julia. BA, Morehouse Coll., 1971; LLD (hon.), Dalhousie U., 1969, U. Bridgeport, 1969, Wesleyan U., Conn., 1969, U. Oreg., 1969, Syracuse U., 1970, Eastern Mich. U., 1971, Tuskegee Inst., 1971, Howard U., 1971, Morgan State U., 1971, Wilberforce U., 1971, Patterson State Coll., 1972, N.H. Coll., 1973, Detroit Inst. Tech., 1973; DCL (hon.), Lincoln (Pa.) U., 1970, Bates Coll., 1998, Northeastern U., 1999, Edward Waters Coll., 1995, Gonzaga Sch. Law, 1997, Calif. State U., Monterey Bay, 1998, Washington U., 2000; LLD (hon.), Audrey Cohen Coll., New York, 2001. A founder Com. Appeal for Human Rights, 1960, exec. sec., 1961; a founder Student Nonviolent Coordinating Com., 1960, communications dir., 1961-66; reporter, feature writer Atlanta Inquirer, 1960-61, mng. editor, 1963; mem. Ga. Ho. of Reps., from Fulton County, 1965-75, Ga. State Senate, 1975-87. Vis. prof. history and politics Drexel U., 1988-89; Pappas fellow U. Pa., 1989; vis. prof. Harvard U., fall 1989, 91; prof. U. Va., fall 1990, 1993—, Am. U., 1991—, Williams Coll., fall 1992. So. corr. Reporting Racial Equality Wars; narrator Pts 1 and 2, Eyes on the Prize. Mem. adv. bd. Harvard Bus. Sch., Initiative on Social Enterprise; bd. dirs. So. Conf. Edn. Fund, So. Poverty Law Ctr., Coun. for Liveable World; pres. emeritus So. Poverty Law Ctr.; chmn. bd. dirs. NAACP, 1998—; chmn. Premier Auto Group Diversity Coun.

BOND, MARC DOUGLAS, lawyer; b. Spokane, Wash., July 3, 1954; s. Richard Milton and Patricia (Hendrickson) B.; m. Cathy Sue Kasner, July 16, 1977; children: Travis Eliot, Carly Mariah, Katie McKenzie, Juli Sierra. BA in Polit. Sci., Willamette U., 1975, JD cum laude, 1978. Bar: Wash. 1978, Alaska 1979, U.S. Dist. Ct. Alaska 1979, U.S. Ct. Appeals (9th cir.) 1984, U.S. Supreme Ct. 1991. Law clk. to presiding judge Alaska Ct. System, Anchorage, 1978-79; assoc. Delaney, Wiles, Hayes, Reitman & Brubaker, Inc., Anchorage, 1979-83; shareholder Delaney, Wiles, Hayes, Gerety, Ellis & Young, Inc., Anchorage, 1983-97; gen. counsel Mount Roberts Tramway Ltd. Partnership, 1995-98; asst. counsel Union Oil Co. of Calif., 1997—; gen. counsel Alaska Nitrogen Products, LLC, 1998-2001. Co-founder, bd. dirs. Arctic Power!, 1992—; spl. counsel Alaska Ski Areas Assn., 1992—97. Author: Alaska from Leasing to Production, 2000. Legal advisor Alaska div. Nat. Ski Patrol System Inc., Denver, 1982-89, dir. Alaska div., 1988-90, asst. nat. legal counsel, 1990-91, nat. legal counsel, 1991-97; dir. Sourdough Ski Patrol, Girdwood, Alaska, 1983-86; bd. dirs. ARC, Anchorage, 1983-86, Alaska Health Fair, Inc., 2001—; asst. scoutmaster Boy Scouts Am. Troop 209, 2001—. Mem. Wash. State Bar Assn., Alaska Bar Assn. (co-chair corp. counsel sect.), Federalist Soc., Asia Pacific Lawyers Assn. Republican. Avocations: skiing, hiking, camping, soccer. Office: Union Oil Co of Calif Unocal Alaska 909 W 9th Ave Anchorage AK 99501-3339 E-mail: mbond@unocal.com.

BOND, MEREDITH, medical educator; b. Sydney, N.S.W., Australia, Mar. 3, 1955; d. Kenneth Arthur and Jean Yvonne Bond; m. Antonio Scarpa, Mar. 3, 1998. BA, Macquarie U., Sydney, Australia, 1976; PhD, U. Pa., 1984. Assoc. staff to staff Cleve. Clinic Found., Molecular Cardiology Dept., 1992—2003; assoc. prof. to prof. Case Western Res. U., Physiology, Biophysics Dept., 1994—2002; prof. and chair U. Md. Sch Medicine, Physiology Dept, Balt., 2003—. Cons. NIH Peer Rev. Study Sect., Bethesda, Md., 1992—; com. chair Am. Heart Assoc., Rsch. Programs and Eval Com., Dallas; exec. com. mem. Biophysical Soc., Bethesda, Md., 1999—2002. Contbr. articles various profl.

jours. (Rsch. Award of the Am. Heart Assn., 2002). Com. mem., chair sub. com. Am. Heart Assn. Rsch. Program and Edn. Com., Dallas, 1997—2002. Grantee R01 Rsch. awards, NIH, 1996-2004. Mem.: Biophysical Soc., Am. Physiol. Soc. Achievements include research in identified genes involved in development of heart failure; identified proteins which regulate contractility of the heart. Avocations: hiking, travel.

BOND, NILES WOODBRIDGE, cultural institute executive, former foreign service officer; b. Newton, Mass., Feb. 25, 1916; s. George Wood and Clara Mehitabel (Bonney) B.; m. Julia Rice Folsom, June 25, 1940 (dec. Sept. 1986); children: Ellen Dudley, Nancy Kenneth; m. Pamela Guest Bird, Sept. 17, 1988 (dec. Sept. 2002). AB, U. N.C., 1937; A.M., Fletcher Sch. Law and Diplomacy, Medford, Mass., 1938. U.S. fgn. service officer, 1939-68; vice consul, 1939-40, Yokohama, Japan, 1940-41; 3d sec., vice consul Madrid, Spain, 1942-45; 2d sec., 1945-46; adviser to U.S. delegation to 4th session Econ. and Social Council, 1947; 2d sec., vice consul Bern, Switzerland, 1947; 1st sec. and consul, 1947; asst. chief div. N.E. Asian affairs Dept. State, 1947-49, officer in charge Korean affairs, 1949-50; adviser to U.S. delegation to 4th session UN Gen. Assembly, 1949; 1st sec. Office of U.S. Polit. Adviser to Supreme Comdr. Allied Powers, Tokyo, Japan, 1950; acting chmn. Allied Council for Japan, 1952, counselor embassy Tokyo, 1952, Seoul, Korea, 1953-54, Rome, Italy, 1956-58; dir. Office UN Polit. and Security Affairs, Dept. State, 1954-56; counselor of embassy, vis. lectr. Bologna Center, Johns Hopkins U., 1957-58; research fellow Ctr. for Internat. Affairs, Harvard, 1958-59; minister-counselor embassy Rio de Janeiro, Brazil, 1959-63; coordinator interdeptl. seminar Dept. State, 1963; minister, consul gen. São Paulo, Brazil, 1964-68; sec. bd. trustees Corcoran Gallery Art, Washington, 1973-86; pres., bd. dirs. Brazilian Am. Cultural Inst., 1976-86; mem. ct. sys. study com. D.C. Bar, 1979-81, exec. dir. fee arbitration bd., 1981-87. Exec. dir. Project Orbis, 1972; adviser São Paulo Bienal, 1969; dir. internat. exhbns. com. Am. Fedn. Art, 1976-77. Author: poetry Arcanum, 1965, Elegos, 1967, Dreams From a Wintry Night, 1993. Decorated commendatore Al Merito della Repubblica Italiana, grand officer Order So. Cross (Brazil). Mem. Univ. Club, Army and Navy Club (Washington), Harvard Club (N.Y.C.). Interned in Japan upon outbreak of war, repatriated on S.S. Gripsholm, Aug. 1942. Home: 14 Ferry Rd Apt E-2 Old Lyme CT 06371-2338

BOND, PATRICIA B. camping accessories company executive; b. N.Y.C., Sept. 1, 1928; m. Joseph N. Bond, July 15, 1950; children: Kathleen, Thomas, Jay, Randy. BA, CUNY, 1973; MA, Adelphi U., 1977. Tchr. Northport (N.Y.) H.S., 1973-93; adminstr., v.p. Bondco, Inc., Commack, N.Y., 1993—. Adj. instr. Syracuse (N.Y.) U., 1986-93; mem. Nat. Bd. Rev. (film screening group; presenter in field. Contbr. poetry to various publs. Bd. dirs. Northport Arts Coalition, 1998. Mem. AAUW, Nat. Mus. Women in Arts. Home: 28 Sarina Dr Commack NY 11725-1815

BOND, PETER DANFORD, physicist; b. Providence, Jan. 30, 1940; s. Douglas D. and Helen H. (Cannon) B.; m. Sandra E. Salim, Aug. 3, 1968; children: Jennifer, Colin; stepchildren: Anthony Shane, John Shane. BA, Harvard U., 1962; MA, Western Res. U., 1963; PhD, Case Western Res. U., 1969. Rsch. assoc. Stanford U., Palo Alto, Calif., 1969-72; from asst. physicist to acting chief Brookhaven Nat. Lab., Upton, NY, 1972—2002, acting chief info. officer, 2002—. Chmn. exec. com. Holifield Heavy Ion Rsch. Facility, 1981; mem. program adv. com. Super Heavy Ion Linear Accelerator, 1977-81, chmn., 1981; mem. program com. on heavy ions SUNY, Stony Brook; mem. panel to rev. maj. nuclear physics facilities Dept. Energy, 1987; mem. siting panel for Gammasphere, 1989; reviewer physics program SUNY Grad. Sch.; mem. physics divsn. adv. com. Oakridge Nat. Lab., 1992-97; mem. com. of visitors to NSF, 1994; mem. nuclear sci. adv. com. to Dept. Energy/NSF, 1994-97; mem. dean's adv. com. MIT/Lab. Nuclear Sci., 1994-99. Contbr. numerous articles to profl. jours. FOM fellow (the Netherlands), 1983-84. Fellow AAAS (steering com. on physics 2001-03), Am. Phys. Soc. (nuclear physics div. 1977-79, program com. 1989-90, mem. selection com. Tom Bonner Prize 2000-01, chair 2001); mem. Sigma Xi. Avocation: athletics. Home: 7 Simpson Pl Stony Brook NY 11790-1744 Office: Brookhaven Nat Lab Directors Office Bldg 460 Upton NY 11973 E-mail: bond@bnl.gov.

BOND, PHILLIP J. federal agency administrator; Grad., Linfield Coll. Spl. asst. Sec. of Def. for Legis. Affairs, 1987—90; chief of staff, rules com. assoc. Congressman Bob McEwen, 1990—92; prin. dep. asst. sec. Def. for Legis. Affairs, 1992—93; chief of staff Congresswoman Jennifer Dunn, 1993—98; sr. v.p. for govt. affairs, treas. Info. Tech. Industry Coun.; dir. fed. pub. policy Hewlett-Packard Co.; chief of staff to sec. commerce Dept. Commerce, Washington, 2002—, under sec. tech. adminstrn., 2001—. Com. mem. Pres. Nat. Sci. and Tech. Coun. Republican. Office: Dept Commerce Tech Adminstrn 14th & Constitution Ave NW Washington DC 20230

BOND, RICHARD LEE, lawyer, state senator; b. Kansas City, Kans., Sept. 18, 1935; s. Clarence Ivy and Florine (Hardison) B.; m. Sue S. Sedgwick, Aug. 23, 1958; children: Mark, Amy. BA, U. Kans., 1957, JD, 1960. City atty., Overland Park, Kans., 1960-62; adminstrv. asst. to Congressman Robert Ellsworth, Washington, 1961-66, Congressman Larry Winn, Washington, 1967-85, Congressman Jan Meyers, Washington, 1986; chmn. bd. dirs. Home State Bank, Kansas City, 1983-94; ptnr. Bennett, Lytle, Wetzler et al, Prairie Village, Kans., 1986-89; senator State of Kans., Topeka, 1985-2001, senate pres., 1997-2001. Vice chmn. Guaranty Bank and Bancshares, Kansas City, Kans., 1995-2002. Mem. Kans. Bd. Regents, 2002—. Named State Legislator of Yr. Governing Mag., 2002. Republican. Presbyterian. Avocations: gardening, tennis, hunting, fishing. Home: 9823 Nall Ave Shawnee Mission KS 66207-2915

BOND, ROBERT HAROLD, electrical engineering educator; b. Denver, July 27, 1936; s. James Lowell Bond and Clara Ferguson; m. Wilda Rae Gilbert, June 1, 1958; childen: James, Steven, Kevin. BSEE, Colo. State U., 1958; MSEE, Calif. Inst. Tech., 1959, PhD in Elec. Engring., 1965. Assoc. prof. elec. engring. Va. Poly. Inst. and State U., Blacksburg, 1965-71; test set design engr. Western Electric, Winston-Salem, N.C., 1971-80; engring. mgr. AT&T, Winston-Salem, 1980-93; mem. tech. staff Bell Labs., Princeton, N.J., 1993-94; assoc. prof. elec. engring. N.Mex. Tech., Socorro, 1994 . Patentee sealed contact test apparatus, nest for connector assembly tool. Mem. IEEE, Am. Soc. Engring. Edn. Avocations: sailing, car restoration. Office: NMex Tech 801 Leroy Pl Socorro NM 87801-4681

BOND, VICTORIA ELLEN, conductor, composer; b. L.A., May 6, 1945; d. Philip and Jane (Courtl) B.; m. Stephan Peskin, Jan. 27, 1974. B Mus. Arts, U. So. Calif., L.A., 1968; M Mus. Arts, Juilliard Sch. Music, 1975, D Mus. Arts, 1977; DFA (hon.), Washington and Lee U., 1992, Hollins Coll., 1995, Roanoke Coll., 1995. Condr., composer. Mem. N.Y. State Coun. Arts Music Panel, 1987-90; bd. dirs. N.Y. Women Composers. Guest condr. Cabrillo Music Festival, Calif., 1974, White Mountains Music Festival, N.H., 1975, Aspen (Colo.) Music Festival, 1976, Shenandoah Music Festival, W.Va., 1977, Colo. Philharm., 1978, Houston Symphony, 1979, 86, Buffalo Philharm., 1979, Pitts. Symphony, 1980, N.W. Chamber Orch., Seattle, 1980, Anchorage Symphony, 1980, 82, Ark. Symphony, 1981, Hudson Valley Philharm., N.Y., 1981, 98, Newton Symphony, Boston, 1982, Hartford Symphony, 1982, RTE Symphony, Dublin, Ireland, 1983, Albany Symphony Orch., 1984-85, Houston Symphony Orch., 1986, Richmond Symphony Orch., 1987, Williamsburg Symphony Orch., Greenville Symphony Orch., Des Moines Symphony Orch., Utah Symphony Orch., Cape Cod Symphony Orch., Tallahassee Symphony Orch., Va. Symphony Orch, 1988-90, Shanghai Symphony, 1993, 94, Erie (Pa.) Philharmonic, 1995, Amarillo (Tex.) Symphony, 1996, Opera Carolina, N.C., 1997, 99, Harrisburg (Pa.) Opera, 1997, 98, 99, 2000, 2001, 2002, Norwalk Symphony, 2002, Cutting Edge Concerts, 2002, Wuhan Symphony, China, 1997, 99, Hunan Symphony, Changsha, China, 1998, Honolulu Symphony, 1998, Louisville Symphony, 1998, Flagstaff Symphony, 1998, Greenville Symphony, 1998, 1998, Ray Charles 70th Birthday Concert, Warsaw (Poland) Symphony, York (Pa.) Symphony, Music from Penn's Woods (Pa.), 1999-2000, NY City Opera Showcasing Am. Composers, 2001; artistic dir. Cutting Edge Concerts, N.Y.C., 1999-2000, Hanisburg Opera, 1998-2003; music dir. New Amsterdam Symphony Orch., N.Y.C., 1978-80, Pitts. Youth Symphony Orch., 1978-80, Empire State Youth Orch., 1982-86, Southeastern Music Ctr., 1983-84, Bel Canto Opera, 1983-86, Roanoke (Va.) Symphony Orch., 1986-95; artistic dir. Bel Canto Opera Co., 1986-88, artistic adv., Wuhan Symphony (China), 1997—, Opera Roanoke, 1989-95; Exxon/Arts Endowment condr., Pitts. Symphony, 1978-80, recs. include Twentieth Century Cello, Two American Contemporaries, The Frog Prince, An American Collage, Live from Shanghai, Victoria Bond: Compositions, The American Piano Concerto, Yes, 2003; commd. by Pa. Ballet, 1978, Jacob's Pillow Dance Festival, 1979, Am. Ballet Theater, 1981, Empire State Inst. Performing Arts, 1983, 84, Stage One, Louisville, 1986, Ga. State U., 1986, L'Ensemble, 1990, Renaissance City Winds, 1990, Audubon String Quartet, 1990, Women's Philharm., San Francisco, 1993, Va. Explore Park and The Shanghai Symphony, 1994, D Day Found., 1994, Linda Plaut, 1994, The Billings (Mont.) Symphony, The Elgin (Ill.) Symphony, The Elements String Quartet, The Indpls. Chamber Orch., The Composers' Conf., The Jade String Trio; others. Bd. dirs. Am. Music Ctr. Recipient Victor Herbert award 1977, Perry F. Kendig award, 1988, ASCAP Composition award 1973—; Nat. Inst. for Music Theater grantee in opera conducting N.Y.C. Opera, 1985, Martha Baird Rockefeller grantee, 1978-79, Meet-The-Composer grantee in Composition, 1973—; Juilliard scholar, 1972-77; Juilliard fellow, 1975-77, Aspen Music Festival fellow, 1973-76; named Exxon/Arts Endowment Conductor, 1978-80, Woman of Yr. in Va., 1990, 91; featured on NBC Today show, 1990, profiled in C.S. Monitor, 1987, Wall Street Jour., 1987, other mags. and shows. Mem. ASCAP (awards 1975—), Am. Symphony Orch. League, Am. Fedn. Musicians, Condrs. Guild (bd. dirs. 1994—), Internat. Alliance Women in Music, N.Y. Women Composers, Mu Phi Epsilon. Avocations: horseback riding, sailing, hiking. E-mail: victoriabond@earthlink.net. *I believe that our life's work is in sharing our talents and gifts with others. Our own happiness and fulfillment are in direct proportion with the amount we give of ourselves.*

BOND, WILLIAM JENNINGS, JR., retired air force officer, scholar, educator; b. Boyce, La., Mar. 12, 1953; s. William Jennings and Iris Elizabeth (Chenault) B.; m. Karen Lynne Lloid, May 20, 1975 (dec. Aug. 1980); m. Mary Dean Clark, Nov. 19, 1983; 1 child, William Seth. B in Music Edn., Northwestern State U. La., 1974, MusM, 1978; MS in Adminstrn., Ctrl. Mich. U., 1992; grad., Joint Mil. Intelligence Coll., 1994; postgrad., Nova Southeastern U.; grad., Armed Forces Staff Coll. Choral dir. Fairview (La.) H.S., 1975-80; commd. 2d lt. USAF, 1980, advanced through grades to maj., 1991; comdr. sect. squadron 23d Civil Engrs., Alexandria, La., 1983-85; tng. flight comdr. USAF Officer Tng. Sch., San Antonio, 1985-87, chief student adminstrn., 1987-88; missile crew evaluator comdr. 321st Missile Wing, Grand Forks, 1990-92; mem. missile combat crew 448th Missile Squadron, Grand Forks, 1988-90, instr., evaluator flight comdr., 1992—, internat. treaty implementation officer, 1992-93; chief, mil. prodn. analysis br. Def. Intelligence Agy., Washington, 1994-96; mem. Bosnian task force Office Sec. of Def., Washington, 1997-98; chief inteligence ops. HQ 8th Air Force, 1998-99, ret., 1999; ind. scholar, 2000—. Vol. fireman Town of Boyce, La., 1968-71; res. police officer Natchitoches (La.) Police Dept., 1973; combined fed. campaign dir. USAF Officer Tng. Sch., 1986; trustee, choral dir. Calvary Bapt. Ch., Emarado, N.D., 1992; choral dir. South Run Bapt. Ch., Springfield, Va., 1993-97, Haughton (La.) H.S., 2000—. T.H. Harris Edn. scholar State of La., 1971-74. Mem.: ASPA, NRA, Assn. Former Intelligence Officers, Acad. Polit. Sci., Nat. Mil. Intelligence Assn., Nat. Assn. Scholars, Kiwanis Internat., Sigma Iota Epsilon. Republican. Avocations: shooting sports, photography. Home: 201 Ridgefield Dr Bossier City LA 71111-2370 E-mail: bondwj@worldnet.att.net.

BOND, WILLIAM L. career officer; b. Roseburg, Oreg. Commd. U.S. Army, advanced through grades to brig. gen., 1998; comdg. gen. Simulations, Tng. and Instrumentation Command, Orlando, Fla., 1998—. Office: Simulations Tng and Instrumentation Command 12350 Research Pkwy Orlando FL 32826-3261

BOND, ZINNY SANS, linguistics educator; b. Riga, Latvia, Sept. 1, 1940; came to U.S., 1950; d. Rudolf and Maria Johanna (Didrichson) Sans; divorced, 1978; children: Erica Lenora, Mark Michael. BA, U. Akron, 1962; MA, Ohio State U., 1967, PhD, 1971. Asst. prof. linguistics U. Alta., Can., 1971-74; rsch. assoc. Wright-Patterson AFB, Ohio, 1974-75; asst. prof. Ohio U., Athens, 1975-80, assoc. prof., 1981-85, 85—, prof., 1988—, chairperson dept. linguistics, 1992-94. Cons. SRL, Dayton, Ohio, 1985-88. Author: Slips of the Ear: Errors in the Perception of Casual Conversation, 1999; contbr. articles to profl. jours. Mem. Linguistic Soc. Am., Acoustical Soc. Am. (mem. tech. com. 1976-78), Assn. for Advancement of Baltic Studies (mem. program com. 1978-82). Lutheran. Avocations: hiking, reading, travel. Office: Ohio U Dept Linguistics 367 Gordy Hall Athens OH 45701

BONDAR, RICHARD JAY LAURENT, biochemist; b. N.Y.C., Sept. 4, 1940; s. Kelliher H. and Helen (Halper) B.; m. Enid Sue Teicher, Dec. 21, 1961; children: Randal, Karen. BS, McGill U., Montreal, Que., Can., 1962; MS, Calif. Inst. Tech., 1965; PhD, U. Calif., Riverside, 1969. Tech. dir. Worthington Biochem. =Corp., Freehold, N.J.; prin. devel. chemist Beckman, Brea, Calif.; mgr. Abbott Labs, South Pasadena, Calif.; v.p. Internat. Medication Systems, South El Monte, Calif.; mgr. pharm. devel. Banner Pharmacaps, Chatsworth, Calif.; mgr. quality control John Wayne Cancer Inst., Santa Monica, Calif., CancerVax, Marina del Rey, Calif., 3M Pharms. Contbr. over 30 refereed articles to profl. jours. Fellow Am. Inst. chemists; mem. Am. Chem. Soc., Am. Assn. Pharm. Scientists, Sigma Xi.

BONDAREFF, WILLIAM, psychiatry educator; b. Washington, Apr. 29, 1930; s. Leon and Gertrude Bondareff; children by previous marriage: Hyla, Sarah; m. Rifa Haber Kassoy, Jan. 2, 1988. BS in Zoology, George Washington U., 1951, MS in Zoology, 1952; PhD in Anatomy, U. Chgo., 1954; MD, Georgetown U., 1962. Diplomate Am. Bd. Psychiatry and Neurology with added qualifications in geriatric psychiatry. Rsch. assoc., instr. anatomy U. Chgo., 1955; rotating intern USPHS Hosp., Balt., 1962-63; resident in psychiatry Northwestern Meml. Hosp. Inst. Psychiatry, Chgo., 1978-80; asst. prof. anatomy Northwestern U., Evanston, Ill., 1963-65, assoc. prof., 1965-69, prof., 1969-78, chmn. dept. anatomy, 1970-78; prof. psychiatry and gerontology U. So. Calif., L.A., 1981—; mem. staff U. So. Calif. Univ. Hosp., L.A., 1991—; mem. attending staff L.A. County/U. So. Calif. Med. Ctr., L.A., 1981—; mem. Hosp. Good Samaritan, L.A., 1981-96; mem. staff Norris Cancer Hosp., 1987—; mem. attending staff Cedars-Sinai Med. Ctr., 2001—. Physician/cons. VA Hosp., Downey, Ill., 1969-80, Jewish Home for Aged, Reseda, Calif., 1981-90; vis. staff mem. medicine Passavant Pavilion Northwestern Meml. Hosp., 1972-80; dir. div. geriat. psychiatry U. So. Calif., 1981—; dir. U. So. Calif.-St. Barnabas Alzheimer Disease Ctr., 1985-2001; acting dir. dept. Gerontology Research Inst. Andrus Gerontology Ctr.-U. So. Calif., 1982; staff psychiatrist Los Angeles County Hosp., 1981—; past holder various com. offices Northwestern U. Editor Mechanisms of Aging and Devel., 1970—; assoc. editor Am. Jour. Anatomy, 1970-76; mem. editl. bd. Alzheimer Disease and Associated Disorders-An Internat. Jour., 1985-95, Neurbiology of Aging, 1980-94, The Jour. of Gerontology, 1981-84, Internat. Rev. Jour. of Psychiatry, 1988—, Jour. Alzheimer's Disease, 1997-2001; contbr. articles to profl. jours. Mem. sci. adv. bd. Alzheimer's Disease & Related disorders Assn. L.A., bd.dirs., 1989 ; mem. rsch. rev. com. treatment, devel. and assessment Nat. Inst. Mental Health, 1987-92. Served with USPHS, 1955-63. USPHS fellow, 1955, U. Cambridge Clare Hall vis. fellow, 1980, Hughes Hall vis. fellow, 1988; scholar Allergy Found., 1960, U. Chgo., 1953; recipient Career Devel. award Nat. Inst. Neurol. Disease and Blindness, 1966-69, Sesquicentennial award Hobart and William Smith Colls., 1972, Sandoz prize Internat. Assn. Gerontology, 1983, Alzheimer Disease and Related Disorders Assn. award, 1984; Fulbright Lectr., U. Goteborg, Sweden, 1967-68. Fellow AAAS (councilor 1970-74), Am. Psychiat. Assn. (geriatrics task force 1981), Gerontol. Soc.; mem. Am. Assn. Anatomists (chmn. local com. ann. meeting 1969), Electron Microscope Soc. Am., Am. Soc. Cell Biology, Am. Acad. Neurology (chmn. neuroanatomical scis. sect. 1971-77), Soc. Neurosci., Assn. Anatomy Chmn. (councilor 1975-77), Am. Assn. Geriat. Psychiatry (program com. 1984-89, bd. dirs. 1985-89), So. Calif. Psychiat. Soc., Internat. Psychogeriat. Assn., Cajal Club, Cosmos Club, Sigma Xi. Office: U So Calif Sch Medicine MOL 203 1237 N Mission Rd Los Angeles CA 90033-1018

BONDAROOK, NINA, public relations consultant; b. N.Y.C., Sept. 19, 1955; d. Peter and Lydia Bondarook; m. Earl S. Belofsky, Apr. 14, 1989. BA in Journalism, Ariz. State U., 1977; MS in Applied Comm., U. Denver, 1990. Founder Premium PR, Millbrae, Calif., 2002. Mem. Pub. Rels. Soc. Am., Soc. Profl. Journalists. Office: 595 Market St Fl 26 San Francisco CA 94105-2802 E-mail: nina@premiumpr.com.

BONDE, COUNT PEDER CARLSSON, investment company executive; b. Stockholm, Sept. 2, 1923; came to U.S., 1992; s. Carl Gustaf and Ebba (Wallenberg) B.; m. Ylva M. Jenssen, June 18, 1948 (div. Jan. 1956); children: Johan, Ulrika, Hans; m. J. Madeleine Rouchier, Sept. 27, 1957 (div. May 1988); m. Clarissa Leggett, July 2, 1989; children: Helena, Amelie, Sophia. Student exam, Sigtunaskolan, Sigtuna, Sweden, 1942; res. officer, Royal Horse Guard, Cavalry, Stockholm, 1946; Lic.Jur., Uppsala U., 1948. Asst. judge Dist. Ct. Askim, Göteborg, Sweden, 1948-51; banking trainee U.S., France, Germany, 1952-56; from asst. v.p. to exec. v.p. Stockholms Enskilda Bank, 1957-71; dep. chief exec. Skandinaviska Enskilda Banken, Stockholm, 1972-73, Salén Shipping Group, Stockholm, 1973-76; spl. rep. Skandinaviska Enskilda Banken, Zürich, Switzerland, 1977; pres., CEO Banque Scandinave en Suisse, Geneva, 1978-82; exec. vice-chmn. Investor AB, Providentia AB, Stockholm, 1983-91; vice-chmn. Investor AB, Stockholm, 1992-93; chmn., CEO Investor Internat. AB, Washington, 1993-98. Bd. dirs., vice-chmn., chmn. Alfa-Laval AB, Stockholm, 1961-91; vice-chmn. Stora AB, Falun, Sweden, 1985-91, Skandia Ins. Group AB, Stockholm, 1985-92, Astra AB, Sodertalje, Sweden, 1987-92; chmn. Forestal Valdivia, Santiago, Chile, 1991-94; chmn. European-Am. Bus. Coun., Washington, 1994-99. Mem. governing bd. Nat. Cathedral Sch. for Girls, Washington, 1999—2002. Capt. Cavalry, Sweden, 1952—76. Decorated Knight Royal Order of Vasa, 1972, The King's Gold Medal, 1994, grand officer Portuguese Order of Henry the Seafarer by Pres. of Portugal, 1991, grand cross Order of St. Gregorius the Great by His Holiness the Pope, 1991, grand cross Order of Leopold II by H.M. the King of the Belgians, 1994; named Lord in Waiting, Ct. of His Majesty the King of Sweden. Mem.: Nat. Press Club, Chevy Chase Club, Met. Club, Royal Swedish Yacht Club, Royal Bachelors Club (Göteborg). Home: Oak View 3201 36th St NW Washington DC 20016-3143

BONDI, BERT ROGER, accountant, financial planner; b. Portland, Oreg., Oct. 2, 1945; s. Gene L. and Elizabeth (Poynter) B.; m. Kimberley Kay Higgins, June 18, 1988; children: Nicholas Stone, Christopher Poynter. BBA, U. Notre Dame, 1967. CPA, Colo., Calif., Wyo. Sr. tax acct. Price Waterhouse, L.A., 1970-73; ptnr. Valentine Adducci & Bondi, Denver, 1973-76; sr. ptnr. Bondi & Co., Englewood, Colo., 1976—. 50 for Colo.-1998 dir. Citizens Bank. Bd. govs. Met. State Coll. Found.; bd. dirs. Am. Cancer Soc. Denver, Colo. Youth Symphony Orch.; mem. adv. bd. Jr. League of Denver. Mem. C. of C., Cmty. Assns. Inst., Govt. Fin. Officers Assn., Colo. Soc. Assn. Execs. (edn. com.), Home Builders Assn., Am. Inst. CPAs., Rotary (Denver), Notre Dame Club, Metropolitan Club (Denver), Castle Pines Country Club. Roman Catholic. Home: 49 Glenalla Pl Castle Rock CO 80104-9026 Office: Bondi & Co 44 Inverness Dr E Englewood CO 80112-5410 E-mail: bbondi@bondico.com.

BONDI, JOSEPH CHARLES, JR., education educator, consultant; b. Tampa, Fla., Aug. 15, 1936; s. Joseph C. and Virginia B.; m. Patsy L. Hammer, Aug. 6, 1960; children: Pamela, Beth, Bradley. BS, U. Fla., 1958, M.Ed., 1964; Ed.D., U. Fla, 1968. Tchr., adminstr. Hillsborough County (Fla.) Pub. Schs., 1958-65; instr. U. South Fla., Tampa, 1965-66, asst. prof., 1966-68, assoc. prof., 1968-74, prof. edn., 1974—; ptnr. Wiles, Bondi & Assocs., edn. cons. Cons. in field, South Africa, Hong Kong, China, Taiwan, Can., Am. Internat. Schs. Author 25 textbooks including Developing Middle Schools, 1972, Curriculum Development, 1979, 6th edit., 2002, Practical Politics for School Administrators, 1981, The Essential Middle School, 1981, 93, 00, Supervision: A Guide to Practice, 6th edit., 2002. Councilman City of Temple Terrace, Fla., 1970-74, mayor, 1974-78; ruling elder Presbyn. Ch. With USNR, 1958-63. Mem. Fla. ASCD (pres.), Am. Ednl. Rsch. Assn. Democrat. Office: U South Fla Coll Edn Tampa FL 33620

BONDINELL, STEPHANIE, counselor, academic administrator; b. Passaic, NJ, Nov. 22, 1948; d. Peter Jr. and Gloria Lucille (Burden) Honcharuk; m. Paul Swanstrom Bondinell, July 31, 1971; 1 child, Paul Emil. BA, William Paterson U., 1970; MEd, Stetson U., 1983. Cert. elem. educator Fla., guidance counselor grades K-12 Fla. Tchr. Bloomingdale (N.J.) Bd. Edn., 1971-80; edn. dir. Fla. United Meth. Children's Home, Enterprise, 1982-89; guidance counselor Volusia County Sch. Bd., Deltona, Fla., 1988—. Coord. sch. improvement svcs., Deltona Lakes, 1996—98, Deltona Lakes, 2002—03. Sec. adv. com. Deltona Jr. HS, 1996—98, sec. PTA, 1982; vice-chmn. adv. com. Deltona Mid. Sch., 1988, chmn., 1991—92, 1991—92; mem. adv. com. Deltona HS, 1995—96; secondary sch. task force Volusia County Sch. Bd., 1986—; mem. exec. com. Volusia County Reps.; mem. Rep. Presdl. Task Force; mem. state adv. bd. Fla. Future Educators Am., 1990—92. Named Girls State Rep., Am. Legion, 1966, Deltona Lakes Tchr. of Yr., 1991; recipient Outstanding Ednl. Partnership award, S.W. Volusia C. of C., 1998, Sunshine State Medallion award, Fla. Pub. Rels. Assn., 1998, award, Volusia/Flagler Alcohol and Drug Abuse Prevention Coun., 1998—2003, Fla. Lottery Creative Tchg. award, 2002, Deltona Lakes Tchr. of Yr., 1996; Acad. scholar, Becton, Dickinson & Co., 1966, N.J. State scholar, 1966—70. Mem.: AAUW, ASCD, Internat. Platform Assn., Volusia Tchrs. Orgn., N.J. Edn. Assn., Fla. Assn. Counseling and Devel., Disvn. Learning Disabilities, Coun. Exceptional Children, Stetson U. Alumni Assn., Deltona Civic Assn., 4 Townes Federated Rep. Women's Club (sec., v.p.), Deltona Rep. Club (v.p. 1991—93). Avocations: painting, creative writing, dancing. Home: 1810 W Cooper Dr Deltona FL 32725-3623 Office: Volusia County Sch Bd 2022 Adelia Blvd Deltona FL 32725-3976 E-mail: sbondine@mail.volusia.k12.fl.us.

BONDOC, ROMMEL, lawyer; b. June 23, 1938; s. Nicholas Rommel and Gladys Sue (Buckner) Bondoc; m. Ariel Guiberson, Aug. 20, 1960 (div. 1963); m. Alberta Linnea Young, Dec. 13, 1967; children: Daphne, Patience, Margaret, Nicholas. AB, Stanford U., 1959, JD, 1963. Bar: Calif. 1964, U.S. Ct. Appeals (9th cir.) 1965, U.S. Supreme Ct. 1969. Assoc. Melvin Belli, San Francisco, 1964—66, Vincent Hallinan, San Francisco, 1966—69; sole practice San Francisco, 1969—. Mem.: Calif. Attys. for Criminal Justice (bd. dir. 1975—80), No. Calif. Criminal Trial Lawyers Assn. (bd. dir. 1972—, pres. 1978—79), San Francisco Bar Assn. (judiciary com. 1982—85). Democrat. Methodist. Home: 509 Canyon Rd Novato CA 94947-4330 Office: 819 Eddy St San Francisco CA 94109-7701

BONDS, BARRY LAMAR, professional baseball player; b. Riverside, Calif., July 24, 1964; s. Bobby Bonds. Student, Ariz. State U. With Pitts. Pirates, 1985—92, San Francisco Giants, 1993—. Named Most Valuable Player, Baseball Writer's Assn. Am., 1990, 1992, 1993, Maj. League Player of Yr., Sporting News, 1990, Nat. League Player of Yr., 1990, 1991; named to All-Am. team, Sporting News Coll., 1985, All-Star team, 1990, 1992—96; recipient Gold Glove award, 1990 94, 1996, Silver Slugger award, 1990—96. Achievements include leading the Nat. League in intentional walks, 1992-94. Office: San Francisco Giants Candlestick Point 24 Willie Mays Plz San Francisco CA 94107-2199

BONDS, GEORGIA ANNA, writer, lecturer; b. N.Y.C., Dec. 30, 1917; d. Alex Matthews and Mattie Ethel (Stephens) Arnett; m. Alfred Bryan Bonds Jr., Feb. 23, 1939; children: Anna Belle, Alfred Bryan III, Alexandra Burke, Stephen Arnett. BA, U. N.C., Greensboro, 1938; MA, La. State U., 1940; postgrad., U. N.C., 1940-42, Baldwin-Wallace Coll., 1960s. Editl. asst. The So. Rev., Baton Rouge, 1938-39; editor Abstracts of Theses La. State U., Baton Rouge, 1940; editl. asst. pub. sch. curricula State of La., 1941; freelance writer, lectr., 1943—; editor dist. newspaper United Meth. Ch., Cleve., 1979-91. Lectr. on Egyptian days and ways, 1956-70, internat. concerns, 1970-85, Cherokee Indian heritage, 1985—. Editor: (English transl.) Wheat Growing in Egypt, 1954; author: The Lake Erie Girl Scout Council, the First Seventy-five Years, 1987; contbr. articles to popular mags. Active Girl Scouts USA, 1928—, leader, organizer troop 1, Cairo, 1953-55, mem. Lake Erie coun., Cleve., 1956—, leader, organizer Mounted troop, 1957-80, coun. bd. dirs., 1966-70, 79-87, coun. pres., 1979-84, mem. nat. coun., 1966-72, 78-83, troop leader internat. encampment, 1968, condr. world tour nat. and internat. ctrs., 1972, world conf. asst., 1984, organizer troops, Volgograd, Russia, 1991—; mem. Dist. United Meth. Women, Cleve., 1956—, bd. dirs., 1965-78, pres., 1974-78, com. on dist. superintendency, 1977-81, chair, 1978-81, mem. World Meth. coun., London, 1966; mem. Ch. Women United in Ohio, 1960—, state bd. dirs., 1966-72; active YWCA, Little Rock, 1950—, bd. dirs., 1950-53, bd. dirs. Cleve. chpt., 1977-79; active Philanthropic Ednl. Orgn., 1950—, bd. dirs. Ohio state chpt., 1965-71, pres., 1971. Recipient Outstanding and Dedicated Svc. award Girl Scouts of Lake Erie Coun., 1979, Thanks Badge, 1971, Thanks Badge II, 1997, World Friendship and Understanding Through Girl Scouting award Girl Scouts of Lake Erie Coun., 1984, award of honor for fund raising S.W. Gen. Hosp. Found., 1996,

Outstanding Intellectual of the 20th Century Internat. Biographical Ctr., Cambridge, England. Mem. AAUW (bd. dirs. 1984-89), Baldwin-Wallace Coll. Women's Club (hon. life mem.), Order of Ea. Star, Delta Zeta, Kappa Phi, Phi Beta Kappa (Cleve. assn. bd. dirs. 1964-69, pres. 1968). Avocations: swimming, travel. Home: PO Box 768 Berea OH 44017-0768

BONDS, JOHN BLEDSOE, musician, educator; b. Meridian, Miss., Dec. 16, 1939; s. Fay and Virginia Bledsoe Bonds; m. Elizabeth Hutson Rollins, June 9, 1962; children: John Bledsoe Jr., Margaret Lynn Podlich. BA in History, Rice U., 1957—62; MS in Internat. Affairs, George Wash. U., 1972—73; MA in Polit. Sci., Brown U., 1973—76; PhD in History, U. of S.C., 1995—2000. Offshore Operator Sail and Power USCG, 1986, Master Skipper USN, 1986. Surface line officer USN, RI, 1962—88; exec. dir. U.S. Sailing Assn., Newport, RI, 1988—94; grad. student U. of S.C., 1995—2000; vis. prof. of history The Citadel, 1997—. Safety at sea cons., Charleston, SC, 1995—; dir. U.S. Sailing Assn., Newport, RI, 1996—2000, Boat/US, Alexandria, Va., 1998—. Author: (scholarly book) Bipartisan Strategy, Westport CT, 2003, (S.C. Hist. Assn. mag.) Opening the Bar at Charleston - first dredging, (art., USN Inst. proceedings) Punishment, Discipline and the Naval Profession, The Navy Needs More Sailors, All Work and No Play. Mem.: Charleston Ocean Racing Assn., Coaster's Harbor Navy Yacht Club (commodore 1973—75), South Atlantic Yacht Racing Assn. (bd. mem. 1998—2003), Royal Naval Sailing Assn. (hon.), Hobcaw Yacht Club, Royal Ocean Racing Club, Storm Trysail Club, Cruising Club of Am., N.Y. Yacht Club, U.S. Naval Sailing Assn. (life; vice commodore 1998—2003). Avocations: sailing, racing, cruising. Home: 253 Hobcaw Dr Mount Pleasant SC 29464-2568 Office: History Dept The Citadel 171 Moultrie St Charleston SC 29409 Personal E-mail: john.bonds@bigfoot.com. E-mail: bondsj1@citadel.edu.

BONDS, JOHN WILFRED, JR., lawyer; b. Jackson, Tenn., May 6, 1943; s. John Wilfred Sr. and Louise (Robinson) B.; m. Mary Anne Hatchett, July 18, 1969; children: Kathleen Lucile, Mary Julia. BS, U.S. Air Force Acad., 1965; JD, Vanderbilt U., 1973. Bar: Ga. 1973. Commd. 2nd lt. USAF, 1965, advanced through grades to capt., 1965-70, resigned, 1970; assoc. Sutherland, Asbill & Brennan, Atlanta, 1973-79, ptnr., 1979—. Editor in chief Vanderbilt Law Rev., 1973. Mem. ABA, Ga. Bar Assn., Atlanta Bar Assn., Lawyers Club Atlanta, Order of Coif. Presbyterian. Office: Sutherland Asbill & Brennan 999 Peachtree St NE Atlanta GA 30309-3996

BONDURANT, EMMET JOPLING, II, lawyer; b. Athens, Ga., Mar. 16, 1937; s. John Parnell and Mary Claire (Brannon) B.; m. Jane E. Fahey, Aug. 12, 1990; children by previous marriage: Emmet Jopling III, Katherine Elizabeth, Melissa Eileen, Christopher Scott, Miles Stephen. AB cum laude, U. Ga., 1958, LL.B. magna cum laude, 1960; LL.M., Harvard U., 1962. Bar: Ga. 1959. Law clk. to Judge Clement Haynsworth, Jr. U.S. Ct. Appeals, 4th Circuit, 1960-61; assoc. Kilpatrick, Cody, Rogers, McClatchey & Regenstein, Atlanta, 1962-68, ptnr., 1968-77; ptnr. firm Bondurant, Mixson & Elmore and predecessor, Atlanta, 1977—. Vis. lectr. in antitrust law U. Ga., spring 1971; pres. Atlanta Legal Aid Soc., 1972-73; vice chmn. Ga. Gov.'s Commn. on Criminal Justice Standards and Goals, 1974 Contbr. articles on antitrust and reapportionment, right to counsel, bankruptcy, and local govt. issues to profl. jours.; co-editor: Antitrust Law Developments, 1974. Mem. Joint Atlanta-Fulton County Citizens Adv. Com. on Consolidation, 1969; chmn. Atlanta Charter Commn., 1971-72; co-chmn. Com. for Sensible Rapid Transit, Atlanta, 1971-72; trustee Am. Inns of Ct., 2002--; pres. Common Cause of Ga., 2002--; chmn. bd. Ga. Appellate Resource Ctr. Named 1 of 5 Outstanding Young Men, Atlanta Jaycees, 1970; recipient Ga. Trial Lawyer of Yr., Am. Bd. Trial Advocates (Ga. chpt.), Good Govt. award, LWV Atlanta-Fultin County, 1980, Dufree award, Calif. Western Sch. Law, 1984, Elbert P. Tuttle Jurisprudence award, 2001, Harold G. Clarke award, Ga. Indigent Def. Coun., 2001. Fellow Am. Bar Found.; mem. ABA (exec. com. Atlanta lawyers com. for civil rights), Ga. Bar Assn., Atlanta Bar Assn. (exec. com. 1975-81, Leadership award 1992), State Bar Ga. (chmn. sect. antitrust law 1972-73, chmn. jud. sys. comm. 1991—), Am. Law Inst., Am. Coll. Trial Lawyers, Am. Acad. Appellate Lawyers, Am. Judicature Soc., Ga. Law Sch. Alumni Assn. (pres. 1996-97), Lawyers Club Atlanta (sec. 1971-72), Phi Beta Kappa, Phi Delta Phi, Phi Kappa Phi, Kappa Alpha. Methodist. Home: 2930 Habersham Rd NW Atlanta GA 30305-2846 Office: Bondurant Mixson & Elmore Ste 3900 1201 W Peachtree St NW Atlanta GA 30309-3417

BONDURANT, STUART, physician, educational administrator; b. Winston-Salem, N.C., Sept. 9, 1929; s. Stuart Osborne Bondurant; m. Susan Haughton Ehringhaus, May 5, 1991; children from previous marriage: Stuart, Margaret Lynn, Nancy Vance. BS, Duke U., 1952, MD, 1953; DSc (hon.), Ind. U., 1980. Intern Duke Hosp., Durham, NC, 1953—54, resident in internal medicine, 1954—55; resident Peter Bent Brigham Hosp., Boston, 1958—59; asst. prof. medicine Ind. U. Sch. Medicine, Indpls., 1959—61, assoc. prof., 1961—66, prof., 1966—67; assoc. dir. Ind. U. Cardiovascular Research Ctr., 1961—67; chief med. br. artificial heart-myocardial infarction program NIH, Bethesda, Md., 1966—67; prof. medicine, chmn. dept., physician in chief Albany Med. Ctr. Hosp., NY, 1967—74; pres., dean Albany Med. Coll., 1974—79; prof. medicine U. N.C., Chapel Hill, 1979—, dean Sch. Medicine, 1979—94, interim dean, 1996—97; dir. Ctr. for Urban Epidemiology Studies N.Y. Acad. Medicine, N.Y.C., 1994—96. Contbr. articles to med. jours. Named Citizen Laureate, Univ. Found., Albany, 1979; recipient Disting. Alumnus award, Duke U. Sch. Medicine, 1974, Merit award, Am. Heart Assn., 1975, Thomas Jefferson award, U. N.C.-Chapel Hill, 1998. Fellow: ACP (regent, pres. 1980), Royal Coll. Physicians London, Royal Coll. Physicians Edinburgh; mem.: Am. Clin. and Climatological Assn. (pres. 1996), Assn. Am. Med. Colls. (exec. com. 1977, chmn. coun. deans 1979—82, chmn. 1993—94), Inst. of Medicine (interim pres. 1992, David Rall award 2000), Assn. Am. Physicians (pres. 1985—86), Am. Soc. Clin. Investigatio (v.p. 1974). Office: U NC Sch Medicine CB # 7000 Office of Dean Chapel Hill NC 27599-7000 E-mail: sbondurant@med.unc.edu.

BONDURIS, THAD SANTIKOS, music educator; b. San Antonio, Feb. 16, 1952; s. James Bonduris and Kiki Santikos Pringle; m. Lynette Mateu Bonduris, May 20, 1977 (div. Nov. 30, 1992); children: Nicole, Heather; m. Melody Pride Bonduris, Dec. 30, 1994 (div. Feb. 1997). BA, Trinity U., San Antonio, 1974; postgrad., U. N. Tex., Denton, 1974—80. Performing musician, San Antonio, 1970—74; bartender San Francisco Steakhouse, Dallas, 1975—76; music instr. Hammond Music Co., Denton, 1976—82, Bonduris Music Instrn., Denton, 1982—, Richardson, Tex., 1982—. Contract instr. mini-courses U. North Tex., Denton, 1979—; contract instr. Perry Middle Sch./N. Smith H.S., Carrollton, Tex., 1980—83; bandleader, sole proprietor Fabulous Echoes/Fanatix, Dallas, 1981—, Denton, 1981—; creative advising/recording Poundhouse-Boadrape Band, Dallas, 1997—98, Joe Miller Band, Dallas, 2001—02; tech. support Mark Austin Band, Dallas, 2001—02; instr. Nat. Guitar Summer Workshop, 2003—. Composer: (jazz instrumental) Kryptic, 1986, (song) Town Without a Main Street, 1988. Friend, supporter Greater Denton Arts Coun., 1999—, Denton Arts Guild, 2001—. Mem.: Am. Fed. of Musicians, Dallas-Ft. Worth Musicians Union, Tex. Music Tchr. Assn., Music Tchr. Nat. Orgn. Greek Orthodox. Office: Bonduris Music Instrn 106 Austin Denton TX 76201

BONDY, PHILIP KRAMER, physician, educator; b. N.Y.C., Dec. 15, 1917; s. Eugene Lyons and Irene (Kramer) B.; m. Sarah B. Ernst, Mar. 18, 1949; children: Jonathan L., Jessica, Steven M. AB, Columbia U., 1938; MD, Harvard U., 1942; MA (hon.), Yale U., 1961. Intern Peter Bent Brigham Hosp., Boston, 1942-43; mem. staff Grady Meml. Hosp., Atlanta, 1943, 46-48, chief resident in medicine, 1947-48; mem. faculty Emory U., 1947-48, 49-52, asst. prof. medicine, 1951-52; Alexander Browne Coxe fellow physiol. chemistry Yale U., New Haven, 1948-49, mem. faculty, 1948-49, 52-74, 77-88, prof. medicine, 1961, 77-88, prof. emeritus, 1988—, C.N.H. Long prof. medicine, 1965-74, chmn. dept. internal medicine, 1965-72, assoc. dean for vets. affairs, 1983-89, chmn. com. outpatient svcs., 1960-62; chmn. med. divsn. Royal Marsden Hosp., 1972-77; Cancer Rsch. Campaign prof. Inst. Cancer Rsch., London; cons. Ludwig Inst. Cancer Rsch., Zurich, Switzerland, 1972-77; assoc. chief of staff for rsch. West Haven VA Med. Ctr., 1977-83, chief of staff, 1983-89. Mem. med. vis. com. Brookhaven Nat. Labs., 1969-73, chmn., 1973; mem. program project com. NIH-Nat. Inst. Arthritis and Metabolic Disease, 1964-68, chmn., 1966-68; mem. exptl. biol. sect. breast cancer task force NIH-Nat. Cancer Inst., 1973-76; mem. adv. coun. NIDDK, 1990-94; mem. planning com. Med. Rsch. Svc. VA, 1985-88, chmn., 1986-88; mem. N.E. region planning com. VA. Editor-in-chief Jour. Clin. Investigation, 1957-62, Yale Jour. Biology and Medicine, 1978-92; editor: Diseases of Metabolism, 6th, 7th, 8th edits, Yearbook of Endocrinology and Metabolism, 1963-64; editorial bd. Conn. Medicine, 1959-61, Yearbook of Medicine, 1954-84, Medicine, 1963-85, Merck Manual, 1969—, Clinics in Endocrinology and Metabolism, 1973-84, Cancer Topics, 1975-79. Sec. libr. bd. City of Woodbridge, Conn., 1960-67; sec. bd. dirs. Southbury Tng. Sch. Found.; sec., bd. trustees Southbury Tng. Sch.; mem. governor's Coun. on Mental Retardation, Conn., 1997—. Capt. M.C., AUS, 1943-46. Recipient Edward Sutliffe Brainard prize Columbia U., 1938, Sigma Xi prize Emory U., 1949, Rsch. Career award NIH, 1962, 66. Fellow AAAS (chmn. sect. N on med. sci. 1979), Royal Coll. Physicians, Royal Soc. Medicine (v.p. sect. oncology 1975-77); mem. ACP (master), Endocrine Soc. (councillor 1964-67, mem. publs. com. 1965-72, chmn. 1968-72), Assn. Am. Physicians, Assn. Physicians Gt. Britain and Ireland, Am. Soc. Clin. Investigation, Am. Fedn. Clin. Rsch., Nat. Assn. VA Chiefs of Staff (mem. exec. com. 1986-88), Soc. Exptl. Biology and Medicine, Interurban Clin. Club, Inst. Cancer Rsch. (London, hon.). Home: 9 Chestnut Ln Woodbridge CT 06525-1701

BONE, LAWSON MITCHELL, songwriter, poet; b. Fayetteville, Tenn., Feb. 13, 1954; s. John Davis and Ester Eugene Bone. BA in Bus. Lit., Ala. A&M U., 1976. 1st asst., mgr. Big K Dept. Stores, Nashville, 1976-90; underwriter Prudential Ins. Co., Huntsville, Ala., 1990-91; songwriter Columbine Records, Hollywood, Calif., 1995—, HillTop Records, Hollywood, 1995—. Songwriter: Hey Writer-Keep It Up, Song Business, Flesh Tight, Got To Be The One; author: (screenplays) Make Bones About It, 1994, Disaster Relief, 1994; author numerous poems. Sponsor Children Internat. Honduras, Kansas City, Mo., 1995—, Childreach, Cali, Colombia, Warwick, R.I., 1995—. Named Famous Poet for 1996, 98-2002, Famous Poets Soc., 1996, Poet of the Yr., 1999-2002; Poetry Gem award, 2000-02; recipient Prometheus Muse of Fire Poetry award, 2001, Poem of Yr. award, 2002, Shakespeare Trophy of Excellence, 2002, Internat. Writer of Yr. 2003. Home: 306 Hamilton St Fayetteville TN 37334-3316

BONE, ROBERT WILLIAM, writer; b. Gary, Ind., Sept. 15, 1932; s. Robert Ordway and Georgia Juanita (Clapp) B.; m. Sara Ann Cameron, Aug. 14, 1965; children: Christina Ann, David Robert. BS in Journalism, Bowling Green State U., 1954. Editor, tng. literature The Armor Sch., Ft. Knox, Ky., 1954-56; reporter, photographer Middletown (N.Y.) Daily Record, 1956-59, San Juan (Puerto Rico) Star, 1959-60; news editor Popular Photography Mag., N.Y.C., 1960-62; editor-in-chief Brazilian Bus. Mag., Rio de Janeiro, 1962-63; picture editor Time-Life Books, N.Y.C., 1963-68; sr. writer Fielding's Travel Guide to Europe, Mallorca, Spain, 1968-71; staff writer Honolulu Advertiser, 1971-84; free-lancer Honolulu, 1984—. Stringer Time-Life News Svc., 1981-86. Author: Maverick Guide to Hawaii, 1977, Maverick Guide to Australia, 1979, Maverick Guide to New Zealand, 1981, Fielding's Alaska and the Yukon, 1989; travel editor Honolulu mag., 1985-88, R.S.V.P. mag., 1988-89. 1st lt., U.S. Army, 1954-56. Named to Journalism Hall Fame Bowling Green State U., 1990. Mem. Soc. Am. Travel Writers, Am. Soc. Mag. Photographers. Democrat. Home and Office: 1053 Lunaai St Kailua HI 96734-4633 E-mail: travelwriter@robertbone.com.

BONEAU, C. ALAN, psychology educator, researcher; b. Cin., Feb. 2, 1926; s. Charles A. and Virginia Louise (Kircher) B.; m. Ann Mallin, Sept. 2, 1955; children: Denise Lynn, Jonathan Alan, Paul Charles. BA in Psychology with high honors, U. Cin., 1950, MA in Psychology, 1951; PhD in Exptl. Psychology, Duke U., 1957. Supr. employment testing aircraft gas turbine divsn. Gen. Electric Co., 1952-53; grad. asst., rsch. asst., univ. fellow Duke U., Durham, N.C., 1953-57, USPHS rsch. fellow, 1957-58, from asst. prof. to assoc. prof., 1958-66, asst. to dean, 1962-64; ednl. affairs officer Am. Psychol. Assn., 1966-71, dir. programs and planning, 1971-76, exec. officer, 1974-75; sr. assoc. Devel. Assocs., Inc., Arlington, Va., 1977-78; program mgr. Essex Corp., Alexandria, Va., 1978-80; prof. psychology George Mason U., Fairfax, Va., 1980-98, chair psychology dept., 1980-82, emeritus prof., 1998—; rsch. prof. Krasnow Inst. for Advanced Studies, 1998—. Faculty senate Duke U., 1962-64; rsch. psychologist Army Rsch. Inst., 1980-89. Contbr. articles to profl. jours. Treas. Sci. Manpower Commn., 1976. With USN, 1944-46. USPHS Spl. fellow Stanford U., 1965-66, citation classic recognition Current Contents, 1986. Fellow AAAS, APA (cons. editor Jour. Applied Psychology 1981-86, exec. com. editor newsletter 1981, rep. to Coun. Social Sci. Assns. 1975-76, liaison to Nat. Adv. Mental Health Coun.), Soc. for Gen. Psychology (pres. 1987), Am. Psychol. Soc., Washington Acad. Sci.; mem. Psychonomic Soc., Soc. for Computers in Psychology, Soc. for Studying Unity Issues in Psychology (pres. 1987-88), Phi Beta Kappa, Sigma Xi. Office: Dept of Psychology George Mason U Fairfax VA 22030 E-mail: aboneau@gmu.edu.

BONEE, JOHN LEON, III, lawyer; b. Hartford, Conn., Dec. 16, 1947; s. John Leon, Jr. and M. Elaine (Sheridan) B. BA, Trinity Coll., Hartford, 1970; JD, Suffolk U., Boston, 1974; postgrad., Hague Acad. Internat. Law, The Netherlands, 1975. Bar: Conn. 1974, U.S. Dist. Ct. Conn. 1974; U.S. Ct. Appeals (2d cir.) 1975, U.S. Supreme Ct. 1979. Assoc. McCook, Kenyon and Bonee, Hartford, 1974-78; ptnr. Bonee Law Offices, LLP, Hartford, Conn., 1979—. Contbr. articles to profl. jours. Mem. bd. edn. Town West Hartford, 1981-83, corp. counsel, 1983, mem. community planning adv. com., 1984, mem. town coun., 1985-89; bd. dirs. World Affairs Coun., Hartford, 1980-91. Mem. ABA (litig. gen. practice and internat. law sects., mem. ho. dels. 1996—), Conn. Bar Assn. (editor-at-large jour. 1978-84, probate, litigation and family law sects., mem. ho. of dels. 1995—, com. on professionalism 2000—), Hartford County Bar Assn. (bd. dirs. 1991-97, treas. 1992-93, sec. 1993-94, pres. elect 1994-95, pres. 1995-96, past pres. 1996-97, co-chair bench/bar leadership conf. com. 1992-93). Office: 1 State St Hartford CT 06103-3100 E-mail: boneelaw@aol.com.

BONELLO, MICHAEL C. economist; Gov. Ctrl. Bank of Malta. Gov. for Malta Internat. Monetary Fund. Office: Ctrl Bank of Malta Castille Place Valletta CMR 01 Malta

BONEMERY, ANNE M. language educator; b. Springfield, Mass., Nov. 1, 1950; d. Alley and Radie Bonemery. BA, Am. Internat. Coll., 1972, MAT, 1974; AS, Springfield Tech. C.C., 1993. Cert. tchr. in English and Bilingual English Mass., tchr. French and Bilingual French Mass., tchr. Spanish and Bilingual Spanish Mass. Tchr. Northampton Pub. Schs., Mass., 1972—85; prof. Springfield Tech. C.C., 1985—; acct., office mgr. Emery Devel., Ltd., Mass., 1985—. English lang. cons. Springfield Instn. Savings (now First Mass. Bank), 1996—97; treas. Emery Devel., Ltd., 1985—, bd. dirs. Vol. U.S. citizenship studies and English lang. studies Springfield Literacy Network, 1987—; bd. dirs. Am. Internat. Coll. Alumni Bd., Mass., 1997—2000, bd. dirs. Springfield chpt., 2000—. Recipient Nat. Inst. Staff and Orgnl. Devel. Excellence award, U. Tex. Austin, 1997, 2000, Ptnr. in Philanthropy award, We. Mass. chpt. Assn. Fundraising Profls., 2001. Mem.: TESOL, MLA, NEA, Springfield Tech. C.C. Profl. Assn. (bldg. rep.), We. Mass. Fgn. Lang. Assn., Mass. Fgn. Lang. Assn., Mass. Assn. TESOL, Mass. Tchrs. Assn., Am. Coun. Tchg. Fgn. Langs., Am. Assn. Tchrs. French, Springfield Libr. and Mus. Assn., Sigma Lambda Kappa (sec. 1985—2000). Avocations: travel, reading, photography, hiking. Office: Springfield Tech CC One Armory Sq Springfield MA 01105

BONEPARTH, PETER, retail executive; Sr. mng. dir., head investment banking Mabon Securities, 1990—94, Rodman & Renshaw, 1994—97; COO Norton McNaughton, Inc., 1997—99, pres., 1997—, CEO, 1999—2002; CEO, pres. Jones Apparel Group, Inc., 2002—. Office: 250 Rittenhouse Cir Bristol PA 19007*

BONESIO, WOODROW MICHAEL, lawyer; b. Hereford, Tex., Dec. 27, 1943; s. Harold Andre and Elizabeth (Ireland) B.; m. Michaele Ann Dougherty; children: Elizabeth Eaton, Jo Kristin, William Michael. BA, Austin Coll., 1966; JD, U. Houston, 1971. Bar: Tex. 1971, U.S. Dist. Ct. (we., no., so., and ea. dists.) Tex. 1973, U.S. Ct. Appeals (5th cir.) 1973, U.S. Ct. Appeals (11th cir.) 1981. Law clk. to U.S. dist. Judge Western Dist. Tex., San Antonio, 1971-73; ptnr. Akin, Gump, Strauss, Hauer & Feld, Dallas, 1973-92, Kuntz & Bonesio LLP, Dallas, 1992—2002, Shackelford, Melton & McKinley L.L.P., Dallas, 2003—. Speaker profl. confs. Precinct chmn. Dallas County Dems.; bd. dirs. Grace Presbytery Devel. Bd., 1986—89; ruling elder First Presbyterian Ch., Dallas, 1999—2001. Fellow: Dallas Bar Found., Tex. Bar Found.; mem.: FBA, ABA, Nat. Assn. Rec. Artists, Vocal Majority (bd. dirs., 1990—, pres. 2002—03), U. Houston Law Alumni Assn. (chpt. pres. 1982), Austin Coll. Alumni Assn. (bd. dirs. 1983, Disting. Alumni award 2001), Common Cause Tex. (bd. dirs. 1999—), Dallas Assn. Def. Counsel, Tex. Bar Coll., Dallas Bar Assn., Am. Judicature Soc., Assn. Atty. Mediators, Am. Arbitration Assn., Lake Highlands Exch. Club, Soc. for Preservation and Encouragement Barber Shop Quartet Singing in Am. (internat. chorus champions 1975, 1979, 1982, 1985, 1988, 1991, 1994, 1997, 2000, 2003), Order of Barons, Phi Alpha Delta. Office: Shackelford, Melton & McKinley LLP 10100 N Central Expressway Ste 600 Dallas TX 75231 E-mail: mbonesio@shacklaw.net.

BONESSA, DENNIS R. lawyer; b. Uniontown, Pa., Jan. 15, 1948; s. Arthur V. and Josephine A. (Sierzega) B.; m. Bernadine Kopec, May 1, 1976; children: Dirk Arthur, Andrew Edward. BA, Pa. State U., 1969; JD, Georgetown U., 1972. Bar: Pa., U.S. Dist. Ct. (we. dist.) Pa., U.S. Ct. Appeals (3rd cir.), U.S. Tax Ct. Ptnr. Reed Smith LLP, Pitts., 1972—. Mem. Pa. Bar Assn., Allegheny County Bar Assn. Office: Reed Smith PO Box 2009 Pittsburgh PA 15230-2009 E-mail: dbonessa@reedsmith.com.

BONESTEEL, MICHAEL JOHN, lawyer; b. L.A., Dec. 22, 1939; s. Henry Theodore Samuel Becker and Kathleen Mansfield (Nolan) B.; children: Damon Becker, Kirsten Kathleen; m. Susan Elizabeth Schaaf, June 1, 1980. AB in History, Stanford U., 1961; JD, U. So. Calif., 1966. Bar: Calif. 1967, U.S. Dist. Ct. (ctrl. and so. dists.) Calif, 1967, U.S. Ct. Appeals (9th cir.) 1967, U.S. Dist. Ct. (no. dist.) Calif. 1969, U.S. Dist. Ct. (ea. dist.) Calif. 1983, U.S. Supreme Ct. 1989. Assoc. Haight, Brown & Bonesteel, and predecessors, L.A., 1967—71, ptnr., 1972—. Fellow Internat. Acad. Trial Lawyers, Am. Coll. Trial Lawyers; mem. ABA, State Bar Calif., Los Angeles County Bar Assn., Def. Rsch. Inst., Assn. So. Calif. Def. Counsel, Am. Soc. Most Venerable Order of Hospitaller St. John of Jerusalem, Hospitaller Order St. Lazarus of Jerusalem, Grand Priory of Am., Bel Air Bay Club, L.A. Country Club. Office: Ste 800 6080 Center Drive Los Angeles CA 90045-1574 Address: PO Box 45068 Los Angeles CA 90045-0068 Fax: 310-215-7300. E-mail: bonesteelm@hbblaw.com.

BONFANTE, LARISSA, classics educator; b. Naples, Italy; came to U.S., 1939, naturalized, 1951; d. Giuliano and Vittoria (Dompé) B.; m. Peter B. Warren, Sept. 1950 (div. 1962); children: Sebastian Raditsa, Alexandra Bonfante-Warren; m. Leo Ferrero Raditsa, May 2, 1973 (dec. 2001). Student, Radcliffe Coll., 1950, U. Rome, 1951; BA, Barnard Coll., 1954; MA, U. Cin., 1957, PhD, Columbia U., 1966. Mem. faculty NYU, 1963—, prof., 1978—, chmn. dept. classics, 1978-84, 87-90. Cons. in field; vis. mem. Inst. for Advanced Study, 1980. Author: Etruscan Dress, 1975, paperback, 2003, Out of Etruria, 1981, Reading the Past, Etruscan, 1990; author: (with Giuliano Bonfante) The Etruscan Language (transl. into Italian 1985, into Romanian 1995), 1983, 2d edit., 2002; author: Corpus Speculorum Etruscorum, N.Y. The Metropolitan Museum of Art, 1997; editor: Etruscan Life and Afterlife: Handbook of Etruscan Studies, 1986; translator (into Romanian), 1996; editor (with Francesco Roncalli): Antichità dall'Umbria a New York, 1991; editor: (with Judith Sebesta) The World of Roman Dress, 1994; translator: Chronology of the Ancient World (E.J. Bickerman), 1967, The Plays of Hrotswitha of Gandersheim, 1979; editor (with Vassos Karageorghis): Italy and Cyprus in Antiquity: 1500-450 BC; contbr. articles to profl. jours. Mem. Archaeol. Inst. Am. (gov. bd. 1982-88), Istituto di Studi Etruschi (fgn.), German Archaeol. Inst. (corres. mem.). Home: 50 Morningside Dr New York NY 10025-1739 Office: NYU Classics Dept 25 Waverly Pl New York NY 10003-6701 E-mail: lb11@nyu.edu .

BONFIELD, ARTHUR EARL, lawyer, educator; b. New York City, May 12, 1936; s. Louis and Rose (Lesser) B.; m. Doris (Harfenist), June 10, 1958 (dec. 1995); 1 child, Lauren; m. Eva (Tsalikian), Apr. 8, 2000. BA, Bklyn. Coll., 1956; JD, Yale Univ., 1960, LLM, 1961, post grad. (sr. fellow), 1961-62; DHL (hon.), Cornell Coll., 1999. Bar: Conn., 1961; Iowa, 1966. Asst. prof. U. Iowa Law Sch., 1962-65, assoc. prof., 1965-66, prof., 1966-69, Law Sch. Found. disting. prof., 1969-72, John Murray disting. prof., 1972—2003, Alan D. Vestal disting. chair, 2003—, assoc. dean for rsch., 1985—; summer vis. prof. law U. Mich., 1970; summer vis. prof. U. Tenn., 1972, U. N.C., 1974, Hofstra U., 1977, Lewis and Clark U., 1984. Vis. prof. law U. Mich., 1970, U. Tenn, 1972, U. N.C., 1974, Hofstra U., 1977, Lewis and Clark U., 1984; gen. counsel spl. joint com. state adminstrv. procedure act Iowa Gen. Assembly, 1974-75; spl. counsel adminstrv. procedure exec. br. State of Iowa, 1975; chmn. com. constl. law Nat. Conf. Bar Examiners Multi-State Bar Exam, 1977-2003; reporter 1981 Model State Adminstrv. Procedure Act, Nat. Conf. Commn. Uniform State Laws, 1979-81; cons. Ark. State Constl. Conv., 1980; chmn. Iowa Governor's Com. State Pub. Records Law, 1983; Iowa Commn. Nat. Conf. Commn. on Uniform State Laws, 1984-2000; chmn. Iowa Governor's Task Force on Uniform Adminstrv. Rules, 1985-92; chmn. Iowa Governor's Task Force Team on Regulatory Process, Rule Making, and Rules Rev., 1999-2000. Prin. draftsman Iowa Civil Rights Act, 1965; Iowa Fair Housing Act, 1967; Iowa Adminstrv. Procedure Act, 1974,; Iowa Open Meetings Act, 1978; Iowa Civil Rights Act, 1978; Amendments to Iowa Pub. Records Law, 1984; Amendments to Iowa Adminstrv. Procedure Act, 1998; author: State Adminstrv. Rule Making, 1986; State and Federal Adminstrv. Law, 1989; contbg. numerous articles to law jour. Recipient Outstanding Svc. to Civil Liberties Award, Iowa Civil Liberties Union, 1974; Hancher Finkbine Outstanding Faculty Mem. Award, U. Iowa, 1980; Faculty Excellence Award, Iowa Bd. Regents, 1995; Outstanding Law Sch. Tchg. Award, U. Iowa, 1996; Frederick Klocksiem fellow Aspen Inst. Humanistic Studies, summer 1978. Mem. ABA (chmn. divsn. state adminstrv. law 1976-80, coun. 1980-84, chmn. sect. 1987-88, sect. adminstrv. law and regulatory practice); Am. Law Inst. (life mem.); Iowa State Bar Assn. (chmn. com. adminstrv. law 1971-85, coun. sect. adminstr. law 1990-93, 94-97, 98-99, 2000-03, reporter and mem., task force on state adminstrv. law reform 1994-96; Pres. Award Outstanding Svc. to Bar and Public 1996); Am. Coun. Learned Soc. (del. from Assn. Am. Law Sch. 1984-94). Home: 206 Mahaska Dr Iowa City IA 52246-1606 Office: U Iowa Sch Law Iowa City IA 52242

BONFIELD, BARBARA GOLDSTEIN, non-profit organization administrator; b. Lincoln, Ala., Jan. 12, 1937; d. Samuel Jacob and Margaret (Embry) Goldstein; m. Robert Lawrence Bonfield, Feb. 26, 1959; children: Barney, Susan. BA, Ala. Coll., 1958; MSW, U. Ala., 1976. Lic. cert. social worker, Ala. Social worker Jefferson County Dept. Pub. Welfare, Birmingham, Ala., 1958-59; child welfare worker Children's Aid Soc., Birmingham, 1960-71; human resources officer Jefferson County Commn., Birmingham, 1976-77, dir. area agy. on aging, 1977-96; founder, dir. Human and Natural Resources, Inc., Birmingham, 1996—. Freelance writer Builder/Architect Mag., 2000—. Dir. Ms. Sr. Am. Ala., Inc., 1995-99; bd. dirs. Jewish Family Svcs. Birmingham, 1996—, chmn. sr. svcs. com. 1999, 2000, mem. exec. bd., 1999—, v.p., 2001-02, 2002-03; bd. dirs. Am. Classics, Inc., 1997-98, Birmingham Jewish Found., 2003; advisor Assistance League of Birmingham. Recipient Cmty. Svc. award B'nai B'rith Women, Birmingham, 1983, Social Worker of Yr. award Ala. Conf. Social Work, 1993, CARTS Transp. award; named to State of Ala. Sr. Citizen Hall of Fame 1993, Ala. Social Work Hall of Fame, 2002. Mem. NASW (chairperson PACE com. 1997—, Social Worker of Yr. Birmingham chpt. 1978, 99, Lifetime Achievement in Social Work Ala. chpt. 1999), Ala. Gerontol. Soc. (Profl. of Yr. 1986), Nat. Assn. Area Agys. on Aging, Southeastern Assn. Area Agys. on Aging (sec., bd. dirs. 1981), Acad. Cert. Social Workers, Hadassah (nominating com. 2002, fundraising com. 2002, exec. bd. asst. treas. 2003). Democrat. Jewish. Avocations: reading, gardening, interior decorating. Home and Office: 233 Beech Cir Birmingham AL 35213-2021 E-mail: BBonfield@aol.com.

BONFIGLIO, THOMAS ALBERT, pathologist, educator; b. Rochester, N.Y., Oct. 17, 1942; s. Charles P. and Minnie C. (Argentiere) B.; m. Mary Barat Rice, July 2, 1966; children: Susan Marie, Amy Elizabeth, Megan Lynn. BS magna cum laude, St. John Fisher Coll., 1964; MD, U. Rochester, 1969. Diplomate Am. Bd. Pathology; cert. Nat. Bd. Med. Examiners, Internat. Bd. Cytopathology, N.Y.S. lab. dir.; lic. Ohio, N.Y. Intern in pathology U. Hosps. Cleve., 1969-70, resident in pathology, 1969-71; tchg. fellow pathology Case Western Res. U., 1969-71; chief resident in pathology Strong Meml. Hosp., Rochester, N.Y., 1971-72; instr., pathology fellow U. Rochester Med. Ctr., 1971-72, asst. prof. pathology, 1972-76, assoc. dir. cytopathology lab., assoc. dir. sch. cytotech., 1973-76, acting dir. surg. pathology, divsn., dir. cytopathology lab., 1975-76; asst. prof. pathology Case Western Reserve U., 1976-77; asst. pathologist, chief divsns. cytopathology and surg. pathology Mt. Sinai Hosp., Cleve., 1976-77; assoc. prof. pathology U. Rochester Med. Ctr., 1977-84, prof. pathology, 1984-89, prof., acting chmn. dept. pathology and lab. medicine, 1989-90, prof., chair dept. pathology and lab. medicine, 1990-97, clin. prof.

pathology, 1997—2003, prof. pathology, dir. cytopathology, 2003—. Chmn. Internat. Bd. Cytopathology, 1998—; cons. pathology Rochester Gen. Hosp., 1978-97, Genesee Hosp., 1979-97; attending pathologist, dir. surg./pathology unit, 1984-85, Strong Meml. Hosp., attending pathologist, dir. anatomic pathology divsn., 1985-97, pathologist in chief, 1989-97; sr. attending pathologist, head pathology divsn. Genesee Hosp., 1997-99; dir. pathology divsn. ViaHealth, 1999-2003; sr. attending pathologist Strong Meml. Hosp., 2003—; mem. Cytotechnologist Exam. Com., 1980-83, Biol. Stain Commn., 1981-91, cytopathology exam com. Am. Bd. Pathology, 1984-89, spl. ad hoc com. cytopathology N.Y. State Dept. Health, 1988, others; v.p. Intersoc. Pathology Coun., 1988, pres., 1989; bd. dirs. Univs. Assoc. Rsch. and Edn. in Pathology; presenter papers, abstracts; participant, invited spkr., dir., panelist numerous workshops, meetings, seminars, confs., teleconfs. in field; vis. prof., guest lectr. Med. Coll. Ohio, Toledo, 1980, Dartmouth-Hitchcock Med. Ctr., Hanover, N.H., 1982, William Beaumont Army Med. Ctr., El Paso, 1984, Med. U. N.J., Newark, 1984, New Eng. Deaconess Hosp., Boston, 1985, Henry Ford Hosp., Detroit, 1989, Loyola U. Sch. Medicine, Chgo., 1990, St. Francis Hosp., Hartford, Conn., 1991, Marshall U. Sch. Medicine, Huntington, W.Va., 1991, U. Iowa Sch. Medicine, Huntington, W.Va., 1991, U. Iowa Sch. Medicine, Iowa City, 1991, U. Mass. Sch. Medicine, 1994. Author: Cytopathologic Interpretation of Transthoracic Fine-Needle Biopsies, 1983, (with others) Histologic Typing of Female Genital Tract, 1994; editor: Gynecologic Cytopathology, 1997, Fine Needle Aspiration of Subcutaneous Organs and Masses, 1996; mem. editl. bd. Human Pathology, 1982-92, Am. Jour. Clin. Pathology, 1985—, Lab. Medicine, 1984-90; mem. N.Am. rev. bd., editl. adv. bd. ACTA Cytologica; contbr. articles to profl. jours.; author video Cytopathology of Fine Needle Biopsies of the Abdomen, 1985. Fellow Am. Soc. Clin. Pathologists (v.p. 1990-91, pres.-elect 1991-92, pres. 1992-93, clin. pathologists commn. on continuing edn., bd. dirs. 1985-94, chmn. nominating com. 1988, 92, rsch. and devel. com. 1985-89, chmn. quality assurance steering com. 1987-92, dep. commr. commn. on continuing edn. 1984-90, chmn. coun. cytopathology 1983-84, coun. on cytopathology 1979-84, Disting. Svc. award 1988, Ward Burdick award 2002), Coll. Am. Pathologists, Internat. Acad. Cytology (sci. program com. 1988-89, terminology com. 1992); mem. AMA, Am. Soc. Cytology (Cert. of Merit for outstanding svcs. 1987, Papanicolaou award 1991, v.p. 1984-85, pres.-elect 1985-86, pres. 1986-87, chmn. sci. program com. 1982-84, exec. com. 1980-88, numerous others), Arthur Purdy Stout Soc. Surg. Pathologists, Assn. Dirs. Anat. and Surg. Pathology (coun. 1989-95), Assn. Pathology chmn., Internat. Soc. Gynecol. Pathologists, Monroe County Med. Soc., N.Y. State Soc. Pathologists, Rochester Area Assn. Pathologists (v.p. 1978-79, pres. 1979-80), U.S. and Can. Acad. Pathology, Papanicoleau Soc. Cytology (Educator of Yr. award 2003), Alpha Omega Alpha. Roman Catholic. Avocations: fishing, boating. Home: 3666 Nibawauka Bch Canandaigua NY 14424-9725 Office: 601 ELmwood Ave Box 626 Rochester NY 14642 E-mail: tabonf@aol.com., tom_bonfiglio@urmc.rochester.edu.

BONFIGLIO, THOMAS PAUL, literature and linguistics educator; s. Anthony Paul and Frances Bonfiglio. BS, U. Rochester; MA, U. Toronto, U. Wis.; PhD, Ind. U., 1984. Asst. prof. Kalamazoo (Mich.) Coll., 1982—84; from asst. prof. to assoc. prof. U. Richmond, Va., 1984—2002, prof., 2003—. Author: Race and the Rise of Standard American, 2002, Achim von Arnims Novellensammlung 1812, 1987; contbr. articles to profl. jours. Mem.: MLA, German Studies Assn. Office: Univ Richmond Dept Modern Lang Richmond VA 23173 Business E-Mail: tbonfigl@richmond.edu.

BONFILS, DARCY REYNE, television producer; b. Washington, Sept. 20, 1957; d. James Robert and Marjorie (Stemm) Bonfils. BA, Middlebury Coll., 1979; MA, U. Colo., 1983. Exec. asst. Internat. Student Movement of UN, Geneva, 1980; anchor, reporter KYCU-TV, Cheyenne, Wyo, 1984-86; asst. news dir. WUFT-TV, Gainesville, Fla., 1986-87; prodr. WPEC-TV, West Palm Beach, Fla., 1987-89, WFSB-TV, Hartford, Conn., 1989-91, WBBM-TV, Chgo., 1991-92, WCBS-TV, N.Y.C., 1992-95; sr. prodr. Court TV's: Inside Am.'s Cts., N.Y.C., 1995-97; prodr. WABC-TV, N.Y.C., 1997—. Co-author: The Elvis Presley Family and Friends Cookbook, 1999; prodr.: (documentaries) Elvis: Precious Memories, 2000, (news feature) Grounding of the Golden Venture, 1993 (Emmy nomination, 1993), (news spls.) Hurricane: Eyewitness to a Storm, 2000 (Writers Guild Am. award, 2001, Emmy nomination, 2001). Mem.: NATAS, Am. Women in Radio and TV, Writers Guild Am. E-mail: darcylbon@aol.com.

BONGIORNO, JAMES WILLIAM, electronics company executive; b. Westfield, N.Y., Apr. 2, 1943; s. Samuel Salvatore and Marjorie Ruth (Hardenburg) B. Student public schs. Profl. musician, 1961—65; engr. Hadley Labs., Pomona, Calif., 1965—66, Marantz Co., Woodside, NY, 1966—67; chief engr. Rectilinear Rsch. Corp., Bklyn., 1967—68; profl. musician, writer Popular Electronics, also Audio mag., 1968—71; dir. engring. Dynaco Inc., Phila., 1972, S.A.E. Inc., Los Angeles, 1973—74; founder, pres. Gt. Am. Sound Co. Inc., Chatsworth, Calif., 1974—77; founder, 1977; pres. Sumo Electric Co. Ltd., West Hollywood, Calif., 1977—82; ind. electronic cons. Lompoc, Calif., 1982—88; founder, pres. Spread Spectrum Techs., Inc., Lompoc, Calif., 1988—. Ind. electronic cons. Patentee class A audio amplifier, FM IF-detector. Recipient State of Art Design award, Stereo Sound mag., Tokyo, 1976, 1980, 2003, High End Audio Best of CES Show award, 2003. Mem. Audio Engring. Soc., Am. Fedn. Musicians. Republican. Home and Office: 716 N G St Apt 2 Lompoc CA 93436-4530 E-mail: sstinc@earthlink.net. *Aside from the fact that my lifetime goal has always been to design the world's finest amplifier, I also wanted it to be affordable by as many people as possible. I am happy that I have achieved this goal as there are a lot more poor people than rich people.*

BONGIORNO, JOSEPH JOHN, JR., electrical engineering educator; b. Bklyn., Aug. 3, 1936; s. Joseph John and Mildred Rose (LoPinto) B.; m. Carol Marie Olsen, Nov. 22, 1958; children: James Michael, Peter Joseph, Richard Edward, Cathryn Mary BEE, Poly. Inst. Bklyn., 1956, MEE, 1958, DEE, 1960. Asst. prof. Poly. Inst. N.Y., Bklyn., 1960-64, assoc. prof., 1964-74, prof., 1974-96, prof. emeritus, 1996—. Cons. Unisys (formerly Sperry Systems Mgmt.), Gt. Neck, N.Y., 1963-93. Contbr. articles to profl. jours. Mem. St. Aidan's Parish Sch. Bd., Williston Park, N.Y., 1967-70, 73-76, pres. 1975-76. Rsch. grantee NSF, Washington, 1972, 82, 85, Army Rsch. Office, Durham, N.C., 1993. Fellow IEEE (Control Systems Soc. best paper award 1977) Roman Catholic. Home: 36 Park Ave Williston Park NY 11596-1628 Office: Poly U 105 Maxess Rd Melville NY 11747 E-mail: jbongior@rama.poly.edu.

BONHAG, THOMAS EDWARD, insurance company executive, financial consultant, financial planner; b. Bronxville, N.Y., Jan. 19, 1952; s. Herman Arthur and Anne Elizabeth (Sage) B.; m. Noreen Patricia Early, Apr. 24, 1976 (div. Dec. 1981); m. Cornelia Hackett Lyons, Oct. 8, 1983. BS, Fordham U., 1973; MBA, St. John's U., 1979; postgrad., Am. Coll., 1979-84. CLU; cert. fin. planner, chartered fin. cons. Field sales rep. Colgate-Palmolive Co., N.Y.C., 1973-74; employee relations officer Chase Manhattan Bank, N.Y.C., 1974-78; agt., dist. mgr. Equitable Life Assurance Soc., N.Y.C., 1979-83; v.p. northeastern region mktg. Edison, N.J., 1984-90; sr. v.p. Kornreich Life Assocs., Inc., N.Y.C., 1990-94; CEO Winged Keel Group, Inc., N.Y.C., 1994-95; dir. advanced planning/markets Equitable Life, N.Y.C., 1995-98, mng. dir. The deBart Group, Inc., N.Y.C., 1999—. Fin. cons. Am. Geriatrics Soc., N.Y.C., 1983-86; bd. dirs. Fin. Assurance Fed. Credit Union, 2001-. Mem. Hoboken (N.J.) Environ. Com., 1983-90; mayoral appointee citizens' budget adv. com. Twp. of Cranford, N.J., 1991-92; mem. Cranford Bd. Edn., 1991-94, pres., 1992-94. Mem. Soc. Fin. Svc. Profls., Nat. Assn. Ins. and Fin. Advisors, Fin. Planning Assn., Estate Planning Coun. N.Y.C., Assn. for Advanced Life Underwriting. Avocations: golf, walking, bicycling, sailing. Home: 406 Monmouth Ave Spring Lake NJ 07762-1131 E-mail: tombonhag@prodigy.net.

BONHAM, HAROLD FLORIAN, research geologist, consultant; b. L.A., Sept. 1, 1928; s. Harold Florian and Viola Violet (Clopine) B.; m. Sally Mae Reimer, Sept. 6, 1952 (dec. July 1999); children: Cynthia Jean Kimball, Douglas Craig, Gary Stephen; m. Linda Jean Shipp, June 14, 2000. AA in Physics, U. Calif. Berkeley, 1951; BA in Geology, UCLA, 1954; MS in Geology, U. Nev., 1963. Geologist So. Pacific Co., 1955-61; mining geologist Nev. Bur. Mines and Geology, Reno, 1963-93, acting dir., state geologist, 1993-95; cons. geologist, 1996—. Cons. UN, Can., Australia, Peoples Republic of China, 1980-90; cons. in field. Contbr. articles to profl. jour. V.p. Palomino Valley Gen. Improvement Dist., Nev., 1986-88. With USN, 1946-49, PTO. Fellow Geol. Soc. Am., Soc. Econ. Geologist, Assn. Exploration Geochemists (councillor 1988-94); mem. Geol. Soc. Nev. (hon.). Republican. Avocations: reading, computers, photography, oenology. Home: 265 Mia Dr Sparks NV 89436-7912

BONHAM, JOHN DWIGHT, retired lawyer; b. Tuscaloosa, Ala., Sept. 13, 1928; s. Harry Dwight and Mamie Marie (Griffith) B.; m. Bobbye Claire Maxwell, Sept. 13, 1952; 1 child, Mary Bonham Ward. BS in Commerce, U. Ala., 1950, JD, 1952. Bar: Ala. 1952, U.S. Dist. Ct. (so. dist.) Ala. 1960. Staff atty. Legis. Ref. Svc., Montgomery, Ala., 1952-55; ptnr. Hare & Bonham Attys., Monroe County, Ala., 1955-60; asst chief, trial atty. Ala. Conservation Dept., Montgomery, 1960-70; asst. dir., chief atty. Ala. Legis. Ref. Svc., Montgomery, 1970-95. 1st lt. USAR, 1953-60. Presbyterian. Avocations: hunting, fishing.

BONHAM-CARTER, HELENA, actress; b. Eng., May 26, 1966; Ed., Westminster. TV appearances include A Pattern of Roses, Miami Vice, A Hazard of Hearts, The Vision, Arms and the Man, Beatrix Potter, Dancing Queen, Fatal Deception, A Dark Adapted Eye; films include Lady Jane, A Room with a View, Maurice, Francesco, The Mask, Getting It Right, Hamlet, Where Angels Fear to Tread, Howard's End, Mary Shelley's Frankenstein, A Little Loving, Mighty Aphrodite, Margaret's Museum, 1994, Portraits Chinois, 1995, Twelfth Night, 1995, Wings of a Dove, 1996, Revengers Comedies, 1996, Keep the Aspidistra Flying, 1997, The Theory of Flight, 1997, Fight Club, 1998, Women Talking Dirty, 1999, Novacaine, 2000, Til Human Voices Wake Us, Planet of the Apes, 2001, Heart of Me, 2001, Live from Baghdad, 2002, Big Fish, 2003, Henry VIII, 2003. Office: Adam Isaccs United Talent 9560 Wilshire Blvd Beverly Hills CA 90212-2427 also: Conway Van Gelder 18-21 Jermyn St London SW1Y 6HP England

BONHAM-YEAMAN, DORIA, retired law educator; b. L.A., June 10, 1932; d. Carl Herschel and Edna Mae (Jones) Bonham; widowed; children: Carl Q., Doria Valerie-Constance. BA, U. Tenn., 1953, JD, 1957, MA, 1958; EdS in Computer Edn., Barry U., 1984. Instr. bus. law Palm Beach Jr. Coll., Lake Worth, Fla., 1960-69; instr. legal environment Fla. Atlantic U., Boca Raton, 1969-73; lectr. bus. law Fla. Internat. U., North Miami, 1973-83, assoc. prof. bus. law, 1983—2001; ret., 2001. Editor: Anglo-Am. Law Conf., 1980; Developing Global Corporate Strategies, 1981; mem. editl. bd. Attys. Computer Report, 1984-85, Jour. Legal Studies Edn., 1985-97; contbr. articles to profl. jours. Bd. dirs. Palm Beach County Assn. for Deaf Children, 1960-63; mem. Fla. Commn. on Status of Women, Tallahassee, 1969-70; mem. Broward County Dem. Exec. Com., 1982-2000; pres. Dem. Women's Club Broward County, 1981; mem. Marine Coun. of Greater Miami, 1978-94, Svc. award, 1979. Recipient Faculty Devel. award Fla. Internat. U., Miami, 1980; grantee Notre Dame Law Sch., London, summer 1980. Mem. AAUW (pres. Palm Beach county chpt. 1965-66), U.S. Coun. for Internat. Bus., No. Dade C. of C., Acad. Legal Studies in Bus., Alpha Chi Omega (alumnae club pres. 1968-71), Tau Kappa Alpha. Episcopalian.

BONI, MIKI, artist; b. Bklyn., Nov. 10, 1938; Children: Andrew, Viki. BA, U. Guanajuato, 1974. Tchr. painting and drawing U. Guanajuato, Mex., 1974-76; exec. dir. Kreativ Assocs., Watertown, Mass., 1976-82; prin. Miki Boni Assocs., 1982-86; editor, graphic designer publ. Interface Found., Watertown, 1987-89, program dir., 1989-91; founder, propr. Silk Road, 1991-94; founder, artist in residence Kaos Studios & Fine Art Gallery, Wilmington, Vt., 1998—2002. Owner Kaos Gallery S. in Village of Arts, Bradenton, Fla., 2002—. Exhbns. include Russian-Am. Cultural Ctr., Boston, Art on the Mountain, Vt., 1995—(People's Choice award), Ringling Sch. Art and Design; contbr. poetry to anthology Searching for Soft Voices (Editor's Choice award 1998). Named to Internat. Poetry Hall of Fame, 1997; recipient spl. painting award, Lincoln Ctr., 1978, painting award, Longboat Key Ctr. for Arts, 2001. Mem.: Longboat Key Ctr. Arts, Art Coun. Sarasota, Art League Manatee County, Women Contemporary Artists, Women Art Profls. (co-founder, v.p.).

BONIFACHO, BRATSA, artist; b. Belgrade, Yugoslavia, 1937; arrived in Can., 1973, naturalized, 1976. Student, Sumatovachka Sch. Art, Belgrade, 1957-59, U. Belgrade, 1960-65, Acad. di Belle Arti, Italy, 1966-68, Atelier Kruger, West Germany, 1966-68. Tchr. painting and drawing Sch. Fine Arts, Belgrade, 1967-68; pvt. tutor, 1979-87. One-person shows Gallery Scollard, Toronto, 1978, Contemporary Art Gallery, Vancouver, 1979, Richmond (B.C.) Art Gallery, 1982, 93, 97, Heffel Gallery Ltd., Vancouver, 1988, 90, 91, Quan-Schieder Gallery, Toronto, 1989, 90, Fran Willis Art Gallery, Victoria, B.C., Can., 1992, 93, 94, 95, 2000, Patrick Doheny Fine Art Gallery, Vancouver, 1992, 93, 94, Artropolis, 1993, Seattle Art Fair, 1993, Threshold Gallery, Vancouver, 1993, Bau-Xi Art Gallery, Vancouver and Toronto, 1995, 96, 99, 2001, 02, 03, Kimzey Miller Gallery, Seattle, 1996, Mus. History and Art, Anchorage, 1997, Gallerijk Progres, Belgrade, 2000, Contemporary Art Gallery, Zrenjanin, Yugoslavia, 2001, Gallery of the Matica Srpsick, Novi Sad, Yugoslavia, 2002; juried group exhibits in B.C., 1974-93; represented in numerous pub. and pvt. collections. Grantee, B.C. Arts Coun., 1996, 1998, 2000; travel grantee, Can. Coun., 2000, 2001, 2002, B.C. travel grantee, 1999. Office: PO Box 549 Sta A Vancouver BC Canada V6C 2N3 E-mail: preview@portal.ca.

BONIFAZI, STEPHEN, chemist; b. Hartford, Conn., Oct. 31, 1924; s. Camillo and Carrie (Mortensen) B.; m. Joan Rose Dunlop, Dec. 19, 1959; 1 child, Karen Stephanie Brooks. BS, Trinity Coll., Hartford, 1949; postgrad., Okla. U., 1943-44, Rensselaer Poly. Inst., 1955-58. Sr. chemist Pratt & Whitney Aircraft Co., East Hartford, Conn., 1950-56, supr. chemistry, 1956-58, project chemist West Palm Beach, Fla., 1958-63, gen. supr. chemistry, 1963-78, fuels and lubricants specialist, 1978-86, cons., 1986—. Contbr. articles to sci. jours. Served with inf. AUS, 1943-45, ETO. Decorated Bronze Star medal. Mem. ASME, ASTM, Am. Chem. Soc., Am. Soc. Lubrication Engrs., Internat. Assn. for Hydrogen Energy, Coordinating Rsch. Coun., Sigma Pi Sigma. Home and Office: 237 Eagleton Lake Blvd Palm Beach Gardens FL 33418-8059 E-mail: stevepga@aol.com.

BONILLA, HENRY, congressman, broadcast executive; b. Jan. 2, 1954; children: Alicia, Austin. BJ, U. Tex., 1976. Reporter KTVV, Austin, Tex., 1976-78, reporter, prodr. KENS-TV News, 1978-80; asst. Press sec. for Gov. Dick Thornburgh, Phila., 1981; news producer WABC-TV, N.Y.C., 1982-85; asst. news dir. WTAF-TV, Phila., 1985-86; TV exec. prodr. KENS-TV, San Antonio, 1986-89; mem. appropriations com. 103rd-106th Congress from 23rd Tex. dist., Washington, D.C., 1993—. Mem. appropriations; chair agr. appropriations subcom., fgn. ops. appropriations subcom., def. appropriations subcom. Bd. v.p. San Antonio Crimestoppers; mem. adv. bd. United Way Vol. Ctr.; mem. adv. coun. Univ. Tex. Women's Athletics Dept., San Antonio Mus. Assn. Mex. Splendors Media; bd. dirs. Careers Info. and Referral Svc., San Antonio Pub. Library Found. Recipient San Antonio Hispanic C.of C. Leadership award, 1989, Corp. Community Svc. award, 1990. Republican. Office: US Ho of Reps 2458 Rayburn Washington DC 20515-4323

BONIN, PAUL JOSEPH, real estate and banking executive; b. Malden, Mass., Mar. 6, 1929; s. Honoré Auguste and Yvonne Adrienne (Vuillaumié) B.; m. Annette Kagey, Jan. 19, 1968; children: Adam Spencer, Christopher Paul, Page Alexandra. Student, Bentley Coll., 1948-50, NYU, 1950-52, New Sch. for Social Rsch., 1962. Lic. real estate broker, N.Y. Acct. Henry W.T. Mali & Co., N.Y.C., 1951-58; budget contr., asst. account exec., developer budget control system Young & Rubicam, N.Y.C., 1958-60; v.p. Wm. Alfred White, Inc., N.Y.C., 1960-65; pres. Bonin & Barringer, Inc., N.Y.C., 1964-65; v.p. Wm. B. May & Co., Previews, Inc., N.Y.C., 1965-69; dir. acquisitions Nationwide Real Estate Co., N.Y.C., 1969-74; v.p. Landauer Assocs., Inc., N.Y.C., 1974-79, Citibank, N.A., N.Y.C., 1979-82; pres. Assocs. Mgmt., Inc., Dallas, 1982-84; dir. acquisitions The Hendrix Cos., N.Y.C., 1984-85, The Ziegelman Orgn., N.Y.C., 1985-86; sr. v.p. Crossland Svs. Bank, Bklyn., 1987-89; pres. asset mgmt. group Team Cos., N.Y.C., 1989-93; asset valuation rev. team leader, portfolio mgr. FDIC, Franklin, Hartford, Mass., Ct., 1990-2000; fin. analyst, 2000—02; loss control cons. to ins. cos., 2003—. Asset mgr. Shell Pension Fund of The Hague, The Netherlands, Electricity Coun. of Eng., London, N.Y.C.; real estate cons. Pan Am World Airways, N.Y. State Dept. Housing and Cmty. Renewal. With USN, 1946-48. Mem. Mortgage Bankers Assn., Nat. Assn. Realtors (cert. property mgr.), Inst. Real Estate Mgmt. Roman Catholic. Avocations: tennis, skiing. Home: 81 Larch St Providence RI 02906 E-mail: paulnet4@cox.net.

BONIN, SUZANNE JEAN, artist; b. Oakland, Calif., Nov. 12, 1955; d. Charles Freeman and Dorice Ruth (Brown) B.; m. Donald George Winchester, May 16, 1986 (div. Nov. 1990); m. Joseph Bogusis, Nov. 2, 1996. Grad. h.s., Alton, N.H. Owner, mgr. Bonin Gallery, Wolfeboro, NH, 1983-94, Bonin Studio, Wolfeboro, NH, 1994—. Spl. needs art instr. Kingswood Regional Sch. System, Wolfeboro, 1982. Designer logo Audubon Soc. of NH, 1982; exhbn. The Art Place, Wolfeboro; illustrator: The Best Plants for NH Gardens and Landscapes, 2003. Charter mem. Gov. Wentworth Arts Coun., Wolfeboro, 1980, vol., 1980—; donor N.H. Public TV, Durham, N.H.; initiator of art collection for silent auction Hospice, Wolfeboro, 1982—; donor Lakes Region Humane Soc., 1999—; mem. Cmty. Ch. of Alton, 1962—. Mem. League of NH Craftsmen, Washington Area Printmakers, No. NH Arts Alliance. Avocations: gardening, fishing, swimming, cross-country skiing, basketball. Studio: Bonin Studio 713 Beach Pond Rd Wolfeboro NH 03894-0801

BONINA, MARY, poet; b. Worcester, Mass., Nov. 2, 1950; d. Biagio John Bonina and Mary Cecilia Feeherry; m. Mark Joseph Pawlak, Aug. 21, 1982; 1 child, Gianni Bonina-Pawlak 1 stepchild, Andrai Pawlak Whitted. AB in English Lit., Anna Maria Coll., Paxton, Mass., 1972; MFA in Creative Writing, Warren Wilson Coll., 1985. Cert. tchr. Mass. Co-editor, writer The Little Apple (mag.), Worcester, 1975—82; tchr. English and social studies secondary schs., Worcester, 1978—81; instr. comm. skills Quinsigamond C.C., Worcester, 1981; statewide dir. Mass. Conservation Assistance Fund Office Cmtys. and Devel., Commonwealth of Mass., Boston, 1982—85; workplace instr. English Lang. Interchange, Inc., Concord, Mass., 1988—90; program developer, dir. Pub. Libr.: The Literacy Project, Cambridge, Mass., 1990—98; writer, 1999—. Poet in the Schs. resident Worcester County Poetry Assn., 1974—76; poet in residence Cambridge Pub. Libr./Schs./Mass. Bd. Libr. Commrs., Cambridge, 1988; cons. Oksner, Inc., N.Y.C., 1992. Author (poetry collections): Hanging Loose, 1991, Red Brick Review, 1992, City River of Voices, 1992. Founding com. mem. Abby's House (women and children's shelter), Worcester, 1975; selection and organizing coms. Oxfam, Am., Harvard U., 1988—89; rschr., writer, prodr. Mental Health Care for Women (radio documentary), 1977. With VISTA, 1972—74. Fellow Fiction Writing, Vt. Studio Ctr. Colony, Johnson, Vt., 1990. Fellow: Va. Ctr. Creative Arts; mem.: Nat. Writers Union (Boston local), PEN New Eng., Acad. Am. Poets. Avocations: photography, creative gourmet cuisine, hiking, canoeing. Home: 44 Thingvalla Ave Cambridge MA 02138

BONINA, SALLY ANNE, secondary school educator; b. Stamford, Conn., Jan. 30, 1951; d. Salvatore Edward and Mary Dolores (Giancola) Bonina; children: Vincent Salvatore, Michael Christopher. BA in Spanish with honors, Coll. New Rochelle, 1972; MS in Reading Cons., Bridgeport U., 1975; 6th yr. degree adminstrn., So. Conn. State U., 1994. Spanish tchr. Westhill H.S., Stamford, 1973-78; pvt. tutor John Jay Middle and High Schs., Katonah, N.Y., 1978-89; substitute tchr. Katonah (N.Y.)/Lewisboro Schs., 1990-91; Spanish tchr. Cloonan Middle Sch., Stamford, 1991-2001, Shelton (Conn.) H.S., 2001—. Scheduling com. mem. Cloonan Sch., Stamford, 1992-95, student-of-the-month com., 1993-94, character counts com., 1998—; active middle sch. confs., Champion Internat., Stamford, 1991-94; mem. fgn. lang. curriculum writing team Stamford Pub. Schs., 1997-99, character counts com., 1998-2001, prof. devel. com., 1999—2001; ednl. adv. Nat. Young Leaders Conf., Washington, D.C. Religious edn. tchr. St. Aloysius Ch., New Canaan, Conn., 1984-91; pub. ctr. coord. Meadow Pond Sch., Katonah, 1988-90, book fair co-chairperson, 1989-90; schedule co-coord. Westchester (N.Y.) Putnam Baseball Assn., 1992-94; mem. Cloonan Site Based Com., 1997-98; mentor Connecticut BEST program, 2000—. Mem.: ASCD, Stamford Edn. Assn. (negotiations team 1999—2000), Shelton Edn. Assn. (negotiations team 2002), Am. Coun. Tchg. Fgn. Langs., N.E. League Mid. Schs., Adminstrn. and Supervision Assn. So. Conn. State U. Roman Catholic. Avocations: swimming, reading, walking, cooking, theatre. Office: Shelton H S 120 Meadow St Shelton CT 06484

BONINI, JAMES, federal court official; BA in Criminal Justice, Indiana U. of Pa., 1986; MPA, U. So. Calif., 1988. Administrv. asst. South Bay Mcpl. Ct. Los Angeles County, Calif., 1987—88, sr. adminstrv. asst., 1988—89, divsn. head budget and mgmt. svcs., 1989; chief dep. ct. adminstr. Ct. Common Pleas, Montgomery County, Pa., 1990—91, dist. ct. adminstr. Berks County, Pa., 1991—96; clk. of ct. U.S. Bankruptcy Ct. No. Dist. Ind., South Bend, 1996—. Office: US Bankruptcy Ct PO Box 7003 401 S Michigan St South Bend IN 46634-7003

BONINI, WILLIAM EMORY, geophysics educator; b. Washington, Aug. 23, 1926; s. John Emory and Thelma (Scrivener) B.; m. Rose Rozich, Dec. 4, 1954; children: John Allen, Nancy Mara, James Prior, Jennifer Adra. BS in Engring, Princeton, 1948, MS, 1949; PhD, U. Wis., 1957. Mem. faculty Princeton, 1953-96, prof. civil and geol. engring., 1966-70, George J. Magee prof. geophysics and geol. engring., 1970-96; prof. emeritus, 1996—; chmn. water resources program Princeton, 1971-74, chmn. geol. engring. program, 1973-96; ret., 1996. Author articles in field. Pres. Yellowstone-Bighorn Research Assn., Red Lodge, Mont., 1959-60, 71-73, v.p., 1966-71, 85-87. Served with USNR, 1945-46. Nat. Acad. Sci. exchange scientist to Yugoslavia, 1974; NSF sr. postdoctoral fellow U. Newcastle upon Tyne, Eng., 1963-64 Fellow Geol. Soc. Am. (sec.-treas. geophysics div. 1981-83, chmn. geophysics div. 1985-86); mem. Am. Assn. Petroleum Geologists, Soc. Exploration Geophysicists, Nat. Assn. Geosci. Tchrs. (councilor-at-large 1981-83, v.p. 1983-84, pres. 1984-85), Sigma Xi (v.p. Princeton chpt. 1988-89, pres. 1989-90). Achievements include research on gravity and magnetic anomalies and crustal structure, seismic crustal studies, geophys. exploration engring. and groundwater studies, environmental geology. Home: 74 Robert Rd Princeton NJ 08540-5333 E-mail: bonini@princeton.edu.

BONIOR, DAVID EDWARD, congressman; b. Detroit, June 6, 1945; s. Edward John and Irene (Gaverluk) B.; children: Julie, Andy BA, U. Iowa, 1967; MA in History, Chapman Coll., Calif., 1972. Mem. Mich. Ho. of Reps., 1973-77, U.S. Congress from 10th Mich. dist., 1977—2002; mem. com. on rules; Dem. whip, 1991—2002; prof. Wayne St. Univ., Coll. Urban, Labor & Met. Affs., Detroit, 2003—. Mem. VA, passport svs. and social security coms. U.S. Congress, 1999-2002. Author: The Vietnam Veteran: A History of Neglect, 1984 Served in USAF, 1968-72. Democrat. Roman Catholic. Office: Wayne St Univ 656 W Kirby St 3198 CULMA/FAB Detroit MI 48202*

BONIS, LASZLO JOSEPH, business executive, scientist; b. Budapest, Hungary, May 31, 1931; came to U.S., 1957; s. Joseph and Ilona (Hunvald) B.; m. Eva Markovich, July 31, 1955 (div. 1981); children: Andrea Christine, Peter Anthony Laszlo; m. Cheryl E. Olsen, Dec. 28, 1985. DM Ing. Mech. Engring., U. Tech. Sci., Budapest, 1953; MSc in Metallurgy, MIT, 1959, postgrad., 1959-60. Registered profl. engr., Calif., Mass.; cert. chemist Nat. Cert. Commn. Assoc. dir. material research Electronics, Inc., Budapest, 1953-56; prof. U. Tech. Sci., 1953-56; rsch. asst. MIT, Cambridge, 1957-60; exec. v.p., tech. dir. Ilikon Corp., Natick, Mass., 1960-62, pres., tech. dir., 1962-74; mgmt. cons. Tech. Fin. and Mktg., Inc., Natick, Mass., 1974—; pres., chmn., tech. dir. Composite Container Corp., Medford, Mass., 1977-88; pres. T.F.M. Cons., Dover, Mass., 1988—. Editor: (4 vols.) Fundamental Phenomena in the Material Science; contbr. articles to profl. jours.; patentee in field. Bd. dirs. The Opera Co., Boston, 1962-85, pres., 1966-85; pres. Boston Arts Coun., 1974—, Boston Opera House, 1991-94. Recipient Muse award Pub. Action for the Arts, 1984, George Washington award Am. Hungarian Found., 1984, Golden Door award Internat. Inst., 1980; named One of Outstanding Young Men of Greater Boston C. of C., 1966. Fellow Am. Inst. Chemists; mem. N.Y. Acad. Scis., MIT Club. Office: TFM Cons 52 Haven St Dover MA 02030-2131 E-mail: dr.bonis@tfmconsultants.com.

BONJACK, STEPHANIE, music librarian; b. Cleve. d. Brian and Linda Bonjack. MusB in Vocal Performance, Butler U., Indpls., 1999; MS in Libr. and Info. Sci., Dominican U., River Forest, Ill., 2001. Libr. asst. VanderCook Coll. of Music, Chgo., 2000—02, music libr., 2002—. Mem.: Am. Musicological Assn., Music Libr. Assn. Green Party. Office: VanderCook College of Music 3140 S Federal St Chicago IL 60616 Office Fax: 312-225-5211. E-mail: sbonjack@vandercook.edu.

BONJEAN, CHARLES MICHAEL, foundation executive, sociologist, educator; b. Pekin, Ill., Sept. 7, 1936; s. Bruno and Catherine Ann (Dancey) B. BA, Drake U., 1957; MA, U. N.C., 1959, PhD in Sociology, 1963. Mem. faculty U.

Tex., Austin, 1963—2003, Hogg prof. sociology, 1974—2003, chmn. dept., 1972-74; exec. assoc. Hogg Found., 1974-79; v.p., 1979-93; exec. dir. Hogg Found., 1993—2003. Sociology editor Chandler Pub. Co., 1967-73, Crowell Pub. Co., 1973-77, Dorsey Press, 1979-88, Wadsworth Pub. Co., 1988-93; mem. coun. Intern-Univ. Consortium Polit. and Social Rsch., 1972-76; mem. steering com. Coun. Social Sci. Jour. Editors, 1975-81; 2d v.p. Conf. S.W. Found., 1984-85, 1st v.p., 1985-86, pres., 1986-87; exec. com. Grantmakers Evaluation Network, 1994-98; mem. exec. com. Grantmakers in Health, 1995-98, bd. dirs., 1993-2000; chmn. rsch. com. Coun. Founds., 1991-94, bd. dirs., 1998-2003; mem. adv. com. Am. Sociol. Found., 1992-97, chmn., 1995-97. Co-author: Sociological Measurement, 1967, Sociology: A Core Text with Adapted Readings, 1990; co-editor: Blacks in the United States, 1969, Planned Social Intervention, 1969, Community Politics, 1971, Political Attitudes and Public Opinion, 1972, The Idea of Culture in the Social Sciences, 1973, Social Science in America, 1976, The Mexican Origin People in the United States, 1985, Community Care of the Chronically Mentally Ill, 1989, Mental Health Research in Texas, 1990; editor Social Sci. Quar., 1966-94; cons. editor Am. Jour. Sociology, 1974-76, The Am. Sociologist, 1990-96; contbr. to profl. jours. Bd. dirs. Lake Travis Ednl. Found., 1986-91. Recipient tchg. excellence award U. Tex. Students Assn., 1965, Alumni Disting. Svc. award Drake U., 1979, Disting. Svc. award Southwestern Social Sci. Assn., 2001; Sigma Delta Chi scholar, 1957. Mem. Am. Sociol. Assn. (chmn. cmty. sect. 1976-78, publs. com. 1978-81, chmn. 1979-81, pres. sect. on orgns. 1983-84, chmn. dist. scholarship com. 1992-84, coun. 1985-88, exec. office and budget com. 1994-97), Southwestern Sociol. Assn. (pres. 1972-73), Southwestern Social Sci. Assn. (exec. com. 1966-97, v.p. 1992-93, pres.-elect 1993-94, pres. 1994-95, Disting. Svc. award 2001), Philos. Soc. Tex. Home: 16310 Clara Van St Austin TX 78734-3928 E-mail: bonjean@mail.utexas.edu.

BONK, SHARON CATHERINE, librarian; b. North Tonawanda, N.Y., Nov. 28, 1943; d. Joseph J. and Ann (Danylow) B. BS in Edn., SUNY, Geneseo, 1965; MA in Am. Studies, MA in Libr. Sci., U. Minn., 1969. High sch. libr. Sch. Dist. 3, Huntington, N.Y., 1965-67; social scis. selector Northeastern U. Librs., Boston, 1969-81, head, periodicals dept., 1978-82; head acquisitions dept. SUNY Albany Librs., Albany, 1978-83; asst. dir. tech. svcs. SUNY Librs., Albany, 1984-88, interim dir., 1988-89, asst. dir. rsch. svcs., 1989-90; asst. direct user svcs. Albany, 1990-93, dir. Queens Coll. Librs. CUNY, 1993—. Contbr. articles to profl. jours.; author chpts. in monographs; assoc. editor Serials Rev. Trustee Sand Lake (N.Y.) Town Libr., 1987-89; mem. users coun. OCLC, 1994-2000; mem. adv. coun. N.Y.S. Regents LSCA, 1995-97, vice chair 1996-97. Recipient Fulbright Fellowship, 1989, Chancellor's Award for Excellence in Librarianship, SUNY, 1986, Lambert Scholarship, Blackwells Coll. of Libr. Wales, U.K., 1981. Mem. ACRL (bd. dirs. univ. librs. sect. 2001—), Assn. for Libr. Collections and Tech. Svcs./ALA (bd. dirs. 1989-92), Beta Phi Mu. Office: Rosenthal Library Queens Coll Kisseha Blvd Flushing NY 11367

BONN, ETHEL MAY, psychiatrist, educator; b. Cin., Oct. 14, 1925; d. Stanley Ervin and Ethel May (Cliffe) B. BA, U. Cin., 1947; MD, U. Chgo., 1951. Asst. chief, then chief women's neuro-psychiat. services VA Hosp., Topeka, 1956-61, chief north service, 1961-62; assoc. dir. for clin. services Ft. Logan Mental Health Ctr., Denver, 1962-67, dir., 1967-76; clin. instr. psychiatry U. Colo. Sch. Medicine, 1963-76; field rep. Joint Commn. on Accreditation of Hosps., 1976-78; assoc. clin. prof. psychiatry UCLA Sch. Medicine, 1978-81; chief of quality assurance VA Med. Ctr.-Brentwood, L.A., 1978-81; chief psychiatry service VA Med. Ctr., Albuquerque, 1981-89; assoc. prof. psychiatry U. N.Mex. Sch. Medicine, 1981-89; prof. emeritus psychiatry sch. medicine U. N.Mex., 1989—. Cons. Fitzsimons Army Hosp., Denver, 1963-67, U. Calif. Dept Biobehavioral Scis., Los Angeles, 1978-81, VA Hosps., Ft. Lyon, Colo., Sheridan, Wyo., Tuscaloosa, Ala., 1963-67. Contbr. chpts. to books, articles to profl. jours. Recipient Dirs. commendation, VA, 1962, 81, 89, Psychiat. Adminstrs. award Am. Assn. Psychiat. Adminstrs., 1976. Fellow Am. Coll. Psychiatrists (emeritus), Am. Psychiat. Assn. (life; program com. insts. for hosp. and cmty. psychiatry 1977-81), Am. Coll. Mental Health Adminstrn. (founding), Am. Coll. Utilization Rev. Physicians; mem. AMA, Am. Hosp. Assn. (chmn. psychiat. sect. 1972-74). Avocations: travel, gardening, oil and watercolor painting, collecting rocks and minerals, photography.

BONN, RONALD SHELDON, TV news producer, journalism educator; b. N.Y.C., June 5, 1930; s. Roy S. and Rose (Trilling) B.; m. June Weinstein, Sept. 9, 1962; children: Julia, David, Daniel. BA in Journalism, Pa. State U., 1952; postgrad., Columbia U., 1962-63. Writer, prodr. CBS News, N.Y.C., 1960-63, CBS Evening News with Walter Cronkite, N.Y.C., 1963-73, co-prodr., 1973-78; creator, exec. prodr. Universe—CBS News, N.Y.C., 1979-80; prodr. NBC News, N.Y.C., 1981-83; prodr. in charge spl. segments NBC Nightly News with Tom Brokaw, N.Y.C., 1983-88; prodr. in charge The New Cold War NBC News, 1984, medicine and sci. prodr. Sunday Today, 1989-92, line prodr. Tel Aviv, 1991; ind. prodr. various prodns. including NBC News Dateline, ABC News 20/20, Discovery Channel, A&E, CNN, 1993—. Guest lectr. various univs., 1965—; adj. prof. journalism U. San Diego, 2000—. Co-author: How to Help Children through a Parent's Serious Illness, 1994. Docent Maritime Mus. San Diego, 2000—. Sgt. U.S. Army, 1952-54. CBS News fellow Columbia U., 1962-63; recipient 3 Emmy awards Nat. Acad. TV Arts and Scis., 1970, 74, 84, Edward R. Murrow award Overseas Press Club Am., 1985, Edward R. Murrow Brotherhood award B'nai B'rith, 1986, Nat. Headliner award Press Club Atlantic City, 1991, White House Press Photographers award, 1991, Silver Gavel award ABA, 1992, Disting. Alumnus award Pa. State U., 1989, Am. Women in Radio and TV Commendation awards, 1991, 92. Avocations: sailing, travel. Home: 11075 Viacha Dr San Diego CA 92124 Office: Dept Comm U San Diego 5998 Alcala Park San Diego CA 92110 E-mail: ronbonn@sbcglobal.net.

BONN, THEODORE HERTZ, computer scientist, consultant; b. Phila., May 27, 1923; s. Norman Eugene and Matilda (Rickliss) B.; m. Edith Jeanette Sindell, Apr. 7, 1946; children: Suzanne, Miriam, Matthew. BSEE, U. Pa., 1943, MSEE, 1947. Rsch. asst. U. Pa., Phila., 1943-47; sr. engr. Eckert Mauchly Computer Corp., Phila., 1947-49; chief sonar components U.S. Naval Air Devel. Ctr., Johnsville, Pa., 1949-50; chief engr. rsch. and peripheral devel. UNIVAC, Blue Bell, Pa., 1950-64; dir. applied rsch. and standards Honeywell Info. Svc., Waltham, Mass., 1964-70; dir. Computer Rsch. Lab. Sperry Rsch. Ctr., Sudbury, Mass., 1970-83; mgr. C3I Systems Dept. Sperry Corp., Waltham, 1983-85; pres. Bonn Cons., Falmouth, Mass., 1985-90. Contbr. articles to profl. jours.; holder 45 patents in electronics field. Fellow IEEE (vice chmn. computer soc., chmn. tech. program com. Spring Joint Computer Conf., 1969, exec. com., fin. com., U.S. Activities bd. 1980-81, v.p. publs. 1980-82, bd. dirs. 1982-84, ednl. activities bd. 1984, Richard E. Merwin award Computer Soc. 1987). Jewish. Avocations: tennis, photography, music, travel, reading. Home (Winter): 1601 Pelican Point Dr HA213 Sarasota FL 34231 Home (Summer): 98 Shoreland Path East Falmouth MA 02536-5828 E-mail: tedbonn@aol.com.

BONNARD, RAYMOND, theater director; b. Chambersburg, Pa., May 13, 1951; m. Ricki Whitacre, Jan. 22, 1977; children: Christopher David, Alexander Whitacre. BS cum laude, Indiana (Pa.) U., 1973; MFA cum laude, Ohio U., 1976. Prodn. mgr. Mo. Reparatory Theatre, Kansas City, 1978-79; assoc. prodr. Tiffany's Attic Theatre, Waldo Astoria Theatre, Kansas City, 1979-81; prodn. stage mgr. Folly Theatre, Kansas City, 1981; mng. dir. Del. Theatre Co., Wilmington, 1981-84; producing dir. Studio Area Theatre, Buffalo, 1984-95. Asst. prof. U. Mo., Kansas City, 1978-79; respondent Am. Coll. Theatre Festival. Active Buffalo Fin. Planning Commn., Leadership Buffalo. Mem. League Regional Theatres (exec. com. 1988-91), Theatre DIst. Assn. (v.p. 1993—).

BONNE, ULRICH, chemical physicist; b. London, Mar. 10, 1937; came to U.S., 1965; s. George and Hildegard (Stubbe) B.; m. Colleen M. Traxinger, Aug. 5, 1967; children: Alex, George, Marc. BS, U. Freiburg, Germany, 1957; MS, U. Göttingen, Germany, 1960, PhD, 1964. Rsch. assoc. U. Göttingen, 1960-65; prin. rsch. scientist Honeywell, Mpls., 1965-67, prin. rsch. fellow, 68—; prin. rsch. scientist Factory Mut. Rsch. Corp., Norwood, Mass., 1967-68; lead microsensor tech. devel. Honeywell Labs., Plymouth, Minn. Divisional cons. Honeywell HESA, Brussels, 1980-81. Contbr. articles to profl. jours.; patentee in field. Judge Minn. Sci. Fair, 1966—. Recipient Engring. award Minn. Soc. Profl. Engrs., 1978. Mem. ASHRAE, Internat. Combustion Inst., Am. Chem. Soc., Honeywell Fellows (chmn. 1987-88). Avocations: gardening, tennis, snorkeling. Office: Honeywell Labs 12001 State Hwy 55 Plymouth MN 55441 E-mail: ubonne@msn.com.

BONNEFOUX, JEAN-PIERRE, artistic director, choreographer, dancer; b. Bourg-en-Bresse France, Apr. 9, 1943; s. Laurent and Marie-Therese (Noel) Bonnefoux; m. Patricia McBride, Sept. 8, 1973. Ed., Paris Opera Sch.; ArtsD(hon.), Goucher Coll., 1987. Tchr. Sch. of Am. Ballet, N.Y.C.; choreographer, 1977—80; artistic dir. N Carolina Dance Theatre, Charlotte, NC, 1996—. Ballet artist-in-residence Goucher Coll., Towson, Md., 1984—94; artistic dir. ballet dept. Ind. U., Bloomington, 1985—96. Dancer N.Y.C. Ballet, 1970—81. Decorated Officier L'Ordre du Merite France. Office: N Carolina Dance Theatre 800 N College St Charlotte NC 28206-3227

BONNELL, VICTORIA EILEEN, sociologist, educator; b. N.Y.C., June 15, 1942; d. Samuel S. and Frances (Nassau) B.; m. Gregory Freidin, May 4, 1971. BA, Brandeis U., 1964; MA, Harvard U., 1966, PhD, 1975. Lectr. politics U. Calif., Santa Cruz, 1972-73, 74-76, asst. prof. sociology Berkeley, 1976-82, assoc. prof., 1982-91, prof., 1991—. Chair Berkeley Ctr. for Slavic and East European Studies, U. Calif.-Berkeley, 1994—. Author: Roots of Rebellion: Workers' Politics and Organizations in St. Petersburg and Moscow, 1900-1914, 1983; editor: The Russian Worker: Life and Labor Under the Tsarist Regime, 1983, (with Ann Cooper and Gregory Freidin) Russia at the Varricades: Eyewitness Accounts of the August 1991 Coup, 1994, Iconography of Power: Soviet Political Posters Under Lenin and Stalin, 1997, Identities in Transition: Eastern Europe and Russia After the Collapse of Communism, 1996, Beyond the Cultural Turn: New Directions in the Study of Society and Cultyre, 1999; contbr. articles to profl. jours. Recipient Heldt prize in Slavic women's studies, 1991; AAUW fellow, 1979; Regents Faculty fellow, 1978, Fulbright Hays Faculty fellow, 1977, Internat. Rsch. and Exch. Bd. fellow, 1977, 88, Stanford U. Hoover Instn. nat. fellow, 1973-74, Guggenheim fellow, 1985, fellow Ctr. Advanced Study in Behavioral Scis., 1986-87, Pres.' Rsch. fellow in Humanities, 1991-92; grantee Am. Philos. Soc., 1979, Am. Coun. Learned Socs., 1976, 90-91. Mem. Am. Sociol. Assn., Am. Assn. Advancement Slavic Studies, Am. Hist. Assn.

BONNELL-MIHALIS, PAMELA GAY, library director; b. Monterey, Calif., Feb. 2, 1948; d. Dewey L. and Marlyce I. (Hansen) Scoggins; m. Verneil S. Henerson, June 18, 1966 (div. 1971); 1 child, V. Samuel Henerson III; m. Chrisman E Bonnell, Mar. 2, 1974 (div. 1983); m. Hugh R. McElroy, Nov. 10, 1990 (div. 1996); m. Stephan S. Mihalis, Oct. 5, 2002. BA, Cameron U., Lawton, Okla., 1972; MLS, U. Okla., 1972-73; CPM, S.W. Tex. State U., 1990. Libr. Met. Libr. Sys., Oklahoma City, 1974-75, Office of City Mgr., Dallas, 1977-80; dir. audience devel. Dallas Symphony Orch., 1980-81; libr. Dallas Morning News, 1981-83; libr. mgr. Plano (Tex.) Pub. Libr. Sys., 1983-91; dir. libr. svcs. Waco-McLennan County Libr. System, Waco, Tex., 1992—2001; exec. dir. Elyria (Ohio) Pub. Libr., 2002—. Author: (book) Fund Raising for Small Libraries, 1983; contbr. chapters to books, articles to profl. jours. Gala chair Easter Seal Soc., Dallas, 1988; bd. dirs. Women's Shelter, Plano, 1991; exec. bd. Am. Heart Assn., 1997—99; chmn. Lorain County Librs. Coun., 2003—; trustee Dallas Symphony Orch., 1981, Freedom to Read Found., 1999—; pres. Townbluff Homeowners Assn., Plano, 1984—90, Hippodrome Theatre Guild, 1996; treas. YWCA, 1995—96. Recipient Telecom. Excellence award, Ctrl. Tex. Edn., 1997. Mem.: ALA (councilor-at-large 1990—99, pres. Intellectual Freedom Round Table 1993—94, constn. and bylaws chair 1994—97, Shirley Olofson Meml. award 1974, cert. of Spl. Thanks 1986, John Phillip Immroth award 1990), Ctrl. Tex. Women's Alliance (bd. dirs. 1992—96), Tex. Libr. Assn. (chmn. Adminstrs. Roundtable 1994—95, trustee Leroy C. Merritt Trust Fund 1997—2000, chair intellectual freedom com. 2000—02, SIRS Intellectual Freedom award 1990), Tex. Mcpl. Librs. Dirs. (pres. 1994—95), Jr. League, Leadership Waco Alumni Assn., Rotary. Avocations: reading, travel. Home: 164 Arrow Ct Elyria OH 44035 Office: Elyria Pub Libr 320 Washington Ave Elyria OH 44035

BONNELLY, CLAUDE, library director; b. Quebec, Can., Feb. 4, 1946; s. Emmanuel and Gabrielle (Lepine) B.; m. Lise Lebeuf, Dec. 29, 1969; children: Mathieu, Simon. PhB, U Laval, Quebec, 1966, Lic. Philosophy, 1968; MLS, U. Montreal, Que., Can., 1973. Ref. libr. Libr. U. Laval, Sainte-Foy, Que., 1968-75, head ref. dept., 1975-78, assoc. libr., 1978-88, dir., 1988—. Can. Inst. Hist. Microprodns., Ottawa; chair Can. Initiative on Digital Librs. Contbr. articles to profl. jours. Mem. Assn. Rsch. Librs., Can. Assn. Rsch. Librs. (dir. 1990-91), Assn. Pour L'Advancement des Scis. et des Techniquer de la Documentation, Corp. des Bibliothecaires Profls. du Que., Can. Libr. Soc., Internet Soc. Home: 929 Brown Quebec QC Canada G1S 2Z6 Office: U Laval Libr Pavillon Bonenfant Sainte-Foy QC Canada G1K 7P4 E-mail: claude.bonnelly@bibl.ulaval.ca.

BONNER, BESTER DAVIS, school system administrator; b. Mobile, Ala., June 9, 1938; d. Samuel Matthew and Alma (Davis) Davis; m. Wardell Bonner, Nov. 28, 1964; children: Shawn Patrick, Matthew Wardell. BS, Ala. State Coll., 1959; MS in Library Sci., Syracuse U., 1966; PhD, U. Ala., 1982. Cert. tchr. Librarian Westside High Sch., Talladega, Ala., 1959-64; librarian, tchr. lit. Lane Elem. Sch., Birmingham, Ala., 1964-65; head librarian Jacksonville (Ala.) Elem. Lab. Sch., 1965-70; asst. prof. library media Ala. A&M U., Huntsville, 1970-74; adminstv. asst. to pres. Miles Coll., Birmingham, 1974-78, chmn. div. edn., 1978-85; specialist media Montgomery County Pub. Schs., Md., 1987-88; dir. libr. and media svcs. div. curriculum and ednl. tech. Dist. of Columbia Pub. Schs., 1988—. Forum leader Nat. Issues Forum, Domestic Policy Assn. U. Ala., Birmingham, 1983-84; mem. Libr. Svcs. Construction Act Adv. Com. Contbr. writer The Developing Black Family, 1975. Chmn. ethics commn. St. Ala., Montgomery 1977-81; radiothorn site coordinator United Negro Coll. Fund, Birmingham 1981. Mem. ALA, Ala. Instructional Media Assn. (pres. dist. II 1971-72), Assn. Women Deans and Adminstrs., Com. 100, D.C. Assn. Sch. Librs., D.C. Libr. Com., Am. Assn. Sch. Librs., Nat. Assn. State Ednl. Profls. Democrat. Methodist. Avocations: writing, speaking, consulting, piano. Home: 9601 Burgess Ln Silver Spring MD 20901-4701

BONNER, BILLY EDWARD, physics educator; b. Oak Grove, La., Dec. 12, 1939; s. James Wilbur and Julia (Deer) B. BS, La. Tech. U., 1961; MA, Rice U., 1963, PhD, 1965. Prin. scientific officer Rutherford High Energy Lab., Didcot, Berkshire, England, 1966-70; postdoctoral fellow U. Calif., Davis, 1971-72; physicist Los Alamos (N.Mex.) Nat. Lab., 1972-85; scientific assoc. CERN, Geneva, 1983-84; prof. physics Rice U., Houston, 1985—, chmn. dept. physics, 1986-91, dir. Bonner Nuclear Lab., 1987—. Editor 3 books; contbr. articles to profl. jours. Avocations: squash, fishing, cooking. Office: Rice Univ Bonner Nuclear Labs Houston TX 77005-1892 E-mail: bonner@rice.edu.

BONNER, DARLENE E. minister, writer; b. Reed City, Mich., July 12, 1956; d. William Gilbert Washington and Margaret Louise Taylor, William P. Taylor (Stepfather) and Phyllis Marie Washington(Stepmother); m. Algin Bonner Jr., Sept. 24, 1994; children: Marcus Lamont Washington, Clinton Lee Washington, Antonio Leshawn Washington, William Lorenzo Tate. Grad., Oceanside Coll. Cosmetology, 1980; cert. cosmetology, Ferris State Coll., 1981. Lic. cosmetology State of Mich., 1982, cert. nurses aide State of Mich., 1996. Cert. nurses aide Hurley Home Care and Hospice, Flint, Mich., 1996—99; founder Bonnerhouse Pub. Inc., Flint, 2002—. Pres. Young Teen Prayer Warriors, Flint, Mich., 2000—02. Author (publisher): (book of poetry) Bible Rhymes and Revelations (na, na), (novel) Distractions Decoys and The Truth, (poetry series) Prayer Warriors. Ministry, tchr., vol. River Of God Tabernacle Min, Flint, 2002—03. Avocations: swimming, writing, travel. Office: Bonnerhouse Pub Inc 445 Harriet St Flint MI 48505

BONNER, FRANCIS TRUESDALE, chemist, educator, university dean; b. Salt Lake City, Dec. 18, 1921; s. Walter Daniel and Grace (Gaylord) B.; m. Evelyn Hershkowitz, Jan. 17, 1946 (dec. 1990); children: Michael David, Joan Alisa (dec.), Rachel Pearl; m. M. Jane Carlberg, Dec. 31, 1994. BA, U. Utah, 1942; MS, Yale U., 1944, PhD, 1945. Chemist Manhattan Project S.A.M. Labs. Columbia U., 1944-46; chemist Clinton Labs., Oak Ridge, 1946-47; scientist Brookhaven Nat. Lab., Upton, N.Y., 1947-48, research collaborator, 1958-88; asst. prof. chemistry Bklyn. Coll., 1948-54; Carnegie vis. fellow Harvard, 1954-55; research phys. chemist Arthur D. Little, Inc., Cambridge, Mass., 1955-58; prof. dept. chemistry SUNY-Stony Brook, 1958—, founding chmn. dept., 1958-70, dean for internat. programs, 1983-86, prof. emeritus, 1992—. Cons. editor Addison-Wesley Pub. Co., Reading, Mass., 1956-77; Rockefeller Found. adviser on curriculum, instl. devel. Universidad Del Valle, Cali, Colombia, 1961-62, 64, Ford Found. adviser, 1968; Ford Found. adviser to Universidad de Antioquia, Medellin, Colombia, 1962-64; dir. N.Y. Met. Area Ctr. Chem. Edn. Materials Study for NSF 1961-62; mem. com. for chemistry Coll. Entrance Exam. Bd., 1962-63; mem. NSF-sponsored Adv. Coun. on Coll. Chemistry, 1967-70; mem. Coll. Proficiency Exam. Com. Chemistry, N.Y. State Edn. Dept., 1963-64, 66-70; NSF sr. postdoctoral fellow Svc. des Isotopes Stables, Centre d'Etudes Nucleaires de Saclay, Gif-Sur-Yvette, France, 1964-65; vis. scientist Swiss Fed. Inst. for Water Resources and Water Pollution Control, Swiss Fed. Inst. Tech., Zurich, 1973, Kings Coll. U. London, 1987; Nat. Acad. exch. visitor, Romania, 1975; mem. grants adv. panel Fund for Overseas Grants and Edn., 1968-76; bd. dirs. Rsch. Found. State U. N.Y., 1976-88; cons. L.I. Power Authority, 1998-2003. Author: (with Melba Phillips) Principles of Physical Science, 1957, 2d edit., 1971; Contbr. numerous articles profl. jours. Mem. Ind. Rev. Panel for Decommissioning of Shoreham Nuc. Power Sta., 1992-95; mem. bd. edn. Ctrl. Sch. Dist. 6, Huntington, N.Y., 1968-72. Fellow: AAAS; mem.: AAUP, Am. Chem. Soc., Sigma Xi. Home: PO Box 2063 Setauket NY 11733-0707 Office: State U NY Dept Chemistry Stony Brook NY 11794-3400

BONNER, HERBERT DWIGHT, construction management educator; b. Lakewood, Ohio, Sept. 5, 1942; s. Herbert C. and Ruth (H.) B.; m. Marilyn Anne Seidel, Sept. 18, 1965. BArch, Ohio State U., 1969, MArch, 1971. Registered architect, Ohio; cert. profl. constructor. Tng. engr. H.K. Ferguson Co., Cleve., 1961-62, U.S. Steel Corp., Cleve., 1962-64, Hausman Steel Corp., Grandview, Ohio, 1964-65; tng. architect Kellam & Foley Architects, Columbus, Ohio, 1965-68; rsch. assoc. bldg. rsch. lab. Ohio State U., Columbus, Ohio, 1968-71, asst. prof., 1971-74; prof. Columbus State C.C., 1974-95; owner Bonner Constrn. Svcs., Patagonia, Ariz., 1971—. Cons. Aubon Ednl. Svcs., Columbus, 1980-85; adj. faculty mem. Caiptal U., Columbus, 1986-95; exec. dir. Associated Two Yr. Sch. Constrn., Edmonds, Wash., 1989-95. Author: Building Plans and Working Drawings, 1981; editor: Scheduling Construction Projects, 1984, Construction Equipment Operators, 1992; contbr. articles to profl. jours. Trustee Am. Coun. for Constrn. Edn., Monroe, La., 1990-95. Recipient Disting. Svc. award Assn. Bus. and Profl. Women, 1982, Nat. Assn. Women in Constrn., 1984; grantee Dept. of Def., 1970-71, 1st Community Village, 1974, Owens Corning Fiberglass, 1981-82. Mem. AIA, Am. Inst. Constructors, Ohio Horeman's Coun., Tenn. Walking Horse Beaders and Exhibitors Assn., Mid-Ohio Walking Horse Assn., Hocking County Trail Blazers. Avocations: competitive horse riding and showing, endurance riding. Office: Bonner Constrn Svcs PO Box 1060 Patagonia AZ 85624

BONNER, JACK WILBUR, III, psychiatrist, educator, administrator; b. Corpus Christi, Tex., July 30, 1940; s. Jack Wilbur and Irldene (Turner) B.; m. Myra Lynn Taylor; children: Jack Wilbur, IV, Katherine Lynn, Shelley Bliss. AA, Del Mar Coll., Corpus Christi, 1960; BA with honors, U. Tex., Austin, 1961; MD, S.W. Med. Sch., U. Tex., Dallas, 1965. Diplomate Am. Bd. Psychiatry and Neurology. Intern U. Ark. Med. Center, 1965-66; resident Duke U. Med. Center, 1966-69; assoc. in psychiatry Highland Hosp. divsn. Duke U. Med. Center, Asheville, N.C., 1971, asst. prof. psychiatry, 1972-80, dir. outpatient services, 1972-75, med. dir., 1975-81; chmn. bd. dirs., CEO, med. dir. Highland Hosp., Asheville, N.C., 1981-92; med. dir. The Oaks Psychiat. Health Sys., Austin, Tex., 1992-93, exec. med. dir., 1993-94; med. dir. Behavioral Health Svcs. Greenville (S.C.) Hosp. Sys., 1994—, adminstr. Behavioral Health Svcs., 1996-2000, acad. chair, 1999—. Asst. clin. prof. Duke U. Med. Ctr., Durham, N.C., 1982-87, asst. cons. prof. psychiatry, 1987—; clin. assoc. prof. U. N.C. Sch. Medicine, Chapel Hill, 1986-92, Quillen-Dishner Coll. Medicine, Johnson City, Tenn., 1989-92, U. Tex. Health Sci. Ctr., San Antonio, 1993-94, U. S.C. Sch. Medicine, Columbia, 1995—. Author: (with others) The Psychology of Discipline, 1983, Unmasking the Psychopath: Antisocial Personality and Related Syndromes, 1986; contbr. articles to profl. jours. Chmn. bd. dirs. The Highland Found., 1980-93; bd. dirs. Western N.C. Med. Peer Rev. Found., 1975-78; trustee La Amistad Found., Maitland, Fla., 1985-95, N.C. Symphony, 1987-92, Cooper Riis Found., Mill Spring, N.C., 2000—. Fellow Am. Psychiat. Assn. (Disting. Life Fellow; trustee 1999—, Warren Williams award 2002), So. Psychiat. Assn. (v.p. 1984-85, chmn. bd. regents 1988-89, pres.-elect 1991-92, pres. 1992-93), Am. Coll. Psychiatrists (treas. 1992-95, 2d v.p. 1999-2000, 1st v.p. 2000-01, pres.-elect 2001-02, pres. 2002-03, E.B. Bowis award 2000); mem. AMA, Nat. Assn. Psychiat. Health Sys. (trustee 1989-94, 1st v.p. 1990-91, pres.-elect 1991-92, pres. 1992-93), Am. Group Psychotherapy Assn., Nat. Acads. Practice, Buncombe County (NC) Med. Soc. (pres.-elect 1982, pres. 1983), NC Psychiat. Assn. (pres.-elect 1981-82, pres. 1982-83), Nat. Anorexic Aid Soc. (nat. anorexia adv. coun. 1979-86), So. Med. Assn. (sec. sect. on neurology, neurosurgery and psychiatry 1977-80, chmn.-elect 1980-81, chmn. 1981-82), Ctrl. Neuropsychiat. Hosp. Assn. (councillor 1981-85, pres.-elect 1982-83, pres. 1983-84), Group Advancement Psychiatry (treas. 1991-99, pres.-elect 1999-2001, pres. 2001-03), U. Tex. Southwestern Med. Sch. Alumni Assn. (bd. dir. 1988-95, pres. 1989-91), Benjamin Rush Soc., Phi Theta Kappa. Home: Four Brookside Way Greenville SC 29605-1212 Office: Greenville Hosp Sys Behavioral Health Svcs 701 Grove Rd Greenville SC 29605-5601 E-mail: jbonner@ghs.org.

BONNER, JOHN TYLER, biology educator; b. N.Y.C., May 12, 1920; s. Paul Hyde and Lilly Marguerite (Stehli) B.; m. Ruth Anna Graham, July 11, 1942; children: Rebecca, Jonathan Graham, Jeremy Tyndall, Andrew Duncan. Grad., Phillips Exeter Acad., 1937; BSc, Harvard U., 1941, MA, 1942, PhD (Jr. fellow 1942, 46-47), 1947; DSc (hon.), Middlebury Coll., 1970. Asst. to assoc. prof. Princeton U., 1947-58, prof., 1958-90, emeritus prof., 1990—, chmn. dept. biology, 1965-77, 83-84, 87-88. Lectr. embryology Marine Biol. Lab., Woods Hole, Mass., 1951-52; spl. lectr. U. London, 1957, Bklyn. Coll., 1966; Arnold Bernhard vis. prof. Williams Coll., 1989; Raman prof. Indian Acad. Scis., 1990; trustee Biol. Abstracts, 1958-63; mem. bd. editors Princeton U. Press, 1965-68, 71, trustee, 1976-82. Author: Morphogenesis, 1952, Cells and Societies, 1955, The Evolution of Development, 1958, The Cellular Slime Molds, 1959, The Cellular Slime Molds, rev. edit., 1967, The Ideas of Biology, 1962, Size and Cycle, 1965, The Scale of Nature, 1969, On Development, 1974, The Evolution of Culture in Animals, 1980; author: (with T.A. McMahon) On Life and Size, 1983; author: The Evolution of Complexity, 1988, Researches on Cellular Slime Molds, 1991, Life Cycles, 1993, Sixty Years of Biology, 1996, First Signals, 2000, Lives of a Biologist, 2002; editor: Growth and Form, 1961, Evolution and Development, 1981; assoc. editor: Am. Scientist, 1961—69, mem. editl. bd.: Am. Naturalist, 1958—60, 1966—68, Jour. Gen. Physiology, 1962—69, Growth, 1955—89, Differentiation, 1976—90, Oxford Surveys in Evolutionary Biology, 1982—93. Pvt. to 1st lt. USAC, 1942-46; staff aero. med. lab. Wright Field, Dayton, Ohio. Sheldon traveling fellow Panama, 1941; Rockefeller traveling fellow France, 1953; Guggenheim fellow Scotland, 1958, 71-72; recipient Selman A. Waksman award for contbns. to microbiology Theobold Smith Soc.; NSF sr. postdoctoral fellow, 1963 Fellow Am. Acad. Arts and Scis., Indian Acad. Scis. (hon.); mem. NAS, Am. Soc. Naturalists, Soc. Growth and Devel., Am. Philos. Soc., Phi Beta Kappa, Sigma Xi. E-mail: jtbonner@princeton.edu.

BONNER, JOSIAH ROBINS, JR., (JO BONNER), congressman; b. Selma, Ala., Nov. 19, 1959; s. Josiah Robins Bonner; m. Janée Lambert Bonner; children: Jennifer Lee, Josiah Robins III. JB, U. Ala., 1982. Chief of staff U.S. Rep. Sonny Callahan, press sec., 1984, Congl. press sec., 1985; congressman 1st Dist. Ala. U.S. Ho. Reps., 2003—. Mem. pres. adv. coun. U. Mobile; mem. bd. cmty. advisors Jr. League Mobile. Named Outstanding Alumnus in Pub. Rels., U. Ala. Coll. Comm., 2000. Mem.: Mobile Area C. of C. (bd. dirs.), U. Ala. Alumni Assn. (Mobile chpt., bd. dirs.), Leadership Mobile (bd. dirs.), Rotary Club (bd. dirs.). Republican. Episcopalian. Office: 315 Cannon HOB Washington DC 20515-0101*

BONNER, ROBERT CLEVE, federal agency administrator, lawyer; b. Wichita, Kans., Jan. 29, 1942; s. Benjamin Joseph and Caroline (Kirkwood) B.; m. Kimiko Tanaka, Oct. 11, 1969; 1 child, Justine M. BA magna cum laude, Md. U., 1963; JD, Georgetown U., 1966. Bar: D.C. 1966, Calif. 1967, Ct. Appeals (4th, 5th, 9th, 10th cirs.), U.S. Supreme Ct. Law clk. to judge U.S. Dist. Ct., L.A., 1966-67; asst. U.S. atty. U.S. Atty's Office (cen. dist.) Calif., L.A., 1971-75, U.S. atty., 1984-89; judge U.S. Dist. Ct. (cen. dist.) Calif., L.A., 1989-90; ptnr. Kadison, Pfaelzer, et al, Los Angeles, 1975-84; dir. Drug Enforcement Adminstrn., Washington, 1990-93; ptnr. Gibson, Dunn & Crutcher, L.A., 1993—2001; commr. U.S. Customs Svc., Washington, 2001—. Chair Calif. Commn. on Jud. Performance, 1997-99. Served to lt. comdr. JAGC, USN, 1967-70 Fellow Am. Coll. Trial Lawyers, Fed. Bar Assn. (pres. Los

Angeles chpt. 1982-83); mem. L.A. C. of C. (bd. dirs. 1999-2001). Republican. Roman Catholic. Office: US Customs Svc Hdqr 1300 Pennsylvania Ave NW Washington DC 20229 Office Fax: 202-927-1380.

BONNER, ROBERT WILLIAM, lawyer, director; b. Vancouver, B.C., Can., Sept. 10, 1920; s. Benjamin York and Emma Louise (Weir) B.; m. Barbara Newman, June 16, 1942; children: Barbara Carolyn (Mrs. Massie), Robert York, Elizabeth Louise (Mrs. McPhee). BA in Econs. and Polit. Sci. U. B.C., 1942, LL.B., 1948. Bar: B.C. 1948, created Queen's counsel 1952. With firm Clark Wilson White Clark & Maguire, Vancouver, 1948-52; atty. gen. Province of B.C., 1952-68; sr. v.p. adminstrn. MacMillan Bloedel Ltd., 1968-70, exec. v.p. adminstrn., 1970-71, vice chmn., 1971-72, pres., chief exec. officer, 1972-73, chmn. bd., 1973-74, ret., 1974; chmn. B.C. Hydro & Power Authority, 1976-85; ptnr. Bonner & Fouks, 1974-84, Robertson, Ward, Suderman, Vancouver, 1985-89. Mem. B.C. Legislature, 1952-69; mem. Energy Supplies Allocation Bd., bd. dirs. Served to maj. Royal Canadian Army, 1942-45; lt. col. Res. (ret.). Mem. Canadian Bar Assn., Law Soc. B.C. (life bencher), Delta Upsilon. Mem. Social Credit Party. Clubs: Mason, Vancouver; Union (Victoria). Home: 5679 Newton Wynd Vancouver BC Canada V6T 1H6 Office: Box 18162 2225 W 41st Ave Vancouver BC Canada V6M 2A3 Fax: 604-264-6142. E-mail: rwbonner@attcanada.ca.

BONNER, SHIRLEY HARROLD, business communications educator; b. Pitts., July 22, 1929; d. William DeWitt Jr. and Erma Dorothy (Ruppert) Harrold; m. Joseph A. Bonner, Apr. 21, 1956; children: Margaret Leslie, Joseph Edward. BS in Edn., U. Pitts., 1951, MEd, 1971, PhD, 1981. With Gulf Oil Corp., Pitts.; tchr. Three Rivers Bus. Sch., Pitts., Antwerp (Belgium) Internat. Sch., Duff's Bus. Sch., Pitts., C.C. of Allegheny County, Pitts., Learning Ctr. Chatham Coll., 1994—. Pres. Chatham Coll. literacy bd., 1997—. Author: Margaret of Austria, Governess of the Low Countries, 1507-1530, 2 vols.; contbr. articles to The Balance Sheet. Mem. Baltzer Meyer Hist. Soc.; past bd. dirs. Am. Protestant Ch. of Antwerp. Mem.: AAUW (pres. DuBois area br. 1967—69), Assn. for Bus. Comm., World Affairs Coun. Pitts. (consul), Delta Zeta. Republican. Avocations: travel, mysteries, biographies. Home: 403 Denniston Ave Pittsburgh PA 15206-4411

BONNER, THOMAS, JR., English language educator; b. New Orleans, Sept. 19, 1942; s. Thomas and Mercedes Mary (Vulliet) B.; m. Judith Ann Hopkins, Aug. 27, 1966; children: Ashley Elizabeth, Laura Vulliet. BA, Southeastern La. U., 1965; MA, Tulane U., 1968, PhD, 1975. English instr. U. Southwestern La., Lafayette, 1966-68; prof. Xavier U. La., New Orleans, 1971—, Kellogg prof. English, 2001—, chair dept. English, 1976—82, 2003—. Disting. vis. prof. English USAF Acad., 1991-92, 2000-02; reader-evaluator Ednl. Testing Svc., Princeton, N.J.; writer-judge Varsity Quiz Bowl, WYES-TV, New Orleans, 1982-92; book reviewer Times-Picayune, New Orleans, 1980-89; editor Xavier Rev. Press, 1988—. Author: William Faulkner, 1980, The Kate Chopin Companion, 1988, The Epistolary Poe, 2001; editor Xavier Rev., 1982—, Above Ground, 1993; editor and contbr. John Faulkner Issue of Miss. Quarterly, 2001; author numerous poems; contbr. articles to profl. jours. Dir. lit. series, New Orleans Pub. Libr. and NEH, 1979. Recipient Bush Found. award, 1990; United Negro Coll. Fund-Mellon fellow, 1982. Mem. MLA, South Ctrl. MLA (pres. 1996, exec. com. 1990-92), South Atlantic MLA, Soc. Study So. Lit. (exec. com. 1983-85, 93—), Conf. on Christianity and Lit., South Ctrl. Conf. on Christianity and Lit. (exec. com. 1979—), So. Am. Studies Assn. (pres. 2002—). Roman Catholic. Avocations: tennis, hiking, fishing, travel.

BONNESON, PAUL GARLAND, lawyer; b. Milw., May 12, 1959; s. Garland Waldemar and Marilyn Adah (Giese) B. BA cum laude, Marquette U., 1981; JD, Drake U., Des Moines, 1984. Bar: Wis. 1984, U.S. Dist. Ct. (ea. dist.) Wis. 1984, U.S. Ct. Appeals (7th cir.) 1991, U.S. Supreme Ct. 1992. Assoc. Riemer Law Offices, Delavan, Wis., 1984-87, Tikalsky, Raasch & Tikalsky, Waukesha, Wis., 1987-90, Rudolph Law Offices, Elm Grove, Wis., 1990-91; pvt. practice Wauwatosa, Wis., 1991—. Mem. Badger State Vettes, Ltd., 1990—. Mem. Rep. Party of Waukesha County, 1996—; active Elmbrook Ch., Brookfield, Wis. Mem. State Bar of Wis. (pres. young lawyers divsn. 1994-95, exec. com. 1995-96, bd. govs. 1995-96, continuing legal edn. com. 1996-2000, chair mentor coun. com. 2000-02), Waukesha County Bar Assn. (bd. dirs. 1998-2001, sec.-treas. 2001-02, pres.-elect 2002-03, pres. 2003—), Corvette Club. Republican. Home: 20185 A Independence Dr Brookfield WI 53045-5385 Office: 631 N Mayfair Rd Wauwatosa WI 53226-4249 E-mail: vettlaw@execpc.com.

BONNETT, THOMAS W. political scientist, writer; b. Hanover, N.H., Nov. 21, 1952; s. Robert Wilcox Bonnett and I. Joyce Smith; m. Karen Elizabeth Kahn, May 30, 1982; 1 child, Stephen Kahn. BA, Bennington Coll., 1975; M in Pub. Policy, U. Calif., Berkeley, 1980. City planner City Planning, N.Y.C., 1985-87; policy analyst Human Resources Adminstrn., N.Y.C., 1987-91; policy dir. Coun. Gov.'s Policy Advisors, Washington, 1992-97; pres. Pub. Policy Consulting, Bklyn., 1997—2002; asst. commr. for policy and rsch. Dept. of Homeless Svcs., N.Y.C., 2002—. Author: Rural Competitiveness, 1993, Telewars in the States, 1996, Competing in the New Economy, 2000. Mem. Assn. Pub. Policy Analysis & Mgmt., Bklyn. Poker Club. Deist. Avocations: basketball, poker, reading. Office: Dept of Homeless Svcs 33 Beaver St New York NY 10004 E-mail: TWBPARKSLO@aol.com.

BONNEVILLE, KATHERINE ANN, human resources specialist, consultant; b. Duluth, Minn., Apr. 21, 1960; d. Charles Albert and Patricia Jean Bonneville; children: Daniel Thomas Barthell, Sarah JoAnn Barthell. BA in Psychology, Sociology, U. Minn., Duluth, 1982; MA in Indsl. Rels., U. Minn., 1986. Compensation mgr. ING Group (formerly NWNL Co. Inc.), Mpls., 1984—91; dir. compensation NW Airlines, St. Paul, 1991—99; compensation practice leader Orgnl. Concepts Internat., Mpls., 1999—. Mem.: Nat. Assn. Stock Plan Profls., WorldatWork. Avocations: reading, travel, oil painting. Office: Organizational Concepts International 730 2nd Avenue South Suite 730 Minneapolis MN 55402 Office Fax: 612-399-0052. Personal E-mail: kbonneville@oci-hr.com. E-mail: kbonneville@oci-hr.com.

BONNEVILLE, RICHARD BRIGGS, retired petroleum exploration and production executive; b. Chgo., July 15, 1942; s. Alfred Briggs and Grace Estelle (Burke) B.; B.S. in M.E., U. Notre Dame, 1964; M.B.A., Harvard U., 1967; m. Mary Ann E. Pittman, July 17, 1976; children: Ann M., John B. Project engr. Hamilton Standard div. United Technologies, 1964-65; asst. to pres. Strathmore Paper div. Hammermill Paper, Springfield, Mass., 1966; mgr. planning Union Oil Co., Schaumburg, Ill., 1967-72; asst. to exec. v.p. Santa Fe Industries, Inc., Chgo., 1972-77, mgr. planning, 1977-79, dir. planning, 1979-84; corp. sec. Santa Fe So. Pacific Corp., 1984-88;, v.p. planning, Santa Fe Energy Resources, Inc., Houston, 1988-95, ret., 1995. Mem. Tau Beta Pi, Pi Tau Sigma. Home: 920 Cranberry Hill Ct Houston TX 77079-5010

BONNEY, HAL JAMES, JR., federal judge; b. Norfolk, Va., Aug. 27, 1929; s. Hal J. and Mary (Shackelford) B.; m. Marie McBee, July 4, 1963 (div. 1979); children: David James, John Wesley. BA, U. Richmond, 1951, MA, 1953; JD, Coll. William and Mary, 1969. Bar: Va. 1969. Instr. Norfolk public schs., 1951-61; supt. Douglas MacArthur Acad., 1961-67; practiced law, 1969-71; law clk. U.S. Dist. Ct., 1969; prof. U. Va., 1964-71, Coll. William and Mary, 1969-71; U.S. bankruptcy judge Norfolk, 1971-95; ret., 1995. Adj. prof. law Regent U. Law Sch., 1987—97; prodr. Hal Bonney Prodns. Author: Overturning Applecarts, 2002. Tchr. Wesleymen Bible Class Sta. WTAR-AM, 1962-98, tchr. emeritus, 1998; tchr. Good News TV Network, 1989—; treas. Wesleymen Found., Inc., Billy Graham Crusades, 1974-76; pres. adv. coun. CBN U., 1986-95; vice-chmn. Va. Meth. Bd. Edn., Inc., 1991-99; bd. visitors Duke Div. Sch., 1991—; 1st v.p., bd. dirs. Norfolk Union Mission, 1994—, 1st v.p.; v.p. The Tidewater Winds; mem. City of Norfolk Task Force on Pub. Housing, 1995-96; advisor Film Sch., Regent U., 1996-2000, assoc. prodr. 2000—; mem. City of Norfolk Parks and Recreation Commn.; vice chair rules com. Va. United Meth. conf., 1996—; bd. ordained ministry United Meth. Ch., Va; commr. City of Norfolk Parks and Recreation, 2003—; active World Affairs Coun. Recipient S.A.R. Good Citizenship medal, Woodmen of the World History medal, U. Richmond Gold medal, George Washington honor medal Freedoms Found., Alli award Cultural Alliance Greater Hampton Rds., 1998; Judge Hal Bonney Day named in honor by City of Norfolk, Jan. 27, 1998. Mem. Nat. Conf. Bankruptcy Judges (pres. 1983, chmn. editl. bd. The Am. Bankruptcy Law Jour.), Va. State Bar, Norfolk and Portsmouth Bar Assn., Nat. Film Soc., Am. Film Inst. (Second Decade coun.), Brit. Film Inst., Am. Cinematheque (moving picture ball benefit com.), James Kent Inn of Ct. (hon., pres. 1994-96), Phi Alpha Theta, Pi Sigma Alpha, Phi Alpha Delta, Masons, Shriners, Elks, Kiwanis (dir.). Methodist. Home: 1357 Windsor Point Rd Norfolk VA 23509-1311 Office: The Wesleymen 408 Boush St Norfolk VA 23510-1215 E-mail: bonney@erols.com.

BONNEY, JOHN DENNIS, retired oil company executive; b. Blackpool, Eng., Dec. 22, 1930; s. John P. and Isabel (Evans) B.; six children. BA, Hertford Coll., Oxford U., Eng., 1954, MA, 1959; LL.M., U. Calif., Berkeley, 1956. Oil adviser, Middle East, 1959-60; fgn. ops. adviser, asst. mgr., then mgr. Chevron Corp. (formerly Standard Oil Co. of Calif.), San Francisco, 1960-72, v.p., from 1972, vice chmn., dir., 1987-95. Mem.: Commonwealth; World Affairs Coun. of No. Calif., World Trade (San Francisco); Oxford and Cambridge (London). Office: 345 California St 30th Fl San Francisco CA 94104

BONNIE, RICHARD JEFFREY, law educator, lawyer; b. Richmond, Va., Aug. 22, 1945; s. Herbert Herman and Helene Selma (Berz) B.; m. Kathleen Ford, June 15, 1967; children: Joshua Ford, Zachary Andrew, Jessica Katherine. BA, Johns Hopkins U., 1966; LLB, U. Va., 1969. Var: Va. 1969, U.S. Dist. Ct. (ea. dist.) Va. 1969; U.S. Ct. Appeals (4th cir.) 1969, U.S. Supreme Ct. 1986. Asst. prof. law U. Va., Charlottesville, 1969-70, assoc. prof., 1973-77, prof., 1977-87, John S. Battle prof., 1987—; dir. Inst. Law, psychiatry, and Pub. Policy, 1979—. Vis. prof. Cornell Law Sch., 1993-94; assoc. dir. nat. Commn. Marijuana and Drug Abuse, 1971-73; reporter Nat. Conf. Commrs. on Uniform State Laws, 1972-74; cons. Spl. Action Office for Drug Abuse Prevention Exec. Office of the Pres., 1973-75; spl. asst. to U.S. Atty. Gen., 1975; mem. and sec. Nat. Adv. Coun. on Drug Abuse, 1975-80; mem. Com. on Problem of Drug Dependence, Inc., 1979-84; charter fellow Coll. Problems of Drug Dependence, 1992—; cons. Am. Psychiat. Assn., Coun. Psychiatry and Law, 1979—; mem. U.S. State Dept. Del. to investigate psychiat. practices in the Soviet Union, 1989; mem. World Psychiat. Assn. rev. team to investigate Soviet psychiatry, 1991; mem. adv. bd. permanent coordination office Reforms in psychiatry in Ctrl. and Ea. Europe, former Soviet Union, 1993—; bd. dirs. Geneva Initiative on Psychiatry, 1996—; pres. Am. Friends of Geneva Initiatives on Psychiatry, 1997—, mem. MacArthur Found. Network on Mental Health and the Law, 1988-96; bd. dirs. Va. Capital Representation Resource Ctr., 1994-97, 2002—; mem. MacArthur Found. Network on Mandated Treatment, 2000—. Author: The Marijuana Conviction: The History of Marijuana Prohibition in the United States, 1974, 2d edit. 1999, Legal Aspects of Drug Dependence, 1975, Psychiatrists and the Legal Process: Diagnosis and Debate, 1977, Marijuana Use and Criminal Sanctions: Essays in the Theory and Practice of Decriminalization, 1980, Criminal Law: Cases and Materials, 1982, 2d edit., 1986, The Trial of John W. Hinckley, Jr.: A Case Study in the Insanity Defense, 1986, rev. edit. 2000, Criminal Law, 1997, Growing Up Tobacco Free, 1994, Mental Disorder, Work Disability and the Law, 1997, Reducing the Burden of Injury, 1999, The Evolution of Mental Health Law, 2001, Elder Mistreatment, 2002, Adjudicative Competence, 2002. Chmn. Va. Human Rights Com., Dept. mental Health and Mental Retardation, 1979-85; bd. dirs. Coll. on Problem of Drug Dependence, 1996-2000. Served to capt. USAF, 1970-73. Inst. Criminology fellow Cambridge U., 1977. Fellow Va. Law Found.; mem. Inst. Medicine of NAS (mem. bd. neurosci. and behavioral health, 1992-2001, mem. com. on preventing nicotine dependence in children and youths, 1993-94, mem. membership com. 1995-98, chair com. on opportunities in drug abuse rsch. 1995-96, chair com. injury prevention control 1997-98, mem. com. to assess sci. base for tobacco harm reduction 1999-2001, mem. com. to assess the sys. for the protection of human rsch. subjects 2000-2002, chair com. to propose strategy to prevent and reduce underage drinking 2002-03, divsn. behavioral and social scis. and edn. 2003—), Nat. Rsch. Coun. (mem. comm. on data and rsch. for policy on illicit drugs 1998-2000, chair com. elder abuse and neglect 2001-02, mem. common law and justice com. 2002—. chair com. underage drinking, 2002—, mem. div. com. behavioral and social scis. and edn. 2003—), ABA (mem. criminal justice-mental health stds. project adv. bd. 1981-87), NAS, Am. Psychiat. Assn. (Isaac Ray award 1998, Spl. Presdl. Commendation 2003), Va. Bar Assn. (chmn. com. mentally disabled 1981-90, mem. criminal law sect. coun. 1992-96), World Psychiat. Assn. (rev. team to investigate Soviet Psychiatry 1991), Am. Acad. Psychiat. Law (Amicus award 1994), Inst. Medicine (Yarmolinsky medal 2002), Va. Law Found. (fellow), Nat. Acad. Sci. (nat. assoc.). Office: U Va Sch Law 580 Massie Rd Charlottesville VA 22903

BONNY, HELEN LINDQUIST, music therapist; b. Rockford, Ill., Mar. 31, 1921; d. Gustavus Elmer Emmanuel and Ethel Mae (Geer) Lindquist; m. Oscar E. Bonny, Aug. 17, 1943 (div. 1980); children: Beatrice Starrett, Erich Lind, Francis Albert. B in Music, Oberlin Conservatory, 1943; B in Music Edn., Kans. U., 1961-64, M in Music Edn., 1968; PhD in Music and Psychology, Union Grad. Sch., 1976. Instr. string dept. Anthony (Kans.) Pub. Schs., 1948-50; instr. violin St. Mary Coll., Xavier, Kans., 1958-60; music therapist Parsons (Kans.) State Hosp., 1965; research investigator VA Hosp., Topeka, Kans., 1966-69; coordinating sec. Nat. Assn. Music Therapy, Lawrence, Kans., 1967-69; research asst. Md. Psychol. Research Ctr., Balt., 1969-73, research fellow, 1973-75; dir. music therapy Cath. U. Am., Washington, 1975-80; founder, dir. Inst. for Cons. & Music, Port Townsend, Wash., 1973-86; owner Music Rx, Port Townsend, Wash., 1985-89; pres., dir. The Bonny Found., Salina, KS, 1989-2001. Lectr. U. Md., Balt., 1974-75; mem. adv. bd. Salina Symphony Orch., 1990-96; rsch. advisor Walden U., Mpls., 1982-88; field advisor Antioch Coll., Seattle, 1983; co-dir. Coun. Grove Conf., Kans., 1989-90; external examiner The Fielding Inst., Santa Barbara, Calif., 1986-87. Author: Music and Consciousness: The Evolution of Guided Imagery and Music, 2002; co-author: Music and Your Mind, 1973; contbr. articles to profl. jours. Founder Council Grove Conf., Topeka, 1968; mem. edn. com. Peninsula Coll., Port Townsend, 1985-88. NIMH grantee, 1964. Mem. Am. Assn. Music Therapy, Nat. Assn. Music Therapy (pres. 1976-77), Assn. Music and Imagery. Mem. United Ch. of Christ. Avocations: playing quartets, swimming, traveling. Home: 1166 6th Ave 4C Vero Beach FL 32960 E-mail: helenbonny@CS.com.

BONO, MARY WHITAKER, congresswoman; b. Cleve., Oct. 24, 1961; d. Clay and Karen Whitaker; children: Chesare Elan, Chianna Maria; m. Glenn Baxley, Nov. 2001. BFA in Art History, U. So. Calif., 1984. Cert. personal fitness instr. Mem. U.S. Congress from 44th Calif. dist., 1998—; mem. energy and commerce com. Bd. dirs. Palm Springs Internat. Film Festival. Active D.A.R.E. Program, Olive Crest Home Abused Children, Tiempos de Los Ninos, Named Woman of the Yr., San Gorgonio (Calif.) chpt. Girl Scouts U.S., 1993. Republican. Avocations: outdoor activities, computer technology. Office: US House of Reps 404 Cannon Ho Office Bldg Washington DC 20515-0545*

BONOMETTI, ROBERT JOHN, technology management and strategy executive; b. N.Y.C., Sept. 29, 1953; s. Joseph Patrick and Fortunata Mary (Barba) B.; m. Virginia Anne Scyphers, Oct. 26, 1997; stepchildren: Jessica, Michael. BS summa cum laude, U.S. Mil. Acad., 1975; MS in Physics, MIT, 1981, PhD in Physics, 1985; MBA, L.I. U., 1987. Registered profl. engr., Va. Assoc. prof. physics U.S. Mil. Acad., West Point, N.Y., 1985-88; program mgr. Def. Advanced Rsch. Projects Agy., Arlington, Va., 1988-93; sr. policy analyst White House Sci. and Tech. Office, Washington, 1993-95; exec. dir. technology strategy Bell Atlantic Corp., Arlington, 1995-98; pres. MGB Enterprises, LLC, Winchester, Va., 1998—; prof. info. sys. and computer tech. Shenandoah U., Byrd Sch. Bus., 1999—. Industry adv. bd. Ctr. for Satellite and Hybrid Comm. Networks, U. Md., 1994-2000; chmn. rev. com. commercialization of space NASA, Washington, 1996; exec. dir. info. and comm. R&D com. Nat. Sci. and Tech. Coun., Washington, 1993-95; adj. prof. various univs., 1981—; chmn. Tek-Xam content exec. com. Va. Found. for Ind. Colls., 2000-01 Contbr. articles to profl. jours. Chmn. Tek-Xam content exec com. Va. Found. for Ind. Colls., 2000-01; active animal rights and environ. orgns. Lt. col. U.S. Army, 1975-95. Recipient Laurel award Aviation Week and Space Tech., 1990; Sci. and Tech. fellow Dept. Commerce, 1993-94; Hertz Found. fellow, 1981-85. Mem. IEEE (sr.), AIAA (sr.), Am. Phys. Soc., Am. Astron. Soc. Avocations: music, weightlifting, tennis, running. Home and Office: Majestik Global Bus Enterprises LLC 260 Golds Hill Rd Winchester VA 22603-3129 E-mail: athenswv@aol.com.

BONOMI, FERNE GATER, public relations executive; b. Council Bluffs, Iowa, July 27, 1923; d. Roy Winfield and Leona Hazel (Bays) Gater; m. Robert Foch Bonomi, Sept. 3, 1949 (div. 1974); children: Robert Duff, David Scott; m. Wayne P. Davis, Apr. 20, 1991. BA magna cum laude, U. Iowa, 1948. Editor Silver City (Iowa) Times, 1940-41; reporter, photographer, Sunday editor Cedar Rapids (Iowa) Gazette, 1943-47; dir. pub. info. Iowa Devel. Commn., Des Moines, 1950-51; pub. info. officer Gov. William S. Beardsley, Des Moines, 1951-53; v.p. Bonomi Assocs. Inc., Des Moines, 1954-72; adminstr. Mid-Iowa Drug Abuse Coun., Des Moines, 1972-74; cons. Plain Talk Pub. Co., Des Moines, 1974-75; communications dir. Iowa Assn. Sch. Bds., Des Moines, 1975-86; owner, operator Bonomi & Co., Des Moines, 1986—. Chmn. pubs. evaluation Am. C. of C. Execs., Washington, 1977-81; mem. Universal Accreditation Bd., 2003—; presenter in field. Author: Show Me A Man, 1969; editor Iowa Sch. Bd. Dialogue, 1975-86; assoc. editor Leader's Mag., 1964-72. Active Gov.'s Com. on Employment Handicapped, 1968—74; chmn. comms. Des Moines Area Religious Coun., 1980—82. Named Iowa Sch. Communicator of Yr., Iowa Sch. Pub. Rels. Assn., 1997. Fellow Pub. Rels. Soc. Am. (developer mentoring program 1994-97, chmn. 1995, pres. Iowa chpt. 1980-82, chmn. accreditation 1982-2001, writer nat. curriculum for accreditation 1998, rev. 2003, Outstanding Contbr. award 1983, commendation for meaningful rsch. Bronze Anvil competition 1997); mem. Nat. Sch. Pub. Rels. Assn. (cert., Gold medallion 1987), Phi Beta Kappa, Alpha Delta Pi (nat. editor 1959-62, Outstanding Alumna award 1977). Mem. United Ch. Christ. Avocations: canoeing, horseback riding, church choir, dancing, theater. Office: Bonomi & Co 1003 Kennedy St Ames IA 50010-4247

BONOMI, JOHN GURNEE, retired lawyer; b. N.Y.C., Aug. 13, 1923; s. Felix A. and Bessie (Gurnee) B.; m. Patricia Updegraff, Aug. 22, 1953; children: Kathryn, John. BA, Columbia U., 1947; JD, Cornell U., 1950; LL.M., N.Y.U., 1957. Bar: N.Y. 1952, U.S. Supreme Ct. 1966, U.S. Dist. Ct. (so. dist.) N.Y. 1975, U.S. Ct. Appeals (2d cir.) 1978. Asst. dist. atty., N.Y. County, 1953-60; spl. counsel subcom. antitrust and monopoly, for hearings on organized crime and monopoly in profl. boxing, Kefauver Com. U.S. Senate, 1960-61; spl. asst. atty. gen. investigating 1961 N.Y.C. mayor race N.Y. State, 1961-62; chief counsel com. grievances Assn. Bar City N.Y., 1963-76; vis. scholar Harvard U. Law Sch., 1976-77; counsel firm Anderson, Russell, Kill & Olick, N.Y.C., 1977-80; practice law N.Y.C., 1980-96; mem. com. grievances and admissions U.S. Ct. Appeals (2d cir.), from 1983. Lectr. Fordham U. Law Sch., 1973; mem. N.Y. state judicial conf. com. on disciplinary enforcement, 1971-72. Columnist: N.Y. Law Jour. 1978-83; contbr. articles to legal jours. Trustee Village of Tarrytown, N.Y., 1965-67, 68-72; councilman, dep. supr. Town of Greenburgh, 1974; spl. counsel to Village of Irvington, N.Y., 1972. With USAAF, 1943-45, ETO. Mem. ABA (spl. com. on evaluation disciplinary enforcement Clark Com. 1967-70, cons. spl. com. on evaluation ethical stds. 1967-69), N.Y. State Bar Assn. (vice-chmn. com. grievances 1970-71, com. profl. discipline 1988-93), Am. Law Inst. (spl. com. peer rev. 1978-80), New York County Lawyers Assn. (com. profl. discipline 1993—), Assn. of Bar of City of N.Y. (cons. spl. com. on free press and fair trial, Medina com. 1966-67, com. profl. discipline 1983-88), Inst. Jud. Adminstrn., Nat. Orgn. Bar Counsel (pres. 1970-71, chmn. spl. com. on Watergate discipline 1974-76). Clubs: Harvard (N.Y.C.). Democrat. Home: Irvington, NY. Died Nov. 6, 1999.

BONOMO, JOSEPH RALPH, naval officer; b. N.Y.C., Mar. 20, 1951; s. Ralph J. and Anita R. (Curiale) B.; m. Janet M. Storace, Apr. 6, 1991. BBA, Iona Coll., 1973; MPA, SUNY, Albany, 1975; student, USN Officer Candicate Sch., Newport, R.I., 1976, Navy Supply Corps Sch., Athens, Ga., 1976, USN Submarine Sch., Groton, Conn., 1977; MS, Naval Postgrad. Sch., 1985. Data adminstr. Welfare Research Inc., Albany, N.Y., 1975-76; advanced through grades to comdr. USN; supply officer USS Henry Clay (Blue Crew) USS Henry Clay (SSBN-625), Charleston, S.C., 1977-79; supply officer Fighter Squadron 101, Oceana, Va., 1979-81; aviation support officer USS Constellation, San Diego, 1981-83; info. systems officer Comdr. Naval Air Force, U.S. Atlantic Fleet, Norfolk, Va., 1985-88, USS Saratoga, 1988-90; with COMNAVSUPSYSCOM, Washington, 1990-93; supply/comptroller officer U.S. Naval Air Facility-ATSUGI JA, 1993-96; staff NAVSUBSUPPFAC, New London, Conn., 1996-97; ret. USN, 1997; mgmt. analyst Town of Wilton, Conn., 1999—. Vol. WHRO Pub. TV, Norfolk, 1987-88; mem. Smithsonian Resident Assocs., Washington, 1984—; mem. Planetary Soc., Pasadena, Calif., 1983—, Nat. Geog. Soc., Washington, 1986—. Mem.: NRA, Govt. Fin. Officers Assn., Am. Soc. Pub. Adminstrs., Ret. Officers Assn., Nat. Air and Space Soc., U.S. Naval Inst. (life), SUNY Albany Alumni Assn., Iona Coll. Alumni Assn., Supply Corps Sch. Alumni Assn., Am. Legion, Delta Lambda Kappa. Roman Catholic. Avocations: shooting sports, sailing, painting, photography, microcomputers. E-mail: bonstor@optonline.net.

BONOMO, TIMOTHY PAUL, education educator, consultant; b. Corning, NY, July 6, 1960; s. Robert Paul Bonomo and Rebecca Ann Cart; m. Doreen Kelly, Aug. 28, 1988; children: Nicholas Robert, Kelly JoAnne. AAS, Corning C.C., 1978—80; BS, NY State U. Coll. at Brockport, 1982—84; EdM majors in adult and gen. edn., Elmira Coll., 2002—03. Dist. mgr. Cinema North Corp., Painted Post, NY, 1985—93; pres. Concepts in Comm., Corning, NY, 1987—; co-host tv show WYDC-TV, Corning, NY, 1993—94; corp. spl. assignment Wegmans Food Markets, Corning, NY, 1995—2002; instr. Corning C.C., NY, 2003—. Author: (book) Customer Service: Aiming for Excellence, (movie content rating system) AAI: The Appropriate Age Index. Mem. Rotary Internat., Corning, NY, 1980—82. Recipient Robert J. Uplinger Disting. Svc. award, Lions Internat. Found., 1993. Home: 12023 Birch Dr Corning NY 14830 Personal E-mail: tympbo@aol.com.

BONOSARO, CAROL ALESSANDRA, professional association executive, former government official; b. New Brunswick, N.J., Feb. 16, 1940; d. Rudolph William and Elizabeth Ann (Betsko) B.; m. Donald D. Kummerfeld, Sept. 8, 1962 (div. Jan. 1970); m. Athanasios Chalkiopoulos, Nov. 21, 1976 (div. Dec. 1991); 1 child, Melissa. BA, Cornell U., 1961; postgrad., George Washington U., 1961-62. Analytical statistician Office Mgmt. and Budget, Exec. Office of Pres., Washington, 1961-66; asst. dir. fed. programs div. U.S. Commn. on Civil Rights, Washington, 1966-68, dir. Office Fed. Programs, 1968-69, dir. tech. assistance div., 1969-71, spl. asst. to staff dir., 1972, dir. women's rights program, 1972-79, asst. staff dir. for program planning and evaluation, 1979-80, asst. staff dir. congressional and public affairs, 1980-86; pres. Sr. Execs. Assn., Washington, 1986—. Mem. adv. com. Asian Am. Govt. Execs. Network, 1996—; mem. Nat. Partnership Coun., 1997-2001. Vice chmn. Nat. Com. on Asian Wives of U.S. Servicemen, 1975-85; pres. Catholics for a Free Choice, 1980-83; chmn. bd. dirs. William Jump Found., 2003—. Mem. Exec. Women in Govt., Sr. Exec. Assn. (dir. 1981-86, chmn. bd. dirs. 1983-86) Democrat. Home: 5504 Jordan Rd Bethesda MD 20816-1366 Office: Sr Execs Assn PO Box 44808 Washington DC 20026-4808

BONOVITZ, SHELDON M. lawyer; BS, U. Pa.; JD, Harvard U. Bar: Pa. Ptnr. Duane Morris LLP, Phila., 1969—, chmn. tax dept., 1972-93, mem. ptnrs. bd., 1976—, vice chmn., 1994-97, chmn., 1998—. Atty.-advisor to Honorable Arnold Raum, U.S. Tax Ct.; bd. dirs. Comcast Corp., eRsch. Tech., Inc.; lectr. in law U. Pa. Law Sch., 1979-86, 93, 95, Temple U. Sch. Law, 1967-78; spkr. in field. Contbr. articles to profl. jours. Bd. trustees Curtis Inst. Music, Phila. Mus. Art. Fellow Am. Coll. Tax Counsel; mem. ABA (chair com. on corp. tax 1987-88), Pa. Bar Assn. (tax law sect.), Phila. Bar Assn. (chair tax sect. 1987-88), Am. Law Inst. (tax adv. group). Office: Duane Morris LLP One Liberty Pl Philadelphia PA 19103-7396

BONOW, ROBERT OGDEN, medical educator; b. Camden, N.J., Mar. 11, 1947; m. Patricia Jeanne Hitchens, Sept. 12, 1982; children: Robert Hitchens, Samuel Crawford. BS in Chem. Engring. magna cum laude, Lehigh U., Bethelehem, Pa., 1969; MD, U. Pa., Phila., 1973. Diplomate Am. Bd. Internal Medicine, subspecialty bd. on cardiovascular disease. Intern in medicine Hosp. U. Pa., Phila., 1973-74, resident, 1974-76; clin. assoc. cardiology br. Nat. Heart, Lung and Blood Inst., Bethesda, Md., 1976-79, sr. investigator, attending physician cardiology br., 1979-92, chief nuclear cardiology sect., 1980-92, dep. chief, 1989-92; Goldberg prof. medicine Northwestern U. Med. Sch., Chgo., 1992—; chief divsn. cardiology Northwestern Meml. Hosp., Chgo., 1992—; attending physician dept. medicine VA Lakeside Med. Ctr., Chgo., 1993—, Evanston (Ill.) Hosp., 1994—. Pfizer vis. prof. cardiovasc. medicine Yale U., 1992, U. Mass., 1998; AHA/ACC Task Force on Practice Guidelines Com. on Cardiac Radionuclide Imaging, 1993-95; chair com. on mgmt. of patents with valvular heart disease, 1996—; vis. prof. various univs., 1982-99; mem. bd. extramural adivsors NHLBI, NIH, 2000—; mem. clin. rsch. roundtable Inst. of Medicine, Nat. Acad. Sci.; working group on methods/technologies Nat. Heart Attack Alert Program, 1994—; invited presenter at sci. sessions, symposia and acad. med. ctrs. Mem. editl. bd. Am. Jour. Cardiology, 1983—, Jour. Am. Coll. Cardiology, 1983-87, 91-95, Circulation, 1986—, Cardiovascular Imaging,

1988—, Am. Jour. Cardiac Imaging, 1990-95, Internat. Jour. Cardiac Imaging, 1990-95, Jour. Heart Valve Disease, 1982-95, Jour. Nuclear Cardiology, 1993—, Jour. Nuclear Medicine, 1994-2000, Cardiologia, 1995—, Am. Heart Jour., 1998—; contbr. over 300 publs. in med. jours. and textbooks. Recipient NIH Director's award, 1986, USPHS Commendation medal, 1990, USPHS outstanding svc. medal, 1991. Fellow ACP, Am. Coll. Cardiology (exhibits com. 1986-92, 1999-2000, program com. 1991-92, chair extramural edn. com., 1998—, bd. trustees 1999—, Disting. fellow 2000), Am. Heart Assn. (chmn. sci. session program com. 1998-2000, bd. dirs. 1999—, chmn. Coun. on Clin. Cardiology, 1999-2001, pres. 2002-03, Nat. Leadership award 2003); mem. AAAS, Am. Bd. Internal Medicine (subsplty. bd. cardiovasc. disease 1996-2001), Am. Soc. Clin. Investigation, Assn. Am. Physicians, Am. Heart Assn. Met. Chgo. (bd. govs. 1992-98, rsch. coun. 1992-98, pres. 2001-02), Am. Soc. Nuclear Cardiology (bd. dirs. 1994-98, chmn. edn. com. 1994-2000, nominating com. 1994-96), Assn. Profs. Cardiology (nominating com. 1993—, councillor 1994—, sec., treas. 1996-99, v.p. 1999-2000, pres. 2000-01), Chgo. Cardiology Group (pres. 1994-96), Soc. Nuclear Medicine (chmn. Cardiovascular Coun. 1990-91, publs. com. 1994-2000), Am. Fedn. Clin. Rsch., Assn. Am. Physicians, Assn. Univ. Cardiologists, Ctrl. Soc. Clin. Rsch., Alpha Omega Alpha. Office: Northwestern U Med Sch Cardiology Divsn 201 E Huron St Ste 10-240 Chicago IL 60611-2958

BONSELL, THOMAS ALLEN, journalist, publisher; b. Lusk, Wyo., Mar. 17, 1935; s. Dee V. and Neoma Vada (Bevens) B. BBA, Woodbury U., 1963; postgrad., Georgetown U., 1964-65. Journalist, reporter The Portland (Oreg.) Reporter, 1963-64; intelligence analyst Nat. Security Agy., Ft. Meade, Md., 1964-65; journalist, editor The Utica (N.Y.) Daily Press, 1965-67, The Denver Post, 1967-80; journalist, writer Port Orchard, Wash., 1980—. Founder, editor Country Cottage Pub., Port Orchard, 1995—. Author: The Un-Americans, 1995. With USAF, 1956-60. Mem. Phi Gamma Kappa. Avocations: art (drawing, painting), gardening. Home and Office: Country Cottage Pub 285 SE Rim Rd Port Orchard WA 98367-7708

BONSER, QUENTIN, retired surgeon; b. Sedro Wooley, Wash., Nov. 1, 1920; s. George Wayne and Kathleen Imogene (Lynch) B.; m. Loellen Rocca, Oct. 20, 1945; children: Wayne, Gordon, Carol, Patricia Bonser Sanford. BA in Zoology, UCLA, 1943; MD, U. Calif., San Francisco, 11947. Diplomate Am. Bd. Surgery. Intern U. Calif. Hosp., San Francisco, 1947-49, resident in gen. surgery, 1949-56; pvt. practice, Placerville, Calif., from 1956; now ret. Surgeon King Faisal Splty. Hosp., Saudi Arabia, Sept.-Oct., 1984; vis. prof. surgery U. Calif., San Francisco, 1968. Vol. physician, tchr. surgery, Vietnam, 1971, 72, 73. Capt. M.C., USAF, 1950-51. Fellow ACS; mem. H.C. Naffziger Surg. Soc. (pres. 1974-75). Home: 2590 Northridge Dr Placerville CA 95667-3416 Fax: 530-622-5748. E-mail: qbonser@ns.net.

BONSKY, JACK ALAN, lawyer; b. Canton, Ohio, Mar. 12, 1938; s. Jack H. and Pearl E. Bonsky; m. Carol Ann Portmann, Sept. 2, 1960; children: Jack Raymond, Cynthia Lynn. AB, Ohio U., 1960; JD, Ohio State U., 1964. Bar: Ohio 1964, U.S. Dist. Ct. (so. dist.) Ohio 1969. With Metcalf, Thomas & Bonsky, Marietta, Ohio, 1964-69, Addison, Fisher & Bonsky, Marietta, 1969-70; asst. counsel GenCorp., Inc. (formerly Gen. Tire & Rubber Co.), Akron, Ohio, 1970-75, assoc. gen. counsel, 1975-86, asst. sec., 1977-86, v.p., sec., 1986; v.p., sec., gen. counsel DiversiTech Gen., Inc., 1986-87; v.p., gen. counsel GenCorp Polymer Products, 1988-94; asst. gen. counsel, dir. environ. affairs GenCorp, Inc., 1994-96; pvt. practice, 1996—. Solicitor City of Marietta, 1966-67; legal advisor City of Marietta Bd. of Edn., 1966-67; police prosecutor, Belpre, Ohio, 1969-70; comml. law instr. Am. Inst. Banking, 1969; dir. Frontier Holdings, Inc., Denver, Frontier Airlines, Denver, 1985 (merged with People Express Airlines, 1985). Mem. Marietta Income Tax Bd. of Rev., 1966-67; mem. Traffic Commn., 1966-69, chmn., 1967; mem. Marietta Civil Svc. Commn., 1969; trustee Urban League, Akron, 1978-81, pres., 1980-81; trustee Akron Comty. Svc. Ctr., 1978-81, United Way of Summit County, 1982-89; mem. Bath (Ohio) Twp. Merger Commn., 1995-96; v.p. Bath Twp. Homeowners' Assn., 1999; pres. Bath Twp. Homeowners Assn., 2000-2003; bd. dirs. Washington County Soc. for Crippled Children, 1964-70, S.E. Ohio unit Arthritis Found., 1967-70, chmn., 1968-70; mem. Washington County (Ohio) Health Planning Com., 1968-70; ho. of dels. Ohio Easter Seal Soc., 1968-70; mem. econ. devel. revenue com. Bath Twp., 1999-2000. Recipient Akron Comty. Svc. Ctr. and Urban League Leadership award, 1981. Mem. Ohio Bar Assn. Home and Office: 4234 Idlebrook Dr Akron OH 44333-1726

BONTA, MARCIA MYERS, freelance nature writer, researcher, columnist; b. Camden, N.J., July 11, 1940; d. Harold Chester and Leona (Deibert) Myers; m. Bruce Drace Bonta, Aug. 25, 1962; children: Steven Christopher, David Jeffrey, Mark Andrew. BA, Bucknell U., 1962. Tchr. history Danville (Pa.) H.S., 1962-63; editor Pitt Series on Nature and Natural History, U. Pitts. Press, 1991-98; columnist Pa. Wildlife, Pa. Wildlife Fedn., Harrisburg, 1983-2000; columnist Pa. Game News, Pa. Game Commn., Harrisburg, 1993—. Author: Escape to the Mountain, 1980, Outbound Journeys in Pennsylvania, 1988 (award Pa. Outdoor Writers Assn. 1988), Appalachian Spring, 1991 (award Outdoor Writers Assn. Am. 1991), Women in the Field, 1991, Appalachian Autumn, 1994, More Outbound Journeys in Pennsylvania, 1996, Appalachian Summer, 1999; editor: American Women Afield, 1995; contbr. over 300 articles to state and nat. mags. and jours. Mem. Pa. Outdoor Writers Assn., Pa. Soc. Ornithology, Juniata Valley Audubon Soc. (v.p. 1982-84, pres. 1984-88, bd. dirs. 1988-98). Avocations: walking, reading, travel to natural places, cooking, listening to 20th century classical music and italian opera. Home and Office: PO Box 68 Tyrone PA 16686 E-mail: marciabonta@hotmail.com.

BONTE, FREDERICK JAMES, radiology educator, physician; b. Bethlehem, Pa., Jan. 18, 1922; s. Frederick R. and Harriett (Stoudt) B.; m. Cecile Poetzel; children: Frederick W., Stephen J., John A., Therese A., Suzanne M., Ann E. BS, Western Res. U., 1942, MD, 1945. Diplomate: Am. Bd. Radiology (trustee 1969-75), Am. Bd. Nuclear Medicine. Intern Huntington Meml. Hosp., Pasadena, Cal., 1945-46; resident Univ. Hosp., Cleve., 1948-52; practice medicine, specializing in radiology and nuclear medicine Dallas, 1956—; mem. faculty Western Res. U. Sch. Medicine, 1952-56, asst. prof., 1952-56, chief radiotherapy and nuclear medicine, 1954-56; prof. U. Tex. Southwestern Med. Sch., Dallas, 1956—, chmn. dept. radiology, 1956-73, dean, 1973-80; dir. Nuclear Medicine Research Center, 1980—, Effie and Wofford Cain disting. chair in diagnostic imaging; Dr. Jack Krohmer prof. in radiation physics. Mem. bd. Nat. Council Radiation Protection and Measurements, 1966-71; radiology tng. com. Nat. Insts. Gen. Med. Scis., USPHS, 1966-70, residency rev. com. radiology AMA, 1966-69, adv. and rev. coms. VA, 1972— ; Founding trustee Am. Bd. Nuclear Medicine, 1971-73, chmn., 1977-80; internat. cons. on med. edn. Contbr. articles to profl. jours. Capt. USAAF, 1946-48. Fellow Am. Coll. Radiology, Am. Coll. Nuclear Physicians (Pres.'s award 1997); mem. AMA (del., chmn. grad. med. edn. com., Roentgen Centennial Hartman medal 1995), Soc. Nuclear Medicine (De Hevesy Nuclear Pioneer award 1995), Am. Roentgen Ray Soc. (exec. com.), Radiol. Soc. N.Am., Sigma Xi, Alpha Omega Alpha. Achievements include research on experimental nuclear medicine and radiology. Home: 11138 Wonderland Trl Dallas TX 75229-3943 Office: 5323 Harry Hines Blvd Dallas TX 75390-9061

BONTOYAN, WARREN ROBERTS, chemist, state laboratories administrator; b. Balt., Aug. 2, 1932; s. Cesario Baron and Dorothy Bertha (Hunter) B.; m. Gladys Frances Daughaday, May 3, 1958; children: Warren Wendel, Suzanne Cheri. BS, U. Md., 1956. Food and drug insp. FDA, Balt., 1956-58; rsch. chemist USDA, Beltsville, Md., 1958-60; head chemist methods devel., tng., standards and quality control lab. EPA, Beltsville, 1960-78, chief chem. and biol. investigation br., 1978-89, also dir. labs., 1978-89; the md. state chemist, chief state chemistry sect. Md. Dept. Agriculture, Annapolis, 1990—. Mem. vector and biol. control expert panel WHO.; U.S. rep. to Collaborative Internat. Pesticide Adv. Coun.; mem. expert panel pesticide chemistry FAO; cons. World Bank, 1987, Chesapeake Rsch. Consortium Inc.; chmn., organizer, participant numerous scientific symposiums. Editor: EPA Manual of Chem. Analysis of Pesticides and Devices, 1975; Contbr. articles to profl. jours. Fellow Assn. Ofcl. Analytical Chemists (pres. 1983, gen. referee pesticide formulation analysis, bd. dirs. 1978-84), Am. Inst. Chemists; mem. Am. Chem. Soc., Assn. Am. Control Ofcls., Alpha Chi Sigma. Office: 50 Harry S Truman Pkwy Annapolis MD 21401-8960

BONURA, JACQUELINE, special education educator; b. Middle Island, N.Y., Sept. 6, 1975; d. Anthony James Bonura and Joann Lentini. A, Suffolk C.C., 1995; B in Mgmt., Dowling Coll., 2000, M in Spl. Edn., 2003. Sales asst. David Lerner Assoc., Syosset, NY, 1995—97; client assoc. Merrill Lynch, Smithtown, NY, 1997—2000; writer, editor Long Island Entertainment, Oceanside, NY, 2000—01; tchr. asst. Develop. Disabilities Inst., Huntington, NY, 2001—. Freelance editor, Oakdale, NY, 2000. Author: (poem) Lost Souls, 1993 (Dickinson award, 1993), (book of poetry) The Soul of My Youth, 1998. Mem. Amenesty Internat., Dix Hills, NY, 1991—92, Natural Helpers, Dix Hills, NY, 1992—93. Avocations: writing, sketching, running, bicycling, painting.

BONURA, LARRY SAMUEL, writer; b. Galveston, Tex., Jan. 4, 1950; s. Leo Bonura and Beatrice Sadie (Maiorka) Immel; m. Marilyn Esther Ward, Feb. 17, 1990; 1 child, Sean Joseph Sullins. BS in Journalism, U. Kans., 1977; MA in Am. History, Emporia (Kans.) State U., 1982. Asst. libr. U. Kans. Librs., Lawrence, 1975-77; instr. Butler County Community Coll., El Dorado, Kans., 1982-83; dir. bikelibrary, Emporia, 1977—84; mng. editor Agora Assocs., Balt., 1983-84; dir. Word Workers, Richardson, Tex., 1984—; mgr. editorial svcs. Convex Computer Corp., Richardson, 1987-94; sr. instr. No. Telecom Meridian Info. Products, Richardson, 1994-95; sr. tech. writer DSET Corp., 1999—2001; tech. writer Multigen-Paradigm Inc., 2001—. Instr. Richland C.C., Dallas, 1988-91; leader seminar Solutions Inc., Boston, 1991-93; participant 2d World Congress on Sports Documentation, Vienna, Austria, 1982. Author: Fruit of a Fleeting Joy, 1975, Desktop Publisher's Dictionary, 1989, Desktop Publisher's Thesaurus, 1990, Indexing Technical Documents, 1991, The Art of Indexing, 1994, Engulfed from Within, 2002. Mem. Pearce High PTA, 2000-03; coach Richardson Sports Inc., 1990-95. Mem. Am. Soc. Indexers (pres. D.C. chpt. 1985), Soc. for Tech. Comm. (sr. mem.), Dallas Hist. Soc., Dallas Geneal. Soc., Italian Club of Dallas, Nat. Trust for Hist. Preservation, N.Am. Soc. Sports History, Soc. for Am. Baseball Rsch., So. History Assn., USS Forestal Assn., Learning Disabilities Assn. Richardson, U. Kans. Alumni Assn., Pi Gamma Mu, ESU Alumni Assn. Avocations: walking, history, music, reading, computers. Home: 806 Clearwater Dr Richardson TX 75080-5032 Office: PO Box 831038 Richardson TX 75083-1038 E-mail: lbonura@hotmail.com.

BONUTTI, BORIS PAUL, medical company executive; b. Cleve., Feb. 21, 1959; s. Karl B. and Hermina J. (Rijavec) B. Student, U. Chgo., 1976-80, Gilmour Acad., 1973-76. Project mgr. ACME Consolidated, Inc., Chgo., 1981-85, v.p., gen. mgr. Atlanta divsn., 1985-89; v.p. ops., CFO Bonutti Orthop. Clin., Effingham, 1989—; v.p., COO Biomax Rehab., Inc., Effingham, Ill., 1991—, Bonutti Rsch., Inc., Effingham, 1989—, 1989—. V.p., CFO Joint Active Sys., Inc., 1995—, Multi Tak Suture Sys., Inc., 1996—; pres. Village Wine Shop, Inc. Avocations: yacht racing, flying. Office: Bonutti Orthopedic Clinic Inc 1303 W Evergreen Ave Effingham IL 62401-1619

BONVILLIAN, WILLIAM BOONE, lawyer; b. Honolulu, Mar. 7, 1947; s. William Doughty and Florence Elizabeth (Boone) B.; m. Janis Ann Sposato, Apr. 12, 1980; children: Raphael William Boone, Marcus Doughty. AB, Columbia U., 1969; MA in Religion, Yale U., 1972; JD, Columbia U., 1974. Bar: Conn. 1975, D.C. 1976, U.S. Supreme Ct. 1983. Law clk. to Hon. Jack B. Weinstein U.S. Dist. Ct. (ea. dist.) N.Y., 1974-75; assoc. Steptoe & Johnson, Washington, 1975-77; dep. asst. sec., dir. congl. affairs, liaison officer U.S. Dept. Transp., Washington, 1977-81; ptnr. Brown, Roady, Bonvillian & Gold, Washington, 1981-85, Jenner & Block, Washington, 1985-89; chief counsel, legis. dir. to Sen. Joseph Lieberman U.S. Senate, Washington, 1989—. Bd. editors Columbia Law Rev. 1973-74; contbr. articles to law and sci. jours. Recipient 2 outstanding Performance awards U.S. Sec. Transp., Washington, 1979, 80. Mem. Conn. Bar Assn., D.C. Bar Assn. Democrat. Episcopalian. Home: 930 Hickory Run Ln Great Falls VA 22066-1903 Office: Office Sen Lieberman 706 Hart Senate Office Bldg Washington DC 20510-0001

BONZAGNI, VINCENT FRANCIS, lawyer, program administrator, analyst, researcher; b. Boston, Dec. 10, 1952; s. Augustine Joseph and Augusta M. (Giarla) B.; m. Marie T. Rainville, Aug. 27, 1972 (div. Sept. 1982); 1 child, Gina Theresa; m. Donna J. Bachtell, May 14, 1988; stepchildren: Allison, Neil. BS in Math., Lowell (Mass.) Tech. Inst., 1974; JD, George Mason U., 1998. Bar: Va. 1998, U.S. Supreme Ct., 2002; notary pub. Claims adminstr. Social Security Adminstrn., 1976-79, quality assurance specialist, 1979-83, disability analyst Arlington, Va., 1983-88; program adminstr. Corp. for Open Systems, McLean, Va., 1988-91; sr. hearings and appeals analyst Social Security Adminstrn., Falls Church, Va., 1991—2003; pvt. practice, 1998—. Self-employed researcher and crossword puzzle cons., 1982-2003. Author: The Mensa Book of Lists, 1992, The Mensa Book of Lists II, 1997; co-author: A History of Mensa, 1990. Treas. Maplewood Village Condo. Assn., 1989-93, 1998-2001. Mem. ABA, NRA, Mensa (local treas. 1986-90, local pres. 1990-91, 2000-2002, nat. historian 1989-2003, nat. SIGs officer 1989-91, internat. archivist 1992—), Nat. Puzzlers League, Phi Alpha Delta. Avocations: crossword puzzles, contests, games, trivia, genealogy. Home: 147 Mountain Top Rd Front Royal VA 22630-6013 Office: Bonzagi Law Firm PO Box 2281 Front Royal VA 22630 E-mail: bonzagni@shentel.net.

BOO, KATHERINE, newswriter; AB (summa cum laude), Columbia U., 1988. Writer, editor Wash. City Paper, 1988—92, Wash. Monthly, 1988—92; staff writer Wash. Post, 1992—; writer New Yorker. Recipient Pulitzer prize, 2000; fellow MacArthur Found. fellow, 2002. Office: Washington Post 1150 15th St NW Washington DC 20071*

BOOBYER, DON J. computer operator, bookkeeper; b. Phoenix, Dec. 1, 1953; s. Gordon Boobyer and Lois Eileen (Martz) Evans. AA, Pasadena City Coll., 1973. Computer operator Aircloom Bedding, El Monte, Calif., 1973-79, Miller Dial Corp., El Monte, 1981—; bookkeeper Franklin Computer Systems, South Pasadena, 1980. E-mail: dboobyer@concentric.net.

BOOCHEVER, ROBERT, judge; b. N.Y.C., Oct. 2, 1917; s. Louis C and Miriam (Cohen) Boochever; m. Lois Colleen Maddox, Apr. 22, 1943 (dec.); children: Barbara K, Linda Lou, Ann Paula, Miriam Deon; m. Rose Marie Borden, Aug. 31, 2001. AB, Cornell U., 1939, JD, 1941; HD (hon.), U. Alaska, 1981. Bar: N.Y. 1944, Alaska 1947. Law clk. Nordlinger, Riegel & Cooper, 1941; asst. U.S. atty. Juneau, 1946—47; partner firm Faulkner, Banfield, Boochever & Doogan, Juneau, 1947—72; assoc. justice Alaska Supreme Ct., 1972—75, 1978—80, chief justice, 1975—78; judge U.S. Ct. Appeals (9th cir.), Pasadena, Calif., 1980—86; sr. judge U.S. Ct. Appeals, Pasadena, Calif., 1986—. Mem. 9th cir. rules com. U.S. Ct. Appeals, 1983—85, chmn. 9th cir. libr. com., 1995—2001; chmn. Ala. Jud. Coun., 1975—78; mem. appellate judges seminar NYU Sch. Law, 1975; mem. Conf. Chief Justices, 1975—79, vice chmn., 1978—79; mem. adv. bd. Nat. Bank of Ala., 1968—72; guest spkr. Southwestern Law Sch. Disting. Lecture Series, 1992. Contbr. articles to profl. jours. Chmn. Juneau chpt. ARC, 1949—51, Juneau Planning Commn., 1956—61; mem. Alaska Devel. Bd., 1949—52, Alaska Jud. Qualification Commn., 1972—75; mem. adv. bd. Juneau-Douglas C.C. Capt. U.S. Army, 1941—45. Named Juneau Man of Yr., Rotary, 1974, The Boochever & Bird Chair for Study and Tchg. of Freedom and Equality, U. Calif. Sch. Law, Davis, 2000; recipient Disting. Alumnus award, Cornell U., 1989. Fellow: Am. Coll. Trial Attys.; mem.: ABA, Am. Law Inst., Am. Judicature Soc. (dir. 1970—74), Juneau Bar Assn. (pres. 1971—72), Alaska Bar Assn. (pres. 1961—62), Alaskans United (chmn. 1972), Juneau C. of C. (pres. 1952, 1955), Altadena Town and Country Club, Cornell Club L.A. Office: US Ct Appeals PO Box 91510 125 S Grand Ave Pasadena CA 91105-1652 E-mail: boochever@ca9.uscourts.gov.

BOOCOCK, STEPHEN WILLIAM, lawyer; b. Wilkinsburg, Pa., Sept. 25, 1948; s. William Samuel and Zelda Elizabeth (Heginbotham) B.; m. Carol Ann Bennett, July 11, 1970; children: Eric Alan, Allison Anne, Megan Leigh. BS in Acctg., Pa. State U., 1970; JD, U. Pitts., 1973. Bar: Pa. 1974, U.S. Dist. Ct. (we. dist.) Pa. 1973. Supervising tax specialist Coopers & Lybrand (now part of PricewaterhouseCoopers), Pitts., 1973-76; tax counsel Incom Internat., Inc., Pitts., 1977-81; asst. treas., dir. tax Allegheny Ludlum Corp., Pitts., 1981—94, asst. v.p. taxes, 1994-96; asst. v.p. taxes, chief tax officer Allegheny Technologies, Inc., Pitts., 1996—2002; dir. tax controversy svcs. Deloitte & Touche LLP, Chgo., 2003—. Treas. Meadow Wood Homeowner's Assn., 1990-2001. Served to capt. U.S. Army, 1970-79; with USAR. Mem.: ABA, AICPA, Tax Execs. Inst. (treas. Pitts. chpt. 1985—86, sec. 1986—87, sr. v.p. 1987—88, pres. 1988—89, nat. inst. dir. 1989—91, v.p. region VI, 50th ann. task force 1993—95, membership com. 1993—97, mem. IRS adminstrv. affairs com. 1993—2003, nominating com. 1994—95, vice chmn. 1995—97, mem. alternative tax sys. com. 1995—97, tax info. sys. com. 1995—97, nominating com. 1997—98, chmn. 1997—99, nat. inst. dir. 1999—2001, mem. nat. exec. com. 1999—2003, nat. treas. 2001—02, nat. sec. 2002—03), Pa. Inst. CPAs, Allegheny County Bar Assn., Pa. Bar Assn. Republican. Avocation: golf. Home: 1350 N Lake Shore Dr # 1904 Chicago IL 60610-5149 Office: Deloitte & Touche LLP Tax Svcs 200 E Randolph St Chicago IL 60601-7002

BOODELL, THOMAS JOSEPH, JR., lawyer; b. Chgo., Sept. 29, 1935; s. Thomas J. and Mary Elizabeth (Houze) Boodell; m. Beata Bergman, Aug. 4, 1962; children: Beata, Mary, Peter, David. BA, Princeton U., 1957; JD, Harvard U., 1964. Bar: Ill. 1964. Assoc. Boodell, Sears et al, Chgo., 1964—68; fellow Adlai Stevenson Inst. Internat. Affairs, Chgo., 1968—71; ptnr. Boodell, Sears, Giambalvo & Crowley, Chgo., 1971—84, Kck, Mahin & Cate, Chgo., 1984—; pub., contr. articles New York City Mag., 1967—71. Lt. j.g. USN, 1957—60. Recipient Disting. Svc. award, Chi Psi, 1984, Dist. Svc. award, Princeton Club Chgo., 1979; fellow Am. Bar Found. Mem.: Ill. State Bar Assn., Chgo. Bar Assn., ABA, Law in Am. Soc. Found. (mem., Chgo. 1972), Chi Psi Ednl. Trust (trustee 1978—84), Wendy Will Case Cancer Fund (bd. dir. 1983), Chgo. Children's Choir (pres. bd. dir. 1979), Univ. Club, Legal Club Chgo., Law Club City Chgo. Democrat. Home: 1229 E 56th St Chicago IL 60637-1616 Office: Keck Mahin & Cate 77 W Wacker Dr Ste 4900 Chicago IL 60601-1604

BOODEY, CECIL WEBSTER, JR., political science educator; b. Yonkers, N.Y., June 10, 1931; s. Cecil Webster and Dorothy (Mitchell) B.; m. Phyllis Ann Stensland, July 9, 1955; children: William Mitchell, John Barton, Pamela D. Ellen. BA, U. N.H., 1953; postgrad., Princeton U., 1953-54; MA, NYU, 1960. Tng. program Arabian-Am. Oil Co., Dhahran, Saudi Arabia, 1954; with N.Y. Telephone Co., Westchester, 1957-62; instr. polit. sci. Fashion Inst. Tech., N.Y.C., 1964-68, from asst. prof. to prof., 1968-95, adj. prof., 1996—. Chmn. dept. social sci. Fashion Inst. Tech., N.Y.C., 1971—73; vis. prof. fgn. langs. Inner Mongolia U., Huhhot, China, 1989—90, 1996—97, 2001; lectr., China, 2000—03. Treas. Richards Boys Club, Yonkers, 1962-63; v.p. Manasquan-Brielle Little League, N.J., 1969; sec. Manasquan Babe Ruth League, 1972-96; Democratic municipal chmn., Manasquan, 1970-78; pres. 11th Ward Democratic Club, Yonkers, 1962; bd. dirs. Manasquan Area Human Rels. Coun., 1973-98, Brookdale C.C., Lincroft, N.J., 1979-88; pres. Squan Soccer Club, 1980. With U.S. Army, 1954-56. Fellow Ford Found., 1953-54; Penfield scholar NYU, 1960. Mem. Am. Polit. Sci. Assn., Assn. Asian Studies, Internat. Studies Assn., Asia Soc., China Inst. in Am., Am. Profs. for Peace in the Middle East (nat. vice chmn. 1989-90), Phi Beta Kappa, Phi Kappa Phi, Pi Mu Epsilon, Pi Gamma Mu. Methodist. Home: 80 Allen Ave Manasquan NJ 08736-3426 Office: Fashion Inst Tech 7th Ave At 27th St New York NY 10001 E-mail: pcboodey@bytheshore.com. *To assist young adults to develop their qualities for critical thinking and to encourage them to participate in extra-curricular activities— these are the goals of my life.*

BOODRAM, MOHAN DAVID, academic administrator; b. N.Y.C., N.Y., Oct. 18, 1964; s. Mohanlal Davendrenath Boodram and Sylvia Edith Blackett, Claudius Augustus Blackett (Stepfather); life ptnr. Robert Francis Morris. BS, Yale U., 1986; MA, Harvard U., 1988. Dir. admissions and fin. aid Harvard Med. Sch., Boston, 2000—. Treas. Neighborhood Action, Inc., Boston, 1998—2002; ch. vestry St. John the Evangelist Episcopal Ch., Boston, 1999—2002. Recipient AT&T Coop. Rsch. fellowship, AT&T Bell Labs., 1985—88, Nat. Achievement scholarship, Nat. Merit Scholarships, 1982. Mem.: Assn. of Am. Med. Colls. Group on Student Affairs, Nat. Assn. of Student Fin. Aid Adminstrs. Office: Harvard Med Sch 25 Shattuck St Boston MA 02115 Personal E-mail: mboodram@aya.yale.edu. E-mail: mboodram@hms.harvard.edu.

BOOHER, ALICE ANN, lawyer; b. Indpls., Oct. 6, 1941; d. Norman Rogers and Olga (Bonke) B. BA in Polit. Sci., Butler U., 1963; LLB, Ind. U., 1966, JD, 1967. Bar: Ind. 1966, U.S. Dist. Ct. (so. dist.) Ind. 1966, U.S. Tax Ct. 1970, U.S. Ct. Customs and Patent Appeals 1969, U.S. Ct. Mil. Appeals 1969, U.S. Ct. Appeals (D.C. cir.) 1969, U.S. Supreme Ct. 1969; cert. tchr., Ind. Rsch. asst., law clk. Supreme and Appellate Cts. Ind., Indpls., 1966; legal intern, atty., staff legal advisor Dept. State, Washington, 1966-69; staff legal adviser Bd. Vets. Appeals, Washington, 1969-78, sr. atty., 1978—, counsel, 1991—. Former counselor D.C. Penal Facilities and Shelters. Author: The Nuclear Test Ban Treaty and the Third Party Non-Nuclear States, also children's books; contbr. articles to various publs., chpts. to Whiteman Digest of International Law; exhibited crafts, needlepoint in juried artisan fairs; originator U.S. postage stamps Women in Mil. Svc., 1980-97, POWs/MIAs, 1986-96. Bd. dirs. community groups including D.C. Women's Commn. for Crime Prevention, 1980-81, Friends of Nat. Vets Mus.; pres., legal adviser VA employees Assn. Recipient various awards; named Ky. Col., 1988. Mem. DAV (life), VFW Aux. (life), D.C. Sexual Assault Coalition (chmn. legal com.), Life Mem. Judge Advocates Assn., Butler U. Alumni Assn., Nat. Mus. Women in Arts, Kennedy Ctr. Stars, Sackler/Freer Galleries (patron), Women in Mil. Svcs. to Am. Found., Bus. and Profl. Women (pres. D.C. 1980-81, nat. UN fellow 1974, nat. bd. dirs. 1980-82, 87-94, Woman of Yr. award D.C. 1975, Marguerite Rawalt award D.C. 1986), USO, Navy League U.S.A. (life), Am. Legion Aux. (life), Women Officers Profl. Assns., Nat. Vets. Mus. Task Force, Nat. Task Force on Women of the Mil. and Women Mil. POWS (chair Esther Peterson Tribute 1995, panel, paper moderator conf. 1997, book reviewer, contbr. to Stars & Stripes, Ex POWs Bull., others), Assn. Former Intelligence Officers (assoc.), Army Women Officers Profl. Assn., Am. News Womens Club, Cons., Saigon Tourist, Inc., Alliance Nat. Defense.

BOOK, EDWARD R. consultant, retired association executive; b. Cleve., May 9, 1931; s. Raymond John and Grace Elizabeth Book; m. Inga M. Scheyer, Feb. 14, 1953; children: Sandra Book Liddick, Edward R. Jr., Frederick A. BS in Hotel Adminstrn, Pa. State U., 1954. Mgr. restaurant Howard D. Johnson Co., Harrisburg, 1950-54; mgr. food and beverage, asst. mgr. Hotel Harrisburger, Harrisburg, 1956-60; v.p., gen. mgr. Hotel Bethlehem, Pa., 1960-68; gen. mgr. Hospitality Motor Inn, Cleve., 1968-69, Hotel Hershey, Pa., 1969; mng. dir. Hotel Hershey and Country Club, 1970; dir. hostelry div. HERCO, Inc. (formerly Hershey Estates), 1971, v.p., 1973-74, exec. v.p., asst. to pres., 1974, chmn. bd., pres., CEO, 1974-80, chmn., CEO, 1980-87; vice chmn. bd. dirs. Hershey Trust Co., 1985-87; exec. v.p. Travel Industry Assn. Am., Washington, 1987-89, pres., 1989-94, ret. Interim pres. USA Nat. Tourism Orgn., 1996-97; mem. travel and tourism industry adv. com. U.S. Senate Commerce Com., 1989-94; mem. adv. com. travel and tourism caucus U.S. Ho. of Reps., 1989-94; charter mem. adv. bd. HRIM program U. Del., 1990-2000; mem. nat. adv. bd. Acad. Travel and Tourism, 1994-97. Chmn. adv. com. Milton S. Hershey Med. Ctr., 1977—82; campaign chmn. Tri-County United Way, 1980, pres., 1982—83; mem. Ams. for Competitive Enterprise Sys., 1977—82; mem. devel. coun. Pa. State U., 1982—89; mem. Ctrl. Pa. SCORE; mem. bd. mgrs. Milton Hershey Sch., 1974—87, Milton S. Hershey Found., 1974—87, chmn., 1981—87; trustee Pa. State U., 1977—85, vice chmn. bd., 1982—85; trustee Harrisburg Area YMCA, 1978—87; mem. exec. bd. Keystone Area coun. Boy Scouts Am., 1975—87, Capital Area coun. Boy Scouts Am., 1988—89; bd. dirs. Hwy. Users Fedn., 1993—95, Palmer Art Mus. Friends. With U.S. Army, 1954—56. Named Pa. Travel Man of Year, 1976, Disting. Alumnus, Pa. State U., 1986; recipient order of achievement Lambda Chi Alpha, 1976; elected to Travel Industry Hall of Leaders, 1986. Mem. VFW (life mem. post 8896), Pa. Travel Industry Adv. Coun. (chmn. 1972-76), Pa. State Hotel and Restaurant Soc. (pres. 1964), Harrisburg Area C. of C. (pres. 1975-76), Am. Hotel and Motel Assn. (industry adv. coun., long range planning com., trustee ednl. inst., resort com. 1975-87), Nat. Inst. for Food Svc. Industry (trustee 1979-82), Travel Industry Assn. Am. (bd. dirs. 1976—, chmn. 1981-82), Pa. State U. Alumni Assn. (life, pres. 1977-79), Pa. Soc. (life), Am. Legion, Lambda Chi Alpha (bd. dirs. 1998-2002). Presbyterian (elder). Home: 305 Village Hts Dr Apt 221 State College PA 16801-7685

BOOK, JOHN KENNETH (KENNY BOOK), retail store owner; b. Hillsboro, Ill., June 26, 1950; s. Vern Ray Book and Pearl Iva (Foster) Book Alford Carroll (dec. Sept., 2001); m. Betty L. Christy, Dec. 23, 1981; children: Elizabeth Marie Dunn Rose, Leslie Michelle Dunn. Assoc. in Acctg., Ky. Bus. Coll., 1974. Laborer Lexington (Ky.) Army Depot, 1968-70; machine operator A.O. Smith, Mt. Sterling, Ky., 1971-72; laborer Irvin Industries, Lexington, Ky., 1973-75; owner Kenny's Signs & Bus. Svcs., Winchester, Ky., 1977-90, Book's

Bookkeeping & Tax Svc., Winchester, Ky., 1990—; rsch. bd. advisors ABI, 1990—. Rsch. bd. advisors ABI. Active Winchester Sch. Bd., 1976, 78; candidate for commr. City of Winchester, 1977, 79, 81, 83, 87, elected commr., 1989, re-elected, 1993, 96, 98, 2000, 02, candidate of mayor, 1985; bd. dirs. Blue Grass Rails to Trails. Named to Hon. Order Ky. Cols., 1973; Road scholar Ky. Dept. Transp., 2002, Road Master, 2003. Mem. Ky. Sheriff's Assn. (hon.). Democrat. Office: Book's Bookkeeping & Tax Svc PO Box 840 Winchester KY 40392-0840

BOOK, KEVIN, information technology executive, consultant; b. Washington, May 16, 1972; s. David Lincoln and Gail Stephanie (Ross) Book. BA in Econs. and English, Tufts U., 1993, MA in Law and Diplomacy, 2003. Sr. dir. tech. The Motley Fool, Inc., Alexandria, Va., 1998—2001; pres. Enigmatics, Inc., College Park, Md., 2001—. Lead guitarist/composer: Waiting For Jane, Waiting for Jane II; musician: Songs of Joy. Recipient Premier 100 IT Leader award, Computerworld Mag., 2001. Republican. Episcopalian. Avocations: squash, music, dogs, cooking, travel. E-mail: kevinbook@enigmatics.com.

BOOKBINDER, HYMAN H(ARRY), public affairs counselor; b. Bklyn., Mar. 9, 1916; s. Louis and Rose (Palger) B.; m. Bertha Losev, Dec. 25, 1938 (dec. 1976); children: Ellen, Amy. BSS., CCNY, 1937; postgrad., NYU, New Sch. Social Research; LHD (hon.), Hebrew Union Coll., 1989. Economist Amalgamated Clothing Workers, 1938-43, 46-50; labor adv. Nat. Prodn. Authority, 1951-53; legis. rep. CIO, 1953-55, AFL-CIO, 1955-60; spl. asst. to sec. commerce, 1961-62; mem. President's Commn. on Status of Women, 1961-63; dir. Eleanor Roosevelt Meml. Found., 1963-64; exec. officer President's Task Force on Poverty, 1964; asst. dir. OEO, also spl. asst. to vice president U.S. Hubert Humphrey, 1964-67; Washington rep. Am. Jewish Com., 1967-86, rep. emeritus, 1986—; mem. President's Commn. on Holocaust, 1979-80, U.S. Holocaust Meml. Council, 1980-87. Mem. Com. on Conscience, 1996—; Washington chmn. Ad Hoc Coalition for Ratification of Genocide Treaty, 1970-87; chmn. public policy adv. com. Corp. Public Broadcasting, 1972-77; spl. advisor to Gov. Michael Dukakis, 1988; chmn. bd. advisers Nat. Jewish Dem. Coun., 1990—. Author: To Promote the General Welfare, 1950, Off the Wall, 1991; co-author: Through Different Eyes, 1987, also articles; editor: Washington Letter, 1970— ; moderator: Washington Scene radio series, 1971-75. Bd. dirs. Ctr. for Nt. Policy, Friends of VISTA, Am. Jewish-Israeli Rels. Inst., Am. Jewish World Svcs., Multi-Issue Polit. Action Com., Found. for Mid. East Comm., Internat. Inst. for Study of Prejudice, Project Nishma (Let Us Listen), Washington Inst. for Jewish Leadership and Values, Mid. East Human Rights Watch, Jewish Fund for Justice, Israel Policy Forum, Operation Understanding. Recipient Nat. Brotherhood citation NCCJ, 1977, Lifetime Achievement award Thomas Jefferson H.S. Alumni Assn., 1982, Honored Am. award Americans by Choice, 1986, Franklin Roosevelt Four Freedoms medal Franklin and Eleanor Roosevelt Inst., 1990, Jewish Nat. Fund Sholom Peace award, 1992, Hubert Humphrey Humanitarian award Nat. Jewish Dem. Coun., 1994, Am. Jewish Com. Nat. Leadership award 1997. Mem. Am. Vets. Com., People for Am. Way, Common Cause, Friends of Histadrut, Americans for Dem. Action, Washington Hebrew Congregation Brotherhood Club. Clubs: B'Nai B'rith, Workmen's Circle. Democrat. Home: 6308 Bannockburn Dr Bethesda MD 20817-5404 Office: Am Jewish Com 1156 15th St NW Washington DC 20005-1704 *Born into a world that soon exposed me to depression, war, and the Holocaust, I fast acquired an almost compulsive interest in public affairs. It has been my good fortune to be able to combine career development with opportunities to help shape public policy. Government's principal purpose must indeed be to implement the great promise of America— the securing of life, liberty, and the pursuit of happiness. Above all, this has meant for me the lifting of discriminatory barriers to self-fulfillment— race, religion, gender, national origin. The Hebrew sage Rabbi Hillel, has provided the guideline for my life's work: "If I am not for myself, who will be for me? But if I am only for myself, what am I?"*

BOOKBINDER, ROBERT MAX, superintendent of schools; b. Newark, Apr. 28, 1923; s. Harry and Pearl (Barenberg) B.; m. Natalie Sonya Gelfand, Sept. 10, 1946 (dec. Feb. 1996); children: Howard, Susan Blauel, Pamela Spears. BA, U. Ky., 1947; MA, Columbia U., 1948, profl. diploma, 1952; EdD, East Coast U., 1971. Owner, dir. summer day camp Camp Gelfand, Mountaindale, NY, 1947—66; tchr. BOCES 3d Dist., Huntington, N.Y., 1948-50, Harborfields C. Sch. Dist., Greenlawn, N.Y., 1950-54, elem. prin., 1954-61, jr. h.s. prin., 1961-64, curriculum and adminstrv. coord., 1964-67, asst. supt., 1967-73; supt. East Stroudsburg (Pa.) Sch. Dist., 1973-87; prof. East Stroudsburg U., 1987-90; supr. student tchrs. Lynn U., Boca Raton, Fla., 1996-99. Ednl. cons. Careers/Cons. in Edn., Pompano Beach, Fla., 1977—; arbitrator Am. Arbitration Assn., N.Y.C., 1987—. Author: (textbook) Critical Issues in Education, 1972, The Principal, 1992; (books) Amusing Definitions, 1999, Witty Remarks, 1999, Noteworthy Proverbs, 1999, Concise Quotations, 1999, The Keys to the Classroom, 1999, Funny School Excuses, 1999, An Educator's Scrapbook, 2000, Toasts for All Occasions, 2000, Best of Satire and Wit, 2002, Golf's Best Jokes and Quips, 2002, The Colonel's Combat Team 343 in WWII; (weekly article) Pocono Today, 1975-84. Pres. Monroe Arts Coun., 1980-81, United Way of Monroe County, 1983-84. 1st lt. U.S. Army, 1943-46, 51-52, ETO. Decorated Bronze Star; recipient Combat Infantryman's badge. Mem. ASCD, Am. Assn. Sch. Adminstrs., 86th Blackhawk Divsn. Assn. (pres. 2000—), B'nai B'rith (pres. 1996-2000), Phi Delta Kappa, Zeta Beta Tau. Democrat. Jewish. Avocations: golf, theater, public speaking, writing, swimming. Home and Office: Careers/Cons in Edn 3050 N Palm Aire Dr Apt 310 Pompano Beach FL 33069-3424

BOOKER, BETTY MAE, poet; b. Allentown, Pa., Nov. 26, 1948; d. Harold George and Bessie (Bealer-Miller) Bartholomew; m. Samuel Efford Booker III, June 27, 1970 (dec. May 1998); children: Liesel Tamarah, Dacey Justin, Jaeson Bartholomew. BA in English, Millersville (Pa.) State Coll., 1970. Contbr. poetry to jours. and lit. mags., including Plainsong, America, Christian Century, Poetry Now. Home: 27826 Island Dr Salisbury MD 21801-2350 E-mail: sebefford@aol.com.

BOOKER, BRUCE ROBERT, rabbi; b. St. Paul, Dec. 14, 1951; s. Robert Max Booker and Elaine Mae Hinzie; m. Barbara Jean Toelaer, Oct. 28, 1971 (div. Aug. 1982); children: Justin Eric, Rebecca Lynn; m. Patricia Gardner, Nov. 26, 1983; 1 child, David Ray. B in Bibl. Studies, Bibl. Life Coll. & Sem., 1981; MA in Bus. Edn., Columbia Pacific U., 1985, PhD, 1988; postgrad., Union Messianic Jewish Congregations Yeshiva, 1990-93. Ordained rabbi 1989. Tech. instr. Mitel Corp., Irvine, Calif., 1980-85; chief engring. Johnston Telcom., Walnut, Calif., 1985-87; messianic rabbi Beth Shalom Messianic Congregation, Colton, Calif., 1989-91, Etz Chaim Messianic Fellowship, 1991—94, Beth Shalom Messianic Fellowship, Sandpoint, Idaho, 2000—03; mktg. analyst Norstar Telcom., Wilkes-Barre, Pa., 1991-94; pres. Sar Shalom Ministries, Inc., Scranton, Pa., 1991-94, Booker Ednl. Svcs. Corp., Memphis, 1997-98; dir. tng. and tech. support Genesis Comm., Memphis, 1994-97; dir. tng. Hartford Comm., 1998—2002; messianic rabbi Beth Yeshua Messianic Fellowship, Priest River, Idaho, 2003—. Exec. dir. N.E. Pa. Christian Task Force Against Anti-Semitism, Scranton, 1993—94. Author: Mitel ARS Made Easy, 1988, Mitel Generic 1000 Automatic Route Selection Made Easy, 1989, To the Jew First, 1989, Towards a Jewish Evangelism, 1991, The Lie - The Satanic Origins of Anti-Semitism, 1993, A Call to Holiness, 1994, A Merciful Severity - A History of the Christian Persecution Against the Jew, 1995. Staff sgt. USMC, 1972—80. Mem.: SAR, DAV (life), NRA (life), Vietnam Vets. Am., Messianic Bur. Internat., Internat. High IQ Soc. (life), Jews for Preservation of Firearms Ownership, Mensa, Am. Legion. Republican. Avocations: computer studies, biblical studies. Home and Office: PO Box 1946 Priest River ID 83856-1946 E-mail: brucebooker@msn.com.

BOOKER, HENRY MARSHALL, economics educator; b. Newport News, Va., Jan. 12, 1935; s. William Henry and Mary Evelyn (Wheeler) B.; m. Sarah Porter Cheatwood Phillips, June 22, 1963; children: Mary DeMott Booker Campbell, Sharon Sinclair McCracken, Paige Meriwether Shoun, Marshall Phillips. BA in Bus. and Fin., Lynchburg Coll., 1959; PhD in Econs., U. Va., 1965. Instr. econs. Salem Coll., Winston-Salem, N.C., 1962-64; asst. prof. econs. Frederick Coll., Portsmouth, Va., 1964-65; assoc. prof., dir. grad. studies Old Dominion, Norfolk, Va., 1965-69; prof. econs. Christopher Newport U., Newport News, 1969—2003; dean Christopher Newport Coll., Newport News, 1969-74, emeritus prof. econs., 2003—, chmn. econs., 1974-79, dir. bur. bus./econ. rsch., dir. univ. grad. studies, 1980—; prof. George Washington U., Washington area, 1969-89. Fulbright scholar Azerbaijan State Econ. U., Baku, 2003—; cons. Bank of Lancaster, Va., 1988-89, also various law firms, 1970—. Author: The Role of the Chesapeake Bay in the American Revolution, 1981; contbr. articles to profl. publs. Mem. Parks and Recreation Commn., Poquoson, Va., 1984-88; mem. Commn. on AIDS in Schs., Poquoson, 1987-88; mem. Chem. People-Drug program, Poquoson, 1988; mem. adv. bd. Jr. League of Hampton Roads, Va., 1987 ; chmn. commn. to reorganize Poquoson Sch. System, 1987-89. Recipient Nat. award for Excellence in Teaching Free Enterprise, Joint Coun. Econ., 1985, Gibson Hobbs Alumni award Lynchburg Coll., 1991. Mem. Va. Assn. Economists (pres. 1986), Atlantic Econs. Soc., N.C. Assn. Gifted and Talented, Lions (pres. 1987), Sigma Pi (alumni advisor), Omicron Delta Epsilon, Phi Theta Kappa. Republican. Episcopalian. Avocations: sailing, woodworking, reading, music. Home: 5 Insley Cir Poquoson VA 23662-1260 Office: Christopher Newport U 1 University Pl Newport News VA 23606-2998

BOOKER, JAMES DOUGLAS, retired lawyer, government official; b. Columbus, Ohio, June 27, 1933; s. Homer Newton and Grace Bernice (Hermann) Booker; m. Onda Lee Minshall, Aug. 31, 1958; children: Christine E. Booker Garrett, Linda K. Booker Stanek, Molly A. Booker Lary, Andrew W. JD, Ohio State U., 1961. Bar: Ohio 1961, U.S. Dist. Ct. (so. dist.) Ohio 1962, U.S. Ct. Appeals (6th cir.) 1972, U.S. Supreme Ct. 1971. Asst. atty. gen. State of Ohio, Columbus, 1961-62; ptnr. Williams, Deeg, Ketcham, Booker & Obetz, Columbus, 1962-75; adminstrv. law judge SSA, Columbus, 1975-98. Former PTA officer, ch. deacon and Sunday Sch. tchr. Served with U.S. Army, 1953-55. Mem. Ohio State Bar Assn. Republican. Avocations: chess, music, history. Home: 1290 Smallwood Dr Columbus OH 43235-2503 E-mail: jamesdbooker@prodigy.net.

BOOKER, LARRY FRANK, accountant; b. Mobile, Ala., May 22, 1950; s. Frank and Helen Louise Booker; m. Prudence E. Porter, Sept. 1, 1972; children: Jennifer Erin, Meggan Leah. BA, U. South Ala., 1972; student, U. N.C., 1976-77. Lic. pub. acct., Ala. Rsch. economist Rsch. Triangle Inst., Durham, N.C., 1974-76; with Providence Hosp., Mobile, 1978-80; pvt. practice acctg. Mobile, 1981-2000; sr. acct. Mobile Area Water and Sewer System, Ala., 2000—. Enrolled IRS; lectr. in field. Author: Sales and Use Taxes in Alabama, 1999; co-author: State and Local Taxation in Alabama, 2000. Vol. Jr. Achievement. Mem. Nat. Assn. Accts., Nat. Assn. Tax Practitioners, Nat. Soc. Pub. Accts., Ala. Assn. Pub. Accts. (past dist. pres., bd. dirs.), Accreditation Coun. in Acctg. and Taxation (accredited in taxation and accountancy). Home: 6436 Brindlewood Ct Mobile AL 36608-3837 Office: 1409 Government St Mobile AL 36604

BOOKER, LEWIS THOMAS, lawyer; b. Richmond, Va., Sept. 22, 1929; s. Russell Eubank and Leslie Quarles (Sessoms) B.; m. Nancy Electa Brogden, Sept. 29, 1956; children: Lewis Thomas Jr., Virginia Frances, Claiborne Brogden, John Quarles. BA, U. Richmond, 1950, LLD, 1977; JD, Harvard U., 1953. Bar: Va. 1953, U.S. Ct. Mil. Appeals 1954, U.S. Supreme Ct. 1958, D.C. 1980, N.Y. 1985. Assoc. Hunton & Williams, Richmond, Va., 1956-63, ptnr., 1963-95, sr. coun., 1995—; substitute Judge 13th Dist., Va., 1996—. Lectr. in law Seinan Gakuin U., Fukuoka, Japan, 1985; vis. lectr. in law St. Thomas U., Miami, Fla., 1993; maj. gen., sr. mil. aide to Gov. of Va., 1997-2001. Mem. Va. Coun. on Human Rights, 1987; commr. chmn. Richmond Redevel. and Housing Authority, 1961-70; mem., v. chmn. Richmond Sch. Bd., 1971-80; trustee U. Richmond, 1972-2002, emeritus, 2002—, rector, 1973-77, 81-85, 91-94, vice rector, 1985-87, chmn. exec. commn., 1977-81; trustee Va. Inst. Sci. Rsch., 1981-94, Richmond Symphony, 1987-92, Rouse-Bottom Found., 1989—; mem. Coun. Richmond Symphony, 1995, Westminster-Canterbury Found. Richmond, 1995-2001, chmn., 1998-2001; mem. Robins Found., 1996—, Richmond Symphony Orch. Found., 1999—, Christian Children's Fund, 2000—, Christian Children's Fund Internat., 2002-, CCF Internat., 2002—, Richmond Eye and Ear Hosp., 2000—, Homeward, 2001—; chmn. Richmond Eye and Ear Fedn., 2001—. Fellow Am. Coll. Trial Lawyers, Am. Bar Found.; mem. ABA, Va. Bar Assn., Va. Law Found. (chmn. fellows coun. 1996-2001), Richmond Bar Assn., Westwood Racquet Club. Democrat. Baptist. Office: Hunton & Williams East Tower Riverfront Pla PO Box 1535 Richmond VA 23218-1535 E-mail: lbooker@hunton.com.

BOOKER, NANA LAUREL, art gallery owner, consul; b. Waco, Tex., Aug. 5, 1946; d. Karl and Helen Dorothy (Keene) B. BA, Baylor U., 1968; MA, U. Fla., 1970; MBA, Pepperdine U., 1980. Asst. prof. comm. U. New Orleans, 1970-74, 1977-78; pub. rels. cons. New Orleans, 1974-78; dir. pub. rels. Touro Infirmary, New Orleans, 1976 78; dir. comm. Lifemark Corp., Houston, 1978-81; pres. Comm. Alliance, Houston, 1981-82; dir. internat. rels., comm. Mayor's Office, City of Houston, 1982-84; pres. Nana Booker & Assocs. (now Booker/Hancock & Assocs.), Houston, 1984—; owner Booker-Lowe Gallery of Australian Aboriginal Art, 2002—. Hon. consul of Australia, State Tex., 1999—. Co-author: Introduction to Theatrical Arts, 1972. Mem. South Tex. Dist. Export Coun., Houston, 1988-92; press aide campaign K. Whitmire for Mayor, Houston, 1982; mem. exec. adv. bd. coll. bus. adminstrn. U. Houston, 1990—; bd. dirs. Escape Ctr., 1990-93, YWCA, Houston, 1991-92. Recipient Internat. Assn. Bus. Communicators awards, Women in Comms. awards, Crystal award Am. Mktg. Assn., Outstanding Pub. Rels. Practitioner award Tex. Pub. Rels. Assn., 1996, Vol. of the Yr. award Houston Area Women's Ctr., 1998. Mem. Pub. Rels. Soc. Am. (accredited, chairperson internat. sect. 1993-95, Excalibur award 1988, Cert. of Appreciation 1993, 94, 95; mem. U.S. coun. 1994-96), Internat. Pub. Rels. Assn., Houston World Trade Assn. (bd. dirs. 1986—), Houston-Shenzhen Sister City Assn. (bd. dirs. 1987-94), Swiss-Am. C. of C. (bd. dirs. 1987-90), River Oaks Breakfast Club (bd. dirs. 1997), The Asia Soc. of Tex. (bd. dirs. 1995—). Avocations: hot air ballooning, photography, design, collecting art. Fax: 713-863-8364. E-mail: bookerlowegallery@houston.rr.com.

BOOKHAMMER, EUGENE DONALD, state government official; b. Lewes, Del., June 14, 1918; s. William and Winifred (Jenkins) B.; m. Catherine Williams, Jan. 31, 1942; children: Joy, Jean. Student, Am. Tech. Soc., 1938. Owner-pres. Bookhammer Lumber Mill, Lewes, 1939—71, Joy Beach Devel. Co., Lewes, 1955—76, Rehoboth Bay Dredging Co., Lewes, 1963—75; mem. Del. Senate, 1962—68; lt. gov. Del., 1969 76; mem. Del. Health Planning Council, 1976—84. Mem. Del. Coastal Zone Appeals Bd.; bd. dirs. Mellon Bank, Del. Life mem. Boy Scouts Am.; del. Rep. Nat. Conv., 1952, 56, 60, 80; chmn. Sussex County Rep. Com., 1964-66; Rep. nat. committeeman from Del., 1977—; chmn. bd. dirs. Beebe Hosp., 1976—; trustee Wilmington Med. Ctr., 1971—, Wesley Coll., 1982—, trustee emeritus; bd. trustees, Beebe Med. Found., 1992—. Served with AUS, 1944-46, ETO. Decorated Purple Heart. Mem. Am. Inst. Banking, Am. Legion, Del. C. of C., VFW, DAV, 40 and 8, Masons (32 deg.), Shriners (potentate nurtemple 1972), Lions, Rehoboth Beach Country Club. Home: 2073 John J Williams Hwy Lewes DE 19958

BOOKHARDT, FRED BARRINGER, JR., architect; b. New Orleans, May 14, 1934; s. Fred B. and Leticia (Chevez) B. BArch, Tulane U., 1959; postgrad., U. Pa., 1960-61. Designer Freret and Wolf, Architects, 1959-60, Kenneth Ripnen, Architect, 1961-63, Francis X. Gina, Architects, 1963-64, Smith, Smith, Haines, Lundberg and Waehler, N.Y.C., 1965; ptnr., v.p. William F. Pedersen & Assocs., N.Y.C. and New Haven, 1965-77; prin. Fred B. Bookhardt, Architect, N.Y.C., 1977—. Dir. 28 E. 4th St. Housing Corp.; cons. Engring. Cons. Group, Cairo, Heliopolis and Alexandria, Egypt, 1983—; dir. The Network of Bus. & Profl. Orgns. Contbg. editor Uptown mag., New Orleans; archtl. works include: Superior Cts. Bldg., New Haven, 1974, Hall Minerals and Gems of Am. Mus. Natural History, 1976, Fed. Office Bldg., New Haven, 1978, Restaurant Claire, Key West, Fla., 1978, Woodmere Kingdom of Minerals, 1980, exec. offices So. Container Corp., Hauppauge, N.Y., 1981, Mus. Shop Am. Mus. Natural History, N.Y.C., 1982, renovation of pub. spaces lower level, 1984, employees cafeteria, 1984, Children's Reception Ctr., 1986, Sadowsky residence, Northport, N.Y., 1987, Kaufman residence, N.Y.C., 1987, Grossman residence, Montauk, N.Y., 1983, St. Barts, W.I., 1990, Zweibel residences, N.Y.C., 1983, Ft. Lauderdale, Fla., 1984, exec. offices Bon Temps Employment Agy., N.Y.C., 1984, Dieckmann residence, Manhasset, N.Y., 1985, master plan Am. Mus. Natural History, N.Y.C., 1989, space analysis The Trotting Horse Mus., Goshen, N.Y., 1989, addition and renovation, 1990, De Roy residence, N.Y.C., 1991, Zweibel residence, Boca Raton, Fla., 1993, Kelley residence, St. James, N.Y., 1983, HIV Law Project, 1994, Hinlein residence, 1995, Price/Uribe Residence, East Northport, N.Y., 1996, Branford (Conn.) H.S. with David M. Chin, 1996-97, Mancini Residence, N.Y.C., with Charles Burke, 1998, Fitz Simons Residence, 1999, Cary Grossman Residence, 1999, Bookhardt-Gaskell Residence, New Orleans, 2000. With U.S. Army, 1954-56. Recipient Lumen award Illuminating Engrs. Soc., 1977, 1st pl. award Home Mag. ceramic tile competition. Mem. AIA, N.Y. State Assn. Architects, Architects Coun. N.Y.C., N.Y. Soc. Architects, Am. Assn. Mus., N.E. Mus. Conf., Nat. Cert. Archtl. Rev. Bd. (cert.) Home and Office: 819 Marigny St New Orleans LA 70117-8525

BOOKMILLER, ROBERT JAMES, political science educator; b. Danville, Pa., Apr. 6, 1963; s. Robert Curry and Betty (Schott) B.; m. Kirsten Nakjavani, May 27, 1989. BA, Ind. U. of Pa., 1985; MA, U. Va., 1989, PhD, 1992. Vis. asst. prof. Salisbury (Md.) State U., 1993-94, U. Va., Charlottesville, 1992, Lebanon Valley Coll., Annville, Pa., 1995-96; adj. asst. prof. Franklin and Marshall Coll., Lancaster, Pa., 1994—2002; asst. prof. Millersville (Pa.) U., 1997—. Contbr. articles to profl. jours. including Jour. South Asian and Mid. Eastern Studies, Current History, Mid. East Policy. Rsch. fellow Govt. Can., 1999; rsch. visitorship U. Ottawa, 1999; Younger scholar grantee NEH, 1984. Mem. LWV, Assn. for Can. Studies in U.S., Pa. Can. Studies Consortium (exec. bd. dirs. 1999—, assoc. dir. 2002—), Soc. for Historians Am. Fgn. Rels. Democrat. Avocations: photography, collecting stamps, collecting political memorabilia. Office: Millersville U Dept Govt Juniata House Millersville PA 17551 E-mail: robert.bookmiller@millersville.edu.

BOOKOUT, JOHN FRANK, JR., oil company executive; b. Shreveport, La., Dec. 31, 1922; s. John Frank and Lena (Hagen) B.; m. Mary Carolyn Cook, Dec. 21, 1946; children: Beverly Carolyn, Mary Adair and John Frank III (twins). Student, Iowa Wesleyan Coll., 1943, Centenary Coll., 1946-47, LLD (hon.), 1987; BSc, U. Tex., 1949, MA, 1950; DSc (hon.), Tulane U., 1978. Geologist Shell Oil Co., Tulsa, 1950-59, div. exploration mgr., 1959-61, area exploration mgr. Denver, 1961-63, The Hague, Netherlands, 1963-64, mgr. exploration and prodn. econs. dept. N.Y.C., 1965, v.p. Denver exploration and prodn. area, 1966, v.p. Southeastern exploration and prodn. region New Orleans, 1967-70; pres., chief exec. officer, dir. Shell Can. Ltd., Toronto, Ont., 1970-74; exec. v.p., dir. Shell Oil Co., Houston, 1974-76, pres., chief exec. officer, dir., 1976-88; dir., mem. exec. com. Shell Petroleum Inc., 1988—; dir. Royal Dutch Petroleum Co., 1988-93. Bd. dirs. Investment Co. Am., McDermott Internat., Inc.; past chmn. adv. bd. Inst. Bioscis. and Tech.; chmn. Tex. A&M U. Active chancellor's coun., mem. devel. bd. U. Tex.; chmn. bd. dirs. Meth. Hosp., Houston; mem. regional adv. bd. Inst. Internat. Edn.; co-chmn. media com. Econ. Summit, Houston, 1990. With USAAF, 1942-46. Decorated Air medal with 3 oak leaf clusters; comdr. Order of Orange-Nassau (The Netherlands), 1988; recipient Disting. Service award Nat. Assn. Secondary Sch. Prins., John Rogers award Southwestern Legal Fedn., 1986; named Outstanding Chief Exec. Domestic Integrated Oil Co. Wall St. Transcript, 1982-84, Disting. Alumnus U. Tex., 1981; named to Offshore Energy Ctr. Industry Pioneer Hall of Fame, 2001. Mem. Am. Assn. Petroleum Geologists (Excellence in Exploration Leadership award 1990), Nat. Petroleum Coun. (former chmn.), Houston C. of C., The Conf. Bd. (bd. dirs.), Am. Petroleum Inst. (bd. dirs., past chmn. bd., mgmt. com.), 25 Yr. Club Petroleum Industry (bd. govs. SW dist.), Internat. C. of C. (U.S. Coun., trustee), Coun. on Fgn. Rels. Inc., All-Am. Wildcatters Assn., Bus. Roundtable (mem. policy com.), Am. Coun. on Edn. (bus.-higher edn. forum mem.), The 1001 World Wildlife Fund (life). Home: PO Box 2463 Houston TX 77252-2463 Office: JKJ LLC One Shell Plz 910 Louisiana Ste 5050 Houston TX 77002

BOOKS, ROBERTA PAULA, real estate finance executive; b. Boston, Apr. 4, 1943; d. Leonard and Mary (Karsh) Books; m. Jay S. Negin, May 20, 1973; children: Martha Alice Books Negin, Samuel Benjamin Books Negin. AB in Math., Bryn Mawr Coll., 1964, AM in Physics, 1969; MBA, Harvard U., 1971; postgrad., NYU, 1966. Acct. mktg. rep. IBM, N.Y.C., 1966-69; v.p. Morgan Stanley, N.Y.C., 1971-81; spl. asst. to comptroller Office of the Comptroller of the Currency, Washington, 1977-79; mng. dir. Prudential Ins. Co. Am., Newark, 1982-86; v.p., co-head real estate capital markets Salomon Bros., N.Y.C., 1986-90; v.p. Citicorp Real Estate, N.Y.C., 1991-94; mng. dir. Chem. Bank, N.Y.C., 1994-96, Landauer Assoc., 1997—; pres. Books Realty Capital, 1999—. Author pamphlet. Mem. fin. com. The Geren Meadow Waldorf Sch., 2001—; bookshop chair Bryn Maur Club NY. Mem.: Comml. Mortgage Securitization Assn., Fin. Women's Assn. N.Y. Office: Books Realty Capital 6 Demarest Ct Englewood Cliffs NJ 07632-1904

BOOKSTEIN, JOSEPH J. radiologist, educator; b. Detroit, Mich., July 25, 1929; s. Harry Bookstein and Judith Yetta Safran; m. Edith S. Bookstein; children: Robert Eric, Elizabeth Cheryl, Kenneth Harry. MD, Wayne State U., 1954. Lic. physician Mich., Calif. Chief cardiovasc. radiology U. Mich., Ann Arbor, 1974—96, U. Calif., San Diego, 1974—96, prof. emeritus, 1996—. Contbr. articles to profl. publs., and books. Capt. USAF, 1954—56. Recipient Gold medal, Western Angiography Soc. Fellow: Soc. Cardiovasc. and Interventional Radiology (Gold medal 2002). Avocations: tennis, skiing, bicycling. Home: 7810 Lookout Dr La Jolla CA Office: U Hosp Dept Radiology 200 W Arbor St San Diego CA 92103

BOOM, WILLEM HENRY, physician, biomedical researcher; b. L.A., Nov. 5, 1952; s. Willem B.K. and Florence Ann (Hopper) B.; m. Anne Louise Batzell, July 7, 1984; children: Alexander, Katherine. Cert. d'Etudes Politiques, Inst. D'Etudes Politiques, Paris, 1972; BA, Amherst Coll., 1975; MD, U. Rochester, 1979. Bd. cert. in internal medicine and infectious diseases Am. Bd. Internal Medicine. Intern and resident in internal medicine George Washington U. Sch. Medicine, Washington, 1979-82, chief resident in medicine, 1982-83; clin. and rsch. fellow in infectious diseases Harvard U., Boston, 1983-88; asst. prof. Case Western Res. U., Cleve., 1988-95, assoc. prof., 1995-2000, vice chmn. rsch. dept. medicine, 1999—, dir. Tuberculosis Rsch. Unit, 1999—, prof., 2000—. Editor Jour. Immunology, 1995-99; contbr. articles to profl. jours. Recipient grants NIH, 1985—. Mem. AAAS, Am. Assn. Immunologists, Infectious Diseases Soc. Am. Avocations: playing squash, gardening, travel, cinema. Office: Case Western Res U 10900 Euclid Ave Cleveland OH 44106-1712 E-mail: whb@po.cwru.edu.

BOOMER, DENNIS KEITH, college official, clergyman; b. Hobbs, N.Mex., Oct. 30, 1951; s. Earl Ralph and Eva Mae Boomer; m. Nancy Claire Bellamy, Mar. 12, 1983. BA, Hardin-Simmons U., 1974; MDiv, Southwestern Bapt. Theol. Sem., Ft. Worth, 1977; PhD, Baylor U., 1989. Ordained to ministry Bapt. Ch., 1974. Pastor Oplin Bapt. Ch., Clyde, Tex., 1973-74, S.W. Bapt. Ch., Belton, Tex., 1981-89; vis. asst. prof. W.Va. U., Morgantown, 1989-90, 91-92; dir. Albany (Ga.) Campus, Brewton-Parker Coll., 1999-2000; pastor Carey Heights Bapt. Ch., Oklahoma City, 2002—. Instr. U. Mary Hardin Baylor, Belton, 1981—87; founder, dir. Religious Rsch. Svc., Oklahoma City, 1992—; adj. prof. New Orleans Bapt. Theol. Sem., 1999, Okla. Bapt. U., 2003. Mem.: Am. Acad. Religion. Republican. Avocations: reading, visiting historical sites, computers, cooking. Home: 4509 Sunnyview Dr Apt 1134 Oklahoma City OK 73135-3166

BOOMERSHINE, DONALD EUGENE, bureau executive, development official; b. Brookville, Ohio, Oct. 5, 1931; s. Harold Everett and Elsie (Rhoads) B.; m. Marilyn Sullivan, Aug. 29, 1953 (dec.); children: Jeffrey, Alan; m. Patti Watson, May 29, 1985. BS, Bowling Green (Ohio) State U., 1953; grad., Northwestern U. Bank Mktg. Grad. Sch., 1965; M in Banking, Rutgers U. Stonier Sch. Banking, 1969-72; postgrad., U. Okla. Nat. Comml. Lending Sch., 1974. With jr. exec. program Frigidaire div. Gen. Motors Corp., Dayton, 1955-57; sr. sales rep. IBM, Dayton, 1957-61; bus. devel. rep., asst. cashier Exchange Security Bank, Birmingham, 1961-65; asst. v.p. charge nat. accounts divsn. Birmingham Trust Nat. Bank, 1965-78, v.p., 1968-71, v.p., sales mgr. Circle S div., 1978-80; v.p. community devel. Met. Devel. Bd., 1980-82; pres. Better Bus. Bur. of Cen. Ala., Birmingham, 1982—. Chmn. Bus. Tomorrow Conf. Auburn U., 1975; ednl. chmn. Assoc. Industries Ala., 1975—77; pres. Better Bus. Bur., Birmingham, 1982—; mem. Atlanta-Birmingham br. Fed. Res. Bd., 1990—97, chmn., 1993, 96; mem. bus. adv. coun. Sorrell Coll. Bus., Troy State U. Pres. North Central Ala. chpt. Muscular Dystrophy Found., 1964; trustee Birmingham YWCA, 1972—; gen. chmn. U.S. World Youth Game, 1973; charter mem. Downtown Action Com., 1966; bd. dirs. ARC, 1968—; mem. steering com. Mobile Coll., 1987—; mem. adv. bd. U. South Ala., 1975-78; chmn. Am. Cancer Crusade, 1976; bd. dirs. Birmingham Children's Theatre, 1974-78, Downtown YMCA, Met. YMCA, 1992-97; mem. adv. bd. Ala. State Bd. Edn., 1976—; bd. dirs., 2d v.p. Birmingham Better Bus. Bur.,

1980-82; bd. govs. Ala. Assn. Ind. Colls. and Univs.; v.p. Nat. Vet's Day, 1972—; active Leadership Birmingham; mem. Blue and Gold Bd. U.S. Naval Acad., designated info. officer, 1982—; mem. exec. com. Birmingham Cmty. Svc. award; founding bd. dirs. Ala. Jump Start Coalition, 2002; mem. Ala. com. Employers Support of the N.G. and Res. With USMCR, 1953-84; now col. Ret. Recipient Comdt. award U.S. Naval Acad., 1994, Comdts. Dir. award, 1999, Outstanding Broadcasters Cooperation award Ala. Broadcasters Assn., 1998, Alumni Cmty. Svc. award Bowling Green State U., 2001; Res. Day proclaimed in his honor, 1983. Mem. Bank Mktg. Assn. (nat. dir. 1971-75, nat. v.p. devel. 1971), Ala. Indsl. Devel. Coun., So. Indsl. Coun., World Trade Assn. Ala., Diplomats of Birmingham (founder, chmn. 1973), Marine Corps Res. Officers Assn. (nat. dir. 1974-76), Operation Native Sons and Daus. (chmn. 1972), Newcomen Soc. of U.S., Birmingham C. of C. (life), Vestavia Country Club, The Club, Touchdown Club (Birmingham, founder, dir., treas), Kiwanis (officer, dir., Birmingham 1971, Hixson fellow 2003), Vestavia Country Club, The Club, Summit Club, Sigma Chi. Home: 3801 Cromwell Dr Birmingham AL 35243-5512 Office: Better Bus Bur PO Box 55268 Birmingham AL 35255-5268

BOONE, ANTHONY GERARD, healthcare educator; b. N.Y.C., May 23, 1961; s. Robert Colin and Annie Mae Boone; children: Jordan Alexander, Jacquelyn Izora. AS, City Coll. San Francisco, 1993; student, San Francisco State U., 2001—. Cert. environ. inspector Environ. Assessment Assn. Hazardous materials tech. Lawrence Livermore (Calif.) Lab., 1985—88; radiation safety technician U. Calif., San Francisco, 1988—89; aircraft maintenance technician United Airlines, San Francisco, 1989—91, health and safety instr., 1991—. Cons. Regional Tech. Tng. Ctr., Oakland, Calif., 1999—. Tchr. Third Bapt. Ch., San Francisco, 1983—. With USN, 1979—85. Avocations: comic book collecting, photography, music, baseball. Office: United Airlines SFOED Bldg 47 3rd Fl MOC San Francisco CA 94128

BOONE, BILLY WARREN, lawyer, judge; b. Perryton, Tex., Feb. 6, 1955; s. Kermit George and Verna Jean (Thomas) B.; m. Celia Trimble, 1990; children: Billy Warren II, Carol Ann. BA with honors, Tex. Tech U., 1977, JD cum laude, 1980. Bar: Tex. 1980, U.S. Dist. Ct. (no. dist.) Tex. 1982, U.S. Ct. Appeals (5th cir.) 1990, U.S. Supreme Ct. 1993. Assoc. David P. Hooper & Assocs., Abilene, Tex., 1980-82; prin. Billy W. Boone, Abilene, 1982—. Part-time U.S. magistrate U.S. Dist. Ct. (no. dist.) Tex., Abilene, 1987—. Mem. ABA, Tex. Bar Assn., Abilene Bar Assn., Nat. Coun. U.S. Magistrates. Home: 49 Cypress Point St Abilene TX 79606-5130 Office: US Dist Ct 104 Pine St #705 PO Box 2797 Abilene TX 79604-2797

BOONE, CELIA TRIMBLE, lawyer; b. Clovis, N.Mex., Mar. 3, 1953; d. George Harold and Barbara Ruth (Foster) T.; m. Billy W. Boone, Apr. 21, 1990. BS, Ea. N.Mex. U., 1976, MA, 1977; JD, St. Mary's U., San Antonio, 1982. Bar: Tex. 1982, U.S. Ct. Appeals (5th cir.) 1985, U.S. Supreme Ct. 1986; cer. family law Tex. Bd. Legal Specialization, 1987, family law examination commn., 2002. Instr. English Ea. N.Mex. U., Portales, 1977-78; editor Curry County Times, Clovis, 1978-79; assoc. Schultz & Robertson, Abilene, Tex., 1982-85, Scarborough, Black, Tarpley & Scarborough, Abilene, Tex., 1985-87; ptnr. Scarborough, Black, Tarpley & Trimble, Abilene, Tex., 1988-90, Scarborough, Black, Tarpley & Boone, Abilene, Tex., 1990-94; of counsel Scarborough, Tarpley, Boone & Fouts, Abilene, Tex., 1994-96; prin. Law Office of Celia Trimble Boone, Abilene, Tex., 1996—. Instr. legal rsch. and writing St. Mary's Sch. Law, 1981-82; mem. family law exam. com. Tex. Bd. Legal Specialization, 2002--. Legal adv. bd. to bd. dirs. Abilene Kennel Club, 1983-85; landmarks commn. City of Abilene, 1989-90. Recipient Outstanding Young Lawyer of Abilene, 1988. Mem. ABA, State Bar Tex. (disciplinary rev. com. 1989-93), Am. Trial Lawyers Assn., Tex. Trial Lawyers Assn., Tex. Criminal Def. Lawyers Assn., Tex. Acad. Family Law Specialists, Abilene Bar Assn. (bd. dirs. 1985-88, sec.-treas. 1985-86), Abilene Young Lawyers Assn. (bd. dirs. 1985-89, treas. 1985-86, pres.-elect 1987-88, pres. 1988-89). Avocations: needlework, gardening. Office: 104 Pine St Ste 316 Abilene TX 79601-5930

BOONE, DANIEL LEE, retired music educator; b. Chelsea, Mass., Feb. 1, 1966; s. MaryLou and Frank Doebler(Stepfather); m. Lori Sanders, July 7, 2000; 1 child, Stephen Daniel. MusB in Theory and Composition, Mansfield U., 1989. Cert. Music Edn. Pa. 1989. Music tchr. Williamsport (Pa.) Area Sch. Dist., 1989—91, Canton (Pa.) Area Sch. Dist., 1991—99; piano sales Robert M. Sides Family Music Ctr., Williamsport, 1999—. Mem.: Masons. Home: PO Box 3174 Williamsport PA 17701 Office: Robert M Sides 201 Mulberry St Williamsport PA 17701 Personal E-mail: dlboone66@hotmail.com. E-mail: piano1@ rms.com.

BOONE, DAVID EASON, lawyer; b. Raleigh, N.C., July 5, 1948; s. Devan Duke and Virgil (Eason) B.; m. Beverly Ann Deem, Feb. 3, 1968; children: Rebecca Ann, Jacob Elisha, Courtney Keriann. BA, U. Va., 1970; JD, U. Richmond, 1975. Bar: Va. 1976, U.S. Dist. Ct. (ea. dist.) Va. 1976, U.S. Ct. Appeals (4th cir.) 1976, U.S. Supreme Ct. 1982. Law clk. Hon. Judge D. Dortch Warriner U.S. Dist. Ct., Richmond, Va., 1976-78; assoc. Francis, Hubard & Tice, Richmond, 1978-80; ptnr. Boone, Beale, Cosby & Long, Richmond, 1980—. Adj. instr. J. Sargeant Reynolds Community Coll., Richmond, 1977—. Served to lt. USN, 1970-73, Vietnam. Recipient NAACP Freedom Fund award, Richmond, 1982. Mem. ABA, Richmond Criminal Bar Assn., Nat. Assn. Criminal Def. Lawyers, Va. Coll. Criminal Def. Attys., Lawyers Pilots Bar Assn. Republican. Baptist. Avocations: flying, travel. Office: Boone Beale Cosby & Long 27 N 17th St Richmond VA 23219-3607 E-mail: deboone27n17st@yahoo.com.

BOONE, DONNA CLAUSEN, physical therapist, biostatistician, researcher; b. Nebraska City, Nebr., Dec. 12, 1932; d. Otto Ralph and Hallie Rae Clausen; m. Robert William Boone, Apr. 3, 1965. BA in Zoology, U. Wyo., 1954; MS in Phys. Therapy, U. So. Calif., 1980, MS in Biometry, 1983. Lic. phys. therapist, Calif. Phys. therapist Ill. Hosp. Sch., Chgo., 1955-59, Calif. Hosp., L.A., 1959-63; hemophilia specialist in phys. therapy Orthopaedic Hosp., L.A., 1963-78, rsch., project dir. Hemophilia Ctr., 1967-78; rsch. methods instr. U. So. Calif., L.A., 1982-83, Calif. State U., Long Beach, 1982-83; biostatistician immunulogy U. So. Calif., L.A., 1983-87, coord., statistician Nat. Clin. Trial, The Silicone Study, 1987-93; phys. therapist Huntington Meml. Hosp., Pasadena, Calif., 1993-98; cons. Hemophilia, Continuous Quality Improvement, Lompoc, Calif., 1998—. Internat. lectr., cons. World Fedn. Hemophilia, Montreal, Can., 1970-78; cons. biostatis. dentistry and pharmacology U. So. Calif., L.A., 1982-83, cons. orthopaedics, U. Buffalo, 1982-83; continuous quality improvement coach Doheny Eye Inst., L.A., 1990-92, Huntington Meml. Hosp., Pasadena, Calif., 1993-97; cons. physical therapy working group Nat. Hemophilia Found., 2000—. Editor: Comprehensive Management of Hemophilia, 1976, (internat. newsletter) World Hemophilia AIDS Ctr., 1984-93; contbr. articles to profl. jours. including Phys. Therapy, Archives Phys. Medicine, Bone and Joint Surgery, Western Medicine, Pharmacology, Diagnostic Immunology, Ophthalmology, Archives of Ophthalmology, Controlled Clin. Trials; mem. editl. bd. Am. Phys. Therapy Assn., 1975-82. Co-chair United Way Campaign Orthopaedic Hosp., L.A., chair, 1975—75; mem. Lompoc Rep. Women, 1998—, legis. chair, 2000—; vol. Rep. Campaign for Ho. of Reps., Glendale, Calif., 1996; recording sec. Santa Barbara County Rep. Women, 2000—01; lay leader St. Mary's Episcopal Ch., 1998—; bd. dirs. World Hemophilia Alliance, sec., 1996—; mem. alumni com. U. Wyo., 1999—; mem. med. adv. bd. Hemophilia Found. So. Calif., L.A., 1974—78. Grantee Fed. Govt. Agys., 1967, 73; recipient Dr. Murray Thelin award Nat. Hemophilia Found., 1976, Disting. Alumna award U. Wyo., 1979, Achievement award Alpha Chi Omega, 1980, Spl. Achievement award for treatment advances 50th Anniversary of the Nat. Hemophilia Found., 1998, Donna Clausen Boone ann. award Nat. Hemophilia Found. to Phys. Therapist, 1999—. Mem. Village Country Club, Antique Automobile Club. Republican. Episcopalian. Avocations: gardening, antique autos, travel, reading, jazz music clubs. Office: Hemophilia Continuous Quality Improvement 266 Oakwood Cir Lompoc CA 93436-1300 E-mail: boone266@impulse.net.

BOONE, EARLE MARION, business executive; b. Panama City, Fla., Apr. 25, 1934; s. Earle Alpha and Lucy Marian (Jerkins) B.; m. Birthe Schnohr Kristensen Boone, Oct. 16, 1979; children: Tina Boone Broderick, Darlene Boone Bauer, Earle Marion Jr. BS in Aviation Mgmt., So. Ill. U., 1977; MS in Pub. Adminstrn., Calif. State U., 1983. Lic. airline transport pilot. USAF pilot, 1954-75; corp. pilot pvt. practice, 1975-78, aviation mgmt. cons., 1978-80; mktg. dir. Northrop Corp., Hawthorne, Calif., 1980-92; v.p. mktg. Cognitive Neurometrics, Scottsdale, Ariz., 1992-95; pres., CEO Cognitive Neurometrics Inc., Scottsdale, Ariz., 1995-2001; ind. investor Dripping Springs, Tex., 2001—. SR-71 pilot 9th Strat Recon Wing, Beale AFB, Calif., 1966-68; F4-E combat fighter pilot 388 Tactical Fighter Wing, Thailand, 1970-71; mktg. dir. Northrop Corp., Hawthorne, 1980-92. Lt. col. USAF, 1954-75, Vietnam. Recipient The Disting. Flying Cross, The Air medal, Bronze Star medal, Meritorious Svc. medal, Sec. Air Force, Vietnam, 1970-71,. Mem. Ret. Officers Assn., Order of Daedalians, Sierra Club, Phi Alpha Alpha. Republican. Avocations: reading, hiking, foreign travel, language study, computers.

BOONE, ELWOOD BERNARD, JR., physician, urologist; b. Petersburg, Va., May 7, 1943; s. Elwood Bernard Sr. and Antoinette (Brown) B.; m. Carol Ann Fraser, June18, 1968; children: Elwood Bernard III, Melanie Lynn. AB, Colgate U., 1965; MD, Meharry Med. Coll., 1969. Diplomate Am. Bd. Urology. Intern Med. Coll. Va., 1970-72, resident in surgery, 1972-75, resident in urology, 1975; pvt. practice urology, Richmond, Va., 1975—. Baptist. Home: 209 Chickahominy Bluffs Rd Richmond VA 23227-1707 Office: 111 N Robinson St Ste 403 Richmond VA 23220 E-mail: ebbojr@cs.com.

BOONE, HAROLD THOMAS, retired lawyer; b. Oak Hill, W. Va., Dec. 14, 1921; s. Thomas Thumb and Cora Anna (McGlamery) B.; m. Ferne Miller, July 31, 1948; 1 dau., Cheryl Ann. BS, W. Va., 1943; JD, U. Va., 1948. With Md. Casualty Co., Balt., 1948-87, v.p., gen. counsel, corp. sec., 1979-87, dir., 1979-89. Dir. N.C. Guaranty Fund, Calif. Def. Counsel; arbitrator Def. Research Inst., Inc., v.p. ins., 1986-87; part time freelance arbitrator. Served to 2d lt. USAAF, 1943-46. Mem. Internat. Assn. Ins. Counsel (v.p. 1979-81), Am. Arbitration Assn. Clubs: Hunt Valley Golf. Republican.

BOONE, MORELL DOUGLAS, information and communications technology educator; b. Londonderry, Northern Ireland, Dec. 15, 1942; arrived in U.S., 1946; s. Paul J. and Margaret (Hill) B.; m. Carolyn June Gallagher, July 6, 1968; children— Ian Charles, Megan Elizabeth BS, Kutztown State Coll., Pa., 1964; MS, Syracuse U., 1968, PhD, 1980. Librarian Pennridge Schs., Perkasie, Pa., 1964-66; reference librarian Hobart and William Smith Colls., Geneva, N.Y., 1968-70; lectr. Syracuse U., N.Y., 1970-72; dean learning resources U. Bridgeport, Conn., 1973-80, prof. interdisciplinary tech. Eastern Mich. U., Ypsilanti, 1998—, dean learning resources and techs., 1980-2001. Cons. for internat. ednl. devel. Iran, Swaziland, Yemen, others. Presenter at profl meetings;, co-author book; contbr. articles to profl. jours.; mem. editl. bd. The Tech. Source, Libr. Hi Tech. Chmn. Community Cablecasting Commn., Ypsilanti, 1981-84, Ypsilanti Ednl. Found., 1988-94; pres. bd. dirs. Meals on Wheels, Ypsilanti, 1998—. Named to Pennridge H.S. Wall of Fame, 2001. Mem. ALA, EDUCAUSE, Soc. Coll. and Univ. Planning, Kiwanis. Democrat. Presbyterian (elder). Avocations: gardening, reading, travel. Home: 5774 Pineview Dr Ypsilanti MI 48197-8983 Office: Eastern Mich U Bruce T Halle Library Ypsilanti MI 48197 E-mail: morell.boone@emich.edu.

BOONE, RICHARD WINSTON, SR., lawyer; b. Washington, July 19, 1941; s. Henry Shaffer and Anne Catherine (Huehne) B.; m. Jean Knox Logan, Dec. 17, 1966; children: Elizabeth Anne, Richard Winston, Jr., Katheryn Jeanne. BA with honors, U. Ala., 1963; JD, Georgetown U., 1970. Bar: Va. 1970, D.C. 1970, Md. 1984, U.S. Ct. Appeals (D.C. cir.) 1970, U.S. Ct. Appeals (2nd cir.) 1973, U.S. Ct. Appeals (4th cir.) 1972, U.S. Supreme Ct. 1974, U.S. Ct. Claims 1975. Ptnr. Carr, Jordan, Coyne & Savits, Washington, 1977-81; shareholder, dir. Wilkes, Artis, Hedrick & Lane, P.C., Washington, 1984—95; pres. Richard W. Boone, P.C., McLean, Va., 1984—95, The Law Offices of Richard W. Boone, 1995-97, Boone & Assocs., P.C., 1998—. Capt. USAR, 1964-67. Mem. D.C. Def. Lawyers Assn., Va. Trial Lawyers Assn., Va. Assn. Def. Attys., Barristers Assn. Avocations: model railroading, photography. E-mail: rwboone@aol.com.

BOONE, ROBERT RAYMOND, former professional baseball coach; b. San Diego, Nov. 19, 1947; m. Susan Boone. 3 children, Bret, Aaron, Matt. BA in Psychology, Stanford U., 1969. Baseball player Phila. Phillies, 1969-81, Calif. Angels, 1981-88, Kansas City Royals, 1988-93, Oakland Athletics, 1993; minor league mgr. Pacific Coast, Tacoma, 1992-93; major league baseball mgr. Kansas City Royals, 1995—97, Cin. Reds, 2000—03. Player Nat. League All-Star Game, 1976, 78, 79, Am. League All-Star Game, 1983, World Series, 1980. Recipient Nat. League Gold glove, 1978-79, Am. League Gold glove, 1986-89; named Catcher, Sporting News Nat. League All-Star Team, 1976.

BOONE, STEPHEN CHRISTOPHER, retired neurosurgeon; b. Navasota, Tex., Mar. 18, 1938; s. Berrill Harrison and Joyce (Taylor) Boone; m. Elizabeth Thompson, Apr. 9, 1960 (div. June 1979); children: Stephen, Michael, Laura; m. Susan Pate, Nov. 3, 1979; children: Christopher, Emily. BS, Duke U., 1960, MD, PhD, Duke U., 1965. Diplomate Am. Bd. Neurological Surgery. Surg. intern Duke Hosp., Durham, NC, 1965, resident in neurosurgery, 1967-72; chief neurosurgeon Brooke Army Med. Ctr., 1973-75; asst. chief neurosurgery Walter Reed Army Med. Ctr., Washington, 1975-77; from assoc. prof. to prof. neurosurgery U. N.C., 1977-82; neurosurgeon Raleigh (N.C.) Neurosurgery Clinic, 1982—2002; ret., 2002. Brig. gen. USAR, 1962—87. Republican. Episcopalian. E-mail: scboone38@earthlink.net.

BOONE, WILLIAM ROGERS, health facility administrator, educator, researcher; b. Greenville, S.C., Apr. 5, 1948; s. Merritt Anderson and Dorothy (Rogers) B.; m. Edna T. Boone, July 30, 1977 (div.); children: Joseph A. Gambrell, Bonnie B. Jennings, Becky B. Keck, Michael S. Gambrell. BS, U. Ga., 1970; MS, Clemson U., 1972, PhD, 1977. Asst. prof. Ga. Coll., Milledgeville, 1977-81; dir. R&D Maplehurst Ova Transplants, Inc., Keota, Iowa, 1981-86; dir. ART and andrology labs. U. Wis., Madison, 1986-90, Greenville (S.C.) Hosp. Sys., 1990—; adj. prof. Clemson (S.C.) U., 1996—; assoc. prof. Med. U. S.C., Charleston, 1992-2000, prof., 2000; assoc. prof. U. S.C. Med. Sch., Columbia, 1995-2000, prof., 2000. Co-author: 113 Calhoun Street: The Early Years of the Beta Zeta Chapter of Alpha Gamma Rho; contbr. articles to profl. jours. including Jour. Dairy Sci., Am. Jour. Obstets. and Gynecol., Jour. Assisted Reprodn. and Genetics, Animal Reprodn. Bd. dirs. Bears Inc., Simpsonville, S.C., 1993—, Wesleyan Found. Ga. Coll., Milledgeville, 1985-86; mem. adv. com. for high tech. Indian Hills Cmty. Coll., Ottumwa, Iowa, 1985-86 Mem. Am. Soc. for Reproductive Medicine, Am. Soc. Andrology, Am. Zoo and Aquarium Assn., Internat. Assn. for Bear Rsch. and Mgmt., Soc. for the Study Reprodn., S.C. Acad. Sci. Methodist. Avocation: bear research. Office: Reproductive Endocrinology and Infertility 890 W Faris Rd Ste 470 Greenville SC 29605-4281

BOONSHAFT, HOPE JUDITH, public affairs executive; b. Phila., May 3, 1949; d. Barry and Lorelei Gail (R ienzi) B. BA, Pa. State U., 1972; postgrad. Del. Law Sch, Kellogg Inst. Mgmt. Tng. Program writer Youth Edn., N.Y.C., 1972; legal aide to judge Phila., 1975; dir. spl. projects Guiffre Med. Ctr., Phila., 1975; senatorial campaign fin. dir. Arlen Specter, Phila., 1975; presdl. campaign fin. dir. Jimmy Carter, Atlanta, 1976; fin. dir. Dem. Nat. Com., 1977—79; dir. devel. World Jewish Congress, N.Y.C., 1978, Yeshiva U., L.A., 1979; dir. comm. Nat. Easter Seal Soc., Chgo., 1979-83; CEO Boonshaft-Lewis & Savitch Pub. Rels and Govt. Affairs, L.A., 1983-93; sr. v.p. Edelman Worldwide, 1993-95; exec. v.p. external affairs Sony Pictures Entertainement, L.A., 1995—. Spl. adv. cmty. rels. The White House, 1977-80; guest lectr. U. Ill., 1982, May Co.'s Calif. Women in Bus. Bd. dirs. L.A. Arts Coun., Los Angeles County Citizens for Economy and Efficiency in Govt. Commn., Calif. Film Commn., Spkrs. Commn. Calif. Initiative. Home: 1967 Mandeville Canyon Rd Los Angeles CA 90049-2235 Office: Sony Pictures Entertainment 10202 Washington Blvd Culver City CA 90232-3119

BOOR, MYRON VERNON, psychologist, educator; b. Wadena, Minn., Dec. 21, 1942; s. Vernon LeRoy and Rosella Katharine (Eckhoff) B. BS, U. Iowa, 1965; MA, So. Ill. U., 1967, PhD, 1970; MS, U. Pitts., 1981. Lic. psychologist, Mo. Research psychologist Milw. County Mental Health Ctr., 1970-72; asst. prof. clin. psychologist Ft. Hays State U., Hays, Kans., 1972-76, assoc. prof., 1976-79; NIMH postdoctoral fellow in psychiat. epidemiology U. Pitts., Western Psychiat. Inst. and Clinic, 1979-81; research psychologist R.I. Hosp. and Butler Hosp., Providence, 1981-84; clin. psychologist Newman Meml. County Hosp., Emporia, Kans., 1985-93, Heartland Health Sys., St. Joseph, Mo., 1994—. Clin. psychologist Ft. Hays State U., 1972-79; asst. prof. psychiatry and human behavior Brown U., Providence, 1981-84; adj. faculty Emporia State U., 1985-94. Contbr. articles to profl. jours. U.S. Pub. Health Service fellow, 1965-67, NIMH fellow 1979-81. Home: 3018 Cambridge St Saint Joseph MO 64506-1164 E-mail: mboor@ccp.com.

BOORKMAN, JO ANNE, librarian; b. San Jose, Calif., July 21, 1947; d. Charles John and Ruth Ellen (Reuss) B. BA, Scripps Coll., 1969; MS, U. Ill., 1971. Bibl. search analyst biomed. library UCLA, 1971-73, reference librarian Darling biomed. library, 1973-77; head pub. svcs. health scis. library U. N.C., Chapel Hill, 1977-80, head collections devel. health scis. library, 1980-84; head pub. svcs. Carlson health scis. library U. Calif., Davis, 1985-86, acting asst. univ. librarian health scis., 1986-87, head Carlson library, 1988—. NSF fellow, 1969-70. Fellow Spl. Librs. Assn., Med. Libr. Assn. (bd. dirs. 1988-91); mem. No. Calif. and Nev. Med. Libr. Group (pres. 1988-89, award profl. excellence 1996), Mid-Atlantic chpt. Med. Libr. Assn. (pres. 1983-84), P.E.O. Office: U Calif Carlson Health Scis Libr Davis CA 95616-5291 E-mail: jaboorkman@ucdavis.edu.

BOORMAN, GARY ALEXIS, veterinary pathologist; b. Leonard, Minn., June 30, 1942; s. George Henry and Winifred Emogene (Forbragd) B.; m. Natalie Ruth Campe, Oct. 8, 1965; children: Beth Mary Boorman McClure, Sonja Louise. DVM, U. Minn., 1967; MS in Pathology, U. Mich., 1971; PhD in Pathology, U. Calif., Davis, 1978. Diplomate Am. Bd. Toxicology, Am. Coll. Lab. Animal Medicine, Am. Coll. Vet. Pathologists. Pathologist Inst. for Exptl. Gerontology, Rijswijk, The Netherlands, 1971-74; resident in pathology U. Calif., Davis, 1974-78; pathologist Nat. Inst. Environ. Health Sci., Research Triangle Park, N.C., 1978-83, chief chem. pathology br., 1983-89, chief chem. carcinogen br., 1989—93, pathologist, 1993—. Advisor cancer evaluaton com. FDA, Rockville, Md., 1986-89; exec. com. Am. Coll. Lab. Animal Medicine, Washington, 1979-82. Author, editor: Pathology of the F344/N Rat, 1990; contbr. over 150 articles to profl. jours. Mem. Am. Assn. Cancer Rsch., Soc. Toxicol. Pathologists, ACLU, Sierra Club. Home: 1505 Cumberland Rd Chapel Hill NC 27514-2622 Office: Nat Inst Environ Health Sci PO Box 12233 Research Triangle Park NC 27709-2233

BOORMAN, HOWARD LYON, history educator; b. Chgo., Sept. 11, 1920; s. William Ryland and Verna (Lyon) B.; m. Mary Houghton, Jan. 20, 1972 (dec.), 1 child by previous marriage: Scott A. BA, U. Wis., Madison, 1941; postgrad., Yale U., 1946-47. Divisional asst., divsn. def. materials Dept. of State, Washington, 1942-43; fgn. service officer to Peking, Hong Kong, 1947-54; rsch. assoc. Sch. Internat. Affairs, Columbia U., N.Y.C., 1955-67; prof. history Vanderbilt U., Nashville, 1967-84, prof. emeritus, 1984—. Vis. scholar Univ. Ctr. of Va., 1963. Gen. editor: Biographical Dictionary of Republican China, 4 vols, 1967-71; contbr. articles to profl. jours. Lt. USNR, 1943-46. Recipient Rockefeller Public Service award, 1954-55 Mem.: Assn. Asian Studies, Am. Polit. Sci. Assn., Am. Hist. Assn., Univ. Club (Nashville). Home: 12 Redbud Dr Nashville TN 37215-2423 Office: Vanderbilt U Dept History Nashville TN 37235

BOORNE, RYAN, ballet dancer; b. Toronto, Ontario, Can. Student, National Ballet Sch., Quinte Ballet Sch. Mem. Nat. Ballet Co., Toronto, Canada, 1992—, first soloist, 1997—, principal soloist, 1999—. Dancer (ballets) Romeo and Juliet, Coppélia, The Sleeping Beauty, Giselle, Swan Lake, 1999; performer: (ballets) A Disembodied Voice, Terra Firma, The Four Seasons, Cruel World, Voluntaries. Office: Walter Carsen Ctr Nat Ballet of Canada 470 Queens Quay West Toronto ON Canada M5V 3K4

BOORSTEIN, BEVERLY WEINGER, judge; b. Chgo., Apr. 25, 1941; d. Morris Aaron and Bess (Meisel) Weinger; m. Sidney L. Boorstein, July 3, 1962; children: Robin Anne, Michelle Loren. BA, Brandeis U., 1961; JD, Boston U., 1964. Bar: Mass. 1964, U.S. dist. Ct. Mass. 1967. Assoc. Siskind & Siskind, Boston, 1965-70; sole practice Boston, 1971-79; ptnr. Beverly Weinger Boorstein, P.C., Boston, 1980-92; assoc. justice Middlesex County Probate and Family Ct., 1992—2003; first justice Middlesex Divsn. Probate and Family Ct., Cambridge, 2003—. Commr. Jud. Conduct Commn.; pres. Mental Health Legal Advisors Com. Contbr. articles to legal publs. Mem. Mass. Bar Assn., Middlesex County Bar Assn., Mass. Assn. Women Lawyers (adv. bd.), Boston Bar Assn. Office: The Trial Ct Probate & Family Dept Middlesex County Divsn 208 Cambridge St Cambridge MA 02141-1202

BOORSTEIN, LAURENCE, economist, educator; b. Neuilly, France, Jan. 22, 1951; s. Edward and Regula (Simons) B. BA, Columbia U., 1972, MS, 1974; CE, 1978, MBA, 1988. Sys. analyst Frederic R. Harris, Inc. engring. divsn. Planning Rsch. Corp., N.Y.C., 1974-77, prin. sys. engr. Frederic R. Harris, Inc. divsn., 1977-79; sr. systems planner Frederic R. Harris Engring. Div., N.Y.C., 1979-83; sr. economist Frederic R. Harris, Inc. divsn. Planning Rsch. Corp., N.Y.C., 1983-86; sr. economist Soros Assocs., N.Y.C., 1988-94; prin. economist DMJM Harris Inc. divsn. AECOM Tech. Corp., N.Y.C., 1994—. Mem.: Soc. Civil Engrs. Home: 1 Ipswich Ave Apt 112 Great Neck NY 11021-3260 Office: DMJM Harris 20 Exchange Pl New York NY 10005-3262 E-mail: larry.boorstein@dmjmharris.com., lboorstein@att.net.

BOORSTIN, DANIEL JOSEPH, historian, lecturer, educator, author, editor; b. Atlanta, Ga., Oct. 1, 1914; s. Samuel and Dora (Olsan) Boorstin; m. Ruth Carolyn Frankel, Apr. 9, 1941; children: Paul Terry, Jonathan, David West. AB summa cum laude, Harvard U., 1934; postgrad., Inner Temple, London, 1934—37; BA with honors, Oxford U., 1936, BCL with honors, 1937; JSD, Yale U., 1940; LittD (hon.), Cambridge U., 1967; LLD (hon.), Harvard U., 1993; other hon. degrees. Cert.: Inner Temple (barrister-at-law) 1937, bar: Mass. 1942. Instr., tutor history and lit. Harvard and Radcliffe Coll., 1938—42; lectr. legal history Harvard Law Sch., 1939—42; asst. prof. history Swarthmore Coll., 1942—44; from asst. prof. to prof. Am. history U. Chgo., 1944—64, Preston and Sterling Morton disting. svc. prof., 1964—69; Walgreen lectr. Am. instns., 1952; dir. Nat. Mus. History and Tech., Smithsonian Instn., Washington, 1969—73, sr. historian, 1973—75; libr. of Congress Libr. of Congress, 1975—87, libr. of Congress emeritus, 1987—. Vis. lectr. U. Rome, 1950—51, Kyoto U., Japan, 1957; cons. social sci. rsch. ctr. U. P.R., 1955; lectr. in field; 1st incumbent of chair Am. history U. Paris, 1961—62; prof. U. Cambridge, 1964—65; sr. fellow Huntington Libr., 1969; mem. Commn. on Critical Choices for Ams., 1973—77; mem. Indo-Am. joint subcommn. edn. and culture Dept. State, 1974—81; mem. Japan-U.S. Friendship Commn., 1978—84; mem. Am. Revolution Bicentennial Commn.; sr. atty. office lend lease adminstrn. Dept. Justice, Washington; fellow Trinity Coll., 1964—65; mem. task force on exploration NASA, 1989. Author: The Mysterious Science of the Law, 1941, 1996, Delaware Cases, 1792-1830, 1943, The Lost World of Thomas Jefferson, 1948, The Genius of American Politics, 1953, The Americans: The Colonial Experience, 1958 (Bancroft award, 1959), America and the Image of Europe, 1960, The Image or What Happened to the American Dream, 1962, The Americans: The National Experience, 1965 (Francis Parkman prize, 1966), The Landmark History of the American People, 1968, 1987, The Decline of Radicalism, 1969, The Sociology of the Absurd, 1970, The Americans: The Democrtic Experience, 1973 (Pulitzer prize, 1974, Dexter prize, 1974), Democracy and Its Discontents, 1974, The Exploring Spirit, 1976, The Republic of Technology, 1978; author: (with Brooks M. Kelley) A History of the Untied States, 1981, 1991; author: The Discoverers, 1983 (Watson-Davis prize History of Sci. Soc., 1986), 1991, Hidden History, 1987, The Creators, 1992, Cleopatra's Nose, 1994, The Daniel J. Boorstin Reader, 1995, The Seekers, 1998, Daniel J. Boorstin: A Comprehensive and Selectively Annotated Bibliography, 2000; editor: An American Primer, 1966, American Civilization, 1972, Am. History, Ency. Britannica, 1951—55; mem. bd. editors:, 1981—; contbr. articles and book revs. to various publs. Trustee Colonial Williamsburg, Kennedy Ctr., Cafaritz Found., Woodrow Wilson Ctr., Thomas Gilcrease Mus.; mem. bd. visitors USAF Acad., 1968—70. Named to, Japanese Order of Sacred Treasure, 1st class, Grand Officer, Portugal, Legion of Honor, France, Order of Cultural Merit, Belgium; recipient Younger prize, 1936, Charles Frankel prize, NEH, 1989, Nat. Book award, Nat. Book Award Com., 1989, numerous others; scholar Rhodes scholar, Balliol Coll., Oxford U., 1936. Fellow: Royal Hist. Soc. (corr.), Am. Geog. Soc. (hon.); mem.: Colonial Soc. Mass., Orgn. Am. Historians, Am. Studies Assn. (pres. 1969—71), Am. Antiquarian Soc., Am. Philos. Soc. (Thomas Jefferson medal 1999), Am. Acad. Arts and Scis., Elizabethan Club (Yale U. chpt.), Nat. Press Club, Internat. House Japan,

Cosmos Club, Phi Beta Kappa (Disting. Svc. to Humanities award 1988). Jewish. Home: 3541 Ordway St NW Washington DC 20016-3173 Office: Libr Congress Libr Emeritus Washington DC 20540-0001 Home Fax: (202) 966-1783.

BOOSINGER, TIMOTHY R. dean; DVM, Purdue U., 1976, PhD, 1983. Cert. vet. pathologist Am. Coll. Vet. Pathologists. Assoc. dean for acad. affairs Auburn (Ala.) U. Coll. Vet. Medicine, 1993—95, interim dean, 1993—95, dean, 1997—. Office: Auburn U Coll Vet Medicine Auburn University AL 36849*

BOOT, JOHN C.G. economics educator; b. Semarang, Java, Indonesia, June 10, 1936; came to U.S. 1965; s. Frederik Rutger and Maria (den Tex) B.; m. A.M. Hinke Tuinman, May 22, 1965; children— Maren Caroline, Mark Frederik Abe. Ph.D., Netherlands Sch. Econs., Rotterdam, 1964. Prof. econs. and stats. SUNY-Buffalo, 1965— . Author: Quadratic Programming, 1964, others. Home: 177 Beard Ave Buffalo NY 14214-1729 Office: SUNY Amherst Campus Jacobs 341 Buffalo NY 14260-4000 E-mail: jboot@buffalo.edu.

BOOTE, ALFRED SHEPARD, marketing researcher, educator; b. N.Y.C., May 21, 1929; s. Alfred Denton and Katharine (Kerrison) B.; m. Joan Peterson, July 9, 1960 (div. Sept. 1963); m. Heath Drury, June 1, 1973. BA, Colgate U., 1951; MBA, Columbia U., 1953, MPhil, 1974, PhD, 1975; MA, Stanford U., 1957. Research mgr. design and market research labs., Container Corp. of Am., 1961-63; assoc. dir. mktg. research Pepsi-Cola Co., 1963-65; dir. mktg. research Far East area, PepsiCo Internat., 1965-67, dir. mktg. rsch. Worldwide, 1967-70; pvt. practice mktg. research cons. clients include Singer Co., McDonald's Corp., GTE, Gen. Elec. Co., Magic Chef Corp., and others. N.Y.C., 1970-75, 90—; cons. Arthur D. Little, Inc., Cambridge, Mass., 1975-76; gen. mgr., dir. research Decision Research Corp., Lexington, Mass., 1976-78; dir. mktg. research Singer Co., Stamford, Conn., 1978-81; mng. dir., founder Psychographics Research Corp., Inc., Bedford, N.Y., 1981-86; v.p. research Smith Stanley & Co., Inc., Darien, Conn., 1983-87. Adj. assoc. prof. sociology Hunter Coll., 1983; adj. lectr. mktg. rsch. Nichols Coll., 1985; vis. prof. mktg. Clark U., 1985-89; presenter in field. Author: An Evil Trust, 2001; mem. editl. rev. bd. Jour. of Advt., 1982-87; mem. editl. bd. Psychology and Mktg., 1983-85; contbr. articles to bus. and profl. jours. Mem. Planning Commn., Woodstock, Conn., 1985-91; mem. Regional Planning Commn. N.E. Conn., 1987-91; founder, 1st chmn. Mktg. Rsch. Soc. of Hong Kong, 1967; justice peace, Woodstock, Conn., 2001—. Served to lt. (j.g.) U.S. Navy, 1953-56. Sr. rsch. fellow Robert C. Fischer Inst., 1999—. Mem. Am. Sociol. Assn., Alpha Kappa Delta, Alpha Kappa Psi. Home: 73 Bull Hill Rd Woodstock CT 06281-2311 Office: Robert C Fischer Inst Dudley MA 01571 E-mail: asb103@columbia.edu.

BOOTH, ANNA BELLE, accountant; b. Homesville, Ohio, Jan. 15, 1912; d. John Wilson and M. Pearl (Toomey) B.; m. Guy DiAmbrosio, Apr. 29, 1930; 1 child, Guy Booth. BA, Taylor Coll., 1930. Office mgr. in charge of mfg. Jacobs Tailored Clothes, Inc., Phila., 1931-41; acct., corp. cashier Lehigh Coal and Navigation Co., Phila., 1941-55; acct. Bishop & Hedberg, Phila., 1955-57; acct., office mgr. The Camax Co., Phila., 1957-60; office mgr., cashier New Eng. Mutual Life Ins. Co., Phila., 1960-67; acct. Wall & Ochs, Inc., Phila., 1967-71; comptr. Bisler Packaging Div./Pet, Inc., Phila., 1971-82; ret. Mem. Am. Soc. Women Accts. (Phila. pres. 1956-58, dir. 1952-54, 62-64, 73-75), LWV (Phila.). Home: 135 S 20th St Apt 1002 Philadelphia PA 19103

BOOTH, BARBARA RIBMAN, civic worker; b. N.Y.C., May 2, 1928; d. Benjamin C. and Ceclia (Lowe) Ribman; m. Mitchell B. Booth, July 13, 1952; 1 child, Brian S. AA, Centenary Jr. Coll., Hackettstown, N.Y., 1948; BA, Barnard Coll., 1950. Pres. women's alliance, chmn., Christmas fair 1st Congl. Ch. of City of N.Y., 1959-63; mem. vol. com. Sheltering Arms Children's Svc., N.Y.C.; vol., coord. high sch. visits, pres. aux. N.Y. Hosp., 1989-91, co-chmn., 1995—; trustee Florence K. Griswold Meml. Fund. Com., All Souls Unitarian Ch., N.Y.C., United Hosp. Funds Auxiliary for N.Y. Hosp., 1996; bd. dir. women's div. Jefferson Dem. Club. N.Y.C.; committeewoman N.Y. County Dem. Com.; bd. govs., v.p. N.Y. Fruit and Flower Mission, Inc.; del. city conv., chmn. East Manhattan br. LWV. Recipient Auxilian of N.Y. Hosp. award, 1996. Mem. City Gardens Club N.Y.C. (mem. grants com.). Home: 75 E End Ave New York NY 10028-7909

BOOTH, BETTY JEAN, daycare administrator, poet; b. St. Louis County, Mo., Dec. 27, 1944; d. Richard Augustus and Leoma Thelma (Atchison) Woods; m. Alfred Lee Pope Jr., Aug. 20, 1962 (div. Apr. 14, 1975); children: Wayman Maurice Pope, Aundrea Denise Pope, Juanita Rosetta Pope, Victoria Lynn Pope, Daniel Jerome Pope, Alfred Lee III Pope; m. Robert Lee Booth, Mar. 3, 1984; 1 stepchild, David Griffin. Cert., United Bus. Coll., North St. Louis, Mo., 1987. Baby nurse, Ladue, Mo., 1984—89; home care worker and provider Clayton, Mo., 1989; adminstrv. asst. Grateful Home Homeless Shelter, Detroit, 1992; day care asst. Time for Happy Land Care, Detroit, 1999—. Contbr. poetry. Avocations: writing, gardening, taping, reading, creating. Home: 14503 Hazelridge St Detroit MI 48205-3619

BOOTH, DAVID LAYTON, retired chemicals executive; b. Aurora, Ill., July 20, 1939; s. Harry Edward and Inez Nellie Booth; m. Nancy Ann Baker, June 30, 1962; children: Edward Layton, Andrew Dale. BS, Beloit Coll., 1957—61; PhD, U. of Oreg., 1961—65. V.p. of dyes and organic specialities Morton Internat., Inc., Chgo., 1989—97, v.p. of sci. and tech., 1997—2001; ret., 2001. Contbr. articles to profl. jours. Mem.: Informex, Synthetic Organic Chem. Manufacturers Assn., Comml. Devel. and Mktg. Assn., Comml. Devel. Assn., Chem. Manufacturers Assn., The Royal Soc. of Chemistry, Am. Chem. Soc. (life). R-Consevative. Achievements include patents for 60 US and foreign patents. Home: 652 Kendallwood Ct Crystal Lake IL 60014 Personal E-mail: dbooth@mc.net.

BOOTH, DONALD RICHARD, economist, educator; b. Marble, Minn., June 1, 1931; s. Floyd James and Maude (Marquart) B.; m. Louise Hitt, Aug. 22, 1953; 1 child, David. BA, Whittier Coll., 1955; MA, Claremont Coll., 1956; PhD, UCLA, 1970. Grad. dean Chapman Coll., Orange, Calif., 1973-77, acad. dean, 1977-78, exec. v.p., 1978-79, dean, sch. of bus., 1979-81, prof. econs., 1959—, v.p. fin., 1988-89; sr. economist Claremont (Calif.) Inst., 1989—. Bd. dirs. United Am. Bank, Westminster, Calif., Consumer Credit Counseling of Orange County, Calif. Recipient Eliot Jones award, We. Econs. Assn., 1958; Danforth Teaching fellow, Danforth Found., 1962, NSF fellow, 1970. Avocations: chess, stamp collecting, swimming. Office: Chapman U One University Dr Orange CA 92866-1011

BOOTH, EDGAR HIRSCH, lawyer; b. Bklyn., June 8, 1926; s. Benjamin H. and Lee (Benzman) B.; m. Joan E. Blumberg, Oct. 7, 1956; children— Charles, Janet. Student, U. Va., 1944, 46-47; BA, Stanford, 1949; JD, Harvard, 1953. Bar: N.Y. State bar 1954. Since practiced in, N.Y.C.; assoc. Booth, Lipton & Lipton, N.Y.C., 1954-65, ptnr., 1965-84, Booth, Marcus & Pierce, N.Y.C., 1984-87, Myerson & Kuhn, N.Y.C., 1988-89, Warshaw Burstein Cohen Schlesinger & Kuh, N.Y.C., 1989-2000, of counsel, 2000—02; ret. Mem. mediators panel U.S. Bankruptcy Ct. So. Dist. N.Y. Mem. Glen Rock Bd. Edn., 1971-77, pres., 1973-74; bd. dirs. S.M. Louis Fund, Inc., N.Y.C. Served with AUS, 1944-46. Mem. Am. Bankruptcy Inst., N.Y. State Bar Assn., Assn. Bar City N.Y. Home: 25 Belmont Rd Glen Rock NJ 07452-2305 Office: 555 5th Ave New York NY 10017-2416 E-mail: ebooth@wbcsk.com.

BOOTH, GEORGE, cartoonist; b. Cainsville, Mo., June 28, 1926; s. William and Norene B.; m. Dione Babcock; 1 child, Sarah. Student, Chgo. Acad. Art, 1948-49, Corcoran Sch. Art, Washington, Adelphi U., Sch. Visual Arts, N.Y.C.; DFA (hon.), Stonybrook State U., 2003. Staff cartoonist Leatherneck Mag., USMC, 1946-52; art dir. Bill Communications, N.Y., 1958-64. Cartoons appearing regularly in The New Yorker mag., 1969—; author: Think Good Thoughts About a Pussycat, 1975; illustrator: Rehearsal's Off, 1976, Dogs, Henry Morgan and George Booth, 1976, 1,001 Logical Laws, Profound Principles, Trusty Truisms, Homey Homilies, Colorful Corollaries, Quotable Quotes and Rambunctious Ruminations for all Walks of Life, 1979, Pussycats Need Love, Too!, 1981, Omnibooth, 1984, Booth Again!, 1989, Wacky Wednesday, 1974, Possum Come a' Knockin', 1990, Self-Editing for Fiction Writers, 1993, It's Not My Turn to Look for Grandma!, 1995, The Ballymara Flood, 1996, The Essential George Booth, 1999, Who Invited You?, 2002, Cosbyology, 2002. Recipient N.Y. Film Festival Animation award, 1994, Reuben Mag. Cartoon award Nat. Cartoonists Soc., 1994; named Hon. Mem. Class of 1939, Colgate U., 2003. Address: PO Box 1539 Stony Brook NY 11790-0830 E-mail: BoothWorks@aol.com.

BOOTH, GEORGE KEEFER, financial service executive; b. Rockville Centre, N.Y., July 23, 1943; s. David Conover and Nan (Tracy) B.; m. Jeanne Marie Storey, May 12, 1979; 1 child, Sarah. BA, C.W. Post Coll., 1970; MBA, Fordham U., 1973. Asst. cashier Franklin Nat. Bank, N.Y.C., 1970-74; mgr. facilities leverage leasing Gen. Electric Credit Co., Stamford, Conn., 1974-77; corp. mgr. sales fin. Harris Corp., Melbourne, Fla., 1977-83; exec. v.p. Internat. Capital Equipment Co., N.Y.C., 1983-85; exec. v.p., CFO, bd. dirs. Phoenixcor, South Norwalk, Conn., 1985-94; founder, mng. dir. Black Rock Capital LLC, 1994—. Contbr. articles to Leasing Digest, Monitor, ELA. Served with USN, 1967—69. Mem. United Assn. Equipment Lessors, Equipment Leasing Assn. (industry future con. 1982-84, captive com. 1981, acctg. com. 1988), Internat. Assn. Diemaking and Diecutting, Eastern Assn. Equipment Lessors, Am. Mgmt. Assn., KC, Black Rock Yacht Club (Bridgeport, Conn.; past commodore). Republican. Roman Catholic. Home: 41 Grist Mill Ln Southport CT 06890 Office: Black Rock Capital LLC PO Box 416 Fairfield CT 06824 E-mail: gkbooth@blackrockcapital.com.

BOOTH, GORDON DEAN, JR., lawyer; b. Columbus, Ga., June 25, 1939; s. Gordon Dean and Lois Mildred (Bray) B.; m. Katherine Morris Campbell, June 17, 1961; children: Mary Katherine McCormick, Abigail Kilgore Curvino, Sarah Elizabeth, Margaret Campbell, Celecia. BA, Emory U., 1961, JD, 1964, LLM, 1973. Bar: Ga. 1964, D.C. 1977, U.S. Supreme Ct. 1973. Pvt. practice, Atlanta, 1964-96; ptnr. Schreeder, Wheeler & Flint, Atlanta, 1995—. Bd. dirs., v.p. Stallion Music Inc., Nashville, BAA USA, Inc.; trustee, sec. Inst. for Polit. Econ., Washington. Contbr. articles to profl. jours. Trustee Met. Atlanta Crime Commn., 1977-80, chmn., 1979-80; mem. assembly for arts and scis. Emory Coll., 1971-86, chmn., 1983. Mem. Internat. Bar Assn. (coun. sect. bus. law 1974-88, chmn. aero. law com. 1971-86), State Bar Ga., Capital City Club, Piedmont Driving Club, Univ. Club (N.Y.C.), Advocates Club, Sigma Chi. Home: 3226 Paces Mill Rd SE Atlanta GA 30339-3787

BOOTH, HAROLD WAVERLY, lawyer, finance and investment company executive; b. Rochester, N.Y., Aug. 8, 1934; s. Herbert Nixon and Mildred B. (Anderson) B.; m. Flo Rae Spelts, July 4, 1957; children: Rebecca, William, Eva, Harold, Richard. BS, Cornell U., 1955; JD, Duke U., 1961. Bar: Nebr. 1961, Ill. 1967, Iowa 1974; CLU; chartered fin. counselor; cert. fin. planner. Staff atty. Bankers Life Nebr., Lincoln, 1961-67; pres. First Nat. Bank, Council Bluffs, Iowa, 1970-74; exec. v.p., treas. Blue Cross-Blue Shield Ill., Chgo., 1974-77; pres., chief exec. officer, chmn. Bankers Life Nebr., Lincoln, 1977-84; exec. v.p. Colonial Penn Group, Phila., 1985-87; chmn., chief exec. officer VGVR Cos., 1985—. Served to 1st lt. USAF, 1955-58. Fellow Life Mgmt. Inst. (pres. 1981-84); mem. Ins. Fedn. Nebr. (past pres.) Home: 1000 Stony Ln Gladwyne PA 19035-1128

BOOTH, JANE SCHUELE, real estate company executive, real estate broker; b. Cleve. d. Norman Andrew and Frances Ruth (Hankey) Schuele; m. George Warren Booth, Dec. 6, 1968. AA, Stephens Coll., 1946; student, U. Mo., 1946-47. Lic. real estate broker, Fla. Assoc. J.M. Mathes Inc., N.Y.C., 1947-48; dept. supr. Lord and Taylor, Scarsdale, N.Y., 1948-50; art coord. J. Walter Thompson, Inc., N.Y.C., 1953-58; art buyer SSC&B Inc. Advt., N.Y.C., 1959-80; pres. Jane Schuele Booth Realty, Ocala, Fla., 1982—. Mem. Fla. Thoroughbred Fillies, Ocala, 1980—; charter mem., trustee Royal Dames for Cancer Rsch., Inc., Ocala, 1986—; treas. Ladies Aux. Fla. H.C.H. Inc., Ocala, 1986-90; bd. visitors Fla. Horsemen's Children's Home, Inc., 1983-90. Mem. Ocala/Marion County Assn. Realtors, Ocala/Marion County C. of C. (agribus./equine com.), Nat. Assn. Realtors, Fla. Assn. Realtors, Estates Club. Home: 1771 SW 55th Street Rd Ocala FL 34474-5933 Office: PO Box 5538 Ocala FL 34478-5538 E-mail: janeschuelebooth@aol.com.

BOOTH, JOHN NICHOLLS, minister, writer, photographer; b. Meadville, Pa., Aug. 7, 1912; s. Sydney Scott and Margaret (Nicholls) B.; m. Edith Kriger, Oct. 1, 1941 (dec. Sept. 22, 1982), 1 child, Barbara Anne Booth Christie. BA, McMaster U., 1934; MDiv, Meadville/Lombard Theol. Sch., 1942; LittD, New Eng. Sch. Law, 1950. Ordained to ministry Unitarian Ch., 1942. Profl. magician, 1934-40; min. Unitarian Ch., Evanston, Ill., 1942-48, 1st Ch., Belmont, Mass., 1949-57, 2d Ch. (now 1st and 2d Ch.), Boston, 1958-64, Unitarian Ch., Long Beach, Calif., 1964-71; interim pastor N.Y.C., Gainesville, (Fla.), Detroit, 1971-73. Celebrity platform lectr. and performer on conjuring and mentalism, 1942-58; ministerial adviser to liberal students MIT, 1958-63; mem. books selection com. Gen. Theol. Library, Boston, 1960-63. Author: Super Magical Miracles, 1930, Magical Mentalism, 1931, Forging Ahead in Magic, 1939, Marvels of Mystery, 1941, The Quest for Preaching Power, 1943, Fabulous Destinations, 1950, Story of the Second Church in Boston, 1959, The John Booth Classics, 1975, Booths in History, 1982, Psychic Paradoxes, 1984, Wonders of Magic, 1986, Dramatic Magic, 1988, Creative World of Conjuring, 1990, Conjurians' Discoveries, 1992, The Fine Art of Hocus Pocus, 1995, Keys to Magic's Inner World, 1999, Extending Magic Beyond Credibility, 2001; contbr. articles to mags. and newspapers; photographer full length feature travel documentary films for TV, lecture platforms made in India, Africa, S.Am., Indonesia, South Seas, Himalayas; presented first color travelogue on TV in U.S. over NBC in N.Y.C., 1949; panel mem. radio program Churchmen Weigh The News, Boston, 1951-52; spl. corr. in Asia for Chgo. Sun-Times, 1948-49; by-line writer Boston Globe, 1954-66; producer, photographer motion pictures Heart of Africa, 1954, Golden Kingdoms of the Orient, 1957, Indonesia: Pacific Shangri La, 1957, Treasures of the Amazon, Ecuador and Peru, 1960, Adventurous Britain, 1962, South Seas Saga in Tahiti, Australia and New Guinea, summer 1966, The Amazing America of Will Rogers, 1970, Spotlight on Spain, 1975. Co-founder Japan Free Religious Assn., Tokyo, 1948; co-founder Mass. Meml. Soc., 1962, dir., 1962-64; organizer Meml. Soc. Alachua County (Fla.), 1972; pres. Long Beach Mental Health Assn., 1964-66; adv. coun. Fair Housing Found. Recipient John Nevil Maskelyne prize London Magic Cir., 1987; placed on former N.Y. Town Hall Travelogue Cinematographers Wall of Fame, 1967; named Disting. Alumnae, Gallery of McMaster U.; lit. fellow Acad. Magical Arts, 1977, lifetime achievement fellow, 1990, masters fellow, 2001. Mem. Unitarian-Universalist Mins. Assn. (past dir.), Am. Unitarian Assn. (past com. chmn.), Unitarian Mins. Pacific S.W. Assn. (v.p.), Clergy Counseling Svc. So. Calif., Soc. Am. Magicians (inducted into Hall of Fame 1983), Magic Castle Hollywood, Internat. Brotherhood Magicians (hon. life), L.A. Adventurers Club (pres. 1983), Evanston (Ill.) Ministerial Assn. (pres. 1947-48). Achievements include having the first regularly scheduled TV broadcasts in U.S. by clergyperson, WBKB, Chgo., mid-1940s. Home and Office: 12032 Montecito Rd Los Alamitos CA 90720-4511 *Success often greets an imaginative, innovative approach to that which has been done in a settled way too long. An ability to time change properly and accept philosophically that which does not yield is to live maturely with one's own struggles and hopes. Bertrand Russell guides wisely in suggesting that a person living in a spirit that aims at creating rather than possessing has a certain fundamental happiness. Such a way of life is thereby freed from the tyranny of fear, since what one values most in one's existence is not at the mercy of outside power.*

BOOTH, JOHN THOMAS, investment banker; b. N.Y.C., Oct. 21, 1929; s. John E. and Katherine (Keeler) B.; m. Anne C. Mott, Feb. 26, 1960; children: Alison Booth Cramer, Miven Booth Trageser, Roxanna Booth Cistulli. Grad. cum laude, Deerfield Acad., 1947; BA cum laude, Amherst Coll., 1951; LLB, Harvard U., 1957. Bar: N.Y. 1957. Assoc. firm Dewey Ballantine Bushby Palmer & Wood, N.Y.C., 1957-61; mem. buying dept. Eastman Dillon, Union Securities & Co., N.Y.C., 1961—, ptnr., 1963—; exec. v.p., dir. Blyth Eastman Dillon & Co., Inc., 1972-81; chmn. bd. Eastdil Realty, Inc., 1979-81, Am. Health Capital, Inc., 1982-86, Am. Health Capital Ventures, Inc., 1986-89; chmn. Franklin Venture Capital Inc., 1990-97, Greystone Communities, Inc., 1990—, Coleman, Swenson, Booth, Inc., 1997—. Bd. dirs. Wells Hill Ptnrs. Ltd., Litchfield Bancorp; adv. bd. Saugatuck Capital, Inc.; dir., mem. Eli Whitney investment adv. bd. Conn. Innovations, Inc.; asst. to dir. Harvard Def. Studies Program, 1956-57; counsel N.Y. State Assembly Com. on N.Y.C., 1960, Com. on Judiciary, 1961. Trustee Litchfield Hist. Soc., White Meml. Found.; mem. major gifts com. Capital Program for Amherst Coll., mem. Litchfield H.S. scholarship com. Lt. (j.g.) USNR, 1951-54. Mem. Newcomen Soc., Pilgrim Soc., Delta Kappa Epsilon, Delta Sigma Rho. Clubs: Links, University (N.Y.C.); Litchfield (Conn.) Country. Republican. Episcopalian. Office: Box 25 182 Whites Wood Rd Litchfield CT 06759-0025

BOOTH, LINDA LEIGH, vocational educator, homemaker; b. Dallas, May 12, 1953; d. Federico Rose and Gladys Ruth (Petty) Buenrostro; m. Joe Henry Booth Jr., May 24, 1985; children: Kathryn Leigh, Elizabeth Rose. BS in Home Econs., Abilene Christian U., 1985. Instr. Abilene (Tex.) Ind. Sch. Dist., 1988-99; instr. in family and consumer sci. Memphis City Schs., 2001—02. Mem. edn. vocat. adv. bd. Abilene Ind. Sch. Dist., Abilene, 1991-99, mem. textbook selection com., 1990-91. Judge Future Homemakers of Am., Abilene, 1987—88; mem. citizens rev. panel ofr child care United Way Abilene, 1997, 1998; trainer Girl Scout Coun. of Mid-South, 0199—; troop leader Girl Scouts of USA, 1997—; mem. children's ministries com. U. Ch. of Christ, 1993, co-dir. children's worship; co-dir. Children's Worship and Presch. Bible Hour, 1998; share time leader Sycamore View Ch. of Christ Children's Ministries, 2001—, tchr. bible camp jr. week, 2001—. Mem. Am. Vocat. Assn., Tex. Vocat. Spl. Needs Assn., Vocat. Home Econs. Tchrs. Assn. of Tex. (alt. dir. 1996-98), Tex. Restaurant Assn., Abilene Restaurant Assn., Tex. Classroom Tchrs. Assn., Assn. Tex. Profl. Educators (faculty campus rep. 1997-99, state conf. del.), Memphis Area Home Edn. Assn., Hospitality Educators Assn. Tex., Future Homemakers Am. Avocations: reading, gardening, sewing, home improvements, counted cross-stitch. Home: 2237 Goldbrier Ln Memphis TN 38134-5953

BOOTH, MITCHELL B. lawyer; b. N.Y.C., June 26, 1927; s. Samuel and Rose (Waxman) B.; m. Barbara C. Ribman, July 13, 1952; 1 son, Brian S. AB, Clark U., 1949; JD, N.Y. U., 1952. Bar: N.Y. 1952. Assoc. I. Moldauer, N.Y.C., 1952-54, Sol A. Rosenblatt, N.Y.C., 1954-67; pvt. practice law N.Y.C., 1967—. Minority counsel joint legis. com. unsatisfied judgments N.Y., 1958-59, joint legis. com. preservation restoration hist. sites N.Y., 1960-64; med. malpractice mediator First Jud. Dept. Supreme Ct. State N.Y., 1980-91; bd. dirs., treas. East Hampton Mews Tenants Corp., Burgos Art Galleries Ltd., Dorolyat Corp. Asst. to chmn. Dem. law com., N.Y. County, 1961-65; rep. admissions for states of N.Y., N.J. and Conn. Clark U., 1968-71. Served to lt. USNR, 1945-46, 49-83. Mem. ABA, N.Y. State Bar Assn., Assn. of Bar of City of N.Y. (mem. com. profl. discipline 1986-89), N.Y. Commandry, Mil. Order Fgn. Wars U.S. (life, judge advocate), Univ. Club. Home: 75 E End Ave New York NY 10028-7909 Office: 111 W 57th St Ste 1120 New York NY 10019

BOOTH, PENELOPE PARTRIDGE, educator, school principal, author; b. Niskayuna, N.Y., Dec. 7, 1943; d. Leonard Charlton and Elizabeth Jane (Russ) Partridge; m. John Robert Booth, Sept. 10, 1966 (div. 1975); children: Elizabeth Ashley, Patricia Anne. BS in Math., Mary Washington Coll., 1965; MEd, Towson State U., 1981. Comml. supr. Chesapeake & Potomac Telephone Co., Washington, 1965-66, Richmond, Va., 1967-68; math. tchr. Havelock (N.C.) High Sch., 1966-67, Jack Jouett Jr. High Sch., Charlottesville, Va., 1968-70, Baltimore County Pub. Schs., Towson, Md., 1974-81, supr. math., 1987-93; prin. Catonsville (Md.) Middle Sch., 1993-96; tchr. gifted and talented resource Office Of Math., Towson, 1981-84; chmn. math. dept. Hereford Mid. Sch., Monkton, Md., 1984-87; coord. office of maths. Baltimore County Pub. Schs., 1996—. Instr. Baltimore county Pub. Schs., 1976-88, Md. Acad. Scis., Balt., 1984-86, Inst. for the Gifted Talented, Towson, 1983-85; cons. Md. State Dept. Edn., Balt., 1981—, Sylvan Learning, 2002-; adj. prof. Johns Hopkins U., 1996—, Coll. Notre Dame Md., 1997—, Loyola Coll. Md., 2002-; co-owner Conversation Pieces, 1997—. Author: Essentials of Mathematics, 1988, Consumer Mathematics, 1988, Foundations of Algebra and Geometry, 1998, (booklet) First Book of Testing. Adult leader troop 336, Girl Scouts U.S.A., Towson, 1972-88; mem. Lutherville (Md.) Recreation Coun., 1979-89; cons. Md. Math. League, 1982-87; chmn., co-founder Christa McAuliffe Scholarship Found., 1986—; mem. alumni adv. coun. Towson State U.; mem. adv. bd. MAT Program Johns Hopkins U., 1992-2002. Recipient Presdl. award NSF, 1985, Disting. Alumni award Towson State U., 1989, Educator of Yr. award Md. Coun. Tchrs. of Maths., 2002. Mem. ASCD, Nat. Coun. Suprs. Math. (sec.-treas. Md. coun. 2000—), Nat. Coun. Tchrs. Math., Coun. Presdl. Awardees (scholarship chmn.), Optimists, Phi Delta Kappa, Delta Kappa Gamma (v.p.) Republican. Presbyterian. Avocations: traveling, needlepoint. Home: 135 Greenridge Rd Lutherville Timonium MD 21093-6124 E-mail: pbooth@bcps.org.

BOOTH, RACHEL ZONELLE, nursing educator; b. Seneca, S.C., Feb. 10, 1936; m. Richard B. Booth, Feb. 13, 1957; 1 child, Kevin M. Student, Furman U., 1953-54; diploma in nursing, Greenville (S.C.) Gen. Hosp., 1956; student, U. Alaska, 1964-66; BS in Nursing, U. Md., Balt., 1968; MS in Nursing, U. Md., 1970, PhD in Adminstrn. Higher Edn., 1978; D of Nursing Sci. (hon.), Chiang Mai U., Thailand, 1999. RN. Staff nurse VA Hosp., Murfreesboro, Tenn., 1956-57, U. Colo. Med. Ctr., Denver, 1957-58; nurse psychiatry dept. Patton State Hosp., Calif., 1958-59; staff nurse USAF Dispensary, Iraklion, Greece, 1959-60; charge nurse psychiatry Santa Rose Med. Ctr., San Antonio, 1961; staff nurse Shannon S.W. Tex. Meml. Hosp., San Angelo, 1962; supervisory clin. nurse, head nurse U.S. Dept. Health, Edn., and Welfare/USPHS/Indian Health Service, Anchorage, 1962-66; staff nurse U.S. Dept. Health, Edn., and Welfare/USPHS, Balt., 1966, 68; assoc. dir. dept. nursing U. Md. Hosp., 1970-76, dir. primary care nursing svc., 1976-81; asst. prof. Sch. Nursing U. Md., 1972-76, asst. prof. Sch. Pharmacy, 1972-80, acting assoc. dean Sch. Nursing, 1979-81, assoc. prof. Sch. Nursing, 1979, assoc. prof. clin. pharmacy, 1980-83, assoc. dean for undergrad. studies Sch. Nursing, 1981-83, co-dir. nurse practitioner program Sch. Nursing, 1972-76, chairperson grad. program dept. primary care, 1974-79; dean, Sch. of Nursing and asst. v.p. for health affairs Duke U., Durham, N.C., 1984-87; dean Sch. Nursing U. Ala. at Birmingham, University Station, 1987—. Instr. Sch. Medicine U. Md., 1972-83, program dir. primary care nurse practitioner program continuing edn., 1976-82, project dir. Robert Wood Johnson Nurse Faculty Fellowship program, 1977-82; mem. joint practice com. Med. and Surg. Faculty Md., 1974-77, mem. tech. adv. com. for physician's assts. Bd. Med. Examiners Md., 1975-80; mem. adv. com. nursing program Community Coll. Balt., 1976-79; mem. Joint Commn. on Accreditation of Hosps., pres. Md. Council Dirs. of Assoc. Degree, Diploma, and Baccalaureate Programs, 1982-83; mem. adv. bd. nursing Essex Community Coll., 1983; mem. peer rev. panel advanced nurse edn. nursing div. U.S. Dept. Health and Human Services, 1987—. Editor (with others) Hospital Pharmacy, 1971-72; asst. editor Jour. Profl. Nursing, 1984-87; contbr. articles on nursing to prof. jours. Bd. dirs. Health and Welfare Coun. Ctrl. Md., Inc., 1974-78, v.p., 1975-78; mem. health adv. com. to Pres. of Pakistan, 1981—. Recipient numerous grants for nursing adminstrn., 1972—. Mem. ANA (mem. nat. rev. com. 1975-78, v.p. 1977, chair 1978), Internat. Coun. Nurses (observer conf. 1981), Nat. Acad. Practice for Nursing (vice chairperson 1984-89), Nat. Orgn. for Nurse Execs., Nat. League for Nursing, Coun. Nat. Acad. Practice, Am. Assn. Colls. in Nursing (dean's summer seminar com. 1984-85, edn. and credentialing com. 1985-86, nominating com. 1986-87, bd. dirs. 1989-96, pres.-elect 1992-94, pres. 1994-96), N.C. Orgn. Nurse Execs. (bd. dirs. 1986-87), So. Coun. Collegiate Edn. for Nursing (exec. com. 1986-91, v.p., bd. dirs. 1991-94, pres. 1997-99), Sigma Theta Tau (chairperson nominating com. 1974, mem. 1975, rec. sec. 1980-83). Avocations: genealogy, travel, swimming. Office: U Ala at Birmingham 1530 3rd Ave S Birmingham AL 35294-0002

BOOTH, ROBERT ALAN, artist, educator; b. Mt. Kisco, N.Y., Apr. 22, 1952; s. George Warren and Ellen (Cooley) B. BFA, Mass. Coll. Art, 1976; MFA, Syracuse U., 1978. Prof. visual arts SUNY, Fredonia, 1978—, dept. chmn., 1988-96. Lectr. coll. and univ. art programs. Numerous exhbns. Faculty Rsch. Fellow SUNY 1982, 83; grantee Ford Found. Syracuse U., 1977, 78. Mem.: Mid. Am. Coll. Art Assn. (bd. dirs. 1999—2003), Internat. Sculpture Ctr. Democrat. Home: 3197 Route 83 Fredonia NY 14063-9784 E-mail: booth@fredonia.edu.

BOOTH, ROBERT WARD, lawyer; b. Chgo., June 21, 1918; s. Robert N. and Florence E. (Ward) Booth; m. Elizabeth V. Engelhardt, Oct. 17, 1943; children: Elizabeth A. (Poor), Barbara S. (Goesel). BS, U. Ill., Urbana, 1939; JD, 1941. Bar: Ill. 1941. Atty. Internat. Harvester Co., Chgo., 1946—63; asst. gen. atty., 1963—65; gen. atty., 1965; assoc. gen. atty., 1965—80; v.p., asso. gen. atty., 1980—83; v.p. law, 1983—; mem. lawyers coun. Machinery & Allied Products Inst., 1981; mem. adv. bd. Southwestern Legal Found., 1981—. Capt. USAAF, 1942—46. Mem.: Chgo. bar Assn., Ill. State Bar Assn., ABA, U. Ill. Coll.

Commerce and Bus. Adminstrn., Chgo. Heights (Ill.)Pub. Libr. Bd., Chgo-Kent Bd. Overseers, Chgo. Crime Commn., Chgo. Better Bus. Bur., Olympia Fields Country, Chgo. Heights Country. Republican. Presbyn.

BOOTH, STEPHEN WALTER, English language educator; b. N.Y.C., Apr. 20, 1933; s. Frank and Ruth Joan (Friedman) B.; m. Susan Patek, June 20, 1959; children: Jason Michael, Mary. AB, Harvard U., 1955, PhD, 1964; BA, Cambridge (Eng.) U., 1957; LHD, Georgetown U., 1991. Asst. prof. U. Calif., Berkeley, 1962-69, assoc. prof., 1969-74, prof., 1974—. Author: An Essay on Shakespeare's Sonnets, 1969, paperback, 1972, The Book Called Holinshed's Chronicles, 1969, Shakespeare's Sonnets, Edited with Analytic Commentary, 1977, rev. edit., 1978, paperback, 1979, King Lear, Macbeth, Indefinition and Tragedy, 1983, (pamphlet) Liking Julius Caesar, 1991, Precous Nonsense: The Gettysburg Address, Ben Jonson's Epitaphs on His Chidren, and Twelfth Night, 1998; mem. editorial bd. S.E.L., 1978—, Assays, 1979—, Mississippi Studies in English, 1979—, Shakespeare Quar., 1981—. Decorated Order Brit. Empire; recipient Marshall scholarship British govt., Cambridge, 1955-57; Guggenheim fellow, 1970-71. Mem. MLA (James Russell Lowell prize 1978). Democrat. Episcopalian. Home: 98 The Uplands Berkeley CA 94705-2815 Office: Univ of Calif Dept English 322 Wheeler Hall Berkeley CA 94720-1030

BOOTH, WAYNE CLAYSON, English literature and rhetoric educator, author; b. American Fork, Utah, Feb. 22, 1921; s. Wayne Chipman and Lillian (Clayson) B.; m. Phyllis Barnes, June 19, 1946; children: Katherine, John Richard (dec.), Alison. AB, Brigham Young U., 1944; MA, U. Chgo., 1947, PhD, 1950; DLitt (hon.), Rockford Coll., 1965, St. Ambrose Coll., 1971, U. N.H., 1977; DHL (hon.), Butler U., 1984, Lycoming Coll., 1985, SUNY, 1987, Wabash Coll., 1990; DHL (hon.), Kalamazoo Coll., 1991; DHL (hon.), Ball State U., 1992; DHL (hon.), DePaul U., 1994; DHL (hon.), Earlham Coll., 1995, Carleton Coll., 1995, Villanova U., 2002. Instr. U. Chgo., 1947-50; asst. prof. Haverford Coll., 1950-53; prof. English, chmn. dept. Earlham Coll., 1953-62; George M. Pullman prof. English U. Chgo., 1962-91, dean Coll., 1964-69, prof. emeritus, 1992—, chmn. com. on ideas and methods, 1972-75. Vis. cons. (with wife) South African schs. and univs., 1963; Amnesty Internat. lectr. Oxford U., 1992. Author: The Rhetoric of Fiction, 1961 (Christian Gauss prize Phi Beta Kappa, 1962, David H. Russell award Nat. Coun. Tchrs. English, 1966), Now Don't Try To Reason With Me: Essays and Ironies for a Credulous Age, 1970, A Rhetoric of Irony, 1974, Modern Dogma and the Rhetoric of Assent, 1974, Critical Understanding: The Powers and Limits of Pluralism, 1979 (Laing prize, 1981), The Company We Keep: An Ethics of Fiction, 1988; author: (with M. Gregory) Harper & Row Reader, 1984; author: The Vocation of a Teacher: Rhetorical Occasions, 1967-88, 1988, The Art of Growing Older, 1992; author: (with J. Williams and Gregory Colomb) The Craft of Research, 1997, 2003; author: For the Love of It: Amateuring and Its Rivals, 1999; editor: The Knowledge Most Worth Having, 1967; co-editor: Critical Inquiry, 1974—85. Trustee Earlham Coll., 1965-75. Served with inf. AUS, 1944-46. Recipient Disting. Alumni award Brigham Young U., 1975, Lifetime Achievement award Assn. for Mormon Letters, 1995, Lifetime Achievement award Conf. on Christianity and Literature, 1995, Quantrell prize for undergrad. tchg. U. Chgo., 1971, lifetime tchg. award, 1997, award for contbns. to edn. Am. Assn. Higher Edn., 1986; Ford Faculty fellow, 1952-53, Guggenheim fellow, 1956-57, 69-70, NEH fellow, 1975-76, Rockefeller Found. fellow, 1981-82; Phi Beta Kappa vis. scholar, 1977-78. Fellow Am. Acad. Arts and Scis., Am. Philos. Soc.; mem. MLA (exec. coun. 1973-76, pres. 1981-92, Francis Andrew March award for Disting. Svc. of Profession of English 1991), Coll. Conf. on Composition and Comm., Nat. Commn. on Educating Undergrads. in Rsch. Univs. Democrat. Mem. Lds Ch. Home: 5411 S Greenwood Ave Chicago IL 60615-5103

BOOTHBY, LISA ANNE, pharmacist, drug information specialist; b. L.I., May 11, 1969; d. Vincent Joseph Muscarnera and Virginia Margaret McCarthy; m. David Charles Boothby, Jan. 28, 1995; children: Joshua, David. PharmD, U. Fla., 2000; BA, New Coll. Fla., 1993; A in Sci., Suffolk Coll., Selden, N.Y., 1991. Accredited drug info. practice residency ASHP, bd. cert. pharmacology specialist. Tchg. asst. New Coll., Sarasota, Fla., 1993; substance abuse counselor First Step of Sarasota, 1994; drug info. practice resident Columbus (Ga.) Regional Healthcare Sys., 2000—01; drug info. coord. Columbus Regional Healthcare Sys., 2001—; affiliate clin. asst. prof. Auburn (Ala.) U. Harrison Sch. Pharmacy, 2001—; preceptor drug info. clerkship U. of Ga. Coll. Pharmacy, Athens, 2001—. Dist. dir. Ga. Soc. of Health Sys. Pharmacists, Columbus, Ga., 2001—; adj. clin. asst. prof. Mercer U. So. Sch. Pharmacy, Atlanta, 2001—. Editor: GSHP Newsletter, 2002—; contbr. articles to profl. jours. (Nat. Hosp. Pharmacy Quality award, 2001). Mentor Ptnrs. in Edn. Clubview Elem. Sch., Columbus, 2001—02. Recipient Outstanding Newsletter, Ga. Soc. of Health Sys. Pharmacists, 2000, 2d pl. Advances in Drug Info., Facts and Comparisons, 2000; grantee Undergraduate Rsch. grantee, NIH, 1997, NSF, 1992. Mem.: Ga. Soc. Health Sys. Pharmacists, Am. Soc. of Health Sys. Pharmacists, Am. Coll. of Clin. Pharmacy, Am. Pharm. Assn., U. of Fla. Alumni Assn., Kappa Epsilon (chaplain 1997—98). Democrat. Roman Catholic. Avocation: music. Home: 6219 Canterbury Dr Columbus GA 31909 Office: Columbus Regional Healthcare Sys 710 Center St Columbus GA 31902 Home Fax: 706-571-1625; Office Fax: 706-571-1625. Personal E-mail: lisaboothby@yahoo.com. E-mail: lisa.boothby@crhs.net.

BOOTHBY, WILLARD SANDS, III, bank executive; b. N.Y.C., Nov. 18, 1946; s. Willard Sands Jr. and Florence (Clifford) B.; m. Linda Kent, Sept. 8, 1973; children: Elizabeth, Willy. BA, Princeton U., 1969; MBA, Harvard U., 1972. Asst. treas. Morgan Guaranty Trust Co., N.Y.C., 1975-78, asst. v.p., 1978-80, v.p., 1980-86, sr. v.p., mng. dir., 1986-2000, vice chmn. investment banking, 2000—. Mem.: River (N.Y.C.). Office: 277 Park Ave Fl 15 New York NY 10172-0003 Fax: 646-534-1770.

BOOTHBY, WILLIAM MUNGER, mathematics educator; b. Detroit, Apr. 1, 1918; s. Thomas Franklin and Florence (Munger) B.; m. Ruth Robin, June 8, 1947; children— Daniel, Thomas, Mark. AB, U. Mich., 1941, MA, 1942, PhD, 1949. Mem. faculty Northwestern U., Evanston, Ill., 1948-59; fellow Am.-Swiss Found. for Sci. Exchange, Swiss Fed. Inst. Tech., Zurich, 1950-51; assoc. prof. Washington U., St. Louis, 1959-62, prof. math., 1962-88, ret., 1988—. NSF sr. postdoctoral fellow Inst. for Advanced Study, Princeton, N.J., 1961-62, U. Geneva, Switzerland, 1965-66; professeur associe U. Strasbourg, France, 1971, 77 Author: Introduction to Differentiable Manifolds and Riemannian Geometry; co-editor: Symmetric Spaces; contbr. articles to profl. jours. Served with USAAF, 1942-46. Mem. Am., London math. Socs., Math. Assn. Am., Soc. Indsl. and Applied Math., Sigma Xi. Home: 6954 Cornell Ave Saint Louis MO 63130-3128 Office: Washington U Dept Math Saint Louis MO 63130-4899

BOOTHE, LEON ESTEL, academic administrator emeritus, consultant; b. Carthage, Mo., Feb. 1, 1938; s. Harold Estel and Merle Jane (Hood) B.; m. Nancy Janes, Aug. 20, 1960 (dec. Jan. 1997); children: Cynthia, Diana and Cheri (twins); m. Karen Ball, Nov. 11, 2000. BS (Curators' scholar), U. Mo., 1960, MA, 1962; PhD in History, U. Ill., 1966; LLD, Kyung Hee U., Korea, St. Thomas Inst. Advanced Study, 1985, Hebrew Union Coll., 1994. Tchr. history Valparaiso (Ind.) H.S., 1960-61; asst. prof. history U. Miss., Oxford, 1965-68, assoc. prof., 1968-70; assoc. prof. history George Mason Coll., U. Va. (now George Mason U.), Fairfax, 1970-73, prof. history, 1973-80, assoc. dean, 1970-71, dean, 1971-72, dean coll. arts and scis., 1972-80; provost, v.p. acad. affairs Ill. State U., Normal, 1980-83; pres. No. Ky. U., Highland Heights, 1983-96, pres. emeritus, 1996—; sr. advisor Nat. Underground R.R. Freedom Ctr., 1997-2000; prof. history No. Ky. U., 1983—. Bd. dirs. Fifth Third Bank No. Ky.; chmn. Am. Assn. of State Colls. and Univs., 1993; bd. dirs. Commn. on Internat. Edn. of Am. Coun. Edn., Nat. Underground Railroad Freedom Ctr., exec. com., 2001. Former mem. adv. bd. Cin. Coun. World Affairs; trustee Cin.-Kharkiv Project, hon. mem., 1995-96; bd. dirs. Met. YMCA, Cinn., 1984—, Met. Cin. chpt. ARC, former mem., McLean County Heart Assn., McLean County United Way, INROADS/Cin., Inc., NCCJ, 1983—, Cin.'s Enjoy the Arts, 1988-90, Cin. Music Festival, Cin. Nat. Classical Music Hall Fame, Cin. Ballet, 1999—, No. Ky. U. Found., Sr. Citizens No. Ky., 1996—, May Festival, 1998—; vice chmn. No. Ky. United Way, chmn., 1988; Greater Cin. YMCA; mem. steering com. Cin. Bicentennial; chmn. Multiple Sclerosis Soc. Gifts Campaign; mem. steering and exec. coms. Cin. Youth Collaborative; co-chair blue ribbon econ. devel. study No. Ky. Area Devel. Dist.; mem. Leukemia Soc.; bd. dirs. Greater Cin. Conv. and Visitors Bur., 1989—, Kids Helping Kids, 1998—, Merc. Libr., 1998—, Festival of Arts, 1998—; bd. dirs., mem. exec. com., vice-chair cmty. edn. svcs., 1989-90, Cin. chpt. ARC, Wood Hudson Cancer Rsch. Lab. Inc., 1987-92; chmn. Ky. Bicentennial Com., 1990, chmn. steering com., 1992; chmn. Leadership Ky. Class; trustee Greater Cin. United Way and Cmty. Chest, 1991; steering com. greater Cin. summit on racism, 1994; sr. advisor Nat. Underground Railroad freedom Ctr., 1997; mem. Underground R.R. Freedom Ctr. Bd., 2000—; former bd. dirs. Am. Music Scholarship Assn., Cin. Scholarship Found., Leadership Ky. Found.; lifetime advisor to pres. Nat. Coun. for Cmty. and Justice; advisor Cin. Hispanic C. of C.; bd. dirs. Sr. Svcs. of No. Ky., 1996. NEH fellow, 1967-68; scholar Diplomat Seminars Dept. State; recipient Coll. Liberal Arts and Scis. award U. Ill., 1988, Alumni Coun. Pres.'s Spl. Recognition award No. Ky. U., 1989, Alumni award U. Mo., 1989, Walter R. Dunlevey Frontiersman award, 1994, Disting. Citizens Citation award NCCJ, Disting. Pub. Svc. award No. Ky. U. Found., 1995, Character award YMCA, 1997, Kinsman award Urban Appalachian Coun., 1998, Pres. award Pub. Rels. Soc., 2000, Lighthouse Beacon Light award, 2001. Mem. Soc. Historians for Am. Fgn. Rels., McLean County Assn. for Commerce and Industry, Am. Assn. State Colls. and Univs. (internat. programs com. 1986-94), No. Ky. C. of C. (Walter R. Dunlevey-Frontierman award 1994), Greater Cin. C. of C. (asst. sec.-treas. 1989-93), Rotary, Masons, Leon Boothe Soc. (svc. award No. Ky. 2002), Sigma Rho Sigma, Omicron Delta Kappa, Phi Alpha Theta, Phi Delta Kappa. Home: 1378 Collinsdale Ave Cincinnati OH 45230-2308 E-mail: boothel@nku.edu.

BOOTHROYD, GEOFFREY, industrial and manufacturing engineering educator; b. Radcliffe, Eng., Nov. 18, 1932; arrived in U.S., 1967; s. Arthur and Annie (Fletcher) Boothroyd; m. Shirley Lewis, Apr. 10, 1954; children: Janet Kaye, Lynda Jean. BS in Engring., U. London, 1956, PhD in Engring., 1962, DSc in Engring., 1974. Apprentice Mather & Platt Ltd., Manchester, 1948—56, designer, 1956—57, English Electric Co. Ltd., Leicester, England, 1957—58; lectr., reader Salford (Eng.) U., 1958—67; prof. U. Mass., Amherst, 1967—85, U. R.I., Kingston, 1985—97, prof. emeritus. Vis. prof. Ga. Inst. Tech., Atlanta, 1964—65; cons. mfg. industries U.K. and U.S., also various pubs.; pres. Boothroyd Dewhurst, Inc. Author: Fundamentals of Metal Machining, 1965; author: (with A.H. Redford) Mechanized Assembly (Japanese edit. 1969), 1968; author: Fundamentals of Metal Machining and Machine Tools (Spanish 1978, internat. student edit. 1979), 1975; co-author: Introduction to Engineering, 1975; author (with C.R. Poli): Applied Engineering Mechanics, 1980; author: (with C.R. Poli, L.E. Murch) Automatic Assembly, 1986; author: Handbook of Feeding and Orienting Techniques for Small Parts; author: (with L. Alting) Manufacturing Engineering Processes, 1982; author: (with P. Dewhurst) Design for Assembly Handbook, Design for Robot Assembly, 1985; author: (with W.A. Knight) Metal Machining and Machine Tools, 1991; author: Assembly Automation and Product Design, 1992; author: (with P. Dewhurst and W.A. Knight) Product Design for Manufacture and Assembly, 1994. Recipient Teaching award, Western Electric, 1969, Sr. Scholar award, U. Mass., 1982, Sci. and Tech. award, R.I. Gov., 1989, Nat. medal of Technology, U.S. Dept. Commerce Technology Admin., 1991, Providence Engring. Soc., 1991, U.K. Mensforth Internat. Gold medal, IEE, 1993; grantee NSF, 1967—87, GE, 1967, 1969, 1981, 1983, AMP Inc, 1978, 1981—84, IBM, 1983—85, AT&T, 1985, Ford Motor Co., 1984, 1986. Fellow: Soc. Mfg. Engrs.; mem.: NAE. Avocation: squash, tennis, golf, painting.. Office: Boothroyd Dewhurst Inc 138 Main St Ste 2 Wakefield RI 02879-3574 E-mail: gboothroyd@dfma.com.

BOOTHROYD, HERBERT J. insurance company executive; b. Mason City, Iowa, Dec. 23, 1928; s. Herbert L. and Clara (Schmitt) B.; m. Barbara Elizabeth Dunne, Feb. 9, 1961; children: Diane Lea, John Herbert. AB, U. Mich., 1952, AM, 1953. Enrolled actuary, 1976. With Mass. Mut. Life Ins. Co., 1953-57; with New Eng. Mut. Life Ins. Co., Boston, 1957-87, v.p., 1967-77, sr. v.p. pension ops., 1977-82, exec. v.p. group ops., 1983-87; dir. New Eng. Pension and Annuity Co., 1980-87, pres., 1981-87; pres., dir. New Eng. Gen. Life, 1983-85. Dir. New Eng. Mut. Life Ins. Co., 1984-87, New Eng. Variable Life Ins. Co., 1984-97. Author: (book) Hammett Families, 1983, Cockrill Families of No. Virginia, 2002; contbg. author: Life and Health Insurance Handbook, 1973. Bd. dirs. New Eng. chpt. Am. Diabetes Assn., 1979-84; bd. govs. Handel and Haydn Soc., 1984-94, sec., 1986-94, overseer, 1994—; mem. nat. campaign com. U. Mich., 1983-90; bd. dirs. Better Bus. Bur. Ea. Mass., 1980-88, vice chmn., mem. exec. com., 1985-88. Fellow Soc. Actuaries; mem. SAR, Am. Acad. Actuaries, Internat. Congress Actuaries, New Eng. Hist. Geneal. Soc., Ky. Hist. Soc., U. Mich. Alumni Assn. (v.p. 1st dist. 1989-91, pres. 1991-93, nat. bd. dirs. 1997-2000, chair nat. clubs coun. 1999-2000), Phi Beta Kappa, Theta Delta Chi. Home and Office: 4205 SW 96th Dr Gainesville FL 32608 E-mail: herbbooth@aol.com.

BOOTY, JOHN EVERITT, emeritus educator; b. Detroit, May 2, 1925; s. George Thomas and Alma (Gamauf) B.; m. Catherine Louise Smith, June 10, 1950; children: Carol Holland, Geoffrey Rollen, Peter Thomas, Catherine Jane. BA, Wayne State U., 1952; B.D., Va. Theol. Sem., 1953, DD, 1994, U. of the South, 1997; MA, Princeton U., 1957, PhD, 1960. Ordained to ministry Episcopal Ch., 1953. Curate Christ Episcopal Ch., Dearborn, Mich., 1953-55; asst. prof. ch. history Va. Theol. Sem., 1958-64, assoc. prof., 1964-67; prof. ch. history Episcopal Theol. Sch., Cambridge, Mass., 1967-82; acting dir. Inst. Theol. Rsch., 1974-76; dean Sch. Theology U. of South, Sewanee, Tenn., 1982-85, prof. Anglican studies, 1984-90, prof. emeritus, 1990—, historiographer Episc. Ch., 1988-99. Vis. prof., rsch. Yale Div. Sch., 1985-86; Disting. vis. prof. Episcopal Divinity Sch., 1990-91, prof. emeritus, 1991—; vis. prof. Anglican studies Gen. Theol. Seminary, 1992; Trotter vis. prof. Va. Theol. Sem., 1993, 98. Author: John Jewel as Apologist of the Church of England, 1963, Yearning to be Free, 1974, Three Anglican Divines on Prayer: Jewel, Andrewes, and Hooker, 1978, The Church in History, 1979, 2d edit., 2003, The Spirit of Anglicanism, 1979, The Godly Kingdom of Tudor England, 1981, The Servant Church, 1982, What Makes Us Episcopalians, 1982, Anglican Spirituality, 1982, Meditating on Four Quarters, 1983, 2d edit., 2003, Anglican Moral Choice, 1983, The Christ We Know, 1987, The Episcopal Church in Crisis, 1988, Mission and Ministry: A History of the Virginia Theological Seminary, 1996, An American Apostle: A Biography of Stephen F. Bayne, 1997, Reflections on the Theology of Richard Hooker: An Elizabethan Addresses Modern Anglicanism, 1999; editor: The Book of Common Prayer, 1559: The Elizabeth Prayer Book, 1976, John Jewel: The Apology of the Church of England, 1963, 74, 2002, John Donne: Divine Poems, Sermons, Meditations and Prayers, 1990, The Works of Richard Hooker, vol. 4, 1982; co-editor, contbr.: The Study of Anglicanism, 1988; contbr. articles to profl. jours. Chmn. Nat. Youth Commn., P.F. Ch., 1948-50; chmn. bd. St. Luke's Jour. Theology, 1987-91, Sewanee Theol. Rev., 1991-99. Recipient Am. Philos. Soc. award, 1964; Folger Shakespeare Libr. fellow, 1964, NEH fellow, 1978-79 Mem. Soc. for Promoting Christian Knowledge (vice chmn. 1984-87). Home: 612 Mt Israel Rd Center Sandwich NH 03227-3710

BOOTY, MICHAEL RICHARD, mathematician educator; b. London, Aug. 12, 1957; came to the U.S., 1984; s. Maurice John and Drusilla Fraser (Bryan) B. MA, Trinity Coll., Cambridge, Eng., 1978, part III math. tripos, 1978-79; diploma, PhD, Imperial Coll., London, 1982. Overseas rsch. fellow Sci. & Engring. Rsch. Coun., U.K., 1982-84; rsch. fellow Northwestern U., Evanston, Ill., 1984-87; asst. prof. So. Meth. U., Dallas, 1987-93; assoc. prof. N.J. Inst. Tech., Newark, 1993—. Contbr. articles to profl. jours. Grantee NSF, State of N.J., State of Tex. Mem. Soc. for Indsl. and Applied Math., Am. Phys. Soc.

BOOZ, GRETCHEN ARLENE, marketing executive; b. Boone, Iowa, Nov. 24, 1933; d. David Gerald and Katherine Bevridge (Hardie) Berg; m. Donald Rollett Booz, Sept. 3, 1960; children: Kendra Sue (dec.), Joseph David, Katherine Sue. AA, Graceland Coll., 1955. Med. asst. Robert A. Hayne M.D., Des Moines, 1955-61; mktg. dir. Herald Pub. House, Independence, Mo., 1975—. Author: (book) Kendra, 1979. Mem. Citizens Adv. Bd., Blue Springs, Mo., 1979-91, Independence Mayor's Christmas Concert Com., 1987-91; bd. dirs. Comprehensive Mental Health, 1981-83, Child Placement Svcs., Independence, 1987-94, Hope House, Inc., Independence, 1987-91, Ctr. for Profl. Devel. and Life-long Learning, Inc., 1995-96; trustee Graceland U., Lamoni, Iowa, 1984-96. Mem. Leadership Edn. Action Devel. (L.E.A.D.), Independence C. of C. (diplomat, Outstanding Mem. award 1981), Rotary. Republican. Mem. Community of Christ Ch. Avocation: writing and presenting monologues of women in history. Home: 1200 Crestview Dr Blue Springs MO 64014-2312 Office: Herald Pub House 1001 W Walnut PO Box 390 Independence MO 64051-0390 E-mail: gbooz@heraldhouse.org., gbooz3@comcast.net.

BOOZE, THOMAS FRANKLIN, toxicologist; b. Denver, Mar. 4, 1955; s. Ralph Walker and Ann (McNatt) B.; children: Heather N., Ian T. BS, U. Calif., Davis, 1978; MS, Kans. State U., 1981, PhD, 1985. Registered environ assessor, Calif. Asst. instr. Kans. State U., Manhattan, 1979-85; consulting toxicologist Chevron Corp., Sacramento, 1985-92; sr. toxicologist URS/Radian Internat., Sacramento, 1992-2000; toxicologist Dept. Toxic Substances Control Calif EPA, Sacramento, 2000—. Cons. in field, Manhattan, Kans., 1981-83. Contbr. articles to profl. jours. Vol. Amigos de las Americas, Marin County, Calif., 1973, Hospice Care, Manhattan, 1985. Mem. Soc. Toxicology, Soc. for Risk Analysis, Sigma Xi. Home: 8338 Titian Ridge Ct Antelope CA 95843-5627 Office: HERD 8810 CalCenter Dr Sacramento CA 95826 E-mail: tbooze@dtsc.ca.gov.

BOOZMAN, JOHN, congressman; b. Shreveport, La, Dec. 10, 1950; m. Cathy Marley; 3 children. Student in pre-optometry, So. Coll. Optometry, 1977. Pvt. practice eye clinic, 1977; mem. U.S. Congress from 3d Ark. dist., 2002—. Served Rogers Sch. Bd.; establisher low vision program Ark. Sch. for Blind for Little Rock; vol. optometrist area clinic. Republican. Office: 1708 Longworth HOB Washington DC 20515-0403*

BOPP, JAMES, JR., lawyer; b. Terre Haute, Ind., Feb. 8, 1948; s. James and Helen Marguerite (Hope) B.; m. Cheryl Hahn, Aug. 8, 1970 (div.); m. Christine Marie Stanton, July 3, 1982; children: Kathleen Grace, Lydia Grace, Marguerite Grace. BA, Ind. U., 1970; JD, U. Fla., 1973. Bar: Ind. 1973, U.S. Supreme Ct. 1977. Dep. atty. gen. State of Ind., Indpls., 1973-75; ptnr. Bopp & Fife, Indpls., 1975-79, Brames, Bopp, Abel & Oldham, Terre Haute, Ind., 1979-92, Bopp, Coleson & Bostrom, Terre Haute, 1992—; of counsel Webster, Chamberlain and Bean, Washington, 1997—. Dep. prosecutor Vigo County, Terre Haute, 1979-86; gen. counsel Nat. Right to Life Com., Washington, 1978—; pres. Nat. Legal Ctr. for Medically Dependent and Disabled, 1984—; gen. counsel James Madison Ctr. Free Speech, 1997—; instr. law Ind. U., 1977-78. Editor: Human Life and Health Care Ethics, 1985, Restoring the Right to Life: The Human Life Amendment, 1984; editor-in-chief Issues in Law and Medicine, 1985—. Mem. Pres.'s Com. on Mental Retardation, 1984-87, mem. congl. biomed. ethics adv. com., 1987-89; Vigo County Election Bd., 1991-93; vice chmn. Early for Gov., 1995-96; del. Rep. State Conv., Indpls., 1980, 82, 84, 86, 90, 92, 94, 96, 98, 2000, 2002; alt. del. Rep. Nat. Conv., 1992, 96, del., 2000; chmn. Vigo County Rep. Ctrl. Com., 1993-97, White House Conf. on Families, Washington, 1980, White House Conf. on Aging, Mpls., 1981; bd. dirs. Leadership Terre Haute, 1986-89, Nat. Rep. Pro-Life Com., Washington, 1988-91, Alliance for Growth and Progress, Terre Haute, 1993-97; chmn. bd. dirs. Hospice of Wabash Valley, Terre Haute, 1982-88; mem. The Federalist Soc., Free Speech & Election Law Practice Group, co-chmn. election law subcom., 1996—. Mem. Ind. State Bar Assn., Terre Haute Bar Assn., Terre Haute Rotary (bd. dirs. 1984-86). Roman Catholic. Home: 1124 S Center St Terre Haute IN 47802-1116 Office: Bopp Coleson & Bostrom 1 S 6th St Terre Haute IN 47807-3510 E-mail: jboppjr@bopplaw.com.

BOPPE, CHARLES WILLIAM, aeronautical engineering educator; b. Winfield, Kans., Jan. 27, 1948; s. William Bruce and Mary Augusta (Johnson) B.; m. Ann Bernadette Carrig, July 18, 1970; children: Thomas, Claire, Sarah. BS in Aero. Engring., NYU, 1970, MS in Aero. Engring., 1972. Engr. Grumman Corp., Bethpage, N.Y., 1970-75; rsch. assoc. NASA-Langley Rsch. Ctr., Hampton, Va., 1975-76; sr. engr. Grumman Corp., Bethpage, 1976-78, engring. specialist, 1978-82; tech. specialist Grumman Aerospace Corp., 1982-85, prin. engr., mgr. tech. devel., 1985-95; sr. lectr. aero. engring. MIT, 1995—2003, dir. A&A Master of Engring. program, 1998—2003; sys. engring. tech. dir. Draper Lab., 2003—. Yacht tech. design cons. Sail Am. Found., San Diego, 1985-87; pres. Internat. Numerics Corp., Smithtown, N.Y., 1987-92; lectr. Purdue U., AGARD. Contbr. articles to profl. jours.; patentee in field. Recipient Lawrence Sperry award AIAA, 1981, Pub. Svc. medal NASA, 1980, Wright Bros. medal SAE, 1986, 90. Fellow AIAA (assoc.); mem. SAE, Internat. Coun. Systems Engring.

BOPRY, JEANETTE, education educator; b. Traverse City, Mich., Sept. 22, 1951; d. Robert Edwin and Barbara Jean (Trobaugh) B. MA, Mich. State U., 1978; MS, Ind. U., 1989, PhD, 1998. Instr. Tokyo YMCA Coll. of English, Tokyo, 1983-85, Temple U., Tokyo, 1985-86; lectr. Nagoya U. of Commerce and Bus. Adminstrn., Nagoya, Japan, 1991-95; postdoctoral rschr. U. Jyvaskyla, Finland, 1998-99; asst. prof. U. N.D., Grand Forks, 2000—03, Nat. Inst. Edn., Singapore, 2003—. Contbr. articles to profl. jours. and publs.; editor: Teaching and Learning Jour., 2001—, others; assoc. editor: Cybernetics & Human Knowing jour., 2002—. Mem. Ednl. Rsch. Assn., Assn. for Ednl. Comms. and Technology. Office: NIE 1 Nanyang Walk 2-03-60 Singapore 637616

BORAH, KRIPANATH, pharmacist; b. Calcutta, India, Mar. 1, 1931; s. Ambicanath and Gunabati (Barooah) B.; married; children: Shambhunath, Arun. BS, Calcutta U., 1952, MS, 1956; PhD, U. Munich, 1961. Mgr. R&D Ciba-Geigy, Bombay, 1962-76; rsch. assoc. Boston Coll., 1976-77; group leader W.H. Rorer & Co., Ft. Washington, Pa., 1977-80; dir. pharm. devel. Organon Inc., West Orange, N.J., 1980-91; assoc. dir. Enzon Inc., South Plainfield, N.J., 1991-92; sci. dir. G & W Labs., South Plainfield, 1992-96; dir. R & D Tomer Labs., Somerset, 1997—2002; sr. cons. Pharm. Ops., Phillipsburg, NJ, 2002—. Adj. prof. Temple U. Sch. Pharm., Phila., 1991—. Fellow Alexander von Humboldt Found., 1959-61. Mem. Am. Chem. Soc., Am. Assn. Pharm. Sci., Am. Assn. Indian Pharm. Scientists. Home: 1028 Deerhaven Ter Stewartsville NJ 08886-2919 Office: Pharm Ops 101 Broad St Phillipsburg NJ 08865

BORAN, ROBERT PAUL, JR., orthopedic surgeon; b. Pottsville, Pa., May 21, 1952; s. Robert Paul Sr. and Ellen Elizabeth (Reisig) B.; m. Catherine Virginia Kling, Oct. 18, 1980; children: Catherine, Ellen, Mary. BS, St. Joseph U., 1974; MD, Jefferson Med. Coll., 1978. Diplomate Am. Bd. Orthop. Surgery. Lab. technician Pottsville Hosp., 1972-74; disc jockey WPPA-AM and WAVT-FM, Pottsville, 1972-75; intern Pa. Hosp., Phila., 1978-79; resident in orthop. surgery Thomas Jefferson U. Hosp., Phila., 1979-83; chief resident Alfred I. DuPont Inst. of Nemours Found. Crippled Children, Wilmington, Del., 1981, U.S. VA Hosp., Wilmington; pvt. practice Pottsville, 1983—. Mem. clin. adj. faculty dept. allied health sci. Kings Coll., Wilkes Barre, Pa. Bd. dirs. Schuylkill Rehab. Ctr., 1987-2002, chmn. bd. dirs., 1988-2002. Fellow: ACS, Am. Acad. Orthop. Surgeons, Internat. Coll. Surgeons; mem.: AMA, Del. Valley Orthopaedic Trauma Consortium, Jefferson Orthop. Soc., N.Am. Faculty of Swiss Assn. for Study of Internal Fixation of Fractures, So. Med. Assn., So. Orthop. Assn., Pa. Orthop. Soc., Ea. Orthop. Assn. (nominating com. 2001—02), Assn. Arthritic Hip and Knee Surgeons, Am. Assn. Hip and Knee Surgeons, Schuylkill County Med. Soc., Internat. Soc. for Technology in Arthroplasty, Pa. Med. Soc., The Pa. Soc., Union League of Phila., Thomas Bond Soc. of Pa. Hosp., AO Alumni N.Am., Alfred I. DuPont Inst. Alumni Assn., Skytop Club, Pottsville Club, Vesper Club, Schuylkill Country Club, Elks, Ancient Order of Hibernians, Alpha Sigma Nu. Republican. Roman Catholic. Avocations: golf, cards. Home: 146 Glenworth Rd Pottsville PA 17901-8888 Office: Bldg 100 101 Schuylkill Medical Plz Pottsville PA 17901-3661 E-mail: rpboranmd@losch.net.

BORCHARD, WILLIAM MARSHALL, lawyer; b. N.Y.C., Nov. 19, 1938; s. Bernard Philip and Helen (Marshall) B.; m. Myra Cohen, Dec. 13, 1969; children: Jillian, Thomas. BA, Princeton U., 1960; JD, Columbia U., 1964. Bar: N.Y. 1964, U.S. Dist. Ct. (so. and ea. dists.), U.S. Ct. Appeals (2d, 3d, fed. cirs.), U.S. Supreme Ct. Assoc. Kaye, Scholer, Fierman, Hays and Handler, N.Y.C., 1964-74, ptnr., 1974-83, Cowan, Liebowitz and Latman, N.Y.C., 1983—. Mem. editl. bds. Art and the Law, 1982—, The Trademark Reporter, 1983-99 Author: Trademarks and the Arts, 1999, A Trademark is Not a Copyright or a Patent, 2003. Staff sgt. USAFR, 1961-67. Stone scholar Columbia Law Sch. N.Y.C., 1962. Mem. ABA (coun. 1987-90), Am. Law Inst. (adv. com. 1986-92), Internat. Trademark Assn. (legal counsel 1988-91). Democrat. Jewish. Avocations: tennis, boating, biking. Office: Cowan Liebowitz & Latman 1133 Ave of Americas New York NY 10036-6799 E-mail: wmb@cll.com.

BORCHARDT, BETSY OLK, artist; b. Clintonville, Wis., June 5, 1953; d. James Howard and Bernice Durben (Olk); m. Andrew Peter Borchardt, Dec. 27, 1980. Student, Lawrence U., 1971; BA in Sociology, St. Norbert Coll., De Pere, Wis., 1980; postgrad., U. Tenn., 1981. Home health aide Upjohn, Oshkosh, Wis., 1989, Oshkosh, 90; pvt. practice, Omro, 1990—93; program aide United Cerebral Palsy, Oshkosh, 1996—97; participant electronic tramission art Ariz. State U. project shown at UN 4th World Conf. on Women, Beijing, 1995;

recruiting asst. U.S. Census Bur., Stevens Point, Wis., 2000; line therapist Autism and Behavioral Cons., Fond du Lac, Wis., 2002—03. Author: (poetry) A Personal Struggle, 1987; solo exhbn. U. Wis. Ctr., Marinette, Wisc., 2003;one woman show at U. Wis. Ctr.-Marinette, 2003; exhibited in groups shows at Kansas City Kans. Civic Ctr., Pub. Libr., The Country Club Plz., Kansas City, Mo., 1987-88, Neville Pub. Mus., Green Bay, Wis., 1990, The Art Barn Gallery, Green Lake, Wis., 1995, Wis. Ctr., Madison, 1996, Our Savior Luth. Ch., Oshkosh, Wis., 1998, Art for All, Menominee, Mich., 2002. Vol. Franklin Ctr. Coffee Shop, Kansas City, 1984; activity aide Omro Care Ctr., 1988—89; visual arts leader Winnebago County 4-H, Omro, 1991, 1992; vol. tutor Redgranite Elem. Sch., 1995—2000; mem. chorus, drama cast, handbell choir Maestro Prodns., Inc., Oshkosh, 1991—2000; scientist pen-pal Sci. By Mail Mus. Sci., Boston, 1996—2000; founding mem. Wildlife Land Trust Humane Soc. U.S., Wildlife Guardian for Defenders of Wildlife, 1999—, Nat. Trust for Hist. Preservation, 2000—03; mem. and legis. activist Nat. Wildlife Fedn., 2000—; charter mem. Smithsonian Nat. Mus. of Am. Indian, 2000—. Mem. Nat. Mus. Women in Arts (charter), Planetary Soc., Wis. Regional Artists Assn. (Kenneth and Marie Kuemmerlein award 1992, Obermiller Edn. award, 1996), Wis. Regional Writers Assn., Lions (sec. 2001—). Avocations: reading, camping, fishing, bird watching. Home: 231 Wood St Redgranite WI 54970-9342 E-mail: betsyborchardt@hotmail.com.

BORCHARDT, DONALD ARTHUR, visual and performing arts educator; b. St. Paul, June 4, 1931; s. Herbert Friedrich Gustav and Rosalie Bertha Hulda (Sahnow) B.; m. Audrey Anne Rayfield, June 15, 1957. BA, U. Minn., 1953, MA, 1958; PhD, U. Utah, 1960. Instr. U. Minn., St. Paul, 1953, asst. prof. U. Wis., River Falls, 1960-61, Macalester Coll., St. Paul, 1961-64, U. Fla., Gainesville, 1964-67, Rutgers U., Newark, 1967-73, assoc. prof., 1973-93, prof. emeritus, 1993—. Pres. East Ctrl. Theatre Conf., 1982-84; adjudicator Am. Coll. Theatre Festival, 1972-86. Author: Think Tank Theatre, 1984; artist exhibit Forms in Space and Movement, 1991. With U.S. Army, 1953-55. Recipient AMOCO gold medallion award of excellence for svc. Am. Coll. Theatre Festival, Washington, 1977. Fellow: Internat. Soc. Exploring Tchg. Alternatives (pres. 1985—86); mem.: AAUP (pres. emeriti assembly Rutgers chpt. 1999—2003), Assn. Theatre in Higher Edn. (treas. 1987—89), Internat. Soc. Individualized Instrn., Phi Gamma Delta, Phi Kappa Phi.

BORCHARDT, DUKE, federal labor relations professional; b. Pinneberg, Germany, Mar. 29, 1941; came to the U.S., 1954; s. Karl Heinrich and Martha (Kreuzfeld) B.; m. Nancy Ann Saskas, Dec. 26, 1964; children: Lisa Marie Borchardt Baker, Marc. JD, La Salle U., 1968. Adminstrv. specialist N.Y. N.G., Rocky Point, 1964-74, Fla. N.G., Orlando, 1974-78, recruiting and retention specialist St. Augustine, 1978-83, pers. mgmt. specialist, 1983, labor rels. mgr., 1983-2001; human resources cons. for Fla. N.G. Express Pers. Svcs., St. Augustine, 2001—. Discipline and adverse action appeal hearing examiner Nat. Guard Bur., 1989—, chmn. labor rels. adv. coun., 1995—; mediator 7th jud. cir. small claims ct. St. Augustine, 1997—. Arbitrator 1st time juvenile offenders 7th Jud. Cir. State's Atty., St. Augustine, 1984—, guardian ad litem, 1989—, vice chair, 1992—; bd. dirs. St. Johns County Blood Bank, St. Augustine, 1994—; vice chair St. Johns County Juvenile Justice Com., St. Augustine, 1994—; mem. mental health/substance abuse adv. com. St. Johns County, 1988—, mem. health & human svcs. adv. coun., 1995—. Republican. Roman Catholic. Avocations: antique collecting, walking, working with and representing abused and neglected children. E-mial. Home: 7 Grandview Rd Saint Augustine FL 32080-5339 Office: Fla NG St Francis Barracks PO Box 1008 Saint Augustine FL 32085-1008 E-mail: dandnborch@aol.com., duke.borchardt@fl.ngb.army.mil.

BORCHARDT, KENNETH ANDREW, microbiology consultant, educator; b. Chgo., Sept. 20, 1928; s. Leo Arthur and Edith R. (Peterson) B.; m. C. Joyce Truitt, Feb. 6, 1954; children: Gregory David, Kimberly Jo, Jeffrey Andrew. BS, Loyola U., Chgo., 1950; MS, Miami U., Oxford, Ohio, 1951; PhD, Tulane U., 1961. Chief clin. microbiologist Fitzsimmons Army Hosp., Denver, 1957-58, Letterman Army Hosp., San Francisco, 1961-65; commd. USPHS, 1965, advanced through grades to capt., 1983, ret., 1982; prof., cons. microbiology San Francisco State U., 1982—; chief rsch. Biomed Diagnostics, San Jose, Calif., 1990—. Contbr. articles to med. jours. Fellow in Tropical Medicine, La. State U., 1970. Fellow Am. Acad. Microbiology, Royal Acad. Tropical Medicine and Hygiene (London); mem. N.Y. Acad. Scis., Sigma Xi. Republican. Lutheran. Avocation: organ. Home: 15 Capilano Dr Novato CA 94949-5824 Office: San Francisco State U 1600 Holloway Ave San Francisco CA 94132-1722

BORCHERS, ROBERT REECE, physicist and administrator; b. Chgo., Apr. 4, 1936; s. Robert Harley and Rena Josephine (Reece) B.; m. Mary Bridget Hennessy, Nov. 26, 1960; children: Patrick Joseph, Anne Marie, Robert Edward BS in Physics, U. Notre Dame, 1958; MS in Physics, Math., U. Wis., 1959, PhD in Nuclear Physics, 1962. Prof. physics U. Wis., Madison, 1961-76, vice chancellor, 1976-77, U. Colo., Boulder, 1977-79; dep. assoc., dir. MFE Program Lawrence Livermore (Calif.) Nat. Lab., 1979-83, assoc. dir. computation, 1983-91, asst. to dir. for univ. rels., 1991-93; divsn. dir. advanced sci. computing NSF, Arlington, Va., 1993—2001; chief tech. officer Maui High Performance Computing Ctr., 2001—; CEO R.R. Borchers & Assocs., 2001—. Mem. com. NSF, Washington, 1973-93, Nat. Acad. Sci., Washington, 1983-93. Editor Computers in Physics jour., 1987-91, chmn. editorial bd., 1991-95; contbr. numerous chpts. in books, articles on physics and computing. NSF postdoctoral fellow, 1964; A.J. Schmidt Found. fellow and scholar, 1954-60; Sloan Found. fellow, 1964-68; Guggenheim Found. fellow, 1970; recipient W.H. Kiekhofer Disting. Teaching award U. Wis., Madison, 1966; Centennial of Sci. Alumnus award U. Notre Dame, 1966 Fellow Am. Phys. Soc.; mem. IEEE Computer Soc. Avocations: golf, music. Office: MHPCC 550 Lipoa Ste 100 Kihei HI 96753

BORCHERT, CAROL ANN, school librarian; b. Rochester, Mich., 1968; d. Richard Howard and Sheila Borchert. Student, U. Va., 1988; B in Bus. Adminstrn., Coll. William and Mary, 1990; MLS, U. Ky., 1991; MA in Spanish, U. South Fla., 2001. Dept. head cataloging Furman U. Libr., Greenville, SC, 1991—95, reference/govt. docs. libr., 1995—97, U. South Fla., Tampa, 1997—99, reference/latin am. and caribbean studies libr., 2000—. Editor: (newsletter) FLA News Digest. Bd. mem., treas. Unity Ch. Greenville, SC, 1995—97. State U. Sys. Grant-In-Aid, U. South Fla., 2000—01. Mem.: REFORMA (chpt. pres. 2000—01), Fla. Libr. Assn., ALA, Phi Kappa Phi, Beta Phi Mu.

BORCHERT, CATHERINE GLENNAN, minister; b. L.A., Dec. 6, 1936; d. Thomas Keith and Ruth Haslup Adams Glennan; m. Frank R. Borchert Jr., Sept. 12, 1959 (dec. Sept. 1997); children: Frank R. III, Anne Matthews, Thomas Adams. BS, Swarthmore Coll., 1958; MSLS, Western Res. U., 1959; MDiv, McCormick Theol. Sem., 1991; postgrad., Case Western Res. U. Ordained to ministry, Presbyn. Ch., 1991. Serial records libr. U. Chgo. Libr., 1959-61; ref. libr., head outreach Cleveland Heights (Ohio) Pub. Libr., 1979-86; stated clk. Presbytery of Western Res. U., Cleve., 1984-94; interim pastor Lyndhurst (Ohio) Cmty. Presbyn. Ch., 1993-94; coord. adv. com. social witness policy Gen. Assembly of Presbyn. Ch., Louisville, 1994-97; adj. faculty McCormick Theol. Sem., Chgo., 1987—, interim dean doctoral programs and continuing edn., 2000-01. Mem. exec. com. Permanent Judicial Commn. Contbr. articles to profl. jours. Bd. dirs. United Protestant Campus Min., Cleve., 1999—2002, History Assocs., Cleve., 1999—; mem. steering com. Woman 2000 Case Western Res. U., 1998—2000; alumni interviewer Swarthmore (Pa.) Coll., 1965—; mem. exec. com. Chs.' Ctr. for Theology and Pub. Policy, Washington. Mem.: Mortar Bd., Phi Alpha Theta, Beta Phi Mu. Democrat. Avocations: reading, birdwatching, choir, bike riding. Home: 13415 Shaker Blvd #9C2 Cleveland OH 44120

BORCHERT, DONALD MARVIN, philosopher, educator; b. Edmonton, Alta., Can., May 23, 1934; s. Leo Ferdinand and Lillian Violet (Bucholz) B.; m. Mary Ellen Cockrell, Dec. 27, 1960; children: Carol Ellen, John Witherspoon. AB, U. Alta., Edmonton, 1955; BD, Princeton Theol. Sem., 1958, PhD, 1966; ThM, Ea. Bapt. Theol. Sem., 1959. Teaching fellow Princeton (N.J.) Theol. Sem., 1960-61; asst. prof. Juniata Coll., Huntingdon, Pa., 1966-67, Ohio U., Athens, 1967-71, assoc. prof., 1971-75, prof. philosophy, 1975—, assoc. dean Coll. Arts and Scis., 1980-86, chmn. dept. philosophy, 1987—2002. Author: Being Human in a Technological Age, 1979, Introduction to Modern Philosophy, 1981, 7th edit., 2001, Exploring Ethics, 1986, Medical Ethics, 1992, Philosophy of Sex and Love, 1997; editor in chief: Encyclopedia of Philosophy Supplement, 1996, Compendium of Philosophy and Ethics, 1999; contbr. articles to profl. jours. Assoc. Danforth Found. Nat. Humanities Inst. fellow, 1976-77; NEH Implementation grantee, 1981. Mem. Ohio Philos. Assn. (v.p. 1983-85, pres. 1985-90), Ohio Humanities Council (vice chmn. 1981-83, chmn. 1983-85). Presbyterian. Home: 9 Coventry Ln Athens OH 45701-3717 Office: Ohio U Dept Philosophy Ellis Hall Athens OH 45701 E-mail: borchert@ohio.edu.

BORCOVER, ALFRED SEYMOUR, journalist; b. Bellaire, Ohio, May 1, 1931; s. Joseph and Kate (Florman) B.; m. Doris E. Wellner, Sept. 13, 1958 (div. 1966); m. Linda A. Gredig, Oct. 11, 1989. B.Sc. in Journalism, Ohio State U., 1953; MSJ., Northwestern U., 1957. Writer Northwestern U., Evanston, Ill., 1957-58; reporter, copy editor Chgo. Tribune, 1959-63, asst. travel editor, 1963-73, assoc. travel editor, 1973-79, editor travel sect., 1979-81, travel editor, columnist, 1981-93; ret., 1994. Freelance travel columnist/writer, 1994—. Author: Dollarwise Guide to Chicago, 1967; contbg. editor Fodor's Chicago, 1985-88; contbr. to Around the World with the Experts, 1970, WGN Travel Show, 1986-93; travel columnist Prodigy On-line Svc., 1990-96. Served to 1st lt. USAF, 1953-55 Recipient spl. citation George Hedmon Awards, 1965, Outstanding Achievement in Travel Writing award N.Y. Travel Writers Assn., 1976, Econ. Impact Writing award Travel Industry Assn. Am., 1983, Lowell Thomas Writing award, 1986; Gold Medal Writing award Pacific Asia Travel Assn., 1987, Cen. States Consumerism Reporting award, 1987, Alumni Svc. award Northwestern U., 1991, Cen. States Best Fgn. Series award, Cen. States Henry E. Bradshaw Sweepstakes Writing award, 1991, Cen. States Fgn. Series and U.S. Article awards, 1992, Earl R. Lind Consumer Edn. award Better Bus. Bur. of Chgo., 1993. Mem. Soc. Am. Travel Writers (pres. 1973-74), Chgo. Headline Club (pres. 1983-84), Medill Sch. Journalism Alumni Assn. (bd. dirs. 1984-89, pres. 1989-91), Northwestern U. Alumni Assn. (bd. dirs. 1986-90), Soc. Profl. Journalists. Democrat. Jewish. Avocations: tennis, music, photography. Home and Office: 1022 Michigan Ave Evanston IL 60202-1436 E-mail: aborcover@aol.com.

BORDA, RICHARD JOSEPH, retired insurance company executive; b. San Francisco, Aug. 16, 1931; s. Joseph Clement and Ethel Cathleen (Donovan) B.; m. Judith Maxwell, Aug. 30, 1953; children: Michelle, Stephen Joseph. AB, Stanford U., 1953, MBA, 1957. With Wells Fargo Bank, San Francisco, 1957-70, mgr., 1963-66, asst. v.p., 1966-67, v.p., 1967-70, exec. v.p. adminstrn., 1973-85; asst. sec. Air Force Manpower Res. Affairs, Washington, 1970-73; vice chmn., chief fin. officer Nat. Life Ins. Co., Montpelier, Vt., 1985-90, also bd. dirs.; chmn., chief exec. officer Sentinal Group Funds, Inc., 1985-90, also bd. dirs.; bd. dirs. Info. USA. Former pres. Air Force Aid Soc., Washington; mem. bd. visitors Monterey Inst. Internat. Studies; govs. coun. Boys and Girls Club of Monterey Peninsula; bd. dirs. Sunset Ctr. for the Arts Found., Marines' Meml. Assn., San Francisco, Info USA, Omaha. Recipient Exceptional Civilian Svc. award, 1973, 95. Mem. USMC Res. Officers Assn., Bohemian Club, Monterey Peninsula Country Club, Old Capital Club, Air Force Aid Soc. (disting. counselor), Phi Gamma Delta, Cypress Point Club. Republican. Episcopalian.

BORDAGE, GEORGES, physician, medical education educator; b. St.-Louis-De-Kent, N.B., Can., May 30, 1947; came to U.S., 1992; s. Edmond and Rita (Gionet) B.; m. Joanne R. Fisher, Dec. 9, 1978; children: Anna, Daniel. BA, Coll. Bathurst, N.B., 1969; MD, U. Laval, Quebec City, Que., Can., 1973; MSc in Biometry, Case Western Res. U., 1976; PhD in Ednl. Psychology, Mich. State U., 1982; PhD (hon.), U. Sherbrooke, Can., 1999; DSc (hon.), U. Moncton, Can., 2002. Intern Hotel Dieu de Que. Hosp., Quebec City, 1973-74; rsch. fellow dept. biometry Case Western Res. U., Cleve., 1974-76; rsch. fellow office med. edn. R&D Mich. State U., East Lansing, 1976-78; prof. U. Laval, 1978-92, founding dir. MA degree, 1984; prof., dir. grad. studies U. Ill., Chgo., 1992—. Hon. cons. Greenwich Dist. Hosp., London, 1987-88; cons. WHO, Brussels, Karachi, 1982-83, 93, Eli Lilly, Awashima, Hakone, Tokyo and Kobe, 1994-97. Recipient John P. Hubbard award Nat. Bd. Med. Examiners, 1994, Disting. Career award in health professions edn. Am. Edn. Rsch. Assn., 2002. Mem. Assn. Am. Med. Colls. (chmn. rsch. in med. edn. 1991, chmn. group on ednl. affairs 1995-96, Merrel Flair award 1999), Assn. for Surg. Edn., Assn. for Study Med. Edn., Soc. Tchrs. in Family Medicine, Friends of Osler Libr., Club Pedagogie Med. Que. (chmn., exec. sec. 1989-92). Avocations: reading, music, cooking. Office: U Ill Chgo Dept Med Edn 808 S Wood St Dept Med Chicago IL 60612-7300

BORDALLO, MADELEINE MARY (MRS. RICARDO JEROME BORDALLO), congresswoman; b. Graceville, Minn., May 31, 1933; d. Christian Peter and Mary Evelyn (Roth) Zeien; m. Ricardo Jerome Bordallo, June 20, 1953; 1 daughter, Deborah Josephine. Student, St Mary's Coll., South Bend, Ind., 1952; AA, St. Katherines Coll., St. Paul, 1953; AA hon. degree for community service, U. Guam, 1968. Presented in voice recital Guam Acad. Music, Agana., 1951, 62; mem. Civic Opera Co., St. Paul, 1952-53; mem. staff KUAM Radio-TV sta., Agana, 1954-63; freelance writer local newspaper, fashion show commentator, coordinator, civic leader, 1963; nat. Dem. committeewoman for Guam, 1964-98; 1st lady of Guam, 1974-78, 81-85; senator 16th Guam Legislature, 1981-82, 19th Guam Legislature, 1987-88, 20th Guam Legislature, 1989-90, 21st Guam Legislature, 1991-92, 22nd Guam Legislature, 1993-94; Dem. Party candidate for Gov. of Guam, 1990, lt. gov. of Guam, 1994; lt. gov. of Guam, 1994—2002; at-large repr. U.S. Ho. of Reps. from Guam, 2003—. Del. Nat. Dem. Conv., 1964, 68, 72, 76, 80, 84, 88-92, 96, pres. Women's Dem. Party Guam, 1967-69; rep. Presdl. Inauguration, Washington, 1965, 77, 85; del. Dem. Western States Conf., Reno, 1965, L.A., 1967, Phoenix, 1968, conf. sec., 1967-69; del. Dem. Women's Campaign Conf., Wash., 1965, Dem. Inauguration, 1992. Pres. Guam Women's Club, 1958-59; del Gen. Fedn. Women's Clubs Convs., Miami Beach, Fla., 1961, New Orleans, 1965, Boston, 1968; v.p. Fedn. Asian Women's Assn., 1964-67, pres., 1967-69, pres. 1996-98; pres. Guam Symphony Soc., 1967-73, del. convs., Manila, Philippines, 1959, Taipei, Formosa, 1960, Hong Kong, 1963, Guam, 1964, Japan, 1968, Taipei, 1973; chmn. Guam Christmas Seal Drive, 1961; bd. dirs. Guam chpt. ARC, 1963, sec., 1963-67, fund dr. chmn., 2000; pres. Marianas Assn. For Retarded Children, 1968-69, 73-74, 84—; bd. dirs. Guam Theatre Guild, Am. Cancer Soc.; mem. Guam Meml. Hosp. Vols. Assn., 1966—, v.p., 1966-67, pres., 1970-71; chmn. Hosp. Charity Ball, 1966; pres. Women for Service, 1974—, Beauty World Guam Ltd., 1981—, First Lady's Beautification Task Force of Guam, 1983-86; pres. Palace Restoration Assn., 1983—; nominee Dem. party for Gov. of Guam, 1990. Mem. Internat. Platform Assn., Guam Rehab. Assn. (assoc.), Guam Lytico and Bodig Assn. (pres. 1983-98), Spanish Club of Guam, Inetnon Famalaoan Club (pres. 1983-86), Guam Coun. of Women's Club (pres. 1993-95), Nat. Conf. Lt. Govs. (exec. com. 1998—). Democrat. Home: PO Box 1458 Agana GU 96932-1458 Office: PO Box 2950 Agana GU 96932-2950 also: 427 Cannon Ho Office Bldg Washington DC 20515-5301 Business E-Mail: lt.gov.@mail.gov.gu .*

BORDAO, RAFAEL, educator, writer, poet; b. Havana, Cuba, June 17, 1951; came to U.S., 1980; s. Mario and Marta (Herrera) B.; m. Miriam Parajon, Dec. 30, 1971 (div. Jan. 1980); 1 child, Aisné; m. Laura Garcia, Nov. 25, 1995. MA, Columbia U., 1988, MPh, PhD, Columbia U., 1999. Cert. tchr., N.Y. Founder, pub. La Nuez, N.Y.C., 1988-93, Editl. Arcas, N.Y.C., 1988—; adj. prof. Mercy Coll., N.Y.C., 1988-89, Columbia U. Tchrs. Coll., N.Y.C., 1989-90; tchr. N.Y.C. Pub. Sch. Sys., 1991—; founder, pub. Editl. Palmar, 1993—; pub. Sinalefa, 2002—. Adj. prof. Columbia U., 2002—. Author: La Revolucíon de Castro, 1999, (poetry): Proyectura, 1986, Acrobacia del Abandono, 1988, Escurriduras de la Soledad, 1995, El Libro de Las Interferencias, 1995, Propinas para la Libertad, 1998, El Lenguaje del Ausente, 1998, Los descosidos labios del Silencio, 2000, The Debris of Dreams, 2001, La Satira, la ironia y el carnaval literario en Leprosorio de Reinaldo Arenas, 2002; contbr. works to lit. mags. and poetry anthologies. Named Homme de Lettres, Acad. Francaise, Paris, 1998, Premio de Poesia Fernand Esquio, Galicia, Spain, 1998, others. Mem. PEN, Interam. Acad. Poetry (sec. N.Y. chpt.). Avocations: reading, walking, tennis. Home: PO Box 26751 Brooklyn NY 11202-3617

BORDEAUX, CHRISTI RENEE, government agency administrator; b. Spencer, Iowa, Mar. 25, 1957; d. Charles Russel Dunn and Joyce Faye Bobzien Dunn; m. Harold Paul Bordeaux, Dec. 9, 1984 (div. Dec. 1993); children: Aaron Kie Froemming, André Charles. BA, Prescott (Ariz.) Coll., 1986; M in Pub. Mgmt., East Tenn. State U., 1999. Freelance writer, editor, Milford, Conn., 1986-90; child support enforcement officer State of Conn. Jud., Bridgeport, 1990-94; editor Vets. Health Sys. Jour., Balt., 1995-97; exec. analyst Office of Commr. Social Security Adminstrn., Balt. and Washington, 1999, spl. asst. to dep. commr., 1999-2000; pub. health analyst Cmty. Access Program U.S. Dept. Health and Human Svcs., Bethesda, Md., 2000—02; FEMA program specialist Cadre Mgmt. Group FEMA HR, Washington, 2002—. Mem. Phi Kappa Phi. Democrat. Avocations: flute, gardening, whitewater rafting, writing. Office: Cadre Mgmt Group FEMA HR 500 C St SW Washington DC 20472 E-mail: christi.r.boreeaux@fema.gov.

BORDELON, CAROLYN THEW, elementary school educator; b. Shelby, Ohio, Dec. 28, 1942; d. Burton Carl and Opal Mae (Harris) VanAsdale; m. Clifford Charles Spohn, Aug. 28, 1965 (div. Feb. 1982); m. Al Ramon Bordelon, Oct. 26, 1985. BA in History and Polit. Sci., Otterbein Coll., 1966; MA in Edn., Bowling Green State U., 1972; postgrad., Ohio State U., 1986—. Cert. tchr. grades 1-8, Ohio. Elem. tchr. Allen East Schs., Harrod, Ohio, 1966-68, Marion (Ohio) City Schs., 1968-78, chpt. I reading tchr., 1978-86, reading recovery tchr., 1986-88, Dublin (Ohio) City Schs., 1988—. Adj. instr. reading dept.grad. studies Ashland (Ohio) U., 1996. Author: The Parent Workshop, 1992, Octopus Goes to School, 1995. Vol. Am. Heart Assn., Worthington, Ohio, 1991; mem. Rep. Nat. Com., Washington, 1994-95; mem. Royal Scots Highlanders, Mansfield, Ohio, 1976—. Recipient Excellence in Edn. award Dublin City C. of C., 1991-93, 96, 97; Dublin City Schs./Ohio Dept. Edn. Tchr. Award grantee, 1993; Martha Holden Jennings Found. scholar, 1978. Mem. Archaeol. Inst. Am., Ohio Edn. Assn., Reading Recovery Coun. N.Am., Opera/Columbus, Mus. of Art, Columbus, Phi Delta Kappa, Phi Alpha Theta. Presbyterian. Avocations: bagpiping and scottish activities, archaeology, interior design, harpsichord. Home: 3958 Fairlington Dr Columbus OH 43220-4531 Office: Griffith Thomas Elem Sch 4671 Tuttle Crossing Blvd Dublin OH 43017-3575 E-mail: cbordelonread@aol.com.

BORDEN, DAVID, composer, educator; b. Boston, Dec. 25, 1938; s. Raymond Borden and Natalie Mallard; m. Rebecca Lee Simmons, Dec. 8, 1994; 1 child, Gabriel. MusB, Eastman Sch. of Music, Rochester, N.Y., 1963; MusM, Eastman Sch. of Music, 1963; MA, Harvard U., 1965. Scholarship/hochschule für musik Fulbright Com., West Berlin, Germany, 1965—66; composer-in-residence Ithaca City Sch. Dist., NY, 1966—68; composer/pianist for dance Cornell U., Ithaca, 1968—87, dir., digital music program, 1987—. Dir. and rec. artist Earthquack Records, Ithaca, 1972—78; rec. artist Cuneiform Records, Silver Spring, Md., 1987—, Arbiter Records, N.Y.C. Composer: (music composition) C-A-G-E Parts 1, 2 & 3 for synthesizer ensemble, (electroacoustic music in 12 parts) The Continuing Story of Counterpoint, (electroacoustic pieces and soloists) Anagram Portraits, (choral and electroacoustic) Angels, (electroacoustic variations plus soloists) Earth Journeys, (electroacoustic cantus firmus pieces) Synergy Soundscapes. Home: 227 Enfield Falls Rd Ithaca NY 14850 Office: Cornell University Dept Music Lincoln Hall Ithaca NY 14853-4101

BORDEN, DAVID M. state supreme court justice; b. Hartford, Conn., Aug. 4, 1937; BA magna cum laude, Amherst Coll., 1959; LLB cum laude, Harvard U., 1962. Bar: Conn. 1962, U.S. Dist. Ct. Conn. 1962, U.S. Ct. Appeals (2d cir.) 1965, U.S. Supreme Ct. 1969. Pvt. practice, Hartford, Conn., 1962-77; judge Conn. Ct. Common Pleas, 1977-78, Conn. Superior Ct., 1978-83, Conn. Appellate Ct., 1983—90; assoc. justice Conn. Supreme Ct., 1990—. Chief counsel joint com. on judiciary Conn. Gen. Assembly, 1975-76; lectr. Law U. Conn. Sch. Law, 1968-70, 85-92, 94—; exec. dir. Conn. Commn. to Revise Criminal Statutes, 1963-71. Mem. Conn. Bar Assn., Hartford County Bar Assn., Phi Beta Kappa. Democrat. Jewish. Avocations: hiking, reading. Office: PO Drawer N Sta A Hartford CT 06106

BORDEN, DIANE LYNN, communications educator; b. Chgo., Jan. 25, 1947; d. H. Frederick and Vera L. Borden; m. Robert Easley (div. 1970). BA, Colo. State U., 1972; MA, Stanford U., 1989; PhD, U. Wash., 1993. Mng. editor Bellingham (Wash.) Herald, 1977-80; dep. mng. editor Tribune, Oakland, Calif., 1981-85; pres. Santa Fe (N.Mex.) New Mexican, 1986-87; assoc. prof. Temple U., Phila., 1993-95; project dir. Am. Soc. Newspaper Editors, Reston, Va., 1995-96; asst. prof. George Mason U., Fairfax, Va., 1996-98; prof. San Diego State U., 1998—. Gannett profl. in residence U. Kans., Lawrence, 1985-86; cons. and expert witness in communication law and ethics. Co-editor: The Electronic Grapevine, 1997; co-author: Creative Editing, 4th edit., 2003; contbr. articles to scholarly and profl. jours.; editor: (book) Women and Language, 1997-99. Active NOW, Habitat for Humanity, World Wildlife Fund, Washington. Profl. journalism fellow Stanford U., 1980-81, fellow in telecomm. policy Annenberg Washington Program, 1995; rsch. grantee Temple U., 1994, San Diego State U., 1999, 2000. Mem. Assn. for Edn. in Journalism and Mass Communication, AAUW, Am. Journalism Historians Assn. Avocations: hiking, golf, reading biographies of women. Office: San Diego State U Office of Pres 5500 Campanile Dr San Diego CA 92182-8000

BORDEN, ENID A. public relations executive; b. Bklyn., Feb. 15, 1950; d. Jack Harry and Eleanor (Miller) Borden. BA, Alfred U., N.Y., 1972; MA, Adelphi U., Garden City, N.Y., 1973. Editor/pubr. Wings Mag., Colorado Springs, Colo., 1975-76; press. sec. Guidera for Congress, Waterbury, Conn., 1977-78; press sec. Reagan for Pres., N.Y.C., N.Y., 1979-80; dir. pub. affairs U.S. Dept. HHS, N.Y.C., 1981-83; dir. pub. affairs/dir. policy and legis. Office Human Devel. Svcs. HHS, Washington, 1983-86; dep. commr. for policy and external affairs Social Security Adminstrn., Balt., 1986-88; pres. The Borden Group, Inc., Alexandria, Va., 1988—. Cons. on pub. rels., govt. rels. assn. mgmt. primarily in human svcs.; mem. U.S. adv. bd. on child abuse and neglect, 1992-95; faculty Ctr. for Grad. and Continuing Studies, Goucher Coll., Balt. 1998-2001. Trustee Alfred U., 1985-88; CEO Meals on Wheels Assn. Am., 1993—. ceo 2002-. Recipient Citation Alfred U. Alumni Assn. Office: The Borden Group Inc 1414 Prince St Alexandria VA 22314-2853 E-mail: enid@mowaa.org.

BORDEN, JOHN HARVEY, entomologist, educator; b. Berkeley, Calif., Feb. 6, 1938; s. Charles Edward Borden and Alice Victoria Witkin; m. Edna Rosalind McEachern, June 23, 1962; children: Patrick Carl, Ian McEachern. BS, Washington State U., 1963; MS, U. Calif., Berkeley, 1965, PhD, 1966. Bd. cert. entomologist Entomol. Soc. Am. Rsch. and tchg. asst. dept. entomology U. Calif., Berkeley, 1963-66; asst. prof. dept. biol. scis. Simon Fraser U., Burnaby, Canada, 1966-69, assoc. prof., 1969-75, prof., 1975—2003, dir. chem. ecology rsch. group, 1981—2002, NSERC Indsl. Rsch. chair, 1991-2001, emeritus, 2003—; rsch. dir. Phero Tech Inc., Delta, 2003—. Vis. scientist Forestry Commn. Rsch. Sta., Alice Holt Lodge, Wrecclesham, Farnham, Surrey, Eng., 1976-77; cons. to UN Devel. Program, 1989-97. Contbr. chpts. to books and over 350 articles to profl. jours.; patentee in field. With USMC, 1957-61. Coop. Grad. fellow, NSF, 1964-66, Travelling fellow Nat. Rsch. Coun., 1976-77, Killam Rsch. fellow Can. Coun., 1990-91; recipient Gold medal Sci. Coun. B.C., 1985, Hewlett Packard Can. Forum award, 1997. Fellow Entomol. Soc. Can. (C.G. Hewitt award 1977, Gold medal 1988), Royal Soc. of Canada, Entomol. Soc. Am. (cert., J.E. Bussart Meml. award 1984); mem. Entomol. Soc. B.C. (hon. life), Nat. Assn. Advancement of Sci. (life), Can. Inst. Forestry (Sci. Achievement award 1986), Profl. Pest Mgmt. Assn. B.C. (Excellence award 1986), Internat. Soc. Chem. Ecology (life), Assn. B.C. Profl. Foresters, Assn. Profl. Biologists B.C. Office: Simon Fraser U Dept Biol Scis Burnaby BC Canada V5A 1S6 Business E-Mail: borden@sfu.ca.

BORDEN, THOMAS ALLEN, urologist, educator; b. Richmond, Ind., Aug. 31, 1937; s. William C. and Mildred (Duffill) B.; m. Joan Mattmiller (div. 1988); married; children: Christopher, Catherine. BA, Earlham Coll., 1959; MS, MD, U. Chgo., 1963, cert., 1969. Chmn. Dept. of Urology, program dir. U. N.Mex., Albuquerque, 1973—. Pres. N.Mex. Med. Found., 1985-88. Author: (textbook) Genitourinary Cancer Surgery, 1982; contbr. articles to profl. jours. Maj. USAF, 1969-71. Fellow ACS; mem. AMA, Soc. Pediatric Urology, Am. Urology Assn. Republican. Avocations: hunting, fishing, art. Office: U NMex Sch Medicine 2211 Lomas Blvd NE Albuquerque NM 87106-2745

BORDEN, WESTON THATCHER, chemistry educator; b. N.Y.C., Oct. 13, 1943; s. Martin L. and Doris (Weston) B.; m. Marcia E. Robbins, May 15, 1971 (div. 1987); children: Alice, Michael; m. Shelia R. Buxton, Mar. 1, 2002. BA, Harvard U., 1964, MA, 1966, PhD, 1968. Instr. Harvard U., Cambridge, Mass., 1968-69, asst. prof., 1969-73; assoc. prof. U. Wash., Seattle, 1973-77, prof.,

1977—. Author: Modern Molecular Orbital Theory, 1975; editor: Diradicals, 1982; contbr. articles to profl. jours. Bd. dirs. Itteki Zendo Assn., 1995—. Fellow Fulbright Found., Sloan Found., Guggenheim Found., Japan Soc. for Promotion of Sci.; recipient Humboldt Scientist award. Mem. AAAS, Am. Chem. Soc. Buddhist. Avocation: traditional japanese arts. Office: U Wash Dept Chemistry Bg 10 Seattle WA 98195-0001 E-mail: borden@chem.washington.edu.

BORDER, GLADYS LOUISE, piano educator; b. Cleve., Feb. 11, 1926; d. Frederick August and Edith Elliot (Spellman) Schnell; m. Tondra Harrison Border, Nov. 16, 1946; children: David, Thomas, Calvin. Diploma, Wilcox Coll. Commerce, Cleve., 1944; student, Baptist Bible Inst., Cleve., 1944-46. Sales clk. part time F.W. Woolworth Co., Cleveland Heights, Ohio, 1942-44; office sec. part time Wilcox Coll. Commerce, Cleve., 1944; sec. Standard Oil Co., Cleve., 1944-47; temporary office work Ballou Svcs., Cleve., 1954; piano tchr. pvt. practice, Cleve., 1955-59, Hollywood, Fla., 1959—; sec. indsl. and pub. rels. Food Fair Offices, Miami, 1961-62; piano tchr. pvt. practice, Hollywood, Fla., 1997—. Ch. pianist First Brethren Ch., Cleveland Heights, Ohio, 1941-46; regular pianist Phi Gamma Fishing Club, Cleve., 1944-46; asst. pianist Youth For Christ, Cleve., 1945; 2nd v.p., corr. sec., awards chmn. Broward County Music Tchrs., Ft. Lauderdale, Fla., 1970-90; pianist in churches Nazarene, Bapt. Hollywood Christian Sch., Cleve., 1947-58; accompanist for band solos McArthur H.S., Driftwood Jr. H.S., Hollywood, Fla., 1961-69; regular pianist 1st Bapt. Choir and Ch., W. Hollywood, Fla., 1971-89, part time 1993—. Author: (life story) On the Life of Gladys Louise (Schnell) Border. Den mother Boy Scouts Am. Cub Scouts, Cleve., 1958-59; Sunday sch. tchr. Ch. of Nazarene, Cleve., 1947-48, 57-58; treas. Band Parents Driftwood Jr. H.S., Hollywood, Fla., 1962, 63; recording sec. Women;s Soc. 1st Meth., Hollywood, Fla., 1962, 64; Sunday Sch. tchr. 1st Meth., Epworth Meth., Hollywood, Fla., 1960, 71. Recipient Electronic Metronome McArthur High Band Soloists, Hollywood, Fla., 1967, Bowling trophies Bapt. Fellowship League, Hollywood, Fla., 1973-86, music min. plaques (2) 1st Bapt. W. Hollywood, Fla., 1980, 89; named Fairest of the Island Mother's Banquet 1st Bapt. W. Hollywood, Fla., 1994. Mem. Nat. Guild of Piano Tchrs., Jolly Srs., Fla. Fedn. Music Clubs, Broward County Music Tchrs. Assn. Republican. Baptist. Avocations: piano playing, reading, sewing, bowling, writing letters. Home: 7091 Scott St Hollywood FL 33024-3849

BORDERS, JAMES MATTHEW, music educator, dean; b. Chgo., Apr. 28, 1953; s. Robert Ottis Borders and Ruth Ann Avis; m. Ann Marie Ossler, Aug. 17, 1974; children: Jacqueline, Julia. BM, DePaul U., 1974; PhD, U. Chgo., 1983. Curator Stearns Collection U. Mich., Ann Arbor, Mich., 1980—95; assoc. prof. U. of Mich., Ann Arbor, Mich., 1990—2000, prof., 2000—. Curator Stearns Collection U. of Mich., 1980—95, assoc. dean for grad. studies sch. music, 1996—2003, rep. u. senate, 1988—91, sr. assoc. dean, 2001—03. Author: (book) Early Medieval Chants from Nonantola, 1996; contbr. articles to profl. jours. Grantee, NEH, 1990. Mem.: Huron Valley Aikikai (yudansha 2001—). Roman Catholic. Avocations: iaido, Aikido, kenjutsu, jodo. Office: Univ Mich Sch Music 1100 Baits Dr Ann Arbor MI 48109-2085 Office Fax: 734-763-5097. E-mail: jborders@umich.edu.

BORDERS, JOHN GILLESPIE, psychotherapist, former corporate executive; b. St. Louis, June 12, 1946; s. William Alexis and Kate (Thompson) B.; children: Alexandra, Clara. AB in Econs., Princeton U., 1969; MSW, Washington U., 1993. Asst. treas. Chase Manhattan Bank, N.Y.C., 1972-77; group v.p. Centerre Bank, St. Louis, 1977-86; founding ptnr. Axium Inc., St. Louis, 1987-88; pres., CEO, HealthScan, Inc., St. Louis, 1988-93; psychotherapist Youth Emergency Svc., 1992-94, St. Louis Mental Health Ctr., 1994-97, The Child Ctr., St. Louis, 1997—; actor Neighborhood Playhouse, 1971—72. Mem. psychiat. diversion term Divsn. Family Svcs., State of Mo.; field instr. Washington U., St. Louis, St. Louis U., Webster U. Author: Conglomerate Merger: Corporate Growth Strategy, 1969, Hound with One Red Ear, 1992; contbr. articles to profl. jours. Mem. ops. com. St. Louis Tech. Ctr., 1986-87; bd. dirs. Jefferson Nat. Expansion Meml. Assn., St. Louis, Kammergild Chamber Orch., St. Louis, Altenheim Retirement Ctr., The Thompson Ctr.; mem. exec. com., bd. dirs. Princeton U. Alumni Coun.; mem. exec. com. Project for Peaceful Sch. Learning Environment; steering com., chmn. external rels. cmty. svc. initiative Veiled Prophet Orgn. Served with U.S. Spl. Forces (Airborne) Group, 1969-70. Named one of Nation's Fifty Most Eligible Bachelors, Town & Country Mag., 1968; Eleanor Roosevelt fellow, 1993. Mem. Advance Psychoanalytic Psychotherapy Assn. (treas., bd. dirs.), Adventure Club (past pres.), Lunch Club (past pres.), Hall Commn.(past chmn.), St. Louis Country Club, Princeton Club of St. Louis (exec. com., bd. dirs.). Home: Twelve Highgate Rd Saint Louis MO 63132 Office: The Child Ctr 7900 Natural Bridge Rd Saint Louis MO 63121

BORDERS, WILLIAM ALEXANDER, journalist; b. St. Louis, Jan. 11, 1939; s. William Alexis and Kate (Thompson) B.; m. Barbara D. Burkham, June 17, 1967 (div. 1984); 1 son, William Borders. BA, Yale U., 1960. Staff N.Y. Times, N.Y.C., 1960—, corr., 1970-72, 1972-75, 1975-79, 1979-82, dep. fgn. editor, 1982-83, editor Week in Rev., 1983-89, sr. editor, 1989-90, news editor, 1990—. Home: 227 E 57th St New York NY 10022-2828 Office: NY Times Co 229 W 43rd St New York NY 10036-3959

BORDES, JANE S. lawyer; b. New Orleans, La., Sept. 3, 1973; d. Bruce Gerald and Judith Mathews Bordes. BA in English summa cum laude, Loyola U. of New Orleans, 1994; JD, Tulane U., 1997. Bar: La. 1998. Assoc. Schafer and Schafer, New Orleans, 1997—. Office: Schafer and Schafer 328 Lafayette St New Orleans LA 70130-3244

BORDIE, JOHN GEORGE, linguistics educator; b. Chgo., Apr. 3, 1931; s. John and Helena Jozefin (Kozubal) B.; m. Margaret Lyne Miller, July 22, 1950 (div. Dec. 1955); 1 child, Ruth Claire; m. Camilla May Berkley, Feb. 11, 1956; children: Helena Robin, Ralph Leon. BA, U. Chgo., 1949; PhD, U. Tex., 1958. Asst. prof. linguistics and English Georgetown U., 1958-61; coord. linguistics and literacy Electronic Teaching Labs., Washington, 1961-63; dep. dir. tng. Peace Corps, North and East Africa, also South Asia, 1963-66; mem. faculty U. Tex.-Austin, 1966-95, prof. linguistics, curriculum and instrn., 1974-95, prof. emeritus, 1995—, Fgn. Lang. Edn. Center, 1996—. Vis. prof. Cornell U., 1965, Karachi U., 1980-81; mem. solar and wind energy adv. com. Tex. Energy and Natural Resources Coun., 1979; Fulbright sr. lectr., Pakistan, 1980-81, 82-83, Pakistan, 1991-92, Iraq, 1989-90. Author: The Teaching of African Languages, 1961, English Structure Drills, 1963, A Dari Course, 1968; editor: Jour. Linguistic Assn. S.W, 1976-82. Am. Coun. Learned Socs. fellow, 1954-55; Rockefeller Found. fellow, 1956-57. Mem. Tchrs. English to Speakers Other Langs., Am. Oriental Soc., AAAS. Home: PO Box 1217 Dripping Springs TX 78620-1217 Office: U Tex Dept Linguistics Austin TX 78712

BORDIGA, LORD BENNO, art dealer; arrived in U.S., 1940; s. Adolph and Grace V. Bordiga; m. Edna Bordiga (div. 1960); children: Robert S., Jeff; m. Melva E. Leftwich (div. 1986). BSME, U. Vienna, 1938. V.p. mfg. Olympic Radio and TV, L.I., 1943-58; pres., chmn. bd. Allomatic Industries, Woodside, NY, 1958—, Allstar Automotive Co., Hyde Park, NY, 1962-80, All-O-Matic Instrument and Sys., New Hyde Park, NY, 1967-79; pres. William R. Davis Fine Arts, N.Y.C., 1967—. V.p., dir. Hotel Comdr., N.Y.C., 1955—97; pres., dir. Fogel Mfg. Corp., Bklyn., 1959—64, W&B Industries, 1961—68; pres. Hotel Endicott, N.Y.C., Allomatic U.K. Ltd., Parzen Rsch. Co. Contbr. articles to profl. jours. Pres., bd. dirs. 1050 Park Ave. Tenants Corp., 1970—96. With U.S. Army, 1944—46. Home: 1050 Park Ave New York NY 10028-1031 Office: Allomatic Industries Inc 737 Park Ave New York NY 10021-4256

BORDLEY, JAMES, IV, surgeon; b. Balt., Nov. 24, 1942; s. James III and Julia (Ross) B.; m. Dianne Redmond; children: Jessica, James V. BA, Yale U., 1965; MD, Columbia U. Physicians/Surgeon, 1970. Surg. intern Bassett Hosp., Cooperstown, N.Y., 1970-71, surg. resident, 1971-75, att. surgeon, 1978—; staff surgeon Naval Regl. Med. Ctr., Newport, R.I., 1975-77; fellow biliary and pancreatic surgery U. Wash., Seattle, 1977; instr. surgery Columbia U., N.Y.C., 1978-80, asst. prof. clin. surg., 1980—. Contbr. articles to profl. jours./publs. Lt. cmdr. USN, 1975-77. Fellow Am. Coll. Surgeons; mem. Soc. Surgery of the Alimentary Tract, Soc. Am. Gastrointestinal Endoscopic Surgeons. Office: Bassett Hosp 1 Atwell Rd Cooperstown NY 13326-1301

BORDNER, GREGORY WILSON, chemical engineer; b. Buffalo, Aug. 16, 1959; s. Raymond Gordon and Nancy Lee (Immegart) B.; m. Margaret Patricia Toon, June 14, 1981; children: Eric Lawrence, Heather Rae. BSChemE, Calif. State Poly. U., 1982; MS in Sys. Mgmt., U. So. Calif., 1987. Registered profl. engr., Calif., Ariz., environ. assessor, cert. hazardous materials mgr. Commd. 2nd lt. USAF, 1983, advanced through grades to capt., 1987; engr., mgr. various air launched missile, anti-satellite and strategic def. initiative projects Air Force Rocket Propulsion Lab., Edwards AFB, Calif., 1983-86; asst. mgr. space transp. Air Force Astronautics Lab., Edwards AFB, 1986-87; chief small intercontinental ballistic missiles ordnance firing system br. Hdqrs. Ballistic Missile Orgn., San Bernardino, Calif., 1987-90; sr. plant environ. engr. Filtrol Corp./Akzo Chems. Inc., L.A., 1991-92; water/soils project engr. TABC, Inc., Long Beach, Calif., 1992-98, prodn. engr., 1998-99, asst. project mgr., 1999—2002, asst. mgr. environ. engring., health and safety, 2002—03, mgr. environ. engring., health and safety, 2003—. Author: (manual) Pyrotechnic Transfer Line Evaluation, 1984, (with others) Rocket Motor Heat Transfer, 1984. Mem. AIChE, Am. Water Works Assn. Avocations: jogging, weight lifting, bowling. Home: 10841 Ring Ave Alta Loma CA 91737-4429

BORDNER, MARJORIE RICH, educator, civic worker; b. McDonough Conty, Ill., Dec. 1, 1914; d. HarryR. and Merle (Turner) Rich; m. Lawrence Inman Bordner, Apr. 21, 1946; children: Larry Richard, Larrilyn Louise. BEd, Western Ill. U., 1936; EdM, U. Mo., Columbia, 1940. Tchr. various elem. and secondary schs., Ill.; instr. Western Ill. U. and Spoon River Coll.; acct., receptionist Bordner Air Conditioning-Refrigeration Co.; pres. New Eng. Women Ill. Prairie Colony, 1974-76, Fulton County Hist. and Geneal. Soc., 1974-75, 80—, Spoon River Scenic Drive Assn., 1971-74; sec. found. bd., exec. com. Western Ill. U., 1972—. Appointed by Ill. Gov. to First Western Ill. Univ. Bd. Trustees, 1996—, Western Ill. U. Centennial Com., 1999-2000; mem. Western Ill. U. Alumni Coun., 1972—, sec., 1981—; mem. Fulton County Planning Commn., 1971—, Canton Bicentennial Constn. Commn., 1986—, Canton Hist. Preservation and Devel. Commn., 1986—; chmn. Fulton County Bicentennial Constn. Commn., 1973-76, 86—; sec. County Resource Devel. Exec. Coun. Fulton County, 1979—. Author: A Spoon River Portrait, 1983 (Ill. State award for excellence 1983), Fulton County, Illinois Heritage, 1987, From Cornfields to Marching Feet, Camp Ellis, Ill., 1993; contb. articles to periodicals. Recipient Disting. Alumni award Western Ill. U., 1971, Achievement award, 1980, Jefferson award, 1981, Martha Washnigton award, 1986; named hon. parade marshal Canton Friendship Festival Parade, 1976, 87, Canton July 4, 2000 parade. Mem. Ill. Hist. Soc. (life), Ill. Geneal. Soc. (life), DAR (divsn. dir., regent 1971—, sec., bd. dirs. Ill. chpt. 1977), Nat. Soc. Daus. Founders Patriots (life), Nat. Soc. Daus. Am. Colonists. E-mail: mbordner@winco.net.

BORDNER, PATRICIA ANNE, insurance agent, writer; b. Red Wing, Minn., Mar. 29, 1946; d. Harold Arthur and Cecilia Helen Rodman; m. Thomas Ottis Bordner, May 18, 1981. AA, U. Minn., 1966. Cert. commercial rater U.S. Fidelity and Guaranty Co. Tchr. St. Albert the Great Elem. Sch., Mpls., 1967—68; tchr. Epiphany Edn. Ctr., Coon Rapids, Minn., 1968—70; comml. rater and acctg. clk. U. S. Fidelity and Guaranty Co., Mpls., 1971—85; comml. ins. rater Independent, Coon Rapids, 1985—. Author: (songs) (Poetry Book) Hands of Time, 2000; contbr. Named to Internat. Poetry Hall of Fame, 1996; recipient Golden Poet award, 1990, 1991, 1992, Editor's Choice award, 1993—98. Roman Catholic. Home: 1010 94th Ave NW Coon Rapids MN 55433-5501

BORDO, GUY VICTOR, conductor; MusB, MusM, U. Mich.; studied with Gustav Meier, Tanglewood Music Ctr.; studied with Carl St. Clair, PhD in Orchestral Conducting; student of Victor Yampolsky, Northwestern U. Music dir., conductor Sheboygan Symphony Orch., Wis., 1992; musical dir. Richmond Symphony Orch., 1997—. Guest conductor Orch. Lithuania, St. Christopher Chamber Orch., Kansas Opera, Elmhurst Symphony (Ill.) Orch., Light Opera Works Chgo., Lexington Philharmonic and the Waterloo/Cedar Falls (Iowa) Symphony, 1997. Office: Richmond Symphony Orch PO Box 982 Richmond IN 47375 Business E-Mail: rso1@skyenet.net.

BORDOGNA, JOSEPH, engineer, educator; b. Scranton, Pa., Mar. 22, 1933; s. Raymond and Rose (Yesu) B. BSEE, U. Pa., 1955, PhD, 1964; SM, MIT, 1960. With RCA Corp., 1958-64; asst. prof. U. Pa., Phila., 1964-68, assoc. prof., 1968-72, prof., 1972—, assoc. dean engring. and applied sci., 1973-80, acting dean, 1980-81, dean, 1981-90, dir. Moore Sch. Elec. Engring., 1976-90, Alfred Fitler Moore chair, 1979—; dir. engring. Nat. Sci. Foundation, Washington, 1991-96; COO, acting deputy dir. Nat. Sci. Found., Washington, 1996-99, dep. dir., COO, 1999—. Bd. dirs. Indsl. Imaging Corp., Weston Inc. (chmn. 1996-97), Univ. City Sci. Ctr.; master Stoufer Coll. House, 1972-76; cons. industry, govt., founds.; mem. Nat. Medal of Sci. com., 1989-91; chair adv. com. for engring. NSF, 1989-91. Author: (with H. Ruston) Electric Networks, 1966, (with others) The Man-Made World, 1971; chmn. editorial bd. Engring. Edn., 1987-90 With USN, 1955-58. Recipient commendation for first space capsule recovery, 1957, Lindback award for disting. teaching U. Pa., 1967, Centennial medal Phila. Coll. Textiles and Sci., 1988, Am. Indsl. Modernization Leadership award Nat. Coalition for Advanced Mfg., 1993, Chmn.'s award Am. Assn. Engring. Socs., 1994, Engr. of Yr. award NSPE Phila., 1984, George Washington medal Engrs. Club. Phila., 1997, Gold medal Soc. Mfg. Engrs., 2001, Leadership in Tech. Mgmt. award Portland Internat. Conf. on Mgmt. of Engring. and Tech., 2003; inducted into Engring. Educators Hall of Fame, 1993. Fellow AAAS (chair engring. sect. 1998-99), IEEE (chmn. Phila. sect. 1987-88, Centennial medal 1984, pres. 1998), Am. Soc. Engring. Edn. (George Westinghouse award 1974), Internat. Engring. Consortium; mem. Sigma Xi, Eta Kappa Nu, Tau Beta Pi, Phi Beta Delta. Office: Nat Sci Found Office Dir 4201 Wilson Blvd Ste 1205 Arlington VA 22230-1859

BORDY, BILL (WILLIAM JAMES BORDY), publisher; b. Pitts., Nov. 2, 1930; s. Samuel Alexander and Susan (Elischer) B. BA, Emerson Coll., 1958; cert., La Sorbonne, Paris, 1964. Dir. drama Suffolk U., Boston, 1955-58; pub., founder, pub. emeritus Drama-Logue, Hollywood, Calif., 1969-98; producer, writer, dir. Bill Bordy Prodns., Hollywood, 1980-99; ret., 1999. Producer, actor (TV comedy spl.) Une Soirée élegante, 1984 (Silver medal N.Y. Film and TV Festival 1985); producer, writer, dir., actor (TV movie) Twilight Blues, 1986, (motion picture) Side Roads, 1988; exec. prodr. (motion picture) Healer, 1994. With USMC, 1952-54. Recipient Alumni Recognition award Emerson Coll., 1985, 88, Issachar Hoopes Eldridge award, 2003, Cesar award Pan Am. Theatrical Assn., 1981, 90. Mem. AFTRA, Actors Equity Assn., Screen Actors Guild.

BORDY, MICHAEL JEFFREY, lawyer; b. Kansas City, Mo, July 24, 1952; s. Marvin Dean and Alice Mae (Rostov) B.; m. Marjorie Enid Kanof, Dec. 27, 1973 (div. Dec. 1983); m. Melissa Anne Held, May 24, 1987; children: Shayna Robyn, Jenna Alexis, Samantha Falyn. BA, Hamilton Coll., 1974; PhD, U. Kans., 1980; JD, U. So. Calif., 1986. Bar: Calif., 1986, US Dist. Ct. (cen. dist.) Calif., 1986, (so. dist.) Calif., 1987, US Ct. Appeals (9th cir.), 1986. Tchg. asst. biology U. Kans., Lawrence, 1975-76, rsch. asst. biology, 1976-80; post-doctoral fellow Johns Hopkins U., Balt., 1980-83; tchg. asst. U. So. Calif., LA, 1984-86; assoc. Thelen, Marrin, Johnson & Bridges, LA, 1986-87, Wood, Lucksinger & Epstein, LA, 1987-89, Cooper, Epstein & Hurewitz, Beverly Hills, Calif., 1989-93; ptnr. Jacobson, Runes & Bordy, Beverly Hills, 1994-96, Jacobson, Sanders & Bordy, LLP, Beverly Hills, 1996-97, Jacobson White Diamond & Bordy, LLP, Beverly Hills, 1997—2001, White, Bordy & Levey, LLP, 2002—. Bd. gov. Beverly Hills (Calif.) Bar Barristers, 1988-90, chair real estate law sect. 1998-2000, exec. com. 2000—; bd. govs. Cedars-Sinai Med. Ctr., LA, 1994—; bd. dir. Sinai Temple, 1998-2003; cabinet United Jewish Fund/Real Estate, LA, 1995—; mem. exec. com. Moriah Soc. for U. Judaism, 2002—; mem. planning com. Am. Cancer Soc., 1996-2000; mem. Guardians of the Jewish Home for the Aging, 1995—, Fraternity of Friends, 1997-99; active Lawyers Against Hunger, 1995—. Pre-Doctoral fellow NIH, Lawrence, 1977-80; post-doctoral fellow Mellon Found., Balt., 1980-83. Mem. ABA, State Bar Calif., LA County Bar Assn., Beverly Hills Bar Assn. (gov., barrister 1988-92, chair real estate sect. 1998-00), Profl. Network Group. Democrat. Jewish. Avocations: running, triathlons, reading. Office: White Bordy & Levey 1880 Century Park E Ste 200 Los Angeles CA 90067-1602 E-mail: mjbordy@wbllaw.com.

BOREEN, HENRY ISAAC, computer company executive; b. Warsaw, Mar. 7, 1927; came to U.S., 1949; s. Isaac and Grina (Goldstein) B.; m. Lois Adele Golwyn, June 22, 1958; children: Stuart Michael Boreen, Susan Tobey Hailman. *Wife Lois, BS 1957 Temple University; taught at junior high school, was therapeutic dietician at Germantown Hospital in Philadelphia, Pennsylvania. Son Stuart, BA 1981 University of Pennsylvania; MD 1986 Jefferson University; Anesthesia Residency 1990, currently employed as Anesthesiologist at St. Luke's Hospital, Bethlehem, Penna. Daughter-in-law Joan Lustig Boreen BS 1980 U. Pennsylvania; MBA 1985 Temple University. Daughter Susan Hailman, BA 1985 U. Pennsylvania; MA 1988 Harvard University, cum laude; MBA 1993 Pace University. Son-in-law Eric Peter Hailman, AB 1988 Harvard, Magna Cum Laude, PhD 1997 Rockefeller University, MD 1998 Cornell University, currently doing post doctorate at Washington University in St. Louis, Misso. Grandchildren: Kevin Andrew Boreen, Michael Alexander Boreen, Joshua Michael Hailman,Alexander Daniel Hailman.* BSEE, Drexel U., 1956, MSEE, 1958, DrEngring.Sci, D Engring. Sci., Drexel U., 2002. Asst. prof. Drexel Univ., Phila., 1958; v.p. engr. Vector Mfg. Co., Inc., Trevose, Pa., 1958-64; chmn., CEO Solid State Sci., Inc., Montgomeryville, Pa., 1964-86; chmn. US-Tech, Inc., Valley Forge, Pa., 1987—; chmn., CEO AM Comm., Inc., Quakertown, Pa., 1990-99; chmn. Integrated Circuit Systems Inc., Valley Forge, Pa., 1993-99; with Combex, Inc., Rydal, Pa., 2000—. Bd. trustees Cardiovascular Found. New Rochelle, NY, 2002—; chmn. Combex, Inc., San Jose; bd. dirs. Integrated Cir. Sys., Inc. Co-author: Aerospace Telemetry, 1961. Recipient Centennial medal Drexel Univ., 1991. Avocations: gardening, photography, car racing, hiking, bird watching. Office: Combex Inc PO Box 4070 Rydal PA 19046

BOREI, KARIN ELISABET, librarian; b. Stockholm, Mar. 7, 1939; came to U.S., 1953; d. Hans Georg and Maj Ellen (Osterlin) Borei; children: Susan Elizabeth Hodges, Erich Michael Hodges. BA, Brown U., 1961; MLS, Drexel U., 1972; postgrad., Boston U., 1982--. Asst. libr. Univ. Mus. Libr., Phila., 1966-68; Anglo-Germanic cataloger U. Pa., Phila., 1968-72, catalog editor, 1973-76; circulation libr. U. Va., Charlottesville, 1977-79; copy cataloging coord. Boston U., 1980, systems libr., 1980-83, assoc. dir. librs., 1983-87, mem. instnl. rev. bd., 1984-91; asst. univ. libr. Boston Coll., Chestnut Hill, Mass., 1987-91, assoc. univ. libr., 1991-92; cons. Boston Libr. Consortium, 1992, Mass. State Libr., 1993; libr. dir. Trinity Coll. Vt., Burlington, 1993-98; univ. libr. Millikin U., 1999—. Organizer libr. confs.; presenter at confs., 1982—. Contbr. articles to libr. jours. Mem. ALA, Assn. Coll. and Rsch. Librs. (bd. dirs. 1990-94, White House Conf. com. 1990-92, pres. New Eng. chpt. 1988-89), Libr. Adminstrn. and Mgmt. Assn. (chmn. women adminstrs. group 1984-85), New Eng. Libr. Assn. (chmn. acad. librs. sect. 1984-85), Libr. and Info. Tech. Assn., Beta Phi Mu, Pi Lambda Theta. Office: Staley Libr Millikin U 1184 W Main St Decatur IL 62522-2039 E-mail: kborei@mail.millikin.edu.

BOREI, SVEN HANS EMIL, translator; b. Stockholm, Dec. 21, 1941; s. Hans Georg and Maj Ellen (Österlin) B.; m. Gisela Wilms Möller; children: Bethany, Rolf, Emil. AA, Valley Forge Mil. Acad., 1961; BA in English, U. Pa., 1964; postgrad., Syracuse U. English and writing tchr. Meadowbrook Sch. for Boys, Phila., 1964-65; basic skills instr. adult edn. Syracuse (N.Y.) Pub. Schs., 1965-67; assoc. dir. Ednl. and Cultural Ctr. Onondaga and Oswego Counties, Syracuse, 1966-67; English instr. Maria Regina Jr. Coll., Syracuse, 1967-68; pres., founder, trustee, CEO Ctr. for Literacy, Inc., Phila., 1968-78; literacy project coord. Appalachia Ednl. Lab., Charleston, W.Va., 1980-81; founder, pres., CEO Literacy Inst., Inc., Syracuse, 1981-88; co-prop. H.E.S. Konsult AB, Transförlag, Lerum, Sweden, 1986—; English lang. coord. Språkverket AB, Göteborg, 1987-89. Mem. Nat. Adv. Coun. on Interpreting and Translating, 2001-03; cons., presenter workshops, seminars in field. Author: Appalachian Adult Literacy Programs Survey, 2 vols., 1981, LLA Finance Handbook, 1982, A Measure of Freedom, 1995; editor: Quality Thinking, 1998; translator: Art at Astra, 1997, Jan Johansson, a Visionary Swedish Musician, 1998, Travel Guide for Westmanland, 2000, Jazz Facts, 1999, 2000, 01, Lena Mattson, a small fairy tale, 2001, Olle Kåks, Paintings 1970-2002, 2002, The Savour of Alsace, 2003; contbr. articles to profl. jours. Supervisory tutor trainer Laubach Literacy Action, Syracuse, 1975, master tutor trainer, 1977, regional trainer cons., 1985, bd. dirs. 1972-80; co-founder, chair Tutors for Literacy in Pa., 1975-76, W.Va. Literacy Coalition, 1980-82, Tenn. Literacy Coalition, 1982-85; mem. Lerum Mcpl. Coun., 1991-98, mcpl. exec. com., 1995-98, mcpl. bldg. bd. 1999—; bd. govs. Am.-Swedish Hist. Found., 1973-80, v.p., 1975-77, treas., 1977-78. Mem. Swedish Assn. Profl. Translators (bd. dirs. 1997-2003, vice chmn. 1998-99, chmn. 1999-2003). Avocations: music, local history, poetry, renovating furniture. Home and Office: PL 3181 Koksås S-443 38 Lerum Sweden E-mail: heskon@algonet.se.

BOREL, JAMES DAVID, anesthesiologist; b. Chgo., Nov. 15, 1951; s. James Albert and Nancy Ann (Sieverson) B. BS, U. Wis., 1973; MD, Med. Coll. of Wis., 1977. Diplomate Am. Bd. Anesthesiology, Nat. Bd. Med. Examiners, Am. Coll. Anesthesiologists. Research asst. McArdle Lab. for Cancer Research, Madison, Wis., 1972-73, Stanford U. and VA Hosp., Palo Alto, 1976-77; intern. The Cambridge (Mass.) Hosp., 1977-78; clin. fellow in medicine Harvard Med. Sch., Boston, 1977-78, clin. fellow in anesthesia, 1978-80, clin. instr. in anaesthesia, 1980; resident in anesthesiology Peter Bent Brigham Hosp., Boston, 1978-80; anesthesiologistt Mt. Auburn Hosp., Cambridge, 1980; fellow in anesthesiology Ariz. Health Scis. Ctr., Tucson, 1980-81; research assoc. U. Ariz. Coll. Medicine, Tucson, 1980-81, assoc. in anesthesiology, 1981—; active staff Mesa (Ariz.) Luth. Hosp., 1981—; courtesy staff Scottsdale (Ariz.) Meml. Hosp., 1982—. Vis. anesthetist St. Joseph's Hosp., Kingston, Jamaica, 1980. Contbr. numerous articles to profl. jours. Mem. AMA, AAAS, Ariz. Anesthesia Alumni Assn., Ariz. Soc. Anesthesiologists, Am. Soc. Regional Anesthesia, Can. Anesthetists' Soc., Internat. Anesthesia Rsch. Soc., Am. Soc. Anesthesiologists. Office: Valley Anesthesia Cons 2200 N Central Ave Ste 203 Phoenix AZ 85004-1431

BORELLI, FRANCIS J(OSEPH) (FRANK BORELLI), insurance brokerage and consulting firm financial executive; b. Bklyn., Sept. 2, 1935; s. Anthony and Ida Borelli; m. Madlyn Quadrino, June 25, 1960; children: Frank, Richard. BBA, Baruch Coll. CUNY, 1956. CPA, N.Y. With Deloitte Haskins & Sells, 1956-79, ptnr., 1968-79, mng. ptnr. in charge Bergen County, N.J. office, 1976-79; sr. v.p. fin. and adminstr., dir. Airco, Inc., Montvale, N.J., 1980-84; sr. v.p., chief fin. officer, dir. Marsh & McLennan Cos., Inc., N.Y.C., 1984-2000, sr. advisor, 2001—. Bd. dirs. The Interpub. Group, Express Scripts. Bd. dirs., chmn.-emeritus Nat. Multiple Sclerosis Soc., Sedgwick Claims Mgmt. Svcs.; dir. emeritus pvt. sector coun.; trustee St. Thomas Aquinas Coll.; former dir. Mid Ocean Reinsurance and United Water Resources; former nat. chmn. Fin. Execs. Internat.; active numerous pub. svs. orgns.; chmn. Nyack Hosp. Mem. Fin. Execs. Inst., AICPAs, N.Y. State Soc. CPAs, Ridgewood Country Club, Columbus Found. Club. Office: Marsh & McLennan Cos Inc 1166 Avenue Of The Americas New York NY 10036-2728

BOREN, CLARK HENRY, JR., general and vascular surgeon; b. Marinette, Wis., Nov. 23, 1947; s. Clark Henry and Maryon Lillian (Peterson) Boren; children: Jenna Marie, Matthew William, Nathan Clark. BMS, Northwestern U., 1971, MD with distinction, 1973. Diplomate Am. Bd. Surgery. Resident in gen. surgery U. Calif.-H.C. Moffitt Hosp., San Francisco, 1973-79; rsch. fellow in vascular surgery Ft. Miley VA Hosp., 1976-77; vascular fellow Med. Coll. Wis./Milwaukee County Med. Complex, Milw., 1979-80; mem. staff Fox Valley Surg. Assocs., Ltd., Appleton, Wis., 1980—, pres., 1997—. Chmn. bd. United Health Wis., 1995—99. Contbr. articles to profl. jours. Mem.: AMA, ACS, Am. Assn. Vascular Surgery, Wis. Surg. Soc., Midwest Vascular Soc., Peripheral Vascular Surgery Soc., Wis. State Med. Soc., Phi Kappa Psi, Phi Eta Sigma, Phi Beta Pi, Alpha Omega Alpha. Democrat. Home: 519 E Timberline Dr Appleton WI 54913-7102 Office: Fox Valley Surg Assocs 1818 N Meade St Appleton WI 54911-3454

BOREN, JAMES EDGAR, lawyer; b. New Orleans, Nov. 16, 1949; s. John E. and Katherine (Savage) B.; m. Teresa Anne Berlin, Mar. 7, 1971; children: Anna Blynn, Katherine Lenore, Rebecca Camille. BA, La. Tech U., 1971; JD, La. State U., 1975. Bar: La. 1975, U.S. Dist. Ct. (mid. dist.) La. 1975, U.S. Ct. Appeals (5th cir.)1975, U.S. Dist. Ct. (we. dist.) La. 1976, U.S. Dist. Ct. (ea. dist.) La. 1977, U.S. Supreme Ct. 1979, U.S. Ct. Appeals (11th cir.) 1981. Asst. dist. atty. Parish of East Baton Rouge, 1975-76; ptnr. Boren, Holthaus & Perez, Baton Rouge, 1976-88; pvt. practice Baton Rouge, La., 1988—. Chair La. Atty. Discipline Bd. Hearing Com., 1994-2000. Contbr. articles to profl. publs. Mem.

ACLU (bd. dirs. 1988-92), La. State Bar Assn. (ho. of dels. 1998—), La. Assn. Criminal Def. Lawyers (bd. dirs. 1985—, pres. commendation 1986, pres. 1990-91, chair edn. com. 1997—, Tate award 2000), Nat. Assn. Criminal Def. Lawyers (bd. dirs. 1992-95, chmn. death penalty com. 1994-98, indigent def. co-chair 1998-2002). Democrat. Home: 2035 E Lakeshore Dr Baton Rouge LA 70808-1464 Address: 830 Main St Baton Rouge LA 70802-5597 E-mail: jimboren@bellsouth.net.

BOREN, KENNETH RAY, endocrinologist, nephrologist; b. Evansville, Ind., Dec. 31, 1945; s. Doyle Clifford and Jeannette (Koerner) B.; m. Rebecca Lane Wallace, Aug. 25, 1967; children: Jennifer, James, Michael, Peter, Nicklas, Benjamin. BS, Ariz. State U., 1967; MD, Ind. U., Indpls., 1972; MA, Ind. U., Bloomington, 1974. Diplomate Am. Bd. Endocrinology, Am. Bd. Nephrology, Am. Bd. Internal Medicine, Hypertension Soc. Intern in pathology Ind. U. Sch. Medicine, Indpls., 1972, intern in medicine, 1972-73, resident in medicine, 1975-77, fellow in endocrinology, 1977-79, fellow nephrology, 1979-80, instr., 1980; physician East Valley Nephrology, Mesa, Ariz., 1980—. Chief medicine Mesa Luth. Hosp., 1987—89, chief staff, 1990—91; med. dir. RenalWest, 1996—, regional med. dir., 1996—99. Bd. dirs. Ariz. Kidney Found., Phoenix, 1984—, pres. 1993-94. Lt. USN, 1973-75. Fellow: ACP, Am. Coll. Clin. Endocrinology; mem.: AMA, Am. Diabetes Assn., Am. Endocrine Soc., Internat. Soc. Nephrology, Am. Soc. Nephrology, Ariz. Med. Assn., Maricopa County Med. Assn. Republican. Latter Day Saints. Home: 4222 E Mclellan Rd Ste 10 Mesa AZ 85205-3119 Office: East Valley Nephrology 560 W Brown Rd Ste 3006 Mesa AZ 85201-3225

BOREN, LYNDA SUE, gifted education educator; b. Leesville, La., Apr. 1, 1941; d. Leonard and Doris (Ford) Schoenberger; m. James Lewis Boren, Sept. 1, 1961; 1 child, Lynda Carolyn. BA, U. New Orleans, 1971, MA, 1973; PhD, Tulane U., 1979. Prof. Northwestern State U., Natchitoches, La., 1987-89; propr. Colony Country House, New Llano, La., 1992-94; tchr. of gifted Leesville (La.) H.S., 1992—. Vis. prof. Newcomb Coll., Tulane U., New Orleans, 1979-83, U. Erlangen-Nuremburg, Germany, 1981-82, Middlebury (Vt.) Coll., 1983-84, Ga. Inst. Tech., Atlanta, 1985-87, Srinakharinwirot U., Bangkok, 1989-90; mem. planning com. 1st Kate Chopin Internat. Conf., Natchitoches, La., 1987-89; Fulbright lectr. USIA and Bd. Fgn. Scholars, 1981-82, 89-90. Author: Eurydice Reclaimed: Language, Gender and Voice in Henry James, 1989; co-editor, author: Kate Chopin Reconsidered, 1992; contbg. author: Encyclopedia of American Poetry, 1998; contbr. numerous articles to profl. jours. Founding mem. John F. Kennedy libr. Recipient awards for watercolors; Mellon fellow Tulane U., 1977-78; NEH seminar fellow Princeton U., 1986. Mem. MLA, AAUW, DAR, AFT, Fulbright Alumni Assn. Avocations: painting, video film documentaries, photography. Home: 1492 Fords Dairy Rd Newllano LA 71461-4530 E-mail: alborn@peoplepc.com.

BOREN, ROBERT REED, communication educator; b. Burley, Idaho, Nov. 8, 1936; s. Gilbert Reed Boren and Olive Chambers McBride; m. Marjorie Jean Dixon, Sept. 9, 1958; children: David, Michael, Elisabeth, Stephen. BA, Brigham Young U., 1958, MA, 1964; PhD, Purdue U., 1965. Instr. Purdue U., Lafayette, Ind., 1959-61; asst. prof. Brigham Young U., Provo, Utah, 1961-67; assoc. prof. U. Mont., Missoula, 1967-71; prof. Boise (Idaho) State U., 1971—, chair, 1971-95; pres. Insight Cons., Boise, 1995—. Author: The Human Transaction, 1975, Communication Behavior, 1975, Communication Experiments, 1975, Conducting the Council's Business, 1976, Wildflowers of the Sawtooth Mountains, 1979, Facilitator's Guide for Public Meetings, 1981, Effective Business Writing, 1985, Effective Communication, 1985, Effective Business Communication, 1986, Mountain Wildflowers of Idaho, 1989. Mem. Nat. Comm. Assn., Western States Comm. Assn. (v.p., pres. 1971-73, Disting. Svc. award 1998), Western Forensics Assn. (v.p., pres. 1968-70), Phi Kappa Delta. Avocations: hiking, rafting, fishing, hunting. Home: HC 67 Box 742 Clayton ID 83227-9801 Office: Boise State U 1910 University Dr Boise ID 83725-0399 E-mail: rboren@custertel.net.

BOREN, ROGER W. judge; b. Bingham Canyon, Utah, Sept. 11, 1941; m. Winifred A. Scott, Feb. 4, 1965; 6 children. BA, U. Calif., Berkeley, 1966; MA, San Jose State U., 1968; JD, UCLA, 1973. Bar: Calif. 1973, U.S. Dist. Ct. (ctrl. dist.) Calif. 1973. Dep. atty. gen. State of Calif., 1973-84; judge Mcpl. Ct., Newhall Jud. Dist., 1973-84; judge Superior Ct., L.A. County, Calif., 1985-87; assoc. justice 2 Appellate Dist., Calif. Ct. Appeals, L.A., 1987-93, presiding justice, 1993—. Bd. dirs. Henry Mayo Newhall Meml. Hosp., 1985—. Mem. Lds Ch.

BOREN, WILLIAM MEREDITH, manufacturing executive; b. San Antonio, Oct. 23, 1924; s. Thomas Loyd and Verda (Locke) B.; m. Molly Brasfield Sarver, Dec. 3, 1976; children: Susan, Patricia, Janet, Jenny, Burton, Cliff. Student, Tex. A&M U., 1942-43, Rice U., 1943-44; BS in Mech. Engring., Tex. U., 1949. Vice pres., gen. mgr. Rolo Mfg. Co., Houston, 1949-54; mgr. sales engring. Black, Sivalls & Bryson, Houston, Oklahoma City, 1955-64; vice chmn., dir., mem. exec. com. Big Three Industries, Inc., Houston, 1965—; chmn. Bowen Tool Co., Houston. Bd. dirs. Engring. Adv. Coun., Tex. U.; dir. Air Liquide Am. Corp.; dir. Electric Reliability Coun. Tex. Inventor Classic Bridge game. Trustee S.W. Rsch. Inst., San Antonio; bd. dirs. Coun. Econ. Edn.; mem. chancellor's coun. U. Tex. Lt. (j.g.) USN, 1943-46. Named Disting. Grad. Engring. Dept., U. Tex., 1992. Mem. Internat. Oxygen Mfrs. Assn. (chmn.), French-Am. C. of C. (bd. dirs.), Tau Beta Pi, Pi Tau Sigma. Republican. Home: 2906 Midlane St Houston TX 77027-4912

BORENSTEIN, DANIEL ASA, newspaper political editor; b. Berkeley, Calif., Sept. 23, 1955; s. Martin and Betty (Aron) B.; m. Marian Dabney Scott, Feb. 14, 1999. BA in Journalism, BA in Polit. Sci., U. Calif., Berkeley, 1978, Master of Journalism, Master of Pub. Policy, U. Calif., Berkeley, 1985. Reporter Antioch (Calif.) Daily Ledger, 1980-83; reporter, asst. city editor Valley Times, Pleasanton, Calif., 1983-85, Contra Costa Times, Walnut Creek, Calif., 1986-90, polit. editor, 1990—. Free-lance commentator Sta. KRON-TV, San Francisco, 1995-97, Sta. KQED-TV, San Francisco, 1994—; free-lance writer Calif. Jour., Sacramento, 1986, 91. Mem. Better Govt. task force Contra Costa County, 1995-96. Recipient Pub. Svc. award Calif. Newspaper Pubs. Assn., 1993, Investigative Reporting award, 1994, Third place pub. svc. award Nat. Headliner Club, 1994, Golden Medallion award for legal reporting State Bar of Calif., 1985, 93, Third place investigative reporting award Nat. Newspaper Assn., 1987, numerous others. Mem. Soc. of Profl. Journalists (co-chair Freedom of Info. com. No. Calif. Chpt., 1996-99, invesigative reporting award 1992-93, James Madison Freedom of Info. award 1994). Office: Contra Costa Times 2640 Shadelands Dr Walnut Creek CA 94598-2578

BORENSTEIN, DANIEL BERNARD, psychiatrist, educator; b. Silver City, N.Mex., Mar. 31, 1935; s. Jack and Marjorie Elizabeth (Kerr) B.; m. Bonnie Denice Ulland, June 11, 1967; 1 child, Jay Brian. BSChemE, MIT, 1957; MD, U. Colo., 1962. Diplomate Am. Bd. Psychiatry and Neurology. Intern U. Hosp. U. Ky., 1962-63; resident in psychiatry U. Colo. Med. Ctr., 1963-66; chief resident, psychiatry instr. U. Colo. Sch. Medicine, 1965-66; psychiatry instr. U. So. Calif. Sch. Medicine, 1966-67; asst. clin. prof. psychiatry UCLA Sch. Medicine, 1972-84, assoc. clin. prof., 1984-96, clin. prof., 1996—. Founder, dir. UCLA Mental Health Program for Physicians In Tng., 1980—84; clin. assoc. L.A. Psychoanalytic Soc. and Inst., 1967—71, pres. clin. assocs., 1970—71, faculty, 1973—83, sr. faculty, 1983—; pvt. practice medicine specializing in psychoanalysis and psychiatry, West L.A., 1966—; assoc. vis. psychiatrist UCLA Ctr. Health Scis., 1973—90; cons. Medicare Program, 1995—; examiner Am. Bd. Psychiatry and Neurology; reviewer various med. and psychiat. jours., 1991—. Author: Manual of Psychiatric Peer Review, 1985, Psychiatric Peer Review: Prelude and Promise, 1985; contbr. articles to profl. jours. Bd. dirs. L.A. Child Devel. Ctr., 1981—85, Found. Advancement Psychiat. Edn. and Rsch., 1991—, Coop. Am. Physicians/Mutual Protective Trust, 1994—. Lt. AUS, 1957—58. Fellow: Am. Coll. Psychiatrists (com. on hon. fellowship 2002—), Am. Psychiat. Assn. (life; coun. area VI 1977—79, com. to rev. psychiat. news 1979—81, coun. area VI, dep. rep. assembly dist. brs. 1981—82, work group on competition and legis. 1981—83, nominating com. 1982—83, assembly liaison to peer rev. com. 1982—86, assembly rep. dist. brs. 1982—89, assemly liaison to fin. and mktg. com. 1986—87, assembly corr. group on subspecialization 1986—89, assembly liaison to coun. on econ. affairs 1987—89, med. student edn. com. 1987—90, bd. liaison jud. action commn. 1989—91, bd. trustees 1989—, com. managed care 1990—92, com. mem., bd. liaison to managed care com. 1992—99, bd. liaison econ. affairs coun. 1992—99, chmn. bd. ethics appeals, sec. 1995—97, v.p. 1997—99, pres.-elect 1999—2000, pres. 2000—01, chair med. dir. contract negotiating com. 2001, cons. bus. rels. com. 2001—02, chair nominating com. 2001—02, past pres. 2001—, bus. rels. com. 2002—, disting. fellow); mem.: AMA (ho. dels., alt. 1998—2002, del. 2003—), Internat. Psychoanalytic Assn., Am. Psychoanalytic Assn. (com. on confidentiality 1983—96, com. on govt. rels. and ins. 1983—2000), L.A. Psychoanalytic Soc. and Inst. (co-chmn. ext. divsn. 1973—74, chmn. peer rev. com. 1975—78, curriculum com. 1980—84), Calif. Psychiat. Assn. (exec. coun. 1977—79, 1981—95, chmn. jud. com. 1986—88, bd. trustees 1989—95, Spl. Recognition award 1995), Calif. Med. Assn. (ho. of dels. psychiat. specialty rep. 1979—84, com. on mental health and mental disabilities 1979—85, alt. del. ho. del. 1984—86, del. 1986—88, com. on mental health and mental disabilities 1987—88, com. mental health and mental disabilities 1987—88, bd. trustees, del. 1992—2001, chmn. physicians benevolence operating com. 1996—2001, chmn. bldg. com. 1999—2001, del. 1992—2001), L.A. County Med. Assn. (chmn. mental health com. Bay dist. 1980—85, com. on substance abuse 1981—86, Bay Dist. bd. dirs. 1981—, Bay Dist. v.p. 1985—86, pres.-elect 1986—87, com. on well-being 1986—89, pres. 1987—88, exec. coun. 1988—91), So. Calif. Psychiat. Soc. (chmn. peer rev. com. 1974—77, Outstanding Svc. citation 1975, exec. coun. 1976—89, ethics com. 1977—85, pres. 1978—79, chmn. fellowship and awards com. 1979—85, chmn. Commn. on Psychiatry and the Law 1980—81, Appreciation award 1979, 1st recipient Disting. Svc. award 1984, Outstanding Achievement award 1993). Office: 151 N Canyon View Dr Los Angeles CA 90049-2721

BORENSTEIN, DAVID GILBERT, physician, author; b. Bklyn. s. Murray and Mollie (Koren) B.; m. Dorothy Regina Fait, Aug. 6, 1972; children: Sylvia, Elizabeth, Rebecca. AB, Columbia U., 1969; MD, Johns Hopkins U., 1973. Diplomate Am. Bd. Internal Medicine, Am. Bd. Rheumatology. Intern in medicine Johns Hopkins Hosp., 1973-74, resident in medicine, 1974-76; fellow in rheumatology Johns Hopkins U., 1976-78; asst. prof. medicine George Washington U., Washington, 1978-83, assoc. prof. medicine, 1983-89, prof. medicine, 1989-96, prof. neurosurgery, 1991-96, clin. prof. neurosurgery, 1997-98, clin. prof. medicine, 1997—. Cons. Vaccine Injury Compensation Program, Dept. HHS, Washington, 1993-2002, Sulzer Medica, Austin, Tex., 1997-2002, Searle, Skokie, Ill., 1997-2002, Merck-Medco, Rahway, N.J., 1997-99, OSHA, Dept. Labor, 1998-99, Merck, 1999—, Pfizer, 2003. Author: Low Back Pain: Medical Diagnosis, 1995, Neck Pain: Medical Diagnosis, 1996, Back in Control! A Conventional and Complementary Prescription for Eliminating Back Pain, 2001; contbg. author: Low Back Pain in Rheumatology, 1997. Mem. Appellate Jud. Nominating Commn., State of Md., 1986-94; mem. med. adv. bd. Arthritis Found. D.C., 1986-88, bd. dirs., 1999—; mem. med. adv. bd. Lupus Found. Greater Washington, 1992—. Fellow: Am. Coll Rheumatology (govt. affairs com. 1998—, chmn. govt. affairs com. 2001—), Am. Coll. Medicine; mem.: Rheumatism Soc. D.C. (pres. 1992—93), Internat. Soc. Study Lumbar Spine (membership com. 1999, chmn. 2002), Cosmos Club. Jewish. Avocations: skiing, stereo equipment, squash. Office: Arthritis and Rheum Assocs 2021 K St NW Washington DC 20006-1003

BORENSTEIN, EUGENE REED, lawyer; b. Bklyn., July 19, 1944; s. Charles H. and Gloria (Seiden) B.; m. Maxine Herold, June 25, 1978. B.S., Mich. State U., 1966; J.D., New York Law Sbb., 1969. Bar: N.Y. 1969, U.S. Dist. Ct. (so. dist.) N.Y., 1969. Dep. chief housing and real estate divsn. Law Dept., City of N.Y., 1976-78, asst. chief comml. litigation, 1978-79, dep. chief affirmative litigation, 1979-81, chief worker compensation divsn., 1981-83, dep. chief tort divsn., 1981-92, chief tort divsn., 1992—. Home: 301 E 75th St New York NY 10021-3010 Office: City of NY Law Dept 100 Church St New York NY 10007-2601

BORENSTEIN, MARK A. lawyer; b. Bklyn., June 26, 1951; BA, SUNY, Buffalo, 1973; JD, George Washington U., 1976; LLM, Georgetown U., 1978. Bar: Va. 1976, D,C, 1977, Calif. 1978. Law clk. to Hon. Irving Hill U.S. Dist. Ct. (cen. dist.), Calif., 1976-77; mem. Tuttle & Taylor, L.A., 1978-2000, Shapiro, Borenstein & Dupont, Santa Monica, Calif., 2000—02, Overland & Borenstein, L.A., 2002—. Lectr. U. So. Calif., 1980—82, vis. prof. law, 1997, adj. prof., 1999—. Exec. editor: George Washington Law Review, 1975-76. Inst. for Pub. Interest Representation Law fellow Georgetown U. Law Ctr., 1977-78. Mem. Phi Beta Kappa, Order of the Coif. Office: Overland & Borenstein 6060 Ctr Dr 7th Fl Los Angeles CA 90045 E-mail: mborenstein@overlandborenstein.com.

BORENSTEIN, MILTON CONRAD, lawyer, manufacturing company executive; b. Boston, Oct. 21, 1914; s. Isadore Sidney and Eva Beatrice B.; m. Anne Shapiro, June 20, 1937; children: Roberta, Jeffrey. AB cum laude, Boston Coll., 1935; JD, Harvard U., 1938. Bar: Mass. 1938, U.S. Dist. Ct. 1939, U.S. Ct. Appeals 1944, U.S. Supreme Ct. 1944. Pvt. practice law, Boston, 1938—; officer, dir. Sweetheart Paper Products Co., Inc., Chelsea, Mass., 1944-61, pres., 1961-83, chmn. bd., 1984; with Sweetheart Plastics, Inc., Wilmington, Mass., 1958—, v.p., 1958-84, also dir.; v.p. Md. Cup Corp., Owings Mills, 1960-77, exec. v.p., treas., 1977-84, also dir.; ptnr. Concorde Assocs., Boston. Bd. dirs. Am. Assocs. Hebrew U., 1968—; trustee Combined Jewish Philanthropies, Boston, 1969—, N.E. Sinai Hosp., Stoughton, Mass., 1974—, Ben-Gurion U., 1975-85, 87—, Boston Coll., 1979-87, chmn. estate planning coun., 1981-83, mem. coun. exec. com. 1984—, assoc. trustee, 1987-96; mem. pres.'s coun. Sarah Lawrence Coll., 1970-79; bd. overseers Jewish Theol. Sem. Am., 1971—; mem. pres. Congregation Kehillath Israel, Brookline, Mass., 1977-79, hon. pres., 1979—; mem. pres's coun. Brandeis U., 1979-81, fellow, 1981—; v.p. Assoc. Synagogues of Mass., 1980-81; exec. com. New Eng. region Anti-Defamation League, 1980—; bd. dirs., nat. governing coun. Am. Jewish Congress, 1984—; assoc. chmn. scholarship com. Harvard Law Sch., 1964-66, mem. spl. gifts com., 1990, mem. Langdell com., 1991, 92, 93, 94, 95, 96, 97, 98, 99, Boston regional campaign com., 1992, chmn. class reunion gift, 1993, 98. Recipient Community Svc. award Jewish Theol. Sem. Am., 1970, Am. Jewish Congress, 1993, Bald Eagle Outstanding Alumnus award Boston Coll., 1991; named Rofeh Internat. Man of Yr., 1996. Fellow Mass. Bar Found.; mem. ABA, Mass. Bar Assn., Boston Bar Assn. (mem. bicentennial com. 1986-87), Harvard Club (Boston and N.Y.C.), Harvard Faculty Club.

BORENSTEIN, NATHANIEL SOLOMON, computer programmer, inventor, educator; b. Pitts., Sept. 23, 1957; s. Stanley Russell and Deborah (Kandall) B.; m. Trina Rae Glasser, June 24, 1978; children: Shayna Nova, Rachel Leah, Miriam Eve. BA, Grinnell Coll., 1980; MS, Carnegie Mellon U., 1981, PhD, 1985. Lectr. Carnegie Mellon U., Pitts., 1985-89, sys. designer, 1985-89; mem. tech. staff Bellcore, Morristown, N.J., 1989-94; chief scientist First Virtual Holdings, San Diego, 1994-98; mem. faculty Sch. Info. U. Mich., Ann Arbor, 1998—; chmn., chief scientist NetPOS.com., 2000—02; disting. engr. IBM, 2002—. Author: Multimedia Applications Development with the Andrew Toolkit, 1988, Programming as If People Mattered, 1990. Dir. Peace Action, 1992, Inst. for Global Comm., 1996, Computer Profls. for Social Responsibility, 1996. Named one of Top 100 Internet Gurus, Web World Mag., 1996; NSF fellow, 1980. Mem. Assn. for Computing Machinery (mem. adv. bd. publs. 1996—), Electronic Frontier Found. Democrat. Avocations: guitar, singing, hiking, canoeing, camping.

BORENSTINE, ALVIN JEROME, search company executive; b. Kansas City, Mo., Dec. 14, 1933; s. Samuel and Ella C. (Berman) B.; m. Roula Alakiotou, Dec. 31, 1976; children: Mana an dSami (twins). BS in Econs., U. Kans., 1956; MBA, U. Pa., 1960. Analyst Johnson & Johnson, New Brunswick, N.J., 1961-62; systems mgr. Levitt & Sons, Levittown, N.J., 1962-66; dir. mgmt. info. svcs. Warren Bros. Co., Cambridge, Mass., 1966-71; mgr. fin. & adminstrv. systems Esmark, Inc., Chgo., 1971-72; pres. Synergistics Assocs. Ltd., Chgo., 1972—. Mem. bus. adv. coun. Program Able, Hellenic Dimensions; mem. civic com. El Valor; mem. North Shore Cultural Ctr. Sys. and Procedures Assn. Systems and Procedures Assn. rsch. fellow, 1959-60, Eddie JAcobson Found. scholar, 1958-60. Mem.: Soc. Info. Mgmt., Assn. Sys. Mgmt. (pres Boston chpt. 1969, Disting. award 1970), Assn. Exec. Search Cons., B'nai B'rith, Carlton Club. Home: 6033 N Sheridan Rd Chicago IL 60660-3003 Office: Synergistics Assocs Ltd 400 N State St Ste 400 Chicago IL 60610-4624 E-mail: ajbsynerg@aol.com.

BORER, JEFFREY STEPHEN, cardiologist; b. Deland, Fla., Feb. 22, 1945; s. Lee Norton and Rita Doris (Feldt) B.; m. Brondi Beth Topchik, Sept. 16, 1978; children: Justine Isolde, Jon Andrew. BA in Govt., Harvard U., 1965; MD, Cornell U., 1969. Diplomate Am. Bd. Internal Medicine, Am. Bd. Cardiovascular Disease; cert. Bd. Nuclear Cardiology. Intern, then resident in medicine Mass. Gen. Hosp., Boston, 1969-71; clin. fellow in medicine Harvard U. Sch. Medicine, Boston, 1969-71; clin. assoc. in cardiology Nat. Heart, Lung and Blood Inst., NIH, Bethesda, Md., 1971-74, chief resident physician, 1973-74, sr. investigator, cardiology br., 1975-79; sr. Fulbright-Hays scholar, Glorney-Raisbeck fellow med. scis Guy's Hosp., U. London, 1974-75; assoc. prof. medicine Cornell U. Med. Coll., N.Y.C., 1979-82, prof., 1982—, Gladys and Roland Harriman prof. cardiovascular medicine, 1983—; prof. cardiovascular med. in radiology Cornell Univ. Med. Coll., N.Y.C., 1990—, prof. cardiovascular medicine in cardiothoracic surgery, 1996—; chief divsn. cardiovascular pathophysiology N.Y. Hosp./Cornell Med. Ctr., 1996—; dir. Howard Gilman Inst. for Valvular Heart Diseases, Weill Med. Coll. of Cornell U., 2000—. Chmn. cardiac and renal adv. com. FDA, Washington, 1981—82, 1983—87, 2001—, cons., 1989—2000, mem., 1977—87, 2001—; mem. life scis. adv. com. NASA, Washington, 1984—88, mem. aero. med. adv. com., 1993—96, life and microgravity scis. and application adv. com., 1996—2001, biological and physical rsch. adv. com., 2001—; chmn. NASA/Mir Peer Rev. adv. com., 1993—95, NASA-NIH Biomed. and Behavioral Rsch. adv. com., 1995—; mem. NASA Adv. Coun., 1995—99; vis. prof. Chinese Acad. Med. Scis., Beijing, 1993—; chief divsn. cardiovascular pathophysiology N.Y. Hosp.-Cornell Med. Ctr., 1996—. Author 4 books; editor-in-chief Advances in Cardiology, 2001—; mem. editl. bds. 11 med. jours.; contbr. more than 300 articles on cardiovascular disease to med. jours.; patentee in field. Trustee N.Y.C. Historic Properties Fund, 1984-90; mem. steering com. Assocs. of the Jewish Bd. of Family and Children Svcs., 1989-91; pres. Am. Friends of Israel Nat. Heart to Heart Assn., 1991—; adv. com. The N.Y. Pub. Library Dance Collection, 1999—; pres., bd. trustees Glorney Found. N.Y.C., 2000—. Sr. surgeon USPHS, 1971-79. Recipient Investigator's award prize, European Cardiol. Soc., 1978, spl. award for contbns. to cardiology, Assn. Thoracic and Cardiovascular Surgeons of India, 1985, Wiliam A. Johnston award, Internat. Soc. Heart Rsch., 1986, spl. citation contbn. to Mir program, NASA, 1997, Pub. Svc. medal, 1999, Thomas W. Smith Meml. Lecturer, 7th World Cong. on Heart Failure, 2000, Hans-Peter Krayenbeuhl Meml. award for disting. rsch. in cardiac function, Internat. Acad. Cardiology, 2002; travelling fellow, Am. Physicians Fellowship, 1981. Fellow: ACP, N.Y. Cardiol. Soc. (pres. 1990—91), Am. Coll. Chest Physicians (chmn. cardiology forum 1985—86, exec. com. clin. cardiology sect. 1991—95), Am. Coll. Cardiology (governing coun. N.Y. chpt. 1991—93, pres. N.Y. State chpt. 1997—98, gov. 1997—2000, bd. govs. 1998—2000, bd. govs. task force on cardiovasc. econs. 1999—2000, steering com., chmn.), Am. Soc. Clin. Investigation, Am. Heart Assn. (established investigator 1979—84, coun. clin. cardiology and circulation), Argentine Heart Assn. (hon.); mem.: Cert. Bd. Nuclear Cardiology (bd. trustees 1996—2002, chmn. com. due process and appeals 2002—), Am. Soc. Nuclear Cardiology (fin. com. 1995—95), Soc. Cardiac Angiography and Interventions (gov. 1995—2000), Soc. Nuclear Medicine (trustee cardiovasc. coun. 1991—94), Harvard Club N.Y.C. Avocations: athletics, theater, opera, chinese and japanese calligraphy, ancient greek history. Office: NY Hosp 525 E 68th St New York NY 10021-4885 E-mail: memontal@med.cornell.edu.

BORER, KATARINA T. exercise endocrinologist; b. Tuzla, Bosnia-Herzegovina, Sept. 17, 1940; arrived in US, 1961; d. Juraj and Borka Tomljenovic; m. Paul E. Wenger, Aug. 11, 1990; children: Elizabeta H., Robert C. BA, U. Pa., 1962; PhD, U. Pa., Phila., 1966. Assoc. prof. divsn. kinesiology U. Mich., Ann Arbor, 1981—88, prof. divsn. kinesiology, 1988—. Mem. editl. bd.: Kinesiology, 2002—. Fulbright Rsch. fellow, Sweden, 1991. Mem.: Soc. for the Study Ingestive Behavior, Soc. for Rsch. on Biol. Rhythms, Soc. for Neurosci., Endocrine Soc., Am. Physiol. Soc., Am. Coll. Sports Medicine. Avocations: painting, art collecting. Office: Univ Mich Divsn Kinesiology 401 Washtenaw Ave Ann Arbor MI 48109-2214 Office Fax: 734-936-1925. E-mail: katarina@umich.edu.

BORESI, ARTHUR PETER, writer, educator; b. Toluca, Ill. s. John Peter and Eva B.; m. Clara Jean Gordon, Dec. 28, 1946; children: Jennifer Ann Boresi Hill, Annette Boresi Pueschel, Nancy Jean Boresi Broderick. Student, Kenyon Coll., 1943-44; BSEE, U. Ill., 1948, MS in Mechanics, 1949, PhD in Mechanics, 1953. Research engr. N. Am. Aviation, 1950; materials engr. Nat. Bur. Standards, 1951; mem. faculty U. Ill., Urbana, 1953—, prof. theoretical and applied mechanics and nuclear engring., 1959-79; prof. emeritus U. Ill. at Urbana, Urbana, 1979; Disting. vis. prof. Clarkson Coll. Tech., Potsdam, N.Y., 1968-69; NAVSEA research prof. Naval Postgrad. Sch., Monterey, Calif., 1978-79; prof. civil engring. U. Wyo., Laramie, 1979-95, head, 1980-94, prof. emeritus, 1995—. Vis. prof. Naval Postgrad. Sch., Monterey, Calif., 1986-87.; cons. in field. Author: Engineering Mechanics: Statics, 2001, Engineering Mechanics: Dynamics, 2001; Elasticity in Engineering Mechanics, 4th edit., 2000, Advanced Mechanics of Materials, 6th edit., 2002, Approximate Solution Methods in Engineering Mechanics, 1991, 2d edit., 2002; also articles. Served with USAAF, 1943-44; Served with AUS, 1944-46. Fellow ASME, ASCE, Am. Acad. Mechanics (founding, treas.); mem. Am. Soc. Engring. Edn. (Archie Higdon Disting. Educator award 1993), Soc. Exptl. Mechanics. Office: U Wyo Box 3295 Univ Station Laramie WY 82071 E-mail: boresi@uwyo.edu.

BORETZ, AVRON A. anthropologist, educator; b. Boston, Mass., Jan. 22, 1956; s. Benjamin Aaron and Naomi Messinger Boretz; m. Yingyue Li, Mar. 24, 1997. PhD, Cornell U., Ithaca, NY, 1996. Asst. prof. Hobart and William Smith Colls., Geneva, NY, 1994—98, U. Tex., Austin, 1998—. Post-doctoral Fellow, Chiang Ching-kuo Found. for Internat. Scholarly Exch., 2001-2002. Mem.: Assn. for Asian Studies, Am. Anthrop. Assn. (councillor East Asian sect. 2001—03), Nat. Com. on US-China Rels. (hon.). Avocation: martial arts (student of Taiwanese golden eagle master cheng jia-miao; 2nd-degree black belt, uechi-ryu karate-do). Office: Univ Tex at Austin 1 University Station G9300 Austin TX 78712 E-mail: boretz@mail.utexas.edu.

BORETZ, NAOMI MESSINGER, artist, educator; b. Bklyn. BA, Bklyn. Coll.; MA in Fine Arts, CUNY; MA in Art History, Rutgers U.; postgrad., Art Students League N.Y. Exhibitions include Westminster Arts Coun. Arts Ctr., London, 1971, Hudson River Mus., N.Y., 1975, Katonah Gallery, 1976, Condeso Lawler Gallery, N.Y.C., 1987, Carnegie-Mellon Art Gallery, Pitts., 1989, The Nelson Atkins Mus. of Art, St. Louis, 1994, Westbeth Gallery, N.Y., 1996, Mishkin Gallery, Baruch Coll., 1997, Rutgers (N.J.) U. Art Gallery, 1998, Hillwood Art Mus., N.Y., 2000, Muhlenburg Coll. Art Gallery, 2002, others, Represented in permanent collections Met. Mus. Art, N.Y.C., Solomon R. Guggenheim Mus., DeLand Art Mus., Fla., Brit. Mus., London, Nat. Mus. Am. Art, Washington, Yale U. Art Gallery, Joslyn Art Mus., Omaha, Walker Art Ctr., Mpls., Miami U. Art Mus., Oxford, Ohio, Fogg Art Mus. Harvard U., Cambridge, Mass., Glasgow (Scotland) Mus., San Jose (Calif.) Art Mus., Asheville (N.C.) Art Mus., Whitney Mus. Am. Art, N.Y., Mus. Modern Art, Princeton U. Graphic Arts Collection, N.J., Mus. S.W., Midland, Tex., Swope Art Mus., Terre Haute, Ind., others; contbr. to arts publs. Artist-fellow Va. Ctr. Creative Arts, 1973, 86, Ossabaw Found., 1975, Tyrone Guthrie Arts Ctr., Ireland, 1987, Writers-Artists Guild Can., 1988; grantee N.J. State Coun. on Arts, 1985-86. Studio: Princeton NJ

BORG, MALCOLM AUSTIN, publishing executive; b. N.Y.C., Jan. 28, 1938; s. Donald Gowen and Flora (Austin) B.; m. Sandra Jean Agemian, Sept. 9, 1961; children— John Austin, Jennifer Ann, Stephen Agemian. BS, Columbia U., 1965; postgrad., Harvard Bus. Sch., 1970; LHD (hon.), Ramapo (N.J.) Coll., 1985. Editl. trainee The Record, Hackensack, NJ, 1959-60, gen. assignment reporter, 1960-62, adminstrv. asst. to pub., 1963-64, asst. pub., 1965-66, v.p., 1967-68, exec. v.p., 1968-70, pres., 1971-78, CEO, 1971—, chmn. bd., 1975—; chmn. bd., CEO Macromedia, Inc., Borg Family holding co., Hackensack, 1971—; chmn., CEO North Jersey Media Group, Inc., 2000—. Active numerous civic orgns., 1965—; bd. dirs. Wolfeboro (N.H.) Camp Sch., 1970—; mem. Palisades Interstate Park Commn., 1974—; chmn. Submarine Meml. Assn., Hackensack, 1974—; mem. adv. bd. Sch. Gen. Studies, Columbia U., 1981—, chmn. 1997—, mem. nat. campaign com. Fund for Columbia, 1983-87, 92-98, mem. alumni adv. bd., 1987-95. Recipient 1st William H. Spurgeon III award Bergen council Boy Scouts Am., 1972, 1st Whitney M. Young award, 1986; Torch of Liberty award Anti-Defamation League, B'nai B'rith, 1973, ann. communications and leadership award Greater N.Y. dist. 46 Toastmasters Internat., 1976, Service to Others award N.J. div. Salvation Army, 1977, ann. community leadership award NO. N.J. Interprofl. Council, 1977, Man of Yr. award Holy Name Hosp., 1977, Editor of Yr. award Nat. Press Photographers

Assn., 1985, Owl award Sch. Gen. Studies, Columbia U., 1986, Citizen's award Acad. Medicine N.J., 1986; Alumni Fedn. medal Columbia U., 1991. Mem. Newspaper Assn. Am., Am. Soc. Newspaper Editors, N.J. Press. Assn., Bergen County C. of C. (bd. dirs. 1967-74), N.J. C. of C. (bd. dirs. 1977-79), Hill Sch. Alumni Assn. (pres. 1973-76), Advt. Coun. (bd. dirs. 1978-85), Harvard Bus. Sch. Alumni Assn. (pres. 1976-78), N.J. Srs. Golf Assn., Arcola Country Club (Paramus, N.J.), Columbia Club (N.Y.C.), Englewood Field (N.J.) Club, Mid Ocean Club (Tucker's Town, Bermuda), Harvard Club (N.Y.C.), Bath and Tennis Club (Spring Lake, N.J.), Knickerbocker Country Club (Tenafly, N.J.), Manasquan River Golf Club (Brielle, N.J.), Moselem Springs Golf Club (Fleetwood, Pa.). Avocations: golf, travel. Office: North Jersey Media Group Inc 150 River St Hackensack NJ 07601-7172 E-mail: mac@northjersey.com.

BORG, ROBERT FREDERIC, civil engineer; b. N.Y.C., Jan. 10, 1923; s. Herman Leo and Pauline (Leibman) F.; children: Christina Borg-Gordon, Lisa Borg-Broe, Eric (dec.), Kiri Borg-Henry, Neil, Dean. B in Civil Engring., NYU, 1944, JD, 1949. Bar: N.Y. 1950; lic. profl. engr., N.Y., 1950, Ohio, 1950. Field engr. Turner Construction Co., Rome, N.Y., 1942; structural engr. Chance Vought Aircraft, 1944; field engr. Spencer White & Prentis, N.Y.C., 1946-48; office engr. various gen. contractors, N.Y.C., 1948-55; co-founder, ptnr., chmn. Kreisler Borg Florman Gen. Construction Co. & affiliates, Scarsdale, N.Y., 1955--; co-founder Kensico Construction Co., Scarsdale, 1957--, pres., 1966--. Mem. bldg. rsch. adv. bd. Nat. Acad. Engring., Washington, 1963; adj. prof. NYU, 1971-79, Pratt Inst., Bklyn., 1983-86, Columbia U., N.Y.C., 1987-90; mem. US/USSR joint com. on coop. in housing and other forms construction U.S. Dept. Housing and Urban Devel., Washington, 1976-87; mem. Sino-US Trade Delegation to China, 1993. Author (contbg.): (handbook) Building Design and Construction, 1999, Construction Project Management, Temporary Structures in Construction, 1996, Technical and Business Practices; founder (bull.) Photo Bull., De Witt Clinton H.S., N.Y.C.; editor (photo): (newspaper) Clinton News, 1940; editor-in-chief (mag.) Quadrangle, NYU Coll. of Engring., 1943; one-man shows include photography shows in various locations, 1980—2001, Gallery Show in Soho, N.Y.C., 1985, Show on Cuba, Scarsdale, N.Y., 2001, Show on World Trade Ctr., 2003. Chmn., founder Garth Woods Conservancy, Scarsdale, N.Y., 1991— co-developer, ptnr. Bethune Tower Apts., N.Y.C., 1970, Heywood Tower Apts., 1972, Univ. Riverview Apts., 1973, Cooper Gramercy Apts., 1975, Marcus Garvey Park Village, 1976, Cora Club Apts., 1992; staff mem., docent Internat. Ctr. Photography, N.Y.C., 1994—. Served with USN, 1944-46. Finalist Entrepreneur of the Yr. award, So. New Eng., 1996, 1997, 1998, Entrepreneur of the Yr. Inst.; recipient Outstanding Builder Developer award, Associated Builders and Owners Greater N.Y., 1989—90, 1991, Builder of Yr. award, 1996, Emma Lazarus award, 1997, Disting. Alumni Recognition award, DeWitt Clinton H.S., 2001. Fellow: ASCE (mem. com. on contract administrn. 1952, 1963—67, founder, 1st chmn. constrn. group met. sect. 1962, chmn. tech. activities met. sect. 1963, met. sect. bd. dirs. 1962—67, mem. exec. com. nat. constrn. divsn. 1971, chmn. exec. com. nat. constrn. divsn. 1973—74, founding chmn. com. on social and environ. concerns in constrn. 1971, chair 2001—), Am. Arbitration Assn. (mem. nat. panel arbitrators 1957—, mem. nat. constrn. industry arbitration com. 1972—, chmn. 1974—76, nat. bd. dirs. 1974—84, mem. du Jur Mediation Ctr. 1974—); mem.: Harbor Consortium, N.Y. Acad. Scis. Office: Kreisler Borg Florman Gen Constrn Co 97 Montgomery St Scarsdale NY 10583-5104 Fax: 914-725-0346. E-mail: kbfgeneral@aol.com.

BORG, RUTH I. home nursing care provider; d. Axel Gunner and Charlotte (Benston) B. Diploma, West Suburban Sch. Nursing, 1956; tchr.'s degree, Chgo. Conservatory, 1958; BSN, Alverno Coll., 1981. Staff nurse Boath Meml. Hosp., Chgo.; head nurse psychiatry, head nurse long-term medicine VA North Chgo. Med. Ctr.; staff nurse, night supr. intermediate care VA Clement Zabiocki Med. Ctr., Milw.; pool nurse, in-home nursing care provider Milw. County Mental Health Complex; home nurse care provider Dr. Ghonsham Sooknandan, Kenosha, Wis., 1994—99. In-home nursing care provider. Contbr. 2 articles to profl. jours. Recipient Mary D. Bradford Disting. Alumni award, 1998. Avocation: teaching and performing music.

BORGAONKAR, DIGAMBER SHANKARRAO, cytogeneticist, educator; b. Hyderabad, India, Sept. 24, 1932; came to U.S., 1959, naturalized, 1971; s. Shankarrao Apparao and Kumudinibai (Jatar) B.; m. Manda Purandare, Dec. 27, 1963; children: Rajendra, Sonya. BS in Agr., Osmania U., 1953; diploma, Indian Agrl. Rsch. Inst., 1955; PhD, Okla. State U., 1963. Rsch. asst. agr. dept. Hyderabad and Parbhani, 1955-59; lectr. Agrl. Coll., Parbhani, 1956-57; asst. prof. biology U. N.D., Grand Forks, 1963-64; faculty and head of chromosome lab. Johns Hopkins U., 1964-78, assoc. prof. medicine, 1972-78, lectr. dept. environ. health, 1975-78; prof. biol. scis., rsch. scientist, dir. rsch. Genetics Ctr. North Tex. State U., Denton, 1978-80; dir. Cytogenetics Lab., Christiana Care Health Sys., Newark, Del., 1980—99; vis. scientist Mayo Clinic, Jacksonville, Fla., 1999—2001; vol. rsch. scientist Lab. Neurogenetics Nat. Inst. Aging, NIH, Bethesda, Md., 2001—. Rsch. prof. pediatrics (med. genetics) Thomas Jefferson U., Phila.; adj. prof. life and health scis. U. Del. Author: Chromosomal Variation in Man: A Catalog of Chromosomal Variants and Anomalies, 8th edit., 1998; co-author: Repository of Human Chromosomal Variants and Anomalies: International Registry of Abnormal Karyotypes, 14th Listing, 1993; editor: (with Bergsma, McKusick, Scott) The First Conference on the Clinical Delineation of Birth Defects, vol. 5, 1969; (with Bergsma, Shah) Advances in Human Genetics and Their Impact on Society, Birth Defects, 1972 (with Applewhite and Busbee) Genetic Screening and Counseling: A Multidisciplinary Perspective, 1981. Hyderabad State Rsch. scholar Indian Agrl. Rsch. Inst., 1955; recipient Haldane award Soc. Bionaturalists, Bhopal, India, 1988. Fellow Indian Soc. Genetics, Am. Genetic Assn. (v.p. 1973), Hercules Country Club. Office: Lab Neurogenetics NIH 9000 Rockville Pike Bethesda MD 20892

BORGATTA, EDGAR F. social psychologist, educator; b. Milan, Sept. 1, 1924; came to U.S., 1929, naturalized, 1934; s. Edgar A. and Frances (Zinelli) B.; m. Marie Lentini, Oct. 5, 1946; children: Lynn, Kim, Lee. BA, N.Y. U., 1947, MA, 1949, PhD, 1952. Cert. psychologist, N.Y., Vt., Wis. Instr. NYU, 1949-51, lectr., prof., 1954-59; lectr., research assoc. Harvard U., 1951-54; social psychologist, asst. sec. Russell Sage Found., 1954-59; prof. sociology Cornell U., Ithaca, N.Y., 1959-61; Brittingham rsch. prof. U. Wis., Madison, 1961-72, chmn. dept. sociology, 1962-65, chmn. div. social studies, 1965-68; disting. prof. sociology Queens Coll., CUNY, 1972-77, prof Grad. Ctr., 1972-82, dir. Italian Social Sci. Ctr., 1972-77; rsch. CUNY Case Ctr. for Gerontol. Studies, 1978-81; dir. data svc. CUNY Case Center for Gerontol. Studies, 1981-82; prof. sociology U. Wash., Seattle, 1981—93, chmn. dept., 1992—93, prof. emeritus, 1994—; dir Inst. on Aging U. Wash., Seattle, 1981-86. Cons. to bus. and govt., 1953—, Russell Sage Found., 1970-72; lectr., prof., adj. prof. sociology NYU, 1954-59; cons. editor Rand McNally & Co., 1961-74; chmn. bd. F.E. Peacock Pubs., Inc.; Nat. Inst. Gen. Scis.; spl. research fellow, 1972 Editor: Research on Aging, Sociol. Methodology, Sociol. Methods and Research; co-editor: Handbook of Personality Theory and Research; editor-in-chief: Encyclopedia of Sociology, 2d edit.; contbr. articles to profl. jours. Fellow Am. Psychol. Assn., Am. Psychol. Soc.; mem. Psychometric Soc., Sociol. Research Assn., Am. Sociol. Assn. (v.p. 1983), Pacific Sociol. Assn. (pres. 1985), Internat. Inst. Sociology (pres. 1984-89). Office: U Wash Dept Sociology 98 Union St #608 Seattle WA 98101

BORGATTA, ISABEL CASE, sculptor; b. Madison, Wis., Nov. 21, 1921; d. Harold Clayton and Naomi Olive (Newburn) C.; m. Robert Edward Borgatta, Apr. 24, 1948 (div. Mar. 1976); children: Francesce, Paola, Mia. Student, Smith Coll., 1939-40; BFA, Yale U., 1944; postgrad., New Sch., N.Y.C., 1944-48, Art Students League, 1944-48. Tchr. Halsted Sch., Yonkers, N.Y., 1948-50; lectr. CCNY, 1959-65, adj. prof., 1965-70; adj. prof. Coll. New Rochelle, 1973-77, prof., dept. chairperson, 1977-80. One-women shows include Village Art Ctr., N.Y.C., 1951, Galerie St. Etienne, N.Y.C., 1954, 57, Tyrringham (Mass.) Gallery, 1955, Gallery 10, N.Y.C., 1960, Mus. Hastings-on-Hudson, N.Y.C., 1961, Hudson River Mus., Briarcliff, N.Y., 1961, Frank Rehn Gallery, N.Y.C., 1968, 71, 75, 77, Briarcliff Coll. Mus., 1970, Laurel Gallery, N.Y.C., 1970, Roko Gallery, N.Y., 1972, Seton Coll., Yonkers, 1974, Elaine Benson Gallery, Bridgehampton, N.Y., 1974, 79, 83, Bridge Gallery, White Plains, N.Y., 1975, County Exec. Bldg., White Plains, 1977, Mus. in the Mall, Bridgeport, Conn., 1975, Cathedral Mus., St. John the Divine, 1978, City U. Grad. Ctr., N.Y.C., 1977, Galerie Coach, Paris, 1978, Sid Deutsch Gallery, N.Y.C., 1984, 86,, 87, Camp Gallery Sweet Briar Coll., Va., 1986, Shulman Sculpture Garden, White Plains, 1986, Va. Ctr. for the Arts, 1987, Closson Gallery, Cin., 1987, Westbeth Gallery, N.Y.C., 1988, Rockland Art Ctr., Nyack, N.Y., 2001; group exhbns. include Whitney Mus., Bklyn. Mus., Nat. Acad., Met. Mus., Hartford Atheneum, Women Choose Women, N.Y. Cultural Ctr., Pa. Acad. Fine Arts, Union Coll., San Francisco Mus. Modern Art, Walker Art Ctr., Mpls., Lever House Sculpture Ctr., GE Hdqrs., Fairfield, Conn., others; represented in permanent collections Nat. Sculpture Soc., Hartford Atheneum, Norfolk Mus., Yeshiva U., Kranert Mus., U. Ill., Benton Mus., U. Conn., Coll. New Rochelle, City U. Grad. Ctr., Okla. Art Ctr., Smith Coll. Mus., Book of the Month Club, Galina Co. Milan, Italy, Miller Assocs., N.Y., Collins & Aikman, N.Y.C., NYNEX Hdqrs., Grand Hyatt Hotel, N.Y.c., Zolfital Spa, Rome, H.I. Feldman Corp., N.Y.C., Transnational Devel. Corp. Sculpture grantee Govt. of Greece, Delphi, 1990, 93, Govt. of Greece, Crete, 1995, 96, 2000; Edward MacDowell fellow The Macdowell Colony, Peterborough, N.H., 1968, 73, 74, Yaddo fellow, Saratago Springs, N.Y., 1971, 73, Va. Ctr. for the Creative Arts fellow, 1985, 86, 89, 90, 91, 92. Mem. Nat. Sculpture Soc. (Alex J. Ettl grant for lifetime achievement in Am. sculpture 1995, Victor Meml. prize 1997, exhibit 2002), Sculptors Guild (exec. bd.,), Women's Caucus for Art. Democrat. Home: 463 West St Apt 1105 New York NY 10014

BORGEN, IRMA R. music educator; b. McPherson, Kans., Jan. 15, 1911; d. Nels J.W. Nelson and Ida Elizabeth Shallene; m. Clifford E. Borgen, July 6, 1942 (dec. Oct. 1967); children: David John, Elizabeth Marie. BA, Gustavus Adolphus Coll., St. Peter, Minn., 1932; postgrad., U. Colo., 1964—65. Tchr. Am. Sch. for Dependents, Essen, Germany, 1950—51; pvt. music tchr. Colorado Springs, Colo., 1969—. Mem.: Mil. Widows, Fountain Valley Sr. Orgn. Democrat. Lutheran. Avocations: music, fitness classes. Home: 114 Harvard St Colorado Springs CO 80911

BORGER, JOHN PHILIP, lawyer; b. Wilmington, Del., Apr. 19, 1951; s. Philip E. and Jane (Smyth) B.; m. Judith Marie Yates, May 24, 1974; children: Jennifer, Christopher, Nicholas. BA in Journalism with high honors, Mich. State U., 1973; JD, Yale U., 1976. Bar: Minn. 1976, U.S. Dist. Ct. Minn. 1976, U.S. Ct. Appeals (8th cir.) 1979, U.S. Supreme Ct. 1983, N.D. 1988, U.S. Dist. Ct. N.D. 1988, Wis. 1993. Editor-in-chief Mich. State News, East Lansing, 1972-73; assoc. Faegre & Benson, LLP, Mpls., 1976-83, ptnr., 1984—. Bd. dirs. Milkweed Edits., 1995-01; adj. prof. U. Minn. Sch. Journalism and Mass Comm., 1999. Contbr. articles to profl. jours. Recipient Freedom of Info. award, Minn. Soc. Profl. Journalists, 2002, First Amendment Award, St. Cloud State U. Dept. Mass. Comms., 2001. Mem. ABA (chmn. media law and defamation torts com. torts and ins. practice sect. 1996-97), Minn. Bar Assn., State Bar Assn. N.D., Wis. Bar Assn., Hennepin County Bar Assn. Office: Faegre & Benson LLP 2200 Wells Fargo Ctr 90 S 7th St Ste 2200 Minneapolis MN 55402-3901 E-mail: jborger@faegre.com.

BORGER, MICHAEL HINTON IVERS, osteopathic physician, educator; b. Kirksville, Mo., Nov. 10, 1951; s. Donald L. Borger and Dorothy M. Hinton. BA in Sociology, U. Akron, 1974; DO, Coll. Osteo. Medicine and Surgery, Des Moines, 1977. Diplomate Nat. Bd. Examiners in Osteo. Medicine and Surgery, Am. Coll. Osteopathic Family Physicians; ordained elder Presbyn. Ch., 1969. Rotating extern Youngstown (Ohio) Osteo. Hosp., 1976; extern in family medicine Dietz Diagnostic Clinic, Des Moines, 1977; rotating intern South Bend (Ind.) Osteo. Hosp. (now St. Mary's Cmty. Med. Ctr.), 1977-78, active staff, 1978-79, assoc. staff, 1979-82; pvt. practice Nappanee, Ind., 1978--; mem. staff Elkhart (Ind.) Gen. Hosp., 1978—, Goshen Gen. Hosp., 1981—; clin. asst. prof. gen. practice Kirksville (Mo.) Coll. Osteo. Medicine, 1990-93; apptd. clin. preceptor Kansas City U. of Health Scis. Coll. of Osteo. Medicine, 1993—, asst. clin. prof. family practice, 1995—; pres. Northwood Physicians, Inc., 1992—; asst. prof. clin. medicine Pikeville (Ky.) Coll. Sch. Osteo. Medicine, 2000—, asst. prof. osteo. manipulative medicine, 2000—. Assoc. manuscript reviewer Jour. Respiratory Diseases, 1986-88, Jour. Musculoskeletal Medicine, 1989—; pres. Northwood Profl. Assocs., Inc., 1995—; mem. quality improvement com. Ptnrs. Health Plan, 1996-99, mem. physician credentialling com., 2002-2003; founder Circle of Care Healthcare Sys., 1996, manuscript reviewer, Jour. of Musculoskeletal Medicine, 1981-. Bd. dirs. Nappanee C. of C., 2001—, Nappanee chpt. Families in Action, 1980-82; bd. dirs., chmn. Mission and Svcs. Commn., 1st Mennonite Ch., Nappanee, 1984-90, chmn. pastoral search com., 1989-90; mem. screening com. for elem. prin. Wa-Nee Sch. Dist., 1988; med. advisor United Presbyn. Ch. Nursery Sch., Nappanee, 1995—. Recipient Physician of Yr. award Ind. Assn. Emergency Med. Technicians, 1981, Good Citizens award Tower Savs., 1982, 1st degree black belt Tae Kwon Do, 1988, Tae Kwon Do Student of Yr. award, Hong's USA Tae Kwon Do, 1988; Burroughs-Wellcome Osteo rsch. fellow, 1980-81. Mem. Am. Osteo. Assn., Ind. Assn. Osteo. Physicians and Surgeons, Am. Acad. Applied Osteopathy, Nat. Honor Soc., Masons (3d degree), York Rite. Home: 353 N Hartman St Nappanee IN 46550-1417 E-mail: northwood@fourway.net.

BORGES, WILLIAM, III, management consultant; b. Long Beach, Calif., Nov. 21, 1948; s. William Borges Jr. and Dorothy Mae (Raymond) Morris; m. Rosalind Denise Marye, Nov. 23, 1968; children: William IV, Blake Austin. BA in Geography, Calif. State U., Sonoma, 1973; MBA, U. Phoenix, 1997. Environ. planner Mendocino County Planning Dept., Ukiah, Calif., 1976; project mgr. Engring. Sci., Inc., Berkeley, Calif., 1976-79, Santa Clara County Planning Dept., San Jose, Calif., 1979-81, Internat. Tech. Corp., San Jose, 1985-88; mgr. sales ops. Adac Labs., Milpitas, Calif., 1983-85; prin. WT Environ. Cons., Phoenix, 1988-91; project mgr. Dynamac Corp., Newport Beach, Calif., 1991-93; prin. environ. scientist Midwest Rsch. Inst., Scottsdale, Ariz., 1993-96; gen. mgr. Fitness Care, Inc., Yorba Linda, Calif., 2000—02; bus. process specialist Washoe Health Sys., Reno, 2002—. Adj. faculty U. Phoenix, Reno, 2003—. Contbr. photographs to various mags. Coord. pub. rels. Stellar Acad. for Dyslexics, Fremont, Calif., 1988. With M.I., U.S. Army, 1967-70. Mem.: Mensa. Avocations: photography, traveling. E-mail: wborges6@earthlink.net.

BORGMAN, GEORGE ALLAN, journalist; b. St. Louis, Jan. 22, 1928; s. Herman Francis and Martha Vivien (Wecker) B.; m. Janet Claire Ferroli, Feb. 27, 1957; children: Carole Elaine (dec.), Paul Allan, Eric Bruno; 1 child by previous marriage, Andrea Vivien Hancock (dec.). Student, U. Mo., 1945-46, 48; MusB in Music History and Lit., St. Louis Inst. Music, 1952; MusM in Musicology, Ind. U., Bloomington, 1953. Musician dance bands various locations, 1945-46, 48-50; enlisted bandsman U.S. Army, 1946-48, spl. agent mil. intelligence, 1958-79, advanced through grades to chief warrant officer 3, 1971, retired, 1979; music educator various sch. systems in Colo. and Nev., 1953-57; freelance asst. cinematographer N.Y.C., 1957-58; film editor, TV cameraman Sta. KOMU-TV, Columbia, Mo., 1958; investigator Wackenhut Corp., Boston, 1980-81; personnel security specialist (civilian) U.S. Army, Alexandria, Va., 1981-85; sportswriter Suburban World (newspapers), Needham, Mass., 1988-94; freelance jazz writer, 1988—; New England corr. and jazz writer T-J Today, 1991-92; corr., photographer, contbg. editor, columnist, reviewer Mississippi Rag, 1991—; record reviewer Cadence Mag., 1994-95; reviewer IAJRC jour., 1995—2000, The Jazz Messenger, 1994-96. Contbr. articles to profl. jours. including Joslin's Jazz Jour.; author: notes on jazz CD's. Musician Met. Wind Symphony, Boston, 1981, Fairfax (Va.) City Band, 1982-83, Canton (Mass.) Mcpl. Band/Am. Legion Band, 1980-81; assoc. mem. Westwood (Mass.) Rep. Com., 1988-89. Rated #12 Favorite Jazz Critic, Jazzbeat, 1995. Mem.: Assn. for Recorded Sound Collections, Starr-Gennet Found., Jazz Journalists Assn., Internat. Assn. Jazz Record Collectors, Disabled Am. Vets., Am. Legion. Republican. Home and Office: 158 Burgess Ave Westwood MA 02090-3010

BORGS, CHRISTIAN H. mathematical physicist; b. Dusseldorf, Germany, Apr. 12, 1957; came to U.S., 1997; s. Herwarth J. and Anneliese Borgs; m. Jennifer Tour Chayes, Sept. 2, 1993; 1 child, Claudio Ahlefelder. Diploma, Ludwigs Maximilians U. Munich, 1982, PhD, 1987; habilitation, Free U. Berlin, 1992. Postdoctoral fellow ETH Zürich, Switzerland, 1986-89; asst. prof. Free U. Berlin, 1989-93, Heisenberg prof., 1993-95; prof., head of group U. Leipzig, Germany, 1995-99; prof. math. U. Wash., Seattle, 1999—; mgr. theory group Microsoft Rsch., Redmond, Wash., 1997—. Trustee Inst. Pure and Applied Math., L.A., 1999—. Contbr. articles to profl. jours. Recipient Karl-Scheel prize German Phys. Soc., 1993; PhD fellow Max Planck Soc., 1983-85, Heisenberg fellow Deutsche Forschungsgemeinschaft, 1993-95; undergrad. scholar Found. of the German People, 1978-82. Mem. AAAS, Am. Math. Soc., German Phys. Soc., Internat. Orgn. Math. Physics. Avocations: travel, classical music, skiing. Office: Microsoft Rsch One Microsoft Way Redmond WA 98052 E-mail: ci.c.borgs@microsoft.com.

BORGSTAHL, KAYLENE DENISE, health facility administrator; b. Hampton, Iowa, May 21, 1951; d. Harry Dell and Berniece Irene (Muhlenbruck) Crabb; children: Elliot Michael, Brett Andrew. BS in Nursing, U. Iowa, 1973; MPA, Iowa State U., 1986. Asst. adminstr. Linn County Vis. Nurse Assn., Cedar Rapids, Iowa, 1975-85; v.p. program svcs. Voluntary Hosps. Iowa Home Health Care, Cedar Rapids, 1985-86; adminstr. Norell Home Health Svcs., Edina, Minn., 1986-87; case mgr. In Home Health Svcs., Mpls., 1987-88; adminstr. Sundance Med. Clinic Ltd., Shakopee, Minn., 1988-94, Apple Valley (Minn.) Med. Ctr., 1995—2003, Resource Mgmt., Shakopee, Minn., 1997—2003; IS mgr. Hutchinson Area Heath Ctr., Hutchison, Minn., 2003—. Mem. Sigma Theta Tau. Republican.

BORGSTROM, HOWARD GUSTAVE, federal agency administrator; b. Morristown, N.J., Feb. 16, 1948; s. Howard P.M. and Elsa Troedson B.; m. Carol Spurgat, Aug. 17, 1974; children: Eric, Christine. BA, Wesleyan U., 1970; MPA, George Washington U., 1977, PhD, 1992. Acting dep. asst. sec. mgmt. Office of Fossil Energy U.S. Dept. Energy, Washington, 1994, dir. bus. mgmt. Office of Mgmt. and Adminstrn., 1995—2001; mgr. Working Capital Fund Office of Mgmt., Budget and Evaluation, Washington, 2001—. Pres. Belle Haven Citizens Assn., Alexandria, Va., 1994-95. Recipient Presdl. Meritorious Exec. award, 1990, 98. Mem. Am. Soc. Pub. Adminstrn. Office: US Dept Energy 1000 Indpeendence Ave SW Washington DC 20585 E-mail: howard.borgstrom@hq.doe.gov.

BORHI, CAROL, data processing executive, finance company executive; b. N.Y.C., Oct. 23, 1949; d. Carl and Elsie Elizabeth (Varady) Chaky; m. Nicholas Anthony Borhi, Sept. 23, 1972; children: Christy Nicole, Nicholas James. Assoc. in Applied Sci., Manhattan Community Coll., 1970; student, Hunter Coll., 1967-68, 70-71. Programmer asst. N.Y. Telephone, N.Y.C., 1970-73, programmer, 1974-76, programmer analyst, 1976-83; staff analyst Nynex Svc. Co., N.Y.C., 1984-87; systems analyst Nynex Corp., N.Y.C., 1987, assoc. dir., 1987-90, staff dir., 1991—97, Bell Atlantic, 1997—2000; sr. staff cons. Verizon, 2000—. Pres. Personal Touch Computing, N.Y.C., 1981-86. Mem. Telephone Pioneers Am. (charter), Creative Investors Am. Clubs: Sacred Heart. Republican. Roman Catholic. Avocations: real estate investing, coin collecting, dancing, guitar, piano. Office: Verizon Comms 1095 Ave of the Americas New York NY 10036

BORIE, BERNARD SIMON, JR., retired physicist, educator; b. New Orleans, June 21, 1924; s. Bernard simon and Ruth (Lastrapes) B.; m. Martine Edith Descamps, May 2, 1957 (div. May 1964); children: Kathleen, Fabienne, Marianne. BS, U. S.W. La., 1944; MS, Tulane U., 1949; PhD, MIT, 1956; Fulbright fellow, U. Paris, 1956-57. Rsch. physicist metall. divsn. Oak Ridge Nat. Lab., 1949-53, group leader x-ray diffraction Metals and Ceramics Divsn., 1957-60, head fundamental rsch. sect., 1960-69, sr. scientist, 1969-85; prof. U. Tenn., 1963—; ret. Vis. prof. Cornell U., 1971-72, U. Calif., Berkeley, 1980. Lt. USNR, 1944-45. Fellow AAAS; mem. AIME, Am. Soc. Metals, Am. Crystallographic Assn., Sci. Rsch. Soc. Am. Achievements include research in diffraction effects of thermal motion, x-ray diffraction studies of imperfect solids; order-disorder effects in solid solutions. Home: 13 Brookside Dr Oak Ridge TN 37830-7616

BORIN, JEFFREY NATHAN, real estate developer; b. Detroit, Jan. 10, 1949; s. Ralph and Phyllis (Robinson) B.; m. Barbara Shapiro, Sept. 4, 1988; 1 child, Samuel. BS, U. Pa., 1971. Ptnr. Borin Investment Co., Livonia, Mich., 1971—. Owner Jeffrey N. Borin Constrn. Co., Livonia, 1973—, Jeffrey N. Borin & Co. Real Estate Brokerage, Livonia, 1980—; pres. Borin Constrn. Mgmt., Inc., Livonia, 1987—, Turov Imports, Inc., Livonia, 1990—. Author: Turover Residences and Other Landmarks of Interest in Detroit, 1991, The Turover Aid Society of Detroit and the Turover Shul: Congregation B'nai Jacob, A Pictorial and Documentary History, 1993. Pres. jr. divsn. Jewish Welfare Fedn., Detroit, 1977-78; pres. Jewish Hist. Soc. of Mich., 1979-81. Mem. Western Wayne Oakland Assn. Realtors, Kiwanis, Skyline Club, Alpha Kappa Psi. Avocation: antiquing. Office: Borin Investment Co 11900 Globe St Ste 100 Livonia MI 48150-1152

BORIS, JAMES R. investment company executive; Chmn. bd., CEO Everen Securities Inc., Chgo., until 2000; chmn. JB Capitol Mgmt., Chgo., 2000; bd. dirs. Corp, Inc., Irvine, Calif., 2000—. Office: Core Inc Ste 1750 18881 Von Karman Ave Irvine CA 92612

BORIS, RUTHANNA, dancer, choreographer, dance therapist, educator; b. Bklyn., Mar. 17, 1918; d. Joseph Jay and Frances (Weiss) B.; m. Frank W. Hobi (dec.) Student, Profl. Children's Sch., N.Y.C. Dir. Boris-Hobi Concert Co., 1955-57. Prin. dancer Am. Ballet, N.Y.C., 1934, Ballet Caravan, N.Y.C., 1936; prima ballerina Met. Opera Co., N.Y.C., 1939-41, Ballet Russe de Monte Carlo, N.Y.C., 1942-49; prima ballerina, choreographer-in-residence Royal Winnipeg Ballet of Can., 1957-59, dir. 1957-58; choreographer Ballet Russe de Monte Carlo, 1947, N.Y.C. Ballet, 1951; prof. dance U. Wash., Seattle, 1965-83, prof. emeritus, 1983—; adj. prof. psychiatry U. Wash., 1982; pres. exec. dir. Ctr. for Dance Devel. & Research, Albany, Calif., 1986— ; choreographer: Cirque de Deux, 1947, Quelques Fleurs, 1948, Cakewalk, 1951, Kaleidoscope, 1951, Will O' The Wisp, 1951, Pasticcio, 1955, Wanderling, 1957, Ragtime, 1975, Tape Suite, 1976, Four All, 1980. Mem. adv. bd. Seattle Psychoanalytic Inst., 1975-82. Mem. Am. Guild Mus. Artists (award 1964, gov. 1942-64), Am. Dance Therapy Assn. (pres. Calif. chpt. 1986-88, mem. dance therapy credentials com. 1990-92). Office: Ctr Dance Devel & Rsch 555 Pierce St Apt 1033 Albany CA 94706-1009 *I have always believed that each one of us has some specific mission to perform. My mission, to clarify my work and my human connections, keeps me very busy, active, curious and productive.*

BORISH, IRVIN MAX, b. Phila., Jan. 21, 1913; s. Max and Rose (Gimson) Borish; m. Beatrice Evelyn Silver, June 28, 1936; 1 child, Frances Borish Goldman. Student Temple U., 1930—31; student, Ill. IKnst. Tech., 1935—36; OD, No. Ill. Coll. Optometry, 1934, DOS, 1935; LLD, Ind. U., 1968; DSc (hon.), Pa. Coll. Optometry, 1984; DOS (hon.), So. Calif. Coll. Optometry, 1984, So. Coll. Optometry, Memphis, 1984; DSc (hon.), SUNY, 1984; DSO (hon.), Ill. Coll. Optometry, 1999; DHL (hon.), U. Houston, 2001. Diplomate Am. Acad. Optometry, lic. optometrist Ill., Ind. Instr. to prof. optometry No. Ill. Coll. Optometry, 1935—43; dir. No. Ill. Eye Clinic, 1935—43; practice optometry Kokomo, Ind., 1944—79; vis. lectr. Ind. U., 1955—64, part-time prof., 1965—72, prof., 1972—83; Benedict Prof. Optometric Practice U. Houston, 1983—88. Bd. dirs. PMC Capital Corp. Author: Clinical Refraction, 5 edits. (named Optometric Text of Century, Prentice Soc., 1999); author: (with Clifford Brooks) System of Ophthalmic Dispensing; contbr. articles to profl. jours., chapters to books. Bd. dirs., pres. Kokomo Art Assn., 1950—72; bd. dirs. Civic Music Assn., Kokomo Civic Theatre, 1950—72. Recipient Alumni Scholarship award, No. Ill. Coll., 1934, Benjamin Franklin award, SUNY, 1976, Vision Svc. award, Heart of Am. Contact Lens Congress, John Martin award, Iowa Optometric Assn., 1969, Disting. Svc. award, P.R. Optometric Assn., 1979, Disting. Practitioner award, Nat. Acad. Practice, 1982, Borish Ctr. Ophthalmic Rsch. established, Ind. U. Sch. Optometry, 1996, Irvin M. Borish Reading Rm. established in libr., U. Houston Coll. Optometry, 1996, Irvin M. Borish Chair in Optometric Practice established, 2002, Herman B. Wells Visionary award, Ind. U., 2002. Mem.: AAUP, Am. Optometric Assn. (Apollo award 1968, Contact Lens Person of Yr. 1988, Disting. Svc. award 1989), Am. Acad. Optometry (William Feinbloom award 1985, Max Schapero Invited Meml. Lectr. 1987, Donald R. Korb Lectr. 2001, established Irvin M. Borish Award for promising young rschr. in visual sci., hon. life), Am. Optometric Found., Ind. Optometric Assn., So. Coun. Optometry, Rotary, Beta Sigma Kappa (Gold medal 1982). Jewish.

BORISLOW, ALAN JEROME, hospital dental department chairman; b. Phila., Sept. 22, 1936; s. Nathan and Thelma (Kuperstein) B.; m. Susan Marcia Cohen, June 25, 1961; children: Lisa Anne Nadel, Steven Mark, Deborah Lynne. Student, Temple U., 1954-57, DDS, 1961; Cert. in Orthodontics, Albert Einstein Med. Ctr., 1967. Diplomate Am. Bd. Orthodontics. Gen. dentist U.S. Army Dental Corp, Ft. Knox, Ky., 1961-63; dental practice assoc. Dr. Leonard Opack, Marcus Hook, Pa., 1963-64; resident in orthodontics Albert Einstein Med. Ctr., Phila., 1964-67; orthodontic practice assoc. Dr. Joseph Bernstein, Havertown, Pa., 1967-68; dir. dental externships Temple U., Phila., 1969-85; pvt. practice orthodontics Doylestown, Pa., 1969-87; orthodontic program dir. Albert Einstein Med. Ctr., Phila., 1978—, chmn. Maxwell S. Fogel Dept. of

Dental Medicine, 1980—. Clin. assoc. prof. Temple U. Sch. Dentistry, Phila., 1986—; adj. assoc. prof. U. Pa. Sch. Dental Medicine, Phila., 1989—. Co-author: (book) A Tradition of Excellence, 1993; contbr. to book The Combination Technique, 1972; referee, cons. Am. Jour. of Orthodontics and Dentofacial Orthopedics, 1995. Mem. B'nai Brith Svc. Orgn., Montgomery County, Pa., 1972—; exec. bd. Andorra Valley Civic Assn., Whitemarsh Twp., Pa., 1972-82; mem. Citizens Coun., Whitemarsh Twp., 1974-2000; mem. Residents Assn., Whitemarsh Twp., 2001-; bd. dirs. Greater Phila. Health Care Congress, 1991—. Recipient Outstanding Resident award Albert Einstein Med. Ctr., 1967, Maimonides Soc. honoree, 2001, Disting. alumnus award Temple U. Dental Alumni Soc., 1994, Physician Leadership award, Albert Einstein Soc., 2002; inducted into Hall of Fame Greater Phila. Health Care Congress, 2001. Fellow Am. Assn. Hosp. Dentists, Am. Coll. Dentists, Internat. Coll. Dentists; mem. Am. Dental Assn., Am. Assn. Orthodontists, Temple U. Dental Alumni Soc. (bd. dirs. 1990—), Am. Dental Edn. Assn. Democrat. Avocations: photography, architectural history, gardening. Office: Albert Einstein Med Ctr 5501 Old York Rd Philadelphia PA 19141-3018

BORISOFF, RICHARD STUART, lawyer; b. Rochester, N.Y., May 4, 1945; s. Samuel M. and Ida B.; m. Risa W. Polgar, Aug. 17, 1967; children: Mindy, Dara. AB, U. Pa., 1967; JD, Columbia U., 1970. Bar: N.Y. 1971, D.C. 1981, U.S. Dist. Ct. (so. dist.) N.Y. 1973, U.S. Ct. Appeals (2nd cir.) 1973. Assoc. Paul, Weiss, Rifkind, Wharton & Garrison, N.Y.C., 1970-78, ptnr., 1978—. Mem.: ABA. Office: Paul Weiss Rifkind Wharton & Garrison Ste 2320 1285 Avenue Of The Americas New York NY 10019-6064 E-mail: rborisoff@paulweiss.com.

BORISOV, GEORGE P. music educator; b. Krasnodar, Russia, Mar. 27, 1954; arrived in U.S., 1992, naturalized, 2000; s. Peter Vasilievich and Maria Savcichna Borisov; children: Tatiana, Basil. MA in piano performance, State Inst. Music and Tchg., Rostov-on-Don. Russia, 1976; DMA piano performance, M.Ivanovich Glinka State Conservatory, Novosibirsk, Russia, 1982; PhD in Musicology, All-Russian Inst. Arts, 1992. Cert. music tchr. Dept. Edn., N.J. Piano tchr. N.A. Rimsky Korsakov State Musical Coll., Krasnodar, Russia, 1976—86; sr. lectr. State Inst. Arts, Krasnodar, 1978—92; lectr. Ocean County Coll., Toms River, NJ, 1995—97; music dir. Immaculate Conception Roman Catholic Ch., Eatontown, NJ, 1993—2000; piano tchr. Westminster Conservatory of Rider U., Princeton, NJ, 2000—02; dir. C. Musik Sch., Colts Neck, NJ, 2000—. Author: (book) Kuban Cossack Choir, 1988, Music Culture of South Russia, 1989; contbr. articles to profl.jours.; prodr.(and narrator): (TV series, featuring musical programs) Ctrl. TV USSR and Krasnodar TV, 1984—89; founder and prodr. Music-Art Festivals, NJ, NY areas, 2002—. Recipient Cert. of Excellence, Internat. Concert Alliance, 2000. Mem.: Cecilian Music Club (Laura Conover Pedagogy award 1998, 1999), Nat. Assn. Music Tchr., Am. Guild of Piano Tchr. (Nat. Piano Auditions Honor Roll 1996—2003). Home: 81 five Points Rd Colts Neck NJ 07722

BORJA, MARIANNE E. healthcare educator; b. Oct. 19, 1946; BS, Coll. Misericordia, Dallas, Pa., 1968; MS, Cornell U., 1971; EdD, Temple U., 1985. Prof., co-chair dept. nutrition and dietetics Marywood U., Scranton, Pa., 1985—. Contbr. articles to Jour. Am. Dietetic Assn., Jor. Assessment of Higher Edn., others. Mem. health profl. com. March of Dimes, 1992—. Office: Marywood U Dept Nutrition and Dietetics Scranton PA 18509 E-mail: borja@ac.marywood.edu.

BORJAS, GEORGE J(ESUS), economics educator; b. Havana, Cuba, Oct. 15, 1950; came to U.S., 1962; s. Juan V. Borjas and Edita F. Diaz; m. Jane Maureen Walsh, Nov. 11, 1989; children: Sarah Jane Irene, Timothy Jorge, Rebecca Kathryn. BS, St. Peter's Coll., Jersey City, 1971; MA, M in Philosophy, PhD, Columbia U., 1975; LHD (hon.), St. Peter's Coll., 2003. Asst. prof. Queens Coll., Flushing, N.Y., 1975-77; research assoc. Nat. Bur. Econ. Research, Cambridge, Mass., 1983—; prof. econs. U. Calif., Santa Barbara, 1978-90, San Diego, 1990-95; prof. pub. policy Kennedy Sch. Govt., Harvard U., Cambridge, Mass., 1995-97, Pferzheimer prof. pub. policy, 1998—2002, Robert W. Scrivner prof. of econ. and social policy, 2002—. Cons. Unicon Rsch. Corp., Santa Monica, Calif., 1982-94; econs. adv. panel NSF, 1988-90; mem. Gov.'s Coun. of Econ. Advisers, 1993-98 Author: Wage Policy in the Federal Bureaucracy, 1980, International Differences in the Labor Market Performance of Immigrants, 1988, Friends or Strangers: The Impact of Immigrants on the U.S. Economy, 1990, Labor Economics, 1995, Heaven's Door: Immigration Policy and the American Economy, 1999; editor: Hispanics in the United States, 1985, Immigration and the Work Force: Economic Consequences for the United States and Source Areas, 1992, Issues in the Economics of Immigration, 2000, Rev. of Econs. and Statistics, 1998—; mem. editl. bd. Quar. Jour. Econs., 1992-98, Internat. Migration Rev., 1992—, Review of Economics and Statistics, 1997-98; contbr. articles to profl. jours. Fellow Columbia U. Alumni Fund, 1973, NIMH, U. Chgo., 1977; grantee Rockefeller Found., 1983-85, Sloan Found., 1986-93, NSF, 1986—, Russell Sage Found., 1991-93, Smith Richardson Found., 2001—; vis. scholar Harvard U., 1988-89. Fellow Econometric Soc.; mem. NAS (panel 1984-85, 95-97, Estrada fellow in immigration studies 2000), Am. Econ. Assn., Soc. Labor Econs., Assn. for Pub. Policy Analysis and Mgmt. (exec. coun. 2000-2005). Roman Catholic. Office: Kennedy Sch Govt Harvard U 79 Jfk St Cambridge MA 02138-5801 E-mail: gborjas@harvard.edu.

BORK, ROBERT HERON, lawyer, author, educator, former federal judge; b. Pitts., Mar. 1, 1927; s. Harry Philip and Elizabeth (Kunkle) B.; m. Claire Davidson, June 15, 1952 (dec. 1980); children: Robert Heron, Charles E., Ellen E.; m. Mary Ellen Pohl, Oct. 30, 1982. BA, U. Chgo., 1948, JD, 1953; LLD (hon.), Creighton U., 1975, Notre Dame Law Sch., 1982; LHD, Wilkes-Barre Coll., 1976; JD (hon.), Bklyn. Law Sch., 1984; ThD, DeSales Sch. Theology, 1990; LLD honoris causa, Adelphi U., 1990. Bar: Ill. 1953, D.C. 1977. Assoc., then ptnr. Kirkland, Ellis, Hodson, Chaffetz & Masters, Chgo., 1955-62; assoc. prof. Yale Law Sch., 1962-65, prof. law, 1965-75, on leave, 1973-75; solicitor gen. U.S. Dept. Justice, Washington, 1973-77, acting atty. gen., 1973-74; Chancellor Kent prof. law Yale Law Sch., 1977-79, Alexander M. Bickel prof. pub. law, 1979-81; ptnr. Kirkland & Ellis, Washington, 1981-82; judge U.S. Ct. Appeals for D.C. Cir., 1982-88, resigned, 1988, resident scholar Am. Enterprise Inst. for Pub. Policy Rsch., Washington, 1977, adj. scholar, 1977-82, John M. Olin scholar in legal studies, 1988-99, sr. fellow, 2000—; prof. law Ave Maria Sch. Law, 2000—03. Mem., trustee Woodrow Wilson Internat. Ctr. for Scholars, 1973-78; nominated for position assoc. justice U.S. Supreme Ct., 1987, confirmation denied by U.S. Senate; Tad and Dianne Taube Disting. vis. fellow Hoover Instn., 2003. Author: The Antitrust Paradox: A Policy at War with Itself, 1978, 2d edit., 1993, The Tempting of America: The Political Seduction of the Law, 1990, Slouching Towards Gomorrah: Modern Liberalism and American Decline, 1996, Coercing Virtue: The Worldwide Rule of Judges, 2002. With USMCR, 1945-46, 50-52. Recipient Francis Boyer award Am. Enterprise Inst., 1984, Henry Salvatori prize Intercollegiate Svcs. Inst., 1998. Fellow AAAS; mem. Federalist Soc. (co-chmn., bd. trustees). E-mail: rbork@aei.org.

BORKAN, WILLIAM NOAH, biomedical electronics company executive; b. Miami Beach, Fla., Apr. 29, 1956; s. Martin Solomon and Annabelle (Hoffman) Borkan; m. Vivienne Eliane; children: Martin, Kenneth. Student, Carnegie Mellon U., 1977; PhD, Sussex Coll. Tech., 1979. Tech. Dominicks' Radio & TV Co., Miami Beach, 1971-74; computer programmer Mt. Sinai Hosp., Miami Beach, 1973-74; chief studio engr. WGMA, Hollywood, Fla., 1973-74; disc jockey WBUS-FM, Miami Beach, 1974; chief rec. engr. Dukoff Recording Studios, Miami, Fla., 1974-75; rec. studio design and constrn. TSI, Hollywood, 1975-77; chief design engr. Lumonics Co., Miami, 1974; svc. mgr. 21st Century Electronics Co., Miami, 1975; lab. tech. Carnegie-Mellon U.; mgr. Tech. Electronics Co., Pitts., 1976; pres. Borktronics Co., Miami, 1974-84; cons. specialist in neurobiometrics St. Barnabas Hosp., N.Y.C., 1978-83; pres., CEO NeuroMed, Inc., 1980-85, Nice Tech., Inc., 1989-96; pres. Master Angler, Inc., 1990—. Dir. Saints Venutres Ltd, 1999—; pres. Electrovest Inc., 1985—; cons. specialist in home automation, home theater and audio; mem. curriculum coms. EE Dept. Author publs in field. Named Entrepreneur of the Yr, Fla Inc Mag, 1992; grantee, Carnegie Corp, Carnegie Mellon Univ. Mem.: AAAS, NY Acad Scis, Audio Eng Soc, Asn Advancement Med Instrumentation, Refrigeration and Air Conditioning Engrs, Am Soc Heating. Achievements include numerous US and foreign patents in field; patents pending in field. Home: 3142 NE 166th St Miami FL 33160-3840 Office: Electrovest 12000 Biscayne Blvd Ste 502 Miami FL 33181-2725 E-mail: bbbillfish@aol.com.

BORKO, HAROLD, information scientist, psychologist, educator; b. N.Y.C., Feb. 4, 1922; s. George and Hilda (Karpel) B.; m. Hannah Levin, June 22, 1947; children: Hilda, Martin. Student, Coll. City N.Y., 1939-41; BA, U. Calif. at Los Angeles, 1948; MA, U. So. Calif., 1949, PhD in Psychology, 1952. System tng. specialist Rand Corp., 1956-57; with System Devel. Corp., Santa Monica, Calif., 1957-68, asso. staff head lang. processing and retrieval staff, 1965-68; instr. psychology U. So. Calif., 1957-65; instr. Sch. Library Service UCLA, 1965-68, prof. Grad. Sch. Library and Info. Sci., 1968-93; ret., 1993. Author: Computer Applications in the Behavioral Sciences, 1962, Automated Language Processing, 1967, Targets for Research in Library Education, 1973, (with H. Sackman) Computers and the Problems of Society, 1972, (with C. Bernier) Abstracting Concepts and Methods, 1975, (with C. Bernier) Indexing Concepts and Methods, 1978; Asso. U.S. editor: Information Processing and Management, 1963— ; editorial bd.: Education for Information; editor: Academic Press Library and Information Science series, 1970— ; book rev. editor: Jour. Ednl. Data Processing, 1963-75. Served with AUS, 1942-46; to capt., Med. Service Corps AUS, 1950-56. Mem. Am. Soc. for Info. Sci. (pres. 1966), Assn. Computing Machinery, Am. Psychol. Assn., Assn. Library and Info. Service Edn., Am. Soc. Indexers, Phi Beta Kappa, Sigma Xi, Phi Gamma Mu. Home: 11507 National Blvd Los Angeles CA 90064-3827 *It is unrealistic to expect a person to decide, at age twenty or thereabout, on a career to be followed for the rest of one's life. One should try to attain as good and as general an education as is possible and not be afraid to change professions. The world is changing, and we must be prepared to change with it; only then can we seize the opportunities presented.*

BORKOVEC, VERA Z. Russian studies educator; b. Brno, Czechoslovakia, Aug. 13, 1926; came to U.S., 1952; d. Josef Zanda and Jarmila (Tuscher) Martinasek; m. Alexej B. Borkovec, Aug. 29, 1951. BA, Charles U., 1949; MA, Hollins Coll., 1961, The Am. U., 1966; PhD, Georgetown U., 1973. Secondary sch. tchr. English, French Montgomery County Pub. Schs., Md., 1961-64; from asst. prof. to assoc. prof. Russian studies The Am. Univ., Washington, 1966-91, prof. emerita. Mem. Czechoslovak Soc. of Arts and Scis. (v.p. 1994—). Avocations: theater, music, poetry. Home: 12013 Kemp Mill Rd Silver Spring MD 20902-1515

BORKOWSKI, FRANCIS THOMAS, university chancellor; b. Weirton, W.Va., Mar. 16, 1936; s. Francis Thomas and Felicia Josephine (Pawlowski) B.; m. Kay Kaiser, Aug. 22, 1959; children: Stanley, Anne-Marie, Christian. BS, Oberlin (Ohio) Coll., 1957; M.Mus., Ind. U., 1959; PhD, W.Va. U., 1967; LLD (hon.), St. Leo (Fla.) Coll., 1989. Clarinetist Indpls. Symphony Orch., 1957-59; music dir. Bishop Kenny High Sch., Jacksonville, Fla., 1959-61; dir. bands W.Va. U., 1961-67; assoc. prof. music edn. Ohio U., Athens, 1967-69, asst. dir. Sch. Music, 1969-70, assoc. dean faculties, 1970-75; prof. music, vice chancellor, dean faculty Ind. U.-Purdue U., Ft. Wayne, 1975-78; v.p. Ft. Wayne Philharmonic Orch., 1976-78; provost U. S.C. System, 1978-83, exec. v.p., provost, 1983-88; pres. U. South Fla., Tampa, 1988-93; chancellor Appalachian State U., Boone, NC, 1993—. Bd. dirs. Fla. Nations Bank. Author articles. Mem. nat. adv. coun. John F. Kennedy Ctr., 1978-80; pres. S.C. Orch. Assn., 1982; bd. dirs. United Way of Columbia, 1981; chmn. Moffitt Cancer Ctr. Bd., United Way Bd., Tampa; mem. urban affairs com. Nat. Assn. Land Grant Colls. Recipient Amicus Poloniae award Poland mag., 1971, award for research Sigma Xi; named Polonian of Yr., 1989, Gold medal with Diamond, INTERPROM, 1997, Commdr. of the Cross of the Rep. of Poland, 2001. Mem. Am. Coun. Edn. (bd. dirs.), Am. Assn. Higher Edn., Music Educators Nat. Conf., Phi Beta Kappa, Mortar Bd., Omicron Delta Kappa, Eta Sigma Gamma, Golden Key, Phi Beta Delta. Roman Catholic. Office: Applalachian State U Office Chancellor Boone NC 28608-0001 E-mail: borkowskif@appstate.edu.

BORLAND, KATHRYN KILBY, author; b. Pullman, Mich., Aug. 14, 1916; d. Paul Melbourne and Vinnie (Bensinger) Kilby; m. James Barton Borland, May 16, 1942; children— James Barton, Susan Lee. BS in Journalism, Butler U., 1937. Editor North Side Topics, Indpls., 1938-42. Author: (all with Helen Ross Speicher) Southern Yankees, 1960, Allan Pinkerton, 1962, Miles and the Big Black Hat, 1963, Everybody Laughed, 1964, Eugene Field, 1964, Phillis Wheatley, 1968, Harry Houdini, 1969, Clocks from Shadow to Atom, 1969, Good-Bye to Stony Crick, 1975, The Third Tower, 1974, Stranger in the Mirror, 1974, Good-bye, Julie Scott, 1975, To Walk the Night, 1976, These Tigers' Hearts, 1978, Irena, 1979, Pseudonyms: Alice Abbott, Jane Land. Co-recipient award for most distinguished children's book pub. by Ind. author Ind. U., 1969 Mem. P.E.O., Theta Sigma Phi, Kappa Alpha Theta. Home: 1050 S Maish Rd Frankfort IN 46041-3213

BORLAND, RAYMOND M. researcher; b. Chester, Pa., Nov. 23, 1948; s. Raymond Milton Jr. and Eleanor D. Borland. BS in Biology, St. Joseph's Coll., Phila., 1969; PhD in Developmental Biology, U. Del., 1974; MD, Harvard U., 1980. Postdoctoral fellow Harvard Med. Sch., Boston, 1974-77; asst. dir. clin. rsch. ICI Ams., Wilmington, Del., 1983-84; assoc. dir. clin. rsch. DuPont Pharm. Co., DuPont/Merck Pharm. Co., Wilmington, 1984-93; self-employed rschr., 1993—. Contbr. articles to profl. jours. Home: 695 Colora Rd Colora MD 21917-1121

BORLAUG, NORMAN ERNEST, agricultural scientist; b. Cresco, Iowa, Mar. 25, 1914; s. Henry O. and Clara (Vaala) Borlaug; m. Margaret G. Gibson, Sept. 24, 1937; children: Norma Jean, William Gibson. BS in Forestry, U. Minn., Minneapolis, 1937, MS in Plant Pathology, 1940, PhD in Plant Pathology, 1942; ScD (honoris causa), Punjab (India) Agrl. U., 1969, Royal Norwegian Agrl. Coll., Norway, 1970, Luther Coll., 1971, Kanpur U., India, 1972, Uttar Pradesh Agrl. U., 1971, Mich. State U., 1971, U. de la Plata, Argentina, 1971, U. Ariz., 1972, U. Fla., 1973, U. Católica de Chile, Chile, 1974, U. Hohenheim, Germany, 1976, Punjab Agrl. U., Pakistan, 1978, Columbia U., 1980, Ohio State U., 1981, U. Minn., 1982, U. Notre Dame, 1987, Oregon State U., 1988, U. Tulsa, 1991, Washington State U., 1995, Andhra Pradesh Agrl. U., India, 1996, Indian Agrl. Rsch. Inst., 1996, De Montfort U., U.K., 1997, Emory U., 1999, U. Philippines, 1999; LHD, Gustavus Adolphus Coll., 1971, Iowa State U., 1992; LLD (hon.), New Mexico State U., 1973; D. of Agr. (hon.), Tufts U., 1982; D. of Agrl. Scis. (hon.), U. Agrl. Scis., Godollo, Hungary, 1980, Tokyo U. Agriculture, 1981, U. Nacional Pedro Henríquez Turena, Dominican Republic, U. Cen. del Estes, Dominican Republic, 1983; D. Honoris Causa, U. Mayor de San Simón, Bolivia, U. de Buenos Aires, 1983, U. de Cordoba, Spain, U. Politécnica de Catalunya, Barcelona, Spain, 1986, Colegio Postgraduados, Montecillo, Mexico, 1990; PhD (hon.), U. degli Studi di Bologna, Italy, 1991, Warsaw Agrl. U., Poland, 1993, Bangladesh Agrl. U., 1998, U. LaSalle-Noroeste, Mex., 1999, U. Politécnica de Madrid, Spain, 2000, U. Américas Puebla, Mex., 2000; D. Honoris Causa, U. Autónoma Nuevo León, 2001; PhD (hon.), U. Autónoma de Chapingo, 2001, Rector U. Dubuque, 1992-93; PhD (hon.), U. Studi de Bologna, Italy, 1991, Warsaw Agrl. U., Poland, 1993. With U.S. Forest Service, 1935—38; instr. U. Minn., 1941; microbiologist E.I. DuPont de Nemours, 1942—44; rsch. scientist in charge wheat improvement Coop. Mexican Agrl. Program, Mexican Ministry Agr. Rockefeller Found., Mexico, 1944—60, assoc. dir. assigned to Inter-Am. Food Crop Program, 1960—63; assoc. dir. CIMMYT, 1964-82; dir. wheat research and prodn. program Internat. Maize and Wheat Improvement Ctr., Mexico City, 1964—79, acting dir., 1981, cons., 1980—; disting. prof. internat. agr. dept. soil & crop scis. Texas A&M U., College Station, Tex., 1984—. Cons., collaborator nst. Nacional de Investigationes Agricolas, Mexican Ministry Agr, 1960—64; cons. FAO, North Africa and Asia, 1960; ex-officio cons. wheat research and prodn. problems to govts. in Latin Am., Africa, Asia, 1960—; mem. Citizen's Commn. on Sci. Law and Food Supply, 1973; mem. Commn. Critical Choices for Am, 1973, Council Agr. Sci. and Tech., 1973—, Presdl. Commn. on World Hunger U.S.A., 1978—79, Presdl. Coun. Advisers Sci and Tech., 1990—93; dir. Population Crisis Com., 1971—92; asesor especial Fundacion para Estudios de la Poblacion A.C., Mexico, 1971—80; mem. adv. council Renewable Natural Resources Found., 1973; A.D. White Disting. prof.-at-large Cornell U., 1983—85; Disting. prof. Internat. Agr., Dept. Soil & Crop Scis. Tex. A&M U., 1984—; adj. prof. dept. biology Emory U., Atlanta, 1991—92; advisor The Population Inst., U.S.A., 1971—78; bd. trustees Winrock Internat. U.S.A.; life fellow Rockefeller Found., 1983—; sr. cons. CIMMYT, 1979—; hon. vis. prof. U. Minn., 1980; adj. prof. dept. biology Emory U., Atlanta, 1991—92. Named Uncle of Paul Bunyan, 1969; named to Hall of Fame, Oreg. State U. Agrl., 1981, Agrl. Nat. Ctr., Bonner Springs, Kans., 1984, Scandinavian-Am., U.S.A., 1986, Nat. Wrestling, 1992; recipient Disting. Service awards, Wheat Producers Assns., and state govts. Mexican States of Guanajuato, Queretaro, Sonora, Tlaxcala and Zacatecas, 1955—60, Recognition award, Agrl. Inst. Can., 1966, Instituto Nacional de Tecnologia Agropecuaria de Marcos Juarez, Argentina, 1968, Sci. Service award, El Colegio de Ingenieros Agronomos de Mexico, 1970, Outstanding Achievement award, U. Minn., 1959, Elvin Charles Stakman award, 1961, Disting. Citizen award, Cresco Centennial Com., 1966, Nat. Disting. Service award, Am. Agrl. Editors Assn., 1967, Genetics and Plant Breeding award, Nat. Council Comml. Plant Breeders, 1968, Star of Distinction, Govt. of Pakistan, 1968, citation and street named in honor, Citizens of Sonora and Rotary Club, 1968, Internat. Agronomy award, Am. Soc. Agronomy, 1968, Distinguished Service award, Wheat Farmers of Punjab, Haryana and Himachal Pradesh, 1969, Nobel Peace prize, 1970, Diploma de Merito, El Instituto Tecnologico y de Estudios Superiores de Monterrey, Mexico, 1971, medalla y Diploma de Merito, Antonio Narro Escuela Superior de Agricultura de la U. de Coahuila, Mexico, 1971, Diploma de Merito, Escuela Superior de Agricultura Hermanos Escobar, Mexico, 1973, award for service to agr., Am. Farm Bur. Fedn., 1971, Outstanding Agrl. Achievement award, World Farm Found., 1971, Medal of Merit, Italian Wheat Scientists, 1971, outstanding Achievement award, Minn. Athletic Club, 1971, Service award for outstanding contbn. to alleviation of world hunger, 8th Latin Am. Food Prodn. Conf., 1972, Nat. award for Agrl. Excellence in Sci., Agri-Mktg. Assn., 1982, Disting. Achievement award, Council for Agrl. Scis. and Tech., 1982, inaugural lectr., medal, Dr. S.B. Hendrick's Meml. Lectureship., 1981, other honored lectureships, dedicated in his name, Norman E. Borlaug Centro de Capitación y Formación de Agrs., Santa Cruz, Bolivia, 1983, Borlaug Hall U. Minn., 1985, Borlaug Bldg. Internat. Maize and Wheat Improvement Ctr., 1986, numerous other honors and awards from govts., ednl. instns., citizens groups. Fellow: Indian Soc. Genetics and Plant Breeding; mem.: NAS, Acad. Nat. Agronomía and Veterinaria Argentina, Chinese Acad. Agrl. Sci., Royal Soc. Eng., Internat. Food Policy Research Inst. (trustee 1976—82), Am. Council on Sci. and Health (trustee 1978—), N.I. Vavilov Acad. Agrl. Scis. Lenin Order (USSR.), Adv. Coun. Renewable Natural Resources Acad. Found. (mem. adv. coun. 1973), Coun. Agrl. Sci. and Tech., Soil Sci. Soc. Am. (hon.), Sociedad de Agronomia do Rio Grande do Sul Brazil (hon.), Royal Agrl. Soc. Eng. (hon.), Royal Soc. Edinburgh (hon.), Hungarian Acad. Sci. (hon.), Indian Nat. Sci. Acad. (hon.), Am. Acad. Arts and Scis. (hon.), Hungarian Acad. Scis. (hon.), Mexican Acad. Scis. (hon.), Am. Assn. Cereal Chemists (hon.; life, Meritorious Service award 1969), Crop Sci. Soc. Am. (hon.), Population Crisis Com., Chinese Acad. Agrl. Scis. (hon. prof. 1994), Sasakawa Africa Assn. (pres. 1986), Academia Nat. de Agronomia y Veterinaria (Argentina), Royal Swedish Acad. Agr. and Forestry (fgn. 1971), India Nat. Sci. Acad., Am. Soc. Agronomy (1st Internat. Svc. award 1960, 1st hon. life), Sigma Xi, Xi Sigma Pi, Alpha Zeta. Office: Tex A&M U 2474 Tamu Dept Soil & Crop Scis College Station TX 77843-2474

BORLING, JOHN LORIN, military officer; b. Chgo., Mar. 24, 1940; s. Edward Gustav and Vivian K. (Strietelmeir) B.; m. Myrna Lee Holmstedt, June 22, 1963; children: Lauren, Megan. BS, U.S. Airforce Acad., 1963; grad., Armed Forces Staff Coll., 1975, Nat. War Coll., 1980, Harvard U., 1991, White House fellow, 1998. Commd. 2d lt. USAF, 1963, advanced through grades to maj. gen., 1989, prisoner of war, 1966-73, fighter pilot, comdr., 1974-80, asst. dir. ops. HQ Pentagon, 1981-82, comdr. 86th Combat Support Group Ramstein, Ger., 1982-83, comdr. 86th Fighter Group, 1983-84, exec. officer to COS NATO Mons, Belgium, 1984-86, dep. plans/analysis HQ/SAC Jt. Stategic Target Planning Staff Omaha, 1986-87, comdr. HQ 57th Air Divsn. Minot, N.D., 1987-88, dep. ops. HQ SAC Omaha, 1988-91; dir. operational reg(s) HQ Pentagon, 1991-92; dep. chief of staff NATO, Norway, 1992-94, chief of staff, sr. U.S. mil. officer in Scandinavia, 1994-96; pres., CEO United Way, Chgo., 1997-98; dir. The 5th Media, Chgo., 1999—. Bd. dirs. Hyperfeed Tech., 1999—; chmn. Performance Cons. Group, 2000—; pres., CEO, SOS Am., 2000—; advisor AMSAM Biotechnologies Inc.; mem. Armed Forces Policy Coun., Chgo., Coun. Fgn. Rels., Chgo. Com.; mem. adv. com. Ill. Fatherhood Initiative, Chgo. Founder, charter mem. Ramstein Coun. Internat. Rels., 1983; v.p., dir. Opera Omaha, 1988-91; treas., dir. White House Fellow Fund, 1991—; mem. adv. com. Kellogg Sch., Northwestern U.; mentor Harris Sch., U. Chgo.; adv. bd. Stanton Chase Int., Maritime Trust Co.; bd. govs., Chgo. Mil. Acad.; adv. com. Maritime Trust Co.; bd. dirs. Nat. Jazz Mus., 2000; vice-chmn. Chgo. Meml. Day Parade Com., 2000; dir. Stars & Stripes Relief Fund, 2001 . Decorated Def. Disting. Svc. medal with oak leaf cluster, Air Force Disting. Svc. medal, Silver Star, Def. Superior Svc. medal, Legion of Merit with oak leaf cluster, D.F.C. with oak leaf cluster, Bronze Star medal with V device and 2 oak leaf clusters, Air medal with 5 oak leaf clusters, Purple Heart with one cluster; White House fellow, 1974; recipient George Washington medal Freedom Found., Valley Forge, Va., 1975, Good Scout award Boy Scouts Am., Chgo., 1974, Eagle Am. Hero award Benedictine U., 2001, Patriot's award C. of C., 2001;named Gen. John Logan Chgo, Patriot of Yr., 2002. Mem. Assn. Grads. USAF Acad., VFW, Daedalians, Air Force Assn., Comml. Club Chgo., Execs. Club Chgo. Avocations: music, sports, reading. Office: SOS America Box 1543 Rockford IL 61110-1543 E-mail: forsosamerica@yahoo.com.

BORMAN, JOHN, trial lawyer, arbitrator, mediator; b. Little Falls, Minn., Mar. 21, 1946; s. Myron Francis and Bernadette Mary (Burggraff) B.; 1 child, Mac A. Nelson II. BA in Political Sci., U. Minn., 1973; JD, Notre Dame, 1979. Bar: Minn. 1979, Wis. 1987, U.S. Dist. Ct. Minn. 1980, U.S. Dist. Ct. (we. dist.) Wis. 1990, U.S. Dist. Ct. (we. dist.) Mich. 1996, U.S. Ct. Appeals (8th cir.) 1986, U.S. Ct. Appeals (6th cir.) 1996, U.S. Supreme Ct. 1986; cert. civil trial specialist Minn. State Bar Assn. Law clk. to Hon. Glenn E. Kelley Minn. Dist. Ct., Winona, 1979-80; ptnr. Robins, Kaplan, Miller & Ciresi LLP, Mpls., 1981-97, Streater & Murphy PA, Winona, Minn., 1997-99. Researcher, organizer Minn. Pub. Interest Research Group, Mpls., 1973-76; bd. govs. Minn. Trial Lawyers Assn., 1990—; pres. Minn. Consumer Alliance, Mpls., 1995-97; bd. dirs. Minn. Advocates for Human Rights, Mpls., 1991—, Diversity Found., 2000—. Contbr. to profl. jours. Troop com. chair Boy Scouts of Am., Golden Valley, Minn., 1990-95; Served sgt. USMC, 1964-68. Named Super Lawyer Minn. Jour. Law & Politics, 1998, Leading Am. Atty. Am. Rsch. Corp., 1999, 2000. Mem. ATLA, ABA, Minn. Bar Assn., Wis. State Bar, Ramsey County Bar Assn., Winona County Bar Assn., Hennepin County Bar Assn., Minn. Trial Lawyers Assn. (bd. govs. 1981—, Excellence award 1997), Acad. Cert. Trial Lawyers. Office: Trial Lawyer 502 West Broadway Winona MN 55987 Fax: 507-454-8862. E-mail: johnborman@mymailstation.com.

BORMASTER, LISA KAY, publisher; b. Greeley, Colo., Mar. 21, 1960; d. Arnold Raymond and Karen Denise (Wetig) Napoleon. BSBA summa cum laude, Ariz. State U., 1983. Assoc. account exec. DBG&H Mktg., Advt., Phoenix, 1983-84; advt. rep. Ind. Newspapers, Inc., Phoenix, 1984-85, advt. mgr., 1985-86, mktg. dir., 1986-88, publ., gen. mgr., 1988-90, dir. sales and mktg., 1990-91; display advt. mgr. Ariz. Bus. Gazette, Phoenix, 1991-92; dir. advt. Washington Bus. Jour., 1992-94; pub. Austin (Tex.) Bus. Jour., 1995-97, City Bus./The Bus. Jour., Mpls., 1997—. Mem. Bd. of Trade. Bd. dirs. BBB, 1991-92, Austin Quality Coun., United Way, Jr. Achievement Minn. Mem.: Turnaround Mgmt. Assn. (bd. dirs.), Mpls. Downtown Coun. (bd. dirs.), Better Bus. Bur. (bd. dirs. 1999—), Mpls. C. of C. (chair 2002, bd. dirs.), Scottsdale C. of C., Paradise Valley C. of C. (bd. dirs. 1989—90), Jr. Achievement (bd. dirs. 1998—), Phoenix Advt. Club (bd. dirs. 1988—92, pres. 1991—92). Republican. Avocations: reading, inline skating, strength training. Office: City Bus/The Bus Jour 527 Marquette Ave Ste 300 Minneapolis MN 55402-1306 E-mail: lbormaster@bizjournals.com.

BORN, BROOKSLEY ELIZABETH, lawyer; b. San Francisco, Aug. 27, 1940; d. Ronald Henry and Mary Ellen (Bortner) Born; m. Alexander Elliot Bennett, Oct. 9, 1982; children: Nicholas Jacob Landau, Ariel Elizabeth Landau, Andrew E. Bennett, Laura F. Bennett, Peter J. Bennett. AB, Stanford U., 1961, JD, 1964. Bar: DC 1966. Law clk. U.S. Ct. Appeals, Washington, 1964—65; legal rschr. Harvard Law Sch., 1967—68; assoc. Arnold and Porter, Washington, 1965—67, 1968—73, ptnr., 1974—96, 1999—2002; chair U.S. Commodity Futures Trading Commn., Washington, 1996—99. Lectr. law Columbus Sch. Law, Cath. U. Am., 1972—74; adj. prof. Georgetown U. Law Ctr., Washington, 1972—73. Pres.: Stanford Law Rev., 1963—64. Chair bd. visitors Stanford Law Sch., 1987; trustee Ctr. for Law and Social Policy, Washington, 1977—96, Women's Bar Found., 1981—86; bd. dirs. Nat. Legal Aid and Defenders Assn., 1972—79, Washington Legal Clinic for Homeless, 1993—96, Lawyers Com. for Civil Rights Under Law, 1993—96, Am. Bar Found., 1989—99, Washington Lawyers Com. for Civil Rights and Urban Affairs, 1992—96; chair bd. dirs. Nat. Women's Law Ctr., 1981—96, 2003—; bd. dirs., 1997—2002. Mem.: ABA (chair sect. ind. rights and responsibilities 1977—78, chair fed. judiciary com. 1980—83, chair consortium on legal svcs.

and the pub. 1987—90, bd. govs. 1990—93, chair resource devel. coun. 1993—95, chair coun. Fund for Justice and Edn. 1995—96, state del. from DC 1994—), Southwestern Legal Found. (trustee 1993—96), Am. Law Inst., DC Bar (sec. 1975—76, mem. bd. govs. 1976—79), Order of Coif. Office: Arnold & Porter 555 12th St NW Washington DC 20004-1206 E-mail: brooksley_born@aporter.com.

BORN, ETHEL WOLFE, religious writer; b. Kasson, W.Va., Jan. 6, 1924; d. Otto Guy and Nancy Grace (Nestor) Wolfe; m. Harry Edward Born, Apr. 4, 1944 (dec. Aug. 1992); children: Rosemary Ellen (dec.), Barbara Anne Born Craig. Student, Ecumenical Inst., Geneva, 1983; BA, Mary Baldwin Coll., 1991. Author: A Tangled Web--A Search for Answers to the Question of Palestine, 1989, By My Spirit, Methodist Protestant Women in Mission, 1879-1939, 1990, From Memory to Hope, A Narrative History of the Areas of the World Federation of Methodist Women, 2000; contbr. articles to religious publs. Va. pres. United Meth. Women, 1972-76; bd. dirs. United Meth. Gen. Bd. Global Ministries, N.Y.C., 1976-84, v.p. women's divsn., 1980-84, v.p. com. on relief, 1980-84, Mid. East cons. women's divsn., 1984-88; chmn. N.Am. Coordinating Com. for Non-govtl. Orgns. UN Symposium, N.Y.C., 1986, 87; pres. N.Am. area, asst. world treas. World Fedn. Meth. Women, 1986-91, archivist, 1992-2001; mem. United Meth. Gen. Comm. Christian Unity and Inter-Religious Concerns, N.Y.C., 1988-96; mem. interfaith commn. Nat. Coun. Chs. of Christ, 1996-2000; mem. Pan-Meth. Commn. on Cooperation, 1996-2000. Recipient Stanley S. Kresge award, 1995. Mem. AAUW, Nat. League Am. Pen Women, Nat. Assn. Parliamentarians. Avocation: crafts.

BORN, JAMES E. art educator, sculptor; b. Toledo, Nov. 16, 1934; s. Elmer Arthur and Dorthy (Halstead) B.; m. Donna Jones; children: Karl, Anna Born Ross, Thomas, Christopher, Tanya. BA, Toledo U., 1959; MFA, U. Iowa, 1962. Grad. teaching asst. U. Iowa, Iowa City, 1964-65; asst. prof. Calif. State U., Arcata, 1962-65, Calif. Western U., San Diego, 1965-67, Calif. State U., Turlock, 1967-69; prof. art Ctrl. Mich. U., Mt. Pleasant, 1969—. Bronze sculptures exhibited in group and one-man shows; represented in permanent collections Outdoor Sculpture Exhibit, Southfield, Mich., 1991; exhibited in one-man show Gallery Abbott Kinney, Venice, Calif., 1992, Mich. Competition, Birmingham, Bloomfield Art Ctr., 1992, Commn. Trans World Airlines, L.A. Airport, Watercolor Paintings, All Calif., San Diego Mus. of Art, 1995, Mich. Exhibition, Mt. Clemens, Mich., Art Mus., 1993-95, Mich. Art Exhibition, Saginaw Art Mus., 1993-94. Recipient honor award Battle Creek Art Mus., 1982, 1st award sculpture Ball State U., 1982, grand award S.W. Ark. Art Mus., 1982, 1st award sculpture Mt. Clemens Art Mus., 1989, sculpture award Saginaw Art Mus., 1992. Home: 2716 Greenfield Ave Los Angeles CA 90064-4032 Office: Ctrl Mich U Art Dept Mount Pleasant MI 48859-0001

BORN, ROBERT HEYWOOD, consulting civil engineer; b. L.A., Nov. 7, 1925; s. Robert Bogle and Mignon Mary (Heywood) B.; m. Marilyn Alice Simpson, Aug. 15, 1947; 1 child, Stefanie Born. Student, Stanford U., 1943; BE, U. So. Calif., 1949, MSCE, 1956. Registered civil engineer Calif., Ariz., Nev., Utah, Tenn., Guam; registered agriculture engr. Calif. Assoc. hydraulic engr. Calif. Dept. of Water Resources, L.A., 1949-58; chief engr., county hydraulic engr. County Flood Control/Water Conservation Dist., San Luis Obispo, Calif., 1958-70; dir., exec. v.p., regional mgr. Camp, Dresser & McKee, Inc., Pasadena, Calif., 1970-78; v.p., regional mgr. Born, Barrett & Assoc./Barrett Cons. Group, Newport Beach, Calif., 1978-86, Memphis, 1978-86; prin. Robert H. Born Cons. Engrs., Memphis, 1986—88, Irvine, Laguna Niguel, Calif., 1986—88, Asheville, N.C., 1997—. Chmn. World Affairs Coun., San Luis Obispo, 1965. 1st lt. U.S. Army, 1943-47. Decorated Bronze star medal, 1944. Fellow: ASCE (life Engr. of Merit 1994); mem.: Am. Pub. Works Assn. (Floodplain Mgmt. Assn. Calif., cert. outstanding pub. works achievement 1969), U.S. Com. on Large Dams, Am. Water Works Assn. (com. chmn.), Am. Acad. Environ. Engrs. (life; diplomate). Democrat. Presbyterian. Avocations: historical research, travel. Office: Robert H Born Cons Engrs 15 Little Cedar Ct Asheville NC 28805-2487

BORN, ROSCOE CONKLIN, writer; b. Topeka, Sept. 4, 1920; s. Roscoe Conklin Sr. and Lillian (Gibby) B.; m. Dorothy Jean Anstaett, Aug. 9, 1941; children; Barbara, Karen B., Roscoe III, Nelson Flint, Lynne B. Student, U. Kans., 1937-41. Reporter Ind. Daily Reporter, Independence, Kans., 1941, Topeka State Jour., 1941-42, city editor, columnist, 1945-57; corr. Wall St. Jour., Washington, 1957-61; vice editor Nat. Observer, Washington, 1961-77; Washington editor Barron's Mag., 1977-82. Writing cons. Detroit News, 1983-85; editor-in-residence U. Kans. Sch. Journalism, Lawrence, 1976; mem. editl. bd. Bicentennial State History Series, 1974-78; lectr. in field. Author: The Suspended Sentence: A Guide for Writers, 1993. 2d lt. U.S. Army, 1942-45. Mem.: William Allen White Found. (trustee 1972—97). Avocations: observing wild life, music, photography. Home: 7200 Third Ave C-62 Sykesville MD 21784

BORN, SAMUEL ROYDON, II, lawyer; b. Atwood, Ill., Apr. 19, 1945; s. Samuel Roydon and Mary Elizabeth (Derr) B.; m. Brenda Alice Anderson, June 18, 1988; children: Samuel R. III, Holly Jean; 1 stepchild, Julie Chamberlain Sipe. Student, Northwestern U., 1963-64, Am. U., fall 1966; BA, Simpson Coll., 1967; JD, Ind. U., 1970. Bar: Ind. 1970, U.S. Dist. Ct. (so. dist.) Ind. 1970, U.S. Ct. Appeals (7th cir.) 1975, U.S. Dist. Ct. (no. dist.) Ind. 1990, U.S. Supreme Ct. 2003. Ptnr. Ice Miller, Indpls., 1970—. Mem. safety com. Associated Gen. Contractors Ind., 1988—. Co-author: Safety and Health Guide for Indiana Business, 1999, 4th edit., 2002; mem. bd. editors: Ind. Law Jour., 1969—70; contbr. articles to profl. jours. Mem. bd. visitors Ind. U. Sch. Law, 1988-89, 95-98; chmn. ch. cmty. athletics First Bapt. Ch., Indpls., 1975-78, trustee, 1978-80. Mem. ABA (mem. nat. conf. bar pres. 1987-99, ho. of dels. 1988-98, labor and employment law sect.), Am. Bar Found., Ind. State Bar Assn. (bd. govs. 1990-99, pres. 1997-98, labor law sect.), Ind. Bar Found., Indpls. Bar Assn. (bd. mgrs. 1987-95, pres. 1988), U.S. C. of C. (occupl. safety and health adminstrv. coun. 1981-86, 2000—), Ind. C. of C. (past chmn. occupl. safety health com.), Ind. Mfrs. Assn. (pers. labor rels. com. 1982-99), Highland Golf and Country Club, Crooked Stick Golf Club, Univ. Club, Indpls. Lawyers Club, Masons, Shriners, Kiwanis, Phi Eta Sigma, Sigma Alpha Epsilon. Presbyterian. Avocations: downhill skiing, golf, fly fishing, public speaking. Home: 5202 Grandview Dr Indianapolis IN 46228-1938 Office: Ice Miller 1 American Sq Indianapolis IN 46282-0020 E-mail: born@icemiller.com.

BORNEMAN, JOHN PAUL, pharmaceutical executive; b. Darby, Pa., Oct. 18, 1958; s. John A. III and Ann (Conway) B.; m. Anne Marie Albert, July 18, 1980; 1 child, Elizabeth Anne. BS in Chemistry, St. Joseph's U., Phila., 1980, MS in Chemistry, 1983, MBA in Fin., 1986. V.p. Boiron-Borneman Inc., Norwood, Pa., 1980-86; dir. mktg. Standard Homeopathic Co., L.A., 1986-89, v.p., 1989-96, exec. v.p., 1996-99, chmn., CEO, 1999—; pres. P&S Labs, now Hyland's Inc., L.A., 1996—; dir. Hyland's, Inc. Chmn. FDA liaison com. Am. Assn. Homeopathic Pharmacists, 1986—; chmn., CEO Standard Homeopathic Co., 1999—. Editor Homeopathic Pharmacopoeia U.S., 1983—, mem. bd., 2000—; columnist Resonance mag., 1986-95; contbr. articles to homeopathic jours. Bd. dirs. Internat. Found. for Homeopathy, 1986-92, Nat. Ctr. for Homeopathy, 1987—. Mem. Am. Chem. Soc., Am. Pharm. Assn., Nat. Nutritional Foods Assn. (mem. legis. affairs com. 1996—), Sigma Xi. Avocations: photography, boating. Office: Standard Homeopathic Co Box 61067 210 W 131st St Los Angeles CA 90061-1618

BORNET, VAUGHN DAVIS, former social science educator, research historian; b. Phila., Oct. 10, 1917; s. Vaughn Taylor and Florence Davis (Scull) Bornet; m. Mary Elizabeth Winchester, Dec. 28, 1944; children: Barbara Bornet Stumph, Stephen Folwell. BA with honors, Emory U., 1939, MA, 1940; postgrad. fellow, U. Ga., 1940-41; PhD, Stanford U., 1951. Staff Mercer U., 1946; instr. history U. Miami, 1946-48; research assoc. Inst. Am. History, Stanford U., 1951-53; dir. welfare research project Commonwealth Club of Calif., 1953-56; assoc. editor Ency. Britannica, 1958; rsch. assoc. med. econs. AMA, 1958-59; staff RAND Corp., Santa Monica, Calif., 1959-63; chmn. social scis. div. So. Oreg. U., Ashland, 1963-74, prof. history and social sci., 1963-80. Vis. prof. World Campus Afloat, spring 1969. Author: Struggle for Governmental Power in Georgia, 1754-1757, 1940, Labor and Politics in 1928, 1951, California Social Welfare, 1956, Welfare in America, 1960, Labor Politics in a Democratic Republic, 1964, Speaking Up for America, 1975; (with E.E. Robinson) Herbert Hoover: President of the United States, 1975, The Presidency of Lyndon B. Johnson, 1983 (nominee Pulitzer Prize); (juvenile) It's a Dog's Life and I Like It, 1991; (memoir) An Independent Scholar In Twentieth Century America, 1995; co-author The Heart Future, 1961; articles United States, Ency. Brit. Yearbooks, 1957, 58; contbr. The Federal Campaing of 1864 in East Florida, 1956, Ideas in Conflict, 1958, Herbert Hoover Reassessed, 1981, The Quest for Security, 1982, Essays in Economics and Business History, 1988; pub. Bornet Books. Pres. So. Oreg. Symphony Assn., 1973-75; mem. U.S. Com. on Civil Rights, Oreg., 1985— . Served to lt. USNR, 1941-45, ret. comdr. Recipient Disting. Svc. awards Am., Oreg. Heart Assns., 1964, Disting. Svc. award Southern Oreg. U. Alumni Assn., 1985, Freedoms Found. award 1986. Mem. Rotary, Sigma Chi. Republican. Home: 365 Ridge Rd Ashland OR 97520-2830 E-mail: bornetvd@ashlandhome.net.

BORNHEIMER, ALLEN MILLARD, lawyer; b. Brewer, Maine, June 10, 1942; s. Millard Genthner and Gertrude Evelyn (Kinney) B.; m. Deborah Russell Hill, June 17, 1967; children: Anneliese, Charles, Elizabeth. Student, Phillips Exeter Acad., 1961; AB, Harvard U., 1965, LLB, 1968. Bar: Mich. 1968, Mass. 1971. Assoc. Dickinson, Wright, McKean & Cudlip, Detroit, 1968-70, Choate, Hall & Stewart, Boston, 1970-76, ptnr., 1976-99, mng. ptnr., 1988-95; principal, gen. counsel Cargex Properties, Inc., Boston, 2000—. Bd. dirs. Cargex Properties, Inc. and affiliated cos., Portland, Maine. Town moderator, Duxbury, Mass., 1982—, chmn. fin. com., 1974-76, mem. capital budget com., 1977; bd. dirs. Jordan Hosp., Plymouth, Mass., 1974-81; trustee North Yarmouth (Maine) Acad., 1976-79. Mem. ABA, Mass. Bar Assn., Boston Bar Assn., Am. Coll. Investment Counsel, Mass. Moderators Assn., Duxbury Yacht Club (bd. dirs. 1982-84), Harvard Club (Boston). Republican. Avocations: golf, piano, sailing. Home: 15 Summerhouse Lane Duxbury MA 02332-3930 Office: 20th Fl 50 Milk St Boston MA 02109-5003 E-mail: allen.bornheimer@cargex.com.

BORNHOLDT, LAURA ANNA, university administrator; b. Peoria, Ill., Feb. 11, 1919; d. John and Barbara (Kohl) B. AB, Smith Coll., 1940, MA, 1942; PhD, Yale U., 1945. Asst. prof. history Smith Coll., Northampton, Mass., 1945-52; internat. relations asso. AAUW, Washington, 1952-57; dean Sarah Lawrence Coll., Bronxville, N.Y., 1957-59; dean women, adj. prof. history U. Pa., Phila., 1959-61; dean coll., prof. history Wellesley (Mass.) Coll., 1961-64; v.p. Danforth Found., St. Louis, 1964-73; sr. program officer Lilly Endowment Inc., Indpls., 1973-76, v.p. for edn., 1976-84; dir. office univ.-sch. rels. U. Chgo., 1984-94. Nat. adv. com. on black higher edn. and black colls. and univs. Dept. Edn., 1977-82; mem. Yale U. Council, 1977-82; emerita life trustee Coll. of Wooster, Ohio, 1967-77; trustee St. Louis U., 1971-75. Recipient Yale U. Wilbur Cross medal, 1976, Smith Coll. Alumnae medal, 1987. Mem. Am. Assn. Higher Edn., Phi Beta Kappa. Home: 925 Juniper Pl Bloomington IN 47408-1285

BORNHORST, KENNETH FRANK, electromagnetics and systems engineer; b. Detroit, Feb. 5, 1929; s. Leo John and Alvina Anna (Laufersweiler) B.; m. Patricia Lucille Drayer, July 3, 1954; children: Kenneth Jr., David L., Patricia A. BEE, U. Dayton, 1951, PhD in Engring., 1985; MEE, Poly. Inst. N.Y., 1954. Project engr. monopulse radar receiver devel. Sperry Gyroscope Co., Great Neck, N.Y., 1951-54; project engr. autopilot, motor, timer, gyroscope devel. Globe Industries Inc., Dayton, Ohio, 1954-60; project engr. devel. of servo guided shoe machinery United Shoe Machinery Co., Xenia, Ohio, 1960; engring. sect. head mil. equipment divsn. locator and telemetry beacon and automatic direction finder devel. NCR, Dayton, 1960-74; br. chief, analyst electromagnetic threat analysis, radar, advanced weapon sys. Nat. Air Intelligence Ctr. USAF, Wright-Patterson AFB, Ohio, 1974-94; cons., 1995—. Radar Cross section measurement of troops and vehicles for U.S. Army, 1954-56. Mem. Tau Beta Pi. Achievements include patents for flight control system, UHF bypass capacitor, pulsed carrier radio beacon, UHF radio direction finder, low loss millimeter waveguide.

BORNHURST, ROBERT ALLAN, radiologist; b. Syracuse, N.Y., 1932; BS, LeMoyne Coll., 1954; MD, SUNY, Syracuse, 1960. Diplomate Am. Bd. Radiology. Intern St. Joseph's Hosp., Syracuse, 1960-61; resident in radiology SUNY-Upstate Med. Ctr., Syracuse, 1961-64; pvt. practice St. Joseph's Imaging Assocs., Syracuse, 1989—2001; clin. asst. prof. SUNY-Upstate Med. Ctr., 1970—2001; pvt. prac. Syracuse, 1970-89; retired. Mem. AMA, Am. Coll. Radiology, Radiol. Soc. N.Am. Home: 118 Ruskin Ave Syracuse NY 13207-1325 E-mail: drbobxray@aol.com.

BORNIER, EVELYNE M, language educator; b. Chaumont, France, Aug. 26, 1969; d. Robert Raoul Philippe Bornier and Martine Jeanpierre. PhD, La. State U., 1999; DEA, Universite de France-Comte, 1994; Maitrise with highest honors, Universite de Franche-Comte, 1993, licence with honors, 1992; DEUG, Universite de France-Comte, 1991. Undergraduate adv. Universite de Franche-Comte, 1992—93; tchg. asst., dept. of French and Italian La. State U., 1994—99; instr. of French Baton Rouge French Club, 1996—2000, Friends of French Studies at La. State U., 1998—2000; asst. prof. of French Southeastern La. State U., 2001—. Tchg. asst. Bilborough Coll., Nottingham, England, 1991—92, Fernwood Comprehensive Sch., Nottingham, England, 1991—92; instr. of French Holy Family Cath. Sch., Port Allen, La., 1998—99. Coun. for the Devel. of French in La., 1998, grant, French Consulate, New Orleans, Tchg. Enhancement grant, Karen Domingue Maillet and Denis Maillet endowed scholarship, Southeastern La. State U., 2003, Maria Wloch and Pierre Marius Bornier endowed scholarship. Mem.: La. State Fgn. Lang. Teachers Assn., Friends of French Studies at La. State U., Northeastern Modern Lang. Assn., Modern Lang. Assn. of Am. Office: Southeastern Louisiana University 219 D Vickers SLU 10719 Hammond LA 70402 Office Fax: 985-549-3088. E-mail: ebornier@selu.edu.

BORNMANN, JOHN ALBERT, JR., electrical engineer; b. Daytona Beach, Fla., Nov. 12, 1945; s. John Albert and Lucille Bolger (Briggs) B.; m. Priscilla Sams Gautier, July 26, 1969; children: Kirsten Lee, John Albert III. BS, U.S. Mil. Acad., 1967; MSEE, Ga. Inst. Tech., 1972; MBA, So. Ill. U., 1985; D in Bus. Adminstrn., Nova U., 1989. Registered profl. engr., Va. Commd. 2d lt. U.S. Army, 1967, advanced through grades to lt. col., 1988; program mgr. Office of Sec. of Def., Washington, 1984-88; v.p. Joseph A. Pecar & Assocs., Potomac, Md., 1988-91; dep. program mgr., program mgr., sr. prin., bus. program mgr. Systems Rsch. and Applications Corp., Fairfax, Va., 1991—. Scoutmaster, cubmaster, dist. chmn., mem. dist. staff, v.p. coun. staff Boy Scouts Am., 1956—. Recipient Silver Beaver award Boy Scouts Am., 1976. Mem. Soc. Am. Mil. Engrs. (v.p. 1976-80), Am. Def. Preparedness Assn. (life). Democrat. Episcopalian (sr. warden). Avocations: racquetball, hiking, coin collecting. Home: 1903 Sword Ln Alexandria VA 22308-2446 Office: Systems Rsch & Applications 4300 Fair Lakes Ct Fairfax VA 22033-

BORNMANN, LEWIS JOSEPH, computer scientist; b. Atlantic City, N.J., Oct. 12, 1936; s. Lewis Joseph and Sue (Berish) B.; m. Helen Patricia O'Brien, Dec. 19, 1942 (div. Mar. 1974); children: Siobhan, Kathleen, Lewis Joseph, Christopher Brendon; m. Barbara Nelle Long, Feb. 14, 1975. BS in Math. and Physics, Ind. Inst. Tech., Ft. Wayne, 1965; MS in Computer Sci., U. Wis., 1969; PhD in Computer Sci, Columbia Pacific U., 1986. Analyst, programmer Boeing Co., Renton, Wash., 1965-66; project mgr. Control Data Corp., Sunnyvale, Calif., 1969-72, 73-75; tech. staff Calma Co., Sunnyvale, Calif., 1972-73; sr. analyst Stanford U., Palo Alto, Calif., 1975-76; sect. mgr. EG&G Idaho Inc., Idaho Falls, Idaho, 1976-78; mgr. info. processing STD Rsch. Crop., Arcadia, Calif., 1978-80; systems engr. Space Sys. Divsn. Gen. Electric, San Jose, 1980-91; asst. prof. Mesa State Coll., Grand Junction, Colo., 1992—2003. Instr. Calif. State U., San Jose, 1981. With USAF, 1958-61. Mem. IEEE, Assn. Computing Machinery (coun., Pacific regional rep., chair chpt. com. 1965—). Avocations: computers, jogging, skiing, backpacking, amateur radio. Home: 629 19 1/2 Rd Grand Junction CO 81503-9501

BORNS, HAROLD WILLIAM, JR., geologist, educator; b. Cambridge, Mass., Nov. 28, 1927; s. Harold William and Olive Blanche (Stevens) B.; m. Phyllis Clare Kuehl, May 23, 1954 (div. 1982); children— Harold William III, Donna Jean; m. Margaret Parker, Mar. 11, 1982 BS, Tufts U., 1951; MS, Boston U., 1955, PhD, 1959. Prof. geol. scis. U. Maine, Orono, 1971-74, chmn. dept. geol. scis., 1971-74, dir. inst. quaternary & climate studies, 1974-88, prof. geological scis. inst. for quaternary studies, 1974—; program mgr. polar glaciology Office of Polar Programs NSF, Washington, 1988-90. Contbr. articles to profl. jours. With USCG, 1946-48. Recipient Borns Glacier Antarctica award U.S. Bd. Geog. Names, 1962; Antarctic Service medal U.S. Antarctic Research Program, 1962; Research and Creative Achievement award U. Maine, 1984. Fellow Geol. Soc. Am., AAAS; mem. Explorers Club, Sigma Xi, Phi Kappa Phi Office: U Maine Inst Quaternary & Climate Studies Orono ME 04469-0001

BORNS, ROBERT AARON, real estate developer; b. Gary, Ind., Oct. 24, 1935; s. Irving Jonah and Sylvia (Mackoff) B.; m. Sandra Solotkin, Mar. 30, 1958; children: Stepahnie, Elizabeth, Emily. BS, Ind. U., 1957; hon. degree, U. indpls., 1987. Account exec. Reynolds & Co., Chgo., 1957-59, Francis I duPont co., Indpls., 1960; owner, operator Borns & Co., Indpls., 1960-63; chmn. Borns Mgmt. Corp., Indpls., 1963—, Correctional Mgmt. Co., L.L.C., 1996—. Bd. dirs. Artistic Media Ptnrs. L.L.C., Standard Mgmt. Corp. Bd. dirs. Barbara Sinatra Children's Ctr., Indpls. Mus. of Art, Ind. U. Found., Va. Waring Internat. Piano Competition; past bd. dirs. Ind. Symphony Orch.; mem. bd. visitors Borns Jewish Studies Program, Ind. U.; past bd. dirs. Indpls. Children's Mus., I.W.C. Resources Corp., Indpls. Water Co.; past mem. adv. bd. St. Vincent's Hosp.; past trustee St. Vincent's Hosp. Found. Recipient Enterprise award Indpls. Bus. Jour., 1982, Peace award State of Israel, 1979. Mem. Confrerie des Chevaliers du Tastevin, Econ. Club (bd. dirs.), Thunderbird Country Club (Rancho Mirage, Calif.). Office: Borns Mgmt Corp 21 Beachway Dr Indianapolis IN 46224-8566

BORNSTEIN, ELI, artist, sculptor; b. Milw., Minn., Dec. 28, 1922; dual citizen, U.S. and Can. m. Christina Bornstein; children: Sarah, Thea. BS, U. Wis., 1945, MS, 1954; student, Art Inst. Chgo., U. Chgo., 1943, Academie Montmartre of Fernand Leger, Paris, 1951, Academie Julian, 1952; DLitt, U. Sask., Can., 1990. Tchr. drawing, painting and sculpture Milw. Art Inst., 1943-47; tchr. design U. Wis., Wis., 1949; tchr. drawing, painting, sculpture, design and graphics U. Sask., Canada, 1950-90, prof., 1963-90, prof. emeritus, 1990—, head art dept., 1963-71. Painted in France, 1951-52, Italy, 1957, Holland, 1958; exhibited widely, 1943— ; retrospective exhbn. (works 1943-64), Mendel Art Gallery, Saskatoon, 1965, one man shows, Kazimir Gallery, Chgo., 1965, 67, Saskatoon Pub. Library, 1975, Can. Cultural Center, Paris, 1976, Glenbow-Alta. Inst. Art, Calgary, 1976, Mendel Art Gallery, Saskatoon, 1982, York U. Gallery, Toronto, 1983, Confedn. Ctr. Art Gallery, Charlottetown, P.E.I., 1983, Owens Art Gallery, Mt. Allison U., Sackville, N.B., 1984, Fine Arts Gallery, U. Wis.-Milw., 1984, Mendel Art Gallery, Saskatoon, 1996; represented in numerous pvt. collections; executed marble sculpture now in permanent collection, Walker Art Center, Mpls., 1947; commns. include aluminum constrn. for Sask. Tchr. Fedn. Bldg., 1956, structurist relief in painted wood and aluminum for, Arts and Sci. Bldg., U. Sask., 1958, structurist relief in enamelled steel for, Internat. Air Terminal, Winnipeg, Man., Can., 1962, four-part constructed relief for, Wascana Pl., Wascana Ctr. Authority, Regina, Sask., 1983, and six panel structurist relief for exterior of Can. Light Source Bldg., U. Sask, 2002; also structurist reliefs exhibited, Mus. Contemporary Art, Chgo., Herron Mus. Art, Indpls., Cranbrook Acad. Art Galleries, Mich., High Mus., Atlanta, Can. House, Cultural Centre Gallery, London, 1983, Can. Cultural Ctr., Paris, 1983, Brussels, 1983, Bonn, 1984, Milw. Art Mus., 1984; model of aluminium construction, 1956 and model version of structurist relief in 5 parts, 1962, now in collection, Nat. Gallery, Ottawa, Ont., others in numerous collections.; Co-editor: periodical Structure, 1958; founder, editor: The Structurist, ann. publ. 1960-72, biennial, 1972—; Contbr. articles, principally on Structurist art to various publ. Recipient Allied Arts medal Royal Archtl. Inst. Can., 1968; hon. mention for 3 structurist reliefs 2d Biennial Internat. Art Exhbn., Colombia, S.Am., 1970 Address: 3625 Saskatchewan Cres S Corman Park SK Canada S7T 1B7 Office: U Sask Box 378 RPO U Saskatoon SK Canada S7N 4J8 Home Fax: 306-652-9741. E-mail: eli.bornstein@usask.ca.

BORNSTEIN, GEORGE JAY, literary educator; b. St. Louis, Aug. 25, 1941; s. Harry and Celia (Price) B.; m. Jane Elizabeth York, June 22, 1982; children— Benjamin, Rebecca, Joshua. AB, Harvard U., 1963; PhD, Princeton U., 1966. Asst. prof. MIT, Cambridge, 1966-69, Rutgers U., 1969-70; assoc. prof. U. Mich., Ann Arbor, 1970-75, prof. English, 1975—, C.A. Patrides prof. lit., 1995—. Cons. various univ. presses, scholastic jours., funding agys., 1970—; mem. adv. bd. Yeats: An Annual, 1982—, South Atlantic Rev., 1985-88, Rev., 1991—, Text, 1993—, Paideuma, 2003—. Author: Yeats and Shelley, 1970, Transformations of Romanticism, 1976, Postromantic Consciousness of Ezra Pound, 1977, Poetic Remaking, 1988, Material Modernism: The Politics of the Page, 2001; editor: Romantic and Modern, 1977, Ezra Pound Among the Poets, 1985, W.B. Yeats: The Early Poetry, vol. 1, 1987, vol. 2, 1994, W.B. Yeats: Letters to the New Island, 1990, Representing Modernist Texts, 1991, Palimpsest: Editorial Theory in the Humanities, 1993, W.B. Yeats: Under the Moon, the Unpublished Early Poetry, 1995, Contemporary German Editorial Theory, 1995, The Iconic Page in Manuscript, Print, and Digital Culture, 1998. Cubmaster Wolverine council Boy Scouts Am., 1977-79. Recipient good teaching award Amoco Found., 1983, Warner Rice prize for rsch. in humanities, 1988, Rosenthal award for Yeats studies W.B. Yeats Soc., 2000; fellow Am. Coun. Learned Soc., 1972-73, NEH fellow, 1982-83, fellow Old Dominion Found., 1968, fellow Guggenheim Found., 1986-87. Mem. MLA (exec. com. Anglo-Irish 1976-80, exec. com. 20th Century English 1980-85, exec. com. Poetry 1987-92, exec. com. bibliography and textual studies 1993-98, exec. com. methods of rsch. 1998-2003), Soc. Textual Scholarship (program chair 1997, exec. com. 1998-), Am. Conf. on Irish Studies (book prize judge 1991), Racquet Club, Princeton Club (N.Y.C.), Phi Beta Kappa. Home: 2020 Vinewood Blvd Ann Arbor MI 48104-3614 Office: U Mich Dept English Ann Arbor MI 48109-1003 E-mail: georgeb@umich.edu.

BORNSTEIN, JAN MARTIN, computer engineer; b. Göteborg, Sweden, Nov. 9, 1960; s. Sim and Ulla Britt (Flodén) B. MSEE, Chalmers U. Tech., Göteborg, 1984. Microsoft cert. profl. solution developer, 2000. Specialist in measurement Volvo, Göteborg, 1984-85; designer software Teletron, Kungsbacka, Sweden, 1985-86; designer hardware Televerket, Göteborg, 1986-89; sys. designer Teli, Göteborg, 1989-93; designer mobile data Ericsson, Göteborg, 1993-94; developer MoAr PC-based system for mobile police work Swedish Nat. Police, 1994-96; designer Ericsson, 1997-98, head designer, 1998-99, sr. software architect, 1999—. Patentee in field. Mem. Avancez Chalmersska Ingenjôrs-Fôreningen. Avocations: jujutsu (black belt), floorball, juggler. Office: Ericsson AB Lindholmspiren 11 417 56 Göteborg Sweden E-mail: jan.bornstein@ericsson.com., janne_bornstein@hotmail.com.

BORNSTEIN, LESTER MILTON, retired medical center executive; b. Boston, Feb. 19, 1925; s. Harry and Celia (Adlestein) B.; m. Marilyn Goldstein, Aug. 22, 1948; children: Aura Lynne, Michael Scott, Karen Jane. BS, Boston U., 1948; M.P.H. in Hosp. Adminstrn, Yale U., 1955. Adminstrv. resident Charles S. Wilson Meml. Hosp., Johnson City, N.Y., 1953-54; asst. dir. Barnert Meml. Hosp., Paterson, N.J., 1954-57, Newark Beth Israel Hosp., 1957-68; pres. Newark Beth Israel Med. Center, Newark, 1968-96. Served with AUS, 1943-45, ETO; to maj., Korean War 1950-53. Decorated Bronze Stars. Fellow Am. Coll. Hosp. Adminstrs., N.J. Hosp. Assn. (chmn. bd. trustees 1978-79) Home: 6 Aherne Way West Orange NJ 07052-2102 E-mail: lestb@aol.com.

BORNSTEIN, MYER SIDNEY, obstetrician, gynecologist; b. Boston, Sept. 7, 1938; s. Abram and Celia (Stein) B.; m. Janet L. Difonzo, July 15, 1977; two children: three children by previous marriage. BS, Northeastern U., 1961; MD, U. Vt., 1965; Grad., N.Y. Inst. Photography, 1988; M in Med. Mgmt., Tulane U., 2000. Diplomate Am. Bd. Ob-Gyn., Am. Bd. Utilization Rev. and Quality Assurance Physicians, Am. Coll. Physicians Exes.; cert. advanced hysterectomy and laparascopy, obstet. crit. care; cert. physician exec., med. mgmt. Intern Rochester (N.Y.) Gen. Hosp., 1965-66, resident, 1966-69, practice specializing in gyn., laparoscopy, infertility, 1969—, drug and alcohol treatment, 1984-87; chief ob-gyn Kinchloe AFB, Mich., 1969-71; asst. chief Weisbaden (Germany) Regional Hosp., 1971-74; attending physician Charleton Meml. Hosp., Fall River, Mass., 1974-83, New London (N.H.) Hosp., 1983-87, Morton Hosp., 1987—; dir. Assocs. in Women's Health, 1988—; chief ob-gyn., 1991—; med. dir. substance abuse treatment ctr. Seminole Point Hosp., N.E. Alcohol and Drug Ctr., 1984-87; med. dir. Greater Fall River Family Planning, 1981-87. Chair by-laws com., chmn. laparoendoscopy com.; chair perinatal com., med. dir. substance abuse treatment ctr. Seminole Point Hosp., N.E. Alcohol and Drug Svcs., 1984-87; med. dir. Greater Fall River Family Planning, 1981-83; owner SEMASS Photography, SEMASS Med. Cons.; cons. ob-gyn Fall River Cmty. Devel. Ctr., 1976-83, Taunton State Hosp., 1988—, Stanley Street Alcohol Rehab. Ctr., Fall River, Mass.; guest lectr. dept. social work Providence Coll., 1980; vis. prof. Facility CMH Physician Tng. Ctr., Nashville; freelance nature photographer; reviewer MassPro Blue Cross and Blue Shield; Mass. rep., chmn. sect. alt. to hysterectomy Ob-gyn. Net; bd. dirs. Morton Physician

Assocs.; med. dir., COO Assocs. in Women's Health; med. dir. HyGenia Biomed. Products; assoc. adj. clin. prof. Mass. Coll. Pharmacy. Contbr. photographs to jours. and books. Bd. dirs. Kersang chpt. Am. Cancer Soc., Greater Fall River Children's Protective Svcs., Pilgrim Found. Med. Care; bd. dirs., coach, pres. Wattupa Youth Hockey Assn., 1978-81. Lt. col. USAF, 1969-74. Recipient STARR award for help in program for pregnant addicted women, 1989; named Cmty. Clinican of the Yr., Bristol County Med. Soc. and Mass. Med. Soc., 1999. Fellow Am. Coll. Ob-Gyn., Am. Coll. Physician Exec.; mem. AMA, Am. Coll. Healthcare Execs., Am. Soc. Gynecol. Laparascopy, Am. Soc. Colposcopy, Mass. Med. Soc. (asst. sec. treas. 1997-98,tax support medicare com., managed care com., chair perinatal welfare com. 1998—, vice-chair nominating com. 1994-96, chair 1996-99, trustee, Clinician of Yr. 1999), Bristol North Med. Soc. (pres. 1994-98), Am. Coll. Ob-Gyn., Southeastern New Eng. Ob-Gyn Soc., Am. Inst. Ultrasound in Medicine, Am. Fertility Soc., N.H. Med. Soc. (trainer Origin Medisys., trainer Ethicon Endosurg.), Merrimack County Med. Soc. N.H. Ob-Gyn Soc., Am. Legion, Rotary (New London). Home: 5 Lang St Lakeville MA 02347-1807 Office: 72 Washington St Taunton MA 02780-2470 E-mail: mborn@massmed.org.

BORNSTEIN, PAUL, physician, biochemist; b. Antwerp, Belgium, July 10, 1934; came to U.S., 1947, naturalized, 1952; s. Abraham and Mina (Ginsburg) B. BA, Cornell U., 1954; MD, NYU, 1958. Intern in surgery Yale-New Haven Hosp., 1958-59, intern in medicine, 1959-60, asst. resident in medicine, 1960-62; sr. fellow Arthritis Found. Pasteur Inst., Paris, 1962-63; research asso. NIH, Bethesda, Md., 1963-65, research investigator, 1965-67; asst. prof. biochemistry and medicine U. Wash., 1967-69, asso. prof., 1969-73, prof., 1973—, attending physician, 1968—. Mem. editl. bd. Jour. Biol. Chemistry, 1972-78, 80-85, Jour. Cell Biology, 1988-91, 94-97, Matrix Biology, 1993—; assoc. editor Arteriosclerosis, 1980-90, Collagen Related Rsch., 1981-88; contbr. articles to profl. jours. Served to sr. surgeon USPHS, 1963-67. Recipient Lederle Med. Faculty award USPHS, 1968; Rsch. Career Devel. award NIH, 1969; Macy Faculty Scholar award, 1975; Merit award NIH, 1989; Guggenheim fellow, 1985. Mem.: Internat. Soc. Matrix Biology (pres. 2001—03), Am. Soc. Matrix Biology (v.p. 2001—02, pres. 2002—03), Assn. Am. Physicians, Western Soc. Clin. Rsch., Am. Soc. Biol. Chemistry, Am. Soc. Clin. Investigation. Home: 602 34th Ave E Seattle WA 98112-4306 Office: U Wash Sch Medicine Dept Biochemistry PO Box 357350 Seattle WA 98195-7350 E-mail: bornsten@u.washington.edu.

BORNSTEIN, RITA, academic administrator; b. N.Y.C., Jan. 2, 1936; d. Carl and Florence (Gates) Kropf, m. Harland G. Bloland; children from previous marriage: Rachel, Mark, Per. BA in English, Fla. Atlantic U., 1970, MA in English, 1971; PhD in Ednl. Leadership and Instrn., U. Miami, 1975. Tchr., adminstr. Dade County Pub. Schs., Fla., 1971-75; adminstr. dept. edn. U. Miami, Coral Gables, Fla., 1975-81, adminstr. divsn. devel., 1981-85, v.p., 1985-90; pres. Rollins Coll., Winter Park, Fla., 1990—. Bd. dirs. tupperware Corp. Author: (book) Freedom or Order: Must We Choose?, 1976, Title IX Compliance and Sex Equity: Definitions, Distinctions, Costs and Benefits, 1981; contbr. articles to profl. jours. Mem.: So. Univ. Conf. (exec. com. 1998—2003, pres. 2001—02), So. Assn. Colls. and Schs. (commn. colls. 1998—2000, exec. coun. 1999—2000, appeals com. 2002—), Ind. Colls. and Univs. of Fla. (coun. pres. 1990—, chair 1997—98), Fla. Coun. of 100, Assoc. Colls. of the South (bd. dirs. 1992—2001, treas. 1993—95, sec. 1995—97, vice chair 1997—99, chair 1999—2001), Nat. Assn. Ind. Colls. and Univs. (bd. dirs. 1992—95, chair govt. rels. com. 1994—95), Am. Coun. on Edn. (com. leadership devel. 1991—93, bd. dirs. 1995—98), Annapolis Group (exec. com. 1999—2001). Office: Rollins Coll Office of Pres 1000 Holt Ave # 2711 Winter Park FL 32789-4499

BORNSTEIN, SANDRA, science educator; d. Robert Lawrence Kassel and Alberta Sarah Donahue; m. Gerald Bernard Bornstein, June 1, 1967; children: Lisa Rachel, Danica Robyn. BA in Biology and Chemistry, Barnard Coll., 1967; MSc in Teratology, McGill U., Montreal, Can., 1969; EdM in Math., CUNY, 1995. Cytogenetic technologist. Cytogenetic technician Brookdale Hosp., Bklyn., 1974—76; cytogenetic technologist NYU Med. Ctr., N.Y.C., 1976—83; sci. tchr. Woodward Park Sch., Bklyn., 1983—90, Columbia Prep. Sch., N.Y.C., 1990—97, Young Women's Leadership Sch., N.Y.C., 1997—98, Great Neck (N.Y.)-North Shore Hebrew Acad., 1998—99; sci. tchr., dept. head Poly Prep Country Day Sch., Bklyn., 1999—, Livingston chair lectr., 2000—01. Vis. fellow Am. Antiquarian Soc., Worchester, Mass., 1996; inst. assoc. Bard Coll. Writing and Thinking Inst., Annandale-on-Hudson, NY, 2002—. Author: What Makes You What You Are, 1989; co-author: What is Genetics, 1979, New Frontiers in Genetics, 1984. Named mus. assoc., NSF, 1987—88, Summer Seminar Darwin, NEH, 1995; Access Excellence fellow, Access Excellence, 1996. Mem.: AAAS, N.Y. Acad. Sci., Nat. Sci. Tchrs. Assn. Office: Poly Prep Country Day Sch 9216 7th Ave Brooklyn NY 11228

BORNSTEIN, STEVEN M. broadcast executive; b. Fair Lawn, N.J., Apr. 20, 1952; BS, U. Wis., 1974. Mgr. program coordination ESPN, Inc., Bristol, Conn., 1980—81, dir. program planning and qcauisitions, 1981, dir. programming, 1981—83, v.p. programming, 1983—85, sr. v.p. programming and prodn., 1985—88, exec. v.p. programming and prodn., 1988—90, pres., CEO, 1990—98, also bd. dirs.; pres. ABC Sports, N.Y.C., ABC Inc., Go.com. Mem.: Cable TV Advt. Bur., European Sports Network (dir. Lafayette Beveer bd.), Nat. Acad. Cable Programming (bd. govs.). Office: ABC Corp 77 W 66th St Fl 16 New York NY 10023-6201

BORNTRAGER, JOHN SHERWOOD, principal; b. Oak Harbor, Wash., July 3, 1953; s. George H. and Norma E. Borntrager; m. Linda Diane, Aug. 30, 1975; children: Melissa, Shanna. BA, San Diego State U., 1975; MA, U. Ctrl. Ark., 1984. Cert. elem. educator, Ariz., Mo., Ark.; cert. prin., Mo., Ark. Tchr. Alhambra Pub. Schs., Phoenix, 1976-79; tchr., prin. Norfork Pub. Schs., Ark., 1979-87; prin. Cedarville Pub. Schs., 1987—2003. Mem. ASCD, Ark. Edn. Assn., Ark. Christian Educators Assn., Ark. Assn. Elem. Sch. Prins., Phi Delta Kappa.

BOROCHOFF, IDA SLOAN, artist; b. July 29, 1922; d. Louis and Eva (Bistrick) Sloan; m. Charles Zachary Borochoff, Jan 11, 1942 (dec. July, 1990); children: Lynn Borochoff Gould, Jean Sue Borochoff Shapiro, Toby Ann Borochoff Bernstein, Lance Mark. Student, U. Ga., 1939-40, Ga. State U., 1940, Chgo. Sch. Interior Decorating, 1966, Allegro Sch. Ballet, Chgo., Atlanta Ballet, 1948-54, Emory U., 1971-72. Investor, owner real estate, 1941—; v.p. Designs Unltd., Inc., Atlanta, 1964—; pres. Sloan Borochoff Gallery, Atlanta, 1970—; art lectr. Met. Ednl. Svc.; art tchr. Ga. Inst. Tech., 1991. Prodr. live talk health show on cable TV, Atlanta, 1983-87. One woman shows include Lovett Sch., 1972, 75, Ga. Inst. Tech., 1972, 75, Atlanta Mdse. Mart, Saginaw Art Mus., 1998-99; group shows include Gwinnett Art Mus., Duluth, Ga., 1999, Ind. U., 1999, Purdue U., Indpls., 1999; art rev. columnist Northside Neighbor Newspapers; columnist Around Ga. with Ida. Bd. dirs. Atlanta Ballet, 1950-57, bd. dirs. Atlanta Music Club, co-editor newsletter; hostess Atlanta Arts Festival; capt. Heart Fund, 1968-76, area chmn. dr.; elected to bd. dirs. Am. Cancer Rsch. Ctr. Atlanta chpt.; active various multi-media groups; artistic dir. Atlanta Playhouse Theatre, chmn., trustee; artistic dir. Little Miss Ga. Pageant, Little Mr. Dogwood Festival Pageant; judge 17th Internat. Dogwood Festival Art Show, 1989; mem. U.S. cong. adv. bd. Am. Security Coun., 1983—; archivist nat. oral history nat. Coun. Jewish Women, 1990—; Ga. dir., chairperson Levi Hosp. Art Auction, Hot Springs, Ark., 1993-94; with Archives Exhibit Atlanta Jewish Fedn., 1994; donor Borochoff Libr. of A.A. Synagogue; com. mem., patron AJCC Book Festival, 1995-96. Recipient several art awards including Caber award, 1984; named hon. alumnus Atlanta Art Inst., 1968, One of Ten Leading Ladies of Atlanta, J.C. Singles, 19876, honored by Barbara Bush, White House, Washington, 1989, 90; City grantee, 1985. Mem. Atlanta Press Club, Atlanta Writers Club (membership com.), Atlanta Artists Club, Atlanta Women's C. of C. (chmn. fine arts 1977-78), LVW, High Mus. Art, Ga. Writers Assn., Arts High Mus. (patron), Corcoran Gallery (patron), Nat. Mus. Women in Arts (charter mem.), Internat. Platform Assn., B'nai B'rith Women (pres. chpt. 1975, mem. S.E. regional bd.), Ga. Hist. Soc., AAUW, Women in the Arts, Jockey Club, Progressive Club, Capitol Hill Club (Washington). Home: 3450 Old Plantation Rd NW Atlanta GA 30327-2426 Office: 733 Glendale Rd Scottdale GA 30079-1409

BOROD, DONALD LEE, lawyer; b. Cleve., June 22, 1947; s. Jules Arthur and Hortense Edith (Cowan) B.; m. Jane Duclos Hudson, Nov. 11, 1978; children: James Hudson, Catherine Duclos. B.A., U. Mich., 1969; J.D., Columbia U., 1972. Bar: N.Y. 1973, Conn. 1984. Assoc. firm Dewey, Ballantine, Bushby, Palmer & Wood, N.Y.C., 1972-81; assoc. gen. counsel Kollmorgen Corp., Hartford, Conn., 1981-83, gen. counsel, 1983-86, v.p., gen. counsel, 1986-91; counsel Pepe & Hazard, Hartford, 1992—. Harlan Fiske Stone scholar Columbia U., 1971. Mem. ABA, Conn. Bar Assn., Am. Corp. Counsel Assn., Assn. Bar City N.Y. Club: Hartford Golf. Office: Kollmorgen Corp 2099 Pennsylvania Ave NW Washington DC 20006-6800

BORODIN, ALEXEI, mathematician; b. Donetsk, USSR, June 25, 1975; s. Mikhail Alekseevich Borodin and Gita Yur'evna Rudakova. Diploma in Math. (with honors), Moscow State U., 1997; MSE in Computer Sci., PhD in Math., U. Pa., 2001. Prof. math. Calif. Inst. Tech., Pasadena, 2003—. Vis. fellow Courant Inst. Math. Scis., N.Y.C., 2002; mem. Inst. for Advanced Study, Princeton, NJ, 2001—02. Mem. editl. bd. Internat. Math. Rsch. Notices, 2002, Jour. Stats. Physics, 2003. Long Term Prize fellow, Clay Math. Inst., 2001—. Mem.: Am. Math. Soc. Office: California Insitute of Technology Mathematics 253-37 Pasadena CA 91125

BORONICO, JESS STEPHEN, management science educator, academic dean; b. Bronx, N.Y., Oct. 23, 1956; s. Stelio and Helen (Michaels) B. BS in Math., Fairleigh Dickinson U., 1978, MS in Math., 1980; PhD in Ops. Rsch., U. Pa., 1992. Prof. mgmt. scis. Rutgers U., Camden, N.J., 1987-88, Phila. Coll. Textiles and Scis., 1988-92, Monmouth U., West Long Branch, 1993—2001, assoc. dean Sch. Bus., 1998-2000, dean Sch. Bus., 2000-01; prof. mgmt. scis., dean Cotsakis Coll. Bus., William Paterson U., Wayne, NJ, 2001—. Cons. United Postal Svc., 1990-92, Reality Techs., 1991, N.J. Hwy. Authority, 1991-92, Kennedy Western U., Calif., 1994-97; mem. adv. bd. to various jours., 1993—. Author: Computer Simulation in Operations Management, 1996; contbg. author: The Service Productivity and Quality Challenge, 1995; editor: Studies in the Strategy and Tactics of Competitive Advantage, 2000; contbr. articles to profl. jours. Fellow U. Pa. Wharton Sch., 1983-87; recipient three Anbar citations of excellence for refereed publs., 1996-98. Mem. Inst. for Ops. Rsch. and Mgmt. Scis., Decision Scis. Inst., Am. Statis. Assn., Mensa. Avocations: softball, computer simulations. Home: 525 East St Long Branch NJ 07740-6815 Office: Cotsakos Coll of Bus William Paterson U 1600 Valley Rd Wayne NJ 07470 E-mail: jboronic@monmouth.edu.

BOROS, JEROME S. lawyer; b. N.Y.C., Apr. 28, 1926; s. Edwin N. Boros and Margaret G. Guttman; m. Elayne N. Nossiter, Nov. 23, 1969; stepchildren: Richard, Ronald, Jill LeVine. AB, Syracuse U., 1947, MA, LLB, Syracuse U., 1950; LLM, Yale U., 1951. Bar: N.Y. 1950, D.C. Bar 1966, U.S. Dist. Ct. (so. dist.) N.Y. 1950, U.S. Ct. Appeals (D.C. cir.) 1966. Atty. CAB, Washington, 1950-53, FCC, Washington, 1953-55; assoc. Fly, Shuebruk, Gaguine, Boros & Braun, N.Y.C., Washington, 1955-62, ptnr., 1962-88, Rosenman & Colin, N.Y.C., 1988—96; of counsel Robinson, Silverman, Pearce, Aaronsohn & Berman, N.Y.C., 1996—2002; chmn. telecomm. group of counsel Bryan Cave, 2002—; of counsel Bryan Cave, 2002—. Faculty sch. speech Syracuse U., 1947; adj. prof. law NYU Sch. Law, 1971-95; chmn. Workshop on Broadcasting Practising Law Inst., 1969, lectr., 1969-76; gen. counsel Internat. Radio and TV Soc., N.Y.C., 1973-93, sec., 1973-93, gov., 1973-93; co-trustee radio sta. WYRM. New Britain, Conn., 1987-96. Acting village justice Village of Sands Point, N.Y., 1988-2000, village justice 2000—; chmn. Sands Point Cable Com., 1993—. With U.S. Army, 1944-45. Mem. City Athletic Club (gov., chmn. legal legis. com. 1959-02), Harmonie Club, 2002—. Republican. Jewish. Office: Bryan Cave 1290 Ave of Americas New York NY 10104-0199

BOROVETZ, HARVEY SELWYN, biomedical engineer, educator; b. Pitts., May 21, 1947; s. Hyman and Rose (Dortman) Borovetz; m. Frances Presser, June 22, 1969; children: H. Michael, Roberta Lyn, Sharon Ilene. BA, Brandeis U., 1969; MS, Carnegie-Mellon U., 1973, PhD of Bioengring., 1976. Mem. tech. staff N.Am. Rockwell, Anaheim, Calif., 1969; rsch. asst. Carnegie-Mellon U., Pitts., 1970—76; rsch. assoc. Sch. Medicine and Sch. Engring. U. Pitts., 1976—77, rsch. asst. prof. surgery and civil engring., 1977—82, rsch. assoc. prof. surgery and civil engring., 1982—. Cons. univs. and hosps., 1984—; assoc. prof. surgery and civil engring. U. Pitts., 1986—90; sr. lectr. engrin. in medicine Carnegie-Mellon U., Pitts., 1986—; prof. surgery and civil engring. U. Pitts., 1990—, Robert L. Hardesty prof. surgery, 2000—, prof., chmn. bioengring., 2002—. Contbr. . Health sci. adminstr. NIH, 1999—2000. With USAR, 1970—76. Recipient numerous fellowships and grants. Mem.: AIChE, Internat. Soc. Artificial Organs, Am. Soc. Artificial Internal Organs, Bioengring. Soc., Sigma Xi. Achievements include research in devel. of artificial internal organs for adult and pediatric patients; devel. mechanisms of pulmonary injury, blood flow and arterial disease, the total artificial heart and ventricular assist devices, and membrane blood oxygenation. Home: 5667 Beacon St Pittsburgh PA 15217-2011 Business E-Mail: borovetzhs@msx.upmc.edu.

BOROVICKA, MARSHA LORRAINE, music educator; b. Ls Vegas, Nev., July 21, 1951; d. Arlo Fielding and Carrie Graff Beatty; m. Robert L. Borovicka. BA, U. Nev., 1973, MEd, 1979. Music tchr. CCSD/Jo Mackey Elem. Sch., La Vegas, Nev., 1973—75; dir. choral activities CCSD/Basic H.S., Henderson, Nev., 1975—82, CCSD/Cannon Mid. Sch., Las Vegas, Nev., 1983—85, Clark County Sch. Dist./Chaparral H.S., Las Vegas, Nev., 1985—. Choral dir. LDS Ch., Las Vegas, Nev., 1971. Musician (conductor) various choral groups. Named Tchr. of the Yr., Clark County Sch. Dist./Southland Corp., 1991. Mem. Lds Ch. Avocation: golf. Office: Chaparral HS 3850 Annie Oakley Dr Las Vegas NV 89121 Personal E-mail: marsha_borovicka@interact.ccsd.net.

BOROWIEC, ANDREW, art educator, photographer; BA in Russian, Haverford Coll., 1979; MFA in Photography, Yale U., 1982. Instr. Parsons Sch. Design, Paris, 1980-82, 83-84; tchr. photography and art Germantown Acad., Ft. Washington, Pa., 1982-83; instr. New Sch. Social Rsch., N.Y.C., 1982-84; instr. fashion photography Lab. Inst. Merchandising, N.Y.C., 1984; dir. Sch. Art U. Akron, Ohio, 1990-95, prof. art Mary Schiller Myers Sch. Art, 1995—. Guest lectr. contemporary Am. photography U. d'Aix-Marseille, France; vis. assoc. prof. art history Oberlin (Ohio) Coll., 1990. One-man shows include Club House, UN, Geneva, 1978, Galerie Un Moment En Plus, Paris, 1981, Le Poisson Banane, Arles, France, 1981, Galerie Les Arcenaulx, Marseille, France, 1982, Radnor Gallery, Bryn Mawr Coll., Pa., 1983, Perkins Gallery, U. Akron, 1984, Midtown Y Photography Gallery, N.Y.C., 1984, Dishman Gallery, Lamar U., Beaumont, Tex., 1986, Vox Gallery, Akron, 1988, Rose Gallery, St. Edwards U., Austin, Tex., 1988, Dillingham Gallery, Ithaca (N.Y.) Coll., 1988, Exit Gallery, Reno, 1988, Canton (Ohio) Art Inst., 1989, Fla. Internat. U., North Miami, Fla., 1990, Coll. Wooster (Ohio) Art Mus., 1991, Blue Sky Gallery, Portland, Oreg., 1994, Soc. Contemporary Photography, Kansas City, Mo., 1995, 99, Regis U., Denver, 1996, O.K. Harris, N.Y.C., 1997, So. Light Gallery, Amarillo, Tex., 1999, The Print Ctr., Phila., Pa., numerous others; exhibited in group shows at Images Gallery, Cin., 1991, Ea. Mich. U., Ypsilanti, 1992, Photospiva 93, Joplin, Mo., 1993, Contemporary Artists Ctr., North Adams, Mass., 1994, U. Cin., 1995, Blue Sky Gallery, Portland, 1996, Open Space Gallery, Allentown, Pa., 1997, Cleve. Mus. Art, 1998, numerous others; represented in pub. collections Akron Art Mus., Can. Ctr. Arch., N.Y.C., Montreal, Can., Canton Art Inst., Chgo. Art Inst., Midtown Y. Photography Gallery, N.Y.C., Yale U., New Haven, others; staff photographer Internat. Ctr. Photography, N.Y.C., 1979-80; freelance photography The Chronicle for Higher Edn., 1987-93; commn. by Nat. Trust Historic Preservation and Soc. Photo graphic Edn., 1987, Canton Art Inst., 1988-89; contbr. photography to numerous publs. Recipient Excellence award Kansas City Art Inst., 1987, Hon. Mention and Purchase award Cleve. Mus. Art, 1988, Third prize N.Mex. Photographer, 1994, Purchase prize Nat. Mus. Am. Art, 1996, Fellowship award Soc. Contemporary Photography, 1998; Nat. Endowment Arts/Arts Midwest Photography fellow, 1985; Summer Rsch. fellow U. Akron, 1988, 90, 97, 2000; Individual Artist fellow Ohio Arts Coun., 1988, 98; John Simon Guggenheim Meml. Found. fellow, 1998; Faculty Rsch. grantee U. Akron, 1986; Instl. Support grantee Ohio Arts Coun., 1988; Visual Artists Forums grantee Nat. Endowment Arts, 1988; Folk Endowment grantee U. Akron Sch. Art, 1993; Folk Endowment grantee U. Akron Mary Schiller Myers Sch. Art, 1998. Address: 1062 W Market St Akron OH 44313-7128 Fax: (330) 972-5960. E-mail: borowiec@uakron.edu.

BOROWITZ, ALBERT IRA, lawyer, author; b. Chgo., June 27, 1930; s. David and Anne (Wolkenstein) B.; m. Helen Blanche Osterman, July 29, 1950; children: Peter Leonard, Joan, Andrew Seth. BA in Classics summa cum laude, Harvard U., 1951, MA in Chinese Regional Studies, 1953, JD magna cum laude, 1956. Bar: Ohio 1957. Assoc. firm Hahn, Loeser, Freedheim, Dean & Wellman, Cleve., 1956-62, ptnr., 1962-83, Jones, Day, Reavis & Pogue, Cleve., 1983-90, of counsel, 1991-94; cons., 1994—99. Author: Fiction in Communist China, 1954, Innocence and Arsenic: Studies in Crime and Literature, 1977, The Woman who Murdered Black Satin: The Bermondsey Horror, 1981, A Gallery of Sinister Perspectives: Ten Crimes and a Scandal, 1982, The Jack the Ripper Walking Tour Murder, 1986, The Thurtell-Hunt Murder Case: Dark Mirror to Regency England, 1987, This Club Frowns on Murder, 1990, Jones, Day, Reavis & Pogue: The First Century, 1993, Unhappy Endings, 2001, Blood and Ink: An International Guide to Fact-Based Crime Literature, 2002; author: (with H.O. Borowitz) Pawnshop and Palaces: The Fall and Rise of the Campana Art Museum, 1991; series editor: True Crime, Kent State Univ. Press. Hon. consul of France in Cleve., 1990-95; v.p. French-Am. C. of C. of No. Ohio, 1993-99; co-founder Borowitz True Crime Collection at Kent State U. Librs. Recipient Cleve. arts prize for lit., 1981 Mem. Am. Law Inst., Rowfant Club (Cleve.), Union Club (Cleve.), Harvard Club (N.Y.C.), Vidocq Soc. Phila. (hon.). E-mail: alborowitz@aol.com.

BOROWITZ, JOSEPH LEO, pharmacologist, educator; b. Columbus, Ohio, Dec. 19, 1932; s. Joseph Peter and Anna Louise (Grundei) B.; divorced, 1985; children: Jon Joseph, Peter Joseph, Lynn Anne. BS in Pharmacy, Ohio State U., 1955; MS in Pharmacology, Purdue U., 1957; PhD in Pharmacology (NIH fellow), Northwestern U., 1960. Chief biokinetics br. Sch. Aerospace Medicine, San Antonio, 1960—62; postdoctoral fellow dept. pharmacology Harvard U. Med. Sch., Boston, 1963—64; instr., then asst. prof. pharmacology Bowman Gray Sch. Medicine, 1964—69; assoc. prof. pharmacology and toxicology Purdue U., 1969—74, prof., 1974—; sabbatical leave to Basel, Switzerland, 1984; vis. prof. sch. pharmacy U. P.R., 2001; sabbatical leave to Cambridge, England, 1976. Contbr. articles to profl. jours. Treas. Tippecanoe County (Ind.) Comprehensive Health Planning Coun., 1971-76. Capt. USAR, 1960. Recipient award for excellence in teaching Bowman Gray Sch. Medicine, 1969, Henry Heine award for excellence in teaching Purdue U. Coll. Pharmacy, 1983; named NIH postdoctoral fellow, 1962-64; grantee NSF, 1965-68, NIH, 1971-74, 86-89, 89-94, 94-98, 99—, U.S. Army Med. Rsch., 1989-96, 97-2000. Mem.: Rho Chi. Roman Catholic. Office: Purdue U Dept Med Chem and Molec Pharmacology West Lafayette IN 47907 E-mail: borowitz@pharmacy.purdue.edu.

BOROWITZ, SIDNEY, retired physics educator; b. N.Y.C., N.Y., June 12, 1918; s. Morris and Rose (Cohen) B.; m. Ruth Aaron Meyer, June 20, 1943; children: Michael, Elizabeth. BS, CCNY, 1937; MS, NYU, 1941, PhD, 1948. Physicist David Taylor Model Basin, 1942-43; indsl. engr. Western Electric Co., 1943-45; instr. NYU, N.Y.C., 1946-48, asst. prof., 1950-55, assoc. prof., 1955-59, prof. physics, 1959-84, prof. emeritus, 1984—, dean, 1969-71, chancellor, 1971-77; instr. Harvard U., Cambridge, Mass., 1948-50; chief exec. officer Cistron Biotech., Pine Brook, N.J., 1981-84. Chmn. bd. dirs. Aesculapius Internat. Medicine, N.Y.C., 1987-90, Inst. for Sch. of the Future, N.Y.C., 1987—; cons. NYU, 1987-97; exec. dir. N.Y. Acad. Scis., N.Y.C., 1977-81; mem. investment adv. com. Am. Inst. Physics, 1992-97. Author: Fundamentals of Quantum Mechanics, 1967, Farewell Fossil Fuels, 1998; co-author: Essentials of Physics, 1966, A Contemporary View of Elementary Physics, 1968, Farewell Fossil Fuels, 1999. Avocation: squash. Home: 70 E 10th St New York NY 10003-5102 Office: NYU Physics Dept Washington Sq N New York NY 10003 E-mail: sb8@nyu.edu.

BOROWSKI, JENNIFER LUCILE, corporate administrator; b. Jersey City, Oct. 23, 1934; d. Peter Anthony and Ludwika (Zapolska) B. BS, St. Peter's Coll., 1968; postgrad., Pace Coll., 1976-77. Mgr. benefits Amerada Petroleum Corp., N.Y.C., 1951-66, Mt. Sinai Hosp., N.Y.C., 1966-67; mgr. payroll and payroll taxes Haskins & Sells, N.Y.C., 1967-74, Cushman & Wakefield, Inc., N.Y.C., 1975-89. Mem. Am. Payroll Assn. (bd. dirs. 1979-81, cert.), Am. Mgmt. Assn., Am. Soc. Payroll Mgrs., Internat. Platform Assn. (hon.), Am. Soc. Profl. Exec. Women, NAFE. Avocations: golf, opera, boating. Home: 36 Front St North Arlington NJ 07031-5822

BOROWSKY, PHILIP, lawyer; b. Phila., Oct. 9, 1946; s. Joshua and Gertrude (Nicholson) B.; m. Judith Lee Goldwasser, Sept. 5, 1970 (div. 1996); children: Miriam Isadora, Manuel, Nora Jo. BA, UCLA, 1967; JD, U. San Francisco, 1973. Bar: Calif. Pres. and mng. ptnr. Cartwright, Slobodin, Bokelman, Borowsky, Wartnick, Moore & Harris, San Francisco, 1987-95; pres. Law Offices Philip Borowsky, Inc., San Francisco, 1996—2002; mng. ptnr. Borowsky & Hayes LLP, San Francisco, 2002—. Mem. faculty Practicing Law Inst., N.Y.C., 1983-84; mem, adj. faculty Hastings Coll. Law, San Francisco, 1982-83; arbitrator Superior Ct., San Francisco, 1982—, Am. Arbitration Assn., 1982—, Nat. Assn. Securities Dealers, 1994—. Co-author: Unjust Dismissal and At-Will Employment, 1985; mem. bd. editl. cons. Bad Faith Law Update, 1986—. With U.S. Army, 1968-70, Vietnam. Mem. Consumer Attys. Calif. Democrat. Office: 1 Market Plz San Francisco CA 94105-1420 E-mail: borowsky@borowsky.com.

BORREE, YVONNE, dancer; Student, Sch. Am. Ballet, 1985. Apprentice N.Y.C. Ballet, 1987—88, mem. corps de ballet, 1988—93, soloist, 1993—97, prin., 1997—. Dancer with Mikhail Baryshnikov (ballets) Duo Concertant, 1992, Apollo, Coppelia, The Four Temperaments, The Nutcracker, Stravinsky Violin Concerto, Symphony in Three Movements, The Sleeping Beauty, Romeo and Juliet, Mercurial Manoeuvres, The Chairman Dances, Sinfonia, Sleeping Beauty, Slonimsky's Earbox, Danses de Cour, Correlazione, 1994. Office: NYC Ballet NY State Theatre 20 LIncoln Ctr Plz New York NY 10023-6913

BORRELLI, JOHN FRANCIS, architect; b. Buffalo, Nov. 6, 1955; s. Peter and Maria (Raimondo) B. BSCE, Columbia U., 1977; postgrad., Pratt Inst., 1977-81. Registered arch., N.Y., N.J., Conn., Vt., Ill., Va., Pa., Fla., Md., Mich., Mass., Calif., Tex. Project coord. C. Raimondo and Sons, Ft. Lee, N.J., 1971-78; project mgr. DAT Cons., N.Y.C., 1978-81, Litchfield Grosfeld Assocs., N.Y.C., 1981-83; project arch. Design Mgmt., Inc., N.Y.C., 1983-87; ptnr. Sys. Collaborative, Inc., N.Y.C., 1987-88, Davis Borrelli Assocs., N.Y.C., 1987-91; exec. v.p. Karco-Davis, Inc., N.Y.C., 1987-91; v.p. Rampart Constrn. Assocs., N.Y.C., 1987-91; prin. Meli Borrelli Assocs., N.Y.C., 1991-94; pres. John Francis Borrelli Arch., P.C., N.Y.C., 1991—; prin. MBA Mcpl., Inc., 1993, MBA Internat., Inc., 1991, SPGA MBA, Inc., 1993, Walter M. Ballard, Ltd., 1993, MBA&A, Inc., 1995, Vici Group, Ltd., N.Y.C., 1995. Prin. works include ING/Barings Securities, Inc.Hdqs., N.Y.C., Credit Suisse Hdqs., Schonfeld Securities LLC (various offices in Chgo., L.A., N.Y.C., Miami Beach, others), Jericho L.I. Hdqs., Netscape Comms. Corp., N.Y., Chgo., Detroit, and Bethesda, Md., HS for Environ. Scis., N.Y.C., Burlington Industries Hdqrs., Walt Disney Book and Product Licensing Offices, Jefferson Ins. Corp. Hdqs., N.J., Western Union Corp. Hdqrs., Parade Publs. Corp. Hdqrs., N.Y.C., Covington Fabrics Corp. Hdqrs., Otterbourg, Steindler, Houston and Rosen, Lalique, Macromedia, Inc., N.J., Wilson, Elser, Moskowitz, Edelman & Dicker LLP, White Plains, N.Y., Boston. N.Y.C. Recipient 1st prize Gabriel Industries, 1976; Columbia U. scholar, 1973-77. Mem. AIA, ASCE, Nat. Trust for Hist. Preservation, World Wildlife Fund, Greenpeace. Avocations: woodworking, antique collecting, book collecting, gardening, tennis. Office: John Francis Borrelli Architect PC 13 E 37th St New York NY 10016-2821 E-mail: jfbarchitect@aol.com.

BORROFF, MARIE, English language educator; b. N.Y.C., Sept. 10, 1923; d. Albert Ramon and Marie (Bergersen) B. Ph.B., U. Chgo., 1943, MA, 1946; PhD, Yale U., 1956. Teaching asst. U. Chgo., 1946-47; instr. dept. English Smith Coll., 1948-51, asst. prof., 1956-59, asso. prof., 1959; vis. asst. prof. English Yale U., 1957-58, vis. asso. prof., 1959-6O, asso. prof. English, 1960-65, prof., 1965-71, William Lampson prof., 1971-92, Sterling prof. English, 1992-94; Sterling prof. English emeritus, 1994—; Phi Beta Kappa vis. scholar, 1973-74. Fellow Ezra Stiles Coll., Yale. Author: Sir Gawain and the Green Knight: A Stylistic and Metrical Study, 1962, (with J. B. Bessinger, Jr.); recorded dialogues read in Middle English, 1965, Sir Gawain and the Green Knight: A New Verse Translation, 1967, Pearl: A New Verse Translation, 1977, Language and the Poet: Verbal Artistry in Frost, Stevens, and Moore, 1979, Sir Gawain and the Green Knight, Patience and Pearl: Verse Translations, 2000, Stars and Other Signs: Poems, 2002; essay collection: Traditions and Rewewals Chaucer, the Gawain-Poet, and Beyond, 2003; editor: Wallace Stevens, A

Collection of Critical Essays, 1963; videotaped lectures: To Hear Their Voices, Chaucer, Shakespeare and Frost, Assn. of Yale Alumni Great Tchrs. Series, Chapter Headings: Remarks Made at the Annual Initiation Ceremonies of Phi Beta Kappa, Alpha Chapter of Connecticut, 1989-1994, 1996. Bd. Govs. Yale U. Press, 1988-98. Recipient James Billings Fiske poetry prize U. Chgo., 1943; Eunice Tietjens Meml. prize Poetry mag., 1945; Margaret Lee Wiley fellow AAUW, 1955-56; Guggenheim fellow, 1969-70 Fellow Am. Acad. Arts and Scis.; mem. MLA, Acad. Am. Poets, Medieval Acad. Am., Phi Beta Kappa. Home: 311 St Ronan St New Haven CT 06511-2328 E-mail: marie.borroff@yale.edu.

BORROR, DOUGLAS G. construction company executive; b. 1955; Grad., Ohio State U., 1977. With Huntington Nat. Bank, Columbus, 1977-79, Borror Corp. (now Borror Realty Co. Inc.), Dublin, Ohio, 1979—; pres., CEO, COO Borror Corp. (now Dominion Homes, Inc.), Dublin, Ohio, 1994—; pres., CEO, chmn. bd. Office: Dominion Homes Inc 5501 Frantz Rd Dublin OH 43017-7502

BORROWDALE-COX, DEBORAH ELIZABETH, museum curator; b. San Francisco, Calif., July 21, 1949; d. Clifford Ryder and Elsie Mason Tufts; m. Peter W. Borrowdale-Cox, July 12, 1980; children: Elizabeth, Genevieve. BA, Scripps Coll., 1971; MA, George Washington U., 1982. Cert. humanities tchr., Calif. Educator Escola Americana de Brasilia, 1980-81; mus. specialist Yokohama (Japan) Internat. Sch., 1982-84; program coord. Cultural Coun. of Santa Cruz County, 1984-85; dir. edn. Santa Barbara (Calif.) Mus. of Art, 1986-98; head edn. U. Ky. Art Mus., Lexington, 1998—. Cons. lectr. Mus. of Contemporary Art, L.A., 1989; guest lectr. U. Calif., Santa Barbara, 1995, Nat. Docent Symposia, Atlanta, 1993, Corcoran Gallery of Art, Washington, 1982. Prodr. (video) Ukiyo-e, 1989, Augusto Torres Interview, 1987, Current 4 Artists, 1991. Recipient Ikebane Sensei award Ohara Ikebane Group, 1982. Mem. Nat. Assn. of Art Educators, U.S. Pony Club (sec. 1998-2000), U. Ky. Art Mus. Friends (liaison 1998—). Avocations: riding, travel, music.

BORSARI, GEORGE ROBERT, JR., lawyer, broadcaster; b. Washington, July 30, 1940; s. George Robert and Sara Totton (Dunning) B.; m. Regis Ann Herron, Oct. 23, 1964 (div. Jan. 1985); children: George Robert, III, William Grant. BS, Va. Poly. Inst., 1962; LL.B., George Washington U., 1965. Bar: D.C. 1966. Since practiced in Washington; ptnr. Borsari & Paxson, 1969—. Pres. Local TV Systems, Inc., 1981-89, Outdoor Inst., Inc., 1978—; chmn. Core Group Inc., 1991—. Councilman Town of Glen Echo, Md., 1969-74, mayor, 1977-81, 89-91; mem. Montgomery County (Md.) Muncipality Advisory Bd., 1972-74, Montgomery County CATV Task Force, 1973-74, 80-85, Cable TV Adv. Com., 1979-85; pres. Montgomery County chpt. Md. Mcpl. League. Served to lt. col. JAG USAR. Decorated Army Meritorious Service medal with oak leaf cluster, Army Commendation medal with 2 oak leaf clusters; recipient Presdl. commendation, 1970; St. George award Roman Catholic Archdiocese Washington, 1970; Silver Beaver award Nat. Capital Area council Boy Scouts Am., 1974 Mem. ABA (chmn. cable TV com. sect. sci. and tech. 1982-86, chmn. Broadcast Com. 1986-90, chmn. Mass Media Com. 1990-92, mem. coun. sect. sci. and tech.), D.C. Bar Assn., Fed. Comms. Bar Assn., Isaac Walton League, Kenwood Golf and Country Club, Phi Delta Phi. Democrat. Home: 6107 Princeton Ave Glen Echo MD 20812-1125 Office: Borsari & Paxson 4000 Albemarle St NW Ste 100 Washington DC 20016

BORSCH, FREDERICK HOUK, bishop; b. Chgo., Sept. 13, 1935; s. Reuben A. and Pearl Irene (Houk) B.; m. Barbara Edgeley Sampson, June 25, 1960; children: Benjamin, Matthew, Stuart. AB, Princeton U., 1957; MA, Oxford U., 1959; STB, Gen. Theol. Sem., 1960; PhD, U. Birmingham, 1966; DD (hon.), Seabury Western Theol. Sem., 1978, Gen. Theol. Sem., 1988; STD (hon.), Ch. Div. Sch. of Pacific, 1981, Berk Div. Sch. Yale U., 1983. Ordained priest Episcopal Ch., 1960; curate Grace Episcopal Ch., Oak Park, Ill., 1960-63; tutor Queen's Coll., Birmingham, Eng., 1963-66; asst. prof. N.T. Seabury Western Theol. Sem., Evanston, Ill., 1966-69, assoc. prof. N.T., 1969-71; prof. N.T. Gen. Theol. Sem., N.Y.C., 1971-72; pres., dean Ch. Divinity Sch. of the Pacific, Berkeley, Calif., 1972-81; dean of chapel, prof. religion Princeton U., 1981-88; bishop Episc. Diocese, L.A., 1988—2002; interim dean Berkeley Div. Sch. at Yale, New Haven, 2002—. Rep. Faith and Order Commn., Nat. Coun. Chs., 1975-81; mem. exec. coun. Episc. Ch., 1981-88, Anglican Cons. Coun., 1984-88; chair bd. govs. Trinity Press Internat., 1989—; bd. adv. UCLA Sch. Pub. Policy & Social Rsch., 1998—, Ctr. for the Study Religion, Princeton U., 2000—; trustee Princeton U., 1998—. Author: The Son of Man in Myth and History, 1967, The Christian and Gnostic Son of Man, 1970, God's Parable, 1976, Introducing the Lessons of the Church Year, 1978, Coming Together in the Spirit, 1980, Power in Weakness, 1983, Jesus: The Human Life of God, 1987, Many Things in Parables, 1988, Christian Discipleship and Sexuality, 1993, Outrage and Hope, 1996; editor: Anglicanism and the Bible, 1984, The Bible's Authority in Today's Church, 1993, The Magic Word, 2001. Trustee Princeton U., 1998—. Keasbey scholar, 1957-59 Fellow Soc. Arts, Religion and Contemporary Culture; mem. Am. Acad. Religion, Soc. Bibl. Lit., Studiorum Novi Testamenti Societas, Phi Beta Kappa Home: 2930 Corda Ln Los Angeles CA 90049-1105 E-mail: fhborsch@earthlink.net.

BORSKI, ROBERT ANTHONY, former congressman; b. Phila., Oct. 20, 1948; s. Robert Anthony and Rita (Savage) B.; children: Jill Michele, Dorothy Lynn, Jennifer Marie, Robert A. III, Margaret Rita. BA, U. Balt., 1971. Floor mgr. Raymond James & Assoc., Phila., 1971-77; mem. Pa. Ho. of Reps., 1977-82, U.S. Congress from 3rd Pa. dist., Washington, 1983—2002; mem. transp. and infrastructure com. Democrat. Roman Catholic. Office: Borski and Associates 1001 G St NW Washington DC 20001*

BORSODY, ROBERT PETER, lawyer; b. N.Y.C., Oct. 6, 1937; s. Benjamin F. and Edith Nora (Corcoran) B.; m. Paula Jane Bercutt, Oct. 14, 1973; children: Lisa M., Daniel B., Sarah E., Alexander S. B.E.E., U. Va., 1961, LL.B., 1964; diploma, U. Teheran, Iran, 1959. Bar: N.Y. 1965, D.C. 1978. Assoc. firm Sullivan & Cromwell, N.Y.C., 1964-69; founder, dir. Legal Services for Elderly Poor, 1969-71, Community Health Law Project, 1971-73; pvt. practice law N.Y.C., 1973-78; ptnr., founder Epstein Becker Borsody & Green, N.Y.C., 1978-87; of counsel Epstein, Becker & Green, N.Y.C., 1987-99, Fischbein, Badillo, Wagner & Harding, N.Y.C., 1999—. Adj. prof. Manhattan Coll., 1978-82, Pace U. Sch. Law, 1986-90; mem. N.Y. State Coun. Health Care Financing, 1978—; sec. N.Y. Statewide Health Coordinating Coun., 1978-87; chmn. bd. dirs. N.Y. Bus. Group on Health, 1984-87. Bd. dirs. N.Y.C. Mental Health Assn. Mem. ABA, N.Y. State Bar Assn. Health Law Section (chmn. pub. health com. 1974-78), Assn. of Bar of City of N.Y. Health Law Com., Am. Health Lawyers Assn., Hosp. Fin. Mgmt. Assn. (advanced), Yale Club. Home: 23 Winged Foot Dr Larchmont NY 10538-1124 Office: 17th Fl 909 3rd Ave New York NY 10022-5508

BORSON, DANIEL BENJAMIN, lawyer, educator, physiologist, researcher; b. Berkeley, Calif., Mar. 24, 1946; s. Harry J. and Josephine F. Borson. BA, San Francisco State Coll., 1969; MA, U. Calif., Riverside, 1973; PhD, U. Calif., San Francisco, 1982; JD, U. San Francisco, 1995. Bar: Calif. 1997, U.S. Dist. Ct. (no. dist.) Calif. 1997, U.S. Patent and Trademark Office 1998; lic. comml. pilot, flight instr. FAA. Musician Composer's Forum, Berkeley, San Francisco, 1961-70; flight instr. Buchanan Flying Club, Concord, Oakland, Calif., 1973-77, pres., 1975-77; physiology U. Calif., San Francisco, 1984-92, asst. rsch. physiologist Cardiovascular Rsch. Inst., 1988-92; assoc. Fliesler Dubb Meyer and Lovejoy LLP, 1997—2003, of counsel, 2003—. Vis. scientist Genentech Inc., South San Francisco, Calif., 1990—92; founder Biosci. Forum, 2002, pres., 2002—. Contbr. articles, rev. chpts. and abstracts to profl. jours., legal periodicals and law rev. Fellow NIH, 1976-84, grantee, 1988-93; fellow Cystic Fibrosis Found., 1985, grantee, 1989-91; fellow Parker B. Francis Found., 1985-87; grantee Am. Lung Assn., 1985-87. Mem.: State Bar Calif. (patent standing com., exec. com., coun. of sects.), No. Calif. Pharm. Discussion Group (bd. dirs., chmn. 2000—02), Fed. Cir. Bar Assn., San Francisco Intellectual Property Law Assn., Am. Intellectual Property Law Assn., Am. Chem. Soc., Am. Soc. Cell Biology, Am. Physiol. Soc. (editl. bd. Am. Jour. Physiology 1990—92), ABA, Bay Flute Club (pres. 1978). Avocations: mountain climbing, aviation, music. Office: Ste 400 4 Embarcadero Ctr San Francisco CA 94111 E-mail: dbb@fmdl.com.

BORST, PHILIP CRAIG, veterinarian, councilman; b. Columbus, Ohio, May 19, 1950; s. Lawrence M. and Eldoris B.; m. Jill Patrice Alexander, Sept. 12, 1980; children: Alex, Eric. BS, Purdue U., 1972, DVM, 1975. Vet. Shelby St. Animal Clinic, Indpls., 1975—. Bd. dirs. Ind. Sports Corp., Indpls. Mem. Indpls. City-County Coun., 1980—, pres.; del. Ind. State Rep. Convention, 1982; bd. dirs. Indpls. Conv. and Visitors Assn.; mem. Marion County Capital Improvement Bd.; mem. exec. com. 2000 NCAA Final Four. Named Best City-County Councilman Indpls. Mag., 1986; recipient Svc. to Mankind award Southside Indpl. Sertoma Club, 1987. Mem. Cen. Ind. Vet. Med. Assn. (pres. 1990), Purdue Vet. Med. Alumni Assn. (pres. 1988). Republican. Methodist. Avocations: golf, basketball, purdue athletics. also: City-County Coun Office 200 E Washington St Ste 241 Indianapolis IN 46204-3310

BORST, PHILIP WEST, academic administrator; b. Fullerton, Calif., Feb. 11, 1928; s. Richard Warner and Beatrice Ione (West) B.; m. Marguerite A. Bruns, Mar. 21, 1959; children— David, Kristin, Pamela; m. Barbara Paul, Oct. 24, 1998. AA, Fullerton Coll., 1947; BA, Stanford U., 1949, MA, 1950; postgrad., U. Calif., 1950-54; PhD (Sch. fellow), Claremont Grad. Sch., 1968. Tchr. history Carlmont High Sch., Belmont, Calif., 1954-57; asst. prof. polit. sci. and history Fullerton Coll., 1957-60, asso. prof., 1960-62, prof., 1962-67, asst. to pres., 1967-70, asst. dean instrn., 1970-72, asso. dean instrn., 1972-73, v.p. instrn., 1973-77, pres., 1977-94; retired, 1994. Mem. Assn. Calif. Community Coll. Adminstrs., Phi Delta Kappa. Democrat.

BORSTEIN, LEON BAER, lawyer; b. Camden, N.J., Mar. 21, 1939; s. Isadore and Mildred (Barr) B.; m. Virginia Henneberry; 1 child: Joseph Isaiah. BS, MIT, 1961; LLB, Columbia U., 1964. Bar: N.Y. 1968, U.S. Dist. Ct. (ea. and so. dists.) N.Y. 1974, U.S. Ct. Appeals (2d cir.) 1975, U.S. Supreme Ct. 1978. Prof. econs. Peace Corp, Santa Cruz, Bolivia, 1964-66; expert USAID, La Paz, Bolivia, 1966-68; atty. Jacobs Persinger & Parker, N.Y.C., 1968-69; asst. dist. atty., Bklyn., 1971-75; chief spl. asst. atty. gen. nursing home investigation, N.Y.C., 1975-76; ptnr. Borstein & Sheinbaum, N.Y.C., 1976—, adj. prof. NASD Arbitration & Mediation, U. San Francisco Cal. Law Sch., 2001. Editor: Lawyers Guide to International Business Transaction, 1963; Transactional Guide to UCC, 1964. Author: Population and Housing Census of Santa Cruz Bolivia, 1967. Mem. edn. coun. MIT, 1975—. Home: 120 E 34th St New York NY 10016-4609 Office: 420 Lexington Ave New York NY 10170-0002

BORSTING, JACK RAYMOND, business administration educator; b. Portland, Oreg., Jan. 31, 1929; s. John S. and Ruth B.; m. Peggy Anne Nygard, Mar. 22, 1953; children: Lynn Carol, Eric Jeffrey. BA, Oreg. State U., 1951, MA, U. Oreg., 1952, PhD, 1959. Instr. math. Western Wash. Coll., 1953-54; teaching fellow U. Oreg., 1956-59; mem. faculty Naval Postgrad. Sch., 1959-80, prof. ops. research, chmn. dept., 1964-73, provost, acad. dean, 1974-80; asst. sec. def. (comptroller) Washington, 1980-83; dean Sch. Bus. U. Miami, Fla., 1983-88; Robert Dockson prof. and dean bus. adminstrn. U. So. Calif., Los Angeles, 1988-94; E. Morgan Stanley prof. bus. adminstrn. and exec. dir. Ctr. for Telecomms. Mgmt./U. So. Calif. Marshall Sch. Bus., Los Angeles, 1994—2001, prof., 2002—. Vis. prof. U. Colo. summers 1967, 69, 71; vis. disting. prof. Oreg. State U., summer 1968; bd. dir. Ivax Diagostios, Whitman Edn. Group, Ivax Diagnostics, Northrop Grumman, 1991-2001, coast Fed. 1989-93; bd. visitors Def. Sys. Mgmt. Coll., 1985-91, chmn., 1988-91; trustee Met Life Investor, 2000—, mem. adv. bd. Naval Postgrad. Sch., 1982-86, 98—; bd. overseers Ctr. Naval Analysis, 1984-94; trustee Aerospace Corp., 1986-92, Inst. Def. Analysis, 1990—; bd. advisors Elec. Power Rsch. Inst., 1999—. Contbr. to profl. jours. Trustee Orthop. Hosp. Found., L.A., 1992—, chmn., 1996-98, chmn. bd. dirs. 1999-2002; trustee Rose Hills Found. 1996—; gov. Town Hall of Calif., 1988-94. Recipient Disting. Pub. Service medal Dept. Def., 1980, 82 Fellow AAAS, Mil. Ops. Rsch. Soc. (bd. dirs. 1965-72, pres. 1970-71), Internat. Engring. Consortium, Informs; mem. Inst. Mgmt. Sci., Am. Statis. Soc., Ops. Rsch. Soc. Am. (mem. coun. 1969-79, sec. 1972-74, pres. 1975-76, Kimball medal 1982, Koopmans award 2000), Internat. Fedn. Ops. Rsch. Socs. (treas. 1980-88), Calif. Club, 100 Club L.A., Sigma Xi, Pi Mu Epsilon, Beta Theta Pi. Episcopalian. Office: Marshall Sch Bus DCC 217 USC Los Angeles CA 90089-0871

BORTMAN, DAVID, lawyer; b. Detroit, Sept. 17, 1938; s. Erwin Arne and Miriam Elaine (Shapiro) B. BA, U. Mich., 1962, JD, 1965. Bar: Mich. 1965, Ill. 1971. Asst. prosecutor Wayne County, Detroit, 1965-71; staff atty. Fed. Defender, Chgo., 1971-73; trial atty. SEC, Chgo., 1974-77; sole practice Chgo., 1977-79; ptnr. Bortman, Meyer & Barasa, Chgo., 1980-90; pvt. practice L.A., 1990—. Mem. Fed. Ct. Jury Instrns. Com., Chgo., 1984—85; mem. adv. bd. Air Force Office of Pub. Affairs. Chmn. telethon com. Muscular Dystrophy Assn., Chgo., 1984; pres. Met. Chgo. Air Force Comty. Coun., 1985-88; mem. World Affairs Coun. Mem. ABA, ATLA, Acad. of TV Arts and Scis., State Bar Calif., Los Angeles County Bar Assn. (mem. lawyer referral com.), Fed. Bar Assn. (bd. dirs. Chgo. chpt. 1985-90), Rotary, U. Mich. Club of L.A., U. Mich. Club of Chgo. (bd. govs. 1987-89), Union League of Chgo. (bd. dirs. 1986-89), Variety Club Children's Charities, Jonathan Club, Thalians Charity, West L.A. C. of C. (bd. dirs.), Century City C. of C. (bd. dirs., co-chmn. Entertainment Industry Coun.). Jewish. Home: 11908 Dorothy St Apt 102 Los Angeles CA 90049-5330

BORTOLOT, GARY, writer, educator; b. Norwalk, Conn., Jan. 12, 1951; s. Richard V and Victoria P Bortolot. BA, Providence Coll., Providence, RI, 1973; MA, U. Bridgeport, Bridgeport,CT, 1977. Dir. GWB Enterprises, Norwalk, Conn., 1995—; instr. Gibbs Coll., Norwalk, Conn., 2000—; actor, 1985—95. Bd. dirs. Norwalk Cmty. Health Ctr. Mem.: Affiliated Writing Programs, MLA. Home: 501 Westport Ave Apt 294 Norwalk CT 06851

BORTON, GEORGE ROBERT, retired airline captain; b. Wichita Falls, Tex., Mar. 22, 1921; s. George Neat and Travis Lee (Jones) B.; m. Anne Louise Bowling, Feb. 5, 1944 (dec.); children: Trudie T., Robert B., Bruce M. AA, Hardin Coll., Wichita Falls, 1940. Cert. airline transport pilot, FAA flight examiner. Flight sch. operator Vallejo (Calif.) Sky Harbor, 1947-48; capt. S.W. Airways, San Francisco, 1948-55; check capt. Pacific Airlines, San Francisco, 1955-68, Hughes Air West, San Francisco, 1968-71; capt. N.W. Airlines, Mpls., 1971-82, ret., 1982. Col. USAF, 1943-73, ret. Decorated Air medal. Mem. Airline Pilots Assn., Res. Officers Assn., Air Force Assn., Horseless Carriage Club, Model T of Am. Club (San Jose, Calif.). Republican. Home: 325 Denio Ave Gilroy CA 95020-9203

BORTON, JOHN CARTER, JR., (TERRY BORTON), theatrical producer; b. Washington, Aug. 25, 1938; s. John Carter and Mary (Newlin) B.; m. Deborah H. Borton, June 18, 1960; children: Lynn, Mark. BA, Amherst Coll., 1960; MA, U. Calif., Berkeley, 1962; EdD, Harvard U., 1970. Cert. gen. tchr., Calif. Asst. dir. vol. program Berkeley Unified Schs., 1962-63; tchr. English, co-chmn. dept. Richmond (Calif.) Union H.S., 1963-66; cons. Phila. Bd. Edn., 1966-67, acting dir. Office Affective Devel., 1970-71, dir. dual audio TV project, 1971-77; editorial dir. Xerox Edn. Publs., Middletown, Conn., 1977-80, editor in chief, 1980-86; v.p., editor in chief Field Publs. (formerly Xerox Edn. Publs.), Middletown, 1986-91, Weekly Reader Corp. (formerly Field Publs.), Middletown, 1991-92; prodr., lead performer Am. Magic Lantern Theater, 1992—. Lectr. U. Pa., Phila., 1971-76, Phila. Coll. Art, 1976-77; cons. various sch. systems, univ./colls., founds., profl. orgns., govt. agys., 1975-77. Author: Reach, Touch and Teach: Student Concerns and Process Education, 1970, Emotionales und Soziales Lernen in der Schule, 1976; also numerous articles in profl. jours., including Weekly Reader; performer 2 records and tchr.'s manuals introducing poetry to high sch. students; author 20 scripts for The Storyphone, 1976, 80 scripts for Dual Audio, Sta. WUHY-FM, 1972-73, 12 prodns. for Am. Magic Lantern Theater. Bd. dirs. Oddfellow's Theater. Mem. League Hist. Am. Theaters, N.E. Performing Arts Assn., Magic Lantern Soc. Avocations: carpentry, sculpture, writing, gardening. Office: Am Magic Lantern Theater PO Box 44 East Haddam CT 06423-0044 E-mail: tborton@magiclanternshows.com.

BORUCHOWITZ, STEPHEN ALAN, health policy analyst; b. Plainfield, N.J., Sept. 24, 1952; s. Robert and Earla Louise (Sloat) B.; m. Linda Susan Grant, Sept. 16, 1989; 1 child, Grant Stephen. BA in Internat. Affairs, George Washington U., Washington, 1974; MA in Sci., Tech. and Pub. Policy, George Washington U., 1981. Food prog. specialist U.S. Food & Nutrition Svc., Washington, 1978-81; internat. affairs specialist Office Internat. Cooperation & Devel., Washington, 1981-87; legis. analyst Wash. State Senate, Olympia, 1986-89; project dir. Wash. 2000 Project, Olympia, 1989-92; sr. health policy analyst Wash. Dept. Health, Olympia, 1992—. Mem. Pew Commn. task force on regulation of health professions, 1994-95. Editor newsletter: Project Update, 1990-92. Study team mem. Gov.'s Efficiency Commn., 1990-91; com. mem. Coun. of State Govts. Strategic Planning Subcom., Lexington, Ky., 1990-92; chmn. Montclair Divsn. IV Neighborhood Assn., 1989-92, Shadywood Homeowner's Assn., 1992-94; bd. dirs. Classical Music Supporters, Seattle, 1987-89. Recipient Superior Performance award, U.S. Dept. Agr., 1986. Mem. World Future Soc., Internat. Health Futures Network, Internat. Soc. of Tech. Assessment in Health Care, Health Svcs. Rsch. Assn. Avocations: writing, travel, cooking, classical music. Office: Wash Dept Health PO Box 47851 Olympia WA 98504-7851

BORUM, OLIN HENRY, realtor, former government official; b. Spencer, N.C., Nov. 3, 1917; s. Oscar Henry and Marjorie Mae (Leigh) B.; m. Beatrice Star Comulada, Nov. 14, 1944; children: Pamela Leigh, Robin Olin, Denis Richard. BS, U. N.C., 1938, MA, 1947, PhD, 1949; postgrad., U. Md., 1940-41. Rsch. chemist E.I. du Pont de Nemours & Co., Phila., 1949-50; interim rsch. asst. prof. Cancer Rsch. Lab. U. Fla., 1950; instr., asst. prof. chemistry U.S. Mil. Acad., 1952-55; rsch. adminstr. U.S. Army Chem. Corps R&D Command, Washington, 1956-60, U.S. Army Material Command, Washington, 1964-76; realtor assoc. Unique Properties, Alexandria, Va., 1974-79; realtor, assoc. broker The J. Edwards Co., Inc., Alexandria, Va., 1979-82; prin. broker Olin H. Borum Realty, 1982—. Tchr. chemistry U. Va., Arlington, Va., 1966-68. Contbr. articles to profl. jours. Adult scouter Nat. Capital Area coun. Boy Scouts Am., 1964-75, unit commr., 1968-75; sec. Mt. Vernon (Va.) Civic Assn., 1965-66; mem. Com. of 33 (nat. adv. group Nat. Sojourners, Inc.), 1962-71, chmn., 1969-71, Nat. trustee Nat. Sojourners, Inc., 1971-73. Maj. AUS, 1941-46; maj. USAF, 1951-56, lt. col., 1960-64. Recipient cert. Achievement Dept. Army, 1971; Teaching fellow U. Md., 1940-41, U. N.C., 1946-49. Fellow Am. Inst. Chemists; mem. Am. Chem. Soc., Masons, Shriners, Phi Beta Kappa, Sigma Xi. Presbyterian. Home: 9002 Volunteer Dr Alexandria VA 22309-2921 Office: 9002 Volunteer Dr Alexandria VA 22309-2921

BORUM, RODNEY LEE, financial business executive; b. High Point, N.C., Sept. 30, 1929; s. Carl Macy and Etta (Sullivan) B.; m. Helen Marie Rigby, June 27, 1953; children: Richard Harlan, Sarah Elizabeth. Student, U. N.C., 1947-49; BS, U.S. Naval Acad., 1953. Design-devel. engr. GE, Syracuse, N.Y., 1956-58, Cape Kennedy, Fla., 1956-58, missile test condr., 1958-60, mgr. ground equipment engr., 1960-61, mgr. ea. test range engring., 1961-65; adminstr. Bus. and Def. Svcs. Adminstrn.-Dept. Commerce, 1966-69; pres. Printing Industries Am., Arlington, Va., 1969-85, staff cons., 1985-86, mem. exec. com., 1969-85, dir., pres. W.H. Rigby Cons., 1985-86; exec. v.p. Amasek Inc., Cocoa, Fla., 1986-87; assoc. Fin. Svcs. Orgn., Cocoa, Fla., 1987—. Sec. Graphic Arts Show Corp.; dir. Inter-Comprint Ltd., Strangers Cay, Ltd.; mem. governing bd. Comprints Internat.; Rep. candidate 11th dist. U.S. congress, Fla., 1988-90; ops. mgr. COVIX Corp.; mgmt. cons. 1990—; exec. v.p. Pearl of Va., Inc. Mem. exec. coun. Cub Scouts Am., 1965; bd. dirs., v.p. Brevard County (Fla.) United Fund, 1964-65; bd. dirs. Brevard Beaches Concert Assn., 1965; mem. edn. coun. bd. dirs. Graphic Arts Tech. Found., Pitts., 1970-86; trustee, founder Graphic Arts Edn. and Rsch. Trust Fund, Arlington, Va., 1978-85; candidate for U.S. Ho. of Reps. from llth dist. Fla., 1988. lst lt. USAF, 1953-56. Named Boss of Yr., C. of C., 1965; recipient Bausch and Lomb Sci. award, 1947, Am. Legion award, 1952. Mem. U.S. Naval Inst., U.S. Naval Acad. Alumni Assn., Graphic Arts Coun. N.Am. (bd. dirs. 1977—), Phi Eta Sigma. Methodist.

BORUS, DAVID MURRAY, college dean; b. Chgo., Ill., Apr. 28, 1946; s. Joseph and Rosalie (Bierman) B.; m. Judith Rhoda Krams, June 16, 1968; children: Matthew G., Zachary A. BA, Trinity Coll., Hartford, Conn., 1968; MA, DePaul U., Chgo., 1972; PhD, U. Mich., 1975. Tchr. Blue Island (Ill.) Pub. Schs., 1968-72; admissions asst. U. Mich., Ann Arbor, 1973-74, adminstr. resdl. coll., 1975-76; rschr. Formative Evaluation Rsch., Inc., Ann Arbor, 1976-77; assoc. dean admissions Earlham Coll., Richmond, Ind., 1977-80, dir. admissions, 1980-81, Kalamazoo Coll., 1981-88; dean admissions and fin. aid Trinity Coll., Hartford, 1988—. Mem. regional exec. coun. Midwest Region, Coll. Bd., Chgo., 1984-88, nat. nominating com., N.Y.C., 1987. Author: (journal article) in On Target: Enrollment Management Strategies for the New Millennium, The College Board., (chapter in book) in Making Enrollment Management Work, New Directions for Student Services, (book review in professional magazine) Review of Applying Market Research in College Admissions, in Change Magazine, (article in professional journal) in Community College Review. Bd. dirs. Congregation B'nai Moshe, Kalamazoo, 1986-88; pers. com. Congregation Beth El, West Hartford, Conn., 1994—. Recipient Disting. Svc. Award, Nat. Merit Scholarship Corp., 1996; fellow U. Fellowship, U. of Mich., 1972-1975; grantee Dissertation Rsch. Grant, 1974-1975; scholar Ill. Scholar, Trinity Coll., 1964-1968. Mem. Nat. Assn. Coll. Admission Officers (chief assembly del. 1983-88), Am. Assn. Collegiate Registrars and Admission Officers, Mich. Assn. Coll. Admission Officers (exec. bd., nat. del. 1983-88, Disting. Svc. award 1988). Jewish. Home: 20 Overhill Rd West Hartford CT 06117-2034 Office: Trinity College 300 Summit St Hartford CT 06106-3186

BORWEIN, DAVID, mathematics educator; b. Kaunas, Lithuania, Mar. 24, 1924; s. Joseph Jacob and Rachel (Landau) B.; m. Bessie Flax, June 30, 1946; children— Jonathan, Peter, Sarah. B.Sc. in Engring, Witwatersrand (South Africa) U., 1945, B.Sc. Hons., 1948; PhD, University Coll. London, 1950, D.Sc., 1960. Lectr. St. Andrews U., Scotland, 1950-63; vis. prof. U. Western Ont., London, Can., 1963-64, prof., 1964-89, head math. dept., 1967-89, prof. emeritus, 1989—. Contbr. articles to profl. jours. Served with South African Forces, 1945. NSERC grantee, 1966— Fellow Royal Soc. Edinburgh; mem. London Math. Soc., Am. Math. Soc., Math. Assn. Am., Canadian Math. Soc. (chmn. research com. 1970-73, v.p. 1973-75, pres. 1985-87) Home: 1032 Brough St London ON Canada N6A 3N4 Office: Dept Math U Western Ont London ON Canada N6A 5B7 E-mail: dborwein@uwo.ca.

BORWICK, SUSAN HARDEN, musicologist, educator; d. Clyde and Edythe Brown Harden; m. Douglas Bruce Borwick, Aug. 14, 1976 (div. Apr. 20, 1996); 1 child, John Harden. MusB, MusEdnB, Baylor U., Waco, TX, 1968; PhD, Univ. NC, Chapel Hill, 1972. Asst. prof. music Baylor U., Waco, Tex., 1972—77, Eastman Sch. Music, Rochester, NY, 1977—82; assoc. prof. music Wake Forest U., Winston-Salem, NC, 1982—88, prof. music, 1988—. Chair dept. music Wake Forest U., Winston-Salem, NC, 1982—94, dir. women's studies, 1997—2000; program devel. and adminstrn. coun. Nat. Women's Studies Assn., 2000—, chair contemporary curriculum transformation project, 2001—. Author: (compact disc program notes) American Romantics: Arthur Foote and Amy Cheney Beach; composer: (sacred choral work) Morning Light, Hope: An Advent Choral Introit, (solo for voice, flute, piano) The Song of Mary and Elizabeth, (sacred choral work) Benediction, (incidental music) Much Ado about Nothing; contbr. articles to profl. jours. Chair bd. of deacons Knollwood Bapt. Ch., Winston-Salem, NC, 1994—95; sec. Bapt. Women in Ministry, NC, 2000—; pres., v.p., sec. NC Assn. Music Schs., 1987—94. Grantee R. J. Reynolds Rsch. Leave, Wake Forest U., 2003-2004, 1996, 1986; Travel to Collections grant, Nat. Endowment for the Humanities, 1986, William C. Archie Rsch. grant, Wake Forest U., 2002-2003, 2000-2001. Mem.: Soc. for Am. Music, Am. Musicological Soc., Coll. Music Soc. (life), Omicron Delta Kappa, Mu Phi Epsilon. Avocations: gardening, travel. Home: 4101 Mill Creek Rd Winston Salem NC 27106-2917 Office: Dept of Music Wake Forest Univ 7345 Reynolda Station Winston Salem NC 27109-7345 Office Fax: 336-758-4935. E-mail: borwick@wfu.edu.

BORYS, THEODOR JAMES, state agency data center administrator; b. Buffalo, N.Y., June 17, 1954; s. Svyatoslav and Lorenza Natalie (Bertolino) B.; m. Melissa Joy Ares, June 12, 1976; children: Tasha Rose, Leda Marie. BA in Math., SUNY, Albany, 1976, MS in Computer Sci., 1977. Computer programmer N.Y. State Dept. of Tax & Fin., Albany, 1976; programmer/analyst SUNY, Albany, 1976-78; data base adminstr. N.Y. State Dept. Mental Hygiene, Albany, 1978-81; software engr. Gen. Elec., Schenectady, N.Y., 1981; dir. tech. svcs. N.Y. State Office Mental Health, Albany, 1981-82, dir. systems devel., 1982-84, data adminstr., 1984-96, dir. tech. svcs. and ops., 1996-99, asst. dir. info. sys., 1999—2001, dep. dir. info. sys., 2001—. Lectr. SUNY, Albany, 1978—. Republican. Home: 125 E Poplar Dr Delmar NY 12054-2224 Office: State Office Mental Health 44 Holland Ave Albany NY 12229- E-mail: tedborys@nycap.rr.com.

BORYSENKO, JOAN, psychologist, biologist; b. Boston, Oct. 25, 1945; d. Edward and Lillian Zakon; children: Natalia, Justin, Andrei. BA in Biology, Bryn Mawr Coll., 1967; PhD, Harvard Med. Sch., 1972. Lic. psychologist. Asst. prof. anatomy and cellular biology Tufts U., 1973-78; instr. in medicine Harvard Med. Sch., Boston, 1981-88; pres., founder Mind/Body Health Scis., Boulder,

Colo., 1988—. Author: Minding the Body, Mending the Mind, 1987, Guilt is the Teacher, Love is the Lesson, 1990, Fire in the Soul, 1993, (with Miroslav Borysenko) The Power of the Mind to Heal, 1994, Pocketful of Miracles, 1995, A Woman's Book of Life, 1996, Seven Paths to God, 1997, A Woman's Journey to God, 1999, Inner Peace for Busy People, 2001; others; mem. adv. bd. several jours. and Web sites in field. Achievements include pioneering work in the study of psychoneuroimmunology. Office: Mind/Body Health Scis 393 Dixon Rd Boulder CO 80302-9769 E-mail: luziemas@aol.com.

BORYSEWICZ, MARY LOUISE, editor; b. Chgo. d. Thomas J. and Mabel E. (Zeien) O'Farrell m. Daniel S. Borysewicz, June 11, 1955; children: Mary Adele, Stephen Francis (dec. 1997), Paul Barnabas. BA, Mundelein Coll., 1970; postgrad. in English lit., U. Ill, 1970-71; grad. exec. program, U. Chgo., 1981-82. Editor sci. publs. AMA, Chgo., 1971-73; exec. mng. editor Am. Jour. Ophthalmology, Chgo., 1973-95; media cons. Fox-Wahls Design, Chgo., 1999—. Asst. sec., treas. Ophthalmic Pub. Co., 1985—95; guest lectr. U. Chgo. Med. Sch., 1979, Harvard U. Med. Sch., 1978, Northwestern U. Med. Sch., 1979, Am. Acad. Ophthalmology, 1976, 81, Northwestern U. Joseph Medill Sch. Journalism, 2002. Editor: Opthalmology Principles and Concepts, 7th edit., 1992, 8th edit., 1996, Documenta Ophthalmologica History Issue, 1997, 98; contbg. writer Chicago Shops, 2002, 03; contbr. articles to sci. publs. Mem. Coun. Biol. Editors (bd. dirs. 1988-91, mem. fin. com. 1985-88, mem. teller com. 1992-95). Office: 2018 W Chicago Ave Chicago IL 60622 E-mail: mbory@aol.com.

BORZAK, STEVEN, cardiologist; s. Donald and Lenore Borzak; m. Deena Sue Borzak, Feb. 17, 1985; 4 children. AB, Oberlin Coll., 1980; MD, U. Ill., Chgo., 1984. Diplomate Am. Bd. Internal Medicine, Am. Bd. Cardiovascular Diseases, Nat. Bd. Med. Examiners. Dir. Cardiac ICU, Henry Ford Hosp., Detroit, 1992—2001, assoc. head cardiovascular divsn., 1998—2001; pvt. practice Atlantis, Fla., 2001—; from intern to chief med. resident Michael Reese Med. Ctr., U. Chgo. Sch. Medicine, Chgo., 1984—88; rsch.-clin. fellow in cardiology Brigham and Women's Hosp., Harvard Med. Sch., Boston, 1988—91. Mem. editl. bd. sci. jours.: ; contbr. articles to profl. jours. Fellow: Am. Coll. Chest Physicians, Am. Coll. Physicians, Am. Coll. Cardiology, Am. Heart Assn. Office: Fla Cardiology Group 110 JFK Dr Ste 110 Atlantis FL 33462

BORZOVA, ALLA ALEKSANDRA, composer, conductor; b. Minsk, Belarus, Feb. 28, 1961; arrived in U.S., 1993, naturalized, 2001; d. Alexander A Lis and Klara A Borzova; m. Alexander Igor Dmitriev, July 9, 1983; 1 child, Vladena Aleksandra Dmitriev. BA and MA, Moscow State Conservatory, 1986, D in Musical Arts, 1991. Prof. Belarussian Music Coll., Minsk, Belarus, 1983—93. Composer: (voice and piano) Forest Ball, 1976, Five Songs to the Poems of Ivan Bunin, 1981, (piano solo) Fairy Tale Pictures, 1986, (chamber) Majnun Songs, 1996, Scherzo, 1980, Pinsk & Blue, 1998, Images Françaises, 2002, (symphony orchestra) Symphony, 1986; composer: (librettist) Songs for Lada, 1991; composer: To The New World, 2002, (mixed chorus) When The Wind Is Blowing, 1986, The Ballad of Barnaby, 2000, (ballet) When Reason Sleeps & Wakes: Goya Images, 1995, (songs) Mother Said, 1997 (First Prize, Delius Composition Contest, 1998), (theatrical work) The Animal That Drank Up Sound, 2000. Recipient performances, Da Capo Chamber Players, 2001—, performance, Cassatt String Quartet, 1998, New Amsterdam Singers, 2002, The NY Concert Singers, 2000, Gregg Smith Singers, 2003, performances, Guggenheim Mus., 1999, William Schimmel(renowned Am. accordionist), 1998—, Residencies, Yaddo artist colony, performance, Aspen Music Festival (Aspen, Colo.), 1999, Delius Music Festival (Jacksonville, Fla.), 1999, Sonic Boom Music Festival(New York City), 2002; grantee commn., St. Luke's Chamber Ensemble, 2002;, Belarus Radio-TV Symphony Orch., 1991, Paul Sperry (renowned Am. tenor), 1997, Dale Warland Singers, 1999, The Susan Rose Rec. Grant, Nat. Found. for Jewish Culture, 1999, commn., Tales & Scales, 2000, Renee B. Fisher Found., 2001, Goddard Lieberson fellowship, AAAL, 2002, Rec. grant, NYSCA, 2002, grant, Meet the Composer's Global Connections, 2003, Trust for Mut. Understanding, 2003. Mem.: Am. Guild Organists, Am. Choral Dirs. Assn., Am. Soc. Composers Authors Publs., Am. Composers Forum, Coll. Music Soc., Am. Music Ctr. Home: 305 6th Avenue #6H Pelham NY 10803 Home Fax: 914-738 5847.

BOS, JOHN ARTHUR, retired aircraft manufacturing executive; b. Holland, Mich., Nov. 6, 1933; s. John Arthur and Annabelle (Castelli) B.; m. Eileen Tempest, Feb. 15, 1974; children: John, James, William, Tiffany. BS in Acctg., Calif. State Coll., Long Beach, 1971. Officer 1st Nat. Bank, Holland, Mich., 1954-61; dir. bus. mgmt. Boeing Commercial MD-80 and Mil. Airlift and Tanker Programs, Long Beach, 1962-99. CFO Classic of Calif. Reformed Ch. in Am., 1970—. Mem. Inst. Mgmt. Accts. (cert. mgmt. acct. 1979), Nat. Assn. Accts. Avocations: automobile marketing, golf, consulting. E-mail: bjabos@hotmail.com.

BOSAH, FRANCIS N. molecular biochemist, educator; b. Onitsha, Anambra, Nigeria, Sept. 13, 1959; s. Michael and Comfort (Odiari) Bosah. BS, Shaw U., 1985; MS, N.C. Ctrl. U., 1988; PhD, Clark Atlanta U., 1995. Rsch. asst. N.C. Ctrl. U., Durham, 1985-88, instr., 1988-90; rsch. assoc. Rsch. Triangle Inst., Research Triangle Park, NC, 1989-90; rsch. assoc. dept. biochemistry Morehouse Sch. Medicine, Atlanta, 1990-95, NASA postdoctoral rsch. fellow dept. medicine, 1995-98, rsch. instr. dept. biochemistry, 1998—. Coord. health career Atlanta Met. Coll., 1993—94, instr., 1993—, DeKalb Coll., Clarkston, Ga., 1998—; presenter in field. Contbr. abstracts and articles to profl. jours. Recipient Minority Biochemical Rsch. Support award, 1990—93. Mem.: AAAS, Soc. Exptl. Biology and Medicine, Minority Biomedical Rsch. Soc., N.Y. Acad. Scis., Am. Chem. Soc., Am. Physiol. Soc. (predoctoral fellow 1993—95), Am. Soc. Cell Biology, Beta Kappa Chi. Roman Catholic. Avocations: photography, table and lawn tennis, handball, racquetball, basketball. Home: 5056 Rails Way Norcross GA 30071-4514 Office: Morehouse Sch Medicine Dept Medicine 720 Westview Dr SW Atlanta GA 30310-1458 E-mail: BosahF@msm.edu.

BOSARGE, RICK ANTHONY, health facility administrator; s. Jerries Frances and Barbara Mae Bosarge; m. Kit Root, Dec. 2, 1978; children: Sabrina Elizabeth, Brittany Francis. AS in Nursing, Miss. Gulf Coast C.C., Gulfport, 1980. RN Miss. RN U. Miss. Med. Ctr., Jackson, 1980—89, Meml. Hosp., Gulfport, 1989—95, mgr. sch. based clinics, 1995—. Contbr. Pres. Biloxi Girls Softball League, 1999—2000. Mem.: Miss. Nurses Assn. Achievements include first to opened the first, and 11 more, hosp. sponsored sch. based health clinics in Miss. Office: Meml Hosp 4500 Thirteenth St Gulfport MS 39502-1810 Office Fax: 228-865-3217. E-mail: rbosarge@mhg.com.

BOSCH, BRIAN JAMES, retired military officer; b. Hartford, Conn., Mar. 4, 1937; m. Polly A. Bosch, Aug. 22, 1959; children: Leslie, Andrea. AB in History, Duke U., 1957; MA in History, U. N.C., 1960; grad., Army Command/Gen. Staff Coll., 1970, Inter-Am. Def. Coll., Washington, 1978. Commd. 2nd lt. U.S. Army, 1960, advanced through grades to col., 1980; U.S. def. attaché U.S. Embassy, El Salvador, 1980-81; chief mil. attaché ops. L.Am. Def. Intelligence Agy. U.S. Army, 1985-90, ret., 1990. Author: The Salvadoran Officer Corps and The Final Offensive of 1981, 1999. Recipient Bronze Star, Vietnam, 1968. Mem. Def. Intel Alumni Assn., Duke Alumni Assn. Avocation: history. Home: 1001 26th St S Arlington VA 22202-2101

BOSCH, SAMUEL HENRY, computer company executive; b. Waupun, Wis., Dec. 24, 1934; s. Henry Samuel and Emma (Elgersma) B.; m. Corinne Marilyn Aardema, June 21, 1958; children: Michelle, Jonathan, David, Sara. BS in Physics, San Diego State U., 1961; MS in Physics, UCLA, 1962. Sr. rsch. engr. Gen. Dynamics, San Diego, 1962-69; mgr. mktg. Digital Equipment Corp., Maynard, Mass., 1969-77; dir. mktg. Sys. Engring. Lab., Ft. Lauderdale, Fla., 1977-79; mgr. mktg. Intel, Hillsboro, Oreg., 1979-81; dir. mktg. Metheus, Hillsboro, 1981-82; pres. ATM Techs., Beaverton, Oreg., 1982-86; pres., owner Peregrin Techs., Inc., Portland, Oreg., 1986—, Peregrin Med. Rev. Inc., Portland, 1987—. Served with U.S. Army, 1955-57. Mem. Concord Coalition, N.W. China Coun. Mem. Oreg. Hist. Soc. Republican. Mem. Christian Ref. Ch. Achievements include patent in ATM processing. Home: 20055 NW Nestucca Dr Portland OR 97229-2821 Office: Peregrin Techs Inc 14279 NW Science Park Dr Portland OR 97229-5416

BOSCHETTI, PHILIP J. oil company executive; b. Yonkers, N.Y., Apr. 11, 1944; s. Anthony and Santina (Taccetta) B.; m. Linda Marie Liggio, June 11, 1966; children: Keith Philip, Scott Alan. BBA in Mktg., Iona Coll., 1966. Sales mgr. Firestone Tire and Rubber Co., N.J., 1966; fin. adminstr. William S. Paley & Co., N.Y.C., 1969-91; v.p., CFO Burnett Oil Co., Inc., Ft. Worth, 1991—. Asst. sec., treas. The Greenpark Found., Inc., N.Y.C., 1978-91, William S. Paley Found., Inc., N.Y.C., 1978-91; v.p. Burnett Ranches, Inc., Ft. Worth, 1991—, Burnett Aviation Co., Inc., Ft. Worth, 1991—, Exec. Protective Systems, Ft. Worth, 1991—; v.p., CFO Burnett Ranches, Ltd., Ft. Worth, 1992—; v.p., dir. Burnett Svcs., Inc., Ft. Worth, 1992—, Burnett Security Systems, Inc., Ft. Worth, 1994—; v.p. AJJM Capital Corp., Ft. Worth, 1996—; treas., dir. K&M, Inc., Ft. Worth, 1998-2000, Cookworks of Santa Fe, Inc., 1998-2000, Cookworks, Tex., Inc., Ft. Worth, 1998-2002; pres., dir. CW Beverages, Inc., Ft. Worth, 1999-2002, Addison Warehouse Beverages, Inc., Ft. Worth, 1999-2002; mgr. of bd. Burnett Land, LLC; bd. dirs. Club Pro Clearinghouse Corp. Bd. dirs., v.p., treas. Westwood Baseball Assn., 1977-88; v.p. Westwood Babe Ruth, 1985-88; treas. Tommy League, 1984-86; dir. Westwood Recreation Youth Football, 1984-86; mem. Westwood Inds. Club, 1976-80. Decorated Bronze star, Air medal with oak leaf cluster, Vietnamese Honor medal, Vietnamese Svc. medal, Vietnamese campaign medal w/four svc. stars, Nat. Def. Svc. medal. Mem. River Crest Country Club. Office: Burnett Oil Co Inc Burnett Plz Ste 1500 801 Cherry St Unit 9 Fort Worth TX 76102-6881

BOSCHMANN, ERWIN, chemistry educator; b. Chaco, Paraguay, Jan. 1, 1939; came to U.S., 1959; s. David J. and Anna (Kaethler) B.; children: Heidi, Tonya, Eric. PhD, U. Colo., 1968. Asst. prof. Ind. U.-Purdue U., Indpls., 1968-74, assoc. prof., 1974-77, prof. chemistry, 1977—, assoc. dean faculties, 1988—99, assoc. v.p., 1999—2002, Ind. U., 1998—2002; vice chancellor for acad. affairs (interim) Ind. U. East, 2003. Cons. Ford Found., Peru, 1968-73, Asian Devel. Bank, Indonesia, 1985-87. Author: Ten Teaching Tools, 1987, Foundations of Life, 1991. Recipient Disting. Alumnus award Bethel Coll., 1998; Lilly Endowment faculty open fellow, Indpls., 1988. Mem. Am. Chem. Soc. Mennonite. Office: Ind U Purdue U 902 W New York St Indianapolis IN 46202-5157

BOSCIA, JAMES DOMINIC, lawyer; b. Elkhart, Ind., Aug. 26, 1948; s. James Matthew and Edith Theresa (Dente) B.; m. Susan Lee Brewer, Apr. 24, 1971; children— James E., Theresa L. B.S., Ind. U., 1970, J.D., 1975. Bar: Ind. 1975, U.S. Dist. Ct. (so. dist.) Ind. 1975, U.S. Dist. Ct. (no. dist.) Ind. 1977, Wis. 1986. Atty. student loan adminstrn. Ind. U., Bloomington, 1976-77; assoc. firm Borns, Quinn, Kopko & Lindquist, Merrillville, Ind., 1977-83; ptnr. firm Bowman & McPhee, P.C., Merrillville, 1983-85, treas., 1983-87, pres. 1987—; ptnr. firm Borns & Quinn, P.C., 1985—; mem. State Bur. Wis.. Asst. soccer coach Southlake YMCA, Crown Point, Ind., 1983-84, head soccer coach, 1986—; treas. Cub Scout Pack, 1987—. Mem. ABA, Lake County Bar Assn., Comml. Law League Am. Justinian Soc. N.W. Ind., Am. Bankruptcy Inst. Roman Catholic. Home: 10699 Hanley St Crown Point IN 46307-2825 Office: Borns & Quinn Heintz Bowman & McPhee 1000 E 80th Pl Gary IN 46410-5608

BOSCIA, JON ANDREW, insurance company executive; b. Pitts., Apr. 15, 1952; s. Louis C. and Stella (Weryha) B.; m. Donna M. Lowar, Aug. 18, 1973; children: Nicole Marie, Brandon Jon. BA, Point Park Coll., 1973; MBA, Duquesne U., 1979. Corp. planner Consolidated Nat. Gas, Pitts., 1974-79; fin. sales rep. Westinghouse, Pitts., 1979-80; asst. v.p. Mellon Bank, Pitts., 1980-83; sr. v.p. Lincoln Nat. Pension, Ft. Wayne, Ind., 1983—; ceo, pres., Lincoln Nat. Corp., Phila., 1998—. Sr. v.p. Lincoln Nat. Life, Ft. Wayne, 1984—; bd. dirs. Lincoln Nat. Investment Mgmt. Co., Ft. Wayne, 1985—. Contbr. articles to profl. jours. Mem. coms. Pitts. Bd. Edn., 1974-79; chmn. coms. Arlington Park, Ft. Wayne, 1983-86; mem. START program Ft. Wayne Community Schs., 1985. PPC Found. scholar, 1973. Mem. Nat. Assn. Bus. Economists, Planning Forum. Democrat. Methodist. Avocations: jogging, racquetball, playing drums, swimming, reading. Office: Lincoln Nat Corp 1500 Market St Ste 3900 Philadelphia PA 19102-2100

BOSCO, ANTHONY GERARD, bishop; b. New Castle, Pa., Aug. 1, 1927; s. Joseph M. and Theresa (Pezo) B.. BA, St. Vincent Sem., Latrobe, Pa.; juris canonici licentiatus, Lateran U., Rome; LLD (hon.), Duquesne U., 1971; LHD (hon.), St.Vincent Coll., 1988. Ordained priest Roman Cath. Ch., 1952. Asst. chancellor Diocese of Pitts., 1955—65, vice chancellor, 1965—67, chancellor, 1967—85, aux. bishop, 1970—87; bishop Diocese of Greensburg, Pa., 1987—. Chmn. chmn. Cath. Comms. Found., 1984—; hon. chmn., trustee Seton Hill Coll., Greensburg, 1987; ex officio mem., bd. regents St. Vincent Sem., Latrobe, Pa., 1987—. Named Pitts.'s Man of Yr. in Religion, Pitts. Jaycees, 1975; recipient Leonardo Da Vinci award for Religion, Order of Italian Sons and Daughter, 1970. Mem.: Christian Assocs. S.W. Pa., Nat. Conf. Cath. Bishops. E-mail: abosco@dioceseofgreensburg.org.*

BOSCO, FREDERICK J. language and linguistics educator; b. Bay City, Mich., May 13, 1929; s. Felix and Rosalie Bosco. AB, Ctrl. Mich. U., 1951; MA, U. Mich., 1956; EdD, Calif. Coast U., 1996, PsychD, 2002. Prof. linguistics and Italian Georgetown U., Washington, 1961—89, chmn. dept. Italian, 1965—80. Cons. learning sys. design W and B Assocs., Washington, 1990—. Author: Incontro Con L'Italiano, 1967, Punti Di Partenza, 1975, The Romance of Italian, 2001. Chmn. Cmty. Release Orgn., Washington, 1985. Sgt. USMC, 1951—53. Grantee, Coun. Am. Studies, Rome, 1957—58. Avocations: Roman archaeology, genealogy. E-mail: frederickbosco@aol.com.

BOSCO, JAY WILLIAM, optometrist; b. Bay City, Mich., May 6, 1951; s. Frank Carl and Jeanette (Frontiera) B.; m. Mary Lou Roth, Jan. 22, 1972; children: Angela, Jason, Andrea. BS, Saginaw Valley State Coll., 1977; OD, Ill. Coll. Optometry, 1982. Pvt. practice, Bay City, Mich., 1982-83; dir. vision care services Blue Care Network of East Mich., Saginaw, 1983—2002; pvt. practice Bay City, Mich., 2002—. Served with USAF, 1969-73. Mem. Am. Optometric Assn., Mich. Optometric Assn., Lions (chmn. Site-Mobile, Bay City, 1984—), Beta Sigma Kappa. Roman Catholic. Home: 1382 N Wagner Rd Essexville MI 48732-9532 Office: Ctr Vision Clinic 1415 Center Ave Bay City MI 48708

BOSCO, PHILIP MICHAEL, actor; b. Jersey City, Sept. 26, 1930; s. Philip Lupo and Margaret Raymond (Thek) B.; m. Nancy Ann Dunkle, Jan. 2, 1957; children: Diane, Philip, Christopher, Jennifer, Lisa, Celia, John. BA in drama, Catholic U. Am., 1957. Roles include Brian O'Bannion in Auntie Mame, City Ctr., N.Y.C., 1958; Angelo in Measure for Measure, Belvedere Lake Amphitheatre, N.Y.C., 1960; Heracles in The Rape of the Belt, 1960 (Tony nomination); Will Danaher in Donnybrook, 1961; Hawkshaw in The Ticket-of-Leave Man, 1961; King Henry in Henry IV Part 1, Shakespeare Festival, Stratford, Conn., 1962; Kent in King Lear; Rufio in Antony and Cleopatra: Pistol in Henry V; Aegeon in Comedy of Errors, 1963; Benedick in Much Ado About Nothing: Claudius in Hamlet, 1964; title role in Coriolanus, 1965; Lovewit in The Alchemist, 1967; appeared in Galileo, 1967, Saint Joan, 1968, Amphitryon in 3 Zones, Tiger at the Gates, 1968, Cyrano de Bergerac, 1968, Camino Real, 1970, Operation Sidewinder, 1970, The Playboy of the Western World, 1971, An Enemy of the People, 1971, Antigone, 1971, Mary Stuart, 1971, Narrow Road Into the Deep North, 1972, Twelfth Night, 1972, The Crucible, 1972, Enemies, 1972, The Plough and the Stars, 1973, The Merchant of Venice, 1973, A Streetcar Named Desire, 1973, Mrs. Warren's Profession, 1976, Man and Superman, 1978, Whose Life Is It Anyway?, 1979, A Month In The Country, 1979, Major Barbara, 1980, Inadmissable Evidence, 1981, Hedda Gabler, 1982, Ah! Wilderness, 1983, Misalliance, 1983, Come Back, Little Sheba, 1984, Eminent Domain, 1984, Caine Mutiny, 1984, Be Happy For Me, Masterclass, 1986, You Never Can Tell, 1986, A Man For All Seasons, 1986,The Devil's Disciple, 1988, (Broadway) Lend Me A Tenor, 1989, (Antoinette Perry award 1989), The Miser, 1990, Breaking Legs, 1991, (Broadway) An Inspector Calls, 1994, The Heiress, 1995, Moon Over Buffalo, 1995-96 (Tony nomination), Twelfth Night, 1998; films include: Requiem For a Heavyweight, A Lovely Way To Die, The Pope of Greenwich Village, Walls of Glass, Heaven Help Us, The Money Pit, Trading Places, 1983, Children of a Lesser God, 1986, Suspect, 1987, Three Men and a Baby, 1987, The Luckiest Man in the World, 1988, Working Girl, 1988, Dream Team, 1988, Another Woman, 1988, Blue Steel, Quick Change, FX-2, 1990, True Colors, 1990, Straight Talk, 1991, The Return of Eliot Ness, 1991, Shawdows and Fog, 1992, Attica: Line of Fire, 1993, Angie, 1993, Safe Passage, 1993, Milk Money, 1994, Nobody's Fool, 1994, It Takes Two, 1995, The First Wives Club, 1995, My Best Friend's Wedding, 1997, Critical Care, 1997, Deconstructing Harry, 1997, Shaft II, 1998, The Time Machine, 1999, Kate and Leopold, 2000; TV shows include: The Prisoner of Zenda, The Nurses, O'Brien, Hawk, The NET Play of the Month, Tribeca, Grandpa and the Globetrotters, 1987, Echoes in the Darkness, Internal Affairs, 1988, Murder in Black and White, 1989, Return of Eliot Ness, 1991, Law and Order, 1993, 96-98, Cosby, 1998, Spin City, 1999, Criminal Intent, 2001, S.V.U., 2002; (TV movie) Carriers, 1997. Served with U.S. Army, 1951-54. Recipient Critic's Circle award N.Y. Drama Critics, 1960-61; recipient Clarence Derwent award, 1966-67, Tony award nominations, 1961, 84, 87, 96, OBIE award, 1987, Emmy award, 1988, Tony award, Drama Desk award, Outer Critic's Circle award all for best leading actor, 1988-89; inductee Theater Hall of Fame, 1998. Mem. Actor's Equity Assn., Screen Actor's Guild, AFTRA Roman Catholic.

BOSCOV, ALBERT, retail executive; b. Sept. 22, 1929; D in Pub. Svc.(hon.), Kutztown Univ., 2003. With Boscov's Dept. Stores, Reading, Pa., 1954—, CEO, chmn. Recipient gold medal, Pa. Soc., 2002. Office: Boscov's Dept Stores 4500 Perkiomen Ave Reading PA 19606-3946*

BOSE, ANJAN, electrical engineering educator, academic administrator; b. Calcutta, India, June 2, 1946; s. Amal Nath and Anima (Guha) B.; m. Frances Magdelen Pavlas, Oct. 30, 1976; children: Rajesh Paul, Shonali Marie, Jahar Robert. B Tech with honors, Indian Inst. Tech., Kharagpur, 1967; MS, U. Calif., Berkeley, 1968, PhD, Iowa State U., 1974. Systems planning engr. Con Edison Co., N.Y.C., 1968-70; instr., research assoc. Iowa State U., Ames, 1970-74; postdoctoral fellow IBM Sci. Ctr., Palo Alto, Calif., 1974-75; asst. prof. elec. engring. Clarkson U., Potsdam, N.Y., 1975-76; mgr. EMSD, Control Data Corp., Mpls., 1976-81; prof. elec. engring. Ariz. State U., Tempe, 1981-93; disting. prof. Wash. State U., Pullman, 1993—, dir. Sch. Elec. Engring. and Computer Sci., 1993-98, dean Coll. Engring. and Architecture, 1998—. V.p. Power Math Assocs., Tempe, 1981-84; program dir. power sys. NSF, Washington, 1988-89. Contbr. over 60 articles to engring. jours. Fellow: IEEE; mem.: Nat. Acad. Engring.

BOSE, BIMAL KUMAR, electrical engineering educator; b. Calcutta, India, Sept. 1, 1932; came to U.S., 1971; s. Rajendra and Nirmala (Ghosh) B.; m. Arati Ghosh, June 26, 1961; children: Papia, Amit. BE, Calcutta U., 1956, PhD, 1966; MS, U. Wis., 1960. Asst. engr. Tata Hydro Power Co., Bombay, 1956-59; asst. prof. Bengal Engring. Coll., Calcutta, 1960-71; assoc. prof. Rensselaer Poly Inst., Troy, N.Y., 1971-76; rsch. engr. GE R & D Ctr., Schenectady, N.Y., 1976-87; prof. Condra Chair of Exellence U. Tenn., Knoxville, 1987—. Disting. scientist Power Electronics Appliance Ctr., Knoxville, 1987—; cons. PCI Ozone Corp., N.J., 1971-73, GE, 1971-76, Rsch. Triangle Inst., N.C., 1991-95, Bendix Corp., Electric Power Rsch. Inst., Lutron Electronics, UN for tech. devel. in People's Republic China and India; ; sr. advisor to Beijing Power Electronics R&D Ctr.; lectr. in field; hon. prof. Shanghai U. Tech., 1991, China U. of Mining and Technology, 1996, Xi'an Mining Inst., 1998. Author: Power Electronics and AC Drives, 1986, Modern Power Electronics and AC Drives, 2002; editor; Adjustable Speed AC Drive Systems, 1981, Micro Computer Control of Power Electronics and Drives, 1987, Modern Power Electronics, 1992, Power Electronics and Variable Frequency Drives, 1996; patentee in field; contbr. articles to profl. jours. Recipient Mouat Gold medal Calcutta U., 1967, Publ. award GE, 1982, Silver Patent medal GE, 1983. Fellow IEEE (life, chmn. power electronics, chmn. indsl. power converter com., Trans. Rev. chmn., static power converter com., assoc. editor Trans., neural network coun., Industry Applications Soc. outstanding achievement award 1993, Region 3 outstanding engr. award, 1994, Lamme Gold medal 1996); mem. IEEE Indsl. Electronics Soc. (Eugene Mittlemann Achievement award 1994, chmn. power electronics coun., Cont. Edn. award 1997, Millennium medal 2000). Hindu. Avocations: travel, gardening. Home: 404 Dixieview Rd Knoxville TN 37922-2609 Office: Univ of Tenn Dept Elec Engring 419 Ferris Hl Knoxville TN 37996-0001 E-mail: bbose@utk.edu.

BOSE, KINGSHUK, research engineer; b. Calcutta, India, Aug. 5, 1968; came to U.S., 1988; s. Kulada Prasad and Bina Bose; m. Minakshi Bose, July 4, 1991; children: Shounak, Alok. B in Tech., Indian Inst. Tech., Kharagpur, 1988; MS, Johns Hopkins U., 1990; PhD, U. Pa., 1995. Rsch. asst. Johns Hopkins U., Balt., 1988-90, U. Pa., Phila., 1990-94; sr. devel. engr. Abaqus, Inc., Pawtucket, RI, 1994—. Contbr. articles to profl. jours. Avocation: travel. Office: Abaqus Inc 1080 Main St Pawtucket RI 02860-4847

BOSE, NIRMAL KUMAR, electrical engineering, mathematics educator; b. Calcutta, West Bengal, India, Aug. 19, 1940; came to U.S., 1961; s. Dhruba Kumar and Roma (Guha) B.; m. Chandra Bose, June 8, 1969; children: Meenekshi, Enakshi. B.Tech., Indian Inst. Tech., Kharagpur, West Bengal, 1961; MS, Cornell U., 1963; PhD, Syracuse U., 1967. Asst. prof. U. Pitts., 1967-70, assoc. prof., 1970-76, prof., 1976-86; Singer prof. elec. engring. Pa. State U., University Park, 1986-91, HRB-Systems prof. elec. engring., 1992—; vis. assoc. prof. U. Calif., Berkeley, 1973-74. Cons. RCA, Meadowland, Pa., 1968-69; spl. lectr. Coll. of Steubenville, Ohio, 1968-70; vis. assoc. prof. Am. U. Beirut, 1971, U. Md., College Park, 1972; vis. fellow Princeton U., 1996; apptd. vis. prof. Israel Inst. Tech., 1996; UN expert in neural networks to instns. and ctrs., India, 1994-95; rschr. Japan Soc. for Promotion of Sci., 1998; Humboldt guest prof. Ruhr U., Bochum, Germany, 2000-03. Author: Applied Multidimensional Systems Theory, 1982, Digital Filters: Theory and Applications, 1985, rev. edit., 1993; co-author: Neural Network Fundammentals, 1996; editor: Multidimensional Systems: Theory and Application, 1979, Multidimensional Systems; Progress, Directions and Open Problems, 1985; founding editor-in-chief Multidimensional Sys. and Signal Processing, 1990-; co-editor: Handbook of Statistics vol. on Signal Processing and Its Applications, 1993; assoc. editor Cirs., Sys., and Signal Processing Jour., IEEE Trans. of Cirs. and Sys., Jour. Franklin Inst.; adv. com. Internat. Jour. Smart Engring. Sys. Design. Recipient Invitational fellow for rsch. in Japan, Japan Soc. for Promotion of Sci., 1998, Charles H. Fetter Univ. Endowed fellow in elec. engring., 2001—, Alexander von Humboldt Sr. U.S. Scientist Rsch. award, 1999. Fellow IEEE (chmn. cirs and systems tech. com. on edn. 1979-85, Merit award 2000); mem. AAAS, ASEE, Am. Math. Soc., N.Y. Acad. Scis., Am. Soc. Elec. Engrs. Sigma Xi. Hindu. Avocations: table-tennis, stamp collecting. Home: 1312 W Park Hills Ave State College PA 16803-3250 Office: Pa State U Dept Elec Engring University Park PA 16802 E-mail: nkb1@psu.edu. *Development and cultivation of spiritual and intellectual resources to the best of one's ability supported by parental blessings and encouragement provide the foundation on which the edifice of an individual's contributions to science and society is constructed.*

BOSEKER, BARBARA JEAN, education educator; b. Milw., Dec. 2, 1944; d. Edward Herbert and Alice Margaret (Maas) B.; m. Dale Leslie Sutcliffe, Aug. 8, 1975. Student, U. Nigeria, Nsukka, 1966; BS (hon.) in secondary edn., U. Wis., Milw., 1968; MA in Anthropology, U. Wis., 1971, PhD in edn., 1978, cert Intermediate and secondary English tchr. Wis. Chemistry lab. technician Allen-Bradley Corp., Milw., 1963; coordinator Neighborhood Youth Corps., Madison, 1970; program devel. specialist Tchr. Corps., Madison, 1976-77; asst. prof. edn. Occidental Coll., 1978-80, Moorhead State U., 1980-86, assoc. prof., 1986-90, prof., 1990-95, Winona State U., 1995—. Adv. bd.: Annual Editions: Teaching English as a Second Language, 1999—; cons. Inst. Latin Am. Studies U.Tex, Austin, 1980. Grant writer Fargo-Moorhead (N.D.) Indian Center, 1980; evaluator Indian edn. grant Fargo Pub. Schs., 1985-90; contbr. articles to profl. jours. Elks Nat. and State Youth scholar U. Wis.; fellow Ford Found., 1968-69, NDEA, 1970-71, 78. Mem. NEA, Minn. Edn. Assn., Nat. Women's Studies Assn., Mortar Bd., Phi Kappa Phi, Pi Lambda Theta, Kappa Delta Pi, Sigma Tau Delta, Sigma Epsilon Sigma. Democrat. Christian Scientist. Home: 1317 Ridgewood Dr Winona MN 55987-5421 Office: Winona State U Winona MN 55987 E-mail: bboseker@winona.edu.

BOSGRAAF, PETER JOHN, music educator; b. Glendale, Ariz., Apr. 27, 1976; s. David A and Susan F Bosgraaf. MusB in Music Edn., Viterbo U., La Crosse Wiconsin, 1994—99. Vocal Music K-12 Wis. Dept. of Pub. Instrn. H.s. vocal tchr. Aquinas H.S., La Crosse, Wis. Musical dir. Aquinas H.S., La Crosse, Wis. Author: (poetry) Appalachian Spring, I Need You, etc. Musician St. Patrick's Ch., Mauston, Wis., 1990. Mem.: Nat. Cath. Educators Assn., Music Educators Nat. Conf., Wis. State Music Assn. D-Liberal. Roman Catholic. Avocations: travel, music, writing, gardening.

BOSHES, LOUIS D. physician, scientist, educator, historian, author; b. Chgo. s. Jacob and Ethel (London) B.; children: Arlene Phyllis Boshes Hirschfelder, Judi Myrl; m. Natalie A. Boshes. BS, Northwestern U., 1931, MD, 1936, postgrad., 1947-51; HHD (hon.), 1976. Diplomate neurology, psychiatry, and child neurology Am. Bd. Psychiatry and Neurology. Intern Michael Reese Hosp., Chgo., 1935-36, Cook County Hosp., 1936-37; fellow psychiatry Ill. Neuro-psychiat. Inst., Chgo., 1941-42, 46-47; sr. attending neurologist and psychiatrist, chief neurology clinic Michael Reese Med. Center, 1940—; sr. attending neurologist, psychiatrist emeritus Michael Reese Hosp. Med. Ctr.; prof. neurology and psychiatry Northwestern U., 1955-63; prof. neurology U. Ill. Coll. Medicine, Chgo., 1970-78, prof. emeritus, 1978—, historian and archivist in neurology; emeritus Cook County Hosp.; attending neurologist Ill. Research and Ednl. Hosps., 1963—, dir. consultation clinic for epilepsy, 1963-78; assoc. and attending neurologist, cons. neurology Cook County Hosp., 1947—; sr. cons. neurology Downey VA Hosp., 1952-60; prof. neurology Cook County Grad. Sch. Medicine, 1970—; practice medicine specializing in neurology and psychiatry, 1975—. Med. adv. com. Cook County chpt. Nat Found., 1947-55, March of Dimes, 1956—; med. adv. com. Epilepsy Assn. Am., 1964— ; bd. dirs., med. adv. com. Epilepsy Found. Am., 1964— ; ambassador Internat. Bur. Epilepsy, 1969— ; profl. adv. com. Nat. Parkinson Found., 1960—, Nat. Myasthenia Gravis Found., 1972— ; profl. adv. bd. United Cerebral Palsy; adv. bd. Cognitive Neurology and Alzheimer's Disease Ctr. Northwestern U., 2002--. Author, contbr. to books, med. jours.; assoc. editor Diseases of the Nervous System, 1962—; editor Chgo. Neurol. Soc. Bull., Behavioral Neuropsychiatry; mem. editorial bd. Excerpta Medica, Internat. Jour. Neurology and Neurosurgery. Historian, curator, archivist neurology U. Ill. Coll. Medicine at Chgo., 1990—, historian to Central Neuropsychiatric Assn, 1975—, Lt. comdr. M.C., USNR, 1941-46. Fellow ACP, Am. Acad. Neurology, Am. Psychiat. Assn. (disting. life); mem. AMA (cons. JAMA, bd. govs. 1991—), Inst. Medicine Chgo., Pan Am. Med. Assn. (pres. sect. neurology 1973—, hon. D.Hum. 1976), Ctrl. Neuropsychiat. Assn. (pres. 1973-74, historian, curator), Ill. Psychiat. Soc. (life, sec.-treas., acting pres. 1949-50), Chgo. Neurol. Soc. (pres. 1965-66, historian 1965—, curator), Michael Reese Hosp. and Med. Ctr. Alumni Assn. (pres. 1961-62), Assn. for Rsch. in Nervous and Mental Diseases, Internat. League Against Epilepsy, Am. League Against Epilepsy, Ill. League Against Epilepsy (med. adv. com.), Ill. Med. Soc. (chmn. sect. neurology and psychiatry 1961—), Chgo. Med. Soc., World Fedn. Neurology, AAAS, Am. Med. Soc. Vienna (life), Ctrl. Assn. Electroencephalographers, Sigma Xi, Phi Delta Epsilon, Alpha Omega Alpha. Home: 3150 N Lake Shore Dr Chicago IL 60657-4829 E-mail: l.boshes@uic.edu.

BOSHIER, MAUREEN LOUISE, health facilities administrator; b. Elizabeth, N.J., Oct. 1, 1946; d. John Henry and Mary Hanora (McGarry) B.; m. Robert Hall Rea, May 23, 1987. BSN, Coll. Misericordia, Dallas, Pa., 1968; MS in Psychiat. Nursing, U. Colo., 1973; MBA, U. Phoenix, 1987. Cert. healthcare exec. Clin. specialist psychiat. nursing Denver Gen. Hosp., 1973-74; dir. rehab. svcs. N.Mex. Cancer Control, Albuquerque, 1976-80; exec. dir. N.Mex. State Bd. Nursing, Albuquerque, 1980-84; exec. v.p. N.Mex. Hosp. Assn., Albuquerque, 1984-88; adminstr. surg. svcs., sr. nursing adminstr. U. N.Mex. Hosp., Albuquerque, 1988-94; CEO, pres. N.Mex. Hosps. and Health Sys. Assn., Albuquerque, 1995—. Dir. Profl. Seminar Cons., Inc., Albuquerque, 1982—; v.p. exec. bd. N.Mex. Health Resources, Albuquerque, 1981—, pres., 1989; vice chmn., bd. dirs. Hosp. Home Health Care, Albuquerque, 1978—; dir. Acad. Seminars, Inc., 1982—; mem. governing coun. for small and rural hosps. Am. Hosp. Assn., 1996—, women's dir. devel. program Kellogg Sch. Mgmt. Ctr. for Exec. Devel., 2003. Mem. adv. bd. N.Mex. Bus. Jour., 1995—; contbr. articles to profl. jours. Sec. N.Mex. Ballet Co., Albuquerque, 1982-87; vice chmn. Gov.'s Task Force on Nursing Issues, Albuquerque, 1982-88; adv. bd. Sub-area Coun. Health Sys., Albuquerque, 1980-84; mem. Leadership N.Mex. Class of 2000, alumni com. 2001—. Capt. U.S. Army, 1967-71. Recipient Woman on the Move award YWCA, 1992, Wharton Sch. of Bus. fellowship for health care execs., 1993, Gov.'s award for Outstanding N.Mex. Woman, 1997; named Nurse of Yr., March of Dimes, 2002; fellow Johnson & Johnson, 1993 Mem. Am. Orgn. Nurse Execs. (vice chmn. legis. advocacy com. 1992-94, chmn. 1993-94), Am. Coll. Healthcare Execs. (diplomate, Regent's award 2000), N.Mex. Orgn. Nurse Execs. (treas. 1988-89, pres. 1990), N.Mex. League for Nursing, N.Mex. Nurses Assn. (Nurse Adminstr. award 1984), Rotary (Albuquerque bd. dirs. 2001—), Albuquerque C. of C. (mem. quality of life com. 1994—), Sigma Theta Tau (pres.-elect 1994, pres. 1995—, Mentor award Gamma Sigma chpt. 1994). Democrat. Avocations: music, dance, travel. Home: 9520 Kandace Dr NW Albuquerque NM 87114-4131 Office: N Mex Hosps and Health Sys Assn 2121 Osuna Rd NE Albuquerque NM 87113-1001

BOSKEY, ADELE LUDIN, biochemistry educator, researcher; b. N.Y.C., Aug. 30, 1943; d. Benjamin and Anne (Monoson) Ludin; m. James Bernard Boskey, June 30, 1970 (dec. 1998); 1 child, Elizabeth Rona. BA, Barnard Coll., N.Y.C., 1964; PhD, Boston U., 1970. Editor Cambridge Data Base, England, 1969-70; rsch. fellow The Hosp. Spl. Surgery, N.Y.C., 1970-71, asst. scientist, 1971-75, assoc. scientist, 1975-79, sr. scientist, 1985, chief mineralized tissue rsch. sect., 1984—, dir. rsch., 1993—2002, Starr chair in mineralized tissue rsch.; asst. prof. biochemistry Cornell U. Med. Coll., N.Y.C., 1975-78, assoc. prof. Ithaca, NY, 1978-85, prof., 1986—. Mem. editl. adv. bd. jour. Orthop Rsch., J. Bone and Min. Rsch., Calcif Tissue Internat., Bone and Min., J. Dental Rsch. contbr. articles to profl. jours. Recipient Disting. Rsch. award Kappa Delta, 1979, Career Devel. award NIH-Nat. Inst. Dental Rsch., 1975, NIH merit award Nat. Inst. Dental Research, 1987. Fellow Am. Inst. Chemists; mem. Am. Chem. Soc., Orthopaedic Rsch. Soc. (mem. at-large, newsletter editor 1989—, pres. 1997), Internat. Assn. Dental Rsch. (chair constrn. com., Biol. Basic Rsch. award 1994), Am. Crystallographic Assn., Am. Acad. Orthopaedic Surgeons, Am. Soc. Bone and Mineral Rsch., NIH (Nat. Adv. Coun. 1993— and numerous other coms.) Sigma Xi. Avocations: music, theatre. Office: The Hosp Spl Surgery 535 E 70th St New York NY 10021-4872 Business E-Mail: boskeya@hss.edu.

BOSKEY, BENNETT, lawyer; b. N.Y.C., Aug. 14, 1916; s. Meyer and Janet (Lauterstein) B.; m. Shirley Ecker, July 3, 1940 (dec. 1998). AB, Williams Coll., 1935; LL.B., Harvard U., 1939. Bar: N.Y. 1940, U.S. Supreme Ct. 1943, D.C. 1949. Spl. asst. to Atty. Gen. U.S. Dept. Justice, Washington, 1943; advisor on enemy property U.S. Dept. State, Washington, 1946-47; atty. U.S. Atomic Energy Commn., Washington, 1947-49, dep. gen. counsel, 1949-51; ptnr. firm Volpe, Boskey & Lyons (and predecessors), Washington, 1951-96. Law clk. Judge Learned Hand, 1939-40, Justice Stanley Reed, 1940-41, Chief Justice Harlan F. Stone, 1941-43; trustee Analytic Svcs. Inc., Arlington, Va., 1962-91; adv. bd. internat. legal studies program Am. U., 1987-99. Chmn. bd. trustees Primary Day Sch., Bethesda, Md., 1969— . Served with U.S. Army, 1943-46. Mem. ABA, Am. Law Inst. (treas. 1975—, mem. coun., Am. Law Inst.-ABA com. on continuing profl. edn. 1985—), Am. Soc. Internat. Law (bd. rev. and devel. 1973-88). Office: Ste 600 1800 Massachusetts Ave NW Washington DC 20036-1222

BOSKIN, CLAIRE, psychotherapist; b. Bklyn., Apr. 25, 1933; d. Benjamin and Frieda (Brofman) G.; m. Joseph Boskin, Aug. 5, 1955 (div. Feb. 1982); children: Julie Lise, Lori Kem, Deborah Jo. BA, Bklyn. Coll., 1956; MSW, U. Minn., 1959. Tchr. Ctr. for Tng. of U. So. Calif., L.A., 1965-69; program developer, trainer Dept. Urban Affairs, UCLA, L.A., 1962-65; pvt. practice spiritually oriented tchg. and counseling Newton, Mass., 1973—. Mem. adv. coun. Vt. Healing Tools Project, Brattleboro, 1993—; mem. steering com. Transcultural Network for Global Psychology and Edn., Newton, 1993—96; bd. dirs. internat. traveling chorus Sharing a New Song, 1987—. Avocations: choral singing, photography, gardening. Office: 18 Quincy Rd Chestnut Hill MA 02467-3935 E-mail: clairebenf@aol.com.

BOSL, PHILLIP L. lawyer; b. Feb. 27, 1945; BA, U. Calif., Santa Barbara, 1968; JD, U. So. Calif., 1975. Bar: Calif. 1975. Ptnr. Gibson, Dunn & Crutcher LLP, L.A., 1983—. Mem. U. So. Calif. Law Rev., 1973-75. Officer USCG, 1969-72. Mem. ABA, Los Angeles County Bar Assn., Fed. Bar Assn., Assn. Bus. Trial Lawyers Am., Securities Industry Assn. (compliance and legal divsn.), Inst. Corp. Counsel (gov.), Nat. Assn. Securities Dealers (arbitrator), Order of Coif. Home: 6226 Napoli Ct Long Beach CA 90803-4800 Office: Gibson Dunn & Crutcher LLP 333 S Grand Ave Ste 5300 Los Angeles CA 90071-3197 E-mail: pbosl@gibsondunn.com.

BOSLAND, PAUL WILLIAM, agriculture educator; b. Paterson, N.J., Jan. 6, 1953; s. William and Maudine Bosland; m. Judith Marie Golden, Sept. 3, 1977; children: Emily, William. BS, U. Calif., Davis, 1976, MS, 1977; PhD, U. Wis., 1986. Staff rsch. assoc. U. Calif., 1980-82; grad. rsch. asst. U. Wis., Madison, 1983-86; prof. agr. N.Mex. State U., Las Cruces, 1986—2003, Regents prof., 2003—, dir. Chile Pepper Inst., 1991—. Author: Pepper Garden, 1993, Peppers of the World, 1996, Peppers: Vegetable and Spice Capsciums, 1999. Avocations: gardening, photography, fishing. Office: NMex State U MSC 3Q Las Cruces NM 88003-8003 Fax: 505-646-6041. E-mail: hotchile@nmsu.edu.

BOSLEY, KAREN LEE, English and journalism educator; b. Beech Grove, Ind., Sept. 23, 1942; d. Lowell Holmes and Kathryn Gertrude (Drake) Foley; m. Norman Keith Bosley, Dec. 21, 1964; children: Mark Harold, Rachael Kathryn, Keith Lowell, Sidney Clark. AB in Lang. Arts summa cum laude, U. Indpls., 1965; MA in English, Northwestern U., 1967; MA in Journalism, Ball State U., 1984; postgrad. (Newspaper Fund fellow), U. Mo., 1973; postgrad., Ohio U., 1977. Copy editor, reporter Indpls. News, 1963-65; English tchr., yearbook adviser Beech Grove (Ind.) Jr. H.S., 1965-66; English tchr. So. Regional H.S., Manahawkin, N.J., 1967-68; prof. humanities, journalism, and English Ocean County Coll., Toms River, N.J., 1971—, student newspaper adviser, 1971—, yearbook adviser, 1999—. Part-time reporter Daily Times-Observer, Toms River, 1972-77, part-time copy editor, 1993. Contbr. articles to publs. in field. Trustee Long Beach Island Hist. Assn., Friends of Island Libr., 1975-79; pres. Long Beach I PTA; chmn. Long Beach Twp. Dem. Mcpl. Com., 1971-78; Dem. committeeman Long Beach Twp. Dist. 2, 1971-78, 85—; mem. Long Beach Twp. Recreation Commn., 1972-75; bd. dirs. Ocean County Red Cross, 1972-78, Ocean County Family Planning, Inc., 1972-78, Student Press Law Ctr., 1987-2002, sec., 1998-2000, mem. adv. coun., 2002—; chmn. Cub Scout pack 32, Ocean County Coun. Boy Scouts Am.; founder, bd. dirs. Long Beach I Hist. Assn., Island Dems., Inc.; mem. adminstrv. bd. First United Meth. Ch. Beach Haven Terrace (N.J.); So. Regional H.S. Band Parent Orgn., 1995-96, pres., 1996-97, corr. sec; So. Regional Jazz Band Parents Assn., charter mem., 2001—. Mem. AAUW (pres., dir. Barnegat Light Area br.), NEA, N.J. Edn. Assn., Ocean County Edn. Assn., Faculty Assn. Ocean County Coll. (v.p. 1984-85), Coll. Media Advisers, Inc. (disting. newspaper adviser for U.S. 2-yr. colls. 1978, dir., sec.), Assn. Edn. in Journalism and Mass Comms., C.C. Journalism Assn. (dir., v.p.), Soc. Profl. Journalists, Internat. Platform Assn., Sigma Delta Chi. Home: 9 E Old Whaling Ln Long Beach Township NJ 08008-2930 Office: Ocean CC PO Box 2001 College Dr Toms River NJ 08754-2001 E-mail: kbosley@mac.com.

BOSMAJIAN, HAIG ARAM, speech communication educator; b. Fresno, Calif., Mar. 26, 1928; s. Aram and Aurora (Keosheyan) B.; m. Hamida Just, Feb. 27, 1957; 1 child, Harlan. BA, U. Calif., Berkeley, 1949; MA, U. of Pacific, 1951; PhD, Stanford U., 1960. Instr. U. Idaho, Moscow, 1959-61; asst. prof. U. Conn., Storrs, 1961-65; prof. speech comm. U. Wash., Seattle, 1965—. Author: Language of Oppression (Orwell award), 1983: editor: Censorship, Libraries and the Law, 1983; Justice Douglas, 1980, Freedom of Speech, 1983, First Amendment in the Classroom Series, 1987: vol. 1, The Freedom to Read, 1987, vol. II, The Freedom of Religion, 1987, vol. III, Freedom of Expression, 1988, vol. IV, Academic Freedom, 1989, vol. V, Freedom to Publish, 1989, Metaphor and Reason in Judicial Opinions, 1992, The Freedom Not to Speak, 1999. Recipient Bicentennial of the Bill of Rights award Western States Communication Assn., 1991.

BOSS, AMELIA HELEN, law educator, lawyer; b. Balt., Apr. 3, 1949; d. Myron Theodore and Loretta (Oakjones) B.; m. Roger S. Clark, Mar. 3, 1979; children: Melissa, Seymour, Edward, Ashley. Student, Oxford (Eng.) U., 1968; BA in Sociology, Bryn Mawr, 1970; JD, Rutgers U., 1975. Bar: N.J, Pa., U.S. Dist. Ct. (ea. dist.) N.J., U.S. Dist. Ct. (ea. dist.) Pa., U.S. Supreme Ct., U.S. Ct. Appeals (3d cir.). Law clk. Hon. Milton B. Cranford N.J. Supreme Ct., 1975-76; assoc. Pepper, Hamilton & Scheetz, Phila., 1976-78; assoc. prof. law Rutgers U. Sch. Law, Camden, N.J., 1983-87, Temple U., Phila., 1989-91; prof. law Temple U. Sch. Law, Phila., 1991—, Charles Klein prof. law, 1999—. Vis. prof. law U. Miami Sch. Law, Coral Gables, Fla., 1985—86; Leo Goodwin disting. vis. prof. law Nova U., Sch. Law, 1998; mem. coms. Nat. Conf. Commrs. on Uniform State Laws; U.S. rep. to UN Commn. on Internat. Trade Law; dir. Inst. for Internat. Law and Pub. Policy, 2001—. Author: (books) Electronic Data Interchange Agreements: A Guide and Sourcebook, 1993, ABCs of the UCC: Article 2A, ABCs of the UCC: Article 5; editor-in-chief The Data Law Report, 1993-97, The Business Lawyer, 1998-99, ABCs of the UCC; mem. permanent editl. bd. Uniform Comml. Code; contbr. articles to profl. jours. Named among top 50 women lawyers in U.S. Nat. Law Jour., 1998. Fellow Am. Bar Found.; mem. ABA (chmn. bus. law sect. 2000-01, chmn. sect. officers conf. 2001—), Internat. Bar Assn., Am. Law Inst. (coun. 2000—), Am. Bankruptcy Inst., Am. Coll. Comml. Fin. Lawyers, Nat. Assn. Women Lawyers. Home: 309 Westmont Ave Haddonfield NJ 08033-1714 Office: Temple U Sch Law 1719 N Broad St Philadelphia PA 19122-6002

BOSS, LENARD BARRETT, lawyer; b. Passaic, N.J., Mar. 6, 1960; s. Lawrence Steven and Laura (Ziegler) Boss. BA in Rhetoric, Bates Coll., 1982; JD with high honors, George Washington U., 1985. Bar: Pa. 1985, DC 1986, Md. 1995, US Ct Appeals (4th and 11th cirs) 1986, US Dist Ct DC 1987, US Ct Appeals (DC cir) 1987, US Ct Appeals (3d cir) 1988, US Supreme Ct 1989. Assoc. Asbill, Junkin, Myers & Buffone, Washington, 1986-91; ptnr. Asbill, Junkin & Myers, Washington, 1991-95; asst. fed. pub. defender Fed. Pub. Defender's Office, Washington, 1995-2000; ptnr. Asbill, Junkin, Moffitt & Boss, Washington, 2000—02, Asbill, Moffitt & Boss, Washington, 2002—. Adj. prof. George Washington U. Law Sch., 1999—; co-chair practitioners adv. group U.S. Sentencing Commn., 2000—. Avocations: films, music, sports. Office: Ste 200 1615 New Hampshire Ave NW Washington DC 20009-2520 E-mail: boss@ambdc.com.

BOSS, MANLEY LEON, plant physiologist; b. Atlanta, Dec. 24, 1924; s. Herman Beryl and Florence Clara Boss; m. Helen Phyllis Ellins, Nov. 20, 1956; children: Valerie Jolly(dec.) children: Brian, Daniel. BS, U. Miami, 1949; MAgr, Inter-American Inst. Agrl. Scis., Costa Rica, 1951; PhD, Iowa State Coll., 1954. Asst. then assoc. prof. dept. botany U. Miami, Coral Gables, Fla., 1954—63; prof. dept. biology Fla. Atlantic U., Boca Raton, 1963—91, chmn. biology dept., 1968—72, asst. dean Coll. Liberal Arts, 1991—93, dean Coll. Liberal Arts, 1993—94; ret., 1994. Ecol. cons., Boca Raton, Fla., 1965—94; biostatistician/consultant, 1955—94. With U.S. Army, 1943—45, ETO. Achievements include research in cellular senescence. Home: 3308 Perimeter Rd Palm City FL 34990

BOSSE, DENISE FRANCES, educational administrator, education educator; b. Syracuse, N.Y., Apr. 27, 1953; d. Rufus Elmer Nicholson and Vivian Margaret Herb; m. Philip Roger Bosse, Mar. 27, 1976; children: Matthew R., Jeannine M. BS in Elem. Edn., U. Maine, 1975, MEd, 1987. Cert. tchr./adminstr., Maine. Tchr. prin. Union #122 Stockholm (Maine) Elem. Sch., 1988; ind. ednl. cons. Caribou, Maine, 1988-93; human resource mgr., ednl. materials buyer Mementos Inc., Caribou, Maine, 1988-93; edn. coord., head tchr. Little Feathers Head Start, Presque Isle, Maine, 1995-96; local advisor Nat. Early Childhood Accreditation Assn., Washington, 1996—; adj. faculty U. Maine, Presque Isle, 1993-98; coord. Aroostook Coun. on Transition, Presque Isle, 1996-97; secondary resource rm. tchr. Caribou H.S., 1997—. Bd. dirs. Youth Network, Caribou, 1996-97; mem. steering com. St. John Valley Sch.-to-Work Partnership, Frenchville, Maine, 1996-97, participant Com. on Transition, Augusta, Maine, 1996-97; mem. Coords. Alliance of Maine, Augusta, 1996-97. Grantee State of Maine and U.S. Dept. Edn., Ashland, Maine, 1987. Mem. Vol. Dirs. Assn. Northern Maine, Maine Support Network, KC Ladies Auxiliary, Alpha Delta Pi (permanent alumni sec. 1985—). Roman Catholic. Avocations: travel, reading, creative writing, music. Home: PO Box 594 Caribou ME 04736-0594 Office: Caribou HS Sweden St Caribou ME 04736 E-mail: dbosse@mail.cariboustchools.org.

BOSSE, MARGARET FISHER ISHLER, education educator; b. Bellefonte, Pa., Oct. 19, 1934; d. Fred Raymond Fisher and Margaret (Hoffmeister) Fisher Hess; m. Richard Eves Ishler, Dec. 27, 1956 (div. June 1978); children: Frederick, Theodore; m. Richard C. Bosse, June 26, 1999. BA in English Edn., Pa. State U., 1956, MA in English, 1960; EdD, U. Toledo, 1972. English tchr. Bald Eagle (Pa.) H.S., 1956-57, Marion (N.Y.) Ctrl. Sch., 1957-59, York (Pa.) Suburban H.S., 1959-60; adj. instr. English Pa. State U., York, 1962-64; instr. York Coll., 1964-65; adj. inst. English U. Toledo, 1966-68, grad. asst., 1968-71; from asst. prof. to prof. Bowling Green (Ohio) State U., 1972-90, dir. field experiences and stds. compliance, 1985-90; head dept. curriculum and instrn., prof. U. No. Iowa, Cedar Falls, 1990-96, prof. curriculum and devel., 1997-2000, acting dir. teacher edn., 1998-99, prof. emeritus, 2000—. Mem. Nat. Coun. for Accreditation of Tchr. Edn. Bd. Examiners, 1998—. Co-author: Creating the Open Classroom, 1974, Teaching in a Competency-Based Program, 1977, Dynamics of Effective Teaching, 5th edit., 2003; contbr. articles to profl. jours. Bd. dirs. Wittenberg (Ohio) U., 1984-86, Luth. Student Chapel, Bowling Green, 1988-91, Ohio Luth. Campus Ministry, Columbus, 1986-87, Christian Cmty. Devel. Bd., Waterloo, Iowa, 1992-96. Recipient Christa McAuliff Showcase for Excellence award, 1990. Mem.: Iowa Assn. Tchr. Educators (pres. 1992—94), Ohio Assn. Tchr. Educators (exec. sec. 1980—87, pres. 1982, Disting. Educator 1982), Am. Assn. Colls. Tchr. Edn. (rep. 1985—, cons. 2000—), Assn. Tchr. Educators (nat. pres. 1996—97, named One of 70 Top Tchr. Educators 1990), Mortar Board, Phi Gamma Mu, Pi Lambda Theta, Phi Kappa Phi. Avocations: travel, golf, poetry. E-mail: mishlerbosse@msn.com.

BOSSEN, EDWARD HECHT, pathologist; b. Jacksonville, Fla., Aug. 9, 1939; s. Morris William and Sarah B.; m. Roxana Mack, Aug. 11, 1963; children: Deborah, Barbara, Rebecca. BS, U. Fla., 1961; MD, Duke U., 1965. Intern, resident Duke U., Durham, N.C., 1965-70; prof. pathology Duke U. Med. Ctr., Durham, N.C., 1972—. Maj. U.S. Army, 1970-72. Home: 2811 Wade Rd Durham NC 27705-5622 Office: Duke Univ Med Ctr Dept Pathology Ctr Durham NC 27710-0001

BOSSEN, WENDELL JOHN, retired financial consultant; b. Vienna, S.D., Nov. 11, 1933; s. Hans Simonsen and Clara Patrina (Vorseth) B.; m. Jean Davidson, Jan. 6, 1956; children: Mark, Monica. Student, S.D. Sch. Mines, 1952. CLU. Agt. Northwestern Nat. Life Ins. Co., Mpls., 1957-61, dist. mgr., staff mgr., 1961-68, br. mgr., 1968-72, div. v.p., 1972-77; exec. v.p., chief operating officer Inter-Ocean Ins. Co., Cin., 1977-84; exec. v.p. corp. mktg. Mut. Benefit Life Ins. Co., Newark, 1984-92; pres. Internat. Corp. Mktg. Group, Hartford, Conn., 1992-99, retired, 1999. Cons. Newark Performing Arts Corp., 1986. Author: Businessmens Guide to Insurance, 1981; contbr. articles to profl. jours. Chmn. ARC, Waterstown, S.D., 1962, Northeast S.D. chpt. United Way, Watertown, 1962, Watertown County Reps., 1963-64; mem. exec. com. S.D. Reps., Pierre, 1964; bd. dirs. Am. Luth. Ch., Cin., 1979, Apostles' House, 1989. Recipient Danforth Found. award, 1952. Mem. Nat. Assn. Life Underwriters (pres. Watertown chpt. 1960-61, v.p. state chpt. 1961-62), Chartered Life Underwriters, Life Ins. Mktg. Research Assn. (com. chmn. 1975). Clubs: Golden Valley Country (Mpls). Lodges: Elks (pres. 1962-63), Lions (pres. 1961, 73), Kiwanis. Avocations: golf, tennis, photography. Home: 111 Sugarberry Ln Hendersonville NC 28739-6933 Office: Internat Corp Mktg Group 100 Campus Dr Florham Park NJ 07932-1006 E-mail: wbossen@aol.com.

BOSSERT, PHILIP JOSEPH, information systems executive; b. Indpls., Feb. 23, 1944; s. Alfred Joseph and Phyllis Jean (Cashen) B.; m. Jane Elisabeth Shade, June 29, 1968 (div. Dec. 1990); m. ChaoYing Deng, May 22, 1992; 1 child, Lian Brittni. BA in Econs., Rockhurst Coll., 1968; cert. in Philosophy, U. Freiburg, Fed. Republic Ger., 1970; MA in Philosophy, Washington U., St. Louis, 1972, PhD in Philosophy, 1973. Asst. prof. philosophy Hawaii Loa Coll., Honolulu, 1973-76, pres., 1978-86; dir. Hawaii com. for the humanities NEH, Honolulu, 1976-77; dir. long range planning Chaminade U., Honolulu, 1977-78; pres. Strategic Info. Solutions, Honolulu, 1986-99; mgr. strategic info. systems GTE Hawaiian Telephone, Honolulu, 1987-91; asst. supt. info. and telecom. svcs. Hawaii State Dept. Edn., 1991-94; project dir. Hawaii Edn. and Rsch. Network, 1994-97; chmn. bd. dirs., dir. Media Design & Devel., Inc., 1996-99; chmn. bd. dirs., CEO Baden Wines Internat., Ltd., 1997-2000; dep. dir. Hawaii State Dept. Bus., Econ. Devel. and Tourism, 2000-01; chmn., CEO China Hawaii Investment Corp., Honolulu, 2001—; pres., CEO Hawaii High Tech. Devel. Corp., 2003—. Cons. Sangyong Bus. Group, Seoul, Korea, 1987-90, Nat. Assn. Colls. Univs. and Bus. Officers, Washington, 1980-90, Nat. Inst. for Edn. Rsch., Japan, 1999-2000. Author: Strategic Planning and Budgeting, 1989; author, editor numerous books on philosophy; contbr. articles to profl. jours. Bd. dirs. Hawaii Childrens Mus., 1994-99, Friends of the East West Ctr., 1996-2000, Hawaii Alliance for the Arts, 1996-99, Hanahaùoli Sch., 1999-2000. Fulbright-Hays fellow, 1968-70, Woodrow Wilson fellow, 1972-73, Nat. Endowment for Humanities fellow, 1976. Office: China Hawaii Investment Corp PO Box 2172 Honolulu HI 96805 E-mail: pbossert@china-hawaii-invest.com.

BOSSES, STEVAN J. lawyer; b. Bronx, N.Y., July 29, 1937; s. Fred and Frieda (Picard) B.; m. Abbye Z. Bosses, May 24, 1964; children: Donna Lynne, David Keith, Gary Philip. BME, Cornell U., 1960; LLB, Columbia U., 1963. Bar: N.Y. 1963, U.S. Dist. Ct. (so. dist.) N.Y. 1964, U.S. Dist. Ct. (ea. dist.) N.Y. 1964, U.S. Patent Office 1964, U.S. Ct. Appeals (2d cir.) 1970, U.S. Ct. Appeals (3rd cir.) 1979, U.S. Ct. Appeals (fed. cir.) 1982, U.S. Supreme Ct. 1989. Assoc. Watson Leavenworth Kelton & Taggart, N.Y.C., 1963-71, ptnr., 1972-81, Fitzpatrick, Cella, Harper & Scinto, N.Y.C., 1981—. Mem. ABA, ASME, N.Y. State Bar Assn., Am. Intellectual Property Law Assn., Fed. Bar Coun. (trustee 1989-94), Fed. Cir. Bar Assn. N.Y. Intellectual Property Law Assn. Home: 19 Springdale Rd Scarsdale NY 10583-7330 Office: 30 Rockefeller Plz New York NY 10112-0002 E-mail: sbosses@fchs.com.

BOSSIO, SALVATORE, lawyer; b. Salvatore N. and Rosa; m. Joan S. Smith, Feb. 16, 1957; children: Lora Jo, Deborah, Amy, Stephen, Bruce. BA, Stanford U., 1951, JD, 1953. Assoc. firm Hassard, Bonnington, Rogers & Huber, San Francisco, 1955-64, partner, 1964—. Dir., sec. Swinerton & Walberg Co., San Francisco, 1988—. Served with U.S. Army, 1953-55. Recipient Pres.'s award for outstanding service Assn. Def. Counsel, 1979 Fellow Am. Coll. Trial Lawyers; mem. Am. Bar Assn., Bar Assn. San Francisco, State Bar Calif., Marin County Bar Assn., Am. Bd. Trial Advs., Internat. Assn. Ins. Counsel, Nat. Assn. R.R. Trial Counsel, Calif. Med.-Legal Assn. (chmn. 1978-79), Assn. Def. Counsel (dir. 1979-80), Am. Bd. Profl. Liability Attys.

BOST, ERIC M. federal agency administrator; B in Psychology, U. N.C., 1974; M, U. South Fla., 1985. Dept. dir. Ariz. Dept. Econ. Security, 1994—97; chief exec. & adminstrv. officer Tex. Dept. Human Svcs., 1997—2000; under sec. food, nutrition and consumer svcs. USDA, Washington, 2001—. Office: USDA 1400 Independence Ave SW Washington DC 20250

BOST, MIKE, state legislator; Ill. state rep., 1995—. Office: 300 E Main St Carbondale IL 62901-3029*

BOST, RAYMOND MORRIS, retired college president; b. Maiden, N.C., Aug. 18, 1925; s. Loy Robert and Virginia (Anderson) B.; m. Margaret Martha Vedder, Aug. 16, 1947; children: Timothy Lee, Penelope Ruth, Peter Raymond, Jonathan Otto. AB, Lenoir-Rhyne Coll., Hickory, N.C., 1949, DD (hon.), 1976; BD, Luth. Theol. So. Sem., 1952; MA, Yale U., 1959, PhD, 1963. Ordained to ministry Luth. Ch., 1952; pastor in Spartanburg, S.C., 1952-53, Raleigh, N.C., 1953-57; prof. ch. history, dir. field work Luth. Theol. So. Sem., 1960-66; acad. dean Lenoir-Rhyne Coll., Hickory, 1966-68, pres., 1968-76, Luth. Theol. Sem., Phila., 1976-85; synod historian N.C. Synod, Luth. Ch. in Am., 1985-87; v.p. acad. affairs Newberry (S.C.) Coll., 1987, dean, 1988-89; dir. Ctr. Ethical Devel., Newberry Coll., 1990-92, pres., 1992-95; pres. emeritus, 1995—. Contact min. Nat. Luth. Coun., N.C. State U., 1953-57, Yale U., 1957-59; part-time instr. sociology Columbia Coll., 1962-65; mem. Com. to Implement Refugee Act, 1953; mem. bd. theol. edn. Luth. Ch. Am., 1969-70, mem. standing com. on approaches to unity, 1971-72, del. convs., 1970-76, mem. bd. publs., 1976-84, v.p., 1983-84; pres. Ind. Coll. Fund N.C., 1974-75; v.p. commn. on future Luth. Ednl. Conf. N.Am., 1972-75; trustee Luth. Theol. So. Sem., 1969-76, 98-2001, sec. bd., 1975-76; sec. N.C. Found. Ch. Related Colls., 1969-71; adv. coun. Ctr. on Regligion in the South, Luth. Theol. So. Sem., 1989—, mem. S.C. Tuition Grants Commn., 1993-95, chmn., 1994-95; vis. prof. Inst. Confucian Studies, Qufu (China) Tchrs. U., Shandong, 1993—; advisor Inst. Advanced Profl. Ethics, Jinan, Shandong, 1993—; chmn. archives com. region 9 Evang. Luth. Ch. in Am., 1991-95; interim pastor Christ's Luth. Ch., Stanley, N.C., 1998; bd. dirs. Ea. Cluster Luth. Theol. Sems., 1998-2001, sec., 2000-01. Co-author: (with J.L. Norris) All One Body: The Story of the North Carolina Lutheran Synod, 1803-1993, 1994; editor: Lutheranism. . .With a Southern Accent, 1998 (Commendation from Concordia Hist. Inst. 1999); contbg. author: A History of the Lutheran Church in South Carolina, 1971,

Essays and Reports of Lutheran Historical Conference, Vol. 5, 1977, Vol. 9, 1980, editor vol. 16, 1994; contbr. A Truly Efficient School of Theology, 1981, Luth. Quar., 1988, 89. Pres. bd. dirs. James R. Crumley Jr. Archives, 1995-96; com. on hist. work N.C. Synod Evang. Lutheran Ch. in Am., 1999—, chair, 2000—; 200th ann. task force N.C. Synod, E.L.C.A., 2001-. Luth. Brotherhood Sem. Grad. scholar, 1957-58; Martin Luther fellow Nat. Luth. Ednl. Conf., 1959; faculty fellow Am. Assn. Theol. Schs., 1959-60 Mem. So. Hist. Assn., Luth. Hist. Conf. (bd. dirs. 1994-2000, v.p. 1998-2000), Am. Soc. Ch. History, Rotary (bd. dirs. Newberry 1990-92, 95-96, treas. 1992, 95-96).

BOST, THOMAS GLEN, lawyer, educator; b. Oklahoma City, July 13, 1942; s. Burl John and Lorene Bell (Croka) B.; m. Sheila K. Pettigrew, Aug. 27, 1966; children: Amy Elizabeth, Stephen Luke, Emily Anne, Paul Alexander. BS in Acctg. summa cum laude, Abilene Christian U., 1964; JD, Vanderbilt U., 1967. Bar: Tenn. 1967, Calif. 1969. Instr. David Lipscomb Coll., Nashville, 1967; asst. prof. law Vanderbilt U., Nashville, 1967-68; ptnr. Latham & Watkins, Los Angeles, 1968-99; prof. law Pepperdine U., 2000—. Lectr. on taxation subjects. Chmn. bd. regents, law sch. bd. visitors Pepperdine U., Malibu, Calif., 1980-2000; chmn. bd. trustees Pacific Legal Found., 2000-02. Mem. ABA (chmn. standards of tax practice com., sec. taxation 1988-90), State Bar of Calif., Los Angeles County Bar Assn. (chmn. taxation sect. 1981-82), Calif. Club (L.A.), Beach Club (Santa Monica). Republican. Mem. Ch. of Christ.

BOSTAIN, NANCY S. psychologist, educator; b. Cin., Feb. 5, 1959; d. Claude Warren and Marie Gertrude Bostain; m. David Eugene Wood, June 16, 1990; m. Frank Thomas Addrisi, Dec. 5, 1981 (div. June 1985). BA, U. Cin., 1981; MS, Highlands U., 1986; PhD, Walden U., 2000. Lic. profl. counselor Colo., 1989. Psychiatric social worker Wyo. State Hosp., Evanton, Wyo., 1981—83; dir. Colo. West Regional Mental Health Ctr., Glenwood, Colo., 1984—89; substance abuse coord. Centennial Mental Health Ctr., Ft. Morgan, Colo., 1989—90; dir. Lockeed Martin, Denver, 1990—2001; orgnl. psychologist Apex Solutions, Pine, Colo., 2001—. Trustee Labors Cmty. Agy., Denver, 1991—2000. Book photographer: Cowboy & Gunfighter Collectibles, 1989. Recipient Deitweiler award, Colo. Employee Assistance Profl. Assn., 2000. Mem.: APA, Soc. Indsl. Orgn. Psychologists. Avocations: hunting, photography, camping, ATV riding. E-mail: nbostain@earthlink.net.

BOSTED, DOROTHY STACK, public relations executive; b. Newark, Apr. 6, 1953; d. Richard Joseph and Dorothy Marie (Irvin) Stack; divorced, 2000; 1 child, Danielle Whitney. Student, Lyndon State Coll., 1971-73; BA, NYU, 1975. Reporter The Daily Advance, Succasunna, N.J., 1974-75; producer, tech. intern Manhattan Cable TV, N.Y.C., 1975; editorial asst. Calif. Sch. Employees Assn., San Jose, 1975-76; news dir., anchor UA-Columbia Cablevision, Oakland, N.J., 1977-79; dir. pub. relations Overlook Hosp., Summit, N.J., 1981-84; pres. Dorothy Bosted Pub. Relations, Harding Twp., N.J., 1984-86; dir. pub. relations, communications Middlesex County Coll., Edison, N.J., 1986-88; mgr. corp. communications Hoechst Celanese Corp., Bridgewater, N.J., 1988-89. Ptnr. Bosted-Burton Assocs., Plantation, Fla., 1986—; cons. Plantation, 1986—. Co-author: Writing with Impact, 1986; contbr. articles to N.Y. Times, various mags. Seminar leader Kinnelon (N.J.) Enrichment Program, 1978; trustee Middlesex County Coll. Found., Edison, N.J., 1986-88; bd. dirs. Middlesex County Coll. Alumni Assn., 1986-88. Recipient News Program ACE award Nat. Cable TV Assn., 1979, Spectrum of Talent merit award Internat. Assn. Bus. Communicators, 1982, Percy award N.J. Hosp. Mktg. and Pub. Relations Assn., 1982, 84, Tribute to Women and Industry award YWCA, Ridgewood, N.J., 1979; Mennen Co. scholar, 1971, Neighborhood House scholar, 1971, KP scholar, 1971. Mem. Tribute to Women and Industry Mgmt. Forum (v.p. pub. rels. Ridgewood chpt. 1986-87, bd. dirs. cen. N.J. chpt. 1989-91), Pub. Rels. Soc. Am. (editor N.J. chpt. newsletter 1987-89, bd. dirs. N.J. chpt. 1989-91). Home: 485 N Pine Island Rd #204A Plantation FL 33324-1378 E-mail: dbosted@aol.com.

BOSTER, DAVIS EUGENE, retired ambassador; b. Rio Grande, Ohio, Sept. 14, 1920; s. Ernest Gordon and Nelle (Davis) B.; m. Mary Elizabeth Shilts, 1942 (div. 1977), m. Constanza Helena Gamero, 1978 (div. 1986); children: Davis, Janis, James, Thomas, Barbara, Valerie. AB, Mt. Union Coll., 1942, LLD, 1977. Newspaper reporter Canton Repository, 1939-42; polit. officer U.S. Embassy, Moscow, 1947-49; fgn. affairs specialist U.S. Dept. State, 1949-54; polit. officer U.S. Embassy, Bonn, Germany, 1954-58; staff asst. Sec. State, Washington, 1958-59; officer in charge Soviet Union Polit. Affairs State Dept., 1959—62; assigned to State Dept. Sr. Seminar Sec. State, 1962; polit. officer U.S. Embassy, Mexico City, 1962-63; spl. asst. Asst. Sec. Inter-Am. Affairs U.S. Dept. State, 1964-65, spl. asst. to Under Sec. Econ. Affairs, 1965; polit. counselor U.S. Embassy, Moscow, 1965-67, dept. chief misson Kathmandu, Nepal, 1967-70, Warsaw, 1970-73; head U.S. Del. European Security Conf., Geneva, 1973-74; U.S. amb. Bangladesh, 1974-76; U.S. amb. Guatemala, 1976—79; dir. Radio Liberty, Munich, 1979-80; internat. rels. officer U.S. Dept. State, 1980-81. Career min., 1977; active in Japanese Peace Conf., San Francisco, 1951. With USN, 1942-47, ret. comdr. USNR. Recipient Order of Quetzal for Disting. Svc. Guatemalan Govt., 1978. Home: 1600 N Oak St Apt 912 Arlington VA 22209-2755

BOSTETTER, MARTIN V. B., JR., bankruptcy court judge; b. Balt., Mar. 11, 1926; s. Martin V.B. Bostetter and Louella Jane (Smith) Rice; m. Joanne Rushworth, March 28, 1955; children: Martin III, David W., Jonathan A., Lisa A. BA, U. Va., 1950, LLD, 1952. Bar: Va. 1952, Md. 1953, D.C. 1962. City prosecutor City of Alexandria, Va., 1953-57; chief judge U.S. Bankruptcy Ct. for Ea. Dist. Va., Alexandria, 1985-99. Bd. dirs. Fed. Jud. Ctr., Washington, 1984-87, chmn. edn. com. for all bankruptcy judges, Washington, 1986-89; mem. Fed. State Jud. Rels. Com. of Commonwealth of Va.; chmn. Juvenile Detention Com., Alexandria, 1957-74. Recipient Distinguished Svc. awd. Jr. C.of C., Alexandria, 1959; U.S. Courthouse named Martin V.B. Bostetter U.S. Courthouse by act of Congress, Alexandria, Va., 1998. Office: 200 N Fairfax St Alexandria VA 22314

BOSTIC, JEFF Q. child psychiatrist; b. Ft. Worth, Mar. 6, 1957; s. Foy Danny Bostic and Roseann Crawford; m. Robin Roberts; children: Loren, Basie. MD, EdD, Texas Tech., 1991. Sch. psychiatrist Mass. Gen. Hosp., Boston, 1996—.

BOSTIC, MARY JONES, librarian; b. Durham, N.C., June 20, 1939; d. Isaac William and Jennie Mae (Edwards) Jones; m. Charles Thomas Bostic Sr., Aug. 4, 1970; 1 child, Precious Jennifer. BA, N.C. Ctrl. U., 1964, MLS, 1969; MS, L.I. U., 1975, cert. advanced studies, 1980. Sec. Randolph County Home Econs. Agt., Asheboro, N.C., 1958-60; adminstrv. asst. chief libr. N.C. Ctrl. U., Durham, 1964-69; asst acquisitions libr. L.I. U., Bklyn., 1969-75, acquisitions libr., 1975—. Contbr. articles to profl. jours. Active Coun. Bd. #13, Queens, 1975—. Mem. Assn. Coll. and Rsch. Librs., N.Y. Tech. Svcs. Librs., N.C. Libr. Assn., N.C. Ctrl. U. Sch. Lib. Sci. Alumni Assn., Palmer Grad. Libr. Sch. Alumni Assn., L.I. U. Faculty Fedn., Beta Phi Mu (Beta Mu chpt.), United Block Assn., Dem. Club (Queens). Presbyterian. Avocations: reading, writing, theater, bowling, walking. Home: 10416 198th St Jamaica NY 11412-1216 Office: Long Island Univ 1 University Plz Brooklyn NY 11201-5372 E-mail: mbostic@liu.edu.

BOSTIC, RONALD DAVID, music educator; b. Atlanta, Aug. 26, 1949; s. Lester Owen and Grace (O'Farrell) Bostic; m. Polly Ann Thomas, June 27, 1971; children: Christopher, Benjamin, Kathryn. MusB, Stetson U., 1971; MusM, Fla. State U., 1973; Mus D, Southwestern Bapt. Theol. Sem., 1976. Asst. prof. of ch. music Golden Gate Bapt. Theol. Sem., Mill Valley, Calif., 1976—78; prof. of music Wingate U., NC, 1978—. Pres. Wingate Elem. Sch. Adv. Bd., 1994—95, Forest Hills Athletic Boosters, Marshville, NC, 1999; vice pres. Wingate Cmty Recreation, 1995. Mem.: Coll. Music Soc., Music Educators Nat. Conf., Am. Choral Dir. Assn. Democrat. Baptist. Avocation: golf. Office: Wingate U Campus Box 3059 Wingate NC 28174 E-mail: robost@Wingate.edu.

BOSTICK, CHARLES DENT, retired lawyer, educator; b. Gainesville, Ga., Dec. 28, 1931; s. Jared Sullivan and Charlotte Catherine (Dent) B.; m. Susan Oliver, Sept. 8, 1956; children: Susan, Alan. Student, Emory-at-Oxford U., 1948-49; BA, Mercer U., 1952, JD, 1958. Bar: Ga. 1957, Tenn. 1974, U.S. Dist. Ct. (no. dist.) Ga. 1958, U.S. Ct. Appeals (5th cir.) 1959. Pvt. practice, Gainesville, Ga., 1958-66; asst. prof. law U. Fla., Gainesville, 1966-68, assoc. prof., 1968, Vanderbilt U., Nashville, 1968-71, prof., 1971-92, assoc. dean, dir. admissions, 1975-79, acting dean, 1979-80, dean, 1980-85; ret., 1992. Vis. prof. law U. Leeds, Eng., 1985-86, prof. law emeritus, dean emeritus Sch. Law, 1992. Served to lt. USNR, 1952-55. Mem. Tenn. Bar. Assn. Episcopalian. Office: Vanderbilt U Sch Law 21st Ave S Nashville TN 37240-0001

BOSTIN, MARVIN JAY, hospital and health services consultant; b. Toronto, July 3, 1933; came to U.S., 1956; s. Samuel and Rose (Mandel) B.; 1 child, Shepard Craig. BS, U. Toronto, 1955; MS in Hosp. Adminstrn., Columbia U., 1958; PhD in Pub. Adminstrn., NYU, 1972. Pharmacist New Mt. Sinai Hosp., Toronto, 1953-56; asst. adminstr. L.I. Jewish Hosp., New Hyde Park, N.Y., 1958-62; assoc. dir. Mt. Sinai Med. Ctr., Miami Beach, Fla., 1962-65; exec. v.p. E.D. Rosenfeld Assocs. Inc., hosp. and health svcs. cons., White Plains, N.Y., 1965-78; pres. M. Bostin Assocs., Inc., Stamford, Conn., 1979—. Guest scholar Brookings Instn., Washington, 1965; lectr. Sch. Pub. Health and Adminstrv. Medicine, Columbia U., N.Y.C., 1965-78, Grad. Sch. Pub. Adminstrn., 1967; lectr. Grad. Sch. Architecture and Planning, Columbia U., 1975-78; cons. to Bur. of Hearings and Appeals, Social Security Adminstrn., HEW, 1967-68; cons. task force on guidelines for constrn. and equipment of hosp. and med. facilities, USPHS, DHHS, 1987; mem. implementation work group on improving health Nat. Commn. on Children, 1992; spl. cons. to Office of Equal Health Opportunity, Office of Surgeon Gen., USPHS, 1966-67. Mem. Dade County (Fla.) Welfare Planning Coun., Miami, 1962-65; bd. dirs. South Fla. Hosp. Coun., Miami, 1963-65. Gottlieb Meml. scholar. Fellow APHA, Royal Soc. Health (London), Am. Assn. Healthcare Cons. (chmn. monograph series com. 1970-71, exec. com. 1972-75, profl. standards com. 1974-76); mem. Am. Hosp. Assn., Forum for Health Care Planning (dir. 1982-95, treas. 1988-89, sec. 1989-90), Am. Coll. Healthcare Execs., Can. Coll. Health Svc. Execs. (fgn. affiliate), Internat. Hosp. Fedn. Address: M Bostin Assoc Inc 800 Summer St Ste 315 Stamford CT 06901-1023 E-mail: marvin@bostin.com.

BOSTOCK, ROY JACKSON, advertising agency executive; b. Glen Ridge, N.J., Sept. 25, 1940; s. James Franklin Bostock and Jane (Ritter) Bostock Addis; m. Merilee Huser, 1962; children: Victoria, Matthew, Kate. AB, Duke U., 1962; MBA, Harvard U., 1964. Asst. account exec. Benton & Bowles, N.Y.C., 1964-66, account exec., 1966-68, account supr., v.p., 1968-70, sr. v.p., from 1970, group exec., 1976-81, exec. v.p., gen. mgr., 1981-84; pres. Benton & Bowles, Inc., N.Y.C., 1984-85, D'Arcy Masius Benton & Bowles, Inc., N.Y.C., 1985-88, pres., COO, 1988-89, pres., CEO, from 1989, chmn., CEO, 1990-96, BCom3/McManus Group, N.Y.C., 1996—. Mem. Am. Assn. Advt. Agys., Phi Beta Kappa. Clubs: Apawamis (Rye, N.Y.); Manursing Island (Rye) (pres. 1983-85); Racquet & Tennis (N.Y.C.). Republican. Presbyterian. Home: S Manursing Island Rye NY 10580 Office: BCom 3/MacManus Group 1675 Broadway Fl 2R New York NY 10019-5820

BOSTON, BETTY LEE, investment company executive, financial consultant, financial planner; b. Agana, Guam, Dec. 21, 1935; d. Homer Laurence and Bessie Margarete (Leech) Litzenberg; m. Filibert Roth Boston, Aug. 12, 1956; children: William Litzenberg, Beth Boston Tedesco, Brent Litzenberg. BA, U. Mich., 1958. CFP®. Stockbroker I.M. Simon & Co., Murray, Ky., 1976—78, 1st of Mich. Corp., Murray, Ky., 1978—86; fin. cons. J.J.B. Hilliard, W.L. Lyons, Inc., Murray, Ky., 1986—; v.p. Hilliard Lyons Inc., Murray, Ky., 1998—. Instr. adult edn. investment classes Murray State U., 1977—2000; investment commentator Sta. WKMS, Murray, 1987—. Fin. columnist Murray Ledger and Times, 2000—. Chmn. Inter-Faith Coalition Congregations, Ann Arbor, 1971-73; pres. Need Line Ch. and Cmty. Ministry, Murray, 1981-83; mem. Murray regional bd. Ky. Coun. on Econ. Edn., 1987—. Recipient Woman of Yr. award Murray Bus. and Profl. Women, 1988. Mem. AAUW (treas. Murray br. 1982-87, pres. 1991-97), Rotary (sec. Murray club 1990-95, pres. 1998-99, Paul Harris fellow). United Methodist. Home: 917 N 16th St Murray KY 42071-1523 Office: JJB Hilliard WL Lyons Inc 414 Main St Murray KY 42071-2059

BOSTON, BILLIE, costume designer, costume history educator; b. Oklahoma City, Sept. 22, 1939; d. William Barrett and Margaret Emeline (Townsend) Long; m. William Clayton Boston, Jr., Jan. 20, 1962; children: Kathryn Gray, William Clayton III. BFA, U. Okla., 1961, MFA, 1962. Asst. to designer Karinski of N.Y., N.Y.C., 1966-67; prof. costume history Oklahoma City U., 1987—. Rep. Arts Coun., Oklahoma City, 1987-90, Arts Festival, Oklahoma City, 1972-80; dir. ETC Theater, Oklahoma City SW Coll., 1979-83; actress Lyric Theatre, Oklahoma City, 1979-81; designer Casa Mahara Theatre, Ft. Worth, 1998. Exhibited in group shows at Taos, N.Mex., Santa Fe; represented in permanent collections in Dallas, Taos, Santa Fe, Tulsa, N.Y.C., La Jolla; costume designer Ballet Okla., Oklahoma City, 1979-84, Agnes DeMillie's Rodeo Ballet Okla., 1982, Royal Ballet Flanders, 1983, Pitts. Ballet, 1983, BBC's Childrens Prodn., 1984, 86, Lyric Theatre, Oklahoma City, 1987-95, Red Oak Music Theatre, Lakewood, N.J., 1988, Winter Olympics, 1988, Miss Am. Pageant, 1988, for JoAnne Worley in Hello Dolly, San Francisco Opera Circus, 1991, Jupiter (Fla.) Theatre, 1991-92, Mobile (Ala.) Light Opera, 1992, The Boy Friend, Temple U., Japan, 1995, The Sound of Music, Lyric Stage, Dallas, 1995, Annie Get Your Gun, Guys and Dolls with Vic Damone, 1995, Westbury Flash Valley Forge Music Fair, Oklahoma and Sound of Music, Casa Manana, Theatre, Ft. Worth, 1997, Singing in the Rain, Lone Star Theatre, Galveston, Tex., 1997, Most Happy Fellow, Lyric Stage Dallas, 1997, To Gillian on her 37th Birthday, Watertower Theatre, Dallas, 1998, Carousel, Annie Get Your Gun, Cinderella, Casa Manana, 1998; designer Titanic, Irving, Tex., 2003, Specture Bridegroom, Irving, 2003. Rep. Speakers Bur. Oklahoma City for Ballet, 1979-85; judge State Hist. Speech Tournament, Oklahoma City, 1985-87; chmn. State of Okla. Conf. on Tchr./Student Relationships, Oklahoma City, 1981. Recipient Gov.'s Achievement award, 1988, Lady in the News award, 1987; Excellence in Costume Design award Kennedy Ctr. Am. Coll. Theatre Festival XXXIV, 2001. Mem. Alpha Chi Omega (house corp. bd. 1986-90). Methodist. Avocation: watercolorist. Home: 1701 Camden Way Oklahoma City OK 73116-5121

BOSTON, BRUCE DAVID, writer, book designer; b. Chgo., July 16, 1943; s. John Edmund Boston and Lillian Rosen; m. Margaret Ballif Simon, Apr. 7, 2001. MA, U. Calif., Berkeley, 1967. Assoc. prof. creative writing John F. Kennedy U., Orinda, Calif., 1980—84. Author: (fiction collection) Jackbird, 1976, She Comes When You're Leaving, 1982, Skin Trades, 1988, Houses, 1990, Night Eyes, 1990, Hypertales & Metafictions, 1993, Dark Tales & Light, 1999, (novelette) After Magic, 1990, (prose poem collection) Short Circuits, 1991, (poetry collection) All the Clocks Are Melting, 1984, Alchemical Texts, 1985, Nuclear Futures, 1985, Time, 1985, The Nightmare Collector, 1985, Faces of the Beast, 1990, Cybertexts, 1991, Chronicles of the Mutant Rain Forest, 1992, Accursed Wives, 1993, Specula, 1993, Sensuous Debris, 1995 (Dragon's Breath Award - Best Genre Poetry Collection, 1996), Conditions of Sentient Life, 1996, Cold Tomorrows, 1998, White Space, 2001, Pavane for a Cyber-Princess, 2001 (Rhysling Award - 2nd Pl. - Best Long Sci. Fiction Poem - Sci. Fiction Poetry Assn., 2002), Quanta: Award-Winning Poems, 2001, Night Smoke, 2002, Head Full of Strange, 2003, (long narrative poem) She Was There for Him the Last Time, 2002, (novel) Stained Glass Rain, 1993, (fiction and poetry collection) The Complete Accursed Wives, 2000, Masque of Dreams, 2001. Recipient Pushcart prize for Fiction, 1976, Asimov's Readers' Choice award for poetry, 1989, 1993, 1997, 2002, Best of Soft SF award, 1993. Mem.: Horror Writers Assn., Sci. Fiction Poetry Assn. (sec./treas. 1980—84, Rhysling award for Speculative Poetry 1985, 1988, 1989, 1994, 1996, 1999, 2001, Grand Master 1999), Sci. Fiction Writers of Am. (chmn. Nebula awards jury 1993). Home: 1412 NE 35th St Ocala FL 34479 Personal E-mail: bruboston@aol.com.

BOSTON, BRUCE ORMAND, writer, editor, publications consultant; b. New Castle, Pa., Aug. 11, 1940; s. John Ormand and Williamina (Loudon) B.; m. Sandra Waymer, June 8, 1963 (div. 1973); children: Aaron Clark, Nathan Waymer, Kyle Richard; m. Jean Nelson, Dec. 23, 1989. BA, Muskingum Coll., 1962; BDiv, Princeton Theol. Sem., 1968, PhD, 1973. Instr. theology St. Joseph's Coll., Phila., 1972-73; assoc. Colloquy of Reston, Va., 1973-78; pres. Wordsmith, Inc., Reston, 1976—. Publs. developer Coun. for Exceptional Children, Reston, 1973-75; asst. chief clk. com. on vets. affairs U.S. Senate, Washington, 1976; communications coun. Reston Assn., 1986-89. Author: The Sorcerer's Apprentice, 1976, (with Fortna) Testing the Gifted Child, 1976, (with Orloff) Preparing to Teach the Gifted and Talented, 2 vols., 1980, (with Cox and Daniel) Educating Able Learners, 1985, Language on a Leash, 1988, The Cutting Edge of Common Sense, 1993, Arts Education for the 21st Century American Economy, 1994, The Arts and Education: Partners in Achieving Our National Education Goals, 1995, Connections: Integrating the High School Curriculum through the Arts, 1996; editor: A Resource Manual on Educating the Gifted and Talented, 1975, Gifted and Talented: Developing Elementary and Secondary School Programs, 1975, STET! Tricks of the Trade for Writers and Editors, 1986, Perspectives on Implementation: Arts Education Standards for America's Students, 1994, Their Best Selves, 1997, Every Student a Citizen, 2000, Before It's Too Late, 2000, No Dream Denied, 2003, also numerous articles and scripts. Pres. Fairfax Farms Cmty. Assn., 1980-81; mem. Reston Task Force on Town Governance, 1988-89; lay preacher Episc. Diocese Va., 1984—; sr. warden St. Anne's Episc. Ch., Reston, 1990-92; bd. dirs. Episc. Awareness Ctr. on Handicaps, Washington, 1986-89, Cmty. Svc. Learning Ctr., Springfield, Mass., 1992-96; mem. faculty Learning in Retirement Inst., George Mason U., 1999—; docent Washington Nat. Cathedral, 2000—; gen. editor: Habits of the Heart Project, Ind. Humanities Coun., 1999-2001. Recipient Achievement award Edn. Press Assn., 1986, 91, 1st place award Editor's Forum, 1986, 2d place award, 1991, Golden Eagle awards Coun. for Internat. Non-Theatrical Events, 1977, 84; Danforth Found. fellow, 1962-64, United Presbyn. Grad. fellow, 1968, Kent fellow in religion. Mem. Washington Ind. Writers (bd. dirs. 1982-84), Rotary (bd. dirs. Reston chpt. 1988-90). Democrat. Avocation: collecting books of quotations.

BOSTON, DAVID, football player; b. Humble, Tex., Aug. 19, 1978; Attended, Ohio State U. Wide receiver Ariz. Cardinals, 1999—2003, San Diego Chargers, 2003—. Office: San Diego Chargers PO Box 609609 San Diego CA 92160-9609*

BOSTON, GRETHA, vocalist, actress; b. Crossett, AK; B of Music, N Tex. State U., Denton; vocal study with vocal tech. and coaches, John Wustman, Bill Riley. Carnegie Hall debut Mozart's Coronation Mass, 1991, concert performances Beethoven's Ninth Symphony (Carnegie Hall), Handel's Messiah (Madison, Wis. & Arlington, Tex.), roles (Operas) Carmen in Bizet's Carmen, The Mother in Menotti's The Consul, Ciesca in Puccini's Gianni Schicchi, Delilah in Saint-Saens's Samson et Delilah, Maddalena in Verdi's Rigoletto (N.Y. Grand Opera), Amneris in Verdi's Aida, Azucena in Verdi's Il Trovatore, Queenie in Kern & Hammerstein's Show Boat (Tony award Best Supporting Actress in a Musical, 1995), Maria & Strawberry Woman in Gershwin's Porgy and Bess, 1993, It Ain't Nothin' But The Blues, 1999 (Tony award), appeared (TV series) Law and Order, Rosie O'Donnel, David Letterman, PBS, Today Show. Recipient 3rd place D'Angelo Young Artist Internat. Competition, 1984. Address: 250 W 57th St Ste 2223 New York NY 10107-2210

BOSTON, HOLLIS BUFORD, JR., retired military officer; b. Athens, Ala., Sept. 29, 1930; s. Hollis Buford Sr. and Opie (Hargrove) B.; m. Nancy Thomas Delbridge, Dec. 27, 1955; children: Elizabeth Lynn Boston Chesnutt, James Warren, John David. BBA, Baylor U., 1958; M Polit. Sci., Auburn U., 1972. Commd. 2d lt. USAF, 1953, advanced through grades to col., 1972, ret., 1975; sr. assoc. Program Control Corp., Van Nuys, Calif., 1977-89. Author: Estate Papers of Jones Boston, 1995. Chmn. planning com. City of Montgomery, Ala., 1983; pres. Capital City Kiwanis Club, Montgomery, 1987. Mem. Natchez Trace Geneal. Soc., Smith County Tenn. Hist. Assn., Sons of the Republic of Tex., First Families Ala., Sigma Alpha Epsilon. Republican. Episcopalian. Avocation: historical research and writing. Home: 8360 Wexford Trace Montgomery AL 36117-8212

BOSTON, WILLIAM CLAYTON, lawyer; b. Hobart, Okla., Nov. 29, 1934; s. William Clayton and Dollie Jane (Gibbs) B.; m. Billie Gail Long, Jan. 20, 1962; children: Kathryn Gray, William Clayton III. BS, Okla. State U., 1958; LLB, U. Okla., 1962; LLM, NYU, 1967. Bar: Okla. 1961. Assoc. Mosteller, Fellers, Andrews, Snider & Baggett, Oklahoma City, 1962-64; ptnr. Fellers, Snider, Baggett, Blankenship & Boston, Oklahoma City, 1968-69, Andrews, Davis, Legg, Bixler, Milsten & Murrah, Oklahoma City, 1972-86; pvt. practice Boston & Boston PLLC, Oklahoma City, 1986—. Contbr. articles to profl. jours.; mem. adv. bd. The Jour. of Air Law and Commerce, 1995—. Past pres. and trustee Ballet Okla.; past v.p., bd. dirs. Oklahoma City Arts Coun.; past trustee Nichols Hills (Okla.) Methodist Ch.; past trustee, chmn. Okla. Found. for the Humanities; past trustee, vice-chmn., sec. Humanities in Okla., Inc., 1992-95. With U.S. Army, 1954-56. Mem. ABA (former chmn. subcom. on aircraft fin., former chmn. aircraft fin. and contract divsn. forum on air and space law), FBA, Internat. Bar Assn., Inter-Pacific Bar Assn., Okla. State Bar Assn., Oklahoma County Bar Assn. Home: 1701 Camden Way Oklahoma City OK 73116-5121 Office: 4005 NW Expressway St Oklahoma City OK 73116-1691

BOSTROM, ROBERT EVERETT, lawyer; b. Hartford, Conn., Nov. 20, 1952; m. Elizabeth Mitchell Leys, July 14, 1979; children: Leys, Ashley, Allison. BA, Franklin and Marshall Coll., 1974; M in Internat. Affairs, Columbia U., 1976; JD cum laude, Boston Coll., 1980. Bar: N.Y. 1981, U.S. Dist. Ct. (ea., so. dist.) N.Y. Atty. Fed. Res. Bank, N.Y.C., 1980-82; assoc. Windels, Marx, Davies & Ives, 1982-84, Brown & Wood, N.Y.C., 1984—; mng. ptnr., head fin. instns. practice. Exec. v.p. legal and regulatory affairs, gen. counsel Nat. Westminster Bancorp, 1992-96; mem. bd. advisors Mergers and Acquistions SNL Securities, 1994—; lectr., moderator, spkr., and chairperson in field; co-chmn. Strategic Rsch. Inst. Capital Markets Activities of Interant. Banks, 1994, 95. Contbr. articles to profl jours. and mags; editor-in-chief: Boston Coll. Internat. and Comparative Law Review, 1979-80; co-editor: Internat. Practioner's Notebook, 1988-93. Mem. Internat. Lawyers Assn. (exec. com. Am. br. 1992-94), ABA, N.Y. County Lawyers Assn. (banking com.). E-mail: rbostrom@winston.com.

BOSTWICK, GEORGE WALLACE, family practice physician, geriatrician; b. New Haven, June 6, 1927; s. Wallace Robert and Eunice Ellen (Clapp) B.; m. Anne Goodspeed, June 22, 1952 (dec. Jan. 1977); m. Mary Ann Coombs, Dec. 3, 1977; children: Stephen (dec.), Richard, William, Elisabeth, Nanette L., Matthew C. BA, Yale U., 1950, MD, 1954. Diplomate in family practice and geriatric medicine Am. Bd. Family Practice. Pvt. practice, Newcastle, Maine, 1956-80, Bangor, Maine, 1980—; chief family practice svc. Ea. Maine Med. Ctr., Bangor, 1988-96; med. dir. Ross Manor Nursing Facility, Bangor, 1991—, Bangor Area Vis. Nurses, 1988—, Treats Falls House, Orono, Maine, 1983 ; pvt. practice Bangor. With USNR, 1945-47. Mem. AMA, Am. Acad. Family Physicians, Am. Soc. Anaesthesiologists, Am. Med. Dirs. Assn., Maine Med. Assn. (pres. 1981-82). Office: Ea Maine Med Ctr Employee Health Office 489 State St Bangor ME 04401-6616

BOSTWICK, JAMES STEPHEN, lawyer; b. Pasadena, Calif., Jan. 15, 1943; s. Jack Raymond and Rhoda Loraine (Fox) B.; children from a previous marriage: Brenton Reid, Grant Evan, Blake Powell; m. Marti Philips; children: Taylor, Carter. MS, U. Wash., 1965; JD, Hastings Coll. Law, 1968. Bar: Calif. 1968, Hawaii 1981. Pvt. practice, San Francisco, 1968; assoc. Walkup, Downing, Sterns & Poore, 1968-73; ptnr. Walkup, Downing & Sterns, 1973-77, Sterns, Bostwick & Tehin, 1977-79; sr. ptnr. Bostwick & Tehin, 1979-96, Bostwick & Assocs., 1996—. Faculty Coll. Advocacy, 1976—, Hastings seminar on trial practice; lectr. in field. Recipient Trial Achievement award San Francisco Trial Lawyers Assn., 1979, Presidential Award of Merit, CAOC. Fellow Internat. Acad. Trial Lawyers (sec. internat. rels. 1997-99, bd. dirs. 1993—, dean 2000—, v.p. 2001, pres. elect 2002, pres. 2003); mem. Consumer Attys. Calif. (Presdl. Merit award), Inner Circle Advocates (chmn. profl. liability legis. com. 1975-77, bd. dirs. 1978-85), Am. Bd. Profl. Liability Attys. (diplomate, founding mem.), Hawaii Acad. Plaintiff's Attys., San Francisco Trial Lawyers Assn. (bd. dirs., chmn. patients litigation fund com., chmn. jud. liaison com., nat. cert. com., Best Lawyer Am. personal injury litigation sect 1987—). Democrat. Office: 4 Embarcadero Ctr Ste 750 San Francisco CA 94111-4171 E-mail: james@bostwickfirm.com.

BOSTWICK, RANDELL A. retired retail food company executive; b. Niles, Ohio, Oct. 24, 1922; s. Clifton A. and May (Lloyd) B.; m. Jane Elizabeth Foster, Aug. 28, 1948; children: Suzanne Elizabeth, Sherrard, Randell A. Ed., U. Mich., Westminster Coll. Asst. traffic mgr. A&P, Youngstown, Ohio, 1948-50, asst. to div. traffic mgr. Pitts., 1952-58, div. traffic mgr., 1958-60, div. ops., 1960-69, asst. to nat. dir. ops. N.Y. hdqrs., 1969-75; pres. subs. Super Market Service Corp., Montvale, N.J., 1975-88; corp. v.p. The Gt. A & P Tea Co., 1981-88; chmn. Supermarket Service Corp., 1988-91, ret., 1992. Served to capt. Med. Service Corps U.S. Army, 1943-46, 50-52. Presbyterian. Home: 39 Dale Dr Summit NJ 07901-3104

BOSTWICK, ROBERT LEWIS, architect; b. Chardon, Ohio, Nov. 13, 1955; s. Lewis Robert and Rose Nanovic Bostwick; m. Nancy Hungerford Bostwick, Oct. 11, 1980; children: William, Emily, Thomas. BA, Bucknell U., 1978; MArch, Yale U., 1985. Registered Ohio, Conn. Designer Kohn Pedersen Fox, N.Y.C.; sr. assoc. Cesar Pelli & Assocs., New Haven; prin. for design Collins Gordon Bostwick Arch., Cleve. Bd. dirs. Nature Ctr. Shaker Lns., Shaker Heights, Ohio, Spaces Art Gallery, Cleve.; bd. trustees CMA Contemporary Art Soc., Cleve., 2001—. Editor: (jour.) Perspecta: The Yale Jour. Arch., 1986. Recipient William Wirt Winchester fellowship, Yale U., 1985. Mem.: City Club Cleve. Office: Collins Gordon Bostwick Archs 2729 Prospect Ave Cleveland OH 44115 Office Fax: 216-621-4632.

BOSTWICK, ROBERT OTIS, municipal staff member; b. Mobile, Ala., Apr. 9, 1946; B, U. South Ala., 1967. Supr. Texaco Oil, Mobile, 1979-83; v.p. Midtown Restaurant Corp., Mobile, 1983-85; v.p., CEO, Signs Now, Mobile, 1985-87; v.p., dir. franchising CHECKERS Drive-In Restaurants, Mobile, 1987-89; exec. asst. to mayor Mobile, 1989—. Office: Office of the Mayor Govt Plaza 205 Government St Mobile AL 36602-2613

BOSTWICK, TODD WILLIAM, city archaeologist; b. Seattle, Dec. 18, 1952; s. Michael and Roxie Marilynn (Byers) B.; m. Heidi Bostwick. BA, U. Nev., Reno, 1979; MA, Ariz. State U., 1985; PhD, Ariz. State Univ., 2003. Rsch. asst. Nev. Archaeol. Survey, Reno, 1977; archaeol. technician U.S. Forest Svc., Plumas Nat. Forest, Calif., 1978; asst. crew chief Black Mesa project So. Ill. U., Carbondale, 1980-81; project dir. Northland Rsch., Inc., Flagstaff, Ariz., 1981-85; staff archaeologist, dept. anthropology Ariz. State U., Tempe, 1985-87; asst. city archaeologist City of Phoenix, 1987-90; city archaeologist City of Phoenix, Pueblo Grande Mus., 1990—. Adv. com. Deer Valley Rock Art Ctr., Phoenix, 1994-2000; exec. com. Ariz. Archaeol. Coun., Phoenix, 1994-97, Ariz. Archeol. Council (pres., 1998-99). Co-author: First Street and Madison: Historical Archaeology of the Second and Phoenix Chinatown, 1992, Landscape of the Spirits: Hohokan Rock Art at South Mountain Park, 2002; co-editor, co-author 3 books; contbr. articles to profl. jours. Bd. dirs. Ariz. Preservation Found., Phoenix, 1991-96, Pioneer Cemetery Assn., Phoenix, 1993—. With USAF, 1972-74. Recipient Gov.'s awards in hist. preservation State of Ariz., 1996, Spl. Recognition award State of Ariz., 1995, City Mgr.'s Excellence award City of Phoenix, 1996, others. Mem. Soc. for Am. Archaeology, Ariz. Archaeol. Soc., Ariz. Archaeol. and Hist. Soc., Sigma Xi. Democrat. Avocations: photography, hiking. Office: Pueblo Grande Mus 4619 E Washington St Phoenix AZ 85034-1909 E-mail: todd.bostwick@phoenix.gov.

BOSWELL, DAN ALAN, health maintenance organization executive, health care consultant; b. Upland, Calif., July 25, 1947; s. Paul Leslie and Jana Delores Boswell; m. Lona Kathalene Bentley, Dec. 26, 1969; children: Bethanie Laurel, Daniel Alan II. Grad. in Mktg. and Sales Mgmt., UCLA. Mktg. dir. Maxicare Co., L.A., 1974-78; v.p. Gen. Med, Santa Ana, Calif., 1978-81; exec. v.p. IMC Health Maintenance Orgn., Miami, Fla., 1981-83, Protective Health Providers, San Diego, 1981-83; CEO U.S. Health Plan, San Diego, 1982-84; pres., CEO Serra Health Plan, Sun Valley, Calif., 1984-85, Amerimed (formerly Serra Health Plan), Burbank, Calif., 1985; pres. The Wellstarr Group, Inc., Upland, Calif., 1986-89, pres., CEO, 1990-93, Humantics Managed Care Corp., 1989-92; pres. The Garvey Group, Calif., Upland, 1993-97, Managed Care Specialists, Upland, 1993-97; nat. dir. corp. devel. Axiom Inc., Canoga Park, Calif., 1997-99; pres., CEO AmexUS, Upland, 1999—. Faculty fellow Nat. HMO George Washington U., 1982-83; tech. asst. expert market devel., fed. rev. health maintenance qualification HHS, Rockville, Md., 1982-84. Mem. governing body Healthsys. Agy., San Diego and Imperial Counties, Calif., 1981-85, pres. trauma task force, San Diego, 1984; mem. adv. bd. Calif. Med. Asst. Commn., San Fernando Valley, 1986; dist. dir. Pony Baseball, Inc.; mgr. Upland Black Am. Legion Baseball, 1992-94. Mem. Am. Mgmt. Assn., Am. Mktg. Assn., Group Health Assn. Am., Marine Corps Assn. Am., El Prado Men's Club (Chino, Calif.; bd. dirs. 1985-86), Sierra Laverne Country Club, Towns Club (Pomona, Calif.). Republican. Avocations: golf, writing, cooking, camping, fishing, youth sports. Office: AmexUS 188 N Central Ave Ste B Upland CA 91786-5600 E-mail: dboswell@amexus.org.

BOSWELL, GARY TAGGART, investor, former electronics company executive; b. Ft. Worth, Dec. 24, 1937; s. David W. and Marjory (Taggart) B.; m. Margaret Ruth Yelvington, Sept. 8, 1957 (dec. Jan. 1997); m. Tommie Jean Horn, Dec. 19, 1998; children: Michael David, Margaret McQuiston, Susannah Ruth. BA, Tex. Christian U., 1958, MS, 1965; postgrad., San Diego State Coll., 1960-61. Scientist U.S. Govt. White Sands (N.Mex.) Missile Range, 1958-59; rsch. engr. Gen. Dynamics, San Diego, 1959-60; programmer Bell Helicopter, Hurst, Tex., 1960-63; sect. head Collins Radio Co., Dallas, 1963-68; mgr. software devel. Tex. Instruments, Inc., Austin, 1968-72; mgr. ASC (Advanced Sci. Computer) Mktg., 1973-75, mgr. ASC divsn., 1975-76, mgr. computer sys., 1976-80, mgr. global positioning sys., 1980-81, mgr. TI engring. sys., 1981-83, v.p. equipment group, mgr. intelligent sys. divsn., 1983-86; pres. Aydin Monitor Sys., Ft. Washington, Pa., 1987-88, Aydin Computer and Monitor, Horsham, Pa., 1988-95, investor, 1995—. Mem. Am. Nat. Fortran Standards Com., 1970-74. Designer several fortran compliers. Winner Western Hemisphere Snipe championship, 1970, others. Mem. Snipe Class Internat. Racing Assn. Home and Office: 107 Clubhouse Dr Lakeway TX 78734-4608 E-mail: gtb@hilltopcafe.net.

BOSWELL, G(EORGE) HARVEY, federal judge; b. Medina, Tenn., July 8, 1947; m. Jenny Lynn Butler; one child. BS, U. Tenn., 1969; JD, U. Memphis, 1979. Pvt. practice, Milan, Tenn., 1980-83; atty. Kizer, Bonds, Boswell & Crocker, 1983-93; bankruptcy judge U.S. Bankruptcy Ct. (we. dist.), Tenn., 1993—. Fellow Tenn. Bar Found.; mem. Nat. Conf. Bankruptcy Judges, Am. Bankruptcy Inst., Tenn. Bar Assn. Office: US Bankruptcy Ct 111 S Highland Ave Ste 324 Jackson TN 38301-6107

BOSWELL, GEORGE MARION, JR., orthopedist, health care facility administrator; b. Dallas, May 12, 1920; s. George Marion and Viola (Scarbrough) B.; m. Veta M. Fuller, Oct. 30, 1958; children: Brianna Boswell Brown, Kama Boswell Koudelka, Maia Boswell. *Father and mother both educational administrators with postgraduate degrees. Great grandfather Prickett, surgeon in confederate army from Alabama. Grandmother, Mary Prickett Boswell was very early, strongly influential in the spread of Methodism to the north Texas area. Maternal grandfather Scarborough with some Native American ancestry was a rancher and racehorse breeder in west Texas. Married Veta Fuller Boswell, 1958. Daughters: Brianna Boswell Brown, Kama Boswell Koudelka, and Maia Boswell-Penc. Grandchildren: Hannah, Sarah and Matthew Brown; Bobby, Danny and Teddy Koudelka; Thatcher Boswell-Penc.* BS, Tex. Tech U., 1940; MD, U. Tex., Southwestern Dallas, 1950. Diplomate Am. Acad. Orthopaedic Surgery. Intern Parkland Hosp., Dallas, 1950-51; resident gen. surgeryand orthopedic surgery Parkland, Baylor and Scottish Rite Hosps., Dallas, 1951-55; practice medicine specializing in orthopedics Dallas, 1955—; v.p. med. affairs Baylor Health Care System, Dallas, 1982-86; dir. orthopaedic clin. studies Baylor U. Med. Ctr., 1995—. Owner Bee Aviation Inc., Dallas, 1968—, Boswell Realty Inc., Dallas, 1971—; lectr., cons. on health care delivery. *Active duty as line officer USNR July 1941 to September 1945. Pearl Harbor survivor. Amphibious Warfare Division. Eight combat landings, Europe-African and Pacific theaters. Received two Purple Hearts and two Fleet Admiral Commendations. Continued in inactive reserve throughout medical school and residency in Dallas area. Private practice orthopedic surgery forty years with compulsive desire to "care for the patient." Innovative surgeon who designed several new operative procedures. Private practice included 95,000 + new patient entities and 37,000 + operative procedures. Reduced private practice in 1994 and joined the orthopedic staff of Baylor University Medical Center. Professor of an endowed chair; the George M. Boswell, Jr., M.D. Chair in Orthopedic Surgery named in his honor in 1997.* Contbr. articles to profl. jours. Prof. George M. Bowell, Jr. chair in orthopaedic surgery named in his honor Baylor U. Med. Ctr. Fellow ACS; mem. AMA, Am. Acad. Orthopaedic Surgery (Key Man U.S. Congress 1980—), Am. Hosp. Assn., Tex. Hosp. Assn. (Key Man Tex. Legislature 1980—, council on hosp. staffs), Flying Physicians (pres. Tex. 1960-64). Clubs: Cresent (Dallas). Republican. Methodist. Avocations: flying, photography, fishing, saddle making. Home: 7249 Wabash Cir Dallas TX 75214-3535 Office: Baylor U Med Ctr Dept Orthopaedic Surgery 3500 Gaston Ave Dallas TX 75246-2096

BOSWELL, JAMES AURTHUR, JR., English language educator; b. Pitts., Mar. 21, 1953; s. James A. and Pauline R. B.; m. Olivia. BA summa cum laude, Slippery Rock U., 1975, MA, 1980. Ops. mgr. Hills Dept. Store, York, Pa., 1975-77; fin. trainee GE, Erie, Pa., 1977-78; mgmt. trainee Montgomery Ward, Meadville, Pa., 1978-79; educator Harrisburg (Pa.) Area C.C., 1981—. Writing lab. coord. Harrisburg C.C., 1981-88, 93—; presenter at numerous ednl. seminars and workshops, 1984—. Contbr. articles to profl. jours., poetry to mags; editor: (poetry) The World According to Siggy, 1988. Vol. instr. reading, writing, Melrose Project; instr. in report writing to high sch. engring. students; mem. United Way Com., Harrisburg; active Adult Choir, deacon Ch. Brethren. Recipient Recgnition Svc. cert. Faculty Coun., Harrisburg C.C., Gratitude award from Black Student Union mems, Nat. Instr. award of merit Internat. Assn. Automotive Svc. Ednl. Program, 1998. Mem. MLA, Pa. Assn. Devel. Educators, Nat. Coun. Tchrs. English, Mid-Atlantic Writing Ctrs. Assn., Assembly for Tchg. English Grammar. Home: 676 S 82nd St Harrisburg PA 17111-5533 Office: Harrisburg Area CC 1 Harrisburg Area CC Dr Harrisburg PA 17110

BOSWELL, LEONARD L. congressman; b. Harrison County, Mo., Jan. 10, 1934; s. Melvin and Margaret B.; m. Dody Boswell; 3 children. BA in Bus. Adminstrn., Graceland Coll., 1969. Commd. 2d lt. U.S. Army, 1956, advanced through grades to lt. col., resigned, 1976; mem. Iowa Senate, 1984-96, pres., 1993-97; mem. U.S. Ho. of Reps. from 3d Iowa dist., 1997—; mem. transp. and infrastucture com., agr. com., select copm. on intelligence, 1999—. Grain and livestock farmer Decatur County, 1976—. Past pres., bd. dirs. local Coop. Elevator, Lamoni. Decorated DFC (2), Bronze Star (2). Mem. VFW, Am. Legion, Cattleman's Assn., Lamoni Lions Club. Democrat. Office: US Ho of Reps 1427 Longworth HOB Washington DC 20515-0001 E-mail: Rep.Boswell.ia03@Mail.house.gov.*

BOSWELL, RUPERT DEAN, JR., retired academic administrator, math educator; b. Marshall County, Miss., Aug. 11, 1929; s. Rupert Dean and Mary Exyah (Ellis) B.; m. Grace Hadaway, Apr. 11, 1952; children: James Elton, Deanna Grace. BS, Miss. State U., 1950, MS, 1951; PhD, U. Ga., 1957. Grad. asst. Miss. State U., Mississippi State, 1950-51; instr. math. Reinhardt Coll., Waleska, Ga., 1951-53; grad. asst. U. Ga., Athens, 1953-56; assoc. prof. math. Miss. State U., 1957-61, prof., 1961-62; prof. math. Monmouth (Ill.) Coll., 1962-77, v.p. acad. affairs Rocky Mountain Coll., Billings, Mont., 1977-85; provost, prof. math. Upper Iowa U., Fayette, 1985-89; prof. math. Jacksonville (Ala.) State U., 1989-94. Mem.: AAUP, Math. Assn. Am. (chmn. com. on vis. lectrs. 1967—69, chmn. Ill. sect.), Am. Math. Soc., Fayette C. of C. (sec. 1985—87), Rotary (pres. Monmouth club 1972—73). Presbyterian. Home: PO Box 181 Jacksonville AL 36265-0181

BOSWELL, TOMMIE C. retired middle school educator; b. Gainesboro, Tenn., Nov. 8, 1942; d. Tommy and Ethel (Draper) Cassetty; m. Neal Stanley Boswell, Aug. 28, 1965; children: Brian Andrew, James Travis. AA, Cumberland U., Lebanon, Tenn., 1962; BS, Tenn. Technol. U., 1965; MAT, Rollins Coll., Winter Park, Fla., 1980, EdS, 1984. Cert. tchr. English, social studies; cert. adminstrv. supr. Tchr. English and social studies Beaumont Middle Sch., Kissimmee, Fla., 1965-72, tchr. social studies, 1978-89, Neptune Middle sch., Kissimmee, 1989-99; ret. Team leader 8th Grade Acad. Team "Challengers", Kissimmee, 1994—. Founding pres. Canterbury Lane Neighborhood Assn., Kissimmee, 1988; mem. N.M.S. Program Improvement Coun., Kissimmee, 1994—. Named Social Studies Tchr. of the Yr., Fla. Coun. for Social Studies, 1984, 86, 89, Outstanding Tchr. of Am. History, Joshua Stevens chpt. DAR, Kissimmee, 1982; Delta Kappa Gamma scholar, 1980. Mem. Fla. Trails Assn. Appalachian Trail Conf., Jackson County Tenn. Hist. Soc. Republican. Methodist. Avocations: geneology, reading, bottle and stamp collecting, hiking.

BOSWELL, VIVIAN NICHOLSON, protective services official; b. Brewton, Ala., Mar. 27, 1950; d. Nathaniel Irving Nicholson, Ethel Mae Nicholson; m. Leonard Boswell, Jan. 30, 1981. BA in Sociology, Stillman Coll., 1972. Correctional officer D.C. Dept. Corrections, Washington, 1973—2000. Recipient award of excellence, 9-5 Working Women's Assn., 1997, Lifetime Achievement award, 9 to 5 Working Women, 2002. Mem.: Mothers Against Drunk Driving, AARP, NAACP, Women's World Peace Family, Working Women's Assn., Am. Assn. Retired Persons, Harriet Tubman Assn., Diabetic Assn. Democrat. Baptist. Avocations: singing, art, mentoring, cooking, philantropic activities. Home: 1912 Rochelle Ave #1423 District Heights MD 20747

BOSWELL, WENDY R. finance educator, researcher; b. Santa Barbara, Calif., May 9, 1972; d. Thomas and Carolyn Hoffman; m. Steven M. Boswell, Aug. 17, 1996. BS, Calif. State U., Fresno, 1994; MS, Cornell U., 1997, PhD, 2000. Human resource asst. Regency Bank, Fresno, Calif., 1994—95; instr. Cornell U., Ithaca, NY, 1999—99; asst. prof. mgmt. Tex. A&M U., College Station, Tex., 2000—. Contbr. articles to profl. jours. Mem.: APA, Indsl. Rels. Rsch. Assn. (Hon. Mention - Best Dissertation Competition 2001), Soc. for Indsl. and Orgnl. Psychology (program com., subcom. chairperson 2001—03), Acad. of Mgmt. (program com. 1999—, Best student paper, best paper procs. 2001). Avocations: travel, reading, exercising. E-mail: wboswell@tamu.edu.

BOSWELL, WILLIAM PARET, lawyer; b. Washington, Oct. 24, 1946; s. Yates Paret and Mary Frances (Hyland) B.; m. Barbara Stelle Schroeder, Sept. 6, 1969; children: Susan Anne, Sarah Mary, Christina Catherine. BA cum laude, Cath. U., 1968; JD, U. Va., 1971. Bar: Va. 1971, D.C. 1972, U.S. Ct. Mil. Appeals 1972, U.S. Supreme Ct. 1975, Pa. 1978. Atty. Peoples Natural Gas Co., Pitts., 1978-82, asst. sec., gen. atty., 1982-85, sec., gen. counsel, 1985-88, v.p., gen. counsel, sec., 1985-99; gen. counsel Hope Gas, Inc., Pitts., 1998—99; dep. gen. counsel Consol. Natural Gas Co., Pitts., 1999-2000, Dominion Resources, Inc., Pitts., 2000; ptnr. McGuireWoods LLP, Pitts., 2000—. Mem. exec. com. Gas Industry Stds. Bd., 1994—97, chmn., 2001, N.Am. Energy Stds. Bd., 2002—03, named founding chmn. Pres. Borough Coun., Osborne, Pa., 1984-97, mayor, 1998—; bd. dirs. Mendelssohn Choir Pitts., 1986-2001, pres. 1997-98; trustee Laughlin Found., 1995—. Capt. JAGC, USAF, 1971-78, col. USAFR, 1978-98, ret. Decorated Legion of Merit; knight Order of Malta, knight Equestrian Order of Holy Sepulchre (Vatican). Mem. ABA (chair gas com. 1995-2003, chair infrastructure security com. 2003—), Pa. Bar Assn., D.C. Bar Assn., Va. Bar Assn., Am. Gas Assn. (chair regulatory com. 1996-98), Pa. Gas Assn. (chmn. 1989-90), Am. Corp. Counsel Assn. (pres. Pa. chpt. 1991-92, Excellence in Corporate Practice award 1998), Am. Soc. Corp. Secs., City Club Pitts., Army and Navy Club D.C. Republican. Roman Catholic. Avocations: reading, walking. Home: 405 Hare Ln Sewickley PA 15143-2050 Office: Dominion Tower 23 Fl 625 Liberty Ave Pittsburgh PA 15222-3142

BOSWORTH, BRUCE LEIGHTON, school administrator, educator, consultant; b. Buffalo, Mar. 22, 1942; s. John Wayman and Alice Elizabeth Rodgers; children: David, Timothy, Paul, Sheri, Skyler. BA, U. Denver, 1964; MA, U. No. Colo., 1970; EdD, Walden U., 1984. Elem. tchr. Littleton (Colo.) Pub. Schs., 1964-67, 70-81; bldg. prin. East Smoky Sch. Divsn. 54, Valleyview, Alta., Can., 1967-70; pres., tchr. St. Michael's-of-the-Mountains Sch., Littleton, 1981—. Adoption cons. hard-to-place children; ednl. cons. spl. needs children Warren United Meth. Ch. Mem. ASCD, Coun. Exceptional Children, Masons, Shriners, York Rite. Home and Office: 3500 S Lowell Blvd Apt 316 Denver CO 80236-6168 E-mail: misterb@yahoo.com.

BOSWORTH, DOUGLAS LEROY, international company executive, educator; b. Goldfield, Iowa, Oct. 15, 1939; s. Clifford Leroy and Clara (Lonning) Bosworth; m. Patricia Lee Knock, May 28, 1961; children: Douglas, Dawn. BS in Agrl. Engring, Iowa State U., 1962; MS in Agrl. Engring, U. Ill., 1964. With Deere & Co., Moline, Ill., 1959-94; pres. WorkSpan, Inc., Mahomet, Ill., 1994—2001, Ill. Tech. Ctr., Savoy, Ill., 1995-97; div. engr. disk harrows Deere & Co., Moline, Ill., 1971-76, mgr. mfg. engring., 1976-80, works mgr., 1980-85, mgr. mfg., 1985-89, engring. test mgr., 1989-94. Mem. Engring. Accreditation Commn., 1985—90; v.p. Skills, Inc.; mem. Assoc. Employers Bd., 1989—91; adj. engring. prof. U. Ill., Champaign-Urbana, 1996—. Active Am. Cancer Soc., Rock Island Unit; bd. dirs. United Med. Ctr., 1984—95; exec. com. Quad-City United Way, 1984—89. Mem.: Am. Soc. Agrl. Engrs. (chmn. Ill.-Wis. 1973—74, nat. bd. dirs. 1974—76, 1979—82, v.p. 1979—82, pres. elect 1991—92, pres. 1992—93, Engring. Achievement Young Designer award 1973), Rotary, Gamma Sigma Delta, Alpha Epsilon, Sigma Xi. Lutheran. Home and Office: WorkSpan Inc 1111 E Briarcliff Dr Mahomet IL 61853-9558 E-mail: dlbos@mchsi.com.

BOSWORTH, HAYDEN B. health psychologist; married. PhD, Penn. State U., University Park, 1992—96. Assoc. dir. Durham VAMC, NC, 1997—; assoc. rsch. prof. Duke U., 2001—. Scholar study to lower blood pressure: patient/physician intervention, 2001-2005. Office: Durham VAMC/Duke U 508 Fulton St Durham NC 27705 Office Fax: 919-416-5839. Business E-Mail: hayden.bosworth@duke.edu.

BOSWORTH, STEPHEN WARREN, ambassador; b. Grand Rapids, Mich., Dec. 4, 1939; s. Warren Charles and Mina (Phillips) B.; m. Christine Holmes, June 7, 1984; children— Andrew, Allison. AB, Dartmouth Coll., 1961; LLD, Darmouth Coll., 1986. Joined U.S. Fgn. Service; service in Panama, Colon, Madrid and Paris; dep. asst. sec. state, 1976-79; ambassador to Tunisia, 1979-81; dep. asst. sec. Inter-Am. affairs, 1981-82; dir. policy planning staff coun. U.S. Fgn. Svc., 1983-84; ambassador Manila, Philippines, 1984-87; pres. U.S.-Japan Found., 1988-96; exec. dir. Korean Energy Devel. Orgn., 1995-97; amb. to Republic of Korea Seoul, 1997-2001; dean Fletcher Sch. Law and Diplomacy, Tufts U., Medford, Mass., 2001—. Adj. prof. Columbia U., 1990-94. Trustee Dartmouth Coll., 1992-2002, chmn. bd. trustees, 1996-99. Recipient Dept. State Disting. Honor award, 1976, 86, Arthur S. Flemming award, 1976; named Diplomat of Yr., Am. Acad. Diplomacy, 1986 Office: Fletcher Sch Law and Diplomacy Tufts Univ Medford MA 02155 E-mail: stephen.bosworth@tufts.edu.

BOSWORTH, THOMAS LAWRENCE, architect, architecture educator; b. Oberlin, Ohio, June 15, 1930; s. Edward Franklin and Imogene (Rose) B.; m. Abigail Lumbard, Nov. 6, 1954 (div. Nov. 1974); children: Thomas Edward, Nathaniel David; m. Elaine R. Pedigo, Nov. 23, 1974; stepchildren: Robert Haden Pedigo, Kevin Ian Pedigo. BA, Oberlin Coll., 1952, MA, 1954; postgrad., Princeton U., 1952-53, Harvard U., 1956-57; MArch, Yale U., 1960; PhD Honoris Causa (hon.), Kobe U., Japan, 2003. Draftsman Gordon McMaster AIA, Cheshire, Conn., summer 1957-58; resident planner Tunnard & Harris Planning Cons., Newport, R.I., summer 1959; designer, field supr. Eero Saarinen & Assocs., Birmingham, Mich., 1960-61, Hamden, Conn., 1961-64; individual practice architecture Providence, 1964-68, Seattle, 1968—; asst. instr. architecture Yale U., 1962-65, vis. lectr., 1965-66; asst. prof. R.I. Sch. Design, 1964-66, asso. prof., head dept., 1966-68; prof. architecture U. Wash., Seattle, 1966-98, prof. emeritus, 1998—, chmn. dept., 1968-72; chief architecture Peace Corps Tng. Program, Tunisia, Brown U., summers 1965-66; archtl. cons., individual practice Seattle, 1972—; dir. multidisciplinary program U. Wash., Rome, Italy, 1984-86. Vis. lectr. Kobe U., Japan, Oct., 1982, Nov., 1990, Apr., 1993, May, 1995, June, 1998; Pietro Belluschi Disting. Vis. Prof. U. Oreg., 1996; dir. arch. in Rome program U. Wash., Rome, 1996. Bd. dirs. N.W. Inst. Arch. and Urban Studies, Italy, 1983-90, pres., 1983-85; dir. Pilchuck Glass Sch., Seattle, 1977-80, trustee, 1980-91, adv. coun., 1993—; mem. Seattle Model Cities Land Use Rev. Bd., 1969-70, Tech. Com. Site Selection Wash. Multi-Purpose Stadium, 1970, Medina Planning Commn., 1972-74, steering adv. com. King County Stadium, 1972-74, others; chmn. King County (Wash.) Environ. Devel. Commn., 1972-74, King County Policy Devel. Commn., 1974-77; bd. dirs. Arcade Mag., 1988-2002, pres. 1988-2000; bd. mgrs. YMCA Camping Svcs., 1998-2002; adv. bd. U. Wash Rome Ctr., 1999—. With U.S. Army, 1954-56. Winchester Traveling fellow Greece, 1960; assoc. fellow Ezra Stiles Coll. Yale U.; mid-career fellow in arch. Am. Acad. in Rome, 1980-81, vis. scholar, Spring 1988. Fellow AIA (Seattle medal 2003); mem. Monday Club (Seattle), Bohemian Club (San Francisco), Tau Sigma Delta. Home: 2411 25th Ave E Seattle WA 98112-2610 Office: U Wash Dept Architecture PO Box 355720 Seattle WA 98195-5720

BOSWORTH, WILLIAM POSEY, physician, physical education educator; b. Valdosta, Ga., Mar. 23, 1935; s. Paul Brooks and Myra Mae (Posey) B.; m. Wanda Marie Grimm; 1 child, Lynne Marie. BS, U. Tampa, 1957; MEd, Springfield (Mass.) Coll., 1961; postgrad., Orlando (Fla.) Jr. Coll., 1968; DO, U. Health Scis., Kansas City, Mo., 1972. Phys. edn. tchr., jr. high sch. tchr. Duval County Sch. Bd., Jacksonville, Fla., 1959—62; intern U.S. Naval Hosp., Phila., 1972—73; gen. practice medicine Jacksonville, 1974—. Physician athletic team, 1975—. Mem. Duval County Sch. Bd., Jacksonville, 1986—90, Jacksonville Sports Com., 1981—86, chmn., 1986; mem. Duval County Hosp. Authority, 1982—86, chmn., 1986; mem. Fla. Gov.'s Coun. on Phys. Fitness and Sports, 1985—93, Fla. Sunshine State Games Found., 1990—99, Sports in Fla. Found., 2000—. With USMCR, 1953—58, with USNR, 1969—99, capt. M.C., 1988—. Decorated Navy Commendation medals (2), Meritorious Svc. medal; named Gen. Practitioner of Yr., Fla. Soc. Am. Coll. Family Physicians, 1982, Health Educator of the Yr., Duval County Coalition Against Tobacco, 1991; recipient Physician's Recognition award, AMA, 1988, 1991, 1994, 1997, 1999, 2002, Vol. Svc. 35 yr. gold pin award, AAU/USA, 1988. Mem.: PTA (hon. life), Freedoms Found. at Valley Forge (pres. Jacksonville chpt. 1995—97), Assn. Mil. Surgeons U.S., Duval County Acad. Family Physicians (pres. 1984), Duval County Med. Soc., Fla. Soc. Sons of Am. Revolution (pres. 1980, 2000, Meritorious Svc. medal 1986, Disting. Svc. medal 2001), Fla. Med. Assn., Rotary Club of San Jose (charter), Am. Legion 40/8 Honor Soc. (Voyageur of Yr. 1990). Office: 5743 San Jose Blvd Jacksonville FL 32257-4402

BOT, ADRIAN ION, immunologist; b. Teregova, Romania, June 4, 1968; came to U.S., 1994; s. Vasile and Calina B.; m. Simona Rodica, Sept. 2, 1994; 1 child, Celine. MD, U. Medicine, Timisoara, Romania, 1993; PhD, Mt. Sinai Sch. Medicine, 1998. Prin. scientist, group leader autoimmunity/vaccination dept. Alliance Pharm. Corp., San Diego, 1999—. Guest scientist Scripps Rsch. Inst., La Jolla, Calif., 1998-99; cons. in field. Contbr. articles to profl. jours.; inventor in field. Rsch. fellow Alliance Pharm. Corp., 1998-99. Mem. AAAS, Am. Assn. Immunologists, Am. Soc. Microbiology, PhD Alumni Assn. CUNY. Avocations: philosophy, physics, skiing, tennis. Office: Alliance Pharm Corp 3030 Sci Park Rd San Diego CA 92121

BOTELHO, BRUCE MANUEL, former state attorney general, mayor; b. Juneau, Alaska, Oct. 6, 1948; s. Emmett Manuel and Harriet Iowa (Tieszen) Botelho; m. Guadalupe Alvarez Breton, Sept. 23, 1988; children: Alejandro Manuel, Adriana Regina. Student, U. Heidelberg, Federal Republic of Germany, 1970; BA, Willamette U., 1971, JD, 1976. Bar: Alaska 1976, U.S. Ct. Appeals (9th cir.) 1976, U.S. Supreme Ct. 1979. Asst. atty. gen. State of Alaska, Juneau, 1976—83, 1987—89, dep. commr., acting commr. Dept. of Revenue, 1983-86; mayor City, Borough of Juneau, 1988—91, dep. atty. gen., 1991—94; atty. gen. State of Alaska, 1994—2002. Chmn. Alaska Resources Corp., 1984—86; exec. com. Conf. of Western Attys. Gen., 1997—2002. Editor: Willamette Law Jour., 1975—76; contbr. articles to profl. jours. Pres. Juneau Human Rights Commn., 1978—80, Alaska Coun. Am. Youth Hostels, 1979—81, Juneau Arts and Humanities Coun., 1981—83; pres. S.E. Alaska Area Coun. Boy Scouts Am., 1991—93, 2001—, commr. S.E. Alaska Area Coun., 1993—2000; pres. Juneau World Affairs Coun., 2000—; chmn. Gov.'s Conf. on Youth and Justice, 1995—96, Gov. Task Force on Confidentiality of Childrens Procs., 1998—2002; trustee Alaska Children's Trust, 1996—2000, Alaska Permanent Fund, 2000—02; co-chmn. Alaska Justice Assessment Commn., 1997—2002; active Commn. for Justice Across the Atlantic, 1999—; chmn. Alaska Criminal Justice Coun., 2000—02; Assembly mem. Borough of Juneau, 1983—86; bd. dirs. Found. for Social Innovations, Alaska, 1990—93, Alaska Econ. Devel. Coun., 1985—87; chmn. adminstrv. law sect. Alaska Bar Assn., 1981—82. Recipient Silver Beaver award, Boy Scouts Am., 2000. Mem.: Nat. Assn. Attys. Gen. (exec. com. 1998—). Democrat. Methodist. Avocation: dancing.

BOTEZ, DAN, physicist; b. Bucharest, Romania, May 22, 1948; s. Emil and Ecaterina (Iacob) B.; m. Lynda Diane Arnold, Sept. 25, 1976; children: Anca, Adrian. BSEE with highest honors, U. Calif., Berkeley, 1971, MSEE, 1972, PhD, 1976, U. Politechnica, Bucharest, Romania, 1995. Fellow IBM Thomas J. Watson Rsch. Ctr., Yorktown Heights, N.Y., 1976-77; tech. staff RCA David Sarnoff Rsch. Ctr., Princeton, N.J., 1977-82, rsch. leader, 1982-84; dir. device devel. Lytel Inc., Somerville, N.J., 1984-86; chief scientist TRW Electro-Optic Rsch. Ctr., Redondo Beach, Calif., 1986, lab dir., 1986-87; sr. staff scientist TRW Rsch. Ctr., Redondo Beach, Calif., 1987-93, TRW tech. fellow, 1990-93; Philip Dunham Reed prof. elec. engring. U. Wis., Madison, 1993—; founder, bd. dirs. AlfaLight Inc., Madison, 2000—. Author: Electro-Optical Communications Dictionary, 1983, Diode-Laser Arrays, 1994; contbr. over 230 articles to profl. jours.; holder 40 U.S. patents. Named Outstanding Young Engr., IEEE Lasers and Electro-Optics Soc., San Jose, 1984, recipient Key to Future award, 1984. Fellow IEEE (chmn. tech. com. on semiconductor lasers 1989-90),

Optical Soc. Am.; mem. Phi Beta Kappa. Republican. Mem. Ea. Orthodox Ch. Avocations: racquetball, travel, photography, skiing. Home: 200 N Prospect Ave Madison WI 53726-4027 Office: U Wis Dept Elec Engring 1415 Engineering Dr Madison WI 53706-1607

BOTH, ROBERT ALLEN, recording engineer, record producer; b. Montclair, N.J., Nov. 10, 1952; s. Jacob Jr. and Anna May (Mollen) B.; m. Karen Sue Cody, Mar. 2, 1987; 1 child, Michael. With Polydor Records, N.Y.C., 1971-72; rec. engr., Artist & Repertory dir. James Brown Enterprises, N.Y.C., 1972-76; staff engr. Delta Rec., N.Y.C., 1976-77, Quadrasonic Sound, N.Y.C., 1979; studio owner, engr., producer Twain Rec., West Milford, N.J., 1976—. Contbg. writer Pro Music mag., N.Y.C., 1982-83, Sound Track Mag., 1990, EQ Mag., 1997; instr. audio engring. courses Ramapo Coll. N.J., 1993—, William Paterson U., 1995—; audio instr. County Coll. Morris, N.J., 1997—. Freelance songwriter, 1978; rec. engr. with James Brown (3 Gold records); contbr. articles to various mags. Semi-finalist Am. Song Festival, 1982. Lutheran. Avocations: record collecting, guitar playing, golf, photography. Home and Office: 18 Hiawatha Pass West Milford NJ 07480-3606 E-mail: bobboth@warwick.net.

BOTHA, MARIA MAGDALENA, education educator, researcher; b. Johannesburg, S. Africa, Aug. 23, 1949; d. Frederick Jacobus and Alida Jacoba Dietz (De Villiers) B.; m. James Richard Anders, Dec. 6, 1969 (div. Feb.,1986), 1 child, Christopher; m. Johannes Jurie Botha, Dec. 7, 1991. BA, U. Pretoria, S. Africa, 1969; BEd, U. S. Africa, 1983; MEd, U. of the North, S. Africa, 1985, EdD, 1987. Libr. Pietersburg (S. Africa) Pub. Libr., 1971-73; tchr. Tech. H.S. Tom Naude, Pietersburg, 1973-75; lectr. Setotolwane (S. Africa) Tchrs.' Tng. Coll., 1975-80, head of math. dept., 1981; lectr. U. of the North, Pietersburg, South Africa, 1982-86, sr. lectr., 1986-87; edn. planner (math.) Dept. Nat. Edn., Windhoek, Namibia, 1988; from sr. lectr. to prof. Vista U., Port Elizabeth, South Africa, 1989-94, prof., 1994—, prof. dept. edn., 1997, prof. dept. postgrad. edn., 1998, dean faculty edn., 1998—. Freelance translator, S. Africa, 1986-91. Contbr. articles to profl. jours., chpt. to book. Mem. World Assn. of Ednl. Rsch., S. African Assn. for Rsch. and Devel. in Higher Edn., Edn. Assn. S. Africa. Avocations: classical music, wine. Home: PO Box 28361 Sunridge Park Ea Cape Port Elizabeth 6008 South Africa Office: Vista Univ Private Bag X613 Ea Cape Port Elizabeth 6000 South Africa

BOTHMER, DIETRICH FELIX VON, museum curator, archaeologist; b. Eisenach, Thuringia, Oct. 26, 1918; came to U.S., 1939, naturalized, 1944; s. Wilhelm Friedrich Franz Carl and Marie Julie Auguste Karoline (Freiin von und zu Egloffstein) von B.; m. Joyce de la Bégassière, May 28, 1966; children: Bernard Nicholas, Maria Elizabeth Villalba. Student, Friedrich Wilhelms U., Berlin, 1937-38, Wadham Coll., Oxford, 1938-39; diploma classical archaeology, Oxford U., 1939; PhD in Classical Archaeology, U. Calif., Berkeley, 1944; DPhil (hon.), U. Trier, 1997. Asst. curator Greek and Roman art Met. Mus. Art, 1946-51, assoc. curator, 1951-59, curator, 1959-73, chmn., 1973-90, Disting. rsch. curator, 1990—. Adj. prof. NYU, 1966— Book rev. editor: Am. Jour. Archaeology, 1950-57; assoc. editor, 1970-76; author: Amazons in Greek Art, 1957, Ancient Art from New York Private Collections, 1961, An Inquiry into the Forgery of the Etruscan Terracotta Warriors, 1961, Corpus Vasorum Antiquorum, USA fasc. 12, 1963, Greek Vase Painting: An Introduction, 1972, Corpus Vasorum Antiquorum, USA fasc. 16, 1976, Greek Art of the Aegean Islands, 1979, A Greek and Roman Treasury, 1984, The Amasis Painter and His World, 1985, Greek Vase Painting, 1987, Glories of the Past, Ancient Art from the Shelby White and Leon Levy Collection, 1990, Euphronios, Peintre á Athènes au VI siècle avant Jesus Christ, 1990. Mem. Chancellor's Ct. of Benefactors, Oxford U. With AUS, 1943-45. Decorated Bronze Star, Purple Heart; Rhodes scholar Wadham Coll., 1938-39; Internat. House fellow U. Calif., Berkeley, 1940, Alfred B. Jordan fellow, 1940-41, Univ. fellow, 1941-42; Martin Ryerson fellow U. Chgo., 1942-43; Guggenheim Meml. Found. fellow, 1966, hon. fellow Wadham Coll.; Chevalier Légion d'Honneur, 1997. Mem. Archaeol. Inst. Am. (benefactor), Soc. Promotion Hellenic Studies (hon.), Deutsches Archaeol. Inst., Vereinigung der Freunde Antiker Kunst (Basle, Switzerland), Archaeologische Gesellschaft zu Berlin, Institut de France, Académie des Inscriptions et Belles-Lettres (fgn. assoc.), Piping Rock Club. Home: 401 Centre Island Oyster Bay NY 11771-5011 Office: Met Mus Art Fifth Ave at 82nd St New York NY 10028-0198

BOTHNER-BY, AKSEL ARNOLD, chemist, horseman; b. Mpls., Apr. 29, 1921; s. Aksel Conrad and Merle Marie (von Hagen) Bothner-B.; m. Christine Treuner, Oct. 15, 1949; children: Peter Ole, Anne Sigrun. Student, U. Nanking, China, 1939; B Chemistry, U. Minn., 1943; MS, NYU, 1947; PhD, Harvard U., 1949. Scientist Brookhaven Nat. Lab., 1949-53; fellow Am. Cancer Soc., Zurich, 1952-53; instr., lectr. Harvard U., 1953-58; cons. Retina Found., 1957-58; staff fellow Mellon Inst., 1958-71, dir., 1960-61, mem. adv. com., 1962-71; prof. chemistry Carnegie-Mellon U., 1967-77, chmn. dept., 1967-70; dean Mellon Inst. Sci., 1971-75, Univ. prof., 1977—, acting head, 1987-91, Univ. prof. emeritus, 1991—. Fulbright lectr. U. Munich, Germany, 1962-63; adj. prof. U. Pitts., 1964— ; vis. prof. U. Calif. at San Diego, 1976-77; trustee MPC Corp., 1972-80; Bd. dirs. Pa. Jr. Acad. Scis., 1975-86. Author papers in field of theoretical organic chemistry. With AUS, 1943-45. Recipient Disting. Achievement award, U. Minn., 1975, IR-100 award, 1978, Pitts. award, 1988, G. Laukien award, 2002, EAS award for Achievements in Magnetic Resonance, Ea. Analytical Symposium, 2002. Mem.: Am. Soc. Biochemistry and Molecular Biology, Am. Chem. Soc., U.S. Dressage Fedn. Home: 6317 Darlington Rd Pittsburgh PA 15217-1835 Office: Mellon Inst 4400 5th Ave Pittsburgh PA 15213-2683 E-mail: ab6d@andrew.cmu.edu.

BOTHWELL, ANTHONY PEIRSON XAVIER, SR., lawyer, educator; b. Washington, Aug. 12, 1944; s. Frederick Charles Jr. and Catherine Hannon Bothwell; m. Chung Thi Nguyen, Dec. 22, 1973 (div. Nov. 1999); children: Anthony Peirson Xavier Jr., Thomas Theodore Nguyen. BS in Fgn. Svc., Georgetown U., 1966; MS, Boston U., 1968; JD, John F. Kennedy Sch. Law, 1998; LLM with highest honors, Golden Gate U., 2000. Bar: Calif. 2000, U.S. Dist. Ct. (no. dist.) Calif., U.S. Ct. Appeals D.C. 2003. Editor AP, Miami, Fla., 1970-73; comms. coord. Fla. Power and Light Co., Miami, 1973-78; cmty. rels. mgr. Wis. Power and Light Co., Madison, 1978-83; dir. pub. affairs Lawrence Livermore Nat. Lab., Livermore, Calif., 1983-85; cons. Livermore, 1985-88; tax specialist IRS, Oakland, Calif., 1988—2001; pvt. practice San Francisco, 1999—; law prof. John F. Kennedy U. Sch. Law, Walnut Creek, Calif., 2000—. Newsroom clk. The Washington Post, 1969-70; acting news dir. Radio Sta. WBRK-AM, Pittsfield, Mass., 1967; cons. Atomic Indsl. Forum, Washington, 1981-83. Contbr. studies to profl. publs.; asst. editor: Computer World, 1967-68. City campaign chmn. Jesse Jackson for Pres., Livermore, 1988; cons. policy ethics Ams. for Energy Independence, Washington, 1980-82; cons. energy ethics com. Nat. Conf. of Cath. Bishops, Washington, 1981-83; chmn. City Coun. Adv. Com. on Energy and Environment, Livermore, 1985-87; asst. to chmn. Mass. Rep. Fin. Com., 1967-68. Recipient 1st pl. award on Commemoration of 50th Anniversary of Universal Declaration of Human Rights, San Francisco chpt. UN Assn. of USA, 1999. Mem. Internat. Bar Assn., State Bar Calif., Hist. Soc. of U.S. Dist. Ct. for No. Calif., San Francisco Bay Area chpt. Nat. Lawyers Guild (exec. bd. 1995-98), Chinese for Affirmative Action, U.S. Holocaust Mus., Rotary Internat. Democrat. Avocation: philately. Office: Law Offices of Anthony P X Bothwell Ste 100 PMB 314 350 Bay St San Francisco CA 94133 E-mail: esquire001@msn.com.

BOTHWELL, JOHN CHARLES, retired archbishop; b. Toronto, June 29, 1926; s. William Alexander and Anne (Campbell) B.; m. Joan Cowan, Dec. 29, 1951; children— Michael, Timothy, Nancy, Douglas, Ann. BA with honors in Modern History, U. Toronto, 1948; BD, Trinity Coll., Toronto, 1950, DD (hon.), 1972, Huron Coll., U. Western Ont., Wycliffe Coll. U Toronto, 1989; hon. sr. fellow, Renison Coll., U. Waterloo, 1988. Ordained priest Anglican Ch., 1952; curate St. James Cathedral, Toronto, 1951-53, Christ Ch. Cathedral, Vancouver, B.C., 1953-56; rector St. Aidan's Ch., Oakville, Ont., 1956-60, St. James' Ch., Dundas, Ont., 1960-65; canon missioner Niagara Diocese, 1965-69; nat. exec. dir. Anglican Ch. Can., 1969-71; co-adjutor bishop Niagara, 1971-73; bishop Diocese of Niagara, 1973-92, archbishop, 1985-91; Met. of Ont., 1985-91; ret., 1991; chancellor Trinity Coll., U. Toronto, 1991—2003. Hon. sr. fellow Renison Coll., U. Waterloo, 1988. Co-author: Theological Education for the 70's, 1969; author: Taking Risks and Keeping Faith, 1985, Living Faith Day By Day, 1990, Old-Time Religion or Risky Faith?, 1992; contbr. articles to various newspapers. Active numerous nat. and ecumenical coms.; Dir., com. chmn. Hamilton (Ont.) Social Planning Council, 1965-69, 71-75, v.p., 1975-77, pres., 1977-79; v.p. United Way, 1982, 83, pres., 1984-86; bd. dirs. Hamilton Found., 1982, v.p., 1983, pres., 1985 Inducted into City of Hamilton (Ont., Can.) Gallery of Distinction, 1993. Anglican.

BOTHWELL, MARCELLA ROPER, pediatrician, educator, otolaryngologist; b. Springfield, Mo., Mar. 6, 1966; d. Wilbur Clarence and Marcella Lester Bothwell; m. Larry Albert Scroggins, Sept. 7, 1996; stepchildren: Joseph, Rebecca, Micah. BA, Drury U., 1988; MD, U. Mo., 1993. Diplomate Am. Bd. Otolaryngology, 2000. Intern U. Mo., 1993—94, resident in otolaryngology, 1994—98; fellow in pediat. otolaryngology Washington U., St. Louis, 1998—2000; asst. prof. Dept. Surgery U. Mo., Columbia, Mo., 2000—. Curriculum coord. U. Mo., 2000—, mem. various coms., 2000—; bd. dirs. Ears, Nose, Throat Polit. Action Com., Arlington, Va. Co-author: Pediatric Nasal and Sinus Disorders, 2003; contbr. articles to profl. jours. Grantee Outcomes Rsch. Small Project grant, 1999. Mem.: Am. Acad. Otolaryngology (mem. outcomes rsch. com., mem. pediat. otolaryngology com., com. on residents and fellows in tng. 1996—2000, chmn. com. on residents and fellows in tng. 1996—97, bd. dirs. liaison 1996—98, gov. bd. govs. 1996—97), Soc. Advances in Ear, Nose and Throat Advances in Children (mem. credentials com.), Alpha Omega Alpha. Avocations: photography, reading. Office: Univ Mo Health Care One Hospital Dr MA314 DC027 OO Columbia MO 65212 Office Fax: 573-884-4205.

BOTKIN, DANIEL BENJAMIN, biologist, environmental scientist, writer; b. Oklahoma City, Aug. 19, 1937; s. Benjamin Albert and Gertrude (Fritz) B.; m. Ellen Chase, Dec. 22, 1962 (div. 1976); children: Nancy, Jonathan; m. Erene Victoria Youngberg, Apr. 7, 1978 (dec. Mar. 1994); m. Jane M. O'brien (dec. Feb. 2002). BA, U. Rochester, 1959; MA, U. Wis., 1962; PhD, Rutgers U., 1968. From asst. to assoc. prof. Yale U., New Haven, 1968-76; assoc. scientist Marine Biol. Lab., Woods Hole, Mass., 1976-78; prof. biology U. Calif., Santa Barbara, 1978-92, chmn. environ. studies program, 1978-85; dir. program on global change biology dept. George Mason U., Fairfax, Va., 1993-97, prof. biology, 1993-99; pres. The Ctr. for the Study of the Environment, 1992—; rsch. prof. biology U. Calif., Santa Barbara, 1999—. Author: Discordant Harmonies: A New Ecology for the 21st Century, 1990, Forest Dynamics: An Ecological Model, 1993, Our Natural History: The Lessons of Lewis and Clark, 1995, Passage of Discovery: The American Rivers Guide to the Missouri River of Lewis and Clark, 1999, No Man's Garden: Thoreau and a New Vision for Civilization and Nature, 2001; (software) JABOWA, 1970, Timber: model of forest growth, 1983, 87, JABOWA-II, 1992, JABOWA-3 for Windows, 1999; co-author: Forest Succession, 1981, Environmental Studies, 1982, 87, Changing the Global Environment, 1989, Environmental Science: Earth as a Living Planet, 1995, 4th edit., 2002, The Blue Planet, 1999; contbr. articles to profl. jours., popular mags. and newspapers. Trustee Santa Barbara Bot. Garden, 1987-93; bd. dirs. Environ. Literacy Coun., Washington, 2003-. Recipient Fernow prize for Internat. Forestry, 1995, First Prize, Mitchell Internat. Prize for Sustainable Devel., 1991; named to Environ. Hall of Fame, Calif. Polytechnic U., 1995; fellow Rockefeller Bellagio (Italy) Inst., 1985, East-West Ctr., Honolulu, 1985-87, Woodrow Wilson Internat. Ctr. for Scholars, Washington, 1977-78; grantee EPA, NSF, NASA, NOAA, Mellon Found., Pew Charitable Trusts, W. Alton Jones Found., World Wildlife Fund, SOHIO Alaska Corp. Fellow AAAS; Cosmos Club, Sigma Xi (lectr. 1981-83). Avocations: aircraft piloting, photography, hiking, music. Home: 290 9th Ave Apt 20 C New York NY 10001 E-mail: dbotkin@silcom.com.

BOTKIN, JAMES W. leadership and life coach; b. Long Branch, N.J., May 15, 1943; s. Harold M. and Julia (Bishop) B.; m. Karin S. Bartow, Aug. 20, 1999; m. Rosvita Botkin; children: Alexander, Christopher. BA, Harvard U., 1965, MBA, 1968, DBA, 1973; grad., The Coaches Trng. Inst., 2003. Cert. profl. co-active coach 2003. Pres. InterClass, Cambridge, Mass., 1990—2001; fellow U. Tex., Austin, 1985—. Bd. dirs. Lancaster U., England; internat. advisor New Horizons for Learning, Seattle, 1986—; internat. recognized pub. spkr. Author (with M. Elmandjra and M. Malitza): No Limits to Learning: A Report to the Club of Rome, 1979; author: (with D. Dimancescu and R. Stata) Global Stakes: The Future of High Technology in America, 1982; author: The Innovators: Rediscovering America's Creative Energy, 0184; author: (with D. Dimancescu) The New Alliance: Industry-University Partnerships, 1986; author: (with J. Matthews) Winning Combinations: Entrepreneurial Partnerships Between Large and Small Companies, 1992; author: (with Stan Davis) The Monster Under the Bed: How Business is Mastering the Opportunities of Knowledge for Profit, 1994; author: Smart Business: How Knowledge Communities Can Revolutionize Your Company, 1999. Named Hon. Citizen, Salzburg, Austria, 1977; recipient Innovator award, Rausing Fund, Lund, Sweden, 1990, Alliance award, Carnegie Corp., N.Y.C., 1986. Mem.: ICF (Internat. Coaching Fedn.), Club of Rome. Avocations: hiking, fishing, travel. Office: 26 Grozier Rd Cambridge MA 02138-3315 E-mail: jbotkin@comcast.net.

BOTKIN, MONTY LANE, computer company executive; b. Lubbock, Tex., Mar. 26, 1951; s. Louis A. and Geneva O. (Marlin) B.; 1 child, Nicholas L.; m. Ayami Honda, Oct. 26, 1996. BA, Tex. Tech U., 1975. Supr. Tex. Instruments, Inc., Lubbock, 1976-77, Abilene, Tex., 1977-78; electronic ctr. mgr. Tex. Instruments Supply Co., Palo Alto, Calif., 1978-81; mfg. mgr. home computers Tex. Instruments, Inc., Lubbock, 1981-83, mfg. mgr. calculator, 1983-87, mfg. mgr. ednl. products, 1987-90, Semi-Conductor Grp. photolithography ops. mgr., 1990-91, total quality control mgr. Lubbock Mos Memory, 1991-93; dir. mfg. Brother Industries U.S.A., Bartlett, Tenn., 1993-96, also bd. dirs.; dir. ops. Taiwan Semiconductor Mfg. Co., San Jose, Calif., 1996-2000; v.p. and gen. mgr. LAM Rsch. Corp., 2000—02; oper. officer Fujikin Inc., 2002—; exec. v.p., mng. dir., bd. dirs. Fujikin Am., Santa Clara, Calif., 2002—. Bd. dir. Fujikin of Am., exec. v.p.; bd. dir. Carten Controls Inc. and European Ops., exec. v.p. Mem. Inst. Indsl. Engrs. (sr.), Am. Soc. for Quality Control (chmn. West Tex. sect.), Am. Prodn. and Inventory Control Soc. Avocations: racquetball, photography, golf.

BOTSAI, ELMER EUGENE, architect, architecture educator, retired dean; b. St. Louis, Feb. 1, 1928; s. Paul and Ita May (Cole) B.; m. Patricia L. Keegan, Aug. 28, 1955; children: Donald Rolf, Kurt Gregory.; m. Sharon K. Kaiser, Dec. 5, 1981; 1 dau., Kiana Michelle. AA, Sacramento Jr. Coll., 1950; AB, U. Calif., Berkeley, 1954; D of Architecture, U. Hawaii, 2000. Registered architect, Hawaii, Calif. Draftsman, then asst. to arch. So. Pacific Co., San Francisco, 1953-57; designer H.K. Ferguson Co., San Francisco, 1955; project arch. Anshen & Allen Arch., San Francisco, 1957-63; prin. Botsai, Overstreet & Rosenberg, Arch. and Planners, San Francisco, 1963—, Elmer E. Botsai FAIA, Honolulu, 1979—; of counsel Groupe 70 Internat., 1998—; chmn. dept. arch. U. Hawaii, Manoa, 1976-80, dean Sch. Arch., 1980-90, prof., 1990-99, prof. emeritus, 2000—. Lectr. U. Calif., Berkeley, 1976, dir. Nat. Archtl. Accrediting Bd., 1972-73, 79; adminstrv. and tech. cons. Wood Bldg. Rsch. Ctr., U. Calif., 1985-90, mem. profl. preparation project com. at U. Mich., Ann Arbor, 1986-87; co-author water infiltration seminar series for Bldg. Owners and Mgr. Rsch. Ctr., 1986-87; chief investigator effects of Guatemalan earthquake for NSF and AIA, Washington, 1976; steering com. on structural failures Nat. Bur. Standards, 1982-84; chmn., dir. gen. svc. Adv. Com. State of Calif. Co-author: Architects and Earthquake, Rsch. Needs, 1976, ATC Seismic Standards for Nat. Bur. of Standards, 1976, Arch. and Earthquakes; A Primer, 1977, Seismic Design, 1978, Wood-Detailing for Performance, 1990, Wood as a Building Material, 2d edit., 1991; contbr. articles and reports to profl. jour.; prin. works include expansion of Nuc. Weapons Tng. Facility at Lemoore Naval Air Sta., Calif., LASH Terminal Port Facility Archtl. Phase, San Francisco, Incline Village (Nev.) Country Club, 1365 Columbus Ave. Bldg., San Francisco, modernization Stanford Ct. Hotel, San Francisco; monument area constrn. several Calif. cemeteries. With U.S. Army, 1946—48. Recipient Cert. Honor Fedn. Archtl. Coll. Mex. Republic, 1984; named to Wisdom Hall of Fame, 1998; NSF grantee for investigative workshop project, San Diego, 1974-80. Fellow AIA (bd. dir., 1966-71, treas. No. Calif. chpt. 1968-69, pres. 1971, nat. v.p., 1975-76, nat. pres. 1978, pres. Hawaii 1985); hon. fellow Royal Can. Inst. Arch., NZ Inst. Arch. (hon.), Royal Australian Inst. Arch. (1st arch., 1st Am.), La Societe de Arquitectos Mexicano; mem. Archtl. Sec. Assn. (hon.), Soc. Wood Sci. and Tech., Internat. Conf. Bldg. Ofcl. Home: 321 Wailupe Cir Honolulu HI 96821-1524 Office: 925 Bethel St Fl 5 Honolulu HI 96813-4393

BOTSFORD, DAVID L. lawyer; b. Phila., Aug. 18, 1952; s. Thomas C. and Lois A. (Yarrison) B. BA, U. Conn., 1974; JD, So. Meth. U., 1977. Bar: Tex., 1977, U.S. Supreme Ct., 1981, U.S. Ct. Appeals (5th & 9th cir.), 1982, U.S. Dist. Ct. (we. dist.) Tex., 1983, U.S. Dist. Ct. (no. dist.), Tex., 1979; cert. Tex. Bd. Legal Specialization, criminal law. Law clerk Emmett Colvin, Dallas, 1974-77; assoc., ptnr. Emmet Colvin, Dallas, 1978-81; briefing atty. Hon. Truman Roberts Ct. Criminal Appeals Tex., 1977-78; treas. bond trader Chgo. Bd. Trade, 1981-82; assoc. Frank Maloney, Austin, Tex., 1982-88; ptnr. Alvis, Carssow, Cummins, Hoeffner & Botsford, P.C., 1988-93, Botsford & Sauer, L.L.P., 1993-96; pvt. practice Austin, 1996—. Contbr. articles to profl. jours. Tex. Criminal Def. Lawyers Ednl. Inst. fellow, 1990. Mem.: Travis Bar Assn., Tex. Criminal Def. Lawyers Assn. (assoc. dir. 1985, 1986, dir. 1987—91, asst. sec.-treas. 1991—92, sec.-treas. 1992—93, 2d v.p. 1993—94, 1st v.p. 1994—95, pres.-elect 1995—96, pres. 1996—97, Presdl. Excellence award 1989, 1990, 1993, 1994, 1995), Tex. Assn. Bd. Cert. Specialists Criminal Law (pres. 1991—92), State Bar Tex. (criminal law exam. commn. 1985—, Coll. State Bar 1991, criminal justice sect.Outstanding Criminal Def. Lawyer of Yr. 1993), Nat. Assn. Criminal Def. Lawyers, Barristers, Order of Coif. Office: 1307 W Ave Austin TX 78701-2948

BOTSKO, RONALD JOSEPH, business and engineering consultant; b. Youngstown, Ohio, Sept. 4, 1937; s. Joseph and Lucile Marie (Donaldson) B.; m. Billie Lou Colton. BS in Engring., Case Inst. Tech., 1959, Rsch. engr Youngstown Sheet & Tube Co., 1959-60; sr. rsch./project engr. N. Am. Aviation, L.A., 1960-67; gen. mgr. Microwave Instruments Co., Corona del Mar, Calif., 1967-71; pres., chmn. bd. NDT Instruments, Inc., Huntington Beach, Calif., 1971-88; prin. cons. DuPont, NDT Instruments Div., Huntington Beach, 1988—93 Lectr. in field. Author 2 booklets, handbook sects.; contbr. over 50 articles to profl. jours. Fellow Am. Soc. for Nondestructive Testing (Tech. Achievement award 1968, Gold medal 1983). Achievements include several patents for development of a variety of nondestructive testing instruments and methods, including ultrasonic and electromagnetic principles. Home: 6512 Frampton Cir Huntington Beach CA 92648-6620

BOTSTEIN, DAVID, geneticist, educator; b. Zurich, Switzerland, Sept. 8, 1942; naturalized, 1954; AB in Biochem. Scis. cum laude, Harvard U., 1963; PhD in Human Genetics, U. Mich., 1967. Woodrow Wilson fellow, 1963; instr. dept. biology MIT, Cambridge, 1967-69, asst. prof. genetics, 1969-73, assoc. prof. genetics dept. biology, 1973-78, prof., 1978-88; v.p. sci. Genetech, Inc., 1988-90; Stanford W. Ascherman prof. Stanford U., Palo Alto, Calif., 1997—. Sci. adv. bd. Collaborative Research, Inc., 1978-87. Editor in chief Nat. Acad. Scis., 1981, Inst. Medicine, 1993, Molecular Biology of Cell, 1992—; contbr. over 230 articles to profl. jours. Recipient Career Devel. award NIH, 1972-74; Eli Lilly and Co. award in microbiology and immunology, 1978, Rosenstiel award Brandeis U., 1992, Allen award Am. Soc. of Human Genetics, 1989, Inst. of Medicine, 1993. Mem. NAS, Genetics Soc. Am. (bd. dirs. 1984), Inst. Medicine. Office: Stanford U 300 Pasteur Dr Dept Genetics Palo Alto CA 94304-5120*

BOTSTEIN, LEON, academic administrator, conductor, historian; b. Zurich, Switzerland, Dec. 14, 1946; s. Charles and Anne (Wyszewianski) Botstein; m. Jill Lundquist, 1970 (div.); children: Sarah, Abigail(dec.); m. Barbara Haskell, 1982. BA (Woodrow Wilson fellow, Danforth Found. fellow, Sloan Found. fellow, Rockefeller fellow), U. Chgo., 1967; MA, Harvard U., 1968, PhD, 1985. Teaching fellow Harvard U., 1968—69; lectr. history Boston U., 1969; asst. to pres. N.Y.C. Bd. Edn., 1969—70; pres. Franconia Coll., 1970—75, Bard Coll., Annandale-On-Hudson, 1975—, Simon's Rock Coll. Bard, Great Barrington, Mass., 1979—; founder, artistic dir. Bard Music Festival, 1990—; music dir. Am. Symphony Orch., N.Y.C., 1992—, Jerusalem Symphony Orch., 2003—; artistic dir. Am. Russian Young Artists Orch., 1995—. Founder, prin. condr. White Mountain Music and Art Festival, NH, 1973—75; condr. Hudson Valley Philharm. Chamber Orch., 1989—92; guest condr. London Philharmonic, 1986—99, Philharmonia Orch., 1986, Pro Arte Chamber Orch. of Boston, 1988—89; other guest conducting appearances in Korea, Japan, Czech Republic, Philippines, Austria, Brazil, Lithuania, Romania, Scotland, Germany, Switzerland, Russia; past chmn. N.Y. Coun. Humanitites, Assn. Episc. Colls., Harper's Mag. Found.; vis. prof. Hochschule fur angewandte Kunst, Vienna, 1988; vis. faculty Manhattan Sch. Music, 1986; chmn. Salzburg Seminar, 1987; mem. nat. adv. com. Yale-New Haven Tchrs. Inst. Author: (novels) Jefferson's Children: Education and the Promise of American Culture, 1997; editor: (book) The Compleat Brahms, 1999, Musical Quar., 1992—; contbr. articles; conductor: albums. Recipient Berlin Prize Fellowship; grantee Rockefeller fellow. Fellow: Am. Acad. Arts & Scis. Office: Bard Coll Office of Pres Annandale On Hudson NY 12504

BOTT, HAROLD SHELDON, accountant, management consultant; b. Chgo., Dec. 12, 1933; s. Harold S. and Mary (Moseley) B.; m. Audrey Anne Connor, May 15, 1964; children: Susan, Lynda. AB, Princeton U., 1955; MBA, Harvard U., 1959; postgrad., U. Chgo., 1960-62. Adminstrv. asst. to exec v.p. Champion Paper, Hamilton, Ohio, 1959-61; mgmt. cons. Arthur Andersen & Co., Chgo., 1961-65, mgr., 1965-71, ptnr., 1971-89. Mng. dir. mgmt. info. cons., ptnr. Andersen Cons., 1988-91; ptnr. Strategic Tng. and Recruiting Svcs. Ctr.; vice-chmn. The Assn. Mgmt. Cons., 1982-84; bd. dirs. Harvard Bus. Sch. Assocs.; faculty Grad. Sch. Bus., U. Chgo., 1994-2000; of counsel Omnitech Cons., 1994-96; pres. H.S. Bott Co., 1994-2003. Officer, pres., dir. Urban Gateways, 1965—90; treas., dir. sch. bd., pres. Kenilworth Caucus, 1990; dir. The Cradle, 2000—, Kenilworth United Fund, 1983—89; pres.'s vis. com. Chgo. Theol. Sem., 2002—; bd. dirs. Orch. of Ill., 1988—89, The Joseph Sears Found., 2000—, co-pres., 2001—. With USN, 1955—56. Mem. AICPA, Ill. Soc. CPA's, Harvard Bus. Sch. Club. Chgo. (officer 1967-98, bd. dirs.), Am. Mktg. Assn., French-Am. C. of C. (bd. dirs.), Alliance Francaise (bd. dirs.), Kenilworth Sailing Club (commodore 1970-88), Kenilworth Club (treas., bd. dirs. 1975-79), Kenilworth Hist. Soc. (bd. dirs. 1995—), Indian Hill Club, Chgo. Club. Republican. Congregationalist. Home: 305 Kenilworth Ave Kenilworth IL 60043-1132 E-mail: pete.bott@gsb,uchicago.edu.

BOTT, JAY CORDELL, oncologist, hematologist; b. Salt Lake City, 1947; s. Leroy J. and Blanche T. Bott; m. Julie Christiansen, 1992. BA in Chemistry, U. Utah, 1971, BA in Med. Biology, 1974, MD hons. program in internal medicine, 1975. Cert. internal medicine, hematology, oncology. Intern Naval Regional Med. Ctr., San Diego, 1975-76, resident, 1976-78, fellow in oncology, hematology, 1979-80, 81-82; fellow in oncology U. Utah Med. Ctr., Salt Lake City, 1980-81; with Utah Valley Regional Med. Ctr., Provo, 1983—, Mountain View Hosp., Payson, Utah, 1983 —, Castleview Hosp., Price, Utah, 1984—; Timpanogos Regional Hosp., Orem, Utah, 1998—; founder Oxbow Ranch, Hanna, Utah. V.p. Ctrl. Utah Med. Clinic; prin. investigator Nat. Surg. Adjuvant Breast Bowel Project; est. one of the largest found. Quarter Horse breeding programs in the U.S. Mem. Nat. Rep. Com.; missionary LDS Ch., Germany, 1967—69; tchr. Sunday Sch.; with High Cou. and Bishopric, LDS Ch. Cmdr. USNR, 1973—84. Named Utah Rep. Businessman of Yr., 2000, 2001. Fellow: ACP; mem.: Am. Cancer Soc. (past. pres. Utah Vly. chpt.), Utah County Med. Assn. (past pres.), S.W. Oncology Group, Am. Soc. Hematology, Am. Soc. Clin. Oncology, Phi Kappa Phi, Phi Beta Kappa. Avocations: ranching, hunting, classical piano, outdoorsports. Office: Ctrl Utah Med Ctr 1055 N 500 W Provo UT 84604-3305 also: Oxbow Ranch PO Box 24 Hanna UT 84031-0024 E-mail: cbott@cumcmds.com.

BOTT, SIMON GREGORY, chemistry educator, researcher; b. Leicester, Eng., Oct. 7, 1962; s. Ronald William and Vivienne Mary Bott; m. Angie Rene McGuffey; 1 child, Alexandra McGuffey. BSc, U. Bristol, Eng., 1983; PhD, U. Ala., 1986. Rschr. Oxford (Eng.) U., 1987, MIT, Cambridge, Mass., 1988—89; asst. prof. U. North Tex., Denton, 1990—97; rsch. assoc. prof. U. Houston, 1997, advisor, 2002. Cons. Rimkus Cons., Houston, 1998. Mem.: Am. Chem. Soc. (pres. local chpt. 2002—04), Sigma Xi (local pres. 1995—97). Office: U Houston Dept Chemistry Houston TX 77204 Office Fax: 713-743-2709. Business E-Mail: sbott@uh.edu.

BOTTELLA, TAMMY ANN, lawyer; b. Cranston, R.I., Dec. 7, 1968; d. Ronald John and Louise Marie Bottella. AS, C.C. of R.I., 1989; BS, Bryant Coll., 1991; JD, Tulane U., 1994. Assoc. atty. Law Office of Charles Kirwan, Pawtucket, R.I., 1994-95, Law Office of Arlene Violet, East Providence, R.I., 1995-96; corp. counsel Great Am. Nursing Ctrs., Warwick, R.I., 1996-97; assoc. atty. Law Offices Winfred Eckenreiter, Fairhaven, Mass., 1997-99; pvt. practice Warwick, 1999—. Recipient Outstanding Bus. Student award Am. Mgmt. Soc.,

1986. Mem. ABA, Million Dollar Advocates Forum, Assn. of Trial Lawyers of Am., R.I. Bar Assn., Conn. Bar Assn., Delta Mu Delta. Roman Catholic. Home: 1108 Chopmist Hill Rd Scituate RI 02857-1046 Office: 255 Quaker Ln Ste 600 West Warwick RI 02893

BOTTENBERG, JOYCE HARVEY, social services executive; b. Melrose, Mass., June 29, 1945; d. Robert Willis and Amy Sheppard (Wood) Harvey; 1 child, Joanne Harvey; m. Norman G. Bottenberg, 1985. BA, U. Mass., 1967, diploma grad. journalism program, 1969; diploma, Simmons Coll. Grad. Sch. Mgmt., 1984. Lic., cert. social worker, Mass. Sr. tech. writer Itek Corp., Lexington, Mass., 1967-70; dir. pub. info. Walla Walla (Wash.) C.C., 1970; profl. interviewer McGraw Hill Rsch., N.Y.C., 1971-73; coord. pub. rels. James B. Rendle Assocs., Malden, Mass., 1973-76; exec. dir. ARC, Melrose, Mass., 1976-80, regional mgr., 1980-84, Lynn, Mass., 1984-85; tech. writer Municipality of Met. Seattle, 1985-86; exec. dir. Epilepsy Assn. Western Wash., Seattle, 1986-87; dir. devel. ARC, Seattle, 1988-97, mgr. svc. ctr., 1994-95; exec. dir. Medic One Found., Seattle, 1997-2000; devel. dir. Success Mktg. Inc., Seattle, 2000—. Chief devel. officer Child Care Resources, Seattle, 2001-03; v.p. resource devel. Boys and Girls Clubs of King County, 2003—. Chmn. adv. bd. Mass. Dept. Pub. Welfare Community Service Area; mem. Melrose Mayor's Energy Commn.; civic adv. bd. Met. Bank and Trust; instr. 1st aid, CPR, ARC; merit badge counselor Boy Scouts Am. Recipient Cert. of merit ARC, 1981; named Profl. Fund Raiser of Yr., ARC, 1994; New Eng. Newspaper fellow, 1969. Mem. AAUW, DAR, NAFE, Soc. Mayflower Descs., Soc. Tech. Comms., Nat. Ski Patrol System, N.W. Devel. Officers Assn., Washington Planned Giving Coun., Puget Sound Grantwriters Assn., Alpha Phi Gamma. Episcopalian. Avocation: amateur radio. Home: 2205 197th Ave SE Sammamish WA 98075-9644 Office: 603 Stewart St # 300 Seattle WA 98101 E-mail: jbottenberg@positiveplace.org., bberg@oz.net.

BOTTI, JOHN JOSEPH, obstetrician-gynecologist; b. Middletown, N.Y., 1948; MD, Albany Med. Coll., 1974. Diplomate Am. Bd. Ob-Gyn. Resident ob-gyn. U. Health Ctr., Pitts., 1974-77, fellow maternal fetal medicine, 1977-79; mem. hosp. staff Hershey Med. Ctr., Pa., 1979-94; prof. ob-gyn. Pa. State U.-Hershey Med. Ctr., 1994—. Fellow: ACOG; mem.: Soc. Maternal Fetal Medicine, Nat. Perinatal Assn. (past pres.). Office: Pa State U Milton S Hershey Med Ctr Dept Ob-Gyn Hershey PA 17033 E-mail: jbotti@psu.edu.

BOTTI, OLENIO T. retired transporation executive, writer; b. Bklyn., Oct. 23, 1927; s. Ettore and Filomena (DiLucia) Botti; m. Frances D. Lomonte, June 10, 1950; children: Stephen, Lorraine. Student, Bklyn. Coll., 1952—54, Northwestern U., 1968. Prin. Botti Transp. Orgn., Lincroft, NJ; dir. internat. traffic Dept. of Def., NJ, with. Author: Sam, Pat & Tico, Lions, Lambs and Sleeping Dogs, 1997. With U.S. Army, 1945—46. Named to U.S. Army Transp. Corp. Hall of Fame, 2000. Roman Catholic. Avocations: golf, fishing, walking. Home: 41 Stonehenge Dr Lincroft NJ 07738

BOTTIGLIA, FRANK ROBERT, bank executive; b. S.I., Jan. 12, 1946; s. Hugo and Rose (Renzi) B.; children: Christine Ann, Catherine Rose, Elizabeth Mary, Laura Michele. BBA, CCNY, 1968; MBA, Baruch Coll., 1976. Adv. profl. cert. pub. acctg. Fin. analyst corp. human resources Chase Manhattan Bank, N.Y.C., 1971-73, mgr. fin. controls corp. human resources, 1974-75, mgr. fin. and adminstrn. corp. human resources, 1976-77, sr. fin. mgmt. officer real estate fin., 1978-83, v.p., contr. U.S. regional comml. sector, 1984-89, v.p., budge dir. N.Am. sector, 1990-93, v.p., fin. mgr. global corp. fin., 1994-95, v.p., contr., 1995-96, v.p., contr. client access, 1997-98, v.p., contr. global treasury mgmt., 1998—; dir. Chase Access Svcs. Inc. Bd. mgr. Town and Country Villas Home Owners Assn., S.I., 1991. Sgt. U.S. Army, 1968-70. Mem. Internat. Platform Assn. Roman Catholic. Avocations: tennis, travel. Home: 481 Mill Rd Staten Island NY 10306-4537 Office: Chase Manhattan Bank 4 Chase Metrotech Ctr Brooklyn NY 11245-0005

BOTTIGLIA, WILLIAM FILBERT, humanities educator; b. Bernardsville, N.J., Nov. 23, 1912; s. Vincent Richard and Quintilia (Mastrobattista) B.; m. Mildred MacDonald, Dec. 21, 1943 (dec. Oct. 1966); children: Martha (Mrs. Milton Morris), Janet. AB, Princeton U., 1934, AM, 1935, PhD, 1948. Instr. modern langs. Princeton U., 1934-42; engaged in industry, 1942-47; gen. mgr. J & S Tool Co., East Orange, N.J., 1946-47; asst. prof. English, St. Lawrence U., 1948; prof. Romance langs. and lits., chmn. dept. Ripon Coll., 1948-56; faculty MIT, 1956—, prof. fgn. lit. and humanities, 1960-74, head dept. fgn. lit. and linguistics, 1964-73, prof. mgmt. and humanities, 1974-78, prof. emeritus and sr. lectr. mgmt. and humanities, 1978-91. Author: Voltaire's Candide: Analysis of a Classic, 2d edit., 1964, (with others) Voltaire (Twentieth Century Views), 1968, Heroic Symphony, 1997-99, 4 vols.; editor: Reports of N.E. Conf. on the Teaching of Fgn. Langs, 1957, 62, 63. Mem. Soc. Palmes Académiques, Dante Soc. Am., Phi Beta Kappa. Home: 34 Mary Chilton Rd Needham MA 02492-1138

BOTTITTA, JOSEPH ANTHONY, lawyer; b. Mar. 9, 1949; s. Anthony S. and Elizabeth (Bellisano) B.; m. Lynda Joan Kloss, Apr. 14, 1979;children: Michelle Emma, Gregory Joseph. BSBA, Seton Hall U., 1971, JD, 1974. Bar: U.S. Dist. Ct. N.J. 1974, U.S. Supreme Ct. 1981. Ptnr. Rusignola & Pugliese, Newark, 1974-78; sr. ptnr. Joseph A. Bottitta, West Orange, N.J., 1979-88, Gilbert, Gilbert, Schlossberg and Bottitta, 1988-89; pvt. practice, 1989-95; with Bottitta and Bascelli, 1995-99. Chmn. Supreme Ct. Fee Arbitration Com. Dist. V-B., 1984-85; mem. N.J. Uniform Law Commn., 1987-91; mem. N.J. Commn. on Professionalism in Law, 1997—; pres. N.J. Lawyers Svc., 2000—; pres., E-Law.com, 2000—. Fellow: Am. Bar Found.; mem.: ABA, Essex County Bar Assn. (sec. 1983—84, treas. 1984—85, pres.-elect 1985—86, pres. 1986—87), NJ State Bar Assn. (trustee 1988, treas. 1994—95, v.p. 1995—97, pres.-elect 1997—98, pres. 1998—99). Republican. Roman Catholic. Office: c/o NJ Lawyers Svc 2333 Route 22 W Union NJ 07083-8517 E-mail: joeb@njls.com.

BOTTJER, DAVID JOHN, earth scientist, biologist, educator; b. NYC, Oct. 3, 1951; s. John Henry and Marilyn (Winter) B.; m. Sarah Ranney Wright, July 26, 1973. BS, Haverford Coll., 1973; MA, SUNY, Binghamton, 1976; PhD, Ind. U., 1978. NRC postdoctoral rsch. assoc. US Geol. Survey, Washington, 1978-79; asst. prof. dept. geol. sci. U. So. Calif., LA, 1979-85, assoc. prof. dept. geol. sci., 1985-91, prof. dept. earth sci., 1991—, prof. dept. biol. sci., 2003—. Rsch. assoc. LA County Mus. Natural History, 1979—; vis. scientist Field Mus. Natural History, Chgo., 1986; Paleontol. Soc. Disting. lectr., 1992-93; mem. Nat. Sci. Found. panel on earth systems history, 1997-99; sr. fellow UCLA Ctr. for the Study of Evolution and Origin of Life, 2000. Editor Palaios, 1989-96; assoc. editor Cretaceous Rsch., 1988-91; mem. editl. bd. Geology, 1984-89, 95-2000, Hist. Biology, 1988-93; co-editor Columbia U. Press Critical Moments and Perspectives in Paleobiology and Earth History (book series), 1990—; editor-in-chief Palaeo-3, 2000—. Recipient Disting. Scientist award, Ctr. for Study of Evolution and Origin of Life, UCLA, 2002. Fellow AAAS, Geol. Soc. Am., Geol. Soc. London; mem. Paleontol. Soc. (pres.-elect 2002—), Soc. Sediment Geology (pres. Pacific sect. 2001-02), Internat. Paleontology Assn. Office: U So Calif Dept Earth Scis Los Angeles CA 90089-0001 E-mail: dbottjer@usc.edu.

BOTTO, ROBERT IRVING, analytical chemist, antique dealer; b. Buffalo, Apr. 22, 1949; s. Melvin Robert and Marjorie Elaine (Becker) B.; m. Kathleen Rebecca Abbey, July 26, 1975; children: Catherine Elaine Violet, Elizabeth Mary Rose. BA, SUNY, Buffalo, 1971; MS, Cornell U., 1973, PhD, 1976. Various tech. positions Exxon Rsch. and Engring. Co., Baytown, Tex., 1975-95, head analytical ops., 1987-95, rsch. assoc., 1991—; head analytical lab. Exxon Chem. Co., 1995-99, ExxonMobil Chem., 1999—. Contbr. articles to profl. jours. Mem. Am. Chem. Soc. (chmn. S.W. regional meeting 1986, chmn. S.W. region 1987; chmn. Greater Houston sect. 1989, award 1982, 94), Soc. for Applied Spectroscopy, Houston Vintage Radio Assn. (pres. 1990). Republican. Mem. Assembly of God Ch. Avocations: collecting, restoring, buying and selling vintage phonographs and radios, collecting ancient coins and edison memorabilia, marathon runner. Home: 3505 Del Sur D Baytown TX 77521-9181 Office: ExxonMobil Chem Co 4500 Bayway Dr Baytown TX 77522 E-mail: vintagesounds@altavista.net.

BOTTOM, DALE COYLE, management consultant; b. Columbus, Ind., June 25, 1932; s. James Robert and Sarah Lou (Coyle) B.; m. Frances Audrey Wilson, June 6, 1954 (div.); children: Jane Ellen, Steven Dale, Sharon Lynn, Carol Ann; m. Elaine McAuliffe, Aug. 20, 1988. BS, Ball State U., Muncie, Ind., 1954. Admissions counselor Stephens Coll., Columbia, Mo., 1958-61; exec. asst., then staff v.p. Inst. Fin. Edn., Chgo., 1961-67, pres., 1967-92; exec. v.p., chief fin. officer U.S. League Savs. Instns., 1985-89; chmn., dir. SAF-Systems & Forms Co.; sec.-gen. Internat. Union Fin. Instns., Chgo., 1989-95; cons. Resource Strategies Internat., Hinsdale, Ill., 1995—. Bd. dirs. Savs. Instn. Ins. Group, Ltd., v.p., chief fin. officer. Chmn. bd. Barrington (Ill.) United Meth. Ch., 1981. Served as officer USAF, 1955-58; comdr. USNR (ret.), 1967-78. Recipient Award of Distinction, Ball State U., 2003. Mem. Fin. Mgrs. Soc. (dir.), Savs. Instns. Mktg. Soc. Am., Navy League, Ind. Soc. Chgo., Tavern Club (v.p. 1993), Medinah. Republican. Home and Office: 606 Burr Ridge Clb Burr Ridge IL 60527-5209 E-mail: dbottom@attbi.com.

BOTTOMS, ROBERT GARVIN, academic administrator; b. Birmingham, Ala., June 28, 1944; s. Dalton Garvin and Mary Inez (Cruce) Bottoms; m. Gwendolynn Jean Vickers, June 14, 1968; children: David Timothy, Leslie Clair. BA, Birmingham So. U., 1966; BD, Emory U., 1969; D of Ministry, Vanderbilt U., 1972. Chaplain Birmingham (Ala.) So. Coll., 1973—74, asst. to pres., 1974—75; asst. dean, asst. prof. church and ministry Vanderbilt U., Nashville, 1975—78; v.p. for univ. rels. DePauw U., Greencastle, Ind., 1978—79, exec. v.p. external rels., 1979—83, exec. v.p. of univ., 1983—86, acting pres., 1985, pres., 1986—. Cons. Arthur Vining Davis Found., Jacksonville, Fla., 1978—79, Luth. So. Sem., Columbia, SC, 1979—80; cons. theol. edn. The Lilly Endowment, Indpls., 1979—82; cons. Fund for Theol. Edn., N.Y.C., 1981—82; chmn. audit com. Centel Cable TV Co., Oak Brook, Ill., 1987—89; Am. ctr. for internat. leadership organizer Edn. Policy Commn. U.S.-USSR Emerging Leaders Summit, Phila., 1988. Author: Lessons in Financial Development, 1982. Chmn. com. on ch. and coll. Episcopal Diocese Ind., 1979—84; bd. advisors Vanderbilt Div. Sch., 1980—93; bd. trustees Seabury-Western Theol. Sem., 2001—; bd. dirs. Joyce Found., 1994—2002, G.M. Constrn. Inc., Indpls., 1998—, The Posse Found., 2001—, Women in Govt., Washington, 2001—. Recipient CASE V Chief Exec. Leadership award, 2000. Mem.: NCAA (coun. 1989—95, subcom. eligibility appeals), Ind. Colls. Ind. Found. (bd. dirs. 1987—, nominating com. 1990—), Women in Govt. (bd. dirs. 2001—), Great Lakes Colls. Assn. (bd. dirs. 1987—, chair 1994—96), Ind. Colls. of Ind. (bd. dirs. 1987—, exec. com. 1991—), Am. Coun. Edn. (commn. on women in higher edn. 1990—91), Assn. Governing Bds. Univs. and Colls. (coun. pres. 1997—), Nat. Assn. Schs. and Colls. United Meth. Ch. (bd. dirs. 1987—91), Nat. Assn. Ind. Colls. and Univs. (task force increasing participation of minorities in ind. higher edn. 1989—95), Nat. Coun. Chs. (governing bd. 1985—91), Chgo. Club., Cosmos Club (Washington), Univ. Club of N.Y.C., Columbia Club (Indpls.). Avocation: boating. Home: 125 Wood St Greencastle IN 46135 Office: DePauw Univ Office of Pres 313 S Locust St Greencastle IN 46135-0037

BOTTORFF, GARALD L. retired military officer, foundation administrator; b. New Albany, Ind., Nov. 30, 1939; s. Franklin L. and Mildred L. (Liley) Bottorff; m. Mary Patricia Rewtz; children: Terri Lee, Branch. BS in Bus., U. S.C., 1963; MS in Edn., U. So. Calif., 1968; student, Cath. U., 1983—84. Commd. lt. USAF, 1963, advanced through grades to col., ret., 1987; pres. The Capital Group, Fairfax, Va., 1987—2002; exec. dir. Am. Mil. Spouse Edn. Found., Manassos, Va., 2002—. Congl. liaison USAF, Washington, 1980—84, White House liaison, 1984—86, mem. star wars program, 1986—87; bd. dir. Cold War Mus. Active Dem. Com., Fairfax, 1988—. Mem.: Army Navy Century Club (bd. mem. 1985—87, house com. liaison 1985—87), Army Navy Club, Kappa Sigma (officer 1963—). Avocations: fox hunting, golf, horseback riding. Home: 9912 Great Oaks Way Fairfax VA 22030 Office: American Military Spouse Edn Found 10648 Wakeman Court Manassas VA 20110 Fax: 703-591-8333. E-mail: garybottorff@aol.com.

BOTTS, JACK CHESTER, journalist; b. Ludden, N.D., Oct. 11, 1924; s. Dwight Chellis and Velcia Myrtle (Swafford) B.; m. Dorris Maxine Everhart, Sept. 10, 1950; children: Jeffrey, Christian, Melanie, Michael. AB, U. Nebr., 1949; MS, Northwestern U., 1950. City desk reporter Lincoln (Nebr.) Jour., 1948-49, city editor, 1951, telegraph editor, 1952-66, editl. writer, 1957-60; asst. prof. journalism U. Nebr., 1966-68, assoc. prof., 1968-73, prof., 1973-90, chmn. dept., 1972-90; manuscript editor, 2002—. Author: The Language of News, 1994, A Pocketful of Plums, 1995, Straight and Level, 1996, Play Action, 2001, Home Place 2002, Whitestone, 2003. Sgt. USAAF, 1943-45, ETO. Named Disting. Journalist of Yr., Kappa Tau Alpha, 1990. Mem. Soc. Profl. Journalists (state pres. 1973), AP Mng. Editors (com. chmn. 1978), Phi Beta Kappa. Avocations: writing novels, building furniture, raising roses. Home: 1240 N 42d St Lincoln NE 68503 E-mail: jacandorbotts@aol.com.

BOTWAY, LLOYD FREDERICK, computer scientist, consultant; b. Flushing, NY, June 18, 1947; s. Albert Harold and Alice Rebecca (Halperin) B. BS, Tufts U., 1968; MS, U. Colo., 1970. Programmer Anaconda Co., Butte, Mont., 1970-72; systems analyst U. Mo., Columbia, 1972-77; tech. dir. Dataphase Systems, Inc., Kans. City, Mo., 1977-80; pres. Liberty Logic Corp., Pasadena, Md., 1980-84; computer scientist Computer Sci. Corp., Balt., 1984-86; dir. MIS Internat. Clin. Labs., Nashville, 1986-88; dir. info. systems Nat. Health Labs., Nashville, 1988-94; v.p., chief arch. Quest Diagnostics, San Juan Capistrano, Calif., 1994-2000; actor, writer, musician LA, 2000—. Cons. Internat. Clin. Labs., Nashville, 1981-85; grad. asst. Dale Carnegie. Contbr. articles to profl. jour., co-author: (reference pamphlet) Latex Command Summary, 1985. Libertarian candidate for U.S. Ho. of Reps. from 5th Tenn. Dist., 1994. Recipient Nominated "Best Actor", Orange County, 2002. Mem. Toastmasters. Avocations: composing music, flying, foreign languages, electronics, acting. E-mail: botwayl@juno.com.

BOTWINICK, MILTON EDWARD, genealogist, researcher; b. Phila., Feb. 25, 1942; s. Joseph J. and Beatrice R. (Miller) B. Cert. proficiency Elec. Engring. Tech., Temple U., 1962; BA, Rowan U., 1970. Genealogist, Phila., 1982—. Columnist (newsletter) Chronicles. With USAF, 1962-66. Mem. Geneal. Soc. Pa., Assn. Profl. Genealogists, Assn. Profl. Jewish Genealogists, Phila. Jewish Geneal. Soc. (founder), Hist. Soc. Pa. Home: PO Box 13464 Philadelphia PA 19101-3464 E-mail: botwinick@alumni.rowan.edu.

BOU, ENRIC, language educator; b. Barcelona, Mar. 3, 1954; arrived in U.S., 1986; s. Agustt Bou and Maria Maqueda; m. Chiara Bertola; children: Sarah, Victor. Lic., U. Autonoma, Barcelona, 1977, PhD, 1981. Prof. U. Barcelona, 1981—86, Wellesley (Mass.) Coll., 1987—96, Brown U., Providence, 1996—. Author, editor. Office: Brown Univ Box 1961 Providence RI 02912

BOUBELIK, HENRY FREDRICK, JR., retired travel company executive; b. Chgo., Aug. 16, 1936; s. Henry Fredrick and Anna Mabel (Short) B.; m. Jane V. Boubelik, Oct. 27, 1978; children— Debra Ann, Henry Fredrick III, Steven W., Catherine Earle. Student, U. Ill., 1954-55, Trinity U., 1957-59. Asst. mgr. Avis Rent-A-Car, San Antonio, 1957-60; city mgr. Hertz Rent-a-Car, Corpus Christi, Tex., 1960-67; regional mgr. Nat. Car Rental System, Inc., Mpls., 1967-69, sr. v.p., 1969-92; chmn. Meyer-Boubelik and Assocs., Mpls., 1992-95; pres. Leisure divsns. Northwestern Travel Svc., Minnetonka, Minn., 1995-98; v.p. industry rels. TransGlobal Tours, Inc., Mpls., 1998-2001; ret., 2001. Mem. adv. bd. Corpus Christi Bayfront, 1963-66. Served with AUS, 1955-57. Mem. Car and Truck Rental and Leasing Assn. (v.p. 1973, dir. 1974-77), Am. Car Rental Assn. (pres. 1980-81) Clubs: Civitan (dir., pres.-elect 1963-66). Home: 9400 Woodbridge Dr Minneapolis MN 55438

BOUCEK, MARK MANSFIELD, pediatric cardiologist; b. Rochester, Minn., Apr. 29, 1949; BS, Fla. State U., 1971; MD, U. Miami, 1977. Resident Vanderbilt U., Nashville, 1977-79; fellow U. Utah, Salt Lake City, 1979-81, asst. prof. pediats., 1981-88; assoc. prof. Loma Linda (Calif.) U., 1988-92; prof. Children's Hosp. U. Colo., Denver, 1992—; dir. transplant program Children's Hosp., Denver, 1992—, dir. pediats. cardiology, 1992—. Co-author: Handbook of Cardiac Drugs, 1992. Grantee NIH, 1986, St. Jude Med., 1987-88, Utah Heart Assn., 1987-88, Bugher Physician Scientist Tng. Porgram, 1990-97. Mem. Am. Soc. Transplant Physicians (mem. pediatric com. 1996—), United Network Organ Sharing (chmn. 1996—), Pediatric Heart Transplant Working Group, Colo. Heart Assn. Avocations: running, diving. Office: Childrens Hosp 1056 E 19th Ave # 100 Denver CO 80218-1088

BOUCHARD, JAE ARLENE, writer, poet, interior designer; b. Norwalk, Conn., July 30, 1937; Student, Endicott Coll., Beverly, Mass., 1967-68, N.Y. Sch. Interior Design, 1969-71. Justice of the peace. Draftswoman Samuel Lakow, N.Y.C., 1971-72; owner Bouchard & Co., N.Y.C., 1975-88; mus. curator Foxwood's Indian Mus., Mashantucket, Conn., 1997-98; Justice of the Peace, 2000—. Contbr. poems to Isle of View, 1997, Rhymes of Greatness, 1998, Perceptions in Harmony, 1998, Best Poems of 1998, Promises to Keep, 1998, A Time to be Free, 1999. Mem.New London City Beautification com., 1997—. Mem. Nat. Soc. Interior Designers (cert.). Home: 98 Plant St New London CT 06320-4442

BOUCHARD, JAMES PAUL, steel manufacturing and planning executive; b. Kansas City, Kans., May 2, 1961; s. Robert Clayton and Helen (Clancy) B.; m. Carolyn Keegan, July 19, 1986. BBA, Loyola U., Chgo., 1984. Asst. to dist. mgr. Inland Steel Co., Chgo., 1983-85; sales rep. Denver br. Westinghouse Electric, 1985-87, U.S. Steel (divsn. USX Corp.), Milw., 1987-91, Midwest area sr. rep. Oak Brook, Ill., 1987-94, resident mgr., 1994-97, strategic planning and devel. mgr. Pitts., 1997-98, mgr. mktg., 1998, nat. mgr. pipe, tube, and container group, 1999-2000; v.p. comml. U.S. Steel-Kosice, Pitts., 2000—02; COO Mars Industries, Chgo., 2002—03; CEO Esmark, Chgo., 2003—. Bd. dirs. Esmark, Oak Brook, Ill., Electric Coating Tech., East Chicago, Ind., Bouchard Group, LLC, Hinsdale, Ill., Quaker Valley Recreation Assn., Sewickley, Pa. Co-inventor patented light weight concrete, 1983. Mem. Evans Scholars Found., Strategic Leadership Forum, Pitts. Mem. Loyola U. Alumni Assn., Chgo. Dist. Golf Assn., Edgewood Valley Country Club, mem. Art Inst. of Chgo., Edgeworth Club (Pa.), Sewickley Heights Golf Club (Pa.), Edgewirth Club (Serwickley, Pa.). Republican. Roman Catholic. Avocations: golf, basketball, baseball, football. Home: 3 Beaver St Sewickley PA 15143-1217

BOUCHARD, PAUL EUGENE, artist; b. Providence, Sept. 26, 1946; s. Marcel Paul and Anna Theresa (Dullea) B., m. Ann Marie Jones, Nov. 18, 1972 (div. 1977); 1 child Michael Paul; m. R. Jane Bouchard, Apr. 11, 1997. BFA, Calif. State U., Long Beach, 1978. Bd. dir, Angeles Gate Cultural Ctr., San Pedro, Calif., 1983-85. One-man show at Rogue Coll., Grants Pass, Oreg., 1996, El Camino Coll., 1997, City of Carlsbad, Calif. 1998; exhibited in group shows at Rental Gallery, Oakland Mus., 1984, Rental Gallery, L.A. County Mus. of Art, 1985, Sixth St. Gallery, San Pedro, Calif., Aquarius Gallery, Cambria, Calif., 1986, St. Andrew's Priory, Valyermo, Calif., Riverside (Calif.) Art Mus., Rental Gallery, 1987, Vietnam Vet.'s Art Exhibit, 1988, Coos Art Mus., Coos Bay, Oreg., 1989, Grants Pass Mus. of Art, 1991, Eastern Wash. U., 1992, Dept. Vets. Affairs Hdqrs., Sydney, Australia, 1992-93, Australian Nat. Gallery, Brisbane County Hall Gallery, Nat. Vietnam Vets. Art Mus., Chgo., others. Recipient Contribution to the Arts, City of Torrance, Calif., 1985; grantee Franklin Furnace, N.Y.C., 1989-90, Artist Space, N.Y.C., 1989-90. Home: 166 Denton Rd Saratoga Springs NY 12866 E-mail: paulandjane1@earthlink.net.

BOUCHARD, THOMAS JOSEPH, JR., psychology educator, researcher; b. Manchester, N.H., Oct. 3, 1937; s. Thomas and Florence (Charest) B.; m. Pauline Marina Proulx, Aug. 13, 1960; children: Elizabeth, Mark. BA, U. Calif., Berkeley, 1963, PhD, 1966. Asst. prof. U. Calif., Santa Barbara, 1966-69, U. Minn., Mpls., 1969-70, assoc. prof., 1970-73, prof., 1973—, chmn. dept. psychology, 1985-91. Dir. Minn. Ctr. Twin and Adoption Rsch., U. Minn., 1980—. Editor (assoc.): (jour.) Jour. Applied Psychology, 1977—80, Behavior Genetics, 1982—86; contbr. articles jours. With USAF, 1955-58. Fellow AAAS, APA, Am. Psychol. Soc.; mem. Phi Beta Kappa, Sigma Xi. Home: 1860 Shoreline Dr Wayzata MN 55391-9771 Office: Univ of Minn Dept Psychology 75 E River Rd Minneapolis MN 55455-0280 E-mail: bouch001@tc.umn.edu.

BOUCHER, BRADLEY ALBERT, pharmacist, educator; b. Mpls., Dec. 21, 1955; s. Dwaine Edmund and Betty Jean Boucher; m. Barbara Sue Opitz, Oct. 27, 1979; children: Alexander Albert, Andrew Bradley, Adam Nicholas. BS in Pharmacy, U. of Minn., 1979, PharmD, 1983. Registered pharmacotherapy specialist Bd. of Pharm. Specialties, 1992. Fellow U. of Ky., Lexington, Ky., 1983—84; prof. of pharmacy U. of Tenn., Memphis, 1996—, assoc. prof. of neurosurgery, 1997—. Mem. editl. bd.: Critical Care Medicine, 2000—; contbr. articles to profl. jours., chapters to books. Treas. Germantown Youth Athletic Assn. Football Program, Germantown, Tenn., 1995—2002. Recipient Merck award, U. of Minn. Coll. of Pharmacy, 1979. Fellow: Am. Coll. of Clin. Pharmacy (hon.; treas. 1992—97, pres. 2001—02), Am. Coll. of Critical Care Medicine (hon.); mem.: Am. Soc. of Health-Systems Pharmacists (fellow 1983—84), Soc. of Critical Care Medicine, Am. Assn. of Colls. of Pharmacy, Soc. of Infectious Diseases Pharmacists, The Rho Chi Soc. (hon.), Phi Lambda Sigma Leadership Soc. (hon.). Episc. Avocations: coaching, golf. Office: University of Tennessee 26 South Dunlap Room 210 Memphis TN 38163 Office Fax: 901-448-6064. E-mail: bboucher@utmem.edu.

BOUCHER, FREDERICK C. congressman, lawyer; b. Abingdon, Va., Aug. 1, 1946; s. Ralph E. and Dorothy (Buck) B. BA, Roanoke Coll., 1968; JD, U. Va., 1971. Bar: Va. 1971, N.Y. 1972. Assoc. Milbank, Tweed, Hadley, McCloy, N.Y.C., 1971-73; ptnr. Boucher & Boucher, Abingdon, Va.; state senator Va. Gen. Assembly, Richmond, 1975-79, 79-82; mem. U.S. Congress from 9th Va. dist., Washington, 1983—; mem. energy and commerce com., judiciary com.; assist. whip H. of Reps., 1985—; founder, co-chmn. house internet caucus, 1996—. Recipient Disting. Service award Va. Highlands Community Coll., Abingdon, 1984, Beamer award for Contributions to Vocational Edn., 1986, Legislator of Yr. award Vietnam Vets. Am., 1993. Mem. ABA, Assn. Bar of N.Y.C., Va. Bar Assn. Democrat. Methodist. Office: US Ho of Reps 2187 Rayburn Ho Office Bldg Washington DC 20515-4609*

BOUCHER, JACK EDWARD, architectural photographer, writer; b. Buffalo, Sept. 4, 1931; s. John L. and Alma L. (Hookey) B.; m. Mary M. Sullivan, Sept. 25, 1965; children: Jack J., Paul E. Student, Winona Sch. Profl. Photography, Nat. Trust Eng. Summer Sch. Photographer, writer Atlantic City Tribune, 1949-52; chief photographer, exhibits specialist N.J. Hwy. Authority, 1952-58; sr. photographer U.S. Nat. Pk. Svc., 1958-66; chief historic sites State of N.J., 1966-69; free-lance archtl. photographer, writer, lectr., 1969-70; supr. archtl. photog. documentation Nat. Park Svc., Hist. Am. Bldg. Survey, 1971—. Photographs exhibited at Libr. of Congress, AIA NAt. Hdqrs., Washington; author: Absegami Yesteryear, 1963, Of Batsto and Bog Iron, 1964, History of the Atlantic City Lighthouse, 1965, History of Margate Elephant, 1970, A Record in Detail, 1988. Recipient commendation N.J. Senate, 1964, award of merit Am. Assn. State and Local History, 1961, commendation, 1965, AIA ann. medal, 1980, Pres.'s award, 1986, ann. award N.J. Hist. Commn., 1982, Meritorious Svc. award Dept. Interior, 1986. Fellow Royal Photog. Soc. Gt. Britain; mem. Atlantic County Hist. Soc. (trustee, past pres.). Office: Nat Park Svc-HABS 1849 C St NW # Nc300 Washington DC 20240-0001

BOUCHER, JOSEPH W(ILLIAM), lawyer, accountant, educator, writer; b. Menominee, Mich., Oct. 28, 1951; s. Joseph W. and Patricia (Coon) B.; m. Susan M. De Groot, June 4, 1977; children: Elizabeth, Bridget, Joseph William III. BA, St. Norbert Coll., 1973; JD, U. Wis., 1977, MBA in Fin., 1978. Bar: Wis. 1978, U.S. Dist. Ct. (we. dist.) Wis. 1978; CPA, Wis. Adminstrv. aide to Senator Wis. Senate, Madison, 1977; from assoc. to ptnr. Murphy, Stolper et al., Madison, 1977-84; ptnr. Stolper, Koritzinsky, Brewster & Neider, Madison, 1985-94; mng. ptnr. Stolper, Koritzinsky, Brewster, Neider, Madison, 1989-92, Neider & Boucher, S.C., 1995—. Lectr. bus. U. Wis., Madison, 1980—. Co-author: Organizing a Wisconsin Business Corporation, 1995, 3d edit., 2003, Wisconsin LLCs and LLPs Handbook, 1996, 3d edit., 2003; contbr. articles to Wis. Bar Assn. Bd. dirs. Jackson Found., 1994—99, West Met. Bus. Assn., 1990—95, Dane County United Way., 1986—89, Wis. Chamber Orch., 1990—94, pres., 1993—94; bd. dirs. St. Coletta's, 1997—2001, Edgewood H.S., 1997—2003, chair, 2001—03; mem. bd. advisors St. Mary's Med. Ctr., Madison, 1989—91. Named one of Outstanding Young Men of Am., 1979; named Wis. Lawyer Advocate of Yr., SBA, 1983. Mem. ABA, AICPA (mem. bd. examiners, mem. bus. law subcom. 1987-90), Wis. Bar Assn., Wis. State Bar Assn. (mem. corp. com. 1991—, co-chairperson interprofl. com. 1992-95, chair ltd. liability co. subcom.), Dane County Bar Assn., Wis. Inst. CPAs, U. Wis. Bus. Alumni Assn. (bd. dirs. 1980-87). Roman Catholic. Avocations: sports, reading. Office: Neider & Boucher SC 440 Science Dr Madison WI 53711-1064

BOUCHER, LARRY GENE, sports association commissioner; b. Bowling Green, Ky., Jan. 23, 1947; s. Larry Gene and Virginia Elizabeth (Miller) B.; m. Paula Ann Feeback, Oct. 4, 1949 (div. Feb. 1996); children: Brooke Renee, Brenna Ann. BS in Bus. Edn., Ea. Ky. U., 1970. Unemployment ins. examiner Human Resource Cabinet Ky., Frankfort, 1972-73; budget/policy analyst Ky. Transp. Cabinet, Frankfort, 1973-87, br. mgr. mgmt. svcs., 1987-91; asst. commr. Ky. H.S. Athletic Assn., Lexington, 1991—. Mem. Am. Govtl. Accts., Frankfort, 1984-87. Mem. allocation com. Frankfort/Franklin County United Way, 1987-91. Mem. Church of Christ. Home: 3248 Hunters Point Dr Lexington KY 40515-1079 Office: Ky H S Athletic Assn 2280 Executive Dr Lexington KY 40505-4808

BOUCHER, LAURENCE JAMES, educator, chemist; b. Yonkers, N.Y., Sept. 16, 1938; s. Edward Joseph Boucher and Matilda Ann (Klicska) Higgins; m. Susan Ann Calkins, Aug. 15, 1964; children: Amy Elizabeth, Stephen Edward. AAS in Indsl. Chemistry, Westchester C.C., White Plains, N.Y., 1958; BS in Chemistry, Mich. State U., 1960; MS in Chemistry, U. Ill., 1962, PhD Inorganic Chemistry, 1964. Resident rsch. assoc. Argonne (Ill.) Nat. Lab., 1964-66; asst. prof. chemistry Carnegie-Mellon U., Pitts., 1966-71, assoc. prof., 1971-76; titular prof. U. Autonoma Metropolitana, Mexico City, 1976-78; prof. chemistry, head dept. Western Ky. U., Bowling Green, 1978-85; dean Coll. Arts and Scis., Ark. State U., Jonesboro, 1985-90; dean Coll. Natural and Math. Scis. Towson (Md.) U., 1990-97, prof. chemistry, 1997—. Prof. Exxon Rsch. Co., Linden, N.J., 1973; rsch. chemist U.S. Dept. Energy, Bruceton, Pa., 1976; Fulbright lectr., Colombia, 1981. Contbr. numerous articles to profl. jours. Mem. Am. Chem. Soc., Sigma Xi, Phi Kappa Phi, Alpha Sigma Lambda. Democrat. Episcopalian. Avocation: latin american studies. Office: Towson U Dept Chemistry 8000 York Rd Towson MD 21252-0001 E-mail: laurenceboucher@netscape.net., lboucher@towson.edu.

BOUCHER, LOUIS JACK, retired dentist, educator; b. Ashland, Wis., May 24, 1922; s. Louis Napoleon and Clara (Rappatta) B.; m. Mary Lynn Phyllis Elsner, Nov. 5, 1949; children: Lynn Marie, Ellen Lou, Carol Joy, John Charles. Student, Northland Coll., 1945-48, U. Wis., 1948-49; D.D.S., Marquette U., 1953, PhD, 1961. Dir. grad. studies and research Marquette U. Sch. Dentistry, 1955-65, U. Ky. Coll. Dentistry, 1965-66; assoc. dean Med. Coll., Ga. Sch. Dentistry, 1966-71; dean Sch. Dentistry, Fairleigh Dickinson U., 1971-75; assoc. dean Coll. Medicine and Dentistry, N.J. Sch. Dentistry, Newark, 1976-77; dir. prosthodontics Sch. Dental Medicine, SUNY-Stony Brook, 1978-89, assoc. dean, 1978-82. Cons. VA hosps., U.S. Army, Ft. Jackson, S.C., also Ft. Gordon, Ga.; cons. USAF Aerospace Medicine, Surgeon Gen. USAF, Nat. Inst. Dentistry, USPHS, Am. Dental Assn. Council on Dental Edn. Author: (with A.O. Rahn) Maxillofacial Prosthetics, 1970, A Comprehensive Review of Dentistry, 1979, Occlusal Articulation, 1979, (with T.W. Slaughter) Impacted Teeth and Occlusion, 1980, Treatment of Partially Endentulous Patients, 1982, (with R.P. Renner) Removable Partial Dentures, 1987. Served with AUS, 1942-45. Recipient Nat. Inst. Dental Research Spl. Research fellowship and Career Devel. award, 1961-65 Mem. Am., Internat. colls. dentists, Am. Bd. Prosthodontics, Am. Acad. Maxillofacial Prosthodontics (pres. 1965), Am. Acad. Plastics Research in Dentistry (pres. 1967), Am. Coll. Prosthodontists (pres. 1971), Fedn. Prosthodontics Orgns. (pres. 1967-68), Am. Equilibration Soc. (pres. 1976), Greater N.Y. Acad. Prosthodontics (pres. 1988), Sigma Xi, Omicron Kappa Upsilon. Home: 4 Lyme Pl Avon CT 06001-4577 *I always tried to do my best.*

BOUCHER, RICHARD A. federal agency administrator; b. Bethesda, Md., Dec. 13, 1951; s. Melville J. and Ellen (Kaufmann) B.; m. Carolyn L. Brehm, June 19, 1982; children: Madeleine Brehm, Peter Brehm. BA cum laude, Tufts U., 1973; postgrad., George Washington U., 1976-77. Vol. Peace Corps, Senegal, 1973-75; with Agy. Internat. Devel., Guinea, 1975-76; various positions Fgn. Svc., 1977-84; econ. officer U.S. Consulate Gen., Shanghai, 1984-86; sr. watch officer Dept. of State, 1986-87, dep. dir. polit. affairs office European security and polit. affairs, 1987-89, dep. spokesman, 1989-92, acting spokesman, 1992-93; U.S. amb. to Cyprus, 1993-96; U.S. consul gen. to Hong Kong, 1996-99; U.S. sr. ofcl. Asia Pacific Econ. Cooperation Forum, 1999—; asst. sec. for public affairs Dept. of State, Washington, 2000—. Office: APEC Bur East Asian & Pacific Affairs US Dept State 2201 C St NW Washington DC 20520-0001

BOUCHER, THOMAS OWEN, engineering educator, researcher; b. Providence, June 25, 1942; s. Joseph William and Anne Marie (Byrne) B.; m. Unn Gunnerus Jermstad, Mar. 30, 1974. BSEE, U. R.I., 1964; MBA, Northwestern U., 1970; PhD in Indsl. Engring., Columbia U., 1978. Sr. project engr. Continental Can Co., Chgo., 1967-69; sr. staff cons. ABEX Corp., N.Y.C., 1970-72; asst. prof. Cornell U., Ithaca, N.Y., 1978-81, Rutgers U., New Brunswick, N.J., 1981-87, assoc. prof., 1987-94; prof., 1994—. Author: Computer Automation in Manufacturing, 1996; co-author: Analysis and Control of Production Systems, 2d edit., 1994; dept. editor IIE Transactions, 1987-91; area editor Engring. Economist, 1989-93; assoc. editor Jour. Productivity Analysis, 1989-91; mem. editl. bd. Internat. Jour. Flexible Automation and Integrated Mfg., 1992-2000, Jour. Engring. Valuation and Cost Analysis, 1995—. 1st lt. U.S. Army, 1965—67, Vietnam. Grantee NSF, Def. Logistics Agy. Mem. IEEE (sr.), SME (sr.), Am. Soc. for Engring. Edn. (chmn. engring. econ. dir. 1986-87), N.Y. Acad. Scis., Inst. Indsl. Engrs. (sr. mem., Wellington award 2002), Sigma Xi. Roman Catholic. Achievements include research in manufacturing automation, computer integrated manufacturing systems, production planning and control, and engineering economics. Home: 65 Douglas Rd Glen Ridge NJ 07028-1227 Office: Rutgers U Sch Engring 96 Frelinghuysen Rd Piscataway NJ 08855-0909

BOUCHER, WAYNE IRVING, policy analyst; b. Bay City, Mich., Dec. 12, 1934; s. Harold Oscar and Mildred Christine (Born) B.; m. Donna Lou Collins, June 12, 1961 (div. 1972); children: Michèle Annette, Robert Alain. BA in English Lang. and Lit., U. Mich., 1956, MA in English Lang. and Lit., 1960; postgrad. in philosophy, U. Mo., 1959-61. Instr. English U. Mo., Columbia, 1958-63; asst. to pres. Rand Corp., Santa Monica, Calif., 1963-69; rsch. assoc. Inst. for the Future, Middletown, Conn., 1969-71; co-founder, v.p. The Futures Group, Glastonbury, Conn., 1971-76; dept. dir., dir. rsch. Nat. Commn. on Electronic Fund Transfers, Washington, 1976-78; sr. rsch. assoc. Ctr. for Futures Rsch., U. So. Calif., Los Angeles, 1978-84; exec. v.p. Benton Internat., Torrance, Calif., 1984-93; pres. The Ark. Inst., Little Rock, 1993-94; pres., chief ops. officer Electronic Funds Transfer Assn., Herndon, Va., 1994-95; co-founder, mng. dir. Strategic Futures Internat., Harpers Ferry, W.Va., 1995—. Author: (with J.L. Morrison and W.L. Renfro) Futures Research and Strategic Planning, 1984; Spinoza in English, 1991, 2d edit., 1999, Spinoza: 18th and 19th Century Discussions, 6 vols., 1999; editor: (with J.L. Morrison and W.L. Renfro) Applying Methods and Techniques of Futures Research, 1983; author, editor: The Study of the Future, 1977; editor (with E.S. Quade) Systems Analysis and Policy Planning, 1968; mem. editorial bd. Technol. Forecasting and Social Change, 1978-82, Futures Rsch. Quar., 1984—; contbr. articles to profl. jours. Home: RR 2 Box 667 Harpers Ferry WV 25425-9414 Office: Strategic Futures Internat Shannodale Lake 3 Lakeside Dr Rte 2 Box 667 Harpers Ferry WV 25425-9414 E-mail: wib@sfutures.com.

BOUCHILLON, JOHN RAY, education coordinator; b. Covington, Ga., Sept. 3, 1943; s. John Ray and Mary Reid (Death) B.; m. Martha Jo Logue, Dec. 18, 1965; children: Trey, Monica, Beth. BA, LaGrange Coll., 1965; MEd, Ga. Coll., 1969. Tchr. chemistry Baldwin County, Milledgeville, Ga., 1965-71, career coord., 1971-72; dir. career edn. Liberty County, Hinesville, Ga., 1972-75; career edn. cons. Ga. Dept. Edn., Atlanta, 1975-86, quality basic edn. field adminstr., 1986-87, coord. local strategic planning, 1987-92, sch. support team leader, 1992-98, ret., 1998. Dir. sch. support svcs., asst. dir. sch. improvement and tng. divsn. Ga. Dept. Edn., 1996-98; chmn. career edn. adv. com. Ga. So. Coll., Statesboro, 1972-73; dir.-at-large guidance div. Ga. Vocat. Assn., Atlanta, 1976; sec.-treas. Ga. Vocat. Guidance Assn., 1976, pres., 1979. Co-editor: (newsletter) Ga. Pupil Personnel, 1975; editor: (newsletter) Ga. Personnel and Guidance, 1977-78; mem. editl. bd. Jour. Career Edn., 1978-80, Future Mag., 1978, Chronicle Guidance Corp., 1987-89. Mem. Ga. Sch. Counselors Assn. (Gov.'s award for Govt. Svc.), Internat. Soc. Ednl. Planners (bd. dirs. 1987-91). Democrat. Methodist. Avocations: photography, woodworking. Home: 4276 Village Green Cir Conyers GA 30013 E-mail: raybou@worldnet.att.net.

BOUCKAERT, CARL M. manufacturing executive; CEO Beaulieu of Am. Group. Office: Beaulieu of Am LLC 1502 Coronet Dr Dalton GA 30720*

BOUDART, MICHEL, chemical engineer, chemist, educator, consultant; b. Belgium, June 18, 1924; came to U.S., 1947, naturalized, 1957; s. Francois and Marguerite (Swolfs) B.; m. Marina D'Haese, Dec. 27, 1948; children: Mark, Baudouin, Iris, Philip. BS, U. Louvain, Belgium, 1944, MS, 1947; PhD, Princeton U., 1950; D honoris causa, U. Liège, U. Notre Dame, U. Nancy, U. Ghent. Research asso. James Forrestal Research Ctr., Princeton, 1950-54; mem. faculty Princeton U., 1954-61; prof. chem. engring. U. Calif., Berkeley, 1961-64, adj. prof. chem. engring., 1994—; prof. chem. engring. and chemistry Stanford U., 1964-80, Keck prof. engring., 1980-94, Keck prof. engring. emeritus, 1994—. Co-founder Catalytica, Inc.; Humble Oil Co. lectr., 1958; AIChE lectr., 1961; Sigma Xi nat. lectr., 1965; chmn. Gordon Rsch. Conf. Catalysis, 1962. Author: Kinetics of Chemical Processes, 1968, (with G. Djéga-Mariadassou) Kinetics of Heterogenous Catalytic Reactions, 1983; editor: (with J.R. Anderson) Catalysis: Science and Technology, 11 vols., 1981-96, (with Marina Boudart and René Bryssinck) Modern Belgium, 1990; mem. adv. editl. bd. Catal. Letters, 1989—, Catalysis Rev., 1968—, Jour. Molecular Catalysis, 1995—, Cattech, 1996—. Recipient Curtis-McGraw rsch. award Am. Soc. Engring. Edn., 1962, R.H. Wilhelm award in chem. reaction engring., 1974, Chem. Pioneer award Am. Inst. Chemists, 1991; Belgium-Am. Ednl. Found. fellow, 1948, Procter fellow, 1949; Fairchild disting. scholar Calif. Tech. Inst., 1995. Fellow AAAS, Am. Acad. Arts and Scis., Calif. Acad. Scis.; mem. NAS, NAE, Am. Chem. Soc. (Kendall award 1977, E.V. Murphee award in indsl. and engring. chemistry 1985), Catalysis Soc., Am. Inst. Chem. Engrs., Chem. Soc., Académie Royale de Belgique (fgn. assoc.), French Nat. Acad. Pharmacy (fgn.). Home: 228 Oak Grove Ave Atherton CA 94027-2218 Office: Stanford U Dept Chem Engring Stanford CA 94305 Fax: 650-723-9780. E-mail: mboudart@stanford.edu.

BOUDIN, MICHAEL, federal judge; b. N.Y.C., Nov. 29, 1939; s. Leonard and Jean Boudin; m. Martha Field, Sept. 18, 1984. BA, Harvard Coll., 1961, LLB, 1964. Bar: N.Y. 1964, D.C. 1967. Law clk. U.S. Ct. Appeals (2d cir.), 1964—65, U.S. Supreme Ct., 1965—66; assoc. firm Covington & Burling, Washington, 1966—72, ptnr., 1972—87; dep. asst. atty. gen. anti-trust divsn. Dept. Justice, Washington, 1987—90; judge U.S. Dist. Ct. (D.C. dist.), Washington, 1990—92, U.S. Ct. Appeals, Boston, 1992—98. Vis. prof. Harvard Law Sch., 1982—83, lectr., 1983—98, U. Pa. Law Sch., 1984—85. Contbr. articles to profl. jours. Mem.: ABA, Am. Law Inst. Office: US Ct Appeals 1st Cir 1 Courthouse Way Ste 7710 Boston MA 02210-3009

BOUDINOT, FRANK DOUGLAS, dean; b. New Brunswick, NJ, Mar. 31, 1956; s. Frank Lins and Dorothy Jean (Libourel) B.; m. Sarah Garrett, Sept. 1992; 1 child, Frank Garrett. BS in Biology, Springfield Coll., 1978; PhD in Pharmaceutics, SUNY, Buffalo, 1986. Vet. technician Afton Animal Hosp., Williamsville, N.Y., 1978-79; rsch. technician SUNY-Millard Fillmore Hosp., Buffalo, 1979-80; grad. asst. SUNY, 1980-85; asst. prof. pharmaceutics U. Ga., Athens, 1986-90, assoc. prof., 1990-98, head dept. pharm., 1992-98, prof., head dept. pharm. & biomed. scis., 1998-99, prof. dept. pharm. and biomed. scis., 1998—, assoc. dean grad. sch., 1999—2001, sr. assoc. dean Grad. Sch., 2001—02; dean Sch. Grad. Studies Va. Commonwealth U., Richmond, 2002—, prof. Dept. Pharmaceutics, 2002—. Scientific adv. bd. Pharmassett Ltd., 1999—; adj. prof. Dept. Pharma. and Biomed. Scis., U. Ga., 2002—. Mem. editl. bd.: Jour. Pharmacy Tchg., 1989—2001, Biopharm. and Drug Disposition, 1994—, Antimicrobiol. Agts. and Chemotherapy, 1998—2001, Archives of Pharmacal Rsch., 1999—2001, referee: Jour. Pharm. Scis., 1988—, Jour. Pharm. Rsch., 1989—, N.Am. editor: Jour. Biopharmaceutics and Drug Disposition, 1998—; contbr. over 100 articles to profl. jours. Vice chair govt. svcs. subcom. Oconee 2000, Watkinsville, Ga., 1986—87; vol., event svcs. agt. Summer Olympics, Athens, Ga., 1996; rollerhockey coach Athens YMCA, 2001—02; Little League baseball coach Midlothian, Ga., 2003—; del. Ga. State Rep. Conv., Atlanta, 1989, 1991, 1992; bd. dirs. Oconee Animal Shelter, Watkinsville, Ga., 1986—88. Named one of Outstanding Young Men of Am., 1987. Mem. AAAS, Am. Assn. Pharm. Scientists (mem. abstract screening com., 2001-02, rsch. achievement com., 2002), Am. Assn. Coll. Pharmacy (del. 1989-90, profl. affairs com. 1990-91, tchr. mentoring com., 2002—), Am. Soc. Microbiology, Coun. Grad. Sch., So. Conf. Grad. Sch. (award com. 2002), mem. Rho Chi: Pharmaceutical Hon. Soc.; mem. Phi Kappa Phi (v.p. for scholarships and awards, 2003-). Episcopalian. Achievements include research in pharmacokinetics of antiviral drugs, effects of age in drug disposition, veterinary pharmacokinetics, and drug pharmacodynamics. Office: Va Commonwealth U Sch Grad Studies PO Box 843051 Richmond VA 23284-3051 E-mail: fdboudinot@vcu.edu.

BOUDON, HENRY LAWRENCE, social sciences educator, editor; b. Olean, N.Y., Feb. 3, 1960; s. Henry Lawrence and Mary Shevak Boudon; m. Laura Elizabeth Besseyre, June 25, 1994. BA in Polit. Sci. and Spanish, U. Rochester, 1983; MA in Govt., U. Va., 1986; PhD in Internat. Studies, U. Miami, Fla., 1997. Abstracter Info-South, Coral Gables, Fla., 1992—95; adj. prof. Fla. Internat. U., Miami, 1995; vis. prof. U. of the Andes, Bogota, Colombia, 1996—97; adj. prof. George Washington U., Washington, 1998—99, George Mason U., Fairfax, Va., 1998—99; editor EFE News Svcs., Coral Gables, 1999; adj. prof. Am. U., Washington, 2000—; editor Handbook of Latin Am. Studies Libr. of Congress, Washington, 2000—. Contbr. articles to profl. jours. Recipient Barrett prize, U. Miami, 1998. Mem.: Seminar on Acquisition of Latin Am. Libr. Materials, Latin Am. Studies Assn., Am. Polit. Sci. Assn. Democrat. Avocations: golf, cooking, travel, wine, culture. Home: 2932 Huntington Grove Sq Alexandria VA 22306 E-mail: lbou@loc.gov.

BOUDOULAS, HARISIOS, physician, educator, researcher; b. Velvendo Kozani, Greece, Nov. 3, 1935; married; 2 children. MD, U. Salonica, Greece, 1959. Resident in internal medicine Red Cross Hosp., Athens, Greece, 1960-61, U. Salonica First Med. Clinic, 1962-66, resident in internal medicine and cardiology, 1962-66, lectr., 1969-70; postgrad. fellow, instr. div. cardiology Ohio State U. Coll. Medicine, Columbus, 1970-73, asst. prof. medicine, 1975-78, assoc. prof., 1978-80, dir. cardiac non-invasive lab., 1978-80, prof. medicine div. cardiology, 1980—, prof. pharmacy, 1984—, dir. cardiovascular rsch. div., 1983-86, dir. cardiovascular teaching and rsch. lab., 1992—; prof. medicine div. cardiology Wayne State U., Detroit, 1980-82, chief clin. cardiovascular rsch., 1980-82, acting dir. div. cardiology, 1982; chief cardiovascular diagnostic and tng. center VA Med. Ctr., Allen Park, Mich., 1980-82; chief sect. cardiology Harper-Grace Hosps., Detroit, 1982. Mem. antepistelon Athens Acad., 1998—; dir. Ctr. for Clin. Rsch., pres. sci. coun. Inst. Biomed. Rsch., Acad. of Athens. Editor in chief Hellenic Jour. Cardiology; mem. editl. rev. bd. jours. cardiology; contbr. numerous articles to med. jours. Named Disting. Research Investigator, Cen. Ohio chpt. Am. Heart Assn., Columbus, 1983. Fellow ACP, Am. Coll. Angiology, Am. Coll. Clin. Pharmacology, Am. Coll. Cardiology (trustee Ohio chpt. 1993-97), Am. Heart Assn. (coun. clin. cardiology 1989-93, coun. exec. com. 1991-93, sci. com. 1991-93), European Soc. Cardiology (sci. com. 1991-93, valvular heart disease working group 1993—), Greek Heart Assn., Am. Fedn. Clin. Rsch., Laeneck Soc. (chmn. 1991-93), Hellenic Cardiol. Soc. (pres. 2002). Office: Ohio State U Div Cardiology 1655 Upham Dr Columbus OH 43210-1251

BOUDREAU, A. ALLAN, historian, writer, educator; b. Albany, N.Y., Aug. 1, 1936; s. Alexander and Lillian (Allan) B.; children: Kirstin Rosamund, Andrew Allan. Student, Albany Law Sch., 1955; BS, Russell Sage Coll., 1958; MS, Columbia U., 1972; MBA, NYU, 1964, PhD, 1973. Rockefeller intern N.Y. State Dept. Edn., 1958-59; adminstr. officer N.Y. State Libr., 1959-62; pub. acct. N.Y. State, 1961—; dep. dir. NYU Librs., 1962-73; sec. N.Y. State Libr. Found., 1973—93; sr. rsch. assoc. NYU, 1973-74. Cons. to colls. and univs., govt., industry. Author: The Research Resources at Washington Square 1831-1970, 1972, 200 Years of Freemasonry in New York, 1981, George Washington in New York (state), 1987, George Washington and New York City, 1989; contbr. articles to profl. jours. Vol. fireman N.Y. State; sec. N.Y. State Libr. Trustee Found., 1973-93; trustee Allan Found., 1970—. With AUS, 1953-55, Korea. Recipient Founders Day award NYU, 1973. Mem. ALA (life), DAV (life), NRA (life). N.Y. Civil and Criminal Courts Bar Assn., Am. Philatelic Soc., N.Y. State Ret. Tchrs. Assn. (life), Am. Orchid Soc., Am. Legion (life), N.Y. Athletic Club, Collectors Club (N.Y.C.), Masons (N.Y.C.). Home: 1 Washington Square Vlg New York NY 10012-1632

BOUDREAU, ALICE BENJAMIN, artist, educator; b. Mpls., May 2, 1936; d. Edwin Grimshaw and Marian (Jones) Benjamin; m. Maurice Louis Boudreau, Feb. 9, 1974. Student, Wellesley Coll., 1954-56; BA in Studio Art, U. Minn., 1958, BA in Art Edn., 1963; BFA, San Francisco Art inst., 1961; MS in Art Edn., SUNY, New Paltz, 1967. Zoology artist U. Minn., Mpls., 1958—61; elem. art instr. Onteora Pub. Schs., Boiceville, N.Y., 1963-66; jr. high art instr. Mpls. Pub. Sch., 1967-69; elem. art instr. Northrop & Blakes Schs., Hopkins, Minn., 1969-75; instr. painting, drawing and design Cambridge (Minn.) C.C., 1978-93. Mem. artists' collective West Lake Gallery, Mpls., 1969-81. Illustrator: General Biology-Laboratory Guide, 1960; one-woman exhibit Iris Gallery, Lindstrom, Minn., 1996, Joan Peters Gallery, Bradenton Village of the Arts, 2000-2002; featured exhibitor Plymouth Congl. Ch., Mpls., 1967, 82, 92, 95, Vern Carver Gallery, Mpls., 1993, invitational group exhbn. Art League of Manatee County, 2001— (1st and other awards). Bd. mem. Minn. Organic Merchandise, Cambridge, 1989-93; mem. friends of the libr. East Ctrl. Regional Libr., Cambridge, 1993-97. Recipient Higgins Ink award Scholastic Mag., 1954, 1st, 2d and Best of Show awards East Cen. Arts Coun., Mora, Minn., 1988, 90, 92, 95; travel grantee to France East Cen. Arts Coun., Mora, 1995. Mem. Nat. League Am. Pen Women (pres. Sarasota br. 2000-2002), Art Target, Isanti County Arts Guild (pres. 1984-93), Women Contemporary Artists, Art Ctr. Sarasota, Arts Couns. of Manatee and Sarasota Counties, Art League Manatee County. Democrat. Avocations: reading, swimming, gardening, cooking, correspondence. Home: 10816 Forest Run Dr Bradenton FL 34211-9742 E-mail: boud@kudos.net.

BOUDREAU, BEVERLY ANN, health care professional; b. Chgo., Mar. 1, 1940, d. Alvernon Holmberg and Mildred Catherine (Thomson) Hayes; m. Frederick Joseph Boudreau, Apr. 26, 1958 (div. Jan. 1971); children: Kenneth Joseph, Cynthia Lynn, Susan Marie. Student, Chgo. City Coll., 1967-72, Moraine Valley C.C., Palos Hills, Ill., 1974-77. Cert. med. asst., Chgo., 1974. Tech. sales rep. Diagnostic Tech., Inc., Hauppauge, N.Y., 1979-83; sec., technician Northwestern Meml. Hosp., Chgo., 1984-86; med. sec., asst. Howard Schachter, M.D., Chgo., 1986-95; med. billing staff Rush Presbyn. St. Lukes Medical Ctr., Chgo., 1995-96; med. sec. Rehab. Medicine Clinic, Wheaton, Ill., 1997—. Developer/implementor Operation Beach Camp, USAR Drug Demand Reduction Edn. Program for Children, 1995-96; instr. USAR Family Program Activity Planning, 1994-96, Family Program Drug Demand Reduction, 1997. Mem. Chgo. Coun. Fgn. Rels., 1986-89; participant Ulster Project-DuPage/No. Ireland, Great Lakes, Ill., 1996-2002, Logos After Sch. Program, Glen Ellyn, Ill., 1996-97; charter mem. USAR Family Program, Atlanta, 1991-96, Family Program Adv. Coun., Washington; deacon First Presbyn. Ch. of Glen Ellyn, 1996-99, peacemaking/mission planning activities, 1999, elder missions coun., 2000-01. Recipient Cert. of Achievement, USAR, 1995. Mem. 416th ENCOM Assn. (assoc.), Am. Biog. Inst. (mem. rsch. bd. advisors). Avocation: drug prevention programs for children. Office: Rehabilitation Med Clinic 26w171 Roosevelt Rd Wheaton IL 60187-6078

BOUDREAU, FRANCIS HELIER, obstetrician-gynecologist; b. Cambridge, Mass., Aug. 29, 1934; m. Laura M. O'Brien, Feb. 23, 1963; children: Francis, Laura, Renée, Nicole, Jacques, Jean Paul, Micheline, Andre, Danielle. AB, Harvard U., 1956; MD, Boston U., 1962. Cert. in ob-gyn. Intern St. Vincents Hosp., N.Y.C., 1962-63, resident in surgery, 1963-64, resident in ob-gyn., 1964-68; vice chmn. ob-gyn. dept. St. Elizabeths Hosp., Brighton, Mass., 1998-2000; chmn. St. Elizabeth Ob/Gyn., 2000—. Fellow ACOG (chmn. Mass. sect. 1999-2002); mem. AMA, Am. Fertility Soc., Mass. Med. Soc., Boston Obstetrical Soc. (pres. 1999-2002). Office: 1180 Beacon St Brookline MA 02446-3885

BOUDREAU, ROBERT JAMES, nuclear medicine physician, researcher; b. Lethbridge, Alta., Can., Dec. 27, 1950; came to U.S., 1983; s. George Joseph Boudreau and Eleanor Joyce (Dalzell) Hamilton; m. Francine Suzanne Archambault, Jan. 16, 1982. BSc with highest honors, U. Sask., Saskatoon, Can., 1972; PhD, U. B.C., Vancouver, Can., 1975; MD, U. Calgary (Alta.), 1978. Diplomate Am. Bd. Nuclear Medicine. Resident in diagnostic radiology and nuclear medicine McGill U., Montreal, Que., Can., 1978-82; asst. prof. U. Minn., Mpls., 1983-87, assoc. prof., 1987-93, prof., 1993-99, prof. emeritus, 2000—, dir. grad. studies dept. radiology, 1987-91, dir. nuclear medicine divsn., 1987-2000. Author book chpts.; contbr. articles to profl. jours. Recipient Gold Key award Soc. Chem. Industry, 1972, Soc. Clin. Investigation Young Investigator award, 1978; Can. Heart Found. Med. Scientist fellow, 1976-78. Fellow Royal Coll. Physicians; mem. Soc. Chiefs of Acad. Nuclear Medicine Sects. (treas. 1989-93), Soc. Nuclear Medicine (edn. and tng. com. 1983-91, trustee 1994-95, bd. govs. ctrl. chpt. 1989—, treas. 1992-94, pres. 1994-95), Radiol. Soc. N.Am. Avocations: skiing, boating, travel, computers. Office: U Minn FUMC 500 Harvard St SE Minneapolis MN 55455-0363

BOUDREAUX, JOHN, public relations/internet specialist; b. Franklin, La., July 28, 1946; s. Abel John and Dorothy (Bourgeois) B. BA, La. State U., 1969. Reporter, copy editor Morning Advocate, Baton Rouge, 1969-71; successively reporter, copy editor, asst. city editor Houston Post, 1971-76, city editor, 1976-84; pub. rels. cons., 1984-85; sr. communications specialist IBM, Dallas, 1985-87, comm. mgr. San Francisco, 1987-88, program mgr. Westchester County, N.Y., 1988-2000; mng. editor IBM.com, 2000—03; pres. EJB Comms., 2003—. Named Outstanding Journalism Grad., La. State U., 1969. Mem. Soc. Profl. Journalists, Sigma Delta Chi (bd. dirs. Houston chpt. 1975, 83).

BOUDREAUX, KENNETH JUSTIN, economics and finance educator, consultant; b. New Orleans, Dec. 22, 1943; s. Aldwin John and Beverly Estelle (Swanton) B.; m. Carole Jean Barnette, May 28, 1966; 1 child, Beau Justin AB, Princeton U., 1965; MBA, Tulane U., 1967; Ph.D, U. Wash., 1970. Asst. prof. Sch. Bus., Tulane U., New Orleans, 1970-73, assoc. prof., 1973-78, prof., 1978—, assoc. dean faculty, 1981-83. Cons. City of New Orleans Author: Basic Theory of Corporate Finance, 1977, Finance, 1990; editorial bd. Jour. Econs. and Bus., Jour. Fin. Rsch.; contbr. articles to scholarly jours. AACSB fellow, 1969-70; recipient Wissner award Tulane U., 1972, 75, Outstanding Prof., 1972, 75, Disting. Prof., 1973 Fellow Fin. Analysts Fedn.; mem. Am. Econ. Assn., Am. Fin. Assn., Western Fin. Assn., Western Econ. Assn. Clubs; Cannon (Princeton U.), Pickwick, So. Yacht Club. Office: Tulane U Sch Bus New Orleans LA 70118

BOUDRIA, DON, Canadian government official; b. Hull, Quebec, Can., Aug. 30, 1949; s. Roy and Jacqueline (Lavergne) B.; m. MaryAnn Morris, Aug. 28, 1971; children: Daniel, Julie. BA in History, U. Waterloo, 1999. With Fed. Govt., 1966, chief purchasing agent; mem. Legis. Assembly, Ont., 1981; M.P.P., 1981; opposition critic of govt. svcs., 1982—83; opposition critic of cmty. and social svcs., 1981-83; opposition critic of consumer and comml. rels., 1983-84; M.P. Ho. of Commons, 1984—. Critic Fed. supply and svcs.; official opposition, mem. standing com. on Agriculture, 1984; dep. chmn. Ont. Liberal Caucus, 1984; Public Works critic, 1985; critic Can. Post. and Govt. Ops., 1988; dep. oppositon whip, 1989, asst. House leader for the Official Opposition; Sworn to the Privy Coun., 1996; Min. Internat. Cooperation, Min. Responsible La Francophonie, 1996-97; dep. govt. whip, 1993-94, chief govt. whip, 1994-96; min. of state, leader govt., House of Commons, 1997—. Mem. L'Assn. Internat. des Parlementaires de Langue Française (founding pres. Ont. sect.), Cumberland Twp. Housing Corp. (founding pres.), Sarsfield Optimist Club (founding pres.). Achievements include languages spoken and written; French, English. Avocations: history, music, skiing. Office: House of Commons 215-S Ctr Block Ottawa ON Canada K1A 0A6

BOUÉ, DANIEL ROBERT, pediatric pathologist, neuropathologist, educator; b. N.Y.C., June 22, 1958; s. Robert Charles and Dorothea Anna B.; m. Julie Marie Borgerding; children: Rachel Hope, Jenna Elizabeth, AnnaMarie Monique, Sarah Jane. BA cum laude, Carleton Coll., 1980; PhD, U. Minn., 1988, MD, 1991. Diplomate in anat. and clin. pathology and pediatric pathology Am. Bd. Pathology. Intern U. Calif., San Diego, 1991-92, resident in pathology, 1992-94, chief resident-elect, 1994-95; attending physician U. Calif./San Diego Med. Ctr., 1994-95; clin. instr. U. Calif., San Diego, 1994-95; fellow pediat. pathology Columbus Childrens Hosp., 1995-96; clin. instr. Ohio State U., Columbus, 1995—97, clin. asst. prof. pathology, 1998—; fellow pediat. neuropathology Columbus Childrens Hosp., 1996; staff pathologist, dir. Neuropathology program Childrens Hosp., Columbus, 1997—; dir. surg. and autopsy neuropathology, muscle and nerve biopsy svcs. Interim dir perinatal pathology and autopsy svc. U. Calif., San Diego, 1994-95; rev. pathologist

Biopathology Ctr., Children's Hosp. Rsch. Found.; presenter in field. Contbr. articles to profl. jours. Med. Scientist scholar U. Minn., 1982-91, G.T. Evan scholar Dept. Lab. Medicine and Pathology, 1982-85, Life & Health Ins. Med. Rsch. Fund, scholar, 1985-90; recipient J.T. Livermore Hematology award Minn. Med. Found., 1988, undergrad. med. student rsch. award 1991, Dr. Vernon D.E. Smith award, 1990. Fellow Am. Coll. Pathology, Am. Soc. Clin. Pathologists (Sheard-Sanford award 1988), Coll. Am. Pathologists; mem. Soc. Pediat. Pathology, Alpha Omega Alpha. Office: Columbus Childrens Hosp Dept Lab Med 700 Childrens Dr Columbus OH 43205-2664

BOUFFORD, JO IVEY, health and human services administrator; b. Durham, N.C., July 2, 1945; BA in Psychology magna cum laude, Wellesley Coll., 1965; MD with distinction, U. Mich., 1971; DSc(hon.), SUNY, Bklyn., 1992. Diplomate Nat. Bd. Med. Examiners, Am. Bd. Pediats. Resident in social pediats. medicine Montefiore Hosp. and Med. Ctr., Bronx, N.Y., 1971-74, asst. attending physician, 1975-97, co-dir. Inst. for Health Team Devel., 1975-82, dir. residency program in social medicine, 1975-82; adminstrv. dir. Valentine Lane Family Practice, Yonkers, N.Y., 1975-82; v.p. med. ops. N.Y.C. Health and Hosps. Corp., 1982-83, v.p. med. and profl. affairs, 1983-85, exec. v.p., 1985, acting pres., 1985, pres., 1985-89; internat. fellow in comparative health sys. mgmt. King's Fund Coll., London, 1989-91, dir., 1991-93; prin. dep. asst. sec. for health Dept. Health and Human Svcs., Washington, 1993-97; dean Robert F. Wagner Grad. Sch. of Pub. Svc., New York Univ., 1997—; prof. pub. admin., clin. prof. peds. New York Univ., 1997—; asst. prof. dept. pediats. Albert Einstein Coll. of Medicine, Bronx, N.Y., 1976-87, clin. assoc. prof. dept. epidemiology and social medicine, 1982-94. Acting Asst. Sec. Health, Jan.-June 1997; adj. prof. Lehman Coll. Nursing, Bronx, 1974-80; mem. Nat. Adv. Coun. for Health Professions Edn. US-DHHS, 1976-80; mem. tech. panel on the ednl. environ. Grad. Med. Edn. Nat. Adv. Coun., 1979-80; cons. on manpower programs divsn. medicine bur. Health Professions Edn. HRSA-DHHS, 1980-88; mem. N.Y. State Coun. on Grad. med. Edn., 1987-89, N.Y. State Commn. on Grad. Med. Edn., 1985-86; mem. adv. bd. residency program in gen. preventive medicine and occupl. health Mt. Sinai coll. Medicine, 1986-89; mem. Nat. Vis. Coun. for the Health Scis. Faculty Columbia U., N.Y.C., 1988-90; mem. vis. faculty The New Sch. for Social Rsch., 1989; rep. of U.S. on exec. bd. WHO, 1994-97; mem. joint coordinating com. for Radiation Health Effects Rsch. 1994-97; U.S. staff dir. Gore-Chernomyrdin Commn. Health Com., 1994-97; various consulting positions. Mem. editl. bd. Jour. Med. Edn., 1980-86; mem. editl. adv. bd. The New Physician, 1979-89; contbr. articles to profl. jours.; presenter in field. Mem. Nat. Adv. Coun. of Agy. for Healthcare Quality and Rsch., 2000—; bd. dirs. United Hosp. Fund, 1999—; chair sub-bd. on health, Open Soc. Inst., 1998—; mem. N.Y. State Coun. on Grad. Med. Edn., 1987-89. Fellow Am. Acad. Pediats.; mem. APHA, NAS Inst. Medicine Coun. (Robert Wood Johnson health policy fellow 1979-80), Am. Med. Women's Assn., Ambulatory Pediats. Assn., Soc. for Health and Human Values, Soc. Med. Adminstrs., Med. Adminstrs. Conf. Office: NYU Robert F Wagner Grad Sch Pub Svc 4 Washington Sq N New York NY 10003-6671 E-mail: jo.bouffard@nyu.edu.

BOUGAS, JAMES ANDREW, physician, educator, surgeon; b. Bismarck, N.D., Jan. 25, 1924; s. Andrew James and Mary (Psaltiras) B.; m. Tiina Parlin, June 27, 1953; children: Karen Louise, Tiina Maria. MD, Harvard U., 1948. Diplomate Am. Bd. Surgery, Am. Bd. Thoracic Surgery. Intern Columbia U. Svc., Bellevue Hosp., N.Y.C., 1948-50, chief resident in surgery, 1952-53; resident Presbyn. Hosp., N.Y.C., 1950-52, chief resident surgery, 1953; fellow Overholt Clinic, Boston, 1953-55, assoc., 1955-65; chief thoracic surgery U. Hosp., Boston, 1965-70; assoc. prof. surgery Boston U. Sch. Medicine, 1965—. Lectr. Tufts U. Sch. Medicine, Boston, 1965-70; chmn. Gordon Rsch. Confs., 1967-68. Contbr. articles to profl. jours. Pres. Heart Assn., Boston, 1967-69; chmn. Mass. Rehab. Commn. Adv. Com.; trustee Boston Tb Assn. With U.S. Army, 1942-44. Fellow AAAS; mem. ACS, Am. Coll. Cardiology, Am. Assn. Thoracic Surgeons, Soc. Thoracic Surgeons, Am. Coll. Cardiology, Mass. Med. Soc. (legis. com., coun.), Norfolk Dist. Med. Soc. (pres. 1989-90, Tri-State regional planning com.). Achievements include development of combined cardiac catheterization; porous metal prostheses fabrication and cardio-pulmonary physiology. Office: NE Bapt Hosp 125 Parker Hill Ave Boston MA 02120-2847 E-mail: jbougas@caregroup.harvard.edu.

BOUGHAN, ZANETTA LOUISE, music educator; b. Grantham, Eng., Mar. 22, 1959; arrived in U.S., 1964; d. Peter Leonard and Alyda Venita Maria (Bellord) Snowden; m. Robert William Boughan, Nov. 3, 1995. Student, George Mason U., 1977—78, U. Alaska, 1985—87, Cochise Coll., 1999—, Wayland Bapt. U., Sierra Vista campus, 2003—. Pvt. piano and violin instr., Sierra Vista, Ariz., 1988—. Concertmaster Cochise Coll. Orch., Sierra Vista, 1999—2001, Pima Coll. Orch., Tucson, 2001—02; first violinist Sierra Vista Sym. Orch., 2001—02. Vol. Sierra Vista Police Dept., 2002—; ct. apptd. spl. adv. vol. State Ariz., 2002—; vol. in Police Svc., 2002—; mem. Citizens Police Acad. Assocs., 2003—. With USN, 1979—84. Mem.: Ariz. Music Tchrs. Assn., Nat. Music Tchrs. Assn., Cochise Music Tchrs. Assn. (chmn. fundraising com. 1997—, sec. 1998—2000, treas. 2001—03, pres. 2003—, Profl. Develop. grant 2001). Home: 4924 Marconi Dr Sierra Vista AZ 85635 E-mail: zboughan@earthlink.net.

BOUGHTON, JAMES MURRAY, economist; b. Chgo., Apr. 8, 1944; s. Stanley R. and Erminie (Bloyd) B.; m. Lesley Anne Simmons. BA, Duke U., 1966; MA, U. Mich., 1967; PhD, Duke U., 1969. Asst. prof. Ind. U., Bloomington, 1970-73, assoc prof., 1973-81, prof., 1981-83; economist Orgn. Econ. Coop. and Devel., Paris, 1973-75, cons., 1976-79; economist IMF, Washington, 1981-86, advisor, 1986-92, historian, 1992-2001; sr. assoc. mem. St. Anthony's Coll., U. Oxford, 2000-01; asst. dir. PDR, 2001—. Author: Monetary Policy and Federal Funds Market, 1971, Silent Revolution, 2001; co-author: Principles of Monetary Economics, 1975; co-editor: Fifty Years After Bretton Woods, Future of SDR; contbr. articles to profl. jours. V.p. Ind. Civil Liberties Union, Indpls., 1978-79; chmn. bd. dirs. Bretton Woods, Germantown, Md., 1990-93. Mem.: Am. Econ. Assn., Cosmos Club. Office: Internat Monetary Fund 700 19th St NW Washington DC 20431-0001 E-mail: jboughton@imf.org.

BOUGHTON, LESLEY D. library director; b. New Haven, Conn., Jan. 21, 1945; d. Robert and Marjorie (Anderson) D.; m. Charles E. Boughton, Sept. 5, 1964 (dec. 1991); children: Michael, James, Gregg. AB, Conn. Coll., 1971; MLS, So. Conn. State U., 1978. Dir. Platte County Library, Wheatland, Wyo., 1980-88, Carbon County Library, Rawlins, Wyo., 1988-93, Natrona County Pub. Library, Casper, Wyo., 1993—99; state libr. Wyo. State Libr., Cheyenne, 1999—. Mem. Gov's. Telecommunications Coun., Wyo., 1994—. Mem. ALA (chpt. councilor 1988, 91), Wyo. Library Assn. (pres. 1985, Disting. Svc. award 1991). Office: Wyo State Library 2301 Capitol Ave Cheyenne WY 82002

BOUGNOL, MARIE-LAURE, finance educator; b. Marrakech, Morocco, Apr. 30, 1974; arrived in U.S., 1992; d. Jacques and Jacqueline Bougnol. BBA, U. Miss., 1996, MBA, 1997, PhD in Bus. Adminstrn., 2001. Vis. asst. prof. bus. adminstrn. U. Miss., Oxford, 2001—. Mem.: Decision Sci. Inst., Inst. Ops. Rsch. and Mgmt. Scis. Office: U Miss Sch Bus Adminstrn University MS 38677 E-mail: mbougnol@bus.olemiss.edu.

BOUILLIANT-LINET, FRANCIS JACQUES, global management consultant; b. Garches, France, Aug. 20, 1932; came to U.S., 1977; s. Jacques Achille and Virginia Sutton (McKee) B.-L.; m. Carolyn Jeanine Taylor, Nov. 17, 1978. Diploma in sci., Admiral Farragut Acad., 1948; postgrad., Duke U., 1949-50. Mgmt. trainee Harry Ferguson Cos., Europe, 1951-53; sales promotion mgr. Massey-Harris-Ferguson, Paris, 1957-59; gen. programs mgr. Massey Ferguson Ltd., Coventry, Eng., 1959-63, coord. office of pres. Toronto, Ont., Can., 1963-65, group product mgr., 1966-68; dir. internat. logistics Allis Chalmers Corp., Milw., 1968-71; joint mng. dir. LePiol, s.a.r.l., Cannes, France, 1971-77; chmn. bd., chief exec. officer FBL, Inc., Hurtsboro, Ala., 1977—, also bd. dirs. Exec. dir. H.J. Crawley, Ltd., Leamington, Eng., 1961-66; bd. dirs. F.J.B., Inc., Thermal, Calif. Author: (manual) The New Product Process, 1963; trademark registrant for "Rent-a-Boss." Charter founder Ronald Reagan Rep. Ctr., Washington, 1987. With French Armed Forces, 1953-54, 56-57. Mem. Ala. Sheriff's Assn. (hon.), Capital City Club (life), Midland (Ga.) Fox Hounds. Office: FBL Inc PO Box 298 Hurtsboro AL 36860-0298

BOUJU, JEAN-MARC, photojournalist; Photojournalist Daily Texan, 1991—93, AP, 1993—. Co-recipient Pulitzer prize, 1995, 1999. Office: AP 221 S Figueroa St Los Angeles CA 90012*

BOUKERCHI, AZZEDINE, adult education educator, computer scientist, researcher; MSc, Sch. of Computer Sciences, McGill U., 1989—90; PhD, Sch. of Computer Sci., McGill U., 1990—95. Sr. scientist Metron Inc., San Diego, 1997—98; prof., computer sciences U. of North Tex., 1998—. Achievements include research in Developed The First Synchronization Algorithm For Wireless Multimedia. Office: Dept of Comp Sc Univ of North Texas Ave C & Mulberry St P O Box 311366 Denton TX 76203 Business E-Mail: boukerche@cs.unt.edu.

BOUKIS, KENNETH, lawyer; b. Cleve., Aug. 28, 1940; s. John and Georgia Boukis; m. Pascalia Mageros, Sept. 8, 1968; children: John Paul, Peter M., Elayna G., Andrew C. BBA, Fenn Coll., Cleve., 1963; JD, Case Western Res. U., 1966; LLM, Cleve. State U., 1976. Bar: Ohio 1966. Ptnr. Strangward, Marshman, Lloyd & Malaga, Cleve., 1966-69, Schaaf, Chalko & Boukis, Cleve., 1970-71, Hohmann, Boukis & Boukis, Cleve., 1971-98, Hohmann, Boukis & Curtis, Cleve., 1998—. Mem. adv. com. Fed. Ct. Mem. Nat. Lawyers Assn., Ohio Bar Assn., Cleve. Bar Assn., Am. Hellenic Edn. and Progressive Assn. (pres.), Cleveland Met. Area Intl. Orthodox Christian Charities (chmn.). Republican. Greek Orthodox. Avocations: bible study, church work, fishing, health foods, exercise. Home: 8230 W Ridge Dr Broadview Heights OH 44147-1033 Office: Hohmann Boukis Curtis Co LPA 520 Standard Bldg 1370 Ontario St Cleveland OH 44113-1701 E-mail: kboukis@clevelandlawyers.cc.

BOULANGER, DONALD RICHARD, financial services executive; b. Berlin, N.H., May 28, 1944; s. Romeo James and Jeanette A. (Valliere) B.; m. Wendy Elwell, Nov. 26, 1990 (div. Sept. 1996). BA, Harvard U., 1966, PhD, 1972. V.p. First Interstate Bank, L.A., 1972-76, Kaufman and Broad, L.A., 1976-80, sr. v.p. Los Angeles, 1983-89; v.p. Transam. Corp., San Francisco, 1981-83; exec. v.p. Far West Savs., Newport Beach, Calif., 1983; pres. Nat. Deposit Fin. Corp., Universal City, Calif., 1989—. Bd. dirs. Nat. Deposit Life Ins. Co., Phoenix, Citadel Holding Corp, Am. Stock Exch., Glendale, Calif. Republican. Roman Catholic. Avocation: scuba diving. Office: Nat Deposit Fin Corp 10 Universal City Plz North Hollywood CA 91608-1009

BOULAY, MARC NORMAN, civil engineer, engineering executive; b. New Bedford, Mass., Sept. 14, 1958; s. Norman N. and Aline C. (Dextradeur) B.; m. Debra A. MacIntyre, Aug. 10, 1985. Student, Cape Cod Community Coll., Hyannis, Mass., 1978; AS in Civil Engring., Bristol Community Coll., Fall River, Mass., 1981; student, So. Mass. U., 1980. Constrn. inspector Linenthal, Eisenberg, Anderson, Boston, 1981-83; chief inspector New Eng. Tech. Svc., Boston, 1983-84; chief engr. (civil) Engring. Svcs. Group, Inc., South Yarmouth, Mass., 1984—2002; chief engr. Northridge Cons. Engrs., 2002—. Mem. Firestone Adv. Coun., 2000—01. Editor, contbr. Comml. Roofing and Masonry Jour., 1985. Mem. Constrn. Specification Inst., ASCE, Am. Cons. Engring. Coun. Avocations: camping, travel, weightlifting, motorcycling. Office: Northridge Consulting Engrs Ste 5E 1645 Falmouth Rd Centerville MA 02632

BOULDIN, CHAPMAN WHITFIELD, JR., educator, consultant; b. Mt. Hope, W.Va., June 28, 1937; s. Chapman Whitfield Sr. and Ann Marie Bouldin. BA in History, Lincoln U., Pa., 1959; MA in Am. History, U. Pitts., 1967, PhD in Curriculum Devel. & Supervision, 1980. Tchr. Pitts. Bd. Edn., 1963-93, dept. chmn., 1967-93; instr. Carnegie-Mellon U., Pitts., 1969-71. Author, co-author: Social Studies Curriculum 7th to 12th Grades, 1967-93; cons.: (documentary videos) American Revolution, 1973-74; (textbook) African History, 1992. Mem. Mount Ararat Bapt. Ch., Pitts. With U.S. Army, 1961—62. Mem.: NAACP, Pitts. Fed. Tchrs. Retiree Chpt., Pitts. Assn. Sch. Retirees (bylaws chmn. 1997, exec. bd. 1997—), Western Pa. Coun. for Social Studies, Assn. for Study of African-Am. Life and History, U. Pitts. Team Pitts., U. Pitts. Alumni Assn., Lincoln U. Alumni Assn. (life). Democrat. Avocations: reading, music, sports. Home: 511 Holmes St Pittsburgh PA 15221-2015

BOULDING, ELISE MARIE, sociologist, educator; b. Oslo, July 6, 1920; came to U.S., 1923, naturalized, 1929; d. Joseph and Birgit (Johnsen) Biorn-Hansen; m. Kenneth Boulding, Aug. 31, 1941; children: John Russell, Mark David, Christine Ann, Philip Daniel, William Frederic. BA, Douglass Coll., 1940; MS, Iowa State Coll., 1949; PhD, U. Mich., 1969. Research asso. Survey Research Inst., U. Mich., 1957-58, Mental Health Research Inst., 1959-60; research devel. sec. Center for Research on Conflict Resolution, 1960-63; prof. sociology, project dir. Inst. Behavioral Sci., U. Colo., Boulder, 1967-78; Montgomery vis. prof. Dartmouth Coll., 1978-79, chmn. dept. sociology, 1979-85; prof. emerita, 1985; sec. gen. Internat. Peace Rsch. Assoc., 1989-91; pres. IPRA Found., 1992-96. Mem. program adv. council Human and Social Devel. Program, UN Univ., 1977-80; mem. governing council, 1980-86. Author: (with others) Handbook of International Data on Women, 1976, Bibliography on World Conflict and Peace, 1979, Social System of Planet Earth, 1980, Women and the Social Costs of Economic Development, 1981; author: The Underside of History: A View of Women Through Time, 1975, rev. edit., 1992, Women in Twentieth Century World, 1977, Children's Rights and the Wheel of Life, 1979, Building a Global Civic Culture: Education for an Interdependent World, 1988, 90, One Small Plot of Heaven, 1990, Cultures of Peace: The Hidden Side of History, 2000; (with Kenneth Boulding) The Future: Images and Processes, 1994; editor: Peace Culture and Society: Transnational Research and Dialogue with Clovis Brigagao and Kevin Clements (eds.), 1990; New Agendas for Peace Research: Conflict and Security Reexamined (ed.), 1992; Building Peace in the Middle East: Challenges for States and Civil Society, (ed.), 1993. Internat. chair Women's Internat. League for Peace and Freedom, 1967-70; mem. Exploratory Project on Conditions for Peace, 1984-90; mem. U.S. Commn. for UNESCO, 1978-84; mem. UNESCO Peace Prize jury, 1980-87; chair bd. Boulder Cmty. Parenting Ctr., 1988-92; bd. dirs. Am. Friends Svc. Com., 1990-94, Wayland MA Coun. on Aging, 1988-2000; councillor Interfaith Peace Coun., 1995—. Recipient Disting. Achievement award Douglass Coll., 1973, Ted. Lentz Peace award, 1976, Athena award, 1983, Nat. Women's Forum award, 1985, Inst. of Def., Disarmament, Peace and Democracy award, 1990, Jack Gore Meml. Peace award Denver Am. Friends Svc. Com., 1992, Global Citizen award Boston Rsch. Ctr., 1995, Peacemaker of Yr. award Rocky Mountain Peace and Justice Ctr., 1996, World Futures Studies Fedn. award, 1997, Jane Addams Peace Activist award Women's Internat. League for Peace and Freedom, 2000; named to Rutgers Hall of Disting. Alumni, 1994; Danforth fellow, 1965-67; named Peacemaker Elder, Nat. Conf. on Peacemaking and Conflict Resolution, 1999. Mem. Am. Sociol. Assn. (Jessie Bernard award 1982, Peace and War sect. award 1994), Internat. Peace Rsch. Assn. (newsletter editor 1983-87), World Future Studies Fedn., Colo. Women's Forum. Mem. Soc. Of Friends. Home: N Hill 865 Central Ave Apt I 301 Needham MA 02492-1361

BOULDIN-PAYOR, ELIZABETH GAI, educator (K-12); d. Roger Washington Bouldin and Embry Vivio Lee Bouldin; m. Louis George Payor, Aug. 19, 1967 (dissolved Oct. 1976); children: L. George Payor II, Jason Bouldin Payor. AS cum laude, Columbia State, 1997, AAS cum laude, 1998; BS cum laude, Middle Tenn. State, 1999, MEd cum laude, 2000, EdS cum laude; student doctoral candidate, U Memphis, 2002; MA in Edn., cum laude, U North Ala., 2003. Substitue tchr. Hickman County Bd. of Edn., Columbia, Tenn., 2001—, Lewis County Bd. of Edn., Columbia, 2001—, Maury County Bd. of Edn., Columbia. Donor Am. Red Cross Two Gallon Donor; mem. Friends of Cheekwood. Mem.: Nat. Assn. of U Women (assoc.), Nat. Assn. of Female Exec. (assoc.), DAR, Nat. Museum of Women in the Arts, Nat. Trust for Historic Preservation, Friends of Cheekwood, Nature Conservancy, Col. Williamsburg Founders Soc., Gamma Beta Phi, Phi Kappa Phi, Sigma Kappa Nat. Sorority. Republican. Luth. Avocations: sailing, tennis, horsemanship. Office: PO Box 681132 Franklin TN 37068-1132 Home: 117 Village Lane Hohenwald TN 38462-2501

BOULET-GERCOURT, PHILIPPE, journalist; b. Paris, June 24, 1960; s. Jacques and Edith (Bourboulon) Boulet-G.; m. Jill Krantzow, Feb. 4, 1997. Diploma, I.E.P. Paris, 1985. Journalist L'Express, Paris, 1985-87, Liberation, Paris, 1987-89, Le Nouvel Observateur, Paris, 1989-91, Germany corr. Berlin, 1991-95, U.S. corr. N.Y.C., 1995—. Office: Le Nouvel Observateur 383 Lafayette St #403 New York NY 10003 E-mail: pbg@pipeline.com.

BOULEY, JOSEPH RICHARD, pilot; b. Fukuoka, Japan, Jan. 7, 1955; came to U.S., 1955; s. Wilfrid Arthur and Minori Cecelia (Naraki) B.; m. Sara Elizabeth Caldwell, July 6, 1991; children: Denise Marie, Janice Elizabeth, Eleanor Catherine, Rachel Margaret. BA in English, U. Nebr., 1977; MAS, Embry Riddle Aeronautical U., 1988. Cert. athletics ofcl. U.S.A. Track and Field, 2001. Commd. 2d lt. USAF, 1977, advanced through grades to maj., 1988, F-117A Stealth Fighter pilot, 1991; ret. lt. col. USAFR, 2000; pilot United Airlines, 1992—. Cert. athletics ofcl. USA Track and Field, 2001—. Ct. apptd. spl. advocate Office of Guardian Ad Litem, Salt Lake City, 1996-99. Decorated Disting. Flying Cross, Def. Meritorious Svc medal, 4 Air medals, 3 Meritorious Svc. medals, 2 Aerial Achievement medals, Joint Svc. commendation medal, 3 Air Force Commendation medals, Air Force Achievement medal; recipient Alumni Achievement award U. Nebr., 1998. Mem. VFW, Am. Legion, Disting. Flying Cross Soc., Airline Pilots Assn., Red River Valley Fighter Pilots Assn., Aircraft Owners and Pilots Assn. Roman Catholic. Avocations: flying, golf, running, photography. Home: 952 E Springwood Dr North Salt Lake UT 84054

BOULEZ, PIERRE, composer, conductor; b. Montbrison, nr. Clermont-Ferrand, France, Mar. 26, 1925; s. Leon and Marcelle (Calabre) Boulez. Student, recipient 1st prize, Olivier Messiaen at Paris Conservatory. Apptd. dir. music Jean-Louis Barrault's Theater Co., 1948; tchr., lectr., condr.; musical adviser, prin. guest condr. Cleve. Symphony Orch., 1970—71; chief condr. BBC Symphony Orch., 1970—75; musical dir. N.Y. Philharm. Orch., 1971—77; prof. Coll. de France, 1976—95; dir. Inst. de Recherche et de Coord. Acoustique/Musique, 1976—91; apptd. prin. guest condr. Chgo. Symphony Orch., 1995. Pres. The Ensemble Intercontemporain, 1976—97. Composer: toured Europe, North and South Am.; conducting appearances include: Edinburgh Festival, Bayreuth Festival, Salzburg Festival, Lucerne Festival, 1965; composer: Sonatina for flute and piano, 1946, Three Piano Sonatas, 1946, 1950, 1957, Le Soleil des eaux for voice and orchestra, 1947, Structures, 1952, Le Marteau sans maître, 1955, Deux improvisations sur Mallarmé, 1957, Tombeau (on text of Mallarmé), 1959, Pli selon pli, 1960, Structures II, 1962, Eclat, 1964, Domaines, 1968, Eclat/Multiples, 1970, cummings ist der dichter, 1970, explosante-fixe, 1973, Rituel, 1975, Messagesquisse, 1976, Notations I-IV, 1980, Répons, 1981, Dialogue de l'ombre double, 1986, Mémoriale, 1985, Visage nuptial, 1989, Dérive I, 1985, Anthèmes pour violin solo, 1992, explosante-fixe for large ensemble and electronics, 1993, Anthèmes for Violin Solo and Electronics, 1997, sur Incises, 1998, Notations VII, 1999, Dérive 2, 2002; author: Relevés d'apprenti, 1966, Points de Repère, 1981, le pays fertile-Paule Klee, 1989, Jalon-10 ans d'enseignement au Collège de France, 1989; musical criticism and analysis including: Penser la musique aujourd'hui, 1963. Recipient Praemium Imperiale, Japan Art Assn., 1989, Grosses Verdienstkreuz RFA, 1990, Polar Music prize, Sweden, 1996. Office: Ensemble Intercontemporain 223 Av Jean-Jaures Cite de la Musique F-75019 Paris France

BOULGER, WILLIAM CHARLES, lawyer; b. Columbus, Ohio, Apr. 2, 1924; s. James Ignatius and Rebecca (Laughlin) B.; m. Ruth J. Schachtele, Dec. 29, 1954; children: Brigid Carolyn, Ruth Mary. AB, Harvard Coll., 1948; LLB, Law Sch. Cin., 1951. Bar: Ohio, 1951, U.S. Dist. Ct. (so. dist.) Ohio 1952, U.S. Supreme Ct. 1957. Ptnr. with Thomas A. Boulger, Chillicothe, Ohio, 1951-73; ptnr. Boulger and Boulger, Chillicothe, 1974— . Pres. Ross County Welfare Assn., Chillicothe, 1954-60; mem. Chillicothe. ARC, 1958-84, chmn., 1959-63, 1985—; mem. Democratic Exec. Com., Chillicothe, 1950s. Served as pfc. U.S. Army, 1943-45, ETO. Mem. Ross County Bar Assn. (pres. 1971), Ohio Bar Assn., ABA, Sunset Club, Symposiarchs Club (past pres.). Roman Catholic. Avocations: tennis, golf. Home: 31 Club Dr Chillicothe OH 45601-1129 Office: PO Box 204 Chillicothe OH 45601-0204

BOULOS, EDWARD NASHED, transportation specialist; b. Damanhour, Egypt, May 19, 1941; arrived in U.S., 1979; s. Nashed Boulos and Lila (Habib) Georgy; m. Mervet Saleh, Aug. 31, 1967; children: Nermine E., Yasmine E. BS in Chemistry and Physics, Cairo U., 1963; MS in Solid State Sci., Am. U., Cairo, 1966; PhD in Ceramic Engring., U. Mo., 1970, profl. doctorate degree, 1997. Supr., cons. Ministry of Industry, Cairo, 1963-79; assoc. prof. Am. U., Cairo, 1972-79; vis. prof. Cath. U. Am., Washington, 1979-81; sr. scientist Anchor Hocking Co., Lancaster, Ohio, 1981-84; sr. tech. fellow Ford Motor Co./Visteon Glass Sys., Dearborn, Mich., 1984—. Cons. USAF, Boston, 1984—89; liaison bd. mem. Alfred (N.Y.) U., 1985—, chmn.-elect, 1992; pres. Glass Mfrs. Indsl. Coun., 2003. Co-editor: Advances in the Fusion of Glass, 1988, PAC RIM Glass and Optical Materials Issues, 2 vols., 1994; contbr. articles on glass tech. to profl. jours.; patentee in field. NSF rsch. grantee, 1967-71, 72-79. Fellow Am. Ceramic Soc. (chair Glass and Optical Materials Div., 1996-98); mem. ASTM, Materials Rsch. Soc., Deutsche Glastechnische Gesellschaft, Sigma Xi. Avocations: travel, sports. Office: Visteon Corp 17333 Federal Dr Ste 230 Allen Park MI 48101-3647

BOULOUKOS, THEODORE, II, writer, editor, actor; b. Albany, N.Y., Jan. 2, 1962; s. Charles Theodore and Johanna Costas (Lecakes) B. AB, Columbia U., 1994. Freelance writer, editor, N.Y.C., 1990—. Author (Collaborating): Hiding My Candy, 1996; contbg. author: Sit! The Paintings of Thierry Poncelet, 1993; contbr. ; actor: (plays) Debbie Does Dallas, 2001. Co-chair, mem. jr. com. Am. Assocs. Royal Acad. Art London; mem. jr. com. English-Speaking Union, N.Y.C.; mem. Guild of the Princess Grace Found./U.S., Young Friends of Save Venice, Inc. Mem.: Authors Guild, Albany Acad. Alumni Assn. (bd. dirs.), Columbia Club N.Y. Episcopalian. Home: 53 E 97th St Apt 1D New York NY 10029-7048 E-mail: TBII62@hotmail.com.

BOULTBEE, JOHN ARTHUR, publishing executive; b. Can., July 4, 1943; s. Thomas Edward and Helene Marion (Pattison) B.; m. Eleanor Rose Moore, Nov. 2, 1968 (div. 1985); children: Paul Keith, Leslie Elizabeth; m. Sharon Ann Whitby, Dec. 28, 1985; 1 child, Michael James Edward. B in Commerce, U. Toronto, Ont., Can., 1967, CA, 1970. Mgr. Coopers & Lybrand, Toronto, 1973-77, ptnr., 1977-85, ptnr. in charge of tax group, 1985-86; v.p., CFO Hollinger Inc., Toronto, 1986-98, exec. v.p., CFO, 1999—2002; exec. v.p. Hollinger Internat. Inc., Toronto, 2002—; pub. Saturday Night Mag., Toronto, 1988-89; pres. Saturday Night Mag. Inc., Toronto, 1989-94; vice-chmn. Saturday Night Mag. Ltd., Toronto, 1994-96, vice-chmn., pres., 1996-98. Bd. dirs. Hollinger Inc., Toronto, Argus Corp. Ltd., Toronto, Consol. Enfield Corp., Toronto, Iamgold Corp., Toronto; bd. govs. Royal St. George's Coll., Toronto. Editor, contbr. Can. Tax Jour., 1980-86. Mem.: Can. Inst. Chartered Accts., Osler Bluffs Ski Club. Avocations: cycling, tennis, running, skiing, golf. Office: Hollinger Inc 10 Toronto St Toronto ON Canada M5C 2B7

BOUMA, JOHN JACOB, lawyer; b. Ft. Dodge, Iowa, Jan. 13, 1937; s. Jacob and Gladys Glennie (Cooper) B.; m. Bonnie Jeanne Lane, Aug. 15, 1959; children: John Jeffrey, Wendy Sue, Laura Lynne, Jennifer Ann. BA, U. Iowa, 1958, JD, 1960. Bar: Iowa 1960, Wis. 1960, Ariz. 1962, U.S. Ct. Appeals (9th cir.) 1971, U.S. Ct. Appeals (D.C. cir.) 1971, U.S. Ct. Appeals (10th cir.) 1982, U.S. Tax Ct., 1983, U.S. Supreme Ct. 1975. Assoc. Foley, Sammond & Lardner, Milw., 1960, Snell & Wilmer, Phoenix, 1962-66, ptnr., 1967—, chmn., 1983—. Contbr. articles to profl. jours. Chmn. Phoenix Human Rels. Commn., 1972-75; mem. Phoenix Commn. on LEAP, 1971-72, Phoenix Cmty. Alliance, 1991—; bd. dirs. Phoenix Legal Aid Soc., 1970-76, Ariz. Econ. Coun., 1989-93, Mountain States Legal Found., 1977-95; trustee Ariz. Opera Co., 1984-2002, pres., 1989-91; trustee Phoenix Art Mus., 1994-2000, 2002-, pres., 1996-98. Capt. JAGC, U.S. Army, 1960-62. Recipient Walter E. Craig Disting. Svc. award, 1998, Cmty. Legal Svcs. Decade of Dedication award, 1998, Disting. Achievement medal Ariz. State U. Coll. Law, 1998, Dist. Alumni Award U. Iowa, 2003. Fellow Am. Coll. Trial Lawyers; mem. ABA (Ho. of Dels. 1989—, bd. govs. 1998-2001, editl. bd. 1996-98), Maricopa County Bar Assn. (pres. 1977-78), Nat. Conf. Bar Pres. (exec. coun. 1984-91, pres. 1989-90), Western States Bar Conf. (pres. 1988-89), Ariz. Bar Assn. (pres. 1983-84), Ariz. Bar Found. (pres. 1987-88), Iowa Bar Assn., Wis. Bar Assn., Phoenix Assn. Def. Counsel (pres. 1972), Attys. Liability Assurance Soc. Ltd. (bd. dirs. 1987—, chair 2002-), Iowa Law Sch. Found. (bd. dirs. 1986-2003), Phoenix C. of C. (bd. dirs. 1988-94), Ariz. State Coll. Law Soc. (bd. dirs., pres. 1997-2000), Ariz. Suprme Ct. Spl. Com. on Lawyer Discipline and Profl. Conduct, Order of Coif, Phi Beta Kappa, Phi Eta Sigma, Omicron Delta Kappa. Avocations: fishing, hunting, skiing, travel, golf. Home: 800 E Circle Rd Phoenix AZ 85020-4144 Office: Snell & Wilmer One Arizona Ctr Phoenix AZ 85004-2202

BOUMENIR, AMIN, mathematician, educator; s. Ahmed Boumenir and Toumi; m. Asma; children: Sabrina, Yasser, Yasmina, Zackaria. PhD, U. Oxford, U.K., 1986. Assoc. prof. Sultan Qaboos U., Muscat, Oman, 1998—2000; asst. prof. U. West Ga., Carrollton, Ga., 2000—. Recipient Shumman award, Shumman Ednl. Trust, 1998. Mem.: Am. Math. Soc. Office: State Univ of West Ga 1600 Maple St Carrollton GA GA 30 E-mail: boumenir@westga.edu.

BOUMIL, MARCIA MOBILIA, legal educator, mediator, writer, lawyer; b. Boston, Apr. 1958; d. Nicholas J. and Eleanor A. (Fuschetti) M.; m. S. James Boumil, Jr., Aug. 10, 1986; children: S. James III, Gregory M. BS cum laude, Tufts U., 1979, MS in Pub. Health, 1982; JD with honors, U. Conn., 1983; LLM, Columbia U., 1984. Bar: Mass. 1983, U.S. Dist. Ct. Mass. 1985, U.S. Ct. Appeals (1st cir.) 1987. Assoc. Herrick & Smith, Boston, 1984-85, Parker, Coulter, Daley & White, Boston, 1985-89; asst. prof. family medicine and cmty. health Tufts U. Sch. Medicine, Boston, 1986—; founder, dir. Comprehensive Family Evaluation Ctr., New Eng. Med. Ctr., Boston, 1999—. Lectr. psychology, Boston Coll., 1992—, lectr. law, 1987-89; instr., grad. program in pub. health, Tufts U., 1984-92; vis. asst. prof. law, 1989-91; presenter and lectr. in field. Author: (textbook) Law, Ethics and Reproductive Choice, 1994; co-author: (textbook) Medical Liability: Cases and Materials, 1990, Medical Liability: Teachers Manual, 1990, Women and the Law, 1992, Sexual Harassment, 1992, Date Rape: The Silent Epidemic, 1993, (textbook) Law and Gender Bias, 1994, (textbook) Medical Liability in a Nutshell, 1995, 2d edit., 2003, Betrayal of Trust: Sex and Power in Professional Relationships, 1995, Deadbeat Dads: A National Child Support Scandal, 1996; author (videotape) Sexual Harassment, 1995; contbr. articles to profl. jours. Avocation: child care. Home: 11 Keystone Way Andover MA 01810-3217 Office: Dept Fam Med & Cmty Health Tufts U Sch Medicine 136 Harrison Ave Boston MA 02111 E-mail: mboumil@aol.com., marcia.boumil@tufts.edu.

BOUNDS, JORDAN T. military officer; b. Knoxville, Tenn., July 24, 1979; s. Thomas Steven and Patti Lou Bounds. BS, USAF Acad., 2000. Commd. 2nd lt. USAF, 2000. Republican. Baptist. Home: 913 N Meadows Blvd Knoxville TN 37938-4646

BOUNDS, SARAH ETHELINE, historian; b. Nov. 5, 1942; d. Leo Deltis and Alice Etheline (Boone) Bounds. AB, Birmingham-So. Coll., 1963; EdS in History, U. Ala., 1971, PhD, 1977. Tchr. social studies Huntsville City Sch., 1963, 65-66, 1971-74; residence hall adv., dir. univ. housing U. Ala., Tuscaloosa, 1963-65, 68-71; instr. history N.E. State Jr. Coll., Rainsville, Ala., 1966-68, U. Ala., Huntsville, 1975, 78-80,85—. Dir. Weeden House Mus., 1981-83, com. mem., 1981-2000; asst. prof. edn., supr. student tchr. U. North Ala., Florence, 1978. Mem. NEA, AAUW, Assn. Tchr. Educators, Nat. Coun. Tchr. Social Studies, Ala. Hist. Assn., Ala. Assn. Historians, Ala. Assn. Tchr. Educators, Huntsville Hist. Soc., Historic Huntsville Found., Alpha Delta Kappa (state pres. Ala. 1990-92, regional sec. 1991-93, internat. mem. com. 1993-97, chmn. 1995-97), Kappa Delta Pi, Phi Alpha Theta, Hunstville Pilot Club (pres. 1990-91, club builder 1991-93, Ala. dist. lt. gov. 1995-96, Ala. dist. gov.-elect 1996-97, gov. 1997-98), Huntsville Music Study Club, Aladdin Club. Methodist. Home: 1100 Bob Wallace Ave SE Huntsville AL 35801-2807

BOUNDS-SEEMANS, PAMELLA J. artist; b. Milton, Del., Nov. 5, 1948; d. James Wilson Bounds and Marguerite Edna (Rickards) Bounds Carey; m. Jeffrey Wayne Seemans, Mar. 20, 1984; children: Misty Autumn, Sterling Hunter, Jordan Windsor. BA, N.Mex. Highlands U., 1971, MA, 1972. Tchr. elem. art Indian River Sch. Dist., Frankford, Del., 1973-79. Lectr. U. Md., 1981, U. Del., 1986, Del. Tech. and C.C., 1988, 75th Del. Women's Day Conf. at U. Del., U. Del. Coll. Arts and Mineralogy, 1999. Exhibited in group shows including Rehoboth (Del.) Art League, 1980, 89, 90, 92, 93, Tideline Gallery, Rehoboth Beach, Del., 1980—, Greenville, Del., 1993, Wicomico Art League, 1980, Del. Tech. and C.C., Georgetown, 1981, U. Md., 1981, Bluestreak Gallery, Wilmington, Del., 1989—, Blue Streak Art Gallery, Wilmington, 1993, Jamison Gallery, Santa Fe, 1993—, Del. Art Mus., 1996, Biennal 96 and 98 Del. Art Mus., U. Del., 1999, Am. Mus. Visionary Arts, Balt., 2000, numerous others; represented in permanent collections including Wilmington (Del.) Trust Co., Del. Nat. Bank, Sussex County Courthouse, Del. Parks and Recreation Bldg., Del. State Folklore Collection, also numerous pvt. collections; poster for mayor's office Clifford Brown Jazz Festival, Wilmington, 1998; mem. cmty. adv. editl. bd. News Jour., Gannett Papers, Wilmington, 1997-98; artist Dino Doys Rennaissance Corp. Donated art work to oncology ctr. Beebe Hosp. Found., 1995, Multiple Sclerosis Found. Del., Ronald McDonald House Del.; mem. cmty. adv. bd. News Jour. editl. Staff, 1997—. Recipient award for outstanding body of work Torpedo Factory, Alexandria, Va., 1982; fellow State of Del. Divsn. of the Arts, 1995. Mem. Nat. Mus. of Women in the Arts, Del. Art Mus., Tunnel 2d place award for most outstanding work in exhibit 1990, Popular Vote award 1980, 93, 94, 95, 96, 1st place award 1993, hon.), Del. Ctr. for Contemporary Arts, Del. Ctr. for Creative Arts, Newark Arts Alliance, Del. Nature Soc., Mothers Multiple Births (v.p. 1987), Wicomo Art League (hon. mention 1981), Univ. and Whist Club (Wilmington). Avocations: criminology, fashion, study of primitive art, psychology, gourmet cooking. Home: 1203 Greenbank Rd Wilmington DE 19808-5842

BOUNDY, DAVID ERIC, patent lawyer, computer engineer; b. Puyallup, Wash., July 14, 1957; s. Bruce K. and Henriette E. Boundy. BS cum laude, Hope Coll., 1980; MS, U. Mich., 1983; postgrad., MIT, 1984-90; JD with honors, Columbia U., 1997. Sr. software engr. Pixel Computer, Woburn, Mass., 1983—85; engr. Apollo Computer/Hewlett Packard, Chelmsford, Mass., 1986-92; patent agt. Fish & Richardson, Boston, 1992—95; patent atty. Morgan & Finnegan LLP, N.Y.C., 1994-99; patent atty., head patent prosecution practice group Shearman & Sterling, N.Y.C., 1999—2001; patent atty. Schulte Roth & Zabel, N.Y.C., 2001—03, Wilkie Farr & Gallagher, N.Y.C., 2003—. Lectr. Merrimack Coll., North Andover, Mass., 1987—90. Author: A Taxonomy of Programmers, 1991, Prosecuting the High-Value Patent Application, 2001. Condr. Ars Canticorum, Renaissance Choir, Cambridge, Mass., 1988-90. Mem. ABA, Am. Intellectual Property Law Assn., N.Y. Intellectual Property Law Assn., Assn. for Computing Machinery, IEEE Computer Soc. E-mail: dboundy@willkie.com.

BOURCIER, RICHARD JOSEPH, French language and literature educator; b. New Bedford, Mass., Dec. 25, 1930; s. Adrien and Alida (Richard) B.; m. Florence Rita Michaud, June 17, 1961 (dec. Nov. 26, 1994); children: Michelle, Camille, Jeanine, Normand, Paul. AB, Assumption Coll., 1958; MA in French, Laval U., 1959; PhD in Comparative Lit., SUNY, Binghamton, 1983. Instr. New Bedford (Mass.) Pub. Sch. Sys., 1959-60, Coll. of the Holy Cross, Worcester, Mass., 1961-68; asst. then assoc. prof. U. Scranton (Pa.), 1968—83, prof., 1983—. Dir. French house U. Scranton, 1989-94. Cantor Ch. St. Gregory, Clarks Green, Pa., 1973—. Sgt. U.S. Army, 1953-55. Decorated chevalier/knight Order of Acad. Palms (France). Mem. MLA, AAUP, Am. Assn. Tchrs. French, Institut Français, Assn. des Amis de Georges Duhamel, U.S. Amateur Ballroom Dancers Assn. Avocations: woodworking, music, dancing. Home: 103 Belmont Ave Clarks Green PA 18411-1101 Office: U Scranton Dept Fgn Langs Scranton PA 18510

BOURDON, CATHLEEN JANE, professional society administrator; b. Sparta, Wis., July 13, 1948; d. Cletus John and Josephine Marie (Bourdon) Scheurich; children: Jill Krzyminski, Jeff Krzyminski. BA in Polit. Sci., U. Wis., 1973, MLS, 1974. Tchr. Peace Corps, Arba Minch, Ethiopia, 1969-72; asst. prof., dir. Alverno Coll. Libr., Milw., 1974-83; dep. exec. dir. Assn. Coll. and Rsch. Librs., Chgo., 1983-93; exec. dir. Ref. and User Svcs. Assn. divsn. ALA Assn. Specialized and Coop. Libr. Agys., Chgo., 1993—. Mem. ALA (pres. Staff Assn. 1987-88). Avocations: reading mystery fiction, 1940s movies, building model doll house furniture. Office: Assn Specialized & Coop Libr Agys 50 E Huron St Chicago IL 60611-5295 E-mail: cbourdon@ala.org.

BOURET, PIERRE GEORGE, brokerage house executive; b. Feb. 15, 1924; m. Marie Elizabeth O'Halloran; children: Gregory Pierre, Marc Patrick, Colleen Marie. AB, Stanford U., 1948, MBA, 1949. V.p. major accounts, Dictaphone Corp. Divsn. Pitney Bowes, Rye, N.Y., 1952-89; sr. v.p. Whitehall-Parker Securities, San Francisco, 1995—. 1st lt. mil. intelligence USAR, 1943—54. Mem.: Phi Beta Kappa. Home: 1035 White Gate Rd Alamo CA 94507-2831

BOURGAIZE, ROBERT G. economist; BA, U. Wash., 1949. Dir., sr. v.p. Peoples Nat. Bank, Seattle; pres. Central Bank, N.A., Tacoma, University Place Water Co., Epsilon Econ. Inc. Mem. Nat. Assn. Bus. Economists, English-Speaking Union U.S.A. (nat. dir.), Royal Commonwealth Soc., Am. Waterworks Assn. (life), Pacific Northwest Writers Conf., Adam Smith Econ. Found., Adam Smith Soc. (founder 1976). Office: 3502 Bridgeport Way W University Place WA 98466

BOURGELAIS, PAUL, music educator; b. Exeter, N.H., July 9, 1966; s. Frederick Nelson Bourgelais and Jean Jackson; m. Jennifer Descoteaux, July 16, 1997; 1 child, Addison. MA, U. Of N.H., 2000. Guitar instr. Syms U. Of N.H., Durham, NH, 1990—, Plymouth (N.H.) State Coll., 1997—. Staff guitarist Currier Gallery Of Art, Manchester, NH, 1997—. Composer: (albums) John's Vacation. Nominee Jazz Artist of Yr., Jam Mag. Home: 50 Sunrise Circle Plymouth NH 03264 Office: Plymouth State College Silver Hall Cultural Arts Center Plymouth NH 03264 Personal E-mail: pbourgelais@mail.plymouth.edu.

BOURGEOIS, JAMES HONORÉ, landscape company executive; b. Thibodaux, La., Apr. 24, 1967; s. Honoré George Jr. and Sandra (Ulmer) Bourgeois; m. Kristina Bourgeois, Aug. 24, 1996; children: Lauren Elizabeth, James Honoré II, Carolyn Kristina. BA, Tulane U., 1989; postgrad., We. State U. Law Sch., 1991-94. Cert. arborist Internat. Soc. Arborculture. CEO Bourgeois, Inc., Santee, Calif., 1989—. Capt. N.G. U.S. Army. Recipient Achievement medal, 1997—99, Commendation medal, 2000. Mem.: NRA, Calif. Landscape Contractors Assn. (v.p. 2000—01), U.S. Field Arty. Assn., Golden State Flying Club. Avocations: flying small planes, shooting. Office: Bourgeois Inc PO Box 713083 Santee CA 92072

BOURGEOIS, LOUISE, sculptor; b. Paris, 1911; came to U.S., 1938, naturalized, 1953; Student, Sorbonne U., 1932-35; baccalaureate, Ecole des Beaux Arts, 1936-38; postgrad., Ecole du Louvre, 1936-37, Acad. Grande Chaumiere; D.F.A. (hon.), Yale U., 1977, Calif. Coll. Arts and Crafts, 1988, Moore Coll. Art, Mass. Coll. Art, 1983, Md. Art Inst., 1984, The New Sch., 1987. Instr. Md. Art Inst., Balt., 1984, New Sch. Social Rsch., N.Y.C., 1987. One-woman shows include Norlyst Gallery, 1947, Peridot Gallery, 1949, 50, 53, Allan Frumkin Gallery, Chgo., 1953, White Art Mus., Cornell U., Ithaca, N.Y., 1959, Stable Gallery, 1964, Rose Fried Gallery, 1963, 112 Greene St., N.Y.C., 1974, Xavier Fourcade Gallery, N.Y.C., 1978-80, Max Hutchinson Gallery, N.Y.C., 1980, Renaissance Soc., 1981, Mus. Modern Art, N.Y.C., 1982, retrospective Contemporary Art Mus., Houston, 1983, Daniel Weinberg Gallery, L.A., 1984, Robert Miller Gallery, 1982, 84, 87-89, 91, Serpentine Gallery, London, 1985, Maeght-Lelong, Zurich, 1985, Paris, 1985, Taft Mus., Cin., 1987-89 (travelled to The Art Mus. at Fla. Internat. U., Miami, Fla., Laguna Gloria Art Mus., Austin, Tex., Gallery of Art, Washington U., St. Louis, Henry Art Gallery, Seattle, Everson Mus. Art, Syracuse, N.Y.), Mus. Overholland, Amsterdam, The Netherlands, 1988, Dia Art Found., Bridgehampton, N.Y., retrospective Frankfurter Kunstverein, Frankfurt, Fed. Republic Germany, 1989 (travelled to Städtische Galerie im Lenbachhaus, Munich, 1990, Riverside Studios, London, 1990, Musée d'Art Contemporain, Lyon, 1990, Fondacion Tapies, Barcelona, Spain, Kunstmuseum, Berne, Switzerland, Kröller-Müller Mus., Otterlo, The Netherlands), Linda Cathcart Gallery, Santa Monica, Calif., 1990, Barbara Gross Gallerie, Munich, 1990, Karsten Schubert, London, 1990, Galerie Krinzinger, Vienna, 1990, Karsten Greve Gallery, Cologne, 1990, Ginny Williams Gallery, 1990, Monika Spruthe Galerie, Cologne, 1990, Robert Miller Gallery 1986, 1987, 1988, 1989, 1991, Galerie Lelong, Zurich, 1991; solo exhbns. include Parrish Art Mus., Southampton, N.Y., Ydessa Hendeles Found., Toronto, 1991, 92, Milwaukee Art Mus., 1992, The Fabric Workshop, Phila., Galerie Karsten Greve, Paris, Linda Cathcart Gallery, Santa Monica, Calif., Second Floor, Reykjavik, Iceland; exhibited in numerous group shows, U.S., Europe including Sculpture Ctr., 1997, Jim Kempner Fine Art, 1997, Steinbaum Krauss Gallery, 1998, Mary Boone Gallery, 1998, Am. Craft Mus., 1998; represented in permanent collections Mus. Modern Art, N.Y.C., Whitney Mus., Met. Mus. Art, Hirshorn Mus., Musée Nat. D'Art Moderne, Paris, R.I. Sch. Design, NYU, Albright-KnAustralian Nat. Gallery, Canberra, Musée d'Art Moderne, Paris, Mus. Fine Arts, Houston, Guggenheim Mus., N.Y.C., Kunstmus. Bern, stmus. Lucerne, Albertina, Vienna, Mus. Modern Art, Vienna, Walker Art Ctr., Mpls., Storm King Art Ctr., Mountainville, N.Y., New Mus. Contemporary Art, N.Y.C., DC Moore Gallery, N.Y.C., Cheim & Read Gallery, N.Y.C.; appeared in Limited Edition Artists Books 1990—. Recipient Outstanding Achievement award Women's Caucus, 1980, Pres.'s Fellow award R.I. Sch. Design, 1984, Skowhegan medal sculpture Skowhegan (Maine) Sch. Painting, and Sculpture, Gold medal of honor Nat. Arts Club, 1987, Creative Arts Medal award Brandeis U., 1989, Grand Prix Nat. de Sculpture French Ministry of Culture, 1991, Nat. medal arts, 1999, Wolf prize, 2003; recipient Lifetime Achievement award Coll. Art Assn., 1989, Internat. Sculpture Ctr., 1991; named Officer of Arts and Letters French Ministry of Culture, 1984. Fellow Am. Acad. Arts and Scis.; mem. Am. Acad. and Inst. Arts and Letters, Sculptors Guild, Am. Abstract Artists, Coll. Art Assn. (Disting. Artist award for lifetime achievement 1989). Office: Robert Miller Gallery 524 W 26th St Ground Fl New York NY 10001-5541

BOURGEOIS, MARILYN ANN, piano educator, pianist; b. Bonne Terre, Mo., May 24, 1949; d. Newell Kirkwood and Pauline (Donnell) Jones; m. Arthur Paul Bourgeois, Dec. 21, 1974; children: Paul J., Jeanne Marie. BFA, Stephens Coll., 1971; MusM, Ind. U., 1973. Cert. Music Tchrs. Nat. Assn. Adj. prof. music, recitalist Govs. State U., University Park, Ill., 1978—98; symphony pianist Ill. Philharm. Orch., Park Forest, 1983—; instr. piano, humanities, accompanist, recitalist South Suburban Coll., South Holland, Ill., 1988—. Chamber music performances grantee Ill. Arts Coun., 1985-89. Mem. Nat. Guild Piano Tchrs. (faculty 1979—, bd. judges 1988—), S. Suburban Music Tchrs. Assn. (rec. sec.), P.E.O. (corr. sec., chaplain), Pi Kappa Lambda, Mu Phi Epsilon. Avocations: swimming, hiking, reading. Office: South Suburban Coll Music Dept 15800 State St South Holland IL 60473-1200

BOURGET, EDWIN ROBERT, marine ecologist, educator; b. Senneterre, Que., Can., July 6, 1946; s. Jean-Paul and Myrtle (O'Malley) B.; m. Paule Reny, June 16, 1969; children: Frédéric, Virginie. BSc, U. Laval, Que., 1969, MSc, 1971; PhD, U. Wales, 1974. Oceonology rschr. U. Que., Rimouski, 1974-76; adj. prof. U. Laval, 1976-80, assoc. prof., 1980-84, prof., 1984—, dir. biology dept., 1997-98, vice dean rsch. faculty sci. engring., 1998-2001; vice rector rsch. U. Sherbrooke, Que., 2001—. Author/co-author 6 books or book chpts.; contbr. numerous articles to profl. jours. Recipient Michel-Jurdant prize Can.-French Assn. Advancement Sci., 1996; grantee in field. Mem. Groupe Interuniversitaire de recherches oceanographiques du Que. (dir. 1993-96), Natural Sci. and Engring. Rsch. Coun. (adv. bds. 1987-91), Fonds pour la Formation de Chercheurs et l'Aide a la Recherche. Office: Pavillon Central Sherbrooke QC Canada J1K 2R1

BOURGOIN, DAVID L. lawyer, real estate broker, trade broker, educator, video/television producer; b. Jersey City, Mar. 5, 1946; s. Louis Joseph and Irene Mary Bourgoin. BS, St. Peter's Coll., Jersey City, 1968; MBA, UCLA, 1970; JD, U. San Diego, 1987. Bar: Hawaii 1988, Pa. 1989, U.S. Ct. Appeals (fed. cir.) Hawaii 1988, U.S. Internat. Ct. Appeals. Fin. mgr. Mattel Toys, Hawthorne, Calif., 1969—71; music prodr. Topanga Canyon Records, Redondo Beach, Calif., 1971-76; stock broker Dean Witter, L.A., 1976-78, 2003; prof. U. Hawaii, Honolulu, 1978-80; trade broker Hawaii chi Trading Co., Honolulu, 1978—; pvt. practice Honolulu, 1988—; real estate broker Realty Offices of D.L.B., Honolulu, 1991—. Prof. U. Md., Heidelburg, Germany, 1983-95; vis. prof. mgmt. & internat. studies U. Hawaii, 2003; prodr. TCR Prodns. Capt. USAR, 1973-85. Mem. Hawaii State Bar, Japanese C. of C., K. of C. Avocations: culture, music, sports. Office: 1188 Bishop St Ste 2010 Honolulu HI 96813-3308 E-mail: theofficesnet@yahoo.com.

BOURGUIGNON, ERIKA EICHHORN, anthropologist, educator; b. Vienna, Feb. 18, 1924; d. Leopold H. and Charlotte (Rosenbaum) Eichhorn; m. Paul H. Bourguignon, Sept. 29, 1950. BA, Queens Coll., 1945; grad. study, U. Conn., 1945; PhD, Northwestern U., 1951; DHL, CUNY, 2000. Field work Chippewa Indians, Wis., summer 1946; field work Haiti; anthropologist Northwestern U., 1947-48; instr. Ohio State U., 1949-56, asst. prof., 1956-60, assoc. prof., 1960-66, prof., 1966-90, acting chmn. dept. anthropology, 1971-72, chmn. dept., 1972-76, prof. emeritus, 1990—; dir. Cross-Cultural Study of Dissociational States, 1963-68. Bd. dirs. Human Relations Area Files, Inc., 1976-79 Author: Possession, 1976, rev. edit., 1991, Psychological Anthropology, 1979, Italian transl., 1983; editor, co-author: Religion, Altered States of Consciousness and Social Change, 1973, A World of Women, 1980; co-author: Diversity and Homogeneity in World Societies, 1973; adv. editor: Behavior Sci. Rsch., 1976-79; assoc. editor Jour. Psychoanalytic Anthropology, 1977-87; mem. editl. bd. Ethos, 1979-89, 97—, Jour. Haitian Studies, 2000—, Anthropology of Consciousness, 2002—; editor: Margaret Mead: The Anthropologist in America—, Occasional Papers in Anthropology, No. 2, Ohio State U. Dept. Anthropology, 1986; (with Barbara Rigney) Exile: A Memoir of 1939 by Bronka Schneider, 1998; contbr. articles to profl. jours. Fellow Am. Anthrop. Assn.; mem. Ctrl. State Anthrop. Soc. (treas. 1953-56, exec. com. 1995-98), Ohio Acad Sci., World Psychiat. Assn. (transcultural psychiatry sect.), Am. Ethnol. Soc., Current Anthropology (assoc.), Soc. for Psychol. Anthropology (nominations com. 1981-82, bd. dirs. 1991-93, lifetime achievement award 1999), Soc. for the Anthrop. of Religion, Phi Beta Kappa, Sigma Xi. E-mail: bourguignon.1@osu.edu. *It is more important to enjoy doing what you do, and to be able to do what you want to do, than to be successful. Success, if it comes, is only a by-product, nothing more.*

BOURHAM, MOHAMED ABDELHAY, nuclear and electrical engineering educator; b. Mehalla, Gharbeia, Egypt, Apr. 18, 1944; arrived in U.S., 1987; s. Abdelhay Mohamed Bourham and Badria Ahmed Ghida; m. Laila Gadel Hak, Mar. 22, 1966 (div. 1977); 1 child, Ahmed Mohamed; m. Doria Mahmoud Wafa, Mar. 22, 1987; 1 stepchild, Samir Sami. BSc, Alexandria (Egypt) U., 1965; MSc, Cairo U., 1969; PhD, Ain Shams U., Cairo, 1976. Registered profl. engr. Sr. researcher, asst. prof., then prof. Nuclear Rsch. Ctr., Cairo, 1965-91; vis. assoc. prof. N.C. State U., Raleigh, 1987-91, rsch. assoc. prof. nuclear engring., 1991-95, assoc. prof., 1995-97, prof., 1997—, undergrad. adminstr., 1999. Contbr. scientific papers to sci. publs. Maj. arty. Egyptian Army, 1968—74. Recipient George Blessis Outstanding Undergrad. Advisor award, 2003; grantee, U.S. Army, 1989—, U.S. Dept. Energy, 1992, USN, 1995—, Nat. Textile Ctr., 1999—, USDA, 2001—. Mem.: AAAS, AIAA, IEEE (publs. chair Internat. Conf. Plasma Sci. 1998), Am. Assn. for Engring. Edn., Nat. Assn. of scholars, Am. Assn. Engring. Edn., Am. Soc. Engring. Edn., Nat. Assn. Scholars, Electric Launcher Assn., Fusion Power Assocs., Univ. Fusion Assn., N.Y. Acad. Scis., Am. Nuc. Soc. (tech. chair fusion meeting 1998, exec. com. 1998—), Am. Phys. Soc., U.S. Naval Inst. (life), Nat. Def. Indsl. Assn. (life), Sigma Xi. Moslem. Achievements include research in in plasma microinstabilities and electromagnetic emission from core plasmas in magnetically confined fusion devises; plasma torches for waste disposal; development of of magnetically collimated electron beams for microeletronics; techniques in pulsed power systems for eletrothermal and electro thermal chemical launchers; of diagnostics methodology and techniques for hyper-velocity plasma launchers; database on plasma-facing components; of database for plasma-material interactions under combustion environment; methodology for disruption parameters and surface erosion of fusion tokamaks and methodology for accident scenarios in future large magnetic fusion reactors; research and development of plasma treatment of material surfaces and textile fabrics and non-wovens; research in on plasma-fabric treatment at atmospheric pressures and surface sterilization and decontamination, nano structures and nanoparticulates implantation, x-ray sources for imaging; plasma application to insects control. Office: NC State U Dept Nuclear Engring Raleigh NC 27695-0001 E-mail: bourham@ncsu.edu.

BOURI, MICHAEL, civil servant; b. Maghnia, Algeria, May 5, 1943; s. Hamida and Zoulikha (Senhadji) B.; m. Janet Elizabeth Powell, Feb. 1, 1965 (div.); children: Leila, Hamid; m. Naima Bouri, Mar. 1, 1994. BA, U. Algiers, 1973; MA, Am. U., Washington, 1978. Diplomatic attache Min. of Fgn. Affairs, Algiers, 1967-71, adminstr. Washington, 1972-79; asst. prof. U. Algiers, 1979-81; civil servant dept. children and families econ. self sufficiency State of Fla., Fla., 1988—. Mem. Acad. of Arts and Scis., Assn. of Govt. Economists, Inst. of Polit. Sci. Democrat. Moslem. Avocations: reading, travel. Home: 332 NE 3d St Apt 3 Hallandale FL 33009-3405 Office: State of Fla Dept of Miami 7900 NW 27th Ave Miami FL 33147

BOURKE, THOMAS ANTHONY, librarian, writer; b. N.Y.C., Aug. 19, 1945; s. Anthony Francis and Nora Christina (Bulman) B.; m. Graciela Adelaida Rodriguez, Aug. 18, 1990; children: Isabella A., Nora R. BA, Fordham Coll., 1966; MA, Fordham U., 1967; MS, Columbia U., 1968. Clerical aide N.Y. Pub. Libr., 1963-68, rsch. libr., 1968-80, chief microforms divsn., 1980-95; spl. asst. Ctr. for Humanities, 1995-2000; libr. Gulport (Fla.) Pub. Libr., 2001—. Reviewer Baseball History, Libr. Jour., Microform Rev., RQ, Reprint Bull., Spl. Librs. Editor-in-chief Microform Rev., 1985-90, mem. editl. bd., 1991—; asst. editor Libr. Resources and Tech. Svcs., 1991-93, cons., reviewer, 1990—; contbr. articles to profl. jours.; pub. translations from Spanish lang. to profl. libr. jours. Mem. ALA, Assn. for Info. and Image Mgmt., Libr. and Info. Tech. Assn., Assn. for Libr. Collections and Tech. Svcs. (preservation microfilming com. 1987-89, exec. com. reproduction of libr. materials sect. 1988-91), Soc. for Am. Baseball Rsch. Democrat. Roman Catholic. Avocations: writing, reading, sports. Office: Gulfport Pub Libr 5501 28th Ave S Gulfport FL 33707 E-mail: tbourke2000@yahoo.com.

BOURLAND, D(ELPHUS) DAVID, JR., linguist, educator; b. Wichita Falls, Tex., June 6, 1928; s. Delphus David and Margaret (Hawley) B.; m. Elizabeth Jagush, Oct. 16, 1981; children by previous marriages: David III, Meda, Ruskin, Ileana. AB, Harvard U., 1951, MBA, 1953; lic. in English linguistics, U. Costa Rica, 1973. Ops. analyst Ops. Evaluation Group MIT, Washington, 1955-61; with various corps., 1961-65; pres. IR Assocs., Inc., San Diego, 1965-69, Semantics Rsch. Corp., Washington, 1969-71; from instr. to assoc. prof. U. Costa Rica, San Jose, 1971-80; pres. Semantics Rsch. Corp., Wichita Falls, Tex., 1994—. Trustee Inst. Gen. Semantics, 1964-89. Author: Introduccion a la Tagmemica, 1974; co-author: An Advanced Course in Squirrelly Semantics: A Coloring Book for Some Adults, 1993, Not So Great Moments in the Lives of Great Men and Women, 1994; editor Gen. Semantics Bull., 1964-70; co-editor: To Be or Not: An E-Prime Anthology, 1991, More E-Prime: To Be or Not II, 1994, E-Prime III!, 1997; contbr. numerous articles to profl. publs. Lt. USNR, 1953-65. Korzybski fellow Inst. Gen. Semantics, 1949-50. Mem. Inst. Gen. Semantics, Internat. Soc. Gen. Semantics (contbg. editor Et Cetera, bd. dirs. 1993—, v.p. devel. 1995-97, pres. 1998—, assoc. editor 2000—), Am. Legion (comdr. dept. Panama Canal 1979-81, post comdr. Costa Rica 1980-84), Sons Am. Legion (nat. adjutant 1985, 86), Forty and Eight (nat. exec. com. 1983-86), Harvard Faculty Club, Harvard Club Boston, Wichita Falls Country Club, Sons Confederate Vets., Wichita Falls Yacht Club. Republican. Avocation: power lifting. Home: 1517 Celia Dr Wichita Falls TX 76302-3515

BOURNE, CAROL ELIZABETH MULLIGAN, biology educator, phycologist; b. Rochester, N.Y., May 4, 1948; d. William Thomas and Ruth Townsend (Stevens) Mulligan; m. Godfrey Roderick Bourne, Dec. 21, 1968. BA in Botany/Bacteriology, Ohio Wesleyan U., 1970; MS in Botany, Miami U., Oxford, Ohio, 1978; PhD in Natural Resources, U. Mich., 1992. Lab. asst. Ohio Wesleyan U., Delaware, 1968-70; biol. lab. tech. USDA-Forest Svc., Delaware, 1970-73; grad. rsch. asst. botany dept. Miami U., Oxford, 1973-75; electron microscopist coll. medicine U. Cin., 1975-76; rsch. asst. sch. pub. health U. Mich., Ann Arbor, 1978-80, rsch. assoc. coll. medicine, 1981-83, grad. rsch. asst. sch. natural resources, 1983-86, grad. teaching asst. dept. biology, 1987; postdoctoral scientist U. Fla., Ft. Lauderdale, 1990-92; adj. instr. ecology Fla. Atlantic U. Coll. Liberal Arts, Davie, 1992-93. Adj. asst. prof. dept. biology U. Mo., St. Louis, 1994—, Washington U., St. Louis, 1994—2000, Pierre Laclede Honors Coll., U. Mo., St. Louis, 1997—; bd. dirs. CEIBA Biol. Ctr., Inc. Contbr. articles to scholarly jours. Grantee NSF, 1987-89. Mem.: Soc. for Study of Evolution, Internat. Soc. for Diatom Rsch., Phycological Soc. Am., Am. Inst. Biolog. Scis. Office: U Mo at St Louis Dept Biology 8001 Natural Bridge Rd Saint Louis MO 63121-4499 E-mail: BourneC@msx.umsl.edu.

BOURNE, CHARLES PERCY, information scientist, educator; b. San Francisco, Sept. 2, 1931; s. Frank Percy and Edith (Dunlap) B.; m. Elizabeth A. Scheidtmann, Aug. 15, 1953; children— Glen Wade, Holly Ann. BS in Elec. Engring., U. Calif. at Berkeley, 1957; MS in Indsl. Engring., Stanford, 1963. Sr. research engr. Stanford Research Inst., Menlo Park, Calif., 1957-66; v.p. Information Gen. Corp., Palo Alto, Calif., 1966-70; pres. Charles Bourne & Assos., Menlo Park, 1970—; prof. in residence Sch. Library and Info. Studies; dir. Inst. Library Research U. Calif.-Berkeley, 1971-77; v.p. gen. info. div. Dialog Info. Svcs., Inc., Palo Alto, 1977-92. Research in info. scis. for libraries, schs., acads., including Library of Congress, Nat. Agrl. Library, U.S. Patent

Office, Nat. Acad. Sci.; Guest lectr. univs. including U. Calif. at Berkeley, 1963-66; Sarada Ranganathan lectr., Bangalore, India, 1978; cons. corr. Nat. Acad. Sci. com. on sci. and tech. information, 1968-70; mem. adv. bd. Chem. Abstracts, 1965-68, Ency. Library and Information Scis., 1967—, Documentation Abstracts, 1968-69, Ann. Rev. Information Sci. and Tech., 1966; mem. adv. bd. World Affairs Report, 1987-90; U.S. rep. to a com. of Internat. Fedn. for Documentation, 1966-76; UNESCO cons. to Indonesia and Tanzania; Nat. Acad. Scis. cons. to Ghana, 1976; mem. U.S.-Egyptian Task Force on Tech. Info. Problems, 1976, U.S. del. UNESCO Intergovtl. Conf. Sci. and Tech. Info. for Devel., 1979; mem. Network Adv. Com. Library of Congress, 1987-92; delegate -at-large White House Conf. Lib. and Info. Svcs., 1991. Author: Methods of Information Handling, 1963, Technology in Support of Library Science and Information Service, 1980; co-author: A History of Online Information Services, 2003; contbr. articles profl. jours. Served with USMCR, 1950-51. Recipient ann. award of merit Am. Documentation Inst., 1965 Mem. Am. Soc. Information Sci. (pres. 1970), ALA (dir. information scis. and automation div. 1966-67), Nat. Info. Standards Orgn. (bd. dirs. 1987-90). Home: 1619 Santa Cruz Ave Menlo Park CA 94025-5761

BOURNE, HENRY CLARK, JR., electrical engineering educator, former academic official; b. Tarboro, N.C., Dec. 31, 1921; s. Henry Clark and Marion (Alston) B.; m. Margaret Barr Thomas, Aug. 15, 1953; children: Katherine Wimberley, Henry Clark III, Thomas Franklin, Margaret Alston. S.B., MIT, 1947, S.M., 1948, Sc.D., 1952. Registered profl. engr., Calif., Tex. Asst. prof. Mass. Inst. Tech., 1952-54; asst. prof., then asso. prof. U. Calif. at, Berkeley, 1954-63; prof. elec. engring. Rice U., Houston, 1963-77, chmn. dept., 1963-74; sect. head engring. div. NSF, Washington, 1974-75, div. dir. engring., 1977-79; dep. asst. dir. Directorate Engring. and Applied Sci., 1979-81; v.p. for acad. affairs Ga. Inst. Tech., Atlanta, 1981-86, 87-88, acting pres., 1986-87, prof. elec. engring., 1988-92, prof. elec. engring. emeritus, 1992—. Cons. editor Harper & Row, N.Y.C., 1961-67; cons. elec. engring., 1952— Author tech. papers in field of magnetics. Served to 1st lt. C.E. AUS, 1943-46. Sci. Faculty fellow NSF, 1960-61; hon. research asso. Univ. Coll. London; Eng., 1961 Fellow IEEE, AAAS; mem. Am. Phys. Soc., Am. Soc. Engring. Edn., Sigma Xi, Tau Beta Pi, Eta Kappa Nu, Phi Kappa Phi, Omicron Delta Kappa, Beta Gamma Sigma, Delta Tau Delta. Episcopalian. Home: 173 Windrush Rd Winston Salem NC 27106

BOURNE, JOHN DAVID, retired city finance executive; b. Barbados, West Indies, July 6, 1937; s. Daniel E. and Clarissa M. (Foster) B. BBA, CUNY, 1972; MBA, L.I. U., 1974. Mgr. Household Fin. Corp., N.Y.C., 1963-72, N.Y.C. Off-Track Betting Corp., 1972-92; prof. bus. adminstrn. St. Josephs Coll., Bklyn., 1982-2000, Coll. Adelphi U., 1986-2000; ret., 2000. With USAF, 1959-63. Mem. Baruch Coll., L.I. U. Alumni Assn. Democrat. Home: 249 Fiddlers Point Dr Saint Augustine FL 32080

BOURNE, KATHERINE DAY, journalist, educator; b. Lynn, Mass., Sept. 11, 1938; d. Schuyler Vandervort and Elsie Marie (Mayo) Day; m. William Nettleton Bourne; children: William Alexander, Katherine Loring. BS in Edn., Keene Tchrs. Coll., 1960; MEd, Harvard U., 1984. Tchr. Wachusett Regional High Sch., Holden, Mass., 1960-61; arts editor Bay State Banner, Boston, 1966—; dir. edn. Suffolk County House of Correction, Boston, 1979-84; edn. coord. Dept. Transitional Asst., Mass., 1984—2002, ret., 2002—. Contbr. music revs. to Christian Sci. Monitor. Dir. rels. Crime-out, Boston, 1983; mem. Gov.'s Commn. on Status of Women, 1970-74; co-founder, dir. Harvard-Radcliffe Forum Theatre, Cambridge, 1964-68; bd. dirs., mem. ARC Greater Boston, 1987-95, NAACP Boston, 1978-81. NEH journalism fellow, 1978; recipient Melnea A. Cass award Greater Boston YMCA, 1984. Mem. NAACP (life). Avocations: collecting african-american literature, aerobics, photography, stamps, art relating to black history and life. Home: 52 High St Brookline MA 02445-7707 Office: Bay State Banner The Fargo Bldg 68 Fargo St Boston MA 02210-2122

BOURNE, LYLE EUGENE, JR., psychology educator; b. Boston, Apr. 12, 1932; s. Lyle E. and Blanche (White) H. BA, Brown U., 1953; MS, U. Wis., 1955, PhD, 1956. Asst. prof. psychology U. Utah, 1956-61, assoc. prof., 1961-63; vis. assoc. prof. U. Calif.-Berkeley, 1961-62, vis. prof., 1968-69; assoc. prof. psychology U. Colo., Boulder, 1963-65, prof., 1965—, chmn. dept. psychology, 1983-91, dir. Inst. Cognitive Sci., 1979-83; clin. prof. psychiatry U. Kans. Med. Ctr., 1967-90. Vis. prof. U. Wis., 1966, U. Mont., 1967, U. Hawaii, 1969; cons. in exptl. psychology, VA, 1965-93. Author: Human Conceptual Behavior, 1966, Psychology of Thinking, 1971, Psychology: Its Principles and Meanings, rev. edits., 1976, 79 82, 85, Cognitive Processes, 1979, rev. edit., 1986, Psychology: A Concise Introduction, 1988, Psychology: Behavior in Context, 1998; acad. editor: Basic Concept Series, Learning-Cognition Series, Scott, Foresman Pub. Co., 1970-76, Charles Merill Co., 1980-84, Advanced Psychological Texts Series, Sage Publications, 1992—; editor Jour. Exptl. Psychology: Human Learning and Memory, 1975-80; cons. editor Jour. Clin. Psychology 1975-97, Jour. Exptl. Psychology: Learning, Memory and Cognition, 1984-92, Memory and Cognition, 1984-89. Recipient Research Scientist award NIHM, 1969-74 Mem.: APA (coun. editors 1975—80, coun. reps. 1976—79, chmn. early awards com. 1978—79, bd. sci. affairs 1978—81, coun. reps. 1986—89, bd. sci. affairs 1989—92, pres. divsn. 3 1992, publ. and commn. bd. 1995—), Coun. Grad. Depts. Psychology (exec. bd. 1985—89), Soc. Gen. Psychology (pres. 2001), Rocky Mountain Psychol. Assn. (pres. 1987—88), Fedn. Behavioral Psychol. and Cognitive Scis. (v.p. 1994—95, pres. 1995—97), Soc. Exptl. Psychologists (chmn. 1987—88), Psychonomic Soc. (governing bd. 1976—81, chmn. 1980—81), Sigma Xi. Home: 785 Northstar Ct Boulder CO 80304-1088

BOURNE, MATTHEW, performing company executive, artistic director; Degree in Dance/Theatre, Laban Centre, 1985. Dir., choreographer and artistic dir. Adventures in Motion Pictures, London, 1987—. Founder mem. Lea Anderson's The Featherstonehaughs, 1988. Stage works include : Overlap Lovers, 1987; Spitfire, 1988; Buck and Wing, 1988; The Infernal Gallop, 1989; Town & Country, 1991; The Nutcracker, 1992; Deadly Serious, 1992; The Percys of Fitzrovia, 1992; Highland Fling, 1994; Swan Lake, 1996; Cinderella, 1997; TV work includes Late Flowering Lust, 1993, Drip-A Narcissistic Love Story, 1993; choreographer As You Like It, 1989, Children of Eden, 1990, A Midsummer Night's Dream, 1991—92, The Tempest, 1991, Show Boat, 1991, Peer Gynt, 1994, Watch With Mother, 1994, Oliver!, 1994, Watch Your Step, 1995, Boutique, 1995, Roald Dahl's Red Riding Hood, 1995. Recipient Bonnie Bird award, A Place Portfolio commn. and a Barclays New Stages award for choreography. Office: Adventure in Motion Picture 140A Gloucester Mansions Ste 3 Cambridge Circus London WC2H 8HD England

BOURNE, PETER GEOFFREY, physician, educator, author; b. Oxford, Eng., Aug. 6, 1939; s. Geoffrey Howard and Gwen (Jones) B.; m. Mary Elizabeth King, Nov. 9, 1974. MD, Emory U., 1962; MA in Anthropology, Stanford U., 1969. Fellow dept. psychiatry Med. Sch.; co-dir. Alcoholism Project, Emory U., 1962-63; intern King County Hosp., Seattle, 1963-64; rsch. psychiatrist Walter Reed Army Inst.; rschr. Washington, 1964-67; chief neuropsychiat. br. U.S. Army Med. Research Team, Vietnam, 1965-66; cons. S.E. Asia Health Br. (AID), Dept. State, 1966-67; resident dept. psychiatry, Stanford U. Med. Center, 1967-69; dir. mental health unit Southside Comprehensive Health Center, Atlanta, 1969-71; founder, dir. Atlanta S Ctrl. Cmty. Mental Health Ctr., 1970-71; dir. Ga. Office Drug Abuse, 1971-72; spl. adviser for health affairs to Gov. Jimmy Carter of Ga., 1971-73; asst. dir. White House Spl. Action Office for Drug Abuse Prevention, 1972-74; cons. Drug Abuse Coun., Washington, 1974-76; pres. Found. for Internat. Resources, 1975-76; Mid-Atlantic coord., dep. campaign dir. Jimmy Carter Presdl. Campaign, 1975-76; spl. asst. for health issues to U.S. Pres., Washington, 1976-78; mem. U.S. del. to Exec. Coun. UNICEF, 1977; asst. sec. gen. UN, N.Y.C., 1979-81; pres. Global Water, 1981-98; exec. v.p., pub. Devel. Internat., 1986-90; mem. U.S. Pres. Commn. on White House Fellows; head U.S. del. UN Devel. Program Governing Coun., 1978; emergency rm. physician Casualty Hosp., Washington, 1966-67; emergency room physician Kaiser Permanente Hosp., Santa Clara, Calif., 1967-69; psychiat. cons. Santa Clara County Hosp., 1968-69, San Mateo County Hosp., 1969; cons. WHO, Geneva, 1972, UN Divsn. on Narcotic Drugs, 1976; asst. prof. dept. psychiatry Emory U. Med. Sch., 1969-72, asst. prof. dept. preventive medicine and cmty. health, 1969-72; lectr. dept. psychiatry Harvard U. Med. Sch., 1974; v.p. Nat. Coordinating Coun. on Drug Abuse Edn., 1971-72; prof. psychiatry, chmn. dept. St. Georges Med. Sch., Grenada, 1979-98; pres. Peter Bourne Assocs., Washington, 1985-98. Mem. of jury The Lasker Awards, 1978—79; vice chancellor St. Georges U., Grenada, 1998—2001, vice chancellor emeritus, Grenada, 2001—; chmn. Med. Edn. Coop. with Cuba, 2000—; vis. scholar Green Coll., Oxford, England, 2001—. Author: Men, Stress and Viet Nam, 1970; editor: Psychology and Physiology of Stress, 1969, (with R. Fox) Alcoholism: Progress in Research and Treatment, 1973, Addiction, 1974, Acute Drug Abuse Emergencies, 1976, Water Resources: Social and Economic Aspects, 1983, Fidel, A Biography of Fidel Castro, 1986, Jimmy Carter: A Comprehensive Biography from Plains to the Post-Presidency, 1997; mem. editorial bd. Psychiatry, 1968—, Am. Jour. Drug Alcohol Abuse, 1973— ; contbr. articles to profl. jours. and chpts. to books. Bd. dirs. Save the Children Fedn., Inst. for So. Studies; chmn. global bd. dirs. Hunger Project; chmn., bd. trustees Council on Hemispheric Affairs, 1986—; chmn. bd. dirs. Am. Assn. World Health, 1982-98, Health and Devel. Internat., 1997—, Youth Advocate Program, 1998—, Med. Edn. Collaboration with Cuba, 1998—, Inst. Caribbean and Internat. Studies, Windward Islands Rsch. and Edn. Found. Served to capt. U.S. Army, 1964-67. Decorated Bronze Star medal, Air medal, Combat Medics badge; recipient William C. Menninger award Central Neuropsychiat. Assn., 1967, Pub. Svc. award Nat. Assn. State Drug Abuse Program Coordinators, 1974, Pub. Svc. award Assn. Chinese Ams., 1978; named one of Five Outstanding Young Men, Atlanta Jaycees, 1971, one of Five Outstanding Young Men in Ga., Ga. Jaycees, 1972. Fellow Am. Psychiat. Assn. (disting. life, chmn. task force on drugs and drug abuse edn. 1969-73); mem. AAAS, Ga. Psychiat. Assn., Washington Psychiat. Soc., Royal Soc. Medicine, Med. Assn. Ga., Soc. for Internat. Health (pres. 1988-92), Am. Med. Soc. on Alcoholism, Am. Anthrop. Assn., World Fedn. for Mental Health. Democrat. Home and Office: 2119 Leroy Pl NW Washington DC 20008-1848 E-mail: pbourne@sgu.edu. *I have always felt that my training as a physician was only a starting point in using my life to touch, for the better, the lives of as large a number of people as possible, whether formulating national health policy for the President of the United States, through the United Nations, through the private voluntary agencies or the academic world. I believe that ultimate gratification can only come from the sense that one has left the world a better place than when one arrived.*

BOURNE, RUSSELL, publisher, author; b. Boston, Oct. 10, 1928; s. Standish T. and Sylvia (Russell) B.; m. Miriam Anne Young, Aug. 22, 1953 (dec.); children: Sarah Perkins, Jonathan, Louise Taber, Andrew Russell; m. Dora Grabfield Flash, Oct. 31, 1992. AB magna cum laude, Williams Coll., 1950. Reporter Life mag., 1950-53, asst. to Henry R. Luce, 1953-56; assoc. editor Archtl. Forum, 1956-59; editor Am. Heritage Jr. Library, 1959-64, Time-Life Books, Great Ages of Man, 1964-69; assoc. chief Nat. Geog. Book Service, 1969-72; partner Bourne-Thompson & Assocs., Washington, 1972-77; sr. editor Smithsonian Exposition Books, Washington, 1977-80; pub. Hearst Gen. Books, N.Y.C., 1980-81; pub., editor Am. Heritage Books, N.Y.C., 1981-83; pub. cons., 1984—. Author: View From Front Street, 1989, Red King's Rebellion, 1990, Floating West, 1992, Best of the Best Sparkman and Stephens Designs, 1995, Americans on the Move, 1995, Invention in America, 1996, Rivers of America, 1998, Gods of War, Gods of Peace, 2002. Served with CIC, U.S. Army, Berlin, 1950-52. Home and Office: 2 Fairway Dr Ithaca NY 14850-2764

BOURNEUF, HENRI JOSEPH, JR., librarian; b. Beverly Farms, Mass. s. Henri and Elizabeth (McKean) B.; m. Susan Peterson, June 19; 1 child, Anne Peterson. BA, Harvard U., 1969; MLS, Simmons Coll., Boston, 1980. Ref. libr. Widener Libr., Harvard U., Cambridge, Mass., 1980—, head ref. libr., 1995—. Democrat. Home: 119 Huron Ave Cambridge MA 02138-1366 Office: Widener Library Harvard Univ Cambridge MA 02138 E-mail: bourneuf@fas.harvard.edu.

BOURQUE, RICHARD MICHAEL, foundation administrator; b. Omaha, Nebr., Mar. 9, 1967; s. Adrian Richard Bourque and Kathleen Marrie Van Ackeren; m. Kathy J. Green, June 26, 1993. BS in Agr., U. Mo., 1990. Mgr. Grandmother's, Omaha, 1990-91, Lute Ranch, Ogallala, Nebr., 1991—; owner, pres. Functional Agr. Resource Techs., Inc., Ogallala, 1993—; exec. dir. Lute Family Found., Inc., Ogallala, 1994—; pres. Packaging and Crating Svcs., Inc., North Platte, Nebr., 1996—. Cons. Law Office of McGinley, O'Donnell, Ogallala, 1998—; engr. Ogallala Fire and Rescue; pres. Keith County Housing Devel. Inc., Ogallala, 1997-98. Pres. Tech. Renovation Com., Ogallala, 1995-96; mem., bd. dirs. Comty. Redevel. Authority, Ogallala, 1996-98; bd. dirs. Nebr. Nat. Trails Mus., Keith County, 1996—, Western Nebr. Comty. Found. Inc., Keith County, 1996—. Recipient Outstanding Contbn. award Ogallala Sch. Bd., 1996. Mem. Nebr. Cattlemen's Assn., Ogallala Yacht Club. Roman Catholic. Avocations: skiing, hunting, boating, off-road trail riding, fishing. Office: Lute Family Found Inc PO Box 187 Ogallala NE 69153-0187 E-mail: lfound@atcjet.net.

BOUSFIELD, KENNETH HAROLD, civil engineer; b. L.A., Nov. 14, 1946; s. William Harold and Shirley (Burgess) B.; m. Gail Nuttall, Sept. 2, 1970; children: Tara Lee, Julie, Timothy Kenneth, Kelly Jean. BSCE, Brigham Young U., 1971; postgrad., U. Utah, 1976-80. Registered profl. engr., Utah. Engr. Utah Dept. Health, Salt Lake City, 1971-72; assoc. engr. Nielsen Maxwell & Wangsgard, Salt Lake City, 1973-76; compliance mgr. Utah Dept. Environ. Quality, Salt Lake City, 1976—. Contbr. articles to profl. jours. Fellow EPA; mem. Am. Water Works Assn. Republican. Mem. Lds Ch. Office: Utah Dept Environ Quality 150 N 1950 W Salt Lake City UT 84114-4830

BOUSON, J. BROOKS, English educator; b. Washington, Pa. m. Roberts Bouson Jr. BA, U. Ill., Chgo.; PhD, Loyola U., 1979. Asst. prof. English Mundelein Coll., Chgo., 1980-86, assoc. prof., 1986-91, Loyola U., Chgo., 1991-2000, prof., 2000—. Author: Brutal Choreographies: Oppositional Strategies and Narrative Design in the Novels of Margaret Atwood, 1993, The Empathic Reader: A Study of the Narcissistic Character and the Drama of the Self, 1989, Quiet As It's Kept: Shame, Trauma and Race in the Novels of Toni Morrison, 2000; contbr. articles to profl. jours. and chpts. to books. Edmund J. James scholar U. Ill. Mem. Margaret Atwood Soc., Toni Morrison Soc., MLA, Midwest MLA, Women's Caucus, Phi Kappa Phi, Alpha Sigma Nu. Office: Loyola U Chgo Dept English-Crown Ctr 6525 N Sheridan Rd Dept English Chicago IL 60626-5344

BOUSQUET, DANIEL WILLIAM, forester, educator; b. Southbridge, Mass., Sept. 23, 1942; s. Daniel Touisaint Bousquet and Sabina Anna Skowton; m. Ann Marie Swartz, Feb. 4, 1967 (dec. May 1992); children: Christopher, Matthew, Justin. BS in Forestry, U. Mass., 1964, MS in Forestry and Wood Tech., 1966; MBA in Ops. Mgmt., Pa. State U., 1973. Grad. rsch. asst. U. Mass., Amherst, 1964—66; specialist Forestry W.Va. U., Morgantown, 1966—67; rsch. officer Forest Products Lab. Environment Can., Ottawa, 1967—74; commerce officer Can. Dept. Industry, Trade and Commerce, Ottawa, 1974—75; assoc. prof. Forest Resources U. Vt., Burlington, 1975—. Bd. dirs. Vt. State Sustain Forestry Commn., Montpelier; mem. adv. bd. Vt. Forestry Found., Montpelier, 1990—; mem. adv. coun. Vt. Forest Resources, Montpelier, 1978—82. Author: Timber Harvesting: A Summary of Laws, 2003, Structural Wood Composites, 1994; contbr. Com. mem. Trails and Bikeways, Essex Junction, Vt., 1999—2000. Grantee, USDA, 1999—2000, 1996—99, 1997—98. Mem.: Soc. Wood Sci. and Tech., Forest Products Soc. (sec. 1993—94). Independent. Roman Catholic. Avocations: hiking, canoeing, fishing, bicycling, reading. Home: 2 Greenwood Ave Essex Junction VT 05452 Office: Univ Vermont 194 S Prospect St Burlington VT 05401-3596*

BOUSQUET-CHAVANNE, PATRICK, cosmetics executive; married; 2 children. MBA, Purdue U., Ecole Supérieure de Commerce, Marseilles, France; degree in advanced mgmt., Stanford U. Mng. dir. Elizabeth Arden, England; v.p., gen. mgr. Aramis Internat. divsn. Estée Lauder Cos. Inc., N.Y.C., NY, 1989—92, sr. v.p., gen. mgr. travel retail divsn., 1992—96, pres. Estée Lauder Internat. Inc. divsn., 1998—2001, group pres., 2001—; exec. v.p., gen. mgr. internat. ops. Parfums Christian Dior, Paris, 1997—98. Chmn. bd. dirs. Fragrance Found. Mem.: Coun. Asia-Pacific Econ. Coop., Bus. Coun. Internat. Understanding, Franco-Am. Bus. Coun. Office: Estée Lauder Co Inc 767 5th Ave New York NY 10153*

BOUSVAROS, ATHOS, pediatric gastroenterologist; b. London, May 5, 1960; came to U.S., 1966; s. George and Olga Bousvaros; m. Margaret Marie Lotz, Oct. 29, 1958; 1 child, George. BA magna cum laude, Williams Coll., 1981; MD, Duke U., 1985. Intern Duke U. Med. Ctr., Durham, N.C., 1985-86, resident in pediatrics, 1985-88; fellow Boston Children's Hosp., 1988-91, asst. in medicine, 1991—. Mem. adv. bd. Kids With Tubes, Boston; editor internat. seminars infield. Contbr. articles to profl. jours. Recipient clin. assoc. physician award NIH, 1994. Mem. N.Am. Soc. Pediat. Gastroenterology (young clin. investigator award 1998), Crohn's & Colitis Found. Greek Orthodox. Office: Children's Hosp 300 Longwood Ave Boston MA 02115-5737

BOUTAUD, OLIVIER GILLES, biochemistry research educator; b. Sartrouville, France, Dec. 24, 1966; BS, U. Louis Pasteur, Strasbourg, France, 1990, MS, 1991, PhD, 1994. Postdoctoral fellow Vanderbilt U., Nashville, 1994—98, rsch. instr. biochemistry, 1998—2001, rsch. asst. prof., 2001—. Contbr. articles to sci. jours. Office: Vanderbilt Univ Dept Pharmacology Nashville TN 37232-6602 E-mail: olivier.boutaud@vanderbilt.edu.

BOUTELLE, ANN EDWARDS, poet, educator; b. Aberfeldy, Scotland, Oct. 8, 1943; arrived in U.S., 1965; d. Alexander Wishart and Jean Fulton Edwards; m. William E. Boutelle, June 17, 1967; children: Jonathan, Laura, Alexander. MA, Univ. St. Andrews, Scotland, 1965; PhD, NYU, 1972. Vis. assoc. prof. Mt. Holyoke Coll., South Hadley, Mass., 1980—84; sr. lectr. Smith Coll., Northampton, Mass., 1984—, founder, chair Poetry Ctr., 1997—. Author: (book) Thistle and Rose: A Study of Hugh MacDiarmid's Poetry, 1980; contbr. poems to profl. jours. Founder Poetry Ctr. Smith Coll., 1997; trustee First Congl. Ch., Chesterfield, Mass., 2001—. Finalist Walt Whitman award, Acad. Am. Poets, 1999, Kathryn A. Morton prize, Sarabande Books, 2001; recipient German medal, U. St. Andrews, 1964. Mem.: MLA. Avocation: painting. Office: Smith College Elm St Northampton MA 01063 Office Fax: 413-585-7611.

BOUTELLE, STEVEN W. army officer; b. Pasco, Wash., Feb. 24, 1948; BA in Bus. and Fin., U. Puget Sound, Tacoma; MBA, Marymount U., Arlington, Va. Commd. 2d lt. U.S. Army, 1970, advanced through grades to maj. gen.; program exec. officer Army Task Force XXI, 1996-97, Command, Control and Communications Systems, Ft. Monmouth, N.J., 1997—. Decorated Legion of Merit with oak leaf cluster, others. E-mail: sbout74947@aol.com.

BOUTET, JANE GILMOUR, retired social worker; b. Mt. Kisco, N.Y., Feb. 11, 1932; d. John Wesley and Marie Rose (Nelson) Gilmour; m. James Edward Boutet, Apr. 12, 1958; children: Elizabeth, Simone. MSW, Columbia U., 1955. Lic. social worker. Caseworker Family Svc., Beloit, Wis., 1955-59; St. Vincent's Group Home, Milw., 1959-60; sex edn. educator Dist. 107, Highland Park, 1973-78; sch. social worker Spl. Edn. Dist. of Lake County, Gurnee, Ill., 1978—2000. Mem. LVW, 1973-77; founding bd. dirs. After Sch. Ctr., 1975-78; bd. dirs. Highland Park Cmty. Nursery Sch., 1967-70; bd. dirs. Tri-Con Child Care Ctr., 1975-78, 99—, pers. chair, 1999-2002, pres., 2002—; chmn. budget allocation com. United Way Highland Park, 1990-93; co-chmn. Immaculate Conception Soup Kitchen, 2000—; founding bd. dirs. Cmty. Family Ctr. of Highland Park and Highwood, 2000—. Mem. NASW, Ill. Assn. Sch. Social Workers. Avocations: tennis, bridge, gardening, travel, swimming. Home: 1761 Clifton Ave Highland Park IL 60035-2315

BOUTIETTE, VICKIE LYNN, educator, reading specialist; b. Valley City, N.D., Mar. 13, 1950; BS in Elem. Edn., Valley City State U., 1972; MS in Reading, Moorhead State U., 1997; postgrad., U. S.D., 1998—. 4th-5th grade tchr. Pillsbury Pub. Sch., 1973-74; 3rd grade tchr. West Fargo Pub. Schs., 1984-90, remedial reading tchr., elem. tchr., 1993-98, Reading Recovery tchr. leader, 1998—. Sunday sch. tchr., 1975—, ch. newsletter editor, 1993—; vol. U. Minn. Hosps. and Clinics, 1991-93. Recipient Nat. Educator Award Milken Family Found., 1998, Courage award N.D. Edn. Assn., 1994, Disting. Alumni award Minn. State U. Moorhead, 2002, Alumni Merit award Valley City State U., 2000; Christa McAuliffe fellowship, 2000; named N.D. Tchr. of Yr., 1998, West Fargo Tchr. of Yr. 1997-98. Mem. NEA, West Fargo Edn. Assn. (exec. bd. 1989-90, elem. chairperson 1988-89, pub. rels. chairperson 1988-90), N.D. Edn. Assn., Valley Reading Assn. (rec. sec. 1997—), N.D. Reading Assn., Phi Delta Kappa, Alpha Mu Gamma (pres. 1972). Home: 7103 64th Ave S Fargo ND 58104-5715 Office: Westside Elem Sch 945 7th Ave W West Fargo ND 58078-1429 Fax: 701-356-2119.

BOUTIN, PETER RUCKER, lawyer; b. San Francisco, Oct. 6, 1950; s. Frank J. and Charlotte (Downey) B.; m. Suzanne Jones, Aug. 31, 1974; children: Jennifer, Lisa, Kevin. AB, Stanford U., 1972; JD magna cum laude, Santa Clara U., 1975. Bar: Calif. 1975, U.S. Dist. Ct. (no., ea., so. and ctrl. dists.) Calif. 1976, U.S. Ct. Appeals (9th cir.) 1977, U.S. Supreme Ct. 1982. Assoc. Keesal, Young & Logan, Long Beach, Calif., 1975-78, ptnr., 1978-84, mng. ptnr. San Francisco office San Francisco, 1984—. Arbitrator San Francisco Superior Ct., 1989—, Nat. Assn. Securities Dealers, San Francisco, 1980—; mediator San Francisco Superior Ct., 1989—; early neutral evaluation panel U.S. Dist. Ct., 1993—. Co-author: Am. Arbitration Assn. Arbitrator Tng. Materials, 1992; bd. editors: Securities Arbitration Commentator. Mem. Bar Assn. San Francisco, Securities Industry Assn. Compliance and Legal Divsn., Stanford Buck/Cardinal Club. Office: Keesal Young & Logan 4 Embarcadero Ctr Ste 1500 San Francisco CA 94111-4122 E-mail: peter.boutin@kyl.com.

BOUTIS, TOM, artist, painter, print maker; b. N.Y.C., Aug. 25, 1922; s. Athanasios and Olga (Toskos) B.; m. Bertha Peters, Nov. 15, 1953; 1 child, Athanasios. BFA, Cooper Union U. Artist: one-person exhbns. include Drawings, Cooper Union, N.Y.C., 1953, Paintings: Zabriesky Gallery, N.Y.C., 1955, Am. Embassy, Rome, Italy, 1957, Area Gallery, N.Y.C., 1959, 60, Art Ctr. No. N.J., Tenafly, N.J., 1968; Decade on Paper, Landmark Gallery, N.Y.C., 1976, Paper on Paper, 1978, Cylinders, Columns, Circles and Color, 1979, Shadow Drawings, 1989, Monoprints, 1981, Painting, 1972, 75, 77, 81, Paintings and Monoprints, Maurice M. Pine Libr., Fairlawn, N.J., 1985, Works on Paper, Greek Embassy, 1989; 2-man exhbns. (with Alex Katz) Tanager Gallery, N.Y.C., 1958; group exhbns. include Greek Am. artists Noemata, Bklyn. Mus., 1977, Art Callender, Cooper Union Alumni Exhbn., N.Y.C., 1978, Landmark Gallery, N.Y.C., 1972, 82, Contemporary Drawings, Louise Ross Gallery, N.Y.C., 1984, Xmas Invitation, A.I.R., N.Y.C., 1985, Works on Paper, Ann Weber Gallery, Georgetown, Maine, 1987, Gallery Artists and Friends, Am. Acad. Arts & Letters, N.Y.C., 1988, 89, Shapolsky Gallery, N.Y.C., 1988, Arsenal Invitational, Arsenal Gallery, N.Y.C., 1989, Out of the 50's Snyder Fine Art, N.Y.C., 1993, Nat. Acad. Design, N.Y.C., 1992, 93, 95, 97, 99, 2001, 03, Monhegan Island Artists, The Governor's Mansion, Augusta, Maine, 1996, Works on Paper, Bergen Mus., N.J., 1998, Greek Am. Artists Queens Mus., 1999; represented in public collections at NYU, Everson Mus., Syracuse, N.Y., Chem. Bank, N.Y.C., Prudential Bache, N.Y.C., Resource Mgmt., N.Y.C., St. Michel's Hosp., Newark, Calvin Klein Collection, N.Y.C., Calvin Klein Works on Paper, Weisbaden German, Nieully, France, N.Y. Hilton, Broad Nat. Bank of Newark and many others. Recipient scholarship to Skowhegan (Maine) School of Painting, 1951, Fulbright to Rome, 1955-57, Mark Rothko Found. award, 1974; grantee: N.Y. Coun. on Arts, 1975 (painting), 1979 (graphics), Nat. Endowment for the Arts, 1976, Adolf and Esther Gottleib Found., 1983, The Rockefeller Found. Residency, Bellagio, Italy, 1989. Mem. NAD. Home: 162 E 82nd St New York NY 10028-1826 Office: 195 Chrystie St New York NY 10002 E-mail: tboutis@aol.com.

BOUTON, MARSHALL MELVIN, academic administrator; b. N.Y.C., Aug. 8, 1942; s. Percy Marshall and Mary Fuller (Melvin) B.; m. Barbara Elizabeth Linn, Sept. 14, 1968; children: Christopher, Alexander. BA cum laude in History, Harvard Coll., 1964; MA in South Asian Studies, U. Pa., 1968; PhD in Polit. Sci., U. Chgo., 1980. Exec. sec., program dir. The Asia Soc., N.Y.C., 1975-77; spl. asst. to amb. U.S. Embassy, New Delhi, 1977-80; dir. policy analysis, internat. security affairs Dept. Def., Near East, South Asia, Africa, 1980-81; dir. contemporary affairs The Asia Soc., N.Y.C., 1981-87, v.p. pres. program planning external affairs, 1987-90, exec. v.p., 1990-2001; pres. Chgo. Coun. on Fgn. Rels., 2001—. Tng. project dir. Peace Corps, Sacramento, summer 1967, tng. coord., Estes Park, Colo., summer 1968; tng. assoc. in internat. devel. The Ford Found., New Delhi, 1968-69; lectr. divsn. of social scis. U. Chgo., 1973-75; vis. scholar So. Asian Inst. Columbia U., 1975-77; internat. adv. bd. Ctr. Advanced Study India, U. Pa. Internat. Inst. Strategic Studies, Chgo. Sister Cities; internat. program bd. world affairs Coun. Am.; mem. bd. Pacific Coun. Internat. Policy Comml. Club Club, Econ. Club. Chgo.; cons. World Bank, 1980-81. Author: Agrarian Radicalism in South India, 1985, India's Problem is not Politics, 1998, Foreign Affairs, May/June 1998; co-author: Korea at the Crossroads: Implications for American Strategy, 1987;

editor, co-editor: India Briefing; contbr., editor numerous articles to profl. jours. NSF Dissertation Rsch. fellow, 1972-74, U.S. Agy. on Internat. Devel. grantee, 1974-77, Rockefeller Found. travel grantee, 1977. Mem.: Am. Polit. Sci. Assn., Assn. for Asian Studies, Coun. on Fgn. Rels., Mid-Am. Club, Met. Club Washington, Univ. Club of Chgo., Chgo. Club, Harvard Club. Office: Chgo Coun on Fgn Rels 116 S Michigan Ave Chicago IL 60603

BOUTROS, LINDA NELENE WILEY, medical/surgical nurse; b. New Orleans, Aug. 31, 1951; d. Robert Vernon and Marye Dell (Adcock) Wiley; m. Eddy Boutros, Dec. 23, 1972; children: Scott, Mark, Natalie. BS in Nursing, U. S.W. La., 1973. Cert. health care risk mgr. RN, relief charge, charge nurse, med./surgical flr. Bap. Hosp., Beaumont, Tex., 1973—76; RN, coord./supr. of nursing Kelsey Seybold Clinic, Missouri City, Tex., 1982-86; RN, head nurse S.W. Pediatric Ctr., Sugarland, Tex., 1986-87; RN, nursing supr. Westshore Hosp., Tampa, Fla., 1988-89; med.-surg. nurse Centurion Hosp., Carrollwood and Tampa, 1989-90, asst. head nurse med., 1990-91, relief supr., 1991, dir. surg. nursing svcs., 1992-93; nurse mgr. surg. floor, relief house supr. Univ. Cmty. Hosp. Carrollwood, Tampa, Fla., 1993-99, RN adminstrv. supr., 1999—. Mem. ANA, Fla. Nurses Assn., Fla. Soc. Health Care Risk Mgrs. Home: 502 Brooktree Ct Lutz FL 33548-4427 Office: Univ Cmty Hosp Carrollwood 7171 N Dale Mabry Hwy Tampa FL 33614-2670 E-mail: lwboutros@hotmail.com.

BOUTROS-GHALI, BOUTROS, former U.N. secretary general; b. Cairo, Nov. 14, 1922; LLD, Cairo U., 1946; Diploma of Higher Studies in Pub. Law, Paris U., 1947, Diploma of Higher Studies in Econs., 1948, Diploma of Polit. Sci. Ins., PhD in Internat. Law, Paris U., 1949; dr. h.c., René Descartes U., Paris, 1980, Uppsala (Sweden) U., 1986. Prof. internat. law, internat. rels., head dept. polit. scis. Cairo U., 1949-77; min. state Fgn. Affairs, Egypt, 1977-91, dep. prime min., 1991; sec.-gen. UN, N.Y.C., 1992-96, La Francophonie Org., 1997—2002; chmn. South Centre, 2003—. Assoc. dir. First Dag Hammarskjold Seminar, Netherland, 1963; dir. Ctr. Rsch. The Hague Acad. Internat. Law, 1963-64, mem. study group, 1965-66, mem. external program group, 1968-71, mem. curatorium adminstrv. coun., 1978—; vis. prof. faculty of law Paris U., 1967-68; co-dir. first session external program Acad. Internat. Law, Rabat, 1969; dir. first session of the sr. diplomats Union of the Abu Dhabi, 1973; lectr. internat. law, internat. rels. various univs. Author: (books) Contribution à l'Etude des Ententes Régionales, 1949, Cours de Diplomatie et de Droit Diplomatique et Consulaire, 1951, (with Youssef Chlala) Le Problème de Suez, 1957, Egypt and the United Nations: Carnegie Endowment for International Peace, 1957, Le Principe d'Egalité des Etats et les Organisations Internationales, 1961, Contribution à une Théorie Générale des Alliances, 1963, L'Organisation de l'Unité Africaine, 1969, Le Mouvement Afro-Asiatique, 1969, Les Difficultés Institutionelles du Panafricanisme, 1979, La Ligue des Etats Arabes, 1972, Les Conflits de Frontières en Afrique, 1973; co-author: Foreign Policies in a World of Change, 1983, Will We Survive?, 1989; founder, editor Al Ahram Al-Iktisadi, 1960-75, Al Siyassa Ad-Dawliya; mem. editl. bd. Egyptian Rev. Internat. Law, Yearbook of the Assn. of the Attenders, Alumni of the Hague Acad. of Internat. Law. Mem. Com. application of convs. and recommendations Internat. Labour Orgn., 1971-79; mem. cen. com. Polit. Bur. of the Arab Socialist Union, 1974-77; pres. Ctr. for Polit. and Strategic Studies, Al-Ahram, 1975—; mem. Internat. Commn. Jurist, Geneva, 1975-77; mem. Commn. Internat. Law of the UN, 1979-91; mem. secretariat Nat. Dem. Party, 1980-91. Decorated Order of the Nile (Egypt), Grand Croix de l'Ordre de la Couronne (Belgium), Cavaliere di Gran Croce (Italy), Gran Cruz de la Orden de Boyaca (Colombia), Gran Cruz de la Orden de Antonio José de Irisarri (Guatemala), Grand Croix de la Légion d'Honneur (France), Gran Cruz de la Orden Nacional Al Merito (Ecuador), Gran Cruz de la Orden del Liberation San Martin (Argentina), Tishakti Patta (Nepal), Grand Croix de l'Ordre du Mérite du Niger, Grand Officer de l'Ordre du Mérite du Mali, La Condecoracion De Agulia Azteca (Mex.), Grand Croix de l'Ordre Pro Merito Melitensi de l'Ordre Souverain Militaire et Hospitalier de St. Jean de Jerusalem de Rhodes de Malte, Grand Cordon de l'Ordre du Phoenix de Grèce, Grand Cordon du Mérite du Chili, Order of the Crown of Brunei, Grand Cross of the Order of Merit (Germany), Gran Cruz del Sol del Peru, comdr. de l'Ordre du Mérite Nat. de la Côte d'Ivoire, Grand Croix de l'Ordre du Danebrog, Grand Officer Cross of the Order of the Polar Star (Sweden), The Order of Diplomatic Svc. Merit (Gwanghwa, Korea); Fulbright Rsch. scholar Columbia U., 1954-55. Mem. African Soc. Polit. Studies (pres. 1980—), Egyptian Soc. Internat. Law (v.p. 1965—), Inst. Pub. Internat. Law and Internat. Rels. Thessaloniki (curatorium 1976—), Acad. des Scis. morales et politiques (assoc. 1989—), Inst. Internat. Law (pres. 1985-87), Inst. Affari Internazionali (assoc. 1979—), Acad. Mondiale pour la Paix (sci. com. 1975—), Internat. Inst Human Rights (mem. coun., exec. com. 1975—), Assn. Colombiana de Estudios de Politica Internacional Y Diplomacia (hon. 1980—), Malgache Acad., Academia Mexicana de Dir. Internacional. Home: 2 Avenue El-Nil Giza Cairo Egypt Office: CP 228 1211 Geneva 19 Switzerland

BOUVIER, MARSHALL ANDRE, lawyer; b. Jacksonville, Fla., Sept. 30, 1923; s. Marshall and Helen Marion B.; m. Zepha Windle, July 11, 1938; children: Michael A., Debra Bouvier Williams, Mark A., Marshall André III, Suzanne, John A. (dec.), Wendy Bouvier Clark, Jennifer Lynn. AB, Emory U., LLB, 1949. Bar: Ga. 1948, Nev. 1960. Commd. USN, 1949; naval aviator, judge advocate; ret., 1959; atty. State of Nevada, 1959-60; pvt. practice, Reno, 1960-82, 88—; dist. atty. County of Storey, Nev., 1982-88, spl. cons. to Nev. Dist. Attys., 1991-95; pres., CEO A.G.E. Corp., 1997—. Mem. Judge Advocates Assn., Am. Bd. Hypnotherapy, Ancient and Honorable Order Quiet Birdmen, Rotary, E Clampus Vitus, Phi Delta Phi, Sigma Chi.

BOUYOUCOS, JOHN VINTON, research and development company executive; b. Lansing, Mich., Nov. 9, 1926; s. George John and Delia (Bemis) B.; m. Stella Wright, Sept. 29, 1953; children: Anne Stephanie, Peter Johnson, Hope Nicola; m. Kristine Thuesen Hordon, May 26, 1984. Student, U. Mich., 1944; AB, Harvard U., 1949, S.M., 1951, PhD, 1953, Harvard Bus. Sch. Smaller Co. Mgmt. Program cert., 1976. Asst. dir. Harvard Acoustics Research Lab., Harvard U., 1955-59; mgr. hydroacoustics dept. Gen. Dynamics Electronics Div., Rochester, N.Y., 1959-71; pres., chief scientist Hydroacoustics Inc., Rochester, 1972—. Patentee in field. Pres., chmn. bd. Soc. Chamber Music, Rochester, 1977-96, chmn. bd. 1996-99, chmn. emeritus, 1999—; bd. dirs., vice chmn. Rochester Philharm. Orch., 1978-89, hon. bd. dirs., 1990—. Served with U.S. Navy, 1944-46. Recipient Rochester Patent Law Assn. Inventors award, 1973. Fellow IEEE, Acoustical Soc. Am. (v.p. 1970-71; disting. svc. citation 2000); mem. Soc. Exploration Geophysicists, Audio Engring. Soc., Inst. Noise Control Engrs. Clubs: Harvard Bus. Sch. Rochester (pres. 1984). Home: 11 Elmwood Hill Ln Rochester NY 14610-3445 Office: Hydroacoustics Inc PO Box 23447 Rochester NY 14692-3447 E-mail: bcos@sprintmail.com, hai@eznet.net.

BOUZIDE, ABDERRAHIM, chemist, researcher; b. Casablanca, Morocco, Oct. 30, 1966; s. Mohamed Bouzide and Mbarka Laajili; m. Rachida Qassoudi. PhD, U. Pierre and Marie Curie, Paris, 1993. Post doc. fellow, Linkoping, Sweden, 1993—95; research asst. INRS, Canada, 1995—97; prin. scientist Pharmacor, Inc., Montreal, Canada, 1997—2000; sr. scientist Invenux, Inc., Denver, 2000—. Contbr. articles to profl. jours. Mem.: ACS. Achievements include patents for in field. Avocations: classical music, soccer. Home: 8833 Colorado Blvd 305 Thornton CO 80229 Office: Invenux Inc 6840 N Broadway Suite F Denver CO 80221 Office Fax: 720-542-1105. Personal E-mail: abouzide2@yahoo.com. Business E-mail: abouzide@invenux.com.

BOVA, BENJAMIN WILLIAM, author, editor, educator; b. Phila., Nov. 8, 1932; s. Benjamin P. and Giove (Caporiccio) B.; m. Rosa Cucinotta, Nov. 28, 1953 (div. 1973); children: Michael Francis, Regina Marie; m. Barbara Ellen Berson, June 28, 1974. BS in Journalism, Temple U., 1954; MA in Communications, SUNY Albany, 1987; EdD, Calif. Coast U., 1996. Formerly newspaper reporter; mktg. mgr. Avco Everett Rsch. Lab.; formerly tchr. sci. fiction Harvard U.; formerly tchr. sci. fiction, dir. film courses Hayden Planetarium, N.Y.C.; editor Upper Darby (Pa.) News, 1954-56; tech. editor Project Vanguard, 1956-58; motion picture scriptwriter Phys. Sci. Study Com., Ednl. Svcs., Inc., Watertown, Mass., 1958-60; mgr. mktg. Avco Everett Rsch. Lab., Avco Corp., Everett, Mass., 1960-71; editor Analog Sci. Fiction-Sci. Fact mag. Conde Nast Pub. Co., N.Y.C., 1971-78; fiction editor Omni mag., N.Y.C., 1978-79, exec. editor, 1979-81, v.p., editorial dir., 1981-82. Past mem. panel Office Tech. Assessment, U.S. Congress; lectr. Nat. Geog. Soc., major govt. and corp. exec. groups, univs.; adv. bd. Post Coll.; bd. contbrs. USA Today; publ. Galaxy Online.com, 1999-2000. Author: (fiction) The Star Conquers, 1959, Star Watchman, 1964, The Weathermakers, 1967, Out of the Sun, 1968, The Dueling Machine, 1969, Escape!, 1969, Exiled From Earth, 1971; author: (with George Lucas) THX 1138, 1971; author: Flight of Exiles, 1972, As On a Darkling Plain, 1972, When the Sky Burned, 1972, Forward in Time, 1973; author: (with Gordon R. Dickson) Gremlins, Go Home!, 1974; author: End of Exile, 1975, The Starcrossed, 1975, City of Darkness, 1976, Millennium, 1976, The Multiple Man, 1976, Colony, 1978, Maxwell's Demons, 1978, Kinsman, 1979, The Exiles Trilogy, 1981, Voyagers, 1981, Test of Fire, 1982, The Winds of Altair, 1983, Escape Plus, 1984, Orion, 1984, The Astral Mirror, 1985, Privateers, 1985, Promethians, 1986, Voyagers II: The Alien Within, 1986, Battle Station, 1987, The Kinsman Saga, 1987, Vengeance of Orion, 1988, Peacekeepers, 1988, Cyberbooks, 1989, Voyagers III, Star Brothers, 1990, Orion in the Dying Time, 1990, Future Crime, 1990; author: (with Bill Pogue) The Trikon Deception, 1992; author: Mars, 1992; author: (with A.J. Austin) To Save the Sun, 1992; author: Triumph, 1993, Empire Builders, 1993, Challenges, 1993, Sam Gunn, Unlimited, 1993, Orion and The Conqueror, 1994, Death Dream, 1994; author: (with A.J. Austin) To Fear the Light, 1995; author: Orion Among the Stars, 1995, Brothers, 1996, Moonrise, 1997, Moonwar, 1998, Sam Gunn Forever, 1998, Twice Seven, 1998, Return to Mars, 1999, Venus, 2000, Jupiter, 2001, The Precipice, 2001, The Rock Rats, 2002, Saturn, 2003, (nonfiction) The Milky Way Galaxy, 1961, Giants of the Animal World, 1962, Reptiles Since the World Began, 1964, The Uses of Space, 1965, In Quest of Quasars, 1970, Planets, Life and LGM, 1970, The Fourth State of Matter, 1971 (Best Sci. Book award ALA, 1988), The Amazing Laser, 1972, The New Astronomies, 1972, Starflight and Other Improbabilities, 1973, Man Changes the Weather, 1973; author: (with Barbara Berson) Survival Guide for the Suddenly Single, 1974; author: The Weather Changes Man, 1974, Workshops in Space, 1974, Through Eyes of Wonder, 1975, Science: Who Needs It?, 1975, Notes to a Science Fiction Writer, 1975, Closeup: New Worlds, 1977, Viewpoint, 1977, The Seeds of Tomorrow, 1977, The High Road, 1981, Vision of the Future: The Art of Robert McCall, 1982, Assured Survival, 1984, Star Peace, 1986, Welcome to Moonbase!, 1987; author: (with Sheldon Glashow) Interactions, 1988; author: The Beauty of Light, 1988, First Contact, 1990, The Craft of Writing Science Fiction That Sells, 1994, Space Travel, 1997, Immortality, 1998, The Story of Light, 2001. Recipient 6 Sci. Fiction Achievement awards for best profl. editor (Hugo), E.E. Smith Meml. award for imaginative fiction New Eng. Sci. Fiction Soc., 1974, Balrog award, 1983, Inkpot award, 1985, Disting. Alumnus award Temple U., 1982, Isaac Asimov Meml. award, 1996. Fellow AAAS, Brit. Interplanetary Soc.; mem. AIAA, Nat. Space Soc. (pres. 1982-88, pres. emeritus, chmn. bd. 1988-92), N.Y. Acad. Scis., Sci. Fiction Writers Am. (charter, pres. 1990-92), Planetary Soc., Nature Conservancy, Nat. Space Club, Explorers Club, Amateur Fencer's League Am.

BOVA, DAVIDE, radiologist; b. Naples, Italy, Nov. 16, 1961; came to U.S., 1995; s. Bruno Bova and Anna Roncaglia; children: Libby Starbird, Giulia Maria, Gabriella Anna. MD magna cum laude, U. Degli Studi, Florence, Italy, 1986. Cert. specialist in radiology, Italy; diplomate Am. Bd. Nuclear Medicine, Am. Bd. Radiology. Asst. dept. radiology Mil. Hosp., Piacenza, Italy, 1988-90, chief dept. radiology, 1990-95; house staff Loyola U. Med. Ctr., Maywood, Ill., 1995-2000, asst. prof. radiology, 2000—. Contbr. articles to profl. jours. Maj. Italian Army Med. Svc., 1989-2000. Mem. Italians Soc. Med. Radiology, Radiol. Soc. of N.Am., Am. Roentgen Ray Soc. (internat. mem.). Avocation: fusion and correlative imaging. Office: Loyola U Med Ctr Dept Radiology 2160 S 1st Ave Maywood IL 60153-3304 E-mail: dbova@lunis.lumc.edu.

BOVA, VINCENT ARTHUR, JR., lawyer, consultant, photographer; b. Pitts., Apr. 25, 1946; s. Vincent A. and Janie (Pope) B.; m. Breda Murphy, Mar. 20, 1971; 1 child, Kate Murphy Bova. BA in Bus. Adminstrn., Alma (Mich.) Coll., 1968; MPA, Ohio State U., 1972; JD, Oklahoma City U., 1975. Bar: Okla. 1975, N.Mex. 1976, U.S. Dist. Ct. 1976, U.S. Tax Ct., 1976, U.S. Ct. Appeals (10th cir.) 1976, U.S. Supreme Ct. 1979. Mktg. and systems rep., computer systems div. RCA, 1968-70; research analyst Research Atlanta, 1972-73; assoc. Threet, Threet, Glass, King & Maxwell, 1976-78; ptnr. Lill & Bova, P.A., 1978-81; sole practice Albuquerque, 1981—. Past pres. Bare Bulls Investment, 1982, Fumilan Investment, 1983, Toastmasters; rsch. analyst urban affairs Ohio Dept. Urban Affairs, Columbus, 1971; panel mem. N.Mex. Med. Rev. Commn., 1981—, N.Mex. Legal/Dental/Osteopathic Podiatry Com., 1981—; v.p. Albuquerque Com. on Fgn. Rels., 2001—; co-owner Albuquerque Photography Gallery. Contbr. articles on organizational behavior and mgmt. to profl. jours. Bd. dirs. Rio Grande Nature Ctr.; pres., v.p. spl. projects S.W. Arts and Crafts Festival, Albuquerque, 1986-89; pol. cons. Nov. Group; mem. N.Mex. Estate Planning Coun., 1978—; sec.-treas., vice-chmn., pres. adv. bd. Salvation Army, 1987—; contbr. Ctr. for Home for Prevention of Domestic Violence, 1984-85, Ronald McDonald House, 1984; past chmn. N.Mex. Workers' Compensation Monthly; mem. advt. com. Supreme Ct. Panel; pres. Salvation Army Adv. Bd., Albuquerque; mem. Edn. Forum; pres., bd. mem. Albuquerque com. on fgn. rels.; moot ct. judge, Albuquerque. With Air N.G., 1969-75. Recipient Pacesetters award Ohio State U., 1972; named one of Outstanding Young Men of Am., 1975, 76. Mem. ATLA (advanced grad. Nat. Coll. Advocacy), Ct. Practice Inst. (advanced diplomate), ABA, N.Mex. Bar Assn. (pres. small firm and solo sect.), State Bar N.Mex. (mem. med. legal panel, med.-dental podiatry legal panel, rep. probate, wills and trusts ann. report), Nat. Def. Lawyers, Assn. (staff chmn. 1986), N.Mex. Trial Lawyers Assn., Internat. Assn. Fin. Planners, Nat. Assn. Social Security Claimants Reps. (past state chmn.), Business Round Table, Albuquerque Bar Assn., N.Mex. Fin. Planning Assn., Sole Practitioners Assn., Image Profls. of the Southwest (pres., bd. mem.), Internat. Credit Assn. (lectr.), Ohio State U. Alumni Assn. of N.Mex. (pres.), Image Profls. of the S.W. (bd. dirs., print chmn. 1996—, pres.), Image Profls. S.W. (photography award 1996, Best of Show 2000, 10 others, 14 awards 1999), Profl. Photography Assn., Photog. Soc. Am. (pres. chpt.), Toastmasters (past pres., v.p., edn. chmn., Able Toastmaster award), Millionaires Tip Club, Enchanted Lens Camera Club (pres.), Profl. Photographers Am. (assoc. mem.; 8 awards 1999), Albuquerque Knife and Fork (pres., v.p., sec.-treas., bd. dirs.), Inn of the Ct., Zia Scuba Club, Phi Alpha Delta, Sigma Tau Gamma (pres. Albuquerque com. on fgn. rels.), co-owner of Albuq. Photographors Gallery. Democrat. Presbyterian. Avocations: flower gardening, photography - video and still, computers, investing, reading. Office: 5716 Osuna Rd NE Albuquerque NM 87109-2527

BOVAIRD, BRENDAN PETER, lawyer; b. N.Y.C., Mar. 9, 1948; s. John Francis and Margaret Mary (Endrizzi) B.; m. Carolyn Warren Boyle, Dec. 18, 1971; children: Anne Warren, Sarah Grant. BA, Fordham U., 1970; JD, U. Va., 1973. Bar: N.Y. 1974, D.C. 1980, Pa. 1983, U.S. Dist. Ct. (so. and ea. dists.) N.Y. 1974, U.S. Ct. Appeals (2d cir.) 1974. Atty., Dewey, Ballantine, Bushby, Palmer & Wood, N.Y.C., 1973-82; asst. gen. counsel Campbell Soup Co., Camden, N.J., 1982-90; sr. v.p., gen. counsel, sec. Orion Pictures Corp., N.Y.C., 1990-91; counsel, mem. exec. com. Wyeth-Ayerst Internat. Inc., St. Davids, Pa., 1992-95; pres. KDH Inc., 1994—; v.p., gen. counsel UGI Corp., Valley Forge, Pa., 1995—; v.p., gen. counsel AmeriGas Propane, Inc., Valley Forge, 1995—; bd. dirs. Motion Picture Export Assn. Am., Inc., 1990-91, United Valley Ins. Co. Mem. MPAA (legal com. 1990-91), ABA (corp., bus. law sect., internat. law sect.), Aircraft Owners and Pilots Assn., Phila. Country Club, Phi Delta Phi. Office: UGI Corp PO Box 858 Valley Forge PA 19482-0858

BOVASSO, LOUIS JOSEPH, lawyer; b. Jersey City, Aug. 16, 1935; s. Louis S. and Mildred (Blumetti) B.; m. Margaret Ann Wilt, Aug. 18, 1964 (div. Sept. 1977); children— Tracy, Marc, Shelley, Kari; m. Helen Schumow, July 14, 1984. B.S.M.E., Newark Coll. Engring., 1961; J.D., Catholic U. Am., 1966. Bar: Calif. 1973, U.S. Dist. Ct. (cen. dist.) Calif. 1973, U.S. Ct. Appeals (9th cir.) 1973, U.S. Ct. Appeals (5th cir.) 1975. Assoc. Poms, Smith, Lande & Rose, Los Angeles, 1973-79, ptnr., 1979— . Served to sgt. USAF, 1954-58. Mem. U.S. Trademark Assn., Century City Bar Assn., La. Patent Law Assn. Republican. Home: 26081 Baldwin Pl Stevenson Ranch CA 91381-1135

BOVAY, HARRY ELMO, JR., retired engineering company executive; b. Big Rapids, Mich., Sept. 4, 1914; s. Harry E. and Addibelle (Bentley) B.; m. Sue Goldston, Feb. 1, 1977; children: Mark Benson, Susan Stone C.E., Cornell U., 1936. Jr. engring. aide U.S. C.E., 1936-37; jr. metal insp., project engr. Humble Oil & Refining Co., Baytown, Tex., 1937-45; cons. engr. Houston, 1946-62; pres. Bovay Engrs., Inc., Houston, 1962-73, chmn. bd., chief exec. officer, 1974-84. Owner Bovista Farms, Tenn. and Tex.; pres. Mid-South Telecommunications Co., Inc., 1987—; endowed chair Tex. A&M U. and Cornell U. Editor: Mechanical and Electrical Systems for Buildings Pres., Sam Houston Area council Boy Scouts Am., 1963-64, exec. com. South Central region, 1973-76, bd. dirs., 1975-79, v.p., 1980-81, pres., 1981-82, mem. nat. exec. bd., 1981-84, chmn. camping/outdoor com., 1983-85, chmn. nat. audit com., 1982-87, mem. nat. adv. coun., 1985-98; chmn. Houston Commn. Zoning, 1959-60; bd. dirs. Vis. Nurse Assn., Houston, 1970-75, Retina Rsch. Found., 1998—; active United Fund Houston and Harris County; mem. Houston Adv. Council Naval Affairs, 1959; mem. Tex. Water Resources Adv. Com., 1968-71; mem. adv. com. Coastal Engring. Lab., Tex. A&M U., 1969, also mem. adv. council for Pres.; mem. engring. adv. com. Miss. State U., 1974-77; mem. Alumni Council Cornell U. Coll. Engring.; bd. visitors McDonald Obs., 1985—; mem. demand subpanel Energy Research Adv. Bd., 1985-86; mem. adv. com. rsch. programs Tex. Higher Edn. Coordinating Bd., 1992-95. Recipient Silver Beaver award Boy Scouts Am., 1965, Silver Antelope, 1976, Silver Buffalo, 1986, Disting. Svc. award SAR, 1998, George Washington Svc. award Paul Carrington chpt. SAR, 1998; named Disting. Engr., Tex. Engring. Found.; Baden-Powell fellow, World Scouting Orgn.; camping area Bovay Ranch Sam Houston Area Coun. Boy Scouts Am. Fellow ASCE, ASHRAE (ASHRAE-ALCO award); mem. Nat. Soc. Profl. Engrs. (pres. 1976, Achievement award 1987), Tex. Soc. Profl. Engrs. (pres. 1967-68), Am. Inst. Cons. Engrs. (past pres Tex. chpt.), Houston Engring. and Sci. Soc. (past 2d v.p.), Am. Rd. Builders Assn. (exec. com.), Am. Concrete Inst., Am. Wood Preservers Assn., ASTM (councilor 1960-64), Forest Products Research Soc., Tex. Forest Products Mfrs. Assn., SAME (Toulmin medal), Pres.' Assn., Newcomen Soc. N.Am., Nat. Acad. Engring., Houston Livestock Show & Rodeo (life). Clubs: Houston, Kiwanis, Cosmos, Houston Country, Petroleum. Episcopalian. Office: 3355 W Alabama St Ste 1140 Houston TX 77098-1799

BOVE, ALFRED ANTHONY, medical educator; b. Phila., Apr. 28, 1938; s. Alfred Anthony and Adeline Amelia (DeRose) B.; m. Sandra Ann Seltzer, June 25, 1966; children: Jacqueline, Christopher, Andrew. BSEE, Drexel U., 1962; MD, Temple U., 1966, PhD, 1970. Diplomate Am. Bd. Internal Medicine, Am. Bd. Cardiology, Am. Bd. Undersea Hyperb Medicine. Med. intern Temple U. Hosp., Phila., 1966-67, med. resident, 1969-70, postdoctoral fellow, 1967-69, asst. prof. medicine, 1973-81, prof. medicine, 1986—; postdoctoral fellow Mayo Clinic, Rochester, Minn., 1970-71, prof. medicine, 1981-86; chief of cardiology Temple U. Med. Sch., 1986—99, assoc. dean, practice plan affairs, 1999—2001, prof. emeritus, 2001—. Author: Diving Medicine, 4th edit., 1997; co-author: Diving Medicine, 1990, Exercise Medicine, 1982; editor: Skin Diver mag., 1981—; contbr. articles to profl. jours. Capt. USNR, 1971-73, 98, ret. Recipient Established Investigator award Am. Heart Assn., 1975, Paul Dudley White award Assn. Mil. Surgeons of the U.S., 1998, Disting. fellow award, ACC, 2002. Fellow ACP, Am. Coll. Cardiology (state gov. 1989-92); mem. Am. Physiologic Soc., IEEE, Undersea and Hyperbaric Med. Soc. (pres. 1983, Craig Hoffman award 1988, Stover-Link award 1974). Roman Catholic. Avocations: scuba diving, marathon racing. Office: Temple U Med Ctr Cardiology Sect 3401 N Broad St Philadelphia PA 19140-4105 E-mail: fred@scubamed.com., bovea@tuhs.temple.edu.

BOVE, JOHN LOUIS, chemistry and environmental engineering educator, researcher; b. N.Y.C., Apr. 15, 1928; s. Frank and Bridget (Randazzo) B.; m. June Althea Burns, Dec. 28, 1957; children: Adele, Catherine. BA in Chemistry, Bucknell U., 1949, MSA. in Chemistry, 1954; PhD in Chemistry, Case Western Res. U., 1973. Asst. prof. chemistry Cooper Union, N.Y.C., 1958-67, prof. chemistry and environ. engring., chmn. dept. chemistry, 1970—, dir. environ. program, 1970—; v.p. Cooper Union Research Found., 1974-80. Dep. dir. bur. tech. services N.Y.C. Air Resources, 1967-70; dir. Mid-Atlantic Consortium Air Pollution, 1970-76 Contbr. chpts., articles to profl. publs. Served with M.C. U.S. Army, 1950. Recipient Schweinburg Schweinburg Found., 1964; fellow Dow Chem. Co., 1953— ; grantee NSF, 1960— Republican. Home: 125 Richards Rd Ridgewood NJ 07450-1115 Office: The Cooper Union Cooper Union 51 Astor Pl New York NY 10003-7132 E-mail: bove@cooper.edu.

BOVE, PATRICE MAGEE, elementary education educator; b. Fort Madison, Iowa, Apr. 29, 1946; d. Claude and Susie T. Magee; m. Roger E. Bove, Aug. 6, 1983; 1 child, Jonna. MusB, U. Iowa, 1968; M of Music Edn., Temple U., 1976. Tchr. elem. instrumental music Birmingham (Mich.) Sch. Dist., 1968-69; tchr. elem. music T-E Sch. Dist., Berwyn, Pa., 1969—. Co-author: Philadelphia Orchestra Student Concert Books, 1994—; contbr. MENC (Strategies for Teaching Elementary Music), 1996. Educator, writer edn. adv. com. Phila. Orch., 1994—; accompanist chorus, Wayne, Pa., 1995, Suzuki Concerts, Immaculata, Pa., 1994-97. Mem. AAUW, Nat. Assn. Music Therapy, Music Tchrs. Assn., Gordon Inst. Music Learning, Suzuki, Kodaly, Orff, Pa. Music Edn. Assn. (dist. 12 co-host elem. songfest 1995), Music Educators Nat. Conf. Avocations: reading, computers, cooking. Home: 325 Holly Rd West Chester PA 19380-4614

BOVÉ, ROBERT CHARLES, writer, editor; b. Hackensack, July 13, 1951; s. Donald Paul and Maryanna (Evers) B. BA in English Lang. and Lit., U. Va., 1974; MFA with hons. in Creative Writing, Bklyn. Coll., 1998. Freelance writer, editor, Washington, 1978—; news dir. Sta. WXVA/WZFM Radio, Charles Town, W.Va., 1979-80; sr. writer Office of News and Pub. Affairs George Washington U., Washington, 1980-83; assoc. editor Tng. and Devel. Jour., Alexandria, Va., 1983-87; ptnr. Loco-motive Press, Washington, 1987-91. Faculty tech. cons., adj. asst. prof. English dept. Pace U., 1998—. Author: Cubesteak Canapés, 1990, Nectar, 1991, Nine from Metronome, 1995, The UFO's of October, 2003; editor: Brooklyn Rev. # 15, 1997; contbr. articles to on-line jours. Recipient Good Citizen citation Dept of N.J. Am. Legion, 1966. Avocations: canoeing, camping, swimming. Home and Office: 139 Joralemon St Brooklyn NY 11201-4070 E-mail: rcbove@earthlink.net.

BOVE, VICTOR MICHAEL, JR., media arts and sciences educator, researcher; b. Cape Girardeau, Mo., Dec. 23, 1960; s. Victor Michael and Alice Gloria (Zaharchuk) B.; m. Suzanne Jeannette Frances Sandor, June 13, 1987. BSEE, MIT, 1983, MS in Visual Studies, 1985, PhD in Media Tech., 1989. Asst. prof. MIT, Cambridge, Mass., 1989-93, assoc. prof., 1993-97, Career Devel. Prof. endowed chair Sony Corp., 1991-95, Dreyfoos prof. media tech., 1995-97, undergrad. officer media arts and scis. program, 1996—, prin. rsch. scientist Media Lab., 1997—; co-founder WatchPoint Media, Inc., 1999. Mem. U.S. Com. on Open High-Resolution Sys., 1990-91. Contbr. articles to profl. jours. and periodicals including London Sunday Times. Bd. dirs. Wrentham (Mass.) Hist. Soc., 2000—. Recipient Disting. Alumni award John Piersol McCaskey High Sch., 1997. Fellow SPIE; mem. IEEE, Soc. Motion Picture and TV Engrs. (mgr. New Eng. sect. 1993-95, bd. editors 1995—), Optical Soc. Am., Assn. for Computing Machinery (gen. chair 1996 Multimedia Conf.). Achievements include patents for unrecordable video signals, antialiasing apparatus and method for computer printers, thermochromic ink, volumetric medical imaging. Home: 57 Ray Rd Wrentham MA 02093-1804 Office: MIT 20 Ames St # E15-368B Cambridge MA 02142-1308 E-mail: vmbww@teakettlefarm.com.

BOVÉ-DEWALD, MARYLOU GOODMAN, university director, educator; b. Rock Hill, S.C., Oct. 10, 1958; d. Charles Frank and MaryLou (Brown) Goodman. Student, Coll. Charleston, 1975-78; BA in Sociology, Biology, Winthrop Coll., 1979; MBA in Fin., Emporia State U., 1984. Tech. proofreader Houston Lighting and Power, Wadsworth, Tex., 1980-81; owner Citadel Creek Running Horses, Ottawa, Kans., 1983—; asst. dir. small bus. devel. ctr. Emporia (Kans.) State U., 1984-86; lectr. in bus. Johnson County C.C., Overland Park, Kans., 1986-95; U.S. Disciplinary Barracks, 1991-97; dir. Small Bus. Devel. Ctr. Kansas City (Kans.) Community Coll., 1986-88, Rockhurst Coll., Kansas City, Mo., 1990-92; sr. loan specialist U.S. Small Bus. Adminstrn., 1992—96; lectr. in bus. internat. program Ottawa U., 1990—; owner Dinner Bell Ranch, Eureka Springs, Ark., 1996—; v.p. Commerce Bank, Lawrence, Kans., 2001—. County coord. Kansans for Pari-Mutuel, Lyon County, 1983-86; mem. Jr. League of Kansas City, Cen. Exch., Kansas City, Mo.; docent Nelson Atkins Mus. Art. Named Entrepreneurial Edn. Nat. Instr. of Yr., 1998, Kans. Womens Small Bus. advocate of Yr., 2000, Reg. SBA Minority Advocate of Yr., 2002. Mem. AAUW (v.p. 1983-85, nat. v.p. 1986-87), DAR, Womens C. of C., Kansas City (edn. chair 1987-89, bd. dirs.), Ft. Leavenworth Hunt, Am. Royal Horseshow Com., Mensa. Republican. Episcopalian. Avocations: racing horses, skiing, scuba diving. Home: 610 S Ash St Ottawa KS 66067 Office: US Small Bus Adminstrn 323 W 8th St Kansas City MO 64105-1519

BOVEE, COURTLAND LOWELL, business educator; b. Red Bluff, Calif., Oct. 4, 1944; s. Courtney Van and Shirley Patricia (Safford) B. AA, Shast Coll., 1965; BS, U. N.D., 1967; MS, U. Tenn., 1968. Mem. faculty Grossmont Coll., El Cajon, Calif., 1968—. now prof. business; prin., v.p. Bovee & Thill L.L.C., Las Vegas, Nev., 1997—. Co-author: Bus. in Action, 2004, (textbooks) Bus. Today, 10th edit., 2001, Excellence in Business Communication, 5th edit., 2001, Bus. Communication Today, 7 edit., 2002. Mem. Assn. for Bus. Comm. Avocations: photography, travel. Office: Bovee & Thill LLC 2950 E Flamingo Rd Las Vegas NV 89121-5208 E-mail: bovee@dc.rr.com.

BOVEE, EUGENE CLEVELAND, protozoologist, emeritus educator; b. Sioux City, Iowa, Apr. 1, 1915; s. Earl Eugene and Martha Nora (Johnson) B.; m. Maezene B. Wamsley, May 18, 1942 (div. 1967); m. Elizabeth A. Moss, May 9, 1968; children— Frances, Gregory, Matthew; stepchildren— Lynne, Lisa. BA, U. No. Iowa, 1939; MS, U. Iowa, 1948; PhD, UCLA, 1950. Instr. zoology Iowa U., 1940-41; biology tchr. Greene (Iowa) H.S., Iowa, 1941-42; instr. biology U. No. Iowa, 1946-48; journalist Iowa Rev. Greene, 1945—46; instr. zoology UCLA, 1948-50, research zoologist, 1962-68; asst. prof. biology Calif. Poly. U., 1950-52; assoc. prof. zoology, dept. chmn. N.D. State U., 1952-53; asst. prof. biology U. Houston, 1953-55; assoc. prof. U. Fla., 1955-62; prof. physiology and cell biology U. Kans., Lawrence, 1968-85, prof. emeritus, 1985—. Owner arts and crafts bus., 1985-96; cons. Am. Type Culture Collection, 1980-82, W.C. Brown, Pub., 1978-82. Author: (books of poems) Give Back My Body, 1994, To Tartarus and Back, 1999, Sette Bellos, 2000, A Cinquain Zoo, 2000, Old Olympian Games, 2000, Pundamonium, 2001, Biblical Limericks, 2002, Sonnets for Various Reasons, 2002, Historical Limericks, 2003, The Common Gene Pool, 2003; co-editor, co-author: An Illustrated Guide to the Protozoa, 1985; co-author: How to Know the Protozoa, 2d edit., 1979; Microscop. Anat. Invert., Vol. 1, 1991; editor Kans. Sci. Bull., 1974-79; contbr. chpts. to books, articles to sci. jours.; contbr. to small press lit. jours. 1st lt. U.S. Army, WWII. Research grantee NIH, 1957-62, NSF, 1970-74, NIH, NSF and ONR, 1962-68, Kans. Fed. Water Resources Inst. and U. Kans., 1968-81; recipient Disting. Alumni award U. No. Iowa, 1980. Fellow Iowa Acad. Sci.; mem. Soc. Protozoologists (hon., pres. 1979-80, v.p. 1970-71, treas. 1972-78, exec. com. 1970-81), Am. Microscop Soc. (mem.-at-large exec. com. 1959-62), Western Soc. Naturalists, Kans. Acad. Sci. (life mem., pres. 1979-80, exec. com. 1975-81), Acad. Am. Poets, Kans. State Poetry Soc., Kans. Authors Club (Writing Achievement award 1996), Nat. Woodcarvers Assn., United Amateur Press Assn. Am., Sigma Xi. Home: 808 Mississippi St Lawrence KS 66044-2659

BOVEN, DOUGLAS GEORGE, lawyer; b. Holland, Mich., Aug. 11, 1943; BSE, U. Mich., 1966, JD, 1969. Bar: Calif. 1970. Dir. Reed Smith Crosby, Heafy LLP, San Francisco, 1989—. Arbitrator Fed. and Superior Ct. Panel of Arbitrators, 1980—; panelist Superior Ct. Early Settlement Program, 1987. Mem. ABA (mem. bus. bankruptcy, Chpt. 11 and secured creditors coms.), Am. Bankruptcy Inst., Comml. Law League Am., State Bar Calif. (insolvency law and real estate sects.), Alameda County Bar Assn., Sonoma County Bar Assn., Bay Area Bankruptcy Forum, Bar Assn. San Francisco (comml. law and bankruptcy sect., mem. arbitrator fee disputes com. 1973—), Tau Beta Pi. Office: Reed Smith Crosby Heafey LLP Two Embarcadero Ctr Ste 2000 San Francisco CA 94111 Office Fax: 415-391-8269. Business E-Mail: dboven@reedsmith.com.

BOVEY, TERRY ROBINSON, insurance executive; b. Oregon, Ill., May 13, 1948; s. John Franklin and Frances (Robinson) B.; m. Diana Carmen Rodriguez, Aug. 29, 1970 (div. 1980); 1 child, Joshua; m. Kathy Jo Johnston, Sept. 14, 1985; children: Courtney, Taylor. Student, Ariz. Western Coll., 1966-68, Grand Canyon Coll., 1968-69; BBA, U. Ariz., 1972. Salesman All-Am. Dist. Co., Yuma, Ariz., 1972-76; dist. asst. mgr. Equitable Life Ins., Yuma, 1976-81; gen. sales mgr. Ins. Counselors, Yuma, 1981-83; mng. gen. agt. First Capital Life Ins. Co., Ariz., Calif., Nev., N.C., 1983-90; master gen. agt. Aviva Life Ins. Co., Tucson, 1990—. Regional commr. Ariz. Interscholastic Assn., Yuma, 1972-88; umpire Nat. League, Major League Baseball, 1979, 95, crew chief, 95, Nat. League playoffs, 1984, baseball supr. Ariz. C.C. Athletic Conf., 1992-97. Mem. Century Club, Boy's Club of Yuma. Mem. Million Dollar Round Table, Nat. Assn. Life Underwriters (numerous sales achievement awards, Nat. Quality awards), Life Underwriters Polit. Action Com., Tucson City Assn. Republican. Presbyterian. E-mail: tkbovey@yahoo.com.

BOVINETTE, JAMES THOMAS, musician, educator; b. East St. Louis, Ill., Dec. 10, 1958; s. Everett E and Joan Bovinette; m. Jacqueline Kay Decker, June 10, 1959. Mus D musical arts, U. of Ill., Urbana, 1992—2001; MusM, So. Ill. U., Edwardsville, Ill., 1983—85, MusB ed/performance, 1977—82. Cert. Music Teacher K-12 1982. Prof. of trumpet and jazz Iowa State U., Ames, Iowa, 1995—; trumpet prof. Ill. Wesleyan U., Bloomington, Ill., 1993—95; trumpet instr./jazz dir. St. Louis Visual and Performing Arts H.S., St. Louis, Mo., 1985—92; prin. trumpet St. Louis Philharm. Orch., St. Louis, Miss., 1980—95. Author (arranger): (music) 15 Selections from Arban's The Art of Phrasing. Mem.: Internat. Assn. of Jazz Educators, Internat. Trumpet Guild. Home: 904 Kellogg Ave Ames IA 50010 Office: Iowa State University 245 Music Hall Ames IA 50011

BOW, STEPHEN TYLER, JR., management consultant; b. Bow, Ky., Oct. 20, 1931; s. Stephen Tyler Sr. and Mary L. (King) B.; m. Kathy O'Connor, July, 1982; children: Jerry, Jon; children by previous marriage: Sandra Bow Morris, Deborah Bow Goodin, Carol, Clara. BA in Sociology, Berea (Ky.) Coll., 1953; grad. exec. program bus. adminstrn., Columbia U., 1976. CLU. With Met. Life Ins. Co., 1953-74, 76-89; agt. Lexington, Ky., 1953-55; sales mgr. Birmingham, Ala., 1955-58; field tng. cons., 1958-59; territorial field supr., 1959-60; dist. sales mgr., 1960-64, Lexington, 1964-66; exec. asst. field tng. N.Y.C., 1966-67; regional sales mgr., 1967-72; agy. v.p., officer-in-charge Can. hdqrs., 1972-74; exec. v.p., chmn., chief exec. officer Capital Holding Corp., Louisville, 1974-76; officer-in-charge Midwestern hdqrs. Met. Life Ins. Co., Dayton, 1976-83, sr. v.p., officer-in-charge Western Hdqrs., 1983-89; chmn., CEO Southeastern Group, Inc., Louisville, 1993-94; pres., CEO Anthem Life of Ind., Indpls., 1993-95; chmn., CEO Anthem Life Ins. Cos., 1995-96; exec. v.p. Assoc. Ins. Cos., Inc., Indpls., 1993-96; chmn. Acordia of San Francisco, 1993-96; pres., CEO Delta Dental Ky., Louisville, 1989-94, Blue Cross and Blue Shield Ky., Louisville, 1989-93; vice chmn. DeHayes Group, 1996—; pres. Steve Bow and Assocs., Inc., 1996—; chmn. Victory Tech., Inc., 1998—. Past chmn. Dayton Power and Light Audit Com. Past bd. dirs. San Francisco Visitors and Conv. Bur., 1985-87, Ind. Coll. of No. Calif., Bay Area Coun., Lindsey Wilson Coll.; bd. dirs. Bay Area Boy Scouts Am., Bay Area Council, U. San Francisco; mem. adv. bd. Hugh O'Brian Youth Found.; bd. dirs. Calif. Legis. Adv. Commn. on Life and Health Ins., Metro United Way, Ky. Health Care Access Found., Greater Louisville Econ. Devel. Coun., Leadership Ky., Greater Louisville Fund for the Arts; mem. corp. council San Francisco UN Assn.; mem. bd. dirs. Ky. Home Mut., Ky. Forward, Asian Bus. League, McLaren Coll. of Bus.; past mem. San Francisco Pvt. Industry Council; past chmn. United Negro Coll. Fund of San Francisco, 1985-86; mem. exec. com. bd. dirs., v.p. county ops. United Way of San Francisco Bay Area, 1985-87; vol. chmn. U.S. Savs. Bond Campaign, Bay Area, 1987; trustee Ky. Ind. Coll. Fund, Berea Coll.; bd. dirs. Boy Scouts Am., My Old Ky. Home Coun. Recipient Outstanding Sales Mgmt. award N.Y. Sales Congress, 1972, Frederick D. Patterson award United Negro Coll. Fund San Francisco, 1986, Outstanding County Ops. Vol. award United Way of Bay Area, 1987, Bus. Appreciation award Jeffersontown, Ky. C. of C., 1993, Pres.'s award, 1993, Leadership award Internat. Women's Forum, Washington, 1993; named Citizen of Yr. Wright State U. Med. Sch., Dayton, 1982. Mem. Nat. Assn. Life Underwriters, Gen. Agts. and Mgrs. Assn., Calif. Bus. Roundtable, Nat. Assn. Corp. Dirs. (founder, former pres.), Calif. C. of C. (bd. dirs.), Ky. C. of C., Ky. Home Life Exec. Com., Am. Cancer Soc. Clubs: Lincoln of Northern Calif.; San Francisco Bankers. Republican. Methodist. Avocations: golf, oil painting, reading. Home: PO Box 675905 Rancho Santa Fe CA 92067 Office: 772 W Napa St Sonoma CA 95476-6452 *We achieve goals by thinking positively and focusing on objectives, not on problems. We achieve economic success by concentrating on serving our fellow man and finding new ways to satisfy his needs. We achieve personal satisfaction by doing more than is expected of us, and exceeding even our own expectations through determination and persistency. We achieve happiness by becoming so interested and absorbed in our work that we forget selfish, petty matters. We achieve a successful life by living each day as if our entire life is to be judged by that day alone.*

BOWA, LAWRENCE ROBERT (LARRY BOWA), professional baseball manager; b. Sacramento, Dec. 6, 1945; m. Sheena Bowa; 1 child, Tori. Student, Sacramento City Coll. Player various minor league teams, 1966-69; player with Phila. Phillies, Nat. League, 1970-81, Chgo. Cubs, Nat. League, 1982-85, N.Y. Mets, 1985; mgr. Las Vegas Stars, 1986, San Diego Padres, 1986-88, Phila. Phillys, 2002—. Player All-Star games, 1974-76, 78, 79, World Series, 1980. Holder major league record for highest lifetime fielding percentage for shortstop; winner Gold Glove, 1972, 78. Office: 3501 S Broad St Philadelphia PA 19148

BOWDEN, BOBBY, university athletic coach; b. Birmingham, Ala., Nov. 8, 1929; m. Julia Ann Estock; children: Robyn Hines, Steve, Tommy, Terry, Ginger Madden, Jeff. BS, Howard Coll. (now Samford U.), 1953; grad. degree, Peabody Coll. Coach W.Va. U., 1965-75, head coach, 1969-75; head coach NCAA Divsn. 1A football Fla. State U. Seminoles, 1975—, nat. champions, 1993, 1999. Named So. Ind. Coach of Yr., 1977, 79, Nat. Coach of Yr., ABC-Chevrolet, 1979, Nat. Coach of Yr. (Bobby Dodd), 1980, Region II Coach of Yr., 1987, Walter Camp Coach of Yr., 1991; named to Fla. Sports Hall of Fame, 1983, Ala. Sports Hall of Fame, 1986; recipient Neyland Trophy. Office: Fla State Univ 307 Moore Athletic Ctr Stadium Dr Tallahassee FL 32306-1096

BOWDEN, CHARLES MALCOLM, research physicist, educator; b. Richmond, Va., Dec. 31, 1933; s. Charles Edward and Emma Stevens (Hoover) B.; m. Lou Marquerite Tolbert, Oct. 1, 1960; children: David Malcolm, Steven Mark, Melissa Gail. BS in Physics, U. Richmond, 1956; MS in Physics, U. Va., 1959; PhD in Physics, Clemson U., 1967. Rsch. scientist U.S. Army Aviation and Missile Lab., Huntsville, Ala., 1967-91, sci. and tech. position (S/T) sr. rsch. scientist, 1991-98, S/T E-5, 1998—. Adj. prof. physics U. Ala., Huntsville, 1984—. Contbr. numerous articles to tech. jours. With Gideons, North Camp, Huntsville, 1983—; deacon Univ. Bapt. Ch., Huntsville, 1980—. NASA fellow Clemson (S.C.) U., 1964-67; recipient Paul A. Siple award U.S. Army, West Point, N.Y., 1978, 2000. Fellow Optical Soc. Am.; mem. AAAS, Am. Phys. Soc., Huntsville Athletic Club, Sigma Xi. Avocations: tennis, scuba, backpacking, bicycling, inline skating. Home: 716 Versailles Dr SE Huntsville AL 35803-1728 Office: AMSAM-RD-WS-ST Redstone Arsenal Huntsville AL 35898-0001 E-mail: bowdencm@bellsouth.net., [illegible]@ws.redstone.army.mil.

BOWDEN, DOUGLAS MCHOSE, neuropsychiatric scientist, educator, research center administrator; b. Durham, N.C., Apr. 7, 1937; s. Daniel Joseph and Charlotte (McHose) B.; m. Vivian Lee Bowden, 1966; children: Dana, Julie, Carlos, Luis. BA, Harvard U., 1959; MD, Stanford U., 1965. Staff assoc. NIMH, Bethesda, Md., 1966-69; asst. prof. psychiatry U. Wash., Seattle, 1969-73, assoc. prof. dept. psychiatry & behavioral scis., 1973-79, prof. psychiatry & behavioral scis., 1979—; core staff sci. Regional Primate Rsch. Ctr., U. Wash., 1969—, from asst. dir. to assoc. dir., 1977-88, dir., 1988-94. Adj. assoc. prof. pharmacology U. Wash., 1975-79, adj. prof. pharmacology, 1979-88; rsch. fellow Japan Soc. Promotion of Sci., Japan Assn. Animal Sci., Tokyo, Tsukuba, Inuyama/Kyoto, Japan, 1989. Author: Neuronames (c) Neuroanatomical Nomenclature, 1992; editor: Aging in Nonhuman Primates, 1979; translator Traumatic Aphasia, its Syndromes, Psychology and Treatment, 1970, Primate Models of Human Neurogenic Disorders, 1976; co-author: BrainInfo website, 2001-. Surgeon USPHS, 1966-69. Fellow Gerontol. Soc. Am.; mem. Am. Soc. Primatologists, Soc. Neurosci., Gerontol. Soc., Internat. Primatological Soc. Office: U Wash Natl Primate Rsch Ct Box 357330 1705 NE Pacific St Seattle WA 98195-7330 E-mail: dmbowden@u.washington.edu.

BOWDEN, ELBERT VICTOR, banking, finance and economics educator, author; b. Wrightsville, N.C., Nov. 25, 1924; s. James Owen and Dovie Ellen (Phelps) B.; m. Mary Rose Mariani (div.); m. Doris Adele Fales (div.); children: Elbert V. Jr., Richard Ashley, Doris Ellen, Jack Bryson, William Austin, Joyce Leigh; m. Judith Louise Holbert; children: Kristen R., Amy L. BA in Econs. and Polit. Sci. with high distinction, U. Conn., 1950; MA in Econs., Duke U., 1952, PhD in Econs., 1957. Grad. asst. dept. econs. Duke U., Durham, N.C., 1950-53, instr. dept. econs., 1953-54, 55-56; rsch. assoc. Bur. Bus. Rsch. U. Ky., Lexington, 1954-55; assoc. prof. Norfolk (Va.) Coll. of William and Mary (name now Old Donimion U.), 1956-59, prof., chmn. dept. econs., 1959-63; prof. econs. Elmira (N.Y.) Coll., 1963-64, SUNY, Fredonia, 1970-75; exec. dir. Upper Peninsula Com. for Area Progress, Escanaba, Mich., 1964-65; chief economist, chief of mission Robert R. Nathan Assocs. Trust Terr. Econ. Devel. Team, Saipan, Mariana Islands, 1965-67; assoc. prof., rsch. economist Tex. A&M U., 1967-70; chief econ. adviser, project mgr. Fiji Regional Planning Project UN, Suva, 1975-77; prof. econs. and fin., chair banking Appalachian State U., Boone, NC, 1977—2003, Alfred T. Adams disting. prof., 1992—2003; prof. emeritus, 2003. Dir. Houston-Galveston (Tex.) Area Project Fed. Water Pollution Control Adminstrn. and Tex. Water Quality Bd., 1967-69; testifier Interstate Commerce Commn., U.S. Senate Pub. Works Com., U.S. Senate Com. on Interior and Insular Affairs, 1964-66; asst. Blue Ridge Electric Membership Corp.; speaker Olean (N.Y.) Bus. Inst., 1979; adj. prof. Warsaw Sch. Social Econ. Studies, 1998-2001; cons., presenter seminars, workshops in field. Author: Economics, 1960, rev. edit., 1969, Economics in Perspective, 1974, 7th rev. edit., 2000, Economics: The Science of Common Sense, 1974, 9th edit., 2001, Money, Banking and the Financial System, 1989, revised edit., 2001; co-author: (with Judith Holbert) Revolution in Banking: Regulatory Changes, The New Competitive Environment and the New World for the Financial Services Industry in the 1980s, 1980, rev. 1984, American-Polish Academic Textbook of Macro- and Microeconomics of the Warsaw School of Social and Economic Studies, 2001; contbr. articles, papers, book revs. to profl. publs. and orgns. Mem. fin. com. City of Seven Devils, N.C., 1982-85; asst. N.C. Dept. Marine Fisheries; adv. bd. N.C. Statewide Taxpayers Ednl. Coalition. With U.S. Mcht. Marine, 1943-46, ATO and PTO. Ford Found. fellow, 1960. Mem. AAAS, AAUP, Nat. Assn. Bus. Econs. (U.S. and Carolinas chpts.), Am. Bus. Communication Assn., Am. Econ. Assn., Am. Fin. Assn. (com. 1960-61), Atlantic Econ. Soc., Community Colls. Social Scis. Assn., Ea. Fin. Assn., Fin. Mgmt. Assn., N.Am. Econs. and Fin. Assn., Regional Sci. Assn., So. Econ. Assn., So. Fin. Assn., So. Regional Sci. Assn., Southwestern Social Sci. Assn. (chmn. interdisciplinary symposium on urban and regional problem solving 1970), Western Econ. Assn., Western Regional Sci. Assn. (program planning com.) Avocations: skiing, surfing, guitar playing, singing, fishing, boating, reading. Home: PO Box 1461 Boone NC 28607-1461 Office: Appalachian State U Coll Bus Banking Chair Boone NC 28608-0001 *The world would be better off if more economists were less interested in playing intellectual games amongst themselves and impressing each other with their brilliance and more interested in explaining understandably the ubiquitous economic principles which pervade the lives of all of us.*

BOWDEN, GEORGE NEWTON, judge; b. East Orange, N.J., Nov. 21, 1946; s. W. Paul and Catherine A. (Porter) B. BA, Bowdoin Coll., 1971; JD, U. Maine, 1974. Bar: Wash. 1974, Maine 1975, U.S. Dist. Ct. (we. dist.) Wash. 1978, U.S. Ct. Appeals (9th cir.) 1980, U.S. Supreme Ct. 1982. Asst. county atty. Lincoln County, Wiscasset, Maine, 1974; dep. pros. atty. Grays Harbor County, Montesano, Wash., 1974-76, King County, Seattle, 1976, Snohomish County, Everett, Wash., 1976-79; ptnr. Senter & Bowden, Everett, Wash., 1979-97; judge Snohomish County Superior Ct., Everett, Wash., 1997—. Bd. dirs. Snohomish County Legal Svcs., 2003—. Bd. dirs. Everett Symphony Orch. 1993-2003, pres. 1996-98; v.p. Driftwood Players, Edmonds, Wash., 1978. Sgt. USMC, 1966-68. Mem. ATLA, NADCL, Wash. State Bar Assn. (CLE com., fee arbitration bd., legal aid and pro bono com.), Wash. Assn. Criminal Def. Lawyers (bd. govs., sec. 1993), Wash. State Trial Lawyers Assn., Snohomish County Bar Assn. (pres. 1995), Rotary. Avocations: scuba diving, skiing, bicycling. Office: Snohomish County Courthouse Superior Ct 3000 Rockefeller Ave M/S502 Everett WA 98201-4046

BOWDEN, HENRY WARNER, religion educator; b. Memphis, Tenn., Apr. 1, 1939; s. Warner Hill and Jeannette Evelyn (Winn) B.; m. Karin Violet Svensson, June 9, 1962 (div. Aug. 1989); children: Robin Warner, Annika Hillery; m. Michele Clare Cairns, May 1997. AB magna cum laude, Baylor U., 1961; MA, Princeton U., 1964, PhD, 1966. Instr. faculty of arts and scis. Douglass Coll., Rutgers U., 1964-67, asst. prof., 1967-71, asst. dean acad. affairs, 1969-72, assoc. prof., 1971-79, prof., 1979—. Editor religion books Greenwood Press, 1979—; cons. Funk & Wagnells Revised Ency., 1981-83; cons., author World Book Ency., 1984-94. Author: Church History in the Age of Science: Historiographic Patterns in the United States, 1876-1918, 1971, Church History in an Age of Uncertainty: Historiographical Patterns in the United States, 1906-1990, 1991, American Indians and Christian Missions: Studies in Cultural Conflict, 1981, Dictionary of American Religious Biography, 1977, 2d edit., 1993; author, consulting editor: American National Biography; editor: Religion in America, 1970, Indian Dialogues, 1980, A Century of Church History: The Legacy of Philip Schaff, 1988, Church History: A Centennial Collection of Landmark Studies, 1988; contbr. numerous articles to profl. jours.; assoc. editor Am. Nat. Bibliography, 1989-99. Bd. dirs. Historical Soc. Episcopal Ch., 1999—. Honors fellowship Harvard U. summer session, 1960; religion fellow Princeton U., 1961-62, Roothbert fellow, 1962-64, Lilly Found. fellow, 1964-65, Rutgers Rsch. Coun. fellowship, 1969-70; Rutgers Rsch. Coun. summer grantee, 1967. Mem. Am. Soc. of Ch. History (pres. 1984, exec. sec. 1993-2004), Am. Cath. Hist. Assn., Hist. Soc. of Episcopal Ch. (bd. dirs. 1999—). Democrat. Episcopalian. Office: Religion Dept Rutgers Univ New Brunswick NJ 08903 E-mail: aschnoff@aol.com.

BOWDEN, HOWARD KENT, accountant; b. New Bern, N.C., 1955; s. Paul Franklin and Virginia Belle Bowden; m. Laiad Jitrak; 1 child, Kirk Adam. BSS in Acctg. and Math. summa cum laude, Campbell U., 1976. CPA, Va., N.C. Staff acct. Arthur Andersen & Co., Greensboro, N.C., 1976-78; mgr. McGladrey & Pullen, Fayetteville, N.C., 1978-85; assoc. prin. Thompson, Greenspon & Co., P.C., Fairfax, Va., 1985-91; sr. audit mgr. U.S. Gen. Acctg. Office, Washington, 1991-94, asst. dir., 1994—. Treas. Vander Area Crime Watch, Fayetteville, 1980. Mem. AICPA, Va. Soc. CPAs (chmn. mems. in industry and govt. com. 1993-95, chmn. acctg. and auditing procedures com. 1990-92, Chpt. Pres.'s award 1989-90, Outstanding Mem. in Bus., Industry, and Govt. award 1995-96, chpt. pres. award, 1997-98), N.C. Assn. CPAs, Inst. Mgmt. Accts. (coord. tax symposium 1982, bd. dirs. 1978-84), Assn. Cert. Fraud Examiners (cert.), Assn. Govt. Accts. (cert. govt. fin. mgr.), Lions (bd. dirs. Fairfax club 1986-90, bd. dirs. Fayetteville club 1982-85), Phi Beta Lambda, Phi Kappa Phi. Presbyterian. Avocations: baseball, tennis, softball, other sports. Home: 4337 Farm House Ln Fairfax VA 22032-1613

BOWDEN, JESSE EARLE, newspaper editor, author, cartoonist, journalism educator; b. Altha, Fla., Sept. 12, 1928; s. Jesse Walden and Earlene (Rackley) B.; m. Mary Louise Clark, Feb. 4, 1951; children: Steven Earle, Randall Clark. BS in Journalism and Polit. Sci, Fla. State U., 1951; D.H.L., U. West Fla., 1985. Reporter, columnist Panama City (Fla.) News-Herald, 1950; sports editor Pensacola (Fla.) News-Jour., 1953-57, news editor, 1957-65, editorial page editor, 1965-66, editorial cartoonist, 1965—, editor in chief, 1966-97, v.p., editor, 1969-97, editor emeritus, 1998—; prof. journalist U. West Fla.; Charter mem., chmn. Pensacola Hist. Commn., 1967-2001; chmn. Gulf Islands Nat. Seashore Adv. Com., 1990-93; pres. U. West Fla. Found., 1977-79, Pensacola Hist. Soc., 1978-86. Pres. West Fla. Historic Preservation, Inc., U. West Fla., 2001—. Author: Always the Rivers Flow, 1979, Fla. classic edit., 2002, Iron Horse in the Pinelands, 1982, Pensacola: Florida's First Place City, 1989, The Write Way, 1990, When You Reach September, 1990, Gulf Islands: The Sands of All Time, 1994, Earle Bowden: Drawing from an Editor's Life, 1996, Look and Tremble: A Novel of West Florida, 2000, Texas Desperado in Florida: The Capture of John Wesley Hardin in Pensacola, 1877, 2002, Embrace an Autumnal Heart, 2003; editor Emerald Coast Rev., Vol. V 1993, Vol. VI, 1995, Vol. VII, 1997, Vol. IX, 1999, Vol. X, 2001. Trustee Pensacola Jr. Coll.; bd. dirs. Fla. Hist. Soc. Served to capt. USAF, 1951-53. U. West Fla. Found. fellow, 1982; recipient Disting. Citizen award Pensacola Jr. Coll., 1966, Nat. Editl. Writing award Freedoms Found. at Valley Forge, 1967, 68, 69, 70, 72, 74, awards for editls. and cartoons, 1967, 68, 69, 72, 86, DeLuna award Pensacola Founders' Day, 1979, Pensacola Kiwanis Civic award, 1982, award Am. Assn. State and Local History, 1984, Founder's award Inspiring Pensacola Bus. awards, 1992, Bob Graham Hon. AIA Archtl. Awareness award Fla. Assn. Archs., 1992, Malcolm B. Johnson Fellowship award James Madison Inst., 1994, Spirit of Pensacola award, 1998; named Pensacola Profl. Bus. Leader of Yr., 1980, J. Earle Bowden Jr. Historian award named in honor Pensacola Jr. League, 1983, Preservationist of Yr., Fla. Trust Hist. Preservation, 1985, West Fla. Lit. Hall of Honor, 1989, Dorothy Dodd Lifetime Achievement award Fla. Hist. Soc., 2000; Gulf Island Nat. Seashore Hwy. named J. Earle Bowden Way, 1997, Mary Call Darby Collins award, Fla. Sec. of State, 2002, Lifetime Achievement award Pensacola Heritage Ffound., 2002. Mem. Am. Soc. Newspaper Editors, Nat. Conf. Editorial Writers, Fla. Soc. Newspaper Editors (pres. 1970) Clubs: Rotary. Achievements include establishment of J. Earle Bowden history endowment U. West Fla. Home: 2220 Mccutchen Pl Pensacola FL 32503-3422 Office: One NewsJour Pla Pensacola FL 32501

BOWDEN, RANDALL GLEN, marketing and business development administrator; b. Council, Idaho, Sept. 26, 1959; s. Rocky Smith and Barbara (Chilcott) Loftis; children: Nikki, Sarah. BA, Colo. Christian U., 1987; MA, U. Colo., 1990; PhD, U. Denver, 1999. Glazier All Glass Svc., Lakewood, Colo., 1983-87; sales rep. Kwik Temp Glass, Aurora, Colo., 1988-89; gen. mgr. United Glass Co., Aurora, 1989-90; acad. advisor Colo. Christian Univ., Colorado Springs, 1990-91, acad. coord., 1991-92, dir., 1992-96, exec. dir. Lakewood, 1996-97; dean Colo. Christian U., 1997-98; project mgr. Denver Pub. Schs. Dist., 1997—2000; asst. prof. mgmt. U. Incarnate Word, San Antonio, 2000—03; assoc. dean Saint Leo (Fla.) U., 2003—. Pres. DKDC Enterprises, Inc., Tarron Springs, Fla., 2002—; cons. in field. Co-founding editor: Jour. Hispanic Higher Edn., 2001—, mem. editl. bd.: JOur. Intercultural Desciplines, 2001—; contbr. articles to profl. jours. Adv. Habitat for Humanity Internat., Americus, Ga., 2000; mem. edn. com. Colo. Springs (Colo.) C. of C., 1992—95; media advisor State Rep. Colo., Colo. Springs, 1992. Recipient Best Paper award, Internat. Bus. & Econs. Rsch., 2001, 2002. Mem.: Am. Ednl. Rsch. Assn., Acad. Mgmt., Delta Mu Delta (faculty advisor 2001—03). Avocations: weightlifting, fly fishing. Office: Saint Leo University PO Box 6665 Saint Leo FL 33574

BOWDEN, SALLY ANN, choreographer, teacher, dancer; b. Dallas, Feb. 27, 1943, d. Cloyd MacAnally and Sally Estelle. Student, Boston U., 1960-62. Mem. Paul Sanasardo Dance Co., N.Y.C., 1963-67; pvt. tchr., choreographer N.Y.C., 1968-70; faculty Merce Cunningham Dance Studio, N.Y.C., 1971-76; faculty, co-dir. Constrn. Co. Dance Studio, N.Y.C., 1972-77; choreographer Constrn. Co. Theater/Dance Assocs., N.Y.C., 1972—. Artist-in-residence U. Wis., Madison, fall, 1975, N.C. Sch. of Arts, winter, 1978, U. Minn., Duluth, 1979, 1981-82, Kenyon (Ohio) Coll., fall 1980 Choreographer: Three Dances, 1969, Sally Bowden Dances and Talks at the New School, 1972, The Ice Palace, 1973, White River Junction, 1975, The Wonderful World of Modern Dance or The Amazing Story of the Plie, (1976) Wheat, 1976-77, Kite, 1978, Voyages, 1978, Morningdance, 1979, Crescent, 1980, Diverted Suite, 1983, Baby Dance, 1984. Recipient Creative Artists Public Service award for choreography, 1976-77; Nat. Endowment for the Arts Choreography fellow, 1975 Office: Theater/Dance Assocs 41 E 1st St New York NY 10003-9307

BOWDEN, VIRGINIA MASSEY, librarian; b. Houston, Tex., July 22, 1939; d. Calvin Scott and Juanita Barlow Massey; m. Charles Lee Bowden, July 2, 1960; children: Sharon Scott Bowden Davis, Ellen Maureen. BA, U. Tex., 1960, PhD, 1994; MSLS, U. Ky., 1970. Programmer Texaco Inc., Houston, 1960-64; sr. programmer AMA, Chgo., 1964-65, C.E.I.R. Inc., N.Y.C., 1965-66, Bambergers, Newark, 1967-68; systems analyst, asst. to dir. U. Tex. Health Sci. Ctr., San Antonio, 1970-78, assoc. libr. dir., 1978-85, libr. dir., 1985—. Author: (with others) Handbook of Medical Library Practice, 1983; contbr. articles to profl. jours. Prse. Friends Pub. Libr., San Antonio, 1989-90. Recipient numerous grants Nat. Libr. Medicine, 1982-2000; fellow Coun. Libr. Resources, 1978-79. Fellow Med. Libr. Assn. (Louise Darling medal 1990); mem. ALA, LWV (bd. dirs. 1983-85), Acad. Health Info. Profls, Assn. Acad. Health Sci. Libr. Dirs. (bd. dirs. 1995-98), Nat. Network Librs. Medicine (bd. dirs. South Ctrl. region 1995-97), Amigos Bibliographic Coun. (trustee 1986-89), Nat. Libr. Medicine (cons. 1983-88), Tex. Libr. Assn., Coun. Rsch. and Acad. Librs. (pres. 1986-87), Tex. Coun. State Univ. Librs. (pres. 1996-98), Daus. Rep. Tex., South Ctrl. Acad. Med. Librs. (sec., 1996-98), Phi Beta Kappa (pres. 1979). Unitarian Universalist. Office: U Tex Health Sci Ctr 7703 Floyd Curl Dr San Antonio TX 78229 E-mail: bowden@uthscsa.edu.

BOWDEN, WILLIAM DARSIE, retired interior designer; b. Palo Alto, Calif., Aug. 11, 1920; s. Edmund Robert and Elisabeth (Darsie) B.; m. Anne Minor Lile, July 29, 1948; children: Darsie Minor, Raleigh Anne, Elisabeth Lile. BA, Stanford U., 1942. Jr. exec. Frederick and Nelson Dept. Store, Seattle, 1946-48; v.p., co-owner William L. Davis Co., Seattle, 1948-84. Trustee Found. for

Interior Design Edn. Rsch., Plestcheeff Inst. for Decorative Arts U. Wash. Served to 1st lt. AUS, 1943-46. Fellow Am. Soc. Interior Designers (pres. Wash. chpt. 1966-67, nat. v.p. 1969-71), Furniture History Soc. (London), Phi Beta Kappa, Alpha Delta Phi. Clubs: University, Wash. Athletic. Republican. Episcopalian. Home and Office: 2030 Beans Bight Rd NE Bainbridge Island WA 98110 E-mail: bowdbxx@aol.com.

BOWDEN, WILLIAM P., JR., lawyer, banker; b. East Orange, N.J., Feb. 29, 1944; s. W. Paul and Catherine (Porter) B.; m. Margo Redman, June 8, 1968; children: Jennifer Porter, Peter Chandler. AB, Williams Coll., 1966; JD, Columbia U., 1969. Bar: N.Y. Atty. Davis Polk & Wardwell, N.Y.C., 1969-75, 77-80; gen. counsel, sec. Alaska Interstate Co., Houston, 1976-77; assoc. gen. counsel Citicorp, N.Y.C., 1980-85; dep. gen. counsel Marine Midland Banks, Inc., N.Y.C., 1985-91; chief counsel Office of Comptr. of Currency, U.S. Dept. Treasury, Washington, 1991-94; gen. counsel CS First Boston, Inc., N.Y.C., 1994-96, Société Générale Ams., N.Y.C., 1997—2001, Willis Group Holdings Ltd., N.Y.C. and London, 2001—. Mem. ABA, Assn. of Bar of City of N.Y., Rockaway Hunting Club, Lawrence Beach Club, Univ. Club, The Anglers Club of N.Y. Office: 7 Hanover Sq New York NY 10004-2594 also: 10 Trinity Sq London EC3P 3AX England

BOWDLER, ANTHONY JOHN, physician, educator; b. London, Eng., Oct. 16, 1928; came to U.S., 1967; s. Edward Thomas and Clara (Anthony) B.; m. Eleanor Madeleine Sladen, July 30, 1955; children: Noelle Clare, Jonathan Francis. BSc, U. Coll., London, 1949, MB, BS, 1952, MD (Bilton Pollard fellow), 1962, PhD, 1967; postgrad. (Buswell Sr. fellow), U. Rochester, 1962-64. Intern Univ. Coll. Hosp., London, 1952, Hammersmith Hosp., London, 1953, Brompton Hosp., London, 1956, Dorking Hosp., Surrey, Eng., 1957; registrar and research fellow U. Coll. Hosp., London, 1958-62; sr. instr. U. Rochester, N.Y., 1962-64; sr. lectr. U. Coll. Hosp. Med. Sch., London, 1964-67; assoc. prof. medicine Mich. State U., East Lansing, 1967-70, prof. medicine, 1971-80, Coll. Human Medicine, Marshall U. Sch. Medicine, Huntington, W.Va., 1980-97, prof. medicine emeritus, 1997—. Hon. cons. Univ. Coll. Hosp., 1967. Served as surgeon lt. Royal Navy, 1953-55. Fellow Royal Coll. Physicians, A.C.P., Royal Coll. Pathologists; mem. Am. Fedn. Clin. Research, Central Soc. Clin. Research (emeritus), Am. Soc. Hematology (emeritus), Am. Soc. Clin. Oncology (emeritus), Brit. Med. Assn. Researcher in internal medicine. Home: 4609 Sawgrass Dr E Ann Arbor MI 48108-8644 E-mail: abowdler@comcast.net.

BOWE, RIDDICK LAMONT, professional boxer; b. Bklyn., 1967; s. Dorothy Bowe; children: Riddick Jr., Ridicia, Brenda. Amateur boxer, 1982—89; professional boxer, 1989—; defeated Evander Holyfield for WBA, WBC, IBF titles, 1992; defeated Evander Holyfield for WBA, IBF Titles, 1993; defeated Herbie Hide for WBO Title, 1995; defeated Jorge Luis Gonzalez to retain WBO title, 1995; defeated Evander Holyfield to retain WBO title, 1995. Named ranked Undisputed Heaveyweight Champ, 1992—93; recipient Silver super heavyweight divsn., 1988 Olympics, Seoul, Korea, ranked Undisputed Heaveyweight Champ, 1995—.

BOWE, WILLIAM J(OHN), lawyer; b. Chgo., June 23, 1942; s. William John Sr. and Mary (Gwinn) B.; m. Catherine Louise Vanselow, Nov. 10, 1979; children: Andrew M., Patrick D. BA, Yale U., 1964; JD, U. Chgo., 1967. Bar: Ill. 1967, Tenn. 1984. Assoc. Ross, Hardies, O'Keefe, Babcock, McDougall & Parsons, Chgo., 1967-68; assoc., then ptnr. Roan & Grossman, Chgo., 1971-78; v.p., gen. counsel, sec. The Bradford Exchange Ltd., Niles, Ill., 1979-83; asst. gen. counsel, v.p., gen. counsel United Press Internat. Inc., Nashville, 1984-85; v.p. to exec. v.p., gen. counsel, sec. Ency. Britannica, Inc., Chgo., 1986—; sec. William Benton Found., Chgo., 1987-96; pres. Merriam-Webster, Inc., Springfield, Mass., 1995-96, Ency. Britannica Ednl. Corp., Chgo., 1995-99. Co-chmn. managing the smaller law dept. Corp. Legal Inst., 1995. Mem. bd. editors Intellectual Property Studies, Chinese Acad. Social Studies, Beijing, 1996-99; contbr. articles to legal jours. Mem. The Annenberg Washington Program Anti-Piracy Project, Washington, 1988—89; bd. dirs. Internat. Anticounterfeiting Coalition, Washington, 1993—, chmn., 1994—96; gen. counsel Gov.'s Task Force on Sch. Fin., Chgo., 1975—76; trustee Hull Ho. Assn., Chgo., 1977—79; pres., bd. dirs. Clarence Darrow Cmty. Ctr., Chgo., 1975—84; mem. bd. overseers Ill. Inst. Tech.-Kent Coll. Law, 1982—86; mem. Gov.'s Task Force on Workforce Preparation, 1991—93, Gov.'s Work Group on Early Childhood Care and Edn., 1994—95, Gov.'s Edn. Summit, 2000—02. With U.S. Army, 1968—71. Mem.: ABA, Software and Info. Industry Assn. (govt. affairs coun. 1999—), Software Publs. Assn. (govt. affairs com. 1997—99), Intellectual Property Assn. Chgo., Chgo. Bar Assn., Ill. Bar Assn., Ill. State C. of C. (bd. dirs. 1989—96, mem. edn. com. 1989—99). Office: Ency Britannica Inc 310 S Michigan Ave Ste 900 Chicago IL 60604-4216 E-mail: wbowe@eb.com.

BOWEN, ALICE FRANCES, school system administrator; b. Worcester, Mass., Apr. 14, 1948; d. Vincent Francis and Alice Frances (Gray) B. BS in Edn., Worcester State Coll., 1971, MS in Math. Edn., 1973, MS in Computer Sci. Edn., 1985. Cert. prin., math. and social studies tchr., Mass. Tchr. math. Worcester Pub. Schs., 1971-83, tchr. computer sci., 1983-92, asst. prin., 1992—. Instr. SAT prep. Ctrl. New Eng. Coll., Worcester, 1980-85; mem. Greater Worcester Urban Math. Collaborative Alliance for Edn., 1992-95. Leader Montachusetts coun. Girl Scouts U.S.A., 1968-85. Recipient St. Anne award Montachusetts coun. Girl Scouts U.S.A., 1978. Mem. ASCD, AAUW (bd. dirs. Worcester br. 1972-75, 90-96, Eleanor Roosevelt tchr. fellow 1991, Turtle award Worcester br.), Alliance for Edn., Delta Kappa Gamma, Phi Delta Kappa (Adminstr. of Yr. 2002). Democrat. Roman Catholic. Avocations: travel, crafts, reading. Home: 43 Sheridan Dr Shrewsbury MA 01545-3865 Office: Burncoat Mid Sch 135 Burncoat St Worcester MA 01606-2405

BOWEN, CHESTER EDWARD, financial consultant, financial planner; b. Vienna, Ga., Apr. 23, 1943; s. Chester Allen and Agnes Lee (Hudson) B.; m. Linda Carolyn Polston, Oct. 20, 1962; children: Stephen Todd, Bradley Scott, Geoffrey Edward. BBA, Ga. State U., 1967, M of Profl. Accountancy, 1968. CFP, CPA. Auditor Deloitte & Touche, Atlanta, 1968-73; mgmt. cons. Ernst & Young, Atlanta, 1973-74; auditor, cons. KPMG Peat Marwick, Raleigh, N.C., 1974-76; academician N.C. State U., Raleigh, 1976-80; tax supr. Deloitte & Touche, Durham, N.C., 1980-81; pvt. practice C. Edward Bowen, CPA, Chapel Hill, N.C., 1982-92; sr. trust officer Cen. Carolina Bank, Durham, N.C., 1992-95; investment rep. Edward Jones, Raleigh, 1995—, Merrill Lynch, Raleigh, 2000—02, Wahovia Securities, Inc., Raleigh, 2002—. Bd. dirs. Duke Mgmt. Game, Duke U., Durham, 1988, 89. Rsch. author auditing rsch. project, 1978. Mem. N.C. Assn. CPAs, Chapel Hill/Carboro Kiwanis Club (pres. 1993-94), Chapel Hill Country Club (treas., bd. dirs. 1990). Avocations: golf, travel, swimming. Home: 815 Churchill Dr Chapel Hill NC 27517 Office: Bowen Financial Services Cary NC 27511 E-mail: cedward.bowen@lpl.com.

BOWEN, CLOTILDE MARION DENT, retired career officer, psychiatrist; b. Chgo., Mar. 20, 1923; d. William Marion Dent and Clotilde (Tynes) D.; m. William N. Bowen, Dec. 29, 1945 (dec.). BA, Ohio State U., 1943, MD, 1947. Intern Harlem Hosp., N.Y.C., 1947-48; resident and fellow in pulmonary diseases Triboro Hosp., Jamaica, L.I., 1948-50; resident in psychiatry VA Hosp., Albany N.Y., 1959-62; asst. resident in psychiatry Albany Med. Ctr. Hosp., 1961-62; pvt. practice N.Y.C., 1950-55; chief pulmonary disease clinic, 1950-55; asst. chief pulmonary disease svc. Valley Forge Army Hosp., Pa., 1955—59; chief psychiatry VA Hosp., Roseburg, Oreg., 1962-66, acting chief of staff, 1964-66; asst. chief neurology and psychiatry Tripler Gen. Hosp., Hawaii, 1966-68; psychiatr. lcons. and dir. Rev. Br. Office Civil Health and Med. Program Uniform Svcs., 1968-70; commd. capt. U.S. Army, 1955, advanced through ranks to col., 1968; neuropsychiat. cons. U.S. Army Medcoprs, Vietnam, 1970-71; neuropsychiat. cons. Medcom (USARV Medcom) U.S. Army, Vietnam, chief dept. psychiatry Fitzsimons Army Med. Ctr., 1971-74, chief dept. psychiatry Tripler Army Med. Ctr., 1974-75; assoc. clin. prof. psychiatry U. Hawaii, 1974-75; comdr. Hawley Army Clin., post surgeon U.S. Army, Ft. Benjamin, Harrison, Ind., 1977-78, chief dept. primary care and cmty. medicine, 1978-83, chief psychiat. consultation svc. Fitzsimons Army Med. Ctr., 1983-85; chief psychiatry svc. med./regional office ctr. VA, Cheyenne, Wyo., 1987-90; staff psychiatrist Denver VA Satellite Clin., Colorado Springs, Colo., 1990-96; ret., 1996. Locum Tenens practice psychiatry, 1996—; surveyor Joint Commn. on Accreditation Healthcare Orgns., 1985-92; assoc. clin. prof. psychiatary U. Colo. Med. Ctr., Denver, 1971—; spkr. Vietnam Vets. Meml. Wall, 2001. Decorated Legion of Merit, others; recipient Colo. Disabled Am. Vets. award, 1994-95, Pres.'s 300 Commencement award Ohio State U., 1987, Profl. Achievement award Ohio State U. Alumni Assn., 1998, Cert. of Appreciation, VFW, 2000, Am. Assn. Emergency Psychiat. award, 2001. Fellow Am. Psychiat. Assn. (disting. life), Acad. Psychosomatic Med.; mem. AMA, Nat. Med. Assn., Menninger Found (charter), Ctrl. Neuropsychiat. Assn. (Peter Bassoe fellow). Home: 1020 Tari Dr Colorado Springs CO 80921-2257 *To be successful one must always aspire to a goal just beyond his or her immediate reach.*

BOWEN, DAVID R. science and technology educator, consultant; b. N.Y.C., Sept. 13, 1939; s. Lewis Howard and Nancy (Nichols) B.; m. Joyce Helen Blades, Mar. 12, 1966; children: Peter Scott, Amy Elizabeth Bowen Herhold. BS in Physics, Haverford Coll., 1961; PhD in Physics, U. Pa., 1966. Rsch. assoc. U. Pa., 1967; rsch. assoc., instr. Cornell U., Ithaca, N.Y., 1967-70; asst. prof. Northeastern U., Boston, 1970-73, Nathaniel Hawthorne Coll., Antrim, N.H., 1973-74, assoc. prof., 1974-75, Wayne State U., Detroit, 1975—. Cons. Ford Motor Co., Dearborn, Mich., 1989—. Contbr. chpts. to books, numerous articles to profl. jours. Recipient numerous grants and rsch. awards. Mem. Soc. Of Friends. Avocations: internet and computers, sailing, windsurfing. Home: 4704 Elmhurst Ave Royal Oak MI 48073-1780 Office: Wayne State U 2311 A/AB Detroit MI 48202 E-mail: d.r.bowen@wayne.edu.

BOWEN, DEBRA LYNN, lawyer, state legislator; b. Rockford, Ill., Oct. 27, 1955; d. Robert Calvin and Marcia Ann (Crittenden) Bowen. BA, Mich. State U., 1976; JD, U. Va., 1979. Bar: Ill. 1979, Calif. 1983. Assoc. Winston & Strawn, Chgo., 1979-82, Washington, 1985-86, Hughes Hubbard & Reed, Los Angeles, 1982-84; sole practice Los Angeles, 1984-93; mem. Calif. State Assembly, 1992—98, Calif. State Senate, 1998—. Gen. counsel, State Employee's Retirement System Ill., Springfield, 1980-82; adj. prof. Watterson Coll. Sch. Paralegal Studies, 1985. Exec. editor Va. Jour. Internat. Law, 1977-78; contbr. articles to profl. jours. Mem. mental health law com. Chgo. Council Lawyers, 1980-82. Rotary Internat. fellow Internat. Christian U., Tokyo, 1975; Wigmore scholar Northwestern U. Sch. Law, Chgo., 1976; recipient James Madison Freedom of Information award No. Calif. chpt. Soc. Profl. Journalists, 1995. Mem. Calif. Bar Assn. (exec. com. pub. law sect. 1990-94), Mortar Bd., Phi Kappa Phi. Office: Calif Senate State Capitol Sacramento CA 95814-4906 also: Dist Office 2512 Artesia Blvd Ste 200 Redondo Beach CA 90278-3210

BOWEN, DEREK TYRONE, music educator; b. Columbia City, Ind., Sept. 23, 1969; s. Sheila Irene Aden and Glenn Raymond Bowen; m. Danielle Marie Miner, June 13, 1992; children: Megan, Matthew. MusB Edn., Ind. U., South Bend, 2000. Cert. music K-12 tchr. Ind. Assoc. band dir. Riley H.S., South Bend, 2000—01; head band dir. Heritage Mid. Sch., Middlebury, Ind., 2001—; asst. band dir. Northridge HS, Middlebury, Ind., 2001—. Youth bd. mem. St. Paul's Luth. Ch., Bremen, Ind., 2000; percussionist Sentimental Journey's, Bourbon, Ind., 2002. Mem.: Nat. Forensic League, Ind. Music Educator's Assn., Music Educator's Nat. Conf. Republican. Avocation: reading. Home: 3261 E Shore Dr Bremen IN 46506 Office: Heritage Middle Sch 57697-2 Northridge Dr Middlebury IN 46540-9407 Office Fax: 574-825-9154.

BOWEN, DUDLEY HOLLINGSWORTH, JR., federal judge; b. Augusta, Ga., June 25, 1941; AB in Fgn. Lang., U. Ga., 1964, LLB, 1965; profesor invitado (hon.), Universidad Externada de Bogotá, 1987. Bar: Ga. 1965, U.S. Dist. Ct. (so. dist.) Ga. 1997-. Pvt. practice law, Augusta, 1968-72; bankruptcy judge U.S. Dist. Ct. (so. dist.) Ga., Augusta, 1972-75, judge, 1979-97, chief judge, 1997—; ptnr. firm Dye, Miller, Bowen & Tucker, Augusta, 1975-79. Bd. dirs. Southeastern Bankruptcy Law Inst., 1976-87; mem. Ct. Security Com. Jud. Conf. U.S., 1987-92. Mem. bd. visitors U. Ga. Sch. Law, 1987-90. Served to 1st lt. inf., U.S. Army, 1966-68. Decorated Commendation medal. Mem. State Bar Ga. (chmn. bankruptcy law sect. 1977), Fed. Judges Assn. (bd. dirs. 1985-90), 11th Cir. Dist. Judges Assn. (sec.-treas. 1988-89, pres. 1991-92). Presbyterian. Office: US Dist Ct PO Box 2106 Augusta GA 30903-2106

BOWEN, GARY LEE, social work educator, researcher; b. Greensboro, N.C., Mar. 5, 1953; s. Lynwood C. Sr. and Augusta L. (Whitlow) B.; m. Donna Green, July 22, 1972; children: Christopher L., Natalie T. BS, U. N.C., Greensboro, 1975; PhD, U. N.C., 1981; MSW, U. N.C., Chapel Hill, 1976. House parent Episcopal Child Care, Greensboro, N.C., 1975; area coord. children's svcs. New River Mental Health, Wilkesboro, N.C., 1976-79; sr. rsch. assoc. Family Rsch. and Analyst, Inc., Greensboro, N.C., 1979-81, SRA Corp., Washington, 1981-83; sr. rsch. scientist Westat, Inc., Rockville, Md., 1983-85; asst. prof. U. N.C., Chapel Hill, 1985-88, assoc. prof., 1988-92, prof., 1992-93; disting. prof. William R. Kenan, Jr., 1993—. Rsch. cons. U.S. Dept. Def., Washington, 1979—; work and family cons. E.I. DuPont, Wilmington, Del., 1987-89. Author: (with others) Families in Blue, 1981, The Organizations Family, 1989, Navigating the Marital Journey, 1991, The Work and Family Interface, 1995; contbr. numerous articles to profl. jours. Fellow: Nat. Coun. on Family Rels., Armed Forces Soc.; mem.: NASW. Democrat. Episcopalian. Avocation: tennis. Home: 101 Majestic Ct Chapel Hill NC 27517-8345

BOWEN, GEORGE HAMILTON, JR., astrophysicist, educator; b. Tulsa, June 20, 1925; s. George H. and Dorothy (Huntington) B.; m. Marjorie Evelyn Brown, June 19, 1948; children— Paul Huntington, Margaret Irene, Carol Ann, Dorothy Elizabeth, Kevin Leigh. BS with honor, Calif. Inst. Tech., 1949, PhD, 1952. Asso. biologist Oak Ridge Nat. Lab., 1952-54; asst. prof. physics Ia. State Coll., 1954-57; asso. prof. physics Iowa State U., 1957-65, prof., 1965-92, emeritus prof. astrophysics, 1993—. Served with USNR, 1944-46. Recipient Iowa State U. Outstanding Tchr. award, 1970, Faculty citation Iowa State U. Alumni Assn., 1971 Mem. Am. Astron. Soc., Astron. Soc. Pacific, Am. Assn. Physics Tchrs. (chmn. Iowa sect. 1966-67), Internat. Astron. Union, Sigma Xi, Tau Beta Pi. Home: 1919 Burnett Ave Ames IA 50010-4970 Office: Iowa State U Dept Physics & Astronomy Ames IA 50011-0001

BOWEN, GILBERT WILLARD, minister; b. Muskegon, Mich., Dec. 30, 1931; s. Bruce Oliver and Beatrice Lillian (Sibley) B.; m. Marlene Mary Michell, July 31, 1954; children: Kathryn Leigh, Mark Kevin, Stephen James. BA, Wheaton Coll., 1955; MDiv, McCormick Theol. Sem., 1957, PhD in Ministry, 1976; cert., Ctr. for Religion and Psychotherapy, 1976; DLL (hon.), Nat. Coll. Edn., 1987. Ordained to ministry Presbyn. Ch., 1956. Minister 1st United Presbyn. Ch., Blue Earth, Minn., 1956-63, Faith United Presbyn. Ch., Tinley Park, Ill., 1963-65, Community Presbyn. Ch., Mt. Prospect, Ill., 1965-70, Kenilworth (Ill.) Union Ch., 1970—. Exchange minister Johanneskirche, Neuwied, Fed. Republic Germany, 1961-62; pres. bd. Ctr. for Religion and Psychotherapy; bd. dirs. McCormick Theol. Sem., Chgo., Anatolia Coll., Thessaloniki, Greece, Presbyn. Home, Evanston. Mem. adv. com. North Shore Sr. Ctr., Winnetka, Ill.; bd. dirs. Hospice of North Shore, Wilmette, Ill., Shelter for Battered Women, Evanston; chmn. Instl. Rev. Bd., Evanston. Mem. Am. Assn. Pastoral Counselors, Acad. Parish Clergy, Am. Waldensian Aid Soc. Clubs: Indian Hill. Republican. Avocations: tennis, golf, vocal music. Home: 2 Arbor Ln # 112 Evanston IL 60201 Office: Kenilworth Union Ch 211 Kenilworth Ave Kenilworth IL 60043-1299

BOWEN, HARRY ERNEST, management consultant; b. Elmira, N.Y., Jan. 31, 1941; s. Ernest William and Julia Cora (Forker) B.; m. Sandra Marie Fullerton, June 15, 1962; children: Harry Ernest Jr., Vicki Lynn Bowen Briggs, Nicholas Russel. AS in Gen. Studies, Mt. Wachusetts Coll., Gardner, Mass., 1975; BSBA, Ind. Inst. Tech., 1996. Mem. maintenance officer Intelligence and Security Command U.S. Army, Arlington Hall, Va., 1961-83; ret., 1983; assoc. dir. Martin & Stern, Inc., Chantilly, Va., 1983-89; program mgr. Paragon Sys., Inc., Centreville, Va., 1989-91; program mgr., mem. mgmt. staff Telos Fed. Sys., Sierra Vista, Ariz., 1991-96; regional mgr., project mgr., mem. mgmt. staff FC Bus. Sys., Sierra Vista, 1991-97; mem. tech. staff, dep. program mgr. Telos Corp., Ashburn, Va., 1998; v.p. PDS eastern ops., def programs FC Bus. Sys., Fairfax, Va., 1998—. Sole owner T and L Sys., Sierra Vista. Mem. Soc. Logistics Engrs. (chmn. 1991-94, Sr. Membership award 1993), Kiwanis (pres. 1996-97)_. Republican. Avocations: bowling, swimming, coaching, walking, golfing. Home: 6422 Horn Ln Warrenton VA 20187 Office: FC Bus Sys 8001 Braddock Rd Ste 300 Springfield VA 22151-2110 E-mail: hbowen@fcbs.com.

BOWEN, JAMES THOMAS, career officer; b. Mason City, Iowa, May 4, 1948; s. Stanley Thomas and Marilyn Louise (Ott) B.; m. Joyce Anne Kermabon, Sept. 10, 1977; 1 child, Steven James. BBA, U. Iowa, 1969; MS, U. So. Calif., Los Angeles, 1974. Cert. project mgmt. profl. Commd. 2nd lt. USAF, 1969, advance through grades to col., 1991; student pilot 3575th Pilot Tng. Wing, Vance AFB, Okla., 1969-70; co-pilot 773rd Tactical Airlift Squadron, Clark AFB, Phillipines, 1971; pilot 6594th Test Group, Hickam AFB, Hawaii, 1971-75; acquisition program mgr. Aeronautical Systems Div., Wright-Patterson AFB, Ohio, 1976-82; chief, standoff surveillance and attack systems HQ USAF, Rsch. Devel. and Acquistion, Pentagon, Va., 1984-87; chief, acquistion plans and programs br. Air Force Inspection and Safety Ctr., Norton AFB, Calif., 1988-90; dir. projects joint tactical autonomous weapons Aero. Systems Div., Wright-Patterson AFB, Ohio, 1990-91, dir. devel. and integration F-16, 1991-94; F-16 mgmt. dir. Ogden Air Logistics Ctr., Hill AFB, Utah, 1994-95; custom sys. program mgr. Hewlett Packard and Agilent Tech. Cos., Santa Rosa, Calif., 1996-2001; site mgr. Agilent Techs., Rohnert Park, Calif., 2001—02, program mgr., 2002—. Active Rep. ctrl. com. Sonoma County; bd. dirs. Blood Bank of the Redwoods, Project Mgmt. Inst. Wine Country chpt. Decorated Air medal USAF, 1972. Mem. Air Force Assn., Def. Systems Mgmt. Coll. Alumni Assn., Am. Mgmt. Assn., Ret. Officers Assn., Project Mgmt. Inst. Methodist. Avocations: skiing, deep sea fishing, golf. Office: Agilent Techs 1400 Fountaingrove Pkwy MS 3LS W Santa Rosa CA 95403-4902 E-mail: james_bowen@agilent.com., jbowen@pacbell.net.

BOWEN, JANICE, musician, music educator; b. Duncan, Okla., Dec. 9, 1931; d. Ocie Coleman and Zella Marie (Coulter) King; m. Gayle Bowen, Aug. 27, 1953; children: Tamara, Steve, Tricia. BM, Hardin Simmons U., 1953; MM, Tex. Tech. U., 1970. Piano tchr. Bowen Piano Studio, Lubbock, Tex., 1957-79, Canyon, Tex., 1980—; organist Bacon Heights Bapt. Ch., Lubbock, Tex., 1974-80, First Bapt. Ch., Canyon, Tex., 1980—; tchr. Kindermusik, Canyon, 1985—. Mem. Amarillo Music Tchrs. Assn. (pres. 1992-94), Canyon Fine Arts Club. Republican. Baptist.

BOWEN, JEAN, retired librarian, consultant; b. Albany, N.Y., Mar. 23, 1927; d. John W. and Grace Lester (Quier) B.; m. Henry F. Bloch, June 26, 1962; 1 child, Pamela A. Bloch. AB, Smith Coll., 1948, AM, 1956; MS, Columbia U., 1957. Curator Rodgers & Hammerstein Archives of Recorded Sound, N.Y.C., 1962-67; asst. chief music divsn. N.Y. Pub. Libr., N.Y.C., 1967-85, chief music divsn., 1986-96, dir. Humanities and Social Scis. Libr., 1996-2000. Cons. Rockefeller Bros. Found., N.Y.C., 1963, 67, N.Y. Philharm., N.Y.C., 1984, Schubert Archives, N.Y.C., 1982; mem. faculty Rare Book Sch. Columbia U., N.Y.C., 1984, 87, 91; bd. dirs. Amphion Found., N.Y.C. Contbr. articles to High Fidelity, Opera News, Am. Record Guide, Saturday Rev., MLA Notes, New Grove Dictionary of Am. Music. Mem.: Rare Book Sch. (mem. faculty, Columbia U., NYC 1984, 1987, 1991), Amphion Found. (NYC).

BOWEN, JEWELL RAY, chemical engineering educator; b. Duck Hill, Miss., Jan. 9, 1934; s. Hugh and Myrtle Louise (Stevens) B.; m. Priscilla Joan Spooner, Feb. 4, 1956; children: Jewell Ray, Sandra L., Susan E. BS, MIT, 1956, MS, 1957; PhD, U. Calif., Berkeley, 1963. Asst. prof. U. Wis., Madison, 1963-67, assoc. prof., 1967-80, prof. chem. engring., 1970-81, chmn. chem engring. dept., 1971-73, 78-81, assoc. vice chancellor, 1972-76; prof. chem. engring. U. Wash., Seattle, 1981-2000, prof. emeritus, 2001—, dean coll. engring., 1981-96. Cons. in field; adviser NSF, Dept. Def.; vis. prof. Kyoto U. Internat. Innovation Ctr., 2002. Contbr. articles to profl. jours.; editor: 7th-10th Internat. Colloquia on Dynamics of Explosions and Reactive Systems, 1979, 81, 83, 85, chmn. program com. 18th; bd. dirs. Inst. for Dynamics of Explosions and Reactive Sys., 1989—, pres., 1989-95, treas. 1995—. Bd. dirs. Wash. Tech. Ctr., 1983-97, interim exec. dir., 1989-91; mem. Wash. High Tech. Coordinating Bd., 1983-87. Recipient SWE Rodney Chipp award, 1995; NATO-NSF postdoctoral fellow, 1962-63, sr. postdoctoral fellow, 1968; Deutsche Forschungsgemeinschaft prof., 1976-77. Fellow AIAA, AAAS (com. on coun. affairs 1995-97, sect. chmn. 1996-97), Am. Soc. Engring. Edn. (deans coun. 1985-92, chmn. 1989-91, bd. dirs. 1989-94, 1st v.p. 1991, pres.-elect 1992, pres. 1993); mem. AIAA, AIChE, Am. Phys. Soc., Combustion Inst., Sigma Xi, Tau Beta Pi, Beta Theta Pi. Home: 5324 NE 86th St Seattle WA 98115-3922 Office: U Wash Dept Chem Engring PO Box 351750 Seattle WA 98195-1750 E-mail: bowen@engr.washington.edu.

BOWEN, JOSE ANTONIO, music educator; b. Woodland, Calif., Mar. 11, 1962; s. Wayne Bowen and Celina Engracia Andux; m. Nancy Kirschner, Mar. 28, 1992; 1 child, Naomi. BS, Stanford U., 1984, MA, 1986, PhD, 1993. Dir. jazz ensembles Stanford (Calif.) U., 1983—87; dir. Ctr. for the History and Analysis of Recorded Music U. Southampton, England, 1993—99; Caestecker chair, dir. music Georgetown U., Washington, 1999—. Author: (book) Cambridge Companion to Conducting; composer (and dir.): (cd of compositions for jazz ensemble) Reincarnation; composer: (and pianist) (cd of original compositions) The Garden; composer: (dir.,and pianist) A Klezmer Service; contbr. articles to profl. jours. Recipient Louis Sudler prize in the Arts, Sudler Found., 1985, Koret Israel prize, Koret Found., 1990; fellow, Royal Soc. Art Eng., 1996, NEH, 1999; Grad. fellow, Stanford Humanities Ctr., 1990—91. Mem.: Am. Musicol. Soc. Office: Georgetown Univ Dept Art Music and Theatre Washington DC 20007

BOWEN, JUDITH REINA, fundraising executive; b. Tampa, Fla., Aug. 15, 1940; d. Salvatore and Frances (Tyler) Reina; m. Lowell Wayne Coryell, Jan. 5, 1961 (div. Sept. 1980). BEd, Fla. State U., 1969, EdM, 1972. Program dir. Univ. Union Fla. State U., Tallahassee, 1961-65, dir. orientation, 1965-76, asst. to v.p. univ. rels., 1977-79, dir. South Fla. office Ft. Lauderdale, 1979-96; v.p. for devel. Broward C.C., Ft. Lauderdale, 1996—. Co-author: The College Admissions Game - How to Pay and Win. Active Broward Edn. Found., 1996—, Coun. for Advancement and Support Edn., 1997; mem. Broward Roundtable; grad. Leadership Fla., Leadership Broward. Mem.: Assn. Governing Bds. (program planning com.), Assn. Fundraising Profls. (Broward chpt.), Broward Hist. Soc., Execs. Assn., Tower Club. Democrat. Episcopalian. Avocations: gardening, interior design. Home: 333 Sunset Dr Apt 407 Fort Lauderdale FL 33301-2647 Office: 111 E Las Olas Blvd Fort Lauderdale FL 33301-2208

BOWEN, LOWELL REED, lawyer; b. Prince Frederick, Md., Jan. 29, 1931; s. Perry Gray and Melba (Hutchins) B.; m. Marilyn Sack, June 14, 1958; children: Mark Holdsworth, David Stockbridge. BA, U. Md., 1952; LLB, U. Md., Balt., 1957. Bar: Md. 1957, U.S. Dist. Ct. Md. 1958, U.S. Ct. Appeals (4th cir.) 1959, U.S. Supreme Ct. 1964. Law clk. to chief judge U.S. Dist. Ct. Md., Balt., 1957—58; assoc. Miles & Stockbridge, Balt., 1958—65, ptnr., 1966—, mng. ptnr., 1974—91, chmn., 2001—02. Lectr. U. Md. Law Sch., 1958-63, U. Balt. Law Sch., 1965-70. Mem., chmn. various coms. Md. Commn. to Revise Annotated Code Md., Annapolis, 1973—; mem. Standing Com. on Rules of Practice and Procedure, Md. Ct. Appeals, Annapolis, 1980—; trustee, chmn. Balt. Opera Co., Inc., 1977-92; mem. Md. Humanities Coun., 1992-97; trustee, pres. Lyric Found., Inc., 1997—. 1st lt. USAF, 1952-54. Mem. ABA, Md. State Bar Assn., Maryland Club, Ctr. Club (bd. govs. 1984-93, sec. 1985-93). Office: PC 10 Light St Baltimore MD 21202-1487 E-mail: lbowen@milesstockbridge.com.

BOWEN, MARY LU, ecumenical administrator; b. Wheeling, W.Va., Feb. 14, 1930; d. Walter Philip and Helen Elizabeth (Luthy) Wagenheim; m. Robert Edward Bowen, June 13, 1953; children: Jeanne, Thomas, Robert, David. BS in Edn., Wittenberg U., 1952; MA in Social Scis., SUNY, Binghamton, 1989. Cert. tchr., Ohio, W.Va., Tex., N.Y. Various teaching positions, 1952-80; coord. ministry with the aging Coun. of Chs., Broome County, N.Y., 1979-82, adminstrv. asst., 1982-83, asst. dir., 1984-86; assoc. for ecumenical devel. N.Y. State Coun. of Chs., Albany, Syracuse, N.Y., 1990-94, regional dir. southern tier Albany, 1995-96; dir. of pub. policy N.Y. State Cmty. of Churches, 1997-98, exec. dir., 1998—. Sec. exec. cabinet N.Y. State Coun. Chs., Albany, Syracuse, 1986-91; synodical lay rep. Evang. Luth. Ch. in Am. Region VII Coun., Phila., 1987-91, churchwide leadership team Social Min. Project, Chgo., 1990-91, sec. constituting conv. Upstate N.Y. Synod, Syracuse, 1987. Author: Reclaiming Christianity's Feminist Heritage: Reflections on Patriarchal Teachings and Women's Problems, 1989, Handbook for Clergy on Child Abuse and Neglect, 1995. Active Broome County Coordinating Coun. Child Abuse and Neglect, 1986-88, 96-98, treas. 1997; mem. Luth. Statewide Advocacy Exec. Com., Albany, 1982-90, 2000—, chmn. exec. com., 1991-99; regional adv. bd. Citizen Action N.Y., Binghamton, 1994-98; co-chmn. Interreligious Health and Justice Coalition, N.Y. Ctrl. So. Tier Region, 1994-98; Evang. Luth. Ch. in Am. Coalition for Mission in Appalachia, 1996—, chair, 2000-2001. Recipient Citizen Action N.Y. Phoenix award, 1998, Upstate N.Y. Synod Lay Discipleship award, 1999; Sr. Congl. intern, 1997. Mem.: Nat. Assn. Ecumenical Staff.

Democrat. Lutheran. Avocations: travel, reading. Home: 14 Overbrook Dr Apalachin NY 13732-4234 Office: NY State Cmty Chs 362 State St Albany NY 12210-1202 E-mail: marylubowen@aol.com., nyscoc@aol.com.

BOWEN, MAURICE RICHARD, JR., lawyer, director; b. Vicksburg, Miss., Nov. 21, 1939; s. Maurice Richard and Frances (Seymour) Bowen; m. Mary Keith Hampton, June 4, 1961; 1 child, Jane Hampton. BS, Middle Tenn. U., 1961; JD, Vanderbilt U., 1964. Bar: Tenn. 1964. Gen. practice, Chattanooga, 1964—74; prin. SNC Group, Montreal, Canada, 1979—82; sec., dir. Hensley-Schmidt/SNC Co., 1977—82; sr. v.p. develop. Hensley-Schmidt, Inc. Engr., Architects and Mgr., Chattanooga, 1979—82; pres., chmn. Tandem Internat., Inc., 1982; counsel Grant, Konvalinka & Grubbs, PC, 1984; chmn. bd. dir. Tantex, Inc.; dir. Jasper Bulk Terminals, Inc., 1985—; del. Dem. Nat. Conv., 1968. Recipient Danforth Found. Leadership award, Eagle Scouts Boy Scouts Am.; fellow Scottish Rite Fellowship in Internat. Rels., George Washington U., 1957. Mem.: Walden, AAUP, ABA, Hamilton County Dem. Exec. Com., Tenn. State Dem. Conv., State Govtl. Affairs Council, Chattanooga Area Econ. Develop. Council, Chattanooga/Hamilton County Develop. Corp., Hamilton County Indsl. Develop., Met. Charter Study Commn., Mountain City, Chattanooga Golf and Country, Sigma Club. Presbyn. Office: PO Box PO Box 11263 Chattanooga TN 37401-2263

BOWEN, PATRICK HARVEY, lawyer, consultant; b. Cin., July 7, 1939; s. Albert Vernon and Elsie Matilda (Harvey) B.; m. Karen A. Hunter; 1 child, Harvey Shaw. BA, Marietta Coll., 1961; JD, Duke U., 1964; MBA, Columbia U., 1975. Bar: N.Y. 1965, Conn. 1990. Assoc. Mudge, Rose, Guthrie & Alexander, N.Y.C., 1964-66; atty. Kennecott Copper Corp., N.Y.C., 1966-71, asst. counsel, 1971-79, asst. gen. counsel, 1979-83, asst. sec., 1980-83; sr. assoc. atty. Allied Stores Corp., N.Y.C., 1983-87, v.p., gen. counsel, sec., 1987-88, v.p., 1988-89; pvt. practice Stamford, Conn., 1990—. Mem. ABA, Conn. Bar Assn., N.Y. State Bar Assn., Assn. of Bar of City of N.Y., Am. Soc. Corp. Secs. Avocation: traditional jazz musician. Office: 2001 W Main St Ste 140 Stamford CT 06902-4562 E-mail: phbowen@aol.com.

BOWEN, PAUL HENRY, JR., lawyer; b. Troy, Ohio, Sept. 28, 1948; s. Paul Henry, Sr. and Dorothy Jane (Winters) B.; m. Linda Margaret Mary Eisenhart, Mar. 2, 1974. B.A., Pa. State U., 1970; J.D., U. Pitts., 1973. Bar: Pa. 1973, Fla. 1978, U.S. Dist. Ct. (mid. dist.) Fla. 1978, U.S. Ct. Appeals (5th cir.) 1984, U.S. Supreme Ct. 1983. Assoc., Vernon David, P.A., Winter Garden, Fla., 1980-81, Swann & Haddock, P.A., Orlando, Fla., 1981-85, Trenam, Simmons, Kemker, Scharf, Barkin, Frye & O'Neill, P.A., Tampa, Fla., 1985— . Precinct capt. to re-elect Mayor Frederick of Orlando, 1984. Served to capt. JAGC, USAF, 1975-80. Mem. ABA, Assn. Trial Lawyers Am., Acad. Fla. Trial Lawyers. Democrat. Methodist. Lodge: Kiwanis (citizenship com.). Home: PO Box 814 Tampa FL 33601-0814

BOWEN, PETER GEOFFREY, arbitrator, business educator; b. Iowa City, Iowa, July 10, 1939; s. Howard Rothmann and Lois Berntine (Schilling) B.; m. Shirley Johns Carlson, Sept. 14, 1968; children: Douglas Howard, Leslie Johns. BA in Govt. and Econs., Lawrence Coll., 1960; postgrad., U. Wis., 1960-61, U. Denver, 1963-64, U. Colo., 1994. Cert.: expert witness, Denver. V.p. Perry & Butler, Denver, 1972-73; exec. v.p., dir. Little & Co., Denver, 1973; pres. Builders Agy. Ltd., Denver, 1974-75; CEO, gen. ptnr. The Investment Mgmt. Group Ltd., Denver, 1975—. Arbitrator NASD Regulation, Inc., 1996—, Am. Arbitration Assn., 1996—; adj. prof. bus. Colo. Mt. Coll., 1992-2000; arbitrator Eagle County Colo. Atty.'s Office, 1997; asst. prof. bus. adminstrn. and law Regis U., 2000—; continuing legal edn. lectr. on real estate syndications, 1983. Author: A Small Business Primer for Displaced Corporate Executives, 2000; contbr. articles to profl. publs. Vice-chmn. Greenwood Village (Colo.) Planning and Zoning Commn., 1983-85; mem. Vail Planning and Environ. Commn., 1992-96; chmn. emeritus Vail Partnership Environ. Edn. Programs, Inc., 1993-2000; elected mem. City Council Greenwood Village, 1985-86, also mayor pro tem, 1985-86; trustee Vail Mountain Sch. Found., 1987-88. Mem. Colo. Bar Assn. (legal fee arbitration com.), Denver Bar Assn. (legal fee arbitration com. 1997—), Rotary Club (bd. dirs. Vail chpt., named Rotarian of Yr. 1992), Lawrence U. Alumni Assn. (bd. dirs. 1966-72, 82-86). Home: 16006 Double Eagle Dr Morrison CO 80465-9617 E-mail: jsbowen@pcisys.com.

BOWEN, RAY MORRIS, academic administrator, engineering educator; b. Ft. Worth, Mar. 30, 1936; s. Winfred Herbert and Elizabeth (Williams) B; m. Sara Elizabeth Gibbens, July 5, 1958; children: Raymond Morris, Marguerite Elizabeth. BS in Mech. Engring., Texas A&M U., 1958, PhD in Engring., 1961; MS in Mech. Engring, Calif. Inst. Tech., 1959. Registered profl. engr., Tex., Ky. Assoc. prof. Mech. Engring. La. State U., Baton Rouge, 1965-67; prof. Mech. Engring. Rice U., Houston, 1967-83, chmn. dept., 1972-77; dir. divsn. NSF, Washington, 1982-83, from acting asst. dir., engr. to dep. asst. dir., engr., 1990-91; prof. Engring., dean U. Ky., Lexington, 1983-89; v.p. acad. affairs Okla. State U., Stillwater, Okla., 1991-93, interim pres., 1992—94; pres. Tex. A&M U., College Station, 1994—2002, pres. emeritus, 2002—. Mem. staff Sandia Corp., Albuquerque, summers 1966, 67, 72, cons., 1970-78; cons. U.S. Army Ballistic Rsch. Lab, Aberdeen Proving Ground, Md., 1970, Sun Oil Co., Albuquerque, 1974-75. Author: Introduction to Continuum Mechanics for Engineers, 1989; co-author: Introduction to Vectors and Tensors, Vols. I and II, 1976; contbg. author: Rational Thermodynamics, 1984; contbr. articles to profl. jours. Capt. USAF, 1961-64. Fellow Johns Hopkins U., 1964-65 Sr. Scholars Johns Hopkins U., Nat. Sci. Bd., 2002-, Tau Beta Pi, Phi Kappa Phi, Sigma Xi. Office: Tex A&M Univ Evans Library Annex 252C College Station TX 77843-5000

BOWEN, RICHARD LEE, architect; b. Canton, Ohio, Nov. 1, 1935; s. Raymond Leed and Lillian E. (White) Bowen; m. Robin Herrington (div.); children: Richard Lee, David Herrington, Laurel Ann, Sean Andrew, Scott Andrew; m. Gail Audrey; children: Tabitha Erin, Colin Leed. BA, Case Western Res. U., 1959. Registered arch., 50 states, DC, P.R., Can., Australia, Nat. Coun. Archtl. Registration Bd.s, Archtl. Registration Coun. U.K. Founder, pres. Richard L. Bowen & Assocs. Inc., archtl. engrs., planners, constrn. mgmt., Cleve., Richard L. Bowen & Assocs. Inc., Cleve., 1963—, Richard L. Bowen, Inc., Cleve., 1970—2002; pres. Enerwaste, Inc., 1992-99; mng. ptnr. ComDel, 1970; pres. Richard L. Bowen & Assocs. Fla., Pompano Beach, 1969—. Apptd. mem. Ohio State Archtl. Registration Bd., 2001—, Nat. Coun. Archtl. Registration Bds., mem. internat. registration com., mem. com. for internat. reciprocity. Prin. works include Western Campus, Cuyahoga CC, Akron State Office Bldg., West Jr. HS, John Hay HS, Cleve. Ctrl. Police Hdqs., Cleve. Hopkins Internat. Airport, FAA Regional Office Bldg., classroom and libr. bldgs. Ashtabula Campus, Kent State U., Wade Park VA Hosp., Westerly Sewage Treatment Facility Cuyahoga Regional Sewer Authority, Cuyahoga CC Manpower Skills Ctr. Ohio, others. Mem. Leadership Cleve.; mem. exec. com. Cuyahoga County Rep. Com., Cleve., 1963—; trustee St. Luke's Hosp. Assn., 1996—2000, Cleve. Internat. Air Show; mem. adv. bd. Cleve. Inst. Art. Recipient Energy Conservation Design award, Fla. Power Winter Garden Shoppint Ctr., 1986, Merit award, Cleve. Restoration Soc., 1992, Outstanding Achievement award, Cleve. Growth Assn., 1997. Mem.: AIA (design award excellence 1976, award 1979, 2000), Am. Arbitration Assn., Urban Land Inst., Am. Assn. Planners, Bldg. Ofcls. Coun. Am., Constrn. Specifications Inst., Internat. Coun. Shopping Ctrs., Guild Religious Architecture, Soc. Archtl. Historians, Am. Soc. Ch. Architecture, Royal Inst. Brit. Archs., Royal Archtl. Inst. Can., Nat. Assn. Indsl. and Office Pks. (awards 1985, 1989, 1992, 1994, 1995, 2000), Archs. Soc. Ohio (honor award 1988, 2000, 2001), Hillbrook Club, Ft. Lauderdale Yacht Club, Rowfant Club, Cat Cay Club, Useppa Island Club, Valley Country Club, The Club Chagrin, Union Club, Phi Gamma Delta. Avocations: sailing, skiing, fly and deep sea fishing. Home: 14926 Hillbrook Dr Chagrin Falls OH 44022-2634 Office: 13000 Shaker Blvd Cleveland OH 44120-2063 E-mail: rbowen@RLB.com.

BOWEN, RICHARD LEE, academic administrator, political science educator; b. Avoca, Iowa, Aug. 31, 1933; s. Howard L. and Donna (Milburn) B.; m. Connie Smith Bowen, 1976; children: James, Robert, Elizabeth, Christopher; children by previous marriage— Catherine, David, Thomas. BA, Augustana Coll., 1957; MA, Harvard, 1959, PhD, 1967. Fgn. service officer State Dept., 1959-60; research asst. to U.S. Senator Francis Case, 1960-62; legis. asst. to U.S. Senator Karl Mundt, 1962-65; minority cons. sub-com. exec. reorgn. U.S. Senate, 1966-67; asst. to pres., assoc. prof. polit. sci. U. S.D., Vermillion, 1967-69, pres., 1969-76, Dakota State Coll., Madison, 1973-76; commr. higher edn. Bd. Regents State S.D., Pierre, 1976-80; Disting prof. polit. sci. U. S.D., 1980-85; pres. Idaho State U., Pocatello, 1985—. Served with USN, 1951-54. Recipient Outstanding Alumnus award Augustana Coll., 1970; Woodrow Wilson fellow, 1957, Congl. Staff fellow, 1965; Fulbright scholar, 1957. Office: Idaho State U Office of Pres PO Box 8310 Pocatello ID 83209-0001

BOWEN, STEPHEN STEWART, lawyer; b. Peoria, Ill., Aug. 23, 1946; s. Gerald Raymond and Frances Arlene (Stewart) B.; m. Ellen Claire Newcomer, Sept. 23, 1972; children: David, Claire. BA cum laude, Wabash Coll., 1968; JD cum laude, U. Chgo., 1972. Bar: Ill. 1972, U.S. Dist. Ct. (no. dist.) Ill. 1972, U.S. Tax Ct. 1977. Assoc. Kirkland & Ellis, Chgo., 1972-78, ptnr., 1978-84, Latham & Watkins, Chgo., 1985—. Adj. prof. DePaul U. Masters in Taxation Program, Chgo., 1976-80; lectr. Practicing Law Inst., N.Y.C., Chgo., L.A., 1978-84, N.Y.C., 1986—. Mem. vis. com. U. Chgo. Div. Sch., 1984—, mem. vis. com. Sch. Law, 1991-93; mem. planning com. U. Chgo. Tax Conf., 1985—, chair, 1995-98; trustee Wabash Coll., 1996—. Fellow Am. Coll. Tax Counsel; mem. ABA, Ill. State Bar Assn., Order of Coif, Met. Club (Chgo.), Econ. Club Chgo., Phi Beta Kappa. Office: Latham & Watkins Sears Tower Ste 5800 Chicago IL 60606-6306

BOWEN, STEVEN HOLMES, lawyer; b. Norwood, Mass., Mar. 14, 1946; s. Earl Kenneth and Dorothy Ethel (Holmes) B. B.A. magna cum laude, Harvard U., 1968; J.D., Boston U., 1974. Bar: Mass. 1974, U.S. Dist. Ct. Mass. 1975, U.S. Ct. Appeals, 1st cir. 1979, U.S. Supreme Ct. 1979. Law clk. Mass. Superior Ct., Boston, 1974-75; mem. firm Nicholas Macaronis, Lowell, Mass., 1975—. Served with U.S. Army, 1968-70. Mem. Mass. Bar Assn., Greater Lowell Bar Assn. Home: 356 Gray St Arlington MA 02476-6009

BOWEN, THOMAS EDWIN, cardiothoracic surgeon, retired army officer; b. Lackawanna, N.y., Dec. 16, 1934; m. Margaret Marie Harrington, 1959; children: Matthew, Mark, James, John, Thaddeus, Mary Cristine. BS, St. Bonaventure U., 1961; MD, Marquette U., 1965; diploma, U.S. Army War Coll., 1985. Diplomate Am. Bd. Surgery, Am. Bd. Thoracic Surgery, Nat. Bd. Med. Examiners. Commd. 2d lt. U.S. Army, 1961, advanced through grades to brig. gen., 1988; intern Tripler Army Gen. Hosp., Honoluu, 1965-66, resident in gen. surgery, 1966-70, Vietnam, 1970-71; resident in thoracic surgery Walter Reed Army Gen. Hosp., Washington, 1971-73; dep. dir. Profl. Svcs. Directorate Office of Surgeon Gen., Washington, 1983-87, comdr. surgeon 121st Evacuation Hosp., 1987-88; assoc. prof. dept. surgery Sch. Medicine Uniformed Svcs. U. of Health Scis., Bethesda, Md., 1981—; commanding gen. Fitzsimons Army Med. Ctr., Aurora, Colo., 1988-93; assoc. clin. prof. dept. surgery U. Colo. Sch. Medicine, Denver, 1989—; assoc. prof. surgery U. So. Fla. Sch. Med.; chief of staff James A. Haley VA Med. Ctr., Tampa, Fla., 1993—. Contbr. articles to profl. publs. Chmn. Combined Fed. Campaign, Denver, 1990. Decorated D.S.M., Legion of Merit with three oak leaf clusters, Bronze Star, Alfredo Lezcano Gomez medal for Svc. to Republic of Panama; recipient Raymond Franklin Metcalf award, 1971. Mem. Assn. Mil. Surgeons, Am. Coll. Surgeons, Soc. Thoracic Surgeons, Denver C. of C., Aurora C. of C., Rotary. Roman Catholic. Avocations: beekeeping, woodworking, reading, raising animals and crops. Office: James A Haley VA Med Ctr Tampa FL 33612 Office Fax: 813-903-4871.

BOWEN, WILLIAM AUGUSTUS, financial consultant; b. Greenville, N.C., Jan. 17, 1930; s. Joseph Francis and Dorothy Lee (Simmons) B.; m. Hilda Carolyn Rowlett, June 8, 1952; children: Carol Bowen Bernstein, Elizabeth Lee Bowen Jones, William Augustus Jr., Mary Jane Bowen Sullivan. BS in Bus. Adminstrn, U. N.C., 1951, grad. exec. program, 1965. With Wachovia Bank & Trust Co., Charlotte, N.C., 1955-79, regional v.p., mgr. So. region, 1970-79; pres., chief operating officer, dir. First Tulsa Bancorp., Tulsa, First Nat. Bank & Trust Co., Tulsa, 1980-84; chmn., CEO First Nat. Bank and Trust Co., Tulsa, 1984-87; pres. The Bowen Co., 1987—. Bd. dirs. AAON, Inc., Tulsa. Pres. Met. Tulsa Econ. Devel. Found., 1987-88—; chmn. Tulsa Area United Way,, 1986, campaign chmn., 1985. Lt. USNR, 1951-55. Mem. DeBordieu Club Inc. (Georgetown, S.C.), Phi Beta Kappa, Beta Gamma Sigma (pres. 1950-51). Home: 1484 Wallace Pate Dr Georgetown SC 29440-7185

BOWEN, WILLIAM GORDON, economist, educator, foundation administrator; b. Cin., Oct. 6, 1933; s. Albert A. and Bernice (Pomert) B.; m. Mary Ellen Maxwell, Aug. 25, 1956; children: David Alan, Karen Lee. BA, Denison U., 1955; PhD, Princeton U., 1958. Mem. faculty Princeton (N.J.) U., 1958-88, prof. econs., 1965-88, dir. grad. studies Woodrow Wilson Sch. Pub. and Internat. Affairs, 1964-66, provost, 1967-72, pres., 1972-88, Andrew W. Mellon Found., N.Y.C., 1988—. Bd. dirs. Merck and Co., Inc., Am. Express Co., Univ. Corp. for Advanced Internet Devel. Internet, JSTOR; bd. overseers Tchrs. Ins. and Annuity Assn.-Coll. Ret. Equities Fund.; chmn. bd. dirs. Ithaka Harbors, Inc.; lectr. U. Oxford, 2000. Author: The Wage-Price Issue: A Theoretical Analysis, 1960, Wage Behavior in the Postwar Period: An Empirical Analysis, 1960, Economic Aspects of Education: Three Essays, 1964, (with W. J. Baumol) Performing Arts: The Economic Dilemma, 1966, (with T. A. Finegan) The Economics of Labor Force Participation, 1969, Ever the Teacher, 1987, (with J. A. Sosa) Prospects for Faculty in the Arts and Sciences, 1989, (with Neil L. Rudenstine) In Pursuit of the PhD, 1992, Inside the Boardroom: Governance by Directors and Trustees, 1994, (with T. Nygren, S. Turner, E. Duffy) The Charitable Nonprofits, 1994, (with Derek Bok) The Shape of the River: Long-Term Consequences of Considering Race in College and University Admissions, 1998, (with James L. Shulman) The Game of Life: College Sports and Educational Values, 2001, (with Sarah A. Levin) Reclaiming the Game: College Sports and Educational Values, 2003. Trustee Ctr. for Advanced Study in Behavioral Scis., 1978-84, 89-92, Denison U., 1992-2000; regent emeritus Smithsonian Instn. Recipient Joseph Henry medal Smithsonian Instn., 1996, (with Derek Bok) Grawemeyer award in edn. U. Louisville, 2001. Mem. Am. Econs. Assn., Indsl. Rels. Rsch. Assn., Coun. on Fgn. Rels., Phi Beta Kappa. Office: Andrew W Mellon Found 140 E 62nd St New York NY 10021-8124

BOWEN, WILLIAM HARVEY, banker, lawyer; b. Altheimer, Ark., May 6, 1923; s. Robert James and Lois Ruth Bowen; m. Mary Constance Wanasek, Aug. 31, 1947; children: Cynthia Ruth Bowen Blanchard, William Scott, Mary Patricia Bowen Barker. Student, Henderson State Tchrs. Coll., 1941-42; LL.B., U. Ark., 1949; LL.M. in Taxation, NYU, 1950; postgrad., Stonier Grad. Sch. Banking, Rutgers U., 1974. Bar: Ark. 1949, U.S. Supreme Ct. 1950. Atty. adviser U.S. Tax Ct., Washington, 1950-52; spl. asst. to atty. gen. trial sect., tax div. Dept. Justice, Washington, 1952-54; ptnr. Smith, Williams, Friday & Bowen, Little Rock, Ark., 1954-71; pres., dir. Comml. Nat. Bank, Little Rock, Ark., 1971-83, pres., dir., chief exec. officer, 1975-81, chmn., 1981-83; pres., chief exec. officer 1st Comml. Bank N.A., Little Rock, Ark., 1983-90, chmn., chief exec. officer, 1984-87, First Comml. Corp., 1984-90; chief of staff Gov. Bill Clinton, 1991-92; pres., CEO Healthsource Ark. Ventures, Inc., 1993-95; dean Sch. of Law U. Ark., Little Rock, 1995-97. Mem. staff Stonier Grad. Sch. Banking U. Del., 1976-98, bd. regents, 1977-81; mememb. fed. adv. coun. Fed. Res. Bank, St. Louis, 1984-86; lectr. assemblies for bank dirs., So. Meth. U. Author: (with M. Moore) Arkansas Estate Planners Handbook, 1967. Trustee Ben J. Altheimer Found., Altheimer, Ark., 1973, Philander Smith Coll., Little Rock, 1968-80, Hendrix Coll., 1986-98, Drs. Hosp., U. Ark. Little Rock; chmn. bd. visitors U. Ark., 1979-80; state chmn. com. for employer support of N.G. and Res., nat. chmn., 1994-98; chmn. bd. Ark. Sci. and Tech. Authority, 1986-91; adv. council LWV; past chmn. Radio Free Europe Fund, Pulaski County United Fund. Served with USN, 1943-46, to lt. comdr. Res., ret. Named Little Rock Man of Yr. Ark. Dem., 1963; recipient Sales and Mktg. Exec. Man of Yr. award, 1963, Citizen-Lawyer of Yr. award Ark. Bar Found., 1971, Disting. Alumni award U. Ark., 1976 Mem. ABA (adv. com. to Treasury), Ark. Bankers Assn. (pres. 1982, chmn. legis. com. 1978-79), Am. Bankers Assn. (govt. relations council 1984—), Assn. Res. City Bankers, Ark. Bar Assn., Pulaski County Bar Assn., Beta Gamma Sigma, Sigma Alpha Epsilon, Delta Theta Phi . Clubs: Little Rock, Country of Little Rock. Lodges: Masons. Methodist. Home: 2200 Beechwood St Little Rock AR 72207-2024 Office: care Regions Bank PO Box 1471 Little Rock AR 72203-1471

BOWEN, WILLIAM HENRY, dental researcher, dental educator; b. Enniscorthy, Ireland, Dec. 11, 1933; came to U.S., 1956, naturalized; s. William H. and Pauline (McGrath) B.; m. Carole Barnes, Aug. 9, 1958 children: William, Deirdre, Kevin, David, Katherine BDS, Nat. U. Ireland, Dublin, 1955; MSc, U. Rochester, N.Y., 1959; PhD, U. London, 1965; DSc, U. Ireland, Dublin, 1974; D Odontologiae (hon.), U. Goteborg, Sweden, 1995, U. Oslo, Norway, 1991; D Odontologiae (honoris causa), U. Umeå, Sweden, 1993; MD (honoris causa), Nat. U. Irleland, 1995, Trinity Coll., Dublin, 1999. Diplomate Am. Bd. Dentistry, Inst. Medicine-NAS. Assoc. pvt. dental practice private dental practice, London, 1955-56; Quinten Hogg fellow Royal Coll. Surgeons, London, 1956-59, Nuffield Found. fellow, 1962-65, sr. research fellow, 1965-69, Sir Wilfred Fish fellow, 1969-73; acting chief caries prevention br. Nat. Inst. Dental Research, NIH, Bethesda, Md., 1973-79, chief, 1979-82; chmn. dental research U. Rochester, N.Y., 1982-95. Dir. Cariology Ctr., Rochester, 1984-95. Fellow AAAS (sect. R-Dentistry, chair elect 1989, chair 1990); mem. ADA (Gold medal 2000), European Orgn. Caries Rsch., Internat. Assn. Dental Rsch. (treas. 1982-88, v.p. 1988, pres. elect 1989, pres. 1990), Fedn. Dentaire Internationale, Inst. Medicine, Lab. Animal Sci. Assn., Zool. Soc. Roman Catholic. Home: 315 County Road 9 Victor NY 14564-9710 Office: U Rochester Ctr for Oral Biology 601 Elmwood Ave Rochester NY 14642-0001

BOWEN, WILLIAM JACKSON, retired gas company executive; b. Sweetwater, Tex., Mar. 31, 1922; s. Berry and Annah (Robey) Bowen; m. Annis K Hilty, June 6, 1945; children: Shelley Ann, Barbara Kay, Berry Dunbar, William Jackson. BS, U.S. Mil. Acad., 1945. Registered profl engr, Tex. Petroleum engr. Delhi Oil Corp., Dallas, 1949-57; v.p. Fla. Gas Co., Houston, 1957-60, pres. Winter Park, Fla., 1960-74; pres., chief exec. officer Transco Cos., Inc., Houston, 1974-81; chmn. Transco Cos., Inc. (name changed to Transco Energy Co.), Houston, 1976-92; chief exec. officer Transco Energy Co., Houston, 1981-87; ret., 1992; also bd. dirs. Transco Energy Co., Houston; ret., 1992. Bd dirs J P Poindexter and Co, Inc; mem adv bd Am Indust Partners, NY; hon vice-chmn World Energy Coun. Bd dirs YMCA, Houston, Houston Soc Prevention Cruelty to Animals, Character Educ Partnership; trustee emeritus bd Baylor Col Med, Jesse H Jones Grad Sch Bus, Rice Univ. With AUS, 1945—49. Mem.: US Energy Asn (past chmn). Episcopalian. Office: Williams 2800 Post Oak Blvd Level 4 Houston TX 77056-6100

BOWEN-FORBES, JORGE COURTNEY, artist, author, poet; b. Queenstown, Guyana, May 16, 1937; came to U.S., 1966; s. Walter and Margarita V. (Forbes) Bowen. BA, Queens Coll., Eve Leary, Guyana, 1969; MFA, Chelsea (Eng.) Sch. Design, 1972. Comml. artist Guyana Litographic, Georgetown; art dir. Corbin Advt. Agy., Bridgetown, Barbados; tech. advisor Ministry of Info. and Culture, Georgetown. Nat. juror Nat. Arts Club, N.Y.C., 1985, Nat. Soc. Painters in Casein and Acrylic. Major exhbns. include Expo 67, Can., Nat. Acad. Design, N.Y., Frye Mus., El Paso (Tex.) Mus., Wichita (Kans.) Centennial, Caribbean Festival of the Arts, Newark Mus.; 10-one-man exhbns. worldwide; works in collections including Nat. and Colgrain Collections, Guyana, El Paso Mus. Art, Kindercare Internat., Leon Loards Gallery, The McCreery Cummings Fine Art Collection, Bomani Gallery, San Francisco; poetry and articles pub. various jours.; author: Best Watercolors, 1996, Creative Watercolor, 1996; published in Best in Watercolor, Best in Oil Painting, Best in Acrylic Painting, Creative Watercolor, Splash 11, Best Contemporary Watercolors, American Poetry Annual. Recipient Silver medal of honor Allied Artists of N.Y., 1978, Gold medal of honor, 1975. Mem. Nat. Watercolor Soc. (signature mem.), Nat. Soc. Painters in Casein and Acrylics, Audubon Artists, Knickerbocker Artists (Gold Medal of Honor 1977, 79), Am. Watercolor Soc. (signature mem., High Winds medal 1984, Elsie and David Wu Ject-Key Meml. award 1998).

BOWER, ALLAN MAXWELL, lawyer; b. Oak Park, Ill., May 21, 1936; s. David Robert and Frances Emily Bower; m. Deborah Ann Rottmayer, Dec. 28, 1959. BS, U. Iowa, 1962; JD, U. Miami, Fla., 1968. Bar: Calif. 1969, U.S. Supreme Ct. 1979. Internat. aviation law practice, L.A., 1969—; ptnr. Kern & Wooley, L.A., 1980-85, Bronson, Bronson & McKinnon, L.A., 1985-90, Lane Powell Spears Lubersky, L.A., 1990-99, Bailey & Ptnrs., Santa Monica, Calif., 1999—. Contbr. articles to profl. publs. Mem. Lawyer-Pilots Bar Assn. Republican. Presbyterian. Office: Bailey & Ptnrs 2nd Fl 2828 Donald Douglas Loop N Santa Monica CA 90405-2959 Fax: 310-392-8091.

BOWER, BARBARA JEAN, nurse; b. Akron, Ohio, Aug. 25, 1942; d. William Howard and Maxine (Goodykoontz) Sturm; m. Howard Bower, Aug. 25, 1961 (dec. 1989); children: Nancy, Janet. BA, Elmhurst Coll., 1974, postgrad., 1987—; diploma, Evang. Sch. Nursing, 1970; PhD, U. Chgo., 1993. RN. Critical care nurse, supr. nursing Loyola U. Med. Ctr.; critical care nurse Med. Staffing Services, Oak Park, Ill., 1978-84; pres. Heart Care Unltd., Oak Brook, Ill., 1982—. One of first ind. nurse contractors in Ill., Ind., Ariz. Creator edn. programs for cardiac patients, families and staff, 1971—. Stephen min. Christ Ch. of Oak Brook, Ill.; Republican election judge, DuPage County. Mem. AAUW, ANA, Am. Assn. Critical Care Nurses, Am. Heart Assn., Elmhurst Coll. Alumni Assn., U. Chgo. Alumni Assn., Oak Brook Exec. Breakfast Club. Avocations: rose gardening, cooking, candymaking. Office: Heart Care Unltd PO Box 3275 Oak Brook IL 60522-3275

BOWER, CATHERINE DOWNES, communications, management consultant; b. Balt., Dec. 29, 1947; m. Réjean Pierre Proulx, Apr. 28, 1990. BA, Kent State U., 1969. Editor East Ohio Gas Co., Cleve., 1971-74, Personnel Administrator mag., Berea, Ohio, 1974-79, dir. communications, 1979-84; v.p. communications, pub. Am. Soc. Pers. Adminstrn. (name Soc. Human Resource Mgmt.), Alexandria, 1984-86, v.p. communications and pub. relations, 1986-91; sr. ptnr. Tecker Cons., Trenton, N.J., 1991-96, prin. ptnr., 1996—; pres. Cate Bower Communications, Alexandria and West River, Md., 1991—. Project dir. Work in the 21st Century, 1984. Editor: Work Life Visions, 1987. Pres. Oak Cluster Community Council, Alexandria, 1985-89. Recipient Monument award Great Washington Soc. Assn. Execs., 1996. Fellow Am. Soc. Assn. Execs. (cert.; vice chmn. comms. sect. coun. 1986-87, chmn. 1987-88, planning com. 1989-91, bd. dirs. Found. 1989-93, chair rsch. com. 1995-96, chmn. strategic leadership forum 2003, Best Pub. Rels. Program award 1984); mem. Greater Washington Soc. Assn. Execs. (chmn. visibility task force 1994-95, Monument award 1996), West River Sailing Club. Avocations: sailing, gardening. Office: Cate Bower Comms 5109 Holly Dr West River MD 20778-9744 E-mail: cbower@tecker.com.

BOWER, DAVID NORMAN, music educator, researcher; b. Rochester, NY, Dec. 2, 1965; s. Norman Arthur and Favorite Lucille Bower. BM, SUNY Fredonia, Fredonia, NY, 1985—88; MM, Westminster Choir Coll., Princeton, NJ, 1988—90; MA, NYU, New York, NY, 1991—93; PhD candidate NYU, 2000—. Music dir. Second Presbyn. Ch., Rahway, NJ, 1988—90; organist Princeton U. Chapel, Princeton, NJ, 1988—90; music min. St John's Ch., Hazlet, NJ, 1990—91; music dir. St Peter's Ch., Belleville, NJ, 1991—93, St Ann Ch., Raritan, NJ, 1993—; music educator St Ann Sch., Raritan, NJ, 1993—; writing instr. NYU, N.Y.C., 2000—03. Contbr. articles to profl. jour. Mem.: Nat. Assn. of Music Educators, Am. Guild of Organists, Coll. Music Soc., Organ Hist. Soc. Home: 194 Wayne St #4R Jersey City NJ 07302 Office: Saint Ann Church 45 Anderson St Raritan NJ 08869-1834 Home Fax: 908-707-1915. Personal E-mail: dnb208@nyu.edu.

BOWER, DOUGLAS WILLIAM, pastoral counselor, psychotherapist, clergyman; b. Niagara Falls, N.Y., Jan. 6, 1948; s. Charles Henry Bower and Phyllis June (Rank) Ayres; m. Cheryl Stewart, May 25, 1980; children: Katherine Elizabeth, Erin Colleen. AA, Manatee Jr. Coll., Bradenton, Fla., 1969; BS, Oglethorpe U., 1972; PhD, U. Ga., 1989. RN, Ga.; ordained to ministry United Meth. Ch., 1981; cert. counselor, Ga.; life cert. diplomate Am. Psychotherapy Assn. Nurse Northside Hosp., Atlanta, 1970-80; assoc. pastor 1st United Meth. Ch., Griffin, Ga., 1980-82; pastor, pastoral counselor Oconee Street United Meth. Ch., Athens, Ga., 1982-86; dir. Counseling Ministeries, Athens, 1986—. Adj. faculty Ft. Valley State U., 1999—2001. Author: The Person Centered Approach: Application for Living; From Saddlebags to Satellites; contbr. articles to profl. jours. Active Oglethorpe County Sr. Citizens Adv. Coun., United Way of N.E. Ga., U. Ga. Nat. Alumni Assn.; commr. Oglethorpe County, Dist. 1, 2002. Mem. Am. Psychotherapy Assn., Ga. Sheriffs Assn. (hon.), Person-Centered Assn. Avocations: music, walking, reading. Office: PO Box 143 Bishop GA 30621-0143 *While we may not make an impact on the world, we can and do make an impact on the immediate world around and within us. Persistence in maintaining faith, even in the face of adversity, makes a powerful impact on our immediate world.*

BOWER, GLEN LANDIS, lawyer; b. Highland, Ill., Jan. 16, 1949; s. Ray Landis and Evelyn Ferne Bower. BA, So. Ill. U., 1971; JD (hon.), Ill. Inst. Tech., 1974. Bar: Ill. 1974, US Ct. Mil. Appeals 1975, US Ct. Appeals (7th cir.) 1976,

US Dist Ct. (so. dist.) Ill. 1977, US Dist. Ct. (cen. dist.) Ill. 1992, US Supreme Ct. 1978, US Tax Ct. 1984, US Ct. Claims 1986, US Dist. Ct. (no. dist.) Ill. 1994, US Ct. Veterans Appeals 1995. Sole practice, Effingham, Ill., 1974-83; prosecutor Effingham County, Ill., 1976-79; mem. Ill. House of Reps., Springfield, 1979-83; asst. dir., gen. counsel Ill. Dept. Revenue, Springfield, Ill., 1983-90; Presdl. apptd. chmn. US R.R. Retirement Bd., Chgo., 1990-97; asst. to Ill. Sec. of State, Chgo., 1998-99; apptd. dir. revenue State of Ill., 1999—2003. Mil. aide to Gov. of Ill., 1999-2003; liaison mem. Adminstrv. Conf of US, 1991-95; mem. Nat. Adv. Com. for Juvenile Justice and Delinquency Prevention, Washington, 1976-80, US Econ. Adv. Bd. of US Dept. Commerce, Washington, 1981-85, Ill. Gen. Assembly State Adv. Com. on Cir. Ct. Fin., Springfield, 1984; mem. Revenue Bd. Appeals, Chgo., 1985-87, chmn., 1986-87; mem. Com. of 50 on Ill. Constn., 1987-88; adv. com. on electronic tax adminstrn. IRS, 2000-2003, So. Ill. U. Pub. Policy Inst., 2000. Co-editor: Handbook on State Taxation, 1991; contbr. articles to profl. jour. Alt. del. Rep. Nat. Conv., Miami Beach, Fla., 1972, Rep. Nat. Conv., New Orleans, 1988, Rep. Nat. Conv. Houston, 1992, Phila., 2000; vice chmn. Effingham County Rep. Ctrl. Com., Ill., 1976-90; bd. dir. Dana-Thomas House Found., Springfield, Ill., 1989-90, So. Ill. U. at Carbondale Found., 1993-2002, pres.'s coun.; trustee McKendree Coll., Lebanon, Ill., 1978-81; chmn. State of Ill. Organ and Tissue Donors Adv. Bd., 1993-98. Lt. col. USAFR, 1974-99, ret. Recipient The Univ. Disting. Svc. award, 1971, Recognition citation Am. Legion, 1980, Outstanding Svc. cert. to tchg. profession Ill. Edn. Assn., 1981, Disting. Svc. award Am. Vets., 1980, 82, Presdl. citation Navy League US, 1981, Constitution award Mus. of Our Nat. Heritage, 1988, Silver Good Citizenship medal Ill. Soc. SAR, 1990, Profl. Achievement award Ill. Inst. Tech., 1993, Friend of History award Ill. State Hist. Soc., 1994, Alumni Achievement award So. Ill. U., 1994, Disting. Alumnus award So. Ill. U. Coll. Liberal Arts, 2000, Outstanding Civilian Svc. Medal, Dept. Army, 2003, named Outstanding Freshman Legislator, Ill. Edn. Assn., 1980, Legislator of Yr., Ill. Assn. Rehab. Socs., 1981, 82, One of 10 Dels. to China, Am. Coun. Young Polit. Leaders, 1988. Fellow: Am. Bar Found. (life), Ill. Bar Found. (life); mem.: ABA (employment taxes com. 1990, adminstrv. practice com. of taxation sect., ct. procedure com., mem. exec. com. nat. assn. state tax bar sects.), Judge Advs. Assn., Am. Coun. Young Political Leaders, US Capitol Hist. Soc. (charter), Effingham County Mental Health Assn. (pub. affairs com. 1977—78), SBA Adv. Coun., Effingham Regional Hist. Soc. (bd. dir. 1973—77), Ill. State Hist. Soc. (v.o, 1979—81, Ralph C. Francis award 1967), Nat. Assn. Tax Adminstrs. (vice chmn. attys. sect. 1985—86, chmn. 1986—88, vice chmn. attys. sect. 1988—89), Effingham County Bar Assn. (sec. 1976—77, pres. 1983—84), Ill. State Bar Assn. (labor law sect. coun. 1976—77, sec. state taxation sect. coun. 1987—88, vice-chair 1988—89, 1988—89, chair 1989—90, sect. coun. on employee benefits 1991—98, 1991—98, sect. coun. on adminstrv. law 2000, Bd. Gov.'s award 1999), Rep. Nat. Lawyers Assn., Fed. Tax Adminstrs. (bd. trustees 2001—03), Fed. Bar Assn., Sons of Am. Revolution, Art Inst. of Chgo., So. Ill. Univ. Alumni Assn. (life), Res. Officers Assn. (life), Effingham County Old Settlers Assn. (pres., bd. dir. 1983—86), Abraham Lincoln Assn., U.S. Supreme Ct. Hist. Soc., The Nat. Sojourners, Smithsonian Assocs., Am. Legion, So. Ill. U. Carbondale Found. (bd. dir. 1993—2002), Field Mus. of Natural History, Army and Navy Club Washington D.C., Kiwanis (pres. 1977—78), Phi Alpha Delta. Republican. Methodist. Home: PO Box 1106 Effingham IL 62401-1106

BOWER, JANET ESTHER, writer, educator; b. National City, Calif., Apr. 14, 1943; d. Murvel and Esther Eva (Clark) Newlan; m. Robert S. Bower Jr., Nov. 23, 1968; children: Llance Clark, Esther Elizabeth. BA in History and Psychology, Calif. Western U., San Diego, 1965; MA in History, UCLA, 1966; MA in Edn., U.S. Internat. U., San Diego, 1970. Std. jr. coll. credential, elem. credential, Calif. Instr., mem. adj. faculty San Diego C.C. Dist., 1969—, Grossmont/Cuyamaca Coll. Dist., El Cajon, Calif., 1973, 97—, Palomar Coll. Dist., San Marcos, Calif., 1993, 97—, Midlands Tech. Coll., Columbia, S.C., 1995-96, Mira Costa Coll., 2001—. Adj. faculty mem. Nat. U., 1999—, Union Inst., 2000—; hist. cons. pub. Contbg. author: Women in the Biological Sciences, 1997; contbr. articles to periodicals; pub. editor Friends of the Internat. Ctr. Newsletter, U. Calif., San Diego, 1984-85. Bd. dirs. Women of St. Paul's Episcopal Ch., San Diego, 1983-86, Oceanids, U. Calif., San Diego, 1980-85. Grantee U.S. Dept. Edn., 1968-69. Mem. Am. Hist. Assn., Calif. Hist. Soc., Project Wildlife (hon. life mem.). Republican. Avocations: cooking, travel. E-mail: jbower@miracosta.cc.ca.us., jbower@sdeed.net.

BOWER, JEAN RAMSAY, lawyer, writer; b. N.Y.C., Nov. 25, 1935; d. Claude Barnett and Myrtle Marie (Scott) Ramsay; m. Ward Swift Just, Jan. 31, 1957 (div. 1966); children: Jennifer Ramsay, Julia Barnett; m. Robert Turrell Bower, June 12, 1971 (dec. June 1990). AB, Vassar Coll., 1957; JD, Georgetown U., 1970. Bar: D.C. 1970. Exec. dir. D.C. Dem. Ctrl. Com., Washington, 1969-71; pvt. practice Washington, 1971-78, 94—; dir. Counsel of Child Abuse and Neglect Office D.C. Superior Ct., 1978-94. Mem. Mayor's Com. on Child Abuse and Neglect, 1973-94, vice chmn., 1975-79; mem. Family Div. Rules Adv. Com., 1977-94; pres., bd. dirs. C.B. Ramsay Found., 1984—; cons. child welfare issues, writer. Contbr. poetry to In a Certain Place. Active D.C. Child Fatality Rev. Com., 1992-; bd. dirs. Friends D.C. Superior Ct., 1994—, pres. bd. dirs., 2002-; Family & Child Svcs., D.C., 1995-2003; Folger poetry bd. (chair 2002-), Folger Shakespeare Libr., 1998-. Named Washingtonian of the Yr. Washington Mag., 1978. Mem. Women's Bar Assn. (bd. dirs. 1993-96, found. 1986-91, Woman Lawyer of Yr. 1986), D.C. Bar Assn. (election bd. 1994-96, Beatrice Rosenberg award sect. com. 1994—), Women's Bar Assn. Found. (bd. dirs. 1986-91).

BOWER, JOHN, retired fluid mechanics engineer, commissioner; b. Somerset, Mass., Sept. 16, 1920; s. Matthew H. and Alice (Winterbom) Bower; m. Marion Louise Cadorette, Aug. 2, 1948; children: John C., Jeffrey J., Douglas J. BS, Brown Univ., Providence, RI, 1938—41. Cert. WPI, Water Works Op. & Mgmt., Worcester, Mass., 1962. Sales & engr. WW Grainger, Chgo., 1949—86; commr. Somerset Indsl. Fin. Authority, 1980—. Commr. Town of Somerset, Somerset, Mass.; chmn. Bd. of Sewer and Water Commissioners, Somerset, Mass. Warrant officer USAAF, 1942—45. Recipient State Award, Mass Consulting Engr./ Mass., 1999, Nat. Award, Nat. Assoc. Cons. Engr./ Seattle, Wash., 1999. Mem.: NY Acad. of Sci., New Eng. Water Works (life mem. for 40 yrs. svc.), Am. Water Works (life mem. for 30 yrs. svc.), RI Shriners Club (Legion of Honor), Pioneer Lodge (Master 1955). Republican. Episcopalian. Avocation: ski patrol. Home: 2742 Riverside Ave Somerset MA 02726 E-mail: JBower8175@aol.com.

BOWER, JOHN RICHARD FENN, archaeologist, educator; b. Newton, Iowa, May 5, 1935; s. John Oates and Lillian Keithen Bower; m. Andrea Garcia Montero, Feb. 1961 (div. Aug. 1965); m. Janice Sophie Johnson, Sept. 26, 1966; 1 child, Jennifer Keithen. BA, Harvard U., 1957; MA, Northwestern U., Evanston, Ill., 1968; PhD, Northwestern U., 1973. Editor Rand McNally & Co., Skokie, Ill., 1962—67; asst. prof. Lake Forest Coll., Lake Forest, Ill., 1970—73; from asst. prof. to full prof. Iowa State U., Ames, 1973—92, prof. emeritus, 1992—; part-time lectr. U. Minn., Duluth, 1992—. Rsch. fellow Brit. Inst. of History and Archaeology in East Africa, Nairobi, Kenya, 1971; dir. archaeol excavations Serengeti Park; condr. 1st trans-Atlantic archaeol. investigations with Polish collaboration. Author: In Search of the Past, 1986; co-sr. editor Prehistoric Cultures and Environments in Africa, 1988, co-sr. author A Comparative Study of Prehistoric Foragers in Europe and North America, 2002. Lt. USN, 1957—62. Recipient Wilton Park award for internat. svc., Iowa State U., 1989; fellow Fulbright fellow, 1982. Fellow: Am. Anthropol. Assn.; mem.: AAAS, Soc. for Am. Archaeology, Duluth Cmty. Sailing Assn. (bd. dirs. 2000—), No. Lakes Archaeol. Soc. (bd. dirs. 2002—), Duluth Yacht Club (vice commodore 2002—). Democrat. Unitarian Universalist. Avocations: sailing, fly fishing, music, poetry. Office: Univ of Minn-Duluth 10 University Dr Duluth MI 55812

BOWER, JOSEPH LYON, business administration educator; b. N.Y.C., Sept. 21, 1938; s. Morris L. and Florence (Turitz) B.; m. Nancy Milender, Feb. 16, 1958; children: Jonathan, Deborah. AB, Harvard U., 1959, MBA, 1961, D Bus. Adminstrn., 1963. Asst. prof. Grad. Sch. Bus. Adminstrn. Harvard U., Boston, 1963-68, assoc. prof. Grad. Sch. Bus. Adminstrn., 1968-71, Donald K. David prof. bus. adminstrn. Grad. Sch. Bus. Adminstrn., 1972—, sr. assoc. dean for external rels. Grad. Sch. Bus. Adminstrn., 1986-89, chmn. doctoral programs, dir. of rsch. Grad. Sch. Bus. Adminstrn., 1989-95, faculty mem. John F. Kennedy Sch. Govt. Cambridge, Mass., 1969—. Bd. dirs. Anika Rsch. Inc., Woburn, Mass., Brown Shoe Inc., St. Louis, Sonesta Internat. Hotels Corp., Boston, ML-Lee Acquisition Fund, L.P., Boston, New Am. High Income Fund, Boston, Loews Corp., N.Y.C.; trustee TH Lee, Putnam Emerging Portfolio, Boston; chair gen. mgr. program Grad. Sch. Bus. Adminstrn., 1996—. Author: Managing Resource Allocation Process, 1971 (McKinsey Found. award 1971), Two Faces of Management, 1983, When Markets Quake, 1986; co-author: Public Management: Text and Cases, 1978, Business Policy: Text and Cases, 7th edit., 1991, Business Policy: Managing Strategic Processes, 8th edit., 1995. Vice chair New Eng. Conservatory Music, Boston, 1984—; trustee DeCordova and Dana Mus. and Pk., Lincoln, Mass., 1987—. Co-recipient (with C.M. Christensen) McKinsey Found. award, 1995. Mem. Am. Econ. Assn., Coun. Fgn. Rels., St. Botolph Club (Boston), Harvard Club (N.Y.C.). Avocations: tennis, boating. Office: Harvard Business School Sch Bus Morgan # 467 Boston MA 02163 E-mail: jbower@hbs.edu.

BOWER, KATHLEEN ANNE, nurse consultant; b. Detroit, Oct. 9, 1946; d. Richard Edward and Edith M. (Enright) B. BSN, Georgetown U., 1968; MSN, Boston Coll., 1972; DNSc, Boston U., 1991. Staff nurse NYU Med. Ctr., N.Y.C., 1968-70; nurse leader, vice chair nursing New Eng. Med. Ctr., Boston, 1972-89; prin. The Ctr. for Nursing Case Mgmt., South Natick, Mass., 1989-91; co-owner, prin. The Ctr. for Case Mgmt., South Natick, Mass., 1991—. Author: Case Management by Nurses, 1991; contbr. articles to profl. jours. Fellow Am. Acad. Nursing; mem. ANA, Am. Orgn. Nurse Execs., Mass. Orgn. Nurse Execs., Sigma Theta Tau. Office: Ctr for Case Mgmt 6 Pleasant St Natick MA 01760

BOWER, KENNETH FRANCIS, electrical engineer; b. Fostoria, Ohio, June 16, 1942; s. Carl Albert and Carmia June (Butzier) B.; m. Vicki Marie Lambert, Feb. 14, 1975; children: Candi Marie, Jillian June, Brett Kenneth, Michael Courtland, Daniel David. BSEE, Purdue U., 1965. Registered profl. engr., Ohio, Fla. Aerospace engr. NASA Manned Spacecraft Ops., Kennedy Space Center, Fla., 1965-67, NASA Unmanned Launch Ops., Kennedy Space Center, 1967-73; systems engr. Cin. Electronics, 1973-76; programmer AMF, Vandalia, Ohio, 1976-77, Access Corp., Cin., 1977-78; mgr. GTE Compact, Cin., Anaheim, Calif., 1978-81; cons. Telos Cons. Svcs., Hughes Aerospace, Irvine, Calif., 1982-83, Telos Fed. Systems, Jet Propulsion Lab., Pasadena, Calif., 1983-86; lead engr. GE Aircraft Engines, Cin., 1987-93; propr. software cons. bus. Quality Used Profls., Batavia, Ohio, 1993-96, pres., chmn. bd. dirs., 1996-2000; also chmn. bd. dirs. Quality Used Profls., Inc.; sr. engr. Tellabs, Inc., Germantown, Md., 2001; owner The Software Launchpad, Batavia, Ohio, 2003—. V.p., bd. dirs. Gedanken Systems, Inc., Cin., Keane, Inc., 1998-99 Patentee in field. Bd. trustees First Ch. of God, Rubidoux, Calif., 1982-83, 86. Named Father of Yr. First Ch. of God, Cin., 1978. Mem. Mensa (local sec. 1963-83), Purdue Alumnus, Hon. Order Ky. Cols. Democrat. Avocations: Judo, designing computerized games. Home and Office: 248 Seton Ct Batavia OH 45103 E-mail: KennethBower@fuse.net.

BOWER, LAUREL LEE, education educator, researcher; b. San Antonio, Tex., Jan. 8, 1951; d. James Hamilton and Carol Doris Hunt; m. Stephen Paul Bower, Apr. 2, 1970; children: Shawn Matthew, Angela Rose Watts. AA, Great Falls C.C., 1972; BA, Boise State Univ., Idaho, 1996, MA, 1998; PhD, Univ. Nev., Reno, Nev., 2003. Office mgr. House of Flowers, Boise, Idaho, 1974—76; bus. owner Riding Instr., Boise, Idaho, 1985—88, Words Unlimited, Boise, Idaho, 1987—90; acctg. supr. Warm Springs Ctr., Boise, Idaho, 1990—93; acad. adv. Coll. of Bus. Boise State Univ., Boise, Idaho, 1993—96; tchg. asst. Boise State Univ., Boise, Idaho, 1996—98, Univ. Nev., Reno, 1998—2002. Basic writing coord. Univ. Nev., 2000—01, corewriting com., 2000—01, editl. bd., 2000—01. Contbr. articles to numerous profl. jour., to numerous profl. conf. Mem.: Modern Language Assn., Nat. Coun. of Tchrs. of English, Sigma Tau Delta, Phi Kappa Phi. Republican. Christian.

BOWER, RICHARD JAMES, minister; b. Somerville, N.J., June 9, 1939; s. Oneil A. and Mildred R. (Goss) B.; m. Helen Ann Cheek, Dec. 29, 1962 (div. 1985); 1 child, Christopher Scott. Student, Sorbonne, Paris, 1959-60; BA, Wesleyan U., 1961; M.Div., Drew U., Madison, N.J., 1965; student, Oxford U., Eng., 1983; DD, Piedmont Coll., 1999. Ordained to ministry, Congregational Christian Ch., 1965. Minister Community Congl. Ch., Kewaunee, Wis., 1965-67; sr. minister Congl. Ch., Bound Brook, N.J., 1967-78, Congl. Ch. of the Chimes, Sherman Oaks, Calif., 1978-95; preaching min. Congl. Ch. Messiah, L.A., 1995-96, First Congl. Ch., L.A., 2002. Mem. exec. com., dir. Nat. Assn. Congl. Christian Chs., 1973-77, chmn., 1976-77,asst. moderator, 1981-82, moderator, 1982-83, exec. search com., 1990-91, nominating com., 1991-93, chmn., 1992-93; mem. World Christian Rels. Commn., 1993-97. Appeared on TV programs; contbr. poetry and articles to periodicals. Organizer, pres. Am. Field Service, Kewaunee, 1966-67; dir. Children's Bur., Los Angeles, 1981-88; bd. fellows Hollywood Congl. Ctr., 1979-82; bd. dirs. Heritage Playhouse, 1986-96. Recipient Citation for Disting. Svc., Nat. Assn. Congl. Christian Chs., 1997. Mem. Cal-West Assn. (dir., moderator 1986-87) Lodges: Bound Brook Rotary (pres. 1975-76). Republican. Home: 365 W Alameda Ave Apt 302 Burbank CA 91506-3339 E-mail: rijabo@juno.com.

BOWER, RICHARD STUART, economist, educator; b. N.Y.C., Aug. 1, 1928; s. Jacob and Elsie (Vander Beugle) B.; m. Dorothy Ann Hagberg, June 23, 1953; children— Gari Ellen, Laura Jane, Nancy Lynne. AB, Kenyon Coll., 1949; MBA, Columbia, 1955; PhD, Cornell U., 1962. Instr. econs. Kenyon Coll., 1949-50, Alfred U., 1955-57; asst. prof. econs. and bus. Vanderbilt U., 1959-62; prof. bus. econs. Dartmouth, 1962—99; ptnr. Bower Rohr and Assocs., Hanover, 1981—2001. Author: Investment and Liquidity: A Case Study of Clay Construction Products, 1965; Contbr. articles to profl. jours. Served with USNR, 1951-55. Mem. Am. Econ. Assn., Am. Finance Assn., Phi Beta Kappa, Beta Gamma Sigma, Phi Kappa Phi. Democrat. Jewish. Home: South Esker Hanover NH 03755 Office: Amos Tuck Sch Hanover NH 03755

BOWER, ROBERT HEWOTT, surgeon, educator, researcher; b. Omaha, Aug. 20, 1949; s. John Walter and Dorothy May (Sibert) B.; m. Debra Lea Goettsche, July 4, 1980; children: Timothy Conrad, Michael Harvey, Emily Frances. BA, Grinnell Coll., 1971; MD, U. Nebr., 1975. Diplomate Nat. Bd. Med. Examiners, Am. Bd. Surgery (dir. 1995-2001, sr. examiner 2001—). Intern U. Nebr., 1975-76, resident surgery, 1976-80, chief resident, 1979-80; clin. and rsch. fellow U. Cin., 1980-81, asst. prof. surgery, 1981-85; dir. dept. parenteral and enteral nutrition U. Hosp., 1981—, assoc. prof. surgery, 1985-95, prof. surgery, 1995—, dir. surg. residency, 1986—, vice chmn. edn., 1995—. Chief surgical svc. Cin. VA Med. Ctr., 1994—. Contbr. chpts. to books and articles to profl. jours. Pres., trustee, chmn. bd. trustees Vocal Arts Ensemble of Cin.; elder, trustee Knox Presbyn. Ch. Fellow ACS, Am. Surg. Assn.; mem. Ctrl. Surg. Assn., Am. Coll. Nutrition, Soc. Am. Gastrointestinal Endoscopic Surgeons, Assn. Acad. Surgery, Am. Soc. Parenteral and Enteral Nutrition, Ohio Med. Assn., Surg. Infection Soc., Acad. Medicine Cin. (pres. 2002-03), Soc. Univ. Surgeons, Soc. Surgery of Alimentary Tract, Cin. Surg. Soc., Halsted Soc. Office: U Cincinnati Dept Surgery PO Box 670558 231 Albert Sabin Way Cincinnati OH 45267-0558

BOWER, SHELLEY ANN, business management consultant; b. Catskill, N.Y., Jan. 31, 1954; d. Edward Philip and Antoinette (Post) B.; m. Richard D. Connors, Aug. 28, 1976 (div. Mar. 1984); m. Paul Allan Benfatto, Oct. 2, 1999. BA, Mich. Technol. U., 1977; JD, Detroit Coll., 1984. Bar: N.Y. Coord. Cadillac Motorcar, Detroit, 1980-84, employee in tng., 1984-85, supr. EEO, 1985-86; divsn. mgr. property profl. Saugerties, NY, 1986-88; engring. tech., dir. corp. tng. and program adminstrn. Troy, Mich., 1988-92; cons. Electronic Data Sys., Southfield, Mich., 1992-95; dir. planning & devel., corp. counsel C.T. Male Assoc., PC, Latham, NY, 1995-96; prin. Oracle Corp., 1996-97, IBM Global Cons. Svc. Mfg. Industries, White Plains, NY, 1998—2000, non-exec., 2001—; customer relationship mgmt. prin., exec. IBM, 2001—02; offering mgr. IBM Lotus Div., 2002—. Mem. NAFE, N.Y. State Bar Assn. Avocations: skiing, hiking.

BOWER, WARD ALAN, management consultant, lawyer; b. Carlisle, Pa., Feb. 10, 1947; s. Dale Luther and Margaret Louise (Chapman) B.; m. Linda Elliott; children: Miles Robert, Chase Batchelor, Reid Alan, Seth Elliott. BA in Econs., Bucknell U., 1969; JD, Dickinson Sch. Law, 1975. Bar: Pa. 1975. Group pension adminstr. Prudential ins. Co., Newark, 1969-70; methods analyst Liberty Mut. Ins. Co., Boston, 1971—72; prin. Altman Weil, Inc., Newtown Square, Pa., 1977—, pres., 1989—, also bd. dirs. Cons. Liberty Mut. Ins. Co., Boston, 1975—77. Author: (with Frank Arentowicz, Jr.) Law Office Automation and Technology, 1980. Bd. govs. Dickinson Sch. Law of Pa. State U., 1994—. With U.S. Army, 1970-71. Recipient Outstanding Alumni award Dickinson Sch. Law, 1997. Fellow Am. Bar Found., Coll. of Law Practice Mgmt.; mem. ABA (law practice mgmt. sect. divsn. chair 1986-92, coun. 1990-94), Internat. Bar Assn. (chair com. practice mgmt. and tech. 1992-96, working group on multidisciplinary practices 1996—, coun. sect. on legal practice 1996 2002), Pa. Bar Assn. Office: Altman Weil Inc PO Box 625 Two Campus Blvd Newtown Square PA 19073 E-mail: wbower@altmanweil.com.

BOWERFIND, EDGAR SIHLER, JR., physician, medical administrator; b. Cleve., May 7, 1924; s. Edgar Sihler and Edna (Strong) B.; m. Maria Washington Tucker, Apr. 28, 1956; children— Edgar Sihler III, Ellis Tucker, Jane Strong, William Minor Lile Student, Creighton U. Med. Sch., 1945-47; MD, Western Res. U., 1949. Diplomate Am. Bd. Internal Medicine. Intern Univ. Hosps. of Cleve., 1950-51, resident in medicine, 1954-56; practice medicine specializing in internal medicine Cleve., 1957-92; mem. faculty Case Western Res. U. Sch. Medicine, Cleve., 1956-92, asst. prof. medicine, 1965-92, dir. health clinics, utilization rev., 1965-92, asst. prof. emeritus, 1992—; chief med. services Horizon Ctr. Hosp., Cleve., 1981-83. Sec. Citizens Commn. on Grad. Med. Edn., 1961 66 Sub-deacon Episcopal Diocese Ohio, 1970—; trustee The Sihler Mental Health Found. Served with AUS, 1943-46, to capt. USAF, 1951-53. Decorated Bronze Star; Ogelbay fellow in medicine U. Hosps. Cleve., 1955-56 Home: Ste 915 2181 Ambleside Dr Cleveland OH 44106

BOWERING, GEORGE HARRY, writer, English literature educator; b. Penticton, B.C., Can., Dec. 1, 1936, s. Ewart Harry and Pearl Patricia (Brinson) Bowering; m. Angela May Luoma, Dec. 14, 1962; 1 child, Thea Claire. Student, Victoria Coll., 1953-54; BA, U. B.C., 1960, MA, 1963; postgrad., U. Western Ont., 1966-67. Asst. prof. Am. lit. U. Calgary, 1963-66; writer in residence Sir George Williams U., Montreal, 1967-68, asst. prof., 1968-71; prof. Simon Fraser U., Burnaby, 1972—2001; poet laureate of Can. Author: Mirror on the Floor, 1967, Autobiology, 1972, Flycatcher and Other Stories, 1974, Concentric Circles, 1977, A Short Sad Book, 1977, Protective Footwear, 1978, Another Mouth, 1979, Burning Water, 1980, A Place to Die, 1983, Caprice, 1987, Harry's Fragments, 1990, The Rain Barrel, 1994, Shoot!, 1994, Parents From Space, 1994, Piccolo Mondo, 1998, Diamondback Dog, 1998; poetry Points on the Grid, 1964, The Man in Yellow Boots, 1965, The Silver Wire, 1966, Rocky Mountain Foot, 1968, The Gangs of Kosmos, 1969, Touch, 1971, In the Flesh, 1973, The Catch, 1976, Particular Accidents: Selected Poems, 1981, Smoking Mirror, 1984, Kerrisdale Elegies, 1984, 71 Poems for People, 1985, Delayed Mercy, 1986, Sticks & Stones, 1989, Quarters, 1991, Urban Snow, 1992, George Bowering Selected, 1993, The Moustache, 1993, Blonds On Bikes, 1997; (poetry) His Life: A Poem, 2000; (essays) The Mask in Place, 1982, A Way with Words, 1982, Craft Slices, 1985, Errata, 1988, Imaginary Hand, 1988, A Magpie Life, 2001, Cars, 2002; (history) Bowering's B.C., 1996, Egotists and Autocrats, 1999; editor Taking the Field: The Best of Baseball Fiction, 1990, 92, Likely Stories: A Postmodern Sampler, 1992, And Other Stories, 2001, (history) Stone Country, 2003. Served with RCAF, 1954-57. Mem.: Assn. Can. TV and Radio Artists. Home: 2499 W 37th Ave Vancouver BC Canada V6M 1P4 E-mail: bowering@sfu.ca.

BOWERMAN, ANN LOUISE, writer, genealogist, educator; b. Branch County, Mich., June 4, 1933; d. George Allen and Mary (Thomas) Hubbard; m. Virgil Lee Bowerman, June 4, 1954 (div. 1977); children: William Lee, Sally Ann; m. Virgil Wayne Dunkel, Jr., May 23, 1987 (div. Dec. 1996). BA, Western Mich. U., 1966, MSLS, 1971, MA, 1976. Cert. tchr. K-8, Mich., libr. sci. Tchr. Bethel #6 Sch. Dist., Coldwater, Mich., 1953—55; tchr. kindergarten Union City (Mich.) Schs., 1963-64; children's libr. Sturgis (Mich.) Pub. Libr., 1971-72; libr./media specialist Coldwater H.S., 1972-91; field rep. U.S. Census Bur., 2000—02; media specialist libr. Union City (Mich.) Schs., 2002—03; retired, 1991. Mem. programming com., mem. ann. scholarships telethon com., camera staff, video editor Cable TV Channel 31, Coldwater, 1983-90. Author: The Bater Book, 1987, A Bowerman Family History, 1998, Historic Howe, Indiana Walking Tour, 1998, The William (6) Bowerman Family of Conneaut Township, 1998; co-author: Recommendations for High School Media Centers in Michigan, 1980 (booklet); contbr. articles to profl. jours. Mem., chair governing bd. Woodlands Libr. Coop., Albion, Mich., 1973-74, 83-86; adv. coun. Calhoun and Branch Counties Regional Ednl. Media Ctr., Marshall, Mich., 1972-91; com. mem. So. Mich. Region of Coop., Albion, 1989-91; leader All Around 4-H Club, Union City, 1954-74; mem. Sullivan Lady's Aid Soc., Union City, 1955-74, Twin Lakes Cmty. Assn., 1997—; chair winter program com. Tibbits Arts Found., Coldwater, 1980-90; mem. Coldwater Hist. Preservation Assn., 1978-86; del. Mich. Rep. State Conv., Detroit, 1986; candidate for Branch County Commr., Coldwater, 1988; mem. Mich. Assn. for Computer Users in Learning, 1975-91; mem. cultural arts com., mem. walking tour com. Howe (Ind.) Cmty. Assn., 1996—. Recipient Cert. of Appreciation, Mich. Assn. for Media in Edn., 1980, 91, Golden Apple Retirement award Coldwater H.S., 1991. Mem. Soc. of Genealogists (London), New England Hist. Geneal. Soc., Descendants of Founders of Ancient Windsor, Ctrl. N.Y. Geneal. Soc., DAR (good citizen selection com., treas. Coldwater br. 1997-2002), Mich. Assn. Ret. Sch. Pers., Schenectady County Hist. Soc., Old Brutus Hist. Soc., Union City Geneal. Soc., St. Joseph County Hist. Soc. (advisor to Land Office Mus. com. 1997—), Crawford County Geneal. Soc., Coldwater Edn. Assn. (sec. 1980-90), Beta Phi Mu. Avocations: travel, coin collecting, tennis. Home: 1820 W 600 N Howe IN 46746-9406 E-mail: abowerma@ligtel.com.

BOWERMAN, RICHARD HENRY, utility company executive, lawyer; b. Apr. 29, 1917; s. Arthur Lewis and Constance Dorothea (Riehman) B.; m. Frances Annette Whitney, Mar. 7, 1942; children: Judith Condon, Richard Whitney Bowerman, Frances B. Gingrich. BA, Yale U., 1939, LLB, 1942; LLD, U. New Haven, 1982. Bar: Conn. 1946. Assoc. Gumbart, Corbin, Tyler & Cooper, New Haven, 1946-69; ptnr. Gumbart, Corbin, Tyler, Cooper and Tyler, Cooper, Grant, Bowerman & Keefe, New Haven, 1949-69; pres., chmn., CEO Conn. Energy Corp. & So. Conn. Gas Co., New Haven, 1969-80, chmn. bd., 1972-88, pres., 1988; chmn. sci. Park Devel. Corp., New Haven, 1981-94. Bd. dirs. Conn. Agrl. Sta. Judge Mcpl. Ct. of Orange, Conn., 1951-55; 1st chmn. United Way of Greater New Haven; chmn. Yale New Haven Hosp., 1976-83. Capt. USNR, 1941-45, ATO, PTO. Decorated Bronze Star; recipient Disting. Pub. Svc. award New Haven C. of C., 1973, Disting. Pub. Svc. award YMCA, New Haven, 1982, Disting. Pub. Svc. award Lions Club of New Haven, 1981, others; named to Hall of Fame Jr. Achievement, 1984. Mem. New Eng. Gas Assn. (dir., chmn.), Assn. Gas. Distbrs. (nat. chmn.), Am. Gas Assn., Conn. Bar Assn. (pres.). Roman Catholic. Home and Office: 612 Thornhill Ln West Haven CT 06516-7914

BOWERS, BEGE K. English educator, academic administrator; b. Nashville, Tenn., Aug. 19, 1949; d. John and Yvonne Bowers. BA in English cum laude, Vanderbilt U., 1971; student, U. Mich., 1985; MACT, U. Tenn., 1973, PhD, 1984. Asst. loan officer Ctr. for Fin. Aid and Placement, Baylor U., Waco, Tex., 1975-76; editorial asst. Wassily Leontief, NYU, N.Y.C., 1976-78; instr. bus. English Florence-Darlington Tech. Coll., Florence, S.C., 1979-80; tchr. English and French St. John's High Sch., Darlington, S.C., 1980-82; teaching asst. dept English U. Tenn., Knoxville, 1982-84; asst. prof. English Youngstown (Ohio) State U., 1984-88, assoc. prof., 1988-92, prof., 1992—, composition coord. dept. English, 1985-94, acting chmn. dept., 1989, asst. to dean Coll. Arts and Scis., 1992-93, dir. profl. writing and editing, 1996-2000, assoc. to the dean Coll. Arts and Scis., 2001—02, asst. provost acad. programs and planning, 2002—. Part-time freelance editor MLA, N.Y.C., 1978-80; cons. Project Arete, Youngstown and Mahoning County Pub. Schs., 1984-87, Youngstown Pub. Schs., 1986, 87-88, 90-91, Macmillan Pub. Co., 1986, Trumbull (Ohio) County Schs., 1988, Akron Beacon Jour., 1994-95, Ohio Dept. Edn., 1998-2001; mem. Ohio Bd. Regents, 2002—. Co-editor: CEA Critic, 1998-2002, CEA Forum 1988—, (with Barbara Brothers) Reading and Writing Women's Lives: A Study of the Novel of Manners, 1991, (with Chuck Nelson) Internships in Technical Communication, 1991, (with Mark Allen) Annotated Chaucer Bibliography 1986-1996, 2002; mem. editl. bd. South Atlantic Review, 1987-89; editor: of more than 40 pamphlets, 7 children's books, and 1 videoscript. Alumni Found. Rsch. fellow U. Tenn., 1978, dissertation fellow U. Tenn., 1983, Davis editl. fellow U. Tenn., 1984; Grad. Rsch. Coun. grantee Youngstown State U. Mem.: MLA, Gould Soc. (pres. faculty com. 1991—93), No. Ohio Soc. for Tech. Comm., Soc. for Tech. Comm. (Jay R. Gould award for excellence in tchg. tech. comm. 1999, Disting. Chpt. Svc. award 2001, Assoc. fellow award 2002), Assn.

Tchrs. Tech. Writing, New Chaucer Soc. (asst. bibliographer 1986—), Coll. English Assn. Ohio, Coun. Editors of Learned Jours., Coll. English Assn. (exec. bd., Disting. Svc. award 1996), Phi Beta Kappa, Phi Kappa Phi (pres. 1991—92, sec. 1994—98, exec. bd. 1998—). Office: Youngstown State U Office of the Provost Youngstown OH 44555-0001 E-mail: bkbowers@ysu.edu.

BOWERS, CHARLES RICHARD, surgeon; b. Frederick, Md., 1924; MD, Johns Hopkins U., 1947. Diplomate Am. Bd. Surgery. Intern Union Meml. Hosp., Balt., 1947-48; resident in surgery Baylor U. Med. Ctr., Dallas, 1948-49, 50-52, resident in pathology, 1949-50; clin. instr. U. Tex. Sch. Medicine, San Antonio, 1952-54; mem. staff emeritus St. Johns Med. Ctr., Anderson, Ind., 1954-98. Clin. instr. USAF Lackland AFB, San Antonio, 1952-54. Active Vol. Physicians for Vietnam, 1966-72. Capt. M.C. USAF, 1952-54. Fellow Am. Coll. Surgeons; mem. AMA. Home: 8734 Grey Oaks Ave Sarasota FL 34238-4371

BOWERS, CURTIS RAY, JR., chaplain; b. Lancaster, Pa., Feb. 6, 1933; s. Curtis Ray and Oleita (Geisler) B.; m. Doris Jean, June 18, 1955; children: Sharon, William, Stephen. BA, Asbury Coll., 1958; MDiv, Asbury Theol. Sem., 1960. Pastor Methodist Ch., Cynthiana, Ky., 1956-60, Ch. of the Nazarene, Cape May, N.J., 1960-61; chaplain U.S. Army, 1961-84; dir. chaplaincy ministries Ch. of the Nazarene, Kansas City, Mo., 1984-2000. Author: Forward Edge of the Battle Area: A Chaplain's Story. Col. U.S. Army, 1961-84. Decorated Silver Star; named Srs. Double Inter-Svc. Tennis Champion, 1982; named to 327th Infantry Regimental Hall of Fame, 1998; recipient Outstanding Chaplain of Yr. award, Ch. of the Nazarene, 2000. Mem. Ch. Of The Nazarene. Avocation: tennis. Home: 3523 Portland Ave Nampa ID 83686-7993 E-mail: crbowers11@juno.com.

BOWERS, DAVID PAUL, operations analyst; b. San Jose, Calif., Dec. 29, 1961; s. Ken H. and Vicki Z. Bowers; m. Lisa L. Olsen, Sept. 9, 1988; children: Zachary, Nicholas. Student, U. Calif., Berkeley, 1981-82. Copy operator Kinko's, Reno, 1984—85, with customer svc. dept. L.A., 1985—86; sr. ops. analyst Pitney Bowes Mgmt. Svcs., 1986—. Chmn. region 65 Libertarian Party Calif., Los Angeles County, 1998—. Avocations: fishing, tennis, gardening, golf, cooking. Home: 10620 Dolan Ave Downey CA 90241 Office: 1149 S Broadway # 101 Los Angeles CA 90015-2213 E-mail: [illegible]@aol.com.

BOWERS, FRANCIS ROBERT, literature educator; b. N.Y.C., May 4, 1920; s. William Leo and Catherine (Callahan) B. BA, Cath. U. Am., 1946, PhD, 1959; MA, Fordham U., 1952. Tchr. Ascension Sch., N.Y.C., 1946-48, St. Augustine's High Sch., Bklyn., 1948-51, St. Peter's High Sch., Staten Island, 1951-53; instr. De La Salle Coll., Washington, 1953-59; assoc. prof. English and world lit. Manhattan Coll., 1959-70, 85-89, chmn. dept., 1967-70, chmn. grad. English dept., 1961-70, dean arts and scis., 1970-80, provost, 1980-85, acad. advisor to intercollegiate athletes, 1988—. Author: Characterization in Narrative Poetry of George Crabbe, 1959. Trustee scholarship Cath. U., 1953-58. Finn grantee, 1962; Manhattan Coll. grantee, 1966 Mem. Phi Beta Kappa. Office: Manhattan College Acad Support Svcs Dept Bronx NY 10471

BOWERS, FREDALENE BARLETTA, education educator, consultant; b. Indiana, Pa., Oct. 2, 1948; d. Fred Matthew and Ruth Ellen (Isenberg) Barletta; m. Samuel David Bowers, Oct. 27, 1973; children: Adam Troy, Cody Alan, Justin David. BA, Indiana U. Pa., 1970, MEd, 1973; PhD, U. Pitts., 1985. Cert. Pa. Dept. of Corections Trainer; elem. guidance counselor Pa., elem./secondary sch. prin. Edn. coord., tchr. Indiana County Child Day Care Program, 1970-77; coord. spl. projects Indiana U., 1985—89, asst. prof. child development, 1992—2003, assoc. prof., 2003—; elem. guidance counselor Indiana Sch. Dist., 1990; coord. at-risk programs ARIN Intermediate Unit 28, Indiana, 1990-98. Sr. fellow Ctr. for Study of Correctional Edn., Calif. State U., San Bernardino; cons., trainer in field. Contbg. editor Resource Manual for Pregnant and Parenting Teen Programs, 1995, Best Practices for Pregnant and Parenting Teen Programs, 1999; co-editor: (jour.) Nat. Orgn. for Adolescent Parenting, Pregnancy & Prevention. Chairperson exec. com. Indiana County Human Svcs., 1990—, Children's Adv. Coun., 1996—; exec. com., 1996—; co-chairperson, 2000—; pvt. provider Pa. Student Assistance Program, 1991—; mentor IVP Mortor Bd. Nat. Honor Soc., 2002. Recipient R.O.S.E. award, 2000, 2001, IVP Grad. Deans award for Outstanding Commitment to Sponsored programs, 1999—2000. Mem. PEO (officer), Am. Assn. Family and Consumer Scis., Nat. Assn. Edn. Young Children, Pa. Sch. Counselors Assn., Phi Delta Kappa, Kappa Delta Pi. Methodist. Avocations: organ, piano. Office: Indiana U Pa Ackerman Hall Rm 207 Indiana PA 15701

BOWERS, GLENN LEE, retired professional society administrator; b. York, Pa., May 7, 1921; s. Elmer Frederick and Naomi Mae (Shellenberger) B.; m. Betty June Lehr, Apr. 21, 1943; children— Tina, Timothy BS, Pa. State U., 1946, MS, 1948. Wildlife biologist Pa. Game Commn., various locations, 1948-57, chief div. research Harrisburg, 1957-59, dep. exec. dir., 1959-65, exec. dir., 1965-82. Chmn. bd. dirs. Worldwide Furbearer Conf., Frostburg, Md., 1976-80 Contbr. articles to profl. jours. Served to capt. USMCR, 1942-45, PTO Recipient John Pearce Meml. award N.E. sect. Wildlife Soc., 1982; Nat. Wildlife Conservationist award Nat. Wildlife Fedn., 1982 Mem. Wildlife Soc., Internat. Assn. Fish and Wildlife Agys. (exec. com. 1972-80, pres. 1978-79, gen. counsel 1983-95, Seth Gordon award 1982), N.E. Assn. Fish and Wildlife Agys. (various offices, v.p., pres. 1965-82). Lodges: Masons. Republican. Methodist. Avocations: fishing; hunting. Home: 221 Mountain Rd Dillsburg PA 17019-1514

BOWERS, JEROME DAVID, II, history educator, consultant; b. Sunbury, Pa., Mar. 21, 1967; s. Jerome David Bowers and Lyn Fetter Cupp; m. Kristy Sue Wilson, Dec. 27, 1997. BA, Coll. of William and Mary, 1989; MA, Ind. U., 1994, PhD, 2002. Admissions counselor Ball State U., Muncie, Ind., 1989-90, Haverford (Pa.) Coll., 1990-92; fin. aid counselor Ind. U., Bloomington, 1992-95, vis. lectr., 1995-97; adj. prof. Oakland City U., Bedford, Ind., 1995-97; social studies tchr. Punahou Sch., Honolulu, 1997-2000; history tchr. The Madeira Sch., McLean, Va., 2000—02; asst. prof. history, coord. tchr. cert. No. Ill. U., DeKalb, 2002—. Cons. Joseph Priestly House and Mus., Northumberland, Pa., 1994-98, NEH, 1994-97; cons., adv. placement reader Coll. Bd./E.T.S., Princeton, N.J., 1998—. Sec., mem. sch. bd. St. Patrick Sch., Honolulu, 1998-2000. Democrat. Roman Catholic. Avocations: sailing, rowing/paddling, baseball/softball, skiing. Office: No Ill U Dept History Zulauf Hall Dekalb IL 60115 Home: 527 E Roosevelt St Dekalb IL 60115

BOWERS, JOHN CARL, minister, lawyer; b. L.A., Oct. 7, 1943; s. John Gordon and Georgene (Kendie) Bowers; m. Prathima Christdas, July 26, 2003. BA in Philosophy, Occidental Coll., 1965; MDiv, Union Theol. Sem., N.Y.C., 1972; DMin, Drew U, 1995; JD, Bklyn. Law Sch., 2000. Bar: N.Y. 2001, U.S. Dist. Ct. (so. and ea. dists.) N.Y. 2001; ordained to ministry Presbyn. Ch. (USA), 1973. Interim supply pastor United Presbyn. Ch. of St. Andrew, Groton, Conn., 1972-73; asst. pastor Trinity Presbyn. Ch., East Brunswick, N.J., 1973-75; pastor Ft. Schuyler Presbyn. Ch., Bronx, N.Y., 1976-85, Presbyn. Ch. in Elmont (N.Y.), 1985-92, Homecrest Presbyn. Ch., Bklyn., 1992—. Co-chair regional conf. Nat. Student Christian Fedn., Berkeley, Calif., 1965; commr. Synod of N.E., 1980-82; bd. dirs. Ft. Schuyler House, Bronx, 1981-84; mem. com. on ministry Presbytery of N.Y.C., 1980-85, 93-97, mem. permanent jud. commn., 2000—, pers. com., 2002—. Mem. sch. bd. Elmont Union Free Sch. Dist., 1988-92; treas. Stanforth Action Com., Elmont, 1987-92; chair subcom. Citizens Adv. Com., Elmont, 1987; bd. dirs. Homecrest Cmty. Svcs., 1996—, v.p., 1997—; bd. mgrs. Bklyn. Coun. Chs., 1996—; commr. 214th Gen. Assembly, 2002. Recipient Bausch and Lomb Sci. medal, 1961, cert. of appreciation Greater N.Y. coun. Girl Scouts U.S., 1985, appreciation plaque Elmont Union Free Sch. Dist., 1987, award as Ecumenical Pastor of Yr., Bklyn. Coun. Chs., 1998; Nat. Merit scholar, 1961-65; Sparer fellow in pub. interest law, 1997-2000 Mem. ABA, N.Y. State Bar Assn., Assn. of Bar of City of N.Y., So. Bklyn. Clergy Assn., Phi Delta Phi (magister 2000). Democrat. Home: 2048 E 14th St Brooklyn NY 11229-3314 Office: Homecrest Presbyn Ch 2048 E 14th St Brooklyn NY 11229-3314 E-mail: carl.bowers@verizon.net. *"Who knows? Who cares? What's the difference?"—that's what we hear, as we enter the third millenium. But that's wrong. We should know, because we can; we should care, because we are people of justice and faith; and we can make a difference—the question is: will we? The truth of our faith, the integrity of our justice, the depth of our love, will be judged by just that: whether our faith and justice and love made any difference to anyone else.*

BOWERS, KLAUS D(IETER), retired electronics research development company executive; b. Stettin, Germany, Dec. 27, 1929; s. Franz A. and Elisabeth (Schneider) B.; m. Roswitha U. Rau, June 15, 1964; children: Pamela, Colin. BA, Oxford (Eng.) U., 1950, MA, PhD, 1953. Research lectr. in physics Christ Ch., Oxford U., 1952-56; with AT&T, 1956-90; researcher Bell Telephone Labs., Murray Hill, N.J., 1956-59, mgr. electronics devel., 1959-66, Allentown, Pa., 1966-71; mng. dir., v.p. Sandia Nat. Labs., Albuquerque, 1971-75; exec. dir. Pa. Labs. Bell Telephone Labs., Allentown, 1975-79, v.p. Murray Hill, 1979-90. Bd. dirs. Semiconductor Research Corp., 1985-88, chmn., 1987-88 Contbr. sci. articles to profl. jours.; patentee in field. Trustee Cedar Crest Coll., 1983-87. Fellow IEEE (Frederik Philips award 1989); mem. Nat. Acad. Engring. Home: 2890 Golf Cir Emmaus PA 18049-1735

BOWERS, LARRY DONALD, chemistry and pathology educator; b. York, Pa., Nov. 29, 1950; s. Phares Aven and Evanna Lucille (Grass) B.; m. Janet Mary Pietruch, June 9, 1973; children: Geoffrey Mark, Kimberly Ann. BA in Chemistry, Franklin and Marshall Coll., 1972; PhD in Analytical Chemistry, U. Ga., 1975. Cert. Am. Bd. Clin. Chemistry. Prof. lab. medicine and pathology U. Minn., Mpls., 1977-92; prof. pathology and lab. medicine Ind. U. Med. Ctr., Indpls., 1992—2000, dir. athletic drug testing and toxicology lab., 1992—2000; prof. chemistry Sch. Sci. Purdue U., Indpls., 1993—2000; sr. mng. dir. U.S. Anti-Doping Agy., 2000—. Gen. chmn. 18th Internat. Symposium on Column Liquid Chromatography, Mpls., 1994. Author: Immobilized Enzymes in Analytical and Clinical Chemistry, 1980. Recipient L. S. Palmer award in Chromatography Minn. Chromatography Forum, 1985. Fellow Nat. Acad. Clin. Biochemistry; mem. Am. Assn. for Clin. Chemistry (bd. dirs. 1989-91, Outstanding Contbns. in Selected Area of Rsch. award 1990). Avocation: golf.

BOWERS, MICHAEL JOSEPH, former state attorney general; b. Jackson County, Ga., Oct. 7, 1941; s. Carl Ernest and Janie Ruth (Bolton) Bowers; m. Bette Rose Corley, June 8, 1963; children: Carl Wayne, Bruce Edward, Michelle Lisa. BS, U.S. Mil. Acad., 1963; MS, Stanford U., 1965; MBA, U. Utah-Wiesbaden, Germany, 1970; JD, U. Ga., 1974. Bar: Ga. 1974. Sr. asst. atty. gen. State of Ga., Atlanta, 1975—81, atty. gen., 1981—97, candidate for gov., 1998; of counsel Meadows, Ichter & Trigg, Atlanta. Capt. USAF, 1963—70. Mem.: ABA, Decatur-DeKalb Bar Assn., State Bar Ga., Lawyers Club, Kiwanis. Republican. Methodist. Home: 5147 Roswell Rd NE Apt 3 Atlanta GA 30342-2255 Office: Meadows Ichter & Trigg Eight Piedmont Ctr Ste 300 3525 Piedmont Rd NE Atlanta GA 30305

BOWERS, MICHAEL WAYNE, political science educator, writer; b. Santa Paula, Calif., Aug. 6, 1955; s. Vernon Bowers and Wanda Lorene Whittaker. BA in History with highest honors, Cameron U., 1977; PhD in Polit. Sci., U. Ariz., 1983. Prof. polit. sci. U. Nev., Las Vegas, 1984—, assoc. dean liberal arts, 1988-99, chairperson polit. sci., 2003—. Author: The Nevada Constitution: A Reference Guide, 1993, The Sagebrush State: Nevada's History, Government and Politics, 1996, 2nd edit., 2002; editor Nev. Hist. Soc. Quar., 2000, Nev. Pub. Affairs Rev., 1990; editl. adv. bd. U. Nev. Press. Recipient Liberty Bell award Clark County (Nev.) Bar Assn., 1989, Disting. Faculty Mem. of Yr. award Alumni Assn. U. Nev., Las Vegas, 2000Schmiedel Svc. award; grantee Am. Participants Program to Sri Lanka and India, USIA, 1988, Group Study Exch. Program to Germany, Rotary Found., 1991; rsch. fellow Nev. Humanities Com., 1987, 92. Mem. Nat. Soc. Collegiate Scholars (disting. mem.), Western Polit. Sci. Assn. (exec. coun. 1994-97), Nev. Jud. Hist. Soc. (trustee 1994—). Office: U Nev Las Vegas 4505 Maryland Pky Las Vegas NV 89154-5029 Fax: (702) 895-1065.

BOWERS, PATRICIA ELEANOR FRITZ, economist; b. N.Y.C., Mar. 21, 1928; d. Eduard and Eleanor (Ring) Fritz. Student scholar, Goucher Coll., 1946-48; BA, Cornell U., 1950; MA, NYU, 1953, PhD, 1965. Statis. asst. Fed. Res. Bank N.Y., N.Y.C., 1950-53; lectr. Upsala Coll., East Orange, N.J., 1953-59; researcher Fortune mag., N.Y.C., 1959-60; teaching fellow NYU, N.Y.C., 1960-62, instr., 1962-64; mem. faculty Bklyn. Coll., CUNY, 1964-00, prof. econs., 1974-2000, chair dept. econs., 1996-99, prof. emerita, 2000—. Author: Private Choice and Public Welfare, 1974. Sec. Friends of the Johnson Mus., Cornell U., 1989-91. Mem. Am. Econ. Assn., Econometric Soc., Met. Econ. Assn. (sec. 1963-68, pres. 1974-75), Am. Statis. Assn. (univs. chmn. ann. forecasting confs. 1970-71, 71-72), Cornell Club N.Y., Kappa Alpha Theta. Home: 145 E 16th St Apt 11-L New York NY 10003-3405

BOWERS, PATRICIA NEWSOME, communications executive; b. Baton Rouge, June 21, 1944; d. Carl Allen and Sue Mayre (Powell) Newsome; m. Robert Lloyd Bowers Jr., Aug. 19, 1967 (div. Nov. 1979); children: Paige Ivy, Katherine Elizabeth. BJ, La. State U., 1967. Sr. writer, editor Litton Industries, Pascagoula, Miss., 1978-80; sr. presentations supr. Martin Marietta Aerospace, Orlando, Fla., 1980-81, mgr. presentations Balt., 1981-85, mgr. pub. rels., 1985-90; dir. pub. rels. and corp. comm. Contraves USA, Pitts., 1990-92; sr. mgr. sector comms. Harris Electronic sys. sector Harris Corp., Melbourne, Fla., 1992-95; dir. mktg. and pub. rels. Intracoastal Health Systems, Inc., West Palm Beach, Fla., 1995-99; dir. mktg. and comms. Northside Hosp., Atlanta, 1999-2000, The Bowers Group, Inc., 2000—01; chief comms. officer Atlanta Pub. Schs., 2001—. Coach Parkville Recreation Council, Balt., 1985-87; bd. dirs. Salvation Army, Human Resources Devel. Agy. Balt. County, Brevard Symphony Youth Orch.; adv. bd. Nat. Aquarium in Balt.; active Brevard Leadership; mem. corp. bd. Boys and Girls Club of Palm Beach County; mem. Osteoporosis Leadership Coun. Atlanta. Mem. Pub. Rels. Soc. Am. (bd. dirs. Chesapeake conf. 1987, Silver Anvil Judge, 1991, 92), Healthcare Forum for Strategic Planning and Mktg. Execs., Nat. Press Club, Navy League (bd. dirs. Balt. council 1986-87), Balt. County C. of C. (leadership program 1986-87), Pitts. Press Club, Forum Club of Palm Beach. Republican. Episcopalian. Avocations: golf, reading, photography.

BOWERS, PAULA JEAN, medical/surgical nurse; b. Allendale, S.C., July 10, 1956; d. Paul Ford and Jessie (King) Bowers. Student, U. S.C., 1974-75; A in Dental Assisting, Midlands Tech. Coll., 1975-76; BS in Nursing, U. S.C., 1979-82; MSN, Tex. Woman's U., 2001. RN, Tex., S.C.; cert. med.-surg. nurse, nephrology nurse, nursing adminstr. Asst. head nurse Richland Meml. Hosp., Columbia, S.C., 1982-84; asst. head nurse Dorn Vets. Hosp., Columbia, S.C., 1984-91; unit mgr. weekends Hermann Hosp., Houston, 1992-94, unit mgr., 1994-95; head nurse VA Hosp., Biloxi, Miss., 1995-96, performance mgmt. coord., 1996-97; clin. dir. Hermann Hosp., Houston, 1997-2000; nursing dir. Meml. Hermann S.E. Hosp., Houston, 2000—. Mem. procedure com. Dorn Vets. Hosp., Columbia, 1989-91, nurse quality control, 1990-91; preceptor hemodialysis unit Dorn Vets. Hosp., Columbia, 1989-91; instr. cardiopulmonary resuscitation ARC, Columbia, 1985-91; CPR instr., Houston, 1991-97, unit guideline com., 1991-97. Contbr. articles to profl. jours. Blood pressure screening ARC, Columbia, 1985-91. Mem. AACN (pub. rels. com. mid-state chpt. 1989-90, pres.-elect 1990-91, pres. 1991-92), Sigma Theta Tau. Republican. Baptist. Home: 11526 Sage Valley Dr Houston TX 77089- Office: Meml Hermann S E Hosp 11800 Astoria Blvd Houston TX 77089-6041 E-mail: Paula_Bowers@mhhs.org., mpaulabowers@earthlink.net.

BOWERS, RAY LANDIS, editor; b. Lehighton, Pa., Sept. 28, 1927; s. Ray Landis and Ella Elizabeth (Smith) B.; m. Helen Fay McFatter, Mar. 3, 1956; children: Norman Landis, Steven Reginald. BS, U.S. Naval Acad., 1950; MA in History, U. Wis., 1960. Commd. 2nd lt. USAF, 1950, advanced through grades to col., 1977, navigator 84th bomb squadron, 1951-58; instr., assoc. prof. history USAF Acad., Colo., 1960-67; chief navigator 345th airlift squadron USAF, S.E. Asia, 1967-68, historian Office Air Force History, 1969-77; editor, publs. officer Carnegie Inst. Washington, 1977-96. Boys tennis coach Thomas Jefferson H.S. Sci. and Tech., Va., 2000—. Author: The Air Force in Southeast Asia: Tactical Airlift; 1969-77; (booklets) Mr. Carnegie's Plant Biologists, 1992, The Earth's Core, 1981, How Galaxies Rotate, 1983; contbr. articles to profl. jours, 1963-75; columnist Tennis Server, 1998—. Decorated Disting. Flying Cross USAF, Legion of Merit. Avocations: tennis, bridge. Home: Apt 1417 900 N Taylor St Arlington VA 22203

BOWERS, RICHARD PHILIP, manufacturing executive; b. Reading, Pa., July 27, 1931; s. Clarence Philip and Lottie Rose (Linkowski) B.; married; children: Richard P., Karen M., Lisa Ann, Julie L. Student, St. Bonaventure U., Olean, N.Y., 1949-51. Sales engr. Bowers Battery and Spark Plug Corp., Reading, Pa., 1952-57; v.p. sales Gen. Battery Cord, Reading, Pa., 1957-64; v.p. sales and mktg. East Penn Mfg. Co., Lyon Station, Pa., 1964-67, exec. v.p., 1967-95; also bd. dirs. E. Penn Mfg. Co., Lyon Station, Pa. Pres. TBS Systems of Ala., Birmingham, 1986—, Pioneer Auto Parts, Phila., 1980—, electro Battery Co., St. Louis; chmn. bd. Taylor Battery Co., Louisville, 1986—; chmn. bd. Power Battery Toronto, Can. Pres. Green Hills Lake Recreational Assn., Green Hills, Pa., 1984-87. Served with U.S. Army, 1962-64. Named Man of Yr., Automotive Merchandising, Chgo., 1984, 89. Mem. Battery Council Internat. (chmn. convention planning com. 1986-91), Ind. Battery Mfrs. Assn. (past pres., bd. dirs.). Democrat. Roman Catholic. Office: East Penn Mfg Co 1070 Lake View Dr Mohnton PA 19540-7965

BOWERS, ROGER PAUL, radiologist; b. Rome, N.Y., May 5, 1951; s. Paul Roger and Cassie Ann (Evans) B.; m. Denise Rae Lyon, Aug. 2, 1976; children: Leslie Ann, Rebecca Jane, Matthew Paul. SB in Math., MIT, 1973; MD, SUNY, Buffalo, 1978. Diplomate Am. Bd. Radiology, Am. Bd. Nuclear Medicine. Internship U. Mich., 1978-79; resident in radiology U. Mich. Hosps., Ann Arbor, 1979-82, chief resident nuclear medicine dept., 1981-82; radiologist Guthrie Clinic, Sayre, Pa., 1982-89, St. Elizabeth Hosp., Utica, N.Y., 1989—; chief radiologist Little Falls (N.Y.) Hosp., 1995-99. Contbr. articles to Guthrie Jour., Jour. Thoracic Cardiovascular Surgery, others, chpts. to book CRC Manual of Nuclear Medical Procedures, 1982. Trustee Athens (Pa.) Wesleyan Ch., 1986-88; chmn. fin. resource CNY Wesleyan Dist., Syracuse, N.Y., 1990—92. Mem. Am. Coll. Radiology, Soc. Nuclear Medicine, Radiol. Soc. N.Am., Soc. Magnetic Resonance in Medicine, Sigma Xi. Republican. Home: 10 Hubbardton Rd New Hartford NY 13413-2743 Office: St Elizabeth Hosp 2209 Genesee St Utica NY 13501-5999

BOWERS, TONI M. literature educator; d. Anthony Anthony G. Maffucci, Jr, and Clara Bowers Maffucci; life ptnr. Thomas McLean; 1 child, Graham. BA, Houghton (NY) Coll., 1980; AM, U. So. Calif., LA, 1985; MA, Stanford U., Calif., 1987, PhD, 1991; MA (hon.), U. Penn., Phila., 1997. Asst. prof. U. Penn., Phila., 1991—97; vis. sr. lectr. Edinburgh U., Scotland, 1999—2000; prof. U. Penn., Phila., 1997—. Am. Soc. Eng. Lit. Studies del. Am. Coun. of Learned Soc., 2002—; del. Modern Lang. Assn., NYC, 2000—; vis. fellow Ill. Program for Rsch. in the Humanities, Urbana, Ill., 2001—02; NEH fellow Newberry Libr., Chgo., 1994—95. Author: (book) Politics of Motherhood, 1996; contbr. articles to profl. jours. (Best Essay award, Eng. Lit. Hist., 1995); guest lectr. (at universities). Vol. Phila. Food Bowl Episc. Comm. Svcs., 1998—2001; vol. tutor Phila. Pub. Sch., 1995—97. Mem. AAUW, Modern Lang. Assn., Am. Soc. for 1st Lang. Studies, Anti-War Anti-Racism Network. Avocations: singing, hiking, cooking. Office: Univ of Pennsylvania Dept of English Lit Philadelphia PA 19104-6273 Home Fax: 215-573-2063. Business E-Mail: tbowers@english.upenn.edu.

BOWERS, ZELLA ZANE, real estate broker; b. May 24, 1929; Real estate broker Haley Realty Inc, Colorado Springs. Home: 128 W Rockrimmon Blvd Apt 104 Colorado Springs CO 80919-1876 Office: Haley Realty Inc 109 E Fontanero St Colorado Springs CO 80907-7494 E-mail: zane@321.net.

BOWERSOCK, GLEN WARREN, historian, educator; b. Providence, Jan. 12, 1936; s. Donald Curtis and Josephine (Evans) Bowersock. AB, Harvard U., 1957; BA, Oxford U., Eng., 1959, MA, DPhil, 1962; Dr h.c., U. Strasbourg, 1990, Ecole Pratique Hautes Etudes, Paris, 1999. Lectr. ancient history Oxford U., 1960-62, vis. lectr., 1966; instr. Harvard U., 1962-64, asst. prof., 1964-67, assoc. prof. classics, 1967-69, prof. Greek and Latin, 1969-80, chmn. dept. classics, 1972-77, assoc. dean faculty arts and scis., 1977-80; prof. hist. studies Inst. Advanced Study, Princeton, N.J., 1980—. Sr. fellow Dumbarton Oaks Ctr. for Byzantine Studies, Washington, 1984—93, Ctr. for Hellenic Studies, Washington, 1976—90; cons. Ednl. Svcs., Inc., 1964, NEH, 1971—; mem. sci. com. Scuola Normale Superiore di Pisa, Italy, Istituto di Studi Umanistici, Florence, Italy; chmn. sci. com. Maison de l'Orient Mediterraneen, Lyon, France; mem. Internat. Colloquium on the Classics in Edn., 1964—66; vis. prof. Australian Nat. U., 1972, Princeton U., 1986—87, Coll. France, 1997; Sather prof. U. Calif., Berkeley, 1991; Jerome lectr. U. Mich. and Am. Acad. in Rome, 1989; syndic Harvard U. Press, 1977—81; lectr. Thompson Lectures, Pomona, 1993, Wiles Lectures, Queens U., Belfast, Northern Ireland, 1993. Author: Augustus and the Greek World, 1965, Pseudo-Xenophon, Constitution of the Athenians, 1968, Greek Sophists in the Roman Empire, 1969, Julian the Apostate, 1978, Roman Arabia, 1983, Hellenism in Late Antiquity, 1990, Fiction as History from Nero to Julian, 1994, Studies on the Eastern Roman Empire, 1994, Martyrdom and Rome, 1995, Selected Papers on Late Antiquity, 2000; editor: Philostratus' Life of Apollonius, 1970, Approaches to the Second Sophistic, 1974; editor: (with J. Clive and S. Graubard) Edward Gibbon and the Decline and Fall of the Roman Empire, 1977; editor: (with C. P. Jones) L. Robert-Martyre de Pionios, 1994; editor: (with T. J. Cornell) Momigliano-Studies on Modern Scholarship, 1994; editor: (with P. Brown and O. Grabar) Late Antiquity-A Guide to the Postclassical World, 1999; mem. editl. bd.: Arabian Archaeology and Epigraphy, Ancient Civilizations from Scythia to Siberia (Russian Acad. Scis.), Berytus, Am. Jour. Philology, 1987—95, Am. Scholar, 1981—93; editor (gen.): Revealing Antiquity. Trustee Am. Schs. Oriental Rsch., 1984—90; bd. dirs. Met. Opera Guild; adv. dir. Met. Opera Assn.; mem. nat. coun. Glimmerglass Opera. Recipient James H. Breasted prize, Am. Hist. Assn., 1992; Rhodes scholar, 1957—60. Fellow: Acad. Nat. dei Lincei, Am. Numis. Soc. (coun. 1983—96), Am. Acad. Arts and Scis.; mem.: Accad. Nazionale dei Lincei, Soc. Straniero, Acad. des Inscriptions et Belles-Lettres, German Archaeol. Inst. (corr.), Russian Acad. Scis. (fgn.), Soc. Promotion Roman and Hellenic Studies (hon. Am. sec. Roman Soc.), Leschetizky Assn. Am., Am. Philol. Assn., Am. Philos. Soc. (coun. 1992—98), Johnsonians, Century Club (N.Y.C.), Knickerbocker Club (N.Y.C.), Phi Beta Kappa. Office: Inst Advanced Study Sch Hist Studies Princeton NJ 08540

BOWERSOX, KENNETH D. astronaut; b. Portsmouth, Va., Nov. 14, 1956; BS in Aerospace Engring., U.S. Naval Acad., 1978; MS in Mech. Engring., Columbia U., 1979. Commd. ensign USN, 1978, advanced through grades to capt.; fleet A-7E pilot USS Enterprise; test pilot Naval Weapon Ctr., China Lake, Calif.; astronaut NASA, 1987—, flight software testing Shuttle Avionics Integration Lab., tech. asst. to dir. flight crew ops., Astronaut Office rep. for Orbiter landing and rollout issues, chief Astronaut Office Safety Br., chmn. Spaceflight Safety Panel. Achievements include 4 space flights; logged 50 days in space; pilot STS-50 Columbia (1992) and STS-61 (1993); spacecraft comdr. STS-73 (1995) and STS-82 (1997), Expedition-6 crew. Office: Astronaut Office/CB NASA Johnson Space Ctr Houston TX 77058

BOWERSOX, THOMAS H. lawyer; b. Beatrice, Nebr., May 1, 1941; s. William H. Bowersox and Fairy (Casey) Huff; m. Barbara Mathieson, Aug. 23, 1963; children: William T., Christopher T., Elizabeth A. BBA, U. Houston 1965, JD, 1969. Bar: U.S. Dist. Ct. (so. and ea. dists.) Tex., U.S. Ct. Appeals (5th and 11th cirs.). Instr. South Tex. Jr. Coll., Houston, 1967-72; assoc. prof. Sam Houston State U., Huntsville, 1972-74; assoc. Baker & Botts, Houston, 1975-76; from assoc. gen counsel to pres. subs. co. Zapata Corp., Houston, 1976-93, exec. v.p., 1993-94; ptnr. Bowersox, Herron & Williamson, Houston, 1996-98; of counsel Hope & Causey, Conroe, Tex., 1998—. Adv. com. energy trade policy, U.S. trade rep. industry sector Dept. of Commerce, 1989-93. Bd. dirs. Offhore Energy Ctr., Houston, 1988-92, mem. adv. bd. 1992-98; mem. adv. com. Sam Houston State U. Coll. Bus., 1985—. Mem. Internat. Assn. Drilling Contractors (vice chmn. contracts and risk mgmt. com. 1984-85, chmn. govt. affairs com. 1986-87, v.p. Tex. gulf coast 1989, v.p. offshore 1990-91, chmn., bd. dirs., 1992), Am. Bureau of Shipping. Avocations: golf, camping, reading. Office: Hope & Causey PO Box 3188 Conroe TX 77305-3188 Fax: 936-441-4674. E-mail: thbowersox@earthlink.net.

BOWERY, WARREN E. music educator; b. Wheeling, W. Va., May 11, 1959; s. Warren E. and Gertrude (Gross) B.; m. Susan C. Waybright, Aug. 10, 1985. BA with hons., West Liberty State Coll., 1981. Substitute tchr. Marshall County Schs., Moundsville, W.Va., 1982-84; band, choir and music tchr. Ottoville (Ohio) Local Schs., 1985—. Com. mem. Putnam County Music Edn. Com., Ottawa, Ohio, 1986, 91, 96, 2001. Composer (musical theater): The Bloody Bridge, 1994, You Can't Get There From Here!, 1995. Mem. Music Educator's Nat. Conf., Ohio Music Edn. Assn., Ohio Edn. Assn. (Outstanding Treas. award 1995), Ottoville Local Edn. Assn. (treas. 1989-90, 2002—). Lutheran. Avocations: pub. svc. monitoring, musician, All-Ohio Scanner Club, target shooting. Office: Ottoville HS PO Box 248 Ottoville OH 45876-0248

BOWES, ARLENE DANNENBERG, dentist; b. Phila., Aug. 8, 1950; d. Arthur Milton Jr. and Aileen (Hart) Dannenberg; m. Stephen Mallory Bowes III, Apr. 21, 1979; 2 children. AB, Swarthmore (Pa.) Coll., 1972; DMD, U. Pa., 1977. Pvt. practice, 1979—, 1991—, 1991—. Clin. instr. U. Pa. Sch. Dental Medicine, 1994—. EMT, 1993—; hist. dist. treas. Lutherville Community Assn., 1986-91; zoning chmn., 1989-91. Lt. USPHS, 1977-79. Home: 7917 Clifton Hunt Ct Clifton VA 20124-

BOWES, FREDERICK, III, publishing executive, consultant; b. Norwalk, Conn., Dec. 20, 1941; s. Frederick Jr. and Mary Priscilla (Herron) B.; m. Margaret Anne Hathaway, Sept. 17, 1966; children: Heather Hathaway Ezzy, Catherine Herron. AB, Dartmouth Coll., 1963; MBA, Columbia U., 1965. Fin. staff Perkin-Elmer Corp., Norwalk, Conn., 1965-70; v.p. ops. and fin. South Shore Pub. Co., North Scituate, Mass., 1970-77; cons. Graphics Mgmt., Inc., Duxbury, Mass., 1977-79; pres. Info-Graphics Inc., Braintree, Mass., 1979-80; v.p. pub. New Eng. Jour. Medicine, Mass. Med. Soc., Waltham, Mass., 1981-90; pres. Macmillan New Media, Cambridge, Mass., 1990-94, Cadmus Digital Solutions, 1995-96; pres., CEO Bowes & Assocs., Inc. dba Publist.com, 1996-2000; cons. Electronic Pub. Assocs., 2000—. Dir. Ctr. for Applied Spl. Tech. CAST, Peabody, Mass., 1999—2000. Sr. warden Parish of St. John the Evangelist, Duxbury, 1981-84; trustee, treas. Soc. St. Margaret, Boston, 1984—; trustee Mass. Bible Soc., Boston, 1983-88. Mem. Soc. Scholarly Pub. (pres. 1998), Am. Assn. Pub. Episcopalian. Avocations: Christian svc., ornithology.

BOWES, HENRY EDWARD, retired communications executive; b. Merchantville, N.J., Sept. 7, 1915; s. Henry Joseph and Evaline Sarah (Humphreys) B.; m. Lauretta Helen Schultz, July 17, 1965; children by previous marriage: Henry, Shirley. Grad., Valley Forge Mil. Acad., 1932; student, U.S. Naval Acad., 1934-35; DBA (hon.), North Cen. Coll. With Philco Corp., 1936-62, gen. mgr. home radio div., 1955-56, v.p., gen. mgr. TV div., 1956-58, v.p. mktg., 1958-61; v.p., dir. mktg. for N.Am., dir. govt. rels. ITT, 1962-64, v.p. indsl. mktg. worldwide, 1964-66, dir. sales and distbn. ITT System, 1966-67, sr. v.p., 1967; pres., chief exec. officer McCall Corp., 1967-68; exec. v.p. Bell & Howell Co., 1969, pres., chief oper. officer, 1970-73, also bd. dirs. Chmn. exec. com. Docutel Corp.; bd. dirs. Beloit Mfg. Co., No. Telecom Corp., Embosograph Corp., Ngrton Simon, Inc. Served from 2d lt. to col. USAAF, World War II. Decorated Legion of Merit; recipient Disting. Alumni award Valley Forge Mil. Acad. Mem. Valley Forge Mil. Acad. Alumni Assn. (past chmn. bd.), Lost Tree Club (North Palm Beach, Fla.). Republican. Episcopalian.

BOWIE, APRIL DENE'T, lawyer, arbitrator; b. Bronx, N.Y., May 09; d. A. D. and S. T. Bowie; m. K. B. Mena; 1 child, A Bowie Mena. BA, NYU, 1989; JD, Nova Southea. U., 1992; postgrad., Fordham U. Law Sch., 1992. Bar: Fla. 1997, D.C. 1998, U.S. Dist. Ct. (so. dist.) Fla. 1998, U.S. Dist. Ct. (so. and ea. dists.) NY 2002, NY 2002. Intern Hon. Cornelius Blackshear U.S. Bankruptcy Ct. (so. dist.), N.Y.C., 1992; rsch. asst. Justice George Bundy Smith Ct. of Appeals of N.Y., N.Y.C., 1994—95; atty. The Brown Law Group, P.A., Miami, Fla., 1996—2001; mng. atty. The Bowie Law Ctr., P.A., Ft. Lauderdale, Fla., 2000—02; atty. The Brown Law Group, N.Y.C., 2003—. Adj. prof. Fla. Meml. Coll., Miami, Fla., 1998—2000; arbitrator Nat. Assn. Securities Dealers, N.Y.C., 2001—; asst. prof. Mercy Coll., White Plains, NY, 2003—. Mem.: Westchester Bar Assn. (assoc.), N.Y. State Bar Assn. (assoc.), Am. Inns of Ct. (assoc.). Avocations: dancing, singing, travel, reading, sports. Office: The Bowie Law Ctr PA PO Box 407 Hartsdale NY 10530 E-mail: bowiemenalaw@yahoo.com.

BOWIE, DARREN A. legal adviser; b. Washington, D.C., Sept. 30, 1967; s. Warren A. and Jeanne Robey Bowie. BA, Coll. of William and Mary, 1989; JD, U. Pa., 1992. Staff atty. FTC, Washington, 1992—2000, asst. dir., 2000—01, legal adviser to chmn., 2001—. Bd. dirs. Dupont Cir. Citizens Assn., Washington, 2000—. Mem.: ABA, D.C. Bar Assn., Phi Beta Kappa. Home: #4 1529 Q St NW Washington DC 20009 Office: FTC 600 Pennsylvania Ave NW Washington DC 20580

BOWIE, E(DWARD) J(OHN) WALTER, hematologist, researcher; b. Church Stretton, Shropshire, Eng., Mar. 10, 1925; came to U.S., 1958; s. Edgar Ormond and Ann Brown (Lorrimer) B.; m. Gertrud Susi Ulrich, Dec. 22, 1948; children— Katherine Ann, Christopher John, John Walter, James Ulrich MA, Oxford (Eng.) U., 1950, BM, BCh, 1952, DM, 1981; MS, U. Minn., 1961. House physician Univ. Coll. Hosp., London, 1953; sr. house officer Bethlem Royal and Maudsley Hosps., London, 1953-54; pvt. practice medicine Treherne, Man., Can., 1954; fellow in medicine Mayo Clinic, Rochester, Minn., 1958-60, cons. in internal medicine and hematology, 1961-90, head sect. hematology research, 1971-89; prof. medicine and lab. medicine Mayo Med. Sch., Rochester, Minn., 1974-90, prof. emeritus, 1990-96, ret., 1996. Invited spkr. Gordon Confs., 1973, 76, 78, Royal Soc., London, 1980; chmn. thrombosis coun. Internat. Soc. and Fedn. Cardiology, 1991; internat. dir. Thrombosis Vascular Tng. Ctrs. Co-author 6 books; assoc. editor Jour. Lab. and Clin. Medicine, 1976-80; contbr. chpts. to books, numerous articles to profl. jours. Recipient Judson Daland travel award Mayo Found., 1963, named Disting. Investigator, 1988, Disting. Alumnus Mayo Found., 1996. Fellow ACP, AMA, Royal Coll. Pathology; mem. AAAS, Am. Heart Assn. Internat. Soc. on Thrombosis and Haemostasis (v.p. 1980-81, Disting. Career award 1991), Am. Soc. Hematology, Internat. Com. on Thrombosis and Haemostasis (chmn. 1989-90), Ctrl. Soc. for Clin. Rsch., Am. Fedn. for Clin. Rsch., World Fedn. Haemophilia. Office: Emeritus Section Mayo Clinic Rochester MN 55905

BOWIE, NORMAN ERNEST, university official, educator; b. Biddeford, Maine, June 6, 1942; s. Lawrence Walker and Helen Elizabeth (Jacobsen) B.; m. Bonnie Jean Bankert, June 11, 1966 (div. 1980); children: Brian Paul, Peter Mark; m. Maureen Burns, Sept. 19, 1987. AB, Bates Coll., 1964; PhD, U. Rochester, 1968. Mem. faculty Lycoming Coll., Williamsport, Pa., 1968-69; asst. prof. philosophy Hamilton Coll., Clinton, N.Y., 1969-74, assoc. prof., 1974-75, U. Del., Newark, 1975-80, prof., 1980-89, dir. Ctr. for Study of Values, 1977-89; Elmer L. Andersen chairperson corp. responsibility U. Minn., Mpls., 1989—, chair dept. strategic mgmt. and orgn., 1992-95; fellow in ethics and professions Harvard U., 1996-97; Dixons prof. bus. ethics and social responsibility London Bus. Sch., 1999-2000. Lynette S. Autrey vis. prof. bus. ethics Rice U., spring 1986; vis. prof. Sch. Mgmt. U. Scranton, 1986-87, Sch. Bus. Adminstrn., Georgetown U., 1988-89; exec. v.p. seminars The Aspen Inst., 1998-99. Author: Towards a New Theory of Distributive Justice, 1971, Business Ethics, 1982, (with Ronald Duska) 2nd edit., 1990, Making Ethical Decisions, 1985, University Business Partnerships: An Assessment, 1994, Business Ethics: A Kantian Perspective, 1999; co-author: The Individual and the Political Order, 1977, 3d edit., 1998; editor: Ethical Issues in Government, 1981, Ethical Theory in the Last Quarter of the Twentieth Century, 1983, Equal Opportunity, 1988; co-editor: Ethical Theory and Business, 1979, 7th edit., 2003, Ethics, Public Policy and Criminal Justice, 1982, The Tradition of Philosophy, 1986, Ethics and Agency Theory, 1992, Guide to Business Ethics, 2001; co-editor Bus. and Profl. Ethics Jour., 1981-88. Mem. N.Y. Coun. for Humanities, 1974-75. NDEA fellow, 1965-68 Mem. AAUP, Acad. Mgmt., Am. Philos. Assn. (nat. exec. sec. 1972-77), Am. Soc. for Value Inquiry (pres. 1980-81), Am. Soc. Polit. and Legal Philosophy, Soc. Bus. Ethics (pres. 1988), Phi Beta Kappa. Home: PO Box 508 Trappe MD 21673-0508 Office: Carlson Sch Mgmt 321 19th Ave S Minneapolis MN 55455-0438

BOWIE, PETER WENTWORTH, judge, educator; b. Alexandria, Va., Sept. 27, 1942; s. Beverley Munford and Louise Wentworth (Boynton) B.; m. Sarah Virginia Haught, Mar. 25, 1967; children: Heather, Gavin. BA, Wake Forest Coll., 1964; JD magna cum laude, U. San Diego, 1971. Bar: Calif. 1972, D.C. 1972, U.S. Dist. Ct. D.C. 1972, U.S. Dist. Ct. Md. 1973, U.S. Dist. Ct. (so. dist.) Calif. 1974, U.S. Ct. Appeals (D.C. cir.) 1972, U.S. Ct. Appeals (9th cir.) 1974, U.S. Supreme Ct. 1980. Trial atty. honors program Dept. of Justice, Washington, 1971-74; asst. U.S. Atty. U.S. Atty.'s Office, San Diego, 1974, asst. chief civil div., 1974-82, chief asst. U.S. atty., 1982-88; lawyer rep. U.S. Ct. Appeals (9th cir.) Jud. Conf., 1977-78, 84-87; judge U.S. Bankruptcy Ct., San Diego, 1988—. Lectr. at law Calif. Western Sch. Law, 1979-83; exec. com. mem. 9th Cir. Judicial Conf., 1991-94; mem. com. on codes of conduct Jud. Conf. of U.S., 1995—. Bd. dirs. Presidio Little League, San Diego, 1984, coach, 1983-84; mem. alumni adv. bd. Sch. Law U. San Diego, 1998-2002. Lt. USN, 1964-68, Vietnam. Mem. State Bar Calif. (hearing referee ct. 1982-86, mem. rev. dept. 1986-90), Fed. Bar Assn. (pres. San diego chpt. 1981-83), San Diego County Bar Assn. (chmn. fed. ct. com. 1978-80, 83-85), Assn. Bus. Trial Lawyers (bd. govs.), San Diego Bankruptcy Forum (bd. dirs.), Phi Delta Phi. Republican. Mem. Unitarian Ch. Office: US Bankruptcy Court 325 W F St San Diego CA 92101-6017

BOWKER, ALBERT HOSMER, retired university chancellor; b. Winchendon, Mass., Sept. 8, 1919; s. Roy C. and Kathleen (Hosmer) B.; m. Elizabeth Rempfer, June 14, 1942; children: Paul Albert, Nancy Kathleen, Caroline Anne; m. Rosedith Sitgreaves, Sept. 26, 1964. BS, Mass. Inst. Tech., 1941; PhD, Columbia U., 1949; D.H.L., City U. N.Y., 1971; LL.D., Brandeis U.; D.H.L., N.Y. Bd. Regents, 1972. Asst. statistician Mass. Inst. Tech., 1941-43; asst. dir. statis. research group Columbia, 1943-45; asst. prof. statistics Stanford, 1947-50, assoc. prof., 1950-53, exec. head statistics dept., 1948-59, dean grad. div., 1959-63, prof. math. and statistics, 1953-63, dir. applied math. and statistics labs., 1951-63; chancellor City U. N.Y., 1963-71, U. Calif., Berkeley, 1971-80, chancellor emeritus, 1980—; asst. sec. for postsecondary edn. Dept. Edn., Washington, 1980-81; dean Sch. Pub. Affairs U. Md., 1981-84, exec. v.p. univ., 1984-86; v.p. research found. CUNY, 1986—. Mem. com. grad. edn. Am. Assn. Univs.; mem. Sloan Commn. on Govt. and Higher Edn.; mem. exec. com. div. math. Nat. Acad. Scis.-NRC, 1963-65 Author: (with Henry P. Goode) Sampling Inspection by Variables, 1952, (with Gerald J. Lieberman) Handbook of Industrial Statistics, 1955, Engineering Statistics, 1972; also articles profl. jours.; Asso. editor: Jour. Am. Statis. Assn, 1949-52. Mem. Corp. Mass. Inst. Tech., 1967-72; mem. Centennial Commn. Howard U., 1965; bd. dirs. San Francisco Bay Area Council, 1972-77; trustee Bennington Coll., U. Haifa. Fellow Am. Statis. Assn. (pres. 1964), Am. Soc. Quality Control, Inst. Math. Statistics (pres 1961-62), AAAS; mem. Math. Assn. Am., Biometric Soc., Operations Research Soc. Am., Soc. for Indsl. and Applied Math., Am. Assn. Univs. (com. grad. edn.), Phi Beta Kappa (hon.), Sigma Xi (exec. com. 1963-66) Office: U Calif Dept Stats 367 Evans Hall Spc 3860 Berkeley CA 94720-3860 E-mail: bowker@stat.berkeley.edu.

BOWKER, LEE HARRINGTON, sociologist, educator, writer; b. Bethlehem, Pa., Dec. 19, 1940; s. Maurice H. Bowker and Blanche E. Heffner; m. Nancy Bachant, 1966 (div. 1973); 1 child, Kirsten Ruth; m. Dee C. Thomas, May 25, 1975; children: Jessica Lynn, Gwendolyn Alice. BA, Muhlenberg Coll., 1962; MA, U. Pa., 1965; PhD, Wash. State U., 1972. Instr. in Sociology Lebanon Valley Coll., Annville, Pa., 1965-66, Allbright Coll., Reading, Pa., 1966-67; assoc. prof. Whitman Coll., Walla Walla, Wash., 1967-77; prof., assoc. dean U. Wis., Milw., 1977-82; dean grad. sch. and research Ind. (Pa.) U. of Pa., 1982-85; provost, v.p. Augustana Coll., Sioux Falls, S.D., 1985-87; dean behavioral and social scis. Humboldt State U., Arcata, Calif., 1987-97, emeritus dean, prof. sociology, 1997—. Cons. various pubs., colls., univs. and state agys; expert witness. Author: Prison Victimization, 1980, Humanizing Institutions for the Aged, 1982, Masculinities and Violence, 1997, The Role of the Department Chair, revised edit., 1997, Ending the Violence, rev. edit., 1998; assoc. editor Pacific Sociol. Rev., 1975-78, Justice Quar., 1983-85, Criminal Justice Policy Rev., 1984-95; contbr. articles to profl. jours. Pres. Blue Mountain Action Coun., OEO, Walla Walla, 1969-71; dir. social therapy program, Wash. State penitentiary, Walla Walla, 1971-73; bd. dirs. Milw. Bur. Community Corrections, 1979-81, Sioux Falls Symphony, 1985, United Way of Humboldt County, 1988-91. Grantee NIMH 1973, 79, 81, Washington Arts Commn. 1972, Washington Office Community Devel. 1974, Fulbright Found. 1985, Nat. Retired Tchrs. Assn./Am. Assn. Retired Persons Andrus Found. 1980; Law Enforcement Assistance Adminstrn. co-grantee, 1978. Mem.: Am. Soc. Criminology, Am. Sociol. Assn., Pacific Sociol. Assn. Home: 3513 H St Eureka CA 95503-5358 Office: Humboldt State U Sociology Faculty Arcata CA 95521 E-mail: lhb3@humboldt.edu.

BOWKER, MARGARET SHEARD, artist; b. Dordrecht, South Africa, Oct. 31, 1938; BA, Rhodes U., Grahamstown, S. Africa, 1960. Tchr. Cape Edn. Dept., E. London, 1961—64, Natal Edn. Dept., Durban, 1965—97. Office: Margie Bowker Art 429 Monterey Rd Santa Maria CA 93055

BOWKER, NANCY ANNE, writer, bookseller; b. Riverside, N.J., May 27, 1956; d. James Sinclair and Marianne Bernice Souder; m. Russell Bowker Jr., May 12, 1979; 1 child, Jessica. Degree in journalism, Burlington County Coll., 1989. Bookseller Barnes & Noble, Moorestown, N.J., 1999—; freelance writer Burlington County Times, Willingboro, N.J., 1986-90. Workshop leader Phila. Writers Conf., Phila., 2000; presenter Assn. Univ. Women, Medford, N.J., 1998. Author: John Rarey: Horse Tamer, 1996; co-author: The Wild Horse: An Adopter's Manual, 1992; contbr. articles to profl. jours. Vol. handicapped riding program Double R Spl. Riders, Berlin, N.J., 1984-91. Recipient Lit. award Burlington County Cultural and Heritage Assn., 1997. Mem. Am. Mustang and Burro Assn., Soc. Children's Book Writers and Illustrators, Civil War Preservation Trust, Ulysses S. Grant Network. Avocations: horses, films, civil war re-enactments, art museums. Home: 1441 Monmouth Rd Eastampton Township NJ 08060

BOWLBY, LEYMOND AMBROSE, linguist, translator; b. Oklahoma City, June 5, 1922; s. Leymond Leroy and Victoria Maria (Bradshaw) B.; m. Eunice Jacquelyn Kelley, Apr. 17, 1949 (div. June 1958); children: Linda Ley, Victoria Lynn. BA in Journalism/Edn., Oklahoma City U., 1950; MEd, Okla. U., 1960; PhD in Applied Linguistics, Pacific Western U., L.A., 1986. Cert. tchr., Conn.; cert. tchr., media specialist, Okla. Tchr. Mansfield (Conn.) Ctr. Pub. Schs., 1950-51, Oklahoma City Pub. Schs., 1952-57, audio-visual film libr., 1957-61, instrnl. media cons., 1963-74; grad. asst. Okla. U., Norman, 1961-62; owner, operator nursery Trees 'n Things, Tuttle, Okla., 1975-87; ind. lang. translator Tuttle, 1987—. Author: Audio-Visual: A Manual for Teachers, 1965; photo illustrator: Social Studies for Today's Children, 1964; text contbr. various pamphlets, 1961-73; translator: Disorder and Early Sorrow, 1988, historic German essays for Am. poultry archives. Sgt. ETO U.S. Army, 1942—45. Decorated French Liberation medal. Mem. Nat. Coalition Ind. Scholars (assoc.), Am. Lit. Translators Assn., Nat. Assn. Scholars; mem. Okla. State Retired Tchrs. Assn., Soc. for Preservation Poultry Antiquities, Normandy Vets. Assn. of Gt. Britain (life), Phi Delta Kappa (local v.p.). Republican. Roman Catholic. Avocations: genealogy, mycology, horticulture, arboriculture, culinary arts. Home and Office: 7501 W Britton Rd #105 Oklahoma City OK 73132-1603

BOWLBY, RICHARD ERIC, retired computer systems analyst; b. Detroit, Aug. 17, 1939; s. Garner Milton and Florence Marie (Russell) B.; m. Gwendoline Joyce Coldwell, Apr. 29, 1967. BA, Wayne State U., 1962. With Ford Motor Co., Detroit, 1962-65, 66-94; computer sys. analyst; ret., 1994. Pres. 1300 Lafayette East-Coop., Inc., 1981-82. Mem. Antiquaries, Friends Detroit Pub. Libr., Detroit Symphony Orch. Vol. Coun., Founders Soc. Club (Detroit).

BOWLDEN, HENRY JAMES, computer science consultant; b. Hamilton, Ont., Can., Apr. 5, 1925; came to U.S. 1946; s. James Henry and Lilian (Callaghan) B.; m. Agnes Rebecca Stringer, Aug. 25, 1948; children: Sara Anne, Peter. BS in Math. and Physics, McMaster U., Hamilton, 1946; MS in Physics, U. Ill., 1947, PhD in Physics, 1951. Asst. prof./assoc. prof. Wayne State U., Detroit, 1950-57; rsch. physicist Union Carbide Corp., Parma, Ohio, 1957-63; adv. scientist Westinghouse Sci. and Tech. Ctr., Pitts., 1963-90, tech. activity area leader, 1981-90; cons. scientist Intelligent Integrated Systems, Monroeville, Pa., 1990—. Cons. physicist U.S. Naval Rsch. Labs., Washington, 1956-61; chmn. Westinghouse R&D Senate, Pitts., 1977-78. Contbr. articles to profl. jours. Mem. ACM, Am. Def. Preparedness Assn., Internat. Fedn. for Info. Processing (sec. ALGOL working group 1970-75), Am. Assn. for Artificial Intelligence, Coop. Users of Burroughs Equip. (chmn. 1963-70). Avocation: organ playing. Home and Office: 1156 Bucknell Dr Monroeville PA 15146-4320

BOWLEN, PAT(RICK)(DENNIS), professional sports team executive, holding company executive, lawyer; b. Prairie du Chien, Wis., Feb. 18, 1944; s. Paul Dennis and Arvella (Woods) B. BBA, U. Okla., 1966, JD, 1968. Bar: Alta. 1969. Read law Saucier, Jones, Calgary, Alta., Can., assoc., 1969-70; asst. to pres. Regent Drilling Ltd., 1970-71; pres. Batoni-Bowlen Enterprises Ltd., 1971-79, Bowlen Holdings Ltd., Edmonton, Alta., Can., 1979—; pres., chief exec. officer, owner Denver Broncos, 1984—. Mem. Law Soc. Alta., Can. Bar Assn., Young Presidents Orgn., Edmonton Club Roman Catholic. Avocations: golf, skiing, surfing. Office: Denver Broncos 13655 Broncos Pkwy Englewood CO 80112-4150

BOWLER, MARIANNE BIANCA, judge; b. Boston, Feb. 15, 1947; d. Richard A. and Ann C. (Daly) B. BA, Regis Coll., 1967; JD cum laude, Suffolk U., 1976, LLD (hon.), 1994; LD (hon.), Regis Coll., 2003. Bar: Mass. 1978. Rsch. asst. Harvard Med. Sch., Boston, 1967-69; med. editor Mass. Dept. of Pub. Health, Boston, 1969-76; law clk. Mass. Superior Ct., Boston, 1976-77, dep. chief law clk., 1977-78; asst. dist. atty. Middlesex Dist. Atty.'s Office, Cambridge, Mass., 1978; asst. U.S. atty. U.S. Dept. of Justice, Boston, 1978-90, exec. asst. U.S. atty., 1988-89, sr. litigation counsel, 1989-90; magistrate judge U.S. Dist. Ct. Mass., Boston, 1990—2002, chief U.S. magistrate judge, 2002—. Chmn. bd. trustees New England Bapt. Hosp., Boston, 1990-95. Trustee Suffolk U., Boston, 1994—, Discovering Justice, 2003—; bd. dirs. The Boston Found., 1995—; dir. South Cove Nursing Facilities Found., Inc., 1995—; co-pres. Boston Coll. Inn of Ct., 1998—; bd. dirs. Discovering Justice, 2003-. Mem. Jr. League Boston, Suffolk Law Sch. Alumni Assn. (pres. 1979-80), Vincent Club, Isabel O'Neil Found., Save Venice. Democrat. Roman Catholic. Avocations: faux finishing, trompe l'oeil painting. Office: 1 Courthouse Way Ste 8420 Boston MA 02210-3010

BOWLES, BARBARA LANDERS, investment company executive; b. Nashville, Sept. 17, 1947, d. Corris Raemone Landers and Rebecca (Bonham) Jennings; m. Earl Stanley Bowles, Nov. 27, 1971; 1 son, Terrence Earl. BA, Fisk U., 1968; MBA, U. Chgo., 1971. Chartered fin. analyst. From bank official to v.p. First Nat. Bank of Chgo., 1968-81; asst. v.p. Beatrice Cos., Chgo., 1981-84, v.p. investor rels. Kraft Inc., Chgo., 1984-86; pres., founder The Kenwood Group Inc., Chgo., 1989—. Bd. dirs. Black & Decker Corp., Hyde Pk. Bank. Bd. dirs. Children's Meml. Hosp., Ga. Pacific Corp. and Dollar Gen. Corp. The Chgo. Urban League. Scholar United Negro College Fund, 1989. Mem. NAACP (life), Assn. for Investment Mgmt. and Rsch., Chgo. Fisk trustee(1998-), University (Chgo.). Mem. United Ch. of Christ. Avocations: tennis, bridge. E-mail: kenwoodg@aol.com.

BOWLES, CRANDALL CLOSE, textiles executive; m. Erskine Bowles. B in Econ., Wellesley Coll.; MBA, Columbia U. Fin. analyst Springs Industries, Inc., 1973—78, exec. v.p. growth and devel., 1992, exec. v.p. textile prodn., 1993, pres. bath fashions group, 1995, pres., COO, 1997—98, CEO, chmn., 1998—; exec. v.p. Springs Co., 1978—82, pres., 1982; also bd. dirs. Bd. dirs. Deere & Co. Bd. trustees African Wildlife Found.; bd. dirs. Juvenile Diabetes Rsch. Found., Charlotte Inst. for Tech. Innovation. Mem.: Palmetto Bus. Forum, Bus. Roundtable, Bus. Coun., Am. Textile Mfrs. Inst., Excellence in Edn. Coun. Office: 205 N White St Fort Mill SC 29715-1654

BOWLES, DAVID STANLEY, engineering educator, engineering consultant; b. Romford, Essex, Eng., June 30, 1949; m. Valerie Rosina Curd; children: Penny, Simon, Amy. BSc, City U., Eng., 1972; PhD, Utah State U., 1977. Registered profl. engr., Utah; cert. profl. hydrologist. Jr. civil engr. George Wimpey & Co., Hammersmith, London, 1967-72; rsch. asst. prof. Utah State U., Logan, 1976-80, rsch. assoc. prof., 1980-81, adj. rsch. assoc. prof., 1981-83, rsch. prof., 1983-85, prof., 1985—, assoc. dir., 1986-91, dir., 1992-96. Vis. scientist Internat. Inst. Applied Systems Analysis, Laxenburg, Austria, 1979; br. mgr., engr. Law Engring., Denver, 1981-83; prin. Risk Assessment Cons. Engrs. and Economists (RAC), 1986—; mem. Australian Com. on Large Dams. Contbr. numerous articles to profl. jours. Bd. dirs. U.S. Soc. on Dams. Fellow ASCE, Am. Water Resources Assn.; mem. Soc. Risk Analysis, Am. Geophys. Union, Am. Inst. Hydrology, Assn. State Dam Safety Ofcls. Home: 1520 Canyon Rd Providence UT 84332-9431 Office: Utah Water Rsch Lab Utah State Univ Logan UT 84322-8200 E-mail: bowles@cache.net.

BOWLES, ERSKINE, White House staff member; b. 1945; s. Hargrove "Skipper" Bowles; m. Crandall Bowles; 3 children. With Morgan Stanley & Co., N.Y.C., Bowles Hollowell Conner & Co., Charlotte, N.C., 1975-93; adminstr. Small Bus. Adminstrn., Washington, 1993-94; from dep. chief of staff to chief of staff The White House, Washington, 1994-98; ptnr. Forstmann Little & Co., N.Y.C., 1999—. Pres. Juvenile Diabetes Found. Office: Forstmann Little & Co 767 5th Ave Ste 4402 New York NY 10153-4499

BOWLES, L. THOMPSON, retired medical association administrator; b. Mineola, N.Y., Sept. 23, 1931; m. Judith E. Bowles, July 10, 1965; children: Julia, Amy, Lauren. AB, Duke U., 1953, MD, 1957; MS, NYU, 1964, PhD, 1971. Intern 4th surgery divsn. Bellevue Hosp., N.Y.C., 1957; acad. dean George Washington U. Med. Ctr., Washington, 1975—87, v.p., exec. dean, 1987—92; pres. Nat. Bd. Med. Examiners, Phila., 1992—2000; ret., 2000. Pres. Med. Licensing Bd., Washington, 1977—79. Founding editor: AAMC Curriculum Directory, 1973. Recipient Disting. Svc. award, D.C. Med. Soc., 1981. Fellow: ACS, Am. Assn. for Thoracic Surgeons, Soc. Thoracic Surgeons; mem.: Alpha Omega Alpha.

BOWLES, LIZA K. construction executive; Pres. NAHB Rsch. Ctr., Upper Marlboro, Md., 1991—. Office: NAHB Rsch Ctr 400 Prince Georges Blvd Upper Marlboro MD 20774-8759 E-mail: lbowles@nahbrc.org.

BOWLES, MARGO LA JOY, lawyer; b. Stillwater, Okla., Jan. 26, 1949; d. Joseph Worth and Vivian Alice (Sears) B.; m. Francis E. Jones Jr., Dec. 22, 1987. BS, Okla State U., 1971; JD, U. Tulsa, 1983. Bar: Okla. 1985, U.S. Dist. Ct. (no. dist.) Okla. Sole practice, Tulsa, 1985—. Instr. U. Ctr. Tulsa, Langston U., 1988-90, Northeastern State U., 1992—. Precinct officer Tulsa Dem. Party, 1987. Mem. ABA, Okla. Bar Assn., Tulsa County Bar Assn. (pres. solo practice/small firm sect. 1993-94). Methodist. Avocation: travel. Office: 1821 E 71st St Ste 200 Tulsa OK 74136 Fax: 918-491-2055. E-mail: mbowlesattorney@aol.com.

BOWLES, NEWTON ROWELL, United Nations executive; b. Chengdu, Szechuan, China, Dec. 4, 1916; Canadian citizen. s. Newton Ernest and Muriel Olive (Wood) B.; m. Augusta Davis, Mar. 29, 1946 (div. July 1969); m. Jean Presley Vaudrin, Dec. 4, 1970 (dec. July 1996). BA, U. Toronto, Ont., Can., 1939, MA, 1940; postgrad., Johns Hopkins U., 1941-42. Chief China desk United Nations Relief Rehab. Adminstrn, Washington, 1945-46, dept. dir. programs China Mission Shanghai, 1946-48; chief China desk UNICEF, N.Y.C., 1948-50, chief Asia sect., 1951-60, dir. program divsn., 1961-76, chief program policy, 1977-85, sr. policy cons., 1986—. Mem. UN Task Force for Child Survival Force, Atlanta, 1986-98, UN rep. Can. UN Assn., Can. Group of 78, Can. Pugwash Group; rep. Sci. for Peace, Internat. Peace Bur. Economists Against Arms Race, NGO Disarmament Com. Author: The Diplomacy of Hope, 2001. Decorated Order of Can. Mem. Soc. for Internat. Devel., Arms Control Assn., Soc. for Internat. Devel. Office: UNICEF 3 United Nations Plz New York NY 10017-4486

BOWLES, PATRICIA MARY, secondary education educator; b. Reading, Pa., Jan. 15, 1950; d. Charles Worthington Doane and Mary Augusta (Kershner) B. BS, Kutztown (Pa.) U., 1971; MEd, Temple U., 1987. Cert. elem. tchr. and elem. prin., Pa. Tchr. visually impaired Reading (Pa.) Sch. Dist., 1972-75, adminstrv. intern, 1986-87, tchr. Berks County Intermediate Unit, Reading, 1973-93; tchr. visually impaired Reading Sch. Dist., 1993—. Account exec. United Way, Berks County, 1988—; bd. dirs. Leadership Berks, Reading, 1988—, Nat. Coun. on Alcoholism, Berks County, 1988—; pres. Leadership Berks Alumni Assn., Reading, 1987, bd. dirs., 1987—. Eleanor Long Tchr. of the Yr., Pa. Div. Visually Impaired, 1984. Mem. Assn. for Edn. and Rehab. Visually Impaired, Assn. for Supervision and Curriculum Devel., Flying Dutchmen Ski Club (trip dir. Reading chpt. 1975-76), Phi Delta Kappa, Delta Kappa Gamma. Republican. Lutheran. Avocations: snow and water skiing, dancing, theatre. Home: 5 Eagle Ct Reading PA 19605-3215 Office: Reading High Sch 801 N 13th St Reading PA 19604-2451

BOWLES, SUZANNE GEISSLER, history educator; b. Somerville, N.J., Nov. 12, 1950; d. Alfred Henry and Suzanne Judith (Golembeski) Geissler; m. Arthur Graham Bowles, Oct. 15, 1994. BA, Syracuse U., 1971; MA, Rutgers U., 1972; PhD, Syracuse U., 1976; MTS, Drew U., 1979. Instr. history SUNY, Cortland, N.Y., 1975-77; lectr. history Drew U., Madison, N.J., 1977-79; adj. prof. history Upsala Coll., Sussex, N.J., 1979-95, William Paterson U., Wayne, NJ, 1995—99, asst. prof., 1999—. Cons. in field. Author: Jonathan Edwards to Aaron Burr, 1981, Lutheranism and Anglicanism in Colonial New Jersey, 1988, A Widening Sphere of Usefulness: Newark Academy, 1993. Mem. Am. Soc. Ch.

History, Am. Hist. Assn., U.S. Naval Inst., Orgn. Am. Historians, Hist. Soc. Episcopal Ch., Soc. Mil. History, Phi Beta Kappa. Office: William Paterson U History Dept Wayne NJ 07470 E-mail: sgbowles@compuserve.com.

BOWLES, WALTER DONALD, economist, educator; b. Seattle, Dec. 28, 1923; s. Walter Alexander and Minnie Ellen (Martin) B.; m. Vincenza Pompea Galasso, Dec. 22, 1955; children: Ellen Maria, Walter Donald. BA in Econs, U. Wash., 1949; MA in Econs, Columbia U., 1952, PhD in Econs., 1958; cert. in Soviet economy, Russian Inst., 1952. Editor Research Program on USSR, N.Y.C., 1953-55; fellow Air U., 1955-57; faculty Am. U., Washington, 1957-94, prof. econs., chmn. dept., 1962-65, prof. econs., dean Coll. Arts and Scis., 1965-69, prof. econs., v.p. acad. affairs, 1969-73, prof. econs., 1974—93; on leave as prof. econs., sr. fellow Columbia U., 1973-74; on leave as economist U.S. AID, 1983-85, cons., 1985-89; prof. econs. Graz Center, Austria, summers 1971-73; prof. emeritus, 1994. Acad. dir. Am. U. London Semester Program, spring, 1991; lectr., dir. African seminars, 1964. With U.S. Army, 1943—46. Mem. AAUP, Am. Econ. Assn., Assn. Study Comparative Econ. Systems, Assn. for Advancement Slavic Studies, Soc. for Internat. Devel. Home: 329 Roosevelt Ave Ventura CA 93003-2589

BOWLIN, GLORIA JEAN, artist; b. Middletown, Ohio, May 18, 1949; d. Leonard William and Margaret May (Hughes) Creager; m. Jerry Edward Bowlin, Mar. 3, 1969; children: Amy Beth, Jeremy Scott. Grad. high sch., Carlisle, Ohio, Ohio. Owner, designer The Crow & The Weasel, New Carlisle, 1994-2000; artist Penny Lane Pub., New Carlisle, 1995—; designer, artist Primitives by Kathy Reproduction Co., 2002—. Author, creator (doll patterns/instrns.) Winter '95 Collection, Spring '96 Collection, Winter '96 Collection, Spring '97 Collection, Fall/Winter '97 Collection, Summer/Fall Collection, 98, Spring '98, 99, Fall/Winter Collection '99; holder copyrights for various doll/soft sculpture designs; lic. prodn. of artwork on greeting cards, rugs, pillows, ornaments, furniture, others; exhibitor Gallery of Am. Craftsmen, 2000-2001. Vol. ABLE Literacy Program, Piqua, Ohio, 1993; student Am. Sign Lang., Cmty. Svcs. for Deaf, Dayton, Ohio, 1993-94. Avocations: herb gardening, antiques, writing simple verse, decorating. Home: 207 W Madison St New Carlisle OH 45344-1925 E-mail: jbowlin950@aol.com.

BOWLIN, MICHAEL RAY, retired oil company executive; b. Amarillo, Tex., Feb. 20, 1943; m. Martha Ann Rowland; 1 child, John Charles. BBA, North Tex. State U., 1965, MBA, 1967. Scheduler prodn. and transp. A. Brant Co., Ft. Worth, 1965—66; mktg. rep. R.J. Reynolds Tobacco Bo., 1967—68; personnel generalist Atlantic Richfield Co., Dallas, 1969—71, coll. relations rep. Los Angeles, 1971—72, mgr. internal profl. placement, 1973, mgr. corp. recruiting and placement, 1973—75, mgr. behavioral sci. services, 1975, sr. v.p. ARCO resources adminstrn., 1985, sr. v.p. ARCO internat. oil and gas acquisitions, 1987, sr. v.p. L.A., 1987—, employee relations mgr., 1975—77; v.p. employee relations Anaconda Copper Co. (divsn. Atlantic Richfield Co.), Denver, 1977—81; from v.p. employee rels. to v.p. fin. planning and control ARCO Oil & Gas (div. Atlantic Richfield Co.), Dallas, 1981—84, v.p. fin. planning and control, 1982—84; sr. v.p. Atlantic Richfield Co., 1985—92; pres. ARCO Coal Co., 1985—87, ARCO Internat. Oil & Gas Co., 1987—92; CEO Atlantic Richfield Co., 1994—2000, chmn., CEO, 1998—2000; pres., COO ARCO Internat. Oil & Gas Co., 1993, pres., CEO, 1994—95, chmn., CEO, 1995—2000.

BOWLING, JOHN ROBERT, osteopathic physician, educator, academic administrator; b. Columbus, Ohio, Feb. 18, 1943; s. Ardyce Saul and Wilma Garcia (Snider) B.; m. Janet Lou Bowman, July 10, 1965; children: Jack Robert, James Richard, Jason Russell. BS, Ohio U., 1965; DO, Kirksville (Mo.) Coll. Osteopathic Medicine, 1969. Diplomate Am. Osteo. Bd. Family Practice; cert. Am. Osteo. Bd. Family Practice. Rotating intern Drs. Hosp., Columbus, 1969—70; gen. practice osteo. medicine Lancaster, Ohio, 1970—88; clin. assoc. prof. Ohio U. Coll. Osteo. Medicine, Athens, 1977—88; med. dir. Lancaster Health Care Ctr., 1980—88; assoc. prof. dept. family medicine U. North Tex. Health Sci. Ctr. Coll. Osteo. Medicine, Ft. Worth, 1988—, interim chmn. dept. family medicine, 1991, vice chmn. dept., 1991—95, course dir. core clin. clerkship in family practice, 1991—, mem. steering com. Catchum project, mem. exec. coun. of faculty, 1992, 1996, mem. curriculum com., 1993—, mem. admissions com., 1989—97, dir. student health svcs., 1992—, dir. rural curriculum track-family medicine, 1996—2001, dir. predoctoral and rural edn. dept. family medicine, phase dir. for integrated clin. curriculum experiences, 1995—. Civ. sr. attending staff Doctors Hosp., 1970—88, co-dir. family practice residency program, 1979, acting dir., 80; chmn. dept. medicine Lancaster Fairfield Cmty. Hosp., 1975, sec. med. staff, 1982—83, pres., 1985; active staff Osteo. Med. Ctr. Tex., 1988—; team physician Bloom Carool (Ohio) Sch., 1973—88; health care workgroup Tex. Tele. Intrastructure Bd., 2001—. Pres., bd. dirs. Montessori Presch., Lancaster, 1975; chmn. youth basketball com. YMCA; former youth coord., tchr., mem. adminstrv. bd. United Meth. Ch.; mem. chancel chour, men's chorus 1st United Mech. Ch., Grapevine, Tex., 1997—; staff parish rels. com. 1st United Meth. Ch., Grapevine, Tex., 2000—01. Named Outstanding Advisor, Tex. Coll. Osteo. Medicine, 1992; recipient Clyde Gallehugh Meml. award, 2002. Fellow Am. Coll. Osteo. Family Physicians (com. on evaluation and edn. 1991—, program chmn. nat. conv. 1995, chmn. resident intern com. 1995-99, Family Physician of Yr. 1996, Clyde Gallehugh Meml. faculty award 2002); mem. Am. Osteo. Assn., Ohio Osteo. Assn., Tex. Osteo. Med. Assn. (program chmn. state conv. 1994, 95), Tex. Med. Assn. (preventive medicine task force 1993-94), Tex. Soc. Am. Coll. Osteo. Family Phsyicians (pres. 1999-00). Methodist. Avocations: tennis, golf, photography, music. Home: 550 Timber Ridge Dr Roanoke TX 76262 Office: U North Tex Health Sci Ctr College Osteo Medicine 3500 Camp Bowie Blvd Fort Worth TX 76107-2644 E-mail: jbowling@hsc.unt.edu.

BOWLING, KELLY K, management consultant; d. Garth Edward and Linda Kay Bowling. BS, Mary Wash. Coll., 1997—2001. Cons. Booz Allen Hamilton, McLean, Va., 2001—. Mem. Friday Morning Music Club, Washington D.C. Recipient Booz Allen Hamilton Team Appreciation award, Booz Allen Hamilton, 2002. Mem.: Music Teachers Nat. Assn., Friday Morning Music Club. Avocation: piano.

BOWLING, LANCE CHRISTOPHER, record producer, publishing executive; b. San Pedro, Calif., May 17, 1948; s. Dan Parker and Sylvia Lois (Van Devander) B. BA in Polit. Sci. and History, Pepperdine U., 1966-70, MPA, 1973. Owner, founder Cambria Master Recordings, Palos Verdes, Calif., 1972—. Editor: Joseph Wagner: A Retrospective of Composer-Conductor 1900-74, 1976, Hazards Pavilion, Jour of Soc for Preservation of South Calif. Mus. Heritage, 1985—; author: Eugene Hemmer: Composer-Pianist, 1983; prodr. more than 150 classical records including works by Charles W. Cadman, Madeleine Dring, Mary Carr Moore, John Crown, Ed Bland, Florence Price, Elinor Remick Warren, Miklos Rozsa, Erich W. Korngold, Max Steiner, Ernst Gold, William Grant Still, Arthur Lange, also classical music radio station documentaries, programs for Taz Libr. Congress; contbr. Opera News. Active allocation com. Region V, United Way, L.A., 1978-85; bd. dirs. Elinor Remick Warren Found., Film Music Soc., Hollywood, Calif., New World Ctr. for Arts, L.A., L.A. Ballet. Recipient Golden Rose award Pi Iota chpt. Phi Beta, 1988. Mem. ASCAP, Nat. Acad. Recording Arts and Scis. (classical com.), Assn. Recorded Sound Collections, Music Libr. Assn., Soc. for Preservation of Film Music, Sonneck Soc., Variety Arts Club (L.A.), Mus. Arts Club (Long Beach, Calif.), Zamorano Club (L.A.). Episcopalian. Avocations: collecting early Calif. books and ephemera, restoration of 78 RPM recordings and antique automobiles. Home: 2625 Colt Rd Palos Verdes Peninsula CA 90275-6578 Office: Cambria Master Recordings 1659 W 7th St San Pedro CA 90732-3421 E-mail: cambriamus@aol.com.

BOWLSBY, BOB, athletic director; b. Jan. 10, 1952; m. Candice Bowlsby; children: Lisa, Matt, Rachel, Kyle. BS, Moorhead State U., 1975; MS, U. Iowa, 1978. Asst. athletic dir. Northern Iowa Univ.; athletic dir. Univ. Northern Iowa, 1984-91, Univ. Iowa, 1991—. Chair NCAA Divsn. I Mgmt. Coun., 1997-99; mem. NCAA Divsn. I Basketball com., 2000—. Chmn. Big Ten Championships and awards com.; chair NCAA Olympic Sports Liaison Com., NCAA/USOC liaison com., Olympics com. mem; bd. dirs. Iowa Games. Mem. Nat. Assn. Collegiate Dir. of Athletics (exec. com.). Office: U Iowa Dir Athletics 338 Carver Hawkeye Arena Iowa City IA 52242-1020 E-mail: robert-bowlsby@uiowa.edu.

BOWMAN, BARBARA TAYLOR, early childhood educator; b. Chgo., Oct. 30, 1928; d. Robert Rochon and Dorothy Vaugn (Jennings) Taylor; m. James E. Bowman, June 17, 1950, 1 child, Valerie Bowman Jarrett. BA, Sarah Lawrence Coll., 1950; MA, U. Chgo., 1952; DHL (hon.), Bankstreet Coll., 1988, Roosevelt U., 1998, Dominican U., 2002, Gov.'s State U., 2002. Tchr. U. Chgo. Nursery Sch., 1950-52, Colo. Women's Coll. Nursery Sch., Denver, 1953-55; mem. sci. faculty Shiraz (Iran) U. Nemazee Sch. Nursing, 1955-61; spl. edn. tchr. Chgo. Child Care Soc., 1965—67; mem. faculty Erikson Inst., Chgo., 1967—, dir. grad. studies, 1978—94, pres., 1994—2002, prof. early edn., 2002. Mem. early childhood com. Nat. Bd. Profl. Tchg. Stds., 1992-2002; cons. early childhood edn., parent edn.; chair com. on early childhood pedagogy NRC, 1998-99. Contbr. articles to profl. jours. Bd. dirs. Ill. Health Edn. Com., 1969—71, Inst. Psychoanalysis, 1970—73, Ill. Adv. Coun. Dept. Children and Family Svcs., 1974—79, Child Devel. Assoc. Consortium, 1979—81, Chgo. Bd. Edn. Desegregation Commn., 1981—84, Bus. People in Pub. Inst., 1980—, High Scope Ednl. Rsch. Found., 1986—93, Gt. Books Found., 1988—, Cmty.-Corp. Sch., 1988—90; mem. Family Resource Coalition, 1992—96, mem. nat. bd. profl. tchr. stds., 1996—2002. Mem. Ill. Assn. Edn. Young Children, Nat. Assn. Edn. Young Children (pres. 1980-82), Chgo. Assns. Edn. Young Children (pres. 1973-77), Black Child Devel. Assn., Am. Ednl. Rsch. Assn. Achievements include research in early education teaching and school improvement. Office: Erikson Inst 420 N Wabash Ave Chicago IL 60611-3568

BOWMAN, BETSEY JEAN, social worker; b. Knoxville, Tenn., June 12, 1923; d. Eugene Taylor and Frieda Evangeline (Harmon) B. BA, Tusculum Coll., 1945; MSW, U. Tenn., 1957. Child welfare worker Tenn. Dept. Pub. Welfare, Johnson City, 1946-57, child welfare cons., 1958-64; clin. social worker VA Ctr., Mountain Home, Tenn., 1965-71; dir. area project on aging East Tenn.-Va. Devel. Dist., Johnson City, 1973-74. Author: People and Places of the Past, 1983, Nostalgia Is...And Other Bits and Pieces, 1989, The Six Senses of Christmas, 1990, A Walk Through Greeneville, 1991, The World of Flickering Light and Shadow, 2002. V.p., sec., corr. sec. Greene County Heritage Trust, pres. 1992—; alderman 1st Ward Town of Greeneville, 1988-97; mem. Airport Authority, 1988-97, Parking Authority, 1988-97, Mayor's Disability Commn., Greeneville, 1989-97; bd. dirs. Roby Fitzgerald Adult Ctr., Greeneville, 1989—; mem. Greeneville Hist. Zoning Commn., 1995-; sec. Main Street: Greeneville, 1997-; trustee Nathanael Greene Mus., 2002; mem. Heritage Network, 2001-. Recipient Outstanding Contbn. and Preservation award Greene County Heritage Trust, 1986, L.E. Coolidge Humanitarian award Citizens of Greene County Takoma Hosp., Greeneville, 1990, Gov.'s award Main St., Greeneville, 1992. Mem. Pilot Club (bd. dirs. Greeneville chpt. 1983-90, Outstanding Pilot of Yr. 1980). Republican. Presbyterian. Avocations: creative writing, swimming. Home: 104 E Spencer St Greeneville TN 37745-3902

BOWMAN, BRUCE, art educator, writer, artist; b. Dayton, Ohio, Nov. 23, 1938; s. Murray Edgar Bowman and Mildred May (Moler) Elleman; m. Julie Ann Gosselin, 1970 (div. 1980); 1 child, Carrie Lynn. AA, San Diego City Coll., 1962; BA, Calif. State U.-Los Angeles, 1964, MA, 1968. Tchr. art North Hollywood Adult Sch., Calif., 1966-68; instr. art Cypress Coll., Calif., 1976-78, West Los Angeles Coll., 1969— ; tchr. art Los Angeles City Schs., 1966—; seminar leader So. Calif., 1986—. Author: Shaped Canvas, 1976; Toothpick Sculpture and Ice Cream Stick Art, 1976; Ideas: How to Get Them, 1985, (cassette tape) Develop Winning Willpower, 1986, Waikiki, 1988. Contbr. articles to profl. jours. One-man shows include Calif. State U.-Los Angeles, 1968, Pepperdine U., Malibu, Calif., 1978; exhibited in group shows McKenzie Gallery, Los Angeles, 1968, Trebor Gallery, Los Angeles, 1970, Cypress Coll., Calif., 1977, Design Recycled Gallery, Fullerton, Calif., 1977, Pierce Coll., Woodland Hills, Calif., 1978, Leopold/Gold Gallery, Santa Monica, Calif., 1980. Served with USN, 1957-61. Avocation: karate (black belt Tang Soo Do). Home: 28322 Rey De Copas Ln Malibu CA 90265-4463

BOWMAN, BRUCE ALAN, civil engineer; b. Garmisch-Partenkirchen, Bavaria, Germany, Mar. 12, 1959; s. Walter Earl and Ingeborg Marie Bowman; m. Leslie Suzanne Thompson, Sept. 19, 1981; children: Gregory, Douglas. BS Chemistry, Ind. U., 1981; MS Ops. Rsch., USAF Inst. Tech., 1988; PhD Civil Engring., Columbia U., 1995. Analyst Office of the Dep. Chief of Staff for Pers., Hdqs., US Army, Washington, 1990—92; asst. prof. US Mil. Acad., West Point, NY, 1996—99; sect. chief and divsn. chief, joint warfighting analysis divsn. (j8) Office of the Chmn. of the Joint Chiefs of Staff, Washington, 1999—2001; prin. cons. PricewaterhouseCoopers Mgmt. Consulting LLP, Fairfax, Va., 2001—01; sr. profl. staff Johns Hopkins U. Applied Physics Lab., Laurel, Md., 2001—. Co-chairman, systems dynamics in nat. security conf. Nat. Def. U., Washington, 2000—00. Contbr. book. Coo and founding exec. dir. The ACE Mentor Program of the Greater Wash. DC Met. Area, Inc., 2000; mem., bd. of directors Learning & Leadership in Families, Inc., Washington, 2001; elder Presbyn. Ch. U.S.A., 1991; youth soccer coach Springfield, Va., 1989—91, Rockland County, NY, 1992—95. Lt. col. US Army, 1981—2001. Mem.: Am. Soc. Engring. Mgmt., ASCE, Mil. Ops. Rsch. Soc. (chmn. weapons of mass destruction nat. symposium 2001—01), Soc. of Am. Mil. Engineers, Inst. for Ops. Rsch. & Mgmt. Sci. (INFORMS). Protestant. Avocation: reading, pastels, chess, soccer, jogging. Office: Johns Hopkins U Applied Physics Lab 11100 Johns Hopkins Road Laurel MD 20723-6099 Personal E-mail: drbrucebowman@cs.com. E-mail: bruce.bowman@jhuapl.edu.

BOWMAN, C. MICHAEL, physician; married; two children. BS in Chemistry (with honors), U. Ill., 1968; PhD in Genetics, U. Wis., 1972, MD, 1975. Diplomate Am. Bd. Pediatrics, Am. Bd. Pediatric Pulmonology. Pediat. resident Vanderbilt U., 1975-78, chief resident, 1978-79; dir. comprehensive cystic fibrosis ctr. Med. U. S.C.; divsn. head Divsn. Pediat. Pulmonolgy, Allergy & Immunology; prof. pediats. Med. U. S.C., Charleston, 2000—. Fellow Am. Acad. of Pediat., mem. Am. Bd. of Pediat., Am. Thoracic Soc. Achievements include research in lung disorders in children. Office: Med U S C Ste 281 PO Box 250561 135 Rutledge Ave Charleston SC 29425 Fax: (843) 876-1583. E-mail: bowmanm@musc.edu.

BOWMAN, CARL BYRON, music educator, composer; b. Philomath, Or., Dec. 14, 1913; s. Otto Bechtel Bowman and Mary Susan Morehous. MusB, Willamette U, Salem, OR, 1942; MusM, U of Wash., Seattle, Wash., 1952; PhD, NYU, New York, NY, 1971. Prof. NYUCC, Manhattan, NY, 1966—83; prof. emeritus NYU, New York, NY, 1983—2003. Musician: (songs) Three Spokes of One Wheel; composer Tripsych Symphony, Concerto for the Tuba. Mem.: ASCAP (life), Soc. of Composers, Inc. (life), Am. Music Ctr. (life), Phi Kappa Lambda (hon.). Protestant. Achievements include publ. and performed original compos./argmnt. for orchestra, band, chorus & chamber ensembles at Bklyn. Philharm.,Indpls. Symp. Orchestra, Julliard Sch.of Music, Eastman Sch. of Music. Home: 140 W 69th St 94-B New York NY 10023 Office: City U of New York 199 Chambers St New York NY 10007

BOWMAN, CATHERINE MCKENZIE, lawyer; b. Tampa, Fla., Nov. 10, 1962; d. Herbert Alonza and Joan Bates (Baggs) McKenzie; m. Donald Campbell Bowman, Jr., May 21, 1988; children: Hunter Hall, Sarah McKenzie. BA in Psychology and Sociology, Vanderbilt U., 1984; JD, U. Ga., 1987. Bar: Ga. 1987, U.S. Dist. Ct. (so. dist.) Ga. 1987. Assoc. Ranitz, Mahoney, Forbes & Coolidge, P.C., Savannah, Ga., 1987-91; ptnr. Forbes and Bowman, 1991—. Bd. dirs. Greenbriar Children's Ctr., 1994-98, exec. com. 1995, pres. 1996-98; sustainer Jr. League Savannah; with Leadership Savannah, 1994-96, Savannah Found. Distbn. Com., 1994-2002; ball com. Telfair Arts Acad., 2002, ball com. Historic Savannah Found., 2002; co-chair Savannah Co. Day Sch. Fair, 2004. Mem. Am. Employment Law Coun., Ga. Def. Lawyers Assn., Savannah Young Lawyers Assn. (pres. 1996-97), 2000 Club (membership chair 1990-91, pres. 1992), South Atlantic Found. (bd. dirs. 1992). Home: 17 Franklin Creek S Savannah GA 31411 Office: Forbes and Bowman PO Box 13929 7505 Waters Ave Ste D-14 Savannah GA 31406-3824

BOWMAN, CHARLES HAY, retired engineering educator, petroleum company executive; b. Pitts., Dec. 21, 1935; m. Lynn A. Holleran; 5 children. BS in Petroleum Engring., Pa. State U., 1957; MS in Petroleum Engring., Tex. A&M U., 1959, PhD in Petroleum Engring., 1961. Rsch. engr. Gulf Oil Corp., Pitts., 1960-64, reservoir engr., 1964-66, rsch. assoc., 1966-69, chief reservoir engr., 1969-70, exploitation supt., 1970-73, spl. projects mgr., 1973-74; gen. mgr. crude oil sales Gulf Oil Trading Co., Pitts., 1974-76; v.p. energy and regulation and compliance Gulf Refining and Mktg. Co., 1976-80, sr. v.p., 1980-81, pres., 1981-83, Gulf Oil Products Co., 1983-85; sr. v.p. petroleum products & refining Sohio Oil Co. (a subs. BP Am. Inc.), Cleve., 1985-86; pres. Old Ben Coal Co. (a subs. BP Am. Inc.), Lexington/Cleve., 1986-88; gen. mgr. Europe BP Oil Internat., London, 1988-90; mng. dir. BP Australia Ltd., Melbourne, 1990-94; chmn., CEO BP Am., Inc., Cleve., 1994-97; prof., head of petroleum engring. dept. Tex. A&M U., College Station, 1997-2001; ret., 2001. Bd. dirs. Nat. City Corp. Bd. dirs. Case Western Res. U., Cleve. Initiative for Edn.; chmn. Cleve. Ballet; founding mem. Australian Bus. Higher Edn. Roundtable. Mem. Tau Beta Pi, Phi Kappa Phi, Pi Epsilon Tau. Avocations: antique collecting, model railroading, furniture restoration, woodworking, boating. Fax: 979-690-8069. E-mail: lynn-chuck@spindletop.tamu.edu.

BOWMAN, DANIEL OLIVER, psychologist; b. Holly Hill, S.C., Feb. 1, 1931; s. John Daniel and Pansy (Mizzell) Bowman. BA in Music, Furman U., 1951; MEd, U. S.C., 1952; PhD, U. Ga., 1963. Lic. psychologist, S.C. Tchr., English, French Summerville (S.C.) H.S., 1952-53; chmn. English dept., sr. guidance counselor Boys H.S., Anderson, S.C., 1955-61; instr. psychology U. Ga., Athens, 1961-63; asst. prof. psychology The Citadel, Charleston, S.C., 1963-66, assoc. prof. psychology, counselor to corps cadets, 1966-69, prof. psychology, dir. grad. studies, 1969-77, prof., head dept. psychology, 1977-91, Arland D. Williams prof. psychology, 1991-96, prof. emeritus, 1996—. Cons. Charleston County Sheriff's Dept., 1985-94, Berkeley County Sch. System, Moncks Corner, S.C., 1977-89. Chmn. Charleston County Mental Retardation Bd., 1988-90. Mem. APA, AAUP, NASP, Am. Psychol. Soc. (charter), Southea. Psychol. Assn., S.C. Psychol. Assn. (pres. 1990-91, Outstanding Contbrs. Psychology 1988), Phi Kappa Phi (pres. 1979-80), Phi Delta Kappa. Home: 6 Fort Royal Ave Charleston SC 29407-6012

BOWMAN, DAVID WESLEY, lawyer; b. Mpls., Dec. 14, 1940; s. Burton F. and Eldred (Frudenfeld) Bowman; m. Patricia L. Schlimme, Nov. 26, 1975; children: Christopher B., Sarah K., David W., Tulley B., Ashley B. BA, U. Iowa, 1964; JD, 1967. Bar: Iowa 1967. Asst. counsel Dept. Navy, Washington, 1968—72, Firestone Corp., Akron, Ohio, 1972—77; counsel Harris Corp., Melbourne, Fla., 1977—80; v.p., sec., gen. counsel Harris Graphics Corp., 1983—87; sr. v.p., gen. counsel, sec. MAPCO, Inc., Tulsa, 1987. Mem.: Nat. Security Indsl. Assn., Nat. Contract Mgmt. Assn., Iowa Bar Assn., Fed. Bar Assn., ABA. Episc. Home: 3104 S Columbia Cir Tulsa OK 74105-2329

BOWMAN, DONALD CAMPBELL, accountant; b. Tampa, Fla., Apr. 1, 1935; s. Jackson Harrison and Margaret (McMullen) B.; m. Cynthia Spencer Young, Apr. 8, 1961; children: Donald Campbell Jr., James Andrew. BS, U.S. Mil. Acad., 1957; MSA Indsl. Personnel Mgmt., George Washington U., 1971; grad., U.S. Army War Coll., 1971. CPA. Commd. 2d lt. U.S. Army, 1957, advanced through grades to lt. col., ret., 1977; dir. mktg. Washington Sch. for Secs., 1977-79; pres. Bowman Bus. Svcs. Inc., Columbus, Ga., 1979-86; mgr. Fountain Arrington Hoffman, CPA, Columbus, 1986-93; owner, jprin. Donald C. Bowman, CPA, LLC, Columbus, 1993—. Contbr. articles to profl. jours. Treas. Ranger Meml. Found., 1992—; mem. Columbus Bldg. uthority. Decorated Legion of Merit, Silver Star; Paul Harris fellow, 1999, Will Watt fellow, 2000. Fellow Ga. Soc. CPAs (mem. litigation suport com. 1994—; mem. AICPA, Rotary (asst. gov. 2000-2001, charter pres. Muscogee club 1991-92). Avocations: reading, flyfishing, walking. Office: PO Box 5507 Columbus GA 31906

BOWMAN, DONALD EUGENE, investment counselor; b. Dayton, Ohio, July 9, 1930; s. John Peter and Delia Francis (Sink) B.; m. Mary Louise, Jan. 20, 1984; children: Clark Woodford, Marylouise Chalfant. BA, U. Wis., 1952; MBA, Loyola Coll., Balt., 1982; Exec. Advanced Mgmt. degree, Harvard U., 1974; postgrad., Stanford U., 1976. Chartered investment counselor. CEO, pres. T. Rowe Price Assn., Balt., 1956-79, Bowman Fin. Mgmt. Co., Balt., 1978—. Bd. dirs. Roland Park Girls Sch., 1969-75, U. Wis. Found., Madison, 1978-95, U. Balt. Found., 1978—, 4-H Found., Washington, 1988—, Wis. Alumni Assn., 1995-2000; chmn., bd. dirs. Towson U. Found., Balt., 1989-95; exec. MBA bd. dirs. Loyola Coll., Balt., 1985—; trustee Balt. Opera Co., 1996-2003; chmn. bd. St. Pauls Sch. for Girls, 1992-95; mem. adv. coun. ERISA, 1972-75; bd. govs. Investment Coun. Assn. Am., Washington, 1968-78; mem. No Load Mut. Fund Bd., 1970-78; trustee Alliance for Chesapeake Bay, 2002—; hon. chmn. Md. Nat. Rep. Bus. Adv. Coun., Presdl. Bus. Adv. Coun.. Capt. USNR, 1952-90. Recipient Bus. of Yr. award, Nat. Rep. Congl. Com., 2003, Bus. Man of the Yr. award, 2003. Republican. Avocations: tennis, fitness. Office: Bowman Fin Mgmt Co Inc 1013 N Calvert St Baltimore MD 21202-3823 E-mail: dobow2000@aol.com.

BOWMAN, DOROTHY LOUISE, artist; b. Hollywood, Calif., Jan. 20, 1927; d. Bruce L. and Dorothy L. (Kalkman) B; m. Howard Hugh Bradford, Dec. 30, 1949 (div. 1965); children: Brock, Cyndra, Tal Scott, Heather, Delia, Callia. Student, Chouinard Art Inst., Calif., 1945-48, Jepson Art Inst., L.A., 1948-49; BA, Webster U., 1979. One-woman show Ventana Gallery, Big Sur, 1998; serigrapher, printmaker, painter: represented in permanent collections: Immaculate Heart Coll., L.A. County Mus., Bklyn. Mus., Long Beach Mus., Crocker Art Gallery, Mus. Modern Art, Phila., Mus. Fine Arts, San Jose State Coll., De Cordova and Danna Mus., Boston Pub. Libr., Boston Mus. Fine Arts, N.Y. Pub. Libr., Rochester Meml. Gallery, U. Wis., U. Hawaii, U. Ill., U. Kans., Santa Barbara Mus., Achenbach Found. Legion of Honor, Mus. Modern Art, Monterey, Calif., Libr. Congress, Calif. State Libr. Archives, Arquivos Historicos De Arte Contemporanea Museu De Arte Moderna, San Paulo, Brazil, Ch. of Latter Day Saints History Mus., Salt Lake City, 1987, Nat. Mus. of Women in the Arts, Washington, 2000—; twice juried internat. show 27 countries, 1987; creator animation films The Mobius World, 2000, Really O'Reiley, 2002; Traveling show Smithsonian Inst., Nat. Colleciton of Fine Arts, 1952; movie producer historical film, Big Sur, 2002. Address: Nat Mus of Women in the Arts Archives 1250 New York Ave NW Washington DC 20005-3970

BOWMAN, DOUGLAS, business educator; b. Winnipeg, Can., Aug. 16, 1961; s. James Lawrence and Ethel Henderson Bowman; m. Sharon Anne Watson; children: Andrew, Thomas, Christopher. BA in Elec. Engring., U. Waterloo, Can., 1985; MBA, U. Western Ont., 1987; MA, U. Pa., 1992; PhD, U. Pa., Philadelphia, PA, 1993. Cert. mgmt. acct. Analyst Nortel Networks, Bramalea, 1987—89; asst. prof. mgmt. Purdue U., West Lafayette, Ind., 1993—99; assoc. prof. mktg. Emory U., Atlanta, 1999—. Contbr. articles to profl. jours. Recipient Paul A. Green Best Paper award, Jour. Mktg. Rsch., 2001. Mem.: Am. Statis. Assn., Inst. Ops. Rsch. and Mgmt. Scis., Am. Mktg. Assn. Office: Emory U Goizueta Bus Sch Atlanta GA 30322 Business E-Mail: Doug_Bowman@bus.emory.edu.

BOWMAN, FAY LOUISE, artist; b. L.A., Feb. 8, 1936; d. Winfield John and Dorothy Ethel (Lane) Michalsky; m. George Arthur Bowman; children: John Winfield, David Lawrence. BA, UCLA, 1958; BFA, Art Inst. So. Calif., 1987. Cert. tchr. La., 1958. Elem. tchr., Alhambra, Calif., 1958-59, Costa Mesa, Calif., 1959-63. One-woman show includes Art Inst. So. Calif., 1987; exhibited in group show at Irvine Valley Coll., 1991; numerous pvt. collections. Sec. President's Club Art Inst., Laguna Beach, Calif., 1990; discussion leader of worldwide Bible Study Fellowship Laguna Beach Presbyn. Ch., 1994-95; active Ebell Club, 1973—; mem. Visionaires of Orange County Mus. Art, 1999—2003. Mem. Designing Women of Art Inst., Assocs. Art Inst. So. Calif. (pres. 1988—).

BOWMAN, FRANK LEE (SKIP BOWMAN), admiral and director naval nuclear propulsion; b. Chattanooga, Tenn., Dec. 19, 1944; m. Linda Anne Rich, June 10, 1966; children: Greg, Christy. BS, Duke U., 1966; MS in Nuclear Engring., Naval Arch., MIT, 1973. Commd ensign USN, 1966, advanced through grades to admiral, 1996; naval officer at sea on USS Simon Bolivar, USS Pogy, USS Daniel Boone, 1966-77; exec. officer USS Bremerton USS Bremerton, 1978-80; comdr. USS City of Corpus Christi USN, 1983-86, comdr. USS Holland, 1988-90, dep. dir. ops. joint staff, 1991-92, dir. polit.-mil. affairs joint staff, 1992-94, dep. chief naval ops., chief naval pers., 1994-96, dir. naval nuclear propulsion, 1996—. Decorated Disting. Svc. medal, Defense Disting. Svc. medal, Legion of Merit with 3 gold stars, Meritorious Svc. medal with 2 gold stars, Battle E Efficiency award, four times, Navy Expeditionary medal twice, Humanitarian Svc. medal twice. Office: NAVSEA-08 SE Bldg 104 1240 Isaac Hull Ave Washington DC 20376-8010

BOWMAN, FRANK PAUL, retired humanities educator; b. Portland, Oreg., June 12, 1927; s. Frank George Bowman and Mary Dorothea Pahl. BA, Reed Coll., 1949; MA, Yale U., 1952, PhD, 1955. Asst. prof. U. Calif., Berkeley, 1954—62; assoc. prof. U. Pa., Phila., 1963—65, prof., 1965—91; vis. prof. U. Paris III, 1973—75, U. Paris VII, 1990, Princeton (N.J.) U., 1993. Mem. editl. bd. French Forum, 1976—, 19th Century French Studies, 1978—, Romantisme, Paris, 1983—. Author: Le Christ des Barricades, 1987, French Romanticism, 1990, Gerard de Nerval, 1997. Vestryman, warden St. Clement's Ch., Phila., 1982—. Cpl. U.S. Army, 1945—46. Recipient Chevalier des Palmes academiques, French Govt., 1979, Officier des Palmes Academiques, 1991; fellow, Guggenheim Found., 1968—69, 1986—87. Mem.: Soc. Etudes Romantiques (mem. governing bd. 1982—), Soc. Etudes Staeliennes (mem. governing bd. 1978—), Phi Beta Kappa. Democrat. Mem. Anglican Ch. Avocation: music. Home: 3300 Darby Rd #4108 Haverford PA 19041

BOWMAN, GEORGE ARTHUR, JR., b. Milw., Dec. 1, 1917; s. George Arthur and Edna Oral (Hunter) B.; m. Rose Mary Thorpe, Aug. 8, 1947 (dec. 1980); children: George A. III, Daniel Andrew. Student, U. Wis., 1936-39; JD, Marquette U., 1943. Bar: Wis. 1943, U.S. Supreme Ct. 1943. Asst. dist. atty. Milw. County, 1947-48, children's ct. judge, 1967-72; asst. city atty. City of Milw., 1948-67; adminstrv. law judge Office of Hearing and Appeals Social Security Adminstrn. Dept. HHS, Chgo., 1973-97, adminstrv. law judge emeritus, 1997; pvt. practice, 1997—. Appointed Pres.'s Task Force, Law Enforcement Assistance Adminstrn., 1972; former counsel Milw. Police Dept.; advisor Nat. Council of Juvenile Ct. Judges, Nat. Conv., Atlanta; chmn. conv. com. Nat. Council of Juvenile Ct. Judges, Milw., 1972; chmn. State Task Force on Juvenile Delinquency, 1970-71; legis. com. Wis. Bd. Juvenile Ct. Judges, 1970-71; former mem. numerous legis. coms., Milw.; pioneered Legal Defender System in Children's Ct.; lecturer, Marquette U. Co-author: LEAA Uniform Standards for Police Departments, 1973 (Pres.'s citation). Bd. dirs. Am. Indian Info. and Action Group, Inc. "Project Phoenix", Juneau Acad.; chmn. Milw. County Rep. Party, 1961-62; active supporter numerous community juvenile programs, including Milw. Boys' Club, St. Joseph's Home for Children, Mt. Mary Coll. Proglram for Truant and Delinquent Girls, Operation Outreach, others; Social Security judge. With USN, 1943-46. Recipient Continious Svc. award Office of Hearings and Appeals Soc. Security Adminstr., 1991. Mem. Fed. Assn. Adminstrv. Law Judges, Assn. Office of Hearing and Appeals Adminstrv. Law Judges, Wis. State Bar Assn., Milw. Bar. Assn., Nat. Council Juvenile Ct. Judges, Am. Judicature Soc., Nat. Council of Sr. Citizens, Inc., Internat. Juvenile Officers Assn., Am. Legion (former post comdr.), Nat. Probate Judges Assn., New Trier Rep. Orgn., Committeeman's Club, Hawthorne Turf Club, Sigma Alpha Epsilon. Roman Catholic. Home: 2824 Orchard Ln Wilmette IL 60091-2144

BOWMAN, HAZEL LOIS, retired English language educator; b. Plant City, Fla., Feb. 18, 1917; d. Joseph Monroe and Annie (Thoman) B. AB, Fla. State Coll. for Women, 1937; MA, U. Fla., 1948; postgrad., U. Md., 1961-65. Tchr. Lakeview H.S., Winter Garden, Fla., 1939-40, Eagle Lake Sch., Fla., 1940-41; welfare visitor Fla. Welfare Bd., 1941-42; specialist U.S. Army Signal Corps, Arlington Hall, Va., 1942-43; recreation work, asst. procurement officer ARC, CBI Theater, 1943-46; lab. technician Am. Cyanamid Corp., Brewster, Fla., 1946-47; instr., asst. prof. gen. extension divsn. U. Fla., Fla. State U., 1948-51; freelance writer, editor, indexer N.Y., Fla., 1951-55; staff writer Tampa (Fla.) Morning Tribune, 1956; staff writer, telegraph editor Winter Haven (Fla.) News-Chief, 1956-57; registrar, admissions officer U. Tampa, 1957-59; coll. counselor Atlantic States, 1959-60; registrar, freshman advisor Towson State Tchrs. Coll., Balt., 1960-62; dir. student pers., guidance, admissions Harford Jr. Coll., Bel Air, Md., 1962-64; instr., asst. prof. York (Pa.) Coll., 1965-69, asst. prof. English, journalism, 1966-69; tchr. S.W. Jr. H.S., Lakeland, Fla., 1969-70; tchr. learning disabled Vanguard Sch., Lake Wales, Fla., 1970-82; libr. asst. Polk County Hist. and Geneal. Libr., Bartow, Fla., 1986-91. Editor, Tampa Altrusan, 1958-60, Polk County Hist. Calendar, 1986-90. Mem. Polk County Hist. Commn., 1992-99. Recipient Mayhall Music medal, 1933, Excellence in Cmty. Svc. award Nat. Soc. DAR, 1994, Outstanding Achievement award Fla. State Geneal. Soc., 2002. Mem. AAUW (hon. 50 yr. life), NOW, Nat. Geneal. Soc., Mortar Board, Polk County Hist. Assn. (editor Newsletter 1990-94), Imperial Polk Genealogical Soc., Alpha Chi Alpha, Chi Delta Phi. Home: 511 NE 9th Ave Mulberry FL 33860-2620

BOWMAN, JAMES EDWARD, physician, educator; b. Washington, Feb. 5, 1923; s. James Edward and Dorothy (Peterson) B.; m. Barbara Taylor, June 17, 1950; 1 child, Valerie June. BS, Howard U., 1943, MD, 1946. Intern Freedmen's Hosp., Washington, 1946-47; resident pathology St. Lukes Hosp., Chgo., 1947-50; chmn. dept. pathology Provident Hosp., 1950-53, Shiraz (Iran) Med. Ctr. Nemazee Hosp., 1955-61; vis. prof., chmn. dept. pathology faculty of medicine U. Shiraz, 1959-61; dir. labs. U. Chgo., 1971-80, prof. dept. pathology, medicine, com. on genetics, biol. scis., collegiate div., 1972-93, dir., 1973-93, prof. emeritus, 1993—. Cons. pathology, div. hosp. and med. facilities HEW, USPHS, 1968; mem. Health and Hosps. Governing Commn., Cook County, 1969-72; mem. exec. com. hemalytic anemia study group NHLI, NIH, Bethesda, Md., 1973-75, Sabbatical fellow Ctr. for Advanced Study in Behavioral Scis., Stanford U., 1981-82, Ethical, Legal & Social Issues, Nat. Human Genome Program NIH/DOE. Contbr. to books and articles to profl. jours. Capt. M.C., AUS, 1953-55. Spl. rsch. fellow NIH Galton Lab., Univ. Coll., London, 1961-62. Mem. Coll. Am. Pathologists, Am. Soc. Clin. Pathologists, Am. Soc. Human Genetics, Cen. Soc. Clin. Rsch., Am. Soc. Hematology, Am. Assn. Phys. Anthropologists, Acad. Clin. Lab. Physicians and Scientists. Home: 4929 S Greenwood Ave Chicago IL 60615-2815 Office: U Chgo Dept Pathology 5841 S Maryland Ave Chicago IL 60637-1463 Fax: 773-285-1549. E-mail: jbowman@uchicago.edu.

BOWMAN, JAMES KINSEY, publishing company executive, rare book specialist; b. Strongsville, Ohio, Nov. 1, 1933; s. Benjamin H. and Margaret A. (Kinsey) B.; m. Judith Ann Lofton, Mar. 29, 1957; children: J. Reed, Eustacia L., Todd K. BA, Denison U., Granville, Ohio, 1956. With McGraw-Hill Book Co., N.Y.C., 1956-90, gen. mgr., v.p. coll. div., 1965-68, group v.p. higher edn., 1968-73, v.p. marketing, 1973-82, sr. v.p. adminstrn., 1982-84, sr. v.p. internat., 1984-87, v.p. gen. mgr. bookstores, 1987-90; chief exec. officer Judith Bowman Books, 1990—. Bd. dirs. Catskill Fly Fishing Ctr. and Mus., 1998—. Mem. Am. Assn. Pubs. (pres. coll. div. 1971-72), Slagle Trout Club (Mich.), Bedford Chowder and Marching Club (pres. 1976-77), Atlantic Salmon Fedn., Theodore Gordon Flyfishers Club (N.Y.C.), Campfire Club Am. (N.Y.), Anglers Club of N.Y., Phi Gamma Delta. Democrat. Presbyterian. Home and Office: 98 Pound Ridge Rd Bedford NY 10506-1241

BOWMAN, JEAN LOUISE, lawyer, civic worker; b. Albuquerque, Apr. 3, 1938; d. David Livingstone and Charlotte Louise (Smith) McArthur; children: Carolyn Louise, Joan Emily, Amy Elizabeth, Eric Daniel. Student, U. N.Mex., 1956-57, U. Pa., 1957-58, Rocky Mountain Coll., 1972-74; BA in Polit. Sci. with high honors, U. Mont., 1982, JD, 1985. Dir. Christian edn. St. Luke's Episcopal Ch., 1979-80; law clk. to assoc. justice Mont. Supreme Ct., 1985-87; exec. v.p. St. Peter's Cmty. Hosp. Found., 1987-91; exec. dir. Harrison Hosp. Found., Bremerton, Wash., 1991-93, St. Patrick Hosp. and Health Found., 1993—2001, Missoula Symphony Bd., 1993-99; pres. Missoula Symphony Assn., 1996-98; dir. devel. Five Valleys Land Trust, 2002—. Bd. dirs. 1st Bank West. Trustee Rocky Mountain Coll., 1972-80; bd. dirs. Billings (Mont.) Area C. of C., 1977-80; mem. City-County Air Pollution Control Bd., 1969-74, chmn., 1970-71; del. Mont. State Constnl. Conv., 1971-72, sec., 1971-72; chmn. County Local Govt. Study Commn., 1973-76; mem. long range planning com. Billings Sch. Dist., 1978-79; bd. dirs. Billings LWV, 1970-72; pres. Helena LWV, 1988, 2d v.p. Mont. LWV, 1987-91; bd. dirs. Internat. Choral Festival, 1999—, Mont. Justice Found., 1999—. Named one of Billings' most influential citizens Billings Gazette, 1977; Bertha Morton scholar, 1982. Mem. Mont. State Bar, Missoula Rotary (pres. 1997-98). Republican. Home: 1911 E Broadway St Missoula MT 59802-4901 E-mail: jmbmslamt@msn.com.

BOWMAN, JEFFREY NEIL, podiatrist; b. Detroit, Apr. 25, 1957; s. Harry and Helen (London) B.; m. Carol Jane Bartlett, Apr. 12, 1986; 1 child, Dana. BS in Biology/Zoology, U. Mich., 1979; DPM, Ill. Coll. Podiatric Medicine, Chgo., 1983. Diplomate Am. Coun. Cert. Podiatric Physicians and Surgeons, Am. Acad. Pain Mgmt., Am. Bd. Podiatric Orthopedics. Resident Harris County Podiatric Surg. Found., Houston, 1983-84; physician Houston Foot Specialists, 1983-86, pres., CEO, 1986—. Bd. dirs. West Houston Surgicare, 1994—, dept. chmn. surgery, 1995—; mem. residency selection com. Houston Podiatric Residency Found., 1990—. Mem. adv. bd. KTRH Radio Sta., Houston, 1994—; physician Houston Marathon, 1984—; health care advisor Houston Ind. Sch. Dist., 1992-94. Recipient Cert. of Excellence, Disting. Physicians Am., 1994—. Fellow Internat. Soc. Podiatric Laser Surgery, Acad. Ambulatory Foot Surgery; mem. Am. Podiatric Med. Assn., Tex. Podiatric Med. Assn. (bd. dirs. 2001—), Harris county Podiatric Med. Assn. Republican. Jewish. Avocations: reading, golf, computers, investments. Office: 8945 Long Point Rd Ste 209 Houston TX 77055-3009 E-mail: drbowman@swbell.net.

BOWMAN, JERRY WAYNE, artist, research scientist; b. Columbia City, Ind., Aug. 3, 1952; s. Wayne Austin and Patricia Ann Bowman; m. Susan Jolie Alexander, Feb. 12, 1988; children: Rachel, Lily. BA magna cum laude, Kalamazoo Coll., 1974. Rsch. scientist Pfizer Inc., Kalamazoo, 1978—. Exhibited in group shows at San Diego Watercolor Soc., 1994, N.W. Watercolor Soc., 1994, Phila. Watercolor Soc., 1995, Grand Exhbn., 1993, 95, Watercolor USA, 1994-96, 98, 2000, 01, 03, Watercolor West, 1992, 94, 96, 97; Rocky Mountain Nat., 1992, 96, 98, 2000, 03, Watercolor Now!, 2003; paintings published in book: Splash 5: Best of Watercolor, 1998, (mag.) Manhattan Arts Internat., 1995. Recipient 1st prize Best of Mich. Show, 1999, 2003, cash prize Watercolor USA, 2000, 03. Mem. Watercolor West (signature, Nat. Watercolor Soc. prize 1997), Rocky Mountain Watermedia Soc. (signature, prize 1998, Daniel Smith award 1991, Golden Palette award 2000), Kalamazoo Inst. Arts, Watercolor USA Honor Soc. Avocations: ornithology, travel, primitive art. Home: 83626 Waldron Dr Lawton MI 49065-7609 E-mail: jerrywbowman@earthlink.net.

BOWMAN, JOHN STEWART, writer, editor; b. Cambridge, Mass., May 30, 1931; s. John Russell and Anne Marie (Stewart) B.; m. Marion Palmedo, Dec. 17, 1957 (div. Sept. 1965); m. Francesca Maria DiPietro, Feb. 11, 1967; children: Michela Anne, Alexander Russell. BA, Harvard U., 1953; postgrad., Cambridge (Eng.) U., 1953-54, U. Munich, 1958-59. Assoc. editor Natural History Mag., N.Y.C., 1961, Book of Knowledge, N.Y.C., 1962-63. Vis. lectr. continuing edn. U. Mass., Amherst, 1978-90. Author: Guide to Crete, 1963-92; co-author: Diamonds in the Rough, 1989; editor: Cambridge Dictionary of American Biography, 1995, Facts About American Wars, 1998, Columbia Chronologies of Asian History and Culture, 2000, Wiley's Encyclopedia of North American Exploration, 2003; librettist operas: The Face, 1978, Emperor Norton, 1981. With U.S. Army, 1954-56. Mem. Soc. for Am. Baseball Rsch., Phi Beta Kappa, Alpha Sigma Lambda. Avocations: reading, walking, music. Home and Office: 53 Massasoit St Northampton MA 01060-2015 Fax: 413-584-0720. E-mail: jsbowman@comcast.net.

BOWMAN, JOSEPH LEONARD, music educator; b. Warren, Ohio, July 2, 1975; s. Terrence Lee and Christine Holloway Bowman. MusB, U. of Cin., 1997; MusM, Ariz. State U., 1999, MusD, 2002. Grad. tchg. asst. Ariz. State U., Tempe, Ariz., 1999—2001; asst. prof. of music U. of Tenn., Martin, Tenn., 2001—. Youth website editor Internat. Trumpet Guild, 2002—; performing artist Yamaha Corp. of Am., Grand Rapids, Mich., 2002—; artist faculty Nat. Trumpet Competition, Washington, 2002—. Musician: Faculty Recital; contbr. articles to profl. jours. Musician Arts in the Desert Cmty. Outreach Program, Tempe, 1998—2001, various Chs., 1993. Mem.: Internat. Assn. of Jazz Educators, The Coll. Music Soc., Internat. Trumpet Guild, Phi Mu Alpha Sinfonia (chpt. pres. 1995—97). Independent. Roman Catholic. Achievements include completed first annotated bibliography of Published Twentieth-Century Sonatas for Trumpet and Piano, 2002. Avocations: golf, travel, softball, baseball. Home: 459 Lackey Road E1 Martin TN 38237 Office: 102 Fine Arts Building The Univerisity of Tennessee at Martin Martin TN 38238 Fax: 731-587-7415. E-mail: jbowman1993@yahoo.com.

BOWMAN, LAIRD PRICE, retired foundation administrator; b. Topeka, Jan. 28, 1927; s. Herbert Douglas and Marion Martha (Price) B.; m. Betty Lou Pote, Dec. 24, 1950; children: Bruce Pote, Susan Bowman Adams. BS, U. Kans., 1950, LLB, 1952. Bar: Kans. 1952, Mo. 1956. Law clk. chief judge U.S. Dist. Ct. Kans., 1952-53; assoc. firm McAnany, Van Cleave & Phillips, Kansas City, Kans., 1953-55; mem. firm Gage Hodges, Park & Kreamer, Kansas City, Mo., 1955-64; with Gas Service Co., Kansas City, Mo., 1964-83, asst. gen. counsel, 1968-70, sec., asst. gen. counsel, 1970-83, v.p., 1978-83, dir., 1979-83; asst. to the pres. Kans. U. Endowment Assn., U. Kans., Lawrence, 1983-91, ret., 1991. With USMC, 1945-47. Mem. Kans. Bar Assn., Mo. Bar Assn., Sigma Chi, Phi Delta Phi. Congregationalist. Home: 1120 Jana Dr Lawrence KS 66049-4418

BOWMAN, LARRY WAYNE, investigator, English and criminal justice educator; b. Mansfield, Ohio, Feb. 8, 1952; s. Ted L. Bowman and Mary Lou (Devore) Dessenberg. B in Criminal Justice, U. Md., 1978, M in Criminal Justice, MA English Lit., U. Md., 1980, PhD in Psychology, 1998; PhD in ESL, Am. Internat. U., 1999. Lic. pvt. investigator. Pvt. investigator, Ohio and Mont., 1974—; English and criminal justice prof. Yeung Jin Coll., Taegu, South Korea, 1992-97; prof., investigator, guidance counselor Kwajalein Police Dept., 1997—2002; prof. criminal justice U. Great Falls, Mont., 2002—. Drug awareness educator, 1974-92; prof./investigator, counselor Kwajalein Police Dept., Republic of Marshall Islands, 1997—. Served with USAF, with Mont. Army N.G., 1970—. Named Outstanding Young Man of Am., 1988. Mem. VFW (life), Air Force Assn. (life), Air Force Security Police Assn., Am. C. of C. (Korea), Am. Legion (life), Amvets (life), Lions, Optimist, Elks. Democrat. Presbyterian. Avocations: hunting, fishing, trapping.

BOWMAN, MARJORIE ANN, family practice physician, educator; b. Grove City, Pa., Aug. 18, 1953; d. Ross David and Freda Louise (Smith) Williamson; m. Robert Choplin; children: Bridget Williamson Foley, Skyler Weston Williamson Choplin. BS, Pa. State U., 1974; MD, Jefferson Med. Coll., 1976; MPA, U. So. Calif., L.A., 1983. Intern, then resident in family practice Duke U., Durham, N.C., 1976-79; med. officer USPHS, Hyattsville, Md., 1979-82; clin. instr. uniformed svcs. U. Health Scis., Bethesda, Md., 1980-83; dir. family practice residency, prof. Georgetown U. Sch. Medicine, Washington, 1983-86; chmn. dept. family practice, prof. Wake Forest U., Winston-Salem, N.C., 1986-96; chmn. dept. family practice U. Pa., Phila, 1996—. Author: (Book) Stress and Women Physicians, 1985, 1990, Women in Medicine: Life and Career, 2002; editor: Archives Family Medicine, 1992—2000, Jour. Women's Health, 2001; contbr. articles to profl. jours. Fellow Am. Acad. Family Physicians; mem. AMA, Soc. Tchrs. Family Medicine (bd. dirs. 1984-88, bd. dirs. Found. 1984-99, v.p. 1988-91, pres. 1991-92), Am. Pub. Health Assn. Republican. Unitarian Universalist. Office: Univ Pa 2 Gates 3400 Spruce St Philadelphia PA 19104-4283

BOWMAN, NED DAVID, medical administrator; b. Chattanooga, Tenn., July 15, 1948; s. Ned Turner and Ernie June (White) B. and Charlotte Bramblett B. (stepmother); m. Linda Carol Eggers, Sep. 18, 1970; children: Robert, Jean, Elizabeth, Scott, Benjamin. BS, U. Tenn., 1971; MBA, Vanderbilt U., 1982. Participant exec. program Managing Ambulatory Health Care Orgns., Harvard Sch. Pub. Health, 1987. Adminstr. Oak Ridge (Tenn.) Orthopedic Ctr., 1971-91, pres., CEO Ancillary Physicians Svcs., Inc., 1976-85; adminstr. Charlotte (N.C.) Eye, Ear, Nose and Throat Assn., 1991-96; chief adminstrv. officer Bond Clinic, Winter Haven, Fla., 1996-99; CEO Richmond Radiological Cons., LLC, 1999—. Pres. Anderson County Health Coun., Clinton, Tenn., 1980-81, 94, 88; v.p. Knoxville Soc. for Advancement of Mgmt., Knoxville, 1974; bd. dirs. Tng. and Tech. Ctr., Oak Ridge, 1976-78; pres., CEO Ctrl. Fla. Physician's Network, Inc., 1998—; founding pres. Polk County Health Improvement Coun., 1997-99. Bd. dirs. C. of C., Oak Ridge, 1972-76, Boys Club Am., Oak Ridge, 1982-86, DRI, Knoxville, 1982, Great Smoky Mtn. coun. Boy Scouts Am., Knoxville, 1984-86, Piedmont Health Care Preferred Provider Orgn., 1992-94, Citrus Boys Club, Winter Haven, Fla., 1996—, Boys and Girls Club, Winter Haven, Fla., 1997-99; mem. gov. bd. dirs. Am. Soc. Ophth. Adminstrs., 1995-98; mem. local exec. com. LDS Ch., Charlotte, 1991-96, Winter Haven, 1997; treas. UN com., Oak Ridge, 1980-86; trustee health plan Mechlenburg County Med. Soc., 1992-96; exec. bd. Indian Waters coun. Boy Scouts Am., Columbia; exec. com. Church of Jesus Christ of Latter-day Saints. Recipient Certs. of Appreciation Vocat. Edn. Dept., Oak Ridge H.S., 1978, Anderson County Health Coun., Oak Ridge, 1980, Soc. for Advancement of Mgmt., Knoxville, 1976, Oak Ridge Human Resource Bd., 1975, Rotary Found. Dist. Svc. award. Mem. AAAS, Am. Coll. Healthcare Execs., Am. Soc. Ophthalmic Adminstrs. (Outstanding Contbn. award 1995-97), Am. Coll. Med. Practice Execs., Med. Group Mgmt. Assn., Fla. Med. Group Mgmt. Assn., Tenn. Med. Group Mgmt. Assn., S.C. Med. Group Mgmt. Assn., Radiology Bus. Mgrs. Assn., Healthcare Fin. Mgmt. Assn., Rotary, Winter Haven C. of C. (bd. dirs. 1998). Avocations: geneaology, basketball, organizing activities for youth, river rafting, hiking. Office: Richland Radiol Cons Columbia SC 29223 Home: 10 S Fork Pl Columbia SC 29223 E-mail: ndbowman@aol.com.

BOWMAN, PASCO MIDDLETON, II, judge; b. Timberville, Va., Dec. 20, 1933; s. Pasco Middleton and Katherine (Lohr) Bowman; m. Ruth Elaine Bowman, July 12, 1958; children: Ann Katherine, Helen Middleton, Benjamin Garber. BA, Bridgewater Coll., 1955; JD, NYU, 1958; LLM, U. Va., 1986; LLD (hon.), Bridgewater Coll., 1988. Bar: N.Y. 1958, Ga. 1965, Mo. 1980. Assoc. firm Cravath, Swaine & Moore, N.Y.C., 1958—61, 1962—64; asst. prof. law U. Ga., 1964—65, assoc. prof., 1965—69, prof., 1969—70, Wake Forest U., 1970—78, dean, 1970—78; vis. prof. U. Va., 1978—79; prof., dean U. Mo., Kansas City, 1979—83; judge U.S. Ct. Appeals (8th cir.), Kansas City, Mo., 1983—98, sr. judge, 1999—, chief judge, 1998—99. Mng. editor: NYU Law Rev., 1957—58, reporter, chief draftsman: Georgia Corporation Code, 1965—68. Col. USAR, 1959—84. Scholar Root-Tilden scholar, 1955—58; Fulbright scholar, London Sch. Econs. and Polit. Sci., 1961—62. Mem.: Mo. Bar, N.Y. Bar. Office: US Ct Appeals 8th Circuit 10-50 US Courthouse 400 E 9th St Kansas City MO 64106-2607

BOWMAN, PHILLIP BOYNTON, lawyer; b. Ames, Iowa, Feb. 28, 1936; s. Alfred Boynton and Susan Jean (Foxworthy) B.; m. Elizabeth Wales Porter, June 20, 1959; children: Susan Foxworthy, William Porter, Peter Wales. BS in Engring., Princeton U., 1958; JD, U. Mich., 1961. Bar: Ill. 1961, U.S. Dist. Ct. (no. dist.) Ill. 1962, U.S. Ct. Appeals (7th cir.) 1965. Assoc. then ptnr. Gorham, Adams, White & DeYoung, Chgo., 1961-75; ptnr. Gorham, Metge, Bowman & Hourigan, Chgo., 1976— . Pres., commr. Northbrook Park Dist., Ill., 1968-76; pres., bd. dirs., referee, coach, Northbrook Hockey League, 1962-86. Mem. ABA, Ill. Bar Assn., Chgo. Bar Assn., Chgo. Soc. Assn. Execs. (edn. com. 1984—), Ill. Bankers Assn. Republican. Episcopalian. Clubs: Skokie Country (Glencoe, Ill.) (golf com. 1984); Chgo. Curling (Northbrook) (bd. dirs., sec. 1980-87), Tavern (Chgo.), Law, Legal. Home: 2060 Plymouth Ln Northbrook IL 60062-6064 Office: 300 W Washington St Chicago IL 60606-1707

BOWMAN, RANDALL HUNTER, reference and instruction librarian; b. Sanford, N.C., Dec. 4, 1966; s. Jimmy Tiree and Kay (Laferney) B. AA summa cum laude, Louisburg Coll., 1990; BA, U. N.C., 1992; MLIS, U.N.C., Greensboro, 1997. Info. desk asst. U. N.C., Greensboro, 1996-97; libr. intern Ctr. for Creative Leadership, Greensboro, 1996; desk supr. U. N.C., Chapel Hill, 1997; ref. libr. Gardner-Webb U., Boiling Springs, NC, 1997-2000; reference and instrn. libr. Elon U., 2000—. Lit. tutor Boiling Springs (N.C.) Elem. Sch., 1998-99; pub. coord., mem. ch. coun. Ctrl. United Meth. Ch., Shelby, N.C., 1999-2000; libr. coord. 1st United Meth. Ch., Elon, 2001—. Mem. ALA, ACRL, N.C. Libr. Assn., Louisburg Coll. Alumni Assn. (pres., bd. dirs. 2003—). Home: 6336 Hibiscus Ct Whitsett NC 27377 Office: Belk Libr Elon U Box 2550 Elon NC 27244

BOWMAN, RICHARD CARL, defense consultant, retired air force officer; b. Chgo., July 5, 1926; s. Carl Elias and Lucile (Rutan) B.; m. Lois Jean Hassenauer, June 10, 1950; children: Mary Bowman Millikin, Kristin Bowman Spencer, Margaret Bowman Flaherty, Victoria Bowman Smoke, Richard Carl. BS, U.S. Mil. Acad., 1949; MS, Okla. State U., 1954; MPA, Harvard U., 1958, PhD, 1964. Enlisted in U.S. Army, 1943; commd. 2d lt. USAF, 1949, advanced through grades to maj. gen., 1975; pilot, flight comdr. Korea, 1951; mem. initial staff Air Force Acad., 1955-57, assoc. prof. polit. sci., 1959-63; mem. staff Nat. Security Council, 1964-66, Office Sec. Air Force, 1967-73; dep. def. adviser to Am. ambassador to NATO, 1973-75; dir. European and NATO affairs Office Sec. Def., 1975-81, ret., 1981. Contbr. to mil. jours. Decorated Def. D.S.M. (2), Air Force D.S.M., Def. Superior Service medal, Legion of Merit (2), D.F.C., Air medal (3), Commendation medal (2); Grand Service Cross with Star W. Ger.; comdr. Order of St. Olaf (Norway, with star). Mem.: Harvard U. Alumni Assn., West Point Assn. Grads., KC (assoc. marshall, past grand knight). Roman Catholic. Home: 7824 Midday Ln Alexandria VA 22306-2724

BOWMAN, RICHARD FREDERICK, banker; b. Evanston, Ill., Jan. 16, 1952; s. Donald Wallace and Elizabeth Mary (Hauser) B.; m. Mary Jane Sweeney, May 10, 1975. BA, Coll. William and Mary, 1972. Cert. bank auditor; CPA, Va. Staff acct. A.M. Pullen & Co., Richmond, Va., 1972-73; sr. acct. Laventhol & Horwath, Norfolk and Washington, 1973-75; v.p., contr. First Va. Banks, Inc., Falls Church, 1975-92, exec. v.p., treas., CFO, 1992—. Tchr. Am. Inst. Banking, 1979— . Bd. dirs., sec-treas. Laurel Mews Condominium Assn., 1980-86; bd. dirs Arlington County Indsl. Devel. Authority, 1982-86. Mem. AICPA. Home: 2710 Oak Valley Dr Vienna VA 22181-5340 Office: 1st Va Banks Inc One First Virginia Plaza 6400 Arlington Blvd Falls Church VA 22042-2336

BOWMAN, ROGER MANWARING, real estate executive; b. Duluth, Minn., Dec. 3, 1916; s. Lawrence Fredrick and Gladys (Manwaring) B.; m. Judith Claypool, Apr. 10, 1942 (dec. 1993); Ann, David, Mary Bowman Johnson, Lawrence II. Attended, U. Mich., 1934-36; student, Wayne State U., 1937. Pres. N. Star Airways, Duluth, 1946-50, North Star Engring. Co., Duluth, 1946-50, Superior (Wis.) Aero, 1946-50, Lawrence F. Bowman Co., Duluth, 1950-70, Gen. Cleaning Corp., Duluth, 1954-92, Bowman Corp., Duluth, 1970-83, Bowman Properties, Duluth, 1983-92; chmn. Deltona Corp., Miami, Fla., 1985-89. Cons. Topeka Group, Duluth, 1985-89; bd. dirs. Parish Corp., Minn. Power, Norwest Bank; chmn. Bowman Properties, 1988-96, Gen. Cleaning Corp., 1985—; mng. gen. ptnr. 6 ltd. partnerships, 1990—. Chmn. St. Louis County Welfare, Duluth, 1964-69, chmn. Govs. Real Estate Adv. Commn., 1968-70; pres. Duluth Devel. Corp., 1960-68; trustee Ordean Found., 1968-92; bd. dirs. Duluth Bd. Realtors, 1958-62; pres. Duluth Bldg. Owners and Mgrs. Assn. Internat., 1963-65. Lt. col. USMCR, 1940-45. Recipient Silver Beaver award Boy Scouts Am., 1959, Mayor's Commendation, City of Duluth, 1976. Mem. Duluth Steam Coop. (bd. dirs. 1970-86), Duluth Bldg. Owners and Mgrs. Internat., Duluth Bd. Realtors, Real Property Adminstrs. Clubs: Kitchi Gammi (dir. 1974-78), Northland Country, Boca Raton Resort and Club, Delray Beach Yacht Club. Republican. Episcopalian. Avocation: cooking. Office: 575 Wells Fargo Ctr Duluth MN 55802 E-mail: rbowman16@aol.com.

BOWMAN, SCOTT MCMAHAN, lawyer; b. Shaker Heights, Ohio, Mar. 16, 1962; s. George Henry and Patricia (McMahan) B.; children: Chad Marshall, David Chandler, Elizabeth Brooks; stepchildren: Garrett Richard Sevek, Grant Allen Sevek. AA in Bus., Fullerton Coll., 1987; BBA, Calif. State U., Fullerton, 1989; JD, U. Cin., 1992. Pvt. practice, Salem, Ohio, 1992—. Asst. city solicitor Salem, 1992-94; advisor YWCA Salem, 1994—; advisor Butler Inst. Art, Salem, 1994—; intermediary, counsel Unorganized Militia, 1996—. Author: The Turning Point, A Personal Account of the Montana Freemen Standoff, 1997. Mem. Design Review Bd. City of Salem (Ohio), 1993-95, v.p., 1995; mem. Salem Planning and Zoning Commn., 1993-95, v.p., 1995; co-founder, trustee Salem Preservation Soc., 1993-95. Epsicopal. Avocations: camping, hunting, surfing, coaching football, politics. Office: PO Box 558 Salem OH 44460-0558 E-mail: SBowmanEsq@aol.com.

BOWMAN, STEPHEN WAYNE, quality assurance engineer, consultant; b. Charlotte, N.C., Oct. 3, 1949; s. John Wayne and Dagmar Katharine (Hege) B.; m. Patricia Faye Waldron, June 17, 1972 (div. 1988); 1 child, Jennifer Leigh. BS in Physics, Ga. Inst. Tech., 1972, MS in Nuclear Engring., 1974. Registered profl. engr., Tex.; cert. quality sys. lead auditor (RAB). Quality assurance engr. GE, Schenectady, N.Y., 1978-81; mgr. IEEE qualification program Stewart and Stevenson Svcs., Houston, 1981-86, mgr. nuclear projects, 1984-86; sr. engr. Pacific Engring. Corp., Portland, Oreg., 1988-89; pres. Bowman and Assocs., Kingwood, Tex., 1986—; project quality assurance mgr. M.W. Kellogg Co., Houston, 1990-96; sr. ptnr. Internat. Mgmt. Systems Co., Midvale, Utah, 1992—; quality assurance mgr. Intec Engring., Inc., Houston, 1997-99; v.p. ops. Tex. Air Corps, 2000—; quality assurance coord. SparTEC, Houston, 2002—03; v.p. engring. TIEC, Inc., Houston, 2003—. Chmn. curriculum adv. bd. dept. mfg. tech. Houston C.C., 1984-87. Contbr. articles to profl. jours. 1st lt. U.S. Army, 1975-78. Mem. Am. Nuclear Soc., Am. Soc. Quality. Home and Office: Bowman & Assocs 1915 Crystal Springs Dr Kingwood TX 77339-3339 E-mail: swbowman@swbell.net.

BOWMAN, WILLIAM SCOTT (SCOTTY BOWMAN), professional hockey coach; b. Montreal, Sept. 18, 1933; s. John and Jane Thomson (Scott) B.; m. Suella Belle Chitty, Aug. 16, 1969; children— Alicia Jean, David Scott, Stanley Glen, Nancy Elizabeth and Robert Gordon (twins). Student, Sir George Williams Bus. Sch., 1954. Scout exec. Club de Hockey Canadien, Montreal, 1956-66, coach, 1971-79; coach, gen. mgr. St. Louis Blues Hockey Club, 1966-71; coach, gen. mgr., dir. hockey ops. Buffalo Sabres Hockey Club, 1979-86; TV analyst Hockey Night in Can., 1987-90; dir. player devel. Pitts. Penguins Hockey Club, 1990-91, interim head coach, 1991-92, head coach, 1992-93; head coach Detroit Red Wings Hockey Club, 1993—2002, dir. player pers., 1993—2002. Recipient Jack Adams award, 1977, 96, Victor award for NHL Coach of Yr., 1993, 96, 2002, Stanley Cup Championship, 1973, 1976-79, 1992, 1997-98, 2002, Lester Patrick award, 2001, Can. Soc. N.Y. award, 2001; named NHL Exec. of Yr. Sporting News, 1979-80, NHL Coach of the Yr. Sporting News, 1995-96, NHL Coach of the Yr. Hockey News, 1976, 77, 93-97, NHL Exec. of the Yr. Hockey News, 1996-97, NHL Coach of the Yr., 1967-68, Hockey News Coach of Yr., 1968, 76, 95-96, Exec. of Yr., 1997; inducted into Hockey Hall of Fame, 1991, Mich. Sports Hall of Fame, 1999, Buffalo Sports Hall of Fame, 2000, mem. Hockey Hall of Fame Selection Com.; holder NHL career regular season records for wins (1,244) and winning percentage (.670); holder NHL career playoffs records for wins (223) and games (353); recipient Stanley Cup as head coach Montreal Canadiens, 1973, 76-79, Pitts. Penguins, 1992, Detroit Red Wings, 1997-98, 2002; only coach in NHL history to win Stanley Cup with 3 different teams. Mich. Sports Hall of Fame, 2001 Office: Detroit Red Wings Joe Louis Arena 600 Civic Center Dr Detroit MI 48226-4419

BOWMAN-DALTON, BURDENE KATHRYN, education testing coordinator, computer consultant; b. Magnolia, Ohio, July 13, 1937; d. Ernest Mowles and Mary Kathryn (Long) Bowman; m. Louis W. Dalton, Mar. 13, 1979. BME, Capital U., 1959; MA in Edn., Akron U., 1967, postgrad., 1976-87. Profl. vocalist, various clubs in the East, 1959-60; music tchr. East Liverpool (Ohio) City Shcs., 1959-62, Revere Local Schs., Akron, Ohio, 1962-75, elem. tchr., 1975-80, elem. team leader/computer cons., 1979-85, tchr. middle sch. math., gifted-talented, computer literacy, 1981-92, dist. computer specialist, 1987-93, dist. statis. for standardize local testing, 1987-91, dist. tech. coord., 1993-98, ret., 1998. Local and regional dir. Olympics of Mind, also World Problem Captain for computer problem, 1984-86; cons., workshop presenter State of Ohio, 1987-91, dist. test. coord., 1991-98; coord. for Revere Schs., Ednl. Mgmt. Info. Sys., 1992-98; mem. Citizen Com., Akron, 1975-76; profl. rep. Bath Assn. to Help, 1978-80; mem. Revere Levy Com. 1986, Revere Bond Issue Com., 1991; audit com. BATH, 1977-79; vol. chmn. Antique Car Show, Akron, 1972-81; dist. advisor MidWest Talent Search, 1987-93; dist. statistician of standardized rech. test results. Martha Holden Jennings Found. grantee, 1977-78; Title IV ESEA grantee, 1977-81. Mem. Assn. for Devel. Computer-Based Instrnl. Sys. (dir. 1992-94), Ednl. Mgmt. Info. Sys. and Proficiency Test (coord. for Revere Schs. 1992-2003), Phi Beta. Home: 353 Retreat Dr Akron OH 44333-1623 Office: 3195 Spring Valley Rd Bath OH 44210-0339

BOWNE, SHIRLEE PEARSON, finance and housing consultant; b. High Shoals Twp., N.C., Mar. 11, 1936; d. Lloyd E. Pearson and Parnell (James) Garland; divorced; 1 child, Gregory Charles. Grad. h.s., Gaffney, S.C. Various secretarial positions, 1955-64; sales repr., pres. Real Estate Marketers, Inc., Tallahassee, 1964-80; chief exec. officer Shirlee Bowne Mktg. & Devel. Inc., Tallahassee, 1980-91; vice chmn. Nat. Credit Union Adminstrn., Washington, 1991-97. Cons. in field. Treas. Rep. Party Fla., 1988-91. Episcopalian. Avocation: bridge.

BOWNES, HUGH HENRY, judge; b. N.Y.C., Mar. 10, 1920; s. Hugh Gray and Margaret (Henry) Bownes; m. Irja C. Martikainen, Dec. 30, 1944 (dec. Jan. 1991); m. Mary Davis, July 12, 1992. BA, Columbia U., 1941, LLB, 1948. Bar: N.H. 1948. Since practiced in, Laconia; ptnr. firm Nighswander, Lord & Bownes, 1951—66; assoc. justice N.H. Superior Ct., 1966—68; judge U.S. Dist. Ct. N.H., Concord, 1968—77, U.S. Ct. Appeals (1st cir.), 1977—90, sr. judge, 1990—. Chmn. Laconia chpt. ARC, 1951—52; pres. bd. Laconia Hosp. Assn., 1963—64; mem. Laconia City Coun., 1953—57; chmn. Laconia Dem. Com., 1954—57; mayor Laconia, 1963—65; mem. Dem. Nat. Com. for N.H., 1963—66. Maj. USMC, 1941—46. Decorated Silver Star, Purple Heart. Mem.: ABA, Belknap County Bar Assn. (pres. 1965—67), N.H. Bar Assn., Am. Law Inst., Laconia C. of C. (past pres.), Lions Club (past pres. Laconia). Office: US Ct Appeals 1st Cir US Courthouse 1 Courthouse Way Ste 6730 Boston MA 02210-3008

BOWRON, EDGAR PETERS, art museum curator, administrator; b. Birmingham, Ala., May 27, 1943; s. James Edgar Bowron and Dorothe Peters Lowles; children: James Edgar III, Clara Beatrice, St. John Grenfell. BA, Colgate U., 1965; MA, Inst. Fine Arts, NYU, 1969, PHD, 1979. Edn. lectr. Met. Mus. Art, N.Y.C., 1969-70; registrar Mpls. Inst. Arts, 1970-73; curator Renaissance and Baroque art Walters Art Gallery, Balt., 1973-78; adminstrv. asst. to dir. and curator Renaissance and Baroque art Nelson Gallery-Atkins Mus., Kansas City, Mo., 1978-81; dir. N.C. Mus. Art, Raleigh, 1981-85; Elizabeth and John Moors Cabot dir., prof. fine arts Art Mus. Harvard U., Cambridge, Mass., 1985-90; sr. curator paintings Nat. Gallery of Art, Washington, 1991-96; Audrey Jones Beck curator of European art Mus. Fine Arts, Houston, 1996—. Art adv. panel IRS, 1994—. Author: Pompeo Batoni and His British Patrons, 1982; European Paintings before 1900 in the Fogg Mus., 1990; Masterworks of European Painting in Museum of Fine Arts, Houston, 2000; editor: Selected Writings of Anthony M. Clark: Studies in Eighteenth Roman Painting, 1981, The North Carolina Museum of Art: Introduction to the Collections, 1983, Anthony M. Clark, Pompeo Batoni, A Complete Catalogue of his Works with an Introductory Text, 1985, Bernard Bellotto and the Capitals of Europe, 2001; co-editor: Art in Rome in the Eighteenth Century, 2000; contbr. articles to profl. jours. Trustee Mus. Fine Arts, Boston, 1988-90; mem. art adv. panel IRS, 1994-. Mem. NEA (arts and artifacts indemnity adv. panel 2000—), Assn. Art Mus. Dirs. (trustee 1987-90), Master Drawings Assn. (bd. dirs. 1987—) Office: Mus Fine Arts PO Box 6826 Houston TX 77265-6826

BOWRON, LEE MATTHEWS, actuary, consultant; b. Birmingham, Ala., Nov. 4, 1966; s. Richard Anderson and Ruth Matthews Bowron; m. Molly Johnson Bickley, June 12, 1999. BS, U. of the South, 1989. Actuarial asst. Alfa Ins. Cos., Montgomery, Ala., 1990-93; actuary Permanent Gen. Cos., Nashville, 1993-98, v.p., chief actuary, 1998—2001; mem./mgr. Kerper and Bowron LLC, Birmingham, Ala., 2001—. Mem. Am. Acad. Actuaries, Casualty Actuarial Soc. (assoc.), Conf. of Cons. Actuaries, Rotary. Home: 2625 Montevallo Rd Birmingham AL 35223 Office: 3045 Independence Dr Ste B Birmingham AL 35209 E-mail: lbowron@yahoo.com.

BOWSHER, CHARLES ARTHUR, retired government official, business executive; b. Elkhart, Ind., May 30, 1931; s. Matthew A. and Ella M. (West) B.; m. Mary C. Mahoney, Dec. 14, 1963; children: Kathryn M., Stephen C. BS, U. Ill., 1953; MBA, U. Chgo., 1956; DSc in Bus. Adminstrn. (hon.), Bryant Coll., 1984; D Pub. Svc. (hon.), George Washington U., 1993; DSc (hon.), U. Ill.-Chgo., 1994; Dr. Pub. Svc. (hon.), St. Joseph's U., 1994; DSc in Pub. Svc. (hon.), Am. U., 1996. C.P.A., Ill. Ptnr. Arthur Andersen & Co., Chgo., 1956-67, Washington, 1971-81; asst. sec. of Navy for fin. mgmt. Dept. Def., Washington, 1967-71; comptroller gen. U.S., 1981-96. Bd. dirs. Am. Express Bank, DeVry Inc., Washington Mutual Investors Fund, SI Internat.; trustee Ctr. Naval Analysis, Logistics Mgmt. Inst., U.S. Navy Meml. Found., Hitachi Found., Concord Coalition, Com. for a Responsible Fed. Budget; bd. trustees, treas. Nat. Cathedral., Washington. Mem. bus. adv. coun. U. Ill.; mem. vis. com. Sch. Bus., selection com. Roger W. Jones award for Exec. Leadership; mem. nat. adv. bd. Pvt. Sector Coun.; active Bus. Execs. for Nat. Security Commn. With U.S. Army, 1953-55. Recipient Enduring Lifetime Achievement award Am. Acctg. Assn., 1996, Integrity award Office of Insp. Gen., 1996; named to Acctg. Hall of Fame, 1996. Mem. AICPA, Nat. Acad. Pub. Adminstrn., Nat. Assn. Govt. Accts., Burning Tree Club (Washington), Met. Club (Washington), Beta Alpha Psi, Pi Kappa Alpha. Home: 4503 Boxwood Rd Bethesda MD 20816-1815

BOWSHER, DENNIS JAMES, internist, cardiologist, pharmacologist; b. Beech Grove, Ind., 1953; s. Donald Andrew and Jacqueline (Brock) Barker; m. Marcia Ann Peyton, July 1, 1978; children: Karla Ann, Peyton James. BS in Chemistry cum laude, Rose Hulman Inst. Tech., Terre Haute, Ind., 1975; MD with honors, Ind. U., 1979. Intern Northwestern U., Chgo., 1979-80, resident in internal medicine, 1980-82, fellow in clin. pharmacology, 1982-84; fellow in cardiology Ind. U. Sch. Medicine, Indpls., 1984-86; mem. staff Ind. U. Med. Ctr., 1987-91, North Broward Med. Ctr., 1991—, North Ridge Med. Ctr., 1991—. Chmn. Pharmacy Com., Rsch. IRB North Broward Hosp. Dist., 1991-94, 1999—. Mem. ACA, Am. Coll. Cardiology, Am. Coll. Chest Physicians. Office: 440 E Sample Rd Ste 102 Pompano Beach FL 33064-4432

BOWYER, R. TERRY, science educator; s. Darrell V. and Lois M. Bowyer; m. Karolyn M. Johnson, May 24, 1974; children: Bryan D., Jeffrey W. BS in Wildlife Mgmt., Humboldt State U., 1970, MS in Wildlife Mgmt., 1976; PhD in Natural Resoruces, U. of Mich., 1985. Asst. prof. Unity (Maine) Coll., 1980—86; prof. of wildlife ecology U. of Alaska Fairbanks, 1986—2002. Dept. head biology and wildlife U. of Alaska, 1995—96, dep. dir. Inst. of Arctic Biology, 1998—99. Author: (monograph) Wildlife Monographs (Outstanding publ. in wildlife ecology and mgmt. The Wildlife Soc., 1998, Disting. Moose Biologist award, 2001); contbr. sci. and rsch. articles to profl. jours. (Authur S. Einarsen award northwest sect. The Wildlife Soc., 2000);, author (researcher) ; researcher. With U.S. Army, 1972. Fellow: AAAS, Arctic Inst. of N.Am.; mem.: The Wildlife Soc. (pres. 1983—84, v.p. 2002—03, N.W. sect., Alaska chpt., pres. 1989—90). Avocations: upland game bird hunting, fishing. Office: U Alaska Inst Arctic Biology Fairbanks AK 99775-7000

BOX, JOHN HAROLD, b. Commerce, Tex., Aug. 18, 1929; s. E.O. and Mary Emma (Haynes) B.; m. Dorothy Jean Baldwin, Jan. 19, 1952 (div. Jan. 1971); children: Richard B., Kenneth W., Gregory V.; m. Eden Van Zandt, Apr. 9, 1977; stepchildren: William D., Kate V.Z. BArch, U. Tex., 1950. Apprentice O'Neil Ford (architects), San Antonio, 1948; designer Broad & Nelson (architects), Dallas, 1954-56; assoc. Harrell & Hamilton (architects), Dallas, 1956-57; ptnr. Pratt, Box, Henderson & Ptnrs. (architects), Dallas, 1957-83, Box Architects, Austin, 1983—; prof., 1st dean Sch. Architecture and Environ. Design, U. Tex., Arlington, 1971-76; prof., dean Sch. Architecture, U. Tex., Austin, 1976-92, Moody prof., 1983—88. Chmn. design of city task force Goals for Dallas, 1968-70; chmn. Goals Achievement Com., 1970— ; chmn. design com. Greater Dallas Planning Council, 1969; v.p. Save Open Space, 1970 Prin. works include: St. Stephen's Meth. Ch., Dallas, 1962, Great Hall of Apparel Mart, Dallas, 1965, Quadrangle Shopping Ctr., Dallas, 1965, Garden Ctr., Dallas, 1970; master plan Griffin Sq., Dallas, 1971; Marsh House, Austin, 1982; Co-author: Prairies Yield, 1962, Goals for Dallas Proposals for Design of City 1970. Bd. dirs. Dallas Chamber Music Soc., 1960-76, Austin Symphony, 1982-90, Laguna Gloria Art Mus., 1984-90, Austin History Ctr., 1984-88; regional dir. Assn. Collegiate Schs. Architecture, 1975-78. Served to lt. C.E. Corps, USNR, 1955. Co-recipient Enrico Fermi Meml. Archtl. Competition prize, 1957; recipient Grand prize Homes for Better Living Competition, 1959, Edward Rominec award, 1992, Llewelen W. Pitts award, 1998, Disting. Alumnus award U. Tex., 2003, others; Tex. Architecture Found. grantee, 1957 Fellow AIA (pres. Dallas 1967, nat. dir. 1975-78); mem. Tex. Soc. Architects (v.p., commr. edn. and research 1971, design awards 1964-66, 68, 70, 71, 82), Phi Kappa Phi, Alpha Rho Chi, Sigma Nu. Episcopalian. Avocation: flute. Office: U Tex Goldsmith Hall Austin TX 78712-1160 Home: Callejon Blanco # 11 San Miguel Allende 37700 Mexico Mailing: 521 Logan PMB 151A Laredo TX 78040-6633 E-mail: halbox@mail.utexas.edu.

BOXER, ALAN LEE, accountant; b. Denver, Sept. 9, 1935; s. Ben B. and Minnette (Goldman) B.; m. Gayle, Dec. 21, 1958; children: Michael E., Jodi S., Richard S. BSBA in Acctg., U. Denver, 1956. CPA, Colo. Audit mgr. Touche, Ross & Co. CPAs, Denver, 1956-60, Ballin, Milstein & Feinstein CPAs, Denver, 1960-61; prin. Alan L. Boxer, CPA, Denver, 1961-69; v.p and treas. Pawley Co., Denver, 1969-78; pres. Sci-Pro Inc., Denver, 1978-82; regional mgr. A.T.V. Systems, Inc., Denver, 1982-83; prin. The Enterprise Group, Denver, 1983-86; shareholder, pres. Allerdice, Baroch, Boxer & Co., CPAs, Denver, 1986-87; prin. Alan L. Boxer, CPA, Denver, 1987-97; dir. Boxer & Assocs. CPAs PC, 1997—. Bd. dirs. Anti-Defamation League, Denver, 1986-90, BMH Congregation, Denver, 1986-90, treas. 1990-93, v.p. 1993-98. Mem. Am. Inst. CPAs, Colo. Soc. CPAs, Bnai Brith #171 (pres. 1982, trustee 1983-89). Democrat. Jewish.

BOXER, BARBARA, senator; b. Bklyn., Nov. 11, 1940; d. Ira and Sophie (Silvershein) Levy; m. Stewart Boxer, 1962; children: Doug, Nicole. BA in Econ., Bklyn. Coll., 1962. Stockbroker, econ. rschr. N.Y. Securities Firm, N.Y.C., 1962-65; journalist, assoc. editor Pacific Sun, 1972-74; congl. aide to rep. 5th Congl. Dist. San Francisco, 1974-76; mem. Marin County Bd. Suprs., San Rafael, Calif., 1976-82, 98th-102d Congresses from 6th Calif. dist., mem. armed services com., select com. children, youth and families; majority whip at large; co-chair Mil. Reform Caucus; chair subcom. on govt. activities and transp. of house govt. ops. com., 1990-93; senator from Calif. U.S. Senate, 1993—, mem. banking, housing and urban affairs com., mem. budget com., mem. environ. and pub. works com. Pres. Marin County Bd. Suprs., 1980-81; mem. Bay Area Air Quality Mgmt. Bd., San Francisco, 1977-82, pres., 1979-81; bd. dirs. Golden Gate Bridge Hwy. and Transport Dist., San Francisco, 1978-82; founding mem. Marin Nat. Women's Polit. Caucus; pres. Dem. New Mems. Caucus, 1983. Recipient Open Govt. award Common Cause, 1980, Rep. of Yr. award Nat. Multiple Sclerosis Soc., 1990, Margaret Sanger award Planned Parenthood, 1990, Women of Achievement award Anti-defamation League, 1990. Democrat. Jewish. Office: US Senate 112 Hart Senate Office Bldg Washington DC 20510-0001*

BOXER, JASON T. title company executive; b. 1970; BA, U. Pa.; JD, NYU. Bar: N.Y. 1995. Real estate atty. Battle Fowler LLP; v.p. real estate Loews Corp., N.Y.C., 2000—. Office: 75 E 55th St New York NY 10022*

BOXER, JEROME HARVEY, computer and management consultant, vintner, accountant; b. Chgo., Nov. 27, 1930; s. Ben Avrum and Edith (Lyman) B.; m. Sandra Schaffner, June 17, 1980; children by previous marriage: Michael, Jodi. AA magna cum laude, East L.A. Coll., 1952; AB with honors, Calif. State U., L.A., 1954. CPA, Calif.; cert. computing profl. Lab. instr. Calif. State U., L.A., 1953-54; staff acct. Dolman, Freeman & Buchalter, L.A., 1955-57; sr. acct. Neiman, Sanger, Miller & Beress, L.A., 1957-63; ptnr. Glynn and Boxer, CPAs, L.A., 1964-68; v.p., sec. Glynn, Boxer & Phillips Inc., CPAs, L.A. and Glendale, Calif., 1968-90; pvt. practice cons., 1990—. Owner Oak Valley Vineyard; instr. viticulture Cuesta Coll.; pres. Echo Data Svcs. Inc., 1978-90; instr. data processing L.A. City Adult Schs.; tchr., lectr., cons. wines and wine-tasting; instr. photography. Contbr. to Wine World Mag., 1974-82, also cons. Mem. Cuesta Coll. North County Ambassadors; founding pres. Congregation Ohr Tzafon; mem. ops. bd. Evrywoman's Village; bd. dirs., v.p. So. Calif. Jewish Hist. Soc.; bd. dirs. Calif. Mid-State Fair; v.p. Jewish Hist. Soc. of Ctrl. Coast; co-founder Open Space Theatre; former officer Ethel Josephine Scantland Found.; past post advisor Explorer scouts Boy Scouts Am., Eagle Scout. Recipient Youth Svc. award Mid-Valley YMCA, 1972-73. Mem.: AICPA, Paso Robles Wine Festival Steering Com., Clowns of Am., Inc., World Clown Assn., Paso Robles Vintners and Growers Assn., Cellarmasters, Wines and Steins, Ctrl. Coast Winegrowers Assn., Am. Wine Assn., Am. Jewish Hist. Soc., Data Processing Mgmt. Assn., Assn. for Systems Mgmt., Calif. Soc. CPAs, Assoc. Students Calif. State U. L.A. (life) (hon.), Profl. Musicians of Am. (life), Cuesta Coll North County Ambs., Scottish Rite Rsch. Soc., L.A.-Bordeaux Sister City Affiliation, L.A. Photog. Ctr., Acad. Model Aeros., Nat. Model Railroad Assn., Maltose Falcons Home Brewing Soc., San Fernando Valley Silent Flyers, San Fernando Valley Radio Control Flyers, Acad. Magical Arts, Internat. Brotherhood of Magicians, Soc. Preservation of Variety Arts, Friends of Photography, Soc. Bacchus Am., Paso Robles Shrine Clowns, Western Region Clown Assn., Western Region Clown Assn., Internat. Shrine-Clown Assn., South Coast Corinthian Yacht Club (former dir., officer), German Shepherd Dog Club Los Angeles County, German Shepherd Dog Club Am., Verdugo Club, Pacific Mariners Yacht Club, Braemar Country Club, Exch. Club, The Invisible Lodge, Paso Robles Masons (32 degree), Kiwanis (pres. Sunset-Echo Park 1968), B'nai Brith, Shriner, The Invisible Lodge, So. Calif. Research Lodge, Blue Key, Alpha Phi Omega. Home and Office: 1660 Circle B Rd Paso Robles CA 93446-9595 E-mail: jhboxer@yahoo.com.

BOXER, LEONARD, lawyer; b. N.Y.C., Feb. 11, 1939; s. Max Boxer and Sally (Grill) Koffler; m. Enid Feuer, Nov. 24, 1965; children: Michael, Jason, Douglas. BS, NYU, 1960, LLB, 1963. Bar: N.Y. 1963, U.S. Dist. Ct. (so. and ea. dists.) N.Y. 1985, U.S. Supreme Ct. Assoc. Eisenberg & Weiss, Bklyn., 1964-65; ptnr. Olnick, Boxer, Blumberg, Lane & Troy, N.Y.C., 1965-86, Stroock & Stroock & Lavan, N.Y.C., 1987—. Mem. adv. bd. Chgo. Title Ins. Co., N.Y.C., 1980—; mem. exec. com., gov. NY Real Estate Bd. Trustee NYU Law Sch., 1994—, Nat. Jewish Ctr. Immunology and Respiratory Medicine, Jewish Assn. Svcs. for the Aged, Children's Hearing Inst.; bd. of trustees Lenox Hill Hosp.; trustee NYU, 2000—, Cancer Rsch. Inst., 2001. Mem. N.Y. State Bar Assn., Bklyn. Bar Assn., Tax Certiorari Bar Assn. (bd. dirs. 1983-97), Beta Alpha Psi. Home: 875 Park Ave New York NY 10021 Office: Stroock & Stroock & Lavan 180 Maiden Ln Fl 17 New York NY 10038-4937

BOXER, LESTER, lawyer; b. N.Y.C., Oct. 19, 1935; s. Samuel and Anna Lena (Samovar) B.; m. Frances Barenfeld, Sept. 17, 1961; children: Kimberly Brett, Allison Joy. AA, UCLA, 1955, BS, 1957; JD, U. So. Calif., 1961. Bar: Calif. 1962; U.S. Dist. Ct. (cen. dist.) Calif. 1962. Assoc. Bautzer & Grant, Beverly Hills, Calif., 1961-63; pvt. practice Beverly Hills, 1963-65, 69—; ptnr. Boxer & Stoll, Beverly Hills, 1965-69. Mem. Calif. Bar Assn., L.A. County Bar Assn., Beverly Hills Bar Assn. Office: 1801 Century Park E Ste 2513 Los Angeles CA 90067-4703

BOXILL, EDITH HILLMAN, music therapist, educator, writer; b. Providence, Nov. 8, 1916; d. Maurice and Lillian Hillman; m. Roger Evan Boxill, 1965; children by previous marriage: Paul R. Epstein, Emily H. Duby. Bd. cert. music therapist. Music instr., composer, performer, N.Y.C., 1954—; dir. music therapy Manhattan Devel. Ctr., N.Y.C., 1974-87, clin. supr. music therapy interns, 1975—; lectr. then asst. prof. music therapy dept. NYU, N.Y.C., 1976-79, prof., 1980—. Adj. prof. NYU, 1980—; participant music therapy confs.; participant profl. confs.; presenter UN Conf. Internat. Yr. Disabled Persons, 1981, World Congress Music Therapy, Genoa, Italy, 1985, III Congreso Mundial del Niño Aislado, Buenos Aires, 1987, Conf. Can. Assn. Music Therapy, Vancouver, 1988; participant UN Internat. Day of Peace for Children, 1988, World Summit for Children, 1988, Music Therapists for Peace, Inc. presentation Nat. Conf. Peacemaking, Montreal, 1989, UN Pacem in Terris Soc., 1989; conducted plenary session IV World Congress of Music Therapy, Spain, 1993; originator Annual Universal Music Therapists forPeace Day Worldwide, 1990—95, World Congress Music Therapy, Rio de Janeiro, 1990, Vitoria, Spain, 93, 9th World Congress Music Therapy, Washington, 1999; originator Music Therapists for Peace presentation and cont. edn. tng. course Golden Anniversary Music Therapy Conf., St. Louis, 2000; originator Joint N.Am. Music Therapy Conf., Toronto, 1993, Peace Sch. Curriculum Through Music Therapy, 1993; originator music therapy workshops Teach for America UCLA, 1993, 94, adj. faculty, 94; originator Edith Hillman Boxill Scholarship Fund for music therapy students, Music Therapy Lifetime Achievement award, 1995, V World Congreess on Isolated Child, Buenos Aires, 1994, Creative Arts Therapies Conf., St. Petersburg, Russia, 1994; founder, dir. Music Therapists for Peace, Inc., Students Against Violence Everywhere-S.A.V.E.-Through Music Theraphy; originator Music Therapists for Peace UN Project, Music Therapy for War-Traumatized Children, 2000, Worldwide Candlelight Peace Vigil; presenter Am. Music Therapy Assn. Conf., Pasadena, Calif., 2001, 10th World Congress of World Fedn. of Music Therapy, Oxford (Eng.) U., 2002, others; originator of worldwide Candlelight Peace Vigil Oxford Univ., England, 2002; and Global Candlelight Peace Vigil, 03; presenter World Fedn. Music Therapy Congress, Oxford, England, 2002. Archives of audiocasettes of music therapy sessions at NYU; composer, arranger, prodr. album: Music Therapy for the Developmentally Handicapped, Folkway Records, 1976, issued on cassette by The Smithsonian Inst./Folkways Cassette Series, 1993; editor (jour.) Music Therapy, PeaceNotes; author: (books) Developing Communication with the Autistic Child Through Music Therapy, 1977, A Continuum of Awareness: Music Therapy with the Developmentally Handicapped, 1981, The Miracle of Music Therapy, 1997, Drumming Circles for Peace, 2002, Developing the Use of Peaceful, Nonviolent Language Through Music Therapy, 2003; (textbook) Music Therapy for the Developmentally Disabled, 1985 (translated into Italian, Japanese, and Korean), Manual: Students Against Violence Everywhere-S.A.V.E.-Through Music Therapy, 1998; co-author: Basic Music Therapy Competencies, 1981; videotape: A Continuum of Awareness: Music Therapy with Developmentally Handicapped, 1979; monograph: Music Therapy for Living: Principle of Normalization Embodied in Music Therapy, 1987; co-prodr. Earth Concert 1989, N.Y.C.; contbr. articles to profl. jours. Originator of Ann. Universal Music Therapists for Peace Day, celebrated UN Ch. Ctr., 1990-94; adv. bd. Potential Unltd. Prodns.; bd. dirs. Symphony for UN.; dir., coord. pilot project for UN: Music Therapy for War-Traumatized Children. Recipient Peace and Cooperation award for Citizens of the World Internat. anthem, UN, 1998, DeWitt Clinton award, 2003. Mem. ASCPA, Am. Music Therapy Assn. (hon. life mem., bd. dirs., chmn. legis. com., editor Music Therapy Jour. 1987-88, conf. of music therapy 1989, presentation Pasadena), Nat. Assn. Music Therapy, Am. Assn. Mental Deficiency (chair creative arts therapies), Nat. Soc. Autistic Children, Coun. Exceptional Children, Assn. Musicians Greater N.Y., Music Therapists for Peace, Inc. (founder-dir., bd. dirs. 1988), Students Against Violence Everywhere (SAVE)-Through Music Therapy (founder, bd. dirs. 1995). Home: 375 Riverside Dr New York NY 10025-2180 E-mail: ehb2@nyu.edu.

BOXWILL, HELEN ANN, primary and secondary education educator; b. Washington, Feb. 28, 1946; d. Melvin E. and Ann (Magnotta) Dorenbaum; children: Hope, David, Andre. BA, Dickinson Coll., Carlisle, Pa., 1967; MA, New Sch. Social Rsch., 1976; MS in Adminstrn. and Supervision, Coll. New Rochelle, 1995. Cert. in staff devel.; lic. reading specialist, elem. tchr., English tchr., sch. adminstr., N.Y. Caseworker City of N.Y., 1967-71; dir. Harriet Tubman Day Care Ctr., Bklyn., 1971-73; family counselor Family Inst. for More Effective Living, Westbury, N.Y., 1976-80; elem. tchr. Carousel Day Sch., Hicksville, N.Y., 1980-82, Pub. Sch. 160 Elem. Sch., Queens, N.Y., 1982-83; reading specialist Soterios Ellenos Parochial Sch., Bklyn., 1983-84, Hempstead (N.Y.) Pub. Schs., 1984-90; tchr. SAT The Sch. for Student Achievement, Jericho, N.Y., 1991-93; reading specialist L.I. U., Greenvale, N.Y., 1984-93; reading tchr. Robert Moses Mid. Sch., North Babylon, NY, 1990—93, North Babylon H.S., 1993—; reading coord. Island Park (N.Y.) Pub. Schs., 1999—; prin. Huntington (N.Y.) Sch. Dist., 2001—; prof. Tchr. Tng. Inst., Ethiopia. Advisor Sch. Improvement Planning Com., Hempstead, N.Y., 1987-89; mem. Dist. Planning Com., 1993—, Curriculum Adv. Com., 1993—; advisor/advisee com., staff devel. com., lang. arts com., site based mgmt. com. renaissance coord. North Babylon Sch. Dist., 1991-99; tchr., trainer Nassau Tract Tchrs. Ctr., 1985-89, North Babylon Schs., 1991—, Hempstead Schs., 1985-90, insvc. courses Owl Tchrs. Ctr., 1991, 93—; tchr. trainer in Ethiopia through IFESH. Contbr. articles to profl. jours. Advisor Youth of Distinction, Huntington, N.Y., 1991-92; leader Girl Scouts Am., Westbury, 1978; mem. Town of Babylon Anti-Bias Task Force, 1999; mem. 21st Century com. Anti-Defamation League. Grantee City of N.Y. Children's Aid Soc., Tract Ctr., Owl Ctr.; recipient Commty. Svc. award, N.Y. State Tchrs., 1999, award AntiDefamation League Project 21st Century, 2000, Pathfinder award L.I. Bus. Assn. Mem. ASCD, Internat. Reading Assn., Nat. Coun. Tchrs. English, Orton Dyslexia Soc., Nassau Reading Coun. Avocations: swimming, reading, writing, guitar, public speaking on anti-racism. Home: 44 Foxwood Dr E Huntington Station NY 11746-2126 E-mail: helenbox@optonline.net.

BOXX, RITA MCCORD, banker; b. Greenwood, S.C., Aug. 10, 1930; d. John Thomas Logan and Dempsie (Dixon) McCord; m. John Douglas Boxx, Apr. 17, 1949; children: John Stephen, Eric Wesley, Merry Christine. Student, pub. schs. Asst. mgr. Greenwood Ins. Agy., 1961-65, mgr., 1967-80; with Bankers Trust S.C., Greenwood, 1951—; asst. v.p. charge ins. dept. NCNB (formerly Bankers Trust S.C.), 1980—. Tchr. ins. seminars. Mem. Nat. Assn. Ins. Women, Ind. Ins. Agts. Am., Greenwood Assn. Ins. Women, Greenwood C. of C. (dir. 1974-76, chmn. environ., energy and conservation com. 1974), chmn. edn. com. 1977), Greenwood Country Club. Baptist. Home: 434 Dogwood Dr Greenwood SC 29646-9210 Office: PO Box PO Box 1058 Greenwood SC 29648-1058

BOY, ANGELO V. psychology educator; b. Malden, Mass., June 3, 1929; s. Victor and Philomena Boy; m. Barbara Ann Sarnie, Apr. 14, 1956; children: Stephanie, Eleanor, Bernadette, Monica. BA cum laude, U. Notre Dame, 1953; MEd, Boston U., 1955, EdD, 1960. Lic. psychologist Mass. Tchr. Everett (Mass.) Schs., 1953—56, sch. counselor, 1956—61, Lexington (Mass.) Schs., 1961—65; assoc. prof. U. N.H., Durham, 1965—69, prof., 1969—2002. Co-author: Fostering Psychosocial Development, 1988, Child-Centered Counseling and Psychotherapy, 1995, A Person-Centered Foundation for Counseling and Psychotherapy, 1999. Recipient Rsch. award, Am. Assn. Counselor Edn. and Supervision, 1997. Fellow: Mass. Psychol. Assn.; mem.: Am. Counseling

Assn., Portsmouth (N.H.) Country Club. Achievements include pioneering work and rsch. in application of Rogerion client-centered counseling in schools. Avocations: golf, walking, Notre Dame sports program, Everett (Mass) sports histories. Home: 40 Coe Dr Durham NH 03824-2206

BOYADZHIEV, KHRISTO NONEV, mathematician, educator, researcher; b. Sofia, Bulgaria, Sept. 4, 1948; came to U.S., 1989; s. Nonio Christoff and Maria I. (Doneff) Boyajieff; m. Irina Assenova Dimitrov, May 8, 1982; children: Marinella, Alexandra M. MS in Math., Sofia U., 1972, PhD in Math., 1978. Sr. rsch. fellow Inst. Math. Bulgarian Acad. Scis., Sofia, 1978-90; prof. math. Ohio No. U., Ada, 1990—. Reviewer Math. Revs., Ann Arbor, Mich., 1980—, Zentralblatt fur Mathematik, Berlin, Germany, 1988—. Contbr. articles to profl. jours. Recipient Badge of Honor, Sofia U., 1971. Mem. Am. Math. Soc., Math. Assn. Am. Achievements include research and theorems in functional analysis and operator theory. Home: 625 W Lima Ave Ada OH 45810-1615 Office: Ohio No Univ Dept Math Ada OH 45810 E-mail: k_boyadzhiev@onu.edu.

BOYAJIAN, LEVON ZAKAR, psychiatrist, administrator; b. N.Y.C., Dec. 9, 1929; s. Apkar Zakar and Verkin (Nazarian) Boyajian; m. Gloria Zabel Hogrogian, June 2, 1956; children: Liza Lee, Zachary Levon. BA, Columbia Coll., 1951; MS, U. Ill., 1952; MD, Yale U., 1956. Diplomate Am. Bd. Psychiatry and Neurology. Intern in medicine Maimonides Hosp., Bklyn., 1956-57; resident in psychiatry Yale U. Sch. Medicine, 1957-60; asst. unit chief, then unit chief Hillside Hosp., Queens, NY, 1962—64; clin. dir., then acting dir. Lincoln Hosp. Mental Health Svcs., Bronx, N.Y., 1964-69; dir. clin. svcs. dept. psychiatry Cath. Med. Ctr. Bklyn. and Queens, 1969-71; mem. faculty divsn. cmty. and social psychiatry Columbia U., N.Y.C., 1971-75; chmn. dept. psychiatry St. Joseph's Hosp. and Med. Ctr., Paterson, N.J., 1975-85, dir. Met. Paterson Cmty. Mental Health Ctr., 1977-80; acting med. dir. Mental Health Clinic of Ocean County, Toms River, N.J., 1985-86; acting med. dir., staff psychiatrist Richard Hall Cmty. Mental Health Ctr. of Somerset County, Bridgewater, NJ, 1986—88; staff psychiatrist Cmty. Mental Health Ctr. U. Medicine and Dentistry of N.J., Newark, 1989-91; med. chief adult outpatient, dept. psychiatry Elizabeth (N.J.) Gen. Med. Ctr., 1991-92; dir. med. ops., clin. dir. Greystone Park (N.J.) Psychiat. Hosp., 1993-94; staff psychiatrist Cmty. Ctrs. for Mental Health, Inc., Englewood and Dumont, N.J., 1995-97; clin. assoc. prof. psychiatry N.J. Med. Sch., Univ. Medicine and Dentistry of N.J., Newark, 1976-2001. Psychiat. cons. Altro Health and Rehab. Svcs., N.Y.C., 1965-71, Met. Life Ins. Co., N.Y.C., 1986-88, Prudential Life Ins. Co., Parsippany, N.J., 1988-89; instr. dept. psychiatry Albert Einstein Coll. Medicine, Yeshiva U., 1964-66, asst. prof., 1966-68, asst. clin. prof., 1968-69; asst. prof. clin. psychiatry, Columbia U., 1971-77; assoc. attending, attending psychiatrist Lincoln Hosp., 1964-69, Columbia Presbyn. Med. Ctr., N.Y.C., 1971-77; assoc. attending psychiatrist Cath. Med. Ctr. Bklyn. and Queens, 1969-71; chmn. dept. psychiatry St. Joseph's Hosp. and Med. Ctr., Paterson, 1975-85; presenter, panelist, spkr., moderator in field. Contbr. articles to profl. jours. Lt. comdr. USNR, 1960. Fellow: North Jersey Psychiat. Assn. (coun. 1982—83, corr. sec. 1983—86), N.J. Hosp. Assn. (task force on patients discharged from state mental hosps. 1978, mental health com. 1978—84, co-chmn. 1984—85), N.J. Psychiat. Assn. (dist. br. com. on psychiat. units of gen. hosps. 1982—85), N.Y. Soc. Clin. Psychiatry (N.Y. County dist. br. com. on psychiatry and cmty. 1973—75), Am. Psychiat. Assn. (life; task force on continuing edn. in adminstrn. for psychiatrists, com. on certification in adminstrv. psychiatry, assoc. examiner 1972—73, 1980, 1982, commn. on certification in adminstrv. psychiatry 1974—79, task force on prospective payment clin. adv. group 1984). Office: 163 Engle St 4A Englewood NJ 07631

BOYAJIAN, TIMOTHY EDWARD, public health officer, educator, consultant; b. Fresno, Calif., Feb. 22, 1949; s. Ernest Adam and Marge (Medzian) B.; m. Tassanee Bootdeesri, Apr. 23, 1987. BS in Biology, U. Calif., Irvine, 1975; M of Pub. Health, UCLA, 1978. Registered environ. health specialist, Calif. Rsch. asst. UCLA, 1978-81; lectr. Chapman U., 29 Palms, Calif., 1982-84, 88-89; refugee relief vol. Cath. Relief Svcs., Surin, Thailand, 1985-86; lectr. Nat. Univ., L.A., 1989-91; environ. health specialist Riverside County Health Svcs. Agy., Palm Springs, Calif., 1991-96; sci. tchr. South Gate (Calif.) H.S., L.A. Unified Sch. Dist., 1999—. Mem. adj. faculty U. Phoenix, 1998—; cons. parasitologist S. Pacific Commn., L.A., 1979; pub. health cons. several vets. groups, L.A., 1981-84, 97—; cons. Assn. S.E. Asian Nations, Bangkok, Thailand, 1988. Veterans rights advocate, Vietnam Vet. Groups, L.A., 1981-84. With USMC, Vietnam, 1969-71. Recipient U.S. Pub. Health Traineeship, U.S. Govt., L.A., 1977-81. Mem. VFW, United Tchrs. L.A. Avocation: writing. Home: PO Box 740 Palm Springs CA 92263-0740

BOYAN, NORMAN J. retired education educator; b. N.Y.C., Apr. 11, 1922; s. Joseph J. and Emma M. (Pelezare) B.; m. Priscilla M. Simpson, July 10, 1943; children: Stephen J., Craig S., Corydon J. AB, Bates Coll., Lewiston, Maine, 1943; A.M., Harvard U., 1947, Ed.D., 1951. Instr. U.S. history Dana Hall Sch., Wellesley, Mass., 1946-48; research assoc. Lab. Social Relations, Harvard U., 1950-52; asst. prin. Mineola (N.Y.) High Sch., 1952-54; prin. Wheatley Sch., East Williston, N.Y., 1954-59; assoc. prof. edn., dir. student teaching and internship U. Wis., 1959-61; assoc. prof. edn. Stanford U., 1961-67; dir. div. ednl. labs. U.S. Office Edn., 1967-68, assoc. commr. for research, 1968-69; prof. edn. Grad. Sch. Edn., U. Calif., Santa Barbara, 1969-90, prof. emeritus, 1990—, dean, 1969-80; assoc. in edn. Grad. Sch. Edn., Harvard U., 1980-81; dir. Ednl. Leadership Inst. U. Calif., 1989-91. Vis. scholar Stanford U., 1974, 86; vis. prof. U. Ark. Program in Greece, 1977, Coll. Edn., Pa. State U., summer 1981, Faculty Edn. U. B.C., summer 1983, U. Alta., 1988, UCLA, 1991; cons. numerous U.S. sch. sys., U.S. govt. and Pacific Trust Ters. Co-author: Instructional Supervision Training Program, 1978; mem. editorial bd. Harvard Edn. Rev, 1948-50, Jour. Secondary Edn, 1963-68, Jour. Edn. Research, 1967-82, Urban Edn, 1967-90; cons. editor, contbr. 5th edit. Ency. Ednl. Research, 1982; editor, contbr. Handbook Research on Ednl. Adminstrn., 1988; contbr. articles to profl. jours. Served with USAAF, 1943-46. Recipient Shankland award for advanced grad. study in ednl. adminstrn., 1950, Roald F. Campbell Lifetime Achievement award U. Coun. for Ednl. Adminstrn., 1998. Mem. Am. Ednl. Rsch. Assn. (v.p. div. A 1978-80), Phi Beta Kappa, Phi Delta Kappa. Home: 1031A Calle Sastre Santa Barbara CA 93105-4439 E-mail: nboyan@aol.com.

BOYAR, BENJAMIN, music educator; b. Ny; m. Jeanne Boyar; children: Nathan, Steven. BFA, U. of NY at Buffalo, Buffalo, NY; Masters, Buffalo State Coll., Buffalo, NY. Music educator Gateway Day Sch., Treatment Program, Willamsville, NY, 1988—90, Villa Maria Inst. of Music, Cheektowaga, NY, 1989—99, Buffalo Acad. for Visual and Performing Arts, Buffalo, 1984—2000; dir. of music Hutchinson Ctrl. Tech. H.S., Buffalo, 2000—. All-state music adjudicator NY State Sch. of Music, NY, 1985—. Assoc. Kennedy Centers' Imagination Celebration, Buffalo, 1985—95; dir. Jazz at Arts, Buffalo, 1984—2000. Recipient Music Cons., Disney Tchr. Awards mus. asst., 1994, Festival Chair, NY State Sch. Music Assn., 1988. Mem.: Internat. Jazz Educators Assn., Erie County Music Educator Assn., NY State Sch. Music Assn., Music Educators Nat. Assn. Avocation: magic. Home: 225 Rosedale Blvd Amherst NY 14226 Office: Hutchinson Central Technical High School 256 South Elmwood Avenue Buffalo NY 14201 E-mail: banjam@adelphia.net.

BOYARSKI, ADAM MICHAEL, physicist; b. North Bank, Alberta, Can., Apr. 14, 1935; came to U.S., 1963; s. Albert and Mary (Roskiewich) B.; m. Lorretta Sramek, June 1, 1968; children: Lisa A., Mike A. BA in Sci., U. Toronto, 1958; PhD, M.I.T., 1962. Rsch. assoc. M.I.T., Cambridge, 1962-63; staff physicist Stanford (Calif.) Linear Accelerator Ctr., 1963—. Cons. in field; mem. team discovering psi family of elem. particles. Author: (software) HANDYPAK, A Histogram and Display Package, 1980; contbr. articles to scientific jours. Mem. Am. Phys. Soc. Avocations: woodworking, camping, computers, mechanics. Office: SLAC 2575 Sand Hill Rd Menlo Park CA 94025-7015

BOYARSKY, IGOR, emergency physician; b. Odessa, Russia, Ukraine, Apr. 15, 1962; s. Izyaslav A. and Rada Boyarsky; m. Angela Boyarsky, Aug. 25, 1990; children: Alexia, Nicholas. DO, Comp, 1995; BS, UCLA, 1986. Diplomate Am. Bd. Emergency Medicine. Physician per diem Martin Luther King Jr.-Drew Med. Ctr., L.A., 1996-98; attending physician, asst. prof. Martin Luther King Jr. - Drew Med Ctr., L.A., 1998—; physician specialist per diem Aegis Narcotic Treatment Program, Wilmington, Calif., 1999, Hubert Humphrey's Urgent Care Clinic, L.A., 1999—, Santa Maria Hosp., L.A., 2000—, Calif. Hosp. Med. Care, L.A., 2000—. Author: Emedicine.com, 2000; reviewer profl. jours. Fellow Am. Coll. Emergency Physicians, Am. Acad. Emergency Medicine; mem. AMA, Am. Osteopathic Assn., Soc. Acad. Emergency Medicine. Avocations: classical music, reading, travelling, fishing. Home: 8736 Wonderland Park Ave Los Angeles CA 90046 Office: Martin Luther King Jr - Drew Med Ctr 12021 S Wilmington Ave Los Angeles CA 90059 E-mail: igrek@sbcglobal.net.

BOYARSKY, SAUL, lawyer, forensic urologist, physiologist, educator; b. Burlington, Vt., July 22, 1923; s. Samuel and Ethel (Kaplan) B.; m. Rose Eisman, June 17, 1945; children: Myer William, Terry Linda Boyarsky Alcorn, Hannah Gail Boyarsky Fowler. BS magna cum laude, U. Vt., 1943, MD cum laude, 1946; JD, Washington U., St. Louis, 1981. Bar: Mo. 1983. Instr. in physiology NYU, N.Y.C., 1955-56; assoc. prof. urology Albert Einstein Coll., N.Y.C., 1956-63; prof. urology Duke U., Durham, N.C., 1963-70, head divsn. genito-urinary surgery, 1970-73; prof. Washington U., St. Louis, 1970-89, head divsn. urology, 1970-73; clin. prof. surgery St. Louis U., 1991—; emeritus urologist Barnes-Jewish-Christian Hosp., Washington Hosp. Med. Ctr., St. Louis. Chmn. rsch. and tng. com. NIH, Bethesda, Md., 1968; cons. on med. devices FDA, Washington, 1969—; chmn. biomed. engring. com. AUA, Balt., 1975—90, founder Urology Lawyers Coun.; chmn. steering and curriculum com., facilitator Lifelong Learning Inst., U. Coll., Washington U., St. Louis; instr. and facilitator Duke Inst. for Learning in Retirement, 1999, 2001—03, mem. curriculum com. Author: The Neurogenic Bladder, 1967; (with others) Hydrodynamics of Micturition, 1971, Urodynamics; Hydrodynamics of the Ureter and Renal Pelvis, 1971, Ureteral Dynamics, 1972, The Care of the Neurogenic Bladder Patient, 1979, Goals in Male Reproductive Research, 1981; mem. editl. bd. Jour. of Legal Medicine. Chmn. steering com. Lifelong Learning Inst., Univ. Coll. Washington U., St. Louis. Capt. U.S. Army, 1943-50. Fellow ACS, Am. Acad. Forensic Sci., Am. Coll. Legal Medicine (former bd. govs.); mem. AAAS, AMA, ABA, AAUP, Am. Urol. Assn. (former chmn. biomed. engrng. com.), Am. Assn. Clin. Urologists, Am. Assn. Genitourinary Surgeons, Am Physiologic Soc., Biomed. Urol. Assn., Internat. Continence Soc., Mo. Med. Assn., Mo., Urologic Soc., Pan-Am. Med. Assn., St. Louis Met. Med. Soc., St. Louis Urol. Soc., Societe Internationale D'Urologie, Soc. Univ. Urologists, Urodynamics Soc. (founder, 1st pres.), Am. Arbitration Assn., Am. Coll. Legal Medicine, Mo. Bar Assn., Bar Assn. Met. St. Louis, Mo. Orgn. Def. Lawyers, Urology Lawyers Coun. (founder, pres.). Home: 6412 Mimosa Dr Chapel Hill NC 27514-9059 Fax: 919-493-7207. E-mail: saulboyar@aol.com.

BOYARSKY, TERRY LINDA, music educator; b. Nuremburg, Germany, Aug. 17, 1949; came to the U.S., 1950; d. Saul and Rose Sophie Eisman Boyarsky; m. Robert Watson Alcorn, May 14, 1982; 1 child, Vera Clare Alcorn. BA in Psychology, Reed Coll., 1970; BA in Eurhythmics, Cleve. Inst. Music, 1977; MA in Ethnomusicology, Kent State U., 1998. Freelance pianist, 1970—. Dalcroze eurhythmics tchr. Cleve. Inst. Music, 1976-86; Dalcroze specialist Cleve. Inst. Dance, 1977-86; vis. faculty Chautauqua (N.Y.) Inst., summers 1988-92; music and movement faculty Hathaway Brown Sch., Shaker Heights, Ohio, 1990-94; artist-in-residence Young Audiences of Greater Cleve., 1999—; mem. summer faculty Vander Cook Coll. Music, Chgo., 2001; tchg. artist ICARE, 2002—; cons. tchg. artist Project Start ID, 2002—; presenter in field. Program rev. com. Young Audiences Greater Cleve., 1997—; mem. chorus Cleve. Orch. Blossom Festival, 2001, 2002, 2003, Akron Symphony Chorus, 2001—03; mem. adv. bd., spl. rhythmic cons. Shalhevet Folk Esemble, Cleve., 1991—95. Mem.: Dalcroze Soc. Am. (chmn. nat. conf. 1996, webmaster 1996—2001, bd. mem. 1996—, chmn. nat. conf. 2000, treas. 1996—2002), Am. Orff Schulwerk Assn. (cert. levels I and II), Cleve. Bot. Gardens. Avocations: sewing, gardening, singing. E-mail: touizers@aol.com.

BOYATT, THOMAS DAVID, former ambassador; b. Cin., Mar. 4, 1933; s. Lynn Craig Haven and Florine (Cloar) B.; m. Maxine Lorraine Shearwood, Dec. 30, 1971; children: Thomas Benton, Christopher Lynn, Jessica Allyn, Alexander Shearwood, Catherine Jordan. BA, Princeton U., 1955, MA, 1956. Vice consul Dept. State, Antofagasta, Chile, 1960-62; 2d sec. Am. Embassy, Luxembourg, 1964-66, 1st sec. Nicosia, Cyprus, 1967-70; dir. Cypriot affairs Near East Bur. Dept. State, Washington, 1970-74, assigned to Sr. Seminar, 1974-75; dep. chief mission, minister counselor Am. Embassy, Santiago, Chile, 1976-78; U.S. ambassador to Upper Volta, Ouagadougou, 1978-80, Colombia, Bogota, 1980-84; v.p. market devel. Sears World Trade Inc., Washington, 1984-87; with Dept. Treasury, 1962-64; ptnr. IRC Group, 1988-96; pres. U.S. Def. Systems, 1990-96. Trustee Princeton U., 1984-89; bd. dirs. Patterson Sch./U. Ky., Inst. for Study of Diplomacy/Georgetown U. Served to 1st lt. SAC, USAF, 1956-59. Decorated Legion d'Honneur (Upper Volta), Gran Cruz Order of San Carlos (Colombia); recipient Meritorious Honor award Dept. State, 1969, William R. Rivkin award Am. Fgn. Service, 1970, Christian A. Herter award, 1976 Mem.: Am. Fgn. Svc. Assn. (treas.), Washington Inst. Fgn. Affairs (bd. dirs.), Acad. of Diplomacy (bd. dirs.), Am. Fgn. Svc. Assn. (pres. 1971—74, award for post-retirement contbns. to fgn. affairs 1999, Lifetime Achievement award 2001).

BOYCE, ANDREA ZYGMUNT, nurse; b. Miami, Fla., Sept. 17, 1956; d. Joseph A. and Eleanor F. (Haduck) Zygmunt; m. Brian W. Boyce, Apr. 27, 1985. BS in Nursing, Our Lady of Angels Coll., 1978. RN, Pa., Calif., Utah; cert. ACLS, BCLS, NRP, PALS. Staff nurse, then asst. head nurse pediatric intensive care St. Christopher's Hosp. Children, Phila., 1978-84; head nurse neonatal ICU, pediatrics Osteo. Med. Ctr., Phila., 1985-88, staff nurse pediatrics, emergency rm., 1988-90; staff nurse emergency rm. Doctors Hosp. of Montclair, 1990; mobile intensive care nurse emergency dept. Ontario (Calif.) Community Hosp., 1992-94; staff nurse pediatric intensive care Primary Childrens Med. Ctr., Salt Lake City, 1994-95; pool nurse, emergency rm. Lower Bucks Hosp., Bristol, Pa., 1996—, St. Mary Med. Ctr., Langhorne, Pa., 1997-98. Home: 114 Drew Dr Langhorne PA 19053-1546

BOYCE, CAROLYN, political organization administrator; State chmn. Idaho Dem. Party, 2000—. Office: Idaho Dem Party 710 W Franklin St Boise ID 83701*

BOYCE, CLAYTON WINFRED, magazine publisher, editor; b. Batavia, N.Y., Sept. 13, 1955; s. Sheldon William Boyce and Mary Meddie Riddle; m. Myrtha Kay Coyte, Sept. 13, 1980 (div. Oct. 1998); 1 child, Charles Randolph; m. Tracy Lynn Shaw, Aug. 31, 2002. BS in Psychology, U. Md., 1986. Reporter Saratogian, Saratoga Springs, N.Y., 1979, Daily News-Record, Harrisonburg, Va., 1980; news editor Evening Capital, Annapolis, Md., 1979-87, Knight-Ridder/Tribune News Svc., Washington, 1987-95; news copy editor Detroit Free Press, 1995; exec. editor Nat. Inst. of Bus. Mgmt., 1995; editor, pub. Traffic World mag., Washington, 1996—. Chmn. bd. Nat. Press Bldg. Corp., Washington, 1987—. Named Transp. Editor of Yr., Transp. Consumer Protection Coun. Inc., 2003; recipient Editl. Excellence award, Am. Soc. Bus. Publ. Editors, 1999, 2001; N.Y. State Regents scholar, 1973. Mem. Nat. Press Club (pres. 1993-94, chmn. 1991, gov. 1989-90, treas. 1994, Courage, Leadership and Svc. award 1973), Washington Press Found. (bd. dirs. 1993-94), Friends of Nat. Journalism Libr. Found. (sec., treas. 1992-94). Baptist. Avocations: golf, reading, genealogy, running. Home: 8616 Yardley Drive Alexandria VA 22308 Office: Traffic World 1270 National Press Bldg Washington DC 20045-2200

BOYCE, DANIEL HOBBS, financial planning company executive; b. Flint, Mich., Oct. 19, 1953; s. James Edward and Alice Marilyn (Hobbs) B.; m. Suzanne Kay Williams; children: Kenneth C., Geoffrey A., Stephen J. BA, U. Mich., 1974, MA, 1979. CFP. Rep. Mut. Svc. Corp., Detroit, 1982-87; br. mgr. Investment Mgmt. & Rsch. Inc., Atlanta, 1987—; co-managing ptnr. Ctr. Fin. Planning Inc., Southfield, Mich., 1988—. V.p. Southworth, Boyce & McFawn Planning Corp., Troy, Mich., 1982-85; owner, fin. planner Daniel H. Boyce Fin. Adv. Svcs., Birmingham, Mich., 1985-88; mem. adj. faculty Coll. Fin. Planning, Denver, 1985-90; mem. adv. coun. cert. program in personel fin. planning Oakland U., Rochester, Mich., 1987-2002; edn. cons. Nat. Ctr. for Fin. Edn., Denver, 1985-2001. Bi-weekly columnist Money Matters, Legal News newsletter, 1984-86; monthly columnist Personal Fin. for suburban Detroit newspaper chain, 1987-93. Bd. dirs. Great Lakes Chamber Music Festival, 1996-98, Detroit Chamber Winds and Strings, 1992-2003, chmn. bd., 1995-98; min. music Birmingham Unitarian Ch., 1976-2001, emeritus, 2002—. Cited by Money Mag. and Worth Mag. as One of Top 200 Fin. Planners in U.S., 1987, 96, 97, 98. Mem. Internat. Assn. Fin. Planning (bd. dirs. S.E. Mich. chpt. 1984-87, 89-91), Detroit Soc. Inst. CFPs (pres. 1986-87, chmn. 1987-88), Detroit Chamber Winds (bd. dirs., chmn. 1995-98). Office: Ctr Fin Planning Inc 26211 Central Park Blvd Ste 604 Southfield MI 48076-4164

BOYCE, DAVID CURTIS, retired ophthalmologist; b. Wauwatosa, Wis., June 12, 1918; BS, U. Wis., 1940, MD, 1943. Diplomate Am. Bd. Ophthalmology. Resident in ophthalmology U. Iowa, Iowa City, 1950, instr. dept. ophthalmology, 1950; pvt. practice Grand Rapids, Mich., 1950—. Lt. USN, 1942-46. Fellow ACS, Am. Acad. Ophthalmology; mem. AMA, Mich. Med. Soc., Kent County Med. Soc., Flying Physicians. Assn. Avocations: flying, biking, sailing, skiing. Home: 3623 Cook Valley Blvd SE Grand Rapids MI 49546 E-mail: dboyce@dnx.net.

BOYCE, DAVID EDWARD, transportation and regional science educator; b. Newark, Ohio, June 24, 1938; s. Francis Henry and Martha Ann (Neutzel) B.; m. Nani Kulish, 1992; children: Lynn, Susan, Michael, Anna, Gregory. BSCE, Northwestern U., 1961; M in City Planning, U. Pa., 1963, PhD in Regional Sci., 1965. Registered profl. engr., Ohio. Rsch. economist Battelle Meml. Inst., Columbus, Ohio, 1964-66; asst. prof. U. Pa., Phila., 1966-70, assoc. prof., 1970-74, prof., 1974-77; prof. transp. and regional sci. U. Ill., Urbana, 1977-88, Chgo., 1988—2003, prof. emeritus, 2003—. Sr. vis. fellow Brit. Sci. Rsch. Coun., Leeds, Eng., 1972-73; vis. prof. optimization U. Linkoping and Royal Inst. Tech., Sweden, 1983, 96. Co-author: Metropolitan Plan Making, 1970, Optimal Subset Selection, 1974, Regional Science, Retospect and Prospect, 1991, Modeling Dynamic Transportation Networks, 1996; co-editor Environment and Planning, 1979-88; assoc. editor Transp. Sci., 1978-94. Mem. Regional Sci. Assn. (sec. 1969-78, internat. conf. coord. 1978-86, pres. 1987), Informs (transp. sci. coun. 1978-80).

BOYCE, DENNIS WAYNE, radiologist; b. Pitts., Mar. 30, 1945; BS, Valparaiso U., 1967; MD, St. Louis U., 1971. Diplomate Am. Bd. Radiology added qualifications in neuroradiology. Intern Northwestern U. Med. Ctr., Chgo., 1971-72; resident Rush-Presbyn.-St. Luke's Med. Ctr., Chgo., 1972-75, fellow neuroradiology, 1975-76; radiologist Modesto Doctors Med. Ctr., Calif., 1976—; pres. Modesto Radiol. Med. Ctr., Calif., 1996—, Modesto Radiol. Med. Group, Inc., 1996—2003. Vice-chmn. dept. radiology Meml. Hosp., Modesto, 1986-88, 90-92, chmn., 1988-90, 92-94; dir. MRI scanning Drs. Med. Ctr., Modesto, 1980-90, vice-chmn. dept. radiology; trustee Stanislaus Found. Med. Care, Modesto, 1980-88. Mem. Ctrl. Cath. High Sch. Found., Modesto, 1985-90; dir. bd. lay mins. Grace Luth. Ch., 1978-90. Mem. Am. Soc. Neuroradiology (sr.), Western Neuroradiology Soc. (sr.), Am. Soc. Spine Radiology. Avocations: snow skiing, walking, hiking, swimming, music. Office: Modesto Radiol Med Group 101 Park Ave Modesto CA 95354-0556

BOYCE, DOREEN ELIZABETH, lecturer, civic development foundation executive; b. Antofagasta, Chile, Apr. 20, 1934; d. George Edgar and Elsie Winifred Vaughan; m. Alfred Warne Boyce, Aug. 11, 1956; children: Caroline Elizabeth, John Trevor Warne. BA with hons., Oxford (Eng.) U., 1956, MA with hons., 1960; PhD, U. Pitts., 1983; DHL (hon.), Westminster Coll., 1986, Washington and Jefferson Coll., 1993. Lectr. and tutor in econs. U. Witwatersrand, South Africa, 1960-62; provost and dean of faculty, Mary Helen Marks prof. econs. Chatham Coll., Pitts., 1963-79; prof. econs., chmn. dept. econs. and mgmt. Hood Coll., Frederick, Md., 1979-82; pres. Buhl Found., Pitts., 1982—. Dir. and vice chair DQE Duquesne Light Co., Dollar Bank, FSB, Orbeco Analytical Svcs. Inc., Coun. Ind. Colls.; co-founder, dir. Microbac Labs., Inc.; Pa. Gov.'s Sports and Exposition Facilities Task Force, 1995; del. White House Conf. on Small Bus., 1980; mem. Gov.'s Conf. Small Bus., 1979-82, chmn. bd. dirs. Trustee Franklin and Marshall Coll., 1982—, Frick Edn. Commn., 1980-94, Carnegie Sci. Ctr., 1982—; mem. Fed.Jud. Nominating Commn., 1977-79, Pa. Gov.'s Commn. on Financing of Higher Edn., 1983-85; bd. dirs. World Affairs Coun., 1984-96; mem. appeal com. Somerville Coll., Oxford, Eng., 1986—. Recipient Medallion of Distinction, U. Pitts., 1987; named Disting. Dau. Pa., 1996, Hon. Fellow Somerville Coll., U. Oxford, Women Who Make A Difference award, Internat. Women's Forum, 1998. Mem. Am. Econs. Assn., Am. Assn. Higher Edn., Grantmakers of Western Pa. (pres. 1984), Internat. Women's Forum, Assn. Governing Bds. Univ. and Coll. (coun. bd. chairs 2002—), Duquesne Club (bd. dirs. 2000—). Office: Centre City Tower 650 Smithfield St Ste 2300 Pittsburgh PA 15222-3912

BOYCE, EMILY STEWART, retired library and information science educator; b. Raleigh, N.C., Aug. 18, 1933; d. Harry and May (Fallon) B. BS, East Carolina U., 1955, MA, 1961; MS in Library Sci., U. N.C., 1968; postgrad., Cath. U. Am., 1977. Librarian Tileston Jr. High Sch., Wilmington, N.C., 1955-57; children's librarian Wilmington Pub. Library, 1957-58; asst. librarian Joyner Library East Carolina U., Greenville, N.C., 1959-61, librarian III, 1962-63; ednl. supr. II ednl. media div. N.C. State Dept. Pub. Instrn., Raleigh, 1961-62; assoc. prof. dept. libr. and info. scis. East Carolina U., 1964-76, prof., 1976-92, chmn. dept., 1982-89; retired, 1992. Cons. So. Assn. Colls. and Schs., Raleigh, 1975-92. Active Asheville YWCA, Mediation Ctr., Botanical Gardens, Literacy Coun. Buncombe County. Mem. ALA, AAUW, N.C. Library Assn., Southeastern Library Assn., Assn. Library and Info. Sci. Educators, Spl. Libraries Assn. Democrat. Home: 30 Creekside Way Asheville NC 28804-1763 E-mail: eboyce@buncombe.main.nc.us.

BOYCE, JOSEPH NELSON, retired journalist, consultant, educator; b. New Orleans, Apr. 18, 1937; s. John and Sadie (Nelson) B.; m. Carol Hill, Dec. 21, 1968; children: Leslie, Nelson, Joel, Beverly. Student, Roosevelt U., Chgo., 1955-65, John Marshall Law Sch., 1965-67. Mem. Chgo. Police Dept., 1961-66; reporter Chgo. Tribune, 1966-70; corr. Time mag., 1970-73, chief San Francisco bur., 1973-79, chief So. U.S. bur., 1979-85, dep. chief Eastern U.S. bur., 1985-87; sr. editor Wall St. Jour., 1987-98, ret., 1998; media rels. cons. Dow Jones/Wall St. Jour., 1998—. Rotating faculty mem., summer program for minority journalists U. Calif., Berkeley, 1986, Berkeley, 87, Berkeley, 88, Berkeley, 89; bd. dirs. Jazzmobile, Inc., N.Y.C.; guest lectr. various colls. and univs.; vis. faculty summer program for minority journalists U. Ala.; vis. faculty Poynter Inst., 1993, William Randolph Hearst vis. prof.-in-residence Howard U., 1996; mem. adv. bd. Lyndon B. Johnson Sch. of Public Affairs U. Tex., Austin, 1998—; adj. prof. Sch. Journalism Columbia U., N.Y.C., 1999, Ind. U., Indpls., 2002. Chmn. Marin County Black Leadership Forum, 1974-75; mem. Marin Justice Coun., 1977-78; bd. dirs. Jazzmobile, 1991-95. With USNR. Recipient Outstanding Black Achiever award Met. YMCA, N.Y.C., 1975; co-recipient Unity In Media award Lincoln U., 1975; Time Mag.-Duke U. fellow, 1981-82. Mem. NAACP, Nat. Assn. Black Journalists, Nat. Assn. Minority Media Execs. (bd. dirs. 1991-93), Soc. Profl. Journalists (Indpls. chpt. bd. dirs., pres. 2003—). Episcopalian. E-mail: boycevibe@aol.com.

BOYCE, RALPH L. ambassador; b. Washington, D.C., Feb. 1, 1952; married; 2 children. BA, George Washington U., 1974; MPA, Princeton U., 1976. Staff asst. to amb. U.S. Fgn. Svc., Tehran, Iran, 1977—79, comml. attache Tunis, Tunisia, 1979—81, fin. economist Islamabad, Pakistan, 1981—84; spl. asst. to adv. Dep. Sec. of State U.S. State Dept., Washington, 1984—88, polit. counselor Bangkok, 1988—92, dep. chief of mission Singapore, 1992—93, charge d'affaires, 1993—94, dep. chief of mission Bangkok, 1994—98, dep. asst. sec. for East Asia and Pacific Affairs, 1998—2001; U.S. amb. to Indonesia, 2001—. Office: Jl Merdeka Selatan 4-5 Jakarta Pusat 10110 Indonesia*

BOYD, ALAN MARTIN, lawyer, legal administrator; b. Washington, July 5, 1959; s. Chester Lorenzo Jr. and Pauline Jean Postell (Martin) B. BA magna cum laude, U. Md., 1981; JD, George Washington U., 1984. Bar: Pa. 1984, D.C. 1985, U.S. Ct. Mil. Appeals 1989, U.S. Supreme Ct. 1990. Law clk Hudson, Leftwich & Davenport, Washington, 1982, Pension Rights Ctr., Washington, 1982-84; legal clk. U.S. Small Bus. Adminstrn., Washington, 1983-84; tax cons. MCI Telecommunications Corp., Washington, 1984; commd. 1st lt. U.S. Army, 1985, advanced through grades to capt., 1985, asst. staff judge advocate, then spl. asst. U.S. atty., 1986—88, appellate def. coun. Legal Svcs. Agy. Falls Church, Va., 1988-92, resigned, 1992; fed. jud. clk. U.S. Ct. Mil. Appeals, Washington, 1992-94; asst. U.S. Atty. Washington, 1994—. Lectr. Fayetteville (N.C.) Tech. Inst., 1985-86. Mem. ABA, Nat. Bar Assn., Omicron Delta Kappa. Avocations: basketball, running, softball, computers. Home: 4843 Dodson Dr Annandale VA 22003-6138 Office: US Atty's Office DC 555 4th St NW Washington DC 20001-2733

BOYD, ANN FISHER, office administrator; b. Corpus Christi, Oct. 2, 1933; d. King and Jewel (Tanner) Fisher; m. Waymon Lewis Boyd, July 8, 1956; children: Wayne Allen, Randy Lynn. Student, Durham Bus. coll., 1956. Operator Gen. Telephone Co., Port Lavaca, Tex., 1954-56; bookkeeper Champ Traylor Meml. Hosp., Port Lavaca, 1955-56; sec., payrol clk. King Fisher Marine Svc., Port Lavaca, 1956-58; sec., asst. sec., treas. King Fisher Marine Svc., Inc., Port Lavaca, 1961-64, asst. sec., treas., 1964—2001; ret. 2002. Home: PO Box 27 134 Harbor Dr W Port Lavaca TX 77979

BOYD, ANN LEWIS, biology educator; b. Shreveport, La., Nov. 15, 1944; d. Fletcher Willard and Bess Juanita (Sherman) Lewis; m. James P. Boyd, June 4, 1965 (div. 1973); children: Kathryn Ann, David Gregory. BS, Northwestern State U., 1965, MS, 1968; PhD, La. State U., 1971; postdoctoral fellow, Baylor Coll. of Medicine, 1971-73. Fellow Baylor Coll. Medicine, 1971-73; rsch. scientist Frederick (Md.) Cancer Rsch., 1973-82; assoc. prof. biology Hood Coll., Frederick, 1982-88, prof. biology, 1988—, dean grad. sch., 1994—2002, assoc. v.p. acad. affairs, 1995-97; cons. Frederick Cancer Rsch., 1982—. Chmn. dept. biology Hood Coll., Frederick, 1988-93, designer, tchr., 1992-94. Citizen amb. People to People Internat., 1983, 88, 91, 97; advocate for the homeless, 1989-92; bd. dirs. Girl Scouts USA, 1979-82, United Way Frederick County. Grantee Nat. Cancer Inst., 1983-86, NSF, 1986-88. Fellow Am. Acad. Microbiology; mem. AAUW (panelist 1988-91, chair 1992-94, fellowship panelist 1988-92, chmn. fellowship panel 1992-94), N.Y. Acad. Scis., Am. Soc. Microbiology, Am. Soc. Virology, Phi Kappa Phi, Sigma Xi. Home: 10901 Farrier Rd Frederick MD 21701 Office: Hood Coll Grad Sch 401 Rosemont Ave Frederick MD 21701-8524 E-mail: boyd@hood.edu.

BOYD, ARTHUR BERNETTE, JR., surgeon, clergyman, beverage company executive; b. Durham, N.C., June 29, 1947; s. Arthur Bernette and Mammie Lee (Chalmers) B.; m. Delphine Victoria Huffman, Mar. 14, 1981; children: Arthur III, Vicki. BA, Fla. A&M Univ., 1969; postgrad., NYU, 1970; MD, Meharry Med. Coll., 1978; postgrad., U. N.C., Chapel Hill, 1998. Cert. ATLS instr., PALS. Intern in surgery Howard Univ. Hosp., Washington, 1978-80; resident and chief resident in surgery St. Luke's Hosp., Cleve., 1981-84; fellow in liver transplant U. Pitts., 1984-85; chief adminstrv. fellow trauma/surg. critical care R.A. Cowley Shock Trauma Ctr. U. Md. Med. Sys., Cali, Colombia, 1993-94, clin. instr. surgery, sr. fellow, traumatologist Baltimore County, 1994—, co-traumatologist Prince George Cmty. Hosp., Cheverly, Md., 1994-95; chief surgeon, pres. Phoenix Med. Surgical Svc., Inc., Cleve., Carribean, 1986—; clin. instr. surgery, sr. trauma fellow Shock Trauma Ctr. U. Md. Med. Ctr., Balt., 1995-96; pres., CEO Motown Beverage Co. of Ohio, Cleve., 1988—, Towne Club Internat. of Ohio, Inc., Cleve., 1988—; pres., CEO, vice chmn. Star Beverage Corp., Shaker Heights, Ohio, 1997; chief adminstrv. fellow in trauma/crit. care R.A. Cowley Shock Trauma Ctr./U. Md. Med. Systems, 1993-94, clin. instr., sr. trauma rsch. fellow, 1994-95; sr. trauma fellow, clin. instr. Shock Trauma Ctr./U. Md., 1995; CEO, pres. Nat. Fin. Group, Inc., Cleve., 1997—; vice chair Star Beverage Corp., 1997. Adj. prof. anatomy and physiology Cuyhoga C.C., Cleve., 1988—; cons. surgeon other hosps. and physicians, Cleve., 1988—; continuing med. educator dept. surgery Case Western Res. U. Sch. Medicine, Cleve., 1997-98; faculty med. bd. profl. preparation course U. Mo., Kansas City, 1997. Inventor: wheelchair with mechanism to raise or lower left or right buttocks of person, hemostat that carries two sutures, synthetic covering with zipper to cover bowel when abdomen unable to be closed after surgery. Vol. Cleve. Community Action Against Addiction, 1987-88; mentor Case Western U. Inner City Program, Cleve., 1988—; judge honors sci. projects Shaker Heights Middle Sch., 1998. Fellow ACS (assoc.), Internat. Coll. Surgeons; mem. AAAS, AMA, N.Y. Acad. Scis., Nat. Med. Assn. (mentor 1990—), Assn. of Black Cardiologists, Ohio State Med. Soc., Cleve. Surg. Soc., Nat. Assn. Small Bus. Owners, Internat. Assn. Small Bus. Owners, Assn. Black Cardiologists, Greater Cleve. Ministers Alliance, Masons, Omega Psi Phi, Alpha Phi Omega. Democrat. Methodist. Avocations: reading, sports, golf. Home and Office: Motown Beverage Co 3277 Lee Rd Cleveland OH 44120-3451 also: Star Beverage Corp Ste 107 20475 Farnsleigh Rd Shaker Heights OH 44122-3850 Fax: 216-283-6143.

BOYD, CAROLYN PATRICIA, history educator; b. San Diego, June 1, 1944; d. Peter James and Patricia Mae (de Soucy) B.; m. Frank Dawson Bean, Jan. 4, 1975; children: Peter Justin Bean, Michael Franklin Bean. AB with great distinction and with honors in History, Stanford U., 1966; MA, U. Wash., 1969, PhD, 1974. Tchg. asst. dept. history U. Wash., 1970-71; from instr. to prof. dept. history U. Tex., Austin, 1973-95, prof., 1995-99, assoc. dean Office Grad. Studies, 1986-88, 90-92, chair dept. history, 1994-99; dir. univ. honors program, assoc. prof. dept. history U. Md., College Park, 1989-90; prof. dept. history U. Calif., Irvine, 1999—. Lectr. in field. Author: Praetorian Politics in Liberal Spain, 1979, La política pretoriana en el reinado de Alfonso XIII, 1990, Historia Patria: Politics, History and National Identity in Spain, 1875-1975, 1997, Spanish edit., 2000; mem. editl. bd. Essays, 1992-95; author chpts. to books; contbr. articles to profl. jours. Recipient Summer award U. Tex. Rsch. Inst., 1997; Woodrow Wilson hon. fellow, 1966, Fulbright-Hays fellow, 1966-67, NDEA Title IV fellow, 1968-72, AAUW fellow, 1972-73, ACLS fellow, 1985; ACLS Grant-in-Aid, 1977, Am. Philos. Soc. grant, 1978, URI Rsch. grant, 1985, New Del Amo Program grant, 2000-02; fellow Woodrow Wilson Internat. Ctr. for Scholars, 2002-03. Mem. Am. Hist. Assn. (James Harvey Robinson prize com. 1992-94, John Fagg prize com. 2001—), Soc. Spanish and Portugese Hist. Studies (gen. sec. 2000—, mem. exec. com. 1978-80, 83-85, 96-98, chair local arrangements, program chmn. conf. 1987), Coun. European Studies, Internat. Inst. in Spain. Office: U Calif Irvine Dept History Irvine CA 92697-0001 E-mail: cpboyd@uci.edu.

BOYD, CLAUDE COLLINS, educational specialist, consultant; b. Kent, Tex., May 25, 1924; s. Edward Clarke and Nora (Morris) B.; m. Frances Arline Haley, Jan. 22, 1955; children: David Chand, Anese Nasim Boyd Forsyth, Mark Kevin, Kimberly Ann Boyd Surgeon. BA, Tex. A&M U., 1948; MEd, U. Tex., 1957, EdD, 1961. Cert. elem. tchr., prin., supt., Tex. Elem. sch. tchr. Culberson County Ind. Sch. Dist., Van Horn, Tex.; elem. sch. prin. The Austin (Tex.) Ind. Sch. Dist.; elem sch bilingual tchr. Ector County Ind Sch. Dist., Odessa, Tex.; assoc. prof. Ind. U., Bloomington; curriculum specialist USAID, Guatemala City, Guatemala; project specialist in edn. The Ford Found., N.Y.C.; assoc. prof. edn. Pa. State U., Erie; edn. specialist Devel. Assocs., Inc., Washington; internat. edn. advisor/cons. U.S. Agy. for Internat. Devel., San Salvador, edn. adminstr., curriculum advisor La Paz, Bolivia; Dominican Republic; edn. adminstr., curriculum advisor U.S. Agy. for Internat. Devel., Dominican Republic; free-lance edn. advisor, cons., worldwide svc. Odessa, Tex.; tchr. edn. specialist InterAm. Devel. Bank, Santo Domingo, Dominican Republic. Ednl. supervision specialist InterAmerican Devel. Bank, Santo Domingo, Dominican Republic; substitute tchr. K-12, Ector County ISD, Odessa, Tex. Recipient Grand Order of Edn., Pres. of Rep. of Bolivia. Mem. ASCD, Phi Delta Kappa (past pres. Mu chpt.). Home: 2426 E 21st St Odessa TX 79761-1703

BOYD, CRAIG STEPHEN, lawyer; b. Coatesville, Pa., Jan. 3, 1948; s. Clarence Clifford and Ellen (Hunsicker) B.; m. Pamela Kline, Aug. 30, 1969; children: David C., Jeffrey R., Steven D. B.S., Shippensburg U., Pa., 1970, M.S., Bowling Green State U., Ohio, 1971; J.D., U. Notre Dame, 1974; L.L.M. in Taxation, Villanova U., 1987. Bar: Pa. 1974, U.S. Dist. Ct. (ea. dist.) Pa. 1974. Assoc., E. Kenneth Nyce, Boyertown, Pa., 1974-77; sole practice law, Boyertown, Pa., 1977-83; mng. ptnr. Boyd & Karver, Boyertown, Pa., 1983—; lectr. law Ursinus Coll., Collegeville, Pa., 1974-76, Pa. State U., 1978-80; solicitor Hereford (Pa.) Twp. Zoning Bd., 1978—. Author: Domestic Relations Guide, 1984; research asst. book Lawyers, Law Students and People, 1974. Bd. dirs. Boyertown Area Community Trust, 1984—, Helping Hands, Inc., 1976-87; pres. Boyertown Area YMCA, 1978-83. Spencer Found. grantee, 1973-74; YMCA Service award, 1983, Red Triangle award, 1982, Exec. award, 1980. Mem. Pa. Bar Assn., Berks County Bar Assn., ABA. Democrat. Home: PO Box 114 Boyertown PA 19512-0114 Office: 7 E Philadelphia Ave Boyertown PA 19512-1154

BOYD, DANNY DOUGLASS, financial counselor; b. Olustee, Okla., Oct. 18, 1933; s. Robert and Juanita Henrietta (Crawford) B.; m. Mary Ann Thomas, Jan. 25, 1953; children: Robert Lee, Rebecca Dyann Boyd McCully, Scott Thomas, Douglas Dean. BA magna cum laude, Abilene Christian U., 1954; MA in Linguistics, U. Tex., Arlington, 1976. CLU, chartered fin. cons.; CFP. Min. Chs. of Christ, Ardmore, Okla., 1954-56, Velma, Okla., 1956-57, Cisco, Tex., 1958-60, Utrecht, The Netherlands, 1960-65, Wilmington, Del., 1965-69, Dallas, 1969-71; v.p. Nat. Comp Assocs., Dallas, 1972-77; marriage and family counselor Adaptive Counseling Assocs., Dallas, 1977-94; fin. counselor CIGNA Ind. Fin. Svcs. Co., 1979-92, Dan Boyd & Assocs., 1992—. Assoc. Fin. Edn. Assocs., Tex., 1994—; exec. v.p. WampumWare, Inc., 1996—; br. mgr. SunAmerica Securities, Inc., 1997-2000; founder Chair of Bible, Cisco Jr. Coll., 1959. Bd. dirs. Skyline H.S. PTA, 1971; intervenor for integrated neighborhoods fed. dist. ct. desegregation suit, Dallas, 1977. Mem. Soc. Fin. Svc. Profls. (Dallas chpt.). Republican.

BOYD, DAVID PRESTON, business educator; b. N.Y.C., Oct. 19, 1943; s. David Preston and Mignon (Finch) B.; m. Sally Sparks, Sept. 9, 1989. BA in English Lit., Harvard U., 1965; DPhil in Behavioral Scis., Oxford U., 1973. Asst. headmaster Dedham (Mass.) Country Day Sch., 1965-69; co-owner the Old Cambridge (Mass.) Co., 1973-77; instr. coll. bus. adminstrn. Northeastern U., Boston, 1977-78, asst. prof., 1978-82, assoc. prof., 1982-87, Patrick F. and Helen C. Walsh rsch. prof., 1985-86, chmn. human resources mgmt. dept., 1986-87, prof., 1987—, acting dean, 1987, dean coll. and grad. sch. bus. adminstrn., 1987-94. Author: Elites and Their Education National Foundation for Educational Research, 1973; mem. editl. bd. Internat. Jour. Value-Based Mgmt., Cross-cultural Mgmt., Corporate Governance; contbr. articles to profl. jours. Past trustee Pine Manor Coll.; corporator Brookline Bancorp. Recipient Excellence in Teaching award Northeastern U., 1980; Northeastern U. grantee, 1982-84, Control Data Corp., 1983, NYU, 1985. Fellow Mass. Hist. Soc.; mem. Soc. Colonial Wars, S.R., Oxford Soc., Tennis and Racquet Club, Somerset Club, Mass Hort. Soc. (former trustee), Comml. Club, Beta Gamma Sigma, Phi Kappa Phi. Home: 14 Bristol Rd Wellesley Hills MA 02481-2727 Office: Northeastern U 304 Hayden Hall Boston MA 02115-5000

BOYD, DAVID WILLIAM, mathematician, educator; b. Toronto, Ont., Can., Sept. 17, 1941; s. Glenn Kelvin and Rachael Cecilia (Garvock) B.; m. Mary Margaret Shields, Sept. 26, 1964; children: Deborah, Paul, Kathryn. BS, Carleton U., 1963; MA, Toronto U., 1964, PhD, 1966. Asst. prof. U. Alta., 1966-67, Calif. Inst. Tech., 1967-70, assoc. prof., 1970-71, U. B.C., Vancouver, Can., 1971-74, prof. math., 1974—, dept. head, 1986-89. Recipient E.W.R. Steacie Prize, 1978; I.W. Killam sr. research fellow, 1976-77, 81-82, Coxeter-James prize, 1979, Jeffery-Williams prize, 2001. Fellow Royal Soc. Can.; mem. Am. Math. Soc., Can. Math. Soc. Office: Univ BC Dept Math Vancouver BC Canada V6T 1Z2 E-mail: boyd@math.ubc.ca.

BOYD, DEBORAH ANN, pediatrician; b. Urbana, Ohio, Jan. 30, 1955; d. John A. Sr. and Juanita Jean (Routt) B. BA cum laude, Wittenberg U., 1977; MD, U. Cin., 1982. Diplomate Am. Bd. Pediatrics, Nat. Bd. Med. Examiners. Intern Children's Hosp. Med. Ctr., Cin., 1982-83, pediatric resident, 1982-85; pediatrician Nat. Health Svc. Corps, Springfield, Ohio, 1985-89; former pediatrician Community Hosp. Health Care Ctr., Springfield, 1989-97; staff pediat. primary care ctr., clin. faculty Children's Hosp. Med. Ctr., Cin., 1998—. Mem. Continuing med. edn. com. Mercy Med. Ctr., Springfield, 1989—, infection control com., 1987—. Adv. com. Miami Valley Child Devl. Ctr., Springfield, 1985—, New Parents as Tchrs., 1986—. Mem. Assn. of Clinicians for the Underserved, Am. Acad. Pediats., Ambulatory Pediat. Assn. Democratic. Avocations: bicycling, photography, basketball, music, church activities. Home: 12132 S Pine Dr Apt 240 Cincinnati OH 45241-1743 Office: Dept Gen Com Pediatrics Children's Hosp Med Ctr 3333 Burnet Ave Fl 4 Cincinnati OH 45229-3026

BOYD, DONALD BRADFORD, chemist; b. Syracuse, N.Y., Oct. 23, 1941; s. Howard M. B. BS honors, Pa. State U., 1963; MA, Harvard U., 1965, PhD, 1968. Rsch. assoc. Cornell U., Ithaca, N.Y., 1967-68; sr. phys. chemist Eli Lilly & Co., Indpls., 1968-74; rsch. scientist, 1975-89; sr. rsch. scientist Eli Lilly & Co., Indpls., 1990—93; adj. prof. Ind. U.-Purdue U., Indpls., 1982—93, rsch. prof. chemistry, 1994—. Chmn. Symposium on Molecular Mechs., 1983, Gordon Rsch. Confs. on Computational Chemistry, 1986, 88, Symposium on Molecular Design and Modeling, 1991, Am. Chem. Soc. Symposia on Emerging Technologies in Computational Chemistry, 2000, 01, 02. Editor: Reviews in Computational Chemistry, 1990—, Jour. Molecular Graphics and Modelling, 1998-2001; editl. bd. Structural Chemistry, Modern Drug Discovery; contbr. articles to profl. jours. Mem. Am. Chem. Soc., QSAR and Modelling Soc., Phi Lambda Upsilon, Pi Mu Epsilon, Sigma Xi. Achievements include being early practitioner of computer assisted molecular design; 6 patents in field. Office: Dept Chemistry Ind U-Purdue U at Indpls Indianapolis IN 46202-3274

BOYD, DONALD EDGAR, artist, educator; b. Sparta, Ohio, Feb. 20, 1934; s. Charles William Boyd and Correl Augusta Downing; m. Joyce Martha Hite, June 28, 1964 (div. Mar. 1982); children: Bentley Gale, Laura Dawn, Jonathan Ashley. BFA cum laude, Ohio State U., 1956; MA in Tchg., Harvard U., 1961; MFA in Sculpture, U. Iowa, 1966. Asst. prof., establisher sculpture program Kenyon Coll., Gambier, Ohio, 1966-72; artist-in-residence S.C. Arts Coun., Walterboro, 1973-74; asst. prof. S.D. State U., Brookings, 1974-86; vis. artist Ohio State U., Columbus, 1986-87; adj. prof. Mt. Vernon (Ohio) Nazarene U., 1994—97, adj. prof. art, 2000—; assoc. prof. U. S.D., Vermillion, 1997-98; asst. prof. Muskingum Coll., New Concord, Ohio, 1998-2000. Dir. Fluxus West, 1975—; curator S.D. Exptl. Artists, 55 Mercer St. Gallery, N.Y.C., 1982, Fluxus Columbus, Geoffrey Taber Gallery, 1987; artist in residence S.C. Arts Coun., 1973-74. Exhibited works at Boston Arts Festival, 1962, 64, Dayton Art Inst., 1968 (first prize), Venice Biennale, 1976, Young Fluxus, Artists Space, N.Y.C., catalog, 1982, ArtReach Exptl. Art Gallery, Columbus, 1988, Tulsa U., 1989, Wexner Ctr. for the Arts, 1994, Mus. New Art, 2001, 02; one-man show; Mansfield Art Ctr., Ohio, 2002. Recipient Nat. 1st prize in slides, Buffalo, N.Y., 1970, Best of Show, ArtReach Gallery, Columbus, 1987, All-Ohio Juried Exhbn. at Ohio State U.-Mansfield, 2002, 1st prize, Mansfield Art Ctr., 1990, 2d prize, Zanesville Art Ctr., 1999; grantee, NEA, 1975, S.D. Arts Coun., 1981. Mem. Mansfield Art Ctr., Zanesville Appalachian Art Group. Home: 75 S Main St Fredericktown OH 43019 E-mail: dboyd56@hotmail.com.

BOYD, F. ALLEN, JR., congressman, farmer; b. Valdosta, Ga., June 6, 1945; m. Cissy Boyd; children: David, John, Suzanne. BA, Fla. State U., 1969. Mem. Fla. Ho. of Reps., 1989—97, U.S. Ho. of Reps. from 2d Fla. dist., 1997—; mem. appropriations com. U.S. Congress from 2d Fla. dist., mem. mil. constrn. and the agr. com., mem. rural devel. com., mem. food and drug adminstrn. Chmn. Fla. House Dem. Conservative Caucus. With U.S. Army, 1969—71. Democrat. Office: 107 Cannon Ho Office Bldg Washington DC 20515-0902*

BOYD, FRANCES ARMSTRONG, language educator, writer; b. Norwalk, Conn., June 27, 1950; d. John W. and Jean M. Boyd; m. Carlos Salvador Velazquez, Aug. 29, 1981; children: Alejandro Guillermo Velazquez, Eduardo Carlos Velazquez. AB, Oberlin Coll., Oberlin OH, 1972; MA, U. Wis., 1974; EdD, Columbia U., 1984. Tchr. McBurney Sch., N.Y.C., 1975—79; sr. lectr. Am. Lang. Program Columbia U., N.Y.C., 1980—. Author (with Garrison Keillor): Stories from Lake Wobegon; author: Making Business Decisions, L'italiano con l'opera (Italian through Opera); editor: (10-vol. acad. English series) NorthStar. Recipient award, Mayor's Coun. on Adult Edn., N.Y.C., 1979, Malkemes prize for profl. writing, 1992; fellow, NDEA, 1973—74; scholar, Am. Field Svc., 1967. Mem.: Tchrs. of English to Spkrs. of Other Langs. Avocation: violin. Office: Columbia U 504 Lewisohn Hall New York NY 10027 E-mail: fab1@columbia.edu.

BOYD, GARY DELANE, electro-optical engineer, researcher; b. L.A., Sept. 14, 1932; s. Vroman O. and Bea L. (Crisp) B.; m. Diana Logan, June 13, 1964; children: Eric Logan, Cynthia Melinda. BSEE, Calif. Inst. Tech., 1954, MSEE, 1955, PhD in Elec. Engring. and Physics, 1959. Mem. tech. staff AT&T Bell Labs., Murray Hill, N.J., 1959-66, Holmdel, N.J., 1967—, head electronic devel. rsch. dept., 1972-84. Cons. Lucent Techs., 1994—; lectr. div. engring. and applied physics, Harvard U., Cambridge, Mass., 1966-67. Patentee laser and optical devices, liquid crystal displays, acoustics delay lines. Fellow IEEE (mem. awards bd. 1977-79), Optical Soc. Am. Presbyterian. Home: 56 E River Rd Rumson NJ 07760-1549 Office: Lucent Technologies Crawfords Corner Rd Rm 4B435 Holmdel NJ 07733 E-mail: gdboyd@worldnet.att.net.

BOYD, HERBERT REED, JR., dentist; b. Petersburg, Va., Sept. 15, 1925; s. Herbert Reed and Eula Jesse (Arnold) B.; m. Beverly Jane Lackey, Aug. 5, 1950 (dec. Apr. 13, 1999); children: Herbert Reed III, Stuart Arnold, Amy Lewis; m. Frances Dixon, Feb. 17, 2001. BA, U. Richmond, 1972; DDS, Med. Coll. Va., 1948. Dental intern in oral surgery Med. Coll. Va. Hosps., Richmond, 1948-49; instr. crown and bridge prosthodontics Med. Coll. Va., Richmond, 1951-53, asst. prof., 1953-56, assoc. prof., 1956-61, asst. clin. prof. periodontics, 1964-70; pvt. practice Petersburg, Va., 1961—. Trustee St. Marks United Meth. Ch., 2001; mem. adminstr. bd. OCRAN United Meth. Ch., 2003—. Capt. U.S. Army, 1949—51, lt. col. U.S. Army, 1962. Fellow Va. Dental Assn.; mem. ADA, Southside Va. Dental Assn. (pres. 1977), Am. Coll. Dentists, Internat. Coll. Dentists, Am. Acad. Medicine, Pierre Fauchard Acad., Med. Coll. Va. Alumni Assn. (pres. 1977), U. Richmond Alumni Assn., Boatwright Soc. U. Richmond (bd. dirs., v.p. 1998-99, pres. 1999-2000), U.S. Lighthouse Soc. (adv. bd. Chesapeake chpt. 1992—), Am. Assn. Ret. Persons (chpt. 2d v.p. 1998), Petersburg C. of C., McKee Dental Study Club Richmond, Rotary (pres. 1976-77), Omnicron Kappa Upsilon, Psi Omega, Phi Kappa Sigma. Home: 10960 Bland Ridge Dr Petersburg VA 23805-7143 Office: 23 Goodrich Ave Petersburg VA 23805-2119

BOYD, JOSEPH ARTHUR, JR., lawyer; b. Hoschton, Ga., Nov. 16, 1916; s. Joseph Arthur and Esther Estelle (Puckett) B.; m. Ann Stripling, June 6, 1938; children: Joanne Louise Boyd Goldman, Betty Jean Boyd Jala, Joseph Robert, James Daniel, Jane N. Ohlin. Student, Piedmont Coll., Demorest, Ga., 1936-38, LLD, 1963; student, Mercer U., Macon, Ga., 1938-39; JD, U. Miami, Coral Gables, Fla., 1948; LLD, Western State U. Coll. Law, San Diego, 1981. Bar: Fla. 1948, U.S. Supreme Ct. 1959, D.C. 1973, N.Y. 1982. Practice law, Hialeah, 1948-68; city atty., 1951-58; mem. Dade County Commn., Miami, Fla., 1958-68, chmn., 1963; vice mayor Dade County, 1967; justice Fla. Supreme Ct., Tallahassee, 1969-87, chief justice, 1984-86; assoc. Boyd Lindsey & Sliger P.A., Tallahassee, 1987—99. Mem. Hialeah Zoning Bd., 1946-48; juror Freedoms Found., Valley Forge, Pa., 1971, 73 Bd. dirs. Bapt. Hosp., Miami, 1962-66, Miami Coun. Chs., 1960-64; emeritus trustee Piedmont Coll. Recipient Nat. Top Hat award Bus. and Profl. Women in U.S. for advancing status of employed women, 1967 Mem. ABA, Fla. Bar Assn., Hialeah-Miami Springs Bar Assn. (pres. 1955), Tallahassee Bar Assn., Hialeah-Miami Springs C. of C. (pres. 1956), Am. Legion (comdr. Fla. 1953-54), VFW, Shriners, Masons (33 deg.), Lions, Elks, Wig and Robe, Iron Arrow, Phi Alpha Delta. Democrat. Baptist (deacon). Office: 1407 Piedmont Dr E Tallahassee FL 32308-7943

BOYD, JOSEPH DON, financial services executive; b. Muncie, Ind., Jan. 22, 1926; s. Joseph Corneluis and Waneta May (Barrett) B.; m. Cynthia Reiley, Dec. 28, 1957; children— Jane Elizabeth, Craig Alan, Michael J. AB (Rector scholar), DePauw U., 1948; MA, Northwestern U., 1950, Ed.D., 1955. Ednl. asst. First Meth. Ch., Anderson, Ind., 1948-49; residence hall counselor Northwestern U., Evanston, Ill., 1949-50, univ. examiner, instr. edn., guidance lab. asst., 1952-54, dean men, asst. prof. edn., 1955-61; exec. dir. Ill. Scholarship Commn., 1961-80; dir. instnl. relations and research Nat. Coll. Edn., Evanston, 1981-84; pres. Joseph D. Boyd & Assocs., Deerfield, Ill., 1984—. Residence hall dir., head tennis coach, asst. basketball coach Albion Coll., 1950-52 Mem. Nat. Assn. Adminstrs. State Scholarship Programs, Phi Delta Kappa, Delta Tau Delta, Phi Eta Sigma. Clubs: Rotarian. Methodist. Home: 1232 Warrington Rd Deerfield IL 60015-3145 Office: 600 Deerfield Rd Deerfield IL 60015-3229

BOYD, JULIANNE MAMANA, theater director, educator; b. Easton, Pa., Dec. 22, 1944; d. Joseph and Julia (Cericola) Mamana; m. Norman Wingate Boyd Jr., July 9, 1966; children: Sarah, Norman III, Emily. BA, Beaver Coll., 1966; MA, Adelphi U., 1968; PhD, CUNY, 1986. Lectr. NYU, 1987-91; artistic dir. Berkshire Theatre Festival, Stockbridge, Mass., 1992-94; artistic dir., founder Barrington Stage Co., Great Barrington, Mass., 1995—. Conceiver and dir. Broadway musical Eubie, 1978 (Audelco award Outstanding Dir 1978), off-Broadway play A...My Name is Alice, 1984 (Outer Critics award), A...My Name is Still Alice, 1992. Mem. adv. bd. Women's Project, Inc., N.Y., 1988-92. Recipient Golden Disc award Beaver Coll., 1981, Outstanding Young Entrepreneur award Citicorp, N.Y., 1980, Outstanding Alumni award CUNY, 1995. Mem. Soc. Stage Dirs. and Choreographers (pres. 1992-98). E-mail: jboyd@barringtonstageco.org.

BOYD, KANISHA, nurse manager; d. Eunice Boyd-Ishman and Earnest Ishman(Stepfather); life ptnr. Glenn O. Basden; 1 child, Devin Glenn Basden. BA, Rutgers U., 1995; AD in Nursing, Christ Hosp. Sch. of Nursing, 1998; BSN, Jersey City U., 2003. RN Clara Mass Med. Ctr., Belleville, NJ, 1998—2000, Newark Beth Israel Med. Ctr., 2000—01, asst. nurse mgr., 2001—. Recipient Odessa Chambliss Quality of Life award and scholarship, 2001. Mem.: Sigma Theta Tau Internat. Baptist. Avocation: reading. Office: Newark Beth Israel Medi Ctr 201 Lyons Ave Newark NJ 07112 Office Fax: 973-282-1386. Personal E-mail: kaysosa73@yahoo.com. E-mail: kboyd@sbhcs.com.

BOYD, KATHERINE ANN, clinical therapist; b. Ranson, W.Va., Sept. 7, 1973; d. James J. and Kathleen S. Sisco; m. Glen Jr. Allan Boyd, May 25, 1996. AA in Social Sci., County Coll. of Morris, 1993; BA in Psychology, Rutgers U., 1997; MA in Counseling Psychology, Coll. of Saint Elizabeth, 2000. Behavoirist, tchr. Nat. Acad. for Child Devel., Mountain Lakes, N.J., 1993-95; mental health counselor N.W. Covenant Med. Ctr., Boonton, N.J., 1997-99; clin. therapist The RedCo Group Behavioral Health Svcs., Stroudsburg, Pa., 2000-2001; clin. specialist Newton (N.J.) Meml. Hosp. Sussex House, 2001—; behavior specialist, cons., mobile therapist Youth Advocate Programs, Inc., East Stroudsburg, Pa., 2001—. Adv. bd. for patient satisfaction N.W. Covenant Med. Ctr., 1997; mentor Coll. of Saint Elizabeth, 1999-2000. Vol. Avon Breast Cancer Crusade, N.Y., 1999-2001, Salvation Army, Dover, N.J., 1997-99, The Meth. Manor, Branchville, N.J., 1996—. Mem. ACA (assoc.), Am. Psychol. Assn., N.J. Psychol. Assn. (assoc.), N.J. Counseling Assn. (assoc.), N.J. Mental Health Counselors Assn., Am. Psychol. Soc. Methodist. Avocations: skiing, travel, equestrian, music, hiking. Home: 303 Walnut Grove East Stroudsburg PA 18301

BOYD, KENNETH ANDREW, music educator; b. Cutchogue, N.Y., Jan. 18, 1975; s. Judith Ann Boyd; m. Jennifer Anne Bangert, June 3, 2000. MusB in Edn., U. of Ctrl. Fla., 1998. Cert. tchr. Fla., 1998. Band dir. Meml. Mid. Sch., Orlando, Fla., 1998—99, U. HS, Orlando, 1999—2002, Olympia HS, Orlando, 2002—. Mem.: Fla. Bandmasters Assn. Office: Olympia High School 4301 S Apopka Vineland Rd Orlando FL 32835 Personal E-mail: boydk@ocps.net. E-mail: boydk@ocps.net.

BOYD, KENNETH R. application and web programmer, mathematician; b. Nov. 15, 1970; s. Lonnie and Dorothy Boyd. BS in Math., Kans. State U., 1992, MS in Math., 1998. CEO Zaimoni.com, Linn Valley, Kans., 2000—. Scholar, Barry M. Goldwater Found., 1987—89. Mem.: Am. Math. Soc. E-mail: zaimoni@zaimoni.com.

BOYD, LARRY CHESTER, recruitment manager; b. Newberry, S.C., Nov. 6, 1958; s. Andrew Larkin Sr. and Anna Lee (McMorris) B.; m. Paula Annette Harris, Aug. 19, 1989; 1 child, Larry Jr. BA in Polit. Sci. cum laude, S.C. State U., 1980; MBA in Adminstrn., Cen. Mich. U., 1990. Commd. 2d lt. U.S. Army, 1980, advanced through grades to lt. col., 1999—, adminstrv. officer 800th Materiel Mgmt. Ctr., 1980-82, asst. sec. gen. staff, protocol officer Hdqrs. VII Corps Stuttgart, Fed. Rep. Germany, 1982-83, chief reenlistment Hdrs. and Hdrs. Co. U.S. Army Garrison Ft. Polk, La., 1984; comdr. 5th Adj. Gen. Replacement Co., Ft. Polk, La., 1984-85; chief, officer records 5th Adj. Gen. Co. U.S. Army, Ft. Polk, La., 1985, chief, pers. records 5th Pers. Svc. Co., 1985, chief, Co. Spt. Div., 1986, chief, G-1/Adj. Gen. Plans and Ops. Hdrs. and Hdqrs. Co. 5th Inf. Div., 1986; advisor Readiness Group Dix First U.S. Army, Ft. Dix, N.J., 1987-88; tng. mgmt. officer, asst. ops. officer U.S. Army, Ft. Dix, N.J., 1988-89, chief adminstrn. logistics assistance div., 1989-92; dep. chief mil. awards br. Dept. of The Army, Alexandria, Va., 1993-97; recruitment mgr. INROADS, Phila., 1992—; dir. mil. pers. directorate 1079th U.S. Army Garrison Support Unit, Fort Dix, N.J., 1997-99; battalion comdr. 3rd Signal Battalion, 3rd Brigade, 80th Divsn., 1999—2002. Intern State of S.C. Task Force on Structure of State and Local Govt., 1980; mem. Bush River Bapt. Ch., Newberry, S.C., 1973—; mem. Tabernacle Bapt. Ch., Burlington, N.J., 1988—; vice chmn. Omega Cmty. Devel., Inc., 1999—. Decorated Army Commendation medal with oak leaf cluster, Meritorious Svc. medal with oak leaf cluster, Nat. Def. Svc. medal, Allen W. Reese Meml. scholar, humanitarian svc. medal; named of Outstanding Men of Am., U.S. Jaycees, 1984, 86, 87, 88, 89, 92, 96, 97, 98, 99; Army Res. Achievement medal. Mem. ASTD, NAACP, Assn. U.S. Army, Nat. Black MBA Assn., Nat. Mgmt. Assn., Am. Legion, S.C. State U.

Alumni Assn., Adjutant Gen. Signal Regimental Assn., Ret. Officers Assn., Pi Gamma Mu, Omega Psi Phi (vice basileus 1978-79, basileus 1979-80, dean of edn. 1981-82, 85-86, area coord. 1982-83, keeper of records and seal 1984-86, 92-93, asst. keeper of records and seal 1990-92, basileus 1993-94, dir. pub. rels. 1994-95, 97-98, 98-2000, Omega Man of yr. 1985, 86, 91). Avocations: sports, music. Office: 1601 Market St Ste 1010 Philadelphia PA 19103-2328 Home: 31 Tarnsfield Rd Westampton NJ 08060-2361 E-mail: omega1977@prodigy.net, lboyd@inroads.org.

BOYD, LAURI LOUISE, lawyer, judge; b. Bremerton, Wash., Oct. 10, 1958; d. Eugene L. Gunkel and Valdi Lee Johanson; m. Mark Lawrence McIntire, Nov. 3, 1978 (div. Jan. 1984); 1 child, Cameron Caid; m. Donald Allen Boyd, Aug. 20, 1988; 1 child, Elena Christine. BA cum laude, Western Wash. U., 1982; JD, Seattle U., 1986. Bar: Wash. 1987, U.S. Supreme Ct. 1999. Assoc. Frderick W. Fleming & Assocs., Tacoma, Wash., 1985-88; asst. city atty. City of Yakima, Wash., 1991-95; mcpl. ct. judge City Selah, Wash., 1995—; appellate atty. Yakima County Prosecutor's Office, Yakima, 1989-91, 95—. Mem. Wash. State Bar Assn. (mandatory CLE bd. 1992-95, ct. rules and procedures com. 1995-99, law examiner's com. 1999—). Avocations: skiing, foreign films, opera. Office: Yakima County Prosecuting Atty 128 N 2d St Yakima WA 98901

BOYD, LEONA POTTER, retired social worker; b. Creekside, Pa., Aug. 31, 1907; d. Joseph M. and Belle (McHenry) Johnston; m. Edgar D. Potter, July 16, 1932 (div.); m. Harold Lee Boyd, Oct. 1972. Grad., Indiana (Pa.) State Normal Sch, 1927; student, Las Vegas (N.Mex.) Normal U., 1933; student Sch. Social Work, Carnegie Inst. Tech., 1945, U. Pitts., 1956-57. Tchr. Creekside Pub. Schs., 1927-30, Papago Indian Reservation, Sells, Ariz., 1931-33; caseworker, supr. Indiana County (Pa.) Bd. Assistance 1934-54, exec. dir., 1954-68, ret. Bd. dirs., hon. life mem. Indiana County Tourist Promotion; former bd. dirs. Indiana County United Fund, Salvation Army, Indiana County Guidance Ctr., Armstrong-Indiana Mental Health Bd.; cons. assoc. Cmty. Rsch. Assocs., Inc.; mem. Counseling Ctr. Aux., Lake Havasu City, Ariz., 1978-80; former mem. Western Welcome Club, Lake Havasu City, Sierra Vista Hosp. Aux., Truth or Consequences, N.M. Recipient Disting. Svc. award Indiana Jaycees, 1965, Bus. and Profl. Women's Club award, 1965. Mem. AARP, Daus. Am. Colonists. Lutheran. Home: 520 S Higley Rd Unit 126 Mesa AZ 85206-2274

BOYD, LON VERNON, lawyer, alderman; b. Kingsport, Tenn. s. Lon and Maude Elizabeth Boyd; m. Elizabeth Lee Boyd, Dec. 15, 1956. BS, East Tenn. State U., 1951; JD, U. Tenn., 1957. Bar: Tenn. 1957. Ptnr. Boyd, Lauderback & Snodgrass, Kingsport, 1965-80; pvt. practice, Kingsport, 1957 65, 80—; alderman City of Kingsport, 1997—. Judge Sullivan County, Tenn., 1966-86, county exec., 1980-86. Pres. Sullivan County Rep. Com., 1963. With USN, from 1947, 52-54; capt. USNR, until 1982. Named Young Man of Yr., Kingsport Jr. C. of C., 1963. Mem. Tenn. Bar Assn., Kingsport Bar Assn. (pres. 1998-99), VFW, Am. Legion, Kiwanis (pres. 1964). Presbyterian. Home: 3352 Ft Henry Dr Kingsport TN 37664 Office: 154 Cherokee St Kingsport TN 37660-4308

BOYD, MALCOLM, minister, writer; b. Buffalo, June 8, 1923; s. Melville and Beatrice (Lowrie) B.; life ptnr. Mark Thompson. BA, U. Ariz., 1944; B.D., Ch. Div. Sch. Pacific, 1954; postgrad., Oxford (Eng.) U., 1955; S.T.M., Union Theol. Sem., N.Y.C., 1956; DD (hon.), Ch. Div. Sch. of Pacific, 1995. Ordained to ministry Episcopal Ch., 1955. V.p., gen. mgr. Pickford, Rogers & Boyd, 1949-51; rector in Indpls., 1957-59; chaplain Colo. State U., 1959-61, Wayne State U., 1961-65; nat. field rep. Episcopal Soc. Cultural and Racial Unity, 1965-68; resident fellow Calhoun Coll., Yale U., 1968-71, assoc. fellow, 1971—; writer-priest in residence St. Augustine-by-the Sea Episcopal Ch., 1982-95. Lectr. World Council Chs., Switzerland, 1955, 64; columnist Pitts. Courier, 1962-65; resident guest Mishkenot Sha'ananim, Jerusalem, 1974; chaplain AIDS Commn. Episcopal Diocese L.A., 1989—; poet-in-residence Cathedral Ctr. of St. Paul, L.A., 1996—, hon. canon, 2002. Host (TV) Sex in the Seventies, LA, 1975; author: Crisis in Communication, 1957, Christ and Celebrity Gods, 1958, Focus, 1960, rev. edit., 2001, If I Go Down to Hell, 1962, The Hunger, The Thirst, 1964, Are You Running with Me, Jesus?, 1965, rev. edit., 1990, Free to Live, Free to Die, 1967, Book of Days, 1968, As I Live and Breathe: Stages of an Autobiography, 1969, The Fantasy Worlds of Peter Stone, 1969, My Fellow Americans, 1970, Human Like Me, Jesus, 1971, The Lover, 1972, When in the Course of Human Events, 1973, The Runner, 1974, The Alleluia Affair, 1975, Christian, 1975, Am I Running with You, God?, 1977, Take Off the Masks, 1978, rev. edit. 1993, Look Back in Joy, 1981, rev. edit., 1990, Half Laughing, Half Crying, 1986, Gay Priest: An Inner Journey, 1986, Edges, Boundaries and Connections, 1992, Rich with Years, 1993, Go Gentle Into That Good Night, 1998, Running with Jesus: The Prayers of Malcolm Boyd, 2000, Simple Grace: A Mentor's Guide to Growing Older, 2001, Prayers for the Later Years, 2002; plays Boy, 1961, Study in Color, 1962, The Community, 1964, others; editor: On the Battle Lines, 1964, The Underground Church, 1968, (with Nancy L. Wilson) Amazing Grace: Stories of Gay and Lesbian Faith, 1991; (with Chester Talton) Race and Prayer: Collected Voices, Many Dreams, 2003; book reviewer: LA Times, 1979-85; contbg. editor Episcopal News; columnist Modern Maturity, 1990-2000; contbr. articles to popular mags. including Newsday, Parade, The Advocate, also newspapers. Active voter registration, Miss., Ala., 1963, 64; mem. Los Angeles City/County AIDS Task Force Malcolm Boyd Collection and Archives established Boston U., 1973; recipient Integrity Internat. award, 1978, Union Am. Hebrew Congregations award, 1980, Lazarus Project award, 2002. Mem. Nat. Council Chs. (film awards com. 1965), P.E.N. (pres. PEN Ctr. U.S. West 1984-87), Am. Center, Authors Guild, Integrity, Nat. Gay Task Force, Clergy and Laity Concerned (nat. bd.), NAACP, Amnesty Internat., Episc. Peace Fellowship, Fellowship of Reconciliation (nat. com.). Episcopalian. Office: PO Box 512164 Los Angeles CA 90051-0164 *The years have taught me the cost of getting involved in life. It is all a risk. One is on stage in an ever-new set without a script. The floor may give way without warning, the walls abruptly cave in. One may die at the hand of an assassin acting on blind impulse. Security, for which men sell their souls, is one of the few real jests in life. Yet the cost of not getting involved in life is higher; one has merely died prematurely. When one has stripped power of its mystique, its robes and artifices, it becomes vulnerable. When you stand up to power, you stand up to one or more individuals. Look an individual, then, in the eye, laugh, if you feel like it. This may be rightly received as a much-needed expression of human solidarity.*

BOYD, MARVIN G. electrical engineer; b. Springfield, Ill., Oct. 22, 1933; s. Eugene Boyd and Vincen Gaynell Black-Boyd; m. Thanomsri Sirikul, June 24, 1974; children: Vincinne K. Weathers-Boyd, Vivien P. Degrees in computer tech., Cen. Data Inst., L.A., 1971; BSEE, LaSalle U., 1997; MSc in Gen. Engring., Kennedy-Western U., 2000. Instrument inspector Bendix Corp., Teterboro, N.J., 1959-67; aircraft and space installer McDonald-Douglas Corp., Long Beach and Huntington Beach, Calif., 1968-69; tech. rep. Lear-Spigler Corp., Oklahoma City, 1969-70, Northrop Corp., L.A., 1971-74; electronic technician FAA, Springfield, Ill., 1974-96; semi-ret., from 1996. With USN, 1951-55. Mem. Am. Assn. Ret. Persons, Am. Legion (life mem.). Avocations: sports hunting and fishing, wood working, crafts. Home: Sherman, Ill. Deceased.

BOYD, MICHAEL ALAN, investment company executive, lawyer; b. St. Petersburg, Fla., Aug. 19, 1937; s. Horace Clinton and Celeste Elizabeth (Tarpley) B. AB, Harvard Coll., 1958; postgrad., Queen's Coll., Oxford, Eng., 1958-61; LLB, Harvard U., 1967. Bar: N.Y. 1968. Assoc. Davis Polk & Wardwell, N.Y.C., 1967-71; sr. v.p., gen. counsel Donaldson, Lufkin & Jenrette, Inc., N.Y.C., 1971—2001; mng. dir. Brock Capital Group LLC, 2002—; ptnr. Brock Ptnrs., LLP, 2002—. With AUS, 1962—64, maj. gen. USAR. Rhodes scholar, 1958. Mem. Civil Affairs Assn. (nat. dir. 1983—), Assn. U.S. Army (bd. govs. N.Y. chpt. 1990, pres. 1995-97), Oxford Alumni Assn. of N.Y. (pres. 1996-99). Republican. Home: 33 Greenwich Ave Penthouse 2 New York NY 10014 Office: 400 Madison Ave 11th Fl New York NY 10017

BOYD, RALPH F., JR., federal agency administrator; BA, Haverford Coll., 1979; JD, Harvard U., 1984. Law clk. Hon. Joseph H. Young U.S. Dist. Ct. Md.; asst. U.S. atty. major crimes unit U.S. Attys. Office, Boston; ptnr. Goodwin Procter LLP, Boston; asst. atty. Gen. Civil Rights Divsn. U.S. Dept. Justice, Washington, 2001—. Mem. exec. com. Mass. Jud. Nominating Commn., 1996—2001; mem. U.S. Magistrate Judge Selection and Rev. Panel, 1998. Office: US Dept Justice Civil Rights Divsn 950 Pennsylvania Ave NW Washington DC 20530-0001

BOYD, RICHARD NELSON, physics educator; b. Omaha, Nebr., Apr. 25, 1940; s. Virgil Edward and Berniece Nelson B.; m. Sarah Anderson, July 14, 1962; children: Martha Anne, Carol Deborah, Rebecca Jeanne. BSE in Physics, BSE in Math., U. Mich., 1962; PhD, U. Minn., Mpls., 1967. Postdoctoral rsch. assoc. U. Minn., 1968, Rutgers U., New Brunswick, N.J., 1968-71, Stanford (Calif.) U., 1971-72; asst. prof. U. Rochester, N.Y., 1972-78; assoc. prof. physics Ohio State U., Columbus, 1978-81, prof. physics, 1981-84, assoc. dean, 1994-97, prof. physics, prof. astronomy, 1984—; program dir. physics divsn. NSF, 2002—. Mem. ISOL task force, 1998-99, mem. adv. com. on TRIUMF, Vancouver, B.C., Can., 1999—. Contbr. articles to profl. jours. Recipient Disting. Rsch. award Ohio State U., 1981; Eminent Scientist award RIKEN, The Inst. for Phys. and Chem. Rsch., Tokyo, 1997. Fellow: Am. Phys. Soc. (mem. exec. com. divsn. nuclear physics); mem.: AAAS. Achievements include research on astrophysics, nuclear physics and particle physics. Home: 161 Whieldon Ln Worthington OH 43085-2940 Office: Ohio State U Dept Physics 174 W 18th Ave Columbus OH 43210-1106 E-mail: boyd@mps.ohio state.edu.

BOYD, ROBERT CARR, JR., fire fighter, paramedic, graduate student; b. Charlotte, N.C., June 15, 1973; s. Robert Carr and Louise Boyd; m. Elizabeth Meckley. BA History, Hampden-Sydney Coll., Hampden-Sydney, VA, 1997; M Pub. Adminstrn., U.N.C.C., 2001. Cert. Nat. Registry of Emergency Med. Technicians-Paramedic 1996, Fire Fighter-Level II 1999, Hazardous Materials-Level I 1999, Structural Collapse (Rescue) 1996. Paramedic Mecklenburg EMS Agy., Charlotte, 1997—2000; firefighter Charlotte Fire Dept., 1998—. Level II fire instr. NC Fire & Rescue Commn., Raleigh, 2001—; EMT instr. Va. Office of Emergency Med. Svcs., Richmond, 1996—98. Vol. Habitat for Humanity, Big Brother, Charlotte, NC, 1997—2001; paramedic, 1st Lt. Ops. Prince Edward Vol. Rescue Squad, Farmville, 1993—2002; pres., fire capt. Hampden-Sydney Vol. Fire Dept., 1995—97. Mem.: ASPA, Pi Alpha Alpha. Avocation: sailing, farming, tennis. Personal E-mail: carrb@bellsouth.net.

BOYD, ROBERT GIDDINGS, JR., health facility administrator; b. San Juan, Mar. 16, 1940; s. Robert Giddings and Laura Jean (Stephenson) B.; m. Amanda Gail Rasmussen, July 28, 1967 (div. 1977); 1 child, Stephanie Gail; m. Denise Ann Ryll, Dec. 10, 1978; children: Robert Giddings III., Julianna Clare. BA in Sociology, Coll. William and Mary, 1962; MBA/MHA, Columbia State U., 1997. Lic. in real estate, Ariz.; lic. nursing home adminstr., Calif., N.C. Supr. staff services Bellcomm, Inc., Washington, 1964-67; budget mgr. Goodbody & Co., N.Y.C., 1968-70; bus. mgr. Westminster Sch., Simsbury, Conn., 1970-76; pres., gen. mgr. F & R Enterprises, Inc., Scottsdale, Ariz., 1976-78; mng. dir. San Diego Symphony Assn., 1981-84; exec. v.p. adminstrn. and fin. San Diego Ctr. for Children, 1985-95. Served to 1st lt. U.S. Army, 1962-64. Mem. Am. Coll. Health Care Adminstrs., Am. Coll. Health Care Execs. Republican. Office: Avante at Wilkesboro 1000 College St Wilkesboro NC 28697-2732

BOYD, ROBERT WRIGHT, III, lamp company executive; b. N.Y.C., July 21, 1945; s. Robert Wright and Ruth Simpson B.; m. Heather Riddle, June 7, 1968; children: Amy, Brook, Adam. Student, Universidad de Los Andes, Bogota, Columbia, 1965-66; BA cum laude, Princeton U., 1967; MA in Latin Am. studies, U. Fla., 1968. Sales rep. The Wilbur Ellis Co., N.Y.C., 1968-71; regional sales mgr. NPFC div. Nat. Can Corp., Phila., 1971-72, mktg. svcs. mgr. Lewis Foods div. Long Beach, Calif., 1972-73, western area sales mgr. Lewis Foods div., 1973-75, mgr. mktg. and sales Wells div. Monmouth, Ill., 1975-78; v.p. sales The Jim Dandy Co., Birmingham, Ala., 1978-80; owner R. W. Boyd & Assocs., Cherry Hill, NJ, 1980-81; mktg. dir. CBS spl. products div. CBS Records, CBS Inc., N.Y.C., 1982-85; v.p. mktg. and sales Action Internat. Ltd., div. Action Industries, Cheswick, Pa., 1985-90; pres., chief exec. officer Hi Lite Industries Inc., Greensburg, Pa., 1990—; ptnr. Westmoreland County Combine, GP, 1997—; pres. Tri-verse, Inc., 2002—. Pub.: His Father's Son, 1997. Deacon Trinity United Presbyn. Ch., Cherry Hill, N.J., 1982-84; trustee Ingomar (Pa.) United Meth. Ch., 1988-89, mem. adminstrv. coun., 1994-97. Mem. Colonial Club (Princeton, N.J.). Republican. Methodist. Avocation: physical fitness. Office: Hi Lite Industries Inc RD 6 Box 517 Woodward Drive Ext Greensburg PA 15601 E-mail: macroboud@aol.com.

BOYD, ROGER ALLEN, investment consultant; b. Meadville, Pa., May 30, 1954; s. Willis W. and Ida Elaine (Stewart) B.; m. Susan Janis Auwarter, July 24, 1982; children: Sara Janis, Emily Katherine. BS in Acctg., Gannon Coll., 1976. CFP. Acct. Arthur Andersen & Co., Pitts., 1976-77; investment real estate salesman Lloyd White Co., Realtors, Erie, Pa., 1977-80; fin. cons. Merrill Lynch, Erie, 1980-81; assoc. v.p. Dean Witter Reynolds, N.Y.C., 1981-88; sr. v.p. Morgan Stanley, Toms River, N.J., 1988—. Owner, mgr. Dunnwright LLC, horse and pony boarding and breeding farm, Lakewood, 1999—. Bd. dirs., v.p., chmn. artistic com. Garden State Philharm., Toms River, 1991-98. Mem. Mensa, Island Heights Yacht Club, Kiwanis (bd. dirs. Toms River 1990-93). Republican. Office: Morgan Stanley 1433 Hooper Ave Toms River NJ 08753-2826 also: Dunnwright LLC 1000 Cross St Lakewood NJ 08701-4005

BOYD, STEPHEN MATHER, arbitrator, mediator, lawyer; b. St. Louis, May 1, 1934; s. Ingram Fletcher and Adeline Ely (Smith) B.; m. Susan Brush Forney, May 9, 1964; children: Christopher Fletcher, Elizabeth Barrows, Charles Mather. AB in History with honors, Princeton U., 1955; LL.B., Harvard U., 1958. Bar: Mo. 1958, D.C. 1973. Assoc. Bryan, Cave, McPheeters & McRoberts, St. Louis, 1963-67, ptnr. Washington, 1978-88; atty. adviser Dept. of State, Washington, 1967-69, asst. legal adviser Near East, South Asia, 1970-73; assoc. Surrey & Morse, Paris, 1973-74, ptnr., 1975-77, Washington, 1977-78; pres. Princeton Project 55, 1989-90, bd. dirs., 1989-92; pvt. practice arbitrator and mediator. Mem. Washington Fgn. Law Soc., 1981-90, bd. govs., 1983-85; cons. in field. Contbr. articles to profl. jours. 1st lt. USAF, 1958-61; Taiwan, Japan Mem.: ABA (com. on internat. litigation 1978—81, mem. litigation sect.), Am. Arbitration Assn. (arbitrator, mediator internat. and comml. disputes), D.C. Bar Assn., Am. Soc. Internat. Law, Character Edn. Partnership (bd. dirs. 1993—97), UN Assn. U.S.A. (bd. dirs. 1982—90). Democrat. Unitarian Universalist. Avocations: hiking, sculling, skiing, tennis, classical music, reading history and biographies. Home: 4400 Cathedral Ave NW Washington DC 20016-3563

BOYD, THEOPHILUS BARTHOLOMEW, III, publishing company executive; b. Nashville, May 15, 1947; s. Theophilus B. Jr. and Mable (Landrum) B.; m. Yvette Jean Duke, May 5, 1984; children: Theophilus B. IV, LaDonna Yvette, Shalae Shantel, Justin Marriel. BS, Tenn. State U., 1969; DD, Shreveport Bible Coll., 1980; LittD (hon.), Easonian Bapt. Sem., 1983. Pers. dir. R.H. Boyd Pub. Corp., Nashville, 1969-79; pres., chief exec. officer, 1979—. Chmn. Citizens Bank, Nashville, 1982—. Vice chair Meharry Med. Coll. bd. trustees, Nashville, 1989—; trustee Fla. Meml. Coll., Miami, 1984-86; bd. dirs. Nashville Symphone Assn., 1986-87, Nashville chpt. March of Dimes, 1986—; past pres. 100 Black Men of Mid. Tenn.; v.p. fin., treas. 100 Black Men Am., 1992-94. Named Hon. Citizen, City of Dallas, 1980, Man of Yr., 1990; recipient Key to the City, Denver, 1985, New Orleans, 1986, Great Seal of U.S. award; named man of the yr. 1990 March of Dimes. Mem. Nashville Area C. of C. (exec. bd.), Kappa Alpha Psi, Sigma Pi Phi, Richland Country Club. Democrat. Baptist. Avocations: boating, marathon running. Office: RH Boyd Publishing Corp 6717 Centennial Blvd Nashville TN 37209-1017

BOYD, THOMAS MARSHALL, lawyer; b. Yorktown, Va., Sept. 10, 1946; s. Laurel Barnett and Mildred Warner Wellford (Marshall) B.; m. Torri Carol Tyler, Oct. 2, 1976; children: Brooke Warner, Tyler Randolph. BA in History, Va. Military Inst., 1968; JD, U. Va., 1971. Bar: Calif. 1973, D.C. 1974. Law clk. to fed. judge U.S. Dist. Ct. (cen. dist.) Calif., Los Angeles, 1973-74; trial atty., atty. advisor U.S. Dept. Justice, Washington, 1974-76; assoc. counsel com. on judiciary U.S. Ho. of Reps., Washington, 1976-86; dep. asst. atty. gen. Dept. Justice Office Legis. Affairs, Washington, 1986-88, asst. atty. gen., 1988-89, dir. office policy devel., 1989-91; dep. gen. counsel Kemper Corp., Washington, 1991-93, v.p. and legis. counsel, 1993-96; v.p. for legis. affairs Investment Co. Inst., Washington, 1996-98; ptnr. Ramsey, Cook, Looper & Kurlander LLP, Washington, 1998-99, Alston & Bird, LLP, Washington, 1999—. House counsel Presdl. Transition Com. on Criminal Justice, Washington, 1980-81; pub. mem. Adminstrv. Conf. U.S., 1992-95. Co-editor U.S. Atty.'s Criminal Trial Manual, 1971; contbr. articles to profl. jours. and pub. interest articles to newspapers. Served to capt. USAF, 1968-73. Recipient Nat. Media award Delta Soc., 1985, Edmund J. Randolph award, 1988. Mem. U.S. Supreme Ct. Bar Assn., Calif. Bar Assn., D.C. Bar Assn., Army-Navy Country Club, Leland (Mich.) Country Club, Golf Club of Va. Republican. Episcopalian. Avocations: golf, jogging, writing.

BOYD, WILLARD LEE, academic administrator, educator, museum administrator, lawyer; b. St. Paul, Mar. 29, 1927; s. Willard Lee and Frances L. (Collins) Boyd; m. Susan Kuehn, Aug. 28, 1954; children: Elizabeth Kuehn, Willard Lee, Thomas Henry. BS in Law, U. Minn., 1949, LLB, 1951; LLM, U. Mich., 1952, SJD, 1962. Bar: Minn. 1951, Iowa 1958. Assoc. Dorsey & Whitney, Mpls., 1952—54; from instr. to prof. law U. Iowa, Iowa City, 1954—64, assoc. dean Law Sch., 1964, v.p. acad. affairs, 1964—69, pres., 1969—81, 2002—03, pres. emeritus, 1981—; pres. The Field Mus., Chgo., 1981—96, pres. emeritus, 1996—. Chmn. Nat. Mus. Scis. Bd., 1988—96; adv. com. Getty Ctr. for Edn. in Arts; chair bd. dirs. Harry S Truman Libr. Inst., 1997—2001; past adv. bd. Met. Opera, Ill. Humanities Coun., Ill. Arts Coun., Chgo. Cultural Affairs Bd. Bd. dirs. Nat. Art Inst. Recipient Charles Frankel prize, Nat. Endowment for Humanities, 1989. Mem.: ABA (com. social labor and indsl. legislations 1963—65, chmn. 1965—66, coun. mem. 1975—82, mem. sect. legal edn. and admission to bar chmn. 1980—81, chmn. coun. of sect. on legal edn. and admission), Nat. Commn. Accrediting (past pres.), Am. Assn. Univs. (past chmn.), Nat. Arts Strategies (bd. dirs.), Am. Law Inst., Am. Acad. Arts and Sci., Am. Art Inst., Ill. Humanities Coun., Iowa Bar Assn. Home: 620 River St Iowa City IA 52246-2433 Office: Univ Iowa Law Sch Iowa City IA 52242-1113

BOYD, WILLIAM ARTHUR, II, communications manager, editor, public relations professional; b. Washington, May 29, 1953; s. Donald Edward and Dorothymae (Phillips) B.; m. Cathy Ann Braman, Sept. 30, 1977; children: David James, Robin Elaine. Student, Am. U., 1971-74, George Mason U., 1975-76, U. Wash., 1976; BSS in Comms., Ohio U. Accredited bus. comm. Internat. Assn. Bus. Communicators, 1994. Reporter, anchor Radio Sta. WAVA, Washington, 1973-76; reporter Radio Sta. KIRO, Seattle, 1976-77; press sec. mayoral campaign Seattle, 1977; press sec. congl. campaign, 1978; assignment editor, reporter Sta. KSTW-TV, Tacoma, 1979-86; prin. William Boyd Pub. Rels., Federal Way, Wash., 1986—88; communications mgr., editor Weyerhaeuser, Federal Way, 1988-94; mgr. employee comms. AT&T Wireless Svcs., Seattle, 1994—98; mgr. corp. comms. Recreational Equipment Inc., Kent, Wash., 1999—2000; sr. mgr. comms. Terabeam, Kirkland, Wash., 2000—02; prin., owner The Bill Boyd Group, Federal Way, Wash., 2002—. Contbr. articles to Christian Sci. Monitor; mem. editl. bd. Jour. Employee Comm. Mgmt. Recipient Bronze Anvil award, Pub. Rels. Soc. Am. Mem.: Internat. Assn. Bus. Communicators (named Seattle Chpt. Communicator of Yr. 1992, eight Gold Quill awards, 11 Silver Six awards). Christian Scientist. Avocations: computers, cooking, photography, travel, education. Home and Office: 1134 S 299th Pl Federal Way WA 98003-3751 E-mail: billboydgroup@attbi.com.

BOYD, WILLIAM ELKINS, lawyer; b. San Mateo, Calif., Oct. 13, 1947; s. William Sprott and Katherine (Elkins) Boyd. Stanford U., 1969; JD, Hastings Coll. of Law, 1974. Admitted to Calif. bar, 1975; ptnr. firm Boyd and McKay, San Francisco, 1980—; v.p. Boyd Bros., investments, San Francisco, 1980—. Spl. asst. to chmn. Calif. Republican Com., 1968; bd. dirs. San Mateo County Planned Parenthood, 1971-73, Hastings Child Care Center, 1974-76. Mem. Am. Bar Assn., State Bar Calif. Assn. (bus. law sect.), Stanford U. Alumni Assn., Hastings Alumni Assn. Episcopalian. Clubs: Burlingame Country, Hastings 1066 Club. Home: 590 Remillard Dr Burlingame CA 94010-6740 Office: 3 Embarcadero Ctr Ste 2360 San Francisco CA 94111-4026

BOYD, WILLIAM HARLAND, historian, writer; b. Boise, Idaho, Jan. 7, 1912; s. Harland D. and Cordelia (Crumley) B.; m. Mary Kathryn Drake, June 25, 1939 (dec. Aug. 1997); children; Barbara A. Boyd Voltmer, William Harland, Kathryn L. Boyd Nemeyer. AB, U. Calif., Berkeley, 1935; MA, U. Calif., 1936, PhD, 1942. cert. Am. Assn. State and Local History, 1997. Tchr. Fall River H.S., McArthur, Calif., 1937-38, Watsonville (Calif.) H.S., 1941-42, San Mateo (Calif.) H.S., 1942-44; prof. history Bakersfield (Calif.) Coll., 1946-73, chmn. social sci. dept., 1967-73. Author: Land of Havilah, 1952; co-author: (with G.J. Rogers) San Joaquin Vignettes, 1965, (with others) Spanish Trailblazers in the South San Joaquin, 1957, A Centennial Bibliography on the History of Kern County, California, 1966, A California Middle Border, 1972, A Climb Through History, 1973, Bakersfield's First Baptist church, 1975, Kern County Wayfarers, 1977, Kern County Tall Tales, 1980, The Shasta Route, 1981, Stagecoach Heyday in the San Joaquin Valley, 1983, Bakersfield's First Baptist Church A Centennial History, 1989, Lower Kern River County, 1997, Kern County's Desert Country, 2000; contbr. articles to profl. jours. Pres. Kern County Hist. Soc., 1950-52; adv. com. Kern County Mus., 1955-60; chmn. Ft. Tejon Restoration Com., Bakersfield, 1952-56, sec., 1955-60; mem. Kern County Hist. Records Commn., 1977-92, Bakersfield Hist. Perservation Commn., 1984-87. Recipient Merit award Kern County Bd. Trade, 1960, Doctor-Waddingham award Conf. Calif. Hist. Socs., 1996, commendation Kern County Bd. Suprs., 1982, 76, 78. Mem. Calif. Tchrs. Assn., Am. Hist. Assn., Phi Alpha Theta. Republican. Baptist. Home: Danville, Calif. Died Aug. 22, 2002.

BOYD-BROWN, LENA ERNESTINE, history educator, education consultant; b. New Orleans, July 3, 1937; d. Eugene A. and Rosemary (Lewis) Boyd. BA, Xavier U., 1958; MA, Howard U., 1960; EdD, Rutgers U., 1979. History instr. So. U., New Orleans, 1960-61; tchr. D.C. Pub. Schs., Washington, 1961-62; history instr. So. U., Baton Rouge, 1962-63; residence counselor N.C. Cen. U., Durham, 1963-64; counselor, instr. Howard U., Washington, 1964-65; asst. prof. history Grambling (La.) State U., 1965-68, Tuskegee (Ala.) U., 1968-70; assoc. examiner history Ednl. Testing Svc., Princeton, N.J., 1970-79; assoc. prof. history, edn. Dillard U., New Orleans, 1979-88; dir. testing, assoc. prof. history Hampton (Va.) U., 1988-89, assoc. prof. history, dept. history chairperson, 1989-91; assoc. prof. history div. social and polit. sci. Tex. A&M U., Prarie View, 1991-2000. Testing cons. Lincoln (Pa.) U., 1974, So. U., Baton Rouge, 1979, New Orleans, 1986-89, Hampton U., 1988. Contbg. author, editor profl. jours. Martin L. King Jr. fellow, Rutgers U., 1977-78; fellow Howard U., 1958-60, Carnegie-Mellon U., Pitts., 1966-67. Mem. Assn. for Study Negro Life and History, Nat. Coalition of 100 Black Women (New Orleans chpt.), Orgn. Am. Historians, History Edn. Soc., Assn., Phi Alpha Theta, Phi Delta Kappa, Kappa Delta Pi, Alpha Kappa Alpha (Alpha Beta Omega chpt.). E-mail: LIZ37hb@aol.com.

BOYDSTON, JAMES CHRISTOPHER, composer; b. Denver, July 21, 1947; s. James Virgal and Mary June (Wiseman) B.; m. Ann Louise Bryant, Aug. 20, 1975. BA in Philosophy, U. Tex., 1971. Lutenist and guitarist Collegium Musicum, U. Tex., Austin, 1968-70; tchr. classical guitar Extension div. The New Eng. Conservatory of Music, Boston, 1972-73. Arranger music: S. Joplins, "The Entertainer," 1976; arranger/composer/performer cassette recording: Wedding Music for Classical Guitar, 1988; composer music: International Portraits for Classical Guitar, 1999, Baroque Suites 1 and 2, 2003; inventor classical guitar bridge-saddle, 1990; author original poetry included in The World of Poetry Anthology, 1991. Avocations: astronomy, reading, building clavichords, camping. Home: 4433 Driftwood Pl Boulder CO 80301-3104

BOYDSTUN, CHARLES BRYANT, JR., lawyer; b. Memphis, Sept. 10, 1949. B.A., U. Tenn., 1971, J.D., 1974. Bar: Fla. 1974, Tenn. 1981, U.S. Dist. Ct. (mid. dist.) Fla. 1974, U.S. Ct. Appeals (5th and 11th cirs.) 1981, U.S. Supreme Ct. 1978, U.S. Dist. Ct. (no. dist.) Fla. 1985; cert. civil trial lawyer Fla. Bar and Nat. Bd. Trial Advocacy. Assoc. Bradham, Lyle, Skipper & Cramer, St. Petersburg, Fla., 1974-76, Lyle, Skipper, Wood & Anderson, St. Petersburg, 1977-79; ptnr. Lyle & Skipper, P.A., St. Petersburg, 1979-93, Boydstun, Dabroski & Lyle, P.A., 1993-98; vice chmn. bd. trustees Pinellas County Law Library, St. Petersburg, 1978-98; chmn. 6th Jud. Circuit Unauthorized Practice of Law Com., St. Petersburg, 1983-85; mem. client security fund com. Fla. Bar, 1995-99. Author: How to Find a Good Lawyer, 1980. Pres. New Life Birthing Ctr., St. Petersburg, 1984-86; contbr. articles to profl. jours. V.p. Christian Legal Soc., St. Petersburg, 1982. Mem. Def. Research Inst., Fla. Acad. Trial Lawyers, ATLA, Am. Bd. Trial Advocates, Fla. Def. Lawyers, Fla. Bar Assn., Tenn. Bar Assn., St. Petersburg Bar Assn., St. Petersburg C. of C., Fla. C. of C., Barney Masterson Inn of Ct., Kiwanis (v.p. 1982-83, pres. 1984-85), Phi Alpha Delta. Democrat. Presbyterian. Office: Boydstun Dabroski & Lyle PA 2600 9th St N Saint Petersburg FL 33704-2744

BOYE, ROGER CARL, academic administrator, journalism educator, writer; b. Lincoln, Nebr., Feb. 8, 1948; s. Arthur J. and Matilda J. (Danca) B. BA with distinction, U. Nebr., 1970; MS in Journalism with highest distinction, Northwestern U., 1971. News editor The Quill, Chgo., 1971-73; instr. Medill sch. journalism Northwestern U., Evanston, Ill., 1973-76; vis. prof. journalism Niagara U., Niagara Falls, N.Y., 1976-78; gen. mgr. The Quill, 1980-84, bus. mgr., 1984-86; asst. dean, asst. prof. Medill sch. journalism Northwestern U., 1986-92, asst. dean, assoc. prof., 1992—. Judge various journalism awards and contests, 1970s; master comm. residential coll. Northwestern U., 1989—96. Weekly columnist Chgo. Tribune, 1974-93; contbr. Ency. Britannica Book of the Yr. and the Compton Yearbook, 1982-99; contbg. editor The Numismatist, 2001–. Recipient Maurice M. Gould award Numismatic Lit. Guild, 1981, 92. Mem. Phi Beta Kappa, Kappa Tau Alpha. Office: Northwestern Univ Medill Sch Journalism 1845 Sheridan Rd Evanston IL 60208-0815

BOYEA, EARL ALFRED, bishop; b. Pontiac, Mich., Apr. 10, 1951; s. Earl Alfred and Helen Marie (Connor) B. AB, Sacred Heart Seminary, Detroit, 1973; STL, Gregorian U., Rome, 1980; MA, Wayne State U., 1984; PhD, Cath. U., 1987. Deacon St. Benedict Parish, Waterford, Mich., 1977-78; asst. past. St. Michael Parish, Monroe, Mich., 1978-79, St. Timothy Parish, Trenton, Mich., 1980-84; asst. prof. Sacred Heart Major Seminary, Detroit, 1987-90, assoc. prof., 1990-95, acad. dean, 1990—2000; prof. Sacred Heart Maj. Sem., Detroit, 1995—2000; rector/pres. Pontifical Coll. Josephinum, Columbus, Ohio, 2000—02; auxiliary bishop of Detroit, 2002—. Contbr. articles to profl. jours. Mem. Am. Cath. Hist. Assn., Cath. Bibl. Assn., Nat. Cath. Ednl. Assn., Am. Cath. Hist. Soc. Home and Office: Aux Bishop of Detroit 2701 Chicago Blvd Detroit MI 48206-1704

BOYELL, GLORIA, musician, music educator; b. Chgo., Nov. 29, 1926; d. Joseph J. and Bessie H. Eisenberg; m. Richard S. Boyell, Sept. 12, 1951 (div. Sept. 1991); children: Joseph Jeffrey, Paula Palmer. MusB, Northwestern U., 1947, MusM, 1948. Mem. Evanston Symphony, Ill., 1973—; piano accompanist Savoy-aires Gilbert & Sullivan Co., 1976—; tchr. music pvt. practice, Glencoe, 1980—. Pres. Savoy-aires, Evanston, 1997—2000, treas., 2001—. Mem.; North Shore Musicians Club, Soc. Am. Musicians, North Shore Music Tchrs. Assn., Phi Beta, Pi Kappa Lambda, Alpha Lambda Delta. Avocations: swimming, cross country skiing. Home: 1024 Eastwood Glencoe IL 60022

BOYEN, MARIAN DE See HOUTZAGER, MARIANNE JOHANNA

BOYENGA, CINDY A. secondary education educator; b. Elgin, Ill., Aug. 5, 1957; d. Harley J. and Mary Ellen (Johnson) Carlson. BA, Augustana Coll., 1979; MSEd, No. Ill. U., 1989. Cert. tchr., Ill. Tchr. reading Laraway Sch., Joliet, Ill.; tchr. English Custer Park Sch., Braidwood, Ill., Streamwood High Sch., Elgin; tchr. reading and lang. arts Waldo Middle Sch., Aurora, Ill., 1984—. Mem. NAt. Coun. Tchrs. English, Secondary Reading League, Internat. Reading Assn. E-mail: cboyenga@yahoo.com.

BOYER, A(DELINE) NADINE, guidance counselor; b. Franklin, Pa., May 9, 1946; d. Robert Ellsworth and Jean Lucille (Sadler) B. BS in Edn., Ea. Ill. U., 1968, MS in Phys. Edn., 1981, Cert. Edn. Specialist, 1986. Tchr. phys. edn. Freeport (Ill.) H.S., 1968-80; tchr. phys. edn., asst. volleyball coach Lake Land Coll., Mattoon, Ill., 1980-81; guidance counselor Carlyle (Ill.) H.S., 1986-87, Odin (Ill.) H.S., 1986-91, East Richland H.S., Olney, Ill., 1991—. Mem. NEA, Ill. Edn. Assn., East Richland Edn. Assn. Methodist. Avocations: reading, walking, videos. Office: East Richland HS 1200 E Laurel St Olney IL 62450-2545

BOYER, CALVIN JAMES, librarian; b. Charleston, Ill., Mar. 4, 1939; s. Ernest Zimmerman and Velma Hazel (Childress) B.; m. Roberta Lorraine Davis, July 1, 1957; children— Carmellia Christine, Jeffrey Ernest; m. Ruth Nell Roden, Sept. 1, 1982 BS in Edn, Eastern Ill. U., 1961; M.L.S., U. Tex., 1964, PhD (HEA Title II-B fellow 1969-72), 1972. Libr. Midwestern U., Wichita Falls, Tex., 1967-69; assoc. prof. Ind. U., Bloomington, 1972-75; libr. U. Miss., 1975-80, U. Calif., Irvine, 1980-93; libr. dir. Longwood Coll., 1993—; bd. dirs Southeastern Library Network, (SOLINET), Atlanta, 1977-80, treas., 1979-80. Author: The Doctoral Dissertation, 1973; gen. editor: UMI Research Press, 1977-81. Mem.: ALA. Methodist. Home: 1004 Hurd St Farmville VA 23901-2150 Office: Longwood Coll Library Farmville VA 23901-9999

BOYER, CARL, III, non-profit organization executive, former mayor, city official, secondary education educator; b. Phila., Pa., Sept. 22, 1937; s. Carl Boyer Jr. and Elizabeth Campbell Timm; m. Ada Christine Kruse, July 28, 1962. Student, U. Edinburgh, Scotland, 1956-57; BA, Trinity U., 1959; MEd in Secondary Edn., U. Cin., 1959; postgrad., Calif. State U., Northridge, 1964-72. Tchr. Edgewood High Sch., San Antonio, Tex., 1959-60; libr. U. Cin., Cincinnati, Ohio, 1960-61; tchr. Eighth Avenue Elem. Sch., Dayton, Ky., 1961-62, Amelia High Sch., Amelia, Ohio, 1962-63; instr. Kennedy San Fernando Comm. Adult Sch., San Fernando, Calif., 1964-74, Mission Coll., San Fernando, 1971; tchr. San Fernando High Sch., San Fernando, Calif., 1963-98. Faculty chmn. San Fernando High Sch., dept. chmn.; cons. Sofia (Bulgaria) City Coun., 1991, Bandung Regency, Indonesia, 2003; key spkr. World Mayors' Conf., Jaipur, India, 1998. Author, compiler 17 books on genealogy and family history; contbr. articles to profl. jours. Councilman City of Santa Clarita, Calif., 1987-98, mayor pro tem, 1989-90, 94-95, mayor, 1990-91, 95-96; mem. Nat. League Cities Internat. Mcpl. Consortium, 1992-98; mem. revenue and taxation com. League Calif. Cities, 1992-95; sec. Calif. Contract Cities Assn., 1992-93; trustee Santa Clarita C.C. Dist., 1973-81, pres., 1979-81; bd. dirs. Castaic Lake Water Agy., 1982-84, pres. Newhall-Saugus-Valencia Fedn. Homeowners Assn., 1969 70, 71-72; pres. Del Prado Condo. Assn., Inc., Newhall, Calif.; exec. v.p. Canyon County Formation Com.; chmn. Santa Clarita City Formation Com., 1987; pres. Santa Clarita Valley Internat. Program, 1991-97; treas. Healing the Children Calif., 1994-96, pres., 1996-99, 2003—, nat. pres., 1999-2000. Mem. New Eng. Hist. Geneal. Soc. Republican. Methodist. Avocations: travel, photography. Home: PO Box 220333 Santa Clarita CA 91322-0333

BOYER, DALE KENNETH, English educator; b. Haines, Oreg., Apr. 6, 1936; s. Kenneth Bardwell and Joanne Bond Boyer; m. Grace Choi, Mar. 20, 1959; children: Gina, Julie, Kenneth. BA, U. Oreg., 1958, MA, 1963; PhD, U. Mo., Columbia, 1969. Instr. English U. Mo., Columbia, 1963-68, Boise Coll., 1968-69; asst. prof. English Boise State Coll., 1969-72; assoc. prof. English Boise State U., 1972-76, prof. English, 1976-2001, prof. emeritus English, 2001—, dir. grad. studies dept., English, 1990—95, dir. undergrad. studies, dept. English, 1998-2001. Editor: Winter Constellations (Richard Blessing), 1977, 3d printing, 1988, Stealing the Children (Carolyne Wright), 1978, 4th printing, 1992, (with Marcia D. Liles) To the Natural World (Genevieve Taggard), 1980, Agua Negra (Leo Romero), 1981, 4th printing, 1985, (with Carol Berg) The Clock of Moss (Judson Crews), 1983, Deer in the Haystacks (Dixie Partridge), 1984, 2d printing, 1987, Flights of the Harvest-Mare (Linda Bierds), 1985, 2d printing, 1986, Underground (Corrine Hales), 1986, 2d printing, 1991, The Country of Here Below (Wyn Cooper), 1987, 3d printing, 1995, Men at Work (Bill Witherup), 1990, Going Home Away Indian (Leo Romero), 1990, Sycamore-Oriole (Ken McCullough), 1991, The One Right Touch (Katharine Coles), 1992, 2d printing, 1994, Each Thing We Know is Changed Because We Know It, and Other Poems (Kevin Hearle), 1994, 2d printing, 1996, Prayers for the Dead Ventriloquist (D.J. Smith), 1995, (with Orvis C. Burmaster and Tom Trusky) Ahsahta Anthology: Poetry of the American West, 1996. With U.S. Army, 1958-60, Germany. Mem. Phi Beta Kappa, Pi Delta Phi, Phi Kappa Phi. Democrat. Episcopalian. Avocations: bicycling, motorcycling, walking.

BOYER, DENNIS LEE, lawyer, lobbyist, writer; b. Allentown, Pa., July 13, 1949; s. Erwin A. and Grace Benner (Choyce) Boyer. BA, Kutztown State Coll., 1975; JD, W.Va. U., 1978. Bar: W.Va. 1978, Wis. 1981. Legal counsel W.Va. Dept. Labor, Charleston, 1978—79; govt. rels. counsel Am. Fedn. State, County and Mcpl. Employees, Madison, Wis., 1980—. Author: Public Employee Bargaining, 1978, Prevailing Wages, 1979, Driftless Spirits, 1997, Giants in the Land, 1998, Great Wisconsin Taverns, 2000, Prairie Whistles, 2001, Gone Missing, 2002. Del. Dem. Nat. Conv., Miami, 1972, Rainbow Coalition, 1986, 1st Nat. Green Politics Conf., 1987; candidate for Pa. State Assembly, 1974. Served to sgt. USAF, 1967—71. Grantee, Dept. Labor, 1977. Mem.: VFW, Scottish Rite, Masonic Lodge. Mem. Wis. Green Party. Home: 3302 Bethlehem Rd Dodgeville WI 53533-8526 Office: AFSCME 8033 Excelsior Dr Madison WI 53717-1903

BOYER, GENE T. management consultant; b. Milw., July 11, 1925; d. Nathan and Rene (Hiller) Cohen; m. Burton L. Boyer, Mar. 25, 1945; 1 child, Bari Lynn. Student, U. Wis., 1942-45. Stock clk., cashier Schudson's Clothing Stores, Milw., 1937-41; rschr., writer Wis. Trade News Assn., Milw., 1941-42; copywriter Gen. Merchandise Co., Milw., 1942-45; freelance writer West Bend, Wis., 1945-51; owner Matlin's Furniture Stores, Beaver Dam, Wis., 1951-83; CEO Gene Boyer & Assocs., Inc., Madison, 1982—, Weston, Fla. Featured leader (videotape) Step by Step. Author workshop manuals: Networking for Fun, Profit and Social Change, 1985-86, Circles of Women on World Plan Issues, 1994-95, Jewish Women's Manual on Domestic Violence, 1997; moderator, founder Jewish Women Leaders, online listserve for e-mail readers, 1998—; contbr. articles to profl. publs. Mem. planning com. Women in Poverty Ednl. Initiatives, 1999; founder New Moon Discussion Groups, 1998; founder, past pres. Wis. Women's Network, Wis. Women's Edn. Fund; founder Jewish Women's Conf. Ctr.; past pres. Nat. Women's Conf. Ctr., Legal Def. and Edn. Fund; Hillel Spitzer Forum mentor Jewish Coun. for Pub. Affairs, 1997, 1998, 1999; lay leader Gates of Heaven Congregation Meml. Svcs., 1985—. Named Woman Activist of Yr., Zero Population Growth, 1973, Woman of Yr. in Bus., Wis. State Jour., 1976, Nat. Woman bus. Leader Women's Equity Action League, 1978, Citizen of the Week, Radio Sta. WTTN, 1985, Pioneer Feminist of Yr., Vet. Feminists Am., 1993, Stateswoman of Yr., Wis. Women's Network, 1997; recipient toast and Roast award Nat. Women's Polit. Caucus, 1980, Nat. Advocate for Women in Bus. award Small Bus. Adminstrn., 1985, citation Wis. State Senate, 1985, Wis. State Assembly, 1985, Keynoter Recognition award SUNY, Buffalo, 1994, Disting. Achievement award Western N.Y. Women's History Celebration Com., 1997, Disting. Leader citation Broward County Women's C. of C., 1999, Women's Circle of Excellence award Women's C. of C., 1999. Mem. NOW (founding mem., nat. treas., fin. v.p. 1968-74, state convenor 1970, Founder Recognition award 1973, Woman of Yr. 1979, visionary Leader award 1986, bd. advisors legal def. and edn. fund emerita 1993-97, past pres. legal def. and edn. fund), AAUW, Nat. Assn. Women Bus. Owners (charter), Nat. Fedn. Ind. Bus. (mem. leadership coun.), Am. Bus. Women's Assn., Jewish Women's Coalition (founding pres. 1996—). Democrat. Jewish. Avocations: bridge, mentoring young feminists, travel, writing. Home: 46 Waterford Cir Apt 202 Madison WI 53719-3176 Office: 16100 Golf Club Rd Apt 201 Weston FL 33326-1648 Fax: 954-389-7656., 608-273-9761.

BOYER, HERBERT WAYNE, retired biochemist; b. Pitts., July 10, 1936; m. Grace Boyer, 1959. BA, St. Vincent Coll., Latrobe, Pa., 1958, DSc (hon.) (hon.), 1981; MS, U. Pitts., 1960, PhD, 1963. Mem. faculty U. Calif., San Francisco, 1966—, prof. biochemistry, 1976—, 1976-91, prof. emeritus, 1991—. Co-founder, dir. Genentech, Inc., South San Francisco, Calif. Recipient V.D. Mattai award, Roche Inst., 1977, Albert and Mary Lasker award for basic med. research, 1980, Golden Plate award, Am. Acad. Achievement, 1981, Moet Hennessy-Louis Vuitton prize, 1988, Jerome H. Lemelson-MIT prize for excellence in invention and innovation, 1996, Nat. Tech. medal, 1989, Nat. Sci. medal, NSF, 1990. Fellow: AAAS; mem.: NAS, Am. Soc. Biol. Chemists, Am. Acad. Arts and Scis.

BOYER, JAMES LORENZEN, physician, educator; b. N.Y.C., Aug. 28, 1936; s. Ralph R. and Alice M. B.; m. Phoebe Bennet, Feb. 23, 1963; children: Phoebe Christine, Anna Birch. AB, Haverford (Pa.) Coll., 1958; MD, Johns Hopkins U., 1962. Diplomate: Am. Bd. Internal Medicine. Med. intern N.Y. Hosp., N.Y.C., 1962-63, resident in medicine, 1963-64, Yale-New Haven Hosp., 1966; postdoctoral fellow liver study unit Yale U., 1966-68; mem. faculty U. Chgo. Pritzker Sch. Medicine, 1972-78, prof. medicine, 1976-78, dir. liver study unit, 1972-78; prof. medicine, dir. liver study unit, chief div. digestive diseases Yale U. Med. Sch., 1978-96; dir. Yale Liver Ctr., 1984—, Ensign prof. of medicine, 1996—. Treas., bd. dirs. Am. Liver Found., 1976-85; dep. chmn. Nat. Digestive Disease Adv. Bd., 1981-84; council mem. NIDDK, 1985-90. Author papers, abstracts in field. Chmn. bd. trustees Mt. Desert Island Biol. Lab., Salsbury Cove, Maine, 1995-2003. Lt. comdr. USPHS, 1964-66. Josiah Macey faculty scholar, 1976 Mem. Am. Assn. Study Liver Disease (pres. 1980), Am. Fedn. Clin. Rsch., A.C.P., Am. Gastroenterol. Assn. (councillor 1983-86), Internat. Assn. Study Liver Diseases (v.p. 1982-84, pres.-elect 1986-88, pres. 1988-90), Am. Soc. Clin. Investigation, Assn. Am. Physicians, Soc. Clin. Rsch., Am. Clin. and Climatolgic Assn. Office: Yale U Sch of Medicine 333 Cedar St New Haven CT 06510-3289

BOYER, JOHN WILLIAM, history educator, dean; b. Chgo., Oct. 17, 1946; s. William Dana and Mary Frances (Corbley) B.; m. Barbara Alice Juskevich, Aug. 24, 1968; children: Dominic, Alexandra, Victoria. BA, Loyola U., 1968; MA, U. Chgo., 1969, PhD, 1975. From asst. prof. to assoc. prof. U. Chgo., 1975-85, prof., 1985—, Martin A. Ryerson Disting. Svc. prof., 1996—, acting dean divsn. social scis., 1992-93, dean of the coll., 1992—. Author: Political Radicalism in Late Imperial Vienna, 1981, Culture and Political Crisis in Vienna, 1995, Three Views of Continuity and Change at the University of Chicago, 1999; editor: Jour. of Modern History. Capt. USAR, 1968-80. Recipient Theodor Körner prize Theodor Körner Found., 1978, John Gilmary Shea prize Am. Cath. Hist. Assn., 1982, Ludwig Jedlicka Meml. prize Kuratorium des Ludwig-Jedlicka-Gedächtnispreises, 1996; Alexander von Humboldt fellow, 1980-81. Mem. Am. Hist. Assn. Roman Catholic. Avocation: cooking. Home: 1428 E 57th St Chicago IL 60637-1838 Office: U Chgo 1126 E 59th St Chicago IL 60637-1580 also: U Chgo Press Jour Divsn 5720 S Woodlawn Ave Chicago IL 60637-1603 E-mail: jwboyer@midway.uchicago.edu.

BOYER, LESTER LEROY, JR., architecture educator, consultant; b. Hanover, Pa., Apr. 6, 1937; s. Lester Leroy and Ruth Florence (Kessler) B.; m. Patricia Barbara Hayes, Dec. 28, 1958; children: Douglas Lester, Blane Edward, Darla Mae. B of Archtl. Engring., Pa. State U., 1960, MS in Archtl. Enging, 1964; PhD in Architecture, U. Calif., Berkeley, 1976. Registered profl. engr., Pa. Instr. archtl. engring. Pa. State U., 1960-64; rsch. engr. Armstrong Cork Co., Lancaster, Pa., 1964-68; course dir. Nat. Soc. Profl. Engrs., 1964-74; sr. cons. acoustics and noise control Bolt Beranek and Newman Inc., Cambridge, Mass., 1968-70; faculty Okla. State U., Stillwater, 1970-84, dir. environ. control program, 1970-84, prof. architecture, 1979-84, Tex. A&M U., College Station, 1984—96, chmn. div. design tech. Coll. Arch., 1988-90, prof. emeritus, 1999—. Fulbright scholar U. N.S.W. and U. Queensland, Australia, 1982, Tech. U., Delft, The Netherlands, 1992; dir. daylighting rsch. NSF, 1985-88; vis. researcher Solar Energy Rsch. Inst., Colo., summer 1985; cons. acoustics, environ. comfort and passive energy design, 1970— ; dir. earth-sheltered bldg. rsch. Control Data Corp. and U.S. Dept. Energy, 1979-81; chair energy rsch. rev. panel on fenestration Office Energy Rsch., U.S. Dept. Energy, Washington, 1988; gen. chmn. Internat. Conf. Earth Sheltered Bldgs., Sydney, Australia, 1983; tech. chmn. Internat. Conf. Earth Sheltered Bldgs., Mpls., 1986; vis. prof., chair dept. arch. Kuwait U., 1997-98; mem. design team Benham Blair & Affiliates, Oklahoma City. Author: Earth Shelter Technology, 1987; editor: Building Design for Environmental Hazards, 1973, Earth Sheltered Building Design Innovations, 1980, Earth Shelter Performance and Evaluation, 1981, Earth Shelter Protection, 1983, Design in Geotecture, 1986, Proceedings of 5th Internat. Conf. on Underground Space and Earth Sheltered Structures, Tech. Univ. Delft, The Netherlands, 1992; contbg. author Simulating Daylight with Architectural Models, 1987. Recipient 1st Pl. Design award Nat. Energy Design competition Calif. State Office Bldg., Sacramento, 1983. Mem. ASHRAE (nat. daylighting symposium organizer 1988), Am. Solar Energy Soc. (nat. coord. passive earth cooling program 1981), Am. Underground Space Assn. (bd. dirs. 1989-92), Illuminating Engring. Soc. Lutheran. Home: HC 68 Box 19 Fort Garland CO 81133-9702 E-mail: llb@fone.net.

BOYER, LILLIAN BUCKLEY, artist, educator; b. Paterson, N.J., Mar. 1, 1916; d. George and Adele (Roomy) Buckley; m. Floyd E. Boyer, Jr., Sept. 7, 1935; 1 child, Karen Boyer Lloyd. BA in Art Edn., U. Ky., 1975. Field interviewer Survey Rsch. Ctr., U. Mich., 1963-68; instr. art U. Ky., Lexington, 1976—2002. Ky. reporter for Sunshine Artists mag., 1976-85. Exhibited in group shows at Grand Theater, Frankfort, Ky., 1983, State Capitol, 1983, Lexington Art League, annually, —, Waller Gallery, Lexington, 1986, Headley-Whitney Mus., 1987—88, 1989, 1990, Gallery IO/IO, Knoxville, 1995, Living Arts and Sci. Ctr., Lexington, 1988, 1989, 1995, 1997, Artists Attic, 1989, Opera House Gallery, 1995, Owensboro Mus. Fine Arts, 2001, others. Crusade chmn. Am. Cancer Soc., Anaheim, Calif., 1958, Orange County, Calif., 1959; active, hon. life mem. PTA, 1950-62; mem. Lexington Arts and Cultural Coun., Ky. Citizens for the Arts, Friends of Ky. Ednl. TV, Headley Whitney Mus., Friends of Lexington Pub. Libr.; pres., life mem. Lexington Art League, 1976-80, 82-83, 84-86. Mem. U. Ky. Alumni Assn., Living Arts and Sci. Ctr., Friends of U.K. Art Mus., Nat. Mus. Women in Arts. Methodist. Address: 969 Holly Springs Dr Lexington KY 40504-3119 E-mail: labinart@aol.com.

BOYER, MARK E, public policy expert, Internet company executive; b. St. Louis, Mo., Dec. 6, 1953; s. Shirley Jean McCreary and James L Boyer; m. Mary Kay Brown; children: Dylan, Abigail. BA, U. of Alaska, 1971—75. Legislative asst. US Senate, Washington, 1976—80, Alaska State Senate, Legis. Affairs Agy., 1981—86; state legislator Alaska State Ho. of Representatives, 1986—93; city mgr. City of Fairbanks Alaska, 1993—94; commr., dept. of adminstrn. State of Alaska, 1994—99; dir., internet bus. solutions group Cisco Systems, Inc, Herndon, Va., 1999—. Bd. of directors Alaska State Bond Com., 1994—99; trustee Alaska Permanent Fund Corp., 1996—99. Mem. Fairbanks Rotary Club, 1993—94; dir. Fairbanks Arts Assn., 1993—94, Fairbanks Golf and Country Club, 1993—94, Fairbanks Rehab. Assoc., 1993—94. Henry Toll fellow, Coun. of State Govt., 1998. Democrat-Npl. Avocations: golf, tennis, travel, mandolin. Office: Cisco Systems Inc IBSG 13635 Dulles Technology Dr Herndon VA 20171 Personal E-mail: markboyer53@hotmail.com.

BOYER, NICODEMUS ELIJAH, chemist, consultant; b. Daugavpils, Latgale, Latvia, June 1, 1925; arrived in U.S., 1949; s. Aloizs and Elvira Adele (Buchholz) Bojars. BS in Natural Scis., U. Göttingen, Germany, 1949; PhD in Chemistry, U. Ill., 1955; postgrad., Princeton U., 1955-56. Rsch. chemist Hooker Chem. Corp., Niagara Falls, N.Y., 1956-61; project leader, lectr. Ill. Inst. Tech., Chgo., 1961-63; rsch. fellow Borg-Warner Chems., Washington, 1964-76; sr. staff mem. Raychem Corp., Menlo Park, Calif., 1976-78; asst. prof. Ind. State U., Terre Haute, 1978-80; sr. rsch. assoc. PPG Industries, Chgo., 1980-88; sr. cons. Delta Sci. Cons., Parkersburg, W.Va., 1988-92, Three Rivers, Mich., 1992—. Lectr. evening sch. U. Buffalo, 1958-60; prof. Glen Oaks Coll., Centreville, Mich., 1995-2001. Vol. abstractor Chem. Abstracts Svc., Columbus, Ohio, 1958-71; editor Cosmology Technikas Apskats, Montreal, Que., Can., 1987-93; author: Organophosphorus Chemistry, Vol. 1, 1957, Vol. 2, 1959, Radiation Chemistry: Monomers and Polymers, 1977, A New Theory of Cosmology, 1983, The Physics of Creation, 2 vols., 1990, Fire Retardants: A Review and Selected Patents, 1991, Cosmogony, 1992, The Baltic Civilization, 2003, The Big Bang: Cosmological Evolution Theory from the Dark Matter, 2003; contbr. over 70 articles to profl. jours.; 180 chemistry patents. Founding mem. Latvian Cath. Students' Assn., Germany, 1946-64; vice chmn. Latvian Acad. Soc. Valdemarija, Ill., Calif., Mich., 1964-; life mem. Rep. Presdl. Task Force, 1989-. With U.S. Army, 1945. Internat. Refugee Orgn. scholar U. Göttingen, 1946-49, Nat. Cath. Welfare Conf. scholar U. Ill., 1949-51; recipient Quality Control & Safety award PPG Industries Inc., 1987. Mem. AAAS, Am. Chem. Soc., N.Y. Acad. Scis. (life), Latvian Acad. Scis., U. Ill. Alumni Assn., Phi Lambda Upsilon, Sigma Xi, Am. Legion (life). Republican. Roman Catholic. Achievements include discovery of extremely stable white coatings to heat and ultraviolet radiation for space applications; patent for the first large-scale fire retardant additive for ABS resins; invented a new theory of cosmology. Office: Delta Sci Cons PO Box 312 Three Rivers MI 49093-0312

BOYER, PATRICIA GRACE, education educator; b. New Orleans, La. d. Francis W and Dorothy M Boyer. BS in chemistry, Xavier U. of La., 1980; MA, U. of No. Iowa, 1981; PhD, U. of Mo., 1997. Editl. asst. Jour. of Sch. Leadership, 1995—97; instr. U. of Mo., Dept. of Ednl. Leadership and Policy Analysis, 1997; inst. rsch. asst. Mo. Sch. Boards Assn., 1997—98, U. of Mo., 1997—98, prof., 1999—. Proposal rev. U. of Mo. Rsch. Bd., 2001; dissertation com. U. of Mo. - Columbia, 2000, U. of Mo. - St. Louis, 2000. Contbr. articles to profl. jours. Office: University of Missouris Divsn of Ednl Leadership and Policy Stud 269 Marillac Hall, 8800 Natural Bridge R Saint Louis MO 63121

BOYER, PAUL D. biochemist, educator; b. Provo, Utah, July 31, 1918; s. Dell Delos and Grace (Guymon) Boyer; m. Lyda Mae Whicker, Aug. 31, 1939. BS, Brigham Young U., 1939; MS, U. Wis., 1941, PhD in Biochemistry, 1943; PhD (hon.), U. Stockholm, 1974. Asst. rschr. biochemistry U. Wis., 1939—43; Instr., research assoc. Stanford, 1943—45; from asst. prof. to prof. biochemistry U. Minn., 1945—56; Hill research prof. U. Minn. Med. Sch., 1956—63; prof. chemistry UCLA, 1963—89, dir. Molecular Biology Inst., 1965—83, dir. biotech. program, 1985—88, 1985-89, prof. emeritus, 1989—; chmn. biochemistry study sect. USPHS, 1962—67. Mem. U.S. Nat. Com. for Biochemistry, 1965—71. Editor: Ann. Rev. of Biochemistry, 1965—71; assoc. editor:, 1972—88; editor: Biochemical and Biophysical Research Communications, 1969—79, The Enzymes, 1970—; mem. editl. bd.: Biochemistry, 1969—76, Jour. Biol. Chemistry, 1978—83, 1987—; contbr. Co-recipient Nobel prize for chemistry, 1997; recipient McCoy award chem. rsch., 1976, Tolman award, 1984, Rose award, Am. Soc. Biochem. and Molecular Biology, 1989, UCLA medal, 1998; fellow Guggenheim Found., 1955—56. Fellow: AAAS (council, v.p. biol. scis. 1985—88); mem.: NAS, Biophys. Soc., Am. Chem. Soc. (past div. chmn., enzyme chemistry award 1955), Am. Soc. Biol. Chemists (past pres., council mem.). Home: 1033 Somera Rd Los Angeles CA 90077-2625 Office: Dept Chem-Biochem Paul Boyer Hall 639 607 Charles E Young Dr E Box 951569 Los Angeles CA 90095-0001*

BOYER, PAUL SAMUEL, history educator; b. Dayton, Ohio, Aug. 2, 1935; s. Clarence William and Ethel Marie (French) B.; m. Ann Chapman Talbot, Sept. 15, 1962; children: Alexander Talbot, Laura Kate. AB, Harvard U., 1960, MA, 1961, PhD, 1966. Asst. editor Notable Am. Women, Cambridge, Mass., 1964-67; with U. Mass., Amherst, 1967-80; prof. history U. Wis., Madison, 1980—2002, Merle Curti prof. history, 1985—2002, prof. emeritus, 2002—, sr. mem. Inst. for Rsch. in the Humanities, 1989—2002; dir. Inst. for Rsch. in the Humanities, 1993—2001. Vis. prof. history UCLA, 1987-88; Henry Luce vis. prof. Am. culture Northwestern U., Evanston, Ill., 1988-89; James Pinckney Harrison vis. prof. Coll. of William and Mary, 2002-03. Author: Purity in Print: Book Censorship in America, 1968, Urban Masses and Moral Order in America, 1820-1920, 1978, By the Bomb's Early Light: American Thought and Culture at the Dawn of the Atomic Age, 1985, When Time Shall Be No More: Prophecy Belief in Modern American Culture, 1992; co-author: Salem Possessed: The Social Origins of Witchcraft, 1972, The Enduring Vision: A History of the American People, 5th edit., 2003; bd. editors Jour. Am. History, 1980-83; gen. editor History of Am. Thought and Culture series U. Wis. Press, 1984-94; editor-in-chief Oxford Companion to United States History, 2001. Mem. nat. adv. bd. The Am. Experience (TV series), PBS, Boston, 1988—; mem. Wis. Humanities Coun., 1999—, chair, 2003—. John Simon Guggenheim fellow 1973-74, Rockefeller Found. Humanities fellow, 1982-83; recipient Gov.'s Humanities award, State of Wis., 2003. Mem. Am. Acad. Arts and Scis., Soc. Am. Historians (elected), Am. Antiquarian Soc. (elected), Am. Hist. Assn., Orgn. Am. Historians (nominating coun. 1991-93, exec. bd. 1995-98). Home: 433 Toepfer Ave Madison WI 53711-1659 E-mail: psboyer@wisc.edu.

BOYER, ROBERT ALLAN, business executive; b. Detroit, Mar. 2, 1934; s. Robert Allan and Elizabeth (Szabo) B.; children: Jennifer, Stephen, Lorna. MBA, Cornell U., 1959. Alfred P. Sloan fellow Cornell U. Grad. Sch., Ithaca, N.Y., 1958, 59; exec. asst. to pres. Merck & Co., Inc., Rahway, N.J., 1962-68; dir. fin. TWA Corp., N.Y.C., 1969-72; nat. dir. fin. Coopers & Lybrand, N.Y.C., 1972-79; exec. dir. Sullivan & Cromwell, N.Y.C., 1979-. Chmn., founder Legal Execs. Group, Law Firm Tech. Group, 1979. Mem. congl. support com.; mem. Pres.'s Club Rep. Party, 1990. Fellow Coll. Law Practice Mgmt.; mem. ABA, Assn. Legal Adminstrs. (exec. com. 1986-87), Aircraft Owners and Pilots Assn., Yorktown Bicentennial Com. (bd. dirs., sec.), Echo Lake Country Club (Westfield, N.J.), Cornell Club (N.Y.), Cornell Club (N.J.), India House (N.Y.C.), N.Y. Acad. Scis. Clubs: Echo Lake Country (Westfield, N.J.). Republican. Presbyterian. E-mail: rboyernyc@aol.com.

BOYER, TYRIE ALVIS, lawyer; b. Williston, Fla., Sept. 10, 1924; s. Alton Gordon and Mary Ethel (Strickland) B.; m. Elizabeth Everett Gale, June 9, 1945; children: Carol, Tyrie, Kennedy, Lee. BA, U. Fla., 1953, LLB, JD, 1954. Bar: Fla. Atty. Crawford, May & Boyer, Jacksonville, Fla., 1954-58, Boyer Law Offices, Jacksonville, 1958-60; judge Civil Ct. of Record, Jacksonville, 1960-63; cir. judge 4th Jud. Cir. of Fla., Jacksonville, 1963-67; atty. Dawson, Galant,

Maddox, Boyer, Sulik & Nichols, Jacksonville, 1967-73; appellate judge 1st Dist. Ct. Appeal, Tallahassee, 1973-79; chief judge 1st Dist. Ct. Appeals, Tallahassee, 1975-76; atty. Boyer, Tanzler, Blackburn & Boyer, Jacksonville, 1979-84, Boyer, Tanzler & Sussman, Jacksonville, 1984—. Adj. prof. Fla. Coastal Sch. Law, Jacksonville, 1996—, U. North Fla., 1998—; chmn. Supreme Ct. Com. on Standard Conduct Governing Judges, Tallahassee, 1976-79. Contbr. articles to profl. jours. Chmn. Duval County Hosp. Authority, Jacksonville, 1970-73, Jacksonville Bldg. Fin. Authority, 1980-81; pres. Jacksonville Legal Aid Assn., 1954-61; bd. dirs. Jones Coll., Jacksonville, 1978-85; bd. advs. Fla. Coastal Sch. Law, 1996—; adj. prof. U. North Fla., 1998—. With USN, 1942-45, PTO. Mem. ABA, Am. Judicature Soc., Fla. Bar, Amer. Bar Assn., Jacksonville Bar Assn., Fla. Acad. Trial Lawyers, Am. Bd. Trial Advs., SCV (comdr.), Mil. Order Stars and Bars (comdr.), Masons, dir., Safari Club Internat., Fla. Blue Key, Order of Coif, Phi Beta Kappa, Phi Kappa Phi. Methodist. Avocation: big game hunting. Home: 3966 Cordova Ave Jacksonville FL 32207-6019 Office: Boyer Tanzler & Sussman 210 E Forsyth St Jacksonville FL 32202-3320

BOYES, KARL W. state legislator; b. Erie, Pa., Mar. 1, 1936; s. Walter and Florence (Smith) B.; m. Barbara Jean Clark, June 27, 1964. BS, Edinboro State Coll., 1959; postgrad., Allegheny Coll., 1961. Govt. tchr. Millcreek Twp. Sch. Dist., Erie, 1959-66; town supr. Millcreek Twp., Erie, 1966-69; regional dir. Pa. Criminal Justice Commn., Northwestern, 1969-70, dep. dir. Harrisburg, 1970-73; asst. prof. Mercyhurst Coll., Erie, 1973-74; county commr. Erie County, Erie, 1975-79; mem. Pa. Ho. of Reps., Harrisburg, 1981—, mem. house profl. lic. com., 1981—, mem. ho. appropriations com., 1987-92, majority chmn. ho. fin. com., 1995—. Recipient Guardian of Small Bus. award Nat. Fedn. Ind. Bus., 1989, Outstanding Citizen award Florence Crittenton Svcs., 1991, Jaycees Disting. Svc. award Pa. Health Care Assn., Better Life award, Coun. Ind. Coll. and Univ. Ben Franklin award, Pa. Assn. Nonprofit Orgn. Legis. of Yr., Pa. Assn. Nonprofit Homes for Aging Cmty. Svc. award. Mem. Coun. State Govts., Am. Legis. Exch. Coun. Presbyterian. Avocation: jogging. Office: Pa Ho of Reps 4602 Peach St Erie PA 16509-2045

BOYES, STEPHEN RICHARD, hydrogeologic consultant; b. Evanston, Ill., May 17, 1950; s. Will W. and Beth (Henry) B. AA, U. South Fla., 1972, BA, 1974. Lic. profl. geologist, Fla. Geophys. engr. seismic process ctr. Geophys. Svcs., Inc., Midland, Tex., 1974, geophys. engr. field ops. Chickasha, Okla., 1975, geophys. engr. Saudi, Arabia, 1975-77; geologist Fla. Dept. Environ. Regulation, Tallahassee, 1978-82, hydrogeologist Tampa, 1982-84; sr. hydrogeologist Groundwater Technology, Tampa, 1984-86, Handex Corp., Odenton, Md., 1986; pres. GeoSolutions, Inc., Gainesville, Fla., 1986—. Contbr. to profl. publs. Mem.: Nat. Groundwater Assn. Avocations: canoeing, computers, snorkeling, racquetball.

BOYETT, JOAN REYNOLDS, arts administrator; b. L.A., May 2, 1936; d. Clifton Faris Reynolds and Jean Margaret (Howard) Hauck; m. Harry William Boyett, Oct. 5, 1956; children: Keven William, Suzanne Marie Boyett Liebherr. Student, Occidental Coll., 1954-55, Pasadena Playhouse, 1955-57. Mgr. youth activities L.A. Philharm. Orch., 1970-79; dir., founder edn. divsn. Performing Arts Ctr. L.A. County, 1979-2001, v.p. edn., 1988-2001. Mem. supt.'s task force on arts edn. Calif. State Dept. Edn., 1997; cons. NEA, Washington; chmn. arts edn. task force Calif. Arts Coun., Sacramento, 1993-95; arts edn. mem. Nat. Working Group, Washington, 1992-95; mem. U.S. Sec. of Edns. Com. on Am. Goes Back to Sch. Active various coms. and task forces, L.A., Sacramento. Named Woman of Yr. L.A. Times, 1976; recipient Labor's award of honor County Fedn. Labor, L.A., 1984, Susan B. Anthony award Bus. and Profl. Women, 1986, Gov.'s award Calif. Arts Coun. and Gov., 1989, R.O.S.E. Outstanding Svc. to Edn. award, U. So. Calif., 1999, Outstanding Arts Educator award Calif. Arts Coun., 2001, Music Ctr. Club 100 Spl. Tribute award, 2001, Women in Ednl. Leadership award, 2002, Ovation award for cmty. svc. Theatre League Alliance, 2002. Mem. Calif. Art Edn. Assn. (Behind the Scenes award 1985), Calif. Dance Educators Assn. (Svc. award 1985), Calif. Ednl. Theatre Assn. (Outstanding Contbn. award 1990, nominated for Nat. Medal Arts 1996, 97). Republican. Presbyterian. Avocations: reading, attending arts events, gardening, swimming. Home: PO Box 1805 Studio City CA 91614-0805 E-mail: jarboyett@earthlink.net.

BOYETTE, LISA WYNN, retired research scientist; b. Atlanta, Ga., Feb. 28, 1956; d. William Worthington and Minnewil Story McNeal; m. James Edward Boyette, Mar. 24, 1990; children: James Zachary, Samuel William. BA, U. of Ga., 1978; MEd, Ga. State U., 1983. Lic. School of Psychology Sch. Psychology, Ga. Profl. Stds. Commn., real estate Atlanta Inst. of Real Estate. Aging rschr. Atlanta VA Med. Ctr., Decatur, Ga., 1991—2001. Dir. Contbr. articles to profl. jours. and confs. Publicity profl. Newcomers, Signal Mountain, Tenn., 2002—03; den leader Boy Scouts of Am., Atlanta, 1998—2000. Grantee, Rehab. R & D Svcs., 1994—98. Mem.: Chattanooga Tennis Assn., Atlanta Lawn Tennis Assn. Achievements include development of exercise expert system. Avocations: tennis, hiking, travel, water-skiing. Personal E-mail: lisazac3212@yahoo.com.

BOYINA, RAMANA PRASAD VENKATA, civil engineering educator, researcher; b. Nellore, India, Aug. 28, 1958; s. Narasimha Rao and Bhagyavati Boyina; m. Subba Lakshmi Bandhuvula, Apr. 19, 1982; 1 child, Kaysuv. BTech, Jawaharlal Nehru Technol. U., Anantapur, India, 1982; MTech, Jawaharlal Nehru Technol. U., Hyderabad, India, 1987; PhD, Indian Inst. Sci., Bangalore, 1992. Lectr. Chaitanya Bharati Inst. Tech., Hyderabad, 1982-92, asst. prof. engring., 1992-98, prof. engring., 1998—. Adj. prof. engring., Rensselaer Poly. Inst., Troy, n.Y., 1998—. Contbr. articles to profl. jours. Grantee UN Devel. Program, 1995, UNESCO, 1996, 97; rsch. grantee Govt. India, 1994-97, 97-2000. Mem. AAAS, ASCE (life), Nat. Soc. Fluid Mechs. and Fluid Power India. Hindu. Avocations: swimming, travel, cooking. Home: 50 3d Ave Seymour CT 06483 Office: Rensselaer Poly Inst 5049 JEC/110 8th St Troy NY 12180 E-mail: boyinr@rpi.edu., boyinarp@hotmail.com.

BOYKAN, MARTIN, composer, music educator; b. N.Y.C., Apr. 12, 1931; m. Susan Schwalb, 1983. AB summa cum laude, Harvard U., 1951; student, U. Zurich, Switzerland, 1951—52; MusM, Yale, 1953. Asst. prof. music Brandeis U., Waltham, Mass., 1964-67, assoc. prof. music, 1967-76, prof., 1976—, Irving G. Fine prof., 1986—. Composer-in-residence Composer's Conf., Wellesley, Mass., 1987; vis. prof. composition Columbia U., 1988-89, NYU, 1993, 2000; sr. Fulbright lectr. Bar Ilan U., Israel, 1994. Composer: String Quartets, 1949, 1965, Flute Quintet, 1953, Psalm, 1958, Prelude for Organ, 1959, Chamber Concerto for 13 Instruments, 1971, String Quartet No. 2, 1973, Piano Trio, 1975, Elegy for soprano and 6 instruments, part I, 1979, Elegy for soprano and 6 instruments, part II, 1982, String Quartet No. 3, 1984, Epithalamion for baritone, violin and harp, 1985, Shalom Rav, 1985, Fantasy Sonata for Piano, 1987, Sonata for cello and piano, 1988, Symphony for orch. with baritone solo, 1989, Piano Sonata #2, 1990, Nocturne for Cello, Piano and Percussion, 1990, Eclogue for flute, violin, cello, horn and piano, 1991, Echoes of Petrarch for flute, clarinet and piano, 1992, Voyages for Soprano and Piano, 1992, Sea-Gardens for Soprano and Piano, 1993, Impromptu for Solo Violin, 1993, Three Psalms for Soprano and Piano, 1993, Pastorale for Piano, 1993, Sonata for violin and piano, 1994, Ma'ariv Settings for chorus and organ, 1995, String Quartet No. 4, 1996, 3 Shakespeare Songs for Chorus, 1996, City of Gold for solo flute, 1996, 2d Trio for violin, cello and piano, 1997, Psalm 121 for soprano and string quartet, 1997, Usurpations for piano, 1997, Sonata for Solo Violin, 1998, Flume for Clarinet and Piano, 1998, Romanza for Flute and Piano, 1999, A Packet for Susan for Mezzo-Soprano and Piano, 2000, Motet for Mezzo-Soprano and Viol Consort, 2000, Songlines for flute, clarinet, violin and cello, 2001, concerto for violin and orchestra; author: (book) Silence and Show Time, 2003; mem. editl. bd.: Perspectives of New Music; contbr. articles to profl. jours. Nat. winner Jeunesses Musicales, 1967, League-ISCM, 1983; recipient Martha Baird Rockefeller award, 1974, Fromm Found. commn., 1975, award Internat. Soc. Contemporary Music, 1983, Koussevitzky commn., 1985, AAUL, 1986, 88, rec. award Am. Acad. and Nat. Inst. Arts and Letters, 1986, Walter Hinrichsen Publ. award Am. Acad. and Inst. Arts and Letters, 1988; Paine fellow, 1951, Fulbright fellow, 1953-55, Guggenheim fellow, 1984, Sr. Fulbright fellow, 1994; grantee Nat. Endowment for Arts, 1983, and numerous others. Mem. Am. Music Ctr., Phi Betta Kappa. Home: 10 Winsor Ave Watertown MA 02472-1460 Office: Music Dept Brandeis Univ Waltham MA 02454 E-mail: boykan@brandeis.edu.

BOYKIN, AMY WILLIAMS, librarian; b. Newport News, Va., Aug. 1, 1968; d. Edward Hamilton Williams, Lucy King Williams; m. Mark Julian Boykin. BA in English, Christopher Newport U., 1990; MS in Libr. Studies, U. N.C., Greensboro, 1993. Asst. reference libr. Christopher Newport U. Libr., Newport News, 1995—. Contbr. book. Mem.: ALA, Ch. and Synagogue Libr. Assn., Mid-Atlantic Regional Archives Conf., Va. Libr. Assn., Beta Phi Mu. Baptist. Avocations: reading, cooking, crocheting. Office: Christopher Newport Univ Libr 1 University Pl Newport News VA 23606 Business E-Mail: awboykin@cnu.edu.

BOYKIN, HAMILTON HAIGHT, lawyer; b. N.Y.C., Feb. 3, 1939; s. Samuel Darrington and Alice (Haight) B.; m. Judith Panneton, Aug. 21, 1965; children: Lisa Ann, Samuel Scott, Allison Christine. B.A., Trinity Coll., Hartford, Conn., 1961; J.D., Georgetown U., 1964. Bar: D.C. 1964, Va. 1964. Ptnr. Colton and Boykin, Washington, 1965-93; ptnr. Boykin & Casano PC, Washington, 1994—. Mem. Va. State Bar Assn., DC Bar Ass. Democrat. Roman Catholic. Office: Boykin & Casano PC 1620 L St NW Ste 900 Washington DC 20036-5628 Home: 37 Pearl Reef Ln Hilton Head SC 29926-3004

BOYKIN, JOSEPH FLOYD, JR., librarian; b. Pensacola, Fla., Nov. 7, 1940; s. Joseph Floyd and Delree (Bailey) B.; m. Evelyn Louise Larson, Aug. 3, 1963; children: Suzanne Michelle, Pamela Denise. Student, Pensacola Jr. Coll., 1958-60; BS, Fla. State U., 1962, MS, 1965. Lic. pvt. pilot. Asst. to librarian U. N.C., Charlotte, 1965-68, acting head librarian, 1968-70; dir. library, 1970-81; dean libraries Clemson (S.C.) U., 1981—. Bd. dirs. Southeastern Libr. Network, Inc., 1975-78, 96-98, chmn., 1977-78. Trustee OCLC Online Computer Library Ctr., Inc., 1980-86; trustee OCLC Users Council, 1978-82, 89-92, pres., 1978-80; mem. State Hist. Records Adv. Bd., S.C., 1990—. Mem. S.C. Libr. Assn. (pres. 1990). Democrat. Baptist. Home: 307 Bent Oak Ln Central SC 29630-9460 Office: Clemson Univ Robert Muldrow Cooper Clemson SC 29634-0001

BOYKIN, NANCY MERRITT, academic administrator; b. Washington, Mar. 20, 1919; d. Matthew and Mary Gertrude (White) Merritt; m. Ulysses Wilhelm Boykin, Apr. 17, 1965 (dec. 1987); 1 child from previous marriage, Tauyna Lovell Banks. BS, D.C. Tchrs. Coll., 1939; MA, Howard U., 1940, MSW, 1956; PhD, U. Mich., 1976. Employee rels. counselor Office Chief of Fin., U.S. Army, Washington; adminstrv. asst. to civilian aide Sec. of Def., Washington; policewoman Met. Police Dept., Washington; social worker Dept. Pub. Welfare, Washington; adminstrv. asst. to dir. Active Cmty. Teams, Inc., Detroit, 1965—66; dir. continuing edn. for girls program Detroit Pub. Schs., 1966—87; ednl. cons. and cmty. outreach coord. New Health Ctr., Livonia, Mich., 1988—90. Presdl. appointee Nat. Adv. Coun. on Extension and Continuing Edn., 1973—80; cons. U.S. Dept. Edn., 1982. Mem. Mich. Bd. Examiners of Social Workers, 1978—83; gov.'s appointee Mich. Youth Adv. Com., 1984—87, Commn. on Svcs. to Aging, 1992—; mem. Nat. Black Republicans, 1972—, Mich. Rep. Com., 1975—80, 1983—; sec. 1st Rep. Dist., 1973—77; presdl. appointee to nat. adv. bd. C.C. of Air Force, 1984—. Named Educator of Yr., Nat. Black Women's Polit. Leadership Caucus, 1981, Hon. Lt. Col. Aide De Camp in Ala. Militia, Gov. Wallace, 1986, in her honor, The Nancy Boykin Continuing Edn. Ctr., Detroit Pub. Sch. Bd., 1993; recipient Spirit of Detroit award, 1979, Nat. Kool Achiever's award in Edn., Brown and Williams Tobacco Co., 1987, Outstanding Contbns. to Cmty. award, Assn. Black Judges Mich., 1988—90, Cmty. Svc. award, YWCA, 1992, Pioneer award, Frederick Douglas Soc., 1994, others. Mem.: Detroit Assn. Univ. Mich. Women, Detroit Orgn. Sch. Adminstrs., Nat. Assn. Black Sch. Educators, Nat. Assn. Supervision and Curriculum Devel., Profl. Women's Network, Mich. Assn. Concerned with Sch. Age Parents (past pres., Recognition award 1986, Outstanding Svc. award 1993), Wayne State U. Sch. Edn. Alumni Assn. (bd. govs.), U. Mich. Alumnae Assn., Phi Delta Kappa, Alpha Kappa Alpha, Eta Phi Beta (Outstanding Profl. Women award 1992). Home and Office: 1316 Fenwick Ln Apt 513 Silver Spring MD 20910-3503

BOYKIN, RICHARD RENARDA, legislative staff member, lawyer; b. Jackson, Miss., Sept. 9, 1968; s. George Albert and Burnette (Knight) B. BA, Ctrl. State U., 1990; JD, U. Dayton, 1994. Bar: Ill. 1994. Tchg. asst. U. Dayton (Ohio), 1993-94, legal intern, 1994; legis. fellow office of Sen. Carol Moseley Brown (Ill.) U.S. Congress, Washington, 1994-95; contract atty. Attys. Per Diem, Washington, 1995-96, Aspen Sys. Corp., Washington, 1996-97; chief of staff office of rep. Danny K. Davis Ho. of Reps., Washington, 1997—. Assoc. min. Met. Bapt. Ch., motivational spkr. Stennis fellow Sen. John C. Stennis Fellowship, 1999-00. Mem. ABA, Chgo. Bar Assn., Ill. State Soc. (bd. dirs.). Baptist. Avocations: reading, racquetball, basketball. Home: 6600 Lake Park Dr #302 Greenbelt MD 20770-3096 Office: US Ho of Reps Office of Rep Danny Davis 1222 Longworth Hob Washington DC 20515-0001

BOYKIN, ROBERT HEATH, banker; b. Carlsbad, N.Mex., Jan. 10, 1926; s. Calvin Clay and Ruby (Heath) B.; m. Camille Inkman, Nov. 26, 1948; 1 child, Robert Heath. BBA, U. Tex., 1950, LL.B., 1953; student, Park Coll., 1943-44; spl. courses, La. State U., Tex. A. and M. Coll., Am. Mgmt. Assn. Bar: Tex. bar 1952. Tabulating supr. Tex. Edn. Agy., 1948-52; with Fed. Res. Bank of Dallas, 1953-91, asst. counsel, 1959-61, asst. counsel, asst. sec. bd., 1961-65, asst. v.p., asst. sec. bd., 1965-67, asst. v.p., sec. bd., 1967-68, v.p., sec. bd., 1968-70, sr. v.p., sec. bd., 1971-75, sr. v.p., 1976, 1st v.p., 1976-80, pres., 1981-91; ret., 1991. Sec. Conf. Pres.'s of Fed. Res. Banks, 1963-64, chmn., 1980; instr. negotiable instruments Dallas chpt. Am. Inst. Banking, 1959-61 Served as lt. (j.g.) USNR, 1943-47. Mem. Tex. Bar Assn., Tex. Bankers Assn., Delta Tau Delta, Phi Alpha Delta. Methodist.

BOYKIN, WILLIAM G. career officer; b. Wilson, N.C., Apr. 19, 1948; Commd. U.S. Army, 1971, advanced through grades to maj. gen., 1999, comdg. gen. Spl. Forces Command, 1998-2000, comdg. gen. Spl. Warfare Ctr. & Schs., 2000—. Office: US Army Spl Warfare Ctr And Schs Fort Bragg NC 28310-0001

BOYKO, CHRISTOPHER ALLAN, lawyer, judge; b. Cleve., Oct. 10, 1954; s. Andrew and Eva Dorothy (Zepko) B.; m. Roberta Ann Gentile, May 29, 1981; children: Philip, Ashley. B in Polit. Sci. cum laude, Mt. Union Coll., 1976; JD, Cleve. Marshall Coll. Law, 1979. Bar: Ohio 1979, Fla. 1985, U.S. Dist. Ct. (no. dist.) Ohio 1979, U.S. Ct. Appeals (6th cir.) 1990, U.S. Tax Ct. 1986, U.S. Supreme Ct., 1988. Prin. Boyko & Boyko, Parma, Ohio, 1979—95; asst. prosecutor City of Parma, 1981-87, dir. of law, 1987-93; exec. v.p., gen. counsel copy Am., Inc., 1993-94; judge Parma Mcpl. Court, 1993, Ct. Common Pleas, Cuyahoga County, Ohio, 1996—, Judicial Corrections Bd., 1999—; chair Ct. Vet. Svc. Com., 2000—. Guardian ad litem Juvenile Ct., 1979-93; legal advisor spl. weapons and tactics divsn. City of Parma Police Dept., 1984-93; chief counsel S.W. Enforcement Bur., 1991-93; mem. faculty Ohio Jud. Coll., Nat. Jud. Coll., lectr. FBI Nat. Acad. jud. editor Law and Fact Com., 1999—. Active Citizens League of Greater Cleve., 1985—; trustee Cops & Kids, Inc., Cleve. Bar Assn., 2000—, County Bar Assn.; mem. Parma Drug Task Force, 1987—; mem. adv. com. Parmadale Children's Svcs., 1991—; mem. St. Anthony's Sch. Commn. Mem.: Nat. Inst. Trial Advocacy (steering com. 2003—), Mt. Union Coll. Alumni Assn., Cleve. Am. Mid. Eastern Orgn., Am. Inns of Ct. Found. (master of bench 2001—, William K. Thomas Inn of Ct.), Narcotics Law Officers Assn., Ukrainian Bar Assn., Parma Bar Assn. (pres., trustee), Cleve. Bar Assn. (bd. trustees, lectr. in law), Cuyahoga County Bar Assn., Ohio Bar Assn., Fla. Bar Assn., ABA, Cuyahoga County Police Chiefs Assn. (assoc.), Elks. Byzantine Catholic. Avocations: martial arts, phys. fitness. Office: Justice Ctr 1200 Ontario St Cleveland OH 44113-1604

BOYKO, IHOR NESTOR, lawyer; b. Winnipeg, Man., Can., Nov. 9, 1951; came to U.S. 1966; s. Maksym and Katherina (Huminilowych) B. BA, Ind. U., 1972, JD, 1975; MS, Purdue U., Indpls., 1989. Bar: Ind. 1975, U.S. Dist. Ct. (so. dist.) Ind. 1983. Law clk. Ind. Employment Security Divsn., Indpls., 1975-76; dep. pub. defender State Pub. Defender, Indpls., 1976-82, spl. dep. pub. defender, 1982-85; staff atty. Legal Aid Soc., Indpls., 1983-85; pvt. practice Indpls., 1985-86; atty. Ind. Dept. Environ. Mgmt., Indpls., 1986-92; corp./environ. counsel PWI Environ., Inc., Indpls., 1992-96; legal counsel Divsn. Reclamation, Divsn. Oil and Gas Ind. Dept. Natural Resources, Indpls., 1996-98, sr. bur. counsel, 1998—. Adj. prof. Sch. Pub. and Environ. Affairs, Ind. U., Indpls., 1990—. Contbr. articles to profl. jours. Sec. Ukrainian-Am. Cultural Soc., Indpls., 1985—, now pres.; Ukrainian and Russian interpreter Internat. Ctr. of Indpls., 1987—. Mem. Com. for Environ. Concerns in Ukraine. Ukrainian Orthodox Ch. Avocations: foreign languages, music. Home: 6224 N Tuxedo St Indianapolis IN 46220-4444 Office: Dept Natural Resources Office of Leagl Counsel/Ind Govt Ctr S W-255L / 402 W Washington St Indianapolis IN 46204 E-mail: iboyko@dnr.state.in.us.

BOYLAN, MERLE NELSON, librarian, educator; b. Youngstown, Ohio, Feb. 24, 1925; s. Merle Nelson and Alma Joy (Kepple) B. BA, Youngstown U., 1950; M.L.S., Carnegie-Mellon U., 1956; postgrad., U. Ariz., 1950-51, Ind. U., 1952. Librarian Pub. Health Library U. Calif., Berkeley, 1956-58; sci. librarian U. Ariz., Tucson, 1958-59; engring. librarian Gen. Dynamics/Convair, San Diego, 1959-61, Gen. Dynamics/Astronautics, 1961-62; assoc. librarian Lawrence Radiation Lab., U. Calif., Livermore, 1962-64, library mgr., 1964-67; chief librarian NASA Ames Research Center, Moffett Field, Calif., 1968-69; asso. dir. libraries U. Mass., Amherst, 1969-70, dir. libraries, Univ. librarian, 1970-72; dir. libraries U. Tex., Austin, 1973-77, U. Wash., Seattle, 1977-89, dir. emeritus, 1989—, prof. Sch. Librarianship, 1982-89; exec. bd. Amigos Bibliographic Council, 1974-77; mem. fin. com., governance com., user's council, computer service council Wash. Library Network, 1978—. Del. Gov.'s Conf. Libraries and Info. Services, 1979; sec. Texas State Bd. Library Examiners, 1974-77; mem. bibliographic networking and resource sharing advisory group Southwestern Library Interstate Coop. Endeavor, 1975-77; sec., chmn. exec. bd. Pacific N.W. Bibliographic Center, 1977-83; mem. com. centralized acquisitions of library materials for internat. studies Center for Research Libraries.; del. OCLC Users Council, 1981-86. Sec. bd. trustees Littlefield Fund for So. History, 1974-77, Fred Meyer Charitable Trust; mem. adv. bd. Library and Info. Resources for Northwest, 1984 87. Mem. ALA, Assn. Coll. and Research Libraries (legis. com. 1977-81), Assn. Research Libraries (bibliographic control com. 1979 83), Spl. Libraries Assn., Am. Soc. Info. Sci., Beta Phi Mu. Home: 1354 Bellefield Park Ln Bellevue WA 98004-6854 Office: Univ of Wash Libraries Suzzallo Library Seattle WA 98195-0001

BOYLAN, MICHAEL A. philosophy educator, writer; b. Sept. 21, 1952; m. Rebecca Warburton Boylan; children: Arianne, Seán, Éamon. BA, Carleton Coll., 1974; MA, U. Chgo., 1976, PhD, 1979. Asst. prof. Marquette U., Milw., 1979-85; vis. asst. prof. Georgetown U., Washington, 1985-87; prof. Marymount U., Arlington, Va., 1987—. Author: Method and Practice in Aristotle's Biology, 1983, The Process of Argument, 1988, Perspectives in Philosophy, 1993, Ethical Issues in Business, 1995, Gewirth: Critical Essays on Action, Rationality and Community, 1999, Biomedical Ethics, 2000, Basic Ethics, 2000, Business Ethics, 2001, Environmental Ethics, 2001, Genetic Engineering: Science and Ethics on the New Frontier, 2002, Ethics Across the Curriculum, 2003, (novels) Far Into the Sound, 1973, Slipknot, 1989, (poetry) Chambers in a House of Stone, 1975, The Dance of Life, 1987, (children's book) When the Elephants Came, 1988; contbr. articles to profl. jours. Office: Marymount U Dept Philosophy 2807 N Glebe Rd Arlington VA 22207 Home: 8100 Hawthorne Ct Besthesda MD 20817

BOYLAN, RICHARD JOHN, psychologist, psychotherapist, researcher, anthropologist, educator; b. Hollywood, Calif., Oct. 15, 1939; s. John Alfred and Rowena Margaret (Devine) Boylan; m. Charnette Marie Blackburn, Oct. 26, 1968 (div. June 1984); children: Christopher J., Jennifer April, Stephanie August; m. Judith Lee Keast, Nov. 21, 1987; stepchildren: Darren Andrew Keast, Matthew Grant Keast. BA, St. John's Coll., 1961; MEd, Fordham U., 1966; MSW, U. Calif., Berkeley, 1971; PhD in Psychology, U. Calif., Davis, 1984. Cert. clin. hypnotherapist. Assoc. pastor Cath. Diocese Fresno, 1965-68; asst. dir. Berkeley Free Ch., 1970-71; psychiat. social worker Marin Mental Health Dept., San Rafael, Calif., 1971-77; dir. Calaveras Mental Health Dept., San Andreas, Calif., 1977-85; prof., coord. Nat. U., Sacramento, 1985-86; lectr. Calif. State U., Sacramento, 1985-90, 98-99; instr. U. Calif., Davis, 1984; assoc. prof. Chapman U., Sacramento, 1997-98; instr. Heald Coll., Sacramento, 2000; clin. social worker Dialysis Clinic, Inc., Sacramento, 2000—01. Dir. U.S. Behavioral Health, Sacramento, 1988—89; pvt. practice, Sacramento, 1974—; clin. social worker South Sacramento Dialysis Ctr., 2000—01; clin. cons. Ctr. for Behavioral Health, Sacramento, 2000; adminstrv. supervising social worker Kair In-Home Social Svcs., Inc., 2001—03. Author: (book) Extraterrestrial Contact and Human Responses, 1992, Close Extraterrestrial Encounters, 1994, Labored Journey to the Stars, 1996, Project Epiphany, 1997. Bd. dirs. Marin Mcpl. Water Dist., 1975—77; cons. Calif. State Legis., Sacramento, 1979—80; chmn. Calaveras County Bd. Edn., Angels Camp, Calif., 1981—84; dir. Star Kids Project, 2002—. Recipient Geriatric Medicine award, NIH, 1984; Expt. Sta. grantee, USDA, 1983. Mem.: Acad. Clin. Close-Encounter Therapists (founder, v.p.), Nat. Resources Def. Coun., Sacramento Soc. Profl. Psychologists (past pres.), Sacramento Valley Psychol. Assn. (past pres.), Nat. Bd. Hypnotherapy and Med. Anaesthesiology. Democrat. Avocations: hiking, jogging, UFOs, camping. Office: PO Box 22310 Sacramento CA 95822-0310 E-mail: drboylan@sbcglobal.net.

BOYLE, ANNE C. state commissioner; b. Omaha, Dec. 22, 1942; m. Mike Boyle; children: Maureen, Michael, James, Patrick, Margaret. Chmn., co-chmn. various polit. campaigns, Omaha, 1974-78; office coord. for U.S. Senator James Exon., 1979-81; corp. and polit. fundraiser, 1983-85, 88; campaign mgr. pub. rels. firm, Omaha, 1990-91; pres. Universal Rev. Svcs., Omaha, 1992—; mem. Nebr. Pub. Svc. Commn., Lincoln, 1996—. Active Clinton for Pres. Campaign, organizer fund raisers, host open house, Omaha, 1992; cons., lobbyist, 1994-95. Former nat. committeewoman Nebr. Young Dems.; chmn. Douglas County Dem. Ctrl. Com.; mem. jud. nominating com. for Douglas County Juvenile Ct.; chmn. inaugural ball invitation com. for gov. of Nebr., 1982; co-chmn. Midwestern Govs. Conf., 1984, Jefferson-Jackson Day Dinner, 1976, 82; del. Dem. Nat. Conv., 1988, 92, 96; mem. Nebr. Rev. com. for Fed. Appts. to U.S. Atty., U.S. Marshall and 8th Dist. Ct. Appeals Fed. Judgeship, 1993-95; mem. Nebr. Dem. Ctrl. Com.; mem. Fin. Com. to Reelect Gov. Ben Nelson; mem. Nebr. Interagy. Coun. on Homeless, President's Adv. Com. on Arts, 1995; Nebr. authorized rep. '96 Clinton-Gore Campaign; Bd. dirs. Bemis Ctr. for Contemporary Arts, Omaha; chmn. Nebr. Dem. Party, 1999-2001. Mem. Nat. Assn. Regulatory Utility Commrs. and Mid-Am. Regulatory Commrs. Democrat. Office: PO Box 94927 Lincoln NE 68509-4927

BOYLE, BARBARA DORMAN, motion picture company executive; b. N.Y.C., Aug. 11, 1935; d. William and Edith (Kleinman) Dorman; m. Kevin Boyle, Nov. 26, 1960; children: David Eric, Paul Coleman. BA in English with honors, U. Calif., Berkeley, 1957; JD, UCLA, 1960. Bar: Calif. 1961, N.Y. 1964, U.S. Supreme Ct. 1964. Atty. bus. affairs dept. corp. asst. sec. Am. Internat. Pictures, L.A., 1960-65; ptnr. Cohen & Boyle, L.A., 1967-74; exec. v.p., gen. counsel, chief op. officer New World Pictures, L.A., 1974-82; sr. v.p. prodn. Orion Pictures Corp., L.A., 1982-85; exec. v.p. prodn. RKO Pictures, L.A., 1986-87; pres. Sovereign Pictures, Inc., L.A., 1988-92, Boyle and Taylor Prodns., 1993-99, Valhalla Motion Pictures, L.A., 2000—03; chair film, TV and digital media dept. UCLA, 2003—. Lectr. in field. Exec. prodr. (film) Eight Men Out, 1987, Bottle Rocket, 1995, Campus Man; prodr. (films) Mrs. Munck, 1995, Phenomenon, 1996, Instinct, 1999; exec. prodr. The Hi Line, 1998. Bd. dirs. UCLA Law Fund Com., L.A. Women's Campaign Fund; pres. Ind. Feature Project/West; founding mem. entertainment adv. coun. sch. law UCLA, co-chmn. 1979-80. Named UCLA Law Sch. Alumni of Yr. 1999, Women in Film Crystal award, 2000, Mem. Acad. Motion Picture Arts and Scis., Women in Film (pres. 1977-78), Hollywood Women's Polit. Com., Calif. Bar Assn., N.Y. State Bar Assn. Office: Valhalla Motion Pictures Ste 400 8530 Wilshire Blvd Beverly Hills CA 90211

BOYLE, BRADLEY CHARLES, civil engineer; b. St. Paul, Dec. 18, 1959; s. Fosten Annett and Beverly Ann (Rehbein) B.; m. Dana Satenick Ramezzano, Aug. 20, 1983. BSCE, U. Minn., 1984, MBA, 1995. Rsch. asst., environ. engring. dept. U. Minn., Mpls., 1984-85; project mgr. Ramsey Engring. Co., St. Paul, 1985-87, N.W. Airlines, Inc., St. Paul, 1987-91; mktg. dir. M.A. Mortenson Co., Mpls., 1991-93; internat. sales mgr. Continental Hydraulics, Mpls., 1995—2002; v.p. sales and mktg. AgMotion, Inc., St. Paul, 2002—. Mem. ASCE, U. Minn. Alumni Assn., Minn. Surveyors and Engrs. Soc., Chi Epsilon, Beta Gamma Sigma. Republican. Episcopalian. Achievements include patent pertaining to load cell technology. Home: 1565 Tamberwood Trl Woodbury MN 55125-3364 Office: AgMotion Inc 444 Cedar St Ste 1000 Saint Paul MN 55101

BOYLE, BRUCE JAMES, publisher; b. Mpls., Aug. 31, 1931; s. Lorille James and Norma Elizabeth (Blish) B.; m. Betty Jean Tucker, May 28, 1960; children: Katherine Ann, Julia Caroline, Amy Elizabeth. B.J., U. Mo., 1958. Copywriter

Sta. KFRU, Columbia, Mo., 1958; continuity dir. KOMO-TV, Columbia, 1959; advt. salesman Better Homes & Gardens mag., 1960; advt. dir. Successful Farming mag., Des Moines, 1969-73, pub., 1973-80, Meredith Pub. Svcs., 1976-80, Meredith Video Pub., 1981-92, dir. mag. devel., 1984-92. Mem. faculty Grandview Coll., 1993-95. Bd. dirs. Youth Homes Mid-Am., 1993-99. With USN, 1951-54. Mem. Nat. Agri-Mktg. Assn. (pres. 1973-74), Farm and Indsl. Equipment Inst., Farm Equipment Mfrs. Assn. (chmn. bd. govs. 1971-72), Agrl. Pubs. Assn. (bd. dirs. 1979-81), Alpha Delta Sigma. Clubs: Wakonda Country, Okoboji Yacht, Rio Verde Country Club. Home: 718 55th St Des Moines IA 50312-1827 E-mail: bjb718@msn.com.

BOYLE, BRYAN DOUGLAS, computer and network systems architect; b. Fall River, Mass., June 11, 1956; s. Edwin Clayton and Lucille Annemarie (Gouin) B.; m. Paula DeAngelis, Jan. 19, 1980 (div. 1983). BA in Comm., Fordham U., 1978. Computer designer ABC, N.Y.C., 1979-85; sys. engr. IMR Sys., Leavenworth, Kans., 1985-86; sr. engr. Data Gen. Corp., 1986-89; sr. sys. cons. Nations, Inc., 1989; sr. cons., sr. arch. Exxon Rsch. & Engring. Co., Florham Park, N.J., 1991-99; sr. mem. tech. staff, lab. mgr. AT&T Labs., Florham Park, N.J., 1999—. Editor Globecom Pub., Prairie Village, Kans., 1981-85; pres. Beta Processing, Bronx, 1981-87; computer cons. Soc. Broadcast Engrs., Indpls., 1983-86, Roncom Broadcast Design, Fairfield, N.J., 1984-87. Software author Bi-Tech Enterprises, Bohemia, N.Y., 1980-83; computer editor Broadcast Comm. mag., 1981-84; contbg. editor Broadcast Mgmt./Engring. mag., 1984-86; editor Broadcast Comm. mag., 1981-83; contbr. Internet Firewalls Frequently Asked Questions. Decorated Sovereign Mil. and Hosp. Order of St. John of Jerusalem, Knight of Malta, Knight of Honor and Merit. Republican. Roman Catholic. Avocations: automobile restoration, living history (civil war), commercial pilot, flight instructor. E-mail: bdboyle@bdboyle.com.

BOYLE, CAROLYN MOORE, public relations executive, marketing communications manager; b. L.A., Jan. 29, 1937; d. Cory Orlando Moore and Violet (Brennan) Baldock; m. Robert J. Ruppelt, Oct. 8, 1954 (div. Aug. 1964); children: Cory Robert, Traci Lynn; m. Jerry Ray Boyle, June 1, 1970 (div. 1975). AA, Orange Coast Coll., 1966; BA, Calif. State U., Fullerton, 1970; postgrad., U. Calif., Irvine, 1970 71; program coord. Newport Beach (Calif.) Cablevision, 1968-70; dir. pub. rels. Fish Comm. Co., Newport Beach, 1970-74; mktg. rep. Dow Pharm. divsn. Dow Chem. Co., Orange County, Calif., 1974-77, Las Vegas, Nev., 1980-81; mgr. product publicity Dow Agrl. Products divsn. Dow chem. Co., Midland, Mich., 1977-80; mgr. mktg. comm. Dowell Fluid Svcs. Region divsn. Down Chem. Co., Houston, 1981-84; adminstr. mktg. comm. Swedlow, Inc., Garden Grove, Calif., 1984-85; cons. mktg. comm., 1985-86; mgr. mktg. comm. Am. Convertors divsn. Am. Hosp Supply, 1986-87; mgr. sales support Surgidev Corp., Santa Barbara, Calif., 1987-88; owner Barrel House, Victorville, 1988-91; pub. info. officer, mgmt. analyst II, Clark County, Las Vegas, 1996—, Saratoga Fences, Las Vegas, 1991; pub. info. officer Clark County Comprehensive Planning, Las Vegas, 1992-96. Bd. dirs. 3CMA; guest lectr. Calif. State U., Long Beach, 1970; seminar coord. U. Calif., Irvine, 1972; mem. Western White House Press Corps, 1972; pub. rels. cons. BASF Wyandotte, Phila., 1981-82. Author: Agricultural Public Relations/Publicity, 1981; editor Big Mean AG Machine (nternal mag.), 1977; contbg. editor Dowell Mktg. Newsletter, 1983; contbr. numerous articles to trade pubs.; creator, designer Novahistine DMX Trial Size nat. mktg. program, 1977. Com. mem. Dow Employees for Polit. Action, Midland, 1978-80; bd. dirs. Dowell Employees for Pub. Action Com., Houston, 1983-84, Clark County Leadership Forum Alumni. Recipient PROTOS award, 1985, 1st rights to televise Pres. Nixon in Western White House; ; World Campus Afloat scholar U. Seven Seas, 1966-67. Mem. Pub. Rels. Soc. Am. (cert.), Soc. Petroleum Engrs., Internat. Assn. Bus. Communicators, Clark County Leadership Forum Alumni Assn. (bd. dirs.). Episcopalian. Office: 2301 Bear Valley St Las Vegas NV 89128 E-mail: vegasboyle@aol.com.

BOYLE, CHRISTOPHER GEORGE, English educator, counselor; b. Binghamton, N.Y., July 27, 1930; s. Edward George and Mary Giblyn B.; m. Mary Ella Morris, Dec. 30, 1951; children: Catherine Flowers, Anne Butler, Russell, Elizabeth O'Brien. AB, Amherst Coll., 1952; EdM, Harvard U., 1960. Cert. secondary tchr., Ariz., cmty. coll. tchg. cert., Ariz. English tchr., coach St. Stephen's Sch., Austin, 1952-54, Worcester (Mass.) Acad., 1954-55; English tchr., dept. head, coach St. Andrew's Sch., Middletown, Del., 1955-80; Fulbright tchr. of English U.S. Dept. of State, Helsinki, Finland, 1962-63; English dept. head, dean of studies, tchr., coach, counselor St. Gregory Coll. Preparatory Sch., Tucson, Ariz., 1980-94. Instr. Freshman English U. Del., Newark, 1970-71; part-time coll. counselor, cons. Catalina Foothills H.S., Tucson, 1997-99; advanced placement English lit exam. reader, cons., Coll. Bd./Ednl. Testing Svc., Princeton, N.J., 1965-96, workshop leader for AP English tchrs., San Jose, Calif., 1989-97; reader Scholastic Assessment Test English essays, 1967-2003. Contbr. articles to profl. jours. Mem. Del. Coun. of Tchrs. of English (pres. 1969-71). Episcopalian. Avocations: scuba diving, choral music, reading. Home: 4820-L E Fort Lowell Rd Tucson AZ 85712-1262 E-mail: cboyle727@aol.com.

BOYLE, DANIEL ROBERT, musician, delivery service executive; b. Bowling Green, Ohio, Dec. 5, 1973; s. Robert Theodore Boyle and Linda Marie (Goris) Boyle; m. Leslie Kathleen Gilbert; 1 child, Frederic Joseph. B magna cum laude, Bowling Green State U., 1996; postgrad., U. Toledo, 1997—98. Cert. music K-12 Ohio. Choir dir. Evergreen Local Schs., Metamora, Ohio, 1996—2000; mid. sch. choral dir. Maumee City Schs., Ohio, 2000—02; sales rep. Verizon Wireless, Findlay, Ohio, 2002—03; driver FedEx Ground, Toledo, 2003—. Organist, choir dir. St. Louis Cath. Ch., Custar, Ohio, 1981—97, Grace Luth Ch., Elmore, Ohio, 1997—. Advisor 4-H, Portage, Ohio, 1991—97. Recipient Man of Yr., Sigma Alpha Iota, Bowling Green State U., 1994; scholar Pres.'s scholar, Bowling Green State U., 1991—95. Mem.: Am. Guild Organists, Music Educators Nat. Conf., Evergreen HS FFA (hon.), Phi Eta Mu, Golden Key, Phi Mu Alpha Sinfonia (music/ritual dir. warden 1994—95). Lutheran. Avocations: bicycling, composing music. Home: 6638 N Texas St Whitehouse OH 43571 Personal E-mail: DanandLeslie@wcnet.org.

BOYLE, E. THOMAS, federal magistrate judge; b. Paterson, N.J., Apr. 30, 1939; m. Mary Lou Kelly; two children. BS in English, Holy Cross Coll., 1961; LLB, U. Va., 1964. Bar: N.Y. 1965, U.S. Ct Appeals (2d cir.) 1974, U.S. Dist. Ct. (ea. and so. dists.) N.Y. 1974. Assoc. Mendes & Mount, N.Y.C., N.Y., 1965-66; trial counsel Legal Aid Soc. Suffolk County, N.Y., 1966-72; appellate counsel Fed. Defender Svcs., N.Y.C., 1972-75; pvt. practice Smithtown, N.Y., 1975-88; county atty. Suffolk County, Hauppauge, N.Y., 1988-92; ptnr. Boyle, Shea & Nornes, Hauppauge, N.Y., 1992-95; magistrate judge for ea. dist. N.Y. U.S. Dist. Ct., Uniondale, 1995—. Office: Alfonse M D Amato US Courthouse Rm 834 Central Islip NY 11722

BOYLE, FRANCIS ANTHONY, law educator; b. Chgo., Mar. 25, 1950; AB in Polit. Sci., U. Chgo., 1971; JD magna cum laude, Harvard U., 1976, AM, 1978, PhD, 1983. Bar: Mass. 1977. Tchg. fellow, assoc. Harvard U. and Ctr. Internat. Affairs, 1976-78; tax atty. Bingman, Dana & Gould, Boston, 1977-78; prof. law U. Ill., Champaign, 1978—. Prof. USSR Summer U. Jurists, 1989; Parhad lectr. U. Calgary, 2001. Author: World Politics and International Law, 1985 (Outstanding Acad. Book, Choice mag. 1985-86), Defending Civil Resistance Under International Law, 1987, The Future of International Law and American Foreign Policy, 1989, The Bosnian People Charge Genocide, 1996, Foundations of World Order, 1999, The Criminality of Nuclear Deterrence, 2002, Palestine, Palestinians and International Law, 2003; contbr. articles to profl. jours. Mem. bur. polit.-mil. affairs (scholar-diplomat program) U.S. Dept. State, 1981; bd. dirs., coordinating coun. Lawyers Com. on Nuclear Policy, 1981—; cons. Amnesty Internat., 1983—; chmn., panel of jurists IPO Brussels Tribunal on Reagan Adminstrns. Fgn. Policy, 1984; advisor Coun. for Responsible Genetics, 1985—; cons. UN Com. on the Exercise of the Inalienable Rights of the Palestinian People, 1987—; bd. dirs. Amnesty Internat. USA, 1988-92; gen .agent Republic of Bosnia and Herzegovina Internat. Ct. Justice with E&P Powers, 1993-94. Mem. Am. Soc. Internat. Law (ad hoc guidelines com. 1978-80, Lieber group on laws of war 1979—), Phi Beta Kappa, Sigma Xi (award and prize in biology). Office: U Ill Coll Law 504 E Pennsylvania Ave Champaign IL 61820-6909 Business E-Mail: fboyle@law.uiuc.edu.

BOYLE, JOHN EDWARD WHITEFORD, cultural organization administrator; b. Milw., Mar. 8, 1915; s. Herman Edward and Margaret Lauretta (Casey) B.; m. Renée Colin Kent, Feb. 2, 1950; children: Vanessa Whiteford Wayne, Christopher Whiteford, Andrea Heller, Alexandra Whiteford. PhB, Marquette U., 1937; postgrad., Harvard U., 1946-47, Inst. Franco-Iranien, 1959-60, U. Tehran, 1960-62, George Washington U., Georgetown U., UCLA; Doctorandus Lettres et Arts Persanes, Jungian Inst., Zurich, Switzerland, 1997. Journalist Hearst Mags., N.Y.C., 1937, WISN, Milw., 1937-38, Milw. Jour., 1938-40; exec. CIA, Washington, L.A., Frankfurt am Main, Germany, 1947-58, Washington, 1964-67; dir. Am. Friends of the Middle East, Tehran, 1958-62, 1962-64, Whiteford Internat. Enterprise, Switzerland, 1967-72, 1972-74; fgn. corr. mag. Viewpoints, 1962-64, Middle East Mag., Beirut, Lebanon, 1963; pres. Fgn. Svcs. Rsch. Inst./Wheat Forders (press), Washington, 1974-99, pres. emeritus, 1999—, Internat. Acad. Ind. Schs. Cons. to embassies on edn., 1974—; cons. on edn. Shah of Iran, 1958-62; prof. Nat. U. Iran, 1960-62; co-founder in cooperation with Ministry of Ct., Iran. Author: Primers for the Age of Inner Space: I-Beyond the Present Prospect, 1977, II-The Indra Web, 1983, III-Graffiti on the Wall of Time (poetry), 1983, IV-Of the Same Root: Heaven, Earth and I, 1990, V-The Way of the Essentialist: Contra Sartres Existentialism, 1993, VI-The Unperceived Revolution: Cracking the Code of the Ultimate Enigma, 1997; VII-Structuring Private Spirituality: Essentialism*A Philosophy of the Presence, 2000. Campaign mgr. Roosevelt for Pres., No. Wis., 1940, John F. Kennedy for Pres., Iran, 1960; mem. Fulbright Commn., 1959-62; bd. dirs. Iran-Am. Soc., 1960-62, Pahlavi Found., Iran, 1959-62, Washington Humane Soc.; vol. Dem. Nat. Com., 1982. Served with USAAF, 1940-45. Recipient Prix Teilhard/Londres, 1982-83, Silver Poet award World of Poetry, 1990, Golden Poet award, 1992, Outstanding Alumni Scholar award Marquette U., 1991, 97, Editor's Choice award for Outstanding Achievemnt in Poetry Nat. Libr. Poetry, 1993. Mem. Acad. Ind. Scholars (pres.), Expt. in Internat. Living (hon. life), Essentialist Philos. Soc. (pres. 1991—), Homer Hon. Soc. Internat. Poets. Mem. Soc. Of Friends. Home: 340 Eastern Promenade Apt 158 Portland ME 04101-2785

BOYLE, JOHN ROBERT, internist; b. Mass., Feb. 28, 1951; BA, Ohio State U., 1973, MD, 1976. Diplomate Am. Bd. Internal Medicine. Intern, resident Ind. U., Indpls., 1976-79; internist Miami Valley Assocs. Internal Medicine, Dayton, Ohio, 1979—. Mem. AMA, Ohio State Assn., Dayton Soc. Internal Medicine, Alpha Omega Alpha. Roman Catholic. Home: 738 Stanbridge Dr Dayton OH 45429-1330

BOYLE, KAMMER, estate planner, financial analyst; b. New Orleans, June 17, 1946; d. Benjamin Franklin and Ethel Clair (Kammer) B.; m. Edward Turner Barfield, July 23, 1966 (div. 1975); children: Darren Barfield, Meloe Barfield. BS in Mgmt. magna cum laude, U. West Fla., 1976; PhD in Indsl./Organizational Psychology, U. Tenn., 1982. Lic. psychologist, Ohio, Tenn.; reg. securities rep. InterSecurities, Inc., Nat Assn. Securities Dealers. Pvt. practice mgmt. psychology, Knoxville, 1978-81; tchg. and rsch. asst. U. Tenn., Knoxville, 1977-81; mgmt. trainer U.S. State Dept., Washington, 1978; cons. PRADCO, Cleve., 1982-83; pres., cons. Mgmt. and Assessment Svcs., Inc., Cleve., 1983-90; pres. Kammer Investment Co., Cleve., 1989-96; fin. advisor O'Donnell Securities Corp., Cleve., 1997-98. Registered securities prin., investment advisor rep. and retirement specialist Wealth Charter Group of InterSecurities, Inc., 1998-. Mem. editl. rev. bd. Jour. of Managerial Issues, 1987; author and presenter ann. Conf. APA, 1980, Southeastern Psychol. Conf., 1979, ann. Conf. Soc. Indsl./Orgnl. Psychologists, 1987, ann. conf. Am. Soc. Tng. and Devel., 1988. Mem. Jr. League Am., Pensacola, Fla., 1970-75; treas. Bar Aux., Pensacola, 1971. Recipient Capital Gifts Stipend U. Tenn., 1976-80; Walter Bonham fellow, 1980-81. Mem. APA, Cleve. Psychol. Assn., Orgn. Devel. Inst., Acad. of Mgmt., Soc. Advancement Mgmt. (pres. 1974-75), Am. Soc. Tng. and Devel. (chpt. rep. career devel. 1984-86), Cleve. Psychol. Assn. (bd. dirs. 1987-88), Real Estate Investor's Assn. (Cleve., trustee/sec. 1992-94), Mensa. Office: Wealth Charter Group Ste 200 6100 Oak Tree Blvd Independence OH 44131

BOYLE, KEVIN GERARD, historian, educator; b. Detroit, Oct. 7, 1960; s. Kevin C. and Anne Boyle; m. Victoria Lynn Getis, Jan. 4, 1992; children: Abigail Grace, Hannah Claire. BA, U. Detroit, 1982; PhD, U. Mich., 1990. Asst. prof. history U. Toledo, 1990—94; asst./assoc. prof. history U. Mass., Amherst, 1994—2002; assoc. prof. history Ohio State U., Columbus, 2002—. Author: (history) The UAW and the Heyday of American Liberalism, 1945-1968, 1995; co-author: Muddy Boots and Ragged Aprons: Images of Working-Class Detroit, 1900-1930, 1997; editor: Organized Labor and American Politics, 1894-1994: The Labor-Liberal Alliance, 1998. Fellow, Rockefeller Found., 1990—91, Mary Ball Wash. Chair in Am. History, J. William Fulbright Found., 1997—98, Am. Coun. Learned Socs., 2001—02, NEH, 2001—02, John Simon Guggenheim Found., 2001—02. Home: 173 N Stanwood Rd Bexley OH 43209 Office: Ohio State Univ Dept History Dulles Hall Columbus OH 43210

BOYLE, KEVIN JOHN, economics educator, consultant; b. Montgomery, Ala., Sept. 15, 1955; s. John Farley and Eliane Ruth (Keaney) B.; m. Nancy Jean Becraft, June 12, 1983; children: Lindsey Jean, Grady John. BA in Econs., U. Maine, 1978; MS in Econs., Oreg. State U., 1981; PhD in Econs., U. Wis., 1985. Rsch. asst. Oreg. State U., Corvallis, 1979—80; economist U.S. Forest Svc., Corvallis, 1981; rsch. asst. U. Wis., Madison, 1982—85, rsch. assoc., 1985—86; asst. prof. econs. U. Maine, Orono, 1986-91, assoc. prof., 1991-97, Libra prof. environ. econ., 1997—2002, chair dept. econs., 2003—, disting. prof., 2003—. Faculty assoc. Ctr. for Econs., Rsch. Triangle Inst., 1992-94; pres. regional project benefits and costs in natural resource planning USDA, 1988-89; vis. scientist Rocky Mt. Rsch. Sta., U.S. Forest Svc., 1999-2000; adj. prof. dept. econs. Andrew Young Sch. Pub. Policy, Ga. State U., 1999. Assoc. editor Jour. Environ. Econs. and Mgmt., 1995-99, Marine Rsch. Econs., 1996-98. Fish and Wildlife Svc. grantee, 1989—, Oak Ridge Nat. Labs. grantee, 1989-90, Exxon, USA grantee, 1989-92, Maine Dept. Inland Fisheries and Wildlife grantee, 1994—, Bangor Hydro-Electric Co. grantee, 1991-93, EPA, 1993-94, Econ. Rsch. Svc. grantee USDA, 1995—; recipient Merit cert. USDA, 1981, Outstanding Rsch. award Coll. Natural Scis. Forestry and Agr., U. Maine, 1999, Presdl. Rsch. and Creative Achievement award U. Maine, 2001. Mem. Am. Econ. Assn., Nat. Rsch. Coun. (com. on valuation of aquatic and related terrestrial ecosystem), Am. Agrl. Econs. Assn., Assn. Environ. and Resource Economists, Northeastern Agrl. and Resource Econs. Assn. (bd. dirs. 1993-96, pres. 1998-2000). Avocations: running, biking, canoeing, reading. Home: 322 Main Rd S Hampden ME 04444-1103 Office: U Maine Econs Dept Winslow Hall Orono ME 04469

BOYLE, LARA FLYNN, actress; b. Davenport, IA, Mar. 24, 1970; Actress: appeared in films made for TV and for movie house distbn.: Amerika, 1987, Poltergeist III, 1988, Terror on Highway 91, 1989, How I Got into College, 1989, The Preppie Murder, 1989, The Rookie, 1990, Mobsters, 1991, Wayne's World, 1992, Where the Day Takes You, 1992, The Temp., 1993, Three of Hearts, 1993, Red Rock West, 1993, Threesome, 1994, Baby's Day Out, 1994, The Road to Wellville, 1994, Three IFS and a Maybe, 1996, Dogwater, 1997, Twin Peaks, 1989, Dead Poets Society, 1989, Men in Black II, 2002; TV appearances include The Practice, 1997-; host Saturday Night Live, 2001. Office: Internat Creative Mgmt c/o Chris Andrews 8942 Wilshire Blvd Beverly Hills CA 90211-1934*

BOYLE, LESTER JOSEPH, marketing and broadcast executive; b. Stamford, Conn., Sept. 1, 1933; s. Lester J. and Mary Katherine (Flanagan) B.; m. Mary Lou Abernethy, June 22, 1957; children: Lester Joseph, Katherine Margaret. BSBA, U. Conn., 1959. Mgr. of advt., mktg. rsch. Getty Oil Co., N.Y.C., Tulsa, 1959-84; mgr. advt., sales promotion Texaco, U.S.A., Houston, 1984-85; exec. v.p. J.L. Media, Inc., Tulsa and Union, N.J., 1985—. Bd. dirs. Doctors Med. Ctr., Tulsa, 1980—; guest lectr. in field. Bd. dirs. ARC, Tulsa, 1980—; pres. bd. dirs. Roy Clark Charity Golf, Tulsa, 1979-84. With U.S. Army, 1952-54. Recipient Disting. Alumnus award U. Conn., 1985. Mem. Am. Mktg. Assn., Am. Advt. Fedn. (v.p. 1981-83, recipient Silver Addy award 1984), Broadcast Execs. of Tulsa (hon. life), Okla. Assn. of Broadcasters. Republican. Home: 4923 E 75th St Tulsa OK 74136-8212 Office: JL Media Inc 401 S Boston Ave Tulsa OK 74103-4016 E-mail: mail@jlmedia.tul.com.

BOYLE, LISA C. marketing and communications executive; m. Kenneth J. Boyle. BA in Social Studies magna cum laude, Montclair State Coll., 1978. Cert. K-12 tchr., N.J. Adminstrv. asst. Scholastic Inc., N.Y.C., 1978, ops.-mktg. mgr., 1978—86; acct. exec. Mokrynski and Assocs. Inc., Creskill, N.J., 1986, Alvin Zeller, Inc., N.Y.C., 1986-87; sr. acct. exec. Am. List Counsel, Princeton, N.J., 1987-90; with Phillips Pub., Potomac, Md., 1990-91; sr. planner Craver Mathews Smith & Co., Falls Church, Va., 1991-94; founder, pres., CEO, Am. Mktg. and Comm. Corp., Frederick, Md., 1994—; founder, pres. Classic Entertainment, 2002—. Cons. direct mail Lisa C. Boyle, Elmwood Park and Howell, N.J., 1986-90, Boyle Group, Germantown, Md., 1990-94; chmn. bd. dirs. Fields for the Future, Inc.; founder, pres., CEO Am. Mktg. d Comm. Corp., 1994—; spkr. in field. Contbr. articles to profl. jours. Polit. campaign organizer Candidate Sch. Bd., Fair Lawn, N.J., 1976; chmn. bd. dirs. People's Network, Inc., 1999—; chmn. bd. dirs. Fields for the Future Inc., 2002-. Mem. Direct Mktg. Assn. Washington (founder, pres. FR coun. 1990-92, plaque 1994, super mem. 1998), Direct Mktg. Assn., Direct Mktg. Assn. N.J. (founder, pres. 1987-89). Office: Am Mktg Comm Corp Ste B 61 Thomas Johnson Dr Frederick MD 21702

BOYLE, MARYLOU OLSEN, nursing administrator; b. Butte, Mont., Aug. 8, 1937; d. Paul Bogvang and Rose Patricia Olsen; m. John Anthony Boyle, July 8, 1978 (dec. Apr. 2000). Diploma, Sacred Heart Sch. Nursing, Spokane, Wash., 1958; BSN, U. Wash., 1969, MA Nursing, 1971; MS in Counseling Psychology, Pepperdine U., Quantico, Va., 1978. Dir. perioperative nursing Alexandria (Va.) Hosp., 1982-87; dir. surg. svcs. Arroyo Grande (Calif.) Community Hosp., 1987-89; DON Cottage Care Ctr., Santa Barbara, Calif., 1989-90, Marian Extended Care Ctr., Santa Maria, Calif., 1990-91; crisis intervention specialist, psychiat. assessment team Vista Del Mar Hosp., 1992-97; nurse CDR USNR, 1972—93. Tchr. religious edn. St. Mary's Assumption Ch. Mem. Assn. Oper. Rm. Nurses (past pres. Coastal Valley chpt. and No. Va. chpt.), Naval Res. Assn. (life), The Ret. Officers Assn. (life), Marine Corps Assn. (life), U. Wash. Alumni Assn. (life).

BOYLE, MICHAEL FABIAN, lawyer; b. Lynwood, Calif., Apr. 11, 1949; s. Erwin Francis Boyle and Phanelphia (Gibson) Brunkow; 1 child, Conor Francis; m. Judy Pettigrew, May 14, 1986. B.A., San Diego State U., 1972; J.D., U. Calif., 1975. Bar: Calif. 1975, U.S. Dist. Ct. (no. dist.) Calif. 1975. Assoc. Connolley, Hothem & Flint, San Francisco, 1975-77; ptnr. Higgs, Flectcher & Mack, San Diego, 1978— , Deans adv. com. Coll. Art & Letters, 2002—. Contbr. articles to profl. jours. Bd. dirs. San Diego Hospice Corp. Bd., 1989-91, mem. The Mayor and City Coun. Citizens Fin. Com., 1990. Capt. USAR, 1971-82. Mem. ABA, Calif. Bar Assn., San Diego County Bar Assn. (chmn. ins. com.), San Diego State Univ. Alumni Assn. (officer, bd. dirs. 1984-89), Construction Fin. Mgnt. Assn. (officer, bd. dirs. 1986-92), San Diego County Taxpayers Assn. (officer, bd. dirs. 1997) Democrat. Roman Catholic. Home: 13482 Caminito Carmel Del Mar CA 92014-3847 Office: Higgs Fletcher & Mack 401 W A St Ste 2600 San Diego CA 92101-7913 Business E-Mail: boylem@higgslaw.com.

BOYLE, MICHAEL FREDERICK, retired television producer, actor; b. Salem, Mass., Mar. 20, 1938; s. Francis Xavier Boyle and Marion Rose (McGannon) McGannon-Boyle; m. Linda Lou Ruff, June 3, 1960 (div. 1974); children: Audrey, Brian. Student, Fordham U., 1956—58. News and program dir. Radio Sta. KFM, Denver, 1961—71; program dir., host Radio Sta. KBUZ, Phoenix, 1971—75; news dir., host Radio Sta. WOI, Ames, Iowa, 1975—79; program host, prodr. Pub. TV Sta. KTCA, Mpls., 1979—81; prodr., reporter TV Sta. KSTP-TV, Mpls., 1981—85; arts prodr. TV Sta. KUAT-TV, Tucson, 1985—97; ret., 1997. Dir. theatre program Denver Model Cities, 1971. Author: That, 1966; actor: numerous theatre companies. Founding mem. Colo. Coun. Arts & Humanities, Denver, 1969. Avocations: writing, reading, music. Home: 3323 E 2d St Tucson AZ 85716

BOYLE, PATRICK KEVIN, journalist; b. Bklyn., July 14, 1959; s. Kenneth and Lola B. BA in Comm. Arts magna cum laude, U. Dayton, 1981. From reporter to mng. editor Bridgehampton (N.Y.) Sun, 1981-83; reporter Watertown (N.Y.) Daily Times, 1984; metro reporter N.Y.C. Tribune, 1984-86; metro reporter, desk editor Washington Times, 1986-92; freelance journalist, sr. editor Car & Travel Mag., 1994-98; editor Youth Today, 1998—; columnist A Father's Place, 2000—. Cons. for one Day One segment, ABC News, 1993; spokesman Am. Automobile Assn., 1994-98. Author: Scouts Honor, 1994. Recipient 3d Place award for Humorous Commentary, L.I. Press Club, 1998, 1st Place award for series Md.-Del.-D.C. Press Assn., 1991, 3d Place award Nat. Headliner Awards, 1991, 1st place award for spot news coverage Soc. Profl. Journalists, 1991, 3d Place award for investigative reporting Nat. Newspaper Assn., 1988, 3d place award for column writing N.Y. Press Assn., 1981, 1st place Opinion, L.I. Press Club, 2001, Bronze award Soc. Bus. Publ. Editors, 2003, others. Office: Youth Today 1200 17th St NW Washington DC 20036-3006

BOYLE, PATRICK OTTO, lawyer; b. St. Louis, Nov. 15, 1935; s. Otto William and Wilma Louise (Bowers) B.; m. Jane Adeline Roberts, Nov. 22, 1966; children— Laura Jane, Daniel Patrick. B.S.B.A., Washington U., 1957, J.D., 1960. Bar: Mo. 1960, Ill., 1970. Assoc. firm Lucas & Murphy, St. Louis, 1963-67; assoc. counsel Interco Inc., St. Louis, 1967-69; counsel Energy Systems divsn. Olin Corp., East Alton, Ill., 1969-74; assoc. Winchester Group Counsel, 1974-77; asst. sec., 1970-77; ptnr. Boyle & Stillwell, East Alton, 1977-80; sole practice, St. Louis and E. Alton, 1980—2001; mgr. The Boyle Law Firm, LLC, 2002--. Bd. dirs. Ferguson-Florissant Sch. Bd., 1981-96. Served to comdr. USCGR, 1960-82. Mem. Mo. Bar Assn., Ill. Bar Assn., Madison County Bar Assn., Metro. Bar St. Louis, Beta Gamma Sigma. Club: Mo. Athletic. Office: 755 Rue Saint Francois Florissant MO 63031-4921 Home: 3715 Greengrass Dr Florissant MO 63033-6634

BOYLE, PETER, actor; b. Phila., Oct. 18, 1935; m. Loraine Alterman, Oct. 1977. Ed., LaSalle Coll., Phila. Monk in Christian Bros. order, until early 1960's. Actor in Off-Broadway shows, N.Y.C., also Second City group, Chgo., and TV commls.; appeared in films including Medium Cool, 1969, Joe, 1970, Diary of a Mad Housewife, 1970, T.R. Baskin, 1972, The Candidate, 1972, Steelyard Blues, 1973, Slither, 1973, The Friends of Eddie Coyle, 1973, Kid Blue, 1973, Crazy Joe, 1974, Young Frankenstein, 1974, Taxi Driver, 1976, Swashbuckler, 1976, F.I.S.T. 1978, The Brink's Job, 1978, Hardcore, 1979, Beyond the Poseidon Adventure, 1979, In God We Trust, 1980, Where the Buffalo Roam, 1980, Hammett, 1980, Outland, 1981, Yellowbeard, 1983, Johnny Dangerously, 1984, Turk 182, 1985, Surrender, 1987, Walker, 1987, The In Crowd, 1988, Speedzone, 1989, Funny, 1989, The Dream Team, 1989, Men of Respect, 1991, Kickboxer 2, 1991, Honeymoon in Vegas, 1992, Malcolm X, 1992, The Shadow, 1994, The Killer, 1994, Exquisit Tenderness, 1994, The Santa Clause, 1994, Katie, 1995, While You Were Sleeping, 1995, Death and Compass, 1996, Final Vendetta, 1996, That Darn Cat, 1997, Milk and Money, 1997, Species II, 1998, Dr. Doolittle, 1998, Species 2, 1998; (TV movies) Tail Gunner Joe, 1977, From Here to Eternity, In the Lake of the Woods, 1996, A Deadly Vision, 1997, That Darn Cat, 1997; (TV series) Joe Bash, 1986, Comedy Tonight, 1970, Everybody Loves Raymond, 1996— (nominee Outstanding Supporting Actor in Comedy Series Emmy award 1999-2001, nominee Funniest Supporting Male Performer in TV Series Am. Comedy award 2000); TV guest appearances include NYPD Blue, Lois & Clark: The New Adventures of Superman, The X Files, The Single Guy, Cosby, The King of Queens, Tribeca, others. Recipient Emmy award, 1996. Office: Everybody Loves Raymond c/o CBS/MTM Studios 4020 N Radford Ave Studio City CA 91604

BOYLE, R. EMMETT, metal products executive; b. 1937; BS in Engring., MS in Engring. With Kaiser Aluminum Corp., Oakland, Calif., 1965—85; pres. Ravenswood (W.Va.) Aluminum Corp., 1989—92; chmn. Ormet Corp., Wheeling, W.Va., 1990—.

BOYLE, RICHARD EDWARD, lawyer; b. Westville, Ill., Mar. 27, 1937; s. Kelley George and Florence (Weisert) B.; m. Janet E. Peskar, Nov. 22, 1968; children: Kevin, Douglas, Leslie. BA, U. Ill., 1959, LLB, 1961. Bar: Ill. 1962, Mo. 1985, U.S. Dist. Ct. (so. dist.) Ill. 1962, U.S. Dist. Ct. (cen. dist.) Ill. 1962, U.S. Dist. Ct. (ea. dist.) Mo. 1991, U.S. Ct. Appeals (7th cir.) 1975, U.S. Supreme Ct. 1985. Assoc. Costello, Wiechert, Roberts & Gundlach, 1962-68; ptnr. Gundlach, Lee, Eggmann, Boyle & Roessler, Belleville, Ill., 1968—. With USAFR. Fellow Am. Coll. Trial Lawyers, Am. Bar Found. (mem. Adv. Group Civil Justice Reform Act 1990—); mem. Nat. Assn. R.R. Trial Counsel (pres. 1991-92), St. Clair County Bar Assn. (pres. 1979-80). Home: 13 Oak Knoll Pl Belleville IL 62223-1817 Office: Gundlach Lee Eggmann Boyle & Roessler Box 23560 5000 W Main St Belleville IL 62226-4727

BOYLE, RICHARD JAMES, banker; b. Bklyn., Dec. 4, 1943; s. James F. and Marie E. Boule; m. Denise T. Burke, Feb. 21, 1944; children: Ann Marie, Richard J. BA, Holy Cross Coll., 1965; MBA in Bus. Fin., NYU, 1969. V.p. Bank of Commonwealth, Detroit, 1971-72; vice pres. Chase Manhattan Bank, N.Y.C, 1971-75, sr. v.p., 1975-84, exec. v.p., 1984-87, vice-chmn. global banking, 1987-90, chief credit and investment officer, 1990-96; ret., 1996. Bd. dirs. Foundling Hosp., St. Vincents Hosps. Recipient Humanitarian award Nat. Jewish Hosp., Denver, 1978, Man of Yr., Cystic Fibrosis Found., N.Y., 1975 Mem.: Beacon Hill (Summit), Baltusrol Golf (Springfield). Republican. Roman Catholic.

BOYLE, ROBERT DANIEL, information technology executive; b. Havre de Grace, Md., June 27, 1965; s. Vincent Michael Sr. and Margaret Kathleen (Helton) B. BS, U. Md., 1987; MBA, Loyola Coll., Balt., 1989, MS in Fin., 1990. CPA, cert. mgmt. acct., cert. fellow in prodn. and inventory mgmt., cert. integrated resource mgmt., cert. mgmt. cons. Pres. Sunquest of Md., Inc., Aberdeen, Md., 1985-88; adj. prof. Loyola Coll., Balt., 1989-90; rsch. fellow David D. Lattanze Ctr., Balt., 1989-92; prin. Sandlot Strategists, Balt., 1989-91; cons. Anderson Cons., Tampa, 1991-92; mgr. Deloitte Cons., Atlanta, 1992-96; sr. prin. Diamond Technology Ptnrs., Inc., Chgo., 1996-99; COO CarrierPoint, Inc., Atlanta, 1999—2001; dir. New Ventures, Deere & Co., Roswell, Ga., 2001—. Cons., speaker in field. Contbr. articles to profl. publs. David D. Lattanze Ctr. fellow, 1989-92. Mem. Am. Prodn. and Inventory Control Soc., Inst. Cert. Mgmt. Accts., Inst. Cert. Mgmt. Cons., Mensa, Phi Theta Kappa, Alpha Sigma Lambda, Phi Kappa Phi, Alpha Sigma Nu, Beta Gamma Sigma. Avocations: reading, movies, fitness, travel, target shooting. Home: 5020 Ridge Oak Walk SE Mableton GA 30126-5922

BOYLE, SUSAN JEAN HIGLE, social studies educator; b. Tarrytown, N.Y., June 15, 1956; d. George Edward and Barbara Jean (Deverill) Higle. BA in Psychology, Elem. Edn., Ladycliff Coll., 1978; MS in Learning Disabilities, Fordham U., 1980; EdS in Ednl. Leadership, Stetson U., 1988. Cert. tchr. Fla., social studies tchr. Fla. Tchr. St. Ursula Sch., Mt. Vernon, N.Y., 1978-81, Blue Lake Elem. Sch., DeLand, Fla., 1982-86, Deltona (Fla.) Lakes Elem., 1986-88, Discovery Elem. Sch., Deltona, 1988-89, Tomoka Elem. Sch., Ormond Beach, Fla., 1989-90, Ormond Beach Mid. Sch., 1990—. Eucharistic minister St. Brendan Ch. Named Tchr. of the Quarter, C. of C., Fall 2000, OBMS Tchr. of Yr., 2003; TOPS grantee, 1985, 86, CITE grantee, 2001, Bright Ideas in Newspapers in Edn. grantee, 2001. Mem. Phi Delta Kappa. Avocations: reading, collecting boyd's bears. Office: Ormond Beach Mid Sch 151 Domicilio Ave Ormond Beach FL 32174-3918

BOYLE, TATIANA GENNADIEVNA, research scientist; b. Khabarovsk, Russia, June 15, 1969; arrived in U.S., 1995; d. Gennadyi Petrovich Sapozhnikov and Tamara Mikhailovna Sapozhnikova; m. David Edward Boyle, Nov. 29, 1997; 1 child, Austin Michael. MS in Biology and Chemistry, Khabarovsk State U., 1991; PhD in Biology, Russian Acad. Scis., Ecology Rsch. Inst., Khabarovsk, 1995. Sr. scientist Russian Acad. Scis., Khabarovsk, 1991—99; rsch. scientist USDA Forest Svc., Sitka, Alaska, 1997—98; sr. scientist North Pacific Flora Rsch., Portland, Oreg., 1997—. Scientist Tahoe-Baikal Inst., Lake Tahoe, Calif., 1995—97; sr. project advisor Sustainable Ecosystems Inst., Portland, Oreg., 1999—2001. Author: Rare Plants of Khabarovsk Region, 1998; author, editor: tv program Path in the Forest, 1998. Active New Parents Group, Portland, 2002—. Mem.: Am. Inst. Biol. Scis. Achievements include research in new species habitats in Siberia and Alaska; new classification for rare plants species. Avocations: skiing, photography, ink drawing, writing, chess.

BOYLE, WILLARD STERLING, physicist, researcher; b. Amherst, N.S., Can., Aug. 19, 1924; naturalized, 1969; s. Ernest Sterling and Bernice Teresa (Dewar) B.; m. Elizabeth Joyce, June 15, 1946; children— Robert, Cynthia, David, Pamela. B.Sc., McGill U., Montreal, Que., Can., 1947, M.Sc., 1948, PhD, 1950; LL.D. (hon.), Dalhousie U.; DSc (hon.), UHBSJ. Asst. prof. Royal Mil. Coll., Kingston, Ont., 1951-53; mem. staff Bell Labs., 1953-62, 64-79, exec. dir. semiconductor device devel. div., 1968-75, exec. dir. communications scis. div., 1975-79. Dir. space sci. Bellcommunications, 1962-64 Author, patentee in field; co-inventor charge coupled device and 1st continuously pumped ruby laser. Served with Canadian Navy, 1942-45. Recipient Ballantine medal Franklin Inst., Progress medal Photog. Soc. Am., 1986, Computing and Comms. Found. prize, Tokyo; Nat. Research Council Can. fellow, 1949 Fellow IEEE (Morris Liebman medal 1974, Breakthrough award Device Rsch. Conf. 1999), Am. Phys. Soc.; mem. Nat. Acad. Engring., Soc. Sci. and Tech. (Edwin Land medal 2001). Address: Wallace NS Canada B0K 1Y0

BOYLE, WILLIAM CHARLES, civil engineering educator; b. Mpls., Apr. 9, 1936; s. Robert William and Daphne Jennette (Connell) B.; m. Nancy Lee Hahn, Apr. 11, 1959; children: Elizabeth Lynn, Michele Jenette, Jane Lynette, Robert William. CE, U. Cin., 1959, MS in Sanitary Engring., 1960; PhD in Environ. Engring., Calif. Inst. Tech., 1963. Registered profl. engr., Wis., Ohio. With Milw. Sewerage Commn., 1955-56; civil engr. O. G. Loomis & Sons, Covington, Ky., 1956-59; asst. engr. Ohio River Valley Water Sanitation Commn., summer 1959; asst. prof. dept. engring. U. Wis., Madison, 1963-66, assoc. prof., 1966-70, prof. dept. civil and environ. engring., 1970-96, chmn. dept. civil and environ. engring., 1984-86, assoc. chair, 1988-96, emeritus prof., 1996—. Vis. prof. Rogaland Distriktshogskole, Stavanger, Norway, 1975-76; vis. prin. engr. Montgomery Engrs. Inc., Pasadena, Calif., 1988-89; cons. Procter & Gamble Co., Monsanto Co., S.B. Foot Tanning Co., Wis. Canners & Freezers Assn., Wis. Concrete Pipe Assn., Oscar Mayer & Co., Bartlett-Snow, Hide Service Corp., W.R. Grace & Co., Lake to Lake Dairies, Milw. Tallow, Wausau Paper Co., Packerland Packing Co., Ray-O-Vac, U.S. Army CERL, Owen Ayres & Assocs., Donohue Engrs., Davy Engrs., Carl C. Crane, Green Engring., RSE div. Ayres & Assocs., Schreiber Corp. Inc., Sanitaire, J.M. Montgomery, Engrs., Polkowski, Boyle, & Assocs., Rust E&I; mem. peer rev. panel on environ. engring. EPA; accreditation visitor Accreditation Bd. for Engring. and Tech., 1990—. Contbr. articles to profl. jours. Sr. warden St. Andrews Episcopal Ch., Madison, 1972-74, treas., 1979-85 Recipient Engring. Disting. Alumnus award U. Cin., 1986, Founders award U.S.A. nat. com. Internat. Assn. Water Pollution Rsch. & Control, 1988, commendation EPA, 1989; Mills Found. scholar U. Cin., 1954-59; USPHS trainee, U. Cin., 1959-60; fellow Ford Found., Calif. Inst. Tech., 1960-61, USPHS, Calif. Inst. Tech., 1961-63 Mem. ASCE (life, Wis. chpt., advisor U. Wis. student chpt. 1968-71, chmn. student affairs com. 1970-72, chmn. profl. activities com. 1972-74, nat., control mem. tech. council on codes and standards-environ. standards 1999—, chmn. environ. stds. devel. cou. 1998-2001; chair oxygen transfer standards com., 1975-2002, mem. history and heritage com., reviewer EED Jour., Rudolf Hering medal 1975, Engring. Achievement award from Wis. chpt. 1986, Engr. of Yr. award Wis. sect. 1998), Water Environment Fedn. (life, research com., joint task force-pretreatment of wastewater, tech. practice com.-energy in treatment plant design, author chpt. Manual of Practice Design Wastewater Treatment Plants, author chpt. Ops. Manual on Activated Sludge, chmn. program com., bd. control, 1996-98, jour. reviewer, chmn. tech. practice com. task force on aeration, Radebaugh award 1978, Eddy award com. 1992-98, Harrison Prescot Eddy Rsch. medal 1989, chmn. rsch. symposia, Gordon Maskew Fair medal for environ. engring. edn., 1992, Arthur Sydney Bedell award 2001), Am. Water Works Assn. (life, chmn. task group on oxygen transfer, editl. bd.), Am. Acad. Environ. Engrs. (diplomate, life, accreditation vis. for Accreditation Bd. Engring and Tech., chmn. edn. com. 1993, trustee 1994-97, pres.-elect 1998, pres. 1999-2000, rep. bd. dirs. ABET, 1994-2000, commr. Engr. Accreditation comm. 2001-, Stanley E. Kappe award 2002), Am. Foundrymen's Soc. (com. on waste disposal, Outstanding Rsch. Paper award environ. cen. div. 1989), Sigma Xi, Theta Tau, Phi Eta Sigma, Chi Epsilon, Tau Beta Pi (advisor U. Wis. student chpt. 1994-96). Episcopalian. Avocations: photography, travel. Home: 105 Carillon Dr Madison WI 53705-4614 Office: Univ Wis 2256 Engineering Hall 1415 Engineering Dr Madison WI 53706-1607 E-mail: boyle@engr.wisc.edu.

BOYLE, WILLIAM LEO, JR., educational consultant, retired college president; b. Utica, N.Y., July 23, 1933; s. William Leo and Gladys (Kuney) B. AB, Colgate U., 1955; postgrad., Cornell U. Law Sch., 1960—61; MA, Columbia U., 1964, Profl. Diploma in Ednl. Adminstrn., 1967, EdD, 1969; LLD (hon.), Hawthorne Coll., 1979; postdoctoral, Harvard U., 1979—81; LHD (hon.), Mercy Coll., 1983; LittD (hon.), Curry Coll., 1992. Participant advanced mgmt. program, recruiter, ednl. adviser Procter & Gamble Co., Cin., 1958-60; legis. aide higher edn. com. N.Y. State Senate, Albany, 1961-62; account exec., ednl. cons. Batten, Barton, Durstine & Osborn, N.Y.C., 1962-64; assoc. dir. devel., presdl. asst. Wesleyan U., Middletown, Conn., 1964-65; program cons. Coun. for Aid to Edn., N.Y.C., 1965-70, asst. v.p., 1970-72, v.p., 1972-75; pres. Keuka Coll., Keuka Pk., NY, 1975—78, Curry Coll., Milton, Mass., 1978—92, pres. emeritus, 1992—; part-time practice as ednl. cons. to pvt. colls. and univs., Utica, 1992—. Author: The National Corporate Educational Support Movement, 1954-1966, 1969; contbr. articles to ednl. and profl. jours. Ednl. cons. to Pres. Ford Com., Washington, 1976; vice chmn. nat. bus. and industry com. Colgate U., Hamilton, NY, 1974—, mem. nat. coun., 1975—, ann. fund exec. com., 1975—, Colgate '55 class agt., 1994—, mem. maj. gifts com., established Boyle Scholarship, 1985, Boyle award in polit. sci., 1997; pres., trustee 1036 Park Ave. Corp., N.Y.C., 1970—74; mem. bd. devel. com. Cmty. Found., Utica, 1992—98; established Boyle Individual Fund, Cmty. Found., Utica, 1991, Boyle Parents Meml. Fund, Cmty. Found., Utica, 2002; bd. dirs. Slocum-Dickson Found., Utica, 1991—, Family Svcs. of the Mohawk Valley, Utica, 1992—, House of the Good Shepherd, Utica, 1992—, Oneida County Hist. Soc., Utica, 1994—. Lt. USAF, 1955—58. Decorated Comdr.'s citation USAF. Mem. various ednl. and profl. orgns., also Colgate Univ. Club (N.Y.C.), Columbia Univ. Club (N.Y.C.), Ft. Schuyler Club (Utica) (bd. mgrs.), Sadaquada Golf Club (Utica), Yahnundasis Golf Club (Utica), Rotary. Home: 12 Rose Pl Utica NY 13502-5614

BOYLES, FREDERICK HOLDREN, historian; b. Gainesville, Fla., Nov. 9, 1954; s. Eugene Harry and Frances Louise (Holdren) B.; m. Deborah Anne Beverly, Aug. 21, 1976; children: Cynthia Beverly, Joseph Holdren. A in Edn. and History, Abraham Baldwin Coll., 1974, BS in Edn. and History, U. Ga., 1976; M in Recreation and Parks Adminstrn., Clemson U., 1981. Dir. trail camp Goshen (Va.) Scout Camps, 1975-79; tchr. history and geography Waycross (Ga.) City Schs., 1976-78; instr. grad. students Clemson (S.C.) U., 1978-79; outdoor recreation planner Nat. Park Svc., Atlanta, 1979-81; historian Cumberland Gap Nat. Hist. Park, Middlesboro, Ky., 1981-85; supt. Moores Greek Nat. Battlefield, Currie, N.C., 1985-89, Andersonville (Ga.)-Jimmy Carter Nat. Hist. Sites, 1989—. Adj. faculty Lincoln Meml. U., Harrogate, Tenn., 1983-84, U. N.C., Wilmington, 1987, Scoutmaster troop 231 Boy Scouts Am., Americus, Ga., 1994; elder 1st Presbyn. Ch., Americus, 1991—. Comdr. USNR, 1987, comdg. officer navy cargo handling bn. 11, Jacksonville, Fla. Named Supt. of Yr., Nat. Pk. Svc., 1998; recipient Superior Achievement award, U.S. Dept. Interior, 1980, Good Citizenship award, SAR, 1989; scholar Grad. alumni scholar, Clemson U., 1979. Mem. Sumter C. of C. (bd. dirs. 1992—), Americus Rotary Club, Burgaw N.C. Rotary Club (bd. dirs. 1988, 90), Burgaw Area C. of C. (pres. 1989). Home: 200 Webber Rd Americus GA 31719-2136 Office: Nat Park Svc RR 1 Box 800 Andersonville GA 31711-9707 E-mail: fred_boyles@nps.gov.

BOYLES, HARLAN EDWARD, former state official; b. Lincoln County, N.C., May 6, 1929; s. Curtis E. and Kate S. B.; m. Frankie Wilder, May 17, 1952; children— Phyllis Godwin, Lynn Boyles Butler, Harlan Edward Jr. Student, U. Ga., 1947-48; BBA in Acctg, U. N.C., 1951. C.P.A., N.C. Corp. tax auditor N.C. Dept. Revenue, 1951-56; exec. sec., local govt. com. N.C. Tax Rev. Bd., 1956-76, dep. treas., 1960-76; treas. State of N.C., 1977-2001; ret. Mem. Council of State; mem. mcpl. securities rulemaking bd. SEC, 1975-77 Mem. adv. bd. Raleigh Salvation Army; chmn. Local Govt. Commn.; chmn. State Banking Commn., Tax Rev. Bd.; mem. State Bd. Edn., State Bd. Community Colls., N.C. Capital Planning Commn., others. Mem. N.C. Assn. CPAs, Nat. Assn. State Auditors, Comptrs. and Treas. (past pres., exec. dir.), Raleigh C. of C. (past bd. dirs.), N.C. State Employees Assn., N.C. Young Dems. Club, Execs. of Raleigh Club (past pres.), Rotary (past pres.). Democrat. Presbyterian (Deacon, Elder, Treas., Clk.). Home: 1924 Fairfield Dr Raleigh NC 27608-2720

BOYLES, JAMES KENNETH, retired banker; b. Louisville, Jan. 27, 1916; s. Forrest Lee and Florence (Glenn) B.; m. Hilda Margaret Rose, Sept. 13, 1940; children: Margaret, James, Douglas, Kevin. Student, Columbia U., Am. Inst. Banking, Rutgers U. With Guaranty Trust Co., N.Y.C., 1933-37; loan officer Chem. Bank, N.Y.C., 1937-50; exec. v.p. The Nat. State Bank, Elizabeth, N.J., 1950-83, dir., 1965-88. Trustee emeritus Union Coll., Cranford N.J. Served to 1st lt., inf., U.S. Army, 1942-46, ETO. Decorated 2 Bronze stars, Purple Heart. Mem. Robert Morris Assocs. (pres. 1963) Republican. Episcopalian.

BOYLES, S. KAY, pianist, music educator; b. Oklahoma City, Jan. 14, 1953; d. J. W. and Louise Boyles. MusB, U. Okla., 1976, MusM, 1977; postgrad., U. Colo., 1985. Instr. dept. continuing edn. U. Colo., Boulder, 1980-85; pianist Clark United Meth. Ch., Oklahoma City, 1985-95; piano tchr. pvt. studio Oklahoma City, 1985—; accompanist Oklahoma City U., 1991—; pianist Epworth United Meth. Ch., Oklahoma City, 1995—2000, N.W. Christian Ch., 2000—. Adjudicator Okla. Music Tcrhs. Assn. Auditions, 1996, 98; accompanist Canterbury Choral Soc. Children's Choirs, 2002. Musician (pianist): (musical theatre prodn) Forever Plaid, 1999, Annie Get Your Gun, 2000, Cotton Patch Gospel, 2001, Mozart Impresario, 2001, Working, 2003; musician: (handbells) (rec. artist (CD) Angels Singing/Nowells Ringing Canterbury Choral Soc., 1994. Mem.: Music Tchrs. Nat. Assn., Nat. Guild Piano Tchrs. (adjudicator 2000—, Paderewski medal 1971). Home: 3219 N Portland Ave Oklahoma City OK 73112-6734

BOYLES, WILLIAM ARCHER, lawyer; b. Lakeland, Fla., Aug. 16, 1951; s. Jesse V. and Louise B.; m. Laura M. Rose, June 12, 1977; children: William Archer Jr., John H. BSBA, U. Fla., 1973, JD, 1976, LLM in Taxation, 1978. CPA Fla.; bar: Fla. 1977, U.S. Tax Ct. 1978, U.S. Dist. Ct. (mid. dist.) Fla. 1979. Assoc. Gray, Harris & Robinson, P.A., Orlando, Fla., 1978-82, shareholder, 1982—. Mem. Cen. Fla. Estate Planning Coun. Bd. dirs. Christian Family Svcs., Inc., Gainesville, Fla., 1977-86, Ctrl. Fla. YMCA, Orlando, 1979-81; treas. Univ. Blvd. Ch. of Christ, Orlando, 1979-88; bd. dirs., treas. Orlando Shakespeare Festival, Inc., 1989-97, bd. dirs., 1992, 2d v.p., 1992-95; bd. dirs. Better Bus. Bur. Ctrl. Fla., 1994-02, chair-elect, exec. com. 1994, 95, chmn., 1996-97; chmn. Leadership Orlando, Leadership Fla.; mem. Planned Giving Coun. Ctrl. Fla. Mem. ABA, Fla. Bar (exec. coun. tax sect.), Orange County Bar Assn., AICPA, Fla. Inst. CPA's, Am. Assn. Atty.-CPA's, Small Bus. Coun. Am. (polit. action com.), Citrus Club. Republican. Office: Gray Harris & Robinson PA 301 E Pine St Ste 1400 Orlando FL 32801-2798

BOYLL, DAVID LLOYD, broadcasting company executive; b. Terre Haute, Ind., Aug. 17, 1940; s. Lloyd A. and Stella Elizabeth (Ellinger) B.; m. Margie R. Coker, Apr. 14, 1962; children: Elizabeth Marie, Kelli Renae. BS in Edn., Abilene Christian U., 1964. Announcer Sta. KWKC, Abilene, Tex., 1959-64; program dir. Sta. KWKC-AM-FM, Abilene, 1964-68; sta. mgr. Sta. KFMN-FM, Abilene, 1968-74, owner, operator, 1974-80, ptnr., gen. mgr., 1980-82, Sta. KEYJ-AM-FM, Abilene, 1982-92; pres., mgr. Sta. KHXS/EZ106, Abilene, 1992-96; ptnr. KMPC-AM/KWKC-AM, Abilene, 1998—. Part-owner Sta. KYYD (now KWKC-AM), Abilene, 1995—; owner KMPC-EZ 1560, 1997—; ptnr., owner KWKC-AM, KZQQ-AM, 1998—. Pres. Abilene Downtown Assn., 1980-83; pres. Chisholm Trail coun. Boy Scouts Am., 1985-87; chmn. adv. com. Taylor County Juvenile Bd.; chmn. Abilene State Sch. Vols., 1987-90, named Vol. of Yr., 1990; chmn. local emergency planning com. Taylor County. Recipient Silver Beaver award Boy Scouts Am., 1987, Leadership and Comms. award Toastmasters Internat., 2003. Mem. Rotary (past pres., bd. dirs. Abilene club). Republican. Home: 3949 N 9th St Abilene TX 79603-5543 Office: KZQQ/KWKC-AM 1749 N 2nd St Abilene TX 79603-7409

BOYLSTON, SCOTT THOMAS, graphic design educator; b. N.Y.C., Nov. 6, 1963; s. Dale James and Deirdre B.; m. Kristin Catapano, May 17, 1997. BS in Art Edn., SUNY, New Paltz, 1985; MS in Comm. Design, Pratt Inst., 2000. Free-lance designer, N.Y.C., 1990—; owner, designer Sea Bob Surf Wear, N.Y.C., 1992-95; designer Garrett Clifford Design, N.Y.C., 1990-94; art dir. Garrett Cliford Design, N.Y.C., 1994-98; prof. graphic design Savannah (Ga.) Coll. Art & Design, 1998—. Rep. Ga. Poetry Ctr., Atlanta, 1999—. Author: Creative Solutions for Unusual Projects, 2001; author of short stories. Recipient The Writers Voice award, 1998, Nantucket Writing award, Midnight Mind Books, 2000. Mem. Sierra Club. Avocations: scuba diva, sailing. Home: 133 Summer Winds Dr Savannah GA 31410 Office: PO Box 3146 Savannah GA 31402-3146 E-mail: sboylsto@scad.edu.

BOYNE, WALTER JAMES, writer, former museum director; b. East St. Louis, Ill., Feb. 2, 1929; s. Walter William and Emily (Campbell) B.; m. Jeanne Quigley, Dec. 26, 1952; children: Mary Louise, Katherine Elizabeth, William James, Margaret Ann. BBA, U. Calif., Berkeley, 1958; MBA, U. Pitts., 1963; PhD (hon.), Salem Coll., 1985. Commd. 2d lt. USAF, 1952, advanced through grades to col., 1971, ret., 1974; asst. curator Nat. Air and Space Mus., Washington, 1974-75, curator, 1975-78, exec. officer, 1978-80, asst. dir., 1980-82, acting dir., 1982-83, dir., 1983-86; ret., 1986. Chmn. bd. dirs. Wingspan TV Channel; aerospace expert in residence Discover Comms.; v.p. Fighter Pilot Prodns. Author: Boeing B-52, 1981, Messerschmitt Me-262, 1980, Treasures of Silver Hill, 1982, Flying, 1979, Jet Age, 1979, De Havilland DH-4, 1983, McDonnell Douglas F-4, 1983, Vertical Flight, 1983, Leading Edge, 1986, (novel) The Wild Blue, 1986, The Smithsonian Book of Flight, 1987, The Power Behind the Wheel, 1988, Trophy for Eagles, 1989, Weapons of Desert Shield, 1991, Gulf War, 1991, Eagles of War, 1991, Air Force Eagles, 1992, Classic Aircraft, 1992, Art in Flight, 1992, Silver Wings, 1993, Clash of Wings, 1994, Clash of Titans, 1995, Beyond the Wild Blue, 1997, Beyond the Horizons, 1998, Brassey Air Combat Reader, 1999, Aces in Command, 2001, Classic Aircraft, 2001, Best of Wings, 2001, Aviation 100, 2001, Encyclopedia of Air Warfare, 2002, The Two O'Clock War, 2002, Dawn Over Kitty Hawk, 2003, Chronicle of Flight, 2003, The Influence of Air Power on History, 2003, Rising Tide, 2003, Operation Iraqi Freedom, 2003, Today's Best Military Writing, 2003; prodr., writer: (video) Beyond the Wild Blue; author, host, narrator: (video) Clash of Wings, 1998, The Sculptures of John Safer, 1998. Recipient Best Fgn. Book award Aero Club de France, 1982, Robert A. Brooks award Smithsonian Instn., 1980, Best Fiction and Non-Fiction awards Aviation Space Writers, 1987, Thomas McKean Meml. Cup, 1989, Cliff Henderson Trophy 1986, Gil Robb Wilson award AIA, 1997; named Elder Statesman of Aviation Nat. Aviation Assn., 1998. Mem. Daedalians, Am. Aviation Hist. Soc. (nat. advisor), Author's Guild, Sons of the Desert, Cosmos Club. Home: 21028 Starflower Way Ashburn VA 20147-4700 E-mail: wboyne@cgi.com. *There is a pleasure in work: it is doubled if appreciated by a peer.*

BOYNTON, FREDERICK GEORGE, lawyer; b. Yokohama, Japan, May 9, 1948; s. Fred Wenderoth and Buelah Eleanor (Nygaard) B.; m. Nancy Jeanne McLendon, Aug. 3, 1985; children: Emily Margaret, Charlotte Clayton, Susan Jeanne. BA, The Citadel, 1970; JD, Tulane U., 1973. Bar: S.C. 1973, Ga. 1976, U.S. Dist. Ct. Ga. 1976, U.S. Ct. Appeals (5th and 11th cirs.). Assoc. Smith, Gambrell & Russell, and predecessors, Atlanta, 1976-82, ptnr., 1982-88; sole practice law Atlanta, 1988—2002; of counsel Jackson and Hardwick, 2002—. Author: Criminal Defense Techniques, 1976; editor articles Tulane Sch. Law Rev. Exec. com. Southside Progress Assn., Atlanta, 1983-84, Leadership Sandy Springs, 1989-90; bd. dirs. Atlanta Union Mission, 1990-97, exec. com., 1991, sec., 1992, adv. bd., 1998—; mem. Local Advisory Coun., Ridgeview Mid. Sch, 2001-03. Served to capt. JAGC, U.S. Army, 1973-76. Fellow Lawyers Found. Ga.; mem. ABA, Fed. Bar Assn. (pres. Atlanta chpt. 1981-82, mem. exec. com. 1982—, dep. chmn. adminstrv. law sect. 1986-87, bd. dirs. younger lawyers divsn. 1981-84, v.p. 11th cir. 1985-87), State Bar Ga. (chmn. adminstrv. law sect. 1987-88), Order of Coif. Home: 4860 Northway Dr NE Atlanta GA 30342-2424 Office: 2325 Lakeview Parkway Ste 275 Alpharetta GA 30004 E-mail: fboynton@jhlaw.net.

BOYNTON, IRVIN PARKER, retired educational administrator; b. Chgo., Mar. 27, 1937; s. Ben Lynn and Elizabeth (Katterjohn) B.; m. Alyce Jane Coyle, Sept. 3, 1964; children: Gregory Allen, Cathy Lynn, Julie Marie, Michael Irvin, Jonathan David. BA, Ohio Wesleyan U., 1959; BS, U. Akron, 1964; MEd, Wayne State U., 1968; counseling endorsement, Siena Heights Coll., 1988. Cert. tchr., Ohio, Mich. Spl. edn. tchr., acting prin. Sagamore Hills Children's Psychiat. Hosp., Cleve., 1961-64; spl. edn. tchr. Fairlawn Ctr., Pontiac, Mich., 1964-68, Walled Lake (Mich.) High Sch., 1968-71; asst. prin. Oakland Tech. Ctr./Southwest Campus, Wixom, Mich., 1971-98; ret., 1998. Mem. spl. needs guideline com. Mich. Dept. Edn., Lansing, 1973-78; keynote speaker Utah Secondary Conf., Salt Lake City, 1978; evaluator North Cen. Accreditation Assn., Waterford, Mich., 1971-73; adv. com. State Tech.Instn. and Rehab. Ctr., Plainwell, Mich., 1978-85. Pres. Roger Campbell Ministries, Waterford, 1987—. Cited as exemplary spl. needs program U. Wis. Mem. ASCD, Am. Vocat. Assn., Mich. Occupational Edn. Assn., Mich. Occupational Spl. Needs Assn. (Outstanding Spl. Needs Educator), Nat. Assn. Vocat. Spl. Needs Personnel (Outstanding Spl. Needs Program 1975), Phi Delta Kappa. Republican. Home: 4901 Juniper Dr Commerce Township MI 48382-1545 E-mail: irvinboynton@comcast.net.

BOYNTON, JAMES STEPHEN, lawyer; b. Stamford, Conn., Apr. 3, 1946; s. Horace William and Lorraine Anne (Nelsen) B.; m. Caroline Foster Cochran, May 9, 1970 (div. Nov. 1996); children: Caroline Lorraine, James Cochran; m. Kathleen Mary Peluso, Jan. 1, 2001. BA, Williams Coll., 1968; JD, U. Pa., 1971. Bar: N.Y. 1973, U.S. Dist. Ct. (so. dist.) N.Y. 1973. Assoc. Debevoise & Plimpton, N.Y.C., 1971-80; ptnr. Tung, Drabkin & Boynton, N.Y.C., 1980-85, Salans, N.Y.C., 1985—. Trustee The Norfolk (Conn.) Land Trust, 1990—, Cushing Acad., 1993—. 1st lt. U.S. Army, 1972. Mem. Norfolk Country Club (pres. 1985-87). Congregationalist. Home: 626 Winchester Rd Norfolk CT 06058-1365 Office: Salans 620 5th Ave New York NY 10020-2402 E-mail: jboynton@salans.com.

BOYNTON, ROBERT MERRILL, retired psychology educator; b. Evanston, Ill., Oct. 28, 1924; s. Merrill Holmes and Eleanor (Matthews) B.; m. Alice Neiley, Apr. 9, 1947 (dec. Oct. 15, 1996); children: Sherry, Michael, Neiley, Geoffrey; m. Sheleah Maloney, Oct. 17, 1998. Student, Antioch Coll., 1942-43, U. Ill., 1943-45; AB, Amherst Coll., 1948; PhD, Brown U., 1952. Asst. prof. psychology and optics U. Rochester, N.Y., 1952-57, asso. prof., 1957-61, prof., 1961-74, founder, dir. Ctr. for Visual Sci., 1963-71, chmn. dept. psychology, 1971-74; prof. psychology U. Calif., San Diego, 1974-91, assoc. dean grad. studies and research, 1987-91; ret., 1991. Guest researcher Nat. Phys. Lab., Teddington, Eng., 1960-61; vis. prof. physiology U. Calif. Med. Center, San Francisco, 1969-70 Author: Human Color Vision, 1979, 2d edit., 1996; chmn. bd. editors Vision Research, 1982-86; contbr. articles to profl. jours. Served with USNR, 1943-45. Recipient Charles F. Prentice award Am. Acad. Optometry, 1997. Fellow AAAS, Optical Soc. Am. (dir.-at-large 1966-69, Frederick Ives medal 1995), APA, Assn. for Rsch. in Vision and Ophthalmology (trustee 1984-89); mem. NAS. Home: 376 Bellaire St Del Mar CA 92014-2207 E-mail: rboynton@ucsd.edu.

BOYNTON, WILLIAM LEWIS, retired electronic manufacturing company official; b. Kalamazoo, May 31, 1928; s. James Woodbury and Cyretta (Gunther) B.; m. Kei Ouchi, Oct. 8, 1953. Asst. mgr. Speigel J&R, Kalamazoo, 1947-48; with U.S. Army, 1948-74, ret., 1974, with Rockwell/Collins div., 1974-78, supr. material, investment recovery coord., 1974-81, coord., 1981-88, investment recovery supr., coord. Rockwell/CDC Santa Ana, Calif., 1981-88, coord. investment recovery, 1982-86, shipping supr., investment recovery, environ. coord., 1982-88, 87-88, material coord., 1988, environ. coord. Rockwell/CDC Newport Beach, 1988-89, ret. Trustee Corp. Bd., 1993, pres., 1993-94, mem. exec. bd. dirs.; adv. panelist bus./econ. devel. Calif. State Legis., 1979-86; trustee Orange County Vector Control Dist., 1980—. Decorated Bronze Star.8 Mem. Assn. U.S. Army, Assn. U.S. Army, Non-Commd. Officers Assn., Mosquito and Vector Control Assn. Calif. (v.p. 1992, pres. 1993), Nat. Geog. Soc. Republican. Roman Catholic. Home: 5314 W Lucky Way Santa Ana CA 92704-1048

BOYSEN, MELICENT PEARL, finance company executive; b. Houston, Dec. 1, 1943; d. William Thomas and Mildred Pearl (Walker) Richardson; m. Stephen M. Boysen, Sept. 10, 1961 (dec. 1973); children: Marshella, Stephanie, Stephen. Student, Cen. Mo. State, 1973-75. Owner, pres. Boysen Enterprises, Kansas City, Mo., 1973-93; fin. cons., underwriter New Eng. Life Ins. Co., Kansas City, 1978-81; owner, pres. Boysen Agri-Svcs., Kansas City, 1984-94; pres. Boysen & Assocs., Inc., Kansas City, 1987—; stockholder, pres. Am. Crumb Rubber, Inc., Kansas City, 1996—; stockholder, v.p. Initiatives Worldwide, Inc., 2002—. Cons. San Luis Rey (Calif.) Tribal Water Authority, Wind River (Wyo.) Reservation, Cheyenne River (S.D.) Sioux, Iroquois Nations (N.Y.), 1983—; founding bd. dirs., pres. Am. Indian Youth Orgn., Visible Horizons, 1987—, stockholder, v.p. Initiatives Worldwide, Inc., 2002-. Founding bd. dirs. Rose Brooks Ctr. Battered Women, Kansas City, 1979-87, treas., 1979-81; exec. dir. The Flame Spirit Run, 1992; citationist, 1993; mem. Pres.'s Vol. Action Awards Program; mem. Pres.'s Bus. Adv. Coun., 2001. Recipient Women of Conscience award Panel Am. Women of Greater Kansas City. Mem.

DAR, Kans. C. of C. and Industry, Kansas City C. of C. Methodist. Avocations: stamp collecting, sports cars. Office: Boysen & Assocs 4112 Pennsylvania Ave Ste 202 Kansas City MO 64111-3057 E-mail: mboysen@boysencompanies.com.

BOYSEN, THOMAS CYRIL, educational association administrator; b. Sioux Falls, S.D., Nov. 16, 1940; s. Cyril Joseph and Dolores Margaret (Parry) B.; m. PoChan Mar, Aug. 25, 1964 (div. 1980); children: Thomas C., Anne-Marie Lee; m. Laurie Louise Shaffer, June 25, 1983. BA in History, Stanford U., 1962; diploma in grad. edn., Makerere U., Kampala, Uganda, 1964; EdD in Edn. Adminstrn., Harvard U., 1969. Geography master Kabaa H.S., Thika, Kenya, 1964-66; dir. adminstrn. Bellevue (Wash.) Pub. Schs., 1968-70; supt. schs. Pasco Sch. Dist., Wash., 1970-73, Pelham (N.Y.) Pub. Schs., 1973-77, Redlands United Sch. Dist., Calif., 1977-80, Conejo Valley Unified Sch. Dist., Thousand Oaks, Calif., 1980-87, San Diego County Schs., 1987-90, Ky. Commn. Edn., 1991-95; sr. v.p. edn. Milken Family Found., Santa Monica, Calif., 1995.

BOYSON, MICHAEL ANDREW, investment consultant; b. Bangor, Maine, Dec. 18, 1953; s. Edward William and Gloria Patricia B.; m. Nancy Lewis Grant Boyson, May 10, 1980; children: Oscar Andrew, Elise Cook. BA, Colby Coll., Waterville, Maine, 1976. Cert. investment mgmt. analyst. Vol. U.S. Peace Corps., Rabala, Sierra Leone, 1980-82; cons. UN Devel. Program, Rabala, Sierra Leone, 1982-84; v.p. E.F. Hutton & Co., Inc., Portland, Maine, 1984-88, Shearson Lebanon Bros., Portland, Maine, 1988-95; sr. v.p. Sobmon Smith Barney, Portland, Maine, 1995—. Mem. Investment Mgmt. Cons. Assn., Chgo., 1998—. Mem. Maine Coll. Savings Bd., Augusta, 1998—, United Way Found., Portland, Maine, 1996—; pres. Greely Ski Boosters, Cumberland, Maine, 1998—, Ctr. for Cultural Exchange, Portland, Maine, 1996-99. Recipient 2nd Pl. Bradbury Mountain Hill Climb, Pownal, Maine, 2000. Mem. Woodlands Club, Bay Club, Maine Track Club. Episcopalian. Avocations: running, skiing, hiking, sailing, golf. Home: 24 Colonial Dr North Yarmouth ME 04097 Office: Solomon Smith Barney 100 Middle St Portland ME 04101 E-mail: mike_boyson@hotmail.com.

BOYSON, WILLIAM ALBERT, retired obstetrician, gynecologist; b. Gettysburg, Pa., 1920; BA, Gettysburg Coll., 1941; MD, U. Pa., 1950; MS in Ob-Gyn., Baylor U., 1957. Diplomate Am. Bd. Ob-Gyn. Intern Walter Reed Gen. Hosp., Washington, 1950-51; resident obs. Herman Kiefer Hosp., Detroit, 1951; resident gynecology Detroit Receiving Hosp., 1952; resident in ob-gyn. Brooke Gen. Hosp., Ft. Sam Houston, Tex., 1954-57; gynecologist Brooke Army Med. Ctr., San Antonio, 1983-90. Fellow Am. Coll. Surgeons; mem. Am. Coll. Ob-Gyn.

BOYTE, GEORGE GRIFFIN, lawyer; b. Humboldt, Tenn., Mar. 10, 1925; s. Hubert C. and Olga (Hogan) Boyte; m. Carol Dent, June 20, 1953; children: Bonnie Carol (Capsuto), George Griffin Jr. 1 stepchild, Katherine (Dent). BA, Vanderbilt U., 1949; JD, 1952. Bar: Tenn. 1952. Mem. firm J. Frank Warmath, Humboldt, 1952—54; ptnr. Warmath & Boyte, Humboldt, 1954—; city atty. City of Humbold, 1973—83; mem. Tenn. Gen. Assembly, 1961—62; del Tenn. Constl. Conv., 1959, 1965. Served USMCR, 1943—45. Recipient Pub. Trust award, Humboldt Courier-Chronicle, 1976; fellow Am. Bar Found., Tenn. Bar Found. Mem.: Humboldt C. of C. (pres. 1971—72), Gibson County Bar Assn. (pres. 1968—69), Tenn. Bar Assn. (pres. 1978—79, mem. ho. of dels. 1979—82), Tenn. Def. Lawyers Assn. (v.p. 1980—), Am. Law Inst., ABA (mem. council gen. practice sect. 1974—79, ho. of del. 1980—86), Golf and Country Club (pres. local club), Rotary (pres. 1968—69). Bapt. Office: Warmath and Boyte 314 N 22nd Ave Humboldt TN 38343-3010 Home: PO Box 406 Humboldt TN 38343-0406

BOYTER, SCOTT M. academic administrator; b. Cedar City, Utah, June 19, 1947; s. Neil K. and Mae (Macfarlane) Boyter; m. Sherrie L. Bowen, Aug. 2, 1974; children: Laura Michelle, Tonia Leigh, Diana Lynn. BS, Brigham Young U., 1973, MS with high distinction, 1987. Adminstrv. asst. coll. fine arts and communications Brigham Young U., Provo, Utah, 1973-76, bus. mgr. Sch. Music, 1976-82, bus. mgr. Coll. Fine Arts and Comm., 1982-94, asst. dean, contr. Coll. Fine Arts and Comm., 1995—. Missionary Ch. Jesus Christ LDS, Ohio, 1967—69, 1967—69. With USAR, 1971—2003. Recipient 1st Sgt. of the Yr. award, 96th Regional Support Command, USAR, 1996. Mem.: Assn. Cert. Fraud Examiners, Am. Assn. Univ. Adminstrs., Am. Philatelic Soc., Key Club, Beta Gamma Sigma. Republican. Mem. Lds Ch. Avocations: philately, WWII history. Home: 331 N 875 E Orem UT 84097-5075 Office: Brigham Young U Coll Fine Arts & Communications Provo UT 84602 E-mail: scott_boyter@byu.edu.

BOZA, CLARA BRIZEIDA, marketing and communications executive; b. Havana, Cuba, Apr. 18, 1952; came to U.S., 1957; d. Eduardo Otmaro and Hubedia Marta (Garcia) B. BA in English summa cum laude, Barry Coll., 1973, MA in Comm. Media, 1988. Program adminstr. Dade County Coun. Arts and Scis., Miami, Fla., 1980-82; dir. program devel. Nat. Found. for Advancement in Arts, Miami, 1982-85; exec. dir. Bus. Vols. for Arts/Miami, 1985-86; legal asst. supr. Steel Hector & Davis, Miami, 1978-80, dir. mktg., 1986-96; dir. practice devel. Arnold & Porter, Washington, 1996-98; chief mktg. officer Kirkpatrick & Lockhart, LLP, Washington, 1998—. S.E. regional cons. Arts and Bus. Coun., N.Y.C., 1986-88; panelist and spkr. various local, state and nat. orgns. and assns. Recipient ednl. scholarship Barry Coll., Miami, 1969-73, Fla. Bd. Regents, 1969-73. Mem. ABA (mem. commn. on advt. 1994-97), Legal Mktg. Assn. (bd. dirs. and officer 1993, 94, 96, bd. dirs. Mid-Atlantic chpt. 1997-99), Am. Mktg. Assn. (bd. dirs. Miami chpt. 1992-96), Fla. Bar (standing com. on advt. 1993-96). Office: Kirkpatrick & Lockhart 1800 Massachusetts Ave NW Washington DC 20036-1806

BOZDECH, MAREK JIRI, physician, educator; b. Wildflecken, Bavaria, Federal Republic Germany, Oct. 12, 1946; s. Jiri Josef and Zofia Jadwiga (Swiatecka) B.; m. Frances Barclay Craig, Dec. 22, 1967; children: Elizabeth, Andrew, Matthew. AB, U. Mich., 1967; MD, Wayne State U., 1972. Diplomate Am. Bd. Internal Medicine, Am. Bd. Med. Oncology, Am. Bd. Hematology. Intern and resident in internal medicine U. Wis. Hosps., Madison, 1972-75, dir. clin. hematology lab., 1978-82, dir. bone marrow transplantation, 1984-85; asst. prof. medicine U. Wis., Madison, 1978-84, assoc. prof. medicine, 1984-85; clin. fellow in hematology Moffitt Hosp. U. Calif., San Francisco, 1975-76, postdoctoral fellow in hematology Cancer Research Inst., 1976-78, research assoc. Cancer Research Inst., 1977-78, assoc. prof., 1985-89; dir. adult bone marrow transplantation U. Calif. Med. Ctr., San Francisco, 1985-89; chief oncology Kaiser Permanente Med. Ctr., Santa Rosa, Calif., 1989-91; pvt. practice specializing in oncology Hematology Redwood Regional Oncology Ct., Santa Rosa, 1991—. Contbr. articles to profl. jours. Scout leader Boy Scouts Am., Novato, Calif., 1985; bd. trustees Pacific Found. Med. Care, 1995—. Recipient Nat. Research Service award NIH, 1977-78; Wayne State U. scholar, 1971. Mem. ACP, Am. Soc. Hematology, Am. Soc. Clin. Oncology, Assn. No. Calif. Oncologists (bd. dirs. 1994-97), Sonoma County Med. Assn. (bd. dirs. 1994-96). Avocations: skiing, gardening, music, films, theatre. Home: 50 La Placita Ct Novato CA 94945-1244 Office: U Calif Med Ctr A502 M Redwood Regional Oncology 121 Sotoyome St Ste 203 Santa Rosa CA 95405-4822 E-mail: mbozdech@mindspring.com., mbozdech@yahoo.com.

BOZE, BETSY VOGEL, university dean, marketing educator; b. Shreveport, La., Sept. 18, 1953; d. Leroy Vogel and Betty Gray (Garrett) Vogel McDonald; children: Christopher Lee Boze, Broox Garrett Vogel Boze, Lee Gray Boze. BS in Psychology, So. Meth. U., 1974; postgrad., Am. Grad. Sch. Internat. Mgmt., 1975; MBA, So. Meth. U., 1975; PhD, U. Ark., 1984. Lectr. U. Md., 1975, 78-80; asst. prof. St. Bonaventure U., Olean, N.Y., 1977-78; instr. U. Ark., Fayetteville, 1979-83; asst. prof. Centenary Coll. of La., Shreveport, 1983-89; assoc. prof., chair U. Alaska, Anchorage, 1989-94; dean, prof. mktg. U. Tex., Brownsville, 1994—; pres. Boze & Assocs., Shreveport and Anchorage, 1983-94. Dir. Women in Mgmt. Conf., Shreveport, 1983-89; mem. continuing edn. com. Hispanic Ednl. Telecomms. Sys., San Juan, P.R., 1995—; co-dir. Tex. Transp. Inst. Ctr. for Ports and Waterways, 1994—, HERS/Mid-Am. Summer Inst., 1996; vis. faculty Portland State U. in Khaborosk, Russia, 1994. Mem. editl. bd. Jour. for Not-for-Profit Mktg., 1990—; contbr. articles to profl. jours., chpts. to textbooks. V.p. Atlantic Mktg. Assn., Orlando, Fla., 1988-90; pres. Susitna coun. Girl Scouts U.S., Anchorage, 1992-94; pres. Wish Upon a Star, Shreveport, 1988-90; mem. program com. Commonwealth North, Anchorage, 1989-94; Tex. coord. Nat. Identification program Am. Coun. on Edn. U.S. Dept. Edn. Internat. fellow U. Hawaii, 1990. Mem. AAUP, AAUW, Am. Coun. Edn., Am. Assn. State Colls. & Univs., Leadership Tex., Petroleum Club of Anchorage, Delta Delta Delta (pres. alumnae chpt. 1989-92). Methodist. Avocations: reading, swimming, backgammon. Home: 1409 Avenida Santa Ana Rancho Viejo TX 78575 Office: U Tex Brownsville 80 Fort Brown St Brownsville TX 78520-4956

BOZEMAN, FRANK CARMACK, lawyer; b. Greenwood, Miss., Oct. 16, 1933; s. Frank Carmack and Mamie Hyatt (Pyle) B.; m. Mary Ireland Callcott, Dec. 29, 1961; children: Frank C. III, William Pyle, Thomas Anderson. BA, U. of South, 1955; MA, U. Va., 1956; JD, Washington and Lee U., 1960. Bar: Fla. 1960, Va. 1960. Assoc. Beggs and Lane, Pensacola, Fla., 1960-65; ptnr. Harrell, Wiltshire, Bozeman, Clark & Stone, Pensacola, 1965-75, Carlton, Fields, Ward, Emmanuel, Smith & Cutler, P.A., Pensacola, 1975-93, Bozeman, Jenkins & Matthews, Pensacola, 1993—. Editor Washington and Lee Law Rev., 1960. Chmn. Eagle Scout rev. com., Boy Scouts Am., Pensacola, 1961-63; trustee U. Of South, 1990-96. Capt. USAF, 1956-57. Mem. Am. Bd. Trial Advs. (pres. Pensacola chpt. 1989-90), Fla. Def. Lawyers Assn., Fedn. Ins. and Corp. Counsel, Register of Pre-Eminent Lawyers, Def. Rsch. Inst., Phi Delta Phi (Grad. of Yr. award 1960). Republican. Episcopalian. Avocations: sailing, gardening, civil war history and research. Home: 122 W Lloyd St Pensacola FL 32501-2637 Office: Bozeman Jenkins & Matthews PO Box 13105 Pensacola FL 32591-3105

BOZEMAN, LAURA BETH, military officer, educator; b. Florrisant, Mo., Feb. 21, 1970; d. Boyd Benjamin and Dorothy Louise Carmichael; m. James Michael Bozeman, Nov. 26, 1993. MA, U. of Minn., 2001—01; BA, Tex. Christian U., 1992; diploma, Adj. Gen.'s Corps Officer Basic Course, Ft. Benjamin Harrison, Ind., 1992, Adj. Gen.'s Corps Officer Advanced Course, Ft. Jackson, S.C., 1996; cert., Combined Arms Staff and Svc. Sch., Ft. Leavenworth, Kans., 1999. Co. comdr. Alpha Co., 43d Adj. Gen. Bn., Fort Leonard Wood, Mo., 1997—99; instr. Dept. of English, West Point, NY, 2001—. Dep. adj. gen. hdqs. U.S. Army Element, Allied Land Forces Cen. Europe, Heidelberg, Baden-Wuerttemburg, Germany, 1995—96, co. exec. officer hdqs. co., 1994—95; adj./brigade s1 (pers. officer) 2d Signal Brigade, Mannheim, Baden-Wuerttemburg, Germany, 1992—94. Sponsor internat. mil. exch. program participant U.S. Army Maneuver Support Ctr., Ft. Leonard Wood, 1998—99; sponsor 4th class cadets U.S. Mil. Acad., West Point, NY, 2001—03; mem. rite of Christian initiation of adults team; host family participant, eucharistic min. Most Holy Trinity Cath. Parish, West Point, 2002—03. Capt. U.S. Army, 1992—2003. Decorated Def. Meritorious Svc. Medal, Meritorious Svc. Medal, ; recipient Advanced Civil Schooling fellowship, U. S. Army, 1999—2001, 4-Yr. Army ROTC scholarship, Hdqs., U. S. Army Cadet Command, 1988. Mem.: MLA, Spaatz Assn., Adj. General's Corps Regtl. Assn. (v.p. for publicity Ozarks chpt. 1997—99, Adj. General's Corps Achievement medal 1999), Longaberger Basket Collectors Club, Sigma Tau Delta (pres. Tex. Christian U. chpt. 1991—92), Alpha Lambda Delta, Phi Beta Kappa. Roman Catholic. Avocations: travel, classic films, French language and culture. Home: 122 Delafield Ln Newburgh NY 12550 Office: US Mil Acad Dept English 607 Cullum Rd West Point NY 10996 Office Fax: 845-938-2562. Personal E-mail: mlbozeman@yahoo.com. E-mail: cl6892@usma.edu.

BOZEMAN, ROSS ELLIOT, engineering executive; b. New Orleans, Feb. 16, 1967; s. Robert Ray and Rita (Findley) B. BS cum laude, La. Tech. Inst., 1990. Registered profl. engr., Tex., 1998, La., 1999, Ariz., 2002. Assoc. vessel engr. Litwin Engrs. and Constructors, Houston, 1990-94, vessel engr., 1994-96; engring. mgr. Bergaila Engring. Svcs., Inc., Houston, 1996-99; engring. mgr., owner Bozeman Engring., Houston, 1999—. Mem. ASME (assoc.), Tau Beta Pi. Avocations: country and western dancing, drag racing, study of vehicle dynamics, finite element analysis. Office: 2640 Fountain View Ste 212 Houston TX 77057 Home: Ste 212 2640 Fountain View Dr Houston TX 77057-7610 Fax: 928-833-5381. E-mail: ross@bozemanengineering.com.

BOZEMAN, THEODORE D. religion educator; b. Gainesville, Fla., Jan. 27, 1942; s. Simuel Bozeman and Kathleen Ford; m. Hannelore Bozeman, July 29, 1973. BA, Eckerd Coll., 1964; BD, Union Theol. Sem., N.Y.C., 1968; ThM, Union Sem., Richmond, Va., 1970; PhD, Duke U., 1974. Prof. U. Iowa, 1974—. Author: Protestants in an Age of Science, 1977, To Live Ancient Lives, 1988. NEH fellow, 1982, 95; recipient James Henley Thornwell award Presbyn. Hist. Assn., 1975. Mem. Am. Soc. Ch. History, Orgn. Am. Historians, So. Hist. Assn., Am. Hist. Assn. Office: U Iowa Dept Religious Studies Iowa City IA 52242

BOZINOVSKI, STEVO, computer science educator, researcher; b. Bitola, Macedonia, May 24, 1949; s. Misko and Goluba Bozinovski; m. Liljana Bulakovska Bozinovska, Apr. 12, 1975; children: Nevena, Adrian. BEE in Computer Sci., U. Zagreb, Croatia, 1973; MSc in Electronics, U. Zagreb, 1975, PhD in Computer Sci., 1982; Diploma in Robotics and FMS, State Acad. Sci., Krems, Austria, 1993. Vis. rschr. U. Mass., Amherst, 1980—81; prof. U. Cyril and Methodius, Skopje, Macedonia, 1983—2001; assoc. prof. S.C. State U., Orangeburg, 2001—. Vis. scholar Kanazawa Inst. Tech., Japan, 1984, U. Mass., Amherst, 1995—96; vis. rschr. German Info. Tech. Ctr., Sankt Augustin, 1999, 2000; conf. organizer Biocybernetics Soc., Skopje, 1978—84; session organizer SCI Multiconf., Orlando, Fla., 2001; guest editor Jour. Automatika, Zagreb, 1985. Author: Consequence Driven Systems, 1995; contbr. Recipient Award for best paper in robotics, ETAN (Electronics, Telecommunications, Automation, and Nuclear Engineering Soc.), Nis, Yugoslavia, 1985; Fulbright Found. grantee, 1980, 1995. Mem.: IEEE, N.Y. Acad. Sci., Macedonian Biocybernetics Soc. Achievements include first one solving delayed reinforcement learning problem using neural network; first one introducing a neural feeling-based self-reinforcement mechanism; research in finding field theory equation between emotion, motivation, behavior; predicting active role of rRNA in molecular genetics. Avocation: history of Macedonians and comic arts. Home: 241 Wannamaker St Orangeburg SC 29115 Office: South Carolina State Univ 300 College St Orangeburg SC 29117

BOZIWICK, GEORGE E. music librarian, composer, curator; b. Rockville Centre, N.Y., Aug. 23, 1954; s. George Emil Boziwick and Jean Constance Kuch; m. Stephanie Doba, July 26, 1986; children: Anna, Emily. BA, SUNY, Oneonta, 1976; MA in Music Composition, Hunter Coll., 1981; M in Libr. Svc., Columbia U., 1987. Music libr. circulating collections The N.Y. Pub. Libr. for the Performing Arts, N.Y.C., 1986—88, music libr. music divsn., 1988—91, curator Am. Music Collection, 1991—. Composer: (chamber music) Opus One Records #135, 162; contbr. articles to profl. jours. Sec. parish adv. coun. Oratory Ch. of St. Boniface, Bklyn., 2000—02, archives cons., 2003, composer, musician, performer, 2003—. Mem.: Am. Music Ctr., Music Libr. Assn. (mem. Dena Epstein award com. 1998—99, coord. Music Publs. Assn./Music Libr. Assn./Maj. Orch. Libr joint com.), Soc. for Am. Music (bd. dirs. 2001—). Avocation: blues harmonica player. Home: 614 10th St Brooklyn NY 11215 Office: NY Pub Libr for the Performing Arts Music Divsn 40 Lincoln Center Plaza New York NY 10023

BOZOZUK, MICHAEL, civil engineer; b. Poland, Nov. 10, 1929; married Marcelle F. M. Daoust, July 20, 1957; children: Lyne, Sylvie, Camille. BSc in Civil Engring., U. Man., Winnipeg, Can., 1952, MSc in Soil Mechanics, 1954; PhD in Geotechnical, Purdue U., 1972. Rsch. officer geotechnical section, divsn. building rsch. Nat. Rsch. Coun. Can., 1953-89; pvt. practice, 1989—; exec. dir. Engring. Inst. Can., 1994-99. Com. soil and rock instrumentation Transp. Rsch. Bd., 1972-81, com. on founds. of bridges and other structures, 1972-81; chmn. adv. com. civil tech. Algonquin Coll., Ottawa, 1972-76; adv. com. Beaufort Sea artificial island Dept. Indian and No. Affairs, Govt. Can., 1981-84; rsch. com. silo founds. Ont. Silo Assn., 1978-82; Can. Gen. Stds. Bd. Geotextiles, 1980-85; chmn. adv. com. environ./geotechniques Sir Sanford Fleming Coll., Lindsay, Ont., 1983-87; tech. com. on founds. Can. Stds. Assn., 1983-90; mem. Can. Geosci. Coun., 1985-91; S.E. China Tour Lectr., 1986; hon. prof. Chengdu U., China, 1986; sci. advisor various orgns. and univs. Recipient Hon. award Caisse Populaire St. Genevieve, Ottawa, Can. Engring. Centennial Silver Medal, 1987, Cert. Citizenship City Calgary, 1987. Fellow Engring. Inst. Can. (govt. liaison com. 1989-90, strategic planning and adv. com. 1986-91, chmn. engring. liaison com. 1993-94, Can. Paper award 1960, John B. Stirling medal 1990), Can. Soc. Civil Engrs., Can. Acad. Engring., NRC Can. (assoc. com. geotech. rsch., tech. advisor 1985-89, sec. 1989-91); mem. Geocontbns. (founding v.p. 1993-95, pres. 1999—), Assn. Profl. Engrs. Ont., Can. Geotech. Soc. (cross Can. tour lectr. 1979, v.p. tech., pres. bd. dirs. no. and ea. Ont. 1984-85, past pres. 1985-90, chmn. award com. 1986-90, assoc. editor Can. Geotech. Jour. 1982-86, prize for best paper 1973, svc. award 1988, R. F. Legget award 1994), Ottawa Geotech. Group (sec. 1957-59, chmn. 1976-78), Internat. Soc. Soil Mechanics and Found. Engring., Can. Geotech. Fund (treas. 1985-88), Ottawa Lapsmith Club (pres. 1995). Roman Catholic. Home and Office: 691 Sandra Ave Ottawa ON Canada K1G 2Z7

BOZZUTO, MICHAEL ADAM, wholesale grocery company executive; b. Waterbury, Conn., 1956; s. Adam John and Lillian B. BBA, Stetson U., 1978. Pres., CEO, treas. Bozzuto's, Inc., Cheshire, Conn., 1978—. Former mem. adv. bd. Bank of Boston-Conn.; bd. dirs. IGA USA. Trustee Cheshire Acad. Mem. Food Mktg. Inst., New Eng. Wholesale Food Distbrs. Assn. (former chmn.), Food Distbrs. Internat. (bd. govs.), Conn. Food Assn. (bd. dirs., Person of Yr. 1999), Lambda Chi. Roman Catholic. Office: Bozzuto's Inc 275 Schoolhouse Rd Cheshire CT 06410-1257

BRAAKSMA, JOHANNA, educational consultant, researcher; b. The Netherlands, Apr. 15, 1956; Student, State U. Groningen, The Netherlands, 1984. Rschr. RION, Groningen, The Netherlands, 1984-85, U. Amsterdam, 1985-88; ref. libr., information specialist U. Twente, The Netherlands, 1988-2000. Mem. exam. com. GO, 1990—93; chair adv. com. NVB, Netherlands, 1992—98; mem. adv. com. Sch. for Librs., Deventer, 1998—2000; advisor HBO-raad (Netherlands Assn. Univs. Profl. Edn.), 2000—01; ednl. advisor Dinkel Inst., U. Twente, 2001—03; advisor IOWO, Cath. U. Nymegen, 2003—. Recipient Victorine van Schaick award Stichting Victorine van Schaick Fonds, The Hague, 1996, 97. Office: IOWO PO Box 6540 6503 GA Nymegen Netherlands E-mail: j.braaksma@iowo.kun.nl.

BRAASCH, BARBARA LYNN, banker, consultant; b. Santa Monica, Calif., Apr. 14, 1958; d. C. Duane and René Barbara (Siegel) B. Student, Golden Gate U., 1989-91. Cert. Compensation Professional, 1999. Ops. officer Bank of Am., Fresno, Calif., 1976-87; v.p., mgr. Wells Fargo Bank, San Fransisco, 1987-96; v.p., mgr. fin. MIS Bank of Am., San Fransisco, 1996-2000, catalyst bus. cons., owner, 2000—; mgr. investment sys.; mgr. devel. Wells Fargo Bank, 2000—. Mentor Jr. Achievement, L.A., 1980-83. 1st class scout Girl Scouts Am., 1976, leader, asst. leader, 1976-79, 84-87; vol. Open Hand, San Francisco, 1991-92, San Francisco AIDS Found., various women's groups, 1989—. Mem. Am. Compensation Assn., Bay Area Compensation Assn., Fin. Tech. Forum. Democrat. Jewish. Avocations: music, movies, theatre. Office: Wells Capital Mgmt 525 Market St 10 B Fl San Francisco CA 94105 E-mail: braascba@wellscap.com.

BRABEC, ROSEMARY JEAN, retail executive; b. St. Paul, Apr. 5, 1951; d. Peter Michael and Mary Jane (Nigro) Jacovitch; m. Loren W. Brabec, Sept. 16, 1972; children: Brenda Marie, Daniel Joseph. BS in Elem. Edn., St. Cloud State U., 1973. Tchr. Ind. Sch. Dist. 314, Braham, Minn., 1975-78; owner, mgr. Rosemary's Quilts and Baskets, Braham, 1988-97. Dir. Community Edn. Adv. Coun., Braham, 1978-95, chmn., 1992-95. Designer quilt block representing Minn. div. AAUW for display at Internat. Fedn. Univ. Women conv., Calif. Chmn. P.I.C.K. Immunization Clinic, Braham, 1978-85; vol. driver coord. Home Delivered Meals, Braham, 1984—; vol. coord. Com. to Build Robert Leathers Playground, Braham, 1985; mem. Braham City Park Bd., 2001—, chmn., 2002--. Mem. AAUW (sec.Cambridge Area Branch, 1985-87, 98-99, v.p. 1987-88, historian 1997-98, pres. 1999-2002), Minn. Quilters.

BRABON, DAVID LAWRENCE, plastic reconstructive surgeon; b. Medellín, Antioquia, Colombia, Aug. 6, 1947; s. Harold Arthur and Margaret Balfour (Round) B.; m. Gloria Patricia Martinez, Sept. 1, 1990; children: Daniel, Harold. BA, Asbury Coll., Wilmore, Ky., 1969; MD, U. Louisville, 1973. Resident gen. surgery Wayne State U., Detroit, 1973-76; staff physician Good Samaritan Hosp., Lexington, Ky., 1976-80; fellow plastic surgery Straith Hosp., Southfield, 1980-82; staff physician Garrard Meml. Hosp., Lancaster, Ky., 1982-84; rural physician Hosp. Simon Bolivar, Bogotá, Colombia, 1984-85, chief clinics, 1985-96, chief plastic, reconstructive surgery and burn unit, 1993-96; staff physician Rockcastle Hosp., Mt. Vernon, Ky., 1996—. Recipient Alumni A award Asbury Coll., Wilmore, Ky., 1994. Mem. AMA, Am. Coll. Emegency Physicians, Am. Sci. Affiliation, N.Y. Acad. Sci., Ky. Med. Assn. Methodist. Avocations: history, philosophy, art, music.

BRACCO, LORRAINE, actress; b. Bklyn., 1955; m. Harvey Keitel (div.); m. Edward James Olmos, Jan. 28, 1994; children: Margaux, Stella. Studied, Actors Studio; studied with Stella Adler, Ernie Martin, John Strasberg. Model in Europe. Films include The Pick-Up Artist, 1987, Someone to Watch Over Me, 1987, Sing, 1989, The Dream Team, 1989, Goodfellas, 1990 (Acad. award nominee for best supporting actress 1990, LA Film Critics Assoc. award for best sup. actress, 1990), Talent for the Game, 1991, Switch, 1991, Medicine Man, 1992, Radio Flyer, 1992, Traces of Red, 1992, (Showtime movie) Scam, 1993, Being Human, 1994, Even Cowgirls Get the Blues, 1994, The Basketball Diaries, 1995, Hackers, 1995, Les Menteurs, 1996, Ladies Room, 1999, Tangled, 2000, Your Aura is Throbbing, 2000, Riding in Cars With Boys, 2001; on TV in Getting Gotti, 1996, Lifeline, 1996, The Taking of Pelham One Two Three, 1998, The Sopranos, 1999-; off-Broadway play Goose and Tom-Tom. Mem.: bd. of dir. Riverkeeper, NY Council for the Humanities.

BRACE, C. LORING, anthropologist, educator; b. Hanover, N.H., Dec. 19, 1930; s. Gerald Warner and Huldah (Laird) B.; m. Mary Louise Crozier, June 8, 1957; children: Charles L., Roger C., Hudson H. BA, Williams Coll., 1952; MA, Harvard U., 1958, PhD, 1962. Instr. U. Wis., Milw., 1960-61; asst. prof., then assoc. prof. U. Calif., Santa Barbara, 1961-67; assoc. prof. anthropology U. Mich., Ann Arbor, 1967-71, prof., 1971—, curator phys. anthropology Mus. Anthropology, 1967—. Author: Human Evolution, 1965, 2d edit., 1977, Stages of Human Evolution, 1967, 5th edit., 1995, Atlas of Human Evolution, 1971, 2d edit., 1979, Evolution in an Anthropological View, 2000. With U.S. Army, 1954-56. Fellow AAAS (chmn. sect. H); mem. Am. Ahthrop. Assn., Am. Assn. Phys. Anthropology, Dental Anthropology Assn. (pres. 1988-90), History of Sci. Soc. Home: 1020 Ferdon Rd Ann Arbor MI 48104-3631 Office: U Mich Mus Anthropology 1109 Geddes Ave Ann Arbor MI 48109-1079 E-mail: clbrace@umich.edu.

BRACERAS, JENNIFER C. commissioner; BA Phi Beta Kappa, Magna Cum Laude, U. Mass., 1989; JD cum laude, Harvard Law Sch., 1994. Bar: Mass., Hispanic Nat. Atty. Ropes & Gray, Boston, 1996—2000; law clerk to the Hon. Ralph K. Winter, US Court of Appeals 2nd Circuit, 1995—96, to the Hon. William G. Young, US Dist Court, Dist Mass., 1994—95; staff asst. to Chief of Staff, VP Dan Quayle. Contbr. articles weekly column, various profl. jours. Grantee Charles Hamilton Houston, Harvard Law Sch., 2000—01. Mem.: Nat. Adv. Bd of Indep. Women's Forum, Civil Rights Practice Group of Federalist Soc. Law & Pub. Policies Studies. Office: 624 9th St NW Washington DC 20425*

BRACEWELL, GAYNOR LEE, hydro electric plant owner, developer; b. Dublin, Ga., Oct. 26, 1924; s. Ira Lee and Lola Belle (Morton) B.; m. Ruth Lee, July 1956 (div. July 1983); m. Carol Davis, July 25, 1964; children: Gaynor Lee II, Carol Victoria. BS in Agr., U. Ga., 1948. Agr. tchr. H.S., Blairsville, Ga., 1948; soil scientist Soil Conservation Svc., Tifton, Ga., 1948-49; bldg. contractor Bracewell Constrn., Plant City, Fla., 1950-73; owner, operator Sarge's War Surplus, Plant City, Fla., 1961-78, 574 Trailer Park, Plant City, 1963-83, Paradiso Falls & Beach, High Shoals, Ga., 1968—, High Shoals Hydro, 1988—. Dir. rep. Aviation Authority, Tampa, 1956-63. Author: (with others) High Shaols Then and Now, 1978. Sgt. U.S. Army, 1943-44. Mem. Sons Confederate Vets., S.E. Energy Assn. Baptist. Avocations: flying, sky diving, scuba diving, water and snow skiing. Home: 110 Frazier Hill Rd High Shoals GA 30645 Office: High Shoals Hydro PO Box 1 High Shoals GA 30645-0001

BRACEWELL, RONALD NEWBOLD, engineering educator; b. Sydney, Australia, July 22, 1921; s. Cecil Charles and Valerie Zilla (McGowan) Bracewell; m. Helen Mary Lester Elliott; children: Catherine Wendy, Mark Cecil. BSc in Math. and Physics, U. Sydney, 1941, B in Engring., 1943, M in Engring. with 1st class honors, 1948; PhD, Cambridge (Eng.) U., 1950. Sr. rsch. officer Radiophysics Lab., Commonwealth Sci. and Indsl. Rsch. Orgn., Sydney, 1949—54; vis. asst. prof. radio astronomy U. Calif., Berkeley, 1954—55; mem. elec. engring. faculty Stanford U., 1955—, Lewis M. Terman prof. and fellow

in elec. engring., 1974—79, now Terman prof. emeritus elec. engring. Pollock Meml. lectr. U. Sydney, 1978; Tektronix Disting. Visitor, 81; Christensen fellow St. Catherine's Coll., Oxford, 1987; sr. vis. fellow Inst. Astronomy; fellow commoner Churchill Coll., Cambridge U., 1988; Bunyan lectr. Stanford U., 1996; mem. adv. panels NSF, Naval Rsch. Lab., Office Naval Rsch., NAS, Nat. Radio Astronomy Obs., Jet Propulsion Lab. Adv. Group on Radio Experiments in Space, Advanced Rsch. Projects Agy. Author: The Fourier Transform and Its Applications, 1965, 2000, The Galactic Club: Intelligent Life in Outer Space, 1974, The Hartley Transform, 1986, Two-Dimensional Imaging, 1995; co-author: Radio Astronomy, 1955; translator: Radio Astronomy (J.L. Steinberg and J. Lequeux); editor: Paris Symposium on Radio Astronomy, 1959; former mem. editl. bd.: Internat. Jour. Imaging Sys. and Tech., Planetary and Space Sci., Proceedings of the Astron. Soc. Pacific, Cosmic Search, Jour. Computer Assisted Tomography, mem. bd. ann. rev.: Astronomy and Astrophysics, 1961—68; contbr. articles and revs. to jours., chapters to books. Recipient Duddell Premium, Instn. Elec. Engrs., London, 1952, Inaugural Alumni award, Sydney U., 1992; Fulbright travel grantee, 1954, William Gurling Watson traveling fellow, 1978, 1986. Fellow: AAAS, IEEE (life Heinrich Hertz Gold medal 1994, Jim Wolfensohn Suguna award 1996), Am. Acad. Arts and Scis., Astron. Soc. Australia, Royal Astron. Soc.; mem.: Order of Australia (officer), Internat. Sci. Radio Union, Astron. Soc. Pacific (life), Internat. Astron. Union, Am. Astron. Soc. (past councilor), Inst. Medicine of NAS (fgn. assoc.). Achievements include patents in field. Home: 836 Santa Fe Ave Stanford CA 94305-1023 Office: Stanford U 367 Packard Stanford CA 94305-9515 E-mail: bracewell@star.stanford.edu.

BRACEY, COOKIE FRANCES LEE, minister; b. Phila., Mar. 14, 1945; d. John Daniels and Evelyn (Jarvis) Bracey. B in Social Work, Temple U., 1983; MDiv, Wesley Theol. Sem., 1990. Administrv. asst. United Meth. Ch., Phila., 1963—66, parish cmty. devel., 1984—86, local pastor Catonsville, Ellicott City, Md., 1986—90; chaplain Meth. Hosp., Phila., 1990—; pastor St. Luke Snyder Ave United Meth. Ch., Phila., 1990—92, St. Matthews United Meth. Ch., Trevose, Pa., 1992—99; sr. pastor, dir. after sch. program Mt. Carmel United Meth. Ch., 1999—; chaplain Vet. Affairs Med. Ctr., Phila., 2003. Missionary, Brazil, 1988, Costa Rica, 1989, Dominican Republic, 1992, Zim Babwe, Africa, 1998, El Salvador, 1998; pastor St. Matthews United Meth. Ch., Trevose, Pa., 1992; Meth. mission tour, London, 1992, Israel, 1994; adj. faculty Ea. Bapt. Theol. Sem., Wynnewood, Pa., 1994—, Henry George Sch., Phila., 1996—; mem. faculty Phila. Sch. Devel. Mins., 1997, fac. mem. Sch. of Devel. Ministries, 1997; vol. reading specialist Howe Elem. Sch., Phila., Rowen Elem. Sch., Phila., 2001; supr. Pioneers Internat., Inc., Phila., 2001; chaplain VA Med. Ctr., Phila., 2003. Mem. Multi-Cultural Task Force, Phila. 1980, Victims and Crime Task Force, Phila. Ministers Law Enforcement Support Unit, Phila. Cmty. Assistance Network; del. World Meth. Conf., Rio Janero, Brazil, 1996; chaplain CAP Aux. USAF, 1996—, Phila. Prison Sys., 1996—; mem. Phila. Mayor's Commn. on Literacy, World Affairs Coun. of Phila., Spell Binders Storytellers; missionary Zimbabwe, Africa, 1998; faculty Phila. Sch. of Developing Ministries, 1997; bd. dirs. Archives and History United Meth. Ch., 1997; del. Clergywoman Convocation, Atlanta, 1997, San Diego, 2002; cert. mentor for supr. for ministry candidates; del. Billy Graham Conv., Amsterdam, 2000, World Meth. Conf., Brighton, Eng., 2001; bd. dirs. Youth Build Charter Sch. of Phila., 1999-. Recipient Outstanding Clergywoman award Nat. Assn. Clergywomen, 1990, Peace & Justice award Ch. Women United, 1992, Ministry award Harry Hosier United Meth. Ch., 1992, Preacher of Yr. award, 1998. Mem. AAUW, Am. Assn. Christian Counselors, Temple Univ. Soc. Adminstrn. Alumni Assn., Asian Am. Youth Assn., Nat. Fellowship Local, Black United Meth. Preachers (v.p.), Black Clergy Phila. and Vicinity (corr. sec.), Phila. Police Clergy, Coalition Prison Evangelists, Good Shepherd Mediation Program, Chaplaincy Coalition of Greater Phila., Wesley Theol. Sem. Alumni Assn., Mil. Chaplains Assn. Democrat. Avocations: music, opera, historical researcher, board games, traveling. Home: 337 Christian St Apt 3 Philadelphia PA 19147-3219 Address: 5909 North Park Ave Philadelphia PA 19141

BRACEY, EARNEST NORTON, political science educator; b. Jackson, Miss., June 8, 1953; s. Willard and Odessa Manola (Ford) B.; m. Atsuko Konuma, Apr. 2, 1995; children: Dominique, Princess, Omar. MPA, Golden Gate U., 1979; MA, Cath. U., Washington, 1983; D of Pub. Adminstrn., George Mason U., 1993; PhD in Edn., Capella U., 1999. Commd. 2d lt. U.S. Army, 1975, advanced through grades to lt. col., 1992; ret., 1995; prof. polit. sci. C.C. of So. Nev., Las Vegas, 1996—. Adj. prof. Ctrl. Tex. Coll., Camp Zama, Japan, 1993-95; mem. Nev. faculty alliance C.C. of So. Nev., Las Vegas, 1996—, past chair dept. polit. sci. and history. Author: Choson, 1994, Prophetic Insight, 1999, Daniel "Chappie" James, 2003. Mem. NAACP, Am. Soc. of Mil. Comptrs., Assn. of the U.S. Army, Retired Officer Assn. Avocations: jazz trumpeter, marathon runner, writing, poetry, american historian.

BRACH, PAUL HENRY, artist; BFA, U Iowa, 1948, MFA, 1950. Tchr. U. Mo., Columbia, 1950-51, New Sch. Social Rsch., N.Y.C., 1952-55, NYU, 1954-67, 86-90, Parsons Sch. Design, 1956-67, The Cooper Union, 1960-62, 79-82, Cornell U., 1965-67; chair dept. visual arts. U. Calif., San Diego, 1967-69; dean Sch. Art Calif. Inst. Arts, Valencia, 1969-75; chair divsn. arts Fordham U., N.Y.C., 1975-79, Empire State Coll., N.Y.C., 1979—95; Milton Avery disting. prof. Bard Coll., N.Y.C., 1993. Vis. artist U. N.Mex, Albuquerque, 1965; guest critic U. Minn., Mpls., Sarah Lawrence Coll., Bronxville, N.Y., Montclair (N.J.) State Coll., Art Forum Mag., 1976; vis. critic N.Y. studio program Empire State Coll., 1976—; cons. Rutgers U., New Brunswick, 1977; guest critic Bard Coll., Empire State Coll., N.Y.C., 1977; contbg. critic Art Forum Mag., 1977; vis. artist Banff (Can.) Art Ctr., 1979; contbg. critic Art in Am., 1979-2002; guest lectr. Pratt Inst., N.Y.C., 1980, Tuscon Mus. Art, 1992; vis. artist Litho Workshop, Ariz. State U., Tempe, 1981, U. N.Mex., Albuquerque, 1981; guest lectr. Tuscon Mus. Art, 1992. One-man shows at Leo Castelli, N.Y.C., 1957, 59, Cordier Ekstrom Gallery, N.Y.C., 1961-63, Kornble Gallery, N.Y.C., 1971, Andre Emmerich Gallery, N.Y.C., 1974, Jean Millant Gallery, L.A., 1974, Benson Gallery, Bridgehampton, N.Y., 1975, Lerner Heller Gallery, N.Y.C., 1978, 80, Yares Gallery, L.A., 1979, Janus Gallery, L.A., 1980, Yares Gallery, Scottsdale, Ariz., 1981, Bernice Steinbaum Gallery Ltd., N.Y.C., 1983, 85, 87, 90, 91, Elaine Horwitch Galleries, Palm Springs, Calif., 1987, Benton Gallery, Southampton, N.Y., 1987, Vered Gallery, East Hampton, N.Y., 1989, Rancho Linda Vista Gallery, Oracle, Ariz., 1992, Steinbaum Krauss Gallery, N.Y.C., 1994, McAllen (Tex.) Internat. Mus., 1995, Tucson (Ariz.) Mus. Art, 1995, Guild Hall, East Hampton, 1995, Bernice Steinbaum Gallery, Miami, Fla., 2000, others; exhibited in group shows at Wake Forest U. Art Gallery, Winston-Salem, N.C., 1988, Rose Art Mus., Brandeis U., Waltham, Mass., 1988, Anderson Gallery, Va. Commonwealth U., Richmond, 1988, Temple U., Phila., 1988, Alexandra Monet Fine Arts, New Orleans, 1989, Bernice Steinbaum Gallery, N.Y., 1990, Guild Hall Mus., East Hampton Ctr. Contemporary Art, 1990, Weatherspoon Art Gallery, Greensboro, N.Y.C., 1990, Tyler Art Gallery, Oswego, N.Y., 1990, Albright-Knox Art Gallery, Buffalo, 1990, LewAllen/Butler Gallery, Sante Fe, N.Mex., 1993, Vered Gallery, East Hampton, 1993, Steinbaum Krauss Gallery, N.Y.C., 1993, Kent (Conn.) Gallery, 1994, Andre Zarre Gallery, N.Y.C., 1995, U. Iowa, Iowa City, 2002, others; represented in permanent collections at Mus. Modern Art, N.Y.C., Whitney Mus. Am. Art, N.Y.C., L.A. County Mus. Art, St. Louis Art Mus., Smith Coll. Mus., Nebr. Art Mus., Albuquerque Mus. Art, Mus. Fine Art, Santa Fe, Phoenix Art Mus., NYU, U. Iowa, others; contbr. articles to profl. jours. Fellow Djerassi Found., Woodside, Calif., 1987, 90.

BRACHFELD, JONAS, cardiologist, educator; b. Antwerp, Belgium, Dec. 1, 1924; came to U.S., 1943; s. Chaskiel and Rosa (Spira) B.; m. Rosalind Roth, Apr. 3, 1955; children: Claude A., Renée K., Eric L. BS, Calif. Inst. of Tech., 1947; MD, U. Pa., 1952. Diplomate Am. Bd. Internal Medicine, Am. Bd. Cardiovascular Disease. Chmn. dept. internal medicine Rancocas Hosp., Willingboro, N.J., 1961-94, dir. CCU, 1972-93; founder, CEO Brachfeld Med. Assocs., Willingboro, 1969-94; prof. clin. medicine U. Medicine and Dentistry N.J., Camden, 1993—; dir. Fellows' Clinic, dept. cardiology Univ. Med. Ctr., 1997—. Founder Brachfeld Day Care Ctr. Jewish Geriatric Home, Cherry Hill, N.J., 1972. Fellow Am. Coll. Cardiology, Am. Heart Assn. Avocation: languages (Dutch, Spanish, French, German, and Hebrew). Home: 227 Nicholson Dr Moorestown NJ 08057-2909 Office: U Med Ctr 1103 Kings Hwy N Cherry Hill NJ 08034-1983

BRACHMAN, MALCOLM K. oil company executive; b. Ft. Worth, Dec. 9, 1926; s. Solomon and Etta (Katzenstein) B.; m. Minda Fay Delugach, Sept. 4, 1951 (dec.); children: Lynn, Malcolm K. Jr., Lisa. BA, Yale U., 1945; MA, Harvard U., 1947, PhD, 1949. CLU. Asst. prof. So. Meth. U., Dallas, 1949-50; assoc. physicist Argonne Nat. Lab., Chgo., 1950-53; rsch. staff Tex. Instruments, Inc., Dallas, 1953-54; v.p. Pioneer Am. Ins. Co., Ft. Worth, 1954-61, pres., 1961-73, chmn. bd., CEO, 1973-79; pres. N.W. Oil Co., Dallas, 1956—. Chmn. adv. coun. Econ. Growth Ctr. Yale U. Capt. USAF, 1950—57. Recipient Yale Presdl. medal, 1999, Hon. Alumnus award, Tex. Christian U., 1999, Yale medal, Assn. Yale Alumni, 2002. Fellow Am. Phys. Soc., Soc. Petroleum Engrs., Am. Math. Soc.; sr. mem. IEEE, Soc. Exploration Geophysics; mem. Dallas Petroleum Club, Century Assn. (N.Y.C.). Jewish. Avocation: bridge. Home: 3510 Turtle Creek Blvd Apt 16F Dallas TX 75219-5545 Office: NW Oil Co 3811 Turtle Creek Blvd Ste 330 Dallas TX 75219 E-mail: mkb@nwoil.net.

BRACHMAN, RICHARD JOHN, II, financial services consultant, banking educator; b. Madison, Wis., Oct. 30, 1951; s. Richard John and Joan Katherine (Harrington) B.; m. Connie Beth Ten Haken, May 14, 1977; children: Samantha Joan, Richard John. BS, U. Wis., 1974. With The Rural Cos., Madison, 1975-83; v.p. CBI Ins. Svcs., Inc., Middleton, Wis., 1983-84, exec. v.p., 1984-85, pres., 1985-87; sr. v.p. Valley Bank Ins., Madison, 1987-94; pres. Cmty. Life Ins. Co., divsn. Valley Bancorporation, Madison, 1987-94; owner, v.p., dir. Lexlawn, Inc., Lexington, Ky., 1993-98; pres., CEO, The Brachman Group, Ltd., Madison, 1994—; owner Midwest Lawn Care, Inc., 2000—. Mem. faculty Iowa Sch. Banking, U. Iowa, 1998—; bd. dirs. Ins. Svcs. Inc., Cmty. Life Ins. Co., Madison, Career Mgmt. Group. Mem. parish coun. Our Lady Queen of Peace Ch., Madison, 1989—; bd. dirs. U. Wis. Meml. Union. Mem. U. Wis. Alumni Assn. (bd. dirs. 1988-94, Spark Plug award 1987), Mendota Gridiron Club (bd. dirs.), KC. Roman Catholic. Avocations: photography, reading, golf. Home and Office: 3882 Cardinal Point Trail Verona WI 53593-5551

BRACHNA, GABOR (SAMUEL), elementary school educator; b. Cleve, May 14, 1941; s. Gabor and Ethel Brachna; m. Susan Chamberlin, Dec. 24, 1987; children: Christopher, Jonathan. BA, Kent State U., 1963; postgrad., London Sch. Econs., 1964—65; grad. elem. sch. adminstrn., Case Western Reserve State U., Cleve., 1973; moral devel. cert., Harvard U., 1983. Tchr. Cleve. Pub. Sch., 1966—71, adminstrv. intern, 1971—74, peer advisor, 1994—96; rschr. Cleve. C. of C., 1998. Advisor Tchr. Adv. Bd. for Natural History Mus., Cleve., 1988—89; rschr. Intellicor, NYC, 1977; curriculum developer Cleve. Lang. Arts Curriculum Devel. Com., 1971—74. Author (contbg. author): (novels) Whatever Happened to the Paper Rex Man?, 1993, (encyclopedia) Encyclopedia of Cleveland History, 1987, World East Pubs., 1999. V.p. Cleve. Cultural Gardens, 1993; liason rep. Buckeye Woodland Sch. Cmty. Coun., Cleve., 1971—74; moderator Great Decisions Coun. on World Affairs, Lakewood, Ohio. With U.S. Army Nat. Guard, 1965—71. Recipient cert. of appreciation, Kiwanis Club, 1979. Mem.: Knights of St. John of the Hosp. of Jerusalem (Malta). Republican. Lutheran. Avocations: tropical fish, stamps. Home: 2954 Eaton Rd Shaker Heights OH 44122-2516

BRACK, O. M., JR., English language educator; b. Houston, Nov. 30, 1938; s. O. M. and Olivia Mae (Rice) B.; 1 child, Matthew Rice. Student, U. Houston, 1956-57; BA, Baylor U., 1960, MA, 1961; PhD, U. Tex., Austin, 1965. Asst. prof. William Woods Coll., 1964-65; asst. prof. English lit. U. Iowa, Iowa City, 1965-68, assoc. prof., 1968-73, dir. center textual studies, 1967-73; prof. English lit. Ariz. State U., Tempe, 1973—. Chmn. 18th Century Short Title Catalogue Com., 1970-73; pres. Arete Publs., Ltd., 1976-81; Albert H. Smith Meml. lectr. bibliography Birmingham (Eng.) Bibliog. Soc., 1983 vis. fellow U. Oxford Wolfson Coll., 1986-87; mem. adv. bd. 18th-Century Brit. Periodical Subject Indiex, 1996—, Soc. for Textual Scholarship, 1998; bd. dirs. 18th-Century Short-Title Catalogue, Inc., 1999-2000. Author: Bibliography and Textual Criticism, 1969, Samuel Johnson's Early Biographers, 1971, Hoole's Death of Johnson, 1972, Henry Fielding's Pasquin, 1973, A Catalogue of the Leigh Hunt Manuscripts, 1973, The Early Biographies of Samuel Johnson, 1974, American Humor, 1977, Twilight of Dawn, 1987, Writers, Books and Trade, 1994, Samuel Johnson in New Albion, 1997; textual editor: Works of Tobias Smollett, 1966—; gen. editor: Works of Tobias Smollett, 1973-86; editor: English Literature in Transition, 1981-82, mem. editl. com., 1982—91; editor: Studies in Eighteenth Century Culture, 1981-86; mem. editl. com.: Yale edit. Works of Samuel Johnson, 1977— ; editl. cons. The Literature of England, Scott, Foresman & Co., 1977-79, Works of David Hume, Princeton U. Press, 1990-91, Oxford U. Press, 1995-97; asst. editor: Eighteenth-Century Bibliography, 1964-73, Books at Iowa, 1966-73; editor Eighteenth Century: A Current Bibliography, 1983-90; mem. editl. com.: Age of Johnson, 1985-2003, Rocky Mountain Rev. of Lang. and Lit., 1980-98, Clarissa Project, 1987-2000. Mem. Salvation Army Coun., South Mountain Corps, 1996-2002, chair, 1999-2002. Named Grad. Coll. Outstanding Mentor, 2000; recipient Grad. Coll. Disting. Rsch. award, 1981—82, Rocky Mountains MLA Huntington Libr. award, 1986, Humanities Rsch. award, 1989—90, Faculty Achievement award, Ariz. State U. Alumni Assn., 1991; fellow, Huntington Libr., 1978, Am. Coun. Learned Soc., 1979—80, Newberry Libr., 1982, Andrew W. Mellon Fund, Huntington Libr., 1994, Huntington Libr., 1996, 1997; grantee, Am. Philos. Soc., 1967, NEH, 1993—95, 1995—98; scholar Disting. scholar, Phi Kappa Phi, 1975. Mem. Am. Soc. 18th Century Studies, South Central 18th Century Soc. (pres. 1982-83). Western Soc. for 18th Century Studies (pres. 2000-01), Rocky Mountain MLA, Bibliog. Soc. Am., Bibliog. Soc. U. Va., Bibliog. Soc. (London), Printing Hist. Soc., Am. Printing History Assn., Samuel Johnson Soc. So. Calif. (bd. dirs. 1989—, pres. 1994-95). Clubs: Grolier, The Johnsonians. Episcopalian. Office: Ariz State U Dept English Tempe AZ 85287-0302 E-mail: om.brack@asu.edu.

BRACK, ROBERT LOUIS, retired music educator; b. Brownsville, Tenn., June 8, 1944; s. Cobon Walton and Opal Virginia Brack; m. Lavell L Lawson, Nov. 23, 1974. BS in Music Edn., Tenn. State U., 1966; MEd in Music Edn., U. of Ark., 1972. Cert. music tchr. Ark. State Dept. of Edn., 1998. Choral music tchr. Emanuel County HS, Swainsboro, Ga., 1967—67; choral music dir. Wash. HS, El Dorado, Ark., 1967—69; dir. of choral activities Horace Mann High and Jr. HS, Little Rock, 1969—73, Hall HS, Little Rock, 1973—75, Ctrl. HS, Little Rock, 1975—. Ch. organist St. Peter's Rock Bapt. Ch., Little Rock, 1982—2002. Mem.: Ark. Music Educators Assn. (Ark. Music Educators Assn. Hall of Fame 2000), Am. Choral Directors Assn. (region chmn. ctrl. region choral dirs. assn. 1984—86, Ctrl. Region Choral Dir. of the Yr. award 1994—95, 1996—97, 2001—02). Democrat. Baptist. Avocation: community choral group. Home: 14217 Longtree Drive Little Rock AR 72212-1961 Office: Central High School 1500 Park Street Little Rock AR 72202 Personal E-mail: llbrack@aristotle.net. E-mail: rlbrack@central.lrsd.k12.ar.us.

BRACKEN, CHARLES HERBERT, banker; b. Corry, Pa., June 5, 1921; s. Olin Williams and Vellah (Morgan) B.; m. Barbara E. Barton, June 19, 1948; children: Betsy Louise, Sally Anne, Charles Herbert, Barton William, Douglas Morgan. BS, U. Pa., 1948; student spl. banking courses. Successively asst. to pres., v.p., exec. v.p. and trust officer, pres., dir. Citizens Nat. Bank, Corry, 1948-64; pres., dir. Marine Bank, Erie, Pa., 1964-74, chmn. bd. dirs., chief exec. officer, 1974-87. Dir. Country Fair Inc., 1965-85; vice chmn. PNC Bank, 1984-85. Bd. dirs. Eric Conf. Cmty. Devel.; trustee Hamot Med. Ctr., 1970-79, corporator, 1980—, pres., 1977-78; pres., trustee Erie Cmty. Found., 1970-96; treas. Erie Episc. Diocese, 1969-87; bd. govs., treas. Erie unit Shriners Hosp. Crippled Children, 1967-79; corporator St. Vincent Health Ctr., 1965—; adv. bd. Titusville campus U. Pitts., 1967-84, Gannon Coll., 1971-88, Mercyhurst Coll., 1968-97, trustee. Mem. Pa. Bankers Assn. (pres. 1966-67), Newcomen Soc. N.Am. (dir.), Masons, Shriners, Yacht Club, Rotary, Univ. Club, Erie Club, Kahkwa Club, Sigma Alpha Epsilon. Episcopalian. Home: 5060 Saybrook Pl Erie PA 16505-1324 Office: 901 State St Erie PA 16501-1414 also: PO Box 8480 Erie PA 16553-8480

BRACKEN, HARRY MCFARLAND, philosophy educator; b. Yonkers, N.Y., Mar. 12, 1926; s. Harry S. and Grace M. (McFarl) B.; m. Eva Maria Laufkotter, Dec. 24, 1949 (div.); children— Christopher, Timothy; m. Elisabeth van Gelderen, June 19, 1985 BA, Trinity Coll., Hartford, Conn., 1949; MA, Johns Hopkins, 1954; PhD, U. Iowa, 1956. Instr. U. Iowa, Iowa City, 1955-57, asst. prof., 1957-61; asso. prof. U. Minn., Mpls., 1961-63; prof. Ariz. State U., Tempe, 1963-66; prof. philosophy McGill U., Montreal, Que., Can., 1966-91. Prof. U. Calif., San Diego, 1970; vis. prof. Trinity Coll., U. Dublin, Ireland, 1972-73, 79-80; vis. prof. metaphysics U. Coll., Nat. U. Ireland, Dublin, 1972-73, 79-80; adj. faculty philosophy Erasmus U., Rotterdam, 1988-95, Rijksuniversiteit Groningen, 1990 95; adj. prof. philosophy Ariz. State U., 1995—. Author: The Early Reception of Berkeley's Immaterialism: 1710-1733, 1959, 2d edit., 1965, Berkeley, 1974; Mind and Language: Essays on Descartes and Chomsky, 1984, Freedom of Speech: Words Are Not Deeds, 1994, Descartes, 2002. Served with USNR, 1943-46, PTO. Recipient Acad. Freedom award Ariz. Civil Liberties Union, 1965; Edn. award J. I. Segal Found. for Jewish Culture, 1972 Mem. Am. Philos. Assn., Internat. Berkeley Soc., The Hume Soc., USS Lauderdale Assn. Home: 9107 E Avenida Las Noches Apache Junction AZ 85218-4676 E-mail: hbracken@imap2.asu.edu.

BRACKEN, KATHLEEN ANN, nurse; b. Chgo., Mar. 14, 1947; d. Thomas James and Catherine Anastasia (Cowal) B. Diploma, Little Company of Mary Hosp., Evergreen Park, Ill., 1968; BSN, Lewis U., 1984, MBA, 1989. RN, Ill. Mem. staff Little Company of Mary Hosp., Evergreen Park, Ill., 1968-69, 71-73, supr. ICUs, 1976-79, dir. ICU's, 1979-91; v.p. patient care svcs. South Chgo. Cmty. Hosp., 1991-93; staff nurse Chgo. Lying-In Clinic, U. Chgo., 1970-71; nurse mgr. VA Chgo. Healthcare Sys., 1994-98, assoc. chief nurse, 1998—. Bd. dirs., chmn. nursing cardiovascular com. South Cook Heart Assn., 1977-83. Recipient Meritorious Svc. award, 1979, 81, 82, 83, 84, 85, 86. Mem. NAFE, NOVA, Beverly Area Planning Assn., Am. Orgn. Nurse Execs., Chgo. Heart Assn., Assn. Critical Care Nurses (pres. southside Chgo. Area chpt. 1983-84, rec. sec. 1984-85), Am. Heart Assn. (cardiovasc. nursing coun.), Brain Injury Assn. Ill., Chgo. Healthcare Exec. Forum, Sigma Theta Tau. Home: 10321 S Campbell Ave Chicago IL 60655-1016 Office: VA Chgo Health Care Sys Lakeside Divsn 333 E Huron St Chicago IL 60611-3004

BRACKEN, NANETTE BEATTIE, lawyer; b. Poughkeepsie, N.Y., Mar. 12, 1950; d. John Lindley and Margaret Jane (Brickner) Beattie; m. Paul Bracken, May 25, 1974; children: Kathleen John, James Beattie, Margaret Logue. BA, Vassar Coll., 1972; JD, U. Balt., 1975. Bar: N.Y. 1976, Conn. 1978, U.S. Dist. Ct. Conn. 1980. Chief clk. estate tax dept. Surrogate's Ct. Westchester County, N.Y. Dept. Taxation and Fin., White Plains, N.Y., 1976-78; assoc. Crehan & Fricke, Ridgefield, Conn., 1978—87; vol. Children's Ctr. Bedford Hills Correctional Facility, 1988—. Active Birthright, Danbury, Conn., 1978—80, Housatonic Mental Health Commn, Conn., 1980—83, Ridgefield Youth Commn., 1978—81; vice-chmn. Ridgefield Housing Commn., 1996—; trustee Wooster Sch., 2001—. Mem. ABA, N.Y. State Bar Assn., Conn. Bar Assn. Avocations: travel, gardening, golf, tennis, dude ranching. Home and Office: 22 Green Ln Ridgefield CT 06877-3017

BRACKEN, PEG, writer; b. Filer, Idaho, Feb. 25, 1918; d. John Lewis and Ruth (McQuesten) B.; m. John Hamilton Ohman, June 15, 1991; 1 child from previous marriage, Johanna Bracken. AB, Antioch Coll., 1940. Author: The I Hate to Cook Book, 1960, The I Hate to Housekeep Book, 1962, I Try to Behave Myself, 1963, Peg Bracken's Appendix to The I Hate to Cook Book, 1966, I Didn't Come Here to Argue, 1969, But I Wouldn't Have Missed It for the World, 1973, The I Hate to Cook Almanack - A Book of Days, 1976, A Window Over the Sink, 1981, The Compleat I Hate to Cookbook, 1986, On Getting Old for the First Time, 1996.

BRACKEN, THOMAS, bank executive; Pres., CEO N.J. Nat. Bank (named changed First Union Core States Bank), Pennington, 1993—; head govt. and comml. banking of N.J. First Union Core States Bank, Pennington, 1998—2001; CEO, pres. Sun Bank Corp., 2001—. Office: Sun Bank Corp 266 Candis Ave Vineland NJ 08360*

BRACKEN, THOMAS ROBERT JAMES, real estate investment executive; b. Spokane, Wash., Jan. 1, 1950; s. James Lucas and Frances (Cadzow) B.; m. Linda Jacobson, Sept. 9, 1972; children: Karl Forest, David Erskine. BS, Yale U., 1971; MBA, Columbia U., 1972. Sr. appraiser Prudential Ins., N.Y.C., 1972-74, mgr. real estate N.Y.C. and Newark, 1974-76, assoc. gen. mgr. Seattle, 1977-78; v.p. First City Investments, Seattle, 1978-80; pres. Fenix, Inc., Seattle, 1980-86; v.p. Washington Mortgage Corp., Seattle, 1982-85, exec. v.p., 1986-88; sr. v.p. Pioneer Bank, Lynwood, Wash., 1985-86; pres.real estate financing USL Capital, San Francisco, 1988-97; sr. v.p. real estate fin. group Orix, USA, San Francisco, 1997-98; pres. Presidio Interfunding Corp., San Francisco, 1998-99; dir. L.J. Melody & Co., San Jose, Calif., 2000—03; mem. Crossbow Capital, LLC, Los Altos, Calif., 2000—; mng. dir. The Broe Cos., San Francisco, 2003—. Mem. Nat. Assn. Indsl./Office Parks (v.p. Seattle chpt. 1981-83), Yale Assn. Western Wash. (pres. 1984-86), Urban Land Inst., Mortgage Bankers Assn. Presbyterian. Avocations: running, sports. Office: The Broe Cos 110 Sutter 8th Fl San Francisco CA 94104 E-mail: tombracken@msn.com.

BRACKENRIDGE, N. LYNN, not-for-profit developer; b. Youngstown, Ohio, Sept. 9, 1957; d. John Bruce Brackenridge and Mary Ann Rossi; m. Harry Lee Carrico, July 1, 1994. BA, Lawrence U., 1978; MS, Georgetown U., 1980. Tchg. asst. Georgetown U., Washington, 1979-81, admissions officer, 1984-85, editor, writer devel., 1985-87, asst. dir. devel., 1987-89; dir. devel. Cath. Charities U.S.A., Washington, 1989-91, Johns Hopkins U. Bologna (Italy) Ctr., 1991-92; dir. devel. and pub. rels. Nat. Ctr. for State Cts., Williamsburg, Va., 1993-97; v.p. for devel. Gateway Homes Greater Richmond (Va.), Inc., 1998-99, pres., 1999—. Vol. Richmond Ballet, 1993-95, Leukemia Soc. Am., Hampton, Va., 1996—; bd. dirs. Nat. Alliance for Mentally Ill (Va. chap.), 2000—, Chesterfield Alternatives, Inc., 2000—. Georgetown U. fellow, 1979-81; recipient diplome d'etudes Inst. d'Etudes Francaises de Touraine, 1976. Mem. Nat. Soc. Fund Raising Execs. (cert. fund raising exec., chmn. program com., pres. 1997). Democrat. Avocations: flying small aircraft, running, reading, films, languages. Home: 9303 Cragmont Dr Richmond VA 23229-7610 Office: Gateway Homes Greater Richmond Inc PO Box 11303 Richmond VA 23230-1303 E-mail: lbrackenridge@gatewayhomes.org.

BRACKETT, COLQUITT PRATER, JR., judge, lawyer; b. Norfolk, Va., Feb. 24, 1946; s. Colquitt Prater Sr. and Antoinette Gladys (Cacace) B.; m. Carol Ann Roberts, Dec. 29, 2000; 1 child, Susan Elizabeth Brackett Brooks. BS, U. Ga., 1966, MA, 1968, JD, 1973, LLM, 1976; travel mktg. profl. diploma, S.E. Tourism Soc. Mktg. Coll., 1999. Bar: Ga. 1973, U.S. Dist. Ct. (so. dist.) Ga. 1974, U.S. Dist. Ct. (mid. dist.) Ga. 1977, U.S. Supreme Ct. 1980, Tenn. 1987. Assoc. Surrett & CoCroft, Augusta, Ga., 1972-74; ptnr. Surrett & Brackett, Augusta, 1974-76; faculty Sch. Law, U. Ga., Athens, 1977-82; mng. ptnr. Brackett, Prince & Neufeld, Athens, 1982-90; adminstrv. law judge Ga. Dept. Med. Assistance, Athens, 1990-98. Hearing officer Ga. State Bd. Edn., 1979-91; v.p. Mus. Dolls & Gifts, Inc., Watkinsville, Ga., 1983—; pres. Bear Country Lodge and Conf. Ctr., Pigeon Forge, Tenn., 1996—, chmn. bd. Adventures in Toy Land, 1999-2000; CEO Toy Mus. at Natural Bridge Va., 2002-; exec. dir. Soc. Preservation of Am. Childhood Effects, 2002-; curator Toy Mus., Natural Bridge, Va., 2002-. Author: Court Administration, 1972; (monograph) The Security Inventors Protection Corporation and the Operations of SIPC, 1976; (musical play) Americanization of Mary Poppins, 1995. Pres. Athens/Clarke Mental Health Assn., 1985; chmn. bd. dirs. N.E. Ga. Mental Health Assn., 1989-90; bd. dirs. Coalition for The Blue Ridge Pkwy., 1994-2000, Oconee Cultural Arts Found., 1995-97, Blue Ridge Pkwy. Assn., 1997-2001, Shennandoah Valley Travel Assn., 2003—. Mem. ABA, Ga. State Bar Assn., Ga. Assn. Adminstrv. Law Judges (bd. dirs. 1990-91), Ga. Trial Lawyers Assn., Shenandoah Valley Travel Assn. (bd. dirs. 2003—), Internat. Platform Assn., Blue Ridge Pkwy. Assn., S.E. Tourism Soc., Rotary Internat., Ea. Nat. Parks Assn., Sevier County Bar Assn., Soc. Am. Poets, Soc. Magna Carta Barons, Phi Alpha Delta (justice A.H. Stephens chpt. 1973). Episcopalian. Avocations: reading, music, golf, cross-country skiing. E-mail: smokymts@ntelos.net.

BRACKETT, MARTIN LUTHER, JR., lawyer; b. Charlotte, N.C., Feb. 23, 1947; s. Martin Luther and Helen Virginia (Smith) B.; m. Lisa Nichol; children— Martin Hunter, Alexander Jones, Amelia Kathleen, Lauren Hart. B.A., Davidson Coll., 1969; J.D., U. N.C., 1972. Bar: N.C. 1972, U.S. Dist. Ct. (we. dist.) N.C. 1973, U.S. Ct. Appeals (4th cir.) 1975. Ptnr. Bailey, Brackett & Brackett, P.A., Charlotte, N.C., 1973-83, Brackett & Sitton, Charlotte, 1983-85, Robinson, Bradshaw & Hinson, P.A., 1985—. Mem. Auditorium-Coliseum-Conv. Ctr. Authority, Charlotte, 1981-87, chmn., 1985-87. Served to capt. U.S. Army, 1972-73. Recipient Van Hecke-Wettach award U. N.C., 1972. Fellow

Am. Coll. Trial Lawyers; mem. N.C. Acad. Trial Lawyers (bd. govs. 1980-86, 88-95, v.p. 1984-86). Democrat. Presbyterian. Office: 1900 Independence Ctr 101 N Tryon St Charlotte NC 28246-0100

BRACKETT, ROBERT CLARK, business valuation specialist; b. Elmhurst, Ill., Apr. 12, 1953; s. Robert Chase and Lillis Margaret Brackett; m. Deborah Francine Brackett, May 20, 1978; 1 child, Robert Beck. BS in Indsl. Engring., Iowa State U., 1975; M in Mgmt., Northwestern U., 1982. CPA, Mass. Cons. Ernst & Whinney, Boston, 1982-85, Killingsworth Assocs., Cambridge, 1986-87, Brackett Consulting, Natick, Mass., 1987-89; mgr. Glenn Ingram & Co., Chgo., 1989-91; pres. Crandall & Brackett, Ltd., Winfield, Ill., 1991—. Mem. adv. bd. DuPage Area Small Bus. Devel. Ctr., Glen Ellyn, Ill., 1994—. Mem. Nat. Assn. Cert. Valuation Analysts (cert., mem. emeritus, exec. adv. bd. 1993-96, amb. 1999—, mem. stds. com. 1996—), Inst. Indsl. Engrs., Winfield (Ill.) C. of C. (pres. 1995). Avocations: backpacking, woodworking. Office: Crandall & Brackett Ltd 2100 Manchester Bldg B Ste 900 Wheaton IL 60187 E-mail: Robert@crandall-Brackett.com.

BRACKETT, RONALD E. investment company executive, lawyer; b. Rockford, Ill., May 10, 1942; s. F. Earl Brackett and Anne (Christenberry) Townsend; m. Susan Catherine Stichnoth, May 31, 1975; 1 child, Charles William. BA, Trinity Coll., 1964; JD, U. Mich., 1967. Bar: N.Y. 1968. Assoc. Rogers & Wells, N.Y.C., 1968-74, ptnr., 1974-91, mng. ptnr., 1984-85, cons., 1992-94; founder, prin. Associated Growth Investors, L.P., Babylon, NY, 1992—. Bd. dirs. King Kullen Grocery Co., Inc., Westbury, NY. Mem. ABA, N.Y. State Bar Assn., Phi Beta Kappa. Office: Associated Growth Investors LP 1801 House Argyle Square Babylon NY 11702-2711

BRACKMANN, DERALD E. otolaryngologist; b. Buckley, Ill., Feb. 13, 1937; s. Otto Henry Brackmann and Anna Mina Abraham; m. Charlotte Joyce Boyden, June 21, 1959; children: David, Douglas, Mark, Steven. Student, U. Ill., 1958, MD, 1962. Diplomate Am. Bd. Otolaryngology. Intern Ill. Ctrl. Hosp., Chgo., 1962—63; resident in ob-gyn. Ill. Rsch. Hosp., Chgo., 1963—64; resident in Otolaryngology L.A. County/U. So. Calif. Med. Ctr., 1966—70, chief otology, 1981—98; staff physician House Ear Clinic, L.A., 1970—85, pres., 1985—. Chief ENT svc. St. Vincent Med. Ctr., 1971—98; clin. prof. otolaryngology U. So. Calif., clin. prof. neurologic surgery, clin. instr. House Ear Inst. Editor: Otologic Surgery, Neurotology, Neurological Surgery of the Ear & Skull Base; editl. bd.: jour. Advances in Otolaryngology-Head and Neck Surgery, Laryngoscoope, Neurotology; co-author (chpt.): Electrocochleography, 1976, Hearing Disorders, 1976, Acoustic Tumors: Diagnosis and Management, 1979, Acoustic Tumors Vol. 1 Diagnosis, 1979, Otolaryngology, 1980, Controversy in Otolaryngology, 1980, Butterworth International Medical Reviews: Otology, 1982, Disorders of the Facial Nerve, 1982, Essential Otolaryngology Head & Neck Surgery, 1983; author: Surgery of the Skull Base, 1983, Meniere's Disease: A Comprehensive Appraisal, 1983; contbg. editor: Neurological Surgery of the Ear and Skull Base, 1982; co-author: Gerald M. English Otolaryngology, Sensory Evoked Potentials, 1984, Cochlear Implants, 1985; author: The Facial Nerve, 1986; co-author: Ear and Skull Base, 1986, Conn's Current Therapy, 1988, Otologic Medicine and Surgery, 1988, Advances in Otolaryngology-Head and Neck Surgery, 1989; author: Operative Challenges in Otolaryngology Head and Neck Surgery, 1990, Neurosurgery Update 1: Diagnosis, Operative Technique and Neuro-Otology, 1990, Operative Techniques in Otolaryngology-Head and Neck Surgery, 1991, Surgery of Cranial Base Tumors, 1993; author: Handbook of Intraoperative Monitoring, 1994; co-author: Essential Otolaryngology, 1995, Otolaryngology, 1996; author: Atlas of Head & Neck Surgry-Otolaryngology, 1996, Disorders of the Vestibular System, 1996, Head and Neck Surgery Volume 2: Ear, 1996; co-author: Acoustic Tumors Diagnosis and Management, 1997, Diseases of the ear, 1998, Essential Otolaryngology, 1998, Head and Neck Surgery-Otolaryngology, 1998, Surgery of the Skull Base, 1998, Textbook of Clinical Neurology, 1998, Cranial Base Surgery, 1999; author: The Facial Nerve, 2000; co-author: Operative Techniques in Neurosurgery, 2001, Controversies in Otolaryngology, 2001, Surgery of the Ear 5th, 2002, Essential Otolaryngology, 2003; contbr. articles to profl. jours.; editor: Neurologic Surgery of the Ear and Skull Base, 1982; contbg. editor: Otologic Surgery, 1994, 2001; co-editor: Neurotology, 1994. Capt. USAF, 1964—66. Recipient Alumni Achievement award, U. Ill., 1997, Gold medal, Prosper Meniere's Soc., 2000; fellow, House Ear Inst. and Clinic, 1970—71. Fellow: AMA, Am. Laryngol. Rhinological Otological Soc., Am. Acad. Olotaryngology Head and Neck Surgery (pres. 1988, com. facial nerve disorders, pres. 1987—88); mem.: ACS, Asian Conf. Neurol. Surgeons, N.Am. Skull Base Soc. (pres. 1995—96), Rsch. Study Club, L.A. Soc. Otolaryngology (pres. 1986—87), Otolaryngology Soc. Australia (hon.), Royal Soc. Medicine (hon.), L.A. County Med. Assn., Calif. Med. Assn., Am. Otological Soc. (task force sub-certification, pres. 1995—96), Am. Neurotology Soc. (exec. coun., pres. 1984—85), Centurion Club, Alpha Omega Alpha. Republican. Achievements include research in neurotology; cochlear implant; auditory brainstem implant. Avocations: fishing, hunting. Office: House Ear Clinic 2100 W 3rd St Los Angeles CA 90057 Office Fax: 213-484-5900. E-mail: dbrackmann@hei.org.

BRACKNEY, WILLIAM HENRY, archivist, historian; b. Washington, Jan. 30, 1948; s. Samuel Harp and Mildred (Pointer) B.; m. Kathryn Godfrey Edens, May 23, 1970; children— Noel Christian, Erin Anne, Godfrey Raphe. BA, U. Md., 1970; MA, Eastern Bapt. Theol. Sem., 1972, Temple U., 1974, PhD, 1976. Ordained to ministry, 1971. Minister United Meth. Ch., Bryn Mawr, Pa., 1971-73, Hellertown, Pa., Machias, N.Y., Limestone, N.Y.; research fellow dept. history Temple U., 1975-76; asst. prof. Houghton Coll., N.Y., 1976-79; exec. dir. Am. Bapt. Hist. Soc., Rochester, N.Y., 1979-86; archivist Am. Bapt. Chs., U.S.A., 1980-86; v.p., dean Eastern Bapt. Theol. Seminary, Phila., 1986-89, prof. history of Christianity, 1986-89; prin., prof. eccles. history McMaster Divinity Coll., Hamilton, Ont., Can., 1989—. Adj. prof. Colgate-Rochester Div. Sch., 1979-84; curator Samuel Colgate Bapt. Hist. Collection, 1979-86; cons. hist. preservation. Author: Traveller's Guide to American Baptist Historical Sites, 1982; Baptist Life and Thought 1600-1980: A Source Book, 1983; Dispensations of Providence: The Journal and Selected Letters of Luther Rice, 1984, Festschrift in Honor of Norman H. Maring, 1985, A Guide to the Manuscripts in the American Baptist Historical Society, 1986, The Baptists, 1988, Faith, Life and Works: Papers of the B.W.A. Study and Research Division, 1990; contbr. articles to profl. jours. Recipient Elmore prize in ch. history Eastern Bapt. Sem., 1972; Cooke award Temple U., 1973; Houghton Coll. faculty award, 1978. Mem. Soc. Am. Archivists, Am. Soc. Ch. History, Am. Assn. State and Local History, Roger Williams Fellowship, Lake Ontario Archives Conf., Phi Alpha Theta. Baptist. Home: 65 San Pedro Dr Hamilton ON Canada L9C 2C4 Office: McMaster Divinity Coll Hamilton ON Canada L9C 2C4

BRADBEER, CLIVE, biochemistry and microbiology educator, research scientist; b. Tynemouth, Northumberland, Eng., Feb. 20, 1933; came to U.S., 1962, naturalized, 1994; s. Joseph Walter and Mary (Hall) B.; m. Wilma Jean Youngert, Sept. 1, 1960; children: Suzanne Mary, Thomas Clive. BSc with first class honors, Durham U., Newcastle Upon Tyne, Eng., 1954, PhD, 1957. Jr. rsch. biochemist U. Calif., Berkeley, 1957-59, Davis, 1959; postdoctoral fellow U. Wis., Madison, 1959-60; lectr. Queen Mary Coll., London U., 1960-62; asst. prof. Sch. Medicine, U. Va., Charlottesville, 1964-69, assoc. prof., 1969-79, prof., 1979—. Vis. scientist NIH, Bethesda, Md., 1962-64, ad hoc mem. study sect., 1980-84; vis. prof. U. Otago, Dunedin, New Zealand, 1982-83, 93. Contbr. articles to profl. jours. Mem. Am. Soc. for Biochemistry and Molecular Biology. Episcopalian. Achievements include contbns. in elucidation of the molecular mechanisms involved in utilization of vitamin B12 in microbial and animal cells. E-mail: cb7f@virginia.edu.

BRADBERRY, EDWARD, opera company executive; b. Augusta, Ga., June 6, 1941; BMus, U. Ga., 1961; postgrad., Ind. U. Pianist, tchr., Augusta, Ga., 1964-74; bd. dirs. Augusta Opera, 1972-74, gen. dir., from 1975. Recipient award in arts Gov.'s Office, 1978, Disting. Svc. award Opera Am., 1995. Died Feb. 2002.

BRADBURN, DAVID DENISON, engineer, retired air force officer; b. Hollywood, Calif., May 27, 1925; s. Clarence Earl and Florence Lyle (Easton) B.; m. Bertha Evelyn Stout, Nov. 3, 1956; children: Carol (Mrs. Patrick V. Navagato), Susan (Mrs. Ronald G. Inloes), David Stout, Robert Easton. BS, U.S. Mil. Acad., 1946; MSE., Purdue U., 1952; MS in Internat. Affairs, George Washington U., 1966. Commd. 2d lt. U.S. Army, 1946; advanced through grades to maj. gen. USAF, 1974; pilot, flight comdr. Korea, 1950-51; research and devel. staff officer, 1952-57; mil. space research project officer Los Angeles, 1957-65; space program mgr., 1966-71; dir. space systems, 1971-73; dir. spl. projects Office Sec. Air Force, Los Angeles, 1973-75; vice-comdr. Electronic Systems Div., Boston, 1975-76; ret., 1976. Mem. U.S. del. Joint Chiefs Staff rep. to U.S.-Soviet Anti-Satellite Negotiations, Helsinki, 1978, Bern, Vienna, 1979; sr. staff scientist TRW Def. Systems Group, 1980-84, dir. engring., 1984-87; chmn. bd. Beach Cities Symphony Assn., 1978-84, pres., 1984-87. Decorated D.S.M. (2), Legion of Merit (3), D.F.C., Meritorious Service medal, Air medal (4). Mem. Sigma Xi, Tau Beta Pi, Eta Kappa Nu. Mem. United Ch. of Christ. Achievements include pioneering mil. applications space vehicles. Home: Apt C117 860 Morningside Dr Fullerton CA 92835-3563

BRADBURN, NORMAN M. behavioral science educator; b. Lincoln, Ill., July 21, 1933; s. Hubert Benjamin and Mary Celeste (Marshall) B.; m. Wendy McAneny, Dec. 15, 1956; children: Isabel Stuart, Andrew Marshall, Laura Humphreys. BA, U. Chgo., 1952, Oxford U., Eng., 1955; MA, Harvard U., 1958, PhD in Social Psychology, 1960. From asst. prof. to assoc. prof. behavioral sci. U. Chgo., 1960-67, prof., 1967—, chmn. dept. behavioral sci., 1973-79, Tiffany and Margaret Blake Disting. Service prof., 1977-99, provost, 1984-89, prof. emeritus, 1999—. Sr. study dir. Nat. Opinion Research Center, Chgo., 1961—, dir., 1967-71, 79-84, 89-92, rsch. dir., 1992-2000; asst. dir. NSF, 2000—. Author: (with D. Caplovitz) Reports on Happiness, 1967, The Structure of Psychological Well-Being, 1970, (with S. Sudman, G. Gockel) Side by Side: A Study of Integrated Neighborhoods, 1971, (with S. Sudman) Response Effects in Surveys, 1974, Asking Questions: A Practical Guide to Questionnaire Construction, 1982, Polls and Surveys: Understanding What They Tell Us, 1988, (with others) Improving Questionnaire Design and Interview Method, 1979, (with S. Sudman and N. Schwarz) Thinking About Answers, 1996. Alexander von Humboldt scholar U. Cologne (Germany), 1970-71 Fellow AAAS, Am. Statis. Assn.; mem. Internat. Statis. Inst., World Assn. Pub. Opinion Rsch., Am. Assn. Pub. Opinion Rsch. (pres. 1991-92), Am. Acad. Arts and Scis. Home: 502 N Abingdon St Arlington VA 22203-2049 Business E-Mail: nbradbur@nsf.gov.

BRADBURY, DANIEL JOSEPH, library administrator; b. Kansas City, Kans., Dec. 7, 1945; m. Mary F. Callaghan, May 10, 1967 (div. 1987); children— Patricia, Tracy, Amanda, Anthony, Sean, m. Jobeth Baile Cannady, Nov. 23, 1988. BA in English, U. Mo., Kansas City, 1971; M.L.S., Emporia State U., 1972; LittD, Baker U., 1992. Assoc. dir. extension service Waco-McLennan Library, Tex., 1972-74; library dir. Rolling Hills Consol. Library, St. Joseph, Mo., 1974-77, Janesville Pub. Library, Wis., 1977-83; dir. leisure services City of Janesville, 1982-83; library dir. Kansas City Pub. Library, Mo., 1983—; interim exec. dir. Kansas City Sch. Dist., Mo., 1985. Faculty Baylor U., Waco, 1973-74; participant Gov.'s Conf. on Library and Info. Sci., Wis., 1979; mem. council Kansas City Metro Library Network, 1984—, pres., 1987, mem. coordinating bd. for higher edn. library adv. com., 1984—, chmn., 1986-87, pres. 1991—; bd. dirs. Greater Kansas City Coun. Philantrophy. Bd. dirs. Arrowhead Library System, Janesville, 1978-83, Mid-Town Troost Assn., Kansas City, St. John's Sch., Janesville, 1980-83, Pub. Sch. Retirement Fund, Kansas City, 1995—, treas., 1996—; bd. dirs. Jackson County Hist. Soc., 1998—, treas., 1999-2000, v.p.-elect, 2000—. Named Libr. of Yr. Libr. Jour., N.Y.C., 1991; recipient Disting. Grad. award Emporia State U., 1985, Cornerstone award Kansas City Econ. Devel. Corp., 1988, Achievement award U. Mo. Alumni Assn., 2000; Hon. Doctorate, Baker U., 1991. Mem. ALA (various offices 1972—), Am. Soc. Pub. Adminstrs. (bd. dirs. Kansas City chpt. 1994—), Mo. Libr. Assn. (legis. chmn. 1984-85), Libr. Adminstrn. and Mgmt. Assn. (sec. 1983-85), Wis. Libr. Assn. (pres. 1982). Lodges: Rotary. Roman Catholic. Home: 3318 Karnes Blvd Kansas City MO 64111-3628 Office: Kansas City Pub Libr 311 E 12th St Kansas City MO 64106-2412

BRADBURY, RAY DOUGLAS, b. Waukegan, Ill., Aug. 22, 1920; s. Leonard Spaulding and Esther Marie (Moberg) B.; m. Marguerite Susan McClure, Sept. 27, 1947; children: Susan Marguerite, Ramona, Bettina, Alexandra. DLitt, Whittier Coll., 1979. First pub. short story, 1941; stories pub. pulp mags., 1941-45. Author: (short story collections) Dark Carnival, 1947, The Illustrated Man, 1951, The Golden Apples of the Sun, 1953, Fahrenheit 451, 1953 (Commonwealth Club Calif. gold medal 1954), The October Country, 1955, A Medicine for Melancholy, 1959 (pub. in Eng. as The Day It Rained Forever, 1959), The Ghoul Keepers, 1961, The Small Assassin, 1962, The Machineries of Joy, 1964, The Vintage Bradbury, 1965, The Autumn People, 1965, Tomorrow Midnight, 1966, Twice Twenty-Two, 1966, I Sing The Body Electric!, 1969, (with Robert Bloch) Bloch and Bradbury: Ten Masterpieces of Science Fiction, 1969 (pub. in Eng. as Fever Dreams and Other Fantasies, 1970), (with Bloch) Whispers From Beyond, 1972, Harrap, 1975, Long After Midnight, 1976, The Best of Bradbury, 1976, To Sing Strange Songs, 1979, The Stories of Ray Bradbury, 1980, Dinosaur Tales, 1983, A Memory of Murder, 1984, The Toynbee Convector, 1988, Kaleidoscope, 1994; (poetry) Old Ahab's Friend, and Friend to Noah, Speaks His Piece: A Celebration, 1971, When Elephants Last in the Dooryard Bloomed: Celebrations for Almost Any Day in the Year, 1973, That Son of Richard III: A Birth Announcement, 1974, Where Robot Mice and Robot Men Run Round in Robot Towns, 1977, Twin Hieroglyphs That Swim the River Dust, 1978, The Bike Repairman, 1978, The Author Considers His Resources, 1979, The Aqueduct, 1979, The Attic Where The Meadow Greens, 1979, The Last Circus, 1980, The Ghosts of Forever, 1980, The Haunted Computer and the Android Pope, 1981, The Complete Poems of Ray Bradbury, 1982, The Love Affair, 1983, Forever and the Earth, 1984, Death has Lost Its Charm for Me, 1987; (novels) The Martian Chronicles, 1950 (pub. in Eng. as The Silver Locusts, 1951), Dandelion Wine, 1957, Something Wicked This Way Comes, 1962, Death is a Lonely Business, 1985, A Graveyard for Lunatics, 1990, Green Shadows, White Whale, 1992; (juvenile novels) Switch on the Night, 1955 (Boys Club Am. Jr. Book award 1956), R is for Rocket, 1962, S is for Space, 1966, The Halloween Tree, 1972, The April Witch, 1987, The Other Foot, 1987, The Foghorn, 1987, The Veldt, 1987, Fever Dream, 1987, The Smile, 1991; (non-fiction) Teacher's Guide: Science Fiction, 1968, Zen and the Art of Writing, 1973, Mars and the Mind of Man, 1973, The Mummies of Guanajuato, 1978, Beyond 1984: Remembrance of Things Future, 1979, Los Angeles, 1984, Orange County, 1985, The Art of Playboy, 1985, Yestermorrow: Obvious Answers to Impossible Futures, 1991, Ray Bradbury On Stage: A Chrestomathy of His Plays, 1991, Journey to Far Metaphor: Further Essays on Creativity, Writing, Literature, and the Arts, 1994, The First Book of Dichotomy, The Second Book of Symbiosis, 1995; (plays) The Meadow, 1960, Way in the Middle of the Air, 1962, The Anthem Sprinters, and Other Antics, 1963, The World of Ray Bradbury, 1964, Leviathan 99, 1966, The Day It Rained Forever, 1966, The Pedestrian, 1966, Dandelion Wine, 1967, Christus Apollo, 1969, The Wonderful Ice-Cream Suit and Other Plays, 1972, Madrigals for the Space Age, 1972, Pillar of Fire and Other Plays for Today, Tomorrow, and Beyond Tomorrow, 1975, That Ghost, That Bride of Time: Excerpts from a Play-in-Progress, 1976, The Martian Chronicles, 1977 (5 L.A. Drama Critics Circle awards), Farenheit 451, 1979, A Device Out of Time, 1986, Falling Upward, 1988; prodr. one-act plays, Royal Shakespeare Festival Theatre, The Pandemonium Theatre Co., 1963; screenwriter: (films) It Came from Outer Space, 1953, The Beast from 20,000 Fathoms, 1953, Moby Dick, 1956, Icarus Montgolfier Wright, 1962 (Academy award nomination best short film 1963), An American Journey, 1964, Picasso Summer, 1972, Something Wicked This Way Comes, 1983; (TV scripts for series) Alfred Hitchcock Presents, Jane Wyman's Fireside Theatre, steve Canyon, Trouble Shooters, Twilight Zone, Alcoa Premiere, Curiosity Shop, Ray Bradbury Television Theatre; editor: Timeless Stories for Today and Tomorrow, 1952, The Circus of Dr. Lao and Other Improbable Stories, 1956, A Day in the Life of Hollywood, 1992. Recipient O. Henry prize, 1947, 48, Benjamin Franklin award best story, 1954, Nat. Inst. Arts and Letters award, 1954, Golden Eagle award, 1957, Mrs. Ann Radcliffe award Count Dracula Soc., 1965, 71, Writers Guild award 1974, World Fantasy award for lifetime achievement, 1977, Balrog award best poet, 1979, Aviation and Space Writers award, 1979, Gandalf award, 1980, PEN Body of Work award, 1985. Mem. Screen Writers Guild, Sci. Fantasy Writers Am., Pacific Art Found. (v.p.), Writers Guild Am. (mem. screen writers bd.) Office: Bantam Doubleday Dell 1540 Broadway New York NY 10036-4039 Home: c/o Avon Books 1350 Avenue Of The Americas New York NY 10019-4702*

BRADBURY, WILLIAM CHAPMAN, III, state official; b. Chgo., May 29, 1949; s. William L. and Lorraine (Patterson) B.; m. Betsy Harrison (Sept. 1984); children: Abby, Zoe; m. Kathleen P. Eymann, June 7, 1986. Student, Antioch Coll., 1967-69. News reporter KQED-TV Newsroom, 1969-70; dir. pub. affairs Sta. KMPX-FM, San Francisco, 1970; mem. video prodn. group Optic Nerve, San Francisco, 1970-73; project dir. Coos Country TV, Bandon, Oreg., 1973-75; reporter, anchor Sta. KVAL-TV, Eugene, Oreg., 1975-76; news dir. Sta. KCBY-TV, Coos Bay, Oreg., 1976-78; prodr., writer, editor video news feature svc. Local Color, Langlois, Oreg., 1978-79; field prodr. PM Mag., Sta. KGW-TV, Portland, Oreg., 1979-80; mem. Oreg. Ho. of Reps., Salem, 1980-84, Oreg. Senate, Salem, 1984-95, pres., 1993-95; exec. dir. Sake of the Salmon, Gladstone, Oreg., 1995-99; sec. of state State of Oreg., Salem, 1999—. Chmn. Western Legis. Conf., Coun. State Govs., 1991, mem. ocean resources com.; founder, former chmn. Pacific Fishery Legis. Task Force. Prodr. documentaries Gorda Ridge—Boom or Bust for the Oregon Coast?, The Tillamook Burn—From Ruin to Rejuvenation, Not Guilty by Reason of Insanity, Child as Witness, Local Color, Salmon on the Run, The First Perennial Poetic Hoohaw, TV Town Hall Meetings, Common Sense, also prodr. mktg. videos and commls. for polit. candidates, hosp. Democrat. Mem. Soc. Of Friends. Avocation: white water kayaking. Office: Sec of State 141 State Capitol Bldg Salem OR 97310-0722 E-mail: bill.bradbury@state.or.us.

BRADDOCK, DAVID LAWRENCE, health science educator; b. Glendale, Calif., Mar. 10, 1945; s. Mark Perry and Christina Bain Braddock; m. Laura Stanlye Haffer, May 1, 1976; children: Gabriel, Autumn, Adam. BA, U. Tex., 1967, MA, 1970, PhD, 1973. Spl. asst. to dir. sec.'s com. on mental retardation HEW, Washington, 1972; prin. investigator Coun. for Exceptional Children, Reston, Va., 1973-77; cons. White House Conf. on the Handicapped, Washington, 1977-78; rsch. prof., program dir. Inst. Study Devel. Disabilities U. Ill., Chgo., 1979-88, prof. cmty. health scis. Sch. Pub. Health, 1985—2001, prof. human devel., founding head dept. disability and human devel., 1988—2001, assoc. dean for rsch., 1997-98; assoc. v.p. rsch. U. Colo. Sys., 2001—; exec. dir. Coleman Inst. for Cognitive Disabilities U. Colo., 2001—; Coleman-Turner chair in cognitive disability, prof. psychiatry U. Colo. Health Scis. Ctr., Coll. Medicine, 2001—. Cons. U.S. Dept. HHS, Washington, 1972—. Author: Federal Policy Toward Mental Retardation, 1987, Residential Services and Developmental Disabilities in U.S., 1992, The State of the States in Developmental Disabilities, 7 edits., Disability at the Dawn of the 21st Century, 2002; co-author: State Law and the Education of Handicapped Children, 1972; contbr. more than 200 articles to profl. jours., monographs in field. Cons. Joseph P. Kennedy Jr. Found.; active in promoting civil and human rights of people with mental retardation and other disabilities.; bd. dirs. Spl. Olympics Internat. Fellow, Nat. Inst. on Disability and Rehab. Rsch., 1988—89; grantee U.S. Dept. HHS, U.S. Dept. Edn., Nat. Inst. on Disability and Rehab. Rsch., 1999—2000; univ. scholar, U. Ill., 1998—2001. Fellow: Am. Assn. on Mental Retardation (pres. 1993—94, editor books and monographs 1997—2002, Career Rsch. award 1998), Delta Omega; mem.: AAAS, Assn. for Retarded Citizens of U.S. (sci. adv. bd. 1987—, Disting. Rsch. award in mental retardation 1987, Franklin Smith award for disting. nat. svc. 2000). Office: Coleman Inst Cognitive Disabilities U Colo SYS 586 4001 Discovery Dr Boulder CO 80309

BRADDOCK, DONALD LAYTON, lawyer, accountant, real estate broker, investor; b. Jacksonville, Fla., Dec. 14, 1941; s. John Reddon and Harriet Braddock; children: Stella Helene Knowlton, Leslie Ann Meshad, Donald Layton Jr. BS in Bus. Adminstrn., U. Fla., 1963; JD, 1967. Bar: Fla. 1968, U.S. Dist. Ct. (mid. and no. dists.) Fla. 1968, U.S. Ct. Appeals (5th cir.) 1968, U.S. Ct. Appeals (4th and 11th cirs.) 1968, U.S. Supreme Ct. 1976, U.S. Tax Ct. 1970; CPA; registered real estate broker. Staff acct. Coopers and Lybrand, CPAs, 1964-65, Keith C. Austin, CPA, 1965-67; assoc. Kent, Durden & Kent, attys. at law, 1967-71; sole practice, 1971-73; ptnr. Howell, Kirby, Montgomery, D'Aiuto & Dean, attys. at law, 1974-76; pres., dir. Howell, Liles, Braddock & Milton, attys. at law, Jacksonville, Fla., 1976-88; ret., 1988. Bd. dirs., mem. exec. com. Fla. Lawyers Mutual Ins. Co.; pres., dir. Donald L. Braddock Chartered dba Mandarin Realty, 1970—; mgr. Wildcat Venture, LLC, 2000—; mgr. Bryant Hill, LLC, 2000—. Bd. dirs. Jacksonville Vocat. Edn. Authority, 1971-75; mem. Jacksonville Bicentennial Commn., 1976; bd. govs. Fla. Bar Found., 1984-86, sec.-treas., 1986-88; sec., dir. Laurel Grove Plantation, Inc., 1988—. Served with Air N.G., 1963-69. Mem. Fla. Bar (bd. govs. young lawyers sec. 1972-77), Fla. Inst. CPAs, Jacksonville C. of C. (com. of 100), Jacksonville Bar Assn. (pres. 1983-84, bd. govs. 1978-84), U Fla. Alumni Assn. (pres. 1975, bd. dirs. 1968-75), Fla. Blue Key, Friars Club, Phi Delta Phi, Alpha Tau Omega. Republican. Office: PO Box 57385 Jacksonville FL 32241-7385

BRADDOCK, RICHARD S. internet company executive; b. Oklahoma City, Nov. 30, 1941; s. Robert L. and Mary Alice (Krueger) B.; m. Susan Schulte, Feb. 14, 1978; 1 child, Christina; children by previous marriage: Jennifer, Richard, Derek BA, Dartmouth Coll., 1963; MBA, Harvard Bus. Sch., 1965. Mem. mktg. staff General Foods, White Plains, N.Y., 1965-73; mem. staff Citicorp, N.Y.C., 1973-92, sector exec. in charge of worldwide consumer fin. svcs., info. bus., investor rels., corp. pub. affairs, customer affairs, corp. advt., 1985-90, also bd. dirs.; pres. Citibank/Citicorp, N.Y.C., 1990-92; chief exec. officer Medco Containment Svcs., Montvale, N.J., 1992; spl. advisor Gen. Atlantic Ptnrs. LLC, 1996-97; non-exec. chmn. True North Communications Inc., 1997; chmn., CEO Priceline.com, 1998—2002. Bd. dirs. Eastman Kodak, Lotus Devel. Corp.; chief exec. officer Medical Mktg. Group, Synetics. Bd. dirs. Cancer Rsch. Inst., N.Y.C., Lincoln Ctr., N.Y.C. Partnership; mem. Coun. on Fgn Rels. Mem. N.Y. C. of C. (bd. dirs.). Office: Priceline dot com 5 High Ridge Park Ste 14 Stamford CT 06905-1355

BRADDOCK, STEPHEN E. not-for-profit executive, priest; b. Port Chester, N.Y., July 25, 1964; s. Eugene S. and Nora C. Braddock. At, Westchester CC, NY, Sacred Heart Sch. of Theology, Hales Corners, Wis.; PhD, Cardinal Stritch U., 1994. Ordained into priesthood Archdiocese of Milw., 1998. Chmn. of the bd. St. Camillus Campus, Milw., 1995—99; priest Order of St. Camillus, Milw., 1998—; pres., exec. dir. Fla. Keys Outreach Coalition, Inc., Key West, 1999—. Chmn. of the bd. Southernmost Homeless Assistance League, Inc., Key West, 2003—. Bd. officer SHAL, Inc., Monroe County, Fla., 1999—2003. Recipient Alumni award for Profl. Distinction, Cardinal Stritch U., 1997. Mem.: Fla. Coalition for the Homeless, Nat. Coalition for the Homeless, Monroe County Emergency Food and Shelter Program (chmn. 2000—03), Key West Sunset Rotary. Independent. Office: Florida Keys Outreach Coalition Inc PO Box 4767 Key West FL 33041 Office Fax: 305-293-8276. Personal E-mail: frbraddock@cs.com. E-mail: frbraddock@cs.com.

BRADDOCK, STEPHEN ROBERT, pediatrician, educator; b. Newark, Apr. 28, 1962; s. LeRoy Ildefonze and Eleanor Shaheen Braddock; m. Barbara Ann Wheeler, Apr. 21, 1990; children: Robert Joseph, Matthew Thomas. B.S., U. Notre Dame, 1984; M.D., U. Mo., 1988. Assoc. prof. clin. child health U. Mo.-Columbia Sch. Medicine, 1994—. Dir. pediatric genetics Craniofacial Ctr., U. Mo., Columbia, 1994—; dir. Mo. Teratogen Info. Svc., Columbia, 1995—. Contbr. articles to profl. jours. Grantee Mo. Teratogen Info. Svc., Mo. Dept. Health, 1995—2003, March of Dimes, 2000—02, Establishment of Regional FAS Tng. Ctr., Ctrs for Disease Control, 2002—. Fellow: Am. Coll. Med. Genetics, Am. Acad. Pediat.; mem.: AMA, Orgn. Teratology Info. Svcs., Boone County Med. Soc., Mo. State Med. Soc., Am. Cleft Palate and Craniofacial Assn., Am. Soc. Human Genetics, Teratology Soc. Roman Catholic. Avocations: sports, travel, movies. Office: U Mo - Columbia 1 Hospital Dr DC05800 Columbia MO 65212 E-mail: braddocks@missouri.edu.

BRADDOCK, WALTER DAVID, III, economist; b. Chgo., Sept. 3, 1936; s. Walter David and Marian (Lee) B.; m. Zoe Skalafuris, Dec. 27, 1962; children: Walter David IV, Demetrios Thomas, Christopher Timothy. BS, MIT, 1958; MBA, U. Chgo., 1961; MA in Math., East Tenn. State U., 1966; PhD in Econs., No. Ill. U., 1984. Programmer U. Minn., Mpls., 1966-71; analyst State of Ill., Springfield, 1971-74; instr. fin. Ill. State U., Normal, 1974-75; asst. prof. grad. fin. Sangamon State U., Springfield, 1976-80; instr. fin. Pa. State U., Middletown, 1980-82, Ind. U., South Bend, 1982-83; asst. prof. fin. and econs. Miss. State U., Starkville, 1983-86; asst. prof. fin., bus. and econs. Averett Coll., Danville, Va., 1986-87; staff economist Dept. Commerce and Community Affairs State of Ill., Springfield, 1989-92; econ. prof. Delta State Univ., Cleveland, Miss., 1992—96; ret. Patentee automated stock exch. With U.S. Army, 1959-60. Avocation: sports.

BRADDOM, RANDALL LEE, physician, medical educator; b. Monarch, Va., Oct. 29, 1942; s. Audy Lee and Ruth Janet Braddom; m. Diana Verdun, 2001; children from previous marriage: Eric C., Steven R., Karen L. BA, DePauw U., 1964; MD, Ohio State U., 1968, MS, 1971. Diplomate Am. Bd. Electrodiagnostic Medicine, Am. Bd. Phys. Medicine and Rehab. Rotating intern Mt. Carmel Hosp., Columbus, Ohio, 1968-69; resident in phys. medicine and rehab. Ohio State Univ. Hosps., Columbus, 1969-72; physiatrist, electromyographer Rancocas Valley Hosp., Willingboro, N.J., 1972-74, Phila. Naval Med. Ctr., 1972-74; asst. prof. phys. medicine and rehab. U. Cin., 1974-75, assoc. prof., dir. phys. medicine and rehab., 1975-81; med. dir. phys. med. and rehab. St. Francis-St. George Hosp., Cin., 1987-89, Providence Hosp., Cin., 1982-89; assoc. prof., dep. chmn. rehab. medicine Temple U., Phila., 1989-91; chmn. rehab. medicine Albert Einstein Hosp., Phila., 1989-91; v.p. med. affairs Moss Rehab. Hosp., Phila., 1989-91; practitioner Rehab. Assocs., Indpls., 1991-96; med. dir. Hook Rehab. Ctr., Indpls., 1991-98; prof., chmn. phys. medicine and rehab. Ind. U. Sch. Medicine, Indpls., 1991-98. Dir. Wishard Health Svcs., Indpls., Ind.; physiatrist Albert Einstein Med. Ctr. N., Phila., 1973; clin. instr. rehab. medicine Thomas Jefferson Coll. Med., Phila., 1972-74; assoc. in medicine Jewish Hosp., Cin., 1974-89; cons. phys. medicine and rehab. VA Hosp., Cin., 1975-81; dir. phys. med. and rehab. U. Hosps., U. Cin., 1975-81; assoc. clin. prof. phys. med. Ohio State U., Columbus, 1984-90; clin. assoc. prof. phys. medicine and rehab. U. Cin., Coll. Medicine, 1982-89; cons. St. Francis Hosp., Indpls., 1991-97; phys. med. and rehab. svc. chief Wishard Meml. Hosp., Indpls., 1991-2000; dir. phys. medicine and rehab. svc. Richard Roudebush VA Hosp., Indpls., 1991-97; vis. prof. Dept. Phys. Medicine and Rehab. U. Ark., 1992, U. Ky. Dept Phys. Medicine and Rehab., 1992, Dept. Internal Medicine Dvsn. Phys. Medicine & Rehab. La. State U. Sch. Medicine, New Orleans, La., 1994, Baylor Coll. Medicine Dept. Physical Medicine & Rehab., 1994, N.J. Sch. Medicine and Dentistry Dept. P.M. & R.; presenter in field; lectr. in field. Author: (with others) Physical Medicine & Rehabilitation Review, 1980; editor: Sports Medicine and Rehabilitation: A Sport-Scientific Approach, 1994, Physical Medicine and rehabilitation, 1996; contbr. articles to profl. jours. Founder, med. dir. ECCO Family Health Ctr., Inc., Columbus, 1970-72; bd. dirs. Nat. Paraplegia Found., 1975-80; med. adviser Easter Seals Soc. Southwestern Ohio, 1980-82; asst. scoutmaster Troop 291, Boy Scouts Am., 1982-84; chmn. Citizens for Our Schs. Tax Levy Campaign, Forest Hills Sch. Dist., Cin., 1985; trustee Total Living Concepts, Inc., Cin., 1977-85, Disability Svcs. Group, Inc., Cin., 1985-89; bd. examiners The Henry B. Betts award, 1991-94. Lt. comdr. USNR, 1972-74. Recipient Kiwanis Club Citizenship award, Dayton, 1960, Rsch. award Am. Paralyzed Vets. Assn., 1968, Am. Therapeutic Soc., 1968, Landacre Soc. award Ohio State U., 1978, Sidney Licht Lectureship Ohio State U., 1985, Alumni Achievement award Ohio State U., 1993, Sidney Licht Lectureship U. Minn., 1993, Randy Braddom award U. Cin. Coll. Medicine, 1989; named Man of Yr. Columbus Citizen-Jour., 1970, Landwerlen award Muscular Dystrophy Found. Ind., 1994. Mem. Indpls. Med. Soc., Ind. Soc. Phys. Med. and Rehab., Nat. Stroke Assn., Am. Kinesiotherapy Assn. (mem. adv. bd. 1993—), Am. Acad. Phys. Med. and Rehab. (med. edn. com. 1983-86, membership recruitment group 1987, career brochure devel. group 1987, joint annual meeting planning subcom. 1987-88, chairperson continuing med. edn. subcom. 1982-86, sci. program com. 1982-86, mktg. and comms. com. 1987-89, chairperson med. edn. com. 1986-88, sec. bd. govs. 1988-90, third-mem.-at-large 1990-91, 2d mem.-at-large 1991-92, 1st mem.-at-large 1992-93, chair awards com. 1992-93, v.p. 1994-95, fin. com. 1994-95, chair annual meeting task force 1994-95, pres. elect 1994-95, pres. 1995-96, past pres. 1996-97, Disting. Clinician award 1997), Am. Assn. Electrodiagnostic Medicine (com. on edn. 1974-76, exam. com. 1975-76, liaision to assn. of acad. physiatrists 1988, chairperson courses com. 1986-89, pres.-elect 1989-90, bd. dirs. 1989-92, pres. 1990-91, immediate past pres.-chairperson long-range planning com. 1991-92, chmn. long range planning com. 1991-92, alt. del. AMA House of Dels. 1993-95, nominating com. 1993-94, chmn. 1994-95), Am. Assn. Electrodiagnostic Medicine, Assn. Acad. Physiatrists, Ohio State Med. Alumni Assn., AMA, Am. Bd. Electrodiagnostic Medicine (bd. dirs. 1994, long-range planning com. 1994, treas. 1995-98), Cin. Soc. of Phys. Medicine and Rehab. (pres., founder 1987-88), Internat. Med. Med. Assn. (U.S. counselor 1986-95). Office: 35 Bamm Hollow Rd Middletown NJ 07748 E-mail: rbraddom@earthlink.net.

BRADDY, VANESSA F. civil engineer; b. Richmond, Va., June 18, 1959; d. Joseph L. and Rosetta Watkins; m. Mozell Braddy, Dec. 3, 1988. BSCE, Carnegie-Mellon U., 1982; MS in Mgmt., Frostburg State U., 1986; MS in Pub. Policy, U. Md., 1993. Design engr. Bechtel Power Corp., Gaithersburg, Md., 1982-84; engr. Tracor Applied Scis., Inc., Rockville, Md., 1984-85; asst. project engr. State Hwy. Adminstrn., Balt., 1985-87, project engr., 1987—98, asst. to dep. adminstr., chief engr. ops, 1998—. Newsletter editor Women's Transp. Seminars, Balt., 1987-90, sec., 1988-89. Recipient Pres.' Transp. award, Am. Assoc. of State Hwy. and Trans. Officals, 1998, Woman of Color in Tech. award, U.S. Black/Hispanic Engr. and Info. Tech. Mag., 2001. Mem. Delta Sigma Theta. Office: State Hwy Adminstrn 211 E Madison St Baltimore MD 21202-3709

BRADEN, BERWYN BARTOW, lawyer; b. Pana, Ill., Jan. 10, 1928; s. George Clark and Florence Lucille (Bartow) B.; m. Betty J.; children— Scott, Mark, Mathew, Sue, Ralph, Ladd, Brad Student, Carthage Coll., 1946-48, U. Wis., 1948-49, JD, 1959. Bar: Wis. 1959, U.S. Supreme Ct. 1965. Ptnr. Genoar & Braden, Lake Geneva, Wis., 1959-63; individual practice law Lake Geneva, Wis., 1963-68, 72-74; ptnr. Braden & English, Lake Geneva, Wis., 1968-72, Braden & Olson, Lake Geneva, Wis., 1974—2002, Gagliardi O'Brien Braden Olson and Kapelli, Lake Geneva, 2002—. City atty. City of Lake Geneva, 1962-64; tchr. Law Sch., U. Wis., 1977 Bd. dirs. Lake Geneva YMCA. Mem. ABA, Walworth County Bar Assn. (pres. 1962-63), State Bar Wis. (chmn. conv. and entertainment com. 1979-81, chmn. adminstrn. Justice and Judiciary com., 1986-87, bench bar rels. com., 1987-90, mem. exec. com. Wis. Bicentennial Com. on Constn.), Wis. Acad. Trial Lawyers (sec. 1975, treas. 1976, dir. 1977-79), Assn. Trial Lawyers Am. Home: 1031 W Main St Lake Geneva WI 53147-1700 Office: 716 Wisconsin St Lake Geneva WI 53147-1826 also: PO Box 940 Lake Geneva WI 53147-0940 E-mail: buzzb@genevaonline.com.

BRADEN, BETTY JANE, legal association administrator; b. Sheboygan, Wis., Feb. 5, 1943; d. Otto Frank and Betty Donna (Beers) Huettner; children: Jennifer Tindall, Rebecca Leigh; m. Berwyn Bartow Braden, Nov. 5, 1983. BS, U. Wis., 1965. Cert. elem. tchr., Wis. Tchr. Madison (Wis.) Met. Sch. Dist., 1965-70, 71-72, sub. tchr., 1972-75; adminstrv. asst. ATS-CLE State Bar Wis., Madison, 1978, adminstrv. asst. Advanced Tng. Seminars-Continuing Legal Edn., 1979, coordinator, 1980, adminstr. coordinator, 1980-84, adminstrv. dir., 1984-87, dir. adminstrn., bar svcs., membership, 1987—; mem. rels. and pub. svcs. dir. Legal Edn., 1992—. Speaker Bar Leadership Inst. of ABA. Mem.: LWV, Nat. Assn. Bar Execs. (program chair 1995—96, sec. 1996—98, v.p. 1998—99, pres. elect 1999—2000, pres. 2000—01), Wis. Soc. of Assn. Execs., Am. Soc. of Assn. Execs., Am. Soc. for Personnel Adminstrn., Am. Mgmt. Assn., Adminstrv. Mgmt. Soc., Meeting Planners Internat. (sec. Wis. chpt. 1981—82, pres. 1982—83). Avocations: tennis, scuba diving, reading, skiing. Home: 41 Golf Pkwy Madison WI 53704-7003 Office: State Bar of Wis 5302 Eastpark Blvd Madison WI 53718-2101

BRADEN, CHARLES HOSEA, physicist, university administrator; b. Chgo., Mar. 21, 1926; s. Charles Eugene and Rachel Irene (Atchison) B.; m. Sara Caroline McKinley, Sept. 7, 1952; children— Patsy Irene, Jack David. BS in Engring, Columbia U., 1946; PhD in Physics, Washington U., St. Louis, 1951. Asst. prof. physics Ga. Inst. Tech., 1951-53, assoc. prof., 1953-59, prof., 1959-71, Regents prof. physics, 1971-91; assoc. dir. Sch. Physics, 1971-80, interim dir., 1980-82; assoc. program dir. for physics NSF, Washington, 1959-60; cons. Fernbank Mus. Natural History, 1989-96. Contbr. articles to Phys. Rev., Sys. Dynamics Rev. Served with USNR, 1943-47. Episcopalian. Achievements include research in exptl. nuclear physics, modeling of socio-econ. systems.

BRADEN, JAMES DALE, former state legislator; b. Wakefield, Kans., Aug. 2, 1934; s. James Wesley and Olive (Reed) B.; m. Naomi Carlson, July 3, 1952 (div. Jan. 1982); children: Gregory, Michael, Ladd, Amy; m. Margie Clark Tidwell, Sept. 17, 1983; stepchildren: Richard, Lon, Dale. Grad. high sch., Wakefield. CLU, The Am. Coll. Meat cutter, Wakefield, 1952-64; ins. agt., securities broker Braden Fin. Svcs., Clay Ctr., Kans., 1964—; state rep. Kans. Ho. of Reps., Topeka, 1974-91, house majority leader, 1985-87, speaker of the house, 1987-91. Past chmn. econ. devel. com. Nat. Conf. State Legislatures, legis. coordinating council, calendar and printing com.; past chmn. assessment and taxation com.; mem. Council of State Govts. intergovtl. affairs com.; past chmn. taxation task force of Midwestern Conf. of Council State Govts.; chmn. Interstate Cooperation Commn.; former mem. State Fin. Council, Kans. Inc.; past chmn. Legis. Commn. on Kans. Econ. Devel.; past mem. Kans. Pub. Agenda Commn. Active St. Paul's Episcopal Ch., Clay Ctr.; mem. Rep. Party Exec. Com. Mem. NALU, Kans. Assn Ins. and Fin. Advisors (past pres.), Million Dollar Round Table (life), Rotary, Masons, Shriners, Elks. Episcopalian. Avocations: hunting, fishing, flying, sailing. Home: PO Box 58 Clay Center KS 67432-0058 Office: Braden Fin Svcs 1101 5th St # 58 Clay Center KS 67432-2021 E-mail: jbraden@classicnet.net.

BRADEN, JOHN ALAN, accountant; b. Houston, Feb. 9, 1945; s. John Earl and Marjorie (Wilson) B.; m. Leilani D. Fowler, Dec. 9, 1972; children: Meredith, Alana. BBA, U. Houston, 1967. CPA, Tex.; cert. fin. planner. Sr. acct. Haskins & Sells, Houston, 1967-71; pres. John A. Braden, Houston, 1971-86, Braden & Kikis, Houston, 1986-96, John A. Braden & Co., Houston, 1996—, Braden, Bennink, Goldstein, Gazaway & Co., PLLC, 1996—. Mem. behavioral enforcement com. Tex. State Bd. Pub. Accountancy, 1998—2001; mem planned giving adv. com. U. Houston, 1998—. Contbr. articles to profl. jours. Bd. dirs., treas. Northampton Mcpl. Utility Dist., Spring, Tex., 1986—; pres., commr. Harris County Rural Fire Protection Dist. # 1, 1989-92; officer parent orgn. Klein Oak H.S., 1986-94; chmn. audit com., mem. adminstrv. bd., fin. com., found. trustee, choir pres. Klein United Meth. Ch., Spring. Mem. AICPA, Tex. Soc. CPAs (bd. dirs., com. chmn. 1969—), Houston Chpt. CPAs (bd. dirs., com. chmn. 1969—, v.p. 1990-91), Houston Estate and Fin. Forum, Planned Giving Coun. Houston, Fin. Planning Assn. Republican. Home: 6107 Knollview Dr Spring TX 77389-3748 Office: John A Braden & Co Ste 422 12941 North Fwy Houston TX 77060-1242

BRADEN, MARTHA BROOKE, concert pianist, educator; b. Sturgis, Mich., July 19, 1936; d. Frederick Richard and Laura Clemens (Brooke) B.; m. Edmund Sanford Jones, Mar. 14, 1959 (div. Aug. 1983); children: Carrie Brooke, David Sanford, Christopher Braden, Charles Clemens, Mary Evelyn Reilley. Studied with Frances Oman Clark, Kalamazoo, 1942-60; student, Kalamazoo Coll., 1954-55; MusB, Westminster Choir Coll., Princeton, N.J., 1959; studied with Dr. Julius Hereford, N.Y.C., 1957-59; studied with, David Kraehenbuehl, Princeton, 1959-61, 84-97, Erno Balogh, Washington, 1976-79, Ross Lee Finney, N.Y.C., 1987-88, Madame Ming Tcherepnin, 1979-91, Madeline Bruser, 1999-2000. Cert. directress Montessori primary edn. ages 2 1/2 to 6 Washington Montessori Inst.; cert. of attendance advanced course in Montessori edn. ages 6-12 State Ctr. for Montessori Studies, Bergamo, Italy. Piano tchr. Frances Clark Studios, Kalamazoo, 1951-54; piano faculty piano and prep. depts. Westminster Choir Coll., Princeton, 1956-60; founding faculty mem. New Sch. for Music Study, Princeton, 1960-61; co-founder, Montessori primary dir. Hope Montessori Sch., Annandale, Va., 1963-68; co-founder New City Montessori Sch., Washington, 1969-74; piano faculty New Sch. for Music Study, Princeton, 1978-80; piano tchr./coach Braden Piano Studio, Washington, 1975-78, N.Y.C., 1979—. Artistic dir. The David Kraehenbuehl Soc., 2001—. Featured artist Kalamazoo Symphony, South Bend (Ind.) Symphony, 1954; recitalist (with Doris Martin) Frances Clark Piano Workshops for Piano Tchrs., nationwide, summers 1948-58; N.Y. debut solo recital Carnegie Recital Hall, 1977, Lincoln Ctr. debut solo recital Alice Tully Hall, 1980; solo recitals include Carnegie Recital Hall, N.Y.C., 1979, Abraham Goodman House, N.Y.C., 1981, Merkin Concert Hall, N.Y.C., 1984, 85, NYU Maison Francaise, 1996; artist roster Circum-Arts Found., Inc., 1999—; (recs.) Ross Lee Finney, 1988, Alexander Tcherepnin, 2002, David Kraehenbuehl, 2000, Pocketful of Music, 2003; author, pub.: (with Nancy M. Connors) David Kraehenbuehl, American Composer, 2000; editor, pub.: The Collected Works for Solo Piano by David Kraehenbuehl, 1999, Pocketful of Music, 2003; contbr. articles to Piano and Keyboard, Keyboard Companion. Performer benefit concerts UN Internat. Sch., N.Y., St. Luke's Sch., N.Y., 1999—, Kent Pl. Sch., N.J., 2002. Recipient 2d place award Bartok-Kabalevsky Internat. Piano Competition, Radford Coll., 1992; recipient Tcherepnin award Ibla Internat. Piano Competition, Ragusa, Italy, 1993; grantee concert and tchg. tour of mainland China, Ministry of Culture and Conservatories of Music/The Tcherepnin Soc., 1982, Irving S. Gilmore Found., 1987, Warren Studios, 1998.. Mem.: MENC, Montessori Internat., Nat. Assn. for Music Edn., Music Tchrs. Nat. Assn. Avocations: family, friends, forests. Office: Martha Braden Studio 780 W End Ave Apt 7A New York NY 10025-5548 E-mail: futurenote@earthlink.net.

BRADEN, THOMAS WARDELL, news commentator; b. Greene, Iowa, Feb. 22, 1917; s. Thomas Wardell and Louise (Garl) Braden; m. Joan E. Ridley, Dec. 18, 1948 (dec.); children: David, Mary, Joan, Susan, Nancy, Elizabeth, Thomas Wardell III(dec.), Nicholas R. AB, Dartmouth Coll., 1940, AM, 1964; LittD, Franklin Coll. Ind., 1979. Newspaperman, instr. English Dartmouth, 1946, asst. to pres. and asst. prof., 1947—48; exec. sec. Mus. Modern Art, N.Y.C., 1949; dir. Am. Com. on United Europe, 1950; editor, pub. Blade Tribune, Oceanside, Calif., 1954—68; columnist Los Angeles Times Syndicate, 1968—86; commentator CNN, CBS, NBC, 1978—89. Author (with Stewart Alsop): Sub-Rosa, 1946; author: Eight is Enough, 1975. Mem. Calif. Bd. Edn., 1959—67; past pres. Trustee Calif. State Coll., 1961—64, Dartmouth, 1964—74, Carnegie Endowment, 1970—82. With King's Royal Rifle Corps Brit. Army, 1941—44, Africa and Italy, trans. to inf. AUS, 1944.

BRADEN, VICTORIA JANE, small business owner; b. Phoenix, Oct. 23, 1955; d. Harlo Clark and Suzanne (Moore) Sartorius; m. Scott J. Karasek, Aug. 26, 1978 (div. 1989); 1 child, Lauren Suzanne; m. James D. Braden, June 1, 1991; children: Kelly, Karen, Stephen, Paula, John. BS, Western Ill. U., 1976. With McNeil Consumer Products Co., 1977-83, sales trainer, 1979-80, unit mgr., 1980-82; sales planner Borden Cons. Products, Atlanta, 1982-83; div. mgr. Shasta Beverages, Atlanta, 1984-86; dist. mgr. The Pillsbury Co., Atlanta, 1986-88, market mgr., 1988-89; with Priority Mgmt., 1990-92; ins. lic. Braden Benefit Strategics Inc. Mem. North Point Cmty. Ch. Republican. Home: 5726 Fairley Hall Ct Norcross GA 30092-1425

BRADFORD, BARBARA REED, lawyer; b. Cleve., June 13, 1948; d. William Cochran and Martha Lucile (Horn) B.; m. Warren Neil Davis, Oct. 9, 1976 (div. 1989); m. S. Jack Odell, Dec. 12, 1991. BA, Pitzer Coll., 1970; JD, Georgetown U., 1975, MBA, 1985. Bar: N.Y. 1976, D.C. 1976. Staff asst. Sen. Edward M. Kennedy, Washington, 1970-71; assoc. Breed, Abbott & Morgan, N.Y.C., 1975-76, Verner, Liipfert Law Firm, Washington, 1976-78; atty. AID, Washington, 1978-83; pres. Georgetown Export Trading, Inc., Washington, 1984-86; regional dir. U.S. Trade & Devel. Agy., Washington, 1986-2000, dep. dir., 2000—. Bd. dirs. Jr. League, Washington, 1977-78. Democrat. Avocations: art, golf, reading.

BRADFORD, BARBARA TAYLOR, writer, journalist, novelist; b. Leeds, Eng. came to U.S., 1964; d. Winston and Freda (Walker) Taylor; m. Robert Bradford, Dec. 24, 1963. Student pvt. schs., Eng.; D of Letters (hon.), Leeds (Eng.) U., 1990, U. Bradford, West Yorkshire, Eng., 1995; D of Humane Letters (hon.), Teikyo Post U., Waterbury, Conn., 1996. Women's editor Yorkshire (Eng.) Evening Post, 1951-53, reporter, 1949-51; editor Woman's Own, 1953-54; columnist London Evening News, 1955-57; exec. editor London Am., 1959-62; editor Nat. Design Center Mag., 1965-69; syndicated columnist Newsday Spls., L.I., 1968-70; nat. syndicated columnist Chgo. Tribune-N.Y. (News Syndicate), N.Y.C., 1970-75, Los Angeles Times Syndicate, 1975-81. Author: Complete Encyclopedia of Homemaking Ideas, 1968, A Garland of Children's Verse, 1968, How to Be the Perfect Wife, 1969, Easy Steps to Successful Decorating, 1971, Decorating Ideas for Casual Living, 1977, How to Solve Your Decorating Problems, 1976, Making Space Grow, 1979, Luxury Designs for Apartment Living, 1981, (novels) A Woman of Substance, 1979, Voice of the Heart, 1983, Hold the Dream, 1985, screen adaptation, 1986, Act of Will, 1986, To Be the Best, 1988, The Women in His Life, 1990, Remember, 1991, Angel, 1993, Everything to Gain, 1994, Dangerous to Know, 1995, Love in Another Town, 1995, Her Own Rules, 1996, A Secret Affair, 1996, Power of a Woman, 1997, A Sudden Change of Heart, 1999, Where You Belong, 2000, The Triumph of Katie Byrne, 2001, Three Weeks in Paris, 2002. Recipient Dorothy Dawe award Am. Furniture Mart, 1970, 71, Matrix award N.Y. Women in Comms., 1985, Spl. Jury prize for body of lit. Deauville Festival of Am.Film, 1994. Mem. Coun. Authors Guild, Nat. Soc. Interior Designers (Disting. Editl. award 1969, Nat. Press award 1971), Authors Guild Am. (mem. coun. 1989—), Am. Soc. Interior Designers. Office: Bradford Enterprises 450 Park Ave New York NY 10022-2605

BRADFORD, CARL O. judge; b. Dallas, Nov. 16, 1932; s. Montie Leroy and Vivian Ila (Milan) B.; m. Claire Solange Chaloux, Jan. 15, 1955 (dec. 1972); children: Timothy, Kathleen, Elizabeth; m. Mary Ellen Sanborn, July 7, 1973; children: Bethany, Michael. Student, U. Detroit, 1956-59; JD, U. Maine, Portland, 1962. Bar: Maine 1963, U.S. Dist. Ct. Maine 1963, U.S. Ct. Appeals (1st cir.) 1963, U.S. Supreme Ct. 1978. Asst. atty. gen. State of Maine, Augusta, 1963-64, justice Superior Ct., 1981-98, active-ret. justice Superior Ct., 1998—. Ptnr. Powers & Bradford, Freeport, Maine, 1964-81; commr. Uniform State Laws, 1972-76; mem. drafting com. Uniform Exemptions Act, 1974-76. Bd. dirs. Nat. Ctr. State Cts., Williamsburg, Va., 1997—2000; trustee Nat. Jud. Coll., Reno, 2001—. With USN, 1951—55. Fellow Am. Bar Found., Maine Bar Found.; mem. Maine Bar Assn. (bd. govs. 1970-78, pres. 1977-78), Maine Trial Lawyers Assn. (bd. govs., sec. 1970-81), ABA (ho. of dels. 1978-81, 90-95, state bar del. 1978-81, bd. govs. 1st dist. 1990-93, bd. lisiaon to Nat. Conf. Spl Ct. Judges 1990-91, liaison to Criminal Justice Sect. 1990-93, liaison to Nat. Conf. State Trial Judges 1991-93, chair subcom. nominations and awards com. 1991-93, bd. govs. program com. 1990-91, mem. oper. com. 1991-93, project 2000 subcom. 1991-93, bd. govs. chair compensation com. 1993, bd. govs. exec. com. 1993, bd. govs. exec. dir. search com. 1990, mem. comm. on multi-disciplinary practice 1998-2000), Nat. Conf. State Trial Judges (del. 1982-97, jud. immunity com. 1984-97, chair 1991-96, conf. vice chair 1993, chair-elect 1994-95, chair 1995-96), Am. Judicature Soc. Home: 225 Sea Meadows Ln Yarmouth ME 04096-5523 Office: Superior Ct PO Box 287 Portland ME 04112-0287

BRADFORD, C.O. protective services officer; b. La., Aug. 25, 1955; BA, Grambling U.; JD, U. Houston; MBA, Tex. So. U. Patrolman Houston Police Dept., 1979-91, asst. chief police, 1991-97, chief of police, 1997—. Office: Houston Police Dept 1200 Travis St Houston TX 77002-6001

BRADFORD, DANA GIBSON, II, lawyer; b. Coral Gables, Fla., Sept. 29, 1948; s. Dana Gibson and Jeanette (Ellis) B.; m. Mary E. Bradford, June 20, 1970 (div. Jan. 1982); 1 child, Jeffrey Dana; m. Donna P. Bradford, Apr. 14, 1984; 1 child, Shannon Claire. BA, U. Fla., 1970; JD, Duke U., 1973. Bar: Fla. 1973, U.S. Dist. Ct. (mid. dist.) Fla. 1974, U.S. Dist. Ct. (so. and no. dists.) Fla. 1979, U.S. Ct. Appeals (5th cir.) 1974, U.S. Ct. Appeals (11th cir.) 1982, U.S. Supreme Ct. 1977. Lawyer, ptnr. Mahoney, Hadlow & Adams, Jacksonville, Fla., 1973-82, Baumer, Bradford & Walters, Jacksonville, 1982—2000, Smith, Gambrell & Russell, LLP, Jacksonville, 2000—. Mem. Fla. Bd. Bar Examiners, 1989-94, chmn. bd., 1992-93; mem. Fla. Supreme Ct. Commn. on Professionalism, 1996-98; seminar lectr. Contbr. chpt. to book, articles to profl. jours. Mem. Leadership Jacksonville, 1982; spl. counsel Jacksonville Sports Authority. Capt. U.S. Army Res., 1972-80. Mem. ABA, ATLA, Jacksonville Bar Assn. (bd. govs. young lawyers sect. 1976-78, chmn. trial sects. 1989-90), Jacksonville Assn. Def. Counsel (pres. 1978-79). Republican. Methodist. Office: Smith Gambrell & Russell LLP 50 N Laura St Ste 2600 Jacksonville FL 32202-3625 E-mail: dgbradford@sgrlaw.com.

BRADFORD, DAVID FRANTZ, economist; b. Cambridge, Mass., Jan. 8, 1939; s. Mark Waldo and Matilda (Frantz) B.; m. Gunthild Klaerchen Huober, Feb. 20, 1964; children: Theodore Huober, Catherine Louise. BA magna cum laude (Nat. Merit scholar 1956-60), Amherst Coll., 1960, LHD (hon.), 1985; MS in Applied Math., Harvard U., 1962; Ford Found. dissertation fellow, Churchill Coll., Cambridge U., 1963-64; PhD in Econs, Stanford U., 1966. Econ. cons. Office Asst. Sec. of Def., Germany, Eng. and; Washington, 1964-65; acting instr. econs. Stanford U., 1965-66; asst. prof. econs. Princeton U., 1966-71, assoc. prof. econs. and public affairs, 1971-75, prof. econs. and public affairs, 1975—; assoc. dean Woodrow Wilson Sch., 1974-75, 78-80, 85-88, 89-91, acting dean, 1980, 87. Vis. prof. law Harvard U., 1991; adj. prof. Sch. Law NYU, 1993—; vis. scholar Am. Enterprise Inst., 1993; mem. Pres.'s Coun. Econ. Advisers, 1991-93; dep. asst. sec. for tax policy U.S. Treasury Dept., 1975-76; dir. rsch. in taxation Nat. Bur. Econ. Rsch., 1977-91, rsch. assoc., 1977—. Author: Blueprints for Basic Tax Reform, 1984; Untangling the Income Tax, 1986; contbr. articles to profl. jours. Vice chair N.J. State and Local Expenditure and Revenue Policy Commn., 1985-88; mem. Econ. Policy Coun. N.J., 1985-88, Nat. Commn. on R.R. Retirement Reform, 1989-90. Recipient Exceptional Svc. award U.S. Treasury Dept., 1976; Woodrow Wilson fellow Stanford U., 1960-61, Fulbright fellow Belgium, 1977, fellow Ctr. Advanced Study in Behavioral Scis., Stanford, 1988-89. Mem. Am. Econ. Assn., Econometric Soc., Nat. Tax Assn., Phi Beta Kappa. Office: Princeton U Woodrow Wilson Sch Princeton NJ 08544-1013

BRADFORD, DAVID PAUL, psychotherapist; b. Lynwood, Calif., Mar. 23, 1955; s. William H. and Barbara E. (O'Leary) Johnson. AA, Citrus Coll., Azusa, Calif., 1975; BA in Polit. Sci., UCLA, 1978; postgrad., Calif. State U., L.A., 1984-85, U. West L.A., 1990-91; MA in Psychology, Antioch U., 2003. Prin. clerk UCLA Brain Rsch. Inst., 1977-81; adminstrv. asst., supr. UCLA Hosp. and Clinics, 1977-81; dep. to atty. in residence matters office of registrar UCLA, 1981-85; office of clerk L.A. County Bd. Suprs., L.A., 1987-88; jud. asst., ct. clerk L.A. Superior Ct., L.A., 1988—; assoc. prodr. "Full Disclosure Network, Pub. Access TV of So. Calif., 2001; psychotherapist Marriage and Family Therapy, L.A. Founder Bradford & Assocs., L.A., 1987—; rsch. dir. citizens Protection Alliance, Santa Monica, 1992—. Active L.A. County Domestic Violence Coun. Recipient Cert. of Appreciation, Domestic Violence Coun., 1990, commendation Los Angeles County Bd. Suprs., 1993, L.A. Police Dept. and Assn. Threat Assessment Profls. award, 1994. Mem. N.Y. Acad. Scis., Los Angeles County Superior Ct. Clks. Assn. (local 575 AFSCME pres. 1993, 94), N.Y. Acad. Polit. Scis. E-mail: DavidBradford@uclalumni.net.

BRADFORD, DENNIS DOYLE, real estate broker, developer; b. Tulsa, Sept. 5, 1945; s. Doyle Earl and Elta (Price) B.; m. Richie Deloris Dawson. BSBA in Econs., U. Tulsa, 1969. Sales and mktg. rep. Xerox Corp., Oklahoma City, 1969-72; comml. loan officer Mager Mortgage Co., Oklahoma City, 1973-74; pvt. practice real estate Oklahoma City, 1973—; pres., owner Bradford Oil Co., Oklahoma City, 1977-80; pres. Blazer Oil Co., Oklahoma City, 1980—; v.p. Petro So., Inc., Tampa Fla., 1983-84; ptnr. Coachman Inns, Oklahoma City, 1981-86; chmn., CEO Coachman Inc., Oklahoma City, 1985-98; dir. Coachman Inc, San Juan, P.R., 1998—; pres., CEO Olympic Mills Corp., Guaynabo, P.R., 1995-97; pres. West Coast Ptnrs., Inc., Bradenton, Fla., 1997—. Mem. nat. adv. coun. to U.S. SBA, Washington, 1982-92, del. to White House Conf. on Small Bus., 1986, adv. bd. Nat. SBDC, Washington, 2003—. Bd. dirs. Okla. Med. Ctr. Found., 1989-94, Salvation Army of P.R., 1996-97; bd. dirs., sec. Okla. Air and Space Mus., 1989-95, v.p. 1991-92, pres. 1992-93; mem. Local Selective Svc. Bd., Oklahoma City, 1988-94, Rep. Eagles, 1979-92, Rep. Presdl. Round Table. Mem. Nat. Cowboy Hall of Fame, Okla. Heritage Assn., Okla. County Hist. Soc., Air Force Assn., Navy League, Young Pres.'s Orgn. (chmn. 1993-94, N.Am. spl. projects officer 1993-94), World Pres.'s Orgn. (Oklahoma City chpt. chmn. 2002-03), Oklahoma City C. of C., Balloon Fedn. Am., Oklahoma City Golf and Country Club, Summit Club (Tulsa), Bradenton Country Club. Republican. Methodist. Home: Pointe Tarpon 1574 Pointe Tarpon Blvd Tarpon Springs FL 34689-5887 Office: West Coast Ptnrs Incn 301 NW 63rd St Ste 500 Oklahoma City OK 73116-7989 E-mail: ddb@westcoastpartners.com.

BRADFORD, JAMES C., JR., brokerage house executive; b. Nashville, July 25, 1933; s. James C. and Eleanor (Avent) B.; m. Lillian Frances Robertson, Nov., 1967; children: Jay, Bryan. BA, Princeton U., 1955. Trainee Lehman Bros., N.Y.C., 1958; ptnr. J.C. Bradford & Co., Nashville, 1959-2000; sr. mng. dir. U.B.S. PaineWebber, Nashville, 2001—. Chmn. dist. com. Nat. Assn. Securities Dealers, Atlanta, 1970-73; dir. Securities Industry Assn., N.Y.C., 1972-75; gov. Am. Stock Exch., 1986-87; bd. dirs. N.Y. Stock Exch., 1987-93, Nat. Assn. Securities Dealers Regulation. Trustee Mongomery Bell Acad., Nashville, 1968—; pres. Nashville Symphony Assn., 1969-70; pres. bd. trustees Ensworth Sch., Nashville, 1988-89. 1st lt. USAF, 1955-57. Mem. Belle Meade Country Club (bd. dirs. 1987-89), Nat. Assn. of Securities (gov. Washington 1996). Republican. Episcopalian. Office: UBS PaineWebber 3102 West End Nashville TN 37203

BRADFORD, LOUISE MATHILDE, social services administrator; b. Alexandria, La., Aug. 3, 1925; d. Henry Aaron and Ruby (Pearson) B. BS, La. Poly. Inst., 1945; cert. in social work, La. State U., 1949; MS, Columbia U., 1953; postgrad., Tulane U., 1962, 64, La. State U., 1967; cert., U. Pa., 1966. Diplomate NASW, Am. Bd. Clin. Social Work; cert. social worker Acad. Cert. Social Workers. With La. Dept. Pub. Welfare, Alexandria, 1945-78, welfare caseworker, 1950-53, children's caseworker, 1957-59, child welfare cons., 1959-73, social svcs. cons., 1973-78, state cons. day care, 1963-66; dir. social svcs. St. Mary's Tng. Sch., Alexandria, 1978-2000; adoption splst. Vols. of Am., 2000—. Del. Nat. Day Care Conf., Washington, 1964; mem. early childhood edn. com. So. States Work Conf., Daytona Beach, Fla., 1968; mem. La. adv. com. 1970 White House Conf. on Children, also del.; mem. So. region planning com. Child Welfare League Am., 1970-73; mem. profl. adv. com. Cenla chpt. Parents Without Partners, 1970-95; adj. asst. prof. sociology La. Coll. Pineville, 1969-85; lectr. Kindergarten Workshop, 1970-72; mem. La. 4-C Steering Com.; social svcs. cons. La. Spl. Edn. Ctr., Alexandria, 1980-86; del. Internat. Conf. on Social Welfare, Nairobi, 1974, Jerusalem, 1978, Hong Kong, 1980, Brighton, 1982, Montreal, 1984. Bd. dirs. Cenla Cmty. Action Com., Alexandria, 1966-68; mem. kindergarten bd. Meth. Ch., 1967-87, ofcl. bd., 1974-75, 77-81, 83-85, 96-98, 2000-03. Recipient Social Worker of Yr. award, Alexandria br. NASW La. Conf. Social Welfare, 1974. Mem.: DAR, NASW (Lifetime Achievement award, La. chpt. 2003), Ctrl. La. Pre-Sch. Assn. (dir. 1967—70), Am. Assn. on Mental Retardation (La. social work chair 1989—94, Meritorious Contbn. award 1999, La. chpt. Svc. award 2001, Region V Svc. award 2001), Internat. Coun. on Social Welfare, La. Conf. Social Welfare (George Freeman award 1987, Hilda C. Simon award 1987), So. La. Assn. Children Under Six, Acad. Cert. Social Workers, Alexandria Golf and Country Club, Lions. Home: 5807 Joyce St Alexandria LA 71302-2510

BRADFORD, MARY PINKNEY, music educator; b. Austin, Tex., June 21, 1941; d. Charles Coatsworth and Evelyn (Robinson) Pinkney; m. Halley O. Bradford, 1967 (div. Sept. 1990); children: Katie Elizabeth, Peter Pinkney, John David Robinson; m. Ralph Lee, 1994. MusB, U. Tex., 1964, MusM, 1992. Cert. Music Tchrs. Nat. Assn. Music tchr. Austin Ind. Sch. Dist., 1964-67; substitute tchr. Conroe (Tex.) Ind. Sch. Dist., 1982-84; choral asst. to choir dir. Conroe High Sch., 1984-85; music tchr. Austin Ind. Sch. Dist., 1985-86; pvt. piano instr. Austin, 1986—; piano instr. St. Edward's U., Austin, 1990—. Home: 10300 Aspen St Austin TX 78758

BRADFORD, MATTHEW SILAS, music educator; b. Denver, Mar. 22, 1968; s. Roderick Moyer and Rae Ellen (Sterwart) Bradford; m. Shelly Diane Wray, June 10, 1989; children: Morgan, Blake. BA in Musical Edn., Washburn U., Topeka, Kans., 1996. Cert. Tchr. K-12 music Colo., 1996. Tchr. 5-12 instrumental and choral music Holyoke (Colo.) Schs., 1996—99; tchr. 5-12 instrumental music Clay Center (Kans.) Cmty. HS, 1999—. Worship team mem. Evang. Covenant Ch., Clay Center, 1999—2002. Mem.: Kans. Band Masters Assn., Kans. Music Educators Assn.

BRADFORD, PETER COREY, design consultant; b. Boston, May 24, 1935; s. Edward Allison and Marjorie (Bennett) B.; m. Mary Anne McLean, Nov. 21, 1959; children: Anne Elisia, Mary Lauriston. BFA, R.I. Sch. Design, 1957. Designer Time/Life Inc., N.Y.C., 1957-60; art dir. Indsl. Design mag. Whitney Publs., N.Y.C., 1960-63, CBS Inc., N.Y.C., 1963-65; owner Peter Bradford & Assocs., N.Y.C., 1965—, Peter Bradford Pub., N.Y.C. and Boston, 1978-90, Cement Boat Co. Inc., N.Y.C., 1990—99; instr. Phila. Coll. Art, 1977—92, Sch. Visual Arts, N.Y.C., 1977—; prof. Cooper Union Sch. Art, N.Y.C., 1983-85; prin. Wingspan Inc., N.Y.C. and Boston, 1987—90. Vis. prof. Am. U. in Cairo, 1997; dir. design programs Urban Am. Inc., AIA, Fawcett Publs., USIA, Ford Found., Random House Reference; designer instructional programs Xerox Corp., Random House, McGraw-Hill, Macmillan; dir. Documents Am. Design, N.Y.C.; advisor Silver Mt. Found., N.Y.C., 1982-86, Visible Lang. Quar.; spkr. in field; co-creator TV awareness films, Emmy Awards, ABC TV, 1993. Author: Chair, 1978 (design award 1979), The Design Art of Nicos Zographos, 2000; author, editor: Information Architects, 1996; editor: Jackie Tales, 1998; co-creator: The Curriculum Dictionary, 1989; creator: The Animated Encyclopedia, Cosmic Comics, 1990; visualist: The Age of Science, 2001. Recipient numerous awards including Jesse H. Neal award Assoc. Bus. Publs., 1960, Silver medal N.Y. Art Dirs. Club, 1977. Mem. Alliance Graphique Internat., Am. Inst. Graphic Arts.

BRADFORD, REAGAN HOWARD, JR., ophthalmology educator; b. Lawton, Okla., July 31, 1954; s. Reagan Howard Sr. and Conita Ann (Hargraves) B.; m. Cynthia Ann McGough, Apr. 22, 1988. BS, U. Okla., 1976; MD, U. Okla., Oklahoma City, 1980. Diplomate Am. Bd. Ophthalmology. Intern Bapt. Med. Ctr., Oklahoma City, 1980-81; resident Dean A. McGee Eye Inst. U. Okla., 1981-84; fellow in vitreo retina Bascom Palmer Eye Inst. U. Miami, Fla., 1984-85; assoc. clinical prof. Dean A. McGee Eye Inst., U. Okla., Oklahoma City, 1985—. Author: (with others) Basics of Neurophthalmology; contbr. articles to profl. jours. Fellow Am. Acad. Ophthalmology; mem. Okla. County Med. Soc., Okla. State Med. Assn., AMA, Okla. State Acad. Ophthalmology. Republican. Baptist. Avocations: tennis, softball. Office: Dean A McGee Eye Inst 608 Stanton L Young Blvd Oklahoma City OK 73104-5065

BRADFORD, ROBERT ERNEST, motion picture producer, financier; b. Berlin; came to U.S., 1946, naturalized, 1953; s. Siegfried and Doris (Herzberg) B.; m. Barbara Taylor, Dec. 24, 1963. Student, Marie Curie Coll., Paris, 1937; AB, U. Geneva, 1945. Prodn. cons. Distbn. Corp. Am., N.Y.C., 1946-53; exec. v.p. Jesse L. Lasky Prodns., Beverly Hills, Calif., 1953—; exec. v.p., dir. Samuel Bronston Prodns., N.Y.C., 1955—; exec. v.p. Franco London Films Internat., Ltd., Montreal; pres. Franco London Film S.A., Paris, Franco London Music, Ltd., London; head feature prodn., exec. producer Hal Roach Studios, Hollywood, Calif., 1959—. Bd. dirs. Hy-Ford Prodns., Inc., Hy-Ford Europea, Rome, Jack London Prodns.; lectr. internat. affairs and interracial problems, 1950—; cons., dir. Nat. Found. for Good Govt. Prodr. (films) John Paul Jones, 1958, The Scavengers, 1959, If You Remember Me, 1959-60, The Golden Touch, 1959-60, To Die of Love, 1971, Sweet Deception, 1972, Impossible Object, 1973, Hold the Dream, 1986, Voice of the Heart, 1988, Act of Will, 1988, To Be the Best, 1989, The Women in His Life, 1990, Remember, 1992, Angel, 1993, Everything to Gain, 1994, Dangerous to Know, 1995, Love in Another Town, 1995, A Secret Affair, 1996. Pub. rels. dir. one-world award com. Am. Nobel Anniversary Com. With French Intelligence, 1940-45. Recipient citation for outstanding work and civic achievements Greater N.Y. Citizens Forum, 1952 Office: 450 Park Ave New York NY 10022-2605 E-mail: bradford.ent@att.net.

BRADFORD, SUSAN ANNE, broadcast journalist, writer; b. Pasadena, Calif, Dec. 2, 1969; d. Wesley Gene and Nancy Cornelia (Dixon) B. Student, Coll. Cevenol, Le Chambon Sur Lignon, France, 1985, St. Andrews U., Scotland, 1989-90; BA in English, U. Calif., Irvine, 1992; MA in Internat. Rels., Essex U., Eng., 1996, postgrad. Editor-in-chief Gandalf's Gazette, Irvine, Calif., 1987-88; news editor New Univ., Irvine, Calif., 1987-88; intern Sta. CBS-TV News, LA, 1989; host, exec. producer Witness the News TV show, Irvine, 1990-92; prodn. asst. PBS Red Car Film Project, LA, 1992-93; intern in news writing Sta. KNX News, LA, 1993; reporter City News Svc., LA, 1994-95; founder/editor European Rev., 1995-98. Sr. rsch. fellow, polit. cons., councillor Atlantic Coun. of U.K., 1996—2002; speechwriter U.K. Shadow Fgn. Sec. Michael Howard, 1998; sr. councilor Atlantic Coun. of US, 1999—2001; prodr. Fox News Channel, 2000; prodr., founder Internat. Prodn., 2000—; instr. Fairfax Pub. Access, 2002. Author poems; contbr. articles to profl. jour.; founding editor: European Rev., 1995-98. Bd. dir. HWPC Scholarship Found., Hollywood, Calif., 1992-93; mem. NATO Univ. Adv. Com., 1996-99. Recipient Writing awards Palos Verdes Nat. Bank, 1987, AFL-CIO, 1987, 3d Pl. award Nat. Fedn. Press Women, 1992. Mem. Calif. Press Women (pub. rels. chair 1991-92), Hollywood Women's Press Club (bd. dir. 1989-94), European Movement (com./London strategy group media coord.1995-98), Irvine Women's Crew (founder, pres.), Women's Fgn. Policy Group, Eng. Speaking Union, Federalist Soc. (internat. law com.), UN Assn. (media cons., spkr., writer), Woodrow Wilson Ctr. for Internat. Scholars (assoc.), Capitol Speakers Club. United Ch. Of Christ. Avocations: student of history, travel, nature, classical music. E-mail: susanbradford7@aol.com.

BRADFORD, TUTT SLOAN, retired publisher; b. Apr. 30, 1917; s. Tutt S. and Zula (Bowen) B.; m. Elizabeth Hendley, June 30, 1941 (dec.); children: Nancy, Debbie; m. Mercedes F. Bradford, Dec. 14, 2001. Student, Wofford Coll., 1934; LLD, Maryville Coll., 1987. Pub. Cleve. Daily Banner, 1948-51; asst. to pres. Gen. Newspapers, 1951; pub. Bristol (Va.) Herald Courier, 1951-55, Maryville (Tenn.) Alcoa Daily Times, 1955-85. Bd. dir. humanities, Tenn., 1971-73; mem. devel. coun. U. Tenn., 1980-83; bd. dirs. Maryville Coll., 1974-79, 81-2003, Knoxville Symphony, Knoxville Mus. of Art, Thompson Ctr. for Cancer Survival, Lakeshore Mental Hosp., Tenn. Tech. Found.; Tenn. Resource Valley, 1988-91, 92-95, East Tenn. Found.; pres. Blount Meml. Hosp. Found., Boy's Club Found., Blount Hearing and Speech Found., 1991, Blount County Libr. Found., 1999. Pres. Blount County Indsl. Devel. Bd., 1970-72. With 9th AF AUS, 1943-45, ETO. Recipient Disting. Svc. award Bristol Jr. C. of C., 1952, Maryville-Alcoa Jr. C. of C., 1958, 73, Sequoyah Literacy award Tenn. Hist. Com., 1995, Tenn. Vol. Cmty. award Gov. Don Sunquist, 2003; named to East Tenn. Hall of Fame, Jr. Achievement, 1990; named Vol. Yr., U. Tenn., 1994, Outstanding Philanthropist Nat. Soc. Fund Raising Execs., 1991. Mem. So. Newspaper Pubs. Assn. (bd. dirs. 1968-70), Tenn. Press Assn. (pres. 1974), Knox Arts Coun. (award 1988), Blount County C. of C. (pres. 1960), Kiwanis (pres. Maryville 1967). Home: 1401 Broad Run Dr Maryville TN 37803

BRADFORD, WILLIAM DALTON, pathologist, educator; b. Rochester, N.Y., Nov. 2, 1931; s. William Leslie and Lenora Dee (Dalton) B.; m. Anne Bevington Harden, July 8, 1961; children— Scott Harden, Lisa Graham BA, Amherst Coll., 1954; MD, Western Res. U., 1958. Diplomate Am. Bd. Pediatrics, Am. Bd. Anatomic Pathology. Intern in pathology Boston Children's Med. Ctr., 1958-59, resident in pediatrics, 1959-61; teaching fellow in pathology Harvard Med. Sch., 1963-64; asst. prof. pathology Duke U., Durham, N.C., 1966-70, assoc. prof., 1970-81, prof., 1981—, assoc. dean, 1970-71, 74-78, 84-87, asst. to chancellor for health affairs, 1987-89, dir. pediatric pathology, 1966—, dir. pathology tng. program, 1974-2001. Pres. Durham YMCA, 1978, bd. dirs., 1976-83, 90-95; faculty chmn. of athletics Duke U., 1979-85. Lt. comdr. USN, 1961-63. Recipient Golden Apple award Student Med. Assn., 1969, 93, 95, 98, Layman of Yr. award YMCA, 1974, 78, Disting. Tchr. award Duke Med. Alumni Assn., 1989; Mead Johnson fellow, 1963-64. Mem. Internat. Acad. Pathology, Am. Assn. Pathologists, Soc. Pediatric Research, Group for Rsch. in Pathology Edn., Soc. for Pediatric Pathology (pres. 1987-88), Nat. Collegiate Athletic Assn. Council, Nat. Faculty Athletics Reps. Forum (chmn. 1985), Atlantic Coast Conf. (pres. 1982-83), Duke Med. Alumni Coun. (pres. 2000-01). Office: Duke U Med Ctr PO Box 3712 Durham NC 27710-0001 E-mail: bradf001@mc.duke.edu.

BRADFORD, WILLIAM EDWARD, oil field equipment manufacturing company executive; b. Dallas, Jan. 8, 1935; m. JoDeane Browning, Aug. 18, 1955; children: William B., A. Kathleen, Jon E. BS in Geology, Centenary Coll., 1958; grad., Tex. A&M U., 1975. Salesman Hycalog, Inc., 1958-61; v.p., gen. ptnr. Analytical Logging, Inc., 1961-70; product mgr. Oilfield Products Group Dresser Industries, Inc., Dallas, 1970-72, mgr. Mid-cont. Oilfield Products Group, 1972-73, mgr. Europe, Africa, Middle East Oilfield Products Group, 1973-76, v.p. security divsn., 1976-78, pres. security divsn., 1980-83, group pres. Oilfield Products Group, 1983-84, v.p. ops., 1984-92, sr. v.p., 1988-92; pres. CEO Dresser-Rand Co., Corning, N.Y., 1992-95; pres., COO and dir. Dresser Industries, Inc., Dallas, ., 1995-96, pres., CEO, dir., 1996-98, chmn. pres., 1998-2000; chmn. Halliburton Co. (formerly Dresser Industries, Inc.), Dallas, 2000—. Bd. dirs. Kerr-McGee Corp., Valero Energy Corp. Mem. Soc. Petroleum Engrs., Am. Assn. Petroleum Geologists, Petroleum Equipment Suppliers Assn., Northwood Country Club (Dallas), Double Eagle Club, Rolling Rock Club. Office: 5500 Preston Rd Ste 210 Dallas TX 75205-2699

BRADIE, PETER RICHARD, lawyer, engineer; b. Bklyn., Feb. 19, 1937; s. Alexander Robert and Blanche Isabelle Bradie; m. Anna Barbara Corcoran, Jan. 22, 1960; children: Suzanne J., Barbara L., Michell S. BSME, Fairleigh Dickinson U., 1960; JD, South Tex. Coll. Law, 1978. Bar: Tex. 1978, U.S. Dist. Ct. (so. dist.) Tex. 1981; registered profl. engr., Ala. Performance engr. Pratt & Whitney Aircraft, West Palm Beach, Fla., 1961-63; sr. engr. Hayes Internat. Corp., Huntsville, Ala., 1963—68, Lockheed Missiles and Space, Huntsville, 1964—68; fluidics engr. Double A Products Co., Manchester, Mich., 1968-69; cons. Spectrum Controls, Montvale, N.J., 1969-72; sr. project mgr. Materials Research Corp., Orangebury, N.Y., 1972-74; sr. contracts adminstr. Brown & Root Inc., Houston, 1974-85; sole practice Houston, 1985-91; ptnr. Bradie, Bradie & Bradie, Houston, 1991—. Counsel Inverness Forest C.A, Houston., 1978-80; sr. counsel Raymond-Brown & Root-Molem, J.V., Houston, 1982-84. Contbr. articles on fluidic controls to mags.; patentee. Dem. committeeman Bergen County, Haworth, N.J., 1959; del. Harris County Reps., Houston, 1984; officer, bd. dirs. Inverness Forest Civic Assn., Houston, 1975-78. Served to 2d lt. USMCR, 1958-61. Mem.: ATLA, Comml. Law League Am., Houston N.W. Bar Assn. (treas. 1986, bd. dirs. 1988, pres.-elect 1988—89, pres. 1990—91), Tex. Bar Assn., N.W. Houston Sunrise Rotary Club, Montvale Rotary Club (bd. dirs. 1973—74), Rotary Internat., Am. Inn of Ct. Republican. Jewish. Avocations: classical music, history, computers. Home: 22007 Kenchester Dr Houston TX 77073-1315 Office: Bradie Bradie & Bradie 3845 Fm 1960 Rd W Ste 330 Houston TX 77068-3519 E-mail: bradiex3@bradie-law.com.

BRADISH, WARREN ALLEN, internal auditor, operations analyst, management consultant; b. Adrian, Mich., June 9, 1937; s. Calvin Gamber and Florence Helen (Schulze) B.; m. Setsuko Arimatsui, May 18, 1959 (div.); children: Donna, John, Bradly, Jacqueline; m. Robert Mary Kalil, Sept. 26, 1969. BA in Bus. Adminstrn. summa cum laude, St. Leo Coll., 1977; MA in Bus. Mgmt., Ctrl. Mich. U., 1980. Commd. officer U.S. Army, 1956, advanced through grades to maj., 1976; ret., 1976; edn. and tng. officer State of Ga., 1977-80; dir. investigations Sec. of State, Ga., 1980-82, dir. surveillance, specialized investigative svcs., 1982-83; internal auditor, ops. analyst Ga. Dept. Revenue, 1983-84; govt. security specialist McPherson, Ga., 1984-88; intelligence ops. specialist MacDill AFB, Fla., 1988-99. Adj. prof. St. Leo Coll. Decorated Bronze Star. Mem. DVA, Assn. Former Intelligence Officers, Spl. Forces Decade Assn., Sigma Iota. Home: 4841 Foxshire Cir Tampa FL 33624-4309

BRADLEE, BENJAMIN CROWNINSHIELD, executive editor; b. Boston, Aug. 26, 1921; s. Frederick J. and Josephine (deGersdorff) B.; m. Jean Saltonstall, Aug. 8, 1942; 1 son, Benjamin Crowninshield; m. Antoinette Pinchot, July 6, 1956; children: Dominic, Marina; m. Sally Quinn, Oct. 20, 1978; 1 son, Josiah Quinn Crowninshield. AB, Harvard U., 1943. Reporter N.H. Sunday News, Manchester, 1946- 48, Washington Post, 1948-51; press attachè embassy Paris, France, 1951-53; European corr. Newsweek mag., Paris, 1953-57, reporter Washington bur., 1957-61, sr. editor, chief bur., 1961-65; mng. editor Washington Post, 1965-68, v.p., exec. editor, 1968-91, v.p. at large, 1991—. Chmn. Hist. St. Mary's City Commn., 1992—. Author: That Special Grace, 1964, Conversations with Kennedy, 1975, A Good Life--Newspapering and Other Adventures, 1995. Served to lt. USNR, 1942-45. Home: 3014 N St NW Washington DC 20007-3404 Office: care Washington Post 1150 15th St NW Washington DC 20071-0001

BRADLEY, AMELIA JANE, lawyer; b. Columbia, S.C., Apr. 18, 1947; d. Hugh Wilson and Amelia Jane (Wylie) B.; m. Richard Bancroft Hovey, Apr. 1, 1977. BA, U. Va., 1968; MA, George Washington U., 1971. Bar: Va. 1976, D.C. 1985. Budget and mgmt. analyst NLRB, Washington, 1968-71, 72; clk. Cohen and Vitt, PC, Alexandria, Va., 1972-76; assoc. Cohen, Vitt & Annand, PC, Alexandria, 1976-80; White House fellow USDA, Washington, 1980-81, Office U.S. Trade Rep., Exec. Office of Pres., Washington, 1981, asst. gen. counsel, 1981-82, assoc. gen. counsel, 1982-84, legal advisor to U.S. GATT del. Geneva, 1984-87; prin. dep. gen. counsel Office U.S. Trade Rep., Exec Office of Pres., Washington, 1989-92; asst. U.S. trade rep. for dispute resolution Office U.S. Trade Rep., Exec. Office of Pres., Washington, 1994; assoc. dir. for global environment White House Office on Environ. Policy, Washington, 1994-95; assoc. dir. internat. trade and devel. Coun. on Environ. Quality, Washington, 1994—95; asst. U.S. trade rep. for monitoring, enforcement Exec. Office of Pres., Washington, 1996—2002. Chief negotiator U.S. GATT Uruguay Round Dispute Settlement Negotiating Group, 1986-87, 89-93; chmn. interagy. Sect. 301 Com., Washington, 1988-92; vis. rsch. assoc. Fletcher Sch. Law and Diplomacy, Tufts U., Medford, Mass., 1987-88; vis. rschr. Harvard U. Law Sch., Cambridge, Mass., 1988. Mem., chmn. Alexandria Human Rights Commn., 1975-80; pres., trustee Alexandria Law Libr., 1978-80; founding mem. Lawyer Referral Svc., Alexandria, 1978. NEH fellow, 1978. Mem. ABA, Va. State Bar (mem., chmn. com. on legal edn. and admission to bar 1977-84), D.C. Bar (chmn. internat. trade com. 1989-90). Episcopalian.

BRADLEY, ANN WALSH, state supreme court justice; married; 4 children. BA, Webster Coll., 1972; JD, U. Wis., 1976. Tchr. HS; pvt. law practice; former judge Marathon County Circuit Ct., Wausau, Wis.; justice Wis. Supreme Ct., Madison, Wis., 1995—. Office: Wis Ct Sys PO Box 1688 Madison WI 53701-1688*

BRADLEY, BARBRA BAILEY, musician, educator, accompanist; b. Windsor, Ont., Can., Dec. 27, 1944; d. Charles David Bailey and Mary Alice Calow; m. Joseph Patrick Bradley, Sept. 19, 1981. BA in Honours Music Edn., U. Western Ont., London, Can., 1967; A of Music in Piano, West. Ont. Conservatory Music, London, 1967; MM in Piano, Ind. U., 1969. Freelance performer piano and harp, adjudicator, 1974-81; tchr. piano, performer Brigham Young U., Provo, Utah, 1973-74; accompanist concert tour Mu Phi Epsilon Found., various cities, 1974-76; tchr. piano, performer St. Clair divsn. Royal Hamilton Coll. Music, Windsor, Ont., 1975-79; tchr. piano, performer music dept. St. Clair Coll., Windsor, 1979-81; freelance performer Washington, 1981—; tchr. piano, performer Leidzen Sch. Music, Fairfax, Va., 1987-88, Nat. Cathedral Sch., Washington, 1988—. Composer (music for children's theater): Cricket on the Hearth, 1989, Goldilocks and the Christmas Bears, 1991. Fellow doctoral fellow for grad. study Ind. U., Can. Coun., 1970. Mem.: Am. Fedn. Musicians, Fri. Morning Music Club (chamber music performer 1986—), Mu Phi Epsilon (internat. officer, alumni advisor 1996—, pres. Washington alumni chpt. 1990—94, dist. dir. Atlantic-2 dist. 1994—96, Sterling Staff Internat. Competition winner 1974). Mem. Lds Ch. Avocations: ballet, photography, walking, genealogy. Office: Nat Cathedral Sch Mount St Albans Washington DC 20016 E-mail: bradley@cathedral.org.

BRADLEY, BILL, former senator; b. Crystal City, Mo., July 28, 1943; s. Warren W. and Susan (Crowe) B.; m. Ernestine Schlant, Jan. 14, 1974; 1 dau., Theresa Anne. BA, Princeton U., 1965; MA, Oxford (Eng.) U., 1968. Player N.Y. Knickerbockers Profl. Basketball Team, 1967-77; U.S. senator from N.J., 1979-96; mem. fin., energy coms., spl. com. on aging; Disting. leadership scholar, chair U. Md., College Park; Payne Disting. prof. Inst. for Internat. Studies, Stanford U., 1997-98; campaigned for Dem. Presdl. Nomination, 1999-2000. Bd. advisors acad. leadership U. Md., College Park; chair advt. couns. adv. com. on pub. issues; essayist CBS TV Weekend Evening News; sr. advisor, vice chair internat. coun. J.P. Morgan and Co., Inc., 1997-99; vis. prof. pub. affairs Univ. of Notre Dame, 1998; bd. trustee Princeton U.; mem. Coun. Fgn. Rels. Author: Life on the Run, 1976, The Fair Tax, 1984, Time Present, Time Past, 1996, Values of the Game, 1998. Chmn. Nat. Civic League, Ams. Promise (co-chmn. task force on safe spaces, structured activities). Served with USAFR, 1967-78. Rhodes scholar, 1965-67; named three-time basketball All-Am.; recipient Sullivan award as the country's outstanding amateur athlete. Democrat. Achievements include being a mem. NBA championship team, 1970, 73, gold medal team Tokyo Olympics.

BRADLEY, BOB, professional soccer coach; b. Montclair, N.J., Mar. 3, 1958; B.History, Princeton U.; M.Sports Adminstrn., Ohio U. Head coach soccer Ohio U., Athens, 1980-81; asst. coach U. Va., 1982-83; head coach Princeton U., 1984-95; asst. coach D.C. United, 1995-97; head coach Chgo. Fire, 1997—. Named Major League Soccer's 1998 All Sport Coach of the Yr., NCAA Divsn. I Men's Coach of the Yr., 1993. Office: Chicago Fire # 1998 980 N Michigan Ave Chicago IL 60611-4501

BRADLEY, CHARLES HARVEY, lawyer; b. Indpls., July 17, 1923; s. Charles Harvey and Carolyn (Coffin) Bradley; m. Mary Jo Albright, Aug. 26, 1944; children: Sally A., Jane C. AB, Yale U., 1945, LLB, 1949. Bar: Ind. 1949. Ptnr. Thomson, O'Neal & Smith, Indpls., 1950—60; mgr. legal dept. Eli Lilly and Co., Indpls., 1960—63, asst. sec., dir. legal div., 1963, sec., gen. counsel, 1964—84, v.p., gen. counsel, 1984—86, sr. v.p., gen. counsel, 1986—87. Mem. com. on character and fitness Ind. Supreme Ct., 1965—87; Supreme Ct. Com. on Continuing Legal Edn., 1984—87; bd. dirs. Mountain Lake Corp. Trustee Hussey-Mayfield Meml. Pub. Libr., Zionsville, Ind., 1990—96. Served to 2d lt. USMC, 1943—45, to capt. USMC, 1952—53. Decorated Air medal with 8 oak leaf clusters, D.F.C. with 3 oak leaf clusters; recipient Sagamore of Wabash award, Gov. Ind. Fellow: Ind. Bar Found.; mem.: Yale Law Sch. Assn. (pres. 1977—79, pres.'s commn. mgmt. agy. for internat. devel. 1991—92, mem. exec. com.), Indpls. C. of C. (dir. emeritus), Assn. Gen. Counsel, Indpls. Bar Assn., Ind. Bar Assn., Mountain Lake Corp. Golf Club, Yale of Ind. Club (past pres.), Indpls. Lawyers Club. Home: 1310 S Us Highway 421 Zionsville IN 46077-9762

BRADLEY, CHARLES WILLIAM, podiatrist, educator; b. Fife, Tex., July 23, 1923; s. Tom and Mary Ada (Cheatham) B.; m. Marilyn A. Brown, Apr. 3, 1948 (dec. Mar. 1973); children: Steven, Gregory, Jeffrey, Elizabeth, Gerald. Student, Tex. Tech., 1940-42; D. Podiatric Medicine, Calif. Coll. Podiatric Medicine U. San Francisco, 1949, MPA, 1987, D.Sc. (hon.). Pvt. practice podiatry, Beaumont, Tex., 1950-51, Brownwood, Tex., 1951-52, San Francisco, San Bruno, Calif., 1952—; assoc. clin. prof. Calif. Coll. Podiatric Medicine, 1992-98. Chief of staff Calif. Podiatry Hosp., San Francisco; mem. surg. staff Sequoia Hosp., Redwood City, Calif.; mem. med. staff Peninsula Hosp., Burlingame, Calif.; chief podiatry staff St. Luke's Hosp., San Francisco; chmn. bd. Podiatry Ins. Co. Am.; cons. VA; assoc. prof. podiatric medicine Calif. Coll. Podiatric Medicine. Mem. San Francisco Symphony Found.; mem. adv. com. Health Policy Agenda for the Am. People, AMA; chmn. trustees Calif. Coll. Podiatric Medicine, Calif. Podiatry Coll., Calif. Podiatry Hosp.; mem. San Mateo Grand Jury, 1989. Served with USNR, 1942-45. Mem. Am. Podiatric Med. Assn. (trustee, pres. 1983-84), Calif. Podiatry Assn. (pres. No. div. 1964-66, state bd. dirs., pres. 1975-76, Podiatrist of Yr. award 1983), Nat. Coun. Edn. (vice-chmn.), Nat. Acads. Practice (chmn. podiatric med. sect. 1991-96, sec. 1996—), Am. Legion, San Bruno C. of C. (bd. dirs. 1978-91, v.p. 1992, bd. dir. grand jury assoc. 1990), Olympic Club, Commonwealth Club Calif., Elks, Lions. Home: 2965 Trousdale Dr Burlingame CA 94010-5708 Office: 560 Jenevein Ave San Bruno CA 94066-4408 E-mail: bradlee2@aol.com.

BRADLEY, COURTNEY JENE, researcher; b. Lansdale, Pa., Jan. 8, 1969; d. Frederick Richard and Jo-Anne Gervais Brown. BA in Psychology, Duke U., 1990; MPH, U. N.C., 1995; postgrad., Columbia U., 2000—. Student athletic trainer Duke U., Durham, N.C., 1986-90; sales specialist Parke-Davis, A Warner-Lambert Co., Asheville, N.C., 1990-93, intern, healthcare systems Morris Plains, N.J., summer 1994; rsch. asst. dept. health promotion and disease prevention U. N.C., Chapel Hill, 1995; healthcare econs. specialist Parke-Davis, A Warner-Lambert Co., Morris Plains, 1995-96, product mgr., atherosclerosis disease team, 1996-98; program officer The Dorothy Rider Pool Health Care Trust, Allentown, Pa., 1998-2000; rsch. asst. Ctr. for Psychosocial Study of Health & Illness Mailman Sch. Pub. Health Columbia U., N.Y.C., 2000—02, program coord. Ctr. for Psychosocial Study of Health and Illness, Mailman Sch. Pub. Health, 2002—. Roundtable mem. The Morning Call's A Change of Heart Initiative, Allentown, 1999-2000; curriculum devel. com. mem. The Morning Call's A Change of Heart for Kids, Allentown, 1999. Author publs. in field. Vol. tutor The Learning Club, Inc. of the Girls' Club, Inc., Allentown, 1998-2000; vol. Jersey Cares, N.J., 1997-98; vol. Activities Asst./Charles House Adult Day Care, Chapel Hill, N.C., 1994-95, The Health Adventure, Asheville, N.C., 1990-93. Recipient Lucy S. Morgan fellowship U. N.C. Sch. of Pub. Health, Chapel Hill, 1994; doctoral fellow sociomed. scis. Mailman Sch. Pub. Health, Columbia U. Mem. Am. Pub. Health Assn., Delta Omega Soc. Avocations: music/jazz, cooking, hiking. Office: Ctr for Psychosocial Study Health and Illness 100 Haven Ave Ste 6A New York NY 10032 E-mail: cjb133@columbia.edu.

BRADLEY, DAMON FREDERIC, headmaster; b. Chelsea, Mass., Oct. 20, 1942; s. Damon Herbert and Helen Louise (McKinnon) B.; m. Odette Marguerite Bradley, Aug. 9, 1969; children: Nathaniel Damon, Benjamin Laycock. AB, Boston U., 1964; MDiv, Yale U., 1968; MPhil, Syracuse U., 1976. Ordained to ministry, Bapt. Ch., 1970; cert. as edn. dir., elem. edn., secondary edn., Md. Religion instr. Cheshire (Conn.) Acad., 1965-66; instr. English Friends' Boys' Sch., Ramallah, Jordan, 1966-67; instr. humanities Am. Cmty. Sch., London, 1972-73; adj. instr. English Bentley Coll., Waltham, Mass. 1973-74; head upper sch. (boys) Head-Royce Sch., Oakland, Calif., 1974-79

headmaster Elliott-Pope Sch., Idyllwild, Calif., 1979-90, Landon Sch., Bethesda, Md., 1990—. Asst. minister Eastwood Bapt. Ch., Syracuse, 1968-71; assoc. minister Am. Ch. in Paris, 1971-72. Contbr. articles to profl. jours. Mem. Montgomery County Cmty. Partnership, Bethesda, 1992-94; trustee Norwood Sch., 1991-97, Assn. of Ind. Sch. Greater Washington, 1993-95, v.p. 2002—; trustee Internat. Coalition of Boys Schs., 1999—, treas., 2001—; trustee McLean Sch., Potomac, Md., 2001—. Recipient Exec. Leadership award Black Student Fund, Washington, 1998, Disting. Ednl. Leadership award Washington Post, 2000. Mem. Headmasters Assn., Assn. of Ind. Md. Schs. (trustee 1995-2000, pres. 1998-2000), City Tavern Club, Rotary (trustee 1992-94). Avocations: travel, cooking, boating, home renovation. Home: 6210 Poe Rd Bethesda MD 20817-3182 Office: Landon Sch 6101 Wilson Ln Bethesda MD 20817-3199 E-mail: damon_bradley@landon.net.

BRADLEY, DANA BURR, education educator, consultant; d. Daniel Burr and Madeline Haynes Bradley; m. J. Krist Schell, 1997; children: Saralinda E. Schell, Daniel R. Schell. BA with high distinction, U. of Rochester, 1983; MS, Carnegie-Mellon U., 1987; PhD, Carnegie Mellon U., 1987. Asst. prof. of polit. sci. and gerontology U. of NC at Charlotte, 1997—; dir. of UNCC-Duke partnership Duke U., 1994—. Contbr. articles to jours. Co-chair health coun. United Way of Ctrl. Carolinas. Rockefeller Humanities fellowship, Rockefeller Found., 1983—85, Svc. Learning grant, US Corp. for Pub. Svc., AGHE, 1998, Nonprofit Rsch. and Capacity Bldg. grant, Sisters of Mercy of NC Found., INC, 1999, Sisters of Mercy of NC Found., Inc., 2000, 2001, Faculty Rsch. grant, The U. of NC at Charlotte, 2002. Mem.: Gerontol. Soc. of Am. (chair-elect humanities and arts com. 2002—03), Assn. for Gerontology in Higher Edn. (program devel. com., awards com.; advancement com.). Avocations: yoga, spinning, gardening, cooking. Office: University of NC at Charlotte 9201 University City Blvd Charlotte NC 28223 Office Fax: 704-687-3497. E-mail: dbradley@email.uncc.edu.

BRADLEY, DAVID MICHAEL, mathematician, educator; b. Kitchener, Ont., Can., 1966; arrived in U.S., 1998; B in Math., U. Waterloo, Ont., Can., 1990; PhD, U. Ill., 1995. NSERC postdoctoral fellow Ctr. for Exptl. and Constructive Math., Simon Fraser U., Burnaby, Canada, 1995—97; postdoctoral fellow dept. math. and stats. Dalhousie U., Halifax, Canada, 1997—98; asst. prof. math. U. Maine, Orono, 1998—. Contbr. articles to profl. jours. Grantee, Natural Scis. and Engring. Rsch. Coun. Can., 1988, 1989, U. Maine, 1999, Am. Math. Soc., 2000. Mem.: Sigma Xi (sec.-treas. U. B.C. chpt. 1996—97, sec.-treas. U. Maine chpt. 2002—03), Internat. Assn. for Math. and Computers in Simulation, Math. Assn. Am., Can. Math. Soc., Am. Math. Soc., U. Ill. Alumni Assn. (life), Phi Kappa Phi. Office: Univ Maine 5752 Neville Hall Orono ME 04469-5752 Office Fax: 207-581-3902.

BRADLEY, DONALD EDWARD, lawyer; b. Santa Rosa, Calif., Sept. 26, 1943; s. Edward Aloysius and Mildred Louise (Kelley) B.; m. Marianne Stark, Apr. 22, 1990; children: Evan Patrick, Matthew Jordan, Andrea Phelps. AB, Dartmouth Coll., 1965; JD, U. Calif., San Francisco, 1968; LLM, N.Y.U., 1972. Bar: Calif. 1968, U.S. Dist. Ct. (no. dist.) Calif. 1968, U.S. Ct. Appeals (9 cir.) 1968, U.S. Tax Ct. 1972, U.S. Ct. Claims 1973, U.S. Supreme Ct. 1981. Assoc. Pillsbury, Madison & Sutro, San Francisco, 1972-77, ptnr., 1978-84; mem. Wilson Sonsini Goodrich & Rosati, Palo Alto, Calif., 1984—. Mng. dir. Wilson Sonsini Goodrich & Rosati, Palo Alto, 1995—; adj. prof. Golden State U., San Francisco, 1973-82; pres., chmn. bd. dirs. Atty.'s Ins. Mut. Risk Retention Group, Honolulu, 1986—. Capt. U.S. Army, 1969-70. Recipient Charles M. Ruddick award N.Y.U., 1972, award Bureau of Nat. Affairs, Washington, 1968. Mem. ABA, Internat. Bar Assn., Santa Clara Bar Assn., San Francisco Bar Assn., Internat. Tax Club, Peninsula Tax Club. Office: Wilson Sonsini Goodrich & Rosati 650 Page Mill Rd Palo Alto CA 94304-1050 E-mail: dbradley@wsgr.com.

BRADLEY, E. MICHAEL, lawyer; b. N.Y.C., Apr. 13, 1939; s. Otis Treat Bradley and Marian Booth (Alling) Ward; m. Judith Allen Thompson, June 29, 1962; children: Jennifer Treat, Michael Thompson, Thomas Alcott, Samuel Allen. BA, Yale U., 1961; LLB, U. Va., 1964. Bar: N.Y., 1965. Assoc. Davis, Polk & Wardwell, N.Y.C., 1964-72, Brown & Wood, N.Y.C., 1972-73, ptnr., 1974-95, mem. policy com., 1981-94, mem. exec. com., 1989-94; ptnr. Jones Day, N.Y.C., 1995—. Lectr. Practicing Law Inst., N.Y.C., 1970-79; 86, Am. Law Inst.-ABA, Phila., 1977-78; arbitrator Am. Arbitration Assn., N.Y.C., 1975—. Contbg. editor: The Use of Experts in Corporate Litigation, 1978, Securites Law Techniques, 1985. Bd. dirs. Bennett Coll. Found., N.Y.C., 1984—, Inst. of Ams., La Jolla, Calif., 2001—; trustee Salisbury (Conn.) Sch., 1987—. Mem. ABA, N.Y. State Bar Assn., Fed. Bar Assn., Assn. of Bar of City of N.Y., River Club, Union Club, Coral Beach Club, Quogue Field Club, Shinnecock Yacht Club, Nat. Golf Links of Am., L.I. Wyandanch Club. Republican. Presbyterian. Office: Jones Day Reavis & Pogue 222 E 41st St New York NY 10017- E-mail: embradley@jonesday.com.

BRADLEY, EDWARD JAMES, state official, computer programmer and analyst; b. Syracuse, N.Y., Jan. 3, 1946; s. Robert Carroll and Hazel Irene (Malone) B.; m. Gwen Eileen Coats, Sept. 3, 1977 (div. 1984); 1 child, Edward James II. BA cum laude, SUNY, Albany, 1971, MPA, 1980; grad., Citizens Police Acad., 1992. Specialist N.Y. State Dept. Social Svcs., 1973-78; pub. adminstr. N.Y. State Dept. Transp., Albany, 1978-81; pub. mgmt. intern N.Y. State Dept. Civil Svcs., 1981-82; personnel adminstr. N.Y. State Dept. Taxation & Fin., 1982-83; computer programmer, analyst N.Y. State Dept. Transp., 1983—. Commr. City of Albany Mcpl. Civil Svc. Commn., 1992-93, chmn., 1992-93. Author: Child and Family Genealogy Reporting System. Pres. Child and Family Enterprises, Inc., Albany, 1978-84, Traditional Am. Values, Albany, 1984-2003, Books Unbound, 1991-2003, V.O.T.E.S., 1992-2003; fundraiser United Way Am./Northeastern N.Y., Inc., 1976-78, Capital Are Coun. Chs., 1978, Birthright of Albany, Inc., 1984-88; mem. Albany County Dem. Com., 1985-93; active Pro-life Dems., Inc., 1984-94, Nat. Right-to-Life Com., Inc., 1984—, N.Y. State Right-to-Life, 1984—, Human Life Internat., 1992—; mem. nat. nominating com. Outstanding Young Ams., 1997—. With USN, 1963-66. Named one of Outstanding Young Men Am., 1982. Mem. DAV, ASPA, Am. Mgmt. Assn., Am. Pub. Welfare Assn., N.Y. State Forum for Info. Resources Mgmt., Vietnam Era Vets., Am. Legion, N.Y. Assn. Transp. Engrs., Capital Dist. Geneal. Soc. (pres. 1982-84), Nat. Spkrs. Assn., Toastmasters, Elks. Roman Catholic. Home: 1941 Western Ave Apt 1403 Albany NY 12203-7014 Office: State Office Campus Computer Svcs Bur Rm 218 Albany NY 12232-0001

BRADLEY, EDWARD R. news correspondent; b. Phila., June 22, 1941; s. Ed. R. and Gladys Bradley; divorced. BA in Edn., Cheyney (Pa.) State Coll., 1964. Radio news reporter Sta. WDAS, Phila., 1963-67, Sta. WCBS, N.Y.C., 1967-71; with CBS Television News, 1971—, stringer, 1971-73, prin. corr., 1971, Saigon, 1972-74, Washington, 1974—75, Phnom Penh, 1975, Saigon, 1975; White House corr. CBS News, 1976—78; prin. corr. CBS Reports, 1978-81, 60 Minutes, 1981—; anchorman CBS Sunday Night News, 1976-81; anchor CBS News magazine "Street Stories", 1992—93. Anchorman: various documentaries including What's Happening to Cambodia, 1978, The Boat People, 1979, The Boston Goes to China, 1979. Recipient Du Pont award, 1978, 80, 97, George Foster Peabody Broadcasting award U. Ga., 1979, 97, George Polk journalism award, 1980, Emmy award, 1979 (3), 1983 (2), 1985, 86, 92, 93, 95. Office: CBS News 60 Minutes 555 W 57th St New York NY 10019-2925*

BRADLEY, EDWARD WILLIAM, sports foundation executive; b. Milltown, N.J., Aug. 12, 1927; s. William Ernest and Hilda (Schwendeman) B.; m. Eleanor A Massing, Apr. 12, 1952; children: Scott Richard, Gail Sharon Bradley Klewsaat, Lisa June Bradley LaMarca. BE, Panzer Coll., 1950. Dir. athletics, supr. phys. edn. and health Milltown Pub. Schs., 1951-69; owner, pres. The Exec. Health Club, East Brunswick, N.J., 1965 84; apptd. by Gov. Florio chmn., CEO N.J. Fitness and Sports Found., Milltown, 1984—; writer Middlesex County Govt., North Brunswick, N.J., 1985—. Dir. activities Playboy Club Resort Hotel at Great Gorge, 1972; founder first sch. bicycle safety edn. program curriculum State of N.J., 1996; apptd. exec. coun. Cancer Rsch. Inst. Am. Cancer Soc., 1998; served Nat. Coalition Com. prostrate cancer, Wash., 2002-; cons. World WIOC, 2000. Apptd. by Gov. Kean chmn. CEO Gov.'s Coun. on Phys. Fitness and Sports, 1983—; state dir. for fight against abolishing phys. edn. in N.J. schs.; chmn. CEO Middlesex County Coun. on Phys. Fitness and Sports divsn. Pres.' Coun. on Phys. Fitness, 1992, N.J. Youth Fitness Coalition; mem. N.C. Prostate Cancer Coalition, 2002; chmn. N.J. Olympic XXIII Torch Relay Com., 1984; asst. torch relay U.S. Olympics XXVI, N.J. and Atlanta, 1996; dist. coord., cons. Nat. Assn. Disabled Athletes; founder, chmn. Gov.'s Blue Ribbon Panel on Fitness and Sports, David A. Sonny Werblin, pres., N.J. Health Am. Fitness Leaders Award Program; mem. State of N.J. Blue Ribbon Com. for Baseball in N.J.; dir. Phys. Fitness and Sports for U.S. Job Corp., Edison, N.J.; state-county coord. Nat. Park Svc., N.J. Trails Relay, 1996; mem. Mission Possible task NEA-AAPERD; supt. recreation Borough of Milltown, 1951-64; active Pres.' Coun. on Phys. Fitness and Sports, 1964—; cons. Pres. Kennedy, Johnson, Carter, Nixon, Ford, Reagan, Bush; master cons., adv. Pres.' Coun. The White House, 1988; nat. dir., founder sch. Stay Way project Gen. Jones (Pentagon); meeting with Pres. Clinton (invitation by The White House) nat. project Stay Way, 1994; nat. dir. U.S. Army and NFL, 1993; Chief of Staff Colin Powell meeting at the White House; founder sch. bicycle safety edn. prog. curriculum, N.J., 1996, nat. dir. No-Shows for Charity Shows, 1996; VIP del. Pres.' Summit, White House, 1997; VIP del. Pres.' Summit, Washington, 1997; N.J. chmn. Nat. Network on Volunteerism, 1997; mem. Nat. Com. for George W. Bush Pres., 2000; regional coord. Winter Olympic Games 2002, Salt Lake City; patnership with Arnold Schwarzenegger's Inner City Games and Mayor Oscar Goodman's Needy Youth Program, Las Vegas, 2003; mem. exec. bd. Make A Wish Found., N.C., 2003. Recipient U.S. Outstanding Phys. Leadership award Pres.' Coun. on Phys. Fitness and Sports by Pres. Kennedy and U.S. Jaycees, The White House, 1962, U.S. Healthy Am. Fitness Leaders award Pres.' Coun., U.S. Jaycees and Allstate, 1985, Svc. in Phys. Fitness and Sports award Montclair State Coll., 1988, Phys. Edn. award for Excellence Panzer Coll., Svc. Award Ea. Dist. AAHPERD, N.J. Award for People to Watch, 1984, Jerseyan of Week award Newark Star Ledger, 1988, Honor Fellow award N.J. Assn. Health, Phys. Edn. and Recreation, 1964, Young Man of Yr. award Milltown Jaycees, 1962, Sports Master award by Pres. Reagan, 1987, Svc. to the Cmty., State and Nation Award, Pres. Bush, 1992, Pres. Clinton, 1997, Pub. Svc. award State N.J. and Pres.' Summit, 1997, Daily Point of Light award The White House and Point of Light Found., 1999, Pres.'s Svc. award, The White House, 2000, Outstanding Alumni award Montclair State Coll., 2000, Outstanding Gov.'s award Vol. Svc., Trenton, N.J., 2000, Outstanding Gov.'s award Vol. Svc., Raleigh, N.C., 2000; honored guest Pres. Nixon, 1975, Pres. Reagan, 1987, Richard Nixon Libr., 1990, Pres. Reagan Libr., Pres. Bush-the White House, 1991, 92, State of N.J., Pres.' Historic Summit for 55 Yrs. Pub. Svc., Pres. Clinton, The White House, 1947-2000, Govs. N.J. Leadership award Gov. Whitman, 2000, Gov. Vol. award N.C. Gov. Hunt, 2000, Outstanding Alumni award Montclair State U., 2000, Pres.' Svc. award, Pres. Bush, 2001, Martin Luther King Jr. award for Outstanding Cmty. Svc., 2002; named Leader of N.J. State of N.J., 1998, Mem.: Internat. Assn. Approved Basketball Ofcls., Nat. Fitness Leadership Assn., Outstanding Phys. Fitness Leadership Congress, N.J./N.C. Youth Fitness Coalition Pres.' Club (corr. Honored Lifetime citation 2001), Amblers Walking Club, Court Club, Am. Legion, U.S. Jayvees, VFW (N.C., N.J.). Avocations: bicycling, reading, sports, Volksmarch programs. Office: NC Fitness & Sports Foundation Lambeth Walk Complex Pinkerton Corner Fairview NC 28730 also: PO Box 2510 Wachovia Bank Complex Asheville NC 28802 also: PO Box 2145 Fairview NC 28730-2145 also: NJ Fitness & Sports Found 35 Pinkerton Cor Fairview NC 28730-7737 also: Nat Office Vols PO Box 1253 Asheville NC 28802-1253 also: NC Fitness & Sports No-Shows for Charity-Shows PO Box 2510 Asheville NC 28802-2510 also: NJ Found Office PO Box 311 Whiting NJ 08759-0311 Address: No-Shows for Charity Shows Found Office 314 De Armond Rd Kingston TN 37763

BRADLEY, ELIZABETH CLAY, financial planner, educator; b. Dayton, Ky., Feb. 6, 1948; d. Glenn Washington and Margaret Elizabeth Clay; m. James D. McPhail, Aug. 16, 1970 (dec. Sept. 1990); m. Julian Bradley, May 4, 1996. BS in Home Econs., U. Ky., 1970; MS in Family Econs., Kans. State U., 1977. CFP, cert. in personal fin. planning. Tchr. Bourbon Co. Jr. H.S., Paris, Ky., 1970—71, Manhattan (Kans.) H.S., 1974—84; investment rep. Edward Jones, Cary, NC, 1984—2001; ret., 2001; cons. Wachovia Sec., Raleigh, NC, 2002—. Author: (workbook) Motivation Plus, 1982, The Good Life, 2001. Chairperson Expanding the Circle-Glenaire, Cary, 2001; trustee Glenaire Presbyn. Home, Cary, 2002; mem. Cary C. of C.; bd. dirs. Glenaire Found. Named Young Educator, Kans. Assn. Vocat. Home Econs. Tchrs., 1984. Presbyterian. Avocations: walking, writing, reading, quilting, designing clothes. Home: 119 W Park St Cary NC 27511

BRADLEY, GILBERT FRANCIS, retired banker; b. Miami, Ariz, May 17, 1920; s. Ever and Martha (Piper) B.; m. Marion Bebb, June 21, 1941; children: Larry Paul, Richard Thomas, Steven Ever. Grad., LaSalle Extension U., 1942, U. Wash., 1953; Advanced Mgmt. Program, Harvard U. With Valley Nat. Bank, Ariz., Miami, Globe, Clifton, Nogales and Phoenix, 1937—, pres., 1973-76, chmn. bd., chief exec. officer, 1976-82, ret., 1982, dir., vice chmn. exec. com., 1982—, Valley Nat. Corp., 1982—. Mem. adv. council Fed. Res. Bd., Comptroller of the Currency, Denver; instr. Am. Inst. Banking. Mem. Tucson Airport Authority, 1960— ; mem. adv. council Ariz. State U. Sch. Bus., pres. dean's adv. council; dean's adv. council U. Ariz., Tucson. Served to capt. USAAF, 1942-45. Decorated D.F.C., Air medal with three oak leaf clusters. Mem. Ariz. Bankers Assn. (pres.), Assn. Res. City Bankers, Ariz. C. of C. (v.p., dir.), Tucson C. of C. (dir.), Better Bus. Bur. (dir.), Tucson Clearing House Assn. (past pres.), Navy League, Air Force Assn., Beta Gamma Sigma. Clubs: Masons, Rotary. Home: Apt 1102 7500 N Calle Sin Envidia Tucson AZ 85718-7349

BRADLEY, J. F., JR., retired manufacturing company executive; b. Wagoner, Okla., July 7, 1930; s. Jacob F. and Ilsa (Ellington) B.; m. Mary Joan Oberc, June 7, 1952 (div. 1978); children: Jeffrey F. (dec.), Michael B., Michelle J.; m. Angela C. Cutrone, Aug. 14, 1981; 1 child, Adam C.C. BBA, U. Mich., 1952; MBA, U. Detroit, 1959. Fin. analyst Ford Motor Co., Detroit, 1956-60; v.p. corp. fin. TRW Inc., Cleve., 1960-72; exec. v.p. adminstrn. and fin. Scott Fetzer Co., Lakewood, Ohio, 1972-83, dir., 1971-83; pres. Scott Fetzer Fin. Svcs. Group, Westlake, Ohio, 1983-86; chmn. Kadee Metalfab Inc., Bedford, Ohio, 1986-89, K.B.B. Enterprises Inc., Cleve., 1988-93. Trustee Ohio Coll. Podiatric Medicine, chmn., 1990-94; trustee Animal Protective League, Cleve. 1st lt. AUS, 1952-56. Mem. Masons, Shriners, Jesters, Elks, Knights Templar. Home: 7050 Lassiter Dr Cleveland OH 44129-6351 E-mail: jbradley@ocpm.edu.

BRADLEY, JAMES ALEXANDER, software engineer, researcher; b. Van Nuys, Calif., May 16, 1965; m. Alyson Wait, July 11, 1992. BA in Math., Computer Sci., U. Colo., 1988, postgrad., 1991—. Software developer Sci. Computer Systems, Inc., Boulder, Colo., 1982-84; teaching asst. Boulder Valley Pub. Schs., Boulder, Colo., 1984-87; software engr. Martin Marietta Aerospace, Littleton, Colo., 1988-94; dir. software engring. Intelligent Energy Corp., Golden, Colo., 1994—2002; software and systems engring. Advanced Solutions, Inc., 2003—. Recipient NASA New Tech. award, Martin Marietta Aerospace, 1990. Mem. Am. Math. Soc., Math. Assn. Am., Golden Key Honor Soc. Achievements include design of LASER engraving system, high-speed target tracking and aquisition system. Office: Advanced Solutions Inc 6901 S Pierce St Ste 301 Littleton CO 80128 E-mail: James.Bradley3@comcast.net.

BRADLEY, JAMES HAROLD, public relations consultant; b. Manchester, N.H. s. James B. and Mary T. (Fitzpatrick) B.; children: Elizabeth M. Bradley Ewing, Adele V. AB in English, St. Anselm Coll., Manchester, 1953. Accredited in pub. rels. Asst. to treas. St. Anselm Coll., Manchester, 1950-55; asst. dir. admissions and aid U. Chgo., 1955-67; dir. admissions and aid Siena Coll., Loudonville, N.Y., 1967-75; dir. pub. rels. The Moore Ctr., Manchester, 1975-80; account exec. Mann Advt., Inc., Manchester, 1980-87; exec. dir. Tri-State Gasoline and Automobile Dealers Assn., Concord, N.H., 1987-89, Cathedral of the Pines, Rindge, N.H., 1989-91; sr. counsel Bradley & Assocs., Manchester, N.H., 1978—. Dir., pub. rels. chmn. N.H. Travel Coun., 1980-91. Author, editor, producer promotional brochures, radio and TV spots. Fellow Pub. Rels. Soc. Am. (assembly del. 1987, founding pres. Yankee chpt. 1982, lectr. ethics, jud. panel N.E. dist., dist. chmn., treas., sr. advisor to edn. com.); mem. Greater Manchester Child Care Assn. (dir., mem. exec. com., chmn. pub. rels. and nominating coms.), N.H. Travel Coun. (dir., mem. fin. com., past chmn. membership com., past chmn. mktg. and pub. rels. com.), Monadnock Travel Coun. (dir., chair spl. events com.), Ad Club N.H. (past v.p. membership). Avocations: travel, writing, cooking. Home and Office: PO Box 128 Manchester NH 03105-0128

BRADLEY, JEB E. U.S. Congressman; b. Rumford, Maine, Oct. 20, 1952; m. Barbara Bradley; 4 children. BA, Tufts U., 1974. Painter, contractor; owner Natural Food Store; former mem. from dist. 8 N.H. State Ho. of Reps., former mem. environ. and agr. com., former chmn. sci., tech. and energy com.; mem. 108th U.S. Congress, 1st Dist., 2003—; mem. armed servs. com., small bus. com., veterans affairs com. Mem. Wolfeboro (N.H.) Planning Bd., 1986-90, Wolfeboro Budget Com., 1989—; mem. Chap Lakes Region Conservation Trust, 1989-90; v.p. Carpenter Sch. PTO, 1989-90. Office: 1218 Longworth HOB Washington DC 20515*

BRADLEY, JENNETTE, lieutenant governor; m. Michael C. Taylor. BA in Psychology, Wittenberg U. Lic. registered rep. Nat. Assn. Securitites Dealers. Exec. dir. Columbus Met. Housing Authority; sr. v.p. pub. fin. banker Kemper Securities; sr. v.p., pub. funds mgr. Huntington Nat. Bank; councilwoman Columbus (Ohio) City Coun., 1991—2002, chair parks and recreation com., chair utilities and energy generation coms., chair safety com., mem. safety and judiciary com., mem. adminstrn. com., mem. recreation and parks com., mem. health, housing and human svcs. com., mem. zoning com.; lt. gov. State of Ohio, Columbus, 2003—. Dir. Ohio Dept. Commerce, 2003—; mem. fin., adminstrn. and intergovernmental rels, steering and policy coms. Nat. League Cities. Grad. Leadership Columbus; trustee Wittenberg U.; bd. mem., former chair Joint Columbus and Franklin County Housing Adv. Bd. Recipient Woman of Achievement award, YWCA. Republican. Office: 23rd Fl 77 High St Columbus OH 43215*

BRADLEY, JOHN A. military officer; b. Lebanon, Tenn. BS in Math., U. Tenn., Knoxville, 1967; postgrad., Indsl. Coll. Armed Forces, 1978, Harvard U., 1996, Syracuse U., 2000. Commd. 2d lt. USAF, 1967, advanced through grades to maj. gen., 1999; mathematician, program analyst Hdqrs. Strategic Air Command, Offutt Air Force Base, Nebr., 1967—69; pilot combat tng. Sheppard Air Force Base, Tex., 1969—70; fighter pilot 8th Spl. Ops. Squadron, Bien Hoa Air Base, Vietnam, 1970—71; instr. pilot 50th Flying Tng. Squadron, Columbus Air Force Base, Miss., 1971—73, 47th Tactical Fighter Squadron, Barksdale Air Force Base, La., 1973—78; chief standardization and evaluation 917th Tactical Fighter Group, Barksdale Air Force Base, La., 1978—81; asst. ops. officer, ops. officer 47th Tactical Fighter Squadron, Barksdale Air Force Base, La., 1981—83; dep. commdr. ops. 917th Tactical Fighter Group, Barksdale Air Force Base, La., 1983—85; comdr. 924th Tactical Group, Bergstrom Air Force Base, Tex., 1985—88; dep. chief of staff ops. 10th Air Force, Bergstrom Air Force Base, Tex., 1988—89; comdr. 442d Fighter Wing, Richard-Gebaur Air Force Base, Mo., 1989—93; dep. to chief of Air Force Res. Hdqrs. USAF, Washington, 1993—98; comdr. 10th Air Force, Naval Sta. Joint Res. Base, Ft. Worth, 1998—2002; dep. comdr. Joint Task Force-Computer Network Ops., U.S. Space Command, Arlington, Va., 2002—. Decorated DSM, Legion of Merit, DFC, Air medal with 15 oak leaf clusters. Office: US Space Command 250 S Peterson Blvd Ste 116 Cheyenne Mountain AFB CO 80914-3190

BRADLEY, JOHN ANDREW, hospital management company executive; b. Hammond, Ind., Aug. 3, 1930; s. Andrew C. and Florence (Wolfe) B.; m. Judith E. Salmi, June 1, 1955; children: John Michael, Kerry Kathleen, Kelly Ann. BS, Loras Coll., 1952; MHA, St. Louis U., 1955, PhD, 1962. Asst. adminstr. Incarnate Word Hosp., St. Louis, 1958-61; from assoc. adminstr. to adminstr. Santa Rosa Med. Ctr., San Antonio, 1961-69; from v.p. to sr. v.p. Am. Medicorp, Inc., San Antonio, 1969-78; with Am. Healthcare Mgmt., Dallas, 1978-89, pres., 1978-84, chmn., chief exec. officer, 1985-89, Chancellor Health Systems Inc., Dallas, 1989—. Capt. AUS, 1953-57. Home: 4228 Winding Way Ct Dallas TX 75287-2767

BRADLEY, KATHERINE, librarian; b. Glendale, Calif., Oct. 24, 1964; d. Homer and Maryella B. BA in English, Calif. State U., 1987; MLS, U. Az., 1990. Refrence libr. Kern Co. Libr., Bakersfield, Calif., 1990—. Staff assn. treas. Kern Co. Libr., Bakersfield, Calif., 1991, sec. libr. students orgn., U. Az., Tucson, 1990. Mem. Order Eastern Star. Republican. Protestant. Avocations: sketching, sewing, basketball, hiking. Office: Kern Co Libr 701 Truxtun Ave Bakersfield CA 93301-4800

BRADLEY, KIM ALEXANDRA, sales and marketing specialist; b. Glen Cove, N.Y., Aug. 27, 1955; d. Harold William and Helen Doris (Rosenthal) Shepard; m. Gary Morgan Bradley, Oct. 2, 1982; children: Hunter Morgan, Parker Davis, Preston Carter. BS, U. Ill., 1977. Media estimator Lee King & Ptnrs., Chgo., 1977-78; asst. buyer Grey North Advt., Chgo., 1978; broadcast negotiator J. Walter Thompson, Chgo., 1978-80; acct. exec. Katz Communications, Inc., Chgo., 1980-84, sales mgr., 1984-88, v.p. sales mgr., 1988-93; prin., pres. The Encore Group, Inc., Chgo., 1993; pres., owner Bradley Mktg. Group, Northbrook, Ill., 1993—2002; prin., owner Bradley and Thomas, Lake Forest, Ill., 2002—. Mem. mktg. com., bd. dirs. Child Abuse Prevention Svcs.; alliance mem. Art Inst. of Chgo.; vol. Infant Welfare Soc.; aux. bd. dirs. Juvenile Protection Assn. Mem.: Nat. Bur. Profl. Mgmt. Cons. (cert. profl. cons. to mgmtl.), Nat. Assn. Women Bus. Owners, Am. Mktg. Assn., Inst. Mgmt. Cons., Am. Mgmt. Assn., Rotary (pres.-elect Lake Forest/Lake Bluff chpts.), The Exec. Club, Broadcast Advt. Club (bd. dirs., v.p., exec. v.p., pres., chair for Child Abuse Prevention Svcs. charity com.). Home: 30 Barnswallow Ln Lake Forest IL 60045-2984 Office Fax: 847-295-3345. E-mail: kbradley@bradleyandthomas.com.

BRADLEY, LAURENCE ALAN, psychologist; b. Cleve., Sept. 13, 1949; s. Irving and Jeanne (Weil) B.; m. Gifford Weary, Dec. 28, 1974 (div. 1979); m. Elizabeth Wrenn, Oct. 3, 1981 (div. 1991). *Father, Irving Bradley, is an engineer, inventor, and management consultant with 26 product and process patents. Mother, Jeanne Weill Bradley, was an Executive Security and homemaker. Paternal grandfather, David Bradley built homes and apartment complexes in New Haven, Connecticut and Cleveland, Ohio and was elected to the Shaker Heights, Ohio 100 in recognition of his community contributions. Maternal grandfather, Leo Weill, was a prominent Attorney and prosecutor on Cleveland, Ohio who also served as commissioner of purchases and supplies for the City of Cleveland. I am engaged to be married to Dr. Virginia Wadley, Assistant Professor of Psychology at University of Alabama at Birmingham and mother of Mallory Wadley, an Interior Designer, and Rachel Wadley, student at Auburn University.* BA in Psychology, Vanderbilt U., 1971, PhD, 1975. Clin. intern Duke U. Med. Ctr., Durham, N.C., 1975-76; asst. prof. U. Tenn., Chattanooga, 1976-77, Fordham U., Bronx, 1977-80, Bowman Gray Sch. Med., Winston-Salem, NC, 1980-82, assoc. prof., 1982-89, adminstrv. head sect. med. psychology, 1981-89; assoc. prof., dir. epidemiology, edn. & health svcs. rsch. Multipurpose Arthritis & Musculoskeletal Disease Ctr U. Ala., Birmingham, 1989-92, prof., dir. epidemiology, edn. & health svcs. rsch., 1992-99, prof., dir. neuro-behavioral medicine rsch., 1999—. Adj. assoc. prof. U. N.C., Greensboro, 1983-89; vis. behavioral scientist Orebro Med. Ctr. Hosp., Sweden, 1986-92. Co-author: Health Psychology: Clinical Methods and Research, 1991; co-editor: Medical Psychology: Contributions to Behavioral Medicine, 1981, Coping with Chronic Disease: Research and Applications, 1983; assoc. editor: Clin. Psychology, Pain, 1995—2000, editl. bd.: Health Psychology, 1999—2001, Arthritis Care & Rsch., 1995—, Jour. Back and Musculoskeletal Rehab., 1999—. Rsch. grantee Robert Wood Johnson Found., 1983-86, Am.-Scandinavian Found., 1986, NIH, 1989—; Disting. scholar Arthritis Health Professions Assn. Fellow APA, Soc. Personality Assessment; mem. Internat. Assn. Study of Pain, Am. Pain Soc., Sigma Xi, Phi Beta Kappa. Democrat. Achievements include research to determine that relaxation training and psychological therapy reduces pain behavior and number of painful joints among patients with rheumatoid arthritis, and that functional brain activity abnormalities are associated with chronic pain. Home: 3831 Clairmont Ave S Birmingham AL 35222-3607 Office: U Ala Divsn Clin Immunol and Rheumatol 805 Faculty Office Tower 510 20th St S Birmingham AL 35294-0001 E-mail: Larry.Bradley@ccc.uab.edu., painsensation@aol.com.

BRADLEY, LAWRENCE D., JR., lawyer; b. Santa Monica, Calif., Feb. 19, 1920; s. Lawrence D. Bradley and Virginia L. Edwards; m. Joan Worthington, Feb. 1, 1945; children— Gary W., Brooks, Eric Scott BS, U.S. Coast Guard Acad., 1942; LL.B., Stanford U., 1950. Bar: Calif. 1950, U.S. Dist. Ct. (cen. dist.) Calif. 1950, U.S. Dist. Ct. (so. dist.) Calif. 1967. Assoc. Pillsbury, Madison & Sutro, L.A., 1950-59, ptnr., 1959—90; ret. ptnr. Pillsbury Winthrop LLP, 1990—. Lectr. admiralty and ins. law U. So. Calif., 1952-80 Pres. Stanford Law Rev., 1949-50; assoc. editor Am. Maritime Cases, 1990-2000. Mem. adv. bd. Tulane Admiralty Law Inst., 1990—. With USN, 1942-48; to lt. comdr. Res.

Mem. ABA, Calif. Bar Assn., Maritime Law Assn. U.S. (mem. exec. com. 1974-78, chmn. cruise line com. 1991-94), Inst. Navigation, Order of Coif, Calif. Club, Chancery Club, Calif. Yacht Club, San Diego Yacht Club, Propeller Club, Transpacific Yacht Club, Tutukaka South Pacific Yacht Club. Office: Pillsbury Winthrop LLP 725 S Figueroa St Ste 2800 Los Angeles CA 90017-5443

BRADLEY, LEON CHARLES, musician, educator, consultant; b. Battle Creek, Mich., Sept. 8, 1938; s. Leon Harvey and Sigrid Pearl (Anderson) B.; m. Mary Elizabeth, Dec. 23, 1968; children: Kyle Newman, Shannon Sigrid, Karl Norman, Charles Nathan. BA, Mich. State U., 1961; MM Brass Splst., 1967; postgrad., U. Okla., summer 1974, U. Wis., summer 1975. Band dir. Owosso-St. Paul, Mich., 1958-61, Hopkins (Mich.) Pub. Schs., 1961-62, Cedar Springs (Mich.) Pub. Schs., 1962-65; grad. asst. music theory-aural harmony Mich. State U., East Lansing, 1965-67; asst. prof., asst. dir. bands Minot (N.D.) State Coll., 1967-69; assoc. prof. instrumental music, music edn., dir. bands. Coll. of the Ozarks, Point Lookout, Mo., 1969-93, dept. chmn., 1987-89; ret., 1993. Clinician low brass instruments Selmer, Inc., 1979—; founder instrumental ensembles including Am. Concert Band, Xian Conservatory of Music, China, fall 1995; vis. prof. S.W. Bapt. U., 1998—. Performed with Springfield (Mo.) Symphony Orch., 1969-72, 81-98, Springfield Regional Opera Orch., 1981-98, Branson Brass Quintet, 1982—, Coll. of the Ozarks, Mozark Brass Quintet, SMSU Cmty. Band, others; dir. Abou Ben Adhem Shrine Band, 1978-80; contbr. articles to profl. jours. Condr. Republic (Mo.) Cmty. Band, 1999. Recipient Jess Cole Jazz Edn. award, Mo. Jazz Educators Assn., 2003. Mem. Coll. Band Dirs. Nat. Assn. (nat. chmn. Sacred Wind Music commn.), Music Educators Nat. Conf., Internat. Assn. Jazz Educators (state treas. 1980—), Nat. Assn. Wind and Percussion Instrs. (new music reviewer, assn. jour. 1968-71), Mo. Music Edn. Assn., Mo. Bandmasters Assn., Ducks Unltd. (mem. com. 1978-81, chmn. 1981), Masons (Scottish Rite), Shriners, Lions (pres. 1983-84), Phi Mu Alpha. Home: 119 South Dr Branson MO 65616-3708

BRADLEY, LISA M. artist; b. Columbus, Ohio, Dec. 15, 1951; d. Phillip Raymond Bradley and Jean Lichtenstein. BA, Boston U., 1973. Assoc. dir. Pace Primitive, N.Y.C., 1977-84, dir., 1984—2002. One-woman shows include Boston City Hall, 1973, Harvard U., Cambridge, Mass., 1976, Boston Ctr. for the Arts, 1977, Ludlow Hyland Gallery, N.Y.C., 1978, 79, Bette Stoler Gallery, N.Y.C., 1979, Major-Saxbe Gallery, Urbana, Ohio, 1986, Phillip Dash Gallery, N.Y.C., 1987, Donahue Gallery, N.Y.C., 1989, Ratner Gallery, Chgo., 1991, Donahue Gallery, 1993, Galerie Kaj ForsBlom, Helsinki, Finland, 1995, Donahue Gallery, N.Y.C., 1996, 98, Brenau U. Galleria, Gainsville, Ga., 2003; exhibited in group shows Essex Inst., Salem, Mass., 1972, Cambridge Art Assn., 1972, 73, New Bertha Schaeffer Gallery, N.Y.C., 1975, Gallery 200, Columbus, 1975, Galeria Rosanna, Boston, 1976, Baak Gallery, Cambridge, 1977, 78, Betty Parsons Gallery, N.Y.C., 1978, 79, 80, 81, Bette Stoler Gallery, N.Y.C., 1979, 80, 81, 1st Women's Bank, N.Y.C., 1981, Fay Gold Gallery, Atlanta, 1982, Deicas Art, La Jolla, Calif., 1982, Elayne Marquis Gallery, San Francisco, 1982, Soker-Kaseman Gallery, San Francisco, 1983, Phillipe Guimiot Gallery, Brussels, 1983, Kouros Gallery, N.Y.C., Leonarda Di Mauro Gallery, N.Y.C., 1985, Chronocide Gallery, 1986, Mokotoff Gallery, 1986, Jan Baum Gallery, L.A., 1986, Phillip Dash Gallery, N.Y.C., 1986, Lavrov Gallery, Paris, 1987, Sensibilities Contemporaines, Cie Moderne & Contemporaine, Paris, 1991, Musee de Nationale de Dakar, Senegal, 1992, E.M. Donahue Gallery, N.Y.C., 1993, Solway Gallery, Cin., 1993, Face to Face Artists on Artists Gallery, 1995, Blue Broadway Gallery, N.Y.C., 1996, Women Artists in Vogel Collection, Brenau U. Mus., 1998, Material Perception, Charlotte, N.C., 1999, Wako Gallery, Tokyo, 2002, The Work Space Celestial, N.Y.C., 2003; pub., The Art of Seeing, Fisher & Zelanski, "The Spiritual in Art", 1993. Jewish. Home: 356 W 20th St Apt 3B New York NY 10011-3385

BRADLEY, MARILYNNE GAIL, advertising executive, advertising educator; b. Rockford, Ill., Apr. 12, 1938; d. Sherwin S. and Lillian (Leopold) Gersten; m. Charles S. Bradley, 1959 (div. Feb., 1994); children: Suzanne, Scott. BFA, Washington U., 1960; MAT, Webster U., St. Louis, 1975; MFA, Syracuse U., 1981; postgrad., St. Louis Tchrs. Acad., 1990. With Essayons Studio, St. Louis, 1968-69; tchr. Webster Groves (Mo.) H.S., 1970-98; instr. Webster Univ., Webster Groves, 1973-82, 97—, supr., 2002; instr. U. Mo., 1980—, St. Louis U., 1978-99, Washington U., St. Louis, 1984-87. Sec. Mo. Art Edn., State of Mo., 1986-87; mem. Tchrs. Acad. 1990-92. Author, illustrator: Arpens and Acres, 1976, Packets on Parade, 1980, illustrator: St. Louis Silhouettes, 1977; editor: (videos) 12 Water Color Lessons, 1987, Techniques of American Watercolor, 1990, The Santa Fe Trail Series, 1993, Over Gauguin's Shoulder, 1994, Aboriginal Art Techniques, 1994, City of Century Homes, 1995, Australian Dreamings, 1996, Aboriginal Art - Past, Present and Future, 1996, Drawing and Painting Techniques, 1997, Line, Shape, Value, 1998, Molas, Snip and Sew: The Kuna Indians, Molas: Panamanian Traditions, 1999, The Katy Trail Series, 2000, Art Along the Katy Trail, 2000, Apre's Paris, 2001, Lewis and Clark Trail, 2001, It's Somewhere in St. Louis, 2002. Bd. govs. Webster Groves Hist. Soc., 1965-72, 94—, v.p., 2002—; mem. St. Louis Philharm. Soc., 1956-72; commr. City of Webster Groves, 1995—; co-chair Hist. Preservation Com., 2002. Named Tchr. of Yr., 1987, Best of Show, Mo. Watercolor Soc., 2000, Southern Watercolor Soc. Silver Brush award, award of Excellence Salute to the Masters. Mem.: Mo. Watercolor Soc. (bd. mem. 2001—), St. Louis Artist Guild (sec. 1985—86, pres. 1989—92, v.p. pres.'s coun. 1995—, Disting. Woman 1987), St. Louis Woman Artists, So. Watercolor Soc. (sec. 1978—80, v.p. 2002—, chair 26th ann. exhibit, Silver Brush award, Exceptional Salute to the Masters award), Monday Club (chmn. 1979—83). Avocations: music, art, travel. Home and Office: Bradley & Assocs 817 S Gore Ave Saint Louis MO 63119-4023 E-mail: mgbrad@aol.com.

BRADLEY, MELVIN LEROY, communications company executive; b. Texarakana, Tex., Jan. 6, 1938; s. S.T. and David Ella (Garth) B.; m. Ruth Ann Terry, Mar. 3, 1958; children: Cheryl, Eric, Jacqueline, Tracy. Student, Los Angeles City Coll., 1955, Compton Coll., 1965; BS, Pepperdine U., 1973; LLD (hon.), Shaw U., 1982, Bishop Coll., 1984, Lane Coll., 1986. Real estate broker, Los Angeles, 1960-63; dep. sheriff Los Angeles County, 1963-70; asst. to Gov. Ronald Reagan, 1970-75; dir. public relations Drew Med. Sch., Los Angeles, 1975-77; asst. v.p. United Airlines, 1977-81; sr. policy advisor to Pres. U.S., White House, 1981-82, asst. to Pres. U.S., 1982-89; pres. Garth & Bradley Assocs., Washington, 1989—. Bd. dirs Essex Savs. Bank, SMA MicroSys. Republican. Baptist. Office: 9300 Livingston Rd Ste 213 Fort Washington MD 20744 E-mail: garthbrad@yahoo.com.

BRADLEY, NOLEN EUGENE, JR., personnel executive, educator; b. Memphis, Nov. 29, 1925; s. Nolen Eugene and Anice Pearl (Luther) B.; m. Eloise Mullins, Jan. 7, 1947; children: Sharon (Mrs. Edward W. Vanderpool), Diana (Mrs. Wiley M. Rutledge), Nolen Eugene III, David Lee. BS, Memphis State U., 1951, MA, 1952; EdD, U. Tenn., 1966. Instr. polit. sci. Memphis State U., 1951-52; tchr. English Messick High Sch., Memphis, 1952-56; asst. dean admissions Memphis State U., 1956-64; dir. State Agy. for Title I, Higher Edn. Act, 1965, Div. Continuing Edn., U. Tenn., 1966-70; dean instrn. Vol. State Community Coll., Gallatin, Tenn., 1970-78; tutor, ednl. cons., 1978-79; pers. asst. Hoeganaes Corp., Gallatin, 1979-80, pers. mgr., 1980-82; dir. pers. Music Village U.S.A., Hendersonville, Tenn., 1984—. Contbr. articles to profl. jours. Deacon Bapt. ch., 1966—. With AUS, 1944-46, ETO. Mem. Am. Assn. Sch. Adminstrs., Tenn. Adult Edn. Assn., Tenn. Edn. Assn., Omicron Delta Kappa, Pi Delta Epsilon, Phi Delta Kappa, Phi Kappa Phi. Democrat. Lion. Avocations: writing, travel, movies, reading. Home: 907 Harris Dr Gallatin TN 37066-3462 E-mail: geneloise@comcast.net.

BRADLEY, PAUL N. special education educator; b. Jackson, Miss., Mar. 10, 1950; s. Nathaniel and Amy (Bennet) Bradley; m. Karen Marie Bradley, June 17, 1989; 1 child, Kimberly Denise. BS in Social Wk., Spl. Edn., Adminstr. Leadership, Ctrl. State U., Wilberforce, Ohio, 1972; MS, U. Wis., Milw., 1977, U. Wis., 1990; JD, John Marshall Law Sch., Atlanta, 1980; MBA, Cardinal Stritch U., Milw., 1998; postgrad., Walden U., Mpls., 2002—. Cert. K-12 learning disabled tchr. Wis., lic. dir. spl. edn./pupil svcs. Wis., secondary adminstr. Wis., ins. agt. Wis. Tchr.'s aide Juneau Acad., Milw., 1973—76; tchr. Milw. Pub. Schs., 1976—79, Atlanta Pub. Schs., 1979—81; vol. tchr. trainer U.S. Peace Corps, Kingston, Jamaica, 1981—83; supr. student tchrs. Purdue U., West Lafayette, Ind., 1983—84; supr. exceptional edn. Milw. Pub. Schs., 1984—96; tchr. Holy Redeemer Acad., Milw., 1996—97, Waukegan Pub. Schs., Ill., 1997—98; social worker Lacausa, Inc., Milw., 1998—2000; tchr. spl. edn. Racine Unified Sch. Dist., Wis., 2000—. Cons. Big Bro. Big Sister for Pub. Edn., Milw.; coord. youth group YMCA, Milw., 2001; mem. ACLU; bd. dirs. Gray's Child Devel. Ctr., Milw. Mem.: Acad. of Mgmt. Jour. Mem. Assn., The PhD Project Mgmt. Doctoral Students Assn., The Gideon Assn. Home: 9600 W Debbie Ln Milwaukee WI 53224-4618 Office: 1901 12th St Racine WI 53403

BRADLEY, PAULA E. former state legislator; b. New Haven, Conn., Oct. 11, 1924; d. Richard Travis and Harriett (Bogenhagen) Elliott; m. William L. Bradley, 1947; children: James R. Choukas-Bradley, Dwight C., Paul W. BA, Hiram Coll., 1945; postgrad., Middlebury Coll., 1946, Hartford Seminary, 1963-64. Ret. rsch. assoc. univ. devel. Yale U.; mem. N.H. Ho. of Reps., 1992—98, 2000—02. Treas. Coos County Dem. Party, 1998—, N.H. State Dem. Com., 1992—; treas. Randolph Dem. Party, 1992—; bd. dirs. Coos County Family Health Svcs., Berlin, N.H., 1993-2001, Weeks Meml. Hosp., Lancaster, N.H., 1993-95, No. Forest Heritage Park, Berlin, N.H., 2001—; mem. Gorham (N.H.) Congregational Ch.; chair bd. adjustment Town of Randolph, 2000-01. Mem.: AAUW (Androscoggin br. 1990—), Randolph Mountain Club (bd. dirs. 1986—91, 1992—97, treas. 1989—91, pres. 1995—96). Democrat. Avocations: walking, gardening, choral singing. Office: RR 1 Box 1060 Randolph NH 03570-9714

BRADLEY, PHILLIP ALDEN, lawyer; b. Madison, Wis., Dec. 2, 1954; s. Sterling Gaylen and Lois Evelyn (Lee) B. B.A. with honors, St. Andrews Coll., 1975; J.D., Antioch Sch. Law, 1978. Bar: Ga. 1978, U.S. Dist. Ct. (no. dist.) Ga. 1978, U.S. Dist. Ct. (mid. dist.) Ga. 1985, U.S. Dist. Ct. (so. dist.) Ga. 1987, U.S. Dist. Ct. (no. and so. dists.) Tex. 1991, U.S. Tax Ct. 1989, U.S. Ct. Appeals (5th cir.) 1978, U.S. Ct. Appeals (11th cir.) 1981, U.S. Ct. Appeals (4th cir.) 1992. Staff atty. Atlanta Legal Aid Soc., 1978-79; supervising atty. Ga. Legal Services, Conyers, 1980-81; assoc. Long, Aldridge & Norman, Atlanta, 1981-84, ptnr., 1985-94, mng. ptnr. sect. litigation, 1994—. Mem. Atlanta Bar Assn. Office: Long Aldridge & Norman 303 Peachtree St NE Ste 5300 Atlanta GA 30308-3251

BRADLEY, RICHARD, chemist, consultant; s. Francis J. and Ann (DeRogatis) B.; m. Nancy Donovan (div.); children: Erin, Dennis, Tara, Kelly; m. Marianne Arentz, June 22, 1980; children: Sean P., Rachel. BS in Chemistry, St. Francis Coll., 1968. Rsch. chemist Exxon Rsch. and Engring. Co., Linden, N.J., 1969-74; chemist CIBA-Geigy Co., Ardsley, N.Y., 1974-76; scientist Betz Labs., Inc., Trevose, Pa., 1976-77; tech. mgr. Norton Co., Trenton, N.J., 1977-79; dir. technology Monsanto Radiation Dynamics, Melville, N.Y., 1979-83; dir. R&D Bristol-Myers Squibb Corp., Princeton, N.J., 1983-89; v.p. Internat. Info. Assocs., Yardley, Pa., 1989—96; pres. Lifetech Systems Inc., Palm Harbor, Fla., 1996—. Mgmt. adv. bd. Modern Plastics Mag., 1981. Author: Radiation Technology Handbook, 1984, Entrepreneurial R&D Management, 1991, Design Controls for Medical Industry, 2003; editor: Jour. Indsl. Irradiation Tech., 1985-87. Adv. bd. N.J. State Sch. for Deaf, Trenton, 1988-89. Fellow Am. Inst. Chemists (pres. 2003—); mem. TAPPI, Am. Chem. Soc., Soc. Plastics Engrs., N.Y. Acad. Scis. Independent. Roman Catholic. Achievements include patent in field; research in radiation effects on plastics. Office: Lifetech Systems Inc 36181 E Lake Rd Ste 300 Palm Harbor FL 34685

BRADLEY, RICHARD EDWIN, retired college president; b. Omaha, Mar. 9, 1926; s. Louis J. and Betsy (Winterton) B.; m. Doris I. McGowan, June 8, 1946; children— Diane, Karen, David. Student, Creighton U., 1946-48; BSD., U. Nebr., 1950, D.D.S., 1952; MS, State U. Iowa, 1958. Instr. State U. Iowa, 1957-58; asst. prof. Creighton U., 1958-59; asst. prof., chmn. dept. periodontics U. Nebr., 1959-62, assoc. prof., 1962-65, prof., 1965-67; assoc. dean Coll. Dentistry, 1967-68, dean, 1968-80; pres., dean Baylor Coll. Dentistry, 1980-90, pres., dean emeritus, 1990—; clin. prof. Coll. Dentistry U. Nebr. Med. Coll., Lincoln, 1990—; cons. dental edn., 199-93. Mem. Commn. A, Coun. on Dental Edn., 1986-93; pres. Am. Assn. Dental Schs., 1977-78; mem. nat. adv. com. on health professions edn. Dept. Health and Human Resources, 1982-86; pres. Am. Fund for Dental Health, 1986-87; mem. bd. of vis. Temple Univ. Sch. of Dentistry, 2001—. Editor: The New Dentist, 1992-94; contbg. editor Orban's Textbook of Periodontics, 1963; contbr. Clark's Clin., 1980. Mem. bd. visitors Temple U. Sch.Dentistry, 2001--. Served with USNR, 1944-46. Fellow AAAS, Internat. Coll. Dentists; mem. ADA, Am. Acad. Peridontology Found. (bd. dirs., pres. 1994-96), Am. Coll. Dentists (regent 1992-96, v.p. 1997-98, pres. Found. 2001-02), Sigma Xi, Omicron Kappa Upsilon. Home: 6831 Northridge Rd Lincoln NE 68516-2955 Office: U Nebraska Coll Dentistry Lincoln NE 68583-0740

BRADLEY, RICHARD T. state representative; b. Chgo., May 18, 1955; m. Cynthia Santos; children: Meghan, Julianne. BS, Concordia Tchrs. Coll., 1979. Dep. dir. Mayor's Inquiry and Info. Office; liason cmty. rels., office mgr. Chgo. Ward 35; social worker Crisis Intervention, Chgo.; asst. supr. Dept. Streets and Sanitation; chief of staff Chgo. Alderman Joe Kotlarz, 1983—91, Chgo. Alderman Mike Wojcik, 1991—92; CEO Art Specialty Co.; mem. Ill. Ho. of Reps., 1997—. Past adv. bd. Independence Pk.; past bd. dirs. Alvernia H.S., Belmont Cmty. Hosp., Irving Park Food Pantry, Madonna H.S., Neighbors United Civic Orgn., St. Viator's Grammar Sch. Mem.: Portage Pk. C. of C., Friends Independence Pk. Libr., Lions, Kiwanis. Democrat. Roman Catholic. Office: 290-S Stratton Office Bldg Springfield IL 62706 Address: 3520 N Pulaski Rd Chicago IL 60641*

BRADLEY, ROCHELLE ELAINE, music educator; b. Corona, Calif., July 24; d. Edward Lawrence and Ethelreda Jane Feist; m. Christopher Allen Bradley, July 24, 1982; children: Paul Edward, Angie Rene, Jennifer Ann. AA, El Camino Coll., 1979; BA, Calif. State U, Dominguez Hills, 1982. Music tchr. Holy Rosary Acad., San Bernardino, Calif., 1994—96; band, piano, tchr. Holy Name of Mary Sch., San Dimas, Calif., 1997—98; music tchr. Fontana (Calif.) Unified Sch., 1998—2000, Our Lady of the Assumption Sch., Claremont, Calif., 2000—. Contbr. articles. Grantee Claremont Chamber of Commerce Award, 2003. Mem.: Nat. Piano Found., Music Tchr. Assn. of Calif. (telephone chair), Calif. Assn. of Prof. Music Tchr. (assoc.), Music Edn. Nat. Conf. (assoc.). Cath. Avocations: family time, internet rsch., non-fiction books. Office: Our Lady of the Assumption Sch 611 W Bonita Ave Claremont CA 91711

BRADLEY, ROGER WILLIAM, lawyer; b. N.Y.C., Sept. 25, 1944; s. Joseph Wilson and Alyce (Halferty) B.; m. Ann Marie Cummings, Aug. 27, 1977; children: Daniel, Brendan. BA, Colgate U., 1966; JD (magna cum laude), Syracuse U., 1969. Bar: N.Y. 1970, U.S. Ct. Appeals (2d cir.) 1975, U.S. Dist. Ct. (no. dist.) N.Y. 1974, U.S. Dist. Ct. (so. dist.) N.Y. 1975, U.S. Dist. Ct. (we. dist.) N.Y. 1979. Law asst. Appellate div. 3d jud. dept. N.Y. Supreme Ct., Binghamton, N.Y., 1969-71; spl. asst. atty. gen. State of N.Y., Albany, 1971-73; ptnr. Melvin & Melvin, L.L.P., Syracuse, N.Y., 1973—. Mem. panel of medicators U.S. Dist. Ct. (no. dist.) NY. Bd. dirs. Syracuse Boys and Girls Club; mem. fin. Onondaga County Rep. Party. Mem. ABA (forum of constrn. industry 1989—, litigation sect. 1989—, tort and ins. practice sect., bus. law sect.), Am. Arbitration Assn. (panel of arbitrators 1980—), Constrn. Specifications Inst., N.Y. State Bar Assn. (fed. comml. litigation sect., com. on constrn. 1989—), Onondaga County Bar Assn. Republican. Roman Catholic. Avocations: swimming, skiing, Aikido. Office: Melvin & Melvin LLP 217 S Salina St Ste 700 Syracuse NY 13202-1390

BRADLEY, RONALD JAMES, neuroscientist; b. Enniskillen, No. Ireland, Feb. 17, 1943; s. Samuel John and Mary Elizabeth (Irvine) B.; m. Doris Brown, Mar. 5, 1966; children— Nicola, Jason, Steven. B.Sc., Queens U., Belfast, No. Ireland, 1964; PhD, U. Edinburgh, Scotland, 1967. Mem. faculty Yale U., 1967-69, U. NMex., 1969-71, U. Ala., Birmingham, 1972-92, prof. psychiatry and neuroscis., 1976-92; prof. psychiatry and pharmacology La. State U. Med. Sch., Shreveport, La., 1992—. Assoc. dean for instnl. devel., La. State U. Med. Sch.; guest prof. U. Saarlands, Fed. Republic of Germany, 1977-81. Editor: Internat. Rev. Neurobiology, 1974—. Recipient A. E. Bennett award Soc. Biol. Psychiatry, 1967 Mem. AAAS, Biophys. Soc., Neuroscis. Soc., Soc. Biol. Psychiatry. Home: 2407 Lakecrest Dr Shreveport LA 71109-3003 Office: LSU Med Ctr Dept Psychiatry PO Box 33932 Shreveport LA 71130-3932

BRADLEY, SALLY SUE, registered nurse; b. LaGrange, Ga., Nov. 17, 1944; children from previous marriage: Patricia Anne, Elizabeth Sue, James Burton Jr. AA, DeKalb Coll. Nursing, 1973; BA, Ga. State U., Atlanta, 1971, MEd, 1978; EDS, U. Ga., 1987; BSN, Clayton State Coll., 1994. RN. Sr. health educator Ga. Dept. Human Resources, Lawrenceville, 1975-88; asst. dir. staff devel. ARC, Atlanta, 1988; with Atlanta Eye Screening, 1988-89; outreach coord. Cataract Inst., Atlanta, 1989-90; tng. coord. S.E. Regional Ctr. For Drug-Free Schs. & Communities, 1990; tng. planner Atlanta Community Prevention Coalition, 1991-92; sole propr. Health Lifestyles, 1992-95; nursing instr. Griffin Tech. Sch., 1992-93; sr. nurse Clayton Ctr., Jonesboro, Ga., 1993-95; adminstrv. supr. Peachtree Regional Hosp., 1994-98; clin. nursing instr. Gordon Coll. Nursing Students, 1995-97; supr. Healthways, Morrow, Ga., 1995; health svcs. adminstr. Correctional Healthcare Solutions, 1996; adminstrv. supr. Fayette Comm. Hosp., 1997-98; exec. dir. Canine Vision, Inc., Villa Rica, Ga., 1997-2000; cmty. health nurse Ft. McPherson, Ga., 2001—. Chmn. bd. dirs. Canine Vision, Inc., 1993—96. Author: 6 manuals; contbr. articles to profl. jours. Founder, treas., bd. dirs. Georgia Guides, Inc., 2000—. Recipient Significant Contributions to Healthcare award State of Ga., 1998. Mem. NAFE, ASTD, AAPHERD, UDC (state chmn. 1988-90, nat. chmn. of pages 1989), Ga. Fedn. Profl. Health Educators, Internat. Platform Assn., Daus. of 1812 (local officer 1989-2001, state officer 1992-94), Continental Soc., Daus. of Indian Wars (nat. officer, state officer 1990-99), DAR (organizing regent chpt. 1982-84, nat. spkrs. staff 1986-89), Daus. Am. Colonists (chpt. regent 1988-91, state officer 1991-2000), Colonial Dames of XVII Century (local registrar), Ga. Soc. Magna Chart Dames (state officer 1986-2000), First Families of Ga., Lions (1st female mem. Atlanta club, chmn. sight and vision 1989-90, officer 1990-91), Sigma Theta Tau. Episcopalian. Avocations: gardening, reading. Home: 2305 Luther Bailey Rd Senoia GA 30276-2972 E-mail: Sallysue@mindspring.com.

BRADLEY, SCOTT M. surgeon; b. Palo Alto, Calif., July 10, 1958; s. Frank W. and Ann M. Bradley; m. Robyn A. Alexander, July 15, 1989; children: Luke A., Emma M., Gwyneth W. AB, Harvard U., 1976—80; MD, Harvard Med. Sch., 1981—85. Pediatric cardiac surgeon Med. U. of SC., 1995—. Mem.: Am. Assn. for Thoracic Surg., Congenital Heart Surgeons Soc., So. Thoracic Surg. Assn., Soc. of Thoracic Surgeons. Office: Med U of SC 96 Jonathan Lucas Str Charleston SC 29425 Office Fax: 843-792-8286.

BRADLEY, TERRANCE LEE, retired music educator; b. Rolla, Nd, Feb. 12, 0941; s. Lawrence Joseph and Mary Orpha Bradley; m. Linda Ann Heller, Jan. 18, 1944; children: Kimberly Ann, Patrick Shay. BS, Minot State U., Minot, ND, 1963—67; MS, Bemidji State U., Bemidji, MN, 1975. Music educator Palo Verde Schools, Blythe, Calif., 1967—68, Mt. Pleasant Sch., Rolla, ND, 1968—72, Ind. Sch. #31, Bemidji, Minn., 1972—2001. Adjudicator Minn. H.S. League, Brooklyn Park, Minn., 1974—2002; music advisor Region 8AA Governing Cmty., Alexandria, Minn., 1991—95. Mem. Rolla Civic Club, Rolla, ND, 1968—72. E-8 U.S. Army, 1981—2001. Recipient Outstanding Young Educator, Jaycees, 1970. Mem.: Am. Legion, Elks (sec. 1985—86). Methodist. Avocations: camping, hunting, golfing. Home: 1925 Chippewa Drive Northeast Bemidji MN 56601

BRADLEY, THOMAS PAUL, internist; b. S.I., N.Y., June 21, 1954; MD, U. Monterrey, Nuevo Leon, Mex., 1982. Diplomate Am. Bd. Internal Medicine, Am. Bd. Hematology, Am. Bd. Oncology. Resident, fellow hematology-oncology SUNY, Bklyn., 1984-91, asst. prof., 1991—, vice chair medicine for clin. affairs, 2001—02; program dir. hematology/oncology fellowship North Shore U. Hosp., Manhasset, NJ, 2002—. Dir. medicine U. Hosp. Bklyn.; assoc. program dir. internal medicine SUNY Health Scis. Ctr., Bklyn Fellow ACP; mem. Am. Soc. Clin. Oncology, Am. Soc. Hematology. Office: North Shore U Hosp 300 Community Dr Manhasset NY 11030 E-mail: tbradleymd@yahoo.com.

BRADLEY, VINCENT GERARD, judge; b. Kingston, N.Y., Oct. 3, 1939; s. Vincent and Mary (McGowan) B.; m. Dorothy Maureen Roach, Jan. 4, 1964; children— Brigid, Vincent, Barney, Meghan, Rian, Caitlin. B.S., N.Y. State Maritime Coll., 1962; J.D., Fordham U., 1967. Bar: N.Y. Ptnr. Ryan, Bradley, Kerr, Dall Vechia & Roach, P.C., Kingston, N.Y., 1967-81; justice State N.Y. Supreme Ct., Kingston, 1981— . Mem. N.Y. State Bar Assn., N.Y. Assn. Supreme Ct. Justices, Ulster County Bar Assn. Democrat. Roman Catholic. Home: 215 N Manor Ave Kingston NY 12401-2503 Office: Ulster County Courthouse 285 Wall St Kingston NY 12401-3817

BRADLEY, WALTER D. lieutenant governor, real estate broker; b. Clovis, N.Mex., Oct. 30, 1946; s. Ralph W. and M. Jo (Black) B.; m. Debbie Shelly, Sept. 17, 1977; children: Tige, Lance, Nicole, Kristin. Student, Eastern N.Mex. U., 1964—67. Supr. Tex. Instruments, Dallas, 1967—73; mgr., salesman Nat. Chemsearch, Irving, Tex., 1973—76; real estate broker Colonial Real Estate, Clovis, 1976, Realtors Assn. N.Mex., Clovis, N.Mex., 1976—; state senator Curry County, State of N.Mex., 1990—92; lt. gov. State of N.Mex., Santa Fe, 1995—. V.p., bd. dirs. Clovis Indsl. Commn., 1983—86, pres. econ. devel., 1987; bd. dirs. United Way, Clovis, 1984—86, Curry County Blood Adv. Bd., Clovis, 1980—85; chmn. Curry County Reps., Clovis, 1984—88, Cosmos Soccer, Clovis, 1984. Named Man of Yr., Progressive Farmer Mag., 1998; recipient Leadership award, Albuquerque NAACP, 1997, Disting. Svc. award, N.Mex. Farm and Livestock Bur., 1997, Leadership Beatification award, Keep N.Mex. Beautiful, 2000, Mark Weidler Disting. Pub. Servant award, N.Mex. Petroleum Marketers Assn., 2000, Outstanding N.Mex. Small Bus. Supporter, N.Mex. Small Bus. Devel. Ctr., 1997, Outstanding Leadership award, N.Mex. Cattle Growers' Assn., 1996. Mem.: N.Mex. Jaycees, Curry County Jaycees, Clovis C. of C., Clovis Bd. Realtors (pres. 1982, 1993), Realtors Assn. N.Mex. (v.p., bd. dirs. 1982—85, v.p. 1987—88), Lions. Republican. Baptist. Office: Office of Lt Gov State Capitol Bldg Rm 417 Santa Fe NM 87501

BRADLEY, WANDA LOUISE, librarian; b. Havre de Grace, Md., June 6, 1953; d. William Smith and Josephine Viola (Miller) B. BA, U. Md., 1975; MSLS, Atlanta U., 1976; postgrad., Cath. U.; MPA (scholar), U. Balt., 1986. Libr. Harford County Pub. Libr., Bel Air, Md., 1976, Harford County Bd. Edn., Bel Air, Md., 1977-81, Nat. Grad. U., Arlington, Va., 1982, Md. State Dept. Edn., Balt., 1982-83, U.S. Dept. Labor, Washington, 1984, Balt. Gas and Electric Co., 1984-85, Morgan State U., Balt., 1985, Coppin State Coll., Balt., 1985-86, Montgomery County Pub. Sch. System, Rockville, Md., 1985-86, Community Coll., Balt., 1987-88; grant adminstr. Howard County Pub. Libr., 1988; libr., media specialist Balt. City Pub. Sch. System, 1992—. Acad. advisor George Mason U., Fairfax, Va., 1981-82. Dept. Edn. fellow, 1983-84; U. Balt. Merit scholar, 1984, Atlanta U. scholar, 1976, U. Md. scholar, 1971; Howard County Pub. Libr. grantee, 1988. Mem. ALA, ASIS, Md. Libr. Assn., Spl. Librs. Assn., Med. Libr. Assn. Methodist. Office: Dr Roland N Patterson Sr Acad Greenspring Ave Baltimore MD 21231

BRADLEY, WAYNE BERNARD, lawyer; b. Decatur, Ga., Oct. 11, 1944; s. Bernard Bell and Frances Eleanor (Copelan) Bradley. Student, Young Harris Jr. Coll., 1963—64; AB in Econs., U. Ga., Athens, 1966; JD, John Marshall U., Atlanta, 1972. Bar: Ga. 1972, US Supreme Ct. 1975. Asst. dist. atty. Ocmulgee Jud. Cir., Milledgeville, Ga., 1972—74; assoc. Peugh and Bradley, 1975—85; pvt. practice Milledgeville, 1985—. Mem.: Baldwin County Bar Assn. (past pres.), Ocmulgee Bar Assn. (past pres.), Ga. Bar Assn. (bd. govs.). Home: 160 Tanya Rd NE Milledgeville GA 31061-7826 Office: 201 S Wilkinson St Milledgeville GA 31061-3351

BRADLEY, WESLEY HOLMES, physician; b. Chaumont, N.Y., Aug. 7, 1922; s. William Holmes and Margaret Jane (Bartrem) B.; m. Barbara Jean Sawyer, Sept. 23, 1945; children: James, Douglas, William, David. AB, Syracuse U., 1944, MD, 1946. Diplomate Am. Bd. Otolaryngology (exec. com. 1972, 74, 78). Intern Mass. Meml. Hosp., Boston, 1946-47; resident in otolaryngology U. Mich., 1949-53; practice medicine specializing in otolaryngology Syracuse, N.Y., 1953-75; mem. faculty SUNY Coll. Medicine, 1953-75, clin. prof., 1974-75; dir. communicative disorders program Nat. Inst. Neurol and Communicative Disorders and Stroke, NIH, Bethesda, Md., 1975-78; med dir. Commd. Corps UPSHS, 1975-78; prof. otolaryngology Albany (N.Y.) Med Coll., 1978—; chief otolaryngology VA Med. Center, Albany, 1978—. Mem nat. adv. council Boys Town Nat. Inst. for Communicative Disorders in Children Bd. editors: Rhinology and Laryngology, 1978— ; contbr. articles to profl. jours. Served with USN, 1947-49. Mem. AMA, ACS, Am. Acad Otolaryngology-Head and Neck Surgery (v.p. 1970, exec. v.p. 1979-81, exec council 1972-76), Am. Laryngological Rhinological and Otological Soc. (v.p 1982, exec. council 1983-85, pres. 1985-86), Otosclerosis Study Group (pres 1976), Am. Otological Soc. (pres. 1974), Assn. Research in Otolaryngology Deafness Research Found. (bd. dirs. 1967-75, 78—, exec. com. 1970-75, dir

med. affairs), Am. Council Otolaryngology (assoc. exec. dir. 1969-72, exec. com. 1972), Alpha Omega Alpha, Alpha Kappa Kappa, Lambda Chi Alpha. Republican. Methodist. Office: 113 Holland Ave Albany NY 12208-3410 *As I think about my life, these are a few of the feelings which seem to have a recurring consistency: maintaining a sense of awe and respect for the wonders of creation around us; keeping faith in oneself, in others, and in the ongoing pageant of life; and having fun each day while not taking oneself too seriously.*

BRADLEY, WILLIAM BRYAN, cable television regulator; b. Charleston, W.Va., Feb. 12, 1929; s. Floyd England and Florence Clara (O'Bryan) B.; m. Virginia Vanderhoof Logan, Oct. 27, 1951; children: Christopher, Thomas, Michael, John, Mary Clare (dec.), Mary Ellen, Ann. BA in Journalism cum laude, U. Notre Dame, 1950. Supr., indsl. engr. Martin Co., Denver, 1958-61, 62-65; cons. Reynolds, Ward & Carey, Denver, 1961-62; analyst Denver City Coun., 1965-69, staff dir., 1969-82; dir. Office of Telecommunications, Denver, 1982-94; sr. assoc. Media Mgmt. Svcs., Inc., 1994-99. Co-founder, dir., vice-chmn. Greater Metro Cable Consortium, 1992; initiated joint city-industry cable TV Tech. Stds., 1987, adopted by FCC, 1992. Participant Japanese-Am. conf. on Globalization and Cable TV, Suwa, Japan, 1991. Co-founder Nat. Assn. Telecomm. Officers and Advisors, Washington, 1980, bd. dirs., 1983-88, pres., 1985-87; chmn. telecomm. subcom. Colo. Mcpl. League, Denver, 1985-86; bd. dirs. Denver Cmty. TV, 1996 98; charter mem. The Cable Ctr., 1998. Line Officer USN, 1950-53. Roman Catholic. Avocations: chess, books.

BRADLEY, WILLIAM LEE, retired foundation executive, educator; b. Oakland, Calif., Sept. 6, 1918; s. Dwight Jaques Bradley and Kathryn Lee (Culver) Bradley/Bovard; m. Paula Anne Elliott; children: James Richard Choukas-Bradley, Dwight Culver, Paul William. BA, Oberlin Coll., 1941; PhD, Edinburgh (Scotland) U., 1949; BD, Andover Newton Theol. Sch., 1950. Instr. to prof. Hartford (Conn.) Theol. Sem., 1950-66; temporary field staff Rockefeller Found., N.Y.C., 1964-66; vis. prof. Thammasat U., Bangkok, Thailand, 1964-66; asst. to assoc. dir. Rockefeller Found., N.Y.C., 1966-70; pres. Edward W. Hazen Found., New Haven, 1970-84; ret., 1984. Editor Mountain View Publs., 1990-99; bd. dirs. Obor Inc. Author: (book) P.T. Forsyth-The Man and His Work, 1952, The Meaning of Christian Values Today, 1964, Siam Then, 1982. Mem. Gov.'s Commn. on Human Svcs., Hartford, 1962-64, Gov.'s Commn. on Libraries, Hartford, 1962, Gov.'s Commn. on Equity and Excellence in Edn., Hartford, 1984-85; pres. Randolph Found., 1991-96; bd. dirs. Arts Alliance No. H.H., 1999—; bd. dirs. No. Forest Heritage Park, Perkin, N.H., 1999—. Tech. sgt. USAF, 1942-45. Mem. Coun. on Fgn. Rels. Democrat. United Ch. of Christ. Avocations: reading, writing, hiking, travel. Home and Office: RR 1 Box 1060 Randolph NH 03570-9714

BRADLOW, DANIEL DAVID, law educator; b. Johannesburg, Oct. 23, 1955; s. Basil Arnold and Daphne Bradlow; m. Karen Joanne Hofman, May 22, 1983; children: Benjamin H., Adam H. BA, U. Witwatersrand, 1977; JD, Northeastern U., 1982; MLIC, Georgetown U., 1985. Bar: N.Y. 1983, D.C. 1984. Rsch. assoc. Internat. Law Inst., Washington, 1983-85; assoc. Reichler & Appelbaum, Washington, 1985-88; asst. prof. Washington Coll. Law/Am. U., Washington, 1989-92, assoc. prof., 1992-95, prof., 1995—, dir. internat. legal studies program, 1996—. Vis. prof. Cmty. Law Ctr./U. Western Cape, Cape Town, South Africa, 1996; sr. spl. fellow UN Inst. for Tng. and Rsch., Geneva, 1995-96, 2000—, cons., 1990—; cons. World Commn. on Dams, 1999-2000. Contbr. articles to profl. jours. Mem. ABA, Am. Soc. Internat. Law. Office: Am U Washington Coll Law 4801 Massachusetts Ave NW Washington DC 20016-8196

BRADNA, JOANNE JUSTICE, manufacturer's representative; b. Evergreen Park, Ill., May 1, 1952; d. John George and Virginia Dorothy (Breault) Justice; m. William Charles Bradna, Aug. 20, 1972 (dec. Aug. 2000); children: Trevor William, Cameron Jon. Student, North Cen. Coll., Naperville, Ill., 1970-72; BS, Northwestern U., 1974; MS, U. Ill., Chgo., 1981. Med. technologist Northwestern U. Med. Sch., Chgo., 1974-76, Good Samaritan Hosp., Downers Grove, Ill., 1977-78; instr. med. lab. scis. U. Ill., Chgo., 1976-81, asst. prof., 1984-89, clin. coord., 1984-89, admissions coord., 1988-89; tech. sales rep. Analytab Products, Plainview, N.Y., 1981-84; owner, mgr. Rochelle Sci., mfr.'s reps. lab. equipment and supplies, Lisle, Ill., 1989—. Ednl. cons. Hinsdale (Ill.) Hosp., 1979-80; mem. adv. com. Moraine Valley C.C., Palos Hills, Ill., 1982-92. Contbr. articles and abstracts to profl. jours. Vp. St. Isaac Jogues Home Sch. Assn., 1990-91, pres., 1991-92; mem. youth commn. St. Isaac Jogues Ch., Hinsdale, 1986-90, mem. edn. commn., 1988-92; bd. dirs. Care and Counseling Ctr., Downers Grove, Ill., 1993-95, treas., 1994-95; treas. Hinsdale Jr. Women's Club, 1983-85, 88-89, pres., 1985-86; 3d v.p. 5th dist. Ill. Fedn. Women's Clubs, 1986-88, treas., 1988-90; mem. alumni bd. U. Ill. Coll. Assoc. Health Professions, 1992-96, v.p. alumni bd., 1993-95; eucharistic min. St. Elizabeth Seton Ch., Naperville, Ill., 1994—, chmn. women's network, 2002—. Recipient Outstanding Mem. award Hinsdale Jr. Woman's Club, 1981, 82, lifetime svc. award 5th-6th Dist. Jr. Orgn., 1990, Ill. Fedn. Women's Club, 1990, Heart of Gold citation United Way, 1994, Excaliber Tchg. award, 1989, Outstanding Sales awrads, 1990, 91, 93, 94, 97, 98, 99. Mem. Am. Soc. Clin. Pathologists, Am. Soc. Med. Technologists (cert. of appreciation 1977), Chgo. Soc. Med. Technologists (bd. dirs. 1977-80, cert. of recognition 1978-80), Am. Soc. Microbiology, Ill. Soc. Microbiology (sec. 1981-83, bd. dirs. 1985-87, 92-94, nominations com. 1987-89, tellers com. 1994-95, pres.-elect 1995-96, pres. 1996-98, awards chmn. 1998-2000, newsletter editor 2000—, Tanner Shaughnessy merit award 1992), Ill. Med. Technologists Assn. (cert. of recognition 1978, 79), South Ctrl. Assn. Clin. Microbiology, West Point Parents Club of Ill. (newsletter editor 1998-2001). Roman Catholic. Avocations: children and family, sports. Office: Rochelle Sci PO Box 637 Lisle IL 60532-0637

BRADSELL, KENNETH RAYMOND, minister; b. N.Y.C., Mar. 9, 1948; s. Robert Husted and Doris Mildred (Pennie) B.; m. Marcia Ann Van Dyke, June 25, 1971; children: Adam, Mark, Rachel. BA, Hope Coll., 1970; MDiv, New Brunswick Sem., 1974; STM, Union Theol. Sem., N.Y.C., 1983. Cert min. edn. Ref. Ch. in Am., 1982. Assoc. pastor Community Ch. Douglaston, N.Y., 1974-76; pastor Blawenburg (N.J.) Ref. Ch., 1976-81; co-pastor 1st Ch. in Albany, N.Y., 1981-84; min. for edn. Ref. Ch. in Am., N.Y.C., 1984—95, dir. congl. svcs., 1992-95, dir. policy planning, adminstrv. svcs., 1995—2002, asst. sec., 1997—, dir. ops. and support, 2002—, acting gen. sec., 2002. Chmn. Ministries in Christian Edn., Nat. Coun. Chs. of Christ, U.S.A., N.Y.C., 1989-95; chmn. Presbyn. and Ref. Edn. Ministry, Louisville, 1990-95. Editor: Designs for Teacher and Leader Education, 1990; also articles. Mem. Christian Educators Ref. Ch. in Am. (pres. 1981-84, Educator of Yr. award 1988), Assn. Presbyn. Educators, Religious Edn. Assn. Office: Ref Ch in Am 475 Riverside Dr New York NY 10115-0122 E-mail: kbradsell@rca.org.

BRADSHAW, BEVERLY JEAN, psychotherapist, consultant, educator; b. Denver, Dec. 25, 1946; d. William Heartsel and Shirley Marie (Powell) B. BA, U. No. Colo., 1970; MA, U. Denver, 1984; postgrad., U. Colo., Regis U. Cert. Type B profl. tchr., Colo. Recreation supr. City of Englewood (Colo.), 1968-76; communications bd. chmn. U. No. Colo., Greeley, 1968-70; tchr. Englewood Schs., 1970-83, counselor, tchr., 1984-87, counselor, 1987-92; pvt. practice, Englewood, Colo., 1991-96. Adj. prof. Arapahoe C.C., 1993—. Mayor pro tem Engelwood City Coun., 1980-87, 2000-01; mem. South Suburban Parks and Recreation Found., 1984—, chmn., 2000-02. Mem. NEA, AARP. Republican. Roman Catholic. Avocations: theater, reading, writing, carving, jewelry making. Home: 5165 S Bird Cir Englewood CO 80110-6712 E-mail: bev5165@aol.com.

BRADSHAW, BILLY DEAN, retired retail executive; b. Decatur, Ill., June 25, 1940; s. Lester H. and Gertrude (Davis) B.; children: Deborah, Amanda. Grad., Lakeview High Sch., Decatur, Ill., 1959. Retail div. supr. Schnepps Assocs., Decatur, 1964-74; store mgr. Firestone Tire & Rubber Co., Decatur, 1975—, ret., 2001. Coach Decatur's Boys Baseball, 1965-69. With USAF, 1960-64. Mem. Am. Motorcyclist Assn., Tennesse-Squire, Am. Legion. Avocations: boating, golf. Home: 24 Lake Grove Clb Decatur IL 62521-2321 Office: Firestone Store 2605 N 22nd St Decatur IL 62526-4745

BRADSHAW, CLAUDETTE, federal government official, parliamentarian; married; 2 children. Dir. girl's program Moncton's Boy's and Girl's Club, 1968-74; exec. dir. Moncton Headstart Early Family Intervention Ctr., 1974-97; mem. Ho. of Commons, Govt. of Can., 1997; parliamentary sec. to Minister of Internat. Cooperation and Minister Responsible for Francophonie, 1997; Minister of Labour Govt. of Can., 1998—, fed. coord. on homelessness, 1999—. Mem. parliament Moncton-Riverview-Dieppe, 1997-2000, re-elected, 2000—, Standing Com. of Fgn. Affairs and Internat. Trade, Standing Com. on Human Resources Develop. Recipient Muriel Fergusson award Greater Moncton C. of C, Ann Bell award N.B. Child Welfare Assn., Paul Harris award Moncton-West Riverview Rotary, Family Svc. Can.'s 1998 Leadership award. Office: Phase 2 11 Fl Place Portage 165 Hotel de Ville St Hull QC Canada K1A-OJ2

BRADSHAW, CONRAD ALLAN, lawyer; b. Campbell, Mo., Dec. 22, 1922; s. Clarence Andrew and Stella (Cashdollar) B.; m. Margaret Crassous Sanderson, Dec. 31, 1959; children— Dorothy A., Lucy E., Charlotte L. AB, U. Mich., 1943, JD, 1948. Bar: Mich. bar 1948. Since practiced in Grand Rapids with firm Warner, Norcross & Judd. Served to lt. USNR, 1943-46. Mem. Am. Bar Assn., State Bar Mich. (chmn. corp., fin. and bus. law sect. 1976), Grand Rapids Bar Assn. (pres. 1970) Home: 3261 Lake Dr SE Grand Rapids MI 49506-4320 Office: 900 Fifth Third Ctr 111 Lyon St NW Grand Rapids MI 49503

BRADSHAW, CYNTHIA HELENE, educational administrator; b. S.I., N.Y., May 9, 1954; d. Frederick Thomas and Audrey Helene (Stetter) B. BS in Elem. Edn., Wagner Coll., 1975; MS in Edn., U. Miami, 1979, Cert. elem tchr, adminstr., and supr. Tchr. Young Scholars Montessori Sch., S.I., 1975-76, Luth. Schs., Mo. Synod, S.I., 1976, Hialeah and North Miami, Fla., 1976-80, Dade County Pub. Schs., Miami, Fla., 1980-88, Rahway (N.J.) Pub. Schs., Bayonne (N.J.) Pub. Schs., 1988-91; tester, field worker, classroom surveyor Prospects-Chgo., Bklyn., 1991—; prin. Christ Luth. Sch., 1997-98, Calvary Luth. Sch., 1998-99; prin. Calvary Luth. Sch. Luth Scs., Mo. Synod; prin. Balt. City Pub. Schs., 2000—. Reliability study subject Fla. Dept. Edn., Tallahassee, 1984—; participated in 3 videos in cooperation with Wagner Coll., S.I., N.Y., Bayonne (N.J.) Bd. Edn.; co-produced videos with Wagner Coll. and S.I. Continuum, 1988—. Sch. chairperson United Way, Miami, 1983—. Recipient Cert. of Recognition Dade County Pub. Schs., 1984. Mem. United Tchrs. Dade, United Tchrs. Dade Polit. Orgn., Order Ea. Star, U. Miami Sch. Edn. Allied Professions Alumni Assn. (mem. alumni telephone funding campaign 1984), Wagner Coll. Alumni Assn. (alumni telephone funding campaign 1988—), Alpha Delta Kappa. Republican. Lutheran. Avocation: music. Office: Balt City Pub Schs Baltimore MD 21202 E-mail: CBrad45090@aol.com.

BRADSHAW, DOVE, artist; b. NYC, Sept. 24, 1949; d. David Nelson and Jean Katherine (Cormack) B. BFA, Boston Mus. Sch. Fine Arts, 1973. Co-artistic advisor The Merce Cunningham Dance Co., N.Y.C., 1984—. Artist in residence Pier Ctr., Orkney, Scotland, Sirius Art Ctr., Cork, Ireland, Statens Vaerksteder for Kunst, Copenhagen, 2000. One-man shows include Alan Stone Gallery, N.Y.C., 1979, S. Gering Gallery, N.Y., 1988-89, 91, 93, 95, 98, Graham Gallery, N.Y.C., 1979, Ericson Gallery, 1982, N.Y. Wave Hill, N.Y., 1983, PSI Mus., N.Y.C., 1991, Mattress Factory Mus., Pitts., 1990, 99, Pier Ctr., Orkney, Scotland, 1995, Stalke Gallery, Copenhagen, 1995, 96, 98-99, 2001, Barbara Krakow Gallery, 1997, Mus. Contemporary Art, L.A., 1998, Larry Becker Contemporary Art, Phila. 2000, Stark Gallery, N.Y., 2001, many others; group shows include Am. Ctr., Paris, Science Mus., Tokyo, 1982, Mus. Modern Art, N.Y.C., 1989, Carnegie Internat., Pitts., 1991, Mct. Mus. N.Y., 1992, Art Inst. Chgo., 1992, 96, Aldrich Mus., Ridgefield, Conn., 1993, Phila. Mus., 1993, 98, 2000, Swiss Inst., N.Y.C., 1995, Baumgartner Gallery, Washington, 1998, Carnegie Mus. Art, 1997, Whitney Mus. Am. Art, N.Y., 1997, Millennium Film Theatre, 1998, Mus. Contemporary Art, L.A., 1998, U. Calif., San Diego, U. Mass. Amherst, 1999, UBU Gallery, N.Y.U., Baruch Coll., N.Y.C., Bayley Art Mus., U. Va., Charlottsville, 2000, Mus. Contemporary Art, Roskilde, Denmark, Rooseum Contemporary Art Ctr., Malmo, Sweden, Nikolaj Contemporary Art Ctr. Copenhagen, 2002, Baruch College, CUNY, Diferenca Gallery, Lisbon, Volckers and Preunde Gallery, Berlin, Tanya Bonakdar, NY, 2003, others; represented in permanent collection at Met. Mus. Art, N.Y.C., Mus. Modern Art, N.Y.C., Bklyn. Mus. Art, Whitney Mus. Am. Art, Art Inst. Chgo., Phila. Mus. Art, Ark. Art Ctr., Little Rock, Fogg Art Mus., Cambridge, Mass., Harvard U., Getty Ctr., L.A., Mus. Contemporary Art, L.A., Nat. Gallery, Washington, Carnegie Mus Art, Pitts., Mattress Factory Mus., Pitts., Internat. Le Pompidou Ctr., Paris, Pier Ctr. Orkney, Scotland, Mus. Art, Bilboa, Spain, Kunst Mus., Dusseldorf, Germany, Moderna Mus., Stockholm, Oxygen, 2002, Self Interest, 1999; prodr., dir., artist: (film) Indeterminacy, 1995; prodr.: Metropolitan Mus. postcard, 1976-1992, Met. Mus. guerilla postcard, 1978; artist, prodr. handmade books, including Plain Air (installation with live birds 1969, 88, 91, documentation 1991), 1969-91; author: Indeterminacy, Contingency, Equivalents, Removal, Riverstone, 1991-99. Recipient Pollock-Krasner award, 1985; grantee Nat. Endowment Arts, 1975. Mem.: Larry Becker Contemporary Art Gallery (Phila.), Barbara Krakow Gallery (Boston), Sandra Gering Gallery (N.Y.). Avocations: meditation, yoga, running, reading. Home and Studio: 924 W End Ave New York NY 10025-3534 E-mail: dbradshaw1@nyc.rr.com.

BRADSHAW, ELAINE A. pediatrician; b. Allentown, Pa., Mar. 2, 1966; d. Howard Holt and Rae Allen B. BA, Harvard U., 1987; MD, Stanford U., 1992. Diplomate Am. Bd. Pediatrics. Intern Duke U. Med. Ctr., Durham, N.C., 1992-93; resident Children's Nat. Med. Ctr., Washington, 1993-95. Mem. staff pediats., asst. prof. U. N.Mex. Mem. N.Mex. Med. Soc., Am. Acad. Pediatrics. Office: U NMex Dept Pediats 2211 Lomas Blvd Acc Fl 3 Albuquerque NM 87131-0001

BRADSHAW, JAMES EDWARD (JIM BRADSHAW), consultant; b. Waco, Tex., Aug. 18, 1940; s. Leo Herman Sr. and Eleanor Rose (Cogdell) B.; m. Ouida P. Massey; children: Robin Louise, Dorenda and Dorette (twins), James E. Jr., Cogdell O'Neal. BBA in Mktg. and Fin., Baylor U., 1963. Ptnr. Cogdell's Westview, Waco, 1960-64, Kennedy-David & Assocs., Waco, 1966-68; sales rep. Fed.-Mogul Corp., Detroit, 1964-66; pres. Cogdell Auto Supply Co., Inc., Ft. Worth, 1968-77; chmn. bd. dirs. Auto Supply Co., Inc., Ft. Worth, 1979-91; mayor pro tem City of Ft. Worth, 1976-79; cons. pvt. practice, Fort Worth, Tex. Bd. dirs. Sr. Transp. Network, Geriatric Ctr. of Excellence; adv. bd. Betty Ford Ctr., Tarrant County Coun. on Alcoholism and Drug Abuse. Former bd. dirs. Big Bros./Big Sisters Tarrant County, United Way, Jr. Achievement, Tex. Mcpl. League, Austin, 1976-78; mem. adv. bd. dirs. Betty Ford Ctr.; mem. cmty. devel. steering com. Nat. League Cities, 1978-79; chmn. Tarrant County March of Dimes, Ft. Worth, 1979, Future Pres. Orgn., Kansas City, Mo., 1974; councilman City of Ft. Worth, 1975-79, mayor pro tem 1976-79, mem. zoning commn., 1974-75; Republican. candidate 12th Congl. Dist., 1980; mem. exec. com. Tarrant County Rep. Party. Named to Ten to Watch, D mag., 1977. Mem. Colonial Country Club, Masons. Methodist. Avocations: golf, reading, astronomy. Home: 4613 Briarhaven Rd Fort Worth TX 76109-4609 Office: PO Box 100338 Fort Worth TX 76185-0338

BRADSHAW, JAMES R. business educator; b. Beaver, Utah, Oct. 26, 1938; s. Lafey LaVel and Ilynn (Christensen) B.; m. Jeanie Bok Dong Chung, Sept. 4, 1964; children: Scott, Lisa, Jonathan, Mibi. BSBA in Edn., CSU, Cedar City, 1968; MS in Bus. Adminstrn./Edn., Utah State U., Logan, 1969; EdD in Bus. Report Writing, Brigham Young U., 1974. Missionary, dist. supr. Latter-Day Ch. Korea, 1958-61; with Mountain Fuel Supply co., Salt Lake City, 1964-66, State Bank of So. Utah, Cedar City, 1966-68, Cache Tractor & Implement Co., 1968-69; vis. prof. MBA program Chaminade U., 1977-85; vis. lectr. Cen. Mich. U., 1983—; prof. internat. bus. Brigham Young U., Hawaii, 1969—. Lectr., presenter Japan, Korea, Hong Kong, Taiwan, Singapore, Jakarta, 1986-92, U.S., Mex., 1982-96; vis. prof. Ctrl. China Normal U., Wuhan, 1997. Contbr. articles to profl. jours. With U.S. Army, 1961-64. Decorated U.S. Army Commendation medal; recipient David L. Sargent Manhood of Yr. award, 1968, NEA Title V fellow Utah State U., 1969, David O. McKay Lectr. award, Brigham Young U., Hawaii, 1987, Disting. Teaching award, Cen. Mich. U., 1987, Outstanding Faculty of Yr. award/Bus. Div., Brigham Young U., Hawaii, 1988, Outstanding Tchr. of Yr. award/Bus. Div., 1988, 90, Disting. Scholar award Korean Acad. Internat. Commerce, 1995. Mem. Acad. Internat. Bus., Acad. Bus. Adminstrn., Nat. Bus. Edn. Assn., Am. Bus. Communications Assn., Hawaii Bus. Edn. Assn., Western Bus. Edn. Assn. Mem. Lds Ch. Avocation: family. Office: Brigham Young U PO Box 1808 Laie HI 96762

BRADSHAW, JEAN PAUL, II, lawyer; b. May 12, 1956; married; children: Andrew, Stephanie. BJ, JD, U. Mo., 1981. Bar: Mo. 1981, U.S. Dist. Ct. (we. dist.) Mo. 1982, U.S. Dist. Ct. (so. dist.) Ill. 1988, U.S. Ct. Appeals (8th cir.) 1986, U.S. Supreme Ct. 1987. Assoc. Neale, Newman, Bradshaw & Freeman, Springfield, Mo., 1981-87, ptnr., 1987-89; U.S. atty. we. dist. Mo. U.S. Dept. Justice, Kansas City, 1989-93; of counsel Lathrop & Gage, Kansas City, 1993-99, mem., 2000—, chair dept. health law, 2000—. Named Spl. Asst. Atty. Gen. State of Mo., 1985-89; mem., chmn. elect U.S. Atty. Gen.'s adv. com., office mgmt. and budget subcom., sentencing guidelines subcom. Chmn. Greene County Rep. cen. com., 1988-89; pres. Mo. Assn. Reps., 1986-87; bd. dirs. Greene County TARGET, 1984-89; mem. com. on resolutions, family and community issues and del, 1988 Rep. Nat. Conv.; mem. platform com. Mo. Reps., 1988; chmn. Greene County campaign McNary for Gov., 1984, co-chmn. congl. dist. Dole for Pres., 1988, regional chmn. Danforth for Senate, 1988, co-chmn. 7th congl. dist. Webster for Atty. Gen., 1988; county chmn. U. Mo.-Columbia Alumni Assn., 1985-87; bd. dirs. Springfield Profl. Baseball Assn., Inc.; past mem. Mo. Adv. Coun. for Comprehensive Psychiat. Svcs., former bd. dirs. Ozarks Coun. Boy Scouts Am.; pres. bd. trustees St. Paul's Episcopal Day Sch., 1997-2002. Named Outstanding Recent Grad. U. Mo.-Columbia Sch. Law, 1991. Mem. ABA, Mo. Bar Assn., Kansas City Met. Bar Assn., U. Mo.-Columbia Law Sch. Alumni Assn. (v.p. 1988-89, pres. 1990-91), Law Soc. U. Mo.-Columbia Law Sch. Office: 2345 Grand Blvd Ste 2800 Kansas City MO 64108-2612 E-mail: jpbradshaw@rathropgage.com.

BRADSHAW, JOHN ROBERT COVINGTON, III, internet service company executive; b. Carthage, N.Y., Aug. 4, 1942; s. John Covington and Selma Pauline Bradshaw; children: Sean C., Heather Hodgson. BS, U. Mo., 1968, MBS, 1970. Pres., CEO UniGlobe Fin. Inc., Clearwater, 1998—, UniGlobe Leasing., UniGlobe Multimedia; pres., owner ATM Nat. Svcs., Clearwater, Fla., 1989—. Mem. Clearwater C. of C. (chmn. resource com.), Rotary, SCORE. Avocations: boating, travel, model trains. E-mail: jbradshaw@uniglobemultimedia.com.

BRADSHAW, MURRAY CHARLES, musicologist, educator; b. Hinsdale, Ill., Sept. 25, 1930; s. Murray Andrew Bradshaw and Marie (Novak) Orth; m. Doris Hogg; children: Jean Marie, Murray Edward, Thomas Andrew; m. Sharon Ann Sitton, Apr. 19, 1997. MusM in Piano, Am. Conservatory Music, Chgo., 1955, MusM in Organ, 1958; PhD in Musicology, U. Chgo., 1969. Prof. UCLA, 1966—. Organist and choirmaster various chs. in Illinois, Ind., Calif., 1948—; music critic Gary Post Tribune, Ind., 1962-64; chair dep. musicology, UCLA, 1993-95. Author: The Origin of the Toccata, 1972, The Falsobordone, 1978, Francesco Severi, 1981, Girolamo Diruta The Transylvanian, 1984, Giovanni Luca Conforti, 1985, Gabriele Fattorini, 1986, Emilio de' Cavalieri, 1990, Conforti, "Breve et facile", 1999; gen. editor Musicol. Studies and Documents and Miscellanea, 2000—; contbr. articles to profl. jours. Served with U.S. Army, 1954-56. Grantee: Am. Philos. Soc., 1987, NEH (travel), 1994. Mem. Am. Musicol. Soc. (pres. local chpt. 1979-81), Am. Guild Organists, Ctr. for Medieval and Renaissance Studies. Avocations: reading, jogging, yoga, bridge. Home: 17046 Burbank Blvd Apt 3 Encino CA 91316-1830 Office: UCLA Dept Musicology 405 Hilgard Ave Los Angeles CA 90095-9000 E-mail: mbrads3486@aol.com.

BRADSHAW, OTABEL, retired primary school educator; b. Magnolia, Ark., Oct. 27, 1922; d. Grover Cleveland and Mae (Staggs) Peterson; AA, Magnolia A&M Coll., 1950; BS in Edn., So. State Coll., 1953; MS in Edn., Henderson State U., 1975; postgrad. U. Ark.; PhD, Kensington U., 1983; m. Charles Howard Bradshaw, Aug. 14, 1948; children: Susan Charla, Michael Howard. Tchr., English and drama Walkers Creek Schs., Taylor Ark., 1945-46, primary grades Locust Bayou Schs., Camden, Ark., 1946-52, 2d grade Fairview Sch., Camden, 1962-73; tchr. 1st grade Harmony Grove Sch., Camden, 1973-83, coordinator Title IX, gifted children and handicapped; tchr. East Camden Accelerated Sch., 1983-96, ret., 1996; cons. econ. edn. workshop U. Ark., Fayetteville. Life mem., sec., historian chmn. bicentennial com. PTA; active vol. fund-raising drives Am. Cancer Soc., Birth Defects Soc.; leader Missionary Soc., Camden 1st United Methodist Ch.; mem. Camden and Ouachita County Library bd., 1974-77; active Boys Club Aux. Recipient Disting. Alumni Award So. Ark. U., 1981, Valley Forge Tchr. medal and George Washington Honor medal Freedom Found., 1973; Achievement citation Kazanian Found., 1969, citation for ednl. leadership Pres. of U.S., 1976, 77; profl. achievement citation Internat. Paper Co. Found., 1981. Mem. Assn. Supervision and Curriculum Devel. (speaker San Francisco conf.), NEA, Ark. Edn. Assn. (speaker 1969), Harmony Grove Edn. Assn. (pres. 1978-79), Nat. Council for Social Studies (mem. sexism com.), Am. Assn. Adminstrs, Alpha Delta Kappa (outstanding mem.). Club: Tate Park Garden (sec.). Home: 3188 Roseman Rd Camden AR 71701-5533

BRADSHAW, PETER, engineering educator; b. Torquay, Devon, Eng., Dec. 26, 1935; came to U.S., 1988; s. Joseph Newbold and Frances Winifred (Finch) B.; m. Aline Mary Rose, July 18, 1959 (div. 1968); m. Sheila Dorothy Brown, July 20, 1968. BA, Cambridge U., Eng., 1957; DSc (hon.), Exeter U., Eng., 1990. Sci. officer Nat. Phys. Lab., Teddington, Eng., 1957-69; prof. Imperial Coll. Sci. and Tech., London, 1969-88; Thomas V. Jones prof. engring. Stanford U., 1988-95, prof. emeritus, 1995—. Cons. various engring. cos. Author: Introduction to Turbulence, 1971, Momentum Transfer, 1977, Convective Heat Transfer, 1984; author nearly 200 journ. articles on aerodynamics. Recipient Bronze medal Royal Aero. Soc., London, 1971, Busk prize, 1972, Fluid Dynamics award AIAA, 1994. Fellow Royal Soc. London. Avocations: cycling, walking.

BRADSHAW, RALPH ALDEN, biochemistry educator; b. Boston, Feb. 14, 1941; s. Donald Bertram and Eleanor (Dodd) B.; m. Roberta Perry Wheeler, Dec. 29, 1961; children: Christopher Evan, Amy Dodd. BA in Chemistry, Colby Coll., 1962; PhD, Duke U., 1966. Asst. prof. Washington U., St. Louis, 1969-72, assoc. prof., 1972-74, prof., 1974-82; prof., chair dept. U. Calif., Irvine, 1982-93, prof., 1993—. Study sect. chmn. NIH, 1979, mem., 1975-79, 80-85; mem. sci. adv. bd. Hereditary Disease Found., 1983-87, ICN Nucleic Acids Rsch. Inst., 1986-87; rsch. study com. physiol. chem. Am. Heart Assn., 1984-86, mem. Coun. on Thrombosis, 1976-90; fellowship screening com. Am. Cancer Soc. Calif., 1984-87; chmn. adv. com. Western Winter Workshops, 1984-88; dir., chmn., mem. organizing com. numerous symposia, confs. in field including Proteins in Biology and Medicine, Shanghai, Peoples Republic of China, 1981, Symposium Am. Protein Chemists, San Diego, 1985, mem. exec. com. Keystone Symp. Mol. Cell. Biol., 1991-97, chmn., 1991-94, bd. dirs., 1997—, treas., 1997—; trustee Keystone Ctr., 1991-97; mem. exec. com. Internat. Union Biochem. Mol. Biol., 1991-97, U.S. Nat. Commn. Biochem., 1987-96, chmn., 1992-96; bd. dirs. Fed. Am. Soc. Exptl. Biology, 1992-96, v.p., 1994-95, pres., 1995-96. Mem. editl. bd. Archives Biochemistry and Biophysics, 1972-88, Jour. Biological Chemistry, 1973-77, 78-79, 81-86, assoc. editor, 1989-2002, Jour. Supramolecular Structure/Cellular Biochemistry, 1980-91, Bioscience Reports, 1980-87, Peptide and Protein Reviews, 1980-86, Jour. Protein Chemistry, 1980-90, IN VITRO Rapid Com. in Cell Biology, 1984—; editor Trends in Biochem. Scis., 1975-91, editor-in-chief, 1986-91, J. Neurochem, 1986-90, Proteins: Structure, Functions & Genetics, 1988-92; assoc. editor Growth Factors, 1989—; assoc. editor Protein Sci., 1990-92, 1997-2002, mem. editl. bd., 1992-2002; mem. editl. bd. Biotech. Appl. Biochem., 1995—; co-editor-in-chief Molecular Cell Biol.-Rsch. Comms., 1998-2002; editor-in-chief Molecular and Cellular Proteomics, 2000—; contbr. numerous articles to sci. jours. Recipient Young Scientist award Passano Found., 1976. Fellow AAAS; mem. Am. Chem. Soc. (Sect. award 1979), Am. Soc. Biochem. Molecular Biology (coun. 1987-90, treas. 1991-97), Am. Peptide Soc., N.Y. Acad. Scis., Protein Soc. (acting pres. 1986-87), Am. Soc. for Cell Biology, Soc. for Neuroscience, The Endocrine Soc., Am. Soc. Bone Mineral Rsch., Assn. Biomolecular Rsch. Facilities, Sigma Xi. Home: 25135 Rivendell Dr Lake Forest CA 92630-4134 Office: U Calif Irvine Coll Medicine Dept Physiol & Biophysics D238 Med Sci I Irvine CA 92697-4560

BRADSHAW, RICHARD EUGENE, government relations, energy and environment consultant; b. Rocky Mount, N.C., Jan. 15, 1950; s. Harvey Edmond and Grace Darling (Cowley) B.; m. Pamela Anne Lacey, June 3, 1989. BA in Polit. Sci., U. N.C., 1974; MA in Internat. Rels., East Carolina U., 1977; postgrad., U. S.C., 1977-78. Fgn. svc. officer U.S. Dept. of State, Washington, Paris, 1978-82; dir. rsch. North Am. Telecomm. Assn., Washington, 1982-83; R&D policy cons. Washington Nichibei Cons., Washington, 1983-87; asst. prof. George Mason U., Fairfax, Va., 1987-93; sr. S & T policy analyst NSF, Washington, 1988-92; v.p. North Atlantic Rsch., Inc., Washington, 1993-94; asst. to sec. IMF, Washington, 1995-96; spl. asst. to sec. Energy U.S. Dept. Energy, Washington, 1997-2001; v.p. Columbus Newport LLC, Arlington, Va., 2001; ptnr. Dykema Gossett PLLC, Washington, 2001—. Vis. fellow George Mason U., Arlington, Va., 1996-98. Policy coord. for sci. and tech. issues Bill

Clinton for Pres. Campaign, 1992; campaign staff, Clinton/Gore '96; fin. com. staff, 1997 Presdl. Inaugural. Office: Dykema Gossett 1300 I St NW Ste 300W Washington DC 20005 E-mail: rbradshaw@dykema.com.

BRADSHAW, RICHARD JAMES, general director of opera company; b. Rugby, England, Apr. 26, 1944; s. Alfred James and Florence Mary B.; m. Diana Hepburne-Scott, June 30, 1977; children: Jenny Alexandra, James Edward Merton. BA with honors, U. London, 1965. Dir. Music at Higham, 1967-77, New London Ensemble, 1972-77; internat. freelance condr. symphonies & operas, 1972—; chorus dir. Glyndebourne Festival Opera, 1975-77; resident condr. San Francisco Opera, 1977-89; chief condr., head music Can Opera Co., Toronto, 1989—, artistic & music dir., 1994—, gen. dir., 1998—. Disting. vis. faculty music U. Toronto, 1999. Decorated chevalier Order Arts and Letters (France); Conducting fellow Royal Liverpool (Eng.) Philharm. Orch., 1972; assoc. fellow Massey Coll., U. Toronto, 1995—, sr. fellow 1998—. Office: Can Opera Co 227 Front St E Toronto ON Canada M5A 1E8 E-mail: rbradshaw@coc.ca.*

BRADSHAW, RICHARD ROTHERWOOD, engineering executive; b. Phila., Sept. 12, 1916; s. Joseph Rotherwood and Rosanna (Jones) B.; m. Audrey Grace Skinn, Oct. 3, 1940 (dec. Jan. 1981); children— Linda M., Barbara A., Vicki; m. Chanin Hale, Feb. 14, 1986. BS, Calif. Inst. Tech., 1939; MS, U. So. Calif., 1950. Pres. Richard R. Bradshaw, Inc., Van Nuys, Calif., 1946—, pres. br. office Honolulu. Contbr. articles to tech. jours., Important works include, Disneyworld Hotels, Orlando, Fla., U.S. embassy, Warsaw, Poland, U.S. Exhbn. Bldg., Moscow USSR, Taraara Hotel, Tahiti, Gulf Life Bldg., Jacksonville, Fla., Los Angeles City Airport. Recipient Alfred Lindau award Am. Concrete Inst., 1968, many others for structural design. Mem. ASCE, Internat. Assn. Bridges and Structural Engring., Am. Seismol. Soc., Cons. Engrs. Assn., Internat. Assn. Thin Shells, Am. Concrete Inst., Am. Arbitration Assn. Office: Richard R Bradshaw Inc 17300 Ballinger St Northridge CA 91325-2005

BRADSHAW, ROD ERIC, personnel consultant; b. Washington, May 29, 1957; s. Howard Vernon and Ona A. (Joyce) Bradshaw; m. Rebecca Lynn Bell, Mar. 20, 1974 (div. Jan. 1981); m. Pierrette A. Newman, Dec. 2, 2000. BS, U. Md., 1973; M in Human Resource Mgmt. with honors, Pepperdine U., 1981. Pers. cons. Career Devel. Corp., Atlanta, 1977-79, regional office mgr., 1979-82, prin., mgr., 1982-93; pres. Bradshaw & Assocs., 1993—. Served as envoy to coms. during 1996 Atlanta Olympic Games; asst. to pres. Christopher's Corner Cmty. Assn., Marietta, Ga., 1978—79, chmn. planning com., 1979; rep. Gov.'s Environ. Symposium Smithsonian Inst., 1971; fund raiser, charter mem. High Mus. Art, Atlanta, 1979—; sponsor, adv. bd. rep. Sch. Bd. Coop. Bus. Edn. Adv. Bd.; merit badge counselor Boy Scouts Am.; nominating com. bd. mem. Buckhead Bus. Assn., Young Bucks, Outstanding Ams.; dir. cmty. affairs Atlanta Games Legacy Orgn., 1998—2000; pres. bd. dirs. Jefferson Twp., 1998—; mem. Pub. Schs. Work Bd. Learning Adv. Bd. Named One of Outstanding Young Men of Am., Atlanta C. of C., 1985; recipient J.P. Rice Scholarship, 1971. Mem.: Am. Mgmt. Assn., Nat. Assn. Pers. Cons., Am. Legion, Internat. Platform Assn., Atlanta Ski Club, Delta Tau Delta, Omicron Delta Kappa. Republican. Avocation: Avocations: yachting, home improvement projects, sports, politics. Home: 5717 Windsor Gate Ln Fairfax VA 22030- Office: Bradshaw & Assocs 400 Galeria Pkwy Ste 1500 Atlanta GA 30339-

BRADSHAW, TERRY, sports announcer, former professional football player; b. Shreveport, La., Sept. 2, 1948; Ed., La. Tech. U. With profl. football team Pitts. Steelers, 1970-84; sports analyst CBS Sports Inc NFL Today, 1987-94, Fox Sports, 1995—. Author, country and western singer, entertainer, appears in numerous commls., pub. speaker; author: It's Only a Game, 2001 (NY Times Best Selling Book), Keep It Simple, 2002 (NY Times Best Seller). Named Most Valuable Player, Super Bowl XIII, 1978, Super Bowl XIV, 1979, Most Favorite TV Sportscaster TV Guide, 1999; named to Pro Bowl, 1978, 79; inducted into Hall of Fame, 1989; recipient Emmy award for sports studio analyst, 2000, 02; named Father of Yr. L.A., 2000; recipient Star on Hollywood Walk of Fame, 2001. Achievements include being the quarterback in Super Bowl win, 1974, 75, 78, 79. Office: care Fox Network PO Box 900 Beverly Hills CA 90213-0900 Address: 1925 N Pearson Ln Roanoke TX 76262-9018

BRADSHAW, TROY WAYNE, nurse educator; b. Midland, Tex., May 2, 1948; s. Troy Carlton and Melba Alyene (Franklin) B.; divorced; 1 child, Carlton Allen. BSN, Baylor U., 1970; MS, Tex. Woman's Univ., 1978; student, Tulane U., 1982. Commd. officer U.S. Army, advanced through grades to lt. col.; dir. nursing svc. Martin County Hosp. Dist., Stanton, Tex.; instr., AD nursing Grayson Coll., Denison, Tex., 1974-80; chief preventive medicine U.S. Army MEDDAC, Vicenza, Italy, 1984-87, Ft. Leonard Wood, Mo., 1988-92, chief cmty. health nursing Ft. Hood, Tex., 1992-94; asst. prof. nursing Angelo State U., San Angelo, Tex., 1994-98; instr. Midland (Tex.) Coll., 1998—. Lt. col. U.S. Army, 1968-73, 1981-94. Home: 3101 Mark Ln # A Midland TX 79707-5320 Office: Midland Coll Health Scis Divsn 3600 N Garfield St Midland TX 79705-6329 E-mail: tbradshaw@midland.edu.

BRADSHAW, WILLIAM ELBERT, lawyer; b. Kingsport, Tenn., Oct. 7, 1947; s. Hugh Lowell and Margaret Louise (Wolfe) Bradshaw; m. Grace Currie Bradshaw, Jan. 27, 1973; children: Sara Elizabeth, Rachel Margaret. BA, U. Va., 1970; JD, 1973. Bar: Va. 1973, Pa. 1979. Sole practice, 1973—75; with Westmoreland Coal Co., 1975—; counsel ea. ops. Big Stone Gap, Va., 1975—78; dir. legal and govtl. affairs, 1978—79; gen. counsel, 1979—; sec., 1982. Mem.: Am. Soc. Corp. Sec., Pa. Bar Assn., Va. Bar Assn., ABA, Racquet (Phila.). Republican. Presbyn. Office: Westmoreland Coal Co 2500 Fidelity Bldg Philadelphia PA 19109

BRADSHER, NEAL CLIFTON, investment company executive; b. Moscow, July 1, 1965; s. Henry St. Amant and Monica (Pannwitt) B.; m. Elizabeth Martin Johnson, Apr. 28, 1991. BA cum laude, Yale Coll., 1987. Rsch. assoc. Fred Alger Mgmt., N.Y.C., 1987-89; sr. analyst Hambrecht & Quist, N.Y.C., 1989-91; v.p., equity analyst Alex, Brown & Sons, N.Y.C., 1991-94; mng. dir., COO, co-owner Campbell Advisors, Inc., N.Y.C., 1994-99; mng. dir. Whitehall Asset Mgmt., N.Y.C., 1999—2002; founder, pres. Broadwood Capital, Inc., N.Y.C., 2002—. Mem. Assn. Investment Mgmt. and Rsch. (charterd fin. analyst), N.Y. Soc. Securities Analysts. Avocations: swimming, history, hiking, travel. Office: Broadwood Capital Inc 767 Fifth Ave 50th Fl New York NY 10153 Fax: 212-508-5756. E-mail: neal@broadwoodcapital.com.

BRADSTOCK, JOHN, advertising executive; Pres., N.Am., Pacific Am. DDB Needham Worldwide, Inc., N.Y.C., 1994—. Office: DDB Needham Worldwide Inc 437 Madison Ave New York NY 10022-7001

BRADT, HALE VAN DORN, physicist, x-ray astronomer, educator; b. Colfax, Wash., Dec. 7, 1930; s. Wilber Elmore and Norma (Sparlin) B.; m. Dorothy Ann Haughey, July 19, 1958; children— Elizabeth, Dorothy Ann. AB in Music, Princeton U., 1952; PhD in Physics, MIT, 1961. Mem. dept. physics MIT, 1961—, prof., 1972-2001, prof. emeritus, 2001—; sci. investigator Small Astronomy Satellite, NASA, 1975-79; co-prin. investigator High Energy Astronomy Obs., 1977-79; prin. investigator Rossi x-ray timing explorer ASM, 1995—2001. Co-editor: X and Gamma Ray Astronomy, 1973, The Active X-ray Sky, 1998; mem. editl. bd. Astrophys. Jour. Letters, 1974-77; auhor: Astronomy Methods, 2003. With USNR, 1952—54. Recipient Exceptional Sci. Achievement medal NASA, 1978, Buechner Tchg. prize, 1990. Mem. Am. Astron. Soc. (sec.-treas. high energy astrophysics divsn. 1973-75, chmn. 1981, Rossi prize HEAD divsn. 1999), Am. Phys. Soc., Internat. Astron. Union, Sigma Xi. Office: MIT 37-587 Cambridge MA 02139

BRADTKE, PHILIP JOSEPH, architect; b. Chgo., Aug. 13, 1934; s. Felix Anthony and Frances Agnes (Mach) B.; m. Diane Gloria Westol, Oct. 19, 1963 (div. July 1987); children: Michael, Christine; m. Catherine Adler, Nov. 25, 1989. BArch cum laude, U. Notre Dame, 1957. Registered architect, Ill. Project architect Belli & Belli, Chgo., 1957-64; project mgr., v.p. A.M. Kinney Assoc., Inc., Evanston, Ill., 1964-80, v.p., pres., 1987-96; v.p., sr. assoc. Kober/Belluschi Assoc., Chgo., 1980-87; archtl. divsn. mgr., v.p. Patrick Engring. Inc., Glen Ellyn, Ill., 1996—. Lectr. U. Notre Dame, 1975. Commr. bldg. dept. Village of Glenview, Ill., 1980-83, commr. appearance commn., 1983—. Recipient Hon. Mention award Beaux Arts Inst. Design, 1955, 1st prize award Ch. Property and Adminstrn. Mag., 1956, 1st Mention award Indpls. Home Show Archtl. Competition, 1956, Hon. Mention award, 1959, Modernization Excellence award Bldgs. Mag., 1985. Mem. AIA (corp., housing com. 1968, chmn. honor awards com., 1973, treas., 1975-76), Notre Dame Club, Glenview Shoreline Tennis Team (capt. 1976—). Roman Catholic. Avocations: tennis, golf, basketball. Home: 1441 Canterbury Ln Glenview IL 60025-2252

BRADY, ADELAIDE BURKS, public relations agency executive, giftware catalog executive; b. N.Y.C., June 27, 1926; d. Earl Victor and Audrey (Calvert) Burks; m. James Francis Brady, Jr., June 22, 1946 (div. 1953); 1 child, James Francis. BS, Boston U., 194. Exec. v.p. Media Enterprises, 1952—55; dir. group rels. Save the Children Fedn., N.Y.C., 1955-59; dir. pub. affairs divsn. Girl Scouts U.S.A., N.Y.C., 1959-69; pres. Comm. Internat., Inc., Washington, 1969-73, Burks Brady Comm., Washington, 1972—, Adelaide's Angel Shopper Catalog Inc., Wilton, Conn., 1976—. Exec. v.p. Arts in Parks Inc., Washington, 1971—. Past bd. dirs. Lenox Hill Hosp., N.Y.C., Achievement Rewards for Coll. Scientists Found.; pres. Animal Lovers Inc. Decorated comdr. Order of St. John of Jerusalem (Eng.); recipient Silver Reel award for film The Children of Now, Save the Children Fedn. Mem. NAFE, NEA, AAUW, Nat. Assn. Women Bus. Owners, Pub. Rels. Soc. Am., Am. Women in Radio and TV, Nat. Ednl. Broadcasters Assn., Am. Soc. Profl. and Exec. Women, Women Execs. in Pub. Rels., N.Y. Press Women, Nat. Fedn. Press Women (state pres.),Women's Econ. Roundtable, DAR, Capitol Hill Club (Washington), Yacht and Country Club (Fla.), MDW Officers Club (Washington). Republican. Episcopalian. Home: 312 Harvest Commons Westport CT 06880-3954 also: Yacht Country Club 3664 SE Fairway E Stuart FL 34997-6116 Office: 785 Park Ave New York NY 10021-3552

BRADY, CARL FRANKLIN, retired aircraft charter company executive; b. Chelsea, Okla., Oct. 29, 1919; s. Kirty A. and Pauline Ellen (Doty) B.; m. Carol Elizabeth Sprague, Mar. 29, 1941; children: Carl Franklin, Linda Kathryn, James Kenneth. Ed., U. Wash., 1940. Co-owner Aero Cafe, Yakima, Wash., 1946-47; pilot Central Aircraft, Yakima, 1947-48; partner Economy Helicopters, Inc., Yakima, 1948-60; pres. ERA Helicopters, Inc., Anchorage, 1960-85, ERA Aviation Center, Inc., 1977-85, Livingston Copters, Inc., 1977-85. Exec. v.p. Rowan Companies, Inc., Houston, 1973-85, also bd. dirs.; owner, pres. Brady Investments Ltd. Mem. Alaska Ho. of Reps., 1965-66, Alaska Senate, 1967-68; pres. Alaska Crippled Childrens Assn., 1963; mem. Nat. Advisory com. Oceans and Atmosphere, 1981-86. Served with USAAF, 1943-46. Named Alaskan of Yr., 1989; named to Alaska Bus. Hall of Fame, 1990. Mem. Helicopter Assn. Am. (pres. 1953, 57, Larry D. Bell award 1976), Anchorage C. of C. (pres. 1963-64), Alaska Air Carriers Assn., Am. Helicopter Soc., Commonwealth North, Petroleum Alaska Club, Elks. Republican. Methodist. Home: 510 L St Anchorage AK 99501-1964 Office: 1031 W 4th Ave Ste 502 Anchorage AK 99501-5906 also: Apt 806 510 L St Anchorage AK 99501-1960

BRADY, CHRISTINE ELLEN, education coordinator; b. Manchester, N.H., Feb. 23, 1943; d. George Lewis and Lucy Eleanor (Broderick) B. BA in English, Manhattanville Coll., 1964; MA in English, U. Pa., 1966; EdD in Curriculum and Instrn., No. Ariz. U., 1987. Cert. tchr., N.Y., Ariz., Mass.; cert. adminstr., N.Y., Ariz. English instr. Bryn Mawr (Pa.) Coll., 1966-67; lang. arts tchr. Tuba City (Ariz.) H.S., 1978-82; asst. dir. Reading/Learning Ctr., Flagstaff, Ariz., 1982-83; supervisory home living specialist Apache Agy. Dept. Indian Affairs, Whiteriver, Ariz., 1983-85; English and edn. lectr. Cortland (N.Y.) State Coll., 1988-89; asst. dir. Tchr. Ctr. Broome County, Binghamton, N.Y., 1990-91; English instr. Broome Cmty. Coll., Binghamton, N.Y., 1989-91; labor svc. rep. N.Y. State Dept. Labor, Ithaca, 1992-94; Title I lang. arts tchr. Highland Residential Ctr. N.Y. State Office Children and Family Svcs., Highland, 1994-98, edn. coord. S.I. Residential Ctr., 1998—2003; edn. supr. Arthur Kill Correctional Facility N.Y. State Dept. Corrections, Staten Island, 2003—. Mem.: AAUW, Assn. Bus. and Profl. Women, Phi Delta Kappa (exec. bd. 1998). Office: Arthur Kill Correctional Facility NY State Dept Correctional Svcs Staten Island NY 10309

BRADY, DANIEL P. state representative; b. Bloomington, Ill., July 4, 1961; m. Teri Brady; children: Danielle, Thomas. AA, Southern Ill. Univ., 1982; BA, St. Ambrose Univ., 1983. State Rep. House of Rep., Dist. 88, 2000—; owner and operator Brady Funeral Home, 1987—91. Coroner McLean County, 1992—2000; rep. Ill. State House, 2001—; pres. McLean County Elected Officials, 1996—; co-chmn. Campaigns for City County, State and Fed. Campaigns, 1984—; elected mem. Precinct 10 comm., 1997—98; pres. McLean County Young Rep., 1984—88; mem. Appropriations - Higher Ed., Elections & Campaign Reform; spokesperson Gov. accountability & Streamlining; Higher Ed.; Ins.; State Gov. Admin. Mem.: McLean County Funeral Dir. Assoc. (mem. 1987), Parish Council (elected mem. 1988—90), Holy Trinity, St. Clare Sch. (elected Sch. Bd. mem. 1997—), McLean County Lincoln Club (pres. 1990—91), Numerous Civic and Fraternal (mem. 1984—), Bloomington Young Mens Club (mem. 1984—), Bloomington Sunrise Rotary, Kiwanis Club, Bloomington Elks Lodge #281 (mem. 1985). Republican. Catholic. Office: Capitol 200-8N Stratton Office Bldg Springfield IL 62706 also: District 514 East Locust St Bloomington IL 61701*

BRADY, DAVID JONES, engineering educator, entrepreneur; b. Billings, Mont., Aug. 28, 1961; s. Verl Brady and Norma Melzer; m. Rachael Buhse, Aug. 30, 1986; children: Katherine, Alexander. BA, Macalester Coll., 1984; PhD, Calif. Inst. Tech., 1990. Prof. elec. and computer engring. U. Ill., Urbana, 1990—2001; dir. Fitzpatrick Ctr. for Photonics and Comm. Sys. Duke U., Durham, NC, 2001—. Fellow, David and Lucile Packard Found., 1990—95. Mem.: Optical Soc. Am. Achievements include invention of reference structure tomography. Avocation: running. Office: Duke Univ ECE Dept Box 90291 Durham NC 27708 Office Fax: 919-403-5005. E-mail: david.brady@duke.edu.

BRADY, EDMUND MATTHEW, JR., lawyer; b. Apr. 24, 1941; s. Edmund Matthew and Thelma (McDonald) B.; m. Marie Pierre Wayne, May 14, 1966; children: Edmund Matthew III, Meghan, Timothy BSS, John Carroll U., 1963; JD, U. Detroit, 1966; postgrad., Sch. Law, Wayne State U., 1966—69; DHL (hon.), U. Detroit, 1998. Bar: Mich. 1966, U.S. Dist. Ct. (ea. dist.) Mich. 1966, U.S. Ct. Appeals (6th cir.) 1973, U.S. Supreme Ct. 1974. Sr. ptnr. Vandeveer & Garzia, 1973-90, Plunkett & Cooney, P.C., 1990—. Village clk. Grosse Pointe Shores, Mich., 1975-80; trustee St. John Hosp. and Med. Ctr., Detroit, 1992-2000, chmn., 1994-2000, Grosse Pointe Acad., Mich., 1977-83, adv. trustee, 1983-89; vice chmn. St. John Physicians Hosp. Orgn., 1994-95; supr. Grosse Pointe Twp., 1994-2000, trustee, 1989-2000; pres., dir. Grosse Pointe Hockey Assn., 1969-70; bd. dirs., chmn. maj. gifts divsn. 1st Fund, St. John Hosp. Guild; bd. dirs., pres. Friends of Bon Secours Hosp.; trustee, mem. exec. com., mem. fin. com. St. John Health Sys., 1998-2000. Recipient award of distinction U. Detroit Law Alumni, 1981, Michael Franck award State Bar of Mich. Rep. Assembly, 1998, Respected Advocate award Mich. Trial Lawyers Assn., 1998; named U. Detroit Mercy Alumnus of Yr., 2003. Fellow Am. Bar Found, Mich. State Bar Found. (life); mem. ABA, Am. Coll. Trial Lawyers, Inter. Soc. Barristers, Am. Bd. Trial Advocates, Internat. Assn. Def. Counsel, Assn. Def. Trial Counsel (dir. 1975-80, pres. 1980-81), Mich. Def. Trial Counsel (dir. 1980-81), Def. Rsch. Inst. (Exceptional Performance citation 1981), Cath. Lawyers Soc., Soc. Irish-Am. Lawyers (founding dir. 1979-81), Mediation Tribunal Assn. (mem. panel Wayne County, Macomb County mediator 1989-98), Detroit Bar Assn. (dir. 1986-91, sec.-treas. 1988, pres.-elect 1989-90, pres. 1990-91), State Bar Mich. (commr. 1991-98, treas. 1994, v.p. 1995, pres.-elect 1996, pres. 1997-98), Country Club of Detroit, Detroit Athletic Club, Delta Theta Phi. Republican. Roman Catholic. Office: Plunkett & Cooney 535 Griswold St Ste 2400 Detroit MI 48226 E-mail: ebrady@plunkettcooney.com.

BRADY, GEORGE CHARLES, III, lawyer; b. Darby, Pa., Mar. 13, 1947; s. George Charles Jr. and Lillian (Foster) B.; m. Joan Ann Kilkenny, Apr. 27, 1973; children— Jeffrey, Stephanie, Brent. A.B., Holy Cross Coll., 1969; J.D., Villanova U., 1972. Bar: Pa. 1972, U.S. Dist. Ct. (ea. dist.) Pa. 1972. Assoc. McDonnell & McDonnell, Drexel Hill, Pa., 1972-74; asst. dist. atty. Montgomery County, Pa., 1974-76; ptnr. Cox & Brady, Conshohocken, Pa., 1976-81; sole practice, Conshohocken, 1981-83; ptnr. Baughman & Brady, Conshohocken, 1983-85, Pizonka & Brady, Norristown, Pa., 1985—; dir. Personnel Data Systems, Conshohocken. Mem. Villanova Law Sch. Alumni Assn. (pres. 1980). Republican. Roman Catholic. Club: Whitemarsh Valley Country. Home: 1417 Uxbridge Way North Wales PA 19454-3683

BRADY, GERALDINE, mathematician, educator; d. Richard Joseph Brady and Mary Veronica Lally. BA, U. Chgo., MA, 1990; PhD, U.Oslo, 1997. Lectr. U. Chgo., 1999—2002, asst. prof., 2002—, math. advisor, 2001—. Presenter in field. Author: (book) From Peirce to Skolem, 2000; contbr. articles to profl. jours. Mem.: Nat. Trust (UK), English Heritage. Office: Dept Computer Sci U Chgo Chicago IL Office Fax: 773-702-8487. Business E-Mail: brady@cs.uchicago.edu.

BRADY, GORDON LEONARD, JR., economist; b. Washington, Sept. 2, 1945; s. Gordon Leonard and Sally (Hart) Brady; m. Sara Crickenberger, 1985. BA in Econs., U. N.C., Chapel Hill, 1967; MA in Econs., U. N.C., Greensboro, 1973; PhD in Econs., Va. Poly. Inst. and State U., 1976. MSL (grad. fellow) Yale U. Law Sch., New Haven, 1981; lectr. econs. Va. Poly. Inst. and State U., 1975—76; Rockefeller postdoctoral fellow Law and Econs. Ctr., U. Miami Law Sch., 1976—77; econ. policy fellow Brookings Instn., 1978—79; chief econ. analysis divsn. Nat. Commn. Air Quality, 1979—80; lectr. econs. Yale U., 1980—81; sr. econs. policy advisor Pres.'s Coun. on Environ. Quality, 1982—85; bd. visitors econs. dept. U. N.C., Chapel Hill, 1987—91; staff asst. to adminstr. energy info. adminstrn. U.S. Dept. Energy, 1985—89; sr. advisor environ. econs. U.S. Dept. of State, 1989—90; assoc. prof., dir. environ. studies program Sweet Briar Coll., 1990—95. Sr. rsch. fellow Pub. Choice Ctr. George Mason U., Fairfax, Va., 1995—2002; com. econ. corrs. Media Inst., Washington; profl. assoc. East-West Ctr., Honolulu; prof. econ., Wayne D. Angell Disting. Chair in Econ. Ottawa Univ., 2003—. Contbr. articles and revs. to profl. jours., chapters to books. Fellow, Ford Found., Salvatori fellow, fellow, Heritage Found., 1991—93. Mem.: Henry Simons Soc. (co-founder, sec. 1987—), Pub. Choice Soc., Am. Econ. Assn. Office: Ottawa Univ 1001 S Cedar St Ottawa KS 66067-3399 E-mail: gbrady6430@aol.com.

BRADY, JAMES JOSEPH, economics educator; b. Jersey City, Mar. 2, 1936; s. James and Anna (Shine) B.; m. Sheila Hartney, July 24, 1965; children: Matthew, Michael, James. BA, U. Notre Dame, 1959, MA in Econs., 1963, PhD in Econs., 1969. Profl. baseball player Detroit Tigers, 1955-60; asst. prof. econs. Ind. U., South Bend, 1965-69; asst. prof., assoc. prof., prof. econs. Old Dominion U., Norfolk, Va., 1969-79; dean Coll. Arts and Scis. Jacksonville (Fla.) U., 1979-83, dean Coll. Bus., 1983-84, v.p. acad. affairs, 1984-88, pres.-elect, 1988-89, pres., 1989-95, prof. econs., 1995—. Spl. master Fla. Pub. Employees Rels. Commn., Tallahassee, 1985—; pvt. labor cons., Jacksonville, 1978-88; mem. Fed. Mediation and Conciliation Svc. Labor Panel, 1986—; perm. arbitrator State Fla. dept. mgmt. svcs., 1999-, Social Security Adminstrn. Warner-Ribbins AFB, Fla. Author: Arbitration Principles: Layoffs, 1989; co-author: Transportation Noise Pollution, 1970. With U.S. Army, 1959-61. NASA grantee, Norfolk, Va., 1970. Mem. Am. Arbitration Assn. (labor arbitrator 1965—, comml. arbitrator 1987-89), Indsl. Rels. Rsch. Assn., Soc. Profls. in Dispute Resolution, Jacksonville C. of C. (bd. dirs. 1989—). Avocations: fishing, cooking, tennis. Home: 4454 Maywood Dr Jacksonville FL 32277-1036 E-mail: leftybrady@attbi.com.

BRADY, JEAN STEIN, retired librarian; b. Concord, Mass., Nov. 4, 1930; d. Walfred and Mary Selina (Jussila) Stein; m. Maurice Goodrich Klein, Feb. 22, 1957 (div. 1982); 1 child, Audrey Elaine; m. Lawrence Kevin Brady, Oct. 15, 1988. BS, Simmons Coll., 1952; cert. d'Etudes, U. Grenoble, France, 1954; MA, Northwestern U., 1957. Cert. pub. libr., N.Y. Sr. libr. N.Y. Pub. Libr., 1952-53, 57-60; cataloger Columbia U., N.Y.C., 1954-55; reference asst. Northwestern U., Evanston, Ill., 1955-57; cataloger U. W.Va., Morgantown, 1960-61; book reviewer ALA, Chgo., 1961-63; sr. cataloger Cleve. Pub. Libr., 1964-70; sr. catalog libr. Yale U. Libr., New Haven, Conn., 1970-92; cataloger Columbia U., N.Y.C., 1993-95; ret., 1995. Revision asst. Bibliographical Guide to Romance Langs. and Lits., 1956-57; reviewer: Booklist and Subscription Books Bulletin, 1961-63. Mem. Simmons Coll. Club of Cape Cod. Democrat. Episcopalian. Avocations: reading, travel, walking, swimming.

BRADY, JOHN PATRICK, JR., electronics educator, consultant; b. Newark, Mar. 20, 1929; s. John Patrick and Madeleine Mary (Atno) B.; m. Mary Coop, May 1, 1954; children: Peter, John P., Madeleine, Dennis, Mary G. BSEE, MIT, 1952, MSEE, 1953. Registered profl. engr., Mass. Sect. mgr. Hewlett-Packard Co., Waltham, Mass., 1956-67; v.p. engring. John Fluke Mfg. Co., Inc., Mountlake Terrace, Wash., 1967-73, Dana Labs., Irvine, Calif., 1973-77; engring. mgr., tech. advisor to gen. mgr. Metron Corp., Upland, Calif., 1977-78; ptnr. Research Assocs., Newport Beach, Calif., 1978-86; prof. electronics Orange Coast Coll., Costa Mesa, Calif., 1977-99, emeritus, 1999, faculty fellow, dean tech., 1983-84, chmn. electronics tech. dept., 1994-96, chmn. acad. rank com., 1988-98. Instr. computers and elec. engring. Calif. State U., Long Beach, 1982-84; dir. measurement sci. conf. MIT, L.A., 1982-83. Contbr. articles to profl. jours. Mem. evaluation team Accrediting Commn. for Cmty. and Jr. Colls., 1982-92; mem. blue ribbon adv. com. on oversees tech. transfer U.S. Dept. of Commerce, 1974-76. With USN, 1946-48. Mem. Eta Kappa Nu, Tau Beta Pi, Sigma Xi. Office: Orange Coast Coll Costa Mesa CA 92626

BRADY, JOHN PAUL, psychiatrist; b. Boston, June 23, 1928; s. James Henry and Evelyn Louise (Rice) B.; m. Christeen Nelson, Mar. 19, 1963; children— James Palmer, Pamela Eros, June Pamela, David Duncan. AB, Boston U., 1951, MD, 1955; MA (hon.), U. Pa., 1967. Intern Gorgas Hosp., Panama, 1955-56; resident in psychiatry Inst. of Living, Hartford, 1956-59; rsch. psychiatrist Ind. U. Med. Sch., Indpls., 1959-63; faculty U. Pa. Med. Sch., Phila., 1963—, prof. psychiatry, 1968—, Kenneth Appel prof., 1974—, chmn. dept., 1974-82. Co-founder, asso. editor Behavior Therapy, 1970— Author: An Introduction to the Science of Human Behavior, 1963, Classics of American Psychiatry, 1975, Psychiatry: Areas of Promise and Achievement, 1977, Voyage to Inishneefa, 1987; co-editor: Controversy in Psychiatry, 1978, Behavioral Medicine; Theory and Practice, 1979, Psychiatry at the Crossroads, 1980, also articles. Recipient Research Scientist award NIMH, 1963-74; Strecker award Inst. of Pa. Hosp., 1972 Fellow Am. Psychiat. Assn., Indian Psychiat. Soc.; mem. Assn. Advancement Behavior Therapy (past pres.), Soc. Biol. Psychiatry (pres. 1979-80), Psychiat. Research Soc. (program chmn. 1973), Soc. Behavioral Medicine (dir. 1980-81), Soc. Interam. de Psicologia, Am. Psychosomatic Soc. Office: 300 E Lancaster Ave Ste 207 Wynnewood PA 19096-2142 E-mail: chpabrady@home.com.

BRADY, JOSEPH VINCENT, behavioral biologist, educator; b. N.Y.C., Mar. 28, 1922; s. James J. and Mary F. (Michaelson) B.; m. Nancy Heaton; children: Barbara Ann, Michael Joseph, Kathleen Theresa, Nancy Marie, Joanne Cecelia, Jessica Lea, Margaret Mary. BS, Fordham U., 1943; PhD, U. Chgo., 1951. Dep. dir. div. neuropsychiatry Walter Reed Inst. Research, 1951-71; prof. psychology U. Md., 1955-69; prof. behavioral biology Johns Hopkins Sch. Medicine, Balt., 1967—, prof. neurosci., 1982—; dir. Behavioral Biology Rsch. Ctr. Johns Hopkins U., Balt., 1992—; pres., chmn. bd. trustees Inst. for Behavior Resources, Balt., 1988—. Cons. pres. sci. adv. com. Merck Inst. for Therapeutic Rsch., U.S. Army Med. Rsch. and Devel. Command, NASA; assoc. chmn. Nat. Commn. for Protection Human Subjects of Biomed. and Behavioral Rsch., 1974-79; chmn. sci. adv. com. New Eng. Regional Primate Rsch. Ctr., Harvard Med. Sch., Boston, com. on problems of drug dependence NRC, com. on space biology and medicine, com. on toxicology NAS; mem. adv. com. NASA/NIH; mem. space medicine com. NAS Inst. Medicine. Contbr. articles to profl. jours. Col. M.C., U.S. Army. Fellow AAAS, APA (div. pres.), Am. Coll. Neuro-psycho-pharmacology, Coll. Problems Drug Dependence (pres.), Acad. Behavioral Med. Rsch.; mem. Eastern Psychol. Assn. (pres.), Soc. Behavioral Medicine (pres.), Pavlovian Soc. (pres.), Behavioral Pharmacology Soc. (pres.). Home: Unit 610 1000 Fell St Baltimore MD 21231-3554 Office: Johns Hopkins U Behavioral Biology Rsch Ctr 5510 Nathan Shock Dr Baltimore MD 21224-6823 E-mail: jvb@jhmi.edu.

BRADY, JULES MALACHI, philosopher, educator, priest; b. St. Louis, Mo., Feb. 17, 1919; s. Jules Musik and Laura Catherine Brady. BA, St. Louis U., 1939, PhD, 1949. Ordained Jesuit, 53. Prof. philosophy Rockhurst Univ., Kansas City, Mo., 1955—2000, retired, 2000. Roman Catholic. Home: Fusz Pavilion 3601 Lindell Blvd Saint Louis MO 63108-3301

BRADY, KATHLEEN DEMING, psychologist, occupational therapist, educator; b. Enid, Okla., Jan. 8, 1920; d. Leon J. and Lola Faye (Hendryx) Deming; m. Roland Anderson (dec.); children: Virginia, Leon; m. Frederick S. Brady (dec. Jan. 1999); 1 child, Faye Lillian Burnaman. Student, William & Mary Coll., 1937-38, Arts Student League, NYC, 1938-39; BS cum laude, NYU,

1943; student, Pennsylvania U., 1945, Wayne State U., 1957-59; MA in Exceptional Edn., U. Fla., 1964, EdD in Psychology and Exceptional Edn., 1967. Registered Occupational Therapist, Phila., 1945; Cert. Sch. Psychologist, Occupational Therapist, Guidance. Art tchr., N.Y., Ohio and Mich.; occupational therapist U.S. Army Hosp., 1944-45; dir. occupational therapy Perry Point V.A. Hosp., 1946-55; coord. exceptional edn. program Brevard County, Fla., 1960-64; dir. guidence and counseling Satellite H.S., Brevard County, Fla., 1965-68; dir. guidence Brevard County, 1968-69; dir. guidance and counseling Orange County, 1969; psychologist Learning Disability Ctr. and Gateway Sch., 1970-72; dir. Pupil Personnel Services, High Point, N.C., 1972-73; psychologist Exceptional Edn. Program, Orlando, Fla., 1973-78; dir. Bureau Indian Affairs Special Edn. Program, Washington, 1978-80; psychologist Western Navajo Agency, Tuba City, Ariz., B.I.A. Eastern Navajo, 1983. Tchr. Brevard C.C. Fla., 1964-68, U. Fla. Gainesville, Fla., 1966-68, Fla. Ctrl. U. Orlando, 1969, U. So. Fla. Tampa, Fla., 1971-72, Rollins Coll. Orlando, 1976-77. Author: (booklet on VA rsch.) Occupational Therapy, 1950, Reflections Poems and Pictures, 2001, Renaissance Journey Poetry Book. Pres. Brevard County Coun. Exceptional Children, Brevard County Guidance Assn.; vol., greeter program James A. Haley VA Hosp. Scholar United Cerebral Palsy, U. Fla.; recipient Outstanding Achievement award Veterans Adminstrn. Mem. Nat. Assn. State Dirs. Special Edn. Home: 4000 E Fletcher Ave C-302 Tampa FL 33613-4890 E-mail: k63007@aol.com.

BRADY, KEVIN, congressman; b. Vermillion, S.D., Apr. 11, 1955; m. Cathy Brady. BS, Univ. S.D., 1990. Mem. Tex. House of Reps., 1990-96, U.S. Congress from 8th Tex. dist., 1997—; mem. ways and means com. Active Saints Simon and Jude Cath. Ch. Mem.: Rotary. Republican. Office: 428 Cannon Bldg Washington DC 20515-4308*

BRADY, KYLE JAMES, football player; b. Jan. 14, 1972; Attended, Penn State U. Football player Jacksonville Jaguars, 1999—. Guest appearance Politically Incorrect, 1999. Recipient Bobby Dodd award, Touchdown Club Atlanta. Office: Jacksonville Jaguars One ALLTEL Stadium Pl Jacksonville FL 32202

BRADY, LAWRENCE LEE, geologist; b. Topeka, Nov. 6, 1936; s. Bosker B. and Anna B.; m. Mary Elizabeth; children: Beth Ann, Geoffrey Scott. BS in Geology, Kans. State U., 1958; MS in Geology, U. Kans., 1967, PhD in Geology, 1971. Registered geologist, Mo., Kans. Engring. geologist U.S. Army Corps of Engrs., Kansas City, Mo., 1958-63; tchg. & rsch. asst. U. Kans., Lawrence, 1963-70; asst. prof. geology Okla. State U., Stillwater, 1971; from rsch. assoc. to sr. scientist Kans. Geol. Survey, Lawrence, 1971—. Mem. Am. Assn. Petroleum Geologists (past pres. energy minerals divsn. 1998-99), Geol. Soc. Am., Assn. Engring. Geologists. Avocations: canoeing, running, gardening. Home: 913 W 28th St Lawrence KS 66046-4625 Office: Kans Geol Survey 1930 Constant Ave # Campus W Lawrence KS 66047-3724 Business E-Mail: lbrady@kgs.ku.edu.

BRADY, LAWRENCE PETER, lawyer; b. Jersey City, July 26, 1940; s. Lawrence Peter and Evelyn (Mauro) B.; div; children: Deegan, Tara, Kerry, Melissa, James; m. Mary Helen Reynolds, Mar. 28, 1984. BS in Acctg., St. Peters Coll., 1961; JD, Seton Hall U., 1964; LLM, Bklyn. Law Sch., 1966. Bar: N.J. 1964, U.S. Dist. Ct. N.J. 1964, U.S. Supreme Ct. 1969, U.S. Ct. Appeals (3rd cir.) 1972, N.Y. 1991; cert. civil trial atty. State of N.J. 1982; cert. Nat. Bd. Trial Advocacy 1989. Asst. prosecutor Hudson County, Jersey City, 1964-70; prosecutor Town of Kearny, N.J., 1971-74; sr. ptnr. Doyle & Brady, Kearny, 1974—. Dir. and founding incorporator Growth Bank, New Vernon, N.J. Mem. ATLA, Nat. Bd. Trial Advocacy, N.J. State Bar Assn., Hudson County Bar Assn., West Hudson Bar Assn. (sec. 1980, treas. 1981, v.p. 1982, pres. 1983), Am. Trial Lawyers N.J. (bd. govs.), Roxiticus Golf Club (Mendham, N.J.), Sandalfoot Country Club (Boca Raton, Fla.), Ocean Reef Club (Key Largo, Fla.), Ocean Reef Yacht Club. Roman Catholic. Avocations: golf, tennis, travel, fishing, boating. Office: Doyle & Brady 377 Kearny Ave Kearny NJ 07032-2600

BRADY, LUTHER W., JR., physician, radiation oncology educator; b. Rocky Mount, NC, Oct. 20, 1925; s. Luther W. and Gladys B. AA, George Washington U., 1944, AB, 1946, MD, 1948; DFA (hon.), Colgate U., 1988; DSc (hon.), Lehigh U., 1990; MD (hon.), Toyama U., Japan, 1996; Dr. med. honoris causa, U. Heidelberg, Germany, 1997. Diplomate: Am. Bd. Radiology (treas. 1980-82, v.p. 1982-84, pres. 1984-86). Intern Jefferson Med. Coll. Hosp., Phila., 1948-50, resident in radiology, 1954-55; resident radiology Hosp. U. Pa., Phila., 1955-56; fellow Nat. Cancer Inst., 1954-57; practice medicine, specializing in radiation oncology Phila. Asst. instr. radiology Jefferson Med. Coll. Hosp., 1954-55, U. Pa., Phila., 1955, instr., 1956-57, assoc. radiology, 1957-59; asst. prof. radiology Coll. of Physicians and Surgeons, Columbia U., NYC, summer, 1959; assoc. prof. radiology Hahnemann Med. Coll. and Hosp., Phila., 1959-62, prof., 1963—97, Disting. Univ. prof., 1997-, chmn. dept. radiation oncology, 1970—97; asst. prof. radiology Harvard Med. Sch., Boston, 1962-63; mem. med. radiation adv. com. Bur. Radiation Health, HEW, 1971-74; cons. radiation therapy various hosp.; mem. US del. to Interam. Congress Radiology, 1975, Internat. Congress of Radiology, 1981; sec. gen. Internat. Congress Radiology, 1985; med. adv. radiation therapy, med. affairs com., 1984-97; dir. Pa. Blue Shield, Camp Hill; chair Pa. Cancer Control Bd., 1989-97. Author: Tumors of the Nervous System, 1975, Cancer of the Lung, Clinical Applications of the Electron Beam; editor Cancer Clin. Trials (Am. Jour. Clin. Oncology), (with C. Perez) Principles and Practice of Radiation Oncology; editorial bd. Cancer; assoc. editor: Gynecologic Oncology, Am. Jour. Roentgenology, Cancer Research; sr. editor: Internat. Jour. Radiol. Oncology; contbr. articles on radiation therapy to profl. jour. Bd. dir. Assn. Artists Equity of Phila., Welcome House, 1974-94, Settlement Music Sch., 1973—, Phila. Art Alliance, 1977-84; mem. oriental art com., trustee Phila. Mus. Art, 1974—, chmn. exec. com., 1968-72, mem. print, contemporary art and Indian art coms., 1974—; trustee Fleisher Art Meml., 1997-, Founders Award, 2003; trustee curtis Institutde of Music, 1997-, trustee- the Phillips Collection, 2003 Served to lt. M.C. USN, 1950-54. Recipient Grubbe award Chgo. Radiol. Soc., 1977, Gold medal Gilbert Fletcher Soc., 1984, Albert Soiland Gold medal U. So. Calif., 1985, del Regato Gold medal, 1986, Disting. Alumni award George Washington U., 1991, Padro Pio medal, 1993, Founder's award Fleisher Art Meml., 1997. Fellow Am. Coll. Radiology (Gold medal 1983); mem. AMA (Gold medal Disting. Svc. award 1999, Am. Roentgen Ray Soc., Am. Radium Soc. (Gold medal 1981), Am. Cancer Soc., Am. Fedn. Clin. Rsch., Am. Bd. Radiology, Am. Soc. Clin. Oncology, Am. Coll. Radiation Oncology (Gold medal 1996), Am. Soc. for Therapeutic Radiology and Oncology (Gold medal 1987), Am. Assn. for Cancer Rsch., Soc. Chmn. Acad. Radiation Oncology Program, Soc. Chmn. Acad. Radiology Dept., Assn. Pendergrass Fellows, Internat. Soc. for Radiation Oncology, Internat. Skeletal Soc., Internat. Club Radiotherapists, James Ewing Soc., Radiation Rsch. Soc., Soc. Surg. Oncology, Assn. Univ. Radiologists, Radiation Rsch. Soc., Radiol. Soc. N.Am. (Gold medal 1989), Del. Med. Soc., Med. Soc. State Pa., Pa. Radiol. Soc., Phila. County Med. Soc., Phila. Roentgen Ray Soc. Clubs: Merion Cricket; Racquet, Union League (Phila.), Phila., Peale. Office: 230 N Broad St Philadelphia PA 19102-1121 also: Hahnemann U Hosp Broad & Vine MS-200 Philadelphia PA 19102

BRADY, M. JANE, state attorney general; b. Wilmington, Del., Jan. 11, 1951; m. Michael Neal. BA, U. Del., 1973; JD, Villanova U., 1976. Dep. atty. gen. Wilmington and Kent County, 1977—90; chief prosecutor Sussex County, 1987—90; solo law practice, 1990—94; atty. gen. State of Del., Wilmington, 1994—. Bd. dirs. Nat. Dist. Attys. Assn., Kent/Sussex Industries. Past chair Rep Attys. Gen. Assn.; bd. dirs. Nat. Org. Victim Assistance; founder KINfolk; bd. dirs. Del. Children's Trust Fund; advisory bd. Big Bros./Big Sisters Sussex County. Named Delaware's Top Fraud Fighter, AARP Delaware, 1998. Mem.: Nat. Assn. Attys. Gen. (exec. com.). Republican. Office: Office of Atty Gen Carvel State Office Bldg 820 N French St Wilmington DE 19801-3509 E-mail: jbrady@state.de.us.*

BRADY, MARK A. cinematographer, photographer; b. Palm Beach, Fla., Oct. 4, 1953; s. Robert Austin Brady and Carol King Bailley. BFA, Sch. of Visual Arts, NYC, 1980. Photographer Lincoln Ctr. Libr. of Performing Arts, NYC; cameraman Dialogues for the NY Pb. Libr. Dir. Brads Film and Tape. Cinematographer: (films) Foreplay, Fish, 1980; (documentaries) Rock and Roll Hall of Fame series, Musical Tribute to Stiv Bators, Hey is Dee Dee Home, (music videos) Slowdrive, The Fleshtones, The Boredoms, The Mekons, Cheetah Chrome, Elliott Murphy, Sonny Vincent All Stars, also TV commercials, (with Michael Drexler): (films) The Date (winner Houston Film Festival, 1994), (with Ellen Cornfield): (documentaries) Sidewalk Sonata, (with Emma Diamond) Six Metamorphoses, (title sequence) Rock Soup (best documentary San Francisco Film Festival, 1992); dir.: (music videos) Dee Dee Ramone; dir. of photography : (films) What About Me?; Rex Justice; War is Menstrual Envy. Democrat. Mailing: #1 20 E 14th St New York NY 10003-3150

BRADY, NORMAN CONRAD, lawyer, corporate executive; b. Dallas, June 29, 1934; s. Conrad and Louise Mabel (Norman) B.; m. Joyce Johnson, Sept., 1958 (div. 1967); 1 dau., Brigitte; m. Kornelia Jefferies Sichol, July 3, 1969; 1 son, Adam Conrad; step-children— Arthur, Tom, Timothy. B.A., Baylor U., 1956; J.D., U. Tex.-Austin, 1964. Bar: Tex. 1964, U.S. Dist. Ct. (no. dist.) Tex. 1967, U.S. Supreme Ct. 1984. Assoc. firm Rogers, Sayers & Brady, Austin, 1964-65; assoc. atty. Tex. Wholesale Beer Distbrs., Austin, 1965-67, Biesel, Zwieg, Diamond, Brady, Dallas, 1967-68; v.p. Service Corp. Internat., Houston, 1968— . Harris County campaign mgr. Gov. Preston Smith, 1968-70; mem. Harris County Fin. Com., Gov. Mark White, 1982. Served as 1st lt. USAF, 1956-58. Mem. SCV, SAR. Baptist. Clubs: Champions Golf, Houston, Inns of Court (Houston); Onion Creek Country, (Austin). Home: 14118 Kiamesha Ct Houston TX 77069-1344

BRADY, PATRICIA G. volunteer; b. Lafayette, La., Dec. 4, 1933; d. Samuel Cooper and Camille Cora (Donlon) Grunewald; m. Robert Stratton Brady, Oct. 8, 1960; children: Sheila K. Barth, Michael S., Mary F. DeVerter. Student, U. Tex., 1951-53, U. Madrid, Spain, 1954-55; BS in Fgn. Svc., Georgetown U., 1956, MA, 1961. Bibliographer Hispanic Found. Libr. Congress, Washington, 1956-58, rsch. asst. Hispanic Law divsn., 1958-61; rep. Springfield dist. Fairfax (Va.) County Group Resdl. Facilities Commn., 1981-90; pres. LWV (nat. capital area), Washington, 1989-91; dir. LWV U.S., Washington, 1992-96, LVW liaison to ABA, 1997—; mem. adv. com. to ABA Commn. on 21st Century Judiciary, 2002—. Mem. The Constitution Project, ABA Coalition for Justice, 1999—. Vice chair Fairfax County Bicentennial Commn., 1987-91; Va. coord. Belfast Children's Summer Program, Gaithersburg, Md., 1986-93. Mem. LWV. Roman Catholic. Avocations: reading, needlework. Office: LWV US 1730 M St NW Ste 1000 Washington DC 20036-4508

BRADY, PATRICIA MARIE, nurse; b. Taylor, Pa., Feb. 6, 1946; d. Herman John and Regina Theresa (Yonushka) Kovalan; m. Edward Joseph Brady, June 22, 1968 (dec. Mar. 1996); children: Maureen C., Edward M. RN, St. Joseph's Hosp., Carbondale, Pa., 1966. Cert. emergency nurse, ACLS; cert. diabetes educator. Staff nurse med.-surg. Wilkes-Barre (Pa.) Gen. Hosp., 1966; staff nurse med. Dept. VA Med. Ctr., Wilkes-Barre, 1966-72, staff nurse ambulatory care and emergency rm., 1977—. Mem. diabetes adv. com. Dept. VA Med. Ctr., 1993—. Assisted in formation diabetes edn. program VA, 1994; established and facilitated VA Med. Ctr. Pain Clinic, 1996—. Mem. Pittston (Pa.) Area Taxpayers Assn., 1995—; parishner Sacred Heart of Jesus Ch., Dupont, Pa., 1968—. Mem. Am. Assn. Diabetes Educators (by-laws com. 1995—), Electric City Swing Dance Soc. Democrat. Roman Catholic. Avocations: wreath and flower crafts, country, ballroom, and swing dancing, golf. Home: 1289 Suscon Rd Pittston PA 18640-9596 Office: Dept VA Med Ctr 1111 E End Blvd Wilkes Barre PA 18711-0030

BRADY, PATRICK, French literature educator, novelist; b. Broken Hill, New South Wales, Australia, Oct. 27, 1933; came to U.S., 1969; naturalized, 1993; s. Patrick and Frances (Minahan) B. BA with first class honors, U. Sydney, Australia, 1953-56; D., Sorbonne, 1960. Asst. in English Poitiers (France) Tchr.'s Coll., 1957-58; lectr. in English U. Lille (France), 1959-60; lectr. in French U. Melbourne (Australia), 1961-64; sr. lectr. U. Queensland, Brisbane, Australia, 1964-68, reader in French, 1968; assoc. prof. Fla. State U., Tallahassee, 1969-72; prof. French Rice U., Houston, 1972-83, Favrot prof. French, 1983-88; Shumway chair of excellence U. Tenn., Knoxville, 1988—. Vis. prof. comparative lit. Harvard U., Cambridge, Mass., 1978; Disting. Humanities lectr. S.W. Conf. Humanities Consortium, 1980-81; state rep. Australasian Univs. Lang. and Lit. Assn., 1967-68; founder New Paradigm Press, 1991, Synthesis jour., 1995. Author: L'Oeuvre d'Emile Zola, 1967, Structuralist Perspectives, 1978, Rococo Style, 1984, Chaos in the Humanities, 1995, Feminism, 1995, (novel) Guruwari, 1995, also others; contbr. over 100 articles to profl. jours. Decorated Ordre Palmes Académiques (France); travelling scholar U. Sydney, 1958-60; Mellon Found. rsch. grantee, 1982. Mem. Am. Comparative Lit. Assn., Tenn. Writers' Alliance. Office: U Tenn Dept Modern Fgn Languages & Lit Knoxville TN 37996-0001

BRADY, PATRICK, advertising executive; Pres., COO Cyrk, Inc., Gloucester, Mass., 1999—, CEO, 1999—. Office: Cyrk Inc Ste 225 201 Edgewater Dr Wakefield MA 01880-6216

BRADY, PHILLIP DONLEY, lawyer; b. Pasadena, Calif., May 20, 1951; s. Donley L. and Evelyn M. (Dorweiler) B.; m. Kathleen Ryan; children: Ryan Donley, Conor Phillip, Sean Patrick. BA cum laude, U. Notre Dame, 1973; JD cum laude, Loyola U., Los Angeles, 1976. Bar: Calif. 1976, U.S. Ct. Appeals (D.C. cir.) 1978, U.S. Supreme Ct. 1980, U.S. Ct. Mil. Appeals 1990. Assoc. atty. Spray, Gould & Bowers, L.A., 1976-78; dep. atty gen. State of Calif., L.A., 1978-79; legis. counsel U.S. Rep. Daniel E. Lungren, Washington, 1979-81; regional dir. ACTION Agy., San Francisco, 1981-82; dir., Congl. Affairs, Immigration and Naturalization Svc. Dept. of Justice, Washington, 1982-83, assoc. dep. atty. gen., 1983-84, acting asst. atty. gen., 1984-85; dep. asst. to V.P. The White House, Washington, 1985-88, dep. counsel to Pres., 1988-89; gen. counsel Dept. Transp., Washington, 1989-91; asst. to Pres. and staff sec. The White House, Washington, 1991-93; v.p, gen. counsel Am. Automobile Mfrs. Assn., Washington, 1993—99; COO ind. rels. Nat. Automobile Dealers Assn., McLean, Va., 1999—2001, pres., 2001—. Mem. Coun. of the Administrv. Conv. of the U.S., 1988-93. Mem. ABA, Calif. State Bar Assn., FBA (chair gen. counsels sect. 1989-91, nat. coun. 1989—). Home: 5916 Colfax Ave Alexandria VA 22311-1024 Office: Nat Automobile Dealers Assn 8400 Westpark Dr Mc Lean VA 22102-3522

BRADY, RICHARD ALAN, lawyer; b. Newark, Sept. 17, 1934; s. Andrew Joseph and Katherine (Bogan) B.; m. Kathleen R. Sweeney, June 12, 1965; children: Cecilia, Kathleen, Andrew, Joshua. BS, Yale U., 1956, LLB, 1959. Bar: D.C. 1960. Ptnr. Covington & Burling, Washington, 1959—. Office: Covington & Burling 1201 Pennsylvania Ave NW PO Box 7566 Washington DC 20044-7566

BRADY, ROBERT A. congressman; b. Phila., Apr. 7, 1945; m. Debra; 2 children: Robert, Kimberly. Grad. H.S., Phila. Carpenter, Phila., 1963-65; official Carpenter's Union, Phila., 1965-98; mem. U.S. Congress from 1st Pa. dist., 1998—; mem. armed svcs. com., small bus. com. Mem. Pa. Dem. State Com., Dem. Nat. Com.; instr. Organizational Dynamics course, U. Pa. Voted in as mem. 34th Ward Dem. Exec. Com., 1967; elected 34th Ward leader, 1980, chmn. Phila. Dem. Party, 1986 ; appointed asst. sgt.-at-arms for Phila. City Coun., 1975-83, Phila. dep. mayor for labor in the W. Wilson Goode adminstrn., cons. to the Pa. State Senate, Pa. Turnpike commr., mem. bd. dirs. Phila. City Redevel. Authority. Democrat. Office: 206 Cannon Ho Office Bldg Washington DC 20515-3801*

BRADY, RODNEY HOWARD, holding company executive, broadcast company executive, former college president, former government official; b. Sandy, Utah, Jan. 31, 1933; s. Kenneth A. and Jessie (Madsen) B.; m. Carolyn Ann Hansen, Oct. 25, 1960; children: Howard Riley, Bruce Ryan, Brooks Alan. BS in Acctg. with high honors, U. Utah, MBA with high honors, 1957; DBA, Harvard U., 1966; postgrad., UCLA, 1969-70; PhD (hon.), Weber State Coll., 1986, Snow Coll., 1991, Univ. Utah, 1997. Missionary Ch. Jesus Christ of Latter-day Saints, Great Britain, 1953-55; teaching assoc. Harvard U. Bus. Sch., Cambridge, Mass., 1957-59; v.p. Mgmt. Systems Corp., Cambridge, 1962-65, Center Exec. Devel., Cambridge, 1963-64, v.p., dir. Boston, 1964-65; v.p. Tamerand Reef Corp., Christiansted, St. Croix, V.I., 1963-65; v.p., dir. Am. Inst. Execs., N.Y.C., 1963-65; v.p., mem. exec. com. aircraft div. Hughes Tool Co., Culver City, Calif., 1966-70; asst. sec. adminstrn. and mgmt. Dept. HEW, Washington, 1970-72; chmn. subcabinet exec. officers group of exec. br., 1971-72; exec. v.p., chmn. exec. com., dir. Bergen Brunswig Corp., Los Angeles, 1972-78; chmn. bd. Uni-mgrs. Internat., Los Angeles, 1974-78; pres. Weber State Coll., Ogden, Utah, 1978-85; pres., CEO Bonneville Internat. Corp., Salt Lake City, 1985-96, also dir.; pres., CEO Deseret Mgmt. Corp., Salt Lake City, 1996—. Bd. dirs. Amerisource Bergen Corp., 1st Security Bank Corp., 1985-2000, Mgmt. and Tng. Corp., Deseret Mut. Benefit Assn., chmn.; bd. dirs. Maximum Svc. Television, Inc., Intermountain Health Care Found., Nat. Assn. Broadcasters TV Bd., 1993-96, bd. advisors Mountain Bell Telephone, 1983-87; chmn. Nat. Adv. Com. on Accreditation and Instl. Eligibility, 1984-86, mem., 1983-87; chmn. Utah Gov.'s Blue Ribbon Com. on Tax Recodification, 1984-90; cons. Dept. Def., Dept. State, Dept. Commerce, HEW, NASA, Govt. of Can., Govt. of India (and indsl. firms), 1962—. Author: An Approach to Equipment Replacement Analysis, 1957, Survey of Management Planning and Control Systems, 1962, The Impact of Computers on Top Management Decision Making in the Aerospace and Defense Industry, 1966, (with others) How To Structure Incentive Contracts— A Programmed Text, 1965, My Missionary Years in Great Britain, 1976, An Exciting Start Along an Upward Path, 1978; contbr. articles to profl. jours. Mem. exec. com. nat. exec. bd. Boy Scouts Am., 1977—; chmn. nat. Cub Scout commn., 1977-81, pres. Western region, 1981-83, chmn. nat. ct. of honor, 1984-88; mem. adv. com. program for health sys. mgmt. Harvard U., 1973-78, mem. nat. adv. coun. U. Utah, 1971—, chairperson, 1974-76, nat. adv. bd. Coll. Bus., 1985—, chmn., 1989-93, mem. adv. com. Brigham Young U. Bus. Sch., 1972—; mem. dean's round table UCLA Grad. Sch. Mgmt., 1973-78; trustee Ettie Lee Homes for Boys, 1973-79; mem. gov. bd. McKay Dee Hosp., Ogden, Utah, 1979-87; bd. dirs. Utah Endowment for Humanities, 1978-80, Nat. Legal Ctr. for the Pub. Interest, 1991—, vice chmn., 1994-95, chmn., 1995-97, Utah Shakespeare Festival, 1992-2001, Ogden C. of C., 1978 83; bd. dirs. Utah Opera Co., 1997—, Utah Symphony Orch., 1985--. 1st lt. USAF, 1959-62. Recipient Silver Antelope award Boy Scouts Am., 1976; recipient Silver Beaver award Boy Scouts Am., 1979, Silver Buffalo award Boy Scouts Am., 1982, Disting. Alumni award U. Utah, 1990. Mem. Nat. Assn. TV Broadcasters (bd. dirs.), Am. Mgmt. Assn. (award 1969), L.A. C. of C. (tax structure com. 1969-70), Salt Lake Area C. of C. (bd. dirs. 1985-88), SAR (pres. Utah chpt. 1986-87), Sons of Utah Pioneers, Freedoms Found. at Valley Forge (nat. bd. dirs. 1986—), L.A. Country Club, Alta Club, Rotary, Phi Kappa Phi, Tau Kappa Alpha, Beta Gamma Sigma. Mem. LDS Ch. (past pres. L.A. stake). Office: Deseret Mgmt Corp Eagle Gate Tower 60 E South Temple Ste 575 Salt Lake City UT 84111-1016

BRADY, ROSCOE OWEN, neurogeneticist, educator; b. Phila., Oct. 11, 1923; s. Roscoe O. and Martha (Roberts) Brady; m. Bennet Carden Manning, 1972, 2 children. Student, Pa. State U., 1941-43; MD, Harvard U., 1947; postgrad., U. Pa., 1948 49. Intern Hosp. U. Pa., 1947-48; NRC fellow U. Pa., 1948-50, USPHS spl. fellow, 1950-52; sect. chief Nat. Inst. Neurol. Diseases and Blindness, NIH, 1954-67, asst. lab. chief neurochemistry, 1967-72; chief developmental and metabolic neurology br. Nat. Inst. Neurol. Disorders and Stroke, 1972—; pres., CEO Targeted Techs., Inc., Rockville, Md. Professorial lectr. George Washington U. Sch. of Medicine, 1963—73; mem. faculty Georgetown U. Sch. of Medicine, 1965—; mem. med. staff Children's Hosp., Washington, 1992—; chmn. sci. adv. bd. Therascope, A.G., Heidelberg, Germany. Author (with Donald B. Tower): Neurochemistry of Nucleotides and Animo Acids, 1960; author: Basic Neurosciences, 1975; author: (with John A. Barranger) Molecular Basis of Lysosomal Storage Disorders, 1984; author: numerous articles. Recipient award, Gairdner Found., 1973, Lasker Found., 1982, Passano Found., 1982, Warren Alpert Found. award, 1992, Myrtle Wreath award, Hadassah, 1993, Exec. Excellence award, Sr. Execs. Assn., 1993. Mem.: NAS (J.S. Kolvenko medal 1991), Inst. of Medicine, Am. Soc. Human Genetics, Am. Soc. Clin. Investigation, Am. Acad. Mental Retardation, Am. Acad. Neurology (Kotzias award 1980), Am. Soc. Biol. Chemists. Achievements include first demonstration of enzyme system for fatty acid synthesis; development of biosynthesis of myelin sheath lipids, nature of metabolic defects in Gaucher's disease, Neimann-Pick disease,Fabry's diseases and Tay-Sachs disease; enzyme replacement and gene therapy for lipid storage diseases; discovery of aberrant metabolism of sphingolipids in neoplastic diseases; role of antigenic sphingolipids in neurological diseases. Home: 6026 Valerian Ln Rockville MD 20852-3410 Office: NIH 9000 Rockville Pike Bethesda MD 20892-1260 E-mail: bradyr@ninds.nih.gov.

BRADY, RUPERT JOSEPH, lawyer; b. Washington, Jan. 24, 1932; s. John Bernard and Mary Catherine (Rupert) B.; m. Maureen Mary MacIntosh, Apr. 20, 1954; children: Rupert Joseph Jr., Laureen Zegowitz, Kevin, Warren, Jeanine Hartnett, Jacqueline Rada, Brian, Barton. BEE, Cath. U. Am., 1953; JD, Georgetown U., 1959. Bar: Md. 1961, U.S. Ct. Appeals (D.C. cir.) 1964, U.S. Patent Trademark Office 1961, D.C. 1962, U.S. Supreme Ct. 1969, U.S. Ct. Appeals (fed. cir.) 1961. Elec. engr. Sperry Gyroscope Co., L.I., 1953-56; patent specifications writer John B. Brady, patent atty., 1956-59; patent agt. B.P. Fishburne, Jr., Washington, 1959-61; pvt. practice patent agt. Washington and Md., 1961; practice Washington, Md. and Va., 1961—; sr. ptnr. Brady, O'Boyle & Gates, Washington & Chevy Chase, Md., 1963-95; of counsel Birch, Stewart, Kolasch & Birch, LLP, Va., 1996—. V.p. Ministr-O-Media Inc. Patentee crane booms, moldboard support assembly. Mem. ABA, Am. Intellectual Property Law Assn., Md. Patent Law Assn., Senator's Club Alumni. Republican. Roman Catholic. Home: 7201 Pyle Rd Bethesda MD 20817-5623 Office: 8110 Gatehouse Rd Ste 500E Falls Church VA 22042-1210

BRADY, SALLY RYDER, writer, literary agent; b. Boston, May 26, 1939; d. Francis Clark and Dorothy Childs Ryder; m. Upton Birnie Brady, Nov. 17, 1962; children: Sarah, Andrew, Nathaniel, Alexander. Student, Barnard Coll., 1956-57, 59-60. Freelance writer, Hartland Four Corners, Vt., 1970—; lit. agt. Brady Lit. Mgmt., Hartland Four Corners, 1988—. Educator Harvard U., Cambridge, Mass., 1978-86. Author: (novel) Instar, 1976, (non-fiction) A Yankee Christmas, Vol. I, 1992, Vol. II, 1993.

BRADY, STEPHEN R.P.K. physician; b. New London, Conn., Oct. 13, 1955; s. Richard Harris and Jeanne Margaret (Halpin) B.; m. Marsha Anne Erickson, June 18, 1978 (div. Jan. 1993); 1 child, Ericka Anuhea; m. Elizabeth Ada Rewick, Dec. 27, 1994. AB cum laude, Harvard U., 1977; MPH, U. Hawaii, 1978, postgrad., 1979; MD, U. Pa., 1982. Diplomate Am. Bd. Internal Medicine. Intern U. Hawaii, 1982-83, resident in internal medicine, 1983-85, clin. instr. Sch. Medicine, 1986-99, clin. asst. prof. Sch. Medicine, 1999—; physician Kaiser Clinics, Honolulu, 1985-86; physician, med. dir. Kokua Kalihi Valley, Honolulu, 1986-89; physician Waianae (Hawaii) Coast Health Svc., 1989-94; asst. med. dir., physician Am. Hawaii Cruises, Honolulu, 1989-95; physician Straub Clinic and Hosp., Honolulu, 1984—. Founding chair Hawaii Consortium for Continuing Med. Edn. U. Hawaii Sch. of Medicine, 1993—. Host weekly Ask the Dr. program KHON-Fox 2 News, Hawaii, 1996—, (weekly TV program) Health in Paradise 'Olelo Channel 52, 2001—. Cubmaster Boy Scouts Am., Kailua, Hawaii, 1995-2000; bd. dirs. Straub Found. Comdr. U.S. Mcht. Marine, 1989—. Recipient Po'okela awards, 1991, 93, 95, 99, Guy Milnor award for cmty. svc., 1999; Cub Scouter award Aloha coun. Boy Scouts Am., 1999, Cubmaster award, 2000; rsch. grantee Kuakini Med. Rsch. Inst., Honolulu, 1971, Pacific Health Rsch. Inst., Honolulu, 1972-78, Children's Hosp., Phila., 1979; Paul Harris fellow, 1995; named Scot of Yr., State of Hawaii, 1999, Physician of Yr., Honolulu County Med. Soc., 2002; listed Best Doctors in Am., 2001-02. Fellow: ACP-Am. Soc. Internal Medicine; mem.: Ahahui O Na Kauka (v.p.), Soc. Epidemiologic Rsch., Hawaii Med. Assn. (chair cont. med. edn. com. 1987—, councillor), Hawaii Soc. Internal Medicine, Am. Soc. Internal Medicine, APHA, ACP, AMA, Aumoana Cmty. Assn. (v.p. 1996—), Plaza Club, Soroptimist (pres. 1998—99), Rotary, Kaneohe Yacht Club, Delta Omega. Congregationalist. Avocations: singing, running, sailing, scuba diving, music. Home: 758 Kapahulu Ave PMB 309 Honolulu HI 96816-1196 Office: Straub Clinic & Hosp 888 S King St Honolulu HI 96813-3083 E-mail: kaukaoli@hotmail.com.

BRADY, STEVEN L. civil engineer, consultant; b. Ash Grive, Mo., Nov. 29, 1944; s. Lawrence Emery and Avia Brady; m. Carolyn Sue Brady, Jan. 22, 1967 (div. June 1997); children: Tamera L. Jones, Michelle L. Harper, Neil S.; m. Elena Villescas Brady, Sept. 12, 1998. BSCE, U. Mo., Rolla, 1967; M in Engring., U. Fla., 1971. Registered profl. engr., Mo., Kans., Okla., Ark.; registered land surveyor, Mo. Structural design engr. Phillips Petroleum Co., Bartlesville, Okla., 1967-68; assoc. engr. Anderson Engring., Inc., Springfield, Mo., 1971-79, v.p., 1979-92, pres., 1992—, also chmn. bd., bd. dirs. Chmn. Salvation Army, Springfield, Mo., 1975; mem. Ozark Greenways, Springfield, 1998. 1st lt. U.S. Army Corps Engrs., 1968-70, Vietnam. Named Outstanding

Young Man Jr. C. of C. Springfield, 1978. Mem. NSPE, ASCE, Mo. Soc. Profl. Engrs. (pres. Ozark chpt. 1980, chmn. 1983-84, Young Engr. of Yr. 1975). Baptist. Avocations: running, weight training, bike riding, tennis. Home: 3552 E Loren St Springfield MO 65809-1449 Office: Anderson Engring Inc 730 N Benton Ave Springfield MO 65802-3702

BRADY, TERRENCE JOSEPH, judge; b. Chgo., Dec. 24, 1940; s. Harry J. and Othele R. Brady; m. Debra René, Dec. 6, 1969; children: Tara René, Dana Rose. BA cum laude, Coll. St. Thomas, 1963; JD, U. Ill., 1968. Bar: Ill. 1969, U.S. Dist. Ct. (no. dist.) Ill. 1970, U.S. Ct. Appeals (7th cir.) 1971. Pvt. practice, Crystal Lake, Ill., 1969-70, Waukegan, Ill., 1970-77; assoc. judge 19th Jud. Cir., Ill. Cir. Ct., Waukegan, 1977—. Lectr. Ann. Ill. Assoc. Judge Seminars, Statewide Ill. Traffic Conf., 1982, Lake County Bar Assn. Seminar, 1983, 88, others; invited participant Law and Econs. Seminar, U. Kans., 2000, Judicial Faculty Development, Ill. Judicial Conf., 2000; vis. jud. faculty Nat. Jud. Coll., U. Nev. Reno, 1997, condr. seminar civil mediation, 1999; materials author and lectr. in field, 1997; author, presenter, lectr. in field, 1998-; long range planning com. 19th Jud. Circuit, Lake County, Ill., 1999; alt. faculty mem., Chancery and Miscellaneous Remedies, 2000, Settlement Techniques, 2002; mem. delegation of Am. judges, Mexican Govt. Jud. Visitation Program, Mex.,2001. Author: Settle It, The Docket, 1998, The Six Steps of a Jury Trial, 1999, Civil Discovery-Rule 213-Keys to Compliance, 1999; author and lectr., SCR 213-2000 Update, The Docket, 2000; mem. editl. bd. The Docket; contbr. articles to profl. jours. Served with U.S. Army, 1963-64, 68-69. Mem. ISBA (bench and bar sect. coun., adv. polls com.), LCBA (civil trial, med., legal coms.), Ill. Bar Assn. (com. on jud. adv. polls 1994—, vice-chair adv. polls 1998, task force on domestic violence 1998—, chair jud. adv. polls, 1999, sec. com. on jud. adv. polls 1997-99, bench and bar coms., judicial polls), Ill. Judges Assn. (bd. govs.), Ill. Bar Found., Lake County Bar Assn., Libertyville Racquet Club, Am. Inns of Ct. Avocations: tennis, golf, writing, reading. Office: Lake County Courthouse 18 N County St Waukegan IL 60085-4304 E-mail: tbrady@co.lake.il.us. *Notable cases include: Wiegman vs. Hitch-Inn Post, 721 N.E. 2d 614, 2d Dist, 1999, affirmed in allowing case to go to jury on strong circumstantial evidence of wet floors and stairs in motel swimming pool and recreational areas; Benitez vs. KFC Nat. Mgmt. Co., 714 N.E., 2d 1002, 2d Dist, 1999, affirmed in entering judgment for three pls-waitresses, and against for df-employees and mgrs. of KFC; Nowak vs. Coghill, 693 N.E., 2d 332, 2d Dist., 1998, affirmed trial ct. of df's motion of summary judgment in its finding no evidence of unnatural accumulation of snow, nor such accumulation as a proximate cause of pl's fall and injuries; Gantz vs. McHenry County Sheriff, 694 N.E., 2d 1078, 2d Dist, 1998, petition for leave to appeal denied at 699 N.E., 2d 1031, Ill. S. Ct., 1998, affirmed trial courts dismissal of pl's complaint on essential grounds of courts lack of subject matter jurisdiction via the preemption of collective bargaining issues under the Illinios Public Labor Relations Act; Koules vs. Euro-American Arbitrage, Inc., 689 Ill. 2d 411 2d Dist., 1998, affirmed trial court's grant of df'a motion for summary judgment against pl's employment contract claims of payment of guaranteed salary and vacation benefits; Lenz vs. Julian, 657 Ill. 2nd 712 2d Dist., 1995, affirmed trial ct. allowing the jury to decide pl's automobile negligence claims against a state trooper although the defendant claimed bars of sovereign immunity and public official immunity; Adams vs. Adams, 133 Ill. 2d 457 S. Ct., 1989, which involved the Ill. Appellate Ct., in a divided opinion, affirmed, Adams vs. Adams, 174 Ill. App. 3d 595 2d Dist., 1988. The Ill. Supreme Ct. reversed and remanded, holding the issues of paternity and consent must be determined under Fla. law; Agazim vs. Agazim, 176 Ill. App. 3d 225 2d Dist., 1988, which affirmed the trial ct.'s distbn. of marital property requiring the husband to pay off substantial marital debts which he had incurred of his own purposes; Chapman vs. Chapman, 162 Ill. app. 3d 308 2d Dist., 1987; which affirmed trial ct.'s denial of husband's motion to vacate a marital property settlement agreement, without an evidentiary hearing; Peppers vs. FNB of Lake Forest, 151 Ill. App 3d 909 2d Dist., 1987, which affirmed trial ct.'s enjoining the defendant bank, as trustee, from seeking forfeiture of a real estate purchase installment contract; People ex. rel. Foreman vs. Sojourner's Motorcycle Club Ltd., 134 Ill. App. 3d 448 2d Dist., 1985, which affirmed trial ct.'s denial of defendant's motion to quash adminstrv. search warrant processed by sheriff's dep. on behalf of, and executed by, the County Zoning officer.*

BRADY, THOMAS CARL, lawyer; b. Malone, N.Y., Sept. 5, 1947; s. Francis Robert and Rosamond Ethel (South) B.; m. Joan Marie Murray, Dec. 4, 1971; children: Erin Marie, Ryan Thomas, Trevor Michael. BA, Niagara U., 1969; JD, SUNY, Buffalo, 1972. Bar: N.Y. 1973, U.S. Dist. Ct. (we. dist.) N.Y. 1973, Fla. 1981. City ct. judge City of Salamanca, N.Y., 1973; atty. County of Cattaraugus, Little Valley, N.Y., 1973-76; ptnr. Eldredge, Brady, Peters & Brooks, Salamanca and Ellicottville, NY, 1976-82; sr. ptnr. Brady, Brooks & Smith, Salamanca, 1982—96, Brady, Brooks & O'Connell, L.L.P., Salamanca, 1996—2001, Brady & O'Connell, L.L.P., Salamanca, 2001—02, Brady & Swenson, Salamanca, 2002—. Trustee St. Patrick's Roman Cath. Ch., Salamanca, 1991—; mem. N.Y. State Office Parks, Recreation and Hist. Preservation Allegany Region Commn., 1998—, vice chair, 1999—; mem. 8th Dist. Atty. Grievance Com., 1994-2000. Capt. USAR, 1969-76. Mem.: ATLA, N.Y. State Trial Lawyers Assn., Cattaraugus County Bar Assn. (pres. 1984), N.Y. State Bar Assn. (mem. ho. of dels. 2003), Fla. Bar Assn., Kiwanis (pres. Salamanca club 1983—84). Republican. Roman Catholic. Avocations: skiing, golf, swimming, boating. Home: 6894 Woodland Dr Great Valley NY 14741-9752 Office: Brady & Swenson 41 Main St Salamanca NY 14779-0227 Fax: 716-945-3566. E-mail: tbrady@bradyandswenson.com.

BRADY, TOM, football player; b. San Mateo, Calif., Aug. 3, 1977; Degree in orgnl. studies, Mich. State U. Profl. football New Eng. Patriots, 2000—. Office: New Eng Patriots 60 Washington St Foxboro MA 02035

BRADY, UPTON BIRNIE, editor, literary agent; b. Washington, Apr. 17, 1938; s. Francis Ignatius and Sue (Birnie) B.; m. Sally Ryder, Nov. 17, 1962; children— Sarah Schenck, Andrew Upton Birnie, Nathaniel Francis Ryder, Alexander Childs. AB, Harvard Coll., 1959. Coll. field editor Random House, N.Y.C., 1961-63; editor McGraw Hill, N.Y.C., 1963-65; mng. editor Atlantic Monthly Press, Boston, 1965-72, assoc. dir., 1972-79, dir., 1979-84, exec. editor, 1984-88; free-lance editor, cons., literary agt., 1988—. Served to lt. (j.g.) USNR, 1959-61 Mem.: PEN. Roman Catholic. Home and Office: Town Farm Hill PO Box 164 Hartland Four Corners VT 05049-0164

BRADY, WILLIAM E. state legislator; m. Nancy Brady; children: Katie, William, Duncan. Grad., Ill. Wesleyan U., 1983. Founder, pres., oper. officer Brady Weaver Realtors/Better Homes & Gardens, 1984—, Brady Property Mgmt., 1984—; co-founder, sec. Brady & Assocs. Constrn. & Devel., 1986—; pres. Decade 200 Mortgage Svcs., Inc., 1991—; mem. from 88th dist. Ill. Ho. of Reps. Bd. dirs. YMCA, 1990—; v.p. bd. dirs. Ctrl. Cath. H.S. Found., 1980-94; mem. Rep. Ctrl. Com., 1986—; active in polit. campaigns of Ed Madigan and Jim Edgar. Mem. Bloomington/Normal Assn. Realtors (bd. dirs. 1990—), Bloomington/Normal Homebuilders Assn., McLean County Young Reps. (bd. dirs. 1986—), McLean County C. ofC. (bd. dirs. 1987-90, sec. 1990-91). Office: 2203 Eastland Dr Ste 3 Bloomington IL 61704-7924 Home: 1202 Elmwood Rd Bloomington IL 61701-3319*

BRADY, WRAY GRAYSON, mathematician, educator; b. Benton Harbor, Mich., July 20, 1918; s. Wray Grayson and Mildred (Sauters) B.; m. Emilie Peterson, Apr. 30, 1943; children— Susan, Wray Gordon; m. Mildred Sheir, Dec. 2, 2000. BS, Washington and Jefferson Coll., 1940, MA, 1942; PhD, U. Pitts., 1953. Prof., chmn. dept. math. Washington and Jefferson Coll., 1951-65, U. Bridgeport, Conn., 1965-69; dir. rsch., dean Slippery Rock U., 1969-72, prof. math., 1972-87, prof. emeritus, 1987—. Cons. Bettis Plant, AEC, 1955-60; prof. math NSF U. Ariz., 1963-67. Co-author: Calculus, 1960, Analytic Geometry, 1961. Lt. USNR, 1943-46. Fellow AAAS; mem. Am. Math. Soc., Math. Assn. Am., Fibonacci Soc., AAUP. Democrat. Presbyterian. Home: Apdo 330 45900 Chapola Jalisco Mexico

BRADY-BORLAND, KAREN, retired reporter, columnist; b. Buffalo, Mar. 13, 1940; d. Charles A. and Mary Eileen (Larson) B.; m. Gregg Robinson Borland, Sept. 6, 1969 (div. July 1985); children: Caitlin Luise, Kristin Robinson, Leila Nell. BA in English, Daemen Coll., 1961; MS in Journalism, Columbia U., 1962. Summer reporter Buffalo News, 1961, reporter, 1965-68, columnist, 1968-81; editor Prentice-Hall, Inc., Englewood, N.J., 1962-65; press officer for Rep. Max McCarthy U.S. Ho. Reps., Washington, 1967; gen. assignment & features reporter Buffalo News, 1981—91, higher education reporter, 1991—2002; ret., 2002. Recipient numerous awards Buffalo Newspaper Guild, 1969-79, N.Y. State award for Major Dailies Mag. Writing AP, 1982, numerous community awards, Hilbert Coll. medal, 2002.

BRAECKMANS, PAUL, advertising executive; Chmn., pres. Huntsinger & Jeffer, Richmond, Va. Office: Huntsinger & Jeffer 809 Brook Hill Cir Richmond VA 23227

BRAENDEL, DOUGLAS ARTHUR, hotel executive; b. Highland Park, Mich., Dec. 9, 1939; s. Helmuth Gunther and Constance Leah (Drysdale) B.; m. Cameron Lawry, Nov. 30, 1968; children: Jennifer Braendel Miller, Eric, Heike Lawry Batluck. BSBA, Lehigh U., 1961, MBA, 1971; Grad., Army Command and Gen. Staff, Coll., Army War Coll. Commd. U.S. Army, 1966, advanced through grades to col., 1989; bn. supply officer 24th Med. Bn., Fed. Republic of Germany, 1966-68; patient adminstr., detachment comdr. 3d Mobile Army Surg. Hosp., Vietnam, 1968-69; CFO Noble Army Community Hosp., Ft. McClellan, Ala., 1972-75; asst. prof. health adminstrn. Baylor U. Grad. Sch., San Antonio, 1975-79; exec. officer 45th Med. Battalion, Hanau, Fed. Republic Germany, 1980-82; adminstr. Army Regional Med. Lab., Landstuhl, Fed. Republic Germany, 1982-84; comdr. 10th Mobile Army Surg. Hosp., Ft. Meade, Md., 1984-86; dir. programs and evaluation Army Surgeon Gen., Washington, 1986-89; spl. asst. Office Managed Care, Health Care Fin. Adminstrn., Washington, 1989-90; CFO U.S. Army Health Svcs. Command, San Antonio, 1990-93; dir. capitation financing Office Asst. Sec. Def., Falls Church, Va., 1993-96; ret. U.S. Army, 1996; health care mgmt. cons., 1996—2000; bus. mgr. White Sulphur Springs Hotel, 2000—. Adj. instr. Park Coll., San Antonio, 1976—79, Gadsdon (Ala.) State Jr. Coll., 1973—74, Allegany (Md.) Coll., 1997—98. Vol. income tax asst. IRS, Falls Church, Va., 1986-90, Bedford, Pa., 1994—; unit commr. Boy Scouts Am., Kaiserslautern, Fed. Republic Germany, 1982-84, scoutmaster, Rochester, N.Y., and Augsberg, Fed. Republic Germany, 1965-68. Col. U.S. Army, 1966—. Decorated Def. Superior Svc. medal, Legion of Merit with oak leaf cluster, others; recipient Outstanding Author award Am. Soc. Mil. Comptrollers, 1994. Fellow Am. Coll. Healthcare Execs. (Regents award for leadership in health care 1994); mem. Assn. U.S. Army, Beta Gamma Sigma. Avocations: sailing, skiing. Office: White Sulphur Springs Hotel 4499 Milligans Cove Rd Manns Choice PA 15550

BRAENDLE, DONALD HAROLD, geneticist, researcher; b. Flushing, N.Y., Nov. 8, 1927; s. Harold Anthis and Alouise Dorothy Braendle; m. Carolyn Hartwell; 1 child, Thomas Allen. BA, Rice U., 1955; PhD, Rutgers U., 1957. Rsch. scientist Abbott Labs., North Chicago, Ill. Cpl. U.S. Army. Home: 239 E Washington Ave Lake Bluff IL 60044-2156

BRAEUTIGAM, RONALD RAY, economics educator; b. Tulsa, Apr. 30, 1947; s. Raymond Louis Braeutigam and Loys Ann (Johnson) Henneberger; m. Janette Gail Carlyon, July 27, 1975; children: Eric Zachary, Justin Michael, Julie Ann. BS, U. Tulsa, 1969; MSc, Stanford U., 1971, PhD, 1976. Petroleum engr. Standard Oil Ind., Tulsa, 1966—70; staff economist Office of Telecomm. Policy, Exec. Office of Pres., Washington, 1972—73; from asst. to prof. econs. Northwestern U., Evanston, Ill., 1975—; dir. bus. instns. program, 1995—; Harvey Kapnick prof. Bus. Instns. dept. econs. Northwestern U., Evanston, Ill., 1990—, Charles Deering McCormick prof. tchg. excellence, 1997. Vis. prof. Calif. Inst. Tech., Pasadena, 1978-79. Co-author: The Regulation Game, 1978, Price Level Regulation for Diversified Public Utilities, 1989, Microeconomics: An Integrated Approach, 2002; assoc. editor Jour. Indsl. Econs., Cambridge, Mass., 1987-90; mem. editorial bd. MIT Press Series on Regulation, Cambridge, 1980-90, Jour. Econ. Lit., 1987-91, Rev. Indsl. Orgn., 1991—. Coach Skokie (Ill.) Indians Little League, 1985-91, Evanston Youth Baseball Assn., 1991-96. Grantee, Dept. Transp., NSF, Ameritech, Sloan Found., Mellon Found., others; sr. rsch. fellow Internat. Inst. Mgmt., Berlin, 1982-83, 91. Mem. Am. Econ. Assn., Econometric Soc., Internat. Telecommunications Soc. (bd. dirs. 1990-97), European Econ. Assn., European Assn. for Rsch. in Indsl. Econs. (exec. com. 1992—, pres. 1997-99). Soc. Petroleum Engrs. Avocations: travel, music, German lang., French lang. Home: 731 Monticello St Evanston IL 60201-1745 Office: Northwestern U Dept Econs Evanston IL 60208-0001

BRAFF, HOWARD, brokerage house executive, financial analyst, solar energy consultant; b. Bklyn., July 18, 1952; s. Emanuel and Rose (Schlamberg) B.; m. Cindi Louise Sansone, Mar. 25, 1975; 1 child, Shana. BA in Math. and Psychology summa cum laude, Hofstra U., 1974, MBA in Fin., 1984. Fin. mgr. Save On Oil, Inc., Merrick, NY, 1974-83, Laidlaw, Adams & Peck, Inc., Westbury, NY, 1983-86; ind. investment adv. Merrick, NY, 1977-83; account exec., portfolio mgr. high tech and health care industry analyst Investors Ctr. Inc., Farmingdale, NY, 1986-87; health care industry analyst, portfolio mgr. Strasbourger Pearson Tulcin Wolff Inc., N.Y.C., 1987-88; br. mgr. Olde Discount Corp., Hicksville, NY, 1988-91; pres., chmn., chief exec. officer Save on Discount Stockbrokers Corp., Bellmore, NY, 1991-93; br. mgr. Scottsdale Securities, Inc., Lake Grove, NY, 1993-2000; v.p. Kimberly Securities, Inc., Huntington, NY, 2000—02; solar cons. Prime Energy Techs., Inc., Northport, NY, 2003—. Mem. Phi Beta Kappa. Home: 4 Mews Ct Holtsville NY 11742-1900 Office: 4 Mews Ct Holtsville NY 11742 E-mail: hbraff@optonline.net.

BRAFFORD, WILLIAM CHARLES, lawyer; b. Pike County, Ky., Aug. 7, 1932; s. William Charles and Minnie (Tacket) B.; m. Katherine Jane Prather, Nov. 13, 1954; children— William Charles III, David A. JD, U. Ky., 1957; LLM (fellow), U. Ill., 1958. Bar: Ky. 1957, Ga. 1965, Tax Ct. U.S 1965, Ct. Claims 1965, Ohio 1966, U.S. Ct. Appeals 1966, U.S. Supreme Ct. 1970, Pa. 1973. Trial atty. NLRB, Washington and Cin., 1958-60; atty. Louisville & Nashville R.R. Co., Louisville, 1960-63, So. Bell Telephone Co., Atlanta, 1963-65; asst. gen. counsel NCR Corp., Dayton, Ohio, 1965-72; v.p., sec., gen. counsel Betz Dearborn, inc., Trevose, Pa., 1972-97, ret., 1997. Former dir. Betz Process Chems., Inc., Betz, Ltd. U.K., Betz Paper Chem. Inc., Betz Energy Chems., Inc., Betz S.A. France, B.L. Chems., Inc., Betz GmbH, Germany, Betz Entec, Inc., Betz Ges. GmbH, Austria, Betz NV Belgium, Betz Sud S.p.A., Italy, Betz Internat. Inc., Betz Europe Inc., Primex Ltd., Barbados. Served as 1st lt. C.I.C. AUS, 1954-56. Mem. Am. Soc. Corp. Secs., Nat. Assn. Corp. Dirs., Atlantic Legal Found. Republican. Presbyterian.

BRAGDON, CLIFFORD RICHARDSON, city planner, educator; b. St. Louis, June 30, 1940; s. Dudley Acton and Ruth (Butler) B.; m. Sarah Vaughn, Aug. 21, 1965; children: Katherine, Rachel, Elizabeth. BA, Westminster Coll., 1962; MS, Mich. State U., 1965; PhD, U. Pa., 1970. Urban planner West Philadelphia Cmty. Mental Health Consortium, U. Pa., 1967-69; environ. specialist, acting chief bio-acoustics div. U.S. Environ. Hygiene Agy., Edgewood, Md., 1969-72; prof. dept. city planning Ga. Inst. Tech., Atlanta, 1972-93, asst. dean, dir. of extension, 1979-82, dir. continuing edn., 1982—, assoc. v.p., 1983-90, special asst. office of pres., 1990-93, head sensory spatial systems group, 1993; dean Sch. Aviation and Transp., v.p. and dir. Nat. Aviation and Transp. Ctr., Dowling Coll., 1993-2001, dir., 1999; clin. prof. Sch. of Pub. Health Emory U., Atlanta, 1979—; disting. prof. Fla. Atlantic U., Boca Raton, 2001—. Disting. vis. prof. Fla. Atlantic U., 2001-2002; disting. full prof., dir. ctr. intermodel transp. safety and security, 2002—; adj. prof. Auburn U., 1981—; pres. C.R. Bragdon & Assocs., environ. planning; bd. dirs. Transp. Rsch. Forum, U. Transp. Rsch. Ctr. Region II; chmn. edn. adv. bd. U. Transp. Rsch. Ctr., 1999—. Author: Noise Pollution: The Unquiet Crisis, 1972, Noise Pollution: A Guide to Information Sources, 1979; General Aviation Airport Noise and Land Use Planning, 1979; Municipal Noise Legislation: 1980, Installation Compatability Use Zone Planning: ICUZ Guide, 1987, Airport Land Use Planning and Noise Control, 1997; contbr. chpt. to Environ. Health, 1979, Politics of Neglect, 1974, Airport Noise Planning Transp. Noise Ctrl. Handbook; contbg. editor Sound and Vibration, 1974—; columnist Airport Press, 1994—; cable TV Host Transpo 2000, 1994-97; adv. bd. Airport Noise Reporter; editl. bd. FAA Aviation Topics; chmn. STAR USA; patentee in field. Cons. to office noise abatement U.S. EPA, 1972—, also FAA; constrn. engr. rsch. lab. U.S. Army C.E., 1973—; pres. Friends of Redan, 1985-93; chmn. Specialized Tng. Transp. and Aeronautics Rsch., 1994—; bd. dirs. Opportunity Skyway, Inc., 1998-99, mem. council advs. Nat. Sci. Ctr. for Communications and Electronics, 1984-89; bd. dirs. Network Instrnl. TV, 1983-86; mem. Lincoln Inst. for Land Policy, Harvard U., 1985-93; mem. Intermodal Transp. Task Force, Intelligent Transp. Soc. of Am., 1995—; chmn. Aviation Consortium for Edn. and Tng., 1992—; 1996 Summer Olympics Transp. Atlanta Regional Commn., 1993—. Served to capt. U.S. Army, 1969-72. Fellow Acoustical Soc. Am. N.Y. State (engr. achievement of yr. award 1998); mem. Nat. Acad. Sci. (mem. adv. bd. high speed rail and ITS coms.), Am. Indsl. Hygiene Assn. (pres. Ga. chpt. 1973-74), Am. Nat. Standards Inst. (com. chair 1979-81), Am. Planning Assn. (pres. Ga. chpt. 1979-81), Am. Inst. Cert. Planners, Assn. Energy Engrs. (dir.), ASCE, Transp. Research Bd. (adv. coms. transp. edn., simulation, airport compatibility, acoustics), Nat. Trust Hist. Preservation, Sigma Xi, Omicron Delta Kappa, Kappa Alpha Order. Home: 110 Resort Ln Palm Beach Gardens FL 33418 E-mail: cbragdon@fau.edu.

BRAGDON, PAUL ERROL, educator; b. Portland, Maine, Apr. 19, 1927; s. Errol Freemont and Edith Lillian (Somerville) B.; m. Nancy Ellen Horton, Aug. 14, 1954; children: David Lincoln, Susan Horton, Peter Jefferson. BA magna cum laude, Amherst Coll., 1950, DHL (hon.), 1980; JD, Yale U., 1953; LLD (hon.), Whitman Coll., 1985; DLitt. (hon.), Pacific U., 1988; DHL (hon.), Reed Coll., 1989. Bar: N.Y. 1954. With firm Dewey, Ballantine, Bushby, Palmer & Wood, N.Y.C., 1953-58, Javits, Trubin, Sillcocks, Edelman & Purcell, N.Y.C., 1961-64; counsel Tchrs. Ins. and Annuity Assn. Coll. Retirement Equities Fund, N.Y.C., 1958-61; asst. to mayor City of N.Y., 1964-65, exec. sec. to mayor, 1965, exec. asst. to pres. City Council, 1966-67; v.p. NYU, 1967-71; pres. Reed Coll., Portland, Oreg., 1971-88; pres. emeritus, 1988—; asst. for edn. to gov. State of Oreg., 1988-91; dir. Office Edn. Policy and Planning Oreg., 1990-91; pres. Med. Rsch. Found. Oreg., Portland, 1991-94, Oreg. Grad. Inst. Sci. and Tech., Portland, 1994-98; interim pres. Lewis & Clark Coll., Portland, 2003—. Trustee Amherst Coll., 1972-78, Multnomah (Oreg.) County Libr. Bd., 1994—, The Oreg. Garden, 1994—; The Libr. Found., Multnomah County, 1995—. Recipient Torch of Liberty award Anti-Defamation League of B'nai B'rith, 1985, Presdl. Leadership award Marylhurst U., 1988, award of excellence Kaul Found., 1994, Aubrey Watzek award Lewis and Clark Coll., 1999, Simon Benson award Portland State U., 1999, Libr. Leadership award Libr. Found. Multnomah County, 2001. Mem. Phi Beta Kappa, Phi Beta Kappa Assocs., Beta Theta Pi, Arlington Club, Univ. Club. E-mail: bragdon@admin.ogi.edu.

BRAGG, DARRELL BRENT, nutritionist, consultant; b. Sutton, W.Va., May 24, 1933; s. William H. and Gertrude (Perrine) B.; m. Elizabeth Hosse, Dec. 28, 1957; children: Roger, Larry, Teresa. BSc, W.Va. U., 1959, MSc, 1960; PhD, U. Ark., 1966. Instr. dept. animal sci. U. Ark., Fayetteville, 1965-67; asst. prof. U. Man., Winnipeg, Can., 1967-68, assoc. prof., 1968-70; assoc. prof. dept. poultry sci. U. B.C., Vancouver, Can., 1970-74, prof., head dept., 1976-86; industry cons., Vancouver, 1986-89; nutritionist, dir. quality assurance Rangen Aquaculture Feeds, Buhl, Idaho, 1990-92; sr. rsch. scientist Rangen Aquaculture Rsch. Ctr., Hagerman, Idaho, 1991-92. Indsl. biochem. cons. AB Scis., Payette, Idaho. Contbr. numerous articles to sci. jours. With U.S. Army, 1954-56. Recipient numerous rsch. grants from industry, univs. and govts. Mem. Poultry Sci. Assn. (nat. bd. dirs., v.p., pres. 1978-84), World Poultry Sci. Assn. (bd. dirs., v.p. 1975-86), Sigma Xi, numerous others. Avocations: hunting, fishing, travel. Home: PO Box 38 Payette ID 83661-0038 Office: PO Box 38 Payette ID 83661-0038 E-mail: db1@fmtc.com.

BRAGG, ELLIS MEREDITH, JR., lawyer; b. Washington, Jan. 30, 1947; s. Ellis Meredith Sr. and Lucille (Tingstrum) B.; m. Judith Owens, Aug. 18, 1968; children: Michael Andrew, Jennifer Meredith. BA, King Coll., 1969; JD, Wake Forest U., 1973. Bar: N.C. 1973, U.S. Dist. Ct. (we. and mid. dists.) N.C. 1974, U.S. Ct. Appeals (4th cir.) 1980, U.S. Supreme Ct. 2002. Assoc. Bailey, Brackett & Brackett, P.A., Charlotte, N.C., 1973-76; ptnr. Howard & Bragg, Charlotte, 1976-77, McConnell, Howard, Johnson, Pruitt, Jenkins & Bragg, Charlotte, 1977-79; pvt. practice,, Charlotte, 2002—. Dist. chmn. Mecklenburg County Dems., Charlotte, 1978; coach youth soccer program YMCA, Charlotte, 1982-83; mem. Headstart Policy Council, Charlotte, 1985. Mem. ABA, N.C. Bar Assn., N.C. Acad. Trial Lawyers. Presbyterian. Avocations: reading, jogging, gardening. Home: 6407 Honegger Dr Charlotte NC 28211-4718 Office: 500 E Morehead St Ste 210 Charlotte NC 28202-2694 E-mail: Bragglaw@aol.com.

BRAGG, LINCOLN ELLSWORTH, application developer; b. Buffalo, Jan. 25, 1936; s. Lester William and Helen Aleetah (Rich) B.; m. Martha Lee Householder, June 24, 1961 (div. Sept. 1972); m. Betty Jean Marquiss, Nov. 4, 1972 (div. Mar. 1983); children: Willa Guenevere, Henry Elsworth, Angela Rachael. BS in Elec. Engring., Carnegie-Mellon U., 1959, MS in Math., 1960, PhD in Applied Math., 1964. Rsch. asst. prof. U. Md., College Park, 1963-65; spl. instr. math. U. Minn., Mpls., 1965-67; asst. prof. math. U. Ky., Lexington, 1967-71, Fla. Inst. Tech., Melbourne, 1971-75; programmer, mathematician Sea Automated Data Sys. Agy., Indian Head, Md., 1976-80; sr. mem. tech. staff Computer Scis. Corp., Falls Church, Va., 1980-83; prin. sys. analyst Calspan Corp., Arlington, Va., 1983-85; lead software engr. Quality Sys. Inc., Fairfax, Va., 1985-87; software engring. specialist E-Sys., Garland Divsn., CAC Ops., McLean, 1987—96; lead software engr. Raytheon Corp., CAC Ops., McLean, 1996—. Contbr. chpt. to book and articles to profl. jours. Mem. Am. Assn. Physics Tchrs., Math. Assn. Am., Sigma Xi. Home: 704 Four Mile Rd Alexandria VA 22305-1518

BRAGG, LYNN MUNROE, federal commissioner; b. Ft. Leonard Wood, Mo., June 15, 1954; d. Irving William and Elaine Frances (Heath) Munroe; m. Raymond Frank Bragg, Jr., Aug. 12, 1989; children: Hudson, Rachael, Braxton. BA in English, Mary Washington Coll., 1976; MS in Pub. Rels., Boston U., 1978. Speech and fin. writer Potomac Electric Power Co., Washington, 1978-80; legis. dir., legis. asst. Office of U.S. Senator Malcolm Wallop, Washington, 1981-91; dir. govtl. affairs Edison Electric Inst., Washington, 1991-94; commr. U.S. Internat. Trade Commn., Washington, 1994—, vice chmn., 1996-98, chmn., 1998-2000. Republican. Episcopalian. Avocation: golf. Office: US Internat Trade Commn 500 E St SW Washington DC 20436-0001

BRAGG, MICHAEL ELLIS, lawyer, insurance company executive; b. Holdrege, Nebr., Oct. 6, 1947; s. Lionel C and Frances E (Klinginsmith) Bragg; m. Nancy Jo Aabel, Jan. 19, 1980; children: Brian Michael, Kyle Christopher, Jeffrey Douglas. BA, U. Nebr., 1971, JD, 1975. CLU, ChFC, CPCU; bar: Alaska 1976, Nebr 1976, US Supreme Ct. 2001. Assoc. White & Jones, Anchorage, 1976-77; field rep. State Farm Ins., Anchorage, 1977-79, atty. corp. law dept. Bloomington, Ill., 1979-81, sr. atty., 1981-84, asst. counsel, 1984-86, counsel, 1986-88; asst. v.p., counsel gen. claims dept. State Farm Fire and Casualty Co., Bloomington, 1988-94; v.p., counsel, gen. claims dept. State Farm Ins. Co., Bloomington, Ill., 1994-97, assoc. gen. counsel corp. law dept., 1997—; admitted US Supreme Ct., 2001. Lectr, contbr legal seminars. Contbr, ed: articles to legal and insurnace jour. Pres. McLean County Crime Detection Network, 1988—95. With USNG, 1970—76. Recipient Disting. Legal Svc. Award, Corp. Legal Times, 1998, 2003. Fellow: Am. Bar Found.; mem.: ABA (various offices tort an ins. practices sect. 1981—2003, vice-chmn property ins law com. 1986—91, chmn. ins. coverage litigation com. 1991—92, chmn. task force on ins. staff counsel 2000—02, coun. 2000—03, standing com. on ethics and profl. responsibility 2001), Internat. Assn. Def. Counsel, Fedn. Def. and Corp. Counsel, Def. Rsch. Inst., Am. Corp. Counsel Assn. Republican. Avocations: golf, tennis. Office: State Farm Ins Co Assoc Gen Counsel One State Farm Plz B-3 Bloomington IL 61710 E-mail: buck.bragg.achk@statefarm.com.

BRAGG, ROBERT HENRY, physicist, educator; b. Jacksonville, Fla., Aug. 11, 1919; s. Robert Henry and Lilly Camille (McFarland) B.; m. Violette Mattie McDonald, June 14, 1947; children: Robert Henry, Pamela. BS, Ill. Inst. Tech., 1949, MS, 1951, PhD, 1960. Assoc. physicist rsch. lab. Portland Cement Assn., Skokie, Ill., 1951-56; sr. physicist physics div. Armour Rsch. Found. Ill. Inst. Tech., Chgo., 1956-61; sr. mem., mgr. phys. metallurgy dept. Lockheed Palo Alto Rsch. Lab., Palo Alto, Calif., 1961-69; prof. materials sci. U. Calif., Berkeley, 1969-87, chmn. dept. materials sci. and mineral engring., 1978-81, prof. emeritus, 1987—. Faculty sr. scientist Lawrence Berkeley Lab., 1969-87, emeritus 1987—; mem. materials rsch. adv. com. NSF, 1982-86; program dir. div. materials rsch. U.S. Dept. Energy, 1981-82; cons. IBM, Siemens-Allis, NASA, NIH, NSF, NRC; vis. prof. Musashi Inst. of Tech., Tokyo, 1989, Howard U., 1999; del. 2d Edward Bouchet Internat. Conf., Accra, Ghana, 1990; rschr. Mich. U., Howard U., AT&T Collaborative Access Team, 1999. Contbr. articles to profl. jours. Pres. Palo Alto NAACP, 1967-68. With U.S. Army, 1943-46. Decorated Bronze star (2); recipient Disting. award No. Calif. sect. Am. Inst. Mining and Metall. Engrs., 1970; J. William Fulbright rsch. fellow, Nigeria, 1992-93. Fellow Nat. Soc. of Black Physicists; mem. AAUP, AAAS, Am. Phys. Soc., Am. Ceramics Soc. (chmn. No. Calif. sect. 1980), AIME

(chmn. No. Calif. sect. 1970), Am. Carbon Soc., Am. Soc. Metals, No. Calif. Coun. Black Profl. Engrs., Nat. Tech. Assn., Sigma Xi, Tau Beta Pi, Sigma Pi Sigma., Am. Crystallographic Assn. Democrat. Home: 2 Admiral Dr Ste 373 Emeryville CA 94608-1502 Office: U Calif Dept Materials Sci & Engring Berkeley CA 94720-0001 E-mail: petebragg@aol.com., rbragg@socrates.berkeley.edu.

BRAGIEL, SUE A. social work educator, clinical practitioner; m. Raymond M. Bragiel. BA, Hanover Coll., 1957; MA, Ind. U., 1959. Lic. clin. social worker. Past field instr. Ind. U. Sch. Social Work, Indpls.; clinician Cmty. Hosp. Indpls. Mem. Nat. Assn. Social Workers (past mem. com. on inquiry).

BRAGLE, GEORGE W. criminal justice educator; b. Troy, N.Y., Apr. 4, 1934; s. George W. and Helen C. (Wallace) B.; m. Kathleen E. Burns, Nov. 21, 1970; children: Margaret H., James, John A. AB, St. Bonaventure U., 1955; MS, Siena U., 1958; EdD, SUNY, Albany, 1969, MA, 1984, Colgate, Rochester, N.Y., 1995. Cert. tchr., N.Y. Tchr., chair Waterford (N.Y.) Pub. Sch., 1957-62; prof. Hudson Valley C.C., Troy, 1962-63; prof., chair Coll. Saint Rose, Albany, 1963-73; prof. Empire State Coll., Albany, 1973-98. Cons. N.Y. State Edn. Dept., Albany, Albany-Troy-Schenectady Police Depts., 1993—, Police Fedn. of Eng. and Wales, Israeli Nat. Police. Author: Introduction to Criminal Justice, 1978, 85, 92, Introduction to Juvenile Delinquency, 1983; contbr. poetry to jours. Adv. bd. St. Peter Hosp., Albany, 1982-92, N.Y. State Sen. com. aging, 1987-90, Com. on Crime Victims, Albany, 1993—. Fulbright scholar, 1960; grantee CEEB, Georgetown U., Cornell U. Home: PO Box 401 Slingerlands NY 12159-0401

BRAGONIER, JOHN ROBERT, obstetrician-gynecologist; b. Cedar Falls, Iowa, July 4, 1937. MD, U. Nebr., 1964. Cert. in ob-gyn. Intern U. Nebr. Hosp., Omaha, 1964-65, resident, 1965-66, Jeff Hosp., Phila., 1966-68; attending Harbor-UCLA Med. Ctr., Torrance, Calif., 1970—2002, ret., 2002; dir. maternal health and family planning programs L.A. County Dept. Health Svcs. Adj. prof. ob-gyn. UCLA, 1982—. Fellow ACOG; mem. APHA, Alpha Omega Alpha.

BRAHA, THOMAS I. business executive; b. Austin, Tex., Sept. 3, 1947; s. Jacob and Valentine (Capone) B.; m. Nancy Elizabeth Rowe, Mar. 31, 1973 (div.); children: Nancy Elizabeth, Jeanne Valentine, Travis Ian. BSME, U. Tex., 1969; MBA, Temple U., 1971; postgrad., NYU, 1971-73. Engr. Davis Electronics, Inc., Austin, 1967, Whirlpool Corp., Evansville, Ind., 1968; project engr. ITE Imperial Corp., Phila., 1969-71; sr. supply analyst Mobil Oil Corp., N.Y.C., 1971-74; pres. Western Hemisphere Bulk Oil (U.S.A.), Inc., N.Y.C., 1974-75. Chmn. bd., CEO Braha Holding Corp., Braha Oil Corp. and Subs., Braha Estates, Inc., Braha Farms, Braha Profit and Pension Trusts; adj. faculty The Wharton Sch., U. Pa., 1996-2002. Active Bryn Mawr Presbyn. Ch. Mem. ASME, Am. Mgmt. Assn., Am. Petroleum Inst., Inst. Petroleum (U.K.), Nat. Petroleum Refining Assn., Phila. Country Club. Office: Braha Holding Co PO Box 390 Bryn Mawr PA 19010-0390

BRAHAM, DELPHINE DORIS, accountant, government official; b. L'Anse, Mich., Mar. 16, 1946; d. Richard Andrew and Viola Mary Aho; m. John Emerson Braham, Sept. 23, 1967 (div. Aug. 1988); children: Tammy, Debra, John Jr. BS summa cum laude, Drury Coll., 1983; M in Mgmt., Webster U., St. Louis, 1986. Bookkeeper Cmty. Mental Health Ctr., Marquette, Mich., 1966-68; acctg. technician St. Joseph Hosp., Parkersburg, W.Va., 1972-74; material mgr. U.S. Army, Ft. Leonard Wood, Mo., 1982-86; acct., 1986-92; supervisory acct. Dept. Def., Indpls., 1992—. Instr., adj. faculty Columbia Coll., 1987-92, Park Coll., 1988-92. Leader Girl Scouts U.S., Williamstown, W.Va., 1972-74, Hanau, Germany, 1977-79. Mem. AAUW (treas. Waynesville br. 1986-90), Am. Soc. Mil. Comptrs., NAFE, Assn. Govt. Accts., Waynesville Bus. and Profl. Women's Orgn. Home: 2752 Pawnee Dr Indianapolis IN 46229-1418

BRAHAM, RANDOLPH LEWIS, political science educator; b. Bucharest, Romania, Dec. 20, 1922; came to U.S., 1948, naturalized, 1953; m. Elizabeth Sommer, Dec. 15, 1954; children: Steven, Robert. BA, CCNY, 1948, MS, 1949; PhD, New Sch. for Social Research, 1952. Research assoc. YIVO-Inst. for Jewish Research, N.Y.C., 1954-59; faculty CCNY, N.Y.C., 1959—, prof. polit. sci., 1971—, disting. prof., 1987—, disting. prof. emeritus, 1992—, chmn. dept. polit. sci., 1971-81. Dir. Inst. for Holocaust Studies, Grad. Ctr. CUNY, 1980—; faculty Fairleigh Dickinson U., Hofstra U., Hunter Coll., 1956-59 Author: The Politics of Genocide, 2 vols., 1981, 2d rev. edit., 1994, The Hungarian Labor Service System, 1977, Hungarian Jewish Studies, 3 vols., 1966-73, Soviet Government and Politics, 1965, Human Rights, 1979; writer, editor, contbr. to books in field. Democrat. Home: 11407 Union Tpke Flushing NY 11375-6850 Office: CUNY Graduate Ctr New York NY 10016

BRAHMA, CHANDRA SEKHAR, civil engineering educator; b. Calcutta, India, Oct. 5, 1941; came to U.S., 1963; s. Nalinia Kanta and Uma Rani (Bose) B.; m. Purnima Sinha, Feb. 18, 1972; children: Charanjit, Barunashish. B in Engring., Calcutta U., 1962; MS, Mich. State U., 1965; PhD, Ohio State U., 1969. Registered profl. engr. Calif., Utah, N.H., Tex., Wis. Asst. engr. Pub. Works Dept., Calcutta, 1962-63; rsch. asst. Mich. State U., East Lansing, 1963-65; teaching and rsch. assoc. Ohio State U., Columbus, 1965-69; project engr. Frank H. Lehr Assocs., East Orange, N.J., 1969-70; sr. soils engr. John G. Reutter Assocs., Camden, N.J., 1970-72; asst. prof. Worcester (Mass.) Poly. Inst., 1972-74; prin. soils engr. Daniel, Mann, Johnson & Mendenhall, Balt., 1974-79; sr. engr. Sverdrup Corp., St. Louis, 1979-80, cons., 1980—; prof. Calif. State U., Fresno, 1980—2002, prof. emeritus, 2002—. Cons. Expert Resources, Inc., Peoria Heights, Ill., 1981—, The Twining Labs., Inc., Fresno, 1982—, Law Offices Marderosian and Swanson, Fresno, 1985—, Law Offices Hurlbutt, Clevenger, Long and Vortmann, Visalia, Calif., 1988—, Tech. Adv. Svcs. for Attys., Blue Bell, Pa., 1992—. Author: Fundaciones y Mechanica de Suelos, 1986; contbr. articles to profl. jours. Head sci. judge Calif. Cen. Valleys Sci. and Engring. Fairs, Fresno, 1988-2002. Recipient Outstanding Prof. of Yr. award Calif. State U., 1989, Halliburton award Calif. State U., 1991, Calif. Ctrl. Valley Outstanding Profl. Engr. award Calif. Soc. Profl. Engrs., 1993, Disting. Svc. award, 1994, Claude C. Laval Jr. award Innovative Tech. and Rsch. Calif. State U., 1991, 92, Portrait of Success award KSEE 24, Fresno, Calif., 1997, Std. of Excellence award Tau Beta Pi, 1997, Outstanding Prof. award Tau Beta Pi, 1998, Outstanding Prof. award NSPE, 1998; Brahma St. named in City of Bakersfield, Calif., 1989; Fulbright scholar, 1984; Hugh B. William fellow, Assn. Drilled Shaft Contractors, 1986, others. Fellow ASCE (v.p. 1983-84, pres. 1984-85, Outstanding Engr. award 1985, Disting Svc. award, 1986, Outstanding Prof. award 1985, Edmund Friedman Profl. Recognition award 1993); mem. ASTM, Am. Soc. Engring. Edn. (AT&T Found. award 1991, Outstanding Tchg. award 1997, AT ANDT Found. award for excellence in tchg. and rsch. 1991), Rotary (chair Clovis club 1986—, chair pub. rels. 1987, chair youth svcs. 1989, bd. dirs. 1989). Democrat. Hindu. Avocations: swimming, tennis, music, reading. Home and Office: 561 Houston Ave Clovis CA 93611-7032 E-mail: chandrab@csufresno.edu.

BRAHMBHATT, SUDHIRKUMAR, chemical company executive; b. Dabhoi, Gujarat, India, Apr. 4, 1951; came to U.S., 1973; s. Ramanlal Kalidas and Kamalaben Motilal Barot Brahmbhatt; m. Ashaben Amarsingh, May 22, 1977; children: Tejal Sudhirkumar, Nisha Sudhirkumar. B in Chem. Engring., Nadiad Inst. Tech., India, 1973; M in Chem. Engring., Steven Inst. Tech., 1975; MBA in Internat. Mgmt. and Mktg., Fairleigh Dickinson U., 1982; PhD in Chem. Engring., Kennedy Western U., 1991. Rsch. asst. Stevens Inst. Tech., Hoboken, N.J., 1975-77; chem. engr. Exxon Co. U.S.A., Linden, N.J., 1977-79; sr. process engr. Air Products and Chemicals, Inc., Allentown, Pa., 1979-84; applications engr. MG Industries divsn. of Hoechst, Valley Forge, Pa., 1984-87, sr. project engr., 1987-89, mgr. chems. group, 1989-92, head R&D dept., 1992-96; owner Ashutej Co., Trexlertown, Pa., 1982-84; mgr. chem. group MG Industries divsn. of Hoechst, Valley Forge, 1996-98, team leader global pulp and paper tech., 1996—, dir. tech. and team leader global R&D, 1998—2001, sr. group mgr., 2001—. Patentee in environ. and chem. engring. fields; contbr. articles to profl. jours. Dir., host radio program Music of India, Sta. WMUH, Allentown, 1981-91, Sta. KDHX, St. Louis, 1992-2000; pres. Exxon Volleyball League, Linden, 1978-79; pres. Bal Vihar Assn., Hindu Temple Soc., Allentown, Pa., 1989-91; founder, pres. Bal Vihar (Children's Ethnic Sch.) of St. Louis, 1992—; pres.-elect Lafayette H.S.Sch. Orch. Parents Assn., Ballwin, Mo., 1999—. Recipient Merit cert. Poly-Olefins Industries Ltd., Bombay, India, 1972. Mem. AIChE, TAPPI, Am. Powder Metallurgy Inst. (chmn. Phila. sec. 1987-88), Am. Chem. Soc., Am. Ceramic Soc., Am. Soc. Metals. Avocations: cultural programs, radio, overseas travel. Home: 1700 Countrytop Ct Glencoe MO 63038-1446 Office: MG Industries PO Box 3039 5 Great Valley Pkwy Ste 100 Malvern PA 19355-0739 E-mail: Sudhir_Brahmbhatt@mgind.com.

BRAHMS, THOMAS WALTER, engineering institute executive; b. Brookline, Mass., Mar. 12, 1945; s. Samuel David and Barbara Ann (Robinson) B.; m. Virginia Wahlen, Dec. 30, 1966; children— Theodore S., Anna Elisabeth. BS in Civil Engring, Northeastern U., 1971. Transp. planner Boston Redevel. Authority, 1965-69; sr. traffic engr. aide, traffic and parking dept. Town of Brookline, 1970-71; project engr. (traffic) Tippetts, Abbett, McCarthy & Stratton, Brookline, 1971-73; dir. tech. affairs Inst. Transp. Engrs., Arlington, Va., 1973-76, exec. dir., 1976—; mini-bus officer Reston Commuter Bus, Inc., Va., 1973-76, 77, v.p., 1976-77, 78-79, pres., 1979. V.p. Ward Six Civic Assn., West Somerville, Mass., 1972-73; bd. dirs. Reston Internal Bus System, 1977. Pres. Fairway Cluster Assn., Reston, 1973-75; coach Reston Soccer Assn., 1975-76; mem. Reston Homeowners Assn. Archtl. Bd. Rev., 1977, Inst. Transport Engrs., 2000; rep. Transp. Research Bd., 1976—; sec. Theodore M. Matson Meml. Award Com., 1974—; trustee Transp. Mus., Boston, 1981-84; mem. tech. edn. adv. coun. Fairfax County, 1990-93; sec. Intelligent Vehicle Hwy. Soc. Am., 1991-92, dir., 1991—; bd. regents Eno Ctr. for Transp. Leadership Devel., 1992—. Recipient Burton W. Marsh award for Disting. Svc. Inst. Transportation Engrs., 1988, Adminstr.'s award for outstanding svc. Urban Mass Transp. Adminstrn., U.S. Dept. Transp., 1988 Mem.: ASCE, ITS World Congress (bd. dirs.), Roadway Safety Found. (rsch. subcom. 1995—), World Interchange Network (bd. dirs. 1995—99), Rd. Gang, Am. Soc. Assn. Execs., Coun. Engring. and Sci. Soc. Execs., Inst. Transp. Engrs. (hon.). Office: 1099 14th St NW Ste 300 W Washington DC 20005-3438

BRAHMS, WILLIAM BERNARD, librarian, writer; b. Camden, N.J., Oct. 1, 1966; s. William Arthur and Jane Dilks Brahms; m. Gina-Marie Lugo, Dec. 7, 1996; children: Matthew Frederick, Giovanna Elizabeth. BA with honors, Rutgers Coll., 1989; MLS, Rutgers U., 1993. Cert. profl. libr. N.J. State Dept. Edn., 1993. Libr. intern South Brunswick (N.J.) Pub. Libr., 1992—93; refrence libr. Franklin Twp. Pub. Libr., Somerset, NJ, 1993—95, sr. reference libr., 1995—99, head adult svcs. (reference), 1999—. Com. mem. N.J. Digitization Hwy., Trenton, Highlands Regional Libr. Coop. Info. Svcs. Com., Denville, NJ; twp. historian Twp. of Franklin, Somerset. Author: (book) Images of America: Franklin Township, 1997 (Mayor's Commendation, Franklin Twp., 1998), Franklin Township, Somerset County, NJ: A History, 1998 (Mayor's Commendation, Franklin Twp., 1999); editor: Cap & Skull Centennial History and Biographical Directory, 2000. Bd. mem. Friends of the Franklin Twp. Pub. Libr., Somerset, 1993—2003; mem. Meadows Found., Somerset, 1998, Raritan-Millstone Heritage Alliance, Somerset; bd. mem. Alumni Assn. of the Epsilon Chpt. of Delta Phi (St. Elmo's Club of Rutgers U.), New Brunswick, 1994—2003, Cap and Skull Soc. Alumni Assn., New Brunswick, 1995—2003. Named Author of the Yr., Marconi Found., 1999; recipient Cap & Skull Soc., Rutgers Coll., 1988; Henry Rutgers scholar, 1989. Mem.: ALA, Phi Eta Sigma, N.J. Libr. Assn., Omicron Delta Epsilon, Phi Beta Kappa, Delta Phi. Home: 17 Crammer Ln Hillsborough NJ 08844 Office: Franklin Twp Pub Libr 485 DeMott Ln Somerset NJ 08873 Personal E-mail: gmandwb@patmedia.net. E-mail: wbrahms@franklintwp.org.

BRAIBANTI, RALPH JOHN, political scientist, educator; b. Danbury, Conn., June 29, 1920; s. Daniel Vincent and Jane Helena B.; m. Lucy Kauffman, Feb. 19, 1943; children— Claire, Ralph Lynn. BS, Western Conn. State U., 1941, LHD (hon.), 1995; A.M., Syracuse U., 1947, PhD, 1949. Asst. prof. polit. sci. Kenyon Coll., 1949-52, assoc. prof., 1952-53; adv., civil adminstr. Ryuku Islands, 1950; adj. lectr. George Washington U., 1951; asst. dir. Am. Polit. Sci. Assn., Washington, 1950-51; cons. Govtl. Affairs Inst., 1950-51; assoc. prof. polit. sci. Duke U., Durham, N.C., 1953-58, prof., 1958-68, James B. Duke prof. polit. sci., 1968-90, James B. Duke prof. emeritus, 1990—; vis. asst. prof. Trinity Coll., 1952; adj. lectr. Am. U., 1956; vis. asst. prof. Utica Coll., 1949; dir. Islamic and Arabian devel. studies, 1977-89. Scholar-in-residence Rockefeller Found., Bellagio Ctr., Italy, 1967; cons. AID, 1958-59, Ford Found., 1972, UN, 1974, Govt. Saudi Arabia, 1974—, UNESCO, 1977, Islamic Secretariat, 1980, World Bank, 1987; vis. prof. U. Kuwait, 1984; advisor on adminstrv. reform Pakistan, Malaysia, South Africa, Lebanon, Morocco, Saudi Arabia, Bangladesh; cons.; bd. advisors Nat. Coun. U.S.-Arab Rels., Moroccan-Am. Found., Mid East Policy Coun.; trustee Am. Inst. Pakistan Studies, Am. Inst. Yemeni Studies; bd. dirs. U.S. Mid-East Performing Arts Coun., 1995—; chmn. nat. selection com. Joseph J. Malone Postdoctoral Fellowships in Arabian Affairs; King Faisal Disting. Internat. lectr. Am.-Arab Affairs Coun., 1989-91; mem. internat. adv. com. Global Forum of Spiritual and Parliamentary Leaders on Human Survival, 1996—. Author: Research on the Bureaucracy of Pakistan, 1966, The Nature and Structure of the Islamic World, 1995, revised edit., 2000, Chief Justice Cornelius of Pakistan: Analysis, Letters, Speeches, 1999; co-author, editor: Political and Administrative Development, 1969, Pakistan: The Long View, 1976, Asian Bureaucratic Systems Emergent from the British Imperial Tradition, 1966, Tradition, Values and Socio-Economic Development, 1961, Administration and Economic Development in India, 1963, Evolution of Pakistan's Administrative System: The Collected Papers of Ralph Braibanti, 1987; co-compiler, co-editor: (with Lucy Kauffman Braibanti) The Collected Poems of Charles Henry Kauffman, 2001; gen. editor 7 vol. series on comparative adminstrn., 1968-73; bd. editors Middle East Policy, Studies in Contemporary Islam, Jour. South Asian and Mid. Ea. Studies, Comparative Politics, Politikon, Asian Forum, Jour. Pakistan Studies, Internat. Jour. Islamic and Arabic Studies. Served to capt. U.S. Army, 1942-47. Recipient citation outstanding prof. Duke Student Assn., 1972, alumni award disting. undergrad. teaching, 1979; Maxwell fellow Syracuse U., 1949, Ford Found. fellow, 1955-56, Social Sci. Rsch. Coun. fellow, 1955-56; decorated commendation medal U.S. Army, 1947. Fellow Internat. Assn. Mid. Ea. Studies (mem. exec. com. 1991—); mem. Internat. Studies Assn.-South (pres.), Am. Inst. Pakistan Studies (founding pres. 1975-77, pres. 1986-90), Internat. Cultural Soc. Korea (hon.), Am. Council for Study Islamic Socs. (bd. dirs.) Home and Office: 3805 Darby Rd Durham NC 27707-5004 *The encouragement of a profound understanding of seemingly divergent cultural systems is of critical importance. This must embrace helping newly-developed political systems appreciate their own cultural values. Only the strength of such pride can withstand the dynamic interventionism which characterizes the relations of transitorily dominant superpowers and weak, newer political entities.*

BRAID, FREDERICK DONALD, lawyer; b. N.Y.C., Aug. 10, 1946; s. Donald Michael and Margaret Anna (Fluty) B.; m. Eleanor Mae Friedman, Oct. 23, 1980; children: Andrew Harris, Roy Leal, Josh Perry, David Barnett, Steven Gabriel. BS in Econs., St. John's U., Jamaica, N.Y., 1968; JD, St. John's U., Bklyn., 1971; LLM, NYU, 1979. Bar: N.Y. 1972, U.S. Dist. Ct. (so. and ea. dists.) N.Y. 1973, U.S. Ct. Appeals (2d cir.) 1973, (D.C. and 4th cirs.) 1997, U.S. Supreme Ct. 1975. Assoc. Rains & Pogrebin, Mineola and N.Y.C., N.Y., 1971-77, ptnr., 1978-99; bd. dirs. Rains & Pogrebin, P.C., Mineola and N.Y.C., N.Y.; ptnr. Holland and Knight LLP, 2000—. Mem. adv. bd. NYU Sch. Law Ctr. for Labor and Employment Law, 1997—. Mng. editor St. John's Law Rev., 1970-71; contbr. articles to profl. jours. Served to capt. USAR, 1972-80. St. Thomas More scholar, St. John's U. Sch. Law, 1968-71. Mem. ABA, N.Y. Bar Assn., Omicron Delta Epsilon, Delta Mu Delta. Home: 17 E 96th St New York NY 10128-0783 Office: Holland & Knight LLP 195 Broadway New York NY 10007-3100

BRAILEY, SUSAN LOUISE, quality analyst, educator; b. Omaha, Aug. 28, 1939; d. James Burt and Helen Frances B.; m. Hugh Pelham Whitt, Dec. 29, 1990. BS in Edn. with distinction, U. Nebr., Omaha, 1961; postgrad., U. Nebr., Lincoln, 1977-79; MA in Comm., U. Cin., 1970. Cert. quality analyst Quality Assurance Inst., Orlando, Fla. Instr., dir. debate Omaha Pub. Schs., 1965-67; tchr. Walnut Hills H.S., Cin., 1967-69, U. Cin., 1969-72, U. Nebr., Lincoln, 1978; dir. MIS Wayne (Nebr.) State Coll., 1979-80; sr. tech. writer, analyst 1st Data Resources, Omaha, 1981-82, supr. documentation, 1982-83, tng. specialist, 1983-85, sr. analyst quality assurance, 1988-92; tng. specialist Enron Corp., Omaha, 1985-86, sr. analyst quality assurance Houston, 1986-88. Mem. Dem. Nat. Com., 1995—, Dem. Congl. Campaign Com., 2000—. Mem. AAUW, Arthritis Found., Lupus Found, Pi Kappa Delta, Phi Delta Kappa, Phi Delta Gamma. Congregationalist. Avocations: reading, antiques, bridge, music, politics. Home: 9530 Davenport St Omaha NE 68114-3872

BRAILSFORD, JUNE EVELYN, musician, educator; b. Wiergate, Tex., Apr. 11, 1939; d. Lonnie and Jessie (Coleman) Samuel; m. Marvin Delano Brailsford, Dec. 23, 1960; children: Marvin Delano, Keith, Cynthia. BA in Music, Prairie View A & M U., Tex., 1960; MA in Music, Trenton (N.J.) State Coll., 1981; postgrad., Jacksonville State U., summer 1971, Lamar U., Beaumont, Tex., summer 1963, Juilliard Sch., summer 1994. Jr. high music tchr. Lincoln Jr. High Sch., Beaumont, Tex., 1960-61; organist/choir dir. various chs., various locations, 1962-82; dir. adult edn. Morris County Human Resources, Dover, N.J., 1980-82; band and choral dir. Zweibruecken Am. High Sch., Ger., 1982-84. Vocal soloist and pianist Am. Women's Activities, Ger., 1986-87; dir. female choir U.S. Army War Coll., 1978-79, U.S. Air Force Skylarks, Sembach, Ger., 1976-77. Commr., Beaumont (Tex.) Hist. Landmark Commn., 2003; adv. bd., Conv. and Visitors Bur., Beaumont, 2003; hostess/fundraiser Quad City Symphony Guild 75th Ur., Rock Island, 1989, Links, Inc. Beautillion Scholarship, 1989, Installation Vol. Coord. Cons., Ft. Belvoir, Va., 1990-91; minister music First Bapt. Ch., Vienna, Va., 1995; bd. dirs. S.E. Tex. Cmty. Devel. Corp.; active numerous charitable orgns. Recipient Molly Pitcher award U.S. Army F.A. Officers, 1986, Outstanding Civilian Svc. award Dept. Army, 1990, Disting. Civilian Svc. award Dept. Army, 1992. Mem. NAACP (life mem.), Rock Island Arsenal Hist. Soc. (hon. mem.), The Links, Inc., Just Good Friends, Inc., Bible Study Fellowship Internat. Baptist. Avocations: bridge, bid whist, traveling, reading. Home: 7445 Prestwick Cir Beaumont TX 77707

BRAIN, GEORGE BERNARD, university dean; b. Thorp, Wash., Apr. 25, 1920; s. George and Alice Pearl (Ellison) B.; m. Harriet Gardinier, Sept. 28, 1940; children— George Calvin, Marylou. BA, Central Wash. State U., Ellensburg, 1946, MA, 1949; Ed.D., Columbia Tchrs. Coll., 1957; postgrad., U. Wash., Wash. State U., Harvard U., U. Colo., Stanford U. Tchr. math. and sci. Yakima (Wash.) secondary schs., 1946-49; instr. Central Wash. State Coll., 1949-50; elementary sch. prin. Ellensburg, 1950-51; successively elementary sch. prin., asst. supt. schs., supt. schs. Bellevue, Wash., 1951-59; vis. prof. Central Wash. State Coll., 1953, Wash. State U., 1959, U. Md., 1964; supt. schs. Balt., 1959-66; dean Coll. Edn., also dir. summer schs. Wash. State U., Pullman, 1965-85; fellow Danforth Found., 1986—. Lectr. Columbia, U. Conn., Harvard, U. Ga., U. Del., Johns Hopkins, Morgan U., U. Okla., Towson State U., Stanford, Wash. U.; chmn. Fulbright Group Western European Seminar Comparative Edn., 1959; chmn. ednl. policies commn. N.E.A.; ednl. cons. (Office Edn.), 1962— ; cons. Ednl. Testing Service, Princeton, N.J., 1964-67; dir. Intext Pub. Inc., Scranton, Pa., Worldbook-Childcraft (Scott-Fetzer); bd. dirs. Md. Acad. Sci., 1960-65, Nat. Edn. Found., Field Enterprises Ednl. Corp., 1970—, Pacific Am. Inst., 1977— Mem. editorial adv. bd.: Scholastics Publs, 1963—, Am. Sch. and Univ, 1960-64, Education, USA, 1964-71; mem. editorial bd.: World Book, 1966—, Jour. Tchr. Edn, 1966— . Served with USNR, 1941- 42; Served with USMCR, 1942-46; maj. lt. col. Res. Recipient Disting. Svc. award Wash. State Jr. Assn. Commerce, 1956, Disting. Svc. award in edn. NCCJ, 1963, Disting. Alumnus award Cen. Wash. U., 1989; named Man of Year Met. Civic Assn. Balt., 1962; Fulbright scholar, 1959; library named in his honor, Wash. State U., 1987. Life mem. Am. Assn. Sch. Adminstrs. (exec. com. 1964-66, pres. 1965), NEA; hon. life mem. Wash. State Assn. Sch. Adminstrs. (pres. 1959), Md. Assn. Sch. Adminstrs., Nat. Congress P.T.A.; mem. Wash. Edn. Assn. (pres. dept. adminstrn. and supervision 1957), AAAS (exec. com. commn. elementary and secondary sci. 1963-66), Assn. Supervision and Curriculum Devel., Univ. Council Ednl. Adminstrn., Nat. Joint Council Econ. Edn. (exec. com. 1963—), Nat. Conf. Profs. Ednl. Adminstrn., AAUP, Internat. Platform Assn., Nat. Council for Edn. in Health Professions, Nat. Acad. Sch. Execs., Nat. Council Fgn. Study League, Exec. Hall Fame, Phi Delta Kappa, Kappa Delta Pi. Lodges: Rotary (dir. Balt. 1964-65). Presbyterian.

BRAIN, JESSE, manufacturing executive; b. N.Y.C., Nov. 12, 1921; s. David Brain and Anna Goro; m. Marie Evelyn Richter, Mar. 17, 1951 (dec. Oct. 2002); children: Stephen L., Kenneth A., Dion T., Jeffrey S., John R., Cynthia M. LLB, Blackstone Sch. Law, 1963; MS in Indsl. Mgmt., Bklyn. Poly., 1974. Engr., designer Combustion Engring., N.Y.C., 1948—51; pvt. practice mfg. engring. cons. Farmingdale, NY, 1951—53; prodn. mgr. Republic Aviation, Farmingdale, 1953—66; dep. dir. planning and control Grumman Aerospace, Bethpage, NY, 1966—71; dir. ops. Fairchild Industries, Manhattan Beach, 1971—75; gen. mgr. fabrication Skikorsky Aircraft, Stratford, Conn., 1975—99. Author: Aircraft Parts Manufacturing, 1955, Production Control Management, 1985, Historical Aircraft of WWII, 2002. Skipper Sea Scouts Am., N.Y.C., 1938—51; vol. docent Palm Springs (Calif.) Air Mus., 1996—. With USNR, 1943—46. Named Vol. of Yr., Palm Springs Air Mus., 2003. Fellow: ASME. Avocation: writing. Home: 1924 Navajo Dr Palm Springs CA 92264

BRAIN, JOSEPH DAVID, biomedical scientist; b. Paterson, N.J., Jan. 20, 1940; married, 1961; 3 children. SM, Harvard U., 1962, SMHyg, 1963, SDHyg, 1966. Rsch. assoc. in physiology Harvard U., Boston, 1966—68, from asst. prof. to assoc. prof., 1968—78; prof. physiology Harvard Sch. Pub. Health, Cambridge, Mass., 1978—, Cecil K. and Philip Drinker prof. environ. physiology, dir. Harvard Pulmonary Specialized Ctr. Rsch., 1977—96, dir. respiratory biol. program, 1981—93, dir. physiology program, 1993—98, chair dept. environ. health, 1990—. Mem. com. Cardiovasc. and Pulmonary Study Sect. NIH, 1975-79, program project rsch. rev. com. Nat. Heart, Lung and Blood Inst., 1980-83; bd. sci. counsellors Nat. Inst. Occupl. Safety and Health, 1992-96; dir. NIEHS Ctr. Environ. Health. Bd. trustees Taylor U., 1984—. Fellow AAAS, Am. Physiol. Soc., Am. Thoracic Soc., Reticuloendothelial Soc., Sigma Xi. Office: Harvard U Sch Pub Health 665 Huntington Ave Boston MA 02115-6021

BRAINARD, MELISSA, accountant; b. Buffalo, Jan. 11, 1969; d. Peter Anthony and Mary Agnes (Lazarus) Arena; m. Kevin Joseph Brainard, Sept. 25, 1993; children: Jacob Leon, Zachary Martin. BS, SUNY, Buffalo, 1991. CPA, N.Y., 1993. From staff mem. to mgr. KPMG, Buffalo, 1991-97; CFO Goodwill Industries Western N.Y., 1997-98; mgr. Deloitte & Touche, Buffalo, 1999—2002; cons. Albright-Knox Art Gallery, Buffalo, 2002—. Avocations: animals, family, collecting baskets. E-mail: mbrainard@albrightknox.org.

BRAINARD, PAUL HENRY, musicologist, retired music educator; b. Binghamton, N.Y., Apr. 18, 1928; s. George E. and Frances (Weinhauer) B. BA, U. Rochester, 1949, MA, 1951; postgrad., Heidelberg (Germany) U., 1954; PhD, Goettingen (Germany) U., 1960. Research asst. Deutsches Musikgeschichtliches Archiv, Kassel, Germany, 1960; instr. music Ohio State U., 1960-61; faculty Brandeis U., Waltham, Mass., 1961-81, prof. music, 1974-81, chmn. Sch. Creative Arts, 1965-68, chmn. dept. music, 1969-72, 75-77; prof. music Princeton (N.J.) U., 1981-87, Yale Inst. Sacred Music, 1987-93; ret., 1993. Spl. research music history. Author: Le sonate per violino di Giuseppe Tartini, 1975; editor: Neue Bach-Ausgabe, Vols. II/7, 1977, II/8, 1979, I/16, 1981, Cantatas, Easter and Ascension Oratorios, Italienische Violinmusik der Barockzeit, Vols. I, 1987, II, 1988; contbr. articles to profl. jours. Served with AUS, 1951-53. Home: 7 Dover Dr Englewood FL 34223-4637

BRAINARD, WILLIAM CRITTENDEN, economist, educator, university official; b. Jersey City, July 2, 1935; s. William E. and Eleanor (Holston) B.; m. Ellen Rawlings, Oct. 18, 1958; children: David, Michael, Daniel. BA, Oberlin Coll., 1957; MA, Yale U., 1959, PhD, 1963. Asst. prof. econs. Yale U., 1962-66, assoc. prof., 1966-69, prof., 1969—, provost, 1981-86, chmn. econs. dept., 1992-97; research assoc. Brookings Instn., 1965-66. Dir. Cowles Found., New Haven, 1971—73, New Haven, 1976—81, chmn. dept. econs., 1992—97; chmn. Fed. Reserve Bank, Boston, 1997—2002. Editor: Brookings Papers on Econ. Activity, 1980— ; contbr. articles to profl. jours. Fellow Econometric Soc.; mem. Am. Econ. Assn. Home: 207 Everit St New Haven CT 06511-1335 Office: Yale U Dept Econs PO Box 208268 New Haven CT 06520-8268

BRAINERD, RICHARD CHARLES, human resources executive, consultant, educator; b. L.A., Dec. 22, 1944; s. Calvin Richard and Charlotte Louise (Roethe) B.; m. Phyllis Jean Cottingham Wentzel, July 14, 1966, (div. Dec. 1980); children: Bret, Staci; m. Mary Keith Knopp, Mar. 31, 1984; children: Andrew, Mary Angela. BS in Bus. and Econs., U. Wis., 1968; grad. leadership devel. program, Ctr. for Creative Leadership, Greensboro, N.C., 1985. Pers. analyst Wis. Bur. Personnel, Madison, 1968-74; dir. pers., asst. adminstr. for adminstrn. Wis. Dept. Justice, Madison, 1974-80; dep. commr. pers. Minn. Dept. Employee Rels., St. Paul, 1980-85; dir. pers. Ramsey County, St. Paul, Minn., 1985-97; human resources dir. Met. Coun., St. Paul, 1997—. Instr. U.

Minn. Carlson Sch. Mgmt. Employer Edn. Svc., Mpls., 1985—; co-chair, mem. exec. bd. Twin Cities Area Labor-Mgmt. Coun., Mpls., 1994—; advisor Inst. for Labor Mgmt. Studies, White Bear Lake, Minn., 1997; speaker on human rels., expert witness, 1985—, Coach Mahtomedi (Minn.) Youth Baseball Assn., 1992-97; vice chair Bd. of Pub. Works, Madison, Wis., 1979-80; vice chair, mem. fin. com. City of Mahtomedi, 1994—; pres. Riverside Lions, St. Paul, Minn., 1995-98. Mem. Pub. Employer Labor Rels. Assn., Minn. Pub. Employer Labor Rels. Assn., Internat. Pub. Mgmt. Assn. Human Resources (pres. 1990, bd. dirs.; hon. life, Stockbergen award), St. Paul Pers. Dirs. Assn. (pres., v.p., sec.-treas.). Lutheran. Avocations: skiing, hunting, swimming, reading, writing. Home: 1823 Park Ave Mahtomedi MN 55115-1932 E-mail: richard.brainerd@metc.state.mn.us.

BRAITERMAN, THEA GILDA, economics educator, state legislator, selectman; b. Balt., Sept. 11, 1927; d. Isaac E. and Clara (Fink) Bloom; m. Marvin Braiterman, Mar. 21, 1948; children: Kenneth, Marta, David. BS, Johns Hopkins U., 1949; MA, U. Md., 1966; PhD, Union Inst., 1977. Assoc. prof. econs. Balt. Coll. of Commerce, 1966-73; prof. econs. New England Coll., Henniker, N.H., 1973—; mem. N.H. Ho. of Reps., 1988-94. Cons. on retirement, 1988—; selectman Town of Henniker, 1997—. Author: Workbook on Economic Theory, 1966; contbr. articles to profl. jours. Sec., bd. govs. United Way of Merrimack County, Concord, N.H., 1984-90; v.p., bd. govs. Cmty. Svcs. Coun., Concord, 1980-84. Jane Addams Peace Assn. grantee, 1976-77; Gilmore grantee New Eng. Coll., 1988-90. Mem. Am. Econ. Assn., Ea. Econ. Assn. Home: PO Box 686 Henniker NH 03242-0686 Office: New England Coll Henniker NH 03242 E-mail: theabrait@conknet.com.

BRAITHWAITE, BARBARA J. secondary school educator; BA, Ctrl. Mich. U., 1959; MA, U. Mich., 1960. Geography tchr. grade 7 Pocono Mountain Sch. Dist., Swiftwater, Pa. Recipient 1st Place award Am. Express geography competition for tchrs., 1990, Outstanding Secondary Level Tchr. of the Year award Pa. Coun. Social Studies, 1992, Innovative Tchg. award State Farm Ins. Co., 1995. Mem. Pa. Geog. Alliance (steering com., tchr. cons.), Pocono Regional Geog. Alliance (co-founder, chairperson), Nat. Coun. Geog. Edn., Pa. Geog. Soc. (Tchr. Recognition award 1993, Pa. Tchr. of Yr. 1999). Home: 65 Stones Throw East Stroudsburg PA 18301-9094 Office: Pocono Mt Intermediate Sch Swiftwater PA 18370-0254 also: Pocono Mountain Sch Dist Swiftwater PA 18370-0200

BRAITHWAITE, J. LORNE, real estate executive; b. Dewberry, Alta., Can., July 16, 1941; s. Joseph and Olga (Prill) B.; m. Josie Bey, Feb. 14, 1962; children: Todd, Jodi, Troy, Travis. B in Commerce, U. Alta., 1963; MBA, U. Western Ont., 1969; I.D.A., Investment Dealers' Assn., Calgary, 1970. With T. Eaton Co., Calgary, Canada, 1963—67, 1971—74, group sales and mdse. mgr. Edmonton, Canada, 1971—74; sales mgr., then v.p. and gen. mgr. South Park Industries Assoc. Cos.; project mgr., then sales mgr. ATCO Industries, Calgary, 1969—71; project mgr. Oxford Devel. Group, Edmonton, 1974—76, sr. v.p. devel. Calgary, 1976—78; pres., chief exec. officer Cambridge Shopping Centres Ltd., Toronto, 1978—2001; chmn. Ethan Allen Can., Toronto, 1997—. Bd. dirs. Cambridge Leaseholds Ltd., Jannock Ltd., Can. Inst. Pub. Real Estate Cos., OMERS Realty Corp., Enbridge Inc., Coun. for Can. Unity. Gen. mgr., coach Tornhill Thunderbirds AAA Midget Hockey Team, 1983—85; mem. bd. govs. Jr. Achievement Met. Toronto and York Region; vol. real estate divsn. corp. capital campaign Hosp. for Sick Children, Toronto, 1986; worldwide chmn. I.C.S.C., 1995—96; chmn. Can. Com. I.C.S.C., 1989—93; pres. Can. Inst. Pub. Real Estate Cos., 1995—97. Inducted into Hall of Fame, Can. Inst. Pub. Real Estate Cos., 1995-97, Cirass Henry award, 1996. Mem. Toronto Club, Goodwood Club, Bayview Golf and Country Club, Cambridge Club, World Pres.'s Orgn. Avocations: squash, hockey, golf, tennis. Office: 350 Bay St 6th Fl Toronto ON Canada M5H 2S6 E-mail: lbraithwaite@ethanallen.ca.

BRAITHWAITE, KARL ROYDEN, dean; b. St. George, Utah, Mar. 16, 1942; s. Alice Todd Braithwaite; m. Jane L. Teare; children: Ryan Todd, Scott, Michelle Croasdell. AS, So. Utah U., 1962; BS, U. Utah, 1964; PhD, U. Wis., 1967. Asst. prof. polit. sci. Duke U., Durham, NC, 1967—70; mem. staff Senators Montoya and Moss, 1970—73; profl. staff Environment Subcom. Ed Muskie, U.S. Senate, Washington, 1973—80; staff dir., dir. of govt. rels. Los Alamos Nat. Lab., N.Mex., 1980—2001; dean and prof. of pub. policy and mgmt. Edmund S. Muskie Sch. of Pub. Svc., Portland, Maine, 2001—. Editor: (book) Science, Computers and the Information Onslaught, 1984. Chair, vice chair N.Mex. Environ. Improvement Bd., 1983—88. Recipient N.Mex Disting. Pub. Svc. award, 1997. Mem.: AAAS, Assn. for Pub. Policy and Analysis and Mgmt., Nat. Assn. of Schs. of Pub. Affairs and Adminstrn. Mem. Ch. Latter-Day Saints. Office: Muskie Sch Pub Svc U So Maine 96 Falmouth Portland ME 04104-9300 Office Fax: 207-780-4417. Business E-Mail: kbraithw@usm.maine.edu.

BRAITHWAITE, MARGARET CHRISTINE, retired elementary education educator; b. Toledo, Sept. 9, 1945; d. John William and Eleanor Margaret (Gedert) B. BS in Edn., U. Toledo, 1968. Cert. pvt. glider pilot, adv. ground instr. Tchr. 1-8th Toledo Pub. Schs. Resource facilitator for project S.T.A.R., Toledo Pub. Schs. Mem.: Adrian Soaring Club (past pres.), Toledo Fedn. Ret. Tchrs., Lucas Co. Ret. Tchrs. Assn., Ohio Ret. Tchrs. Assn., Soaring Soc. Am., Women Soaring Pilots Assn., Delta Kappa Gamma (chair program of works com.). Avocations: soaring, photography. Home: 3710 Wrenwood Rd Toledo OH 43623

BRAITHWAITE, WILFRED JOHN, physics educator; b. Ferndale, Wash., Apr. 11, 1940; s. John Alfred and Joyce Elinor (Gunderson) B.; m. Wanda Pearl Chism, June 3, 1961 (div. 1975). BS in Physics with honors, Seattle Pacific U., 1962; MS in Physics, U. Wash., 1965, PhD in Physics, 1971; postgrad., U. Tex., 1988-89. Instr. physics Princeton (N.J.) U., 1970-72; asst. prof. physics U. Tex., Austin, 1972-79, rsch. scientist faculty, 1979-81; tech. and sci. cons. Austin, 1981-89; assoc. prof. physics U. Ark., Little Rock, 1989-95, prof. physics, 1995—. Vis. staff mem. Los Alamos (N.Mex.) Nat. Lab., 1975-76, 78-79; vis. scientist Ind. U., Bloomington, 1990-96; affiliate prof. physics U. Wash., Seattle, 1991-96; sci. assoc. PPE divsn. CERN, Geneva, Switzerland, 1992—; guest scientist Brookhaven Nat. Lab., Upton, N.Y., 1992—; lectr. in field; grant referee Ark. Sci. and Tech. Authority, 1990—; cons. for GE Corp. R&D, 2002—. Numerous unedited contbns.; jour. referee Phys. Rev. C and Phys. Rev. Letters, 1970—, Found. Physics, Assoc. Ed. Ark. Acad. Sci., 2000—. U.S. Dept. Energy rsch. grantee, 1992-95, 99—, Ark. Sci. and Tech. Authority rsch. grantee, 1993-94, 96-98; numerous grants from NSF, Dept. of Energy, Robert A Welch Found. Mem. IEEE, Am. Phys. Soc., Nat. Assn. for Rsch. in Sci. Teaching, N.Y. Acad. Sci., Ark. Acad. Sci. Achievements include rsch. of time reversal invariance; high excitation neutron particle-hole states; charge-dependent matrix elements in light nuclei; method for determining rotational symmetries of nuclear states using heavy ions; multiply-excited atomic states in helium-like and lithium-like oxygen; strength of the 3-alpha process in stellar helium burning; method for identifying antimatter stars; large isospin mixing in light nuclei via scattering comparisons of positive and negative pions near the pion-nucleon resonance; measurement limits on source sizes formed in symmetric collisions of ultra-relativistic heavy nuclei; method for separating charged kaons and pions in Time Projection Chambers via in-flight decays; instrument design for high-energy nuclear physics. Home: 1 Broadmoor Dr Little Rock AR 72204-4818 Office: Univ of Ark at Little Rock Dept Physics and Astronomy 2801 S University Ave Little Rock AR 72204 E-mail: wjbraith@comcast.net.

BRAKAS, JURGIS (GEORGE) HOEGH, philosopher, educator; b. Copenhagen, Nov. 14, 1944; arrived in U.S., 1952; s. Martin and Gunhild Hoegh (Bryoe) B. AB in phil., Princeton U., 1968; PhD in phil., Columbia U., 1984. Assoc. prof. philosophy Marist Coll., Poughkeepsie, NY, 1990—. Author: Aristotle's Concept of the Universal, 1988; contbr. articles to profl. jours. Recipient Princeton U. scholarships, 1962-68; Columbia U. fellow, 1972-74; NEH Summer Seminar participant, 2003. Mem. Am.-Scandinavian Found., Am. Phil. Assn., Ayn Rand Soc., Soc. Ancient Greek Phil. Avocations: attending ballets and concerts, films, running, weightlifting. Office: Marist Coll Dept Philosophy Fontaine Hall Poughkeepsie NY 12601 E-mail: jurgis.brakas@marist.edu.

BRAKAS, NORA JACHYM, education educator; b. Schenectady, N.Y., Aug. 9, 1952; d. Thaddeus Michael and Theresa Mary (Patnode) J.; m. Jurgis Brakas, June 15, 1996. BS in Elem. Edn., Plattsburg State U. Coll., 1974; MS in Reading, SUNY, Albany, 1977, Cert. Advanced Study in Reading, 1986, PhD in Reading, 1990. Cert. elem. sch. tchr., reading tchr. Elem. sch. and reading tchr. Lee (Mass.) Ctrl. Sch., 1976-82; reading specialist Guilderland (N.Y.) Sch. Dist., 1988-89; rsch. asst., tchg. asst. SUNY, Albany, 1985-88, instr. reading dept., 1989-90; asst. prof. tchr. edn., reading specialist Southeastern La. U., Hammond, 1990-91, Marist Coll., Poughkeepsie, N.Y., 1991—. Presenter, spkr. in field. Contbr. articles to profl. jours. Student Literacy Corp. grantee U.S. Dept. Edn., 1991, IBM/Marist Joint Study Project grantee, 1992. Mem. Internat. Reading Assn., Soc. Children's Book Writers and Illustrators. Avocations: drawing, writing children's books, collecting antique children's books. Home: PO Box 176 Rhinecliff NY 12574-0176 Office: Marist Coll 388 F Dyson Poughkeepsie NY 12601 E-mail: Nora.Brakas@Marist.edu.

BRAKE, CECIL CLIFFORD, retired diversified manufacturing executive; b. Ystrad, Mynach, Wales, Nov. 14, 1932; came to U.S., 1967; s. Leonard James and Ivy Gertrude (Berry) B.; m. Vera Morris, Aug. 14, 1954; children— Stephen John, Richard Colin, Vanessa Elaine Chartered engr.; B.Sc. in Engring., U. Wales, 1954; M.Sc., Cranfield Inst., Bedford, Eng., 1957; grad. A.M.P., Harvard U. Sch. Bus., 1985. Mgr. research and devel. Schrader Fluid Power, Wake Forest, N.C., 1968-70, engring. mgr., 1970-75; mng. dir. Schrader U.K. Fluid Power, 1975-77; v.p., gen. mgr. Schrader Internat., 1977-78; group v.p. Schrader Bellows, Fluid Power, Akron, Ohio, 1978-82; exec. v.p. Scovill, Inc., Waterbury, Conn., 1982-86; pres. Yale Security, Inc. subs. Scovill, Inc.; group exec. Eagle Industries, Inc., Chgo., 1986—; retired, 1997. Chief oper. officer Mansfield (Ohio) Plumbing Products Inc., Hart and Cooley Inc., Holland, Mich., Caron Internat., Inc., Rochelle, Ill., Caron Internat., Inc., Rochelle, Ill., Chemineer Inc., Dayton, Ohio, Pulsafeeder Inc., Rochester, N.Y., Clevaflex Inc., Cleve., Equality Specialties Inc., N.Y.C., De Vilbiss Co., Toledo, Hill Refrigeration, Trenton, N.J., Air-Maze Corp., Bedford Heights, Ohio, Burns Aerospace Corp., Winston Salem, N.C., Atlantic Industries, Inc., Nutley, N.J., Stimsonite Products, Niles, Ill.; ptnr., owner Prince of Wales Inc.; bd. dirs. CFI Industries. Avocations: sailing; golf. Office: Eagle Industries Inc 2 N Riverside Plz Chicago IL 60606-2600 also: 17 Harborview Rd Westport CT 06880-5061

BRAKE, TIMOTHY L. lawyer; b. St. Joseph, Mo., Apr. 8, 1948; s. Douglas E. and Ruth E. (Fahling) B.; m. Julia Marie Gerkin, Sept. 3, 1977; children: Jennifer L., Douglas M. BA in English, Regis Coll., 1970; JD, U. Mo., 1973. Bar: Mo. 1973, U.S. Dist. Ct. (we. dist.) Mo. 1973. Assoc. Margolin & Kirwan, Kansas City, 1973-79, ptnr., 1979-80; sole practice Kansas City, 1980-2001; of counsel Davis, Bethune & Jones, L.L.C., 2001—. Bd. dirs. Ozanam Home for Boys, 1990—2001, Lantz Welch Charitable Found., 1991—96. Fellow U. Mo. Law Found.; mem. Def. Lawyers Assn. (dir. western sect. 1979-80), Assn. Trial Lawyers Am., Mo. Assn. Trial Attys., Mo. Bar Assn., Kansas City Met. Bar Assn., Friends Art, Friends Zoo, Kansas City Athletic Club (dir. 1986-87), Hallbrook Country Club, Homestead Country Club. Home: 3620 Wyncote Ln Shawnee Mission KS 66205-2739 Office: 1100 Main St Kansas City MO 64105-2105 E-mail: tbrake@dbjlaw.net.

BRAKEBILL, TINA STEWART, historian, writer; b. Muncie, Ind., May 8, 1962; d. Silas and Janey Stewart; m. Brian K. Brakebill, Aug. 23, 1986. BS, MS in History, Ill. State U., 2002. Loan officer Bloomington (Ill.) Mcpl. Credit Union, 1989—98; grad. tchg. asst. Ill. State U., Normal, 1999—2000; Ill. regional archives depository intern State Ill. Archives Divsn., Normal, 2000—01; ind. scholar, writer Bloomington, Ill., 2001—. Archival cons. McLean County C. of C., Bloomington, 2000—00, Ill. State U., Normal, 2001—01. Contbr. articles to profl. jours. Vol. reading asst. for at-risk 3rd graders Sheridan Grade Sch., Bloomington, 2002—. Mem.: McLean County Hist. Soc., Ill. State Hist. Soc., Orgn. Am. Historians, Am. Hist. Assn. Home: 913 West Wood St Bloomington IL 61701 Personal E-mail: tjbrake@aol.com.

BRAKELEY, GEORGE ARCHIBALD, JR., fundraising consultant; b. Washington, Apr. 18, 1916; s. George Archibald and Lillian (Fay) B.; m. Roxana Byerly; children: George Archibald III, Deborah Fay, Joan Keller. BA, U. Pa., 1938. V.p., dir. John Price Jones Co., Inc. (fund-raising counsel), N.Y.C.; pres., treas. John Price Jones Co. (Can.), Ltd., 1950-52; chmn., CEO G.A. Brakeley & Co., Ltd., 1952-61, G.A. Brakeley & Co., Inc., L.A., 1956-69; chmn., chief exec. officer Brakeley, John Price Jones Inc., 1972-83; chmn. Brakeley, John Price Jones, Inc., 1983-87, sr. cons., 1987—. Author: Tested Ways to Successful Fund Raising. Trustee Ctr. for the Study of the Presidency. Capt. C.E. AUS, WWII. Mem. Mayflower Soc., Anglers Club (N.Y.C.), Montreal Racket Club (hon.), Wee Burn Golf Club (Darien, Conn.), Royal Poinciana Golf Club (Naples, Fla.). Episcopalian. Home: 185 South Ave # 26 New Canaan CT 06840-5729 Office: 86 Prospect St Stamford CT 06901-1616

BRAKEMAN, LOUIS FREEMAN, retired university official; b. Kalamazoo, Nov. 9, 1932; s. Louis Freeman and Ruth Adelaide (Parsons) B.; m. Lori Mallett, Aug. 16, 1953; children: David, Mark, Peter, Paul, Amy. BA, Kalamazoo Coll., 1954; MA, Fletcher Sch. Diplomacy, Tufts U., 1955, PhD, 1963; LHD, Denison U., 1985. Lectr. history Brown U., 1958-59; asst. prof. polit. sci. Carroll Coll., Waukesha, Wis., 1959-62; mem. faculty Denison U., Granville, Ohio, 1962-85, prof. polit. sci., 1968-85, chmn. dept., 1965-70, dean Coll., 1970-73, provost, 1973-85, acting pres., 1974-75; dir. research project faculty devel. Gt. Lakes Colls. Assn., 1985-86; provost Stetson U., DeLand, Fla., 1987-93. Vis. prof. polit. sci. Kalamazoo Coll., 1987; vis. scholar center for Study of Higher Edn. U. Mich., 1980; dir. Regional Council Center for Internat. Students, summers 1966-68; chmn. regional selection com. Danforth Found. Assocs. Program, 1971-73; mem. Common Cause, 1972—. Co-author: Research Problems in American Politics, 1969, What One Has Within, What the Context Provides, 1989; contbr. articles to profl. jours. Pres. Volusia County Arts Coun., 1994-96, West Volusia Habitat for Humanity, 1996-98; sec. DeLand Mus. Art, 2000-01. Fulbright scholar India, 1957-58; Danforth grad. fellow, 1954-57 Mem. Nature Conservancy, Phi Beta Kappa. Presbyterian (elder). Home: 522 Princewood Dr Deland FL 32724-8103 E-mail: Lbrakema@aol.com.

BRAKKE, MYRON KENDALL, retired research chemist, educator; b. Fillmore County, Minn., Oct. 23, 1921; s. John T. and Hulda Christina (Marburger) B.; m. Betty-Jean Einbecker, Aug. 16, 1947; children: Kenneth Allen, Thomas Warren, Joan Patricia, Karen Elizabeth. BS, U. Minn., 1943, PhD, 1947; DSc (hon.), U. Nebr., 1996. Rsch. assoc. Bklyn. Bot. Garden, 1947-52; rsch assoc. U. Ill., 1952-55; rsch. chemist U.S. Dept. Agr., Lincoln, Nebr., 1955-86. Prof. plant pathology U. Nebr., Lincoln, 1955-86. Editor: Virology, 1960-66; contbr. articles to profl. jours. Fellow AAAS, Am. Phytopath. Soc. (Award of Distinction 1988); mem. Am. Chem. Soc., Nat. Acad. Scis., Sigma Xi, Phi Lambda Upsilon, Gamma Sigma Delta, Alpha Zeta. Home: 5700 Fremont St Apt 348 Lincoln NE 68507-1686 E-mail: MB13144@alltel.net.

BRALEY, OLETA PEARL, home health care provider; b. Rochester, N.Y., July 19, 1944; d. Horace Everet and Ruby Doris Sullivan; m. Edward Walter Plow, June 24, 1967 (div. Jan. 10, 1990); children: James Edward Plow, John Patrick Plow; m. Franklin John Braley, Mar. 17, 1990. Degree in cosmotology, Continental Beauty, Rochester, 1966; student, Sch. Visual Arts, N.Y.C., 1963. Prodn. Kodak Park, Rochester, 1964—66; hairdresser local salons Rochester, 1966—80; money room oper. AMSA, Rochester, 1986—90; home health aide Tender Loving Care, Rochester, 1990—97; home health caretaker Via Health II, Rochester, 1997—. Author: (poetry book) Best of the 90's, 1996, Best Poetry and Poets, 2002; composer: (songs) Remember, 1997, Wondering, 1997. Recipient Editor's Choice award, 1996, 1997, 1998. Avocations: music, art, writing. Home: 91 B Green Leaf Meadows Rochester NY 14612-4347

BRALEY, RUSSELL NORTON, retired journalist, author; b. Seattle, Nov. 10, 1921; s. Edward Russell and Gladys Bernita (Norton) B.; m. Madeleine Elizabet Karacsony, Mar. 25, 1953 (dec. July 2002). BA, U. Wash., 1944; French cert., Sorbonne U., Paris, 1950. Reporter The Oakland (Calif.) Post-Enquirer, 1947-49, The Stars and Stripes, Darmstadt, Germany, 1951-52; mng. editor Overseas Weekly, Frankfurt, Germany, 1952-55; Germany corr. N.Y. Daily News, 1955-75, UN corr., 1975-82; news editor Voice of Am., Washington, 1984-86; dep. fgn. editor Washington Times, 1986-87. Freelance writer. Author: Bad News: The Foreign Policy of the New York Times, 1984, (Internet publ.) MountNixon.com, 1999; contbr. articles to profl. jours. Lt. (j.g.) USNR, 1944-46. E-mail: rnbraley@erols.com.

BRAM, LEON LEONARD, publishing company executive; b. Chgo., Sept. 20, 1931; s. Samuel and Rose Bram; m. Doris A. Hebel, Apr. 29, 1961 (div. 1972); children: Mark James, Alexander Anton; m. Joanne Frances Casino, Sept. 30, 1978 (div. 1990); 1 child, Victoria Lynn. B.Sc., DePaul U., 1967. Various positions Chgo. Pub. Library, 1949-55, F.E. Compton Co., Chgo., 1955-63; dir. editorial rsch. Standard Ednl. Corp., Chgo., 1963-69; exec. editor F.E. Compton Co., Chgo., 1969-74; v.p., editorial dir. Primedia Reference Corp., Mahwah, NJ, 1974-97, arts adminstr., 1998, non-profit mktg. mgr., 1999—. Mem. ALA.

BRAMANTE, PIETRO OTTAVIO, physiology educator, retired pathology specialist; b. Rome, May 21, 1920; came to U.S., 1952; s. Michele Bramante and Amelia Ferriani; m. Aurora de Valle Medina, June 1, 1957. MD, U. Rome, 1944; MS in Biomed. Engring., Drexel U., 1965. Diplomate Am. Bd. Pathology. Intern to asst. dept. internat. medicine U. Rome, 1945-51; instr. to assoc. prof. St. Louis U. Sch. Medicine, 1952-65; assoc. prof. to prof. dept. physiology U. Ill., Chgo., 1965-75; resident pathology Loyola U., Chgo., 1975-78; pathologist William Beaumont Med. Ctr., El Paso, Tex., 1978-79, Sun Bay Hosp., St. Petersburg, Fla., 1981-82. Cons. Italian Fedn. Sport Medicine, Rome, 1945-51; med. expert Ct. of Justice, Rome, 1948-49; vis. scientist Am. Physiol. Soc., Washington, 1964-67; glossary com. mem. Internat. Union Physiology, Washington, 1969; vis. prof. U. Westfalia, Münster, Germany, 1971-72. Contbr. articles, revs. to profl. publs., 1944-78; editl. reviewer Am. Physiol. Soc.; patentee in field. Pres. Chess Club, Pinellas Park, Fla., 1986-96; tchr. fgn. langs., sci. and math. in local schs. 2d lt. Air Force Italian, 1947-50. Postgrad. fellow Swedish Govt., Stockolm, 1951-52, fellow Nat. Heart Inst., Baylor U., Houston, 1957, spl. fellow Nat. Heart Inst., Drexel U., Phila., 1962-64. Republican. Roman Catholic. Avocation: chess. Home: 2022 Camelot Dr Apt 33 Clearwater FL 33763-4249

BRAME, JOSEPH ROBERT, III, lawyer; b. Hopkinsville, Ky., Apr. 18, 1942; s. Joseph Robert and Atwood Ruth (Davenport) B.; m. Mary Jane Blake, June 11, 1966; children: Rob, Blake, Virginia, John, Thomas. BA with high honors, Vanderbilt U., 1964; LLB, Yale U., 1967. Bar: Va. 1968, D.C. 2001. Assoc. McGuire, Woods, Battle & Boothe, Richmond, Va., 1967-72, ptnr., 1972-97; mem. NLRB, 1997-2000; shareholder Ogletree, Deakins, Nash, Smoak & Stewart, P.C., Washington, 2000—02, McGuire Woods, LLP, 2002—. Lectr. in field. Contbr. articles to profl. jours. Mem. adv. bd. Salvation Army, Richmond, 1980-97, chmn., 1989-91; troop com. chmn. Robert E. Lee coun. Boy Scouts Am., 1980-91; chair 10th Amendment Litig. com., Gov.'s Adv. Coun. on Federalism and Self Determination, 1994-97; gen. counsel Rep. Party Va., 1993-96. Mem. Am. Bar Found., Am. Coll. Labor and Employment Lawyers, Va. State Bar, Phi Beta Kappa. Presbyterian. Office: McGuire Woods LLP Washington Sq 1050 Conneticut Ave NW Ste 1200 Washington DC 20036-5317 E-mail: rbrame@mcguirewoods.com.

BRAME, MARILLYN A. hypnotherapist; b. Indpls., Sept. 17, 1928; d. David Schwalb and Hilda (Riley) Curtin; 1 child, Gary Mansour. Student, Meinzinger Art Sch., Detroit, 1946-47, U. N.Mex., 1963, Orlando (Fla.) Jr. Coll., 1964-65, El Camino Coll., Torrance, Calif., 1974-75; PhD in Hypnotherapy, Am. Inst. Hypnotherapy, 1989. Cert. and registered hypnotherapist. Color cons. Pitts. Plate Glass Co., Albuquerque, 1951-52; owner Signs by Marillyn, Albuquerque, 1952-53; design draftsman Sandia Corp., Albuquerque, 1953-56; designer The Martin Co., Orlando, 1957-65; pres. The Arts, Winter Park, Fla., 1964-66; supr. tech. publs. Gen. Instrument Corp., Hawthorne, Calif., 1967-76; pres. Camart Design, Westminster, Calif., 1977-86, Visual Arts, Lake Forest, Calif., 1978—; mgr. tech. publs. Archive Corp., Costa Mesa, Calif., 1986-90. Adj. instr. Orange Coast Coll., Costa Mesa, 1985-90; hypnotherapist, Mission Viejo, 1986—; bd. dirs. Orange County chpt. Am. Bd. Hypnotherapy. Author: Lemon and Lime Scented Herbs, 1994, (textbook) Folkdancing is for Everybody, 1974, Innovative Imagery, 1996, Changing Your Mood, 1997; inventor, designer dance notation sys. MS Method. Mem. bd. govs. Lake Forest II Showboaters Theatre Group, 1985-88; mem. City of Mission Viejo Cultural Arts Com., 1995—; bd. dirs. Orange County Fine Arts, v.p., pres., 2001. Mem. Soc. Tech. Communication (v.p. programs, 1987, newsletter editor 1986-87, newsletter prodn. editor 1985-86). Avocations: folkdancing, rock collecting, community theater, metaphysics. E-mail: visualarts@mindspring.com.

BRAMLETT, JEFFREY OWEN, lawyer; b. Detroit, Nov. 13, 1953; s. Melvin C. and Edith H. Bramlett; m. Nancy E. Frakes, May 30, 1981; children: Cynthia, Melissa, Robert, Susanna. BA, U. Md., 1975; JD, U. Tex., 1980. Bar: Tex. 1980, U.S. Ct. Appeals (5th and 11th cirs.) 1980, Ga. 1981, U.S. Dist. Ct. (all dists.) Ga. 1981, U.S. Dist. Ct. (we. dist.) Mich. 1995, U.S. Supreme Ct. 1985. Legis. aide Hon. Robert Eckhardt, U.S. Congress, Washington, 1974-77; law clk. to judge Jerre S. Williams U.S. Ct. Appeals (5th cir.), Austin, Tex., 1980-81; assoc., then ptnr. Bondurant, Mixson & Elmore, Atlanta, 1981—. Bd. trustees State Bar Ga. Client Security Fund, Atlanta, 1992—97. Mem. Bar Assn. of Ga. (bd. govs. 1994—), Atlanta Bar Assn. (pres., 2000-01, bd. dirs. 1993—, chmn. litigation sect. 1994-95), ACLU, (bd. dirs. 1993-97, pres. Ga. affiliate 1987-89, bd. dirs. 1983-97). Office: Bondurant Mixson & Elmore 1201 W Peachtree St NW Ste 3900 Atlanta GA 30309-3417 E-mail: bramlett@bmelaw.com.

BRAMLETT, PAUL KENT, lawyer; b. Tupelo, Miss., May 31, 1944; s. Virgil Preston and McDuff (Goggans) B.; m. Shirley Marie Wilhelm, June 14, 1966; children: Paul Kent II (dec.), Robert Preston. AA with honors, Itawamba Jr. Coll., Fulton, Miss., 1962-64; BA, David Lipscomb Coll., 1966; postgrad., George Peabody Coll., 1966; JD, U. Miss., 1969. Bar: Miss. 1969, U.S. Dist. Ct. (no. dist.) Miss. 1969, U.S. Ct. Appeals (5th cir.) 1974, U.S. Supreme Ct. 1974, U.S. Dist. Ct. (we. dist.) Tenn. 1976, Tenn. 1980, U.S. Dist. Ct. (mid. dist.) Tenn. 1980, U.S. Ct. Appeals (6th cir.) 1980, U.S. Ct. Appeals (11th cir.) 1981, U.S. Dist. Ct. (so. dist.) Miss. 1983, U.S. Dist. Ct. (ea. dist.) Tenn. 2003. Pvt. practice, Tupelo, Miss., 1969-80, Nashville, 1980—. Mem. Million Dollar Advs. Forum, 1998. Mem. ABA, Miss. Trial Lawyers Assn. (bd. govs. 1976-79), Tenn. Bar Assn., Miss. Bar Assn. (pub. info. com. 1979-81), Nashville Bar Assn. (fed. ct. com. 1980-81), Am. Arbitration Assn. (comml. panel), Civitan Club (past gov. and legal counsel no. dist. Miss.). Mem. Ch. of Christ. Avocation: music. Office: PO Box 150734 Nashville TN 37215-0734

BRAMLETT, SHIRLEY MARIE WILHELM, interior decorator, artist; b. Scottsboro, Ala., June 14, 1945; d. Robert David and Alta (Reeves) Wilhelm; m. Paul Kent Bramlett, June 5, 1966; children: Paul Kent II (dec.), Robert Preston. BS, David Lipscomb U., 1966; postgrad., U. Miss., 1966-68; pvt. study art, 1976—. Decorator The Anchorage House, Oxford, Miss., 1966-67, Interiors by Shirley, Tupelo, Miss., 1971-80; tchr. Oxford City Schs., 1967-69; decorator, buyer Donald Furniture, Tupelo, 1969-71; owner, importer Bramblewood Interiors & Antiques, Belden, Miss., 1976-80; owner, decorator, artist The Cottage on Caldwell, Inc., Nashville, 1980—. Sec.-treas. Kent Bramlett Found., Inc., 1992—. Represented in art galleries Hundred Oaks Castle, Winchester, Tenn., Lyzon Gallery, Nashville; introduced and presented painting House of Parliament, Luxembourg; commd. for watercolor print fortnightly Musicale of Miss., 1991-92; European representation by Internet Internat. Bd. dirs. Found. for Christian Edn., 1988—, Ea. European Missions, Vienna, Austria, 1986—(commd. for watercolor print used in internat. fundraising); del. Miss. Dem. caucus, 1970; fundraiser Agape Artist, 1991; sec., treas., bd. dirs. Kent Bramlett Found., Inc.; curator Hundred Oaks Castle, Winchester, Tenn. Named Woman of Decade, David Lipscomb Coll., 1986, one of Outstanding Young Women of Am., 1979; selected Centennial Artist, David Lipscomb U., Nashville, 1991, one of ten Master Tenn. Artists, Lyzon Gallery, Nashville, 1991. Mem. Nat. Mus. Women in Arts, Tenn. Watercolor Soc., Nat. Soc. Tole and Decorative Painters, Green Hills Garden Club (cover artist for nat. conv. garden clubs 1985), Assoc. Ladies Lipscomb (bd. dirs. 1991-92). Mem. Ch. of Christ. Avocation: restoring historic castle. Home: 930 Caldwell Ln Nashville TN 37204-4016

BRAMLETTE, DAVID C., III, federal judge; b. New Orleans, Nov. 27, 1939; BA, Princeton U., 1962; JD, U. Miss., 1965. Assoc., then ptnr. Adams, Forman, Truly, Ward & Bramlette, Natchez, Miss., 1975-91; spl. cir. judge Dist. Ct. (6th

dist.) Miss., 1977, 79; fed. judge Dist. Ct. (so. dist.) Miss., 1991—. Trustee Miss. Nature Conservancy, 1990—; pres. BBCHA, 1989-90; active Arcole Hunting Camp, Ducks Unlimited, Nat. Wild Turkey Fedn.; mem. adv. bd. Natchez Lit. Celebration. Office: PO Box 928 Natchez MS 39121-0928 E-mail: connie_davis@mssd.uscourts.gov.

BRAMMER, J. WILLIAM, JR., judge, lawyer; b. Des Moines, Iowa, Sept. 15, 1942; s. James W. and Mary Virginia (Steck) B.; m. Donna Crosby, June 20, 1964; children: Jill S., James W. III. BS, U. Ariz., 1964, JD, 1967. Bar: Ariz. 1967, U.S. Dist. Ct. Ariz. 1968, U.S. Ct. Appeals (9th cir.) 1970, U.S. Supreme Ct. 1970. Law clk. to judge Ariz. Ct. Appeals, Tucson, 1967—68; asst. atty. City of Tucson, 1968; from assoc. to ptnr. DeConcini, McDonald, Brammer, Yetwin & Lacy PC, Tucson, 1968—97; judge Ariz. Ct. of Appeals, Tucson, 1997—. Com. examinations Ariz. Supreme Ct., Phoenix, 1977-84, chmn. 1982-84. Bd. visitors U. Ariz. Coll. Law, Tucson, 1981-84, 88—. Fellow: Ariz. Bar Found.; mem.: ABA, Law Coll. Assn. U. Ariz. (pres. 1990—91), Pima County Bar Assn. (pres. 1993—94), Morris K. Udall Inn of Ct. (pres. 2001—02). Office: Ariz Ct Appeals 400 W Congress St Ste 302 Tucson AZ 85701-1353 E-mail: brammer@apltwo.ct.state.az.us.

BRAMMER, LAWRENCE MARTIN, psychology educator; b. Crookston, Minn., Aug. 20, 1922; s. Martin G. and Edna L. (Thiesen) B.; m. Marian S. Sjolin, Feb. 11, 1945; children: Karin Marie, Kristen Lenore. BS, St. Cloud State U., 1943; MA, Stanford U., 1948, PhD, 1950. Diplomate: Am. Bd. Prof. Psychology. Psychologist Stanford U. Counseling and Testing Ctr., 1948-50; assoc. dean students Sacramento State Coll., 1950-64; prof. ednl. psychology U. Wash., Seattle, 1964-88, prof. emeritus, 1988—. Author: Therapeutic Psychology, 6th edit., 1993, Helping Relationships, 7th edit., 1999, Outplacement and Inplacement Counseling, 1984, How to Cope with Life Transitions, 1991, Caring for Yourself While Caring for Others: A Caregiver's Survival and Renewal Guide, 1999. Lt. M.S.C. AUS, 1944-46. Fulbright fellow, 1961-62 Fellow APA; mem. ACA, Queen City Yacht Club, Elks. Democrat. Lutheran. Home: 7714 56th Pl NE Seattle WA 98115-6329

BRAMMER, T. HAWK, small business owner; b. Person, NC; s. Alfred P. Brammer, Patricia M. Philpott; 1 child, Kilana Hawkins-Brammer. Student, Va. Tech., 1983—85. Registered EMT, CNA N.C. Pres. All Things Considered, Lexington, NC, 1995—. Author, artist Experimental Fiction, 1998; exhibitions include Dark Night, 1983 (2d pl., 1983). Vol. mem. Davidson Humane Soc., Lexington, 1994—; vol. Am. Children's Home, Lexington, 1994—2001, Bapt. Children's Home, Thomasville, NC, 1988—90, 1994—2001. With USN, 1990—94, Okinawa. Mem.: Friends of Libr., Davidson Arts Coun., Davidson Writer's Guild. Democrat. Avocations: art, writing. Office: All Things Considered PO Box 1342 Lexington NC 27293

BRAMNIK, ROBERT PAUL, lawyer; b. N.Y.C., Nov. 17, 1949; s. Abe and Ruth (Richman) B.; m. Sheryl Ann Kalus, Aug. 12, 1973; children: Michael Lawrence, Andrew Martin. BA, CCNY, 1970; JD, Bklyn. Law Sch., 1973. Bar: N.Y. 1974, Ill. 1980, U.S. Dist. Ct. (so. and ea. dists.) N.Y. 1974, U.S. Dist. Ct. (no. dist.) Ill. 1980, U.S. Dist. Ct. (ctrl. dist.) Ill. 1982, U.S. Ct. Appeals (2d cir.) 1974, U.S. Ct. Appeals (4th cir.) 1987, U.S. Ct. Appeals (3d and 7th cirs.) 1992, U.S. Ct. Fed. Claims 1994, U.S. Supreme Ct. 1977. Sr. trial atty. NYSE, Inc., N.Y.C., 1973-75; asst. gen. counsel E.F. Hutton & Co., Inc., N.Y.C., 1975-77, Nat. Securities Clearing Corp., N.Y.C., 1977-79; with Arvey, Hodes, Costello and Burman, Chgo., 1979-86, ptnr., 1982-86, Wood, Lucksinger & Epstein, Chgo., 1987-88, Altheimer & Gray, Chgo., 1988-97, Wildman, Harrold, Allen & Dixon, Chgo., 1997—2003, Duane Morris LLC, Chgo., N.Y.C., 2003—. Lectr. Securities Industry Assn. Compliance and Legal div., N.Y.C., 1980-91, 95-2001. Vice chmn. Ill. Adv. Com. on Commodity Regulation, Chgo., 1985-89, chmn., 1989-95. Fellow: Ill. Bar Found.; mem.: ABA (coms. on futures and derivatives regulation, co-chmn. subcom. on futures commn. merchants), Nat. Futures Assn. (hearing com. 2001—), Nat. Assn. Sec. Dealers, Assn. of Bar of City of N.Y. Jewish. Office: Duane Morris LLP 227 W Monroe St Ste 3400 Chicago IL 60606 E-mail: rpbramnik@duanemorris.com.

BRAMS, MARVIN ROBERT, economist, mental health counselor, interfaith minister; b. Boston, Apr. 16, 1937; s. Leo and Sarah Brams; m. Myrna Berlin, May 15, 1960; children: Adam, Aaron. BS, Northeastern U., 1959, MBA, 1962; PhD, Clark U., 1967; M in Counseling, U. Del., 1984; postgrad., Carl Rogers Inst. Psychotherapy, 1985, Inst. Rational Emotive Therapy, 1987; MS in Spiritual Therapy, New Sem., 1990. Diplomate Am. Bd. Med. Psychotherapists; ordained as interfaith min. Columbia U., 1989; cert. Nat. Bd. Cert. Counselors; lic. mental health counselor; cert. in clin. pastoral edn. Instr. econs. Northeastern U., 1965-67; economist, prof. urban affairs and pub. policy U. Del., Newark, 1967—97, clin. psychotherapist Employee Wellness Program, 1995—97; fellow in psychoanalytic psychotherapy Harvard U., 2002—03. Econ. cons. to legal profession; vis. scholar Harvard U. Divinity Sch., 1997-99; psychiatry intern Med. Ctr. Del., 1996-97; clin. psychotherapist, VA Hosp., 1999-2001. Contbr. chpts. to books and articles to jours. and newspapers. Mem. Gov.'s Com. Del. State Fins., 1969, Gov.'s Econ. Adv. Coun., 1969-72; adv. com. property tax exemption policy Cities of Newark and Wilmington, 1972-75; mem. Del. Revenue Study Comm., 1973, Citizens Task Force on Housing, 1975, Del. Tomorrow Commn., 1974-76, New Castle County Water Supply Adv. Coun., 1975-81, Del. Revenue Study Com., 1977; fed. revenue sharing adv. com. City of Newark, 1976-78; advisor Del. Dept. Natural Resources, 1979. 1st lt. ordinance AUS, 1959-60. Fellow in urban econs. and pub. policy MIT, 1970, NSF fellow Stanford U., 1971. Mem. ACA, Assn. Humanistic Psychology, Am. Mental Health Counselors Assn., Am. Men and Women of Sci., Mass. Inst. for Psychoanalysis, Northeastern Soc. for Group Psychotherapy. Home: 32 Old Oak Rd Newark DE 19711-3653

BRAMS, STEVEN JOHN, political scientist, educator, game theorist; b. Concord, N.H., Nov. 28, 1940; s. Nathan and Isabelle (Tryman) B.; m. Eva Floderer, Nov. 13, 1971; children: Julie Claire, Michael Jason. BS, MIT, 1962; PhD, Northwestern U., 1966. Research assoc. Inst. Def. Analyses, Arlington, Va., 1965-67; asst. prof. polit. sci. Syracuse U., 1967-69; asst. prof. NYU, 1969-73, assoc. prof., 1973-76, prof., 1976—. Vis. prof. U. Rochester, U. Pa., U. Mich., Yale U., U. Calif.-Irvine, U. Haifa, Inst. Advanced Studies, Vienna; cons. in field Author: Game Theory and Politics, 1975, Paradoxes in Politics: An Introduction to the Nonobvious in Political Science, 1976, The Presidential Election Game, 1978, Game Theory and the Hebrew Bible, 1980, rev. edit., 2003; author: (with Peter C. Fishburn) Approval Voting, 1983; author: Superior Beings: If They Exist, How Would We Know?, 1983, Superpower Games: Applying Game Theory to Superpower Conflict, 1985, Rational Politics: Decisions, Games and Strategy, 1985; author: (with D. Marc Kilgour) Game Theory and National Security, 1988; author: Negotiation Games: Applying Game Theory of Moves, 1994; author: (with A.D. Taylor) Fair Division: From Cake-Cutting to Dispute Resolution, 1996; author: The Win-Win Solution: Guaranteeing Fair Shares to Everybody, 1999; co-author: Applied Game Theory, 1979, Modules in Applied Mathematics: Political and Related Models, 1983; mem. editl. bd. Pub. Choice, 1973—90, Am. Polit. Sci. Rev., 1978—82, Jour. Politics, 1968—73, 1978—82, 1991—, Math. Social Scis., 1980—, Theory and Decision, 1982—, Jour. Behavioral Decision Making, 1987—90, Jour. Theoretical Politics, 1988—, Group Decision and Negotiation, 1991—, Control and Cybernetics, 1993—, Rationality and Society, 1999—, patentee in field. Social Sci. Rsch. Coun. fellow, 1964-65, Guggenheim fellow, 1986-87; Russell Sage Found. vis. scholar, 1998-99, grantee NSF, 1968-71, 73-75, 80-91, Social Sci. Rsch. Coun., 1968, Ford Found., 1984-85, Sloan Found., 1986-89, U.S. Inst. Peace, 1988-89. Fellow AAAS, Pub. Choice Soc.; mem. Am. Econ. Assn., Am. Polit. Sci. Assn., Internat. Studies Assn. (Susan Strange award 2002), Policy Studies Orgn., Peace Sci. Soc. (pres. 1990-91). Democrat. Jewish. Home: 4 Washington Square Vlg Apt 17I New York NY 10012-1910

BRAMSON, ROBERT SHERMAN, lawyer; b. NYC, Nov. 11, 1938; s. Oscar David and Gertrude (May) B.; m. Ruth Schaffer, June 27, 1942; children: Jonathan, Jennifer, James, Julia. B.M.E., Rensselaer Poly. Inst., 1959; JD, Georgetown U., 1963; postgrad., U. Chgo. Sch. Bus., 1963-64. Bar: Ill. 1963, Pa. 1968, N.Y. 1984. Patent examiner US Patent Office, Washington, 1959-60; patent agt. Stevens, Davis, Miller & Mosher, Washington, 1960-63; atty. Abbott Labs., North Chgo., Ill., 1963-66, Scott Paper Co., Phila., 1966-68; ptnr., head computer and tech. law group Schnader, Harrison, Segal & Lewis, Phila., 1968-89; v.p., gen. patent and tech. counsel Unisys Corp., Blue Bell, Pa., 1989-90; founder Bramson and Pressman, Conshohocken, Pa., 1991, 95—; pres., CEO InterDigital Tech. Corp., King of Prussia, Pa., 1992-95; pres. VAI Patent Mgmt. Corp., Conshohocken, Pa., 1995—. Adj. prof. Temple U. Law Sch., Phila. Mem. ABA, Internat. Bar Assn., Am. Law Inst., Am. Patent Law Assn., Phila. Patent Law Assn., Phila. Bar Assn. Home: 112 Booth Ln Haverford PA 19041-1752 Office: VAI Patent Mgmt Corp 1100 E Hector St Ste 410 Conshohocken PA 19428-2378 E-mail: rbramson@b-p.com.

BRAMUCCI, RAYMOND L. employment and training executive; b. Ludlow, Mass. Sr. exec. Internat. Ladies' Garment Workers Union, 1957-79; dir. N.J. ops. Senator Bill Bradley, 1979-90; commr. N.J. Dept. Labor, 1990-94; asst. sec. labor Employment and Tng. Adminstrn., Dept. Labor, Washington, 1994—. Exec. dir. Inst. on Work, Seton Hall U.; arbitrator N.J. Bd. Mediation; former spl. advisor to Pres. of Montclair State U.; adj. prof. polit. sci. Rutgers U.

BRAMWELL, BEVIL ROBERT, theology studies educator, priest; b. Windhoek, Namibia, June 7, 1951; PhD, Boston Coll. Ordained priest Roman Cath. Ch., 85. Asst. pastor St. Anne's Sydenham, Durban, South Africa; prof., mem. formation staff Grande Seminaire, French Polynesia; dir. comms. Archdiocese of Tahiti; parochial vicar Ste. Jeanne d'Arc Parish, Lowell, Mass.; dir. grad. theology program Franciscan U., Steubenville, Ohio, 2000—03; tchr. theology St. John Vianney Theol. Sem., Denver, 2003—. Editor: (jour.) Fides Quaerens Intellectum, 2001—. Mem.: U. Faculty for Life, Cath. Theol. Soc. Am., Fellowship Cath. Scholars, Am. Acad. Religion. Office: St John Vianney Theol Sem 1300 S Steele St Denver CO 80210 Personal E-mail: father.bramwell@archden.org.

BRAMWELL, HENRY, federal judge; b. Bklyn., Sept. 3, 1919; s. Henry Hall and Florence Elva (MacDonald) B.; m. Ishbel W. Brown, Jan. 29, 1966. LLB, Bklyn. Law Sch., 1948, LLD (hon.), 1979. Bar: N.Y. bar 1948. Asst. U.S. atty., Bklyn., 1953-61; asst. counsel N.Y. State Rent Commn., 1961-63; judge Civil Ct., N.Y.C., Bklyn., 1966, 69—; asst. adminstrv. judge Kings County, Bklyn., 1974—; judge U.S. Dist. Ct., Bklyn., 1975—; U.S. Sr. Dist. judge, 1987—. Mem. Community Mayors N.Y. State; trustee Bklyn. Law Sch., 1978— Active Bklyn. Old Times Found., Inc. Served with AUS, 1942-44. Profiled in Black Judges on Justice, 1994. Mem. ABA, Nat. Bar Assn. (life), N.Y. State Bar Assn., Bklyn. Bar Assn. (trustee), Fed. Judges Assn. (founding mem.). Home: 101 Clark St Brooklyn NY 11201-2746 Office: US Dist Ct 225 Cadman Plz E Brooklyn NY 11201-1818

BRAMWELL, KATHARINE HONE EMMET, civic worker; b. N.Y.C., Oct. 19, 1914; d. Herman Le Roy and Helen (Dunscomb) Emmet; m. Gerald Ames Bramwell, Sept. 22, 1934 (dec. 1983); children: Heidi Bramwell Humes, Katherine Bramwell Hamilton (dec. 1992), Gerald Ames (dec. 1967); m. Henry Gardiner, June 10, 1989. Student, Smith Coll. Vol. worker for numerous charitable orgns., including Cmty. Chest; operator gift shop Brit. War Relief, World Warr II, later for Cmty. Chest; trustee, head fund raising drive St. Timothy's Sch. Balt.; dist. dir. nat. auditions Met. Opera, N.J.; trustee North Country Sch., Lake Placid, N.Y. Republican. Episcopalian. Home: 7 Meadow Ln Apt U4 Hightstown NJ 08520-3350 also: PO Box 472 Quogue NY 11959-0472

BRAMWELL, MARVEL LYNNETTE, mental health nurse, social worker; b. Durango, Colo., Aug. 13, 1947; d. Floyd Lewis and Virginia Jenny (Amyx) Bramwell. LPN, Durango Sch. Practical Nursing, 1968; ADN, Mt. Hood CC, 1972; BSN, BS in Gen. Studies cum laude, So. Oreg. State Coll., 1980; cert. in edn. grad. sch. social work, U. Utah, 1987, cert. in counselor alcohol, drug abuse, 1988, MSW, 1992. RN Utah, Oreg., Ind., Nev.; cert. social worker Utah, Ind., Nev., LCSW Nev., 2003. Staff nurse Monument Valley (Utah) Seventh Day Adventist Mission Hosp., 1973-74, La Plata Cmty. Hosp., 1974-75; health coord. Tri County Head Start Program, 1974-75; nurse therapist, team leader Portland Adventist Med. Ctr., 1975-78; staff nurse Indian Health Svc. Hosp., 1980-81; coord. village health svcs. North Slope Borough Health and Social Svc. Agy., Barrow, Alaska, 1981-83; nurse, supr. aides Bonneville Health Care Agy., 1984-85; staff nurse LDS Adolescent Psychiat. Unit, 1985-86; coord. adolescent nursing CPC Olympus View Hosp., 1986-87, 91; charge and staff nurse adult psychiatry U. Utah, 1987-88; nurse MSW Cmty. Nursing Svc., Salt Lake City, 1989-90, Willow Springs Ctr., Reno, 1996—2002; resident scvs. coord., dir. nursing Arden Cts., Reno, 1998-99—; med. social worker Meth. Home Health, Indpls., 1994-96; psychiat. nurse Willow Springs Ctr., 1996—2002; DON, resident svc. coord. Arden Cts., Reno, 1998-99; per diem nurse N. Nev. Med. Ctr., 2000—01; discharge planner Carson-Tahoe Hosp., 2003; lic. social worker, 2003—. Cons. design and constrn. 6 high tech. health clinics Alaska Arctic, 1982—83; per diem nurse Reno VA Med. Ctr., N. Nev. Med. Ctr., 1998—99; psychiat. nurse specialist Cmty. Nursing Svc. Contbr. articles to profl. jours. Active Mothers Against Drunk Driving Program U. Alaska Rural Edn., 1981—83. Recipient cert. appreciation, U.S. Census Bur., Colo., 1970, Barrow Lion's Club, 1983, others. Mem.: NASW, NOW, Assn. Women Sci. Avocations: watercolor painting, photography, hiking, horseback riding. Home: Apt 349 6200 Meadowood Mall Circle Reno NV 89502-6621 E-mail: anp3943@aol.com., marvel@bhr.reno.nv.us.

BRANAGAN, JAMES JOSEPH, lawyer; b. Johnstown, Pa., Mar. 5, 1943; s. James Francis and Caroline Bertha (Schreier) B.; m. Barbara Jeanne Miller, June 19, 1965; children: Sean Patrick, Erin MacKay, David Michael. BA in English Lit. with honors magna cum laude (Woodrow Wilson fellow), Kenyon Coll., Gambier, Ohio, 1965; LL.B. cum laude, Columbia U., 1968. Bar: Ohio 1968. Assoc. Jones, Day, Reavis & Pogue, Cleve., 1968-72; with Leaseway Transp. Corp., Cleve., 1972-81, gen. counsel, 1975-80, sec., 1979-81, v.p. corp. affairs, 1980-81; also officer, dir. Leaseway Transp. Corp. (subsidiaries); v.p. Premier Indsl. Corp., Cleve., 1981-82; sr. counsel TRW Inc., 1982-88; pvt. practice Cleve., 1988—; treas., gen. counsel, sec. Biomec Inc., 1998—. Mem. ABA, Ohio Bar Assn., Cleve. Bar Assn., Phi Beta Kappa. E-mail: bizlaw@stratos.net.

BRANAGH, KENNETH, actor, director; b. Belfast, Northern Ireland, Dec. 10, 1960; m. Emma Thompson, Aug. 1989 (div. 1996); m. Lindsay Brunnock, May 2003. Grad., Royal Academy of Dramatic Art, 1981; LittD (hon.), Queens U., Belfast, 1990. Co founder Renaissance Theater Co., Eng., to 1994. Decorated Order of Arts and Letters (France).

BRANAND, CLAIRE DIANE, advertising executive, writer; d. Frank X. Dostal and Clara A. Weidmann; m. David C. Branand, May 12, 1990 (dec. Sept 29, 2001); m. Richard M. Halpert, July 3, 1969 (div. July 20, 1973); 1 child, Wendy C. Student, Chamberlayne Jr. Coll., 1962—63; BFA, Parsons Sch. Design, 1966; student, Sch. Visual Arts, 1966—67. Layout artist R.H. Macy & Co., N.Y.C., 1966—70; freelance art dir. and writer Washington, 1974—77; prin., owner Halpert & Assocs. Advt., Washington, 1978—90; pvt. practice Washington, 1990—. Author Skye Pub., Annapolis, Md., 1996—. Author: Overboard! A Provocative History of the U.S.S. J.P. Kennedy, Jr., 2000, Here's To Your Health! Cooking With Red Wine, 2002, Nat. Assn. Post-Polio Syndrome Newsletter. Sec. bd. dirs. Nat. Assn. Post Polio Syndrome, Washington, 1991—96. Recipient Citation, Assn. for Help of Retarded Children, 1967. Mem.: U.S. Navy League (assoc.), U.S. Naval Inst. (assoc.). Avocations: painting, writing, poetry, cooking, nutrition. Office: Skye Publishing PO Box 4562 Annapolis MD 21403

BRANCA, FRANK JOSEPH, realtor, retired police officer; b. Norwalk, Conn., Dec. 4, 1948; s. Joseph and Angela Ann (Grallo) B.; m. Judy Ann Perry, July 10, 1975; children: Meredith Lynn, Kristin Jane, Ashley Marie. BS in Criminal Justice, Iona Coll., 1983. Police officer Greenwich Police Dept., Greenwich, Conn., 1970-77, youth officer, 1977-78, detective, 1978-87, sgt., 1987-90, lt., 1990-96, capt., 1996-99, ret., 1999; real estate salesperson Prudential Foothills Real Estate, Prescott, Ariz., 2000—03, broker/mgr., 2003. Pres. Fairfield County (Conn.) Police Tng. Officers Assn., 1990-92. Coord. United Way of Greenwich (Conn.), 1989-95. With USNG, 1970-76. Named Police Officer of the Year, Greenwich (Conn.) Lions Club, 1983; recipient Ofcl. Citation, State of Conn. Gen. Assembly, 1983. Mem. Internat. Assn. Chiefs of Police, Am. Soc. Law Enforcement Trainers, Silver Shield Assn. (pres. 1977-78), Greenwich Old Timers Athletics Assn. (dir. 1990-99, pres. 1993-94), Conn. Police Chiefs Assn., Prescott Assn. Realtors, Ariz. Assn. Realtors, Nat. Assn. Realtors (accredited buyer rep.), Prescott C. of C. Republican. Avocations: golf, computers, travel. E-mail: info@thebrancagroup.com.

BRANCA, JOHN GREGORY, lawyer, consultant; b. Bronxville, N.Y., Dec. 11, 1950; s. John Ralph and Barbara (Werle) B. AB in Polit. Sci. cum laude, Occidental Coll., 1972; JD, UCLA, 1975. Bar: Calif. 1975. Assoc. Kindel & Anderson, Los Angeles, 1975-77, Hardee, Barovick, Konecky & Braun, Beverly Hills, Calif., 1977-81; ptnr. Ziffren, Brittenham, Branca & Fischer, L.A., 1981—. Cons. N.Y. State Assembly, Mt. Vernon, 1978 82, various music industry orgns., L.A., 1981—. Editor-in-Chief UCLA-Alaska Law Rev., 1974-75; contbr. articles to profl. jours. Cons., bd. trustees UCLA Law Sch. Com., UCLA Athletic Dept., Occidental Coll., Musician's Assistance Program, 1995. Recipient Bancroft-Whitney award; named Entertainment Lawyer of Yr. Am. Lawyer mag., 1981. Mem. ABA (patent trademark and copyright law sect.), Calif. Bar Assn., Beverly Hills Bar Assn. (entertainment law sect.), Phi Alpha Delta, Sigma Tau Sigma. Avocations: art, antiques, music, real estate. Office: Ziffren Brittenham Branca & Fischer 1801 Century Park W Fl 9 Los Angeles CA 90067-6406

BRANCALEONE, SALVATORE JOSEPH, nutritionist, consultant; b. N.Y.C., Oct. 29, 1943; s. Joseph and Julia (Vitale) B.; m. Rebecca Diann Thornburg; children: Dina, Debra. AS, U. Fla., 1963; BS, Fla. Atlantic U., 1966, MEd, 1976. Cert. nutritionist Agy. for Health Care Admin. Bd. Medicine Dept. of Health. Tchr. H.S. and Broward C.C., Hollywood & Coconut Creek, Fla., 1966-82; pres., clin. nutritionist Palm Lakes Natural Food Market, Margate, Fla., 1980-99; nutritional cons. Parkland, Fla., 1999—. Radio talk show host WDJA-850, West Palm Beach, Fla., WWNN 1470, Boca Raton, Fla., 1991—99, Boca Raton, 2001—; clin. nutritionist specializing in treatment of degenerative diseases such as cancer, heart disease, arthritis, diabetes, immune sys. disfunction, etc; lectr. in field. Contbr. articles to profl. jours. Bd. dirs., v.p. Cypress Head Homeowners Assn. Mem. Nat. Nutritional Edn. Assn., Nat. Health Fedn., Nat. Counselors Assn. Democrat. Roman Catholic. Avocations: tennis, weight training, jogging, swimming. Home and Office: 7600 Marblehead Ln Parkland FL 33067-2336 E-mail: dijesse@aol.com.

BRANCALEONE KENNA, LAURIE ANN, social worker; b. Mineola, N.Y., Oct. 9, 1963; d. Peter and Kathleen (Marsala) B., m. June 20, 1997. B Social Worker, Adelphi U., 1985, MSW, 1986. Cert. clin. social worker. Caseworker III, Nassau County Dept. Social Svcs., Mineola, 1986-88; med. social worker Mercy Med. Ctr., Rockville Centre, N.Y., 1988—; pvt. practice in psychotherapy Garden City, N.Y., 1992—. Cons. counselor St. Vincent De Paul Parish Outreach, Elmont, NY, 1985—87. Bd. dirs. West Nassau Mental Health, Franklin Sq., N.Y., 1988. Mem. NASW, Acad. Cert. Social Workers. Roman Catholic. Avocations: music, poetry writing. Home: 349 Carnation Ave Floral Park NY 11001

BRANCATO, LEO JOHN, manufacturing company executive; b. N.Y.C., Oct. 27, 1922; s. Leo and Josephine (Abbruscato) B. BS in Mech. Engring, Cooper Union, 1950; MS, Columbia U., 1952. Registered profl. engr., Conn. Design engr. Ermold Co., N.Y.C., 1946-51; with Heli-Coil Corp., Danbury, Conn., 1952-70, exec. v.p., 1963-70, pres., 1970; v.p., dir. Mite-Corp., merger co. including Heli-Coil Co., Danbury, 1970-74; pres. Mite-Corp., 1974-88. Incorporator Union Savs. Bank, Danbury, 1967-92. Patentee in field of fastener tech. Trustee Danbury Hosp., 1961—, Union Savs. Bank Found. Inc., 1998; chmn. Housatonic Regional Mental Health Council, 1965-68; commr. conservation, Danbury, 1974-79; mem. bd. visitors U. Conn. Sch. Bus. Adminstrn., 1977-89. Lt. C.E., AUS, 1943-46. Fellow ASME; mem. Princeton Club (N.Y.C.), Ridgewood Country Club (Danbury), Tau Beta Pi.

BRANCH, JOHN CURTIS, biology educator, lawyer; b. Buffalo, Okla., Oct. 1, 1934; s. Ernest Samuel and Ethel Imogene (Parsons) B.; m. Jacqueline Joyce Davis, July 20, 1960; children: Kim Renee, Karla Jean, Kay Lynn. BS, Northwestern Okla. State U., 1959; MS, U. Okla., 1963, PhD, 1965; JD, Okla. City U., 1980. Bar: Okla. 1980. Asst. prof. biology dept. Okla. City U., 1964-67, assoc. prof. biology dept., 1967-75, prof. biology dept., 1975—. With U.S. Army, 1955-57. Mem. Okla. County Bar Assn., Okla. Acad. Sci., Okla. Bar Assn., Beta Beta Beta. Methodist. Avocations: reading, sports, traveling. Home: 2705 Abbey Rd Oklahoma City OK 73120-2702 Office: John C Branch PC 4912 S Western Ave Oklahoma City OK 73109-3838 also: Okla City U Dept Biology 2501 N Blackwelder Ave Oklahoma City OK 73106-1402

BRANCH, MICHAEL PAUL, humanities educator; b. Wyandotte, Mich., Dec. 6, 1963; s. Stuart Elton and Sharon Eileen (Shuck) B. BA in English, Coll. William and Mary, 1985; MA in English, U. Va., 1987, PhD of English, 1993. Tchr. U. Va., Charlottesville, 1986-93; asst. prof. English Fla. Internat. U., Miami, 1993-95; asst. prof. lit. and environment U. Nev., Reno, 1995-96, assoc. prof. lit. and environment, 1997—2003, prof. lit. and environ., 2003—. Pres. Assn. for Study of Lit. and Environment, 1995-96. Book rev. editor Interdisciplinary Studies in Lit. and Environment, 1996—; mem. editl. bd. Am. Nature Writing Newsletter, 1993-95; co-editor: The Height of Our Mountains, 1998, Reading the Earth, 1998; editor: John Muir's Last Journey, 2001; co-editor: The ISLE Reader, 2003; editor, Reading the Roots, 2003; contbr. articles to profl. jours. Fellow State Coun. Higher Edn., 1988, 90; Knapp Found. grant, 1994. Mem. MLA, Am. Lit. Assn., Am. Soc. Environ. History, Soc. Early Americanists, Western Lit. Assn., Sierra Club, Wilderness Soc., Wild Earth, Orion Soc., Phi Beta Kappa. Avocations: hiking, playing blues harp, gardening. Office: Univ Nevada Dept English 098 Reno NV 89557-0001 E-mail: mbranch@unr.edu.

BRANCH, RONALD DREWITT, lawyer; b. Richmond, Va., Jan. 24, 1948; s. Cornell Drewitt and Virgie Ann (Pitts) B. B.A., Va. State U., 1970; J.D., Howard U., 1973. Bar: D.C. 1976, U.S. Dist. Ct. D.C. 1976. Atty., civil rights specialist U.S. Dept. Justice, Washington, 1976-78, GSA, 1978, U.S. Dept. Labor, 1978-79, HUD, Washington, 1979— ; arbitrator D.C. Superior Ct., 1984— . Div. leader Combined Fed. Campaign, Washington, 1982-83. CLEO scholar Howard U., 1970; Danforth intern U. Cin., 1970. Mem. ARC, D.C. Bar Assn. (pro bono), ABA, Wash. Bar Assn., Phi Alpha Delta. Baptist. Club: Nat. Lawyers. Home: 2450 Virginia Ave NW Washington DC 20037-2679

BRANCH, STACY, veterinarian, educator; b. Phila., Dec. 28, 1963; DVM, Tuskegee U., 1990, PhD, N.C. State U., 1995. Diplomate Am. Coll. Forensic Medicine, Am. Coll. Forensic Examiners (fellow). Prof. environ. and molecular toxicology N.C. State U., Raleigh, 1995—. Contbr. articles to profl. jours., chpts. to books. Vol. surgeon Operation Cat Nip, Raleigh, 1997—; mentor Wake County Cmty. Svc. Program, Raleigh, 1996. Recipient Rsch. grant NIEHS, 1998—. Mem. Soc. Toxicology. Home: 307 Riverstone Dr Clayton NC 27520 Office: NC State U Box 7633 Raleigh NC 27695 Fax: 919-515-7169. E-mail: stacy_branch@ncsu.edu.

BRANCH, TAYLOR, writer; b. Atlanta, Jan. 14, 1947; s. Franklin T. and Jane (Worthington) B.; m. Christina Macy; 2 children. AB, U. N.C., 1968; postgrad., Princeton U., 1968-70. Staff member Washington Monthly mag., Washington, D.C., 1970-73, Harper's mag., N.Y.C., 1973-75, Esquire mag., N.Y.C., 1975-76. Author: (with Bill Russell) Second Wind: The Memoirs of an Opinionated Man, 1979, The Empire Blues, 1981, (with Eugene M. Propper) Labyrinth, 1982, Parting the Waters. America in the King Years, 1954-63, 1988 (Pulitzer Prize for history 1989, Nat. Book Critics Circle award for non-fiction 1988, Christopher award 1988, Nat. Book award nomination 1989), Pillar of Fire, 1999; editor, contbr.: (with Charles Peters) Blowing the Whistle: Dissent in the Public Interest, 1972. Office: care Larhansoff & Verrill 179 Franklin St New York NY 10013-2857*

BRANCH, THOMAS BROUGHTON, III, lawyer; b. Atlanta, June 5, 1936; s. Thomas Broughton Jr. and Alfred Iverson (Dews) B.; m. Trudi Schroetter, Dec. 27, 1963; children: Maria Barbara, Thomas B. IV. BA cum laude, Washington and Lee U., 1958, JD, 1960. Bar: Ga. 1960, U.S. Dist. Ct. (no. dist.) Ga. 1960, U.S. Ct. Appeals (5th cir.) 1960, U.S. Dist. Ct. (mid. dist.) Ga. 1980, U.S. Ct. Appeals (11th cir.) 1980, U.S. Dist. Ct. (so. dist.) N.Y. 1984, U.S. Ct. Appeals (2d cir.) 1984, U.S. Supreme Ct. 1991. Assoc. Kilpatrick & Cody, Atlanta, 1960-63; ptnr. Greene, Buckley et al, Atlanta, 1963-79, Wildman, Harrold, Allen, Dixon & Branch, Atlanta, 1979-89, Branch, Pike & Ganz, Atlanta, 1990-95, Holland & Knight, Atlanta, 1995—. Asst. prof. Woodrow Wilson Law Sch., Atlanta, 1964-68; trustee Washington and Lee U., Lexington, Va., 1979-90, trustee emeritus, 1991—; trustee, chmn. Atlanta Lawyers Found., Atlanta, 1980-81, Atlantis Aurora, Inc., 1970-74. Mem. Citizens Adv. Council on Urban Devel., Atlanta, 1977; trustee The Children's Sch., Inc., Atlanta,

1980-85; elder, clk. First Presbyn. Ch., Atlanta, 1967-79, 81-85, 97—. Fellow Am. Bar Found.; mem. ABA, Ga. Bar Assn., Atlanta Bar Assn. (mem. jud. selection and tenure com. 1988—), Am. Jud. Soc., Atlanta Lawyers Club (pres. 1976-77), Bleckley Inn of Ct. (master), Def. Rsch. Inst., Ansley Golf Club (pres., bd. dirs. 1976-87). Home: 85 Montgomery Ferry Dr NE Atlanta GA 30309 E-mail: tbranch@hklaw.com.

BRANCH, WILLIAM BLACKWELL, playwright, producer; b. New Haven, Sept. 11, 1927; s. James Matthew and Iola (Douglas) B.; m. Marie Louise Foster, Aug. 19, 1956 (div.); 1 dau., Rochelle Ellen. BS, Northwestern U., 1949; M.F.A., Columbia U., 1958; ABC fellow, Yale U., 1965-66. Prof. Cornell U., 1985-94. Vis. scholar, lectr. numerous univs.; vis. prof. U. Md., Baltimore County, 1979-82; U. Calif. Regents lectr., spring, 1985; vis. Luce fellow Williams Coll., fall, 1983; vis. disting. prof. William Paterson Coll. N.J., Wayne, 1994-96. Actor appearing in: Anna Lucasta, 1945, Detective Story, 1951; playwright for theatre, TV and motion pictures, 1951—; assoc. in film, Columbia Sch. of Arts, 1968-69; staff writer-producer, Channel 13, Ednl. TV, N.Y.C., 1962-64; dir. The Jackie Robinson Show, NBC, 1958-60; co-author: The Jackie Robinson Column N.Y. Post and syndication, 1959-61; screenwriter Universal Studios, 1968-69, producer, NBC News, 1972-73, pres., William Branch Assos., 1973—; works include (theatre) A Medal for Willie, 1951, In Splendid Error, 1954, A Wreath for Udomo, 1960, To Follow the Phoenix, 1960, Baccalaureate, 1975; (TV) Light in the Southern Sky, 1958 (Robert E. Sherwood TV award 1958), A Letter From Booker T., 1987; TV documentary Still a Brother: Inside the Negro Middle Class, 1968 (Emmy award nominee 1969, Blue Ribbon award Am. Film Festival 1969); documentary TV series Afro American Perspectives, 1974-83; screen Together for Days, 1971; exec. producer: Black Perspective on the News, Pub. Broadcasting System, 1978-79; author: Fifty Steps Toward Freedom, 1959; author, editor: Black Thunder: An Anthology of Contemporary African American Drama, 1992 (Am. Book award 1992), Crosswinds: An Anthology of Black Dramatists in the Diaspora, 1993. Bd. dirs. Am. Soc. African Culture, 1963-70; treas. Nat. Conf. African Am. Theatre, 1987-91; bd. dirs. Nat. Citizens Com. for Broadcasting, 1969-71; mem. nat. adv. bd. Ctr. for Book, Library of Congress, 1979-83, W.E.B. DuBois Found., 1987—. Served with AUS, 1951-53. John Guggenheim fellow, 1959-60; recipient Hannah B. Del Vecchio award Columbia, 1958 Address: 53 Cortlandt Ave New Rochelle NY 10801-2032

BRANCH, WILLIAM TERRELL, urologist, educator; b. Paragould, Ark., Dec. 7, 1937; s. William Owen and Mary Rose (Dempsey) B.; m. Mary Fletcher Cox, Dec. 11, 1965; children: Ashley Tucker, William T., Steven K. BS, Ark. State U., 1964, MD, 1971. Diplomate Am. Bd. Urology. Adminstrv. asst. mental retardation planning project State of Ark., Little Rock, 1964-66; intern U. South Fla. Sch. Medicine Affiliated Hosps., Tampa, 1971-72, resident in surgery, 1972-73, resident in urology, 1973-75, chief resident in urology, 1975-76, clin. prof. urology, chmn. dept. surgery, 1976—; practice medicine specializing in urology Tampa, 1976—; mem. staff, sec. urology Tampa Gen. Hosp., 1976-78, vice chief urology, 1978-80, chief urology, 1980-82; mem. staff, co-chief surgery Meml. Hosp., Tampa, 1978-80, vice chief med. staff, 1980-82, chief med. staff, 1982-84, trustee, 1983-88, bd. dirs. Mem. adv. bd. Suncoast Ednl. Telecommunications Systems, 1982; vice chmn., bd. dirs. Meml. Hosp., 1987-88; cons. in urology James A. Haley VA Hosp., Tampa, 1978—; mem. staff St. Joseph's Hosp., Tampa, 1976—, Tampa Gen. Hosp.; cons. staff Women's Hosp., Tampa; adv. bd. Glendale Fed. Savs., 1983-85, Beneficial Harbour Island Savs. Bank, 1985-87, South Trust Bank, 1988—, also bd. dirs., exec. com., chair audit com.; chief urology, bd. mem. Tampa Outpatient Surgery Facility, 2000—; chmn. vol. faculty com. Dept. Surgery U. South Fla. Coll. Medicine; vice chmn. bd. dirs. Shriners Hosp. for Children, Tampa. Author: (with others) Mental Retardation in Arkansas, 1964-66; A Demographic Study, 1966; cons. editor Jour. Fla. Med. Assn., 1978-93. Bd. dirs. Tampa Ballet, 1980, Tampa Charity Horse Show Bd. Dirs. Assn., 1985-87, Shriners Hosp. for Children, Tampa, 2000, Tampa Outpatient Surg. Facility,,United Way, Tampa, 1983-90, mem. exec. com., 1984-88; mem. med. adv. bd. Nat. Kidney Found. of Fla., Inc., 1983-90; mem. Tampa Bay Super Bowl XXV Task Force, Super Bowl XXXV Task Force; mem. adv. bd. dirs. Salvation Army; founding chmn. Kettle com., vice chmn. adv. bd. dirs., chmn., 1998-2000. Recipient Disting. Alumnus award Ark. State U., 1986. Fellow ACS (credit com. region IV, Fla. chpt. 1982-98, exec. com. Fla. chpt. 1985—, sec., treas. 1987-88, pres.-elect 1989-90, pres. 1990-92, gov. 1990-96, bd. gov. chpt. activities com. 1991-96, alt. 1993, chmn. nomination com. 1995, chmn. applications com. region IV); mem. Am. Urol. Assn., Royal Soc. Medicine (affiliate), Fla. Med. Assn. (del. 1983, 88-96), Fla. Urol. Soc. (Milton Copeland award 1976, exec. com. 1978-82), Hillsborough County Med. Assn. (exec. com. 1978-81, treas. 1981-82, sec. 1983-84), Fla. Quality Med. Assurance, Inc. (bd. dirs., treas., chmn. exec. com. 1995, chmn. bd. govs.), Southeastern Surg. Congress, Greater Tampa C. of C. (dir. 1982-86, 87-90, chmn. med. meetings task force 1983-84, Super Star award 1983), Tampa Bay Surg. Soc. (founding mem., sec., bd. dirs. 1998, pres. 1999-2001), Tampa Hist. Soc., Hillsborough County Med. Soc. (pres. polit. action com. 1986-87, 88-89), Tampa Yacht and Country Club (gov. 1984-87), Centre of Tampa Club (founding mem. 1988-93, bd. dirs., chmn. mem. com.), Univ. Club (treas. 1998-99, sec. 1999-2000, bd. dirs. 1998-99), Ye Mystic Krewe of Gasparilla (bd. dirs. 1991-2000, 1st lt. 1988-89, lord chamberlain 1994-95, chmn. exec. com. 1995-96, capt. 1996-98), King Gasparilla LXXXVI. Home: 1002 Harbour Island Blvd # 1605 Tampa FL 33602 Office: 2919 W Swann Ave Ste 303 Tampa FL 33609-4051

BRANCH, WILLIAM THOMAS, JR., medical educator; b. Montgomery, Ala., Mar. 28, 1941; s. William Thomas and Mary Seibels (Lanier) B.; m. Carolyn Jenkins, June 9, 1967; 1 child, Katherine Mary Seibels Branch. BA, Vanderbilt U., 1963; MD, Med. Coll. Ala., 1967. Resident Peter Bent Brigham Hosp., Boston, 1967-72; staff assoc. NIH, Bethesda, Md., 1969-71; assoc. prof. Med. Sch. Harvard U., Boston, 1972-95; prof. Sch. Medicine, vice chmn. dept. medicine Emory U., Atlanta, 1995—, dir. divsn. gen. medicine, 1995—. Dir. primary care residency program Brigham & Women's Hosp., Boston, 1974-95. Editor: Office Practice of Medicine, 1982, 2d edit., 1987, 4th edit., 2003; contbr. articles to profl. jours. including New Eng. Jour. Medicine, JAMA, among others. Recipient Career award for med. edn. Soc. General Internal Medicine, 1997. Master ACP. Methodist. Home: 99 Inman Cir NE Atlanta GA 30309-3384 Office: Emory U Sch Medicine 1525 Clifton Rd NE Atlanta GA 30322-4200

BRANCH, WINSTON PATRICK, artist; b. Castries, St. Lucia, Mar. 16, 1947; came to U.S., 1998; s. Nicholas and Eugenie Genevieve Branch; Eleni Zaharopoulou, Feb. 26, 1996; 1 child, Polly. Diploma in Fine Art, Univ. Coll., London, 1970; postgrad., Brit. Sch., Rome, 1971-72. Artist-in-residence Fisk U., Nashville, 1973; vis. tutor Kingston Art Sch., London, 1973-82, Chelsea Art Sch., London, 1973-92; vis. tutor Slade Sch. Fine Art, U. Coll., London, 1973-92; asst. adj. prof. U. Calif., Berkeley, 1998-99; assoc. prof. Kans. State U., Manhattan, 2000-01. Exhibited in group shows Transforming the Crown: African Asian and Caribbean Artists in Britain, 1966-96, Bienal of Sao Paulo, 1971, 96, Salon des Jennes Peintures Grand Palais, Paris, 1971, World Festival of African Arts and Culture, Lagos, Nigeria, 1977, Biennale of Paris, 1982, Bienal of Cuenca, 1994, Studio Mus. Harlem, 1997, 25 other mus.; represented in collections Berkeley Art Mus., Brit. Mus., Victoria and Albert Mus., Arts Coun. Gt. Britain; stage designer Hello-Out-There, London, 1968, Village Wooing, London, 1968, Jimmy K Fitsh, Amdsterdam, 1971. Panelist City of Oakland Cultural Arts Dept., 2003. Recipient Brit. Prix de Rome, 1971, Brit. Coun., 1973, purchase award 23d Bienal Sao Paulo, 1996; Guggenheim fellow, 1978; grantee Artists-in-Berlin Program, 1976, OAS, 1994. Mem. Chelsea Arts Club London, Faculty Club U. Calif. Berkeley, Mus. Modern Art (San Francisco). Avocations: music, theater, cultural programmes. Office: PO Box GM 921 Gablewoods Mall Saint Lucia

BRANCHE, ANNA LOUISE, physical education educator, performing arts educator, religious studies educator; b. Chester, Pa., June 6, 1931; d. Florence Layton; m. Stanley Everett Branche Sr. (div.); children: Mark Ivan, Stanley Everett Jr., Wilma Ward, Alexander. BS, Pa. State U., 1953; MA, Temple U., 1966. Ordained min. Universal Ch., 1968, ordained priest Liberal Cath. Ch., London, 1991, ordained archbishop Ethiopian Coptic Ch., Eng., 1993; cert. profl. educator Pa. Phys. edn. instr. Sch. Dist. of Phila., 1955—75, coord. dance instrn., 1975—80; founder, presiding officer The New SEED Sanctuary, Phila., 1983—. Spiritual cons., Phila., 1973—; lectr., workshop facilitator The New SEED Sanctuary, Phila., 1983—. Author: Wisdom from the Motherland; composer music included in the film The Crucible. Choreographer Phila. Cotillion, 1958—62; founding bd. mem. Nat. African Religion Congress, Phila., 1999—2003; vol. ARC, Phila., 1983—95. Achievements include African Initiation featured in television documentary Divine Magic, filmed by the BBC for the Discovery Channel. Avocations: travel, reading, bridge, Scrabble. Office: The New SEED Sanctuary 6000 Overbrook Ave Philadelphia PA 19131

BRANCO, JAMES JOSEPH, estate planner; b. Santa Maria, Azores, Portugal, Mar. 14, 1951; arrived in U.S., 1954; s. Leroy and Michele (Desroches) B.; married, Aug. 27, 1994; children: James II, Natalie, Gabrielle. BA, Brandywine Coll., 1971. Chief exec. officer Profl. Fin. Mgrs., Inc., Spring Lake, N.J., 1974—; ptnr. Atlantic Drilling Co., Sea Girt, 1982—. Pres. Profl. Condo Conversions, Belmar, N.J., 1977-93. Mem. Belmar C. of C. (pres. 1995-98, v.p. 1998, 99, 2000), KC (3d deg.), Pan Am. Club, Phi Epsilon. Republican. Roman Catholic. Avocations: racquetball, whitewater rafting, photography. Office: Profl Fin Mgrs Inc PO Box 460 Manasquan NJ 08736 E-mail: jim@lifebroker.com.

BRAND, CHARLES MACY, history educator; b. Stanford, Calif., Apr. 7, 1932; s. Carl F. and Nan (Surface) B.; m. Mary Joan Shorrock, Aug. 7, 1954; children: Catharine, Stephen. BA, Stanford U., 1953; MA, Harvard U., 1954, PhD, 1961. Asst. prof. history San Francisco State Coll., 1962-64; asst. prof. Bryn Mawr Coll., Pa., 1964-69, assoc. prof., 1969-75, prof. history, 1975-99, chmn. dept. history, 1978-81, 96-97, prof. emeritus, 1999—. Author: Byzantium Confronts the West, 1180-1204, 1968, 2d edit., 1992; editor: Icon and Minaret, 1969; translator: Deeds of John and Manuel Comnenus (by J. Kinnamos), 1976. Served with U.S. Army, 1955-57. Dumbarton Oaks Center for Byzantine Studies fellow, 1961, 1988; Fulbright research fellow, 1968; Gennadius fellow, 1968; Guggenheim fellow, 1972 Mem. U.S. Nat. Com. for Byzantine Studies (1961), Medieval Acad. Am., Am. Hist. Assn., Byzantine Studies Conf. Home: 508 Montgomery Ave Haverford PA 19041-1409

BRAND, EDWARD CABELL, retail executive; b. Salem, Va., Apr. 11, 1923; s. William F. and Ruth (Cabell) B.; m. Shirley Hurt, June 20, 1964; children: Sylvia, Miriam, Liza, Richie, John, Edward, Marshall, Caroline. Grad., Va. Mil. Inst., 1944; HHD (hon.), Roanoke Coll., 1997, Washington and Lee U., 1999. Dept. of State econ. analyst, intelligence office Berlin Mil. Govt., 1947-49; v.p. Ortho-Vent Shoe Co., 1949-62; pres. Brand Edmonds Assocs. Advertising, 1962-66, chmn. bd., 1962-81; founder, pres. Stuart McGuire Co., Salem, Va., 1962-85, chmn. bd., chief exec. officer, 1973-05, chmn. emeritus, cons. Stuart McGuire Co. (merged with Home Shopping (TV) Network), 1985-86; pres. Recovery Systems, Inc., Salem, Va., 1986—. Rsch. assoc., former instr. bus. adminstrn. and sales mgmt. Roanoke Coll. Chmn. Va. State Bd. Health, 1989-93; pres., founder Cabell Brand Ctr. for Internat. Poverty and Resource Studies of Roanoke Coll; former mem. Bus. Leadership Adv. Council.; past bd. dirs. Roanoke Council of Community Services; founder, pres. Total Action Against Poverty, Roanoke Valley, 1965-95; pres. Pvt. Sector Commn. Va. Community Action Agys., 1986-88; mem. Gov.'s Commn. on Fed. Funding of State Domestic Program, 1986-88; former trustee Council on Religion and Internat. Affairs, Ethics Resource Ctr.; past bd. dirs. Woodlands Conf. div. Woodlands Ctr. for Future Research and the Houston Area Research Ctr., Global Water, Washington; bd. dirs. Va. Health Care Found., Richmond, Va., 1993-2000, Va. Found. for the Humanities and Pub. Policy, Charlottesville, 1993-99, Blue Ridge Pub. TV, Roanoke, Va., 1993—, Action Alliance for Va. Children and Youth, Richmond, 1994-2000, Va. Conservation Network, Richmond, 1996—; bd. trustees Western Va. Land Trust, Roanoke, Va., 1995-2000; assoc. World Resources Inst., Washington, 1985. Served from pvt. to capt. AUS, 1942-46, ETO. Decorated Bronze Star. Named Businessman in U.S. who has done most to help disadvantaged people, Vista, 1980; recipient LBJ Humanitarian nat. award, 1989, Outstanding Citizen Rotary Club, 1999. Mem. NAS (coun., pres. circle), Social Venture Network, Direct Selling Assn. (past dir., chmn. named to Hall of Fame), U.S. C. of C., Conf. Bd. (exec. coun.), World Pres. Assn. (past dir., chmn. Argentina Conf. 1988), Newcomen Soc. N.Am., Roanoke Touchdown Club (past pres.), Valley Torch Club (past pres.), Roanoke Sales Execs. (past dir.), Rotary (past. pres. Salem). Home: 701 W Main St Salem VA 24153-3513 Office: Recovery Systems Inc PO Box 429 Salem VA 24153-0429 E-mail: CBC@CBCenter.org. *In addition to trying to do the best job I could— whether in school, business, public service, or in my family— I have felt a continuing need to improve our system and society. This has led to extensive study, travels, and a variety of extra-curricular activities. Today I have great confidence in the future of the United States and the world, but see urgent need for dramatic changes in our value systems, and need for long range planning. Our New Center focuses on inter-relationship between poverty and resource limitation for sustainable development.*

BRAND, GEORGE EDWARD, JR., lawyer; b. Detroit, Oct. 25, 1918; s. George Edward and Elsie Bertie (Jones) B.; m. Patricia Jean Gould, June 7, 1947; children— Martha Christine, Carol Elsie, George Edward. BA, Dartmouth Coll., 1941; postgrad., U. Minn., Harvard U., 1941; JD, U. Mich., 1948. Bar: Mich. 1948, U.S. Supreme Ct. 1958. Mem. firm George E. Brand, Detroit, 1948-63, Butzel, Long, Gust, Klein & Van Zile, P.C., Detroit, 1963—; ptnr., dir., pres. Butzel, Long, Gust, Klein & Van Zile, 1974-89. Served with USNR, 1942-46. Fellow Am. Bar Found., Am. Coll. Trial Lawyers; mem. ABA, Am. Judicature Soc., Detroit Bar Assn., VFW. Clubs: N.S.S.C. Home: 1233 Kensington Ave Grosse Pointe Park MI 48230-1101 Office: 150 W Jefferson Ave Ste 900 Detroit MI 48226-4416

BRAND, GROVER JUNIOR, retired state agricultural official; b. Stark City, Mo., July 5, 1930; s. Grover Cleveland and Ada Neomi (Evans) B.; m. Juanita Sue Warden, Aug. 30, 1952 (div. Oct. 1968); children: Ellen E., Teresa L., Lisa S. B Liberal Studies, U. Okla., 1970. Cert. profl. purchasing agent. Mgr. Crest Drive-In Commonwealth Theatres, Joplin, Mo., 1952-58; buyer Eagle-Picher Ind., Joplin, 1958-65, purchasing mgr., 1965-73; project coord. Atlas Industries, Oswego, Kans., 1973-78; warehouse examiner Kans. State Grain Inspection, Topeka, 1979-92. Recipient 6th pl. award Nat. Amateur Typing Contest, 1948. Mem. Nat. Assn. Purchasing Mgrs. (chmn. value techniques com. 1972-73). Avocation: stock investing. Home: 1990 NW 120th St Columbus KS 66725-3077

BRAND, IRVING, lawyer; b. Wilkes-Barre, Penn., Oct. 22, 1942; s. Nathan H. and Rose (Mitchneck) Brand; m. Marion F. Daitch, Aug. 31, 1967; 1 child, Ross G. BA, Lafayette Col., 1964; LLB, U. Va., 1967. Bar: N.Y. 1968, U.S. Ct. Appeals (2d cir.) 1968, U.S. Dist. Ct. (ea. and so. dists.) N.Y. 1975. Atty. Kelley, Drye & Warren, N.Y.C., 1967-75; v.p. staff labor rels. NBC, Inc., N.Y.C., 1975-2000, 2000—. Dir., v.p. Westfield (N.J.) Basketball Assn., 1979—85; alumni admissions rep. Lafayette Coll., 1989—, mem. steering com., 1997—2000. Named Outstanding Alumni Admissions Rep., Lafayette Coll., 1993. Mem.: ABA, Assn. Bar City N.Y. (labor employment/law com.), Col. Men's Club Westfield (mem. scholarship com., v.p.). Jewish. Avocations: basketball, tennis. Home: 214 Lynn Ave Westfield NJ 07090-1811 Office: NBC Inc 30 Rockefeller Plz Rm 1653E New York NY 10112-0036

BRAND, MYLES, academic administrator; b. N.Y.C., May 17, 1942; s. Irving Philip and Shirley (Berger) B.; m. Wendy Hoffman (div. 1976); 1 child: Joshua; m. Margaret Zeglin, 1978. BS, Rensselaer Poly. Inst., 1964, PhD (hon.), 1991; PhD, U. Rochester, 1967. Asst. prof. philosophy U. Pitts., 1967-72; from assoc. prof. to prof., dept. chmn. U. Ill., Chgo., 1972-81; prof., dept. head U. Ariz., Tucson, 1981-83, dir. cognitive sci. program, 1982-85, dean, social & behavioral scis., 1983-86; provost, v.p. acad. affairs Ohio State U., Columbus, 1986-89; pres. U. Oreg., Eugene, 1989-94, Ind. U., Bloomington, 1994—2002, Nat. Collegiate Athletic Assn., Indpls., 2003—. Author: Intending and Acting, 1984; editor: The Nature of Human Action, 1970, The Nature of Causation, 1976, Action Theory, 1976. Bd. dirs. Ariz. Humanities Coun., 1984-85, Am. Coun. on Edn., Washington, 1992-97. Recipient research award NEH, 1974, 79. Mem. Clarion Hosps. Assn. of Am. Phi, Assn. Am. Univs. (pres. 1999). Office: NCAA PO Box 6222 Indianapolis IN 46206

BRAND, OSCAR, folksinger, writer, educator; b. Winnipeg, Man., Can., Feb. 7, 1920; s. Isidore and Beatrice (Shulman) B.; m. Rubyan Saber (div.); children: Jeannie, Eric, James; m. Karen Lynn Grossman, June 14, 1970; 1 child, Jordan. BA, Bklyn. Coll., 1942; Polit. Sci. Laureate, Fairfield U., 1972; PhD (hon.), U. Winnipeg, 1987. Host, performer Folksong Festival, Sta. WNYC-AM, N.Y.C., 1945—. Pres. Harlequin Prodns., Inc., Gypsy Hill Music, Inc.; trustee Newport Festival Found.; mem. faculty Hofstra U., New Sch., 1970-80; music adviser nat. bd. YWCA; mem. creative bd. Sesame Street, Pres.'s Com. on Nutrition; cons. Bill Moyers, PBS-TV, 1983; curator Songwriters Hall of Fame. Host: (TV show) World of Folkmusic, H.E.W., 1962-82, Oscar Brand's Am. Odyssey, 1970-72, Treasure Chest, The First Look, 1965-68, (radio show) Voices in the Wind, 1974-80, 13 of Segovia, First Person Am.; star: (TV series) Let's Sing Out, Can., 1962-68, Brand New Scene, Can., 1966; artistic dir. Project America, 92d St. Y, 1998-2001; music dir. (TV series) Nat. Geog. Bicentennial, 1974, Sunday, Exploring; music advisor: (TV series) Nuclear Age, 1986-87, (PBS) Liberty, 1998; writer, dir.: (TV spl. and show) Sing, America, Sing, Kennedy Ctr. Bicentennial Celebration, 1975; composer, lyricist: (broadway show) Joyful Noise, 1966, HYMAN KAPLAN, 1968, (off-broadway show) In White America, 1965, How to Steal an Election, 1969, It's a Jungle, Bridge of Hope for lit. conf., 1969, Celebrate for N.Y. Presbytery, 1970, (off broadway show) Thunder Bay, Fun and Games, Protest, 1999, Ready Aim Sing, 1999, Ballads and Ballots, 2000, Me and Woody, 2000, (songs for film) The Fox, Sybil, The Long Riders, Blue Chips, 1994; author: Singing Holidays, 1957, Bawdy Songs, 1960, Folksongs for Fun, 1961, The Ballad Mongers, 1964, Songs of '76, 1974, When I First Came to This Land, 1975, Party Songs, 1983; rec. artist 100 albums; performer (video) At Home, 1988, Campaigns for Smithsonian, 1999; editor: Words About Music, 1980-2002. Program coord. Nat. Hadassah, 1989-98; trustee BMI Found., 1995—; music dir. Rukeyser Guide, 1996. Served as sgt. M.C. AUS, 1942-45. Recipient Radio Pioneers of Am. award, 1986, Venice, Edinburgh, Valley Forge and Cannes Film Festival awards for documentary and ednl. films, 1946, numerous other awards include Emmy, Peabody, Freedoms Found., Scholastic for radio, TV and films, 1962-86, Lifetime Achievement award World Folk Music Assn., 1996, Peabody Personal award, 1996; honoree Coalition Against Domestic Violence (adv. bd. 1993—), United Cmty. Fund, 1997; named Illustrious Alumnus Bklyn. Coll., 2001. Mem. Nat. Acad. Popular Music (bd. dirs. 1969—), N.Y. Folklore Soc., Sheet Music Soc. Avocations: sailing, carpentry. Office: Gypsy Hill Music PO Box 1362 Manhasset NY 11030-6362 E-mail: oscarbrand@oscarbrand.com. *I need more time.*

BRAND, VANCE DEVOE, astronaut; b. Longmont, Colo., May 9, 1931; s. Rudolph William and Donna (DeVoe) B.; m. Joan Virginia Weninger, July 25, 1953; children: Susan Nancy, Stephanie, Patrick Richard, Kevin Stephen; m. Beverly Ann Whitnel, Nov. 3, 1979; children: Erik Ryan, Dane Vance. BS in Bus., U. Colo., 1953, BS in Aero. Engring., 1960; MBA, UCLA, 1964; grad., U.S. Naval Test Pilot Sch., Patuxent River, Md., 1963; DSc (hon.), U. Colo., 2000. With Lockheed-Calif. Co., Burbank, 1960-66, flight test engr., 1961-62, traveling engr. rep., 1962-63, engring. test pilot, 1963-66; astronaut NASA Johnson Space Ctr., Houston, 1966-92, command module pilot Apollo-Soyuz mission, 1975, comdr. STS-5 Mission, 1982, comdr. STS 41-B Mission, 1984, comdr. STS-35 Mission, 1990; chief plans Nat. Aero-Space Plane Joint Program Office, Wright-Patterson AFB, Ohio, 1992-94; asst. chief flight ops. directorate DFRC NASA, Edwards, Calif., 1994-98, dep. dir. aerospace projects, 1998—2002, acting dir. aerospace projects, 2002—. With USMCR, 1953-57. Decorated 2 Disting. Svc. medals NASA, 2 Exceptional Svc. medals, 3 Space medals; indeucted into Internat. Space Hall of Fame, 1996, U.S. Astronaut Hall of Fame, 1997, Internat. Aerspace Hall of Fame, 2001. Fellow AIAA, Am. Astron. Soc., Soc. Exptl. Test Pilots. Office: M/S D2332 DFRC PO Box 273 Edwards CA 93523-0273

BRANDAU, CHRISTIE PEARSON, librarian; b. Boone, Iowa, May 7, 1949; d. Ingemar Nils and Elsa Pearson; m. John Alan Brandau, Dec. 20, 1968; children: Jennifer Brandau Carlson, Kara Brandau Califf, Benjamin John. MA in Libr. Sci., U. of Iowa, 1988; BA in Polit. Sci., Iowa State U., 1975. Asst. state libr. State Libr. of Iowa, Des Moines, 1991—2000; state libr. Libr. of Mich., Lansing, 2000—. Mem.: ALA (SLAS chair 2001—02), Mich. State Hist. Records Adv. Bd., Mich. Humanities Coun. Office: Libr Mich 702 W Kalamazoo Prescott MI 48756 Office Fax: 517-373-4480. E-mail: cbrandau@michigan.gov.

BRANDAUER, FREDERICK PAUL, Asian language educator; b. N.Y.C., Dec. 14, 1933; s. Frederick William and Grace Angeline (Martin) B.; children— Rebekah Susan, Frederick Jonathan. BA, Lebanon Valley Coll., 1955; M.Div., United Theol. Sem., 1958; MA, U. Pitts., 1965; PhD, Stanford U., 1973. Missionary United Meth. Ch., Hong Kong, 1959-69; acting dir. (Christian Study Center), Hong Kong, 1967-69; lectr. Chinese, Stanford (Calif.) U., 1972-73; asst. prof. Chinese U. Wash., Seattle, 1973-78, chmn. dept. Asian lang. and lit., 1978-82, assoc. prof., 1978-97, assoc. prof. emeritus, 1997—. Author: (with M. Berkowitz and J. Reed) Folk Religion in an Urban Setting, 1969, Tung Yueh, 1978; editor (with C.C. Huang) Imperial Rulership and Cultural Change in Traditional China, 1994; contbr. articles to profl. jours. NDEA Title IV fellow, 1969-71; NDFL Title VI fellow, 1971-72; ACLS Chinese Civilization grantee, 1976-77; Alexander von Humboldt fellow U. Munich, 1977-78 Mem. Assn. Asian Studies, Am. Oriental Soc., Soc. Study of Chinese Religions. Roman Catholic. Address: 1816 NE 55th St Seattle WA 98105-3323 E-mail: mariefred@home.com., fbrandau@u.washington.edu.

BRANDEIS, BARRY, corporate executive; b. May 3, 1946; s. Norman and Jennie (Yousin) B.; m. Renee Riesenberg, Apr. 4, 1971; children: Adam, Marisa. BS in Psychology, Pa. State U., 1968, MBA in Mgmt., 1970; MBA in Fin., CUNY, 1974, postgrad. in bus., 1975. Account exec. Meridian Securities Co., Bala Cynwyd, Pa., 1968-70; instr. Pace U. Grad. Sch., Baruch Coll., 1971; assoc. prof. Pace U. Grad. Sch., 1975—99. Asst. to chmn. Wasko Gold Products Corp., N.Y.C., 1975-77, v.p. fin., 1977-80, exec. v.p., 1980-83; group exec. Holding Capital Group, 1984-85; chief exec. officer Budoff, Inc., 1985-88; v.p. Craftex Creations Inc., N.Y.C., 1988-90; prin. Twin Era Ltd., N.Y.C., 1991—. U.S. Senate Bus. Adv. Bd.; alumni bd. Pa. State U., Abington. Mem. AAUP, Internat. Precious Metals Inst. (charter), Assn. MBA Execs., P.R. C. of C. in U.S. (bd. dirs.), Internat. Platform Assn., N.Y. Acad. Scis., Parmi Nous, Omicron Delta Kappa, Psi Chi. Home: 15 Cooper Dr Great Neck NY 11023-1908 Office: Twin Era Ltd 1410 Broadway New York NY 10018-5007 E-mail: bbxny@aol.com.

BRANDEISKY, KATHLEEN SEXTON, social worker, consultant; b. Evergreen Park, Ill., Jan. 23, 1961; d. Stephen Richard Sexton and Margaret Louise (Nemann) Schreibeis; m. Howard Paul Brandeisky, Sept. 6, 1987; children: Kara Veronica, Paul Stephen. BS in Social Welfare, Ohio State U., 1983; MA, U. Chgo., 1985. Lic. clin. social worker, Ill. Med. social worker Westchester County Med. Ctr., Valhalla, N.Y., 1985-87; psychiat. social worker St. Vincents Hosp., Harrison, N.Y., 1987-89, supervising psychiat. social worker, 1989-91; pvt. practice Mt. Kisco, N.Y., 1992-94; mem. staff The Therapy Ctr., Mt. Kisco, 1997—99; sch. social worker Wilmette (Ill.) Dist. 39, 1999—. Coord., cons. Mt. Kisco Drug & Alcohol Abuse Prevention Coun., 1989—99. Mem. NASW (qualified clin. social worker), Nat. Register Clin. Social Workers. Home: 2306 Cambridge Dr Northbrook IL 60062-6936

BRANDEL, RALPH EDWARD, management consultant; b. Cleve., Sept. 15, 1922; s. Wallace Lester Andrew and Marion (Coulton) B.; m. Dorothy Lucille Alspach, Jul. 14, 1945. BS, U. Md., 1954; MS, Rensselaer Polytech. Inst., 1960; postgrad., American U., Washington, 1970-72. With USMC, 1942-69, commd. 2d lt., 1944, advanced through grades to col., 1968, inf. officer, 1944, arty. officer, 1945, photointerpretation intelligence officer, 1945, engr. officer, 1949-67; S-4 logistics, S-3 ops., 1st Engr. Bn., 1st Marine Divsn. Fleet Marine Force Pacific, 1954-56; asst. prof. naval sci. Rensselaer Poly. Inst., Troy, N.Y., 1957-60; cmdg. officer 2d MarDiv engrs. Cuban Crisis, 1962-63; tng. plans officer for 4 Korean Armed Forces, 1963-64; Def. Depot Ogden dir. installation svcs., 1964-67; head officer plans HQMC, 1968-69; ret. USMC Hdqrs., Washington, 1969; v.p., sec., treas. Va. Pharms. Co., Inc., Fairfax, 1974-84; cons., 1984—; dep. dir. Gen. for the Am. Internat. Biog. Ctr., Cambridge, Eng., 1997—. Sci. adviser to dir. gen. Internat. Biog. Ctr., Cambridge, Eng., 2000—. Decorated Joint Svcs. Commendation medal, Navy Commendation medal, Army Commendation medal; recipient Wisdom award of Honor Wisdom Soc.; named Eminent Wisdom fellow Wisdom Hall of Fame, 1998. Mem. VFW (life), Am. Legion (life), Nat. Assn. Atomic Vets. (life), Mil. Officers Assn. of Am. (life), Marine Corps Engr. Assn., Order Internat. Fellowship (life), Toastmasters. Episcopalian. Avocations: furniture restoration, relacquering and gilding antiques, asian art, stamp collecting, photography. Home and Office: Oakdale Park 8606 Janet Ln Vienna VA 22180-6864

BRANDELL, SOL RICHARD, electrical power and control system engineer, research mathematician; Studied with Norman Masloff, Juilliard Sch. Music, 1932-41; studied with Sir John Barbirolli, La Follette Sch. Music, N.Y.C., 1939; student, U. Cin., 1943-44, U. Paris, 1945; BEE, CCNY, 1949; postgrad., Poly. Inst. Bklyn., 1952, CCNY, 1954-58, Oxford U., 1974. Registered profl. elec. engr. and control systems engr., Calif.; lic. profl. engr., N.Y.; registered profl. engr., N.D. Elec. field engr., designer, estimator Rao Elec. Equipment Co., N.Y.C., 1947-50; elec. designer Edward E. Ashley, P.E., N.Y.C., 1950-51; elec. design engr. Wearn, Vreeland, Carlson, and Sweatt, N.Y.C., 1951-52; sr. elec. engr. Bechtel Assocs., N.Y.C., 1952-57; chief elec. engr. Am. Hydrotherm Corp., N.Y.C., 1957-76; supervising elec. engr. Heyward-Robinson Co., N.Y.C., 1976-77; prin. mem. tech. staff Ralph M. Parsons Co., Pasadena, Calif., 1977-91; pvt. cons., electric power rsch. engr., mathematician Alexandria, Va., 1991—. Co-author: Analysis of Harmonic Pollution on Power Distribution Systems, 1989; author: Recollections of a World War II Infantryman, 1994. With U.S. Army, 1942-46, ETO. Decorated Bronze Star medal, Purple Heart medal, ETO Campaign medal with 2 bronze campaign stars; N.Y. State War Vet. scholar, 1949. Mem. IEEE (life, sr.), VFW, DAV, Vets. Battle of the Bulge, Combat Infantrymen's Assn., U.S. Holocaust Meml. Mus. (hon. charter), Am. Math. Soc., N.Y. Acad. Scis., Sigma Xi. Achievements include patents in electric power applications; engineering and design of electrical supervisory control systems for the first atomic reactor prototype power generating station in U.S. for GE Corp.; research in solid state electronic annunciators, analog to discrete variable conversion system for chemical process temperature control, extremely reliable low-voltage electrical power generating stations for the uninterruptible supply of large-scale FAA air-route traffic control center operations throughout the U.S., Puerto Rico, Alaska and Hawaii, mathematical modeling and computational harmonic analysis of nonsinusoidal energy flow in electrical power systems, on the decomposition of harmonic distortion power, in various applications of Bessel's equation including experimental work in low frequency eddy-current heating of process liquids in pipes and vessels. Home: 1250 S Washington St Alexandria VA 22314-4455

BRANDENBURG, DAVID SAUL, gastroenterologist, educator; b. Linz, Austria, Apr. 12, 1948; came to U.S., 1948; s. Mayer and Syda Brandenburg; m. Bette Ellen Hirschberg, Aug. 8, 1971; children: Stacey, Mark, Marci. BA, Rutgers U., 1968; MD, Georgetown U., 1972. Bd. cert. internal medicine; bd. cert. GI. Intern, resident R.I. Hosp.-Brown U. Affiliated, Providence, 1972-75; gastroenterology fellow Emory U., Atlanta, 1975-77; pvt. practice Atlanta Digestive Diseases and Internal Medicine, 1977-82, Brandenburg and Kramer M.D., P.C., Atlanta, 1983-97; clin. asst. prof. medicine Emory U. Sch. Medicine, Atlanta, 1977—; with Atlanta Gastroenterology Assocs., 1997—. Med. dir. North Atlanta Endoscopy Ctr., Atlanta, 1986-2002; sec., v.p., pres. Ga. Soc. GI Endoscopy, Atlanta, 1980 86; chmn., med. adv. com. Ga. chpt. Crohn's and Colitis Found., Atlanta, 1995-97. Bd. trustees Temple Emmanuel, Dunwoody, Ga., 1985-91, 95-96, treas., v.p., 1985-91 . Fellow Am. Coll. Gastroenterology (gov. 1991-95); mem. Am. Gastroenterol. Assn., Am. Soc. Gastrointestinal Endoscopy. Office: 5671 Peachtree Dunwoody Rd Ste 600 Atlanta GA 30342-2311

BRANDENBURG, RICHARD GEORGE, management educator; b. Oak Park, Ill., Feb. 21, 1935; s. George Arthur and Florence (Ream) B.; m. Maxine Toby Newman, Dec. 21, 1957; children: Suzanne Linda, Cynthia Anne. BME, Cornell U., 1958, MBA, 1960, PhD, 1964. Asst. to dean Grad. Sch. Indsl. Adminstrn., Carnegie Inst. Tech., Pitts., 1962-64, asst. dean, asst. prof. indsl. adminstrn., 1964-67; acting dean, assoc. prof. indsl. adminstrn. Grad. Sch. Indsl. Adminstrn., Carnegie-Mellon U., Pitts., 1967-68; dean, prof. mgmt. Sch. Mgmt., SUNY, Buffalo, 1968—76, adj. prof. mgmt., 1976—80; v.p. mfg. and engring. The Carborundum Co., Niagara Falls, NY, 1976-80; chmn. Vt. Health Care Authority, 1992-94; dean, prof. mgmt. Coll. Bus. Adminstrn. Grad. Sch. Bus. and Pub. Mgmt., U. Denver, 1980-87; prof. bus. adminstrn. U. Vt., Burlington, 1987—2002, dean Sch. Bus. Adminstrn., 1987-92, dean divsn. engring., math. and bus. adminstrn., 1987-92, sr. advisor to provost, 2001—02, prof. emeritus, 2002—. Pres. Am. Assembly Collegiate Schs. Bus., 1984—85, Mid. Atlantic Assn. Colls. Bus. Adminstrn., 1974; mem. policy com. regents external degree in bus. adminstrn. N.Y. State Dept. Edn., 1975—80; mem. mfg. coun. Machinery and Allied Products Inst., Am. Mgmt. Assn., 1976—80; trustee arts devel. svcs., Buffalo, 1973—76; bd. dirs., mem. coun., mem. exec. seminar adv. com. Niagara Inst.; trustee N.Y. Coun. for Humanities, 1977—80; vice chmn. Advs. Com. on Mgmt. and Budget for Erie County; bd. regents Canisius Coll., Buffalo, 1974—80; past trustee Daemen Coll., Champlain Coll.; past dir. Assoc. Inns and Restaurants Co. Am., HMO Colo., United Bank of Monaco, Denver, Mentor Corp., Denver; vis. prof. ctr. for the evaluative clin. scis. Dartmouth Med. Sch., 1994—95, adj. prof. cmty. and family medicine, 1995—, mem. clin. microsystems resource group, 2002—; pres. bd. dirs. Vt. Inst. for Sci., Math and Tech., 1998—2003; chmn. bd. dirs. Vt. Ethics Network, 1999—. Author: (with H.I. Ansoff, Fred E. Portner, R. Radosevich) Acquisition Behavior of U.S. Manufacturing Firms, 1946-65, 1971, Japanese edit., 1972; mem. editorial bd.: Calif. Mgmt. Rev, 1967-76, Jour. Gen. Mgmt, 1970; editor mfg. sect.: AMA Mgmt. Handbook, 1983; mem. adv. bd.: Non Profit Mgmt. and Leadership; contbr. articles to profl. jours. Recipient McKinsey award, 1969; named One of 10 Most Disting. citizens, Denver Bus. mag., 1984 Mem. Am. Mgmt. Assn. (president's coun. 1980-83, Rand D coun. 1983-86), Vt. Bus. Roundtable (pub. fin. and budgeting study com., econ. devel. study com.), Vt. C. of C. (bd. dirs. 1988-91), Denver C. of C. (small bus. steering com. 1986-87), Lake Champlain Regional C. of C. (bd. dirs. 1990-92, health care policy com. 1998—, bd dirs. Leadership Champlain program 1988-2000), Phi Kappa Tau, Beta Gamma Sigma, Phi Kappa Phi, Pi Tau Sigma, Tau Beta Pi, Delta Sigma Pi, Mu Kappa Tau. Home: 131 Northshore Dr Burlington VT 05401-1273

BRANDENBURG, STANLEY C. financial company executive; b. Miami, Fla., Jan. 3, 1940; s. Ernest Clay and Abbie R. B.; m. Sandy Sue Bussard, 1965 (div. 1966); children: Lisa, Lee; m. Micki Gruchick, 1967 (div. 1975); children: Stacy Dion, Brian Dean; m. Janiece Parker (div. 2002); m. Nenita De La Cruz, 2002. BA, postgrad., U. Ariz. Lic. tax expert U.S. Treasury Dept.; cert. tax profl., long-term care agt.; enrolled agt.; accredited in fed. taxation Calif. Soc. Acctg. and Tax Profls.; registered rep.; uniform securities agt. Gen. ptnr. Brandenburg Ins., Canoga Park, Calif., Brandenburg Enterprises, Canoga Park, S&J Rentals, Canoga Park; pres. Team Securities Corp., Canoga Park, Brandenburg Inc., Canoga Park. Treas. Art World Ind. Inc. Mem. Nat. Assn. of Enrolled Agts., Nat. Assn. of Tax Cons., Am. Inst. of Tax Studies, Nat. Soc. of Tax Profls., Nat. Soc. of Accts., Calif. Soc. Enrolled Agts. (pres. SFV chpt.). Republican. Methodist. Avocation: investment. Home: 19128 Roscoe Blvd Northridge CA 91324-4237 Office: Brandenburg Inc/Team Securities Corp 200-250 Owens Mouth Trail Canoga Park CA 91303-2040

BRANDENSTEIN, DANIEL CHARLES, astronaut, retired naval officer; b. Watertown, Wis., Jan. 17, 1943; s. Walter C. and Agnes (Holzworth) B.; m. Jane A. Wade, Jan. 2, 1966; 1 dau., Adelle. BS, U. Wis., River Falls, 1965; postgrad., U.S. Naval Text Pilot Sch., Patuxent River, Md., 1971. Commd. officer U.S. Navy, 1965, advanced through grades to capt., 1984, ret., 1993, student aviator, 1965-67, aviator Whidbey Island, Wash., 1967-71, test pilot Patuxent River, Md., 1971-74, aviator Whidbey Island, Wash., 1974-78, astronaut NASA Johnson Space Ctr., Houston, 1978-93, chief astronaut office, 1987-93; dir. program development Loral Space Info. Sys., Houston, 1993-96; exec. v.p. Kistler Aerospace Corp., Kirkland, Wash., 1996-99; v.p. Lockheed Martin Space Ops., 1999—. Decorated Legion of Honor (France), 34 medals and awards USN, 1968-93; recipient Disting. Alumnus award U. Wis., 1982, Yuri Gagarin Gold medal Fedn. Aeronautique Internationale, 1990, Laurel Award, Space/Missiles, Aviation Week & Space Tech., 1993, Haley Space Flight award Am. Inst. of Aeronautics and Astronautics, 1993; named to Astronaut Hall Fame, 2003. Mem. AIAA (Haley Space Flight award 1993), Soc. Exptl. Text Pilots (Ivan C. Kinchloe award 1992), U.S. Naval Inst., Assn. Space Explorers. Office: PO Box 58980 Houston TX 77258-8980 E-mail: dan.brandenstein@csoconline.com.

BRANDER, BRUCE GEORGE, international journalist, author; b. Milw., July 8, 1933; s. George Edwin and Anita Margaret (Laucks) B.; m. Mary Lee Wederath, Apr. 28, 1985; children: Gordon, Ian, Bethany, Breton. BS in Edn. and English, U. Wis., Milw., 1955-59, postgrad., 1981-82, Univ. Coll. Cork, Ireland, 1968-69. Cert. Tchr. Secondary Schs. Wis., New Zealand. Reporter, photographer Christchurch (New Zealand) Star, 1960-61, Waikato Times, Hamilton, New Zealand, 1961-63; reporter Milw. Jour., 1964; writer, editor Nat. Geographic, Washington, 1965-68; internat. journalist self employed, Hawaii, Ireland, New Zealand, 1968-75; editor, journalist World Vision, Monrovia, Calif., 1985-97; internat. journalist Colorado Springs, Colo., 1997—. Cons. in field, Milw., Colorado Springs, 1968—. Author: Hamilton and the Waikato, 1964, New Zealand, 1966, The River Nile, 1966, Canary Islands, 1967, Staring into Chaos, 1998; co-author: Australia, 1968; contbr. numerous articles to periodicals. With U.S. Army, 1953-55. Recipient 1st pl. nat. award Eastman Kodak Co., 1993, Profl. Photographers Am., 1993; named Hon. Knight of Mark Twain, 1967. Mem.: Toastmasters. Avocations: hiking, rock climbing. Office: Brander Comms 2311 Zane Pl Colorado Springs CO 80909-1650

BRANDES, DORIS, artist, art administrator, journalist; b. N.Y.C., Nov. 20, 1923; d. Robert Ralph Pratt and Grace Isabella Mott; m. Walter A. Spiro, July 24, 1948 (div. May 1971); children: Karen L., Pamela A. Gowers, Paul D., Amy E.; m. Gordon A. Brandes, June 13, 1971 (div. Aug. 1986); m. Tor Bjorn Polfelt, Sept. 11, 1993 (dec. Mar. 30, 2001). BFA, Pratt Inst., Bklyn., 1941; postgrad., Art Students League, 1942-43. Owner, ptnr. Witch Craft, N.Y.C., 1945-48; dir., tchr. Hidden House Creative Workshop, Jenkintown, Pa., 1964-69; printmaker, tchr. Abington Art Ctr., Jenkintown, 1971-79; dir. Cheltenham (Pa.) Art Ctr., 1979-81; founder, pub., editor Art Matters, Phila., 1981-93, dir. projects, 1981-93; founding bd. mem. Michener Art Mus., Doylestown, Pa., 1988—. Founding dir. Artsbridge, New Hope, Pa., Lambertville, N.J., 1993—; art columnist New Hope Gazette, 1994—, Lambertville Beacon, Hunterdon County, N.J., 1996-99; video script and prodn. Art of the River Towns, New Hope, 1996. Author: Artists of the River Towns, 2002; columnist: Artbuzz for Prime Time mag., feature writer: Bucks County Herald. Chairperson Alverthorpe Park Bd., Abington, 1964—65; founding mem. Ptnrs. in Progress, New Hope, 1996—98; adv. bd. Hepatitis B Found., Doylestown, Pa., 1994—99; advisor Artist in Residence, New Hope, 1998; trustee James A. Michener Art Mus., 1999; bd. mem. New Hope Hist. Soc. Recipient R. Tate McKenzie medal for svc. Phila. Sketch Club, 1985, Mayor's Citation City of Phila., 1986, 1st pl. for feature articles Pa. Press Assn., 1999, Cmty. Svc. award New Hope Pub. Libr., 1998. Democrat. Mem. Soc. Of Friends. Avocations: swimming, gourmet cooking, knitting, hiking, photography. Home and Office: 10 W Randolph St New Hope PA 18938-1326

BRANDES, JO ANNE, lawyer; BS, U. Wis., Eau Claire; JD, Willamette U. Assoc. Herz, Levin, Teper, Chernof & Sumner, SC, 1978—81; gen. counsel S.C. Johnson Comml. Markets, Sturtevant, Wis. Mem. bd. regents U. Wis., Wis., 1996—; mem. Gov.'s Commn. on Glass Ceiling; chmn. Wis. Child Care Coun.; past president Racine (Wis.) Area United Found. Office: SC Johnson Comml markets 8310 16th St PO Box 902 Sturtevant WI 53177-0902

BRANDES, JOEL R. consultant, publisher, writer; b. Bklyn., Dec. 15, 1943; s. Murray and Evelyn (Levine) B.; children: Bari, Evan. Student, U. Tampa, 1961-62; BA, Queens Coll., 1965; JD, Bklyn. Law Sch., 1968; LLM in Corp. Law, NYU, 1974; postgrad., U. Tampa, 1961-62. Assoc. Wallman & Kramer, N.Y.C., 1972-77; pvt. practice Garden City, N.Y., 1977-87; ptnr. Brandes & Stamler, Garden City, 1987-90, Brandes Weidman & Spatz P.C., N.Y.C. and Garden City, 1991-93; prin. The Law Firm of Joel R. Brandes P.C., N.Y.C., Garden City, 1993—2002. Instr. matrimonial law Adelphi U., Garden City, 1976-88; vis. lctr. Sch. Law Hofstra U., Advanced Practice Inst., 1981. Co-author: Digest of Equitable Distribution Cases, 1981, A Practical Guide to the New York Equitable Distribution Law, 1980, Contemporary Matrimonial Law Issues, 1986, Encyclopedia of Matrimonial Practice, 1992, A Comprehensive Analysis of All Reported Equitable Distribution Cases to Date, 1982, Equitable Distribution Case Law, 1983, Law and the Family, New York, 2d edit. (9 vols.), 1986-98, Law and the Family, New York Forms (4 vols.), 1995; contbr. articles to profl. jours; editor: N.Y. Family Law Reporter; internet pub. New York Divorce and Family Law. Pres. Old Lindenmere Civic Assn., Merrick, N.Y., 1975-80, Community Council Merricks, 1977-80; arbitrator Civil Ct. of City of N.Y. Mem. ABA (family law sect., assoc. editor Family Law Newsletter 1971-78, litigation sect., trial evidence com. 1975-77, exec. mem. child custody com. 1982-83, panel mem. Law in the Fifty States 1986-87), Am. Soc. Writers on Legal Subjects, N.Y. State Bar Assn. (family law sect. 1975-2002, Family Law Rev. Edil. Bd. 1975-2002, sec. com. on legis. 1975-77, com. continuing legal edn. 1980-92, chmn. com. continuing legal edn. 1982-92, fin. officer 1990-92, sec. 1992, mem. com. profl. discipline 1992-93, mem. com. on children and the law 1997-2000, mem. com. on Cts. of Appellate Jurisdiction 1998-2000), Nassau County Bar Assn. (com. matrimonial and family law 1975-2002, mem. newsletter subcom. 1976, chmn. legis. subcom. 1978-80, chmn. continuing legal edn. subcom. 1980-82, chmn. matrimonial and family law 1982-84), Am. Arbitration Assn. (panel mem 1974-87), Internat. Acad. Matrimonial Lawyers, Am. Acad. Matrimonial Lawyers (legal edn. com. 1978, bd. mgrs. 1979-83, bd. examiners 1979-80, chmn. legis. com. 1979-80, com. legal fees in matrimonial matters 1980-81, ad hoc com. on revisions of equitable distbn. law 1980-81). Jewish. Office: 155 Washington St Jersey City NJ 07302 E-mail: divorce@brandeslaw.com. *Notable cases include: Tucker v. Tucker, 55 NY 2d 378, which held that equitable distribution law (EDL) was not retroactive and that an action pending prior to the enactment of the N.Y. EDL could not be discontinued to commence a new action under the EDL; Marone v. Marone 50 NY 2d 481 which held that although N.Y. did not recognize palimony, a meritorious relationship, in and of itself, was not a bar to establishing an oral partnership agreement between a man and woman living together; McSparron v. McSparron, 87 NY 2d 275 which held that a professional (law) license retains its identity as an asset and does not merge into the professional's career or practice.*

BRANDES, JOSEPH, historian, educator; b. Trembowla, Poland, Jan. 23, 1928; came to U.S., 1939; s. Harry and Clara (Neufeld) B.; m. Margot Bernstein, Aug. 16, 1953; children: Cheryl, Lynn, Susan, Aviva. BS in Social Sci., CCNY, 1949; MA, Columbia U., 1950; PhD, NYU, 1958. Cert. tchr. social studies, N.Y. Tchr. social studies N.Y.C. Bd. of Edn., 1950-55, 56-57; lectr. econs. CCNY, 1955; fellow NYU, N.Y.C., 1955-56, 57-58; cons. economist Dept. Commerce, Washington, 1958-59; asst. prof. to prof. history William Paterson U. N.J., Wayne, 1958-92, prof. emeritus, 1992—. Vis. assoc. prof. NYU, summer, 1963-66; manuscript cons. Univ. Presses, Princeton, N.J.; rsch. assoc. Am. Jewish History Ctr., N.Y.C., 1965-75; faculty cons. Coll. Bd. Ednl. Testing Svc., 1990—; mem. N.J. Bd. Mediation; mem. legal ethics com. Supreme Ct. N.J., dist. ethics com., 1997-2001. Author: Herbert Hoover and Economic Diplomacy, 1962, Immigrants to Freedom, 1971, From Sweatshop to Stability, 1976. Acad. coun. Am. Jewish Hist. Soc., Waltham, Mass., 1973—, editl. bd., 1973—; pres. N.J. Coun. for Social Studies, Trenton, 1961-63. N.J. Hist. Soc. History Honors fellow, 1972. Mem. Am. Arbitration Assn., Phi Beta Kappa, Phi Alpha Theta (councillor 1990-92). Avocations: hiking, travel, reading, historical research. Home: 16-36 Raymond St Fair Lawn NJ 07410-1908 Office: William Paterson Univ NJ 300 Pompton Rd Dept History Wayne NJ 07470-2103

BRANDES, MARCIANA WATSON, civic worker; b. Defiance, Ohio, Oct. 24, 1921; d. Lawrence Willard and Ida Marie (Schlumbrecht) Watson; m. Richard Charles Brandes, June 14, 1943; children: Judith, Eric, Jeanne, Robert. BA, Ohio Wesleyan U., 1943. Mem. Upper Arlington (Ohio) City Coun., 1958-62; chmn. Upper Arlington N.W. Bicentennial Commn., 1967—, Commn. chmn. on Aging, 1988—, Upper Arlington Ohio Bicentennial com., 2000—; pres. PTO Upper Arlington Jr. & Sr. High Schs.; trustee Upper Arlington C. of C.; mem. Va. Bd. Health. Named Neighbor of the Month, 1987. Mem. AAUW (pres. Columbus, Ohio chpt. 1972-74), Phi Beta Kappa, Delta Sigma Rho, Kappa Delta Pi, Pi Kappa Alpha, Chi Omega. Clubs: Columbus Monnett (pres. 1971-72). Republican. Episcopalian. Avocations: travel, photography, public speaking, bridge. Home: 2029 Upper Chelsea Rd Columbus OH 43221-4112

BRANDES, RAYMOND STEWART, history educator; b. San Diego, Jan. 2, 1924; s. Theodore C. and María Rosario (Peters) B.; m. Irma Dolores Montijo, Jan. 28, 1961; children: Elena María, Elisa Anne, Laura Raquel, Claudia Reneé, Ramón Antonio, Marta Denise, Paula Nicole. BA, U. Ariz., 1961, PhD, 1965. Asst. prof. history U. San Diego, 1966-67, assoc. prof., 1967-71, prof., 1971-98, univ. archivist, 1992-98, chmn. dept., 1967-73, grad. dean, 1973-91; ret., 1998. Dir. several grants related to hist. preservation and hist. site archaeology in San Diego area. Author: Diario of Miguel Costanso, 1969, Troopers West: Military and Indian Affairs on the American Frontier, 1970, Frontier Military Posts of Arizonia, 1960, San Diego: An Illustrated History, 1982; editor Brand Book 1, San Diego Corral of Westerners, 1970, Masterplanner for Old Town State Historical Park, 1973-74, Old Town San Diego, 1821-1974, 1976, History and Archaeology of New Town, San Diego, 1985, Coronado: The Enchanted Island, 1987, 3d edit., 1999, Coronado: We Remember, 1993, The Pacific Coast League San Diego Padres, 2 vols., 1936-1957, 1997. Mem. Gaslamp Quarter Project Area Com., 1977—, chmn., 1980; v.p. San Diego Sci. Found., 1978-87, Internat. Am. Heritage Found., 2000—. With U.S. Army, 1943-46, USAR, 1950-53. Recipient medal of San Diego de Alcala, U. San. Diego, 1997; NDEA grantee, 1961-64; CETA grantee, 1978, 79; named Outstanding Prof. Social Sci. U. San Diego, 1968, 69, Disting. Historian medal U. Ariz., 1989. Mem. Mex.-Am. Educators, Nat. Coun. Pub. History, Soc. Am. Baseball Rschrs., Pacific Coast League Baseball Hist. Soc., San Diego Baseball Hist. Soc. (1st pres.), Coronado Hist. Soc. & Mus. (bd. dir.). Democrat. Roman Catholic. Home: 230 W Laurel St Apt 406 San Diego CA 92101-1464 E-mail: rb@acusd.edu., raybrandes@sbcglobal.net.

BRANDES, STANLEY HOWARD, anthropology educator, writer; b. N.Y.C., Dec. 26, 1942; s. Emanuel Robert and Annette (Zalisch) B.; m. Jane Brandes; children: Nina Rachel, Naomi Clara. BA, U. Chgo., 1964; MA, U. Calif., Berkeley, 1969, PhD, 1971. Asst. prof. anthropology Mich. State U., East Lansing, 1971-75; asst. prof. anthropology U. Calif., Berkeley, 1975 78, assoc. prof., 1978-82, prof. anthropology, 1982—, chmn. dept., 1990-93, 97-99. Dir. Barcelona Study Ctr., U. Calif. and Ill., Spain, 1981-82, Mexico City Study Ctr., 1995-96, U. Calif. Author: Migration, Kinship and Community, 1975, Metaphors of Masculinity, 1989, Forth: The Age and the Symbol, 1985, Power and Persuasion, 1988, Staying Sober in Mexico City, 2002; co-editor: Symbol as Sense, 1980. NIH fellow, 1967-71; NICHD Rsch. fellow, 1975-77; fellow John Carter Brown Libr., 1994, Am. Council Learned Socs. grantee, 1977 Fellow Am. Anthrop. Assn.; mem. Am. Ethnological Soc., Soc. for Psychol. Anthropology Office: U Calif Dept Anthropology Berkeley CA 94720-0001

BRANDES, STUART DEAN, historian, educator; b. Rockford, Ill., Feb. 4, 1940; s. Herbert Dean and Eula Brown Brandes; m. Polly Hand Powrie, May 21, 1966; children: Carolyn Patricia, Marcia Christine. BS, U. Wis., 1961, MS, 1965, PhD, 1970. Instr. history U. Wis., Janesville, 1967—69, asst. prof., 1969—75, assoc. prof., 1976—81, prof., 1981—98, prof. emeritus, 1998—. Chair dept. history U. Wis. Coll., 1981—84. Author: American Welfare Capitalism 1880-1940, 1976, Warhogs: A History of War Profits in America, 1997. Mem.: Wis. Assn. Scholars (treas. 1991—), Nat. Assn. Scholars, Wis. Hist. Soc., Hist. Soc. Avocations: fly fishing, boating. Home: 1112 Pocahontas Dr Monona WI 53716 E-mail: sbrandes@chorus.net.

BRANDEWIE, RICHARD ANTHONY, laser and optics consultant; b. Sidney, Ohio; s. Leo Peter and Mary Agnes (Doorley) B.; m. Arlene Therese Warner, Aug. 29, 1959; children: Leo Peter, Frances Brandewie Geoffrion. BEE, U. Detroit, 1959; MS, Carnegie Inst. Tech., Pitts., 1960, PhD, 1963. Mem. tech. staff N.Am. Aviation, Anaheim, Calif., 1963-67; supr. lasers Rockwell Autonetics, Anaheim, 1967—79; mgr. lasers Rockwell Rocketdyne, Canoga Park, Calif., 1979-80, dir. rsch., 1980-84, program mgr., 1984-92; ind. cons. Monte Nido, Calif., 1992—. Contbr. articles to profl. jours. Dir. Edenwild Property Owners Assn., L.A., 1983, sec., 1983, pres., 1984. Recipient Esso fellowship Esso Corp., Carnegie Inst. Tech., 1961-63; recipient Nat. Sci. and Tech. award Iris Active Systems Group, 1992. Mem. IEEE, Am. Phys. Soc., Carnegie Mellon U. L.A. Alumni Assn. (dir., sec. 1980, pres. 1995-96), Sigma Xi, Eta Kappa Nu, Tau Beta Pi. Achievements include recognition as a founding father of laser radar and a major early contributor to the field of adaptive optics. Home and Office: 25760 Vista Verde Dr Monte Nido CA 91302-2164 E-mail: richbrand@ieee.org.

BRANDHORST, WESLEY THEODORE, retired information scientist; b. Portland, Oreg., May 9, 1933; s. Wesley Theodore and Mary Margeurite (LaRouche) B.; m. Jane Smythe, Sept. 1, 1962; children— Tristan, Thea BA, U. Calif.-Berkeley, 1955, M.L.S., 1957. Spl. intern Libr. Congress, Washington, 1957-59; libr. Documentation Inc., Washington, 1959-61; asst. dir. NASA Sci. and Tech. Info. Facility, Washington, 1962-69; dir. ERIC Processing and Reference Facility, Washington, 1970-2000; ret., 2000. Chmn. Z39 Nat. Info. Stds. Orgn., 1985-87. Contbr. articles to profl. jours. Mem. ALA, AAAS, Spl. Librs. Assn., Am. Soc. Info. Sci. Unitarian Universalist. Avocations: tennis, running, bicycling, chess, reading. Home: 3346 Yonge Ave Sarasota FL 34235 E-mail: tbrandho@worldnet.att.net.

BRANDIMORE, WADIE MILLER, retired pediatrics nurse; b. Laconia, Tenn., Aug. 19, 1920; d. William and Lillie (Edwards) Miller; m. LeRoy Brandimore, Aug. 24, 1946; children: Geraldine F. Brandimore Anderson, LeRoy William. Student, Murray State Coll., 1939; diploma, Nazareth Sch. Nursing, Lexington, Ky., 1944. Oper. rm. circling nurse St. Joseph Hosp., Lexington, 1944; office nurse Dr. Adoplhus D. Butterworth, Murray, Ky., 1944-45; 1944-46; office nurse Dr. Randall M. McLaughlin, Pasadena, Md., 1955-57; pvt. duty nurse USN Hosp., Annapolis, Md., 1958-67; staff nurse Anne Arundel Med. Ctr., Annapolis, Md., 1967-95; ret., 1995. Ensign, USN, 1945-46. Mem. ANA, Navy Nurse Corps Assn., Washington Metro Area Navy Nurse Corps Assn., Md. Nurses Assn. (bd. dirs. dist. 3). Home: 329 Clifton Ave Arnold MD 21012-1546

BRANDINGER, JAY JEROME, electronics executive; b. N.Y.C., Jan. 2, 1927; s. Abraham and Lillian (Newman) B.; m. Alice Levite, Dec. 23, 1949; children: Paul, Donna, Norman. BS in Elec. Engring., Cooper Union U., 1951; MS in Elec. Engring., Rutgers U., 1962, PhD in Elec. Engring., 1968. Group head display systems Research div. RCA Labs., Princeton, 1966-70, group head televideo systems, 1970-74, v.p. div. TV engring., 1974-79; div. v.p., gen. mgr. RCA SelectaVision VideoDisc Ops., Indpls., 1979-84; staff v.p. systems engring. RCA Electronics Products and Labs., Indpls., 1984-86; v.p. mfg. and materials div. David Sarnoff Rsch. Ctr., 1986-91; exec. dir. N.J. Commn. on Sci. and Tech., Trenton, 1991-95; pres., ceo Ja Brand Ass Inc., Pennington, N.J., 1995-98; chmn., CEO Westar Photonics Inc., 1999—.

BRANDL, JOHN EDWARD, public affairs educator; b. Aug. 19, 1937; m. Rochelle Jankovich; children: Christopher, Mary Katherine, Amy. BA in Econs. with honors, St. John's U., Collegeville, Minn., 1959; MA in Econs., Harvard U., 1962, PhD in Econs., 1963. Lectr. econs. Boston Coll., 1961-62; systems analyst Office of Sec. Def., Washington, 1963-65; asst. prof. econs. St. John's U., Collegeville, 1965-67; asst. prof., rsch. assoc. Inst. for Rsch. on Poverty, dir. Systematic Analysis Program U. Wis., Madison, 1967-68; dep. asst. sec. HEW, Washington, 1968-69; from assoc. prof. to prof. pub. affairs U. Minn., Mpls., 1969—, dir. sch. pub. affairs, 1969-76, dean Hubert H. Humphrey Inst. Pub. Affairs, 1997—2002; rep. State of Minn., Mpls., 1977-78, 81-86, senator, 1987-90. Exec. bd. Ctr. for Policy Rsch. in Edn., 1986-96; vis. lectr. dept. econs. U. Philippines, 1968; vis. prof. pub. adminstrn. and pub. policy U. Sydney, Australia, 1973; teaching fellow dept. econs. Warsaw Sch. Econs., 1992-95. Author: Money and Good Intentions are Not Enough, 1998; (with A. Naftalin) Twin Cities Regional Strategy, 1981; co-editor: Public Policy and Educating Handicapped Persons, 1982; mem. editl. bd. Urban Affairs Quarterly, 1971-74, Sage Profl. Papers Adminstrv. Scis., 1972-76, Jour. Policy Analysis and Mgmt., 1981 ; cons. editor Improving College and University Teaching, 1979-82; contbr. articles to pprofl. jours. Bd. dirs. Tri-Cap Community Action Agy. Inc., Mpls., 1966-67; trustee Mpls. Soc. Fine Arts, 1983-86; pres. Twin Cities Citizens' League, 1993; nat. adv. coun. St. John's U., Minn., 1975-91; chmn. Twin Cities Met. Coun. Cable TV Adv. Com., 1972-73, mem. FCC Cable Adv. Coun., 1972-73, Minn. State Planning Adv. Com., 1971-73, Gov.'s Adv. Com. on Mgmt. and Personnel Devel., 1971-76, Gov.'s Coun. of Econ. Advisors, 1971-76; Mem. study group Nat. Assessment of Student Achievement., 1986, Nat. Tchrs. Coun. Edn. Testing Svc., 1986-92, Nat. Commn. Indsl. Innovation, 1984-86; bd. dirs. policy studies orgns., 1985-90; asst. majority leader Minn. Ho. of Rep., 1983-84, minority caucus steering com., 1985-86; bd. regents St. John's U., Minn., 1991-2000. Recipient Presdl. prize Am. Evaluation Assn., 1988, Disting. Svc. award Nat. Govs. Assn., 1996. Fellow Nat. Acad. Pub. Adminstrn.; mem. NIMH (rsch. edn. adv. com. 1980-84), Assn. for Pub. Policy Analysis and Mgmt. (v.p. 1983-84, pres. 1986-87), Am. Soc. Pub. Adminstrn. (bd. dirs. Minn. chpt. 1975-76), Cath. Econ. Assn. (coun. dirs. 1968), Harvard Grad. Soc. (coun. 1988-91), Delta Epsilon Sigma.

BRANDL, MARY-KATHERINE, mathematics educator; d. John Edward and Rochelle Ann Brandl. BA, U. Calif., Santa Cruz, 1995; MS, U. Oreg., 1997, PhD, 2001. Grad. tchg. fellow U. Oreg., Eugene, 1995—2001; asst. prof.

Centenary Coll. of La., Shreveport, 2001—. Mem.: Assn. for Women in Math. (corr.), Math. Assn. of Am. (corr.), Am. Math. Soc. (corr.). Liberal. Office: Centenary Coll La 2911 Centenary Blvd Shreveport LA 71134 Personal E-mail: kbrandl@centenary.edu.

BRANDMAN, JAMES FRANKLIN, internist, oncologist; b. Chgo., Mar. 14, 1949; MD, Boston U., 1975. Cert. internal medicine 1978, med. oncology 1981, hospice and palliative medicine 1997. Intern Cleveland Clin., 1975-76, resident, 1976-78; fellow oncologist Albany Med. Ctr., 1979-81; MD Riverview Clin., 1981-92, Glen Ellyn Clin., 1992-00, Northwestern U. Hematology-Oncology, 2000—. Office: Northwestern U Divsn Hematology/Oncology 676 N Saint Clair St Ste 850 Chicago IL 60611-2978 E-mail: j-brandman@northwestern.edu.

BRANDNER, CHRISTINE MARIE, art administrator, artist; b. Ocean City, N.J., Aug. 15, 1969; d. Roger Joseph and Judith Ann (Knueven) B. BA in Art Edn., U. Ky., 1991; MFA in Painting, Savannah Coll. Art & Design, 1997, postgrad., 2001, Jackson Hole Artist Workshop, 1999. Cert. art tchr. grades K-12, N.C. Art tchr. grades 7-9 Spring Lake (N.C.) Jr. High, 1992-94; exhibitions mgr. galleries dept. Savannah (Ga.) Coll. Art and Design, 1997-2000; dir. admission Portfolio Ctr. Savannah Coll., 2000—02; dir. undergrad. enrollment Savannah Coll. of Art and Design, 2002—. One-person show, 1996, 97, 98, 99; works exhibited in group shows nationally, including Internat. Soc. Exptl. Artists, Longboat Key, Fla., 1997, Sarah Bain Gallery, Fullerton, Calif., 1997, Savannah Internat. Airport, 1997-98, Flight Safety Internat., Savannah, 1998, Galerie Lumiére, Savannah, Tiverton and Four Corners, R.I., 1998, 99, Roane State C.C., Harriman, Tenn., 1999, Soho Myriad, Inc., Atlanta, 1998—; represented in corp. collections Penns Landing, Phila., Evergreen Conf. Ctr., Stone Mountain, Ga., Westin Hotel, Savannah, Ga., Am. Incontinental U., Savannah Coll. Art and Design, Omni/Chrysler; executed mural painter Lexington Children's Mus., Lexington, Ky., 1991. Supporter Epworth United Meth. Ch., Savannah, 1996-98. Acad. scholar U. Ky., Lexington, 1987. Mem. Internat. Soc. Exptl. Artists, Nat. Art Edn. Assn., Coll. Art Assn. Avocations: avid reader, painter, artist, yoga. Home: 1922 E Henry St Savannah GA 31404-3006 E-mail: christysue32@earthlink.net.

BRANDON, DAVID A. food service executive/restaurant manager; b. 1952; With Procter & Gamble Distbg. Co., 1974-79, GFV Comm., Inc., 1979-83, COO, exec. v.p., dir., 1983-86; COO, exec. v.p., pres., dir. Valassis Inserts, Inc., Livonia, Mich., 1986—99; pres., CEO Valassis Comm., Livonia, Mich., 1989—99, chmn., 1997—99; chmn., CEO Domino's Pizza, Inc., Ann Arbour, Mich., 1999—. Office: 30 Frank Lloyd Wright Dr Ann Arbor MI 48105-9757*

BRANDON, ELVIS DENBY, JR., financial planner; b. Sheridan, Ark., Nov. 28, 1927; s. Elvis Denby and Hazel Ione (Davidson) B.; m. Helen Holt Deupree, Apr. 25, 1953; children: Elvis Denby III, Raymond Wilson. BA with honors, Rhodes Coll., Memphis, 1950; MA, Duke U., 1952. CLU; cert. fin. planner; chartered fin. cons.; registered prin. Nat. Assn. Securities Dealers. Fin. planner, chmn. Brandon Fin. Planning, Inc./Brandon Investments, Inc., Memphis, 1952-. Author: A New Beginning, 1979; prodr., moderator (t.v.) Your Furture Unlimited, 1955, (Sylvania TV award). Tchr. Shady Grove Presbyn. Ch., Memphis, 1989—; mem. pres.'s coun. and heritage soc. Rhodes Coll; coord. Great Millennium Reunion. Named Young Man of Yr., Memphis Jaycees, 1953. Mem. CFP Bd. Stds. (chmn. 1989-90, 1st chmn. internat. CFP coun. 1992), Am. Soc. Fin. Svc. Profls., Econ. Club of Memphis, Racquet Club of Memphis, Rotary, Phi Beta Kappa. Home: 505 West Racquet Club Pl Memphis TN 38117 Office: Brandon Fin Planning Inc 5101 Wheelis Rd Ste 112 Memphis TN 38117 Business E-Mail: edenbybrandonjr@brandonorgs.com.

BRANDON, ELVIS DENBY, III, financial planner; b. Memphis, Aug. 11, 1954; s. Elvis Denby Jr. and Helen (Deupree) B.; m. Sarah Louise Buntin, Mar. 15, 1980; children: Elizabeth Holt, William Denby, Mary Buntin. BBA, So. Meth. U., 1976; MBA, Memphis State U., 1979. Cert. fin. planner; CLU; chartered fin. cons. Mgmt. candidate First Tenn. Bank, NA, Memphis, 1979-80; sr. credit analyst Banc Texas/Dallas NA, 1980-82; asst. v.p., comml. loan officer Banc Texas/Sherman NA, 1982; pres. Brandon Investments, Inc., Memphis, 1982—; v.p. Brandon Fin. Planning, Inc., Memphis, 1982—. Adj. faculty Coll. for Fin. Planning, Denver, 1984-85. Elder Idlewild Presb. Ch. Mem.: NASD (registered prin.), Fin. Planning Assn., Soc. Fin. Svc. Profls. Presbyterian. Home: 5953 Brierdale Ave Memphis TN 38120-2345 Office: Brandon Fin Planning Inc 5101 Wheelis Rd Ste 112 Memphis TN 38117

BRANDON, GARY KENT, physician, health facility administrator; b. Pueblo, Colo; s. Vernon Charles and Eva M. (Hachey) B.; m. D.J. Harris, May 21, 1976; children: Terry, Belinda, John, Tracye, Sherry, Kimberly. BA, U. So. Colo., 1968; MS, N.Mex. Highlands U., 1969; DO, U. Health Scis., 1973; MPH, Johns Hopkins U., 1979; postgrad., Nat. War Coll., 1989-90. Diplomate Am. Bd. Preventive Medicine, Am. Bd. Med. Mgmt. Intern Lake Side Hosp., Kans. City, Mo., 1973-74; resident Johns Hopkins, 1978-79, USAF Sch. Aerospace Medicine, 1979-80; commd. capt. USAF, 1976, advanced through grades to col., 1986; hosp. comdr. Barksdale AFB, Shreveport, La., 1987-89, MacDill AFB, Tampa, Fla., 1990-93; dir. med. inspection USAF, Albuquerque, 1993-95, ret., 1995; med. dir. Valley Wide Health Svc., Alamosa, Colo., 1995-97; pres. Brandon Consulting, Grand Junction, Colo., 1997-98; dir. med. ops. and quality svc. Freeman Hosp. and Health Sys., Joplin, Mo., 1998—2003; dir. Arca Med., Concentra Clinics, Tucson. Sr. examiner Malcolm Baldridge Nat. Quality Award, Washington, 1993-97. Author: Aviation, Space and Environmental Medicine, 1980, co-author 2d edit., 1983. V.p. Rocky Mountain HMO, Grand Junction, Colo., 1975, Western Colo. Physicians, Inc., Grand Junction, 1975; pres. Mesa County Osteo. Assn., Grand Junction, 1976. Recipient Med. Leadership award Strategic Air Command USAF, Aboline, Tex., 1986, USAF award for profl. excellence, Washington, 1994. Fellow Am. Coll. Preventive Medicine; mem. APHA, Am. Coll. Occupl. and Environ. Medicine, Am. Soc. Quality Control, Nat. Assn. Managed Care Physicians. Avocations: flying, scuba diving, photography, horseback riding. Office: Arca Med Dir Concentre Med Ctr 4600 S Pk Ave Tubac AZ 85646

BRANDON, JEFFREY CAMPBELL, physician, interventional radiologist, educator; b. Reynoldsville, Pa., Dec. 5, 1953; s. Milton Boyd and Patricia Alfreda (Steele) B. BS, Allegheny Coll., 1975; MD, Jefferson Med. Coll., 1979. Diplomate Am. Bd. Radiology, Nat. Bd. Med. Examiners. Intern gen. surgery Bryn Mawr (Pa.) Hosp., 1979-80, resident gen. surgery, 1980-81; resident in diagnostic radiology Hahnemann U. Hosp., Phila., 1983-86, fellow interventional radiology, abdominal imaging, 1986-87, clin. instr., 1987-88; asst. prof. U. Calif., Irvine, 1988-94, assoc. prof., chmn. radiol. scis., 1992-95; vice chmn. radiol. scis. U. South Ala., Mobile, 1995—, disting. prof. radiology, 1996—, asst. dean for grad. med. edn., 2000—03, assoc. dean for continuing and grad. med. edn., 2003—. Mem. adv. bd. Baxter Health Care Tech. and Ventures Divsn., Irvine, 1990-92, Laparomed Corp., Irvine, 1991-94, Visioneering, Fullerton, Calif., 1993-95. Author: (chpt.) Common Problems in Gastrointestinal Radiology, 1989, Critical Care Imaging, 1990, Textbook of Gastrointestinal Radiology, 1991, Textbook of Diagnostic Imaging, 1994; contbr. articles to books and profl. jours. Recipient S. Macuen Smith Otolaryngology award Jefferson Med. Coll., 1979, Baxter Healthcare grant Baxter Corp., 1990, Faculty Rsch. grant U. Calif., Irvine Coll. of Medicine, 1990. Mem. Am. Bd. Radiology, Assn. Univ. Radiologists, Soc. Gastrointestinal Radiologists (lectr. 1989—), Am. Inst. Ultrasound in Medicine, Soc. Cardiovascular and Interventional Radiologists, Calif. Med. Assn. (bd. dirs., sci. adv. panel on radiology 1993-95), Phi Beta Kappa. Office: U South Ala Mastin 301 Radiology 2451 Fillingim St Mobile AL 36617-2238

BRANDON, JOHN MITCHELL, physician; b. Pitts., June 28, 1927; s. Albert Given and Adelaide Victoria (Mitchell) B.; m. Phyllis Katherine Wagner, June 22, 1966 (dec.). BS, U. Pitts., 1952, MD, 1956. Diplomate in internal medicine and hematology Am. Bd. Internal Medicine; diplomate Am. Bd. Pathology. Intern Geisinger Meml. Hosp., Danville, Pa., 1956-57; resident in internal medicine Cleve. Clinic, 1957-60, renal fellow, 1960-61; pvt. practice internal medicine Allegheny Valley Hosp., Tarentum, Pa., 1961-66; resident in pathology VA Hosp. of Pitts., Oakland, Pa., 1966-70, resident in immunology, 1970-71; fellow in coagulation Ctrl. Blood Bank, Oakland, 1971-72; dir. lab. Monongahela Valley Hosp., Monongahela, Pa., 1972-94, part-time pathologist, 1994—. Chmn. blood program Monessen (Pa.) Health Ctr., 1972-94; clin. asst. prof. pathology U. Pitts. Med. Sch., 1980—; prof. med. lab. tech. C.C. Allegheny County, Pitts., 1986—. Contbr. chpts. to books, articles to profl. jours. Cpl. USAAF, 1945-46. Recipient Sickman-Levin award for dimensions in medicine Monongahela Valley Hosp., 1993. Fellow ACP, Coll. Am. Pathologists, Am. Soc. Clin. Pathology, Internat. Pathology Soc.; mem. AMA, Pa. Med. Soc. Avocations: fishing, hunting, gardening. Office: Monongahela Valley Hosp Rte 88 Monongahela PA 15063

BRANDON, KATHRYN ELIZABETH BECK, pediatrician; b. Sept. 10, 1916; d. Clarence M. and Hazel A. (Cutler) Beck; children: John William, Kathleen Brandon McEnulty, Karen (dec.). MD, U. Chgo., 1941; BA, U. Utah, 1937; MPH, U. Calif., Berkeley, 1957. Diplomate Am. Bd. Pediats. Intern Grace Hosp., Detroit, 1941-42; resident Children's Hosp. Med. Ctr. No. Calif., Oakland, 1953-55, Children's Hosp., L.A., 1951-53; pvt. practice La Crescenta, Calif., 1946-51, Salt Lake City, 1960-65, 86—. Med. dir. Salt Lake City public schs., 1957-60; dir. Ogden City-Weber County (Utah) Health Dept., 1965-67; pediatrician Fitzsimmons Army Hosp., 1967-68; coll. health physician U. Colo., Boulder, 1968-71; student health physician U. Utah, Salt Lake City, 1971-81; occupational health physician Hill AFB, Utah, 1981-85; child health physician Salt Lake City-County Health Dept., 1971-82; cons. in field; clin. asst. U. Utah Coll. Medicine, Salt Lake City, 1958-64; clin. asst. pediatrics U. Colo. Coll. Medicine, Denver, 1958-72; active staff emeritus Primary Children's Hosp., LDS Hosp., and Cottonwood Hosp., 1960-67. Fellow APHA, Am. Pediat. Acad., Am. Sch. Health Assn.; mem. AMA, Utah Coll. Health Assn. (pres. 1978-80), Pacific Coast Coll. Health Assn., Utah Med. Assn., Salt Lake County Med. Soc., Utah Pub. Health Assn. (sec.-treas. 1960-66), Intermountain Pediat. Soc. Home and Office: PO Box 58482 Salt Lake City UT 84158-0482

BRANDON, LIANE, filmmaker, educator; Student, St. Lawrence U., U. Edinburgh, Scotland; exchange student, U. Moscow; AB, MEd, Boston U. Ski instr., Mt. Tremblant, Que., Can.; actress Children's Theatre, Cambridge, Mass.; film project dir. English dept. Quincy pub. schs., Mass.; prof. film-TV prodn. and media studies Sch. Edn. U. Mass., Amherst, 1973—; co-founder, mem. New Day Films, 1971—; co-dir. UMass Ednl. TV, U. Mass., Amherst, 1994—; dir. Sch. Edn. Ednl. Tech. Program, U. Mass., 1998—. Film cons. Mass. Gov.'s Commn. on Status of Women, 1974; cons. Mass. Artists Found., 1975, 82, WGBH-TV, 1992-97; judge Regional Student Acad. Awards, 1991, New Eng. Regional Emmy Awards,1992; trustee Theaterworks, 1981-83; bd. dirs. Boston Film-Video Found., 1983-87, ACLU of Mass., 1990-97; mem. adv. bd. Children's Media Found. Boston, 1993-97; guest lectr. various confs. on edn. and film to colls. and art schs. in U.S. Exhibited film, Mus. Modern Art, Whitney Mus. Am. Art, Chgo. Art Inst., Nat. Film Theatre, London, Internat. Womens Film Festival, Paris, Mus. Fine Arts, Boston, Libr. Congress, Washington, John F. Kennedy Ctr. Performing Arts, Washington; dir., prodr. (film) Anything You Want to Be, 1971 (Blue Ribbon Am. Film Festival award), Betty Tells Her Story, 1972, Once Upon a Choice, 1980 (Silver medal Houston Internat. Film Festival), How to Prevent a Nuclear War, 1987 (Blue Ribbon award Am. Film Festival 1988); prodr. (video) Goodnight Amherst, 1995, Fine Print, 1995, Try This At Home, 1998 (Judge's Choice award Hometown Video Festival 1999), Fresh Ink, 1998, Try This At Home: Nature Series, 2000 (award of Distinction, Communicator award); still photographer: Murder at Harvard, 2002, Act Your Age, 2002. Recipient Creative Artist award AAUW, 1975, Disting. Alumni award Boston U., 1985; Careth Found. grantee, 1988, Funding Exchange grantee, 1989, Mass. Found. for Humanities and Pub. Policy grantee, 1975, Film Fund grantee, 1985. Try this at Home: Nature Series (Award of Distinction, Communicator Awards), 2000 Mem. New Eng. Screen Edn. Assn. (v.p. 1972-83), Assn. Ind. Video and Filmmakers, Women in Film and Video New Eng. Office: U Mass Sch Edn Furcolo Hall Amherst MA 01003

BRANDON, RAYMOND WILSON, financial planner, securities principal; b. Memphis, Mar. 11, 1959; s. Elvis Denby Jr. and Helen (Deupree) B.; m. Dana Stallings, Sept. 21, 1996. BA, Vanderbilt U., 1981; MBA, U. Tex., 1983. CFA; CLU; cert. fin. planner; chartered fin. cons. Pres., chmn. investment com. Brandon Fin. Planning, Inc., Memphis, 1983—; v.p. ops. Brandon Investments, Inc., Memphis, 1983—. V.p. Brandon Underwriting Specialists, Inc., Memphis. Sord scholar U. Tex., 1983. Mem. Internat. Assn. Fin. Planning (pres. Memphis chpt. 1988-89), Am. Soc. Fin. Svc. Profls., Memphis Inst. Cert. Fin. Planners (bd. dirs.), Rotary (Paul Harris fellow, treas., bd. dirs.), Racquet Club Memphis, Assn. for Investment Mgmt. and Rsch., Phi Beta Kappa. Presbyterian. Avocations: swimming, running, traveling, magic, public speaking. Office: 5101 Wheelis Rd Ste 112 Memphis TN 38117

BRANDON, WALTER WILEY, JR., retired physicist, retired aerospace engineer; b. Gainesville, Ga., Dec. 1, 1929; s. Walter Wiley and Nancy (Logan) Brandon; m. Patricia Donham, May 18, 1957; children: Dean Corbly, Miles Logan, Nancy Lynn. BA, Emory U., 1952, MS, 1953. Scientist Rohm and Haas Co., Huntsville, Ala., 1953—64, 1967—71; aerospace engr. Boeing Co., Huntsville, Ala., 1964—67; analyst U.S. Army Missile Command, Huntsville, Ala., 1972—87; aerospace engr. NASA Marshall Space Flight Ctr., Huntsville, Ala., 1987—98, ret., 1998. Tech. cons. detonation U.S. Army Missile Command, Huntsville, Ala., 1988, Morton-Thiokol Corp., Huntsville, Ala., 1988. Fellow: AIAA (assoc.); mem.: Sigma Pi Sigma (Emory U. chpt. pres. 1952—53), Sigma Xi (assoc.). Methodist. Avocations: photography, model building. Home: 1902 Colice Rd SE Huntsville AL 35801-1640

BRANDON, WILLIAM PEW, JR., social sciences educator; b. Greensboro, N.C. s. William P. and Katherine Wolff Brandon; m. Pamela Sue Fawcett, Dec. 20, 1975 BA in Philosophy and Polit. Sci.with gen. honors, Johns Hopkins U., 1963; MSc in Politics, U. London, 1967; PhD in Polit. Sci., Duke U., 1975; MPH in Health Policy and Adminstrn., U. N.C., 1976. Dir. info. svcs. evaluation and planning Orange-Chatham Comprehensive Health Svcs., Chapel Hill, N.C., 1971-75; asst. prof. preventive medicine and polit. sci. U. Rochester, N.Y., 1976-82; NEH fellow Hastings Ctr., Hastings-on-Hudson, N.Y., 1982-83; from assoc. prof. to prof. polit. sci. and pub. adminstrn. Seton Hall U., South Orange, N.J., 1984-93; Metrolina Med. Found. Disting. prof. U. N.C., Charlotte, 1994—. Vis. prof. health care adminstrn. Bernard M. Baruch Coll., CUNY, 1990; dir. rsch., fin. officer Essex and Union Adv. Bd. for Health Planning Inc., South Orange, 1992-93. Contbr. numerous articles to profl. jours., including New Eng. Jour. Medicine, Polit. Theory, Jour. Health Politics Policy and Law, others. Vol. U.S. Peace Corps, Iran, 1964-66; mem. City Planning Commn., Rochester City Govt., 1979-82; mem. N.J. State Health Planning Bd., Trenton, 1992; active Leadership Charlotte XXII, 2000-01; bd. visitors Miss Hall's Sch., Pittsfield, Mass., 2000—. Faculty fellow in healthcare fin. Robert Wood Johnson Found.-Johns Hopkins Med. Instn., 1985-86; grantee for rsch. on Medicaid, N.C. HHS-U.S. Agy. Healthcare Rsch. and Quality, 1996-2001. Mem. APHA (governing coun. 1984-86), Am. Polit. Sci. Assn., Academy for Health Svcs. Rsch., Charlotte Area Peace Corps Assn. (pres. 2003), Phi Beta Kappa, Sigma Xi. Office: U NC Dept Polit Sci 9201 University City Blvd Charlotte NC 28223 Fax: 704-687-496. E-mail: wilbrand@email.uncc.edu.

BRANDOW, STEPHEN JON, priest; b. Olean, N.Y., Dec. 25, 1960; s. David Arden and Jacqueline Delores (Johns) B. BA, Northwestern State U. La., 1983, BA in Social Work, 1985; MDiv, Notre Dame U., 1996. Ordained to ministry, Cath. Ch., 1996. Social worker Woodview Regional Hosp., Pineville, La., 1986; med. clk. VA Med. Ctr., Alexandria, La., 1986-91; assoc. pastor St. Rita Cath. Ch., Alexandria, La., 1996-97, Immaculate Heart of Mary Cath. Ch., Tioga, La., 1997-2000. Chaplain Ctrl. La. State Hosp., Pineville, 1997—2000, Christus St. Frances Cabrini Hosp., Alexandria, 1997—, 1997—2001, VA Med. Ctr., Alexandria, 1998—; mem. com. continuing formation of clergy Diocese of Alexandria, 1996—, sec., 1996—97. Mem. Cath. Commn. on Scouting, 1997—; bd. dir. Girl Scout Coun. of Ctrl. La., 2001—02; v.p. Attatapac Coun. Boy Scout of Am. Recipient Whitney Young Svc. award, Boy Scouts Am., 2002, Pelican award, Cath. Com. on Scouting, Diocese of Alexandria, 2003; James E. West fellow, Boy Scouts Am., 2002. Mem.: United Assn. Christian Counselors, La. Chaplains Assn. (bd. dirs. 1999—2002). Avocation: yoga. Home: PO Box 39 Tioga LA 71477 Office: VA Med Ctr PO Box 69004 Tioga LA 71306 Fax: 318-483-5053. E-mail: sbran62261@aol.com.

BRANDOW, THEO, architect; b. Phila., Nov. 18, 1925; s. Ralph and Minnie (Weinstock) B.; m. Selma Koss, July 22, 1945; children: Jonathan, Rinna, Shanna. Student, Girard Coll., 1935—43; BArch, U. Pa., 1949. Assoc. Oskar Stonorov, Phila., 1949-52; pvt. practice architecture Phila., 1952-78; project dir. Rochlin & Baran & Assocs., West Los Angeles, Calif., 1978-81; pres. Brandow Design Assocs., 1982-87; pvt. practice architecture Ambler, Pa., 1987—. Cons. urban renewal; vis. speaker sch. system Wellspring Ecumenical Ctr., Phila., 1966—. Prin. works include houses, apt. and office buildings, churches; design architect Benjamin Franklin House; works pub. in various mags. including Life, House and Home, Am. Home; author: Closer to Saturday, 1971, Michla, A Trilogy; also articles and lectures on Israel's Day of Atonement War of 1973; group shows include Chestnut Hill Fine Arts Festival, Phila., 1995 (1st place prize 1995), New Hope Art Festival, Pa., 1995 (award of excellence 1995), Lansdale Festival of the Arts, Pa., 1995 (most unique craft award 1995), Woodmere Art Mus., Phila., 1996, 97, 98. V.p. Erdenheim (Pa.) PTA, 1956; mem. Whitemarsh Valley Fair Housing Coun., 1966—; pack master local coun. Boy Scouts Am.; bd. dirs. local Jewish synagogue. With USNR, 1943-46. Recipient award World Traveling Exhibit Art in Arch., 1949, Homes for Better Living, 1957, 59, state citation Am. Home mag., 1957, nat. citation, 1958, spl. award Am. Builder mag., 1959, McCall's Congress for Better Living award, 1959, awards Nat. Assn. Home Builders, 1961. Mem. AIA (awards 1957, 61). Home: 2601 #1 Market St Camp Hill PA 17001

BRANDRETH, ELIZABETH ANNE, library director; b. N.Y.C., July 8, 1937; d. John Joseph and Edith M. (Mayer) B. AA, Mount Aloysius Jr. Coll., Cresson, Pa., 1957; BA, Coll. Misericordia, 1961; MSLS, Cath. U. Am., 1963; MS in Human Resources Adminstrn., U. Scranton, 1988. Mem. Sisters of Mercy. Asst. libr. Coll. Misericordia, Dallas, Pa., 1963-64; libr. Bishop McCort H.S., Johnstown, Pa., 1964-67; reference libr. Mount Aloysius Jr. Coll., Cresson, Pa., 1967-71, libr. dir., 1971-79; dir. libr. svcs. Mercy Hosp., Scranton, Pa., 1979-95; regional dir. libr. svcs. Mercy Health Ptnrs., Scranton, 1995—. Sec.-treas. bd. dirs. Catherine McAuley Ctr., Scranton, 1986-95; sec. bd. dirs. N.E. Pa. chpt. Susan G. Komen Breast Cancer Found., Scranton, 1989-93; bd. trustees Coll. Misericordia, Dallas, 1990-93. Mem. Med. Libr. Assn., Pa. Libr. Assn. (bd. mem. N.E. chpt. 1985-87), Beta Phi Mu. Roman Catholic. Avocation: reading. Office: Mercy Hosp 746 Jefferson Ave Scranton PA 18510-1697 E-mail: ebrandreth@hotmail.com.

BRANDRUP, DOUGLAS WARREN, lawyer; b. Mitchel, S.D., July 11, 1940; s. Clair L. and Ruth M. (Wolverton) B.; m. Patricia R. Tuck, Dec. 20, 1986; children: Kendra, Monika, Peter. AB in Econs., Middlebury Coll., 1963; JD, Boston U., 1966. Bar: N.Y. 1969, U.S. Dist. Ct. (so. dist.) N.Y. 1970, U.S. Ct. Appeals (2d cir.) 1970. Assoc. Donovan, Leisure, Newton & Irvine, N.Y.C., 1968-72; ptnr. Griggs, Baldwin & Baldwin, N.Y.C., 1972-80, sr. ptnr., 1980—. Chmn. Equity Oil Co., mem. disciplinary com. first dept. appellate divsn. Supreme Ct. State of N.Y., 2003. Mem. Govs. Security Adv. Com., State of N.J., 1975-90. Capt. U.S. Army, 1966-68. Recipient Ellis Island medal of Honor, 1999, Order of St. John, 2002. Mem. ABA, N.Y. County Bar Assn., N.Y. State Bar Assn., Met. Club (N.Y.C., pres.), Mashomack Preserve Club. Republican. Episcopalian. Office: 57 Old Post Rd No 2 Greenwich CT 06830 Fax: 203-629-7983.

BRANDS, JAMES EDWIN, medical products executive; b. Lebanon, Ind., July 5, 1937; s. Edwin Herman and Pearl Irene (Brown) B.; m. Gail Marian Knight, Sept. 12, 1959; children: Jeffrey, Scot, Alan, Susan. AB, Wesleyan U., Middletown, Conn., 1959; MBA, U. Chgo., 1961; JD, Kennedy-Western U., Boise, Idaho, 1992. CPA, Mo. Staff acct., mgr. Arthur Andersen, Chgo., 1961-71, ptnr. St. Louis, 1971-82; sr. v.p. Scherer-Storz, Inc., St. Louis, 1982-86; vice chmn., CFO Scherer Healthcare Inc., Atlanta, 1982-95; exec. v.p. Scherer Sci. Ltd., Atlanta, 1986-95; chmn., CEO Marquest Med. Products, Inc., Denver, 1993-95; CFO Wilson Pest Control, Inc., Atlanta, 1997-99; sr. exec. v.p. Able Telcom Holding Corp., Atlanta, 1999—2001. Bd. dirs., pres. Body-Care Inc., Atlanta, New Products Inc., Atlanta; bd. dirs. Horizon Med. Products Inc., Manchester, Ga.; pres. Brands & Co, 1981—, Throwleigh Techs. LLC, Atlanta, 2000—. Mem. AICPA, Mo. Soc. CPAs, Bellerive Country Club (St. Louis), Country Club of the South (Atlanta). Republican. Home: 4330 Bancroft Valley Alpharetta GA 30022-5175 E-mail: brandsj@bellsouth.net.

BRANDS, ROBERT FRANCISCUS, business executive; b. Tilburg, Holland, June 18, 1957; came to U.S., 1982; s. Robert M. and Jetty Brands. BA, Inst. Tech., Eindhoven, Holland, 1981; student Small Bus. Mgmt. program, NYU, 1984. Rsch. analyst French-Dutch C. of C., Paris, 1981-82; mgr., internat. trade advisor Netherlands C. of C., N.Y.C., 1982-84; v.p. mktg. Airspray Internat., Inc., N.Y.C., 1985-88; pres. Branco Internat., Inc., N.Y.C., 1985-88; new product mgr., market mgr. consumer divsn. Philips Lighting, 1988-89; mktg. mgr., cons. divsn. U.S. Lighting, OSRAM Sylvania, Inc., 1989-93; v.p. mktg. Sterling Plumbing Group, Inc., a Kohler Co., 1993-94, Kohler Plumbing N.A., 1995-98; pres. Airspray Internat., Inc., Pompano Beach, Fla., 1998—. Mng. dir. Airspray NV, Ayaky. Author trade surveys. Past pres. Erie # 4 Fire Assn., Georgetown, Mass.; supporter Netherlands-Am. Cmty. Assn. Sgt. Royal Dutch Mil. Police, 1977-78. Mem. Round Table USA (past nat. bd. dirs., internat. rels. officer), Gen. Mdse. Distbn. Coun. (past adv. bd.). Roman Catholic. Avocations: flying, sailing. Home: 12601 NW 18th Pl Coral Springs FL 33071-5415 Office: Airspray Internat Inc 3768 Park Central Blvd N Pompano Beach FL 33064-2217

BRANDT, ANTHONY SCOTT, free-lance writer, consultant; b. Cranford, N.J., Nov. 21, 1936; s. Axel Elmer and Grace Scott Brandt; m. Barbara L. Rescorla, June 21, 1958 (div. July 1976); children: Katherine Grace, Evan Anthony; m. Lorraine Dusky, Sept. 20, 1981. BA, Princeton U., 1958; MA, Columbia U., 1961. Bus. historian Office of Sherman M. Fairchild, N.Y.C., 1962-71; free-lance writer, 1972—. Judge non-fiction category Nat. Book Awards, 2002. Author: Reality Police, 1975, People Along the Sand, 1992; editor: Pushcart Book of Essays; contbg. editor Men's Jour. mag., 1992-99, Nat. Geographic Adventure mag., 1999—; series editor Nat. Geographic Adventure Classics; contbr. numerous articles to mags. Chmn. Bd. of Historic Preservation and Archtl. Rev., Sag Harbor, N.Y., 1985-90. Recipient Nat. Mag. award Ednl. Writers Assn., 1988. Mem. Princeton Club of N.Y. Home and Office: 54 High St Sag Harbor NY 11963 E-mail: asbrandt@aol.com.

BRANDT, CARL DAVID, research virologist; b. Bridgeport, Conn., Jan. 19, 1928; s. Carl August and Hildur (Wedberg) B.; m. Elsa Lund Erickson, Apr. 25, 1964; children: Karen, Erik. BS, U. Conn., 1949; MS, U. Mass., 1951; PhD, Harvard U., 1958. Rsch. instr. dept. vet. sci. U. Mass., Amherst, 1949-52, 54; rsch. virologist Charles Pfizer & Co., Inc., Ind. and Conn., 1958—62; assoc., dept. epidemiology Pub. Health Rsch. Inst., N.Y.C., 1962—66; rsch. assoc. virology rsch. Children's Nat. Med. Ctr., Washington, 1966-79, sr. rsch. assoc., 1979-86, sr. scientist, 1986-94; ret., 1994. Instr. Georgetown U. Med. Sch., Washington, 1966-69; asst. prof. pediat. George Washington U. Med. Sch., Washington, 1969-74, assoc. prof., 1974-94, emeritus prof., 1994. Contbr. over 125 articles to profl. jours. 1st lt. USAF, 1952-54. Fellow Am. Acad. Microbiology, Infectious Diseases Soc. Am., Am. Coll. Epidemiology; mem. N.Y. Color Slide Club (bd. dirs. 1965-66), Silver Spring Camera Club (pres. 1970-71), Rock Creek Amateur Radio Assn. (pres. 1985-89). Avocations: photography, amateur radio. Home: 819 E Franklin Ave Silver Spring MD 20901-4709

BRANDT, DEAN MYRON, design engineer; b. Mpls., May 2, 1963; s. Norman Rupert and Norma Marion (Ohler) B. AA in Mech. Design, Mpls. Drafting Sch., 1987. Cert. ProE, 1997. With Multitech Sys., Mounds View, Minn., 1982-84, prodn. supr., 1984-86, design engr., 1986-97, design engr., mgr., 1997—. Mentor St. Paul Pub. Schs., 1997-98. Mem. Optimist Club (v.p. 1999, mentor 1998-99). Achievements include patents in data communications, modem design, multifunction personal communication system, design desktop model chassis, portable modem, desktop computer housing, IP telephone, VPN server, CSM. Home: 2708 E 49th St Minneapolis MN 55417 Office: Multi Tech Sys 2205 Woodale Dr Mounds View MN 55112

BRANDT, EDWARD NEWMAN, JR., physician, educator; b. Oklahoma City, July 3, 1933; s. Edward Newman and Myrtle (Brazil) Brandt; m. Patricia Ann Lawson, Aug. 29, 1953; children: Patrick James, Edward Newman III, Rex Carlin. BS, U. Okla., 1954, MD, 1960, PhD, 1963; MS, Okla. State U., 1955; LHD (hon.), Med. U. S.C., Rush U.; DSc (hon.), N.Y. Inst. Tech. Intern Oklahoma City VA Hosp., 1960—61; resident U. Okla. Hosps., 1961; from instr. to prof. preventive medicine and pub. health U. Okla. Med. Center, Oklahoma City, 1961—70; prof., chmn. dept. biostatistics U. Okla. Med. Center (Sch. Health), 1967—68; assoc. dean U. Okla. Med. Center (Sch. Medicine); assoc. dir. U. Okla. Med. Center (Med. Center), 1968—70; dean Grad. Sch., prof. preventive medicine and community health U. Tex. Med. Br., Galveston,

1970—72; acting dean U. Tex. Med. Br. (Grad. Sch.), 1972—74, assoc. dean clin. affairs, 1972—73, prof. preventive medicine and community health, 1970—84, acting dean medicine, 1973—74, prof. family medicine, 1973—84, dean medicine, 1974—76, exec. dean, 1976—77; vice chancellor health affairs U. Tex. System, Austin, 1977—81; asst. sec. health HHS, 1981—84; pres. U. Md.-Balt., 1985—89, also prof. epidemiology and preventive medicine, 1985—89; prof. internal medicine, exec. dean Coll. Medicine U. Okla., Oklahoma City, 1989—92; dir. Ctr. for Health Policy U. Okla., 1992—; prof. health adminstrn. Coll. Pub. Health, 1989—96, Regents prof., 1996—, chair dept. health adminstrn. and policy, 2000—02. Mem. primate ctr. rev. com. NIH, 1975—79, chmn., 1978—79, mem. rsch. career devel. award com., 1968—72, mem. adv. com. on rsch. in women's health, 1995—97; bd. regents Nat. Libr. Medicine, 1985—89, chmn., 1987—89; mem. exec. bd. WHO, 1982—84; chmn. adv. com. on injury control CDC, 1988—93; chmn. adv. coun. on food FDA, 1992—2000. Editor, contbr. Proc. of Conf. at U. Okla. Med. Ctr., 1968, editor Continuing Education for the Family Physician, 1974—77, AIDS and Pub. Polic Jour., 1988—91. Recipient Superior Performance award, VA Hosp., Oklahoma City, 1961, Lloyd M. Southwick Meml. award for med. writing, 1974, 1975, Spl. Appreciation award, Tex. Acad. Family Physicians, 1974, Leone award for adminstrv. excellence, 1976, Outstanding Alumni Svc. award, U. Okla. Coll. Medicine, 1977, Disting. Svc. award, U. Tex. Med. Br., 1977, 19th Ann. Stoneburner lectr., Med. Coll. Va., 1966, Disting. Leadership award, HHS, 1984, Disting. Pub. Svc. award, Dept. Def., 1986, Pub. Health award, Am. Acad. Family Physicians; scholar Triennial, Phi Kappa Phi, 1998—2001. Fellow: AAAS (chair med. scis. sect. 1992—93), Am. Coll. Cardiology (hon.); mem.: AMA (chmn. sect. on med. schs. 1979—81, chmn. com. accreditation continuing med. edn. 1979—81), Inst. Medicine NAS (governing coun. 1986—92), Philos. Soc. Tex., Okla. Acad. Family Physicians, Am. Acad. Family Physicians, Okla. Med. Assn. (chmn. com. on family violence 1993—98, chmn. coun. on state legis. 1994—), Assn. Am. Med. Colls. (exec. coun. 1986—89, Spl. Recognition award 1985), Alpha Omega Alpha, Sigma Xi, Mu Epsilon, Phi Sigma Pi, Phi Kappa Phi (nat. scholar), Alpha Epsilon Delta, Phi Eta Sigma. Office: U Okla Health Scis Ctr PO Box 26901 Oklahoma City OK 73190-0901

BRANDT, GENE STUART, fundraising consultant; b. N.Y.C., Aug. 29, 1950; s. Eugene Charles and Elsie Virginia (Williams) B.; m. Elizabeth Holland, July 20, 1991; children: Cameron Elizabeth, Christopher Holland. AB in Polit. Sci., Knox Coll., 1972. Asst. dir. admission Knox Coll., Galesburg, Ill., 1972-74, dir. alumni affairs, 1974-76; dir. univ. devel. U. Nev., Reno, 1976-79; dir. devel. Lake Forest (Ill.) Coll., 1979-81, v.p. devel., 1981-86; v.p. external affairs Mus. Sci. and Industry, Chgo., 1986-91; pres. sci. and tech. Mus. of Atlanta, 1991-97; prin., cons., pres. TerMolen Brandt & Assocs., Inc., 1997—2003; pres. TerMolen Watkins & Brandt, LLC, 2003—. Bd. dirs., vice-chmn. Pub. Broadcasting Atlanta; bd. trustees Cazenovia Coll., 2001—, McCormick Theol. Sem., 2001—; elder Ctrl. Presbyn. Ch. Named to Outstanding Young Men of Am., 1981. Mem. Am. Assn. Mus., Assn. Fundraising Profls., Coun. for Advancement and Support of Edn., Econ. Club Chgo., Oak Park Country Club, Lahinch Golf Club (Ireland). Office: TerMolen Watkins Brandt & Assocs 500 N Dearborn St Ste 500 Chicago IL 60610-4997

BRANDT, GREGORY ALAN, secondary school educator; b. Carlisle, Pa., Apr. 24, 1963; s. Maynard Leon and Ruth Kyle Brandt. BA in English, Hampden-Sydney Coll., 1985; postgrad., U. Oxford, Eng., 1988; MA in Liberal Arts, St. John's Coll., 1994. Tchr. St. Andrew's Sch., Boca Raton, Fla., 1985—88, Pine Crest Prep. Sch., Ft. Lauderdale, Fla., 1990—92, Ransom Everglades Sch., Coconut Grove, Fla., 1994—96, Phillips Acad. Summer Session, Andover, Mass., 1993—97, Park Sch. of Balt., Brooklandville, Md., 1997—; editl. asst. Coll. Bd., N.Y.C., 1989—90. Mem.: Appalachian Trail Conf. (life), Phi Beta Kappa. Avocations: running, hiking, travel. Home: 106 W University Pkwy Apt J5 Baltimore MD 21210 Office: Park Sch of Balt Old Court Rd Brooklandville MD 21022 E-mail: gbrandt@parkschool.net

BRANDT, HARRY, mechanical engineering educator; b. Amsterdam, The Netherlands, Nov. 14, 1925; came to U.S., 1946, naturalized, 1962; s. Friedrich H. and Henny (Rous) B.; m. Muriel Ruth Harman, Jan. 24, 1953; children: Joyce Estelle, Marilyn Audrey, Robert Alan. BS, U. Calif.-Berkeley, 1949, MS, 1950, PhD, 1954. Supervising research engr. Chevron Research Co., La Habra, Calif., 1954-64; lectr. UCLA, 1962-64; prof. mech. engring. U. Calif., Davis, 1964—, chmn. dept., 1969-74, 86-91; dir. Internat. Pipeline Techs. Inc., Beaverton, Oreg., 1985-91; chmn. bd. Clean Energy Systems, Inc., 1997—. Cons. Lawrence Livermore Nat. Lab., 1969—, State of Calif., 1970-87, State of Alaska, 1972, Los Alamos Nat. Lab., 1988-93. Mem. ASME, Am. Welding Soc., AIAA, Sigma Xi, Tau Beta Pi. Presbyterian. Home: 26934 Middle Golf Dr El Macero CA 95618-1053 Office: U Calif Dept Mech and Aero Engring One Shields Ave Davis CA 95616 E-mail: hbrandt@ucdavis.edu.

BRANDT, HOWARD EDWARD, physicist; b. Emerado, N.D. s. Howard Edward and Mamie Luella (Franklin) B.; m. Marilyn Kay McKinstry, Mar. 25, 1972; children: Karen, Sonja. BS in Physics, MIT, 1962; MS in Physics, U. Wash., 1963, PhD in Physics, 1970. Engr., physicist Boeing Co., Seattle, 1958-64; predoctoral rsch. asst. U. Wash., Seattle, 1964-70; physics tchr. Seattle Prep. Sch., 1971-72; physicist U. Md., College Park, 1972-73, Lulejian and Assocs., Falls Church, Va., 1973-76, Sci. Applications, Inc., McLean, Va., 1976-77, Army Rsch. Lab., Adelphi, Md., 1977—. Editor various books/conf. procs. in field, including Selected Papers on Nonlinear Optics, 1991; contbr. articles to profl. jours. Sloan Found. scholar, 1958-62; recipient Siple Silver medallion U.S. Army, 1980. Mem. Am. Phys. Soc., Am. Optical Soc., Am. Math. Soc., Math. Assn. Am., Am. Assn. Physics Tchrs. Presbyterian. Avocations: mathematics, philosophy. Home: 2713 Shanandale Dr Silver Spring MD 20904-1633 Office: Army Rsch Lab 2800 Powder Mill Rd Adelphi MD 20783-1138 E-mail: hbrandt@arl.army.mil.

BRANDT, IRA KIVE, pediatrician, medical geneticist; b. N.Y.C. s. Charles Zachary and Hilda Eleanor B.; m. Dorothy Godfrey; children— Elizabeth, Laura, William, Rena. AB, NYU, 1942; MD, Columbia U., 1945. Diplomate Am. Bd. Pediatrics, Am. Bd. Med. Genetics. Intern Morrisania City Hosp., N.Y.C., 1945-46; resident Lincoln Hosp., N.Y.C., 1948-50; fellow pediatrics Yale U., New Haven, 1955-57, asst. prof., 1957-61, assoc. prof., 1961-68; chmn. dept. pediatrics Children's Hosp., San Francisco, 1968-70; clin. prof. pediatrics U. Calif., San Francisco, 1970; prof. pediatrics and med. genetics Ind. U. Sch. Medicine, Indpls., 1970-89, prof. emeritus, 1989—. Served to capt. U.S. Army, 1946-47, 52 Mem. Am. Pediatric Soc., Am. Acad. Pediatrics, Soc. Pediatric Rsch., Soc. Inherited Metabolic Disorders, Am. Soc. Human Genetics, Am. Coll. Med. Genetics. Office: Ind U Sch Medicine Dept Pediatrics 702 Barnhill Dr # 0907 Indianapolis IN 46202-5128 E-mail: ibrandt@iupui.edu.

BRANDT, IRENE HILDEGARD, retired secondary education educator; b. Meriden, Conn., June 6, 1942; d. Walter M. and Hildegard E. Brandt. BS, Ctrl. Conn. State U., 1964, cert. 6th yr. degree, 1989, MS, 1969, postgrad., 1989. Cert. 7-12 math. tchr., K-12 adminstrn. and supervision, intermediate supervision, Conn. Tchr. math. Jefferson Jr. H.S., Meriden, 1964-67, Platt H.S., Meriden, 1967-99; ret., 1999. Substitute tchr. Platt H.S. Active Summit Club, Meriden, 1972-99. Yearbook dedicated to her Platt H.S., 1971, named Outstanding Tchr. by Srs., 1990, 91, 92, 96, 98, 99, 2000. Mem. ASCD, Nat. Coun. Tchrs. Math., New Eng. Math. Tchrs. Assn., Assn. Tchrs. Math. in Conn. (conv. presider 1990-98), Am. Fedn. Tchrs., Conn. Fedn. Tchrs., Meriden Fedn. Tchrs. (sec. 1982-90). Avocations: travel, reading, crossword puzzles, gardening. Home: 70 Genest St Meriden CT 06450-4538

BRANDT, JOHN ASHWORTH, fuel company executive; b. Chgo., Oct. 3, 1950; s. William W. and Joan V. (Ashworth) B.; m. Debbie M. Fico, June 2, 1984; children: Briana Ashley, Bryan Ashworth. Student, U. Colo., 1969-72. Mgr. co. accounts Lincoln Wood Commodities, Chgo., 1972-74; pres. Lafayette Coal Co., Burr Ridge, Ill., 1974—, Hoosier King Coal Co., 1993—, Ind. Farms, Inc., 1996—; gen. mgr. Hoyelton LLC, 2002—. Pres. Chgo. Coal Shippers, 1984—; pres. Hoosier King Coal Co.; dir. Muliganeers Non-Profit Orgn. Office: Lafayette Coal Co 200 S Frontage Rd Ste 310 Hinsdale IL 60521-6953

BRANDT, JOHN EDWARD, human services administrator; b. Mason City, Iowa, July 31, 1946; s. Edward Floyd and Sarah Elizabeth (Holdcroft) B.; m. Karen Maurine Hilleman, July 30, 1977. Student, St. Olaf Coll., 1964-66; BA in History, U. Iowa, 1968, JD, 1971, MBA, 1973. Evaluation specialist/legal analyst Integrated Svcs. Project, Des Moines, 1973-77; coord. planning and grants Linn County Health Ctr., Cedar Rapids, Iowa, 1977-86; exec. dir. Linn County Dept. Human Resources Mgmt., Cedar Rapids, 1986—. Bd. dirs. Hawkeye Area Cmty. Action Program, Cedar Rapids, 1986—, Linn County Fed. Emergency Mgmt. Agy. for Emergency Food and Shelter Program, Cedar Rapids, 1988—; mem. adv. coun. Heritage Area Agy. on Aging, Cedar Rapids, 1986-93; mem. grant com. United Way Time Ltd., Cedar Rapids, 1988-97, mem. Linn County Foresight 2020 Cmty. Planning Oversight Com., 1996—; chmn. Mental Health Planning Com., Cedar Rapids, 1989—, Linn County Employee Devel. Com., 1993—, Patch Grant Adv. Com., Cedar Rapids, 1991-95, Healthy Linn Care Network, 1996—; chmn. steering com. Partnership for Safe Families, 1995—; chmn. adv. bd. Linn County Innovation Zone, 1997-98, chmn. cmty. empowerment governance bd., 1998-99; chmn. Linn County Elderly Svcs. Cmty. Planning com.chmn., 2001, Cmty. Indigent/Low Income Svcs. Study Com., 2002—; active State Decategorization Projects Com., 1991—; chmn. 6th Jud. Dist. Ordered Svc. Planning Com., 1998—; co-chmn. AmeriCorp I Can Regional Bd., 1994-96; chmn. exec. com. Linn County Decategorization, 1991—; others. Contbr. articles to profl. jours. Mem. adv. coun. Jr. League Cedar Rapids Community, 1986-89; mem. Linn County Emergency Ops. Ctr. for Duane Arnold Nuclear Plant Evacuation Plan, Cedar Rapids, 1987—; chmn. St. Paul's Meth. Ch. Outreach Task Force, 1987-89, Neighborhood Chs. Task Force, 1989-93; docent Herbert Hoover Mus., 1990—. Recipient award 6th Jud. Dist. Dept. Correctional Svcs., Cedar Rapids, 1985, Gov.'s award for Volunteerism, 1996, Alternative Svcs. Profl. Child Advocate award, 2000. Mem. Herbert Hoover Presdl. Libr. Assn., Iowa State Hist. Soc., Iowa Club Linn County, Family Resource Devel. Assn. (chmn.), Phi Alpha Delta. Avocations: history, museums, theater, travel, music. Office: Linn County Dept Human Resources Mgmt 305 2nd Ave SE Cedar Rapids IA 52401-1215 E-mail: john.brandt@co.linn.ia.com.

BRANDT, JOHN HENRY, physician; b. Cleve., July 30, 1940; s. Harold Paul and Dorothy Helen (Kern) B.; m. Jon Ellison, July 30, 1963 (div. 1971); children: Sylvia Ann, Laura Ann; m. Marilyn Ruth Brandt, July 25, 1980. BA, Yale U., 1962; postgrad., Cambridge (Eng.) U., 1962-64; MD, Harvard U., 1970. Asst. to dir. Harvard Ctr. for Community Health, Boston, 1968-69; clin. fellow Med. Sch. Harvard U., Boston, 1970-73, instr. in psychiatry Med. Sch., 1973-74, 74-99; resident psychiatrist McLean Hosp., Belmont, Mass., 1970-73, dir. Waverley House, 1973-74, attending psychiatrist, 1974-90, Mass. Mental Health Ctr., 1991-99; staff psychiatrist med. dept. MIT, Cambridge, 1979-99. Active Mass. Hist. Soc., New Eng. Hist. Geneal. Soc.; mem. Trinity Ch., Boston, 1988—. Mem.: Chief Execs. Club of Boston, Internat. Inst., N.Y. Acad. Medicine, Mass. Med. Soc., World Boston, Gore Pl., Bostonian Soc., Yale Mory's Assn., Guild of St. Luke, English Speaking Union, Clare Assn., Am. Friends Cambridge U., Harvard Musical Assn. (dir. 1990—93), Russell Trust Assn., Colonial Soc., Nichols House Mus., Soc. for Preservation of New Eng. Antiquities, Lincoln Land Conservation Trust, Trustees of Reservations, Thursday Evening Club, Yale Club of Boston (sec. 1988—90, dir. 1990—93), Harvard Faculty Club, Boston Athenaeum, Harvard Club of Boston (chmn. Ho. com. 1989—91, v.p. 1991—93), Yale Elizabethan Club, Cosmos Club, Phi Beta Kappa. Republican. Episcopalian. Avocation: music. Home and Office: PO Box 530 Lincoln MA 01773-0530

BRANDT, JOHN REYNOLD, editor, journalist; b. Amarillo, Tex., Aug. 25, 1959; s. Reynold Francis Jr. and Patricia Levonne (Wallace) B.; m. Svetlana Stevovich, May 28, 1989; children: Emma Evangeline Stevovich Brandt, Aidan Reynold Stevovich Brandt. BA, Case Western Reserve U., Cleve., 1981. Sales rep. Merrell Dow Pharmaceuticals, Cleve., 1982-84, Miles Pharmaceuticals, Cleve., 1984-88, Tokos Perinatal Nursing Svcs., Cleve., 1988-89; sr. assoc. M. Zunt Assocs., Cleve., 1989-90; dir. mgmt. devel. CSA Health System, Cleve., 1990-91; assoc. editor Corp. Cleve. Mag., 1991-94; from exec. editor to pub. IndustryWeek Mag., Cleve., 1994—2000; chief editl. dir. Exec. Mag., 2000—03, pres., pub., 2001—03, editor-at-large, 2003—; pres. John R. Brandt, Inc., 2000—; CEO MPI Group, Inc., 2003—. V.p. Inst. Environ. Edn., Cleve., 1990-91. Bd. dirs. Work in N.E. Ohio Coun., 1997—; judge Workforce Excellence Awards of Nat. Assn. Mfrs., 1997—, Am. Bus. Media Neal awards, 2000. Recipient numerous awards in field from Am. Bus. Press, Assn. of Area Bus. Publs., The Press Club of Cleve., March of Dimes, Am. Soc. Bus. Press Editors. Mem. Press Club of Cleve. (dir. 1994-2001, v.p. 1996-98, pres. 1998-99). Office: 2835 Sedgewick Rd Cleveland OH 44120-1837

BRANDT, KATHLEEN See WEIL-GARRIS BRANDT, KATHLEEN

BRANDT, LINDA ANN, social worker; b. Evanston, Ill., July 18, 1947; d. Howard Clinton and Arleigh R. (Munderloh) Fauss; m. Bruce Edwin Brandt, Dec. 14, 1968; children: Amanda, James. BA, U. Denver, 1969, MA, 1970, MSW, 1979; PhD in Sociology, S.D. State U., 1999. Cert. social worker, S.D. Caseworker Dept. Social Svc., Denver, 1969-70; dir. patient svcs. Am. Cancer Soc., Boston, 1971-77; mental health counselor Lake Regional Mental Health Ctr., Brookings, S.D., 1979, East Cen. Mental Health Ctr., Brookings, 1980-82; coord., founding mem. bd. dirs. Dakota Care Hospice, Brookings, 1984-87; coord. respite care Easter Seals, Brookings, 1985—87; social worker, sub-acute unit Avera Prince of Peace, Sioux Falls, SD, 2001—. Founding mem. bd. dirs. Brookings Interagy. Coun. for Spl. Needs Children and Their Families, 1982—, pres. bd. dirs., 1987—. Organizer Elderly Transp. Network, Brookings, 1982-84; organizer, trainer Minn-Ia-Kotan coun. Girl Scouts U.S.A., 1988-2000, sec. Sioux Falls Coalition on Aging, 2002—. Mem. NASW (chmn. nominating com. 1983-84, regional rep. 1986-87, treas. 1988-91). Democrat. Home: 304 Dakota Ave Brookings SD 57006-2341

BRANDT, MITZI MARIANNE, retired educational specialist; b. St. Louis, Dec. 21, 1932; d. Vernon Osborn and Kathleen Louisa (Everett) Young; m. William Eugene Brandt Jr., Dec. 16, 1951; children: William Eugene III, Shelley, Susan, Shauna. BS, Wright State U., 1975, M in Reading, 1976; alphabetic phonics therapy cert., Neuhaus Edn. Ctr., Houston, 1993. Tchr. 2d grade Fairborn (Ohio) City Schs., 1975-82; tchr. 3d grade Clear Creek Ind. Sch. Dist., Clear Lake, Tex., 1982-89, editl. specialist, 1989-93; ret., 1994; pvt. tutor dyslexic students. Mem. advanced dyslexia therapist tng. Neuhaus Edn. Ctr., Houston, 1991; tutor dyslexic children grades 3-9. Rep. Leukemia Soc. of Am., Houston, 1985-90. Mem. Tex. Tchrs. Assn. (chairperson Houston chpt. 1984-87), Clear Creek Educators Assn. (rep. 1983-86), Orton Dyslexic Soc. Avocations: reading, bicycling, crocheting, gardening, research. E-mail: Brandtdyslexia@aol.com.

BRANDT, RICHARD PAUL, communications and entertainment company executive; b. N.Y.C., Dec. 6, 1927; s. Harry and Helen (Satenstein) Brandt; m. Helen H. Kogel, May 31, 1975; children: Claudia, David, Matthew, Thomas 1 stepchild, Jennifer. BS with high honors, Yale U., 1948; PhD, of Comm. Arts (hon.), Am. Film Inst., 2002. With Trans-Lux Theatres Corp., 1950-54, v.p., 1952-54; with Trans-Lux Corp., Norwalk, Conn., 1950—2003, v.p., 1959-62, pres., 1962-80, chmn. bd., 1974—, CEO, 1974-92; dir. Am. Book-Stratford Press, Inc., 1962-87, Brandt Theatres, Presdl. Realty Corp.; founding gov. Ind. Film Importers & Distbrs. Am., 1959-63, bd. dirs., 1959-69; v.p., mem. exec. com. Theatre Owners Am., 1962-65; mem. bill of rights com. Council Motion Picture Orgns., 1963-65; bd. dirs. Film Soc. Lincoln Ctr., 1968-71; mem. N.Y. State Bus. Adv. Com. on Mgmt. Improvement, 1966-70. Bd. dirs. Trans-Lux Corp.; chmn. bd. Univ. Settlement Soc., 1964-66, hon. pres., bd. dirs., 1966-77; dir. Am. Theatre Wing, 1970-99, United Neighborhood Houses, 1968-73; bd. dirs., treas. Settlement House Employment Devel., 1969-72; trustee, mem. exec. com. Am. Film Inst., 1971—, vice chmn., 1980-83, chmn. bd., 1983-86, chmn. emeritus 1986—; trustee Mus. Holography, 1979-82; mem. Tony awards mgmt. com., 1986-98; founder Live Poets Soc., 1991—. Vice chmn. bd. Coll. of Santa Fe, 1987-98; trustee Maritime Ctr., Norwalk, 1991-92; treas. bd., exec. com. Coll. of Santa Fe, 1999—; bd. dirs. Taos Talking Pictures Festival, 1998-2003. Named Exhibitor of Yr., ShoWest, 1984. Mem. Nat. Assn. Theatre Owners (dir. 1957-78, exec. com. 1965-78, Sherrill Corwin award 1983), Phi Beta Kappa, Sigma Xi. Office: Trans-Lux Corp 433 Paseo De Peralta Santa Fe NM 87501-1941

BRANDT, ROBERT BARRY, lay worker; b. Lebanon, Pa., Nov. 13, 1948; s. Marlin Jay Brandt and Arlene Hilda (Bowman) Gable; m. Ruth Ann Peterson, June 6, 1970; 1 child, Matthew Scot. BA in Sociology, Lebanon Valley Coll., 1971; postgrad., United Theol. Sem., Dayton, Ohio, 1973. Lic. to ministry Meth. Ch., 1968. Min. Ea. Pa. United Meth. Ch., Harrisburg, Pa., 1968-72, deacon Valley Forge, Pa., 1972-76; local ch. lay leader Ridgewood (N.J.) United Meth. Ch., 1985—87, 2001—; dist. lay leader no. dist. North N.J. Conf. United Meth., Paramus, N.J., 1986-89, lay leader ann. conf. Madison, N.J., 1989-96. Chair No. N.J. Bd. of Laity, Madison, 1989-96; chair coun. on ministries Ridgewood United Meth. Ch., 1988-89; mem. bishop's task force No. N.J. United Meth., Madison, 1989, 96-99; mem. Walk to Emmaus Community, 1987—, Disciplined Order of Christ, Nashville, 1988—; v.p. tech. and corp. svcs. Matrix Info. Consulting, Inc., Rochelle Park, N.J., 1987—; mem. gen. coun. on Ministries United Meth. Ch., 1992-96; lay dir. Skylands Walk to Emmaus Cmty., 1996-97. Mem., sec. gen. com. on gen. conf. United Meth. Ch., 1992-2000, del. gen. conf., 1992, 96, 2000; mem. Episcopacy com., N.E. jurisdiction United Meth. Ch., 1991-99, Greater N.J. Conf. United Meth., 1986—; N.E. regional rep. for Internat. Walk to Emmaus, 1998—, internat. steering com., 1998—. Named Layperson of Yr. Northern N.J. Conf., United Meth. Ch., 1993, Man of Yr. Ridgewood United Meth. Ch., 1996. Mem. Nat. Assn. Ann. Conf. Lay Leader. Democrat. Home: 28 Hoitsma Ct Fair Lawn NJ 07410-2760 Office: Matrix Info Cons Inc 365 W Passaic St Rochelle Park NJ 07662-3017 E-mail: brandty@aol.com., bbrandt@matrixcc.com. *We are each called to a life of service to others. It is in the loosing of ourselves to others that we ultimately find who and what we were meant to be when God placed us on this earth.*

BRANDT, ROBERT FREDERIC, III, retired newspaper editor, journalist; b. Louisville, Sept. 17, 1946; s. Robert Frederic Jr. and Dorothea (Burton) B.; m. Annette Floyd, Aug., 1968 (div.); m. Walda Ruth DuPriest, Sept., 1980. Student, Ea. Ky. U., 1964-66; BA, U. Ky., 1968. Copy editor The Hartford (Conn.) Courant, 1968-69, The Tampa (Fla.) Tribune, 1971-72; news editor The Miami (Fla.) Herald, 1972-78; asst. mng. editor The Washington Star, 1978-81, Newsday, L.I., N.Y., 1981-87, v.p., mng. editor, 1987—2001; ret., 2001. Bd. dirs. Guide Dog Found. for Blind, Inc., Smithtown, N.Y. Mem. AP Mng. Editors Assn., Am. Soc. Newspaper Editors. Presbyterian.

BRANDT, RONALD STIRLING, retired editor, researcher; b. Neligh, Nebr., Aug. 14, 1932; s. Ferdinand B. and Ruth G. (Thornton) B.; m. Dorothy May Rice, May 13, 1951; children: Rhonda, Rebecca, Bonita. BS, U. Nebr., 1955; MA, Northwestern U., Evanston, Ill., 1960; EdD, U. Minn., 1970. Tchr. Racine (Wis.) Pub. Schs., 1957-62, prin., 1962-64; tchr., cons. No. Nigeria Tchr. Edn. Project, Maiduguri, 1965-66; program coord. Upper Midwest Regional Edn. Lab., Mpls., 1966-68; dir. staff devel. Mpls. Pub. Schs., 1968-70; assoc. supt. Lincoln (Nebr.) Pub. Schs., 1970-78; exec. editor Ednl. Leadership, Alexandria, Va., 1978-96; asst. exec. dir. ASCD, Alexandria, 1995-97; adj. faculty George Mason U., Fairfax, Va., 2003—. Co-author: Dimensions of Thinking, 1986, Dimensions of Learning, 1992, the Language of Learning, 1997; editor: Content of the Curriculum, 1988, Assessing Student Learning, 1998, Education in a New Era, 2000; author: Powerful Learning, 1998. 1st lt. U.S. Army, 1955-57. Inductee EdPress (Ednl. Press Assn.) Hall of Fame, Apr. 1996.

BRANDT, WILLIAM ARTHUR, JR., consulting executive; b. Chgo., Sept. 5, 1949; s. William Arthur and Joan Virginia (Ashworth) B.; m. Patrice Bugelas, Jan. 19, 1980; children: Katherine Ashworth, William George, Joan Patrice, John Peter. BA with honors, St. Louis U., 1971; MA, U. Chgo., 1972, postgrad., 1972-74. Asst. to pres. Pyro Mining Co., Chgo., 1972-74; commentator Sta. WBBM-AM, Chgo., 1977; with Melaniphy & Assocs., Inc., Chgo., 1975-76; pres., cons. Devel. Specialists, Inc., Chgo., 1976—. Mem. adv. bd. Sociol. Abstracts, Inc., San Diego, 1979-83. Contbr. articles to profl. jours. Trustee Fenwick H.S., 1991-2000, Comml. Law League of Am., Internat. Coun. Shopping Ctrs., Nat. Assn. Bankruptcy Trustees, Ill. Sociol. Assn., Midwest Sociol. Soc., Urban Land Inst.; mem. Fla. del. to Dem. Nat. Conv., 1996, also mem. Dem. Party Platform Com., 2000. LaVerne Noyes scholar, 1971-74. Mem. Am. Bankruptcy Inst., Am. Sociol. Assn., Amelia Island Plantation Club, Union League Club Chgo., City Club of Miami, gov. mem. Chicago Symphony, Clinton/Gore '96 Natl. Finance Bd., mnging. trustee Democratic Natl. Comm., maj. trust mem. Democratic Senatorial Campaign Comm., life mem. Zoological Soc. of the Miami Metro Zoo. Democrat. Roman Catholic. Home: 2000 S Bayshore Dr Apt 39 Coconut Grove FL 33133-3251 Office: 3 First Nat Plz Ste 2300 Chicago IL 60602 also: Wells Fargo Ctr 333 S Grand Ave Ste 2010 Los Angeles CA 90071-1524

BRANDWEIN, RUTH ANN, social welfare educator, administrator, author; b. Bklyn., Apr. 24, 1940; d. Charles and Kate (Berkowitz) Solin; divorced; children: Lorena Lisa Epstein, Garth Whitman. BA magna cum laude, Bklyn. Coll., 1960; MSW, U. Wash., 1970; PhD, Brandeis U., 1978. Libr. trainee Bklyn. Pub. Libr., 1960-61; substitute tchr. N.Y.C. Bd. Edn., 1961-63; recreation dir. Seattle Park Dept., 1964-66; exec. dir. Cen. Seattle Commn. Coun., 1967-69; rsch. assoc. Harvard U./Lab. Comm. Psychiatry, Boston, 1971-72; asst. prof., chair, comm. org. Boston U. Sch. Social Work, 1973-78; dir., assoc. prof. U. Iowa Sch. Social Work, Iowa City, 1978-81; dean Sch. Social Welfare SUNY, Stony Brook, 1981-89, prof. Sch. Social Welfare, 1981—, dir. Social Justice Ctr., 2001—; commr. Suffolk County Dept. Social Svcs., Hauppauge, NY, 1989-93; holder Spafford Endowed chair U. Utah Sch. Social Work, 1994-96. Vis. prof. U. Wash. Sch. Social Work, 2000-01; co-founder Women's Rsch. Ctr. of Boston, 1971-78; co-dir. Women's Com. of 100, 1995—; cons. U.S. Senate Subcom. on Vets.' Affairs, 1971; guardian ad litem Family Ct., Middlesex County, Mass.; expert witness Grevatt vs. U. Minn., Duluth; vis. assoc. Inst. Policy Studies, 1986-87; lead reviewer Nat. Inst. Justice, 1997-98; spkr. nat. and internat. confs. Author: Battered Women, Children and Welfare Reform: The Ties That Bind, 1999; founding editor Affilia: Jour. of Women and Social Work; contbr. articles to profl. jours. and chpts. to books; mem. editl. bds. Mem. Nat. Adv. Coun. Violence Against Women, 1997—2000; mem. steering com. L.I. Fund for Women and Girls, 1993—2000; mem. N.Y. Gov.'s Mental Health Coun., 1990—2002, chair, 1992—95, Suffolk County Exec. Task Force on Family Violence, 1988—94; bd. dirs., v.p. Kehillath Shalom Synagogue, Cold Spring Harbor, NY, 1987—90, bd. dirs., v.p., chair social action com., 2001—03; bd. dirs. United Way of L.I., Melville, NY, 1982—88, Suffolk Cmty. Coun., Islandia, NY, 1981—97; bd. dirs., mem. exec. com. Am. Jewish Congress, L.I., 1989; bd. dirs. N.Y. Civil Liberties Union, 1994—98; adv. bd. L.I. Progressive Coalition, 1998—; bd. dirs. L.I. Cmty. Found., 1994—96, Hudson-Peconic Planned Parenthood, 1997—, Health and Welfare Coun. L.I., 1996—2001. Recipient Disting. Alumnus award U. Wash. Sch. Social Work, Seattle, 1989, Congrl. award Congressman Mrazek, Suffolk County, N.Y., Hon. Supporter award Women on the Job; Vol. Svc. award, Suffolk County Human Rights Commn., 2003. Mem.: NASW (bd. dirs. 1991—96, 2d v.p. 1994—96, pres.-elect NY state chpt. 1997—98, pres. 1998—2000, nat. com. on women's issues 2000—, Suffolk County Social Worker of Yr. 1989, Lifetime Achievement award 2003), Huntington NY NOW (bd. dirs. 1982—91, chair 1988—91), Coun. Social Work Edn. (chair women's commn. 1980—83, chair internat. commn. 1988—89, bd. dirs. 1987—89), NY Pub. Welfare Assn. (bd. dirs. 1990—93), Phi Beta Kappa. Office: SUNY Stony Brook Sch Social Welfare Health Sci Ctr Level 2 Rm 093 Stony Brook NY 11794-0001

BRANEGAN, JAMES AUGUSTUS, III, journalist; b. Phila., June 6, 1950; s. James Augustus, Jr. and Emmeline Elizabeth (McBurney) B.; m. Stefania Pittaluga, Feb. 4, 1992. BA, Cornell U., 1972; MS in Journalism, Northwestern U., 1973. Reporter Chgo. Today, 1973-74, Chgo. Tribune, 1974-81; with Time Mag., 1981—2001, chief econs. corr. Washington bur., 1986-87, corr., 1987-93, European econ. corr. Brussels, 1993-97, state dept. corr. Washington, 2001, White House corr., 1997-2001; adj. prof. Georgetown U, 2002—03, Northwestern U., 2002—03; profl. staff mem US Senate Com. on Fgn. Rels., Washington, 2003—. Co-recipient Pulitzer prize for spl. local reporting, 1976 Office: c/o Senate Fgn Rels 450 Dirkson Senate Office Bldg Washington DC 20510

BRANHAM, C. MICHAEL, lawyer; b. Columbia, S.C., Nov. 6, 1957; s. Mack C. and Jennie Louise (Jones) B.; m. Teresa Barrett; children: Anthony, Mark. BS, Auburn U., Montgomery, Ala., 1979; JD, U. S.C., 1983. Bar: S.C.; cert. tax law specialist; CPA. Acct. Wilson, Price, Barranco & Billingsley, CPAs, Montgomery, 1979-80; law clk. Atty. Gen.'s Office, State of S.C., Columbia, 1981-82; acct. Price, Waterhouse, Columbia, 1983-86; tax lawyer Young, Clement, Rivers & Tisdale, LLP, Charleston, SC, 1986—, chmn. tax, estate planning and probate group, 1999—, firm mgmt. com., 1999—, asst. mng. ptnr., 1999—2001, mng. ptnr., 2002—. Chmn. taxation law specialization adv. bd. S.C. Supreme Ct., 1995-97; pres. Charleston Tax. Coun., 1993-94; dean's adv. bd. Med. U. S.C. Nursing Sch., Charleston, 1994-97; chmn. MUSC Planned Giving adv. coun., 1993-97; S.C. case reporter ABA sect. real property, probate

and trust law, 1997-2002; mem. Bishop Gadsden Estate Planning Adv. Coun., Charleston, 1998—. Coach Hungryneck Internat. Soccer Assn., Mt. Pleasant, S.C., 1989-99, James Island/Trident United Soccer Assn., Charleston, 1999-2000; sec., bd. dirs. S.C. Youth Soccer Assn., 2000-02; active Charleston Estate Planning Coun. Mem. ABA, AICPA, S.C. Assn. CPAs, S.C. Bar Assn., Charleston Breakfast Rotary. Avocations: soccer coaching, weight lifting. Home: 829 Detyens Rd Mount Pleasant SC 29464-5181 Office: Young Clement Rivers & Tisdale LLP 28 Broad St Charleston SC 29401-3070

BRANHAM, GRADY EUGENE, principal; b. Birmingham, Ala., June 19, 1947; s. Grady B. and Pauline (Kelley) B.; m. Joy Canavan, Mar. 26, 1983; children: Joy Elizabeth, Gralynn. BS, Birmingham (Ala.) So. Coll., 1969; MEd, Montevallo (Ala.) U., 1976; PhD, U.N.A., St. Louis, 1988. Prin. Dallas Christian Sch., Selma, Ala., 1970-84, Briarwood Christian High Sch., Birmingham, Ala., 1984—. V.p. Community Concert Assn., Selma, 1980-84. Named Patriot of Yr., Patriotic Am. Youth, Jackson, Miss., 1982, Outstanding Alumnae of Yr., Jefferson State C.C., 1999. Mem. Am. Soc. Interior Design. Avocations: travel, design, music. Office: Briarwood Christian High 6255 Cahaba Valley Rd Birmingham AL 35242-4915 E-mail: gbranham@briarwood.org.

BRANHAM, GREGORY HARRIS, facial plastic surgeon; b. Columbia, S.C., Mar. 28, 1957; s. Clarence Stevenson and Theodocia (Hearon) B.; m. Cynthia Lynn Nowell, June 7, 1986; children: Allison, Matthew, Grace. BS in Biology, U. S.C., 1979, MD in Medicine, 1983. Instr. Washington U., St. Louis, 1989-90; asst. prof. St. Louis U., 1990-96, assoc. prof., 1996—, assoc. dean, 1995—. Exec. com. mem. St. Louis U. Governing Coun., 1995—. Fellow Am. Coll. Surgeons, Am. Acad. Facial Plastic & Reconstructive Surgery (bd. examiner 1994—), Am. Acad. Otolaryngology. Office: St Louis U Sch Medicine 1402 S Grand Blvd Saint Louis MO 63104-1004

BRANHAM, MACK CARISON, JR., retired theological seminary educator, minister; b. Columbia, S.C., Apr. 20, 1931; s. Mack Carison and Laura Pauline (Sexton) Branham; m. Jennie Louise Jones, Dec. 17, 1953; children: Kenneth Gary, Charles Michael, Keith Robert, Laurie Lynn. BS, Clemson U., 1953; MDiv, Luth. Theol. Sem., 1958, STM, 1963; MS, George Washington U., 1968; PhD, Ariz. State U., 1974; DD (hon.), Newberry Coll., 1990, LLD (hon.), Clemson U., 1991. Ordained to ministry Luth. Ch., 1958. Pastor Providence Nazareth Luth. Ch., Lexington, S.C., 1958-59; commd. 2d lt. USAF, 1953, advanced through grades to col., 1959, ret., 1979; adminstrv. asst., registrar Luth. Theol. So. Sem., 1979-81, v.p. adminstrn., 1981-82, pres., 1982-92, pres. emeritus, 1992—. Instr., counselor. Editor Air Force Chaplain newsletter, 1975-77. Decorated bronze star, Legion of Merit; named to Order of Palmetto (S.C.). Mem.: Greater Chapin C. of C. (bd. dirs. 1998—2000, pres. 2000), Rotary. Lutheran. Home: 2839 Old Lexington Hwy Chapin SC 29036-7913

BRANHAM, MELANIE J. lawyer; b. Kansas City, Mo., Nov. 22, 1960; d. John Francis II and Annette (Bowers) B. BA, U. Kans., 1983, MUP, 1985; JD, We. New Eng. Coll., 1994. Bar: Kans. 1994, Mo. 1995, U.S. Ct. Appeals (10th cir.) 1994, U.S. Ct. Appeals (8th cir.) 1995, U.S. Supreme Ct. 1997. Grad. planner City of Lawrence, Kans., 1984; city planner City of Overland Park, Kans., 1984-85; asst. dir. planning and inspections City of Merriam, Kans., 1985-87; city adminstr. City of Westwood, Kans., 1987-89; town adminstr. Town of Sheffield, Mass., 1989-91; law clk. We. Mass. Legal Svcs., Springfield, Mass., 1992-93; atty./law clk. Kans. Legal Svcs., Olathe, 1993-94; assoc. Johnson County Dist. Atty.'s Office, Olathe, 1994; pvt. practice Olathe, 1994-99; atty. Cohen, McNeile, Pappas & Shuttleworth, P.C., Leawood, Kans., 1999-2001, Branham Law Firm, Overland Park, Kans., 2001—. Active Nelson-Atkins Mus. Art, Kansas City, Mo., 1986—, ACLU of Kans. and Western Mo., Kansas City, Mo., 1992—; mem. adv. bd. Kans. Legal Svcs., 1999—. Lt. col. Aux. Civil Air Patrol USAF, 1972—76. Named to Outstanding Young Women of Am., 1987, Vol. of Yr., United Way, 2001; recipient Am. Jurisprudence award, 1993. Mem.: ABA, Mo. Bar Assn., Kans. Bar Assn. (Pro Bono Atty. of Yr. 2001), Johnson County Bar Assn. (v.p. 2002), Kans. Trial Lawyers Assn. Episcopalian. Office: Branham Law Firm PO Box 11567 Overland Park KS 66207 Fax: 913-652-6517.

BRANIGAN, HELEN MARIE, educational consultant, academic administrator; b. Albany, N.Y., Sept. 24, 1944; d. James J. and Helen (Weaver) B. BS in Bus. Edn., Coll. St. Rose, Albany, 1967, MA in English, 1972; postgrad., SUNY, Albany, 1973-81. Tchr., chair dept. bus. edn. S. Colonie Sch. Dist., Albany, 1968-81; assoc. Bur. Bus. Edn. N.Y. State Edn. Dept., Albany, 1981-87; assoc. Bur. Occupational Edn. Program Devel., Albany, 1987-91, Bur. Occupational Edn. Innovation and Quality, Albany, 1991-93, Cen./So. Regional Field Svcs., Albany, 1993-95, North Country/Regional Field Svcs., 1995-98, Regional Sch. Improvement Team, 1998—2003; facilitator Champlain Valley Ednl. Ctr., Plattsburg, 2003—; ednl. cons. The Inst. for Learning Centered Edn., 2003—. Bd. trustees St. Catherine's Found., 1993-97; sr. cons. Internat. Ctr. for Leadership in Edn., Schenectady, N.Y., 1991—; cons. Inst. for Learner-Centered Edn., Potsdam, N.Y., 2003—; bd. dirs. Adirondack Curriculum Project, 2003—; facilitator Champlain Valley Ednl. Ctr., 2003—. Editor: Glencoe Pub., 1986—; contbr. Lay vol. Archdiocese of Anchorage, 1967-68; mem. N.Y. State Staff Devel. Coun. Mem. ASCD, Bus. Tchrs. Assn. N.Y. State, Delta Pi Epsilon. Roman Catholic. Avocations: skiing, mountaineering, golf, reading. Home: 540 New Scotland Ave Albany NY 12208-2318 E-mail: Hbranigan@aol.com.

BRANIGAN, THOMAS PATRICK, lawyer; b. Detroit, Aug. 6, 1963; s. John Thomas and Nancy May (Palmer) B.; m. Carolyn Marie O'Shea, May 27, 1989; 2 children. BA, Wayne State U., 1985; JD cum laude, Mich. State U., 1988. Bar: Mich. 1988, U.S. Dist. Ct. (ea. dist.) Mich. 1988, U.S. Dist. Ct. (ctrl. dist.), U.S. Dist. Ct. (we. dist.) Mich. 1991, Utah 1995, U.S. Ct. Appeals (6th cir.) 1996, Ohio 1999, Ill. 2000, U.S. Dist. Ct. (no. dist.) Ill. 2000, U.S. Ct. Appeals (10th cir.) 2002; pro hac vice bar admissions as trial counsel in 18 states. Assoc. Plunkett & Cooney, Detroit, 1988-91, Bowman & Brooke, Detroit, 1991-94, ptnr., 1995—, mng. ptnr., 2003—; mediator Oakland County Cir. Ct., Pontiac, Mich. Speaker Def. Rsch. Inst. Young Lawyer's Trial Techniques Seminar, 1992, 93. Editor-in-chief Law Rev., 1987-88. Recipient Trial Advocacy award Am. Jurisprudence, 1987, Louis J. Colombo award Detroit Coll. of Law, 1988, Finch Evidence award 1987, Edward Rakow award Detroit Fed. Bar Assn., 1988; named one of the 40 Most Successful Trial Lawyers in Am. Under Age 40, Nat. Law Jour. Mem. ABA (Automotive Products Subcom.; spkr. litigation ann. meeting 2001), Def. Rsch. Inst., Detroit Bar Assn., Soc. Automotive Engrs. Roman Catholic. Avocations: family, golf, sailing. Office: Bowman & Brooke Ste 600 50 W Big Beaver Troy MI 48084-5293 E-mail: TBraniga@Bowman-Brooke.com.

BRANIN, JOAN JULIA, health services management educator; b. Newark, July 20, 1944; d. Alvin Edwin and Julia (White) B. BA, Newark State Coll., 1966; MA, Calif. State U., 1970; MBA, UCLA, 1979. CFP. Tchr. Los Alamitos (Calif.) Sch. Dist., 1966-70; sales mgr. Calif. Copy Products, 1970-73; pharm. sales rep. Lederle Labs., L.A., 1973-75; med. mktg. analyst Am. Hosp. Supply, Glendale, Calif., 1975-78; corp. loan officer Security Pacific, L.A., 1978-80; v.p. First Interstate Bank, 1980-84; v.p., mgr. Std. Chartered Bank, Chgo., 1984—88; v.p. mgr. Union Bank Pvt. Banking Group, L.A., 1988—89; mgr. Chase Manhattan Pvt. Investment Bank, L.A., 1989—91; fin. planner retirement and estate planning Mass. Mut. Ins. Co., 1991-93; asst. prof. U. La Verne, Calif., 1993—, chmn. grad. programs in gerontology, 1997, chmn. health svcs. mgmt. program, 1999—; dept. chair Dept. Health Svc. Mgmt., 1999—. Contbr. articles to profl. jours. Bd. dirs. Area Dance Alliance, Calif. Conf. Arts, Young Musicians Found., UCLA Internat. Student Ctr., 1983-93, Leadership Coun. United Way Med. div., 1989-93. Am. Diabetes Assn., 1989-93, Am. Heart Assn., 1990-93, Music Ctr. Unified Fund Cabinet and Spl. Gifts Com., CSULP Pres. Assocs. exec. bd., 1991-93, Chgo. chpt. Girl Scouts U.S.A., 1987-88, OxBox Summer Sch. Arts Inst., 1987-88. Recipient Disting. Alumni award Calif. State U. Long Beach, 1990, Women of Achievement award YWCA, 1999. Mem. APA, Am. Coll. Healthcare Execs., Am. Evaluation. Assn., Women Health Adminstrn., Healthcare Fin. Mgmt. Assn. (local chpt.), Soc. Behavioral Medicine, Assn. Health Svcs. Rsch., Acad. Health, Women Scholars, Internat. Assn. for Fin. Planning, Gerontol. Soc. Am., Am. Soc. Aging, Phi Kappa Phi, Pi Lambda Theta, Phi Delta Gamma, Kappa Delta Pi. Democrat. Home: 2043 Allen Ave Altadena CA 91001-3423

BRANMAN, M. JEFFREY, investment fund company executive; b. N.Y.C. m. Elizabeth D. Branman, 1995; children: Alexandra, Matthew. AB, U. Calif., Berkeley, 1976; MBA, Carnegie-Mellon U., 1980. Mgr. Boston Consulting Group, Chgo., 1980-84; v.p. May Dept. Stores Co., Inc., St. Louis, 1984-85, CS 1st Boston, Inc., N.Y.C., 1985-89; mng. dir., ptnr. Financo, Inc., N.Y.C., 1989-96; sr. v.p. corp. devel. Venator Group, Inc., N.Y.C., 1996-2000; CEO Footlocker.com, Inc., N.Y.C., 1999-2000; pres. Interactive Tech. Ptnrs., West Chester, Pa., 2000—. Bd. dirs. GSI Commerce, Inc., Commerce Hub, Inc., Albany, NY. Office: Interactive Tech Ptnrs 1200 Wilson Dr West Chester PA 19380-4262

BRANN, DONALD LEWIS, JR., school superintendent; b. L.A., Nov. 1, 1945; s. Donald Lewis and Shirley June (Scott) B.; m. m. Sari Ellen Donohoe, June 17, 1967; children: Shanonn, Rebecca. AA in Bus. Adminstrn., El Camino Coll., 1966; BS, U. So. Calif., L.A., 1968, EdD in Ednl. Adminstrn., 1982; MA in Elem. Edn., Calif. State U., L.A., 1972. Cert. tchr., sch. adminstr., Calif. Tchr. El Segundo (Calif.) Unified Sch. Dist., 1970-72, reading specialist, 1972-76, program coord., 1976-79; prin. Wilsona Sch. Dist., Lancaster, Calif., 1979-81, supt., 1981-84, Old Adobe Union Sch. Dist., Petaluma, Calif., 1984-91, Mother Lode Union Sch. Dist., Placerville, Calif., 1992-93, Wiseburn Sch. Dist., Hawthorne, Calif., 1993—. Bd. dirs. Schs. Committed To Reducing Utility Bills, Sacramento, 1983—; mem. State Supts. Small Sch. Adv. Com.; coord. El Segundo Jr. Olympics, 1972; bd. dirs. Antelope Valley Fedn. Tchrs. Credit Union, Lancaster, 1983; v.p., bd. dirs. Friends of Antelope Valley Indian Mus., Lancaster, 1982. Named One of Top 100 Sch. Execs. in N.Am., Exec. Educator, 1985. Mem. Am. Assn. Sch. Adminstrs., Sonoma County Supts. Gang of 13, Assn. Calif. Sch. Adminstrs., Small Sch. Dist. Assn. (founder, pres., treas. 1983—), Alpha Kappa Psi. Home: 640 California St El Segundo CA 90245-3216 Office: Wiseburn Sch Dist 13530 Aviation Blvd Hawthorne CA 90250-6498 E-mail: dbrann@wiseburn.k12.ca.us.

BRANN, EVA TONI HELENE, educator; b. Berlin, Jan. 21, 1929; came to U.S., 1942; d. Edgar and Paula (Sklarz) B. BA, Bklyn. Coll., 1950; MA, Yale U., 1951, PhD, 1956; HHD (hon.), Whitman Coll., 1995, Middlebury Coll., 1999. Instr. archaeology Stanford (Calif.) U., 1956-57; tutor St. John's Coll., Annapolis, Md., 1957—, dean, 1990-97; mem. Inst. for Advanced Study, 1958. Mem. U.S Adv. Commn. for Internat. Edn., 1973-77, vis. prof. Whitman Coll., Walla Walla, Wash., 1978-79; honors prof. U. Del., Newark, 1984-86. Author: Protoattic Pottery from the Athenian Agora, 1962, Paradoxes of Education in a Republic, 1979, The World of the Imagination, 1991, What, Then, Is Time, 1999; translator: Greek Mathematics and the Origin of Algebra, 1968; co-translator: Plato's Sophist, 1996, Plato's Phaedo, 1998. Mem. state adv. com. U.S. Commn. on Civil Rights, Md., 1988-96. Woodrow Wilson Ctr. fellow, 1976; NEH grantee, 1987. Mem. Phi Beta Kappa. Democrat. Jewish. Office: St John's Coll PO Box 2800 Annapolis MD 21404-2800

BRANN, RICHARD ROLAND, lawyer; b. Olney, Ill., June 9, 1943; s. Roland John and Margaret (McVay) B.; m. Penny Sue Farrington, June 5, 1965; children: Wesley R., Patrick T. BA, Miss. State U., 1965; JD, U. Tex., 1968. Bar: Tex. 1968, U.S. Dist. Ct. (so., no., ea. and we. dists.) Tex. 1970, U.S. Ct. Appeals (5th and 11th cirs.) 1973, U.S. Supreme Ct. 1973; bd. cert. in labor and employment law Tex. Bd. Legal Specialization. Assoc. Baker & Botts, Houston, 1968-76, ptnr., 1976—. Chmn. fed. judiciary rels. com. State Bar Tex., 1996-98; chmn. Houston Mgmt. Lawyers Forum, Houston, 1981. Editor: Tex. Assn. of Bus. and C. of C. Labor Law Quar. Rev., Tex. Labor Letter; chmn. bd. editors Tex. Bd. Legal Specialization, 2000-2003. With USMC, 1961-66. Fellow Coll. Labor and Employment Lawyers; mem. ABA, Tex. Bar Assn., Tex. Bar Coll., Houston Bar Assn. (chmn. labor and employment law sect. 1997-98), Def. Rsch. Inst., Am. Employment Law Coun., Houston Club, Plaza Club, Order of Coif, Phi Kappa Phi. Republican. Methodist. Avocations: fitness activities, reading. Home: 13 Stonegate Dr Houston TX 77024-2703 E-mail: richard.brann@bakerbotts.com.

BRANNAN, CLEO ESTELLA, retired elementary education educator; b. Turon, Kans., Feb. 22, 1924; d. Jesse Logan and Nancy Elma (Cox) Zink; m. Raymond Eugene Brannan, Aug. 4, 1946 (deceased); children: Raymond Eugene Jr., Nancy Estelle, Tricia Elaine. BS, Ft. Hays State U., 1964. Cert. elem. edn. educator, Kans. Elem. tchr. Pretty Prairie (Kans.) Schs., 1943-45, Meade (Kans.) Elem. Sch., 1945-48, 58-60, 61-87, substitute secondary sch. tchr., 1987; ret., 1987. Contbr. articles to Meadowlark mag. Trustee Meade Pub. Libr., 1961-65, 90-98, rustee, treas., 1990—; state bd. dirs. Friends of Kans. Librs., 1990-96; Silver Haired legislator, 1999—. Named Kans. State Libr. Friend of the Yr., 2002. Mem. AAUW (local pres. 1985-86), Kans. Ret. Tchr. Assn. (bd. dirs. 1991-99, state pres. 1996-97), Delta Kappa Gamma. Avocations: collecting china, traveling, reading, arranging flowers. Home: PO Box 13 Meade KS 67864-0013

BRANNAN, EULIE ROSS, educational consultant; b. Norwood, Ohio, Sept. 6, 1928; s. Olin Hiram and Bernice Cleo (Beall) Brannan; m. Ruby Merle Moore, Dec. 16, 1945 (dec.); children: Stephen Earl, Deborah Brannan Watkins, Rebecca Brannan Hagan, Julie Ross Brannan-Williams; m. Willie Metta Strong, Mar. 7, 1981. AA, Ala. Christian Coll., 1947; BA, Huntingdon Coll., 1949; MS, Auburn U., 1953, EdD, 1960; postgrad., Harding Grad. Sch., 1960-63, Oxford (Eng.) U., 1981. HS tchr., Montgomery, Ala., 1949-51; guidance counselor Montgomery Bible HS, 1951-53; prin. Ala. Christian HS, Montgomery, 1953-55; prof. Ala. Christian Coll., Montgomery, 1953-55, asst. to pres., 1955 56, acad. dean, 1956-69, acad. v.p., 1969-73, pres., 1973-81; field dir. Nat. Edn. Program, Huntsville, Ala., 1981-82; pres. Jefferson Christian Acad., Birmingham, Ala., 1982-90; assoc. J. Robert Clark & Assocs., 1990-91; spl. counsel to pres. Faulkner U., Montgomery, 1991—. Chaplain Madison Police Dept., 1996—. Mem.: Phi Delta Kappa. Home: 103 Manningham Dr Madison AL 35758-7419 Office: Faulkner Univ 5345 Atlanta Hwy Montgomery AL 36109-3390 E-mail: eulieb@aol.com.

BRANNAN, STEPHEN E. health services administrator; b. Montgomery, Ala., Mar. 12, 1947; s. E. R. and Merle Moore Brannan; m. Brenda Brannan, Oct. 22, 1972; children: Brittney, Leigh. BA, David Lipscomb Coll., 1968; MA, Ea. Mich. U., 1981. Spl. agt. FBI, 1972-98; corp. compliance officer U. Ala. Health Svcs. Found., Birmingham, 1998—. Lt. USN, 1968-72. Mem. Kiwanis. Mem. Ch. of Christ. Office: U Ala Health Svcs Found 500 22d St S Ste 504 Birmingham AL 35233 E-mail: sbrannan@uabmc.edu.

BRANNEN, JEFFREY RICHARD, lawyer; b. Tampa, Fla., Aug. 27, 1945; s. Jackson Edward and Tobiah M. (Lovitz) B.; m. Mary Elizabeth Strand, Nov. 24, 1972; 1 child, Samuel Jackson. BA in English, U. N.Mex., 1967, JD, 1970. Bar: N.Mex. 1970, U.S. Dist. Ct. N.Mex. 1970, U.S. Ct. Appeals (10th cir.) 1976, U.S. Supreme Ct. 1978. Law clk. N.Mex. State Supreme Ct., Santa Fe, 1970-71; from assoc. to pres., shareholder Montgomery & Andrews, pa, Santa Fe, 1972-93; pres. Jeffrey R. Brannen, P.A., Santa Fe, 1993—; of counsel Comeau, Maldegan, Templeman & Indall (formerly known as Carpenter, Maldegan, Templeman & Indall), Santa Fe, 1995—. Faculty Nat. Inst. Trial Advocacy, Hastings Ctr. for Trial & Appellate Advocacy, 1980-93; co-chmn. Pers. Injury Inst., Hastings, 1992. Mem. ABA, Am. Bd. Trial Advocates (N.Mex. pres. 1998), Assn. Def. Trial Attys. (state chmn. 1992—), Def. Rsch. Inst. (Exceptional Performance Citation 1989), N.Mex. Def. Lawyers Assn. (pres. 1989). Democrat. Avocations: skiing, soccer, fly fishing, travel. Office: Comeau Maldegan Templeman & Indall 141 E Palace Ave Santa Fe NM 87501-2041 Fax: (505) 982-4611. E-mail: jbrannen@cmtisantafe.

BRANNICK, ELLEN MARIE, retired management consultant; b. Rochester, Minn., Aug. 10, 1934; d. Daniel Ryther and Grace Ellen (Mills) Markham; m. Thomas L. Brannick BS in Health, Phys. Edn., MacMurray Coll., 1956, MS, 1959. Elem. phys. edn. Ritenour Consol. Sch. Dist., Overland, Mo., 1958-61; head tchr., summer dir. Civic League Day Nursery, Rochester, 1961-64; recreation therapist Rochester State Hosp., 1964-68; rehab. dir. Rochester State Hosp., 1968-70; rehab. therapist Napa State Hosp., Calif., 1971, indsl. therapy con., 1971-73, community liaison rep., 1973-00; ret., 2001. Mem. Friends Napa County Library, 1977. Mem. Napa County Hist. Soc., Rogue Valley Geneal. Soc. Democrat. Avocations: antique post cards, philately, bibliophily, military history, traveling.

BRANNMAN, WARD SCOTT, elementary school educator; BA, U. of Wash., 1980—85, BM, ME, 1985. Cert. tchr. State of Wash. Bd. Edn., 1985. Tchr. Lake Wash. Sch. Dist., Kirkland, 1986—.

BRANNON, GUY EMILIO, physician; b. Bossier City, La., June 19, 1968; s. Guy Winford and Ruby Rangel Brannon; m. Shelley Marie Lawson, Apr. 20, 1996; 1 child, Grayson Alarich. BS, La. State U., Shreveport, 1991; MD, La. State U., Health Sci. Ctr., Shreveport, 1995. Diplomate La. State Bd. Med. Examiners, 1996. Intern La. State U. Med. Ctr., Shreveport, 1995—96, resident, 1996—99, chief resident, 1998—99; dir. adult psychiatric unit Brentwood-A Behavioral Health Co., Shreveport, 1999—. Asst. clin. prof. psychiatry La. State U. Health Scis. Ctr., Shreveport, 1999—; adj. prof. psychology La. State U., Shreveport, 2002—. Contbr. chapters to books, articles to profl. jours. Mem.: AMA, Am. Soc. Clin. Pharmacology, La. Group Psychotherapy Soc., Am. Group Psychotherapy Assn., Am. Soc. Addiction Medicine, Am. Med. Polit. Action Com., La. Psychiat. Med. Assn. (N.W. La. chpt. v.p. 2000—01, N.W. La. chpt. pres. 2002—03, Dr. John M Bick award 1995), Am. Psychiat. Assn., So. Med. Assn., Am. Psychotherapy Assn., Am. Acad. Pain Mgmt., Mental Health Assn. Caddo - Bossier (bd. mem. 2000—02). Achievements include research in clinical drug trials. Office: Brentwood - A Behavioral Health Company 1002 Highland Ave Shreveport LA 71101 Office Fax: 318-222-6227. E-mail: brentwoodoffice@aol.com.

BRANNON, PAT, poet; b. Morrilton, Ark., Nov. 6, 1953; d. Ben O. and Mary Ellen Baker; m. Howard Lynn Brannon, July 13, 1956; children: Jason Matthew, Shawn Christopher. Substitute sch. tchr. Amory Sch. Sys., Miss., 1988—99. Author: Walk Softly (You're Steppin' On My Heart), (poetry) Forgiven, 2001 (3rd Pl. Poetry Challenge winner Poetry of Today Pub., 2001), A Heart's Tug Away, 2001 (Adult World Reader's Choice award Poetic Lic. Mag., 2001), A Sacrificial Christmas, 2001 (Hon. Mention for Editor's Choice award Weems Concepts, 2001), Santa In His Place, 2001 (Hon. Mention for Editor's Choice award Weems Concepts, 2001). Vol. Stars Over Miss., Amory, 1994—2002; singer, musician, and revival choir mem. Beverly Health Care Nursing Home, Amory, 1986—2001; vol. Meals on Wheels, 1984—94; ch. clerical worker Food Pantry, Amory, 1996—98; vol. standardized testing Amory Sch. Sys.; band booster vol. & bus chaperone Amory H.S. Band; R.R. festival cmty.-wide ann. ch. svc. choir mem. City of Amory; pre-school dir. Meadowood Bapt. Ch., Amory, adult youth coun. rep., 1991—2001, mission action chairperson Women's Missionary Union, mem. adult choir, 1987, mission friends tchr., youth Sunday sch. tchr., mem. adult fellowship com., 2001, publicity chairperson for Challenge to Build fin. bldg. campaign, publicity chairperson for the Faithful to the Future fin. bldg. campaign, dir. women on mission fundraising projects, numerous positions, 2001—02. Baptist. Avocations: reading, writing, music. Home: 212 Oakdale Dr Amory MS 38821 Personal E-mail: wonderview31@lycos.com.

BRANNON, RONALD ROY, retired minister; b. Aberdeen, S.D., Apr. 16, 1928; s. Walter Carlos and Mary Erma (Snyder) B.; m. Rosalee Vernela Carry, July 20, 1949; children: Rhonda Lee Storer, Rodney Vaughn, Randall Roy. BA, Okla. Wesleyan U., 1950; DD, Southern Wesleyan U., 1987. Ordained to ministry Wesleyan Ch., 1951. Pastor Heber Wesleyan Ch., Miltonvale, Kans., 1949-52, First Wesleyan Ch., Wichita, Kans., 1952-68; dist. supt. Kans. Dist. of the Wesleyan Ch., Miltonvale, 1968-83; gen. sec. Internat. Ctr.-The Wesleyan Ch. Hdqtrs., Indpls., 1982-2000; ret., 2000. Co-founder, coord. police chaplaincy, Wichita. Trustee/sec. bd. dirs. Miltonvale Wesleyan Coll., 1967-72, Okla. Wesleyan U., 1968-84, So. Wesleyan U., 1984-92; mem., sec. Hephzibah Children's Home, 1983-92, chair bd. dirs., 1992—; bd. dirs. Wesleyan Investment Found., 1983—. Mem. Nat. Assn. Evangelicals (bd. dirs. 1970-72), Christian Holiness Assn. (treas. 1984-88). Republican. Mem. Wesleyan Ch. Home: 1412 N Marlin Dr Marion IN 46952-1536

BRANNON-PEPPAS, LISA, chemical engineer, researcher; b. Houston, Sept. 19, 1962; d. James Graham and Patricia Ann (Hightower) Brannon; m. Nicholas A. Peppas, Aug. 10, 1988. BS, Rice U., 1984; MS, Purdue U., 1986, PhD, 1988. Sr. formulations chemist Eli Lilly & Co., Indpls., 1988-91; pres., founder Biogel Tech., Indpls., 1991—2002; rsch. prof. dept. biomed. engring. U. Tex., Austin, 2002—. Author, editor: Absorbent Polymer Technology, 1990, mem. editl. bd.: Jour. Applied Polymer Sci., 1995—2001, Jour. Controlled Release, 1997—2001, Jour. Nanoparticle Rsch., 1998—, Biomaterials, 1999—. Vol. Indpls. Mus. Art, 1990—98, Humane Soc. Indpls., 1990—98, Indpls. Zoo, 1994—2000; trustee Chem. Engring. Found., 1999—2000. Recipient Harold B. Lamport award Biomed. Engring. Soc., 1989; named Outstanding Young Alumna, Kinkaid Sch., 1998-2000. Fellow Am. Inst. of Med. and Biol. Engring.; mem. AIChE (dir. 1998-2000, exec. bd. programming coun., dir. materials divsn., chmn. subcom. biomaterials divsn. 1990-93, dir.-at-large food, pharm. and bioengring. divsn. 1992-94, 2d vice chair materials divsn. 1994-95, 1st vice chmn. materials divsn. 1995-96, chmn. 1996-97, bd. dirs. 1998-2000), Am. Chem. Soc. (membership com. 1990—), Controlled Release Soc. (treas. 1995-98, internat. planning com. 1991, bd. govs. 1992-95), Jr. League Indpls. (bd. dirs. 1992-94). Avocations: fine art, dance, travel. Office: U Tex Austin CPE 3-168a Austin TX 78712

BRANON, M. SUSAN, school system administrator; b. Milan, Tenn., Sept. 3, 1946; d. Howard Brooks and Mary Louise (Black) Branon; divorced; 1 child, Eric Dean Nelson. BS in Elem. Edn., Lambuth U., 1968; MA in Spl. Edn., Memphis State U., 1974; postgrad., Nat. Coll. of Edn., 1977-80, U. Louisville, 1982, Old Dominion U., 1985, Coll. William and Mary, 1987, U. Ctrl. Ark., 1998-99. Elem. edn. tchr., Orlando, Fla., 1968-70; tchr. learning disabilities Memphis City Sch. System, 1970-74; resource and learning disabilities tchr. Am. Dependent Schs., Fed. Republic Germany, 1974-77; team leader learning disability North Suburban Spl. Edn. Dist., 1977-80; elem. and high sch. tchr. learning disabilities Ft. Knox Ind. Sch. System, 1981-83; learning disabilities developer Norge Elem. Sch., Williamsburg, Va., 1984; learning disability resource and itinerant tchr. Williamsburg James City County Schs., 1984-86; learning disabilities resource tchr., ednl. diagnostician Matthew Whaley Elem. Sch., 1984-87; area supr. spl. edn. sect. Ark. Dept. Edn., Little Rock, 1988-94, coord. comprehensive sys. personnel devel. spl. edn., 1994—96, adminstr. state program devel., 1996—. Asst. in planning state and nat. confs. and insvc. workshops; asst. in developing state program for indirect svc. model; coop. cons. for spl. edn. dept.; program chmn. State Edn. Conf., 1992, 94; state contact for Nat. Assn. State Dirs. of Spl. Edn. ann. meeting, 1993, asst. to developing program ann. meeting, 1995; adj. prof. U. Ctrl. Ark., Conway, 2000-2002; developer paraprofl. tng. modules for Ark, 1997-2002; presenter in field. Vol. adv. Ft. Monroe's Family Mem. of the Handicapped; v.p. United Cerebral Palsy Aux., pres.; bd. dirs., past pres. Indian Hill Condo Assn.; mem. edn. com. Sunday sch. class. Mem. CEC (symposium presenter 1990, 96, sec. divsn. for learning disability Va. chpt.), Ark. Assn. Spl. Edn. Adminstrn. Avocations: entertaining, candy making, baking, walking, travel. Home: 1917 Dakota St North Little Rock AR 72116-4481 Office: Ark Dept Spl Edn 4 State Capitol Little Rock AR 72201-1011 E-mail: sbranon@arkedu.k12.ar.us.

BRANSCOMB, HARVIE, JR., lawyer; b. Dallas, Mar. 24, 1922; s. Bennett Harvie and Margaret (Vaughan) B.; m. Mary Josephine Goodearle, Dec. 28, 1951; children: Mary Margaret, Bennett Hill, Richard Lee. AB, Duke U., 1943; LL.B., Yale U., 1948. Bar: Tex. 1948, D.C. 1980, CPA, Tex. Shareholder Matthews & Branscomb, Attys.-at-Law, Corpus Christi, Tex., 1948—. Contbr. articles to profl. jours. Trustee Found. Scis. and Arts, Corpus Christi, Tex. A&M U. Corpus Christi Found.; trustee emeritus Southwestern Legal Found.; trustee, pres. Una Chapman Cox Found. Served with USNR, 1943-46. Fellow Am. Coll. Tax Counsel; mem. ABA, (chmn. tax sect. 1979-80), State Bar Tex. (chmn. sect. taxation 1961-62), Am. Law Inst., Am. Inst. CPA's, Phi Beta Kappa, Phi Delta Phi. Episcopalian. Home: 4500 Ocean Dr Apt 8B Corpus Christi TX 78412-2500 Office: 802 N Carancahua St Ste 1900 Corpus Christi TX 78470-0102

BRANSCOMB, LEWIS CAPERS, JR., librarian, educator; b. Birmingham, Ala., Aug. 5, 1911; s. Lewis Capers and Minnie Vaughn (McGehee) Branscomb; m. Marjorie Berry Stafford, Jan. 15, 1938 (dec. 1999); children: Lewis Capers III(dec.), Ralph Stafford(dec.), Carol Jean, Lawrence McGehee. Student, Birmingham-So. Coll., 1929-30; AB, Duke U., 1933; AB in Libr. Sci., U. Mich., 1939, AM in Libr. Sci., 1941; postgrad., U. Ga., 1940; PhD, U. Chgo., 1954. Clk. Young & Vann Supply Co., Birmingham, 1933-38; order libr. U. Ga., 1939-41; libr. Mercer U., 1941-42; libr., prof. libr. sci. U. S.C., 1942-44; asst. dir. pub. svc. depts., assoc. prof. libr. sci. U. Ill., 1944-48; assoc. dir. librs., prof.,

1948-52; dir. librs., prof. Ohio State U., Columbus, 1952-71, prof. Thurber studies, 1971-81, prof. emeritus, 1981—. Mem. faculty compensation and benefits com. Ohio State U., 1981-90; chmn. Adv. Coun. on Libr. Svcs. and Constrn. Act, Ohio, 1967-70; cons. Punjab Agrl. U., India, 1967, Mansfield (Ohio) Pub. Libr., 1977; mem. adv. coun. Hitachi Found., 1985-88. Author: Ernest Cushing Richardson Research Librarian, Scholar, Theologian, 1993; editor: The Case for Faculty Status for Academic Librarians, 1970; contbr. articles to profl. jours. Mem. Ohio Commn. to Abolish Capital Punishment, 1960-69; bd. dirs. Ctr. for Rsch. Librs., 1953-64, mem. exec. com., 1954-56, chmn. bd. dirs., 1961-62, mem. coun., 1965-71; chmn. bd. trustees Ohio Coll. Libr. Ctr., 1968-70, vice chmn., 1970-72. Mem. AAUP (sec.-treas. U. Ill. chpt. 1947-48; sec.-treas. Ohio State U. chpt. 1948-52, pres. 1953-54; nat. council 1952-55, co-author History of the Ohio Conf. 1949-74, chmn. com. E 1979-91, mem. exec. com. 1981-91), ALA (chmn. nominating com. 1954-55), Assn. Coll. and Research Libraries (dir. 1953-55, v.p. 1957-58, pres. 1958-59), Ohio Library Assn. (chmn. coll. and univ. sect. 1952-53, chmn. library adminstrn. sect. 1969-70, chmn. local conf. com. 1970, chmn. awards and honors com. 1974-75, chmn. notable Ohio librarians com. 1978-79, award of merit 1971, Hall of Fame 1982), Franklin County Library Assn., Acad. Library Assn. Ohio, ACLU (exec. com. Central Ohio chpt. 1958-60, 64-66), Common Cause, Thurber Circle, Thurber House (bd. trustees emeritus 1985—), Friends of Ohio State U. Libraries, Ohio State U. Retirees Assn. (exec. bd. 1983 92), Beta Phi Mu (exec. council 1955-58), Sigma Alpha Epsilon. Democrat. Home: 3790 Overdale Dr Columbus OH 43220-4749 Office: Ohio State Univ Main Libr Columbus OH 43210

BRANSCOMB, LEWIS MCADORY, physicist, researcher; b. Asheville, N.C., Aug. 17, 1926; s. Bennett Harvie and Margaret (Vaughan) B.; m. Margaret Anne Wells, Oct. 13, 1951; children: Harvie Hammond, Katharine C. Branscomb Kelley. AB summa cum laude, Duke U., 1945, DSc (hon.); MS, Harvard U., 1947, PhD, 1949; DSc (hon.), Poly. Inst. N.Y., Clarkson Coll., Rochester U., U. Colo., Western Mich. U., Lycoming Coll., U. Ala., Pratt Inst., Rutgers U., Lehigh U., U. Notre Dame; DEng (hon.), Colo. Sch. Mines, 1999; D Pub. Politics, Carnegie Mellon U., 2000; DSc (hon.), SUNY, Binghamton; LHD (hon.), Pace U. Instr. physics Harvard U., 1950-51; lectr. physics U. Md., 1952-54; vis. staff mem. Univ. Coll., London, 1957-58; chief atomic physics sect. Nat. Bur. Standards, Washington, 1954-60, chief atomic physics div., 1960-62; chmn. Joint Inst. Lab. Astrophysics, U. Colo., 1962-65, 68-69; chief lab. astrophysics div. Nat. Bur. Standards, Boulder, Colo., 1962-69; prof. physics U. Colo., 1962-69; dir. Nat. Bur. Standards, 1969-72; chief scientist, v.p. IBM, Armonk, N.Y., 1972-86, mem. corporate mgmt. bd., 1983-86; dir. sci. and tech. policy program Kennedy Sch. Govt., Harvard U., Cambridge, Mass., 1986-96, Albert Pratt pub. service prof., 1988-94; Aetna prof. pub. policy and corp. mgmt. Harvard U., Cambridge, Mass., 1994-96, prof. emeritus, 1996—. Mem.-at-large Def. Sci. Bd., 1969-72; mem. high level policy group sci. and tech. info. Orgn. Econ. Coop. and Devel., 1968-70; mem. Pres.'s Sci. Adv. Com., 1965-68, chmn. panel space sci. and tech., 1967-68; mem. Nat. Sci. Bd., 1978-84, chmn., 1980-84; mem. Pres.'s Nat. Productivity Adv. Com., 1981-82; mem. standing com. controlled thermonuclear research AEC, 1966-68; mem. adv. com. on sci. and fgn. affairs Dept. State, 1973-74; mem. U.S.-USSR Joint Commn. on Sci. and Tech., 1977-80; chmn. Com. on Scholarly Communications with the People's Republic of China, 1977-80; mem. tech. assessment adv. coun. Office of Tech. Assessment, U.S. Congress, 1990-95; chmn. Carnegie Forum Task Force on Teaching as a Profession, 1985-86; dir. Lord Corp.; mem. pres.'s bd. visitors U. Okla., 1968-70; mem. astronomy and applied physics vis. coms. Harvard U. 1969-83, bd. overseers, 1984-86; mem. physics vis. com. M.I.T., 1974-79; mem. Pres.'s Com. Nat. Medal Scis., 1970-72; bd. dirs. Am. Nat. Standards Inst., 1969-72; trustee Carnegie Instn., 1973-90, mem. Carnegie Commn. on Sci., Tech. and Govt., 1988-93; trustee Poly. Inst. N.Y., 1974-78, Vanderbilt U., 1980-2003, Nat. Geog. Soc., 1984-01, Woods Hole Oceanographic Instn., 1985-92, 93-98, LASPAU, 1999—; chmn. Nat. Info. Infrastructure-2000 steering com. NRC, 1994-95; Harvie Branscomb disting. vis. prof. Vanderbilt U., 1999-2000. Author: Taking Technical Risks, 2001, Empowering Technology, 1993, Confessions of a Technophile, 1995, Korea at the Turning Point, 1996, Investing in Innovation, 1998, Industrializing Knowledge, 1999, Taking Technical Risks, 2000, Making America Safer, 2002; editor Rev. Modern Physics, 1968-73. Trustee Telluride Inst., 1996-97; mem. Commn. on Global Info. Infrastructure, 1995—. USPHS fellow, 1948-49; Jr. fellow Harvard Soc. Fellows, 1949-51; recipient Rockefeller Pub. Service award, 1957-58, Gold medal exceptional service Dept. Commerce, 1961, Arthur Flemming award D.C. Jr. C. of C., 1962, Samuel Wesley Stratton award Dept. Commerce, 1966, Career Service award Nat. Civil Service League, 1968, Vannevar Bush award, nat. Sci. Bd., 2001, Proctor prize Rsch. Soc. Am., 1972, Okawa prize in Info. and Telecomm., 1998, prize for Info. and Telecomms. Ohkawa Found., 1998, Centennial medal, Harvard U., 2002. Fellow Am. Phys. Soc. (chmn. divsn. electron physics 1961-68, pres. 1979), AAAS (dir. 1969-73, 99-2003), Am Acad. Arts and Scis.; mem. NAS (coun. 1972-75, 98-2001), Nat. Acad. Engring. (Arthur Bueche award), Engring. Acad. Japan (fgn. assoc.), Russian Acad. Sci., Washington Acad. Scis. (Outstanding Sci. Achievement award 1959), Nat. Acad. Pub. Adminstrn., Am. Philos. Soc., Phi Beta Kappa, Sigma Xi (pres. 1985-86). Office: Harvard U Kennedy Sch Govt 79 J F Kennedy St Cambridge MA 02138-5801 E-mail: lewis_branscomb@harvard.edu. *No achievement is entirely one's own nor is there satisfaction without sharing. Taking pride in my late wife's professional achievements, my colleagues ideas and my students promise keeps me creative.*

BRANSDORFER, STEPHEN CHRISTIE, lawyer; b. Lansing, Mich., Sept. 18, 1929; s. Henry and Sadie (Kohane) B.; m. Peggy Ruth Deisig, May 24, 1952; children: Mark, David, Amy, Jill. AB with honors, Mich. State U., 1951; JD with distinction, U. Mich., 1956; LLM, Georgetown U., 1958. Bar: Mich. 1956, U.S. Supreme Ct. 1959, U.S. Dist. Ct. (we. dist.) Mich. 1959; cert. mediator U.S. Dist. Ct. (we. dist.) Mich. 1995. Trial atty. Dept. Justice, Washington, 1956—58; atty., editor Office of Public Info., Office of Atty. Gen., 1958—59; spl. asst. U.S. Atty. for D.C., 1958—59; assoc. Miller, Johnson, Snell & Cummiskey, Grand Rapids, Mich., 1959—63, ptnr., 1963—89; dep. asst. atty. gen. civil div. U.S. Dept. Justice, Washington, 1989—92; pres. Bransdorfer & Bransdorfer, P.C., Grand Rapids, 1993—2000; ptnr. Bransdorfer & Russell, LLP, Grand Rapids, 2000—. Pres. State Bar of Mich., 1974-75, commr., 1968-75, chmn. sr. lawyers sect., 1994-95; pres. Grand Rapids chpt. Am. Inns of Ct., 1995-96; trustee Am. Inns of Ct. Found., 1997-2001; chmn. Mich. Civil Svc. Commn., 1977-78, mem., 1975-78; adv. com. 6th Cir. Jud. Conf., 1984-89; co-chair Mich. polit. leadership program Mich. State U., 1992-94; mem. comml. panel Am. Arbitration Assn., 1998-2001. Asst. editor: U. Mich. Law Rev, 1956. Pres. Grand Rapids Child Guidance Clinic, 1969-71; chmn. Kent County Coms., Griffin for Senator, 1972, Lenore Romney for Senator, 1966; mem. council legal advisers Rep. Nat. Com., 1981-89; Rep. candidate for atty. gen., Mich., 1978; trustee, v.p., Mich. State Bar Found., 1985-87, chmn., fellows, 1987-89; chmn. Mich. State Bd. Canvassers, 1985-87, Commn. on Future Directions in Health Care, West Mich., 1987-89; trustee Hist. Soc. for U.S. Dist. Ct. (we. dist.) Mich., 2002—. With U.S. Army, 1951-53. Recipient Spl. award for Superior Performance Civil Divsn. U.S. Dept. Justice, 1990. Fellow Am. Bar Found.; mem. ABA, 6th Cir. Jud. Conf. (life, mem. mems. com., sr. counsel to 6th cir. ct., 1999—), Grand Rapids Bar Assn., FBA (pres. West Mich. chpt. 1984, Disting. Life Svc. award 1989), Rep. Nat. Lawyers Assn. (bd. govs. 1985-89), Mich. Rep. Party (Svc. award 1989), Rotary, Cascade Hills Country Club, Phi Kappa Phi. Presbyterian. *Life is a series of challenges. Do your best and you need not worry about the results.*

BRANSFIELD, JAMES JOSEPH, surgeon; b. Chgo., Nov. 8, 1932; s. James Joseph and Beatrice Catherine (Greene) B.; m. Virginia Kaye Paully, Dec. 17, 1967; 1 child, Helena Theresa. BS, Loyola U., 1955, MD, 1957. Diplomate Am. Bd. Emergency Medicine. Am. Bd. Surgery, Am. Bd. Emergency Medicine. Pvt. practice specializing in surgery, Chgo., 1968—. Chief surgeon Chgo. Police Dept., 1983-94. Lt. comdr. USNR, 1960-63. Avocations: swimming, sailing. Home: 6200 N Knox Ave Chicago IL 60646-5030

BRANSON, ALBERT HAROLD (HARRY BRANSON), judge, educator; b. Chgo., May 20, 1935; s. Fred Brooks and Marie (Vowell) B.; m. Siri-Anne Gudrun Lindberg, Nov. 2, 1963; children: Gunnar John, Gulliver Dean, Hannah Marie, Siri Elizabeth. BA, Northwestern U., 1957; JD, U. Chgo., 1963. Bar: Pa. 1965, Alaska 1972. Atty. Richard McVeigh law offices, Anchorage, 1972-73; ptnr. Jacobs, Branson & Guetschow, Anchorage, 1973-76, Branson & Guetschow, Anchorage, 1976-82; pvt. practice Law Offices of Harry Branson, Anchorage, 1982-84, 85-89; atty. Branson, Bazeley & Chisolm, Anchorage, 1984-85; U.S. magistrate judge U.S. Dist. Ct., Anchorage, 1989—. Instr., adj. prof. U. Alaska Justice Ctr., 1980—93; U.S. magistrate, Anchorage, 1975—76; mem. 9th Cir. Magistrate Judges Exec. Bd., 2001. Mem. steering com. Access to Civil Justice Task Force, 1997-98. With U.S. Army, 1957-59. Mem. Alaska Bar Assn. (bd. dirs., v.p. bd. govs. 1977-80, 83-86, pres. bd. govs. 1986, Disting. Svc. award 1992, Spl. Svc. award 1988, editor-in-chief Alaska Bar Rag 1978-86), Anchorage Bar Assn. (bd. dirs., bd. govs. 1982-86), Anchorage Inn of Ct. (pres. 1995). Democrat. Avocations: book collecting, cooking, poetry. Office: US Dist Ct 222 W 7th Ave Unit 33 Anchorage AK 99513-7504

BRANSON, BRANLEY ALLAN, biology educator; b. San Angelo, Tex., Feb. 11, 1929; s. Branley Allan and Era Elizabeth (Rogers) B.; m. Mary Louise Lewis, June 3, 1964; 1 son, Rogers McGowan. AA, Northeastern Okla. A. and M. Coll., 1954; BS, Okla. State U., 1956, MS, 1957, PhD, 1960. Asst. prof. biology Kan. State Coll., Pittsburg, 1960-64; prof. biology Eastern Ky. U., Richmond, 1964—, found. prof., 1989-90. Contbr. articles to mags. Recipient Sci. award Okla. A. and M. Coll., 1953; named Disting. Scientist of Ky., 1984 Fellow Okla. Acad. Sci., AAAS; mem. Southwestern Assn. Naturalists (bd. govs. 1965—), Am. Malacological Union, Soc. for Study Evolution, Kan. Acad. Sci., Ky. Acad. Sci. (editor transactions), Soc. Systematic Zoologists, Am. Soc. Zoologists, Am. Soc. Ichthyologists and Herpetologists, Sigma Xi, Phi Theta Kappa, Phi Kappa Phi. Achievements include research and numerous publs. on description several species unknown animals; described structural workings lateral-line system in various fishes; olfactory system, geog. distbn. fishes and mollusks. Home: 100 Walnut Hill Dr Richmond KY 40475-3620 Office: Eastern Ky U Richmond KY 40475 *I've had a long-term love affair with the nature of things, and the fervor doesn't seem to be lessening any with the passage of time. And strongly supported by the very real love affair with my wife and son, I've simply had the best of conditions for being creative.*

BRANSON, HARLEY KENNETH, finance executive; b. Ukiah, Calif., June 10, 1942; s. Harley Edward and Clara Lucile Branson; 1 child, Erik Jordan. BS in Acctg. and Fin., San Jose State U., 1965; JD, Santa Clara U., 1968. Bar: Calif. 1969-98. Law clk. to judge U.S. Ct. Appeals (9th cir.), San Diego, 1968-69; pvt. practice San Diego, 1969-78; div. counsel Ralston Purina Co., San Diego, 1978-83; group gen. counsel Castle & Cooke, Inc., San Diego, 1983-85; exec. v.p., gen. counsel, corp. sec. Bumble Bee Seafoods, Inc., San Diego, 1985-89; pres., CEO Flying Palms LLC, San Diego, 1995—. Bd. dirs. Wind and Weather, Inc., JetQue, Inc.; gen. ptnr. Hankins Ptnrs., LLC, 1997—. E-mail: kennethbranson@earthlink.net.

BRANSON, ROBERT EARL, marketing economist; b. Dallas, Dec. 3, 1918; s. R. Earl and Gertrude (Smith) B.; children: Donald, Richard. BS, So. Meth. U., 1941; MPA, Harvard U., 1948, MA, 1949, PhD, 1954. Economist War Food Adminstrn., USDA, Dallas, 1941-43; economist, statistician USDA, Washington, 1943-55; assoc. prof., prof. Tex. A&M U., College Sta., Tex., 1955-80, dir., Tex. Agr. Mkt. Research Ctr., 1969-88; pres. Branson Research Assoc., Inc., Bryan, Tex., 1985—, Agribusiness Analysts, Bryan, 1985—; prof. emeritus Tex. A&M U., College Sta., 1987—. Mktg. economist research cons. U. P.R., 1949-51, Argentina Eco Planning Staff, Foreign Agr. Service, USDA, Bryan/College Station Tex. 2020 Vision Area Planning Com. Author: Intro Agriculture and Marketing, 1983; contbr. articles to profl. jours. With U.S. Army, 1944-45. Mem. Am. Mktg. Assn., So. Agr. Econ. Assn. (Life Mem. award 1989), Kiwanis (College Station pres. 1982, 97). Methodist. Home: 2511 Broadmoor Dr Bryan TX 77802-2804 Office: Branson Rsch Assoc Inc 1807C Briar Oaks Bryan TX 77802 E-mail: brai@tca.net.

BRANSTAD, TERRY EDWARD, former governor, lawyer; b. Leland, Iowa, Nov. 17, 1946; s. Edward Arnold and Rita (Garl) B.; m. Christine Ann Johnson, June 17, 1972; children: Eric, Allison, Marcus. BA, U. Iowa, 1969; JD, Drake U., 1974. Bar: Iowa. Sr. ptnr. firm Branstad-Schwarm, Lake Mills, Iowa, until 1982; farmer Lake Mills; mem. Iowa Ho. of Reps., 1973-78; lt. gov. State of Iowa, 1979-82, gov., 1983-99. Bd. dirs. Am. Legion of Iowa Found. With U.S. Army, 1969. Mem. Nat. Govs. Assn. (past chmn.), Rep. Govs. Assn. (task chair), Midwestern Govs. Assn., Am. Legion, Farm Bur. Lodges: Lions, KC. Republican. Roman Catholic. Office: Regency West 2 1401 50th St Ste 325 West Des Moines IA 50266-5924

BRANSTETTER, CECIL DEWEY, SR., lawyer; b. Deer Lodge, Tenn., Dec. 15, 1920; s. Miller Henry and Lillie Mae (Adams) B.; m. Charlotte Virginia Coleman, Aug. 5, 1944; children: Kay Frances Johnson, Linda Charlotte Mauk, Kathy Jane Stranch, Cecil Dewey Jr. BA, George Washington U., 1947; JD, Vanderbilt U., 1949. Bar: U.S. Supreme Ct. 1957, U.S. Ct. Appeals (6th cir.) 1963. Ptnr. Branstetter, Kilgore, Stranch & Jennings, Nashville, 1990—. Chmn. Bd. Profl. Responsibility Supreme Ct. Tenn. Contbr. articles to profl. jours. Mem. Gen. Assembly Tenn., Nashville, 1950-53; chmn. Charter Commn. and Charter Revision Commn., Nashville, 1957-62, 78-90; mem. Met. Action Commn., Nashville, 1964-68; pres. Coun. Community Agys. and Tenn. Environ. Coun., Nashville, 1970, 71-73. Sgt. U.S. Army, 1943-46, lt. Res., 1946-52, ETO. Mem. ACLU (bd. dirs.), ABA, Met. Human Rels. Commn., Am. Judicature Soc., Tenn. Conservation League (Carter Patten award), Am. Trial Lawyers Assn., Tenn. Bar Assn., Tenn. Trial Lawyers Assn., Nashville Bar Assn., Davidson County Sportsman Club, Order of Coif. Democrat. Baptist. Avocations: farming, fishing, hunting, raising angus cattle.

BRANSTUTTER, JOSEPH WAYNE, research scientist; b. Kokomo, Ind., July 26, 1975; s. Larry Wayne and Freda Ann Branstutter. BS, Ind. Wesleyan U., Marion, 1997; MS, Ball State U., 1999. R&D scientist Micronix Innovative Diagnostics, Carmel, Ind., 2000—. Avocations: drawing, reading, piano, golf. Home: 617 E 625 N Windfall IN 46076 Office: Micronix Innovative Diagnostics 14950 Greyhound Ct Ste 307 Carmel IN 46032

BRANT, DONNA MARIE, journalist; b. N.Y.C., Oct. 17, 1955; d. Earl Evans and Catherine Marie (Schatz) B. BA in Philosophy, George Washington U., 1977; MS in Broadcast Journalism, Boston U., 1979. Desk asst. nat. news desk NBC News, N.Y.C., 1979, news and feature asst. presdl. campaign, 1979-80, bur. coord. nat. news bur. Pitts., 1980-82, futures editor nat. news desk Washington, 1982-83, polit. assignment editor presdl. campaign, 1983-84, assignment editor nat. news desk, 1984-89; West Coast reporter, prodr. Am.'s Most Wanted, Fox Broadcasting Co., Washington, 1989-95, N.Y. reporter, prodr., 1995-96, mng. editor, 1996-99, sr. prodr. spl. projects, 1999—. Sr. rschr.: Barter, 1978. Contbr. mem. Smithsonian Instn., Washington, 1982. Recipient citation Internat. Assn. Asian Crime Investigators, Davis (Calif.) Police Dept., Multnomah County (Oreg.) Sheriff's Office, Riverside County (Calif.) Sheriff's Office, U.S. Marshals Svc., Ariz. Law Enforcement Fraternal Order of Police. Mem. Washington Hist. Soc., Sigma Delta Chi. Avocations: photography, travel, history, swimming, designing and building furniture. Office: America's Most Wanted 5151 Wisconsin Ave NW Washington DC 20016-4124 E-mail: donnabrant@aol.com.

BRANT, HENRY, composer; b. Montreal, Que., Can., Sept. 15, 1913; s. Saul and Bertha (Dreyfuss) B.; children: Piri, Joquin, Linus; m. Katu Wilkovska, 1989. Student, Juilliard Sch. Music, N.Y.C., 1930-34; DFA (hon.), Wesleyan U., 1998. Mem. faculty Juilliard Sch. Music, 1947-55; dept. music Columbia U., 1943-53; mem. faculty Bennington (Vt.) Coll., 1957-80. Composer, condr. documentary films, U.S. Govt. OWI, State Dept., Dept. Agr. 1940-47; composer, condr. various radio network program series for NBC, CBS, ABC, 1942-46; large ensemble works include Angels and Devils, 1931, Origins: Percussion Symphony, 1952, Signs and Alarms, 1953, Antiphony 1, 1953, Millenium 2, 1954, Encephalograms 2, 1954, Ceremony, 1954, Galaxy 2, 1954, December, 1954, spatial opera Grand Universal Circus, 1956, Hieroglyphics, 1957, The Children's Hour, 1958, Mythical Beasts, 1958, Atlantis, 1960, Concerto with Lights, 1961, Barricades, 1961, Headhunt, 1962, Voyage 4; Total Antiphony, in 83 Parts, 1963, Odyssey-Why Not?, 1965, Kingdom Come, 1970, Crossroads, 1971, Immortal Combat, 1972, American Requiem, 1973, Prevailing Winds, 1974, Solomon's Gardens, 1974, Homage to Ives, 1975, A Plan of the Air, 1975, Spatial Piano Concerto, 1976, Antiphonal Responses, 1977, Trinity of Spheres, 1978, Orbits: 80 Trombones, 1979, The Secret Calendar, 1980, The Glass Pyramid, 1980, Meteor Farm, 1982, Western Springs, 1984, Fire in the Amstel, 1984, Desert Forests, 1985, Northern Lights Over the Twin Cities, 1986, Ghost Nets, 1988, Rainforest, 1989, 500: Pathways to Security, 1990, Prisons of the Mind, 1990, Hidden Hemisphere, 1992, Fourscore, 1993, Homeless People, 1993, Trajectory, 1994, Plowshares and Swords, 1996, Mergers, 1998, Ice Field, 2001 (Pulitzer prize in music 2002), Crystal Antiphonies, 2000, Glossary, 2000, Prophets, 2000, others; recs: Columbia, Desto, CRI, New World, Nonesuch, Sonic Arts, AmCam, Newport Classic. Recipient Prix Italia, 1955, Alice M. Ditson award, 1962, 64, ASCAP/Nissim award 1985, Mcpl. citations: Boston, 1983, N.Y.C., 1992; Guggenheim fellow 1946, 55, Thorne fellow, 1972; grantee: Inst. Arts and Letters, 1955, Copley, 1960, Huber, 1960, Dollard 1966, N.Y. State Coun. for Arts, 1974, NEA, 1976, ASCAP/Nissim 1984, Fromm, 1992, Koussevitzky Found., 1996. Mem. Am. Acad. Arts and Letters (life) Achievements include pioneering in development of spatial-antiphonal music. Office: 1607 Chino St Santa Barbara CA 93101-4757 *Undoubtedly, the answer to the riddle of existence must be: perpetual discovery.**

BRANT, JOHN GETTY, lawyer; b. Apr. 13, 1946; BBA, U. Okla., 1968; JD, U. Tex., 1972. Bar: US Dist. Ct. Colo. 1974, US Tax Ct. 1974. Atty. IRS, Houston, 1972—74; ptnr. Bradley, Campbell & Carney, Golden, Colo., 1975—83, Doussard, Brant, Hodel & Markman, Lakewood, Colo., 1983—86; pvt. practice Lakewood, Colo., 1986—2000; ptnr. Brant, Stevens & Graf, Lakewood, 2000—02. Arbitrator Nat. Assn. Securities Dealers. Bd. dirs. U. Tex. Law Sch. Assn., Austin, 1983-86, Nat. Multiple Sclerosis Soc., Denver, 1975-91. Mem.: Centennial Estate Planning Coun. (pres. 1976). Office: 710 Kipling St Ste 305 Lakewood CO 80215-8006

BRANTIGAN, CHARLES OTTO, surgeon; b. Balt., Jan. 24, 1943; s. Otto Charles and Edith May (Reinhart) B.; m. Linda Anne Reynolds, 1972 (dec. 1978); m. Kathleen Sharon Aylsworth, July 16, 1983; 1 child, Charles Aylsworth. BA in Chemistry, Cornell U., 1964; MD, Johns Hopkins U., 1968. Intern U. Colo., 1968-69, resident, 1969-70, 72-73, fellow in cardiovascular surgery, 1973-74; resident in thoracic surgery Denver Gen. Hosp., 1974-75; sr. resident U. Colo. Med. Ctr., 1975-76; pvt. practice Denver, 1976—. Assoc. clin. prof. surgery U. Colo., 1976—; chief of surgery Presbyn. St. Lukes Med. Ctr., Denver, 1994—2002; dir. Denver Vascular Diagnostic Ctr., 1984—; med. dir. Denver Wound Care Ctr., 1991—2001; chief thoracic surgery Denver Gen. Hosp., 1976; asst. dir. surg. tng. program St. Joseph Hosp., Denver, 1984—86; chmn. nutritional support com. Presbyn. Med. Ctr., 1983—87; vis. prof. Mostafa Kamel Hosp., Alexandria, Egypt, 2000, El Maadi Hosp., Cairo, 2000—02. Contbr. articles to profl. jours.; author 4 books. Chmn. Hosp. Dist. Urban Design Forum, Denver, 1993—; participated in creation of Lafayette St. Historic Dist., Denver, 1987. Lt. comdr. USN, 1970-72. Recipient Spl. Citizen award Planning Office City of Denver, 1995, Historic Preservation award Historic Denver, 1988, Stephen H. Hart award Colo. State Hist. Soc., 1988, People's Choice award Capitol Hill United Neighborhoods, 1997, Ann. Love award for Hist. Preservation, Hist. Denver, 2002. Mem.: ACS, AMA, Soc. Critical Care Medicine, Am. Coll. Chest Physicians, Internat. Soc. for Cardiovasc. Surgery, Western Thoracic Surgery Soc., Am. Assn. Vascular Surgery, Am. Heart Assn., Colo. Med. Soc., Rocky Mountain Traumatologic Soc., Denver Med. Soc., Denver Brass Inc. (chmn. bd. dirs.). Lutheran. Avocations: urban land use planning, architectural historical research. Home: 2105 Lafayette St Denver CO 80205-5337 Office: 2253 Downing St Denver CO 80205-5234 E-mail: cbrantigan@drbrantigan.com.

BRANTINGHAM, BARNEY, journalist, writer; b. Chgo., Feb. 26, 1932; s. Carl Brantingham and Frances Bell; m. Angela Mendez, Oct. 30, 1957 (div.); children: Barclay Carl, Frances, Wendy, Kenneth. Grad., U. Ill., 1954. Reporter Star Newspapers, Chicago Heights, Ill., 1957-59; editor San Clemente (Calif.) Sun-Post, 1959-60; reporter Santa Barbara (Calif.) News-Press, 1960—, columnist, 1977—. Commentator Sta. KTMS, Santa Barbara, 1989-91, Sta. KIST, Santa Barbara, 1991, SAM, 1990, 92; radio sta. feature and travel commentator KQSB, 1994-97; co-host Around the World with Arthur and Barney, Sta. KTMS, 1998, KEYT-AM, 1998-2003, Around the World, Sta. KXBN, 2003—; founding dir. Opinionated Traveler internet site www.opinionatedtraveler.com. Prodr. TV program Santa Barbara Traveler; author: The Pro Football Hall of Fame, 1988, Barney's Santa Barbara, 1989, Around Santa Barbara County with Barney, 1992; co-dir. The Opinionated Traveler Internet Site. With U.S. Army, 1955-57. Mem. Internat. Food, Wine and Travel Writers Assn. (dir. 1991-95), Am. Travel Media Assn. (bd. dirs.). Avocation: travel. Office: Santa Barbara News-Press PO Box 1359 Santa Barbara CA 93102-1359 E-mail: bbrantingham@newspress.com.

BRANTINGHAM, PAUL JEFFREY, criminology educator; b. Long Beach, Calif., June 29, 1943; s. Charles Ross and Lila Carolyn (Price) B.; m. Patricia Louise Matthews, Aug. 26, 1967; 1 child, Paul Jeffrey Jr. BA, Columbia U., 1965, JD, 1968; Diploma in Criminology, Cambridge U., 1970. Bar: Calif. 1969. Asst. prof. Fla. State U., Tallahassee, 1971-76, assoc. prof., 1976-77, Simon Fraser U., Burnaby, B.C., Can., 1977-85, assoc. dean faculty interdisciplinary studies, 1980-82, prof., 1985—; dir. spl. revs. Pub. Svc. Commn. Can., Ottawa, Ont., 1985-87. Editor: Juvenile Justice Philosophy, 1974, 2d edit. 1978, Environmental Criminology, 1981, 2d edit. 1991; author: Patterns in Crime. Recipient Eisenhower Watch award Columbia U., 1966; Ford Found. fellow, 1969-70, Western Soc. Criminology fellow, 1996, Sr. fellow Fraser Inst. Mem. ABA, Calif. Bar Assn., Am. Soc. Criminology (chmn. nat. program 1978), Acad. Criminal Justice Scis., Canadian Criminal Justice Assn., Soc. for Reform of Criminal Law, Western Soc. Criminology (v.p. 2000-01, pres. 2001-02). Home: 4680 Eastridge Rd North Vancouver BC Canada V7G 1K4 Office: Simon Fraser U Sch Criminol 8888 University Dr WMC 2630 Burnaby BC Canada V5A 1S6 E-mail: branting@sfu.ca.

BRANTL, SISTER CHARLESMARIE, economics educator; b. Bklyn., Apr. 30, 1929; d. Charles Justin and Edna Marie (Muir) B. BA, Albertus Magnus Coll., 1951; MA, Fordham U., 1959, PhD, 1963. Tchr. N.Y. Diocesan Sch. System, N.Y.C., 1953-61; tchr. Dominican Acad., N.Y.C., 1962-65; prof. Ohio Dominican U., Columbus, 1965-76, Albertus Magnus Coll., New Haven, 1976-90, v.p. acad. affairs, 1990—2002, dir. assessment and instnl. rsch., 2002—. Trustee Ohio Dominican U., Columbus, 1988—; arbitrator Hartford Diocese Arbitration Bd., Hartford, Conn., 1982-88; chmn. bd. dirs. INternat. Assembly Collegiate Bus. Edn., 2003—. Mem. Am. Econ. Assn., Assn. Social Econs., Ea. Econ. Soc., Dominican Order, Tau Pi Phi (nat. gov. 1986-89, trustee 1989-91). Republican. Roman Catholic. Home and Office: Albertus Magnus Coll 700 Prospect St New Haven CT 06511-1224

BRANTLEY, JEFFREY GARLAND, health science facility administrator; b. Rocky Mount, N.C., Nov. 4, 1949; s. Roy Garland and Irene (Cockrell) B.; m. Mary Mathews, Nov. 21, 1981. BA in History, Davidson Coll., 1971; MD, U. N.C., 1977. Diplomate Am. Bd. Psychiatry. Resident in psychiatry U. Calif., Irvine, 1981; pvt. practice psychiatry Laguna Niguel, Calif., 1981-82, Durham, N.C., 1985-87; med. dir. Hospice Orange County, Laguna Niguel, 1982; clin. dir. Durham County Mental Health Ctr., Durham, N.C., 1982-89; freelance cons., educator Durham, 1990—; dir. mindfulness-based stress reduction program Duke Ctr. for Integrative Medicine, 1998—. Clin. assoc. dept. psychiatry U. Calif., Irvine, 1981-82; consulting assoc. Dept. Psychiatry Duke U., 1983—. Mem.: N.C. Psychiat. Assn., Am. Psychiat. Assn. Democrat. Buddhist. Avocations: spectator sports, golf, jogging, music. Home and Office: 1109 Huntsman Dr Durham NC 27713-2370 E-mail: brant006@mc.duke.edu.

BRANTLEY, LEE REED, chemistry educator; b. Herrin, Ill., Sept. 23, 1906; s. Homer L. and Blanche R. (Reed) B.; m. Audrey Ryan, June 25, 1930 (dec. 1983); m. Ruth Thomas, Aug. 21, 1984 AB, UCLA, 1927; MS, Calif. Inst. Tech., 1929, PhD, 1930. Registered profl. engr., Calif.; registered chem. engr., Calif. Instr. physics and chemistry Occidental Coll., L.A., 1930-36, asst. prof. chemistry, 1936-40, assoc. prof., 1940-42, prof., 1942-67, head dept. chemistry, 1940-62, prof. emeritus, from 1967; rsch. fellow physics Calif. Inst. Tech., 1936-42; rsch. asst., cons. chemistry Nat. Def. Rsch. Com. Contract, 1942-44; vis. prof. Lehigh U., 1958-59; prof. chemistry U. Hawaii, Honolulu, 1962-63, vis. prof. chemistry, 1965-66, rsch. prof. edn. Curriculum R&D Group, 1967—72, emeritus prof. chemistry, from 1972, phys. sci. dir. edn. Found. Approaches in Sci. Tchg., 1966-72, cons., 1972—, rsch. prof. dept. chemistry, 1985—, cons. chemistry Sch. Architecture, 1986-88. Dir. contract Office Naval Rsch. on Principles of Adhesion, 1949-58, Q.M. Rsch. and Devel. Environ. Protection, 1953-58; dir. Corn Industries Rsch. Found. Adhesion Contract, 1957-59; cons. on protective coatings Nat. Bur. Standards, 1951-53; writer Commn. on Sci. Edn., AAAS. Author: Chemistry for Architects, 1986, Chemistry of Building Materials, 1986, Building Materials Technology: Structural Performance and Environmental Impact, 1996; contbr.: Standard Hand-

book for Civil Engineers, 4th edit., 1996, 5th edit., 2003, Time-Saver Standards for Architectural Design Data, 4th edit., 1996; contbr. articles to profl. publ. Past chmn. environ. health adv. com. Am. Lung Assn. Hawaii, 1968-93; past chmn. air com. Oahu chpt. Conservation Council of Hawaii.; Served as sr. gas officer Glendale (Calif.) Citizens Def. Corps, 1943-45. Recipient Petroleum Research award for advanced study Am. Chem. Soc., 1958-59; John R. Kuebler award Alpha Chi Sigma, 1973. Fellow AAAS; mem. Pacific S.W. Assn. Chemistry Tchrs. (past pres.), Calif. Acad. Sci., Am. Chem. Soc. (pres. So. Calif. sect. 1947-48, chmn. Hawaii sect. 1970-71, 50-year emeritus mem.), Electrochem. Soc. (emeritus), Nat. Ret. Tchrs. Assn., Hawaii Acad. Sci., Rotary, Sigma Xi, Alpha Chi Sigma (pres. 1958-60), Kappa Sigma. Home: Honolulu, Hawaii. *Each day I look forward to learning more about the many wonders of our world.* Died Aug. 14, 2003.

BRANTLEY, STEPHEN GRANT, pathologist; b. Raleigh, N.C., Nov. 27, 1957; s. Herbert and Juanita (Grant) B. BS with honors, U. N.C., 1980; MD, Med. U. S.C., 1984. Diplomate Am. Bd. Pathology. Residency in pathology U. Pitts. Med. Sch., 1984-88; pathologist Tampa (Fla.) Gen. Hosp., 1988—. Med. dir. labs. Kindred Hosp., Tampa, 1990—; clin. assoc. prof. U. South Fla. Coll. Medicine, Tampa, 1988—. Bd. dirs. Tampa Bay Chamber Orch., Tampa, 1993-2000; exec. com. mem. Rep. Party of Hillsborough County, Tampa, 1989-96; hon. bd. advisors Chamber Orch. Fla., 2000-. Mem. Coll. Am. Pathologists, Am. Soc. Clin. Pathologists, Am. Soc. Transplant Physicians, Internat. Soc. for Heart Transplantation. Republican. Episcopalian. Office: Ruffolo Hooper and Assocs Ste 300 4511 Woodland Corporate Blvd Tampa FL 33614-2423 E-mail: SBrantley@tgh.org.

BRANTLEY, WILLIAM ALBERT, information architect, consultant; b. Louisville, Nov. 16, 1967; s. William Albert Brantley Sr. and Louella Caudill. B Speech Comm., Ea. Ky. U., 1990; M Polit. Mgmt., George Washington U., 1996. Sr. paralegal Ky. Natural Resources Cabinet, Frankfort, 1991-95; computer specialist Social Security Adminstrn., Balt., 1997-98; intergovtl. policy analyst Gen. Svcs. Adminstrn., Washington, 1998-99; database engr. Digicove, Inc., Louisville, 2000—. Instr. U. Louisville, 2000—. Author manual: Information, Coordination and Persuasion, 1996; creator website The Campaigner*First Political Opposition Research Website, 1995. Tour guide NASA Goddard Spaceflight Ctr., Greenbelt, Md., 1995-97. Presdl. Mgmt. intern U.S. Govt., 1997. Mem. Golden Key Nat. Honor Soc. Democrat. Home: 1046 E Kentucky St Louisville KY 40204-1936 Office: Brantley Rsch 1046 E Kentucky St Louisville KY 40204-1936 Fax: (502) 636-1064. E-mail: wabranty@mindspring.com.

BRANTZ, GEORGE MURRAY, retired lawyer; b. Phila., Oct. 19, 1930; s. Louis Paul and Jeannette (Vinitz) B.; m. Joan Nadler, Mar. 29, 1953; children: Nancy Brantz Ginsberg, Amy L. Brantz Bedrick. AB, Princeton U., 1952; LLB magna cum laude, Harvard U., 1957. Bar: Pa. 1957, U.S. Dist. Ct. (ea. dist.) Pa., U.S. Ct. Appeals (3rd cir.). Ptnr. Wolf, Block, Schorr and Solis-Cohen, Phila., 1966-93; ret., 1993. Pres. Council Migration Service, Phila., 1971-73; bd. dirs. Phila. Port Corp., 1982-84. With U.S. Army, 1952-54. Mem. Am. Law Inst., Jane Austen Soc. (treas. 1993-98), Locust Club. Jewish. Avocation: sailing.

BRANYAN, CHERYL MUNYER, museum administrator, consultant; b. Vincennes, Ind., Apr. 27, 1970; d. Edward A. and Janet E. Munyer; m. Richard R. Branyan, Oct. 4, 1997. BA, Ea. Ill. U., 1992, MA, 1995. Asst. curator Coles County Hist. Soc., Charleston, Ill., 1994-95; intern Nat. Pk. Svc., Natchez, Miss., 1995; asst. curator Manship Ho. Mus., Jackson, Miss., 1995-96, The Hermitage, Nashville, 1996-97; cons. Lower Lodge Conservation and Mus. Svcs., Natchez, 1997—; mus. adminstr. Rosalie Miss. State Soc. DAR, Natchez, 1999—; v.p. bd. dirs. Miss. Museums Assn., 2001—. Newsletter editor Historic House Museums Affinity Group, 2000—; bd. dirs. Natchez Hist. Soc., 2000—. Editor SERA News, 1998—, Hist. House Mus. Affinity Group, 2000—; copy editor, contbr. (newsletter) History at Eastern, 1995; co-founder, contbr. (jour.) Historia, 1992. Vol. Lincoln Meml. Gardens, Springfield, Ill., 1993, U. Fla., Gainesville, 1994, Miss. Arts Pavillion, Jackson, 1996; bd. dirs. Natchez Hist. Soc., 2001—. Mem. Am. Assn. Museums (Kay Paris Meml. award, registrar's com. 1997), Am. Assn. State and Local History (vol. Saratoga Springs, N.Y. 1995), Nat. Assn. Jr. Aux., Miss. Mus. Assn. (v.p. of bd. dirs. 2001—), Southeastern Registrars Assn. (comm. chair 1998—), Southeastern Museums Conf. (spkr.), Phi Alpha Theta, Sigma Tau Delta. Democrat. Lutheran. Avocation: visiting museums. Office: Rosalie House Mus MSDAR 100 Orleans St Natchez MS 39120-3452 E-mail: manager@rosalie.net.

BRANYAN, W. DAVID, novelist, real estate broker; b. Orleans, France, May 16, 1965; born U.S. citizen; s. William Henry and Bessie May Day Branyan. Student, Yale U., 1984, Columbia U., 1988. Editor Random House, N.Y.C., 1989-91; mem. editl. staff Paris Rev., N.Y.C., 1991-94; sec. Lloyd Richards, N.Y.C., 1994-95; editor Mark Sullivan Literacy Agy., N.Y.C., 1998—; broker Bellmarc Brokerage, 2001—02, The Corcoran Group Real Estate, 2002—. Evaluator Eugene O'Neil Theater Ctr., N.Y.C., 1992—. Author: The Vile Beginners, 1993, Finessing Meadowhampton, 1998; co-author, editor: (with Barr McClellan) Blood, Money and Power, 2003; contbr. articles to Newman Jour., Nat. Rev. Bd. dirs. L.I. Opera, Oyster Bay, N.Y., 1998—. Mem. Civitas. Avocation: guitar. E-mail: wdbranyan@earthlink.net.

BRAR, BERINDER PAL SINGH, engineer; b. Kasauli, Himachal Pradesh, India, May 17, 1964; s. Surjit Singh Brar; m. Theresa Lynnette Brar; children: Karinn Kaur, Karissa Kaur children: Ranjit Singh. BS, CSU, Fresno, 1986; MSc, UC, Santa Barbara, CA, 1992; PhD, UC, Santa Barbara, 1995. Engr. PG&E, Fresno, Calif., 1986—87, Rockwell Sci. Ctr., Thousand Oaks, Calif., 1987—99; rsch. asst. UCSB, 1989—95; engr. Tex. Instruments, Dallas, 1995—99, Rockwell Sci. Ctr., Thousand Oaks, Calif., 1989—. Mem.: IEEE. Avocations: golf, tennis, hiking, basketball.

BRAR, GURDARSHAN SINGH, soil scientist, researcher; b. Fazilka, Punjab, India, Dec. 25, 1946; came to U.S., 1983; s. Mall Singh and Gurnam Kaur (Aulakh) B.; m. Kuldeep Kaur Sran; children: Ramandeep, Samrita, Yashmeen. BS, Punjab Agrl. U., Ludhiana, 1969, MS, 1972; PhD, Indian Inst. Tech., Kharagpur, West Bengal, 1986. Soil sci. extension specialist dept. soils Punajb Agrl. U., Ludhiana, India, 1973-77; soil physicist dept. soil sci. Punabj Agrl. U., 1977-83; soil scientist environ. firm. Va., 1985-88; rsch. assoc. Tex. Tech. U., Lubbock, 1988-89; soil scientist agrl. rsch. svc. USDA, Bushland, Tex., 1989-92; rsch. phys. scientist U.S. Army C.E., Hanover, N.H., 1992-96; pres. EarthCare, Dallas, Tex., 1995—. Contbr. articles to profl. jours. Mem. Agronomy Soc. Am., Crop Sci. Soc. Am., Soil Sci. Soc. Am.

BRAS, RAFAEL LUIS, engineering educator; b. San Juan, P.R., Oct. 28, 1950; s. Rafael and Amalia Antonia (Muniz) B.; m. Patricia Ann Brown, June 29, 1974; children— Rafael Edmundo, Alejandro Luis. BSCE, MIT, 1972, MSCE, 1974, ScD in Water Resources and Hydrology, 1975; Laurea honoris causa, U. Perugia, Italy, 1991. Registered profl. engr., Mass., P.R. 1992. Asst. prof. U. P.R., Mayaguez, 1975-76; from asst. prof. hydrology to assoc. prof. MIT, Cambridge, 1976-82, prof., 1982—, head water resources and environ. engring. divsn., 1983-91, dir. Ralph M. Parsons Lab., 1983-91, dir. Minority Intro. to Eng. and Sci., 1987, William E. Leonhard prof. engring., 1988-95, Bacardi & Stockholm Water Founds. prof., 1995—, head dept. civil and environ. engring., 1992—2001, chmn. faculty, 2002—; assoc. dir. Ctr. for Global Change Sci., 1990—. Cons. to govt. and industry; vis. assoc. prof. Universidad Simon Bolivar, Caracas, Venezuela, 1982-83; vis. scholar Internat. Inst. Applied Systems Analysis, Vienna, 1983; vis. prof. Iowa Inst. Hydraulic Rsch., U. Iowa, 1989-90; mem. adv. bd. engring. divsn. NSF, 1988-91; bd. atmospheric scis. and climate NRC, 1989-93; earth scis. and applications divsn. adv. subcom. NASA, 1990, sci. team TRMM mission, 1991-94, chair Earth Sys. Sci. and Applications Adv. com.(ESSAAC), 1998-2002; sci. steering group GCIP-Global Energy and Water Cycle Experiment, 1991-95; adv. coun. for com. Nat. Insts. for Environ.; ASCE task com. on edn. initiatives, 1996-97, Science Adv. Com., ISAC, 1999, Johns Hopkins Adv. Com, Civil Egring. Dept., 1998, Adv. Coun., Princeton U., 1999-; nominating com. mem. Stockholm Water Prize, 1996—; mem. adv. coun. dept. civil engring. Rensselaer Poly. Inst., 2000-02; mem. adv. com. dept. civil and environ. engring. Cornell U., 2001—; bd. dirs. Fundacion Chile, 2000-02, MIT Alumni Assn., 2002; exec. com. mem. Clarke Prize, 2002—; mem. bd. on atmospheric scis. and climate NAE, 2001—. Author: (with I. Rodriguez-Iturbe) Random Functions and Hydrology, 1985, 94, Hydrology: An Introduction to Hydrologic Science, 1990; editor: The World at Risk: Natural Hazards and Climate Change, 1993; editor Nonlinear Processes in Geophysics, 1996-2000; contbr. articles to profl. jours.; assoc. editor Water Resources Rsch., 1980-88, Jour. Geophys. Rsch.-Atmospheres, 1996-98; mem. editl. bd. Jour. Hydrology, Internat. Jour. Environ. Tech.; mem. editl. adv. bd. SERRA, 1998—. Recipient: Walter L. Huber Civil Engring. prize, 1993, Giants in Sci. award Quality Edn. for Minorities Math., Sci. and Engring. Network, 2001, Albert Baez Jr. award and Outstanding Educator award Hispanic Engr. Nat. Achievement Awards Conf., 1999, MLK-MIT Leadership award, 2000, Clarke prize, 1998; named to Top 100 Most Influential Hispanics, Hispanic Bus., 1997; Guggenheim fellow, 1982; P.R. Econ. Devel. Adminstrn. fellow; Gilbert Winslow Career Devel. chair MIT; Horton lectr. AMS, 1997, 1999, Kisiel Disting. lectr., 2002, William Mong Disting. lectr. U. Hong Kong, 1999-2000. Fellow: ASCE (task com. 1996—97, Huber prize 1993), Am. Meteorol. Soc. (Robert E. Horton lectr. 1999), Am. Geophys. Union (chmn. bd. jous. editors 1984—88, chair budget and fin. 1990—94, assoc. editor, pres.-elect Hydrology sect. 2002, nominating com. 2002—04, Horton award 1981, James B. Macelwane award 1982); mem.: AMS, AAAS, NAE, Boston Soc. Civil Engrs., Chi Epsilon, Tau Beta Pi, Sigma Xi. Roman Catholic. Office: MIT Rm 48-213 Dept Civil Environ Engring Cambridge MA 02139 E-mail: rlBras@mit.edu.

BRASCH, WALTER MILTON, journalist, educator; b. San Diego, Mar. 2, 1945; s. Milton and Helen (Haskin) B.; m. Ila Wales (div. 1980); m. Vivian Laughrey (div. 1982); m. Rosemary Renn, Dec. 31, 1983; children: Jeffrey Gerber, Matthew Gerber. AB in Sociology, San Diego State U., 1966; MA in Journalism, Ball State U., 1969; PhD in Mass Comm. and Journalism, Ohio U., 1974. Reporter, editor various daily newspapers, Calif., Ind., Iowa, Ohio, 1965-72; exec. dir. MID Prodns., 1971-74; asst. prof. Temple U., Phila., 1974-76; editor-in-chief Tribune Pubs., L.A., 1976-80; prof. Bloomsburg (Pa.) U., 1980—. Part-time copywriter Maushake Advt., L.A., 1974-85; media analyst Jackson-Walsh, L.A., 1975-84; media cons. to polit. and entertainment clients; media and social issues commentator United Broadcasting Network, 1995-2000; v.p. Scripts Destitute, 1996—; columnist Spectrum Features Syndicate, 1992—; PIO, exec. bd. Columbia County Emergency Mgmt. Agy., 1990—; mem. Pa. Local Emergency Planning Commn., 1995—; mem. regional task force counter terrorism, 2000-. Author: A Comprehensive Annotated Bibliography of American Black English, 1974, Black English and the Mass Media, 1981 (Choice award 1981), Columbia County Place Names, 1983, 2nd edit., 1997, Cartoon Monickers: An Insight into the Animation Industry, 1983, The Press and the State: Sociohistorical and Contemporary Interpretations, 1987 (Choice award 1988), Forerunners of Revolution: Muckrakers and the American Social Conscience, 1990, With Just Cause: Unionization and the American Journalist, 1991, Before the First Snow, 1994, Enquiring Minds and Space Aliens : Wandering Through The Mass Media and Popular Culture, 1996, Brer Rabbit, Uncle Remus and the Cornfield Journalist: The Tale of Joel Chandler Harris, 2000, The Joy of Sax: America During the Bill Clinton Era, 2001 (award Nat. Fedn. of Press Women, 2002), (with Dana Ulloth) Social Foundations of the Mass Media, 2001, Voices from the Couch, 2001, Sex and the Single Beer Can, 2003; editor: A ZIM Self-Portrait, 1988; author (play) Tremor at Sand Creek, 1971, The Face of the Battle, 1972; producer (movie) Ride the Wild Wind, 1976; author, producer In the Beginning (the Indian), 1972, Sounds of the Battle, 1973; contbr. more than 200 articles. Recipient 1st pl. award for column Press Club So. Calif., 1977, for sports, 1980, for revs., 1982, for news feature, 1984, for HM Commentary, 1984, 2nd feature, 1977, 5 awards 2002; 1st pl. award for edn. writing Pacific Coast Press Club, 1982, 2d column award Nat. Soc. Newspaper Columnists, 1995, 96, Herb Caen Meml. award, 2000, 2d col., 2001, 3rd col. award Nat. Fed. Press Women, 2d feature, 2001, 1996, 3rd Feature Story award, 1995, 3rd Feature award, 1995, Outstanding adviser coll. pub., 1996, 99, 2001, 2002, 1st journalism res award, 1997, 2002, 2nd journalism res. award, 1999, 2nd non-fiction book award, 1996, 1st nonfiction book award, 2002, 3rd chpt. in book award, 1999; 1st col. award Pa. Press Club, 1996, 98, 99, 2002, 2nd col. award, 1995, 97, 2000, 2003, 1st feature award, 1995, 96, 2nd feature award, 1997, 2002, 1st, 2002, HM social issues award, 1996, 1st, 2002, 2003, 2nd, 2001, 3rd profile award, 1999, 2nd profile award, 2000, 2nd spl. series award, 1999, 2000, 2nd edn. award, 1996, 1st govt./politics, 2003; HM bus. award, 1996, HM environ. award, 1995, 1st radio talk show award, 1998, 99, 3rd brochure award, 2000, 2nd col. award Pa. Womens Press Assn., 1998, 3rd col. award, 1997, HM, 2002; 1st opinion award Internat. Assn. Bus. Communicators, 1994, 2nd Opinion award, 1999, 2nd media kits award, 1997, San Diego State (Calif.) U. Points of Light award, 1997, 2nd articles award Pennwriters, 1998, Creative Arts award, Bloomsburg (Pa.) U. Dean's Salute to Excellence, 2002, Civil Liberties award ACLU, 1998, Spl. Merit award Lowe Syndrome Soc., 2001. Mem. Soc. Profl. Journalists (pres. Keystone State profl. chpt. 1991-98, dep. regional dir. 1995-97, Dir.'s award 1993, 2d place award for column 1993, 94, 1st pl. sports 1995, HM commentary 1996, 97, 99, 2nd commentary, 1995, 2000, Nat. Freedom Info. award 1994), Pa. Journalism Educators (pres. 1992-94), Pa. Women's Press Assn. (v.p. 2001-, award 2002), Nat. Soc. Newspaper Columnists, Nat. Writers Union, Newspaper Guild, Author's Guild, Pa. Press Club (Social Issues Reporting award, Govt. Reporting award, Arts and Enterainment Reporting award, Column and General Reporting 2d pl. award, Column and Humor 2d pl. award), Phi Kappa Phi, Kappa Tau Alpha, Alpha Kappa Delta. Jewish. Avocation: collecting political buttons and campaign items. Office: Bloomsburg U 400 E 2nd St BCH # 106 Bloomsburg PA 17815 E-mail: brasch@bloomu.edu.

BRASFIELD, EVANS BOOKER, lawyer; b. Richmond, Va., Sept. 21, 1932; s. George Frederick and Minna (Booker) B.; children: Evans Booker, John McDonald, Elizabeth Lee; m. Anne Dobbins Heilig, June 28, 1980; stepchildren: J. Randall Heilig, Mollie P. Heilig. BA, U. Va., 1954, LLB, 1959. Bar: Va. 1959. Pvt. practice, Richmond; ptnr. Hunton & Williams, Richmond, 1965-99; gen. counsel Va. Electric & Power Co., Richmond, 1976-94, Dominion Resources, 1983-91. Pres. Children's Home Soc. Va., 1972-73, bd. dirs., 1965-91; chmn. Cen. Va. Ednl. TV Corp., 1978-84, bd. dirs., 1965—; bd. dirs. Richmond Cmty. Action Program, 1974-76, Richmond Area Cmty. Coun., 1973-75, Big Bros. Richmond, 1970-75, Sheltering Arms Hosp., 2001--. With USNR, 1954-56. Fellow Am. Bar Found., Va. Law Found.; mem. ABA (chmn. sect. pub. utility law 1996-97), Va. Bar Assn. (exec. com. 1981-86, pres. 1985), Richmond Bar Assn.,, Va. State Bar, Phi Beta Kappa (pres. Richmond chpt. 1982-83). Clubs: Country of Va., Commonwealth, (Richmond). Presbyterian. Home: 2 Ampthill Rd Richmond VA 23226-2233

BRASHEAR, CHARLES ROSS, English educator, retired, writer; b. Martin County, Tex., Dec. 11, 1930; s. George A. and Sallie Louise (Whitaker) B.; m. Kerstin Birgitta Brorson, June 13, 1959 (div. July 7, 1987); children: Erik Ross, Bart Alan, Per Whitaker; m. L. Lenore Arnew Shepherd, Jan. 1, 2000. BA, U. Calif., Berkeley, 1956; MA, San Francisco State U., 1960; PhD, U. Denver, 1962. Cert. secondary tchr., Calif. Tchr. Maxwell (Calif.) Union H.S., 1957-59; Fulbright lectr. in Am. philology Royal U. Stockholm, 1962-65; asst. prof. English, U. Mich., Ann Arbor, 1965-68; prof. English, San Diego State U., 1968-92, prof. emeritus, 1992—. Lectr. in field. Author: (novel) Killing Cynthia Ann, 1999 (2d pl. award San Diego Book Awards 1999), Elements of Creativity, 2001, Elements of Dialog, Dialect, and Conversational Style, 2001, Elements of the Novel, 2001, A Writer's Toolkit-Elements of Writing Poems, Essays, Stories, 2001, Elements of Form and Style in Expository Essays, 2001, and others; author (textbook) Creative Writing: Fiction Drama, Poetry, the Essay, 1968, The Structure of Essays, 1973; author short stories; contbr. articles to profl. jours. Coll. rep., bd. dirs. Greater San Diego Coun. Tchrs. of English, 1971-75; mem. statewide legis. com. Calif. Assn. Tchrs. of English, San Diego and Sacramento, 1973-75. Cpl. U.S. Army, 1953-55. Mem.: Writers' League Tex., Western Writers Am., WordCraft Circle of Native Am. Writers (sec. 1998—99), Calif. Writers' Club. Avocations: genealogy, travel, reading. Home: 1718 Arroyo Sierra Cir Santa Rosa CA 95405 E-mail: brashear@mail.sdsu.edu.

BRASHEAR, JAMES THOMAS, lawyer; b. Cleve., Dec. 17, 1934; s. Charles O'Niel and Jessi Lee (Drugoo) B.; m. Carol Ann Rowely, Jan. 1, 1956 (div. Sept. 1974); children: Barbara Alice, John Thomas; m. Lori Joan Becker, Mar. 7, 1989. Student, El Camino Coll., Torrance, 1977-78; BA, Calif. State U., Dominguez Hills, 1980; JD, Loyola U., 1984. Bar: Calif., 1989. Dep. pub. defender, Madera, Calif., 1990-92; supr. atty. Fresno (Calif.) Juvenile Ct. Office, Fresno, Calif., 1992-94; asst. chief def. atty. Fresno, Calif., 1993-96; trial atty. Superior Ct., Fresno, 1994-95; supr. atty. Juvenile Hall, Fresno, 1996; chief def. atty. Alt. Def. Office, Fresno, 197-99; Madera alt. John A. Barker & Assocs., Madera, 1999—2000, dep. pub. def., 2000—. Mem. Christian Businessmen'c Com., Nat. Rifle Assn. (life), Calif. Bar Assn., Fresno County Bar Assn., Madera County Bar Assn. Republican. Avocations: history, model trains, oil painting, gardening. Office: 210 S D St Madera CA 93638-3735

BRASHEAR, JERRY PAUL, management consultant; b. Oklahoma City, July 11, 1945; s. Henry Paul and Bonnie Genung Brashear; m. Judith Caroline Brinkley, Dec. 29, 1967 (div. 1976); children: Judith Corbin, Regan Pretlow; m. Pamela Ann Newton, Aug. 25, 1979. AB magna cum laude, Princeton U., 1967; MBA, Harvard U., 1969; PhD in Urban, Technol. & Environ. Planning, U. Mich., 1975. Project mgr. Cmty. Sys. Found., Ann Arbor, Mich., 1969—72, Riverside Rsch. Inst., N.Y.C., 1972-75; v.p. Lewin & Assocs., Inc., Washington, 1975-87, bd. dirs., 1980-87; sr. v.p. ICF Kaiser Internat., Inc., Fairfax, Va., 1987-96; mng. dir. The Brashear Group LLC, Potomac, Md., 1996—; provisional dir. Ctr. for Petroleum Asset Risk Mgmt. U. Tex., Austin, 2002—. Bd. dirs., mem. exec. com. ICF Resources, Inc., Fairfax, 1987-96. Mem. editl. bd. Jour. Petroleum Scis. and Engring., 1987-91. Usher Cedar Lane Unitarian Universalist Ch., Bethesda, Md., 1998—. Mem. Soc. Petroleum Engrs. (disting. lectr.), Am. Assn. Petroleum Geologists, Internat. Assn. for Energy Econs., Phi Beta Kappa. Avocations: movies, symphony. Office: The Brashear Group LLC 10121 Donegal Ct Potomac MD 20854-4340 E-mail: jpb@brashear-group.com.

BRASHEAR, WILLIAM RONALD, lawyer, writer; b. Royal Oak, Mich., Oct. 8, 1932; s. William Wilson and Theresa Elizabeth (Briggi) B.; m. Lydia Mary Rothman Brashear, Jan. 1961 (dec. Apr. 1988); children: Ruth Margot, Lydia Louise. BA, U. Mich., Ann Arbor, 1953, MA, JD, U. Mich., Ann Arbor, 1956; MA, Princeton U., N.J., 1958, PhD, 1959. Bar: Mich., 1957, U.S. Dist. Ct. (so. dist.) Mich. 1957, U.S. Ct. Appeals (6th cir.) 1973, U.S. Supreme Ct., 1977. Ptnr. Brashear, Tangora & Spence, Livonia, Mich., 1958—; adj. lectr., English Wayne State U., Detroit, 1959-71. Author: The Living Will, 1969, The Gorgon's Head, 1977, The Desolation of Reality, 1995; contbr. articles to profl. jours. Fellow Mich. State Bar Found.; mem. 6th Cir. Judges' Conf. (life).

BRASHEARS, SUMNER, funeral director; b. Paris, Ark., Dec. 11, 1949; s. Felix Sumner and Mary Jo (Boomer) B.; m. Jackie Sue Taylor, Feb. 11, 1988; children: Stacy K. Easterling, Gara M. Mosier. Diploma, Dallas Inst. Mortuary Sci., 1971; AS, N.Ark. C.C., 1976; BS, U. of the State of N.Y., Albany, 1980. Lic. funeral dir. and embalmer, Ark., cert. funeral svc. practitioneer Acad. Profl. Funeral Svc. Practice. Exec. v.p. Brashears Funeral Home, Inc., Huntsville, Ark., 1971-91, pres., CEO, 1991—. Bd. dirs. Selected Funeral and Life Ins. Co., Hot Springs, Ark., chmn. bd. dirs., 1996—; vice chmn. bd. Selected Fin. Svc. Corp., Hot Springs, 1982—. Alderman Huntsville City Coun., 1974-88; pres. Ark. State Bd. Embalmers and Funeral Dirs., 1986-94; commr. Huntsville Water and Sewer Commn., 1976—. Named Funeral Dir. of Yr., Morticians of the S.W., 1987. Mem. Nat. Funeral Dirs. Assn. (pres. 1995), Ark. Funeral Dirs. Assn. (pres. 1987), Masons (life, master), Kiwanis Club of Huntsville (life, pres. 1981), Western Ark. Scottish Rite Bodies (33d degree, past comdr.), York Rite (grand high priest 1985, grand master 1994). Democrat. Presbyterian.

BRASHER, EARLENE D. music educator, church organist; b. Albertville, Alabama, May 2, 1932; d. David Frank and Luna (Pearson) Decker; m. Francis Eugene Brasher, 1956 (div. 1976); children: Julia Brasher Thorn, Celia Kay(dec.). MusB, Alabama Coll., 1952; MusM in Sacred Music, New Orleans Seminary, 1959; MusM, Ga. State U., 1981; PhD, U. So. Miss., 1988. Choral dir. Tuscaloosa Sr. H.S., Tuscaloosa, Ala., 1953—54; organist First Bapt. Ch., Columbia, SC, 1954—56; music tchr. Whitesburg Elem. and Jr. H.S., Huntsville, Ala., 1965—69; music supr. Thomasville City Sch., Thomasville, Ga., 1969—70; music resource tchr. New Orleans Pub. Sch., New Orleans, 1970—79; elem. music specialist DeKalb County Sch. Sys., Decatur, Ga., 1979—2001; organist Briarcliff Bapt. Ch., Atlanta, 1979—2002; coord. of choral music DeKalb County Sch. Sys., Decatur, Ga., 1989—2002. Edn. adv. bd. Clayton State U., Morrow, Ga., 1990—; adv. bd. Atlanta Boy Choir, Atlanta, 1995—, Young Singers of Callanwolde, Atlanta, 1989—2002. Author: (dissertation) The Contributions of Robert Shaw and the Atlanta Symphony Orch., 1988, (periodical) To the Ednl. Cultural Climate of Atlanta. Mem. Atlanta Symphony Orch. Chorus, Atlanta, 1979—96. Recipient Life Time Achievement Award, Ga. Music Educators Assn., 2001, Mary Clark Award, Decatur Civic Chorus, 2003, Student Govt. Assn., Alabama Coll., 1951—52, Miss Ala Coll., 1952. Mem.: Music Educators Nat. Conf., Am. Choral Dir. Assn, Alpha Delta Kappa. Presbyterian. Achievements include listed in Who's Who in Am. Colleges and U., 1952; listed in Two Thousand Notable Am. Women, 1992; listed in The World Who's Who of Women, 1992. Home: 3910 Stonbriar Ct Duluth GA 30097 E-mail: earlenebrasher@aol.com.

BRASHER, GEORGE WALTER, physician, consultant; b. Jackson, Tenn., Dec. 7, 1936; s. George W. and Verla S. Brasher; m. Martha S. Brasher, Dec. 23, 1960; children: Suzanne Cheshier, George Brasher, John Brasher, David Brasher. BA, Lambuth U., 1959; MD, U. Tenn., 1961. Diplomate Am. Bd. Allergy and Immunology, Am. Bd. Pediatrics. Cons. Scott & White Clinic & Hosp., Temple, Tex., 1966—. Dir. Allergy and Immunology Scott & White Clinic and Hosp., Temple. Tex., 1975—; prof. Medicine and Pediatrics Tex. A&M U. Coll. of Medicine, Temple, Tex., 1977—. Contbr. articles to profl. jours. Fellow Am. Acad. Allergy and Immunology, Am. Acad. Pediatrics, Am. Coll. Allergy and Immunology; mem. AMA, Tex. Med. Assn., Bell County Med. Soc., Tex. Allergy Soc. Avocations: civil war history, amateur radio. Office: Scott & White Clinic & Hosp 2401 S 31st St Temple TX 76508-0001

BRASIER, ALLAN R. medical educator; BA in Biomed. Engring., U. Calif., San Diego, 1979; MD, U. Calif., San Francisco, 1983. Diplomate Am. Bd. Internal Medicine. Intern, med. resident Brigham & Women's Hosp., Boston, 1983—86; endocrinology/ metabolism fellow Mass. Gen. Hosp., Boston, 1986—87, clin. & rsch. fellow dept. molecular endocrinology, 1987—89, rsch. assoc. Howard Hughes Med. Inst., 1988—91; assoc. prof. medicine Sealy Ctr. Molecular Sci. U. Tex. Med. Br., Galveston, 1991—98, prof., 1998—, sr. scientist, 1996. Contbr. articles to profl. jours. Recipient Acad. Excellence award, U. Calif. San Francisco Alumni Faculty Assn., 1993, Established Investigator award, Am. Heart Assn., 1995. Mem.: Alpha Omega Alpha, Phi Beta Kappa. Office: U Tex Med Br Sealy Ctr Molecular Sci S104 Med Rsch Bldg Galveston TX 77555-0001

BRASKET, CURT JUSTIN, systems analyst, chess player; b. Tracy, Minn., Dec. 7, 1932; s. Curt John and Mary Ann (Jenniges) B.; m. Rita Ann Bronk, July 20, 1963; children: Monica, Barbara, Rebecca. Student, U. Minn., 1950-51; BA in Math, St. John's U., Collegeville, Minn., 1954. Systems analyst Unisys (Sperry, Univac), St. Paul, 1957-88. Served with AUS, 1955-57. Mem. U.S. Chess Fedn. (life master, life mem.), Internat. Chess Fedn. (master 1983—) Achievements include being U.S. Chess master, 1953—; U.S. jr. champion, 1952; 16 times Minn. champion, 4 times North Central champion. Home: 220 Spring Valley Dr Minneapolis MN 55420-5540

BRASLOW, DEAN GERALD, lawyer; b. Mt. Vernon, NY, Mar. 10, 1934; s. Samuel and Evelyn Rose (Adler) Braslow; m. Ingrid Smedresman, Mar. 19, 1964; children: Nina, Michele, Kenneth. BA, Yale Coll., 1955; JD, Columbia U., 1961. Bar: NY 1961, US Dist. Ct. (so. and ea. dist.)/NY 1962, Ariz. 1989. Dep. asst. atty. gen. State of NY, 1961—63; asst. atty. gen., 1963; legal asst. Surrogate's Ct., Westchester County, NY, 1963—66; assoc. Parker, Duryee, Rosoff & Haft, NYC, 1966—68, Parker, Duryee, Zunino, Malone & Carter, NYC, 1966—68; ptnr. Parker, Duryee, Rosoff & Haft, NYC, 1969—. Contbr. articles. Served U.S. Army, 1956—58. Fellow Am. Coll. Trust and Estate Counsel, Am. Coll. Trust and Estate Counsel. Mem.: Westchester Women's Bar Assn., NYC Bar Assn., White Plains Bar Assn., Westchester County Bar Assn., State Bar Ariz., NY Bar Assn., White Plains Dem. party, Estate Planning Council NYC, Estate Planning Council Westchester, Yale. Jewish. Office: Parker Duryee Rosoff & Haft 529 5th Ave New York NY 10017-4608

BRASS, DICK, information technology executive; m. Regina Brass. Student, Cornell U. Reporter N.Y. Post, The Wall St. Jour., WNBC-TV; features editor The Daily News, N.Y.C.; founder Gen. Info. Inc.; various positions Oracle Corp.; corp. v.p. tech. devel. Microsoft, Redmond, Wash., 1997—. Dir. electronic pub. Wang. Achievements include development of first dictionary based spelling checker software; first electronic thesaurus-The Random House Thesaurus, 1981. Office: One Microsoft Way Redmond WA 98052-6399

BRASSARD, VIRGINIA, educator; b. Clinton, Mass., Sept. 13, 1924; d. Patrick Francis and Anne Elizabeth (McIlveen) Hynes; m. Roland Ronald Brassard, Dec. 26, 1948; children: Anne Brassard Wharen (dec.), Patricia Brassard Small. BS, U. Mass., Boston, 1945; student, R.I. Coll., 1959, 61. Cert. tchr., Mass., R.I. Tchr. City of Boston, 1945-47; asst. to curator Mus. R.I. Sch. Design, Providence, 1947-49; tchr. City of Pawtucket, R.I., 1957-67; treas. Brassard & Co., Inc., 1972-85, ret.; internat. tchr. in San Salvador, Guatemala, Uruguay, Morocco Internat. Exec. Svcs. Corps, Stamford, Conn., 1985-96. Mem. Doric Dames State House, Boston, 1975-90. Mem. United Ostomy Assn. (treas. 1990—, membership chair 1999—), VFW Aux., KC Aux. (function chair 1999, KC aux. pres. 2000). Roman Catholic. Avocations: genealogy, world travel. Home: 3360 Sheffield Cir Sarasota FL 34239-6716 E-mail: VBrassard@aol.com.

BRASSINGTON, GLENN SIDNEY, psychologist, educator; BA in Humanities, St. Joseph's Coll., 1985; MA in Psychology, San Jose (Calif.) State U., 1993; PhD in Psychology, U. of Mo., 2000. Contbr. articles to profl. jours. Office: Sonoma State University 1801 E Cotati Ave Rohnert Park CA 94306

BRASUNAS, ANTON DE SALES, retired metallurgical engineering educator; b. Elizabeth, N.J., Mar. 11, 1919; s. Anthony J. and Stefana (Žekus) B.; m. Ellen Lydia Wirth, Nov. 16, 1946; children: James Anton, Kay Ellen, Anne Elizabeth. BS, Antioch Coll., Yellow Springs, Ohio, 1943; MS, Ohio State U., 1946; Sc.D., M.I.T., 1950. Cert. advanced metric specialist. Research engr. Battelle Meml. Inst., Columbus, Ohio, 1943-46; research metallurgist Oak Ridge Nat. Lab., 1950-53; ret. Assoc. prof. metallurgy U. Tenn., Knoxville, 1953-55; dir. cdn. ASM Internat. (formerly Am. Soc. Metals), Metals Park, Ohio, 1955-64; mem. faculty U. Mo., Rolla, St. Louis, 1964-84, assoc. dean engr., prof. metall. engrng., 1964-84, prof. emeritus, 1984-2001; cons. in field; guest lectr. U. Antioquia, Colombia, 1986. Author, editor in field. Recipient Alumni award U. Mo., Rolla, 1971, Fullbright award, 1986. Fellow Am. Soc. Metals, U.S. Metric Assn. (nat. sec. 1988-92, chmn. Cert. Metrication Specialist Bd. 1992-96); mem. Alpha Sigma Mu (pres. 1968-69). Avocations: sports, tennis. Home: 8030 Daytona Dr Saint Louis MO 63105-2510

BRASWELL, EDWIN MAURICE, JR., lawyer; b. Fayetteville, N.C., Mar. 6, 1952; s. Edwin Maurice Sr. and Ruth (Cox) B.; children: Edwin Maurice III, Anna Elizabeth. BSBA, U. N.C., 1973; JD cum laude, N.C. Cen. U., 1978. Bar: N.C. 1978, U.S. Dist. Ct. (ea. dist.) N.C. 1978, U.S. Ct. Appeals (4th cir.) 1985. Law clk. to hon. judge Burley Mitchell N.C. Ct. of Appeals, Raleigh, 1978-79; asst. dist. atty. 8th Prosecuting Dist., Kinston, N.C., 1979-82; ptnr. Wallace, Morris & Barwick, P.A., Kinston, 1982—. Vice pres. legis. affairs com. Lenoir County C. of C., Kinston, 1987-88; mem. coun. Village Walnut Creek, 2003—. Mem. N.C. Assn. Def. Attys., Def. Rsch. Inst., 8th Dist. Bar Assn. (pres. 1988-89), Lenoir County Bar Assn. (pres. 1985). Methodist. Avocations: boating, tennis. Home: 120 Walnut Creek Dr Goldsboro NC 27534-8942 Office: Wallace Morris & Barwick PA PO Box 3557 Kinston NC 28502-3557 E-mail: edbraswell@justice.com.

BRASWELL, LOUIS ERSKINE, lawyer; b. Selma, Ala., Mar. 11, 1937; s. Erskine McKinley and Leota (Grubb) B.; m. Anne, June 1, 1985 (dec. Feb. 20, 1996); children by previous marriage: Margaret, Anne, Helen. AB, Birmingham So. Coll., 1959; JD, Harvard U., 1962. Bar: Ala. bar 1962. Assoc. firm Hand, Arendall, Bedsole, Greaves & Johnston, Mobile, Ala., 1963-68; ptnr. Hand Arendall LLC, Mobile, 1968—. Participant Nat. Conf. on Discovery Reform, U. Tex. Law Sch., 1982; program participant 11th Cir. Jud. Conf., 1984, others Bd. dirs. Children's Dental Clinic, Mobile, 1965-75; past pres. Friends of Mobile Public Library; bd. dirs. Jr. Achievement of Mobile; past pres. YMCA Rockies Alumni Assn.; bd. dirs. Kidney Found. South Ala., 1978-85, Ecumenical Ministries, Inc., 2001-. With U.S. Army, 1962-63. Mem. ABA, Am. Law Inst., Ala. Law Inst., Ala. Bar Assn., Ala. Def. Lawyers Assn., Athelstan Club, Rotary Internat., Point Clear Rotary Club (bd. dirs. 1997-2000, pres. 1998-99). Presbyterian. Home: 107 Keifer Ave Fairhope AL 36532 Office: PO Box 123 Mobile AL 36601-0123

BRASWELL, PAULA ANN, artist; b. Decatur, Ala., May 6, 1955; d. Andrew Leon and Dorothy Faye (Fretwell) B.; m. Roger Armand Robichaud, June 22, 1990. BA, Jacksonville State U., 1978; postgrad., New Orleans Acad. Fine Arts, 1987, U. New Orleans, 1987-88; MFA, Fla. State U., 1990. Instr. art Butler Sch., Marrero, La., 1984, Fla. Keys Coll., Tavernier, 1985; grad. instr. Fla. State U., Tallahassee, 1989-90; adj. prof. Calhoun Coll., Decatur, Ala., 1990, Chattanooga State Coll., 1991, Cleveland (Tenn.) State Coll., 1991; studio artist Knoxville, Tenn., 1991-96, Toronto, Ont., Can., 1996—. One-man shows include Propeller Gallery, 2001, Loop Gallery, Toronto, 2002—03, Windsor (Ont.) Gallery Art, 2002, Kabat Wrobel Gallery, Toronto, 2003, WARC Gallery, Toronto, 2003, exhibited in group shows at Contemporary Arts Ctr., New Orleans, 1992, Knoxville (Tenn.) Mus. Art, 1994—95, Combined Talents Fla. Nat., 1995, Transforming Tradition, 1996, New American Talent, 1996, ARC Gallery, 1997, Fla. State U., Mus. of the Ams., Washington, 1997, Mus. of the Ams., 1997, Mus. of Fine Arts, 1998, FSU Mus., 1998, Propeller Gallery, Toronto, 2000—02, WARC Gallery, 2000, 2003, Sculpture Soc. Can., 2000—01, Gallery 121, Toronto, 2000, Soul Ecology Exhibit, 2000, Propeller Ctr. for the Visual Arts, 2000—01, Sculpture Soc. Gallery, 2001, John B. Aird Gallery, 2001, John B. Aird Gallery traveling exhibit, 2003. Grantee, Nat. Endowment Arts, 1991, Ont. Arts Coun., 1997, 2000, 2001—02, 2003, Can. Coun., 2002, Can. Coun. Individual Arts, 2003. Mem. AAUW, NOW, Women's Caucus for Arts (exhibitor), Knoxville Mus. Art (exhibitor), Knoxville Arts Coun. (exhibitor), Coll. Art Assn., Contemporary Arts Ctr. (exhibitor), People for Protection of Animals, Humane Soc. U.S. Democrat. Mem. Ch. of Christ. Avocations: gardening, environmental concerns, animal care, skiing, camping. Address: 806 Huron Terr Kincardine ON Canada N2Z 2Y1 E-mail: paulabrasw@aol.com.

BRASWELL, RONALD LEE, music educator, tenor; b. Goldsboro, N.C., July 10, 1950; s. Ralph Lee and Etta Edwards Braswell. BS, Old Dominion U., 1973, MS, 1991. Music tchr., choral dir. Dunbar Sch., Newport News, Va., 1974—80, Larrymore Elem., Norfolk, Va., 1981—86; choral dir. Lake Taylor Middle, Norfolk, 1986—98; music tchr., choral dir. Ghent Sch., Norfolk, 1998—. Tenor soloist, choir dir. St. Andrews Episcopal/Larchmont Meth., Norfolk, 1970—; soloist Hampton Roads Men's Chorus, Norfolk, 1999—; music tchr. Summer Gifted, Norfolk, 1982—95; instr. Old Dominion U., Norfolk, 1995—97; choral dir. DePaul Hosp. Choir/Nurses Choir, Norfolk, 1985—95. Contbr. articles to profl. jours. Named Citizen of the Yr., Lafayette/Winona Civil League, Norfolk, 1990, 1994. Mem.: Norfolk Fedn. Tchrs. (v.p. 1996—), Va. Choral Dirs. Assn. (treas., v.p., pres. 1992—2000), Va. Music Educators Assn. (exec. bd. 1988—2000). Roman Catholic. Avocations: crafts, swimming, rollerblading, reading. Home: 1604 Lafayette Blvd Norfolk VA 23509

BRATCHER, JUANITA, journalist; b. Columbus, Ga. d. Benjamin Pickens and Tommie (English) Forte; m. Neal Archie Bratcher; children: Pamela, Angela, Sonya, Neal Jr. AA, Olive Harvey Coll.; BA in Journalism, Columbia Coll., 1976. News reporter South End Rev., Chgo., Roseland Rev., Chgo., Chgo. Defender; editor, publ. Southeast Alliance, Chgo., Copyline Mag., Chgo., 1990—. Bd. dirs. Provident Found.; host cable talk show One on One; host internet talk show PCC Network. Author: Harold: The Making of a Big City Mayor, 1993, I Cry for a People: In Their Struggle for Justice, 1996, Crooked Curves: The Last of the Red Hot Mamas, 1999, A Celebration of Love, 2001, Love Me One More Time, 2001, The Best Poems and Poets of 2001, The Best Poems and Poets of 2002, Chasing the Good Times, 2003; works appear in Nat. Libr. of Poetry Best Poems of 1997, A Celebration of Poets, 1998, The Best Poems and Poets of 2001, Under a Quick Silver Moon, 2002, recordings include Too Many Memories, 1996, Everything But Love, 1996, I'm Here for You, 1997, You've Been Gone Too Long, 1997, God Can Ease the Pain, 1999, Glorious Day in Heaven, 1999, America, The Land of Freedom, 1999, Freedom, Our Birthright, 1999, That Twinkle In Your Eyes, 2001, Overdose of Love, 2001, CD recordings include God Can Ease the Pain, 1999, A Glorious Day in Heaven, 1999, The Sound of Poetry, album recordings include America, The Land of Freedom, 1999, Freedom, Our Birthright, 1999, Everything But Love, 2001, That Twinkle in Your Eyes, 2001, An Overdose of Love, 2001, A Toast To Christmas, 2001, Can't Make It Without Him, 2001, CD recordings include The Sound of Poetry, 2002, mem. editl. com. One City, Chgo. Coun. Urban Affairs, guest panelist, guest host for numerous TV and radio programs. Mem. Regional Aux. Coun. Atlas Ctr.; press aide Cook County bd. campaign John S. Stroger; press aide Alderman Lorraine Dixon. Recipient certs. of merit Chgo. Pub. Schs., everyday hero award Ill. Sec. State George Ryan, 1993, Kizzy award The Kizzy Found., 1983, Probation Challenge Portraits of Achievers award, 1983, 87, Editor's Choice award (6) Nat. Libr. Poetry, svc. award Boy Scouts Am., U.S. Dept. Edn. Region V, Outstanding Support of Human Rights award Ill. Dept. Human Rights, 1985, Cmty. Svc. award Ada Park Adv. Coun., 1990, exemplary civic svc. award Dorcas Care Ctr., 1988, Excellence in Achievement award Zeta Phi Beta, Oustanding Svc. in Media and Telecomm. award Delta Sigma Theta, press award Chgo. and No. Dist. Assn. of Club Women, Inc., Par Excellence Journalism award Coalition for United Cmty. Action, 1987, Dedicated Svc. to Cmty. award Firefighters for Justice and Equality, 1987, The Good Spirit of Excellence award, 2000, From Whence We Came award, Allstate Ins., 2002.; named black bus. woman of yr. Parkway Cmty. House, Chgo., 1993; inductee Internat. Poetry Hall of Fame, Probation Challenge's Hall of Fame, 1991. Mem. Internat. Soc. Poets. Baptist. Home: 9026 S Cregier Ave Chicago IL 60617-3533 Fax: 773-375-7461. E-mail: JuanitaBratcher@yahoo.com., Copyfine.Magazine@oneononetelevision.com.

BRATER, D. CRAIG, dean, educator; m. Stephanie Brater; 1 child, Aimee. Postgrad. tng., Duke U., U. Calif. Med. Ctr.; grad., Duke U., 1971; postgrad. tng., U. Calif. Med. Ctr. Mem. faculty Southwestern Med. Sch.; dir. divsn. clin. pharmacology Ind. U. Sch. Medicine, chmn. dept. medicine, John B. Hickam prof. medicine, prof. pharmacology and toxicology, Walter J. Daly prof., 2001—, dean, 2001—. Pres. U.S. Pharmacopoeia. Office: Ind U Sch Medicine 1120 W South Dr Fesler Hall Indianapolis IN 46202-5114

BRATT, HERBERT SIDNEY, lawyer; b. Milw., Sept. 8, 1931; s. Ishmael and Freda (Nelson) B.; m. Rosalee Bender, Dec. 22, 1957; children: Jay, Annie, Jennifer. BS, U. Wis., 1953; JD, Yale U., 1956. Bar: Wis. 1956, N.Y. 1981. Assoc. M.J. Levin, Milw., 1956-61; ptnr. Bratt & Shapiro, Milw., 1961-64, Zubrensky, Padden, Graf & Bratt, Milw., 1964-80, Laikin, Bratt & Laikin, Milw., 1980-81; pvt. practice Milw., 1981-91; ptnr. Churchill, Duback & Smith, Milw., 1991-94; pvt. practice Milw., 1994—. Chpt. 7 panel trustee U.S. Trustee's Office for Ea. Dist. Wis., Milw., 1984-90. Trustee, Congregation Sinai, Milw., 1972-86, pres., 1979-81. Recipient William Gorham Rice Civil Liberties award Wis. Civil Liberties Union, 1968. Mem. ABA, Am. Judicature Soc., State Bar Wis., N.Y. Bar Assn., Milw. Bar Assn. Avocation: running. Home: 1610 N Prospect Ave Apt 201 Milwaukee WI 53202-2402 Office: 735 N Water St Ste 704 Milwaukee WI 53202-4104

BRATT, NICHOLAS, investment management and research company executive; b. Gerrards Cross, Eng., June 6, 1948; came to U.S., 1976; s. Guy Maurice and Francoise Nelly (Girardet) B.; m. Kuniko Matsui, Aug. 10, 1976; 1 child, Emi Margaret Matsui. Degree in Politics and Econs., Oxford U., 1970; MIA, Columbia U., 1972. Rsch. analyst Morgan Grenfell & Co. Ltd., London, 1972-75; portfolio mgr. Morgan Grenfell S.A., Geneva, 1976, Scudder, Stevens & Clark, N.Y.C., 1976—2002, mng. dir., 1984—, Deutsche Asset Mgmt., N.Y.C., 2002—03; portfolio mgr. Lazard Asset Mgmt. LLC, 2003—. Pres. Scudder Internat. Fund, N.Y.C., 1982, Korea Fund, N.Y.C., 1984-2003, Scudder New Asia Fund, N.Y.C., 1987-2003, Brazil Fund, N.Y.C., 1988-2003, Scudder New Europe Fund, N.Y.C., 1990, Argentina Fund, N.Y.C., 1991-98, First Iberian Fund, N.Y.C., 1991-98, Scudder Greater Europe Fund, 1994—. Mem. N.Y. Assn. for Fgn. Investment (chmn. 1978-80), Japan Soc., Korea Soc. (bd. dirs.). Avocations: mountain climbing, skiing, tennis, paddle tennis, sailing, golf. E-mail: nicholas.bratt@db.com.

BRATTEN, WILLIAM P. music educator; b. Bklyn, Dec. 7, 1966; s. William G. and Dolores M. (Jalsevac) Bratten. B in music, Wilkes U., 1995. Cert. Teaching (secondary) Penn., NJ. Assoc. Roxbury HS, NJ, 1995—. Guest conductor Wilkes U., Wilkes Barre, Pa., 1996, NJSMA Region 1 J. Band, NJ, 2000; guest conductor, lectr. Wilkes U., 2002; bd. of dir. Roxbury HS Band Patron Assn., 1995—. Composer: (ensemble piece) Aggressions, 1994. Recipient Presser Music award, Wilkes U., Theodore Presser Co., 1995. Mem.: Internat. Assn. of Jazz Educators, NJ Edn. Assn., Music Educators Nat. Conf. Roman Catholic. Achievements include selected to perform at Avery Fisher Hall in Lincoln Ctr. N.Y.C. Avocation: baseball coach, player and manager. Home: 78 Overlook Dr Hackettstown NJ 07840

BRATTON, IDA FRANK, retired secondary school educator; b. Glasgow, Ky., Aug. 31, 1933; d. Edmund Bates and Robbie Davis (Hume) Button; m. Robert Franklin Bratton, June 20, 1954; 1 child, Timothy Andrew. BA, Western Ky. U., 1959, MA, 1962. Cert. secondary tchr., Ky. Tchr. math. and sci. Gottschalk Jr. H.S., Louisville, 1959-65; tchr. math. Iroquois H.S., Louisville, 1965-79; tchr. Waggener H.S., Louisville, 1979-2000, chair dept. math., 2000, ret., 2000. Mem. NEA, AAUW, Ky. Edn. Assn., Jefferson County Tchrs. Assn. Democrat. Methodist. Avocations: travel, needle crafts. Home: 304 Paddington Ct Louisville KY 40222-5541 Office: Waggener High Sch 330 S Hubbards Ln Louisville KY 40207-4099

BRATTON, JAMES HENRY, JR., lawyer; b. Pulaski, Tenn., Oct. 9, 1931; s. James Henry and Mabel (Shelley) B.; m. Alleen Sharp Davis, Oct. 15, 1960; children: Susan Shelley McGonigle, James Henry III, Margaret Alleen Schilling. BA optime merens, U. South, 1952; BA, Oxford (Eng.) U., 1954, MA, 1978; LL.B., Yale U., 1956. Bar: Tenn. 1956, Ga. 1957. With antitrust div. Dept. Justice, summer 1955; since practiced in Atlanta; sr. ptnr. firm Smith, Gambrell & Russell. Vis. lectr. U. Ga. Law Sch., 1967; adj. prof. law Emory U., 1984— Editor Yale Law Jour.; contbr. articles to profl. jours. Mem. Gov.'s Citizens Adv. Council on Environ. Affairs, 1970-74; trustee Trust Fund for Sibley Park, Ga. chpt. Multiple Sclerosis Soc., U. of the South, 1984-87, 95-98, Pembroke Coll. Found., Peachtree Rd. United Meth. Ch., chmn. bd. trustees; bd. dirs. Soccer in the Streets, Buckhead Christian Ministry, pres., 1996; pres. Peachtree Heights West Civic Assn., 1984-99; co-chmn. Sewanee Parents Council, 1987-88; v.p. Pembroke Coll. Soc. of N.Am.; mem. Williams Parents' Fund, 1984-86; mem. parents adv. coun. Hamilton Coll., 1988-91. Named Alumnus of Yr., Sewanee Club Atlanta, 1990. Fellow Lawyers Found. Ga., Am. Law Inst.; mem. ABA (standing com. on aero. law 1962-84, chmn. 1977-80), Ga. Bar Assn. (founding chmn. environ. law sect. 1970-73), Fed. Bar Assn., Atlanta Bar Assn., Lawyers Club Atlanta, Old Warhorse Lawyers Club, Am. Acad. Polit. and Social Scis., Am. Judicature Soc., Associated Alumni U. of South (v.p. admissions 1993-95, pres. 1995-97), Yale Law Alumni Assn. (exec. com. 1976-79), Phi Beta Kappa, Phi Delta Phi, Pi Gamma Mu, Gridiron. Democrat. Methodist. Home: 63 N Muscogee Ave NW Atlanta GA 30305-3542 Office: 1230 Peachtree St NE Atlanta GA 30309-3592 E-mail: jbratton@sgrlaw.com.

BRATTON, WILLIAM EDWARD, electronics executive, management consultant; b. Dallas, Oct. 25, 1919; s. William E. and Edna (Walker) B.; m. Betty Thume, May 30, 1942; children: Dale, Janet, Donna. AB in Econs., Stanford U., 1940; MBA, Harvard U., 1945. From v.p. to pres. Librascope, Glendale, Calif., 1947-63; v.p., gen. mgr. Ampex, Culver City, Calif., 1963-66; pres. Guidance Tech., Santa Monica, Calif., 1967-68; v.p. electronics div. Gen. Dynamics, San Diego, 1969-72, pres. Theta Cable T.V., Santa Monica, 1974-82; pres., chief exec. officer Stagecoach Properties, Salado, Tex., 1959-99, ret., 1999. Served to lt. (j.g.) USNR, 1944-46. Mem.: El Niguel Country (Laguna, Calif.) (pres. 1978-79). Republican. Episcopalian. Avocations: golf, skindiving.

BRATTON, WILLIAM J. chief of police, former police commissioner; m. Cheryl A. Fiandaca, 1986; 1 child, David. B, B, postgrad., Boston State Coll.; grad. Sr. Execs. and Sr. Exec. Fellows Program, Harvard U.; grad., FBI Nat. Exec. Inst., New Eng. Inst. Law Enforcement Mgmt. Command Program, Police Exec. Rsch. Forum Sr. Mgmt. Inst. for Police. Various positions to exec. supt. Boston Police Dept., 1970-83; chief of police Mass. Bay Transp. Authority, 1983-86; supt. Met. Police Dept., Boston, 1986-90; chief N.Y.C. Transit Police Dept., 1990-92; police commr. City of Boston, 1992-94, City of N.Y., 1994-96; exec. v.p. First Security Consultants, N.Y.C., 1996—98; pres., COO Carco Group Inc, St. James, NY, 1998—2001; chief of police City of Los Angeles, 2002—. Mem. exec. session of policing Kennedy Sch. Govt. Harvard U., 1985-92 mem. policing in 21st century work group Nat. Inst. Justice, Washington. Mem. Internat. Assn. Chiefs of Police (major cities chiefs group), Police Exec. Rsch. Forum (pres. 1994—). Office: Office of the Chief of Police 150 N Los Angeles St Los Angeles CA 90012

BRATTSTROM, BAYARD HOLMES, biology educator; b. Chgo., July 3, 1929; s. Wilber LeRoy and Violet (Holmes) B.; m. Cecile D. Funk, June 15, 1952 (div. May 1975); children: Theodore Allen, David Arthur.; m. Martha Isaacs Marsh, July 8, 1982. BS, San Diego State Coll., 1951; MA, UCLA, 1953, PhD, 1959. Dir. edn. Natural History Mus., San Diego, 1949-51, asst. curator herpetology, 1949-51; assoc. zoology UCLA, 1954-56; research fellow paleoecology Calif. Inst. Tech., Pasadena, 1955; instr. biology Adelphi U., Garden City, N.Y., 1956-60; asst. prof. Calif. State U., Fullerton, 1960-61, assoc. prof., 1961-66, prof., 1966-94, prof. emeritus, 1994—. Co-owner Horned Lizard Ranch, Horned Lizard Press; rschr., author publs. in osteology, ecology, conservation, zoogeography of vertebrates, social behavior; hon. rsch. assoc. herpetology, vertebrate paleontology Los Angeles County Mus., 1961—; pres. Fullerton Youth Mus. and Natural Sci. Ctr., 1962-64, dir., 1962-66; assoc. prof. zoology UCLA, summers 1962-63; vis. prof. zoology Sydney U., Australia, 1978, U. Queensland, Brisbane, Australia, 1984; vis. rschr. James Cook U., Townsville, Australia, 1993-94; ecol. cons. to numerous govtl. agys. and pvt. corps. Co-author: The Talon Digs Deeply Into My Heart, 1974; co-author: (with M.A. Brattstrom) Aussie Slang, 2000. Recipient Disting. Teaching award Calif. State U., Fullerton, 1968, Dean's award for Outstanding Teaching and Rsch., 1992; Am. Philos. Soc. grantee to Mex., 1958, to Panama, 1959; NSF grantee, 1964-66; NSF fellow Monash U., Australia, 1966-67. Fellow AAAS (mem. coun. 1965-90), Herpetological League; mem. Am. Soc. Ichthyologists and Herpetologists (bd. govs. 1962-66, v.p. western div. 1965), Orange County Zool. Soc. (mem. bd. 1962-65, pres. 1962-64), So. Calif. Acad. Sci. (dir. 1964-67), Ecol. Soc. Am., Soc. for Study Evolution, Soc. Systematic Zoology, San Diego Soc. Natural History, Soc. Vertebrate Paleontology, Am. Soc. Mammalogists, Cooper Ornithol. Soc., Am. Ornithol. Soc., Am. Soc. Zoologists, Sigma Xi. Home: Horned Lizard Ranch PO Box 166 Wikieup AZ 85360 *My life and research has been based on an insatiable curiosity about the natural world, especially as seen in the evolutionary adaptations of animals to their environment and their interactions with each other.*

BRATVOLD, THOMAS ERIK, physicist; b. Seattle, July 17, 1968; s. Owen Gerald and Bodil Alma (Petersen) Bratvold; m. Melissa Charlene Finch, June 25, 1994; children: Thomas Erik II, Evan August, Owen Daniel. BS in Physics, Wash. State U., 1993. Health physicist Westhinghouse Hanford Co., Richland, Wash., 1993-96, Fluor Daniel Hanford Co., Richland, 1996-98, mgr., 1999-2000; radiol. control mgr. Duke Engrng. & Svcs. Hanford Co., Richland, 1998-99; sr. rsch. scientist Batelle Meml. Inst., Pacific N.W. Nat. Lab., Richland, 2000—02; radiol. control mgr. Fluor Hanford, Inc., Richland, 2002—. Mem.: Health Physics Soc. (mem. lab accreditation com. Columbia chpt.), Am. Acad. Health Physics. Home: 2965 Sonoran Dr Richland WA 99352-2927 Office: PO Box 1000 Richland WA 99352-1000

BRATZLER, MARY KATHRYN, desktop publisher; b. Albuquerque, Sept. 16, 1960; d. William James and Nancy Jane (Hobbs) Colby; m. Zim Emig, May 30, 1987 (div. Nov. 1990); 1 child, Aeriel Kaylee Emig; m. Steven James Bratzler, Mar. 16, 1996, 1 child, Cody Benjamin. B of Univ. Studies, U. N.Mex., 1995. Comml. artist Modern Press, Albuquerque, 1978—80; asst. composition supr. Graphic Arts Pub., Albuquerque, 1980—84, composition supr., 1984—85, asst. plant mgr., 1985—86; typesetter Universal Printing and Graphics, Albuquerque, 1986—87, Bus. Graphics, Albuquerque, 1988—90; office asst. UNM Gen. Honors, Albuquerque, 1992—93; desktop pub., 1990—; computer specialist NEDA Bus. Cons., Inc., 1996—98; electronic prepress Acad. Printers, Albuquerque, 2002—. Cons. Mary Kay Cosmetics, 1991—96. Participant N.Mex. Pub. Utilities Commn., Santa Fe, 1993; coord. clothing bank PTA, Zia Elem. Sch., 1995-96; parent rep. Unified Student Centered Classroom, 1996-98; gen. bd. mem. Albuquerque Acad. Parent Assn., 2000—. Mem. Golden Key, Phi Beta Kappa. Avocations: piano playing, bicycling, hiking, camping.

BRAUDE, EDWIN SIMON, manufacturing company executive; b. Chgo. s. Simon Arthur and Marie (Selz) B.; m. Olga Bergstad, May 4, 1951 (dec. Dec. 1992); children: Mitchell, Edwin S. Jr., Bradford, Timothy, Tammy, Teena; m. Dorothy Herzberg, Sept. 10, 1998. BSCE, U. Colo., 1949; postgrad., Chgo. Tech., 1959; MBA, Rockford (Ill.) Coll., 1967. From pipefitter to sr. plant layout engr. Fisher Body Div. Gen. Motors, Willow Springs, Ill., 1954-61; materials mgr., mgr. mfg. Ingersoll Milling Machine Co., Rockford, 1961-71; factory mgr., v.p. mfg. NATCO, Richmond, Ind., 1972-73; plant mgr. Graphic Systems div. Rockwell Internat., Chgo. and Cedar Rapids, Iowa, 1973-76; pres. Barth Industries subs. NESCO, Cleve., 1976-82; chmn. bd. Lester Engrng. subs. NESCO, Cleve., 1976-82; pres. Hiram & E.S.D. subs. NESCO, Mich., N.C. and Calif., 1976-82, Lexington Switch, Flex Cable & Kirkhof, Mich. and Ohio, 1982-84, Nat. Acme, Cleve., 1984—; v.p. ops. Acme Cleve., 1984—; pres. A.A. Gage, Ferndale, Mich., 1990—. Work with cos., Magdeburg, Germany, 1992, Novosibirsk, Siberia, 94; cons. Wolverine Diecast, 1998; chmn. bd. Wiscon Co., Memphis, 2001—. Chmn. City of Roscoe (Ill.) Zoning Commn.; mem. Roscoe Planning Bd. With USCG, 1944-46, PTO; with USAF, 1950. Mem.: Univ., Cleve. Athletic. Republican. Lutheran. Avocations: racquetball, scuba diving. Home: 2995 Farnham Rd Richfield OH 44286 E-mail: endbraude@worldnet.att.net.

BRAUDE, MICHAEL, retired commodity exchange executive; b. Chgo., Mar. 6, 1936; s. Sheldon and Nan B.; m. Linda Rae Miller, Aug. 20, 1961; children— Peter, Adam BS, U. Mo., 1957; MS, Columbia U., 1958. Vice pres. Commerce Bank, Kansas City, Mo., 1960-73; vice pres. Mercantile Bank, Kansas City, Mo., 1966-73; exec. v.p. Am. Bank, Kansas City, Mo., 1973-84; pres., CEO Kansas City Bd. Trade, Mo., 1984—. Bd. dirs. Country Club Bank, Kansas City, Mo., Midwest Grain Products, Inc., Atchison, Kans. Author: Managing Your Money, 1975, also 12 childrens books Pres. Metr. Cmty. Coll. Found., Kansas City, Mo., 1982-84; mayor City of Mission Woods, Kans., 1982-84; trustee Kans. Pub. Employee Retirement Sys., 2001—, chmn. Mem. U. Mo. Alumni Assn. (bd. dirs. 1985-87). Jewish. Avocations: running; public speaking. Home: 5319 Mission Woods Ter Shawnee Mission KS 66205-2013

BRAUDE, ROBERT MICHAEL, retired medical library administrator; b. L.A., Sept. 27, 1939; s. Aaron and Dorothy (Lishner) B.; m. Sharon Helene Katz, Dec. 16, 1961; children— Michael, Daniel, Julianne BA, UCLA, 1962, MLS, MA, 1964; PhD, U. Nebr., 1987. Reference librarian Biomed Library Ctr. for Health Scis., UCLA, Los Angeles, 1964-65, head Medlars search sta., 1965-68; assoc. dir. U. Colo. Med. Library, Denver, 1968-75, dir., 1975-77, U. Nebr. Med. Library, Omaha, 1978-86; asst. dean for info. resources, Frances and John Loeb librarian Weill Med. Coll./Cornell U., 1986—; ret., 2001. Adj. faculty U. Denver, 1972-78; vis. assoc. prof. Sch. Libr. Sci., Pratt Inst., 1988—; del. White House Conf. on Libraries and Info. Services, 1979; mem. biomed. library rev. com. Nat. Library Medicine, Bethesda, Md., 1980-84, mem. panel on med. informatics long range planning project, 1985-86, mem. planning panel on outreach programs, 1988-89. Author: (continuing edn. syllabus) Planning: Strategic and Tactical, 1983, also articles and book chpts.; mem. editorial adv. bd. Bibliography of Bioethics; mem. editorial bd. ann. Statis. of Med. Sch. Librs. and U.S. and Can., 19887-93; mem. editorial bd. Jour. Am. Med. Informatics Assn. Sec.-treas. Children's Chorale, Denver, 1974-75, trustee, 1975-77 Fellow N.Y. Acad. Medicine, Med. Libr. Assn. (sec., bd. dirs. 1972-75, Janet Doe lectr. 1996, chmn. numerous coms. N.Y.-N.J. chpts., Outstanding Achievement award Midcontinental chpt. 1986, Noyes award 2002), Am. Coll. Med. Informatics; mem. ALA, Acad. Health Info. Profls. (disting.), Health Scis. Libr. Dirs. (stds. and practices com. 1980-83), Assn. Western Hosps. (chmn. hosp. librs. sect. 1976-77, membership com. 1976-77), Am. Med. Informatics Assn. (mem. editl. bd.).

BRAUDY, DOROTHY MCGAHEE, artist, educator; b. L.A., Dec. 10, 1930; d. Clarence Leland and Dorothy (Shacker) Wood; m. George Harbeson Fitzgerald, May 23, 1951 (div. 1965); children: George Fitzgerald, David Fitzgerald; m. Leo Braudy, Dec. 24, 1974. BA, U. Ky., 1952; MA, NYU, 1963; ABD, Tchr.'s Coll. Columbia, 1975. Asst. prof. art edn. Pratt Inst., Bklyn., 1972-78; asst. prof. visual arts Goucher Coll., Towson, Md., 1977-83. Guest Beijing, Xian, Shanghai, China, 1990. One-person shows include 2d Story Spring St. Soc., Soho, N.Y., 1975, Viridian Gallery, N.Y., 1977-78, B.R. Kornblatt Gallery, Balt., 1979, Mason County Mus., Maysville, Ky., 1982, Clark County C.C., Las Vegas, Nev., 1985, Orlando Gallery Sherman Oaks, Calif., 1986, 88, Pvt. View, L.A., 1991, 871 Fine Arts Gallery, San Francisco, 1993, Fisher Gallery, U. So. Calif., L.A., 1994; retrospective show Ellen Kim Murphy Gallery, Santa Monica, Calif., 2000; exhibited in group shows Pratt-Phoenix Gallery, N.Y.C., 1975, Pratt Inst. Gallery, 1977, Goucher Coll.,

1982, 84, UPB Gallery, Berkeley, 1986, 871 Fine Arts Gallery, San Francisco, 1989, 90, 92; represented in pub. collections Am. Embassy, Vienna, Jane Zimmerli Mus. Art, Rutgers U., New Brunswick, N.J., Fed. Res. Bank, Richmond, Va., Mason County Mus., Maysville; represented in numerous pvt. collections featured in publs. Atlas of Southern Californa; publs. Dorothy Braudy, Finishing the Hat; contbr. revs. and articles to periodicals.

BRAUDY, SUSAN ORR, writer; b. Phila. d. Bernard and Blanche (Malin) Orr. BA cum laude, Bryn Mawr Coll.; postgrad., U. Pa., Yale U. Editor, writer The New Jour. Yale U., New Haven; assoc. editor Newsweek Mag., N.Y.C.; editor, writer Ms. Mag., N.Y.C.; freelance writer N.Y. Times, N.Y.C.; v.p. Warner Bros., N.Y.C., L.A., Michael Douglas Prodns., N.Y.C., L.A. Author: (novels) Between Marriage and Divorce, 1975, Who Killed Sal Mineo, 1984, What the Movis Made Me Do, 1984, This Crazy Thing Called Love, 1991, Family Circle: The Boudins and the Aristocracy of the Left, 2003; screenwriter : (films) Scorsese Co.; Am. Zeotrope; Ixtlan; Disney. Mem.: NOW, Writers Guild of Am., PEN Club Internat., Vet. Feminists Am., Nat. Bd. Rev., Bryn Mawr Alumni Club (class v.p.). Home: 240 Central Park S Apt 16B New York NY 10019-1413

BRAUER, CAMILLA THOMPSON (KIMMY THOMPSON BRAUER), civic leader; b. St. Louis, Apr. 8, 1946; m. Stephen F. Brauer; children: Blackford, Rebecca, Stephen Jr. Grad., Mary Inst., Bennett Coll., Millbrook, N.Y., 1966. Dir. St. Louis Arts & Edn. Coun., 1988—; dir., exec. com. Opera Theater of St. Louis, 1986—; dir. exec. com. Sheldon Arts Found., 1991—; trustee St. Louis Art Mus., 1989-94, chmn. bd. trustees, 1991-94, commr., 1996—; trustee Webster U., 1994—; exec. com., 1995—; chair Alexis de Tocqueville Soc., 1995, 96, 2001; v.p. exec. com. United Way of St. Louis, 1996—; bd. trustees St. Louis Symphony, 1994—, exec. com., 1995—. Recipient Internat. Barker award Variety Club, 2000; named St. Louis Post Dispatch Woman of Achievement, 1996. Mem. Naat. Soc. Fund Raising Execs. (Vol. of Yr. St. Louis 1994, Vol. of Yr. U.S. 1996), Variety Club (exec. bd. dirs. 1992—, Woman of Yr. 1992, Mo. Hist. Soc. (dir. 1991—, exec. com. 1991—). Home: 9630 Ladue Rd Saint Louis MO 63124-1311 Fax: (314) 994-1441. E-mail: camillabrauer@aol.com.

BRAUER, DONNA JEANNE, nursing educator, researcher; b. Harrisburg, Pa., Aug. 4, 1946; d. Fred William and Jeanne Esther Herman; m. Ralph Allen Brauer, Aug. 26, 1967; 1 child, Max Frederick. BA, U. Wyo., 1968; BSN, Bowling Green State U., 1980; MS, U. Minn., 1989, PhD, 1993. RN Minn., 1980. Asst. scientist U. Minn. Sch. Medicine, Mpls., 1968—76; staff nurse Mercy Hosp., Coon Rapids, Minn., 1980—82; asst. head nurse St. Mary's Hosp., Mpls., 1982—87; rsch. fellow U. Minn. Sch. Nursing, Mpls., 1990—93; rsch. nurse Mpls. Med. Found., 1993—96; asst. prof. U. Minn., Mpls., 1996—. Contbr. articles to profl. jours. Vol. Little Bros./Friends of the Elderly, Mpls., 2002—; election judge City of Ramsey, Minn., 2002. Mem.: Minn. Horticultural Soc., AAUP, Midwest Nursing Rsch. Soc. (coun. 1999—), Sigma Theta Tau (faculty advisor Zeta chpt. 1998—2002, chair rsch. com. 2002—, Tchg.-Mentoring award 2000). Avocation: horticulture. E-mail: braue002@umn.edu.

BRAUER, GWENDOLYN GAIL, real estate broker; b. Middletown, Ohio; d. Robert J. and Mary M. (Kurry) Flynn; 1 child, John. CFP. Sales assoc. Better Homes Realty, Fairfax County, Va., 1976-81, Town & Country Properties, Fairfax County, 1981-84; asst. broker ReMax Xecutex Real Estate, Fairfax County, 1984—. Mem. Nat. Assn. Realtors (cert. residential specialist, Million Dollar Sales Club 1980—), Employee Relocation Coun. (cert. relocation profl.), Internat. Bd. CFPs, No. Va. Assn. Realtors (Top Producers Club 1985—), Va. Assn. Realtors, Remax 100 Club (Hall of Fame 1994—). Office: ReMax Xecutex Real Estate 2911 Hunter Mill Rd Ste 101 Oakton VA 22124-1700 Home: 6715 Tomlinson Ter Cabin John MD 20818-1328

BRAUER, HARROL ANDREW, JR., broadcasting executive; b. Oct. 17, 1920; s. Harrol Andrew and Bertie (Gregory) B.; m. Elizabeth Anne Hill, May 18, 1946; children: Harrol Andrew III, William Lanier, Gregory Hill. BA, U. Richmond, 1942; LLD, Christopher Newport U. Chief announcer, program dir., account exec. various radio stas. in Va., 1939-42, 45-49; v.p. Sta. WVEC Radio, Hampton, Va., 1949-80; v.p., dir. sales Sta. WVEC-TV, Hampton, 1953-82; v.p. Peninsula Cable Corp., 1966-82; chmn. Wyatt Bros., 1983-90. Pres. Hampton Cmty. Chest, 1951-52; crusade chmn. Peninsula unit Am. Cancer Soc., 1960—; mem. Hampton Sch. Bd., 1963—, vice-chmn., 1964-68, chmn., 1968-70; pres. Hampton Parking Authority, chmn., 1988—; bd. dirs. YMCA, Va. USO; bd. dirs., vice-chmn. Va. Pub. Telecomms. Bd., chmn., 1985—; chmn. Soc. Founders of Mace Christopher Newport U., 1989—; chmn. bd. trustees Hampton Roads Ednl. TV Assn., 1965-70; rector Christopher Newport U., 1976-82; co-chmn. for 375th Anniversary Celebration City of Hampton, 1985. Lt. USNR, 1942-45. Recipient Thomas P. Chisman award Va. Air and Space Ctr., Disting. Svc. medallion Christopher Newport U., NCCJ award, Am. Advt. Fedn. Silver Medal award, Disting. Citizen award City of Hampton, Outstanding Man of Yr. award Peninsula Ad Club, 1993. Mem. Hampton Retail Mchts. Assn. (past pres., bd. dirs.), Chesapeake Acad. Found. (vice-chmn. 1988—), Jamestowne Soc., Peninsula C. of C. (past bd. dirs.), Broadcast Pioneers, James River Country Club, Hampton Yacht Club, Peninsula Exec.'s Club (past pres., bd. dirs.), Town Point Club, Kiwanis (past bd. dirs., pres., lt. gov.), Sigma Alpha Epsilon. Home: 35 N Boxwood St Hampton VA 23669-2401

BRAUER, RHONDA LYN, lawyer; b. Gary, Ind., Nov. 23, 1959; d. Hugh Donald and Charlotte Gloria (Danzig) B.; m. Gregory John Holch, Sept. 7, 1989; children: Jillian Brauer Holch, Justin Brauer Holch. BA magna cum laude, Cornell U., 1981; JD magna cum laude, Ind. U., 1984. Bar: N.Y. 1985, U.S. Dist. Ct. (so. and ea. dist.) N.Y. 1991, U.S. Supreme Ct. 1992. Assoc. Cleary, Gottlieb, Steen & Hamilton, N.Y.C., 1984-86, 89-92, Brussels, 1986-88; counsel The New York Times Co., N.Y.C., 1992—94, sr. counsel, 1994—, asst. sec., 1996—2002, sec., 2002—. Contbr. articles to profl. jours. Pro bono work Lawyers Com. for Human Rights, N.Y.C., 1984-86, ACLU, 1989-90, Vol. Lawyers for the Arts, N.Y.C., 1989-92, N.Y. Lawyers for the Pub. Interest, 1992-95. Recipient Anne MacIntyre Litchfield prize of history Cornell U. Coll. Arts and Scis., 1981; Salzburg (Austria) Seminar fellow, 1988. Mem. Assn. Bar City N.Y., N.Y. Women's Bar Assn. Avocations: swimming, hiking, film, jogging.

BRAUER, RIMA LOIS, psychiatrist; b. Bklyn., Feb. 5, 1938; d. Gerald and Freeda (Rubin) Rubenstein; m. Lee David Brauer, Dec. 29, 1959; children: Samuel, Jennifer, Nathan. BA, Goucher Coll., 1959; MD, U. Md., 1964. Biochemistry researcher Sinai Hosp., Balt., 1958-60; med. intern Montefiore Hosp., Bronx, N.Y., 1964-65; psychiatry resident Yale Sch. Medicine, New Haven, Conn., 1966-69, child fellow, 1969-72; psychoanalyst Western New England Inst. for Psychoanalysis, New Haven, 1977-84; pvt. practice Hartford, Conn., 1984—. Clin. faculty Yale Sch. Medicine, New Haven, 1973-84, U. Conn. Sch. Medicine, Hartford, 1984-2003, Inst. of Living, 2003--. Mem. Am. Psychoanalytic Assn. (com. on analytic practice 1991-2000), Western New Eng. Inst. Psychoanalysis (pres. 1998-2000), N.Y. Acad. Sci. Office: 2 Hartford Sq W Hartford CT 06106-5105

BRAUER, SASHA GERRITSON, church musician, music educator; b. North Hampton, Mass., July 9, 1972; d. Stephen Lawrence Gerritson and Alicen Jean McGowan; m. Todd Lawrence Brauer, Sept. 22, 2000. MusB, Northeastern Ill. U., 1991, MusM, 1996; post master's cert., DePaul U., 1999. Exec. dir., founder L'Opera Piccola, Chgo., 1995—; dept. chair, faculty Merit Sch. Music, Chgo., 1996—; asst. to Daniel Barenboim Chgo. Symphony Orch., 1999—2001; part-time faculty Harold Washington Coll., Chgo., 2000—01; artistic dir. Happiness Club for Kids, Chgo., 2000—; part-time faculty Northeastern Ill. U., Chgo., 2000—; min. music Park Ridge Cmty. Ch., Ill., 2000—. Composer: (musical theatre work) Rumpelstiltskin, 1996. Recipient Talent award for artistic achievement, MacDowell Artists Assn., Chgo., 1991, Joan Sachs/Neill Found., Chgo., 1994, Harold Berlinger/Neill Found., 1996. Mem.: The Nation, Am. Choral Dirs. Assn. Democrat. United Church Of Christ. Avocations: professional opera singer, writing, reading. Office: L Opera Piccola 5239 N LaCrosse Ave Chicago IL 60630 E-mail: sasha@loperapiccola.org.

BRAUER, STEPHEN FRANKLIN, diplomat, manufacturing company executive; b. Sept. 3, 1945; s. Arthur John, Jr. and Jane (Franklin) B.; m. Camilla Cary Thompson, June 12, 1971; children: Blackford Fitzhugh, Rebecca Randolph, Stephen Franklin, Jr. Student, Washington and Lee U., 1963-64; BA, Westminster Coll., 1967; LLD (hon.), 1997. Sales and mktg. ofcl. Hunter Engring. Co., St. Louis, 1971-78, exec. v.p., 1978-81, pres., 1981-2001; U.S. amb. to Belgium, 2001—. Bd. dirs. Boatmen's Trust Co., St. Louis, 1986-96; ptnr. St. Louis Cardinals baseball club, 1996—; pvt. client bd. Bank of Am., 1996—. Civilian aide Sec. Army, 1991-95; trustee Mo. Bot. Garden, 1988—; trustee Washington U., St. Louis, 1991—; mem. Mo. 21st Jud. Dist. Commn., 1992-96; hon. consul Govt. Belgium, 1987-2001; mem. St. Louis Consular Corps; mem. nat. bd. Smithsonian Instn., Washington, 1993-99. 1st lt. C.E., AUS, 1968-70. Recipient St. Louis Regional Commerce Growth Assn. Tech. award, 1993, Recognition of Outstanding Bus. Leadership award U.S. Ho. of Reps., 1993, Dean's award Washington U. Sch. Engring., 1998, Spirit of Enterprise award Mo. Rep. Party, 1999. Mem. St. Louis Country Club, St. Louis Club, Log Cabin Club, Bellerive Country Club, Bath & Tennis Club (Palm Beach), Everglades Club (Palm Beach). Republican. Episcopalian. Home: 9630 Ladue Rd Saint Louis MO 63124-1311 Office: 11250 Hunter Dr Bridgeton MO 63044-2306 E-mail: sfbrauer@hunter.com.

BRAULT, G. LORAIN, healthcare executive; b. Chgo., Jan. 3, 1944; d. Theodore Frank and Victoria Jean (Pribyl) Hahn; m. Donald R. Brault, Apr. 29, 1971; 1 child, Kevin David. AA, Long Beach City Coll., 1963; BS, Calif. State U.-Long Beach, 1973, MS, 1977. RN, Calif; cert. nurse practitioner. Dir. nursing Canyon Gen. Hosp., Anaheim, Calif., 1973-76; dir. faculty critical care masters degree program Calif. State U., Long Beach, 1976-79; regional dir.. nursing and support svcs. Western region Am. Med. Internat., Anaheim, Calif., 1979-83; v.p. Hosp. Home Care Corp. Am., Santa Ana, Calif., 1983-85; pres. Hosp. Home Health Care Agy. Calif., Torrance, 1986-92; v.p. Healthcare Assn. So. Calif., L.A., 1993—98; dir. student health svc. Fullerton Coll., 1999—. Invited lectr. China Nurses Assn., 1983; cons. AMI, Inc., Saudi Arabia, 1983; guest lectr. dept. pub. health UCLA, 1986—87; assoc. clin. prof. U. So. Calif., 1988—93; chair editl. adv. com. RN Times, Nurseweek, 1988—2000; advisor Nursing Inst., 1990—91; lectr. Calif. State U., L.A., 1996—99, Fullerton, Calif., 1999—; bd. dirs. Health and Human Svcs., Long Beach, Calif., 1997—, chmn., 2002—. Contbr. articles to profl. jours., chpts. to books. Commr. HHS, Washington, 1988, chmn., 2002—. Grantee Health and Human Svcs. Advanced Nurse Tng. Mem. Women in Health Adminstrn. (sec. 1989, v.p. 1990), Nat. Assn. Home Care, Am. Orgn. Nursing Execs., Calif. Assn. Health Svcs. at Home (task force chmn. 1988, bd. dirs. 1988-93, chmn. bd. dirs. 1990-93), Calif. League Nursing (bd. sec. 1983, program chmn. 1981-82), Am. Coll. Health Care Execs., ASAE, AONE (pres.2002-), HSACCC (pres.2002-, chair-elect 2002-), Phi Kappa Phi, Sigma Theta Tau, Soroptomist Internat. Republican. Methodist.

BRAULT, GERARD JOSEPH, French language educator; b. Chicopee Falls, Mass., Nov. 7, 1929; s. Philias J. and Aline E. (Rémillard) B.; m. Jeanne Lambert Pepin, Jan. 23, 1954; children: Francis Gerard, Anne-Marie Welsh, Suzanne Eveline Dannenmueller. AB, Assumption Coll., Worcester, Mass., 1950, DLitt, 1976; AM cum laude, Laval U., 1952; PhD, U. Pa., 1958. Teaching fellow U. Pa., 1954-56, assoc. prof. Romance langs., 1961-65, vice dean Grad. Sch., 1962-65; instr. French Bowdoin Coll., Brunswick, Maine, 1957-59, asst. prof. French, 1959-61; prof. French Pa. State U., University Park, 1965-90, Disting. prof. French and medieval studies, 1990, Edwin Erle Sparks prof. French and medieval studies, 1990-97, head dept. French, 1965-70, Edwin Erle Sparks prof. emeritus French and medieval studies, 1998—. Fellow Inst. Arts and Humanistic Studies, 1976—; dir. NDEA Summer Insts., Bowdoin Coll., 1961, 62, Assumption Coll., 1964; Fulbright fellow, Strasbourg, France, 1956-57, Fulbright rsch. scholar and Guggenheim fellow, Strasbourg, 1968-69; sr. fellow in Can. studies, Quebec City, 1984, Camargo Found. fellow, Cassis, France, 1987, 94. Author: Celestine: A Critical Edition of the First French Translation (1527) of the Spanish Classic La Celestina, 1963, Cours de langue française destiné aux jeunes Franco-Américains, 1963, rev. edits., 1965, 69, Early Blazon, 1972, rev. edit., 1997, Eight Thirteenth-Century Rolls of Arms in French and Anglo-Norman Blazon, 1973 (prix Paul Adam-Even), The Song of Roland: An Analytical Edition (named outstanding book Choice 1979), 2 vols., 1978, La Chanson de Roland: Student Edition, 1984; The French-Canadian Heritage in New England, 1986, Rolls of Arms of Edward I (1272-1307) (Aspilogia III), 2 vols., 1997 (Bickersteth medal, Riquer prize); mem. editl. bd. French Forum, 1975—, Purdue U. Monographs, 1978— ; contbr. articles to profl. jours. Mem. Cath. Commn. on Intellectual and Cultural Affairs, also, Comité de Vie Franco-Américaine, Société Historique Franco-Américaine. Served with CIC, U.S. Army, 1951-53. Decorated Palmes Académiques French Ministry Edn., 1965, officer, 1975; officer, Ordre National du Mérite, 1980, Ordre des Francophones d'Amérique, 1980; recipient Faculty Scholar medal Pa. State U., 1981, Class of 1933 Humanities award, Pa. State U., 1987 Fellow Soc. Antiquaries of London, Heraldry Soc. London, Medieval Acad. Am. (adv. bd. Speculum 1972-75), Académie Internationale d'Héraldique; mem. MLA, Société Rencesvals pour l'étude des épopées romanes (pres. 1985-88, pres. Am.-Canadian br. 1970-73, editorial bd. Olifant 1975—), Am. Assn. Tchrs. French, Middle Atlantic Conf. Canadian Studies (pres. 1981-83), Internat. Arthurian Soc., Harleian Soc. (council 1987-98). Home: 705 Westerly Pky State College PA 16801-4227 Office: Pa State U Burrowes Bldg Rm 325 University Park PA 16802 E-mail: gjb2@psu.edu.

BRAUMAN, JOHN I. chemist, educator; b. Pitts., Sept. 7, 1937; s. Milton and Freda E. (Schlitt) B.; m. Sharon Lea Kruse, Aug. 22, 1964; 1 dau., Kate Andrea. BS, MIT, 1959; PhD (NSF fellow), U. Calif., Berkeley, 1963. NSF postdoctoral fellow UCLA, 1962-63; asst. prof. chemistry Stanford (Calif.) U., 1963-69, asso. prof., 1969-72, prof., 1972-80, J.G. Jackson-C.J. Wood prof. chemistry, 1980—, chmn. dept., 1979-83, 95-96, cognizant dean phys. scis. Cons. in phys. organic chemistry; adv. panel chemistry divsn. NSF, 1974-78; adv. panel NASA, AEC, ERDA, Rsch. Corp., Office Chemistry and Chem. Tech., NRC; coun. Gordon Rsch. Confs., 1989-95, trustee, 1991-95. Mem. editl. adv. bd. Jour. Am. Chem. Soc., 1976-83, Jour. Organic Chemistry, 1974-78, Nouveau Jour. de Chimie, 1977-85, Chem. Revs., 1978-80, Chem. Kinetics, 1987-89, Accts. Chem. Rsch., 1995-97, 98-2001; bd. trustees Ann. Revs., 1995—, mem. editl. adv. bd.; dep. editor for phys. scis. Sci., 1985-2000, chair sr. editl. bd., 2000—. Alfred P. Sloan fellow, 1968-70, Guggenheim fellow, 1978-79; Christensen fellow Oxford U., 1983-84. Fellow AAAS (chmn. sect. 1996-97, mem.-at-large sect. 1997-99), Calif. Acad. Scis. (hon.); mem. NAS (home sec. 2003—, Award in Chem. Scis. 2001), Am. Acad. Arts and Scis., Am. Chem. Soc. (award in pure chemistry 1973, Harrison Howe award, 1976, R.C. Fuson award, 1986, James Flack Norris award 1986, Arthur C. Cope scholar, 1986, Linus Pauling medal 2002, J. Willard Gibbs medal 2003, exec. com. phys. chemistry divsn., com. on sci. 1992-97), Sigma Xi, Phi Lambda Upsilon. Home: 849 Tolman Dr Palo Alto CA 94305-1025 Office: Stanford U Dept Chemistry Stanford CA 94305-5080

BRAUMILLER, ALLEN SPOONER, oil and gas exploration company executive, geologist; b. Texarkana, Tex., Feb. 1, 1934; s. Jack and Jenie (Spooner) B.; m. Patsy Lois McCoy, Dec. 23, 1955; children: Allen Spoonr, Dana Ruth Braumiller Nance, Adrienne Brevard, Colin McCoy. Student, Tulane U., 1952-53; BS, U. Miss., 1955; MS, U. Ill., 1957. Sr. exploration geologist Carter Oil Co. (merged into Humble Oil & Refining Co. 1961), 1957-69; v.p., exploration geologist Helmerich & Payne, Inc., Tulsa, 1969-96, ret., 1996; pres. Braumiller & Braumiller, Inc., Tulsa, 1995—; mgr. Est Tex. Seismic Data, LLC, Tulsa, 1996—. Geol. cons. No. Ill. Natural Gas, Urbana, 1956-57. Elder area Presbyn. ch.; mem. Philbrook Mus. Art, Tulsa, Thomas Gilcrease Mus., Tulsa. Mem. Am. Assn. Petroleum Geologists, Geol. Soc. Am., Am. Assn. Profl. Landmen, Ill. Geol. Soc., Oklahoma City Geol. Soc., Tulsa Geol. Soc., Soc. Petroleum Engrs., Archaeol. Inst. Am., Internat. Assn. Energy Advs., Internat. Platform Assn., Internat. Wine and Food Soc., Tulsa C. of C., U.S. C. of C., Nat. Trust for Historic Preservation, Knife and Fork Club, Petroleum Club (bd. dirs. 1989-92). Republican. Avocations: reef diving, cycling, swimming, gardening, music. E-mails. Home: 4979 E 113th St Tulsa OK 74137-7607 also: Braumiller & Braumiller Inc Philtower Bldg 427 S Boston Ave Ste 500 Tulsa OK 74103-4118 Address: 5105 E Belle Fontaine Beach Rd Ocean Springs MS 39564 E-mail: etsd@webzone.net., patbrau@cs.com.

BRAUN, ARTUR, physicist; D of Natural Sci., Swiss Fed. Inst. of Tech., Switzerland, 1999; Diplom-Physiker, RWTH Aachen, Aachen, Germany, 1989—96. Rsch. assoc. Philips Rsch. Labs., Aachen, Germany, 1994, KFA Juelich Nuc. Sci. Rsch. Ctr., 1994—96; rsch. asst. Paul Scherrer Inst. Swiss Fed. Inst. of Tech., Villigen, 1996—99, Lab. for Neutron Scattering, Villigen, 1999; physicist Lawrence Berkeley Nat. Lab., Berkeley, Calif., 1999—2001, Consortium for Fossil Fuel Sci., Lexington, Ky., 2001—. Spokesperson Amnesty Internat., Aachen, 1994—95. Recipient Erdoesz Number 3 award, Erdoesz Project, 2002. Mem.: Am. Chem. Soc. Achievements include research in Application and Promotion of Lambert's W function in science and engineering; first to Establishment of in-situ small angle X-ray scattering in lithium battery research; development of Various analytical mathematical models for magnetic storage and thin film growth. Office Fax: 859-257-7215.

BRAUN, DANIEL, physicist, researcher; b. Tuttlingen, Germany, Aug. 18, 1967; s. Klaus and Elisabeth Braun. Diploma in physics, 1992; MA, SUNY, 1990; PhD, U. Paris, 1995. Postdoctoral fellow, asst. prof. U. Essen, Germany, 1995-2000; devel. engr. Infineon Techs., Yorktown Heights, N.Y., 2000—. Author: Dissipative Quantum Chaos and Decoherence, 2000. Mem. extended bd. Fulbright Alumni Assn., Frankfurt, 1997-98. Fulbright scholar, 1989-90, German Nat. Scholarship Found. scholar, 1989-92. Mem.: Am. Phys. Soc., German Phys. Soc. E-mail: vzbraun@us.ibm.com.

BRAUN, DAVID A(DLAI), lawyer; b. N.Y.C., Apr. 23, 1931; s. Morris and Betty Braunstein; m. Merna Feldman, Dec. 18, 1955; children: Lloyd Jeffrey, Kenneth Franklin, Evan Albert. AB, Columbia U., 1952, LLB, 1954. Bar: N.Y. 1955, Calif. 1974. Assoc. Ellis, Ellis and Ellis, N.Y.C., 1954-56, Davis and Gilbert, 1956-57; ptnr. Pryor, Cashman, Sherman and Flynn, 1957-73, Hardee, Barovick, Konecky & Braun, N.Y.C., 1973, L.A., 1974-81; pres., CEO Polygram Records, Inc., N.Y.C., 1980-81; counsel Wyman, Bautzer, Rothman, Kuchel & Silbert, L.A., 1982-85; ptnr. Braun, Margolis, Burrill & Besser, L.A., 1985-87; counsel Silverberg, Rosen, Leon & Behr, 1987-89, Silverberg, Katz, Thompson & Braun, 1989-91; spl. counsel Proskauer, Rose, Goetz & Mendelsohn, 1991-93; ptnr. Monasch Plotkin & Braun, 1993-94; pvt. practice, 1994-98; sr. counsel Akin, Gump, Strauss, Hauer & Feld, L.L.P., 1998—. Adj. prof. U. So. Calif. Sch. Cinema-TV; guest lectr. UCLA Ext.; adv. com. Ctr. for Law, Media and the Arts, Columbia U. Sch. Law; internat. adv. bd. Nat. Inst. Entertainment and Media Law, Southwestern U. Sch. Law. Bd. visitors Columbia Coll., 1980-86, Columbia Law Sch., 1992-94; bd. dirs. Reprise! Broadway's Best in Concert, Musician's Assistance Program, 1994-98, Tu 'Um EST Cmty. Drug Rehab. Ctr., Rock and Roll Hall of Fame, 1985-93. Mem. Assn. of City of N.Y., L.A. County Bar Assn., Beverly Hills Bar Assn., Nat. Acad. TV Arts and Scis. (pres. N.Y. chpt. 1972-73), NARAS, Am. Arbitration Assn., Hollywood Radio and TV Soc. (bd. dirs. 1983-86), Sigma Chi, Phi Alpha Delta. Jewish. Home: 211 S Spalding Dr Apt 401S Beverly Hills CA 90212-3664 Office: Akin Gump Strauss Hauer & Feld LLP 24th Fl 2029 Century Park St Los Angeles CA 90067 E-mail: dbraun@akingump.com.

BRAUN, EUNICE HOCKSPEIER, religious order executive, author, lecturer; b. Alta Vista, Iowa; d. George Phillip and Lydia (Reinhart) Hockspeier; m. Leonard James Braun, May 29, 1937. Student, Gates Coll., 1932-34, Coe Coll., 1941-43, Northwestern U., 1944-47. Freelance writer for mags., newspapers, 1947-52; bus. mgr. Baha'i Publishing Trust, Wilmette, Ill., 1952-55, mng. dir., 1955-71; internat. news editor Baha'i News, 1952-70; tchr. Baha'i schs., Alaska, Can., Europe and U.S., 1958—. Lectr. Baha'i Faith in U.S., Central Am., Europe, Africa, Asia, 1953— ; cons. Baha'i Pub. Trust, New Delhi, India, 1972; mem. aux. bd. Continental Bd. Counselors, Baha'i Faith in the Ams., 1972-86. Author: Know Your Baha'i Literature, 1959; The Dawn of World Peace, 1963; Baha'u'llah: His Call to the Nations, 1967; From Strength to Strength, Half Century of the Formative Age of the Baha'i Faith, 1978; A Crown of Beauty, 1982; The March of the Institutions, 1984; A Reader's Guide: The Development of Baha'i Literature in English, 1986; From Vision to Victory, 1993; contbr. essays to Baha'i World, Internat. Record. Mem. Nat. League Am. Pen Women, Baha'i Faith, Iota Sigma Epsilon. Home: 1025 Forestview Ln Glenview IL 60025-4433 E-mail: sprucelawn@aol.com.

BRAUN, FREDERICK B. lawyer, food company executive; b. Cin., Aug. 4, 1942; s. Roger K. and Ruth (Sherperd) B.; m. Susan Braun, Nov. 23, 1967 (div. 1983); 1 child, Roger Tracy. B.A., U. Cin., 1967; M.S., Case Western Res. U., 1969, J.D., 1973. Bar: Ohio, 1973, Ill., 1980, U.S. Dist. Ct. (so. and we. dists.) Ohio 1973, U.S. Ct. Appeals (6th cir.), U.S. Dist. Ct. (no. dist.) Ill. 1981, U.S. Ct. Appeals (7th cir.) 1981. Assoc. Beckman, Lavercombe Fox & Weil, Cin., 1973-78; ptnr. Buechner, Braun & Haffer, Cin., 1979-80; chief labor counsel Sara Lee Corp., Chgo., 1980-85, asst. counsel, 1985—. Assoc. editor Internat. Law Rev., 1972. Chmn. Title XX Social Security Adv. Bd., Columbus, Ohio, 1977-80. Mandell fellow Case Western Res. U., 1978. Mem. ABA, Ill. Bar Assn., Chgo. Bar Assn., Cin. Bar Assn., Ohio Bar Assn. Episcopalian. Club University (Cin.). Home: 728 Cutter Ln Barrington IL 60010-1535 Office: Sara Lee Corp 3 1st Nat Plz Chicago IL 60602

BRAUN, GUSTAV MILAN, facial plastic surgeon, otolaryngologist; b. Mar. 8 1938; BA in Chemistry, Wayne State U., 1962; MS, U. Iowa, 1971; MD, U. Mich., 1965. Diplomate Am. Bd. Otolaryngology. Intern UCLA Affiliated Hosps., 1965-66; resident in surgery Wadsworth VA Hosp., L.A., 1966-67 resident in ear, nose, throat and facial plastic surgery U. Iowa Hosps., Iowa City 1967-71; asst. prof. facial plastic surgery and otolaryngology Sch. Medicine U Calif., San Diego, 1974-76; pvt. practice Calif., 1977-78, Harlingen, Tex. 1979-91, Houston, 1992-2000, Mineral Wells, Tex., 2001, Palo Pinto Meml Hosp., Mineral Wells, 2001—. Clin. asst. prof. Baylor Coll. Medicine, Houston 1992-2001. Maj. U.S. Army, 1966-73. Fellow ACS, Am. Acad. Facial Plastic and Reconstructive Surgery, Am. Acad. Otolaryngology-Head and Neck Surgery; mem. Tex. Med. Assn, Rotary Internat. (Paul Harris fellow). Office: PO Box 1527 218 SW 26th Ave Mineral Wells TX 76067 E-mail: gmbraun@cox-internet.com.

BRAUN, JANET LARSON, nurse; BSN, U. Iowa, 1974; MSPH, U. Minn. 1980. Instr. U. Minn. Coll. Nursing, Mpls., 1980-81; health cons. Control Data Corp., Mpls., 1981-82; dir. extended care Home Health Plus, Mpls., 1982-86; sr health cons. Options and Choices Inc., Rockville, Md., 1987-94; dir. Ctr. for Women's Health, Lexington, Ky., 1995-98; assoc. dir. Women's Health Ctr. Lexington, 1998—. Bd. dirs. Planned Parenthood, Lexington, 1997-2002. Mem AWHONN, APHA, Sigma Theta Tau. Office: U Ky Women's Health Ctr A30 Ky Clinic Ctr Lexington KY 40536-0284

BRAUN, JANICE LARSON, language arts educator; b. Cook, Minn., Mar. 4 1949; d. Roy Woodrow and Hazel Vivian (Huff) Larson; m. Joseph Edmund Braun, July 17, 1975; 1 child, Elizabeth. BA in English and German, Concordia Coll., Moorhead, Minn., 1971; MEd, St. Mary's U. Minn., 2000. Lang. arts tchr Dist. 742 Cmty. Schs., St. Cloud, Minn., 1971—, mem. K-12 lang. arts com. 1984—, mem. Tech. H.S. site com., 1988-92. Mem., writer assessment gran com. State of Minn. and Dist. 742, 1993-97, mem. graduation stds. panel 1997—, mem. dist. gifted and talented task force, 1999—, advisor cultural awareness and racial equity com., lang. arts dept. chair, 2002—; advisor Tech H.S. chpt. Amnesty Internat., 1987—. Leader Wide Horizons 4-H Club, Benton County, Minn., 1990-98; catechist Bethlehem Luth. Ch., St. Cloud, 1994-96 mem. Archie Givens Origins project St. Cloud State U., 1993-96. Mem. NEA Minn. Edn. Assn., St. Cloud Edn. Assn., Nat. Coun. Tchrs. English. Democrat Avocations: reading, walking, skiing, canoeing, camping. Office: Tech HS 23 12th Ave S Saint Cloud MN 56301-4286 E-mail: jbraun@cloudnet.com.

BRAUN, JEFFREY LOUIS, lawyer; b. N.Y.C., Oct. 2, 1946; s. Arthur and Berta (Freimark) B.; m. Beth Essig, June 6, 1982; children: Arthur Paul, Emily Claire. BA, Rutgers U., 1968; JD, Yale U., 1971. Bar: N.Y. 1974, U.S. Dist. Ct. (so. and ea. dists.) N.Y., U.S. Tax Ct., U.S. Ct. Appeals (2d cir.), U.S. Ct. Appeals (9th cir.), U.S. Supreme Ct. Law clk. to Judge Harry Pregerson U.S. Dist. Ct. (cen. dist.) Calif., L.A., 1971—72; assoc. Paul, Weiss, Rifkind Wharton & Garrison, N.Y.C., 1972—74, Rosenman & Colin LLP, N.Y.C. 1974—80, ptnr., 1980—2002; of counsel Kramer Levin Naftalis & Frankel LLP, N.Y.C., 2002—. Mem. Assn. of the Bar of the City of N.Y. (com. on internat. human rights 1985-88, com. on mcpl. affairs 1988-91, com. on recruitment and retention of lawyers 1992-94, long-range planning com. 1994-97), Fed. Bar Coun. (com. on cts. of the second cir. 1995—). Home: 15 Park Rd Irvington NY 10533-2008 Office: Kramer Levin Naftalis & Frankel LLP 919 Third Ave New York NY 10022-3852 E-mail jbraun@kramerlevin.com.

BRAUN, JEROME IRWIN, lawyer; b. St. Joseph, Mo., Dec. 16, 1929; s. Martin H. and Bess (Donsker) B.; children: Aaron, Susan, Daniel; m. Dolores Ferriter, Aug. 16, 1987. AB with distinction, Stanford U., 1951, LLB, 1953. Bar: Mo. 1953, Calif. 1953, U.S. Dist. Ct. (no. dist.) Calif., U.S. Tax Ct., U.S. Ct. Mil. Appeals, U.S. Supreme Ct., U.S. Ct. Appeals (9th cir.). Assoc. Long & Levit, San Francisco, 1957-58, Law Offices of Jefferson Peyser, San Francisco, 1958-62; founding ptnr. Farella, Braun & Martel (formerly Elke, Farella & Braun), San Francisco, 1962—. Instr. San Francisco Law Sch., 1958-69; mem. U.S. Dist. Ct. Civil Justice Reform Act Adv. Com., 1991—; spkr. various state bar convs. in Calif., Ill., Nev., Mont.; requent moderator/participant continuing edn. of bar programs; past chmn. 9th Cir. Sr. Adv. Bd., past chmn. lawyer reps. to 9th Cir. Jud. Conf.; mem. appellate lawyers liaison com. Calif. Ct. Appeals 1st dist.; jud.conf. U.S. Com. Long Range Planning; founder Jon Samuel Abramson Scholarship Endowment Stanford U. Law. Revising editor: Stanford U. Law Rev.; contbr. articles to profl. jours. Mem. Jewish Community Fedn. San Francisco, The Peninsula, Marin and Sonoma Counties, pres., 1979-80; past pres. United Jewish Community Ctrs. 1st lt. JAGC, U.S. Army, 1954-57, U.S. Army Res., 1957-64. Recipient Lloyd W. Dinkelspiel Outstanding Young Leader award Jewish Welfare Fedn., 1967, Professionalism award 9th cir. Am. Inns of Ct., 1999. Fellow Am. Acad. Appellate Lawyers, Am. Coll. Trial Lawyers (teaching trial and appellate advocacy com.), Am. Bar Found., mem. ABA, Calif. Bar Assn. (chmn. adminstrn. justice com. 1977), Bar Assn. San Francisco (spl. com. on lawyers malpractice and malpractice ins.), San Francisco Bar Found. (past trustee), Calif. Acad. Appellate Lawyers (past pres., mem. U.S. Dist. Ct. Civil Justice Reform Act adv. com., Calif. Ct. of Appeals 1st Dist. Appellate Lawyers liaison com., jud. conf. of the U.S., com. on long-range planning, panelist 1994), Am. Judicature Soc. (past dir.), Stanford Law Sch. Bd. of Visitors, U.S. Dist. Ct. of No. Dist. Calif. Hist. Soc. (past pres., bd. dirs.), 9th Cir. Ct. of Appeals Hist. Soc. (past. pres.), Mex.-Am. Legal Def. Fund (honoree), Order of Coif. E-mail: jbraun@fbm.com.

BRAUN, KAZIMIERZ PAWEL, theatrical director, writer, educator; b. Mokrsko Dolne, Kielce, Poland, June 29, 1936; came to U.S., 1985; s. Juliusz and Elzbieta (Szymanowska) B.; m. Zofia M. Reklewska, July 15, 1962; children: Monika Braun Beres, Grzegorz, Justyna. M in Letters, U. Poznan, Poland, 1958, PhD, 1971; MFA in Directing, Theater Acad., Warsaw, Poland, 1962; PhD in Theatre, Wroclaw (Poland) U., 1975; PhD in Directing, Theater Acad., Warsaw, 1988. Prof. Polish State Title, 1992. Prof., dir. Teatr Polski, Warsaw, 1962-64, Teatr Horzycy, Torun, Poland, 1965-67; artistic dir., gen. mgr. Teatr Osterwy, Lublin, Poland, 1967-74, Contemporary Theatre, Wroclaw, 1975-84; head of acting program SUNY, Buffalo, 1987—89, prof. dept theater and dance, 1989—. Prof. Wroclaw U., 1974-85, Sch. Drama, Wroclaw, 1978-85; vis. prof. NYU, 1985, Swarthmore Coll., Pa., 1985-86; regents prof. U. Calif., Santa Cruz, 1986. Dir. 130 plays U.S., Poland, Can., Germany, and Ireland; pub. 31 books theater history, novels, plays, Polish, English transls. Recipient Japanese Found. award, Tokyo, 1981, Guggenheim Found. award, 1990; Best Dir. award, Critics Com., Wroclaw, 1976, 80, 84, 85, Artie award, Buffalo, 1996, Aurum award, Can., 2000, Fulbright award. 2001. Mem. Internat. Theatre Inst. (Young Dir. award 1961), Actors Union Poland, Writers Union Poland, PEN Club. Roman Catholic. Avocation: travel. Office: SUNY Dept Theater and Dance 278 Alumni Arena Amherst NY 14260-5030

BRAUN, LLOYD, broadcast executive; Entertainment atty. Silverberg, Katz, Thompson & Braun; pres. Brillstein-Grey Entertainment; chmn. Buena Vista TV Prodns., 1998—99; co-chmn. ABC TV Entertainment Group, 1999—. Office: ABC Inc 2040 Avenue Of The Stars Fl 3 Century City CA 90067-4785

BRAUN, LUDWIG, educational technology consultant; b. Bklyn., May 14, 1926; s. Ludwig and Wetie (Schmidt) B.; m. Eva Margaret Taylor, Sept. 7, 1947; children: Barbara Ann, Edith Elizabeth, Anne Catherine, John Ludwig. BEE, Poly. Inst. Bklyn., 1950, MEE, 1955, DEE, 1959. Elec. engr. Allied Control Co., N.Y.C., 1950-51; head electronics dept. Anton Electronics Labs., Inc., Bklyn., 1951-55; from instr. elec. engring. to prof. sys. and elec. engring. Poly. Inst. Bklyn., 1955-72; prof. engring. SUNY, Stony Brook, 1972-82, dir. bioengring. program, 1976-79, dir. personal computers in edn. lab., 1979-82; prof. computer sci., dir. acad. computing lab. N.Y. Inst. Tech., Central Islip, 1982-87; rsch. prof. NYU, N.Y.C., 1987-89; ret., 1989. Sr. fellow C.W. Post Campus, L.I.U., 1998—; dir. Nat. Inst. Microcomputer Based Learning, 1981-87, Intercounty Tchr. Resource Ctr., 1985-87, Mecklenburger Group, 1993-96; lectr., med. scientist Downstate Med. Ctr., 1970-82; cons. ednl. tech., 1990—, Vertol divsn. Boeing Co., GE, Ford Found., NSF, Nat. Inst. Edn., IBM, NET Schs., Inc.; tech. advisor Orton Soc., Suffolk. Author: (with E. Mishkin) Adaptive Control Systems, 1961; contbg. author: Signals and Systems in Electrical Engineering, 1962, Perry's Chemical Engineering Handbook, 1961, System Engineering Handbook, 1965, Computer Techniques in Biomedicine and Medicine, 1973, Vision Test Recommendations for American Education Decision Makers, 1990, Celebrating Success, 1995. Mem. Women's Action Alliance, 1985-88; bd. dirs. Playing To Win, Inc., 1983-90, Internat. Coun. for Computers in Edn., 1987-89. With AUS, 1944-46. First recipient Paul Pair award for contbns. to edn. through tech., Nat. Ednl. Computing Assn. Pioneer award in Ednl. Tech., 1999; fellow Global Village Schs. Inst., 1996-98. Mem. IEEE (sr. 1990), Internat. Soc. for Tech. in Edn. (bd. dirs. 1989-90), Sigma Xi, Tau Beta Pi, Eta Kappa Nu. Home: 11 Parsons Dr Dix Hills NY 11746-5217 E-mail: ludbraun@optonline.net.

BRAUN, MARY LUCILE DEKLE (LUCY BRAUN), therapist, consultant, counselor, educator; b. Tampa, Fla. d. Guthrie "Gus" J. and Lucile (Culpepper) Dekle; children: John Ryan, Matthew Joseph, Jeffrey William, Douglas Edwin. AB, Brenau Coll.; MA, U. Cen. Fla.; EdD, U. Fla. Cert. disability mgmt. specialist, rehab. counselor, victim advocate; lic. mental health counselor; lic. marriage and family therapist; nationally cert. counselor. Coord. Orange County Child Abuse Prevention, Orlando, Fla., 1983-88; cons. Displaced Homemaker Program, Orlando, 1989-94, DCS, Oviedo, Fla., 1990-92. Adj. prof. U. Ctrl. Fla., Orlando, Troy State U.; clin. dir. Response Sexual Abuse Treatment Program, 1993—95; mem. adv. bd. Fla. Hosp. Women's Ctr., Orlando, 1989—; bd. dirs. Parent Resource Ctr., Orlando, Children With Attention Deficit Disorders, Orlando, 1989—91; cons. program devel. for children and adolescent treatment svcs., 1997—98; dir. clin. svcs. Rehab. and Indsl. Counseling, 1997—; cons., counselor contractor VA; counselor Share the Care Program. Author: Someone Heard, 1987, Humor Us Soup, 1989, Child Abuse and Neglect: Resource Guide for Orange County Schools, 1985, 2d edit., 1987; contbg. author: Death from Child Abuse, 1986, Personality Types of Abusive Parents, 1993, Why Children Fight, 1992. Sustaining mem. Jr. League of Greater Orlando. Program recipient Cmty. Svc. award Walt Disney World, 1987. Mem. ACA, Fla. Counseling Assn., Nat. Bd. Cert. Counselors, Phi Kappa Phi, Kappa Delta Pi, Chi Sigma Iota, Alpha Delta Pi: Avocations: scuba diving, sailing, puzzles. E-mail: dr.lucybraun@juno.com.

BRAUN, ROBERT ALAN, lawyer; b. Bronx, N.Y., Mar. 6, 1950; s. George and Sylvia (Feuerstein) B.; children: Alison, Scott, Brianna, Benjamin, Amanda; m. Laura Rosemarie Icolari. BA, Queens Coll., 1972; JD, St. Johns U., 1976. Bar: N.Y. 1977, U.S. Dist. Ct. (ea. and so. dists.) N.Y. 1977, U.S. Ct. Appeals (2d cir.) 1978, U.S. Supreme Ct. 1982. Asst. dist. atty. Kings County Dist. Atty., Bklyn., 1976-80; assoc. Robert Rivers PC, Hempstead, N.Y., 1980, Singer & Braun PC, Hempstead, N.Y., 1980-82, Sarisohn, Sarisohn, et al, Commack, NY, 1982-85, ptnr., 1985—. Mem. Suffolk County Dem. Com., 1982—; trustee Temple Beth Sholom of Smithtown, 1999-2000, corr. sec., 2000-01, exec. v.p., 2001-02, pres., 2002—. Staff sgt. USANG, 1970-76. Mem. ABA, N.Y. State Bar Assn., Suffolk County Bar Assn. (com. mem. profl. ethics, grievences and fee disputes), Soc. Am. Magicians Assembly #1 (pres. 1981-82), Rotary. Democrat. Jewish. Office: Sarisohn Sarisohn et al 350 Veterans Hwy Commack NY 11725-4330 E-mail: rbraun@lawteam-ny.com.

BRAUN, ROBERT CLARE, retired association and advertising executive; b. Indpls., July 18, 1928; s. Ewald Elsworth and Lila (Inman) B. BS in Journalism-advtg., Butler U., 1950; postgrad., Ind. Univ., 1957, 66. Reporter Northside Topics Newspaper, Indpls., 1949; advt. mgr., 1950; asst. mgr. Clarence E. Crippen Painting Co., Indpls., 1951; corp. sec. Auto-Imports, Ltd., Indpls., 1952-53; pres. O.R. Brown Paper Co., Indpls., 1953-69; pres., chief exec. ofcr. Robert C. Braun Advt. Agy., 1959-70; with Zimmer Engraving Inc., Indpls, IN, 1964-69; former chmn. bd. O.R. Brown Paper, Inc. Advtg. cons. Rolls Royce Motor Cars, 1957-59, exec. dir., chief exec. ofcr. Historic Landmarks Found., Ind., 1969-73, exec. v.p. Purchasing Mgmt. Assn., Indpls., 1974-85, Midwest Office Systems abd Equipment Show, 1974-85, Grand Valley Indsl. Show, 1974-85; Evansville Indsl. Show, 1982-85, Ind. Bus. Opportunity Fair, 1985-88. Author: The Mr. Eli Lilly That I Knew, 1977. Editor: Historic Landmarks News, 1969-74; Hoosier Purchaser mag., 1974-85, I.R.M.S.D.C. News, 1985-88. Contbr. articles to profl. jours. Chmn. Citizens' Adv. Com. to Marion County Met. Planning Dept., 1963; pres. museum com. Indpls. Fire Dept., 1966-76, mem. adv. com. Historic Preservation Commn. Marion County, 1967-73; Midwestern artifacts cons. to curator of White House, Wash., 1971-73; mem. chmn. Mayor's Contract Compliance Adv. Bd., 1977-91; mem. Mayor's subcom. for Indpls. Stadium, 1981-83; adv. bd., exec. com. Indpls. Office Equal Opportunity 1982—; mem. Ind. Minority Bus. Opportunity Counc., 1985-88; mem. Met. Mus. Art, Indpls. Mus. of Art bd. dirs. Historic Landmarks Found. Ind., 1960-69; dir., sec. Ind. Arthritis and Rheumatism Found., 1960-67, pres., 1969, dir., 1970-90, hon. lifetime dir., 1992—, dir. Assoc. Patient Svcs., 1976-91, dir. emeritus, 1992; pres. Amanda Wasson Meml. Trust, 1961-72. Recipient Meritorious Svc. awd. St. Jude's Police League, 1961; citation for meritorious svc. Am. Legion Police Post 56, 1962; Tafflinger-Holiday Park appreciation awd., 1973; Nat. Vol. Svc. Citation, Arthritis Found., 1979; Margaret Egan Meml. awd. Ind. Arthritis Found., 1980; Indpls. Profl. Fire Fighters meritorious svc. awd., 1982. Mem. Marion County Hist. Soc. (dir. 1964—, pres. 1965-69, 74-76, 1st v.p. 1979), Am. Guild Organists (mem. Indpls. chpt., charter mem. Franklin Coll. br.), Indpls. Humane Soc., Ind. Mus. Soc. (treas., dir. 1967-74), Internat. Fire Buff Assocs., Indpls. Second Alarm Fire Buffs (sec.-treas. 1967, pres. 1969), Ind. Hist. Soc., Nat. Hist. Soc., Nat. Trust Historic Preservation, Smithsonian Assn., Friends of Cast Iron Architecture, Soc. Archtl. Historians, Am. Heritage Soc., N.A.P.M. Editors Grp. (nat. sec. 1979-81, nat. chmn./pres. 1981-84), Am. Assn. State and Local History, Decorative Arts Soc. Indpls., Ind. Soc. Assn. Execs., Nat. Assn. Purchasing Mgmt. (W.L. Beckham internat. pub. rels. awd. 1983), purchasing Mgmt. Assn. Indpls. (dir. 1974—), Victorian Soc. Am. (nat. sec. 1971-74), Lambda Chi Alpha, Alpha Delta Sigma, Sigma Delta Chi, Tau Kappa Alpha. Club: Indpls. Press, Rolls-Royce Owners. Home: 1415 W 52nd St Indianapolis IN 46228-2316

BRAUN, STEPHEN BAKER, academic administrator; b. Cleve., Nov. 3, 1942; s. William B. and Louise M. (Baker) B.; m. Retta F. Kriefall, June 16, 1974; children: Elizabeth Rachel, Christopher Baker. BS, Xavier U., 1964; MBA, Fairleigh Dickinson U., 1976; postgrad., Imperial Coll., U London, 1996—. Regional mgr. Northwest Airlines, Inc., St. Paul, 1967-72; v.p. Inflight Motion Pictures, Inc., N.Y.C., 1972-78; v.p., gen. mgr. Columbia Pipe & Supply, Inc., Portland, Oreg., 1978-79; exec. v.p. Golby Mfg. Co., Portland, 1979-80; v.p. fin. Timberline Software, Inc., Portland, 1980-82; pres., founder Computer Systems Supplyware, Inc., Portland, 1982-87; dean Sch. Bus. Concordia U., Portland, 1987-92, exec. v.p., 1993—; COO Concordia U. Found., Portland, 1993-2000, vice chmn., dir., 1985-2000. Mem. bd. regents Concordia U., 1986-87, 92-2000; bd. dirs. Alameda Resources Co., Tigard, Oreg.; vis. scholar grad. sch. bus. Univ. Washington, 2000—; founder, chmn. CEO Roundtable, 1994—; mem. adv. bd. Oreg. Bus. mag., 2002—.. Com. chmn. United Way, Boston, 1966; bd. dirs. German Am. Found., 1990-2000. With USN, 1964-67. Mem. Oreg. Ctr. for Entrepreneurship (pres., founder, 1986), Oreg. Enterprise Forum, Am. Mktg. Assn. (panelist 1985-88), Assn. Data Processing Systems Orgn., Rotary (long-range planning com. 1985-96, judge Oreg. Enterprise Forum, Entrepreneur of Yr. award 1998). Lutheran. Office: Concordia U 2811 NE Holman St Portland OR 97211-6099 also: Imperial Coll/Mgmt Sch 53 Princes Gate Exhibition Rd London SW7 2PG England

BRAUN, STEPHEN HUGHES, psychologist; b. St. Louis, Nov. 20, 1942; s. William Lafon and Jane Louise Braun; 1 son, Damian Hughes. BA, Washington U., 1964, MA, 1965; PhD, U. Mo., Columbia, 1970. Fellow in clin. psychology USPHS, U. Mo., Columbia, 1970; asst. prof. psychology Calif. State U., Chico, 1970-71, Ariz. State U., 1971-79; dir. social learning divsn. Ariz. State Hosp., Phoenix, 1971-74; chief bur. planning and evaluation State of Ariz., Dept. Health Svcs., Phoenix, 1974-79; pres. Braun and Assocs., Scottsdale, 1979-95; v.p. Ariz. Healthcare, 1991-95; dir. clin. svcs. Cmty. Partnership So. Ariz., 1995-97; asst. prof. psychology Ariz. State U., 1971-79; v.p. ValueOptions, Phoenix, 1997—. Vis. asst. prof. Ctr. of Criminal Justice, 1974-79, Ctr. for Pub. Affairs, 1979-81; cons. Law Enforcement Assistance Adminstrn., NIMH, Alcohol, Drug Abuse and Mental Health Adminstrn., State of Ariz. Dept. Health Svcs., Dept. Corrections, Dept. Econ. Security, and local and regional human svc. agys. Editl. cons.; contbr. articles to sci. and profl. publs. Grantee NIMH, 1971-74, State of Calif., 1971. Mem. APA, Sigma Xi. Home: 9724 E San Salvador Dr Scottsdale AZ 85258-5621

BRAUN, SUSAN, foundation administrator; BA in English and Sociology with honors, George Mason U.; MA in Health Scis. with honors, U. Md.; postgrad. in Internat. Mktg., U. Muenster, Germany. Exec. Pracon Inc. and Ctr. Econ. Studies in Medicine; various positions, Oncology/Immunology Divsn. Bristol-Myers Squibb, Princeton, NJ; pres. and CEO Susan G. Komen Breast Cancer Found., 1996—. Office: Susan G Komen Breast Cancer Found 5005 LBJ Freeway Ste 250 Dallas TX 75244

BRAUN, THOMAS W. academic administrator; b. Pitts., Pa. BS in biology, U. Pitts., 1969, DMD summa cum laude, MS in pharmacology, U. Pitts., 1973, PhD in anatomy, 1977. Resident in oral and maxillofacial surgery Presbyterian U. Hosp., Pitts.; instr. in anatomy at Sch. Dental Medicine U. Pitts., 1975—90, assoc. prof. and chmn., Dept. Oral and Maxillofacial Surgery, 1990—93, assoc. dean hospital affairs, 1991—96, prof., 1993—, sr. assoc. dean, 1996—99, interim dean, Sch. Dental Medicine, 1999—2000, dean, Sch. Dental Medicine, 2000—. Contbr. articles to profl. jours. Mem.: Pa. Soc. Oral and Maxillofacial Surgeons (past pres.), Am. Assn. Oral and Maxillofacial Surgery (mem. House of Delegates), Am. Bd. Oral and Maxillofacial Surgery (past pres.). Office: 3501 Terrace St Pittsburgh PA 15261

BRAUN, WILHELM, retired educator; b. June 29, 1921; PhD, U. Toronto, 1953. Prof. U. Rochester, N.Y., 1956-91, emeritus prof., 1991—. Author articles in fields of German lit. and criticism. Home: 415 Hillside Ave Rochester NY 14610-2918

BRAUN, WILLIAM JOSEPH, life insurance underwriter; b. Belleville, Ill., May 21, 1925; s. Walter Charles and Florence (Lauer) B.; m. Elizabeth Ann Braun, July 7, 1951; children: Brian William (dec.), Roger Edward, Christopher Burnes, Thomas Barrett, Maura Tracey. BS in Mktg, U. Ill., 1949; grad., Inst. Life Ins. Mktg., So. Methodist U., 1950. CLU; chartered fin. cons.; accredited estate planner Nat. Assn. Estate Planners. Life underwriter Mass. Mut. Life Ins. Co., Decatur, Ill., 1949—. Pres. Am. Soc. C.L.U.s, 1976-77; bd. dirs. Am. Coll. C.L.U.s, Bryn Mawr, Pa., 1975-78 Served with USNR, 1943-46. Decorated Navy Air medal. Life mem. Million Dollar Round Table; Nat. Assn. Life Underwriters, Nat. Assn. Estate Planning Couns. (pres. 1985-86), KC, Decatur Club, Country Club Decatur, Decatur Athletic Club. Roman Catholic. Home: 4606 E Powers Blvd Decatur IL 62521-2549 Office: Mass Mutual Decatur Club Bldg 158 W Prairie Decatur IL 62523-1230

BRAUN, ZEV, motion picture and television producer; b. Chgo. s. Julius and Charlotte (Brandau) B.; children: Benjamin, Jonathan, Jeremy; m. MayLing Cheng, Mar. 22, 1972; 1 child, Sue-Ling. Student, Roosevelt U., Chgo., Marquette U., U. Chgo. Producer: Goldstein, 1964 (U.S. rep. Cannes Film Festival, recipient Prix de la Nouvelle Critique), Wanted: Babysitter, 1974-75, The Little Girl Who Lives Down the Lane, 1976 (Best Horror Film, Acad. Sci-Fi, Fantasy and Horror Films), Freedom Road, 1978, The Fiendish Plot of Dr. Fu Manchu, 1979-80, Marlene, 1984 (Acad. award nomination, N.Y. Film Critics award Nat. Bd. Rev. award, Nat. Soc. Film Critics award), Where Are the Children, 1985, (TV mini-series) Menendez: A Killing in Beverly Hills, 1994, Edges of the Lord, 2000; exec. prodr.: Madron, 1970, Angela, 1977, Murphy's Law, 1987, Stillwatch, 1987, Murder Ordained, 1987, Tour of Duty, 1987, 88, 89, Father Clements, 1987, (TV movie) Abducted: A Father's Love, 1996, Lethal Vows, 1999; co-prodr.: The Pedestrian, 1973 (Acad. award nomination, Nat. Bd. Rev. award, Golden Globe award), Bagdad Cafe, 1990, Seduction in Travis County, 1991, Split Images, 1992. Bd. dirs. Little City Found., Palatine, Ill., 1962-63; v.p., dir. Gastro-Intestinal Research Found., U. Chgo., 1964-65; v.p. City of Hope, 1970— ; gen. chmn. Ann. Salute to Med. Research, 1969; chmn. bd. dirs. Internat. Kidney Inst., UCLA, 1981-83; bd. dirs. Am. Found. AIDS Rsch., 1995, Albert B. Sabin Inst. at Georgetown U., 1996, Heart Touch Project. Jewish. Office: Braun Entertainment Group 280 S Beverly Dr Ste 500 Beverly Hills CA 90212-3908

BRAUND-ALLEN, JULIANNA ELISE, librarian; b. Anchorage, Nov. 11, 1953; d. Melvin Arnold and Gertrude Evelyn Johansen Braund; m. George Robert Allen, Sept. 9, 1978; stepchildren: Quentin Christine, Shelley Leigh, Cindy Elaine, Kathleen Diane 1 child, Missa Melaina. BA, U. Alaska, Fairbanks, 1977; MLS, La. State U., 1986. Ref. libr. Anchorage Mcpl. Librs., 1986—88; rsch. libr. Environment & Natural Resources Inst. U. Alaska, 1988—; program mgr., arctic environ. info. & data ctr. Environment & Natural Resources Inst. U. of Alaska, 1993—; mgmt. team libr. Alaska Resources Libr. & Info. Services, 1997—; reference libr., assoc. prof., consortium libr. U. Alaska, 2000—, acting program mgr., Alaska state climate ctr., environment & natural resources inst., 2002—. Editor Vizual Dog, Anchorage, 1994—; spl. librs. rep. Gov.'s Libr. Adv. Coun., 1998—2002. Editor: Icebreakers: Alaska's Most Innovative Artists, The Health of the Inuit of North America: A Bibliography from the Earliest Times through 1990; contbr. articles to profl. jours. Recipient Hammer award, Nat. Performance Rev., V.P. Gore, 1997, cert. of Appreciation, U.S. Dept. of Interior, 1997, Nat. award Libr. Svc., U.S. Inst. Mus. & Libr. Svcs., 2001, citation Exceptional Svc. Citizens of Alaska, Alaska State Legis., 2002. Mem.: United Acads., Alaska Libr. Assn., Polar Librs. Colloquy, Beta Phi Mu, Phi Kappa Phi. Office: ENRI U Alaska 707 A St Anchorage AK 99501 Office Fax: 907-257-2707. E-mail: anjb1@uaa.alaska.edu.

BRAUNER, DAVID A. lawyer; b. N.Y.C., Mar. 4, 1942; s. Herman M. and Mary (Trachtenberg) B.; m. Amy Jo Kaplan, May 3, 1981; children: Sara Lynne, Jesse Howard. AB, Dickinson Coll., Carlisle, Pa., 1963; JD, Columbia U., 1966. Bar: N.Y. 1968. Vol. VISTA, Denver, 1966-67; staff atty. Mobilization for Youth, N.Y.C., 1967-68; ptnr. Brauner Baron et al, N.Y.C., 1968—. Bd. dirs. Helen M. DeMario Found. Bd. dirs. Herman Goldman Found., N.Y.C., 1981—; dir. The Bridge, Inc., N.Y.C., 1980—. Mem. N.Y. State Bar Assn. Democrat. Jewish. Avocations: travel, squash, carpentry. Home: 315 W 106th St New York NY 10025-3445 Office: Brauner Baron et al 61 Broadway New York NY 10006-2701 E-mail: dbrauner@braunerbaron.com.

BRAUNER, RONALD ALLAN, religion educator; b. Phila., Aug. 5, 1939; s. Samuel Joseph Brauner and Ann Ruth (Soloner) Levin; m. Marcia Faith Silver, Sept. 9, 1962; children: Yaakov Baruch, Miriam Aliza. Cert. in teaching, Greenberg Inst., Jerusalem, 1960; BS in Edn., Temple U., 1962; PhD, Dropsie Coll., 1974. Cert. tchr., Pa. Assoc. prof. Gratz Coll., Phila., 1967-78; acad. dean Reconstructionist Rabbinical Coll., Phila., 1972-83; dir. Brandeis-Bardin Inst., L.A., 1983-85; exec. dir. Hebrew Inst. Pitts., 1985-91; pres. Found. for Jewish Studies, Inc., Pitts., 1991—. Prof. Jewish studies Siegal Coll. Jewish Studies, 1994—. Editor Jewish Civilization: Essays and Studies, 1979-85, Straightalk, 1991—; author: Being Jewish in a Gentile World: A Survival Guide, 1995, Thinking Jewish: The Art of Living in Two Civilizations, 2001. Mem. Coalition Alternatives in Jewish Edn., Am. Oriental Soc., Soc. Biblical Lit., Assn. Jewish Studies. Democrat. Office: Found for Jewish Studies 1531 S Negley Ave Pittsburgh PA 15217-1419 E-mail: rbrauner@Torah.com., rbrauner@siegalcollege.edu.

BRAUNGARD III, CHARLES W. music educator; b. Lancaster, Pa., Nov. 12, 1964; s. Freda B. Braungard and Charles W. Braungard Jr.; m. Sharon Faye Kuhns, Aug. 3, 1991. BS, Millersville U. of Pa, Millersville, PA, 1987. Music educator Ea. Lebanon County Sch. Dist., Myerstown, Pa., 1988—89, Harford County Sch. Dist., Bel Air, Md., 1990—. Recipient Advanced Profl. Cert., Md. State Dept. of Edn., 2000. Mem.: Music Educators Nat. Conf.

BRAUNGART, MARGARET MITCHELL, psychology and bioethics educator; b. Washington, Jan. 1, 1942; d. Nelson Paul and Isabel (Carney) Mitchell; m. Richard G. Braungart, Aug. 29, 1964; children: Julia, Katherine, Elizabeth. BS in Elem. Edn., U. Md., 1964, MA in Human Devel., 1972; PhD in Psychology, Syracuse U., 1980. Instr. Syracuse (N.Y.) U., 1978-79, SUNY Upstate Med. Ctr., Syracuse, 1976-79, asst. prof. psychology, 1979-84; assoc. prof. psychology SUNY Health Sci. Ctr., Syracuse, 1984-90, prof. psychology, 1990—2000, chair dept. health scis. and human studies, 1991-97; prof. Ctr. Bioethics and Humanities, Coll. Medicine Upstate Med. U., 2000—. Pres. gen. faculty assembly, SUNY Health Scis. Ctr., 1984-86; mem. exec. adv. com. for geriat., SUNY Health Scis. Ctr., 1982-95, mem. adv. bd. geriat. patients, 1987-89; co-dir. Life Course Rsch. Ctr., Syracuse U., 1985—; cons. WETA-TV, Washington, 1989, 91; lectr., cons. UN, N.Y.C., 1995—2000; lectr. SUNY Upstate Med. U. Coll. Medicine, 1996-2000; mem. SUNY Pres. Tchg. award com., 1997-2002; exec. dir. Consortium for Culture and Medicine, 2001-. Author: Global Survey of Youth Attitudes and Behavior, 2000; editor: Political Sociology of the State, 1990; editor, author: Life Course and Generational Politics, 1993; editor, author (rsch. series) Research in Political Sociology, 1985-89; contbr. over 80 articles to profl. jours., chpts. to books; mem. editl. bd. Rsch. in Polit. Sociology, 1990—. Citizen rep. Town of Manlius (N.Y.) Environ. Com., 1982-85. Rsch. grantee U.S. Dept. HEW, 1977-78, Ctr. Study Vietnam Generation, Washington, 1987. Mem.: Am. Soc. Bioethics & Humanities, Am. Psychol. Assn. Democrat. Avocations: walking, travel, reading. Home: 4783 Armstrong Rd Manlius NY 13104-1418 Office: SUNY Upstate Med U 750 E Adams St Syracuse NY 13210-2306

BRAUNGART, RICHARD GOTTFRIED, sociology and international relations educator; b. Balt., Apr. 21, 1935; s. Paul Peter and Jean Mary (Stanton) B.; m. Margaret Lombard Mitchell, Aug. 29, 1964; children— Julia, Katherine, Elizabeth. BA, U. Md., College Park, 1961, MA, 1963; PhD, Pa. State U., State College, 1969. Rsch. asst. Bur. Social Sci. Rsch., Washington, 1964; instr. sociology Pa. State U., State College, 1966-69; asst. prof. sociology U. Md., College Park, 1969-72; assoc. prof. sociology Syracuse U., NY, 1972—76, prof. sociology, 1976—2002, prof. internat. rels., 1993—2002, prof. polit. sci., 1998—2002, prof. emeritus, 2003—. Rsch. dir. President's Commn. on Campus Unrest, 1970; vis. lectr. USIA, 1971; prof. assoc. East-West Ctr., Honolulu, 1978; lectr., cons. Nat. U. Mex., 1980, USSR Acad. Scis., Moscow, 1989; German Marshall Fund U.S., Berlin and Fed. Republic Germany, 1990, China Youth Coll. for Politics, Beijing Acad. Social Scis., Shanghai Ctr. Youth Rsch., Shanghai Acad. Social Scis., Ewha U., Seoul, Han Nam U., Taejon, Republic of Korea, 1991, Vista U., U, Pretoria, Potchefstroom U., U. Orange Free State, U. Port Elizabeth, Witwatersrand U., South Africa, 1992, UN, N.Y.C., 1995, 98. Author: Family Status, Socialization and Student Politics, 1979; editor: Society and Politics, 1976, Jour. Polit. and Mil. Sociology, 1983; editor: (assoc.), 1984—; editor: Life Course and Generational Politics, 1984, 1993, The Political Sociology of the State, 1990, Critical Issues in the U.S., 1997—98; editor: (series) Research in Political Sociology, 1985—89; mem. editl. bd.:, 1989—; editor (assoc.): Western Sociol. Rev., 1976—82, Sociol. Spectrum, 1980—83; editor: (book rev.) Jour. Polit. and Mil. Sociology, 1977—84; mem. editl. bd.: Sociol. Symposium, 1972—77, Polit. Behavior, 1978—84, Micropolitics, 1980—84, Quar. Jour. Ideology, 1983—90. With U.S. Army, 1954—56, with USAR, 1956—62. Mem. Am. Sociol. Assn. (polit. sociology sect. co-founder, treas. 1982-84, sect. coun. 1985-88, collective behavior sect. coun. 1984-86), Internat. Soc. Polit. Psychology (nominating com. 1983-84, chmn. nominating com. 1989-90. governing coun. 1989-91, chmn. search com. 1990-91), Internat. Sociol. Assn. (v.p. rsch. com. 1982-90, 98-2002, pres. com. polit. sociology 1994-98), Soc. Study Social Problems (chmn. internat. conflict and coop. divsn. 1984-86, chmn. com. stds, rsch., tchg. 1996-98), Internat. Polit. Sci. Assn. (pres. com. on polit. sociology 1994-98, v.p. rsch. com. 1998-2002). Democrat. Avocations: gardening, jogging, travel. Home: 4783 Armstrong Rd Manlius NY 13104-1418 Office: Syracuse U Dept Sociology Syracuse NY 13244-1090 E-mail: rgbraung@maxwell.syr.edu., rbraung1@twcny.rr.com.

BRAUNSCHWEIG, KARL DAVID, education educator, performing arts educator, humanities educator; b. Madison, Wis., Mar. 8, 1969; s. David Lee and Rhoda Dora Braunschweig; m. Kelly Marie Foreman, June 18, 1994. BA, St. Olaf Coll., 1991; MusM, U. Mich., 1993, PhD, 1997. Computer programmer, editor U. Wis., Madison, 1987—91; tchg. asst. St. Olaf Coll., Northfield, Minn., 1988—91, U. Mich., Ann Arbor, 1991—96; asst. prof. Wayne State U., Detroit, 1997—. Mem. editl. bd. In Theory Only, 1998—; contbr. articles to profl. jours. Pres. Mich. Music Theory Soc., Ann Arbor, 1993—95. Deans Rsch. grant,

Wayne State U., 2002. Mem.: Internat. Musicol. Soc., Am. Musicol. Soc., Soc. for Music Theory, Pi Kappa Lambda, Phi Beta Kappa. Office: Wayne State Univ Music Dept 4841 Cass Ave Detroit MI 48202

BRAUNSDORF, JAMES ALLEN, physics educator; b. South Bend, Ind., Apr. 13, 1938; s. Walter Louis and Ruth Harriet (Tuttle) B.; m. Donna Lou Munson, June 10, 1960; children: Kevin Scott, Allen Keith, Walter James. AB in Physics, De Pauw U., 1960; MS in Math., Purdue U., 1965. Cert. secondary tchr., Ind. Tchr. physics Greencastle Schs., 1960-62, Mishawaka (Ind.) Sch., 1962—2002. Tax preparer, Mishawaka, 1967—; adj. lectr. Ind. U., South Bend, 1981-89. Pres. Beiger Heritage Corp., Mishawaka, 1981-86, 2003—; active Youth for Understanding, 1990—. Mem. NEA, Ind. State Tchrs. Assn., Am. Assn. Physics Tchrs. (Ind. Disting. Physics Tchr. 1984), Nat. Sci. Tchrs. Assn., Mishawaka Edn. Assn. (pres. 1970-74), Phi Beta Kappa. Methodist. Avocations: computing, genealogy. Home: 449 Edgewater Dr Mishawaka IN 46545-6909 E-mail: jbraunsdorf@msn.com.

BRAUNSDORF, PAUL RAYMOND, lawyer; b. South Bend, Ind., June 18, 1943; s. Robert Louis and Marjorie (Breitenstein) Braunsdorf; m. Margaret Buckley, June 18, 1966; children: Christopher, Mark, Douglas, Amy. BA magna cum laude, U. Notre Dame, 1965; LLB, U. Va., 1968. Bar: NY 1968, US Dist Ct (western dist) NY 1969, US Dist Ct (northern dist) NY 1980, US Ct Appeals (2d cir) 1975, US Supreme Ct 1980. Assoc. Harris Beach LLP, Rochester, 1968-75; ptnr., 1976—. Instr Nat Inst Trial Advocacy, Rochester, 1988; lectr in field. Author (contbg auth): (book) Antitrust Health Care Handbook II, 1993, Antitrust Law in New York, 1995, 2d edit., 2002. Bd dirs McQuaid Parent's Club, 1984—90, pres, 1986—87; bd dirs Mercy Parent's Club, 1989—90, Brighton Baseball, 1987—90. Republican. Roman Catholic. Avocations: tennis, photography, music. Office: Harris Beach LLP 99 Garnsey Rd Pittsford NY 14534

BRAUNSTEIN, ETHAN MALCOLM, skeletal radiologist, paleopathologist, educator; b. Chgo., June 16, 1945; BA, Dartmouth Coll., 1967; MD, Northwestern U., Chgo., 1970. Instr. radiology U. Mich., Ann Arbor, 1976-81, assoc. prof., 1983-87; asst. prof. radiology Harvard U., Cambridge, Mass., 1981-83; prof. radiology Ind. U., Indpls., 1987-2000, No. Ariz. U., Flagstaff, 2000—, Adj. prof. anthropology Ind. U., Indpls., 1990-00; cons. radiologist Mayo Clinic, Scottsdale, Ariz., 2001—. Contbr. numerous articles to profl. jours., chpts. to books. Bd. dirs. Kelsey Mus. Archeology, Ann Arbor, 1983-87. Mem.: Radiol. Soc. N.Am., Am. Assn. Phys. Anthropologists, Internat. Skeletal Soc. Office: No Ariz U Flagstaff AZ 86011-5200

BRAUNSTEIN, GLENN DAVID, physician, educator; b. Greenville, Tex., Feb. 29, 1944; s. Mervin and Helen (Friedman) B.; m. Jacquelyn D. Moose, July 5, 1965; children: Scott M. Braunstein, Jeffrey T. Braunstein. BS summa cum laude, U. Calif. San Francisco, 1965, MD, 1968. Diplomate Am. Bd. Internal Medicine, subspecialty endocrinology, diabetes, metabolism. Intern, resident Peter Bent Brigham Hosp., Boston, 1968-70; clin. fellow in medicine Harvard U. Med. Sch., Boston, 1969-70; clin. assoc., reproduction rsch. br. NIH, Bethesda, Md., 1970-72; chief resident in endocrinology Harbor Gen. Hosp. UCLA, 1972-73; dir. endocrinology Cedars-Sinai Med. Ctr., L.A., 1973-86, chmn., dept. medicine, 1986—; asst. prof. medicine UCLA Sch. Medicine, 1973-77, assoc. prof., 1977-81, prof., 1981—, vice chair dept. medicine, 1986—. Cons. for AMA drug evaluations, 1990—; mem. internat. adv. com. Second World Conf. on Implantation and Early Pregnancy in Human, 1994; mem. endocrinologic and metabolic drugs adv. com. FDA, 1991-95, chmn., 1994-95, spl. advisor, 1995-2001, chmn., 2001—; bd. mem. Am. Bd. Internal Medicine Endocrinology, Diabetes, Metabolism Subspecialty, 1991-99, chmn., 1995-99, bd. dirs., 1995-99; bd. dirs. Cedars-Sinai Med. Ctr., 1997-2002, Am. Bd. Emergency Medicine, 2002--. Mem. editl. bd. Mt. Sinai Jour. Medicine, 1984-88, Early Pregnancy: Biology and Medicine, 1998, Am. Family Physician, 1995—, The Am. Jour. Medicine, 1996—, Clin. Endocrinology & Metabolism, 1978-80; assoc. editor Integrative Medicine: Integrating Allopathic, Alternative and Complementary Medicine, 1997-2000. Bd. dirs. Israel Cancer Rsch. Fund, 1991-94, Cedars-Sinai Med. Ctr., 1997—; mem. Jonsson Comprehensive Cancer Ctr., 1991—. Recipient Gold Headed Cane Soc. award U. Calif. San Francisco Med. Ctr., 1968, Merck scholarship, 1968, Mosby scholarship, 1968, Soc. of Hacham award Cedars-Sinai Med. Ctr., 1976, Morris Press Humanism award Cedars-Sinai Med. Ctr., 1984, outstanding achievement and cmty. svc. award Anti-Defamation League, 1997, James R. Klinenberg Chair in Medicine, 2000—, Sherman M. Mullinkoff Faculty award UCLA Sch. Medicine, 2002. Fellow ACP (mem. adv. com. to gov., So. Calif. region 1989—, credentials com. So. Calif. region 1993); mem. AAAS, Am. Diabetes Assn., Cross Town Endocrine Club (chmn. 1982-83), Endocrine Soc. (publs. com. 1983-89, long range planning com. 1986-87, recent progress hormone rsch. com. 1993-98, ann. meeting steering com. 1993-98, spl. programs com. 1998—, media adv. com. 1999—, chmn. 2002), Pacific Coast Fertility Soc. (pres. 1988), Western Soc. for Clin. Rsch., Am. Fedn. for Clin. Rsch., Am. Thyroid Assn., Am. Fertility Soc., Western Assn. Physicians (pres. 1998-99), Assn. Am. Physicians, Am. Soc. Clin. Investigations (mem. nominating com. 1989), USCF Sch. Medicine Alumni Faculty Assn. (regional v.p. so. Calif., mem. bd. dirs. Israel Cancer Rsch. Fund 1991-94, mem. Jonsson Comprehensive Cancer Ctr. 1991—), Phi Delta Epsilon, Alpha Omega Alpha. Office: Cedars Sinai Med Ctr Dept Med Pla Level Rm 2119 8700 Beverly Blvd Los Angeles CA 90048-1865 E-mail: braunstein@cshs.org.

BRAUNSTEIN, HERBERT, pathologist, educator; b. N.Y.C., Jan. 10, 1926; s. Max and Ida (Meyerson) B.; m. Frances Toomey, Aug. 1, 1954; children: Sheila, Mary, John, Anne. BS, CCNY and CUNY, 1944; MD, Hahnemann Med. Coll., 1950. Intern Montefiore Hosp., N.Y.C., 1950-51; resident in pathology U. Mich., Ann Arbor, 1951-52, U. Cin., 1952-55, from asst. prof. to assoc. prof. pathology, 1956-64; chmn. dept. pathology Michael Reese Hosp., Chgo.; also prof. pathology Chgo. Med. Sch., 1964-65; from assoc. prof. to prof. pathology U. Ky., Lexington, 1965-70; chmn. dept. labs. San Bernardino (Calif.) County Med. Ctr., 1970-91, also dir. sch. med. tech.; clin. prof. pathology Loma Linda (Calif.) U., 1970-91, UCLA, 1980-83; prof. in residence biomed. scis. U. Calif., Riverside, 1979-83. Author book; mem. editorial bd. Modern Pathology; contbr. articles to sci. jours., chpts. to books. Served with USNR, 1944-46, PTO. Recipient numerous research grants, Career devel. award USPHS, 1958-64. Mem. AMA, Calif. Med. Assn., San Bernardino County Med. Soc., Am. Soc. Clin. Pathologists, Coll. Am. Pathologists, U.S.-Can. Acad. Pathology, Am. Assn. Pathologists, Histochem. Soc., Phi Beta Kappa, Sigma Xi, Alpha Omega Alpha. Home: 28372 Via Anzar San Juan Capistrano CA 92675-2936

BRAUNSTEIN, MYRON LEE, psychology educator; b. N.Y.C., Sept. 3, 1936; s. Hyman and Anne B.. BS, Bklyn. Coll., 1956; MS, U. Mich., 1959; PhD, U. Mich., Ann Arbor, 1961. Rsch. psychologist Cornell Aero. Lab., Buffalo, 1960—63, Flight Safety Found., Phoenix, 1963—65; asst. prof. U. Calif., Irvine, Calif., 1965—67, assoc. prof., 1967—73, prof., 1973—. Author: (research text) Depth Perception Through Motion; editor: Perception & Psychophysics, 1994—98. Fellow: APA, Am. Psychol. Soc.; mem.: Human Factors and Ergonomics Soc. Office: U Calif 3151 Social Science Plz Irvine CA 92697-5100

BRAUNWALD, EUGENE, physician, educator; b. Aug. 15, 1929; m. Nina H. Starr (dec.); m. Elaine R. Smith, 1993; children: Karen G., Allison Jill. AB, NYU, 1949, MD, 1952; AM (hon.), Harvard U., 1972; MD (hon.), U. Lisbon, 1984, MD (hon.), 1985; ScD (hon.), Mt. Sinai Med. Ctr., 1991; MD (hon.), U. Rome, 1991, U. Portg, 1992, U. Vienna, 1995, U. La Plata (Argentina), 1995, U. Rio de Janeiro, 1998, Carol Davila U., 2002, U. Athens, 2003, U. Padua, 2003, Bates Coll., 2003. Diplomate Am. Bd. Internal Medicine, Am. Bd. Cardiovascular Disease. Intern, fellow Mt. Sinai Hosp., N.Y.C., 1952—54; research fellow Columbia U. Coll. Physicians and Surgeons, N.Y.C., 1954—55; clin. assoc. cardiovascular physiology lab. Nat. Heart Inst., Bethesda, Md., 1955—57; asst. resident Osler Med. Service, Johns Hopkins Hosp., Balt., 1957—58; chief cardiology sect., chief cardiology br., clin. dir. Nat. Heart and Lung Inst., Bethesda, 1958—68; prof., chmn. dept. medicine U. Calif.-San Diego, 1968—72; Hersey prof. of theory and practice of medicine Harvard U. Med. Sch., Boston, 1972—96, Herrman Blumgart prof. Medicine, 1980—89, chmn. study group, 1984—, Disting. Hersey prof., 1996—, faculty dean for acad. programs, 1996—2003. Chmn. dept. medicine Brigham and Women's Hosp., 1972—96, Beth Israel Hosp., 1980—89; lectr. physiology George Washington U., 1959—62; from asst. clin. prof. to clin. prof. Georgetown U. Sch. Medicine, 1960—68; lectr. medicine Johns Hopkins U., 1960—68; trustee McLear Ptnrs., 1993—96; vis. prof. numerous U.S. and fgn. univs.; lectr. in field. Co-editor: Year Book of Cardiovascular and Renal Diseases, 1965—72, Year Book of Medicine, 1973—93, Harrison's Principles of Internal Medicine, 1967—; editor: Heart Disease, 1980—; mem. editl. bds.: Ciculation, Jour. Clin. Investigation, 1964—71, Jour. Cardiovascular Pharmacology, Am. Jour. Medicine, Am. Jour. Cardiology, New Eng. Jour. Medicine, numerous others. Bd. visitors Rockefeller U., 1978—82; mem. vis. com. MIT, 1979—85, Technion U., 1979. Recipient Arthur S. Fleming award, 1965, Superior Svc. award, HEW, 1967, Disting. Achievement award, Modern Medicine, 1968, Gustav Nylin award, Swedish Med. Soc., 1970, Williams award Outstanding Chmn. and Medicine, 1987, Bristol Myers Squibb Excellence in Cardiovascular Rsch. award, 1993, J. Allyn Taylor Internat. prize, Robarts Rsch. Inst., 1993. Fellow: ACP (Phillips award 1991), Am. Coll. Cardiology (v.p. 1967, trustee 1967, 1970—75, Disting. Scientist award 1987), Am. Acad. Arts and Scis.; mem.: NAS, Internat. Soc. Cardiology, Royal Soc. Medicine, Harvey Soc., Am. Heart Assn. (bd. dirs. 1966—75, v.p. 1966—70, Rsch. Achievement award 1972, Herrick award 1981), Am. Soc. Pharmacology and Exptl. Therapeutics (John Jacob Abel award 1965), Am. Physiol. Soc., New Eng. Cardiovascular Soc. (pres. 1987—88), Assn. Univ. Cardiologists, Western Soc. for Clin. Rsch. (pres. 1971—72), Am. Fedn. Clin. Rsch. (pres. 1969—70), Am. Soc. Clin. Investigation (pres. 1974—75), Western Assn. Physicians, Assn. Am. Physicians (Kober medal 1998), Assn. Profs. Medicine (pres. 1974—75), Johns Hopkins Soc. Scholars, Alpha Omega Alpha. Office: Timi Study Group 350 Longwood Ave 1st Fl Boston MA 02115

BRAUSE, BARRY DAVID, infectious diseases physician; b. N.Y.C., Apr. 15, 1945; s. Jack and Ruth (Heiman) B.; m. Geraldine Hersh, June 13, 1970; children: Juliet, Melissa, Jacqueline. BA, NYU, 1966; MD, U. Pitts., 1970. Diplomate Am. Bd. Internal Medicine, Infectious Diseases. Intern Boston City Hosp., 1970-71; resident N.Y. Hosp., 1971-73; fellow infectious diseases Cornell U. Med. Coll., N.Y.C., 1973-75, clin. assoc. prof. medicine, 1983-95, clin. prof. medicine, 1995—. Assoc. attending physician Hosp. Spl. Surgery, N.Y.C., 1984-96, attending physician, 1996—; assoc. attending physician N.Y. Hosp., 1983-95, attending physician, 1995—. Editl. reviewer Jour. AMA, 1990—, Jour. Bone and Joint Surgery, 1989—; relevance reviewer Am. Bd. Internal Medicine, 1995—; contbr. chpts. in books. Bd. dirs. N.Y. County Soc. Internal Medicine. Recipient Andrew Mellon Tchr.-Scientist award Andrew W. Mellon Found., 1977-79, Frank Stinchfield award The Hip Soc., 1985. Fellow ACP; mem. Infectious Diseases Soc. Am. Office: 215 E 68th St New York NY 10021-5718

BRAUTIGAM, DAVID CLYDE, lawyer, judge; b. Westfield, N.Y., Nov. 11, 1950; s. Frank C. and Edna M. Brautigam; m. Amy S. Konz, Apr. 30, 1988; children: Sarah, Susanna, Sharon. BA, Houghton Coll., 1972; JD, U. Pitts., 1979. Bar: N.Y. 1980, U.S. Dist. Ct. (we. dist.) N.Y. 1983. Assoc. Shane & Franz, Olean, N.Y., 1979-84; ptnr. Richardson, Pullen & Brautigam, Fillmore, N.Y., 1984-93; town justice Town of Rushford, N.Y., 1997—; pvt. practice Houghton, N.Y., 1993—. Bd. dirs. So. Tier Legal Svcs., Bath, N.Y., 1981-85, Odosagih Bible Conf., Inc., Mchias, N.Y., 1990-93; chmn., bd. dirs. 1st Bapt. Ch., Rushford, N.Y., 1996-2000, deacon, 1988-2000, 2002--. Mem. Nat. Lawyers Assn., Allegany County Bar Assn. (sec.), Christian Legal Soc. Republican. Baptist. Avocations: hunting, gardening, farming, reading. Office: 9888 County Road 23 Houghton NY 14744-8742

BRAUTIGAN, JUNE MARIE, artist, poet; b. Syracuse, N.Y., Apr. 2, 1952; d. Ward Ernest Shaut and Frances Mary Craig; m. Thomas Francis Brautigan, Nov. 24, 1995; children: Timothy, Chad, Nathan, Crystal. Assoc. Degree, Corning C.C., Corning, N.Y., 1994. Author: (poetry) Goldenrod, 1993 (Winner in SCOP jour., 1993), Hometown, 1995, Perpetuate, 1997, Seacast, 1997, Purgation, 1998, Reign, 1999, the coming of Age, 2000, Unify, 2001, I Can See Things I Cannot See, 2002, Weathering The Layoff, 2002, The Same Sameness, 2002, (short stories) A Room I Remember, 1992 (First place in Scop jour., 1992), Judgments, 2002. Mem.: Internat. Poet Soc. Avocations: interior decorating, gardening. Home: 2850 Dunn's Mountain Rd Salisbury NC 28146 Personal E-mail: jmbrautigan@yahoo.com.

BRAUTIGAN, MARK W. emergency physician; b. Detroit, 1952; MD, Wayne State U., 1978. Diplomate Am. Bd. Emergency Medicine. Intern Wayne State U., Detroit, 1978-79; resident in emergency medicine Detroit Gen. Hosp./Wayne State U., 1979-81; chief dept. emergency medicine Sinai-Grace Hosp., Detroit, 1992—; assoc. prof. Wayne State U. Mem. Am. Coll. Emergency Physicians, Soc. Acad. Emergency Medicine. E-mail: mbrautig@dmc.org.

BRAVERMAN, ALAN N. lawyer; b. Mass. BA, Brandeis U., 1969; JD, Duquesne U., 1975. Bar: D.C. 1976. Assoc. Wilmer, Cutler & Pickering, 1976-82, ptnr., 1983-93; exec. v.p., gen. counsel ABC, Inc., NYC, 1993-2000; deputy, gen. counsel The Walt Disney Co., Burbank, Calif., 2000—03; exec. v.p & gen. coun. Disney, 2003—. Office: ABC Inc 500 S Buena Vista St Burbank CA 91521-0922

BRAVERMAN, AMY JOAN, statistician, researcher; b. L.A., May 2, 1960; d. Jerome David and Judith Margret Braverman. PhD, U. Calif., L.A., 1999. Sr. analyst Nat. Econ. Rsch. Assocs., L.A.; rsch. dir. Micronomics, Inc., L.A., 1987—90; post doctoral scholar Calif. Inst. Tech., Pasadena, 1999—2001; statistician Jet Propulsion Lab., Pasadena, 2001—. Mem.: IEEE, Am. Geophys. Union, Am. Statis. Assn. (pub. officer statis. graphics sect.), Interface Found. of N.Am. (sec. 2001—, bd.dirs.). Office: Jet Propulsion Lab MS 169 237 4800 Oak Grove Dr Pasadena CA 91109-8099 E-mail: amy.braverman@jpl.nasa.gov.

BRAVERMAN, BURT ALAN, lawyer; b. N.Y.C., Apr. 20, 1946; BA, Miami U., Oxford, Ohio, 1966; JD with honors, George Washington U., 1969. Bar: Va. 1969, D.C. 1970, U.S. Supreme Ct. 1972. Ptnr. Cole, Raywid & Braverman, Washington, 1969—. Author treatise Information Law, 1985, Getting and Protecting Competitive Business Information, 1997; editor-in-chief Jour. Law and Econ. Devel., 1968-69; contbr. articles to profl. jours. Office: Cole Raywid & Braverman 2d Fl 1919 Pennsylvania Ave NW Washington DC 20006-3404 E-mail: bbraverman@crblaw.com.

BRAVERMAN, HERBERT LESLIE, lawyer; b. Buffalo, Apr. 24, 1947; s. David and Miriam P. (Cohen) B.; m. Janet Marx, June 11, 1972; children: Becca Danielle, Benjamin Howard. BS in Econs., U. Pa., 1969; JD, Harvard U., 1972. Bar: Ohio 1972, U.S. Dist. Ct. Ohio 1972, U.S. Supreme Ct. 1975, U.S. Ct. Appeals (6th cir.) 1980, U.S. Ct. Claims 1980. Assoc. Hahn, Loeser, Freedheim, Dean & Wellman, Cleve., 1972-75; sole practice Cleve., 1975-87; ptnr. Porter, Wright, Morris & Arthur, Cleve., 1987-95, Walter & Haverfield LLP, Cleve., 1996—. Councilman Orange Village, Ohio, 1988—, pres., 1998-2001. Capt. USAR, 1970-82. Fellow Am. Coll. Trust and Estate Counsel; mem. ABA, Ohio Bar Assn., Bar Assn. Greater Cleve. (former chmn. estate planning trust and probate sect.), Suburban East Bar Assn. (pres. 1978-80), Rotary (Cleveland Heights pres. 1980), B'nai Brith (local pres. 1978-84), Wharton Club Cleve. (pres. 1991—), Am. Jewish Congress (Ohio pres. 1992—). Avocations: golf, symphony, reading. Home: 3950 Orangewood Dr Cleveland OH 44122-7406 Office: Walter & Haverfield LLP 1300 Terminal Tower 50 Public Sq Ste 1300 Cleveland OH 44113-2253 also: 2000 Auburn Dr Ste 200 Beachwood OH 44122 E-mail: hbraverman@walterhav.com., hbraverman@ameritech.com.

BRAVERMAN, IRWIN MERTON, dermatologist, educator; b. Boston, Apr. 17, 1929; s. Morris and Molly (Singer) B.; m. Muriel S. Freedman, June 5, 1955; children: Paula, David, Michael. AB, Harvard U., 1951; MD, Yale U., 1955. Diplomate: Am. Bd. Med. Examiners, Am. Bd. Dermatology, Am. Bd. Pathology. Practice medicine specializing in dermatology New Haven; asst. prof. dermatology Yale U., New Haven, 1962-68, assoc. prof., 1968-73, prof., 1973—. Author: Skin Signs of Systemic Disease, 1970, 3d edit., 1997; contbr. articles to profl. jours. Served to capt. U.S. Army, 1956-58. Recipient Mr. and Mrs. J.N. Taub Internat. Meml. award for research in psoriasis Baylor Med. Coll., 1980 Mem. AMA, New Eng. Dermatol. Soc. (v.p. 1990-91, pres. 1991-92), Am. Dermatol. Assn., Am. Acad. Dermatology (dir. 1980-83, Sulzberger Internat. lectr. 1989, Master of Dermatology 1993, Everett C. Fox Meml. lectr. 2001), Soc. Investigative Dermatology (bd. dirs. 1982-87, pres. elect 1991-92, pres. 1992-93, David M. Carter award for mentorship 1999), Am. Fedn. Clin. Rsch., Am. Assn. Physicians. Office: Yale U Med Sch 333 Cedar St New Haven CT 06510-3289 E-mail: irwin.braverman@yale.edu.

BRAVERMAN, JANIS ANN BREGGIN, lawyer; b. Rochester, N.Y., Mar. 5, 1955; d. Arnold H. and Eleanor (Wingo) Breggin; m. Joseph T. Braverman; children: Rachel Tyler, Cadiz Safira, Theo Socrates, Arielle. BA, U. Denver, 1976, JD, 1980. Bar: Colo. 1980, U.S. Ct. Appeals (10th cir.) 1980. Assoc. Sherman & Howard, Denver, 1980-82, Jeffrey M. Nobel & Assocs., Denver, 1982-84; assoc. in house counsel Bill L. Walters Cos., Englewood, Colo., 1984-85; assoc. Deutsch & Sheldon, Englewood, 1985-87; ptnr. Breggin & Assocs. P.C., Denver, 1987-95, The Breggin Law Firm, P.C., Denver, 1995—. Mem. Denver Women's Commn., 1990-93, chmn. 1991-92. Mem. Colo. Bar Assn., Denver Bar Assn., Colo. Women's Bar Assn. Office: The Breggin Law Firm PC 9145 E Kenyon Ave 301 Denver CO 80237

BRAVERMAN, JORDAN, columnist; b. Boston, July 4, 1936; s. Morris and Molly (Singer) B. BA, Harvard Coll., 1958; MPH, Yale U., 1963; MS of Fgn. Svc., Georgetown U., 1968. Urban planner, economist City Govt. of Quincy, Mass., 1959-61; adminstr. Nat. Blue Cross Assn., Chgo., 1963-65; economist U.S. Dept. Health Edn. and Welfare, Pub. Health Svc., Washington, 1965-67; mgmt. cons. EBS Mgmt. Cons., Washington, 1967-69; asst. to the exec. dir. Am. Pharm. Assn., Washington, 1969-72; dir. pub. policy rsch. Pharm. Mfrs. Assn., Washington, 1972-74; mng. editor Topics in Health Care Financing, Rockville, Md., 1974-75; dir. legis., policy analysis divsn. Health Policy Ctr., Georgetown U., Washington, 1975-77; cons. editor, author Washington, 1978—. Appeared numerous TV and radio shows; speech writer, lectr., pub. spkr., jour./mag. book reviewer, cons. editor VA, Washington, 1986-88, FMAS, Inc., Rockville, 1990—, others; columnist The Balt. Sun, 1990, Am. Weekly News, Washington, 1988—, Capital Jester, Washington, 1993, Internat. Med. News Svc., Washington, 1982—, Consumer Health Reporter, Washington, 1983-84, World Media Reports, 2001—, others; manuscript book referee, reviewer U. Press Am., 1982—, Rowman & Littlefield Publs. Inc., 1995—. Author: Pharmaceutical Payment Plans: An Overview, 1973, Crisis in Health Care, 1978, rev. 1980 (nominated Kulp Book award 1978), The Consumer's Book of Health: How to Stretch Your Health Care Dollar, 1982, The Education of the Osteopathic Physician, 1985, Health Maintenance Organizations: New Choices for Paying and Receiving Medical Care, 1980, Nursing Home Standards: a Tragic Dilemma in American Health, 1970, State Health Insurance Plans: Is Anyone Listening?, 1977, To Hasten the Homecoming: How Americans Fought World War II Through the Media, 1996, others; contbr. Echoes of Yesterday, 1994 (anthologies) Best Poems of 1995, Best Poems of the 90s, 1996, Best Poems of 1997, Best Poems of 1998, Thoughts by Candlelight, 1998, Outstanding Poets of 1998, A Celebration of Poets: Showcase Edition, 1998, The Blush of Morning, 1999, Nature's Echoes, 2000 (poetry anthology) The Falling Rain, 2000 (poetry anthology) American at the Millennium: The Best Poems and Poets of the 20th Century (anthology), 2000, (poetry anthology) Poetry's Elite: The Best Poets of 2000, Poetry's Elite, 2001 (poetry anthology), Under a Quicksilver Moon (poetry anthology), 2002; contbr. poetry to Poetry.com, 2000; (cassette) The Sound of Poetry, 1995-2003, (photog. anthologies) Cherished Moments in Time, 1997, Candid Captures, (photog. anthology), 2001, Shadows of Thought (photography anthology), 2001, (photog. anthology) photography exhibited World Sci., Washington, 1997, photograph included in Editor's Choice Desk Calendar, Internat. Libr. Photograpy, 1999, Reflections from the Past, 1998, America at the Millennium: The Best Photos of the 20th Century, 1999, The Best Photos of 2000, 2000, Best Photos of 2003, Hidden Treasures, 2000 (photog. anthology), Poetry's Elite Award, 2000 (Editor's Choice award, 2001); contbr. articles to profl and popular jours., govt. publs., univs.; photog. exhibited in Internat. Photo. Hall of Fame Mus., 1997-2001; photography featured in Internat. Libr. Photography Desk Calendar, 1999 (Editor's Choice award 1998-99). Column submitted for nomination of Pulitzer Prize, 1994; William Stoughton scholar Harvard U., 1958-59; name inscribed on Nat. Wall of Tolerance, Montgomery, Ala., 2001; recipient Editors Choice award N.Am. Open Poetry Contest, 1994, 97, Editor's Choice award, 2001; candidate Robert F. Kennedy Journalism award 1994; nominated Pulitzer Prize in Letters, 1996; candidate John H. Dunning prize in U.S. History, Am. Hist. Assn., 1997, Albert J. Beveridge award in Am. History Am. Hist. Assn., 1997, The PEN/Amazon.com Short Story award, 2000. Mem. Internat. Soc. Poets (Poet of Yr. 1996, Internat. Poet of Merit, 1997, 99, 2000, elected Hall of Fame 1997, nomination Poet of Yr. 1999, 2000), Internat. Soc. Photographers (nominated disting. mem.), Friends of Statue of Liberty and Ellis Island, Inc. (charter), Harvard Club of Washington, Yale Club of Washington, Georgetown Club of Washington. Avocations: trumpet, old time radio collector, theatre, sports, cmty. affairs. Home: 2401 H St NW Washington DC 20037-2564

BRAVERMAN, RAY HOWARD, secondary school educator; b. Bklyn., Feb. 28, 1947; s. Irving Leonard and Josephine (Segan) B.; divorced; 1 child, Christopher Marc; m. Barbara Diane Braverman, July 30, 1994. BA in History, U. Del., 1969; MA in History, Wash. Coll., 1979; postgrad., U. Del., 1979-85. Cert. tchr., Del. Chmn. history dept., history instr. Dover (Del.) H.S., 1970—. Chmn. history dept. Dover H.S. Recipient Cert. of Appreciation U. Del., 1987, Nat. Coun. History Edn., 1991. Mem. NEA, Nat. Coun. for the Social Studies, Del. Coun. for Social Studies, Nat. Coun. for History Edn., World History Assn., Del. Edn. Assn., Capital Educators Assn., Orgn. of Am. Historians, Am. Hist. Assn. Home: 33 Elizabeth Ave Dover DE 19901-5803 Office: Dover HS One Pat Lynn Dr Dover DE 19904-2853 E-mail: rbraver@capital.k12.de.us.

BRAVERMAN, ROBERT JAY, international consultant, public policy educator; b. N.Y.C., Mar. 4, 1933; s. Arthur and Ruth Edith (Beck) B.; m. Alice Glantz, Dec. 24, 1954; 1 son, John Nachem; m. Claire Hurney, Dec. 31, 1964; children: Sam, Amy. AB with honors and distinction, Columbia U., 1954, postgrad., Harvard U. Sch. Law, 1956-57, Sch. Bus., 1963. With Harbridge House, Inc. (Mgmt. Cons.), Cambridge, Mass., 1957-66; with ITT, N.Y.C., 1966-86; sr. v.p., CEO ITT Coins Inc., 1986—. Chief exec. officer Braverman Adv. Svcs., 1986—91; prof. practice of pub. policy studies Duke U.; adj. prof. NYU, 1999—2002. Served with U.S. Army, 1954-56. Mem. Phi Beta Kappa. Home and Office: 235 W 76th St New York NY 10023-8210

BRAVO, IRENE MARIA, psychologist, educator; b. Bayamo, Cuba, Jan. 24, 1949; arrived in U.S., 1966; d. Edmundo Pedro Bravo and Irene Manuela Castro; m. Robert Quintero, Feb. 14, 1968 (div. Oct. 27, 1987); children: Robert Francis Quintero, Giselle Christine Quintero, Marguerite Irene Quintero. B in Psychology, Fla. Internat. U., 1990, M in Psychology, 1994, PhD in Psychology, 1998. Lic. psychologist Fla., mental health counselor, hypnotherapist. Crisis counselor Miami Mental Health Ctr., 1994; mental health therapist South Shore Hosp., Miami, 1994—96; clin. intern Miami Heart Inst. and Cedars Med. Ctr., Miami, 1996—97; clin. coord. Adult Day Treatment Ctr., Miami, 1997—98; asst. prof. Carlos Albizu U., Miami, Fla., 1999—; pvt. practice Miami, 1998—. Adj. instr. Fla. Internat. U., Miami, 1994—2001; presenter in field. Contbr. articles to profl. jours. Mem.: APA, Florida Psychol. Assn., Soc. Child and Adolescent Psychology. Roman Catholic. Avocations: classical music, interior decorating, films. Office: Carlos Albizu U 2173 NW 99th Ave Miami FL 33172 Business E-Mail: ibravo@albizu.edu.

BRAVO, KENNETH ALLAN, lawyer; b. Cleve., July 27, 1942; BS, Rutgers U., 1964; JD cum laude, Ohio State U., 1967. Bar: Ohio 1967, D.C. 1967. Trial atty. Criminal Divsn., U.S. Dept. Justice, 1967-69, spl. atty., 1969-79; ptnr. Benesch, Friedlander, Coplan & Aronoff, Cleve., 1979-94; of counsel Ulmer & Berne LLP, Cleve., 1994-96, ptnr., 1997—. Mem. ABA, Ohio State Bar Assn. (coun. of dels. 1992-2001, bd. govs. 2001—), Cleve. Bar Assn. (chmn. fed. ct. com. 1984-85, trustee 2001-02), Cuyahoga County Bar Assn. (chmn. fed. ct. com. 1980-82, chmn. cert. grievance com. 1986-88), Nat. Assn. Criminal Def. Lawyers, Lawyer-Pilots Bar Assn., Jud. Conf. 8th Dist. Ohio (life). Office: Ulmer & Berne LLP 1300 E 9th St Ste 900 Cleveland OH 44114-1583 E-mail: kbravo@ulmer.com.

BRAWER, CATHERINE COLEMAN, foundation executive, curator; b. NYC, Feb. 19, 1943; d. Joseph A. and Beatrice R. Coleman; m. Robert A. Brawer, Sept. 7, 1962; children: Christopher Paul, Nicholas Andrew. BA, Sarah Lawrence Coll., 1964; MA in Art History, NYU, 1966. Publicity coord. Evehjem Mus. Art, Madison, Wis., 1970-75, curator Liebman Collection, 1974-75; mktg. mgr. Maidenform, Inc., NYC, 1975-78; ind. curator NYC, 1978; v.p. Ida and William Rosenthal Found., NYC, 1981-90, pres., 1990—; dir.

pub. affairs Maidenform Inc., NYC, 1990-97, bd. dir., 1970-97. Curator Maidenform Mus., 1992-97; trustee Katonah (NY) Mus. Art, 1982-2000, Ind. Curators, Internat., NYC, 1989—, vice chmn., 1998—, Inst. Fine Arts, NYU, 1993—, Musica Viva, 1995-2002. Author: (catalogues) The Auspicious Dragon in Chinese Decorative Arts, 1978, Many Trails: Indians of the Lower Hudson Valley, 1983, Trade Winds: The Lure of the China Trade, 1985; (book) Making Their Mark: Women Artist Move into the Mainstream 1970-85, 1989, Chinese Export Porcelain from the Liebman Porcelain Collection, 1992. Trustee Plymouth (Mass.) Plantation, 2002—, Pk.-McCullough House, North Bennington, Vt., 2001—. Mem. NY Regional Assn. Grantmakers (mem. com. 1990-91), Art Table NY, Soc. Mayflower Descs. (sec. 2000--).

BRAWLEY, JOEL VINCENT, mathematician, educator; b. Mooresville, NC, Feb. 2, 1938; s. Joel Vincent Brawley Sr. and Dorothy Cavin Brawley; m. Mary Frances Owen, Aug. 23, 1959; children: Albert Vincent, Daniel Owen, Frances Brawley Barnes. BS, N.C. State U., 1956—60, MS, 1960—62, PhD, 1962—64. Instr. N.C. State U., 1964—65; asst. prof. Clemson U., 1965—68, assoc. prof., 1968—72; vis. assoc. prof. N.C. State U., 1971—72; prof. of math. sciences Clemson U., 1972—82; vis. prof. U. of Tenn., 1979—80; alumni disting. prof. of math. sciences Clemson U., Clemson, 1982—. Author: (book) Infinite Algebraic Extensions of Finite Fields; contbr. numerous jour. articles. Recipient Southeastern Sect. Award for Disting. Coll. or U. Tchg. of Math., Math. Assn. of Am., 1998, Deborah and Franklin Tepper Haimo Award for Disting. Coll. or U. Tchg. of Math., 1999, SC Governor's Prof. of the Yr., 2001—02. Office: Clemson U Dept of Math Sci Clemson SC 29634-0975 Office Fax: 864-656-5230. E-mail: brawley@clemson.edu.

BRAWNER, LEE BASIL, retired librarian, consultant; b. Seguin, Tex., May 1, 1935; s. Lee Basil and Thelma (Davenport) B.; m. Nancy Jayne Wallis, Dec. 6, 1958; children: Betsy Lynn, Allen Lee. Student, Tex. A. and M. U., 1953-55; BA, North Tex. State U., 1957; MA, George Peabody Coll. Tchrs., 1960. Head popular libr. and circulation dept. Dallas Pub. Libr., 1958-60, head Lakewood br., 1961-62, chief br. svcs., 1964-67; dir. Waco (Tex.) Pub. Libr., 1962-64; asst. state libr. Tex. State Libr., 1967-71; dir. Met. Libr. System, Oklahoma City, 1971-99; owner Brawner Assocs., L.L.C. Trustee AMIGOS Bibliog. Coun., 1987—90; panelist libr. bldg. awards AIA-ALA, 1990—92; mem. state adv. bd. U. Okla. Sch. Librs. and Info. Studies, 1994—. Co-author: (with Donald K. Beck, Jr.) Determining Your Public Library's Future Size: A Needs Assessment and Planning Model, 1996, Disaster Response and Planning for Libraries, 1998, In Celebration of Intellectual Freedom, 1999. Trustee, v.p. Okla. Ctr. for the Book, 1987-93; trustee Okla. Humanities Com., 1977-78; mem. Leadership Oklahoma City Alumni, 1994—; chmn. Okla. Found. for Humanities; trustee Freedom to Read Found., 1982-85, pres., 1985-86; mem. Murrah Fed. Bldg. Meml. Com., 1995—. Recipient Alumni award U. North Tex., 1989, First Amendment award Okla. Soc. Profl. Journalists, 1997-98, Downtown Now Pioneer award, 1997, Hugh M. Hefner 1st Amendment award, 1998, Angie Debo Civil Libertarian of Yr. award ACLU Union of Okla. Found., 1999, Libr. Endowment Trust 1st Lee B. Brawner Lifetime Achievement award, 2003; named to 30th Anniversary Honor Roll, ALA Intellectual Freedom to Read Found., 1999. Mem.: ACLU, ALA (coun. 1978—81, intellectual freedom com. 1979—82), Okla. Libr. Assn. (chmn. libr. devel. 1982—83, pres. 1984—85, chmn. legis. com. 1990, chmn. awards com. 1992—93, Disting. Svc. award 1983, SIRS Intellectual Freedom award 1997), Pub. Libr. Assn. (effectiveness com. 1992), Libr. Adminstrn. and Mgmt. Assn. (libr. bldg. awards com. 1987—90, 1992—93, chmn. 1990, chmn. libr. bldgs. and equipment sect. 1992), Sigma Phi Epsilon.

BRAWNER, NANCY JAYNE, social worker, psychotherapist; b. Dallas, July 29, 1937; d. Hal J. and Irma M. (Harrison) Wallis; m. Lee B. Brawner, Dec. 6, 1958; children: Betsy Lynn, Allen Lee. BS in Med. Tech. with high honors, U. North Tex., 1969; MSW with high honors, U. Okla., 1979. Lic. clin. social worker, marital and family therapist, Okla. Co-dir. Golden Agers Ctr. Salvation Army Sr. Citizens' Ctrs., Oklahoma City, 1975-76; assoc. dir. recruitment and placement Ret. Sr. Vol. Program, Oklahoma City, 1976-79; dir. social svcs., oncology social worker Mercy Health Ctr., Oklahoma City, 1979-82; pvt. practice clin. social work, psychotherapy Oklahoma City, 1982—. Clin. asst. prof. dept. psychiatry Okla. U. Health Scis. Ctr., Oklahoma City, 1986—2001 mem. ARC disaster mental health team, Oklahoma City, 1989-99; cons. in field; presenter seminars; presenter at profl. confs. Co-author: Psychosocial Issues in Heart Transplantation, 1997, (chpt.) The Transplantation and Replacement of Thoracic Organs, 2d edit., 1996. Co-organizer Bethlehem Ctr. Clinic for Low Income, Oklahoma City, 1972; chair vol. tng. com. Am. Cancer Soc., Oklahoma City, 1986; group leader post-mastectomy support group Mercy Health Ctr., 1988. Mem. NASW, Mental Health Assn. Oklahoma County, Am. Assn. Mental Retardation. Avocations: rock collecting, hiking.

BRAWNER, SHARON LEE, bilingual education educator, researcher; b. Marietta, Ga. d. Robert Felton and Ruby Lee B.; div.; 1 child, Marion Eugene Sealy III. BA, Clemson U., 1975; MEd, U. S.C., 1987; EdD, U. Ga., 1994. ESL cert., gifted and talented tchg. cert. English tchr. grades 7-12, Columbia, S.C., 1981-88; English instr. U. Ga., Athens, 1990, grad. asst., 1990-94; asst. prof. No. Ariz. U., Yuma, 1994-96; sr. faculty English U. Ariz., 1997-2000, ESOL specialist, 2000—. Pres. English Assets; presenter Ga. Children's Lit. Conf., Athens, 1991, Ga. Coun. Tchrs. English Conf., 1991, TESOL Nat. Conf., Balt., 1994; founder, dir. Connections Tutoring Program, 1997-99. Author: New Ways in Teaching Listening, 1995. Pres., governing bd. Yuma County Juvenile Ct. Sys. Charter Sch., 1995-96; mem. San Luis, Ariz./San Luis, Sonora, Mex. Edn. Commn., 1994-96; essay judge Ga. Acad. Decathlon, Athens, 1991; vol. tutor Athens Regional Libr., 1993-94. Mem. Internat. Reading Assn. (rsch. com. No. Ariz. U. 1994-96), Nat. Council for Tchrs. of English, mem., Tchrs. of English to Speakers of other Languages. Avocations: foreign languages, computers, baseball cards, travel, piano.

BRAX, GHAZI FOUAD, editor, writer; b. Jazzine, Lebanon, May 2, 1936; s. Fouad and Mahiba (Abuabdallah) B.; m. Najwa M. Salam, June 24, 1981. BA in Arabic Lit. and Liguistics, Lebanese U., Beirut, 1957, MA, 1958; PhD, St. Joseph U., Beirut, 1973. Prof. Lebanese U., Beirut, 1973-86; mng. editor Daheshist Pub. Co., N.Y., 1986—; editor Dahesh Voice Mag., N.Y., 1995—. Author: Kahlil Gibran, 1973, Pathways of Fire & Light, 1985, Lights Upon Dr. Dahesh and Daheshism, 1986; editor (mag.) Dahesh Voice, 1995. Daheshist. Avocation: chess. Office: Daheshist Pub Co 1775 Broadway Ste 501 New York NY 10019-1903 E-mail: gnbrax@earthlink.net.

BRAXTON, TONI, popular musician; b. Severn, Md., Oct. 7, 1967; m. Keri Lewis; 1 child, Denim Lewis. Albums Toni Braxton, 1993, Heat, 2000, Snow Flakes, 2001, More Than a Woman, 2002, appeared in (films) Kingdom Come, 2000, contbr. Boomerang soundtrack, 1992, Secrets, 1997; actor: (Broadway musical) Aida, 2003. Recipient Grammy award Best Female R&B Vocal, 1994, 1995, 2001, Aretha Franklin Soul Train award, 2000, BET Black Oscar, 2000, 3 time Amer. Music award . Office: Arista Records care LaFace 6 W 57th St New York NY 10019-3999*

BRAY, AUSTIN COLEMAN, JR., lawyer, investor; b. Dallas, Oct. 25, 1941; s. Austin Coleman and Mary Thelma (Pettigrew) B.; m. Sherrill Ann Farr, Nov. 28, 1964 (div. 1970). Diploma, U. Vienna, Austria, 1962; BA cum laude, Washington and Lee U., 1963; LLB, Columbia U., 1967. Bar: Tex. 1967, U.S. Dist. Ct. (no. dist.) Tex. 1967, U.S. Ct. Appeals (5th cir.) Tex. 1967, U.S. Supreme Ct. 1970, U.S. Dist. Ct. (we. dist.) Tex. 1978, U.S. Ct. Appeals (11th cir.) Tex. 1981. Assoc. Gardere, Wynne & Sewell, Dallas, 1967-69; asst. atty. gen. State of Tex., Austin, 1969-73; subcom. counsel U.S. Rep. Richard White, Washington, 1973-74; exec. asst. to State Senator Mike McKinnon, Austin, 1974-76; atty. Tex. R.R. Commn., Austin, 1977-78; exec. asst. to State Rep. Bob Close, Austin, 1978-79; sr. staff atty. Tex. Sec. State, Austin, 1979-82, sole practice, 1982-87; asst. gen. counsel Tex. Sec. of State, Austin, 1987-98; pvt. practice Austin, 1998—. Editor-in-chief Columbia Law Sch. News, 1966-67. Mem. ABA, State Bar Tex., English-Speaking Union, Kent Ct., Kappa Alpha Order. Episcopalian. Office: Ste 106 1218 Baylor St Austin TX 78703-4140

BRAY, CAROLYN SCOTT, education educator; b. May 19, 1938; d. Alonzo Lee and Frankie Lucile (Wood) Scott; m. John Graham Bray Jr., Aug. 24, 1957 (div. May 1980); children: Caron Lynn, Kimberly Anne, David William. BS, Baylor U., 1960; MEd, Hardin-Simmons U., 1981; PhD, U. North Tex., 1985. Registered med. technologist. Dir. career placement Hardin-Simmons U., 1979-82, adj. prof. bus. comm., 1981-84, assoc. dean students, 1982-85; assoc. dir. career planning and placement U. North Tex., Denton, 1985-95, adj. prof. higher edn. adminstrn., mem. Mentor program; dir. Career Ctr., U. Tex. at Dallas, Richardson, 1995-2000, prof. edn., project mgr. TExES/ExCET, 2000—. Mem. Consortium State Orgn. Tex. Tchr. Edn., 1999—; mem. adv. bd. TxBESS, 2000—. Adult Bible study tchr. 1st Bapt. Ch., Richardson, Tex., 2000—. Mem.: North Ctrl. Tex. Assn. Sch. Pers. Adminstrs. and Univ. Placement Pers. (pres. 1987—88, sec. 1988—95), Nat. Assn. Colls. and Employers (co-chair nat. conf. planning com. 1996—98), Tex. Assn. for Employer Edn. and Staffing (v.p. 1986—87, pres. 1987—88), Am. Assn. for Employment in Edn. (bd. dirs. 1989—94, treas. 1994—95, nat. conf. com. 1999, conf. com. local arrangements 1999, Priscilla A. Scotlan award for disting. svc. 1999), S.W. Assn. Colls. and Employers (life; chair ann. conf. registration 1991—92, vice chair ops. 1992—93, 4-yr. coll. dir. 1998—99, pres.-elect 1999—2000, co-chmn. tech. com.), Leadership Denton (co-dir. curriculum 1988—89, chair membership selection com., steering com. 1990, 1993—94), Denton C. of C. (pub. rels. com. 1988—95), Kappa Kappa Gamma (chpt. advisor, chair adv. bd. Zeta Sigma chpt. 1987—93). Republican. Avocations: skiing, tennis, golf, reading. Office: U Tex at Dallas PO Box 830688 GR22 Richardson TX 75083-0688 E-mail: csbray@utdallas.edu.

BRAY, DALE IRVING, civil engineering educator; b. Moncton, Can., June 1, 1940; s. Ivan Simeon and Marion Estella (Irving) B.; m. Carol Velma Cox, June 27, 1964; children: Marnie, Mark. BS in Civil Engring., U. New Brunswick, Fredericton, Can., 1963, MS in Civil Engring., 1965; PhD, U. Alberta, Edmonton, Can., 1972. Asst. prof. U. New Brunswick, Fredericton, 1965-72, assoc. prof., 1972-78, prof., 1978-98. Chmn. dept. civil engring. U. New Brunswick, 1994-98, mem. groundwater studies group, 1988—. Contbr. articles to profl. jours. Mem. Can. Water Resources Assn. (Disting. Svc. award 1995), Can. Soc. Civil Engring. (Camille A. Dagenais award 1998). Baptist. Avocations: hiking, canoeing. Office: Dept Civil Engring U New Brunswick PO Box 4400 Fredericton NB Canada E3B 5A3 E-mail: bray@unb.ca.

BRAY, GEORGE AUGUST, physician, scientist, educator; b. Evanston, Ill., July 25, 1931; s. George A. and Mary H. B.; m. Martha, Aug. 8, 1959 (div. July 1983); children: George, Thomas, Susan, Nancy; m. Marilyn Rice, Jan. 1, 1984. BA summa cum laude, Brown U., 1953; MD magna cum laude, Harvard U., 1957. Diplomate Am. Bd. Internal Medicine; cert. Nat. Bd. Med. Examiners, Mass. Bd. Registration Medicine, Calif. Bd. Med. Examiners, La. Bd. Med. Examiners. Intern Johns Hopkins Hosp., Baltimore, Md., 1957-58; rsch. assoc. NIH, Bethesda, Md., 1958-60; resident U. Rochester, N.Y., 1960-61; rsch. assoc. Mill Hill Nat. Inst. Med. Rsch., London, 1961-62; asst. prof. medicine Tufts U., Boston, 1964-69, assoc. prof., 1969-70, UCLA, 1970-72, prof., 1972-81, U. So. Calif., Los Angeles, 1981-89, prof. medicine and physiology, 1983-89, chief of Diabetes and Nutrition Los Angeles County USC Med. Ctr., 1981-89; prof. medicine, vice chancellor Med. Ctr. La. State U., Baton Rouge, 1989-99; exec. dir. Pennington Biomed. Rsch. Ctr., Baton Rouge, 1989-99; prof., chief clin. sci., 1999—; Boyd prof. La. State U., Baton Rouge, 1999—. Vis. prof. U. Ill., 1981; cons. FDA, 1971, 95, Can. Dept. Health and Welfare, Ottawa, Ont., 1974, Nat. Inst. on Aging; mem. adv. coun. Nat. Inst. Diabetes, Digestive and Kidney Diseases, 1985-90. Author: Obese Patient, 1976; editor: Obesity in America, 1979, Obesity in Perspective, 1976, Treatment of Obesity, 1985, 89, Obesity: Basic Aspects and Clinical Applications, 1989; contbr. articles to profl. jours. Recipient Travel award Am. Thyroid Assn., 1970, Sam E. Roberts award Kans. Nutrition Soc., 1977, Wellcome Vis. Prof. award Mich. State U., 1978, U. Chgo., 1985, Alumni Day spkr. Harvard Med. Sch., Boston, 1982, Osborne and Mendel award Am. Inst. Nutrition, 1989, E.V. McCollum award Am. Soc. Clin. Nutrition, 1989, Joseph Goldberger award in Clin. Nutrition AMA, 1994, TOPS award NAASO, 1999, W. Henry Sebrell award Weight Watchers Found., 2000, Bristol-Myers Squibb/Mead Johnson Nutrition award, 2000; grantee NIH, 1965—, Weight Watchers Found., 1979-81, Kroc Found., 1980-81; fellow NSF, 1961-62, NIH, 1962-64. Master: Am. Coll. Endocrinology (pres. 1993—95, editor Endocrine Practice 1993—95), ACP, APC (chmn.-elect con. med. spltys. 1987—88, bd. regents 1987—91, chmn. 1988—91); fellow: Am. Inst. Nutrition (Osborne-Mendal award 1988), Am. Soc. Nutrition Sci., AAAS; mem.: Johns Hopkins U. Soc. Scholars, Internat. Assn. Study Obesity (pres.-elect 1990—94, pres. 1994—98, Willendorf award 1980), Assn. Am. Physicians (hon.), Am. Soc. Clin. Investigation (hon.), N.Am. Assn. Study Obesity (chmn. organizing com. 1980—82, councilor 1984—88, pres.-elect 1988—89, pres. 1989—90, editor Internat. Jour. Obesity 1974—91, Obesity Rsch. 1991—97, TOPS award 1999), Am. Fedn. Clin. Rsch., Am. Diabetes Assn. (bd. dirs. So. Calif. 1984—88, 1988—89), Endocrine Soc., Am. Soc. Clin. Nutrition (councilor 1982—84, v.p. 1985—86, pres.-elect 1986—87, pres. 1987—88, McCollum award 1989), Am. Assn. Clin. Endocrinology (bd. dirs. 1990—96), Peripatetic Club (hon.), Alpha Omega Alpha, Sigma Xi, Phi Beta Kappa. Avocations: medical history, travel. Office: Pennington Ctr 6400 Perkins Rd Baton Rouge LA 70808-4124

BRAY, GERALD LEWIS, minister, educator; b. Montreal, Quebec, Can., Nov. 16, 1948; arrived in Eng., 1972; s. Leonard Lewis and Catherine Viola (Garnett) B. BA, McGill U., Montreal, 1969; DLitt, Sorbonne, Paris, 1973. Ordained to ministry Anglican Ch., 1978. Lectr. Oak Hill Coll., London, 1980-92; prof. Samford U., Birmingham, Ala., 1993—. Author: Holiness and the Will of God, 1979, The Doctrine of God, 1993, Documents of the English Reformation, 1994, Biblical Interpretation: Past and Present, 1996, The Anglican Canons 1529-1947, 1998, Ancient Christian Commentary on Scripture: Romans, 1998, 1 & 2 Corinthians, 1999, James-Jude, 2000, Tudor Church Reform, 2000. Mem. Tyndale Fellowship. Avocations: swimming, cycling. Home: 16 Manor Ct Pinehurst Grange Rd Cambridge CB3 9BE England Office: Samford Univ Beeson Divinity Sch Birmingham AL 35229-0001 E-mail: glbray@samford.edu.

BRAY, LAURACK DOYLE, lawyer; b. New Orleans, Nov. 13, 1949; s. Laudrack Doyle Bray and Helen Davis. AA, L.A. City Coll., 1969; BA, Long Beach State U., 1972, MS, 1977, MPA, 1981; JD, Howard U., 1984. Bar: Pa. 1986, D.C. 1986, U.S. Ct. Appeals (D.C. and fed. cirs.) 1987, U.S. Dist. Ct. D.C. 1987, U.S. Ct. Appeals (4th cir.) 1991, Md. 1991, U.S. Supreme Ct. 1992. Cmty. rsch. worker Crenshaw Consortium, L.A., 1977-79; adminstrv. intern City of Lawndale, Calif., 1981; legis. intern U.S. Congress, Washington, 1982; law clk. FDIC, Washington, 1983-84; pvt. practice Washington, 1987—. Mem. moot ct. team Howard U., Washington. Contbr. articles to law jours. Recipient Am. Jurisprudence award, 1982, Best Brief award ABA, 1984. Mem. D.C. Bar Assn., Pi Alpha Alpha, Phi Kappa Phi. Democrat. Avocations: sports, dancing, travel. Home and Office: 1019 E Santa Clara St Ventura CA 93001-3034

BRAY, PATRICIA SHANNON, music educator, musician, small business owner; b. Elkton, Md., Sept. 4, 1953; d. Francis William Shannon and Mary Elizabeth Gardner; m. William Joseph Bray Jr., July 31, 1976; children: Mark William, Eric Joseph. BMEd magna cum laude, East Carolina U., 1975; MS summa cum laude, Med. Coll. Va., Va. Commonwealth U., 1995. Lic. tchr. Va. Tchr., dir. orch. Chesterfield County Pub. Schs., Chesterfield, Va., 1975—. Cellist Richmond Philharm. Orch., Va., 1975—82, Petersburg Symphony, Va., 1987—94, Lynchburg Symphony, Va., 1998—; chair dept. music Salem Ch Mid. Sch., Richmond, 1998—; owner Talent Edn. Chesterfield, 2000—; adjucator Richard Bland Lions Club, Music Scholarship Competition, Chester, Va., 2000; adjucator Jr. Festival Va. Fedn. of Music Clubs, 2003; presenter in field, 00; co-presenter Suzuki Assn. of the Ams. Conf., 2002, Chesterfield County Pub. Schs. Leadership Conf., 2002. Faculty sponsor Salem Music Boosters, Richmond, 1998—; sch. crisis team Chesterfield County Pub. Schs., 1995—, sch. improvement planning com., 2002—. Scholarship, Theodore Presser Publ. Co. Scholarship, 1973. Mem.: Va. Mid. Sch. Assn., NEA, Am. String Tchrs. Assn., Music Educators Nat. Conf., Suzuki Assn. Americas, Sigma Alpha Iota, Kappa Delta Pi, Phi Kappa Phi. Avocations: hiking, reading, gardening. Home: 918 Dawnwood Rd Midlothian VA 23114 Office: Salem Ch Mid Sch 9700 Salem Church Rd Richmond VA 23237 E-mail: intuitpsb@aol.com.

BRAY, PIERCE, business consultant; b. Chgo., Jan. 16, 1924; s. Harold A. and Margaret (Maclennan) B.; m. Maud Dorothy Minto, May 14, 1955; children—Margaret Dorothy, William Harold, Andrew Pierce. BA, U. Chgo., 1948, MBA, 1949. Fin. analyst Ford Motor Co., Dearborn, Mich., 1949-55; cons. Booz, Allen & Hamilton, Chgo. and Manila, Philippines, 1955-58; mgr. pricing, then corp. controller Cummins Engine Co., Columbus, Ind., 1958-66; v.p. fin. Weatherhead Co., Cleve., 1966-67; from v.p. to dir. Mid-Continent Tel. Corp. (now ALLTEL Corp.), Hudson, Ohio, 1967—76, dir., 1976—85; chmn. various subs. Mid-Continent Telephone Corp. (now ALLTEL Corp.), Hudson, Ohio. Instr. fin. and econs. U. Detroit, 1952-54; chmn. investor relations com. U.S. Telephone Assn., 1974-85; chmn. exec. com. Inst. Public Utilities, 1981-83. Trustee Beech Brook, Cleve., Ohio, 1972-96, life trustee, 1996—, treas., 1976-79, pres., 1979-81; bd. dirs. Breckenridge Village Retirement Cmty., 1991-2001, chmn. fin. com. 1995-2001; trustee Ohio Presbyn. Retirement Svcs., 1996-2001; chmn. fin. com., 1999-2001; chmn. safety com. Walloon Lake Assn., 1995-2000. With AUS, 1943-46. Mem. Fin. Execs. Inst. (bd. dirs. 1993-96), Cleve. Treasurers Club, Union Club Cleve., Walloon (Mich.) Yacht Club (chmn. bd. 1980-81, 85-86, 93-2003, commodore 1981-82, 87-88, bd. dirs., sec. 1988-2003), Ohio Masters Swim Club (hon., trustee 1985-92, 96-98, 2001-, sec. 1989-93), Lake Erie Local Masters Swim Com. (chmn. 1992-96), Delta Upsilon. Presbyterian. Avocations: competitive swimming, sailing, volunteer and church activities. Home and Office: 1847 Ridgebrook Cir Cleveland OH 44122-1077

BRAY, RONALD EUGENE, obstetrician/gynecologist; b. Seattle, Jan. 26, 1935; MD, U. Wash., 1960. Diplomate Am. Bd. Ob/gyn. Intern King County Hosp., Seattle, 1960-61; resident U. Wash. Hosps., Seattle, 1961-65; staff Stevens Hosp., Edmonds, Wash., pres. med. staff, 1987-88; clin. instr. U. Wash.; pvt. practice Edmonds, Wash., 1968—. With USAF, 1965-68. Mem. Am. Coll. Ob/gyn., Pacific N.W. Ob-gyn. Soc., Seattle Gynecol. Soc. (pres. 1991-92), Wash. State Ob/gyn. Office: Sound Womens Care 21616 76th Ave W Ste 205 Edmonds WA 98026-7512 Fax: (425) 640-4884.

BRAY, RONALD LAWRENCE, sales executive; b. New Haven, May 17, 1956; s. Lawrence William and Abby Christine (Willadsen) B. BA, U. Va., 1978; MA, Syracuse U., N.Y., 1980. Direct mail coordinator G. Fox & Co., Hartford, Conn., 1980-81; advt. mgr. Compumart Corp., Cambridge, Mass., 1981-82; asst. account exec. BBDO/West, Los Angeles, 1982-85; account supr. Smith-Hemmings-Gosden, El Monte, Calif., 1985-87; v.p., mktg. McClellan Corp. Internat., Woodland Hills, Calif., 1987-88; direct mktg. mgr. Ashton-Tate Corp., Torrance, Calif., 1988-91; dir. mktg. Baker and Taylor, Simi Valley, Calif., 1991-94; mktg. comms. mgr. FileNet Corp., Costa Mesa, Calif., 1995-98; v.p. sales Excel Group, Fountain Valley, Calif., 1999—2002; mktg. and customer programs mgr. File Net Corp., Costa Mesa, Calif., 2003. Mem. Direct Mktg. Club So. Calif. Los Angeles, Soc. Internet Advancement Orange Co., Internet Profls. Network Orange Co. Democratic. Avocations: travel, reading, tennis. Home: 18134 Wood Barn Ln Fountain Valley CA 92708 E-mail: ron@xlg.com.

BRAY, SARAH HARDESTY, newspaper editor, writer; b. Fairmont, W.Va., Jan. 12, 1951; d. Charles Howard and Doris (Wilson) Hardesty; m. William Philip Bray, Sept. 1, 1990; 1 child, Elizabeth Hardesty. BA in English and History, Duke U., 1972; MS in Journalism, Northwestern U., 1973. Copywriter J. Walter Thompson, Chgo., 1973-75; reporter-rschr. Forbes mag., N.Y.C., 1976-78; account exec. Hill and Knowlton, N.Y.C., 1978-80; mem. comm. programs staff Mobil Corp., N.Y.C., 1980-81; v.p. Hill and Knowlton, N.Y.C., 1981-87; dir. comm. Coun. for Advancement and Support of Edn., Washington, 1987-89, v.p. comm., 1989-99; sr. editor opinion sect. Chronicle of Higher Edn., 1999—. Co-author: Success and Betrayal: The Crisis of Women in Corporate America; editor: What People Are Saying About College Prices and College Costs; mem. adv. bd. Duke Mag., 1988—; contbr. Family Weekly mag., 1979-80. Bd. dirs. Lit. Vols. N.Y.C., 1981-86, Eric Hawkins Dance Co., N.Y.C., 1983-86, Horizons Theatre, Washington, 1988-92; mem. vol. com. Circle in the Sq. Theatre, N.Y.C., 1982-83; mem. benefit com. CARE, 1991-94. Mem. Edn. Writers Assn. (bd. dirs. 1989-92). Home: 4501 47th St NW Washington DC 20016-4434 Office: Chronicle of Higher Edn 1255 23rd St NW Washington DC 20037-1125 E-mail: Sarah.bray@chronicle.com.

BRAZAITIS, MARK THOMAS, writer, English educator; b. East Cleveland, Ohio, July 23, 1966; s. Thomas Joseph Brazaitis and Sheila Jean Loftus; m. Juliet Susan Penn, June 27, 1998; children: Annabel, Rebecca. BA, Harvard Coll., 1989; MFA, Bowling Green State U., 1995. Tech. trainer World Learning Inc., Santa Lucia Milpas Atlas, Guatemala, 1995-96; English instr. Fordham U., Bronx, 1997-2000, Helene Fuld Coll. of Nursing, N.Y.C., 1996-2000; asst. prof. English W.Va. U., Morgantown, 2000—. Author: The River of Lost Voices: Stories from Guatemala, 1998 (Iowa short fiction award 1998), Steal My Heart, 2000; contbr. articles to profl. publs. Peace corps. vol. U.S. Peace Corps, 1990-93. Individual Lit. fellowship Nat. Endowment for the Arts, 2000-02; recipient Richard M. Devine Meml. award Bowling Green State U., 1994. Mem. Nat. Returned Peace Corps Vols. Avocations: swimming, guitar playing, gardening. Office: WVa U English Dept PO Box 6296 231 Stansbury Hall Morgantown WV 26506-9900 E-mail: MBrazait@wvu.edu.

BRAZAITIS, THOMAS JOSEPH, journalist; b. Cleve., Aug. 8, 1940; s. Joseph R. and Regina G. (Greicius) B.; m. Eleanor Clift, Sept. 30, 1989; children: Mark Thomas, Sarah Jean. BS, John Carroll U., Cleve., 1962. Mng. editor newspapers Collinwood Pub. Corp., Cleve., 1964—71; reporter, then Washington corr. Cleve. Plain Dealer, 1971—79, Washington bur. chief, 1979—98, Washington sr. editor, 1998—2002, columnist, 2003—. Co-author: (with Eleanor Clift) War Without Bloodshed: The Art of Politics, 1996, Madam President: Shattering the Last Glass Ceiling, 2000. 1st lt. USAR, 1962-64. Mem.: Washington Press Club Found. (bd. dirs. 1994—2003), Nat. Press Club, Regional Reporters Assn. (founder), Gridiron Club. Office: 930 National Press Building Washington DC 20045-1928 E-mail: tbrazaitis@msn.com.

BRAZDA, FREDERICK WICKS, pathologist, educator; b. New Orleans, Dec. 17, 1945; s. Fred George and Helen Josephine (Wicks) B.; m. Margaret Mary Hubbell, Sept. 8, 1973; children: Geoffrey Frederick, Gretchen Marie, Gregory Paul. Student, U. Chgo., 1962-64; BS cum laude, Tulane U., 1966; MD, La. State U., 1970. Diplomate Am. Bd. Pathology. Intern, then resident in pathology La. State U. divsn. Charity Hosp., New Orleans, 1970-75; pathologist Hotel Dieu Hosp., New Orleans, 1975-92; dir. Sch. Med. Tech., New Orleans, 1976-83; assoc. med. dir. Am. Bio-sci. Labs., New Orleans, 1985-89; tech. dir. Smith Kline Beecham Clin. Labs., New Orleans, 1990-94; pathologist, tech. dir. U. Hosp. Lab., New Orleans, 1993-95, Med. Ctr. La. at New Orleans U. Campus Lab., 1995—. Cons. St. Tammany Parish Hosp., Covington, La., Riverside Hosp., Franklinton, La, 1976-84; asst. clin. prof. pathology and med. tech. La. State U. Med. Ctr. (now La. State U. Health Scis. Ctr.), New Orleans, 1976-93, prof. clin. pathology, 1994—, dep. dir. labs. health care svcs. divsn., 1998—. Fellow Nat. Acad. Clin. Biochemistry, Coll. Am. Pathologists, Am. Soc. Clin. Pathologists; mem. AMA, AACS, Am. Chem. Soc., Am. Assn. Clin. Chemistry, So. Med. Assn., La. Med. Soc., La. Pathology Soc., Orleans Parish Med. Soc., Greater New Orleans Pathology Soc., Clin. Lab. Mgmt. Assn., La. Civil Svc. League, Friends of City Park, Friends of Zoo, Friends of Aquarium, Friends of Charity Hosp., New Orleans Mus. Art, Les Amis du Vin, Phi Beta Kappa, Alpha Omega Alpha, Phi Beta Pi. Democrat. Roman Catholic. Home: 422 Hector Ave Metairie LA 70005-4412 Office: 2025 Gravier St Ste 200 New Orleans LA 70112-2290 E-mail: fbrazd@lsuhsc.edu.

BRAZEAL, AURELIA ERSKINE, former ambassador; b. Chgo., Nov. 24, 1943; BS, Spelman Coll., 1965; M of Internat. Affairs, Columbia U., 1967; postgrad., Harvard U., 1972. With Foreign Svc., 1968; consular and econ. officer U.S. Embassy, Buenos Aires, 1969-71; econ. reports officer Econ. Bureau U.S. State Dept., 1971-72, watch and line officer Office of Secretariat, 1973-74, desk officer Uruguay, Paraguay, 1974-77; review officer Office of Secretariat U.S. Dept. Treasury, 1977-79; econ. officer Tokyo, 1979-82; officer ECON Bur. U.S. Dept. State, 1982-84; dep. dir. Econ. Office Japan, 1984-86; mem. sr. seminar, 1986-87; min. counselor econ. affairs U.S. Embassy, Tokyo, 1987-90; U.S amb. to Micronesia, 1990-93; U.S. amb. to Kenya, 1993-96; deputy asst. sec. East Asian & Pacific Affairs, 1996-98; dean sr. seminar Fgn. Svc. Inst., Arlington, Va., 1998-99, dean leadership and mgmt. sch. and sr. seminar, 1999—2002; U.S. amb. to Ethiopia, 2002—. Office: Pub Affairs US Dept State 2201 C St NW Rm 2206 Washington DC 20520-2204*

BRAZEAL, DONNA SMITH, psychologist; b. Greenville, S.C., Feb. 10, 1947; d. G.W. Hovey and Ollie Occena (Crane) Smith; m. Charles Lee Brazeal, June 27, 1970 (div. May 1980). BA, Clemson U., 1971, MEd, 1975; postgrad., Western Carolina U., 1974, Furman U., Greenville, 1977; PhD, Columbia Pacific U., 1994. Lic. sch. psychologist, S.C., N.C. Instr., head med. record dept.

Greenville Tech. Coll., 1971-73; N.E. area chief psychologist Greenville County Schs., 1975-80; coord. psychol. svcs. Union County Schs., Monroe, N.C., 1980-97; ret., 1997; pvt. practice psychology, 1986-92. Mem. learning disabilities com. Greenville County Schs., 1978-79; co-founder, bd. dirs. Ctr. for Spiritual Awareness of N.C., Monroe, 1982—. Co-author, co-editor: School Psychologist, 1980. Child find program coord. Union County, 1980-85; mem. various coms. Assn. for Retarded Citizens, Monroe; mem. Union County Assn. for Retarded Citizens; mem. interagy. coun. Piedmont Mental Health, Monroe, 1983-97; mem. adult edn. com. River Hills Cmty. Ch., 1985-86. Catawba Bus. Women scholar, 1965; N.C. Dept. Pub. Instrn. Pre-Sch. Incentive grantee, 1984. Mem. Nat. Assn. Sch. Psychologists, N.C. Assn. Sch. Psychologist (mem. pub. relations com. 1984-85), Greenpeace, Humane Soc. U.S., Delta. Democrat. Interdenominational Christian. Home: PO Box 240173 Charlotte NC 28224-0173 E-mail: donny210@aol.com.

BRAZEAL, EARL HENRY, JR., electrical engineer; b. Springfield, Vt., Aug. 24, 1939; s. Earl Henry and Nellie Mary (Krasofski) B.; m. Jennifer Pease Clark, 1962 (div. 1980); children: Tracy, Suzanne, Jeremy; m. Beverly May Green, Apr. 24, 1982; 1 stepchild, Dulcie. Cert., Ward Tech. Inst., Hartford, Conn., 1959; BSEE, U. Conn., 1964, MSEE, 1966. Engr. electronics United Technologies, East Hartford, Conn., 1965-69; sr. engr. Scan-Optics, East Hartford, 1969-76, mgr. electronic engring., 1976-78; sr. engr. electronics Mediscan/Smith-Kline Instruments, South Windsor, Conn., 1978-81; mgr. surface receiver devel. program Teleco Oilfield Svcs., Meriden, Conn., 1981-82; adv. engr. electronics Scan-Optics, East Hartford, Conn., 1982-85, mgr. imaging electronics, 1985-90, mgr. electronic imaging and hardware support, 1990-94, mgr. mech. and elec. sys. devel., 1994-96, mgr. elec. engring., 1996—2001, dir. hardware engring., 2001—. Instr. Sch. Engring., U. Conn., Storrs, 1974-80. Inventor various systems, 1970—; patentee in field. Mem. stewardship com. United Ch. of Christ, 2d Congl., Coventry, Conn., 1983-86, 89-92, 95-96, 98, treas. deacon's, 1984, 85, asst. fin. sec., 1995-96, chmn. property bd., 1999-2000, sec. property bd., 2000-02. Mem. IEEE (first prize N.E. sect. 1964), Sigma Xi, Eta Kappa Nu. Democrat. Avocations: amateur radio, antique radio collecting and restoring, skiing, reading, scuba diving. Home: 518 Route 169 Woodstock CT 06281-3041 Office: Scan-Optics Inc 169 Progress Dr Manchester CT 06040-2242 E-mail: [illegible]@sigmaxi.org

BRAZELL, JAMES ERVIN, oil company executive, lawyer; b. Cromwell, Okla., Sept. 11, 1926; s. John Edward and Eva May (Black) B.; m. Peggy Lee Carson, Feb. 9, 1951; children: James, Mary Margaret, April Kay. BSMechE, Okla. State U., 1950; JD, U. Tulsa, 1959. Bar: Okla. 1959, U.S. Supreme Ct. 1976. With Texaco, Inc., various locations, 1950—; exec. v.p. Texaco Can. Inc., Toronto, Ont., Can., 1978-80; staff dir. exploration and producing exec. com. Texaco Inc., White Plains, N.Y., 1980—, also bd. dirs. With USAF, 1945. Mem. Am. Petroleum Inst., Soc. Petroleum Engrs., Okla. Bar Assn., Can. Geographic Soc., Granite Club (Toronto), Country Club of Asheville. Home: 503 Cokesbury Lane Asheville NC 28803-2011 Office: Texaco Inc 2000 Westchester Ave West Harrison NY 10604-3692

BRAZELL, KAREN WOODARD, Japanese literature educator; b. Buffalo, Apr. 25, 1938; d. Charles Cary and Josephine Mary (Bordonaro) Woodard; m. James Reid Brazell, Aug. 27, 1961 (div. 1978); children: Katherine Ann Brazell Rivera, Stephen Reid. Student, Coll. Wooster, 1956-58, Internat. Christian U., Tokyo, 1958-60; BA, U. Mich., 1961, MA, 1962; PhD, Columbia U., 1969; D Lit (hon.), Univ. Puget Sound, 1993. Asst. prof. Japanese lit. Princeton U., 1969-74; assoc. prof. Cornell U., Ithaca, N.Y., 1974-79, prof., 1979—, chmn. dept. Asian studies, 1977-82, dir. East Asia program, 1987-91. Vis. prof. U. Calif., Berkeley, 1984, Nat. Inst. Japanese Lit., Tokyo, 1988-89, vis. Shinchosha prof. Columbia U., 1996. Author: Confessions of Lady Nijo, 1973 (Nat. Book Award 1974), Noh as Performance, 1977, Dance in the Noh Theater, 1981; editor: 12 Plays of Noh and Kyogen Theaters, 1988; assoc. editor Jour. Japanese Studies, 1978—; contbr. articles and book revs. to profl. jours. Trustee Cornell U., 1979-83; bd. dirs. U.S.-Japan Soc. Ithaca, N.Y., Japan Soc. N.Y.C. Performing Arts Adv. Com., 1993—, Japan-U.S. Partnership for Performing Arts Inc., N.Y.C., 1994—. Fulbright-Hayes fellow, 1972-73, NEH fellow, summer 1974, Cornell U. Soc. Humanities fellow, 1976-77, Japan Found. fellow, 1978, 85, Nat. Inst. Japanese Lit. rsch. fellow, Tokyo, 1988-89. Mem. Assn. Asian Studies, Assn. Tchrs. of Japanese (exec. com. 1981-83, bd. dirs. 1989-92), Phi Beta Kappa (senator at large 1976-82, trustee found. 1977-82). Office: Cornell U Dept Asian Studies Ithaca NY 14853 Home: 376 Turkey Hill Rd Ithaca NY 14850-2943

BRAZELTON, WILLIAM THOMAS, chemical engineering educator; b. Danville, Ill., Jan. 22, 1921; s. Edwin Thomas and Gertrude Ann (Carson) B.; m. Marilyn Dorothy Brown, Sept. 23, 1943; children— William Thomas, Nancy Ann. Student, Ill. Inst. Tech., 1939-41; BS in Chem. Engring. Northwestern U., 1943, MS, 1948, PhD, 1952. Chem. engr. Central Process Corp., 1942-43; instr. chem. engring. Northwestern U., 1947-51, asst. prof., 1951-53, assoc. prof., 1953-63, prof., 1963-91, prof. emeritus, 1991—, chmn. dept., 1955-56, asst. dean Technol. Inst., 1960-61, assoc. dean, 1961-94, acting asst. dean, 1994-96, ret., 1996. Engring. and ednl. cons., 1949— Mem. Prospect Heights (Ill.) Bd. Edn., 1957-61; bd. dirs., exec. com. Chgo. Area Pre-Coll. Program. Recipient Vincent Bendix Minorities in Engring. award ASEE, 1986. Mem. Am. Inst. Chem. Engrs. (chmn. Chgo. sect. 1966-67), Am. Chem. Soc., Am. Soc. Engring. Edn. (chmn. Ill.-Ind. sect. 1963-64, 73-74, Vincent Bendix Minorities in Engring. award, 1986), Soc. for History of Tech., Soc. for Indsl. Archeology, Sigma Xi, Tau Beta Pi, Phi Lambda Epsilon, Alpha Chi Sigma, Triangle. Home: 10 E Willow Rd Prospect Heights IL 60070-1332 Office: Northwestern U Technol Institute Evanston IL 60208-0001 E-mail: wtb@northwestern.edu.

BRAZER, BARBARA ROBACK, accountant; b. Chgo., Jan. 18, 1950; d. Warren Theodore and Mary Lou (Febel) Rumatz; m. Donald W. Roback, Oct. 21, 1973 (div. Nov. 1984); 1 child, Darren Donald Roback; m. Geoffrey Robert Brazer, Sept. 9, 1995. BSBA, Roosevelt U., 1978, MBA, 1987. Plant acct. Fansteel/VR Wesson, Lake Bluff, Ill., 1979-86; plant contr. Littell Machine, Chgo., 1986-87; contr. Hycor Corp., Lake Bluff, 1987-88, Hertel Cutting Tech., Oak Ridge, Tenn., 1988-91; cost acctg. mgr. EG&G Instruments, Oak Ridge, 1991-95, AAR Powerboss, Aberdeen, N.C., 1995-97; fin. inventory mgr. ANH Refractories Co., Pitts., 1998—. Mem. Inst. Mgmt. Accts. Avocations: golf, skiing. Home: 9811 Fox Chase Dr North Huntingdon PA 15642-6607 E-mail: bbrazer@anhrefractories.com.

BRAZIER, DON ROLAND, retired railroad executive; b. Pittsburg, Kans., Mar. 30, 1921; s. Hosie O. and Lola Frances (Tow) B.; m. June Darla Harr, Nov. 8, 1941. B.C.S., Benjamin Franklin U., Washington, 1950, M.C.S., 1951. Civilian budget officer Ordnance Corps, Dept. Army, 1940-43, 46-53; OFC asst. sec. def., 1953-67; comptroller Def. Supply Agt., 1967; dep. asst. sec. Army, 1967-68; prin. dep. asst. sec. def.-comptroller, 1968-74; treas. AMTRAK, 1974-75, v.p. fin., treas., 1975-82, exec. v.p. fin. and adminstrn., 1982-86. Dir. Washington Union Terminal; pres., dir. Chgo. Union Sta. With USAAF, 1943-46; maj. AUS ret. Decorated Meritorious Service medal; recipient Def. Disting. Civilian Service award, 1971, 73, 74

BRAZIER, JOHN RICHARD, lawyer, physician; b. Olean, N.Y., Mar. 11, 1940; s. John R. and Edith (Martin) B.; children: Mark, Jennifer. AAS, SUNY, Alfred, 1960; BS in Engring. Physics, U. Colo., 1963, MD, 1969; JD, Santa Clara U., 1989. Bar: Calif., 1989. Intern in surgery Downstate Med. Ctr., Bklyn., 1969-70; resident in surgery U. Colo., Denver, 1970-75; fellowship thoracic and cardiovascular surgery NYU, 1975-77; asst. prof. surgery UCLA, 1977-78; pvt. practice Northridge, 1978-84, Newport News, Va., 1984-86, Sacramento, 1989—. Fellowship NIH, UCLA, 1972-74. Mem. AMA, ACS, Calif. Bar. Avocation: law. Home: 1401 36th St Sacramento CA 95816-6606 Office: 915 21st St Sacramento CA 95814-3117

BRAZIER, MARY MARGARET, psychology educator, researcher; b. New Orleans, Feb. 4, 1956; d. Robert Whiting and Margaret Long (Mc Waters) B. BA, Loyola U., New Orleans, 1977; MS, Tulane U., 1985, PhD, 1986. Assoc. prof. Loyola U., 1986—, chair dept. psychology, 1993—, acting assoc. dean Coll. Arts and Scis., 1997-98. Grantee, NSF, 1987, 1999. Mem.: APA, Southwestern Psychol. Assn. (coun. 1988—2000, pres. 2002—), So. Soc. Philosophy and Psychology (exec. coun. 1989—92), Southeastern Psychol. Assn., Am. Psychol. Soc. Roman Catholic. Avocations: gardening, sailing, new orleans cooking and culture, dance. Office: Loyola U Dept Psychology 6363 Saint Charles Ave Dept New Orleans LA 70118-6195 E-mail: brazier@loyno.edu.

BRAZIL, HAROLD EDMUND, political science educator; b. Bearden, Ark., Aug. 24, 1920; s. Paul Brazil and Lavenia (Govenor) Pullen; children: Leslie, Christopher, Susan, Paul, Ernest, Harold, Michael. BS, Tuskegee U., 1942; MA, Ohio State U., 1957; PhD, Ohio State U., Columbus, 1961. Placement officer VA, Columbus, 1946-49; dir. civil personnel Internat. Refugee Orgn., Fed. Republic of Germany, 1949-50; personnel officer USAF, Philippines, 1955-57, dir. research and community relations, 1957-59, command historian, 1959-62; attaché Am. Embassy, Cairo and Monrovia, Liberia, 1962-66; prof., chmn. dept. polit. sci. Sienna Coll., Loudonville, N.Y., 1966-70; co-dean sch. humanities and social sci. Rensselaer Poly. Inst., Troy, N.Y., 1970-72, prof., chmn. dept. history and polit. sci., 1972-75, prof. polit. sci., 1975-90, prof. emeritus, 1990—. Instr. Indsl. Coll. of Armed Forces, Washington, 1964, Fgn. Service Inst. of Dept. of State, Washington, 1965. Author: The Taiwan Straits Crisis of 1958, 1959, The Politics of Philippine Economic Development, 1962, A World Apart: America Military Diplomacy in S.E. Asia, 1976, The Law of the Oceans: Pursuing Order in the Twenty-First Century, 1988, The Third World, Multinationals, and the Law of the Sea Treaty, in Papers in Public Law and Comparative Political Science, 1989. Served as capt. USAF, 1942-46. Mem. Am. Internat. Polit. Sci. Assn., African Studies Assn., Inter-Univ. Seminar on Armed Forces and Soc. Home: PO Box 1560 Troy NY 12181-1560 Office: Rensselaer Poly Inst Dept Sci & Tech Studies Sage Hall Troy NY 12181

BRAZIL, JOHN RUSSELL, academic administrator; b. L.A., Mar. 5, 1946; s. Burton R. and Helen Frances (Douglas) B.; m. Janice Hosking; children: Adrian, Morgan AB, Stanford U., 1968; MPhil, Yale U., 1971, PhD, 1975. Coordinator Am. studies program San Jose (Calif.) State U., 1976-79, from assoc. prof. to prof., 1979-84, spl. asst. to acad. v.p., 1979-81, exec. asst. to pres., 1981-83, assoc. acad. v.p., 1983, acad. v.p., 1983-84; pres. Southeastern Mass. U., North Dartmouth, 1984-92, Bradley U., 1992-99, Trinity U., San Antonio, 1999—. Chmn. S.E. Mass. Partnership, 1988-92; exec. dir. Sourisseau Acad. State and Local History, San Jose, 1977-79; cons. Calif. Coun. for Humanities in Pub. Policy, 1976-78, NEH, chmn. Coun. of Pub. Pres.'s and Chancellors, Mass., 1986-87; hon. adv. bd. SHARE, Inc., 1986-92; mem. Am. Coun. Edn., 1984—; bd. dirs. Caterpillar Inc; exec. com. FIICU, 1992-99 Contbr. articles on Twain, London, Sterling, Bierce, the 1920's, numerous book revs. Bd. dirs. Mass. Ctr. for Excellence in Marine Sci., 1986-92; mem. Fall River Regional Task Force, 1984-92; com. mem. SEMTECH, Mass., 1984-92; trustee Greater New Bedford Indsl. Found., 1984-92; mem. Charlton Meml. Hosp., 1985-92; pres. S.E. Mass. U. Found., 1985-92; bd. govs. Forest Pk. Found., 1995-99; founder, bd. dirs. United Way S.A.; World Affairs Coun., S.A. Med. Found., 1999—. Fulbright Sr. scholar, U. Sydney, 1980; Phi Kappa Phi Disting. Faculty Achievement award, San Jose State U., 1984; S&H Found. lectureship grant. Mem. NCAA (Pres.'s Commn. 1987-92, chair Walter Byers scholarship com. 1991-96), Am. Assn. State Colls. and Univs., Am. Studies Assn., Am. Assn. Higher Edn., New Bedford C. of C. (bd. dirs. 1984-88), No. Calif. Am. Studies Assn. (exec. bd. 1978-80), Soc. Advancement of Mgmt. (adv. rev. bd. 1991-92), Assoc. Colls. of the South (bd. dirs.), nat. Assn. Ind. Colls. and Univs. (bd. dirs.), So. Coll. Athletic Conf. (bd. dirs.), Higher Edn. Coun. San Antonio (pres.-elect), Fall River C. of C. (bd. dirs. 1984-87), Phi Beta Kappa, Phi Kappa Phi, Omicron Delta Kappa. Office: Trinity U Office of Pres 715 Stadium Dr San Antonio TX 78212-7200

BRAZINSKY, IRV(ING), chemical engineering educator; b. NYC, Oct. 27, 1936; s. Israel and Rebecca (Singer) B.; m. Rosalie Seligson, June 14, 1959; children: Howard, Michael. BSChemE, Cooper Union, 1958; MS, Lehigh U., 1960; ScD, MIT, 1967. Chemist Freeport Sulfur Co., Port Sulfur, La., 1957; rsch. engr. NASA, Cleve., 1958, 59-61, Polaroid Corp., Waltham, Mass., 1966-69; sr. rsch. engr. Celanese Corp., Summit, N.J., 1969-76; sr. R & D engr. Halcon Internat., NYC, 1976—81; process devel. mgr. Foster Wheeler Energy Corp., Livingston, N.J., 1981-85, cons., 1985-88; adj. prof. N.J. Inst. Tech., Newark, 1971-81; assoc. prof. chem. engring. Cooper Union, N.Y.C., 1985-91, prof., 1991—, chmn. dept., 1989—. Cons. Gen. Foods Inc., Philip Morris Inc., N.Y.C. Dept. of Pers., 1985-92. Pioneer, patentee processes for heat stabilizing microporous plastic film, improving melt strength of polyester and nylon melts, and rapid chilling of beverages; contbr. articles to profl. jours. Mgr., coach Matawan Little League, 1975-81; active YMCA Indian Guides Program, 1972-80; coach Aberdeen-Matawan Basketball League, 1979-85; v.p. Matawan High Sch. Parents Athletic Assn., 1986-90. Schweinburg scholar, 1954-55; Petroleum Rsch. Fund fellow, 1958-59, A.D. Little fellow, 1963-64, Proctor & Gamble fellow, 1964-66; N.Y. State Regents scholar, 1954-58, Campbell, Reilly, Schiff and O'Rourke scholar, 1955-58. Mem. AIChE, Am. Soc. Engring. Edn., Am. Chem. Soc., Soc. Plastics Engrs., Cooper Union Fedn. of Coll. Tchrs. (v.p. 1997-2003, pres. 2003—), Rheology, N.Y. Acad. Scis., Sigma Xi. Home: 6 Rustic Ln Matawan NJ 07747-2865 Office: Cooper Union 51 Astor Pl New York NY 10003-7132

BRDLIK, CAROLA EMILIE, retired accountant; b. Wuerzburg, Germany, Mar. 11, 1930; came to U.S., 1952; d. Ludwig Leonard and Hildegard Maria (Leipold) Baumeister; m. Joseph A. Brdlik; children: Margaret Louise, Charles Joseph. BA, Oberrealschule Bamberg, Fed. Republic Germany, 1948; MA, Bavarian Interpreter Coll., Fed. Republic Germany, 1949; Cert., Internat. Accts. Soc., Chgo., 1955. Interpreter, exec. sec. NCWC Amberg, Schweinfurt, Ludwigsburg and Munich, Fed. Republic Germany, 1949-52; exec. sec. Red Ball Van Lines, Jamaica, N.Y., 1952; interpreter Griffin Rutgers Inc., N.Y.C., 1952-53; office mgr., exec. sec. Rehab. Ctr. Summit Co., Inc., Akron, 1953-56; pvt. practice acctg. Cuyahoga Falls, Ohio, 1956-61. Uniontown, Ohio, 1961-81; sec., treas. Omaca, Inc., Uniontown and Deerfield Beach (Fla.), 1981-86, pres. Uniontown and Jupiter, 1986-2000, ret., 2000. Sec.-treas. Shipe Landscaping, Inc., Greensburg, Ohio, 1968-92, Sattler Machine Products, Copley, Ohio, 1981-88; asst. treas. Mar-Lynn Lake Park, Inc., Streetsboro, Ohio, 1969-97. Bd. dirs., trustee Czechoslovak Refugees, Cleve. and Cin., 1968. Mem.: Nat. Assn. Tax Profls., Nat. Soc. Accts. Roman Catholic. Avocations: sewing, swimming, travel. E-mail: carola-brdlik@msn.com.

BREAKIRON, LEE ALLEN, astronomer; b. Arlington, Va., July 26, 1948; s. Philip Lewis and Margaret Elisabeth (Jensen) B.; m. Patricia Joy McDonough, June 14, 1975 (div. Aug. 1985); 1 child Jason Lance; m. Teiko Rosemary Hirasawa, May 24, 1987. BA in Astronomy, U. Va., 1970; MS in Astronomy, U. Pitts., 1973, PhD in Astronomy, 1977. Asst. to div. dir. NSF, Washington, 1980-85; rsch. astronomer Wesleyan U., Middletown, Conn., 1976-80, U. Pitts., 1985-86; timekeeping astronomer U.S. Naval Obs., Washington, 1986—. Contbr. rsch. papers to Astron. Soc. of Pacific Publs., Astron. Jour., Astrophys. Jour. Supplement, Astronomy and Astrophys. Supplement, IEEE Std.; rsch. editor Proceedings of Precise Time and Time Interval Meeting. Zaccheus Daniel fellow U. Pitts., 1972-76. Mem. Am. Astron. Soc., Internat. Astron. Union, Sigma Xi.

BREAKSTONE, ROBERT ALBERT, consumer products, e-commerce, information technology and consulting executive; b. N.Y.C., Feb. 20, 1938; s. Morris and Minnie E. (Guon) B.; m. Eileen Fogel, Nov. 5, 1966; children: Warren, Ron, David. BS in Math., CCNY, 1960, MBA in Mgmt., 1964. Sys. engring. mgr. IBM, N.Y.C., 1960-64; dir. mgmt. sys. Continental Copper & Steel Industries, Inc., N.Y.C., 1964-68; v.p., CFO Sys. Audits, Inc., N.Y.C., 1968-70; v.p., group exec. Chase Manhattan Bank, N.Y.C., 1970-74; group v.p., bd. dirs. Chesebrough-Pond's, Inc., Greenwich, Conn., 1974-85; pres., CEO Health-Tex Inc., N.Y.C., 1985-88; exec. v.p., COO GTech Corp., West Greenwich, R.I., 1988-95; pres., CEO Landmark Internat. Group, Inc., Boca Raton, Fla., 1995—. Adj. asst. prof. Pace U. and NYU, 1964-71; adj. prof. Mercy Coll. Grad. Sch. of Bus., 1997—; bd. dirs. State of Conn. Conix Program, OSF, Inc.; bd. advisors Hoffinger Industries, World Entertainment Group, Inc.; spkr. in field. Bd. dirs. Stamford Mus. and Nature Ctr., Bi-Cultural Sch.; pres. United Jewish Fedn. of Stamford, 1996-98. Mem. N.Am. Soc. Corp. Planning, Am. Apparel Mfrs. Assn. (dir.), Mu Gamma Tau (pres.). Mem. N.Am. Soc. Corp. Planning, Am. Apparel Mfrs. Assn., Mu Gamma Tau (pres.). Home: 2432 NW 62nd St Boca Raton FL 33496 Office: Landmark International Group Inc 2432 NW 62nd St Boca Raton FL 33496 also: 95 Lynan Rd Stanford CT 06903

BREALL, SUSAN, judge; Chief criminal divsn. San Francisco Dist. Atty.'s Office, 1984—2001; judge Superior Ct. of Calif., County of San Francisco, San Francisco, 2001—. Mem. adv. bd. Nat. Network for Battered Immigrant Women. Office: Superior Ct of Calif Civic Ctr Courthouse 400 McAllister St San Francisco CA 94102-4519 Address: Volcano Press PO Box 270 Volcano CA 95689-0270

BREAREY, SUSAN WINFIELD, artist, art educator; b. Biddeford, Maine, Sept. 9, 1964; BA, Evergreen State Coll., 1988; MFA, R.I. Sch. Design, 1994; diploma in lithography, Ecole des Beaux Arts, Paris, 1987. Tchg. asst. R.I. Sch. Design, Providence, 1992-94; adj. prof. art Keene (N.H.) State Coll., 1995-96; mem. visual arts faculty The Putney (Vt.) Sch., 1991—; vis. artist grad. painting program Bretton Hall U. Leeds, 2000. Exhbns. include Springfield (Mass.) Mus. Art, 1995, Hood Mus. Art, Dartmouth Coll., Hanover, N.H., 1998, Parrish Art Mus., Southampton, N.Y., 1998; represented by Gerald Peters Gallery, Santa Fe, N.Mex., Carol Craven Gallery, Martha's Vineyard, Mass., N.Y.C., Texann Ivy Fine Art Gallery, Orlando, Fla., Gerald Peters Gallery, Santa Fe. Recipient Purchase award Cheekwood Mus. Art, Nashville, 1993, Grumbacher award, Springfield Mus. Art, 1995. Mem. Nat. Mus. Women in the Arts, Coll. Art Assn., World Wildlife Fedn. Democrat. Avocations: gardening, photography, music, hiking, cross-country skiing.

BREARLEY, CANDICE, fashion designer; b. Trenton, N.J., Jan. 2, 1944; d. Joseph William and Lillian (Mieler) Szalay; m. Purvis Brearley, Sept. 2, 1965. BFA, Mus. Sch., Phila., 1965, MFA, 1968; BFA, Parsons Sch. Design, 1975, New Sch. Social Rsch., 1975. Freelance portrait artist, Trenton, 1965-72; asst. designer Malcolm Starr, N.Y.C., 1974-75; designer Originala, N.Y.C., 1975-77, Vignette, N.Y.C., 1977-78; pres., designer Candice Brearley, Inc., Trenton, 1978—; pres. Wickford Corp. of N.J., Trenton, 1986—. Bd. dirs. Beta Con Corp., Lawrenceville, N.J. One-woman shows Nat. State Bank, N.J., 1971; exhibited in group show at N.J. State Mus., Trenton, 1970. Mem. devel. com. Restoration of "The Brearley House," Lawrenceville, N.J. Recipient award Lane Bryant Design Competition, 1974. Fellow Phila. Mus. Art, Met. Mus. Art, Princeton U. Mus., N.J. State Mus.; mem. Lawrence Hist. Soc. Roman Catholic. Avocations: collecting art, vintage cars, antique refinishing, opera, cooking. Office: Candice Brearley Inc 128 Buckingham Ave Trenton NJ 08618-3314

BREARTON, JAMES JOSEPH, lawyer; b. Troy, N.Y., Aug. 12, 1950; s. James Edward and Lois Marie (Mesnig) B.; m. Margaret Anne Cassidy, Aug. 27, 1977. BA, Coll. Holy Cross, 1972; JD, Albany Law Sch., 1975. Bar: N.Y. 1976, U.S. Dist. Ct. (no. dist.) N.Y. 1976. Assoc. Wager, Taylor, Howd, Brearton & Kessler, Troy, N.Y., 1975-87; ptnr. Wager, Taylor, Howd & Brearton, Latham, NY, 2001—; pvt. practice, Latham, NY, 1987—2001. Mem. bd. arbitrators Nat. Assn. Securities Dealers, Inc., 1992—; mem. Am. Prepaid Legal Svcs. Inst.; mem. examining counsel Monroe Title Ins. Corp.; examining counsel Fidelity Nat. Title Ins. Co.; instr. Am. Inst. Banking, 1994; mem. law guardian liaison com. 3d Jud. Dist., N.Y., 1987-2002. Co-author: Alternate Dispute Resolution, American Jurisprudence, 2nd rev. edit., 1995. Pres. Alumni Assn. LaSalle Inst., Troy, N.Y., 1997-98, mem., ex-officio, Bd.Trustees, 1998. Mem. ABA, N.Y. State Bar Assn., Rensselaer County Bar Ass., Albany County Bar Assn., Capital Dist. Trial Lawyers Assn., Mensa, Uncle Sam Toastmasters, K.C. Democrat. Roman Catholic. Office: PO Box 889 950 New Loudon Rd Latham NY 12110-2116 E-mail: JJBREARTON@aol.com.

BREATHED, BERKELEY, cartoonist; b. Encino, Calif., June 21, 1957; s. John William Breathed and Martha Jane (Martin) de Varennes; m. Jody Boyman, May 10, 1986; children: Sophie, Milo. BA, U. Tex., 1980. Syndicated cartoonist Washington Post Writer's Group, Washington, 1980-95. Cartoonist: Bloom County, 1980-89, Outland, 1989-95; author: (compilations) Loose Tails, 1983, Toons for Our Times,1984, Penguin Dreams and Stranger Things, 1985, Bloom County Babylon: Five Years of Basic Naughtiness, 1986, Billy and the Boingers Bootleg, 1987, Tales Too Ticklish To Tell, 1988, Night of the Mary Kay Commandos, 1989, Classics of Western Literature, 1990, Politically, Fashionably and Aerodynamically Incorrect, 1992, His Kisses Are Dreamy But Those Hairballs Down My Cleavage..., 1994, One Last Peek: The Final Hits, The Special Hits, The Inside Tips, 1995, (children's books) A Wish for Wings that Work (also TV spl., home video), 1991, The Last Basselope, 1992, Goodnight Opus, 1993, Red Ranger Came Calling, 1994, Edwurd Fudwupper Fibbed Big, 2000, Flawed Dogs, 2003. Recipient Pulitzer prize for editorial cartooning Columbia U., 1987. Avocations: travel, animal rights, motorcycling.

BREATHITT, EDWARD THOMPSON, JR., lawyer, railroad executive, former governor; b. Hopkinsville, Ky., Nov. 26, 1924; s. Edward Thompson Sr. and Mary Josephine (Wallace) B.; m. Lucy Alexander Breathitt; children: Mary Frances, Linda Key, Susan Holleman, Edward Thompson III. BS in Commerce, U. Ky., 1947, LLB, 1950, JD, 1970, LLD (hon.), 1965, U. Marshall, 1966, U. Ky., 1967. Bar: Ky. 1950, U.S. Supreme Ct. 1974. Ptnr. Trimble, Soyars & Breathitt, Hopkinsville, 1960-62; gov. State of Ky., Frankfort, 1963-67; ptnr. Trimble, Soyars & Breathitt, Hopkinsville, 1968-72; v.p. Southern Ry. Co., Washington, 1972-82, Norfolk Southern Corp., Washington, 1982-86, sr. v.p., 1986-92; with Wyatt Tarrent & Combs Law firm, Lexington, Ky., 1992—. Mem. adv. bd. Am. Security Bank, Washington, 1987-90; mem. Ky. Econ. Devel. Corp., 1979—; chmn. bd. trustees U. Ky., 1992-99. Mem. legis. State of Ky., Frankfort, 1952-56; chmn. and pres. Commn. on Rural Property, Washington, 1965-67; pres. Commn. to Fulfill These Rights, Washington, 1965-67. With USAAF, 1942-45. Named Conservationist of Yr. Nat. Wildlife Fedn. and Outdoor Life Mag., 1966; recipient Conservationist award U.S. Dept. of Interior, 1967, Lincoln Key award for Civil Rights, 1966. Fellow U. Ky.; mem. Ky. Bar Assn., D.C. Bar Assn., Chevy Chase Club, Pendenis Club. Democrat. Methodist. Avocations: fishing, hunting, golf, tennis, hiking. Home: 1703 Fairway Dr Lexington KY 40502-1648 Office: Wyatt Tarrant and Combs Lexington Fin Ctr 250 W Main St Ste 1700 Lexington KY 40507-1746

BREAULT, KEVIN D. sociology educator, research scientist; b. N.Y.C., May 24, 1954; s. Roland E. and Vera A. Breault; m. Joy Dworkin, June 27, 1982 (div. Sept. 1985); m. Lynn E. Egan, July 30, 1988; 1 child, Lucy. BA, Reed Coll., 1978; MA, U. Wash., 1983; PhD, U. Chgo., 1986. Asst. prof. U. Cin., 1985-87, Washington U., St. Louis, 1988-91, U. Ill., Chgo., 1991-92; assoc. prof. Austin Peay State U., Clarksville, Tenn., 1993-97; assoc. prof. sociology Mid. Tenn. State U., Murfreesboro, 1997-98, prof., 1998—. Author: (monograph) Four Hundred Years of Social Thourhg, 1986, (children's book) With Wings To Fly, 2000; contbr. articles and book revs. to profl. jours., including Am. Jour. Sociology, Jour. Interpersonal Violence, jour. Quantitative Criminology, Social Forces, Brit. Jour. Sociology, Contemporary Sociology, Sociol. Focus, Am. Sociol. Rev., Jour. Marriage and Family, Sociol. Quar., Social Sci. Rsch., also chpts. to books. Grantee U. Cin., 1986, Austin Peay State U., 1994, G.H. Weems Ednl. Found., 1997, Mid. Tenn. State U., 1999; fellow Ctr. for Advanced Study in Behavioral Scis., Ogburn-Stouffer fellow U. Chgo., 1987-88. Mem. Am. Sociol. Assn., Am. Birding Assn. Avocations: birding, travel, chess, writing young adult books. Office: Middle Tenn State U Dept Sociollogy Murfreesboro TN 37132

BREAULT, THEODORE E(DWARD), lawyer; b. N.Y.C., Mar. 7, 1938; m. Gretchen S. Clements, Dec. 10, 1966; children: Victoria Ann, Theodore Edmund, Heidi Sherwin, Edmund Clements. BS, Manhattan Coll., 1960; JD, Cath. U. Am., 1963. Bar: D.C. 1964, Va. 1964, Pa. 1970, U.S. Ct. Appeals (D.C. cir.) 1964, (4th cir.) 1969, U.S. Supreme Ct. 1967. Assoc. Seltzer & Suskind, Washington, 1964-69, Egler & Reinstadtler, Pitts., 1969-77; pvt. practice Fairfax, Va., 1967-69, Pitts., 1977—. Lectr. Cath. U. Am. Sch. Nursing, 1968, Robert Morris Coll., 1973-74; mem. Pa. Workmen's Compensation Sect.; spl. master Allegheny County Ct. of Common Pleas; arbitrator U.S. Dist. Ct. Pres. Sewickley (Pa.) Symphony Orch., 1974-75. Fellow: Pa. Bar Found. (life); mem.: Am. Coll. Legal Medicine (assoc. in law), Am. Arbitration Assn. (arbitrator accident and comml. claims), Pa. Def. Inst., Am. Soc. Law and Medicine, Allegheny County Bar Assn. (health law sect., chmn. workmen's compensation sect. 2001—02), D.C. Bar Assn., Va. State Bar Assn., Pa. Bar Assn. (civil litigation sect.), Matrimonial Inns of Ct. (master). Home: 108 Claridge Dr Moon Township PA 15108-3204 Office: Breault & Assocs PC 428 Forbes Ave 1509 Lawyers Bldg Pittsburgh PA 15219

BREAUX, JOHN B. senator, former congressman; b. Crowley, La., Mar. 1, 1944; s. Ezra H., Jr. and Katherine (Berlinger) B.; m. Lois Gail Daigle, Aug. 1, 1964; children: John B., William Lloyd, Elizabeth Andre, Julia Agnes. BA in

Polit. Sci, U. Southwestern La., 1964; JD, La. State U., 1967. Bar: La. 1967. Ptnr. Brown, McKernan, Ingram & Breaux, 1967-68; legis. asst. to Congressman Edwin W. Edwards, 1968-69, dist. asst., 1969-72; mem. 92d-99th Congresses from 7th Dist. La., 1972-86; U.S. Senator from La. Washington, 1987—; mem. Fin. com., 1990—; chief dep. whip, 1993—. Mem. commerce, sci. and transp. com., aviation subcom., comm. subcom., consumer affairs subcom., oceans and fisheries subcom., surfact transp. and merchant marine subcom., fgn. commerce and tourism, fin. com., internat. trade subcom., taxation and IRS oversight com.; ranking mem. subcom. on Social Security and Fgn. Policy; mem. Senate Dem. steering coord. com., senate dem. tech. comm. com.; ranking mem. spl. com. on aging, fgn. commerce and tourism subcom., social security and family policy subcom.; chmn. Nat. Water Alliance, 1987-88, Nat. Dem. Senatorial Campaign Com., 1989-90, Dem. Leadership Coun., 1991-93; co-chmn. Nat. Bipartisan Commn. on Future of Medicare, 1998-99; co-chmn. Nat. Commn. on Retirement Policy, 1997-98. Co-chair senate Centrist Coalition; mem. Senate New Dems. Recipient Am. Legion award; Moot Ct. finalist La. State U., 1966; Neptune award Am. Oceanic Orgn., 1980 Mem. La. Bar Assn., Crowley Jr. C. of C., La. Jr. C. of C., Pi Lambda Beta, Phi Alpha Delta, Lambda Chi Alpha. Democrat. Office: US Senate 503 Hart Senate Bldg Washington DC 20510-0001*

BREAUX, PAUL JOSEPH, lawyer, pharmacist; b. Franklin, La., Mar. 11, 1942; s. Sidney J. and Irene (Bodin) B.; m. Marilyn Anne Jones, Aug. 21, 1965; children: Jason E., James P. BS in Pharmacy, Northeast La. U., 1965; JD, La. State U., 1972. Bar: La. 1972, U.S. Supreme Ct. 1975. Pharmacist Belanger's Pharmacy, Morgan City, La., 1965-66, Clinic Pharmacy, Morgan City, La., 1966-69; pvt. practice of law Lafayette, La., 1972-73, 93—; assoc. Allen, Gooch, Bourgeois, Breaux, Robison, Theunissen Attys., Lafayette, 1973-75; ptnr. Allen, Gooch, Bourgeois, Breaux, Robison & Theunissen, Lafayette, 1975-93. Sec., bd. dirs. Bank of Lafayette. Bd. dirs. Lafayette Community Health Care Clinic, Inc., 1992-, vice chmn., 1996-2002, pres. 2003-; bd. dirs. Hospice of Acadiana, Inc., 1996-, v.p., 1999-2003, pres. 2003-; bd. dirs. The Hospice Found., pres. 1998-; mem. Gov.'s Universal Health Care Law Reform Commn., 1992-; active Boy Scouts Am., 1984-92. Named Vol. of Yr., Lafayette Cmty. Health Care Clinic, Inc., 2000. Mem.: ABA, Soc. Hosp. Attys. of La. Hosp. Assn., Acad. Hosp. Attys. of Am. Hosp. Assn., Am. Health Lawyers Assn., Am. Soc. Pharmacy Law, Am. Soc. Law & Medicine, Nat. Assn. Retail Druggists, Am. Compliance Inst., La. Pharmacists Assn. (bd. dir. 1991—99, 2001—, Pharmacist of Year award 1992), Am. Pharm. Assn., La. Bankers Assn. (mem. bank counsel com. 1983—85, 1988—90, La. banking code legis. revision com. 1983), Lafayette Parish Bar Assn., La. Bar Assn., Lafayette C. of C., Phi Eta Sigma, Kappa Psi. Republican. Roman Catholic. Office: 600 Jefferson St Ste 503 Lafayette LA 70501-6998

BREAZEALE, HELENE, arts administrator, educator; b. Balt., Sept. 14, 1937; d. Harry Saile and Sophia Himmelfarb Cohen; 1 child, Gregory A. BS in Dance, The Juilliard Sch., 1959; MA in Dance Edn., Columbia U., 1972; PhD in Dance Edn., Union Grad. Sch., 1976. Mem. faculty Case Western Reserve U., Cleve., 1965-69, Cleve. State U., 1969-72; prof., chair dept. dance Towson U., Balt., 1972-90, assoc. dean, 1990-96; exec. dir. World Music Congresses, Balt., 1995—; prodr. World Cello Congress II, Russia, 1997, World Cello Congress III, Balt., 2000. Cons. Md. State Arts Coun., Balt., 1972-80, Balt. Mayor's Adv. Com., 1988—94 Contbr. articles to various mags. Vol. Balt. Mus. of Art, 1987-91, Jewish Mus. of Md., 1998—. Mem. Nat. Assn. Schs. of Dance, Am. Assn. Univ. Adminstrs., Guitar Found. Am., Balt. Classical Guitar Soc. Office: Towson U World Music Congresses 8000 York Rd Admin Bldg 423 Baltimore MD 21252-0001 E-mail: hbreazeale@towson.edu.

BREAZEALE, MACK ALFRED, physics educator; b. Leona Mines, Va., Aug. 15, 1930; s. Carl Samuel and Maude Ella (Moore) B.; m. Joanne Morton O'Dell, Oct. 4, 1952 (dec. Nov. 1989); children: Jennifer Lee, David Mark, William Carl; m. Louise Hanna Scott, Nov. 10, 1990. BA, Berea Coll., 1953; MS, U. Mo. at Rolla, 1954; PhD, Mich. State U., 1957. Asst. rsch. prof. Mich. State U., 1957-62; assoc. prof. U. Tenn., 1962-67, prof. physics and astronomy, 1967—95; cons. solid state div. Oak Ridge Nat. Lab., 1962-71, cons. health and safety research div., 1985-87; cons. Naval Rsch. Labs., 1971-75; prin. investigator contracts Office Naval Rsch., AEC, 1963—95; disting. rsch. prof. U. Miss., 1988—; prin. scientist Nat. Ctr. for Phys. Acoustics, Miss., 1988—. Guest Inst. Basic Tech. Problems, Warsaw, Poland, 1972; vis. prof. Tech. U. of Denmark, 1977; guest U. Paris, 1977; mem. program com. Internat. Symposium on Nonlinear Acoustics, 1975, 76, 78, 81, 84, 87, 90, 93, 96. Contbr. articles to profl. jours. Fulbright rsch. fellow Tech. U., Stuttgart, Fed. Republic Germany, 1958-59; Fulbright travel grantee, 1977-78, NATO rsch. grantee, 1978-81, 92-2001, NSF U.S.-Italy program grantee, 1982-86. Fellow IEEE (adminstrv. com. ultrasonics, ferroelectrics and frequency control soc. 1987-89, program com. 1979—, pres. lectr., 1987, co-chair Atlanta meetings Ultrasonics Symposium 2001, named Disting. Lectr. 1987-88), Acoustical Soc. Am. (assoc. editor Nonlinear Acoustics 1977-2001, Silver medal in phys. acoustics 1988), Inst. Acoustics (U.K.); mem. AAUP, Am. Phys. Soc., Sigma Xi, Phi Kappa Phi, Sigma Pi Sigma. Office: National Center for Physical Acoustics Coliseum Dr University MS 38677 E-mail: breazeal@olemiss.edu. *Scientific progress ultimately depends upon absolute integrity and honesty. A scientist therefore must pursue Truth in such a manner that the path between himself and his goal can never be totally obstructed by any other human being.*

BREBBIA, CARLOS ALBERTO, educator, engineering consultant; b. Rosario, Argentina, Dec. 13, 1948; came to U.S., 1969; s. Carlos Alejandro and Elda (Eiris) B.; m. Carolyn Susan Stones, Oct. 30, 1971; children: Alexander Carlos, Isabel Elena. BS in civil engring., U. Litoral, Rosario, 1968; PhD in Civil Engring., U. Southampton, Eng., 1972; PhD (hon.), U. Bucharest, 1994. Lectr. U. Southampton, 1970-75, reader, 1976-79; assoc. prof. Princeton (N.J.) U., 1975-76; prof. U. Calif., Irvine, 1979-81; dir. Wessex Inst. Tech., Southampton, 1981—; pres. Computational Mechanics Inc., Billerica, Mass., 1984—. Mem. several adv. bds. Author 13 books; editor over 200 books; editor 2 profl. jours. Recipient Ville France medal, 1978; freeman City of London. Fellow Inst. Mech. Engring. (U.K.); mem. Liverymen of Co. of Sci. Instrument Makers, Internat. Soc. Boundary Elements (pres. 1989—). Roman Catholic. Achievements include development of the main concept of the boundary element method, of innovative computational techniques, of an industrial computer aided design code based on boundary element methods; founder of Wessex Institute of Technology. Office: WIT Ashurst Lodge Ashurst Southampton SO407AA England

BRECHBILL, SUSAN REYNOLDS, lawyer, educator; b. Washington, Aug. 22, 1943; d. Irving and Isabell Doyle (Reynolds) Levine; children: Jennifer Rae, Heather Lea. BA, Coll. William and Mary, 1965; JD, Marshall-Wythe Sch. Law, 1968. Bar: Va. 1969, Fed. Bar, 1970. Atty. AEC, Berkeley, Calif., 1968-73, indsl. rels. specialist Las Vegas, 1974-75; atty. ERDA, Oakland, Calif., 1976-77, Dept. Energy, Oakland, 1977-78, dir. procurement divsn. San Francisco Ops. Office, 1978-85, asst. chief counsel for gen. law, 1985-93, acting asst. mgr. environ. mgmt. and support, 1992, acting asst. mgr. def. programs, 1993; chief counsel Dept. Energy Richland Ops. Office, 1994 99; mgr. Ohio field office Dept. of Energy, 1999—. Mem. faculty U. Calif. Extension; speaker Nat. Contract Mgmt. Assn. Ann. Symposiums, 1980, 81, 83, 84, 88, Weapons Complex Monitor Decision Makers forum, 1999, 2000, Fed. Agy. Environ. Clean-up forum, 2001. Contbr. articles to profl. jours. Spkr. on doing bus. with govt. leader Girl Scouts U.S.A., San Francisco area; bd. dirs. Am. Heart Assn. Eastern Wash., 1997-99, Sexual Assault Response Ctr., Tri Cities, Wash., 1997-99; vol. tchr. Jr. Achievement, 1999. Named Outstanding Young Woman Nev., 1974; recipient Meritorious Svc. award Dept. Energy, 1992, 2000. Mem. NAFE, Va. State Bar Assn., Fed. Bar Assn., Nat. Contract Mgmt. Assn. (pres. Golden Gate chpt. 1983-84, N.W. regional v.p. 1984-86). Republican. E-mail: susan.brechbill@ohio.doe.gov.

BRECHER, BERND, management consultant; b. Germany, Oct. 2, 1932; arrived in U.S., 1940; s. Jacob and Betty (Lewinsohn) B.; m. Helen Edith Casel, Feb. 1, 1959; children: Jacalyn Naomi, Alison Fay, Daniel Evan. BA, Columbia U., 1954, MS in Journalism, 1955. Dir. devel., pub. rels. and alumni affairs Coll. Physicians and Surgeons, Sch. Dentistry, Columbia U., N.Y.C., 1954-57; campaign dir., supr. John Price Jones Co., Inc., N.Y.C., 1958-67; v.p. Hamilton Coll. and Kirkland Coll., Clinton, N.Y., 1967-69; exec. v.p. John Price Jones Internat., Inc., N.Y.C., 1969-71; sr. v.p. Brakeley, John Price Jones, Inc., N.Y.C., 1971-73; pres. Bernd Brecher & Assocs., Inc., N.Y.C. and Scarsdale, 1973-93, Instl. Advancement Programs Inc., N.Y.C., Tuckahoe, Becket, Mass., 1979—. Cons., strategic planner for arts, health, edn., youth, religious, cmty., environ. and other not-for-profit instns.; exec. dir. The Grad. Ctr. Found., N.Y.C., 1994—97, Lehman Coll. Found., 2000—; cons. Lilly Endowment, Indpls., 1994—. Pres. Bd. Edn., Greenburgh, N.Y., 1977-78, Woodlands Scholarship Fund, Hartsdale, N.Y., 1965-66, Soc. of Columbia Graduates, 1980-85; mem. exec. com. Columbia Journalism Sch. Alumni, 1981-89; trustee Berkshire Children's Mus., 1998-2000. With U.S. Army, 1957-58. Recipient alumni medal for svc. Columbia U., 1983, Pres.'s Cup, 1981, Lion Awards, 1979, 80, 94, 99. Mem. Coun. for Advancment and Support of Edn. (Quarter Century Svc. award 1981), Assn. Fundraising Profls. (v.p. N.Y. chpt. 1987-89), Am. Assn. Cmty. and Jr. Colls., Am. Hosp. Assn., Am. Assn. Mus., Princeton Univ. Club, Univ. Club of Chgo. Avocations: theatre, tennis, travel, fine dining. Home: 35 Parkview Ave Bronxville NY 10708-2953 Office: Instl Advancement Programs Inc 65 Main St Tuckahoe NY 10707-2908 E-mail: BrecherServices@aol.com.

BRECHER, IRVING, economics educator; b. Montreal, Que., Can., Feb. 1, 1923; m. Toba Brecher, May 11, 1944; children: Richard, Thomas, Ronald, Teresa. BA, McGill U., 1943; MA, Harvard U., 1947, PhD, 1951; JD, Yale U., 1953. Tchg. fellow Harvard U., Mass., 1946—48; asst. prof. econs. McGill U., Montreal, 1948-50; Asst. prof. econs., lectr. law Northwestern U., Evanston, Ill., 1953-55; assoc. prof. McGill U., 1955—62; prof., 1962-84; chmn. dept. McGill U., 1981-84, prof. emeritus, 1985—, founding dir. Centre for Developing-Area Studies, 1963-71. Tchg. fellow Harvard U., 1946-48; joint dir. Pakistan Inst. Devel. Econs., Karachi, 1960-61; bd. govs. Internat. Devel. Research Centre, Ottawa, 1970-73; vice chmn. Econ. Council Can., Ottawa, 1972-74; advisor various Can. and internat. orgns.; mem. staff Royal Commn. on Can.'s Econ. Prospects, Ottawa, 1955-57, Can. Royal Commn. on Banking and Fin., Ottawa, 1964-66; vis. fellow Rsch. Sch. Pacific Studies Australian Nat. U., Canberra, 1972; sr. fellow East-West Ctr. U. Hawaii, 1971-72; hon. lectr. law McGill U., 1964-66. Author: Monetary and Fiscal Thought and Policy in Canada, 1919-1939, 1957, Capital Flows between Canada and The United States, 1965, Canada's Competition Policy Revisited, 1982; co-author: Canada-United States Economic Relations, 1957, Foreign Aid and Industrial Development in Pakistan, 1972; editor: Human Rights, Development and Foreign Policy: Canadian Perspectives, 1989; co-editor: Development Planning and Policy in Pakistan, 1950-70, 1973, Equity and Efficiency in Economic Development, 1992; contbr. numerous articles profl. jours., parliamentary procs., magazines and newspapers. Bd. dirs. Can. Human Rights Found., Montreal, 1988-91, Internat. Ctr. for Human Rights and Dem. Devel., Montreal, 1990-94. Recipient Queen's Silver Jubilee medal, 1978, prize for rsch. on internat. cartels Yale Law Sch., 1962; Leave fellow Can. Council, 1971-72. Mem. Am. Econ. Assn., Can. Econs. Assn., Can. Inst. Internat. Affairs, North-South Inst. (founding com. 1975-76). Office: McGill U-Dept of Econs 855 Sherbrooke St W Montreal QC Canada H3A 2T7

BRECHER, KENNETH, astrophysicist, educator; b. N.Y.C., Dec. 7, 1943; s. Irving and Edythe (Grossman) B.; m. Aviva Schwartz, Aug. 18, 1965; children: Karen, Daniel. BS, MIT, 1964, PhD, 1969. Research physicist U. Calif., San Diego, 1969-72; asst. prof. physics MIT, Cambridge, 1972-77, assoc. prof., 1977-79; assoc. prof. astronomy and physics Boston U., 1979-81, prof., 1981—, dir. Sci. and Math. Edn. Ctr., 1990—. Author, editor: (with G. Setti) High Energy Astrophysics and Its Relation to Elementary Particle Physics, 1974, (with M. Feirtag) Astronomy of the Ancients, 1979; contbr. numerous articles to profl. jours. Mem. Mass. Cultural Coun., 1989-91. Guggenheim fellow, 1979—80, W.K. Kellogg fellow, 1985—88, NRC sr. rsch. assoc., 1983—84, Exploratorium Osher fellow, 2001. Fellow Am. Phys. Soc. (chmn. astrophysics div. 1990-91); mem. Am. Aston. Soc., Internat. Astron. Union, Am. Assn. Physics Tchrs., N.Y. Acad. Scis., Sigma Xi. Home: 35 Madison St Belmont MA 02478-3535 Office: Boston U Dept Astronomy 725 Commonwealth Ave Boston MA 02215-1401

BRECHER, MICHAEL, political science educator; b. Montreal, Mar. 14, 1925; s. Nathan and Gisela (Hopmeyer) B.; m. Eva Danon, Dec. 7, 1950; children: Leora, Diana, Seegla. BA, McGill U., 1946; MA, Yale U., 1948, PhD, 1953. Mem. faculty McGill U., Montreal, 1952—, prof. polit. sci., 1963—, R.B. Angus prof. polit. sci., 1993—. Founder Shastri Indo-Can. Inst., 1968, pres., 1969, 70; vis. prof. U. Chgo., 1963; vis. prof. internat. rels. Hebrew U., Jerusalem, 1970-75, U. Calif., Berkeley, 1979, Stanford U., 1980. Author: The Struggle for Kashmir, 1953, Nehru: A Political Biography, 1959, The New States of Asia, 1963, Succession in India, 1966, India and World Politics, 1968, Political Leadership in India, 1969, The Foreign Policy System of Israel, 1972, Israel: The Korean War and China, 1974, Decisions in Israel's Foreign Policy, 1975, Studies in Crisis Behavior, 1979, Decisions in Crisis, 1980, Crisis and Change in World Politics, 1986, Crises in the 20th Century: Vol. 1, Handbook of International Crises, Vol. 2, Handbook of Foreign Policy Crises, 1988, Crisis, Conflict and Instability, 1989, Crises in World Politics, 1993, A Study of Crisis, 1997, 2000, Millennial Reflections on International Studies, 2002; contbr. over 80 articles in field to profl. jours. Recipient Watumull prize, Am. Hist. Assn., 1960, Killam awards, Can. Coun., 1970—74, 1976—79, Woodrow Wilson Found. award, Am. Polit. Sci. Assn., 1973, Fieldhouse tchg. award, McGill U., 1986, Disting. Scholar award, Internat. Studies Assn., 1995, Léon-Gérin Quebec Prize for Human Scis., 2003, Disting. Rsch. award, McGill U., 2000; Nuffield fellow, 1955—56, Rockefeller fellow, 1964—65, Guggenheim fellow, 1965—66, rsch. grantee, Can. Coun. and Soc. Sci. and Humanities Rsch. Coun. of Can., 1960, 1965, 1968, 1969—70, 1975—76, 1980—87, 1990—92, 1993—96, 2002—05. Fellow Royal Soc. Can.; mem. Internat. Studies Assn. (pres. 1999-2000), Brit. Internat. Studies Assn., World Assn. Internat. Relations, Internat., Am., Can., Israeli polit. sci. assns. Home: 5 Dubnov St Jerusalem 91043 Israel Office: McGill U Dept Pol Sci 855 Sherbrooke St W Montreal QC Canada H3A 2T7

BRECHKA, FRANK TILSON, retired librarian, historian; b. N.Y.C., Sept. 30, 1930; s. Frank August and Marjorie Tilson (Connell) B. AB, Columbia U., 1952, MS, 1954, AM, 1958; PhD, U. Calif., Berkeley, 1968. Libr. N.Y. Pub. Libr., N.Y.C., 1954-57, sr. libr., 1959-61; head libr. S.I. C.C., N.Y.C., 1958-59; reference libr. Wagner Coll., N.Y.C., 1961-63, U. Calif., Berkeley, 1967-71, history libr., 1971-91, retired, 1991. Instr. history and librarianship U. Calif., Berkeley, 1970-77; cons. San Francisco Towers Libr., 1996—. Author: Gerard Van Swieten and His World, 1700-1772, 1970; contbr. articles to profl. jours. Rsch. grantee Librs. Assn. Univ. Calif., Berkeley, 1982; scholar Columbia Univ. Sch. Libr. Svc., N.Y.C., 1952-53, Fulbright, Netherlands and Austria, 1965-66. Mem. Am. Hist. Assn., Inst. for Hist. Study. Avocations: collecting books and antique maps, writing letters, travel. Home: 1661 Pine St Apt 823 San Francisco CA 94109-0409

BRECHT, SALLY ANN, quality assurance executive; b. Trenton, N.J., Aug. 5, 1951; d. Charles L. and Helen (Orfeo) B. BBA, Coll. William and Mary, 1973; MBA, Rider Coll., 1981. Cert. quality engr., software quality engr.; quality auditor, quality mgr., project mgr. Project Mgmt. Inst. Electronic data processing auditor McGraw Hill, Inc., Hightstown, N.J., 1976-79, State of N.J., Mercerville, 1979-80, NL Industries, Hightstown, 1980-84; systems tech. planning specialist Ednl. Testing Svc., Princeton, N.J., 1984-85, acting div. dir. application devel., 1985-87, mgr. computer standards and security, 1987-88, asst. dir. office corp. quality assurance, 1988-98; dir. software quality assurance Y2K Renovation, 1998—; portfolio project mgr. IT Project Mgmt. Office, 2000—02; project mgr. CMM Metrics Implementation, 2002—. Contbr. articles to popular publs. Mem. Am. Soc. for Quality Control (cert. quality engr., mgr., auditor and software quality engr.). Avocation: riding show hunters.

BRECHT, WARREN FREDERICK, retired business executive; b. Detroit, May 21, 1932; s. August F. and Margaret (Roos) B.; m. Barbara Boone, July 31, 1983; children: Amy E., Stephen F., David C., Peter J. BA, DePauw U., 1954; postgrad., U. Mich., 1955; MBA, Harvard U., 1959. Systems analyst W.R. Grace & Co., Cambridge, Mass., 1959—61; v.p., treas. Mgmt. Systems Corp., Cambridge, 1961—65; ptnr. in charge adminstrn. Peat, Marwick, Livingston & Co., Boston, 1965—69; prin. in charge profl. practice, mgmt. cons. dept. Peat, Marwick, Mitchell & Co., N.Y.C., 1969—71; dep. asst. sec. for mgmt. and budget U.S. Dept. Interior, Washington, 1971—72; asst. sec. for adminstrn. U.S. Dept. Treasury, 1972—77; v.p. acctg. and mgmt. info. systems Northeast Utilities, Hartford, Conn., 1977—85; sr. v.p. N. Am. Holding Corp. and Subs., East Hartford, Conn., 1985—89; sr. v.p., sec. Butler Internat. (formerly N.Am. Ventures Inc.), Montvale, NJ, 1985—2001; sr. v.p. adminstrn. and sec. Butler Svc. Group., Inc., Montvale, 1990—2001. Mem. panel deregulationn govt. mgmt. Nat. Acad. Pub. Adminstrn., 1982—83. Exec. bd. coun. BSA, Bergen County, NJ, 1997—98; bd. dirs., treas. Nyack Comty Ctr., 1999—; Trustee Conn. Pub. Expenditure Coun., 1978—84; vice chmn. ch. coun., treas., trustee Riverside Ch., N.Y.C, 1993—2000, 2002—. With USAF, 1955—57. Recipient Outstanding Young Man award Lexington (Mass.) Jaycees, 1968; Exceptional Service award Dept. Treasury, 1976; Alumni citation DePauw U., 1976; Rector Scholar 25th Anniversary Achievement award DePauw U., 1979. Mem. Phi Beta Kappa. Home: 23 Tallman Ave Nyack NY 10960-1605 E-mail: wbbrecht@optonline.net.

BRECHTEL, UNDA JURKA, library director; b. Riga, Latvia, Mar. 3, 1935; came to U.S., 1951; d. Aleksanders and Irene (Stesingers) Jurka; m. Philipp Jack Brechtel Jr., Sept. 3, 1960 (div. Aug. 1986); children: Philipp Jack III, Peter Kevin. BS in Psychology, St. Thomas Aquinas, 1981; MLS, L.I. U., 1982. Reference librarian Haverstraw (N.Y.) Pub. Libr., 1982-83; libr. dir. Sloatsburg (N.Y.) Pub. Libr., 1983-85, Wanaque (N.J.) Pub. Libr., 1985-88, Oakland (N.J.) Pub. Libr., 1988-2000; ret., 2000; libr. L.I. U., Sparkill, N.Y., 2000—. Mem. N.J. Libr. Assn., N.Y. Libr. Assn. Lutheran. Avocations: ballroom dancing, travel, gardening. Home: 1-16 Lawrence Pk Piermont NY 10968 E-mail: undausa@yahoo.com.

BRECKBERG, ROBERT LEE, lawyer; b. Kodiak, Alaska, June 14, 1951; s. Henry and Ruth Lorraine (Davis) B. BA, Amherst Coll., 1974; JD, Lewis and Clark Coll., 1977. Bar: Alaska 1977, U.S. Dist. Ct. Alaska 1978, U.S. Ct. Appeals (9th cir.) 1978, U.S. Ct. Claims 1989. Assoc./ptnr. Robert M. Goldberg, Anchorage, 1978-80; hearing examiner Alaska Transp. Commn., Anchorage, 1980, 81-84; assoc. Lynch, Crosby, Molenda & Sisson, Anchorage, 1985-86, Edgar Paul Boyko, Anchorage, 1986-99; pvt. practice Anchorage, 1999—. Mem. Alaska Bar Assn., Anchorage Bar Assn. Avocations: fishing, biking, skiing, hiking, beachcombing. Office: 750 W 2d Ave Ste 104 Anchorage AK 99501

BRECKEL, ALVINA HEFELI, librarian; b. Chgo., Dec. 6, 1948; d. William Christ and Liselotte (Herrmann) Hefeli; m. Theodore A. Breckel, Feb. 10, 1973. BFA cum laude, Bradley U., 1970; MALS, Rosary Coll. (now Dominican U.), 1973. Cert. art tchr., media libr., Ill. Tchr. art Chgo. Pub. Schs., 1971-84; libr. Oakton CC, Des Plaines, Ill., 1988—. Mem. North Shore Bd. of Gads Hill Ctr., corr. sec., 2000—; nat. seminar spkr. Early Am. Pattern Glass Soc., 1999; spkr. Mid-States conf. Early Am. Pattern Glass Soc., 2001; co chmn. Winnetka Antiques Show, 1999, chmn., 2000, dealer chmn., 2000—; mem. Com. for Gallery 37 in the Schs., 2001—; mem. visual arts com. Chgo. Cmty. Trust Gallery, Northwestern U. Settlement Assn., 2001—. Author: Looking for Glass on the Internet, 1996; editor News & Notes, 1988-89. Rep. election judge New Trier Twp., Ill., 1988; com. mem. Villagers for a Safe Winnetka, 1989; mem. women's bd. Howard Area Cmty. Ctr., 1990-95; chmn. Fuller Lane Cir., Winnetka, 1991-92, 94-95; mem. Midwestern Antiques Club, 1993—; mem. women's bd Winnetka Cmty. House, 1995—03, historian, 1997—2003, mem. steering com., 1999—. Mem. AAUW (bd. dirs. New Trier chpt. 1989-90), Sandwich (Mass.) Hist. Soc., Winnetka Hist. Soc., Art Inst. Chgo. (life), Nat. Greentown Glass Assn., Nat. Am. Glass Club (life, founding mem. James H. Rose chpt., chpt. sec. 1992-97), Greater Chgo. Glass Collectors Club (v.p. 1995-97, pres. 1998-2000, chmn. bylaws com. 2001, chmn. nominating com. 2002), Early Am. Pattern Glass Soc. (nominating com. 1998, spkr. Mid-States conf. 2001), Pi Lambda Theta (life, art editor chpt. Notes 1977-84), Delta Zeta (v.p. Chgo. North Shore chpt. 1987-90), Phi Delta Kappa. Avocation: collecting and researching early American decorative arts, especially glass. Home: 185 Fuller Ln Winnetka IL 60093-4212 Office: Oakton CC 7701 Lincoln Ave Skokie IL 60077-2800

BRECKENRIDGE, JUDITH WATTS, writer, educator; b. Knoxville, Tenn., Jan. 30, 1948; d. William Robert and Mary Kathryn (Ault) Watts; m. Rufus Gentry Breckenridge, June 26, 1977; children: Kathryn Suzanne, Mary Audra, Caroline Irene, Judith Gentry. BA in English, Carson-Newman Coll., 1970; MA in English, West Ga. Coll., 1972. Instr. Augusta (Ga.) Coll., Walter State C.C., Morristown, Tenn., 2002—; columnist Greeneville (Tenn.) Sun, 1993—; freelance writer. Author: Simple Physics Using Everyday Materials, 1993; author, creator (radio spots) Momtrax Minutes, 1999; author: (song) LA Cop: Cop of Lower Alabama, 1991. Mem.: First Families Tenn., Greeneville Arts Coun. (sec. 2001—02), Tuesday Morning Book Club. Baptist. Achievements include copyright Grammar Sticks; copyright Momtrax. Avocations: hiking, photography. Home: 606 Whisperwood Dr Greeneville TN 37743

BRECKENRIDGE, KLINDT DUNCAN, architect; b. Iowa City, Apr. 24, 1957; s. Jack Duncan and Florence (Kmiecik) B.; m. Nancy Ann Dernier, Apr. 19, 1986; children: Wilson Reid, Lauren Alessandra, Carson Duncan. BArch, U. Ariz., 1981. Registered architect, Ariz., Calif., Nev.; cert. NCARB. Architect Finical & Dombrowski, Tucson, 1981-84; pvt. practice Tucson, 1984—. Assoc. faculty Pima Community Coll. Bd. dirs., pres. Mirical Sq. Mem. AIA (treas. So. Ariz. chpt. 1997-99, pres. 1999-2000, state pres. elect 2003, com. arch. edn., pres.-elect). Democrat. Episcopalian. Avocation: running. Home: 5535 N Waterfield Dr Tucson AZ 85750-6473 Office: Brickenridge Group 700 N Stone Ave Tucson AZ 85705-8306 E-mail: breckenridge@breckenridgearch.com.

BRECKER, JEFFREY ROSS, lawyer, educator; b. N.Y.C., June 9, 1953; s. Milton S. and Charlotte (Alpert) B.; m. Phyllis L. Gordon, Oct. 30, 1983. BA in Polit. Sci., NYU, 1975; JD, New Eng. Sch. Law, Boston, 1978. Bar: N.Y. 1979, U.S. Dist. Ct. (so. and ea. dists.) N.Y. 1979, U.S. Supreme Ct. 1982. Atty. Nassau (N.Y.) County Legal Svcs. Commn., 1978-80, Dist. Coun. 37 Legal Svcs., N.Y.C., 1980-82, Wingate & Shamis, N.Y.C., 1982-85; sr. trial atty., unit supr. Jacobowitz & Lysaght, N.Y.C., 1985-89; mng. atty. Damashak Godosky & Gentile, N.Y.C., 1989-95, Godosky & Gentile, N.Y.C., 1995—. Adj. prof. New Coll., Hofstra U., 1981; chairperson tort litigation com. Assn. Bar City of NY. Office: Godosky & Gentile 61 Broadway 20th Fl New York NY 10006-2701 Business E-Mail: JeffreyB@Godosky&Gentile.com.

BRECKER, MICHAEL, saxophonist; Recipient Grammy award Best Jazz Instrumental Performance, 1996, 1997, Grammy award Best Jazz Instrumental Solo, 1996—97, 2002. Office: Dept h of Field Mgmt 1501 Broadway Ste 1304 New York NY 10036-5601

BRECKINRIDGE, JAMES BERNARD, optical engineer; b. Cleve., May 27, 1939; s. Albert Coles and Catherine Rose (Wengler) B.; m. Ann Marie Yoder, July 24, 1965; children: Douglass E., John Brian. BS in Physics, Case Inst. Tech., 1961; MS in Optical Sci., U. Ariz., 1970, PhD in Optical Sci., 1976. Rsch. asst. Lick Obs., Mt. Hamilton, Calif., 1961-64; electron tube engr. Rauland Corp., Chgo., 1967; rsch. asst. Kitt Peak Nat. Obs., Tucson, full time, 1964-66, 68, 75-76, part time, 1969-74; mem. tech. staff Jet Propulsion Lab., Calif. Inst. Tech., 1976—, part-time faculty in applied physics, 1981—, mgr. optics sect., 1981-94; program mgr. for innovative imaging tech. and sys. Flight Projects Office, 1994—99; leader NASA Team to Assess Optics Tech. in Former Soviet Union, 1992-97, mgmt. and tech. cons., 1994—; program dir. advanced tech. and instrumentation, program dir. Nat. Radio Astronomy Obs., NSF, 1999—2002; chief technologist Astron. Search for Origins, NASA, 2002—. Co-investigator NASA Spacelab 3; mem. adv. com. NASA, NSF, Dept. Def.; staff mem. Hubble Space Telescope Failure Bd., 1990, tech. mgr. Hubble Space Telescope Camera Optics Repair; mgr. advanced tech. and instruments and Nat. Radio Astronomy Obs., NSF, 1999-2002. Contbr. articles to jours. in field; 5 patents in field. Scoutmaster Boy Scouts Am.; bd. trustees United Ch. of Christ. Fellow Optical Soc. Am. (bd. dirs.), Royal Astron. Soc., Internat. Soc. Optical Engring. (bd. govs., pres. 1994, George W. Goddard award 2003); mem. IEEE, Am. Astron. Soc., Coun. of Scientific Soc. Pres.'s (bd. dirs. 1996), Internat. Astron. Union (chair U.S. com. internat. congress on optics, G.W. Goddard award), Astron. Soc. of Pacific. Achievements include research in remote optical and infrared sensing instrumentation, interferometry, spectroscopy, image intensifiers and image analysis. Office: Natl Science Fdn 4201 Wilson Blvd Arlington VA 22230

BRECKINRIDGE, MICHAEL FREDERICK, pharmacist; b. Sacramento, May 1, 1947; s. Frederick Allen Breckinridge and Gail K. Breckinridge Beckwith; m. Catherine Tirado, May 15, 1976; children: Raquel, Daniela, Rebecca. BS in Biol. Scis., U. Calif., Davis, 1969; BS in Pharmacy, Oreg. State

U., Corvallis, 1973. Registered pharmacist, Oreg. Staff pharmacist USPHS Hosp., Staten Island, N.Y., 1973-77; chief pharmacy svc. USPHS Bur. Med. Svcs./USPHS Outpatient Clinic, San Juan, 1977-81, USPHS Indian Health Svc./Indian Health Ctr., Wolf Point, Mont., 1981-86; chief pharmacist USPHS Indian Health Svc./Point Pleasant Health Ctr., Perry, Maine, 1986—. Contbr. articles to profl. jours. Mem. Am. Pharm. Assn. Christian. Avocation: amateur radio (call sign n1jxp). Home: 32 Harrison St Calais ME 04619-1106 Office: Pleasant Point Health Ctr PO Box 351 Perry ME 04667-0351 E-mail: nljxp@midmaine.com.

BRECKNER, WILLIAM JOHN, JR., retired air force officer, corporate executive, consultant; b. Alliance, Ohio, May 25, 1933; s. William John and Frances P. (Bertchey) B.; m. Cheryl V. Carmell, Aug. 30, 1963; children: William R., Kristen C. BA, SUNY, 1976; postgrad., Harvard U., 1980. Commd. 2d lt. USAF, 1955, advanced through grades to maj. gen., 1983, various pilot and command positions, 1955-72; comdr. USAF Interceptor Weapons Sch., 1973-75; vice commandant cadets USAF Acad., Colo., 1976-79; comdr. 82d Flying Tng. Wing Williams AFB, Ariz., 1979-80; dep. chief staff logistics Hdqrs. Air Tng. Commd., Tex., 1980-83; chief staff Hdqrs. USAF Europe, 1983-84; commdr. 17th Air Force, Sembach AFB, Germany, 1984-86; ret., 1986. Prisoner of war, Vietnam, 1972-73. Decorated D.S.M., 1986, Silver Star, 1972, Legion of Merit, 1973, Bronze Star medal, 1973, Air medal, 1968, 72, Purple Heart, 1972, 73, Republic of Vietnam Cross of Gallantry with palm, 1973 Mem. Nat. War Coll. Alumni Assn., Order Daedalians, Air Force Assn., Nam Prisoners of War Inc., Red River Valley Fighter Pilots Assn., C. of C. (chmn. mil. affairs coun. 1994-95). Lutheran. Avocations: golf, skiing, tennis. Home: 17865 Fairplay Way Monument CO 80132-8581 Office: 590 Hwy 105 Ste 266 Monument CO 80132 E-mail: brexgroup@earthlink.net.

BREDA, JOHN ALEXANDER, physician, musician; b. Boston, Sept. 9, 1954; s. Alexander John and Eda (Feroli) B.; m. Karen Schultz, Aug. 14, 1988; 1 child, Joseph Samuel. MusB, MusM, New England Conservatory Music, 1972-78; postgrad., Harvard U., 1990; MD, U. Mass., 1996. Diplomate Am. Bd. Internal Medicine, 2000; cert. instrument rated pilot. Symphonic musician Oreg. Symphony, Portland, 1982-89; med. rschr. Harvard Sch. Pub. Health, Boston, 1989-90, Harvard Med. Sch., Boston, 1990-91; intern, resident Metro West Med. Ctr., Framingham, Mass., 1996-97; resident Miriam Hosp., R.I. Hosp., Brown U. Program, Providence, 1997-99; physician in internal medicine Harvard Vanguard Med. Assocs., Medford, Mass., 1999—2001; physician in internal medicine Primary Care and Urgent Care, Harvard U. Health Svcs., Cambridge, Mass., 2001—. Instr. medicine Harvard Med. Sch., 2001—; woodwind instrument builder, cons. clarinet design, Boston, 1978—; guest lectr. New Eng. Conservatory Music, Boston, 1981. Performed with numerous musical orgns. including San Francisco Opera, 1980, Santa Fe (N.Mex.) Opera, 1980, Boston Symphony, 1978-81. Betty Lea Stone fellow Am. Cancer Soc., 1992, Tanglewood fellow Berkshire Music Ctr., 1982, Symphony Orch. Inst. fellow, 1996. Mem. AMA, Mass. Med. Soc. (Charles River dist. scholar 1992), Worcester Med. Soc. Avocations: flying, skiing, bicycling. Office: Harvard Univ Health Svcs 75 Mount Auburn St Cambridge MA 02138-4992

BREDAR, JAMES KELLEHER, judge; b. Omaha, Feb. 6, 1957; s. William Lorenz and Helen Dorothy (Kelleher) B.; m. Stacey Lynn Sewell, July 26, 2002. BA, Harvard U., 1979; JD, Georgetown U., 1982. Bar: Colo. 1983, Md. 1995, U.S. Supreme Ct. 1993. Nat. park ranger U.S. Dept. Interior, Estes Park, Colo., 1976-80; jud. law clk. U.S. Dist. Judge R. Matsch, Denver, 1983; dep. dist. atty. State of Colo., Craig, 1984; asst. U.S. atty. U.S. Dept. Justice, Denver, 1985-89; asst. fed. pub. defender U.S. Courts, Denver, 1989-91, fed. pub. defender Balt., 1992-98; project dir. Vera Inst. Justice, London, 1991-92; U.S. magistrate judge Balt., 1998—. Vis. scholar Yale U., New Haven, 1981-82. Author/editor: Justice Informed, 1992. Office: US Magistrate Judge 8C US Courthouse 101 W Lombard St Baltimore MD 21201-2605

BREDDAN, JOE, systems engineering consultant; b. N.Y.C., Sept. 18, 1950; s. Hyman and Sylvia (Hauser) B. BA in Math. and Psychology, SUNY, Binghamton, 1972; MS in Ops. Rsch., U. Calif., Berkeley, 1975; PhD in Systems Engring., U. Ariz., 1978. Teaching and research assoc. Dept. Systems and Indsl. Engring. U. Ariz., Tucson, 1975-79; project engr. B.D.M. Services Co., Tucson, 1979-80; mem. tech. staff Bell Labs., Am. Bell, AT&T Info. Systems, Denver, 1980-86; staff mgr. AT&T, Denver, 1986-91; pvt. practice cons. Boulder, Colo., 1991—. Patentee in field. Bd. dirs. Colo. Environ. Coalition, 1996—, v.p., 1997—. Home and Office: 2120 Goddard Pl Boulder CO 80305-5616 E-mail: joe11756@msn.com.

BREDE, ANDREW DOUGLAS, research director, plant breeder; b. Pitts., Feb. 4, 1953; s. James Faris and Adele Katherine (Konefal) B.; m. Linda Davis Rudd, Jan. 11, 1992; children from previous marriage: Loralee Elizabeth, Michael Douglas. BS, Pa. State U., 1975, MS, 1978, PhD, 1982. Asst. golf course supt. Valley Brook Country Club, McMurray, Pa., 1975-76; grad. rsch. asst. Pa. State U., University Park, 1976-82; assoc. prof. Okla. State U., Stillwater, 1982-86; dir. rsch. Simplot Turf & Horticulture, Post Falls, Idaho, 1986—. V.p. Turfgrass Breeders Assn., Tangent, Oreg., 1989-91; chmn. variety rev. Lawn Inst., Marietta, Ga., 1990-96; bd. dirs. Nat. Turfgrass Evaluation Program; golf course supr. Assn. Am. Rsch. Com., 1996-97. Author: Turfgrass Maintenance Reduction Manual, 2000; assoc. editor Agronomy Jour., 1993-99; contbr. articles to Agronomy Jour., 150 articles to mags.; prodr. 15 ednl. videos; patentee in field. Rsch. grantee, 1983-86. Mem. Am. Soc. Agronomy. Republican. Achievements include organization of 1st turfgrass conf. in People's Republic of China; developer, patentee 60 plant varieties. Office: Simplot Turf & Horticulture 5300 W Riverbend Rd Post Falls ID 83854-9456

BREDEHOEFT, JOHN DALLAS, geologist; b. St. Louis, Feb. 28, 1933; married, 1958; 3 children. BSE, Princeton U., 1955; MS, U. Ill., 1957, PhD in Geology, 1962. Geologist Humble Oil & Refining Co. divsn. Standard Oil Co., N.J., 1957-59, Desert Rsch. Inst., Nev., 1962; rsch. geologist U.S. Geol. Survey, Menlo Park, Calif., 1962-74, dep. asst. chief rsch. hydrologist Water Resources divsn., 1974-95; cons. in hyrogeology La Honda, Calif., 1995—. Vis. assoc. prof. U. Ill., 1967-68; rsch. assoc. Resources for Future, 1968-70. Mem. Nat. Acad. Engring., Geol. Soc. Am. (Penrose medal 1997), Am. Geophys. Union (R.E. Horton award), Am. Assn. Petrol Geologists, Russia Acad. Nat. Scis. Achievements include research in ground water hydrology, physical properties of ground water systems, physics of ground water motion, transport of chemical constituents in ground-water systems. Home: PO Box 550 Story WY 82842-0550

BREDEHOFT, ELAINE CHARLSON, lawyer; b. Fergus Falls, Minn., Nov. 22, 1958; d. Curtis Lyle and Marilyn Anne (Nesbitt) Charlson; m. Keenan P. Frank; children: Alexandra Charlson, Michelle Charlson. BA, U. Ariz., 1981; JD, Cath. U. Am., 1984. Bar: Va. 1984, U.S. Ct. Appeals (4th cir.) 1984, U.S. Bankruptcy Ct. (ea. dist.) Va. 1987, D.C. 1994, U.S. Ct. Appeals (D.C. cir.) 1994. Assoc. Walton and Adams, McLean, Va., 1984-88, ptnr., 1988-91, Charlson Bredehoft, P.C., Reston, Va., 1991—. Spkr. Fairfax Bar Assn., CLE, 1992—, VB Assn., CLE, 1993—, 12th Ann. Multistate Labor and Employment Law Update, 1993—, Va. Women's Trial Lawyers Assn. Ann. Conf., 1998, Va. Bar. Assn. Labor and Employment Conf., 1994-97, 99—, Va. Trial Lawyers Assn., 1995, 97, Va. Law Found., 1995—, Va. Assn. Def. Attys., 1996, 2001; mem. faculty Va. State Bar Professionalism Com., 1997-2000, Va. State Bar Law Student Professionalism Com., 2001—; invitee 4th Circuit Judicial Conf., 1997-99, permanent mem., 1999—; invitee Boyd Graves Conf., 1999—; substitute judge 19th Judicial Dist., 1998—; chair Fairfax Bar Assn. Diversity Taskforce, 1998-99 (Pres. Vol. award 1998). Bd. dirs. Va. Commn. on Women and Minorities in the Legal System, 1987-90, sec., 1988-90. Mem. Am. Coll. Trial Lawyers, Va. Bar Assn. (mem. exec. com. young lawyers sect., mem. litigation com., mem. nominating com., chmn. model jud. com.), Va. Trial Lawyers Assn. (vice chmn. ann. conv. 1996-98, mem. com. on long-range planning 1996-97, spkr. 1995, 97), Minn. State Soc., Fairfax Bar Assn. (co-chair subcom. on minorities, Pres.'s Vol. award 1998, 99), George Mason Inns of Ct. (master 1996—). Office: Charlson Bredehoft PC 11260 Roger Bacon Dr Ste 201 Reston VA 20190-5252

BREDEHOFT, MICHAEL ROGER, lawyer, mediator; b. Kansas City, Mo. s. Roger and Elaine B. BA Political History, U. Mo. K.C., 1992, MA in History, 1994, JD, 1997. Cert. life/health/casualty/fire and allied lines ins., Mo. Tchg. asst. U. Mo. K.C., 1992-93; atty. Ahmann, Stewart and Nixon, Independence, Mo., 1997-98, Barnett and Jamison, Kansas City, Kans., 1998-99, UAW Legal Svcs., Liberty, Mo., 2000—. Contbr. articles to profl. jours. Mem. ABA, Am. Trial Lawyers Assn., Mo. and Kans. Bar Assn., U. Mo.-Kansas City Alumni Leaders, Phi Delta Phi. Independent. Avocation: cycling.

BREDESEN, PHILIP NORMAN, governor; b. Oceanport, N.J., Nov. 21, 1943; s. Philip Norman and Norma (Walborn) B.; m. Andrea Conte, Nov. 22, 1974; 1 child, Benjamin. AB in Physics, Harvard U., 1967. Computer programmer Itek Corp., Lexington, Mass., 1967-70; dir. systems devel. Searle Medidata, Lexington, 1970-73, div. mgr. London, 1973-75; dir. spl. project Hosp. Affiliates Internat., Nashville, 1975-78; v.p. internat. div. INA Health Care Group, Nashville, 1978-80; chmn. and chief exec. officer HealthAmerica Corp., Nashville, 1980-86; chmn., co-founder Coventry Corp., Nashville, 1986-90; chmn. Clin. Pharms., Nashville, 1986-93; mayor Met. Govt. Nashville and Davidson County, 1991-99; pres. Bredex Corp., Nashville, 2000—02; gov. State of Tenn., Nashville, 2003—. Bd. dirs. Nashville Symphony, 1985-91, Univ. Sch. Nashville, 1986-95, United Cerebral Palsy, 1988-92, United Way of Middle Tenn., 1985-90, Tenn. State U. Found., Nashville Pub. Libr. Found., 1997—; chmn., founder The Land Trust for Tenn., 1999-2001; trustee Frist Ctr. for Visual Arts, 1998—, chair fin. com., 2000—; founder Nashville's Table, 1989, bd. dirs., 1989-91. Democrat. Presbyterian. Avocations: skiing, reading, computers. Home: 1724 Chickering Rd Nashville TN 37215-4908 Office: State Capitol Office Governor Nashville TN 37243-0001 E-mail: phil.bredesen@state.tn.us.

BREDFELDT, JOHN CREIGHTON, economist, financial analyst, retired air force officer; b. Oct. 31, 1947; s. Willis John and Geraldine Elizabeth (Creighton) Bredfeldt; children: Jason Caulter, Bryan Thomas. BBA, Wichita State U., 1969, MA in Econs., 1971; PhD in Pub. Adminstrn., La Salle U., 1995; grad., Air Command and Staff Coll., 1984, Nat. Defense U., 1987. Dir. Brennan Halls Wichita State U., 1969-71; commd. 2d lt. USAF, 1971, advanced through grades to lt. col., 1987, ret., 1993; budget/cost analyst Aero. Sys. Divsn., Dayton, Ohio, 1971-76; insp. Air Force IG, Andrews AFB, Md., 1976-79; chief economist Dir. Programs AF/PRP, Pentagon, Va., 1979-83; chief cost analyst divsn. USAF Europe, 1985-87, dep. dir. program control, engine program office, 1987-89; dir. program control spl. ops. forces USAF, 1989-93; project leader for econs./fin. analyst Modern Techs. Corp., Warner Robins, Ga., 1993—. Instr. econs. Wichita State U., 1969-71, bus. prof. Bowie State Coll., 1980-83; econs. instr. European divsn. U. Md., Germany, 1985-87, Sinclair C.C., Dayton, 1988-93, Macon (Ga.) State Coll., 1994—; adj. prof. Mercer U., 1996—, Wesleyan Coll., 1998—. Contbr. articles to profl. jours. Rep., Sunday sch. tchr. Ramstein Protestant Parish Coun. Germany, 1984-86; asst. scout master Ramstein Coun. Boy Scouts Am., 1984-87, den leader Weblos, 1998, Troop 550 charter rep., 1999—; v.p. St. Timothy Lutheran Ch., Dayton, 1989-91. Mem. Assn. Govt. Accts., soc. cost Estimating and Analysis, Am. Soc. Mil. Comptrollers, Nat. Eagle Scout Assn. E-mail: jcb6@earthlink.net.

BREDHOFF, ELLIOT, lawyer; b. NYC, July 31, 1921; s. Morris and Mamie (Shapiro) Bredhoff; m. Louise H. Bredhoff, Sept. 10, 1950; children: Robert, Nancy. BS, CCNY, 1942; LLB, Yale U., 1949. Bar: NY 1949, DC 1953, US Ct. Appeals (DC and 6th cir.) 1958, US Ct. Appeals (3d cir.) 1961, US Supreme Ct. 1959. Spl. counsel United Steelworkers Am., AFL-CIO, 1965; gen. counsel indsl. union dept AFL-CIO; counsel Nat. Indsl. Group Pension Plan, 1973—93; fgn. svc. grievance bd., 1973—93; currently ptnr. Bredhoff & Kaiser, Washington. Served USAF. Mem.: Am. Arbitration Assn. (bd. dir. 1983—), Commn. on Law and Economy, ABA (chmn. mem. sect. on labor and employment law 1984—85). Democrat. Jewish. Office: 805 Fifteenth St. N.W., Ste 1000 Washington DC 20005

BREDIN, BRENDA ANN, communications educator; b. Waynesboro, Pa., Sept. 22, 1941; d. Paul Franklin Royer and Dolores Lorraine Snurr; children: Brendan(dec.), Elena. BA, Thiel Coll., 1963; MEd, Kutztown U., 1967; MA, U. Ctrl. Fla., 1989. Tchr. Geneva H.S., Ohio, 1963—64, Exeter H.S., Pa., 1964—67, Wyomissing H.S., Pa., 1967—70; adj. prof. U. Ctrl. Fla., Orlando, 1987—89; prof. Valencia C.C., Orlando, 1989—. Fellow, NDEA, 1965. Republican. Episcopalian. Avocations: reading, gardening, poetry. Home: 3881 Becontree Pl Oviedo FL 32765 Office: Valencia Cmty Coll 701 N Econlockhatchee Trl Orlando FL 32801*

BREE, MARLIN DUANE, publisher, author; b. Norfolk, Nebr., May 16, 1933; s. George F. and Luile Bree; m. Loris Bree; 1 child, William Marlin. BA, cert. in journalism, U. Nebr., 1955. Mng. editor Davidson Pub. Co., 1958-61; editor Greater Mpls. mag., 1962-63; pub. rels. specialist Blue Shield, 1964-67; editor Sunday Mag., Star and Tribune, Mpls., 1968-72; columnist Corp. Report, Mpls., 1973-77; publs. cons., 1978-83; co-founder, ptnr., editorial dir. Marlor Press, Inc., St. Paul, 1983-91, co-owner, pub., 1992—. Chmn. Midwest Book Awards, St. Paul, 1992. Author: In the Teeth of the Northeaster: A Solo Voyage on Lake Superior, 1988, Call of the North Wind: Voyages and Adventures on Lake Superior, 1996, Wake of the Green Storm: A Survivor's Tale, 2001; co-author: Alone Against the Atlantic, 1981; columnist River Skipper, 2002. Dir. comm. Mpls. Bicentennial Celebration, 1976. With U.S. Army, 1955-57. Named Pub. of Yr., Midwest Ind. Pubs. Assn., 1994; recipient Golden Web award, 2003-04; honored as one of Best Ind. Pubs. in U.S., Top 101 Ind. Book Pubs., 1997. Mem.: St. Paul Sail and Power Squadron (hon.). Avocation: sailing. Office: Marlor Press Inc 4304 Brigadoon Dr Saint Paul MN 55126-3100 E-mail: marlin.marlor@minn.net.

BREECE, ROBERT WILLIAM, JR., lawyer; b. Blackwell, Okla., Feb. 5, 1942; s. Robert William Breece Sr. and Helen Elaine (Maddox) Breece Robinson; m. Elaine Marie Keller, Sept. 7, 1968; children: Bryan, Justin, Lauren BSBA, Northwestern U., 1964; JD, U. Okla., 1967; LLM, Washington U., St. Louis, 1970. Bar: Oklahoma 1967, Mo. 1970. Pvt. practice, St. Louis, 1968—. Pres., chmn. bd. dirs. Crown Capital Corp., St. Louis. Mem. ABA, Internat. Bar Assn., Mo. Bar Assn., Okla. Bar Assn., Phi Alpha Delta, Beta Theta Pi, Melrose Club, Univ. Club, Forest Hills Country Club (pres. 1978). Home: 35 Crown Manor Dr Chesterfield MO 63005-6805 Office: 540 Maryville Centre Dr Ste 12 Saint Louis MO 63141-5828

BREED, ALLEN FORBES, correctional administrator; b. Wisconsin Rapids, Wis., Oct. 1, 1920; s. Noel Jerub and May Belle (Forbes) B.; m. Virginia Mae Plaskett, June 24, 1945; children: Marla, Eleanor, Carol. BA cum laude, U. Pacific, 1942. With Dept. Youth Authority, State of Calif., 1945-76, supt. correctional schs., 1947-65, chief div. instns., 1965-67; chmn. Youth Authority Bd., State of Calif., 1967-76; dir. Dept. Youth Authority, State of Calif., 1967-76; vis. fellow Dept. Justice, 1976-77; spl. master U.S. Dist. Ct., R.I., 1977-78; dir. Nat. Inst. Corrections, Dept. Justice, Washington, 1978-83; chmn. bd. Nat. Council Crime and Delinquency, Washington, 1983-91, 98-99; spl. master to fed. and state cts. on prison litigation issues, 1983—. Chmn. Task Force on Corrections and mem. Joint Commn. on Juvenile Justice Standards, ABA and Inst. Judicial Adminstrn.; mem. nat. adv. com. on Juvenile Justice and Delinquency Prevention; mem. U.S. del. UN Congress on Prevention of Crime and Treatment of Offenders, Caracas, Venezuela, 1980; mem. UN Congress on Prevention Crime and Treatment of Offenders, Milan, Italy, 1985; del. Internat. Conf. on Criminology, Hamburg, Federal Republic of Germany, 1988, Internat. Conf. on Future of Corrections, Ottawa, Can., 1991—; leader del. on juvenile justice to Russia, 1989—; lectr. 1st Sino-Am. Criminal Justice Inst., People's Republic China, 1986; criminal and juvenile justice del. People's Republic China, 1992; del. Internat. Conf. Corrections, Warsaw, 1993. Contbr. articles to profl. jours., newspapers, mags. Mem. justice programs adv. com. Edna McConnel Clark Found., 1983-89. Served to maj. USMC, 1942-45. Decorated Purple Heart. Mem. Nat. Assn. State Correctional Adminstrs. (state and nat. awards), Nat. Assn. State Juvenile Delinquency Program Adminstrs. (past pres.), Interstate Compact on Probation and Parole (past pres.), Am. Correctional Assn. (v.p. 1984-86, bd. govs. 1986-91), Am. Arbitration Assn., Nat. Coun. Crime and Delinquency (chmn. emeritus bd. dirs.), Calif. Probation, Parole and Correctional Assn. Episcopalian. Home: PO Box 698 San Andreas CA 95249-0698

BREED, HENRY ELTINGE, III, diplomat, educator; b. Trondheim, Norway, Mar. 16, 1961; s. Henry Eltinge and Helen (Illick) B. BA, BS with honors, Ind. U., 1985; MA, Columbia U., 1987; diploma, Grad. Inst. Internat. Studies, Geneva, 1990; MPA, Harvard U., 2000. Internat. programs specialist Am. Coun. for Arts, N.Y.C., 1986-87; consulting editor UNESCO, Paris, 1987-90; drafting expert UN, Geneva, 1991-92, polit. affairs officer, dept. of peace-keeping N.Y.C., 1993-99, program analyst Iraq program, 2000—02, task force reform, 2002—. Adj. prof. pub. policy Duke U., 1998—; coun. on fgn rels. Internat. Inst. of Strategic Studies, London; panelist Nat. Endowment for Arts, 2000—. Concert pianist, U.S. and Europe, 1984-89. Recipient Boursier de la Confedn. Suisse, Swiss Govt., 1988-89; Fulbright scholar, 1987-88; Beale fellow, 1999-2000. Mem. Soc. of Mayflower Descendants (N.Y.), Phi Kappa Lambda. Avocations: music, theatre, skiing, gardening. E-mail: breed@un.org.

BREED, MICHAEL DALLAM, environmental, population, organismic biology educator; b. Kansas City, Mo., Sept. 2, 1951; s. Laurence W. and Loree (Dallam) B.; m. Cheryl A. Ristig, Aug. 9, 1975. BA, Grinnell Coll., 1973; MA, U. Kans., 1975, PhD, 1977. Asst. prof. environ., population, organismic biology U. Colo., Boulder, 1977-83, assoc. prof., 1983-89, prof., 1989—, acting chmn. dept. anthropology, 1991-93, chmn. dept., 1986-90, 97-99, acting assoc. dean, 1991-93, chmn., dept. east asian lang. and civilizations, 2002—. Contbr. articles to sci. jours. Mem. Internat. Union for Study of Social Insects (pres. N.Am. sect. 1984, sec. gen. 1994—), Animal Behavior Soc., Internat. Bee Rsch. Assn., Entomol. Soc. Am. (officer sect. C 1992-95), Sigma Xi. Home: 700 Dahlia St Denver CO 80220-5112 Office: U Colo Dept Biology 102 Boulder CO 80309-0001

BREED, RIA, anthropologist; b. Feb. 5, 1944; d. Jan Mathys and Maria Arnoldina (Gommans) Trienekens; m. David Scranton Breed, Sept. 5, 1976; children: Christian, Genevieve. Med. technologist, Profl. Sch. Venlo (Netherlands), 1962; BA in Social Anthropology, U. Amsterdam, 1972; MA in Phys. Anthropology, NYU, 1977, PhD, 1984. Clin. technologist St. Lambertus Hosp., Helmond, 1962—65, DePaul Hosp., Norfolk, Va., 1965—66; rsch. technician U. Amsterdam, 1968—70; rsch. technician cardiovascular rsch. NYU Med. Ctr., N.Y.C., 1966—68, 1972—77; rsch. assoc. NYU, 1984; head biomechanics dept. Breed Corp., 1984—88; with Automotive Tech. Internat., Denville, NJ. Home: 48 Hillcrest Rd Boonton NJ 07005-9433 Office: Automotive Tech Internat PO Box 8 Denville NJ 07834-0008

BREEDIN, BERRYMAN BRENT, journalist, public relations, historian, consultant; b. Beaufort, S.C., Nov. 3, 1925; s. Berryman Brent Breedin and Jane Cunningham Dixon; m. Allain Crenshaw, Sept. 1959 (div. Jan. 1978); children: David Singleton, Sarah Breedin Chase, Amelia Breedin Twarogowski. BA, Washington and Lee U., 1947. Reporter Caller-Times, Corpus Christi, Tex., 1947-48; sports editor, columnist Daily Mail, Anderson, S.C., 1949-52; publicist, editor Clemson (S.C.) U., 1952-55, 64-66; resident mgr. Hunt Internat. Oil Co., Pakistan, 1955—58, 1996—97; press sec. U.S. Senator Strom Thurmond, Washington, 1958-59; info. specialist DuPont Co., Wilmington, Del., 1960-63; editor Am. Coll. Pub. Rels. Assn., Washington, 1966-71, Coun. Libr. Resources, Washington, 1972-75; dir. pub. rels. Georgetown U., Washington, 1977-79, Rice U., Houston, 1981-87; pvt. practice Columbia, S.C., 1988—; historian White House Weekly, Washington, 1998—. Adv. Washington D.C. Libr., 1972-76, Houston Zoo, 1981-87. Founding mem. Capital Hill Montessori, Washington, 1964, Field Sch., Washington, 1972. With USN, 1944-45. Mem. Nat. Press Club, Sigma Delta Chi. Episcopalian. Avocations: family history, sports history, movie history. Home and Office: 1829 Senate St Apt 4C Columbia SC 29201-3837 E-mail: bbreedin@sc.rr.com.

BREEDING, J. ERNEST, JR., (SUNNY BREEDING), physicist, travel consultant, photographer, web master, webmaster; b. Peoria, Illinois, Mar. 17, 1938; s. J. Ernest Breeding, Sr. and Ruth Irene (Saddoris) Hoffman; m. Barbara Ellen (Walker), June 6, 1970 (div. 1989); 1 child, Della Grace; m. Rebecca (Darden), May 19, 1990; stepchildren: David Benefield, Michael Benefield. Attended, Simpson Coll., 1956-59; BA, Drake U., 1960; post grad., U. Tenn., 1960-61; PhD, Columbia U., 1972. Grad. tchg. asst. U. Tenn., Knoxville, Tenn., 1960-61; physicist Naval Coastal Sys. Ctr., Panama City, Fla., 1962-78; grad. rsch. asst. Lamont - Doherty Earth Obs., Colombia U., Palisades, NY, 1965-70; assoc. prof. oceanography and ocean engring. Fla. Inst. Tech., Melbourne, 1979-87; oceanographer, mathematician Naval Oceanog. Office, Stennis Space Ctr., Miss., 1988; rsch. physicist Naval Rsch. Lab., Miss., 1988-98; owner World Class Travel and Tours, La., 1994—; geophysicist cons., owner World Class Rsch. and Tech., Slidell, La., 1998—. Vis. assoc. prof. Fla. State U., Tallahassee, 1977-79; mem. adv. bd. Summit Travel Group, Inc., Winston - Salem, N.C., 1996-99. Contbg. articles to profl. jour. Trustee, pres., Am. Homesteading Found., Melbourne Village, Fla., 1986-88. Mem. AAAS; Am. Geophys. Union Soc.; Exploration Geophysicists; Am. Meteorol. Soc.; Am. Assn. Physics Tchr.; Nat. Assn. Commd. Travel Agt.; Cruise Lines Internat. Assn.; Sigma Xi; Sigma Pi Sigma; Lambda Chi Alpha. Republican. Avocations: amateur radio, photography. Home and Office: 115 Blackbeard Dr Slidell LA 70461-2721 E-mail: travel@goworldclass.com.

BREEMS, BRADLEY G. sociologist, educator; b. Prinsburg, Minn., Jan. 1, 1948; s. Gordon and Lorraine Ruth Breems; m. Helen J. Veltkamp, June 11, 1971; children: Kara Elen, Daniel Garett Luther, Joel K. BA in English Lit., Dordt Coll., 1970; MPhil in Sociology, Inst. Christian Studies, Toronto, Can., 1975; PhD in Sociology, U. B.C., Vancouver, Can., 1991. Lab. rep. Christian Labour Assn. Can., Toronto, 1975-76, Vancouver, 1976-83; tchg. asst. U. B.C., Vancouver, 1984-88; prof. Trinity Christian Coll., Palos Heights, Ill., 1988—. Adj. prof. Trinity Western U., Langley, B.C., Can., 1986-87. Copy editor U. B.C. Press, 1982-83; co-author: Ethnic Conflict in Vancouver, 1985. Dir., rschr. Neighborhood Action Project B.C. Civil Liberties Assn., Vancouver, 1983-85; mem. econ. subcom. Developing Cmtys. Project, Chgo., 1989-96; mem. study com. Synod Christian Reformed Ch., Grand Rapids, Mich., 1993-96, mem. adv. com., 2000—; mem. com. Main St. Project, Blue Island, Ill., 1993-95; bd. dirs. Roseland Christian Homes Corp., Chgo., 1996-98; mem. bd. curators Inst. Christian Studies, Toronto, 2000—. Mem. Am. Sociol. Assn., Assn. Sociology Religion, Internat. Assn. Promotion Christian Higher Edn. Democrat. Avocations: gardening, reading, hiking, bicycling. Office: Trinity Christian Coll 6601 W College Dr Palos Heights IL 60463 E-mail: brad.breems@trnty.edu.

BREEN, DAVID EDWARD, physicist, researcher; s. Edward Leo and Josephine Breen; m. Cynthia Elizabeth Skripak, June 17, 1989; children: Stefan Andreas Breen Skripak, Ryan Edward Skripak Breen. BA, Colgate U., 1978—82; MS, Rensselaer Poly. Inst., 1982—85, PhD, 1985—93. Rsch. engr. Rensselaer Poly. Inst., 1985—93; mem. of rsch. staff European Computer-Industry Rsch. Centre, Munich, 1994—96; asst. dir., cg lab Calif. Inst. of Tech., Pasadena, 1996—2002, sr. rsch. scientist, 2002—. Editor: (technical reference) Cloth Modeling and Animation; computer art. Recipient Best Paper of the Yr., Literati Club, 1997. Mem.: European Assn. for Computer Graphics, Assn. for Computing Machinery, IEEE Computer Soc. Avocations: skiing, travel, reading, history, bicycling. Office: California Institute of Technology MS 107-79 Pasadena CA 91125

BREEN, DAVID HART, lawyer; b. Ottawa, Ont., Can., Mar. 27, 1960; came to U.S., Aug. 19, 1978; naturalized, 1993; s. Harold John and Margaret Rae (Hart) B.; m. Pamela Annette Mitchell, Sept. 17, 1988; 1 child, Matthew Mitchell. BA cum laude, U. S.C., Columbia, 1982, JD, 1986. Bar: S.C., U.S. Dist. Ct. S.C., U.S. Ct. Appeals (4th cir.), U.S. Bankruptcy Ct. S.C. 1987. Law clk. to Hon. Don S. Rushing Cir. Ct. (6th cir.), S.C., 1986-87; English instr. humanities U. Coastal Carolina Coll., Conway, 1987-88; criminal law instr. Horry-Georgetown Tech. Coll., Conway, 1987-88; sr. ptnr. David H. Breen, P.A., Myrtle Beach, 1988—. C.J.A. panel atty. U.S. Dist. Ct. S.C., 1991-97; mem. family ct. adv. com. 15th Jud. Ct., 1998—. Campaign asst. Joe Clark for Prime Minister, Ottawa, 1975-76. Recipient Province of Ontario Achievement Award, 1976, Nat. Dean's List Award of Merit, 1981—82, Gold Medal - Rifle Shooting, Canada Summer Games, 1977, Provincial Champion Rifle Shooting, Ontario, 1977. Mem. ABA, ATLA, S.C. Trial Lawyers Assn., S.C. Bar Assn., Horry County Bar Assn., Am. Bankruptcy Inst., Oshawa Gun Club, Phi Delta Phi. Methodist. Avocations: swimming, computers. Home: Prestwick Country Club 2187 N Berwick Dr Myrtle Beach SC 29575-5835 Office: 4603 Oleander Dr Ste 6 Myrtle Beach SC 29577-5738

BREEN, JANICE DEYOUNG, health services executive, community health nurse; b. Paterson, N.J., Apr. 15, 1947; d. Corneilius and Catherine (Van Ostenbridge) DeYoung; m. Robert Neal Breen, Aug. 1, 1969; children: Gregory Neal, Karen Elizabeth. BSN, William Paterson Coll., Wayne, N.J., 1970; MEd, Rutgers U., 1976, postgrad.; MSN, U. Pa., 1988; postgrad., Rutgers U. Cert. clin. specialist in community health nursing. Insvc. edn. instr. Cmty. Meml.

Hosp., Toms River, NJ, 1972—75; instr. nursing Ocean County Coll., Toms River, 1977—82, program. coord. for allied health, 1980—82; dir. cmty. svcs. St. Francis Med. Ctr., Trenton, NJ, 1988—94; pres., CEO Advanced Cmty. Health Sys., Verona, NJ, 1994—97; bus. devel. v.p. Sr. Care Ctrs. of Am., 1997—98; clin. asst. prof. divsn. nursing NYU, 2000—02. Vis. asst. prof. William Paterson U., Wayne, NJ, 1996—97; healthcare cons. Care Plus Consulting, Middletown, NJ, 1999—; rsch. fellow Pain Mgmt. Ctr. U. Medicine and Dentistry of N.J., 2002—03. Mem. ANA, N.J. State Nurses Assn., Vis. Nurses Assn. N.J. (treas., chmn., CEO, cons.), Eastern Pain Assn., Sigma Theta Tau. E-mail: jbreen@careplus-consulting.com.

BREEN, JOHN DANIEL, federal judge; b. Jackson, Tenn., July 10, 1950; m. Linda Turnbo; two children. BA summa cum laude, Spring Hill Coll., 1972; JD, U. Tenn., 1975. Bar: Tenn. 1975, U.S. Ct. Appeals (6th cir.) 1977, U.S. Supreme Ct. 1979. Atty. Waldrop and Hall, Jackson, Tenn., 1975—2003; magistrate judge U.S. Dist. Ct. (we. dist.), Tenn., 1991—2003, U.S. Dist. judge, 2003—. Mem. exec. com. West Tenn. Boy Scouts of Am.; lifetime bd. dirs. West Tenn. Cerebral Palsy Ctr. appointed U.S Dist. Judge, Western Dist. of Tenn., 2003. Mem. ABA, Am. Bar Found., Fed. Magistrate Judges Assn. (cir. dir. 6th cir. 2000-2003), Fed. Judges Assn., Tenn. Bar Found. (chair 2002-03), Tenn. Bar Assn. (pres. 1996-97), Jackson-Madison County Bar Assn. (pres. 1983-84), Leo Bearman Inn of Ct. (master). Office: US Dist Ct 345 US Courthouse 111 S Highland Ave Jackson TN 38301-6107 Fax: 901-421-9255.

BREEN, JOHN EDWARD, civil engineer, educator; b. Buffalo, May 1, 1932; s. Timothy J. and Alice C. (Keenan) B.; m. Marian T. Killian, June 20, 1953; children: Mary L., Michael T., Dennis P., Sheila A., Sean F., Kerry T., Christopher D. B.C.E., Marquette U., Milw., 1953; MS in Civil Engring., U. Mo., 1957; PhD, U. Tex., Austin, 1962. Registered profl. engr., Tex., Mo. Structural designer Harnischfeger Corp., Milw., 1952-53; asst. prof. U. Mo., Columbia, 1957-59; mem. faculty U. Tex., Austin, 1959—, prof. civil engring., 1969—, J.J. McKetta prof. engring., 1977-81, Carol Cockrell Curran chair engring., 1981-84, Nasser I. Al-Rashid chair civil engring., 1984—; dir. P.M. Ferguson Structural Engring. Lab., Balcones Research Center, 1967-85. Cons. in field. Contbr. articles to profl. jours. Served to lt. USNR, 1953-56. Recipient Tchg. Excellence award Gen. Dynamics Corp., 1971, Tchg. Excellence award U. Tex. Student Assn., 1963, Teaching Excellence award Std. Oil Found. Ind., 1968, Fedn. Internat. Precontrainte medal, 1990, Internat. award of merit in structural engring. Internat. Assn. Bridge and Structural Engring., 2000; Freyssinet medal Internat. Assn. for Structural Concrete, 2002. Mem.: ASCE (T.Y. Lin medal 1985, 1989, 1991, A.J. Boase Reinforced Concrete Rsch. Coun. award 1987, Croes medal 1999), Swiss Acad. Engring., Nat. Acad. Engring., Am. Concrete Inst. (hon.; bd. dirs. 1974—77, Wason medal 1972, 1983, Raymond C. Reese Rsch. medal 1972, 1979, Kelly medal 1981, Anderson medal 1987, Raymond Davis lectr. 1978, Bloem award 1989, Alfred E. Lindau award 1994, Structural Engring. award 2002), Austin Yacht Club (commodore 1977), Sigma Xi. Democrat. Roman Catholic. Home: 8603 Azalea Trl Austin TX 78759-7501 Office: Univ Tex Ferguson Lab 10100 Burnet Rd Austin TX 78758-4445 E-mail: jbreen@mail.utexas.edu.

BREEN, JOHN WAKEFIELD, personnel services company executive; b. Columbus, Ohio, Sept. 16, 1945; s. John Lawrence and Margaret (Wakefield) B.; divorced; 1 child, John. BS in Bus. Adminstrn., Ohio State U., 1969. Sales mgr. Sherwin Williams Co., Cleve., 1974-76, regional sales mgr., 1976-78; dir. devel. City of Gahanna, Ohio, 1978-80, mayor, 1980-82; dir. Pers. Tng. and Cons., Chillicothe, Ohio, 1983-85; chief oper. officer Health Options Inc., Chillicothe, 1985-88; pres. Enterprises Unltd. Inc., Chillicothe, 1988—, Performance Solutions, 1998—2002, Property Solutions Unltd., 2002. Bd. dirs. Columbus Regional Devel. Coun., 1978-82; mem. Ctrl. Ohio Econ. Devel. Coun., Columbus, 1979-80; bd. dirs. JobPro Inc., Chillicothe. Mem. City Coun., Gahanna, 1976-80, pres., 1979-80. Mem. Gahanna Rotary (founder, pres. 1980-81). Home and Office: 441 Lyncroft Gahanna OH 43230

BREEN, KATHERINE ANNE, speech and language pathologist; b. Chgo., Oct. 31, 1948; d. Robert Stephen and Gertrude Catherine (Bader) Breen. BS, Northwestern U., 1970; MA, U. Mo., Columbia, 1971. Cert. speech pathologist. Speech/lang. pathologist Fulton (Mo.) Pub. Schs., 1971-73; co-dir. Easter Seal Speech Clinic, Jefferson City, Mo., summer 1972, 73; speech/lang. pathologist Shawnee Mission (Kans.) Pub. Schs., 1973-96; staff St. Joseph's Hosp., Kansas City, Mo., 1978-81, Midwest Rehab. Ctr., Kansas City, 1985; pvt. practice speech therapy. Cons. East Ctrl. Mo. Mental Health Center; guest lectr. Fontbonne Coll., St. Louis. Vol., Mid Am. Rehab. Hosp. Mem. NEA, Am. Speech and Hearing Assn., Kans. Speech and Hearing Assn., Mo. State Tchrs. Assn., Kansas City Alumni Assn. of Northwestern U. (dir. alumni admissions coun., Outstanding Leadership award 1981, Svc. award 1991), Friends of Art Nelson/Atkins Art Gallery and Mus. (vol.), Nat. Trust Historic Preservation, Kansas City Hist. Found., Zeta Phi Eta. Methodist. Home: 8318 Mackey St Shawnee Mission KS 66212-2728

BREEN, NEIL THOMAS, publishing executive; b. N.Y.C., Oct. 14, 1944; s. Neil G. and Eileen M. Breen; m. Catherine M. Breen, Dec. 2, 1978. BA, Marquette U., 1966; JD, Creighton U., 1970. Bar: Nebr. 1970, U.S. Dist. Ct. Nebr. 1970. Editor-in-chief Shepard's/McGraw Hill, Colorado Springs, Colo., 1979-86, v.p. devel., 1987-89; Thomson Legal Pub., Stamford, Conn.; pres. Callaghan & Co., Deerfield, Ill., 1989-90; v.p., gen. mgr. litigation and fed. products group, 1991-92; v.p. legal divsn. McGraw Hill Ryerson, Whitby, Ont., Can., 1993-95; pres. Law Bull. Pub. Co., Chgo., 1996—. Author: Texas Law Locator, 1973, Illinois Law Locator, 1975. Mem. ABA, Assn. of trial Lawyers of Am., Ill. State Bar Assn., Chgo. Bar Assn., Can. Bar Assn. Avocations: skiing, snowshoeing, hiking. Office: Law Bulletin Pub Co 415 N State St Ste 200 Chicago IL 60610-4631

BREEN, RICHARD F., JR., law librarian, lawyer, educator; b. Providence, Aug. 1, 1940; s. Richard F. and Elizabeth (Hurlin) B.; children: Stephanie, Jonathan. AB in Econs., Dartmouth Coll., 1962; LLB, U. Maine, Portland, 1967; MLS, U. Oreg., 1973. Bar: Maine, N.H. Asst dean U. Maine Sch. Law, Portland, ., 1967-70; with firm Tesreau and Gardner, Lebanon, N.H., 1970-72; assoc. law libr., assoc. prof. law U. Maine Sch. Law, Portland, 1974-76; law libr., assoc. prof. law Willamette U. Coll. Law, Salem, Oreg., 1976-80, law libr., prof. law, 1980—, interim adminstrv. dean., law libr., 1986-87. Mem. U.S. Olympic Biathlon Tng. Team, 1963. Capt. USAR, 1962-64. Mem. Am. Assn. Law Librs., Oreg. Libr. Assn., Casque and Gauntlet Honor Soc. Democrat. Congregationalist. Avocations: cross-country skiing, hiking. Office: Willamette U Law Libr 245 Winter St SE Salem OR 97301-3916

BREEN, STEPHEN P. editorial cartoonist; Grad., U. Calif., Riverside, 1992. Editl. cartoonist Asbury Park Press, Neptune, NJ. Caricatures, Sunday "Celebs" page, comic strip, Grand Avenue, hundreds of newspapers and nat. mags. Copley News Svc. Recipient John Locher Meml. award, Assn. Am. Editl. Cartoonists, Charles M. Schulz award, Scripps Howard, Pulitzer prize, 1998. Office: c/o Asbury Park Press The Gannett Co PO Box 1550 Neptune NJ 07754-1550

BREESKIN, MICHAEL WAYNE, lawyer; b. Washington, Dec. 25, 1947; s. Nathan and Sylvia (Raine) B.; m. Frances Cox Lively, May 29, 1982; children: Molly Louise, Laura Rose. BA cum laude, U. Pitts., 1969; JD, Georgetown U., 1975. Bar: D.C. 1975, Colo. 1983, U.S. Dist. Ct. D.C. 1977, U.S. Dist. Ct. Colo. 1983, U.S. Ct. Appeals (D.C. cir.) 1978, U.S. Ct. Appeals (10th cir.) 1984, U.S. Supreme Ct. 1995. Mng. atty. Tobin & Covey, Washington, 1977-79; assoc. Donald M. Murtha & Assocs., Washington, 1979-80; counsel NLRB Office Rep. Appeals, Washington, 1980-83; trial atty. NLRB Denver Regional Office, 1983-88; assoc. Wherry & Wherry, Denver, 1989-91; sr. atty. The Legal Ctr. for People with Disabilities and Older People (formerly The Legal Ctr. Serving Persons with Disabilities), Denver, 1991—98; gen. counsel Assn. Cmty. Living Boulder County, Inc. (formerly the Assn. for Retarded Citizens in Boulder County, Inc.), 1998—2000; counsel Fox & Robertson, PC, Denver, 2000—02, Arc of Denver, Inc., 2002—. Presenter, lectr. in field. Adv. com. Domestic Violence Initiative for Women with Disabilities, 1997—. Recipient Outstanding Work for People with Disabilities acknowledgement Very Spl. Arts Colo., 1996; named Profl. of Yr., The Arc of Adams County, 1997; recipient Adv. of the Year award Assn. Cmty. Living in Boulder County Inc., 1996, Schenkein award Arc of Denver, Inc., 1997, award Disability Ctr. Ind. Living and Colo. Cross-Disability Coalition, 1999, Colo. Cross Disability Coalition Meml. award for Civil Rights Legal Advocacy, 2000. Mem. ABA, Colo. Bar Assn. (disability law forum com.), Arapahoe County Bar Assn., Disability Rights Roundtable. Avocations: bicycling, skiing, reading. Office: Arc of Denver 1905 Sherman St Ste 300 Denver CO 80203

BREEZE, WILLIAM HANCOCK, college administrator; b. Cin., Nov. 25, 1923; s. William T. and Nancy (Hancock) B.; m. JoAnne Robertson Watson, Oct. 8, 1949 (dec. Jan. 1983); 1 child, Nancy Louise Breeze; m. Barbara L. Hall, Dec. 15, 1990. Student, Berea Coll., 1943-44; AB, Centre Coll., Danville, Ky., 1945; MA, U. Ky., 1948. Various actuarial positions Ohio Nat. Life Ins. Co., Cin., 1948-56, actuary, 1956-65, asst. to pres., 1965-67, sr. v.p., 1967-72, exec. v.p., 1972-86; v.p., gen. sec. Centre Coll., Danville, Ky., 1987-88, 89-91, acting pres., 1988-89, spl. asst. to pres. for endowment, 1991—. Bd. dirs. Ohio Nat. Life Ins. Co., 1966-88. Bd. dirs. Jr. Achievement Greater Cin., 1974-84; trustee Centre Coll., 1980-86. Served to lt. (j.g.) USNR, 1943-46, PTO. Fellow Soc. Actuaries Republican. Presbyterian. Avocations: reading, classical music. Home: 468 W Broadway St Danville KY 40422-1420 Office: Centre Coll Danville KY 40422 E-mail: breeze@centre.edu.

BREGA, CHARLES FRANKLIN, lawyer; b. Callaway, Nebr., Feb. 5, 1933; s. Richard E. and Bessie (King) B.; m. Betty Jean Witherspoon, Sept. 17, 1960; children: Kerry E., Charles D., Angie G. BA, The Citadel, 1954; LLB, U. Colo., 1960. Bar: Colo. 1960. Assoc. firm Hindry & Meyer, Denver, 1960-62, partner, 1962-75, dir., 1975; dir. firm Roath & Brega, Denver, 1975-89, Brega & Winters, Denver, 1989—. Lectr. in field; guest prof. U. Colo., U. Denver, U. Nev. (numerous states and), Can. Trustee Pres.'s Leadership Class, U. Colo., 1977 . Served with USAF, 1954-57. Mem. Colo. Trial Lawyers Assn. (pres. 1972-73), Assn. Trial Lawyers Am. (gov. 1972-79), ABA, Am. Law Inst., Am. Bd. Trial Advs., Internat. Acad. Trial Lawyers, Internat. Soc. Barristers, Cherry Hills Country Club, Denver Athletic Club. Episcopalian. Home: 4501 S Vine Way Englewood CO 80110-6027 Office: Brega & Winters PC 1700 Lincoln St Ste 1300 Denver CO 80203-4522

BREGA, KERRY ELIZABETH, physician, researcher; b. Denver, Sept. 8, 1961; d. Charles Franklin and Betty Jean Brega. BA, U. Colo., 1983, MD, 1989. Diplomate Am. Bd. Spine Surgery, Am. Bd. Neurol. Surgery. Resident in neurosurgery U. Colo., Denver, 1990-95, asst. prof. neurosurgery, 1995—; dir. neurosurgery Littleton Adventist Hosp., Denver, 1998—; asst. prof. neurosurgery U. Colo., Denver, 1995—. Bd. dirs. Donor Alliance, Denver, 1994—. Mem. Am. Coll. Spine Surgery, Am. Assn. Neurol. Surgeons, Congress Neurol. Surgeons, Colo. Neurol. Soc., Alpha Omega Alpha. Office: Littleton Adventist Hosp 7720 S Broadway Ste 220 Littleton CO 80122-

BREGER, WILLIAM N. architect, educator; b. N.Y.C., Aug. 1, 1922; s. S.A. and B. (Kalvar) B. BArch., MArch., Harvard, 1945. Asst. to Walter Gropius, Cambridge, Mass., 1944-46; tchr. N.Y. Sch. Interior Design, 1945—; chmn. dept. archtl. design Pratt Inst., 1946-69; lectr. Columbia Sch. Pub. Health and Hosp. Adminstrn., 1964-78; practice architecture with with S. Salzman, 1947-55; architect Breger Terjesen Assoc., 1955—; vis. Disting. prof. architecture Pratt Inst., 1983-84, dir. mechs. inst., 1998—. Exhibited, Mus. Modern Art, 1952, 79, 80, Chgo. Art Inst., 1954, Gold Medal Exhbn. Archtl. League, 1960, Bklyn. Mus., 1955; author: (with William Pomeranz) Nursing Home Development, 1985; Mem. editorial bd.: Ency. Philosophy, 1967. Trustee, dir. N.Y. Sch. Interior Design, 1960— . Served with AUS, 1942-43. Recipient Langford Warren prize, 1944, 3d prize Jefferson Nat. Meml. Competition, St. Louis, 1947; Prix de Rome Alternate, 1947; 3d prize N.Y. Pub. Housing Award (with S. Salzman) 1950; Good Design award Mus. Modern Art, 1952; 1st prize House and Garden mag., 1950; 1st prize Carson Pirie Scott Chicago Loop design, 1954; hon. mention hosp. design Rubberoid Competition, 1958; 1st prize Allegheny Sq. competition (with J. Terjesen and W. Winter) Pitts., 1964; hon. mention Fremont Civic Center Master Plan, 1966; AIA award, 1968; Queens C. of C. award; Bard award City Club of N.Y., 1977; N.Y. State Assn. Architects award, 1978, 80; Archi design award L.I. chpt. AIA, 1979 Fellow AIA. Office: 545 8th Ave Fl 17 New York NY 10018-4307

BREGLIO, JOHN F. lawyer; b. N.Y.C., June 5, 1946; s. John N. and Sylvia V. (Calucci) B.; m. Nan K. Proctor, May 22, 1976; children: Eliza Mason, Nola Keene. BA, Yale U., 1968; JD, Harvard U., 1971. Bar: N.Y. 1972, U.S. Dist. Ct. (ea. and so. dists.) 1974, U.S. Ct. Appeals (2d cir.) 1975, U.S. Ct. Appeals (D.C. cir.) 1982. Ptnr. Paul, Weiss, Rifkind, Wharton & Garrison, N.Y.C., 1971—. Adj. prof. Sch. of Arts, Columbia U.; chmn., lectr. on entertainment industry N.Y. Law Jour. Seminars, N.Y.C., 1984—88, Practising Law Inst. Bd. dirs. The Acting Co., N.Y.C., 1982-92, The Golden Fund, N.Y.C., 1989—, The Alliance for the Arts, Inc., 1989—, Am. Found. for AIDS Rsch., N.Y.C., 1994—, Young Playwrights Inc., 1995—; chmn. bd. Theater Devel. Fund, N.Y.C., 1982—; mem. adv. com. Theatre Collection Coun., Mus. of City of N.Y. Mem. ABA, N.Y. State Bar Assn., Assn. of Bar of City of N.Y., Am. Arbitration Assn. (panel arbitrators), The Century Assn. (N.Y.C.), Yale Club (N.Y.C.), Waccabuc Country Club (Westchester, N.Y), Phelps Assn. (New Haven). Home: 1120 5th Ave New York NY 10128-0144 also: 41 School House Rd Waccabuc NY 10597 also: 52 W Miacomet Rd Nantucket MA 02554-4369 Office: Paul Weiss Rifkind Wharton & Garrison Rm 200 1285 Avenue Of The Americas New York NY 10019-6065 E-mail: jbreglio@paulweiss.com.

BREGMAN, ARTHUR RANDOLPH, lawyer, educator; b. Phila., Dec. 9, 1946; s. Nathan and Stella (Husock) B.; m. Patrice Rosalie Gancie, May 30, 1980. BA, Columbia U., 1968; MA, Yale U., 1969; JD, Georgetown U., 1985. Bar: D.C. 1985, U.S. Ct. Appeals (D.C. cir.) 1985, U.S. Dist. Ct. D.C. 1985, U.S. Claims Ct. 1985. Treas. Nat. Coun. for Soviet and E. European Rsch., Washington, 1981-83; law clk. Washington Lawyers' Com. for Civil Rights, 1983-84; assoc. Klores, Feldesman and Tucker, Washington, 1985-86; dir. Soviet and E. European Svcs. APCO, Washington, 1988-91; of counsel Steptoe & Johnson, Washington, Moscow, USSR, 1991-92, ptnr. Washington D.C. and Moscow, 1992-99, Squire, Sanders & Dempsey, Washington, 1999—2003, Salans, Washington, N.Y., 2003—. Adj. prof. Georgetown U. Law Ctr., Washington, 1986-89; program dir. Internat. Law Inst., Washington, 1986-91; chmn. bd. adv. U.S.-Russia Bus. Law Report, 1990—. Editor: U.S.-Soviet Contract Law, 1987. Recipient Civil Procedure prize Lawyers Coop. Pub. Co., Balt., 1982. Mem. ABA (internat. bar sect.), D.C. Bar. Home: 3059 Porter St NW Washington DC 20008-3272 Office: 1330 Connecticut Ave NW Washington DC 20036 also: 620 Fifth Ave New York NY 10020 E-mail: rbregman@salans.com.

BREGMAN, DAVIS, physician, pain management specialist; b. Nov. 21, 1969; BS, MIT, 1990; MD, NYU, 1994. Diplomate Am. Acad. Pain Mgmt. Intern Lenox Hill Hosp., N.Y.C., 1994-95; resident Hosp. U. Pa., Phila., 1996-97; pres. Polo Medgroup, N.Y.C., 1996-98; med. dir. Medplaza Physicians, Huntington, NY, 1998—2002, pres., 1999—2002; med. dir. Medplaza Pain Care Ctr., 2002—. Disease prevention editor Medplaza News, Dix Hills, N.Y., 1998-99; host radio show "Your Health with Dr. Bregman," 1999-2001; developer outpatient healthcare facility, 1998; cons. Ambulatory Surgery Ctr. Devel., 1996-97; pub. spkr. on pain mgmt. topics; pioneer in use of non-surgical spinal decompression therapy. Contbr. articles to profl. jours. Named outstanding intellectual of 20th century for achievement in orthops. and pain mgmt., Hon. Chmn. of the Health Care Bus., Adv. Coun. for U.S. Congressman Tom Delay, 2001, Physician of the Yr. award, Congressman Tom Reynolds; recipient Disting. leadership award for outstanding contbns. to contemporary soc., 1999, 2000, Internat. Order Merit for svcs. to orthops. and medicine, proclamation for cmty. svc., County Exec. Robert J. Gaffney, Presdl. Seal of Honor, 2001, Businessman of the Yr. award for N.Y. State, U.S. Congressman Tom Davis, 2001. Fellow Suffolk Acad. Medicine, Am. Biog. Inst., Am. Biog. Inst. Rsch. Assn. (dep. gov.); mem. Internat. Order of Ambs., Med. Soc. State of N.Y., mem. Suffolk County Med. Soc. Office: Medplaza Pain Care Ctr 152 E Main St ste D Huntington NY 11743-5713 E-mail: drbregman@doctor.com.

BREGMAN, JACOB ISRAEL, environmental consulting company executive; b. Hartford, Conn., Sept. 17, 1923; s. Aaron and Jennie (Katzoff) B.; m. Mona Madan, June 27, 1948; children: Janet, Marcia, Barbara. BS, Providence Coll., 1943; MS, Poly. Inst. Bklyn., 1948, PhD, 1951. Rsch. chemist Fels & Co., 1947—48; head phys. chem. labs. Nalco Chem. Co., Chgo., 1950—59; supr. phys. chemistry rsch. sect. Armour Rsch. Found., Chgo., 1959—63; asst. dir. chemistry rsch. Ill. Inst. Tech. Rsch. Inst., Chgo., 1963—65, dir. chem. scis., 1965—67; dep. asst. sec. U.S. Dept. Interior, 1967—69; pres. Wapora Inc., 1969—82; v.p. Dynamac Corp., 1983—84; pres. Bregman and Co., 1984-2000, CEO, 1984—2001, treas., 2001—. Chmn. N.E. Ill. Met. Area Air Pollution Control Bd., 1962—63; chmn. Ill. Air Pollution Control Bd., 1963—67; chmn. adv. bd. on saline water conversion NATO Parliamentarians Conf., 1963; chmn. Water Resources Rsch. Coun., 1964—67; profl. lectr. George Washington U., 1980—98. Author: Corrosion Inhibitors, 1963, Surface Effects in Detection, 1965, The Pollution Paradox, 1966, Handbook of Water Resources and Pollution Control, 1976, Environmental Regulations Handbook, 1991, Environmental Impact Statements, 1992, 2d edit., 1999, Environmental Compliance Handbook, 1996, 2d edit., 1999; patentee in field; contbr. over 65 articles to profl. jours. Chmn. Montgomery County (Md.) Citizens Task Force on Georgetown Br. Right of Way, 1986—90; mem. Md. Dem. State Ctrl. Com., 1974—78; treas. Montgomery Dem. Ctrl. Com., 1974—76; del. Dem. Conv., 1976; mem. plan commn. Park Forest, Ill., 1956—59; trustee, 1958—62. With AUS, 1943—46, ETO, survivor sunken troop ship "Empire Javelin", 1944. Decorated two Battle Stars, AUS. Fellow: Am. Inst. Chemists; mem.: Am. Chem. Soc., Nat. Def. Ind. Assn. (life), Soc. Am. Military Engrs. (life), VFW, Am. Legion, Phi Lambda Upsilon, Sigma Xi. Home: 5630 Old Chester Rd Bethesda MD 20814-1025 Office: 5272 River Rd Ste 550 Bethesda MD 20816 E-mail: bregman4827@yahoo.com.

BREGMAN, MICHAEL EVAN, urban planner; b. Miami Beach, Apr. 8, 1966; s. Harold and Doris (Brown) B. Cert. in Planning Studies, BS in Geography, Fla. State U., 1988; MA in Urban and Regional Planning, U. Fla., 1993. Intern Miami-Dade Park and Recreation, Miami, 1992; planning technician Miami-Dade Planning and Zoning, Miami, 1993-94, sr. planner, 1994—. Mem. urban design com. Downtown Miami Main St., 1998-99; mem. Urban Environment League, Miami, 1996-97. Contbr. articles to Gold Coast Planner newspaper. Mem. Downtown Miami Citizens on Patrol, 1998-99. Mem. Am. Inst. Cert. Planners (cert. planner), Am. Planning Assn. (sec. Gold Coast 1996-97). Democrat. Avocation: Tae Kwon Do. Office: Miami-Dade Dept Planning and Zoning 111 NW 1st St Ste 1220 Miami FL 33128-1923

BREGMAN, STEVEN HOWARD, library director; b. N.Y.C., Feb. 1, 1951; s. Harry and Sylvia Bregman. BA, Queens Coll., Flushing, N.Y., 1972, MLS, 1973. Cert. pub. libr. N.Y. State Edn. Dept. Asst. dir. Nassau Libr. Sys., Uniondale, N.Y., 1986-90; dir. Bellmore (N.Y.) Meml. Libr., 1990—. Pres. Nassau County Libr. Assn., 1999. Mem. ALA, N.Y. Libr. Assn., Nassau County Libr. Assn., Libr. Dirs. Nassau County (chair 1998-99). Democrat. Jewish. Avocations: music, travel. Office: Bellmore Meml Libr 2288 Bedford Ave Bellmore NY 11710-3615 Fax: 516-785-2798. E-mail: steve.bregman@lycos.com.

BREHL, JAMES WILLIAM, lawyer; BS engring., U. Notre Dame, 1956; JD, U. Mich., 1959. Bar: Wis. 1989; Minn. and various fed. cts. Lawyer Maun & Simon, St. Paul, 1963-2000; law practice and mediation/arbitration Nuetral Svcs., 2000—. Contbr. articles to law jours. Mem. Minn. Bar Assn. (exec. com. 1976-80, 1997-00), Ramsey County Bar Assn. (exec. coun. 1977-80, 87-90, pres. 1993-94). Fax: 651-436-5679.

BREHM, LORETTA PERSOHN, secondary art educator, librarian, consultant; b. New Orleans, Jan. 31, 1954; d. Edwin Joseph and Loretta (Persohn) B. BA, Nicholls State U., Thibodaux, La., 1975, MEd, 1979, postgrad., 1980. Cert. tchr., La. Substitute tchr. Jefferson Parish Sch. Bd., Gretna, La., 1971-74; tchr. art John Ehret Sch., John Ehret High Sch., Marrero, La., 1974-95; art tchr., libr. Westbank Cathedral Acad., 1995-98; cons. Ventures Edn. Sys., 1998—; pub. rels. rep. Jefferson West Higher Edn. Ctr., 1999—. Trustee, chmn. bd. emeritus Jefferson Parish Coun. on Aging; assessor La. State Dept. Edn., 1997—, 1st v.p. Epsilon State, Delta Kappa Gamma Soc. Internat. Ladies aux. Westwego Vol. Fire Co.; historian Westwego Bicentennial; vol. Westwego Com. on Aging, Gumbo Festival, Bridge City, La., ARC, Operation Mainstream, others; founding mem. Jefferson Parish Cmty. Arts Commn.; alumni pres., former sch. advisor Jefferson Parish 4-H Clubs; art dir. Knights of King Arthur Mardi Gras Orgn.; libr. asst. Westbank Cathedral Acad.; choir, set designer Holy Guardian Angels Ch.; trustee Jefferson Parish Coun. on Aging, 1993—; bd. dirs. Westwego Hist. Soc., Jefferson Parish Hist. Soc.; commnr. Westwego Law Enforcement Commn., Westwego Zoning Commn., treas. Westwego Tourist Commn.; treas. Bridge City Cmty. Com. on Aging. Recipient awards from Jefferson Parish Sch. Bd., 1978, Westwego Vol. Fire Co., 1982, 4-H Club, 1983, Am. Automobile Assn. Nat. Sch. Traffic Safety Program, 1987-92, others. Mem. Nat. Art Edn. Assn., La. Art Edn. Assn., Internat. Reading Assn. (chmn. Jefferson Parish coun.), Jefferson Parish Hist. Soc. (charter), New Orleans Mus. Art, La. Children's Mus., Nicholls State U. Alumni Assn., Delta Kappa Gamma, Kappa Kappa Iota, Phi Delta Kappa. Democrat. Avocations: travel, gardening, social work, freelance art work. Home: 250 Louisiana St Westwego LA 70094-4114

BREIDBART, RORY STEVEN, endocrinologist; b. N.Y.C., Mar. 13, 1962; s. Murray Richard and Judith Marcia Breidbart. BS in Chemistry and Biology, Emory U., 1983; MD, Tel Aviv U., 1987. Diplomate Am. Bd. Internal Medicine, Am. Bd. Endocrinology, Diabetes and Metabolism. Resident in medicine L.I. Jewish Med. Ctr., New Hyde Park, N.Y., 1987-90, fellow in gen. internal medicine and primary care, 1990-91; fellow in endocrinology Mt. Sinai Med. Ctr., N.Y.C., 1991-93; pvt. practice, Gt. Neck, N.Y., 1993—. Clin. instr. medicine N.Y. U. Sch. Medicine, N.Shore U. Hosp., St. Francis Hosp., L.I. Jewish Med. Ctr. Fellow: ACP, Am. Coll. Endocrinology; mem.: AAAS, AMA, N.Y. Acad. Scis., Am. Assn. Clin. Endocrinology, Am. Diabetes Assn. Office: 29 Barstow Rd Ste 305 Great Neck NY 11021-2209

BREIDEGAM, DELIGHT EDGAR, JR., battery company executive; b. Fleetwood, Pa., Oct. 3, 1926; s. DeLight Daniel and Helen Mamie (Fenstermacher) B.; m. Helen Merkel, Feb. 28, 1948; children: Daniel, Sally. LLD (hon.), Kurtztown U., 1997; attended, Gettysburg Coll., 1944-45; LLD (hon.), Kutztown U., 1997, Moravian Coll., 1995. Chmn., CEO East Penn Mfg. Co., Inc., Lyon Sta., Pa.; mem. Battery Coun. Internat. Trustee Moravian Coll.; bd. dir. Kutztown U. Served with USAF. Recipient Grow with Berks award Reading Assn. Reators, 1994, Richard J. Caron award of excellence, 1997; named Entrepreneur of Yr., Ea. Pa./Delaware Valley, 1990; named to Jr. Achievement Hall of Fame, 1994, Moravian Coll. Hall of Fame. Mem. Ind. Battery Mfrs. Assn., Reading-Berks C. of C. (Bus. Person of Yr. 1984), Moselem Springs Golf Club, Bonita Bay Country Club, Longleff Golf and Country Club, Saucon Valley Country Club, Huguenot Lodge, Shriners, Mason, lifetime mem. BCI Lutheran. Office: East Penn Mfg Co Inc Deka Rd Lyon Station PA 19536 Home: 214 Deysher Rd Fleetwood PA 19522

BREIDENBACH, MONICA EILEEN, educator, career counselor; b. Dayton, July 2, 1932; d. Clement and Mary (Deschler) B. BS in Music Edn., Mt. St. Joseph Coll., 1969. Music educator St. Bernard Sch., Springfield, Ohio, 1952-54; elem. sch. educator grade schs., Ohio, Mich., 1954-63; music educator St. Mary's H.S., Jackson, Mich., 1963-67, DeKalb (Ill.) Pub. Schs., 1967-68; dir. edn. Diocese of Columbus, Ohio, 1968-75; exec. dir. The Liturgical Conf., Washington, 1975-76; dir. counseling Pierson Assocs., Washington, 1976-78; owner, counselor Career Mgmt. Svcs., Prairie Village, Kans., 1978—. Sr. prof. DeVry U., Kansas City, Mo., 1983—. Author: Career Development, 4th edit., 2001; contbr. articles to profl. jours. Home: 5401 W 80th St Prairie Village KS 66208-4912 E-mail: mbreidenbach@kc.devry.edu.

BREIER, ALAN, pharmaceutical executive; b. Toledo, Ohio, May 22, 1953; m. Diane Rooney, May 30, 1981; children: Michael, Matthew. MD, U. Cin., 1980. Diplomate Am. Bd. Psychiatry and Neurology. Chief outpatient dept. Md. Psychiatric Ctr., Balt., 1987-93; chief pathophysiology and treatment unit NIH, Bethesda, Md., 1993-95, chief sect. clin. studies, 1995-97; v.p. pharm. products, leader NS product team Eli Lilly and Co., Indianapolis, 1998—. Adj. prof. psychiatry U. Md., Balt., 1994—; prof. medicine Ind. U., Indianapolis, 1997—. Mem. editl. bd. Schizophrenia Rsch., 1994—, Biol. Psychiatry, 1999—. Recipient Lustman Rsch. award Yale U. Sch. Medicine, 1982-84, Young Investigator award, Schizophrenia Rsch., 1987, A.E. Bennett award Soc. Biol. Psychiatry, 1988, Joel Elkes Internat. award ACNP, 1997. Office: Eli Lilly and Co Lilly Corp Ctr Indianapolis IN 46285 E-mail: breier_alan@lilly.com.

BREIER, MORTON A. philosopher; b. NYC, June 30, 1934; s. Max M. and Rose (Zucker) Breier; m. Karen M. Sutherland, Mar. 1, 1997; m. Phyllis Benu (div.); children: Nicole C., Damien S., Maximillian D. BSME, CCNY, NYC, NY, 1958. Engr. Gen. Instrument, NYC, 1958—63; dir. advanced design Dortech, Inc., Stamford, Conn., 1967—71; prin./ptnr. Breier Neidle Patrone Assoc., Darien, Conn., 1971—89; pres. Inner Journeys-Outer Worlds, Kailua-Kona, Hawaii, 1994—. Author: (novels) Aleph-Zero, 1976, Masks Mandalas & Meditations, 1996. Pres. New Thought Ctr., Kailua-Kona, Hawaii, 1998—; VP Kona Beth Shalom, Kailua-Kona, Hawaii, 1999—, Habitat for Humanity Kona, Kailua-Kona, Hawaii, 2000—. Home: 73-4548 Mahi St Kailua Kona HI 96740 Office: Inner Journeys-Outer Worlds 73-4548 Mahi St Kailua Kona HI 96740

BREIGER, RONALD LOUIS, social sciences educator; b. N.Y.C., NY, Mar. 19, 1948; s. Lazarus H. and Lillian E. Breiger; m. Linda Ruth Waugh, May 20, 1984; 1 child, David Luis Waugh-Breiger. AB, Brandeis U., 1966—70; PhD, Harvard U., 1970—75. Asst. prof. of sociology Harvard U., 1975—79, assoc. prof. of sociology, 1979—81; prof. of sociology Cornell U., Ithaca, 1981—95, dept. chmn., 1988—93, Goldwin Smith prof. sociology, 1995—2000; prof. of sociology U. of Ariz., 2000—. Vis. prof. U. of Lille-1, France, 2002. Editor: (jour.) Social Networks; author: (collected works) Explorations in Structural Sociology (Harvard Studies in Sociology series); chair (symposium) Nat. Acad. of Sciences workshop on Dynamic Network Models and Analysis. Exec. bd. mem. Internat. Network for Social Network Analysis, 2003—. Grantee Fellowship, Ctr. for Advanced Study in the Behavioral Sciences, 1985-86. Mem.: Nat. Sci. Found. (mem. sociology panel 1988—90), Sociol. Rsch. Assn., Internat. Network for Social Network Analysis (exec. bd. mem. 2003), Am. Sociol. Assn. (exec. com., sect. on math. sociology 2000—02). Office: U of Ariz Dept of Sociology Tucson AZ 85721-0027

BREIMAYER, JOSEPH FREDERICK, patent lawyer; b. Belding, Mich., May 4, 1942; s. Ronald and Crystal Helen (Reeves) B.; m. Margaret Anne Murphy, Aug. 26, 1967; children: Kathleen A., Deborah L., Elizabeth L. BEE, U. Detroit, 1965; JD, George Washington U., 1969. Bar: D.C. 1970, N.Y. 1973, Minn. 1975. Cooperative engr. Honeywell Inc, Mpls., 1962-65; patent examiner U.S. Patent and Trademark Office, Washington, 1965-70; patent atty. Eastman Kodak Co., Rochester, N.Y., 1970-73; sr. patent counsel Medtronic Inc., Mpls., 1973-90; assoc. Fredrikson & Byron, Mpls., 1990-93. Pres. Good Shepherd Home and Sch. Assn., 1984; precinct chmn. Dem. Farmer Labor Party, 1980-82. Mem. Minn. Intellectual Property Law Assn. (treas. 1986). Avocations: boating, skiing, travel. Home: 4700 Circle Down Minneapolis MN 55416-1101 Office: Breimayer Law Office 1221 Nicollet Mall Ste 206 Minneapolis MN 55403-2472

BREINDEL, DAVID SAUL, psychiatrist; b. N.Y.C., Jan. 23, 1948; s. Benjamin and Ida B.; m. Lynn Hollenbeck, Sept. 12, 1982; children: Daniel, Jeremy, Alexander. BS, MIT, 1969; MD, Albert Einstein Coll. Medicine, 1976. Intern straight medicine Met. Hosp., N.Y.C., 1976-77; resident in psychiatry Bronx Mcpl. Hosp. Ctr./Albert Einstein Coll. Medicine, 1977-80; psychiatrist pvt. practice, New Rochelle, N.Y. Clin. lectr. N.Y. Hosp., White Plains, 1991—. Home and Office: 234 Elk Ave New Rochelle NY 10804-4217

BREINER, SANDER JAMES, psychiatry educator, psychoanalyst; b. Fiume, Italy, July 12, 1925; (parents Am. citizens); s. Alfred and Margaret (Steiner) B.; m. Beatrice Marsha Oboler, Mar. 18, 1951; children: Linda Marie, Myles Steven, Robert Ethan. BS, U. Ill., 1948; MB, MD, Chgo. Med. Sch., 1953. Diplomate Nat. Bd. Med. Examiners, Am. Bd. Psychiatry and Neurology, Nat. Bd. of Accreditation in Psychoanalysis. Asst. prof. psychiatry Wayne State U., Detroit, 1957—; assoc. prof. Mich. State U., East Lansing, 1970—; attending staff, mem. psychiatry dept. Harper Grace Hosp., Detroit, 1960—; attending psychiatry dept. William Beaumont Hosp., Royal Oak, Mich., 1968—. Cons. depts. ob-gyn., surgery and medicine Harper Grace Hosp., 1960—; cons. dept. ob-gyn. William Beaumont Hosp., 1982—; cons. in marital/sexual problems; tng./surpervising analyst Mich. Psychoanalytic Coun.; trustee Nat. Bd. Accreditation in Psychoanalysis. Author: Slaughter of the Innocents: Child Abuse Through the Ages and Today, 1990; contbr. more than 80 articles to profl. jours. Cons. Detroit Commn. on Children and Youth, 1957-62; cons. bd. edn. Detroit, Garden City and Bloomfield Hills, 1957-71. With inf. U.S. Army, 1943-45, ETO. Fellow Am. Psychiat. Assn., Am. Soc. Psychoanalytic Physicians; mem. AMA, AAAS, Psychosmatic Medicine, N.Y. Acad. Sci., Internat. Assn. for Psychohistory, Mich. Soc. for Psychoanalytic Psychology, Mich. Psychoanapytic Coun., Tng. and Supervising Psychoanalyst. Democrat. Avocations: gardening, mountain hiking, psychohistory. Home: 7410 Franklin Rd Bloomfield Hills MI 48301-3610 Office: 7457 Franklin Rd Ste 304 Bloomfield Hills MI 48301-3604

BREINIG, JEANE M. English educator, consultant; b. Ketchikan, Alaska, July 5, 1955; d. Perry Christian and Julie Rebeca Coburn; m. Steve W. Bailey, Apr. 8, 1978 (div. Nov. 1985); Christopher Lee Breinig, Nov. 27, 1986; children: Lee Christopher, Luke Coburn. BA in English, U. Wash., 1988, MA in English, 1989, PhD in English, 1995. Program coord. Office Minority Affairs, Seattle, 1991-94; assoc. prof. U. Alaska, Anchorage, 1995—. Co-editor: Alaska Native Writers, Storytellers & Orators: The Expanded Edition, 1999. Alaska regional liaison Ford Found., Anchorage, 1997—; trustee S.E. Alaska Heritage Found., Juneau, 1998—2001; mem., sec. Alaska Native Sisterhood, 1994; bd. dirs. Kasaan Village Corp., Inc., Anchorage, 1996—, Alaska Humanities Forum, Anchorage, 1998—. Ford Found. fellow, 1993-94. Mem. Assn. Study Am. Indian Lits., Assn. Am. Indian & Alaska Native Profs., Soc. Study Indigenous Langs., Alaska Native Educators, Golden Key. Office: U Alaska Anchorage Dept English 3211 Providence Dr Anchorage AK 99508

BREININ, BARTLEY JAMES, lawyer; b. NYC, Nov. 14, 1957; s. Goodwin Milton and Rose-Helen (Kopelman) B.; m. Rachel Gelin Breinin, Sept. 20, 1986; children: Alexander James, Caroline Rebecca. BA cum laude, Yale U., 1979; JD, U. Va., 1983. Bar: NY 1984. Assoc. Simpson Thacher and Bartlett, NYC, 1983-88, Morgan, Lewis and Bockius, NYC, 1988-94; v.p., sr. assoc. counsel Chase Manhattan Bank, NA, NYC, 1994-95; v.p., asst. gen. counsel Cambrian Corp., NYC, 1995-97, sr. v.p., gen. counsel, 1998-99; mng. dir., asst. gen. counsel PricewaterhouseCoopers LLP, NYC, 2000—. Mem. ABA, Bar Assn. City NY, Sunningdale Country Club, Univ. Club Larchmont, Yale Univ. Alumni Interviewer. Office: PricewaterhouseCoopers LLP 1177 Ave of Americas New York NY 10036 E-mail: bartley.j.breinin@us.pwc.com.

BREININ, GOODWIN M. physician; b. N.Y.C., Dec. 10, 1918; s. Louis and Mary (Mirsky) B.; m. Rose-Helen Kopelman, June 22, 1947; children: Bartley James, Constance. BS, U. Fla., 1939; A.M., Emory U., 1940, MD, 1943. Diplomate Am. Bd. Ophthalmology (dir., vice chmn., cons.). Intern U.S. Marine Hosp., Stapleton, N.Y., 1944; resident ophthalmology N.Y. U.-Bellevue Med. Ctr., 1947-51, sr. Heed fellow ophthalmology, 1954, Daniel B. Kirby prof. research ophthalmology, 1957; Daniel B. Kirby profl. ophthalmology Bellevue and U. Hosps., 1959—; chmn. dept. ophthalmology N.Y. U.-Bellevue Med. Ctr., 1959—2000; dir. eye svc. Bellevue and U. Hosps., N.Y.C., 1959—2000; chmn. med. bd. N.Y. U.-Bellevue Med. Ctr., 1975-77. Mem. vision commn. NRC, 1960-65; hon. assoc. U. Coll., London, 1966-67; chmn. vision research tng. com. Nat. Insts. Neurol. Diseases and Blindness, 1963-64; chief cons. Manhattan VA Hosp.; cons. Manhattan Eye, Ear and Throat, St. Vincent's, Beth Israel hosps., Lenox Hills Hosp.; surg. gen. USPHS; chmn. Nat. Res. Rev. Com., 1976-77; vis. prof., cons. Hailie Selassie I Univ. Found., Ethiopia, 1972; lectr. Mem. various adv. coms. relating to field, mem. med. adv. bd. Nat. Council to Combat Blindness; pres. Council for U.S./USSR Health Exchange, 1977; mem. Am. com. Internat. Agy. for Prevention of Blindness, 1980— ; pres. 2d Internat. Symposium in Visual Optics, Tucson, 1982. Author: The Electrophysiology of Extraocular Muscle, 1962; editor: Advances in Diagnostic Visual Optics, 1983; mem. editorial bd. Investigative Ophthalmology, Archives of Ophthalmology; Contbr. articles to profl. jours. Mem. nat. coun. for medicine Emory U., Atlanta; mem. coun. visitors Marine Biol. Labs., Woods Hole, Mass. Recipient Knapp medal for contbn. ophthalmology A.M.A., 1957, Edward Lorenzo Holmes lectr. citation and award for contbns. to med. sci. Inst. Medicine Chgo., 1959, Gifford lectr. and award Chgo. Ophthal. Soc., 1970, Heed Ophthalmic Found. award, 1968, Emory U. medal, 1993; Wright lectr. U. Toronto, 1972; Lloyd lectr. Bklyn. Opthal. Soc., 1971; May lectr. N.Y. Acad. Medicine, 1974; guest of honor Australian Coll. Ophthalmologists, 1974, Japanese Cong. Neuro-ophthalmalogy, 1979; Scobee lectr., 1977. Fellow Am. Acad. Ophthalmology and Otolaryngology (v.p. 1979, Sr. Honor award 1984), ACS, N.Y. Acad. Medicine (sec. sect. ophthalmology 1962-63, chmn. sect. 1967-68); mem. AMA (sec. sect. on ophthalmology 1966-69, chmn. 1970-71), Rsch. Ophthalmology, Am. Ophthal. Soc., N.Y. Ophthal. Soc. (pres. 1980), Harvey Soc., AAAS, Am. Commn. for Optics and Visual Physiology (chmn. 1970—), Am. Orthoptic Coun., Assn. Univ. Profs. Ophthalmology, Pan. Am. Assn. Ophthalmology, Sigma Xi, Alpha Omega Alpha. Clubs: Century Assn., Practitioners, Charaka (N.Y.C.). Home: 912 Fifth Ave New York NY 10021-4159 Office: NYU Med Ctr 550 1st Ave New York NY 10016-6481 E-mail: gb7@nyu.edu.

BREISACH, ERNST A. historian, educator; b. Schwanberg, Austria, Oct. 8, 1923; came to US, 1953; s. Otto and Maria (Eder) B.; m. Herma E. Pirker, Aug. 2, 1945; children: Nora Sylvia, Eric Ernst. PhD in History, U. Vienna, Austria, 1946; D in Econs., Wirtschafts U., 1950. Prof. Realgymnasium Vienna XIV, Austria, 1946-52; assoc. prof. Olivet Coll., Mich., 1953-57; prof. Western Mich. U., Kalamazoo, 1957-96. Author: Introduction to Modern Existentialism, 1962, Caterina Sforza: A Renaissance Virago, 1967, Renaissance Europe, 1300-1517, 1973, Historiography: Ancient, Medieval, and Modern, 1983, 2d edit., 1994, American Progressive History, 1993; editor: Classical Rhetoric and Medieval Historiography, 1985; On the fFuture of History: The Postacodernist Challenge and Its Aftermath, 2003. Recipient fellowship, Nat. Found. for the Humanities, Washington, 1989-90. Mem. Am. Hist. Assn. Home: 228 W Ridge Cir Kalamazoo MI 49009-9108 Office: Western Mich U Dept History Kalamazoo MI 49008 E-mail: breisach@wmich.edu.

BREIT, WILLIAM, economist, educator, writer; b. New Orleans, Feb. 13, 1933; s. Murray and Sylvia (Shor) Breit. BA, U. Tex., 1955, MA, 1956; PhD, Mich. State U., 1961. Asst. prof. La. State U., Baton Rouge, 1961—63, assoc. prof., 1964—65, U. Va., 1965—70, prof., 1970—83; E.M. Stevens disting. prof. econs. Trinity U., San Antonio, 1983—89, Vernon F. Taylor disting. prof. econs., 1999—. Contbr. articles to profl. jours.; author (with others): The Antitrust Penalties, 1976; author: Murder at the Margin, 1978, 1993, The Academic Scribblers, 1982, 1998, The Fatal Equilibrium, 1985, 1986, The Antitrust Casebook, 1982, 1996, A Deadly Indifference, 1998, Lives of the Laureates: Thirteen Nobel Economists, 1997. Recipient Disting. Alumni award, Mich. State U., 1998, Disting. Achievement award, S.W. Social Sci. Assn., 2002. Mem.: Am. Econ. Assn., So. Econ. Assn. (v.p. 1980—81, pres. 1985—86), Mystery Writers Am., Cosmos Club, Phi Beta Kappa (book prize 1977). Avocations: philately, Abyssinian cats. Home: 438 E Hildebrand Ave San Antonio TX 78212-2501 Office: Trinity U 715 Stadium Dr San Antonio TX 78212-7200

BREITENBACH, MARY LOUISE MCGRAW, psychologist, chemical dependency counselor; b. Pitts., Sept. 26, 1936; d. David Evans McGraw and Louise (Schoch) Neel; m. John Edgar Breitenbach, Apr. 15, 1960 (dec. 1963); m. Joseph George Piccoli III, Aug. 15, 1987; children: Cary Plumer Frye and Douglas Plumer (twins), Kirstin Amethyst Gretchen, Leticia Piccoli. Postgrad., Oreg. State Coll., 1960-61; BA, Russell Sage Coll., Troy, N.Y., 1958; MEd, Harvard U., 1983. Lic. profl. counselor, chem. dependency specialist, Wyo.; cert. addiction specialist, level III; nat. cert. addiction counselor II, master addiction counselor. Paraprofessional psychologist St. John's Episc. Ch., Jackson, Wyo., 1963—94; pvt. practice Wilson, Wyo., 1983—. Counselor Curran/Seeley Found. Addiction Svcs., Jackson, 1989-91, Van Vleck House/Tri-County Group Home, Jackson, 1986-89, others; provider multiple employee assistance programs local and nat. cos.; mem. adv. com. The Learning Ctr., 1997—. Trustee Teton Sci. Sch., Kelly, Wyo, 1960-76; pres. bd. govs. Teton County Mus., 1989-91, Jackson; vestry mem. St. John's Ch., Jackson. Mem. APA, LWV, Wyo. Psychol. Assn., Wyo. Assn. Counseling and Devel., Wyo. Assn. Addiction Specialists, Nat. Assn. Alcohol and Drug Addiction Counselors. Democrat. Episcopalian. Avocations: horseback riding, reading, gardening. Home and Office: Star Rte # 2 Cheney Ln Wilson WY 83014

BREITENFELD, FREDERICK, JR., retired educational consultant, former public broadcasting executive; b. N.Y.C., Sept. 26, 1931; s. Frederick and Dorothy (Falk) B.; m. Mary Ellen Fitzgerald, Dec. 27, 1954 (dec. 1998); children: Ann Clark, Kathleen Ellen. BS in Engring., Tufts U., 1953, MEd, 1954; MS in TV-Radio, Syracuse U., 1960, PhD, 1963; LHD (hon.), U. Md., 1976, Salisbury State Coll., 1982, Phila. Coll. Textiles and Sci., 1987, Wesley Coll., 1992. Tchr. physics and chemistry pub. H.S., North Creek, N.Y., 1958-59; program adminstr. U. Coll., Syracuse U., 1960-61; asst. dean Syracuse U., 1961-63; resident cons. in comm. U.S. Air Force, Cape Canaveral, Fla., 1963-64; rsch. project dir. Nat. Assn. Ednl. Broadcasters, Washington, 1964-65, assoc. dir. ednl. TV stas. divsn., 1965-66; exec. dir. Md. Center for Pub. Broadcasting, Owings Mills, Md., 1966-83; CEO, pres. WHYY Inc., 1983-97. Chmn. Ea. Ednl. TV Network, 1974-76; founding chmn. Am. Program Svc., 1991, vice-chmn., 1993; vice-chmn. bd. mgrs. PBS, 1973; cons., lectr. in field; adj. prof. Cath. U. Am., 1967-72, Am. U., 1972-74; vis. prof. Syracuse U., 1976, Johns Hopkins U., 1978-83; charter mem., chmn. Nat. Univ. Consortium for Telecomms. in Tchg. Trustee Thomas Jefferson U., 1988—, Valley Forge Mil. Acad. and Coll., 1992—, Bucks County C.C., 1994—; bd. dirs. Nat. Bd. Med. Examiners, 1995-99; active Lower Makefield Twp. Zoning Hearing Bd., Bucks County, Pa., 1998-99, Pennsbury Bd. Sch. Dirs., 1998-2001. Naval aviator USNR, 1954-58. Recipient Disting. Alumnus award Radio TV dept. Syracuse U., 1967; Andrew White medal Loyola Coll., Balt., 1979; Lord Baltimore medal St. Mary's Coll., 1980; Man of Yr. award Boys and Girls Club of Phila., 1987; Globe and Anchor award USMC Scholarship Found., 1991; Williamson award for excellence in cmty. svc. Williamson Free Sch., 1993. Mem. Screen Actors Guild, AFTRA. Home: 1525 Harvest Dr Yardley PA 19067-4234 E-mail: ricbreit@aol.com. *To live is both to care and to laugh.*

BREITENSTEIN, DAVID E. newswriter; b. Belleville, Ill., Jan. 17, 1975; s. Eugene R. and Linda J. B. BS in Journalism, U. Kans., 1997; postgrad., Fla. Gulf Coast U. Writer, editor Univ. Daily Kansan, Lawrence, Kans., 1996-97; writer Anderson (S.C.) Ind.-Mail, 1997-99, Naples (Fla.) Daily News, 1999—. Vol. Kans. Spl. Olympics, Lawrence, 1997, Anderson Literacy Festival, 1998. Recipient Cert. Pl. Merit, William Randolph Hearst Found., 1997, 2d Pl. award, S.C. Press Assn., 1998, Fla. Press Club, 1999, 3d Pl. award, 1999, 1st Pl. award, 2000, 2d Pl. award, 2000, 1st Pl. award, 2001, 2002, 2nd Pl. award, 2002. Mem. Soc. Profl. Journalists (Mark of Excellence in In-depth Reporting 1997), Am. Assn. Sch. Adminstrs., Nat. Sch. Pub. Rels. Assn., Fla. Press Club, Edn. Writers Assn., Kans. Alumni Assn. Avocations: writing, athletics, reading, vacationing. Home: 27062 S Riverside Dr Bonita Springs FL 34135 Office: Naples Daily News 1075 Central Ave Naples FL 34102-6295

BREITENSTEIN, PETER FREDERIC, lawyer; b. Denver, Mar. 10, 1938; s. Jean Sala and Helen (Thomas) B.; m. Karla Ann Gasser, Jan. 27, 1962; children: Kurt Frederick, Dana Ann, Hugh Thomas. BA in Econs., Amherst Coll., 1960; LLB, U. Calif., Berkeley, 1963. Bar: Colo. 1963. Law clk. to O. Hatfield Chilson U.S. Dist. Ct. for Colo., Denver, 1963-64; assoc. Fairfield and Woods, PC, Denver, 1964-71, ptnr., 1971—, also bd. dirs. Mem. ABA, Colo. Bar Assn., Denver Bar Assn., Law Club, Denver Country Club, Univ. Club. Office: Fairfield and Woods PC 1700 Lincoln St Ste 2400 Denver CO 80203-4524 E-mail: pbreiten@fwlaw.com.

BREITLING, JULIUS, financial executive; b. Apr. 14, 1932; s. Carl and Minnie (Flechman) B.; m. Ariane Henningson, Apr. 18, 1968. BS in Mech. Engring., CCNY, 1959; MBA in Mgmt. Sci., Iona Coll., New Rochelle, N.Y., 1968. Registered profl. engr., N.Y., Mass., Tex., Va. Sr. valuation engr. N.Y. Pub. Svc. Commn., 1959-67; sr. cons. Ebasco Svcs. Inc., N.Y.C., 1967-69, prin. valuation cons., 1970-72; sr. engr. Jackson & Moreland divsn. United Engrs. & Constructors, Boston, 1969-70; exec. cons. Commonwealth Mgmt. Cons., N.Y.C., 1972-73; v.p. fin. mgmt. Ebasco Bus. Cons. Co., N.Y.C., 1973-83; dir. Coopers & Lybrand L.L.P., 1983-94, ret., 1994. Pres. Depreciation Valuation Svcs. Internat. Inc., Centerville, Mass., 1996-2002; ret. 2002. Patentee talking photo album. Mem. Am. Soc. Appraisers (accredited sr. appraiser), Soc. Depreciation Profl., N.Y. State Soc. Profl. Engrs.

BREITMAN, JOSEPH B. prosthodontist, dental educator; b. Phila., Aug. 4, 1952; s. Abraham A. and Natalie (Ketchurin) B.; m. Barbara Susan Beitman, May 13, 1990; children: Ilana Michelle, Ariel Judah, Leela Sivie. BA, LaSalle Coll., 1974; DMD, U. Pa., 1977; Cert. of Tng. in Prosthodontics, Temple U., 1979. Oral biology fellow Temple U., Phila., 1978; practice gen. dentistry Lafayette Hill, Pa., 1978-79; prosthodontist Marlton, N.J., 1979-80; pvt. practice Phla., 1980—. Asst. prof. dental materials Temple U., Phila., 1978-84; assoc. in restorative dentistry U. Pa., Phila., 1985-90; asst. prof. post-doctoral prosthodontics Temple U., 1990. Fellow Internat. Congress Oral Implantologists; mem. ADA, Am. Coll. Prosthodontics, N.E. Dental Soc. (pres. 1988-89), Eastern Dental Soc., Pa. Assn. Dental Surgeons (pres. 1984-85), Masons. Jewish. Avocations: playing bagpipes, Tae Kwon Do. Office: 8021B Castor Ave Philadelphia PA 19152-2733

BREITROSE, HENRY S. communications educator; b. Bklyn., July 22, 1936; s. Charles and Ruth (Leib) B.; m. Prudence Elaine Martin, Oct. 11, 1968; children— Charles Daniel, Rebecca Marjorie. BS, U. Wis., 1958; MA, Northwestern U., 1959; PhD, Stanford U., 1966. Writer Internat. Film Bur., 1958; mgr. Midwest office Contemporary Films Co., 1959; mem. faculty Stanford (Calif.) U., 1959—, prof. communication, 1975—, chmn. dept. communication, 1976-82. Vis. prof. London Sch. Econs., 1976-77; mem. public media panel NEA, 1974—; ednl. adv. com. Am. Film Inst., 1974; v.p. for rsch. and publs. Ctr. Internat. des Liasions des Ecoles du Cinema et du TV, 1989—; Christensen vis. rsch. fellow St. Catherine's Coll., Oxford, 1996. Gen. editor: Cambridge Studies in Film; mem. editorial bd. Calif. Lawyer, 1980-86; author articles, chpts. in books. Bd. dirs. Sta. KQED, San Francisco, 1985-90, vice chmn. 1988; mem. adv. bd. Sta. KCSM. Grantee Rockefeller Found., 1965-66; Lilly Endowment, 1976-77; Stanford U. fellow, 1972-74, Christensen fellow Oxford U., 1996. Mem.: Univ. Film Assn. (exec. v.p. 1987—89). Home: 897 Tolman Dr Stanford CA 94305-1017 Office: Stanford U Dept Communication Stanford CA 94305-2050

BREITWEISER, GARY CHARLES, art dealer, appraiser; b. Alton, Ill., Jan. 28, 1937; s. Wilbur H. and Vera Breitweiser. BA, Northwestern U., 1959; MS, Princeton U., 1961. Chem. engr. Mallinckrodt Chem. Works, St. Louis, 1960-62; rsch. assoc. McDonnell-Douglas, St. Louis, 1962-67; rsch. scientist Sloan Tech. Corp., Santa Barbara, Calif., 1967-70; art dealer, appraiser Studio 2, Santa Barbara, 1970—. Inventor in field of thin-film devices. NSF fellow, 1959-60. Mem.: Am. Assn. Ind. Appraisers (adv. panel). Home: 925 Calle Puerto Vallarta Santa Barbara CA 93103 Office: Studio 2 Box 20026 Santa Barbara CA 93120 E-mail: studio2@west.net.

BREKKE, ALAN LEE, industrial engineer; b. Havre, Mont., Aug. 6, 1946; s. Knute Charles Brekke and Doris Emily Allen. Degree in indsl. and mgmt. engring., Mont. State U., 1974. Constrn. worker Brekke & sons, Harlem, Mont., 1959-70; deliverer and stockperson Merry Mkt., Harlem, 1962-64; intern Western Interstate Commn. for Higher Edn., Sydney, Mont., 1971; indsl. engr. Mont. State U., Bozeman, 1973; indsl. engr., with program planning dept. The Boeing Co., Seattle, 1974-83; constrn. mgr. Harlem H.S., 1986-87; indsl. engr. in pvt. practice Harlem, 1983—. Staff writer (centennial book) Thunderstorms and Tumbleweeds, 1989; author: Kid Curry, 1989. With EMS Blaine County III Ambulance, Harlem, 2000—. Avocations: artist, miner, ancient languages (alphabets), geneaologist, ancient history. Home and Office: PO Box 635 Harlem MT 59526-0635

BREKKE, STEWART ERNEST, retired chemistry and physics educator; b. Chgo., Dec. 28, 1941; s. Herbert and Rebecca Brekke. BA, U. Ill., 1965; MA, Wayne State U., 1971; MS in Edn., Purdue U., 1987. Cert. tchr. Ill. Physics and chemistry tchr. Chgo. Pub. Schs., 1975—2001; ret., 2001. Contbr. articles to profl. jours. Mem.: Am. Assn. Physics Tchrs. (emeritus mem.), Am. Geophys. Union, Am. Phys. Soc. Achievements include invention of mathematical theory of parallelism, divergence and convergence nuclear vibration: the determinant of nuclear barrier heights; research in quark oscillation and oscillating-electron oscillation; a 5th quantum number. Avocations: chess, tennis. Home: 100 W Roosevelt Ave Bensenville IL 60106 E-mail: sbrekke@cs.com.

BRELIS, MATTHEW DEAN BURNS, journalist; b. Boston, Aug. 30, 1957; s. C. Dean Brelis and Nancy Emerson (Burns) Jay; m. Mary Morgan Baker, Sept. 10, 1988; children: Mary Margaret, Elinor Baker. AB, Vassar Coll., 1980. Reporter trainee/clk. The Washington Star, 1980-81; reporter The Pitts. Press, 1981-89, Boston Globe, 1989—. Recipient Pulitzer Prize, Columbia U., 1987, Keystone award Pa. Newspaper Pubs. Assn., 1987, Roy Howard award Scripps-Howard, 1987. Mem.: Boston Vassar, Mt. Auburn, Cambridge Skating. Office: Boston Globe Globe Newspaper Co 135 Morrissey Blvd Dorchester MA 02125-3338

BRELSFORD, EDMUND MUNGER, III, musician, educator; b. Miami, Fla., Apr. 11, 1931; s. Edmund Munger Brelsford and Alice Ashby; m. Veronica Gabrielle Alewyn, Nov. 22, 1960; children: Allegra Alewyn, Oliver Ashby, Wendy Carlotta, Cecelia Van Hook, Alicia Throm. BA, U. of Miami, 1954—57; MA, Middlebury Coll., 1959—60. Prof. of fgn. languages and literatures Marlboro Coll., Marlboro, Vt., 1964—. Internat. lectr., France, Italy, Brazil, China, Cuba, Egypt, Mongolia, Ecuador, et. al. Internat. artist (concert), No., Ctrl., So. Am., Europe, Asia, Middle Ea. Chmn. The Grammar Sch., Putney, Vt., 1976—80. Machinist mate USN, 1950—54, U.S.S. Black. Decorated Korean War Theater/Combat U.S. Govt.; recipient Prix Lafayette, France-Amérique, 1957; Full Academic scholarship, French Govt., 1957—60, Rsch. grant, Partners of the Americas, 1963, Marlboro Coll., 1999. Mem.: Early Music Am., The Marlboro Recorder Workshop, Ensemble Cordiforme, New Eng. Regional Assn. of Lang. Lab. Directors, U.S.Mensa, The Appalachian Mountain Club, The Brattleboro Outing Club, The Putney Ski Club. Avocations: dancing, bicycling, cross-country ski racing, theater. Home: Box 146 Marlboro VT 05344 Office: Marlboro Coll PO Box A Marlboro VT 05344 Office Fax: 802-257-4154. E-mail: ebrel@marlboro.edu.

BREM, HENRY, neurosurgeon, educator, researcher; b. Paterson, N.J., Aug. 14, 1952; s. Jacob and Adele (Machabanski) B.; m. Rachel Frydman, Jan. 28, 1978; children: Andrea, Alisa, Sarah. BA, NYU, 1973; student, Harvard U., 1973-74, MD, 1978. Diplomate Am. Bd. Neurosurgery. Intern in surgery Peter Bent Brigham Hosp., Boston, 1978-79; fellow in neurosurgery Johns Hopkins Hosp., Balt., 1979-80; resident in neurosurgery Neurol. Inst. N.Y. Columbia Presbyn. Med. Ctr., N.Y.C., 1980-84; neurosurgeon Johns Hopkins U. Sch. Medicine, Balt., 1984—, prof. neurosurgery, ophthalmology and oncology, 1991—, dir. Hunterian Neurosurg. Lab., 1995—, assoc. dir. dept. neurosurgery, 1995—, Harvey Cushing profl, chmn. dept. neurosurgery, 2000. Office: Johns Hopkins Hosp Meyer 7-113 600 N Wolfe St Baltimore MD 21287-0005

BREMBECK, WINSTON LAMONT, retired speech communication educator; b. Urbana, Ind., Sept. 28, 1912; s. Paul John and Hulda (Speicher) B.; m. Neva Gloyd, June 20, 1940. BA magna cum laude, Manchester Coll., N. Manchester, Ind., 1936; MA, U. Wis., 1938, PhD, 1947. Instr. Westmar Coll., LeMars, Iowa, 1936-39; tutor Bklyn. Coll., 1939-42; mem. faculty U. Wis., 1947—, prof. communication and pub. address, 1960-83, prof. emeritus, 1983—. Cons. in communications and persuasion to business, profl. and religious groups, 1947— Author: (with W.S. Howell) Persuasion a Means of Social Control, 1952, Persuasion a Means of Social Influence, 1976, also articles. Served with AUS, 1943-46. Recipient A.T. Weaver Outstanding Tchr. award Wis. Speech Assn., 1970 Mem. Speech Assn. Am. (exec. com. 1966-68), Central States Speech Assn. (pres. 1965-66), Wis. Speech Assn. (pres. 1949-50), Delta Sigma Rho, Tau Kappa Alpha, Phi Kappa Phi. Republican. Methodist. Home: 3206 Leyton Ln Madison WI 53713-3405 *Over the years I have noted some people remember themselves selfishly into oblivion, others forget themselves into greatness.*

BREMENSTUHL, DAVID P. elementary school educator; b. Englewood, N.J., Aug. 10, 1942; s. V. Burton and Elsie M. (Dutcher) Bremenstuhl; m. Mary Ann K. Warnock, Sept. 13, 1973; children: Heather, Erin. BS in Edn., SUNY, New Paltz, 1964, postgrad., 1967—73, U. Md., 1967—73. Cert. tchr. N.Y. State Dept. Edn., advanced profl. cert. Md. Bd. Edn. Elem. tchr. Middletown (N.Y.) Pub. Schs., 1964—66, White Plains (N.Y.) Pub. Schs., 1966—70, Irvington Pub. Schs., Irvington-on-Hudson, NY, 1971—73, Montgomery County Pub. Schs., Rockville, Md., 1973—2003, Edn. Cons. Svc., 2003—. Founding mem. Nat. Campaign for Tolerance; profl. assn. leadership councils, 1967—73, 1978—93. Recipient Lifetime Achievement award, George Washington Elem. Sch. PTA, 1970, honor Wall of Tolerance Meml., Ala. Mem.: ACLU, NEA, Montgomery County Edn. Assn., Md. State Tchrs. Assn., Amnesty Internat., Wilderness Soc., So. Pover Law Ctr., Sierra Club. Achievements include name

inscribed on Wall of Tolerance civil rights memorial in Montgomery, Alabama. Avocations: writing poetry, composing music, landscape gardening. Home: 9601 Brink Rd Gaithersburg MD 20882 Office: Potomac Elem Sch 10311 River Rd Potomac MD 20854

BREMER, CELESTE F. judge; b. San Francisco, 1953; BA, St. Ambrose Coll., 1974; JD, Univ. of Iowa Coll. of Law, 1977; EdD, Drake U., 2002. Asst. county atty Scott County, 1977-79; asst. atty. gen. Area Prosecutors Div., Iowa, 1979; with Carlin, Liebbe, Pitton & Bremer, 1979-81, Rabin, Liebbe, Shinkle & Bremer, 1981-82; with legal dept. Deere and Co., 1982-84; corp. counsel Economy Forms Corp., 1985-89; magistrate judge U.S. Dist. Ct. (Iowa so. dist.), 8th cir., Des Moines, 1984—; ed. D. Drake U. Sch. of Edn., 2002. Instr. Drake Univ. Coll. of Law, 1985-96. Mem. ABA, Fed. Magistrate Judge Assn., Nat. Assn. Women Judges, Am. Judicature Soc., Iowa State Bar Assn. (bd. govs., 1987-90), Iowa Judges Assn., Iowa Supreme Ct. Coun. on Jud. Selection (chmn. 1986-90), Iowa Orgn Women Attys., Polk County Bar Assn., Polk County Women Attys. Office: US Courthouse Ste 435 123 E Walnut St Des Moines IA 50309-2036

BREMER, HOWARD WALTER, lawyer, consultant; b. Milw., July 18, 1923; s. Walter Hugo and Lydia Martha (Schmidt) B.; m. Caryl Marie Faust, May 28, 1948; children: Katharine, William (dec.), Thomas, Timothy, Margaret. BSChemE, U. Wis., 1944, LLB, 1949. Bar: Wis. 1949, U.S. Patent and Trademark Office 1954, U.S. Supreme Ct. 1957, U.S. Ct. Appeals (fed. cir.) 1959, U.S. Dist. Ct. (so. dist.) Ohio 1960. Patent atty. Procter & Gamble Co., Cin., 1949-60; patent counsel Wis. Alumni Rsch. Found., Madison, 1960-88; cons., Madison, 1988—. Adv. com. Coun. on Govtl. Rels., Washington, 1975-93; panel mem. Office Tech. Assessment, Washington, 1981-83; mem. Adv. Commn. on Patent Law Reform, Washington, 1991-92. Mem. internat. adv. bd. Industry and Higher Edn. Jour., 1996—; contbr. articles to profl. jours. Pres. Edgewood Campus Sch. PTA, Madison, 1967-69; adv. bd. Edgewood H.S., 1971-80, chmn. adv. bd., 1973-74. With USN, 1944-46. Recipient Alumni Appreciation award Edgewood H.S., 1990, Hon. Recognition award, U. Wis. Coll. Agrl. and Life Scis., 2000. Mem. ABA (chmn. com. 1993-2001), Am. Intellectual Property Law Assn. (chmn. com. 1996-99), State Bar Wis. (chmn. intellectual property sect. 1967-68, 79-80), Wis. Intellectual Property Law Assn. (pres. 1989-90), Assn. Univ. Tech. Mgrs. (trustee 1977-78, 80-82, pres. 1978-80, com. chmn. 1985-93, mem. editl. bd. jour. 1990—, Birch award 1980). Avocations: building furniture, home maintenance, model railroading, travel, reading. Home: 1106 Brookwood Rd Madison WI 53711-3116 E-mail: hwbremer@warf.org.

BREMER, JOANNA CHARLES, journalist; b. Roanoke, Va., Apr. 24, 1947; d. John Clyde Jr. and Ruth Vivian Forman; m. Robert M. Charles, June 3, 1967 (div. 1984); m. James Allen Bremer, Sept. 19, 1987. Student, Orange Coast C.C., Costa Mesa, Calif., 1964-65; BS in Journalism, Wayne State U., 1982. Staff writer Salt Lake Tribune, 1966-69, Mellus Newspapers, Lincoln Park, Mich., 1969; women's editor News-Herald Newspapers, Wyandotte, Mich., 1969-72; various editorial positions Detroit Free Press, 1972-89; pres. Joanna Charles Comms., Detroit, 1989-95, Wharton Enterprises, Galveston, Tex., 1995—; editor Pierpont Comms., Houston, 1996-97, M. Garrett & Assocs., Galveston, Tex., 1997-98. Assoc. dir. devel. stewardship U. of Tex. Med. Br. at Galveston, 1999-2002, adminstr. ctr. for interdisciplinary rsch. in women's health, 2002—; cons. pub. rels. Founders Soc. Detroit Inst. Arts/Art and Flowers Festival, 1992-93, Detroit Sci. Ctr., 1990-91; cons. newsletter Detroit Grand Prix Assn., 1989, cons., race dir., 1990; cons. Identity Com. St. John Health Sys., Detroit, 1994-95; cons. Pierpont Comms., 1997-98, The Hall Group, Houston, 1996-99. Editor, cons. Health Alliance Plan, 1994-97; contbg. editor Hart's Energy Markets, 1997-99. Vice chair Mems. Coun./Internat. Inst. Detroit, 1991-92, chair, 1993; mgr. media ctr. Detroit Grand Prix Assn., 1991-95; mgr. media ctr. Texaco Grand Prix Houston, 1998; ad hoc com. Mich. Women's Studies Assn., Lansing, 1988-95; mem. Beginning Experience/Detroit team, 1985-87, Founders Soc./Detroit Inst. Arts, 1982-95; bd. dirs. Mich. Journalism Hall of Fame, 1991-93; mem. adv. com. St. John. Hosp., Detroit, 1993-95; mem. disaster edn. com. ARC, 1996-97, mem. hist. marker com., 1997, mem. adv. bd. Galveston unit, 1998-2001; bd. dirs. Galveston Econ. Devel. Partnership, 1999-2000, Galveston County Econ. Devel. Alliance, 1999—; bd. dirs. exec. com. Galveston County Econ. Devel. Alliance, 1999-2001; bd. dirs. Cmtys. in Schs.-Galveston, pub. affairs chair 1999-2000, pres., 2000-01; mentor Big Bros./Big Sisters of the Gulf Coast, 2001—. Mem. Houston Profl. Chpt. Assn. Women in Comm. (pres. Detroit chpt. 1991-92), Galveston Hist. Found., Mich. Freedom of Info. Com. (treas. 1991-92), Exec. Career Women (co-chair scholarship com. 1996-2003, rec. sec. 1997), Z Krewe for Galveston Mardi Gras, Galveston C. of C. (econ. devel. com. 1997-98, bd. of dirs. 1998-2001, vice-chair mem. devel. 2000), Friends of Mich. Women's Hall of Fame, Houston Mus. Fine Arts. Avocations: golf, hiking, sailing, sewing, cycling. Office: Univ Tex Med Br 301 University Blvd Galveston TX 77555-0587

BREMER, JOHN M. lawyer; b. 1947; BA, Fordham U., 1969; JD, Duke U., 1974. Bar: Wis. 1974. From atty. law dept. to sr. exec. v.p., COO Northwestern Mutual Life Ins., Milw., 1974—2002, COO, 2002—. Office: Northwestern Mutual Life Ins Co 720 E Wisconsin Ave Milwaukee WI 53202-4703

BREMER, RONALD ALLAN, genealogist, editor; b. South Gate, Calif., May 2, 1937; s. Carl Leonard and Lena Evelyn (Jury) B.; m. Trudy Graham; children: Blindy, Ron, Trina, Rebecca, Melinda, Aaron, Serena, Lorrie, Jennie, Elizabeth, Hans, Adam, Rachel. Student, Los Angeles Trade Tech., Cerritos Coll., Am. U., Brigham Young U.; grad., Nat. Inst. Geneal. Rsch., 1961. Prof. genealogist, 1959—; research specialist Fam. Hist. Libr., Salt Lake City, 1969-72; profl. lectr. on genealogy Salt Lake City, 1973—. Editor Genealogy Digest mag., Salt Lake City, 1983-84, Roots Digest, 1984-85; lectr. in field. Author: World's Funniest Epitaphs, 1983; Compendium of Historical Sources, 1983; (with Bill Dollarhide) America's Best Genealogy Resource Centers, 1999. Office: PO Box 345 Paradise UT 84328-0345 E-mail: RonBremer@juno.com. *Money and things don't matter. Position and education mean little. Genius and slow-normal have the same opportunity. Happiness is achieving your greatest potential. Go for the goose-bumps!.*

BREMER, WILLIAM RICHARD, lawyer; b. San Francisco, Jan. 5, 1930; m. Margaret Herrington; children: Mark Richard (dec.), Karen Elizabeth, William Richard Jr. BS in Bus. Adminstrn., Menlo Coll., 1952; JD, U. San Francisco, 1958. Bar: Calif. 1959, U.S. Dist. Ct. (no. dist.) Calif. 1959, U.S. Ct. Appeals (9th cir.) 1959, U.S. Supreme Ct. 1965, U.S. Ct. Mil. Appeals 1973. Pvt. practice San Francisco Bay area, 1959—. Officer, dir. Marshall Hale Meml. Hosp., 1986-88, Childrens Hosp. San Francisco, 1988-91; bd. dirs. Bridgeway Plan for Health, 1988-92. Bd. dirs. Bay Area USO, 1980-89; arbitrator Marin County and San Francisco County Cts., 1977—; animal control hearing officer Marin County, 1998—; city councilman Town of Tiburon (Calif.), 1966-70, mayor, 1968-69; v.p., bd. dirs. Tiburon Peninsula Found.; regional v.p. No. Calif. Naval War Coll. Found., 1997-2000. Lt. USMC, 1952-54, Korea; col. USMC Res. (ret.), 1954-82. Mem. Am. Arbitration Assn. (panel arbitrator 1965—), ATLA, San Francisco Trial Lawyers Assn., Marin County Bar Assn., Calif. Trial Lawyers Assn., Navy League U.S. (life mem. San Francisco Coun., pres. 1978-80, nat. bd. dirs. 1978-88, no. Calif. state pres. 1981-82, nat. dep. JAG 1997-2001, nat. dir. emeritus 2000), Marine Corps Res. Officers Assn. (life), Res. Officers Assn. (life), Naval Order of U.S. (life, San Francisco commandery, comdr. 1982, 83, comdr. gen., nat. pres. 1993-95), Corinthian Yacht (commodore 1986-87), Montgomery St. Motorcycle (pres. 1974-75), Marines Meml. San Francisco (pres. 1985-86), Kiwanis (bd. dirs. San Francisco chpt. 1981-83), Tiburon-Belvedere Rotary (bd. dirs. 1997—, chair cmty. svc., pres. 2001-02). Office: 120 Taylor Rd Belvedere Tiburon CA 94920-1061 E-mail: BillBrem@aol.com.

BREMER MARTINO, JUAN JOSE, ambassador; b. Mexico City, 1944; Law degree, Nat. Autonomous U. Mex., 1966. Pvt. sec. to Pres. Govt. of Mex., 1972—75; dep. sec. Ministry of Presidency, 1975—76; head Nat. Fine Arts Inst., 1976—82; dep. sec. cultural affairs Ministry Edn., 1982; pres. Cervantino Internat. Festival, 1983; pres. fgn. affairs com. Chamber of Deps., 1985—88; '; amb. to Sweden Mexican Embassy, 1982, amb. to USSR, 1988—90, amb. to Fed. Rep. Germany, 1990—98, amb. to Spain, amb. to U.S., 2001—. Co-chair Mexican delegations XXVI Mex.-U.S. Interparliamentary Commn., Colorado Springs, Colo., 1986, XVII Mex.-U.S. Interparliamentary Commn., New Orleans, 1988; participant Commn. to Study Future of Mexican-Am. Rels., 1988; lectr. in field. Office: Embassy of Mex in US 1911 Pennsylvania Ave NW Washington DC 20006*

BREMNER, JAMES DOUGLAS, psychiatrist, researcher, education educator; b. Topeka, Kans., June 5, 1961; s. James Douglas and Linnea Bremner; m. Laura Viola Vaccarino, Aug. 1, 1991; children: Sabina Francesca, Dylan Vittorio. BS, U. of Puget Sound, 1979—83; MD, Duke U. Sch. of Medicine, 1983—87. Cert. Am. Bd. of Psychiatry and Neurology, 1996, Am. Bd. of Nuc. Medicine, 2001. Assoc. prof. of psychiatry and radiology Emory U. Sch. of Medicine, 2000—; dir. Emory Ctr. for Positron Emission Tomography, 2000—. Asst. and assoc. prof. of psychiatry Yale U. Sch. of Medicine, 1992—2000. Author: (book) Does Stress Damage the Brain?. Achievements include research in brain imaging and neurobiology of mood and anxiety disorders. Home: 2125 Ponce de Leon Ave NE Atlanta GA 30307 Office: Emory U 1256 Briarcliff Rd Atlanta GA 30306 Office Fax: 404-712-8442. E-mail: jdbremn@emory.edu.

BREMNER, JOHN MCCOLL, agronomy and biochemistry educator; b. Dumbarton, Scotland, Jan. 18, 1922; came to U.S., 1959; s. Archibald Donaldson and Sarah Kennedy (McColl) B.; m. Eleanor Mary Williams, Sept. 30, 1950; children: Stuart, Carol. BS, Glasgow U., 1944, DSc, 1987; PhD, U. London, 1948, DSc, 1959. With chemistry dept. Rothamsted Exptl. Sta., Harpenden, Eng., 1945-59; assoc. prof. Iowa State U., Ames, 1959-61, prof. agronomy and biochemistry, 1961-75, C.F. Curtiss disting. prof. agriculture, prof. agronomy, biochemistry, 1975-93; disting. prof. emeritus, 1993—. Tech. expert IAEA, Austria, 1964-65, Yugoslavia, 1964-65. Author or co-author over 300 publs. including 30 chpts in sci. monographs. Recipient Outstanding Research award First Miss. Corp., 1979, Alexander Von Humboldt medal Alexander Von Humboldt Found., Fed. Republic of Germany, 1982, Gov.'s Sci. medal State of Iowa, 1983, Harvey Wiley award U.S. Assn. Ofcl. Analytical Chemists, 1984, Spencer medal Am. Chem. Soc., 1987, Burlington No. Found. Faculty Achievement award for Research, Gamma Sigma Delta award of merit for disting. service to agriculture, Regents award for faculty excellence, 1992, Award for Advancement of Agrl. & Food Chemistry, Am. Chem. Soc.; fellow Rockefeller Found., 1957, Guggenheim Found., 1968. Fellow AAAS, Am. Acad. Microbiology, Am. Soc. Agronomy (Agronomic Rsch. award 1985, Environ. Quality Rsch. award 1990), Soil Sci. Soc. Am. (Achievement award 1967, Bouyoucos Disting. Career award 1982, Disting. Svc. award 1993), Iowa Acad. Sci. (disting.); mem. NAS, Am. Soc. Microbiology, Brit. Soc. Soil Sci., Internat. Soil Sci. Soc., Phi Kappa Phi (centennial medalist 1997), Sigma Xi, Gamma Sigma Delta. Achievements include patent for nitrification inhibitor; development and evaluation of nitrification and urease inhibitors for control of adverse transformations of fertilizer nitrogen in soils; development of methodology for research on the nitrogen cycle and environmental problems related to agriculture; research on microbial, enzymatic, and chemical processes responsible for nitrogen transformations in soils, such as nitrification, denitrification, chemodenitrification, and urease activity. E-mail: bremnerjm@msn.com.

BREMOND, DUANE BENJAMIN, marketing professional; b. San Francisco, Oct. 22, 1961; s. Walter and Bertha B.; m. Harvelin Roberts, Mar. 17, 1985 (div. 1988); 1 child, Diandra. BS in Mgmt., Pepperdine U., 2001. Congrl. aide Congresswoman Maxine Waters, L.A., 1988-95; dir. cmty. rels. AIDS Project L.A., 1995-97; asst. dir. devel. Hospitaller Found., L.A., 1997-2000; dir. mktg. and devel. Ctr. Cmty. & Family Svcs., Padadena, Calif., 2000—02; prin. Bremond & Assoc., Inglewood, Calif., 2002—. Commr. L.A. HIV & Health Svc., L.A., 1995-97. Dir. logistics Nelson Mandela Tour, L.A., 1990. With U.S. Army, 1984-87. Democrat. Home: 6002 Ladera Park Ave Los Angeles CA 90056 E-mail: breme10@yahoo.com.

BREMS, DAVID PAUL, architect; b. Lehi, Utah, Aug. 10, 1950; s. D. Orlo and Gearldine (Hitchcock) B.; m. Johna Devey Brems; children: Stefan Tomas Brems, Beret Alla Brems. BS, U. Utah, 1973, MArch, 1975. Registered architect, Utah, Calif., Colo., Ariz., Wyo., N.Mex., Idaho, Mont., Tex., Wash. Draftsman Environ. Assocs., Salt Lake City, 1971-73; draftsman/architect intern Environ. Design Group, Salt Lake City, 1973-76; architect/intern Frank Fuller AIA, Salt Lake City, 1976-77; prin. Edward & Daniels, Salt Lake City, 1978-83; pres. David Brems & Assocs., Salt Lake City, 1983-86; prin. Gillies, Stransky, Brems, Smith P.C., Salt Lake City, 1986—. Adj. prof. U. Utah Grad. Sch. Architecture, 1990-93; mem. urban design com. Assist, Inc., Salt Lake City, 1982-85, Salt Lake County Planning Commn., 1991-97, chmn., 1992-96; mem. Emigration Twp. Planning Commn., 1997—, chmn. 1997-99; mem. Emigration Masterplan Adv. Com., 1997-99; invited lectr. Wyo. Soc. Archs., 1992, sch. engrng. U. Utah, 1993, 95, Va., 1993, Utah Soc. Archs., 1994, Utah Power and Light, 1994, Utah Soc. Archts., 1994; juror U. Utah Grad. Sch. Architecture, 1975—, Utah Soc. Am. Planning Assn., 1994—, Sunstone Symposium, 1995, Contemporary Arts Group, 1995—; with adv. com. U. Utah Grad. Sch. Architecture, 2000—. Pub. Firm Profile Intermountain Architecture,, 1996, Web Mag., 1997; prin. works include solar twin homes Utah Holiday (Best Solar Design award), Sun Builder, Daily Jour., Salt Lake Tribune, Brian Head Day Lodge, Easton Aluminum, Four Seasons Hotel, Gore Coll. Bus., CMF Tooele, utah Regional Corrections Facility, St. Vincents De Paul Ctr., Steiner Aquatic Ctr., U. Utah Football Support Facility, Sports Medicine West, West Jordan Cmty. Water Park, Utah Nat. Guard Apache Helicopter Hangar & Armory, Kashmitter I Residences, St. Thomas More Cath. Ch., Spanish Fork Cmty. Water Park, Natures Herbs, ABC Office Bldg. Divsn. of Natural Resources Bldg., Kashmitter II Residence, Litton Residence, Elliott Residence, Utah Olympic Speed Skating Oval for 2002 Olympics, Vis. Ctr. Grand Staircase Escalante Nat. Monument, Bennett Fed. Bldg., and others; ALTA Club mem., Great Salt Lake Yacht Club mem., Bear Lake Yacht Club mem., mem. Leadership Utah; mem. 2002 Olympic Energy and Water subcom., 1996—; mem. State of Utah Divsn. of Facilities Mgmt. Com. on Energy Efficient Architecture. Mem. Salt Lake City Bus. Advisory. Recipient three awards Am. Concrete Inst., 1993, Chief Engrs. Honor award U.S. Army Corps Engrs., 1994; Bronze medalist Utah Summer Games, 1991, Silver medalist, 1992, Gold medalist, 1994, Design award Dept. Def., 1995, Blue Seal award, 1995, Outstanding Project award U.S. Dept. Def., 1995, Western Mountain Region Hon. Mention St. Thomas More, 1996, Solar Today award Sun award, Energy Uses News award Dept. Natural Resources, 1996; named Best Pvt. Project by Intermountain Architecture, 1994, Salt Lake County Vol. of Yr. Salt Lake County Planning Commn., 1995, Best Recreation Project Intermountain Arch., 1995. Mem.: AIA (chmn. Western Mountain Regiona honor awards 1983, pres. Salt Lake chpt. 1983—84, chmn. Western Mountain Region conf. 1986, pres. Utah Soc. 1987, chmn. Western Mountain Regional honor awards 1988, com. on design 1990—, juror Colo. West awards 1992, chmn. com. on environment AIA Utah 1993, chmn. Design for Life Workshop at Sundance 1993, Honor awards 1983, Merit awards 1983, 1985, Honor awards 1988, PCI award 1988, IFRAA award 1988, Merit awards 1988, 1993, IFRAA award 1994, Merit awards 1999, Steel Inst. award 2002, Sarnafil award 2002, award Utah sect. IES for St. Thomas More, Honor award 2002), Am. Solar Soc., Am. Solar Energy Soc., Utah Soc. Architects, Black Builder Mesa Water Assn. (sec.), Acorn Hills Water Assn. (trustee), Am. Planning Assn. (juror awards 1994), Illuminating Engrng. Soc. (assoc.), Utah Open Lands (S.W. Utah br.), Salt Lake Olympic Com. (environ. adv. com.), Hobie Fleet 67 (commodore 1985—86). Home: 119 N Young Oak Rd Salt Lake City UT 84108-1601

BREMSER, GEORGE, JR., electronics company executive; b. Newark, May 26, 1928; s. George and Virginia (Christian) B.; m. Marie Sundman, June 21, 1952 (div. July 1979); children: Christian Fredrick II, Priscilla Suzanne, Martha Anne, Sarah Elizabeth; m. Nancy Kay Woods, Oct. 27, 1983 (div. Feb. 1989); m. Betty Glover Lohse, Oct. 8, 1997 (dec. Mar. 2001). BA, Yale U., 1949; postgrad., U. Miami, 1959; MBA, NYU, 1962. With McCann-Erickson Inc., N.Y.C., 1952-61, asst. gen. mgr. Bogota, Colombia, 1955, gen. mgr., 1955-57, account supr. N.Y.C., 1958, v.p., mgr. Miami, Fla., 1959-61; with Gen. Foods Corp., White Plains, N.Y., 1961-71; v.p., gen. mgr. internat. div. Gen. Foods Europe, White Plains, N.Y., 1967; pres. Gen. Foods Internat., White Plains, 1967-71; group v.p. Gen. Foods Corp., White Plains, 1970-71; chmn., pres., chief exec. officer Texstar Corp., Grand Prairie, Tex., 1971-81; exec. v.p. Shaklee Corp., San Francisco, 1981-82; chmn., pres., chief exec. officer Etak Inc., Menlo Park, Calif., 1983-88, 96, chmn., 1989-96, 97—; chmn., pres., CEO Etak, Inc., Menlo Park, Calif., 1996-97, chmn., 1997-2000, CEO, 2000-01; bd. dir. Tele Atlas N.A., Inc., 2000—, chief adminstrv. officer, 2001—02. Bd. dirs. PBI Industries Inc. Trustee Union Ch., Bogota, 1956-57; Dem. county committeeman, Ridgewood, N.J., 1962-63; mem. New Canaan (Conn.) Town Council, 1969-73; founder, past pres. Citizens Com. for Conservation, New Canaan; mem. coun. Save the Redwoods League, 1987—. Served to 2d lt. USMC 1950-52, capt. Res. Mem. New Canaan Country Club, Brook Club, Yale Club (N.Y.C.), Block Island Club, Casino Club (Nantucket, Mass.), Explorers Club, Phi Beta Kappa, Beta Gamma Sigma, Beta Theta Pi. Home: 5575 Hilltop Cres Oakland CA 94618-2605 also: Mansion Beach Rd Block Island RI 02807 Office: Tele Atlas NA Inc 1605 Adams Dr Menlo Park CA 94025-1448

BRENDEL, ALFRED, concert pianist; b. Wiesenberg, Austria, Jan. 5, 1931; s. Albert and Ida (Wieltschnig) B.; m. Iris Heymann-Gonzala, 1960 (div. 1972); m. Irene Semler, 1975; 1 son, 3 daus. Studied piano under, Sofija Dezelic, Zagreb, Yugoslavia, Ludovika V. Kaan, Graz, Austria, Edwin Fischer, Lucerne, Switzerland, Paul Baumgartner, Basel, Switzerland, Edward Steuermann, Salzburg, Austria; studied harmony under Franjo Dugan, Zagreb; studied composition under A. Michl, Graz, Austria; DMus (hon.), U. London, 1978; DLitt (hon.), Sussex U., 1981; DMus (hon.), Oxford U., 1983, Warwick U., 1991, Yale U., 1992; fellow, Royal No. Coll., Manchester, 1988; Bayer, Akademie der Wissenschaften. First piano recital Graz, 1940, concert tours through Europe, Latin Am. and N.Am., 1963—, Australia, 1963, 66, 69, 76, appeared at many music festivals including Salzburg, 1960—, Vienna, Berlin, Montreux, Lucerne, Edinburg, Aldeburgh, Athens, Granada, P.R.; has performed with most maj. orchs. in Europe and U.S. and others; performed all Beethoven piano sonatas in concert cycle Paris, London, Berlin, Amsterdam, Vienna, Hamburg, Basel, Dusseldorf, Freiburg, Vevey, N.Y.C., 1983, 92—; recording The Alfred Brendel Collection. Recipient Premio Citta de Bolzano Concorso Busoni, 1949; recipient Grand Prix du Disque, 1965, 84, Edison prize, 1973, 81, 84, 87, Brit. Music Trade Assn. award 1973, 78, 81, Grand Prix des Disquaires de France, 1975, Deutscher Schallplattenpreis, 1976, 77, 81, 82, 84, Wiener Flotenuhr, 1976, 77, 79, 82, 84, 87, Gramophone award, 1978, 80, 82, 84, Japanese Grand Prix award, 1977, 78, 80, 82, 84, 87, Franz Liszt prize, 1979, 80, 82, 83, 87, Frankfurt Music award 1984, Busoni Found. award, 1990, Diapason D'Or award, 1992, Preis der deutschen Schallplatten-Kritik, 1992, Orden pour le Merite fur Wissenschaften und Kunste, 1991; decorated knight British Empire, 1989. Fellow Exeter Coll.; mem. Am. Acad. Arts and Scis. (hon.), Royal Acad. Music (hon.), Comdr. des Arts et Letters. Office: care Colbert Artists Mgmt Inc 111 W 57th St New York NY 10019-2211

BRENDER, JEAN DIANE, epidemiologist, nurse; b. Bellingham, Wash., Nov. 23, 1951; d. Otto and Jennie Wilma Tolsma; m. Dennis Ray Brender, Aug. 30, 1975; 1 child, Valerie. BSN summa cum laude, Whitworth Coll., 1974; M of Nursing, U. Wash., 1979, PhD of Epidemiology, 1983. RN Tex. Staff nurse, infection control Sacred Heart Med. Ctr., Spokane, Wash., 1974-80; instr. nursing Intercollegiate Ctr. for Nursing Edn., Spokane, 1979-80, asst. prof. nursing, 1982-84; teaching asst. epidemiology U. Wash., Seattle, 1981-82; rsch. health scientist Audie L. Murphy Vets. Hosp., San Antonio, 1984-85; staff epidemiologist bur. epidemiology Tex. Dept. Health, Austin, 1986-87, acting program dir. environ. epidemiology program, 1987, dir. environ. epidemiology program, 1987-93, dir. noncommunicable disease epidemiology and toxicology, 1993-97; infectious disease epidemiologist Bur. Disease Control, 1997-99; also state environ. epidemiologist Tex. Dept. Health, Austin, 1993-97; assoc. prof. health svcs. rsch. S.W. Tex. State U., 1999—. Bd. dirs. Agriculture Resources Protection Authority; adj. instr. allied health scis. and health adminstrn. S.W. Tex. State U., 1988-90; adj. asst. prof. epidemiology U. Tex. Health Sci. Ctr.-Houston Sch. Pub. Health, 1985-93, adj. assoc. prof., 1993—. Contbr. articles to profl. jours. Recipient H.E.A.L.T.H. award, 1994; grantee in field. Mem. APHA, Soc. Epidemiologic Rsch., Coun. State and Territorial Epidemiologists, Am. Coll. Epidemiology, Tex. Pub. Health Assn. (governing coun.). Avocations: reading, computers, church activities, snow skiing. Home: 6902 Alder Cv Austin TX 78750-8161 Office: Tex State U 601 University Dr San Marcos TX 78666-4616 E-mail: jb52@txstate.edu.

BRENDLE, GARY ALLEN, SR., landscape architect; b. Annapolis, Md., Sept. 2, 1952; s. William Glade Sr. and Betty Allen (Basil) B.; m. Barbara Libersky, Sept. 9, 1990; children: Gary Allen Jr., Courtney Paige. AA, Anne Arundel C.C., Arnold, Md., 1972; student, U. Md., 1976-77; B Landscape Arch., U. Ga., 1979. Registered landscape architect, Md. Planner, land arch. Collerado Assocs., Inc., Memphis, 1980; draftsman Lindsay Ervin & Assocs., Crofton, Md., 1981; planner Genstar Stone Products Co., Hunt Valley, Md., 1981-83; landscape architect, planner McCrone, Inc., Annapolis, 1983-91; salesman Brendle Enterprises, Annapolis, 1992-93; owner Gary Brendle, Landscape Arch., Annapolis, 1993—, Chesapeake Distributors, Annapolis, 1995—. With USAF, 1972-76. Mem. Am. Soc. Landscape Architects, Crabtowne Skiers, Inc. Republican. Methodist. Avocations: golf, skiing, volleyball. Home: 221 Meadowgate Dr Annapolis MD 21401-5824 Office: Chesapeake Distributors PO Box 189 Annapolis MD 21404-0189

BRENDLER, CHARLES BURGESS, urologist, educator; b. Charlottesville, Va., June 20, 1944; s. Herbert and Virginia Burgess B.; m. Lucretia Cattley Rock, June 18, 1966; children: Christopher, Amy, Emily, Peter. AB, Harvard Coll., 1966; MD, U. Va., 1974. Instr. urology Johns Hopkins U., Balt., 1980-81, asst. prof. urology, 1981-85, assoc. prof. urology, 1985-93; chief urology Balt. City Hosps., 1981-84; prof., chief urology U. Chgo., 1994—. Mem. surg. exec. com. U. Chgo. Med. Ctr., 1994—, mem. surgery edn. com., 1994—. Assoc. editor: Urologic Surgery, 5th edit., 1998; co-author: Campbell's Urology, 1985, 92, 97, 02; Urologic Surgery, 1983, 91, assoc. editor, 1998, 03; co-author Operative Urology 1990, 97, 02; contbr. articles to profl. jour. Capt. USAF, 1967-71. Mem. Am. Urol. Assn. (2d prize clin. rsch. 1983, 1st prize clin. rsch. Mid-Atlantic sect. 1991, 92), Am. Assn. Genito-Urinary Surgeons, Nat. Urol. Forum, Soc. Basic Urol. Rsch., Soc. Urol. Oncology, Am. Joint Commn. on Cancer (advisor task force on urol. cancer 1997), Alpha Omega Alpha. Democrat. Unitarian Universalist. Avocations: skiing, hiking, jogging, traveling. Home: 6301 S County Line Rd Burr Ridge IL 60527-4856 Office: U Chgo Sect Urology 5841 S Maryland Ave # Mc 6038 Chicago IL 60637-1463 E-mail: cbrendle@surgery.bsd.uchicago.edu.

BRENDLINGER, LEROY R. academic administrator; b. Frederick, Pa., Dec. 14, 1918; s. Claude R. and Elsie May B.; m. Virginia Steltz, Dec. 28, 1941; children: Dawn, Brian, Craig. BS, West Chester State Coll., 1946; MS, U. Pa., 1949; Ed.D., Temple U., 1959. Former tchr., East Greenville, Pa.; Ordnance Officer Candidate Sch., Aberdeen, Md.; former prin. Pottsgrove (Pa.) Schs.; former asst. supt. Montgomery (Pa.) Schs.; pres. Montgomery County Community Coll., now pres. emeritus. Chmn. SCORE, chpt. 594 Tri County area. Author: The Brendlinger Family History 1660-1994, 1995. Past pres. Montgomery County (Pa.) Health and Welfare Coun.; bd. dirs. Montgomery Hosp., Lutheran Children and Family Svc.; pres. Tri-County Area local chpt. Score 594, Pottstown, Pa. With U.S. Army, 1942-46, ETO. Recipient Outstanding Alumnus award West Chester U., 1984. Mem. Am. Assn. Jr. and C.Cs. (past pres. Pa. Commn. C.Cs.). Clubs: Brookside Country (treas. bd. govs.). Office: 340 Dekalb Pike Blue Bell PA 19422-1412

BRENDSEL, LELAND C. former mortgage company executive; b. Sioux Falls, S.D. married. BA, U. Colo., 1967; D in Fin., Northwestern U., 1974. Prof. U. Utah, 1971-76; economist Farm Credit Banks, 1976, Fed. Home Loan Bank, Des Moines, 1978-82; exec. v.p., CFO Fed. Home Loan Mortgage Corp., McLean, Va., 1982-85, acting pres., CEO, 1985-87, pres., CEO, 1987-89; chmn., CEO Fed. Home Loan Mortgage Corp.(Freddie Mac), McLean, Va., 1989—2003. Adv. bd. J. L. Kellogg Grad. Sch. Northwestern U.; chmn. bd. Fed. Home Loan Mortgage Corp. Found.; bd. trustees Nat. Urban League. Named Washingtonian of the Yr., 1991, Children's Champion UNICEF Coun., 1992, Corp. Citizen of the Yr. Nat. Black Child Devel. Inst., 1993, Corp. Advocate of the Yr. Child Welfare League Am., 1995; recipient N.Y. Coun. Adoptable Children's award, 1993, Give Your Heart to Child award Vo. Emergency Families for Children, 1997.

BRENDTRO, LARRY KAY, psychologist; b. Sioux Falls, S.D., July 26, 1940; s. A. Kenneth and Bernice (Matz) B.; m. Janna Agena, July 14, 1973; children: Daniel Kenneth, Steven Lincoln, Nola Kristine. BA, Augustana Coll., 1961; MS, S.D. State U., 1962; PhD, U. Mich., 1965. Prin. Crippled Children's Hosp. and Sch., Sioux Falls, 1962-63; psychology intern Hawthorn Ctr., Northville, Mich., 1964-65; instr. U. Mich., 1965; asst. prof. U. Ill., Urbana, 1966-67; pres., CEO Starr Commonwealth, Albion, Mich., 1967-81; prof. Augustana Coll., Sioux Falls, S.D., 1981-99; pres. Reclaiming Youth Internat., Lennox, SD,

1997—; dean Starr Commowell Rsch. Inst., 2002—. Mem. U.S. Coordinating Coun. on Juvenile Justice and Delinquency Prevention, 1997—. Co-author: The Other 23 Hours, 1969, Positive Peer Culture, 1974, 1985, Re-educating Troubled Youth, 1983, Reclaiming Youth at Risk, 1990, 2002; co-editor: Reclaiming Children and Youth, 1992—, Reclaiming Our Prodigal Sons and Daughters, 2000, No Disposable Kids, 2001, Kids Who Outwit Adults, 2002. Lutheran. Home: PO Box 57 Lennox SD 57039-0057 Office: Reclaiming Youth Internat PO Box 57 Lennox SD 57039-0057 E-mail: courage@reclaiming.com.

BRENEMAN, DAVID CLINTON, II, systems analyst, communications executive, radio director; b. Tacoma, Feb. 13, 1959; s. Robert Weldon and Jane Harriet (Hill) Breneman; m. Lesli Anne Morrow, July 4, 2003. BA in Econs., U. Puget Sound, 1985. Segment prodr. Photo N.W. Video, Tacoma, 1986-87; dir. Spud Goodman Radio Show, Tacoma, 1986-87; owner Rosedale Audio Prodns., Gig Harbor, Wash., 1986—; dir. program syndicated in the N.W. Spud Goodman Radio-Radio Show, Tacoma, 1987-89; asst. dir. & editor The Other Spud Goodman Show, 1991; data sys. adminstr. Tacoma Screw Products, Inc., 1989-93; audio dir., editor The Spud Goodman Show, Sta. KTZZ-TV, Seattle, 1992-95; audio dir., editor, cinematographer The Spud Goodman Show, Fox Net, 1996-98; sr. Unix sys. adminstr. AT&T Wireless Svcs., 1995-97; distributed sys. software analyst Airborne Express, 1998—. Web page designer/adminstr. www.spudgoodman.com, 1999—. Commr. Pierce County (Wash.) Rev. Com. Charter Rev. Commn., 1987; precinct comitteeman Rosedale (Wash.) Reps., 1986—92; mem. Pierce County Rep. Exec. Com., 1989—92; v.p. Rosedale Cmty. Hall Assn., 1996—98, 2000—02. Home: 8520 86th Ave NW Gig Harbor WA 98332-6750 Office: Rosedale Audio Prodns 8520 86th Ave NW Gig Harbor WA 98332-6750 E-mail: dcb@rosedale.seaslug.org.

BRENER, SORIN JAKOB, physician; b. Galatzi, Romania, Aug. 28, 1959; s. Moshe and Ghiza Brener; m. Gratziella Ethel Kraft, Aug. 1, 1982; children: Shirley Rose, Michael Iehoshua. MD, Hebrew U., Jerusalem, 1984. Diplomate Israeli Med. Assn., 1985. Staff cardiologist Cleve. Clinic Found., 1989—, dir., angiography core lab., 2001—. Author: (scientific manuscripts) Treatment of acute myocardial infarction; Anti-platelet agents; contbr. book chapters. Office: Cleve Clinic Found 9500 Euclid Ave Desk F-25 Cleveland OH 44195 Office Fax: 216-444-8050. E-mail: breners@ccf.org.

BRENKEN, HANNE MARIE, artist; b. Duisburg, Germany, July 6, 1923; arrived in U.S., 1977; d. Hermann and Luise (Werth) Tigler; m. Hans Brenken, Mar. 28, 1942 (div. 1985); children: Karin Brenken Schneider-Henn, Berndt; m. Ricardo Wiesenberg, May 20, 1986. Grad., Landschulheim, Holzminden, Germany, 1941; studied in pvt. art schs., Munich and Bonn, Germany. One-person shows include Contra Kreis Gallery, Bonn, Germany, 1958, Galerie Junge Kunst, Fulda, Germany, 1959, Universa-Galerie, Nurenberg, Germany, 1960, Galleria Monte Napoleone, Milan, 1961, Galerie Niedlich, Stuttgart, Germany, 1961, 63, Galerie am Jakobsbrunnen, Stuttgard, 1964, 67, Kunst und Kunstverein Mus. Pforzheim, Germany, 1969, Kunstverein Mus., Munich, 1972, Galerie Dorothea Leonhart, Munich, 1974, I.C.L. Gallery, East Hampton, N.Y., 1980, Anne Reid Gallery, Princeton, N.J., 1981, Adagio Gallery, Bridgehampton, N.Y., 1982, 84, Queens Mus., N.Y., 1983, Ericson Gallery, N.Y.C., 1984, 85, Benton Gallery, Southampton, N.Y., 1986, Vered Gallery, East Hampton, N.Y., 1988, Gallery Rodeo, Lake Arrowhead, Calif., Taos, N.Mex., Beverly Hills, Calif., 1990, Brian Logan Art Space, Washington, 1991, The Gallery, Leesburg, Va., 1992, Amerika Haus, Frankfurt, Germany, 1993, Ganser Haus Gallery, Wasserburg, Germany, 1993, Ann Norton Sculpture Gardens, West Palm Beach, Fla., 1994, Jean Chisholm Gallery, West Palm Beach, 1994, Okuda Internat. Gallery, Washington, 1995, Misia Broadhead Studio/Gallery, Middleburg, Va., 1996, Millennium Gallery, East Hampton, N.Y., 1997, Reynolds Gallery Westmont Coll., Santa Barbara, Calif., 1998, Svitozor Fine Arts, Santa Barbara, Calif., 2000, L.A. Artcore, Los Angeles, 2001; group shows include Duisburg (Germany) Mus., 1959, Baden-Baden Mus., Germany, 1961, 62, Haus der Kunst, Munich, 1963, 64, 69, 70, 71, 72, 73, Kunstgebäude, Stuttgart, 1963, 71, Acad. Fine Arts, Berlin, 1964, 73, Forum Stadtpark, Graz, Austria, 1965, Folkwang Mus., Essen, Germany, 1965, Munich City Mus., 1967, Karlsruhe (Germany) Kunstverein, 1967; permanent collections include Solomon R. Guggenheim Mus., New York, Queens Mus., Phoenix Art Mus., Guild Hall Mus, several mus. in Europe. Avocations: travel, visiting galleries and musuems, reading. Home: 184 Middle Rd Montecito CA 93108-2446

BRENLY, BOB, professional sports team executive, broadcaster; Grad., Ohio U., 1977. Appeared as a catcher 1 All-Star game; catcher nine major league seasons San Francisco Giants; 3d baseman catcher Bobcats; mgr. Ariz. Diamondbacks, 2000—. TV color analyst Ariz. Diamondbacks, broadcaster, Chgo. Achievements include leading Arizona to a 92-70 regular season record; a National League West Division title; National League pennant; became first rookie manager since 1997 to lead his team to the playoffs. Office: Ariz Diamondbacks 401 E Jefferson St Phoenix AZ 85004

BRENMAN, STEPHEN MORRIS, lawyer; b. San Francisco, Mar. 25, 1945; s. Irving I. and Vivian H. (Weiss) B.; m. Laura R. Yocum, Aug. 14, 1968; children: Jeremy S., Sara N. BS, Miami U., Oxford, Ohio, 1967; JD with distinction, Valparaiso (Ind.) U., 1970. Bar: Ind. 1970, U.S. Dist. Ct. (no. and so. dist.) Ind. 1970, U.S. Ct. Appeals (7th cir.) 1970, U.S. Supreme Ct. 1973, U.S. Tax Ct. 1973, U.S. Ct. Claims 1973. Assoc. Saul I. Ruman & Assocs., Hammond, Ind., 1970-73; ptnr. Katz & Brenman, Gary and Merrillville, Ind., 1973-78, mng. ptnr. Merrillville, 1978-99; pvt. practice Merrillville, 2000—; prin. Stephen M. Brenman, P.C. Lectr. Valparaiso U. Sch. Law, 1970; chief pub. defender Gary City Ct., 1973-78, staff coord., 1973-78; dir. and officer Dunes Volkswagen, Inc., Gary, 1977-80, Len Pollak Buick, Inc., Gary, 1977-83, Merrillville Volkswagen, Porshe-Audi, Inc., Merrillville, 1980-83; lectr. alcoholic beverage laws in Ind., miscellaneous trade orgns., 1980—; temp. probate commr., pro-tem and temp. judge Superior Ct. Lake County, Civil Divsn., East Chicago, Ind., 1980—; lectr. estate planning and right to die Congregation Beth Israel, Inc., Hammond, 1989—, Jewish Fedn., Inc., Highland, Ind., 1989—; lect. Alcoholic Beverage Server Tng., 2001-. Editor, publisher Ind. Alcoholic Beverage Laws, Rules, Regulations, Policies, Procedures & Forms, 2001; note editor Valparaiso U. Law Rev., 1969-70; contbr. articles to profl. jours. Co-chmn. Ind. Alcoholic Beverage Commn. Study Com., Rules, Regulations and Forms Rev., 1990, 2000—; election judge and commr. Lake County Election Bd., Crown Point, Ind., 1973-78; dir. Munster (Ind.) Little League, 1980-84, umpire and coach, 1980-84; bd. dirs. Munster Youth Athletic Assn., 1980-84; bd. dirs. Jewish Fedn., Inc., Highland, 1980-85, Congregation Beth Israel, Inc., Hammond, 1980-85, 2000-, chmn. bldg. com., 2000-; dir. Hoosier Boys Town, Inc., Schererville, Ind., 1990-94, dir. and officer Hoosier Boys Town Found., 1990-94; mem. Munster H.S. Booster Club, 1987—; mem., dir., officer Alpha Epsilon Pi Parents Club, Inc., Bloomington, Ind., 1990-94. Recipient Disting. Svc. award Jewish Fedn., 1980, 83, 84, Red and White Club, Munster H.S. Booster Club, 1989, Mustang Club, 1989; Valparaiso U. scholar, 1968-70. Mem. ABA (sect. bus. law, adminstrv. law and regulatory practice, subsect. alcoholic beverage law, real property, probate, trust law sects.), Nat. Assn. Estate Planners and Couns., Nat. Alcoholic Beverage Control Assn., Nat. Acad. Elder Law Attys., Nat. Assn. Criminal Def. Attys., Ind. State Bar Assn. (mem. regulatory practice and alcoholic beverage subcom., govtl. law sect.), Fed. Bar Assn., Assn. Trial Lawyers Am., Ind. Trial Lawyers Assn., Lake County Bar Assn. (chmn. legal forms com.), Am. Judicature Soc. (corp. counsel inst. mem.), Phi Alpha Delta, B'nai B'rith, Miami U. Alumni Assn., Valparaiso U. Sch. Law Alumni Assn., Zeta Beta Tau Alumni Assn. Democrat. Office: 107 West 79th Ave Merrillville IN 46410-5438 Fax: 219-641-7215. E-mail: smbpclaw@aol.com.

BRENNAN, CIARAN BRENDAN, accountant, oil industry executive; b. Dublin, Jan. 28, 1944; s. Sean and Mary (Stone) B. BA with honors, Univ. Coll., Dublin, 1966; MBA, Harvard U., 1973; MS in Acctg., U. Houston, 1976. Lic. real estate broker, Calif.; CPA, Tex. Auditor Coopers & Lybrand, London, 1967-70, Price Waterhouse & Co., Toronto, Canada, 1970-71; asst. contr. Kerr-McGee Corp., Oklahoma City, 1976-80; contr. Cummings Oil Co., Oklahoma City, 1980-82; CFO Red Stone Energies, Ltd., 1982, Leonoco, Inc., 1982-87; treas., chief fin. officer JKJ Supply Co., 1983-87, Saturn Investments Inc., 1983-87, JFL Co., 1984-87, Little Chief Drilling & Energy Inc., 1984-85; pres. Ciaran Brennan Corp., 1990—; CFO Nationwide Industries, 1991-93; mgr. of budget Mission Foods, 1996-98; contr. Hoffy Bacon, 1998—2001; ptnr. CiaranBrennan.com, 2001—. Bd. dirs., cons. small oil cos.; adj. faculty Oklahoma City U., 1977-86; vis. faculty Ctrl. State U., 1977-86. Contbr. articles to profl. jours. Mem. AICPA, Inst. Chartered Accts. Eng. and Wales, K.C. Republican. Roman Catholic. E-mail: ciaranrb@aol.com.

BRENNAN, DONNA LESLEY, public relations company executive; b. Washington, Mar. 13, 1945; d. Don Arthur and Louise (Tucker) B.; m. James L Bergey, Mar. 6, 1999. BA, Denison U., 1967. Tchr. Souderton Area H.S., Pa., 1967-69; mgr. media rels. Ins. Co. N.Am., Phila., 1969-72; dir. press rels. Colonial Penn Group, Phila., 1972-75, 1975-81, dir. comm., 1981-83; v.p. corp. comm. Norstar Bancorp, Albany, N.Y., 1983-85; v.p. comm. Meritor Fin. Group, Phila., 1986-87; prin. Donna Brennan Assocs., 1988—. Bd. dirs. W. Vincent Land Trust, Inc. Mem. Pub. Rels. Soc. Am. (pres. Phila. chpt. 1988), Phila. Women's Network (founder, bd. dirs.), Women's Assn. for Women's Alternatives (vice-chmn., bd. dirs.), Forum of Exec. Women (pres. 1992-93, bd. dirs. 1989-97).

BRENNAN, ELIZABETH LANE, educator, program director; b. Chgo., Mar. 4, 1951; d. John Maurice and Ann Chenoweth (Poust) Lane; m. Edward Michael Brennan, June 16, 1984; children: Ann, Matthew, Edward. BA, Colo. State U., 1973; MEd, Kent State U., 1994, PhD, 1997. Lic. social worker. Investment coord. Sterling Ltd., Shaker Heights, Ohio, 1982-84; mgr. Envirochem Industries, Inc., Cleve., 1984-88, pres., 1988-92; cons. chem. mfg., 1992-94; grant coord. Family Child Learning Ctr. Kent (Ohio) State U., 1994-97; rsch. coord. San Francisco State U., 1996-98; faculty, program dir. St. Mary's Coll. Calif., 1998—. Com. chmn. PTA, Shaker Heights, 1979-83; vice chmn. Kids on Block, Cleve., 1981-83; performer, publicist Hermit Club, amateur theater, Cleve., 1978-96. Mem. Nat. Assn. for Women in Careers (founding bd. dirs. Cleve. chpt. 1989-91), Coun. for Exceptional Children (pres. Calif. divsn. for early childhood), Kappa Kappa Gamma (exec. bd. Cleve. 1979-90, exec. bd. Hudson, Ohio, 1991-95). Republican. Roman Catholic. Avocation: acting.

BRENNAN, FRANCIS PATRICK, banker; b. Somerville, Mass., Jan. 9, 1917; s. John Joseph and Bridget (Sullivan) B.; m. Mary J. Gilhooly, July 23, 1949; children: Mary Ann, Eileen, John, Thomas. AB cum laude, Boston Coll., 1939; postgrad., Bentley Coll. Accounting and Finance, 1941. Loan officer Reconstrn. Finance Corp., Boston, 1941-42, [illegible] v.p. Mass. Bus. Devel. Corp., Boston, 1954-61; chmn., chief exec. officer Union Warren Savs. Bank, Boston, 1961-87; vice chmn. Home Owners Savs. Bank (merger Union Warren Savs. Bank), Boston, 1987-90. Bd. dirs., trustee, chmn. audit com. Boston Co. Funds, Inc.; chmn., pres., treas. Laurel Mut. Funds, 1993—; bd. dirs., exec. and fin. coms., chmn. audit and salary com. Boston Mut. Life Ins. Co., chmn. Dreyfus/Laurel Mutual Funds. Former trustee vice chmn. exec. com., chmn. fin. com. Stonehill Coll.; chmn. Mass. Bus. Devel. Corp.; mem. Sidney Farber Cancer Inst., Boston; mem. Mass. Hist. Soc.; past bd. dirs. Boston Mcpl. Research Bur., Greater Boston Real Estate Bd., Boston met. chpt. ARC. 2d lt. AUS, 1942-45, ETO. Decorated Bronze Star. Mem. Savs. Banks Assn. Mass. (pres. 1972-73), Mass. Bankers Assn. (dir.-at-large), Greater Boston C. of C. (v.p., admitted to Acad. of Disting. Bostonians 1992), Algonquin Club (Boston), Clover Club (Boston), Winchester Country Club, Madison Sq. Garden Club, Knights of Malta, Knights of Holy Sepulchre. Roman Catholic. Home: 36 Central St Winchester MA 01890-2630

BRENNAN, GEORGE GERARD, pediatrician; b. N.Y.C., Nov. 6, 1931; s. George and Bertha (Bradley) Brennan; m. Joan Worfolk, Oct. 31, 1959; children: Jeanne, Gerry, Robert, James, Thomas. AB, Fordham U., 1953; MD, Loyola U., Chgo., 1957. Intern Jersey City Med. Ctr., 1957-58; pediatric resident St. Vincent's Med. Ctr., N.Y.C., 1958—60; pediatrician Old Bridge-Sayneville Med. Group, P.A., 1958—2002; assoc. prof. clin. pediatrics Robert Wood Johnson Med. Sch.-UMDNJ, 1997—. Fellow Am. Acad. Pediatrics; mem. N.J. State Med. Soc., Middlesex County Med. Soc. Republican. Roman Catholic. Avocations: tennis, literature, music, travel. Office: Pediat and Adolescent Assocs of Cen NJ 100 Perrine Rd Old Bridge NJ 08857 E-mail: ggbrennanmd@comcast.net.

BRENNAN, HENRY HIGGINSON, architect; b. Chgo., Nov. 25, 1932; s. Henry D. and Ann (Higginson) Brennan; m. Margaret Butler, 1960; children: Henry Higginson Jr., Kathryn Ann Brennan Smith, Martin Timothy, Jennifer M. B.Arch., U. Ill., 1958. Registered arch., 12 states. Draftsman Westchester Constrn., White Plains, NY, 1958—59; job capt. Ketchum & Sharp, N.Y.C., 1959—61, project architect, dir. prodn., 1961—73; sr. v.p., dir. N.Y. office Welton Becket, 1973—84; ptnr. Brennan Beer Gorman/Archs., 1984—. Prin. works include master plan and design of maj. office bldgs., hotels, retail and mixed-use complexes. Mem.: AIA, Apawamis Club (Rye, NY). Office: Brennan Beer Gorman Architects 515 Madison Ave New York NY 10022-5403

BRENNAN, JAMES JOSEPH, lawyer, banking and financial services executive; b. Chgo., July 14, 1950; s. John Michael and Rosemary (Rickard) B.; m. Donna Jean Blessing, June 2, 1973; children: Michael James, Laura Jessica. BS, Purdue U., 1972; JD, Indiana U., 1975. Bar: Ind. 1975, U.S. Dist. Ct. (so. dist.) Ind. 1975, U.S. Tax Ct. 1975, U.S. Ct. Appeals (6th cir.) 1976 U. S. Ct. Appeals (4th cir.) 1977, Ill., 1978, U.S. Dist. Ct. (no. dist.) Ill. 1978, U.S. Ct. Appeals (7th cir.) 1978, U.S. Supreme Ct. 1981. Law clk. to judge U.S. Dist. Ct. (ea. dist.), Tenn., 1975-77; ptnr. Pope, Ballard, Shepard & Fowle, Ltd., Chgo., 1977-87, Hopkins & Sutter, Chgo., 1987-91; ptnr., co-chmn. fin. svcs. group Barack, Ferrazzano, Kirschbaum & Perlman, Chgo., 1991-99; exec. v.p. corp. affairs, gen. counsel BankFinancial Corp., 2000—. Chmn. legal affairs com. Ill. Bankers Assn., Chgo., 1986, chmn. bank counsel sect., 1987; lectr. programs for bankers, bank examiners, accts and bank counsel; participant drafting of various Ill. banking laws; adj. prof. grad. sch. bank law Ill. Inst. Tech. Kent Coll. Law, 1992-2000. Articles editor Ind. Law Rev., 1974-75; editor: Ill. Bankers Assn. Law Watch, 1988-94; contbr. articles to profl. jours. 1st recipient Disting. Bank Counsel award Ill. Bankers Assn., 1989. Mem. Riverside Golf Club (bd. dirs. 1992-2000, sec.-treas. 1995-98), Western Golf Assn. (bd. dirs. 1998—, Evans Scholars (Purdue chpt. 1968-72, pres. 1970-71). Office: 15 W 60 Frontage Rd Burr Ridge IL 60527 Business E-Mail: jbrennan@bankfinancial.com.

BRENNAN, JAMES PATRICK, SR., lawyer; b. N.Y.C., June 20, 1947; s. Michael Joseph and Mary Patricia (Regan) B.; m. Ellen Margaret Hall, Nov. 6, 1970; children: James Patrick II, Liam Daniel. BS, Pratt Inst., 1969; JD, St. Mary's U., San Antonio, 1975. Bar: Tex. 1975. Atty. IRS, San Antonio, 1975-80, atty, life insurance securities and tax counsel USAA, San Antonio, 1980—, gen. counsel; instr. Am. Soc. CLU's., San Antonio, 1983-84. Assoc. editor law Jour. St. Mary's U., 1974. Mem. ABA, Tex. Bar Assn., Estate Planning Coun. San Antonio, Am. Soc. CLU's., Am. Soc. Charted Fin. Cons., Nat. Assn. Health Underwriters. Republican. Roman Catholic. Office: USAA VP Life Ins C-3-W 7800 Fredericksburg Rd San Antonio TX 78229-3418

BRENNAN, JOHN JOSEPH, lawyer, legal administrator; b. Troy, N.Y., Nov. 1, 1958; s. James Patrick and Grace Marie (Bartolomeo) B. AAS, Schenectady (N.Y) Community Coll., 1978; BA cum laude, Siena Coll., 1981; JD cum laude, Union U., 1985. Bar: N.Y. 1986, U.S. Dist. Ct. (no. dist.) N.Y. 1986, U.S. Supreme Ct. 1999. Law clk. to Appellate Divsn. Justice 4th Dept., Herkimer, N.Y., 1985-86; assoc. law ck. to justice State Supreme Ct., Herkimer, 1986-90; law clk. to U.S. Magistrate-Judge, Utica, N.Y., 1991-92; assoc. law clk. to justice N.Y. Supreme Ct., Utica, 1992—2001, 2002—. Adj. prof. Herkimer County CC, 2003—; mem. panel Surrogate Decision Making Program, 2002—. Bd. dirs. Mohawk Valley Red Cross, Utica Zoo. Mem. ABA, N.Y. State Bar Assn., Oneida County Bar Assn. (bd. dirs.), Herkimer County Bar Assn. (treas. 1990), KC, Pi Gamma Mu. Roman Catholic. Avocations: running, skiing. Home: 119 Court St Herkimer NY 13350-1923 Office: Herkimer County Ct House Utica NY 13350

BRENNAN, JOHN WILLIAM, lawyer, real estate broker; b. Norfolk, Va., May 26, 1940; s. John Leo and Ann Virginia B.; m. Sarah Charlotte Albrecht, July 2, 1966; children: John William, Jr., Anne Alexander, James Rayfield. BA, Duke U., 1963; JD, U. Va., 1966. Staff atty. Fed. Trade Commn., Washington, 1966-70; asst. Washington counsel U.S. Savings and Loan League, Washington, 1970-77; pres., CEO, dir. Mt. Vernon Savings Assn., Alexandria, 1977-80; dir. Va., Md. and D.C. Foremost Guaranty Corp., Madison, Wis., 1980-82; pvt. practice Fairfax, Va., 1982-92; assoc. Scanlon & Assocs., Manassas, Va., 1992-93; pvt. practice Portsmouth, Va., 1993-95; commercial realtor, legal counsel Barrick Tri-City Real Estate, Portsmouth, 1995—. Bd. dirs. Fairfax County United Way, Annandale, Va., 1985-86; pres., dir. Hampton Roads Affordable Housing, Inc., Portsmouth, 1997-2000. Placed 1st Ann. Golf Tournament, Fed. Home Loan Bank Bd., Washington, 1971,75, 79, State Savings and Loan Supprs., Colorado Springs, Colo., 1973, Va. Savings and Loan League, Hilton Head, S.C., 1980; recipient Grand Prize Vince Lombardi Golf Tournament Vince Lombardi Meml. Fund., 1975. Mem. Am. Philatelic Soc., U. Va. Alumni Assn. (life), Va. State Bar Assn., SAR, Olde Towne Civic Assn. Episcopalian. Avocations: antique collecting, golf, stamp collecting, swimming, hiking. Home: 416 North St Portsmouth VA 23704-2522 Office: Barrick Tri-City Real Estate 3403 County St # C Portsmouth VA 23707-3233

BRENNAN, LAWRENCE EDWARD, electronics engineer; b. Oak Park, Ill., Jan. 29, 1927; s. Lawrence John and Lillian Irene (Day) B.; m. Mary Ellen Green, Aug. 9, 1947; children: Kathleen, Marianne, Teresa, James. BS in Elec. Engring., U. Ill, 1948; PhD Elec. Engring., U. Ill., 1951. Mem. tech. staff Rand Corp., Santa Monica, Calif., 1957-67; chief scientist Tech. Service Corp., Santa Monica, 1967-80; v.p. Adaptive Sensors, Inc., Santa Monica, 1980-93; cons. pvt. practice, Orange Beach, Ala., 1993—. Served with USN, 1944-46. Fellow IEEE E-mail: lbrennan@gulftel.com.

BRENNAN, MATTHEW CANNON, English literature educator, poet; b. Richmond Heights, Mo., Jan. 18, 1955; s. William Joseph and Suzanne (Simon) B.; m. Laura Lee Fredendall, Aug. 13, 1977 (div. June 1987); 1 child, Daniel William; m. Beverley Simms, May 21, 1994. AB, Grinnell Coll., 1977; MA, U. Minn., Mpls., 1980, PhD, 1984. Editor Golle and Holmes Fin. Learning, Minnetonka, Minn., 1982-84; vis. asst. prof. U. Minn., Mpls., 1984-85; asst. prof. Ind. State U., Terre Haute, 1985-88, assoc. prof., 1988-92, prof. English, 1992—. Author: (poetry) Seeing in the Dark: Poems, 1993, The Music of Exile: Poems, 1994, American Scenes: Poems on WPA Artworks, 2001, (monograph) Wordsworth, Turner, and Romantic Landscape, 1987, The Gothic Psyche, 1997; co-editor: (exhbn. catalog) Is Poetry a Visual Art?, 1993. Ind. Arts Commn. fellow, 1994; Thomas Merton Ctr. Poetry Prize, 1999, Theodore Dreiser Disting. Rsch./Creativity award, 2002; Univ. Rsch. grantee Ind. State U., Terre Haute, 1991, 96, Univ. Arts grantee, 1993, 98, 2001; named to Acad. Am. Poets, U. Minn., Mpls., 1979, 80, 84. Mem. Wordsworth-Coleridge Assn., Phi Beta Kappa, Phi Kappa Phi. Avocations: travel, film. Home: 1013 Maple Ave Terre Haute IN 47804-2936 Office: Ind State U Dept English Terre Haute IN 47809-0001 E-mail: mbrennan@indstate.edu.

BRENNAN, MAUREEN, lawyer; b. Morristown, N.J., Aug. 7, 1949; BA magna cum laude, Bryn Mawr Coll., 1971; JD cum laude, Boston Coll., 1977. Bar: Pa. 1977, U.S. Dist. Ct. (ea. dist.) Pa. 1978, Ohio 1989. Atty. U.S. EPA, Washington, 1977-80; asst. dist. atty. Phila. Trial and Appellate Divs., 1980-84; in-house environ. counsel TRW, Inc., 1985-87; assoc. Baker & Hostetler, Cleve., 1987-91, ptnr., 1991—. Adj. prof. Case Western Res. U., Cleve., 1990-92, 2000-01. Active Cleve. Tree Commn., 1991-96, co-chair, 1993-95; trustee Clean-Land Ohio, 1990-2000; rep. Canal Heritage Corridor Com., 2000—; mem. Cuyahoga County Greenspace Working Group, 1999—; bd. dirs. Crown Point Ecology Ctr., 2001--. Recipient Bronze Medal for Achievement, U.S. EPA, 1980. Mem. ABA (natural resources and environ. sect., standing com. environ law 1996-98), Pa. Bar Assn. (environ. law com.), Ohio State Bar Assn. (environ. law com.), Cleve. Bar Assn. (environ. law sect., chair wetlands com. 1991-92, sect. chair 1996-97, mem. steering com. adv. OEPA on Brownfield regulations 1995-97). Office: Baker & Hostetler LLP 3200 Nat City Center 1900 E 9th St Ste 3200 Cleveland OH 44114-3475 E-mail: mbrennan@bakerlaw.com.

BRENNAN, NOEL-ANNE GERSON, anthropologist, educator, writer; b. N.Y.C., Apr. 12, 1948; d. Noel Bertram Gerson and Nancy (Hasenwinkle) Hendriks; m. James Beach Brennan, July 27, 1968; 1 child, Anne Wendy. BA in Anthropology, Brown U., 1970; MA in Sociology and Anthropology, U. R.I., 1982. Writer, rschr., 1973—78, 1980—. Tchg. asst. anthropology U. R.I., Kingston, 1978—80, instr. sociology, 1985—, adj. asst. prof. women's studies, 1986—, mem. women's studies adv. bd., 1980—, mem. women's ctr. governing bd., 1981—83; ptnr. Ocean Wind Electric Co., Peace Dale, RI, 1980—86; instr. anthropology YWCA R.I., Saunderstown, 1983. Author: (book) The Goodspeed Opera House, 1974, Winter Reckoning, 1986, The Sword of the Land, 2003; contbr. articles and poetr ty various profl. jours. and mags. Sponsor Ctr. Environ. Edn., 1981—; mem. Internat. Snow Leopard Trust, World Wildlife Fund. Mem.: New Eng. Women's Studies Assn., Nat. Women's Anthropology Caucus, R.I. Animal Rescue League, Planetary Soc., Nature Conservancy. Home: 231 Curtis Corner Rd Peace Dale RI 02879-2129

BRENNAN, NORMA JEAN, professional society publications director; b. Helena, Mont., Apr. 16, 1939; d. Harland Sanford Herrin and Elizabeth (Wardlaw) Brumfield; m. Anthony E. Brennan, Dec. 4, 1964 (div. Mar. 1986); children: Christopher E., Kimberly A. BA, U. Pacific, 1960. Editorial asst. Am. Rocket Soc., N.Y.C., 1961-62, asst. mng. editor, 1962-65; mng. editor AIAA, N.Y.C., 1978-80, publs. divsn. dir. N.Y.C., Washington,Reston, Va., 1980—. Mem. Young Republicans, Stockton, Calif., 1958-60; vol. Mt. Sinai Hosp., N.Y.C., 1962-64. Fellow: AIAA (assoc. Space Shuttle Flag award); mem.: Washington Women's Info. Network, N.Am. Serials Interest Group, Coun. Engring. and Sci. Soc. Execs., Assn. Am. Pubs., Coun. Sci. Editors, Soc. for Scholarly Pub. (bd. dirs.). Avocations: reading, travel, gardening. Home: 11551 Links Dr Reston VA 20190-4820 Office: AIAA 1801 Alexander Bell Dr Reston VA 20191-4344 E-mail: normab@aiaa.org.

BRENNAN, PATRICIA FLATLEY, nursing educator, systems engineering educator; b. July 21, 1953; BSN, U. Del., 1975; MSN, U. Pa., 1979; MS in Indsl. Engring., U. Wis., 1984, PhD in Indsl. Engring., 1986. RN, Ohio. Staff nurse surg. ICU Lankenau Hosp., Phila., 1975-76; clin. nurse mgr./practitioner Friends Hosp., Phila., 1976-80; asst. prof. psychiat. nursing Marquette U., Milw., 1980-83; lectr. quantitative analysis U. Wis., Madison, 1984; asst. prof. nursing and systems engring. Frances Payne Bolton Sch. Nursing, Case Inst. Tech., Case Western Res. U., Cleve., 1986-89, assoc. prof., 1989-92; Lillian Moehlman-Bascom prof. nursing U. Wis., Madison, prof., indsl. engring. Mem. health care study sect. Nat. Ctr. Health Svcs. Rsch., 1989—; participant Coun. Nurse Researchers, 1981—, Nat. Conf. on Nursing Minimum Data Set, Milw., 1985, Nursing Use of Decision Support Workshop, Killarney, Ireland, 1988; guest lectr. Coll. Nursing, U. Wis., 1986, 89; mem. vis. faculty Campus for the Professions, U. Md., 1987, 89, 91, 92, U. Wis., 1989, U. Calgary, Alta., Can., 1989; presenter numerous profl. and edn1. orgns., 1981—. Mem. editorial bd. Computers in Nursing, 1988—; reviewer publs. Symposium on Computer Applications in Med. Care, 1982—, Rsch. in Nursing and Health, 1985—, Tech. MEDINFO86, 1985; contbr. articles to profl. publs. Mem. adv. bd. Sch. Nursing, U. Md., 1986—; active data consortium AIDS Commn. Cleve., 1989; vol. Am. Cancer Soc., 1983-86. Rsch. grantee Marquette U., 1981, Regner Fund, 1982, USPHS, 1982-86, Cleve. Found., 1987, NIH, 1987—, Mellon Found., 1987, Nat. Ctr. Nursing Rsch. 1988-91, Nat. Inst. on Aging, 1989—. Fellow Am. Acad. Nursing; mem. ANA, AACCN (mem. info. systems task force 1986-87), Ohio Nurses Assn. (mem. rsch. assembly, mem. GCNA), Am. Inst. Decision Scis. (mem. membership com., reviewer ann. meetings), Inst. Indsl. Engrs. (chpt. devel. chairperson 1987—), Inst. Medicine, The Mgmt. Sci. Inst.-Ops. Rsch. Soc. Am., Sigma Xi, Sigma Theta Tau. Office: U Wis-Madison Module K4 K6/340 Clin Sci Ctr 600 Highland Ave Madison WI 53792

BRENNAN, PATRICK THOMAS, meteorology company executive, meteorologist; b. Fabius, N.Y., Jan. 29, 1952; s. Thomas William and Mary Patricia (Herlihy) Brennan. BA in Meteorology, SUNY, Oswego, 1974; MS, SUNY, Stony Brook, 1978. Cert. cons. meteorologist. Meteorologist Smith-Singer Meteorologist, Amityville, NY, 1974-76, Meteorol. Evaluation Svcs., Amityville, 1977-81, v.p., 1981-86, pres., 1987—. Contbr. articles to profl. jours. Mem.: AAAS, N.Y. Acad. Sci., Wind Engring. Rsch. Coun., Am. Meteorol. Soc., Am. Nuc. Soc., Clocks Blvd. Yacht Club, Amityville Club. Republican. Roman Catholic. Avocations: sailing, skiing. Home: 201 Trouville Rd Copiague NY 11726-3018 Office: Meteorol Evaluation Svcs Co Inc 165 Broadway Amityville NY 11701-2703

BRENNAN, ROBERT LAWRENCE, educational director, psychometrician; b. Hartford, Conn., May 31, 1944; s. Robert and Irene Veronica (Connors) B. BA, Salem State Coll., 1967; M of Art in Tchg., Harvard U., 1968, EdD, 1970.

Rsch. assoc., lectr. Grad. Sch. Edn., Harvard U., Cambridge, Mass., 1970-71; asst. prof. edn. SUNY, Stony Brook, 1971-76; sr. rsch. psychologist Am. Coll. Testing Program, Iowa City, 1976-79, dir. measurement rsch. dept., 1979-84, asst. v.p. for measurement rsch., 1984-92, disting. rsch. scientist, 1990-94. Dir. Iowa Testing Programs, 1994-2002; adj. faculty Sch. Edn. U. Iowa, 1979-94, E.F. Lindquist prof. edn. measurement, 1994—, dir. ctr. for advanced studies in measurement and assessment, 2002—. Author: Elements of Generalizability Theory, 1983, Test Equating Methods and Practices, 1995, Generalizability Theory, 2001; editor: Methodology Used in Scaling the Act Assessment and P-ACT, 1989, Cognitively Diagnostic Assessment, 1995; assoc. editor Applied Psychological Measurement, 1982—, Jour. Ednl. Measurement, 1978-83, 96—; contbr. articles to profl. jours. Harvard U. prize fellow, 1967. Fellow: APA; mem.: Iowa Acad. Edn. (pres. 1996—99), Psychometric Soc., Nat. Coun. Measurement Edn. (bd. dirs. 1987—90, v.p. 1995, pres. 1997—98, Tech. Contbn. award 1997, Career Contbn. award 2000), Am. Statis. Assn., Midwestern Ednl. Rsch. Assn. (pres. 1987—88), Am. Ednl. Rsch. Assn. (v.p. 1994—96, Divsn. D award 1980). Home: 1925 Liberty Ln Coralville IA 52241-1071 Office: U Iowa 297 Lindquist Ctr N Iowa City IA 52242-1533 E-mail: robert-brennan@uiowa.edu.

BRENNAN, SARA JEAN, retired artist; b. Atlanta, Dec. 25, 1936; d. Donald Patton and Sarah Frances (Wilkerson) Macleod; m. William Raymond Brennan, June 13, 1959; children: Melinda Jean, William Raymond Jr., Stuart Anthony. BS, Fla. State U., 1959. Artist Crisp & Harrison Advt., Jacksonville, Fla., Douglas Printing, Jacksonville; artist, dir. Jeanne Morehead Advt., Tampa, Fla.; artist Bill Hudson Advt., Nashville; freelance artist Conv. and Visitors Bur., Macon, Ga., Southeastern Antiques and Collectibles, Macon, Macon Mag. Artist Antebellum Trail, Macon, Hist. Heartland Travel Assn., Macon; art dir., editor Southeastern Antiques and Collectibles Newspaper. Photo montage, Macon - Looking Up, 1987; illustrator (poster/calendar) Cherry Blossom Festival, Macon, 1989. Artist vol. St. John's Episc. Ch., Tampa, 1970—78, St. George's Episc. Ch., Nashville, 1978—80, Christ Ch., Macon, 1980—2003. Recipient Addy award, Advt. Club of Macon, 1989. Mem.: Healy Point Golf and Country Club. Republican. Episcopalian. Avocations: golf, travel, doll house miniatures, decorating.

BRENNAN, STEPHEN JAMES, physical education educator, consultant; BA in Broadcast Journalism and English, U. Nebr., 1973, MEd in Ednl. Adminstrn., 1978, M in Phys. Edn. and Sport Psychology, 1986; PhD in Performance and Health Psychology, U. Nebr., Lincoln, 2001. Tchr., basketball coach Archbishop Ryan H.S., Omaha, 1974-75; tchr., coach Ralston (Nebr.) H.S., 1975-80, Valley (Nebr.) H.S., 1980-84, U. Nebr., Lincoln, 1984-86; founder, pres. Peak Performance Cons., Omaha, 1986—. Performance cons. Kansas City Royals, 1989-94; head basketball coach East All Star Team, Fremont, Nebr., 1981; founder, exec. dir. Midwest Youth Coaches Assn., 1990—, Nat. Assn. Coll. Athletic Recruiters, 1999; exec. dir. The Recruiters Inst., 1993—, The Recruiters Libr., 1993—; pres. Ctr. for Performance Enhancement Rsch. and Edn., 1999—; adj. faculty U. Nebr.-Omaha, 2002—. Author: The Mental Edge: Basketball's Peak Performance Workbook, 1987, 2nd edit., 1993, 3rd edit., 2002, The Sport Performance Report, 1990, Competitive Excellence: The Psychology and Strategy of Successful Team Building, 1990, Competitive Excellence: The Psychology and Strategy of Successful Team Building, 2nd edit., 1995, (with others) Basketball Resource Guide, 1989, 2nd edit., 1995, The Recruiters Bible, 2000, 6 Psychological Factors for Success, 2001; editor: Inside Recruiting: The Master Guide to Successful College Athletic Recruiting, Vol. I, 1998, Vol. II, 1999, Vol. III, 2000; contbr. numerous articles to profl. jours. Mem. AAHPERD, Assn. for Advancement of Applied Sport Psychology, Nat. Assn. Sport and Phys. Edn., Nat. Assn. Basketball Coaches, Nat. Fedn. State H.S. Assns., Nat. Assn. Sports Ofcls., Nat. Fedn. Interscholastic Ofcls. Assn., Nat. H.S. Athletic Coaches Assn., Nebr. Coaches Assn., Midwest Officials Assn., Omaha Met. Area Basketball Coaches Assn. Home and Office: 14728 Shirley St Omaha NE 68144-2144

BRENNAN, THOMAS EMMETT, lawyer; b. Detroit, May 27, 1929; s. Joseph Terence and Jeannette Frances (Sullivan) B.; m. Pauline Mary Weinberger, Apr. 28, 1951; children: Thomas Emmett, Margaret Ann and John Seamus (twins), William Joseph, Marybeth, Ellen Mary. LL.B., U. Detroit, 1952; LL.D., Thomas M. Cooley Law Sch., 1976. Bar: Mich. 1953. Assoc. Kenny, Radom, Rockwell & Mountain, Detroit, 1952-53; ptnr. Waldron, Brennan & Maher, Detroit, 1953-61; judge Detroit Ct. Common Pleas, 1962-63, Wayne County Circuit Ct., 1963-66; justice Mich. Supreme Ct., 1967-73, chief justice, 1969-70; adj. prof. polit. sci. U. Detroit, 1970-72; founder, pres., dean emeritus Thomas M. Cooley Law Sch., Lansing, 1972—; of counsel Riley, Roumell and Connolly, Detroit, 2002—. Mem. Mich. Commn. Law Enforcement and Criminal Justice, 1969-70; bd. dirs. Motor Wheel Corp., 1987-89. Author: Judging the Law Schools, 1997, The Bench, 2000. Founder, commr. Am. Golf League, 2000; bd. dir. Cath. League for Religious & Civil Rights, 1993—. Fellow Am. Bar Found., Mich Bar Found.; mem. ABA, Ingham County Bar Assn., State Bar Mich. (bd. commrs. 1979-83), Mich. Assn. of Professions (Disting. Citizens award 1982), Assn. of Ind. Colls. and Univs. Mich. (bd. dirs., exec. com., sec. 1990, chmn. 1991), Cath. Lawyers Soc. (Thomas More award 1987), Am. Jurisprudence Soc., Inc. Soc., Irish Am. Lawyers, Cooley Legal Author's Soc. (charter), v.p.-treas. 1990—), Mich. State C. of C. (bd. dirs. 1988-94), Walnut Hills Country Club (bd. dirs. 1992-95), Detroit Athletic Club, KC, Delta Theta Phi. Roman Catholic. Office: Thomas M Cooley Law Sch 217 S Capitol Ave Lansing MI 48933-1503 Home: American Golf League 14150 6th Street Dade City FL 33525

BRENNAN, THOMAS GEORGE, JR., audiologist, speech-language pathologist; b. S.I., N.Y., Jan. 19, 1953; s. Thomas George Sr. and Gladys Kathleen (Atkinson) B. BS in Edn., Stephen F. Austin State U., 1981, MEd, 1984. Cert. clin. competence in audiology and speech-lang. pathology; cert. indsl. audiometric technician Coun. Accreditation on Occupl. Hearing Conservation; registered hearing aid dispenser; registered hearing tester. Piano tuner, technician Brennan's Piano Tuning and Repair, Nacogdoches, Tex., 1972—; pvt. practice audiology assoc. Nacogdoches, 1985-89; pvt. practice speech-lang. pathologist, 1989—; pvt. practice audiologist, 1992—. Computer programmer, Nacogdoches, 1984—. Author: An Introduction to Biofeedback for Speech-Language Therapists, 1985, rev. edit., 1998, Behavior Checklist, 1993, A Guide to Speech-Language-Hearing Screening for Related Service Providers, 1993, rev. 1996, Computer Auditory Test, 1993, Diagnostic Audiometric Tests, 1994, rev. 2000, An Introduction to the Use of Frequency Shifted Ultrasound as an Assessment Tool in Speech Pathology, 1996, rev. 2000, Environmental Sound Test, 1997, The Blind Leading the Blind, 2002, rev. 2002; author, programmer: (computer program, manual) Fear Survey, 1990. Screener East Tex. Cmty. Health Svcs., Nacogdoches, 1991-93; svc. provider Health Fair, Nacogdoches, 1992-94, Child Health Jamboree Com., Nacogdoches, 1992-94. Mem. Am. Speech-Lang.-Hearing Assn., Am. Tinnitus Assn. (referral source), Nat. Fedn. of the Blind, Mensa. Home: 2209 Pearl St Lot 11 Nacogdoches TX 75965-3464

BRENNAN, THOMAS JOHN, city and state official, consultant, educator; b. Bklyn., Mar. 23, 1923; s. Thomas Joseph and Violet Emma (Jurgens) B.; m. Margaret Karen Jensen, Sept. 18, 1948; children: Debra Gail, Mark Kevin, Laurie Kathleen. AB, Wittenberg Coll., 1949; MGA, U. Pa., 1950. Dep. sec. for adminstrn. Dept. Welfare, Commonwealth Pa., Harrisburg, 1957-59; dep. sec. for state properties Pa. Dept. Property and Supplies, 1959-64; exec. officer Del. Dept. Mental Health, Dover, 1965-67; v.p. Exec. Mgmt. Svc., Arlington, Va., 1967-76; exec. dir. Gov.'s Justice Commn. Pa. Commn. on Crime and Juvenile Delinquency, 1976-79; dir. water utility City of New Brunswick, N.J., 1983-91, chief labor negotiator, 1988-91, pers. mgr., 1988-91, exec. officer police dept., 1989-91, pub. mgmt. cons., 1991—. Adj. instr. U. Del., 1965—67; adj. assoc. prof. Rider Coll., Lawrenceville, NJ, 1983—84, Lawrenceville, 1984—85; hearing officer N.J. Dept. Civic Svc., Trenton, 1976—2002; cons. exam. constrn., 1985—2000; cons. to staff com. UN, 1982—84; cons. various municipalities and agys.; presenter papers to profl. orgns. Bd. dirs. Bucks County Opera, Pa., 1975-80, Bucks County Play House, New Hope, Pa., 1970s; elected mem. alumni coun. Wittenberg U., 1989—; mem. Merrill's Mauraders, WWII. Decorated Silver Star, Bronze Star with 2 oak leaf clusters, Combat Infantry badge; recipient various plaques; Fels scholar U. Pa., 1948. Mem. VFW (Post #6393), Internat. Personnel Mgmt. Assn., Am. Pub. Works Assn. (dist. rep. Eastern Pa. bldg. and grounds com.), Am. Water Works Assn., Internat. Chief of Police Assn., Nat. Conf. State Justice Planning Adminstrn. (regional chmn., mem. exec. com.), Criminal Justice Tng. Inst. (chmn. planning com. 1978, 79), Huntington Valley Hunt (Bucks County, bd. dirs. 1975-80), Am. Legion (post #79), Upper Makefield Hist. Soc. (dir.), Wharton Alumni (Phila.), Fraternal Order of Police. Avocations: fox hunting, pleasure riding. Home: 327 Pineville Rd Newtown PA 18940-3111

BRENNAN, TIMOTHY WILLIAM, not-for-profit fundraiser; b. Richmond Heights, Mo., June 29, 1951; s. William Joseph and Suzanne (Simon) B.; m. Nancy Jane Hamann, May 24, 1987. BA, U. Mo., 1972; MA, Wash. U., 1977; MBA, Wharton Sch., 1980. Bus. mgr. Phila. Drama Guild, 1980-83; gen. mgr. South Coast Repertory, Costa Mesa, Calif., 1983-86; mng. dir. Hartman Theatre Co., Stamford, Conn., 1987; first v.p. Silver Screen Mgmt., N.Y.C., 1987-94; CFO Playhouse Internat. Pictures, N.Y.C., 1994—96; prin. Brennan Cons., Norwich, Conn., 1996—2000; dir. devel. CERES, Inc., Boston, 2000—. Part-time faculty, Marymount Manhattan Coll., N.Y.C., 1989. Mem. Phi Beta Kappa, Beta Gamma Sigma. Home: 66 Bullard St Sharon MA 02067-1087 Office: CERES Inc 99 Chauncy Boston MA 02111-1703

BRENNAN, TRACY ELIZABETH, physician; b. 1956; d. John Patrick and Barbara (Kolb) B.; m. Neville J. Graham, Aug. 9, 1986; children: Neville, Dierdre Brennan, Maura, Patrick. BS, U. Conn., 1978; MD, Northwestern U., 1983. Intern Hartford (Conn.) Hosp., 1979-80, resident, 1980-83, with. Elected mem. med. staff Hartford Hosp., 1993-96; co-chmn. Red & Black Ball Hartford Hosp., 1997; bd. dirs. Birthright Conn.; mem. sch. bd. St. Brigid Sch., Conn., 1996—2002; mem. bd. corporators Hartford Hosp. Named to, Best Doctors in Am., 1996—. Fellow Am. Coll. Ob-gyn. Roman Catholic. Office: Hartford Ob-Gyn Group 136 Retreat Ave Hartford CT 06106-2529

BRENNAN, WILLIAM COLLINS, JR., lawyer; b. Northampton, Mass., Nov. 23, 1951; s. William Collins and Doreen Angela (Murphy) B.; m. Ann Marie Simonetta, Aug. 18, 1973; 1 son, James P. B.A. magna cum laude, Boston Coll., 1973; J.D., Cath. U. Am., 1976. Bar: Md. 1976, D.C. 1977, U.S. Supreme Ct. 1980; cert. specialist in criminal trial advocacy Nat. Bd. Trial Advocacy. Assoc. DePaul, Willoner & Kenkel, P.A., College Park, Md., 1976-80; ptnr. Knight, Manzi, Brennan, Ostrom & Ham, P.A., Upper Marlboro, Md., 1980—; counselor Am. Inn of Ct. LXII, Prince George's County. Mem. Addictions Adv. Council Prince George's County, 1984. Mem. ABA, Assn. Trial Lawyers Am., Nat. Assn. Criminal Def. Lawyers, Md. State Bar Assn., Md. Trial Lawyers Assn., Md. Criminal Def. Attys. (bd. dirs. 1987—), Prince George's County Bar Assn., Phi Beta Kappa. Democrat. Roman Catholic. Lodge: KC. Home: 8221 Canning Ter Greenbelt MD 20770-2705 Office: Knight Manzi Brennan Ostrom & Ham PA 14440 Old Mill Rd Upper Marlboro MD 20772-3088

BRENNAN, WILLIAM JOSEPH, manufacturing company executive; b. Buffalo, Feb. 11, 1928; s. Laurence J. and Mary Julia (Scherer) B.; m. Rita Jeanne Brooks, Dec. 27, 1947; 1 dau., Susan. BA, Bryant and Stratton Coll., 1949. With Fedders Corp., 1949—, asst. controller corp., 1962-64, dir. distbn. brs., 1965-67, v.p., dir. sales, 1967-74, v.p., dir. adminstrn., 1974-77; pres. Fedders Fin. Corp., 1977-78, group v.p. diversified products, 1978-80, v.p. fin., chief fin. officer, 1980; exec. v.p., chief fin. officer, dir. Fedders Corp., Peapack, N.J., 1986-87; pres. NYCOR Inc., Peapack, 1987-88; fin. cons. Fedders Corp., NYCOR Inc., 1988—. Bd. dirs. Fedders Corp.; chmn. bd. dirs. CSM Environ.; arbitrator NYSE. Served with AUS, 1946-47. Republican. Roman Catholic. Home and Office: 224 Whispering Woods Ct Little Silver NJ 07739 E-mail: bb842@aol.com.

BRENNAN-SPARKS, JENNIFER ANNE, writer; b. Farnborough, Hampshire, United Kingdom, Aug. 20, 1935; arrived in U.S., 1969; d. Gordon Arthur Thomas and Lucette May (Whitburn) Pritchard; m. Arthur Joseph Sparks; children: Jonathan (dec.), Adam. Diploma, Salisbury (Eng.) Coll. Art, 1956. Woman's editor, columnist The Bangkok World, 1962-64; art dir. Marklin Advt., Bangkok, 1966-69; coord. Pacific chpt. UN Assn. USA, L.A., 1972-76; mng. dir. Pritchard, Ltd., Bangkok, 1974-75; publicity dir. Pacific chpt. UN Assn. USA, L.A., 1976-81; owner, dir. instr. The Asian Experience, Playa del Rey, Calif., 1977-83. Contbg. weekly columnist L.A. Herald-Examiner, 1979-83. Author of numerous books, including Curries and Bugles; A Memoir and a Cookbook of the British Raj, 1990, La Cucina Thailandese, 1989, Encyclopedia of Chinese and Oriental Cookery, 1989, One-dish Meals of Asia, 1986, The Cuisines of Asia, 1984, Thai Cooking, 1981, The Original Thai Cookbook, 1981. Mem. AFTRA, Royal Soc. for Asian Affairs, Am. Legion. Avocations: painting, gardening, cooking, researching. Home: 4634 36th St San Diego CA 92116

BRENNECKE, ALLEN EUGENE, lawyer; b. Marshalltown, Iowa, Jan. 8, 1937; s. Arthur Lynn and Julia Alice (Allen) B; m. Billie Jean Johnstone, June 12, 1958; children: Scott, Stephen, Beth, Gregory, Kristen BBA, U. Iowa, 1959, JD, 1961. Bar: Iowa 1961. Law clk. U.S. Dist. Judge, Des Moines, 1961-62; assoc. Mote, Wilson & Welp, Marshalltown, Iowa, 1962-66; ptnr. Harrison, Brennecke, Moore, Smaha & McKibben, Marshalltown, 1966—. Contr. articles to profl. jours. Bd. dirs. Marshalltown YMCA, 1966-71; mem. bd. trustees Iowa Law Sch. Found., 1973-86, United Meth. Ch., Marshalltown, 1978-81, 87-89; fin. chmn. Rep. party 4th Congl. Dist., Iowa, 1970-73, Marshall County Rep. Party, Iowa, 1967-70. Fellow ABA (chmn. ho. of dels. 1984-86, bd. govs. 1982-86), Nat. Jud. Coll. (bd. dirs. 1982-88), Am. Coll. Trusts and Estates Counsel, Am. Coll. Tax Counsel, Am. Bar Found., Iowa Bar Assn. (pres. 1990-91, award of merit 1987); mem. Masons, Shriners, Promise Keepers. Republican. Methodist. Avocations: golf, travel, sports. Home: 703 Circle Dr Marshalltown IA 50158-3809 Office: Harrison Brennecke Moore Smaha & McKibben 302 Masonic Temple Marshalltown IA 50158

BRENNECKE, HENRY MARTIN, chemical engineer, researcher; b. Saratoga, Tex., July 16, 1924; s. Charles Henry and Mary Eleanora Grace (Carlson) Brennecke; children: Jeff Martin, Joy Alice. BS in Chem. Engring., Tex.A&M, College Station, 1947; PhD, U. Tex., Austin, 1954. Refinery engr. Taylor Refinery, Corpus Christi, Tex., 1947—50; rsch. engr. Carney's Point and Eastern labs. E.I. du Pont, Repauno, NJ, 1954—70, rsch. engr. Wilmington (Del.) Exptl. Sta., 1970—74; tech. specialist E. I. du Pont, Ingleside, Tex., 1974—84. Vol. Corpus Christi Better Govt. Com., 1984—2001; vol. Corpus Christi Mus. Sci. and History, 1984—2002. Seaman 1st class USNR, 1944—46. Democrat. Achievements include patents for 4 new processes. Home: 5261 River Oaks Dr Corpus Christi TX 78413

BRENNEISE, HARVEY RAY, library director; b. Palo Alto, Calif., Jan. 26, 1951; s. Ehud and Verna Sylvesta Brenneise; life ptnr. Richard Edward Lewis, Oct. 23, 1953; children: Bruce Alan, Julie Christine. BA, Andrews U., 1973, MA, 1974; MSLS, U. N.C., 1979. Prof. libr. sci. Andrews U., Berrien Springs, Mich., 1979—98; libr. dir. Mich. Cmty. Health Electronic Libr., Okemos, 1998—. Contbr. articles to profl. jours. Co-chmn. Gay, Lesbian, Straight Edn. Network, Lansing, Mich., 2000; chmn. ManKind Project, Windsor, Canada, 2003. Mem.: APHA, ALA, Mich. Pub. Health Assn. (bd. mem. 2001), Med. Libr. Assn., Mich. Health Scis. Libr. Assn. (chair tech. com. 1998), Michiana Orchid Soc. (pres. 1990), Am. Orchid Soc. (chair libr. com. 1997—2002), Phi Kappa Phi, Alpha Mu Gamma, Phi Alpha Theta. Avocations: travel, reading. Home: 5441 Wild Oak Dr East Lansing MI 48823 Office: Mich Pub Health Inst Ste 389 2436 Woodlake Cir Okemos MI 48864 Office Fax: 517-324-8327. Personal E-mail: harveyb@msu.edu. E-mail: hbrenne@mphi.org.

BRENNEMAN, DELBERT JAY, lawyer; b. Albany, Oreg., Feb. 4, 1950; s. Calvin M. and Velma Barbara (Whitaker) B.; m. Caroline Yorke Allen, May 29, 1976; children: Mark Stuart, Thomas Allen. BS magna cum laude, Oreg. State U., 1972; JD, U. Oreg., 1976. Bar: Oreg. 1976, U.S. Dist. Ct. Oreg. 1977, U.S. Ct. Appeals (9th cir.) 1977. Assoc. Schwabe, Williamson, and Wyatt, Portland, Oreg., 1976-83, ptnr., 1984-92, Hoffman, Hart & Wagner, Portland, Oreg., 1993—. Spkr. Oreg. Self-Ins., 1978, 90; seminar instr. U. Oreg. Law Sch., Eugene, 1980. Mem. ABA, Oreg. State Bar Assn., Multnomah County Bar Assn. (spkr. 1983-84), Order of Coif, Multnomah Athletic Club, Propeller Club of U.S. (bd. dirs. 1983-85), Phi Kappa Phi, Beta Gamma Sigma. Office: Hoffman Hart & Wagner 1000 SW Broadway Fl 20 Portland OR 97205-3035 E-mail: djb@hhw.com.

BRENNEMAN, HUGH WARREN, JR., judge; b. Lansing, Mich., July 4, 1945; s. Hugh Warren and Irma June Brenneman; m. Catherine Brenneman; 2 children. BA, Alma Coll., 1967; JD, U. Mich., 1970. Bar: Mich. 1970, D.C. 1975, U.S. Dist. Ct. (we. dist.) Mich. 1974, U.S. Dist. Ct. Md. 1973, U.S. Ct. Mil. Appeals 1971, U.S. Ct. Appeals (6th cir.) 1976, U.S. Ct. Appeals (D.C. cir.) 1981, U.S. Supreme Ct. 1980. Law clk. Mich. 30th Jud. Cir., Lansing, 1970-71; asst. U.S. atty. Dept. Justice, Grand Rapids, Mich., 1974-77; assoc. Bergstrom, Slykhouse & Shaw PC, Grand Rapids, 1977—80; magistrate judge US Dist. Ct. (we. dist.) Mich., Grand Rapids, 1980—. Instr. Western Mich. U., Grand Valley State U., 1989-92. Mem. exec. bd. and adv. coun. Gerald R Ford coun. Boy Scouts Am., 1984—, v.p., 1988-92; mem. Grand Rapids Hist. Commn., 1991-97, pres., 1995-97; dir. Cmty. Reconciliation Ctr., 1991. Capt. JAGC, U.S. Army, 1971-74. Recipient Disting. Alumnus award Alma Coll., 1998. Fellow Mich. State Bar Found.; mem. FBA (pres. Western Mich. chpt. 1979-80, nat. del. 1980-84), U.S. Dist. Ct. Hist. Soc. (pres. 2002--), State Bar Mich. (rep. assembly 1984-90), D.C. Bar Assn., Grand Rapids Bar Assn. (chmn. U.S. Constn. Bicentennial com., co-chmn. Law Day 1991), Fed. Magistrate Judges Assn., Am. Inns of Ct. (master of bench Grand Rapids chpt., pres.), Phi Delta Phi, Omicron Delta Kappa, Peninsular Club, Rotary (past pres., Charities Found. of Grand Rapids v.p., Paul Harris fellow), Econ. Club of Grand Rapids (past bd. dirs.). Congregationalist. Office: US Dist Ct West Mich 110 Michigan St NW Rm 580 Grand Rapids MI 49503-2313

BRENNEMAN, JAMES ALDEN, biology educator; b. Elida, Ohio, Aug. 26, 1943; s. William Oral and Mabel Esther (Smith) B.; m. Sandra Kay Schloneger, Aug. 5, 1967; children: Kerry, Kent. BA, Goshen (Ind.) Coll., 1965; MS, W.Va. U., 1967; PhD, La. State U., 1970. Prof. biology U. Evansville, Ind., 1970—. Cons. Ind. Poison Control, Indpls. Mem. AAAS, Am. Inst. Biol. Scis., Nat. Audubon Soc., Nat. Assn. Biology Tchrs., Mycol. Soc. Am., N.Am. Mycol. Assn., Population Connection, Sigma Xi, Phi Kappa Phi. Avocations: stamp collecting, nature photography, tennis, hiking, gardening. Home: 4033 Count Fleet Dr Newburgh IN 47630-2261 Office: U Evansville 1800 Lincoln Ave Evansville IN 47714-1506

BRENNEMAN HARRAH, SANDRA, lawyer; b. Charleston, W.Va., Nov. 3, 1970; d. Samuel Lee and Patricia Ruth B. BS in Bus. Adminstrn., BA in Polit. Sci., Alderson-Broaddus Coll., 1993; JD, W.Va. U., 1996. Bar: W.Va. 1996, U.S. Dist. Ct. (so. dist.) W.Va. 1996, (no. dist.) 2000. Assoc. Calwell & McCormick, Charleston, W.Va., 1996-97, Hill, Peterson, Carper, Bee & Deitzler, PLLC, Charleston, W.Va., 1997—. Mem. Assn. Trial Lawyers Am. (bd. govs. new lawyers divsn., 1999—), W.Va. Trial Lawyers Assn. (bd. govs. 2003—). Avocations: skiing, scuba diving. Office: Hill Peterson Carper Bee & Deitzler 500 Tracy Way Charleston WV 25311-1261 E-mail: sandra@hpcbd.com.

BRENNEN, CAROLE J. researcher in human services; b. Pitts., Sept. 3, 1942; d. James J. and Gaynell (Farwell) B.; children: Eric L. Slaney, Erin C. Slaney-Miller. Diploma, Presbyn. U. Hosp. Sch. Nursing, 1963; BSN, U. Pitts., 1969; MSN, Duquesne U., 1977; postgrad., NYU, 1980. Pub. health nurse Bklyn. Vis. Nurses Assn.; vis. nurse Vis. Nurse Assn. Allegheny County, Pitts.; instr. Duquesne U. Sch. Nursing, Pitts.; infection control nurse VA Hosp.-Univ. Dr., Pitts., 1982—. Contbr. articles to profl. jours. With Army Nurse Corps Res., 1990. Mem. VA Soc. Practitioners in Infectious Disease, Assn. for Practitioners in Infection Control, Sigma Theta Tau. Office: Va Med Ctr Infectious Dis (111E) University Dr Pittsburgh PA 15240 E-mail: cbren84435@aol.com.

BRENNEN, STEPHEN ALFRED, international business consultant; b. N.Y.C., July 07; s. Theodore and Margaret (Pembroke) B.; m. Yolanda Alicia Romero, Sept. 28, 1957; children: Stephen Robert, Richard Patrick. AB cum laude, U. Americas, Mexico City, 1956; MBA, U. Chgo., 1959. Supr. Montgomery Ward, Chgo., 1956; credit mgr. Aldens, Chgo., 1956-59; gen. mgr. Purina de Guatemala, 1964-66; pres. Purina Colombiana, Bogotá, 1967-69; founding pres. Living Marine Resources, Inc., San Diego, 1969-70; mng. dir. Central and S. Am. Ralston Purina, Caracas, Venezuela, Coral Gabels, Fla., 1970-74; pres. Van Camp Seafood Co., San Diego, 1974-79; chmn. P.S.C. Corp., Buena Park, Calif., 1979-81; pres. Inter-Am. Cons. Group, San Diego, 1981-85; chmn. Beta Enterprises Inc., 1986-91. Advisor Nat. Productivity Exch.; spl. asst. C.A.O., County of San Diego, Calif., 1987-95; mng. ptnr. Interam. Cons. Group, 1983-95; ptnr. Acad. Interpreting & Translations, Internat., 1995; assoc., owner the Montgomery Group, Inc., La Jolla. Author: Successfully Yours. Past mem. adv. bd. Mexican-Am. Found. Served with USAF. Mem. Am. Soc. Profl. Cons. Clubs: U. Chgo. in San Diego (past pres.). Roman Catholic.

BRENNEN, WILLIAM ELBERT, management consultant; b. Mo., Sept. 30, 1930; s. William E. and Frances (Andrew) B.; m. Natalia Summers, Nov. 14, 1958 (div. 1979); children: William, Natalia Jane, Elizabeth; m. Sharon Russell, Aug. 8, 1987 (dec. Feb. 1991); m. Nancy Wiese, Apr. 6, 1997. BS, U.S. Mcht. Marine Acad., 1952; MBA, U. Chgo., 1964. Ship's officer, traffic and ops. mgr. States Marine Lines Inc., Korea and Japan, 1952-61; with Case & Co./Stevenson Jordan & Harrison, Inc. Mgmt. Cons., Chgo. and N.Y.C., 1961-68; dir. internat. materials mgmt. Internat. Minerals & Chems., Skokie, Ill., 1968-71, Abbott Labs., North Chicago, Ill., 1971-73; pres. W.E. Brennen Cons., Inc. (name changed to Brennen Cons., Inc. 1987), 1987-88; mgmt. cons. Evanston, Ill., 1973-88, South Bend, Ind., 1988—; v.p. mng. prin. Fry Cons., 1982-88. Adj. assoc. prof. mktg. U. Notre Dame, 1991-92. Bd. dirs., v.p. Corvilla, Inc., 1991-94, pres. 1993-94. Lt. (j.g.) USNR, 1953-55. Mem.: Inst. Mgmt. Cons. (dir. Chgo. chpt. 1987—91, 1998—, pres. 2003—, vice chmn. cons. round table South Bend 1998—, chmn. 2000—02), Am. Mktg. Assn. (pres. Chgo. chpt. 1982—83, bus. mktg. coun. 1987—90, ethics com. 1990—92), St. Joseph County Friends of the Libr. (dir. 1997), Rotary Internat. Episcopalian. Office: 300 N Michigan St South Bend IN 46601-1295

BRENNER, ALFRED EPHRAIM, physicist; b. Bklyn., Sept. 11, 1931; s. Hyman and Ricky (Levine) B.; m. Rosamond Deborah Drooker, June 30, 1958 (div. 1987); children: Tamara Jean, Kendra Susan, Lyle Abraham; m. Natalie Levine Leibowitz, Apr. 12, 1997. BS, MIT, 1953, PhD, 1958. Fellow Ctr. for European Nuclear Rsch., Geneva, 1958-59; instr. Harvard U., Cambridge, Mass., 1959-62, asst. prof., 1962-66, sr. rsch. assoc., 1966-70; sr. physicist, head computing dept. Fermilab, Batavia, Ill., 1970-85; pres. Consortium for Scientific Computing, Princeton, N.J., 1985-86; dir. applications rsch. Supercomputing Rsch. Ctr., Bowie, Md., 1986-93; dep. dir. info. tech. and systems divsn. Inst. for Defense Analyses, Alexandria, Va., 1993—. Chmn. Nat. Inst. Standards and Tech. Rev. Panel for Computing and Applied Math., Gaithersburg, Md., 1985-91; sci. computer cons. U.S. Dept. Energy, Germantown, Md., 1980-85, tech. cons., 1972-86. Editor Jour. of Supercomputing, Internat. Jour. High Speed Computing; contbr. over 100 articles to profl. jours.; patentee in field. Fellow Am. Phys. Soc.; mem. AAAS, IEEE (sci. supercomputer com. 1983—, computer soc., chmn. tech. com. on supercomputing applications 1990-94), Assn. for Computing Machinery, Am. Math. Soc., N.Y. Acad. Scis., Soc. for Indsl. and Applied Math. Office: Inst for Defense Analyses 4850 Mark Ctr Dr Alexandria VA 22311-1882 E-mail: abrenner@ida.org.

BRENNER, ANITA SUSAN, lawyer; b. LA, Aug. 18, 1949; d. Morris I. and Lillian F. Brenner; m. Leonard E. Torres, Aug. 19, 1973; children: Andrew, Rachel. BA, UCLA, 1970, JD, 1973. Bar: Calif. 1974, U.S. Dist. Ct. (ctrl. dist.) Calif. 1974. Atty. Grtr. Watts Justice Ctr., L.A., 1974-75; pvt. practice L.A., 1975; dep. pub. defender L.A. County, 1975-84; assoc. Tyre and Kamins, L.A., 1979; ptnr. Torres-Brenner, Pasadena, Calif., 1984—. Lectr. criminal law. Mem. editl. bd., assoc. editor UCLA Law Rev., 1971-73; editor FORUM mag., 1980-83; contbr. articles to profl. jours. Bd. dirs. One Stop Immigration, 1979-81, Lanterman Ho. Mus., 2003—; vol. LA Area Coun. on Child Passenger Safety, 1981; joint com. on med.-legal issues LA County Med. Assn., 1983. Mable Wilson Richards scholar, 1971-72. Mem. Calif. Attys. for Criminal Justice (bd. govs. 1980-86). Office: Torres-Brenner 301 E Colorado Blvd Ste 614 Pasadena CA 91101-1918

BRENNER, BARRY MORTON, physician; b. Bklyn., Oct. 4, 1937; s. Louis and Sally (Lamm) B.; m. Jane P. Deutsch, June 12, 1960; children: Robert, Jennifer. BS, L.I. U., 1958; MD, U. Pitts., 1962; MA (hon.), Harvard U.; DSc (hon.), Long Island U.; D.M.Sc. (hon.), U. Paris, (Pierre et Marie Curie); diploma (hon.), Charles U., Prague; fellow (hon.), Royal Coll. of Physicians, London; MD (hon.), U. Complutense, Madrid. Asst. prof. medicine U. Calif.-San Francisco, 1969-72, asso. prof. medicine and physiology, 1972-75; prof. medicine and physiology U. Calif., San Francisco, 1975-76; Samuel A. Levine prof. medicine Harvard Med. Sch., Boston; with Peter Bent Brigham Hosp., Boston, 1976—; dir. renal div. Brigham and Women's Hosp., Boston,

1979-2001, dir. emeritus, 2001—. Dir. physician-scientist program, Harvard Med. Sch., 1984-90, Harvard Ctr. for Study of Kidney Diseases, 1987—; cons. NIH. Editor: The Kidney, 2 vols., 1976, 7th edit., 2004, Renal Pathology, 2 vols., 1989, 2d edit., 1994, Textbook of Hypertension, 2 vols., 1990, 2d edit., 1995; Acute Renal Failure, 1985, 3d edit., 1994; co-editor Contemporary Issues in Nephrology, 1978-90; founding editor Current Opinion in Nephrology and Hypertension, 1992—; contbr. numerous articles to profl. jours. Recipient Homer W. Smith award N.Y. Heart Assn., 1984, George E. Brown award Am. Heart Assn., 1983, Merit award NIH, 1984, SKF Disting. Scientist award 1985, Donald W. Seldin and David Hume awards NKF, 1995, Am. Acad. Arts and Scis., Philip S. Hench Disting. Alumnus award, U. Pitt., 1995; rsch. grantee NIH, 1969—. Fellow AAAS, Molecular Med. Soc., Am. Acad. Arts and Scis.; mem. Am. Soc. Cell Biology, Am. Physiol. Soc., Assn. Am. Physicians (councillor), Am. Soc. Clin. Investigation (councillor, v.p.), Am. Soc. Nephrology (councillor, pres., John P. Peters award), Am. Soc. Hypertension (exec. com., pres., Richard Bright award), Internat. Soc. Nephrology (councillor, Jean Hamburger award, Amgen Internat. prize), Western Assn. Physicians, Salt and Water Club, Interurban Clin. Club, Alpha Omega Alpha, Phi Sigma. Office: 75 Francis St Boston MA 02115-6110

BRENNER, BERYL H. arts therapist; b. N.Y.C., Dec. 29, 1950; d. David and Ethel Feigenbaum; m. Laurence A. Brenner, Nov. 11, 1979; 1 child, Michael. BFA, Bklyn. Coll., 1971, MA in Art Edn., 1974. Arts and crafts dir. Dept. of the Army, Ft. Hamilton Army Base, Bklyn., 1978—90; creative arts therapist Dept. of VA St. Albans Med. Ctr., NY, 1990—92; rec., creative arts therapist VA Harbor Healthcare Med. Ctr., Rec. Svcs., Bklyn., 1992—. Lectr. Times Sq. Inc., N.Y.C., 2002, Kingsboro C.C., Bklyn., 2002—, Metro Profl. Conf./St. Elizabeth Ann's Adult Day Healthcare, Staten Island, NY, 2003, VA N.Y. Harbor Healthcare Ctr./Grand Rounds, Bklyn., 2003. Artist sculpture (group shows) Gallery of Contemporary Art, N.Y.C., 1976, Artist League Bklyn., Met. Mus. Art Cmty. Gallery, 1976, 1977, Artist League Bklyn., Cork Gallery, Lincoln Ctr., 1977, 1979, (exclusive stained glasswork) Our Lady of Guadelupe, Danbury, Conn., 1986, artist Temple Beth Shalom, Atlanta, 1991, (fused glass works) Robert Lerhman Gallery at Urban Glass, Bklyn., 2001, (fused glass piece) Ann. Wreath Exhbn. Arsenal Gallery, N.Y.C., 2002, (newspaper showcase) Heart as Soul, (mainchance pubs. website gallery), 2002—, Catalyst Prouns. Inc., Website Gallery, 2002—. Recipient Ofcl. Commendation, Dept. of the Army, 1981, Exceptional Performance, 1983, Cert. of Achievement, 1984, Performance award, Dept. of Veteran's Affairs, 1991, 1992, 1993, Outstanding Rating Cert., 1994, 1995, 1996, Manhattan Arts Internat. award of excellence, 2003. Mem.: Artist's League of Bklyn., Am. Fedn. Govt. Employees Union, Metro (conf. com. 2003). Jewish. Avocations: travel, film. Office: VA Harbor Healthcare Med Ctr/Rec 800 Poly Pl Brooklyn NY 11209 Office Fax: 718-630-3793. Personal E-mail: beryl2b@yahoo.com.

BRENNER, BETH FUCHS, publishing executive; Grad., U. Vt., 1980. Sales promotion coordinator Chanel, Inc., 1980-83; promotion mgr. M mag., 1983-86; adv. sales rep. New York mag., 1986-91, adv. dir., 1991-93, SELF mag., 1993-94, pub., 1994-2001, v.p., pub., 2001—. Office: SELF Magazine 4 Times Sq New York NY 10036-6562*

BRENNER, DAVID H. marketing executive; m. Denise Brenner; 3 children. BBA in Mktg. summa cum laude, U. Notre Dame, 1973. With dept. gen. advt. Procter & Gamble, Cinn., 1973-76; sales promotion mgr. divsn. health care Johnson & Johnson, 1976-78, brand mgr. first aid products, 1978-80; new product devel. mgr. Kellogg's, 1980-82, past new product devel mgr., past mng. dir. bus. ops., pres. U.S. subs., 1988-91; sr. v.p. new bus. ventures Amway, Ada, Mich., 1991—. Regent Edison New Products Yr.; guest lectr. Yale U., Notre Dame U., Aquinas Coll., Grand Valley State U. bd. trustees Grand Rapids Art Mus., Cath. Soc. Svcs., Grand Rapids, Killgoar Found. Immaculate Heart Mary Sch.; chmn. ann. fund GRAM, 1995-97. Mem. Am. Mktg. Assn., Cascade Hills Country Club, Beta Gamma Sigma. Office: Amway Corp 7575 Fulton St E Ada MI 49355-0001

BRENNER, DOUGLAS, editor; Exec. editor Archtl. Rec., 1980—88; arts editor House & Garden, 1989—93; exec. editor Travel & Leisure, 1993—94; editor Garden Design; dep. editor Martha Stewart Living, 1999—2000, exec. editor, 2000, editor-in-chief, editor, 2002—. Contbr. articles to newspapers. Recipient award of Excellence, Garden Writers Am., 1996. Office: Martha Stewart Living Omnimedia Advt 20 W 43d St 25th Fl New York NY 10036

BRENNER, EDGAR H. law administrator; b. N.Y.C., Jan. 4, 1930; s. Louis and Bertha B. (Guttman) B.; m. Janet Maybin, Aug. 4, 1979; children from previous marriage— Charles S., David M., Paul R. BA, Carleton Coll., 1951; JD, Yale U., 1954. Bar: D.C. 1954, U.S. Ct. Claims 1957, U.S. Supreme Ct. 1957. Mem. 2d Hoover Commn. Legal Task Force Staff, Washington, 1954; trial atty. U.S. Dept. Justice, Washington, 1954-57; assoc. Arnold & Porter, Washington, 1957-62, ptnr., 1962-89. Co-dir. Inter Univ. Ctr. for Legal Studies, 1999—. Co-editor: Legal Aspects of Terrorism in the United States, Terrorism and the Law, U.S. Federal Legal Responses to Terrorism, The United Kingdom's Legal Responses to Terrorism; contbr. articles to profl. jours. Commr. Fairfax County Econ. Devel. Corp., Va., 1963—78; v.p., bd. dirs. Stella and Charles Guttman Found., N.Y.C.; bd. dirs. Ams. for Med. Progress, Arlington, Va. Recipient Disting. Achievement award Carleton Coll., 2001; fellow Coll. Problems of Drug Dependency. Mem.D.C. Bar Assn., Yale Club, Explorers Club (N.Y.C.). Democrat. Home: 340 Persimmon Ln Washington VA 22747-1845 Office: 4620 Lee Hwy Ste 216 Arlington VA 22207-3400 E-mail: edgarhbrenner@email.com.

BRENNER, EGON, university official, education consultant; b. Vienna, July 1, 1925; s. Aaron and Margarethe (Adler) B.; m. Rhoda Greenberg, Dec. 24, 1950; children: Dorothy, Claudia. B.E.E., CCNY, 1944; M.E.E., Poly. Inst. Bklyn., 1949, D.E.E., 1955. Mem. faculty CCNY, 1946-81, prof. elec. engring., 1966-81, dean engring., 1971-73, acting provost, 1973-74, provost, v.p. acad. affairs, 1974-76; acting vice chancellor for acad. affairs CUNY, 1976-77, dep. chancellor, 1978-81; exec. v.p. Yeshiva U., 1981-93, prof. emeritus, Vis. prof. Tex. Tech. U., summer 1965, U. Okla., 1966 Author: (with M. Javid) Analysis of Electric Circuits, 1959, 2d rev. edit., 1967, Analysis, Transmission and Filtering of Signals, 1963. Served with AUS, 1944-46. Decorated Bronze Star. Fellow IEEE, AAAS; mem. Am. Soc. Engring. Edn., Sigma Xi, Eta Kappa Nu, Tau Beta Pi. Address: 1601 Abaco Dr Coconut Creek FL 33066 E-mail: EB1925@FL1.Powerflite.net.

BRENNER, ELIZABETH (BETSY BRENNER), publishing executive; b. Bellevue, Wash. m. Steven Ostrofsky. BJ, MBA, Northwestern U. City news reporter The Chgo. (Ill.) Tribune, 1977, bus. news reporter, columnist, 1978; with mktg. dept. The New York Times; with retail advt. and circulation posts Miami Herald, Rocky Mountain News, Denver, sr. v.p. sales and mktg., 1994—96; pub. Bremerton Sun, 1996—98, The News Tribune, Tacoma, 1998—. Bd. dirs. Econ. Devel. Bd, Tacoma, Mus. Glass, Greater Tacoma Cmty. Found., exec. coun.; mem. Tacoma adv. coun. U. Wash.; co-chmn. campaign Olympic Coll. Libr. Kitsap County. Office: The News Tribune 1950 S State St Tacoma WA 98405-2817 Mailing: PO Box 11000 Tacoma WA 98411 E-mail: betsy.brenner@mail.tribnet.com.*

BRENNER, ESTHER HANNAH, elementary school educator; b. N.Y.C., Apr. 12, 1940; d. Israel Eli and Elsie (Lipschitz) B. BEd, U. Miami, 1963. Cert. tchr., Fla. Elem. tchr. Dade County Bd. Pub. Instrn., Miami, Fla., 1963-96, ret., 1996; youth coord. Red Cross, 1996-99. Unit chmn. Jackson Meml. Hosp., Miami, 1963-73; instr. trainer first aid and CPR, Greater Miami and The Keys chpt. ARC, 1987—, chmn. safety svcs. Homestead br., 1989-92, chmn. nursing and health programs S.W. br., youth chmn., 1988-90, vol. disaster shelter mgr.; adult trainer South Fla. coun. Girl Scouts USA, 1987—, master trainer, 1995; mem. PTA, editor newsletter, 1999—; historian Richmond Elem., 1983-87, pres. 1987-89; nat. faculty ARC Babysitter's Tng.; mem. Greater Miami Jewish Fedn., Jewish Vol. Ctr., 2000-02; vol. coord. Cmty. Disaster Edn., ARC. Recipient Appreciation plaque Adv. for Victims, 1985, Clara Barton Honor award, 1985, Ayme Carroll Meml. award, 1988, Plaque of Appreciation, PTA, 1989, Health and Safety award ARC, 1989, Spl. Recognition award, 2001, Woman of Yr. award Am. Cancer Soc., 1990—, Sarah Cullipher award, 1992, Appreciation Pin, Girl Scouts U.S., 1992, Honor Pin, 1995; Janet Baker scholarship Red Cross, 1998; named to Eckerd's 100, 1998. Mem. NSTA, Fla. Assn. Sci. Tchrs., Dade County Sci. Tchrs. Assn. (Sci. Tchr. of Yr. award 1994), Dade County Retired Educators Assn., Advs. for Victims (plaque of appreciation 1987), Nat. Assn. of Investment Corp. (Miami and Points South steering com., dir. S.E. Fla. coun. 2000-02), Bulls, Bears and Baloney Investment Club (recording ptnr. 1997, presiding ptnr. 1998-99), Dough Nut Investment Club (presiding ptnr. 1999-2000), Gamma Sigma Sigma (past historian, sec., v.p., pres. Greater Miami chpt., so. region dir. 1975-79, nat. pub. rels. dir. 1979-83, Woman of Yr. award 1973, Outstanding Alumnae award 1977, Disting. Svc. award 1987); bd. dirs. Nat. Assn. Investor Corp. (S.E. Fla. chpt. 1999-2001), Dough Nut Invitation Club (presiding officer 1999-2001). Democrat. Jewish. Avocations: travel, needlepoint, photography. Home: 12310 SW 111th S Canal Street Miami FL 33186-4826 E-mail: eb21604@aol.com.

BRENNER, FRANK, lawyer; b. N.Y.C., Oct. 26, 1927; s. Jack and Betty (Teifer) B.; children: Jay Marlow, Matthew Adam, Amy Rebecca, Diane Rachel. BA cum laude, Lehigh U., 1948; JD, Harvard U., 1951. Bar: N.Y. 1951, U.S. Supreme Ct. 1955, U.S. Tax Ct. 1975. Asst. dist. atty., N.Y. County, 1951-55; pvt. practice, N.Y.C., 1955—83; pvt. practice, 1985—2003; judge N.Y.C. Criminal Ct., 1983-84. Mng. dir. InterEquity Capital Corp., 1991-98; adminstrv. judge Waterfront Commn. N.Y. Harbor, 1994-98; jud. hearing officer N.Y. State Supreme Ct., 2000-03; arbitrator Nat. Assn. Securities Dealers, 2001-03; spl. referee appellate divsn. Supreme Ct., 2002-2003. Mem. mediation and arbitration panel JAMS/Endispute, 1993-99. With USNR, 1945-46. Recipient commendation Brit. Royal Commn. on Capital Punishment, 1950. Fellow Am. Acad. Matrimonial Lawyers; mem. ABA (litig. sect. com. on trial complex crimes 1977-2003, criminal justice sect. com. on def. function 1979-2003, RICO subcom. on white collar crime 1982-84), N.Y. State Bar Assn. (ho. dels. 1978-83, 85-90, 92-96. fellow, bar found. 1992-2003, com. on unlawful practice law 1984-89, criminal justice sect. com. on criminal discovery 1985-2002), Assn. Bar City N.Y. (spl. com. on legal aid inquiry 1971-2, com. on penology 1972-77, com. profl. discipline 1982-85, criminal cts. com. 2002-2003), N.Y. County Lawyers Assn. (dir. 1977-83, pres. coun. of assn. 1992-2002, jud. com. 1991-2002, chmn. Pres. adv. com. criminal law, 1990-2003, chmn. com. criminal law 1968-70, 80-83, com. matrimonial law 1975-80, spl. com. on selection and tenure of judges 1975-77, spl. com. to review jud. discipline 1979-80), Fund for Modern Cts. (com. on ct. facilities 1985-2002), Harvard Club. Home: 7958 Royal Birkdale Cir Bradenton FL 34202

BRENNER, HOWARD, chemical engineering educator; b. N.Y.C., Mar. 16, 1929; s. Max and Margaret (Wechsler) B.; children: Leslie, Joyce, Suzanne; m. Lisa Glucksman, Sept. 8, 1995. BChemE, Pratt Inst., 1950; MChemE, NYU, 1954, D in Engring. Sci., 1957. Instr. chem. engring. NYU, 1955-57, asst. prof. chem. engring., 1957-61, assoc. prof., 1961-65, prof., 1965-66, Carnegie-Mellon U., 1966-77; prof., chmn. dept. chem. engring U. Rochester, N.Y., 1977-81; W.H. Dow prof. chem. engring. MIT, Cambridge, Mass., 1981—. Sr. vis. fellow Sci. Rsch. Coun. Gt. Britain, 1974; Fairchild Disting. scholar Calif. Inst. Tech., 1975-76, Chevron vis. prof., 1988-89; Gulf vis. prof. Carnegie-Mellon U., Pitts., 1991; Lady Davis fellow, Israel, 1995-96; vis. prof. U. Calif., Berkeley, 1996. Author: (with J. Happel) Low Reynolds Number Hydrodynamics, 1965, 2d edit., 1973, Russian edit., 1976; (with D.A. Edwards and D.T. Wasan) Interfacial Transport Processes and Rheology, 1991; (with D. A. Edwards) Macrotransport Processes, 1993; contbr. articles to profl. jours.; co-editor in chief Physico-Chem. Hydrodynamics, 1988-89. Recipient Disting. Alumni award Pratt Inst., 2001, Caribbean Congress Fluid Dynamics award, 2001; Guggenheim fellow, 1988. Fellow AAAS, NAE, AIChE (Alpha Chi Sigma award 1976, Walker award 1985, Lewis award 1999), Am. Acad. Mechanics; mem. NAS, Am. Acad. Arts and Scis., Soc. Rheology (Bingham medal 1980), Am. Phys. Soc. (Fluid Dynamics prize 2001), Am. Chem. Soc. (Kendall award 1988, 11th ann. Honor Scroll Indsl. Engring. Chemistry Divsn. 1961), Am. Soc. Engring. Edn. (Gen. Electric Sr. Rsch. award 1996). Office: MIT Rm 66 564 Dept Of Chem Engring Cambridge MA 02139-4307

BRENNER, JANET MAYBIN WALKER, lawyer; b. Arkansas City, Kans. d. D. Arthur and Maybin (Gardner) Walker; children: Margaret Maybin Jonas, Theodore Kimball Jonas, Amanda Nash Freeman; m. Edgar H. Brenner, Aug. 4, 1979. AB, U. So. Calif.; JD, George Washington U., 1978. Bar: D.C. 1978, U.S. Dist. Ct. (D.C.). Sponsor Brenner Women's Leadership com.; mem. women's com. Corcoran Gallery Art, Washington, 1969—, Pres.'s Cir., Planned Parenthood D.C., 1969—, Found. for Preservation of Hist. Georgetown. Mem. D.C. Bar Assn., Sulgrave Club (Washington). Home: 3325 R St NW Washington DC 20007-2310 also: Shadow Ridge Farm Washington VA 22747

BRENNER, JOHN FINN, lawyer; b. Eglin AFB, Fla., Aug. 18, 1956; s. Theodore Engelbert and Maria Theresa (Finn) B.; m. Lydia Snel, Dec. 29, 1979; children: Meredith R., Corinne J., Elise H. BA, Dartmouth Coll., 1977; JD, U. Va., 1980. Bar: N.J. 1980, U.S. Dist. Ct. N.J. 1980, U.S. Ct. Appeals (3d cir.) 1984, N.Y. 1988. Assoc. McCarter & English, LLP, Newark, N.J., 1980-88, ptnr., 1988—. Contbr.: New Jersey Product Liability Law, 1994. Chmn. planning bd. Borough of Fair Haven, N.J., 1998—. Mem. ABA, Def. Rsch. Inst., N.J. State Bar Assn., Phi Beta Kappa. Office: McCarter & English LLP 100 Mulberry St Newark NJ 07102-4096 E-mail: jbrenner@mccarter.com.

BRENNER, JOHN G. protective services official; b. Mt. Holly, N.J., Oct. 23, 1965; s. John R. and Regina K. Brenner; m. Laurin Ann Mylnek, May 9, 1967; children: Amanda, Kailee. BS, Charter Oak State Coll., 1999; undergrad. cert., U. New Haven, 1997; postgrad., Fairfield U., 2000, Boston U., 2003, U. Va., 2002. FBI Nat. Acad. 210th session; RN Conn.; cert. police cert. Bridgeport Police Acad. Emergency svcs. nurse Yale U., New Haven, 1990—91; police officer Bridgeport (Conn.) Police, 1991—93, detective, 1993—97, sgt., 1997—2001, lt., 2001—. Recipient Decorated police officer (multiple), City of Bridgeport. Mem.: FBI Nat. Acad. Assoc. Quantico, Va., Police Assn. Conn., Police Benevolent Assn. Office: Bridgeport Police 300 Congress St Bridgeport CT 06604 Fax: 203-576-7625. E-mail: brennjo@ci.bridgeport.ct.us.

BRENNER, LAWRENCE, medical librarian, consultant; b. Lynn, Mass., Sept. 19, 1939; m. Ruth Ida Winer. BS in Edn., Northeastern U., 1962; cert. profl. libr., Boston State U./U. Mass., 1965; registered records adminstr., Northeastern U., 1976, MPA, 1981. Registered health info. adminstr. Sr. med. libr. Boston City Hosp., 1962-94; med. record cons. ind. co. Swampscott, Mass., 1994-95; med. record cons., coord. Vencor Corp., Boston, 1995—. Contbr. articles to profl. jours. Recipient Nat. Scholastic Art award, Nat. Scholastic/Boston Globe, 1957. Mem.: ALA, Mass. Health Info. Mgmt. Assn. (contbg. writer Bookshelf and Consultants' Corner columns, Spl. award 1997), Am. Health Info. Mgmt. Assn., Masons (past master 1987, 1999—2000). Avocations: coins, stamps, china, gardening, government. Home: 44 Elwin St Swampscott MA 01907-1065

BRENNER, LYNNETTE MARY, reading specialist, educator; b. Woodbury, N.J., July 20, 1959; d. Bernhard A. and Anna Rose (Rickert) B. BS in Bible and Elem. Edn., Lancaster (Pa.) Bible Coll., 1981; MEd in Reading, Beaver Coll., 1991. Cert. elem. and reading tchr., N.J., Pa. Elem. tchr. Killian Hill Christian Sch., Lilburn, Ga., 1981-83, Bethel Bapt. Ch. Sch., Cherry Hill, N.J., 1984-92; reading specialist, first grade tchr. Cherry Hill Bd. Edn., 1992—. Adj. faculty Ea. Coll., St. Davids, Pa., 1994-96; mem. steering com. Cherry Hill Tchrs. applying Whole Lang., 1993-95. Sec. missions com. Columbus Bapt. Ch., 1992-97, discipleship ministry, 1993—, Sun. sch. tchr., 1992-94, chmn. missions com., 1992; discipleship leader Precepts Bible study. Recipient recognition for geography awareness N.J. Senate, 1990, recognition Gov.'s Tchr. Recognition Program award, 1995, Celebrate Literacy award Internat. Reading Assn., 1999; named Tchr. of Yr., 1995. Mem. NEA, N.J. Edn. Assn., West Jersey Reading Coun. (bd. dirs. 1995-98, Celebrate Literacy award 1999), N.J. Reading Assn., Internat. Reading Assn. Republican. Baptist. Avocations: Bible study, scrapbooking, stamping, crafts, travel. Office: Joyce Kilmer Elem Sch Chapel Ave Cherry Hill NJ 08002

BRENNER, MICHAEL EDWARD, executive search and coaching consultant; b. Bklyn., Apr. 30, 1935; s. Arthur Allen and Edythe (Madoff) B.; m. Elsa Ferda Claman, June 23, 1958 (div. July 1974); children: Deborah Ann, Amy Beth, Gabriel Stephen; m. Roberta Lee Gorsky, Apr. 8, 1976; 1 child, Samantha Allyn. SB in Indsl. Mgmt., MIT, 1957; D Engring., Johns Hopkins U. 1963. Mgr. sys. analysis Bell Telephone Labs., 1962-69; assoc. prof. NYU, N.Y.C., 1969-72; prin. Arthur Young & Co., N.Y.C., 1975-80; pres. Michael Brenner Assocs., N.Y.C., 1980-83; sr. v.p. PA Cons., N.Y.C., 1983-86; ptnr. Canny Bowen, N.Y.C., 1986-91; sr. ptnr. LAI Worldwide, N.Y.C., 1991-99; chief resource Brenner Exec. Resources Inc., N.Y.C., 1999—. Pres. NY chpt. Soc. for Human Resource Mgmt., 1983-84; trustee Columbia Grammar & Prep. Sch., NYC, 1989-94; pres., bd. dir. Fedcap, NYC, 1999—. Capt. US Army, 1957-58. Mem.: Soc. for Info. Mgmt. Democrat. Jewish. Avocations: hiking, roller blading, yoga, opera, travel. Home: 33 Riverside Dr Apt 4C New York NY 10023-8025 Office: Brenner Exec Resources 1230 Avenue of the Americas New York NY 10020 E-mail: mbrenner@brennerresources.com.

BRENNER, RAYMOND ANTHONY, priest; b. Evansville, Ind., Feb. 12, 1943; s. George Frederick and Marie Catherine (Gries) B. BA, St. Meinrad (Ind.) Coll., 1965; MDiv, St. Meinrad Sch. Theology, 1969. Ordained priest Roman Cath. Ch., 1969. Deacon Nativity Ch., Indpls., 1968; assoc. pastor St. John's Ch., Loogootee, Ind., 1969-74, Sts. Peter and Paul Ch., Haubstadt, Ind., 1974-78; pastor St. Mary's Ch., Sullivan, Ind., 1978-86, St. Joan of Arc Ch., Jasonville, Ind., 1982-86, Resurrection Ch., Evansville, 1986—2002, St. Joseph Ch., Jasper, Ind., 2002—. Mem. Cath. Charities Bd., Evansville, 1972-75; v.p. Ministerial Assn., Sullivan, 1985-86; pres. Coun. of Priests, Evansville, 1989; diocesan chaplain St. Vincent de Paul Soc., Evansville, 1990-94. Mem. Wabash Valley Human Svcs., Vincennes, Ind., 1982-86, Sullivan Housing Authority, 1983-85, Fed. Emergency Mgmt. Agy., Sullivan, 1984-86, Emergency Food Bank, Sullivan, 1984-86; spiritual advisor Evansville Cath. Cursillo, 1994—; chaplain German Twp. Vol. Fire Dept., 1998-2002, Cmty. Marriage Builders, 1997—. Mem. Optimists (chaplain Evansville Westside club 1990-2002), Elks. Democrat. Address: St Joseph Cath Ch 1020 Kundek St Jasper IN 47546-1917 E-mail: rbrenner@evansville-diocese.org. *It takes so little time to offer a smile, and the rewards are beyond imagining. Somehow they know you care and that God cares too.*

BRENNER, RENA CLAUDY, communications executive; b. Camden, N.J. d. John Lawler and Louretta (Du Fresene) Morgan; m. Edgar W. Claudy (div. 1968); 1 child, Renee; m. Millard Brenner, Nov. 6, 1971 (dec. 1975); children: Sally, Malcolm, Hugh. Student, U. Pa., 1978, U. Mich., 1983. Reporter Tribune-Telegram, Salt Lake City, 1943-45, Times Chronicle, Jenkintown, Pa., 1950-55; free-lance writer Enfield, Pa., 1955-60; pub. relations dir., advt. mgr. Gen. Atronics/Magnavox, Phila., 1960-70; mgr. corp. pub. relations ITE-Imperial, Phila., 1970-73, dir. corp. comm., 1973-76, Parker-Hannifin Corp., Cleve., 1976-83, v.p. corp. comm., 1983-85; pres. Brenner Assocs., Clearwater, Fla., 1986—, CFO Fla. Sport Dance Fedn. of Am., 1999—. Recipient Creative Direction award Phila. Club Advt. Women, 1970, Clarion award Women in Communications, 1982, Gold Key award Pub. Relations News, 1984. Mem. Bus. Profl. Advt. Assn. (life), Pub. Relations Soc. Am. (life), Nat. Investors Relations Inst.. Office: Brenner Assocs 1501 Gulf Blvd Apt 607 Clearwater FL 33767-2903

BRENNER, RICHARD JAMES, physician; b. Sept. 27, 1949; BA, U. Calif., Santa Cruz, 1971; MD, UCLA, 1975; JD, U. San Francisco, 1981. Dir. breast imaging Cedars-Sinai Med. Ctr., L.A., 1980-92, John Wayne Cancer Ctr. Inst., L.A., 1992—; prof. radiology UCLA, 1995—; with Tower-St. Johns Imaging, 1994—. Editor: The Augmented Breast, 1996, ACR Risk Management Syllabus, 1999. Pres. Upper Mandeville Canyon Assn., L.A., 1992-95; bd. dirs. Ctrl. L.A. divsn. Am. Cancer Soc., 1995—. Mem.: Soc. Breast Imaging (v.p.), Am. Coll. Radiology Comisa (com. on mammography interpretive skills assessment), Am. Coll. Radiology (chair med.-legal com. 1995—, chair task force on mammography practice 2001—). Office: Eisenberg Keefer Breast Ctr 1328 22d St Santa Monica CA 90404

BRENNER, ROBERT DAVID, federal agency administrator; b. Washington, July 26, 1953; s. Norbert and Ruth (Sternheim) B.; m. Barbara Friling, Feb. 18, 1988. AB, Princeton U., 1975, MPA, 1977. Mem. rsch. faculty Ctr. Internat. Studies, Princeton, N.J., 1977-80; energy policy analyst EPA, Washington, 1980-87, dir. Air Policy Office, 1987-99; dep. asst. adminstr. Office of Air and Radiation, EPA, Washington, 1999—. Recipient Gold medal EPA, 1989, Presdl. Meritorious Svc. award, 1991, 98. Avocations: golf, tennis, hiking. Office: EPA Policy Analysis & Review 6103 Washington DC 20460-0002

BRENNER, SYDNEY, molecular biologist, researcher; b. Germiston, South Africa, Jan. 13, 1927; s. Morris and Lena (Blacher) B.; m. May Woolf Balkind, 1952; 3 children; 1 stepchild. MSc, U. Witwatersrand, Johannesburg, South Africa, 1947, MB, BCh, 1951; DPhil, Oxford (Eng.) U., 1954; 10 hon. degrees. Mem. sci. staff Med. Rsch. Coun., Cambridge, Eng., 1957-92, dir. lab. molecular biology, 1979-86, dir. molecular genetics unit, 1986-91; fellow King's Coll., Cambridge U., 1959—; hon. fellow Exeter Coll., Oxford U., 1985; rsch. scientist dept. medicine U. Cambridge Sch. Clin. Medicine, 1992-96; mem. staff Scripps Rsch. Inst., La Jolla, Calif., 1992-94; pres., dir. The Molecular Scis. Inst., Berkeley, Calif., 1996—. Carter-Wallace lectr. Princeton U., 1966, 77; Gifford lectr. U. Glasgow, Scotland, 1978-79; Dunham lectr. Harvard U., 1984; hon. prof. genetic medicine U. Cambridge Clin. Sch., 1989-96; lectr. in field. Contbr. articles to sci. jours. Recipient Warren Triennial prize, 1968, William Bate Hardy prize Cambridge Philos. Soc., 1969, Albert Lasker Med. Rsch. award, 1971, Royal medal Royal Soc., 1974, Charles-Leopold Mayer prize French Acad., 1975, Gairdner Found. ann. award, 1978, Krebs medal FEBS, 1980, CIBA medal Biochem. Soc., 1981, Feldberg Found. prize, 1983, Rosenstiel award Brandeis U., 1986, Prix Louis Jeantet de Medecine, Switzerland, 1987, medal Genetics Soc. Am., 1987, Harvey prize Technion-Israel Inst. Tech., 1987, Hughlings Jackson medal Royal Soc. Medicine, 1987, Waterford Bio-Med. Sci. award Rsch. Inst. Scripps Clinic, 1988, Kyoto prize Inamori Found., 1990, Gairdner Found. Internat. award, Can., 1991, King Faisal Internat. prize, 1992, Disting. Achievement award Bristol-Myers Squibb, 1992, Nobel Prize in physiology or medicine, 2002. Fellow Royal Soc. (Croonian lectr. 1986, Royal medal 1974, Copley medal 1991), AAS, IASc (hon.) RSE (hon.), Royal Coll. Physicians (Neil Hamilton Fairley medal 1985) Royal Coll. Pathologists (hon.); mem. Max-Planck Soc., Deutsche Acad. Natural Sci. Leopoldina (Gregor Mendel medal 1970), Am. Philos. Soc. (fgn.), Real Acad. Ciencias (Spain), Am. Acad. Arts and Scis. (fgn. hon.), NAS (U.S., fgn. assoc.), Royal Soc. South Africa (fgn. assoc.), Acad. Europa, Chinese Soc. Genetics (hon.), Assn. Physicians Gt. Brit. and Ireland (hon.); associé étranger, Académie des Scis.; corr. Scientifique Emérite de l'INSERM. Office: Molecular Scis Inst 2168 Shattuck Ave Berkeley CA 94704-1307

BRENNER, THEODORE ENGELBERT, retired trade association executive; b. N.Y.C., Apr. 18, 1930; s. Engelbert F.J. and Julie M. (Kierschner) B.; m. Maria T. Finn, Sept. 12, 1953; children— John Finn, Elisabeth Ann, Christopher. BCE, Manhattan Coll., 1951; MS, Johns Hopkins, 1954. Registered profl. engr., Pa., N.J. Diplomate Am. Acad. Environ. Engrs. Mgr. waste treatment dept. Permutit div. Sybron Corp., Paramus, N.J., 1959-62; prin. Hydroscience, Inc., Ft. Lee, N.J., 1963; with Soap and Detergent Assn., N.Y.C., 1963-93, v.p., tech. dir., 1970, v.p., dir. govt. affairs, 1971, pres., 1972-93; ret., 1993. Exec. dir. Joint Industry Govt. Task Force Eutrophication, 1968-70; mem. Dept. Interior Water Resources Sci., Info. Center Adv. Group, 1969-70; mem. spl. adv. com. N.Y. Temp. State Commn. on Water Resources Planning, 1964-67 Contbr.: chpt. to Advances in Environmental Sciences, Vol. II, 1969; articles to profl. jours. Mem. Rumson Bd. Edn., 1968-74, 1st v.p., 1973-74; mem. Rumson-Fair Haven Regional Bd. Edn., 1974-77, v.p., 1976-77. Served to capt. USAF, 1952-59; lt. col. ret. Mem. ASCE, AIChE, Am. Soc. Assn. Execs., Union League (N.Y.C.), Seabright (N.J.) Beach Club. Home: 5 Tyson Ln Rumson NJ 07760-1912

BRENT, JULIA DEENER, language educator; b. Searcy, Ark., May 19, 1937; d. Richard Gregory and Elizabeth Sharpe Deener; children: Julia Lytle, Virginia Brent Jones. BA, Mary Baldwin Coll., 1958; MA, George Washington U., 1970, PhD, 1975. Tchr., chmn. dept. English St. Stephen's and St. Agnes Sch., Alexandria, Va., 1987—. Named Tchr. of Yr., Washington POst. Office: St Stephen's and St Agnes Sch 1000 St Stephens Rd Alexandria VA 22304-1727

BRENT, REBECCA KEMP, volunteer, calligrapher and textile artist; b. Columbus, Ga., Sept. 18, 1959; d. John Richard and Pat Kemp; m. James Burkhart Brent, Jan. 11, 1985; children: Patricia Marie, Jonathan Lawrence. BS summa cum laude, U. Ala., Tuscaloosa, 1979; PhD, U. Tenn., 1983. Pattern and design cons. Texsel, Inc., West Point, Ga., 1979; asst. to assoc. dean Coll. Home Econs. U. Tenn., Knoxville, 1981, grad. teaching asst. dept. textiles, merchandising and design, 1979-82; designer, cons. Frey Assocs., Knoxville, 1982; operator Alteration Svc., Knoxville, 1982-83; product devel. and design Vol. Apparel, Inc., Knoxville, 1983-87; freelance writer and instr. machine embroi-

dery, sewing, and quilting, 1995—. Contbr. articles to Creative Machine Embroidery, Sew News and local newspapers. Instr. Children's Mus. of Oak Ridge, 1987; bd. dirs. YWCA Oak Ridge, 1989-95, pres., 1993-94, instr., 1988-95. Named to Group Study Exchg. Pakistan by Rotary Internat., 1992; recipient various awards Smoky Mountain Quilters Show and Competition, Best of Show award Anderson County Fair. Avocations: needlework, calligraphy, reading.

BRENT, ROBERT LEONARD, radiology and pediatrics educator; b. Rochester, N.Y., Oct. 6, 1927; s. Charles and Rose (Katz) B.; m. Lillian H. Hoffman, Aug. 21, 1949; children: David A., James R., Lawrence H., Deborah A. AB, U. Rochester, 1948, MD with honors, 1953, PhD, 1955, DSc (hon.), 1988. Fellow Nat. Found., Strong Meml. Hosp., 1953-54; intern pediatrics Mass. Gen. Hosp., Boston, 1954-55; chief radiation biology Walter Reed Army Inst. Rsch., 1955-57; mem. faculty Jefferson Med. Coll., 1955—, prof. radiology, 1962—, also prof. pediatrics, Louis and Bess Stein prof. pediatrics, 1985—, emeritus chmn. pediats., 1999—; apptd. Disting. prof. Thomas Jefferson U., 1989. Hon. prof. Norman Bethume U. Med. Sci., People's Republic of China, 1992, West China U. Med. Scis., Chengdu, People's Republic of China, 1992; chmn. med. adv. bd. Nat. Found.; mem. fertility and maternal health com. FDA; mem. human embryology study sect. NIH, 1970-74; bd. trustees Health and Environ. Sci. Inst., 1991-94; pres. First Internat. Congress on Birth Defects, People's Republic of China, 1994. Editor in chief Teratology, 1976-93. Pres. Teratology Soc., 1968. Served with U.S. Army, 1955-57. Recipient Richie Meml. prize U. Rochester Med. Sch., 1953, Lindback Found. award for disting. tchg., 1968, Med. Sch. award Alpha Omega Alpha, 1952, Burlington Internat. award, 1990, Landauer award Health Physics Soc., 1995, Robley D. Evans Commemorative medal Health Physics Soc., 2000; travelling fellow Royal Soc. Medicine, 1971-72; vis. fellow FitzWilliam Coll., Cambridge, 1971-72; Lady Davis scholar Hadassah Med. Ctr., Jerusalem, 1983-84. Mem. AAAS, NAS Inst. Medicine, Teratology Soc. (pres. 1967-68), Internat. Life Sci. Inst., Radiation Rsch. Soc., Am. Soc. Exptl. Pathology, Soc. Pediat. Rsch., Am. Pediats. Soc., Am. Acad. Pediats. (Merit citation 2001), Soc. Exptl. Biology and Medicine, Phila. Coll. Physicians, Phila. Pediat. Soc., Am. Assn. Immunology (emeritus), Soc. Developmental Biology, Nat. Coun. Radiation Protection, Nat. Acad. Sci. (elected Inst. Medicine 1996), Japan Teratology Soc., European Teratology Soc., Ambulatory Pediat. Assn., Sigma Xi. E-mail: rbrent@nemours.org.

BRENTANI, PATRICIA BRODIE, social worker; b. N.Y.C., May 11, 1935; d. William Campbell and Marjorie Eve (Englehart) Brodie; m. Giampiero Brentani, June 10, 1961; children: Christine, William, Catherine, Deborah. BA, Cornell U., 1956; MA, Boston Coll., 1980; MSW, Boston U., 1983. Lic. ind. clin. social worker, Mass.; cert. alcoholism and drug counselor, Mass. Rschr. Mass. Mental Health Ctr., Boston, 1957-58; statistician MIT, Cambridge, 1958-60; rschr. dept. psychology U. Calif., Berkeley, 1960-61; social worker Stacey House, Sao Paulo, Brazil, 1973-75; tchr. English Concord-Carlisle High Sch., 1976-79, Dana Hall Sch., Wellesley, Mass., 1979-80; psychotherapist, intern Greater Lynn (Mass.) Community Mental Health Ctr., 1982-84; psychotherapist alcohol svcs. Emerson Hosp., Concord, 1983-84; psychotherapist Herbert Lipton Cmty. Mental Health Ctr., Leominster, 1984-88; pvt. practice, Concord and Leominster, 1984—. Mem. NASW, Soc. Family Therapy and Rsch. Home: PO Box 291 Concord MA 01742-0291 Office: PO Box 291 Concord MA 01742-0291 E-mail: patbr@gis.net.

BRENTLINGER, PAUL SMITH, venture capital executive; b. Dayton, Ohio, Apr. 3, 1927; s. Arthur and Welthy Otello (Smith) B.; m. Marilyn E. Hunt, June 23, 1951; children: Paula, David, Sara. BA, U. Mich., 1950, MBA, 1951. With Harris Corp., Melbourne, Fla., 1951-84, v.p. corp. devel., 1969-75, v.p. fin., 1975-82, sr. v.p. fin., 1982-84; ptnr. Morgenthaler Ventures, Cleve., 1984—. Bd. dirs. Allegheny Techs., Inc., Pitts., Hypres, Inc., Elmsford, N.Y. Trustee Cleve. Inst. Art. Mem. Union Club, Phi Beta Kappa. Home: 2755 Eaton Rd Cleveland OH 44122-1800 Office: Morgenthaler 50 Public Sq Ste 2700 Cleveland OH 44113-2236

BRENTLINGER, WILLIAM BROCK, college dean; b. Flora, Ill., Aug. 21, 1926; s. Arthur Kenneth and Frances (Maxwell) B.; m. Barbara Jean Weir, Dec. 29, 1946; children: Gregory, Gary, Rebecca Anne, Garth, Barbara Sue. Student, Washington U., 1946-47; AB, Greenville Coll., 1950; MA, Ind. State U., 1951; PhD, U. Ill., 1959. Instr. speech Greenville Coll., 1951-59, chmn. dept., 1959-62, dean of coll., 1962-69, dean coll. fine arts and comm., 1969-92; interim pres. Lamar U., Beaumont, Tex., 1992-93, asst. to pres., 1993—. Cons. higher edn. Served with USNR, 1944-46. Recipient tchr. study award Danforth Found., 1957 Mem. Internat. Council Fine Arts Deans, Speech Communication Assn. Am., Tex. Speech Assn., Tex. Assn. Coll. Tchrs., Tex. Council Arts in Edn. (pres.), Phi Kappa Phi. Clubs: Rotary (Beaumont). Baptist. Home: 6530 Salem Cir Beaumont TX 77706-5552 Office: Lamar U PO Box 10001 Beaumont TX 77710-0001 *I have always attempted to treat people as subjects, not objects, as fellow creatures of God, and thus to be worked with not worked upon.*

BRENTON, HATICE, painter, graphics designer; 1 child, Thomas. Student, Cornell U., 1990; MFA, Goddard Coll., 2003. Fine artist, graphic designer Herbert F. Johnson Mus., Cornell U. Mem.: Nat. Mus. Women in the Arts, U.S. Holocaust Meml. Mus., Phi Kappa Phi. Green Party.

BRENY BONTEMPI, JEAN M. health educator; d. Craig N. and Angie C. Breny; m. Christopher D. Bontempi, July 25, 1992. BA in Comm., Western Conn. State U., 1986; MPH in Cmty. Health Edn., San Jose State U., 1994; PhD in Health Behavior and Health Edn., U. N.C., 2000. Qualitative rsch. specialist U. N.C., Chapel Hill, 1999—2000; asst. prof. So. Conn. State U., New Haven, 2000—. Pvt. evaluation cons., Hamden, Conn., 2000—; grad. coun. sec. So. Conn. State U., New Haven, 2002—. Contbr. articles to profl. jours. Elected mem. Orange County Commn. for Women, Chapel Hill, NC, 1997—98. Grantee Evaluation of Conn. HIV Medication Adherence Programs, Conn. State Dept. Pub. Health, 2000—01, HIV/AIDS Needs Assessment, Norwalk Cmty. Health Ctr., 2002—03; Health Sci. scholar, Calif. Parents, Tchrs., and Students, Inc., 1993, Rsch. grantee, Ctr. for AIDS Rsch., U. N.C. Chapel Hill, 2000. Mem.: APHA, Campus Cmty. Partnerships for Health, Soc. for Pub. Health Edn. (membership com. co-chair 2002—03), Eta Sigma Gamma. Avocations: photography, travel, wine enthusiast. Office: So Conn State Univ 144 Farnham Ave New Haven CT 06515 Office Fax: 203-392-6965. Personal E-mail: brenybontej1@southernct.edu. E-mail: brenybontej1@southernct.edu.

BRERETON, SANDRA JOY, engineer; b. Toronto, Ont., Can., Nov. 21, 1960; came to U.S. 1983; d. Frank William and M. Joyce (Mortson) B.; m. Donald Thomas Blackfield, Sept. 22, 1990; children: Danielle Francine Brereton Blackfield, Benjamin William Brereton Blackfield. BASc in Chem. Engring., U. Toronto, 1983; SM in Nuclear Engring., MIT, 1985, PhD in Nuclear Engring., 1987. Fusion systems engr. Ont. Hydro Canadian Fusion Fuels Tech. Project, 1987-90; cons. Pleasanton, Calif., 1990-91; facility mgr. Lawrence Livermore (Calif.) Lab., 1991—. Contbr. articles to profl. jours. Mem. Am. Nuclear Soc. (sec.-treas. fusion energy divsn. 1998-2001), Sigma Xi. Anglican. Office: Lawrence Livermore Nat Lab L-360 PO Box 808 Livermore CA 94551-0808

BRESANI, FEDERICO FERNANDO, business executive; b. Lima, Peru, Apr. 27, 1945; came to U.S., 1964; s. Federico L. and Beatriz (Ferrer) B.; m. Patricia Anne Grannis, Aug. 26, 1972; children: Christina Anne, Vianna Clarissa. BS in Elect. Engring., Milw. Sch. of Engring., 1970; MBA, Fairleigh Dickinson U., 1980. Engr. Cerro Corp., Lima, Peru, 1973-76; supr. Cerro Corp./CMP, N.Y.C., 1976-77, mgr., 1978, purchasing mgr., 1979-80; product mgr. Schumag, Inc., Norwood, N.J., 1980-82, v.p., 1982; sales, mktg. mgr. EVG, Inc., N.Y.C., 1983-85; v.p. EVG, N.Y.C., 1986-92, pres., 1992—. Mem. Wire Assn. Internat., Wire Reinforcement Inst., Latin Am. Iron and Steel Inst., Am. Concrete Inst., Concrete Reinforcing Steel Inst., Rowayton Yacht Club, Omicron Delta Epsilon. Avocations: sailing, ham radio. Home: 77 Chuckanutt Dr Oakland NJ 07436-3728 Office: EVG 220 E 42nd St New York NY 10017-5806 E-mail: f.bresani@evg-usa.com.

BRESCHER, JOHN B., JR., lawyer; b. Elizabeth, N.J., July 8, 1947; BS, Lehigh U., 1969; JD, Georgetown U., 1972, LLM, 1976. Bar: N.J. 1973, D.C. 1975. Atty. McCarter & English, Newark. Adj. prof. law Seton Hall U., 1980-84. Mem. ABA, N.J. State Bar Assn., Essex County Bar Assn. Office: McCarter & English PO Box 652 Four Gateway Ctr 100 Mulberry St Newark NJ 07102-4004

BRESEE, JAMES COLLINS, chemical engineer; b. N.Y.C., Oct. 25, 1925; s. John James and Mabel Elizabeth (Collins) Bresee; m. Mary Kathryn Duncan, July 5, 1952 (dec. Mar. 1973); children: Kathryn Ann Bresee Brooke, Stuart James; m. Susan Lynn Austermiller, Aug. 3, 1974; children: James Michael, Benjamin Carter, Nathan John, Joanna Meghan, Andrew Paul. BSChemE, U. Ill., 1945, MSChemE, 1947; ScDChemE, MIT, 1953; JD, U. Tenn., 1971. Bar: Tenn. 1972, DC 1979. Asst. prof. chem. and nuclear engring. MIT, Cambridge, Mass., 1951-54; br. chief and asst. dir. chem. tech. div. Oak Ridge Nat. Lab., Oak Ridge, Tenn., 1954-64, dir. civil def. rsch. project, 1964-72; asst. dir. for gen. energy devel. div. applied tech. AEC, Washington, 1972-75; dir. div. geothermal energy ERDA, Washington, 1976-77; dir. N.C. Energy Inst., N.C. State Dept. Commerce, Raleigh, 1978-81; supervisory engr. and mgr. geosci. rsch. Geothermal Tech. Div., U.S. Dept. Energy, Washington, 1982-86; mem. sr. exec. svc. Office Civilian Radioactive Waste Mgmt., U.S. Dept. Energy, Washington, 1986-98, dir. repository coordination div., 1986-88; dep. assoc. dir. for program and resources mgmt. Office Civilian Radioactive Waste Mgmt. U.S. Dept. Energy, 1988-94, acting dir. Office Human Resources and Adminstrn., Office Civilian Radioactive Waste Mgmt., 1994-96, dep. dir. Office of Program Mgmt. and Adminstrn., 1996-98, Sr. Tech. Specialist, 1998—; sr. tech. specialist DOE Office Nuc. Energy, Sci. and Tech., 2000—. Adj. prof. chem. engring. N.C. State U., 1978—81. Editor-in-chief: Geothermal Sci. and Tech., 1987—99; contbr. scientific papers to profl. publs. Mem. Oak Ridge Planning Commn., 1963—67. Lt. USNR, 1944—46, CBI. Mem.: DC Bar Assn., Tenn. Bar Assn., Sigma Xi, Phi Kappa Phi, Kappa Kappa Lambda, Beta Theta Pi. Presbyterian. Avocation: music. Home: 3213 Birchtree Ln Silver Spring MD 20906-3041 Office: US Dept Energy 1000 Independence Ave SW Washington DC 20585-0001 E-mail: james.bresee@hq.doe.gov.

BRESLAUER, GEORGE WILLIAM, political science educator; b. N.Y.C., Mar. 4, 1946; s. Henry Edward and Marianne (Schaeffer) B.; m. Yvette Assia, June 5, 1976; children: Michelle, David. BA, U. Mich., 1966, MA, 1968, PhD, 1973. Asst. prof. polit. sci. U. Calif., Berkeley, 1971-79, assoc. prof., 1979-90, prof., 1990—, Chancellor's prof., 1998—2001, chmn. dept., 1993-96, chmn. Ctr. for Slavic and East European Studies, 1982-94, dean of social scis., 1999—. Vice chmn. bd. trustees Nat. Coun. for Soviet and East European Rsch., Washington, 1988-91. Author: Khrushchev and Brezhnev as Leaders, 1982, Soviet Strategy in the Middle East, 1989, Gorbachev and Yeltsin as Leaders, 2002; editor: Can Gorbachev's Reforms Succeed?, 1990, Learning in U.S. and Soviet Foreign Policy, 1991, Russia in the New Century: Stability or Disorder?, 2001. Grantee Ford Found., 1982-84, Carnegie Corp., 1985-94, 97-99. Mem. Am. Assn. for Advancement Slavic Studies (bd. dirs., exec. com. 1990-93). Office: U Calif Dept Polit Sci 210 Barrows Hall Berkeley CA 94720-1950

BRESLAW, CATHY LEE, artist, educator; b. Coral Gables, Fla. d. William Howard and Miriam Roberts (Lasker) B.; m. Paul K. Cohen, Nov. 24, 1986; children: Adam, Micah. BA, George Washington U., 1973; MSW, Howard U., 1978. Educator, artist Lee Press, Encinitas, Calif., 1992—. Instr. fine art in painting and creativity. Exhbns. include Nat. Watercolor Ann. Exhbn. and Travel Show, 1996-97, Gallery Contemporary Art U. Colo., 1997, Tubac Ctr. Arts, 1997, Downey (Calif.) Mus. Art, 1997, Calif. Watercolor Assn., Hilton Corp. Hdqrs., Art Inst., San Francisco, 1997, Nat. Oil and Acrylic Painting Soc., 1998, San Diego Art Inst., 1998, Internat. Soc. Exptl. Painters, 1999, Art Expo, San Francisco, 2000; one-woman shows include Emerald Plaza, San Diego, 1996, Off Track Gallery, 1997, 1st Nat. Bank, San Diego, 1998, 2001, Acme Restaurants, Del Mar, Calif., 1998, San Diego State U., 2000, Falcon Arts Gallery, San Diego, 2000, Escondido Ctr. for the Arts, 2001, William D. Cannon Gallery, Carlsbad, Calif., 2001, Grand Ctrl. Art Ctr., Santa Ana, Calif., 2002-2003; represented in corp. and pvt. collections; pub. in New American Paintings, 2003. Bd. dirs., sec. United Cerebral Palsy Bay Area, San Francisco, 1978-82. Mem. Nat. Watercolor Soc. (signature mem.), San Diego Mus. Fine Arts Guild. Avocations: reading, writing, travel, cooking, skiing. Office: PO Box 231122 Encinitas CA 92023-1122 E-mail: cathy@cathybreslaw.com.

BRESLER, MICHAEL JAY, emergency physician; b. Phila., Oct. 12, 1946; BA, Amherst Coll., 1968; MD, Stanford U., 1973. Diplomate Am. Bd. Emergency Medicine. Intern Santa Clara Valley Med. Ctr., San Jose, 1973-74; resident in emergency medicine Stanford U. Med. Ctr., 1978-79; pvt. practice Emergency Med. Assocs., San Mateo, Calif.; emergency physician Stanford U. Med. Ctr.; chief emergency medicine Mills Hosp.; clin. prof. surgery Stanford U. Mem. AMA, Am. Coll. Emergency Physicians, Calif. Med. Assn. Office: Emergency Med Assocs 100 S San Mateo Dr San Mateo CA 94401-3805

BRESLIN, ELIZABETH WALKER, biological scientist, biomedical consultant; b. Phila., Jan. 10, 1940; d. Edwin Olen and Delphine Jane (Durkin) Walker; m. Michael Joseph Breslin, June 5, 1965; children: Anne Marie B. Sullivan, Michael Joseph Jr., Thomas Edwin. AS, Gwynedd Mercy Coll., 1959; BS, Hahnemann Med. Coll. and Hosp., 1961; postgrad., Bryn Mawr Coll., 1988-94. Lic. med. technologist, Calif., Fla.; registered med. technologist. Rsch. med. technologist dept. gastroenterology Hahnemann Med. Coll. and Hosp., 1961-65, staff supr. dept. gastroenterology, 1962-65; staff technologist Fort Ord Army Hosp., Calif., 1966-67, Meml. Hosp. of Jacksonville, Fla., 1974-78; supr. hematology lab. Daroff Divsn. Albert Einstein Med. Ctr., Phila., 1979-81; rsch. med. technologist Geometric Data Corp., A SmithKline Co., Wayne, Pa., 1981-86; scientist Smith Kline & French R&D, Swedeland, Pa., 1986-88; biol. scientist Zynaxis, Inc., Malvern, Pa., 1988-92, quality assurance/quality control specialist, 1993-94, quality control supr., 1994-95, Intracel Corp., West Chester, Pa., 1995-96, biomed. cons., 1996—. Contbr. articles to profl. jours. Vol. med. technologist U.S. Naval Hosp., Yokosuka, Japan, 1968-69. Mem. Am. Soc. Clin. Pathologists (assoc., cert. med. technologist). Avocations: reading, gardening, wood finishing. Office: 607 Harper Ave Drexel Hill PA 19026-1439

BRESLIN, EVALYNNE LOUISE WOOD-ROBERTSON, retired psychiatric nurse; b. Richmond, Ohio, July 7, 1931; d. Evan P. and Ada Augusta (Huscroft) Wood-Robertson; m. Donald Joseph Breslin, Jan. 30, 1954; children: Lisa Karen, Mark Nathaniel, Paul Andrew Scott. Diploma, Cleve. Met. Gen. Hosp., 1952; student, Case Western Res. U., 1953-55, Akron U.; HHD (hon.), London Inst. of Applied Rsch., 1973. Lic. RN, Ohio, Mass; RN, Ohio, Mass. Head nurse Cleve. Met. Gen. Hosp., 1952-55, Cleve. State Receiving Hosp., 1952-55; cons. mental illness and addictions Mass.; ret., 1986. Ret. bd. dirs. Triple Trouble; ret. vol. monitor state hosp. facilities Alliance for Mentally Ill; vol. nursing/psychiat. work wirh abandonded adolscents, 1968—2001; vol. tour guide Barefoot Beach Preserve, Inc.; tchr. ESL, 1999—.

BRESLIN, MICHAEL JOSEPH, III, social services administrator, educator; b. Fountain Springs, Pa., Feb. 5, 1949; s. Michael Joseph Jr. and Barbara Ellin (Mellet) B. BS in Sociology, U. Scranton, 1971; MS in Adminstrn., Shippensburg (Pa.) U., 1984. Tchr. aide Selinsgrove (Pa.) Ctr., 1968, 69, 70; caseworker Northumberland County Children and Youth Agy., Sunbury, Pa., 1971-73; juvenile probation officer Northumberland County Juvenile Ct., 1973-74, supr., 1974-75, dir., 1976-87; dir. human svcs. Northumberland County Human Svcs., 1987-91; exec. dep. sec. Dept. Pub. Welfare, Harrisburg, Pa., 1992-95; v.p. Northwestern Corp., Harrisburg, Pa., 1995-97; sr. v.p. Northwestern Human Svcs., Harrisburg, 1997—. Adminstr. Northumberland County Mental Health and Mental Retardation Program, 1984-87; mem. adj. faculty Susquehanna U., Selinsgrove, 1989-91; cons. Tng. & Mgmt. Systems, Gibsonia, Pa., 1983-85; mem. Youth Svcs. Tng. Ctr., 1986-90. Mem. adv. bd. White Deer Run Treatment Ctr., Allenwood, Pa., 1975-77; advisor Explorer Pres. Assn., Netami dist. Boy Scouts Am., 1980-81, tng. coord. Explorer program, 1982-86, scouting coord. Explorer Post 2312, 1986-91; coord. high sch. youth program St. Michael's Ch., Sunbury, 1981-91, pres. parish coun., 1989-91; vice chmn. SSS, Sunbury, 1982-89; chmn. Sunbury Govt. Study Commn., 1989-90; bd. dirs. Hemlock coun. Girls Scouts U.S.A., 1990-95; bd. dirs. Pa. Partnerships for Children, 1996-2001, treas., 2001—; mem. parish coun. St. Patrick Cathedral, Harrisburg, 1997-2000; chair citizen rev. panel United Way Capitol Region, 1998-2000, bd. dirs., 2003—; chair Early Childhood Initiative Steering com. United Way, 1999—; bd. dirs. United Way Capital Region, 2003—. Named Chief Probation Officer of Yr., Juvenile Ct. Judges Commn., Harrisburg, Pa., 1985; recipient Liberty Bell award Northumberland County Bar Assn., 1986, Meritorious Svc. award Pa. Foster Parents, 1988, affiliate award Pa. Assn. County Commrs., 1990, Citizen of Yr., City of Sunbury, 1992, Pres.'s award Pa. Assn. County Human Svc. Dirs., 1994, Disting. Svc. award Juvenile Detention Ctr. Adminstrs. Pa., 1994. Mem. Nat. Juvenile Ct. Svcs. Assn. (regional rep. 1989-93), Nat. Coun. Juvenile and Family Ct. Judges (awards com.), Nat. Juvenile Detention Assn., Nat. Juvenile Ct. Svcs. Assn., Mental Health and Mental Retardation Program Adminstrs. Assn., Mental Health and Mental Retardation Adminstrs. Assn. Pa. (chmn. 1989-91). Democrat. Office: Northwestern Human Svcs 1320 Linglestown Rd Harrisburg PA 17110-2822 Home: 4515 Laurelwood Dr Harrisburg PA 17110-2829 E-mail: mikebreslin@comcast.net., mbreslin@nhsonline.org.

BRESLIN, NANCY ANN, psychiatrist, photographer, educator; b. Orange, NJ, Aug. 18, 1957; d. Alfred J. and Joyce L. (Deutsch) B.; m. Peter J. Caws, Nov. 28, 1987; 1 child, Elisabeth Breslin Caws. BA, Rutgers U., 1979; MD, U. Pitts., 1983; MFA, U. Del., 2000. Diplomate Am. Bd. Psychiatry and Neurology. Instr. in psychiatry George Washington U., Washington, 1986-87, asst. prof. psychiatry, 1987-96, assoc. clin. prof. psychiatry, 1996—2002, mem. grad. neurosci. program, 1992-97; sr. staff fellow NIMH, Washington, 1989-90; adj. faculty mem. U. Del., 2001—. Med. bd., NIMH Neuropsychiat. Rsch. Hosp., Washington, 1988-90, dep. med. dir., 1989-90. Co-editor: The Behavioral Sciences in Psychiatry, 1995. Laughlin fellow Am. Coll. Psychiatrists, 1987, Individual Artist fellow Del. Divsn. Arts, 2003. Mem. LWV (bd. dirs. 2003—), Am. Psychiat. Assn. (chair APA/Lilly resident rsch. award com. 1995-97), Soc. for Photographic Edn. (sec. Mid-Atlantic regional bd. 2002—), Alpha Omega Alpha, Phi Kappa Phi. Avocations: painting, travel. Home: 237 Cheltenham Rd Newark DE 19711-3617 E-mail: nbreslin@udel.edu.

BRESLOW, ESTHER MAY GREENBERG, biochemistry educator, researcher; b. N.Y.C., Dec. 23, 1931; d. Harry Daniel and Lillian (Solomon) Greenberg; m. Ronald Charles David Breslow, Sept. 4, 1955; children: Stephanie Ruth, Karen Ann. BS with distinction, Cornell U., 1953; MS in Biochemistry, NYU, 1955, PhD in Biochemistry, 1959; postgrad., Radcliffe Coll., 1954-55. Postdoctoral fellow Cornell U. Med. Coll., N.Y.C., 1959-61, rsch. assoc., 1961-64, asst. prof., 1964-72, assoc. prof., 1972-78, prof. biochemistry, 1978—, acting chmn. dept. biochemistry, 1992-95. Mem. rev. panels NIH, Bethesda, Md., 1973—77, Bethesda, 1994—97, NSF, Bethesda, 1981—84, Mem. editorial bd. Jour. Biol. Chemistry, 1982-87, Internat. Jour. Peptide and Protein Rsch., 1981-97; contbr. articles to profl. jours. Mem. Englewood (N.J.) Bd. Health, 1986-94; mem. Dem. Mcpl. Com., Englewood, 1985-91. Eli Lilly fellow, 1954-55; USPHS fellow, 1959-61; NIH grantee, 1961—. Fellow AAAS; mem. Am. Soc. for Biochemistry and Molecular Biology, Am. Chem. Soc. (sec. div. biol. chemistry 1972-76), Harvey Soc., Sigma Xi. Home: 275 Broad Ave Englewood NJ 07631-4350 Office: Joan and Sanford I Weill Med Coll Cornell U 1300 York Ave New York NY 10021-4805 E-mail: ebreslow@mail.med.cornell.edu.

BRESLOW, LESTER, physician, educator; b. Bismarck, N.D., Mar. 17, 1915; s. Joseph and Mayme (Danziger) Breslow; m. Devra J.R. Miller, 1967; children: Norman, Jack, Stephen. BA, U. Minn., 1935, MD, 1938, MPH, 1941, DSc (hon.), 1988. Diplomate Am. Bd. Preventive Medicine and Public Health. Intern USPHS Hosp., Stapleton, NY, 1938—40; dist. health officer Minn. Dept. Health, 1941—43; preventive medicine officer U.S. Army, 1943—45; chief bur. chronic diseases Calif. Dept. Pub. Health, Berkeley, 1946—60, chief divsn. preventive medicine, 1960—65, dir. dept., 1965—68; lectr. U. Calif. Sch. Pub. Health, Berkeley, 1950—68; prof. pub. health UCLA Sch. Pub. Health, 1968—, chmn. dept. preventive medicine and social medicine, 1969—72, dean, 1972—80, mem. divsn. cancer control, 1980—, dir. health promotion ctr., 1988—91, dean, prof. emeritus, 1980—; dir. study Pres.'s Commn. Health Needs of Nation, 1952. Cons. Office of Technology Assessment, Nat. Heart, Lung, Blood Inst., 1977, Nat. Cancer Inst., 1981—, chmn. bd. sci. counsellors divsn. cancer prevention and control, 1982—84; chmn. Nat. Com. on Vital and Health Stats., 1979—81; mem. U.S.-China Health Scis. Com., Dept. HHS, 1982; bd. dirs., chmn. Calif. Ctr. for Health Improvement, 1998—. Editor: Ann. Rev. Pub. Health, 1979—90, Encyclopedia Pub. Health, 2002; editorial cons. in field:. Active L.A. County Pub. Health Commn., 1996—, chmn., 1997—98. Capt. U.S. Army, 1943—45. Decorated Bronze Star; recipient Lasker award, Mary Lasker Found., 1960, Dana award, Charles A. Dana Found., 1988, Healthtrac Found. prize, 1995, Porter prize, 1998, Outstanding Achievement award, U. Minn., 1970, Thomas Francis, Jr. Meml. award, U. Mich. Fellow: AAAS, ACP, Am. Coll. Preventive Medicine (Disting. Svc. award 1976); mem.: APHA (past pres., Sedgwick medal 1977), Inst. Medicine NAS (council 1978—80, chmn. bd. health promotion and disease prevention 1980—82, Lienhard award 1997), Assn. Schs. Public Health (pres. 1973—74), Am. Cancer Soc. (nat. dir., Calif. dir., chmn. adv. com. on rsch. etiology), Internat. Epidemiol. Assn. (past pres.), Am. Epidemiol. Soc., Public Health Cancer Assn. (past pres.), Am. Heart Assn. (fellow epidemiology sect.). Home: 10926 Verano Rd Los Angeles CA 90077-2224

BRESLOW, NORMAN EDWARD, biostatistics educator, researcher; b. Mpls., Feb. 21, 1941; s. Lester and Alice Jane (Philp) Breslow; m. Gayle Marguerite Bramwell, Sept. 7, 1963; children: Lauren Louise, Sara Jo. BA, Reed Coll., 1962; PhD, Stanford U., 1967; Doctorate (honoris causa), U. Bordeaux II, 2001. Trainee Stanford U., 1965—67; vis. research worker London Sch. Hygiene, 1967—68; instr. U. Wash., Seattle, 1968—69, asst. prof., 1969—72, assoc. prof., 1972—76, prof., 1976—, chmn. dept. biostats., 1983—93; statistician Internat. Agy. Research Cancer, Lyon, France, 1972—74. Mem. Hutchinson Cancer Ctr., Seattle, 1982—; statistician Nat. Wilms' Tumor Study, 1969—2003; cons. Internat. Agy. Rsch. Cancer, Lyon, 1978—79; assoc. prof. U. Geneva, 1994—. Named sr. U.S. Scientist, Alexander Humboldt Found., Fed. Republic of Germany, 1982; recipient Spiegelman Gold medal, APHA, 1978, Preventive Oncology Acad. award, NIH, 1978—83, Snedecor award, Com. of Pres.'s on Statis. Socs., 1995, R.A. Fisher lectr. award, 1995; fellow sr. Internat., Fogarty Ctr., 1990; grantee rsch., NIH, 1984—. Fellow: AAAS, Royal Statis. Soc., Am. Statis. Assn. (com. on fellows 1996—2000, N. Mantel award 2002); mem.: Internat. Biometric Soc. (regional com. 1975—78, coun. 1994—2000, v.p. 2001, pres. 2002—03), Inst. Medicine-Nat. Acad. Scis., Internat. Statis. Inst. Avocations: ski mountaineering, hiking, bicycling. Office: Univ of Wash Dept Biostatistics Seattle WA 98195-7232 E-mail: norm@u.washington.edu.

BRESLOW, RONALD CHARLES, chemist; b. Rahway, N.J., Mar. 14, 1931; s. Alexander E. and Gladys (Fellows) Breslow; m. Esther Greenberg, Sept. 7, 1955; children: Stephanie, Karen. AB summa cum laude, Harvard U., 1952, MA, 1953, PhD, 1955. NRC fellow Cambridge (Eng.) U., 1955—56; mem. faculty Columbia, 1956—, prof. chemistry, 1962—66, S.L. Mitchell prof., 1966—; univ. prof., 1992—. Cons. to industry, 1958—; mem. medicinal chemistry panel NIH, 1964—; mem. adv. panel on chemistry NSF, 1971—; mem. sci. adv. com. GM Corp., 1982—; A.R. Todd vis. prof. Cambridge U., 1982; editor Benjamin, Inc., 1962—. Author: Organic Reaction Mechanisms, 1965, 1969; contbr. articles to profl. jours.; editl. bd. Organic Syntheses, 1964—, Jour. Organic Chemistry, 1969—, Jour. Bio-organic Chemistry, 1972—, Tetrahedron, 1975—, Tetrahedron Letters, 1975—, Procs. NAS, 1984—. Trustee Rockefeller U., 1981—; bd. sci. advisers Alfred P. Sloan Found., 1978—85. Recipient Fresenius award, Phi Lambda Upsilon, 1966, Mark Van Doren award, Columbia U., 1969, Roussel prize, 1978, Great Tchr. award, Columbia U., 1981, T.W. Richards medal, 1984, A.C. Cope award, 1987, G.W. Kenner award, U. Liverpool, Eng., 1988, Paracelsus prize, Swiss Chem. Soc., 1999, Arthur Day award, 1990, Nat. medal of Sci., NSF, 1991, Paracelsus award, New Swiss Chem. Soc., Royal Soc. London, 1990, Mayor's award in Sci., N.Y.C., 2000, Centenary lectr., London Chem. Soc., 1972. Fellow: Indian Acad. Scis. (hon. fgn.), Am. Acad. Arts and Scis., Korean Chem. Soc. (hon.); mem.: NAS (chmn. chemistry divsn. 1974—77, award in chemistry 1989), Royal Soc. Chemistry (London, hon.), New Swiss Chem. Soc. (Paracelsus award 1990), Royal Soc. London (hon.), Chem. Soc. Japan (hon.), Am. Chem. Soc. (pres.-elect 1995—96, pres. 1996, chmn. divsn. organic chemistry 1970, Pure Chemistry award 1966, Baekeland medal 1969, Harrison Howe award 1974, Remsen award 1977, J.F. Norris award 1980, N.Y. sect. Nicholas medal

1989, Priestley medal 1999, Bioorganic Chemistry award 2002), Am. Philos. Soc. (coun. 1987—), Phi Beta Kappa (1st marshall 1952). Home: 275 Broad Ave Englewood NJ 07631-4350 Office: Columbia U Dept Chemistry 116th St & Broadway New York NY 10027

BRESNAHAN, ARTHUR STEPHEN, lawyer; b. Chgo., Dec. 26, 1944; s. Arthur Patrick and Margaret Genevieve (Gleason) B.; m. Patricia Margaret Wetz, June 29, 1968; children: Arthur Patrick, Maureen Justina, Brian Michael, Brendan Robert, Sean Matthew. BA in Psychology, Loras Coll., 1967; JD, Ill. Inst. Tech., 1975. Bar: Ill. 1975, U.S. Dist. Ct. (no. dist.) Ill. 1975, U.S. Ct. Appeals (7th cir.) 1978, U.S. Supreme Ct. 1986, U.S Ct. Claims 1986. Assoc. Garbutt, Jacobson & Lee, Chgo., 1975-77; sr. assoc. atty. Purcell & Wardrope, Chgo., 1977-83; ptnr. Bresnahan & Garvey, Chgo., 1983-88, 1988-98; pvt. practice Arthur S. Bresnahan & Assocs., Chgo., 1998—. Speaker in field. Asst. scoutmaster Boy Scouts Am., Chgo., 1980—, Webelos Den leader. Capt. USMC, 1967-72. Mem. ABA, VFW, Fed. Bar Assn., Ill. Bar Assn., Fed. Trial Bar, Chgo. Bar Assn., Trial Lawyers Club, Vietnam Vets. Am., Lawyer Pilots Bar Assn., Am. Legion. Lodges: KC, Moose. Democrat. Roman Catholic. Avocations: golf, girl/boy scouts. Home and Office: 4715 N Kenneth Ave Chicago IL 60630-4004

BRESNAHAN, JAMES FRANCIS, retired medical educator; b. Springfield, Mass., Dec. 28, 1926; s. James Francis and Margaret Anna Bresnahan. AB, Coll. Holy Cross, 1947; MA, Weston Coll, 1953, STL, 1960; JD, Harvard U., 1950, LLM, 1955; PhD, Yale U., 1972. Bar: Mass. 1955, U.S. Dist. Ct. Mass. 1975; joined Soc. of Jesus, Roman Cath. Ch., 1949. Tchr. Cheverus H.S., Portland, Maine, 1955-56; asst. prof. religious studies Fairfield U., 1962-66, 69-70; vis. prof. ethics Weston Jesuit Sch. Theology, 1971-72; assoc. prof. religious studies and philosophy Regis U., 1972-74; prof. ethics Jesuit Sch. Theology in Chgo., 1975-81; vis. lectr. in med. ethics Northwestern U. Med. Sch., Chgo., 1978-80; vis. lectr. in legal ethics Northwestern U. Law Sch., Chgo., 1979; co-dir. ethics program Northwestern U. Med. Sch., Chgo., 1980-96, prof. med. ethics and humanities, clin. medicine, 1989-97, prof. emeritus, 1997—, ret., 2002—. Ethics cons. Northwestern Meml. Hosp., 1982—2001; cons. palliative care program Dartmouth-Hitchcock Med. Ctr., 2002—03; adj. prof. Dartmouth Med. Sch., 2002—03. Mem. adv. com.: Jour. Law and Religion, mem. edit. bd., Cambridge Quar. Health Care Ethics; contbr. articles to profl. jours. Mem. com. to draft code profl. conduct Canon Law Soc. Am., 1978—79; treas. Chgo. Clin. Ethics Programs, 1989—90, pres.-elect, 1990—91, pres., 1991—92. Mem.: AAUP (v.p. chpt. 1973—74), Inst. Medicine Chgo., Am. Soc. Bioethics and Humanities, Am. Soc. Law, Medicine and Ethics, Ill. Coalition Against Death Penalty, Coun. on Religion and Law, Soc. Christian Ethics (convenor ethics and law task force 1979—80, dir. 1981—85). Office: St Mary's Hall Boston Coll 140 Commonwealth Ave Chestnut Hill MA 02467-3802 E-mail: jfbresnahan@northwestern.edu.

BRESS, MICHAEL E. retired lawyer; b. Mpls., Aug. 23, 1933; s. Michael J. and Anna (Tema) B.; m. Grace Billings, June 3, 1966; 1 child, Anne Ruth. BA, U. Minn., 1954, LLB, 1957. Bar: N.Y. 1958, Minn. 1959. Assoc. Donovan Leisure Newton & Irvine, N.Y.C., 1957-59, Dorsey & Whitney LLP, Mpls., 1959-64; ptnr. Dorsey & Whitney LPP, Mpls., 1964-91, of counsel, 1992-97, ret., 1998. Trustee St. Vladimir's Orthodox Theol. Sem., Crestwood, N.Y. Mem. Minn. Bar Assn., Hennepin County Bar Assn., Phi Beta Kappa. Home: 2007 W Franklin Ave Minneapolis MN 55405-2422 E-mail: mbress@mn.rr.com.

BRESSAN, PAUL LOUIS, lawyer; b. Rockville Centre, NY, June 15, 1947; s. Louis Charles Bressan and Nance Elizabeth Batteley. BA cum laude, Fordham Coll., 1969; JD, Columbia U., 1975. Bar: N.Y. 1976, Calif. 1987, U.S. Dist. Ct. (so., ea. and no. dists.) N.Y. 1976, U.S. Dist. Ct. (no. and ctrl. dists.) Calif. 1987, U.S. Ct. Appeals (2d cir.) 1980, U.S. Supreme Ct. 1980, U.S. Ct. Appeals (1st and 4th cirs.) 1981, U.S. Ct. Appeals (11th cir.) 1982, U.S. Ct. Appeals (9th cir.) 1987, U.S Ct. Appeals (7th cir.) 1991, U.S. Dist. Ct. (ea. dist.) Calif. 1995; U.S. Dist. Ct. (so. dist.) Calif. 1997. Assoc. Kelley, Drye & Warren, N.Y.C., 1975-84, ptnr. N.Y.C. and Los Angeles, 1984—2003; shareholder Buchalter, Nemer, Fields & Younger, LA, 2003—. Served to lt. USNR, 1971-72. Named One of Outstanding Coll. Athletes of Am., 1969; Harlan Fiske Stone scholar Columbia Law Sch. Mem. ABA, Calif. Bar Assn., Phi Beta Kappa. Republican. Roman Catholic. Office: Buchalter Nemer Fields & Younger 601 S Figueroa St Ste 2400 Los Angeles CA 90017 E-mail: pbressan@buchalter.com.

BRESSAN, ROBERT RALPH, accountant; b. Yonkers, N.Y., Feb. 8, 1945; s. Alfred D. and Antionette (Desivo) B.; m. Florence L. Vigna, June 9, 1968 (dec.); children: Anne Marie, Robert A., Tiffany L. BBA in Acctg., Iona Coll., 1967. CPA, Colo.; cert. tax profl. Am. Inst. Tax Studies. Staff to sr. Coopers & Lybrand, N.Y.C., 1967—70; sr. to audit mgr. Fox & Co., Colorado Springs, 1970—80; ptnr., owner Robert R. Bressan, Colorado Springs, 1980—2002. Mem. exec. com. GAO Intergovtl. Audit Forum. Mem. charity rev. com. BBB. Mem. AICPA, Sertoma, Inst. Mgmt. Accts., Govtl. Fin. Officers Assn., Colo. Govtl. Fin. Officers, Nat. Assn. Counties. Avocations: coins, golf, dancing. Office: 2997 Broadmoor Valley Rd Ste 200 Colorado Springs CO 80906

BRESSE-RODENKIRK, ROBERT FRANCIS, journalist; b. Evanston, Ill., Apr. 28, 1952; s. Robert Francis and Joan Marie (Wolter) Rodenkirk. BA in History and Journalism, Ind. U., 1974; postgrad., Northwestern U., 1976. Program dir., pub. affairs dir. WIUS Radio, Bloomington, Ind., 1972-74; reporter City News Bur. of Chgo., 1974-77; news dir. WNUR Radio, Evanston, Ill., 1977; announcer WDHF Radio, Chgo., 1977; news dir. WMET Radio, Chgo., 1977-78; Chgo. corr. AP Radio Network, 1978-79; reporter, anchor WINS Radio, N.Y.C., 1984-88, WMAQ Radio, Chgo., 1979-84, 88-00; reporter WBBM Radio, Chgo., 2000—. Recipient Nat. Broadcast awards AP, 1998, UPI, 1979, 81, 83, 90, 98, Nat. award Sigma Delta Chi, 1996, Max Karant award Aircraft Owners & Pilots Assn., 1997, others. Mem.: Chgo. Headline Club (bd. dirs. 1993—, pres.-elect 1995—96, pres. 1996—97, v.p. 1998—, Peter Lisagor award 1988, 1996, 2000, 2001, 2002), Radio-TV News Dirs. Assn. (Edward R. Murrow Regional award 1998, 2002), Soc. Profl. Journalists, Ill. News Broadcasters Assn. (bd. dirs. 1988—, v.p. 1994—96, pres. 1996—97), Shore Line Interurban Hist. Soc. (sec. 2002—), Fox River Trolley Mus. (publicity dir.), Ill. Rlwy. Mus., Branford Electric Rlwy. Assn. Roman Catholic. Avocations: railroading, bicycling.

BRESSLER, BARRY E. lawyer; b. Phila., Apr. 7, 1947; s. Joseph and Shirley M. (Eiseman) B.; m. Risé Sharon Cohen, June 14, 1970 (dec.); children: Allison Ivy, Michelle Amy. AB, Franklin and Marshall Coll., Lancaster, Pa., 1968; JD, U. Pa., 1971. Bar: Pa. 1971, U.S. Dist. Ct. (ea. dist.) Pa. 1973, U.S. Ct. Appeals (3d cir.) 1977, U.S. Supreme Ct. 1988, U.S. Dist. Ct. (mid. dist.) Pa. 1990. Law clk. to judge Superior Ct. Pa., Phila., 1971-73; assoc. Meltzer & Schiffrin, Phila., 1973-79, ptnr., 1979-86, Fox, Rothschild, O'Brien & Frankel, Phila., 1987-88; mem., sr. lawyer real estate litigation & creditors' rights Pelino & Lentz, P.C., Phila., 1988-2000; ptnr. Schnader, Harrison, Segal & Lewis, LLP, Phila., 2000—. Adj. instr. landlord-tenant law Delaware County C.C., Media, Pa., 1985—, Montgomery County C.C., Blue Bell, Pa., 1987—. V.p. English Ceramic Study Group, Phila.; v.p., sec. Temple Sinai, Dresher, Pa., 1991-97, 2003-; grad. Leadership, Inc., Phila. Mem. ABA (litigation sect.), Pa. Bar Assn. (corp. banking and bus. sect.), Phila. Bar Assn. (real property sect.), Bankruptcy Conf. Ea. Dist. Pa. (treas. 1995-2000), Am. Arbitration Assn. Republican. Jewish. Avocations: tennis, ceramics, bridge. Office: Schnader Harrison Segal and Lewis LLP 1600 Market St Ste 3600 Philadelphia PA 19103-7286 E-mail: bbressler@schnader.com.

BRESSLER, BARRY LEE, theoretical physicist, systems analyst; b. Reading, Pa., Feb. 16, 1936; s. Kenneth Russell and Lillian Mary (Good) B. BS in Physics, Ursinus Coll., 1957; MS in Physics, Va. Poly. Inst. State U., 1979, PhD in Physics, 1986. Tchr., curator insect collection Reading Pub. Mus., 1954-55; data-processing technician Philco Corp., Phila., 1956, jr. engr. Spring City, Pa., 1957-58; physicist Naval Surface Warfare Ctr., Dahlgren, Va., 1958-94, group leader, 1983-89, fellow, 1983-85, sr. scientist, 1989-94; prin. scientist EG&G Tech. Svcs., Inc., Dahlgren, 1994-95, sr. prin. scientist, 1995—. Cons. Windy Knoll Enterprises, Inc., Magnolia, Tex., 1994—; adj. prof. physics Va. Poly. Inst. State U., Blacksburg, 1994—. Bryn Mawr Coll. scholar, 1957. Mem. Am. Phys. Soc., Coleopterists Soc. (jour. referee 1991-95), Sigma Pi Sigma, Sigma Xi. Achievements include mathematical modeling and simulation, and computation of trajectories, for ballistic missiles, reentry vehicles, and interceptor missiles; determination of guidance commands for flight tests of maneuvering reentry vehicles; analysis of simulated engagements between evasively maneuvering reentry vehicles and interceptor missiles; design and optimization of reentry maneuvers; threat analysis; analysis of advanced strategic and tactical weapons systems; formulation of theoretical models for the electromagnetic pulse produced by a high-altitude nuclear burst, and for various other weapons effects; research in the quantum mechanics of many-particle systems, particularly of fermion-boson systems; education of nontraditional graduate physics students. Avocations: ecology, myrmecology, cerambycid taxonomy, Shetland sheepdogs. Home: PO Box 1345 Fredericksburg VA 22402-1345 Office: EG&G Services PO Box 552 Dahlgren VA 22448-0552 E-mail: blbressler@aol.com., bbressler@eggin c.com., bbressle@vt.edu. *Request for EHL.*

BRESSLER, BERNARD, lawyer; b. NYC, Jan. 2, 1928; s. Morris and Masha (Roitman) B.; m. Teresa Stern, June 25, 1950; children: Lisa, Jeanette. BA, Rutgers U., 1949; LLB magna cum laude, Harvard U., 1952. Bar: N.Y. 1953, N.J. 1977. Atty. firm Greenman, Shea, Sandomire & Zimet, N.Y.C., 1952-60; ptnr. Bressler, Amery & Ross, N.Y.C., 1960—, Florham Park, N.J., 1981—. Sec., bd. dirs. Gradco Systems Inc.; dir., chmn. bd. N.J. Pub. Interest Law Ctr., 1996—. Author: (with others) Tax Annotations Nichols Ency. Forms, 1954-59; Editor: (with B. Meislin) New York Lawyers Manual, 1954, Harvard Law Rev., vol. 65. Campaign dir. Summit (N.J.) United Jewish Appeal, 1957-60; chmn. Summit Democrat Club, 1957; trustee Summit Civic Found., 1958-65; chmn. Summit Area United Negro Coll. Fund, 1979-92. With USNR, 1945-46. Mem.: Lotos (N.Y.C.), Park Ave. Club (N.J.). Home: 3 Kimberwick Ct Morristown NJ 07960-6993 Office: 17 State St New York NY 10004-1501 also: 325 Columbia Tpke Florham Park NJ 07932-1212

BRESSLER, H.J. lawyer, judge; b. Balt., Dec. 31, 1939; s. Sam Bressler and Rose Cohen; m. Elizabeth Ann Woodward, Dec. 20, 1959; children: Scott, Erika, Jason. Student, U.S. Army Lang. Sch., 1959; BA, Miami U., Oxford, Ohio, 1964; JD, Salmon P. Chase Law Sch., 1968. Regional credit mgr. Procter & Gamble, Cin., 1964-65, U.S. Shoe Co., Cin., 1965-68; ptnr. Holbrock, Jonson, Bressler and Houser, 1972-85, Bressler, Shanks & Gedling Co. L.P.A., Hamilton, Ohio, 1985-96. Judge Butler County Ct., Ohio, 1981-96, Butler County Common Pleas Ct., 1997—; lectr. Ohio Jud. Coll., Ohio Bar Assn. Chmn. Ohio juvenile sentencing com.; vice-chmn. Ohio criminal sentencing commn.; trustee Ohio common pleas judge assn.; Served with U.S. Army, 1958-61. Mem. Ohio Bar Assn., Butler County Bar Assn. (pres. 1981), Am. Acad. Trial Lawyers, Ohio Acad. Trial Lawyers, Greater Hamilton Trial Lawyers Assn. (pres. 1978), Ohio Muni-County Judges Assn. (pres. 1991), Ohio Common Pleas Judges Assn. (trustee 1999—). Republican. Methodist. Office: Govt Svcs Ctr 315 High St Hamilton OH 45011-6056

BRESSLER, MARCUS NATHAN, consulting engineer; b. Havana, Cuba, July 31, 1929; came to U.S., 1942; s. Isaac and Augustine (Draiman) B.; m. Sondra Kipnes, Nov. 7, 1954; children: Eric L., Lisa A., Karen J. Lee. B of Mech. Engring., Cornell U., 1952; MSME, Case Inst. Tech., 1960. Registered profl. engr., Ohio, Tenn. Stress analysis engr. The Babcock & Wilcox Co., Barberton, Ohio, 1955-66; design engr. Lenape Forge, West Chester, Pa., 1966-70; mgr., product design and devel. engr. Taylor Forge, Cicero, Ill., 1970-71; supr. codes, standards and materials TVA, Knoxville, 1971-79, sr. engring. specialist, 1979-88; pres. M.N. Bressler, PE, Inc., Knoxville, 1988—. 1st lt. U.S. Army, 1952-54, capt. USAR, 1957. Fellow ASME (mem. boiler and pressure vessel stds. com., bd. conformity assessment, bd. nuc. codes and stds., Century Medallion 1980, Bernard F. Langer Nuc. Codes and Stds. award 1992, J. Hall Taylor medal for pressure tech. codes and stds. outstanding contbns. 1996, Dedicated Svc. award 2001). Home and Office: M N Bressler PE Inc 829 Chateaugay Rd Knoxville TN 37923-2017 E-mail: mbresslerpe@juno.com.

BRESSLER, RICHARD J. communications company executive; married; two children. Grad. summa cum laude, Adelphi Coll., 1979. CPA. Ptnr. Ernst & Young, Inc., 1979-88; from asst. controller to exec. v.p., CFO Time Warner, Inc., N.Y.C., 1988—95, CEO, sr. v.p., 1995—98; senior v.p., CFO Viacom Inc, N.Y.C., 2001—. Bd. dirs. Prep for Prep, Outward Bound; mem. Chase Nat. Adv. Bd., CFO Adv. Coun.; trustee Citizen's Budget Commn. Mem. Am. Inst. CPAs, N.Y. State Soc. Cert. CPAs. Office: Viacom Inc 1515 Broadway New York NY 10036

BREST, PAUL A. law educator; b. Jacksonville, Fla., Aug. 9, 1940; s. Alexander and Mia (Deutsch) B.; m. Iris Lang, June 17, 1962; children: Hilary, Jeremy. AB, Swarthmore Coll., 1962; JD, Harvard U., 1965; LLD (hon.), Northeastern U., 1980, Swarthmore Coll., 1991. Bar: N.Y. 1966. Law clk. to Hon. Bailey Aldrich U.S. Ct. Appeals (1st cir.), Boston, 1965-66; atty. NAACP Legal Def. Fund, Jackson, Miss., 1966-68; law clk. Justice John Harlan, U.S. Supreme Ct., 1968-69; prof. law Stanford U., 1969—, Kenneth and Harle Montgomery Prof. pub. interest law, Richard E. Lang prof. and dean, 1987-99; pres. William and Flora Hewlett Found., Menlo Park, Calif., 1999—. Author: Processes of Constitutional Decisionmaking, 1992. Mem. Am. Acad. Arts and Scis. Home: 814 Tolman Dr Palo Alto CA 94305-1026 Office: William and Flora Hewlett Found 2121 Sand Hill Rd Menlo Park CA 94025 E-mail: pbrest@hewlett.org.

BRESTEL, MARY BETH, librarian; b. Cin., Feb. 5, 1952; d. John Wesley and Laura Alice (Knoop) Seay; m. Michael Charles Brestel, Aug. 3, 1974; 1 child, Rebecca Michelle. BS, U. Cin., 1974; MLS, U. Ky., 1984. Libr. asst. history and lit. dept. Pub. Libr. Cin. and Hamilton County, 1974-78, children's asst. Pleasant Ridge br., 1978-81, children's asst. Westwood br., 1981-84, reference libr. sci. and tech. dept., 1984-90, 1st asst. sci. and tech. dept., 1990-92, mgr. dept., 1992—. Mem. Ohio Libr. Coun., Columbus, 2001—03. Mem. United Methodist Ch. Office: Pub Libr Cin and Hamilton County Sci and Tech Dept 800 Vine St Cincinnati OH 45202-2071

BRESTER, GARY W. educator; b. Billings, Mont., Oct. 23, 1958; s. Donald and Norma Brester; m. Colleen Brester, May 22, 1982; children: Erin Marie, Kyle John. BS, Mont. State U., 1980, MS, 1982; PhD, N.C. State U., 1990. Asst. prof. Kans. State U., Manhattan, 1990—95, assoc. prof., 1995—97, Mont. State U., Bozeman, 1997—2000, prof., 2000—. Mem.: Western Agrl. Econs. Assn. (v.p. 2002—03), Am. Agrl. Econs. Assn. Personal E-mail: gbrester@montana.edu.

BRESTLE, DAN, cosmetics executive; m. Cathy Brestle; 2 children. BA, Villanova U., 1967. With Johnson & Johnson, 1973—78; distbn. mgr. Estée Lauder Cos., Oakland, NJ, 1978—79, plant mgr., 1979, dir. mfg., warehousing and distbn., 1979—83, regional mktg. dir. Aramis N.Y.C., 1983—84, v.p., nat. sales mgr. prescriptives, 1984—88, pres. prescriptives, 1988—92, pres. Clinique Labs., 1992—98, pres. Estée Lauder U.S. and Can., 1998—2001, group pres., 2001—. Mem. adv. coun. Coll. Commerce & Fin. Villanova U. With USAF. Mem.: Csometic, Toiletry, and Fragrance Assn. (bd. dirs.). Office: Estee Lauder Co Inc 767 5th Ave New York NY 10153*

BRETHAUER, WILLIAM RUSSELL, JR., claim investigator; b. Pitts., Apr. 5, 1953; s. William Russell and Cecelia Helen Brethauer; m. Barbara L. Summers, Mar. 8, 1980; children: Laura Diane, Stacey Lynn. BA magna cum laude, Thiel Coll., 1975; grad., Inst. Paralegal Tng., Phila., 1976. Cert. paralegal, casualty-property claim law assoc. Claim rep. St. Paul Cos. Inc., Ft. Washington, Pa., 1977-80, claim supr. San Jose, 1980-82, St. Paul, 1982-84, spl. claim investigator Orlando, Fla., 1984—. Intern WQED-TV, Pitts., 1974; mem. Fla. adv. com. arson prevention, Maitland, 1984—. Author: (novel) Boardwalk, 1991, (book) If I Were A Horse, They'd Shoot Me, 1993, My Enemies, Small Devils, 1993, Insurance Fraud: Deceit & Ingenuity, 1992; asst. prodr.: (multimedia program) When to Say When, 1974. Libertarian. Avocations: whitewater rafting, windsurfing, rollerblading, skiing, travel. Home and Office: PO Box 621329 Oviedo FL 32762-1329

BRETT, ANTHONY H. lawyer; b. Ahoskie, N.C., Oct. 11, 1953; BA, Yale U., 1975; JD, Duke U., 1979. Bar: N.C. 1979, U.S. Supreme Ct. 1983. Ptnr. Womble, Carlyle, Sandridge & Rice, PLLC, Winston-Salem, N.C., 1979—. Mem. N.C. Bar Assn., N.C. Soc. Health Care Attys., Am. Health Lawyers Assn. Office: Womble Carlyle Sandridge & Rice PLLC One West Fourth St Winston Salem NC 27102-0084 E-mail: abrett@wcsr.com.

BRETT, ARTHUR CUSHMAN, JR., banker; b. Bronxville, N.Y., Mar. 23, 1928; s. Arthur Cushman and Mary Kathryn (Clark) B.; m. Mary Elizabeth Cunliffe, Aug. 21, 1954; children: Margaret Brett Uzarski, Catherine Brett Main, John, Patricia, Matthew BS, Fordham U., 1953; MBA, NYU, 1959. Asst. v.p. Bowery Savs. Bank, N.Y.C., 1950-68; instl. registered rep. Salomon Bros., N.Y.C., 1968-71, 73-75, Blyth Eastman Dillon, Boston, 1971-73; v.p. Mut. Am. Life Ins. Co., N.Y.C., 1975-78; v.p. investments, sec. East River Savs. Bank, N.Y.C., 1978-80; sr. v.p., treas., chief investment officer Apple Bank for Savs., N.Y.C., 1980-92. Mem. investment com. Social Sci. Rsch. Coun., 1976-86, NYU Fed. Credit Union, 1983-89. Mem.: NY Soc. Security Analysts. Roman Catholic. Home: 2514 Redding Rd Fairfield CT 06824-1745 also: 441 Ocean Ave Stratford CT 06615-7829

BRETT, GEORGE HOWARD, baseball executive, former professional baseball player; b. Glen Dale, W.Va., May 15, 1953; s. Jack Francis and Ethel (Hansen) B. Student, Longview C.C., Mo., El Camino Coll., Torrance, Calif. Former third baseman Kansas City (Mo.) Royals Profl. Baseball Team, v.p. baseball ops. Player Am. League All-Star Game, 1976—88. Named Am. League batting champion, 1976, 80, 90, Am. League Most Valuable Player, 1980; player Am. League All-Star Game, 1976-88; Inductee Baseball Hall of Fame, Cooperstown, N.Y., 1999. Address: care Kansas City Royals attn: vp ops PO Box 419969 Kansas City MO 64141-6969

BRETT, GEORGE WENDELL, retired geologist, philatelist; b. Spirit Lake, Iowa, May 30, 1912; s. John Franklin and Jessie Cary (Cummings) B.; m. Louise Schindler, 1941 (div. 1942). BA, U. Chgo., 1953, MS, 1961. Statistician U.S. Dept. Agr., Spirit Lake, Iowa, 1933; clk. Dickinson County Corn-Hog Control Assn., Spirit Lake, 1934-36; ry. postal clk. U.S. P.O. Dept., on trains Iowa, Ill., Wis., Chgo. terminal, 1936-42; fiscal acctg. clk. U.S. Dept. of Navy, Coco Solo, Canal Zone, Republic of Panama, 1942-45, 46-49; geologist U.S. Geol. Survey, Washington, 1953-72, geologist, cons., 1976-79, ret., 1979—. Author: The Giori Press, 1961, Printing Methods and Techniques, 1985; contbr. several hundred published articles to jours. in field, 1930—. Mem. Coun. Philatelists. With USN, 1945-46. Recipient Nat. Merit award Assoc. Stamp Clubs of Southeastern Pa. and Del., 1964, Phoenix award Ariz. Fed. of Stamp Clubs, Phoenix, 1964, Scroll of Honor, U.S. Geol. Survey, Washington, 1972, Luff award Am. Philatelic Soc., 1978, Writers Hall of Fame, Unit 30, Am. Philatelic Soc., 1979, Meritorious Svc. award The Philatelic Found., N.Y.C., 1981, U.S. Philatelic Rsch. award The Cryer Found., 1983, Lichtenstein Meml. award Collector's Club of N.Y., 1982, McCoy award Am. Philatelic Congress, 1989, Dist. Philatelist award U.S. Philatelic Classics Soc., 1991, Dorothy Colby Meml. award Am. Philatelic Congress, 1993. Mem. Bur. Issues Assn. (Hopkinson Meml. award 1954, 58, 92, spl. award for 20 yrs. svc. as officer 1974, Southgate Disting. Philatelist award, 1980), Bureau Issues Assn., U.S. Stamp Soc. (named to Hall of Fame 2000), Nat. Postal Mus. (coun. of philatelists 1997—). Republican. Avocations: studying postage stamp prodn., travel, photography, mountain climbing. Home: 2412 Lincoln Ave Spirit Lake IA 51360-7032

BRETT, JAMES CLARENCE, retired journalism educator; b. Watertown, N.Y., July 28, 1931; s. Clarence Richard and Justina Leone (Cleland) B. BA, Notre Dame U., 1953. With Watertown Daily Times, 1955-71, author series on Frederick Exley, 1968; chmn. Times Editl. Assn., 1970; adj. assoc. prof. Oswego (N.Y.) State U. Coll., 1970-71, asst. prof., 1971-96; ret., 1996. Mem. organizing com. SUNY Colls. in the North Country, Fort Drum, Watertown, N.Y., 1985; organizer, dir. student internship program New York Times, 1972. Pvt. first class U.S. Army, 1953-55. Mem. Royal Hort. Soc., Am. Hort. Soc., Jefferson County Hist. Soc., Master Gardeners Am., N.Y. State Ret. Tchrs. Assn., Oswego Emeriti Assn., Am. Legion, Ives Hill Country Club, Black River Valley Club. Republican. Roman Catholic. Avocations: gardening, traveling, reading. Home and Office: 146 Ward St Watertown NY 13601-4616

BRETT, JAN CHURCHILL, illustrator, author; b. Hingham, Mass., Dec. 1, 1949; d. George and Jean (Baxter) Brett; m. Daniel Bowler, Feb. 27, 1970 (div. Jan. 1979); 1 child, Lia Bowler; m. Joseph Hearne, Aug. 18, 1980. Student, Colby Jr. Coll., 1968-69, Boston Mus. Fine Arts Sch., 1970; DHL (hon.), Fitchburg State Coll., 1996. Mem. bd. overseers Boston Symphony Orch., 1991—99, trustee, 1999—, Thayer Acad., Braintree, Mass. Mem.: Nat. Soc. Colonial Dames Am., Chilton Club. Office: 132 Pleasant St Norwell MA 02061-2523 E-mail: janbrett@janbrett.com.

BRETT, JOHN BRENDAN, JR., corporate advertising and public relations executive; b. Mar. 28, 1944; s. John Brendan and Vera Mae (Locke) B.; m. Alyene Maybeth Wales, Apr. 30, 1966; children: Heather Allyson, Sean Timothy. Student, U. Md., 1964-65, U. So. Miss., 1965-66; BS in Advt., U. Fla., 1969. Advt. supr. Armstrong Cork Co., Lancaster, Pa., 1969-72; mgr. advt. K-D Mfg. Co., Lancaster, 1972-75; dir. mktg. comm. Brodart Inc., Williamsport, Pa., 1975-78; mktg. comm. supr. E.I. duPont de Nemours & Co., Wilmington, Del., 1978-80, group mgr. mktg. comm., carpet fibers, 1980-85, mgr. corp. advt., 1985-87, group mgr. mktg. comm. electronics, 1987-91, sr. cons., external affairs, 1991-92; mgr. mktg. commn. and pub. affairs Sontara Tech./Dupont Nonwovens, Old Hickory, Tenn., 1992-99, global brand mgr., 1999—2001; dir. alumni rels. and grant programs Aquinas Coll., Nashville, 2001—. Mem. Idea98 & Idea2001 com. INDA Nonwovens Assn., 1997-99; mem. advt. adv. coun. U. Fla., 1984-87. Mem. editl. sounding bd. Advertising Age mag., 1985-87. Vice chmn. Del. all-star football game com. Del. Found. for Retarded Children, 1982-83, chmn., 1984, trustee, 1989-92; bd. govs. Automotive Advertisers Coun., 1975; mem. vestry St. Thomas Episc. Ch., 1974-75, St. David's Episc. Ch., Wilmington, 1989-92, sr. warden, 1991-92; treas. N.E. Missionary Convocation, Diocese of Mid. Tenn., Diocesesan Conv. Del., 1995; chmn. bldg. com. Country Hills Homeowners Assn., 1994-2000, sec. bd. dirs., 2000-02. Recipient Outstanding Advt. Campaign award Am. Bus. Press/Bus.-Profl. Advt. Assn., 1974. Mem. Assn. Nat. Advertisers (corp. advt. com. 1985-86), Mid-Tenn. Classic Chevy Club, Antique Automobile Club of Am., Alpha Delta Sigma, Kappa Tau Alpha. Avocations: outdoor photography, gardening, antique autos. Home: 119 Spy Glass Way Hendersonville TN 37075-8550 Office: Aquinas Coll 4210 Harding Rd Nashville TN 37205 E-mail: brettj@aquinas-tn.edu.

BRETT, KATE M. epidemiologist, researcher; m. Kevin L. Enoch; children: Cora Enoch, Lillian Enoch. AB, U. Chgo., 1980; MA, W.Va. U., 1985; PhD, U. N.C., 1991. Epidemic intelligence svc. CDC and Prevention/Nat. Ctr. for Health Stats., Hyattsville, Md., 1991—93, epidemiologist, 1993—. Decorated Commd. Corp Crisis Response award, Commd. Corp Unit Commendation, Commd. Corp Acheivement medal, Commd. Corp Commendation medal, . Mem.: Commd. Officiers Assn. of USPHS, Am. Coll. Epidemiology. Unitarian Universalist. Office: CDC/Nat Ctr for Health Stats 3311 Toledo Rd Rm 6226 Hyattsville MD 20782 E-mail: kmb5@cdc.gov.

BRETT, NANCY HELÉNE, artist; BFA, Wayne State U., 1969; MFA, Cranbrook Acad. of Art, 1972. One-woman shows include Gallery Seven, Detroit, 1976, Ericson Gallery, N.Y.C., 1980, Harm Bouckaert Gallery, N.Y.C., 1982, Hillwood Art Mus., C.W.Post, Long Island U., N.Y., 1987, L'Ecole Gallery, N.Y.C., Victoria Munroe Gallery, N.Y.C., 1989, 91, 93, Victoria Munroe Fine Art, N.Y.C., 1993, Lake George Arts Project, N.Y., 1996, The Painting Ctr., N.Y.C., 1997, Cranbrook Art Mus., 1998, Hyde Collection Art Mus., Glen Falls, N.Y., 1999; group shows include Mich. Focus, Detroit Inst. of Art and Grand Rapids Mus. of Art (Catalog), 1974, Mus. of Modern Art, Touchstone Gallery, N.Y.C., 1979, Susan Caldwell, N.Y.C., 1979, Landscape Anthology, Grace Borgenicht Gallery, N.Y.C., 1988, Lines of Vision: Drawings by Contemporary Women, Blum Helman Warehouse and Hillwood Art Mus., Long Island U. Catalog, N.Y., 1989, Notions of Place: Paintings and Drawings, Victoria Munroe Gallery, N.Y.C., 1990, The Painters, 1991, Summer Salon, 1992, Celebrating Nature, Champion Internat. Corp. Collection Exhibit., Stamford, Conn., 1991, Landscape Not Landscape, Gallery Camino Real, Boca Raton, Fla. Catalog, 1994, Bklyn. Mus. Art, Gasworks Gallery, London, Cornerstone Gallery, Manchester, U., Gallery Camino Real, Boca Raton, Fla., 1994, U. Art Mus., 1994, Gallery at Hastings-on-Hudson, Mcpl. Bldg., N.Y., 1995, West Eng., Bristol, 1996, Parsons Gallery, 1996, Bklyn. Mus. Art, 1997, Hyde Collection Art Mus., Glens Falls, N.Y., 1998, Exit Art/The first World, N.Y., 1999, Wendy Cooper Gallery, Madison, Wis., 2000, Williamsburg Art and Hist. Ctr., Bklyn., 2000, Akus Gallery, Ea. Conn. State U., Willimantic, Conn., 2000, Exit Art/The First World, N.Y.C., 2002, Sperone Westwater Gallery,

N.Y.C., 2002, Courthouse Gallery, Lake George, N.Y., 2002, A.I.R., N.Y.C., 2002, numerous others; represented in pub. collections: J.P. Morgan, Morgan Guaranty Trust Co., N.Y., Champion Internat., Stamford, Conn., Amerada Hess Corp., GE, Manhattan Savings Bank, Milbank, Tweed, Hadley and McCloy, N.Y.C., Herbert F. Johnson Mus. of Art, Cornell U., Prudential Ins., Best Products, IBM, Morgan Stanley, N.Y.C., Cranbrook Acad of Art Mus., Kidder Peabody, Inc., Hosp. Corp. Am., Power Inst. of Fine Arts, Sydney, Australia, IBM, GE, Princess Cruise Lines, Marsh and McClennan Cos. Inc., Libr. of Congress, Washington. Studio: 457 Broome St New York NY 10013-2681

BRETT, PETER D. writer; b. Jackson, Mich., Apr. 23, 1943; s. Benjamin Thomas Brett and Fanchon (Hillsburg) Eidelman; m. Janet G. Brett; 1 child, Rebecca Hoffman. BS in Biology, Wayne State U., 1965; postgrad., U. Mich., 1970. Writer Peter Brett Assocs., San Rafael, Calif., 1970—. Cons. Sierra Club, San Francisco, 1975; grant writer City of Richmond, 1972; cons., tech. writer Sch. of Holography, San Francisco, 1970-72; lectr. U. Calif., San Diego, 1978. Author: Crossing Paradise, 1970 (Hopwood award 1970), Ghost Rhythms, 1976, Gallery, 1978, Borrowing the Sky, 1978. Fellow U. Colo., 1969-70. Home: PO Box 1771 Ross CA 94957 Office: Peter Brett Assocs 501 B St San Rafael CA 94901 E-mail: bestres@aol.com.

BRETT, THOMAS RUTHERFORD, federal judge; b. Oklahoma City, Oct. 2, 1931; s. John A. and Norma (Dougherty) B.; m. Mary Jean James, Aug. 26, 1952; children: Laura Elizabeth Brett Tribble, James Ford, Susan Marie Brett Crump, Maricarolyn Swab. BBA, U. Okla., 1953, LL.B., 1957, JD, 1971. Bar: Okla. 1957. Asst. county atty., Tulsa, 1957; mem. firm Hudson, Hudson, Wheaton, Kyle & Brett, Tulsa, 1958-69, Jones, Givens, Brett, Gotcher, Doyle & Bogan, 1969-79; judge U.S. Dist. Ct. (no. dist.) Okla., Tulsa, 1979—. Bd. regents U. Okla., 1971-78; mem. adv. bd. Salvation Army; trustee Okla. Bar Found. Col. JAG, USAR, 1953-83. Named to Okla. Heritage Assn. Hall of Fame, 2000. Fellow Am. Coll. Trial Lawyers, Am. Bar Found.; mem. Okla. Bar Assn. (pres. 1970), Tulsa County Bar Assn. (pres. 1965), Am. Judicature Soc., U. Okla. Coll. Law Alumni Assn. (bd. dirs.), Order of Coif (hon.), Phi Alpha Delta. Democrat. Office: Crown & Dunley Kennedy Bldg 4th & Boston Ste 500 Tulsa OK 74103

BRETTELL, RICHARD ROBSON, art historian, museum consultant, educator; b. Rochester, N.Y., Jan. 17, 1949; s. Herbert Robson and Ellen (Sackett) B.; M. Zoe Caroline Bieler, June 9, 1973. BA, Yale U., 1971, MA/PhD, 1977. Acad. program dir., asst. prof. history of art U. Tex., Austin, 1976-80; Searle curator European painting Art Inst. of Chgo., 1980-88; dir. The Dallas Mus. of Art, 1988-92; founding dir. McKinney Ave. Contemporary, 1992-93; prof. visual aesthetic studies U. Tex., Dallas, 1998—. Adj. prof. Northwestern U., Evanston, Ill., 1984-88; vis. prof. Yale U., 1994, Harvard U., 1995; prin. organizer exhbns. The Art of the Edge: European Frames, Art Inst. Chgo., 1986, The Art of Paul Gauguin, Nat. Gallery, Washington, 1988-89, Art Inst. Chgo., Grand Palais, Paris, Pissaro: Urban Series, 1992-93, Dallas Mus. of Art, Royal Acad., Camille Pissarro in the Caribbean 1850-55, St. Thomas and the Jewish us., 1997, Impression: Painting Quickly in France, 1860-1890, Nat. Gallery London, Van Gogh Mus., Clark Inst., 2000-2001; mem. organizing com. Camille Pissarro, The Hayward Gallery, London, 1980-81, Grand Palais, Mus. Fine Arts, Boston. Author: Pisarro and Pontoise, 1990, Modern Art: Capitalism and Representation, 1999, Impression: Painting Quickly in France, 1860-1890; co-author: The Art of Paul Gauguin, 1988, Painters and Peasants in the 19th Century, 1983, A Day in the Country: Impressionism and the French Landscape, 1984, Degas in the Art Inst. of Chgo., 1984, (exhbn. catalogues) Gauguin, 1988. Bd. dirs. Mus. African-Am. Life, Dallas, 1988, DARE, 1991—; mem. Dallas Com. for Internt. Cultural Affairs, 1988. Decorated Chevalier Order of Arts and Letters (France); vis. fellow J. Paul Getty Mus., spring 1985; fellow Nat. Endowment for Humanities, summer 1980, U. Rsch. Inst. U. Tex., Austin, summer 1978, The Whiting Found, 1975-76, Samuel Kress fellow, Yale U., 1974-75. Mem. Coll. Art Assn. Am. (bd. dirs. 1986-89), Midwest Art History Assn., Soc. Archtl. Historians, Am. Assn. Museums, The Getty Grant Program (publs. com. 1987-91), Elizabethan Club. Avocation: piano playing.

BRETTHAUER, ERICH WALTER, chemist, educator; b. Denver, Sept. 12, 1937; s. Walter V. and Lucy E. (Feeley) B.; m. Sharlene Marie Stimpson, Oct. 10, 1966; children: Terrance Magee, Anthony Magee, Heidi, Erich Walter II. BS, U. Nev., 1960, MS, 1962. Various sci. rsch. and mgmt. positions Pub. Health Svc. and EPA, 1962-68; dir. monitoring ops. div. EPA, Las Vegas, 1978-79, dir. nuclear radiation assessment div., 1979-80, detail to U.S. radiation policy coun. Washington, 1980-81, lab. dir. Office Rsch. Devel. Enivron. Monitoring Systems Lab. Las Vegas, 1985-89, asst. administr. Office Rsch. & Devel. Washington, 1990-93; rsch. prof. U. Nev., Las Vegas, 1993-95; pres. Bryce Meadows Devel. Corp., Las Vegas, 1996—. Congl. fellow U.S. Senate Com. on Environ. and Pub. Works, 1982—; recipient Gold medal for directing and monitoring outreach program at Three Mile Island EPA, 1979. Mem. Am. Chem. Soc., Am. Water Works Assn., Sigma Xi.

BRETTON-GRANATOOR, GARY MARTIN, rabbi; b. Bronx, July 20, 1956; s. Jerold Mark and Sylvia Gertrude (Wollowitz) G.; m. Marianne Julia Bretton-Granatoor, May 27, 1978; children: Samantha Ariel, Jacob Daniel, Zachary Hillel. BA, Sarah Lawrence Coll., Bronxville, N.Y., 1978; MAHL, Hebrew Union Coll., N.Y.C., 1982. Ordained rabbi, 1984. Assoc. dir. N.Y. Fedn. Reform Synagogues, N.Y.C., 1984-87; dir. adult studies Union of Am. Hebrew Congregations, N.Y.C., 1987-89, nat. dir. dept. interreligious affairs, 1989-95; sr. rabbi Stephen Wise Free Synagogue, N.Y.C., 1995—. Faculty Sarah Lawrence Coll., Bronxville, 1990-93, NYU U. Continuing Edn., 1986-89; assoc. dir. Commn. on Social Action, 1989—, Commn. on Jewish Edn., 1986-89. Author, editor: Guidelines for Adult Jewish Study, 1989, Challenge of Tzedakah, 1991, A Jewish Guide to Cults, 1997. Chmn. Interfaith Assembly on Homelessness and Housing, N.Y.C., 1984-86; adv. bd. Homes for the Homeless, 1987—. Recipient Horace J. Wolf prize Hebrew Union Coll.-Jewish Inst. Religion, 1984, Jacob Rudin prize in homiletics, 1983. Mem. Cen. Conf. Am. Rabbis, N.Y. Bd. Rabbis. Home: 351 11th St Brooklyn NY 11215-4010 Office: 30 W 68th St New York NY 10023-6005 *In Exodus, we read "Let them make for Me a sanctuary so that I may dwell among them." Notice it does not read, "...so that I may dwell in it." The spirit of God rest upon those who labor for what is good and right. We who build the world that God ordained for us work as God's partners.*

BRETTSCHNEIDER, RITA ROBERTA FISCHMAN, lawyer; b. Bklyn., Nov. 12, 1931; d. Isidore M. and Augusta T. (Singer) Fischman; m. Bertram D. Brettschneider, June 25, 1950 (dec. Nov. 17, 1986); children: Jane Brettschneider, Joseph Brettschneider; m. Bertram D. Cohn, June 30, 1991 (dec. July 2002). BA, CUNY, 1953; JD, Bklyn. Law Sch., 1956; postgrad., NYU, 1968-69, Nat. Inst. Trial Advocacy, 1976. Bar: N.Y. 1961, U.S. Dist. Ct. N.Y. 1971. Pvt. practice, Huntington, NY, 1961. Instr. women and the law C.W. Post Coll., Brookville, N.Y., 1969-70; arbitrator med. malpractice arbitration com. Suffolk County (N.Y.), 1974-76; spl. assoc. prof. philosophy and law New Coll. Hofstra U., Hempstead, N.Y., 1974-76; faculty N.Y. Law Jour. Conf. Changing Concepts in Matrimonial Law, 1976; legal advisor Am. Arbitration Assn., 1977-84; arbitrator night small claims ct. Nassau County, 1978-83; of counsel Nassau County Psychol. Assn., 1987—, Suffolk County Psychol. Assn., 1990-95. Contbr. numerous articles to profl. jours. Pres., bd. dirs. For Our Children and Us, 1992—2001. Mem. Nassau-Suffolk Women's Bar Assn. (chair judiciary com. 1974-80), Nassau County Bar Assn. (demonstrating atty. mock trial contested matrimonial action 1975), Suffolk County Bar Assn. (demonstrating atty. mock trial contested matrimonial action 1976), Am. Arbitration Assn. (legal advisor 1977-84), Nassau-Suffolk Women's Bar Assn. (pres. 1980-81). Home: 2 Crosby Pl Cold Spring Harbor NY 11724-2403 Office: Brettschneider & Brettschneider 83 Prospect St Huntington NY 11743-3306 E-mail: vember@aol.com.

BRETZ, WILLIAM FRANKLIN, retired elementary and secondary education educator; b. Urbana, Ill., May 30, 1937; s. William Franklin and Lois Evelyn (Scheffler) B. AA, Springfield (Ill.) Coll., 1957; BA, Ill. Coll., 1959; MA, Georgetown U., 1972. Cert. tchr., Ill. Chief page Ill. Senate, Springfield, 1957-63; tchr. history Lanphier High Sch., Springfield, 1964-78, Benjamin Franklin Sch., Springfield, 1979—, chmn. social sci. dept., 1989-94; ret., 1994. Staff mem. U.S. Ho. of Reps., Washington, 1975; site interpreter Lincoln's Tomb, Springfield, 1988—. Mem. Animal Protective League, Springfield. Univ. scholar Georgetown U., 1959-60. Mem. NEA, Ill. Edn. Assn., Springfield Edn. Assn., Ctr. for French Colonial Studies in Ill., Nat. Trust for Hist. Preservation, U.S. Capitol Hist. Soc. Home: 2325 S Park Ave Springfield IL 62704-4354

BRETZFELDER, DEBORAH MAY, retired museum staff member; b. Hazelton, Pa., Sept. 21, 1932; d. Joseph and Rose (Smulyan) Hirsh; m. Robert Bretzfelder, Dec. 24, 1955; children: Karl, Marc. Student, Syracuse U., 1950-53. Textile colorist, designer Cohn-Hall-Marx, N.Y.C., 1954-55; fashion coordinator Hecht's Dept. Store, Washington, 1956; freelance artist Washington, 1956-58; exhibits technician Smithsonian Instn., Washington, 1958-59, supr. exhibits prodn., 1959-63, exhibits specialist Nat. Mus. Am. History, 1963-75, visual info. specialist, project mgmt. officer, 1975-83, acting chief design, 1983, chief design, 1983-87, assoc. asst. dir. exhibits and pub. spaces, 1987-88; ret., 1988. Cons. various firms., orgns., mus. personnel; instr. mus. programs; freelance photographer and exhibit designer; project dir. Contbr. works to various publs.; musician: violin sect. George Washington U. Orch., 2003, violin sect. Georgetown Symphony Orch., 2003—. Mem.: Nat. Mus. Women in Arts, Nat. Soc. Hist. Preservation, Am. Assn. Mus., Potomac Appalachian Trail Club, Tau Sigma Delta. Jewish. Home: 2748 Woodley Pl NW Washington DC 20008-1517

BREU, GEORGE, accountant; b. Milw., May 8, 1954; s. George and Grace (Rossmaier) B.; m. Nancy Lee Roblee, June 6, 1987; children: Michael G., Lisa A. BBA in Acctg. cum laude, U. Wis., Milw., 1976. CPA, Wis. Audit staff Reilly, Penner & Benton, Milw., 1976-78; tax mgr. Radke, Schlesner & Wernecke, S.C., Milw., 1978-88; contr. Megal Devel. and Constrn. Corp., Milw., 1988-2000; pres. George Breu CPA, S.C., Brookfield, Wis., 2000—. Treas. Elmbrook Hist. Soc., Brookfield, Wis., 1981-83. Mem. Am. Inst. CPA's (tax div.), Wis. Inst. CPA's, U. Wis. Milw. Tax Assn., Germany Philatelic Soc. (treas. Milw. chpt. 1978—), U. Wis. Milw. Philatelic Soc. (founder, treas. 1972-81), Milw. Philatelic Soc. Inc. (corp. registered agt. 1986—), U. Wis. Milw. Alumni Assn., Beta Gamma Sigma, Phi Eta Sigma. Republican. Roman Catholic. Avocations: stamp collecting, reading history, traveling. Home: 15840 Fieldbrook Dr Brookfield WI 53005-1419 Office: George Breu CPA SC 15840 Fieldbrook Dr Brookfield WI 53005-1419

BREUER, MALA KLEE, artist; b. Oakland, Calif., Dec. 21, 1927; d. Adolph Franz and Louise (Klee) B.; widowed; children: Paul Mayer, Dawn Heiss. Student, San Francisco Art Inst., 1946-48; BFA, Calif. Coll. Arts and Crafts, Oakland, 1966; MA, San Francisco State U., 1970. Exhibited in group shows at Edward Tyler Nahem Gallery, N.Y.C., 1995, Wes Mills Farm Art Space, Missoula, Mont., 2002, Galerie Albrecht, Munich, Germany, 2002, Richard Levy Gallery, Albuquewrquc, 1995-2002. Recipient Polloch-Krasner award, N.Y.C., 1991, Site Santa Fe award, 1995, Western States Art Fedn.-Nat. Endowment for Arts award, Santa Fe, 1996, James Kelly/Contemporary, 1999—, Edward Tyler Nahem Gallery, N.Y.C., 1995—. Home: PO Box 400 Truchas NM 87578

BREUER, RONALD KARL, SR., investment banking executive; b. Glen Cove, N.Y., June 18, 1945; s. Peter George and Charlotte Eleanor (Petersen) B.; m. Eileen Joan Erber, Dec. 29, 1968; children: Ronald, Karen, Bethany. BS, MBA, N.Y. Inst. Tech., 1976. Cert. project mgr., Project Mgmt. Inst. Sr. rep. Scandanavian Airlines System, N.Y.C., 1965-75; v.p. Chase Manhattan Bank, N.Y., N.Y.C., 1975-84, J.P. Morgan Investment Mgmt. Inc., N.Y.C., 1984-2000, v.p., div. exec. planning and cons.; v.p., mgr. Global Program Office J.P Morgan Asset Mgmt. Svcs., N.Y.C., 1998—; pres., chief exec. officer Constantin MVP Consulting, 2000; chmn. adv. com. Constantin Walsh-Lowe LLC, 2001—03; vice chmn. Constantin Info. Tech. Consulting, 2003—. Mem. com. Fifth Ave. Assn., N.Y.C., 1987—, N.Y.C. Downtown Alliance, 2001-. Mem. com. Huntington (N.Y.) Nutrition for Homeless, 1989-92; coun. mem. Boy Scouts Am., Dix Hills, N.Y., 1985-87; v.p. St. Luke's Ch., Dix Hills, 1982-87; br. pres. Aid Assn. for Lutherans, Dix Hills, 1981-83; bd. dirs. Nat. Tech. Inst. Deaf Found., 1995—; mem. Project Mgmt. Inst., 1996; hon. co-chmn. bus. adv. coun. Rep. Party, 2003. Recipient Svc. award United Way, 1982, Nat. Leadership award Nat. Rep. Congl. Com., 2003. Mem.: Am. Mgmt. Assn., Am. Bankers Assn., MBA Execs., Inst. Indsl. Engrs. Republican. Lutheran. Avocations: golf, travel, camping, boating. Home: 46 Candlewood Path Dix Hills NY 11746-5306 Office: Constantin Walsh-Lowe LLC 525 Washington Blvd Hoboken NJ 08830 also: 1575 Madison Ave New York NY 10021

BREUER, STEPHEN ERNEST, religious organization administrator; b. July 14, 1936; came to U.S., 1938, naturalized, 1945; s. John Hans Howard and Olga Marion (Haar) B.; m. Gail Fern Breitbart, Sept. 4, 1960 (div. 1986); children: Jared Noah, Rachel Elise; m. Nadine Bendit, Sept. 25, 1988. BA cum laude, UCLA, 1959; gen. secondary credential, 1960. Tchr. L.A. City Schs., 1960-62; dir. Wilshire Blvd. Temple Camps, L.A., 1962-86; exec. dir. Wilshire Blvd. Temple, L.A., 1980—; dir. Edgar F. Magnin Religious Sch., L.A., 1970-80; instr. Hebrew Union Coll., L.A., 1965-76, 1992—, U. Judaism, 1991; field instr. San Francisco State U., 1970-80, Calif. State U., San Diego, Hebrew Union Coll., 1977-81, U. of Judaism UCLA extension. V.P. L.A. Youth Programs Inc., 1967-77; youth advisor L.A. County Commn. Human Rels., 1969-72, bd. dirs. Cmty. Rels. Conf. So. Calif., 1965-85; bd. dirs. Alzheimer's Disease and Related Disorders Assn., 1984-95, v.p. L.A. County chpt., 1984-86, pres., 1986-88, nat. exec. com., 1987-95, nat. devel. chair, 1992-95, Calif. state coun. pres. 1987-92, chmn. of Calif. gov.'s adv. com. on Alzheimer's disease, 1988-97; mem. goals program City of Beverly Hills, Calif., 1985-91; bd. dirs. Pacific SW regional Union Am. Hebrew Congregations, 1985-88, mem. nat. bd., exec. com., 1993-97; bd. dirs. Echo Found., 1986-88, Mazon-Jewish Response to Hunger, 1993-97, Wilshire Stakeholders exec. com., 1987-94, Internat. Rescue Cmty. West Coast Bd., 1999—; treas. Wilshire Cmty. Prayer Alliance, 1986-88; active United Way. Recipient svc. awards L.A. County Bd. Suprs., 1982, 87, Ventura County Bd. Suprs., 1982, 87, Weinberg Chai Lifetime Achievement award Jewish Fed. Council Los Angeles, 1986, Nat. Philanthropy Day L.A. Medallion, 1993, L.A. County Redevel. Agy. recognition, 1994, L.A. Bus. Coun. award, 1997; Steve Breuer Conference Ctr. in Malibu named in his honor at Wilshire Blvd. Temple Camps, 1990. Mem.: ASCD, NATA, Jewish Profl. Network, So. Calif. Conf. Jewish Communal Workers, Am. Mgmt. Assn., Jewish Communal Profls. So. Calif., Profl. Assn. Temple Adminstrs. (pres. 1985—88), L.A. Assn. Jewish Edn. (bd. dirs.), Nat. Assn. Temple Educators (Kaminker curriculum award 1973), Nat. Assn. Temple Adminstrs. (nat. bd. dirs. 1987—, v.p. 1991—93, pres. 1993—97, Svc. to Judaism award 1989, Svc. to the Cmty. award 1990, Svc. award 1994), So. Calif. Camping Assn. (bd. dirs. 1964—82), Assn. Reform Zionists Am. (bd. dirs. 1993—98), People for the Am. Way, Los Angeles County Mus. Contemporary Art, Maple Mental Health Ctr. of Beverly Hills, Living Desert, Wildlife Fedn., Ctr. for Environ. Edn., Wilderness Soc., UCLA Alumni Assn, World Union for Progressive Judaism, Jewish Resident Camping Assn., Amnesty Internat. Office: Wilshire Blvd Temple 3663 Wilshire Blvd Los Angeles CA 90010-2798

BREUER, WERNER ALFRED, retired plastics company executive; b. Sinn, Hessia, Germany, Jan. 30, 1930; came to U.S., 1959; s. Christian and Hedwig (Cunz) B.; m. Gertrud Ackermann, June 21, 1950 (dec. 1998); children: Patricia, Julia, Eva-Maria. LLB, La Salle Ext. U., 1970; BS in Human Rels. and Orgnl. Behavior, U. San Francisco, 1983; MS in Bus. Mgmt., U. La Verne, 1985, DPA, 1988. Lab. supr. Dayco Corp. (Am. latex divsn.), Hawthorne, Calif., 1959-65; tech. ops. mgr. Olin Corp., Stamford and New Haven, Conn., 1965-69; gen. mgr., exec. v.p. Expanded Rubber and Plastics Corp., Gardena, Calif., 1969-96; ret., 1996; gen. mgr. Schlobohm Co. Inc., Dominguez Hills, Calif., 1989-96; ret. Cons. human resources Stabond Corp., Gardena, 1988-95. Author/composer various recordings, 1970s; contbr. articles to jours. Founder Worls Peace and Diplomacy Forum, Cambridge, England. Recipient Portfolio award, USF, Calif., 1984, Lifetime Achievement award, IBC, 2001, Am. Medal of Honor award, 2002. Mem. ASTM, ASCAP, Am. Soc. for Metals, Soc. for Plastics Engrs., N.Y. Acad. Scis., Nat. Space Soc., Planetary Soc., U. La Verne Alumni Assn. Republican. Avocations: play music, writing, horseback riding, composing, sketching. Achievements include pioneering use of plastics especially polyurethanes in defense missiles and space and communication aviation industry; defense projects from DEW Line N.A. radar defense to Stealth Fighter B-2 Project. Home: 835 Sanctuary Cir Longmont CO 80501-2355

BREUER, WILLIAM BENTLEY, writer; Frequent keynote spkr.; guest numerous radio shows and TV programs; former guest lectr. salesmanship, publicity and promotion seminars. Author: An American Saga, 1982, Bloody Clash at Sadzot, 1982 (transl. into Belgian), Captain Cool, 1983, They Jumped at Midnight, 1983, Drop Zone Sicily, 1984 (transl. into Japanese and French), Hitler's Fortress Cherbourg, 1984, Agony at Anzio, 1985 (transl. into Czechoslovakian), Storming Hitler's Rhine, 1985 (transl. into Serbo-Croatian), Death of a Nazi Army, 1985, Operation Torch, 1986, Retaking the Philippines, 1987, Devil Boats, 1987 (transl. into Japanese), Operation Dragoon, 1988 (transl. into French), The Secret War with Germany, 1988, Sea Wolf, 1989, Nazi Spies in America, 1989, Geronimo!, 1990, Hoodwinking Hitler, 1993, Race to the Moon, 1993 (transl. into Burmese, Choice award ALA 1995), The Great Raid on Cabanatuan, 1994, J. Edgar Hoover and His G-Men, 1995, MacArthur's Undercover War, 1994 (transl. into Polish), Feuding Allies, 1995 (trans. into Polish), Shadow Warriors, 1996, War and American Women, 1997, Unexplained Mysteries of World War II, 1997 (transl. into Polish, Czech and Chinese), Vendetta: Castro and the Kennedy Brothers, 1997 (transl. into Polish), Undercover Tales of World War II, 1998, Top Secret Tales of World War II (transl. into Japanese), 1999, Secret Weapons of World War II (trnasl. into Arabic and Chinese), 2000, Daring Missions of World War II, 2001 (transl. into Polish and Chinese), Deceptions of World War II, 2002 (transl. into Polish), The Air-Raid Warden Was a Spy, 2002, The Spy Who Spent the War in Bed, 2003. Sgt. U.S. Army, WWII. Recipient numerous awards. Hon. mem. numerous vets. assns. Home: 3815 Westview Dr NE Cleveland TN 37312-5057

BREUL, JONATHAN DUTRO, consultant; b. Bridgeport, Conn., Aug. 18, 1947; s. Alvin C. and Helena (Plumb) B.; m. Nancy Mathers, May 4, 1974; children: Hannah P., Sarah M. BA, Colby Coll., 1969; MPA, Northeastern U., 1972. With U.S. Gen. Svcs. Adminstrn., 1973-75, U.S. Dept. of Health and Human Svcs., 1976-82; sr. policy analyst for fin. mgmt. U.S. Office Mgmt. and Budget, Washington, 1983-89, chief evaluation and planning, 1990-93, sr. advisor to dep. dir., 1993—2002; assoc. ptnr. IBM Bus. Consulting Svcs., 2002—; sr. fellow IBM Endowment for Bus. of Govt., 2002—. With USAF, 1969-72. Recipient Mydral Pub. Svc. award Am. Evaluation Assn., 1996. Fellow Nat. Acad. Pub. Adminstrn. (bd. trustees); mem. ASAP. Avocation: fly fishing. Home: 3809 Jenifer St NW Washington DC 20015-1917

BREUNIG, ROBERT GLASS, botanical facility administrator; b. Indpls., Nov. 16, 1945; s. Henry Latham and Nancy (Tyree) B.; m. Karen Enyedy Breunig, Feb. 16, 1979; 1 child, Lydia Ann. BA, Ind. U., 1968; PhD, U. Kans., 1973. Asst. prof. anthropology No. Ariz. U., Flagstaff, 1972-74; educator Mus. No. Ariz., Flagstaff, 1975-77, curator, 1977-81, curator, head dept. anthropology, 1981-82; chief curator, dep. dir. The Heard Mus., Phoenix, 1982-85; exec. dir. Desert Botanical Garden, Phoenix, 1985-94; dir. Santa Barbara (Calif.) Mus. Natural History, 1994-97; exec. dir. Lady Bird Johnson Wildflower Ctr., Austin, 1997—. Vis. asst. prof. anthropology U. Conn., 1974, Denison U., Granville, 1975; trustee Ctr. for Plant Conservation, St. Louis, 1991-94, 99—; mem. bd. dirs. (presdl. appointment) Nat. Mus. Svcs. Bd., Washington, 1992-02. Mem. Am. Assn. Mus. Office: Lady Bird Johnson Wildflower Ctr 4801 LaCrosse Ave Austin TX 78739

BREVE, FRANKLIN STEPHEN, pharmacist; b. Phila., Jan. 25, 1955; s. Albert Francis and Lillian Marie (Di Biase) B.; m. Linda Ruth Maedel, Mar. 16, 1985; children: Christina Lynn, Rebecca Anne, Allison Marie. BA in Psychology, Temple U., 1977, BS in Pharmacy, 1981; MBA in Pharm. Mktg., St. Joseph's U., 1998. Registered Pharmacist. Oncology pharmacist Thomas Jefferson U., Phila., 1981-86, nuclear pharmacist, 1986-87; oncology pharmacist Rancocas Valley Hosp., Willingboro, NJ, 1987-88; night phramacy coord. West Jersey Hosp., Camden, NJ, 1988-97; pres., CEO Pharmatech Cons. Group, Blackwood, NJ, 1992—; CME coord. Kennedy Health Sys., 1997—; pharmacy mgr. Baxter Health Care Renal Divsn., Bridgeport, NJ, 2000—. Cons., instr. in field. Mem. Am. Soc. Hosp. Pharmacists, Am. Pharm. Assn., N.J. Soc. Hosp. Pharmacists, N.Y. Acad. Scis., Am. Soc. Cons. Pharmacists, N.J. Pharm. Assn., N.J. Acad. Cons. Pharmacists, Am. Geriatrics Soc. Republican. Roman Catholic. Avocations: woodworking, science fiction, white-water rafting. Home and Office: 6 Briarwood Dr Blackwood NJ 08012-5387 Fax: (856) 627-5292. E-mail: f.breve@comcast.net., f.breve@kennedyhealth.org., frank_breve@baxter.com.

BREVER, MICHAEL STEPHEN, non-profit executive director, alderman; b. Milw., Apr. 21, 1955; s. Robert Thomas and Dorothy Helen (Schoofs) B.; m. Mary Beth Burns, Aug. 29, 1987; children: Megan Lanie, Timothy Michael, Patrick Burns, Daniel Fredrick. BA in History, U. Wis., Milw., 1979; MS in Mgmt., Cardinal Stritch Coll., 1990. VISTA vol. South Cmty. Orgn., Milw., 1981, exec. dir., 1982-98, Tri Corp Housing Inc., Milw., 1998—. Panelist and lectr. confs. Bd. pres. Southside Housing Coop., Milw., 1987—; alderman City of Oak Creek, Wis., 1993-2001, common coun. pres., 1996-97, temporary acting mayor, 1996; bd. govs. Wis. Ins. Plan, Milw., 1994—; adv. bd. mem. Lincoln Neighborhood Redevel. Corp., Milw., 1994—; commr. Cmty. Devel. Authority, Oak Creek, 1995—; mem. Affordable Housing Task Force, Milw., 1997. Recipient Bronze award United Way Greater Milw., 1991, Disting. Svc. award Southside Civic Assn., Milw., 1994, Am. Hometown Leadership award Nat. Assn. Towns & Twps., 1996, Proclamation of Distinction, Oak Creek Common Coun., 1996, award f distinction for cmty. svc. WHEDA, 1999, MANDI award for leadership in cmty. devel., 1999. Mem. Southside Bus. Assn., Southside Civic Assn. (Disting. Svc. award 1994), U. Wis. Milw. Alumni Assn., St. Josephs Found. (bd. dirs. 1995—), Oak Creek Tax Incremental Fin. Dist. II (chmn. 1997), KC. Avocations: golf, reading, basketball, spectator sports. Home: 615 E Parkway Estates Dr Oak Creek WI 53154-4528 Office: Tri-Corp 1635 S 8th St Milwaukee WI 53204-3455

BREVERMAN, HARVEY, artist; b. Pitts., Jan. 7, 1934; s. Theodore and Sarah (Haffner) B.; m. Deborah Dobkin, June 26, 1960. BFA, Carnegie Mellon U., 1956; MFA, Ohio U., 1960. Tchr. Carnegie Mellon U., summer 1959; tchr. drawing Ohio U., Athens, 1960-61, Ill. State U., Normal, summer 1969, Falmouth (Eng.) Art Sch., 1969; prof. art Univ. at Buffalo, 1961—99, SUNY disting. prof., 1999—. Resident painter, State Acad. Fine Arts, Amsterdam, 1965-66, vis. painter, Kalamazoo Inst. Art, summer 1972, 73, vis. artist, Oxford U., 1974, 77, U. Mich., 1978, Md. Inst. Coll. Art, 1984, 92d St. Y, N.Y.C., 1989, Coll. William & Mary, 1990, Skidmore Coll., 1990, Pont Aven Sch. Art, France, 1995, Jagiellonian U., Poland, 1997; one man shows include Albright-Knox Art Gallery, Buffalo, 1967, 89, U. Oreg., U. Ill., 1970, Canton (Ohio) Art Inst., 1971, 87, Middlebury Coll., 1973, FAR Gallery, N.Y.C., 1974, 79, Gadatsy Gallery, Toronto, 1975, 76, 79, 80, Kalamazoo Inst. Art, 1976, Hackley Art Mus., Muskegon, Mich., 1977, Grand Rapids (Mich.) Art Mus., 1977, Gadatsy Gallery, Toronto, 1978, 81, 84, U. Mich., 1978, Nardin Galleries, N.Y.C., 1980, U. N.H., 1981, Art Gallery of Hamilton (Ont., Can.), 1981, Hollins U., 1982, Niagara U., 1984, Miami (Ohio) U. Art Mus., 1987, Gadatsy Gallery, Toronto, 1987, Meml. Art Gallery, Rochester, N.Y., 1988, Wenniger Gallery, Boston, 1988, St. Lawrence U., 1989, Taller Galeria Ft., Cadaqués, Spain, 1990, Babcock Galleries, N.Y.C., 1990, 91, Brigham Young U., 1993, Nina Freudenheim Gallery, Buffalo, 1994, Butler Inst. Am. Art, 1997, Yeshiva U. Mus., N.Y.C., 1997, 2002, Milton Weill Gallery, N.Y.C., 1997, Gertrude Herbert Inst. Art, Augusta, Ga., 2000, Indiana U. Sch. Fine Arts Gallery, Bloomington, 2001; exhibited in group show at Corcoran Biennial, Washington, 1963, Bklyn. Mus., 1964, Assn. Am. Artists, N.Y.C., 1965, Rijksakademie, Amsterdam, 1968, Boston Mus. Fine Arts, 1968, NAD, 1968, Pa. Acad. Fine Arts Biennial, 1969, 2d and 3d Brit. Internat. Biennial, Bradford, Eng., 1970 72, FAR Gallery, 1972-74, Whitechapel Gallery, London, 1973, Pushkin Mus., Moscow, 1972, 2d Norwegian Internat. Biennial, 1974, Mus. Modern Art, Oxford, Eng., 1974, Honolulu Acad. Fine Arts, 1975, 8th Internat. Art Fair, Basel, Switzerland, 1977, Auslands Institut, Dortmund, W. Ger., 1977, Arte Fiere '78, Bologna, 1978, Art Gallery Ont., Toronto, 1979, Am. Acad. and Inst. Arts and Letters, N.Y.C., 1980, 81, NYU, N.Y.C., 1980, Jewish Mus., N.Y.C., 1982, Queens Mus., N.Y.C., 1983, Rose Art Mus., Brandeis U., 1985, Minn. Mus. Art, St. Paul, 1985, Roger Ramsay Gallery, Chgo., 1986, Va. Mus. Fine Arts, Richmond, 1986, Lever House Gallery, N.Y.C., 1986, Albright-Knox Art Gallery, 1987, Harvard U., Carpenter Ctr., 1987, Mus. Art, San Juan, P.R., 1987, Contemporary Arts Ctr., Cin., 1988, Mus. of Fine Arts, Houston, 1988, Oakland (Calif.) Mus., 1988, 8th Print Internat., Barcelona, 1988, 4th Internat. Print Biennal, Taipei Fine Arts Mus., Taiwan, 1989, Inst. of Contemporary Art, Boston, 1990, La Jolla Mus. of Contemporary Art, 1990, Grand Palais, Paris, 1990, Yurakucho Art Forum, Tokyo, 1991, Denver Art Mus., 1991, Scottsdale Ctr. for the Arts, 1991, Nat. Acad. Design, N.Y.C., 1992, Internat. Print Triennal, Krakow, Nüremberg, 1994, 97, 2000, 03, Mus. Applied Arts. Belgrade, 1995, XIII Premio Internat. Per L' Incisione, Biella, Torino, 1997, Bermuda Nat.

Gallery, 1997, 9th Internat. Print Biennale, Varna, Bulgaria, 1997, Beijing Internat. Ex-Libris Exhbn., China, 1998, Embassy of France, La Maison Française, Washington, 1998, Florean Mus., Carbunari, Romania, 1999, 2001, 02, Mus. Civico Di Grafica, Brunico, Italy, 1999, Chateau du Puget, Alzonne, France, 1999, 12th Deutsche Internat. Grafik Triennale, Frechen, Germany, 1999, De Mini Gravura, Vitoria, Brasil, 2000; 4th Brit. Internat. Miniature print Exhibition Bankside Gallery, London, 2000, Quingdao Internat. Print Biennial, People's Republic of China, 2000, 4th Internat. Triennial Lahti Art Mus., Finland, 2000, Temple Gallery, Rome, 2002, Inst. for Advanced Art and Culture, Aix-en-Provence, France, 2002, 4th Egyptian Internat. Triennial, Cairo and Alexandria, 2003, 1 Er Concours Internat. d'Exlibris, Ankara and Istanbul, Turkey, 2003, Zeichen der Gegenwart, Vienna Art Gallery, Austria, 2003, others, L'Espace Melanie, Rec-Sur-Belon, Brittany and Mona Bismark Found., Paris, 2003, Internat. Print and Drawing Exhbn., Silpakorn U. Art and Culture Ctr., Bangkok, Thailand, 2003, 5th Brit. Internat. Miniature Print Exhbn., Gracefield Arts Ctr., Dumfries, Scotland, 2003-2004; also traveling exhibits in U.S., Europe, Central Am., Japan, paintings for, U.S.embassies, 1976; represented in permanent collections Mus. Modern Art, N.Y.C., Whitney Mus., Albright-Knox Art Gallery, Phila. Mus., Butler Inst. Art, Youngstown, Ohio, Nat. Mus. Am. Art, Washington, Library of Congress, Israel Mus., Jerusalem, Bradford City Art Mus., St. Catharines Dist. Arts Council, Ont., Can., Victoria and Albert Mus., London, Cleve. Mus., Balt. Mus. Art, Nat. Portrait Gallery, Washington, British Mus., London, Met. Mus. Art, N.Y.C., Smithsonian Inst., Washington. Served with AUS, 1956-58, Korea. Grantee Louis Comfort Tiffany Found., 1962, Netherlands Govt., 1965, N.Y. Coun. Arts, 1972; named fellow NEA, 1974-75, 80-81, Va. Ctr. for the Creative Arts, 1992; elected mem. Nat. Acad. Design, N.Y.C., 1992; recipient Hassam-Speicher award Am. Acad. Arts and Letters, 1990, 91, Nat. Alumni Assn. medal of merit Ohio U., 1992, Disting. Tchg. Art award Coll. Art Assn. N.Y.C., 2003. Address: 76 Smallwood Dr Snyder NY 14226-4027

BREVETTI, FRANCINE CLELIA, journalist; b. San Francisco, July 20, 1943; d. Frank Albert and Tecla Puccetti Brevetti. BA in French, U. Calif., Berkeley, 1966; MA in Theater, UCLA, 1969. Staff writer Jour. Commerce, N.Y.C., 1977-85; pvt. practice Hong Kong, 1985-97; bus. writer The Oakland (Calif.) Tribune, 1998—. Dir. Francine Brevetti Prodns., 1981—; West Coast corr., past Hong Kong corr. Seatrade Rev., Seatrade Orgn., 1994—; Hong Kong corr. Pensions & Investments, Crain Comm., 1995—; cons. Renwick-McCormick, Hong Kong, 1995-97. Editor ECA China News, 1995—; contbr. Hobson's Publs., 1996—, The Securities Jour., 1996—. Mem.: NY Fin. Writers Assn., Fgn. Corr. Club (mem. com. 1987—), Hong Kong Journalists Assn., Women in Pub., Soc. Profl. Journalists (bd. dirs. No. Calif. chpt.). Office: The Oakland Tribune Oakland CA 94607 Fax: 510-208-6477. E-mail: francineb@earthlink.net.

BREVETTI, LUCY S, surgeon; d. Rusky and Rose Sun; m. Gregory R. Brevetti, Jan. 7, 1995. MD, SUNY-Health Sci. Ctr of Bklyn, 1989—93. Diplomate surgery Am. Bd. of Surgery, 2000. Rsch. fellow UCSF-Pacific Vascular Rsch. Lab, San Francisco, 1998—; asst. prof. surgery Robert Wood Johnson Med. Sch., New Brunswick, NJ, 2001—. Gen. surg. resident U. of Iowa, 1993—98. Recipient William J. von Liebig Found. award for excellence in Vascular Surg. Rsch. for Residents and Fellows, William J. von Liebig Found., 2000—01, ACS Com. on Trauma-Rsch. Paper, ACS, 1996; Nat. Rsch. Svc. Award, NIH, 1999—2001. Mem.: ACS, Peripheral Vascular Surgery Soc. (assoc.). R-Consevative. Catholic. Achievements include research in study of vascular gene transfer for critical limb ischemia. Avocation: snowboarding.

BREWER, A. BRUCE, university administrator; b. Pasadena, Tex., Oct. 18, 1951; s. Leo Louie and Norma Jane (Nabors) Brewer; m. Patricia Anne Lumley, Mar. 12, 1977; 1 child, April Bruce stepchildren: Frand D Hollifield III, Patrick C M. AB in Am. Studies, U. Ala., 1974, MA in Counseling and Guidance, 1975; PhD in Higher Edn. Leadership, Ga. State U., 1988. Asst. dir. admissions Auburn U., Montgomery, Ala., 1976—79, coord. Career Devel. Ctr., 1979-81; coord. cooperative edn. Placement and Cooperative Edn. Office/West Ga. Coll., Carrollton, Ga., 1981-82; dir. dept. career svcs. State U. of West Ga., Carrollton, 1982—. Mem. psychology faculty, coord. orgn. devel. State U. West Ga., Carrollton, 1990—; architect Ga eFair, 2000, Teacher Staffing eFair, 2001; project dir. Ctr. for Traumatology, U. West Ga., Carrollton, 2002—03. Co-editor: (book) Annual Job Search Handbook for Educators, 2000—. Pres Sertoma Civic Club, Carrollton, 1996—97; dist chmn Boy Scouts Am, Carrollton, 1994—95; pres W Ga Indust Leaders Assn, Carrollton, 1995, W Ga Pers Asn, Carrollton, 1992. Mem.: Ga. Assn. Cols. and Employers (pres 2000—01, Founders award 1999). Baptist. Avocations: music, chess, antiques. Office: State Univ West Ga Maple St Carrollton GA 30118-0001 E-mail: bbrewer@westga.edu.

BREWER, BRETT, lawyer; b. Oklahoma City, Sept. 1, 1966; s. David Louis and Marjorie Joy Brewer; m. Shauna Renee Nowell, Apr. 12, 1997. BA, Baylor U., Waco, Tex., 1989; JD, U. Okla., 1992. Bar: Tex. 1992. Assoc. David Line & Assocs., Dallas, 1993; senate aide U.S. Senator Phil Gramm, Dallas, 1993-97; assoc. Norman, Thrall, Angle, Guy & Day, LLP, Jacksonville, Tex., 1997—. Dist. com. chmn. Boy Scouts Am.; deacon Fellowship Bible Ch. of Jacksonville, 2000—. Fellow Tex. Bar Found.; mem. Christian Legal Soc. (v.p. 1991-92), State Bar Tex., Cherokee County Bar Assn. (v.p. 1998-99, pres. 1999-2000), C. of C. (amb. com. 1997—), Rotary (pres. Jacksonville 2001-2002). Republican. Avocations: literature, music. Office: Norman Thrall Angle Guy & Day 215 E Commerce St Fl 2 Jacksonville TX 75766-4955 E-mail: brettbrewer@normanlawfirm.com.

BREWER, CAREY, retired academic administrator; b. Lynchburg, Va., July 8, 1927; s. James Allen and Esther Goode (Leftwich) B.; m. Betty Ann Brighton, Sept. 3, 1949; children— Mary Elizabeth, Robert Allen, Ruth Ann, Catherine Lee. BA, Lynchburg Coll., 1949; student, Am. U., 1951; M.P.A., Harvard U., 1952, PhD, 1956. Analyst with legislative reference service Library of Congress, 1949-56; sr. def. specialist mil. ops. subcom. Ho. of Reps., 1956-60; mem. staff joint com. atomic energy U.S. Congress, 1960-61; various positions Office Emergency Planning, Exec. Office of Pres., 1961-64; pres. Lynchburg Coll., 1964-83. Lectr. Am. U., 1954-56; Mem. bd. higher edn., also mem. gen. bd., ch. fin. council Christian Ch. (Disciples of Christ); mem. Pres.'s Civil Def. Adv. Council, 1970-72; Bd. dirs. Nat. Lab. for Higher Edn.; pres. Va. Found. Ind. Colls., 1978-80 Author: Civil Defense in the United States, 1951, Implications of a National Service Program, 1952, Science and Defense, 1956, also numerous articles. Served with USNR, 1945-46. Littauer fellow Harvard, 1951-53 Mem. Council Ind. Colls. Va. (pres. 1972-74), Greater Lynchburg C. of C. (past pres.) Mem. Christian Ch. Clubs: Sphex, Waterfront Golf.

BREWER, CHERYL ANN, obstetrician and gynecologist, educator; b. New Rochelle, N.Y., Oct. 31, 1959; d. John Paul and Marie Elizabeth (Royance) B. BS, Miss. U. for Women, 1981; MD, Ind. U., Indpls., 1985. Resident in ob-gyn. SUNY Health Scis. Ctr., Syracuse, 1985-89, asst. prof. ob-gyn., 1989-91; asst. prof. dept. ob-gyn. Ind. U., Indpls., 1991-92; fellow in gynecologic oncology U. Calif., Irvine, 1992-96; asst. prof. ob-gyn., dir. gynecologic oncology Sch. Med. So. Ill. U., 1996-98; asst. prof. U. Ill., Peora, 1998—. Dir. divsn. gyn. oncology U. Ill., Peoria, 2000—02. Fellow Am. Coll. Ob-Gyn. Home: 59 N Shore Dr Petersburg IL 62675-9778 Office: U Ill Chgo Coll Medicine Dept OG/Divsn Gynecology 515 NE Glen Oak Ave # S5e301 Peoria IL 61603-3136

BREWER, DANA, lawyer, educator; b. Concordia, Kans., Jan. 25, 1952; s. Dean Decker and Irma Elaine (Ames) B. BS cum laude, Kans. State U., 1974; JD, Washburn U., 1976. Bar: Kans. 1977, U.S. Dist. Ct. Kans. 1977. Assoc. Baldwin, Paulsen & Buechel, Chartered, Concordia, 1977-82; ptnr. Paulsen, Buechel, Swenson, Uri & Brewer, Chartered, Concordia, 1982—; educator Cloud County Community Coll., Concordia, 1979—. Chmn. United Lutheran Ministries, N. Central Kans., 1981-83; commr. Indsl. Devel. Adv. Commn., Concordia, 1982—; bd. dirs. Pan-Am. Hwy. Assn., 1984—, St. Joseph Hosp., Concordia, 1988—; bd. dirs. Brown Grand Theatre, Concordia, 1988—. Mem. Cloud County Bar Assn. (sec. 1977-79), Kans. Bar Assn. (com. on legal issues affecting elderly 1985—), ABA, Kans. Sch. Attys. Assn. (bd. dirs. 1984-88), Concordia C. of C. (bd. dirs. 1984—, chmn. 1986-88), Jaycees (community devel. v.p. 1983-84), Moose, Lions. Republican. Lutheran. Home: RR 2 Concordia KS 66901-9802 Office: Paulsen Buechel Swenson Uri & Brewer 613 Washington St # 327 Concordia KS 66901-2821

BREWER, DAVID L. sociologist; b. Tucson, Mar. 11, 1933; s. Leslie O. and Nina (Brinkerhoff) B.; m. Sue Mansfield; children: Phillip, Brent, Robin. BS, Brigham Young U., 1957; MS, Purdue U., 1959; PhD in Sociology, U. Utah, 1966. Various teaching and rsch. positions including Fresno (Calif.) State U., Calif. State U./Hayward, Newark State Coll, others, 1964-71; rsch. analyst Calif. Dept. Corrections, Chino, 1972-82, various to assoc. govtl. program analyst Sacramento, 1982-88, correctional counselor, 1988-89, Chino, 1989-90, clin. sociologist, 1990-92, correctional counselor, 1992-94; rsch. assoc. Dem. Processes Ctr., Tucson, 1995—. Contbr. articles to profl. jours., publs. Mem. Soc. for Study of Symbolic Interaction. Office: Dem Processes Ctr 4349 N Linda Lee Dr Tucson AZ 85705-2399 E-mail: manbrew@earthlink.net.

BREWER, DAVID MADISON, lawyer; b. Bordeaux, Gironde, France, July 8, 1953; s. Herbert L and Paulyne B (Ver Benec) Brewer; m. Andrea M Bordiga, May 20, 1978; children: James David Madison, Caroline Elizabeth, Geoffrey Andrew. AB summa cum laude, Yale U., 1975, JD, 1978. Bar: NY 1979. Assoc. atty. Cravath Swaine & Moore, N.Y.C., 1978-84; assoc. gen. tax counsel Union Pacific Corp., N.Y.C. and Bethlehem, Pa., 1984-89; pres. Madison Co., Inc., N.Y.C., 1990—; pres., CEO Madison Oil Co., Dallas, 1993-2000, vice chmn., 2000—01, chmn., 2001—. Bd. dirs. Toreador Resources Corp., Dallas, 2002—. Editor: Yale Law Rev., 1977—78. Spec gifts chmn Yale Univ Class 1975 and Law Sch Class 1978, 1985—; mem Yale Develop Bd, 2000—; nat vice-chmn Smithsonian Friends First Ladies, 1989—92; mem. world bd. USO, 1995—2002; vice chmn Bush/Quayle '92 Fin Comt, 1991—92; policy asst Office Campaign Mgr, Bush-Quayle campaign, 1988; bd. govs. Am. Friends of the Anglican Ctr. in Rome, 2002—; bd dirs Yale Univ Law Sch Fund, 1989—93, Yale Alumni Fund, 1989—95; trustee Pine Ridge Sch, Vt., 1998—. Assoc. fellow, Saybrook Coll., Yale U., 2000—. Mem.: NY Bar Assn., Mory's (New Haven), Cercle de l'Union Interalliée (Paris), Yale Club (N.Y.C.), Phi Beta Kappa. Republican. Episcopalian. Office: Toreador Resources Corp 4809 Cole Ave Ste 108 Dallas TX 75205

BREWER, EDWARD CAGE, III, law educator; b. Clarksdale, Miss., Jan. 20, 1953; s. Edward Cage Brewer Jr. and Elizabeth Blair (Alford) Little; m. Nancy Corr Martin, Dec. 27, 1975 (div. Sept. 1985); children: Katherine Martin, Julia Blair; m. Laurie Carol Alley, June 27, 1993 (div. Dec. 1999); 1 child, Caroline Elizabeth McCarty; m. Korlyn Ann Schnapp; children: Matthew Karl Schnapp, Andrew Cage Schnapp. BA, U. of the South, 1975; JD, Vanderbilt U., 1979. Bar: Ala. 1980, U.S. Ct. Appeals (5th and 11th cirs.) 1981, U.S. Dist. Ct. (so. dist.) Ala. 1981, Ga. 1982, U.S. Dist. Ct. (no. dist.) Ga. 1982, U.S. Dist. Ct. (so. dist.) Ga. 1988, U.S. Ct. Appeals (3d and 8th cirs.) 1983, U.S. Dist. Ct. (mid. dist.) Ga. 1992, U.S. Supreme Ct. 1996. Law clk. to Hon. Virgil Pittman U.S. Dist. Ct. (so. dist.) Ala., Mobile, 1979-81; law clk. to Hon. Albert J. Henderson U.S. Ct. Appeals (5th and 11th cirs.), Atlanta, 1981-82; pvt. practice Atlanta, 1982-96; instr. Coll. of Law Ga. State U., Atlanta, 1992, 94; adj. prof. legal writing Emory U., Atlanta, 1994-96; asst. prof. law No. Ky. U., Highland Heights, 1996-2000, assoc. prof. law, 2000—02, prof. law, 2002—. Co-author: Railway Labor Act of 1926: Legislative History, 1988, Georgia Appellate Practice, 1996, 2d edit., 2002; author: Powerpoint Materials for Morgan and Rotunda, Professional Responsibility, 1997, 2d edit., 2003; contbr. articles to profl. jours. Mem.: Omicron Delta Kappa, Phi Beta Kappa. Episcopalian. Avocations: choral music, guitar, bicycling, hiking, canoeing. E-mail: brewerec@nku.edu.

BREWER, JANICE KAY, state legislator, property and investment firm executive; b. Hollywood, Calif., Sept. 26, 1944; d. Perry Wilford and Edna Clarice (Bakken) Drinkwine; m. John Leon Brewer, Jan. 1, 1963; children: Ronald Richard, John Samuel, Michael Wilford. Med. asst. cert. Valley Coll., Burbank, Calif., 1963, practical radiol. technician cert., 1963; D in Humanities (hon.) L.A. Chiropractic Coll., 1970. Pres., Brewer Property & Investments, Glendale, Ariz., 1970—; mem. Ariz. Ho. of Reps., Phoenix, 1983-86, Ariz. Senate, 1987-96, majority whip, 1993-96; mem. Maricopa County Bd. Suprs., 1997-2002; sec. of state, State of Ariz.,Phoenix, 2003-. State committeeman, Rep. Party, Phoenix, 1970, 1983; legis. liaison Ponderosa Rep. Women, Phoenix, 1980; bd. dirs. Motion Picture & TV Commn. Active NOW. Recipient Freedom award Vets. of Ariz., 1994; named Woman of Yr., Chiropractic Assn. Ariz., 1983, Legislator of Yr., Behaviour Health Assn. Ariz., 1991, NRA, 1992. Mem. Nat. Fedn. Rep. Women, Am. Legis. Exch. Coun. Lutheran. Office: 7th Fl State Capitol 1700 W Washington Phoenix AZ 85007-2808*

BREWER, JESSE WAYNE, education educator, entomologist; b. Rives, Mo., Oct. 10, 1940; s. Jesse J. and H. Faye Brewer; m. Sandra J. Ewald, Jan. 2, 1990; children: Laura E. Davis, Matthew W. PhD, Purdue U., Ind., 1968. Head dept. entomology Mont. State U., Bozeman, 1984—87, Auburn U., Ala., 1987—95, prof., 1995—. Author: about 75 Rrfereed Jjur. articles in Ssi. jurns. Mem. Orgn. of Tropical Studies, Durham, NC, 1988—2000. Grantee Vis. Scientist, Nat. Acad. of Sci., 1968, 1969, 1983, 1987. Mem.: Entomol. Soc. of Am. (exec. com. 2003—). Avocations: sports cars, hiking, skiing, snow shoeing. Home: 2114 Springwood Dr Auburn AL 36830 Office: Dept of Entomology Funchess Hall Auburn Univ Auburn AL 36849 Personal E-mail: brewejw@auburn.edu.

BREWER, JOHN CHARLES, journalist; b. Cin., Oct. 24, 1947; s. Harry Marion and Barbara Ann (Burrier) B.; m. Adeline Laude, Dec. 22, 1973 (div. 1994); children: Andrew John, Jeffrey Joseph; m. Ann Hagen Kellett, 1997. BS, Calif. State Poly. U., Pomona, 1970. Newsman, photographer Daily Report, Ontario, Calif., 1967-69; newsman AP, L.A., 1969-74, news editor, 1974-75, asst. chief bur., 1975-76, chief of bur., 1976-82, L.A., 1982-86, gen. exec. membership dept. N.Y.C., 1986-88; exec. editor news svc. The N.Y. Times, 1988-90, editor in chief news svc., 1990-97; pres. N.Y. Times Syndication Sales Corp., 1990-97; publisher, editor Peninsula Daily News, Port Angeles, Wash., 1998—. Bd. dirs. Port Angeles C. of C., Olympic Meml. Hosp. Found., Port Angeles Downtown Assn. Mem. Fedn. of Fly Fishers, Northwest Steelheaders-Trout Unlimited, Nat. Steelhead Trout Assn., Rotary Internat., Kiwanis. Republican. Roman Catholic. Office: Peninsula Daily News 305 W 1st St Port Angeles WA 98362-2205 *I enjoy very much being a journalist and newspaper executive. Nothing can compare with it. As for finding time for everything— the news and photo reports, relations with advertisers and subscribers, my family, my personnel, problems—always the problems—I am reminded of a woman who had eleven children. She was asked how she had time to take care of all of them. She replied that when she had one child it took 100 percent of her time, and eleven could not take more. I think there's an analogy in this.*

BREWER, JUDITH ANNE, special education educator, consultant; b. Pontiac, Mich., Jan. 25, 1952; d. Lorenz Robert and Jane Francis (Behen) Einheuser; m. Randall Edward Brewer, May 17, 1974; children: Michael E., Julie M. BS in Spl. Edn. summa cum laude, Western Mich. U., 1974; MA in Teaching, Oakland U., 1977. Cert. spl. edn. tchr. for emotionally impaired and learning disabled; cert. Project Adventure; cert. advanced stds. Project Adventure. Spl. edn. resource tchr. Mayfield and Woodside Elem. Sch., Lapeer, Mich., 1974-75; learning disabled tchr. Pine Tree Elem. Sch., Lake Orion, Mich., 1976, elem. self-contained learning disabled tchr., 1977-79; spl. edn. resource tchr. Carpenter and Blanche Sims Elem. Sch., Lake Orion, 1976-77; spl. edn. tchr. Lake Orion Middle Sch., 1983-85; spl. edn. tchr., cons. Lake Orion H.S., 1985—, spl. edn. dept. chair, 1992—, interim asst. prin., fall 1994, MATRIX interdisciplinary block program co-chair, tchr., 1994-98. Jr. class advisor Lake Orion H.S., 1985-87, sophomore class advisor, 1987-88, ski club sponsor, 1990-97, sch. improvement com. mem., 1990-94, mem. bldg. coun., 1992—, mem. new bldg. com., 1994-96, mem. block scheduling com., 1995—, mem. insvc. subcom., 1995—, mem. LOHS blue ribbon schs. com., 1999, blue ribbon schs. program evaluator 2000-01, profl. devel. steering com., 2000—; exec. bd. rep. Lake Orion Edn. Assn., 1987-89, 94-95, 98—; student activities chair, sch. improvement team, 1990; high sch. level steering com. North Ctrl. Accreditation, 1989-90, evaluator, 1991, 2000-01, chairperson for LOHS spl. edn. dept. NCA self-study, 1998-99; mem. Cmty. Svc. Com., 1993, mem. portfolio com., 1991; lectr. in field Cath. Social Svcs., Oakland County, Mich., 1985—. Social chmn. Sylvan Manor Homeowners Assn., West Bloomfield, Mich., 1982-84, pres. 1985; sec. Marina Pk. Estates, Subdiv., Lake Orion, 1987-89, soc. chmn., 1991-92. Grantee Lake Orion Bd. Edn., 1990, Durant Funds, 1998. Mem. Mich. Assn. Learning Disability Educators, Oakland County Educators Learning Disabled, Coun. for Exceptional Children. Roman Catholic. Avocations: reading, sewing, swimming, boating. Home: 365 Bay Pointe Rd Lake Orion MI 48362-2572 Office: Lake Orion High Sch 495 E Scripps Rd Lake Orion MI 48360-2249 E-mail: jbrewer1@lakeorion.k12.mi.us.

BREWER, KAREN, librarian; b. Janesville, Wis., Apr. 29, 1943; d. Gordon A. and Charlotte (Warren) Schultz; m. Eugene N. Brewer, June 22, 1963. BA, U. Wis., 1965, MA, 1966; PhD, Case Western Res. U., 1983. Libr. Middleton Med. Libr. U. Wis., Madison, 1966-67; libr. Med. Libr. U. Tenn., Memphis, 1968-69; libr. Cleve. Health Sci. Libr. Case Western Res. U., Cleve., 1970-76; dir. libr. Coll. Medicine Northeastern Ohio U., Rootstown, 1976-88; dir. libr. Med. Ctr. NYU, 1988—. Mem. editorial bd. Ann. Stats. Acad. Health Sci. Libr., 1986-91. Fellow N.Y. Acad. Medicine; mem. Assn. Acad. Health Sci. Librs. (sec.-treas. 1986-89, pres. 1995), Med. Libr. Assn. (bd. dirs. 1991-94), Acad. Health Info. Profls. (disting. mem.), Am. Med. Informatics Assn. Office: NYU Med Ctr Libr 550 1st Ave New York NY 10016-6402

BREWER, LEWIS GORDON, judge, lawyer, educator; b. New Martinsville, W.Va., Sept. 6, 1946; s. Harvey Lee and Ruth Carolyn (Zimmerman) B.; m. Kathryn Anne Yunker, May 25, 1985. BA, W.Va. U., 1968, JD, 1971; LLM, George Washington U., 1979. Bar: W.Va. 1971, Calif. 1978. Commd. 2d lt. USAF, 1968, advanced through grades to col., 1988, dep. staff judge adv., 1976-78, chief civil law San Antonio Air Logistics Ctr. Kelly AFB, Tex., 1979-83, staff judge adv. MacDill AFB, Fla., 1983-86, chief Air Force Cen. Labor Law Office Randolph AFB, Tex., 1987-88, dep. staff judge adv. Air Tng. Command, 1988-89, staff judge adv. 7th Air Force Osan AFB, Korea, 1989-91, 45 Space Wing Patrick AFB, 1991-93; adminstrv. law judge W.Va. Edn. and State Employee Grievance Bd., Charleston, 1993-2000, mediator, 1994—; legal counsel W.Va. Ethics Commn., Charleston, 2000—. Instr. bus. law No. Mich. U., Marquette, 1972, Solano Coll., Suisun City, Calif., 1978; instr. labor law Webster U., Ft. Sam Houston, 1983. Decorated Air Force Commendation medal, Meritorious Service medal, Legion of Merit. Mem. ABA, Assn. for Conflict Resolution, W.Va. Bar Assn., State Bar Calif., W.Va. U. Alumni Assn., George Washington U. Alumni Assn. Roman Catholic. Home: 528 Sheridan Cir Charleston WV 25314-1063 Office: 1207 Quarrier St Charleston WV 25301-1826 E-mail: Mede8wv@abanet.org., LBrewer@GWMail.state.wv.us.

BREWER, MARK COURTLAND, lawyer; b. Hammond, Ind., Apr. 1, 1955; s. Harold Russell and Carol Joan (Odell) B. BA, Harvard U., 1977; JD, Stanford U., 1981. Bar: U.S. Dist. Ct. (ea. and we. dist.) Mich. 1983, U.S. Ct. Appeals (6th cir.) 1983. Law clk. U.S. Ct. Appeals (5th cir.), Austin, 1981-82; law clk. to justice Mich. Supreme Ct., Lansing, 1982-83; assoc. Sachs, Waldman, O'Hare, P.C., Detroit, 1983-89; mem. Sachs, Waldman & O'Hare, Detroit, 1989-95. Pres. Stanford Pub. Interest Law Found. Palo Alto, Calif., 1980-81; bd. dirs. Interfaith Ctr. for Racial Justice, Warren, Mich., Mich. Protection and Adv. Svc., Lansing, Mich. Contbr. articles on AIDS discrimination, drug testing, and employee privacy to profl. publs. Mem. Macomb County Dem. Com., Mich., 1982—, 12th Congl. Dist. Dem. Com. Macomb County, 1983-93, 10th Congl. Dist. Dem. Com. Macomb County, 1993—; exec. chmn. Mich. Dem. Party; vice chair Dem. Nat. Com. Mem. ABA, FBA (pres. ea. dist. Mich., bd. dirs. 1999-2000), State Bar Mich. (Outstanding Young Lawyer 1988), Assn. State Dem. Chairs (pres.), Sierra Club. Democrat. Lutheran. Office: Mich Democratic Party 606 Townsend St Lansing MI 48933-2313

BREWER, NATHAN RONALD, veterinarian, consultant; b. Albany, N.Y., June 28, 1904; s. William and Rose (Johnson) B.; m. Jean Lees, Apr. 1, 1936; children: Maureen Pasik, Sandra Ginsberg, Jacquelyn Fechter. BS, Mich. State U., 1930, DVM, 1937; PhD in Physiology, U. Chgo., 1936; DSc (hon.), Chgo. Coll. Osteo. Medicine, 1977. Diplomate Am. Coll. Lab. Animal Medicine. Instr. pharmacology U. Ill., Chgo., 1935-36; veterinarian Detroit Bd. Health, 1937-38; prof. physiology Middlesex Vet. Sch., Waltham, Mass., 1938-39; pvt. practice Irvington (now Fremont), Calif., 1940-45; assoc. prof. physiology, dir. lab. animal facilities U. Chgo., 1945-69; pvt. cons. Chgo., 1969—. Contbr. articles to profl. jours. Named Man of Yr., Nat. Soc. Med. Rsch., 1956; recipient Arthur Brown award Delaware Valley Coll., 1983, Disting. Vet. Alumni award Mich. State U., 1997, Centennial award Del. Valley Coll., 1997. Mem. Am. Assn. Lab. Animal Sci. (life, dist. svc. award 2000, pres. emeritus 2003), Am. Vet. Med. Assn. (chmn. various coms., Charles River award 1992, Animal Welfare award 2001), Nat. Acad. Sci. (chmn. parasitism com. 1953-58), Ill. State Vet. Med. Assn. (life), Chgo. Vet. Med. Assn. (life), Am. Physiol. Soc., Conf. Rsch. Workers in Animal Diseases, Ill. State Acad. Sci. (chmn. animals in rsch. com. 1968), Am. Assn. Lab. Animal Sci. (editor 1950-62, pres. 1950-55. editor emeritus, chmn. arrangements com. 1950-53, 59, 62, 66, Griffin award 1960, Ann. Nathan R. Brewer award established in his name 1994—), Nat. Acad. Sci. Inst. Lab. Animal Resources, Am. Coll. Lab. Animal Medicine (pres. 1957-59), Am. Soc. Vet. Physiologists and Pharmacologists, Am. Soc. Lab. Animal Practitioners (chmn. mgmt. practice com.), Ill. Acad. Vet. Practice. Avocation: chess. Home and Office: 10800 Tara Rd Potomac MD 20854-1340

BREWER, NEVADA NANCY, elementary education educator; b. Balt., Jan. 21, 1949; d. Leo and Rebecca (Johnson) Brewer. BS, Coppin State Coll., 1973, MEd, 1974, MEd, 1981; postgrad., C.C. Balt., 1985. Cert. elem. tchr., spl. edn. tchr. Tchr. Balt. County Adult Edn., Towson, Md., 1973-88; coord. Just Say No to Drugs program Balt. City Sch. Sys., tchr., 2000—01, mgr. summer sch., 2000—02, acad. coach math. and sci., 2002—03, coord. math. elem. lab., 2003—. Coord. Heads Up Program, 1980, math-a-thon program St. Jude Rsch. Ctr., 1993—, 24 Challenge Math. Tournament, 1996—, elem. math. lab., 2003—, academic coach math. and sci. grades prek-5, 2002-03; supr. tchr. for student tchrs. Towson State U., Coll. Notre Dame, Coppin State Coll., 1989—; leadership tchr. STARS sci. program, 1995; participant in Project Future Search Phone-a-Thon to recruit minority students U. Md., College Park., Write to Learn Program, Balt. City Sch. Sys., 1990-91; acad. coach math and sci. grades Pre-K-5, 2002—. Coord. Echo Hill Outdoor Sch., 1988—, mem. adv. bd., 2003—. Recipient Freedom Found. award, 1974. Home: 1616 Wentworth Ave Baltimore MD 21234-6125 E-mail: nbrew@unlonnet.net.

BREWER, PAUL HUIE, advertising executive, artist, portrait painter; b. Jan. 24, 1934; s. Ralph Wright and Margot (Riviere) Brewer; m. Anita Hines, May 16, 1953 (div. 1971); children: Anita Joy(dec.), Launa Riviere; m. Carole Lynn Kuhrt, July 8, 1972; children: Nicole Renee, Brett Kuhrt. BA, La. Coll., Pineville, 1956; degree in advt. design, Famous Artists Schs., Westport, Conn., 1959. Artist Ralph Brewer's Studio and Engraving Co., Alexandria, 1952—54; art dir. Sta. KALB-TV, Alexandria, 1954—56; designer New Orleans Pub. Svc. Co., 1956; artist King Studio, Chgo., 1957; asst. art dir. Continental Casualty Co., Chgo., 1957—58; designer, art dir. Field Enterprises divsn. Chgo. Sun-Times, then dir. design; art dir. State Farm Ins. Cos., Bloomington, Ill., 1973, dir. art and design, 1973—77; prodn. mgr., exec. art dir. U.S. Savs. and Loan League, Chgo., 1977—, corp. v.p., 1983—. Cons. Johns Byrne Co., 1991, Darwill, 1992—93; instr. Wilmette (Ill.) Park Dist., 1997—, Glencoe (Ill.) Park Dist., 1997—, Winnetka (Ill.) Park Dist., 1997—, Deerpath (Ill.) Art League, 2003—, Suburban Fine Arts Ctr., 2003—. One-man shows include La. Coll., 1963, Chgo. Pub. Libr., Chgo. Press Club, Who Am I?, 1973, Represented in permanent collections Union League Club, Chgo., Ill. Bell Telephone Co., Standard Rate & Data, Krantzen Studio, Red Buttons, Lee Bolivier, Edward P. Morgan, others, Jack Benny, Danny Kaye, Danny Thomas, Pablo Picasso, Mrs. Marshall Field IV, Phil Silvers, David Susskind, Leonard Bernstein, Chuck Connors, Merve Griffin, Bob Newhart, Mike Singletary, Carol Kuhrt, others, New in the City, Count a Lonely Cadence, Who Am I?. Advt. dir. Artists Guild Bull., 1965; chmn. Artist Guild Chgo. Watercolor Show, 1967; bd. dirs. Artists Guild Chgo. Credit Union, House of Wray Corp. Ill., North Shore Art League, Lake County Art Commn., Deerpath Art League; elder Presbyn. Ch. Recipient award, Am. Newspaper Guild, Artists Guild Chgo., Famous Artists Sch., Graphic Arts Coun. Chgo., Hartford Illustrationaward, 1968, Chgo. III award, 1970, Nat. award, Louisville Rotogravure Assn., 1975, 3 SIMSA nat. awards, 1977, 2 SIMSA nat. awards, 1979, award, Union League Chgo., award of excellence, Hopper Paper Co., 1978, 1979, 2 Addy awards, State of Iowa, 1980, Nat. Merchandising awrad, P.O.P.I.A., 1980, 2 nat. awards, Fin. Insts. Mktg. Assn., 1984, award, Internat. Paper Co., 1984, Fima award, 1989, 1990, award, Chgo. Fin. Advertisers, 1990. Mem.: La. Coll. Alumni Assn., North Shore Art League, Chgo. Soc. Typographic Arts, Chgo. Soc. Communicating Arts (bd. dirs.), Deerpath Art League, Am. Soc. Portrait Artists, Famous Artists Sch. Alumni Assn., Artists Guild Chgo., Am. Watercolor Soc. (assoc.). Home: 1160 S Green Bay Rd Lake Forest IL 60045-4065 also: 3630 Lee St Alexandria LA 71302-3929 also: 1400 S Shore Dr Delavan WI 53115-3627 also: 3630 Lee St Alexandria LA 71302-3929 E-mail: PaulBrewerArt@aol.com.

BREWER, PETER GEORGE, ocean geochemist; b. Ulverston, Eng., Dec. 30, 1940; came to U.S., 1967, naturalized, 1982; s. Frederick and Irene (Clarkson) B.; m. Hilary Williams, Mar. 29, 1966; children: Jillian Anne, Alastair Michael, Erica Christine. BSc, Liverpool (Eng.) U., 1962, PhD, 1967. From asst. scientist to sr. scientist Woods Hole Oceanog. Inst., Mass., 1967—78, sr. scientist, 1978—91; program dir. marine chemistry NSF, 1981—83; exec. dir. Monterey Bay Aquarium Rsch. Inst., Pacific Grove, Calif., 1991—96, sr. scientist, 1996—. Leader of ocean sci. expeditions; mem. Environ. Task Force, 1992-93, NAS Ocean Studies Bd., 1986-94, Com. on Climate Change and the Ocean, 1987-90; convenor NATO A.R.I. on Chem. Dynamics of Upper Ocean, Jouy en Jossas, France, 1983; mem. NAS panel on policy implications of greenhouse gas warming: mitigation, 1989-91; mem. NAS carbon dioxide adv. com., 1982-83; vis. prof. U. Wash., 1979; mem. GEOSECS sci. adv. com., 1972-78. Assoc. editor: Geophys. Rsch. Letters, 1977-79, Jour. Marine Rsch., 1974-81, Deep-Sea Rsch., 1984-87, Jour. of Oceanography, 1994—; contbr. articles to profl. publs. Chmn. Gordon Rsch. Conf. on Chem. Oceanography, 1980; vice-chmn. Joint Global Ocean Fluxes Com., SCOR, 1987-90; mem. adv. bd. Applied Physics Lab., U. Wash., 1991-96. Grantee NSF, NASA, Office Naval Rsch., Dept. Energy. Fellow AAAS, Am. Geophys. Union. Office: Monterey Bay Aquarium Rsch Inst 7700 Sandholdt Rd Moss Landing CA 95039-0628 E-mail: Grpe@mbari.org.

BREWER, PHILIP WARREN, retired civil engineer; b. Hagerstown, Md., Dec. 18, 1923; s. J. Chester and Ruth (Emmert) B.; m. Elizabeth Marvel Wynn, Aug. 29, 1947; children: Dorothy Wynn, Bruce Douglas. BS, U. Md., 1945. Hydraulic engr. Water Resources Br., U.S. Geol. Survey, College Park, Md., 1945-47; designing engr. Wash. Suburban San. Commn., Hyattsville, Md., 1947-53; sanitary engr., civil engr. Bur. Yards and Docks, Dept. Navy, Washington, 1953-68; head spl. design Naval Facilities Engring. Command, 1968-73, chief civil engr., 1973-80. Bd. dirs. Madison County Wildlife Assn., Monument River Sportsmen's Assn. (Houlton, Maine). Mem. Madison County Wildlife Assn. (bd. dirs.), Monument River Sportsmen's Club (Houlton, Maine). Episcopal. Home: 2600 Barracks Rd Apt 271 Charlottesville VA 22901-2193

BREWER, PRISCILLA JOAN, historian, educator; d. William Dodd and Alice Van Ess Brewer. BA, Williams Coll., 1977; PhD, Brown U., 1987. Asst. prof. U. South Fla., Tampa, 1987—92, assoc. prof., 1992—2003, prof., 2003—. Author: From Fireplace to Cookstove, Shaker Communities, Shaker Lives. Office: American Studies Univ of South Florida 4202 E Fowler Avenue CPR 107 Tampa FL 33620 E-mail: brewer@luna.cas.usf.edu.

BREWER, ROBERT ALLEN, physician; b. Inpls., Jan. 29, 1927; s. Robert Dewayne and Viola Mae (Grant) B.; m. Mildred Noreen Barnett, Jan. 1, 1950 (dec. May 1997); children: Robert A. Jr., Raymond, Richard, Brian, Andrew. AA, St. Petersburg Jr. Coll., Fla., 1949; AB, Ind. U., 1952; MD, Ind U., Inpls., 1955. Emergency dept. staff physician Mound Park Hosp., St. Petersburg, Fla., 1960; staff physician Pinellas Hosp., Largo, Fla., 1961-68; pvt. practice Logansport, Ind., 1969—. Mem. Cass County Republican Com., Logansport, Ind., candidate for city coun., 1995. Capt. U.S. Army, 1957-59. Mem. AMA, Am. Acad. Family Practitioners (bd. cert. diplomate), Ind. Med. Assn., Cass County Med. Assn. Republican. Avocations: stamp collecting, coin collecting. Office: PO Box 119 831 E Broadway Logansport IN 46947-3161

BREWER, ROY EDWARD, lawyer; b. Atlanta, Dec. 22, 1949; s. Roy Mullins and Martha Joan (Still) Brewer; m. Catherine Elizabeth Schindler, May 5, 1979; children: Garrett Edward, Alex Winston. BA in Polit. Sci., U. Fla., 1971, MA in Polit. Sci., 1973; JD, U. Pacific, 1982. Bar: Calif. 1984, U.S. Dist. Ct. (ea. dist.) Calif. 1984, U.S. Supreme Ct. 1990. Regional planner North Cen. Fla. Regional Planning Council, Gainesville, Fla., 1975-78; dir. met. affairs Sacramento Met. C. of C., 1978-79; dir. land planning Raymond Vail and Assocs., Sacramento, 1979-84; pvt. practice Sacramento, 1984-89; ptnr. Hunter McCray Richey & Brewer, Sacramento, 1989-95, Hunter, Richey, DiBenedetto & Brewer, Sacramento, 1995—2000, mng. ptnr., 1993—2000; ptnr. The Brewer Law Firm, 2000—. Bd. dirs. Am. River Natural History Assn., 1986—90, pres., 1988—89; bd. dirs. No. Calif. Rugby Football Union, 1985—88, pres., 1985—88; chmn. Sacramento Ad-hoc Charter Comm., 1988—90; bd. dirs. Healthcare, 1987—90, chmn., 1988—89; bd. dirs. Sacramento Met. C. of C., 1985—91, pres., 1990; trustee ARC, 1989—90; chmn. Local Govt. Reorgn. Com., 1988; chair Leadership Sacramento, 2000, co-chair, 2001—03; bd. dirs. Sacramento Symphony Assn., 1987—95, Am. Lung Assn., 1988—92, Sacramento Downtown Partnership, 1997—99. Named among Best and Brightest, Sacramento Mag., 1985; recipient Sacramento Regional Pride award for cmty. devel., 1991, Exceptional Performers award, Air Force Assn., 1991, Sacramentan of the Yr. award, 1991. Mem.: Am. Inst. Cert. Planners. Avocations: rugby, Karate, scuba diving, snowboarding. Office: The Brewer Law Firm 980 Ninth St Ste 2050 Sacramento CA 95814

BREWER, RYAN MATTHEW, financial analyst; s. John Campbell and Emily Grace Brewer. BS in Environ. Health, Purdue U., 1994, BS in Mech. Engring., 1996; MBA, Ind. U., 2001. Safety process engr. AlliedSignal Corp., Huntington, Ind., 1994—96; environ. mgr. United Techs. Corp., South Bend, Ind., 1996—98, environ. specialist Detroit, 1998—2000; fin. analyst Houlihan Valuation Advisors, Indpls., 2002—. Assoc. instr. econs. and strategy Ind. U., Bloomington, 1999—2002. Essay contest co-chair Optimist Internat., Indpls., 2002—03. Recipient Gov.'s award, State Ho. State of Ind., 1998; scholar Rsch. and Tchg. Scholar, Kelley Sch. Bus., 1999—2001. Mem.: Inst. Hazardous Materials Mgmt. (licentiate), Am. Soc. Appraisers (assoc.), Optimist Internat. (assoc.; bd. dirs. 2003, co-chair essay contest 2002—03). Avocations: tennis, basketball, reading, travel. Office: Houlihan Valuation Advisors 320 North Meridian Street Indianapolis IN 46204 Office Fax: 317-833-1047. Personal E-mail: ryanmbrewer@hotmail.com. E-mail: ryanbrewer@houlihan.com.

BREWER, STEPHANIE L. lawyer; b. Newport News, Dec. 8, 1969; d. M. Lynn and Constance Susan Taylor; m. Timothy F. Brewer, Apr. 25, 1998. BA, Ariz. State U., 1992; JD, Ind. U., Indpls., 1996. Bar: Ariz. 1996, U.S. Dist. Ct. Ariz. 1996. Assoc. account exec. Bronner Slosberg & Humphrey, Boston, 1992-93; assoc. Chester A. Yon, P.C., Fountain Hills, Ariz., 1997-98, Rhees Hopkins & Kreamer, Phoenix, 1998—. Editor Internat. and Comparative Law Rev., 1994-96. Mem. ABA, State Bar of Ariz. (constrn. law sect. 1998—), Maricopa County Bar Assn., Ariz. Women Lawyers Assn. Republican. Avocations: golf, hiking, sporting events. Office: Rhees Hopkins & Kreamer 4000 N Central Ave Ste 1750 Phoenix AZ 85012-3511

BREWER, THOMAS BOWMAN, retired university president; b. Ft. Worth, July 22, 1932; s. Earl Johnson and Maurine (Bowman) B.; m. Betty Jean Walling, Aug. 4, 1951; children: Diane, Thomas Bowman Jr. BA, U. Tex., 1954, MA, 1957; PhD, U. Pa., 1962. Instr. St. Stephens Episcopal Sch., Austin, Tex., 1955-56, S.W. Tex. State Coll., San Marcos, 1956-57; from instr. to asso. prof. North Tex. State U., Denton, 1959-66, asst. prof. U. Ky., 1966-67; asso. prof. Iowa State U., 1967-68; prof. history, chmn. dept. U. Toledo, 1968-71; dean Tex. Christian U., Ft. Worth, 1971-72, vice chancellor, dean univ., 1972-78; chancellor East Carolina U., Greenville, N.C., 1978-82; v.p. acad. affairs Ga. State U., Atlanta, 1982-88; pres. Met. State Coll. of Denver, 1988-93; interim provost U. Alaska, Anchorage, 1995-97. Editor: Views of American Economic Growth, 2 vols, 1966, The Robber Barons, 1969; gen. editor: Railroads of America Series. Home: 104 Javelin Dr Austin TX 78734-5016 E-mail: TBBSR@alumni.utexas.net.

BREWER, TIMOTHY FRANCIS, III, retired cardiologist; b. Hartford, Conn., Oct. 30, 1931; s. Timothy F. Brewer Jr. and Catherine Marie (Sullivan) Brewer; m. Norma Rae Flicker, June 14, 1954 (div. Jan. 1980); children: Raymond, Donna, Timothy, Kevin, William; m. Barbara Grace Bagdasarian, May 28, 1983. BA, Yale Coll., 1953; MD, N.Y. Med. Coll., 1957. Diplomate Bd. Internal Medicine Cardiovasc. Diseases. Intern St. Francis Hosp., Hartford, 1957-58; resident in internal medicine VA Ctr., L.A., 1958-60; spl. fellow in cardiovascular diseases Cleve. (Ohio) Clinic, 1960-62; pvt. practice St. Francis Hosp., Hartford, 1962-64; assoc. dir. clin. rsch. Pfizer Inc., Groton, Conn., 1964-71; dir. Clin. Pharmacology Miles Lab., West Haven, Conn., 1971-74; pvt. practice Middlesex Hosp., Middletown, Conn., 1974-96, ret., 1996. Pres. med. staff Middlesex Hosp., Middlesex, Conn., 1981—83, chief cardiology sect., 1988—95. Fellow: ACP, Coun. on Clin. Cardiology, Am. Coll. Chest Physicians (emeritus), Am. Coll. Cardiology (emeritus); mem.: AMA (pres. South Ctrl. Conn. chpt. 1982, bd. dirs. 1980), Am. Heart Assn. (Conn. affiliate). Avocation: golf. E-mail: tfb3@earthlink.net.

BREWER, WILLIAM DANE, lawyer; b. Detroit, Oct. 30, 1961; BA, Yale U., 1983; JD, Harvard U., 1986. Bar: Ill. 1986, N.Y., 1995. Assoc. Kirkland & Ellis, Chgo., 1986-89, Winston & Strawn, Chgo., 1990-94, ptnr., 1994, N.Y.C., 1995—. Mem. ABA, Ill. State Bar Assn., Chgo. Bar Assn, N.Y. State Bar Assn., Assn. Bar City N.Y. Office: Winston & Strawn 200 Park Ave Fl 41 New York NY 10166-4401 Fax: 212 294-4700. E-mail: wbrewer@winston.com.

BREWER, WILLIAM E. city materials manager; b. Centralia, Wash., Apr. 30, 1947; s. Nelson E. and Lillian E. Brewer; m. Nedra Jeanine Brewer, June 8, 1968; children: Gregory E., Lisa A., Traci L. BS, Ariz. State U., 1969. Cert. purchasing mgr., cert. pub. purchasing officer. Buyer aid Shell Oil Co., Long Beach, Calif., 1969-71; buyer-buyer mgr. City of Phoenix, 1972-80; purchasing agt., materials mgr. City of Glendale, Ariz., 1981—. Sch. bd. Paradise Valley Christian Sch., Phoenix, 1980-87, Scottsdale Christian Acad., Phoenix, 1988-94; deacon So. Bapt. Ch., Phoenix, 1989; officer positions Ariz. State Capitol Chpt., 1981-85. Mem. Nat. Inst. of Govtl. Purchasing (nat. bd. mem., Nat. Buyer of Yr. 1984, Nat. Purchasing Mgr. of Yr. 1994, Nat. Disting. Svc. award 1997), Inst. Supply Mgmt., City of Glendale Ariz. C. of C., Grand Canyon Minority Supplier Devel. Coun. Republican. Office: City of Glendale 5850 W Glendale Ave Ste 202 Glendale AZ 85301-2599

BREWER-PECSON, DOROTHY WYNNE, environmentalist; b. Hyattsville, Md., Apr. 24, 1949; d. Philip Warren and Elizabeth (Wynn) Brewer; m. Benjamin Matthew Pecson, Apr. 24, 1994. BS, U. Md., College Park, 1972; computer programming degree, Computer Learning Ctr., Springfield Va., 1985. Forest ranger State of Md., Annapolis, 1973—85; receptionist Wheaton Plz . Mgmt., Md., 1986; arborist Montgomery County Govt., Md., 1986—95, environmental planner, 1995—. Editor: (newsletter) The Transporter, 1994. Mem.: Midatlantic Horror Profls. (founding mem. 2001), Maryland Writers Assn. Democrat. Episcopalian. Achievements include First female forest ranger employed by state of Md; first female arborist employed by Montgomery County. Avocations: art, music, handcrafts, nature, writing. Home: 2614 Wesman Rd Wheaton MD 20902-2149 Office: Dept Environ Protectin Montgomery County 255 Rockville Pike Rockville MD 20850

BREWER-SMYTH, KATHLEEN, nursing researcher, nursing educator; b. Phoenixville, Pa. m. Thomas McKean Smyth. BSN, West Chester U., 1979; MSN, U. Pa., 1985, PhD, 2001. RN, Del., Pa.; cert. rehab. nurse. Staff nurse med.-surg. unit Phoenixville Hosp., 1979-80; staff nurse neurosurgery unit, surg. ICU Hosp. of U. Pa., Phila., 1980-85; clin. nurse specialist, coord. comprehensive epilepsy ctr. Grad. Hosp., Phila., 1985-90; staff devel. coord. Mediplex Rehab.-Camden, N.J., 1990-92; instr. nursing Bryn Mawr Rehab. Hosp., Malvern, Pa., 1992-95; clin. instr. U. Del., Newark, 1996-97, asst. prof. nursing, 2003—; postdoctoral rsch. fellow Sch. Nursing U. Pa., Phila., 2001—03. Lectr. in field; presenter at profl. confs. Contbr. articles to profl. jours. Single adult ministry leader 10th Presbyn. Ch., Phila., 1989-91, deaconess, 1997. Mem. Am. Assn. Neurosci. Nurses, Am. Soc. Neurorehab., Assn. Rehab. Nurses (cert.), Am. Soc. Neurorehab., Nurses Christian Fellowship, Christian Med. and Dental Soc., Sigma Theta Tau. Office: U Pa Sch Nursing Guardian Dr Philadelphia PA 19104 Mailing: PO Box 352 Chadds Ford PA 19317 E-mail: kbsmyth@udel.edu.

BREWINGTON, ARTHUR WILLIAM, retired English language educator; b. Bklyn., Nov. 10, 1906; s. Oscar and Julia (Wenisch) B.; m. Thelma Sherman, Aug. 18, 1955. AB, Asbury Coll., 1928; MA, Cornell U., 1931; PhD, Vanderbilt U., 1941. Head English dept. Tenn. Wesleyan Coll., Athens, 1929-31; instr. English Pa. State U., State College, 1932-33; prof. English and speech Memphis State U., 1940-43; inspector quality control Glenn Martin Co., Balt., 1943-45; head speech dept. Towson State U., Balt., 1945-71. Dir. drama and theater Towson State U., 1946-69. Contbr. rsch. to profl. publs. Fund-raiser, bd. dirs. Am. Heart Assn., Green Valley, 1995-96. Fulbright grantee U.S. State Dept., 1955-56, Danforth grantee, 1963. Mem. Fulbright Assn. (pres. U. Ariz. chpt. 2001-02), Kiwanis (com. chmn. 1971-95), Masons (chaplain lodge 171 1972-75), Cornell Club., Green Valley Shrine Club (pres. 1974). Democrat. Episcopalian. Avocations: theater, movies, tv, opera, symphony. Home: 69 W Cedro Dr Green Valley AZ 85614-4203 E-mail: art1110@cs.com.

BREWSTER, CARROLL WORCESTER, former academic administrator; b. N.Y.C., Mar. 26, 1936; s. Carroll Harwood and Blandina (Worcester) B.; m. Ursula Mary Orange, Mar. 9, 1968 (dec. Apr. 1996); children— Abraham Carroll, Ursula Constant, Blandina Worcester. BA, Yale, 1957, LL.B., 1961; L.H.D. (hon.), Hollins Coll., 1981, Hobart and William Smith Coll., 1991; postgrad., Kings Coll., Cambridge U., 1957-58. Bar: Conn. 1962. Law clk. to chief judge U.S. Dist. Ct., Conn., 1961-62; legal asst. to Hon. Mohamed Ahmed Abu Rannat, Chief Justice of the Sudan, Khartoum, 1962-64; assoc. Tyler, Cooper, Grant, Bowerman & Keefe, New Haven, 1965-69, also U.S. commr., 1966-69; lectr. Yale Law Sch., 1967-69; coll. dean Dartmouth Coll., 1969-75; pres. Hollins Coll., Va., 1975-81, Hobart and William Smith Colls., N.Y., 1982-91; exec. dir. Hole in the Wall Gang Fund, New Haven, 1991-98. Trustee Phillips Exeter Acad., 1970-80, Anatolia Coll, 1990—, U. New Haven, 1995—; chmn., bd. dirs. Presiding Bishop's Fund for Wold Relief, 1986-91, The Episcopal Ch. Found., 1985-93. Editor: Sudan Law Jour. and Reports, 1961-65. Senior Fulbright scholar, U. Khartoum, Sudan, 1981-82. Home: 126 Lounsbury Rd Ridgefield CT 06877-4730

BREWSTER, CHARLES EDWARD, writer, engineer; b. Pulaski County, Ky., Jan. 24, 1941; s. Theodore and Essie Pearl Brewster; m. Norma Ruth Brewster, Nov. 5, 1962; children: Nancy Louise, Carolyn Sue, David Charles, Evelyn Ruth. A with honors in Engring. Sci., Sinclair C.C., 1990; B with honors, Christian Bible Coll., 1990, M with honors, 1995, PhD with honors in Theology, 1996; BS in Engring., Calif. Coast U., 2000. Machine tool builder Nat. Cash Register Co., Dayton, Ohio, 1957—67; machinist Litton Industries, Woodland Hills, Calif., 1967—68, Ocean Tech., Burbank, Calif., 1968—69; tool engr., jr. engr. Inland Divsn. Gen. Motors, Dayton, 1969—73, prodn. engr., 1974—79; plant layout engr. Inland-Delco-Delphi Corp., Dayton, 1979—2000; adminstrv. manf. engr. Delphi Corp., Vandalia, Ohio, 2000—. Owner Scriptural Founds., Miamisburg, Ohio, 1996—. Author: Sophia's Unfaithful Lovers, 1996, Secrets of the Ages: Revealed, 2001, What Did God Say?, 2001. Spkr. Evangelical Edn. Ministries, Rockford, Ill., 1999—2000; New Testament Greek classes various local chs., Dayton, Ohio, 2002. Mem.: Ark Found. Dayton, Concerned Women Am. Avocations: guitar, languages, dobro, banjo. Office: Scriptural Found Pub PO Box 1103 Miamisburg OH 45343

BREWSTER, CHRISTOPHER RALPH, lawyer; b. Passaic, N.J., June 6, 1950; s. Ralph Arthur and Ada Barrett Brewster; m. Jane Eldridge, Sept. 29, 1984; children: William Eldridge, Kathryn Barrett. AB, Dartmouth Coll., 1972; JD, U. Va., 1975. Bar: Mo. 1975, D.C. 1988, U.S. Dist. Ct. D.C. 1991. Asst. atty. gen. State of Mo., Jefferson City, 1975-77; legis. asst. U.S. Sen. John C. Danforth, Washington, 1977-82; minority counsel Subcom. on Fed. Spending Practices U.S. Sen. Com. on Govtl. Affairs, Washington, 1979-81, chief counsel/staff dir. Subcom. on Fed. Expenditures, 1981-82; assoc. dir. Bur. Consumer Protection, FTC, Washington, 1982-84; counsel Kaye, Scholer LLP, Washington, 1984—. Trustee St. John's Child Devel. Ctr., Washington, 1985-91. Republican. Episcopalian. Office: Kaye Scholer LLP 901 15th St NW Washington DC 20005-2327

BREWSTER, CLARK OTTO, lawyer; b. Marlette, Mich., Nov. 5, 1956; s. Charles W. and June V. (Hoff) B.; m. Deborah K. Trowhill, Aug. 3, 1974; children: Cassie Mae, Corbin Clark, Cade Otto. BA cum laude, Cen. Mich. U., 1977; JD with honor, Tulsa U., 1980. Bar: Okla. 1981, U.S. Dist. Ct. (ND,WD,ED) Okla. 1982, Tex. 1993. Assoc. Riddle and Assocs., Tulsa, 1981, Braly and McEachin, Tulsa, 1981-82; ptnr. Brewster & DeAngelis, Tulsa, 1982—. Bd. dirs. Redy Corp., Tulsa, Cottontail Oil Corp., Tulsa. Mem. ABA, ATLA, Okla. Bar Assn., Okla. Trial Lawyers Assn. (pres. 1998), Tulsa County Bar Assn., Order of Curule chair, Order of Barristers. Avocations: golf, hunting, horseback riding. Home: 2109 E 30th Pl Tulsa OK 74114-5429 Office: Brewster & DeAngelis 2617 E 21st St Tulsa OK 74114

BREWSTER, ELIZABETH WINIFRED, English language educator, poet, novelist; b. Chipman, N.B., Can., Aug. 26, 1922; d. Frederick John and Ethel May (Day) Brewster BA, U. N.B., 1946; MA, Radcliffe U., 1947; BLS, U. Toronto, 1953; PhD, Ind. U., 1962; DLitt, U. N.B., 1982. Cataloger Carleton U., Ottawa, Ont., 1953-57; cataloger Ind. U. Library, Bloomington, 1957-58, N.B. Legis. Library, 1965-68, U. Alta. Library, Edmonton, Can., 1968-70; mem. English dept. Victoria U., B.C., 1960-61; reference libr. Mt. Allison U. Libr., Sackville, N.B., 1961-65; vis. asst. prof. English U. Alta., 1970-71; mem. faculty U. Sask., Saskatoon, Can., 1972—, asst. prof. English, 1972-75, assoc. prof., 1975-80, prof., 1980-90, prof. emeritus, 1990—. Author: East Coast, 1951, Lillooet, 1954, Roads, 1957, Passage of Summer, 1969, Sunrise North, 1972, In Search of Eros, 1974, Sometimes I Think of Moving, 1977, The Way Home, 1982, The Sisters, 1974, It's Easy to Fall on the ice, 1977, Digging In, 1982, Junction, 1982, A House Full of Women, 1983, Selected Poems 1944-84, 2 vols., 1985, Visitations, 1987, Entertaining Angels, 1988, Spring Again, 1990, The Invention of Truth, 1991, Wheel of Change, 1993, Away from Home, 1995, Footnotes to the Book of Job, 1995, Garden of Sculpture, 1998, Burning Bush, 2000, Jacob's Dream, 2002. Recipient E.J. Pratt award for poetry U. Toronto, 1953, Pres. medal for poetry U. Western Ont., 1980, Lit. award Can. Broadcasting Corp., 1991, Lifetime award for excellence in the arts Sask. Arts Bd., 1995, Short List award Gov. Gen., 1996. Mem. League Can. Poets (life), Writers' Union Can., Assn. Can. Univ. Tchrs. English, Order of Can.

BREWSTER, FRANCIS ANTHONY, lawyer; b. Foochow, China, Jan. 28, 1929; s. Francis Thoburn and Eva (Melby) B.; m. Susan Brewster, Apr. 6, 1974; 1 dau., Melissa Leigh; children by previous marriage— Sara, Julia, Anne, Ellen, Rebecca. BS, U. Wis., 1950, LL.B., 1955. Bar: Wis. 1955, U.S. Dist. Ct. (ea. and we. dists.) Wis. Corporate counsel Scott Paper Co., Phila., 1955-56, labor counsel, 1957; div. personnel mgr. Scott Paper Co. (Detroit div.), 1958-60; corp. counsel RCA, Camden, N.J., 1961; pvt. practice law Madison, Wis., 1961—. Dir. Nat. Guardian Life Ins. Co., Stephan & Brady, Inc.; lectr. law U. Wis., 1961— . Contbr. articles to profl. jours. Gen. counsel Four Lakes coun. Boy Scouts Am., 1980—94; mem. gen. counsel Wis. Privacy Coun., 1991—95; chair Gov.'s Task Force on Privacy, 1999—2001; pres. Hill Farms Assn., 1999—; counsel John Knox Presbytery, 2001—; Chmn. personnel bd. City of Madison, 1970—75; bd. dirs. Capitol div. A.R.C., 1965—74, chmn. div., 1973; bd. dirs. Madison Symphony, Inc., 1968—75, gen. counsel, 1961—91; bd. visitors U. Wis. System, 1972—85, pres. bd. visitors, 1978—80. Served to capt. USMC, 1950—53, Korea. Recipient Certificate of Merit U. Mich.-Wayne State U., 1959; named Outstanding Madisonian, 1969, Wis. Man of Distinction, 1972, State Atty. of Yr. for Pro Bono Svc., 1998. Mem. ABA, Dane County Bar Assn. (past sec. and program chmn.), State Bar of Wis. (chmn. dist. 2 fee arbitration panel 1978—; mem. lawyer dispute resolution panel 1998—), Wis. Bar Found. (bd. dirs. 1981-87, chmn. investment com.), Interfraternity Alumni Council U. Wis. (pres. 1968-74), Delta Upsilon (pres. Wis. 1965-72, Outstanding Alumnus 1984). Republican. Presbyn. (elder). Club: Kiwanian (Madison) (pres. 1969). Office: PO Box 55418 Madison WI 53705-9218 Fax: 608-231-1163. E-mail: fabrewst@facstaff.wisc.edu.

BREWSTER, GERRY LEIPER, educator, lawyer; b. Balt., Sept. 6, 1957; s. Daniel Baugh and Carole Helme (Leiper) B. AB cum laude, Princeton (N.J.) U., 1979; JD, U. Balt., 1984. Bar: Md. 1985., D.C. 1988. Law clk. to judge State of Md., Towson, 1984-85; asst. state's atty. Baltimore County, Towson, Md., 1985-88, asst. to county exec., 1988-90; legislator Md. State Legislature, Annapolis, Md., 1991-95; tchr. Balt. County Pub. Schs., 1995—2002. Bd. dirs. Md. State Fair, Timonium. Exec. dir. Young Dems. of Md., 1987-88; del. Dem. Nat. Conv., Atlanta; former bd. dirs. Franklin Sq. Hosp., Citizens Outreach of Baltimore County; former mem. adv. bd. Sexual Assault and Domestic Violence Ctr., Inc.; Dem. nominee for Congress, Md. 2d Congl. Dist., 1994. Named 1 of 10 Outstanding Young Marylanders, Towson Jaycees, 1989, Merit award Common Cause Md., 1993, Gold Star award League Conservation Voters, 1993, Humanitarian award Gov. of Md., 1993, Md. Law Enforcement Officers Inc. honoree, 1993, Co-Legis. of Yr. award Md. State Fraternal Order of Police, 1994. Mem. ABA, Md. Bar Assn., D.C. Bar Assn., Baltimore County Bar Assn., Nat. Dist. Attys. Assn., Md. State's Atty. Assn., Gilman Alumni Assn. (bd. dirs. 1986—, pres. 1991-92), W. Towson Neighborhood Assn. Episcopalian. Avocations: steeplechase riding, sailing, golf, skiing. Home: 527 Allegheny Ave Baltimore MD 21204-4233 E-mail: GerryBrewster@comcast.net.

BREWSTER, JAMES HENRY, retired chemistry educator; b. Ft. Collins, Colo., Aug. 21, 1922; s. Oswald Cammann and Elizabeth (Booraem) B.; m. Christine Barbara Germain, Jan. 23, 1954; children— Christine Carolyn, Mary Elizabeth, Barbara Anne. AB, Cornell U., 1942; PhD, U. Ill., 1948. Chemist Atlantic Refining Co., Phila., 1942-43; postdoctoral fellow U. Chgo., 1948-49; instr. Purdue U., 1949-50, asst. prof., 1950-55, assoc. prof., 1955-60, prof., 1960-91, prof. emeritus, 1991—. With Am. Field Service, 1943-45. Fellow AAAS; mem. Am. Chem. Soc., Chem. Soc. (London), Royal Soc. Chemistry, Phi Beta Kappa, Sigma Xi, Phi Lambda Upsilon. Achievements include research in bond molecular orbitals, relation optical rotation and constitution, and origins of life. Home: 334 Hollowood Dr West Lafayette IN 47906-2146 Office: Purdue U Dept Chemistry Lafayette IN 47907 E-mail: jbrewst2@Purdue.edu.

BREWSTER, LINDA JEAN, family nurse practitioner; b. Portland, Maine, Nov. 6, 1956; d. Thomas Stuart and Patricia Noreen (Dixon) Warden; m. James Ernest Brewster, Aug. 20, 1977; children: Ryan James, Seth Thomas. BS summa cum laude, U. So. Maine, 1987, MS, 1992; FNP, U. N.H., 1995. Cert. nurse clinician, cert. family nurse prctitioner; cert. ACLS. Staff nurse II Maine Med. Ctr., Portland, 1987-89, clin. level nurse III, 1989-91, case mgr., 1990-91, asst. head nurse, 1991-94; ICU and emergency rm. nurse So. Maine Med. Ctr., 1994-95; intravenous nurse clinician Homedco, Lewiston, Maine, 1994-95; instr. nursing So. Maine Tech. Coll., South Portland, 1994-95; family nurse practioner Bowdoin Med. Group, Cumberland, Maine, 1995—2003, Royal River Family Care, Yarmouth, Maine, 2003—. Site investigator Multisite Study Harvard Med. Sch., 1993-94; co-investigator Maine Med. Ctr., 1993. Author: Section Review Book for RNC Certification Examination, 1994, 2nd edit., 1998. Bd. dirs. Am. Heart Assn., 1989-93, programs chair, 1991-93. Mem. Am. Acad. Nurse Practitioners, Maine Nurse Practitioner Assn., Sigma Theta Tau (Kappa Zeta chpt.). Methodist. Avocations: women's health, adolescent health, patient education, wellness and preventive care. Home: 27 Old Gray Rd Cumberland Center ME 04021-9778

BREWSTER, OLIVE NESBITT, retired librarian; b. San Antonio, July 19, 1924; d. Charles Henry and Olive Agatha (Nesbitt) B. BA, Our Lady of Lake Coll., 1945, BS in LS, 1946. Asst. librarian aeromed. library U.S. Air Force Sch. Aviation Medicine, Randolph AFB, Tex., 1946-60; chief cataloger aeromed. library Sch. Aerospace Medicine, Brooks AFB, Tex., 1960-83, chief tech. processing, 1983-88; ret., 1988. Mem.: ALA, Am. Soc. Indexers, Mensa. Anglican. Home: 1906 Schley Ave San Antonio TX 78210-4332

BREWSTER, ROBERT CHARLES, diplomat, consultant; b. Beatrice, Nebr., May 31, 1921; s. Charles Lee and Lillian Asenath (French) B.; m. Mary Virginia Blackman, Feb. 22, 1951. Student, Grinnell Coll., 1939-41, AB, U. Wash., 1943; postgrad., U. Mex., 1946, George Washington U., 1947, Columbia U., 1946-48. Fgn. affairs analyst State Dept., Washington, 1948-49, fgn. service officer, 1949-81; 3d sec. Am. Embassy, Managua, Nicaragua, 1949-51, 2d sec., 1951-52; vice consul Am. consulate gen. Stuttgart, Germany, 1952-55; policy briefing officer ICA, staff asst. to under sec. of state for econ. affairs, 1958, spl. asst. to under sec. of state, 1959-60; assigned Nat. War Coll., 1960-61; fgn. service insp., 1961-63; counselor Am. Embassy, Asuncion, Paraguay, 1964-66; dep. exec. dir. Bur. of European Affairs, 1966-67, exec. dir., 1967-69; dep. exec. sec. Dept. State, 1969-71, dir. personnel, 1971-73; amb. Ecuador, 1973-76; coord. for Law of Sea Dept. State, 1976, dep. asst. sec. for oceans and internat. environmental and sci. affairs, 1977-78, insp. gen., 1979-81, cons., 1981-89. Mem. D.C. Commn. on Aging, 1984-85; bd. dirs. Nat. Defense Univ. Found., 1984-87; mem. Com. on Research for Security of Future U.S. Embassy Bldgs. Nat. Acad. Scis., 1985-86. With USNR, 1943-46. Mem. Nat. War Coll. Alumni Assn. (pres. 1981-83), Foggy Bottom Assn. (v.p. 1984-85, pres. 1985-87), Diplomatic and Consular Officers Ret. Clubs: Cosmos (Washington). Home: 3050 Military Rd NW 410 Washington DC 20015

BREWSTER, ROBERT GENE, concert singer, educator; b. Pinson, Ala., July 7, 1938; s. Hubert and Chrisella (Ayers) B.; m. Premala Edwards (div.); 1 child, Ravindra Robert. MusB in Piano Performance with honors, Wheaton Coll., 1958; MusM in Voice with distinction, Ind. U., 1961; PhD in Vocal Performances Practices and Musicology, Washington U., St. Louis, 1967; Konzertreife Diploma, Staatliche Hochschule fuer Musik und Darstellender Kunst, Stuttgart, Fed. Republic Germany, 1970; diploma in Lieder and Opera, Mozarteum, Salzburg, Austria, 1969. Tchr. music and French Westfield (Ala.) High Sch., 1959-60; chmn. dept. music Miles Coll., Birmingham, Ala., 1960-62; chmn. area fine arts Jackson (Miss.) Coll., 1962-63; asst. tchr. voice Washington Univ., 1963-66; touring tenor throughout Europe, 1966-73; chmn. dept. music Dillard Univ., New Orleans, 1974; chmn. dept. voice Univ. Miami, Coral Gables, Fla., 1974-82; past pres. Breff Agy., Inc., N.Y.C.; pres. European Fashion Imports, N.Y.C., 1984-88, Fashion Suite, Inc., 1988—. Guest lectr. Stanford U. in, Germany, Beutelsbach, 1968-70; dozent fur gesang Berliner Kirchenmusikschule, 1970-72 Concert tours throughout, Europe, Asia and, The Ams.; rec. artist (album) I See the Stars, 1960. Seely Mudd fellow, 1964-66; Fulbright fellow, 1966-68; Deutsche Akademische Austausch Dienst award, 1968-70 Mem.: AAUP, Coll. Music Soc., Am. Musicol. Soc., Nat. Assn. Schs. Music, Fla. Vocal Tchrs. Assn., Nat. Assn. Tchrs. Singing, One Hundred Black Men, Inc., Nat. Arts Club, Phi Mu Alpha. Democrat. Episcopalian. Home and Office: 475 W 57th St Apt 18A New York NY 10019-1778 E-mail: robertgbrewster@mindspring.com.

BREWSTER, RUDI MILTON, judge; b. Sioux Falls, S.D., May 18, 1932; s. Charles Edwin and Wilhemina Therese (Rud) B.; m. Gloria Jane Nanson, June 27, 1954; children: Scot Alan, Lauri Diane (Alan Lee), Julie Lynn Yahnke. AB in Pub. Affairs, Princeton U., 1954; JD, Stanford U., 1960. Bar: Calif. 1960. From assoc. to ptnr. Gray, Cary, Ames & Frye, San Diego, 1960-84; judge U.S. Dist. Ct. (so. dist.) Calif., San Diego, 1984—98, sr. judge, 1998—. Capt. USNR, 1954-82 Ret. Fellow Am. Coll. Trial Lawyers; mem. Am. Bd. Trial Advs., Internat. Assn. Ins. Counsel, Am. Inns of Ct. Republican. Lutheran. Avocations: skiing, hunting, gardening. Office: US Dist Ct Ste 4165 940 Front St San Diego CA 92101-8902 Fax: 619-702-9927. E-mail: Rudi_Brewster@casd.uscourts.gov

BREWTON, SAMUEL ALTON, JR., urologist; b. Jacksonville, Fla., Feb. 11, 1931; s. Samuel Alton Sr. and Estelle (Stephens) B.; m. Martha Mullins, Dec. 30, 1956; children: Martha Brewton Reddick, Samuel Alton III, Benjamin Howard. AB, Emory U., 1952; MD, Med. Coll. of Ga., 1956. Diplomate Am. Bd. Urology. Intern Duval Med. Ctr., Jacksonville, 1956-57; resident in gen. surgery Med. Coll. of Ga., Augusta, 1959-61, resident in urology, 1961-64; urologist, mem. staff Upson County Hosp., Thomaston, Ga., 1964—, Colisuem Pk. Hosp., Macon, Ga., 1964—. Bd. dirs. Thomaston Fed. Savs. Bank. Councilman City of Thomaston, 1978-84, mayor pro tem, 1981-83, 90-2000, mayor, 2000-; bd. dirs. Thomaston City Sch. Bd., 1971-78. Lt. comdr. USN, 1957-59. Mem. Med. Assn. Ga., Southeastern chpt. Am. Urol. Assn., Am. Urol. Assn. Baptist. Avocations: travel, reading, fly fishing. Home: 100 Joyner Dr Thomaston GA 30286-4064

BREY, ERIC TRENT, hospitality and tourism educator; b. Loyal, Wis., Aug. 5, 1977; s. Duane Alfred and Paula JoAnn Brey. Master's Degree, U. Wis. Stout, Menomonie, 2003. Rsch. specialist, grad. asst. U. Wis. Stout, Menomonie, 1999—, editor-in-chief Jour. Student Rsch., 2002—, assoc. lectr., 2002—03; food svc. adminstr. Wis. State Fair Pk., Milw., 2003—. Cpl. Wis. Army N.G., 1997—2003. Decorated Army Res. Component Achievement medal, Army Achievement medal; recipient Tourism Career Iniative award; scholar, Travel Industry Assn., Meeting Profls. Internat., Purdue U.; grad. studies fellow, Okla. State U. Mem.: Internat. Coun. on Hospitality, Restaurant, Instl. Edn. (assoc.), Internat. Assn. Travel and Tourism Educators (assoc.), Travel and Tourism Rsch. Assn. (assoc.). Home: 403 N Gwinn St Loyal WI 54446 Office: Univ Wis Stout 404 Home Ec Bldg Menomonie WI 54751 Personal E-mail: ebrey@purdue.edu.

BREYER, NORMAN NATHAN, metallurgical engineering educator, consultant; b. Detroit, June 21, 1921; s. Max and Fannie (Landesman) B.; m. Dorothy Atlas, Feb. 10, 1952 (dec. Sept. 1987); children: Matthew, Richard, Marjorie; m. Claire Shore, Mar. 16, 1989. BS, Mich. Tech. U., Houghton, 1943; MS, U. Mich., 1948; PhD, Ill. Inst. Tech., 1963. Aero. research scientist NACA, Cleve., 1948; chief armor sect. Detroit Tank Arsenal, Warren, Mich., 1948-52; dir. research cast steels and irons Nat. Roll & Foundry, Avonmore, Pa., 1952-54; metallurgist-in-charge armor Continental Foundry & Machine div. Blaw-Knox Co., East Chicago, Ind., 1955-57; mgr. tech. projects LaSalle Steel Co., Hammond, Ind., 1957-64; assoc. prof. metall. engring. Ill. Inst. Tech., Chgo., 1964-69, prof., 1969-91, prof. emeritus, 1991—, chmn. dept., 1976-85. Capt. U.S. Army, 1943-46, ETO. Mem. AIME, Am. Soc. Metals Home: 858 Timber Hill Rd Highland Park IL 60035-5121 Office: Ill Inst Tech Dept Metall & Materials Engring 10 W 33rd St Chicago IL 60616-3730

BREYER, STEPHEN GERALD, United States supreme court justice; b. San Francisco, Aug. 15, 1938; s. Irving G. and Anne R. Breyer; m. Joanna Hare, Sept. 4, 1967; children: Chloe, Nell, Michael. AB, Stanford U., 1959; BA (Marshall scholar), Oxford U., 1961; LLB, Harvard U., 1964; LLD (hon.), U. Rochester, 1983. Bar: Calif. 1966, D.C. 1966, Mass. 1971. Law clk. Justice Goldberg, U.S. Supreme Ct., 1964—65; spl. asst. to asst. atty. gen. U.S. Dept. Justice, 1965—67; asst. prof. law Harvard U., 1967—70, prof., 1970—81, lectr., 1981—, prof. govt. J.F. Kennedy Sch., 1978—81; asst. spl. prosecutor Watergate Spl. Prosecution Force, 1973; spl. counsel U.S. Senate Judiciary Com., 1974—75, chief counsel, 1979—81; judge U.S. Ct. Appeals (1st cir.), Boston, 1981—90, chief judge, 1990—94; Oliver Wendell Holmes lectr. Harvard Law Sch., 1992; assoc. justice U.S. Supreme Ct., Washington, 1994—. Mem. U.S. Sentencing Commn., 1985—89, Jud. Conf. of U.S., 1990—94; vis. lectr. Coll. Law, Sydney, Australia, 1975, Salzburg (Austria) Seminar, 1978, 93; Jud. Conf. rep. to Adminstrv. Conf. U.S., 1981—94; vis. prof. U. Rome, 1993. Author (with Paul MacAvoy): The Federal Power Commission and the Regulation of Energy, 1974; author: (with Richard Stewart) Administrative Law and Regulatory Policy, 1979, Administrative Law and Regulatory Policy, 3rd edit., 1992; author: Regulation and its Reform, 1982, Breaking the Vicious Circle, 1993; contbr. articles to profl. jours. Trustee U. Mass., 1974—81; bd. overseers Dana Farber Cancer Inst., Boston, 1977—. Mem.: ABA, Coun. Fgn. Rels., Am. Acad. Arts and Scis., Am. Law Inst., Am. Bar Found. Office: US Supreme Ct Supreme Ct Bldg 1 1st St NE Washington DC 20543-0001*

BREYTSPRAAK, JOHN, JR., management consultant; b. Chgo., May 24, 1929; s. John and Grace Willets (Merrick) B.; m. Charlotte Helfand, Dec. 27, 1958. BA in Econs., Lake Forest (Ill.) Coll., 1950. Mgr. mktg. communications fibers div. Am. Cyanamid, N.Y.C., 1964-67; merchandising mgr. Vectra Fiber, Standard Oil Co. N.J., N.Y.C., 1967-69; account supr. Doyle Dane Bernbach, N.Y.C., 1969-73; mgr. mktg. svcs. Formica Corp., Am. Cyanamid, Cin., 1973-76; pres. Sanitas Wallcoverings, Am. Cyanamid, Wayne, N.J., 1976-80; gen. mgr. Chem. Light, Am. Cyanamid, Wayne, 1980-81; pres. Simmons Wallcoverings, Gulf & Western, N.Y.C., 1981-84; cons. New Bern, N.C., 1984-96; pres. Composers Music Co., New Bern, 1987-97; cons. Lacey, Wash., 1996—, South Sound Sr. Svcs., 2000—. Composer 12 musical works, 1985-89; contbr. hist. articles to Jour. of New Bern Hist. Soc., 1988-89. Pres., Craven Concerts Inc., Craven County, N.C., 1987-89; instr. U.S. Power Squadron, Craven County, 1985-87; mem. New Bern Hist. Soc., 1986-89. Avocation: landscape design. Home and Office: 1414 Sleater Kinney Rd SE Lacey WA 98503-2537

BREZA, KEVIN S. wellness consultant, writer; b. Washington, May 11, 1966; s. George M. and Sarena M. Breza; m. Veronica A. Stevans, Aug. 25, 1970; children: Katherine G., Gregory C. BA in Anthropology, Pa. State U., 1988. Cert. swimming instr. ARC. Apiculture vol. US Peace Corps, Morant Bay, Jamaica, 1989—91; project acct. TDC/TAC/Adecco at Intel, Rio Rancho, N.Mex., 1994—98; owner, ptnr. Attracted to Magnets, Sterling, Va., 1999—; freelance writer Sterling, 2001—; swimming instr. Herndon (Va.) Cmty. Ctr., 2001—. Co-author: Beekeeping in Jamaica, 1991. Mem.: Pa. State Alumni Assn., Returned Peace Corps Vol. Assn., Loudoun County C. of C. Avocations: swimming, role playing games. E-mail: knrbreza@mindspring.com.

BREZINA, DAVID CHARLES, lawyer, educator; b. Berwyn, Ill., Sept. 11, 1953; s. John Charles and Virginia (Nelson) B.; JD with honors, Chgo.-Kent Law Sch., 1978; LLM in Intellectual Property John Marshall Law Sch., 1988. Bars: Ill. 1978, U.S. Dist. Ct. (no. dist.) Ill. 1978, Trial Bar (no. dist.) Ill. 1982, U.S. Ct. Appeals (7th cir.) 1978, U.S. Ct. Customs and Patent Appeals 1980, U.S. Ct. Appeals (fed. cir.) 1982, U.S. Supreme Ct. 1981, U.S. Dist. Ct. (no. dist.) Ind. 1988; registered patent atty. Assoc. Brezina & Buckingham, P.C., Chgo., 1978-87, Myers and Ehrlich, Ltd., 1987-90; assoc. counsel Lee, Mann, Smith, McWilliams, Sweeney & Ohlson, Chgo., 1990-91, ptnr., 1991—2003, ptnr., Barnes and Thornburg, Chgo., 2003-, chmn. mgmt. com., 1997; adj. prof. John Marshall Law Sch., Chgo., 1992—, chmn. selection com. Gerald Rose Legal Writing, 1998; instr. Columbia Coll., Chgo., 1983-92. Author: Cases and Materials on Intellectual Property Law for AEMMP, 1984; (with others) Management Handbook for Intellectual Property and Law, 1987, Antitrust and Misuse Aspects of Intellectual Property Law, 1987. Intellectual property cons. Ill. Inst. Tech./Chgo. Kent Law Rev., 1979-83; guest commentator Columbia Coll. Chronicle, 1984; patentee composite vehicle manufacture, 1985, ry. freight car shoe, 1991; contbr. articles on trademarks to profl. publs. Mem. staff Dick Clark Senate Campaign, Marion, Iowa, 1972; intern 66th Iowa Gen. Assembly, Des Moines, 1975; incorporator Concerned Citizens of Brookfield, Ill., 1976; election troubleshooter Project LEAP, Chgo., 1977—, dir., 1993-95. Mem. ABA, Ill. State Bar Assn., Chgo. Bar Assn. (chair, patents trademarks & copyright com. 1993-94), Intellectual Property Law Assn. of Chgo. (chair legal edn. commn., 1997), Soc. Naval Architects and Marine Engrs. (assoc.), Bohemian Lawyers Assn. of Chgo. Clubs: Chgo. Area Rugby Football Union (discipline chmn. 1980-81), Union League, Lincoln Park Rugby Football (asst. coach 1981-82), Chgo. Corinthian Yacht, Lawyers Club of the City of Chgo. Office: Barnes & Thornburg 1 N Wacker Dr Chicago IL 60606

BRIACH, GEORGE GARY, lawyer, consultant; b. Youngstown, Ohio, Apr. 11, 1954; s. George William and Donna Jean (Phillips) B.; m. Loretta Ann Lepore, May 17, 1985; 1 child, Rachel Renee. BS magna cum laude, Youngstown State U., 1976; JD, U. Akron, Ohio, 1982. Bar: Ohio 1983, Mahoning County, 1983. Assoc. Flask & Policy, Youngstown, 1983-91; asst. atty. gen. State Atty. Gen.'s Office, Youngstown, 1984-90; solicitor Poland (Ohio) Village, 1988-89, cons., dir. Mahoning County (Ohio) Auditor, 1990—; ptnr. White & Briach, Youngstown, 1991—. Fundraiser United Way, Youngstown, 1989-92; bd. dirs., treas., pres. D&E Counseling Ctr., Youngstown, 1992-98, 2000—; trustee, treas. Children' Challenge Found., Inc., 1998-2000, 2002—; bd. dirs. Interfaith Home Maintenance, 1999—. Mem. Ohio Bar Assn., Mahoning County Bar Assn., Youngstown State U. Alumni Assn., Tippecanoe Country Club. Avocations: aerobic and weight training, golf, reading, travel. Home: 45 Russo Dr Canfield OH 44406-9666 Office: White & Briach 755 Boardman Canfield Rd Youngstown OH 44512-4300

BRIAN, JACKSON, artistic director; Music dir. Victoria Choral Soc., Kingston Choral Soc.; asst. condr. to resident to prin. pops condr. Orch. London, prin. guest condr., artistic advisor, 1998—; guest condr. Internat. Symphony, Kingston Symphony. Organ scholar Oxford. Fellow: Royal Coll. of Organists. Office: London Orchestra Can 520 Wellington St London ON Canada N6A 3R1

BRIAN, MARY H. librarian; b. Breckenridge, Tex., Dec. 17, 1929; d. Thomas Henry and M. Loyce Davis Hailey; m. Jack Brian, Dec. 26, 1953 (dec. Sept. 1983); children: Crystal Lee, Rosemary Hope, Tommy Wilson. BA, North Tex. State U., 1949; grad. in Libr. Sci., U. Tex., 1953. Tchr., libr. Dumas Jr. HS, Tex., 1949-94. Fin. chair Moore County Libr. Bd., Dumas, 1959-60, chair, 1960-62. Named among outstanding leaders in elem. & secondary edn., 1976; Defender of the constitution award. Mem. Tex. Ret. Tchr. Assn. (20th Century tchr. award 1997), Tex. Farm Bur.; Rep. Nat. Com., Eisenhower Commission, 2002, Nat. Rifle Assn., 2003. Republican. Baptist. Avocations: travel, opera, gardening, history. Home: 5278 Fm 722 Channing TX 79018-3312

BRIANT, CLYDE LEONARD, metallurgist, educator; b. Texarkana, Ark., May 31, 1948; s. Clyde Leonard and Bonnie Barbara (Green) B.; m. Jacqueline Louise Duffy, July 16, 1977; children— Paul, Judith, Bonnie. BA, Hendrix Coll., Conway, Ark., 1971; BS, Columbia U., 1971, MS, 1973, Eng. Sc.D., 1974. Postdoctoral fellow U. Pa., Phila., 1974-76; staff metallurgist Gen. Electric Co., Schenectady, NY, 1976—94; prof. engring. Brown U., Providence, 1994—, Otis Randall prof., 2000—, dean engring., 2003—. Vis. scientist Rsch. Inst. for Tech. Physics, Hungarian Acad. Scis., Budapest, 1991. Editor: Embrittlement of Engineering Alloys, 1983; contbr. articles to profl. jours. Recipient Alfred Noble prize, 1980; named one of 100 Most Outstanding Young Scientists in U.S.A., Sci. Digest, 1984; overseas fellow Churchill Coll., Cambridge, Eng., 1987-88. Fellow Am. Soc. Metals; mem. AIME (Robert Lansing Hardy gold medal Metall. Soc. 1977, Rossiter W. Raymond 1979). Democrat. Methodist. Home: 9 Wedgewood Ln Barrington RI 02806-3218 Office: Brown Univ Divsn of Engring Box D Providence RI 02912

BRICE, CHARLES STEVEN, airline executive; b. Columbus, Ohio, Feb. 13, 1951; s. Charles Simonton Jr. and Rita Eva (Kuder) B.; m. Darlene Lynn Call, Sept. 13, 1978 (div. June 1986); m. Sally Ann Minard, Sept. 20, 1997; children: Marissa Kay and Jessica Victoria (twins). BA, San Francisco State U., 1974. Lic. FAA airframe and power plant. Ops. mgr. Lockheed Aircraft Co., San Francisco, 1979-83; mgr. ramp svcs. Northwest Airlines, San Francisco, 1983-88, mgr. passenger svcs., 1988-92, dir. customer svc. and ground ops., 1992—. Vice-chmn. bd. dirs. San Francisco Fgn. Flag Carriers, 1997—; chmn. Sta. Mgrs. Am. Transport/SFO, San Francisco, 1994, chmn. security com., 1995. Bd. dirs. March of Dimes, San Mateo County, Calif., 1994-95; mem., airline advisory bd. Calif. Dept. Agr., Sacramento, 1991-92; mem. adv. bd. San Francisco City Coll., 1988—. Mem. Commonwealth Club. Avocations: skiing, hiking, golf, tennis. Office: NW Airlines San Francisco Inter Airport San Francisco CA 94128 Home: 502 Silver Ave Half Moon Bay CA 94019-1564

BRICE, ROGER THOMAS, lawyer; b. Chgo., May 7, 1948; s. William H. and Mary Loretta (Ryan) B.; m. Carol Coleman, Aug. 15, 1970; children: Caitlin, Coleman, Emily. AB, DePaul U., 1970; JD, U. Chgo., 1973. Bar: Ill. 1973, Iowa 1973, U.S. Ct. Appeals (10th, 4th, 6th and 7th cirs.) 1975, U.S. Dist. Ct. (no. and ctrl. dists.) Ill. 1977, 1995, U.S. Trial Bar (no. dist.) 1982, U.S. Supreme Ct. 1978. Staff atty. Office of Gen. Counsel NLRB, Washington, 1974-76; assoc. Kirkland & Ellis, Chgo., 1976-79, Reuben & Proctor, Chgo., 1979-80, ptnr., 1980-86, Isham, Lincoln & Beale, Chgo., 1986-88, Sonnenschein, Nath & Rosenthal, Chgo., 1988—. Legal counsel, bd. dirs. Boys and Girls Clubs Chgo., 1991—. Fellow Coll. Labor and Employment Lawyers. Roman Catholic. Home: 3727 N Harding Ave Chicago IL 60618-4026 Office: Sonnenschein Nath & Rosenthal 233 S Wacker Dr Ste 8000 Chicago IL 60606-6491 E-mail: rbrice@sonnenschein.com.

BRICE, WILLIAM RILEY, geology educator, planetary science educator; b. Groveland, Fla., Feb. 24, 1936; s. Joseph Vernon and Frances Brice; m. Heather Weidenhofer, Jan. 18, 1964; children: Tania Helen Brice-Coffin, John Armstrong. BS, U. Fla., 1958; Diploma of Edn., U. Tasmania, Australia, 1965; postgrad., Cornell U., 1967-68, MS for Tchrs., 1968, PhD, 1971. Tchr. math., sci. Clermont (Fla.) H.S., 1960-62, 65-67; asst. master sci. Taroona (Tasmania, Australia) H.S., 1962-65; tchg. fellow geol. sci. Cornell U., Ithaca, N.Y., 1968-71; assoc. prof. geology and planetary sci. U. Pitts., Johnstown, Pa., 1971-76, assoc. prof. geology, planetary sci., 1976-88, prof. geology, planetary sci., 1988—, chair divsn. natural sci., 1993-97. Vis. assoc. prof. Cornell U., Ithaca, N.Y., 1977-89, vis. prof. geol. sci., 1990-2002; studio tchr. Australian Broadcasting Commn., Hobart, Tasmania, 1963-65. Author: Cornell Geology Through the Years, 1989, Gilbert D. Harris-Life with Fossils, 1996; contbr. 1st v.p. Drake Well Found., v.p., 2001—03, bd. dirs., 1999—2003. With U.S. Army, 1958—60. Named George F. Matthew Rsch. fellow, New Brunswick Mus, 1992, travel grantee, State U. at Campinas (Brazil), 1992, 2001, charter mem., Clermont H.S. Hall of Fame, 1989. Fellow Geol. Soc. Am. (chair history of geol. divsn. 1996, sec.-treas., editor 1999—), Nat. Assn. Geosci. Tchrs. (sec., treas. eastern sect. 1976-92, chair disting. svc. award com. 2000—, Disting. Svc. award 1999), History of Earth Sci. Soc. (pres.-elect 2001-2002, pres. 2003—), Petroleum History Inst. (pres. 2003—), Drake Well Found. (bd. dirs. 1998-2003, 2d v.p. 2001-2003), Petroleum History Inst. (bd. dirs. 2003—, inaugural pres. 2003—, editor 2003—). Avocations: theater lighting, photography, singing. Office: U Pitts at Johnston Geology and Planetary Sci Johnstown PA 15904 E-mail: wbrice@pitt.edu.

BRICHFORD, MAYNARD JAY, archivist; b. Madison, Ohio, Aug. 6, 1926; s. Merton Jay and Evelyn Louise (Graves) B.; m. Jane Adair Hamilton, Sept. 15, 1951; children— Charles Hamilton, Ann Adair Brichford Martin, Matthew Jay, Sarah Lourena. BA, Hiram Coll., 1950; MS, U. Wis., 1951. Asst. archivist State Hist. Soc. Wis., 1952-56; methods and procedures analyst Ill. State Archives, 1956-59; records and space mgmt. supr. Dept. Adminstrn. State of Wis., Madison, 1959-63; archivist U. Ill., Urbana, 1963-95, asso. prof., 1963-70, prof., 1970—. Contbr. articles in field. Mem. gen. commn. on archives and history United Meth. Ch., 1988-96; bd. chmn. U. Ill. YMCA, 1987-89. With U.S. Navy, 1944-46. Council on Library Resources grantee, 1966-69, 70-71; Nat. Endowment for the Humanities grantee, 1976-79; Fulbright grantee, 1985; Am. Phil. Soc. grantee, 1992. Fellow Soc. Am. Archivists (pres. 1979-80); mem. Ill. Archives Adv. Bd. (chmn. 1979-84) Republican. Methodist. Home: 409 Eliot Dr Urbana IL 61801-6725 Office: 19 Library 1408 W Gregory Dr Urbana IL 61801-3607

BRICK, ANN VETA, lawyer; b. Cheyenne, Wyo., Mar. 17, 1947; d. Gerald John and Margaret (Pasternack) Veta; m. Steven Alexander Brick, Dec. 29, 1968; children: Kate Elizabeth, Rachel Suzanne. B.A., Newcomb Coll., Tulane U., 1969; J.D., U. Calif.-Berkeley, 1975. Bar: Calif. 1975, U.S. Dist. Ct. (no. dist.) Calif. 1975, U.S. Ct. Appeals (5th cir.) 1978, U.S. Ct. Appeals (7th cir.) 1981, U.S. Ct. Appeals (9th cir.) 1988. Law clk. to judge U.S. Dist. Ct. (no. dist.) Calif., San Francisco, 1975-76; assoc. Howard, Rice, Nemerovski, Canady, Robertson & Falk, San Francisco, 1977-81, dir., 1981-84, of counsel, 1984—; dir. Legal Aid Soc. of San Francisco, 1982-87, Equal Rights Advocates, San Francisco, 1984—, ACLU of No. Calif., 1988—. Contbr. article to legal jour. Mem. Bar. Assn. Calif. (panelist Continuing Edn. of Bar 1983), State Bar of Calif. (com. on women in law 1986-88), Lawyers Com. for Urban Affairs, San Francisco Bar Assn. (judiciary com. 1982-84), ACLU (cooperating atty. 1978—), Order of Coif, Phi Beta Kappa. Democrat. Jewish. Office: 3 Embarcadero Ctr Ste 7 San Francisco CA 94111-4074

BRICK, BARRETT LEE, lawyer; b. Middletown, N.Y., Jan. 12, 1954; s. Michael and Barbara Lilian (Rosen) B. BA, Columbia U., 1976, JD, 1979. Bar: N.Y. 1980, U.S. Ct. Appeals (D.C. cir.) 1981, U.S. Supreme Ct. 1984. Atty.-adviser FCC, Washington, 1980—. Contbr. to book, Positively Gay, 1979; book review columnist Washington Blade newspaper, 1982-83; editor National Gay Task Force Action Report, 1975-76. Active Cmty. Bd. Nine, N.Y.C., 1978-80, Gay Men's Chorus, Washington, 1984—; bd. dirs. Congregation Bet Mishpachah, Washington, 1980-84, pres., 1984-85; exec. dir. World Congress Gay and Lesbian Jewish Orgns., Washington, 1987-93. Recipient Advocate 400 award, The Advocate, San Francisco, 1984, Disting. Svc. award Gay and Lesbian Activists Alliance, Washington, 2000, Harvey Milk Chesed award Bet Mishpachah, Washington, 2002; named one of Outstanding Young Men of Am. US Jaycees, 1983-84. Mem. ABA, N.Y. State Bar Assn., Nat. Lesbian and Gay Law Assn. Republican. Jewish. Home: 1901 Wyoming Ave NW Washington DC 20009-5079 Office: FCC 445 12th St SW Washington DC 20554-0001 E-mail: bbrick@fcc.gov.

BRICK, DONALD BERNARD, software company executive; b. Bklyn., Oct. 1, 1927; s. Maxwell B. and Edna (Newman) B.; m. Phyllis Madeline Hahn, Oct. 19, 1952; children: James Laurence, Susan Carol Weinbaum, Howard Andrew. Student, Newark Coll. Engring., 1945-46; AB cum laude, Harvard U., 1950, S.M., 1951, PhD, 1954. Registered profl. engr., Mass. Teaching fellow, research asst., fellow Harvard U., 1950-55; sr. scientist, sci. dir. GTE Sylvania, Waltham, Mass., 1955-65; tech. mgmt. cons. Lexington, Mass., 1954-55, 65-75; founder, pres., chmn., tech. dir. Info. Research Assoc.-Infoton Inc., Burlington, Mass., 1965-71; v.p. Addressograph-Multigraph Corp., 1972-73; tech. dir., dep. for devel. plans Elec. Systems div. U.S. Air Force, Bedford, Mass., 1975-83; pres. D.B. Brick and Co., Inc., Lexington, 1983-99; v.p. Aetna Telecommunications Cons., Centerville, Mass., 1983; CEO ID Vehicle.Com, Inc., Burlington, Mass., 1999-2000; pres. Donald B. Brick & Assocs., Inc./Hi-Tech Solutions USA, 2002—. Cons. in field, 2001—. Contbr. articles to profl. jours.; patentee in field. V.p., bd. dirs. Temple Emunah, Lexington, 1970; assoc. campaign chmn. Combined Jewish Philanthropies of Greater Boston, 1974-78, life trustee, 1985—, mem. exec. bd., 1980-89, chmn. cash collections, 1982-84, chmn. high tech. team, 1984-87; chmn. fundraising Am. Technion Soc., N.E. Region, 1989-93. With U.S. Army, 1946-47. Fellow: IEEE (life; chmn. 1969—70); mem.: N.E. Israel C. of C. (exec. bd. 1993—99). Home and Office: 39 Solomon Pierce Rd Lexington MA 02420-2536 E-mail: pmbdbb@earthlink.net. *Not compromising ideals or moral standards for easy gain. Striving to produce quality work that I am proud of.*

BRICK, JOHN, biological psychologist, educator, researcher; b. NYC, Mar. 18, 1950; m. Laurie Stockton Krulish, May 1, 1976. BA, Queens Coll., CUNY, 1973; MA in Psychology, SUNY, Binghamton, 1979; PhD in Biol. Psychology, SUNY, 1981. Rsch. assoc. Ctr. Alcohol Studies Rutgers U., 1980-82, prof., 1982-94; lab. dir. Rutgers U. Alcohol Behavior Rsch. Lab., 1984-88; chief of rsch. edn. tng. divsn. Ctr. Alcohol Studies Rutgers U., 1988-93, assoc. prof., 1991-94; pvt. practice Forensic Pharmacology, 1985—. Exec. dir. Intoxikon Internat., 1994—; cons. Exec. Office of the Pres. The White House, Washington, 1992—93; tchr. Rutgers Sch. Alcohol and Drug Studies, 1982—. Author: Drugs, The Brain and Behavior; co-author: Presidents Commission on Model State Drug Laws; editor: Medical Consequences of Alcohol and Drug Abuse; Stress and Alcohol Use; sr. editor Neuropharmacology; contbr. over 90 articles to profl. jours. Fellow: APA. Office: 1006 Floral Vale Blvd Yardley PA 19067-5532 E-mail: intoxikon@aol.com.

BRICK, SHIRLEY JEAN, rehabilitation nurse; b. Des Moines, Feb. 6, 1954; d. Leo J. and Margaret I. (Powers) B. BSN, U. Nebr., 1976. Cert. in rehab. nursing and case mgmt. Rehab. staff nurse Immanuel Med. Ctr., Omaha, 1976-80, rehab. team leader, 1980-82, rehab. health care facilitator, 1982-88, rehab. charge nurse, 1988-91; nurse case mgr. Hines and Assocs., Inc., Omaha, 1991-93; med. case mgr. Mutual of Omaha, 1993-96; complex care coord. Blue Cross Blue Shield Nebr., Omaha, 1996—. Lectr. numerous Omaha area workshops, 1982-90. Mem. ANA, Nebr. Nurses Assn., Assn. Rehab. Nurses (cert., local chpt. v.p. 1996-97, pres. 1997-98, bd. dirs. 1997-2000), Case Mgmt. Soc. Am. (bd. dirs. Nebr. chpt. 1994-95, v.p. 1997-98, pres. 1998-99), U. Nebr. Alumni Assn. (bd. dirs. 1990-92), Sigma Theta Tau. Democrat. Roman Catholic. Avocations: golf, bowling, reading. Home: 10604 Hartman Ave Omaha NE 68134-1242 Office: Blue Cross Blue Shield Nebr 7261 Mercy Rd Omaha NE 68124-2349 E-mail: sbrick@ditol.com.

BRICKELL, CHARLES HENNESSEY, JR., marine engineer, retired military officer; b. Memphis, Apr. 13, 1935; s. Charles Hennessey and Mary Ellen (Viau) B.; m. Barbara Virginia Davis, Jan. 4, 1958; children: David Brian, Patricia Ellen, Susan Elizabeth, Timothy Paul, Joel Howard. BS in Marine Engring., U.S. Merchant Marine Acad., 1957; MA in Bus. Mgmt., Cen. Mich. U., 1980. Enlisted USN, 1953, commd. ensign, 1957, advanced through grades to rear adm., 1984; dir. research and devel. Undersea and Strategic Warfare, and Nuclear Energy, 1984-87; dir. USN Strategic Def. Initiative Program, 1984-88; dep. dir. Navy Rsch. Devel., Test and Evaluation, 1987-88; ret. USN, 1988; gen. mgr. advanced technologies Stone & Webster Engring. Corp., Boston, 1988-91; dir. Ops. ea. region N.Am. Energy Svcs., Issaquah, Wash., 1991-93; dir. fluids and structural mechanics Applied Rsch. Lab. Pa. State U., State Coll., 1993—. Mem. bd. advisors Applied Rsch. Lab Pa. State U., 1988-93; cons. NAS. Decorated Def. Superior Service Medal, Legion of Merit with three Gold Stars, Meritorious Service Medal with two Gold Stars. Mem. Sigma Iota Epsilon. Roman Catholic. Avocations: baseball, basketball sports officiating.

BRICKER, GERALD WAYNE, marketing executive; b. York, Pa., Dec. 21, 1947; s. Wayne Gilbert Bricker and Grace Fern (Quickel) Geisler; m. Linda Lee Desenberg, June 21, 1969; children: Kristin Lorraine, Scott Michael. BSME, Drexel U., 1970; MBA, No. Ill. U., 1976. Jr. product engr. Borg-Warner Corp., Ithaca, N.Y., 1970-71, product engr. Aurora, Ill., 1971-72; with Maremont Corp., Chgo., 1972-86, dir. sales divsn., 1981-84, V.P. sales divsn., 1984-86; dir. mtkg. Intelligent Controls, Inc., Novi, Mich., 1986-90, v.p. mktg., 1990-93, v.p. products group, 1993-95; mktg. mgr. Pierburg Instruments, Inc., Clinton Twp., Mich., 1995-96; v.p., gen. sales mgr. Omron Automotive Electronics, Inc., Novi, Mich., 1996—, sec., bd. dirs. Farmington Hills, Mich., 2000—. Pres. Gethsemane Luth. Ch., Berkley, Mich., 1979-80, Cana Luth. Ch., Berkley, 1980-81, chmn. audit com., 1991-95, treas. endowment com., 1998-2000; treas. Hickory Creek Homeowner's Assn., 2001—02. Mem. Soc. Automotive Engrs.

(assoc.), U.S. Golf Assn., Drexel U. Alumni of Mich. (bd. dirs. 1990—, v.p. 2002—), Lambda Chi Alpha, Pi Tau Sigma, Beta Gamma Sigma. Avocations: golf, tennis, reading, cross-country skiing. Home: 47765 Lake View Ct Northville MI 48167-8503 Office: Omron Automotive Electronics Inc 29185 Cabot Dr Novi MI 48377 E-mail: gwllbri@comcast.net.

BRICKER, HARVEY MILLER, anthropology educator; b. Johnstown, Pa., June 29, 1940; s. George Harry and Florence Helen (Miller) B.; m. Victoria Evelyne Reifler, Dec. 27, 1964. BA, Hamilton Coll., 1962; MA, Harvard U., 1963, PhD, 1973. Successively instr., asst. prof., assoc. prof. to prof. anthropology Tulane U., New Orleans, 1969—. Co-author: The Analysis of Certain Major Classes of Upper Palaeolithic Tools, 1969, Excavation of the Abri Pataud: The Perigordian VI Assemblage, 1984; co-editor: Hunting and Animal Exploitation in the Later Palaeolithic and Mesolithic of Eurasia, 1993; editor: La Paléolithique Supérieur de l'abri Pataud (Dordogne), 1995; contbr. articles on French prehistory and Maya archaeoastronomy to profl. jours. Decorated Order Palmes Académiques (France). Fellow AAAS; mem. Soc. Am. Archaeology, Soc. French Prehistory. Office: Tulane U Dept Anthropology 1021 Audubon St New Orleans LA 70118-5238 E-mail: hbricker@tulane.edu.

BRICKER, NEAL S, physician, educator; b. Denver, Apr. 18, 1927, s. Eli D. and Rose (Quiat) B.; m. Miriam Thalenberg, June 24, 1951 (dec. 1974); children: Dusty, Cary, Susan, Dan Baker; m. Ruth T. Baker, Dec. 28, 1980. BA, U. Colo., 1946, MD, 1949. Diplomate Am. Bd. Internal Medicine (bd. govs. 1972-79, chmn. nephrology test com. 1973-76). Intern, resident Bellevue Hosp., N.Y.C., 1949-52; sr. asst. resident Peter Bent Brigham Hosp., Boston, 1954-55, asst. dir. cardio-renal lab., 1955-56; instr. Harvard, 1955-56; fellow Howard Hughes Med. Inst., 1955-56; from asst. prof. to prof. Washington U., 1956-72, dir. renal div., 1956-72; Mem. sci. adv. bd. Nat. Kidney Found., 1962-69, chmn. research and fellowship grants com., 1964-65, mem. exec. com., 1968-71; prof. medicine, chmn. dept. Albert Einstein Coll. Medicine, 1972-76; prof. medicine U. Miami, Fla., 1976-78, vice chmn. dept., 1976-78; Disting. prof. medicine UCLA, 1978-86; disting. prof. medicine, dir. sci. and tech. planning Loma Linda (Calif.) U., 1986-92; exec. v.p. Naturon Pharm., Riverside, Calif., 1992; clin. prof. medicine UCR/UCLA Program in Biomed. Scis., UCR, 1996—. Cons. NIH, 1964-68, chmn. gen. medicine study sect., 1966-68, chmn. renal disease and urology tng. grants com., 1969-71; vis. investigator Inst. Biol. Chemistry, Copenhagen, 1960-61; investigator Mt. Desert Island Biol. Labs.; advisor on behalf Inst. Medicine to Sen. Lowell Weicker. Assoc. editor: Jour. Lab. and Clin. Medicine, 1961-67, Kidney Internat, 1972; editorial com.: Jour. Clin. Investigation, 1964-68, Physiol. Revs, 1970-76, Am. Heart Assn. Publs. Com., 1974-79, Calcified Tissue Internat., 1978-86, Proc. Soc. Exptl. Biology and Medicine, 1978-86; editor: Supplements, Circulation and Circulation Research, 1974-79; contbr. articles to profl. jours., chpts. to books. Served with USNR, 1944-45; Served with U.S. Army, 1952-54. Recipient Gold-Headed Cane award U. Colo., 1949, Silver and Gold Alumni award, 1975; USPHS Research Career award, 1964-72; Skylab Achievement award NASA, 1974; Pub. Service award, 1975; George Norlin Silver medal award U. Colo. 1982; citation Kidney Found. So. Calif., 1984. Fellow A.C.P.; mem. Am. Fedn. for Clin. Research, Central Soc. Clin. Research (council 1970-73), Assn. Am. Physicians, Am. Soc. for Clin. Investigation (pres. 1972-73, chmn. com. nat. med. policy 1973-77, Disting. Service award 1969), Internat. Soc. Nephrology (exec. com. 1966-81, v.p. 1966-69, treas. 1969-81), Internat. Congress Nephrology (pres. 1981-84), Am. Soc. Nephrology (1st pres., John Peters medal 1991), Am. Physiol. Soc., Soc. for Exptl. Biology and Medicine, Western Soc. Clin. Research, So. Soc. Clin. Investigation, Nat. Acad. Scis. (com. on space biology and medicine, ad hoc panel on renal and metabolic effects space flight 1971-72, mem. drug efficacy com. 1966-68, com. space biology, chmn. medicine in space sci. bd. 1972-81, com. chmn. 1978-81, chmn. com. renal and metabloic effects space flight 1972-74, chmn. study com. on life scis. 1976-81, mem. space sci. bd. 1977-81), Inst. Medicine of NAS, Sigma Xi, Alpha Omega Alpha. Home: 4240 Piedmont Mesa Claremont CA 91711-2332 Office: UCR/UCLA Riverside CA 92521-0121

BRICKER, VICTORIA REIFLER, anthropology educator; b. Hong Kong, June 15, 1940; came to U.S., 1947, naturalized, 1953; d. Erwin and Henrietta (Brown) Reifler; m. Harvey Miller Bricker, Dec. 27, 1964. AB, Stanford U., 1962; A.M., Harvard U., 1963, PhD, 1968. Vis. lectr. anthropology Tulane U., 1969-70, asst. prof., 1970-73, assoc. prof., 1973-78, prof., 1978—, chmn. dept. anthropology, 1988-91. Author: Ritual Humor in Highland Chiapas, 1973, The Indian Christ, The Indian King: The Historical Substrate of Maya Myth and Ritual, 1981 (Howard Francis Cline meml. prize Conf. Latin Am. History), A Grammar of Mayan Hieroglyphs, 1986, (with Gabrielle Vail) Papers on the Madrid Codex, 1997, (with Eleuterio Po'ot Yah and Ofelia Dzul de Po'ot) A Dictionary of the Maya Language as Spoken in Hocaba, Yucatan, 1998, (with Helga-Maria Miram) An Encounter of Two Worlds: The Book of Chilam Balam of Kaua, 2002; book rev. editor: Am. Anthropologist, 1971-73; editor: Am. Ethnologist, 1973-76; gen. editor: Supplement to Handbook of Middle American Indians, 1977—. Guggenheim fellow, 1982; Wenner-Gren Found. Anthropol. Rsch. grantee, 1971; Social Sci. Rsch. Coun. grantee, 1972; NEH grantee, 1990. Fellow Am. Anthrop. Assn. (exec. bd. 1980-83); mem. NAS, Am. Philos. Soc., Am. Soc. Ethnohistory (exec. bd. 1977-79), Linguistic Soc. Am., Seminario de Cultura Maya, Societe des Americanistes. Office: Tulane Univ Dept Anthropology New Orleans LA 70118

BRICKEY, KATHLEEN FITZGERALD, law educator; b. Austin, Tex., Sept. 16, 1944; d. Robert Bernard and Ina Marie (Daw) Fitzgerald; m. James Nelson Brickey, Aug. 22, 1969. BA, U. Ky., 1965, JD, 1968. Criminal law specialist/cons. Ky. Crime Commn., Frankfort, Cin., 1968-71; exec. dir. Ky. Judicial Conf. and Coun., Frankfort, 1971-72; adj. prof. law U. Ky., Lexington, 1972; asst. to assoc. prof. law U. Louisville, 1972-76; assoc. prof. to prof. law Washington U., St. Louis, 1976-89, George Alexander Madill prof. law, 1989-93, James Carr prof. of criminal jurisprudence, 1993—, Israel Treiman faculty fellow, 2001—02. Cons. U.S. Sentencing Commn., 1988, 91; witness U.S. Senate Com. on Judiciary, Washington, 1986. Author: Kentucky Criminal Law, 1974, Corporate Criminal Liability, 1984, 2d edit., 1992-94, Corporate and White Collar Crime, 1990, 3d edit., 2002; contbr. articles to profl. jours. Mem. Am. Law Inst., Soc. for Reform of Criminal Law, Assn. Am. Law Schs. (sect. on criminal justice chair 1989, exec. com. 1985 91, 94-95). Office: PO Box 1120 Saint Louis MO 63188-1120

BRICKEY, KRISTIN LYNN, healthcare marketing professional; b. Woodbury, N.J., Jan. 21, 1970; d. William Robert Herzig and Linda Jean Wallace; m. Christopher Patrick Brickey, Mar. 21, 1998. BSBA, Ohio State U., 1992; MBA, St. Louis U., 1994. Account exec. Lida Advt., St. Louis, 1994—95; project coord. Aragon Cons. Group, Clayton, Mo., 1995—97; dir. strategic planning Sisters of Mercy System, St. Louis, 1997—. Mem. St. Louis Soc. for Healthcare Planning and Marketing. Office: Sisters of Mercy Health System 2039 N Geyer Rd Saint Louis MO 63131-3332 E-mail: Kbrickey@corp.mercy.net.

BRICKEY, SUZANNE M. editor; b. Grand Rapids, Mich., Apr. 4, 1951; d. Robert Michael and Elizabeth (Rogers) Stankey; m. Homer Brickey, Jr. BA, Ohio U., Athens, 1973; B.J., U. Mo., Columbia, 1977. Editor Living Today, The Blade, Toledo, 1980-82, Toledo Mag., The Blade, 1982-92; asst. editor Features, Toledo, 1992—. Mem. Toledo Press Club, Toledo Rowing Club. Home: 2510 Kenwood Blvd Toledo OH 43606-3601 Office: The Blade 541 N Superior St Toledo OH 43660-0001

BRICKHILL, WILLIAM LEE, international finance consultant; b. Rahway, N.J., Oct. 13, 1937; s. William Welch and Wilma Eloise (Gay) Mumford; m. Margaret A. Stempel, June 16, 1961 (div. 1971); children: William L., Barbara A., Cynthia A., Robert L.; m. Joan Marie Ward, May 19, 1988. Student, U. Ga., 1957, Sophia U., Tokyo, 1958-60; BBA, George Washington U., 1970. Lic. comml. and instrument rated pilot. Internat. specialist Am. Security & Trust Co., Washington, 1960-62; loan officer Export-Import Bank of U.S., Washington, 1962-90, dep. mgr. contract adminstrn., 1990-91, dep. v.p. contract adminstrn., 1991-94, ret., 1994; cons. internat. fin., 1994—. Contbr. articles to profl. jours. With U.S. Army, 1956-58, Germany. Mem. Nat. Capital Bromeliad Soc. (1st v.p. 1991—), Nat. Capital Orchid Soc., Gem, Mineral and Lapidary Soc. (bd. dirs., v.p. 1965-75). Roman Catholic. Avocations: aviation, botany, horticulture, woodworking. Home and Office: 6338 Phyllis Ln Alexandria VA 22312-6402 E-mail: brickhillb@aol.com.

BRICKLER, JOHN WEISE, lawyer; b. Dayton, Ohio, Dec. 29, 1944; s. John Benjamin and Shirley Hilda (Weise) B.; m. Marilyn Louise Kuhlmann, July 2, 1966; children: John, James, Peter, Andrew, Matthew. AB, Washington U., St. Louis, 1966; JD, Washington U., 1968. Bar: Mo. 1968, U.S. Supreme Ct. 1972, U.S. Dist. Ct. (ea. dist.) Mo. 1974, U.S. Ct. Appeals (8th cir.) 1974. Assoc. Peper, Martin, Jensen, Maichel and Hetlage, St. Louis, 1973-77, ptnr., 1978-98, Blackwell Sanders Peper Martin LLP, St. Louis, 1998—2003, Spencer Fane Britt & Browne LLP, 2003—. Bd. dirs. Concordia Pub. House, St. Louis, 1993-, chmn. 1998-2001. Bd. dirs. Luth. Family and Children's Svcs. Mo., St. Louis, 1988-93, vice chmn., 1988-89. Capt. JAGC, U.S. Army, 1969-73. Mem. ABA, Nat. Assn. Bond Lawyers, Bar Assn. Met. St. Louis. Office: Blackwell Sanders Peper Martin LLP 720 Olive St Fl 24 Saint Louis MO 63101-2338 E-mail: jbrickler@blackwellsanders.com.

BRICKLEY, RICHARD AGAR, retired surgeon; b. Bluffton, Ind., Aug. 15, 1925; s. Harry Dwight and Ina (Agar) B.; m. Suzanne Slusser, Nov. 28, 1964; children: Dinah B. Olson, Sarah Jane, Richard Agar II, Laura Brickley Wakeley, Andrew John. Student, Ind. U., 1943-44; BS, B.M., Northwestern U. Med. Sch., 1947, MD, 1948. Diplomate: Am. Bd. Surgery. Intern Cook County Hosp., Chgo., 1947-49, surg. resident, 1955-56; gen. practice Bluffton, 1949-50; surg. preceptorship with Drs. Gatch and Owen, Indpls., 1950-51, 54; pvt. practice medicine, specializing in surgery Indpls., 1957-86; chmn. gen. surgery div. Meth. Hosp., Indpls., 1962-66, Winona Meml. Hosp., Indpls., 1971-73, chief of med. staff, 1974-75, bd. dirs., 1977-84. Served with M.C. USAF, 1951-53. Fellow ACS; mem. AMA, Ind. Med. Assn., Aerospace Med. Assn., Marion County Med. Soc. (chmn. bd. dirs. 1976-77), Seven-Up Club (Hillman, Mich.) (owner), Beta Theta Pi, Nu Sigma Nu. Home: 4530 Crooked Creek Ridge Dr Indianapolis IN 46228-2859

BRICKLIN, MARK HARRIS, magazine editor, publisher; b. Phila., Apr. 13, 1939; s. Arthur Benjamin and Rose (Gaurd) Bricklin; m. Alice Goddard Terry, Apr. 26, 1963 (div.); children: Deirdre, Brendon. BA, Temple U., 1960; postgrad., Boston U., 1961, Temple U., 1962. Teaching fellow English Boston U., 1960—61; city editor Phila. Tribune, 1962—71; freelance writer, photographer, 1962—71; with Rodale Press, Emmaus, Pa., 1971—, v.p., 1975—; exec. editor Prevention mag., 1974—97; founding editor, editorial dir. Spring mag., 1982—84; edit. dir. Men's Health mag., Emmaus, 1980—, Heart & Soul mag., Emmaus, 1994—; editor-in-chief Pets: Part of the Family, 1997—, founding editor, 1998. Journalism preceptor Pkwy. Exptl. Program Phila. Sch. Dist.; cons. book pub. Author: The Practical Encyclopedia of Natural Healing, 1976, Lose Weight Naturally, 1979, Natural Healing Cookbook, 1981, Rodale's Encyclopedia of Natural Home Remedies, 1982; co-author: Positive Living and Health, 1990, Secrets of Executive Success, 1991. Founder Prevention Walking Club, 1986. Home: 5218 W Hopewell Rd Center Valley PA 18034-9607 Office: Prevention 33 E Minor St Emmaus PA 18098-0001 E-mail: mark.bricklin@rodale.com.

BRICKMAN, KENNETH ALAN, state lottery executive; b. Hannibal, Mo., Sept. 10, 1940; s. Roy Frederick and Nita Wilma (Swearingen) B.; m. Mildred Darlene Myers, Aug. 10, 1963; children: Heather Katherine, Erik Alan. BS in Bus. and Econs., Culver-Stockton Coll., Canton, Mo., 1963; JD, U. Mo., 1970. Bar: Ill. 1970, Mo. 1970, US Supreme Ct. 1975. Ptnr. firm Scholz, Staff & Brickman, Quincy, Ill., 1970-78; pres. real estate brokerage Landmark of Quincy, Inc./Better Homes & Gardens, 1978-79; counsel, chief counsel Ill. Dept. Commerce and Cmty. Affairs, Springfield, 1980—85; gen. counsel, dep. dir. Ill. State Lottery, Springfield, 1986-91; sec.-treas., exec. v.p. La. Lottery Corp., Baton Rouge, 1991-95; exec. v.p. Iowa Lottery, Des Moines, 1995—. Served as capt. USAF, 1963-67. Mem. Culver Stockton Coll. Alumni Assn. (pres. 1979). Office: Iowa Lottery 2015 Grand Ave Des Moines IA 50312-4999

BRICKMAN, MIRIAM, concert pianist; b. Gt. Barrington, Mass., Dec. 6, 1933; d. David Krehl and Anna (Persily) B.; m. Charles H. Birch, Jr., July 1, 1962 (div. 1966); m. Ronald Paul Senator, Oct. 17, 1986. BA, CUNY, 1956; MS, Juilliard Sch. Music, 1967. Adj. asst. prof. CUNY, 1972-78; condr. music theatre, N.Y. State, 1967; free-lance musician; condr. master classes; lecture recitalist, solo concert pianist. Concert pianist with orchs. and chamber groups; performed Lincoln Ctr.-Tully Hall N.Y. Town Hall debut, WQXR, WNYC, WIGMORE Hall, United Kingdom, BBC, TBS, Japan, Radio, Hong Kong, Moscow Philharmonic, Bklyn. Philharmonic, Cruise Ships Internat. (54 Crossings QE 2), 20 different ships, premiered many new works; asst. condr. West Side Story; music dir. Trotsky in New York, 1999, Noel Coward's Centennial prodn. A Mahvelous Pahty. Mem. The. Cath. and Jewish Rels. Coun. of N.E., Queens, N.Y. Recipient Creative Achievement award Theatre of Renewal, 1985, Aaron and Lorraine Addleston award for Excellence in the Arts, 1998. Mem. Bohemians. Avocations: making earrings, bridge, boggle, Scrabble, walking. Home: 81 Hillcrest Ave Yonkers NY 10705-1509 E-mail: miriambrickman@hotmail.com.

BRICKNER, ALICE, painter, illustrator; b. N.Y.C., Feb. 12, 1931; d. Warren and Lillian Smolin Rinenberg; m. Philip Walter Brickner, June 17, 1950; children: Jed Walter, Nell Cecilie Brickner Eakin, Maude Lillian. BA, Sarah Lawrence Coll., 1952; studied with, Kurt Roesch, Ezio Martinelli, Lux Feininger, Theodore Roszak, Seong Moy, Arnold Singer, Erich Monch, Ansei Uchima. One-person shows include Howell Ctr., Beacon, N.Y., 1998; exhibited in group shows Poulsen Gallery, Pasadena, Calif., 1988-89, Elaine Benson Gallery, Bridgehampton, N.Y., 1988, 91, 92, 96, Goat Alley Gallery, Sag Harbor, N.Y., 1991, Hammerquist/FACS Gallery, N.Y.C., 1993, River Gallery, Irvington, N.Y., 1994, 95, 96, 97, Millenium Gallery, Easthampton, N.Y., 1995, Sch. House Gallery, Croton Falls, N.Y., 1997—, Chrysalis Gallery, Southampton, N.Y., 1998—, Donnell Libr., N.Y.C., 1999; represented in pub. collections Johnson & Johnson, Pratt Graphic Art Ctr., Stuttgart U., also pvt. collections; works featured in Soc. Illustrators Annuals, Comm. Arts Mag., Paintingsdirect-.com, others. Mem. N.Y. Artists Equity Assn., Artist's Space. Avocations: grandchildren, theater, reading, traveling. Home: 4720 Grosvenor Ave Bronx NY 10471-3307 E-mail: alicebric@aol.com.

BRICKNER, DAVID, religious organization administrator, consultant; b. Beverly, Mass., Sept. 29, 1958; s. Avi Stanley and Leah Esther (Kendal) B.; m. Patrice Anne Vasataro, Dec. 29, 1979; children: Isaac, Ilana. Diploma in Jewish Studies, Moody Bible Inst., 1981; BA in Jewish Studies, Northeastern Ill. U., 1986; MA in Jewish Studies, Fuller Sem., 1994. Ordained min. Bapt. Gen. Conf., 1993. Mobile team leader Jews for Jesus, USA, 1981-84, chief of station, 1985-89, min.-at-large San Francisco, 1989-95, chief of station N.Y.C., 1995-96, exec. dir. San Francisco, 1996—. Portfolio holder Jews for Jesus South Africa, 1988-96, bd. dirs., 1989—; pres. bd. dirs. Jews for Jesus USA, San Francisco, 1996—; bd. dirs. Jews for Jesus Europe, London, 1996—. Author: Mishpochah Matters, 1996, Future Hope, 1999. Mem. Lausanne Consultation on Jewish Evangelism, Evangelical Theol. soc., Evangelical Missiological Soc. Office: Jews for Jesus 60 Haight St San Francisco CA 94102-5895

BRICKWEDDE, RICHARD JAMES, lawyer; b. Bklyn., Dec. 12, 1944; s. George L. and Rose M. (McCarthy) B.; m. June Minsch Gamber, Sept. 2, 1978; stepchildren: Stephanie, Karen, Frances. AB, Syracuse U., 1966; JD, Fordham U., 1969. Bar: N.Y. 1970, D.C. 1971, U.S. Tax Ct. 1972, U.S. Supreme Ct. 1991. Staff asst. Syracuse (N.Y.) office Senator Robert F. Kennedy, 1965-66; adminstrv. asst. U.S. P.O. and OEO/VISTA, Washington, 1966; mgmt. cons. Washington, 1969-71; gen. counsel The Student Vote, Washington, 1971; pvt. practice law Syracuse, 1971-80; regional counsel N.Y. State Dept. Environ. Conservation, Syracuse, 1980-91, acting regional dir., 1984; with Green, Seifter Attys. PLLC, 1992—. Head environ. law practice; assoc. counsel to majority leader N.Y. State Assembly, 1975, asst. counsel to spkr. N.Y. State Assembly, 1976-77. Author: The Student's Right to Vote, 1971, Duke's Tale, 1991, Interstate Garbage: The Carbone Case and the Commerce Clause, 1994, The Superfund Recycling Equity Act of 1999, 2000; contbg. editor Network, 1975-76; contbr. articles to profl. jours. and trade publs. Treas. Legal Svcs. of Ctrl. N.Y., Inc., 1980—81, pres., 1981—82; Goodwill amb. Internat. Ctr. of Syracuse, 2000; chmn. voting rights task force Dem. Nat. Com., 1970—71; bd. dirs. Legal Svcs. of Ctrl. N.Y., Inc., 1978—83, Internat. Ctr. of Syracuse, 1992—2000, bd. dirs., pres., 1998—99; bd. dirs. N.Y. Alpha Tau Omega Student Aid Fund, Inc., Syracuse, 1972—2000, Huntington Family Ctrs., Inc., Syracuse, 1971—89, v.p., 1980; bd. dirs. Onondaga County (N.Y) Child Care Coun., Inc., 1978—80, Appleseed Trust, 2000—, The Nature Conservancy of Ctrl. and Western N.Y., 2001—. Named Hon. Citizen State of Tex., 1976; recipient Pub. Citizenship award N.Y. Pub. Interest Rsch. Group 1980. Mem. ABA (vice chair spl. com. on solid waste 1998-2002, state and local govt. vice-chair environ. com. 1998—), N.Y. Bar Assn., Onondaga County Bar Assn. (co-chair CLE com. 1999-2000, bd. dirs., 2002—), Nat. Solid Waste Mgmt. Assn. (mem. steering com. N.Y. chpt. 1992—) Democrat. Office: Green & Seifter Attys PLLC 1 Lincoln Ctr Ste 900 Syracuse NY 13202-1387 E-mail: rbrickwedde@greenseifter.com.

BRICKWOOD, SUSAN CALLAGHAN, lawyer; b. Sydney, NSW, Australia, Dec. 6, 1946; d. Graham Callaghan Brickwood and Nan (Cahaley) Nichols). BA, Swarthmore Coll., 1969; postgrad., Harvard U., 1969-71; JD, U. So. Calif., 1980. Bar: Calif. 1980, U.S. Tax Ct. 1981. Controller Howard Smith, Ltd., Sydney, 1972-74; assoc. Rifkind & Sterling, Beverly Hills, Calif., 1980-81, Armstrong, Hendler & Hirsch, Century City, Calif., 1981-82; pvt. practice L.A., 1982—. Author: Start Over!, 1990. Office: 9107 Wilshire Blvd #500 Beverly Hills CA 90210

BRIDEAU, LEO PAUL, healthcare executive; b. Leominster, Mass., Mar. 1, 1947; s. Alfred Joseph and Marie Yvonne (Poulin) B.; m. Kathleen Margaret Quinlan, Oct. 5, 1968; children: Alexander, Elizabeth, Neil, Katherine, William. BS, Georgetown U., 1968; MHA, Med. Coll. of Va., 1980. Counselor vets. benefits VA, Togus, Maine, 1971-73, asst. dist. coord. Richmond, Va., 1975-80; mgmt. analyst VA Med. Ctr., Togus, 1973-75; dep. dir. patient care services Strong Meml. Hosp., Rochester, N.Y., 1980-84, acting exec. dir., 1984, dir. hosp. ops., 1984-89, exec. dir., 1990-94, gen. dir., CEO, 1995-97; pres., CEO Strong Ptnrs. Health Sys. Inc., Rochester, 1997—2001, Columbia-St. Mary's, Inc., Milw., 2001—. Preceptor dept. health svcs. Va. Commonwealth U., Richmond, 1985—; preceptor Washington U. Sch. Medicine, St. Louis; instr. health svcs. U. Rochester, 1985—; mem. N.Y. State Pub. Health Coun., 1996-2001. Author: chpt. Cost Containment in a University Hosp., 1987. Chmn. adv. bd. Lifeline, Rochester, 1982-85; bd. dirs. Monroe County Medicap Inc., Rochester, 1984-87, Finger Lakes Health Systems Agy., Rochester, 1985-92; bd. dirs. Rochester Regional Joint Ventures Corp., 1985—, chmn., 1987-89, bd. dirs. Rochester Area Health Maintenance Orgn., Inc., 1985-88. Fellow Am. Coll. Healthcare Execs.; mem. Am. Hosp. Assn. (trustee 2000-02), Wis. Hosp. Assn. (bd. dirs.), Healthcare Assn. N.Y. State (chmn. bd. dirs. 1996, chair govt. rels. com. 1985-86, trustee 1989-2001, chair strategic planning com. 1991—), Rochester Regional Hosp. Assn. (bd. dirs. 1985-96, chmn. 1987-88), Assn. Univ. Programs in Health Adminstrn., Pi Sigma Alpha. Avocation: music. Office: 2025 E Newport Ave Milwaukee WI 53211

BRIDEAU, ROGER J. microbiologist, researcher; b. Tarrytown, N.Y., Dec. 31, 1954; m. Vickie S. Schwab, July 29, 1978; children: Nick, Claire. BS, SUNY, Plattsburgh, 1976; MSc, Oxford U., Eng., 1979. Immunologist Trudeau Rsch. Inst., Saranac Lake, Mich., 1976—80; virologist Pharmacia, Kalamazoo, 1980—2003, Pfizer, Ann Arbor, Mich., 2003—. Mem.: ASM. Office: Pfizer Corp 2800 Plymouth Rd Ann Arbor MI 48105

BRIDEGAM, WILLIS EDWARD, JR., librarian; b. Pottstown, Pa., Oct. 15, 1935; s. Willis Edward and M. Emma (Eberhart) B.; m. Nathalie J. Bridegam; 1 child, Martha Ann. BMus, Eastman Sch. Music, 1957; MS, Syracuse U., N.Y., 1963; MA (hon.), Amherst Coll., 1985. Med. librarian U. Rochester (N.Y.) Sch. Medicine, 1966-69, asso. dir. univ. libraries, 1969-72; dir. libraries State U. N.Y., Binghamton, 1972-75; librarian Amherst (Mass.) Coll., 1975—. Mem. founding com. Oberlin Group. Author: A Collaborative Approach to Collection Storage: The Five College Library Depository, 2001. Served with AUS, 1957. Mem. ALA, Assn. Coll. and Rsch. Libraries. Clubs: Grolier (N.Y.C.). Home: 53 Memorial Dr Amherst MA 01002-2533 Office: Amherst Coll Robert Frost Libr Amherst MA 01002 E-mail: webridegam@amherst.edu.

BRIDENBAUGH, PETER REESE, industrial research executive; b. Franklin, Pa., July 28, 1940; s. Charles Sumner and Helen Catherine (Reese) B.; m. Mary Ann Ellis, Apr. 17, 1965; children: Matthew B., Gabrielle L. BSME, Lehigh U., 1962, MS in Metallurgy, 1966; PhD in Materials Sci., MIT, 1968. With Alcoa Labs., Alcoa Ctr., Pa., R & D group leader, sect. head, spl. program engr. Warrick Ops., 1968-75, mgr., 1975-78; mgr. quality assurance Alcoa, Tenn., 1978-80; dir. ops. Alcoa Labs., 1980-83, dir., 1983-84, v.p. R & D, 1984-91, exec. v.p., chief tech. officer, 1991-95, exec. v.p.-automotive, 1995—. Mem. adv. bd. Carnegie-Bosch; chmn. Fedn. Materials Socs. 10th Biennial Conf., 1988; bd. dirs. Precision Castparts Corp., 1995—. Patentee in field. Mem. Pa. State Rsch. Found.; mem. vis. com. Carnegie-Mellon U., 1984—, Pa. State U., 1984—, Stanford U., 1987—, Lehigh U., 1989—, Northwestern U., 1991—. Fellow Am. Soc. Metals; mem. AIME, NAE, Indsl. Rsch. Inst., Dirs. Indsl. Rsch., Sigma Xi. Clubs: Duquesne (Pitts.), Fox Chapel Golf (Pitts.).

BRIDENBAUGH, PHILLIP OWEN, anesthesiologist, physician; b. Sioux City, Iowa, Dec. 17, 1932; s. Lloyd Donald and Harriet (Anderson) B.; m. Kathleen Conway, June 22, 1957 (div. Apr. 1980); children: Sue, Tom, Dan; m. Diann Hurd, Mar. 7, 1981; children: Rob, Jeff. BA, U. Nebr., 1954; MD, U. Nebr., Omaha, 1960. Diplomate Am. Bd. Anesthesiology. Staff anesthesiologist Mason Clinic, Seattle, 1965-70, dir. dept. anesthesia, 1970-77; prof., chmn. dept. anesthesiology U. Cin. Med. Ctr., 1977—. Pres. UAA, Inc., Cin., 1977—. Co-editor: Neural Blockade, 1980, 2d edit., 1988, 3d edit., 1997; sect. editor Anesthesia and Analgesia, 1989-95; sr. editor Regional Anesthesia, 1989-97. Trustee Wood Libr. Mus. Anesthesiology, 1992-94. 1st lt. U.S. Army, 1954-56. Mem. Assn. Univ. Anesthetists, Soc. Acad. Anesthesia Chmn. (pres. 1988-90), Am. Soc. Anesthesiology (bd. dirs., v.p. sci. affairs 1992-94, 1st v.p. 1994-95, pres. elect 1995-96, pres. 1996-97, immediate past pres. 1997-98), Am. Soc. Regional Anesthesia (pres. 1990-91), Ohio Soc. Anesthesiologists (pres. 1991-92). Office: U Cin Dept Anesthesia 231 Bethesda Ave Cincinnati OH 45267-0001 E-mail: bridenpo@uc.edu.

BRIDESTOWE, Lord See MOORE, THOMAS

BRIDGE, BOBBE J. state supreme court justice; m. Jonathan J. Bridge; children: Rebecca, Don. BA magna cum laude, U. Wash; MA, PhD in Polit. Sci., U. Mich.; JD, U. Wash., 1976. Superior Ct. judge King County, Wash., 1990-1999; chief judge King County Juvenile Ct., Wash., 1994-97, asst. presiding judge, 1997-98, presiding judge, 1998-99; judge Wash. State Supreme Ct., 1999—; mem. faculty Wash. State Jud. Coll. Chmn. King County Criminal Justice Coun., King County Truancy Steerin Com., Juvenile Justice Operational Master Plan Oversight Com., Pub. Trust and Confidence Com. Bd. Jud. Adminstrn.; co-chmn. Unified Family Ct. Bench-Bar Task Force. Bd. dirs. YWCA, Seattle Children's Home, Families for Kids Permanency Oversight Com., Tech. Adv. Com. Female Juvenile Offenders, Adv. Com. Adolescent Life Skills Program, Street Youth Law Program, Northwest Mediation Svc., Woodland Pk. Zoological Soc., Wash. Coun. Crime and Delinquency, Women's Funding Alliance, Alki Found., Privacy Fund, Seattle Arts Commn., U. Wash. Arts and Sci. Devel., Greater Seattle C. of C., Metrocenter YMCA, Juvenile Ct. Conf. Com.; mem. King County Task Force on Children and Families, Wash. State's Dept. Social and Health Svcs. Children., Youth, Family Svcs. Adv. Com., Child Protection Roundtable, Govs. Juvenile Justice Adv. Com.; chmn. State Task Force on Juvenile Issues, Coun. Youth Crisis Work Group, Families-at-Risk sub-com., Bd. Dirs. Ctr. Career Alternatives, Candidate Evaluation Com. Seattle-King Mcpl. League, Law and justice Com. League Women Voters; co-chmn. Govs. Coun. on Families, Youth, and Justice; pres. Seattle Women's Commn., Seattle Chpt. Am. Jewish Com.,bd. dirs., asst. sec.-treas. Jewish Fedn. Greater Seattle, chmn., vice chmn. Cmty. Rels. Coun. Named Judge of Yr. Wash. Women Lawyers, 1996; recipient Hannah G. Solomon award Nat. Coun. Jewish Women, 1996, Cmty. Catalyst award Mother's Against Violence in Am., 1997, Women Making a Difference award Youthcare, 1998; honored "woman helping women" Soroptimist Internat. of Kent, 1999. Mem. Phi Beta Kappa. Office: Wash Supreme Ct PO Box 40929 Olympia WA 98504-0929

BRIDGE, HERBERT MARVIN, jewelry executive; b. Seattle, Mar. 14, 1925; s. Ben and Sally (Silverman) B.; m. Shirley Selesnick, Jan. 25, 1948; children: Jonathan J., Daniel E. BA in Polit. Sci., U. Wash., 1947. Pres. Ben Bridge Jeweler Inc., Seattle, 1955-76, chmn., 1977—. Bd. dirs. Teledesic. Past pres. Downtown Seattle Assn., 1980-81, Am. Jewish Com.; bd. dirs. Naval Acad. Found., Naval Undersea Mus., Alliance for Edn.; chair Puget Sound USO; chmn. sr. adv. bd. Goodwill Games of 1990; co-chair King County chpt. United

Way, 2000-01. Rear adm. USNR, 1942-85. Decorated Legion of Merit with Gold Star in lieu of 2d award; recipient Israel Bonds Masada award, 1974, Am. Jewish Com. Human Rels award, 1978, Navy League scroll hon., 1980, 96, U. Wash. Alumni Legend award, 1987, Vol. of Yr. award Jewish Fedn., 1991, Privacy Fund Humanitarian award, 1991, Heritage award Mus. History and Industry, 1993, A.K. Guy Cmty. Svc. award YMCA, 1995, Sea 1st Cmty. Svc. award, 1998, Citizen Yr. Seattle-King Co., 2001, medal of achievement Fred Hutchinson Cancer Ctr., 2003; named to Nat. Jewelers Hall of Fame, 1998, Puget Sound Bus. Hall of Fame, 1999. Mem.: Greater Seattle C. of C. (past pres.), Pacific N.W. Jewelers (past pres.), Am. Gem. Soc. (head trustee 1993—2000, cert., Triple Zero award 2001, Shipley award 2003), Rotary, City Club (founder), Wash. Athletic Club (past pres.), Naval Res. Assn. (past pres.), Shriners. Democrat. Office: PO Box 1908 Seattle WA 98111-1908

BRIDGE, JONATHAN JOSEPH, lawyer, retail executive; b. Seattle, Mar. 19, 1950; s. Herbert Marvin and Shirley Geraldine (Selesnick) B.; m. Bobbe Jean Chaback, May 20, 1978; children: Donald, Rebecca. BA with honors, U. Wash., 1972, JD, 1976. Bar: Wash. 1976, U.S. Dist. Ct. (we. dist.) Wash. 1976, U.S. Ct. Mil. Appeals 1977, U.S. Ct. Appeals (9th cir.) 1979, U.S. Supreme Ct. 1980. Legal service officer USN, Oak Harbor, Wash., 1976-79, staff judge adv. Bremerton, Wash., 1979-81; exec. v.p. Ben Bridge Jeweler, Inc., Seattle, 1981-90, gen. counsel, co-chief exec. officer, 1990—. Bd. dirs. Ben Bridge Corp., Seattle, U.S. Bank Wash., Seattle, Jewelers Vigilance Com., N.Y., Jewelers Mutal Ins., Neenah, Wis., Assn. Wash. Bus. Bd. dirs. King County Mental Health Bd., Seattle, 1984; mem. bd. Wash. Retail Assn., 1985-94; vice chmn. Seattle Urban League, 1986-88, chmn., 1988-89; pres. Am. Jewish Com., Seattle, 1986-88; counsel Pacific Northwest Jewelers Assn., 1988—, treas., 1990, pres., 1995-97; bd. dirs. Seattle Alliance Edn., 1990—; mem. bd. Ctr. for Career Alternatives, 1981—; precinct committeeman, 1990-96; bd. dirs. U. Wash. Law Sch. Found., 1994—, pres., 2003—. Served to lt. comdr. USN, 1972-81, Vietnam, with Res., 1981—, comdr., 1988-93, capt., 2003. Mem. ABA, Wash. State Bar Assn., Seattle/King County Bar Assn., Judge Advocates Assn., Greater Seattle C. of C., U. Wash. Alumni Assn. (bd. dirs. 1986-93), U. Wash. Law Sch. Alumni Assn. (pres. 1989-91), Wash. Athletic Club, Columbia Tower Club, City Club. Democrat. Jewish. Home: 2440 Montavista Pl W Seattle WA 98199-3723 Office: Ben Bridge Jeweler Inc PO Box 1908 Seattle WA 98111-1908

BRIDGEMAN, BRUCE, psychobiology educator; b. Glen Ridge, NJ, Sept. 17, 1944; s. Jack and Elsie Pauline (Knorr) B.; m. Diane Laura Turchairelli, Dec. 12, 1970; children: Natalie, Theresa. BA in Psychology with honors, Cornell U., 1967; PhD in Physiological Psychology, Stanford U., 1971. Prof. psychology & psychobiology U. Calif., Santa Cruz, 1973—. Guest prof. Max-Planck Inst., Munich, 1993-99, adv. com., 1985-89, 90-99. Author: The Theory of Binocular Vision, 1977, The Biology of Behavior and Mind, 1988, Psychology and Evolution: The Origins of Mind, 2003; contbr. more than 100 articles to profl. jours. Judge Sci. Fair, Santa Cruz County, 1992-98, 2001; speakers bur. Population Connection, Santa Cruz, 1993—; choir dir. Unitarian Fellowship, Freedom, Calif., 1993-96, Santa Cruz Chorale, 1998—. Postdoctoral fellow Free U. Berlin, 1971-73, U. Calif. Berkeley, 1973; Rsch. grantee Nat. Eye Inst., 1975-78, 82-85, NSF, 1979-81, Air Force Office of Scientific Rsch., Washington, 1990-93, NASA, 1994-99. Fellow APA, Am. Physiol. Soc., Psychonomic Soc.; mem. AAAS (sci. resource panel 1995—), Assn. Rsch. in Vision and Ophthalmology (chair program com. 1986-88). Avocations: choral music, bicycling. Home: 208 Crestview Ter Santa Cruz CA 95060-3332 Office: U Calif Psychology Dept Santa Cruz CA 95064 E-mail: bruceb@cats.ucsc.edu.

BRIDGER, BALDWIN, JR., electrical engineer; b. Savannah, Ga., Sept. 18, 1928; s. Baldwin and Helen Bush (Stubbs) B.; m. Wilma Grace Martz, Mar. 21, 1953; children: Ruth Carson, John Wesley, Mary Gere. BS in Engring., Emory U., 1948; postgrad., U. Iowa, 1966-68. Registered profl. engr., Tex., Pa. Test engr. GE, Lynn, Mass., Trenton, N.J., Ft. Wayne, Ind., Schenectady, N.Y., 1948-50, design engr. Phila., 1953-65, engring. mgr. Burlington, Iowa, 1965-68, Phila., 1968-71, product planner, 1972-73; chief engr. Powell Elec. Mfg. Co., Houston, 1973-83, mgr. engring., 1983-85, mgr. application and new products engring., 1985-90, tech. dir., 1990-96; pres. Bridger Engring. Co., 1996—. Contbr. articles to tech. jours. With USN, 1951-52. Fellow IEEE (dept. chmn. 1987-88, soc. treas. 1989-90, soc. sec. 1991, soc. v.p. 1992, pres. 1993, editor, tech. jour. 1997—); mem. Phi Beta Kappa. Republican. Methodist.

BRIDGER, CAROLYN ANN, pianist, music educator; b. Memphis, Tenn., June 20, 1943; d. Grover Leon and Elizabeth Lou (Everett) B.; m. Waldie Alfred Anderson, Dec. 30, 1983. Student, Mozarteum Akademie, Salzburg, Austria, 1963-64; MusB, Oberlin (Ohio) Coll., 1965; MusM, Ind. U., 1967; postgrad., Boston U., 1970-72; D Mus. Arts, U. Iowa, 1977. Adj. lectr. music Emory U., Atlanta, 1967-70; vis. asst. prof. music U. N.C., Chapel Hill, 1974-75; asst. prof. music Delta State U., Cleveland, Miss., 1975-76; prof. piano and chamber music, coord. accompanying Fla. State U., Tallahassee, 1976—. Artistic advisor The Artist Series, Tallahassee; keyboardist Tallahassee Symphony; violist Big Bend Cmty. Orch., Tallahassee. Piano soloist Atlanta Symphony, Balt. Symphony and other orchs.; concert tours solo and chamber music in Europe, S.Am., S.E. Asia, U.S.A. Rsch. grantee Fla. State U. Mem. Music Tchrs. Nat. Assn., Fla. State Music Tchrs. Assn. (chamber music chair 1988—), P.E.O. Sisterhood, Pi Kappa Lambda. Avocations: travel, birding. Office: Fla State U Sch Music Tallahassee FL 32306-1180 E-mail: cbridger@mailer.fsu.edu.

BRIDGERS, JOHN DAVID, retired pediatrician; b. Greenville, N.C., July 4, 1920; s. Samuel Leon and Essie Sutton (Whichard) B.; m. Edith Holland Hamrick, Aug. 29, 1945 (dec. Aug. 2000); children: John D. Jr., Sam L. II, Carl H., Raymond S., Barbara Jean, Ellen Holland. AB, E. Carolina U., 1940; MD, Duke U., 1950. Diplomate Am. Bd. Pediatrics. Intern USN Hosp., Chelsea, 1950; flight surgeon, aviator U.S. NAS, Atlantic City, N.J., 1952-54; resident pediatrician Children's Hosp. Phila., 1954-56, dir. Out Patient Dept., 1956-62; pvt. practice High Point, N.C., 1962-85; physician field rep. Joint Commn. for Accreditation of Healthcare Orgns., Chgo., 1985-88; med. dir. Burnette Tomlin Meml. Hosp., Cape May Court House, N.J., 1988-93; ret., 1994. Asst. prof. U. Pa., Phila., 1956-62. Comdr. USNR, 1941-60. Fellow Am. Acad. Pediatrics; mem. AMA, Am. Acad. Med. Execs. Democrat. Avocations: investments, writing, reading. Home: # 218 4125 North Point Pkwy Alpharetta GA 30022

BRIDGERS, WILLIAM FRANK, retired physician; b. Asheville, NC, July 26, 1932; s. John Dixon and Ruth (Norberg) B.; m. Judith Ann Ware, Nov. 27, 1974; 1 child, Jana; children from previous marriage: Jeffrey, David, Daniel. BA, U. of the South, 1954; MD, Washington U., St. Louis, 1959, fellow in preventive medicine, 1963-65. Intern Barnes Hosp., Washington U., St. Louis, 1959—60, resident, 1962—63; assoc. prof. medicine U. Miami, Fla., 1968; prof., dir. neurosci. program U. Ala., Birmingham, 1970—72, spl. asst. v.p. health affairs, 1976, chmn., prof. dept. pub. health, 1976—93, former dean, 1981—89, prof., 1981—93, univ. scholar emeritus, 1993—2003, dean emeritus, 2000—03; head Eutaw Health Policy Group, 1993—2001; ret., 2003. Staff mem. NAS, Washington, 1974; mem. governing bd. Nat. Coun. Internat. Health, Washington, 1979-87; dir. Lister Hill Ctr. for Health Policy, 1987-90; mem. com. on vital and health stats. HHS, USPHS, 1990-94. Co-editor (monthly feature) Policy Watch Am. Jour. Medicine and Am. Jour. Surgery, 1990-97; contbr. articles to profl. jours. Mem. APHA, Assn. Schs. Pub. Health (pres., mem. exec. com.), Am. Men and Women of Sci., Am. Inst. Nutrition, Am. Soc. Biol. Chemistry, Phi Beta Kappa. Democrat. Home: 2221 English Village Ln Birmingham AL 35223-1730

BRIDGES, ALAN LYNN, physicist, computer scientist, systems software engineer; BS in Physics, Ga. Inst. Tech., 1972, MS in Physics, 1974, postgrad., 1975—78, postgrad., 1994—95. Cert. C-130J R&M HUD, BIU, MC, FMECA. Asst. research scientist Ga. Tech. Research Inst., Atlanta, 1975-78; asst. product mgr. Humphrey Instruments Inc., San Leandro, Calif., 1978; pres., cons. ETC West Ltd., 1979—; with Lockheed Aero Systems Co., 1983-88; sr. prin. engr. new bus. devel. Lockheed Electronics Co., Atlanta, 1988-90; sr. engr., program mgr. Flat Panel & Graphics Display Systems SCI Tech., Inc., Hunstville, Ala., 1990-92; software engr. specialist life cycle software support and C130JRM & S sys. engring. Lockheed Martin Aeronautical Systems Co., Marietta, Ga., 1992-2001, sr. S.W. software specialist, 1998—; reliability, supportability and safety staff engr., lead engr. vision display server Barcoview LLC, 2001—. Mem. Lockheed Software Process Std. ISO 9000/SEI CMM software and sys. engring. CMM process action team, ACM stds. com. tech. adv. group ISO 9241. Contbg. editor Computer Tech. Rev., PC Graphics & Video Mag.; bi-monthly columnist Hardcopy; contbr. articles to profl. jours. Mem. IEEE (sr., dir. Atlanta sect., 1987-88, sec. 1988-89, treas. 1989-90, chmn. student activities com. 1985-87, sec.-treas. computer soc. chpt. 1985-86, chmn. computer soc. chpt. 1986-89, vice-chmn. 1987-88, gen. chmn. Atlanta software tech. conf. 1987, mem P1226 ABBET com., mem. P1498/12207 stds. com., SW stds. com.), Assn. for Computing Machinery, Optical Soc. Am., Soc. Photo-Optical Instrumentation Engrs., Nat. Security Indsl. Assn. (mem. integrated diagnostic working group, co-chair integrated avionics task group), Soc. for Tech. Communications, Computer Press Assn., Soc. for Info. Display, Nat. Telesystems Conf., Control and Displays Session Orgn., Am. Nat. Standards Inst./Internat. Standards Orgn., Sigma Pi Sigma. Home: 8523 Colony Club Dr Alpharetta GA 30022-5407 Office: Barcoview LLC 3059 Premiere Pkwy Duluth GA 30097

BRIDGES, ANNITA MARIE, lawyer; b. Columbia, S.C., Dec. 21, 1951; d. John R. and Anne M. (Wharton) B.; m. Robert H. Alexander, Jr. B.A., Howard U., 1973; J.D., Georgetown U., 1976. Bar: Okla. 1979, Colo. 1976, U.S. Dist. Ct. Colo. 1976, U.S. Dist. Ct. (we. dist.) Okla. 1980, U.S. Ct. Appeals (10th cir.) 1976. Legal intern SBA, Washington, 1974-75; asst. atty. gen. State of Colo., Denver, 1976-78; staff atty. Kerr-McGee Corp., Oklahoma City, 1978— ; lectr. U. Okla., Norman, 1982. Mem. Colo. Gov.'s Clemency Adv. Bd., 1977-78; mem. Gov.'s Adv. Commn. on Status Women; vol. in Oklahoma City Pub. Schs.; bd. dirs., past pres. Planned Parenthood Assn., Oklahoma City; bd. dirs. YWCA, Oklahoma City N.E. Devel. Corp., Black Liberated Arts Council. Recipient Outstanding Community Service award Community Council Central Okla., 1984. Mem. ABA, Okla. Bar Assn. (sec. labor law sect. 1979-80). Office: Kerr-McGee Corp PO Box 25861 Oklahoma City OK 73125-0861

BRIDGES, B. RIED, lawyer; b. Kansas City, Mo., Oct. 20, 1927; s. Brady R. and Mary H. (Nieuwenhuis) B.; 1 son, Ried George. BA, U. So. Calif., 1951, LLB, 1954. Bar: Calif. 1954. Assoc. Overton, Lyman & Prince, L.A., 1956-58, ptnr., 1958-63, Bonne, Jones & Bridges, L.A., 1963-74, Bonne, Bridges, Mueller & O'Keefe, L.A., Santa Ana, San Luis Obispo, Riverside, San Francisco, 1974—. Served with U.S. Army, 1954-56. Fellow Am. Coll. Trial Lawyers, Internat. Acad. Trial Lawyers; mem.Calif. Bar Assn., Assn. So. Calif. Def. Counsel, L.A. County Bar Assn., Santa Barbara County Bar Assn., Am. Bd. Trial Advs. (diplomate), Pacific Corinthian Yacht Club, Balboa of Mazatlan (Sinaloa, Mex.). Republican. Avocation: sportfishing. Home: 2551 Victoria Ave Oxnard CA 93035-2931 Office: Bonne Bridges Mueller O'Keefe & Nichols 3699 Wilshire Blvd 10th Flr Los Angeles CA 90010 E-mail: rbridges@bbmon.com.

BRIDGES, BERYL CLARKE, marketing executive; b. N.Y.C., Oct. 27, 1941; d. David and Edith (Foster) Clarke; m. R. Shaw Bridges, Sept. 2, 1962 (div. May 1985); children: Robert Shaw Jr., Margaret Clarke, John Morrison; m. Robert A. McMillan, July 25, 1992. BA in English, Philosophy, Wheaton Coll., 1963. Acct. exec. McMoran-Redington Pub. Rels., Greenwich, Conn., 1975-77; mgr. sales promotion Lindenmeyr Graphic Resource Ctr., Greenwich, 1977-79; corp. mgr. promotions Lindenmeyr Paper Corp., Greenwich, 1979-81; mgr. southeastern region Paper Sources Internat. subs. Lindenmeyr Paper Corp., 1981-83, v.p. mktg., 1983-84; pres. Zanders USA, Inc. (subs. Internat. Paper Co.), Wayne, N.J., 1984-95. Cons. and lectr. in field. V.p. Greenwich Hist. Soc., 1974-77; mem. Jr. League, Greenwich, 1971-78; founder Girls Inc. of No. N.J., 2002, bd. dir., 2002 Mem. AAUW. Democrat. Avocations: folk dancing, hiking, choral singing. Home: 18 Lake Dr Boonton NJ 07005-1047 *During difficult times I found inspiration in these words: "A sorrow never held a crocus back. The rigid earth revives - Day breaks; tomorrow comes down the starry track." Anonymous.*

BRIDGES, CARL BRANSON, religious studies educator; b. Knoxville, Feb. 3, 1951; s. Carl Branson and Mary Kate Bridges; m. Glenda Ford, Dec. 26, 1971; children: Cynthia Bridges Coffey, Donald Branson. PhD, Union Theol. Sem., Va., 1990. Lectr., prin. Ghana Christian Coll. and Sem., Accra, Ghana, 1976—83; prof. N.T. Johnson Bible Coll., Knoxville, 1987—. Author: (articles) Stone-Campbell Jour. Mem.: Soc. of Bibl. Lit. Office: Johnson Bible Coll 7900 Johnson Dr Knoxville TN 37998 Office Fax: 865-251-2337. E-mail: cbridges@jbc.edu.

BRIDGES, CHARLES HUBERT, veterinarian, educator; b. Shreveport, La., Feb. 23, 1921; s. Charles Maurice Bridges, Mary Ann Carruth; m. Mildred Louise Kruse, Oct. 14, 1945; children: Charmille, Gary W., Greg A. DVM, Tex. A&M U., 1945, MS, 1954, PhD, 1957. Diplomate Am. Coll. Vet./Pathologists 1954. Vet., Brenham, Tex., 1945—49; instr. La. State U., Baton Rouge, 1949—51; vet. USAF, Edwards AF Base, Calif., 1951—53; rsch. fellow Armed Forces Inst. Pathology, Washington, 1954; assoc. prof., prof. Tex. A&M U., Agrl. Exptl. Sta., College Station, 1954—88; prof. emeritus Tex. A&M U., College Station, 1988—. Recipient Harold W. Casey award, Charles L. Davis Found., 1998, Peter Olafson medal, Cornell U., 1994; grantee, NIH, 1960—67, 1964—77, USDA, 1979—81, Robert J. and Helen C. Kleberg Found., 1980—82. Mem.: AVMA, Conf. Rsch. Workshop in Animal Diseases, Tex. Vet. Med. Assn., Am. Assn. Vet. Diagnosticians, Soc. Human and Animal Mycology, Internat. Acad. Pathology, Gamma Sigma Delta, Phi Kappa Phi, Phi Zeta, Sigma Xi. Lutheran. Avocations: fly fishing, camping, genealogy. Home: 1502 Glade St College Station TX 77840

BRIDGES, DAVID MANNING, lawyer; b. Berkeley, Calif., May 22, 1936; s. Robert Lysle and Alice Marion (Rodenberger) B.; m. Carmen Galante de Bridges, Aug. 16, 1973; children: David, Stuart. AB, U. Calif., Berkeley, 1957, JD, 1962. Assoc. Thelen, Marrin, Johnson & Bridges, San Francisco, 1962-70, ptnr., 1970-94, mng. ptnr. Houston, 1981-91. Served as lt. (j.g.) USN, 1957-59. Mem. ABA, State Bar of Tex., Tex. Bar Assn., Houston Bar Assn., Internat. Bar Assn., Houston Club, Coronado Club, Pacific-Union Club. Office: 700 Louisiana St Ste 4600 Houston TX 77002-2732 E-mail: dbridhou@aol.com.

BRIDGES, DOUGLAS M. musician, small business owner; b. Belleville, Ill., Jan. 22, 1958; s. Donald Miles and Geneva (Verduce) Bridges; m. Laura L. Missey, Oct. 21, 1978. Ordained to ministry Universal Life Ch., 1993. Musician Easy St., Belleville, 1981, Cimmaron, Las Vegas, Nev., 1981-85; co-owner Cimmaron Music Works, Estes Park, Colo., 1990-94. Composer, music advisor Horizon Video Prodn., Denver, 1995—. Author: (book) Banjo Owners Notebook, 1989. Pk. watcher Nat. Pks. Conservation Assn., 1994—. Achievements include patents in field. Avocations: camping, hiking, reading, music, environmental work. Office: DM Bridges PO Box 2235 Estes Park CO 80517-2235 E-mail: douglasmbridges@hotmail.com.

BRIDGES, EILEEN, marketing educator; BS in Engring., Calif. Inst. Tech., 1977; MS in Elec. Engring., Rice U., 1978; MBA, Santa Clara U., 1982; PhD, Northwestern U., 1987. R&D engr. Hewlett-Packard Co., Santa Clara, Calif., 1979-80, product mktg. engr., 1980-82, product mgr. Cupertino, Calif., 1982-83; Hewlett-Packard vis. prof. elec. engring. N.C. A&T State U., Greensboro, 1983-84; asst. prof. adminstrv. sci. Rice U., Houston, 1987-94; asst. prof. mktg. Kent (Ohio) State U., 1994-98, assoc. prof. mktg., 1998—, dept. chair, 2000—. Contbr. articles to profl. jours.; mem. editl. bd. Svc. Industries Jour., 1994—. Rsch. grantee APICS, 1998, Kent State U., 1997. Mem. Am. Mktg. Assn., Inst. for Ops. Rsch. and the Mgmt. Scis.

BRIDGES, GERALD JACKSON, social worker; b. Akron, Ohio, Feb. 25, 1928; s. John Richard and Olive Frances (Cliett) B.; m. Melda Lusk, Dec. 17, 1960; 1 child, Gerald Jackson. BS in Edn./Psychology, Carson-Newman Coll., Jefferson City, Tenn., 1958; MSW, U. Tenn., 1963. Caseworker Clover Bottom Hosp. & Sch., Nashville, 1963; social caseworker Nashville Mental Health Ctr., 1963-64; instr. U. Tenn., Knoxville, 1964-67; casework cons. Wesley House Day Care Ctr., Nashville, 1967-69; casework supr. Monroe Harding Children's Home, Nashville, 1967-69; pres. MacDonell United Meth. Children's Svcs., Inc., Houma, La., 1969—. With USN, 1950-54. Republican. Episcopalian. Office: MacDonell United Meth Svcs 8326 Main St Houma LA 70363-4871

BRIDGES, JEFF, actor; b. Los Angeles, Dec. 4, 1949; s. Lloyd Vernet (dec. 1998) and Dorothy (Simpson) B.; m. Susan Bridges, 1977; 3 children Made acting debut at age 8 in Sea Hunt TV series; appeared in films Halls of Anger, 1970, The Last Picture Show, 1971, Fat City, 1972, Bad Company, 1972, The Iceman Cometh, 1973, Lolly-Madonna XXX, 1973 The Last American Hero, 1973, Thunderbolt and Lightfoot, 1974, Hearts of the West, 1975, Rancho Deluxe, 1975, King Kong, 1976, Stay Hungry, 1976, Somebody Killed Her Husband, 1978, Winter Kills, 1979, The American Success Company, 1979, Heaven's Gate, 1980, Cutter's Way, 1981, Tron, 1982, The Last Unicorn (voice only),1982, Kiss Me Goodbye, 1982, Starman, 1984, Against All Odds, 1984, Jagged Edge, 1985, The Morning After, 1986, 8 Million Ways To Die, 1986, Nadine, 1987, Tucker, 1988, See You In The Morning, 1989, The Fabulous Baker Boys, 1989, Texasville, 1990, The Fisher King, 1991, American Heart(also prod.), 1992, The Vanishing, 1993, Fearless, 1993, Blown Away, 1994, Wild Bill, 1995, White Squall, 1996, The Mirror Has Two Faces, 1996, The Big Lebowski, 1998, Arlington Road, 1999, Forever Hollywood, 1999, The Muse, 1999, Simpatico, 1999, The Contender, 2000, Scenes of the Crime, 2001, K-Pax, 2001, Masked and Anonymous, 2003, Seabiscuit, 2003. TV movies: Silent Night, Lonely Night, 1969, In Search of America, 1971, The Girls in Their Summer Dresses and Other Stories by Irwin Shaw, 1981, Hidden in America (also prod.), 2002; (TV, voice) Raising the Mammoth, 2000, Lewis & Clark: Great Journey West, 2002. Office: Creative Artists Agency care Rick Nicita 9830 Wilshire Blvd Beverly Hills CA 90212-1825*

BRIDGES, JOHN FRANCIS PATRICK, healthcare educator, researcher; b. Orange, NSW, Australia, Dec. 20, 1973; arrived in U.S., 1999; s. Terrence Allen and Margaret Myree Bridges; m. Coatney Charlene Rene, Dec. 27, 2003. B Econs. with honors, Australian Nat. U., Canberra, 1996; M Econs. with honors, U. Sydney, Australia, 1997; PhD, CUNY, 2002. Rsch. asst. Nat. Bur. Econ. Rsch., N.Y.C., 1999—2002; asst. prof. Case Western Res. U., Cleve., 2002—. Robert E. Gilleece fellow CUNY, 1999—2002. Lector, eucharistic min. St. Ann's Cath. Ch., Cleveland Heights, Ohio, 2001. Mem.: Australian Health Economics Soc. (v.p. 1998—99, editor 2000—01). Roman Catholic. Office: Case Western Res U 10900 Euclid Ave Cleveland OH 44106-4945 Office Fax: 216-368-3970. Personal E-mail: healtheconomics@hotmail.com. E-mail: jfb12@po.cwru.edu.

BRIDGES, LEONARD HAL, retired history educator, writer; b. Luling, Tex., Nov. 10, 1918; s. Leonard Harold and Lyda Lois (King) B.; m. Alice Miskjian, Aug. 21, 1949; children: Lois Alice, Stephanie Ann. BJ, U. Tex., 1940; MA, Columbia U., 1947, PhD, 1950. Instr. history U. Ark., Fayetteville, 1950-53; asst. prof. U. Colo., Boulder, 1953-55, assoc. prof., 1955-60, prof., 1960-64, U. Calif., Riverside, 1964-79, prof. emeritus, 1979—. Author: Iron Millionaire: Life of Charlemagne Tower, 1952, Lee's Maverick General: Daniel Harvey Hill, 1961, reprinted, 1991, American Mysticism: From William James to Zen, 1970. Maj. U.S. Army, 1940-45, MTO. Sr. faculty fellow U. Calif., 1965; rsch. grantee Am. Philos. Soc., U. Colo., U. Calif. Avocations: writing, walking, reading.

BRIDGES, ROBERT LYSLE, retired lawyer; b. Altus, Ark., May 12, 1909; s. Joseph Manning and Jeffa Alice (Morrison) B.; m. Alice Marian Rodenberger, June 10, 1930; children: David Manning, James Robert, Linda Lee. AB, U. Calif., 1930, JD, 1933. Bar: Calif. 1933, U.S. Supreme Ct 1938. Pvt. practice, San Francisco, 1933-92; assoc. firm Thelen Marrin Johnson & Bridges, 1933-39, ptnr., 1938-92. Trustee, former chmn. U. Calif. Berkeley Found.; trustee, hon. dir. John Muir Found., 1992—. Mem. ABA, Calif. Bar Assn., San Francisco Bar Assn., Commonwealth Club of Calif., Pacific Union Club, Claremont Country Club (Oakland). Republican. Home: 3972 Happy Valley Rd Lafayette CA 94549-2426 Office: 101 Second St Ste 1800 San Francisco CA 94105-3601

BRIDGES, ROBERT MCSTEEN, mechanical engineer; b. Oakland, Calif., Apr. 17, 1914; s. Robert and Josephine (Hite) B.; m. Edith Brownwood, Oct. 26, 1945; children: Ann, Lawrence, Robert. BS cum laude in Mech. Engring., U. So. Calif., 1940; postgrad., UCLA. Registered profl. engr., Calif. Engr. Nat. Supply Co., Torrance, Calif., 1940-41; design engr. landing gear and hydraulics Lockheed Aircraft Corp., Burbank, Calif., 1941-46; missile hydraulic controls design engr. Convair, San Diego, 1946-48; sr. staff engr. oceanic systems mech. design Bendix corp., Symar, Calif., 1948—. Adv. ocean engring. U.S. Congress; participant confs. in U.S., Japan. Contbr. articles. Com. chmn. Boy Scouts Am., 1961. Recipient award of Service Am. Inst. Aero Engrs., 1965. Mem. Marine Tech. Soc. (charter; com. cables, connectors 1969), Tau Beta Pi. Republican. Achievements include patents for field of undersea devices (54 internat., 14 U.S.); deep ocean rubber band moor; invention of U.S. Navy sonobuoy rotochute. Home: 10314 Vanalden Ave Northridge CA 91326-3326 Office: L-3 Communications Ocean Sys 15825 Roxford St Sylmar CA 91342-3537

BRIDGES, ROGER DEAN, historical agency administrator; b. Marshalltown, Iowa, Feb. 10, 1937; s. Floyd F. and Beatrice Andrea (Pipher) B.; m. Karen Maureen Buckley, June 4, 1960; children: Patrick Sean, Kristin Joy, Jennifer Lynn. BA, Iowa State Tchrs. Coll., 1959; MA, State Coll. of Iowa, 1962; PhD, U. Ill., 1970; LHD, Lincoln (Ill.) Coll., 1987, Tiffin U., 1994. Tchr., libr. Keokuk (Iowa) Pub. Schs., 1959—62; instr. in history Bradley U., Peoria, Ill., 1967; asst. prof. history U. S.D., Vermillion, 1968—69; asst. editor Papers of Ulysses Grant, Carbondale, Ill., 1969—70; dir. rsch. Ill. State Hist. Libr., Springfield, 1970—76, head libr., 1976—85; dir. Ill. State Hist. Libr./Ill. Hist. Preservation Agy., Springfield, 1985—87; dir., editor Lincoln legal papers project, asst. state historian Ill. Hist. Preservation Agy, Springfield, 1987—88; exec. dir. Rutherford B. Hayes Presdl. Ctr., Fremont, Ohio, 1988—2003. Part-time instr. Ill. State U., Normal, Ill., 1974-84; adj. prof. Sangamon State U., Springfield, 1985-88, Bowling Green (Ohio) State U., 1989-2003. Author, editor: Illinois: It's History and Legacy, 1984; asst. editor: Papers of Ulysses S. Grant, vol. 4, 1972. Bd. dirs. Springfield Urban League, 1976-82, Gt. Am. People Show, New Salem, Ill., 1978-85; bd. dirs., sec., v.p. Birchard Pub. Libr. Sandusky County, Fremont, 1988-96, pres., 1996-99; bd. dirs., pres. Conv. and Visitors Bur. Sandusky County, Fremont, 1988-99. Nat. Hist. Publs. Commn. fellow, 1969-70; recipient Disting. Svc. awrd Springfield Urban League, 1977. Mem. Am. Hist. Assn., So. Hist. Assn., Abraham Lincoln Assn. bd. dirs. 1985-2003), Orgn. Am. Historians, Soc. for Historians of Gilded Age and Progressive Era (sec., treas. 1989-2003), Ill. State Hist. Soc. (Disting. Svc. award 1988), Ohio Acad. History (exec. coun. 1996-98), bd. trustees Ohioana Library Assn., 1998-2003, C. of C. of Sandusky County (bd. dirs. 1999-2002), Rotary Internat. Democrat. Baptist. Home: 2804 Mockingbird Ln Bloomington IL 61704 E-mail: rdbridges@nwonline.net.

BRIDGES, ROY DUBARD, JR., federal agency administrator; b. Atlanta; m. Benita Louise Allbaugh; children: 2. BS in Engring. Sci., USAF Acad., 1965; MS in Astronautics, Purdue U., 1966. Commd. 2d lt. USAF, advanced through grades to maj. gen., comdr. 6510th Test Wing, 1986-89, comdr. Ea. Space and Missile Ctr. Patrick AFB, Fla., 1989-90, comdr. Air Force Flight Test Ctr. Edwards AFB, 1991-93, dir. requirements Air Force Materiel Command Wright-Patterson AFB, Ohio, 1993-96, ret., 1996; dir. John F. Kennedy Space Ctr. NASA, 1997—. Achievements include being a NASA astronaut, piloted Space Shuttle Challenger July and August, 1985. Office: Mail Code AA John F Kennedy Space Ctr Kennedy Space Center FL 32899-0001

BRIDGES, WILLIAM BRUCE, electrical engineer, researcher, engineering educator; b. Inglewood, Calif., Nov. 29, 1934; s. Newman K. and Doris L. (Brown) Bridges; m. Carol Ann French, Aug. 24, 1957 (div. 1986); children: Ann Marjorie, Bruce Kendall, Michael Alan; m. Linda Josephine McManus, Nov. 15, 1986. BEE, U. Calif., Berkeley, 1956, MEE (GE Rice fellow), 1957, PhD in Elec. Engring. (NSF fellow), 1962. Assoc. elec. engring. U. Calif., Berkeley, 1957-59, grad. rsch. engr., 1959-61; mem. tech. staff Hughes Rsch. Labs. divsn. Hughes Aircraft Co., Malibu, Calif., 1960-77, sr. scientist, 1968-77, mgr. laser dept., 1969-70; prof. elec. engring. and applied physics Calif. Inst. Tech., Pasadena, 1977—2002, Carl F Braun prof. engring., 1983—2002, Carl F Braun prof. engring. emeritus, 2002—, exec. officer elec. engring., 1978-81. Lectr. U. So. Calif., L.A., 1962—64; Sherman Fairchild Disting. scholar Calif. Inst. Tech., 1974—75; bd. dirs. Phasebridge Corp., Access Laser Corp. Author (with C. K. Birdsall): (book) Electron Dynamics of Diode Regions, 1966; contbr. articles to profl. jours.; assoc. editor: IEEE Jour. Quantum Electronics, 1977—82, Jour. Optical Soc. Am., 1978—83. Mem. sci. adv. bd. USAF, 1985—89. Named Disting. Engring. Alumnus, U. Calif., Berkeley, 1995; recipient L. A. Hyland Patent award, 1969. Fellow: IEEE (Quantum Electronics award 1988), Laser Inst. Am. (Arthur L. Schawlow award 1986), Optical Soc. Am. (objectives and policies com. 1981—86, 1989—91, bd. dirs. 1982—84, v.p. 1986, pres.-elect 1987, pres. 1988, past pres.

1989); mem.: Am. Radio Relay League, Nat. Acad. Scis., Nat. Acad. Engring., Phi Beta Kappa, Eta Kappa Nu (One of Outstanding Young Elec. Engrs. 1966), Tau Beta Pi, Sigma Xi. Achievements include invention of noble gas ion laser; patents in field. Office: Calif Inst Tech Moore Bldg 136-93 Pasadena CA 91125-0001 E-mail: w6fa@caltech.edu.

BRIDGES, WILLIAM LLOYD, radiologist; b. Knightstown, Ind., Aug. 31, 1921; MD, Ind. U., 1944. Diplomate Am. Bd. Radiology. Intern Meml. Hosp., South Bend, Ind., 1945; pvt. practice Markleville, Ind., 1947-50; resident in Radiology Ind. U. Med. Ctr., Indpls., 1950-53; mem. staff Parkview Hosp., Ft. Wayne, Ind., 1953-95. Fellow Am. Col. Radiology; mem. AMA, Radiology Soc. North Am.

BRIDGEWATER, BERNARD ADOLPHUS, JR., retired footwear company executive, consultant; b. Tulsa, Mar. 13, 1934; s. Bernard Adolphus and Mary Alethea (Burton) B.; m. Barbara Paton, July 2, 1960; children: Barrie, Elizabeth, Bonnie. AB, Westminster Coll., Fulton, Mo., 1955; LLB, U. Okla., 1958; MBA, Harvard, 1964. Bar: Okla. 1958, U.S. Supreme Ct. 1958, U.S. Ct. of Claims 1958. Asst. county atty., Tulsa, 1962; assoc. McKinsey & Co., mgmt. cons., 1964-68, prin., 1968-72, dir., 1972-73, 75; assoc. dir. nat. security and internat. affairs Office Mgmt. and Budget, Exec. Office Pres., Washington, 1973-74; exec. v.p. Baxter Travenol Labs., Inc., Chgo. and Deerfield, Ill., 1975-79, dir., 1975-85; pres. Brown Group, Inc., Clayton, Mo., 1979-87, 90-99, CEO, 1982-99, chmn., 1985-99, also dir.; now ret.; cons. TIAA-CREF, N.Y.C. Bd. dirs. FMC Corp., Phila., FMC Techs., Inc., Chgo., Mitretek Sys., Inc., McLean, Va., ThoughtWorks Inc., Chgo.; adv. dir. Schroder Venture Ptnrs. LLC, N.Y.C.; cons. Office Mgmt. and Budget, 1973, 75; pvt. cons. Author: (with others) Better Management of Business Giving, 1965. Trustee Rush-Presbyn. St. Luke's Med. Ctr., 1974-84, Washington U., St. Louis, 1983-94, 95—, Barnes Hosp., St. Louis, 1987-90; bd. visitors Harvard U. Bus. Sch., 1987-93. Served to lt. USNR, 1958-62. Recipient Rayonier Found. award Harvard U., 1963; George F. Baker scholar, 1964 Mem. Beta Theta Pi, Omicron Delta Kappa, Phi Alpha Delta. Clubs: River (N.Y.C.); St. Louis Country, Log Cabin (St. Louis); Indian Hill Country (Winnetka, Ill.). Office: 7701 Forsyth Blvd Ste 1000 Saint Louis MO 63105-1841

BRIDGEWATER, ERLE HENRY, lawyer; b. Chauncey, Ohio, Mar. 27, 1919; BS, Ohio U., 1940; JD, Ohio State U., 1946. Bar: Ohio 1946. Ptnr. Bridgewater, Robe, Brooks & Keifer, and predecessors, Athens, Ohio, 1946—; mem. Bd. Commr. Grievances and Discipline Ohio Supreme Ct., 1968—74; dir. Athens Nat. Bank, 1976—81. Mem.: Order of Coif, Am. Judicature Soc., Am. Law Inst., Ohio Trial Lawyers Assn., Am. Trial Lawyers Assn., Athens County Bar Assn., Ohio Bar Assn. (exec. com. 1959—64), ABA, Am. Coll. Probate Counsel, Ohio Bar Found. (pres. 1963), Am. Bar Found. (fellow), Sheltering Arms Hosp. Found. (trustee 1973—76), Athens City Sch. Bd. (mem. 1958—62). Office: 14 W Washington St Athens OH 45701-2432

BRIDGEWATER, HERBERT JEREMIAH, JR., radio host; b. Atlanta, July 3, 1942; s. Herbert Bridgewater and Mary Sallie (Clark) Bridgewater-Hughes. BA, Clark Coll., Atlanta, 1968; postgrad., Atlanta U.; L.H.D., Faith Coll., 1978; LL.D., Heed U., 1978. Tchr. bus. edn. and English Atlanta Pub. Sch. System, 1964-67; relocation and family svcs. cons. Atlanta Housing Authority, 1967-70; columnist, writer Atlanta Daily World, 1968—, Lovely Atlanta; consumer protection specialist FTC, Atlanta, 1970-83; pres. Bridgewater's Personnel Service, 1971—; assoc. prof. bus. edn. and mass communication Clark Coll., instr., 1983-86, Atlanta Jr. Coll., 1986—, The Univ. System of Ga., 1986—; with reservations sales Delta Airline Inc., Atlanta, 1984—. Host radio program Enlightenment (WGKA-AM), 1975-79; host pub. affairs program Confrontation WZGC FM and WIGO AM, 1975-79, WYZE AM, 1979— ; TV talk show host Bridging the Gap Mem. Epilepsy Found. Am., Nat. Urban League, Big Bros. Council of Atlanta, Met. Boys Clubs of Atlanta, YMCA, NAACP; active So. Christian Leadership Conf., Ga. and nationwide civil rights movements; bd. dirs. Atlanta Dance Theater, Ralph C. Robinson Atlanta Boys Club, Proposition Theater Co., Am. Cancer Soc., Just-Us Theatre Task Force. Recipient Pres.'s award Clark Coll. United Negro Coll. Fund, 1960, 61, Best Citizens award Delta Sigma Theta, 1962, Humanitarian award Future Soc. Orgn., 1975, award Atlanta Dance Theatre, 1978-79, also; Met. Atlanta Boys Club; FTC Superior service medal, 1978; Bronner Bros. Nat. Beauticians Conv. Excellence in Communication award, 1978; named One of Most Outstanding Young Men in Am., Nat. Jr. C. of C., 1969, One of Most Eligible Bachelors in Am., 1970, One of 1,000 Successful Black Americans, 1973; both Ebony Mag.; One of 10 Outstanding Young People of Atlanta, 1977-78; One of 20 Most Progressive Young People in Atlanta, 1977; Herbert Bridgewater Day proclaimed in his honor Atlanta. Mem. Atlanta Jr. C. of C., Young Men on the Go, Clark Coll. Alumni Assn., Clark Coll. Assn., Heritage Valley Community Civic Orgn., Hungry Club Forum, Internat. Assn. for African Heritage and Black Identity (founding) Baptist (founder, chmn. bd. jr. deacons). Home: 2963 Duke Of Windsor East Point GA 30344-5606 Fax: 404 209-7287. *Any success which I may have achieved is attributed to my deeply rooted religious rearing which impels me to put God first in all my undertaking. Applying myself to the task with diligence, being prayerful in all my endeavors, and having a mother who is not only my backbone, but who has also stood steadfastly by my side, are the essential factors which I deem vital in my life's achievement.*

BRIDGEWATER, PAMELA E. ambassador; b. Fredericksburg, Va., Apr. 1947; BA in Polit. Sci., Va. State U., 1968, LLD (hon.), 1997; MA in Polit. Sci., U. Cin., 1970; postgrad., Am. U., 1976. Tchr. Voorhees Coll., Denmark, SC, Bowie (Md.) State U., Morgan State U., Balt.; vice-consul Dept. of State, Brussels, labor attache/polit. officer Kingston, Jamaica, polit. officer Pretoria, South Africa, 1990—93, consul gen. Durban, South Africa, 1993—96, dep. chief of mission Nassau, 1996—99, mem., pres. 42nd Sr. Seminar, 1999—2000, U.S. amb. to Benin, 2000—. Office: DOS Amb 2120 Cotonou Pl Washington DC 20521*

BRIDGFORTH, ROBERT MOORE, JR., aerospace engineer; b. Lexington, Miss., Oct. 21, 1918; s. Robert Moore and Theresa (Holder) B.; student Miss. State Coll., 1935-37; BS, Iowa State Coll., 1940; MS, MIT, 1948; postgrad. Harvard U., 1949; m. Florence Jarnberg, November 7, 1943; children: Robert Moore, Alice Theresa. Asst. engr. Standard Oil Co., of Ohio, 1940; teaching fellow M.I.T., 1940-41, instr. chemistry, 1941-43, research asst., 1943-44, mem. staff div. indsl. cooperation, 1944-47; asso. prof. physics and chemistry Emory and Henry Coll., 1949-51; rsch. engr. Boeing Airplane Co., Seattle, 1951-54, rsch. specialist 1954-55, sr. group engr., 1955-58, chief propulsion systems sect. Systems Mgmt. Office, 1958-59, chief propulsion rsch. unit, 1959-60; founder, chmn. bd. Rocket Rsch. Corp., 1960-69, Explosives Corp. Am., 1966-69. Fellow AIAA (assoc.), Brit. Interplanetary Soc., Am. Inst. Chemists; mem. AAAS, Am. Astronautical Soc. (dir.), Am. Chem. Soc., Am. Rocket Soc. (pres. Pacific NW 1955), Am. Ordnance Assn., Am. Inst. Physics, Am. Assn. Physics Tchrs., Tissue Culture Assn., Soc. for Leukocyte Biology, N.Y. Acad. Scis., Combustion Inst., Sigma Xi. Achievements include U.S. patents for rocket tri-propellants and explosives. Home: 4325 87th Ave SE Mercer Island WA 98040-4127

BRIDGMAN, G(EORGE) ROSS, lawyer; b. New Haven, Dec. 27, 1947; s. George Ross Bridgman and Betty Jean (Soderquist) Burrows; m. Patricia Hess; children: Taylor Wilson, Katharine June, Elizabeth Honey. BA cum laude, Yale U., 1970; JD, Northwestern U., 1973. Bar: Ohio 1973, U.S. Dist. Ct. (so. dist.) Ohio 1974, U.S. Dist. Ct. (no. dist.) Ohio 1976, U.S. Ct. Appeals (6th cir.) 1984, U.S. Supreme Ct. 1990. Assoc. Vorys, Sater, Seymour & Paese, Columbus, Ohio, 1973-80, ptnr., 1980—. Mem. editorial bd. Northwestern U. Law Rev., Chgo., 1972-73. Trustee Columbus Jr. Theatre of the Arts, 1976-80, pres., 1978-80; trustee, v.p. London (Ohio) Pub. Libr., 1979-84; bd. dirs. Ctrl. Ohio Regional Coun. on Alcoholism, Columbus, 1987-89; trustee Kidscope, Columbus, 1988-89, Recovery Alliance, Columbus, 1989-97, Ohio Parents for Drug-Free Youth, 1991-99; mem. exec. bd. Simon Kenton coun. Boy Scouts Am., 1996—; mem. Columbus Symphony Chorus, 1999—. Mem. ABA, Columbus Bar Assn., Ohio Bar Assn., Nat. Assn. Coll. and Univ. Attys., Capital Club, Columbus Country Club. Republican. Episcopalian. Office: Vorys Sater Seymour & Pease PO Box 1008 52 E Gay St Columbus OH 43215-3161 E-mail: grbridgman@vssp.com.

BRIDGMAN, MARY WOOD, lawyer; b. Jacksonville, Fla., Apr. 16, 1957; d. Joseph Gladstone and Clarice Annette (Thomas) W. BA with high honors, U. Fla., 1978, JD with honors, 1980. Bar: Fla. 1981, U.S. Dist. Ct. (no. and mid. dists.) Fla. 1981, U.S. Dist. Ct. (so. dist.) Fla. 1983, U.S. Ct. Appeals (11th cir.) 1982. Law clk. U.S. Dist. Ct. (mid. dist.) Fla., Jacksonville, 1981-82; assoc. Marks, Gray, Conroy & Gibbs P.A., Jacksonville, 1982-87; asst. gen. counsel Blue Cross & Blue Shield Fla., Inc., Jacksonville, 1987-93, v.p. for corp. compliance, 1994-99, v.p. audit and compliance, 1999—2002, v.p. corp. audit risk mgmt. and compliance, 2003—. Instr. bus. law Fla. C.C., Jacksonville, 1988-89. Mem. Hendricks Ave. Bapt. Ch., Jacksonville, 1981—, deacon, 1986—, chmn. diaconate, 1995-96, mem. coordinating coun., 1998-2001; mem. Willing Hands, Inc., Jacksonville, 1985; vol. Legal Aid, Inc., Jacksonville, 1982-95; bd. dirs. Theatre Jacksonville, Inc., 1987-88; nominated for Duval County Ct. Judge, 1991; mem. Leadership Jacksonville, 2002. Named one of Outstanding Young Women of Am., 1985. Mem. Fed. Bar Assn. (pres. Jacksonville chpt. 1986-87), Jacksonville Bar Assn. (bd. govs. young lawyers sect. 1988-93, pres. 1992; bd. govs. 1994-96; editor Jacksonville bar bull, 1993-94), Marjorie Kinnan Rawlings Soc. (charter), Heart of Jacksonville African Violet Soc., Order of Coif. Democrat. Baptist. Avocations: reading, african violets, entertaining, music. Office: Blue Cross Blue Shield Fla Inc 4800 Deerwood Campus Pkwy Jacksonville FL 32246-8273 E-mail: mary.bridgman@bcbsfl.com.

BRIDGMAN, SUSAN R. tax lawyer; b. Hamilton, Bermuda, Aug. 3, 1961; came to U.S., 1964; d. Matthew D. and Margaret A. Reddington; m. Charles J. Bridgman Jr., July 25, 1987; children: Rachael K., Emma C. BA in Italian, Ohio State U., 1984; JD cum laude, U. Dayton, Ohio, 1990. Bar: Ohio 1990. Corp. sales rep. Eastman Kodak Co., Dayton, 1984-87; jud. law clk. Montgomery County Ct. Common Pleas, Dayton, 1989-90; staff atty. 2d Dist. Ct. Appeals of Ohio, Dayton, 1990-93; tax atty. NCR Corp., Dayton, 1993-97, Chernesky, Heyman & Kress, PLL, Dayton, 1997—. Mem. ABA, Ohio State Bar Assn., Dayton Bar Assn. Avocations: physical fitness, cooking travel, reading. Office: Chernesky Heyman & Kress PLL 10 Courthouse Plz SW Ste 1100 Dayton OH 45402-1868 E-mail: Srb@chklaw.com.

BRIDGMAN, THOMAS FRANCIS, retired lawyer; b. Chgo., Dec. 30, 1933; s. Thomas Joseph and Angeline (Gorman) B.; m. Patricia A. McCormick, May 16, 1959; children: Thomas, Kathleen Ann, Ann Marie, Jane T., Molly. BS cum laude, John Carroll U., 1955; JD cum laude, Loyola U., Chgo., 1958. Bar: Ill. 1958, U.S. Dist. Ct. 1959. Assoc. McCarthy & Levin, Chgo., 1958, Baker & McKenzie, Chgo., 1958—96, ptnr., 1962—96. Trustee John Carroll U., 1982-88. Fellow Am. Coll. Trial Lawyers, Am. Bd. Trial Advs. (adv.), Internat. Acad. Trial Lawyers (past pres.), Union Club, Beverly Country Club (Chgo., pres. 1983). Democrat. Roman Catholic. Home: 9400 S Pleasant Ave Chicago IL 60620-5646 Office: Baker & McKenzie 1 Prudential Plaza 130 E Randolph St Ste 3700 Chicago IL 60601-6342

BRIDSTON, PAUL JOSEPH, strategic consultant; b. Grand Forks, N.D., May 28, 1928; s. Joseph and Anna (Pederson) B.; m. Peggy C. Cullen, Aug. 26, 1955; children: Peter, Rebecca, Sarah BA magna cum laude, Yale U., 1950; MBA, Stanford U., 1952. Sec.-treas. First Fed. Savs. & Loan Assn., Grand Forks, N.D., 1955-61, pres., 1962-81, chmn. bd., 1961-82; pres. J.B. Bridston Ins. Co., 1963-80. Chief Housing Guaranties Program Latin Am., AID, Washington, 1964-65; cons. U.S. Dept. State, 1968-70; asst. insp. gen. fgn. assistance, 1970; mem. N.D. Ho. Reps., 1972-74; cons. Bridston Co., 1990—; chmn. Pioneer Mortgage Co., 1980-84; vis. prof. mgmt. U. Okla., 1988-92. Pres. Grand Forks YMCA, 1959-60, GrandForks United Fund, 1961-62; bd. dirs. Tyrone Guthrie Theatre, Mpls., 1963-69, Boys Club Am., 1963-69; chmn. Martin County Atlantic-Pacific Housing, Inc., Fla., 1984-86. With USNR, 1952-55. Mem. Nat. Savs. and Loan League (bd. dirs. 1981), U.S. Savs. League (chmn. internat. devel. com. 1968-69), Yale U. Alumni Assn., Stanford Alumni Assn., Augusta Nat. Club. Lutheran. Home: 6843 Tall Pines Rd NE Bemidji MN 56601-7095

BRIDWELL, CAROLYN ELIZABETH, elementary school educator; b. N.Y.C., Oct. 8, 1969; d. John Dewey and Phyllis Carolyn Bridwell. BS in Elem. Edn., Kans. State U., 1992; MA in Curriculum and Instrn., U. Colo., Denver, 1998. Nat. bd. cert. tchr.-mid. childhood generalist Nat. Bd. for Profl. Tchg. Stds., lic. tchr. Colo., postgrad. profl. tchr. Va. Elem. tchr. Bennett (Colo.) Pub. Schs. 29J, 1994—2001, Loudoun County Pub. Schs., Sterling, Va., 2001—. Mem.: Pi Lambda Theta, Kappa Delta Phi. Home: 20308 Burnley Sq Sterling VA 20165-6454 Office: Lowes Island Elem 20755 White Water Dr Sterling VA 20165-2458 Personal E-mail: cebridwell@worldnet.att.net.

BRIEGER, GERT HENRY, medical historian, educator; b. Hamburg, Germany, Jan. 5, 1932; arrived in U.S., 1938, naturalized, 1943; s. Carl Helmuth and Ylse (Fuchs) Brieger; m. Katharine Crenshaw, July 2, 1955; children: Heidi E., William N., Benjamin C. AB, U. Calif., Berkeley, 1953; MPH, Harvard U., 1962; PhD, Johns Hopkins U., 1968. Intern UCLA Med. Ctr., 1957—58; asst. prof. history of medicine Johns Hopkins U. Sch. Medicine, Balt., 1966—70; assoc. prof. cmty. health scis., assoc. prof. history Duke U., Durham, NC, 1970—75; prof. history of health scis., chmn. dept. U. Calif., San Francisco, 1975—84; William H. Welch prof., dir. Inst. History of Medicine Johns Hopkins U., Balt., 1984—2001, chair dept. hist. sci. med. and tech., 1993—2001, disting. svc. prof., 2002—. Author (with A.M. Harvey, S.L. Abrams and V.A. McKusick): A Model of Its Kind, A Centennial History of Johns Hopkins Medicine, 1989; editor: Medical America in the Nineteenth Century, 1972, Theory and Practice in American Medicine, 1976; co-editor Bull. of the History of Medicine, 1990—. Served to capt. U.S. Army, 1958—61. Mem.: History of Sci., Am. Assn. History of Medicine (pres. 1980—82). Home: 10 E Lee St Baltimore MD 21202-6003 Office: Johns Hopkins U Welch Med Library Rm 320 1900 E Monument St Baltimore MD 21205-2167 E-mail: gbrieger@jhmi.edu.

BRIER, BONNIE SUSAN, lawyer; b. Oct. 19, 1950; d. Jerome W. and Barbara (Srenco) B.; m. Bruce A. Rosenfield, Aug. 15, 1976; children: Rebecca, Elizabeth, Benjamin. AB in Econs. magna cum laude, Cornell U., 1972; JD, Stanford U., 1976. Bar: Pa. 1976, U.S. Dist. Ct. (ea. dist.) Pa., U.S. Tax Ct., U.S. Ct. Appeals (3d cir.), U.S. Supreme Ct. Law clk. to chief judge U.S. Dist. Ct. Pa. (ea. dist.), Phila., 1976-77, asst. U.S. atty. criminal prosecutor, 1977-79; from assoc. to ptnr. Ballard, Spahr, Andrews & Ingersoll, Phila., 1979-90; gen. counsel Children's Hosp. of Phila., Phila., 1990—. Legal counsel Womens Way, 1979—2001; lectr. U. Pa., 1988-95; lectr., speaker various orgns. and seminars. Editor Stanford Law Rev., 1974-76; contbr. articles to profl. jours. Bd. dirs. U.S. Com. for UNICEF, 1994—2000, vice chmn., 1998-2000. Fellow Am. Coll. Tax Counsel; mem. ABA (exempt orgn. com. on tax sect., chair 1991-93, mem. health law sect.), Pa. Bar Assn. (tax sect., health law sect., mem. com. charitable orgn., children's rights), Phila. Bar Assn. (tax sect., health law sect., bd. dir. 1998—, chmn. 2002—), Am. Health Lawyers Assn. Home: 132 Fairview Rd Narberth PA 19072-1331 Office: Children's Hosp of Pa 34th St and Civic Ctr Blvd Philadelphia PA 19104

BRIER, ROBERT M, Egyptologist, educator, documentary presenter; b. New York, NY, Dec. 13, 1943; s. Louis and Clara David Brier; m. Patricia Mahoney Brier, Jan. 6, 1995; children: Elaine, Robin, Ian. PhD, Univ. NC, Chapel Hill, NC, 1970; BA, Hunter Coll., Bronx, NY, 1964. Manuscript editor Am. Inst. of Chem. Engr., New York, NY, 1963—66; rsch. fellow Inst. for Parapsychology, Durham, NC, 1966—70; prof. LI Univ., Greenvale, NY, 1971—. Presenter, TV documentaries The Learning Channel, Bethesda, Md., 1995—. Author: (book) The Murder of Tutankhamen, 1998, Egyptian Mummies, 1994, Ancient Egyptian Magic, 1981. Recipient David Newton Award, LI Univ./ Greenvale, NY, 1982; Salon De L'Egypt Award, Thalassic/ New York City, 2000, Trustees Award, LI Univ./ Greenvale, NY, 2002. Mem.: Pallopathology Assoc., Egypt Exploration Soc., Explorers Club. Avocation: long distance. Home: 4525 Henry Hudson Pkwy #110 Bronx NY 10471 Office: CW Post Coll Philosophy Dept Greenvale NY 11548

BRIERLEY, HAROLD M. advertising executive; Grad., Harvard U., 1968. Co-founder Epsilon Data Mgmt., pres., CEO; cons. Am. Airlines, 1980; v.p. sales and advt. Pan Am. World Airways; sr. v.p. mktg. Continental Airlines, 1983; founder Targeted Marketing Systems, Inc., 1985; founder, chmn. bd. Brierley & Ptnrs., Dallas, 1987. Office: Brierley & Ptnrs 8401 N Central Expressway, Ste 1000 Dallas TX 75202

BRIERLEY, JAMES ALAN, biohydrometallurgy consultant; b. Denver, Dec. 22, 1938; s. Everette and Carrie (Berg) B.; m. Corale Louise Beer, Dec. 21, 1965 BS in Bacteriology, Colo. State U., 1961; MS in Microbiology, Mont. State U., 1963, PhD, 1966. Research scientist Martin Marietta Corp., Denver, 1968-69; asst. prof. biology N.Mex. Inst. Mining and Tech., Socorro, 1966-68, from asst. prof. to prof. biology, chmn. dept. biology, 1969 83; research dir. Advanced Mineral Techs., Golden, Colo., 1983-88; chief microbiologist Newmont Metall. Svcs., Englewood, Colo., 1988-2000; chief rsch. scientist biohydrometallurgy Newmont Mining Corp., 2000-01; cons. Brierley Consultancy, LLC, Highlands Ranch, Colo., 2001—. Vis. fellow U. Warwick, Coventry, Eng., 1976, vis. prof. Catholic U., Santiago, Chile, 1983; adj. prof. dept. metallurgy U. Utah, 1994-96; cons. Mountain State Mineral Enterprises, Tucson, 1980, Sandia Nat. Lab., Albuquerque, 1976, Bechtel Civil and Minerals, Scottsdale, Ariz., 1984. Contbr. numerous articles to profl. jours.; patentee in field. Served to staff sgt. Air N.G., 1956-61. Recipient Wadsorth Extractive Metall. award, Soc. Mining, Metall. & Exploration, 2000, Honor Alumnus award, Colo. State U., 2001; grantee 32 rsch. grants. Fellow: AAAS; mem.: Nat. Acad. Engring., Mining & metall. Soc. Am., Soc. Gen. Microbiology, Am. Soc. Microbiology. Avocations: travel, model railroading, gardening. Home: 2074 East Terrace Dr Highlands Ranch CO 80126-2692 Office: Brierley Consultancy PO Box 260012 Highlands Ranch CO 80163-0012 E-mail: j.brierley@worldnet.att.net.

BRIERLEY, PETER WILLIAM, charitable foundation administrator; b. London, Oct. 30, 1938; s. Joseph Clifford and Anne Sophia (New) B.; m. Cherry Antoinette Goatman, Apr. 3, 1965; children: Stephen, Timothy, Kim, Michael. BSc in Stats., U. London, 1961, diploma in theology, 1964, DLitt, Greenwich U., 1996. Actuarial clk. Prudential Ins. Co., 1957-58; sr. sci. officer War Office, London, 1961-62; tchr. Edn. Authority, Southampton, Eng., 1965-67; statistician Ministry of Def., London, 1967-70, Cabinet Office, London, 1970-78; program dir. Brit. Fgn. Bible Soc., London, 1978-83; European dir. MARC Europe, London, 1983-93; exec. dir. Christian Rsch. Assn., 1993—. Chmn. S.E. Asian Outreach, Gravesend, Eng., 1985-92, vice chmn. 1992-97; mem. fin. com. Evang. Union S.Am., London, 1970-82, Eng. and Wales aux. Leprosy Mission, London, 1970-76, Brit. Inst. Mgmt. Coun., 1985-91, mgmt. com. Evang. Missionary Alliance, 1983-89, 90-99, vice chmn., 1989, exec. com., 1985-89, 90-99; chair Blyth Wood Park Mgmt. Co., 1993—; chmn. Blyth Wood Park Prop. Co., 1993—. Author: Mission to London Phase I, II, 1984, 95; editor: U.K. Christian Handbook, 1973, 76, 77, 78, 81, 82, 84, 86, 88, 91, 93, 95, 97, 99, Beyond the Churches, 1984, World Churches Handbook, 1997, UKCH: Religious Trends, 1997, 99, 2001, 03, Future Church, 1998; compiler: Vision Bldg., 1989, Christian England, 1991, Act on the Facts, 1992, Priorities, Planning and Paperwork, 1992, Reaching and Keeping Teenagers, 1993, Prospects for the Eighties vol 1, 1980, vol. 2, 1983, Prospects for Wales, 1983, Prospects for Scotland, 1985, Prospects for Scotland 2000, 1995, The Tide is Running Out, 2000, Steps to the Future, 2000,Reaching and Keeping Tweenagers, 2003, Turning the Tide, 2003, several MARC monographs, 1984-93, Leaders Briefings, 1994—; cons. editor Strategies for Growing Churches mag., 1990—. Mem. Doughty St. Internat. Students Centre Mgmt. Com., 1971-85, treas. 1973-81; mem. gen. and exec. coms. Brit. & Fgn. Bible Soc., 1976-78, staff mem., 1978-83; rsch. assoc. Lausanne Com. for World Evangelisation, Europe, 1984-92, sr. assoc. for rsch., 1992—, mem. adminstrn. com., 1996—; first gov. Bullers Wood Comprehensive Sch. for Girls, 1989-94; dir. mission Christ Ch., 1994-97; mem. Efang. Alliance Coun., 1994-2000. EUSA Fin. sub-com., 1971-82, Doughty Street Internat. Students Ctr. Mgmt. Com., mem. Inst. Charity and Fundraising Mgrs. (steering com. 1982-83), Royal Statis. Soc. (social sect. 1980-82), Social Research Assn. (exec. com. 1979-82), Christian Booksellers Assn. (bd. dirs. 1984-88), Spinnaker Trust (coun. of reference 1987—) Crusaders (adv. coun. 1995-99, patron Inn Christian 1990—, coun. reference Monarch Pubs. 1992-99, coun. reference Outlook 1991—), Market Rsch. Soc., Brit. Ch. Growth Assn. (gen. and exec. coun. 1994—), Assn. Rsch. Ctrs. in Social Scis. (mem. exec. com. 1998-2001, treas. 2000-01). Mem. Anglican. Avocations: reading, making math models, collecting postmarks and stamps, church activities. Home: 37 Blyth Wood Park Bromley Kent BR1 3TN England Office: Christian Rsch/Vision Bldg 4 Footscray Rd Eltham London SE9 2TZ England E-mail: admin@christian-research.org.uk.

BRIERRE, MAUD, French and Spanish educator; b. Haiti; BSN, Universidad de Antioquia, Medellin, Colombia; PhD, U. Calif., Irvine. Prof. French and Spanish Saddleback Coll., Mission Viejo, Calif., 1982—. Author: (book of poetry) Signpost for Your Road, 1997, Un Bout de Chemin, 2003; contbr. Recipient Excellence in Poetry award, Internat. Soc. Poets, 2001, Saddleback Valley award, 1986, Woman of Achievement award, Dawn Mag., 1985. Office: Saddleback College 28000 Marquerite Pkwy Mission Viejo CA 92692-3635

BRIERRE, MICHELINE, artist; b. Jeremie, Haiti; d. Luc Brierre and Simone Lataillaide; m. Charles Lopez (div.); children: Liza Lopez Camus, Charles Lopez; m. Barry Kaplan. Studied with, Mr. Ramponeau, Haiti, 1951-53; student, Academie Nehemie Jean, Haiti, 1958-60, Miraflores Art Ctr., Peru. Author: I am Eve, 1980, Spanish translation, 1980; solo show Commonwheel, Manitou Springs, Colo., 1995; exhibited in group shows at Galerie Hotel Rancho, Haiti, 1961, Galerie Brochette, Haiti, 1962, Onze Femmes peintres, Haiti, 1963, Galerie Brochette, Haiti, 1964, Brierre/Castera, Haiti, 1965, Musee d'Art, Haiti, 1980, Galeria 70, Bogota, Colombia, S. Am., 1980, Galeria San Diego, Colombia, 1980, Woman's Way, Miami, Fla., 1982, Un Regard Soleil, Port-au-Prince, Haiti, 1983, Reflection On The Past, Aureus, Miami, 1983, Un Mundo Para Compartir, Lima, Peru, 1983, Festival Arts Gallery, Port-au-Prince, 1984, An Evening With The Artists, Naples, Fla., 1986, 87, Art in Jewelry, Island House, Bayside, Fla., 1987, Mixed Media Studio Show, Miami, 1989, 91, Collective Show, Commonwheel, Manitou Spings, Colo., 1994, Douglas County Art Ctr., Roby Mills Gallery and Bus. of Art Ctr., 1995. Mem. Fine Arts Ctr. Colo. Springs, Bus. of Art Ctr., Commonwheel Co-op. Home: All Things Beautiful 8050 Woody Creek Dr Colorado Springs CO 80911-8332 E-mail: michelinbrierre@earthlink.net.

BRIERTON, CHERYL LYNN, lawyer; b. Hartford, Conn., Nov. 11, 1947; d. Charles Greenwood and Elizabeth (Grechko) Wootton; m. David Martin Black, Oct. 12, 1968 (div. 1978); m. John Thomas Brierton, Sept. 6, 1982 (div. 1988); 1 child, John Greenwood. BA, Wellesley Coll., 1969, JD, U. San Diego, 1982. Bar: Calif. 1983. Tchr., libr. Anglican High Sch., Grenada, West Indies, 1972-74; dep. dir. Transalpino Student Travel, Paris, 1975-76; asst. dir. adminstrn. Project OZ, YMCA, San Diego, 1976-78; asst. coord. policy and advocacy Community Congress San Diego, 1978-81; field dir. Calif. Child, Youth and Family Coalition, San Diego, 1981-83; asst. exec. dir. Community Congress San Diego, 1984-85; exec. dir. Calif. Child, Youth and Family Coalition, Sacramento, 1985-86; gen. atty. Def. Logistics Agy., Def. Depot Tracy, Calif., 1986-88; atty.-advisor Dept. of the Navy, Mare Island Naval Shipyard, Vallejo, 1988-89; staff atty. San Diego Superior Ct., 1989—. Mem. faculty Nat. Juvenile Judges Conf. Dispositional Alternatives Serious Offenders, 1982, 6th and 7th Nat. Confs. Juvenile Justice, 1979-80; cons. San Diego Youth Involvement Project, 1983-84, San Diego Youth and Community Svcs., 1983-84, South Bay Community Svcs., Chula Vista, 1983. Mem. Juvenile Justice Commn., Golden Hill Neighborhood Justice Cen. Planning Bd.; mem. com. jud. process Regional Criminal Justice Planning Bd. Scholar U. San Diego 1979. Mem. MENSA. Avocations: yachting, travel. Home: 1329 Bancroft St San Diego CA 92102-2429

BRIESE, MICHAEL W. writer; b. Washington, D.C., Nov. 15, 1956; s. Marion L. and Frances G. Briese. BA, U. Scranton, 1980. Cert. housing counselor via Md. Ctr. for Cmty. Devel., 2000. Ind. living specialist, Silver Spring, Md., 2000—. Author: 101 Poems to Live By, 1998, St. Paul-Disciple, Teacher, Servant of Christ, 1998, CHARISMATA, 2002. Vol. Shepherd's Table, Silver Spring, 1997—; mem. Archdiocese of Washington, D.C., 1999—. Mem.: K.C. Democrat. Roman Catholic. Achievements include patents in field of entomology. Avocations: reading, writing, walking. Home: PO Box 8242 Silver Spring MD 20907-8242

BRIGALDINO, GLENN, social scientist, consultant; b. Regina, Sask., Can., Oct. 19, 1958; s. Klaus Brigaldino and Gisela (Eicher) Bastian; m. Bayush Worku Woldegiorgis, Aug. 12, 1991; children: Jens Worku, Melcamm Worku, Samrawit Worku. MSc in Social Scis., U. Duisburg, Germany, 1986; cert., U. London, 1996, U. Wis., 1996, 98. UN officer UN High Commn. for Refugees, 1988-93; program officer European Ctr. Devel. Policy Mgmt., Maastricht, Netherlands, 1993-96; mgr., owner Glenn Brigaldino Cons., Maastricht, 1996-

2000; cons. to Can. non-govtl. orgns. and agys. and UN, 2000—02; rep. APK Cons, South Africa, 1999—; owner GB-BASE, Ottawa, Canada, 2000—. Bus. ptnr. Shegaw Engring, Addis Ababa, Ethiopia; assoc. TKR Cons., Ottawa. Co-editor: EPO-internet, 1998—; contbr., articles to profl. jours. Mem.: Can. E-Authors, Red R (Registered Engineers for disaster relief). Address: 790 Springland Dr Ste 227 Ottawa ON Ontario Canada K1V 6L7 E-mail: gb-base@2wallet.com.

BRIGANCE, MARCELENA, critical care nurse; b. Mobile, Ala., Sept. 16, 1941; d. Maurice Jr. and Dorothy (Bell) B.; children: Monica Renee Burch, Alana Jeanne Burch. Student, Samford U., 1959-60, 61-62; BSN, U. Wash., 1975; postgrad., U. South Ala., 2000—. RN, Ala.; CEN; cert. ACLS instr. Staff nurse surg. ICU, med. ICU, CCU Harborview Med. Ctr., Seattle, 1975-77; staff nurse, supr. oral surg. U. Wash., Seattle, 1979-81; staff nurse emergency room, mobile intensive care nurse Sequoia Hosp., Redwood City, Calif., 1983-87; staff nurse emergency dept. Springhill Meml. Hosp., Mobile, Ala., 1987-91; staff nurse emergency rm. Thomas Hosp., Mobile, 1992-93; PRN emergency nurse Providence and Knollwood Emergency Rm., Mobile, 1992-95; emergency rm. nurse Springhill Hosp., 1992-95, Knollwood Park Hosp., 1995—. Office: Knollwood Emergency Rm 5600 Girby Rd Mobile AL 36693

BRIGEOIS, EVELYNE BRIGITTE, artist, publisher; b. Troyes, Aube, France, Feb. 18, 1946; came to U.S., 1984. Student, B.E.P.C., Aix-en-Othe, France, 1961. Trilingual exec. sec., Eng., France, Germany, Spain, 1965-79; owner, mgr. Brigeois Pub., Vallejo, Calif., 1987—. Spkr. in field. One-woman shows include Lawrence Gallery, Portland, Oreg., 1984, Scott Gallery, Orinda, Calif., 1985, Leslie Levy Gallery, Scottsdale, Ariz., 1986, 89, Charleston Heights Art Ctr., Las Vegas, Nev., 1987, Horvath Gallery, Sacramento, 1993 ; exhibited in group shows at Transco Gallery, Houston, 1988; contbr. articles to profl. jours. Recipient numerous awards, including Robert Wiegand Meml. award La. Watercolor Soc., 1985, award Detroit Inst. Arts Drawing and Print Club, 1985, award of honor Birmingham Mus. Art, 1986, lst place award Assoc. Artists Southport, N.C., 1986. Mem. Nat. Watercolor Soc. (Helen Wurdeman award 1985), Ala. Watercolor Soc. E-mail: brigeoisfineart@fiberpipe.net., ebrigeois@fiberpipe.net.

BRIGGLE, GARY LEE, singer, actor, director, educator; b. Moorhead, Minn., Oct. 31, 1953; s. Leland Wilson and Harriet Maxine (Dickerson) B.; m. Christine Helen Maloney, Dec. 10, 1977 (div. Apr. 1982); life ptnr. Wendy Lehr, Feb. 14, 1983. MusB, St. Olaf Coll., Northfield, Minn., 1975. Resident artist Minn. Opera Co., Mpls., 1977-82, Children's Theater Co. & Sch., Mpls., 1979-82; artistic assoc. Seaside Music Theater, Daytona Beach, Fla., 1979—, Ariz. Theater Co., Tuscon, Phoenix, 1991-94, LYRIC Opera Cleve., 1984-98, artistic dir., 1995-98. Guest dir. Nat. Theater of Hungary, 1999, Boston U., 1998-99, Valparaiso Univ., 1998, Baldwin-Wallace Conservatory, 1999, St Olaf Coll., 2000. Recipient Carbonell award S. Fla. Critics Assn., 1983; Irene Ryan scholar Am. Coll. Theater Festival, 1975. Avocations: aquatics, painting, drawing, hiking, camping. E-mail: arlecchino@juno.com.

BRIGGS, ALAN LEONARD, lawyer; b. Dayton, Ohio, Oct. 1, 1942; s. Donald M. and Helen (Barker) B.; m. Linda Ann Dobie, Sept. 10, 1966 (div. 1991); children: Jason, Aimee, Anna; m. Christine M. McCormick, 1991; 1 child, Caitlin. AB, Miami U., Oxford, Ohio, 1964; JD, Ohio State U., 1967; LLM in Patent/Intellectual Property Law, George Washington U., 1998. Bar: Ohio 1967, Calif. 1970, Fla. 1989, D.C. 1995, Va. 1995, Md. 1995. Ptnr. Murphey, Young & Smith, Columbus, Ohio, 1970-88, Squire, Sanders & Dempsey, Columbus, 1988-91, Miami, Fla., 1991-94, Washington, 1994—. Trustee Legal Aid Soc. Fellow Am. Coll. Trial Lawyers; mem. ABA, Ohio State Bar Assn. (coun. of dels. 1980-86, chmn. screening com. coun. dels. 1983-84, sect. litigation bd. govs. 1986-90), Columbus Bar Assn. (pres. 1985, chmn. litigation practice inst. 1987-90), Am. Arbitration Assn. Office: Squire Sanders & Dempsey 1201 Pennsylvania Ave NW Washington DC 20004-2491

BRIGGS, BARBARA JEAN HOLMES, real estate developer; b. Toronto, Ont., Can., Apr. 29, 1948; d. Campbell Carlisle and Phyllis (Saunders) H.; m. Thomas L. Briggs, Feb. 8, 1997; 1 child, Bizia Catal. BA, U. Western Ont., London, 1970. Real estate saleswoman, Menorca, Spain, 1972-74; owner Essential Alts., Rutland, 1978-83. Developer East Creek Ctr., 1986-99; v.p. Hedgedale Enterprises, Inc., Toronto; franchise owner Taco Bell, 1991-2002, Residential Renovations, Santa Fe, 1992—. Founder, dir. East Creek Playhouse, Rutland, 1986-87; bd. dirs. Vt. Indsl. Devel. Authority, Montpelier, 1986-92. Mem. Back Country Horsemen (Santa Fe chpt.), Las Jardineras Garden Club. Avocations: sailing, skiing, scuba diving, traveling. Office: BJ BRIGGS LLC PO Box 248 Cerrillos NM 87010-

BRIGGS, CYNTHIA ANNE, educational administrator, clinical psychologist; b. Berea, Ohio, Nov. 9, 1950; d. William Benajah and Lorraine (Hood) B.; m. Thomas Joseph O'Brien, Nov. 28, 1986; children: Julia Maureen, William Thomas. B Music Edn., U. Kans., 1973; MusM, U. Miami, 1976; D. Psychology, Hahnemann U., 1988. Lic. psychology, Mo.; bd. cert. music therapist. Music therapist Parsons (Kans.) State Hosp., 1973-74; grad. asst. U. Miami, Coral Gables, Fla., 1974-76; asst. prof., dir. Hahnemann U., Phila., 1976-85, asst. prof., 1985-91; psychology resident Assocs. in Psychol. and Human Resources, Phila., 1988-91; clin. dir. Child Ctr. of Our Lady, St. Louis, 1991—; adj. faculty Lindenwood U., 2000—. Mem. editl. bd. Jour. Music Therapy, 1997-2001; adj. faculty LIndenwood U., 2000—; contbr. chpts. to books, articles to profl. jours. Mem. Am. Assn. Music Therapy (pres. 1987-89), Nat. Coalition Arts Therapies Assns. (chair 1991-93). Democrat. Avocations: cooking, piano, music, theatre. Office: Child Ctr of Our Lady 7900 Natural Bridge Rd Saint Louis MO 63121-4628

BRIGGS, DOUGLAS D. communications executive; Pres. QVC, West Chester, Pa., 1995—. Office: QVC 1200 Wilson Dr West Chester PA 19380-4262

BRIGGS, EDWARD SAMUEL, naval officer; b. St. Paul, Oct. 4, 1926; s. Charles William and Lois Ione (Johnson) B.; m. Nanette Parks, June 7, 1949; 1 child, Jeffrey Charles. BS, U.S. Naval Acad., 1949. Commd. ensign U.S. Navy, 1949, advanced through grades to vice adm., 1980; commanding officer USS Turner Joy, USS Jouett; asst. chief of staff plans, chief of staff U.S. 7th Fleet, 1972-73; fleet ops. officer, asst. chief staff ops. U.S. Pacific Fleet, Makalapa, Hawaii, 1973-75; comdr. Crusier-Destroyer Group 3, San Diego, 1975-77, Navy Recruiting Command, Arlington, Va., 1977-79, Naval Logistics Command, U.S. Pacific Fleet, Naval Base, Pearl Harbor, Hawaii, 1979-80; dep. comdr.-in-chief U.S. Pacific Fleet, Pearl Harbor, 1980-82; comdr. Naval Surface Force U.S. Atlantic Fleet, 1982-84; ret., 1984. Decorated Bronze Star with combat device and one star, Air medals (2), Navy Commendation medal with combat device and two stars, Legion of Merit with combat device and four stars, D.S.M.; Vietnamese Navy Gallantry medal. Mem. Surface Navy Assn., U.S. Naval Acad. Alumni Assn., Naval Inst., Navy League. Home: 3648 Lago Sereno Escondido CA 92029-7902 *Dedication to our nation and devotion to its ideals are the responsibilities of citizenship.*

BRIGGS, ETHEL D. federal agency administrator; BA, N.C. Ctrl. U.; M in Counseling, U. N.C. Dir. adult svcs. Nat. Coun. on Disability, Washington, 1985—, dep. dir., acting exec. dir., exec. dir. Named One of Top 100 African-Am. Bus. and Profl. Women, Dollars and Sense Mag., 1989. Office: Nat Coun on Disability 1331 F St NW Ste 1050 Washington DC 20004-1138

BRIGGS, FERGUS PAUL, retired military officer, federal government official; b. Pocatello, Idaho, Aug. 2, 1949; s. Fergus and Shirley Briggs; m. Gina Marie Briggs. BA, Idaho State U., 1972, cert. secondary edn., 1982; MA, Naval War Coll., 1996. Commd. 2d lt. USMC, 1972, advanced through grades to col., 1995; exec. officer Res. Support Unit, Camp Pendleton, Calif., 1988-91; plans officer, dep. asst. chief of staff G-3 4th Marine Divsn. (reinforced), New Orleans, Va., 1991-92; ops. officer Marine Forces Res. Hdqs., New Orleans, 1992-94, asst. chief of staff plans, 1994-95; dep. dir. Coll. Continuing Edn. Marine Corps U., Quantico, Va., 1996-99; br. head pers. plans and policy Hdqs. USMC (Res. Affairs), Quantico, 1999-2000; dep. dir. readiness Office of Asst. Sec. Def., Washington, 2000—02; ret., 2002. Air def. control officer USMC, various locations, 1972-85; tng. programs officer Hdqs. USMC, Washington, 1985-87. Marine Corps rep. Fallbrook (Calif.) C. of C., 1989-91; mem. U.S. Mil. Pentathlon Team, 1980, 81, 83, 84. Decorated Legion of Merit (2), 1999, 2000, Meritorious Svc. medal (2), 1991, 96, Def. Superior Svc. medal, 2002. Mem. Res. Officers Assn., Marine Corps Assn., Marine Corps Res. Officers Assn. Avocations: running, cycling, skiing, reading. Home: 7213 Regent Dr Alexandria VA 22307

BRIGGS, FRANKLIN HENRY, retired naval officer; b. Council Bluffs, Iowa, Mar. 7, 1933; s. Edwin Charles Briggs and Anna Maud Brandt; m. Chizuko Imaoka, Aug. 28, 1960. Student, U. Colo., 1951; BA, U. Nebr., 1955. Commd. ensign USN, 1955, advanced through grades to capt., 1976; deck and gunnery USS Essex (CVA-9), San Diego, 1955-58; asst. plans officer Comdr. Naval Forces, Yokosuka, Japan, 1958-61; ops. officer USS Paul Revere (APA-248), San Diego, 1961-63; CIC instr. Anti-Air Warfare Def. Ctr., Dams Neck, Va., 1963-66; ship employment officer Amphibious Force, Pacific, Subic Bay, Philippines, 1966-68; comdg. officer Naval Res. Ctr., Scotia, NY, 1968-70; exec. officer USS Anchorage, San Diego, 1970-72; manpower dir. Comdr. 6th Naval Dist., San Diego, 1970-72; dep. comdr. Naval Res. Readiness Command, Washington, 1974-78; Comdr. Cleve. Readiness Command, 1978—79. Decorated Vietnam Campaign medal with 10 stars, Navy Commendation medal with Combat V, Gold star, Cross of Gallantry, Expeditionary medal, Quemay-Matsu. Mem. Ikenobo Internat. mem. the Dicken's Fellowship Conservative. Avocations: reading, history, travel, opera. Home: 890 Buen Tiempo Dr Chula Vista CA 91910-6555

BRIGGS, HENRY PAYSON, JR., headmaster; b. Boston, Apr. 14, 1932; s. Henry Payson Sr. and Eleanor Temple (Smith) B.; m. Charlin Shoenberger Devanney, Nov. 28, 1987; children from previous marriage: Payson Stewart, Heather Kavanagh. BA, Harvard U., 1954, MAT, 1959. Dir. admissions and fin. aid Harvard U., Cambridge, Mass., 1956-66; headmaster Western Res. Acad., Hudson, Ohio, 1966-76, Seven Hills Sch., Cin., 1976—95; interim head St. James' Sch., L.A., 1995—96; dir. major gifts Cin. Opera, 1996-99; interim head The Potomac Sch., McLean, Va., 1999-2000, The Norfolk (Va.) Acad., 2000-01, The Ft. Worth CDS, 2001—02, St. Timothy's Sch., Balt., 2002—. Steering com. Leadership Cin., 1990—; bd. dirs. Queen City Found.; vestryman, warden, mem. com. Christ Episcopal Ch. Cathedral, Cin., 1977—. 1st lt. U.S. Army, 1954-56. Mem. Headmasters Assn. (officer), Country Day Sch. Headmasters Assn.(v.p.), Literary Club, Univ. Club, Tennis Club Cin. (pres.), Williams Club (N.Y.C.). Avocations: education, sports, outdoors, politics. Home: 7937 Bar Harbor Dr Cincinnati OH 45255-4430

BRIGGS, JAMES HENRY, II, engineering administrator; b. San Francisco, Dec. 25, 1953; s. major James Henry(USMC, retired.) and Barbara (Cordes) S.; m. Niwana Alice Page, Sept. 1, 1979; children: Melanie Shannon, James Henry III, Angelica Robin. AA in Bus. Adminstrn., Albany (Ga.) Jr. Coll., 1976; BS in Computer Sci., U. N.C., Wilmington, 1979; BSEE, So. Tech., Marietta, Ga., 1985. Lic. 1st class radio telephone; registered profl. engr. Chief engr. WECT-TV, Wilmington, 1978-82; maintenance supr. Cable News Network, Atlanta, 1982-85; mgr. engring. ops. KCOP-TV, LA, 1985-87; sr. product support engr. Abekas Video Systems, Redwood City, Calif., 1987-92; dir. engring. D.T.S., Union City, Calif., 1992—97; chief engr. Sta. CSUH-TV Calif. State U., Hayward, 1997—99. Design engr. Stage Front Presentation Sys., Savannah, Ga., 1999—, CEO Charis Constrn. Co., Savannah, 2001-. Editor: Video Prodn. in the 90's. Mem. Soc. Motion Picture and TV Engr., Soc. Broadcast Engr., Greenpeace, Toastmasters Club, Lions. Avocations: biking, model trains, music, camping, sailing, travel.

BRIGGS, JANET MARIE LOUISE, nurse practitioner; b. Pitts, June 11, 1951; RN, Ohio; cert. adult nurse practitioner. Staff nurse neonatal ICU Univ. Hosp. Cleve., 1972-73; staff nurse gen pediat. Mt. Sinai Hosp. Cleve., 1973-76; head nurse health svc. Mt. Sinai Med. Ctr., Cleve., 1976-82; grad. rsch. asst. Case Western Res. U., Cleve., 1983-84; dir. nursing Ashtabula County Health Dept., Jefferson, Ohio, 1984-85; staff nurse, dir. nursing in svc., coord., clin. nurse specialist, coord. infection control Meml. Hosp. Geneva, Ohio, 1985-87; nurse practitioner, unit mgr. Parkside Health Mgmt. Corp., Toledo, 1986-87; nurse practitioner ambulatory surgery. Met. Gen. Hosp., Cleve., 1987; nurse practitioner domiciliary homeless program VA Med. Ctr., Cleve., 1987-91, clin. nurse specialist, nurse practioner AIDS team, 1991—; dir., prin. investigator No. Ohio AIDS Edn. and Tng. Ctr., 2000—. Project dir., chmn. Child and Family Health Svc. Grant, Ashtabula County, Ohio, 1984-85; cons. case mgmt. head injuries subcom. Gov.'s Task Force, Ohio, 1988; nurse practitioner Free Clinic, Cleve., 1988—; mem. ethics com. VA Med. Ctr., 1989—; adj. clin. faculty Kent. State U., 1993—; clin. faculty Frances Payne Bolton Sch. Nursing Case Western Reserve U.; investigator multiple clinically based AIDS rsch. projects; dir., prin. investigator No. Ohio AIDS Edn. and Tng. Ctr., 1999—2002; co-prin./responsible investigator Optima Tri-Nat. Clin. Trials, Cleve. Contbr. chpts. to books and articles to profl. jour. Lectr., group leader Hitchcock House, Cleve., 1981-83. Recipient Fed. Exec. Bd. award, 1995, Hearts and Hands award, Sec. Vet. Affairs, 1995, Most Treasured Vol. award for 1996 Fedn. for Cmty. Planning of Greater Cleve., 1997; grantee Fed. Facility Based HIV/AIDS Edn. Demonstration, 1991, Fed. Facility HIV/AIDS Edn. Rsch., 1992, 93, Dept. Vet. Affairs, Ohio HIV/AIDS svc. award, profl. categorym, 2003. Mem. Frances Payne Bolton Sch. Nursing Alumni Assn. (bd. dir., pres. 2001—), Sigma Theta Tau. Roman Catholic. Avocations: bicycling, reading, photography, classical music, motorcycling. E-mail: rnjan@earthlink.net.

BRIGGS, JOHN MANCEL, III, lawyer; b. Muskegon, Mich., May 24, 1942; s. John M. Jr. and Margaret Jane (Wren) B.; m. Janice R. Dykema, May 20, 1967; children: Jennifer Anne, Jill Margaret. BS, U. Mich., 1964, JD, 1967. Bar: Mich. 1968, U.S. Dist. Ct. (we. dist.) Mich. 1968, U.S. Ct. Appeals (6th cir.) 1974, U.S. Supreme Ct. 2000. Assoc. Parmenter, Forsythe, Rude, Van Epps, Briggs & Fauri and predecessors, Muskegon, 1967-70, ptnr., 1970-92; shareholder Parmenter O'Toole, Muskegon, Mich., 1992—. Active Muskegon United Appeal, 1968-73; bd. dirs. Big Bros., Muskegon, 1969-74; bd. dirs. Y Family Christian Assn., 1970-80, 81-83, 1st v.p., 1973-76, pres., 1977-78; bd. dirs. Muskegon-Oceana Legal Aid Soc., 1970-73, pres., 1972-73; bd. dirs. Berean Ch., 1985-86, 88-90, 93-94, 99-2001, sec., 1988-90, v.p., 1993, pres., 1994, 99, 2000. With USAR, 1967-73. Recipient Disting. Svc. award Muskegon Jaycees, 1977. Fellow Mich. State Bar Assn.; mem. ABA, Muskegon County Bar Assn. (sec. 1970-71, v.p. 1974-75, pres. 1975-76), Rotary (bd. dirs. 1981-85, pres.-elect 1982-83, pres. 1983-84, Presdl. Citation). Republican. Office: Parmenter O'Toole PO Box 786 175 W Apple Ave Muskegon MI 49443-0786

BRIGGS, JOSEPH JAY, communications engineer; b. Wilson, N.C., July 14, 1968; s. J. T. Briggs and Helen Grace Stallings; m. Jamie Kaye Whitfield, Feb. 7, 1965; 1 child, Kennedy. BA in Bus. Mgmt., N.C. State U., 1990; MBA, Campbell U., 1997. Cisco network engr. AT&T, Durham, NC, 1999—2000; Cisco engr. Sprint, Raleight, NC, 2000—01; network engr. 4 Front Sys., Inc., Morrisville, NC, 2002—. Author: (book) Emerge and See the State of Emergency, 2002; contbr. poetry to anthologies. Mem.: Nat. Black MBA Assn. (treas. 1998—99). Democrat. Avocations: jogging, bicycling, reading. Home: 110 White Bloom Ln Morrisville NC 27560

BRIGGS, LESLIE RAY, retired mechanical engineer; b. Knoxville, Iowa, Dec. 18, 1944; s. Raymond Edward and Doris Geraldine Briggs; m. m. Donna Lou Van Dyke, July 1, 1967 (div. July 1990); children: Douglas William, Rebecca Lynn; m. Janis A. Vezzoso, Dec. 27, 1990. AS in Mech. Tech., Iowa State Tech. Inst., Ames, 1966; BSME cum laude, U. Evansville, 1986. Registered profl. engr., Iowa. Engring asst. Alcoa, Davenport, Iowa, 1966-79, tech. asst. Newburgh, Ind., 1979-85, tech. specialist, 1985-86, mech. engr., 1986-93, sr. mech. engr., 1993-96; ret. Mem. NSPE, Phi Beta Chi. Lodges: Masons. Republican. Roman Catholic. Avocation: classic automobiles. Home: PO Box 348 Waveland MS 39576-0348 E-mail: lesandjanis@msn.com.

BRIGGS, MARTHA WREN, publishing executive, writer; b. Princeton, N.J., May 30, 1933; d. Garland Baird Briggs and Mattie Williams. BA, Coll. William and Mary, 1955; MA, NYU, 1962. Art libr. C.W. Post Coll., L.I. U., Greenvale, NY, 1964—87; CEO, owner Dory Press, Sedley, Va., 1992—. Author: The Compass Windows of Blandford Church: A Tribute in Tiffany Glass, 1992, Circle and Square Tracts of the Nottoway Indians, 1995, The Little Ferry's Christmas, 1997, The Little Ferry Goes to the Paper Mill, 1998, The Little Ferry Meets the Colonial Ships, 1999, The Little Ferry, a Ham Sandwich and a Virginia Tradition, 1999, The Little Ferry and the Hiding Peanuts, 2000; contbr. articles to mags. and profl. jours. Mem. fund distbn. United Way Gtr. Williamsburg, Va., 2001—02. Mem.: United Daus. of Confederacy (Jefferson Davis medal 1994), DAR, Jamestown Soc., Omicron Delta Kappa (mem. Eta cir. 2001). Methodist. Avocations: birdwatching, gardening, trivia. Home and Office: Dory Press 13396 Wakefield Rd Sedley VA 23878

BRIGGS, NIWANA PAGE, editor, writer; b. Savannah, Ga., Oct. 6, 1957; d. William Gaines and Carolyn (King) Alexander; m. James Henry Briggs II, Sept. 1, 1979; 1 adopted child, Clinton Evans children: Melanie Shannon(dec.), James Henry. AA magna cum laude, Clayton State U., 1979; student, U. N.C., Wilmington, 1980-82. Freelance editor, San Francisco, 1989-94; legal sec. Wilson Sonsini Goodrich & Rosati, Palo Alto, Calif., 1987-89; editor, tech. writer Abekas Video Systems, Redwood City, Calif., 1989-92; proprietor Willee Gee's Used & Collectible Books, Fremont, Calif., 1992-94; exec. aide to polit. liaison World Savs. and Loan Assn., Oakland, Calif., 1992-94; exec. asst. to pres. Am. Immigation Lawyers Assn., Atlanta, 1995-96; freelance editor Atlanta, 1994-97; editor The Savannah (Ga.) Bus. Jour., 1997-99; freelance editor, writer Savannah, 1999—. Editl. contbns. to six novels. Mem. staff press office U.S. Olympic Com., Atlanta, 1996; lit. tutor, computer instr. to teenage unwed mothers Rayoc Learning Ctr., 1998; fundraiser Savannah Onstage, 2000; mem. United Meth. Women, 1999—; mem. Republican Nat. Com., 1978—. Mem. Telfair Acad. Arts and Scis., Screenwriters Guild Am., Am. Humane Soc. Avocations: reading, travel, antiques, baseball, opera. Home and Office: 2 Johnny Mercer Blvd #209 Savannah GA 31410 E-mail: niwanabriggs@aol.com.

BRIGGS, PHILIP, insurance company executive; b. Paris, Feb. 28, 1928; s. Robert E. and Madeleine (Boell) B. (parents Am. citizens); m. Jean M. Sloan, July 9, 1949; children: Karen, Heather, Peter. AB, Middlebury Coll., 1948. With Met. Life Ins. Co., N.Y.C., 1948-93, v.p., gen. mgr., 1971-73, sr. v.p., 1973-77, exec. v.p., 1977-86, vice chmn. bd. dirs., CFO, 1986-93; chmn. Wellchoice, Inc. (formerly Empire Blue Cross and Blue Shield), N.Y.C., 1993—. Fellow: Am. Acad. Actuaries, Soc. Actuaries, Health Ins. Am. (assoc.; past chmn.); mem.: Life Ins. Coun. NY (assoc.; past chmn.), Mid Ocean Club (Bermuda), Sky Club, Desert Forest Golf Club.

BRIGGS, PHILIP JAMES, political science educator, author, lecturer, researcher; b. N.Y.C., July 28, 1938; s. Philip Edward and Florence Marie (Fulham) B.; m. Candace Rae Kohn, Jan. 30, 1971; children: Nicola Fulham, Adam Kohn. BS, SUNY, Oswego, 1960; MA, Maxwell Sch. Citizenship and Pub. Affairs, Syracuse U., 1962, PhD, 1969. Asst. prof. social sci. SUNY Coll. Tech., Delhi, 1963-65; part-time admissions counselor Syracuse (N.Y.) U., 1967; assoc. prof. polit. sci. East Stroudsburg (Pa.) U., 1968-72, prof. polit. sci., 1972-99, dept. grad. coord.and chmn., 1977-95, faculty Fulbright adviser, 1981-82, disting. prof., faculty emeritus, 2000—. Foxhowe lectr., 1980; Commonwealth spkr. Pa. Humanities Coun., 1984—86, 1996—99; invited del. Sci. Rsch. Coun., Acad. Sci. USSR, 1979; invited participant seminar Georgetown U., 1983; invited scholar Presdl. Conf. Com., Hofstra U., 1984, 85, 87; panel co-chair Internat. Polit. Sci. World Congress, Paris, 1985, panel chair, Berlin, 94; manuscript referee Armed Forces and Soc., Chgo., 1979, Chgo., 93; cons. McGraw-Hill Book Co., N.Y.C., 1981. Author: Making American Foreign Policy, President-Congress Relations from the Second World War to Vietnam, 1991, 1992, Making American Foreign Policy, President-Congress Relations from the Second World War to the Post-Cold War Era, 1994, 1995, 1997; contbg. author: series The Congress of the United States, 1789-1989; editor: Politics in America, Readings and Documents, 1972; contbr. articles and revs. to profl. publs.; (TV appearances on) C-Span, 1987, Blue Ridge Cable and Pennarama, 1991, Action News 24, Erie, Pa., 1999. Exec. sec. Rsch. Com. on Armed Forces, 1985-90, exec. dir., 1990-99; exec. dir. Soc. Internat. Polit. Sci. Assn., 1990-99; panel chmn. rsch. com. Fundacion Jose Ortega y Gasset, Madrid, 1990; mem., panel participant Ctr. for Study of Presidency, 1995, 96; spkr. cmty. groups, Pa., NJ, NY, 2000-02. With USCG, 1962, USCGR, 1962-70. Mem. Pa. Polit. Sci. Assn. (panel chmn. ann. meetings 1993-99), Pi Sigma Alpha.

BRIGGS, RICH, secondary school educator; s. Ross G. and Gail I. Briggs. BA in Comm., Bethany Coll., 1988; postgrad., U. Phoenix Online, Am. Intercontinental U. Customer tng. cons. Reynolds & Reynolds, Pitts.; assembly man ITS Corp., Lawrence, Pa., ADC Telecom., Lawrence, Pa.; permanent substitute tchr. h.s. Ft. Cherry Sch. Dist., McDonald, Pa., 2002—. Asst. jr. high basketball coach Ft. Cherry Sch. Dist., McDonald, vol. asst. varsity boys basketball. Mem.: Ft. Cherry Edn. Assn., Pa. State Edn. Assn. Avocations: reading, writing, sports, exercising, golf. Home: 21 4th St Houston PA 15342-1303

BRIGGS, VERNON MASON, JR., economics educator; b. Washington, June 29, 1937; s. Vernon Mason and Anne Maria (Cox) B.; m. Martijna Antonia Aarts, Dec. 29, 1971; children: Vernon Mason III, Kees Kanen. BS, U. Md., 1959; MA, Mich. State U., 1960, PhD, 1965. Asst. instr. econs. Mich. State U., 1960-64; asst. prof. U. Tex., Austin, 1964-68, asso. prof., 1968-74, prof. econs., 1974-78; prof. indsl. and labor relations Cornell U., Ithaca, N.Y., 1978—. Rsch. dir. Com. on Adminstrn. Tng. Programs, HEW, 1967-68; mem. Nat. Coun. Employment Policy, 1977-87, chmn., 1985-87; bd. dirs. Corp. Pub. and Pvt. Ventures, 1978-83, Ctr. for Immigration Studies, 1987—. Author: (with Ray Marshall) The Negro and Apprenticeship, 1967, The Chicanos and Rural Poverty, 1973, (with Walter Fogel and Fred Schmidt) The Chicano Worker, 1977, (with John Adams, Brian Rungeling and Lewis Smith) Employment, Income and Welfare in the Rural South, 1977, (with Ray Marshall and Allan King) Labor Economics: Wages Employment and Trade Unionism, 1980, rev., 1984, (with Felician Foltman) Apprenticeship Research: Emerging Findings and Future Trends, 1981, Immigration Policy and the American Labor Force, 1984, (with Marta Tienda) Immigration Issues and Policies, 1985, The Internationalization of the U.S. Economy, 1986, (with Leon Bouvier) The Population and Labor Force Future of New York, 1988, (with Ray Marshall) Labor Economics: Theory, Institutions and Public Policy, 1989, Mass Immigration and the National Interest, 1992, 3d edit., 2003, Immigration Policy: A Tool of Labor Economics?, 1993, (with Stephen Moore) Still an Open Door? U.S. Immigration Policy and the American Economy, 1994, Immigration and American Unionism, 2001. Recipient Jean Holloway Tchg. Excellence award, 1974 Mem. Assn. for Evolutionary Econs. (pres.-elect 1994, pres. 1995), Phi Sigma Kappa, Delta Sigma Pi, Omicron Delta Kappa, Omicron Delta Epsilon. Home: 332 Winthrop Dr Ithaca NY 14850-1751

BRIGGS, WARD WRIGHT, classics educator; b. Riverside, Calif., Nov. 26, 1945; s. Ward Wright and Madge Elizabeth (Ravenscroft) B. BA, Washington & Lee U., 1967; MA, U. N.C., 1969, PhD, 1974. Instr. classics U. S.C., Columbia, 1973-74, asst. prof., 1974-80, assoc. prof., 1980-86, prof. classics, 1986—, Carolina disting. prof. classics, 1996—, Louise Fry Scudder prof. humanities, 1996—, interim assoc. provost, 1996-97. Vis. prof. U. Va., Charlottesville, 1988, U. Colo., 1988; fellow Inst. for Advanced Study, Princeton, 1999-2000. Author: Narrative and Simile from the Georgics in the Aeneid, 1980; editor: Letters of B.L. Gildersleeve, 1987; editor: Biographical Dictionary of North American Classicists, 1994, Soldier and Scholar, 1998; co-editor: Classical Scholarship, 1990; editor Vergilius, Jour. of Vergilian Soc. Am., 1986-95. Mem. Am. Philol. Assn., Classical Assn. Middle West and South (pres. 1988-89), Cambridge Philol. Soc., Phi Beta Kappa. Episcopalian. Home: 1904 Pendleton St Columbia SC 29201-3906 Office: Dept French and Classics U Sc Columbia SC 29208-0001 E-mail: wardbriggs@sc.edu.

BRIGGS, WILLIAM BENAJAH, aeronautical engineer; b. Okmulgee, Okla., Dec. 13, 1922; s. Eugene Stephen and Mary Bettie (Gentry) B.; m. Lorraine Hood, June 6, 1944; children— Eugene Stephen II, Cynthia Anne, Julia Louise, Spencer Gentry BA in Physics, Phillips U., 1943, DSc (hon.), 1977; MSME, Ga. Inst. Tech., 1947. Aero. scientist NACA, Cleve., 1948-52; propulsion engr. Chance Vought Aircraft/LTV, Dallas, 1952-64; mgr. advanced planning McDonnell Douglas Co., St. Louis, 1964-80, dir. program devel. fusion energy, 1980-87. Mem. planetary quarantine adv. panel NASA Contbr. articles on aero. engring. and energy to profl. jours.; patentee in field Chmn. Disciples Coun. Greater St. Louis, 1969-73; chmn. bd. Christian Bd. Publs., St. Louis, 1974-91; bd. dirs. Joint Cmty. Ministries, 1987-92, Emergency Childrens Home, 1994-2000; chmn. arrangements gen. assembly/synod Disciples of Christ/United Ch. of Christ, 1993; trustee Phillips U., Enid, Okla., 1996— . With USN, 1943-46, Atlantic and West Pacific. Recipient Svc. award, Emergency Childrens Home, 2003. Assoc. fellow AIAA (dir. region 5 1974-77, v.p. mem. svcs. 1978-79); mem. VFW, Am. Nuclear Soc., Navy League. Mem. Disciples of Christ Ch.

Home: 1819 Bradburn Dr Saint Louis MO 63131-1517 *Facing a problem, size up the situation, determine what needs to be done, then take action. Steadfastly working your plan does produce results; just give serendipity a chance to happen.*

BRIGGS, WINSLOW RUSSELL, plant biologist, educator; b. St. Paul, Apr. 29, 1928; s. John DeQuedville and Marjorie (Winslow) B.; m. Ann Morrill, June 30, 1955; children: Caroline, Lucia, Marion. BA, Harvard U., 1951, MA, 1952, PhD, 1956, U. Freiburg, Germany, 2002. Instr. biol. scis. Stanford (Calif.) U., 1955-57, asst. prof., 1957-62, asso. prof., 1962-66, prof., 1966-67; prof. biology Harvard U., 1967-73, Stanford U., 1973—; dir. dept. plant biology Carnegie Instn. of Washington, Stanford, 1973-93. Author: (with others) Life on Earth, 1973; mem. editl. bd. Ann. Rev. Plant Physiology, 1961-72; contbr. articles on plant growth and devel. and photobiology to profl. jours. Recipient Alexander von Humboldt U.S. Sr. Scientist award, 1984-85, Sterling Hendricks award USDA Agrl. Rsch. Svc., 1995, DeWitt award for partnership Calif. State Pks., 2000, Finsen medal Assn. Internat. Photobiology, 2000; John Simon Guggenheim fellow, 1973-74, Deutsche Akademie der Naturforscher Leopoldina, 1986. Fellow AAAS; mem. NAS, Am. Soc. Plant Physiologists (pres. 1975-76, Stephen Hales award 1994), Calif. Bot. Soc. (pres. 1976-77), Am. Acad. Arts and Scis., Am. Inst. Biol. Scis. (pres. 1980-81), Am. Soc. Photobiology, Bot. Soc. Am., Nature Conservancy, Sigma Xi. Home: 480 Hale St Palo Alto CA 94301-2207 Office: Carnegie Inst Washington Dept Plant Biology 260 Panama St Palo Alto CA 94305-4101 *With gifted students, remarkable things are possible.*

BRIGGS-ERICKSON, CAROL ANN, librarian; b. Muskegon, Mich., Aug. 20, 1952; d. Raymond John and Josephine (Dombrausky) Smith; m. Phillip George Briggs, Sept. 25, 1969 (div. Oct. 1977); 1 child, Christine Jeanette; m. Leif Stanley Erickson, Nov. 29, 1991. AA, Muskegon (Mich.) Cmty. Coll., 1978; BS, Grand Valley State U., 1984; M of Info. and Libr. Studies, U. Mich., 1994. With support staff Muskegon Cmty. Coll., 1985-94, libr., 1994—. Co-author: Environmental Guide to the Internet, 1996, 4th edit., 1998. Mem. Phi Kappa Phi, Beta Phi Mu (Excellence in Scholarship 1994). Office: Muskegon Cmty Coll Libr 221 S Quarterline Rd Muskegon MI 49442-1432

BRIGHAM, HENRY DAY, JR., retired lawyer; b. Pittsfield, Mass., Dec. 12, 1926; s. Henry Day and Gladys M. (Allen) B.; m. Catherine T. Van't Hul, Dec. 16, 1961; children: Henry Day, Johan Van't Hul, Alexander Frederick. BA, Yale U., 1947, JD, 1950. Bar: N.Y. 1951, Mass. 1966. Assoc. Milbank, Tweed, Hope & Hadley, N.Y.C., 1951-52, 54-56, Simpson Thacher & Bartlett, N.Y.C., 1956-66; v.p., gen. counsel, dir. Eaton & Howard, Inc., Boston, 1966-73, pres., 1973-79; v.p., chmn. exec. com. Eaton & Howard, Vance Sanders, Inc., Boston, 1979-81, Eaton Vance Corp., Boston, 1981—96; ret., 1996. Former trustee Eaton Vance Cash Mgmt. Fund, Boston; former v.p., trustee Eaton Vance Tax Free Reserves, Boston; former sec., clk., dir. Investors Bank & Trust Co., Boston; v.p., sec., trustee Wright Managed Income Trust, Boston, Wright Managed Equity Trust, Boston. Pres. Trustees of Donations of Episc. Diocese Mass., 1984-89; sr. warden Ch. of the Redeemer, Chestnut Hill, 1975-79; sec., bd. dirs. Chestnut Hill Assn. (Mass.), 1969—. Lt. USNR, 1952-54. Mem.: Assn. Yale Alumni (bd. govs.), Investment Counsel Assn. Am. (bd. govs.), Somerset Club, Tarratine Club, Harvard Club, Tennis & Racquet Club, The Country Club, Downtown Club, Longwood Cricket Club, Soc. Colonial Wars, Phi Delta Phi, Phi Beta Kappa. Episcopalian.

BRIGHAM, JOHN ALLEN, JR., financial executive, environmentalist, politition; b. San Francisco, June 17, 1942; s. John Allen, Sr. and Susan (Endberg) B.; m. Patricia Katherine Carney, Feb. 4, 1968; 1 child, Jennifer. BS in Acctg., San Jose State U., 1967. Acct. Shell Oil Co. Data Ctr., Palo Alto, Calif., 1963-66; asst. plant controller Brown Co., Santa Clara, Calif., 1966-68; budget mgr. Varian Assocs., Palo Alto, 1968-80; cost acctg. mgr. Adac Labs., San Jose, Calif., 1980-86; contr. Crystal Tech., Palo Alto, 1986-90; contr., v.p. fin., CFO GV Custom Modular Constrn., Inc., Healdsburg, Calif.; contr. GV Contractors, Heraldsburg, Calif., 1994—2001; pvt. practice investor, 2001—02; cost account mgr. ICORE, 2003—. Part-time sci. tchr. Insects and Dinosaurs, 1994-96. Del. League Calif. Cities, 1974-78; mem. Saratoga (Calif.) City Council, 1974-78; vice-chmn. Santa Clara County Polity Planning Use Commn., 1975-78; chmn. Santa Clara Com. on Mass Transit, 1976-78; chmn. Open Space Bond Issue, 1976; treas. Calif. State Solar Bond Issue, 1976; mem. Castle Rock State Pk. Com., 1972-74; vice-chmn. Saratoga Hillside Com. 1978-79. Recipient 10 and 25 Yr. Sierra Club Activist awards, 1989, Chpt. Svc. award, 1990, Spl. Achievement award, 1990; Local Outstanding Young Man of Am. award, 1974, Siemens USA Personality of the Month award, Jan. 1990. Mem. Am. Entomol. Soc., Archeol. Inst. Am., Nat. Acctg. Assn., Sierra Club (vice chmn., treas. Loma chpt. 1985-94, treas. Redwood chpt. 1994-97, internat. chmn. 1989-97, Centennial chmn. 1990-92, liaison to USSR and Mex., co-chair Earth Day 1990, taskforce 1989, chmn. fin. commn. 1985-90), Am. Diabetes Soc. (treas., bd. dirs. Santa Clara County chpt.), Nat. Wildlife Fedn., Cousteau Soc., Planetary Soc., Napoleonic Soc., Bromiliad Soc., Am. Diabetes Assn., Sierra Club. Independent. Roman Catholic. Home: 118 Valley Lakes Dr Santa Rosa CA 95409-6237 E-mail: pat646@earthnet.net., jab642@prodigy.net.

BRIGHAM, JUDITH X. philosophy educator; b. Wingham, Ont., Can., Nov. 17, 1915; d. F. E. Clysdale and Flora Ann (Brigham) Mills; m. N. Burnett Magruder. BA in English and History, U. Toronto, Ont., 1938; degree in philosophy, religion, and edn., Yale U., 1940; MA, PhD, Columbia U., 1943. Lectr. philosophy U. Louisville; lectr. English, world, and bibl. lits. Ind. U. Mem. Acad. Polit. Sci. Columbia U. Author: An Historical Study of the Educational Agencies of the Southern Baptist Convention, 1845-1945, The Thought of Edgar Young Mullins, 1954, American Dialectics in Action, 1966, Twentieth Century Questions. Mem. Nat. Rep. Congl. com., Rep. Senatorial Inner Cir. Recipient Rep. Presdl. Legion of Merit medal, 1992, Medal of Freedom, Rep. mems. of U.S. State Senate, 1994, Rep. Congl. Order of Liberty, Nat. Rep. Congl. Com., 1993, Pres.'s Nat. Medal of Patriotism, Am. Police Hall of Fame, 1994. Mem.: Am. Acad. Polit. and Social Sci. Avocation: international relations.

BRIGHAM, ROBERT ALLAN, surgeon, educator; b. Grosse Pointe, Mich., May 13, 1947; MD, Wayne State U., 1977. Diplomate Am. Bd. Surgery, Am. Bd. Gen. Vasc. Surgery. Intern Walter Reed Army Med. Ctr., Washington, 1977-78, surg. resident, 1978-82, fellow in vasc. surgery, 1982-83; dir. surgery Reading Hosp.-Med. Ctr., West Reading, Pa., 1983—. Clin. assoc. prof. surgery Uniform Svcs. U. Health Scis., Temple U. Mem. ACS, Assn. Acad. Surgery, Am. Coll. Physician Execs., Am. Assn. Surgery of Trauma, Internat. Soc. Cardiovasc. Surgery, So. Assn. Vascular Surgery, Reading Physicians Orgn. (pres.). Office: Reading Hosp and Med Ctr 301 S 7th Ave Ste 1070 Reading PA 19611-1493

BRIGHT, BOBBY, mayor; Mayor, Montgomery, Ala., 1999—. Office: PO Box 1111 Montgomery AL 36101

BRIGHT, CRAIG BARTLEY, lawyer; b. Mineola, N.Y., May 23, 1931; s. Herbert Lester and Gertrude Lillian (Smith) Bright; m. Judith Alice Pollard, July 31, 1955 (dec. Aug. 1956); m. Ann Sharpe, July 18, 1959. BA summa cum laude, Colgate U., 1952; JD magna cum laude, Harvard U., 1955. Bar: N.Y. 1956, U.S. Dist. Ct. (so. and ea. dists.) N.Y. 1961, U.S. Dist. Ct. Conn. 1961, U.S. Ct. Appeals (2d cir.) 1961. Staff judge adv. Judge Adv. Gen.'s Group, 1955—57; assoc. Patterson, Belknap, Webb & Tyler, N.Y.C., 1957—64, ptnr., 1965—92. Co-author: The Law and the Lore of Endowment Funds, 1969, The Developing Law of Endowment Funds, 1974; contbr. Capt. USAF, 1955—57. Mem.: ABA, Assn. of Bar of City of N.Y., N.Y. State Bar Assn. (chmn. com. on profl. ethics 1981—84), Hermitage Club Goochland, Va. Republican. Presbyterian. Home and Office: 21 Hunting Ridge Rd Manakin Sabot VA 23103-2614 E-mail: cbbasb@comcast.net.

BRIGHT, DAVID FORBES, academic administrator, classics and comparative literature educator; b. Winnipeg, Man., Can., Apr. 13, 1942; s. John Hamilton and Pauline Murray (Forbes) B.; m. Marlene Joanne Mayercik, Feb. 20, 1965; children: Jennifer, Sarah. BA (hons.), U. Man., 1962; AM, U. Cin., 1963, PhD, 1967. Asst. prof. classics Williams Coll., Williamstown, Mass., 1967-70; from asst. to assoc. prof. classics U. Ill., Urbana-Champaign, 1970-85, prof. classics and comparative lit., 1985-89, chmn. dept. classics, 1977-81, 85-88, dir. comparative lit. dept., 1986-88, acting dean Coll. Liberal Arts and Scis., 1988-89; dean Coll. Liberal Arts and Scis. Iowa State U., Ames, 1989-91; dean, v.p. for arts and scis. Emory U., Atlanta, 1991-97, prof. classics and comparative lit., 1991—, chmn. dept. classics, 1999—, dir. comparative lit., 1999-2001. Author: Haec mihi fingebam. Tibullus in his World, 1978, Elaborate Disarray: The Nature of Statius' Silvae, 1980, Miniature Epic in Vandal Africa, 1987, The Academic Deanship, 2001; editor: Classical Texts and Their Traditions, 1984. Bd. dirs. Atlanta Ballet Co., Savoyards Light Opera, Coun. of Colls. of Arts and Scis., pres. 1996-97. Woodrow Wilson Found. fellow, 1962, U. Cin. travel fellow Am. Acad. in Rome, 1965-66, Am. Council Learned Socs. fellow, 1981-82; Rsch. scholar Delmas Found., 1987. Mem. Am. Philol. Assn., Classical Assn. Middle West and South (exec. com. 1985-89, pres. 1989), Vergilian Soc. (trustee 1983-86), Soc. of Fellows Am. Acad. Rome. Episcopalian. Home: 2646 Rangewood Dr NE Atlanta GA 30345-1516 Office: Emory U Dept Classics 221F Candler Libr Atlanta GA 30322-0001 E-mail: dbright@emory.edu.

BRIGHT, GARRY MICHAEL, executive; b. San Angelo, Tex., July 20, 1952; Jeryl Thomas Bright and Doris Adelle Thomason; m. Cynthia Ann Hardegree, Aug. 24, 1973; children: Adam Michael, Sarah Eileen. BS in Elem. Edn., Angelo State U., 1974. Exec. dir. Assn. Retarded Citizens, San Angelo, Tex., 1972-74; various positions Assn. Retarded Citizens Tex., Austin, 1974-87; dir. govtl. affairs The Arc of Tex., Austin, 1987-95, exec. dir., 1995—. Mem. Am. Soc. Assn. Execs., Am. Tex. Assn. Mental Retardation, Nat. Conf. Execs. of Arc. Mem. Ch. of Christ. Avocation: reading. Office: The Arc of Tex 8001 Centre Park Dr Austin TX 78754 E-mail: mbright@thearcoftexas.org.

BRIGHT, JOSEPH CONVERSE, lawyer; b. Richmond, Va., July 28, 1940; s. Joseph Elliott and Marion (Converse) B.; m. Jill Giddens, May 5, 1989; children: Thomas Converse, Elizabeth Chase. BA, U. Va., 1962; LLB, U. Ga., 1965. Bar: Ga. 1964, U.S. Dist. Ct. (so. dist.) Ga. 1965, U.S. Dist. Ct. (mid. dist.) Ga. 1967, U.S. Dist. Ct. (no. dist.) Ga. 1983, U.S. Ct. Appeals (5th cir.) 1965, Fla. 1976, U.S. Dist. Ct. (mid. and no. dist.) Fla. 1982, U.S. Supreme Ct. 1976, U.S. Ct. Appeals (11th cir.) 1981, U.S. Dist. Ct. (no. dist.) Fla. 1998. Assoc. Joseph B. Bergen, Savannah, Ga., 1965-67; sole practice Valdosta, Ga., 1967-69; ptnr. Blackburn & Bright, Valdosta, 1969-91; pvt. practice Valdosta, 1991—. Instr. part time Valdosta State U., 1967-81; mem. Ga. Bd. Bar Examiners. Fellow Am. Bd. Criminal Lawyers, Am. Coll. Trial Lawyers; mem. ATLA, Nat. Assn. Criminal Def. Lawyers, Ga. Trial Lawyers Assn. (v.p.). Avocations: riding, English history, skeet shooting. Office: PO Box 5889 Valdosta GA 31603-5889 E-mail: jcblaw@bellsouth.net.

BRIGHT, KEVIN S. producer; b. 1955; With Bright-Kauffman-Crane Prodns., Burbank, Calif. Creator, exec. prodr. Dream On, 1990—, Friends, 1994— (Emmy nominee 1995, 96), Veronica's Closet, 1997—, Jesse, 1998. Office: Bright Kauffman Crane Prodns 4000 Warner Blvd Bldg 160 Burbank CA 91522-0001

BRIGHT, MARGARET, sociologist; b. Bentonville, Ark., Nov. 19, 1918; d. William Ray and Edna May (Woolwine) B.; m. Herman Binder, 1983. AB, U. Calif., Berkeley, 1941; MA, U. Mo., 1944; PhD, U. Wis., 1950. Lectr. rural sociology U. Mo., 1944-47; asst. project dir. U. P.R., 1950-51; acting assoc. prof. Cornell U., 1951-52; social affairs officer population br. UN, N.Y.C., 1952-54; research assoc. Bur. Applied Social Research Columbia U., N.Y.C., 1954-57; sociologist-demographer UN Tech. Assistance, Bombay, India, 1957-59; asst. prof. chronic diseases Johns Hopkins U., Balt., 1959-63, assoc. prof., 1963-68; dir. research Center for Urban Affairs, 1968-72, assoc. prof. behavioral scis., 1968-70, prof., 1970-83, prof. emerita, 1983—. Mem. U.S. Mission Coop. Health and Sanitation to, Brazil, 1960. Author: Cooperativas de Consumo de Puerto Rico: Análisis Socio-Económicó, 1957; co-author: Graduates of American Schools of Public Health, 1976; contbr. articles to profl. jours. Mem. Balt. Mayor's Task Force on Polit. Redistricting, 1971; mem. Rockefeller Commn. on Population and the Am. Future, 1970-72. Mem. Am. Pub. Health Assn. Democrat. Home: 3900 N Charles St Apt 1314 Baltimore MD 21218-1738 Office: 624 N Broadway Baltimore MD 21205-1900

BRIGHT, MYRON H. federal judge; b. Eveleth, Minn., Mar. 5, 1919; s. Morris and Lena A. Bright; m. Frances Louise Reisler, Dec. 26, 1947; children: Dinah Ann, Joshua Robert. AA, Eveleth Junior Coll, 1939; BSL, U. Minn., 1941, JD, 1947. Bar: N.D. 1947, Minn. 1947. Assoc. Wattam, Vogel, Vogel & Bright, Fargo, ND, 1947, ptnr., 1949—68; judge 8th U.S. Cir. Ct. Appeals, Fargo, 1968—85, sr. judge, 1985—; disting. prof. law St. Louis U., 1985—88, emeritus prof. of law, 1989—95. Capt. USAF, 1942—46. Recipient Francis Rawle award, ALI-ABA, 1996, Lifetime Achievement award, U. N.D. Law Sch., 1998, Herbert Harley award, AJS, 2000. Mem.: ABA, U.S. Jud. Conf. (com. on adminstrn. of probation sys. 1977—83, adv. com. on appellate rules 1987—90, com. on internat. jud. rels. 1996—2003), N.D. Bar Assn. Office: US Ct Appeals 8th Cir 655 1st Ave N Ste 340 Fargo ND 58102-4952 also: Thomas F Eagleton US Cthse 111 S 10th St Rm 26 325 Saint Louis MO 63102 E-mail: judge_myron_bright@ca8.uscourts.gov.

BRIGHT, PETER BOWMAN, scientist, engineer, researcher; b. Gallipolis, Ohio, Dec. 27, 1937; s. Warren Harris and Elizabeth (Bowman) B.; divorced; children: Alicia Laurel, Debra Elaine, Michael Murray. BS, Antioch Coll., Yellow Springs, Ohio, 1960; PhD, U. Chgo., 1966; MBA, UCLA, 1989. Asst. research biomathematician UCLA, 1973-75; cons. The Aerospace Corp., Los Angeles, 1975-79, mem. tech. staff, 1980-84, project engr., 1984-88, mgr., 1988-90; asst. prof. math. U. Calif., Northridge, 1977-79; project dir. U. So. Calif., Los Angeles, 1979-80; prin. systems engr. GE, L.A., 1991-93; prin. sys. engr. Martin Marietta, L.A., 1993-94; prin. systems engr. Lockheed Martin, Arlington, Va., 1994-95, sr. staff engr. Sunnyvale, Calif., 1995—98, ret., 1998—; asst. prof. U. Tex., Dallas, 1969—73. Contbr. numerous articles to profl. jours. Mem. AIAA, Mgmt., Computer and Reliability Socs. of IEEE (vice chmn. seminars 1983-86, spl. recognition 1985-86), Soc. Math. Biology, Sigma Xi. Home: 150 Nevada Ave Palo Alto CA 94301-4119

BRIGHT, WILLARD MEAD, manufacturing company executive; b. N.Y.C., Mar. 26, 1914; s. William Van Horn and Bernice Hartwell (Reynolds) B.; m. Martha Norris Land, May 15, 1944 (dec.); 1 child, Willard Mead; m. Virginia L. Jones, Mar. 14, 1981 (div. Aug. 1996). BS, U. Toledo, 1936, MS, 1937; postgrad., U. Pitts., 1937-38; A.M., Harvard U., 1941, PhD, 1942. Research chemist Kendall Co., Boston, Chgo., 1942-52; asst. lab. dir. Kendall Co. (Bauer & Black div.), 1944-48; lab. dir. (Theodore Clark Lab. div.), Cambridge, Mass., 1948-52; asst. research dir. Lever Bros. Co., 1952-54, research dir., 1954-60, v.p. research and devel., 1960-64; chmn. bd. W. H. Norris Lumber Co., Houston, 1957-64; treas. Border Lumber Co., Weslaco, Tex., 1957-64; v.p. R.J. Reynolds Tobacco Co., 1964-68; sr. v.p., pres. profl. products group Warner-Lambert Pharm. Co., 1968-70; pres., chief exec. officer Kendall Co., Boston, 1970-73; pres. Curtiss-Wright Corp., 1973-74, Boehringer Mannheim Corp., 1974-81; chmn. Zoll Med. Corp, 1982-96. Bd. dirs. Zoll Med. Corp.; mem. adv. com. on patents U.S. Dept. Commerce, 1966-69; mem. bd. visitors dept. chemistry Boston U. Recipient Gold T award U. Toledo, 1960 Mem. N.A.M. (chmn. sci. tech. com. dir. 1970-73), Am. Chem. Soc., N.Y. Acad. Scis., Assn. Rsch. Dirs., Indsl. Rsch. Inst. (dir. 1963-69, pres. 1967-68), Dirs. Indsl. Rsch., Sigma Xi, Phi Kappa Phi, Harvard Club (Boston), Comml. Club (Boston), The Country Club (Brookline, Mass.), Bent Pine Golf Club (Vero Beach, Fla.). Home: 112 Prestwick Cir Vero Beach FL 32967-7514 Office: Zoll Med Corp 32 2d Ave Burlington MA 01803-4408

BRIGHTBILL, DAVID JOHN, state legislator, lawyer; Sch. dir. Lebanon (Pa.) Sch. Dist., 1965-67; dist. atty. Lebanon, 1977-81; mem. Pa. Senate, Dist. 48, Harrisburg, 1982—.

BRIGHTBILL, JANET M. music educator; b. Lebanon, Pa., Jan. 8, 1954; d. Gurney I. and Harriet E. Eisenhauer; m. Gary G. Brightbill, Sept. 2, 1972; children: Jeremy J., Jessica M. Brightbill-VonCrist, Jamie L. BA in Music Edn. (magna cum laude), U. of Charleston, W.Va., 1986. Cert. Profl. Tchr. W.Va. Dept. of Edn., 2002. Piano tchr. Grace Christian Sch., Myerstown, Pa., 1977—81, Bible Ctr. Christian Sch., Charleston, W.Va., 1983—86; music tchr., k-12 Cross Lanes Christian Sch., W.Va., 1986—97; piano instr. U. of Charleston, W.Va., 1998—. Accompanist Charleston Civic Chorus, W.Va., 1992—2002; pianist Bible Ctr. Ch., Charleston, W.Va., 1995—; accompanist U. of Charleston Concert Choir/U. Singers, W.Va., 1999—, W.Va. Symphony Chorus, Charleston, 2000—. Home: 5122 Lone Pine Ln Cross Lanes WV 25313 Office: U of Charleston 2300 MacCorkle Ave SE Charleston WV 25304

BRIGHTMAN, ROBERT LLOYD, importer, textile company executive, consultant; b. Rockville Center, N.Y., July 17, 1920; s. Harold Warren and Florence (Pennington) B.; m. Marion Altreuter, Oct. 31, 1942 (dec. Nov. 1989); children: Richard Warren, Shelley Anne, Susan Boyd; m. Vera Elisabet Holmsten, Dec. 5, 1990. Grad. cum laude, Montclair Acad., 1936, Phillips Exeter Acad., 1937; BA, Princeton, 1941. With A. Johnson & Co., Inc., N.Y.C., 1946-48; with Johaneson, Wales & Sparre, Inc., N.Y.C., 1948-67, v.p., 1952-64, pres., 1964-67; v.p. Grangesberg Am. Corp., N.Y.C., 1967-68; pres. R.L. Brightman Co., Verona, N.J., 1967—; dir. purchases West Point-Pepperell, N.Y.C., 1968-76, corporate v.p., 1976-88. Mem. Nat. Council Am. Importers, Inc., 1954-69, dir., 1956-69, v.p., 1959-61, pres., 1961-63, sr. councillor, 1963-69; mem. nat. panel arbitrators Am. Arbitration Assn., 1958— Served with USNR, 1942-46. Home and Office: Claridge House One Apt 318 Verona NJ 07044

BRIGHTMIRE, PAUL WILLIAM, retired judge; b. Washington, Mo., June 12, 1924; s. Quinton Claude and Alvena Matilda (Wehr) B.; m. Lorene E. Edwards, Nov. 7, 1952; children: Deborah Sue, William Paul, Jon Edward, Christina Ann, Thomas Christopher. BA, U. Tulsa, 1949, JD, 1951. Bar: Okla. 1951, U.S. Supreme Ct. 1973. With Rogers & Brightmire, 1954-57, Brightmire & Assoc., Tulsa, 1957-70, judge Okla. Ct. Appeals, Divsn. 2, Tulsa, 1971-94, presiding judge, 1971-75; spl. justice Supreme Ct. Okla.; vice- chief judge Okla. Ct. Appeals, 1989, chief judge, 1990-94. Vis. prof. med. jurisprudence Okla. Coll. Osteo. Medicine and Surgery, 1975-82 Founding editor: Tulsa Lawyer, 1962-64; editor in chief: Advocate, 1967-70. Served to 2d lt. USNR, USAR, 1943-46, 51. Recipient Outstanding Svc. award Okla. Ct. Appeals, 1990. Fellow Internat. Acad. Law and Sci.; mem. Am. Trial Lawyers Assn., Okla. Trial Lawyers Assn. (pres. 1967, Outstanding Service award 1968, Appellate Judge of Yr. award 1991), Okla. Bar Assn. (Outstanding Service award 1969), Tulsa County Bar Assn. (Outstanding Service award 1965, exec. com. 1962-64), Am. Inns of Ct. (master emeritus), Tulsa Press Club, Kappa Sigma, Phi Beta Gamma, Pi Kappa Delta. Lodges: Masons (32 deg., Shriner). Home: 4041 S Birmingham Ave Tulsa OK 74105-8230

BRIGHTON, CARL THEODORE, orthopedic surgery educator; b. Pana, Ill., Aug. 20, 1931; s. Louis Frederick and Helen (Frinke) B.; m. Ruth Louise Krentz, July 27, 1954; children: David Carl, Susan Ruth, Andrew Paul, Joel Theodore. BA, Valparaiso U., 1953, DSc (hon.), 1998; MD, U. Pa., 1957; PhD, U. Ill., 1969; DSc (hon.), Valpraiso U., 1998. Diplomate Am. Bd. Orthopedic Surgery. Intern U.S. Naval Hosp., Phila., 1957-58, resident in orthopedics, 1958-61, U. Pa., Phila., 1961-62; staff orthopedist U.S. Naval Hosp., Phila., 1962-63, Naval Hosp., Great Lakes, Ill., 1963-66, USS Sanctuary, South China Sea, 1966-67; asst. prof. orthopedic surgery U. Pa. Med. Sch., Phila., 1968-70, dir. orthopedic rsch., 1968-93, assoc. prof., 1970-73, prof., 1973—, chmn. dept. orthopedic surgery, 1977-93, Paul B. Magnuson prof. bone and joint surgery, 1977-96, Paul B. Magnuson prof. emeritus bone and joint surgery, 1996—. Cons. orthopedic surgery U.S. Naval Hosp., Phila., 1968-78; attending staff VA Hosp., Phila., 1968-84. Editor-in-Chief Clinical Orthopaedics and Related Rsch., 1993-2002. Lt. comdr. (j.g.) USN, 1957-62. Recipient Kappa Delta award for outstanding research, 1974; spl. postdoctoral fellow NIH, 1967-68; Career Devel. Rsch. award, 1971-76, Shands Lectr. award, 1985, Merit award NIH, 1987, Bristol-Myers Squibb/Zimmer award for Disting. Achievement in Orthopaedic Rsch., 1992. Fellow ACS, Am. Acad. Orthopedic Surgeons; mem. Am. Orthopedic Assn., Orthopedic Rsch. Soc. (pres. 1977), Orthopedic Forum, Can. Orthopedic Rsch. Soc. (hon.), Bioelectric Repair and Growth Soc. (co-founder, pres. 1981, 82), Acad. Orthopaedic Soc., Assn. of Bone and Joint Surgeons. Lutheran. Achievements include first to use electricity in treating nonunion fractures. Home: 14 Flintshire Rd Malvern PA 19355-1108 Office: Univ City Sci Ctr Clinical Opthopaedics 3550 Market St Ste 220 Philadelphia PA 19104-3329

BRIGHTON, GERALD DAVID, accounting educator; b. Weldon, Ill., May 14, 1920; s. William Henry and Geneva (Ennis) B.; m. Lois Helen Robbins, June 7, 1949; children: Anne, William, Joan, John, Jeffrey. BS, U. Ill., 1941, MS, 1947, PhD, 1953. C.P.A., Ill. Instr. accountancy U. Ill., Urbana, 1947-53, prof., 1954-83, Ernst & Whinney Disting. prof., 1983-88, prof. emeritus, 1988—, dir. undergrad. acctg. program, 1978-86; staff acct. Touche, Niven, Bailey & Smart, Chgo., 1953-54. Cons. G.D. Brighton, C.P.A., Urbana, 1954—; vis. prof. U. Tex.-Austin, 1973; program specialist Dept. HUD, Washington, 1979; vice chmn. U. Ill. Athletic Assn., Urbana, 1982-86 Contbr. articles to profl. jours. Alderman City of Urbana, 1967-69; officer, bd. dirs. U. Ill. YMCA, Champaign, 1959-81, 89-95, trustee, 2002—; bd. dirs. Wesley Found., U. Ill., 1986—; treas. John Gwinn for Congress, Urbana, 1982-83, Green Meadows coun. Girl Scouts U.S., 1981-83. Served to maj. U.S. Army, 1941-46. AACSB Faculty fellow, 1978-79; recipient Bronze Tablet for high honors U. Ill., 1941 Mem. AICPA (hon.), Ill. Soc. CPAs (disting.), Am. Acctg. Assn., Assn. Govt. Accts., Govtl. Fin. Officers Assn., Nat. Tax Assn., Tax Inst. Am. Democrat. Methodist. Home: 501 Evergreen Ct Urbana IL 61801-5928 Office: U Ill 1206 S 6th St Champaign IL 61820-6978 *Happiness comes very indirectly. "Seek and ye shall find." That is at best a half truth. If we rely on direct rewards for our happiness we are in trouble. At best, the string of treats will be irregular. The key is to widen one's circle. Try to rejoice in the good fortunes of your colleagues. Sometimes, jealousy gets in the way. What is the greatest satisfaction I have had from teaching? It is the occasional glimpses that I see that former students are doing well.*

BRIGHTON, RUTH LOUISE, lay worker, educator; b. Harrisburg, Pa., Apr. 18, 1931; d. Paul Gerhard and Ruth Genevieve (Lee) Krentz; m. Carl T. Brighton, July 27, 1954; children: David, Susan, Andrew, Joel. BA, Valparaiso U., 1953; MS in Math., U. Wis., 1955. Cert. tchr. Tchr. Sunday sch., adult Bible class Christ Meml. Luth. Ch., Malvern, Penn., 1969—; coord. adult edn., Ea. dist. Luth. Ch.-Mo. Synod, Buffalo, 1986-89, bd. dirs., 1988-90. Bd. dirs. Concordia Pub. House, St. Louis, 1989—2001. Teaching fellow in math. U. Wis., 1953. Home: 14 Flintshire Rd Malvern PA 19355-1108

BRIGHTUP, CRAIG STEVEN, lobbyist; b. Aurora, Ill., Jan. 10, 1954; s. James Roscoe and Neoma Arlene (Thomas) B. BA in Polit. Sci., Pa. State U., 1976; postgrad., Am. U., 1980. Info. specialist Fed. Election Commn., Washington, 1976-78, chief of pub. records, 1978-81; dir. legis. and polit. issues U.S. C. of C., Washington, 1981-83; mgr. polit. affairs and state rels. S&A Restaurant Corp., Dallas, 1983-86; polit. affairs mgr. Southwestern Region, U.S. C. of C., Dallas, 1986-87; dir. congrl. rels. Fed. Trade Commn., Washington, 1987-90; assoc. exec. dir. govt. rels. Nat. Roofing Contractors Assn., Washington, 1990—2001, v.p. govt. rels., 2001—. Mem. labor rels. com. U.S. C. of C., 1991—, mem. regulatory affairs com., U.S. C. of C., 1994-. Dep. voter registrar Dallas County, 1984; participant GOP Conv., Dallas, 1984, New Orleans, 1988, Houston, 1992, San Diego, 1996, Phila., 2000; del. Va. State GOP Conv., 1993. Named to Power 30 Lobbyist List, Fortune Small Bus. mag., 2000. Republican. Avocation: running. Home: 215 N Pitt Street Alexandria VA 22314 Office: Nat Roofing Contractors Assn 324 4th St NE Washington DC 20002-5821 E-mail: cbrightup@nrca.net.

BRIGNANO, RUSSELL CARL, English educator, research specialist; b. Hartford, Conn., June 26, 1935; s. Joseph Frank Brignano and Adelina Alda Accomasso; m. Mary Louise Germann, Jan. 24, 1969. BA, Dartmouth Coll., 1957; MS, U. Wis., 1963, PhD, 1966. Tchg. asst. English U. Wis., Madison, 1961-66; asst. prof., then assoc. prof. English Carnegie Mellon U., Pitts., 1966-75; assoc. prof. English Pa. State U., Monaca, 1975-96, emeritus prof. University Park, 1997—; owner I/D Rsch., Pitts., 1999—. Vis. assoc. prof. U. Pitts., 1970. Author: Richard Wright, 1970, Black Americans in Autobiography, 1974, rev. edit., 1984; contbr. articles to profl. jours. Local election judge, Pitts., 1992-96. With U.S. Army, 1957-59. Recipient Younger Humanist award NEH, 1970-71; Brigano Collection of African american autobiography at Pa. State U. Libr. dedicated in his honor. Mem. MLA. Avocations: travel, gardening, baseball. Home: 150 Hartwood Dr Pittsburgh PA 15208-2702 E-mail: brignano@psu.edu.

BRIHAMMAR, B. NIKLAS, lawyer; b. Stockholm, Apr. 12, 1964; s. Bengt Axel and Solbritt Linnea Elisabeth (Pettersson) B.; m. Marta Kristina Sjoevall, Dec. 21, 1995. BS in Econs., U. South Ala., Mobile, 1989; JD, U. Miami, 1993. Bar: Fla. 1993, U.S. Dist. Ct. (so. dist.) Fla. 1995. Asst. mgr. Daiwa Securities, Ltd., Stockholm, 1990; assoc. atty. John E. Bigler, P.A., Key West, Fla., 1994, John R. Fiore, P.A., Miami, Fla., 1995, Sheri Smallwood, Chartered, Key West, 1995-99; pvt. practice Key West, Fla., 1999—. Mem. Gala Task Force, Key West, 1997-99. Mem. Fla. Bar (family law sect.), Monroe County Bar Assn., Swedish-Am. Bar Assn. Avocations: computers, reading, chess, tennis, film. Office: 417 Eaton St Key West FL 33040-6548 E-mail: brihammar@yahoo.com.

BRILL, AARON BERTRAND, nuclear medicine educator; b. N.Y.C., Dec. 19, 1928; s. Louis And Cecile (Sroge) B.; m. Joan Booth Morrison, Sept. 1, 1950; children: Paul, David, Laurie. AB, Grinnell Coll., 1949; MD, U. Utah, 1956; PhD in Biophysics, U. Calif., Berkeley, 1961. Statistician Contra Costa County Health Dept., Martinez, Calif., 1949—50; res. asst. U. Calif., Donner Lab, 1950—52; biophysicist U. Utah Pediatrics Dept., Salt Lake City, 1952-56; intern Salt Lake City Gen. Hosp., 1956-57; USPHS officer Div. of Radiol. Health, Rockville, Md., 1957-64; asst. prof. radiology dept. radiology scis. Johns Hopkins Hosp. and Sch. of Hygiene, 1961-64; assoc. prof. radiol. Vanderbilt U. Sch. Medicine, Nashville, 1964-72; assoc. prof. medicine, biomed. engring. and physics, 1964-79; prof. radiology Vanderbilt U. Sch. Medicine, Nashville, 1972-79, SUNY, Stony Brook, 1979-87; sr. scientist, nuc. medicine coord. Brookhaven (N.Y.) Nat. Lab., 1979-87; prof. nuclear medicine U. Mass. Sch. Medicine, Worcester, 1987—97. Rsch. affiliate MIT, Cambridge, 1993—; affil. prof. Worcester Polytechnic Inst., Worcester, 1995-97; rsch. prof. radiol. sci. Vanderbilt U. Sch. Medicine, Nashville, 1997—, rsch. prof. physics, adj. prof. biomed. engring., 1998—. Editor: Low Level Radiation Fact Book, 1st edit. 1982, 2d edit., 1985; editor: IEEE Trans Med. Imaging, 1986-92. Med. dir. USPHS, 1957-64, U. Calif. at Berkeley fellow, 1959-61. Fellow Inst. for elec. and electronic engring., Am. Coll. Nuclear Physicians, Am. Inst. Med. and Biol. Engring.; mem. NAS (com. on atomic casualties 1964-70, com. on biol. effects of ionizing radiation 1978-80; nat. coun. on radiation protection and measurement 1972-82, 92-97). Democrat. Unitarian Universalist. Avocations: tennis, sailing, skiing. Office: Vanderbilt U Med Sch Dept Radiol Sci Mcn S1314 Nashville TN 37232-2675

BRILL, ALAN RICHARD, entrepreneur; b. Evansville, Ind., July 5, 1942; s. Gregory and Bernice Lucille (Froman) B.; children: Jennifer Leigh, Katherine Anne, Alison Elizabeth. AB, DePauw U., 1964; MBA, Harvard U., 1968. Mgmt. cons. Peace Corps, Ecuador, 1964-66; sr. acct., cons. Arthur Young & Co., N.Y.C., 1968-71; v.p. ops. Charter Med. Mgmt. Co., Inc., 1972-73; v.p. controller Hosp. Investors, Atlanta, 1972-73; v.p., treas., dir. Worrell Newspapers, Inc., Worrell Broadcasting, Inc., Charlottesville, Va., 1973-79; pres. Brill Assocs., Evansville, Ind., 1979—, Brill Media Co., Inc., Evansville, Ind., 1980—. Bd. visitors U. So. Ind. Sch. Bus. Mem. AICPA, N.Y. State Soc. CPAs, Evansville C. of C. (bd. dirs.), Jobs for S.W. Ind. (bd. dirs.), Beacon Group, Farmington Country Club (Charlottesville), Safari Internat. Club. Republican. Methodist. Home: PO Box 3517 Evansville IN 47734-3517 Office: Brill Media Co Inc PO Box 3353 Evansville IN 47732-3353

BRILL, ARTHUR SYLVAN, biophysics educator; b. Phila., June 11, 1927; s. Edward Abram and Lillian (Milner) B.; m. Patricia Anne Hartig, Feb. 10, 1957; children: Julie Anne, Claire Bernice. AB in Physics with highest honors, U. Calif., Berkeley, 1949; PhD, U. Pa., 1956. Postdoctoral fellow in med. physics U. Pa., Phila., 1956-58; rsch. assoc. dept. engring. physics Cornell U., Ithaca, N.Y., 1959-60; asst. prof. biophysics Yale U., New Haven, Conn., 1961-64, assoc. prof. molecular biophysics, 1964-68; prof. materials sci. U. Va., Charlottesville, 1968-73, mem. Ctr. for Advanced Studies, 1968-71, prof. physics, 1973-97, program dir. interdisciplinary biophysics program, 1989-93, prof. emeritus, rsch. prof. physics, 1997—. Author: Transition Metals in Biochemistry, 1977; assoc. editor Biophys. Jour., 1978-81, publ. com., 1981-84; contbr. numerous articles to profl. jours., books. Cpl. U.S. Army, 1945-46. Predoctoral rsch. fellow NIH, U. Pa., 1950-55, Donner fellow in med. sci. NRC-Nat. Acad. Sci., Oxford U., Eng., 1958-59. Fellow Am. Phys. Soc. (chmn. div. biol. physics 1975-76, 90-91); mem. Biophys. Soc. (charter), Am. Chem. Soc., Microscopy Soc. Am. Office: Univ Va Dept Physics Jw Beams Lab Physics Charlottesville VA 22904-0001 E-mail: asb0x@virginia.edu.

BRILL, DONALD MAXIM, educator, writer, researcher; b. Elk Mound, Wis., Sept. 8, 1922; s. John James and Grace Darling (Mayo) B.; m. Meredith Joy Wright, June 25, 1955; children: John Richard, Rebecca Jean, Linda Marie, Susan Elizabeth. BS, Stout State U., 1947; MA, U. Minn., 1949; PhD, U. Wis., 1973. Tchr. Mpls. Pub. Schs., 1949-50, Eau Claire (Wis.) Pub. Schs., 1950, Chippewa Valley Tech. Coll., 1951-58; supr. Wis. Tech. Colls., Madison, 1958-65; coord. Great Cities Program for Sch. Improvement Rsch. Coun., Chgo., 1965-67; supr. rsch. Wis. Tech. Colls., Madison, 1967-70, asst. state dir., 1970-83. Adj. prof. U. Wis., Stout, 1983-86. Mem. state com. for employment support of Guard and Res., 1983-86; mem. Eau Claire Dist. Sch. Bd., 1989-92; founding bd. dirs. Fourth Dimension, Inc., WHEM-FM, 1994-98; primary candidate 3d Congl. Dist., Wis., 1994. With U.S. Army, 1942-45, ETO. Mem. DAV, VFW, SAR, Am. Vocat. Assn. (life), The Mayflower Soc. Republican. Baptist. Avocations: writing, genealogy, poetry, travel, restored victorian home. Home: W 2745 Mitchell Rd Eau Claire WI 54701-8603 E-mail: dmb316@aol.com.

BRILL, LESLEY, literature and film studies educator; b. Chgo., Sept. 3, 1943; s. Walter Henry and Fay (Trolander) B.; m. Megan Parry, Jan. 18, 1970; children: Benjamin, Calista. BA, U. Chgo., 1965; MA, SUNY, Binghamton, 1967; PhD, Rutgers U., 1971. Asst. prof. English U. Colo., Boulder, 1970-80, assoc. prof., 1981-89, chmn. dept. English, 1981-85, grad. dir., 1985-87; prof. and chmn. dept. English Wayne State U., Detroit, 1989-94. Vis. lectr. U. Kent, Canterbury, Eng., 1978-79; vis. prof. U. Paul Valery, Montpellier, France, 1984, U. de Nantes, France, 1995. Author: The Hitchcock Romance: Love and Irony in Hitchcock's Films, 1988, John Huston's Filmmaking, 1997; contbr. articles on lit. and film to profl. jours. Rockefeller Found. fellow, 1977-78. Mem. Soc. Cinema Studies. Office: Wayne State U Dept English Detroit MI 48202 E-mail: aa4525@wayne.edu.

BRILL, MARLENE TARG, writer; b. Chgo., Sept. 27, 1945; d. Irving and Genevieve (Worshill) Targ; m. Richard Benjamin Brill, Feb. 4, 1973; 1 child, Alison. BS Spl. Edn., U. Ill., 1967; MS Early Childhood Edn., Roosevelt U., 1973. Tchr. spl. edn. Dept. Mental Health, Chgo., 1967-70, Chgo. Bd. Edn., 1970-73, Wayne County Intermediate Sch., Detroit, 1973-75; curriculum specialist Cook County Office of Pub. Instrn., Chgo., 1975-78; media coord. South Metropolitan Assn., South Holland, Ill., 1979-80; writer, author MTB Comms., Wilmette, Ill., 1980—. Author: Hide-and-Seek Safety, 1985, John Adams, 1986, I Can Be a Lawyer, James Buchanan, 1988, Rainy Days and Rainbows, 1989, Why Do We Have To?, 1991, Keys to Parenting a Child with Down Syndrome, 1993, Guatemala, 1993, Allen Jay & The Underground Railroad, 1993, Trail of Tears: A Journey from Home, 1994, Keys to Parenting a Child with Autism, 1994, 2001, Guyana, 1994, Extraordinary Young People, 1996, Building the Capital City, 1996, Illinois, 1996, Honduras, 1996, Journey for Peace: The Story of Rigoberta Menchu, 1996, Let Women Vote, 1996, Women for Peace, 1997, Indiana, 1997, Tooth Tales from Around the World, 1998, Michigan, 1998, The AMA Diary of a Drummer Boy, 1998, The AMA Essential Guide to Asthma, 1998, Sport Success: Winning Women in Ice Hockey, 1999, Sport Success: Winning Women in Soccer, 1999, Sport Success: Winning Women in Baseball/Softball, 2000, Sport Success: Winning Women in Basketball, 2000, Margaret Knight: Girl Inventor, 2001, 25 Most Frequently Asked Questions About Discipline, 2001, Tourette Syndrome, 2001, Raising Smart Kids for Dummies, 2003, Bronco Charlie and the Pony Express, 2003. Mem. Soc. Midland Authors, Soc. Children's Book Writers and Illustrators, Author's Guild. Avocations: reading, music, drawing, crafts, walking. Office: MTB Comm 314 Lawndale St Wilmette IL 60091-3215 E-mail: mtbrill@worldnet.att.net.

BRILL, MICHAEL HENRY, physicist, vision scientist, editor; b. Bay Shore, N.Y., Jan. 26, 1949; s. Henry and Wenonah (Beale) B. BA in English and Physics, Case Western Res. U., 1969; MS in Physics, Syracuse U., 1971, PhD, 1976. Postdoctoral fellow MIT, Cambridge, 1974-77; physicist Perception Tech. Corp., Winchester, Mass., 1977-79; chief scientist Solotest Corp., Framingham, Mass., 1979; sr. scientist Jaycor, Alexandria, Va., 1980-83; sr. staff scientist Sci. Applications Internat. Corp., McLean and Falls Church, Va., 1983-94; mem. tech. staff Sarnoff Corp., Princeton, NJ, 1994—2001, cons., 2001—; book editor Physics Today, College Park, Md., 2002—03; prin. color scientist Datacolor, Lawrenceville, NJ, 2003—. Pres. Inter-Soc. Color Coun., 1998-2000; chmn. tech. com. 1-56 improved color matching functions Internat. Illumination Commn., 1999—. Co-author: Dimensional Analysis through Perspective, 1990; assoc. editor Physics Essays, 1995—, mem. editl. bd. mem. editl. bd. Color Rsch. and Application, 1990—; contbr. some 80 articles to profl. jours. 2d lt. USAF, 1972. Co-recipient Emmy award for outstanding tech. achievement Nat. Acad. TV Arts and Scis., 2000. Mem. Optical Soc. Am., Am. Soc. for Photogrammetry and Remote Sensing, Soc. for Info. Display, Phi Beta Kappa. Achievements include retina model with adaptive contrast sensitivity and resolution; volumetric theory of color constancy; broken-mirror model of acoustic rough-surface scattering; formulation of theories of perspective invariance in images; eight patents on vision modeling. Avocations: poetry writing, table tennis, recreational mathematics. Home: 14 Basin St Kingston NJ 08528 Office: Datacolor 5 Princess Rd Lawrenceville NJ 08468 E-mail: mbrill@datacolor.com.

BRILL, STEVEN CHARLES, financial advisor, lawyer; b. Miami, Fla., Aug. 21, 1953; s. Arthur W. and Joan K. (Caveretta) B. AB, Boston U., 1975; JD, Western New Eng. Coll., 1978; LLM, NYU, 1986. Advanced underwriting cons. Equitable Life Assurance Soc., N.Y.C., 1978-79; sr. advanced underwriting cons. Met. Life Ins. Co., N.Y.C., 1979-85; asst. v.p. personal fin. planning group Dean Witter Reynolds, N.Y.C., 1985-87; v.p., dir. asset allocation group Chase Pvt. Bank, N.Y.C., 1987-98; prin. Spielberger, Dampf, Brill & Levine, LLC, 1998—. Chmn. Cmty. Housing Innovations, Inc.; past pres., dir. Wychwood Owner's Corp., Great Neck, N.Y., Realty of Bay Terr. Inc., Bayside, N.Y. Contbr. articles to Mature Outlook Mag. Avocations: skiing, tennis, golf. Home: 16625 12th Ave Whitestone NY 11357-2261 E-mail: brilladvis@aol.com.

BRILL, WINSTON JONAS, microbiologist, educator, research director, publisher and management consultant; b. London, June 16, 1939; came to U.S., 1949; s. Walter and Irmgard (Levy) B.; m. Nancy Carol Weisburd, June 11, 1964; 1 child, Eric David BA, Rutgers U., 1961; PhD in Microbiology, U. Ill., 1963. Postdoctoral fellow MIT, Cambridge, 1965-67; asst. prof. dept. bacteriology U. Wis., Madison, 1967-70, assoc. prof., 1970-74, prof., 1974-79, Vilas research prof., 1979-83, adj. prof., 1983—; v.p., dir. research Agracetus, 1981-89; pres. Winston J. Brill & Assocs., Madison, 1989—. Panel mem. NSF, USDA, Pontifical Acad. Scis.; mem. recombinant DNA adv. com. NIH, 1979-83; mem. policy adv. com. USDA, 1985— ; mem. genetic engring. adv. panel to U.S. sec. state, 1981; mem. exec. bd. Nat. Inst. Emerging Tech. Pub., editor: Innovative Leader, 1992—; mem. editl. bd. Jour. Biotech., Trends in Biotech., Critical Revs. in Biotech.; contbr. articles to profl. jours. Recipient Eli Lilly award in microbiology and immunology, 1979, Alexander von Humboldt Found. award, 1979, Award of Distinction U. Wis., 1990; Henry Rutgers fellow Rutgers U., 1961. Fellow AAAS, Am. Acad. Microbiology; mem. NAS, Am. Soc. Microbiology, Am. Soc. Plant Physiologists, Am. Soc. Biochemistry and Molecular Biology, Internat. Soc. Plant Molecular Biology. E-mail: wbrill@winstonbrill.com.

BRILL, YVONNE CLAEYS, engineer, consultant; b. St. Norbert, Manitoba, Canada, Dec. 30, 1924; d. August and Julienne (Carette) Claeys; m. William Franklin Brill, Dec. 15, 1951; children: Naomi, Matthew, Joseph. BS, U. Manitoba, Canada, 1945; MS, U. So. Calif., 1951. Mathematician Douglas Aircraft, Santa Monica, Calif., 1945-46; research analyst Rand Corp., Santa Monica, 1946-49; group leader Marquardt Corp., Van Nuys, Calif., 1949-52; staff engr. UTC Research, East Hartford, Conn., 1952-55; project engr. Wright Aeronautical, Wood Ridge, N.J., 1955-58; mgr. propulsion systems RCA AstroElectronics, Princeton, N.J., 1966-81, staff engr., 1983-86; mgr. solid rocket motor NASA Hdqrs., Washington, 1981-83; with space engring segment Internat. Maritime Satellite Orgn., London, 1986-91; cons. Brill Assocs., Skillman, N.J., 1991—. Mem. USAF Sci. Adv. Bd., Washington, 1982-83, Nat. Acad. Engring.; Com. on Internat. Orgns. and Programs, 1992-96; apptd. mem. aerospace safety adv. panel NASA, 1994-2001. Contbr. articles to sci. jours.; patentee in field. Recipient Engr. of Yr. award, Ctrl. Jersy Engring. Couns., 1979, Diamond Superwoman award, Harpers Bazaar/DeBeers Corp., 1980, Disting. Pub. Svc. medal, NASA, 2001, Judith A. Resnik award, IEEE, 2002. Fellow AIAA (Marvin C. Demlar award 1983, WYLD award in rocket propulsion 2002), Soc. Women Engrs. (dir. student affairs 1979-80, 83-84, treas. 1980-81, Engring. Achievement award 1986, Resnik Challenger medal 1993); mem. Nat. Acad. Engring., Internat. Astronautical Acad. (academician, edn. com. 1983-85), Sigma Xi, Tau Beta Pi. Home and Office: 914 Route 518 Skillman NJ 08558-2616

BRILL DE RAMIREZ, SUSAN BERRY, English educator; b. N.Y.C., Apr. 25, 1955; d. Robert M. and Dorothy Ann (Retallack) B. Student, St. Johns Coll., 1974-75; BA in English, U. Wis., 1977; MA in English, U. Chgo., 1978; MBA in Mgmt., U. Wis., 1982; PhD in English, U. N.Mex., 1991. Asst. prof. English Bradley U., Peoria, Ill., 1991-97, assoc. prof. English, 1997—2003, prof. English, 2003—. Author: Wittgenstein and Critical Theory, 1995, Contemporary American Indian Literatures and the Oral Tradition, 1999; mem. editl. adv. bd. Jour. Baha'i Studies; mem. editl. bd. Jour. Comm. and Rels. Mem. MLA, Nat. Women's Studies Assn., Nat. Coun. Tchrs. of English, Semiotic Soc. Am., Internat. Assn. Philosophy and Lit., Assn. Study Am. Indian Lit., Assn. for Study Lit. and Environment, Assn. Baha'i Studies, Phi Kappa Phi. Avocations: weight lifting, running, playing the fiddle. Office: Bradley U English Dept Peoria IL 61625-0001

BRILLIANT, ANDREW PRINCE, lawyer; b. Boston, Mass, Nov. 15, 1946; s. Harold and Charlotte (Prince) Brilliant; m. Beverly Bernstein, June 14, 1974; children: Diana, Natalie. BA, U. Va., 1968; JD, Boston Coll., 1973. Bar: Mass. 1973, NY 1976. Atty. advisor cable TV and common carriers burs. FCC, Washington, 1973—76; with Home Box Office, Inc., NYC, 1976—80, assoc. counsel, 1976—78, chief counsel ops., 1979—80; sr. v.p. internat. and legal rels ESPN, Inc., Bristol, Conn., 1980. USAR, 1968—70. Office: ESPN Inc 605 3rd Ave Fl 8 New York NY 10158-0032

BRILLIANT, ASHLEIGH ELLWOOD, writer, cartoonist, publisher, educator; b. London, Dec. 9, 1933; came to the U.S., 1956, naturalized, 1969; s. Victor and Amelia (Adler) B.; m. Dorothy Low Tucker, June 28, 1968. BA with honors, Univ. Coll., London, 1955; MA in Edn., Claremont Grad. Sch., 1957; PhD in Am. History, U. Calif., Berkeley, 1964. Tchr. English Hollywood H.S., L.A., 1956-57; tchg. asst., reader in history U. Calif., Berkeley, 1960-63; asst. prof. history Ctrl. Oreg. Coll., Bend, 1964-65, Floating Campus divsn. Chapman Coll., Orange, Calif., 1965-67; entertainer in coffeehouses, outdoor spkr. San Francisco, 1967-68; syndicated cartoonist, dir. Brilliant Enterprises, pub. and licensing, San Francisco, Santa Barbara, Calif., 1967—. Creator Pot-Shots postcards, T-shirts, cocktail napkins, tote-bags, other items; mem. faculty Sonoma State U., Santa Barbara City Coll.; vis. scholar Ctrl. Oregon Cmty. Coll., 2002. Author: I May Not Be Totally Perfect, But Parts of Me Are Excellent, And Other Brilliant Thoughts, 1979, I Have Abandoned My Search for Truth and Am Now Looking for a Good Fantasy, 1980, Appreciate Me Now and Avoid the Rush, 1981, I Feel Much Better Now That I've Given Up Hope, 1984, All I Want Is A Warm Bed and A Kind Word, and Unlimited Power, 1985, I Try to Take One Day At A Time, But Sometimes Several Days Attack Me At Once, 1987, The Great Car Craze: How Southern California Collided With The Automobile in the 1920's, 1989, We've Been Through So Much Together and Most of It Was Your Fault, 1990, Be A Good Neighbor and Leave Me Alone, 1992, I Want to Reach Your Mind...Where is it Currently Located, 1994, I'm Just Moving Clouds Today-Tomorrow I'll Try Mountains, 1999; founder, leader Ban Leafblowers and Save Our Town, 1996. Recipient Raymond B. Bragg award, 1987, Disting. Alumnus of Yr. award Claremont Grad. U., 2000; Claremont Grad. Sch. scholar, 1956; Haynes fellow, 1962, Panama-Pacific fellow, 1963. Mem. Newspaper Comics Coun., No. Calif. Cartoonists Assn., Mensa. Jewish. Home and Office: 117 W Valerio St Santa Barbara CA 93101-2927 E-mail: ashleigh@west.net.

BRILLIANT, BARBARA, television host, producer, columnist, consultant, journalist, communications and media consultant, musician; b. Montreal, Que., Canada, Sept. 24, 1935; d. Saul and Esther (Saltzman) Lecker; m. Erwin Brilliant, June 29, 1958; children: Bradley, Todd, Michelle. Student, McGill Tchrs. Coll., 1953, McGill Conservatory of Music; AA, Sir George Williams U., Montreal, 1955; BA in Psychology summa cum laude, Boston Coll., 1975. Tchr. Protestant Sch. Bd., Montreal, 1953-58, dir. drama sch., 1957-58; artist-in-residence City of Boston, 1978-83; TV host, producer Sta. WBZ-TV, Boston, 1979-90; freelance news producer AARP News Network, 1989—; mus. dir. Showtime Singers. Artistic dir. Showtime Singers; freelance writer, composer, lyricist; columnist A&E Picks, Dear Barbara advice for people 40 plus; advisor Radcliff Coll., Cambridge, Mass., 1985—; pres. Speechworks; media and pub. speaking coach and trainer; TV location host New Eng. Cable News "Time For Living" program; freelance journalist Boston Herald, Boston Bus. Jour., Banker and Tradesman, Cape Cod Times, Wedding Day; aerobics instr. various workout ctrs. Actor: Mirrored area, 1957—58, Boston area, 1985—; composer (with Charles Segal): You're Not Alone, —, Time to Care, —, Talk to Me, —; prodr.(, co-host nat. cable TV show): Barbara & Bill, —, : Conversations With the Conductor, — (Best Program award, 1997); composer (lyricist, prodr.): (CD) Brilliant! Better Late Than Never, 2001; artistic dir. (plays) Showtime Singers Proclaimation Newton Mayor David Cohen, 2002. Mem. White House Conf. on Aging, Washington, 1981; advisor Cultural Affairs Commn., Newton, 1980—82, Nat. Com. to Study and Resolve Problems of Older Ams., Boston, 1984—; mem. adv. bd. Radcliffe Coll. Women; spokesperson Alzheimers Disease and Related Disorders Assn., Boston, 1985—; mem. Time Capsule Harvard Schlessinger Libr., Cambridge, 1980; advisor Mass. Sec. Elder Affairs, 1992—93. Named One of Boston's Most Interesting Women, Boston Woman Mag., 1988, Hon. Order Ky. Cols., 1987; recipient Cert. of Recognition, City of Boston, 1979, Media award, AARP, 1980, Lifetime Achievement award, WW Group Internat., 1987, award, Sandoz Gerontol. Found., 1989, 1991, Gov. Michael Dukakis proclamation service in media to elderly, 1989, Mayor Raymond Flynn declared Barbara Brilliant Day, Sept. 24, 1989, Awareness of Aging tree planted in her honor Newton City Hall, Bronze/Nat. Mature Media award for "Barbara Bill" 6 part TV series exec. prodr., co-host Barbara Brilliant, Brilliant Artist Entertainment 2001 award excellence in journalism, Nat. Media award, 2001; fellow, Nat. Press. Found., 1987. Mem.: AFTRA, Cultural Commn. Discover Newton Arts, Screen Actors Guild. Avocation: Avocations: singing, tennis, piano, reading, aerobics. Office: Brilliant Communications PO Box 610310 Newton MA 02461-0310 E-mail: brilliantb@aol.com.

BRILLIANT, ELEANOR LURIA, social work educator; b. Bklyn., Nov. 25, 1930; d. Joseph and Leah (Cohen) Luria; m. Richard Brilliant, June 24, 1951; children: Stephanie, Livia, Franca, Myron. BA, Smith Coll., Northampton, Mass., 1952; MS, Bryn Mawr (Pa.) Coll., 1969; DSW, Columbia U., 1974. Asst. in prodn. course Harvard Bus. Sch., Cambridge, Mass., 1952-54; instr. Bryn Mawr Coll., 1969-71; adminstr., dir. Lower East Side Family Union, N.Y.C., 1974-75; dir. planning/evaluation United Way of Westchester, White Plains, N.Y., 1975-78, assoc. exec. dir., 1978-80; asst. prof. Columbia U., N.Y.C., 1980-84, assoc. prof., 1984-85; assoc. prof. social work Rutgers U., New Brunswick, N.J., 1986-95, prof., 1995—, mem. women's studies faculty, 1992—; dir. BSW program Rutgers U. Livingston Coll., New Brunswick, 1987-89; chair, adminstr. policy and planning area MSW program Rutgers U. Sch. Social Work, New Brunswick, 1992-97. Cons. United Way of Westchester, White Plains, 1980, Family Info. and Referral Svc. Teams, Inc., White Plains, 1980-83, 87, James Bell Assoc., 1994-96. Author: The Urban Development Corporation: Private Interests and Public Authority, 1975, The United Way: Dilemmas of Organized Charity, 1990, Private Charity and Public Inquiry: A History of the Filer and Peterson Commissions, 2000. U.S. Fulbright grantee, 1972-73, NIMH grantee 1968-69; fellow Douglass Coll., Rutgers U., 1992—. Mem. NASW (rep. to del. assembly 1987, 90, nat. treas. 1989-91), Assn. for Rsch. on Non-Profit Orgns. and Vol. Action (v.p. adminstrn./sec. 1997-99, bd. mem.-at-large 1999-01), Internat. Soc. for Third-Sector Rsch., Assn. for Cmty. Orgn. and Social Adminstrn. Avocations: travel, reading, swimming. Home: 10 Wayside Ln Scarsdale NY 10583-2908 Office: Rutgers U Sch Social Work 536 George St New Brunswick NJ 08901-1167

BRILLIANT, RICHARD, art history educator; b. Boston, Nov. 20, 1929; s. Frank and Pauline (Apt) B.; m. Eleanor Luria, June 24, 1951; children: Stephanie, Livia, Franca, Myron. BA magna cum laude, Yale U., 1951, MA, 1957, PhD, 1960; LLB, Harvard U., 1954. Bar: Mass. 1954. From asst. prof. to prof., chmn. dept. art history U. Pa., Phila., 1962-70; prof. art history and archaeology Columbia U., N.Y.C., 1970—, Anna S. Garbedian prof. in the Humanities, 1990—; vis. Mellon prof. fine arts U. Pitts., 1971; vis. prof. Princeton U., 1986. Vis. prof. Scuola Normale Superiore, Pisa, Italy, 1974, 80, 88; chmn. governing bd. Soc. Fellows Columbia U., 1981-84; cons. Sta. WNET-TV, N.Y., 1984-89; dir. Italian Acad. for Advanced Studies in Am., Columbia U., 1996-00. Author: Gesture and Rank in Roman Art, 1966, Arch of Septimius Severus in the Roman Forum, 1967, The Arts of the Ancient Greeks, 1973, Roman Art, 1974, Pompeii: A.D. 79, 1979, Visual Narratives, 1984, Portraiture, 1991, Commentaries on Roman Art, 1994, Facing the New World, 1997, My Laocoon, 2000, Un Americano a Roma, 2000; co-author: (film) The Fayum Portraits, 1988, editor Art Bull., 1990-94; co-curator exhbn. Ctr. for African Art, N.Y.C., 1990; guest curator, exhibitor Jewish Mus., N.Y.C., 1997; guest curator (exhbn.) Mpls. Inst. Arts, 2003—. Fulbright grantee Rome, Italy, 1957-59; fellow Am. Acad. in Rome, 1960-62; Guggenheim fellow, 1967-68; NEH sr. fellow, 1972-73 Mem.: N.Y. Acad. Sci., Conn. Acad. Arts and Scis., Am. Sch. Classical Studies (mng. com. 1974—2001), Coll. Art Assn., Mass. Bar Assn., German Archaeol. Inst. (corr.), Phi Beta Kappa. Democrat. Avocations: reading, travel, wine. Home: 10 Wayside Ln Scarsdale NY 10583-2908 Office: Columbia U Dept Art History New York NY 10027

BRILLSTEIN, BERNIE J. producer, talent manager; b. N.Y.C., Apr. 26, 1932; s. Moe and Tillie Brillstein; m. Deborah Ellen Koskoff, 1975; children: Leigh, David Koskoff, Nick Koskoff, Michael, Kate. BS in Advt., NYU. Mailroom/talent rep. William Morris Agy., N.Y.C., 1955-64; talent rep. Mgmt. III, N.Y.C., 1964-69; packager, owner, producer The Brillstein Co., L.A., 1969—; CEO Lorimar Film Entertainment, L.A., 1996—; co-chair Brillstein-Grey Entertainment, Beverly Hills, Calif., 1991-96, pres. & CEO Beverley Hills, CA. Exec. producer (TV) Alf, 1986, The Boys, 1989, Politically Incorrect, 1997-98, 2000-01, It's The Garry Shandling Show, The Days and Nights of Molly Dodd, The Naked Truth, 1995, Mr. Show, 1995, The Steve Harvey Show, 1996, The Dana Carvey Show, 1996, Just Shoot Me, 1997, The Martin Short Show, 1999, Primetime Glick, 2001, The Wayne Brady Show, 2001; exec. producer (films) Dangerous Liaisons, Up the Academy, 1980, Blues Brothers, 1980, Neighbors, 1981, Continental Divide, 1981, Doctor Detroit, 1983, Ghostbusters I 1984, Summer Rental, 1985, Spies Like Us, 1985, Dragnet, 1987, Ghostbusters II, 1989, Larry Sanders Show, Celluloid Closet, 1995, Cat and Mouse, Happy Gilmore, 1996, The Cable Guy, 1996, Bulletproof, 1996, What Planet Are You From? 2000, Run Ronnie Run, 2002, exec.cons. The Real Ghostbusters, 1986. Served with U.S. Army, 1953-55. Recipient Peabody awards, Emmy nominations, Cable Ace award; honoree L.A. Free Clinic, 1987. Mem. N.Y. Friars Club, Beverly Hills C. of C. (bd. dirs.), Acad. Motion Picture Arts and Scis., TV Acad. Office: Brillstein-Grey Entertainment 9150 Wilshire Blvd Ste 350 Beverly Hills CA 90212-3453*

BRIM, ORVILLE GILBERT, JR., former foundation administrator, author; b. Elmira, N.Y., Apr. 7, 1923; s. Orville G(ilbert) and Helen (Whittier) B.; m. Kathleen J. Vigneron, May 30, 1944; children: John G., Scott W., Margaret L., Sarah M. BA, Yale U., 1947, MA, 1949, PhD in Sociology, 1951. Instr. sociology U. Wis., 1952-53, asst. prof., 1953-55; sociologist Russell Sage Found., N.Y.C., 1955-64, asst. sec., 1959-64, pres., 1964-72, trustee, 1964-72, cons., 1972-74; pres. Found. for Child Devel., 1974-85; mem. core study group MacArthur Found. Rsch. Program Successful Aging, 1985-89; dir. MacArthur Found. Rsch. Network on Successful Mid Life Devel., 1989—2002; pres. Life Trends, Inc., 1991—2002; vis. scholar Russell Sage Found., 1985-86; interim pres. Social Sci. Rsch. Coun., 1998-99. Vice chmn. Am. Inst. for Rsch., 1971-88, chmn. 1988-91; chmn. bd. dirs. Automation Engring. Lab., 1959-67; dir. Consumer Behavior, Inc., 1957-61; chmn. environ. panel U.S. Office Edn., 1962-64; mem. drug rsch. bd. NAS., 1964-66, adv. com. on child devel., 1971-76; mem. mental health tng. com. NIMH, 1959-62; chmn. commn. social scis. NSF, 1968-69; nat. adv. food and drug coun. HEW, 1967-69; chmn. com. on work and personality in mid. years Social Sci. Rsch. Coun., 1972-79; trustee Found. for Child Devel., 1972-85, Ctr. for Creative Leadership, 1972-78, Mental Health Law Project, 1973-77, William T. Grant Found., 1975-84, Greenwich Hosp., 1972-77 Author: Sociology and the Field of Education, 1958, Education for Child Rearing, 1959, Personality and Decision Processes, 1962, Intelligence: Perspectives 1965, 1966, Socialization after Childhood: Two Essays, 1966, American Beliefs and Attitudes Toward Intelligence, 1969, The

Dying Patient, 1970, Learning to Be Parents, 1980, Ambition: How We Manage Success and Failure Throughout Our Lives, 1992; editor: Lifespan Development and Behavior, Vol. 2-6, 1979-83, Constancy and Change in Human Development, 1980, How Healthy Are We? A Nat. Study of Well-Being at Midlife, 2003; cons. editor: Child Devel., 1958-61, Sociology of Edn., 1963-69, Sociometry, 1959-62; mem. publ. com.: The Public Interest, 1967-75. Served as 1st lt. USAAF, 1943-46. Recipient Wilbur Lucius Cross medal Yale Grad. Sch. Assn., 1975; Kurt Lewin Meml. award Soc. Psychol. Study Social Issues, 1979 Fellow APA, AAAS, Am. Sociol. Assn., Am. Acad. Arts and Scis., Am. Orthopsychiat. Assn. (pres. 1974-75), Ea. Sociol. Soc. (pres. 1971-72); mem. Inst. Medicine of NAS, Soc. Rsch. Child Devel. (Disting. Sci. Contbns. award, 1985).

BRIMBLE, ALAN, business executive; b. Langwith, Eng., June 5, 1930; arrived in U.S., 1967; s. Arthur George and May (Emery) B. BA with honors, St. Edmund Hall, Oxford (Eng.) U., 1952, MA, 1956. Asst. sec. Crompton Parkinson Ltd., London, 1960—62; music and arts programmes mgr. BBC-TV, 1962-67; sec., controller St. Louis Art Mus., 1969-79; dir. adminstrn. Conv. and Visitors Bur. Greater Kansas City, Mo., 1979-87; fin. cons., plan adminstr., 1987-2000. Mem. citizens com. Met. St. Louis Zoo-Mus. Dist., 1970-71; bd. dirs. Internat. Inst., St. Louis, 1970-73, Kansas City Arts Coun., 1980-84; v.p., CFO Meridian Residential Assn., 1995-99; pres. Meridian Master Assn., 1997-99. With RAF, 1948-49. Fellow, Chartered Inst. Secs. Home: 6909 Fairway Rd La Jolla CA 92037-5620

BRIMELOW, PETER, journalist; b. Warrington, Eng., Oct. 13, 1947; s. Frank Sanderson and Bessie (Knox) B.; m. Margaret Alice Laws, 1980; children: Alexander James Frank, Hannah Claire Catherine. BA in history and econs. with honors, U. Sussex, Eng., 1970; MBA, Stanford U., 1972. Security analyst Richardson Securities of Can., Winnipeg, Man., 1972-73; asst. editor Fin. Post, Toronto, Ont., Can., 1973-76, columnist, contbg. editor, 1978-80, 88-90; bus. editor Maclean's mag., Toronto, 1976-78; guest writer editorial page Wall St. Jour., N.Y.C., summer 1978; econ. counsel to U.S. Senator Orrin G. Hatch of Utah, Washington, 1979-81; columnist Toronto Sun Syndicate, 1980-82; assoc. editor Barron's, N.Y.C., 1981-83, contbg. editor, 1984-86; assoc. editor Fortune, N.Y.C., 1983-84; sr. editor Forbes, N.Y.C., 1986—2001, Nat. Rev. Mag., 1993-98. Contbg. editor . Chief Exec. mag, N.Y.C., NY, 1984—86; contbg. editor. Influence mag., Toronto, 1984—86; columnist The Times, London, 1986—90; editor vdare.com, 1999—; pres. Ctr. Am. Unity, 1999—; columnist CBS Marketwatch, 2002—. Author: The Wall Street Gurus: How You Can Profit from the Investment Newsletters, 1986, The Patriot Game: Canada and the Canadian Question Revisited, 1987, Alien Nation: Common Sense About America's Immigration Disaster, 1995, The Worm in the Apple: How the Teacher Unions are Destroying American Education, 2003; contbr. articles to profl. jours. Recipient Fulbright award, 1970, Nat. Bus. Writing award Royal Bank Can./Toronto Press Club, 1976, Nat. Bus. Writing citation, 1977, Gerald Loeb award, 1990; Stanford U. scholarship, 1970. Episcopalian. Office: Ctr for Am Unity PO Box 910 Warrenton VA 20188 E-mail: pbrimelow@vdare.com.

BRIMEYER, JAMES LEON, language educator; b. Dubuque, Iowa, July 19, 1947; s. Leon Joseph and Grace Carolyn (Link) Brimeyer; m. Kay Ann Frye, Aug. 8, 1970; children: Joseph, Ellen. BA, Loras Coll., Dubuque, 1969, MA, 1976. Tchr. Beckman HS, Dyersville, Iowa, 1969-70, Wahlert HS, Dubuque, 1970-95; instr. English N.E. Iowa CC, Peosta, 1995—. Edn. presenter numerous confs. Contbr. articles to profl. jours. Named State of Iowa Outstanding Tchr., Iowa Dept. Instrn., 1987—88, Educator of the Yr., U. Notre Dame, 1996; recipient Outstanding Tchr. award, U. Chgo., 1989, Tchg. Excellence award, NISOD, U. Tex., 1997, Iowa Literacy award, 2000. Avocations: reading, walking, golf. Home: 2630 Marywood Dr Dubuque IA 52001-0707 E-mail: brimeyej@nicc.edu.

BRIMMER, ANDREW FELTON, economic and financial consultant; b. Newellton, La., Sept. 13, 1926; s. Andrew and Vellar (Davis) B.; m. Doris Millicent Scott, July 18, 1953; 1 dau., Esther Diane. BA, U. Wash., 1950, MA, 1951; postgrad. (Fulbright fellow), U. Bombay, India, 1951-52; PhD, Harvard U., 1957; LL.D., Nebr. Wesleyan U., 1968, Marquette U., 1968, L.I. U., 1969, Oberlin Coll., 1969, Tufts U., 1970, Colgate U., 1970, Atlanta U., 1970, Middlebury Coll., 1971, U. Notre Dame, 1971, Bishop Coll., 1971, Upsala Coll., 1972, U. Md., 1976, U. Mich., 1979, U. So. Calif., 1980, Washington U., 1982; D.Soc.Sc., Boston Coll., 1971, Temple U., 1974; D.C.L., U. Miami, 1971, U. of the South, 1984; D.H.L., DePaul U., 1975. Economist Fed. Res. Bank, N.Y.C., 1955-58; asst. prof. Mich. State U., 1958-61, Wharton Sch. Finance and Commerce, U. Pa., 1961-66; dep. asst. sec. Dept. Commerce, Washington, 1963-65, asst. sec. for econ. affairs, 1965-66; mem. Fed. Res. Bd., 1966-74; Thomas Henry Carroll Ford Found. vis. prof. Grad. Sch. Bus. Adminstrn. Harvard, 1974-76; pres. Brimmer & Co., Inc., Washington, 1976—; Wilmer D. Barrett prof. econs. U. Mass.-Amherst. Bd. govs., vice chmn. Commodity Exchange, Inc.; bd. dirs. Bank of Am., Am. Security Bank, MNC Fin., Inc., Du Pont Co., Gannett Co., Inc., BellSouth Corp., Conn. Mut., Navistar Internat. Corp., Blackstone Investment Income Trust; mem. Fed. Res. Central Banking Mission to Sudan, 1957; cons. SEC, 1962-63; mem. Trilateral Commn.; trustee Coll. Retirement Equities Fund. Author: Survey of Mutual Funds Investors, 1963, Life Insurance Companies in Capital Market, 1962, Economic Development: International and African Perspectives, 1976, The World Banking System: Outlook in a Context of Crisis, 1985, International Banking and Domestic Economic Policies, 1986; Contbr. articles to profl. jours. Chmn. bd. trustees Tuskegee U., Com. for Econ. Devel.; bd. dirs. Interracial Council for Bus. Opportunity; mem. internat. panel UN Mgmt. and Decision Making Project, 1986-88; panel on fgn. trade stats. NAS. With AUS, 1945-46. Named Govt. Man of Year Nat. Bus. League, 1963; recipient Arthur S. Flemming award, 1966, Russworm award, 1966, Capital Press Club award, 1966, Golden Plate award Am. Acad. Achievement, 1967, Alumnus Summa Laude Dignatus U. Wash. Alumni Assn., 1972, Nat. Honoree Beta Gamma Sigma, 1971, Horatio Alger award, 1974, Equal Opportunity award Nat. Urban League, 1974, One Hundred Black Men and N.Y. Urban Coalition award, 1975, Disting. Svc. award Interracial Coun. Bus. Opportunity, 1986, Pub. Svc. award North Adams State Coll., 1987. Fellow Am. Acad. Arts and Scis., Nat. Assn. Bus. Economists; mem. Am. Econ. Assn. (Richard T. Ely lectr. 1982, v.p. 1989), Am. Fin. Assn., Assn. for Study Afro-Am. Life and History (pres. 1970 73, 89—), Coun. Fgn. Rels., Nat. Economists Club, Am. Statis. Assn., Soc. Govt. Economists (Disting. lectr. on econs. in govt. 1988), Ea. Econ. Assn. (v.p. 1989). Office: Brimmer & Co Inc 4400 Macarthur Blvd NW Washington DC 20007-2521

BRIMMER, CLARENCE ADDISON, federal judge; b. Rawlins, Wyo., July 11, 1922; s. Clarence Addison and Geraldine (Zingsheim) B.; m. Emily O. Docken, Aug. 2, 1953; children: Geraldine Ann, Philip Andrew, Andrew Howard, Elizabeth Ann. BA, U. Mich., 1944, JD, 1947. Bar: Wyo. 1948. Pvt. practice law, Rawlins, 1948-71; mcpl. judge, 1948-54; U.S. commr., magistrate, 1963-71; atty. gen. Wyo., 1971-74; U.S. atty., 1975; chief judge U.S. Dist. Ct. Wyo., Cheyenne, 1975-92, dist. judge, 1975—. Mem. panel multi-dist. litigation, 1992-2000; mem. Jud. Conf. U.S., 1994-97, exec., 1995-97. Sec. Rawlins Bd. Pub. Utilities, 1954-66; Rep. gubernatorial candidate, 1974; trustee Rocky Mountain Mineral Law Found., 1963-75. With USAAF, 1945-46. Mem. ABA, Wyo. Bar Assn., Laramie County Bar Assn., Carbon County Bar Assn., Am. Judicature Soc., Masons, Shriners, Rotary. Episcopalian. Office: US Dist Ct 2120 Capitol Ave Rm 2603 Cheyenne WY 82001

BRIN, DAVID, writer, astronomer; b. Glendale, Calif., Oct. 6, 1950; s. Herbert Henry and Selma (Stone) B; m. Cheryl Ann Brigham; 3 children. BS in Astronomy, Calif. Inst. Tech., 1973; MS in Elec. Engring., U. Calif.-San Diego, 1977, PhD in Space Sci., 1981. Electronics engr. Hughes Aircraft Co., Carlsbad, Calif., 1973-77; profl. novelist Bantam Books, N.Y.C., 1980—; postdoctoral fellow Calif. State Inst., LaJolla, Calif., 1982—85. Instr. physics, astronomy, writing San Diego State U., San Diego CC, 1982—85. Author: (novels) Sundiver, 1980, Startide Rising (Nebula award 1983, Hugo award 1983, Locus award), 1983, The Practice Effect (Balrog award), 1984, (with Gregory Benford) Heart of the Comet, 1986, Earth, 1990 (nominee Hugo award, 1994); (novellas and novellettes) The Tides of Kithrup, 1981, The Loom of Thessaly, 1981, The Postman (runner-up Hugo award 1983), 1982, Cyclops (nominee Hugo award 1985), 1984, Glory Season, 1993, Brightness Reef, 1996 (nominee Hugo award), Infinity's Shore, 1996, The Transparent Society, 1998 (Obeler Freedom of Speech award), (series) Startride Rising (Nebula award), 1983, Sundiver, 1985, The Uplift War, 1987 (Hugo and LOCUS awards for best novel, nominee Nebula award), Heaven's Reach, 1998, Foundation's Triumph, 1999, Forgiveness, 2001, Kiln People, 2002, Contacting Aliens: The Illustrated Guide to David Brins Uplift Universe, 2002; (collections) The River of Time, 1986, Otherness, 1994, Tomorrow Happens, 2003, (stories for anthologies) War of the Worlds: Global Dispatches, 1996; contbr. short stories, sci. fact articles, and sci. papers to profl. publs. Nominated for John W. Campbell award for best new author of 1982 Mem. Am. Assn. Aeronautics and Astronautics, Sci. Fiction Writers Am. (sec. 1982-84) Avocations: backpacking; music, science, general eclecticism. Office: care Phantasia Press 5536 Crispin Way Rd West Bloomfield MI 48323-3405*

BRIN, ROYAL HENRY, JR., lawyer; b. Dallas, Oct. 9, 1919; BA, JD, U. Tex., 1941; postgrad. fellow, Harvard U., 1941-42. Bar: Tex. 1941. Atty. OPA, Washington, 1942; asso. firm Strasburger & Price, Dallas, 1946-56, ptnr., 1956—. Editor-in-chief Tex. Law Rev., 1940-41; contbr. articles to profl. jours. Fellow Am. Bar Found. (life); mem. ABA, Am. Acad. of Appellate Attorneys, State Bar Tex., Tex. Assn. Def. Counsel (pres. 1981-82), Dallas Bar Assn., Dallas Assn. Def. Counsel, Def. Rsch. Inst., Am. Acad. Appellate Lawyers, Internat. Brotherhood Magicians (pres. 1969-70), The Chancellors (grand chancellor), Order of Coif, Phi Beta Kappa, Phi Eta Sigma. Home: 6506 Lupton Dr Dallas TX 75225-2323 Office: 4300 Bank of Am Plz 901 Main St Dallas TX 75202-3714

BRINBERG, HERBERT RAPHAEL, publishing company executive, information management; b. N.Y.C., Jan. 27, 1926; s. Henry and Anna (Stambler) B.; m. Blanche Leiman, July 15, 1945; children: Amy Lynn, Todd Michael. AB, Cornell U., 1947; MS, Columbia U., 1948; PhD, NYU, 1955; DSc (hon.), Syracuse U., 1989. Research economist Conf. Bd., 1948-50; cons. economist Boni Watkins, 1951-54; asst. dir. research Licensed Beverage Industries, 1954-55; mgr. econ. research and planning Canco div. Am. Can Co., 1956-61, dir. comml. research, 1961-66, v.p. planning, 1966-71, v.p. info. tech., 1971-78; pres., chief exec. officer Aspen Systems, Rockville, Md., 1978-85, Panel Pubs., Inc., Greenvale, NY, 1982-85; mng. dir. Wolters Kluwer U.S. Corp., N.Y.C., 1978-85, pres., chief exec. officer, dir., 1986-89; pres., CEO Parnassus Assocs. Internat., Inc., 1990—; chmn. Assoc. Info. Mgrs., 1988-90. Bd. dirs. K&F Industries, Brill Academic Publishers, The Associated Blind; adj. prof. Baruch Coll., 1988—, chmn. bus. adv. coun. Bernard L. Schwartz Comm. Inst., 1998—; chmn. bd. visitors Sch. Info. Studies, Syracuse U., 1996—. Mem. coun. Cornell U., 1998-2003. With USAAF, 1944-45. Mem. Info. Industry Assn. (past chmn., vice chmn. 1994-98), Software and Info. Industry Assn.(bd. dirs. 1999-2001), Cornell Club N.Y.C. E-mail: hrbrinberg@parnassusassociates.com.

BRIND, DAVID HUTCHISON, lawyer, judge; b. Albany, N.Y., Feb. 4, 1930; s. Charles Albert and Laura Stuart (Hutchison) B.; m. Shirley Jean Hodgins, Mar. 6, 1954; children: Susan Brind Morrow, Charles. AB, Union Coll., 1951; LLB, Albany Law Sch., 1954, JD, 1968; LHD, N.Y. Inst. Technology, 1971. Bar: N.Y. 1954, U.S. Supreme Ct. 1970. Atty. law divsn. N.Y. State Dept. Edn., Albany, 1954-55; ptnr. Chacchia & Brind, Geneva, N.Y., 1957-64; sole practice Geneva, 1964-95; presiding judge Geneva City Ct., 1974-95; ret., 1995; apptd. jud. hearing officer N.Y. State Supreme Ct., 1995—. Hearing officer N.Y. State and Local Ret. Sys., 1997—; counsel real estate N.Y. State Dormitory Auth., 1970-86; gen. counsel Geneva Gen. Hosp., 1966-85; local counsel Conrail; spl. counsel N.Y. Tchrs. Retirement Sys., 1959-72. Bd. dirs. Geneva United Way, 1965-89; campaign chmn. United Way Greater Rochester (N.Y.), 1966-69, pres., 1969-71; trustee Geneva Gen. Hosp., 1962-73; pres., 1969-71; trustee Geneva Hist. Soc., 1963-90, pres., 1968-70; chmn. Geneva Hist. Commn., 1969-89; mem. exec. bd. Finger Lakes coun. Boy Scouts Am., 1965—; bd. dirs. 7 Lakes Coun. Girl Scouts U.S.A., 1966-73; bd. dirs. Geneva Gen. Hosp. Nursing Home, pres., 1969-71; v.p. Geneva Bd. Edn., 1962-67; mem. pres.'s coun. Eisenhower Coll., 1972-79, Hobart & William Smith Colls., 1967—. Recipient Geneva Cmty. Chest/Red Cross Svc. citation, 1969, named Man of Yr., Geneva C. of C., 1971. Mem. Am. Assn. Homes for Aging, N.Y. State Sch. Bds. Assn. (law revisions com. and constnl. conv. com. 1964-68), Monroe County Jud. Com., 1976-80, Ontario County Bar Assn., N.Y. State Bar Assn. (jud. coun.), Fedn. N.Y. State Judges (pres. 1989-91), N.Y. State Assn. Jud. Hearing Officers (treas. 1995—), St. Andrews Soc. Albany, Rotary (pres. 1967-68), Finger Lakes Forum (pres. 1991—). Republican. Presbyterian. Home: 43 Delancey Dr Geneva NY 14456-2809 Office: 37 Seneca St Geneva NY 14456-0409 E-mail: judge@novocon.net.

BRIND'AMOUR, ROD JEAN, hockey player; b. Ottawa, Ont., Can., Aug. 9, 1970; m. Kellie Brind'Amour; 2 children. Grad., Mich. State U. With St. Louis Blues, 1988—91; left wing/center Phila. Flyers, 1991—99, Carolina Hurricanes, 1999—. Mem. CCHA All-Rookie Team, 1988—89; player NHL All-Star Game. Recipient CCHA Rookie of Yr. award, 1988—89. Office: Carolina Hurricanes 1400 Edwards Mill Rd Raleigh NC 27607-3624

BRINDLE, LEWIS CARVER, administrator,fundraiser, consultant; b. DuBois, Pa. s. Louis Young Brindle and Etta Lorraine Carver. BS in Edn. magna cum laude, Indiana U. Pa., 1975; MusM, Boston U., 1978. Owner Brindle Fine Catering, Boston, 1980-87; exec. asst. to pres./sec. bd. Union Theol. Sem., N.Y.C., 1988-91, major prospects officer, 1991-92; asst. dir. found. and corp. rels. NYU, 1992-95, assoc. dir. devel., 1996-2001; dir. devel. Parrish Art Mus., Southampton, N.Y., 1995-96; dir. Alberto Vilar Global Fellows Prog. in Performing Arts NYU, 2001—. Freelance opera singer, 1978-87. Republican. Episcopalian. Avocations: cooking, swimming, gardening, singing. Office: NYU 726 Broadway Room 638 New York NY 10003 Fax: 212-995-4727.

BRINDLE, WAYNE ALLAN, religious studies educator; s. Melvin and Gladys Felma Brindle; m. Nancy Ann Stewart; children: Jonathan David, Robert Sean. BA, Kans. Wesleyan U., Salina, 1969; ThM, Dallas Theol. Sem., 1973, ThD, 1988. Dir. sem. ext. UnionMissionera Evangelica Colombiana, Cali, Colombia, 1976—79; prof. bibl. studies Liberty U., Lynchburg, Va., 1981—. Newsletter editor Evang. Theol. Soc., Lynchburg, 1995—. Contbr. articles to profl. jours. Mem. Lynchburg Sch. Bd., 1994—2003. Named Tchr. of the Yr., Who's Who Among Coll. Tchrs., 2000; recipient, 2001. Mem.: Evang. Theol. Soc. (regional chair 2001—02), Soc. Bibl. Lit. Baptist. Avocations: writing, amateur radio operator. Office: Liberty Univ 1971 University Blvd Lynchburg VA 24502

BRINEGAR, CLAUDE STOUT, retired oil company executive; b. Rockport, Calif., Dec. 16, 1926; s. Claude Leroy Stout and Lyle (Rawles) B.; m. Elva Jackson, 1950 (div.); children: Claudia, Meredith, Thomas; m. Mary Katharine Potter, 1983 (dec. 1993); m. Karen Bartholomew, 1995. BA, Stanford U., 1950, MS, 1951, PhD, 1954; LLD (hon.), Elmira Coll., 1997. V.p. econs. and planning Union Oil (now Unocal), L.A., 1965, pres. Pure Oil divsn. Palatine, Ill., 1965-69, sr. v.p., pres. refining and mktg. L.A., 1969-73; U.S. Sec. of Transp. Washington, 1973-75; sr. v.p. adminstr. Unocal Corp., L.A., 1975-85, mem. exec. com., 1968-73, 75-92, exec. v.p., CFO, 1985-91, also bd. dirs., 1968-73, 75-95, vice chmn. bd., 1990 95. Founding dir. Conrail, Inc., 1974-75, 90-98; bd. dirs. CSX Corp., 1998-2002; vis. scholar Stanford U., 1992-97. Author: monograph on econs. and price behavior, 1970; contbr. articles to profl. jours. on statistics and econs. Chmn. Calif. Citizens Compensation Commn., 1990-2002; mem. regional selection panel White House Fellows Program, 1976-83, chmn., 1983. Mem. Am. Petroleum Inst. (bd. dirs. 1976-85, 88-91, hon. life dir. 1992), Georgetown Club, Boothbay Harbor Yacht Club, Southport Yacht Club, Phi Beta Kappa, Sigma Xi. Avocation: collecting first editions of Mark Twain. Home and Office: PO Box 20246 Stanford CA 94309-0246

BRINEGAR, ELIZABETH ANNE, critical care nurse, educator; b. Ottumwa, Iowa, Apr. 26, 1949; d. H.M. and Dorothy Jean (Fitzgerald) Thompson; children: Holly, Adam. ADN, Indian Hills Community Coll., Ottumwa, 1971, AA, 1982; BSN cum laude, N.E. Mo. State U., 1983; MS in Nursing, U. Mo., Columbia, 1994. Cert. critical care nurse; cert. ACLS; cert. family nurse practitioner; cert. geriatric nurse practitioner; CCRN. CCU and emergency room nurse St. Joseph's Hosp., Ottumwa, 1971-87; pub. health nurse Wapello County, Ottumwa, 1981-88; nursing resource pool Ottumwa Regional Health Ctr., 1988-91; instr. nursing Indian Hills Community Coll., 1987-91; clin. supr. med. ICU, U. Mo., Columbia, 1991-97; family and geriatric nurse practioner Shellbina Med. Clinic, Hannibal, Mo., 1994—2003. Family nurse practitioner U. Mo. Sch. Nursing; geriatric nurse practitioner, 1995. Mem. AACN. Home: 5620 Waterfront Dr N Columbia MO 65202-9056

BRINEY, ALLAN KING, retired radiologist; b. Wilkinsburg, Pa., Nov. 17, 1921; s. Alonzo Tripp and Helen Marie (Hardman) B.; m. Gayle Diane Briney, July 4, 1986; children: Ronald A., Nancy E., Barbara A., Douglas C. BS summa cum laude, U. Pitts., 1943, MD, 1945; fellow for Radiology, Hosp. U. for Pa., 1948-51. Diplomate Am. Bd. Radiology. Intern Pitts. Hosp., 1945-46; fellow in radiology Hosp. U. Pa., Phila., 1948 51; radiologist Topeka Med. Ct., 1951-53, Murphy Meml. Hosp., Whittier, Calif., 1953-62, Whittier Radiology Med. Group, 1953-94, Memrad Med. Group, Whittier, 1995-97; chief staff Presbyn. Intercommunity Hosp., Whittier, 1979, chmn. risk mgmt., 1981-91, radiologist, 1959-97; ret., 1997. Capt. USAF, 1946-48. Fellow Am. Coll. Radiology, 1969. Libertarian. Mem. Deist Ch. Avocations: skiing, biking, hiking, swimming, sailing. Home: 220 Cayuse Trl Sedona AZ 86336-9797 E-mail: allanking@earthlink.net.

BRING, MURRAY H. retired lawyer; b. Denver, Jan. 19, 1935; s. Alfred Alexander and Ida (Molinsky) B.; m. Constance Brooks Evert, Dec. 30, 1963 (div. June 1989); children: Beth, Catherine, Peter; m. Kathleen Delaney, May 19, 1990. BA, U. So. Calif., 1956; LLB, NYU, 1959. Bar: N.Y. 1960, D.C. 1963, U.S. Supreme Ct. 1966. Law clk. to Chief Justice Earl Warren U.S. Supreme Ct., Washington, 1959-61; spl. asst. to asst. atty. gen. civil div. Dept. Justice, Washington, 1961-62; spl. asst to dep. undersec. state Dept. State, Washington, 1962-63; dir. policy planning anti-trust divsn., 1963-65; ptnr. Arnold & Porter, Washington, 1965-87; sr. v.p., gen. counsel Philip Morris Cos., Inc., N.Y.C., 1988-94, exec. v.p. external affairs and gen. counsel, 1994-97, vice chmn., gen. counsel, 1997-2000; ret., 2000. Editor-in-chief N.Y. Law Rev., 1958-59. Bd. dirs. Guild Hall East Hampton, NYU Law Sch. Found. Mem. ABA, Assn. Bar City N.Y., D.C. Bar Assn., Order of Coif, Phi Beta Kappa, Phi Kappa Phi. Avocations: fishing, photography, art. Office: Philip Morris Cos Inc 120 Park Ave New York NY 10017-5592

BRINGHURST, ROBERT, poet; b. LA, Oct. 16, 1946; s. George Heber and Marion Jeanette (Large) B.; 1 child, Piper Laramie. Student, MIT, 1963-64, 70-71, U. Utah, 1964-65; BA in Comparative Lit., Ind. U., 1973; MFA, U. B.C., Vancouver, Can., 1975. Vis. lectr. dept. creative writing U. B.C., Vancouver, 1975-77, lectr. dept. English, 1979-80; adj. lectr. Simon Fraser U., Burnaby, B.C., 1983-84; writer-in-residence U. Winnipeg, Man., Can., 1986; Can./Scotland exch. fellow U. Edinburgh, Scotland, 1989-90; Ashley Fellow Trent U., Peterborough, Can., 1994; writer in residence U. Western Ontario, 1998-99; conjunct prof. Trent U., 1998—2003; adj. prof. Simon Fraser U., 2000—. Author: Shipwright's Log, 1972, Cadastre, 1973, Deuteronomy, 1974, Eight Objects, 1975, Bergschrund, 1975, Jacob Singing, 1977, Stonecutter's Horses, 1974, Tzuhalem's Mountain, 1982, Beauty of the Weapons: Selected Poems 1972-82, 1982, Ocean/Paper/Stone, 1984, Tending the Fire, 1985, Shovels, Shoes and the Slow Rotation of Letters, 1986, Blue Roofs of Japan, 1986, Pieces of Map, Pieces of Music, 1987, Conversations with a Toad, 1987, The Black Canoe: Bill Reid and the Spirit of Haida Gwaii, 1991, 1992, The Elements of Typographic Style, 1992, 1996, The Calling: Selected Poems 1970-85, 1995, Elements, 1995, A Story as Sharp as a Knife: The Classical Haida Mythtellers and Their World, 1999, The Book of Silences, 2001, Ursa Major, 2003, The Old in Their Knowing, 2003; editor (translator): Nine Visits to the Mythworld, 2000, Being in Being: Collected Works of Skaay of the Qquuna Qiighawaay, 2001; co-author: The Raven Steals the Light, 1984, 1996, A Short History of the Printed Word, 1999, author numerous poems, stage prodns., works for multiple voices. Guggenheim fellow in poetry, 1988. Home: Box 357 1917 W 4th Ave Vancouver BC Canada V6J 1M7

BRINGMAN, JOSEPH EDWARD, lawyer; b. Elmhurst, N.Y., Jan. 31, 1958; s. Joseph Herman and Eileen Marie (Sheehy) B.; m. Laurie Lynn Cunningham, July 11, 1992; children: Joseph Edward Jr., Elizabeth Grace. BA, Yale U., 1980; JD, Stanford U., 1983. Bar: N.Y. 1984, Wash. 1985, U.S. Dist. Ct. (we. dist.) Wash. 1986, U.S. Ct. Appeals (9th cir.) 1986, U.S. Ct. Appeals (fed. cir.) 1988, U.S. Dist. Ct. (ea. dist.) Wash. 2000. Acting asst. prof. U. Wash. Law Sch., Seattle, 1983-85; assoc. Perkins Coie, Seattle, 1985-91, of counsel, 1992—. Dir. Perkins Coie Cmty. Fellowship, Seattle, 1990-96, chair assoc. tng. com., 1997-2000. Editor: Stanford Jour. Internat. Law, 1980-83; author Fed. Trial Practice chpt. Washington Lawyers' Practice Manual, 2002-03. Mem. Yale Alumni Schs. Com., Seattle, 1980—. Nat. Merit scholar, 1976; recipient Pro Bono Publico award Trumbull Coll. (Yale U.), 1980. Mem. ABA, Wash. State Bar Assn., King County Bar Assn. (jud. screening com. 1993-96, chair fair campaign practices com. 1997-99, judiciary and cts. com. 1999-2003, sec. 2003-, trustee 2003-, membership com. 2003-, CLE com. 2003-). Democrat. Roman Catholic. Office: Perkins Coie LLP 1201 3rd Ave Fl 48 Seattle WA 98101-3099 E-mail: brinj@perkinscoie.com.

BRINK, CHARLES PATRICK, lawyer; b. Mpls., Mar. 26, 1955; s. Charles F. and Bernadine (Fitzpatrick) B. BBA, U. Notre Dame, 1977; JD, MBA, St. Louis U., 1980. Bar: Mo. 1980, U.S. Dist. Ct. Minn. 1981, U.S. Tax Ct. 1982, U.S. Ct. Appeals (8th cir.) 1984. Legal counsel Citicorp, St. Louis, 1980; ptnr. Robins, Kaplan, Miller & Ciresi, Mpls., 1981-89, Hart, Bruner & O'Brien, Mpls., 1989-90; atty. Brink & Brink, Ltd., Mpls., 1991—. Spl. bd. cons. Davis Thomas & Assocs., Mpls., 1985-90; bd. dirs. Patrons of the Arts in the Vatican Mus./Minn. Bd. dirs., exec. com. Minn. High Tech. Coun., 1984-88; chmn. bd. Greater Mpls. Food Bank, 1985-88; bd. dirs. Henn Co. Libr. Found., 1994-2000; participant Leadership Mpls., 1985-86. Named Super Lawyer Minn. Law & Politics and Minn. Bus. Jours, Top Lawyer in Minn. Mpls.-St. Paul Mag., 1999-2002. Mem. ABA, Mo. Bar Assn., Minn. Bar Assn. (bd. dirs. computer law sect.), U. Notre Dame Alumni Assn. (pres. 1986-87), Interlachen Country Club (bd. dirs. 2000—). Roman Catholic. Avocation: sports. Home: 1629 Cedar Lake Pky Minneapolis MN 55416-3613 Office: Brink & Brink Ltd 4700 Wells Fargo Minneapolis MN 55402

BRINK, DAVID RYRIE, lawyer; b. Mpls., July 28, 1919; s. Raymond Woodard and Carol Sybil (Ryrie) B.; m. Irma Lorentz Brink; children: Anne Carol, Mary Claire, David Owen, Sarah Jane. BA with honors, U. Minn., 1940, BSL with honors, 1941, JD with honors, 1947; LLD, Capital U., 1981, Suffolk U., 1981, Mitchell Coll. Law, 1982. Bar: Minn. 1947, U.S. Dist. Ct. Minn. 1947, U.S. Tax Ct. 1967, U.S. Supreme Ct. 1980, U.S. Ct. Appeals (D.C. Cir.) 1982. Assoc. firm Dorsey & Whitney, Mpls., 1947-53, ptnr., 1953-89, head Washington office, 1982-84, ret. ptnr. Trustee Lawyers Com. Civil Rights Under Law, 1978—; bd. dirs. Nat. Legal Aid and Defender Assn., 1978-80; U.S. panelist for Dispute Resolution under Free Trade Agreement with Can.; bd. visitors U. Minn. Law Sch., 1978-81; chmn. trust and estates dept. Dorsey & Whitney, 1956-82 Bd. editors: U. Minn. Law Rev, 1941-42; contbr. numerous articles to law jours. Bd. govs. Am. Coll. Trust and Estate Counsel Found., 1987-95. Served to lt. comdr. USNR, 1943-46. Recipient Outstanding Achievement award U. Minn., 1982 Fellow Coll. Law Practice Mgmt. (hon.), Am. Coll. Trust and Estate Counsel (regent, exec. com.); mem. ABA (gov. 1974-77, 80-83, pres. 1981-82), Ctrl. and Ea. European Legal Initiative, Com. on Law and Nat. Security, Com. on Substance Abuse, 2002—, Adv. Com. to Commn. on Lawyers Assisstance Programs, 2000— Com. on Specialization, Fund for Pub. Edn. of ABA (pres. 1981-82), Am. Bar Found. (state chmn. 1977-80, gov. 1980-83), Am. Bar Retirement Assn. (pres. 1976-77), Am. Judicature Soc. (bd. dirs. 1988—), Nat. Conf. Bar Pres., Inst. Jud. Adminstrn., Am. Arbitration Assn. (trustee 1981—), Can.-U.S. Law Inst. (adv. bd. 1987—), Minn. Bar Assn. (pres. 1978-79), Internat. Mgmt. and Devel. Inst., Hennepin County Bar Assn. (pres. 1967-68), Nat. Inst. Citizen Edn. in Law (nat. adv. bd. 1982-85, chmn. 1983-84), N.W. Athletic Club, Sr. Tennis Players Club, Inc. Office: Dorsey & Whitney # 50 S 6th St Minneapolis MN 55402

BRINK, DAVID SCOTT, clinical pathologist, educator; b. St. Louis, Mo., May 29, 1968; s. Gary Sheldon and Janet Gail Brink. BA magna cum laude, Washington U., St. Louis, 1990; MD, St. Louis U., 1995. Diplomate Am. Bd. of Pathology, 1999. Post-sophomore fellow St. Louis U. Sch. of Medicine, St. Louis, 1992—93, house staff (resident), 1995—99, fellow, 1999—2000, asst. prof., 2000—; pediatric pathologist SSM Cardinal Glennon Children's Hosp., St. Louis, 2000—; locum tenens pathologist Meml. Hosp., Belleville, Ill., 2001—02, part-time staff pathologist, 2002—. Contbr. articles to profl. jours. Fellow: Am. Soc. Clin. Pathology; mem.: AMA, Wagih Bari Soc. of St. Louis Pathologists, St. Louis Met. Med. Assn., Mo. State Med. Assn., Soc. for Pediatric Pathology, Coll. Am. Pathologists, Phi Beta Kappa. Avocations: acting

(special interest in Shakespeare), fencing. Home: 5210 Daggett Ave Saint Louis MO 63110-3026 Office: SSM Cardinal Glennon Children's Hospital 1465 S Grand Blvd Rm GC46 Saint Louis MO 63104-1095 Office Fax: 314-268-6471. E-mail: brinkds@slu.edu.

BRINK, FRANK, JR., biophysicist, former educator; b. Easton, Pa., Nov. 4, 1910; s. Frank and Lydia (Wilhelm) B.; m. Marjory Gaylord, May 1, 1939; children— Patricia Brink Mayer, David Warner BS, Pa. State Coll., 1934; MS, Calif. Inst. Tech., 1935; PhD, U. Pa., 1939; D.Sc. (hon.), Rockefeller U., 1983. Instr. physiology Cornell U. Med. Coll., N.Y.C., 1940-41; instr. biophysics Johnson Research Found., U. Pa., Phila., 1941-49; assoc. prof. biophysics Johns Hopkins U., Balt., 1949-53; prof. biophysics Rockefeller U., N.Y.C., 1953-81, dean grad. studies, 1958-72, Detlev W. Bronk prof., 1974-81, prof. emeritus, 1981—. Cons. to sec. of war Dept. Army, Washington, 1941-44; mem. com. for biology and medicine NSF, Washington, 1953-59; chmn. Pres.'s Com. for Nat. Med. Sci., Washington, 1963-64 Editor Biophysics Jour., 1960-64; mem. editorial bd. various jours., 1955-71; contbr. articles on phys. chemistry of nerve cells to profl. jours. Johnson scholar U. Pa., 1935-38; Lalor Found. fellow U. Pa., 1939-40 Fellow AAAS (life); mem. AAAS, NAS, Biophys. Soc. (charter), Am. Physiol. Soc., Soc. Gen. Physiologists, Am. Acad. Arts and Scis. Avocations: reading; cycling; traveling. Home: Pine Run Community Apt E-1 Ferry and Iron Hills Rds Doylestown PA 18901

BRINK, MARION ALICE, retired human resources specialist; b. Boston, Feb. 15, 1928; d. Martin Bernhard and Astrid Marie (Bjaastad) Windedal; m. A. Rudie Shobaken, Feb. 5, 1947 (div. 1963); children: Richard Michael Shobaken, Ron Eric Shobaken; m. James A. Brink, Jan. 29, 1977. Student, Cambridge Jr. Coll., 1945-47, Framingham State Coll., 1967, Boston U., 1967-69; BA, U. N.H., 1983, MLS, 2001; M in Theol. Studies, Harvard U., 1987. From lab tech. to chemist Liberty Mut. Rsch., Hopkinton, Mass., 1963-77; asst. to mgr. Rec. Sec. Office Harvard U., 1977-79; sec. Sloan Sch. MIT, 1980-82; owner tech. typing svc. New Castle, NH, 1982-84; counseling intern Green Pastures Counseling Ctr., Dover, NH, 1984-85; alcohol educator Freedom From Chem. Dependency Found., Inc., Needham, Mass., 1985-87, dir. devel., editor News Bulletin, 1987-88; ptnr. Palmerbrink, Charlestown, Mass., 1989-90; founder MB Assocs., Charlestown, 1991-96; ret., 1996. Mem. Harvard Inst. Learning in Ret., U. N.H. Marine Docent Program. Bd. dirs. Friends Metro Boston, Inc.; counselor Women's Resource Ctr., Portsmouth, 1980. Democrat. Unitarian Universalist. Avocations: sailing, women's studies, reading, spiritual development. Home: 86 Wentworth Rd New Castle NH 03854

BRINK, MARION FRANCIS, trade association administrator; b. Golden Eagle, Ill., Nov. 20, 1932; s. Anton Frank and Agnes Gertrude B. BS, U. Ill., 1955, MS, 1958; PhD, U. Mo., 1961. Rsch. biologist U.S. Naval Radiol. Def. Lab., San Francisco, 1961-62; assoc. dir. div. nutrition rsch. Nat. Dairy Council, Chgo., 1962-65, dir. div. nutrition rsch., 1965-70, pres., 1970-85; exec. v.p. ops. United Dairy Industry Assn., Rosemont, 1985-88, chief exec. officer, 1988-91. Vice chmn. human nutrition adv. com. USDA, 1980-81. Contbr. articles to prof. jours. Recipient citation of merit U. Mo. Alumni Assn. Mem. Am. Soc. for Nutritional Scis., Am. Soc. Clin. Nutrition, Am. Dietetic Assn., Dairy Shrine Club, Soc. for Nutrition Edn., Chgo. Nutrition Assn., Alpha Tau Alpha, Gamma Sigma Delta. Home: 444 Highcrest Dr Wilmette IL 60091-2358

BRINK, RICHARD EDWARD, lawyer; b. Renwick, Iowa, Apr. 27, 1923; s. John Allyn and Sylvia Lonella (Warman) B.; m. Helen M. Ladwig, Nov. 2, 1946 (dec. Feb. 1987); children: Thomas W., Gretchen K., Sara Jane (dec.), Paul E. (dec.); m. Ruth Brady Cousins, Apr. 22, 1989. BSChemE with distinction, BA in Chemistry with high distinction, State U. Iowa, 1944; JD cum laude, William Mitchell Coll., 1952. Bar: Minn. 1952, U.S. Dist. Ct. Minn. 1962, U.S. Dist. Ct. Mich. 1971, U.S. Ct. Appeals (Fed. cir.) 1982, U.S. Ct. Appeals (6th cir.) 1973. With Minn. Mining and Mfg. Co., St. Paul, 1946-59, mgr., 1955-59; mem. firm Carpenter, Abbott, Kinney & Coulter, St. Paul, 1959-70; ptnr. Alexander, Sell, Steldt & DeLaHunt, St. Paul, 1970-76; sr. patent atty. 3M Co., St. Paul, 1976-78, assoc. patent counsel, 1978-84, sr. assoc. patent counsel, 1986, sr. patent counsel, 1986-90, ret., 1990. Author: (with others) An Outline of U.S. Patent Law, 1959. Pres. Minn. Interprofl. Assn., 1993-94; bd. dirs. Walker Meth., Inc., 1993-96; mem. White Bear Lake United Meth. Ch. (charter), White Bear Lake Sch. Bd., 1960-75, chmn., 1969-75; leader People to People tour, China and Russia, 1985. Served with USNR, 1944-46. Mem. ABA (chmn. pub. info. com. patent, trademark and copyright sect. 1983-84, chmn. sub-com. cooperation with fgn. patent offices com. 1988-89), SAR, Minn. Bar Assn., Minn. Intellectual Property Law Assn. (chmn. pub. info. com., bd. dirs. 1983-90, rep. to Nat. Council of Intellectual Property Law Assns., pres. 1985), Am. Intellectual Property Law Assn., Holland Soc. N.Y., Am. Contract Bridge League, Sons of Norway, Phi Beta Kappa, Tau Beta Pi, Phi Lambda Upsilon, Phi Beta Gamma. United Methodist. E-mail: wbearister@aol.com.

BRINKER, THOMAS MICHAEL, finance executive; b. Phila., Sept. 8, 1933; s. William Joseph and Elizabeth C. (Feeley) B.; m. Doris Marie Carlin, Oct. 11, 1958; children: Thomas Michael, James E., Joseph F., Diane M. Student, St. Joseph's U., Pa.; MS in Fin. Svcs., Am. Coll., 1980; DBA, Heed U., 1990; BA in Orgnl. Mgmt., Ea. Coll., 1991. Registered investment advisor; CLU, ChFC, CFP, AEP. With Ice Capades, 1951-52, 56; with Casa Carioca, Garmisch, Fed. Rep. Germany, 1954-56; profl. ice skating tchr. and mfrs. rep. Ridley Park, Pa., 1956-60; agt., div. mgr. Prudential Ins. Co., Phila., 1960-65; gen. agt. Mut. Trust Life Ins. Co., 1965-70; pres., founder Fringe Benefits Inc., Havertown, Pa., 1970—, Fin. Foresight Ltd., Havertown, Pa., 1983—. Adj. prof. Pa. State U., 1984—, St. Joseph's U., 1985—. Host: (radio) Financial Forum, Sta. WWDB-FM, 1982-90, Sta. WCZN-AM, 1990-91, daily report on fin. foresight Sta. WFLN-FM, 1992-, WCZN-AM, 1994-, children's fin. reports on Dr. Tom on Money Matters, WPWA-AM, 1994-, WWCN, Estero, Fla., 1997, others; co-host: (radio) Fin. Foresight, Sta. WFIL-AM, Phila., 1998-2000, WWDB-AM Phila., 2001-, WPEN-AM Phila., 2003-; author: HI, I'm Tom Brinker, You're on WWDB, 1987; columnist: Financially Yours, 1983-, Dollars and $ense, 1999-; ghostwriter: Nat. Assn. Life Underwriter's Fin. Fitness campaign, 1985; columnist Dollars and $ense, 1999-; contbr., author, condr. of seminars on fin. planning; contbr. articles to profl. jours. Pres., Delaware County Estate Planning Coun., 1979-80, Pipeline Inc., Springfield, Pa., 1970-71; dir. nat. coun. Invest-in-Am., 1986; bd. dirs. Pacific Advisors Fund, Inc., 1992—, Cypress Benefit Svcs., Inc., 1997—. Recipient Nat. Quality award Nat. Assn. Life Underwriters, 1966-2002, Nat. Sales Achievement award, 1970-2000, TransAmerica Fin. Advisors award, 2003. Mem. CLU, Delaware County Life Underwriters (pres. 1975-76, 82-83), Am. Coll. Life Underwriters, Nat. Assn. Life Underwriters, Internat. Platform Assn., Nat. Assn. Ins. and Fin. Advisors (inducted into Hall of Fame, 2003), Internat. Assn. Fin. Planners (v.p. Delaware Valley chpt. 1986-88, pres. 1989-, chmn. 1990-), Million Dollar Round Table (mem. Ct. of the Table 1986-, Top of the Table 1991, 93-95, Twenty-Five Million Dollar Internat. forum 1992-93), Lake Naomi Club (v.p., mem. bd. govs. 1982, pres. 1986), KC, Manor Club, Tom Brinker's Op. Christmas Baskets (pres.), Kingsport Club, Inc. (bd. dirs., treas. 1997-). Roman Catholic. Home: 115 Locust Ave Springfield PA 19064-1619 Office: 1 N Ormond Ave Havertown PA 19083-5010 E-mail: jbrinker@brinkerorg.com.

BRINKLEY, ALAN DAVID, historian; b. Washington, June 2, 1949; s. David and Ann Fischer B.; m. Evangeline Morphos, June 3, 1989; 1 child, Diane Elizabeth. AB, Princeton U., 1971; PhD, Harvard U., 1979. Asst. prof. history MIT, Cambridge, 1978—82; Dunwalke assoc. prof. history Harvard U., Cambridge, 1982—88; prof. history grad. sch. CUNY, 1988—91; prof. history Columbia U., N.Y.C., 1991—98, Allan Nevins prof. history, 1998—, provost, 2003—; Harmsworth prof. Am. history Oxford (Eng.) U., 1998—99. Author: Voices of Protest: Huey Long, Father Coughlin, and the Great Depression, 1982 (Nat. Book award 1983), The Unfinished Nation: A Concise History of the American People, 1993, The End of Reform: New Deal Liberalism in Recession and War, 1995, Liberalism and its Discontents, 1998. Trustee Century Found., N.Y.C., 1996—, chmn. bd. trustees, 1999—; trustee the Dalton Sch., N.Y.C., 1999—. Guggenheim Found. fellow, 1984-85, Woodrow Wilson Ctr. Internat. Scholars fellow, 1985, Nat. Humanities Ctr. fellow, 1988-89; Media Studies Ctr. fellow, 1993-94; Russell Sage Found., 1996-97. Fellow Am. Acad. Arts and Scis.; mem. Century Assn. Home: 211 Central Park W # 6H New York NY 10024-6020 Office: Columbia U 205 Low Libr New York NY 10027 Fax: 212-932-0418. Business E-Mail: ab65@columbia.edu.

BRINKLEY, CHARLES ALEXANDER, geologist; b. Moody, Tex., Oct. 3, 1929; s. Jess Daniel and Vera Allene (Anderson) B.; m. Jeraldine Athalene Skeeter, June 18, 1952 (dec. 1992); m. Patricia Ann McCluney, Jan. 13, 1996. Student, Temple Jr. Coll., 1947-48; BS in Geology, Midwestern State U., 1957; MS in Geology, Pa. State U., 1960. Registered profl. geologist, Ark., Fla. Checker, stock mgr. A & P Tea Co., Temple and Waco, Tex., 1947-50; office asst. John M. Mouser, ind. oil operator, Wichita Falls, Tex., 1957; grad. asst. Pa. State U., 1957-59; geologist Texaco, Inc., New Orleans and Jackson, Miss., 1959-70, dist. geologist, 1970-72, dist. stratigrapher, 1972-75; regional geologist Gen. Crude Oil Co., Houston, 1975-77, exploration mgr. West Gulf dist., 1977-79; exploration mgr. (West Gulf) Mobil-GC Corp., 1979; exploration mgr./chief geologist Maralo, Inc., Houston, 1979-85; ind. petroleum geologist Houston, Kingwood, Tex., 1985; petroleum geologist, co-owner High Star Oil and Gas Exploration Co., Houston, Kingwood, Humble, Tex., 1986—. With USN, 1950-54. Fellow AAAS; mem. Am. Assn. Petroleum Geologists (cert., v.p. divsn. profl. affairs 1980-82), Soc. Econ. Paleontologists and Mineralogists (nat. gulf coast sect. and permain basin sect.), Am. Inst. Profl. Geologists (cert., sec.-treas. Tex. sect. 1985-87), Soc. Ind. Profl. Earth Scientists (cert., treas. Houston chpt. 1990), New Orleans Geol. Soc., Houston Geol. Soc., Miss. Geol. Soc., West Tex. Geol. Soc., Internat. Airline Passengers Assn., Houston Club, Midland Petroleum Club. Baptist. Home and Office: High Star Oil & Gas Exploration 8007 Hurst Forest Ln Humble TX 77346-1704 Fax: (281) 852-8919. E-mail: cabrinkley@hotmail.com.

BRINKLEY, JACK THOMAS, lawyer, former congressman; b. Faceville, Ga., Dec. 22, 1930; s. Lonnie Elester and Pauline (Spearman) B.; m. Alma Lois Kite, May 29, 1955; children: Jack Thomas Jr., Fred Alen II. Student, Young Harris Coll., 1947-49, Okla. A. and M. Coll., 1952; LL.B. cum laude, U. Ga., 1959. Bar: Ga. 1958, D.C. 1973. Sch. tchr., Ga., 1949-51; assoc. firm Young, Hollis & Moseley, Columbus, Ga., 1959-61; ptnr. firm Coffin & Brinkley, Columbus, 1961-66; mem. Ga. Ho. Reps., 1965-66; sr. ptnr. Brinkley and Brinkley, 1983-95, of counsel, 1996-2000, of counsel emeritus, 2001—; mem. 90th-97th Congresses from 3d Ga. dist.; chmn. mil. facilities and installations subcom. 97th Congress. Mem. Ga. Ho. Rep., 1965-66. Trustee Young Harris Coll. Mem. Ga. Bar Assn., Columbus Bar Assn., Young Lawyers Club of Columbus (pres. 1963-64), Blue Key, Civitan Club, Masons. Democrat. Baptist. Office: Corporate Ctr Ste 901 Columbus GA 31902

BRINKLEY, WILLIAM R. dean; V.p. grad. sciences, dean Grad. Sch. Biomed. Sciences Baylor Coll. Medicine, Houston, 1991—. Mem.: Inst. Medicine. Office: Baylor Coll Medicine Grad Sch Biomed Scis One Baylor Plz Houston TX 77030

BRINKMAN, DALE THOMAS, lawyer; b. Columbus, Ohio, Dec. 10, 1952; s. Harry H. and Jean May (Sandel) B.; m. Martha Louise Johnson, Aug. 3, 1974; children: Marin Veronica, Lauren Elizabeth, Kelsey Renee. BA, U. Notre Dame, 1974; JD, Ohio State U., 1977. Bar: Ohio 1977, U.S. Dist. Ct. (so. dist.) Ohio 1979. Assoc. Schwartz, Shapiro, Kelm & Warren, Columbus, 1977-82; asst. tax counsel Am. Elect. Power, Columbus, 1982; gen. counsel Worthington Industries, Inc., Columbus, 1982-99, v.p. adminstrn., gen. counsel, sec., 1999—. Author: Ohio State U. Law Jour.,1975-76, editor, 1976-77. Trustee, officer Friends of Dahlberg Ctr., Columbus, 1980-86; dir., officer Assn. for Developmentally Disabled, Columbus, 1986-94. Mem. ABA, Ohio Bar Assn., Columbus Bar Assn. Republican. Roman Catholic. Office: Worthington Industries Inc 1205 Dearborn Dr Columbus OH 43085-4769 E-mail: dtbrinkm@worthingtonindustries.com.

BRINKMAN, JOHN ANTHONY, historian, educator; b. Chgo., July 4, 1934; s. Adam John and Alice (Davies) B.; m. Monique E. Geschier, Mar. 24, 1970; 1 son, Charles E. AB, Loyola U., Chgo., 1956, MA, 1958; PhD, U. Chgo., 1962. Rsch. assoc. Oriental Inst., U. Chgo., 1963, dir. inst., 1972-81, asst. prof. Assyriology and ancient history, 1964-66, assoc. prof., 1966—70, prof., 1970—84, Charles H. Swift disting. svc. prof., 1984—2001, chmn. dept., 1969—72, Charles H. Swift disting. svc. prof. emeritus, 2001—. Ann. prof. Am. Schs. Oriental Rsch., Baghdad, 1968-69; chmn. Baghdad Schs. Com., 1970-85, chmn. exec. com., 1973-75, trustee, 1975-90; chmn. vis. com. dept. Near Ea. langs. and civilizations Harvard U., 1995-2001. Author: Political History of Post-Kassite Babylonia, 1968, Materials and Studies for Kassite History, Vol. I, 1976; Prelude to Empire, 1984; editorial bd. Chgo. Assyrian Dictionary, 1977—, State Archives Assyria, 1985—; editor in charge Babylonian sect. Royal Inscriptions of Mesopotamia, 1979-91; contbr. numerous articles to profl. jours. Fellow Am. Research Inst., in Turkey, 1971; sr. fellow Nat. Endowment Humanities, 1973-74; Guggenheim fellow, 1984-85 Fellow Am. Acad. Arts and Scis.; mem. Am. Oriental Soc. (pres. Middle West chpt. 1971-72), Am. Schs. of Oriental Rsch., Brit. Inst. Persian Studies, Brit. Sch. Archaeology in Iraq, Deutsche Orient Gesellschaft, Brit. Inst. Archaeology at Ankara. Roman Catholic. Home: 1321 E 56th St Apt 4 Chicago IL 60637-1762 Office: U Chgo 1155 E 58th St Chicago IL 60637-1569

BRINKMAN, MICHAEL OWEN, health care consultant, educator; b. Chgo., May 15, 1936; s. Adam John and Alice Corrine (Davies) B.; m. Mary Judith Zeitz, Jan. 18, 1958; children: Stephen, Daniel, Julie, Amy, Carl, Mary Alice. BEE magna cum laude, Marquette U., 1958. Instr. Marquette U., Milw., 1957-59; engr. Wis. Electric Power, Milw., 1958-59, A.C. Electronics, Oak Creek, Wis., 1959-62; svc. engr. Nuclear-Chgo. Corp., Des Plaines, Ill., 1962-63, dir. of svc., 1963-66, plant mgr., 1966-67; gen. mgr. Electrovac, Melrose Park, Ill., 1968; mktg. analyst A.C. Electronics, Oak Creek, Wis., 1969-70; pres. On-Call Nat., Barrington, Ill., 1970-72, Hosp. Maintenance Cons., Columbus, Wis., 1972—. Co-author: (books) Clinical Engineering, 1975, Managing Your Medical Equipment, 1978, 82; contbr. numerous articles to profl. jours. Dep. committeeman Schaumburg Twp. Rep., Hoffman Estates, Ill., 1964-67; supt. Country Christian Schs., Nashotah, Wis., 1978-90, bd. dirs., 1990-95; bd. dirs. Victory Christian H.S., Neosho, Wis., 1991—, vol. tchr., 1991—; mem. Oconomowoc Bible Fellowship, elder, 1996—. Mem. Med. Equipment Repair Assocs. (exec. dir. 1973—), Eta Kappa Nu, Pi Mu Epsilon, Tau Beta Pi, Alpha Sigma Nu. Avocations: bible teacher, golf, stamp collecting, basketball, antique glassware. Home: 443 W Prairie St Columbus WI 53925 1349 Office: Hosp Maintenance Cons Inc PO Box 309 Columbus WI 53925-0309 E-mail: hmc001@globaldialog.com.

BRINKMAN, PAUL DEL(BERT), foundation executive, university administrator; b. Olpe, Kans., Feb. 10, 1937; s. Paul Theodore and Delphine Barbara (Brown) Brinkman; m. Evelyn Marie Lange, Aug. 5, 1961 (dec. June 1988); m. Carolyn L. Backer, July 27, 1990; children: Scott Michael, Susan Lynnstep-children: Debra, Cynthia, Jeffrey. BS, Emporia State Coll., 1958; MA in Journalism (Newspaper Fund fellow), Ind. U., 1963, PhD in Mass Communications (Scripps-Howard fellow), 1971. Editor, reporter Emporia (Kans.) Gazette, 1954-59; instr. journalism Leavenworth (Kans.) High Sch., 1959-62; lectr. Ind. U., Bloomington, 1962-65, 68-70; asst. prof. Kans. State U., Manhattan, 1965-68; prof., dean Sch. Journalism U. Kans., Lawrence, 1970-86, vice chancellor for acad. affairs, 1986-93; dir. journalism programs John S. and James L. Knight Found., Miami, 1993-2001; dean U. Colo. Sch. Journalism and Mass Comm., Boulder, 2001—02, mem. adv. bd., 2002. Balt. Sun disting. lectr. Coll. Journalism, U. Md., 1993. Bd. dirs. William Allen White Found., 1974; chmn. Big Eight Athletic Conf., 1980-81, 87-88; faculty rep. Nat. Collegiate Athletic Assn., 1978-93; mem. press fellowship adv. com. Knight Internat.; adv. bd. Journalism Sch. U. Colo.; coun. on accreditation of law schs. ABA, 1998—; bd. govs. Kinsey Inst., 2002—. Named Trayes Prof. of Yr. Mass Comm. Soc. divsn. Assn. Edn. Journalism, 1990; recipient Disting. Alumni award Emporia State Coll., 1978, Disting. Svc. award Ind. U., 1986. Mem. Am. Assn. Schs. and Depts. Journalism (pres. 1977-78), Inland Daily Press Assn. (chmn. edn. com. 1980-83), Assn. Edn. Journalism (chmn. publs. com. 1974-75, pres. 1980-81), Soc. Profl. Journalists, Lawrence C. of C. (v.p. 1987-88), Rotary (pres. Lawrence chpt. 1987-88), Bloomington Press Club (bd. dirs. 2002-), Indiana U. Sch. Journalism Alumni (bd. dirs. 2003-), Ernie Pyle Soc., Sigma Delta Chi, Kappa Tau Alpha. Home: 3112 Coppertree Drive Bloomington IN 47401 E-mail: delpdb@aol.com.

BRINKMAN, WILLIAM FRANK, physicist, research executive; b. Washington, Mo., July 20, 1938; s. William F. and Mildred A. (Bocklege) Brinkman; m. Sybille Zeldin, Sept. 17, 2002; children: David, Curtis. BS, U. Mo., 1960, PhD, 1965. Postdoctoral fellow Oxford U., 1966; mem. staff Bell Labs., Murray Hill, N.J., 1966-72, dept. head, 1972-74, dir., 1974-84; v.p. rsch. Sandia Nat. Lab., Albuquerque, 1984-87; v.p. phys. scis. rsch. Lucent Techs./Bell Labs., Murray Hill, N.J., 1987-2000, v.p. rsch., 2000—01; sr. rsch. physicist Princeton (N.J.) U., 2002—. Contbr. articles to profl. jours. on theoretical physics. Fellow AAAS, Am. Phys. Soc. (pres. 2002, George E. Pake prize 1994); mem. Am. Acad. Arts and Scis., Nat. Acad. Sci. (chmn. 8-vol. report Physics Through the 1990s), Am. Philos. Soc. Home: 20 Constitution Hill W Princeton NJ 08540 Office: Princeton Univ Dept Physics 328 Jadwin Hill Princeton NJ 08540

BRINKMANN, ROBERT JOSEPH, lawyer; b. Cin., Dec. 25, 1950; s. Robert Harry and Helen R. (Streuwing) B.; children: Christopher, Julia. BA, U. Notre Dame, 1972; postgrad., Alliance Française, 1974-75; AM, Brown U., 1977; JD, Loyola U., Los Angeles, 1980. Bar: Calif. 1980, D.C. 1981, U.S. Ct. Appeals (D.C. and 9th cirs.) 1981, U.S. Supreme Ct. 1984, U.S. Ct. Appeals (6th cir.) 1987. Tchr. secondary schs., Los Angeles and Paris, 1974-77; assoc. Hedrick & Lane, Washington, 1980-82; gen. counsel Nat. Newspaper Assn., Washington, 1982-92; exec. dir. Red Tag News Publs. Assn., 1990-92; v.p., counsel postal and regulatory affairs Newspaper Assn. Am., Reston, Va., 1992—2003; with Olive, Edwards & Brinkmann, Washington, 2003—. Mem. faculty Am. Press. Inst., Reston, 1982-92; adj. faculty U. Md., 1996—. Mem. ABA, Fed. Communications Bar Assn. (former vice chmn. postal affairs com.). Roman Catholic. Home: 204 Lynn Manor Dr Rockville MD 20850-4431 Office: Olive Edwards & Brinkmann 1101 17th St NW Ste 602 Washington DC 20036 E-mail: robert.brinkmann@olive-edwards.com.

BRINKMEYER, DOTTY STEWART, maternal/child nurse; b. Denver, Sept. 12, 1945; d. Dan and May Irene (Davis) Clark; m. LeRoy Brinkmeyer, Jan. 8, 1977; children: Gail Herin, Brian Stewart, Bruce, Amy. BS in Nursing, U. Colo., Boulder and Denver, 1967, MS in Nursing, 1969. Staff nurse U. Colo. Health Scis. Ctr., Denver, 1967-76, 78-88, flex staff nurse, 1991-96; dir. nursing Plateau Valley Hosp.-Nursing Home, Collbran, Colo., 1976-78; coord., acting clin. supr. Physicians' Home Care, Denver, 1986, 87; nurse cons. HHS, Denver Regional Office Health Care Financing Adminstrn., 1988-90, survey and certification program rev. specialist, 1991—. Mem. Am. Nurses Assn., Colo. Nurses Assn., Sigma Theta Tau. Home: 6760 W 19th Pl 8-103 Lakewood CO 80214 E-mail: dbrinkmeyer@cms.hhs.gov.

BRINSFIELD, JOHN WESLEY, military officer, educator; b. Atlanta, Ga., Feb. 23, 1944; s. John Wesley Brinsfield and Marietta Stout Branson; m. Patricia Tallon Brinsfield, July 6, 2002; m. Patsy Knighton, Dec. 31, 1974 (div. Apr. 2, 1986); children: Casey Marie, Cindee Marietta. BA, Vanderbilt U., 1962—66; MDiv, Yale Div. Sch., 1966—69; PhD, Emory U., 1969—73; D of Ministry, Drew Theol. Sem., 1980—83. Cert. of Ordination North Ga. Conf. of the United Meth. Ch., 1969. Squadron chaplain Third Armored Cav. Rgt., Ft. Bliss, Tex., 1974—75; adj. asst. prof. of history U. of Tex. at El Paso, 1974—75; protestant chaplain Turkish-United States Logistics Detachment, Sinop, Turkey, 1975—76; instr. in world history U. of Md.-Europe, Sinop, 1975—76; instr. in ethics and world religions US Army Aviation Sch., Fort Rucker, Ala., 1976—80; asst. prof., history dept. US Mil. Acad., West Point, 1980—84; protestant pastor Mark Twain Chapel, Heidelberg, Germany, 1985—87; chief, unit and individual tng. US Army Chaplain Sch., Ft. Monmouth, NJ, 1987—90; third army pers. chaplain US Army Ctrl. Command, Riyadh, Saudi Arabia, 1990—91; chief of pers. divsn., forces command chaplain staff US Army Forces Command, Ft. McPherson, Ga., 1991—93; historian/author Office of the Chief of Chaplains, The Pentagon, 1993—95; dir. of ethical program devel. US Army War Coll., Carlisle, Pa., 1995—99; dep. command chaplain US Army Forces Command, Fort McPherson, 1999—2002; sr. historian, us army chaplain corps. US Army Chaplain Sch., Fort Jackson, SC, 2002—. Dir. of the mil. family program for 320 mil. families US Army War Coll., 1995—99; elected mem. Outstanding Young People of Atlanta, Atlanta, 1972—2003. Co-author: (history book) Faith in the Fight: Civil War Chaplains; contbr. article on the ethics of Gen. Sherman, article on a civil war chaplain, twenty articles on ethics and history; author: (history book) Encouraging Faith, Serving Soldiers: A History of the US Army Chaplain Corps, 1975-1995, (article on religion in the military) Oxford Companion to Am. Mil. History, (history book) Religion and Politics in Colonial South Carolina, (essay on human and spiritual needs) The Future of the Army Profession. Mem., bd. of directors Participation Ministries, Campbellsville, Ky., 1999—2003. Grantee grad. fellowship, Yale Divinity Sch., 3 yr. doctoral fellowship, Emory U., Woodrow Wilson fellowship for study at Oxford. Mem.: Yale Alumni Assoc., Yale U., New Eng. Hist. and Geneal. Soc., Soc. of Mayflower Desc. Methodist. Avocations: tennis, genealogy, antiques, travel, scuba diving. Home: 1783 Brewer Blvd SW Atlanta GA 30310 Office: US Army Chaplain School (Historian) 10100 Lee Rd Fort Jackson SC 29207 Home Fax: 803-751-8890. E-mail: brinsfieldj@usachcs.army.mil.

BRINSMADE, AKBAR FAIRCHILD, chemical engineering consultant; b. Puebla, Mex., May 31, 1917; s. Robert Bruce and Helen Steenbock Brinsmade; m. Juanita Phillips, June 16, 1944; children: Anne Hudson DeFelice, Robert Bruce P., Charlotte Lynn Odom. BS in Chemistry, U. Wis., 1939; MS in Chem. Engring. Practice, MIT, 1942; postgrad., Poly. Inst. Bklyn., 1945-46, NYU, 1947-49, Tulane U., 1967-73. Registered profl. engr., N.C., La. Gen. mgr. Cia. Minera SnFrancisco y Anex., San Luis Potosi, Mex., 1939-40; sr. rsch. engr. Shell Oil Co. Inc., Houston and N.Y.C., 1942-48; project mgr. Internat. Indsl. Cons., N.Y.C. and Caracas, Venezuela, 1949-50; mng. dir. Promoters Nacional de Indsl., Caracas, 1952-57; R&D engr. Hercules Power Co., Rocket Center, W.Va., 1959-64; rsch. engring. specialist Chrysler Space Divsn., New Orleans, 1966-69; chem. engring. cons. to maj. U.S. and fgn. corps., 1969—. Author: (book) Travel to the Stars, 1996, (book chpts.) Solid Rocket Technology, 1967; patentee in field. Chmn. Citizens for Goldwater, Allegany County, Md., 1964. Fellow Am. Inst. Chemists; mem. NSPE (profl. engr. mem.), AIChE, Am. Chem. Soc., La. Engring. Soc. (profl. engr. mem.), Phi Eta Sigma, Phi Lambda Upsilon, Sigma Alpha Epsilon. Republican. Lutheran. Avocations: books, history, languages, travel, tennis. Home: # 7 Holly Corner The Oaks Diamondhead MS 39525

BRINSMADE, LYON LOUIS, retired lawyer; b. Mexico City, Feb. 24, 1924; s. Robert Bruce and Helen (Steenbock) B. (Am. citizens); m. Susannah Tucker, June 9, 1956 (div. 1978); children: Christine Fairchild, Louisa Calvert; m. Carolyn Hartman Lister, Sept. 22, 1979. Student, U. Wis., 1940-43; BS, Mich. Technol. U., 1944; JD, Harvard U., 1950. Bar: Tex. 1951. Assoc. Butler, Binion, Rice, Cook & Knapp, Houston, 1950-58, ptnr. in charge internat. dept., 1958-83, Porter & Clements, Houston, 1983-91; sr. counsel Porter & Hedges (formerly Porter & Clements), Houston, 1991-99. Bd. dirs. Houston br. English-Speaking Union of U.S., 1972-75. Served with AUS, 1946-47. Mem. ABA (chmn. com. internat. investment and devel. of sect. internat. law and practice 1970-76, council 1972-76, 81-82, vice chmn. 1976-79, chmn.-elect 1979-80, chmn. 1980-81, co-founder and co-chmn. com. Mex. 1982-85), Internat. Bar Assn., Inter-Am. Bar Assn. (co-chmn. sect. oil and gas laws, com. natural resources 1973-76, council 1984-87), Houston Bar Assn., State Bar Tex. (chmn. internat. law com. 1970-74, mem. council sect. internat. law 1975-78), Am. Soc. Internat. Law (exec. council 1984-86), Houston World Trade Assn. (sec., dir. 1967-70), Houston World Trade Assn. (chmn. legis. com. 1967-72), Houston C. of C. (chmn. legis. subcom. internat. bus. com. 1970-72), SAR, Allegro of Houston, Harvard Club (Houston), Sigma Alpha Epsilon Episcopalian. Home: PO Box 1149 Wimberley TX 78676-1149

BRINSON, GAY CRESWELL, JR., retired lawyer; b. Kingsville, Tex., June 13, 1925; s. Gay Creswell and Lelia (Wendelkin) B.; m. Bette Lee Butter, June 17, 1979; children from former marriage: Thomas Wade, Mary Kaye. Student, U. Ill., Chgo., 1947-48; BS, U. Houston, 1953, JD, 1957. Bar: Tex. 1957, U.S. Dist. Ct. (so. dist.) Tex. 1959, U.S. ct. Appeals (5th cir.) 1962 U.S. Dist. Ct. (ea. dist.) Tex. 1965, U.S. Supreme Ct. 1974; U.S. Dist. Ct. (no. dist.) Tex. 1990; diplomate Am. Bd. Trial Advocates, Am. Bd. Profl. Liability Attys. Spl. agt. FBI, Washington and Salt Lake City, 1957-59; trial atty. Liberty Mut. Ins. Co., Houston, 1959-62; assoc. Horace Brown, Houston, 1962-64, Vinson & Elkins, Houston, 1964-67, ptnr., 1967-91; of counsel McFall, Sherwood & Sheehy, Houston, 1992-2000. Lectr. U. Houston Coll. Law, 1964-65; mem. staff Tex. Coll. Trial Advocacy, Houston, 1978-86; prosecutor Harris County Grievance Com.-State Bar Tex., Houston, 1965-70 Served with AUS, 1943-46, ETO. Fellow Tex. Bar Found. (life); mem. Tex. Acad. Family Law Specialists (cert.), Tex. Assn. Def. Counsel, Tex. Bd. Legal Specialization (cert.), Fedn. Ins. Counsel, Nat. Bd. Trial Advocacy (cert.), Houston Ctr. Club, Phi Delta Phi. Home: 3740 Del Monte Dr Houston TX 77019-3018 E-mail: gbrinson@houston.rr.com.

BRINSON, MONICA E. pharmaceutical sales representative; b. Hackensack, N.J., Feb. 19, 1971; d. Attichous and Gladys Brinson. BA, Rowan U., 1994. Lic. health and life ins. Acct. exec. Total Media, Hackensack, NJ, 1994—98; ins. sales rep. Aetna U.S. Health Care, Fairfield, NJ, 1998—99. Mem.: Women in Careers, Delta Zeta. Avocations: travel, golf, running. Home: Apt C 295 Essex St Hackensack NJ 07601 Office: Sanofi-Synthelabo Pharms 90 Park Ave New York NY 10016 Home Fax: 201-678-0633. Personal E-mail: monbri201@aol.com.

BRINSON, ROBERT MADDOX, lawyer; b. Rome, Ga., May 4, 1940; s. Moses Ebenezer and Ruth (Maddox) B.; children: Robert Jr., Ruth E., D. Brooke, Susan Stegall; m. Margaret Dye, May 15, 1982. AB in Law, Emory U., 1962, LLB, 1963. Bar: Ga., 1963. Assoc., then ptnr. Rogers, Magruder and Hoyt, Rome, 1963-75; sr. ptnr. Brinson, Askew, Berry, Seigler, Richardson and Davis, Rome, 1975—. City atty. City of Rome, 1968—. Mem. Ga. Bd. Edn., 1990-96. Master: Am. Bd. Trial Advocates (adv.), Bleckley Inn of Ct.; fellow: Ga. Bar Found. (life trustee, pres. 1992—94), Internat. Soc. Barristers, Am. Bar Found. (life), Lawyers Found. of Ga., Am. Coll. Trial Lawyers; mem.: ABA, Ga. Inst. Continuing Jud. Edn. (trustee 1988—89), The Advocates, Ltd. (pres. 2000—01), Ga. Inst. Continuing Legal Edn. (chmn. 1987—88), Ga. Mcpl. Assn. (pres. city atty.'s sect. 1976—77), State Bar Ga. (pres. 1986—87, Disting. Svc. award 1996, Tradition of Excellence award 2001), Old Warhorse Lawyers Club. Presbyterian. Avocations: gardening, travel. Home: 19 Shadow Ln SW Rome GA 30165-6663 Office: Brinson Askew Berry Seigler Richardson & Davis 615 W 1st St Rome GA 30161-3036

BRINSTER, RALPH LAWRENCE, biologist, educator; BS, Rutgers U., 1953; VMD, U. Pa., 1960, PhD in Physiology, 1964; D honris causa, U. Basque Country, Spain, 1994; DSc (hon.), Rutgers U., 2000. Tchg.fellow U. Pa., Phila., 1961-64, instr. Sch. Medicine, 1964-65, asst. prof., then assoc. prof. Sch. Vet. Medicine, 1965-70, prof. physiology Sch. Vet. Medicine, 1970—. Rich King Mellon prof. reproductive physiology, 1975—. Lectr. Harvey Soc., 1984, Juan March Found., Madrid, 1992. Recipient Charles-Leopold Mayer prize, French Acad. Scis., 1994, March of Dimes prize, Devel. Biology, 1996, Bower award and prize, Sci., 1997, Disting. Svc. award, USDA, 1989, John Scott award, City Trusts Phila., 1997, Ernst W. Bertner award, 2001, Wolf prize in medicine, 2002—03. Fellow: Am. Acad. Arts. and Scis.; mem.: AVMA, NAS, Inst. Medicine. Office: Univ Pa Sch Vet Medicine Philadelphia PA 19104

BRINT, STEVEN GREGORY, sociologist, educator; b. Albuquerque, May 22, 1951; s. Harold Louis Brint and Shirl F. Grayson; m. Michele Renee Salzman, Aug. 4, 1985; children; Juliana Rose, Benjamin Piero. BA, U. Calif., Berkeley, 1973; PhD, Harvard U., 1982. Asst. dir. rsch. inst. NYU, 1984-85; from asst. to assoc. prof. Yale U., New Haven, Conn., 1985-92; prof. U. Calif., Riverside, 1992—. Cons. Carnegie Found. for Advancement of Tchg., Menlo Park, Calif., 1998-99; dir. Colls. and Univs. 2000 Study. Author: The Diverted Dream, 1989 (Am. Ednl. Rsch. Assn. Outstanding book award 1991), In an Age of Experts, 1994, Schools and Societies, 1998; editor: The Future of the City of Intellect, 2002. Mem. bd. admissions and rels. with schs. U. Calif., 1997-98; v.p. acad. senate U. Calif., Riverside, 1995-96; mem. program adv. com. Spencer Found., Chgo., 1997-99. E-mail: brint@mail.ucr.edu.

BRINTNALL, MICHAEL ARTHUR, association executive, political scientist; b. Milw., Apr. 1, 1946; s. Arthur Kelly and Gladys (Merchant) B.; m. Isabel Victor, June 22, 1968; 1 child, Rachel Isabel. BA, Amherst (Mass.) Coll., 1968; PhD, MIT, 1976. Asst. prof. Brown U., Providence, R.I., 1976-80; rsch. analyst U.S. HUD, Washington, 1981-85; v.p., assoc. prof. Mt. Vernon Coll., Washington, 1985-90; dir. profl. affairs Am. Polit. Sci. Assn., Washington, 1990-96; exec. dir. Nat. Assn. Schs. Pub. Affairs & Adminstrn., Washington, 1996—2002, Am. Polit. Sci. Assn., Washington, 2002—. Mem. coun. Town of Glen Echo, Md., 1991—2001. Home: 44 Wellesley Cir Glen Echo MD 20812-1017 Office: Am Polit Sci Assn 1527 New Hampshire Ave NW Washington DC 20036 E-mail: brintnall@apsanet.org.

BRINTON, RICHARD KIRK, marketing executive; b. Hanover, Pa., Apr. 21, 1946; s. James Henry and Mabel Brinton; m. Joan Marita Brinton, Mar. 21, 1970; children: Katherine, Mark, Michael. BA in Liberal Arts, BS in Indsl. Engring., Pa. State U., 1968. Registered profl. engr., Ohio. From systems engr. to dir. mktg. AccuRay/ABB, Columbus, Ohio, 1968-82, group mktg. dir. London, 1982-84; internat. sales mgr. Flow Systems, Seattle, 1984, v.p. sales and mktg., 1985-87; dir. mktg. and bus. devel. UTILX Corp., Seattle, 1987-90, v.p. mktg. and bus. devel., 1990-93, v.p. internat. ops., 1993-96; chmn. Nippon FlowMole, Tokyo, 1991-93; dir. worldwide mktg. and sales Lamb-Grays Harbor, Hoquiam, Wash., 1996-97; pres. BBD Internat., Edmonds, Wash., 1997—; sr. v.p. Magic Wardrobe, Inc., Edmonds, 2000—; v.p. Asian ops. Global Validators, Troy, Mich., 2001—02; v.p. Sabst Mktg. Novinium, 2003—. Sr. mgmt. advisor Pacific N.W. Advisors, Seattle, 1997—. Mem. World Trade Club Seattle (bd. dirs. 1993-95). Home and Office: 541 Pine St Edmonds WA 98020-4028

BRIODY, L(AURENCE) PATRICK, journalist, consultant; b. N.Y.C., July 27, 1936; s. Thomas M. and Mae (Allen) B.; children: John, Mary, Kevin, Joseph, Patricia, Laurence Jr., Daniel. BA, Villanova U., 1957; postgrad., St. Johns U., 1959-60. Methods analyst Met. Life Ins. Co., N.Y.C., 1958-61; various mgmt. positions IBM Corp., N.Y., N.J., 1962-81, industry mgr. utilities, 1981-89; v.p. Stagg Systems, Phoenix, 1990-94; prin. Briody Assocs., Newtown, Conn., 1989—. Trombonist Catoonah St. Jazz and Blues Soc. Contbr. articles to profl. jours. With USMC, 1957-61. Mem. Toastmasters (pres. 1968). Republican. Roman Catholic. Avocations: golf, music. Home: 41 Flat Swamp Rd Newtown CT 06470-1852 Office: Briody Assocs PO Box 27 Newtown CT 06470-0027 E-mail: lpbriody@earthlink.net.

BRIONES, DAVID, judge; b. El Paso, Tex., Feb. 26, 1943; m. Delia Garcia; four children. BA, U. Tex., El Paso, 1969; JD, U. Tex., Austin, 1971. Ptnr. Moreno & Briones, 1971-91; judge El Paso County Ct. No. 1, El Paso, 1991-94; dist. judge U.S. Dist. Ct. (we. dist.) Tex., El Paso, 1994—. With U.S. Army, 1964-66. Fellow Tex. Bar Found.; mem. State Bar of Tex., El Paso Bar Assn., Mexican-Am. Bar Assn. Office: US Courthouse Courtroom 1 511 E San Antonio Ave El Paso TX 79901 2401 E-mail: David_Briones@txwd.uscourts.gov.

BRIONES, NICK ALCANTARA, writer; b. Ocampo Cam Sur, Philippines, Jan. 28, 1941; s. Pastor B Briones and Fidela Cortes Alcantara. BS in mech. engring., Feati U., 1968. Inventor self-employed, Brandford, Fla.; author self-employment. Achievements include invention of ordinary toothbrush, 2 headed toothbrush with surehold. Avocation: hunting. Home: 8701 NW 35th Pl Gainesville FL 32606 Office: 8701 NW 35th Place Gainesville FL 32606 E-mail: heybianca@netzero.com.

BRISBANE, ARTHUR SEWARD, newspaper publisher; b. N.Y.C., Sept. 30, 1950; s. Seward Scatcherd and Doris Mae (Fauser) B.; m. Jo Ellen Hull, Oct. 16, 1982; children: Allison Faith, Madeline Mariah, Laura Calista. AB, Harvard Coll., 1973. Child care worker McLean Hosp., Belmont, Mass., 1973-74; freelance musician, 1974-76; reporter Glen Cove (N.Y.) Guardian, 1976-77, Kansas City (Mo.) Star & Times, 1977-79, columnist, 1979-84; reporter Washington Post, 1984-87, asst. city editor, 1987-89; columnist Kansas City Star, 1990-92, editor, v.p., 1992-97, pub., pres., 1997—. Author: Arthur Brisbane's Kansas City, 1982. Avocations: tennis, reading. Office: The Kansas City Star 1729 Grand Blvd Kansas City MO 64108-1458

BRISBIN, ROBERT EDWARD, insurance agency executive; b. Bklyn., Feb. 13, 1946; m. Sally Ann Tobler-Norton. BSBA, San Francisco State U., 1968. Cert. safety exec. Field rep. Index Research, San Mateo, Calif., 1969-82; mgr. loss control Homeland Ins. Co., San Jose, Calif., 1982-87; ins. exec. Morris and Garritano Ins. Agy., San Luis Obispo, Calif., 1987—; prin., cons. Robert E. Brisbin & Assocs., Pismo Beach, Calif., 1972—. Mgt. cons.; pres. Profl. Formulas Amino Acid Food Supplements, 1987-90. Author: (non-fiction) Amino Acids, Vitamins and Fitness, 1986, Loss Control for the Small-to Medium-Sized Business, 1989; author: (with Carol Bayly Grant) Workplace Wellness, 1992; author: (e-book fiction) Terminal Resolve, Proprietary Oversight, ...Was Yesterday, (non-fiction) Deadly Errors; composer: (songs) Country Songs and Broken Dreams, 1978, America the Land of Liberty, 1980; pub.: cyberRead.com. Mem. Am. Soc. Safety Engrs., World Safety Orgn. (cert. safety exec.). Republican. Avocations: photography, flying, scuba diving, musical composition. Office: PO Box 341 Pismo Beach CA 93448-0341 E-mail: bbrisbin@morrisgarritano.com.

BRISBIN, STERLING G. engineering executive, consultant; b. Gloversville, N.Y., Apr. 8, 1929; s. Sterling L. and Eleanor (Holly) B.; m. Joan Cooke, Feb. 28, 1954; children: Sterling G. Jr., James C., Elizabeth. SB, MIT, 1950, SM, 1951. Registered profl. engr., N.Y., N.H., Conn., W.Va. Sanitary engr. Chase T. Main, Boston, 1953-55; rsch. & sales engr. Dorr Oliver Inc., Stamford, Conn., 1955-62; mng. ptnr. Stearns & Wheler Engrs., Cazenovia, N.Y., 1962-85; cons. S.G. Brisbin, Nokomis, Fla., 1985—. Adj. prof. Cornell U., Ithaca, N.Y., 1980. Contbr. articles to profl. jours. 1st lt. U.S. Army Corps Engrs., 1951-53. Recipient Engring. Project award Consulting Engrs. Coun. Mem. Am. Water Works Assn. (life), Water Environment Fedn. (life), Masons. Avocations: golfing, woodworking. Home: 420 Picasso Dr Nokomis FL 34275-1497

BRISCOE, AGATHA DONATTO, data processing executive, instructor; m. Edward Gans Briscoe; 1 child, Allison Marie. BS in Math. summa cum laude, Tex. So. U., 1969; student, UCLA, 1967-68, 69-70; cert. project mgmt. profl., Project Mgmt. Inst., 2000. Cert. secondary tchr., Tex. Scientific programmer The Aerospace Corp., El Segundo, Calif., 1971-73; tech. staff TRW Def. and Space Systems Group, El Segundo, 1973-76; instr. data processing Hawaii C.C., Hilo, 1979-86; analyst, programmer Cayman Islands Govt., Grand Cayman, 1986-87; dir. mgmt. info. svcs. V.I. Dept. Health, St. Thomas, 1987-89; systems analyst V.I. Telephone Co., St. Thomas, 1989-90; sr. applications specialist InfoTech (Kapiolani Health Care Systems), Honolulu, 1990-93, new projects coord., 1993-95; sr. programmer/analyst Sutter Health, Sacramento, 1995-96; advanced programmer-analyst Shared Med. Systems, Sacramento, 1996-97; sr. cons. Data Dimensions, Inc., Sacramento, 1997-99; project mgr. Logicon Advanced Technology, Sacramento, 1999—2001, Shooting Star Solutions LLC, Sacramento, 2001—. Pres. Hawaii Vocat. Assn., Hilo, 1983-85; coord. data processing program Hawaii C.C., Hilo, 1979-86. Co-author: Distant Revenge, 2000, Distant Revenge II, 2001, The Dreyre--The Saga of Little Owl and Fox Slayer, 2002. Supr. com. mem. Big Island Ednl. Fedn. Credit Union, Hilo, 1979-86; troop leader Girl Scouts Am., Hilo, 1984-85; cmty. rep. African-Am. adv. com. U. Hawaii, Manoa, 1994; vol. tutor, Honolulu, 1991-94. Equipment grantee U. Hawaii Pres.'s Fund, Honolulu, 1985. Mem. Nat. Coun. Negro Women. Avocations: reading, swimming, snorkeling, Scrabble, internet. Office: Shooting Star Solutions LLC 3831 N Freeway Blvd Sacramento CA 95835

BRISCOE, ANNE M. retired scientist, educator; b. N.Y.C., Dec. 1, 1918; m. William A. Briscoe, Aug. 20, 1955 (dec. Dec. 1985); m. Theodore H. Heinly Sr., Jan. 21, 1989 (dec. Dec. 2002). MA, Vassar Coll., 1945; PhD, Yale U., 1949. From rsch. assoc. to asst. prof. Cornell U. Med. Coll., N.Y.C., 1950-56; faculty Columbia U. Coll. Physicians and Surgeons, N.Y.C., 1956—, prof. emeritus, 1987. Spl. lectr., 1987-89; lectr. Harlem Hosp. Center Sch. Nursing, 1968-77; adj. asst. prof. Hunter Coll., 1951-64, 73-75; mem. N.Y.C. Commn. on Status of Women, 1979-93, vice chair, 1982-93; non-govtl. orgn. del. to UN; adv. coun. Inst. Nuc. Power Ops., 1979-84. Contbr. articles to profl. jours. Sterling Jr. fellow, USPHS fellow, Yale U., 1949; recipient Yale medal, 1986, Susan B. Anthony award, 1989, Wilbur Cross medal Yale Grad. Sch. Sesquicentennial Convocation, 1997, Yale Fund Chmns. award, 2000. Fellow: AAAS (mem. coun. 1982—85, chmn.'s award Yale Alumni Fund 2001), Assn. Women in Sci. (editor newsletter 1971—74, nat. pres. 1974—76), N.Y. Acad. Sci. (chair women in sci. com. 1978—92, bd. govs. 1981), Am. Inst. Chemists (sec. N.Y. chpt. 1981—83); mem.: ACS, Assn. Women in Sci. Ednl. Found. (pres. 1978—82), Fedn. Orgns. for Profl. Women (treas. 1978—80), Harvey Soc., Am. Fedn. Clin. Rsch., Am. Soc. Clin. Nutrition, Yale Grad. Sch. Alumni Assn. (pres. 1981—86), Assn. Yale Alumni (assembly rep. 1978—, bd. govs. 1982—85). Home: 2116 Sea Cres Ruskin FL 33570-6128 E-mail: drannieb@aol.com.

BRISCOE, CLARENCE CONWAY, retired obstetrician-gynecologist; b. Haydenville, Ohio, Nov. 7, 1910; AB, U. Pa., 1931, MD, 1935. Intern U. Iowa Hosp., Iowa City, 1935-36; resident ob-gyn. U. Md. Hosp., Balt., 1936-37, resident gynecology, 1937-38; resident obstetrics Meth. Hosp., Bklyn., 1938-39; ob-gyn. Pa. Hosp., Phila.; ret. Former assoc. clin. prof. ob-gyn. U. Pa.; hon. staff Pa. Hosp. Fellow ACOG, ACS; mem. AMA.

BRISCOE, DAVID LLOYD, academic sociologist, educator; b. Mars Hill, N.C., Oct. 14, 1950; s. David and Marjorie (Ray) B.; m. Pamlir Roshell Smith. BA, U. Ark., 1980, MA, 1985; PhD, So. Ill. U., 1993. Cert. family life educator. Lectr. So. Ill. U., Carbondale, 1990-92; asst. prof. U. Ark., Little Rock, 1992-98, assoc. prof., 1998—. Mem. adv. bd. Ark. Consumer Bd., Little Rock, 1999—. Co-author: Plain Talk, 1997. Mem. exec. bd. Quapaw Coun. Boy Scouts Am., Little Rock, 1995—; mem. Martin Luther King Commn., Little Rock, 2000. Recipient Faculty Excellence award in pub. svc., Outstanding African Am. Faculty award, 2000, Legion of Honor award, 1998, Outstanding Profl. award, 2001, Eagle Scout Boy Scouts Am., 1968, Silver Beaver, 1981, Silver Antelope, 1996. Fellow Soc. Values in Higher Edn., Southwest Soc. on Aging; mem. Assn. Gerontology in Higher Edn. (exec. com. 2001). Democrat. Baptist. Avocations: camping, canoeing, martial arts, basketball. Home: 2909 W 6th Little Rock AR 72205 Office: U Ark 2801 S University Ave Little Rock AR 72204 E-mail: dlbriscoe@ualr.edu.

BRISCOE, JOHN, classical languages educator; b. London, Feb. 10, 1938; s. Emmanuel and Rita Rosie (Simmons) B.; m. Lynden Margaret Moore, Mar. 19, 1966 (div. 1975); children: Celia Patricia, Ivan Terence. BA, U. Oxford, England, 1960, MA, 1963, DPhil, 1965. Lectr. ancient history Corpus Christi Coll., U. Oxford, England, 1967-68; lectr. Greek and Latin U. Manchester, England, 1968-74, sr. lectr. Greek and Latin, 1974-82, reader Latin, 1982-96, hon. rsch. fellow, 1996—. Author: Commentary on Livy, 31-33, 1973, Commentary on Livy, 34-37, 1981; editor: Titi Livi ab urbe condita libri XLI-XLV, 1986, Titi Livi ab urbe Candita libri XXXI-XL, 1991, Valeri Maximi facta et dicta memorabilia, 1998; contbr. articles to profl. jour. Recipient Rsch. awards Brit. Acad., 1976, 78-79, 84, 87, 90; jr. rsch. fellow Corpus Christi Coll., U. Oxford, 1962-67, vis. fellow Wolfson Coll., U. Oxford, 1981-82. Mem. Roman Soc. (mem. coun. 1976-79), Classical Assn. (hon. sec. Manchester br. 1974-81, 84-96, chmn. 1983-84, v.p. 1996—). Mem. Labour Party. Home: 4 Lisburn Ave Chorlton-cum-Hardy Manchester M21 OTQ England Office: Classics/Ancient History Univ of Manchester Manchester M13 9PL England

BRISCOE, JOHN, lawyer; b. Stockton, Calif., July 1, 1948; s. John Lloyd and Doris (Olsen) B.; divorced; children: John Paul, Katherine. JD, U. San Francisco, 1972. Bar: Calif. 1972, U.S. Dist. Ct. (no., ea. and ctrl. dists.) Calif. 1972, U.S. Supreme Ct. 1978, U.S. Ct. Appeals (9th cir.) 1981. Dep. atty. gen. State of Calif., San Francisco, 1972-80; ptnr. Washburn and Kemp, San Francisco, 1980-88, Washburn, Briscoe & McCarthy, San Francisco, 1988—2000, Stoel Rives LLP, San Francisco, 2000—. Author: Surveying the Courtroom, 1984, rev. edit., 1999, Falsework, 1997, Tadich Grill, 2002; editor: Reports of Special Masters, 1991; contbr. articles to profl. and lit. jours. Mem.: ABA, Am. Soc. Internat. Law, San Francisco Bar Asn. Roman Catholic. Office: Stoel Rives LLP 111 Sutter St #700 San Francisco CA 94104 E-mail: jbriscoe@stoel.com.

BRISCOE, MARIANNE GRIER, development professional, educator; b. Orange, Calif., Nov. 25, 1945; d. Nelson Borland and Anne Kathryn Grier; m. Alden Frank Briscoe, Aug. 10, 1968; 1 child, Stacy Anne. AB cum laude, Goucher Coll., 1967; cert. in medieval studies, Cath. U. Am., 1972; PhD, Cath. U., 1975. Advanced cert. fund raising exec. Lectr. English lit. U. Mich., Flint, 1973; pub. info. officer Flint Charter Revision Commn., 1974-75; devel. officer The Newberry Library, Chgo., 1975-78, dir. devel., 1978-81; prin. The Briscoe Co., Chgo., 1981-84; assoc. dir. devel. U. Chgo., 1984-85, dir. corp. rels., 1985-89; centennial campaign dir. Sierra Club, San Francisco, 1989-91; sr. cons. Staley/Robeson/Ryan/St Lawrence, 1989-91; v.p. advancement St. Mary's Coll. Calif., Moraga, 1992-94; founding prin. The Briscoe Group, San Mateo, Calif., 1994—. Author, co-editor: Contexts of Early English Drama, 1989; author: Artes Praedicandi, 1992; author, editor: Ethics and Fundraising; Putting Values into Practice, 1994; contbr. articles to profl. jours. Founder Washington Sq. Consortium, Chgo., 1978-81; grant reviewer NEH, Washington, 1979-82; chair bd. Legacy Found. Brit. Acad. fellow, 1978-80, Newberry Library fellow, 1981, Med. Acad. fellow, 1974; Am. Philos. Soc. grantee, 1981. Mem. MLA, Internat. Diplomacy Coun. (pres. bd. dirs.), Nat. Soc. Fund Raising Execs. (nat. bd. dirs. 1984-93, vice chmn. found. 1989-91), Internat. Women's Forum, Women's Forum West.

BRISCOE, MARY BECK, federal judge; b. Council Grove, Kans., Apr. 4, 1947; m. Charles Arthur Briscoe. BA, U. Kans., 1969, JD, 1973; LLM, U. Va., 1990. Rsch. asst. Harold L. Haun, Esq., 1973; atty.-examiner fin. divsn. ICC, 1973—74; asst. U.S. atty. for Wichita and Topeka, Kans. Dept. Justice, 1974—84; judge Kans. Ct. Appeals, 1984—95, chief judge, 1990—95; judge U.S. Ct. Appeals (10th cir.), Topeka, 1995—. Fellow: Kans. Bar Found., Am. Bar Found.; mem.: ABA, Women Attys. Assn. Topeka, Kans. Bar Assn. (Outstanding Svc. award 1992), Topeka Bar Assn., Nat. Assn. Women Judges, Am. Judicature Soc., U. Kans. Law Soc., Kans. Hist. Soc., Washburn Law Sch. Assn. (hon.). Office: US Ct Appeals 10th Cir 645 Massachusetts Ste 400 Lawrence KS 66044-2235 also: US Ct Appeals 10th Cir Byron White US Courthouse 1823 Stout St Denver CO 80257*

BRISCUSO, RAYMOND J. biotechnologist; Grad., Auburn U.; grad. in Law, Georgetown U., Washington. Lawyer, Annapolis, Md.; exec. dir. George Bush for Pres. Campaign, 1987—88; assoc. dir. Exec. Office of Pres. White House Office of Nat. Svc.; lawyer; exec. dir. Biotech. Industry Orgn., Washington, 1991—. Office: Biotech Industry Orgn Ste 400 1225 Eye St NW Washington DC 20005

BRISEBOIS, MARCEL, museum director; b. Valleyfield, Que., Can., Oct. 25, 1933; s. Marc and Rose-Alma (Emond) B. BA, Coll. Valleyfield, 1954; PhD, La Sorbonne U., Paris, 1967; Lic. in Theology, Grand Seminar, Montreal, Que., 1968; LittD (hon.), McGill U., Montreal, 1999. Prof. French and philosophy Coll. Valleyfield, 1958-61, prof. philosophy, head dept., 1968-71, asst. dir., 1971-79, sec. gen., 1979-85; animator, interviewer Radio-Can., Montreal, 1960—; dir. gen. Mus. of Contemporary Art, Montreal, 1985—. Decorated Legion d'Honneur, Ordre du Canada, Ordre de Malte, Ordre de la Pleiade. Office: Musee d'Art Contemp/Montreal 185 Rue Ste Catherine Quest Montreal QC Canada H2X 3X5

BRISENO, KATHLEEN, education educator; d. Dominick Joseph and Rose Clare Tomaino; m. Jack Richard Briseno, Oct. 21, 1995; children: Matthew, Megan Knops. AA, Wright Coll., Chgo., 1972; BE, Northeastern Ill. Univ., Chgo., 1974; MEd, Northern Ill. Univ., Dekalb, Ill., 1979; EdD, Northen Ill. Univ., Dekalb, Ill., 2001. Cert. tchng. special and elem. edn. Ill. Spl. edn. tchr. Union Ridge Sch. Dist., Harwood Heights, Ill., 1974—79, Roselle (Ill.) Sch. Dist., 1979—80; asst. dir. spl. edn. intern Wheaton (Ill.) Sch. Dist., 1980—81; lectr. Elgin C.C., Ill., 1981; adj. faculty Nat. Coll. of Edn., Evanston, Ill., 1983, Northeastern Ill. Univ., Chgo., 1983—84; supr. student tchrs. Univ. Iowa, Iowa, 1989, Lewis Univ., Romeoville, Ill., 1989; field svc. coord., supr. student tchrs. Loyola Univ. of Chgo., Chgo., 1981—91; faculty North Ctrl. Coll., Naperville, Ill., 1990—93; supr. student tchrs., instr. No. Ill. Univ., Dekalb, Ill., 1991—92, grad. asst., 1992—93; sub. tchr. Woodridge (Ill.) Sch. Dist., 1992—94; resident supr. of student tchr. Western Ill. Univ., Macomb, Ill., 1993—94; program coord. Dekalb County Special Edn. Assn., Dekalb, Ill., 1994—97; part-time faculty Coll. of Dupage, Glen Ellyn, Ill., 1987—; asst. prof. U. Mo., 1996; ctrl. sch. spl. edn. adminstr. Naperville Sch. Dist #203, Naperville, Ill., 1997—. Reviewer and editor Merrill/Macmillan Publ. Co., Columbus, Ohio, 1990—. Author: Fall, 1993, Mandates as Reform: Who's Kidding Whom?, 2001. Legis. designee for cmty. and residential svcs. authority Ill. House of Reps. Mem.: ASCD, Coun. of Exceptional Children, Assn. of Tchr. Educators, Ill. Whole Language, No. Ill. Reading Coun., Internat. Reading Assn., Field Experience Supr. Network, Ill. Alliance of Adminstr. of Spl. Edn., Ronald Mcdonald House, Ray Graham Assn. for People with Disabilities, March of Dimes Birth Defects Found., Little Friends, YMCA, Little City Found., Boys and Girls Clubs of Chgo. Avocations: music, travel, reading. Home: 1821 Princeton Cir Naperville IL 60565 Office: Naperville Cmty Unit Sch Dist #203 203 Hillside Naperville IL 60540

BRISKIN, EFREM, music educator; b. Gomel, Belarus, May 13, 1948; arrived in U.S., 1979; s. Semyon Briskin and Tsilia (Lipkina) Briskina; m. Natalya Sloina-Briskin, Aug. 4, 1973; 1 child, Michael. BMus, MMus, PhD, Leningrad (Russia) State Conservatory (now St. Petersburg State Conservatory). Mem. piano faculty Petrozavodsk (Russia) Br. of Leningrad State Conservatory, 1972—79, Prep. Ctr. for Performing Arts at Bklyn. Coll., 1980—83, Lucy Moses Sch. for Music and Dance, N.Y.C., 1980—; artistic dir. Summit Music Festival, Tarrytown, NY, 1990—; mem. piano faculty Music Conservatory of Westchester, White Plains, NY, 1991—; dir. Internat. Acad. Music, St. Petersburg, Russia, 2000—. Dir. Dobbs Ferry (N.Y.) Piano Studio, 1996—; mem. Emelin Trio, N.Y.C., 1982—. Concert pianist: nat. and internat. performances, 1972—. Office: Dobbs Ferry Piano Studio 145 Palisade St Dobbs Ferry NY 10522 E-mail: musicacad@aol.com.

BRISKIN, MADELEINE, paleo-oceanographer, paleoclimatologist, micropaleontologist; b. Paris, Sept. 4, 1932; came to U.S., 1951, naturalized, 1956; d. Michel and Mina B. BS, CCNY, 1965; MS, U. Conn., 1967; PhD, Brown U., 1973. Prof. geology Geology-Physics Bldg., U. Cin., 1980—. Recipient award Rsch. Support, 1971-72, Support award NSF, 1978. Mem. AAAS, Am. Geophys. Union, Am. Quaternary Assn., Paleontologist Soc., Climap, Cin. Engrs. and Scientists Soc., Planetary Soc., Soc. Sci. Exploration, Woods Hole Oceanographic Instn., Lamont-Doherty Geol. Obs., N.Y. Acad. Scis., Sigma Xi. Achievements include discovery of 430,000 plus years astronomical cycle in deep-sea sediments; development of pulsating earth model. Office: U Cin Dept Geology Cincinnati OH 45221-0001 Home: 3346 Sherlock Ave Cincinnati OH 45220

BRISKIN, MAE, writer; b. Bklyn., Oct. 20, 1924; d. Sam Seidman and Yetta Rubin; m. Herbert Briskin, Dec. 1, 1946 (deceased); children: Jonathan, Lauren, Allen. BA, Bklyn. Coll., 1944; MA, Columbia U., 1946; grad. writing program, Stanford U., 1980. Author: A Boy Like Astrid's Mother, 1988 (Pen/West award for short fiction, 1989), (novels) The Tree Still Stands, 1991, A Hole in the Water, 2002; contbr. stories to various mags. Home: 3604 Arbutus Ave Palo Alto CA 94303-4418

BRISKMAN, ROBERT DAVID, engineering executive; b. N.Y.C., Oct. 15, 1932; s. Nathan S. and Rose L. (Fishman) B.; m. Lenora Heffner, Mar. 30, 1957; children: Laura G., Sharon L., Robert D. Jr., Douglas E. BSE, Princeton U., 1954; MS, U. Md., 1961. Registered profl. engr., D.C. Devel. engr. IBM, Poughkeepsie, N.Y., 1954-55; analyst Army Security Agy., Washington, 1956-58; chief of program support tracking and data acquisition NASA, Washington, 1959-63; asst. v.p. domestic systems Communication Satellite Corp., Washington, 1964-72; asst. v.p. space and info. systems Comsat Gen. Corp., Washington, 1973-76; dir. pre-operational program Satellite Bus. Systems, McLean, Va., 1977-79; v.p. systems implementation Comsat Gen. Corp., Washington, 1980-85; sr. v.p. engring. and ops. Geostar Corp., Washington, 1986-91; exec. v.p. engring. Sirius Satellite Radio Inc., N.Y.C., 1992—2001, tech. exec., 2001—. Contbr. articles on satellite systems and applications, 1956—; telecommunications editor: McGraw-Hill Ency. Sci. and Tech., 1985—; patentee in field. Capt. U.S. Army, 1955-57. Recipient Founders award Electronics and Aerospace Systems Conf., 1980; named to Soc. Satellite Profls. Internat. Hall of Fame, 2001, Space Found. Technology Hall of Fame, 2002. Fellow AIAA, IEEE (v.p. tech. activities, sec.-treas., 1976-78, Centennial medal, 1984), Washington Acad. Sci., Washington Soc. Engrs. (pres. 1988-89); mem. Old Crows, Internat. Acad. Astronautics, Armed Forces Comm. and Electronics Assn., Cosmos, Union League Clubs. Republican. Office: Sirius Satellite Radio Inc 1221 Ave of the Americas New York NY 10020

BRISLAIN, JUDY ANN, psychologist; b. Hawthorne, Nev., Apr. 24, 1947; d. Margaret Johnson; m. Ross Bradford, May 19, 2001. BA in English Edn., U. Nev., 1969; MA in Spl. Edn., Calif. State U., 1972; EdD in Ednl. and Counseling Psychology, U. Pacific, 1984. Lic. ednl. psychologist, marriage, family child therapist; lic. secondary tchr., Calif., learning handicapped tchg. specialist, Calif., pupil pers. svcs., Calif., C.C. instr., Calif. Tchr. English, forensic coach Placer Joint Union High Sch. Dist., Auburn, Calif., 1969-70; diagnostic clinician Melvin-Smith Sch., Sacramento, Calif., 1970-71, tchr., 1971-74, resource specialist, program coord., 1974-75, program and behavior

guidance coord., 1975-77; clin. edn. dir. Brislain Learning Ctr., 1977—; pvt. practice, 1980—. Cons. Dept. Grants and Rsch. Devel. Calif. State U., Chico, others. Author: Diagnosis in the Classroom: Program for Success, 1973, Ready, Set Go: A Language Program, 1974. Bd. dirs. Campfire, Inc., 1984, Chico Mus. Found.; co-chair Chico Tomorrow, 1986; mem. steering com. Sch. Bond Election, 1988, Butte County Literacy Coun., 1990; bd. dirs. Chico Community Found., Project Child; mem. steering com. Chico Unified Sch. Dist. Hall of Fame; apptd. by Gov. Pete Wilson to Calif. State Bd. Behavioral Sci. Examiners, 1992, chair, 1994-96. Mem. Am. Assn. Marriage & Family therapy, P.G. & E. Caribou Group for Women Leaders, Rotary Internat. (bd. dirs., pres. 1998 Chico chpt.), Greater Chico C. of C. (chair edn. com., bd. dirs., chair bus.-sch. partnership subcom., chair bd. dirs. 2002, Athena award 1991). Office: Brislain Learning Ctr 1550 Humboldt Rd Ste 3 Chico CA 95928-9115

BRISLIN, RICHARD WALTER, psychology educator; b. Barre, Vt., May 9, 1945; s. Joseph Anthony and Alice Maranville Brislin; m. Ann Whitman; children: Cheryl Overmaier, Sean, Mark. PhD, Pa. State U., 1969. Rsch. assoc. East-West Ctr., Honolulu, 1972—96; prof. U. Hawaii, Honolulu, 1996—2001. Author: (book) Understanding Culture's Influence on Behavior, 2000, Turning Bricks into Jade: Critical Incidents for Mutual Understanding among Chinese and Americans, 2000, Cross-cultural Encounters: Face-to-Face Interaction, 1981, Intercultural Communication Training, 1994, (newspaper column) Honolulu Star Bulletin, 2001—; musician: (folk music) columns for folk music publications, 1980—. Recipient Book of the Month Club Selection for The Art of Getting Things Done: A Practical Guide to the Use of Power, Book of the Month Club, 1992. Fellow: APA (named G. Stanley Hall Lectr. 1987); mem.: Acad. Mgmt., Am. Psychol. Soc. Office: U Hawaii Coll of Bus Admn 2404 Maile Way Honolulu HI 96822 Business E-Mail: brislinr@hotmail.com.

BRISMAN, LESLIE, English language educator; b. Bklyn., May 22, 1944; s. Benjamin and Madelein (Taruskin) B.; m. Susan Hawt, Mar. 11, 1973; children: Aviad, Shira. AB, Columbia U., 1965; PhD, Cornell U., 1969. From asst. to assoc. prof. Yale U., New Haven, 1969-79, prof., 1979—. Author: Romantic Origins, 1968, Milton's Poetry of Choice, 1973, The Voice of Jacob, 1990. Home: 5 Woodside Ter New Haven CT 06515-2020 Office: Yale Univ PO Box 2502A Yale Sta New Haven CT 06520

BRISMAN, RONALD, clinical neurosurgeon; b. Bklyn., Mar. 5, 1940; s. Benjamin and Madelein Brisman; m. Joan Lillian, June 24, 1965; children: Michael, Jonathan, Jennifer, Aaron. AB summa cum laude, Harvard U., 1961, MD, 1965. Diplomate Am. Bd. Neurol. Surgery, Nat. Bd. Med. Examiners. Intern, resident surgery Johns Hopkins U., Balt., 1965-67; resident, chief resident neurosurgery Columbia Presbyn. Med. Ctr., N.Y.C., 1967-71, mem. attending staff neurosurgery, 1975—; asst. prof., then assoc. prof. clin. neurosurgery Columbia U., N.Y.C., 1979—. With U.S. Army, 1971-73, Vietnam. Decorated Legion of Merit; Tech. Svc. medal (Vietnam Air Force); recipient Commendation cert. Surgeon Gen. Vietnam Air Force. Fellow Am. Coll. Surgeons; mem. AMA, Am. Assn. Neurol. Surgeons, Congress Neurol. Surgeons, Am. Soc. for Stereotactic Neurosurgery, Med. Soc. of the County of N.Y., Med. Soc. of the State of N.Y., N.Y. State Neurosurg. Soc., N.Y. Soc. for Neurosurgery, N.Y. Acad. Medicine, Phi Beta Kappa. Office: 710 W 168th St New York NY 10032-2603

BRISSENDEN, ALAN (ALAN THEO BRISSENDEN), writer; b. Griffith, Australia, Oct. 13, 1932; s. Arthur Piercy and Nellie (Rogers) B.; m. Elizabeth Jane Irwin King, Oct. 15, 1960; children: Roger James, Piers King, Celia Jane. BA with honors, U. Sydney, 1954, diploma in edn., 1955; PhD, U. London, 1962. Tchr. Edn. Dept. of NSW, Sydney, 1955, rsch. officer, 1956-59; lectr. U. Adelaide, Australia, 1963—67, sr. lectr., 1968—81, reader in English, 1982—94, hon. vis. rsch. fellow, 1995—, chmn. dept., 1985—86. Adv. com. for South Australia Australian Broadcasting Commn., 1972-75, com. chmn., 1976-77; dance reviewer ABC-Radio, 1984-88; vis. fellow Wolfson Coll., Oxford, 1987, 92; dance critic Sydney Morning Herald, 1952-55, Advertiser, Adelaide, 1976-84, Dance Mag., 1979-83, Dance Australia, 1980—, Australian, 1990—; convenor awards panel, Australian Dance Awards, 2000, mem. adv. bd., 2003—. Author: Rolf Boldrewood, 1972, Shakespeare and the Dance, 1981; co-editor: They Came to Australia, 1961; editor: A Chaste Maid in Cheapside, 1968, Lawson's Australia, 1973, The Drover's Wife and Other Stories by Henry Lawson, 1974, Aspects of Australian Fiction, 1990, As You Like It, 1993; writer TV series Theatre through the Ages, 1963; gen. co-editor series Studies in Tudor and Stuart Literature, 1973-83; contbr. Spenser Encyclopedia, Reference Guide to English Literature, International Dictionary of Ballet, International Ency. of Dance, Australian Dictionary of Biography; contbr. to profl. jours. South Australian mem. Nat. Lit. Bd. of Review, 1971-74; exec. com. Arts Coun. South Australia, 1971, chmn. and v.p., 1972-74; bd. govs. Adelaide Festival Arts, 1981-94; chmn. Early Imprints Project in South Australia, 1977-2003; exec. mem. Early Imprints Project in Australia and New Zealand, 1979-2003; pres. Friends of State Library S. Australia, 1994-2000; hon. life mem. Friends of Adelaide Festival, 1996. Decorated Order of Australia, 1996; grantee Australian Rsch. Grants Com., 1968-71, 78-82, Brit. Coun., 1974-75, Ian Potter Found., 1979, 92; fellow Huntington Libr., 1979. Mem. Bibliographical Soc. Australia and New Zealand (pres. 1983-86), English Assn. (chmn. Adelaide br. 1970-73), Bibliographical Soc. (Eng.), Australian and New Zealand Shakespeare Assn. (v.p. 1990-92, pres. 1992-94, hon. life 1998). Office: U Adelaide Dept English Adelaide SA 5005 Australia

BRISSMAN, BERNARD GUSTAVE, retired insurance company executive; b. St. Paul, May 10, 1919; s. Gustave Erie and Emma Barbara (Beetsch) B.; m. Frances Irene Shackleton, May 30, 1942; children— Gerald, Jonathan, Joan, Roland, William Student, U. Minn., 1937-52, Butler U., Indpls., 1962-64. CPCU. Spl. agt. Gen. Accident, Mpls., 1945-49; casualty mgr. Fireman's Fund Ins. Co., Mpls., 1949-54; sr. v.p., dir. Am. States Co., Indpls., 1954-84. Capt. U.S. Army, 1941-45. Mem. Minn. CPCU Assn. (pres. 1951-52, Ind. CPCU Assn. (pres. 1958-59). Republican. Roman Catholic. Avocations: sailing, computers, acting, dancing. Home: 3373 S Calle Del Acle Green Valley AZ 85614-4809

BRISTER, BILL H. lawyer, former bankruptcy judge; b. Sieper, La., Mar. 5, 1930; s. Clayton Houston and Era (Price) B.; m. Carolyn Lee McDowell, June 11, 1955; children— Jeff, Julie. B.S. in Chemistry, Northwestern State U. Natchitoches, La., 1948; J.D., U. Tex., 1958. Bar: Tex. 1957, U.S. Dist. Ct. (no. dist.) Tex. 1959, U.S. Ct. Appeals (5th cir.) 1971, U.S. Supreme Ct. 1971. Pvt. practice, Lubbock, Tex., 1958-79; bankruptcy judge U.S. Dist. Ct. (no. dist.) Tex., 1979-85; of counsel Winstead, Sechrest & Minick and predecessor firm, 1986—. Served to col. USMCR, 1951-52. E-mail: billbrist@aol.com. Office: Winstead Sechrest & Minick 5400 Renaissance Tower 1201 Elm St Ste 5400 Dallas TX 75270-2199

BRISTER, PAT, political party executive; m. Joe Brister; 5 children. Chmn. La. Rep. Party, 2000—. V.chmn. Tammany Parish Coun.; v.treas. La. State Museum bd., 1996-2000, chmn., bd. trustees Lasalle U., 1996-2002, chmn. La. Victory 2000; Nat. Committeewoman, La. Rep. Party, 1996-2000. Office: Republican Party of Louisiana 7916 Wrenwood Blvd, Suite E Baton Rouge LA 70809*

BRISTO, MARCA, human services administrator; b. Albany, N.Y., June 23, 1953; d. Earl C. and Dorothy (Moore) B.; m. J. Robert Kettlewell, Oct. 15, 1988; children: Samuel Clayton Kettlewell, Madeline Elizabeth Kettlewell. BA in Sociology, Beloit Coll., 1974; BSN, Rush Coll. Nursing, Chgo., 1976. Cert. nursing. RN Rush Presbyn. St. Luke's Med. Ctr., Chgo., 1976-77, Northwestern Meml. Hosp., Chgo., 1977, family planning nurse specialist, 1978-79; exec. dir., co-founder Access Living Met. Chgo., 1979-84, pres., CEO, 1984—. Chair Nat. Coun. Disability, Washington, 1994-2002, Ill. Pub. Action Coun., 1989-94, U.S. delegate U.N. world summit on urban living and shelter, 1996, bd. dirs. Disability Funders Network, 2002-. Mem. Pres.'s Com. on Employment of People with Disabilities; mem. Pres.'s Task Force on Employment of Adults with Disabilities; bd. dirs. Rehab. Inst. Chgo.; mem. Leadership Greater Chgo.; mem. The Chgo. Network. Avocations: cooking, travel. Office: Access Living of Metropolitan Chicago 614 W Roosevelt Rd Chicago IL 61614

BRISTOL, BARBARA KAMMER, foundation administrator; b. Orange, N.J., Feb. 11, 1949; d. John Webster Bristol and Doris Caroline Kammer; m. Harry Nathan Casto, Oct. 30, 1970 (div. 1975); m. Galway M. Kinnell, Dec. 26, 1997. Editor Alfred A. Knopf, Inc., N.Y.C., 1974-94; dir. writers' awards The Rona Jaffe Found., N.Y.C., 1995—, Mrs. Giles Whiting Found., N.Y.C., 1997—. Bd. dirs. The MacDowell Colony, Peterborough, N.H., 1988—; hon. bd. dirs. Cave Canem, N.Y.C., 1998—. Recipient Roger Klein award editl. excellence Roger Klein Found., 1990. Home: 1218 Town Hwy 16 Sheffield VT 05866 Office: Mrs Giles Whiting Found 1133 Ave of Americas New York NY 10036

BRISTOL, CAROL, retired librarian; b. Jackson, Mich., Sept. 6, 1940; d. Max Delatour and Mary Elisabeth (Grigsby) Strawn; m. William P. Bristol, June, 1962 (div. Aug. 1974); children: Shelley, Steven, Andrew. BA, U. Mich., 1962; MA, We. Mich. U., 1975, MS in Librarianship, 1980. Cert. tchr. K-12 with libr. endorsement, Mich. Tchr. English Ypsilanti (Mich.) Jr. High, 1962-63; elem. libr. Kalamazoo (Mich.) Pub. Schs., 1976—80, 1983—97, 2000—01; bookseller Athena Book Shop, Kalamazoo, 1980-83; libr. Kalamazoo Ctrl. High Sch., 1997—2000; ret., 2002. Bd. dirs. Kalamazoo Folklife Orgn., 1999; elder, deacon First Presbyn. Ch., Kalamazoo, 1975-85. Mem. NEA, Mich. Assn. Media in Edn., Kalamazoo Edn. Assn., Mich. Edn. Assn., PEO Sisterhood, Beta Phi Mu. Avocations: growing flowers, reading and discussing books, folk and acoustic music.

BRISTOL, JOSEPHINE HART, psychiatrist; b. Chgo., May 6, 1937; d. Albert and Ann (Webster) Hart; children: Ann, Benjamin, Peter. AB, Radcliffe Coll., 1959, AM, 1960; MPH, U. Hawaii, 1968; MD, U. Conn., 1975. Diplomate Am. Bd. Psychiatry & Neurology. Intern U. Conn. Hosps., Farmington, 1975-76; resident in psychiatry Yale U., New Haven, 1976-79; pvt. practice psychiatry Danbury, Conn., 1979—. Office: 152 Deer Hill Ave Danbury CT 06810-7766

BRISTOL, LOUISE FITZGERALD, educator, retired nurse; b. Moorestown, N.J., Mar. 24, 1935; d. Edward William and Katherine (D'Arcy) Fitzgerald; children: John Edward, Eric Charles. RN, W. Jersey Hosp., 1956; BSN, U. Pa., 1975, MD, U. Del., 1985; postmasters cert. in nursing adminstrn., Villanova U., 1987. RN, N.J. Nurse West Jersey Hosp., Camden, N.J., 1956-57, Mount Holly (N.J.) Hosp., 1957-59, Good Samaratin Hosp., Syracuse, N.Y., 1959-61, Syracuse VA Med. Ctr., 1961-64; med. staff nurse Phila. VA Med. Ctr., 1967-80, staff nurse ICU, 1969-70, surg. staff nurse ICU, 1970-73, night coord., 1973-80; nurse Wilmington (Del.) VA Med. Ctr., 1980-86; headnurse/supr. Coatesville (PA.) VA Med. Ctr., 1986-89; geriatric gerontol. clin. nurse specialist VA Med. Ctr., Coatesville, Pa., 1991-97; ret., 1997; clin. instr. Owens campus Del. Tech. and C.C., 1999—2002. Bd. dirs. NOVA Nat. Com. Mem. Nurses of VA (bd. dirs., chair chpts. com.). Roman Catholic.

BRISTOL, NORMAN, lawyer, arbitrator, former food company executive; b. Bronx, N.Y., June 14, 1924; s. Lawrence and Bell (Allchin) B.; m. Doreen Kingan, Mar. 28, 1952; children: Charles L., Norman, Alexander, Barnaby. Grad., Phillips Exeter Acad., 1941; AB, Yale, 1944; LLB, Columbia Law Sch., 1949. Bar: N.Y. bar 1950, Mich. bar 1954. Atty. Root, Ballantine, Harlan, Bushby & Palmer, N.Y.C., 1949-53; with Kellogg Co., Battle Creek, Mich., 1954-78, asst. gen. counsel, 1958-64, sec., 1960-78, gen. counsel, 1964-78, sr. v.p., 1968-75, dir., 1972-78, exec. v.p., 1975-78; atty. Howard & Howard, Kalamazoo, 1979-93. Mem. Gull Lake Comty. Schs. Bd. Edn., 1963-70, pres., 1965-67; trustee Kalamazoo Symphony Soc., Inc., 1983-94, pres., 1990-91; bd. dirs. Southwest Mich. Land Conservancy, Inc., 1996-2001. Lt. (j.g.) USNR, 1943-46. Mem. State Bar Mich., Kalamazoo Bar Assn., Am. Soc. Corp. Secs., SCORE (counsellor). Home and Office: 2962 Sylvan Dr Hickory Corners MI 49060-9319

BRISTOL, STANLEY DAVID, mathematician, educator; b. Mankato, Minn., Dec. 30, 1948; s. Robert Frederick Bristol and Ruth Charlotte (Buckeye) Bristol Bond; m. Elaine Metzer, Jan. 30, 1970; children: Thomas Alan, Jennifer Elise. BS, Ariz. State U., 1969, MA, 1970. Cert. secondary tchr. with gifted edorsement. Math. tchr. Saguaro HS, Scottsdale, Ariz., 1973-74, Poston Jr. HS, Mesa, Ariz., 1974-77, Corona del Sol HS, Tempe, Ariz., 1977—, chair math. dept., 1990—2003; math. tchr. Ariz. State U., Tempe, 1989—. Sunday sch. tchr. 1st United Meth. Ch., Tempe, 1983—93. With U.S. Army, 1970—73. Named Tchr. of the Yr., Diablos C. of C., 1987, 1998, Tribune Educator of Yr., 1995, Honored Educator, Flinn Found., 1997, Outstanding Adj. Facult, Rio Salado Coll., 2000; recipient Presdl. award for excellence in math. tchg., 1990. Mem.: NEA, Math. Assn. Am., Ariz. Assn. Tchrs. Math., Nat. Coun. Tchrs. Math., Ind. Order Foresters. Avocations: photography, reading, bowling, computers. Office: Corona del Sol High Sch 1001 E Knox Rd Tempe AZ 85284-3204 E-mail: sbristol.cds@tuksd.k12.az.us.

BRISTOW, CLINTON, JR., academic administrator; b. Montgomery, Ala., Mar. 15, 1949; s. T.C. and Betty Bristow; 1 child, Maya. JD, Northwestern U., 1974, PhD, 1977; postgrad., U. Minn., 1983; MBA, Governor's State U., 1984. V.p. adminstrn. Olive-Harvey Coll., Chgo., 1980-81; dean Coll. Bus. Chgo. State U., 1985-93; pres. Chgo. Bd. Edn., 1990-92, Alcorn State U., Lorman, Miss., 1995—. Cons. in field. Contbr. articles to profl. publs. Chmn. Miss. Rhodes Scholarship Com., 1996; bd. dirs. Miss. Agr./Forestry Mus., Jackson, Chgo., Congl. Award Bd., HBCU Capital Fin. Bd.; mem. exec. com. 1890 Coun. Pres. Fellow Northwestern U. Ctr. for Urban Affairs, 1973-74; recipient Role Model award Top Ladies of Distinction, Inc., 1987, Greater Roseland Area Planning, 1990. Mem. Am. Assn. State Colls. and Univs. (state rep.), So. Assn. Colls. and Schs. (exec. com.), Nat. Collegiate Athletic Assn. (bd. of dir.), So. Edn. Found., Miss. Instns. of Higher Learning (coun. of pres.), Southwestern Athletic Conf. (past pres.). Baptist. Avocations: reading, golf, jogging. Home: 1000 Asu Dr # 719 Alcorn State MS 39096-7510 Office: Alcorn State U 1000 DR # 359 Alcorn State MS 39096

BRISTOW, CYNTHIA LYNN, immunologist; b. Altus, Okla., Aug. 19, 1951; d. Robert O'Neil Bristow and Gaylon Eva Walker; children: Charlie, Bo, Rachel, Mary Ann, Rudy. BA, Winthrop U., 1972; MS, Med. U. SC, Charleston, 1979, PhD, 1986. Postdoctoral assoc. biochemistry Med. U. of SC, Charleston, SC, 1986-88; postdoctoral assoc. dental rsch. ctr. U. NC, Chapel Hill, NC, 1988-94; clin. immunologist pathology and lab. medicine U. N.C. Hosp., Chapel Hill, NC, 1999-2001; rsch. asst. prof. U. NC, Chapel Hill, NC, 1994-98; faculty cellular physiology and immunology Rockefeller U., NYC, 2001—. Mem. editl. bd. Biotechnology and Applied Biochemistry, 1996; contbr. articles to profl. jour., chpts. to books; patentee in biotechnology, UNC Ctr. for AIDS Rsch. Recipient Elsa Pardee Found. award, 1990; grantee NIH., 1994, nominated Internat. personality of the yr., Internat. Biog. Ctr., 2001, 02. Mem. Am. Soc. Microbiology, Am. Assn. Immunologists, Am. Chem. Soc., Am. Diabetes Assn., Assn. Med. Lab. Immunologists, Sigma Xi. Episcopalian. Avocations: running, music, poetry, art, tennis, golf. Office: Rockefeller U 1230 York Ave New York NY 10021 E-mail: cbristow@nyc.rr.com.

BRISTOW, DAVID IAN, lawyer; b. Toronto, May 19, 1931; s. Horace George and Elizabeth (Bourne) B.; m. Suzanne Snow, Sept. 9, 1959; children: Timothy Charles, Julie Anne, Lori Anne. BA, U. Toronto, 1953; LLB, Osgoode Hall, Toronto, 1957. Bar: Ont. 1957, apptd. Queen's counsel 1969. Since practiced in, Toronto; mem. firm Shibley Righton McCutcheon, 1969-74, Bristow, Gilgan & Glaholt, 1974-88, Fraser Milner Casgrain LLP, Toronto, 1988—2003, ADR Chambers, Toronto, 2003—. Tchr. Osgoode Hall Law Sch., 1967-74; mem. Pacific Rim adv. coun. respecting preparation internat. arbitration; chartered mediator accreditation com. Artibration and Mediation Inst. Ont. Co-author: Construction and Mechanics Liens in Canada, 1962, 85; mem. editl. bd. Constrn. Law Letter, Constrn. Law Reports. Bd. dirs. McInnis Undersea Found. Named one of Top 500 Lawyers in Can., Lexpert U.S.A., 2001—03; recipient Law Soc. medal, Ont. L.S.M., 2002, Golden Jubilee medal, Queen Elizabeth II, 2002, Giffen award, 2002. Mem. ATLA, Can. Bar Assn. (founding chmn. constrn. law sect. Ont., Disting. Svc. award 1996), Advs. Soc., Country of York Bar Assn., Internat. Bar Assn., Inter-Pacific Bar Assn., Internat. Acad. Mediators, Am. Arbitration Assn., CPR Inst. for Dispute Resolution, Internat. Ct. of Arbitration, Am. Nuclear Soc., Lawyers Club Toronto, Cambridge Club, Granite Club, Phi Delta Phi. Office: ADR Chambers 1st Canadian Pl 48 Yonge St Ste 1100 Toronto ON Canada M5E 1G6

BRISTOW, LONNIE ROBERT, physician; b. N.Y.C., Apr. 6, 1930; s. Lonnie Harlis and Vivian (Wines) Bristow; m. Margaret Jeter, June 1, 1957 (div. Aug. 1961); children: Mary, Mark; m. Marilyn Hingslage, Oct. 18, 1961; children: Robert, Elizabeth. BS, CCNY, 1953; MD, NYU, 1957. Diplomate Am. Bd. Internal Medicine. Intern San Francisco City and County Hosp., 1957—58; resident VA Hosp., San Francisco, 1959—60, Francis Delafield Hosp., N.Y.C., 1960, VA Hosp., Bronx, NY, 1961; practice medicine specializing in internal medicine San Pablo, Calif., 1964—99; mem. staff Brookside Hosp., San Pablo, 1998—99; vice chmn. Physician Leadership on Nat. Drug Policy, Providence, 1999—. Cons. Calif. Dept. Health Care in Prisons, Sacrament, 1976—77, chmn. sickle cell com., 1976—79; mem. admissions com. U. Calif.-Berkeley, 1972—75; mem. Nat. Coun. Health Care Tech., Washington, 1980; mem. physician discussion group on physician payment Health Care Financing Adminstrn., Washington, 1983—86; chmn. bd. regents Uniformed Svcs. U. Health Scis., Bethesda, Md., 1996—. Recipient ann award of excellence, Calif. Med. Polit. Action Com., 1977. Fellow: ACP (master); mem.: AMA (coun. med. svc. 1976—85, trustee 1985—94, pres.-elect 1994—95, pres. 1995), Am. Soc. Internal Medicine (trustee 1976—83, pres. 1981—82), Inst. Medicine of NAS. Office: PLNDP Ctr Alcohol & Addiction Studies Brown U Box G-BH Providence RI 02912 Address: 1966 Tice Valley Blvd # 411 Walnut Creek CA 94595-2203

BRISTOW, MICHAEL, cardiologist, researcher, medical educator; b. West Palm Beach, Fla., Nov. 8, 1944; s. Julius Cyrus and Rosemary Logsdon Bristow; m. Karyn A. Kowalski, June 28, 1978; children: Justin, Nathan, Jacques. BS in Vet. Scis., U. Ill., 1966; MD, U. Ill., Chgo., 1970, PhD in Pharmacology, 1971. Diplomate Am. Bd. Internal Medicine, cert. Am. Bd. Cardiovascular Disease. Asst. prof. cardiology Stanford (Calif.) U. Sch. Medicine, 1983—84; assoc. prof. cardiology U. Utah Sch. Medicine, Salt Lake City, 1984—88, prof. internal medicine (cardiology), 1988—91; dir. Temple Hoyne Buell Heart Ctr. U. Colo. Health Scis. Ctr., Denver, 1991—; head divsn. cardiology U. Colo. Sch. Medicine, Denver, 1991—, S. Gilbert Blount endowed chair cardiology, 2000—; acting dir. U. Colo. Cardiovascular Inst., Denver, 1998—. Sole practitioner Nat. Health Svc. Field Sta. (USPHS Nat. Health Corps), West Yellowstone, Mont., 1972—74; founder, sci. co-founder Myogen, Inc., Westminster, Colo., 1996, bd. dirs., 1998—, chmn. sci. adv. bd., 2000—; mem. sci. adv. bd. Cardiovasc. Clin. Rsch., 2000—, Genzyme, 2000—, Covalent, 2000—, CVRx, 2000—; founder ARCA Discovery, Inc., Aurora, Colo., 2001. Patentee in field. Named top heart failure investigator, Sci. Watch, 1999; recipient Therapeutic Frontiers award, Am. Coll. Clin. Pharmacy, 1993. Fellow: Am. Coll. Cardiology, Am. Heart Assn. (Desert/Mountain Affiliate Rsch. Com. 2001—, Ed Ricketts award 2000); mem.: Assn. Am. Physicians, Assn. Univ. Cardiologists, Am. Fedn. Clin. Rsch., Am. Soc. Clin. Investigation, Heart Failure Soc. Am. (exec. coun. 1999—, founding), Coun. on Basic Cardiovascular Scis. Avocations: skiing, basketball, hiking. Office: U Colo Health Scis Ctr 4200 E 9th Ave B130 Denver CO 80262

BRISTOW, ROBERT O'NEIL, writer, educator; b. St. Louis, Nov. 17, 1926; s. Jesse Reuben and Helen Marjorie (Utley) B.; children by previous marriage— Cynthia Lynn, Margery Jan Wu, Gregory Scott, Kelly Robert; m. Gail Hamiter Rosen, Aug. 25, 2003. BA in Journalism, U. Okla., 1951, MA in Journalism, 1965. Asst. advt. mgr. Altus (Okla.) Times Democrat, 1951-53; free-lance writer Altus, 1951-60; prof. English Winthrop Coll., Rock Hill, S.C., 1960-87, prof. emeritus, 1987—. Author: Time for Glory, 1968, Night Season, 1970, A Faraway Drummer, 1973, Laughter in Darkness, 1974. Served with USNR, 1944-45. Recipient award for lit. excellence U. Okla., 1969, award for novel Friends of Am. Writers, 1974 Mem. Alpha Tau Omega. Home: 613 1/2 Charlotte Ave Rock Hill SC 29730-3648 E-mail: rbristow@cetlink.net.

BRISTOW, THOMAS COLE, JR., social work educator; b. Orangeburg, S.C., Sept. 4, 1939; s. Thomas Cole and Naomi Alice (Whittington) B.; m. Elizabeth Jane Elwood, Nov. 4, 1943; children: Thomas Cole III, Christopher Francis. BS in Psychology, Wofford Coll., 1961; MSW, U. Tenn., 1966; PhD in Edn., U. S.C., 1977. Tchr. S.C. Pub. Schs., St. George, Columbia, 1961-63; caseworker Berkeley County (S.C.) Dept. Social Svcs., 1963-64; protective svc. supr. Greenville (S.C.) Dept. Social Svcs., 1966-68; psychiatric social worker Greenville Area Mental Health Ctr., 1968-70; asst. prof. U. S.C., Columbia, 1970-73; social work supr., unit dir. S.C. State Hosp., Columbia, 1973-84, dir. social work, 1984-88; adj. prof. U. S.C. Coll. Edn., 1977-99; dir. admissions, ancillary svcs. child adolescent svc. William S. Hall Psychiatric Inst., Columbia, 1988-93, dir. admissions, cmty. rels., 1993-99; asst. prof. U. S.C. Sch. Medicine, 1994—2001; prof. Columbia Coll., 1999—. Mem. adv. bd. Columbia Pastoral Counseling Ctr., Columbia, 1990-98, Stone Soup Storytelling Festival, Woodruff, S.C., 1995-00, Chaplaincy Tng. Program, Columbia, 1997-00. Author: The Real Story of the First Thanksgiving, 1998. Co-founder S.C. Mental Health Players, Columbia, 1985-90; precinct capt. Lexington County Dems., 1995-00. With U.S. Army Res., 1964-70. Mem. NASW, Nat. Storytelling Network (state liaison 1995), Nat. Storytelling Youth Olympics (state coord. 1996), Three Rivers Storytelling Guild (pres. 1999). Presbyterian. Avocations: storytelling, writing, music. Home: 208 Middlesex Rd Columbia SC 29210-4407 Office: Columbia Coll 1301 Columbia College Dr Columbia SC 29203-5949 E-mail: tcbristow@msn.com.

BRISTOW, WALTER JAMES, JR., retired judge; b. Columbia, S.C., Oct. 14, 1924; s. Walter James and Caroline Belser (Melton) B.; m. Katherine Stewart Mullins, Sept. 12, 1952; children: Walter James III, Katherine Mullins (dec.). Student, Va. Mil. Inst., 1941-43; AB, U. N.C., 1947; LLB cum laude, U. S.C., 1949; LLM, Harvard U., 1950. Mem. Marchant, Bristow & Bates, 1953-76, S.C. Ho. of Reps., 1956-58, S.C. Senate, 1958-76; resident judge 5th Cir. Ct. S.C., 1976-88; ret., 1988. Nat. pres. Conf. Ins. Legislators, 1974-75. Trustee Elvira Wright Fund for Crippled Children, 1963-76; mem. bd. visitors ex officio The Citadel, Charleston, S.C., 1967-76. Served with AUS, 1943-45, ETO, brig. gen. S.C. Army N.G. Decorated Meritorious Svc. medal; recipient Order of Palmetto, 1999, Order of Cypress, 1999. Mem. ABA, Wig and Robe, S.C. Law Inst., S.C. Coun. on Holocaust, Capital City Club, Cotillion Club, Forest Lake Club, Palmetto Club, Columbia Ball Club, Sertoma, Alpha Tau Omega. Democrat. Office: PO Box 1147 Columbia SC 29202-1147

BRISTOW, WILLIAM HARVEY, JR., psychiatrist; b. Harrisburg, Pa. s. William H and Rosa Leah (St Clair) Bristow; m. Lillian H Heise; children: Jill Virginia, Lisa Ann, William H III. AB, Harvard U., 1949; MD, NYU, 1953. Diplomate Am Bd Psychiat and Neurology. Intern 4th Med. div. Bellevue Hosp., N.Y.C., 1953-54, resident 4th Med. div., 1954-55; resident dept. psychiatry N.Y. VA Hosp., N.Y.C., 1957-60; VA fellow Bellevue Psychiat. Hosp., N.Y.C., 1959-60; pvt. practice Ridgewood, N.J., 1960—. Chmn dept psychiat Bergen Pines County Hosp, Paramus, NJ, 1961; former chmn dept psychiat St Joseph's Hosp, Wayne, NJ, former pres med bd; former pres. med. bd., clin. dir. Ramapo Ridge Psychiat. Hosp., 1985—98, attending psychiatrist; staff psychiatrist Bergen Regional Med. Ctr., 1998—; mem emeritus staff Valley Hosp. Fellow: Am Psychiat Asn (life); mem.: AMA, NYU-Bellevue Psychiat Soc, Asn Convulsive Therapy, NJ Psychiat Asn, Bergen County Med Soc. Congregationalist.

BRITCHER, E. DREW, lawyer; b. Ridgewood, N.J., Apr. 27, 1959; s. Warren Edwin and Dorothy Mae (Lighthiser) B.; m. Elaine W. Westerfield, Sept. 28, 1985; children: Sean Andrew and Caitlin Anne. BA, Rutgers Coll., 1981; JD, N.Y. Law Sch., 1984. Bar: N.J. 1984, U.S. Dist. Ct. N.J. 1984, N.Y. 1985. Ptnr. Britcher, Leone & Roth LLC, Glen Rock, NJ, 2000—. Lectr. in field. Dem. committeeman State of N.J., 1993-97. Mem. ATLA (bd. govs. N.J. 1994—, v.p.), N.J. Bar Assn., Phi Delta Phi. Democrat. Avocations: golf, soccer. Office: Britcher Leone & Roth LLC 175 Rock Rd Glen Rock NJ 07452

BRITNER, PRESTON ARTHUR, IV, developmental psychologist, educator; b. Washington, Sept. 14, 1968; s. Preston Arthur III and Connie Lou (Holloway) B.; m. Suzanne Jean LaFleur, May 28, 1994; children: Samuel, Serena. BA in Developmental Psychology, U. Miami, 1990; MA in Developmental Psychology, U. Va., 1993, PhD in Developmental Psychology, 1996. Asst. prof. psychology Smith Coll., Northampton, 1996-97; asst. prof. Sch. Family Studies U. Conn., Storrs, 1997—2003, assoc. prof., 2003—. Cons. Child-Parent Attachment Clinic, Charlottesville, Va., 1994-2000, Inst. for Psychiatry, U. London, 1996-99; faculty advisor Kappa Sigma fraternity, 2000—; cons. Conn. Dept. Children & Families, 2000—. Author: Preventing Child Abuse and Neglect through Parent Education, 1997; mem. editl. bd. Jour. Sch. Psychology,

1997-2003, Jour. Child & Family Studies, 1999—; assoc. editor Jour. of Primary Prevention, 2002-2003, editor, 2003—; contbr. over 30 articles to profl. jours. including Child Welfare, Jour. Child and Family Studies. Mem. Commn. on Children, Hartford, Conn., 1997-2000; pres. Barrett Day Care Ctr., Charlottesville, Va., 1996, bd. dirs., 1994-96; bd. dirs. Women's Ctr. NE Conn., 2000-2001. Grantee State of Conn. Office of Policy & Mgmt., 1999-2001, Dept. Children & Famililies, 1999-2000. Mem. APA, Am. Psychol. Soc., Soc. for Rsch. in Child Devel., Raven Soc., Iron Arrow Soc., Sigma Xi. Avocations: soccer, community service, running. Office: U Conn Sch Family Studies 348 Mansfield Rd Unit 2058 Storrs Mansfield CT 06269-2058 E-mail: britner@uconn.edu.

BRITO, DAGOBERT LLANOS, economics educator; b. Mex., Apr. 6, 1941; came to U.S., 1945, naturalized, 1958; s. John L. and Guadalupe G. (Llanos) B.; m. Patricia Ann Kendrick, June 29, 1968. BA, Rice U., 1967, MA, PhD, Rice U., 1970. Asst. prof. econs. U. Wis., Madison, 1970-72; asso. prof. econs. and polit. sci. Ohio State U., Columbus, 1972-75, prof., 1976-79; dir. Murphy Inst. Polit. Economy; chmn., prof. econs. Tulane U., New Orleans, 1979-84; Peterkin prof. polit. econs. Rice U., Houston, 1984—. Cons. Dept. State, Dept. Def. Author: A Dynamic Model of the Armaments Race, 1972, Strategic Nuclear Weapons and the Application of International Rights, 1977, Conflicts and Outbreak of War, 1985, Stock Externalities, Pigovian Taxation and Dynamic Stability, 1987, Richardsonian Arms Race Models, 1989, On the Limits of Economic Control, 1990, Externalities and Compulsory Vaccinations, 1991, The Economic and Political Incentives to Acquire Nuclear Weapons, 1993; (with M.D. Intriligator) The Economics of Disarmament, Arms Races and Arms Control, 1993, Minimizing the Risks for Accidental Nuclear War: An Agenda for Action, 1993; (with P.R. Hartley) Consumer Rationality and Credit Cards, 1995, Proliferation and the Probability of War: A Cardinality Theorem, 1996, Pricing Natural Gas in Mexico, 2002; editor: Strategies for Managing Nuclear Proliferation, 1983; assoc. editor Jour. Optimization Theory and Applications. Served with U.S. Army, 1963-66. NSF grantee, 1972, 74, 77, 78, 81; Mershon Center grantee, 1973, 78; Rice scholar Baker Inst. Mem. Econometric Soc., Public Choice Soc., Houston Philo. Soc. Office: Rice U PO Box 1892 Houston TX 77251-1892

BRITT, DAVID VAN BUREN, retired educational communications executive; b. Needham, Mass., July 30, 1937; s. Paul and Ellen Sibront Britt; m. Marjorie Joan Hoag, Feb. 15, 1958 (div. 1984); children: Pamela, Barbara B. Schaefer, Paul David; m. Sue Cushman, July 22, 1989. AB, Wesleyan U., 1959; MPA, Harvard U., 1967. Ops. mgmt. staff No. Trust Co., Chgo., 1959-62; legis. chief U.S. AID, Washington, 1962-68; chief programs and plans U.S. EEOC, Washington, 1968-69; dep. dir. policy planning U.S. Overseas Pvt. Investment Corp., Washington, 1969-70; ind. cons. Washington, 1970-71; from v.p. to COO Sesame Workshop, N.Y.C., 1971-90, CEO, trustee, 1990-99. Mem. Coun. on Fgn. Rels.; mem. adv. bd. Initiative on Social Enterprise, Harvard Bus. Sch., Hauser Ctr. for Non-Profit Orgns., Kennedy Sch. Govt., Harvard U.; chair bd. dirs. Kids Voting U.S.A., 2002—; trustee New World Found., N.Y.C., 1978—86, Wesleyan U., Middletown, Conn., 1989—92. Recipient Disting. Alumnus award Wesleyan U., 1994. Episcopalian. Home: 1252 Harrison Point Trail Amelia Island FL 32034

BRITT, EARL THOMAS, lawyer; b. Phila., July 14, 1940; s. Earl Francis and Marie Rita (Lawless) B.; m. Maureen Wong, Dec. 26, 1964; children: Denise, Karen, Eileen, Mary, Kevin, Stephen. AB, St. Joseph's U., Phila., 1961; JD, U. Pa., 1964. Bar: Pa. 1964, U.S. Dist. Ct. (ea. dist.) Pa. 1964, U.S. Ct. Appeals (3rd cir.) 1964, U.S. Dist. Ct. Appeals (D.C. cir.) 1981, U.S. Supreme Ct. 1982. Atty. Pa. Mfrs. Assn. Ins. Co., Phila., 1964-67; assoc. Swartz Campbell & Detweiler, Phila., 1967-68; assoc., then ptnr. Duane Morris & Heckscher, Phila., 1968-92; founder, ptnr., chmn. Britt, Hankins, Schaible & Moughan, Phila., 1992—; judge pro tem Ct. Common Pleas, Phila., 1991—. Lectr. Comey Inst. Indsl. Rels. St. Joseph's U., 1961-92; adj. faculty Temple U. Sch. Law-Acad. Advocacy, 1994—. Mem. adv. bd. Norwood-Fontbonne Acad., 1997-2002. Mem. ABA, Pa. Bar Assn., Phila. Bar Assn. (trustee campaign for qualified judges 1989, hon. trustee 1990-91), Phila. Assn. Def. Counsel (bd. dirs. 1983-89, 93-94, pres. 1988-89), Pa. Def. Inst. (lectr. Trial Acad. 1990—), Internat. Assn. Def. Counsel, Def. Rsch. Inst., Lawyer's Club Phila. (bd. dirs. 1988-90). Republican. Roman Catholic. Home: 106 Sparango Ln Plymouth Meeting PA 19462-1115 Office: Britt Hankins Schaible & Moughan 11 E Airy St Norristown PA 19401 E-mail: ebritt@bhsm-pm.com.

BRITT, GLENN ALAN, media company executive; b. Hackensack, N.J., Mar. 6, 1949; s. Walter E. Britt and Helen Crupi; m. Barbara Jane Little, Oct. 25, 1975. AB, Dartmouth Coll., 1971, MBA, 1972. Contr.'s asst. Time, Inc., N.Y.C., 1972-74, fin. dir. Iran project, Time-Life Books Alexandria, Va., 1976-78, dir. video group new bus. devel. N.Y.C., 1980-81, sr. v.p. fin. video group, 1984, v.p., treas., 1986-88, v.p., CFO, 1988-90; sr. v.p., treas. Time Warner Inc., N.Y.C., 1990; exec. v.p. Time Warner Cable Group, Stamford, Conn., 1990-92; pres. Time Warner Cable Ventures, Stamford, Conn., 1992-99, Time Warner Cable, Stamford, 1999—2001, chmn., CEO, 2001—; v.p., treas. Manhattan Cable TV, N.Y.C., 1974-76; v.p. network and studio ops. HBO Inc., N.Y.C., 1978-80, sr. v.p., CFO, 1984-86; sr. v.p. fin. Am. TV and Comm. Corp., Stamford, Conn., 1981-84. Mem. Fin. Exec. Inst., Woodway Country Club, Eastward Ho, Cape Cod National Golf Club and Country Club, Univ. Club. Avocations: skiing, gardening, golf. Office: Time Warner Cable Group 290 Harbor Dr Stamford CT 06902-7475

BRITT, JOHN ROY, banker; b. Los Angeles, Oct. 9, 1937; s. Roy Arthur and Virginia Alice (Vaughn) B.; children: Jeffrey John, Belinda Lynn, Gregory Scott. BA, Claremont McKenna Coll., 1959; grad., Pacific Coast Banking Sch., U. Wash., 1973, Managerial Policy Inst., U. So. Calif., 1978. Fellow Am. Bd. Forensic Examiners (bd. cert. forensic examiner). With Security Pacific Nat. Bank, 1959-83, regional v.p., 1972-74, sr. v.p., 1974-83, adminstr. Mid City-Eastern div., 1978-83; instr. Essentials of Banking Sch., U. Notre Dame, 1979; sr. v.p. Coast Savs. and Loan, Los Angeles, 1983-85; exec. v.p., chief operating officer Pacific Inland Bank, Anaheim, Calif., 1985-86, pres., chief exec. officer, 1986-89; pres. JRB Assocs., 1990—; pres., chief exec. officer United Citizens Nat. Bank, L.A., 1992. Mem. pres.'s adv. coun. Claremont McKenna Coll., 1993; past chmn. bd. dirs., mem. exec. com. Commuter Transp. Svcs., Inc., L.A. Capt USAR, 1959 67. Mem.: Risk Mgmt. Assn., Am. Coll. Forensic Examiners (bd. cert.). Republican. Methodist.

BRITT, MAISHA DORRAH, protective services official; b. S.C. d. Charles Joseph Britt and Versena (Kennedy) Dorrah; m. W. Benjamin Williams, Dec. 14, 1963 (div. June 1976); children: Terri Rochelle, Trina Michelle. AS, BS, Phila Coll. Textiles and Sci.; MA, Antioch U., Phila., 1986; postgrad., Del. State U., 1999; PhD in Bibl. Counseling, Friends Internat. Christian U., Merced, Calif., 2002. Cert. in electronic surveillance. Police officer Phila. Police Dept., 1976-79; sgt., county detective Phila. Dist. Atty's Office, 1979-90; orgn. devel. cons., cert. Christian counselor, 2002—; family devel. specialist Norristown Family Ctr., 1994—. Founder, dir. Creative Awareness Workshop. Poet: (contbr. anthologies) Famous Poems of the Twentieth Century, 1996, Nat. Libr. of Poetry, 1998 (Editor's award). Sec. bd. Horizon House, Phila., 1988—; vol. Women Against Abuse, Phila., 1983—, mem. women's ministry Calvary Bapt. Ch., Dover, trustee Ctr. for Literacy, 1990—, vice chmn.; vol. security team program supr. Atlanta Centennial Olympic Games, 1996; tng. facilatator Ch. Women United-Womens LINC, 1999—; chair Dover Human Rels. Commn., 2002-. Inducted into Murrell Dobbins H.S. Hall of Fame, 1988; named Woman of Yr., Fedn.Bus. and Profl. Women's Clubs Inc., 1991. Mem. AAUW (pres. Dover br. 2002-), Nat. Christian Counselors Assn., County and State Detectives Assn. Pa. (exec. bd. 1990—, Leadership award 1989), Fraternal Order of Police, Internat. Police Assn., Internat. Assn. Women Police (Officer of Yr. 1989), Nat. Women's Hall of Fame, Bus. and Profl. Women's Club. Republican. Avocations: music, creative writing, creative dance, walking, photography. Address: PO Box 1381 Dover DE 19903-1381

BRITT, MARGARET MARY, finance educator; b. Balt., Jan. 21, 1951; d. Joseph John and Lottie Elizabeth (Zielinski) Britt. BA in Elem. Edn., U. Mass., 1972; BSBA, Boston U., 1979, M in Human Resource Edn., 1990; DBA in Human Resource Mgmt., Nova Southeastern U., 2002. Cert. tchr. elem. edn., music Mass., Va., N.C., vocat. tech. educator in bus. mktg. Mass. Internal auditor Digital Equip. Corp., Maynard, Mass., 1979-82, sr. fin. analyst FDP, 1982-83, sr. fin. analyst sales Stow, Mass., 1983-85, cons. trainer Maynard, 1985-87, fin. cons., trainer, 1987-90, mgr. corp. fin. edn., 1990-94; automated office instr. Mass. Job Tng., Worcester, 1995-97; sci. tchr. Holden Christian Acad., Eastern Nazarene Coll., Worcester, 1997—, instr. dept. bus. Quincy, Mass., 1998-2000, assoc. prof. dept. bus., 2000—02, asst. prof. bus. adminstrn., 2002—; assoc. prof. dept. bus. Mt. Vernon (Ohio) Nazarene U., 2003—. Part-time instr. fin. continuing edn. dept. Syracuse U., 1990—91; adj. prof. bus. Eastern Nazarene Coll., Quincy, Mass., 1994—; bd. dirs. Am. Biog. Inst., spkr. in field. Sec. Parsons Hill Homeowners Assn., Worcester, 1985—90; presenter time mgmt. workshop MIT-Soc. Women Engrs. and Alumnae, Cambridge, 1988, 1989. Named Outstanding Young Women of Am., 1984. Mem.: AAUW, NAFE, ASTD, Nat. Mus. Women in the Arts, Inst. Internal Auditors. Avocations: walking, reading, singing, cooking. Home: 387 Nantasket Ave Apt 5 Hull MA 02045-2748 Office: Eastern Nazarene Coll 23 E Elm Ave Quincy MA 02170-2905

BRITT, REBECCA FAE, communications executive; b. Kirksville, Mo., Aug. 23, 1956; d. Aubrey Clarence and Marian LaVeta (Wyatt) Britt; children: Rachel Nicole, Joel Steven. BS in Bus. Mgmt. summa cum laude, Kennesaw State U., 1992. Asst. BellSouth Mobility Inc., Atlanta, 1985-87; mgr. real estate Bell South Mobility, Inc., Atlanta, 1987-91, sr. mgr. real estate and constrn., 1991-94, dir. engring. implementation, 1995 97; dir. real estate and devel. BellSouth Cellular Inc., Atlanta, 1997—98; v.p., gen. mgr. Ga. region Crown Castle Internat., Alpharetta, 1999—2001; pres., founder Britco Mgmt. Svcs., Inc., Woodstock, Ga., 2002—. Mem. Nat. Assn. Corp. Real Estate Execs., Phi Kappa Phi. Republican. Avocations: reading, writing poetry.

BRITT, RONALD LEROY, retired manufacturing company executive; b. Abilene, Kans, Mar. 1, 1935; s. Elvin Elbert and Lona Helen Britt; m. Judith Ann Salter, June 29, 1957; children: Brett Gavin, Mark Damon, Melissa Ann. BSM.E., Wichita State U., 1963. From product engr. to product planner Hotpoint divsn. G.E. Co., Chgo., 1963-68; product planner Norge Co., Chgo., 1968; product mgr., asst. dir. engirng. Leigh Products Inc., Coopersville, Mich., 1968-74; mgr. rsch. and devel. Miami Carey divsn. Jim. Walter Corp., Monroe, Ohio, 1974-84; sr. v.p. mfg. and engring. Belvedere USA Corp., Belvidere, Ill., 1984-2001, ret., 2001. Industry rep. for electric fans Underwriters Labs. Acitve Boy Scouts Am., 1970-73, PTA, 1973-78; exec. adviser Jr. Achievement, 1984-85, Boone County chmn., 1968-88; bd. dirs. YMCA, Belvidere, 1990-96, vice-chmn., chmn. fin. com., 1991, v.p., 1992; trustee Dickinson County Hist. Soc., 2003—; dir. on adv. bd. St. Joseph Hosp., 1990-95, 97-99, chmn. long range planning com., 1991; bd. dirs. Boone County Dist. # 100 Edn. Found., 1991-95, Abilene Kans. Airport, 2003—. Served with U.S. Army, 1958-60. Recipient Inventor's award Gen. Electric Co., 1967. Mem. ASME, Home Ventilation Inst. (engring. com. 1975-84), Belvidere C. of C. (bd. dirs. 1986-89), Air Capital Corvette Club, Air Capital Carnival Glass Club, Rotary (v.p. 1999-2000). Republican. Congregationalist. Home: 619 NW 3d Abilene KS 67410

BRITTAIN, JAMES EDWARD, science and technology educator, researcher; b. Mills River, N.C., May 20, 1931; s. Randall Francis and Velma Hassie (Gillespie) B.; m. Louise Mary Lambert, March 29, 1969 (dec. Mar. 27, 1972); m. Jo Ann Layne, Apr. 14, 1973. BS, Clemson U., 1957; MS, U. Tenn., 1959; MA, Case Western Res. U., 1969, PhD, 1970. Jr. rsch. engr. U. Tenn., Knoxville, 1958-59; asst. prof. elec. engring. Clemson (S.C.) U., 1959-66; asst. prof. history of sci. and tech. Ga. Inst. Tech., Atlanta, 1969-71, assoc. prof., 1972-91, prof., 1992-94; prof. emeritus, 1994—. Author: Engineering the New South, 1985, Alexanderson: Pioneer in American Electrical Engineering, 1992, Scanning The Past: A History of Electrical Engineering and Its Pioneers, 1999, Gun Fights, Dam Sites and Water Rights, 2001; editor: Turning Points in American Electrical History, 1977. With USAF, 1950-54. Smithsonian Instn. rsch. fellow, 1972-73; recipient rsch. contract Nat. Park Svc., 1974-75; grantee NSF, 1979. Fellow IEEE (chmn. history com. 1978-79, 88-89, assoc. editor proceedings 1990—, Centennial medal 1984), Royal Soc. Arts, Radio Club Am. (Batcher Meml. prize 1989); mem. Soc. History of Tech. (mem. exec. coun. 1978-80, 89-91, Usher prize 1971). Baptist. Avocations: trout fishing, hiking, photography of historical industrial sites. Home: 189 Mountain Valley Dr Hendersonville NC 28739-9723

BRITTAIN, MAX GORDON, JR., lawyer; b. Glens Falls, N.Y., Dec. 22, 1947; s. Max Gordon and Eloise (Wilbur) B.; m. Teresa Ann Hochreiter, Sept. 28, 1984; children by previous marriage: Matthew Greer, Amanda Kelly. B.S., Bradley U., 1969; J.D. cum laude, Loyola U., Chgo., 1976. Bar: Ill. 1976, U.S. Dist. Ct. (no. dist.) Ill. 1976, U.S. Ct. Appeals (7th cir.) 1978, U.S. Supreme Ct. 1980, U.S. Ct. Appeals (fed. cir.) 1984. Assoc., Schiff Hardin & Waite, Chgo., 1976-79, Kovar & Smetana, Chgo., 1979-82; ptnr. Kovar, Nelson & Brittain, Chgo., 1982— ; instr. Loyola U., Chgo., 1981— ; lectr. on labor law. Mng. editor Loyola Law Rev., 1975-76; author: Wrongful Discharge Claims. Mem. ABA, Ill. Bar Assn. Republican. Methodist. Club: Union League (Chgo.). Home: 515 S Beverly Ln Arlington Heights IL 60005-2103 Office: Kovar, Nelson, Brittain & Sledz 500 Marquette Bldg 400 S Dearborn St Chicago IL 60605-1107

BRITTAIN, NANCY HAMMOND, accountant; b. Athens, Pa., Oct. 29, 1954; d. Charles Avery Hammond and Leona May (Rolls) Mc Creary; m. Edward M. Brittain, Sept. 6, 1975. AS in Bus., Elmira Coll., 1989, BS in Acctg. summa cum laude, 1994. Legal sec. Friedlander, Friedlander, Reizes, Joch & Littman, P.C., Waverly, N.Y., 1973-84; bus. mgr., bd. dirs., pres. Foundry divsn. Ajax X-Ray, Inc., Sayre, Pa., 1984—; pres., bd. dirs. Ajax Leasing Corp. Mem. Athens Borough Zoning Bd., 1991-97. Mem. Inst. Mgmt. Accts., Alpha Sigma Lambda (mem. exec. com. Beta Tau chpt., various offices 1988-95). Republican. Methodist. Avocations: gardening, skiing. Home: PO Box 948 111 Vista Dr Sayre PA 18840-1107 Office: Ajax X-Ray Inc Foundry Divsn PO Box 98 Sayre PA 18840-0098

BRITTAIN, PAUL S. editor; b. Pitts., Oct. 4, 1950; s. Charles Frederick and Margaret Lorraine Brittain; m. Kathleen Adele Susa, Oct. 3, 1981. Grad. high sch., Alverton, Pa. Mail rm. Daily Courier, Connellsville, Pa., 1970—72; reporter Laurel Group Press, Scottdale, 1972—79; editor Laurel Group Press - Ligonier Echo, 1979—81; photographer Laurel Group Press Gray Studio, Scottdale, 1993—96; editor Laurel Group Press - Mt. Pleasant Jour., 1981—93, 1996—2000, Laurel Group Press - Ind. Observer, Scottdale, 2000—02; coord. editor Laurel Group Press, 2002—. Dir. Scottdale Area Chamber. Author: Tranquility, 2000, Cobwebs, 2001, The Crisp, 2002. Coach, officer Girls Softball League, Mt. Pleasant, 1983—96. Named Golden Quill finalist, We. Pa. Press Assn., Pitts., 2003; recipient Keystone Press award, Pa. Newspaper Pubs., Harrisburg, 1978. Mem.: Elks. Avocation: writing. Office: Laurel Group Press 229 Pitts St Scottdale PA 15683

BRITTAIN, WILLARD WOODSON, JR., (WOODY BRITTAIN), diversified financial services company executive; BA in Econs., Yale U.; MBA, Harvard U. With Price Waterhouse L.L.P. - U.S., 1974, prin., 1983, head Chesapeak Area Consulting Group, 1985, head Office Govt. Svcs., 1990, head, 1993, vice chmn. N.Y.C., 1995; mng. ptnr., key member Global Leadership Team PricewaterhouseCoopers. Mem. policy bd. Price Waterhouse L.L.P. - U.S., 1992. Bd. dirs. Washington Ballet, No. Va. Urban League, Inroads Greater Washington, Greater Washington Bd. Trade, Fed. City Coun., Nat. Assn. Black Accountants (Metro-Washington chpt., Pres.'s Spl. Achievment award), Com. Econ. Devel.; bd. dirs. YMCA, N.Y., bd. liaison teen coun.; bd. dirs., chmn. audit com. Nat. Urban League. Uniroyal Acad. scholar; recipient Spl. Achievement award Nat. Assn. Black Accts.; named Man of Yr. Nat. Coun. Negro Women. Office: Price Waterhouse Coopers LLP 30 S 17th St Ste 1400 Philadelphia PA 19103

BRITTAN, MARTIN R. biologist, educator; b. San Jose, Calif., Jan. 28, 1922; s. Ralph Hinton Brittan and Addie Belle Martin; m. Ruth Marie Luebke, Aug. 10, 1947; children: Penelope, Pamela(dec.). AB, San Jose State U., 1946; PhD, Stanford U., 1951. Cert. fishery scientist Am. Fisheries Soc., 1968. Tchg. asst. Stanford U., Calif., 1946—49; asst. prof. biol. scis. S.D. Sch. Mines and Tech., Rapid City, 1949—50, San Diego State U., 1950—53; from asst. prof. to prof. biol. scis. Calif. State U., Sacramento, 1953—93. Ranger, naturalist U.S. Nat. Pk. Svc., Yosemite, Calif., 1949—52, Glacier, Mont., 1954; environ. cons., Brazil, U.S., 1964, 73, 93-96; mem. numerous adv. bd. Author: Rasbora, 1954, 1998; contbr. articles to profl. jours. With U.S. Army, 1942—46. Recipient award for outstanding ichthyological work, Internat. Fedn. Aquarium Societies, 1958. Mem.: Am. Fisheries Soc. (Svc. award 2002), Am. Soc. Ichthyoligical and Herpotologists (v.p. Pacific divsn. 1946—). Democrat. Avocations: photography, fishing, history, travel. Office: Calif State Univ Dept Biol Sci 6000 J St Sacramento CA 95819

BRITTEN, ROY JOHN, biophysicist; b. Washington, Oct. 1, 1919; s. Rollo Herbert and Marion Hale B.; m. Jacqueline Reid, 1986 (dec. Sept. 2001); children: Gregory, Kenneth. BS, U. Va., 1941; PhD, Princeton U., 1951. Staff mem. dept. terrestrial magnetism Carnegie Instn., Washington, 1951-89; sr. research assoc. Calif. Inst. Tech., Corona del Mar, 1973-81, disting. Carnegie sr. rsch. assoc. biology, 1981-99, emeritus, 1999—. Adj. prof. U. Calif., Irvine, 1991—; discoverer repeated DNA sequences in genomes of higher organisms. Inventor in field. Named Disting. Carnegie Sr. Research Assoc. in Biology, 1981-99. Fellow Am. Acad. Arts and Scis., AAAS; mem. Nat. Acad. Scis. Office: Calif Inst Tech Kerchkhoff Marine Lab 101 Dahlia Ave Corona Del Mar CA 92625-2814

BRITTENHAM, RAYMOND LEE, investment company executive; b. Moscow, Feb. 8, 1916; s. Edward Arthur and Marietta (Wemple) B.; m. Mary Ann Stanard, Nov. 3, 1956; children: Edward C., Carol. AB, Principia Coll., Elsah, Ill., 1936; postgrad., Kaiser Wilhelm U., Berlin, Germany, 1937; LLB, Harvard U., 1940. Bar: Ill. 1940, N.Y. 1946. Assoc. Pope & Ballard, Chgo., 1940-42, Mitchell Carroll, N.Y.C., 1947-56; v.p., gen. counsel ITT and subs., 1962-68, sr. v.p. law, counsel, 1968-80, dir., 1965-80; with Lazard Freres & Co., N.Y.C., 1980-89; pres. Spanish Inst., 1980-82, vice chmn., 1982-90. Maj. AUS, 1942-46. Decorated Bronze Star medal; Croix de Guerre France and Belgium; chevalier Ordre de Leopold Belgium). Mem. ABA, Coun. Fgn. Rels., University Club (N.Y.C.). Home: 925 Park Ave New York NY 10028-0210 also: Skyline Ridge Rd # 184 Bridgewater CT 06752-1729

BRITTINGHAM, JAMES CALVIN, nuclear engineer; b. Hamlet, N.C., Apr. 6, 1942; s. James Calvin and Elizabeth (McCanless) B.; m. Margaret Kitchen, Feb. 12, 1978; 1 child, James Robert. BS in Nuc. Engring., N.C. State U., 1964, MS in Nuc. Engring., 1966; PhD in Nuc. Engring., U. Calif., Berkeley, 1975. Registered nuc. engr., Calif. Engr. Rockwell Internat., Canoga Park, Calif., 1975-80; engr. Pacific Gas and Electric, San Francisco, 1981-85; sr. cons. engr. Ariz. Pub. Svc., Phoenix, 1986—. Assoc. faculty Ariz. State U., 1991-93. Contbr. articles to profl. jours. Recipient Talent for Svc. scholarship N.C. State U., 1960-63, AEC fellowship, 1964-66, NSF traineeship, 1967-69. Mem. Am. Nuc. Soc. Republican. Achievements development of original rod cluster control assembly inventory model for Diablo Canyon power plant and topical reports for Ariz. Pub. Svc. Co. Home: 3367 W Grandview Rd Phoenix AZ 85053-2953 Office: Palo Verde Nuclear Generation Sta Mail Sta 7693 5801 S Wintersburg Rd Tonopah AZ 85354-7529 E-mail: jbrittin@apsc.com.

BRITTON, CLAROLD LAWRENCE, lawyer, consultant; b. Soldier, Iowa, Nov. 1, 1932; s. Arnold Olaf and Florence Ruth (Gardner) B.; m. Joyce Helene Hamlett, Feb. 1, 1958; children: Laura, Eric, Val, Martha. BS in Engring., U. Mich., Ann Arbor, 1958, JD, 1961, postgrad. Bar: Ill. 1961, U.S. Dist. Ct. (no. dist.) Ill. 1962, U.S. Ct. Appeals (7th cir.) 1963, U.S. Supreme Ct. 1970, Mich. 1989. Assoc. Jenner & Block, Chgo., 1961-70, ptnr., 1970-88; pres. Britton Info. Systems, Inc., 1991—. Lectr. DePaul U., 1988. Author: Computerized Trial Notebook, 1991, Trial By Notebook, 2002; asst. editor Mich. Law Rev., 1960. Comdr. USNR, 1952-57. Fellow Am. Coll. Trial Lawyers; mem. ABA (litigation sect., antitrust com., past regional chmn. discovery com. 1961), Ill. State Bar Assn. (chmn. Allerton House Conf. 1984, 86, 88, chmn. rule 23 com. 1985-87, chmn. civil practice and procedure coun. 1987-88, antitrust com.), Chgo. Bar Assn. (past chmn. fed. civil procedure com., mem. judiciary and computer law coms., civil practice com.), 7th Cir. Bar Assn., Def. Rsch. Inst. (com. on aerospace 1984), Mich. Bar Assn., Ill. Assn. Trial Lawyers, Order of Coif, Law Club (Chgo.), Racine Yacht Club (Wis.), Macatawa Yacht Club (Mich.), Masons, Alpha Phi Mu, Tau Beta Pi. Republican. Lutheran. Office: 411 E Washington St Ann Arbor MI 48104-2015 E-mail: britton@ic.net.

BRITTON, EMILY MADDOX, sales executive; b. Harris County, Ga., June 21, 1915; d. Charles Baker Maddox and Sara Brown Hudson; m. Joe Britton, June 25, 1935; children: Charles Wayne, Joe Maddox. Diploma, La Grange Bus. Coll., La Grange, Ga. Retail salesperson J.C. Penney, La Grange, Ga., Ala. Vol. with numerous church missions with United meth. Ch. Mem.: Paint Pushers Art Group, DAR, Anchorage Womans Club. Avocation: homemaker, family activities. Home: 1003 D St Anchorage AK 99501

BRITTON, LAURENCE GEORGE, research scientist; b. Hampton Court, Eng., Sept. 26, 1951; came to U.S., 1981; s. George and Barbara Mavis (Card) B.; m. Helen Lynn Grass, Apr. 16, 1983 (dec. 1989); 1 child, Robert; m. Carol-Ann Kirby, Jan. 6, 1995. BS with 1st class honors, U. Leeds, Eng., 1974; PhD in Fuel and Combustion Sci., U. Leeds, 1977. Chartered engr., Engl.; chartered physicist. Rsch. fellow dept. elec. engring. U. Southhampton, Eng., 1978-81; sr. combustion scientist Union Carbide Corp. Tech. Ctr., South Charleston, W.Va., 1981-84, project scientist process fire and explosion hazards, 1984-89, rsch. scientist, 1990-96, prin. engr., 1997-2000; analytical leader, technology steward (flammability) Dow Chem. Co. Tech. Ctr., South Charleston, 2001—02; cons. scientist Neolytica, Inc., 2003—. Guest lectr. Coll. Grad. Studies, Sch. Engring. and Sci., U. W.Va., 1991-94; mem. fueling systems com. U. K. Ministry Def., 1978-81; speaker at profl. metings and symposia; mem. U.S. Coast Guard/U.S. Dept. Transp. Static Electricity Adv. Group, 1993—. Author: Avoiding Static Ignition Hazards in Chemical Operations, 1999; contbr. articles to sci. jours. Fellow: AIChE (mem. editl. rev. bd. Process Safety Progress 1993—, William H. Doyle award 1986, 1989, Norton H. Walton/Ronald L. Miller award 2003), Inst. Energy; mem.: ASTM (mem. E.27 com. on hazard potential of chemicals 1997—), Inst. Physics, Chem. Mfrs. assn./Am. Petroleum Inst. (reactive hazards tech. task force 1995), Chem. Mfrs. Assn. (flame resistant clothing issues group 1995), Nat. Fire Protection Assn. (explosion protection sys. com., classification and properties of hazardous chems. com., static electricity com.), Ctr. Chem. Process Safety (engring. practices com. 1988—, reactive materials storage and handling com. 1990—, safe handling of hazardous particulate solids com. 2000—), Combustion Inst. Home: Howton Grove House Wormbridge Herefordshire HR2 9DY England Office: Neolytica Inc 3606 W Liberty Rd Ann Arbor MI 48103-9049

BRITTON, M(ELVIN) C(REED), JR., physician, rheumatologist; b. San Francisco, Apr. 11, 1935; s. Melvin Creed and Mathilda Carolyn (Epeneter) B.; m. Mary Elizabeth Phillips, Nov. 2, 1957; children: Elizabeth Carolynne, Lisa Marie. AB, Dartmouth Coll., 1957, MS, 1958; MD, Harvard U., 1960. Diplomate Am. Bd. Internal Medicine, Am. Bd. Rheumatology, Am. Bd. Quality Assurance. Resident Dartmouth Coll. Sch. Medicine, Hanover, N.H., 1964-67; fellow Harvard U. Sch. Medicine, Boston, 1967-69; ptnr. Palo Alto (Calif.) Med. Clinic, 1969—, chmn. dept. medicine, 1990-97. Pres. med. staff Stanford (Calif.) U. Med. Ctr., 1985-87, mem. med. staff bd., 1969-87; bd. dirs. Hosp. Conf. No. Calif., 1988-92, Inst. for Med. Quality, 1998—, treas., 1999-2003, chmn. bd., 2003—; mem. Relative Value Update Commn., 1996—. Contbr. articles to med. jours. Pres. Found. for Med. care Santa Clara county, Campbell, 1983-89; mem. Bay Area Lupus Found., 1978—, chmn., 1987-88, 94-95; v.p. Calif. Founds. for Med. Care, 1996, pres., CEO, 1999-2001. Fellow ACP, Am. Coll. Rheumatology (bd. dirs. 1986-89, Paulding Phelps medal 1994, mastership 2000), Calif. Acad. Medicine (exec. com. 1996-2000, pres. 2001—); mem. AMA (alternate del. 1988—, governing coun., speciality & svcs. soc.), Calif. Med. Assn., Santa Clara County Med. Soc. (pres. 1980-81, Bd. Svc. award 1988), Arthritis Found. No. Calif. (chmn. bd. dirs. 1984-87, Disting Svc. award 1985), Vintners Club (San Francisco, v.p. 1975-78), Commonwealth Club (San Francisco). Republican. Episcopalian. Avocations: skiing, traveling, enology. Office: Palo Alto Med Clinic 795 El Camino Real Palo Alto CA 94301-2726

BRITTON, RUTH ANN WRIGHT, elementary educator; b. Ft. Smith, Ark., Apr. 4, 1943; d. Ralph M. and Margaret E. (Reising) Wright; m. Joseph D. Britton, Sept. 25, 1965; children: Beth, Meg, Jo. BA in Elem. Edn., Concordia Tchrs. Coll., River Forest, Ill., 1965; MS, Kans. State U., 1978. Cert. in reading K-12, elem. 1-6, developmental reading K-12, developmental edn. Tchr. 5th grade Pickens (S.C.) Sch. Dist., 1966-68; Tchr. grades 5 and 2 Manhattan (Kans.) City Schs., 1969, 77-78; Chpt. I reading tchr. Montgomery County Schs., Christianburg, Va., 1982-86; Dir. Jr. HS reading lab. Hillsborough County Schs., Tampa, Fla., 1986-92; Instr., dept. head Cochise Coll., Douglas,

Ariz., 1993—. Co-author: Reading Handbook for Parents, Making Connections, a sociology and reading handbook. Recipient Helping Hands award for vol. svc. U.S. Army 7th Corps in Germany, 1980, Excellence in Edn. by Nat. Inst. for Staff and Organizational Development, 1997-98; named Outstanding Instr. Cochise Coll., 1999-2000, Tchr. of Yr. TCJS, 1989-90. Mem. Internat. Reading Assn., Literacy Vols., Coll. Reading and Learning Assn., Governor's Commn. for Svc. Learning and Volunteerism, 2002-. Office: Cochise Coll 4190 West Highway 80 Douglas AZ 85607

BRITTON, THOMAS WARREN, JR., retired management consultant; b. Pawhuska, Okla., June 16, 1944; s. Thomas Warren and Helen Viola (Haynes) B.; m. Jerlyn Kay Davis, 1964 (div. 1970); 1 child, Natalie Dawn; m. Deborah Ann Mansour, Oct. 20, 1973; 1 child, Kimberly Ann. BSME, Okla. State U., 1966, MS in Indsl. Engring. and Mgmt., 1968. Cert. mgmt. cons. Cons. Arthur Young & Co., L.A., 1972-76, prin., 1976—79, ptnr., 1979—88, office dir. mgmt. svcs. dept. Orange County, Calif., 1979—88; ptnr. Price Waterhouse, L.A., ptnr.-in-charge West Coast mfg. cons. practice Nat. Aerospace and Def. Industry, ptnr.-in-charge west coast products and logistics practice, 1988—95; mng. ptnr. west region MCS Products Practice PricewaterhouseCoopers, L.A., chmn. US MCS Tech. Industry Practice, chmn. Global MCS Tech. Industry Practice, 1995—2000, COO MCS west bus. unit, chmn. global MCS tech. industry practice, 2000—02; ret., 2002. Lectr. in field. Mem. creative growth bd. City of San Dimas, 1976—77, chmn. Planning Commn., 1977—83; trustee World Affairs Coun. Orange County, 1980; benefactor, mem. founders com., v.p. ann. fund, pres., chmn. long range planning, trustee, bd. pres. South Coast Repertory Theater, 1982—92; trustee Providence Speech and Hearing Ctr., 1985—90, Spl. Olympics So. Calif., 1995—97; mem. devel. com. U. Calif.-Irvine Med. Sch.; chmn. Costa Mesa Arts Coun., 1984. Capt. USAR, 1971—86. Mem. L.A. Inst. CPAs, Mgmt. Adv. Svcs. Com., Am. Prodn. and Inventory Control Soc., Am. Inst. Indsl. Engrs., Greater Irvine Indsl. League, Okla. State U. Alumni Assn., Jonathan Club, Ridgeline Country Club, Santa Ana Country Club, Kappa Sigma. Home: 9881 Orchard Ln Villa Park CA 92861-3105 E-mail: Tom_britton@msn.com.

BRITZ, JOHN DOMINIC, II, political scientist, consultant; b. Pueblo, Colo., Oct. 5, 1961; s. John Dominic and Frances Ann (Krasouec) B.; m. Betsy Anne Britz, June 24; children: Samantha, Mallory. BA, U. Denver, 1985. Polit. cons. Monaghan & Assocs., Denver, 1987-89; dep. campaign mgr. Citizens for Denver's Future, 1989-90; exec. dir. House Dem. Majority Fund, Denver, 1990-91; campaign mgr. Welchert for Auditor, Denver, 1991; v.p. Welchert & Britz, Inc., Denver, 1991—. Lectr. in field. Contbr. numerous articles to profl. jours.; author tng. manuals. Mem. Denver Met. Wastewater Bd., 1998—; mem. Denver Cmty. Leadership Forum, 1993. Recipient Friend of Pub. Edn. award Phi Delta Kappa, 1999. Mem. Am. Assn. Polit. Cons. Democrat. Roman Catholic. Avocations: snow skiing, weight lifting, watercolor painting, drawing, fishing. Office: Welchert & Britz Inc 1701 Wynkoop St Ste 215 Denver CO 80202 E-mail: john@welchertandbritz.com.

BRITZ, ROBERT G. stock exchange executive; BS in fin., Manhattan Coll.; cert. advanced mgmt., Harvard Sch. Bus. Various positions N.Y. Stock Exch., 1972—95, group exec. v.p., 1995—2002, pres., co-COO, exec. vice chmn., 2002—. Bd. dirs. The Stanley Works; mem. office chmn. N.Y. Stock Exch., co-chair mgmt. com.; chmn. Securities Industry Automation Corp., Sector, Inc. Office: NY Stock Exch attn Ray Pellecchia 11 Wall St 6th fl New York NY 10005-1905

BRITZ LOTTI, DIANE EDWARD, investment company executive; b. York, Pa, June 15, 1952; d. Everett Frank and Billie Jacqueline (Sherrill) Britz; m. Marcello Lotti, Sept. 9, 1978 (dec. Apr. 1990); children: Ariane Elizabeth Lotti, Samantha Alexis Lotti. BA, Duke U., 1974; MBA, Columbia U., 1982. Asst. mgr. Columbia Artists, NYC, 1974-76; gen. mgr. Ea. Music Festival, Greensboro, NC, 1977-78; v.p. Britz Cobin, NYC, 1979-82; pres. Pan Oceanic Mgmt., Inc., NYC, 1983-90, Pan Oceanic Advisors, Ltd., NYC, 1988-94; chair Pan Oceanic Mgmt. Ltd., NYC, 1994-2001; also bd. dirs Pan Oceanic Advisors, Ltd., NYC; mng. dir. Am. Capital Ptnr., Ltd., NYC, 1996—; chmn. Trinity Investors Fund Inc., NYC; mng. dir. ERAFO Ltd., NYC; founding ptnr. Circle Fin. Group LLC, NYC, 2003—. Bd dirs Pan Oceanic Mgt Inc, Trinity Investors Fund Inc; mem undergraduate bd, mem capital campaign comt Duke Univ. Bd. advisors Turtle Bay Music Sch.; pres. Marcello Lotti Found.; trustee Lorne Weill Trust; mem. Nat. Com. Am. Fgn. Policy; bd. dirs. exec. com. Am. Acad. in Rome; chair Trinity bd. visitors Duke U. Mem.: Doubles Club, Columbia Bus Sch Club NY. Mem. Soc. Of Friends. Office: 45 Rockefeller Plz Ste 2043 New York NY 10111-0100

BRIZZOLARA, CHARLES ANTHONY, lawyer, director; b. Chgo., Nov. 20, 1929; s. Ralph D. and Florence H. (Hurley) B.; m. Audree Doyle, Aug. 24, 1968. BA, Lake Forest (Ill.) Coll., 1951; JD, Ill. Inst. Tech., 1957. Bar: Ill. 1959. Practiced law, Chgo., 1959-67; with Walter E. Heller & Co., also Walter E. Heller Internat. Corp. (later Amerifin Corp.), Chgo., 1967-85; v.p., sec., gen. counsel Walter E. Heller & Co., also Walter E. Heller Internat. Corp., 1974-85, sr. v.p., 1980-85; v.p. Chgo. Bears Football Club, Inc., 1975-88; mem. firm Chadwell & Kayser Ltd., 1985-90; ptnr. Michael Best & Friedrich, LLC, Chgo., 1990—2002; of counsel Berger, Newmark and Fenchel P.C., Chgo., 2003—. Bd. dirs. Abacus Real Estate Fin. Co., Walter E. Heller & Co. S.E., Heller Factoring (Hong Kong) Ltd., Factoring Serfin, S.A., Chandler Leasing Corp., 1975-80; lectr. seminars Am. Mgmt. Assn. Editor: Chgo.-Kent Law Rev, 1956. Bd. dirs. Cath. Charities Archdiocese of Chgo., 1978-99, sec., 1991-94; bd. dirs. Ill. Inst. Tech. Chgo. Kent Alumni Assn., 1980-89. Served with AUS, 1952-54. Mem. Internat. Bar Assn., ABA, Ill. Bar Assn. Roman Catholic. Home: Apt 20G 253 E Delaware Pl Chicago IL 60611-1758 Office: 222 N LaSalle St Chicago IL 60601

BRNA, THEODORE GEORGE, JR., physician; b. Radford, Va., June 22, 1957; s. Theodore George and Marilyn Ann (Dianis) B.; m. Ann DuRant, Aug. 9, 1980; children: Stephanie Ann, Meredith Claire, Andrew Paul. BS, Va. Polytech Inst., 1979; MD, Med. Coll. Va., 1983. Resident Martin Army Cmty. Hosp., Ft. Benning, Ga., 1986; commd. 2d lt. U.S. Army, 1979, advanced through grades to maj., 1990. Fellow Am. Acad. Family Physicians; mem. N.C. Med. Soc., Wilson County Med. Soc. (sec.-treas. 1997, v.p. 1998, pres. 1999). Home: 12046 Simms Rd Sims NC 27880-9115 Office: Bailey Family Practice Ctr 6321 Deans St PO Box 280 Bailey NC 27807-0280

BROAD, BARBARA PRENTICE, retired real estate agent; b. Easton, Pa., Mar. 3, 1920; d. Donald Bishop and Mary Louise (Farnham) Prentice; m. Henry Sawyer Broad, Aug. 16, 1952 (dec. Mar. 1997); children: Louise Broad Lavine, Richard G., William G. BA, Wellesley Coll., 1941; postgrad., Northeastern U., 1951-52. Legal sec. Hutchins & Wheeler, Boston, 1946-48; sec. to Judge Charles Wyzanski U.S. Dist. Ct., Boston, 1948-52; real estate agt., 1975-2000; ret., 2000. Chmn. Princeton (N.J.) Nursery Sch.; pres. Wellesley Club Ctrl. N.J., Class of 1941 Wellesley; bd. dirs. Young Audiences N.J., 1978—93, pres., 1980—83. Lt. USNR, 1943—45. Democrat. Presbyterian. Avocations: singing in choir, tennis, bridge. Home: 33 Hedge Row Rd Princeton NJ 08540-5054

BROAD, ELI, financial services executive; b. N.Y.C., June 6, 1933; s. Leon and Rebecca (Jacobson) B.; m. Edythe Lois Lawson, Dec. 19, 1954; children: Jeffrey Alan, Gary Stephen. BA in Acctg. cum laude, Mich. State U., 1954. CPA, Mich. 1956. Cert. public acct., 1954-56; asst. prof. Detroit Inst. Tech., 1956; co-founder, chmn., pres., CEO SunAmerica Inc. (formerly Kaufman & Broad, Inc.), L.A., 1957-2001, chmn., 2001—, Nat. Anchor Nat. Life Ins. Co., First SunAmerica Life Ins. Co., CalAmerica Life Ins. Co., Kaufman and Broad Home Corp., L.A., 1989-93, chmn. exec. com., 1993-95, founder, chmn., 1993—. Chmn. Stanford Ranch Co.; mem. exec. com. adv. bd. Fed. Nat. Mortgage Assn., 1972-73; active Calif. Bus. Roundtable, 1986-2000; co-owner Sacramento Kings and Arco Arena, 1992-99; trustee Com. for Econ. Devel., 1993-95; mem. real estate adv. bd. Citibank, N.Y.C., 1976-81; bd. dirs. Am. Internat. Group, Inc., L.A. Bus. Advisors, Sacramento Kings and ARCO Arena; co-owner Sacramento Kings & Arco Arena, 1992-99. Mem. bd. dirs. L.A. World Affairs Coun., 1988—, chmn., 1994-97, DARE Am., 1989-95, hon. mem. bd. dirs. 1995—; founding trustee Windward Sch., Santa Monica, Calif., 1972-77; bd. trustees Pitzer Coll., Claremont, Calif., 1970-82, chmn. bd. trustees, 1973-79, life trustee, 1982—, Haifa U., Israel, 1972-80, Calif. State U., 1978-82, vice chmn. bd. trustees, 1979-80, trustee emeritus, 1982—, Mus. Contemporary Art, L.A., 1980-93, founding chmn., 1980, Archives Am. Art, Smithsonian Instn., Washington, 1985-98, Am. Fedn. Arts, 1988-91, Leland Stanford Mansion Found., 1992—, Calif. Inst. Tech., 1993—, Armand Hammer Mus. Art and Cultural Ctr. UCLA, 1994-99; pres. Calif. Non-Partisan Vote Registration Found., 1971-72; chancellor's assoc. UCLA, 1971—, mem. vis. com. Grad. Sch. Mgmt., 1972-90, trustee UCLA Found., 1986-96, exec. com. bd. visitors Sch. of the Arts & Architecture, 1997—; assoc. chmn. United Crusade, L.A., 1973-76; chmn. Mayor's Housing Policy Com., L.A., 1974-75; del., spkr. Fed. Econ. Summit Conf., 1974, State Econ. Summit Conf., 1974; mem. contemporary coun. L.A. County Mus. Art, 1973-79, bd. trustees acquisitions com., 1978-81, trustee, 1995—; bd. fellows, mem. exec. com. The Claremont (Calif.) Colls., 1974-79; nat. trustee Balt. Mus. Art, 1985-91; mem. adv. bd. Boy Scouts Am., 1982-85, L.A. Bus. Jour., 1986-88; mem. adv. coun. Town Hall of Calif., 1985-87; trustee Dem. Nat. Com. Victory Fund, 1988, 92, 96; mem. painting and sculpture com. Whitney Mus., N.Y.C., 1987-89; chmn. adv. bd. ART/LA, 1989; bd. overseers The Music Ctr. of L.A. County, 1991-92, mem. bd. govs., 1996-98; mem. contemporary art com. Harvard U. Art Mus., Cambridge, Mass., 1992—; mem. internat. dirs. coun. Guggenheim Mus., N.Y.C., 1993-98; active Nat. Indsl. Pollution Control Coun., 1970-73, Maeght Found., St. Paul de Vence, France, 1975-80, Mayor's Spl. Adv. Com. on Fiscal Adminstrn., L.A., 1993-94; bd. dirs. UCLA/Armand Hammer Mus. Art And Cultural Ctr., 1994-1999. Recipient Man of Yr. award City of Hope, 1965, Golden Plate award Am. Acad. Achievement, 1971, Housing Man of Yr. award Nat. Housing Coun., 1979, Humanitarian award NCCJ, 1977, Am. Heritage award Anti Defamation League, 1984, Pub. Affairs award Coro Found., 1987, Honors award visual arts L.A. Arts Coun., 1989; Eli Broad Coll. Bus. and Eli Broad Grad. Sch. Bus. named in his honor Mich. State U., 1991; Edythe and Eli Broad Art Ctr. named in his honor at UCLA; knighted Chevalier in Nat. Order Legion of Honor, France, 1994; recipient lifetime achievement award L.A. C. of C., 1999, visionary award Harvard Bus. Sch. Assn. So. Calif., 1999, Julius award U. So. Calif. Sch. Policy, Planning and Devel., 2001, Chmn.'s award Asia Soc. So. Calif., 2000, Visionary award KCET, 1999, Teach for Am. Ednl. Leadership award, 2001, Exemplary Leadership in Mgmt. award, UCLA, The Anderson Sch., 2002, The Alexis de Tocqueville award, United Way, 2002; Fellow Am. Acad. Arts and Scis., 2001. Fellow AAAS; mem. Beta Alpha Psi, Regency Club, Hillcrest Country Club (L.A.), California Club. Office: SunAmerica Inc 10900 Wilshire Blvd 12th Fl Los Angeles CA 90024

BROAD, MARGARET CORBETT (MOLLY BROAD), academic administrator; b. Wilkes-Barre, Pa., Feb. 22, 1941; d. Stanley A. and Margaret (Kelly) Corbett; m. Robert William Broad, Aug. 25, 1962; children: Robert W. Jr., Matthew David. BA in Econs., Syracuse U., 1962, postgrad., 1971; MA in Econs., Ohio State U., 1965. Rsch. assoc. to comptr., v.p. finance Ohio State U., Columbus, 1963—65; budget and planning officer Syracuse U., NY, 1971—76; dep. dir. State Commn. Future of Postsecondary Edn. in N.Y., Albany, 1976—77; v.p. govt. and corp. rels. Syracuse U., 1977—85; exec. dir., chief exec. officer Ariz. Bd. Regents, Phoenix, 1985—92; sr. vice chancellor adminstrn. and fin. Calif. State U., 1992—93, exec. vice chancellor, COO, 1993—97; chair bd., CEO Calif. State U. Inst., 1994—97; pres. U. N.C., Chapel Hill, 1997—. Mem.: Beta Gamma Sigma, Phi Beta Kappa. Roman Catholic. Avocations: tennis, bicycling, gardening. Home: 400 E Franklin St Chapel Hill NC 27514-3707 Office: U NC Gen Adminstrn Bldg 910 Raleigh Rd Chapel Hill NC 27514-3916*

BROAD, ROBIN, political economist, educator, researcher; b. Manchester, N.H., Jan. 26, 1954; d. Edward Margoles and Muriel Yvette (Rooff) B.; m. John Henry Cavanagh, Apr. 26, 1982; 1 child, Jesse Broad-Cavanagh. BA in Econs. and Environ. Studies summa cum laude, Williams Coll., 1977; MPA, Princeton U., 1980, PhD, 1983. Rsch. assoc. Xavier U., Mindanao, The Philippines, 1977-78; econ. rschr. Chulalonghorn U., Bangkok, 1979; vis. rsch. assoc. U. Philippines, Manila, 1980-81; internat. economist U.S. Treasury Dept., Washington, 1983-84, devel. bank desk officer, 1984-85; sr. staff economist U.S. Congressman Charles E. Schumer, Washington, 1985-87; resident assoc. Carnegie Endowment Internat. Peace, 1987-88; asst. prof. Am. U., Washington, 1990-96, assoc. prof., 1996—. Trustee Inst. Food and Devel. Policy, 1990-96, pres. bd. trustees, 1994-95; bd. dirs. Philippine Devel. Forum. trustee, Bank Information Ctr., 2002-. Author: Unequal Alliance: The World Bank, The International Monetary Fund, and the Philippines; co-author: Plundering Paradise: The Struggle for the Environment in the Philippines, 1993; editor: Global Backlash: Citizen Initiatives for a Just World Economy, 2002; contbr. articles to profl. jours. Grantee John D. and Catherine T. MacArthur Found., 1988-90, 96-97, Southeast Asia Coun., Assn. Asian Studies grantee, 1991, NSF grantee, 1971, 74; Henry Luce Found. fellow, 1977-78, Princeton U. grad. fellow, 1978-83, Coun. Fgn. Rels. Internat. Affairs fellow, 1987-88. Mem. Coun. Fgn. Rels. Office: Am U Sch Internat Svc 4400 Massachusetts Ave NW Washington DC 20016-8071

BROADBENT, ARTHUR, III, music educator; b. Hot Springs, Ark., July 29, 1958; s. Arthur Broadbent, Jr. and Blanche Broadbent. MusB Edn., Ouachita Bapt. U., 1976—80, MusM Edn., 1980—82. Lic. postgraduate profl. lic. State Bd. Edn., Commonwealth Va., 2002. Soloist/asst. dir. chancel choir First Presbyn. Ch., Norfolk, Va.; choral dir. J. A. Fair Jr./Sr. H.S., Little Rock, 1982—83, Norview Mid. Sch., Norfolk, 1984—98, Lake Taylor H.S., Norfolk, 1999—. Co-chair, all-city mid. sch. chorus Norfolk Pub. Schools, 1986—91; chair, dist. auditions VA-ACDA, Dist. II, Norfolk, 1996; chmn., dist. ii Va. Music Educators Assn., 1997—2000; chair, all-state auditions VA-ACDA Dist. II, 1997—2001; publicity/pub. rels. chair, Va. music camp 2003 Va. Music Educators Assn., 2002—. Singer: (professional core & soloist) Virginia Symphony Chorus, (opera chorus) Virginia Opera Chorus, (singer & soloist) The Virginia Chorale. Artistic com./singer rep. The Va. Chorale, Norfolk, 1996—99; artistic/edn. com. Va. Childrens Chorus, Norfolk, 1998—2000; chorus rep. Va. Opera Chorus, Norfolk, 1992—94. Mem.: Am. Fedn. Tchrs., Chorus Am., Va. Choral Directors Assn., Am. Choral Directors Assn., Music Educators Nat. Conf., Pi Kappa Lambda, Nat. Music Honor Soc., Phi Mu Alpha, Sinfonia. Home: 159 W Seaview Ave Norfolk VA 23503 Office: Norview Middle Sch 6325 Sewells Point Rd Norfolk VA 23513 Personal E-mail: baritone4u@cox.net.

BROADBENT, PETER EDWIN, JR., lawyer; b. Richmond, Virginia, May 16, 1951; s. Peter Edwin and Nancy Talbot (Norris) B.; m. Mary Anna (Toms), June 5, 1976; children: Peter Edwin III, Christopher Toms, Elizabeth Talbot. BA, Duke U., 1973; JD, U. Va., 1976. Bar: Va. 1976, U.S. Dist. Ct. (ea. dist.) Va., 1976, U.S. Ct. Appeals (fourth cir.), 1976. Assoc. Christian, Barton, Epps, Brent, and Chappell, Richmond, Va., 1976-84; ptnr. Christian and Barton LLP., Richmond, Va., 1984—. Bd. dir. James Monroe Meml. Found. Mem. Richmond City Rep. Com., 1973—; nat. committeeman Young Rep. Nat. Com., Washington, 1974-75; mem. state ctrl. com. Rep. Party of Va., 2001—; former v.p., dir. Richmond Teams for Progress; former deacon First Presbyn. Ch.; chmn., bd. dir. Libr. of Va.; bd. dir. Friends of Va. State Archives, bd. dir. James Monroe Meml. Found. Mem. Va. State Bar Assn. (pub. info. com. 1977-82, 93—, chmn. 1982-85, bd. govs. Bus. Law Sect., 1997-, editor Va. Bus. Law, 1995-98), Va. Bar Assn., Richmond Bar Assn., Greater Richmond Intellectual Property Law Assn., Geneal. Rsch. Inst. Va. (past pres., dir. 1984—), Va. Geneal. Soc. (bd. dirs., pres.), Soc. Colonial Wars in Va. (bd. dir.) Republican. Presbyterian. Avocations: genealogy, politics. Home: 5307 Matoaka Rd Richmond VA 23226-2218 Office: Christian & Barton LLP 1200 Mutual Bldg 909 E Main St Richmond VA 23219-3002

BROADDUS, JOHN ALFRED, JR., bank executive, economist; b. Richmond, Va., July 8, 1939; s. John Alfred Broaddus Sr. and Norma (Coleman) Broaddus; m. Margaret C. Lemley, Apr. 16, 1966; children: John Alfred III, Christopher McRae. BA, Washington & Lee U., 1961; diplome, U. Strasbourg, France, 1962; MA, Ind. U., 1970, PhD, 1972; LLD (hon.), Washington and Lee U., 1993. Intelligence rsch. specialist Def. Intelligence Agy., Washington, 1964-66; economist Fed. Res. Bank Richmond, 1970-72, asst. v.p., 1972-75, v.p., 1975-85, sr. v.p., dir. rsch., 1985-92, pres., 1993—. Author: A Primer on the Fed, 1988; contbr. articles to publs. Pres. Richmond Meml. Hosp. Found., 1980—85; trustee Richmond Meml. Found., 1998—; mem. Gov.'s Adv. Coun. on Revenue Estimates, Va., 1993—; chmn. bd. trustees United Way of Greater Richmond, 1990; chmn. bd. govs. St. Christopher's Sch., 1992—96; bd. assocs. Gallaudet U., 1998—, U. Richmond, 1999—; trustee Va. Coun. Econ. Edn., 1994—, Va. Hist. Soc., 2001—, World Affairs Coun. Greater Richmond, 1996—; exec. com. Richmond Renaissance, 1998—. 1st lt. U.S. Army, 1962—64. Named Fulbright scholar, 1961. Mem.: So. Econ. Assn., Nat. Assn. Bus. Economists, Am. Econ. Assn., Omicron Delta Kappa, Phi Beta Kappa. Avocation: running. Office: Fed Res Bank Richmond 701 E Byrd St PO Box 27622 Richmond VA 23261-7622

BROADFOOT, ALBERT LYLE, physicist; b. Milestone, Sask., Can., Jan. 8, 1930; came to U.S., 1963; s. Morris Alexander and Lydia Georgina (Jacklin) B.; m. Katherine Eileen Deacon, Sept. 26, 1964; children: Alexander Lyle, Marilyn Louise. BE in Engring., Physics, U. Sask., Saskatoon, 1956, M.Sc. in Physics, 1960, PhD in Physics, 1963. Engr. Def. Rsch. Bd., Ottawa, Ont., Can., 1956-58; jr. physicist space div. Kitt Peak Nat. Obs., Tucson, 1963-64, asst. physicist, 1964-68, assoc. physicist, 1968-70, physicist, 1971-79; rsch. scientist, assoc. physicist Earth and Space Scis. Inst., U. So. Calif., 1979-82; sr. rsch. scientist Lunar and Planetary Lab., U Ariz., Tucson, 1982—. Home: 5231 E 17th St Tucson AZ 85711-4429 Office: U Ariz Lunar and Planetary Lab 901 Gould Simpson Blvd Tucson AZ 85721-0001

BROADHEAD, JAMES LOWELL, electrical power industry executive; b. New Rochelle, N.Y., Nov. 28, 1935; s. Clarence James and Mabel Roseader (Bowser) B.; m. Sharon Ann Rulon, May 6, 1967; children: Jeffrey Thornton, Kristen Ann, Carolyn Mary, Catherine Lee. B.M.E., Cornell U., 1958; LL.B., Columbia U., 1963. Bar: N.Y. 1963. Mech. engr. sales dept. Ingersoll-Rand Co., 1958-59; assoc. Debevoise, Plimpton, Lyons & Gates, N.Y.C., 1963-68; asst. sec. St. Joe Minerals Corp., N.Y.C., 1968-70, sec., 1970-77, gen. counsel, 1973-74, v.p. devel., 1976-77, exec. v.p., 1980-81, pres., 1981-82, also dir.; sr. vp. GTE Corp., Stamford, Conn., 1984-88; also pres. GTE Corp. telephone ops., Stamford, Conn., 1984-88; pres., CEO Fla. Power & Light Co., West Palm Beach, Fla., 1989-2001; pres., CEO, chmn. bd. FPL Group, Inc., West Palm Beach, 1989-2000, chmn., 2000-2001. Chmn., CEO Energy Rsch. Corp., Danbury, Conn., 1973-74; v.p. St. Joe Petroleum Co., N.Y.C., 1974-76; pres. St. Joe Zinc Co., Pitts., 1977-80; exec. v.p., dir. U.S. Industries, 1983; dir. Pittston Co., Delta Air Lines, Inc., N.Y. Life Ins. Co. Editor: Columbia Law Rev., 1963. Served with U.S. Army, 1960-61. Office: FPL Group Inc 700 Universe Blvd Juno Beach FL 33408-2657

BROADHEAD, RONALD FRIGON, petroleum geologist, geology educator; BS, N. Mex. Tech. U., 1977; MS, U. Cin., 1979. Geologist Cities Svc. Oil Co., Okla. City and Tulsa, 1979-81; prin., sr. petroleum geologist N. Mex. Bur. Mines, Socorro, 1981—. Mem. adj. faculty N.Mex. Tech. Coll., 1983—; mem. potential gas com. Potential Gas Agy. Union Oil Co. Summer fellow Duke U. Marine Lab., 1977. Mem. Am. Assn. Petroleum Geologists (Cheney award 2002, Levorsen award 2003), Soc. Econ. Paleontologists and Mineralogists, N. Mex. Geol. Soc. (past pres.), Roswell Geol. Soc., Four Corners Geol. Soc., West Tex. Geol. Soc., Sigma Xi. Office: NMex Bur Mines Campus Sta Socorro NM 87801

BROADHURST, AUSTIN, JR., executive recruiter; b. Boston, Aug. 9, 1947; s. Austin and Deborah (Lowell) Broadhurst; m. Janine Boyajian, June 15, 1974; children: Robert James, Lauren Cox. BA, Williams Coll., 1969; MBA, Harvard U., 1972. With sec.'s office HEW, Washington, 1972-76; asst. to corp. exec. v.p. Baxter Labs., Deerfield, Ill., 1976-78, group product mgr., 1978-79; dir. corp. planning Nat. Med. Care, Boston, 1979-80, corp. v.p., 1980-83; sr. v.p. UHA Enterprises, N.Y.C., 1983-84; pres., CEO, dir. OcuSys., Inc., 1985-86; exec. dir. Russell Reynolds Assocs., 1986-88, mng. dir., 1988-96, office mgr., 1990-91, health care practice head, 1991-95; ptnr. LAI Ward Howell, 1996-98; v.p. Korn/Ferry Internat., 1998-99; mng. mem. Dauphin Capital Ptnrs., 2000—02, Calchas Group LLC, Greenwich, Conn., 2002—. Bd. dirs. Cohesive Techs., Endius, Surginex. Dir. Norwalk CC Found., 1996—2000, 2003—; incorporator New Eng. Bapt. Hosp., 1980—83, Greenwich Hosp., 1990—96, trustee, 1996—99. Mem.: Indian Harbor Yacht Club, Stanwich Club, Harvard Club N.Y. Episcopalian. Office: c/o Oracle Ptnrs 200 Greenwich Ave Greenwich CT 06830-4720

BROADHURST, JEROME ANTHONY, lawyer; b. Cleve., Feb. 4, 1945; s. William and Estelle M. (Bozak) B.; m. Annette Lou Wilt, Sept. 3, 1966; children: Stephanie Ann, Jerome A., Elizabeth Marie. BS in Bus., U. Akron, 1967, JD, 1971. Bar: Ohio 1973, Tenn. 1987. Acctg. supr., fin. analyst B.F. Goodrich Co., Akron, Ohio, 1971-73, corp. counsel, 1973-76; counsel, asst. sec. The Weatherhead Co., Cleve., 1976-77; asst. counsel Gen. Tire and Rubber Co., Akron, 1977-80; sr. corp. atty. Holiday Inns, Inc. (subs. Holiday Corp.), Memphis, 1980-81, sec., sr. corp. atty., 1981-84; sec., assoc. gen. counsel Holiday Corp., Memphis, 1984-87, v.p., sec., assoc. gen. counsel, 1987-88; v.p., gen. counsel, sec. Perkins Family Restaurants, L.P., Memphis, 1989-91; pvt. practice law, 1991—; ptnr. Armstrong Allen, PLLC, 2000—. Mediator Tenn. Mediation/Arbitration Svc., 1994-95; adj. prof. MBA program Christian Brothers U. Sch. Bus., Memphis, 1997-99. Bd. dirs. Memphis Urban League, 1987-94; trustee Memphis Urban League Endowment Fund, 1987—. Mem. ABA (mem. bus. law sect. subcoms. on corp. litigation and environ. control 1995—, intellectual property law sect. com. on unfair comp.-trade identity 1996—), Tenn. Bar Assn., Ohio Bar Assn., Memphis Bar Assn., Shelby County Bar Assn., Am. Soc. Corp. Secs. (corp. practices com. 1981-97, 99-2001, public company affairs com. 2003—). Republican. Roman Catholic. Avocations: photography, jogging, fishing, racquetball. Office: Brinkley Plaza Ste 700 80 Monroe Ave Memphis TN 38103-2467 E-mail: jbroadhurst@armstrongallen.com.

BROADHURST, NORMAN NEIL, food products executive; b. Chico, Calif., Dec. 17, 1946; s. Frank Spencer and Dorothy Mae (Conrad) B.; m. Victoria Rose Thomson, Aug. 7, 1976; 1 child, Scott Andrew. BS, Calif. State U., 1969; MBA, Golden Gate U., 1975. With Del Monte Corp., San Francisco, 1969-76, product mgr., 1973-76; product mgr. Riviana Foods, Inc. divsn. Colgate Palmolive, Houston, 1976-78; new products brand devel. mgr. foods divsn. Coca Cola Co., Houston, 1978-79, brand mgr., 1979-82, mktg. dir., 1982-89; v.p. mktg. Beatrice Foods Co., Chgo., 1983-86; pres., COO, Famous Amos Chocolate Chip Cookie Co., Torrance, Calif., 1986-88; corp. sr. v.p., gen. mgr. Kerr Group Inc., L.A., 1988-92; corp. sr. v.p., pres. Kerr Group Consumer Products, 1992-95; chmn. dir. Double Eagle Holding, Inc., Seal Beach, Calif., 1995—; chmn., pres., CEO, Trusted Brands, Inc., 1995-98; chmn., CEO, Double Eagle Market Devel. Co., Seal Beach, 1997—2003; pres., CEO Channel Mktg. Resources Inc., Irvine, Calif., 2003—. Chmn. youth soccer program Cystic Fibrosis Found., Houston, 1982-83; chmn., pres. South Coast Symphony, 1985-88; mem. nat. bd. dirs. Literacy Vols. Am., 1988—, vice chmn., 1993-95, chmn., 1997-99; bd. dirs. Human Options, 1997-2001, mem. strategic planning and mktg. coms., 1998-2001; trustee, bd. dirs. Laguna Presbyn. Ch., 1999—. Mem. Assoc. Sales and Mktg. Co., Am. Mktg. Assn., Am. Mgmt. Assn. Office: Channel Mktg Resources 2102 Business Center Dr Ste 212 Irvine CA 92612 E-mail: nbroadhurst@channelmarketingresources.com.

BROADNAX, WALTER D. public policy educator; b. Starcity, Ark., Oct. 21, 1944; s. Walter and Mary Lee (Cotton) B.; m. Angel LaVerne Wheelock; 1 child, Andrea Alyce. BA, Washburn U., 1967; MPA, Kans. U., 1969; PhD, Syracuse U., 1975; Hon. Degrees, Washburn U., Topeka; Hon. Degree, Ctrl. State U. Ohio. Dir. Svc. Children, Youth and Adults, Kans., 1979-80; prin. dep. asst. sec. HHS, 1980-81; lectr. pub. mgmt. and pub. policy John F. Kennedy sch. govt. Harvard U., 1981-87, dir. innovations state and local govt., 1985-87; pres. NY State Civil Svc. Commn., 1987-90; commr. NY State Dept. Civil Svc., 1987-90; pres. Ctr. Govtl. Rsch., Inc., Rochester, NY, 1990-93; dep. sec. HHS, Washington, 1993-96; prof. school of pub affairs Univ of Md, Coll. Pk., Md., 1996-99; dean Coll. Pub. Affairs Am. U., 1999—2002; pres. Clark Atlanta U., 2002—. Bd. dir. Keycorp, Medecision, Inc., CNA Corp. Contbr. articles to profl. jours. Bd. Trustees Syracuse U., The Coun. for Excellence in Govt. Recipient Maxwell Sch. of Citizenship and Pub. Affairs Spirit of Pub. Svc. award. Whiting scholar Washburn U. Fellow Nat. Acad. Pub. Adminstrn.; pres. ASPA (Outstanding Pub. Svc. award Nat. Capital Area chpt.), Nat. Acad. Pub. Adminstrn. (Nat. Pub. Svc. award) Avocations: reading, jogging, music. Home: 691 Beckwith St SW Atlanta GA 30314- Office: Clark Atlanta U Office of Pres Atlanta GA Office Fax: 404-880-8500.

BROADRICK-ALLEN, SANDRA CAROL, retired city manager, consultant, civic worker; b. St. Louis, May 5, 1940; d. Charles Albert Jr. and Verna Catherine (Yount) Allen; m. King Woodard Broadrick, July 4, 1975. BS, Lindenwood Coll., 1962; MA, U. Denver, 1965; PhD, U. Ill., 1975. Cert. tchr. Ill., Mo. Tchr. home econs. Princeville (Ill.) H.S., 1962-65, guidance counselor,

1965-68; dean faculty, dean students Garland Jr. Coll., Boston, 1971—75, pres., 1975-76; adminstr. Office Arms Control, Disarmament and Internat. Security, Urbana, Ill., 1981-82; campaign mgr. for state rep. from 103d legis. dist. Ill. Ho. of Reps., 1982-84; city mgr. Village of Savoy, Ill., 1985-91; adminstrv.-exec. cons., Champaign, Ill., 1992—. Editor: County Banners of the Illinois Association for Home and Community Education, 2000; mem. editl. rev. bd. Nat. Assn. for Women Deans, Adminstrs. and Counselors Jour., 1972-74. Pres. Princeville High Sch. PTA, 1962—68; moderator Princeville Cmty. Coun., 1966—68; bd. dirs. U. YWCA, Champaign, 1983—89; mem. home econs. coun. Champaign County Coop. Ext. Svc., 1985—87, treas. unit coun., 1988—92; vice chmn., pres. Ext. Edn. Found., 1992—99, Ill. Assn. Home and Cmty. Edn., 1997—2000; mem. president's coun. U. Ill., 1998—, Busey Bank, 1998., 1998—; pres. Ill. Assn. Home and Cmty. Edn., 1997—2000; mem. precinct com. Champaign County Dem. Com, 1982—85; sr. high sch. youth fellowship advisor Princeville Presbyn. Ch., 1965—68. Recipient Leadership award Univ. YWCA, 1985, Outstanding Vol. award United Way Champaign County, 1986, cert. of recognition, Ill. Ho. of Reps., 1991; citizens lay advisor scholar Ritenour Sch. Dist., 1958-62, honors scholar Lindenwood Coll., 1958-62; grantee U.S. Office Edn., 1968-70. Mem. Assoc. Country Women of World (vice chmn. UN com. 1998-2001, chmn. 2001—, bd. dirs. 2001—), Scroll Soc., Rotary (charter pres. Savoy 1989-91, gov. dist. 6490 2001-02, coord. task force and adminstrv. coord. 2000-2001, dir. youth programs 2002-2003, chair R.I. Centennial Com. 2003—, Paul Harris fellow 1993, multiple Spirit of Paul Harris awards, others), Phi Delta Kappa, Kappa Omicron Phi. Avocations: international travel, archaeology of lost civilizations, earth-watch and global volunteer, gardening. E-mail: sandyba@net66.com.

BROADWATER, BRUCE A. mayor; b. Columbus, Ohio, Sept. 1, 1938; m. Peggy Broadwater; children: Josh, Jeremy AA, East L.A. Coll.; BA in Human Rels., U. San Francisco. Owner ins. agy., Garden Grove, Calif.; consumer complaint analyst Calif. Dept. Ins.; elected Garden Grove City Coun., 1992-94; elected mayor City of Garden Grove, 1994—, dep. labor commr., 2003—. Bd. dirs. Am. Host Found.; active scouting programs, Boy Scouts Am. With U.S. Army, 1957-59, Germany. Mem. Garden Grove C. of C. (past pres.). Office: Office of Mayor PO Box 3070 Garden Grove CA 92842-3070 E-mail: pamha@ci.garden-grove.ca.us.*

BROADWATER, DOUGLAS DWIGHT, lawyer; b. Preston, Minn., May 31, 1944; s. George and Marion Elaine (Gleason) B.; m. Beatrice (Kinney), July 8, 1978; children: Ian Dwight, George Francis, Mark Fowler. BA, Harvard U., 1966; JD, Columbia U., 1969. Bar: NY., 1969. Staff atty. employment project Ctr. Social Welfare Policy and Law, N.Y.C., 1969—71; assoc. Cravath, Swaine & Moore LLP, N.Y.C., 1971—78, ptnr., 1978—. Office: Cravath Swaine & Moore LLP Worldwide Plz 825 8th Ave 41st Fl New York NY 10019-7475

BROADWATER, JAMES E. publisher; b. Tacoma, Nov. 5, 1945; s. Robert L. and June J. B.; m. Diane K. Plummer, Apr. 22, 1967; children: James Tegan, Kelly Diane, Robert Charles, Krista Dawn. BS in Journalism, U. Fla., 1967. Acct. mgr. Young & Rubicam, Inc., Detroit, Kansas City, N.Y.C. and Houston, 1968-73; assoc. pub. Tex. Monthly Mag., Austin, 1973-78; pres., pub. Saturday Rev. Mag., N.Y.C., 1978-80; regional pub. dir. Baker Publs., Houston, 1980-85; pres. HBC, Inc., Houston, 1985-87; assoc. pub. Tex. Sportsworld Mag., 1985-86; pub. Washington Journalism Rev., 1987-92; pres. The Broadwater Co., Houston, 1993—. Mem. Mag. Pub. Assn., Nat. Press Club, Am. Mgmt. Assn., Direct Mail Mktg. Assn., Lambda Chi Alpha. Baptist. E-mail: jbroadwater@sbcglobal.net. *All things are possible through Christ. Success requires that one deal in results and not succumb to the desire to rationalize excuses.*

BROADWAY, NANCY RUTH, landscape design and construction company executive, consultant, model and actress; b. Memphis, Dec. 20, 1946; d. Charlie Sidney and Patsy Ruth (Meadows) Adkins. BS in Biology and Sociology cum laude, Memphis State U., 1969; postgrad., Tulane U., 1969-70; MS in Horticulture, U. Calif.-Davis, 1976. Lic. landscape contractor, Calif. Claims adjuster Mass. Mut. Ins., San Francisco, 1972-73; community garden coord. City of Davis, Calif., 1976; seed propagation supr. Bordier's Wholesale Nursery, Santa Ana, Calif., 1976-78; owner, founder Calif. Landscape Co., 1978-88, Design & Mgmt. Consultare, 1988—; pres. N.R. Broadway, Inc., 1998—. Actress: Visions of Murder, 1993, Eyes of Terror, 1994. NDEA fellow Tulane U., 1969-70. Fellow Am. Hort. Soc.; mem. Nat. Assn. Gen. Contractors, Calif. Native Plant Soc., Stockton C. of C. Democrat. Home and Office: 2088 Broderick St San Francisco CA 94115-2156 E-mail: nrbway@aol.com.

BROBECK, JOHN RAYMOND, physiology educator; b. Steamboat Springs, Colo., Apr. 12, 1914; s. James Alexander and Ella (Johnson) B.; m. Dorothy Winifred Kellogg, Aug. 24, 1940; children: Stephen James, Priscilla Kimball, Elizabeth Martha, John Thomas. BS, Wheaton Coll., 1936, LL.D., 1960; MS, Northwestern U., 1937, PhD, 1939; MD, Yale U., 1943. Instr. physiology Yale, 1943-45, asst. prof., 1945-48, asso. prof. physiology, 1948-52; prof. physiology, chmn. dept. U. Pa., Phila., 1952-70, Herbert C. Rorer prof. med. scis., 1970-82, prof. emeritus, 1982—. Editor: Yale Jour. Biology and Medicine, 1949-52; chmn. editorial bd.: Physiol. Revs, 1963-72. Fellow Am. Acad. Arts and Scis.; mem. Am. Physiol. Soc. (pres. 1971-72), Am. Inst. Nutrition, Nat. Acad. Scis., Am. Soc. Clin. Investigation, Halsted Soc., Phila. Coll. Physicians, Sigma Xi, Alpha Omega Alpha. Home: 1343 W Baltimore Pike # C118 Media PA 19063-5519

BROBECK, STEPHEN JAMES, consumer advocate; b. New Haven, Sept. 15, 1944; s. John Raymond and Dorothy Winifred (Kellogg) B.; m. Susan Cheney Williams, May 9, 1971. BA, Wheaton Coll., 1966; PhD, U. Pa., 1972. Asst. prof. Case Western Res. U., 1970-79; exec. dir. Consumer Fedn. Am., Washington, 1980—. Vis. assoc. prof. Cornell U., 1989; adj. assoc. prof. U. Md., 1990-92. Author: The Product Safety Book, 1983, The Bank Book, 1986, The Modern Consumer Movement, 1990, Encyclopedia of the Consumer Movement, 1997; contbr. articles to profl. jours. Bd. dirs. Citizens for Tax Justice, 1980—, Coalition Against Ins. Fraud, 1993—, Alliance to Save Energy, 1994—, Jump Start Coalition, 2002—. Mem. Am. Council Consumer Interests. Home: 4700 Connecticut Ave NW Washington DC 20008-5629 Office: Consumer Fed Am 1424 16th St NW Ste 604 Washington DC 20036 2239 E-mail: sbrobeck@consumerfed.org.

BROBERG, MERLE, retired social worker; b. Eagle Bend, Minn., Sept. 7, 1929; s. Herbit and Goldie (Johnson) B.; m. Hazel Irene Holst, Dec. 16, 1949 (div. Dec. 1979); children: Richard, Robert, Christopher, Rebecca; m. Dolores Elizabeth Melching, Feb. 8, 1980. BA, U. Minn., 1949; M in Social Svc., Bryn Mawr Coll., 1957; PhD, Am. U., 1969. Relocation advisor U.S. Urban Renewal Adminstrn., Phila., 1962-65; vis. asst. prof. Lehigh U., Bethlehem, Pa., 1965-66; from asst. prof. to assoc. prof., assoc. dean Bryn Mawr (Pa.) Coll., 1966-85, assoc. prof. emeritus, 1985—; acting dir. Green Tree Sch., Phila., 1988-89. Author: Barbados, 1989; contbr. articles to profl. publs. Bd. dirs. YMCA Germantown, Phila., 1968-79; v.p. Cmty. Svcs. Planning Coun., Phila., 1978-85; pres. Cmty. Renewal Germantown, 1981-86; vol. Portland Players, 1996—, So. Maine Ret. Sr. Vols. Program, 1996—, City of South Portland Planning Dept., 2000—, RSVP Adv. Coun., 2002-. Mem. NASW.

BROCA, LAURENT ANTOINE, aerospace scientist; b. Nov. 30, 1928; came to U.S., 1957; naturalized, 1963; s. Paul L. and Paule Jeanne (Ferrand) B.; m. Leticia Garcia Guerra, Dec. 18, 1972; 1 child, Marie-There Yvonne. BS in Math., U. Bordeaux, France, 1949; lic. es Scis. in Math. and Physics, U. Toulouse, France, 1957; grad., Inst. Technique Professionnel, France, 1960; PhD in Elec. Engring., Calif. Western U., 1979; postgrad., Boston U., 1958, MIT, 1961, Harvard U., 1961. Tchg. fellow physics dept. boston U., 1957-58; spl. instr. dept. physics N.J. Inst. Tech., Newark, 1959-60; sr. staff engr. advanced rsch. group ITT, Nutley, N.J., 1959-60; examiner math. and phys. scis. univ. Paris and Caen (France) Exam Ctr., N.Y.C., 1959-69; sr. engr. surface radar divsn. Raytheon Co., Waltham, Mass., 1960-62, Hughes Aircraft Co., Culver City, Calif., 1962-64; asst. prof. math. Calif. State U., Northridge, 1963-64; prin. engr. astrionics lab. NASA, Huntsville, Ala., 1964-65; fellow engr. Def. and Space Ctr. Westinghouse Electric Corp., Balt., 1965-69; cons. and sci. adv. electronics, phys. scis. and math. to indsl. firms and broadcasting sats., 1969-80; head engring. dept. Videocraft Mfg. Co., Laredo, Tex., 1974-75; asst. prof. math. Laredo State U., summer 1975; engring. specialist dept. sys. performance analysis ITT Fed. Electric Corp., Vandenberg AFB, Calif., 1980-82; engring. mgr. Ford Aerospace and Comms. Corp., Nellis AFB, Nev., 1982-84, Arcata Assocs., Inc., North Las Vegas, Nev., 1984-85; sr. scientific specialist engring. and devel. EG&G-JT3, Las Vegas, 1985—. With French Army, 1951—52. Recipient Published Paper award Hughes Aircraft Co., 1966; Fulbright scholar, 1957. Mem. IEEE, Am. Nuclear Soc. (vice chmn. Nev. sect. 1982-83, chmn. 1983-84), Am. Def. Preparedness Assn., Armed Forces Comms. and Electronics Assn., Air Force Assn. Home: 5040 Lancaster Dr Las Vegas NV 89120-1445 Office: EG&G Spl Projects Inc PO Box 93747 Las Vegas NV 89193-3747 E-mail: lbroca@worldnet.att.net.

BROCCHINI, RONALD GENE, architect; b. Oakland, Calif., Nov. 6, 1929; s. Gino Mario and Yoli Louise (Lucchesi) B.; m. Myra Mossman, Feb. 3, 1957; 1 child, Christopher Ronald BA in Architecture with honors, U. Calif., Berkeley, 1953, MA in Architecture with honors, 1957. Registered architect, Calif., Nev. Architect, designer SMP, Inc., San Francisco, 1948-53, designer, assoc., 1956-60; assoc. architect Campbell & Wong, San Francisco, 1961-63; prin. architect Ronald G. Brocchini, Berkeley, Calif., 1964-67, Worley K Wong & Ronald G Brocchini Assocs., San Francisco, 1968-87, Brocchini Architects, Berkeley, 1987—. Lectr. Calif. Coll. Arts and Crafts, Oakland, 1981-83; commr. Calif. Bd. Archtl. Examiners, 1961-89; mem. exam. com. Nat. Coun. Archtl. Registration Bds., 1983-85. Author: Long Range Master Plan for Bodega Marine Biology, U. Calif., 1982; prin. works include San Simeon Visitor Ctr., Hearst Castle, Calif., Mare Island Med.-Dental Facillity, IBM Ednl. and Data Processing Hdqrs., San Jose, Calif., Simpson Fine Arts Gallery, Calif. Coll. Arts, Ceramics and Metal Crafts, Emery Bay Pub. Market Complex, Analytical Measurement Facility, U. Calif., Berkeley, Bodega Marine Biology Campus, U. Calif., Berkeley, Fromm & Sichell (Christian Bros.) Hdqrs., The Nature Co., Corp. Offices, Berkeley, Merrill Coll., Athletic Facilities, U. Calif., Santa Cruz, Coll. III Housing, U. Calif., San Diego, Ctr. Pacific Rim Studies, U. San Francisco, married student housing Escondido II, III, IV, Stanford (Calif.) U. With U.S. Army, 1953-55. Recipient Bear of Yr. award U. Calif., Berkeley, 1987, Alumni Citation, 1988; recipient 18 Design Honor awards for architecture, Design award State of Calif. Dept. Rehab., 1995. Fellow AIA (bd. dirs. Calif. coun., pres. San Francisco chpt. 1982); mem. Bear Backers Club (bd. dirs. U. Calif.-Berkeley athletic coun.), Berkeley Breakfast Club (bd. govs.), Order of the Golden Bear, Chi Alpha Kappa. Republican. Roman Catholic. Avocations: auto restoration, photography, sports, art. Office: Brocchini Architects Inc 2748 Adeline St Berkeley CA 94703-2251 E-mail: arcbro@pacbell.net.

BROCK, BARRY JAMES, health services administrator, educator, consultant; b. Grove Hill, Ala., Oct. 1, 1953; s. Ben Jones and Doris (Forehand) B.; m. Denise Defant, Aug. 20, 1976; 1 child, Barry Jason. BS, U. Ala., 1976; MPA, U. W. Fla., 1982; EdD, U. Ctrl. Fla., 1993. Cert. healthcare exec.; cert. profl. in human resources. Dir. human resources Hosp. Corp. Am., Nashville, 1978-85; mktg. adminstr. Orlando (Fla.) Regl. Med. Ctr., 1985-88; adminstrv. dir. Rebound Rehab., Orlando and Nashville, 1988-89; v.p. Healthcare Rsch. & Resources, Orlando, 1989—; acad. chair, asst. prof. Barry U., Miami, Fla., 1993—. Faculty U. Ctrl. Fla., Orlando, 1992—; coord. Health Profl. Inst., Seminole C.C., Sanford, Fla., 1992-93; adv. bd. Seminole C.C., Sanford, 1992-93, bd. dirs. HR & R, Mt. Dora, Fla., 1993—; comdr. U.S. Joint Forces Command, 2000. Author: Analysis of Middle Manager Competencies, 1994. Chmn. United Way, Nashville, 1983-85; advisor Jr. Achievement, Orlando, 1986-87. Comdr. Med. Svc. Corps, USNR, 1987—. Mem. Am. Acad. Med. Adminstrn., Am. Coll. Healthcare Execs., Commerce Execs. Soc., Assn. Med. Svc. Corps Officers, Assn. Vocat. Edn. and Rsch., Toastmasters (pres., Nashville, 1984-85), Pi Kappa Phi. Avocations: golf, tennis. Home: 887 Bentley Green Cir Winter Springs FL 32708-4338 Office: Barry U 1650 Sand Lake Rd Orlando FL 32809-7681

BROCK, CHARLES LAWRENCE, lawyer, business executive; b. Ottumwa, Iowa, Mar. 7, 1943; s. Charles Harlan and Betty Arlene (Ream) B.; m. Mary Jane Hipp, June 17, 1978; children: William Walker, Susanna Lawrence. BA with highest distinction, Northwestern U., 1964; JD, Harvard U., 1967; postgrad. (Rotary Found. fellow), U. Delhi (India) and India Law Inst., 1967-68; grad., Advanced Mgmt. Program, Harvard Bus. Sch., 1979. Bar: N.Y. 1968. Asso. firm Sullivan & Cromwell, N.Y.C., 1969-74; v.p., corp. sec., gen. counsel Scholastic Mags., Inc. (now Scholastic, Inc.), N.Y.C., 1974-80; interim CFO and COO Scholastic Mags., Inc., 1975-76, pub. internat. div., 1976-80; pres. Scholastic Tab Publs. Ltd., Can., 1976-80, Ashton-Scholastic Pty. Ltd., Australia, 1976-80, Ashton-Scholastic Ltd., New Zealand, 1976-80; chmn. Scholastic Publs. Ltd., U.K., 1976-80; sr. v.p., mgmt. dir. Compton Communications, 1980-82; mgr. subsidiaries Compton Advertising, 1980-82; counsel Drinker, Biddle & Reath, N.Y.C., Phila., Washington, 1982-84; ptnr. Carter, Ledyard & Milburn, 1984-95, Brock Silverstein McAuliffe LLC (now Brock Silverstein), 1995—. Bd. dirs., chmn. audit coms. B&H Bulk Carriers Ltd., B&H Ocean Carriers Ltd., B&H Maritime Carriers Ltd.; bd. dirs. Harvard Alumni Assn., 1990-95 (two terms), chmn. grad. schs. com. 1992-95; mem. Harvard Coll. Bd. Overseers Com. on Univ. Resources, 1992—, chmn. Harvard Bd. Overseers Nominating Com. 1996—, coun. Harvard Law Sch. Assn., 1983-85, sec., 1988-90, treas., 1990—, exec. com., 1986—, chmn. membership com., 1987—, internat. sect., 1991—, pres. 1996-98; bd. advisors Coll. Arts and Scis., Northwestern U., 1989—, Campaign for Gt. Tchrs. Com., 1989-90, John Evans Club, Northwestern U. 1989—; guild hall trustee Acad. of the Arts, 1990—, mem. exec. com., chmn. nominating com., 1986-90, chmn. bd., 1990-92; trustee, treas. Family Dynamics, 1981-88. Editorial adv. bd. Minority Law Jour. Reunion gift chmn. Harvard Law Sch. Fund, 1967-68, vice chmn., 1975-77; trustee Harvard Law Sch. Assn. N.Y.C., 1982-85, chmn. placement com., 1983-86, v.p., 1985-96, originator, chmn. summer reception, 1982; chmn. Harvard Community Ptnrs., 1984-86; co-chmn. ann. giving St. Barnard's Ch., 1989-95; mem. adv. bd. Minority Atty. Reporter; deacon Brick Presbyn. Ch., N.Y.C., 1973-76, regent Cathedral St. John The Divine. Recipient Mentor award for pioneering efforts creating opportunities for minorities and women. Mem. ABA, N.Y. State Bar Assn., N.Y. County Lawyers Assn., Assn. Bar City of N.Y., Assn. Am. Pubs., Century Assn., Harvard Bus. Club of N.Y. (v.p. 1984-86), Union Club, N.Y. Yacht Club, Down Town Assn., The Pilgrims, Piping Rock (Locust Valley, N.Y.), Maidstone (East Hampton, N.Y.), Phi Beta Kappa, Kappa Sigma. Home: 765 Park Ave New York NY 10021-4254 Office: Brock Ptnrs 420 Lexington Ave Ste 300 New York NY 10170

BROCK, CHARLES MARQUIS, lawyer; b. Watseka, Ill., Oct. 8, 1941; s. Glen Westgate and Muriel Lucile (Bubeck) B.; m. Elizabeth Bonilla, Dec. 17, 1966; children: Henry Christopher, Anna Melissa. AB cum laude, Princeton U., 1963; JD, Georgetown U., 1968; MBA, U. Chgo., 1974. Bar: Ill. 1969, U.S. Dist. Ct. (no. dist.) Ill. 1969. Asst. trust counsel Continental Ill. Nat. Bank, Chgo., 1968-74; regional counsel Latin Am. Abbott Labs., Abbott Park, Ill., 1974-77, regional counsel Europe, Africa, Mid. East, 1977-81, divsn. counsel domestic legal ops., 1981-88, assoc. gen. counsel internat. legal ops., asst. sec., 1989-92, divisional v.p., assoc. gen. counsel, asst. sec., 1992-2000, divisional v.p., chief ethics and compliance officer, 2000—03, corp. v.p., chief ethics and compliance officer, 2003—. Mem. Coun. Sr. Internat. Legal Officers, The Conf. Bd., N.Y.C., 1999-2000, global coun. bus. conduct, 2000—; bd. dirs. Inst. for Bus. and Profl. Ethics/DePaul U., Chgo. Bd. dirs. Character Matters in Lake County, Ill. With U.S. Army, 1964-66. Mem. ABA, Ethics Officer Assn., Health Care Compliance Assn., Mich. Shores Club, Phi Beta Kappa. Republican. Home: 1440 S Ridge Rd Lake Forest IL 60045-3880 Office: Abbott Labs 100 Abbott Park Rd Abbott Park IL 60064-3502 E-mail: charles.brock@abbott.com., ccmbrock@aol.com.

BROCK, DAVID ALLEN, state supreme court chief justice; b. Stoneham, Mass., July 6, 1936; s. Herbert and Margaret B.; m. Sandra Ford, 1960; 6 children. AB, Dartmouth Coll., 1958; LLB, U. Mich., 1963; postgrad., Nat. Jud. Coll., 1977. Bar: N.H. 1963. Assoc. Devine, Millimet, McDonough, Stahl & Branch, Manchester, N.H., 1963-69; U.S. atty. State of N.H., 1969-72; ptnr. Perkins, Douglas & Brock, Concord, N.H., 1972-74, Perkins & Brock, 1974-76; spl. counsel to gov. and exec. coun. N.H., 1974-76; legal counsel to gov. N.H., 1976; assoc. justice N.H. Superior Ct., 1976-78, N.H. Supreme Ct., 1978-86, chief justice, 1986—. Chmn. State of N.H. Legal Svcs. Adv. Commn., 1977-79; chmn. dist. ct. reform subcom. Gov.'s Commn. for Ct. System Improvement, 1974-75; chmn. N.H. Commn. Ct. Accreditation, 1986—; mem. Select Commn. on Unified Ct. System, 1980-84, chmn. N.H. Supreme Ct. Com. on Jud. Conduct, 1981-89, rules adv. com., 1985-97; mem. State N.H. Jud. Coun., 1979-87; nat. adv. bd. Leadership Inst. for Jud. Edn., 1989-96, Nat. Jud. Coll. long range planning com., 1990-91; mem. Jud. Edn. and Tech. Assistance Consortium, 1989-97; chmn. Interbranch Coun. on Substance Abuse and the Criminal Justice System, 1991-95; vice-chmn. State Justice Inst., 1994-95, co-chmn., 1995-98; v.p. Conf. Chief Justices, 1996-97, pres-elect 1997-98, pres., 1998-99; chmn.-elect Nat. Ctr. for State Cts., 1997-98, chmn., 1998-99; mem. Nat. Criminal Justice Info. Svcs. Adv. Policy Bd., 1999-2002. Bd. dirs. Manchester Cmty. Guidance Ctr., 1966-72, pres., 1969 72, policy bd., 1999-2002; chmn. Manchester Rep. Com., 1967-69; vice chmn. N.H. Rep. State Com., 1968-69; Rep. candidate U.S. Senate, 1972; del. N.H. Constl. Conv., 1974; mem. Gov.'s Commn. for Handicapped, 1978-79. Fellow ABA (edn. com. of appellate judges conf. 1981-97, appellate advocacy com. 1982-84, faculty appellate judges' seminar program 1984-89, del. ho. of dels. 1994-96), N.H. Bar Assn. (chmn. constl. revision com. 1976-77), N.H. Bar Found. (hon.). Office: NH Supreme Ct Noble Dr Concord NH 03301

BROCK, DAVID GEORGE, lawyer; b. Buffalo, Oct. 13, 1945; s. Joseph Louis and Julia Strauss (Amram) B.; m. Marilyn Sandra Katz, May 25, 1969; children: Lauren, Joel. BA in English, Union Coll., 1967; JD, SUNY, Buffalo, 1972. Bar: N.Y. 1973, U.S. Dist. Ct. (we. dist.) N.Y. 1973. Atty. Liberty Mut. Ins. Co., Buffalo, 1973-77; assoc. Jaeckle, Fleischmann & Mugel, Buffalo, 1977-79, ptnr., 1980—. Vice-chair N.Y. State Atty. Grievance Com. (8th judicial dist.), 1994-2000. Author: To Get the Best Result, Prepare for the Worst: Preparing the Witness for Deposition, IADC, 1994; mem. editl. adv. bd. NY Trial Objections, 1998. Bd. dirs. Planned Parenthood Buffalo and Erie County, 1999 , treas., 2001, sec., 2002; bd. dirs. Lower West Side Cmty. Enrichment Ctr.; bd. trustees Temple Beth Zion Buffalo, N.Y., 1988-98, pres., 1994-96. Mem.: ABA, Am. Inns of Ct. (counsel 2002), Charles S. Desmond Inn, Nat. Inst. Trial Adv., Internat. Assn. Def. Counsel (bd. editors Def. Counsel Jour. 1992—), Def. Rsch. Inst., Inc., Western N.Y. Trial Lawyers Assn. (bd. dirs. 1993—95), Erie County Bar Assn. (chmn. profl. ethics com. 1991—95, bd. dirs. 1996—99), N.Y. State Bar Assn. Jewish. Avocations: reading, photography. Home: 49 Northington Dr East Amherst NY 14051-1721 Office: Jaeckle Fleischmann & Mugel LLP 12 Fountain Plz Buffalo NY 14202-2292 E-mail: dbrock@jaeckle.com.

BROCK, DAWN MARIE, counselor; b. Joliet, Ill, May 17, 1977; d. Rick A and Cynthia Lou Hargis. BA, U. of Nevada Reno, 1999; MA, U. of Mass. at Dartmouth, 2003. Homicide bereavement counselor Brockton Family and Cmty. Resources, Inc., Brockton, Mass., 2002—; clin. masters intern U. of Mass., Dartmouth Counseling and Student Devel. Ctr., 2002—03. Grad. tchg. asst. U. of Mass., Dartmouth, 2000—02. Mem.: Mass. Mental Health Counselors Assn., Ea. Psychol. Assn., Am. Psychol. Soc., Assn. for Behavior Analysis, Mass. Psychol. Assn., Am. Psychological Assn., Psi Chi. Home: 9 Randolph Ave Tiverton MA 02878

BROCK, DEE SALA, television executive, educator, writer, consultant; b. Covington, Okla., June 7, 1930; d. Lester Edward and Vera Mae (Bowers) Sala; m. Robert Wesley Brock, June 8, 1952 (div. 1979); children: Baron Sala, Bishop Chapman, Bevin Bowers. BA, U. North Tex., 1950, MA, 1956, PhD, 1985. Tchr. high sch. Dallas Ind. Sch. Dist., 1952-66; dir. Dallas Cowboy Cheerleaders, 1960-75; mem. faculty, adminstr. Dallas County Community Coll. Dist., 1966-74, telecourse writer, producer, adminstr., 1974-75, dir. mktg. info., 1975-80; dir., v.p. PBS, Washington, 1980-89, sr. v.p. edn. Alexandria, Va., 1989-90; pres. Dee Brock & Assocs., Plano, Tex., 1991-98; pub. FAQs Press, 1999—. Bd. dirs. Pub. Svc. Satellite Consortium, U.S. Basics; adv. bd. Learning Link, 1987-90, Telcon Industry, 1990-91; chair exec. coun. U. of the World, 1989-91; adv. coun. Triangle Coalition, 1989-91; spkr. in field. Author: Writing for a Reason: Study Guide, 1974; author: (with Jeriel Howard) Writing for a Reason, 1978; author: (with Laura Derr) The World of F. Scott Fitzgerald, 1980; author: (with Deborah Burkett and Carole Wilson) Troup Goes to War: World War II, A Collection of Memories, 1999; author: (with Linda Resnik) Food FAQs: Substitutions, Yields & Equivalents, 2000; author: (with JoAnna Lewis) 100 Great Fundraising Ideas Celebrating 100 Years of Texas Library, 2002; mem. editl. bd. : Am. Jour. Distance Edn., 1987—90; prodr.: (internat. teleconf.) Out of the Red, 1991; prodr., writer: TV series and workbook Communicating in English in the Healthcare Workplace, 1994; contbr. articles to profl. jours. Trustee Coun. for Adult and Experiential Learning, 1989—99; chair spl. task force Mcpl. Libr. Friends of Libr., 1996, pres., 1997—; lay rep. N.E. Tex. Libr. Sys., 1996—, chair planning to plan com., 1997—98, adv. coun., 1998—, vice chair, 1998—2000, chair, 2000—; chmn. Strategic Planning Com., 1999; fundraising co-chair Komen Tyler Race for the Cure, 1999; active PTA, Dallas; pres. Littera, 2002—, Friends of the Troup Libr., 1998—; chair Libr. Friends, Trustees and Advs., 2001—03; bd. dirs. Tyler Civic Theatre Ctr., Coalition for the Advancement of Citizenship, 1988—90. Reynolds Econ. fellow U. N.C., 1966; Literacy award N. Tex. Reading Coun., 1980, Nat. Person of Yr. award Nat. Coun. on Community and Continuing Edn., 1985, Award for Excellence in TV Programming NEA, 1986; recipient Outstanding Career Achievement award ITC Am. Assn. Community and Jr. Colls., 1990. Mem. NEH (nat. bd. cons. 1980-85), LWV (bd. dirs., v.p. cmty. rels. Tyler chpt. 2002-03, pres. 2003—), U.S. Distance Learning Assn. (bd. dirs. 1989-91, adv. bd. 1989), So. Assn. Colls. and Schs. (project 1990 task force 1984-86), Nat. Assn. Ednl. Broadcasters (steering com. 1979-81), Assn. Ednl. Comms. Tech., Nat. Coun. Tchrs. English (pres. S.W. regional coun. 1972-74), Tex. Libr. Assn. (legis. com. 1999—, chair roundtable 2001—). Methodist. Achievements include being co-patentee video indexing system; design of and management of PBS Adult Learning Service and PBS Adult Learning Satellite Service. Home and Office: 3529 Wood Blvd Tyler TX 75707

BROCK, ERIC JOHN, urban planner, historian, consultant; b. Berkeley, Calif., Sept. 24, 1966; s. Robert Donald and Victoria Claire (Berg) B.; m. Pamela Grace Viviano, Nov. 14, 1988 (div. 1996); m. Julie Beth Van Thof, Jan. 2, 2002 (div. 2003). BA in English and History, Centenary Coll., 1988. Editl. page writer Shreveport Jour., 1992-00; pvt. practice consulting historian and planner Shreveport, 1993—; ptnr. Found. Records, Inc., Shreveport. Adv. bd. Shreveport Regional Arts Coun., 1990-93. Author: The Old Oakland Cemetery, 1988, The Jewish Cemeteries of Shreveport, 1995, Holiday-In-Dixie: 50 Years, 1998, Images of Shreveport, 1998, Shreveport in the 20th Century, 1998, New Orleans Cemeteries, 1999, Steamboats on the Red River, 1999, Images of New Orleans, 2000, Centenary College of Louisiana, 2000, Eric Brock's Shreveport, 2001, Shreveport: Faces of the Past, 2002, Jewish Community of Shreveport, 2003, (mag. column) Shreveport Forum News, 1996—. V.p. ACLU of N.W. La., Shreveport, 1993; bd. mem., McNeill Waterworks Mus., Bd. 1999-2001; bd. dirs. Shreveport Art Guild, 2001-2002, McAneny Mus., 2002-2003. Recipient Key to the City of Shreveport, 1990, 94, 97, 2000, La. Preservation Alliance State Preservation award, 2001SCV Comdr.-in-Chief's award, 2001 . Fellow The Tarshar Soc.; mem. SAR, SCV, Holiday-in-Dixie Ambs. (bd. mem. 1996-2000), La. Preservation Alliance (bd. mem. 1990-94), Hist. Preservation of Shreveport (bd. mem., v.p. 1991-96, pres. 1996-2002), Shreveport Beautification Found. (bd. mem. 1990-92), Highland Area Partnership (bd. mem. 1991-95), Oakland Cemetery Preservation Soc. Bd. (pres. 1999-2002). Jewish. Avocations: photography, writing. E-mail: ericjbrock@aol.com.

BROCK, GLEN PORTER, JR., lawyer; b. Mobile, Ala., Nov. 13, 1937; s. Glen Porter Sr. and Esther Alitha (Goodwin) B.; m. Shirley Ann Forbes, Jan. 7, 1961; children: Glen Porter III, Susan Forbes. BS, Auburn U., 1959; JD, U. Ala., 1963; LLM in Taxation, NYU, 1964. Bar: Ala. 1963. Assoc. Hand, Arendall, Bedsole, Greaves & Johnston, Mobile, 1964-69, ptnr., 1970-94; mem. Hand Arendall, LLC, 1995—. Capt. USAR, 1959-67. Mem. ABA, Ala. Bar Assn. (chmn. tax sect. 1974-75), Mobile Bar Assn., Lions (pres. 1982-83). Baptist. Avocations: travel, computers, photography. Home: 737 Westmoreland Dr W Mobile AL 36609-6132 Office: Hand Arendall LLC 3000 AmSouth Bank Bldg 107 Saint Francis St Mobile AL 36602-3334 E-mail: porterb@handarendall.com.

BROCK, HELEN RACHEL MCCOY, retired mental health and community health nurse; b. Cromwell, Okla., Dec. 10, 1924; d. Samuel Robert Lee and Ire Etta (Pounds) McCoy; m. Clois Lee Brock, Sept. 29, 1963; children: Dwayne, Joyce, Peggy, Ricki, Stacey. AS, Southwestern Union Coll., Keene, Tex., 1968; BS in Nursing, Union Coll., Lincoln, Nebr., 1970; postgrad., Vernon Regional Jr. Coll., Tex., 1972, 76; MPH, Loma Linda (Calif.) U., 1983. Cert. ARC nurse. Dir. nursing Chillicothe (Tex.) Clinic-Hosp., 1970-77, Pike County Hosp., Waverly, Ohio, 1977-79, Marion County Hosp., Jefferson, Tex.; 1979-81; nurse III, nursing unit supr. patient health educator Vernon State Hosp., Maximum

Security for Criminally Insane, 1981-96; retired, 1996; nurse, admissions and assessments Texhoma Community Health Svcs., 1987-94. Mem. Am. Nurses Assn., Tex. Nurses Assn. Home: PO Box 238 Chillicothe TX 79225-0238

BROCK, JAMES RUSH, chemical engineering educator; b. Mission, Tex., Dec. 31, 1930; s. Jerome Dalton and Elizabeth (Beeler) B.; m. Mary Lou Waghorn, July 4, 1964; children: Ianthe, Alison. BA, Rice U., 1952, BS, 1953; MS, U. Wis., 1954, PhD, 1960. Registered profl. engr., Tex. Rsch. engr. Humble Oil & Refining Co., Houston, 1954-55; asst. prof. chem. engring. dept. U. Tex., Austin, 1959-62; postdoctoral fellow at Svc. de Chimie Physique II Université Libre de Belgique, Brussels, 1962-63; asst. prof. chem. engring. dept. U. Tex., Austin, 1963-65, assoc. prof., 1965-69, prof., 1969-73, 73-80, K.A. Kobe prof., 1980—; vis. prof. U. Paris VI Faculty Scis., Paris, 1973, Tokyo Inst. Tech., 1988. Mem. rsch. grants adv. com. EPA, Washington, 1970—; v.p. ONG Producing Inc., Austin, 1986—; cons. to govt. agys. Co-author: The Dynamics of Aerocolloidal Systems, 1970; co-editor Internat. Revs. in Aerosol Physics and Chemistry, 1971-73; assoc. editor Jour. Environ. Sci. and Health, 1978—, Jour. Aerosol Sci., 1986-88; mem. editorial bd. Jour. Colloid Sci., 1965-66, Aerosol Sci. and Tech., 1984-88; contbr. more than 150 articles to profl. jours.; holder 20 patents in field. Recipient Disting. Svc. award U.S. Army Rsch. Devel. Engring. Ctr., 1987; grantee NSF. Mem. Am. Chem. Soc., Am. Assn. Aerosol Rsch. (Sinclair award 1992), Gesellschaft fur Aerosol Forschung, Tau Beta Pi, Alpha Chi Omega, Phi Lambda Upsilon. Office: U Tex Coll Engring Dept Chem Engring Austin TX 78712-1062

BROCK, JOHN MORGAN (JUNO), JR., composer, performer, producer; b. San Angelo, Tex., June 15, 1956; Pres. Alternative Music Prodns., Inc., L.A., 1981—; founder theMusicMinistry.com, 2001. Spl. music instr. City of North Las Vegas, 1995-97. Composer, performer, engr. producer: (records) Ahead Of Your Time, 1981, In Tune With Tomorrow, 1982, Android/A 21st Century Band, 1989; (CDs) Christina-Reminiscence, 1991, Mr. Ectomy, 1992, Entoptic Whores, 1994, Making Waves in the Desert—The New Age Symphony, 1998, Dream Within a Dream—The New Age Orchestra, 1999, Prescription Music, 2000, A Light is Shining, 2000, Incarnata: The Holy Passion, 2001, InnerSanctum, 2001, 2K2, 2001, Heart Beat, 2002, Songs of Worship, Songs of Praise, vols. 1 and 2, 2003, (films) Doin' Time on Planet Earth, Martians Go Home, Repossessed, Mother Goose-Rock and Rhyme; also performed on NBC-TV, 1990; comml. music aired on CNN, 1994; commd. by N.W. Youth Ballet, 1995, Palo Verde Theatre, 2000. Choir dir. Showmens League Am., 1997-98; music dir. Westminster Presbyn. Ch., 1997-99; dir. Las Vegas Cmty. Chorus, 2000—; min. of music UNITY in Green Valley, 2003. Nev. State Coun. on Arts/Commn. on Tourism grant, 1996, Ordained as Min. of Music, 2000. Mem. ASCAP (writer, pub.), NARAS, Internat. Electronic Music Assn. Avocations: graphic design, choreography, video production. E-mail: studio@viawest.net.

BROCK, LOUIS MILTON, JR., engineering educator, researcher; b. Davenport, Iowa, Apr. 16, 1943; s. Louis Milton and Mary Elizabeth (Creech) B.; m. Carolyn Starbuck Pratt, July 22, 1972. BS, Northwestern U. 1966, MS, 1967, PhD, 1972. With Black and Veatch, Kansas City, Mo., 1962, Gen Dynamics/Convair, San Diego, 1963-64, Sargeant-Welch Co., Skokie, Ill., 1964, Am. Can Co., Barrington, Ill., 1965; prof. mech. enging. U. Ky., Lexington, 1971—. Contbr. articles to profl. jours. NSF grantee, 1972, 79, 84, 90, 92, 93; USN/Am. Soc. Engring. Edn. fellow, 1983, 85, 87, 90; recipient rsch. award Rsch. Found. U. Ky., 1977, rsch. prof. award, 1986. Fellow ASME; mem. ASCE (corr. award 1989), Sigma Xi. Avocations: hiking, classical music, riding, history. Home: 133 Sycamore Rd Lexington KY 40502-1841 Office: U Ky Dept Mech Engring Lexington KY 40506-0503

BROCK, LYNMAR, JR., food service executive; b. Bryn Mawr, Pa., Jan. 5, 1934; s. Lynmar and Sarah Pratt B.; m. Claudie J. Brock, Oct. 19, 1963; children: Christopher, Andrew. AB, Dartmouth Coll., 1955, MBA, 1956. Pres. Brock & Co. Inc., Malvern, Pa., 1962—. Chmn. Peirce Coll., Phila., 1991-2003, Kendal Corp., Kennett Square, Pa., 1995—. Chmn., suprs. Edgemont Twp., Pa., 1982-92; chmn. zoning bd., 1970-82. Lt. USN, 1956-62. Republican. Mem. Soc. Of Friends. Avocations: skiing, writing, travel. Office: Brock & Co Inc 77 Great Valley Pkwy Malvern PA 19355 E-mail: lbrock@brockco.com.

BROCK, MARY ANNE, research investigator, consultant; b. June 29, 1932; d. Paul Peter and Helen Anna (Mattas). BA, Grinnell Coll., 1954; MA, Harvard U., 1956, PhD, 1959. Tchg. fellow Harvard U., Cambridge, Mass., 1954-58; rsch. assoc. Harvard Med. Sch., Boston, 1959-60; sr. rsch. biologist Nat. Inst. Aging, NIH, Balt., 1960-95; vol. Nat. Inst. Deafness and Other Comm. Disorders, NIH, Bethesda, Md., 1996—. Vis. scientist Stanford U., Calif., 1977; cons. NASA, 1981-90. Contbr. articles to profl. jours. Bd. dirs. Cross Keys Condo Assn., Balt., 1980-85. Recipient Alumni award for achievement and svc. Grinnell Coll., 2000. Fellow AAAS, Gerontol. Soc. Am. (fellowship com. 1988-90, pub. policy com. 1991-94); mem. Cryobiology Soc. (bd. govs. 1973-76, sec. 1971-72, nominating com. 1982-84), Chesapeake Soc. Electron Microscopy (coun. 1979-82), Am. Soc. Cell Biology (legis. alert com. 1982-92, congl. liaison com. 1992—), Soc. Rsch. Biol. Rhythms, Internat. Soc. Chronobiology, Sigma Xi, Phi Beta Kappa.

BROCK, MITCHELL, lawyer; b. Wyncote, Pa., Nov. 10, 1927; s. John W. and Mildred A. (Mitchell) B.; m. Gioia Connell, June 21, 1952; children: Felicity, Marina, Mitchell Hovey, Laura. AB, Princeton U., 1950; LLB, U. Pa., 1953. Bar: N.Y. 1954. Assoc. firm Sullivan & Cromwell, N.Y.C., 1953-59, ptnr., 1960-92, Paris, 1965-68, ptnr. in charge Tokyo, 1987-90. Bd. dirs. Frost Valley YMCA, Oliverea, N.Y., 1980-87, 1990-2000, Am. Found. Blind, 1967-87; pres., trustee Helen Keller Internat., N.Y.C., 1970-87, 90-94, chmn., trustee, 1994-96, sec., 1996—. Served with USN, 1945-46. Mem. Anglers Club, Princeton Club, Ivy Club, Boca Grande Pass Club. Republican. Episcopalian. Home: PO Box 452 Boca Grande FL 33921-0452 E-mail: gimibrock@ewol.com.

BROCK, RANDALL J. poet; b. Colfax, Wash., Nov. 24, 1943; s. Homer Clarence and Roberta Mildred (Keith) B. Student, Wash. State U., 1962-68; BA in History, BA in Edn., Ea. Wash. U., 1970; MFA, U. Oreg., 1973. Tchr. Christian Action Ministry, Chgo., 1967; mailman Yellowstone (Wyo.) Park Co., 1968; janitor Spokesman-Rev., Spokane, Wash., 1978-79. Author of 20 chapbooks; author numerous poems; author of four audio book tapes; photographer: Pockets of Origin, 1983. Poetry scholar Centrum, Port Townsend, Wash., 1977. Mem.: Poets and Writers, Spokane Open Poetry Assn. Avocations: mysteries, history, anthropology. Home: PO Box 1673 Spokane WA 99210-1673

BROCK, STEPHEN L. supervisor international languages, consultant; s. Daniel Gordon Brock and Alicia Marie Derks; m. Mary Lee Bortnem, Oct. 14, 1989; children: Claudia Wentworth, Etienne Leigh. BA, St. Louis U., 1986; M in English Edn., U. of Minn., 1991; MS, Creighton U., Nebr., 2001. Tchr. Omaha South HS, 1992—99; supr. internat. langs. Omaha Pub. Schs., 1999—2002. Pres., bd. mem. Nebr. Internat. Langs. Assn., Lincoln, Nebr., 1998—; past pres., bd. mem. Nebr. Assn. of Tchrs. of German, Omaha, 1998—2002; dir. Ctrl. States Conf. for the Tchg. of Fgn. Langs., Mpls., 2003—. Co-author: (instructional guide) National German Week Packet; consultant (german textbook) Deutsch Aktuell 1 & 2, presenter (conf.) Using Nonlinguistic Approaches to Improve Student Learning (Best of Nebr. award, 2001), Higher Level Thinking: Activities that Reach the Top (Best of Nebr. award, 1999). Pres. South Omaha Neighborhood Assns., 2002—, Hanscom Pk. Neighborhood Assn., Omaha, 2000—; pac-chair of children's action fund Omaha Edn. Assn., 1997—99; parish pastoral coun. pres. St. John's Parish Coun., Omaha, 1998—2000; dir. Police Adv. Coun., Omaha, 2002—. Recipient Ten Outstanding Young Omahan's, Jaycees, 1997, STAR award, Nebr. Dept. of Edn., 1998—2003, Nebr. Outstanding Fgn. Lang. Tchr., Nebr. Fgn. Lang. Assn., 1999; fellow Fulbright Meml. Fund Tchr. Program, Japan-U.S. Ednl. Commn., 2000—01; scholar Kaufman Scholarship, U. of Minn., 1990. Mem.: South Omaha Optimists (assoc.). Roman Catholic. Avocations: wagnerian opera, haute cuisine, reading. Office: Omaha Publ Schs 3215 Cuming St Omaha NE 68131 Office Fax: 402-557-2499. E-mail: stephenbrock@ops.org.

BROCK, THOMAS DALE, microbiology educator; b. Cleve., Sept. 10, 1926; s. Thomas Carter and Helen Sophia (Ringwald) B.; m. Mary Louise Louden, Sept. 13, 1952 (div. Feb. 1971); m. Katherine Serat Middleton, Feb. 20, 1971; children: Emily Katherine, Brian Thomas. BS, Ohio State U., 1949, MS, 1950, PhD, 1952. Research microbiologist Upjohn Co., Kalamazoo, 1952-57; asst. prof. Western Res. U., Cleve., 1957-59, Ind. U., Bloomington, 1960-61, assoc. prof., 1962-64, prof., 1964-71; E.B. Fred prof. natural scis. U. Wis., Madison, 1971-90, prof. emeritus, 1990—, chmn. dept. bacteriology, 1979-82; pres. Sci. Tech. Pubs., Madison, 1990-94, Savanna Oak Found., 2000—. Found. for Microbiology lectr., 1971-72, 78-79 Author: Milestones in Microbiology, 1961, Principles of Microbial Ecology, 1966, Thermophilic Microorganisms, 1978, Biology of Microorganism, 7th edit., 1994, Basic Microbiology with Applications, 3d edit., 1986, A Eutrophic Lake, 1985, Thermophiles: General, Molecular and Applied Microbiology, 1986, Robert Koch: A Life in Medicine and Bacteriology, 1988, The Emergence of Bacterial Genetics, 1990, Shorewood Hills: An Illustrated History, 1999. Recipient Rsch. Career Devel. award NIH, 1962-68, Waksman award Soc. Indsl. Microbiology, 2003. Fellow AAAS; mem. Am. Soc. for Microbiology (hon. mem., chmn. gen. div. 1970-71, Fisher award 1984, Carski award 1988) Home and Office: 1227 Dartmouth Rd Madison WI 53705-2213

BROCK, WILLIAM ALLEN, III, economist, educator; b. Phila., Oct. 23, 1941; s. William Allen and Margaret Elizabeth (Holcroft) Brock; m. Joan Elaine Loutenshlager, Aug. 31, 1962; 1 child, Caroline Christine. AB in Math. with honors, U. Mo., 1965; PhD, U. Calif., Berkeley, 1969. Asst. prof. econs. U. Rochester, NY, 1969-71; assoc. prof. U. Chgo., 1972-75, prof., 1975-81; from assoc. prof. to full prof. Cornell U., 1974-77; Romnes prof. econs. U. Wis., Madison, 1981—, F.P. Ramsey prof. econs., 1984—, W.F. Vilas rsch. prof., 1990—. Vis. assoc. prof. U. Rochester, 1973; cons. U.S. Dept. Justice, SBA, EPA, FTC. Assoc. editor: Jour. Econ. Theory, Internat. Econ. Rev., 1972—99; contbr. articles to profl. jours.; co-author (with A. Malliaris): (book) Differential Equations, Stability and Chaos in Dynamic Economics, 1989; co-author: (with D. Hseieh, B. LeBaron) Nonlinear Dynamics, Chaos and Instability: Statistical Theory and Economic Evidence, 1991. Recipient Roger F. Murray 3d Pl. prize, Inst. Quantitative Rsch. Fin., 1989; NSF grantee, 1970—2003, Sherman Fairchild Disting. scholar, Calif. Inst. Tech., 1978, Guggenheim fellow, 1987—88. Fellow: Econometric Soc.; mem.: AAAS, NAS. Office: U Wis Dept Econs 1180 Observatory Dr Madison WI 53706-1320

BROCK, WILLIAM ALTON, pediatric urologist; b. Bklyn., Mar. 29, 1946; s. Charles Henry and Mary (Campisi) Brock. BS, Fordham U., 1967; MD, Emory U., 1971. Diplomate Am. Bd. Urology. Intern surgery N.Y. Hosp., N.Y.C., 1971-72, resident surgery, 1972-73; resident urology U. Calif., San Diego, 1975-79; fellow pediatric urology U. Liverpool, Eng., 1979; chmn. dept. pediatric urology Children's Hosp., San Diego, 1984-85; clin. prof. urology Albert Einstein Coll. Medicine, Bronx, N.Y., 1989—; ptnr. Pediatric Urologic Assocs., San Diego, 1979-85, Pediatric Urology Assn., N.Y., 1993—; chief pediatric urology L.I. Jewish Med. Ctr., New Hyde Park, N.Y., 1985-98. Assoc. prof. urology U. Calif., San Diego, 1980-85, SUNY, Stony Brook, 1985-89; sci. advisor Nat. Kidney Found., San Diego, 1981-85; chmn. quality assurance dept. urology L.I. Jewish Med. Ctr., New Hyde Park, N.Y., 1989-92; vis. prof. Wake Forest Sch. Medicine, Winston-Salem, N.C., 1988, Ohio State U. Sch. of Medicine, 1992; clin. adj. prof. urology Cornell U. Med. Coll., 1995-98. Reviewer Jour. Urology, 1990-96; author med. textbooks; contbr. articles to profl. jours. Maj. USAF, 1973-75. Fellow ACS, Am. Acad. Pediatrics, N.Y. Acad. Medicine; mem. AMA, Soc. Pediatric Urology, Am. Urologic Assn., Pediatrics Soc. Dominican Republic (hon.). Roman Catholic. Avocations: computers, gardening, sailing, fly fishing. Office: 833 Northern Blvd Great Neck NY 11021-5315

BROCK-BROIDO, LUCIE, poet, educator; b. Pitts., May 22, 1956; d. David Simon Broido and Virginia Lois Brock. BA, Johns Hopkins U., 1978, MA, 1979; MFA, Columbia U., 1982. Prof. poetry Harvard U., Cambridge, Mass., 1988—93; prof. poetry Sch. of Arts Columbia U., N.Y.C., 1993—, dir. poetry Sch. of Arts, 1993—. Author: A Hunger, 1988, The Master Letters, 1995, Trouble in Mind, 2003; contbg. editor: Zoo Press, Poetry Press, The Boston (Mass.) Rev., The Denver (Colo.) Quar.; mem. editl. bd.: Agni Poetry Mag. Recipient Witter Bynner prize, Am. Acad. Arts & Letters, 1996; fellow, John Sloan Guggenheim Found., 1996, NEA, 1998. Mem.: Poetry Soc. Am., Acad. Am. Poets. Office: Columbia Univ Sch Arts 2690 Broadway Dodge Hall New York NY 10027

BROCKELSBY, JEFFREY LIND, investment executive; b. Rapid City, SD, Oct. 20, 1954; s. Earl John Brockelsby and Maude (Wagner) B. BS in Radio/TV summa cum laude, Bradley U., 1976; MS in Mass Comm., S.D. State U., 1983; Cert. in Biblical Studies, Columbia Biblical Sem., 1996. Reporter KEVN/TV, Rapid City, SD, 1976-77; press aide/campaign press sec. Se. George McGovern, Washington, 1979-81; press sec. Rep. Byron Dorgan, Washington, 1981; program dir. S.D. Democratic Party, Pierre, 1983-85; correspondent Huron Daily Plainsman, Pierre, 1985-86; congl. field rep. Rep. Tim Johnson, Rapid City, 1986-87; investment executive Brockelsby Family Trusts, Columbia, S.C., 1993—; corp. treas. Black Hills Reptile Gardens, Inc., Rapid City, 1991—. Bd. dirs. Black Hills Reptile Gardens, Inc., 1993—; polling dir. O'Connor for Gov., Sioux Falls, S.D., 1982. Author: The Brockelsbys of Crawford County Iowa-A Family History, 1991. State campaign treas. Gary Hart for Pres., 1984; field operative Paul Simon for Pres., Rapid City, 1988; cons. several polit. campaigns. Mem.: Depression and Bipolar Support Alliance. Democrat. Avocations: music, running, geneaology. Home: 164 Heritage Village Ln Columbia SC 29212-3512 Office: Brocklesby Fam Trusts 164 Heritage Village Ln Columbia SC 29212-3512

BROCKENBROUGH, EDWIN CHAMBERLAYNE, surgeon; b. Balt., July 24, 1930; s. Edwin Chamberlayne Sr. and Martha Davis (Coale) B.; m. Jean McClure, May 4, 1968; children: John, Martha, Andrew, Ann, Susan. BA, Coll. William & Mary, 1952; MD, Johns Hopkins U., 1956. Intern Johns Hopkins Hosp., Balt., 1956-57, resident, 1957-59; sr. asst. surgeon Nat. Heart Inst., Bethesda, Md., 1959-61; chief resident surgery U. Wash., Seattle, 1961-64, faculty mem. dept. surgery, 1964-75; pvt. practice Seattle, 1975-98. Clin. prof. surgery U. Wash., 1984—; pres. King County Med. Soc., Seattle, 1992; trustee Health Resources N.W., Seattle; med. dir. Pacific Vasc. Inst., 1996—. Contbr. chpt. to book and articles to profl. jours. Sr. asst. surgeon USPHS, 1959-61. Fellow ACS (pres. Wash. State chpt. 1985), Seattle Surg. Soc. (sec. 1972); mem. North Pacific Surg. Assn. (pres. 1995-96), Pacific Coast Surg. Assn., Am. Rhododendron Soc. (pres. 1977-79, Silver medal 1985). Republican. Episcopalian. Avocations: gardening, hybridizing rhododendrons, photography, culinary arts, fishing. Home and Office: 3630 Hunts Point Rd Bellevue WA 98004-1114 E-mail: nedbro@hotmail.com.

BROCKENBROUGH, HENRY WATKINS, lawyer; b. Richmond, Va., Aug. 28, 1923; s. Benjamin Willard and Kathleen Reading (Watkins) B.; m. Mary Lane Williams, Oct. 30, 1948; children: Henry Watkins, Rebecca Lane, John Reading, Willson Williams. BA cum laude, Hampden-Sydney Coll., 1944; LLB, U. Va., 1948; grad. degree, Rutgers U., 1957. Bar: Va. 1949. With Crestar Bank, Richmond, 1948-88, v.p., trust officer, 1963-67, sr. v.p., trust officer, 1967-88, spl.counsel and trust cons. to Crestar Bank, 1988-91; ptnr.unsel Taylor, Hazen, Kauffman & Pinchbeck, Richmond, 1991—2003; of counsel Pinchbeck, P.C., Richmond2003. Chmn. trust com. Va. Bankers Assn., 1970-71. Past pres. Estate Planning Coun., Richmond; chmn. bd. dirs. Tuckahoe YMCA, 1975; bd. dirs. Good Neighbor Village, Varina, Va. Lt. (j.g.) USNR, 1943-46. Mem. Va. State Bar, Va. Bar Assn., The Cohoke Club (West Point, Va., past pres.), Lambda Chi Alpha, Delta Theta Phi. Presbyterian. Home: 802 Horsepen Rd Richmond VA 23229-6725 Office: 6932 Forest Hill Ave Richmond VA 23225

BROCKENBROUGH, THOMAS WILLIAM, civil engineer, educator; b. Buena Vista, Va., July 14, 1920; s. Bernard Jeremiah and Myrtle (Orr) Brockenbrough; m. Mary Lou Kocher, Aug. 1954; children: Thomas William, Mary Alice. BSCE, Va. Poly. Inst., 1942; MS in Civil Engring., MIT, 1946. Registered profl. engr., Del. Asst. prof. civil engring. Va. Poly. Inst., Blacksburg, 1949—53; assoc. prof. U. Del., Newark, 1953—64, asst. dean Coll. Engring., 1964—74, prof., 1974—87, chmn. dept. engring., 1984—87, prof. emeritus, 1988—. Cons. engr. E.I. DuPont de Nemours, Wilmington, Del., 1980—. Contbr. articles to profl. jours. Chmn. bd. appeals City of Newark, 1973—; elder First Presbyn. Ch., Newark, 1958—. Named Del. Engr. of Yr., Del. Soc. Profl. Engrs., 1979. Mem.: ASCE (pres. 1964), Del. Acad. Scis. (pres. 1978), Am. Concrete Inst., Am. Soc. Engring. Edn., Blue and Gold Club (bd. dirs.), Omicron Delta Kappa, Sigma Xi, Tau Beta Pi, Chi Epsilon. Democrat. Avocations: gardening, photography. Home: 5 S Dillwyn Rd Newark DE 19711-5543

BROCKETT, OSCAR GROSS, theatre educator; b. Hartsville, Tenn., Mar. 18, 1923; s. Oscar Hill and Minnie Dee (Gross) B.; m. Lenyth Spenker, Sept. 4, 1951; 1 dau., Francesca Lane. BA, Peabody Coll., 1947; MA, Stanford U., 1949, PhD, 1953. Instr. English U. Ky., 1949-50; asst. instr. drama Stanford U., 1950-52; asst. prof. drama Stetson U., DeLand, Fla., 1952-56; from asst. to assoc. prof. U. Iowa, 1956-63; from prof. to distinguished prof. Ind. U., 1963-78; Ashbel Smith prof. drama U. Tex., Austin, 1978-80; dean U. Tex. Coll. Fine Arts, 1978-80; DeMille prof. drama U. So. Calif., L.A., 1980-81; Waggener prof. fine arts U. Tex., Austin, 1981-87, Virginia L. Murchison Regents prof., 1987-88, holder Z.T. Scott Family Chair in drama, 1988-99, Univ. Disting. Tchg. prof., 1996—. Author 10 books; contbr. articles to profl. jours. With USNR, 1943-46. Recipient Fulbright award, 1963-64, Medallion of Honor Theta Alpha Phi, 1977, Am. Coll. Theatre Festival Gold Medallion, 1978, Career Achievement award Assn. for Theatre in Higher Edn., 1991, Spl. Citation award U.S. Inst. TheatreTech., 2001; Guggenheim fellow, 1970-71. Mem. Am. Theatre Assn. (past pres., Merit award 1979), Coll. Am. Theatre Fellows (dean. 2002—), Am. Soc. Theatre Rsch., Internat. Fedn. Theatre Rsch., Nat. Theatre Conf., Nat. Comm. Assn., Shakespeare Assn. Am., Lit. Mgrs. and Dramaturgs of the Americas. Democrat. Episcopalian. Home: 901 W 9th St #903 Austin TX 78703 Office: U Tex Theater and Dance Dept Austin TX 78712 E-mail: obrockett@mail.utexas.edu.

BROCKETT, RALPH GROVER, adult education educator; b. Toledo, Ohio, Feb. 22, 1954; s. Ralph Grover and Hazel Anna (Frederick) B.; m. Patricia Anne Roney, Aug. 3, 1979 (div. Jan. 1997); 1 child, Megan Roney Brockett; m. Mary Florence Rowden, July 20, 2002. BA, U. Toledo (Ohio), 1976, MEd, 1977; PhD, Syracuse (N.Y.) U., 1982. Cert. gerontology, 1982. Continuing edn. project asst. SUNY, Albany, 1978-79; adminstrv. asst. adult edn. program Syracuse U., 1979-81, asst. prof. adult edn., 1982-84; project devel. coord. End Stage Renal Disease Network 26, East Syracuse, N.Y., 1981-82; asst. prof. adult edn. Mont. State U., Bozeman, 1984-88; assoc. prof. adult edn. U. Tenn., Knoxville, 1988-96, prof. adult edn., 1996—, coord., 1993—. Editor: Continuing Education in the Year 2000, 1987, Ethical Issues in Adult Education, 1988, Professional Development for Educators of Adults, 1991; co-editor Overcoming Resistance to Self-Direction in Adult Learning, 1994, The Power and Potential of Collaborative Learning Partnership, 1998; co-author: Self-Direction in Adult Learning: Perspectives on Theory, Research, and Practice, 1991, The Profession and Practice of Adult Education (Houle award for outstanding lit. in adult edn. 1997), 1997, Toward Ethical Practice, 2003; mem. editl. bd. Adult Edn. Quar., 1986-93, 2002—; editor-in-chief New Directions for Adult and Continuing Edn., 1989-98; co-editor Adult Learning, 2001—; contbr. articles to profl. jours. Advisor Jr. Achievement of Northwestern Ohio, Toledo, 1972-75. Recipient Charters award Syracuse U. Sch. Edn., 1986. Mem. Am. Assn. Adult and Continuing Edn. (bd. dirs. 1988-90, unit chair 1980-81, 90-91, Meritorious Svc. award 1981, 88, 90), Commn. Profs. Adult Edn. (bd. dirs. 1985-87, chair 1992-94), Mountain Plains Adult Edn. Assn., Juvenile Diabetes Rsch. Found. (bd. dirs. E. Tenn. chpt. 2002—). Avocations: music, reading, writing, history. Home: 6531 Deane Hill Dr Apt 50 Knoxville TN 37919-6012 Office: U Tenn Dept Ednl Psychology and Counseling A520 Claxton Complex Knoxville TN 37996

BROCKHAUS, ROBERT HEROLD, SR., business educator, consultant; b. St. Louis, Apr. 18, 1940; s. Herold August and Leona M. (Stutzke) B.; m. Joyce Patricia Dees, June 13, 1970; children: Cheryl Lynn, Robert Herold. BS in Mech. Engring., U. Mo.-Rolla, 1962; MSIA, Purdue U., 1966; PhD, Washington U., St. Louis, 1976. Mgr. Ralston-Purina, St. Louis, 1962-69; pres. Progressive Mgmt. Enterprises, Ltd., St. Louis, 1969—; asst. prof. mgmt. sci. St. Louis Univ., 1972-78, assoc. prof., 1978-84, prof., 1984—; chair in entrpreneurship Coleman Found., 1991—; dir. Small Bus. Inst., St. Louis Univ., 1976-86, Inst. Entrepreneurial Studies, St. Louis Univ., 1987-90; treas. CORO Found., 1987-92; exec. dir. Jefferson Smurfit Ctr. for Entrepreneurial Studies, 1990—; 1st v.p. Mo. Inventors Assn., 1988-94; state adminstr. Mo. Small Bus. Devel. Ctr., St. Louis, 1982-86; state dir. Mo. Small Bus. Devel. Ctrs., St. Louis, 1987-89. Schoen prof. entrepreneurship Baylor U., 1981; McAninch prof. entrepreneurship Kans. State U., 1985—87; vis. scholar So. Cross U., Australia, 1995; del. White House Conf. on Small Bus., 1986, 95; alderman City of Sunset Hills, 1998—; nat. rsch. adv. SBA, 2003. Co-author: Encyclopedia of Entrepreneur, 1982: Building a Better You, 1982; Nursing Concepts for Health Promotion, 1979, Art and Science of Entrepreneurship, 1985, Entrepreneurship in the 1990's, 1991, The State of the Art of Entrepreneurialship, 1992; editor Journal of Consulting, 1988-90; co-editor: Frontiers of Entrepreneurship Research, 1990, Advances in Entrepreneurship, Firm Emergence and Growth, 1993, 95, Entrepreneurship Education, 2001; editor Family Bus. Rev., 1993-97; also contbr. articles to profl. jours. Bd. dirs. City Venture, St. Louis, 1982-86; v.p. United Ch. of Christ, 1991-92, pres., 1992-93; chair troop 25 Boy Scout Am., 1990-93, vice chair Gravois Trail Coun., 2000—; chair, pres. Eastern Mo. Small Bus. Week, 2002. Named extraordinary prof., Potchefstroom U., South Africa, 2000—03, Lindbergh Leader, 2001; recipient Outstanding Svc. award, Boy Scouts Am., 1994, Disting. Svc. award Gravois Trl. Coun., 2002, award of excellence, NASDAQ; Fulbright fellow, U. Waikato, New Zealand, 1985. Fellow Internat. Coun. for Small Bus. (sr. v.p. 1981-83, internat. pres. 1983-84, bd. dirs. 1983, v.p. 1986, exec. dir. 1987—), Nat. Small Bus. Inst. Dirs. Assn. (nat. v.p. 1980-82, 96-97, nat. pres. 1982-83, Disting. Mentor award 2000), U.S. Assn. for Small Bus. Entrepreneurship; mem. Assn. Collegiate Entrepreneurs (internat. bd. dirs., exec. com. 1991-93, recipient outstanding entrepreneurship educator awd., 1992), Acad. Mgmt. (nat. prog. chmn. 1977-78, exec. com. 1993-95), Inventor's Assn. St. Louis (bd. dirs. 1989-94, 1st v.p. 1991), Family Firm Inst. (internat. conf. chair, 1995), Fenton Jaycees (treas.), Exec. Club (St. Louis, moderator 1973-86), Pi Kappa Alpha (dist. pres. 1969-74, faculty adv. 1990—, recipient disting. svc. award 1972, bd. dirs., treas., endowment found. nat. coun. for youth and religion, 1994—). Avocations: swimming, sailing, camping. Home: 10000 Hilltop Dr Saint Louis MO 63128-1512 E-mail: brockhau@slu.edu.

BROCKHOUSE, BERTRAM NEVILLE, physicist, retired educator; b. Lethbridge, Alta., Can., July 15, 1918; s. Israel Bertram and Mable Emily (Neville) Brockhouse; m. Doris Isobel Mary Miller, May 22, 1948; children: Ann, Gordon, Ian, James, Alice Elizabeth, Charles. BA, U. B.C., 1947; MA, U. Toronto, 1948, PhD, 1950; DSc (hon.), U. Waterloo, 1969, McMaster U., 1984, U. Toronto, 1995, U. B.C., Can., 1996; Doctor of Laws (hon.), Dalhousie U., 1996; D Arts and Scis (hon.), U Lethbridge, 1997. Research officer Atomic Energy of Can., Ltd., Chalk River, 1950—59, br. head, neutron physics, 1960—62; chmn. dept. physics McMaster U., 1967—70, prof. physics, 1962—84, prof. emeritus, 1984—. Contbr. sci. articles on neutron physics and condensed matter physics to profl. jours. Served Royal Can. Navy Vol. Res., 1939—45. Recipient Centennial medal of Can., 1967, Queen's Jubilee medal, 1977, Order of Can., 1982, Companion, 1995, Duddell medal and prize, Inst. Physics and Phys.Soc., 1963, Nobel prize in Physics, 1994; fellow Guggenheim, 1970—71; grantee NRC of Can., 1962—78. Mem.: Royal Swedish Acad. Scis. (fgn. mem. 1984—), Am. Acad. Arts and Scis. (hon. fgn. mem.), Am. Phys. Soc. (Buckley prize 1962), Can. Assn. Physicists (achievement in physics 1967), Royal Soc. London, Royal Soc. Can. (Tory Medal 1973). Roman Catholic. Home: 222 Silverbirch Blvd Mount Hope ON Canada L0R 1W0

BROCKINGTON, DONALD LESLIE, anthropologist, archaeologist, educator; b. Weslaco, Tex., Apr. 28, 1929; s. Buford Maurice and M. Juanita (Young) B.; m. Lolita Gutierrez, Dec. 19, 1955; children: Laura Alicia, John Carlos, Peter Daniel. BA, U. N.Mex., 1954; student, U. Calif.-Berkeley, 1953; MA, Mexico City Coll., 1956-57; PhD, U. Wis., 1965. Nstr., adminstrv. asst. Mexico City Coll., 1956—57; asst. prof. San Diego State Coll., 1963—67; assoc. prof. anthropology to prof. U. N.C., Chapel Hill, 1967—96, chmn. dept. anthropology, 1980—85, prof. emeritus, 1996—; dir. hwy. archaeology Wis. State Hist. Soc., Madison, 1960—62; museum evaluator various pub. cos., 1969—. Cons. Museum Archaeology, Cochabamba, Bolivia, 1982—. Served with U.S. Army, 1951-53. Mexico City Coll. fellow, 1956-57, U. Wis. fellow, 1959-63, 65, Bobbs-Merrill fellow, NSF fellow, 1963, 68, 70, U. N.C. fellow, 1968, 71, 74, 76, 84, 86-89; Nat. Geog. Soc. grantee, 1984—. Fellow Soc. Am. Archaeology. Home: 808 Tinkerbell Rd Chapel Hill NC 27517

BROCKLEY, JOHN P. airport terminal executive; Dir. aviation Port of Portland, Oreg. Home: 2077 Bay Meadows Drive West Linn OR 97068-2288

BROCKMAN, LESLIE RICHARD, social worker; b. St. Paul, Aug. 10, 1940; s. Leslie Blair Brockman and Mary Emma (Miller) Hemenway; m. Rosemarie Lemus, Aug. 18, 1962; 1 child, Christopher Scott. BA, Loyola U. of L.A., 1963; MS, Troy (Ala.) State U., 1977; MS in Social Work, U. Tex., Arlington, 1984. Lic. profl. counselor; lic. chem. dependency counselor, marriage and family therapist, master social worker; advanced clin. practitioner ACSW; diplomate clin. social work; cert. criminal justice specialist. Exec. dir. Family Assessment Consultation Therapy Svc., Ft. Worth, 1984—; commd. 2d lt. USAF, 1963, advanced through grades to maj., retired, 1983. Fellow NASW (diplomate); mem. ACA, Am. Assn. Marriage and Family Therapists, Am. Mental Health Counselors Assn., Am. Assn. Behavioral Therapists. Home: 6400 Trail Lake Dr Fort Worth TX 76133-4810 Office: FACTS Inc 5801 Curzon Ave Ste 2B Fort Worth TX 76107-5896

BROCKMAN, WILLIAM S. librarian; b. Paterson, N.J., June 2, 1950; s. Harry A. and Irene M. Brockman; m. Ann W. Copeland, Aug. 10, 1985; children: Peter, Daniel. AB, Rutgers U., 1972, MLS, 1977; MA, Drew U., 1986. Reference libr. Rutgers U., New Brunswick, N.J., 1976-77, Drew U., Madison, N.J., 1977-89; English libr. U. Ill., Urbana, 1989-2001; Paterno family libr. for lit. Pa. State U., University Park, 2001—. Bibliographer James Joyce Quar., Tulsa, 1990—. Author: Music: a Guide to the Reference Literature, 1987 (rsch. award N.J. Libr. Assn. 1987); contbr. articles to profl. jours., including James Joyce Quar., Joyce Studies Ann., Jour. Modern Lit., Dictionary Lit. Biography, Analytical and Enumerative Bibliography. Mem.: MLA, ALA, Internat. James Joyce Found., Soc. for History Authorship, Reading and Pub., Biblog. Soc. Am. Office: Pa State U W329 Pattee Libr University Park PA 16802

BROCKMANN, STEPHEN MATTHEW, education educator; b. N.Y.C., N.Y., Sept. 4, 1960; s. Karen and Henry Caruthers Brockmann. AB, Columbia U., 1978—82; MA, PhD, U. of Wis., 1983—89. Vis. asst. prof. Columbia U., 1989—90, Mich. State U., 1991—92, Brown U., 1992—93; assoc. prof. German, Carnegie Mellon U., Pitts., 1993—. Mng. editor Brecht Yearbook, Pitts., 2002—. Author: (scholarly monograph) Lit. and German Reunification. Fellow stipend, Alexander von Humboldt Found., 1999, 2002, German Academic Exch. Svc., 1996. Mem.: Internat. Brecht Soc., Am. Assn. of Teachers of German, MLA, German Studies Assn. Avocations: travel, hiking. Office: Carnegie Mellon University BH 160 5000 Forbes Ave Pittsburgh PA 15213

BROCKS, ERIC, ophthalmologist, surgeon; b. N.Y.C., Apr. 24, 1946; s. William Benjamin and Muriel (Welk) B.; m. Irene Loretta Kraut, Dec. 19, 1970; children: Jason Matthew, Daniel Charles. BA with high honors, U. Rochester, 1968, MD, 1972. Diplomate Am. Bd. Ophthalmology, Nat. Bd. Med. Examiners. Intern medicine NYU Sch. Medicine, N.Y.C., 1973, resident, chief resident ophthalmology, 1973-76; chief resident ophthalmology Bellevue Hosp., NYU Hosp., Manhattan VA Hosp., N.Y.C., 1975-76; attending physician St. Francis Hosp., Beacon, N.Y., 1976-89; asst./assoc. attending physician Vassar Bros. Med. Ctr., Poughkeepsie, NY, 1976-80; attending physician Vassar Bros. Hosp., Poughkeepsie, N.Y., 1980—; clin. asst. ophthalmology Tisch (NYU) Hosp., N.Y.C., 1976—; clin. asst. attending physician Bellevue Hosp. Ctr., N.Y.C., 1976 —; eye physician and surgeon Hudson Valley Eye Surgeons, P.C., Fishkill, NY, 1976—, pres., 2000—; med. dir. laser vision correction LCA Vision Laser Assocs., Mt. Kisco, NY, 1996—98; bd. dirs. Fishkill Ambulatory Surgical Ctr., NY, 2001—. Cons. ophthalmology Julia Butterfield Hosp., Cold Spring, NY, 1981—94, West Point (N.Y.) Mil. Acad., Keller Army Hosp., 1989—96; chief surgery St. Francis Hosp., Beacon, 1988—89, dir. ophthalmology sect., 1981—88, chief of staff, 1979—81; dir. dept. ophthalmology Vassar Bros. Hosp., 1992—2000, mem. peer rev. com., 1994—; clin. asst. prof. ophthalmology NYU Sch. Medicine, N.Y.C., 1983—, course dir. ophthalmology elective, 1976—91; so. N.Y. coord. Nat. Eye Care Project, San Francisco, 1985—; adj. clin. asst. prof. ophthalmology Mt. Sinai Sch. Medicine, N.Y.C., 1993—; mem. adv. bd. Fishkill Ambulatory Surgery Ctr., 2000—, mem. med. exec. com., 2001—. Contbr. articles to profl. jours. Vol. admissions network U. Rochester, 1986-2000, co-chmn. 25th reunion com., 1993. Recipient 25 Yr. faculty svc. citation, NYU Sch. Medicine, 2001, Practice of Excellence, Laser Vision Ctr., 2001. Fellow ACS, Am. Acad. Ophthalmology (media coord. N.Y. state Nat. Eye Care projects 1978—, mem. pub. info. coun. 1985—, mem. refractive surgery interest group 1996—); mem. AMA, Am. Soc. Cataract and Refractive Surgery, Med. Soc. State N.Y. (mem. ho. dels. 1984-89, 93-96, mem. subcom. officers and adminstrv. matters 1994, mem. govt. affairs subcom. 1987, mem. fed. legis. com. 1993—), Dutchess County Med. Soc. (mem. exec. com. 1992-96, chmn. legis. liaison com. 1990-92, pres. 1990-91), Boca West Club. Avocations: tennis, golf, reading, family travel. Office: Hudson Valley Eye Surgeons Vassar Bros Med Mall 200 Westage Bus Center Dr Fishkill NY 12524 E-mail: eyes@hves.com.

BROCKWAY, DAVID HUNT, lawyer; b. Paterson, N.J., Dec. 18, 1943; s. George Pond and Lucille (Hunt) B.; m. Marilyn Bofshever, July 29, 1979. AB, Cornell U., 1968; JD, Harvard U., 1971. Bar: N.Y. 1972, Washington 1990. Assoc. firm Donovan Leisure Newton & Irvine, N.Y.C., 1971-76; legis. atty. Joint Com. on Taxation, U.S. Congress, Washington, 1976, internat. tax counsel, 1978, deputy chief of staff, 1981, chief of staff, 1983-87; ptnr. Dewey Ballantine, Washington, N.Y.C., 1987-99, co-chmn. tax dept., 1997-99. Mem. Am. Law Inst. Project on Sub-chpt. C., 1988—; mem. adv. bd. European Am. Tax Inst., 1989—; cons. Am. Law Inst. Project on Tax Treaties, 1989—; bd. dirs. Nat. Fgn. Trade Coun., 1993—; GE (Bermuda) Ltd., 1993-99. With U.S. Army, 1963-66. Recipient Outstanding Achievement award NYU Tax. Soc., 1998—. Mem. N.Y. State Bar Assn. (exec. com. tax sect. 1988-89, 94—). Home: 2829 Woodland Dr NW Washington DC 20008-2743 Office: KPMG LLP 2001 M St NW Washington DC 20036-3310

BROCKWAY, LAURIE SUE, editor, journalist, author, minister; b. N.Y.C., Dec. 18, 1956; d. Lee L. and Shirley Ruth Brockway; 1 child, Alexander Kent Garrett. AA, Laguardia C.C., 1978; student in Arts, Hunter Coll. CUNY, 1978-81; MSC, The New Seminary, 1999. Features editor, crime reporter The Bklyn. Paper, 1978-81; editor-in-chief The Iniator, N.Y.C., 1982-83; pub., editor The Transformer, N.Y.C., 1983-84; co-prodr., writer The Brockway Good News Report, N.Y.C., 1984-85; N.Y. bur. chief Women's News, N.Y.C., 1983-85, Manhattan corr., 1985—2000, mng. editor, 1990; account supr. Brockway Assocs., Inc., N.Y.C., 1985-88. Tchr. women's sexuality, spirituality, 1990—; mem. faculty The Seminar Ctr., 1998—. Author: Network Your Way to Endless Romance, 1998, How to Seduce a Man and Keep Him Seduced, 1999, A Goddess Is a Girl's Best Friend, 2002. Recipient LaGuardia Meml. award, 1978, LaGuardia Student Coun. scholar, 1978, Expository Writing award, LaGuardia English Dept., 1978, Woman of Achievement award Women's News, 1997. Home and Office: 83-27 159th St Jamaica NY 11432

BROCKWAY, STEPHEN SWIFT, psychiatrist, addiction medicine specialist; b. Lansing, Mich., Nov. 22, 1949; s. Carl Bernard and Helen Kenney (Smith) B.; m. Karen Brockway; children: Ross, R.J., Nicole, Ben. BA, Dartmouth Coll., 1971; MD, Med. Coll. Wis., 1975. Diplomate Am. Bd. Adolescent Psychiatry, Am. Bd. Psychiatry and Neurology, Am. Soc. Addiction Medicine, Am. Assn. Psychiatrist in Addiction. Staff psychiatrist The Med. Ctr. Clin., Pensacola, Fla., 1978-83; dir. alcohol dependency treatment program Prescott (Ariz.) VA Med. Ctr., 1983-84; dir. combat stress program Phoenix VA Med. Ctr., 1984-88; dir. adult & chem. dependency programs Charter Hosp. of East Valley, Chandler, Ariz., 1988-92; dir. chem. dependency program East Valley Camelback Hosp., Mesa, Ariz., 1991-92; med. dir. The Meadows, Wickenburg, Ariz., 1992—2002. Med. dir. Lifegate Adolescent Treatment Ctr., Phoenix, 1990-92, Bethany Cmty. Ch. Counseling Ctr., Mesa, 1990-92. Contbr. articles to profl. jours. Bd. dirs. St. Francis Meth. Ch., Tucson, 1975-78. Fellow Am. Psychiat. Assn.; mem. Am. Soc. Addiction Medicine (sec. Ariz. chpt. 1996—), Am. Soc. Psychiatrists in Addiction Medicine. Republican. Avocations: horseback riding, poetry, hiking, writing. Office: The Meadows 1655 N Tegner St Wickenburg AZ 85390-1461 E-mail: docbrock22@aol.com.

BROCKWELL, PETER JOHN, statistics educator; b. Melbourne, Australia, Oct. 12, 1937; s. Jack Ellery and Cardia Leo Brockwell; m. Pamela Audrey B., Feb. 6, 1965; children: Anthony Edward, Matthew James, Harold Peter. BA with honors, B in Elec. Engring., U. Melbourne, 1960, MA, 1962; PhD, Australian Nat. U., Canberra, 1967. Asst. mathematician Argonne Nat. Lab., Chgo., 1967-70; assoc. prof. stats. Mich. State U., East Lansing, 1971-73; prof. stats. LaTrobe U., Melbourne, 1973-76, Colo. State U., Ft. Collins, 1976—. Prof. stats. U. Melbourne, 1988-89, Royal Melbourne Inst. Tech., 1993-96; von Neumann vis. prof. Munich U. Tech., 2001-02. Author: Time Series: Theory and Methods, 1987, 91, Introduction to Time Series and Forecasting, 1996; contbr. over 80 articles to profl. jours.; editor Advances in Applied Probability, 1982-89; editl. bd. Stochastic Models, 1984-97, Annals of Stats., 1998-99, Jour. Time Series Analysis, 1997—, Jour. Japanese Statis. Soc., 2000—. Fellow Am. Statis. Assn., Inst. Math. Stats.; mem. Internat. Statis. Inst. Office: Colo State U Dept Statistics Fort Collins CO 80523 E-mail: pjbrock@stat.colostate.edu.

BROD, EVELYN FAY, foreign language educator; b. Cin., Apr. 23, 1942; d. Joseph Theodore and Freda Edith (Mandell) B. BA in Spanish magna cum laude, BS in Secondary Edn., U. Cin., 1964, MA in Spanish, 1966, MEd, 1975, postgrad. Cert. secondary tchr., Ohio, cert. guidance counselor, Ohio. Teaching asst. U. Cin., 1964-67, 69-70, instr. in Spanish, 1970-75, asst. prof., 1975-80, assoc. prof., 1980-89, prof., 1989—; instr. in Spanish Mount Union Coll., Alliance, Ohio, 1967-69. Vice chair faculty and faculty senate U. Cin., 1989-90, 93-94, 96-98, 98-2000, mem. faculty devel. coun., 1996-2002, mem. provostal search com., 1999, gen. edn. coord. com., 1999-2003; faculty rep. to U. Cin. Bd. Trustees, 1999-2001, 2001-03. Author: (poetry) Mirage, 1978, (book) Viajemos 2001: Repaso y Progreso text, workbook and tchr.'s manual, 1990; contbr. articles to profl. jours. Mem. alumni adv. coun. Walnut Hills High Sch., Cin., 1997—. Mem. AAUP, Am. Assn. Tchrs. Spanish and Portuguese (editor Enlace 1986-90), Ohio Fgn. Lang. Assn., Am. Coun. on Tchg. of Fgn. Langs., Phi Beta Kappa, Alpha Lambda Delta, Sigma Delta Pi, Kappa Delta Pi. Avocations: reading, travel, drawing, painting. Office: U Cin Raymond Walters Coll 9555 Plainfield Rd Cincinnati OH 45236-1007 E-mail: evelyn.brod@uc.edu.

BROD, MORTON SHELVIN, oral surgeon; b. Bklyn., Apr. 19, 1926; s. Joseph and Celina (Fromberg) B.; m. Anne Turville Bigelow, June 3, 1955; children: Brian Seth, Timothy Andrew, Abbe Rena. Student, U.S. Mil. Acad., 1947-48; BA, Adelphi Coll., 1951; DDS, Columbia U., 1955. Diplomate Am. Bd. Oral Surgery, Am. Bd. Forensic Dentistry. Intern oral surgery Columbia Presbyn. Med. Ctr., N.Y.C., 1955-56; resident oral surgery Bronx VA Hosp., N.Y.C., 1956-58; pvt. practice oral surgery Norwalk, Conn., 1958-98. Attending oral surgeon chief dental service Norwalk Hosp.; attending oral surgeon Bellevue Hosp; attending surgeon Seaview Hosp., St. Barnabas Hosp.; cons. Manhattan State Hosp., Bronx State Hosp., Psychiat. Inst. N.Y.; instr. dentistry div. clin. oral physiology Columbia Sch. Dental and Oral Surgery, N.Y.C., 1957-69, asst. prof. denistry, 1969-72, assoc. prof., 1972-84, rsch. assoc. dept. stomatology, 1968-84; mem. dental mission to Govt. Anguilla, West Indies, 1969, 70, 71; assoc. prof. dentistry NYU; dir. clin. rev.-oral surgery Physicians Health Svcs.; lectr., Eng., Russia, China, Japan; assoc. prof. oral and maxiofacial surgery NYU Coll. Dentistry, 1993. Contbr. articles to profl. jours., textbooks. Sec. Westport Flood and Erosion Control Bd.; capt. CAP Flying Sharks Search and Rescu Squadron, Conn., 1968—; exec. com. Boy Scouts Am., Westport; mem. Westport Rep. Town Meeting, chmn. pub. works com.; trustee Westport-Weston br. Am. Cancer Soc.; bd. dirs. Norwalk Bd. Dental Health Clinic; dir. Westport Transit Dist., Precision Closure Corp., Auto-Grip Corp.; v.p., treas. Riverview E. Assocs. Real Estate, Inc.; mem. Southwestern Regional Planning Agy., Fairfield County adv. bd. Bridgeport Hydraulic Co. With USAF, 1943-47. Fellow Am. Coll. Oral Surgeons, Am. Soc. Oral Surgeons, Internat. Soc. Oral Surgeons, N.Y. Acad. Dentistry, Am. Coll. Forensic Examiners; mem. ADA, New Eng. Soc. Oral Surgeons, Conn. Soc. Oral Surgeons, Am. Soc. Dentistry for Children (pres. Fairfield County sect. 1962-63), Am. Acad. History Dentistry, Fedn. Dentaire Internat., N.Y. Acad. Scis., N.Y. State Dental Soc., Norwalk Dental Soc. (exec. com. 1966-67, pres. 1967-68), Christian Dental Soc., Flying Dentists Assn., Airplane Owners and Pilots Assn., Pilots Internat. Assn., Fairways Homeowners Assn. (mem. fin. and audit com.). Home and Office: 10 Rosewood Dr Lakewood NJ 08701-5709

BROD, ROY DAVID, ophthalmologist, educator; b. Phila., Oct. 8, 1957; s. Kenneth Lester and Carlene Marcy (Chalick) B.; m. Janice Hope Prossack, May 7, 1983; children: Jamie, Rebecca. BS in Biochemistry magna cum laude, Tulane U., 1979; MD with honors, Temple U., 1983. Diplomate Am. Bd. Ophthalmology. Intern Presbyn. U. Pa. Med. Ctr., Phila., 1983-84; resident in ophtholmology La. State U. Eye Ctr., New Orleans, 1984-87; fellow in vitreoretinal Bascom Palmer Eye Inst., Miami, Fla., 1987-88; assoc. vitreoretinal surgeon Geisinger Med. Ctr., Danville, Pa., 1988-91; pvt. practice Lancaster, Pa., 1991—. Asst. prof. Thomas Jefferson U. Sch. Medicine, Phila., 1991-92; clin. asst. prof. Pa. State U. Sch. Medicine-Hershey Med. Ctr., 1992-95, clin. assoc. prof., 1995—; presenter in field. Contbr. articles to med. jours., chpts. to books. Recipient Outstanding Tchr. award Geisinger Med. Ctr., 1990, 91; Tulane scholar, 1976, E.J. and Sarah Evans scholar, 1979, scholar Measy Found., 1982; named among Best Doctors in Am., 2000. Fellow Am. Acad. Ophthlmology (Honor award 1998); mem. AMA, Assn. for Rsch. in Vision and Ophthalmology, Vitreous Soc. (exec. com.), Retina Soc., Rsch. To Prevent Blindness, Soc. for Contemplation Fascinating Fluorescein Angiograms, Atlantic Coast Vitreoretinal Study Group, Atlantic Coast Fluorescein Angiography Club, Pa. Med. Soc., Pa. Acad. Ophthalmology, Phi Beta Kappa, Alpha Omega Alpha, Phi Eta Sigma, Alpha Epsilon Delta, Omicron Delta Kappa. Avocations: sailing, tennis, bicycling. Office: PO Box 3200 Ste 310 2108 Medical Offices Lancaster PA 17604-3200 E-mail: RYJN@aol.com.

BROD, STANFORD, graphic designer, educator; b. Cin., Sept. 29, 1932; s. Morris and Rebecca (Mitman) B.; m. McCrystle Wood; children: Deborah, Daniel, Michael. BS in Design, U. Cin., 1955. Graphic designer Rhoades Studio, Cin., 1955-62; tchr. exptl. typography Art Acad. Cin., 1960-75; graphic designer Lipson, Alport & Glass Assocs., Inc. and predecessor firm Lipson Jacob, Assocs. Inc., Cin., 1962-94, Wood/Brod Design, Cin., 1994—; prof. graphic design U. Cin., 1962—. Tchr. illustration and packaging Art Acad. Cin., 1991-92, 94, 96-98, 2001-03, tchr. corp. identity, 1992-97, 2002-03, tchr. advt. design, corp. design, 1994-97, tchr. visual comms., 1997-98, exhbn. design, 1999, 2002. Exhibited in group shows at Mus. Modern Art, N.Y.C., 1966, Urban Walls, Cin., 1972, City Banners, Sao Paulo, Brazil, 1975, ITC Ctr., N.Y.C., 1981, Tel Aviv Mus., 1982, Internat. Art Exhbn., Dusseldorf, Germany, 1982, Calligraphia U.S.A./USSR, 1990-96, UN, 1994; one-man shows include Skirball Mus. Hebrew Union Coll., Cin., 1989. Recipient Communications Arts awards, 1959, 64, 66, 70, 73, 76, Creativity on Paper awards, 1960-67, Internat. Typographic awards, 1965, 70, N.Y. Type Dirs. Club award, 1968, Typographic Composition Assn. awards, 1970-76. Office: 3662 Grandin Rd Cincinnati OH 45226-1117 *The more I design and paint the more I am sensitive to the movement of my pen, computer and brush, and am able to transmit the image of the subject in my head by way of my arm into my hand, and so to my work. I have become aware that pressure demands counter-pressure, and the difference between order and chaos. This points out the importance of the smallest detail, and that order is the basis of all creative work.*

BRODAX, ALBERT PHILIP, writer, film producer and director; b. N.Y.C., Feb. 14, 1926; s. Herman and Lillian H. (Joss) Brodax; m. Joan Francine Greenberg, June 24, 1951; children: Daniel Seth, Douglas Aaron, Jessica. Student, Alfred U.; BA, U. Wis., 1948. Program devel. staff The William Morris Agy., N.Y.C., 1950-60; creator, head motion picture/TV dept. King Features Syndicate, divsn. Hearst Corp., 1960-69; self-employed prodr./writer/lyricist/dir., 1979—80; cons. Marvel Comics, 1980-82, Computer Graphics Labs., Inc., 1983—. Writer : (films, tv) Danger; writer (tv films) Climax; writer : (films, tv) Suspense; co-prodr.: (Broadway plays) Winesburg, Ohio; prodr.(writer): (films) Beatle's Yellow Submarine (32 Best Picture of Yr. awards); (TV series) over 500 animations including 220 Popeyes, Barney Google, Krazy Kat, Beatles Cartoon, (co-creator (with Bob Kane) Cool McCool. With U.S. Army, ETO. Decorated Purple Heart, Bronze Star; recipient award, N.Y. Critics, Bellringer award, Scholastic mag. Home: 45 Cedar Hls Weston CT 06883-2948 E-mail: a.j.brodax@optonline.net.

BRODBECK, WILLIAM JAN, marketing consultant, speaker; b. Platteville, Wis., Feb. 14, 1944; s. Richard W. and Helen (Stoneman) B.; m. Janet Piwonka, Feb. 4, 1967; children: Allison S., Courtney K., Stephanie L. BA, Hillsdale (Mich.) Coll., 1966. Asst. to v.p. Hillsdale Coll., 1966-68; mgr. advt. Brodbeck Enterprises, Inc., Platteville, 1968-72, v.p., 1972-79, pres., CEO, 1980-96; pres. Relationship Mktg., Sanibel, Fla., 1996—. Gov. Uniform Product Code Coun., Dayton, Ohio, 1977-86; chmn. First Nat. Bank, Platteville, 1986-92. Contbr. articles to profl. jours. Chmn. Third Congl. Dist. Reagan Campaign, 1976; pres. Platteville Area Indsl. Devel., 1976-79; bd. dirs. Thursday's Child, Madison, Wis., 1983-96, Wis. Shakespeare Festival, Platteville, 1986-96, CROW (Care & Rehab. of Wildlife), 1999-2002; trustee Hillsdale Coll., 1991—, chmn. presdl. search com., 1999-2000, vice chmn., 2000-2003, chmn., 2003—; bd. dirs. Neenah Springs, Inc., Oxford, Wis., 1997—, Noodles and Co., Boulder, Colo., 1998—; mem. bd. govs. The Sanctuary, 1999-2001, v.p., 2001-2003, pres., 2003—; mem. nat. adv. coun. The Heritage Found., Washington, 2003—. Mem. Nat. Grocers Assn. (bd. dirs. 1977-85), Food Mktg. Inst. (bd. dirs. 1982-96, mem. efficient consumer response exec. com. 1993-96), U. Wis. Platteville Found. (pres. 1980-81), Platteville C. of C. (pres. 1972-73), Omicron Delta Kappa (chpt. v.p. 1966). Office: Relationship Mktg 2964 Wulfert Rd Sanibel FL 33957-2213 E-mail: wjbrod@aol.com.

BRODELL, ROBERT THOMAS, internal medicine educator; b. Rochester, N.Y., Nov. 24, 1953; s. Harold Louis and Alma Jean (Moreland) B.; m. Linda P. Brodell, July 2, 1977; children: Lindsey Ann, Julie Lynn, David William, Erin Elizabeth, Nathan Thomas. BA, Washington and Jefferson Coll., 1975; MD, U. Rochester, 1979. Bd. cert. in dermatology and dermatopathology. Asst. prof. dermatology Washington U., St. Louis, 1984-85; asst. prof. internal medicine Northeastern Ohio U. Coll. Medicine, Rootstown, Ohio, 1986-90, 1990-94, prof. internal medicine, 1994—, master tchr., 1997—. Asst. clin. prof. dermatology Case Western Res. U., Cleve., 1986-94, assoc. clin. prof., 1994—; chmn. Midwest Congress Derm. Socs., Dayton, Ohio, 1995—. Trustee Ohio divsn. Am. Cancer Soc., Columbus, 1992—; bd. dirs. Warren (Ohio) Sports Hall of Fame, 1996. Named Cleve. Cavaliers Profl. Basketball Team Fan of Year, 1997. Fellow Am. Acad. Dermatology, Am. Soc. Dermatopathology; mem. AMA, Ohio State Med. Assn., Wilderness Med. Assn., Ohio Dermatol. Assn. (trustee 1994—), Am. Cancer Soc. (v.p. Ohio divsn. 1999-2000, pres. Ohio divsn. 2000—), Masons (Master Old Erie # 3), Phi Beta Kappa, Alpha Omega Alpha. Home: 2660 E Market St Warren OH 44483-6204 Office: Northeastern Ohio Univ Coll Med PO Box 95 4209 State Route 44 Rootstown OH 44272-9698 E-mail: rtb@neoucom.edu.

BRODEN, JOHN E. state legislator; m. Josephine Broden; children: Ana Marie, John Francis. BA, U. Notre Dame; JD, Ind. U. Atty. Botkin & Leone Attys. at Law; city atty. South Bend; mem. Ind. State Senate, 2000—, mem. corrections, criminal and civil procedures com., mem. environ. affairs com., mem. govtl. and regulatory affairs local govt. subcom., mem. pub. policy, pub. affairs subcom. Councilman South Bend City County, 1995-98; active St. Joseph's H.S. Alumni Bd.; bd. dirs. South Bend Ctr. for the Homeless, CHIARA Home. Mem. Ind. State Bar Assn., South Bend Kiwanis Club. Roman Catholic. Avocations: running, golf, reading. Office: 200 W Washington St Indianapolis IN 46204-2785

BRODER, DAVID SALZER, reporter, writer; b. Chicago Heights, Ill., Sept. 11, 1929; s. Albert I. and Nina M. (Salzer) B.; m. Ann Creighton Collar, June 8, 1951; children: George, Joshua, Matthew, Michael. BA, U. Chgo., 1947, MA, 1951; LittD, Denison U., 1975; LLD (hon.), Wabash Coll., 1977, Kenyon Coll., 1980, Cleve. State U., 1981, Wittenberg Coll., 1982, Yale U., 1984, Ind. U., 1985, Kalamazoo Coll., 1988, Rider Coll., 1989, Dartmouth Coll., 1990, Colby Coll., 1990, Lawrence U., 1991, Bates Coll., 1992; LLD (hon.), Stetson U., 1993, U. Mich., 1994, Coll. of William & Mary, 1995, Am. U., 1997; DLitt, Gov.'s State U., 1994; LLD (hon.), 2001, North Central Coll., 2002; D in Polit. Sci. (hon.), DePauw U., 2003. Reporter Pantagraph, Bloomington, Ill., 1953-55, Congressional Quar., Washington, 1955-60, Washington Star, 1960-65, N.Y. Times, Washington bur., 1965-66; reporter Washington Post, 1966-75, assoc. editor, 1975—; syndicated columnist. Prof. journalism U. Md., 2001—. Author: (with Stephen Hess) The Republican Establishment, 1967, The Party's Over: The Failure of Politics in America, 1972, Changing of the Guard: Power and Leadership in America, 1980, Behind the Front Page: A Candid Look at How the News is Made, 1987, (with Bob Woodward) The Man Who Would be President: Dan Quayle, 1992, (with Haynes Johnson) The System: The American Way of Politics at the Breaking Point, 1996, Democracy Derailed: Initiative Campaigns and the Power of Money, 2000; contbr. articles on pub. affairs to mags. and books. Former mem. U. Chgo. Alumni cabinet. Served with AUS, 1951-53. Recipient Pulitzer prize in journalism, 1973, Common Wealth award, Elijah Parrish Lovejoy award, 1990, William Allen White medal U. Kans., 1997, Lifetime Achievement award Nat. Soc. Newspaper Columnists, 1997; fellow Inst. Politics, John F. Kennedy Sch. of Govt., Harvard U., 1969-70; Poynter fellow Yale and Ind. univs., 1973 Fellow Inst. Policy Scis. and Pub. Affairs of Duke, Am. Acad. Arts and Scis., Sigma Delta Chi; mem. Am. Polit. Sci. Assn. (adv. bd. Congrl. Fellows Program 1964—, Carey McWilliams award 1983), Am. Soc. Pub. Adminstrn., Nat. Press Club (4th Estate award 1988), Gridiron Club. Home: 4024 27th St N Arlington VA 22207-5207 Office: Washington Post 1150 15th St NW Washington DC 20071-0002

BRODER, DOUGLAS FISHER, lawyer; b. Cleve., Sept. 30, 1948; s. Harry M. and Peggy (Fisher) B.; m. Rebecca Northey, Jan. 24, 1976; 1 child, Julia N. BA, Vassar Coll., 1970; JD cum laude, Boston U., 1977. Bar: N.Y. 1978, U.S. Dist. Ct. (so. and ea. dists.) N.Y. 1978, U.S. Ct. Appeals (2d cir.) 1983, U.S. Ct. Appeals (6th cir.) 1986, U.S. Ct. Appeals (4th cir.) 1987, U.S. Dist. Ct. (ea. dist.) Mich. 1987, U.S. Supreme Ct. 1993, U.S. Ct. Appeals (9th cir.) 1997. Assoc. Lord, Day & Lord, N.Y.C., 1977-86; ptnr. Coudert Bros. LLP, N.Y.C., 1986—2002, Nixon Peabody LLP, 2002—. Spkr. and lectr. on continuing legal edn. Author: Antitrust Law Desk Book, 2001; lead editor: "International Joint Ventures" Professional Information Publishing Ltd., 1996; mem. editl. bd. European Competition Law Rev.; contbr. articles to profl. publs. Mem. ABA, Assn. of Bar of City of N.Y. Home: 300 Central Park W New York NY 10024-1513 Office: Nixon Peabody LLP 437 Madison Ave New York NY 10022 Business E-Mail: dbroder@nixonpeabody.com.

BRODER, IRVIN, physician, educator; b. Toronto, Ont., Can., June 27, 1930; married, 1954; 3 children. MD, U. Toronto, 1955, FRCP, 1960. Intern Toronto Gen. Hosp., 1955-56; sr. intern Sunnybrook Hosp., Toronto, 1956-57; asst. resident in medicine Toronto Gen. Hosp., 1958-59, resident physician, 1959-60; clin. instr. allergy U. Mich. Med. Ctr., 1960-62, clin. tchr. medicine, 1963-66, assoc., 1966-68, asst. prof., 1968-71, assoc. prof. medicine, 1971-76, prof. medicine Gage Rsch. Inst., U. Toronto, 1977—. Asst. prof. pharmocology U. Mich., 1965-75, asst. prof. pathology, 1965-80; dir. Gage Rsch. Inst., U. Toronto, 1971-95, prof. pathology, 1980-90, prof. occupl. and environ. health, 1982—; resident fellow endocrinology, dept. pathology U. Toronto, 1957-58; resident fellow immunology, dept. pharmacology U. Coll., London, 1962-63; rsch. scholar Med. Rsch. Coun. Can., 1963-66, career investigator, 1966-94; mem. Inst. Med. Sci., Inst. Immunology, U. Toronto, 1971-82. Mem. Can. Med. Assn., Can. Soc. Allergy and Clin. Immunology, Can. Thoracic Soc., Can. Soc. Clin. Investigation, Can. Soc. Immunology. Achievements include research on occupational lung disease, on human obstructive airways disease, and on environmental health issues. Office: Gage Occupl & Environ 223 College St Toronto ON Canada M5T 1R4

BRODER, JOSEPH ARNOLD, lawyer; b. Hartford, Conn., Jan. 19, 1939; s. Morris H. and Dora (Levine) B.; m. Andrea I. Goldstein, Feb. 23, 1967, 1 child, Michael. AB, Trinity Coll., 1960; JD, Harvard U., 1963. Bar: Conn. 1963, N.Y. 1964, U.S. Dist. Ct. Conn. 1965, U.S. Military Ct. 1968, U.S. Supreme Ct. 1976. Assoc. Dammann, Blank, Hirsh & Heming, N.Y.C., 1964-65, Broder & Broder, Colchester, Conn., 1965; pvt. practice Colchester, 1966-80; sr. ptnr. Broder & Butts, Colchester, 1981—. Dir. Yankee Inst. for Pub. Policy Studies, 1993—; corporator Norwich (Conn.) Savs. Soc., 1982-87; bd. dirs., v.p. Colchester Publs., 1982-88. Mem. Conn. Ho. of Reps., 1981-82; mem. Rep. State Ctrl.Com., 1980-81, 87-93; mem. Glastonbury (Conn.) City Coun., 1993-97. Comdr. USNR ret. Mem. ABA, ATLA, Conn. Bar Assn., Nat. Acad. Elder Law Attys., Am. Legion, Rotary Internat. Avocations: tennis, skiing, hunting, fishing, flying. Home: PO Box 208 East Glastonbury CT 06025-0208 Office: Broder & Butts PO Box 270 188 Norwich Ave Colchester CT 06415-1256

BRODER, MICHAEL S. psychologist; b. Phila., Jan. 7, 1946; m. Arlene Goldman; 1 child, Joanne. BA in Psychology, Goddard Coll., 1974; MEd in Ednl. Psychology, Temple U., 1976, PhD in Psychology, 1980. Lic. psychologist, Pa. Pres. Media Psychology Assocs., Phila., 1983—; pvt. practice Phila. Adj. faculty Rowan U., N.J., 1977, Drexel U., Phila., 1979-80, Temple U., Phila., 1981-88, U. Pa., Phila., 1989—, Chestnut Hill Coll., 1993-94, Union Inst., 1993—; instr. Inst. of Awareness, Phila., 1978-84, Temple U., 1978-79,

Gateway, Lansdale, Pa., 1979-81, C.C. Phila., 1980; lectr. Thomas Jefferson U., Phila., 1981; columnist Business Digest, 1979-82, Chain Reaction, 1983-85, Woman's World, Star Magazine, 1987-92, Universal Press Syndicate, First for Women, 1992; cons. Protection Tech., Inc., 1979—, United States Dist. Ct., Ea. Dist. Pa. Probation Ct., 1981-94, Nat. Employee Assistance, Inc., 1986—, Phila. Police Dept.'s Employee Assistance Program, 1988-94; dir., cons. Phila. Inst. Rational/Emotive Therapy, 1981-93; stress mgr. Phila. Police Dept., 1995—; radio program host WIBF, Phila., 1982, WABC, N.Y.C., 1987, WCAU-AM, Phila., 1983-90, ABC Talkradio, 1986-90, NBC Talknet, 1986-90, WOR, N.Y.C., 1991-92, WWDB, Phila., 1980—, WIOQ, Phila., 1995—; TV script cons. Check It Out, 1983-87; presenter APA conv., 1981, 82, 85, 86, 87, 88, 89, 90, 91, Calif. Psychol. Assn., 1982, Assn. Humanistic Psychology conf., 1982, 84, 91, various others; appeared on various radio and TV programs. Author: (books) An Eclectic Approach to Primal Integration, 1976, translated into Italian, 1977, Living Single After the Sexual Revolution, 1988, The Art of Living Single, 1990, The Art of Staying Together, 1993, 94, (cassette series) Positive Attitude Training, 1992, 93, Self Actualization: Achieving Your Full Potential, 1993, Therapist's Assistant, 2 vols. plus home study course, numerous other audio presentations; contbr. articles to profl. jours. and popular magazines. Recipient Annual Media award Pa. Psychol. Assn., 1987. Fellow Pa. Psychol. Assn. (past. chmn. comm. bd.), Phila. Soc. Clin. Psychologists (bd. dirs.); mem. APA (past pres., divsn. 46), AFTRA, Nat. Assn. Radio Talk Show Hosts, Nat. Spkrs. Assn., Phila. Writers Orgn., Mensa. Home: 1420 Locust St Apt 7F Philadelphia PA 19102-4205 Office: Media Psychology Assocs 255 S 17th St Ste 2900 Philadelphia PA 19103-6201

BRODERICK, ANTHONY JAMES, air transportation executive; b. N.Y.C., Feb. 23, 1943; s. Anthony James and Geraldine (Cummings) B.; m. Sylvia Fantasia, May 30, 1967; children: Sean, Pia. BS in Physics, St. Bonaventure U., 1964. Project mgr. pvt. industry, various locations, 1964-71; physicist U.S. Dept. Transp., Cambridge, Mass., 1971-76; staff chief environment and energy FAA, Washington, 1976-79, tech. advisor aviation standards dept., 1979-82, dep. assoc. adminstr. aviation standards dept., 1982-85, assoc. adminstr. aviation standards dept., 1985-88, assoc. adminstr. regulation and cert., 1988-96; ind. aviation safety cons., 1996—. Author numerous sci. and tech. articles; patentee in field. Recipient Arthur S. Fleming award Jaycees, 1979, Presdl. Meritorious Exec. Rank award, 1982, Sr. Exec. Svc. awards U.S. Govt., 1983-87, 89-90, 92-95, Presdl. Disting. Exec. Rank award, 1991, Aviation Week Laurel award, 1992, 2000, Flight Internat. Aerospace Personality of Yr. award, 1995, Disting. Career Svc. award Aviation Week/Flight Safety Found., 1996, RTCA achievement award, 1999, ATW Joseph S. Murphy Industry Svc. award, 2000. Roman Catholic. Home: 4711 Dumfries Rd PO Box 119 Catlett VA 20119-0119 E-mail: tonyb@compuserve.com.

BRODERICK, CYRIL EMERY, SR., plant physiologist, educator; b. Greenville, Liberia, June 29, 1951; came to U.S., 1974; s. Nelson William and Sylvia Elizabeth Broderick. BS, U. Liberia, Monrovia, 1970-73; MS, Iowa State U., 1976; PhD, U. N.H., 1982. Assoc. prof. U. Liberia, 1982-88; mgr. botanical rsch. Firestone Plantations Co. in Liberia of Firestone/Bridgestone Syntheti Rubber & Latex Co., Akron, Liberia, 1988-91; assoc. prof. plant physiology Del. State U., Dover, 1991—. Fulbright scholar, 1974-76; recipient Grape Germplasm Excellence award USDA, Washington, 1998. Mem. Am. Soc. Hort. Sci., In-Vitro Biology Soc., Liberian Studies Assn. (pres. 2000—). Achievements include research in food crops, medicinal plants, plant science and biotechnology. Office: Del State U 1200 N Dupont Hwy Dover DE 19901-2202 E-mail: cbroderi@dsc.edu.

BRODERICK, DENNIS JOHN, lawyer, retail company executive; BA, U. Notre Dame, 1970; JD, Georgetown U., 1976. Bar: Ohio 1976. Assoc. Hahn Loeser Freidheim Dean & Wellman, 1976-81; from staff atty. to asst. gen. counsel Firestone Tire & Rubber Co., 1982-87; counsel for regions, v.p. Federated Dept. Stores, Inc. (formerly Allied Stores Corp.), Cin., 1987-88, v.p., gen. counsel, 1988-90, sr. v.p., gen. counsel, sec., 1990—. Mem. Am. Corp. Counsel Assn. (dir. NE Ohio chpt. 1986). Office: Federated Dept Stores Inc 7 W 7th St Cincinnati OH 45202-2424

BRODERICK, JOHN CARUTHERS, retired librarian, educator; b. Memphis, Tenn., Sept. 6, 1926; s. John Patrick and Myrtle Vaughn (Newson) B.; m. Kathryn Price Lynch, Sept. 10, 1949; children: Kathryn Price, John Caruthers, Jr. AB, Rhodes Coll., Memphis, 1948; MA, U. N.C., 1949, PhD, 1953. Instr. English U. Tex., Austin, 1952-57; asst. prof. Wake Forest (N.C.) U., 1957-58, assoc. prof., 1958-63, prof., 1963-65; with Library of Congress, Washington, 1964-88, specialist, 1964-65, asst. chief, 1965-74, chief, manuscript div., 1975-79, asst. librarian for research services, 1979-88. Adj. prof. English George Washington U., 1964-84; vis. prof. U. Va., 1959, U. N.C., 1968, Cath. U. Am., 1990-91. Author: Past Imperfect, Present Tense, 2000; compiler: Whitman The Poet, 1961; editor: The Journal of Henry David Thoreau, 1981-90; contbr. to profl. jours. Adv. com. U.S. Senate Hist. Office, 1974-78; mem. Nat. Hist. Publs. and Records Commn., 1978-82, Christopher Columbus Quincentennial Jubilee Commn., 1986-88. Served with U.S. Army, 1945-46. Danforth Found. grantee, 1960; Am. Coun. Learned Socs. grantee, 1962-63; Coun. on Library Resources fellow, 1971 Mem. Acad. Am. Poets, Am. Antiquarian Soc., Cosmos Club, Lit. Soc. Washington, Sigma Alpha Epsilon, Omicron Delta Kappa. Home: 8005 Inspection House Rd Potomac MD 20854-3426

BRODERICK, JOHN T., JR., state supreme court justice; BA magna cum laude, Coll. Holy Cross, 1969; JD, U. Va., 1972. Atty. Devine, Millimet, Stahl & Branch, Manchester, N.H., 1972 89; shareholder Broderick & Dean (formerly Merrill & Broderick), Manchester, 1989-95; assoc. justice N.H. Supreme Ct., Concord, N.H., 1995—. Bd. dirs. Legal Svcs. Corp. Fellow Am. Coll. Trial Lawyers, N.H. Bar Found. (bd. dirs. 1985-91); mem. ABA, Mass. Bar Assn., N.H. Bar Assn. (bd. govs. 1985-91, pres. 1990-91), N.H. Trial Lawyers Assn. (bd. govs. 1977-82, pres. 1982-83). Office: NH Supreme Ct One Noble Dr Concord NH 03301*

BRODERICK, MATTHEW, actor; b. N.Y.C., Mar. 21, 1962; s. James and Patricia (Biow) B.; m. Sarah Jessica Parker May, 1997, 1 child Student high sch., N.Y.C. Actor: (stage prodns.) Valentine's Day, 1980, Torch Song Trilogy, 1982 (Villager award 1982, Outer Critics Circle award 1982), Brighton Beach Memoirs, 1983 (Los Angeles Critics award 1983, Drama League award 1983, Theatre World award 1983, Antoinette Perry award 1983), Biloxi Blues, 1985, The Widow Claire, 1986-87, How to Succeed in Business Without Really Trying, 1995 (Tony award Lead Actor in a Musical, Outer Critics Cir. award, Drama Desk award), The Producers, 2001-02, 2003; (feature films) Max Dugan Returns, 1983, WarGames, 1983, Ladyhawke, 1985, Ferris Bueller's Day Off, 1986, On Valentine's Day, 1986, Project X, 1987, Biloxi Blues, 1988, Torch Song Trilogy, 1988, Glory, 1989, Family Business, 1989, The Freshman, 1990, Out on a Limb, 1992, The Night We Never Met, 1993, The Lion King (voice), 1994, The Road to Wellville, 1994, Mrs. Parker and the Vicious Circle, 1994, The Cable Guy, 1996, Addicted to Love, 1997, Inspector Gadget, 1999, You Can Count on Me, 2000; prodr., dir., actor (film) Infinity, 1996; voice-over (film) Arabian Knight, 1995, Godzilla, 1998, The Lion King II: Simba's Pride, 1998, Election, 1998, Good Boy!, 2003; teleplays: Master Harold...and the Boys, PBS, 1984, A Life in the Theatre, TNT, 1993 (Emmy nomination, Supporting Actor - Special, 1994). Mem. Actors' Equity Assn., SAG. Address: care CAA 9830 Wilshire Blvd Beverly Hills CA 90212-1804

BRODERSON, THELMA SYLVIA, marketing professional; b. St. Louis, Feb. 6, 1932; d. Harry and Lillian (Fishman) B. BA, U. Denver, 1953; postgrad., Washington U., St. Louis, 2001—. Marketer Marsh & McLennan, Inc., St. Louis, 1966-85; account exec. Daniel & Henry Co., St. Louis, 1985-87; marketer G. Steven DeMaster, Inc. at Crane Agy., St. Louis, 1987-99. Prodr. Harry Fender Program Sta. KMOX-CBS, St. Louis, 1968-74; columnist The Oil Can, 1972-75. Tchr. religious sch. United Hebrew Temple, St. Louis, 1956-63. Donor Harry Fender Memorabilia to St. Louis Pub. Libr. Media Archives and Rare Books Collection, 1997. Mem.: Phi Beta Kappa. Avocations: theater, arts.

BRODEUR, ARMAND EDWARD, pediatric radiologist; b. Penacook, N.H., Jan. 8, 1922; s. Felix and Patronyne Antoinette (Lavoie) B.; m. Gloria Marie Thompson, June 4, 1947; children: Armand Paul, Garrett Michael, Mark Stephen, Mariette Therese, Michelle Bernadette, Paul Francis. AB, St. Anselm Coll., 1945; MD, St. Louis U., 1947, M.Rd., 1952; LLD (hon.), St Anselm Coll., 1974. Intern St. Louis U. Hosps., 1947-48, resident in pediat., 1948-49; resident in radiology St. Louis U. Hosps. and St. Louis U. Grad. Sch., 1949-52; asst. dean. St. Louis Sch. Medicine, 1947, assoc. dean, 1950—52; instr. St. Louis U. Sch. Medicine, 1952-60, sr. instr., 1960-62, asst. prof., 1962-65, assoc. prof., 1965-70, prof. radiology, 1970—, chmn. dept. radiology, 1975-78, vice chmn. dept., 1978-88, prof. pediat., 1979—, prof. juvenile law, 1979—; pvt. practice specializing in pediat. radiology St. Louis, 1954-56; radiologist-in-chief Cardinal Glennon Meml. Hosp. for Children, St. Louis, 1956-88, Shriners Hosp. for Children, 1988—; assoc. v.p., bd. govs. Cardinal Glennon Children's Hosp., St. Louis. Lectr. and cons. in field; med. dir. radiography Sanford Brown Coll., 1996—. Radio show host Doctor to Doctor, Sta. KMOX-CBS, St. Louis; host daily To Your Health; health reporter Sta. KMOV-TV, also Sta. WFUN-FM, Sta. KSIV-AM; TV host Sta. WCVB Channel 5, Boston; author: Radiologic Diagnosis in Infants and Children, 1965, Radiology of the Pediatric Elbow, 1980, Radiologic Pathology for Allied Health Professions, 1980, Child Maltreatment, 1993, also monographs; contbr. articles to profl. jours., numerous tchg. tapes. Bd. dirs. ARC, TB Soc., March of Dimes, 15 others. With U.S. Army, 1942-46, with USPHS, 1952-54. Decorated Knight Equestrian Order Holy Sepulchre Jerusalem; recipient Mo. Health Care Communicator of Yr. award, 1991, Welby award Nat. Acad. Radio and TV Health Communicators, Healthcare Leadership award Met. Hosp. St. Louis, 1994, Lifetime Achievement award Nat. Assn. Physician Broadcasters, numerous civic awards; Armand Brodeur Day proclaimed by City of St. Louis; named St. Paul Man of Yr., 1991; ann. lecture named in his honor dept. radiology St. Louis U. Sch. Medicine, 1998; named one of very few Top Radiologists in Am., 2002-03. Fellow Am. Coll. Radiology, Am. Acad. Pediat.; mem. AMA (Bronze medal, Golden Apple), Soc. Pediat. Radiology, Radio. Soc. N.Am., Nat. Assn. Med. Communicators (charter, co-founder, pres. 1987-88), Sigma Xi, Alpha Omega Alpha, Alpha Sigma Nu, Phi Beta Kappa, Rho Kappa Sigma. Roman Catholic. Home: 6 Huntleigh Trails Ln Saint Louis MO 63131-4801 Office: 2001 S Lindbergh Blvd Saint Louis MO 63131-3504 *Success is being pleased with what you see in the mirror— every day. It should not be measured by the size of your home or bank account. What you see in the mirror is all that you can take with you. It is measured by what you do for people!*

BRODEUR, HELEN ANTIONETTE, elementary school educator; b. Alburquerque, N.M., May 20, 1940; d. Jose Patricio Sanchez and Bertha Apodaca; m. Alphonse Maurice Brodeur Jr.; children: Alphonse Maurice Brodeur Jr., Maria Elena. BA in Edn., U N.M., 1964, MA in Edn., 1977. 3rd grade tchr. Catholic Sch., Wichita, Kans., 1962—65; 5th, 7th grade tchr. Archdiocese of Santa Fe Catholic Sch., Alburquerque, N.Mex., 1965—69; tchr. Alburquerque (N.M.) Pub. Tchr., 1969—2002, gifted & talented, ESL, Migrant Tchr., 1969—2002; head sub. Isleta (N.M.) Elem. Sch., 1994. Composer: (songs) Colores en mi Cuerpocito, 2001 (First prize for youth song of the year in the N.M. Hispanic Entertainers Assn., 2001). Vol. Sister Dolly's Kitchen of God, Alburquerque, 1981, Good Shepherd's, Alburquerque, 1988, Veteran's Hosp., Alburquerque, 1991. Mem.: N.M. Retiree Assn. (assoc.). Home: PO Box 80010 Albuquerque NM 87198

BRODEUR, JOHN, public relations executive; BA in Journalism, U. Nev.; MPA, Harvard U. Corr. UP Internat.; pub. affairs dir. Sch. Medicine, Nev.; mgr. congl. staff, press sec. to a U.S. sen. Washington, 1972; founder Brodeur/Martin Co., Nev., 1979, Brodeur Worldwide, 1985, chmn., CEO. Office: Brodeur Worldwide 9th Fl 855 Boylston St Ste 9 Boston MA 02116-2622

BRODEUR, MARTIN, hockey player; b. Montreal, Que., Can., May 6, 1972; Selected 1st round NHL entry draft N.J. Devils, 1994, goalie, 1991—. Mem. QMJ Hockey League All-Star 2d Team, 1991—92, NHL All-Rookie Team, 1993—94; player NHL All-Star Game, 1996; mem. Stanley Cup Championship Team, 1995, 2000, 03. Recipient Calder Meml. Trophy, 1993—94. Office: c/o New Jersey Devils 50 Rt 120 N PO Box 504 East Rutherford NJ 07073-0504

BRODEUR, MICHAEL STEPHEN, dean; b. Jacksonville, Fla., Oct. 15, 1949; s. Victor Edward Jr. and Amy (Ropke) B.; m. Deborah Crystal Cazalas, Aug. 9, 1975 (div. Oct. 1979); m. Cheri Anne Winton, Apr. 10, 1982; children: Trey, Aaron, Dana, Margaret. BA in Econs., BA in Fin., U. South Fla., 1972; MPA, U. North Fla., 1989. Cert. coll. bus. mgr. Acctg. mgr. Raymond James Fin., St. Petersburg, Fla., 1974-78; asst. OMB dir. Pinellas County, Fla., Clearwater, 1978-79; dir. OMB Alachua County, Gainesville, Fla., 1979-83; treas. City of Orlando, Fla., 1983-84; dir. OMB Orange County, Fla., Orlando, 1984-86; dir. of fin. State of Fla., Gainesville, 1986-91; mgmt. analyst v.p. adminstrv. affil. U. Fla., 1991-93; chief of staff U. Fla. Coll. of Pharmacy, Gainesville, 1994-98, asst. dean fin. and adminstrv. affairs, 1999—. Exec. v.p. COP Faculty Practice Assn., Inc., Gainesville. Recipient Davis Productivity award Davis Found. Fla. Taxwatch, Inc., 1993, 98, Disting. Svc. Alachua County Bd. Commrs., 1983. Democrat. Presbyterian. Avocations: watch collecting, golf, target shooting. Home: 4818 NW 37th Way Gainesville FL 32605-1034 Office: U Fla Coll of Pharmacy PO Box 100484 101 S Newell Dr Gainesville FL 32610-0484 Fax: 352-273-6528. E-mail: brodeur@ufl.edu.

BRODHEAD, DAVID CRAWMER, lawyer; b. Madison, Wis., Sept. 16, 1934; s. Richard Jacob and Irma (Crawmer) B.; m. Nancie Christensen, Aug. 17, 1963; children: Compton, Peter, Christoffer. BS, U. Wis., 1956, LLB, 1959. Bar: N.Y. 1960, Wis. 1959, D.C. 1979. Assoc. firm Paul, Weiss, Rifkind, Wharton & Garrison, N.Y.C., 1959-68, ptnr., 1969—. Dir. Centennial Industries, Inc., N.Y.C. Editor-in-chief: Wis. Law Rev, 1958-59. Trustee Collegiate Sch., N.Y.C., 1978-85; vestryman Christ and St. Stephen's Episcopal Ch., 1972-82. Mem. N.Y. State Bar, Assn. of Bar of City of N.Y., Wis. Bar. Assn., D.C. Bar Assn., ABA, Westside C. of C. of City of N.Y. (dir. 1970-83), Order of Coif, Delta Theta Phi Clubs: Washington (Conn.); Holland Soc. of N.Y. *Take life one day at a time. Yesterday is gone forever and tomorrow is not here. That leaves only today to deal with.*

BRODHEAD, JAMES E(ASTON), actor, writer; b. St. Louis, Jan. 30, 1932; s. James Easton II and Martha Pusey (Mithoefer) B.; m. Sue Hawes, June 21, 1963; children: William James Pusey, Daniel Alexander Hawes. BA in Speech, U. Mich., 1954. Announcer/news editor Sta. WNOP, Newport, Ky., 1954-55; actor stage and TV N.Y.C., 1955-62; copywriter/reporter Time Mag., N.Y.C. and Calif., 1963-69; pub. rels. account exec. Laurie & Assocs. and Mahoney & Assocs., L.A., 1971-74; actor Querencia Prodns., L.A. and Santa Barbara, 1974—. Bd. dirs. Western Adv. Bd., Actor's Equity, L.A., 1978-83, ANTA West, L.A., 1978-80, Western Coun. Actor's Fund Am., 1993-95, Santa Barbara Symphony, 1998—. Author: Inside Laugh-In, 1969; appeared in 17 films including Leadbelly, First Monday in October, Frances, Mame, Piranha, 3 Disney comedies; TV films include War & Remembrance, Helter Skelter, Gideon's Trumpet; TV series include The Judge, General Hospital, Here's Lucy, Kraft TV Theatre; more than 100 stage prodns. including Inherit the Wind, First Monday in October. Mem. Ensemble Theatre Co., Pacific Pioneer Broadcasters, Actors' Fund (life), Edwin Forrest Soc. (founding) Am. Atheists, Freedom from Religion Found., Santa Barbara Club, Sakonnet Point Club. Democrat. Avocations: reading, cooking, travel, languages. Home and Office: Querencia Prodns 506 Yankee Farm Rd Santa Barbara CA 93109-1060

BRODHEAD, WILLIAM MCNULTY, lawyer, former congressman; b. Cleve., Sept. 12, 1941; s. William McNulty and Agnes Marie (Franz) B.; m. Kathleen Garlock, Jan. 16, 1965; children: Michael, Paul. AB, Wayne State U., 1965; JD, U. Mich., 1967. Bar: Mich. 1968, D.C. 1983. Tchr., Detroit, 1964-65; atty. City of Detroit, 1969-70; mem. Mich. Ho. Reps., 1971-74, 94th-97th Congresses from 17th Dist., mem. com. on ways and means, 1977-82, mem. budget com., 1979-80; chmn. Democratic Study Group, 1981-82; ptnr. firm Plunkett & Cooney P.C., Detroit, 1982—. Trustee The Skillman Found., Mich.'s Children; chair Focus: Hope-Covenant House of Mich.; dir. Citizens Rsch. Coun. of Mich. Home: 5096 Mirror Lake Ct West Bloomfield MI 48323-1534 Office: Plunkett & Cooney 38505 Woodward Ave Ste 2000 Bloomfield Hills MI 48304 E-mail: wbrodhead@plunketcooney.com.

BRODIE, ALICE VELMA, health and ethics advocate; b. Akron, Ohio, June 20, 1924; d. Charles Alvin and Lillian Snowden (Twentyman) Keller; m. Milton John Brodie, Dec. 8, 1980 (dec. 1983). Student, U.S. Nurse Cadet Corps, 1944-47; grad., Mt. Sinai Sch. Nursing, Cleve., 1947; BSN in Pub. Health Nursing, Western Res. U., 1952; postgrad., U. Wash., 1963-64, U. Calif., Berkeley, 1969-70, 81, 86, U. San Francisco, 1987-89, Calif. State U., Dominguez Hills, 1997—. RN, Ohio, Calif.; cert. pub. health nurse. Nursing supr. Mt. Sinai Hosp., Cleve., 1952-54; sch. nurse Renton (Wash.) Sch. Dist., 1958-60; pub. health nurse, vis. nurse, sch. nurse King County Health Dept., Seattle; with Ministry of Health, England, Ireland, Germany, France, Italy, Switzerland, Netherlands, Can., Mex., 1967; ship nurse numerous voyages to Australia, New Zealand, South Sea Island, Suva, 1968. Rschr. No. State Hosp., Wash., 1963-64. Vol. BSF Internat., 1968-74, 93-99, ARC, Seattle, 1958-67, Buck Ctr. for Rsch. in Aging, Marin County, Calif., 1989, 90, Family Radio Tours to China, Hong Kong, Taiwan, 1985, Siberia, Mongolia, 1990s, Argentina, Brazil; mem. Vision for Progress, Vallejo, Calif., 1996—, Calif. Lawyers for Arts, San Francisco, 1996—; amb. People-to People citizen amb. UN Internat. Red Cross Ministry of Health, U.K., Eng., Germany, Italy, Switzerland, Ireland, Holland, Netherlands, France; family radio tours to China, Siberia, Hong Kong, Taiwan, Argentina, Brazil, 1985-94. Mem. APHA, ANA (founding mem. Calif. chpt. 1996), AAUW, Calif. Nurses Assn. (former del. to ANA conv. Detroit), Nat. Coun. for Aging, Calif. Lawyers for Arts, Vallejo C. of C. Avocations: health policy analysis, world travel, education, health legislation.

BRODIE, ANGELA M. biomedical researcher, educator; b. Manchester, Lancashire, Eng., Sept. 28, 1934; d. Herbert Kent and Ann (Hargreaves) Hartley; m. Harry Joseph Brodie, Apr. 25, 1928; children: Mark, John. BS in Biochemistry with honors, Sheffield (Eng.) U., 1956, MS in Biochemitry, 1958; PhD in Chem. Pathology, Manchester (Eng.) U., 1961. Jr. scientific officer Nat. Blood Transfusion Svc., Manchester, 1956-57; rsch. asst. dept. hormone rsch. Christie Hosp. and Holt Radium Inst., Manchester, 1957-59; predoct. fellow Med. Rsch. Coun., Eng., 1959-61; steroid tng. program NIH, 1961-62; postdoct. tng. program in steroid biochemistry Clark U./Worcester Found. Exptl. Biology, Shrewsbury, Mass., 1962; staff scientist Worcester Found. for Expt. Biology, Shrewsbury, 1962-68, 70-78, sr. scientist, 1978-79; res. assoc. prof. dept. pharmacology and exptl. therapeutics U. Md. Sch. Medicine, Balt., 1979-83, assoc. prof. dept. pharmacology and exptl. therapeutics, 1983-86, prof., 1986—; prof. divsn. reproductive endocrinology dept. physiology U. Md., 1985—. Invited presenter Am. Assn. Cancer Rsch., 1987; program leader prostate cancer divsn. oncology dept. medicine The Marlene and Steart Greenebaum Cancer Ctr. U. Md., 1988—; mem. ad-hoc biochem. endorcrinology study sect. NIH, 1982, 83, 85, spl. cons. social scis. and population dynamics, 1982, 84-88, 91, reproductive endocrinology, 1998—; mem. selection com. Roussel Prize, 1985-92, mem. nominating com. Women in Endocrinology, 1991-94, 97-99; chmn. liaison com. Am. Soc. Andropology, 1988-91; site visitor Cancer Rsch. Campaign Program Projects, Eng., 1993, 94, 95; reviewer Nat. Action Plan on Breast Cancer, 1995; mem. integration panel breast cancer program U.S. Army, 1998; chmn. numerous symposia; cons. in field. Editor, contbr. Jour. Enzyme Inhibition, 1990, proceedings 3rd Internat. Aromatase Conf., 1992, Breast Cancer Rsch. and Treatment, 1994; co-editor: Clin. and Biol. Rsch., 1986; rev. Endocrinology, Sci. Steroids, Biology of Reproduction, Cancer Rsch., Jour. Clin. Endocrinology and Metabolism, numerous others; mem. editl. bd. Steroids, 1964-66, 95—, Jour. Steroid Biochemistry, 1985—, Jour. Enzyme Inhibition, 1992—; abstractor Biol. Abstracts, 1968-70. Recipient Pharmacia Upjohn Internat. award for excellence in clin. rsch., 1998, Brinker Internat. award for breast cancer rsch. The Susan Co. Komen Breast Cancer Found., 2000. Mem. AAAS, Am. Assn. Cancer Rsch. (mem. program com. 1988-89, membership com. 1997—), Internat. Soc. Comparative Oncology, Soc. Study Reproduction (mem. pubs. com. 1985, membership com. 1987, nominations com. 1990, awards com. 1995—), Endocrine Soc., Soc. Andrology. Achievements include 4 patents; research, development of formestane aromatase inhibitors, first selective aromatase and first specifically designed for treatment of breast cancer; research in new treatments for prostate cancer, steroid biochemistry, endocrinology of breast and prostate cancer and other estrogen mediated diseases, reproductive endocrinology. Office: U Md Sch Medicine 655 W Baltimore St Baltimore MD 21201

BRODIE, CATHERINE ANNE, music educator; b. Marshall, Mich., Mar. 11, 1948; d. Stephen Frank and Ernestine Viola (Lake) Trupiano; m. William Brodie, Sept. 4, 1970; children: Matthew Ian, Andrew Benjamin, Brian Patrick. BS in Music Performance, Eastern Mich. U., 1970, MA in Music Edn., 1973. Grad. asst. Ea. Mich. U., Ypsilanti, 1970-73, asst. condr. Madrigal Singers, 1972-73; choir dir. St. Ursulas Cath. Ch., Ypsilanti, 1972-77; pvt. voice and pinao instr. Ypsilanti, 1972-79; music educator Monroe (Mich.) Pub. Schs., 1980—. Choral condr. Oakland Singers, Bloomfield Hills, Mich., 1990—. Vocalist Parker Choral, Grosse Ile, Mich., 1988—95, John Tyner Chorale, 1996, dist. mgr., 1996—98, exec. bd., 2001—; choir mem. St. Paul's Meth. Ch., Monroe, 1984—. Recipient Tchr. of Yr., Mich. Music Educators Assn., 1996—97. Mem.: Mich. Educators Assn., Mich. Music Educators Assn. (Tchr. of the Yr. 1996—97), Am. Choral Dirs. Assn., Music Educators Nat. Conf., Mich. Sch. Vocal Music Assn. (honors choir chmn. 1990—94, honor choir dir. 1994—95, 2001—02). Office: Monroe High Sch 901 Herr Rd Monroe MI 48161-9744

BRODIE, HARLOW KEITH HAMMOND, psychiatrist, educator, past university president; b. Stamford, Conn., Aug. 24, 1939; s. Lawrence Sheldon and Elizabeth White (Hammond) B.; m. Brenda Ann Barrowclough, Jan. 26, 1967; children: Melissa Verduin, Cameron Keith, Tyler Hammond, Bryson Barrowclough. AB, Princeton U., 1961; MD, Columbia U., 1965; LLD hon., U. Richmond, 1987; LHD (hon.), High Point U., 1992. Diplomate Am. Bd. Psychiatry and Neurology. Intern Ochsner Found. Hosp., New Orleans, 1965-66; resident in psychiatry Columbia-Presbyn. Med. Center, N.Y.C., 1966-68; clin. assoc. intramural research program NIMH, 1968-70; asst. prof. psychiatry, dir. gen. clin. research center Stanford U. Med. Sch., 1970-74; prof. psychiatry, chmn. dept. Duke U. Med. Sch., 1974-82, James B. Duke prof. psychiatry and behavioral scis., 1981—, prof. dept. psychology, prof. law, 1980—; psychiatrist-in-chief Duke U. Med. Center, 1974-82; chancellor Duke U., 1982-85, pres., 1985-93, pres. emeritus, 1993—. Mem. Pres. Biomed. Rsch. Panel, 1975; mem. Carnegie Coun. on Adolescent Devel., 1986-97; trustee Com. for Econ. Devel., 1986-93, mem. subcom. on edn. and child devel., 1990; trustee Nat. Humanities Ctr., 1988-93; mem. nat. rev. and adv. panel for improving campus race rels. Ford Found., 1990-94; mem. subcom. on Edn. on Child Devel. Com., 1990; bd. dirs. Inst. of Medicine, Mental Health and Behavioral Medicine, 1981-83, chmn., 1981-82; mem. Com. on Leadership Devel., Am. Coun. on Edn., 1990-93; chmn. Com. on Substance Abuse and Mental Health Issues in AIDS Rsch., 1992-95. Co-author: The Importance of Mental Health Services to General Health Care, 1979, Modern Clinical Psychiatry, 1982; co-editor: American Handbook of Psychiatry, vols. 6, 7 and 8, 1975, 81, 86, Controversy in Psychiatry, 1978, Psychiatry at the Crossroads, 1980, Critical Problems in Psychiatry, 1982, Signs and Symptoms in Psychiatry, 1983, Consultation-Liaison Psychiatry and Behavioral Medicine, 1986, AIDS and Behavior: An Integrated Approach, 1994, Keeping an Open Door: Passages in a University Presidency, 1996; assoc. editor Am. Jour. Psychiatry, 1973-81. Recipient Disting. Med. Alumni award Columbia U., 1985, Disting. Alumnus award Ochsner Found. Hosp., 1984, Strecker award Inst. of Pa. Hosp., 1980, N.C. award for sci., 1990, William C. Menninger Meml. award ACP, 1994. Fellow: Royal Soc. Medicine; mem.: NAS, Internat. Soc. Sport Psychiatry, Soc. Biol. Psychiatry (A.E. Bennet Rsch. award 1970), Royal Coll. Psychiatrists, Inst. Medicine, Am. Psychiat. Assn. (sec. 1977—81, pres. 1982—83). Home: 63 Beverly Dr Durham NC 27707-2223 Office: Duke U Office of Pres Emeritus 205 E Duke Bldg Durham NC 27708

BRODIE, JOHN, music educator; b. Denver, Oct. 16, 1960; s. David and Patricia Brodie; m. Laura Brodie; children: Julia, Rachel, Kathryn. BS, West Chester State Coll.; M, PhD, Cath. U. Band dir. Granada (Colo.) Sch., 1982—84; trumpeter USMC Band, Washington, 1984—88; band dir., prof. Va. Mil. Inst., Lexington, 1988—. Hon. mem. Va. Mil. Inst., Lexington, 1992—. Musician: Shenondoah Symphony. Col. Va. Nat. Guard, 1988—. Avocations: racquetball, hockey, scuba diving, running, weightlifting. Home: 1770 Wesley Chapel Rd Lexington VA 24450

BRODIE, M. J. (JAY BRODIE), architect, city planner, government executive; b. Balt., Md., Sept. 25, 1936; s. Meyer and Sarah (Rachliss) B.; m. Georgene Ann Gonzales, May 30, 1958; children: Kimberly Brodie-Hopkins, Ellen Maria Jarrett. B.Arch., U. Va., 1958; M.Arch., Rice U., 1960. Registered architect, Md. Arch, prin. city planner, chief planner Balt. Urban Renewal and Housing Agy., Md., 1967-69; exec. commr. Dept. Housing and Comm. Devel., Balt., 1969-77, commr., 1977-84; exec. dir. Pa. Ave. Devel. Corp., Washington, 1984-93; sr. v.p. RTKL Assoc., Inc., Washington, 1993-95; pres. Balt. Devel.

Corp., Md., 1996—. Mem. Urban Land Inst., 1980—; mem. Gov.'s Task Force on Housing, Annapolis, Md., 1981-83; mem. real estate adv. bd. Johns Hopkins U.; guest spkr. numerous univs., confs., orgns. Past trustee Balt. City Life Mus's.; past mem. Presidio Coun., San Francisco; past chair adv. bd. U. Va. Sch. Architecture; bd. dirs. Empower Balt. Mgmt. Corp. Recipient Thomas Jefferson award Am. Inst. of Architects, 1994 Fellow AIA (bd. dir. Balt. chpt. 1977-78, Thomas Jefferson award 1994): mem Am. Inst. Cert. Planners, Citizens Planning and Housing Assn. (bd. dir. 1976-77), Am. Planning Assn., Lambda Alpha, Nat. Trust for Historic Preservation. Unitarian Universalist. Avocations: ice dancing, writing, music. Home: 609 Craycombe Ave Baltimore MD 21211-2239 Office: Balt Devel Corp 36 S Charles St Fl 16 Baltimore MD 21201-3020 E-mail: jbrodie@baltimoredevelopment.com.

BRODIE, RONALD, lawyer, author; b. N.Y.C., Sept. 22, 1941; s. S. Robert and Ann Brodie. BA in Econs., U. Pa., 1963; SM in Mgmt., MIT, 1965; JD, U. Miami, Fla., 1967, LLM in Taxation, 1968. Bar: Fla. 1967, U.S. Tax Ct. 1976, U.S. Ct. Appeals (11th cir.) 1981. Sole practice, Miami and Miami Beach, Fla., 1967—; pres. Taxplan, Inc., Miami Beach, 1979—. Lectr. Fla. Bar continuing legal edn. seminars, guest lectr. U Miami Law Sch. Author Real Estate Tax Planning Newsletter, 1981-86; author, editor tax column Jour. Property Mgmt., 1981-99; contbr. numerous articles on taxation to profl. jours. Mem. counsel Conservative Caucus of Dade, Inc., Miami, 1980-86; mem. U. Miami Endowment Com., 1969—. Mem. Miami Beach Bar Assn., Real Estate Assn. of Profls. (founder, pres., counsel 1978-80), Fla. Bar (chmn. tax aspects of real property law com. 1979-90, exec. coun. real property, probate and trust law sect. 1979-90), U. Miami Law Alumni Assn., U. Pa. Dade Alumni Club, MIT Club of Miami, U. Miami Alumni Ass., Wharton Sch. Club, Delta Theta Phi, Mensa, Intertel. Republican. Home: 951 W 47th Ct Miami Beach FL 33140-2906 Office: 134 Mirasol Internat Ctr 2699 Collins Ave Miami Beach FL 33140-4716 E-mail: ronaldbrodie@webtv.net.

BRODIE, THEODORE HAMILTON, construction company executive; b. Newton, Mass., Dec. 16, 1929; s. Theodore E. and Martha Washington (Hamilton) B.; m. Robin Fletcher Garland, May 20, 1978; children by previous marriage: Glenn A., Karen Lee, Beth Sprague. BA, Bowdoin Coll., 1952. Salesman Proctor & Gamble, 1952; sales engr. New Eng. Insulation Co., Canton, Mass., 1956-63, contract mgr., 1963-69, pres., 1969—. Assoc., past chmn. Associated Specialty Contractors; chmn. bd. dirs. A.F. Underhill Co. Inc.; gen. ptnr. Hamilton Leasing Co., Duxbury, Mass. Former moderator Pilgrim Congl. Ch., Duxbury, 1963-64; chmn. sch. com. Town of Duxbury, 1974-75; pres. Duxbury PTA; mem. Gov.'s Commn. on Rail Svcs., Mass., 1974-76; bd. overseers Bowdoin Coll., 1983-95, emeritus, 1995—; trustee Mass. Carpenters Funds, Asbestors Workers #6 & #31 Funds. Served with USNR, 1952-56. Named Honoree for labor rels., Mass. Labor Guild, 1995. Mem. Chief Exec. Orgn., World Press Assn., 49ers of New Eng. (chmn. 1990), Am Arbitration Assn., Nat. Insulation Assn. (past pres., chmn. man-made mineral fiber health task force, Man of Yr. award 1989), Assoc. Gen. Contractors, Assoc. Sub Contractors of Mass., Small Bus. Assn. New Eng., Masons, Ocean Reef Club, N.Y. Yacht Club, Duxbury Yacht Club, Blue Water Sailing Club, Bowdoin of Boston Club. E-mail: hamiltonbro@aol.com.

BRODINE, CHARLES EDWARD, physician; b. Sioux City, Iowa, May 10, 1925; s. Ivar and Dorothy B.; m. Lois Bliss, June 26, 1949; children: Stephanie Kay, Jennifer Leah, Charles Edward. BS, Iowa State U., Ames, 1948, research fellow malaria project, 1948-49; MD, Washington U., St. Louis, 1953. Intern St. Louis County Hosp., 1953-54, resident in internal medicine, 1954-55, U.S. Naval Hosp., Oakland, Calif., 1957-59; fellow in hematology, clin. instr. medicine U. Cin. and Cin. Gen. Hosp., 1955-57; head hematology svc. U.S. Naval Hosp., Oakland, 1959-61, Bethesda, Md., 1961-62, cons. in hematology, 1962-73; head divsn. rsch. hematology Naval Med. Rsch. Inst., Bethesda, 1962-66, chmn. dept. clin. investigation, 1966-70, exec. officer, 1970-73; program mgr. Navy frozen blood and trauma rsch. program research div. Bur. Medicine and Surgery U.S. Dept. Navy, Washington, 1962-71, dir. rsch. divsn., 1973-74; spl. asst. med. rsch. and devel. to Surgeon Gen. U.S. Navy, 1974-77; comdg. officer Naval Med. Rsch. and Devel. Command, Nat. Naval Med. Center, Bethesda, 1974-77; asst. med. dir. environ. health and preventive medicine Office Med. Svcs. Dept. State, Washington, 1977-90; mem. Agt. Orange Working Group, 1982-90; exec. com. Nat. Council Internat. Health, 1982-90. Bd. dirs. Gorgas Meml. Inst. Tropical and Preventive Medicine, 1973-89; mem. Bur. Medicine and Surgery Policy Council, 1974-77; med. adviser ARC, 1975-79; adv. com. Nat. Sickle Cell Disease, NIH, 1974-77; mem. com. on biomed. rsch. U.S.-Egypt Joint Working Group, 1975-77; mem. White House Working Group on Internat. Health, 1977; clin. asso. prof. dept. medicine Georgetown U., Washington, 1971— ; Dept. State mem. Nat. Council for Internat. Health, 1978-89. Contbr. articles in field to med. jours. Exec. com. Gorgas Meml. Inst., 1978-88. Decorated Legion of Merit for blood rsch. project, 1968; recipient Meritorious Service medal for work at Naval Med. Rsch. Inst. U.S. Dept. Navy, 1973; Robert Dexter Conrad award for outstanding sci. achievement Sec. of Navy, 1977 Mem. AMA, Assn. Mil. Surgeons (sustaining membership award 1967), Acad. Medicine of Washington (bd. dirs. 1992—), Soc. for Cryobiology (editorial bd. 1964-66), Soc. Fed. Med. Agys., Western Soc. Clin. Investigation, Soc. Med. Cons. Armed Forces. Home: 9213 Friars Rd Bethesda MD 20817-2313

BRODKEY, ROBERT STANLEY, chemical engineering educator; b. L.A., Sept. 14, 1928; s. Harold R. and Clara (Goldman) B.; m. Martha Mahr, Dec. 22, 1958 (div. Nov. 1971); 1 son, Philip Arthur; m. Carolyn Patch, Dec. 6, 1975. AA, San Francisco City Coll., 1948; B.Chemistry with highest honors, MS in Chem. Engring, U. Calif.-Berkeley, 1950; PhD in Chem. Engring. (Gulf Oil fellow), U. Wis., 1952. Rsch. chem. engr. Esso Rsch. & Engring. Co., Linden, N.J., 1952-56, Esso Std. Oil Co., Bayway, N.J., 1956-57; asst. prof. chem. engring. Ohio State U., Columbus, 1957-60, assoc. prof., 1960-64, prof., 1964-92, prof. emeritus, 1992—. Cons. on turbulent motion, mixing kinetics, rheology, 2-phase flow, fluid dynamics, image processing and analysis; expository lectr. GAMM Conf., 1975; vis. prof. Japan Soc. Promotion Sci., 1978; Clyde chair engring. U. Utah, fall 1994. Author: Transport Phemomena, A Unified Approach, 1988, The Phenomena of Fluid Motions, 1967, reprint edit., 1995; editor: Turbulence in Mixing Operations, 1975; contbr. articles to profl. jours.; patentee in field. Recipient Outstanding Paper of Yr. award Can. Jour. Chem. Engring., 1970; NATO sr. fellow in sci. Max Planck Institut für Strömungsforschung, Göttingen, Fed. Republic Germany, 1972; Alexander Von Humboldt Found. sr. U.S. scientist award, 1975, 83; sr. rsch. award Coll. Engring. Ohio State U., 1983, 86; Disting. Sr. Rsch. award Am. Soc. Engring. Edn., 1985; Chem. Engr. lectureship award Am. Soc. Engring. Edn., 1986; North Am. Mixing Forum award, 1994. Fellow AAAS, AIChE, Am. Phys. Soc., Am. Inst. Chemists, Am. Acad. Mechanics; mem. Am. Chem. Soc., Soc. Engring. Sci., Soc. Rheology, Sigma Xi, Phi Lambda Upsilon, Alpha Gamma Sigma, Phi Beta Delta. Office: Ohio St Univ 140 W 19th Ave Columbus OH 43210-1110 E-mail: brodkey.1@osu.edu.

BRODKIN, ADELE RUTH MEYER, psychologist; b. N.Y.C., July 8, 1934; d. Abraham J. and Helen (Honig) Meyer; m. Roger Harrison Brodkin, Jan. 26, 1957; children: Elizabeth Anne Brodkin Brauer, Edward Stuart. BA, Sarah Lawrence Coll., 1956; MA, Columbia U., 1959; PhD, Rutgers U., 1977. Lic. psychologist N.J. Sch. psychologist pub. schs., 1961—73; assoc. dir. Infant Child Devel. Ctr. St. Barnabas Med. Ctr., Livingston, N.J., 1977-79; clin. asst. prof. dept. psychiatry U. Medicine and Dentistry N.J., Newark, 1979-90, clin. assoc. prof., 1990-2001. Vis. scholar Hasting Ctr. for Life Scis., NY, 1979; sr. child devel. cons.; cons. Scholastic, Inc., 1988—. Author: Fresh Approaches to Working with Problematic Behavior, 2001, The Lonely Only Dog, 1998, Between Teacher and Parent, Supporting Young Children As They Grow, 1994; author: (with A.T. Jersild and E.A. Lazar) The Meaning of Psychotherapy in the Teacher's Life and Work, 1962; contbr. Fellow, NIMH, 1962; Adelaide M. Ayer fellow, Columbia U., 1962—63, Louis Bevier fellow, Rutgers U., 1976—77. Fellow: Am. Orthopsychiat. Assn.; mem.: APA, Am. Sociol. Assn., N.J. Psychol. Assn. Home and Office: 2 Trevino Ct Florham Park NJ 07932-2724

BRODKIN, EDWARD STUART, psychiatrist, geneticist; b. Livingston, N.J., June 15, 1966; s. Roger Harrison and Adele (Meyer) B.; m. Stephanie Allison Heck, Sept. 3, 2000. AB magna cum laude, Harvard U., Cambridge, Mass., 1988; MD, Harvard U., Boston, 1992. Diplomate Am. Bd. Psychiatry and Neurology, Nat. Bd. Med. Examiners. Intern in pediat. Yale U. Sch. Medicine, New Haven, 1992-93, resident in psychiatry, 1993-96, postdoctoral fellow in neurosci., 1996-98; postdoctoral assoc. in genetics Princeton U., 1998—2002; asst prof. dept psychiatry U. Pa. Sch. Medicine, Phila., 2002—. Contbg. author: Handbook of Experimental Pharmacology and Antipsychotics, 1996, Molecular and Genetic Basis of Neurological and Psychiatric Disease, 3d edit., 2003; contbr. articles to med. jours., including Sci., Brain Rsch., Neurosci., Jour. of Neurosci. Grantee NIH, 1998-2000, 03—, Burroughs Wellcome Fund, 1998—, Nat. Alliance for Rsch. on Schizophrenia and Depression, 2003—. Mem. AAAS, Am. Psychiat. Assn., Soc. for Neurosci., Internat. Mammalian Genome Soc., Phi Beta Kappa. Avocation: playing carinet. Office: U Pa Sch Medicine Dept Psychiatry Clin Rsch Bldg 415 Curie Blvd Philadelphia PA 19104

BRODKIN, ROGER HARRISON, dermatologist, educator; b. Newark, July 31, 1932. A.B. Lafayette Coll., Easton, Pa., 1954; M.D., Jefferson Med. Coll., 1958; M.M.S. in Dermatology, NYU, 1967. Diplomate Am. Bd. Dermatology. Intern, Lenox Hill Hosp., N.Y.C., 1958-59; resident in dermatology NYU and Bellevue Hosp., N.Y.C., 1959-62; teaching asst. NYU, 1962-64, instr. dermatology, 1964-66; clin. asst. prof. U. N.J. Med. and Dental Sch., Newark, 1966-69, clin. assoc prof., 1969-79, clin. prof., 1979—; pres. Ctr. Dermatology, West Orange, N.J. Named Best Drs. in N.Y. N.Y. Mag. Fellow ACP, Am. Acad. Dermatology, Royal Soc. Medicine, Sigma Psi. Office: Ctr Dermatology 101 Old Short Hills Rd West Orange NJ 07052-1000

BRODL, RAYMOND FRANK, lawyer, former lumber company executive; b. Cicero, Ill., June 1, 1924; s. Edward C. and Lillian (Cerny) B.; m. Ethel Jean Johnson, Aug. 15, 1953; children: Mark Raymond, Pamela Jean, Susan Marie. Student, Norwich U., Northfield, Vt., 1943, Ill. Coll., 1946-48; JD, Loyola U., Chgo., 1951. Bar: Ill. 1951. Atty. law office Joseph A. Ricker, Chgo., 1951-58, Brunswick Corp., Chgo., 1958-62; sec., gen. atty. Edward Hines Lumber Co., Chgo., 1962-84, atty., cons., 1985—, sr. counselor, 2001. Democratic candidate for local jud. office, 1953, 57. Served with AUS, 1943-46. Mem. Ill. Bar Assn. Home and Office: 366 Lance Dr Des Plaines IL 60016-2628

BRODSKY, BEVERLY, artist; Student, The Bklyn. Mus., 1954; BA in Art, Bklyn. Coll., 1965, postgrad., 1966, Sch. Visual Arts, N.Y., 1969-70, The New Sch., 1969-70. Tchr. Parsons Sch. Design, 1979—, Adelphi U., 1980-85, Vt. Grad. Sch., Vt. Coll., others; lectr. in field. Author, illustrator: The Crystal Apple, A Russian Folktale, 1974, Sedna, An Eskimo Myth, 1975, The Golem, A Jewish Legend, 1976 (Caldecott honor medal 1977, Notable Book award 1977), Jonah, 1977, Secret Places, 1979, The Story of Job, 1986; illustrator: Forest of the Night, 1975), Gooseberries to Oranges, 1982 (Notable Book award 1983), The Purim Players, 1984, Buffalo, 2003; one woman shows include B.E.L. Gallery, Westport, Conn., 1979, Washington (Conn.) Art Assn., 1979, SUNY, Plattsburgh, 1980, Wilson Arts Ctr., Rochester, N.Y., 1982, Open Gallery Parsons Sch. Design, N.Y.C., 1986, Kimberly Gallery, N.Y.C., 1990, Elizabeth Stone Gallery, Birmingham, Mich., 1991, Westbeth Gallery, N.Y.C., 1998, Heller Archives Gallery, Hebrew Union Coll., N.Y.C., 1996; group shows include 92nd St. YMCA, N.Y.C., 1982, N.Y. Pub. Libr., N.Y.C., 1982, Ruth S. Harley U. Ctr. Gallery Adelphi U., 1983, Yeshiva U. Mus., N.Y.C., 1983, City Gallery, N.Y.C., 1984, Houghton Gallery Cooper Union, N.Y.C., 1985, Internat. Gallery, San Diego, 1987, Triangle Artists' Workshop, Pine Plains, N.Y., 1988, Jewish Mus., N.Y.C., 1988, Parsons Sch. Design, N.Y.C., 1989, LÖrhl Gallery, MÖnchengladbach, Germany, 1990, M-13 Gallery, N.Y.C., 1992, Galerie Berhard Steinmetz, Bonn, Germany, 1992-93, Blondies' Contemporary Art, High, N.Y.C., 1992, Janice Scharry Epstein Mus., West Bloomfield, Mich., 1992, Art Ctr. Battle Creek, Mich., 1992, Painting Ctr., Soho, N.Y.C., 1994, 96, ALJIRA Found., Newark, 1994, Elsa Mott Ives Gallery, N.Y.C., 1994, Abney Gallery Internat., Soho, N.Y.C., 1997, Broome Street Gallery, Soho, N.Y.C., 1997-98, Westbeth Gallery, 1997-98, Whitney Mus. Westbeth Gallery, 2001, Guild Hall, East Hampton, 2001, Studio 18 Gallery, 2002-03; reviewed in Print Mag., Art Direction Mag., N.Y. Art Review, NY Times, The Village Voice, Publisher's Weekly, Booklist, Washington Post, Juni Magazin Fur Kultur and Politik, Kirkus, Washington Post; curator: Westbeth Gallery, 1999, Whitney Mus., 2000, Sotheby's Exhbn., N.Y., 2001. Conn. Commn. on the Arts fellow, N.Y. Found. Arts fellow, 2000; Triangle Artists Workshop resident, 1988. Studio: Studio 18 Gallery 18 Warren St New York NY 10007 E-mail: bbrodynyc@aol.com.

BRODSKY, DAVID MICHAEL, lawyer; b. Providence, Oct. 16, 1943; s. Irving and Naomi (Richman) B.; m. Stacey J. Moritz; children: Peter, Isabel, Nell. AB cum laude, Brown U., 1964; LLB, Harvard U., 1967. Bar: N.Y. 1968, U.S. Dist. Ct. (so. dist.) N.Y. 1969, U.S. Ct. Appeals (2d cir.) 1974, U.S. Dist. Ct. (ea. dist.) N.Y. 1977, U.S. Supreme Ct. 1977, U.S. Ct. Appeals (D.C. cir.) 1981, U.S. Ct. Appeals (3d cir.) 1984, U.S. Tax Ct. 1984, U.S. Dist. Ct. (no. dist.) Tex. 1986. Law clk. to U.S. Dist. judge U.S. Dist. Ct. (so. dist.) N.Y., 1967-69; asst. U.S. atty. So. Dist. N.Y., 1969-73; assoc. Guggenheimer & Untermyer, N.Y.C., 1973-75, ptnr., 1976-80; ptnr., chmn. litig. dept. Schulte Roth & Zabel, N.Y.C., 1980-99; mng. dir., gen. counsel-Ams., Credit Suisse First Boston, 1999—2002; ptnr., co-chair securities and profl. liability litigation group Latham & Watkins LLP, 2002—. Lectr. in field. Co-author: Federal Securities Litigation: A Deskbook for the Practitioner, 1997. Chmn., bd. dirs. N.Y. Lawyers for Pub. Interest, Inc., 1991-94, vice-chmn., 1994-96; bd. dirs. Equal Justice Works, N.Y. Lawyers for the Pub. Interest, Assn. of the Bar Fund. Recipient Pathways to Justice award. Fellow Am. Coll. Trial Lawyers (mem. access to justice com., mem. downstate N.Y. com.); mem. ABA, (litig. sect., co-chmn. ann. meeting 1998, co-chmn. trial practice com. 1990-94, task force on jury sys. 1995-2001), Assn. of Bar of City of N.Y., Anti-Defamation League (exec. com., legal com. 1994—), Am. Law Inst., N.Y. County Lawyers Assn., Fed. Bar Coun., Harvard Club, Scarsdale Golf Club. Jewish. Office: Latham & Watkins LLP 885 Third Ave New York NY 10022 E-mail: david.brodsky@lw.com.

BRODSKY, FELICE ADRIENNE, lawyer; b. Utica, N.Y., July 21, 1952; d. Emile Borden and Harriet Maxine (Berman) Skraly; m. Keith E. Brinkley, Nov. 4, 2002. BA, U. Rochester, 1973; MBA, SUNY, Buffalo, 1984, JD, 1993. Bar: N.Y. 1994, Fed. 1994. Claims rep. U.S. Govt./Social Security Adminstrn., Batavia, N.Y., 1976-90; pvt. practice Lockport, N.Y., 1994—. Instr. Nat. Coll., Rapid City, S.D., 1973-75, Niagara U., Niagara Falls, N.Y., 1989. Treas. Temple Beth El, Niagara Falls, 1987-93; adv. bd. Salvation Army, Lockport, 1995—; bd. dirs. Niagara County Legal Aid Soc., 1996—, v.p. 1999-2000, pres. 2000—; mem. adv. bd. Planned Parenthood, 2002—. Mem. ABA, N.Y. State Bar Assn., Erie County Bar Assn., Lockport Bar Assn., Women Lawyers of Western N.Y., Nat. Orgn. Social Security Claimants Reps. (sustaining mem.), Phi Delta Phi. Democrat. Jewish. Avocations: travel, reading, civic activities. Home: 71 Bridlewood Dr PO Box 557 Lockport NY 14095-0557 Office: 556 S Transit St Lockport NY 14094-5933 E-mail: Feliceesq@aol.com.

BRODSKY, MICHAEL CARROLL, ophthalmologist, educator; b. San Francisco, Mar. 4, 1955; s. Carroll M. and Herma Hill (Kay) B. BA in Biology, U. Calif., San Diego, 1977; MD, U. Tex., San Antonio, 1981. Diplomate Am. Bd. Ophthalmology. Intern internal medicine Meth. Hosp., Dallas, 1981-82; resident in ophthalmology Wayne State U., Detroit, 1983-86; fellow in neuro-ophthalmology U. Calif., San Francisco, 1987; fellow pediat. ophthalmology Duke U., Durham, N.C., 1988; asst. prof. ophthalmology U. Ark. for Med. Sci., Little Rock, 1988-92, assoc. prof. ophthalmology and pediat., 1992-97, prof., 1997—, prin. investigator optic neuritis treatment trial, 1989-91, prin. investigator longitudinal optic neuritis study, 1992-97; chief pediat. ophthalmology Ark. Children's Hosp., Little Rock, 1988—. Co-author: Pediatric Neuro-Ophthalmology, 1996; prin. investigator Optic Neuritis Treatment Trial and Longitudinal Optic Neuritis study. Mem. AMA, Am. Assn. Pediat. Ophthalmology and Strabismus, N.Am. Neuro-Ophthalmology Socs. Democrat. Avocations: running, swimming, musical composition. Office: Ark Childrens Hosp 800 Marshall St # 111 Little Rock AR 72202-3591

BRODSKY, ROBERT FOX, aerospace engineer, educator, author; b. Phila., May 16, 1925; s. Samuel H. and Sylvia (Fox) B.; m. Patricia Wess, Jan. 24, 1959; children: Bette W., Robert D., David V., Jeffrey M. BME, Cornell U., 1947; MAero. Engring., NYU, 1948, DSc in Engring, 1950; MS in Math., U. N.Mex., 1957. Registered profl. engr., Calif., Iowa. Instr. NYU, 1948-50; supr. theoretical aerodynamics Sandia Corp., Albuquerque, 1950-56; chief aerodynamics Convair/Pomona, 1956-59; with Aerojet-Gen. Corp., 1959-71; chief engr. Space-Gen., El Monte, Calif., 1963-67; corp. mgr. european ops. Aerojet-Gen., Paris, 1969-70; mgr. systems test Aerojet ElectroSystems Co., 1970-71; prof., head dept. aerospace engring. Iowa State U., Ames, 1971-80; on faculty improvement leave with space and communications group Hughes Aircraft Co., 1978-79; sr. systems engr. TRW Space and Tech. Group, Redondo Beach, Calif., 1980-83, dir. technol. planning, 1982-86, program mgr., 1986-88; chief engr. Microcosm, Inc., Torrance, Calif., 1988-98. Adj. prof. aerospace engring. U. So. Calif., 1982-96, Nat. Technol. U., 1994-96; vis. prof. The Technion, Haifa, Israel, 1989-90, 94; seminar lectrs. on remote sensing from space, Turin, Italy, 1988, Paris, London, Munich, 1991, Washington, 1992, 93, 94, 96, Albuquerque, 1995, L.A. & Cocoa Beach, 1996-98, 2000, Israel, 1999; cons. in field. Author: The Engineering Life, 2000, Annals from a Life, 2002, Mouldy Figge Tales, 2003; assoc. editor: Handbook of Astronautics, 1991—; author chpt. on space payloads: Space Mission Analysis and Design, 1991, 2d edit., 1992; contbr. articles to profl. jours. Songs My Mother Never Taught Me, 2003. Served with USN, 1944-46. Recipient Ednl. Achievement award AIAA/Am. Soc. Engring. Edn. Aerospace Div., 1978; NSF/NATO sr. fellow in sci., 1973 Fellow AIAA (deceleration tech. com. 1963-65, ednl. activities com. 1972-97, spacecraft sys. tech. com. 1978-82, space transp. tech. com. 1985-88, editl. adv. bd. A&A 1977-81, chmn. L.A. sect. 1986-87, Sustained Svc. award 2000), Inst. Advancement Engring; mem. NSPE, Internat. Coun. Sys. Engring., Am. Astronautical Soc., Am. Soc. Engring. Edn. (Centennial Citation 1993), Am. Soc. Aerospace Edn. (v.p. 1979 80, Educator of Yr. 1979), Rotary, Sigma Xi. Achievements include inventor space lifeboat (Time mag., Feb. 1, 1963). Home: 110 The Village Unit 410 Redondo Beach CA 90277-2546 E-mail: rfoxbro@aol.com.

BRODSKY, ROBERT JAY, wholesale executive; b. Chgo., June 1, 1939; s. Victor Robert and Anille (Evans) B.; m. Anna-Marie H. Miller, June 21, 1969; children: Paul, David. AB, U. Chgo., 1961, MBA, 1962. With J.J. Brodsky & Sons, Inc., Chgo., 1962—2003, pres., 1986—2003. Served to 1st lt. C.E., Mil. Police, Ill. Army Reserve N.G., 1962-68. Mem. Am. Wholesale Mktg. Assn., Ill. Assn. Tobacco and Candy Distbrs. (bd. dirs. 1987-93). Republican. Jewish. Avocation: photography.

BRODSKY, SAMUEL, lawyer; b. Kansas City, Mo., June 12, 1912; s. Abraham and Anne (Brodsky) B.; m. Margery J. Bach, Oct. 17, 1944; children: Joan E., Alice E. BA, U. Tulsa, 1933; LL.B., Harvard U., 1936. Bar: N.Y. 1937. Since practiced in, N.Y.C.; law clk. to Fed. Circuit Ct. Judge Julian W. Mack, 1936-37; asst. U.S. atty. So. Dist. N.Y., 1937-43, 46, charge civil div., 1942-43, 46; partner firm Aranow, Brodsky, Bohlinger, Einhorn & Alter, 1947-79, Botein, Hays & Sklar, 1979-89; counsel Robinson, Brog, Leinwand, Greene, Genovese & Gluck, N.Y.C., 1989-97. Lectr. taxation NYU Law Sch., 1953, 56-64, also; Inst. on Fed. Taxation, NYU, Practicing Law Inst. Contbr. articles to profl. jours. Served to lt. USNR, 1943-46. Mem. ABA, N.Y. State Bar Assn. (past chmn. tax sect.), Harvard Law Sch. Assn. N.Y. Jewish (past pres., trustee synagogue). Home: 55 Grasslands Rd Apt B224 Valhalla NY 10595 Office: care Robinson Brog Leinwand Greene Genovese & Gluck 1345 Avenue Of The Americas New York NY 10105-0302

BRODSKY, WILLIAM J. options exchange executive; b. N.Y.C., 1944; Student, Syracuse U., 1965, JD, 1968. Bar: N.Y. 1969, Ill. 1985. Atty. Model, Roland & Co., 1968-74; with Am. Stock Exch., 1974-82, exec. v.p. ops., 1979-82; exec. v.p., COO Chgo. Merc. Exch., 1982-85, pres., CEO, 1985-97; chmn., CEO Chgo. Bd. Options Exch., 1997—. Adv. mem. internat. capital mktgs. adv. com. Fed. Res. Bank N.Y.; mem. adv. coun. J.L. Kellogg Grad. Sch. Mgmt.; bd. dirs. Peoples Energy Corp. Bd. trustees Northwestern Meml. Hosp., chair investment com.; trustee Syracuse U. Recipient inclusion, Jr. Achievement Chgo. Bus. Hall of Fame, 2001, Lifetime Achievement award, Anti-Defamation League, 2003. Mem. N.Y. State Bar Assn., Ill. Bar Assn., Swiss Futures and Options Assn. (bd. dirs.), Futures Industry Assn. (bd. dirs.), Econ. Club Chgo., Comml. Club Chgo. Achievements include: selection for inclusion into Derivatives Hall of Fame, 2000, Jr. Achievement Chgo. Bus. Hall of Fame, 2001. Office: Chgo Bd Options Exch LaSalle at Van Buren Chicago IL 60605-7413

BRODT, BURTON PARDEE, retired chemical engineer, writer, researcher; b. Evanston, Ill., June 3, 1931; s. Harry Snowden and Marjorie Florence (Pardee) B.; m. Virginia Faye Futch, June 20, 1954 (div. Dec. 1999); children: Howard A., Stephen R., Cynthia A., Phillip D.; m. Gail Elizabeth Clark, June 1, 2001. BS in Chem. Engring., U. Fla., 1954, MS in Chem. Engring., 1958. Devel. engr. DuPont Elastomers, Louisville, 1958-62, sr. rsch. engr. Wilmington, Del., 1962-66, tech. supr. Deepwater, N.J., 1966-69; rsch. supr. polymers div. E.I. DuPont de Nemours and Co., LaPlace, La., 1969-83, sr. supr. rsch. Wilmington, 1983-89, sr. rsch., assoc. LaPorte, Tex., 1989-91, tech. fellow LaPlace, 1991-96; tchg. fellow, sr. scientist DuPont Dow Elastomers, LLC, LaPlace, 1996-98, ret., 1998. Pres. TechDoc, Inc., 1998—; tech. cons., Wilmington, Del., 1999—2002; cons. in field. Author: Scientists and Engineers: Achieving Success in Industry, 2003, Miracles Around Us, 2001, Kevlar Technology, 2002, also novels, short stories and travel books; contbr. to profl. jours. Chmn. Citizens for Goldwater, Wilmington, 1964; founder, pres. Del. Conservative Union, Wilmington, 1965-69; pres. Homeowners Assn., Chadds Ford, Pa., 1988; hs track coach, 2002—. Lt. USAF, 1954-56. Mem.: AIChE. Republican. Achievements include patent for accelerator encapsulation, high-viscosity level control, proprietary processes, powder attrition tester; development of chemical processes now in commercial use, Brodt equation for phase transfer catalysis. Home and Office: 6051 Canterbury Dr Easton MD 21601-8555

BRODWIN, MARTIN GEORGE, counselor, educator; b. N.Y.C., June 1, 1944; s. Allen Leonard and Dorothy Elaine Brodwin; m. Sandra Kaye Willadsen, Nov. 9, 1980; 1 child, Erin Rebecca. AB, UCLA, 1966; MS, Calif. State U., L.A., 1969; PhD, Mich. State U., 1973. Cert. rehab. counselor. Coord. rsch. Rancho Los Amigos Hosp., Downey, Calif., 1973—74; dir. Clin. Rehab. Svcs., L.A., 1974—79; counselor, co-owner Image Devel., L.A., 1979—88; prof., coord. rehab. counseling program Calif. State U., L.A., 1988—. Vocat. expert Office of Hearings and Appeals, Social Security Adminstrn., Pasadena, Calif., 1980—; presenter in field. Author: (book) Workshops for the Handicapped: An Annotated Bibliography, Medical Aspects of Disability: A Casebook; editor: Medical, Psychosocial, and Vocational Aspects of Disability (2nd ed.), Medical, Psychosocial, and Vocational Aspects of Disability; contbr. chapters to books, articles to profl. jours. Named Outstanding Prof. of the Yr., Calif. State U., L.A., 1996—97, Rehab. Educator of the Yr., Nat. Assn. Rehab. Profls. in the Pvt. Sector, 1996, Disting. Alumnus of the Yr., Calif. State U. L.A. Alumni Assn., 1997; recipient Second Ann. Cinco de Mayo Career Expn. Recognition, Calif. State Dept. of Rehab., 2000, Recognition Award for Exemplary Efforts Toward Creating Employment Opportunities for Persons with Spl. Needs, Calif. State Dept. of Rehab., Employment Resources, 2000. Mem.: Calif. Rehab. Counseling Assn. (pres. 1997—99), Nat. Rehab. Counseling Assn., Nat. Rehab. Assn. (bd. mem. so. Calif. chpt. 1996—98), Internat. Assn. Rehab. Profls., Calif. Assn. Rehab. Profls. (treas., v.p., pres. 1975—78), Coun. on Rehab. Edn. (vice-chair 1991—95), Calif. Assn. for Counseling and Devel. (exec. coun. 1996—). Office: California State Univ 5151 State University Dr Los Angeles CA 90032

BRODY, AARON LEO, food and packaging consultant; b. Boston, Aug. 23, 1930; s. Nathan and Lillian (Gorman) B. m. Carolyn Goldstein, Apr. 11, 1953; children: Stephen, Glen, Robyn. BS, MIT, 1951, PhD, 1957; MBA, Northeastern U., 1970. Head food rsch. labs. Whirlpool Co., St. Joseph, Mich., 1957-61; packaging and product devel. mgr. Mars, Inc., Hackettstown, N.J., 1961-66; packaging coord. Arthur D. Little, Inc., Cambridge, Mass., 1967-73; new ventures mgr. Mead Packaging, Atlanta, 1973-81; mgr. mktg. devel. Container Corp. Am., Oaks, Pa., 1981-85; v.p. strategic studies Schotland Bus. Rsch. Inc., Princeton, N.J., 1985-91; mng. dir. Rubbright/Brody, Inc., Duluth, Ga., 1991-2001; pres., CEO, Packaging/Brody, Inc., 2001—. Course dir. Mich. State U., East Lansing, 1959—61; adj. assoc. prof. dept. food sci. U. Del., Newark, 1983—86; instr. Emory U., 1979; vis. prof. St. Joseph's U., Phila., 1990; adj. prof. Spring Garden Coll., Phila., 1990, U. Ga., 1995—; sr. instr. Keller Grad Sch. Mgmt., 1996—. Contbr. articles to profl. jours.; author books; patentee in field. Mem. optimal program for edn. DeKalb County (Ga.), 1975, sec., 1975; mem. food svc. adv. com. USN, 1958-62; active Kerry for Congress campaign, 1972, Levitas for Congress campaign, 1974; mem. legis. subcom. on spl. edn. State of Ga., 1974; mem. Nat. Def. Exec. Res., 1978-88; mem. pres.'s coun. Spring Garden Coll., Phila., 1984-89. Served with AUS, 1952-54. William Underwood fellow, 1955-56; recipient Willis H. Carrier award ASHRAE, 1960, Indsl. Achievement award Inst. Food Technologists, 1964, Braverman meml. award Israel Inst. Tech., 1976, Outstanding Alumnus award Northeastern U., 1982; named Packaging Man of Yr. Nat. Inst. Packaging, Handling and

Logistics Engrs.; named to Packaging Hall of Fame, 1995. Fellow AAAS, Packaging Inst., Inst. Food Technologists (Riester-Davis Food Packaging Achievement award 1988, Inds. Scientist award 1994, Nicholas Appert award 2000); mem. Packaging Inst. (v.p. 1973-79), Soc. Packaging Profls., Inst. Packaging Profls. (hon. life, Mem. of Yr. 1994-95; cert.), League Internat. Food Edn., Planning Execs. Inst., N.Y. Acad. Scis., Product Devel. and Mgmt. Assn., MIT Club (pres. 1977-79, exec. com., v.p. ednl. coun.), Toastmasters, Sigma Xi. Home: 4981 Trevino Cir Duluth GA 30096-6072 Office: PO Box 956187 Duluth GA 30095 E-mail: aaronbrody@aol.com.

BRODY, ADRIEN, actor; b. N.Y.C., Apr. 14, 1973; s. Elliot Brody and Sylvia Plachy. Student, LaGuardia H.S. Music and Performing Arts, N.Y.C., 1991. Actor: (plays, off-Broadway prodn.) Family Pride in the '50s; (TV series, Home at Last), 1988; (TV series) Annie McGuire, 1988; (films) New York Stories, 1989; (TV films, Showtime movie) Rebel Highway, 1994; (films) Ten Benny/Nothing to Lose, 1995, The Last Time I Committed Suicide, 1996, Six Ways to Sunday, 1999, Restaurant, 2000, The Thin Red Line, 1998, Oxygen, 1999, Summer of Sam, 1999, Liberty Heights, 1999, Bread and Roses, 2000, Harrison's Flowers, 2000, Love the Hard Way, 2000, The Pianist, 2002 (Golden Globe nomination for Best Actor, BAFTA nomination for leading role, SAG award, Acad. award for Best Actor, Nat. Soc. Film Critics award for Best Actor, 2002).

BRODY, ALAN JEFFREY, investment company executive; b. Newark, Apr. 19, 1952; s. Robert and Marcia (Ostroff) B.; m. Miriam Kahan, May 22, 1977 BA, Northwestern U., 1974; JD, Rutgers U., 1977. Bar: N.Y. 1978, N.J. 1978. Assoc. Baer Marks & Upham, N.Y.C., 1977-80; v.p. counsel Commodity Exchange Inc., N.Y.C., 1980-81, pres., chief exec. officer, 1981-89, chmn., 1987-88; v.p. Commodities Exchange Ctr. Inc., 1981-84, alternate dir., 1984-89; sr. v.p. futures div. Lehman Bros., N.Y.C., 1990-96; mng. dir. Lehman Bros. Futures Asset Mgmt. Corp., N.Y.C., 1991-96; sr. v.p. internat. divsn. Prudential Securities, Inc., N.Y.C., 1997-2000; regional dir. Europe/Middle East/Asia Pacific Prudential-Bache Internat. Ltd., London, 2001—. Mem. commodity policy adv. com. to U.S. trade rep.; past mem. coun. Found. Internat. Futures and Commodities Inst., Geneva. Mem. ABA, N.J. Bar Assn., Assn. of Bar of City of N.Y. (commodities regulation com.), New York County Lawyers Assn., Nat. Futures Assn. (bd. dirs., exec. com. 1986-89), Futures Industry Assn. (past mem. exec. com. law and compliance div.), Am. Copper Council (past bd. dirs.), Copper Club (past bd. dirs.), Swiss Commodities & Futures Assn. (bd. dirs.) Office: Prudential Securities Inc One New York Plaza New York NY 10292

BRODY, ARTHUR, industrial executive; b. Newark, June 30, 1920; s. Samuel A. and Ruth (Marder) B.; m. Sophie Mark, Mar. 5, 1944; children: Janice, Donald. Student, Columbia U., 1939-42. Organizer, operator Library Service, 1940-42; exec. buyer L. Bamberger & Co., Newark, 1942-43; chmn. Brodart Co., Williamsport, Pa., 1946—, BDI Investment Corp., San Diego, Tura Inc., Lake Success, N.Y. Past mem. adv. panel study on librs. and industry Nat. Adv. Com. on Librs.; past pres. Friends of N.J. Librs. Patentee in field. Past trustee Newark Symphony Hall., Ctr. for Book, Libr. of Congress, L.A. County Libr. Found., Friends of Libr. USA, San Diego Community Found.; past commr. San Diego Pub. Libr. With AUS, 1943-46. Mem. ALA, NEA, San Diego Yacht Club, Rancho Sante Fe Golf Club, Masons, Shriners. Office: Brodart Co 990 Highland Dr Ste 100 Solana Beach CA 92075-2409

BRODY, BARUCH ALTER, medical educator, academic center administrator; b. Bklyn., Apr. 21, 1943; s. Lester and Gussie (Glass) B.; m. Dena Grosser, Aug. 15, 1965; children: Todd, Jeremy, Myles. BA, Bklyn. Coll., 1962; PhD, Princeton U., 1967. Asst. prof. MIT, Cambridge, 1967-75; assoc. prof. Rice U., Houston, 1975-77, prof., 1977—, Baylor Coll. Medicine, Houston, 1982—, dir. ctr. ethics, 1982—. Cons. NASA, 1990-91, 94—. Author: Abortion and the Sanctity of Human Life, 1975, Identity and Essence, 1981, Life and Death Decision Making, 1988, Ethical Issues in Drug Testing Approval and Pricing, 1994, The Ethics of Biomedical Research, 1998. Chmn. bd. dirs. Hebrew Acad., Houston, 1976-98; pres. Soc. Health and Human Values, 1995-96. Recipient Disting. Alumnus award Bklyn. Coll., 1991. Mem.: Inst. Medicine. Jewish. Office: Baylor Coll Medicine Ctr Med Ethics & Health Pol Houston TX 77030 also: Rice U PO Box 1892 6100 South Main Houston TX 77251

BRODY, BERNARD B. physician, educator; b. N.Y.C., June 24, 1922; s. Abraham and Sarah (Berman) B.; m. Ruth M. Miller, Jan. 15, 1954; children: Sarah, Rachel. BS, U. Wis., 1943; MD, U. Rochester, 1951. Diplomate Am. Bd. Internal Medicine, Nat. Bd. Med. Examiners. Rsch. chemist U. Chgo. and Monsanto, Dayton, Ohio, 1943-47; resident U. Rochester, N.Y., 1951-53, clin. prof. pathology and medicine, 1981-90, prof. emeritus, 1990—; resident Genesee Hosp., Rochester, 1955-56, dir. clin. labs., 1967-81, sr. v.p. med. affairs, 1975-87; pvt. practice internal medicine Rochester, 1956-67. Cons. Eastman Kodak Co., 1971-92, Robert Wood Johnson Found., 1975-80, ED-MAC Assocs., Inc., 1976-83; trustee Freedom Forum, 1980-98; mem. adv. bd. Freedom Forum Media Studies Ctr., N.Y.C., 1985-98, adv. trustee Freedom Forum, 1998—. Bd. dirs. Rochester Mus. and Sci. Ctr., 1994-2003, Genesee Valley Med. Care, Rochester, 1962-68, Crestwood Children's Ctr., 1985-97; chmn. med. adv. bd. St. Ann's Home, 1964-67; corp. mem. United Way, Rochester, 1980-87; mem. Citizens Com. Human Rels., 1980-85; v.p., mem. exec. bd. Otetiana coun. Boy Scouts Am., 1981-91; bd. dirs. Via Health Rochester Gen. Hosp., 2001—; chmn. stewardship cabinet Lifespan, 2003—. 1st lt. U.S. Army, 1953-55. Mem. AMA, ACP, Am. Soc. Internal Medicine, Acad. Clin. Lab. Physicians and Scientists, Am. Assn. Clin. Chemistry, Sigma Xi, Alpha Omega Alpha Home and Office: 12 Huntington Brk Rochester NY 14625-1811 Fax: 585-381-9836. E-mail: Bbrody@rochester.rr.com. *Stay open-minded and flexible in thinking. It helps to recognize and take advantage of opportunities for adjuncts to or career enhancements or changes. It also makes for an interesting and exciting journey through life.*

BRODY, CAROL Z. artist, educator; b. Bklyn., July 5, 1941; d. Morris and Augusta Zimmerman; m. Elliott Brody, June 30, 1962; children: Evan, Susan, David. BA cum laude, Bklyn. Coll., 1962; postgrad., Parsons Sch. Design, 1982-86. Lic. tchr., N.Y. Tchr. Bd. Edn., N.Y.C., 1963-65, art tchr., 1991-96; instr. watercolor Armory Art Ctr., West Palm Beach, Fla., 1997-98. Instr. watercolor Art Lab. at Snug Harbor, N.Y.C., 1987-96; instr. art edn. Coll. S.I., N.Y.C., 1991-96. (exhibited works at) Nat. Watercolor Soc., Calif., 2001, NAD, N.Y.C., 1994, Nat. Arts Club, 1987—2002, Salmagundi Club, 1987—2002, Pen and Brush Club, 1988—99, Met. Mus. Art, Lever house, Fed. Ct. House, Borough Hall, S.I., St. Johns U., Wagner Coll., Newhouse Gallery, Soc. for the Four Arts, Fla., 1997, Coral Springs City Ctr., 1997—2001, Cornell Mus., 1977—79, Ann Norton Sculpture Garden, 1999, Ga. Watercolor Soc., 1994, 1996, (works appeared in) Watercolor Mag., 1990, Best of Acrylic Painting, 1996, CBS-TV Ctrl. Park West, 1996. Mem. Nat. Collage Soc., Nat. Watercolor Soc., Allied Artists Am., Soc. Layerists in Multi-Media, Pen and Brush Club (chmn. watercolor divsn. 1990-96), Catharine Lorillard Wolfe Art Club (v.p., bd. dirs. 1995-96), Salmagundi Club (jury awards 1990-91, admissions com. 1991-94), Audubon Artists. Avocations: gardening, swimming. Home: 801 Caraway Ct West Palm Beach FL 33414-8211

BRODY, DAVID, history educator; b. Elizabeth, N.J., June 5, 1930; s. Barnet and Ida (Gulker) B.; m. Susan Schapiro, Oct. 30, 1955; children: Sara Beth, Pamela, Jonathan. AB, Harvard U., 1952, MA, 1953, PhD, 1958. Asst. prof. Columbia U., N.Y.C., 1961-65; assoc. prof. Ohio State U., Columbus, 1965-67; prof. U. Calif., Davis, 1967—. Visiting prof. U. Warwick, Coventry, Eng., 1972-73, Moscow State U., USSR, 1975, U. Sydney, Australia, 1984, Wayne State U., 1988-89. Author: Steelworkers in America, 1960, Labor in Crisis, 1965, Workers in Indsl. Am., 1980; co-author: America's History, 1987. Pres. Pacific Coast br. Am. Hist. Assn., 1991-92. Recipient Social Sci. Rsch. Coun. fellowship, 1966, NEH sr. fellowship, 1978, Guggenheim Found. fellowship, 1983, Fulbright sr. professorship, 1975. Fellow Soc. Am. Historians; mem. Am. Hist. Assn., Orgn. Am. Historians (exec. bd. 1976-79). Home: 62 Richardson Rd Kensington CA 94707-1228 Office: Dept History U Calif Davis CA 95616

BRODY, DAVID, artist, educator; b. N.Y.C., Feb. 16, 1958; s. Jules and Roxane (Offner) B. BA, Bennington (Vt.) Coll., 1981; MFA, Yale U., 1983. Vis. prof. Carnegie Mellon U., Pitts., 1990-91; head grad. studies Studio Art Ctr. Internat., Florence, Italy, 1992-96; asst. prof. painting and drawing U. Wash., Seattle, 1996-2000, assoc. prof., chmn. dept., 2000—. One-man shows include Gallery NAGA, Boston, 1989, 92, 94, 96, Hewlett Gallery, Carnegie Mellon U., Pitts., 1991, Galeria Gilde, Guimarães, Portugal, 1996, Esther Claypool Gallery, Seattle, 1999, 2001, 2002; exhibited in group shows Chgo. Ctr. for Print, 1985, FPAC Gallery, Boston, 1986, Bridgewater Gallery, N.Y., SixToSix Gallery, N.Y.C., 1987, Gallery NAGA, Boston, 1989, 95, Mills Gallery, Boston Ctr. for Arts, 1989, 90, 91, Hewlett Gallery, 1990, Fitchburg Art Mus., Mass., 1991, 93, Limner Gallery, N.Y.C., 1992, Tribeca Gallery 148, N.Y., Decordova Mus., Lincoln, Mass., 1994, RipArte Art Fair, Rome, Italy, 1995, FAC Art Fair, Lisbon, Portugal, 1995, Trevi Flash Art Mus., Italy, 1996, The Painting Center, N.Y.C., 1996, The Alternative Mus., N.Y.C., 1996, Mus. Fine Arts, Fla. State U., Tallahassee, 1997, ARCO Art Fair, Madrid, 1996, 97, 99, Ctr. on Contemporary Art, Seattle; selected pubs.: David Brody, Selected Paintings, 1985-1994, David Brody, Selected Paintings, 2001-2002. Grantee Guggenheim Found., N.Y.C., 1991, Fulbright Found., Washington, 1992, Elizabeth Found. for Arts, N.Y.C., 1994, Basil H. Alkazzi award, 1998. Office: U Wash PO Box 353440 Seattle WA 98195-3440 E-mail: brody@u.washington.edu.

BRODY, EUGENE BLOOR, psychiatrist, educator; b. Columbia, Mo., June 17, 1921; s. Samuel and Sophie B.; m. Marian Holen, Sept. 23, 1944; children: Julie Anne, James Clarke, John Holen. AB, MA, U. Mo., 1941, DSc (hon.), 1991; MD, Harvard, 1944; grad., N.Y. Psychoanalytic Inst., 1957. Resident Yale Med. Sch., 1944-46, 48-49, from instr. to assoc. prof., 1949-57; prof. psychiatry U. Md. Sch. Medicine, Balt., 1957-76; chmn. dept., also dir. Inst. Psychiatry and Human Behavior, 1959-76, prof. psychiatry and human behavior, 1976-87, prof. emeritus, 1987—; sr. assoc. sch. of hygiene and pub. health Johns Hopkins U., 1986—. Vis. prof. U. Brazil, 1965-68, U. W.I., Kingston, Jamaica, 1972-75, U. Otago, New Zealand, 1981, James Cook U., No. Queensland, Australia, 1992; vis. prof. psychiatry Harvard Med. Sch., 1997-99; fellow Center for Advanced Studies in Behavioral Scis., Stanford, 1975-76, Inst. for Advanced Studies, Tel Aviv U., 1986; mem. adv. bd. Inst. Social Psychiatry, U. San Marcos, Peru, 1968-70; mem. nat. profl. adv. bd. psychiatry, psychology and neurology service VA, 1963-67; cons. WHO (Pan Am. Health Orgn. and Geneva, Switzerland), 1965-95; program dir. Interam. Mental Health Studies Program, 1967-69; mem. exec. bd. World Fedn. Mental Health, 1969-83, adminstrv. mem., 1972-74, mem.-at-large, 1979-81, pres., 1981-83, sec. gen., 1983-99, sr. cons., 1999—; mem. epidemiol. studies rev. com. NIMH, 1975-79, cons. clin. infant devel. program, 1979-81, hosp. rev. com., 1979-86, AIDS grant rev. com. 1987-92; mem. internat. adv. bd. Peruvian Nat. Inst. Mental Health, 1984-94, mem. editl. bd. jours., 1985-94; mem. adv. coun. Hogg Found., 1986-89; mem. sci. com. Internat. Social Sci. Coun., 1989, exec. com. 1989-91, 92-95; cons. UNESCO, 1986-93; sr. advisor Harvard Program Refugee Trauma, 1989—; cons. Balt. VA Med. Ctr., 1990—. Author: The Lost Ones, Social Forces and Mental Illness in Rio de Janeiro, 1973, Sex, Contraception and Motherhood in Jamaica, 1981, Psychoanalytic Knowledge, 1990, Biomedical Technology and Human Rights, 1993, The Search for Mental Health: A History and Memoir of WFMH, 1948-1997, 1998; editor: (with F.C. Redlich) Psychotherapy with Schizophrenics, 1952, (with R. Monroe and G. Klee) Psychiatric Epidemiology and Mental Health Planning, 1967, Minority Group Adolescents in the United States, 1968, Behavior in New Environments, 1970; cons. editor Jour. Nervous and Mental Disease, 1959-67, editor in chief, 1967— ; adv. editor: Tice Med. Ency., 1967-80, Harper & Row Med. Ency., 1980-86; mem. editorial bd. Psychiatry Digest, 1967-71, Mental Hygiene, 1968-70, Social Psychiatry, 1970-81, Internat. Jour. Psychosomatic Obstetrics and Gynecology, 1984-92, Population and Environment, 1987-92; contbr. numerous articles to profl. jours. Chmn. adv. bd. Balt. chpt. Internat. Students Council, ARC, 1964-67; bd. dirs. Md. Partners of Alliance for Progress, 1965-66, Nat. Assn. Mental Health, 1964-66, mem. profl. adv. bd., 1967-71; mem. adv. bd. Inst. for Victims of Trauma, 1988-97. Served to capt. M.C. AUS, 1946-48. Fellow Am. Psychiat. Assn. (life; chmn. com. transcultural psychiatry 1966-68, rep. interam. council 1965-71, trustee 1968-71, chmn. task force family planning 1973-75, Human Rights award 1999), Am. Coll. Psychiatrists (charter), Am. Coll. Psychoanalysts (charter); mem. Assn. Behavioral Sci. and Med. Edn. (pres. 1981), Am. Psychoanalytic Assn. (life), Internat. psychoanalytic assns., Internat. Coll. Pediatrics (senate 1978-86), Internat. Assn. Psychosomatic Ob-Gyn (exec. bd. 1977-86), Peruvian Psychiat. Assn. (hon.), Peruvian Assn. Psychiatry, Neurology and Neurosurgery (hon.), Cosmos Club (Washington), West River Sailing Assn., 14 W. Hamilton St. Club (Balt.). Home: 70 Olmsted Green Ct Baltimore MD 21210-1508 Office: Jour Nervous/Mental Disease care Sheppard & Enoch-Pratt Hosp PO Box 6815 Baltimore MD 21285-6815 Office Fax: 410-938-3183. E-mail: ebbrody@aol.com.

BRODY, EUGENE DAVID, investment company executive; b. Bklyn., Feb. 6, 1931; s. Leon K. and Ruth (Parkoff) B.; m. Jacqueline Galloway, Apr. 5, 1959; children: Jessica, Leslie. BS, U. Pa., 1952; MBA, NYU, 1963. Gen. ptnr. A.W. Jones Assocs., N.Y.C., 1965-70; v.p., bd. dirs. Downe Communications, N.Y.C., 1970-74; chief exec. officer Founders Mut. Depositor Corp., Denver, 1970-74; pres. Beekman Capital, Inc., N.Y.C., 1974—78; sr. v.p., ptnr. Oppenheimer & Co. Inc., N.Y.C., 1978—86; mng. dir. Oppenheimer Capital, 1986-96; pres. Picanet, Inc., N.Y.C., 1997—. Pub. Print Collectors Newsletter, 1971—96; bd. dirs. Alara, Inc., Pasteurized Eggs Corp.; trustee Manhattan Inst. for Policy Rsch., N.Y.C. Author: Odds-On Investing, 1978. Lt. USNR, 1952-55. Mem. N.Y. Futures & Options Soc. (founding dir., pres. 1978-79), University Club N.Y.C., Stamford Yacht Club, Regency Whist Club (bd. govs. 1985-94), Econ. Club N.Y. Home and Office: Picanet Inc 119 E 79th St New York NY 10021-0339

BRODY, HAROLD, neuroanatomist, gerontologist; b. Cleve., May 15, 1923; s. Julius and Esther (Barowitz) B.; m. Anne Pertz, Mar. 24, 1951; children: David Andrew, Evan Barrett. Student, L.I. U., 1941-43; BS, Western Res. U., 1947; PhD, U. Minn., 1953; MD, U. Buffalo, 1961. Instr. anatomy U. Minn., Mpls., 1949-50; asst. prof. U. N.D., Grand Forks, 1950-54, U. Buffalo, 1954-59; assoc. prof. SUNY (merger with U. Buffalo 1961), 1959-63, prof., 1963-95, disting. tchg. prof., 1995—; asst. dean SUNY, Buffalo, 1968-69; assoc. dean SUNY (merger with U. Buffalo 1961), 1969-70, Buswell rsch. fellow, 1970—, chmn. dept. anat. scis., 1971-92. Acting dir. Ctr. for Study of Aging, SUNY, Buffalo, 1977-80, organizer, curator Mus. Neuroanatomy, 1994—; vis. prof. neurophthalmology St. Mary's Hosp., Rochester, N.Y., 1965-75, U. Copenhagen, 1987, 90, 91, 92, 93, 95; Anthes Wilson Abernathy disting. lectr. U. Toronto, Ont., Can., 1987; mem. com. on rsch. and demonstration White House Conf. on Aging, 1971; mem. biology coun. Canisius Coll., Buffalo, 1969; mem. sci. bd. Buffalo Otol. Found., 1968-73; mem. nat. adv. coun. Nat. Inst. on Aging, NIH, 1975-79. Abstractor, Excerpta Medica Sect. Gerontology and Geriat., 1959—; sci. referee Science, 1956—, Jour. Morphology, 1958—; sci. referee Jour. Gerontology, 1957-73, assoc. editor, 1973-75, editor-in-chief, 1975-80; editor Neurobiology of Aging, 1981—; mem. editl. bd. Gerontology and Geriat. Edn., 1980—, Exptl. Gerontology, 1984—. Trustee Erie County Meals on Wheels, Legal Svcs. for Elderly; pres. Friends of Health Scis. Med. Libr. SUNY, Buffalo, 1999. With M.C., AUS, 1943-46. Recipient NSF travel award, 1957, Robert W. Kleemeier Rsch. award in gerontology Gerontol. Soc. Am., 1978; co-recipient Lyn Millane Cmty. Svc. award Amherst (N.Y.) Sr. Citizens' Found., 1998-99; Fulbright sr. rsch. scholar, Copenhagen, 1963. Mem. AAAS, Roswell Park Med. Club (pres. 1978-79), Am. Assn. Anatomists, Am. Assn. Anatomy Chmn., Am. Geriat. Soc., Am. Aging Assn. (trustee 1970-77), Gerontol. Soc. Am. (mem. exec. com. 1961-63, 68-71, pres. 1974-75), Buffalo Neuropsychiat. Soc. (pres. 1967-68), Alpha Omega Alpha. Achievements include research on effects of aging on human central nervous system. Home: 50 Stahl Rd Apt 301 Getzville NY 14068-1554 Office: SUNY Buffalo Main St Campus Dept Pathology and Anat Scis Rm 204 Sherman Hall Buffalo NY 14214

BRODY, HAROLD JOSEPH, dermatologist; b. Sumter, S.C., Jan. 11, 1949; s. Abram and Sara B. BA in Chemistry, Duke U., 1970; MD, Med. U. S.C., 1974. Intern U. Tex. Med. Ctr., 1974-75; resident Emory U. Med. Ctr., 1975-78. Author: Chemical Peeling, 1992, Chemical Peeling and Resurfacing, 1997; sr. editor Jour. Dermatologic Surgery & Oncology, 1991. Bd. dirs. Theatre in the Square, Atlanta, 1986-89, Onstage Atlanta, 1987-90, Calibre Prodns., Atlanta, 1994; mem. Duke U. Nat. Drama Adv. Bd., Durham, N.C., 1994-96. Mem.: Atlanta Dermatol. Assn. (pres. 1989), Ga. Dermatologic Assn. (pres. 2001), Am. Soc. Dermatologic Surgery (bd. dirs. 1989—91, sec. 1995—, v.p. 1998—, pres. 2000). Avocations: theatre, reading, marathons. Office: Hailey & Brody 550 Peachtree St NE Ste 1135 Atlanta GA 30308-3120

BRODY, JACOB JEROME, art history educator; b. Bklyn., Apr. 24, 1929; s. Aladar and Esther (Kraiman) B.; m. Jean Lindsey, Feb. 13, 1956; children: Jefferson, Jonathan, Allison. Cert. fine arts, Cooper Union, 1950; BA, U. N.Mex., 1956, MA, 1964, PhD, 1970. Curator of art Everhart Mus., Scranton, Pa., 1957-58; curator collections Isaac Delgado Mus. Art, New Orleans, 1958-60; Mus. Internat. Folk Art, Santa Fe, 1960-61; prof. anthropology U. N.Mex., 1965-85, prof. art history, 1972-89; prof. emeritus, 1989—; curator Maxwell Mus., U. N.Mex., Albuquerque, 1962—73, dir., 1973—85. Mem. adv. bd. Ghost Ranch Mus., N.Mex. Mus. Natural History, 1981-84, Wheelwright Mus. of the Am. Indian, 1989-92, Zuni Pueblo Mus., 1992—; rsch. curator Maxwell Mus., sr. rsch. assoc.; rsch. curator Sch. of Am. Rsch., Lab. of Anthropology; mem. fine arts bd. City of Albuquerque, vice chmn., 1970-74; mem. Gov. N.Mex. Task Force Paleontol. Resources, 1978-79. Author: Indian Painters and White Patrons, 1971, Mimbres Painted Pottery, 1977, Between Traditions, 1977, Yazz: Navajo Painter, 1982, The Chaco Phenomenon, 1983, The Anasazi, 1990, Beauty From the Earth, 1990, Anasazi and Pueblo Painting, 1991, Pueblo Indian Painting: Tradition and Modernism in New Mexico 1900-1930, 1997; co-author: Mimbres Pottery: Ancient Art of the American Southwest, 1983, To Touch the Past: The Painted Pottery of the Mimbres People, 1996; featured authorPainters, Patrons, and Identity: Essays in Native American Art to Honor J.J. Brody, 2001. Recipient Tom L. Popejoy Dissertation award U. N.Mex., 1970, Gov.'s award of honor N.Mex. Hist. Com., 1978, Non-Fiction award Border-Regional Libr. Assn., 1972, Art Book award, 1979, Conservation and Preservatin award Am. Rock Art Rsch. Assn., 1998, Disting. Alumni award Coll. Fine Arts, U. N.Mex., 2000, Lifetime Contrbn. to Humanities award N.Mex. Endowment for Humanities, 2001; resident scholar Sch. Am. Rsch., 1980-81; honoree Archeol. Soc. N.Mex., 1990, Native Am. Art Rsch. Assn., 1997. Mem.: Am. Rock Art Rsch. Assn., Native Am. Art Studies Assn., N.Mex. Mus. Assn., Soc. Am. Archaeology. E-mail: jjbrody@umn.edu.

BRODY, JACQUELINE, editor; b. Utica, N.Y., Jan. 23, 1932; d. Jack and Mary (Childress) Galloway; m. Eugene D. Brody, Apr. 5, 1959; children: Jessica, Leslie. AB, Vassar Coll., 1953; postgrad., London Sch. Econs., 1953-56. Assoc. editor Crowell Collier Macmillan, N.Y.C., 1963-67; writer Coun. Fgn. Rels., N.Y.C., 1968-69; mng. editor Print Collector's Newsletter, N.Y.C., 1971-72, editor, 1972-96, art writer, 1996—; dir., v.p. Picanet, Inc., N.Y.C., 1996—. Office: 119 E 79th St New York NY 10021-0339

BRODY, JANE ELLEN, journalist, researcher; b. Bklyn., May 19, 1941; d. Sidney and Lillian (Kellner) B.; m. Richard Engquist, Oct. 2, 1966; children: Lee Erik and Lorin Michael Engquist (twins). BS, N.Y. State Coll. Agr., Cornell U., 1962; MS in Journalism, U. Wis., 1963, LHD (hon.), Princeton U., 1987; LHD (hon.), Hamline U., 1993, SUNY Hlth. Sci. Ctr., 1999; LHD U. Minn. (hon.), 2000. Reporter Mpls. Tribune, 1963-65; sci. writer, personal health columnist N.Y. Times, N.Y.C., 1965—; mem. adv. council N.Y. State Coll. Agr., Cornell U., 1971-77. Author: (with Richard Engquist) Secrets of Good Health, 1970; (with Arthur Holleb) You Can Fight Cancer and Win, 1977, Jane Brody's Nutrition Book, 1981, Jane Brody's The New York Times Guide to Personal Health, 1982, Jane Brody's Good Food Book, 1985, Jane Brody's Good Food Gourmet, 1990; (with Richard Flaste) Jane Brody's Good Seafood Book, 1994, Jane Brody's Cold and Flu Fighter, 1995, Jane Brody's Allergy Fighter, 1997, The New York Times Book of Health, 1997, The New York Times Book of Women's Health, 2000, The New York Times Book of Alternative Health, 2001. Recipient numerous writing awards including Howard Blakeslee award Am. Heart Assn., 1971, Sci. Writers' award ADA, 1978, J.C. Penney-U. Mo. Journalism award, 1978, Lifeline award Am. Health Found., 1978 Jewish. Office: NY Times 229 W 43d St New York NY 10036-3913

BRODY, JAY HOWARD, lawyer; b. Detroit, Jan. 4, 1953; s. Robert David and Rhea Antoinnette (Orley) B.; m. Helene Cheryl Brodsky, Aug. 11, 1974 (div. Nov. 1998); children: Stuart, Rachel; m. Susan Logar, Oct. 15, 1999. BA in Anthropology, U. Mich., 1974; JD, Wayne State U., 1976. Bar: Mich. 1977, U.S. Dist. Ct. (ea. dist.) Mich. 1977, U.S. Ct. Appeals (6th cir.) 1977, U.S. Tax Ct. 1979. Acct. Arther Andersen, Detroit, 1977-79; assoc. Raymond & Dillon, Detroit, 1979-80, Rubenstein & Isaacs, Southfield, Mich., 1980-81; pvt. practice Farmington Hills, Mich., 1981-01; with Kemp, Klein, Umphrey, Endelman & May PC, Troy, Mich., 2001—. Dir. Thomas Found., Farmington Hills, 1984—. Exec. producer (film) KillZone, 1997. Mem. ABA, AICPAs, State Bar Mich., Mich. Assn. CPAs. Office: Kemp Klein Umphrey Endelman & May PC 201 W Big Beaver Rd Ste 600 Troy MI 48084

BRODY, JO-ANN, artist, educator; b. N.Y.C., Feb. 28, 1945; d. Joshua and Evelyn E. Brody; m. Aaron Joseph Kleinmann, Aug. 15, 1971; children: Mikhael G. Kleinmann, Zoe M-S Kleinmann, Silmara S Kleinmann. Cert. of Study, Portland Mus. Art Sch., 1967; BA, Reed Coll., Portland, Oreg., 1968. Roster artist Young Audiences, N.Y.C., NY, 1999—, Westchester Arts Coun., White Plains, NY, 1999—; co-dir. Peekskill Creative Arts Camp, Peekskill, NY, 1996—; roster artist Portchester Arts Coun., NY. Exhibition, Woman Forms (N/A), artist exchange/exhibition, Josei no Mori (Forest of Women) (selected to be Exch. artist with Network Nishijin, 2000), exhibition, Women of the Book (group show), Dialogs in the Garden (one person show), Figuratively Speaking (two person show). Bd. of trustees Mohegan Colony Assn, Crompond, NY, 1986—2002; bd. dirs. Peekskill Arts Coun., 1999—. Mem.: Katonah Mus. Mem. Artist, Ceres Gallery. Jewish. Avocations: Tae Kwon Do, walking. Home: Box 328 Crompond NY 10517 Office: 1006 Brown St Ste 206 Peekskill NY 10566

BRODY, KENNETH DAVID, investment banker; b. Phila., June 30, 1943; s. Herbert Brody and Esther (Forman) Brody Shimberg; m. Judy E. Donahue, Feb. 5, 1964 (div. Feb. 1974); m. Helen M. Tandler, Apr. 6, 1974 (div. Oct. 1978); m. Carolyn J. Schwenker, June 26, 1987. BSE.E. with high honors, U. Md., 1964; MBA with high distinction, Harvard U., 1971. Foreman and staff asst. Chesapeake & Potomac Telephone Co., Washington, 1964-66; with Goldman, Sachs & Co., N.Y.C., 1971-91, ptnr., 1978-91; chmn., pres. Export-Import Bank of U.S., Washington, 1993-96; founding ptnr. Winslow Ptnrs., LLC, Washington, 1996—; co-founder Taconic Capital Advisors, 1999—. Bd. dirs. Fed. Realty Investment Trust, Quest Diagnostics, Inc. Bd. dirs. Alvin Ailey Am. Dance Theater, N.Y.C., 1981-93, ARC, 1994-2000, St. John's Coll., 1996-97; chmn. Presdl. Commn. U.S.-Pacific Trade and Investment Policy, 1996-97; mem. investment com. George Washington U., U. Md., ARC, 2001—. Capt. U.S. Army, 1966-69. Baker scholar, 1970; Loeb Rhoades fellow, 1971 Mem. Coun. Fgn. Rels., Tau Beta Pi, Eta Kappa Nu, Omicron Delta Kappa, Alpha Tau Omega. Clubs: Harvard (bd. mgrs. N.Y.C.). Democrat. Unitarian Universalist. Office: Winslow Ptnrs LLC 1300 Connecticut Ave NW Washington DC 20036-1703 Address: 2991 Woodland Dr NW Washington DC 20008-3542

BRODY, LESLIE GARY, social worker, sociologist; b. Albany, N.Y., Aug. 30, 1944; s. Sanford and Cyrille L. (Kosatsky) B.; m. Marjorie A. Rubin, Feb. 1, 1970; children: Jennifer, Jonathan, David. AA, Corning Community Coll., 1966; BA, U. Maine, 1970; MSW, Ind. U., Indpls., 1972; PhD, Boston U., 1984. Lic. ind. clin. social worker, Mass. Dir. regional- statewide planning &devel. drug abuse div. Indpls., 1972-74; dep. dir. Iowa Drub Abuse Authority, Des Moines, 1974-76, dir., 1976-77; exec. dir. Eliot Community Mental Health Ctr., Concord, Mass., 1977-83; pres. Les Brody Assocs., Acton, Mass., 1983—. Author: Effective Fund Raising, 1994; contbr. chpt. to book and articles to profl. jours. Vice pres. Congregation Beth Elohim, Acton, 1979-81, pres., 1982-84; v.p. campaign Acton-Boxborough Cmty. Chest, 1986-87; pres. Acton-Boxborough United Way, 1990-93. With U.S. Army, 1964-67. Jewish. Avocations: landscaping, running, Karate, tennis. Office: PO Box 1121 Acton MA 01720-0121 Fax: 978-264-3161.

BRODY, MARTIN, food service company executive; b. Newark, Aug. 8, 1921; s. Leo and Renee (Kransdorf) B.; m. Florence Gropper, Nov. 22, 1946; children: Marc, Renee. BA, Mich. State U., 1943. Pres. Indsl. Feeding Co., Newark, 1951-61; pres., dir. A.M. Capital Corp., N.Y.C., 1961-71. Chmn. bd., dir. Waldorf System Inc., Boston, 1963-66, Restaurant Assocs., Inc., N.Y.C., 1964-66; chmn. bd., CEO Restaurant Assocs. Industries Inc., 1966-99; chmn. bd. St. Barnabas Corp.; dir. Jaclyn Inc., several Smith Barney mut. funds, Washington Nat. Life Ins. Co. of N.Y.; bd. dirs. Regional Planning Assn. Trustee St. Barnabas Med. Ctr.; bd. dirs. N.J. Transit Corp. Served to capt. AUS, 1943-45. Mem. Orange Lawn Tennis, Greenbrook Country (North Caldwell, N.J.), Boca Raton Hotel and Resort Club.

BRODY, RICHARD ALAN, political science educator, researcher; b. N.Y.C., Mar. 2, 1930; s. Lee and Felice Auslander; m. Marjorie Jean Brody, Aug. 23, 1964; children: Gordon Christopher, David Eric, Aaron Jed. BA, San Francisco

State U., 1956, MA, 1959; PhD, Northwestern U., 1963. Asst. prof. Stanford (Calif.) U., 1962-66, assoc. prof., 1966-70, prof., 1970-95, chmn. dept., 1972-73, 74-77, prof. emeritus, 1995—. Fulbright prof. U. Leiden, The Netherlands, 1970-71; bd. overseers Am. Nat. Election Study, 1980-87. Author: Simulation Internat., 1963, Assessing the President, 1991; co-author: Reasoning and Choice, 1991 (Woodrow Wilson prize 1992); co-editor: Political Persuasion and Attitude, 1996; editor Polit. Behavior jour., 1990-97. Fellow, Ctr. Advanced Study in Behavioral Sci., 1967-68, Am. Acad. Arts and Scis., 1992; Parthemos fellow U. Ga., 1998. Mem. Am. Polit. Sci. Assn. (coun. 1977-79), Western Polit. Sci. Assn. (pres. 1987-88), Midwest Polit. Sci. Assn. Democrat. Avocations: wines, food, travel, birding. Home: 1636 Edgewood Dr Palo Alto CA 94303-2820 Office: Stanford Univ Dept Polit Sci Stanford CA 94305-6044 E-mail: Brody@leland.Stanford.edu.

BRODY, RICHARD ERIC, lawyer; b. N.Y.C., Sept. 9, 1947; s. Harold I. and Lillian C. (Albert) B.; m. V. Jane Cohen, May 25, 1974; children: Lauren, Erica. BA, Washington and Jefferson Coll., 1969; JD, Boston U., 1975. Bar: Mass. 1975, U.S. Dist. Ct. Mass. 1975, U.S. Ct. Appeals (1st cir.) 1975, U.S. Supreme Ct. 1987. Law clk. Mass. Superior Ct., Boston, 1975-76, chief law clk., 1976-77; assoc. Sisson, Lee & Bloomenthal, Boston, 1977-78; asst. dist. atty. Atty.'s Office Middlesex County Dist., Cambridge, Mass., 1978 82; assoc. Morrison, Mahoney & Miller, Boston, 1982-85, ptnr., 1985-95, Brody, Hardoon, Perkins & Kesten, Boston, 1995—. Lectr. Nat. Inst. Trial Advocacy, trial practice series Harvard U., Mass. Continuing Legal Edn., Def. Rsch. Inst.; evaluator Middlesex Multi-Door Courthouse, Cambridge, 1989—; mediator Arbitration Forums, Inc., Tarrytown, N.Y., 1989—, cons. Liability Cons., Inc., Sudbury, 1988—; mem. nat. adv. bd. Govtl. Liability Ins., Richmond, 1985—. Trustee Mass. Civil Liability Ins., Boston, 1983-89. Mem. Mass. Bar Assn. (civil litigation sect. coun.), Mass. Assn. Trial Lawyers, Boston Bar Assn., Def. Rsch. Inst., City Solicitors and Town Counsel Assn. Office: Brody Hardoon Perkins & Kesten 1 Exeter Plz Fl 12 Boston MA 02116-2848

BRODY, ROBERT, dermatologist; b. Cleve., June 15, 1948; s. Melvin and Nancy Elizabeth Brody; m. Mary Ann Conn, July 23, 1988; children: Ian Hamilton Conn, Hartley Messing Conn, Matthew Grant Hutchinson. AB with distinction, Stanford U., 1970; MD, U. Mich., 1974. Intern in internal medicine, Cleve. Clinic, 1974-75, resident in dermatology, 1975-78; practice medicine specializing in dermatology, Cleve., 1978—; staff physician Kaiser-Permanente Med. Center, 1978-82, mem. profl. edn. com., 1978-82, chmn., 1980-82, also sec. exec. com., 1980; pvt. practice, 1982—; asst. clin. prof. Case Western Res. U. Med. Sch., 1978-80, 83—, clin. instr., 1980-83, dermatology dept. rep. to gen. faculty, 1980-82; asst. physician Univ. Hosps. Cleve., 1979—; chief dermatology divsn. St. Luke's Hosp., Cleve., 1999—. Sec., Cleve. Play House Men's Com., 1979-82; mem. ann. fund com. Stanford U., 1978—, regional co-chmn., 1981-82. Diplomate Am. Bd. Dermatology. Mem. Am. Acad. Dermatology, Cleve. Acad. Medicine. Contbr. articles to med. jours. Club: Cleve. Skating, Rowfant. Home: 2870 Glengary Rd Cleveland OH 44120-1731 Office: 3461 Warrensville Center Rd Cleveland OH 44122-5227

BRODY, SAUL NATHANIEL, retired English literature educator; b. N.Y.C., Mar. 6, 1938; s. Irving Bernard and Ethel (Spiegel) B.; m. Frohma-Esther Besner, Jan. 24, 1960; children: Audrey Rachel (dec.), Ruth Elizabeth. BA, Columbia U., 1959, MA, 1960, PhD, 1968. Lectr. Hunter Coll., N.Y.C., 1962-65, City Coll., N.Y.C., 1965-68, asst. prof., 1968-73, assoc. prof., 1974-78, prof. English, 1979-98, dept. chmn., 1979-85, retired, 1998. Co-prin. investigator Mellon Found. grant, 1978; project dir. NEH Summer Inst. for Tchrs., 1984, 86, 88; project dir. Ford Found. grant, 1987-89, 91-95, Dept. Edn. grant, 1991, Mellon Found. grant, 1989-95. Author: The Disease of the Soul: Leprosy in Medieval Literature, 1974; editor: Readings in Asian Literatures, 1992; contbr. articles to scholarly publs. Mem. Medieval Acad. Am., Univ. Seminar in Medieval Studies (Columbia U.). Home: 20 Glenwood Ave Demarest NJ 07627-2625 E-mail: brody@intac.com.

BRODY, SPENCER JOHN, pediatrician; b. Laconia, N.H., Mar. 14, 1936; s. Nathan and Rose Alice (Kurinsky) B.; m. Carol; children: David, Lynn, Jeffrey, Joshua. BS summa cum laude, Tufts U., 1958; MD, Yale U., 1962. Diplomate Am. Bd. Pediatrics, Nat. Bd. Med. Examiners. Internship and residency in pediatrics Grace-New Haven Community Hosp., 1962-65; capt., chief pediatrics 328th USAF Hosp., Richards-Gebaur AFB, Grandview, Mo., 1965-67; pediatrician Laconia, N.H., 1967-77; ptnr. Lakes Region Pediatrics, Laconia, N.H., 1977-2000; adminstr. Care and Comfort Nursing, 2000—. Active staff Lakes Region Gen. Hosp., Laconia, 1967-2000, hon. staff, 2000—, sec. staff, 1972-74, v.p. staff, 1987, pres. staff, 1975, 88-90, chief of staff, 1976, chief of pediatrics, 1977-78, 89-90. Mem. Belknap County Med. Soc. (sec. 1970-71, v.p. 1972, pres. 1973), N.H. Med. Soc. (mem. coun. on health svcs. 1984-99, chmn. 1985-93), Am. Acad. Pediatrics (N.H. chpt. alternate chpt. chmn. 1979, chpt. pres. 1983-89, exec. com. 1989-97, newsletter editor 1989-96), State of N.H. Dept. Health and Human Svcs. (mem. maternal and child health physician adv. com. 1983-96, AIDS med. adv. com. 1986-89, infant death rev. com. 1988-91). Jewish. Home: 7 Skyview Cir Meredith NH 03253 Office: Care and Comfort Nursing 61 BEacon St W Ste 2 Laconia NH 03246

BRODY, THEODORE MEYER, pharmacologist, educator; b. Newark, May 10, 1920; s. Samuel and Lena (Hammer) B.; m. Ethel Vivian Drelich, Sept. 7, 1947; children— Steven Lewis, Debra Jane, Laura Kate, Elizabeth. BS, Rutgers U., 1943; MS, U. Ill., 1949, PhD, 1952. Instr., prof. dept. pharm. U. Mich. Med. Sch., Ann Arbor, 1952-66; prof. Pharmacology Coll. Medicine, Mich. State U., East Lansing, 1966-90, prof. emeritus, 1990—, founding chmn. dept., 1966-86. Cons. NIH, 1969-73, NIDA, 1975-79, Internat. Soc. Heart Rsch., 1973—2002; mem. sci. adv. com. Pharm. Mfrs. Assn. Found., 1973—2002; U.S. rep. Internat. Union Pharmacology, 1973-76; mem. bd. Fedn. Am. Socs. for Exptl. Biology, 1973-76; mem. Com. Sci. Soc. Presidents. Mem. editl. bd. Jour. Pharmacology and Exptl. Therapeutics, 1965-80, specific field editor, 1981-92; mem. editl. bd. Rsch. Comm. in Chem. Pathology and Pharmacology, Molecular Pharmacology, 1972-90; editor: Human Pharmacology Molecular to Clinical, 1991, 94, 97; cons. Random House Dictionary of English Lang., 1964—; contbr. 300 articles to profl. jours. Served with AUS, 1943-46. Recipient Disting. Faculty award, Mich. State U., 1984; Disting. scholar, NSF-U. Hawaii, 1974. Mem. Am. Soc. Pharmacology and Exptl. Therapeutics (John Jacob Abel award 1955, mem. council 1969-72, sec.-treas. 1970, pres. elect 1973, pres. 1974, past pres. 1975, Torald Sollmann award in pharmacology 1995), Internat. Soc. Biochem. Pharmacology, Am. Coll. Clin. Pharmacology, Assn. Med. Sch. Pharmacologists (sec. 1984-86), Soc. Toxicology, Soc. Neurosci., Japanese Pharmacology Soc., AAUP, Sigma Xi, Rho Chi, Phi Kappa Phi. Home: 842 Longfellow Dr East Lansing MI 48823-2444 Office: Mich State U Dept Pharmacology East Lansing MI 48824 E-mail: brodyt@msu.edu.

BRODY, WILLIAM RALPH, academic administrator, radiologist, educator; b. Stockton, Calif., Jan. 4, 1944; m. Wendy Brody; 2 children. BSEE, MIT, 1965, MSEE, 1966; MD, Stanford U., 1970, PhD in Elec. Engring., 1975. With Nat. Heart, Lung, and Blood Inst., USPHS, Balt., 1973—75; intern, then resident and fellow dept. cardiovasc. surgery Sch. Medicine Stanford U., Calif., 1970—73, tng. med. fellow cardiovasc. surgery, resident diag. radiol., 1975—77, from assoc. prof. to prof. dept. radiology, dir. rsch. labs., 1977—86; prof. Stanford U., 1982—84; founder, pres., CEO Resonex, Inc., 1984—87, chmn. bd. dirs., 1987—89; radiologist-in-chief Johns Hopkins Hosp., Balt., 1987—94; prof. radiology, provost U. Minn. Acad. Health Ctr., 1994—96, spl. asst. to pres., 1996; mem. staff depts. elec., computer engring., biomed. engring. Sch. Medicine Johns Hopkins U., 1987—94, Martin Donner prof., dir. dept. radiology, 1987—94; pres. Johns Hopkins U., 1996—. Contbr. articles to profl. jours. Fellow coun. cardiovasc. radiology Am. Heart Assn.; mem. internat. adv. bd. Inst. Sys. Sci., NAt. U. Singapore, 1994—97; mem. internat. acad. adv. panel, 1997; mem. sci. adv. com. Whitaker Found., 1992—97, governing com., 1997—; bd. dirs. Greater Balt. Com., 1997; trustee Goldseker Found., 1996, Balt. Mus. Art, 1997. Recipient Established Investigator award, Am. Heart Assn., 1980—84. Fellow: NAS (Inst. Medicine), IEEE, Am. Inst. Med. and Biomed. Engring. (founding), Am. Coll. Cardiology, Am. Coll. Radiology. Achievements include patents in field. Office: Johns Hopkins Univ 242 Garland Hall 3400 N Charles St Baltimore MD 21218-2680

BRODY-LEDERMAN, STEPHANIE, artist; b. N.Y.C. d. Maxwell and Ann (Rockett) Brody. Student, U. Mich.; BS in Design, Finch Coll., 1961; MA in Painting, L.I. U., 1975. One-person exhbns. Franklin Furnace, N.Y.C., 1979, Kathryn Markel Fine Arts, N.Y.C., 1979, 81, 83; Katzen/Brown Gallery, N.Y.C., 1988, 89, Real Artways, Hartford, Conn., 1984, Alfred U., 1990, Hal Katzen Gallery, N.Y.C., 1992, Hillwood Art Mus., Brookville, N.Y., 1992, Casements Mus., Ormond Beach, Fla., 1994, Broward Cmty. Coll., Ft. Lauderdale, Fla., 1994, Hebrew Home for the Aged, N.Y.C., 1994-95, Galerie Caroline Corre, Paris, 1995, La. State U., Shreveport, 1995, Marc Miller Gallery, East Hampton, N.Y., 1996, Picrogi 2000, Bklyn., 1996, Arlene Bujese Gallery, Easthampton, N.Y., 1997, 123 Watts Gallery, N.Y.C., 1998, Edison Coll., Ft. Myers, Fla., 2001, Arlene Bujese, E. Hampton, N.Y., 2001, Hudson Opera House, Hudson, N.Y., 2001, Arlene Bujese Gallery, East Hampton, N.Y., 2002, Cleary, Gottlieb, Steen & Hamilton Artists Program, N.Y.C., 2003; exhibited in numerous group shows including Newark Mus., 1983, Met. Mus. Art, N.Y.C., 1986, Queens Mus., 1989, Basel Art Fair, 1989, Caroline Corre, Paris, 1991, R.I. Mus. Art, 1991, Am. Acad. Arts & Letters, N.Y.C., 1992, Guild Hall Mus., East Hampton, N.Y., 1993, Ind. U, Terre Haute, 1993, Jewish Mus., N.Y.C., 1994, Nat. Mus. Women in Arts, Washington, 1994, Ronald Feldman Gallery, N.Y.C., 1995, Alternative Mus., N.Y.C., 1995, Eugenia Cucalon Gallery, N.Y.C., 1995, Rotunda Gallery, Bklyn., 1995, The Museums at Stony Brook, N.Y., 1996, Espace Eiffel-Branly, Paris, 1996, Fotouhi Cramer Gallery, N.Y.C., 1996, 123 Watts Gallery, N.Y.C., 1996, Mediethèque, Les Mureaux, France, 1996, San Francisco State U., 1997, Isis Conceptual Lab., West Branch, Iowa, 1997, Harper Collins Exhbn. Space, N.Y.C., 1997, Bklyn. Mus., 1997, Gasworks Gallery, London, 1997, Parrish Art Mus., Southampton, N.Y., 1998, Neuburger Mus., Purchase, N.Y., 1998, Librairie Nicaise, Paris, 1998, Connecticut Coll., New London, 1998, Montclair (N.J.) Art Mus., 1999, Kutztown State Coll., Kutztown, Pa., 1999, Mpls. Coll. Art, 1999, Musee Bourdelle, Paris, 1999—, U. of the Arts, Phila., 1999, Generous Miraeles Gallery, N.Y.C., 1999, Limn Gallery, San Francisco, Bklyn. Mus., N.Y.C., 2000, Eugenia Cucalon Gallery, N.Y.C., 2000, Arlene Bujese Gallery, East Hampton, 2000, N.Y. Sandusky Cultural Ctr., Sandusky, Ohio, 2000, Nassau Comty. Coll., Garden City, N.Y., 2000, Fla. Atlantic U., Boca Raton, Fla., 2000, Elsa Mott Ives Gallery, NYC, 2001, Hillwood Art Mus., LI, 2001, Hungarian Consulate, NYC, 2001, Coll. Art and Design, Bristol, Eng., 2001, Md. Art Place, Balt., 2002, Woodstock (NY) Guild, 2002, 450 Gallery, NYC, 2002, Metaphor Gallery, Bklyn., 2002, Topkapi Mus, Istanbul, 2002, Snug Harbor Culture Ct., Staten Island, N.Y., 2002, Gracie Mansions Booth, Javits Galleria, N.Y.C., 2003, Chelsea Art Mus., NY, 2003, Berliner Kunstproject, Berlin, 2003, OK Harris Gallery, N.Y.C., 2003, Nat. Mus. Woman in the Arts, Washington, 2003; represented in permanent collections Newark Mus., Mus. Modern Art, Prudential Ins., Bertelsmann Music Group, Guild Hall Mus., East Hampton, L.I., Chase Manhattan Bank, N.Y. Health and Hosp. Corp., Victoria & Albert Mus., London, Doubleday Books, Saks 5th Ave. Corp., Vero Beach Ctr. for the Arts, Vero Beach, Fla., Bklyn. Mus., Montclair Art Mus., N.J., Centre Du Livre D'Artiste, Verderonne, France, Hancock Info. Group, Orlando, Fla., 2002; commd. series of work on paper Cmty. Rsch. Initiative on AIDS, 1999; cover painting Paris Rev. Mag.; Cowparade pub. artwork, 2000; contbg. artist "Fresh" project, 2003; artist portfolio Gastronomica Mag., 2003. Recipient Hassam and Speicher purchase award Am. Acad. and Inst. Arts and Letters, 1988, purchase award Arts in Hosps., Richmond, Va., 1994; grantee Creative Artists Pub. Svc., 1977, Ariana Found. for Arts, 1985, Artists Space, 1987, E.D. Found., 1991, Lancaster Group., U.S. A. Comm. award, 1991, spl. opportunity stipend N.Y. State Coun. Arts, 1992, 94, Heuss House project Lower Manhattan Cultural Coun., 1992. Studio: 85 N 3rd St Brooklyn NY 11211-3944 E-mail: sbrodyl@aol.com.

BROEG, BOB (ROBERT WILLIAM BROEG), writer; b. St. Louis, Mar. 18, 1918; s. Robert Michael and Alice (Wiley) B.; m. Dorothy Carr, June 19, 1943 (dec.); m. Lynette A. Emmenegger, July 23, 1977. BJ, U. Mo., 1941. With A.P., Columbia, Mo., 1939-40, Jefferson City, Mo., 1941, Boston, 1941-42; reporter St. Louis Star-Times, 1942; staff sports dept. St. Louis Post-Dispatch, 1945-85, sports editor, 1958-85, asst. to pub., 1977-85. Author: Don't Bring That Up, 1946, Stan Musial: The Man's Own Story, 1964, Super Stars of Baseball, 1971, Ol' Missou, a Story of Missouri Football, 1974, We Saw Stars, 1976, The Man Stan...Musial, Now and Then, 1977, Football Greats, 1977, The Pilot Light and the Gas House Gang, 1980, Bob Broeg's Redbirds, 1981, My Baseball Scrapbook, 1983, Front Page, 1984, Baseball From a Different Angle, 1988, Baseball's Barnum, 1989, Ol' Mizzou, A Century of Tiger Football, 1990, Bob Broeg's Redbirds, A Century of Cardinals Baseball, 1992, Super Stars of Baseball No. 2, 1993, Autobiography, Bob Broeg, Memories of Hall of Fame Sportswriter, 1995; co-author: That's a Winner, Jack Buck Autobiography, 1997, St. Louis Cardinals' Encyclopedia, 1998, The 100 Greatest Moments in St. Louis Sports, 2000; contbr. articles to profl. publs. Bd. dirs. Vets. com. Baseball Hall of Fame, 1972-2000, bd. dirs. 1975-2000; bd. dirs. Honors Ct., Nat. Football Found., 1975. Served with USMCR, 1942-45. Recipient Nat. Sportscasters, Sportswriters awards Mo., 1962-65, 67; Journalism medal U. Mo., 1971; Faculty-Alumni award U. Mo., 1969, Hall of Fame Writing award, 1980; elected to Mo. Sports Hall of Fame, 1978, Nat. Sportscasters/Sportswriters Hall of Fame, 1997, Nat. Baseball Congress Hall of Fame, 1998, Mo. Sports Legend, 2000. Mem. Baseball Writers Assn. Am. (pres. 1958), Kappa Tau Alpha, Sigma Delta Chi, Sigma Phi Epsilon, Omicron Delta Kappa. Home: 60 Frontenac Estates Dr Saint Louis MO 63131-2602 Office: Pulitzer Pub Co 900 N Tucker Blvd Saint Louis MO 63101-1069 *As a newspaperman, I seek as an epitaph only: "He was fair." Hopefully "fair" as in "just," not as in "mediocre".*

BROEK, HOWARD WINDOLPH, real estate executive; b. N.Y.C., Oct. 1, 1934; s. Howard Yates Broek and Mildred Louise Windolph; m. Berthalene Ann Arber, Mar. 30, 1963; children: Christopher John, Jennifer Louise Schnell, Gillian Sarah Gentile, Catherine Elizabeth Stemple, Alexandra Ann Jantje. B Engring., Yale U., 1956, MS, 1958, PhD, 1961. Staff physicist Argonne (Ill.) Nat. Lab., 1960-63; mem. tech. staff Bell Telphone Labs., Whippany, N.J., 1963-75, Naperville, Ill., 1975-89; sr. engr. Motorola, Arlington Heights, Ill., 1990-95; pres. Windolph Realty Co., St. Charles, Ill., 1995—. *Contributed to Review of Scientific Instruments, Physical Review, Nuclear Physics, Journal of Geophysical Research, Journal of the Acoustical Society of America, and Journal of Physical Oceanography. Wrote final report for Project Artemis.* Author: Broek & Jonker Families, 1993, The Third Millenium, 2000; contbr. articles to profl. jours. Deacon Reformed Ch. in Am. NSF fellow Yale U., 1958-59. Mem. Am. Philatelic Soc., Am. Revenue Assn., Assn. for the Advancement of Dutch Am. Studies, N.Y. Geneal. and Biographical Soc., Joliet Bicycle Club, Life Extension Found. Mem. Reformed Ch. in Am. Avocations: bicycling, match and medicine stamps, skiing, oceanography, Dutch immigration studies.

BROEKER, JOHN MILTON, lawyer; b. Berwyn, Ill., May 27, 1940; s. Milton Monroe and Marjorie Grace (Wilson) B.; m. Linda J. Broeker, Dec. 9, 1983; children: Sara Elizabeth, Ross Goddard; stepchildren: Terrance Mercil Jr., Johnny Mercil, Veronica Mercil. BA, Grinnell Coll., 1962; JD cum laude, U. Minn., 1965. Bar: Minn. 1965, Wis. 1982, U.S. Ct. Appeals (8th cir.) 1966, U.S. Dist. Ct. Minn. 1967, U.S. Tax Ct. 1969, U.S. Ct. Appeals (5th cir.) 1971, U.S. Dist. Ct. (we. dist.) Wis. 1982, U.S. Supreme Ct. 1984. Law clk. to presiding judge U.S. Ct. Appeals (8th cir.), 1965-66; ptnr. Gray, Plant, Mooty, Mooty & Bennett, Mpls., 1966-71, Broeker, Geer, Fletcher & LaFond and predecessor firms, Mpls., 1971 91; v.p., gen. counsel NordicTrack, Inc., Mpls., 1991-94; founder Broeker Enterprises, 1992—; pres. Legal Mgmt. Strategies, Inc., Mpls., 1994—; of counsel Popham, Haik, Schnobrich & Kaufman, Ltd., Mpls., 1995-96, Halleland, Lewis, Nilan, Sipkins & Johnson, Mpls., 1996-97; pvt. practice, 1997—. Instr. U Minn. Law Sch., 1967-72; lectr. convs. and seminars, 1969—; lectr. U. Minn. Ctr. for Long Term Care Edn., 1972-77, Gt. Lakes Health Congress, 1972, Sister Kenney Inst., 1972. Contbr. articles to legal jours. Bd. dirs. Minn. Environ. Scis. Found., Inc., 1971-73; bd. dirs. Project Environ. Found., 1977-83, chmn., 1980-82; mem. alumni bd. Grinnell Coll., 1968-71; chmn. MInnetonka Environ. Quality and Natural Resources Commn., 1971-72; trustee The Writers Project, Inc., 1999-2001. Recipient Outstanding Alumni award Grinnell Coll., 1973. Mem. ABA (forum com. on health law 1978-91), Minn. Bar Assn. (chmn. environ. law com. 1970-72), State Bar Wis., Hennepin County Bar Assn. (chmn. environ. law com. 1976-77, legis. com. 1972-76, health law com. 1977-79), Am. Soc. Hosp. Attys., Minn. Soc. Hosp. Attys., Am. Health Care Assn. (legal coordinating com. 1970-75, labor com. 1973-74), Nat. Health Lawyers Assn., Minn. Thoroughbred Assn. (bd. dirs. 1991-92), Minn. Quarterhorse Racing Assn. (bd. dirs. 1994—, pres. 1997-99), Sierra Club (nat. dir. 1974-76, chmn. chpt. 1971-72, regional v.p. 1973-74). Home: 11402 Burr Ridge Ln Eden Prairie MN 55347-4717 Office: 8120 Penn Ave S Ste 151Q Bloomington MN 55431-1326 E-mail: jbroeker@msn.com.

BROENING, WALTER STEPHENS, JR., journalist, history educator; b. Balt., Aug. 15, 1935; s. Walter Stephens and Evelyne (Powers) B.; m. Christine Zucker, Feb. 3, 1962; children: Alexander (dec.), John, Benjamin, Thomas. BA in Polit. Sci., Johns Hopkins U., 1959. Reporter AP, Balt., 1963-65, corr. Paris, 1965-70, Moscow, 1970-74, Lisbon, Portugal, 1974-76; asst. city editor Balt. Sun, 1976-77, op-ed page editor, 1977-85, diplomatic corr., 1985-90; news editor Internat. Herald-Tribune, Paris, 1990-96; vis. scholar in history Johns Hopkins U., Balt., 1996—. With U.S. Army, 1954-56. Mem. Johns Hopkins Club. Home: 5701 Greenleaf Rd Baltimore MD 21210-1319 Office: Johns Hopkins U Dept History 3400 N Charles St Baltimore MD 21218-2608

BROENNLE, A. MICHAEL, anesthesiologist; b. Elyria, Ohio, Nov. 8, 1941; MD, Ohio State U., 1967; MBA, U. Pa., 1997. Diplomate Am. Bd. Anesthesiology. Intern Cleve. Clinic Found., 1967-68; resident in anesthesiology Mass. Gen. Hosp., Boston, 1968-71, fellow in anesthesiology, 1969-70; sr. anesthesiologist Children's Hosp., Phila.; assoc. prof. anesthesiology U. Pa., Phila., 1973—. Fellow Am. Acad. Pediatrics; mem. AMA, Am. Soc. Anesthesiology, Soc. Pediat. Anesthesia. Office: Childrens Hospital Dept Anesthesia CCM Philadelphia PA 19104-4399 E-mail: broennle@email.chp.edu.

BROERS, SIR ALEC NIGEL, engineering educator; b. Calcutta, India, Sept. 17, 1938; s. Alec William and Constance Amy (Cox) B.; m. Mary Therese Phelan, Dec. 27, 1965; children: Mark, Christopher. BSc, Melbourne U., 1958, 59; BA in Mech. Scis., Cambridge U., 1962, PhD in Elec. Engring., 1965, ScD, 1990; DEng (hon.), Glasgow U., 1996; DSc (hon.), Warwick U., 1997; D. in Tech. (hon.), Greenwich U., 2000; LLD (hon.), Melbourne U., 2000; D in Univ. (hon.), Anglia Poly. U., 2000; Fellow (hon.), U. Wales, 2002; D Eng. (hon.), Peking U., 2002. Mem. rsch. staff IBM Thomas J. Watson Rsch. Ctr., Yorktown Heights, N.Y., 1965-81, mgr. electron beam tech., 1967-72, mgr. photo and electron optics, 1972-81; mgr. advanced tech. IBM East Fishkill Devel. Lab., Hopewell Junction, N.Y., 1981-84; mem. corp. tech. com. IBM Hdqrs., Armonk, N.Y., 1984; prof. elec. engring., head elec. div. dept. engring. Cambridge U., 1984-92, head dept. engring., 1992-96, vice chancellor, 1996—2003; mem. rsch. staff IBM Thomas J. Watson Rsch. Ctr., Yorktown Heights, N.Y., 1965-81. Fellow Trinity Coll., Cambridge, 1985-90; master Churchill Coll., Cambridge, 1990-96; mem. Royal Acad. of Engring. Coun., 1994-96, Engring. and Phys. Scis. Coun. U.K., 1992-2000; non-exec. dir. gen. bd. Lucas Industries, 1995-96; non-exec. dir. Vodafone Group; mem. Coun. for Sci. and Tech. Contbr. numerous articles to profl. jours., chpts. to books; patentee in field. Recipient Am. Inst. of Physics prize for indsl. applications of physics, 1982, Cledo Brunetti award IEEE, 1985; hon. fellow Gonville and C. Coll., Trinity Coll., Cardiff U. Fellow Instn. Elec. Engrs. (hon.), Inst. of Physics, Royal Acad. Engring. (coun. 1992-96, 2000—, v.p. 2000-2001, pres. 2001—, Prince Philip medal 2000), Royal Soc.; mem. U.S. Nat. Acad. Engring. (fgn. assoc.), Australian Acad. Technol. Scis. and Engrs. (hon.), Am. Philos. Soc. (fgn. mem.). Avocations: music, small-boat sailing, skiing, tennis. Home: Saint George Wharf Apt 429 Wandsworth Rd London SW8 England also: 32 Mount Hope Ave Jamestown RI 02835-1466 Office: Royal Acad Engring 29 Great Peter St Westminster SW1P 3LW England E-mail: v-c@admin.cam.ac.uk.

BROFFITT, JAMES DRAKE, professor statistics and actuarial science; b. Indpls., Apr. 8, 1941; s. Wilgus Stanley and Virginia Elizabeth (Drake) B.; m. Barbara Helen Alford, Dec. 20, 1975; children: Daniel James, Virginia Lea. BA in Mathematics, DePauw U., 1963; MS in Statistics, Colo. State U., 1965, PhD in Statistics, 1969. Statis. analyst Computer Technology, Inc., Dallas, 1969-70; asst. prof. stats. and actuarial sci. U. Iowa, Iowa City, 1970-75, assoc. prof., 1975-85, 86-88, prof., 1988—, chmn. stats. and actuarial sci., 1993—. Vis. prof. U. Western Ontario, Can., 1985-86; cons. Soc. Actuaries Part 2 Actuarial Exam, Am. Coll. Testing, 1984-85, Iowa Med. Svcs., 1988. Conducted presentations in field at various univs. and confs. in the U.S. and Can.; Contbr. numerous articles to profl. jours. Mem. Am. Statistical Assn., Inst. Mathematical Statistics, Internat. Actuarial Assn., Soc. of Acutaries (assoc. mem. 1980, academic cons. to com. which constructs compound interest examination 1993-95), Sigma Xi, Phi Kappa Phi. Baptist. Home: 3029 E Court St Iowa City IA 52245-4907 E-mail: james_broffitt@uiowa.edu.

BROFSKY, HOWARD, musician, music educator; b. N.Y.C., May 2, 1927; s. Barney L. and Frances (Reich) B.; m. Robin Westen; children: Alexander, Natasha, Gabriel. PhD, NYU, N.Y.C., 1963. Asst. prof. U. Chgo., Chicago, IL, 60-67; prof. Queens Coll., CUNY, N.Y.C., 1967-92, prof. emeritus, 1992—. Prof. U. B.C., Vancouver, Can., summers 1974, 75, Boston U., summer 1978, U. Oslo, Norway, fall 1993; spl. editor music Harper & Row, Pubs., N.Y.C., 1969-71. Co-author: (with J. Bamberger) The Art of Listening, 5th edit., 1988; contbr. articles to profl. jours.; several jazz recs. Pres. Vt. Jazz Ctr., 1998—. Mem. Am. Musicol. Soc., Internat. Musicol. Soc., Internat. Assn. Jazz Educators. Home: 684 Bonnyvale Rd Brattleboro VT 05301-2573 E-mail: drbebop@sover.net.

BROG, DAVID, consultant, former air force officer; b. Manchester, Conn., Aug. 11, 1933; s. Israel and Pesha (Blonstein) B.; m. Verda Anna Raney, Nov. 9, 1959; children: Kai Ling, Tov Binyamin. BA, U. Pitts., 1955; MS, U. So. Calif., 1967. Commd. 2d lt. USAF, 1956, advanced through grades to col., 1978, dir. readiness and electronic combat, Hdqrs., from 1981, dep. chief staff ops. for command control and communications countermeasures, until 1982, ret., 1982; pres. IRD, Inc. (internat. R & D), domestic and internat. cons. on def. issues, Silver Spring, Md., 1982—. Contbr. articles to profl. jours. Decorated D.F.C., Legion of Merit, Air medal with 12 oak leaf clusters; named Disting. Grad. USAF Air War Coll. Mem. Red River Valley Fighter Pilots Assn. (pres.), Assn. Old Crows, Air Force Assn. Jewish. Home: 9200 Three Oaks Dr Silver Spring MD 20901-3362 Office: PO Box 877 Silver Spring MD 20918-0877

BROGAN, FRANK T. former lieutenant governor; m. Courtney Strickland. BA magna cum laude, U. Cin.; M in Ednl. Leadership, Fla. Atlantic U. m. Courtney Brogan. Supt. schs. Martin County Sch. Dist., Fla., 1988-94; commr. edn. Fla. Dept. Edn., Tallahassee, 1994-99; lt. gov. State of Fla., Tallahassee, 1999—2003; pres. Florida Atlantic U., 2003—. Former tchr., dean of students, asst. prin., prin. Martin County Sch. Dist.; chair task force Fla. Classrooms First; mem. development team Tech Prep program. Named Supt. of yr., Fla. Legislature, 1992. Republican. Office: Florida Atlantic Univ PO Box 3091 777 Glades Rd Boca Raton FL 33431-0991

BROGAN, JOHN ANDREW, III, capital management company executive; b. Jersey City, Mar. 5, 1924; s. John Andrew Jr. and Marie Jeannette (Ferris) B.; m. Edith Maria Eyermann, Oct. 25, 1952; children: Jeannette Gräfin Beissel von Gymnich. Student, Biarritz Am. U., France, 1945; BS in Fgn. Service, Georgetown U., 1948. Fgn. rep. King Features Syndicate, Mex., Colombia, Argentina, France, Sweden, 1948-50; fgn. service officer Dept. of State, Washington, 1951-85, asst. French desk officer, 1957-60, dir. ops. ctr., 1968-70, sr. mem. bd. of examiners, 1971, sr. examiner, 1979-85; spl. asst. to U.S. High Commr., Vienna, Austria, 1951-52; press officer U.S. High Commn., Bonn, Germany, 1952-54; vice consul Am. Consulate, Edinburgh, Scotland, 1954-56; first sec. Am. Embassy, Buenos Aires, 1960-65; Allied Press spokesman U.S. Mission, Berlin, 1965-68; consul gen. Am. Consulate Gen., Hamburg, Germany, 1972-76; advisor on political and security affairs Spl. Session U.N. Gen. Assembly, N.Y.C., 1977-78; dir. Amerika Gesellschaft, Hamburg, 1985—. Served with U.S. Army Air Corps, 1942-46, Europe. Named Hon. citizen of Quito, Ecuadorian Govt.; Decorated Knight Sovereign Mil. Order of Malta. Mem. Am. C. of C., Am. Club, English Speaking Union. Clubs: Hamburg Golf, Übersee (Hamburg), Metropolitan (Washington), Diplomatic and Consular Officers, Ret. (Washington). Roman Catholic. Avocations: golf, skiing. Office: Brogan and Co Schwanenwik 10 22087 Hamburg Germany

BROGAN, KEVIN H. lawyer; b. Pasadena, Calif., Nov. 7, 1953; m. Nena Jones, Aug. 1, 1981. BS, U. Calif., Berkeley, 1976; JD, U. Calif., San Francisco, 1979. Bar: Calif. 1979, U.S. Dist. Ct. (ce., so., ea. and no. dists.) Calif. 1979, Wis. 1988, U.S. Claims Ct., U.S. Supreme Ct. Law clk. to judge U.S. Ct. Appeals (10th cir.), Santa Fe, 1979; assoc. Hill, Farrer & Burrill, LLP, L.A., 1979-86, ptnr., 1986—. Bd. dirs. Nat. Conf., Attys. Ins. Mutual. Fellow: Am. Coll. Trial Lawyers; mem.: ABA, Irish Am. Bar Assn., State Bar of Calif. (real property sect. chmn. inverse condemnation and eminent domain subs

1997—98), L.A. County Bar Assn. (chmn. eminent domain and land valuation com. 1992), Fed. Bar Assn., Beta Theta Pi. Roman Catholic. Office: Hill Farrer & Burrill LLP 300 S Grand Ave Ste 37 Los Angeles CA 90071-3110 E-mail: kbrogan@hfbllp.com.

BROGAN, MARY ROSE, public mental health facility administrator, psychologist; d. John F. and Sally E. Brogan. AB, Marywood Coll., 1970; MS, SUNY, Cortland, 1975; PhD, U. S.D., 1977. Diplomate Am. Bd. Profl. Psychology. Clin. psychologist Conn. Valley Hosp., Middletown, 1977-84, dir. psychol. svcs., 1987-92; pvt. practice Middletown, 1984-87, 92-95; assoc. dir. clin. ops. River Valley Svcs., Middletown, 1995—, mem. adv. bd., 1993-95. Part-time pvt. practice, Middletown, 1995—; lectr. U. Conn., Storrs, 1992-95. Fellow Acad. Clin. Psychology; mem. APA, Conn. Psychol. Assn. (ethics com. 1985-98), Nat. Register Health Svc. Providers in Psychology. Office: River Valley Svcs Silver St PO Box 351 Middletown CT 06457-7023

BROGDEN, STEPHEN RICHARD, library director; b. Des Moines, Sept. 26, 1948; s. Paul M. and Marjorie (Kueck) B.; m. Melinda L. Raine, Jan. 1, 1983; 1 child, Nathan. BA, U. Iowa, 1970, MA, 1972. Caretaker Eya Fechin Branham Ranch, Taos, N.Mex., 1970-72; dir. Harwood Found. U. N.Mex., Taos, 1972-75; vis. lectr. U. Ariz., Tucson, 1975-76; rd. mgr. Bill and Bonnie Hearne, Austin, Tex., 1976-79; head fine arts Pub. Libr. Des Moines, 1980-90; dep. dir. Thousand Oaks (Calif.) Libr., 1990-99, dir., 1999—. Chair Met. Coop. Libr. Sys., 2001. Author book revs., Annals of Iowa, 1980; columnist Taos News, 1973. Bd. dirs. Thousand Oaks Libr. Found., 1999—. Mem. Am. Libr. Assn., Calif. Libr. Assn., Films for Iowa Librs. (pres. 1983-86), Metro Des Moines Libr. Assn. (pres. 1980). Office: Thousand Oaks Libr 1401 E Janss Rd Thousand Oaks CA 91362-2199

BROGDEN-STIRBL, SHONA MARIE, writer, researcher; b. Tuscaloosa, Ala., Sept. 3, 1948; d. Edward Henry Jr. and Esther Ruth (Coleman) Brogden; m. Robert Clark Stirbl, Mar. 30, 1990. *Shona Brogden-Stirbl's husband, Robert, is currently Senior Technical Staff at JPL in the Obervational Instruments Division and a recognized electro-optical systems design expert. Receiving his Ph.D. from CUNY, he has taught EE and EO systems design at the NYU School of Graduate Studies, Pratt Institute, CCNY, and was a Manhattan College professor. For Grumman/FEWS, he was responsible for both Space and Surveillance technology business development and the design of the U.S. Army's NPBSE microradian, optical metrology system for their magnetic telescope. At Riverside Research, he assessed Space Based Laser directed energy weapon acquisition and tracking Active and Passive Sensing technology maturity for SDIO/BMD. He currently holds 14 patents.* BA, U. South Ala., Mobile, 1972; MA in English (Poetics), NYU, 1982. Adult protective social worker Mobile County Dept. Pensions and Security, 1972-74; child protection social worker Cumberland County Child Protective Svcs., Fayetteville, NC, 1975-76; cmty. placement specialist S.I. Devel. Ctr., 1976-78, Manhattan Borough Devel. Svc., NYC, 1978-80; adminstr. Coun. on Internat. Ednl. Exch., NYC, 1981, Office of Univ. Devel., Advt. and Pub. Affairs, NYU, NYC, 1982-85; dir. advt. Office of Advt. and Pub. Affairs, NYU, NYC, 1986; cons. Meml. Sloan-Kettering, NDRI, NYU, NYC, 1986-97. Patentee (photog. films with multiple ASA and associated camera). Voice recorder Book on Tape, Jewish Braille Inst., NYC, 1996; adminstrv. support Gay Men's Health Crisis, NYC, 1986; vol. Serendipity Sch. for Emotionally Disturbed Children, Sacramento, 1975, Strasberg Inst., 1977-1978; founding mem. Tell It Like It Was, 1999. Scholar NYU, 1978-82, U. So. Miss., 1966-68, Strasberg Theatre Inst., 1977-78. Christian. Avocations: poetry, art, acting, baroque violin, writing, options trader. Home and Office: 465 S Madison #109 Pasadena CA 91101 E-mail: s.brogden.1@alumni.nyu.edu.

BROGDON, BYRON GILLIAM, physician, radiology educator; b. Fort Smith, Ark., Jan. 22, 1929; s. Paul Preston and Lela Florence (Gilliam) B.; m. Barbara Walkow Schreiber, June 23, 1978; 1 child, David Pope; stepchildren: William and Diane Schreiber. BS, BS in Medicine, U. Ark., 1951, MD, 1952. Intern Univ. Hosp., Little Rock, 1952-53, resident, 1953-55; resident in radiology N.C. Bapt. Hosp., Winston-Salem, 1955-56; asst. prof. radiology U. Fla., 1960-63; assoc. prof. radiology and radiol. scis., radiologist-in-charge diagnostic radiology div. Johns Hopkins U. and Hosp., 1963-67; prof., chmn. dept. radiology U. N.Mex., 1967-77; prof. radiology U. South Ala., Mobile, 1978-89, chmn. dept., 1985-92, univ. disting. prof. of radiology, 1989-96, emeritus univ. disting. prof., 1996—, asst. dean continuing med. edn., 1981-88. Sabbatical leave Univ. Coll., Galway, Ireland, 1988; cons. in forensic radiology Office Med. Exam. State Ala., 1989—; coord. internat. diagnostic course in Davos, 1984-96; mem. bd. trustees Forensic Sci. Found., 2001—, v.p., 2003. Author: Opinions, Comments and Reflections on Radiology, 1983, Forensic Radiology, 1998, a Radiologic Atlas of Abuse and Torture, Terrorism, and Inflicted Trauma, 2003; contbr. articles to med. jours. Maj. USAF, 1953-60. Recipient Disting. Alumnus award U. Ark., 1978, Ark. Travelers Commn. award Gov. of Ark., 1985, Disting. Achievement award Wake Forest U. Med. Alumni Assn., 1990, medal from city of Brescia, Italy, 1991, Joint Resolution of Commendation for outstanding profl. achievement Ala. Legis., 1994, Medal of Honor Leopold-Franzens U., Innsbruck, Austria, 1997, Republic of Austria Cross of Honor for Science and Arts 1st class, 2002. Fellow Am. Coll. Radiology (pres. 1978-79, gold medal 1987), Am. Acad. Forensic Scis. (John B. Hunt award 1995, Disting. Fellow award 2001); mem. AMA (ho. of dels. 1988-95, Physician-Spkr. award 1979), Am. Roentgen Ray Soc. (life, exec. coun. 1974-75, 77-80, 84-90, 2d v.p. 1979-80, gold medal 1996), So. Radiol. Conf. (life hon., pres. 1967-68, sec. 1984-86, Eskridge lectr. 1994), Radiol. Soc. N.Am., Am. Assn. Acad. Chief Residents in Radiology (faculty advisor 1979—, nat. sponsor 1983-93, Malcolm Jones orator 1996), Soc. Pediat. Radiology, Assn. Univ. Radiologists (pres. 1973-74, gold medal 1985), Soc. Chmn. Acad. Radiol. Depts. (sec.-treas. 1969-70), Swiss Soc. Med. Radiology (hon., Schinz medal 1992), Internat. Skeletal Soc. (medal 2001), Country Club Mobile, Sigma Xi, Alpha Omega Alpha, Sigma Chi (Significant Sig 1999). Office: U South Ala Med Ctr Dept Radiology 2451 Fillingim St Mobile AL 36617-2238 *For the physician-scientist-educator, the mere transference of knowledge or the acquisition of new data is not enough. He must participate fully in the affairs of the larger community and has a duty to help others to think about, or form an opinion on, issues they otherwise might not have considered.*

BROGLIATTI, BARBARA SPENCER, television and motion picture executive; b. LA, Jan. 8, 1946; d. Robert and Lottie Spencer; m. Raymond Haley Brogliatti, Sept. 19, 1970. BA in Social Scis. and English, UCLA, 1968. Asst. press. info. dept. CBS TV, L.A., 1968-69, sr. publicist, 1969-74; dir. publicity Tandem Prodns. and T.A.T. Comm. (Embassy Comm.), L.A., 1974-77, corp. v.p., 1977-82; sr. v.p. worldwide publicity, promotion and advt. Embassy Comm., L.A., 1982-85; sr. v.p. worldwide corp. comm. Lorimar Telepictures Corp., Culver City, Calif., 1985-89; pres., chmn. Brogliatti Co., Burbank, Calif., 1989-90; sr. v.p. worldwide TV publicity, promotion and advt. Lorimar TV, 1991-92; sr. v.p. worldwide TV publicity, promotion and pub. rels. Warner Bros., Burbank, 1992-97; sr. v.p. corp. comm. Warner Bros., Inc., 1997-2000; sr. v.p., chief corp. comm. officer Warner Bros. Entertainment Inc., 2000—. Adv. com. acad. advancement program UCLA; bd. govs. UCLA Found., 2003—. Mem. bd. govs. TV Acad., L.A., 1984-86, UCLA Found., 2003—; bd. dirs. KIDSNET, Washington, 1987—, Nat. Acad. Cable Programming, 1992-94; mem. Hollywood Women's Polit. Com., 1992-93; mem. steering com. L.A. Free Clinic, 1997-98. Recipient Gold medal Broadcast Promotion and Mktg. Execs., 1984. Mem. Am. Diabetes Assn. (bd. dirs. L.A. chpt. 1992-93), Am. Cinema Found. (bd. dirs. 1994-98), Dirs. Guild Am., Publicists Guild, Acad. TV Arts and Scis. (vice chmn. awards com.); adv. com. UCLA Acad. Advancement Prog. Office: Warner Bros Studios 4000 Warner Blvd Burbank CA 91522-0002 E-mail: barbara.brogliatti@warnerbros.com.

BROHAMMER, RICHARD FREDERIC, psychiatrist; b. Rockford, Ill., Nov. 9, 1934; s. Joseph C. and Marthe Marie (Ringuette) B.; m. Shirley Ruth Noble, June 22, 1956; children: Richard Frederic II, Renee Marie, Rory Christopher. PhB, U. Detroit, 1960; MD, U. Fla., 1964; postgrad. basic tng. diving medicine, Internat. Underwater Explorers Soc., 1973; advanced tng. diving medicine, Internat. Underwater Explorers, 1974. Diplomate Am. Bd. Psychiatry and Neurology, Am. Bd. Forensic Medicine. Rsch. fellow tropical medicine La. State U., Costa Rica, Fla., 1963, 93, Ctrl. Am., Costa Rica, 1963; intern Duval Med. Ctr., Jacksonville, Fla., 1964-65; resident psychiatry U. Fla., 1965-68; practice medicine specializing in psychiatry Imperial Point Med. Ctr., Ft. Lauderdale, Fla., 1968—; mem. staff Broward Gen. Med. Ctr., 1968—, Imperial Point Med. Ctr., 1974—, Holy Cross Hosp., 1968—. Chmn. dept. psychiatry Imperial Point Hosp., 1975-80, Holy Cross Hosp., 1981-83. Served with USAF, 1954-58, Korea. Rsch. fellow tropical medicine La. State U., Costa Rica, 1963, Ctr. Am., 1968, Costa Rica, 1993. Mem. AMA (pres. student chpt. 1961-64), Broward County (Fla.) Med. Assn., Broward County Psychiat. Soc., Undersea Adventures, Internat. Soc. Diving Medicine. Republican. Roman Catholic.

BROHMAN, MARK ALLEN, lawyer, biologist; b. McCook, Nebr., Oct. 12, 1963; s. Harold Horatio and Judy Louise (Neben) B.; m. Anessa Jo Schreiner, Aug. 1, 1987. BA in Biology and Chemistry, Chadron (Nebr.) State Coll., 1985; JD, U. Nebr., 1990, MS in Forestry, Fisheries and Wildlife, 1991. Bar: Nebr. 1990, U.S. Dist. Ct. Nebr. 1990. Rsch. biologist Chadron State Coll., 1981-85, Nebr. Game and Parks Commn., Lincoln, Nebr., 1988-91, U. Nebr., Lincoln, Nebr., 1985-87, legal rschr., 1987-88; legis. asst. Nebr. Legislature, Lincoln, Nebr., 1991; wetlands biologist Nebr. Dept. Roads, Lincoln, Nebr., 1991-93; environ. analyst supr. Nebr. Game and Parks Commn., Lincoln, Nebr., 1993-98, divsn. adminstr., legis. liaison, 1998—. Mem.: Lincoln Engrs. Club, Nebr. Bar Assn., Elks. Democrat. Home: 2637 Washington St Lincoln NE 68502-2955

BROHN, WILLIAM DAVID, conductor, orchestrator; b. Flint, Mich. BA in Music, Mich. State U., 1955; MMus, New Eng. Conservatory Music. Played with local ensembles and performed on double bass Boston Pops Orch.; played string bass and piano with numerous musical orgns. including classical, theatrical and jazz groups; condr. nat. tours Robert Joffrey Ballet, Royal Ballet; commd. to adapt and arrange program piece for ann. Christmas concert Cleve. Orch., 1961; recreated sound track for 1938 Russian classic film Alexander Nevsky, 1987; vis. lectr. Oxford U., England. Recipient Tony award for orchestrations for Ragtime, N.Y. Drama Desk award for Miss Saigon, N.Y. Drama Desk award for The Secret Garden. Office: c/o American Fed of Musicians 322 W 48th St New York NY 10036-1308

BROIDE, MACE IRWIN, retired public affairs consultant; b. Burlington, Vt., May 21, 1924; s. Abraham A. and Ida (Rosenberg) B.; m. Gloria Leah Goldsholl, Dec. 24, 1943; children: Cheryl Ruth Broide Light, Beverly Elaine Broide Frye, Sandra Pat Broide Banas. AB (Ernie Pyle scholar 1946), Ind. U., 1947. Polit. editor Evansville (Ind.) Press, 1947-58; senatorial adminstrv. asst., 1959-60, co-owner Dallam and Broide, Inc.; public affairs cons., Washington, 1968-78; exec. dir. com. on budget U.S. Ho. of Reps., 1978-86; pub. affairs cons., 1986-99; retired, 1999. Adj. prof. George Washington U., 1986, 87; lectr. in field. Co-author: Inside the New Frontier, 1963; contbr. articles to newspapers, mags. Sec. Nat. Dem. Senatorial Campaign Com., 1961-62; past bd. dirs. Jewish Community Coun. Evansville; past bd. govs. Nat. Dem. Club. With AUS, 1943-46. Decorated Silver Star, Bronze Star. Mem. Assn. Adminstrv. Assts. U.S. Senate (past pres.), B'nai B'rith (past pres.). Home: 4450 S Park Ave Apt 1111 Chevy Chase MD 20815-3641 E-mail: mbroide@aol.com.

BROIDO, ARNOLD PEACE, music publishing company executive; b. N.Y.C., Apr. 8, 1920; s. Samuel S. and Ruth (Lewis) B.; m. Lucille Janet Tarshes, Mar. 5, 1944; children: Jeffrey, Laurence, Thomas. BS magna cum laude, Ithaca Coll., 1941; MA, Columbia U., 1954; DMus (hon.), Ithaca Coll., 1990. Tchr. instrumental music East Jr. High Sch., Binghamton, N.Y., 1941-42; editor, prodn. mgr. Boosey & Hawkes Inc. (music pub.), 1945-55; v.p., gen. mgr. Century Music & Mercury Music Corp., 1955-57; edn. dir. Edward B. Marks Music Corp., 1957-62; dir. publs. and sales Frank Music Corp., 1962-69; v.p. Boston Music Co., 1968-69; pres. Theodore Presser Co., 1969-95, chmn., 1995—; also dir.; chmn. Elkan-Vogel Inc., 1970—. Pres. Music Industry Coun., 1966-68, v.p., 1969-70; dir., sec. Harry Fox Agy., 1989-2000, treas., 2000—. Co-author: Music Dictionary, 1956, Invitation to the Piano, 1959; Asso. editor: Univ. Soc. Ency. of Piano Music; Contbr. articles to profl. jours. Mem. Nassau County (N.Y.) Dem. Com., 1952-63; bd. dirs. N.Y. Citizens Com. for Pub. Schs., 1963-68, Am. Music Ctr., 1968-72, 78-83, 85-91, Am. Music Conf., 1979-80, Nat. Music Coun., 1979-85, 93—, Music Educators Nat. Conf., 1966-68; trustee ASCAP Found., 1976—, treas., 1990—; trustee Union Free Sch. Dist. 21 Bd. Edn., Rockville Centre, N.Y., 1963-69, sec., dist. clk., 1966-67, v.p., dist. clk., 1967-69. With USCGR, 1942-45. Recipient Disting. Alumnus award Ithaca Coll., 2001; Lowell Mason fellow MENC, 2003. Mem. ASCAP (bd. dirs. 1972—, bd. rev. 1980-82, asst. treas. 1989-90, treas. 1990—), Music Pubs. Assn. U.S. (pres. 1972-74, 80-82, bd. dirs. 1980-82, 83-92, 96—), Nat. Music Pubs. Assn. (bd. dirs. 1980—, sec. 1989—, treas. 2000—), Internat. Pubs. Assn. (v.p. sect. music 1972-73), Internat. Confedn. Music Pubs. (v.p. 1978-88, bd. dirs. 1992—, pres. 1993-94, 96—, chmn. 1994-96, pres. 1996-98, chmn. 1998—), Internat. Fedn. Serious Music Pubs. (v.p. 1978-93, pres. 1993—), Music Industry Mfrs. Assn. (dir. 1980-82), Charles Ives Soc. (bd. dirs. 1985-2003), Phi Mu Alpha Sinfonia. Home: 908 Wootton Rd Bryn Mawr PA 19010-2228 Office: 588 N Gulph Rd King Of Prussia PA 19406 E-mail: abroido@presser.com.

BROITMAN, SELWYN ARTHUR, microbiologist, educator; b. Boston, Aug. 30, 1931; s. Julius Z. and Sara (Sallus) B.; m. Barbara Merle Shwartz, June 13, 1953; children: Caryn Beth, Jeffrey Z. BS, U. Mass., 1952, MS, 1953; PhD, Mich. State U., 1956. Dir. Biotech. Assocs., 1959-62; research instr. dept. pathology Boston U. Sch. Medicine, 1963-64, asst. prof. dept. microbiology, 1965-69, assoc. prof. dept. microbiology, 1969-75, prof., 1975—, prof. pathology and lab. medicine, 1983—, asst. dean med. sch. admissions, 1983—; assoc. prof. nutritional scis. Henry Goldman Sch. Grad. Dentistry Boston U., 1974—. Assoc. medicine dept. medicine Harvard Med. Sch., 1969-74; rsch. assoc. Mallory Inst. Pathology, Boston City Hosp., Gastro Intestinal Rsch. Lab., 1956-71; assoc. in medicine Thorndike Meml. Lab., 1969-74; chair, co-chair of various admission programs Boston U. Sch. Medicine; adv.-at-large Acad. of Advisors, 2003. Contbr. articles to profl. jours. Founding mem. Digestive Disease Found. Served with AUS, 1952-66; advisor Boston U. Sch. Medicine, 2003. Recipient Outstanding Teaching award Boston U. Sch. Medicine 1st Yr. Class, 1976 Fellow Am. Coll. Gastroenterology; mem. AAAS, Am. Soc. for Investigative Pathology, Am. Soc. for Nutritional Scis., Am. Assn. for Cancer Rsch., Am. Fedn. for Med. Rsch., Am. Soc. Microbiology, Soc. Applied Bacteriology (Eng.), Soc. Exptl. Biology and Medicine, Nutrition Today Soc. (founding), Am. Gastroent. Assn., Boston Gastroent. Soc., Nat. Acad. Scis. (com. diet, nutrition and cancer 1980-83), N.Y. Acad. Scis., Boston Bug Club (pres. 1976), Sigma Xi. Office: 80 E Concord St Boston MA 02118-2307 *When problems cannot be resolved by the minds of this generation, the solutions must be sought in the minds of the next. The challenge is to find these young people, encourage them, and wherever possible, remove all obstacles to their learning.*

BROKAW, CLIFFORD VAIL, III, investment banker, business executive; b. N.Y.C., Sept. 17, 1928; s. Clifford Vail and Audrey (Stransom Joel) B.; m. Elizabeth Stokes Rogers, June 29, 1960; children: Clifford Vail IV, George Rogers BA, Yale U., 1950; JD, U. Va., 1956. Bar: NY 1957, U.S. Dist. Ct. 1959, U.S. Supreme Ct. 2002. Assoc. White & Case, N.Y.C., 1956-59; assoc. Blyth & Co., Inc., N.Y.C., 1959-61; assoc., then gen. ptnr. W.E. Hutton & Co., N.Y.C., 1961-67; gen. ptnr., sr. v.p. Eastman Dillon Union Securities & Co. and successor firm Blyth, Eastman, Dillon & Co., Inc., N.Y.C., 1967-77; chmn., CEO Invail Capital, Inc., N.Y.C., 1977-95; CEO IRT Corp., San Diego, 1977-95, chmn. bd., 1986-94. Bd. dirs., chmn. fin. com. Brazos River Gas Co., Mineral Wells, Tex., 1962-91; chmn. bd. Cayman Resources Corp., Tulsa, 1977-88, bd. dirs., 1992-95. Bd. advisors Marine Mil. Acad., Harlingen, Tex., 1985-91; mem. alumni assn. coun. U. Va. Sch. Law, 1976-79; founder Brokaw chair corp. law U. Va. Sch. Law, 1985, mem. dean's coun., 1990—, bus. adv. coun., 1995—; mem. indsl. adv. com. Sch. Engring and Applied Sch. U. Va., 1987-94; vestryman French Ch. du St. Espirit, 1986-88, treas., 1988-92, warden, 1989-93. Lt. col. USMCR, 1950-73. Decorated Purple Heart Mem. ABA, Suffolk County Bar assn., Pilgrims U.S., Mil. Order Carabao, Mil. Order World Wars, Mil. Order Fgn. Wars U.S., Mil. Order of Purple Heart, Nat. Inst. Social Scis. (bd. dirs. 1991-94, pres. 1992-94), Nat. Gavel Soc., Ends of Earth, Huguenot Soc. Am. (coun. 1974-80, v.p. 1986-89, pres. 1989-92), Am. Soc. Order of St. John (comdr.), U. Va. Lawn Soc., Burning Tree Club, The Meadow Club, Bathing Corp. of Southampton, Union Club (N.Y.C.), Masons, Shriners, Yale Club (N.Y.C.), Delta Theta Phi. Republican. Episcopalian. Avocations: tennis, golf. Office: PO Box 5002 Southampton NY 11969-5002

BROKAW, NORMAN ROBERT, talent agency executive; b. N.Y.C., Apr. 21, 1927; s. Isadore David and Marie (Hyde) B.; children: David M., Sanford Jay, Joel S., Barbara M., Wendy E., Lauren Quincy Student pvt. schs., Los Angeles. With William Morris Agy., Inc., Beverly Hills, Calif., 1943—, sr. agt. and co. exec., 1951-74, v.p. world-wide ops., 1974-80, exec. v.p., dir., 1980—, co-chmn. bd., 1986-91, pres., CEO, 1989-91, chmn. bd., CEO, 1991-97, chmn. bd. worldide, 1997—. Pres. Betty Ford Cancer Center, Cedars-Sinai Med. Center, Los Angeles, 1978— ; bd. dirs. Cedars-Sinai Med. Center; industry chmn. United Jewish Welfare Fund, 1975. With U.S. Army, World War II. Mem. Acad. Motion Picture Arts and Scis. Clubs: Hillcrest Country (Los Angeles). Clients include former Pres. and Mrs. Gerald R. Ford, Bill Cosby, Gen. Alexander Haig Jr., Gen. Claudia Kennedy, Tony Randall, Donald Regan, C. Everett Koop, Priscilla Presley, Andy Griffith, Brooke Shields, Juliette Lewis, Marcia Clark, Christopher Darden. Office: William Morris Agy 1 William Morris Pl Beverly Hills CA 90212-2775 also: William Morris Agy Inc 1325 Avenue Of The Americas New York NY 10019-6026

BROKAW, THOMAS JOHN, television broadcast executive, correspondent; b. Webster, S.D., Feb. 6, 1940; s. Anthony Orville and Eugenia (Conley) B.; m. Meredith Lynn Auld, Aug. 17, 1962; children— Jennifer Jean, Andrea Brooks, Sarah Auld. BA in Polit. Sci, U. S.D., 1962, hon. degree, Washington U., St. Louis, Syracuse U., Hofstra U., Boston Coll., Emerson Coll., Simpson Coll., Duke U., 1991, Notre Dame U., 1993. Morning news editor Sta. KMTV, Omaha, 1962-65; news editor, anchorman Sta. WSB-TV, Atlanta, 1965-66; reporter, corr., anchorman Sta. KNBC-TV, Los Angeles, 1966-73; White House corr. NBC, Washington, 1973-76; anchorman Sat. Night News, N.Y.C., 1973-76; host Today show, N.Y.C., 1976-82; anchorman, editor NBC Nightly News, 1982—; corr. Exposé NBC, 1991—. Corr. NBC coverage U.S. Presdl. elections, 1976, 80, anchor, 1984, 88; mem. adv. com. Reporters Com. for Freedom of Press. Corr. numerous NBC News specials, including To Be A Teacher, 1987, Wall Street: Money Greed and Power, 1987, A Conversation with Mikhail S. Gorbachev (Alfred I. DuPont award), 1987, Home Street Home, 1988, To Be An American (George Foster Peabody award); Author: The Greatest Generation, 1998, The Greatest Generation Speaks, 1999, An Album of Memories, 2001. Trustee Norton Simon Mus. Art, Pasadena, Calif., U. S.D. Found.; adviser Asia Soc. Mem. AFTRA (dir. 1968-72), Sigma Delta Chi. Office: NBC News 30 Rockefeller Plz Fl 3 New York NY 10112-0002*

BROKKE, CATHERINE JULIET, mission executive; b. Mpls., Dec. 25, 1926; d. Emil John and Alma (Brye) Eliason; m. Harold Joseph Brokke, Sept. 9, 1949; 1 child, Daniel. Diploma in nursing, Luth. Deaconess Hosp., Mpls., 1947, student Concordia Coll., Moorhead, Minn., 1948-49, Bethany Coll. Missions, Mpls., 1949-51. RN, Minn. Sch. and occupational nurse Bethany Fellowship, Mpls., 1951-75; missions sec. Bethany Fellowship Missions, Mpls., 1963-86, dir., 1986-96; retired, 1996. Instr. Bethany Coll. Missions, 1950-88. Mng. editor Message of Cross, 1990-97; composer hymns. Organist Bethany Missionary Ch., Bloomington, Minn., 1956-89; trustee STEM Ministries, 1995-2000, bd. dirs. Mem. Evang. Fellowship of Mission Agys. (trustee 1987-93), Evang. Missions Info. Svc. (bd. dirs. 1994-96). Avocations: piano, organ. Office: Bethany Fellowship Missions 6820 Auto Club Rd Ste D Bloomington MN 55438-2849 E-mail: cathy.brokke@bethfel.org., cathybrokke@worldnet.att.net.

BROM, LIBOR, journalist, educator; b. Ostrava, Czechoslovakia, Dec. 17, 1923; came to U.S., 1958, naturalized, 1964; s. Ladislav and Bozena (Bromova) B.; m. Gloria S. Mena, Aug. 31, 1961; 1 son, Rafael Brom. Ing., Czech Inst. Tech., 1948; JUC, Charles U. Prague, 1951; postgrad., San Francisco State Coll.; MA, U. Colo., 1962, PhD, 1970. V.p. Brom, Inc., Ostrava, 1942-48; economist Slovak Magnesite Works, Prague, Czechoslovakia, 1948-49; economist, chief planner Vodostavba, Navika, Prague, 1951-56; tchr. Jefferson County Schs., Colo., 1958-67; prof., dir. Russian area studies program U. Denver, 1967-91, prof. emeritus, 1992—; journalist, mem. editorial staff Denni Hlasatel-Daily Herald, Chgo., 1978-96; editorial staff Jour. of Interdisciplinary Studies, 1988—. Pres. Colo. Nationalities Council, 1970-72; comptroller Exec. Bd. Nat. Heritage Groups Council, 1970-72; mem. adv. bd. Nat. Security Council, 1980-85; acad. bank participant Heritage Found. Author: Ivan Bunin's Proteges, Leonid Zurov, 1973, Alexander Zinoviev's Concept of the Soviet Man, 1991; co-author: Has the Third World War Already Started, 1983, Christianity and Russian Culture in Soviet Society, 1990, The Search for Self-Definition in Russian Literature, 1991; translator: Problems of Geography, 1955; author: (in Czech) In the Windstorm of Anger, 1976, Time and Duty, 1981, Teacher of Nations and Our Times, 1982, The Way of Light, 1982, On the Attack, 1983, Between the Currents, 1985, Homeland After 50 Years Nazi & Communist Occupation, 1992. V.p. Colo. Citizenship Day, 1968-69; pres. Comenius World Coun., 1976-85, World Representation of Czechoslovak Exiles, 1976-84; pres. Czech World Union, 1985-94; gen. sec. Czechoslovak Rep. Movement, 1980-91. Recipient Americanism medal DAR, 1969, Disting. Service award Am. by Choice, 1968, Kynewisbov Pioneer award Denver U., 1989; named Tchr. with Superlative Performance MLA, 1961, Outstanding Faculty mem. Omicron Delta Kappa, 1972, The Order of M.R. Stefanik Provisional Czechoslovak Govt. in Exile, Order of Judr. Karel Kramar, Nat. Dem. Party, Czech Republic. Mem. Am. Assn. Tchrs. Slavic and Ea. European Langs. (v.p. 1973-75), Rocky Mountain Assn. Slavic Studies (sec./treas. 1975-78, v.p. 1978-81, pres. 1982-83), Czechoslovak Christian Dem. Movement in Exile (ctrl. com. 1970-79), Dobro Slovo (hon.), Slava (hon.), Nat. Rep. Nationalities Coun. (co-chmn. human rights com. 1979-81), Phi Beta Kappa (hon.). Republican. Roman Catholic. Home: 434 A Woodview Rd Barrington IL 60010-1770 Office: U Denver Denver CO 80208-0001 E-mail: lbrbrm@aol.com.

BROM, ROBERT H. bishop; b. Arcadia, Wis., Sept. 18, 1938; Student, St. Mary's Coll., Winona, Minn., Gregorian U., Rome. Ordained priest Roman Cath. Ch., 1963, consecrated bishop Roman Cath. Ch., 1983. Bishop of Duluth, Minn., 1983—89; coadjutor bishop Diocese of San Diego, 1989—90, bishop, 1990—. Office: Diocese of San Diego Pastoral Ctr PO Box 85728 San Diego CA 92186-5728*

BROMAN, JOHN MICHAEL, music educator; b. Chgo., May 17, 1947; s. John Arthur and Onnolee Broman; m. Kathleen Sue Angus, July 1982 (div. May 1993); children: Elizabeth, Jessica. BA in French, Luther Coll., 1969; MusB in Voice, U. Iowa, 1974, MA in Choral Conducting, 1976. French tchr. Webster City (Iowa) Jr. H.S., 1969—72; dir. choral activities Dakota Wesleyan U., Mitchell, SD, 1976—77, Loras Coll., Dubuque, Iowa, 1977—92, North Ga. Coll and State U., Dahlonega, Ga., 1992—. Choir dir. St. Peter Luth. Ch., Dubuque, 1977—92, Christ the King Luth. Ch., Cumming, Ga., 1994—; chorister Lanier Singers, Gainesville, Ga., 1992—98, Gainesville, 2001—, dir., 1998—2001. Mem.: Ga. Music Educators Assn., Music Educators Nat. Conf., Ga. Choral Dirs. Assn., Am. Choral Dirs. Assn. Republican. Lutheran. Avocation: sports. Home: 3777 N River Dr Gainesville GA 30506 Office: North Ga Coll and State U Fine Arts Dept Dahlonega GA 30597 Fax: 706-864-1429. E-mail: jbroman@ngcsu.edu.

BROMAN, PER FREDRIK, education educator; b. Norrkoping, Sweden, July 26, 1962; s. Allan Fredrik and Marianne Elsa Gunvor Broman; m. Nora Anne Engebretsen, Apr. 22, 1968. M in Music Edn., Ingesund Coll. of Music, Sweden, 1987; Post-Grad. Diploma, Royal Coll. of Music, Stockholm, 1992; MA, McGill U., Can., 1995; PhD, Gothenburg U., 1999. Asst. prof. Lulea U. of Tech., Pitea, Sweden, 1992—97, Butler U., Indpls., 1999. Author: (scholarly articles) Jour. of the Swedish Musicological Soc., Grove Dictionary of Music and Musicians, (scholarly book) Back to the Future: Towards and Aesthetic Theory of Bengt Hambraeus; editor: (book) Crosscurrents and Counterpoints. Sgt. Marines, 1982—83, Sweden. Grantee, Sweden Am. Found., 1990, 1991, 1994. Mem.: Swedish Musicological Soc., Coll. Music Soc., Can. U. Music Soc., Soc. for Music Theory (bd. mem., midwest chpt. 2002—), Am. Musicological Soc. Office: Butler U 4600 Sunset Ave Indianapolis IN 46208 Office Fax: 317-940-9658. Personal E-mail: pbroman@butler.edu.

BROMBAL, DOUGLAS NEREO, retired university official, consultant; b. Windsor, Ont., Can., May 18, 1930; s. Nereo and Johanna (Lausch) B.; m. Margaret Anne Howard, Aug. 1, 1953 (div. Feb. 1980); children: David Scott, Karen Elaine; m. Agnes Calcutt Garrison, May 3, 1986. BA, U. Windsor, 1969. Buyer Ford Motor Co. Can., Windsor, 1949-59; sales engr. F.F. Barber Machinery Co., Toronto, Ont., 1959-60, Gardner-Denver Co., Toronto, 1960-61; purchasing and maintenance mgr. Essex Coll., Assumption U., Windsor, 1961-63; asst. to treas., purchasing mgr. U. Windsor, 1963-67, asst. to v.p. adminstrn., 1967-70, asst. v.p. adminstrn., 1970-72; dir. adminstrv. svcs. Carleton U., Ottawa, Ont., 1972-93, dir. pension fund mgmt., 1993-96; cons.,

1996—; hon. chmn. Comstat Capital Scis., Inc., Can., 1997-99; acting exec. dir. Canadian Assn. Univ. Bus. Officers, 1996-97. Mem. pres.'s adv. com. on campus revs. U. Alta, Edmonton, 1987; cons. Brock U., St. Catherines, Ont., 1989. Treas. Can. Red Cross, Windsor, 1968-72; bd. dirs. Can. Assn. Christians and Jews, Windsor, 1970-72; bd. mgmt. Ch. of the Ascension, Diocese of Huron, Windsor, 1964-72, synod del., 1964-72. Mem. Assn. Can. Pension Mgmt. (treas. 1984-87), Can. Pension and Benefits Conf. (regional coun. 1987-90), Pension Investment Assn. Can., Ea. Assn. Coll. Aux. Svcs. (bd. dirs. 1988-94, pres. 1992-93), Nat. Assn. Coll. Aux. Svcs. (Silver Torch award 1994), Italian Wine Soc. Can. (nat. pres.). Avocations: downhill skiing, reading, wine tasting. Home: 1226 Stanton Rd Ottawa ON Canada K2C 3E2

BROMBERG, JOHN E. lawyer; b. Dallas, May 9, 1946; s. Edward S. and Mildred J. (Rosenberg) B.; children from previous marriage: Spencer Harkness, Whitney Payne, Kemp Howitt, Campbell Wynne; m. Beth Jenkins; children: Susan Elizabeth, Melissa Anne. BA, Columbia U., 1968; JD, U. Tex., 1972. Bar: Tex. 1972. Chmn. Stutzman, Bromberg Esserman & Plifka PC, Dallas, 1984—. Past pres. Preston Hollow Park Assn., pre-sch. playground, Dallas. Mem. Am. Contract Bridge League (past pres. Dallas unit) Home: 9 Hallshire Ct Dallas TX 75225-1824 Office: 2323 Bryan St Ste 2200 Dallas TX 75201-2655 E-mail: bromberg@sbep-law.com.

BROMBERG, MYRON JAMES, lawyer; b. Paterson, N.J., Nov. 5, 1934; s. Abraham and Elsie (Baker) B.; m. Lisa Murtha, Nov. 28, 1987; children—Kenneth Karl, Eric Edward, Bruce Abraham. BA, Yale U., 1956; LLB, Columbia U., 1959. Bar: N.J. bar 1960, N.Y. bar 1981. Law asst. to dist. atty., N.Y. County, 1958; law asst. U.S. atty. So. Dist. N.Y., 1958-59; asso. mem. firm Ralph Porzio, Morristown, N.J., 1960-61; ptnr. Porzio, Bromberg & Newman, Morristown, 1962-77, mng. prin., 1980-96. Atty. Morris County Bd. Elections, 1963-64; town atty., Town of Morristown, 1965-67; lectr. trial practice Rutgers Inst. CLE, 1965-94; mem. faculty Kraft-Eidson trial techniques seminar Emory U., 1997—. Chmn. fund and membership Morristown chpt. ARC, 1965; chmn. retail div. Community Chest Morris County, 1963; chmn. Keep Morristown Beautiful Com., 1963; mem. Morris Twp. Com., 1970-72; committeeman Morris County Democratic Com., 1962-63, 72-77; lay trustee Delbarton Sch., Morristown, 1972-75; trustee Morris Mus., 1973-79. Fellow Am. Coll. Trial Lawyers (chmn. com. on admission to fellowship 1986-91, com. on complex litigation 1992-98, com. on tchg. of trial and appellate advocacy 1998—), Am. Law Inst. (cons. group product libility), Am. Bar Found. (life); mem. ABA, Internat. Acad. Trial Lawyers (chair N.J. 1997-99, regional chair 3d jud. cir. 1997-2000, dir. 2002—), N.J. Bar Assn. (named outstanding young lawyer 1970, chmn. joint conf. com. with N.J. Med. Soc. 1970-72), Morris County Bar Assn., Am. Judicature Soc., Trial Attys. N.J. (pres. 1976-77, Trial Bar award 1989), Internat. Soc. Barristers (N.J. State chmn., bd. govs., sec.-treas. 1996-97, v.p. 1998-00, pres. 2000-01), Found. Internat. Soc. Barristers (pres. 2002—), Internat. Assn. Def. Counsel (chair com. on toxic and hazardous substances 1994-96, dir. Def. Counsel Trial Acad. 1996), Andover Alumni Assn. N.Y.C., Columbia U. Law Sch. Assn. of N.J. (bd. dirs. 1986-95, 2001—), Phillips Acad. Alumni Coun., Yale Club (N.Y.C. and ctrl. N.J.), Park Ave. (N.J.) Club, Chi Phi, Phi Delta Phi. Home: 9 Thompson Ct Morristown NJ 07960-6326 Office: PO Box 1997 100 Southgate Pkwy Morristown NJ 07962-1997 E-mail: mjbromberg@pbnlaw.com.

BROMBERG, ROBERT SHELDON, lawyer; b. Bklyn., May 3, 1935; s. Jack and Bertha (Toskey) B.; m. Barbara W. Schwartz, Apr. 1, 1978; children: Jason, David. AB, Columbia U., 1956, LLB, 1959; LLM in Taxation, NYU, 1966. Bar: N.Y. 1960, D.C. 1972, Ohio 1972, U.S. Ct. Claims 1976, U.S. Supreme Ct 1975. Practiced law, N.Y.C., 1960-66; atty. exempt orgns. br. IRS, Washington, 1966-70, Office Chief Counsel, 1970-72; partner firm Baker, Hostetler & Patterson, Cleve., 1972-79; prin. Robert S. Bromberg, L.P.A., Cleve., 1979-81, Paxton & Seasongood, Cin., 1981-85; sole practice Cin., 1985—. Lectr. tax and health law confs. Author: Tax Planning for Hospitals and Health Care Organizations, 2 vols., 1979; cons. editor: Prentice Hall Tax Exempt Organizations Service, 1973-84; nat. adv. bd. Integrated Healthcare Report; adv. bd. The Exempt Organization Tax Review; contbr. articles to profl. jours. Recipient award (5) Dept. Treasury, 1966-72, citation Am. Assn. Homes for Aged, 1973 Mem. Am. Health Lawyers Assn. (pres. 1986-87, program chmn. Ann. Tax Inst. 1975-95). Home and Office: 1144 E Rookwood Dr Cincinnati OH 45208-3334

BROMBERGER, ALLEN RICHARD, legal association administrator; b. Princeton, N.J., May 1, 1955; s. Sylvain and Nancy (Lilienthal) Bromberger; m. Lauren Goldstein; 1 child, Michael Barrows. BA, U. Calif., Berkeley, 1978; JD, U. Calif., San Francisco, 1982. Bar: Calif. 1982, N.Y. 1983. Dir. legal assistance Coun. N.Y. Law Assocs., N.Y.C., 1983-85, assoc. dir., 1985-88, dir. nonprofit law program, 1988-90; exec. dir. Lawyers Alliance for N.Y., N.Y.C., 1990-99; pres. Power of Attorney, N.Y.C., 1999—. Bd. dirs. Lawyers Com. Against Violence, N.Y.C., 1996-98, Interlegal USA, N.Y.C., 1994—, Cause Effective, N.Y.C., 1994-2000, Coalition for the Homeless, N.Y.C., 1994-96; mem. IRS Exempt Orgns. Liaison Com., 1993-99. Editor, author: Getting Organized, 1986, 5th edit., 2000, Advising Nonprofits, 1988, 4th edit., 1995. Mem. ABA, Assn. Bar City N.Y., Nat. Assn. Pro Bono Coords. (exec. com. 1996-98), N.Y. State Advisory Task Force on Corps., 1997-99. Office: Power of Attorney 330 7th Ave Fl 19 New York NY 10001-5010

BROMBERT, VICTOR HENRI, literature educator, author; b. Germany, Nov. 11, 1923; came to U.S., 1941, naturalized, 1943; s. Jacques and Vera B.; m. Beth Anne Archer, June 18, 1950; children: Lauren Nora, Marc Alexis. BA, Yale U., 1948, MA, 1949, PhD, 1953; postgrad., U. Rome, 1950-51; HHD (hon.), U. Chgo., 1981, U. Toronto, 1997. Faculty Yale U., New Haven, 1951-75, from assoc. prof. to prof., 1958-75, Benjamin F. Barge prof. Romance lits., 1969-75, chmn. dept. Romance langs. and lit., 1964-73; Henry Putnam univ. prof. romance and comparative lit. Princeton (N.J.) U., 1975—, dir. Christian Gauss seminars in criticism, 1984-94, chmn. Coun. Humanities, 1989-94. Summer prof. Middlebury Coll., 1951-53, Institut d'Etudes Françaises, Avignon, 1962, 64, 73, U. Colo., 1965; Christian Gauss Seminar in criticism Princeton U., 1964; vis. prof. Scuola Normale Superiore, Pisa, Italy, 1972, U. Calif., 1978, Johns Hopkins U., 1979, Columbia U., 1980, NYU, 1980, 81, U. P.R., 1983, 84, U. Bologna, Italy, 1984, Yale U., 1985; Phi Beta Kappa vis. scholar, 1986-87, 89-90; lectr. Alliance Française, humanities U. Kans., 1966; lectr. Collège de France, 1991; mem. Fulbright screening com., 1965; dir. fellowships in residence NEH, Princeton U., 1975-76, dir. summer seminar, 1979, 82, 84, 86, 88; mem. adv. com. for humanities Libr. of Congress, 1976; mem. Yale U. Coun., 1977-83; mem. ednl. adv. bd. Guggenheim Found., 1982— Author: (Literary Critiques) The Criticism of T. S. Eliot, 1949, Stendhal et la Voie Oblique, 1954, The Intellectual Hero, 1961, The Novels of Flaubert, 1966, Stendhal: Fiction and the Themes of Freedom, 1968, Flaubert par lui-même, 1971, La Prison Romantique, 1976, The Romantic Prison: The French Tradition, 1978, Victor Hugo and the Visionary Novel, 1984, The Hidden Reader, 1988, In Praise of Antiheroes, 1999, Trains of Thought: Memories of a Stateless Youth, 2002; editor: Stendhal: A Collection of Critical Essays, 1962, Balzac's La Peau de Chagrin, 1962, The Hero in Literature, 1969, Flaubert's Madame Bovary, 1969, The World of Lawrence Durrell, 1962, Ideas in the Drama, 1964, Malraux, 1964, Instants Premiers, 1973, Romanticism, 1973, Literary Criticism, 1974, Die Romanische Novelle, 1977, The Author in His Work, 1978, Essais sur Flaubert, 1979, Writers and Politics, 1983, Flaubert and Postmodernism, 1984, Writing in a Modern Temper, 1984, Literary Theory and Criticism, 1984, Hugo le Fabuleux, 1985, 19th Century Literary Criticism, 1985, Charles Baudelaire, 1987, Albert Camus, 1989, André Malraux, 1989, Gustave Flaubert, 1989, Dilemmes du Roman, 1989, Nineteenth Century French Poetry, 1990, Literature, Culture and Society in the Modern Age, 1991, Literary Generations, 1992, Dix Etudes sur Baudelaire, 1993, George Sand et son temps, 1994, Pratiques d' écriture, 1996, Stendhal et le comique, 1999, 500 Years of Theater History:, 2000; contbr. articles to profl. jours. Served with M.I. AUS, 1943-45. Decorated officer Ordre des Palmes Académiques; recipient Harry Levin prize in comparative lit., 1978, Howard T. Behrman award for disting. achievement in humanities, 1979, Wilbur Lucius Cross medal for outstanding achievement, Yale Univ., 1985, Médaille Vermeil de la Ville de Paris, 1985, The Pres. award for disting. tchg., 1999; fellow Fulbright fellow, 1950—51, Guggenheim fellow, 1954—55, 1970, sr. fellow, NEH, 1973—74, Rockefeller found. resident fellow, Bellagio, Italy, 1975, 1990; grantee Am. Coun. Learned Socs., 1966. Fellow Am. Acad. Arts and Scis.; mem. MLA (editl. adv. comm. 1979-83, pres. 1989), Am. Assn. Tchrs. French, Am. Comparative Lit. Assn., Am. Philos. Soc., Soc. des Etudes Françaises, Soc. des Etudes Romantiques, Acad. Lit. Studies (pres. 1983), Soc. d'Histoire Littéraire de la France, Soc. U. per gli Studi di Lingua e Letteratura Francese, Inst. Romance Studies, Elizabethan Club (pres. 1968-70), Yale Club, Phi Beta Kappa. Office: Princeton U E17 Dillon Ct Princeton NJ 08544-0001 Home: 49 Constitution Hill W Princeton NJ 08540-6774

BROME, THOMAS REED, lawyer; b. NYC, Aug. 24, 1942; s. Robert Harrison and Mary Elizabeth (Reed) B.; m. Marie Olszewski, June 5, 1971; children: Clinton Reed, Bethan, Heather. AB, Harvard Coll., 1964; LLB, NYU, 1967. Bar: DC 1967, NY 1968. Law clk. to hon. Warren E. Burger U.S. Ct. Appeals, Washington, 1967-68; assoc. Cravath, Swaine & Moore, NYC, 1968-75, ptnr., 1975—. Dir. Legal Aid Soc., NYC, 1989-98, pres., 1994-96. Mem. sch. bd., Ridgewood, NJ, 1989—92, pres., 1991—92; trustee NYU Law Ctr. Found., NY, 1992—2003, vice chair, 2001—; pres. Ridgewood Pub. Edn. Found., NJ, 1993—96. Mem. ABA, NY State Bar Assn., Assn. Bar of City of NY Republican. Episcopalian. Home: 500 Knollwood Rd Ridgewood NJ 07450-4700 Office: Cravath Swaine & Moore 825 8th Ave New York NY 10019-7475

BROMELKAMP, DAVID JOHN, investment officer; b. Poughkeepsie, N.Y., Aug. 2, 1960; s. Henry James and Elaine Teresa (Kuhl) B. BS, St. Johns U., Collegeville, Minn., 1982; Masters in intl. mgmt., U. St. Thomas, St. Paul, Minn., 1989. CPA, Minn., 1985-88, cert. invest. mgmt. cons., 1996, investment mgmt. analyst, 2001. Corp. acct., 1982-85; acct. Stirtz, Bernards and Co., Mpls., 1986-88; v.p., investment officer RBC Dain Rausher, Mpls., 1988 . Mem. Investment Mgmt. Cons., Minn. Soc. CPAs Republican. Roman Catholic. Home: 4705 Fremont Ave S Minneapolis MN 55409-2206

BROMKE, CINDY ROSE, geriatrics, rehabilitation and home health nurse; b. Mt. Pleasant, Pa., Aug. 18, 1960; d. Clark Raymond and Sara Ann (Fisher) Hancock; children: Crystal, Craig Jr., Casey. ASN, Westmoreland County C.C., 1992. RN, Pa. Charge nurse Integrated Health Svcs. of Greater Pitts., Greensburg, Pa., 1992-93, supr., 1993-94, RN assessment coord., 1994-95, staff nurse rehab. unit, 1995-96; skilled unit mgr. Integrated Health Svcs. Mt. View, Greensburg, Pa., 1996; RNAC Briarcliff Pavilion, North Huntington, Pa., 1996-97; staff nurse Barclay Inpatient Rehab. Unit Westmoreland Regional Hosp., Greensburg, 1997-99, rehab/restorative nurse Westmoreland Home Health Care divsn., 1999—. Sunday sch. supt. St. John's United Ch. of Christ, Mt. Pleasant, Pa., 1991, 98-2000, sec., 1992—, treas., 1997—, asst. supt., 2001—; mem. program com. Westmoreland Assn. of the Penn West conf. United Ch. of Christ, 1994-99 chair, 1997-98, registrar Westmoreland Assn. Penn West Conf., 1997-02. Home: RR 1 Box 352 Hunker PA 15639-9726 E-mail: crbromke@aol.com.

BROMLEY, BRUCE DITMAS, language educator, writer; b. N.Y.C., Sept. 23, 1956; s. Stephen Baldwin and Patricia Ann B. Student, Berklee Coll. Music, 1976-80; BA in English with honors, Columbia U., 1995; postgrad., NYU, 1995—. Poetry workshop asst. dir. Phillips Brooks House Harvard U., Cambridge, Mass., 1976-80; instr. in compositional analysis Berklee Coll. Music, Boston, 1978-84; poetry reading supr. Shakespeare and Co., Paris, 1985-92; instr. English lit. Columbia U., N.Y.C., 1993-95; instr. expository writing, English lit., 1996—. Mentor in expository writing program NYU, 2000—, lectr., 2003—. Author: (play) Sound for Three Voices, 1996, poems; composer (score and piano) Hamlet; composer, playwright in residence Oxford U. Theatre Troupe, Edinburgh Theatre Festival, Scotland, 1986-87; contbr. poems to Gargoyle Mag. Instr. Earl Hall G.E.D. program Columbia U., N.Y.C., 1995—. Mohlberger fellow in English Lit., 2000-2001; recipient Master Tchr. Award, N.Y.U., 2000--. Mem. Princeton Club, Phi Beta Kappa. Home: PO Box 1573 East Hampton NY 11937-0704 E-mail: bdb4945@nyu.edu.

BROMLEY, DAVID ALLAN, physicist, engineer, educator; b. Westmeath, Ont., Can., May 4, 1926; s. Milton Escort and Susan Anne (Anderson) Bromley; m. Patricia Jane Brassor, Aug. 30, 1949 (dec. Oct. 1990); children: David John, Karen Lynn. BS in Engring. Physics, Queen's U., Kingston, Ont., 1948, MS in Physics, 1950; PhD in Nuclear Physics, U. Rochester, 1952; MA (hon.), Yale U., 1961; D of Natural Philosophy (hon.), U. Frankfurt, 1978; Docteur (Physique) (hon.), U. Strasbourg, 1980; DSc (hon.), Queen's U., 1981, U. Notre Dame, 1982, U. Witwatersrand, 1982, Trinity Coll., 1988; LittD (hon.), U. Bridgeport, 1981; Dott. (hon.), U. Padua, 1983; LHD (hon.), U. New Haven, 1987; DSc (hon.), Rensselaer Polytechnic Inst., 1990; LHD (hon.), Ill. Inst. Tech., 1990; DSc (hon.), Lehigh U., 1991, Bklyn. Polytechnic Inst., 1991, U. Guelph, 1991, Fordham U., 1991, Northwestern U., 1991, Coll. of William and Mary, 1991; D Engring. Tech. (hon.), Wentworth Inst., 1991; DSc (hon.), SUNY, U. Mass., Adelphi U., 1993; DHL (hon.), Mt. Sinai Med. Ctr., 1993; D. Eng. (hon.), Colo. Sch. Mines, 1992; DSc (hon.), Fla. State U., 1993, Mich. State U., 1994, Mt. Sinai Med., 1996, U. Pitts., 1997, U. Toronto, 1998; Tex. Tech. U. (hon.), 2001. Oper. engr. Hydro Electric Power Commn. Ont., 1947—48; rsch. officer Nat. Rsch. Coun. Can., 1948; instr., then asst. prof. physics U. Rochester, 1952—55; sr. rsch. officer, sect. head Atomic Energy Can. Ltd., 1955—60; assoc. prof. physics, asso. dir. heavy ion accelerator lab. Yale U., 1960—61, prof. physics, dir. A. W. Wright Nuclear Structure Lab., 1961—89, chmn. physics dept., 1970—77, Henry Ford II prof. physics, 1972—93, Sterling prof. scis., 1994—, dean engring., 1994—2000; asst. to Pres. for sci. and tech. Washington, 1989—93; dir. Office of Sci. and Tech. Policy, Washington, 1989—93; chmn. Pres.'s Coun. Advisers on Sci. and Tech., Washington, 1989—93, Fed. Coordinating Coun. Sci., Engring. and Tech., Washington, 1989—93, Nat. Critical Materials Coun., Washington, 1990—92. Cons. Brookhaven, Argonne, Berkeley and Oak Ridge Nat. Labs., Bell Telephone Labs., IBM, GTE; mem. panel nuc. physics NAS, 1964, chmn. com. on nuc. sci., 1966—74, chmn. physics survey, 1969—74; mem.-at-large, mem. exec. com. divsn. phys. scis. NRC, 1970—74, mem. exec. com., assembly phys. and math. scis., 1974—78, mem. naval sci. bd., 1974—78; mem. high energy physics adv. panel ERDA, 1974—78; mem. nuc. sci. adv. panel NSF and Dept. Energy, 1980—89; mem. White House Sci. Coun., 1981—89, Nat. Sci. Bd., 1988—89; bd. dirs. MBARI, Monterey, Calif., Echlin Inc., New Haven, Thermo Vision, Cambridge, Mass., Sci. Applications Internat., Paris; founding ptnr. Washington Adv. Group, 1997. Editor: Physics in Perspective, 5 vols., 1972, Large Electrostatic Accelerators, 1974, Nuclear Detectors, 1978, Heavy Ion Science, 8 vols., 1981—84, A Century of Physics, 2001; co-editor: Proceedings of the Kingston International Conference on Nuclear Structure, 1960, Facets of Physics, 1970, Nuclear Science in China, 1979, The President's Scientists: Reminiscences of a Presidential Science Advisor, 1993; assoc. editor Annals of Physics, 1968—89, Am. Scientist, 1969—81, Il Nuovo Cimento, 1970—89, Nuclear Instruments and Methods, 1974—89, Science, Technology and the Humanities, 1978—89, Jour. Physics, 1978—89, Nuclear Science Applications, 1978—89, Technology in Soc., 1981—89, cons. editor McGraw Hill Series in Fundamentals of Physics, 1967—89, McGraw Hill Ency. Sci. and Tech. Oak Ridge Assoc. Univs., 1977—80; U. Bridgeport, 1981—86; Sheffield Scientific Sch., 1995—. Decorated Comdr.'s Cross Order of Merit Fed. Rep. of Germany; recipient Disting. Alumnus award, U. Rochester, 1986, U.S. Nat. medal of Sci., 1988, Presdl. medal, N.Y. Acad. Scis., 1989, Yale medal in Sci. and Engring., 1991, Disting. Svc. award, IEEE, 1991, Louis Pasteur medal of Sci., U. Strasbourg, 1991, Harvey medal, Pierce Found., 1991, Disting. Svc. medal, NSF, 1992, Pub. Svc. medla, Ctr. Study of Presidency, 1992, Exec. Yr. award, R&D Mag., 1992, Disting. Scholar medal, U. Rochester, 1993; fellow Timothy Dwight Coll., 1961, Guggenheim, 1977—78, Humboldt, 1978, 1985, 1986, Benjamin Franklin Royal Soc. Arts, London, 1979, Sheffield, Yale U., 2001. Fellow: Am. Phys. Soc. (mem. coun. 1967—71, v.p. 1995, pres.-elect 1996, pres. 1997, Nicholson medal 2001), Washington Adv. Group (sr.); mem.: NAS, AAAS (chmn. physics sect. 1977—78, pres.-elect 1980, pres. 1981—, chmn. bd. 1982—, William Carey medal 1993, Philip Abelson prize 1997), Am. Assn. Engring. Edn. (bd. dirs. 1995—), Am. Soc. for Engring. Edn. (bd. dirs. 1995—), Coun. Engring. Deans (bd. dirs. 1994—, 1994—), Coun. on Fgn. Rels., Southeastern U. Rsch. Assn. (bd. dirs. 1984—89), Internat. Union Pure and Applied Physics (U.S. nat. com. 1969—, chmn. 1975—76, v.p. 1975—81, pres. 1984—87), Conn. Acad. Sci. and Engring., N.Y. Acad. Arts and Scis. (bd. govs. 1994—), Conn. Acad. Arts and Scis. (coun. 1976—78), European Phys. Soc., Can. Assn. Physicists, Sigma Xi. (pres. Yale 1962—63). Home: 35 Tokeneke Dr North Haven CT 06473-4348 Office: Yale Univ PO Box 208124 New Haven CT 06520-8124 also: Wright Nuc Structure Lab 272 Whitney Ave Rm 207 New Haven CT 06520

BROMLEY, ERNEST W. communications executive; M, UTSA. With Sosa and Assocs. (Bromley Comm.); rsch. dir., acct. mgr., media dir., layout artist, copywriter pvt. practice; pvt. practice as pres., CEO, 2002—. Creator AIG (Acculturation Influence Groups) Segmentation Model. Mem. bd. dirs. KLRN Alamo Pub. Telecommunications Coun., Free Trade Alliance, AVANCE, Christus Santa Rosa Health Futures Task Force. Recipient Silver Medal award, Am. Adv. Fed., 2002. Mem.: Greater San Antonio C. of C. Ctrl. Area Coun., U. Tex. at San Antonio Coll. Bus. Adv. Coun., Adv. Forum U. Tex. Austin Sch. Adv. Office: 401 E Houston St San Antonio TX 78205

BROMLEY, STEPHEN C. zoology educator; b. L.A., Aug. 31, 1938; s. Karl F. and Fae Christensen Bromley; m. Wendy McGarry, Oct. 1968 (div. Oct. 1995); children: John Axel, Anna Ruth, Joseph Jacob, James Asa, Jane Alexis, Stephen Calder. BS, Brigham Young U., 1960; AM, Princeton U., 1962, PhD, 1965. Instr. dept. biology Princeton (N.J.) U., 1964-65; asst. prof. dept. zoology U. Vt., Burlington, 1965-69; rsch. assoc. dept. zoology Mich. State U., East Lansing, 1969-70, assoc. prof. dept. zoology, 1970-76, prof. dept. zoology, 1976—, dir. biol. sci. program, 1970-91, dir. The Conservatory, 1988-90. Mem. AAAS. Avocations: handball, wood working, music, athletic conditioning, target shooting. Home: 1023 Glenhaven Ave East Lansing MI 48823-2622 Office: Dept Zoology Mich State Univ East Lansing MI 48823 E-mail: sbromley@msu.edu.

BROMM, CURT, state legislator; b. Oakland, Nebr., Mar. 19, 1945; m. Vicki Nodlinski, 1968; children: Jason, Jenefer, John, Jina, Jaron. Student, U. Nebr. Past county atty. Saunders County; mem. Nebr. Legislature from 23rd dist., Lincoln, 1992—; mem. bus. and labor com. Nebr. Legislature, Lincoln, mem. natural resources and urban affairs com., vice chmn. rules com., speaker of the legislature, 2002—. Chmn. bd. dirs. Saunders County Sch. Reorgn. Bd.; mem., pres. Wahoo Pub. Sch. Bd. Mem. Nebr. State Bar Assn. Home: 1448 N Pine St Wahoo NE 68066-1449 Office: Nebraska Unicameral Legislature State Capitol PO Box 94604 Lincoln NE 68509-4604*

BROMM, SUSAN ELIZABETH, lawyer, government official; b. Miami Beach, Fla., July 6, 1955; d. H. James and Dorothy (Shea) B.; m. Bernard J. Stoll, Jr., Oct. 20, 1984; 1 child, B. Joseph III. BS, SUNY, Albany, 1976; JD, Georgetown U., 1979. Bar: D.C. 1979, U.S. Dist. Ct. D.C. 1980. Atty., advisor office solid waste EPA, Washington, 1980-84, sect. chief, 1984-86, dep. dir. permits and state programs divsn., 1986-88, dir. Resource Conservation and Recovery Act enforcement div., 1988-93, dir. chem., cmty. svcs. and mcpl. divsn., 1993-95, dep. dir. office site remediation, 1995—2002, dir. office site remediation, 2002—. Mem. Environ. Law Inst., Am. Law Inst. Avocations: herbalist, nature photography. Office: EPA 2271A 1200 Pennsylvania Ave NW Washington DC 20460 E-mail: bromm.susan@epa.gov.

BROMSEN, MAURY AUSTIN, historian, bibliographer, antiquarian bookseller; b. NYC, Apr. 25, 1919; s. Herman and Rose (Eisenberg) B. BSS cum laude with spl. honors, CCNY, 1939; MA, U. Calif., Berkeley, 1941, Harvard U., 1945, doctoral postgrad. in history, 1945-50; LHD (hon.), Northeastern U., 1987. Vis. lectr. Am. history Cath. U., Santiago, Chile, 1942; instr. history CCNY, 1943-44; founding editor Inter-Am. Rev. Bibliography, 1950-53; editor, sect. chief dept. cultural affairs Pan Am. Union, Washington, 1950-54; on leave, 1953-54; adv. editor, U.S. rep. Inter-Am. Rev. Bibliography, 1956—; founder, dir. Maury A. Bromsen Assocs. (rare book, manuscript and fine art dealers), Boston, 1954—; pres., treas. Maury A. Bromsen Assocs., Inc. (rare book, manuscript and fine art dealers), 1963-89; proprietor, dir. Maury A. Bromsen Co., 1990—; hon. curator Latin Americana collections Boston Pub. Libr., 1997; hon. curator, bibliographer Latin Americana John Carter Brown Libr., Brown U., Providence, 1996—. Vis. prof. U. Chile, Santiago, 1947; exec. sec. Medina Centennial Celebration, Washington, 1952; adv. coun. univ. librs. U. Notre Dame, 1981-84, emeritus adviser, 1984—; bd. govs. Am. Jewish Hist. Soc., 1987-92; est. Maury A. Bromsen-Simon Bolivar Room John Carter Brown Libr., Providence, 1999. Author: Simón Bolívar: A Bicentennial Tribute, 1983; editor: José Toribio Medina, Humanist of the Americas: an Appraisal, 1960, Spanish transl., 1969; research and publs. in history and bibliography of Ams. Established Medina and Harrisse rare book collections, U. Fla. Library, 1958, 63. Endowed Archibald Bromsen Meml. scholarship, CCNY, 1964; endowed Bromsen lectureship in Humanistic Bibliography, Boston Pub. Library, 1970, Maury A. Bromsen Latin Am. Acquisitions Fund, 1976, Bromsen Fund, Mass. Gen. Hosp. (Health Scis. Lib.), 1983. Decorated Orden al Mérito Bernardo O'Higgins, Knight Comdr. (Chile), Orden de Francisco de Miranda, First Class (Venezuela); elected Colonial Soc. Mass., 1985; Carnegie Endowment for Internat. Peace and U.S. Govt. Exch. fellow U. Chile, 1942; Harvard Woodbury Lowery Travelling fellow, 1946-47, Social Sci. Rsch. Coun. fellow, 1946-48. Mem. Antiquarian Booksellers Assn. Am., Am. Hist. Assn., ALA, Bibliog. Soc. Am., Manuscript Soc. (charter), Conf. on Latin Am. History, Academia Nacional de la Historia, Buenos Aires (corr.), Latin Am. Studies Assn., Bibliog. Soc. (London), Bibliog. Soc. U. Va., Boston Athenaeum, Harvard Coll. Library Friends, Boston Pub. Library Assocs. (hon.), Boston U. Library Assocs. (life), Iowa Library Assocs. (patron), Bell (Minn.) Library Assocs., Clements (Mich.) Library Assocs., Yale Library Assocs., Am. Hist. Soc., Am. Jewish Hist. Soc., Va. Hist. Soc. (life), N.Y. Hist. Soc., Sociedad Chilena de Historia y Geografía, Filson Club (life), Phi Beta Kappa. Clubs: Harvard (Boston), Boston Athenaeum (Boston). Address: 770 Boylston St Apt 23-F Boston MA 02199-7720 *The true bibliographer should be more than an inventory maker and describer of the physical qualities of books and other printed material. This is but a minimal qualification of the craftsman. He ought rather to know something about the ideas to which a work relates and in what manner it supplements the known history of its field. Thereby he will make a contribution to humanism, and this should be the prime motivator of the scholarly bookman worthy of the name bibliographer.*

BROMWICH, MICHAEL RAY, lawyer; b. L.A., Dec. 19, 1953; s. Leo and Rose (Meyer) B.; m. Felice B. Friedman, Dec. 27, 1980; children: Daniel R., Jonah E., Kira A. AB summa cum laude, Harvard Coll., 1976; MPP, JD, Harvard U., 1980. Assoc. Foley & Lardner, Washington, 1980-83; asst. U.S. atty. U.S. Attys. Office, (so. dist.) N.Y., N.Y.C., 1983-87; assoc. counsel Office of Ind. Counsel, Iran-Contra, Washington, 1987-89; spl. counsel Office Ind. Counsel, Iran-Contra, Washington, 1990, 91; ptnr. Mayer, Brown & Platt, Washington, 1989-93; inspector gen. Dept. Justice, Washington, 1994-99; ptnr. Fried, Frank, Harris, Shriver & Jacobson, Washington and N.Y.C., 1999—. Mem. Pres. Coun. on Integrity and Efficiency, 1994-99. Mem. Phi Beta Kappa. Jewish. Office: Fried Frank Harris Shriver & Jacobson 10001 Pennsylvania Ave NW Ste 800 Washington DC 20004 also: One New York Plz New York NY 10004 E-mail: michael.bromwich@ffhsj.com.

BRONAUGH, DEANNE RAE, home health care administrator, consultant; b. Cameron, Mo., Feb. 3, 1952; d. Myron McMillin and Kathryn Marie (Ogden) Bell; m. Richard N. Bronaugh, July 18, 1987; 1 child, Elisabeth Catherine. BSN magna cum laude, Avila Coll., 1974 Cert. nursing adminstr., ANA. Staff nurse Bapt. Meml. Hosp., Kansas City, Mo., 1974-77; nurse clinician North Kansas City (Mo.) Meml. Hosp., 1977-78; asst. dir. Bethany Med. Ctr., Kansas City, 1978-79, spl. projects dir., 1979-80, dir. critical care, 1980-81; DON Lee's Summit (Mo.) Community Hosp., 1981-84; asst. adminstr. Muskogee (Okla.) Regional Med. Ctr., 1984-86; cons. Creative Nursing Mgmt., Mpls., 1986-87; pres. Liberty Cons., Muskogee, 1992-93; state liaison for accreditation affairs ABC Home Health, 1993-94; regional adminstr. 1st Am. Home Care (formerly ABC Home Health), 1994-96; regional dir. clin. svcs. Integrated Health Svcs., Overland Park, Kans., 1996-97; assoc. Corridor Group, Inc., Overland Park, Kans., 1997; sr. assoc. Curran Care, North Riverside, Ill., 1997-98; gen. mgr. VNA Plus, Lenexa, Kans., 1998-99; design cons. Norwalk Furniture, Lenexa, Kans., 1999—; clin. outcomes specialist St. Luke's South Hosp., Overland Park, Kans., 2001—03; nursing adminstrv. coord. U. Kans., 2002—. Health care cons., 2000—; mem. adv. bd. Am. Heart Assn., Kansas City, Kans., 1979-81; clin. outcomes specialist St. Lukes South Hosp., Overland Park, Kans., 2001—. Mem. Rep. Women's Club, Muskogee, 1988, P.E.O., Muskogee, 1992. Mem. Sigma Theta Tau. Home: 11502 W 127th Ter Overland Park KS 66213-3534

BRONAUGH, EDWIN LEE, electromagnetic compatibility engineer, consultant; b. Salina, Kans., July 22, 1932; s. Edwin and Violet Mary (Dryden) B.; m. Geraldine Kelley, Dec. 10, 1955; children: Cecilia Ann Bronaugh Snodgrass, Dana Lea Bronaugh Weinberg. BA in Physics, Math. and Language, Tex. A&M

U., Commerce, 1955. Commd. USAF, 1955, advanced through grades to capt., 1961, various comm. and ops. assignments, 1955-68; major USAFR, 1968; rsch. scientist Southwest Rsch. Inst., San Antonio, 1968-70, sr. rsch. scientist, 1970-76, rsch. dir., 1976-82; dir. R & D, tech. dir. Electro-Metrics Divsn. Penril, Amsterdam, N.Y., 1982-89; prin. electromagnetic compatibility scientist Electro-Mechanics Co., Austin, Tex., 1989-92; v.p. engring., 1992-94; prin. EdB EMC Cons., Austin, 1994—; lead engr. comm. devices divsn. Siemens Info. and Comm. Products, LLC, Austin, 1997-2000. Author: Electromagnetic Interference Test Methodology and Procedures, 1988; contbr. over 150 articles to profl. jours.; patentee in field. Decorated Bronze Star, Air Force Commendation medal. Fellow IEEE (life; Third Millennium medal 2000); mem. IEEE Stds. Assn. (life), Electromagnetic Compatibility Soc. of IEEE (stds. com. 1980—, dir. tech. svcs. 1981-87, v.p. 1988-90, pres. 1990-92; Cert. of Appreciation 1979, Cert. of Achievement 1983, Cert. of Acknowledgement 1985, Richard R. Stoddart award 1985, Stds. Medallion 1992, Lawrence G. Cumming award 1992), Am. Nat. Stds. Inst. (vice chmn. accredited stds. com. C63 on electromagnetic compatibility 1986-2002, mem. emeritus C63 2002—), Nat. Assn. Radio and Telecom. Engrs. (sr., cert.), Electromagnetic Compatibility Soc. (hon. life.). Avocations: music, model railroads, engineering history, learning additional languages. Home and Office: 10210 Prism Dr Austin TX 78726-1364 Fax: (512) 258-6982. E-mail: ed.bronaugh@ieee.org.

BRONDELLO, SANDY, professional basketball player; b. Australia, Aug. 20, 1968; B.Elem.Tchg., 1990. Guard Blazers, Australia, 1995-96, BTV Wuppertal, Germany, 1996-98, Detroit Shock, 1998-99, Miami Sol, 1999—. Mem. Australian Olympic team, 1988; participant World Championships, 1990, 94; guard Austrlian Nat. Team, Women's World Championship, Germany, 1998. Named Australian Intenrat. Basketball Player of the Yr., 1992, WNBL's Most Valuable Player, 1995; recipient European Cup Most Valuable Player, 1996. Office: Miami Sol Sun Trust Internat Ctr One SE 3rd Ave Ste 2300 Miami FL 33131

BRONFIN, FRED, lawyer; b. New Orleans, Nov. 30, 1918; m. Carolyn Pick; children by previous marriage: Daniel R., Kenneth A. BA, Tulane U., 1938, JD, 1941. Bar: La. 1941, U.S. Dist. Ct. (ea. dist.) La. 1941, U.S. Ct. Appeals (5th cir.) 1951, U.S. Supreme Ct. 1973. Assoc. Rittenberg & Rittenberg, New Orleans, 1946-50; ptnr. Rittenberg, Weinstein & Bronfin, New Orleans, 1950-60, Weinstein & Bronfin, New Orleans, 1960-63, Bronfin, Heller, Steinberg & Berins and precessor firms, New Orleans, 1963-91; of counsel Bronfin & Heller, 1991-98, Heller, Draper, Hayden, Patrick & Horn, 1998—. With USN, 1942-46. Mem. ABA, La. Bar Assn., New Orleans Bar Assn., Order of Coif, Phi Beta Kappa. Office: Heller Draper Hayden Et Al 650 Poydras St Ste 2500 New Orleans LA 70130-6175 E-mail: fbronfin@hellerdraper.com.

BRONFMAN, EDGAR MILES, beverage company executive; b. Montreal, June 20, 1929; s. Samuel and Saidye (Rosner) Bronfman; married. Student, Williams Coll., 1946—49; BA, McGill U., 1951; LHD (hon.), Pace U., 1982; LLD (hon.), Williams Coll., 1986. Chmn. adminstrv. com. Joseph E. Seagram & Sons, Inc., 1955-57, pres., 1957-71; chmn., CEO, pres. Distillers Corp.-Seagram Ltd., Montreal, 1971-75; chmn. The Seagram Co. Ltd. and Joseph E. Seagram & Sons Inc.; dir. Vivendi Universal, 2000—. Bd. dirs. Am. Technion Soc. Mem. citizens com. for N.Y.C. U.S.-USSR Trade and Econ. Coun.; chmn. Samuel Bronfman Found.; pres. N.Am. Consortium for Free Mkt. Study, World Jewish Congress; mem. exec. com. Am. Jewish Congress, Am. Jewish Com.; mem. Bus. Com. for Arts United Jewish Appeals; hon. chmn. Fedn. Jewish Philanthropies; mem. internat. adv. bd. Sch. Internat. and Pub. Affairs, Columbia U.; chmn. Anti-Defamation League, N.Y.C.; bd. dels. Union Am. Hebrew Congregation; bd. dirs., Am. Com. Weizmann Inst. Sci., Israel. Named Chevalier de la Légion d'Honneur, French Govt. Mem.: Fgn. Policy Assn., Com. for Econ. Devel., Ctr. Inter-Am. Rels., B'nai B'rith (bd. overseers), Hundred Yr. Assn. N.Y., Coun. Fgn. Rels. Office: Joseph E Seagram & Sons Inc 375 Park Ave New York NY 10152-0002 also: The Seagram Co Ltd 1430 Peel St Montreal QC Canada H3A 1S9*

BRONFMAN, EDGAR MILES, JR., diversified business executive, producer; b. N.Y.C., NY, May 16, 1955; With Seagram Co., 1983—2000, pres., 1989—2000, CEO, 1994—2000; vice chmn. Vivendi Universal, 2000—03. Prodr. films The Blockhouse, 1973, The Border, 1982; prodr. Braodway play Ladies of the Alamo, 1977.*

BRONIS, STEPHEN JAY, lawyer; b. Miami, Fla., Feb. 23, 1947; s. Larry and Thelma (Berger) B.; children: Jason Michael, Tyler Adam, Kenneth Lawrence. BSBA, U. Fla., 1969; JD, Duke U., 1972. Bar: Fla. 1972, D.C. 1973, U.S. Dist. Ct. (so. dist.) Fla. 1973, U.S. Ct. Appeals (5th cir.) 1977, U.S. Supreme Ct. 1978, U.S. Ct. Appeals (11th cir.) 1981, U.S. Dist. Ct. (mid. dist.) Fla. 1989, Colo. 1994, U.S. Dist. Ct. Colo. 1996, U.S. Ct. Appeals (10th cir.) 1996, U.S. Tax Ct. 1998. Asst. pub. defender 11th Jud. Cir. Fla., Miami, 1972-75; ptnr. Rosen & Bronis, P.A., Miami, 1975-77, Rosen, Portela, Bronis, et al, Miami, 1977-82, Bronis & Potela, P.A., Miami, 1982-90; pvt. practice Miami, 1990-93; ptnr. Davis, Scott, Weber & Edwards, Miami, 1993-95, Zuckerman, Spaeder, LLP, Miami, 1996—. Mem. faculty Nat. Inst. of Trial Adv., U. N.C., Yeshiva U, Nova Sch. Law; appointed to Fla. Supreme Ct. Commn. on Professionalism, 2000—; Fla. Bar rep. to 11th Cir. Jur. Conf., 2001—. Contbr. articles to profl. jours. Recipient Am. Jurisprudence award Bancroft-Whitney Co., 1972. Mem. ABA (ho. of dels. 1999—, Fla. rep. 2000—, chmn. def. function com. of criminal justice sect. 2001--), ATLA, Nat. Criminal Def. Attys. Assn., Am. Bd. Criminal Lawyers (v.p. 1981-82), Fla. Criminal Def. Attys. Assn. (Outstanding Svc. award 1981), Calif. Attys. Criminal Justice, Acad. Fla. Trial Lawyers (criminal law sect. dir.). Democrat. Home: 3 Grove Isle Dr Apt 1506 Miami FL 33133-4103 Office: 201 S Biscayne Blvd Ste 900 Miami FL 33131-4326 E-mail: sbronis@zuckerman.com.

BRONKAR, EUNICE DUNALEE, artist, art educator; b. New Lebanon, Ohio, Aug. 8, 1934; d. William Dunham and Helen Kate (Hypes) Connor; m. Charles William Bronkar, Jan. 26, 1957; 1 child, Ramona. BFA, Wright State U., 1971, M in Art Edn., 1983, postgrad. art studies, 1989, Dayton Art Inst., 1972. Cert. art tchr., Ohio. Part time tchr. Springfield (Ohio) Mus. of Art, 1967-77; adjunct instr. Clark State C.C., Springfield, 1974-84, lead tchr., 1984-94, adj. asst. prof., 1998-2000, asst. prof., 1989-94; ret., 1994; artist private practice, Urbana, Ohio, 1995—. Edn. chmn. Springfield Mus. Art, 1973-74; image banks participant, Ohio Arts Coun., Columbus, Visual Arts Network, Dayton, Ohio, 1994—; affiliated with The Art Ctr. of St. Augustine, Fla. Art Scene, Little Gallery, Springfield, Ohio, The Frame Haven Gallery, Springfield, Ohio. One-woman shows include in Springfield, Ohio: Polo Club, Upper Valley Mall Cinema, Security Nat. Bank, Mr. C's Beauty Salon, Lakewood Beach, Springfield Mus. of Art, Clark State C.C.; Dayton, Ohio: Miami Valley Hosp., High St. Gallery, Stoeffer's Restaurant, Wegerzyn Garden Ctr., Meml. Hall, Wright State Univ., Urbana, Ohio: Champaign County Arts Coun., Urbana Cinema; South Charleston, Ohio: Cmty. Park Dedication, Philip Caldwell spl. guest spkr., Chmn. of the Bd. and CEO Ford Motor Co; 4-person show Springfield Mus. Art, 1999, Zanesville (Ohio) Art Ctr., 2000; accepted in over 100 area, state, regional, and nat. juried exhbns., including Ohio Water Color Soc.'s Ann. Traveling shows 1983-84, 86-87, Western Ohio Watercolor Soc., Hon. Mention 1983, 2001, Chase Patterson award, 1985, Spl. Merit award, 1990, 1st, 1995, 1st, 2000, Merit award 1997, 98; Springfield Mus. of Art: awards 1965, 68; 2d pastel 1972, 2d pastel and 1st drawing 1976, Jurors award pastel 1979, 1st drawing 1986, 3d drawing 1987, 2d drawing 1989, 1st drawing 1990, 1st drawing, 1991, 2d painting 1991, 1st drawing 1992, 2d, 1998, 2d pastel 1998, 1st drawing 2000, 1st painting, 2002; Dayton Soc. Painters and Sculptors: Best of Show 1974, 2000, 1st painting, 2d painting 3d drawing 1978, Hon. Mention 1979, 3d Graphic 1980, Best of Show drawing 1981, 1st pastel 1981, 1st drawing 1991, 3d painting 1993, 2d drawing 1993, Spl. Merit award for balance, 2001, Merit award, 2001, 03; Champaign County Fair: Best of show drawing and 1st pastel 1968; drawings and paintings in Am. Artist Renown, 1981, Shades of Gray, 1983, 84, 86, 87, 90, 91, 93, 94, 97; group shows include Wilson Gallery, Sidney, Ohio; represented in six pub. and numerous pvt. collections. Cleaned and restored art collections at Springfield Pub. Schs., Hist. Soc. in Springfield, Logan County Hist. Soc., Champaign County Hist. Soc., Warder Pub. Libr., Foos Manor Bed & Breakfast and the Masonic Temple, Penn House and Mus. of Art in Springfield, 1970-00, Calumet Antiques, Yellow Springs, Ohio, other groups and numerous pvt. collections, 1970—; mem. adv. com. comml. art, Clark County JVS Sch., Springfield, 1991-2003; judge more than 10 pub. h.s. art shows, 1970s-90s; judge Logan County (Ohio) Fair Fine Art Show profl. and amateur, 1998, Champaign County Fair Art Show, 2001. Recipient medal Bicentennial Com. and 4H Found. of Ohio, Springfield, 1976, Outstanding Tchr. award Clark State C.C., 1992, commd. to paint 2 past pres. Generals of the Natl. Soc. Daughters of the Amer. Revolution, which hangs in Continental Hall, Washington. Mem. Western Ohio Water Color Soc, Springfield (Ohio) Mus. of Art, Dayton Soc. Painters and Sculptors, Cin. Art Club, Ohio Water Color Soc., Nat. Mus. Women in Arts, Ohio Pleen Air Painters, Audubon Artists Soc., Pastel Soc., St. Augustine (Fla.) Art Assn., Portrait Soc. Ames, others. Avocations: swimming, walking, sewing, flower arranging, travel to Europe, Caribbean, Russia, Israel and Ireland.

BRONKESH, ANNETTE CYLIA, public relations executive; b. Vineland, N.J., Dec. 18, 1956; d. Manasha and Miriam (Kutlan) B.; m. Steven Silver Schwartz, Aug. 18, 1985; children: Sarah, Emily, Julie. BA, NYU, 1979. Sr. editor Instnl. Investor, N.Y.C., 1979; chief editor McGraw-Hill, N.Y.C., 1980-85; dir. Am. Stock Exchange, N.Y.C., 1985-87; v.p. pub. rels. Nikko Securities, N.Y.C., 1987-90; pres. Bronkesh Assocs., Clifton, N.J., 1990—. Mem. 100 Women in Hedge Funds. Mem. Securities Industry Assn. (pub. rels. roundtable), Fin. Women's Assn. N.Y., Phi Beta Kappa. Avocation: playing piano. Office: Bronkesh Assocs 23 Virginia Ave Clifton NJ 07012-1222 also: 23 Virginia Ave Clifton NJ 07012-1222

BRONKOWSKI, MARK JOHN, textiles executive, real estate agent; b. Hackensack, N.J., Jan. 21, 1958; s. John and Anna Bronkowski; m. Patricia Claire Bronkowski, Oct. 8, 1983; children: Brittany, James. Grad. h.s., Franklin Lakes. Lic. realtor N.J. Owner Textile Tech., Barnegat, NJ, 1976—; sales mgr. Combined Ins., Voorhees, NJ, 1989—90; sales assoc. Horizon Foods, Wall Township, NJ, 1990—91; nat. sales mgr. Net-tel, Manahawkin, NJ, 1992—97; owner, sales assoc. M & P Distributors, Barnegat, 1998—; sales assoc. TCRC, Egg Harbor Twp., NJ, 1999—, Coldwell Banker, Barnegat, NJ, 2000—; nat. sales mgr. Integrity Comm. and Utilities, LLC, Limport, Pa., 2002—. Creator (boardgame) Neighbors. Republican. Roman Catholic. Avocation: sports. Home: PO Box 715 Barnegat NJ 08005 Office: Integrity Comms and Utilities LLC PO Box 715 Barnegat NJ 08005-0715 Fax: 609-698-1250. E-mail: markb@neighborsthegame.com.

BRONNER, FELIX, physiologist, biophysicist, educator, painter; b. Vienna, Nov. 7, 1921; arrived in U.S., 1937, naturalized, 1943; s. Maurice and Lotte (Vogler) B.; m. Leah Horowitz, Oct. 12, 1947; children: Deborah Rachel, Ethan Samuel. BS, U. Calif., Berkeley and Davis, 1941; PhD (Quaker Oats fellow 1950-52), MIT, 1952; student, Kans. State Coll., 1938; postgrad., U. Minn., 1943, U. Va., 1946; D (hon.), Ecole Pratique des Hautes Etud, Paris, 1996. Rsch. assoc. MIT, 1952-54; Helen Hay Whitney fellow, Arthritis and Rheumatism fellow Rockefeller Inst. Med. Rsch., N.Y.C., 1954-56, asst., 1956; dir. lab. mineral metabolism Hosp. for Spl. Surgery, N.Y.C., 1957-63; asst. prof. Cornell U. Med. Coll., 1961-63; assoc. prof. physiology U. Louisville Sch. Medicine, 1963-69; prof. oral biology U. Conn., 1969-86, prof. nutritional scis., 1976-89, prof. biostructure and function, 1986-89, prof. emeritus, 1989—. Vis. scientist Weizmann Inst., Israel, 1965, 76, Varon vis. prof., 1988; vis. scientist Pasteur Inst., Paris, 1977; vis. scientist U. Cape Town Med. Sch., 1984, 88, MRC disting. vis. scientist, 1991; guest scientist INSERM, Paris, 1972, Lyon, France, 1988; cons. USPHS, 1965-68, 70-71, USDA, 1978-79; vis. prof. Tel Aviv U. Sch. Medicine, 1976. Editor: (with C. L. Comar) Mineral Metabolism: An Advanced Treatise, 1960-69; (with A. Kleinzeller) Current Topics in Membranes and Transport, 1970-90; (with J. Coburn) Disorders of Mineral Metabolism, 1981-82; (with M. Peterlik) Calcium and Phosphate Transport Across Biomembranes, 1981; Epithelial Calcium and Phosphate Transport: Molecular and Cellular Aspects, 1984; Cellular Calcium and Phosphate Transport in Health and Disease, 1988; (with W. D. Stein) Cell Shape Determinants, Regulation, and Regulatory Role, 1989; (with D. Pansu) Calcium Transport and Intracellular Calcium Homeostasis, 1990; Intracellular Calcium Regulation, 1991; (with R. V. Worrell) A Basic Science Primer in Orthopaedics, 1991; (with M. Peterlik) Extra- and Intracellular Calcium and Phosphate Regulation: From Basic Research to Clinical Medicine, 1992; Nutrition and Health-Topics and Controversies, 1996; Nutrition Policy in Public Health, 1997; (with R.V. Worrell) Orthopaedics: Principles of Basic and Clinical Science, 1999; Nutritional Aspects and Clinical Management of Chronic Disorders and Diseases, 2003; (with Mary C. Farach-Carson) Bone Formation, vol. 1, Topics in Bone Biology, 2003; mem. editl. bd. Am. Jour. Clin. Nutrition, 1968-76, Am. Jour. Physiol., 1985-97, Jour. Nutrition, 1986-95; contbr. articles to profl. jours.; exhibited in one-man shows, numerous juried shows, reviewed in July, 2003 ARTnews. Pres. Bur. Jewish Edn., Louisville, 1968-69. Served with AUS, 1942-46. Recipient André Lichwitz prize, Nat. Inst. Health and Med. Rsch., France, 1974. Fellow AAAS, Am. Soc. Nutritional Sci.; mem. Am. Physiol. Soc., Biophys. Soc., Harvey Soc., Soc. Exptl. Biology and Medicine, Orthopedic Rsch. Soc., Am. Fedn. Clin. Rsch., N.Y. Acad. Scis., Am. Soc. Clin. Nutrition, Am. Soc. Bone and Mineral Rsch., Am. Soc. Gravity Space Biology, Austrian Bone Soc. (hon.). Home: 33 Ferncliff Dr West Hartford CT 06117-1013 Office: U Conn Health Ctr BioStructure and Function Pharmacology Farmington CT 06030-6125 E-mail: bronner@neuron.uchc.edu. *This has been a bloody century, one where entire peoples were murdered. But it has also been a period of great intellectual and artistic advances. I feel privileged to have survived and to have participated in the science and art of our time.*

BRONNER, JAMES RUSSELL, retired lawyer; b. Chgo., Nov. 14, 1943; s. Maurice Henry and Elaine R. (Rosenberg) B.; m. Barbara Henley, July 3, 1968; children: Michael, Jamie. BA, U. Mich., 1965; JD, Northwestern U., 1968, LLM, 1970. Bar: Ill. 1968, U.S. Dist. Ct. (no. dist.) Ill. 1968, U.S. Ct. Appeals (7th cir.) 1969. Asst. prof. law sch. Northwestern U., Chgo., 1970-72; ptnr. Davis, Miner, Barnhill & Bronner, Chgo., 1972-75; prin. Ct. Club Cir., Chgo., 1975-82; ptnr. Speakers Sport, Inc., Northbrook, Ill., 1976-2000; exec. v.p. SFX Sports, Northbrook, 2000-01, ret., 2001. Lectr. law sch. Northwestern U., 1972-79; vice chmn. Gov.'s Com. on State Salaries, Chgo., 1978. Exec. v.p. Chgo. Shakespeare Repertory Co., 1988-91; masters chmn. U.S. Team for 1993, open sports chmn., 1997 World Maccabiah Games. Named Northwestern Law Sch. Disting Alumni Sports, 2002; fellow, Ford Found., 1968—70. Mem. ABA, Am. Arbitration Assn. (panel mem. 2001—), Chgo. Bar Assn., Nat. Ct. Club Assn. (pres. 1980).

BRONNER, KEVIN MICHAEL, financial analyst, researcher; b. Albany, N.Y., Apr. 18, 1948; s. David Edward and Marjorie J. (Kairnes) B.; m. Karen Ruth Paparian, Nov. 5, 1949; children: Kevin Michael Jr., William James. AAS in Acctg., Jr. Coll. Albany, 1968; BSBA, U. Albany, 1970, MPA in Pub. Finance, 1984, PhD in Pub. Adminstrn., 1992. Fin. analyst N.Y. State Dept. Pub. Svc., Albany, 1970—2003; chief utility intervenor N.Y. State Exec. Dept. Consumer Protection Bd., 1996-98; pub. svc. prof. SUNY, Albany, 2002—. Part-time faculty Rockefeller Coll. Pub. Affairs and Policy U. Albany, 1995—, prof. pub. svc., 2002—, coun. mem., 2003—; mem. bd. dirs. Colonie (N.Y.) Youth Ctr., 1995-98; pres. Pruyn House, Colonie, 1998-99. Reviewer Fin. Mgmt., 1979; contbr. articles to profl. jours. Advisor on mgmt. audit Albany County,N.Y., 1993—; mem. centennial commn. Town of Colonie, N.Y., 1994; mem. Albany County Rep. Com. Chmn.'s Club, 1994—, Greater Loudonville (N.Y.) Assn., 1991—, Colonie Town Bd., 2000— Mem. ASPA, Fin. Mgmt. Assn., Pi Alpha Alpha. Roman Catholic. Home: 4 Georgian Ter Loudonville NY 12211-1952 E-mail: kbronner@nycap.rr.com.

BRONNER, MICHAEL, advertising executive; CEO, new bus. contact Bronner Slosberg Humphrey, Boston, 1980-96; chmn. Digitas, Boston, 1996-2000, chmn. emeritus, 2000—. Office: Digitas The Prudential Tower 800 Boylston St Boston MA 02199-8001

BRONNER, WILLIAM ROCHE, lawyer; b. N.Y.C., Mar. 13, 1946; s. Leonard and Gloria (Roche) Bronner; m. Nancy L. Bloomgarden, Oct. 14, 1973; children: Gregory R.B., Caitlin L.B. BA, Dartmouth Coll., 1967; JD, Columbia U., 1970. Bar: N.Y. 1970, U.S. Dist. Ct. (so. and ea. dists.) N.Y. 1972, U.S. Ct. Appeals (2d cir.) 1973, U.S. Ct. Claims 1977, U.S. Ct. Appeals (9th cir.) 1986, U.S. Dist. Ct. (we. dist.) N.Y. 1990, U.S. Ct. Appeals (fed. cir.) 1992, U.S. Internat. Trade, 1995. Law clk. to presiding judge U.S. Dist. Ct. (so. dist.) N.Y., N.Y.C., 1970-72; asst. U.S. atty. State of N.Y., N.Y.C., 1972-76; assoc. Burns & Jacoby, N.Y.C., 1977; counsel div. NL Industries, N.Y.C., 1978-80, counsel govt. affairs, 1980-82, group counsel, 1982-84, assoc. gen. counsel, 1984-87; gen. counsel NL Chems., Inc., N.Y.C., 1987-90; v.p., sec., gen. counsel Kronos, Inc., Hightstown, N.J., 1990—; v.p. Electro-Optical Scis., Inc., Irvington, N.Y., 2000—. Office: Kronos Inc 5 Cedarbrook Dr Cranbury NJ 08512-3618 also: Electro Optical Scis Inc One Bridge St Irvington NY 10533 E-mail: william.bronner@nli-usa.com.

BRONSON, CAROL E. administrative health facility coordinator; b. St. Louis, Sept. 11, 1944; d. Whitfield R. and Ruby E. (Graham) B.; m. Andre Pierre Duplessis, Sr. Nov. 16, 1980; children: Carl, Carol Lynne, Sterling, Andre, Jr., William, Andra, K'rin. BBA, Nat. U., San Diego, 1978; MA, U.S. Internat. U., San Diego, 1993; MA in Culture and Human Behavior, Calif. Sch. Profl. Psychology, San Diego, 2000; student, The Fielding Inst., Atlanta. Adminstrv. coord. Calif. Sch. Profl. Psychology, San Diego, 1989—2001; mgr., owner Any Necessary Typing Svc., San Diego, 1988-93; tchr. in bus. Calif. Comty. Colls.; tchr. San Diego City Schs., 2001. Instr. San Diego C.C., 1997, instr. 1979-2000; spkr. Cath. Diocese of San Diego, 1995, San Diego Black Nurses Assn., 1994. Author: (book) A History of Christ: The King Catholic Church 1932-95, 1996. Co-dir. nat. conf. comty. and justice, 1998-2001; probation asst. San Diego Dept. of Probation, 1994-95, tutor, 1987; children's advocate Voices for Children, San Diego, 1992-93; vol. coord. United Negro Coll. Fund, San Diego, 1985-95. Recipient 1st place runner-up award Writers Guild, San Diego, 1992. Mem. Nat. Assn. Multicultural Educators. Democrat. Roman Catholic. Avocations: reading, writing short stories.

BRONSON, CHRISTOPHER HERBERT, financial service company executive, planner; b. Lajes AFB, Portugal, Sept. 4, 1959; (parents Am. citizens); s. Herbert Everton and Barbara Ann Bronson; m. Nancy Ann Davis, Apr. 23, 1983; children: Andrea Marie, Sean Michael, Jessica Nicole, Michael Geoffrey. Student, Citadel; BA, Rice U., 1983; cert. fin. mgr., Merrill Lynch Inst. Fin. cons. Merrill Lynch, Pierce, Fenner & Smith Inc., Vero Beach, Fla., 1989-90; regional sales mgr. James L. Mitchell & Co., Orlando, Fla., 1990; life agt., registered rep. N.Y. Life Ins. Co., Orlando, 1991; sales mgr. Furniture Man, Vero Beach, 1991-92; stewardship cons. James L. Paris Fins. Svcs., Inc., Longwood, Fla., 1993-94; fin. cons. Mercer Global Advisors, Inc., Tampa, Fla., 1994-99, br. mgr. Bala Cynwyd, Pa., 1999—. Campaign mgr. Rep. Candidate State Rep., Indian River County, Fla., 1989; chmn. parish fin. com. St. Sebastian Parish, Fla., 1991; treas. Cypress Meadows Homeowners Assn., Tampa, 1997; asst. scoutmaster Troop 339 Boy Scouts Am., Tampa, Fla., 1999, asst. scoutmaster Troop 19, Bryn Mawr, Pa., 2000. 1st lt. USAR, 1984-2000. Mem. Fin. Planners Assn. Republican. Avocations: outdoor activities, reading. Office: Mercer Global Advisors Inc 401 E City Ave Ste 720 Bala Cynwyd PA 19004-1128 Fax: 610-747-0277.

BRONSON, JOHN ORVILLE, JR., retired librarian; b. Memphis, Apr. 6, 1937; s. John Orville and Elinor (Sutherland) B.; m. Patricia Ann Packer, June 11, 1962; 1 stepchild, Richard Wayne McCoy; children: Victoria Patricia Elizabeth, Glenn Charles. Student, N.E. Miss. Jr. Coll., 1957-59; BS, Miss. State U., 1961; MLS, U. Miss., 1965. Field sec. Miss. Libr. Commn., 1961-63, Acacia Nat. Frat., 1963-65; instr. U. Miss., 1965-66; head libr. Calhoun Jr. Coll., Decatur, Ala., 1965-67, Chesapeake Coll., Wye Mills, Md., 1967-82, telecomms. specialist, 1982-91, coord. media tech., 1991-2000. Pres. Wye Milling Co., Inc. Editor Ala. Jr. Coll. Librarian, 1966-67. Historiographer, Easton diocese Episcopal Ch., 1980-83; pres. Talbot County Dem. Club, 1984-85; v.p., sec. congl. coun. St. Marks Luth. Ch., 1999—; del. Del.-Md. synod ELCA, 1998-99; bd. dirs., Integrity, Cathedral of the Annunciation, Episcopal Diocese of Md., Balt., 1999-2003. Served with USAFR, 1955-63. Mem. ALA, Md. Libr. Assn., Ala. Libr. Assn., Md. Assn. Jr. Colls., Congress Acad. Librs., Old Wye Mill Soc. (treas.) Soc. for Preservation Md. Antiquities (dir.), Upper Shore Geneal. Soc. (founder), Acacia, Masons. Home: 7288 Shirley Dr Easton MD 21601-4804

BRONSON, OSWALD PERRY, SR., religious organization administrator, clergyman; b. Sanford, Fla., July 19, 1927; s. Uriah Perry and Flora (Hollingshed) B.; m. Helen Carolyn Williams, June 8, 1952; children— Josephine Suzette, Flora Helen, Oswald Perry. BS, Bethune-Cookman Coll., 1950; B.D., Gammon Theol. Sem., 1959; PhD, Northwestern U., 1965. Ordained to ministry Meth. Ch., 1957; pastor in Fla., Ga. and Rock River Conf., Chgo., 1950-66; v.p. Interdenominational Theol. Center, Atlanta, 1966-68, pres., 1968-75, Bethune-Cookman Coll., 1975-. Dir. Fla. Bank and Trust Co.; Past trustee Carrie Steel Pitts Home, Atlanta; past pres. and chmn. bd. edn. Ga. Conf., Central Jurisdiction, United Meth. Ch.; now mem. bd. ministry DeLand dist., also Fla. Ann. Conf., mem., univ. senate, past chmn. div. ministry, mem.-at-large bd. global ministries; mem. Pres.'s Bd. Advisors HBCU, USAF Bd. Advisors HBCU. Bd. dirs. United Meth. Com. on Relief; past mem. Volusia County (Fla.) Sch. Bd., Fla. Gov.'s Adv. Council on Productivity; past mem. exec. com. So. Regional Edn. Bd.; mem. adv. com. Fla. Sickle Cell Found., Inc.; past mem. council presidents Atlanta U. Center; mem. Fla. Bd. Ind. Colls. and Univs.; past trustee Hinton Rural Life Center; past bd. dirs. Inst. of Black World, Wesley Community Center, Atlanta, Martin Luther King Center Social Change, Work Oriented Rehab. Center, Inc., Fund Theol. Edn.; mem. nat. selection com. Rockefeller Doctoral Fellowships in Religion; bd. dirs. Am. Nat. Red Cross, United Way, Nat. Assn. Equal Opportunity in Higher Edn., United Negro Coll. Fund; also mem. fund raising strategy adv. com. Ga. Pastors' Sch. Crusade scholar, 1957-64. Mem. Am. Assn. Theol. Schs. (v.p. 1968-70), Ministerial Assn. of Halifax Area, Religious Edn. Assn. (past pres., past chmn. bd. dirs.), Mid-Atlantic Assn. Profs. Religious Edn., Fla. Assn. Colls. and Univs. (pres. 1997—), Atlanta Theol. Assn. (past vice chmn.), AAUP, Daytona Beach area C. of C., NAACP, Theta Phi (past dir. internat. soc.), Alpha Kappa Mu, Phi Delta Kappa, Sigma Pi Phi, Alpha Phi Alpha. Clubs: Rotary, Daytona Beach area Execs, Daytona Beach Quarterback. Methodist. Office: Bethune-Cookman Coll 640 Dr Mary Mcleod Bethune Blv Daytona Beach FL 32114-3012

BRONSON, ROBERT LEE, engineering company inventor, retired; b. Clermont, Fla., Jan. 12, 1932; s. George Washington Bronson and Sarah Margurite Fields; m. Doris Eugenia Powers, June 20, 1954 (div. Sept. 1974); m. Ruby Mayo Bronson, July 25, 2001 (dec.). Design drafting diploma, Draftec Coll. Drafting, Orlando, Fla., 1968. Salesman petroleum products Gulf Oil Corp., Eustis, Fla., 1951—65; owner Bronson Gulf Svc., Eustis, 1965—66; design draftsman Magnavox Def. Cont., Ft. Wayne, Ind., 1966—68; electro-mech. designer Electron Machine, Inc., Umatilla, Fla., 1968—74; chief draftsman design Golden Gem Growers, Inc., Umatilla, 1974—87; ret., 1987; owner Action Enterprises, Eustis, 1987—. Author short stories and poems. Program chair Eustis Kiwanis Club, 1965—66; gold, silver leader Day Comdrs. Club, Washington, 1993—94; deacon First Bapt. Ch., Eustis, 1957. Achievements include invention of state-of-the-art control gate for hydraulic ramps for unloading citrus. Avocations: travel, camping, cooking, research.

BRONSON, WILLIAM CAVOLT, JR., counselor; b. Oklahoma City, Feb. 9, 1937; s. William Cavolt and Mary Jane (Looney) B. BA, Washburn U., 1961. Cert. clin. supr., Okla., internat. alcohol drug counselor, HIV/AIDS prevention counselor, Okla. Social worker Okla. Adolescent Unit, Oklahoma City, 1964-67; supr. counseling svcs. Urban League Oklahoma City, 1967-72; exec. dir. Tulsa Nat. Conf. Christians and Jews, 1972-76; social worker Dept. Human Svcs., Tulsa, 1977-79; dir. drug/alcohol svcs. Archdiocese of Okla., Oklahoma City, 1980-81; coord. Okla. Assn. for Retarded Citizens, Oklahoma City, 1981-82; coord. refugee resettlement Archdiocese of Okla., Oklahoma City, 1982-83; exec. dir. Southwest Okla. Adolescent Treatment, Lone Wolf, 1983-86; social worker Okla. Child Abuse Investigation, Oklahoma City, 1986-90; counselor drug treatment The Referral Ctr., Oklahoma City, 1990-93; clin. coord. Drug Alcohol Youth Svcs., Altus, Okla., 1995—. Author: Etiology of Violence, 2001, short stories, poem. Contbr. Nat. Dem. Conv., 2000; mem. Human Rights Campaign, Washington, 2001. Grantee U.S. Dept. Health, 1984, Kerr Found. Okla, 1982. Mem.: Am. Soc. Drug Counselors, Internat. Soc. Poets. Home: PO Box 283 Mangum OK 73554-0283 E-mail: billbronsonparkonmain@yahoo.com.

BRONSTEIN, ALVIN J. lawyer; b. Bklyn., June 8, 1928; LLD, N.Y. Law Sch., 1951, LLD (hon.), 1990. Bar: N.Y. 1952, Miss. 1967, La. 1971, U.S. Ct. Appeals (D.C., 1st, 2d, 3d, 4th, 5th, 9th, 10th and 11th cirs.), U.S. Supreme Ct. 1961. Ptnr. Bronstein & Bronstein, Bklyn., 1952-63; pvt. practice Elizabethtown, N.Y., 1963-64; chief staff counsel Lawyers Constl. Def. Com., Jackson, Miss., 1964-68; fellow Inst. Politics, Kennedy Sch. Govt. Harvard U., Cambridge, Mass., 1968-69, assoc. dir. Inst. Politics, Kennedy Sch. Govt., 1969-71; ptnr. Elie, Bronstein, Strickler & Dennis, New Orleans, 1971-72; exec. dir. Nat.

Prison Project, Nat. Jail Project ACLU Found., Washington, 1972-96, cons. nat. legal dept., 1996—. Cons., trial counsel CORE, NAACP, NAACP Legal Def. Fund, SCLC, SNCC, Miss. Freedom Dem. Party, Black Panther Party, Nat. Inst. for Edn. in Law and Poverty, and others; guest lectr. various law schs., 1964—; cons. various state corrections depts., 1972—; adj. prof. Am. U. Law Sch., 1973; expert witness in various prison litigations, 1978—; appointed mem. Fed. Jud. Ctr. Adv. Com. on Experimentation in the Law, 1978-81. Contbg. author: The Evolution of Criminal Justice, 1978, Prisoners' Rights Sourcebook, Vol. II, 1980, Confinement in Maximum Custody, 1980, Sage Criminal Justice Annual, Vol. 14, 1980, Readings in the Justice Model, 1980, Our Endangered Rights, 1984, Prisoners and the Courts: The American Experience, 1985; author: (with Rudovsky and Koren) The Rights of Prisoners, 1988; author, editor: Representing Prisoners, 1981; editor: Prisoners' Self-Help Litigation Manual, 1977; contbr. articles to profl. jours. MacArthur Found. fellow, 1989; named one of the 100 most influential lawyers in Am., Nat. Law Jour., 1985, 88, 91, 94; recipient Roscoe Pound award Nat. Coun. on Crime and Delinquency, 1981, Karl Menninger award Fortune Soc., 1982, Pa. Prison Soc. award, 1991. Office: Penal Reform Internat 1120 19th St NW 8th Fl Washington DC 20036

BRONSTEIN, FRED, orchestra executive; b. Boston; MusB, Boston U.; MMus, Manhattan Sch. Music, N.Y.C.; DMus, SUNY, Stony Brook. Co-founder Aequalis, Boston, 1985-93; orch. mgmt. fellow Am. Symphony Orch. League, 1995-96; exec. dir. Civic Orch. Chgo., 1996-98; CEO, pres. Omaha Symphony Orch., 1998—2002; pres. Dallas Symphony Orch., 2002—. Office: 2301 Flora St Ste 300 Dallas TX 75201

BRONSTEIN, JAGODA EWA, pediatrician; b. Lublin, Poland, Sept. 26, 1962; came to the U.S., 1990; d. Zygmunt and Danuta (Celinska) O.; m. Glen Max Bronstein, Feb. 19, 1992; children: Lara Melanie, Sophie Milena. MD, Med. Acad., Lublin, Poland, 1990. Intern pediat. St. Vincent's Hosp. and Med. Ctr., N.Y.C., 1992-93; resident pediat. N.Y. Hosp.-Cornell Med. Ctr., N.Y.C., 1993-95; attending physician N.Y. Meth. Hosp., Bklyn., 1995-99, dir. primary care and gen. pediat., 1996-98; attending physician St. Joseph's Hosp. and Med. Ctr., Paterson, N.J., 1998—. Primary care faculty devel. fellow Mich. State U., East Lansing, 1992-98. Mem. AMA, Am. Acad. Pediat., Ambulatory Pediat. Assn. Office: St Joseph's at Willowbrook 57 Willowbrook Blvd Wayne NJ 07470-7045

BRONSTEIN, LYUDMILA M. chemist; b. Kalinin, Russia, Apr. 27, 1952; arrived in U.S., 1999; d. Michael P. Bronstein and Tatiana S. Kuperwasser; m. Kenneth G. Caulton, Oct. 2, 1998; 1 child, Simon B. Tumansky. PhD, Nesmeyanov Inst. Oganoelement Compounds, Moscow, 1979. Jr. scientist Nesmeyanov Inst., Moscow, 1979—86, rsch. fellow, 1986—89, sr. scientist, 1989—96; leading scientist Nesmeyanov Inst. of Organoelement Compounds, Moscow, 1996—; sr. scientist chemistry dept. Ind. U., Bloomington, 1999—. Contbr. ency. chpt. Grantee, NASA, 2001—04, NATO, 1999—. Mem.: Am. Chem. Soc. Achievements include patents for Colloidal metal composition and its preparation. Office: Ind U Chemistry Dept 800 E Kirkwood Ave Bloomington IN 47405 E-mail: lybronst@indiana.edu.

BRONSTEIN, PHIL, executive editor; m. Sharon Stone (div.). Reporter Sta. KQED-TV, San Francisco; reporter, fgn. corr. San Francisco (Calif.) Examiner, 1980-90; exec. editor San Francisco (Calif.) Chronicle, 1991—2003, exec. v.p., editor, 2003—. Recipient awards Overseas Press Club, AP, World Affairs Coun., Media Alliance, Pulitzer Prize finalist. Office: San Francisco Chronicle 901 Mission St San Francisco CA 94103*

BRONSTEIN, RICHARD J. lawyer; b. Chgo., May 11, 1949; s. Jack and Elaine (Abrams) Bronstein; m. Eileen Silvers, Aug. 24, 1995; children: Steven, Sharron; Andrew, Grace. AB, U. Pa., 1971; JD, U. Chgo., 1974. Bar: Ill. 1974, N.Y. 1977, U.S. Tax Ct., D.C. 1984. Law clk. to Hon. Spottswood W. Robinson III U.S. Ct. Appeals, Washington, 1974-75; law clk. to Hon. William J. Brennan, Jr. U.S. Supreme Ct., Washington, 1975-76; assoc. Paul, Weiss, Rifkind, Wharton & Garrison, N.Y.C., 1976-82, ptnr., 1982—. Lectr. Practising Law Inst., N.Y.C., 1981—, NYU, N.Y.C., 1985. Mem. ABA, N.Y. State Bar Assn. (com. on depreciation), Assn. of Bar of City of N.Y. (com. on taxation). Office: Paul Weiss Rifkind Wharton & Garrison Rm 2301 1285 Avenue Of The Americas New York NY 10019-6064 E-mail: rbronstein@paulweiss.com.

BRONSTEIN, ROBERT, retired lawyer; b. East Chicago, Ind., Dec. 8, 1919; s. Phillip and Sarah (Gross) B.; m. Sonia Zeidman, July 4, 1922; children: Eric, Scott. MA in Sociology, U. Chgo., 1948, JD, 1951. Bar: Ill. 1951, Colo. 1961. Dir. mgmt. analysis State of Colo., 1961-64, dir. budget, 1964-70, coordinator environ. problems, 1970-72; sec. Colo. Environ. Commn., 1970-72; project dir. Boulder (Colo.) Area Growth Study, 1972, mgmt. cons., 1973-75; asst. dept. dir. Colo. Dept. Labor and Employment, 1975-76; assoc. dir. Colo. Div. Employment and Tng., 1976-80; pvt. practice Denver, 1981-2000; ret., 2000. Faculty U. Denver Grad Sch. Pub. Adminstrn., 1973, U. Colo. Grad. Sch. Pub. Affairs, 1973. Writer screenplays, books. Bd. dirs. Colo. Citizens Com. on Govt., 1975-79, Citizens Inquiry into Colo. Constitution, 1977; mem. arbitration panel Am. Arbitration Assn., Better Bus. Bur., Denver County Assessment Appeals, Nat. Assn. Securities Dealers, 1985-95; mediator Ctr. Dispute Resolution, 1984-87. Lt. USAF, 1941—45, lt. col. USAF, 1960, ret. USAF, 1960. Mem. ACLU, Common Cause. Home: 2457 S Dahlia Ln Denver CO 80222-6119

BRONSTER, MARGERY S, state attorney general; b. N.Y., Dec. 12, 1957; married; 1 child. BA in Chinese Lang., Lit. and History, Brown U., 1979; JD, Columbia U., 1982. Assoc. Sherman & Sterling, NY, 1982—87; ptnr. Carlsmith, Ball, Wichman, Murray, Case & Ichiki, Honolulu, 1988—94; atty. gen. State of Hawaii, 1994—99; pvt. practice Honolulu, 1999—. Co-chair planning com. Citizens Conf. Jud. Selection, 1993. Mem.: Am. Judicature Soc. (bd. dirs., chair gov. com. on crime, VAWA planning com.). Office: Bronster Crabtree Hoshibata 23d Fl 1001 Biship St Pavahi Tower Honolulu HI 96813

BRONWELL, NANCY BROOKER, writer; b. Columbia, S.C., Oct. 11, 1921; d. Norton Wardlaw and Lucile Duty (Michaux) Brooker; m. Alvin Wayne Bronwell, June 21, 1943 (div. Mar. 1975); children: Betsy Randolph Bronwell Jones, Cynthia Alison (dec.). BS, Mary Washington Coll., 1942; postgrad., U. Ky., 1942-43, Tex. Tech. U., 1965, 87. Tchr. English, phys. edn. Louisville Pub. Schs., 1943-46; sec. edn. dept. Jos. S. Seagram & Sons Inc., Louisville, 1945-46; sec. to sales mgr. Marshall Field Corp., Chgo., 1946; sec. to dir. purchases Jos. E. Seagram & Sons., Inc., 1946-48; freelance writer Lubbock, Tex., 1978—. Author: Lubbock: A Pictorial History, 1980; contbr. articles to mags. Co-founder, bd. dirs. Young Women's Christian Assn., Lubbock, 1953; vol. Lubbock Jr. League, Lubbock Symphony Orch., Palsy Ctr., ARC, Tech. Mus., St. Paul's Ch. Mem. South Plains Writers Guild, Lubbock Heritage Assn. (Excellence award 1981), DAR, Huguenot Soc., Friends of Libr. (life). Republican. Episcopalian. Avocations: reading, word games. Home and Office: 4108 18th St # A Lubbock TX 79416-6009

BRONZI, PHILLIP A. social worker, educator; s. Guesippi and Gina Bronzi; 1 child, Laura. BS in Social Studies, Villanova U., 1963, MA in Polit. Sci., 1965. Social worker St. Michael Parish, Atlantic City. Mem. Chelsea Neighborhood Assn.; commr. Charter Study, Atlantic City, 1976; mayor Election Bd. Recipient grad. scholarship, Villanova Coun., 1963—65. Mem.: Moose, Elks, KC (recorder 1999).

BRONZINO, JOSEPH DANIEL, electrical engineer; b. Bklyn., Sept. 29, 1937; s. Joseph Rocco and Antoinette (Saporito) B.; m. Barbara Louise McGrath, Dec. 2, 1961; children: Michael J., Melissa J., Marcella J. BSEE, Worcester Poly. Inst., 1959, PhD in Elec. Engring, 1968; MSEE, U.S. Naval Postgrad. Sch., 1961. Registered profl. engr., Conn. Instr. elec. engring. U. N.H., 1964-66, asst. prof. elec. engring., 1966-67; NSF faculty fellow Worcester Found. for Exptl. Biology, Shrewsbury, Mass., 1967-68, mem. cooperating staff, 1968-94; assoc. prof. engring. Trinity Coll., 1968-75, prof., 1975—, Vernon Roosa prof. applied sci., 1977—, chmn. dept. engring., 1981-91. Adj. faculty Boston U. Med. Sch., 1987—; dir. and chmn. biomed. engring. program Hartford (Conn.) Grad. Ctr., 1969-97; clin. assoc. dept. surgery U. Conn. Health Ctr., Farmington, 1971-77; rsch. assoc. Inst. for Living, Hartford, 1968-97; reviewer NSF; panelist NSF Rsch. Initiation Grants; dir. Biomed. Engring. Alliance for Conn., 1997—; pres. Biomed. Engring. Alliance and Consortium, 1997-- lectr., spkr. in field. Author: Technology for Patient Care, 1977, Computer Application in Patient Care, 1982, Biomedical Engineering Basic Concepts and Instrumentation, 1986, Medical Technology: Economic and Ethical Issues, 1990, Expert Systems: Basic Concepts, 1990, Management of Medical Technology: A Primer for Clinical Engineers, 1992, Biomedical Engineering Handbook, 1995, 2d edit., 2000, Introduction to Biomedical Engineering, 1999; contbr. articles to profl. publs. Mem. Simsbury (Conn.) Planning Commn., 1977-82. Served to 1st lt. Signal Corps U.S. Army, 1961-63. Fellow: AAAS, IEEE (sr.; regional dir. group engring. in medicine and biology 1973—78, v.p. tech. activities 1982—85, pres. 1985—86, chmn. health care engring. policy com. 1986—90, vice chmn. tech. policy coun. 1990—91, chmn. tech. policy coun.), Conn. Acad. Sci. and Engring. (v.p. 2000—02, sec. 2002—, editor-in-chief Acad. Press Biomed. Engring. Book Series), Biol. Psychiatry, Neurosci. Soc., Am. Soc. Engring. Edn. (exec. com. divsn. biomed. engring. 1973—82, vice chmn. career devel. 1974—76, vice chmn.profl. devel. 1976—77, divisional newsletter editor 1977—79, chmn.-elect divsn. 1979—80, exec. com. 1990—91, chmn. tech. policy coun. 1992—94), Am. Inst. Med. and Biol. Engrs., Rotary (pres. Simsbury club 1971—89, 1991—93, Hartford Club 1989—91). Republican. Roman Catholic. Achievements include rsch. in signal analysis concepts and applications, basic neurophysiol. concepts involved in identifying specific neural circuits associated with specific functions of the brain. Home: 12 Brenthaven Avon CT 06001-3941 Office: Trinity Coll Dept Engring Hartford CT 06106

BROOK, ADRIAN GIBBS, chemistry educator; b. Toronto, May 21, 1924; s. Frank Adrian and Beatrice Maud (Wellington) B.; m. Margaret Ellen Dunn, Dec. 18, 1954; children— Michael A., Katherine M., David L. BA, U. Toronto, 1947, PhD, 1950. Lectr. chemistry U. Sask., 1950-51; research fellow Imperial Coll., London, 1951-52, Iowa State Coll., 1952-53; lectr. chemistry U. Toronto, 1953-56, asst. prof., 1956-60, assoc. prof., 1960-62, prof., 1962-87, univ. prof., 1987-89, univ. prof. emeritus, 1989—, chmn. dept. chemistry, 1969-74. Vis. prof. U. Sussex, 1974-75, Cambridge (Eng.) U., 1982, Ind. U., 1988. Contbr. articles to profl. jours. Nuffield Overseas fellow, 1951; recipient Izaak Walton Killam Meml. prize for Sci., 1994. Fellow Royal Soc. Can., Chem. Inst. Can. (CIC medal 1985); mem. Am. Chem. Soc. (Frederic Stanley Kipping award 1973) Home: Apt 202 7 Thornwood Rd Toronto ON Canada M4W 2R8 Office: U Toronto Dept Chemistry 80 St George St Toronto ON Canada M5S 3H6 E-mail: abrook@chem.utoronto.ca.

BROOK, CAROL ANN, retired guidance director, school counselor; b. Boston, Dec. 25, 1940; d. Joseph Patrick and Catherine Mori; m. Richard John Brook, Sr., Nov. 14, 1978. BA, Emmanuel Coll., 1969; MEd, Boston Coll., 1973. Cert. social sci. tchr., secondary sch. prin., guidance dir., guidance counselor, social studies tchr., N.H., supr., Mass. Secondary sch. tchr. Bishop Fenwick H.S., Peabody, Mass., 1967-69, St. Gregory's H.S., Dorchester, Mass., 1969-71; asst. rschr. Boston Coll., Chestnut Hill, Mass., 1971-73; secondary sch. tchr. Dedham (Mass.) H.S., 1973-79; sch. counselor Inter-Lakes Jr.-Sr. H.S., Meredith, N.H., 1979-81, guidance dir./sch. counselor, 1983-2001. Chairperson curriculum com. Dedham H.S., 1975-77. Mem. NEA, N.H. Sch. Counselors Assn. (Sch. Adminstr. of Yr. 1988-89), N.H. Career Devel. Assn., N.H. Counseling and Devel. Assn., N.H. Comprehensive Guidance and Counseling Program, Inc. (regional rep. 1987-95, exec. bd., past pres.). Democrat. Avocations: skiing, cooking, reading, hiking, camping. Home: 1829 Dick Brown Rd Plymouth NH 03264-5330 E-mail: carolbruk@aol.com.

BROOK, JUDITH SUZANNE, psychiatry and psychology researcher and educator; b. N.Y.C., Dec. 31, 1939; d. Robert and Helen E. (Zimmerman) Muser; m. David W. Brook, Dec. 15, 1962; children: Adam, Jonathan. BA, Hunter Coll., 1961; MA in Psychology, Columbia U., 1962, EdD in Devel. and Ednl. Psychology, 1967. Lic. psychologist, N.Y. Asst. prof. psychology Queens Coll., CUNY, Flushing, 1967-69; rsch. assoc. Columbia U., N.Y.C., 1969-77, sr. rsch. assoc., 1977-80; assoc. prof. psychiatry Mt. Sinai Sch. Medicine, N.Y.C., 1980-90, adj. prof., 1990-94; prof. N.Y. Med. Coll., Valhalla, N.Y., 1990-94; prof. cmty. and preventive medicine Mt. Sinai Sch. Medicine, 1994—. Rsch. scientist devel. award Nat. Inst. on Drug Abuse, 1982-90, sr. rsch. scientist, 1992—, ad hoc reviewer, 1989—, chair study sect. epidemiology, prevention and rsch., 1995-2000; ad hoc reviewer NIMH, NSF, 1992—; adj. prof. psychiatry N.Y. Med. Coll., 1994-2001. Author: (Psychology book) The Psychology of Adolescence, others; contbr. chpts. to books and more than 200 articles to profl. jours. Recipient 1st ann. Dean's Disting. Rsch. award N.Y. Med. Coll., 1992; grantee Nat. Inst. on Drug Abuse, 1979—. Fellow: Am. Psychopathol. Assn.; mem.: APA, NY State Psychol. Assn., Assn. for Med. Edn. & Rsch. in Substance Abuse, Am. Psychol. Soc. (liaison officer 1989—), Coll. on Problems of Drug Dependence. Office: Mt Sinai Sch Medicine Dept Cmty & PrevMed Box 1044A One Gustave Levy Pl New York NY 10029

BROOK, ROBERT HENRY, health services researcher, physician, educator; b. N.Y.C., July 3, 1943; s. Benjamin and Elizabeth (Berg) Brook; m. Susan Jean Weiss, June 26, 1966 (div. 1980); children: Rebecca, Daniel; m. Jacqueline Barbara Kosecoff Plaut, Jan. 17, 1982; children: Rachel, Davida. BS, U. Ariz., 1964; MD, Johns Hopkins U., 1968, ScD, 1972. Diplomate Am. Bd. Internal Medicine. Intern Balt. City Hosp., 1968—69, resident in medicine, 1969—72; project officer Nat. Ctr. Health Svcs. Rsch., HEW, Washington, 1972—74; vice-chmn. medicine UCLA, 1990—92, dir. clin. scholar program, 1974—, prof. of medicine and pub. health, 1974—; dir. health program RAND Corp., Santa Monica, Calif., 1990—, v.p., 1998—. Mem. editl. bd.: Health Adminstrn. Press, 1986—92, Jour. Gen. Internal Medicine, 1987—89, Health Policy, 1986—; contbr. articles to profl. jours. Asst. surgeon USPHS, 1972—76. Named one of one of 75 pub. health heroes of Johns Hopkins, 1991; recipient Rsch. prize, Baxter Found. Health Svcs., 1988, Glazer award, Soc. Gen. Internal Medicine; fellow Lita Annenberg Biomed. fellow, Inst. Humanistic Studies, 1981. Fellow: ACP (Rosenthal award); mem.: Johns Hopkins Soc. Scholars, Assn. Am. Physicians, Assn. Health Svcs. Rsch. (bd. dirs. 1982—89, Disting. Health Svc. Rschr. award), Am. Soc. Clin. Investigation, Inst. Medicine NAS. Democrat. Jewish. Home: 1474 Bienveneda Ave Pacific Palisades CA 90272-2346 Office: Rand Corp 1700 Main St Santa Monica CA 90401-3297

BROOKBANK, JOHN W(ARREN), retired microbiology educator; b. Seattle, Apr. 3, 1927; s. Earl Bruce and Louise Sophia (Stoecker) B.; m. Marcia Ireland, Sept. 16, 1950 (div. 1978); children: Ursula Ireland, John W. Jr., Phoebe Bruce; m. Sally Satterberg Cahill, Aug. 6, 1983. BA, U. Wash., 1950, MS, 1953; PhD, Calif. Inst. Tech., 1955. Asst. prof. biology U. Fla., Gainesville, 1955-58, assoc. prof., 1958-68, prof. zoology and microbiology, 1972-79, prof. microbiology and cell sci., 1972-85, prof. emeritus, 1985—. Vis. assoc. prof. U. Fla. Coll. Medicine, Gainesville, 1961-63, U. Wash., Seattle, 1965; cons. in field, Friday Harbor, Wash. 1986—. Author: Developmental Biology, 1978, (with W. Cunningham) Gerontology, 1988; editor: Improving Quality of Health Care of the Elderly, 1977, Biology of Aging, 1990; contbr. articles to profl. jours. Pres. Griffin Bay Preservation Com., Friday Harbor, 1985-99, past pres., 2000; pres. Bridge Council on Narcotics Addiction, Gainesville, 1974, Marine Environ. Consortium, 1986 89, San Juan Nature Inst., 1997-98; founding pres. Gainesville Regional Council on Alcoholism, 1976; devel. adv. bd. U. Wash. Friday Harbor Lab., 1995 98. Rsch. grantee, NIH, 1957—80, NSF, 1972—73. Mem. Seattle Tennis Club. Republican. Episcopalian. Avocations: fishing, boating, tennis, skiing. Home: PO Box 2688 Friday Harbor WA 98250-2688 E-mail: johnb@rockisland.com.

BROOKE, AVERY ROGERS, publisher, writer; b. Providence, May 28, 1923; d. Morgan Witter and Lucy Avery (Benjamin) Rogers; m. Joel Ijams Brooke, Sept. 14, 1946; children— Witter, Lucy, Sarah. B.F.A., R.I. Sch. Design, 1945, Union Theol. Sem., 1970. Founder Vineyard Books, Inc., Noroton, Conn., 1971-88; pub., v.p. Seabury Press, N.Y.C., 1980-83. Mentor Annand Program in Spiritual Growth, Yale/Berkeley Div. Sch., 1991—96. Author: Youth Talks with God, 1959, Doorway to Meditation, 1973, How To Meditate without Leaving the World, 1975, Plain Prayers for a Complicated World, 1975, 93, Roots of Spring, 1975, As Never Before, 1976, Hidden in Plain Sight, 1978, Cooking with Conscience (under pseudonym Alice Benjamin), 1975, The Vineyard Bible, 1980, Celtic Prayers, 1981, Trailing Clouds of Glory, 1985, Finding God in the World, 1989, 2d edit., 1994, Plain Prayers in a Complicated World, 1993, Healing in the Landscape of Prayer, 1996; contbr. articles to religious jours. Mem. The Author's Guild, Oblate Order of the Holy Cross, Spiritual Dirs. Internat. Democrat. Episcopalian. Home: 27 Pasture Ln Darien CT 06820-5618 E-mail: AveryRBr@aol.com.

BROOKE, EDNA MAE, retired business educator; b. Las Vegas, Nev., Feb. 10, 1923; d. Alma Lyman and Leah Mae (Ketcham) Shurtliff; m. Bill T. Brooke, Dec. 22, 1949; 1 child, John C. BS in Acctg., Ariz. State U., 1965, MA in Edn., 1967, EdD, 1975. Grad. teaching asst. Ariz. State U., Tempe, 1968-69; prof. bus. Maricopa Tech. Coll., Phoenix, 1967-72, assoc. dean instl. services, 1972 74; prof. bus. and acctg. Scottsdale (Ariz.) Community Coll., 1974-93; ret., 1993. Cons. in field. Author: The Effectiveness of Three Techniques Used in Teaching First Semester Accounting Principles to Tech. Jr. College Students, 1974. Home: 1176 E Northern Hills Dr Bountiful UT 84010-1707

BROOKE, EDWARD WILLIAM, lawyer, former senator; b. Washington, Oct. 26, 1919; s. Edward W. and Helen (Seldon) B. BS, Howard U., 1940, LL.D., 1967; LL.B. (editor Law Rev.), Boston U., 1948, LL.M., 1949, LL.D., 1968, George Washington U., 1967, Skidmore Coll., 1969, U. Mass., 1971, Amherst Coll., 1972; D.Sc., Lowell Tech. Inst., 1967; D.Sc. numerous other hon. degrees. Bar: Mass. 1948, D.C. Ct. Appeals 1979, D.C. Dist. Ct. 1982, U.S. Supreme Ct. 1962. Chmn. Boston Fin. Com., 1961-62; atty. gen. State of Mass., Boston, 1963-66; mem. U.S. Senate from Mass., 1967-79; chmn. Nat. Low-Income Housing Coalition; former ptnr. O'Connor & Hannan, Washington; formerly of counsel Csaplar & Bok, Boston. Former pub. mem. Adminstrv. Conf. U.S.; chmn. bd. dirs. Boston Bank Commerce; bd. dirs. Meditrust, Inc., Wellesley, Mass., Grumman Corp., Bethpage, N.Y. Chmn. Boston Opera Co.; former commr. Pres.'s Commns. on Housing and of Wartime Relocation and Internment of Civilians; bd. dirs. Washington Performing Arts Soc. Served as capt. inf. AUS, World War II, ETO. Decorated Combat Infantryman's Badge; recipient Disting. Svc. award Amvets, 1952, Charles Evans Hughes award NCCJ, 1967, Springarn medal, NAACP, 1967 Fellow Am. Bar Assn., Am. Acad. Arts and Scis. Office: 6437 Blantyre Rd Warrenton VA 20187-7147

BROOKE, FRANCIS JOHN, III, foundation administrator; b. Charleston, W.Va., Mar. 4, 1929; s. Francis John Jr. and Elizabeth (Baird) B.; m. Helen Holmes Morgan, Dec. 20, 1958; children: Francis John, Haynes Morgan, David Tucker. BA, Hampden-Sydney Coll., 1949; MA, U. Chgo., 1951; PhD, U. N.C., 1954. Instr. German Roanoke Coll., Salem, Va., summers 1950-52; teaching fellow, part-time instr. U. N.C., Chapel Hill, 1951-54; mem. faculty, to assoc. prof. German U. Va., Charlottesville, 1956-65, asst. dean. Coll. Arts & Scis., 1959-62, acting chmn. dept. modern langs., 1962-63; exec. dean, prof. German Centre Coll., Danville, Ky., 1965-68; v.p. acad. affairs Va. Commonwealth U., Richmond, 1968-74, provost, acad. campus, 1973-79, spl. asst. to pres., 1979-80, prof. German, 1968-80; pres. Columbus (Ga.) Coll., 1980-87; spl. asst. to chancellor Univ. System of Ga., Atlanta, 1988; Pacific N.W. regional rep. Presbyn. Ch. Found., Seattle, 1989-99, ret., 1999. Vice chmn. So. Humanities Conf., 1965; pres. South Atlantic region Am. Assn. Tchrs. German, 1965-67; exec. com. South Atlantic chpt. MLA, 1963-66. Mem. gen. assembly com. on theol. edn. Presbyn. Ch., 1988-90. With AUS, 1954-56. Old Dominion Found. grantee, 1960; intern acad. adminstrn. Ellis L. Phillips Found., Cornell U., 1963-64. Mem. Assn. State Colls. and Univs. (com. on humanities 1984-86, com. on urban affairs 1986-87), Omicron Delta Kappa.

BROOKE, GEORGE MERCER, JR., historian, educator; b. Tokyo, Oct. 21, 1914; (parents Am. citizens); s. George Mercer and Isabel Elsie (Tilton) B.; m. Frances Fleming Bailey, June 13, 1942; children: George Mercer III, Marion Bailey Brooke Philpott. BA in Liberal Arts, Va. Mil. Inst., 1936; MA in History, Washington and Lee U., 1942; PhD in History, U. N.C., 1955. Spl. agent Md. Casualty Co., Balt., 1936-41; history instr. Va. Mil. Inst., Lexington, 1942-43, from asst. prof. to prof., 1948-80, prof. emeritus, 1980—; history instr. Washington & Lee U., Lexington, 1946-47. Author: John M. Brooke, Naval Scientist, 1980, General Lee's Church, 1984, John M. Brooke's Pacific Cruise, 1986; editor: Ironclads and Big Guns of the Confederacy: The Journal and Letters of John M. Brooke, 2002; contbr. numerous articles to profl. publs. Chmn. Citizen-Soldier Meml. Va. Mil. Inst., 1983-84, Sesquicentennial celebration, 1986-89; unit pres. Am. Cancer Soc., 1980-82; pres. Stonewall Jackson area coun. Boy Scouts Am., 1964-67. 1st lt. U.S. Army, 1943-46, PTO. Fulbright rsch. scholar Keio U., 1962-63; Fulbright teaching grantee Nat. Taiwan U., 1963; recipient Silver Beaver award Boy Scouts Am., 1967, Citizen-Scouter of Yr. award, 1989. Mem. SAR, So. Hist. Assn., Assn. for Preservation Va. Antiquities (br. pres. 1975-77), Soc. of the Cin. (standing com. 1984-87), Rockbridge Hist. Soc. (pres. 1960-62, author procs. 1989), English Speaking Union (br. pres. 1980-82), Soc. Mayflower Descs. in Commonwealth of Va., Internat. House of Japan, Am. Legion, Phi Beta Kappa, Kappa Alpha. Republican. Episcopalian. Avocations: travel, reading, walking. Home: 405 Jackson Ave Lexington VA 24450-1905

BROOKE, JAMES BETTNER, news correspondent; b. N.Y.C., Feb. 21, 1955; s. John Louis Barde and Louisa (Ludlow) B.; m. Elizabeth Heilman Brooke, Sept. 7, 1985; children: James, Alexander, William. BA in Latin Am. Studies, Yale U., 1977. Reporter S.Am. region The Miami Herald, Rio de Janeiro, 1982-84; metro reporter The N.Y. Times, N.Y.C., 1984-86, West Africa bur. chief, 1986-89, Brazil bur. chief Rio de Janeiro, 1989-95, Rocky Mountain bur. chief Denver, 1995-99, Can. bur. chief, 1999-2001, Japan/Korea econ. corr., 2001—. also: NY Times Asahi Shimbun Bldg 3-2 Tsukiji 5-Chome Tokyo 104-8011 Japan E-mail: brooke@nytimes.com.

BROOKE, JOHN L. history educator; b. Mass., May 19, 1953; m. Sara C. Balderston, July 31, 1979. BA in History and Anthropology, Cornell U., 1976; MA in History, U. Pa., 1977, PhD in History, 1982. Vis. asst. prof. Amherst (Mass.) Coll., 1982-83; asst. prof. to prof. Tufts U., Medford, Mass., 1983-2001; dept. chair, 1996-97; prof. Ohio State U., Columbus, 2001—. Author: The Heart of the Commonwealth: Society and Political Culture in Worcester County, Massachusetts, 1713-1861, 1989, The Refiner's Fire: The Making of Mormon Cosmology, 1644-1844, 1994; contbr. articles to scholarly jours. Recipient award Nat. Soc. Daus. Colonial Wars, 1989, E. Harold Hugo Meml. Book prize Old Sturbridge Village Rsch. Libr. Soc., 1989, Merle Curti award for intellectual history, 1991, book prize for Am. history Nat. Hist. Soc., 1991, Bancroft prize Columbia U., 1995, ann. book prize Soc. for Historians of Early Am. Republic, 1995, ann. book award New Eng. Hist. Assn., 1995; S.F. Haven fellow Am. Antiquarian Soc., 1982, faculty rsch. fellow Tufts U., 1983, 88, Charles Warren fellow Harvard U., 1986-87, jr. fellow NEH, 1986-87, sr. fellow Commonwealth Ctr., 1990-91, fellow Am. Coun. Learned Socs., 1990-91, NEH fellow 1997-98, Guggenheim fellow, 1997-98. Mem. AAUP, Am. Antiq. Soc., Am. Hist. Assn., Orgn. Am. Historians, Mass. Hist. Soc. Democrat. Office: Ohio State U Dept History Dulles Hall Columbus OH 43210

BROOKE, PEGAN STRUTHERS, artist, art educator; b. Santa Ana, Calif., July 19, 1950; d. Lee Edwin and Maxine (Jones) Struthers; children: Marshall Payne, Clara Payne. BA in Lit., U. Calif., San Diego, 1972; BFA in Painting, Drake U., 1976; MA in Painting, U. Iowa, 1977; MFA in Painting, Stanford U., 1980. Instr. Sonoma (Calif.) State U., 1983; vis. artist U. Calif., Berkeley, 1982, Davis, 1984; prof. art San Francisco Art Inst., 1985—. Guest artist Calif. Coll. Arts and Crafts, Oakland, 1983. One-woman shows include Hansen Fuller Gallery, San Francisco, 1981, 83, Fuller Goldeen Gallery, San Francisco, 1985, 87, Parnas Gallery, Santa Monica, Calif., 1994, U. Calif., Davis, 1994, Terrain Gallery, San Franciso, 1995, Joan Roebuck Gallery, Lafayette, Calif., 1996, 97, R.B. Stevenson Gallery, La Jolla, Calif., 1996, 98, 99, 2002, Winfield Gallery, Carmel, Calif., 1998, Percival Galleries, Des Moines, 2000, Friesen Gallery, Sun Valley, Idaho, 2002; exhibited in group shows Guggenheim Mus., N.Y.C., 1987, Documenta, Sao Paulo, Brazil, 1994, Washburn Gallery, N.Y.C., 1995, R.B. Stevenson Gallery, 1996, U. Calif., San Diego, 1997, Monterrey (Calif.) Mus. Art 1999, Anne Loucks Gallery, Glencoe, Ill., 2003. Grantee Tiffany Found., 1983-84, Marin Arts Coun., 1992, 1998, U.S. Govt., 1995—. Home: PO Box 857 Bolinas CA 94924-0857 Office: San Francisco Art Inst 800 Chestnut St San Francisco CA 94133-2206 E-mail: pbrooke@sfai.edu.

BROOKE, RALPH IAN, dental educator; b. Leeds, Eng., Apr. 25, 1934; s. Michael and Jeanette (Cohen) B.; m. Lorna Ruth Shields; children: Michael Jeremy Richard, Andrew Timothy. Baccalaureus Chirurgiae Dentium, Licentiate in Dental Surgery, Leeds U., England, 1957. Licentiate Royal Coll. Physicians, 1963. Sr. lectr. Leeds U., 1970-72; prof., chmn. dept. oral medicine U. Western Ont., London, Can., 1972-82, dean dentistry faculty, 1982-97, vice provost health scis., 1987-97. Chief dentistry Univ. Hosp., London, 1973-92. Contbr. articles to profl. jours. Fellow Acad. Dentistry Internat. (hon.), Royal Coll. Dentists Can., Royal Coll. Surgeons; mem. Nat. Dental Exam Bd. (past

chmn. Can. commn. on dental accreditation), Can. Faculties Dentistry (past pres.), Can. Acad. Oral Medicine (past pres.), Can. Dental Assn. (hon.). Avocations: music, cycling. E-mail: rbrooke@julian.uwo.ca.

BROOKE, TAL (ROBERT TALIAFERRO), writer; b. Washington, Jan. 21, 1945; s. Edgar Duffield and Frances (Lea) B. BA, U. Va., 1969; M in Theology/Philosophy, Princeton (N.J.) U., 1986. V.p. pub. rels. nat. office Telecom Inc., 1982-83; pres., chmn. Spiritual Counterfeits Project, Inc., Berkeley, 1989—; founder End Run Pub., 1999—. Guest lectr. Cambridge U., Eng., 1977, 86, 97, 99, Oxford and Cambridge U., 1979, 84. Author: Lord of the Air: The International Edition, 1976, The Other Side of Death, Lord of the Air: The International Edition, 1979, Riders of the Cosmic Circuit, 1986, Millennial Edit., 2002, Avatar of Night, 1987, When the World Will Be As One, 1989, Lord of the Air, 1990, Virtual Gods, 1997, Conspiracy to Silence the Son, 1998, One World, 2000, The Mystery of Death, 2001. Mem. Internat. Platform Assn., Authors Guild, Soc. of The Cincinnati. Office: SCP Inc PO Box 4308 Berkeley CA 94704-0308 E-mail: scp@scp-inc.org., tal7@attbi.com.

BROOKE, WILLIAM WADE, business executive, lawyer; b. Baton Rouge, Apr. 5, 1956; s. Frederick Dixon and Sybil Stringer (Vogtle) B.; m. Margaret Lee Williamson, June 2, 1979; children: William W. Jr., Robert A., Sarah M. BA in Gen. Bus. Mgmt., U. Ala., 1978, JD, 1981. Bar: Ala. 1981. Assoc. Burr & Forman, Birmingham, Ala., 1981-87; mng. ptnr. Wallace, Brooke & Byers, Birmingham, 1987-91; gen. counsel Harbert Corp., Birmingham, 1991-94, COO, 1995—2001; exec. v.p. and mng. dir. Venture Capital, 2001—; chmn. Harbert Realty Svcs., Inc., 1998—. Trustee Bus. Coun. Alabama, 1998—. Trustee Discovery 2000 Mus., Birmingham, 1987-2000; trustee Mountain Brook City Schs. Found., 1993—, pres., 1995-97, chmn., 1997—; trustee Ctrl. Alabama United Way, 1998—, Cornerstone Schs. Ala., 1996—; bd. visitors U. Ala. CXBA Sch., 2001—. Mem. ABA, Ala. Bar Assn., Birmingham Bar Assn., Rotary. Republican. Presbyterian. Avocations: sport fishing, golf, reading. Office: Harbert Mgmt Corp 1 Riverchase Pkwy S Birmingham AL 35244-2008 E-mail: wbrooke@harbert.net., wbrooke@bellsouth.net.

BROOKER, JEFF ZEIGLER, cardiologist; b. Columbia, S.C., Nov. 1, 1941; s. Jefferson Zeigler and Virginia (Ligon) B.; m. Rhoda Arrowsmith, June 12, 1966; children: Jeff III, John, Rhoda. BS, U. S.C., 1962; MD, Med. U. S.C., 1966. Cert. in interventional cardiology, clin. cardiac electrophysiology, cardiovasc. disease and internal medicine Am. Bd. Internal Medicine. Intern, resident Hosp. U. Pa., Phila., 1966-68; resident internal medicine Stanford U. Med. Ctr., Palo Alto, Calif., 1970-71, rsch. fellow cardiology, 1971-73; staff cardiologist Tex. Heart Inst., Houston, 1973-74; assoc. dir. cardiology Providence Hosp., Columbia, S.C., 1974-81; pvt. practice cardiology Columbia, 1981—. Cons. peer rev. Jour. AMA, Chgo., 1976-77; local and regional rsch. com. Am. Heart Assn., Dallas., 1977-86. Mem. editorial bd. Jour. S.C. Med. Assn., Columbia, 1991—; editorial reviewer: Essentials of Echocardiography, 1977. Legis. liaison S.C. Med. Assn., Columbia, 1991-92. Lt. comdr. USN, 1968-70. Recipient Best Sci. Article award Roe Found., Columbia, 1991. Fellow ACP, Am. Coll. Cardiology, Am. Heart Assn. (coun. on clin. cardiology 1975—), Soc. for Cardiac Angiography and Interventions; mem. N.Am. Soc. Pacing and Electrophysiology, Mensa, Phi Beta Kappa, Alpha Omega Alpha. Achievements include improved method for oral dipyridamole testing for ischemic heart disease; devising a percutaneous method for inserting pacing lead into the internal jugular vein yet still implant and pulse generator on the anterior chest wall. Office: 1625 Bernardin Ave Columbia SC 29204-2003

BROOKER, LENA EPPS, human relations diversity management consultant; b. Lumberton, N.C., Oct. 13, 1941; d. Frank Howard and Grace Evelyn (Smith) Epps; m. James Dennis Brooker, July 30, 1966; children: Lora, Lindsey. AB, Meredith Coll., Raleigh, N.C., 1962. Cert. elem. sch. tchr., N.C. Elem. sch. tchr., Charlotte, Robeson County, N.C., Winchester, Va., Chevy Chase, Md., Raleigh, 1962-75; coord. human svcs. program N.C. Commn. Indian Affairs, Raleigh, 1975-78; planner, adminstr. human svcs. program N.C. Dept. Natural Resources and Community Devel., Raleigh, 1978-86; dir. diversity mgmt. The Women's Ctr., Raleigh, 1990-96; mgr. Diversity prog. First Citizens Bank, Raleigh, 1996-97; human rels. and diversity mgmt. cons., 1998-99. Developer model program U.S. Dept. Labor, Raleigh, 1976; presenter Pres.'s Commn. on Status of Women, Raleigh, 1979; facilitator Internat. Yr. of Woman, Winston-Salem, N.C., 1977; speaker on status of Am. Indians to univs., schs., chs. and orgns., 1975—. Contbg. writer The Carolina Call, The Carolinian. Chaplain, entertainment chmn. Dem. Women Wake County, Raleigh, 1989-91; mem. Task Force on Native Am. Ministry N.C. Conf. United Meth. Ch., chmn. ethnic minority local ch. concerns com., 1988-91, mem. bd. evangelism, 1986-91, audit com. coun. fin. and adminstrn., 1990-91, coun. ministries, 1992-94, mem. bishops task force on staff and structure, 1993-95; mem. Wake County Mammography Task Force, 1990-93; mem. cultural diversity com. Wake County Arts Coun., 1990; bd. dirs. Internat. Festival Raleigh, 1990-91, Triangle OIC, 1991-93, N.C. Civil Liberties Union, 1992-94, United Arts Coun. Wake County, 1996-97, sec. 1996; mem. steering com. for Yr. of native Am., N.C. Mus. Natural History, 1986; mem. city of Raleigh Human Resources and Human Rels. Commn., 1990-93; pres. bd. dirs. Women's Fund of N.C., 1993-97; bd. advisors Heritage Arts Found., 1993, N.Am. Health Edn. Fund, 1994-98, Women's Leadership Inst., Bennett Coll., 1995-96; mem. N.C. Coun. on Women, 1999—; bd. dirs. Carteret County Domestic Violence Program, 1999. Recipient Personal Advocacy for Women in N.C. Carpathian award N.C. Equity, 1993, Martin Luther King Jr. Light of Hope award Wake County Pub. Schs., 1998; grantee N.C. Arts Coun., Duke-Seminars Fine Arts Found., 1986. Mem. N.C. Natural Scis. Soc. (bd. dirs. 1987-90), Triangle Native Am. Soc. (past coord. spl. projects), Meredith Coll. Alumne Assn. (bd. dirs. 1994-95),The Women's Forum of North Carolina. Avocations: tennis, reading, writing, collecting american indian art and objects. Address: 120 Leisure Mountain Rd Asheville NC 28804-1117 E-mail: LBrooker00@cs.com.

BROOKER, ROBERT ELTON, JR., retired manufacturing company executive; b. L.A., Apr. 12, 1937; s. Robert Elton and Sarah (Smith) B.; m. Katherine Jones, Mar. 21, 1964; children: Robert III, Carolyn, Christopher, Alison. BS, MIT, 1959; MBA, Harvard U., 1965. With Cummings Engine Co., 1965-81, gen. mgr. Great Lakes Foundry divsn., 1966-69, pres. fleetguard Dallas, 1970-77, v.p. Latin Am. Miami, Fla., 1977-80, v.p. components group Columbus, Ind., 1981; pres. info. svcs. group N.L. Industries, Houston, 1981-86; pres., COO Lord Corp., Erie, Pa., 1987-90, CEO, 1990-91; pres., COO Connell Ltd. Partnership, Boston, 1993-95; dir. Dura Automotive Sys., 1995-98; ret., 1998. Dir. FCI, 1991—, Innovative Components Inc., 1998—, Dura Automotive Sys., 1995—. Author: British Military Pistols, 1603-1887, 1978, Parole Sachen, 1990; contbr. articles to profl. jours. Mem. Sea Space Symposium. Capt. USMC, 1959-63.

BROOKER, SUSAN GAY, employment consulting firm executive; b. Washington, Sept. 4, 1949; d. Robert Morris and Mildred Ruby (Parler) B. BA, St. Mary's Coll., St. Mary's City, Md., 1971. News editor WPGC Radio, Lanham, Md., 1971; mgr. trainee Household Fin. Corp., Silver Spring, Md., 1972; career counselor Place-All, Bethesda, Md., 1972-73; exec. v.p. New Places, Inc./Get-A-Job, Washington, 1973-89; employment cons., owner, pres. SGB Consultants, Reston, Va., 1989—. Mem. Emploibank, Washington, 1978-79; guest condr. LGCW 15th Aniv. Concert, 1999. Conservation chairperson Silver Spring Woman's Club, 1993—94; watch capt. Sawyer's Neighborhood, 1997—2001; crisis crew mem. Avon Breast Cancer, 2000; outreach vestry chair Grace Episcopal Ch., 1992—94. Recipient Cert. Appreciation U.S. Fish and Wildlife Assn., 1985, Cert. of Recognition Chaplaincy Assocs., Howard Gen. Hosp, Letter of Appreciation Pres. Bill Clinton, 1996. Mem. Pell-Capital Pers. Svc. Asssn. (cert.), St. Mary's Coll. (Md.) Alumni Assn. (bd. dirs. 1987-91). Democrat. Avocations: swimming, travel, gardening, golf, snorkling. Home and Office: 2209 Coppersmith Sq Reston VA 20191-2305 E-mail: suebrooker@aol.com.

BROOKER, THOMAS KIMBALL, oil company executive; b. L.A., Oct. 1, 1939; s.Robert Elton and Sally Burton Harrison (Smith) B.; m. Nancy Belle Neumann, 1966; children: Thomas Kimball Jr., Isobel, Vanessa. BA in French Lit., Yale U., 1961; MBA, Harvard U., 1968; MA in Art History, U. Chgo., 1989, PhD in Art History, 1996. Assoc. in corp. fin. Morgan Stanley & Co., Inc., N.Y.C., 1968-73, v.p., 1973-75, mng. dir., 1976-88, head Chgo. office, 1978-88; pres. Barbara Oil Co., Chgo., 1989—, also bd. dirs. Bd. dirs. Arthur J. Gallagher & Co., Miami Corp., Cutler Oil & Gas Corp.; bd. govs. Midwest Stock Exch., 1980-88, vice chmn., 1986-88. Contbr. articles to profl. jours. Chmn. vis. com. libr. U. Chgo., mem. vis. com. visual arts dept.; mem., chmn. com. on libr. Yale U. President's Coun., 1980-84; trustee Pierpont Morgan Libr., Gov. John Carter Brown Libr., Yale U. Libr. Assn.; vice chmn. Newberry Libr.; bd. dirs. Lyric Opera Chgo. Recipient Sir Thomas More medal U. San Francisco, 1992; assoc. fellow Saybrook Coll., Yale U. Mem. Adminstrv. Coun. (v.p.), Assn. Internat. de Bibliophilie, Bibliotheca Wittockiana (mem. sci. com.), Bandar-Log, Caxton Club, Chgo. Club, Comml. Club, Econ. Club, River Club (N.Y.C.), Knickerbocker Club (N.Y.C.), Grolier Club (N.Y.C.), The Casino, Saddle and Cycle Club, Edgartown (Mass.) Yacht Club, The Reading Room (Edgartown), Quadrangle Club, Racquet Club, Rockaway Hunt Club, Wayfarers Club. Home: 1500 N Lake Shore Dr Chicago IL 60610-6657 Office: Barbara Oil Co 21 S Clark St Ste 3990 Chicago IL 60603-2000

BROOKER, TIMOTHY DOUGLAS, social studies educator; s. Richard A. and Lorena Jane Brooker; m. Paulita Sharlene Harp, Aug. 16, 1975; children: Brandon Richard, Nathan Paul. BA in Social Studies, John Brown U., Siloam Springs, Arkansas, 1979; MA in Diplomacy, Internat. Commerce, U. Ky., 1981, M in Pub. Policy Adminstrn., 1983; EdD, U. Ark., 1998. Cert. counselor Nat. Bd. of Cert. Counselors, 1998, residential behavioral therapist Nat. Tchg. Family Assn., 1990, lic. assoc. counselor Ark. Counseling Bd., 1996. Adj. prof. govt., bus. mgmt. Ea. Ky. U., Richmond, 1983—85; co-dir., residential behavioral therapist Ashe County Youth Svcs., Copper Kettle Ho., West Jefferson, NC, 1988—2000, West Oaks Psychiat. Inst., Houston, 1990—93, Dogwood Achievement Ctr., Inc., Siloam Springs, Ark., 1994—98; asst. prof. of govt. Oral Roberts U., Tulsa, 2001—. Adj. prof. govt., econs. John Brown U., Siloam Springs, Ark., 1993—2001; syndicated radio talk show host Demaree Media Inc., Fayetteville, Ark., 1994—2000; chair higher edn. evaluation com. Murphy Commn., Little Rock, 1996—98; vis. prof. govt. Ark. Tech. U., Russellville, 2001. Columnist: newspaper Northwest Arkansas Times. Regional chair Rep. Party Ark., Little Rock, 1993—97. Baptist. Office: Oral Roberts University 7777 S Lewis Tulsa OK 74171

BROOKES, CAROLYN, early childhood education educator; b. Orlando, Fla., June 16, 1946; d. Thomas M. and Hilda Marie (Hanson) Jessen: m. Edward N. Brookes, Aug. 8, 1970 (dec. Oct. 1990); 1 child, Donna Marie. BA, U. So. Fla., 1960; MS, Nova U., 1990. Asst. dir., dir. lower schs. Gables Acad., Winter Park, Fla., 1973-83; tchr. Orange County Pub. Schs., Orlando, 1983-98, early childhood resource tchr., high-scope trainer, 1983-92, coord. edn. homeless children and youth program, 1992-95. Coord. mentor tchr. program U. Ctrl. Fla. and Orange County Pub. Schs., 1993-96; regional specialist State Dept. of Edn., 1997-98; parent educator, adj. instr. U. Ctrl. Fla.; ednl. cons.; literacy first trainer distance educator Ednl. Mgmt. Group, Phoenix, 1994-96; trainer Staff Devel. for Educators, Implications Brain Rsch., Literary First, Loving Guidance; pres. People to People, 1992-99; literacy coach U. North Fla., 1998-2000.; project cons. staff devel. CD programs, Jensen Learning Corp., 2002. Co-author presch. literacy curriculum, 2001. Mem. ASCD, Internat. Reading Assn., Nat. Staff Devel. Coun., Assn. for Childhood Edn. Internat., Nat. Assn. for Edn. Young Children, So. Early Childhood Assn., Orange County Assn. for Edn. Young Children, Delta Kappa Gamma Soc. Internat. for Key Women Educators, Phi Delta Kappa. Home: 6316 Grand Bahama Cir Tampa FL 33615-4204 Office: Carolyn Jessen Brookes Ednl Cons 6316 Grand Bahama Cir Tampa FL 33615-4204 E-mail: cjbrookes@aol.com.

BROOKINS, CAROLE L. federal agency administrator; b. Ind. Grad., U. Okla. Chmn., CEO World Perspectives, Inc., 1980—2001; chair adv. com. U.S. State Dept. Food, Hunger and Agrl. in Devel. Countries, 1984—88; mem. adv. com. U.S. State Dept. Internat. Econ. Policy, 1990—92; exec. dir. Internat. Bank Reconstruction and Devel., Washington, 2001—. Office: The World Bank 1818 H St NW Washington DC 20433

BROOKMAN, ANTHONY RAYMOND, lawyer; b. Chgo., Mar. 23, 1922; s. Raymond Charles and Marie Clara (Alberg) B.; m. Marilyn Joyce Brookman, June 5, 1982; children: Meribeth Brookman Farmer, Anthony Raymond, Lindsay Logan Christensen. Student, Ripon Coll., 1940-41; BS, Northwestern U., 1947; JD, U. Calif., San Francisco, 1953. Bar: Calif. 1954. Law clk. to presiding justice Calif. Supreme Ct., 1953-54; ptnr. Nichols, Williams, Morgan, Digardi & Brookman, 1954-68; sr. ptnr. Brookman & Talbot, Inc. (formerly Brookman & Hoffman, Inc.), Walnut Creek, Calif., 1969-92, Brookman & Talbot Inc., Sacramento, 1992—. Pres. Young Reps. Calif., San Mateo County, 1953-54. 1st lt. USAF. Mem. ABA, Alameda County Bar Assn., State Bar Calif., Lawyers Club Alameda County, Alameda-Contra Costa County Trial Lawyers Assn., Assn. Trial Lawyers Am., Calif. Trial Lawyers Assn., Athenian Nile Club, Masons, Shriners. Republican. Office: 901 H St Ste 200 Sacramento CA 95814-1808 also: Ste B-201 675 Ygnacio Valley Rd Walnut Creek CA 94596 also: 1746 Grand Canal Blvd Ste 11 Stockton CA 95207-8111

BROOKNER, ANITA, writer, educator; d. Newson and Maude B. BA, King's Coll., 1946-49; Ed., U. London; PhD, Courtauld Inst., Paris, 1949-53. Vis. lectr. U. Reading, 1959-64; Slade prof. U. Cambridge, 1967-68; lectr. Courtauld Inst. of Art, 1964. Author: Watteau, 1968, The Genius of the Future, 1971, Greuze: The Rise and Fall of an Eighteenth Century Phenomenon, 1972, Jacques-Louis David, 1980, (novels) A Start in Life, 1981, Providence, 1982, Look At Me, 1983, Hotel du Lac, 1984 (Booker McConnell prize), Family and Friends, 1985, A Misalliance, 1986, A Friend From England, 1987, Latecomers, 1988, Lewis Percy, 1989, Brief Lives, 1991, Fraud, 1992, A Family Romance, 1993, A Private View, 1995, Altered States, 1996, Visitors, 1997, The Visitors, 1998, Soundings, 1998, Falling Slowly: A Novel, 1999, The Bay of Angels: A Novel, 2002; contbr. articles to mags.

BROOKNER, ELI, electrical engineer; b. N.Y.C., Apr. 2, 1931; s. Angel and Fanny Brookner; m. Ethel Bobick, Nov. 20, 1955; children: Lawrence, Richard. BEE, CCNY, 1953; MEE, Columbia U., 1955, DSc, 1962. Jr. engr. radar div. Rome (N.Y.) Air Devel. Ctr., summer 1952; rsch. engr. Columbia U. Electronics Rsch. Lab., N.Y.C., 1953-57, sr. rsch. engr., 1960-62; project engr. Fed. Sci. Corp. (name now Nicolet), N.Y.C., 1957-60; prin. fellow Raytheon Co., Sudbury, Mass., 1962—. Internat. lectr. in radar tech.; served on coms. for Nat. Acad. Sci., DARPA, Air Force Sci. Adv. Bd., Air Force Mil. Space Systems Tech. Workshops. Author, editor: Radar Technology, 1977, Aspects of Modern Radar, 1988, Practical Phased-Array Antenna Systems, 1991, Tracking and Kalman Filtering Made Easy, 1998; achievements include conception and lead technical engr. for the wake measurements radar, first pulse doppler travelling wave tube radar put into space, system engring. for active phase array RADARSAT II-Plus. Recipient Jour. Premium award Franklin Inst., 1966. Fellow AIAA, IEEE (Centennial medal 1984, IEEE Region I award for continuing edn. course devel. 1986, Meritorious Achievement award edn. activities bd. 1990, Centennial medal 2000, Warren White award for excellence in radar engring., 2003); mem. IEEE Aerospace and Electronics Systems Soc. (chmn. Boston chpt. 1972—, Outstanding Chpts. award 1977-78, 83-84, Disting. lectr. 1988—), IEEE Antennas and Propagation Soc. (Disting. lectr. 1983-85, Wheeler Best Applications paper award 1999, chair internat. symposium on phased array systems and tech. 1996), Internat. Union Radio Sci. (commns. B and C, invited session chmn. 1973), Tau Beta Pi, Eta Kappa Nu. Avocations: swimming, dancing, classical music, comedy, photography. Home: 282 Marrett Rd Lexington MA 02421-7009 E-mail: Eli_Brookner@Notes.res.ray.com.

BROOKS, AARON LAFETTE, football player; b. Newport News, Va., Mar. 24, 1976; BA in Anthropology, U. Va. Football player New Orleans Saints, 2000—. Avocations: basketball, reading. Office: New Orleans Saints 5800 Airline Dr Metairie LA 70003

BROOKS, ALAN, publications editor, writer; b. Havre de Grace, Md., Feb. 1, 1949; s. Jimmy Maynard and Edna Lee Brooks; m. Jodie Ann Chatfield, June 20, 1987; children: Kyra Marie, Shane Michael. Cert., Nat. Outdoor Leadership Sch., 1970; BS, U. Del., 1971. Editor Natural Resource Ecology Lab., Ft. Collins, Colo., 1974-76, Colo. State U., Ft. Collins, 1976-85, AT&T, Denver, 1985-94; owner Alan Brooks Comm., Denver, 1994-96; editor Internat. Wood Soc., Albuquerque, 1995—, Am. Inst. Archs., 1998-99. Lectr. Colo. State U., 1977-83; cons. Around the World in 80 Ways, Riner, Va., 1980-81, Colo. Purchasing Assn., Denver, 1992-93; bd. trustee Internat. Wood Soc., Calgary, Can., 1995—. Editor Grassland Biome, 1974-76, Colo. Comments, 1976-83, Denver Views, 1985-94, Trail and Road Encounters, 1994-96, World of Wood, 1995—, AIA New Mexico Perspectives, 1998-99. Recipient Cmty. Svc. award Colo. Environ. Action Exch., 1990. Mem. Intercollegiate Outing Club Assn. (exec. dir. 1969-71). Avocations: natural sciences, history, contra dancing, hiking, road trips. Home and Office: 13105-B Candelaria Rd NE Albuquerque NM 87112-2167

BROOKS, ANDRÉE AELION, journalist, educator, author; b. London, Feb. 2, 1937; d. Leon Luis and Lillian (Abrahamson) Aelion; m. Ronald J. Brooks, Aug. 16, 1959 (div. Aug. 1986); children: Allyson, James. Journalism cert., N.W. London Poly., 1958. Reporter Hampstead News, London, 1954-58; story editor Photoplay mag., N.Y.C., 1958-60; N.Y. corr. Australian Broadcasting Co., N.Y.C., 1961-68; elected rep. Elstree, Eng., 1973-74; columnist N.Y. Times, N.Y.C., 1978-95; free-lance journalist, 1978—; adj. prof. journalism Fairfield U., Conn., 1983-87. Assoc. fellow Yale U., 1989—; founder, pres. Women's Campaign Sch. Yale U., 1993-96; v.p. Minuteman Media, 1995-96; coord.-dir. Out of Spain hist. curriculum, 1997-2000. Author: Children of Fast Track Parents, 1989 (Best Non-fiction Book award 1990), (biography) The Women Who Defied Kings: The Life and Times of Dona Gracia Nasi, 2002 (Mark Twain award 2003). Exec. bd. Am. Jewish Com., 1987-91; trustee Temple Israel, Westport, Conn., 1991-97. Recipient 1st place for news writing Conn. Press Women, 1980, 83, 85-86, 87, 94, Outstanding Achievement award Nat. Fedn. Press Women, 1981, 1st place award Fairfield County chpt. Women in Comms., 1982-83, 86-87, 92, 93, 97, 2d place award in mag. writing Nat. Assn. Home Bldrs., 1983, Spl. Svc. award Conn. chpt. Am. Planning Assn., 1983, 1st place award for mag. writing Nat. Fedn. Press Women, 1983, Mark Twain award Conn. Press Club, 2003; named one of Am. Women of Achievement Am. Jewish Com., 1989; honored by Am. Sephardi Fedn., 2001. Mem. Conn. Press Women (chmn. nominating com. 1983-86), Women in Communications (contest co-chmn. 1983-84). E-mail: andreebrooks@hotmail.com. *Keep true to what you believe and don't become cynical or full of hate - for hate only breeds more hate.*

BROOKS, ANITA HELEN, public relations executive; b. N.Y.C. d. Arthur and Bertha (Stewart) Sayle; m. Arnold Brooks, July 1, 1954 (div.). BA, Hunter Coll., 1950; MA, Columbia U., 1952, MLS, 1954. Tchr. Latin Hunter Coll. H.S., N.Y.C., 1955; publicity rep. WOR Radio, N.Y.C., 1955; writer King Features Syndicate, N.Y.C., 1955-59; pub. rels. exec. NBC-TV, N.Y.C., 1956; dir. pub. rels. N.Y. State Mental Health Fund Campaign, 1956, WMCA Radio, N.Y.C., 1957; account exec. various pub. rels. agys., N.Y.C., 1957-65; pres. Anita Helen Brooks Assocs., Pub. Rels., N.Y.C., 1965—. Lit. agt. Anita Brooks Lit. Agt., N.Y.C., 1956—. Writer radio-TV shows. Vice chmn. Sinatra for Meml. Sloan-Kettering Cancdr Hosp. Benefit; mem. patroness com. Harkness Ballet Found.; mem. benefit com. Mannes Coll. Music, N.Y.C.; mem. legis. adv. com. of Senator Roy M. Goodman, N.Y. State Senate. Decorated dame comdr. Knights of Malta; named hon. citizen Venezuela. Mem. Am. Women in Radio and TV, Pub. Rels. Soc. Am., Internat. Radio and TV Soc., Publs. Publicity Assn., Assn. Motion Picture Advertisers, Mystery Writers Am., Columbia U. Alumni Assn., Sisters in Crime Soc., Smithsonian Assocs., N.Y. Press Club, Eta Sigma Phi, Latin/Greek Honor Soc. Home and Office: 155 E 55th St New York NY 10022-4038

BROOKS, BABERT VINCENT, publisher; b. N.Y.C., Sept. 2, 1926; s. Babert Vincent and Florence (Goodwin) B.; m. Audrey Stephenson, Dec. 6, 1952 (div.); children— Torrey, Scott, Wendy; m. Kathryn Frazer, May 23, 1987. AB magna cum laude, Dartmouth Coll., 1947, MBA with distinction, 1949. Security analyst Arnold Bernhard & Co., N.Y.C., 1952-56; cons. Booz, Allen & Hamilton, N.Y.C., 1956-58; v.p. finance Schine Enterprises, N.Y.C., 1958-61; v.p., treas. Murray Corp. Am., N.Y.C., 1961-62; pres. Brooks, Torrey & Scott, Inc., Westport, Conn., 1962—, Westport Travel Svc., Inc., 1963, chmn., 1988-92; pres. Brooks Community Newspapers, 1974-82, chmn., 1982-99; pub. Westport (Conn.) News, 1964-99, Darien (Conn.) News-Rev., 1973-99, Fairfield (Conn.) Citizen-News, 1973-99, Norwalk Citzen News, 1997-99, Greenwich (Conn.) News, 1983-96, Inside Fairfield County, Westport, 1993-99. Sec.-treas. Airspur Corp., N.Y.C., 1969-70; trustee King Indsl. Properties, Boston, 1965-82; dir. Westfair, Inc., Westport, CFS Corp., County Fed. Savs. & Loan Assn., Westport, 1969-85, United Printing & Litho Corp., Bridgeport, Conn., 1984-89, Warner Investing Corp., Westport; trustee Am. Inst. Econ. Rsch., Great Barrington, Mass., 1997—, vice chmn., 2002, Media Rsch. Ctr., 2002- Bd. dirs., treas. Dartmouth in Greenwich, 1972-81; trustee Conn. Policy and Econ. Coun. Inc., 1989-99, Norwalk Hosp., 1988-93, 95-00, Norwalk Health Svcs., Inc., 1994—, U. Bridgeport, 1991—, Media Rsch. Ctr., Washington, 2002—. With USNR, 1945-47. Mem. Riverside Yacht Club, Phi Beta Kappa.

BROOKS, BETH ANN, physician; b. Feb. 21, 1950; MD, U. Nebr., 1974; MSA, Ctrl. Mich. U., 1993. Dir. med. student edn. in psychiatry Wayne State U., Detroit, 1978-88, residency tng. dir. in child and adolescent psychiatry, 1998—, prof., assoc. chair dept. psychiatry, 1998—, residency tng. dir. in psychiatry, 2001—; div. head child/adolescent psychiatry, vice chair psychiatry Henry Ford Health Sys., Detroit, 1989-97; chief pediatric psychiatry/psychology Children's Hosp. of Mich., Detroit, 1998—2001. Office: Univ Psychiatric Ctr 2751 E Jefferson #400 Detroit MI 48207-4166

BROOKS, CHARLES LEE, III, computational biophysicist, educator; b. Detroit, May 14, 1956; married; 2 children. BS in Chemistry and Physics, Alma (Mich.) Coll., 1978; PhD in Physical Chemistry, Purdue U., 1982. Postdoc. fellow Harvard U., Boston, 1982-85, NIH, 1983-85; from asst. prof. to prof. Carnegie Mellon U., 1985—94, prof., 1994—; prof. molecular biology Scripps Rsch. Inst., 1994—. Mem. spl. rev. panels, site visit coms., mem. reviewers reserve Cell Biology & Biophysics Divsn. A study section, NIH; reviewer, mem. cellular and molecular biophysics panel, NSF; mem. adv. bd. Nat. Biomed. Computation Resource Inst., San Diego Supercomputing Ctr., sr. fellow, 1997; presenter in field. Mem. editl. bd. Proteins, 1995—, Biochimica et Biophysica Acta, 2000—, Physical Chemistry Chemical Physics, 2000—; contbr. over 125 articles to profl. jours.; author 1 book, several book chpts. A.P. Sloan fellow, 1990-93, AAAS, 2000; grantee Swedish Rsch. Coun., 1992. Office: Scripps Rsch Inst Dept Molecular Biology TPC6 10550 N Torrey Pines Rd La Jolla CA 92037-1000 E-mail: brooks@scripps.edu.

BROOKS, DARRELL LEMONT, collections and bad debt manager; s. David and Virginia Brooks. Cert. in acctg., Brookstone Coll. Bus., 1997. Acctg. software specialist, NC. Debt mgmt. specialist Brookstone Coll. Bus., Greensboro, NC, 1999—. Collections specialist Brookstone Coll. Bus., Greensboro, NC, 1999—. Office: Brookstone Coll Bus 7815 National Svc Rd Greensboro NC 27409 Office Fax: 336-668-2717. Personal E-mail: dbrooks@brookstone.edu.

BROOKS, DAVID BARRY, resource economist; b. Easton, Mass., Feb. 15, 1934; s. Abraham and Mae (Fox) B.; m. Toby Judith Haftka, Sept. 11, 1955; children: Michael Jan, Naomi Sara. S.B. in Geology, MIT, 1955; MS in Geology, Calif. Inst. Tech., 1956; PhD in Econs., U. Colo., 1963. Geologist U.S. Geol. Survey, 1956-59; research assoc. Resources for the Future, Washington, 1961-66; asst. prof. econs. Berea Coll., 1966-67; chief div. mineral econs. Bur. Mines, Dept. Interior, 1967-70; chief Mineral Econs. Research div. Can. Dept. Energy, Mines and Resources, 1970-73; dir. Office Energy Conservation, 1974-77; dir. Ottawa office Energy Probe, 1977-82; bd. dirs. Can. Friends of the Earth, pres., 1977-81, 85-88; prin. Marbek Resource Cons. Ltd., Ottawa, Ont., Canada, 1983-88; sr. advisor Internat. Devel. Rsch. Ctr., Ottawa, 1988—2002; dir. rsch. Friends of the Earth, Canada, 2002—. Cons. Can. Internat. Devel. Agy., 1983, 85, 86, 88, UN Conf. on Human Environ., 1971-72, Labrador Resources Adv. Coun., 1979, Dept. Indian and No. Affairs, Ottawa, 1979; mem. study team on non-renewable materials, environ. studies bd. Nat. Acad. Scis., 1972-73; mem. study team on environ. Fed. Task Force and Program Rev.; mem. energy options adv. com. Office of Ministry of Energy, Ottawa, 1986-88; cons. Highlander Rsch. and Edn. Ctr., New Market, Tenn., 1979; exec. dir. Beaufort Sea Rsch. Coalition; bd. dirs. Ont. Hydro; keynote spkr. First Israeli-Palestinian Internat. Academic Conf. on Water in Zurich, 1992. Author: Supply and Competition in Minor Metals, 1965, Peaceful Use of Nuclear Explosives: Some Economic Aspects, 1969, Minerals: an Expanding or a Dwindling Resource?, 1973, Zero Energy Growth for Canada, 1981; co-author: Life After Oil: A Renewable Energy Policy for Canada, 1983, Watershed: The Role of Fresh Water in the Israeli-Palestian Conflict, 1994, Water: Local-Level Management, 2002; also monographs on environ. problems of mining and

energy conservation, energy and internat. devel.; also articles. Chmn. No. Va. chpt. Congress Racial Equality, 1963-65; sec. Fed. Employees for a Democratic Soc. Served with AUS, 1957. Ashley fellow Trent U., Can., 1992. Mem.: Internat. Water Acad. Home: 1-202 Flora St Ottawa ON Canada K1R 5R7 Office: Friends of the Earth Can 260 St Patrick St Ottawa ON Canada K1N 5K5 E-mail: dbrooks@foecanada.org.

BROOKS, DAVID VICTOR, lawyer; b. Sendai, Japan, May 22, 1948; came to U.S., 1951, naturalized, 1975; s. David Kenneth and Mary Victoria (Gooding) B.; m. Deborah Ann Gary, Nov. 14, 1970 (div. 1983); m. Mary Bonnie Kemp, July 7, 1984; children: Meredith Maxwell, Healther Branan, Matthew David, Sarah Rose. BA with high honors, N.C. State U., 1974; JD, U. N.C., 1977. Bar: N.C. 1977, U.S. Ct. Mil. Appeals 1978, U.S. Dist. Ct. (ea. dist.) N.C. 1980. Sr. trial atty. Naval Legal Svc. Office, Pearl Harbor, Hawaii, 1977-78; tort claims atty. Norfolk, Va., 1978-80; assoc. Maupin, Taylor & Ellis, P.A., Raleigh, N.C., 1980-84, ptnr., 1984-85; chmn. N.C. Indsl. Commn., 1985-87; mng. ptnr. Brooks, Stevens & Pope, P.A., Cary, N.C., 1987—. Author: The New Book of Rights, 1998. Bd. dirs. Mid-State Safety Coun., Henderson, N.C., 1983—; gen. counsel N.C. Rep. Party, Raleigh, 1983-85; dist. commr. Boy Scouts Am., Raleigh, 1981—. Capt. USMC, 1966-72, Vietnam; lt. comdr. USN, 1977-80. Decorated Silver Star medal, Navy and Marine Corps medal, Bronze Star, Purple Heart. Mem. ABA, N.C. Bar Assn., Am. Soc. Safety Engrs., Wake County Bar Assn., VFW, Lions. Lutheran. Republican. Office: NC Indsl Commn Dobbs Bldg 2000 Regency Pkwy Ste 150 Cary NC 27511-8581 Home: 1604 Burgess Hill Ct Apex NC 27502-7984

BROOKS, DEBRA L. healthcare executive, neuromuscular therapist; b. Cedar Rapids, Iowa, Dec. 10, 1950; d. Rex L and Phyllis M (Harman) Brooks; children from previous marriage: Brei, Benjamin, Bryan. BA, Coe Coll., 1973; MS, Clayton Coll., 1999, PhD, 2000. Cert. neuromuscular therapy Fla., natural therapeutics specialist N.Mex. Tchr. Cedar Rapids Cmty. Sch. Dist., 1973-92; COO NeuroMuscular Therapy Ctr., Walford, Iowa, 1994—. Educator Helping Hands Seminars, Cedar Rapids, 1992—2000, Debra Brooks' Seminars, Walford, 1993—; bus and educ consult Brooks Consults, Cedar Rapids, 1990—; mem Iowa Bd Examiners, 2001—03; chair adv. bd. ABLE, 2001—02; mem., chair Nat. Alliance State Bds., 2001—02; editl. bd. Momentum Media. Contbr. articles to profl jours and newsletters. Fundraiser, performer in musicals St Luke's Hosp, Cedar Rapids, 1978—91; fundraiser, performer in Follies Cedar Rapids Symphony, 1981—99; fundraiser, performer in telethons Variety Clubs Am, Cedar Rapids, 1989—91; mem Walford Community Develop, 1994—98; editl. bd. Tng. and Conditioning Mag. Named Outstanding Mentor of the Yr, YWCA, 2001; recipient First in Nation in Educ Award, State of Iowa, 1991, Tribute to Women of Achievement Award, YWCA, 2001. Mem.: Profl. Women's Network (chair 2002—03), Am. Massage Therapy Assn. (state v.p., edn. dir. 1992—94, nat. trustee Found. 1994—98, nat. bd. dirs. 1994—2002, cert), Am. Coll. Healthcare Execs. Avocations: singing, painting, pianist, power walking, philosophy. Office: NeuroMuscular Therapy Ctr PO Box 8267 Cedar Rapids IA 52408-8267

BROOKS, DERRICK DEWAN, football player; b. Pensacola, Fla., Apr. 18, 1973; m. CArol Brooks; children: Derrick Jr., Brianna Monai, Darius. Degree, Fla. State U., 1994, M degree, 1999. Linebacker Tampa Bay Buccaneers. Co-hosts weekly minute radio call-in show. Active March of Dimes, D.A.R.E., Audley Evans Ctr.; host Brooks Bunch; founder Derrick Brooks Charities Found.. Named Number One on The Sporting News Good Guys List for cmty. work, Man of Yr., NFL, 2000, Defensive Player of Yr., 2002. Office: Tampa Bay Buccaneers 1 W Buccaneer Pl Tampa FL 33607-5797

BROOKS, EDGAR R. (DICK BROOKS), utility company executive; b. Slaton, Tex., 1937; m. Martha Garrett Brooks; 2 children. BSEE, Tex. Tech U., 1961; postgrad., Harvard U., 1985, U. Mich. Engr. West Tex. Utilities Co., Abilene, 1961-82, v.p. customer svcs., 1980-82; v.p. engring. Ctrl. Power & Light Co., 1982-83; chief engring. officer, sr. v.p. Cen. Power & Light Co., 1983-86, pres., CEO, 1986-87; exec. v.p. elec. ops. Cen. & S.W. Corp., Dallas, 1987, exec. v.p., 1988-89, chmn., CEO, 1990—; also past pres., CEO Cen. & S.W. Svcs., Inc.; also pres., CEO Transok, Inc. Various positions West Tex. U. Engring. Dept. Trustee Dallas Theater Ctr., Dallas Symphony; past chair Tex. Coun. Econ. Edn.; chmn. N.Am. Elec. Reliability Coun., Edison Electric Inst.,, 1997—98; deacon Park Cities Bapt. ch., Dallas; chmn. exec. bd. Cir. Ten Coun. Boy Scouts Am.; exec. bd. United Way of Met. Dallas. Recipient Named Disting. Engr. award, Tex. Tech U., 1988, Disting. Alumni, 1993. Mem.: Tex. Rsch. League, Assn. Elec. Cos. Tex. (mem. exec. bd.), Tex. C. of C. Office: Cen and SW Corp PO Box 660164 Dallas TX 75266-0164 Also: Central & SW Corp 1616 Woodall Rodgers Fwy Dallas TX 75202-1234

BROOKS, EDWARD HOWARD, college administrator; b. Salt Lake City, Mar. 2, 1921; s. Charles Campbell and Margery (Howard) B.; m. Courtaney June Perren, May 18, 1946; children: Merrillee Brooks Runyan, Robin Anne (Mrs. R. Bruce Pollock). BA, Stanford U., 1942, MA, 1947, PhD, 1950. Mem. faculty, adminstrn. Stanford U., 1949-71; provost Claremont (Calif.) Colls., 1971-81; v.p. Claremont U. Center, 1979-81; sr. v.p. Claremont McKenna Coll., 1981-84; provost Scripps Coll., 1987-89, pres., 1989-90; ret., 1990. Trustee EDUCOM, 1978-80, Webb Sch. of Calif., 1979-90, Menlo Sch. and Coll., 1985-88, Albuquerque Acad.; bd. overseers Hoover Instn., 1972-78; bd. dirs. Student Loan Mktg. Assn., 1973-77; mem. Calif. Student Aid Commn., 1984-88, chmn., 1986-88. Served with AUS, 1942-45. Home: 201 N Orange Grov Pasadena CA 91103 *Looking back since retirement, I have concluded that the most useful and, perhaps, enduring contribution an institutional leader can make is clearly committed efforts to make the institution better and the individuals within it better; holding everyone to even higher standards.*

BROOKS, FRANKLIN RAMON, psychologist, army officer; b. Margarita, CZ, Panama, Dec. 2, 1945; s. Sherman C. and Astrea (Bertonini) B.; m. Lenalee Bunch, July 6, 1950; children: Franklin Bryson, Marcus Ramon, Jennifer Jean; m. May 29, 1970. BS, Tex. A&M U., 1967; MS in Clin. Psychology, U. North Tex., 1971, PhD in Clin. Psychology, 1975. Cert. psychologist, Tex. 2d lt. U.S. Army, 1967, advanced through grades to col.; chief psychology svc. Frankfurt (Germany) Army Regional Med. Ctr., 1984-88, Eisenhower Army Med. Ctr., Ft. Gordon, Ga., 1988-89, chief dept. psychology, 1989-93; chief psychology svc. Brooke Army Med. Ctr., Ft. Sam Houston, Tex., 1993-95, chief dept. psychology, 1995-98, chief dept. behavioral medicine, 1998—2001; chief ops. officer Brown Sch., Laurel Ridge, 2001—02; pvt. practice San Antonio, 2002—. Clin. psychology cons. US Army Health Svc. Command, Ft. Sam Houston, 1993-95, Gt. Plains Regional Command, Ft. Sam Houston, 1995-2001. Fellow Am. Coll. Forensic Examiners (diplomate); mem. APA, Am. Psychol. Soc., Assn. Mil. Surgeons US, Am. Soc. Clin. Hypnosis. Roman Catholic. Avocations: movies, racquetball. Home: 2615 Oak Leigh San Antonio TX 78232 E-mail: drfrbrooks@aol.com.

BROOKS, FREDERICK PHILLIPS, JR., computer scientist, educator; b. Durham, N.C., Apr. 19, 1931; s. Frederick Phillips and Octavia Brooks; m. Nancy Lee Greenwood, June 16, 1956; children: Kenneth Phillips, Roger Greenwood, Barbara Brooks LaDine. AB in Physics, Duke U., 1953; SM, Harvard U., 1955, PhD, 1956; D Tech. Sci. (hon.), ETH-Zurich, 1991. Engr. IBM, Poughkeepsie, NY, 1956—59, Yorktown Heights, NY, 1959—60, mgr. devel. computer System/360 Poughkeepsie, 1960—64, mgr. devel. Operating System/360, 1964—65; founder computer sci. dept. U. N.C., Chapel Hill, 1964, prof., 1964—75, chmn. dept. computer sci., 1964—84, Kenan prof., 1975—. Bd. dirs. Triangle U. Computation Ctr., 1966—84, chmn., 1975—77, N.C. Ednl. Computing Svc., 1965—; active Def. Sci. Bd., 1982—86, Nat. Sci. Bd., 1987—92. Author: The Mythical Man-Month-Essays on Software Engineering, 1975, 1995; author: (with K.E. Iverson) Automatic Data Processing, 1963, Automatic Data Processing System/360 Edition, 1969; author: (with G.A. Blaauw) Computer Architecture: Concepts and Evolution, 1997; contbr. articles to profl. jours.; inventor (with D.W. Sweeney) program interruption system, alphabetical read-out device. Trustee Durham Acad., pres., 1977—80; trustee Trinity Sch. Durham and Chapel Hill, 2003—; chmn. exec. com. Ctrl. Carolina Billy Graham Crusade, 1972—73; mem. corp. Inter-Varsity Christian Fellowship, 1968—77. Recipient McDowell award, IEEE Computer Soc., 1970, Man of Yr. award, Data Processing Mgmt. Assn., 1970, Nat. Medal Tech., 1985, Harry Goode Meml. award, Am. Fedn. Info. Proc. Socs., 1989, Bower award and prize for achievement in sci., Franklin Inst., 1975; fellow Guggenheim Found., 1975; grantee, NSF, AEC, NIH, NASA, Def. Advanced Projects Rsch. Agy. Fellow: IEEE (John von Neumann medal 1993), Brit. Computer Soc. (disting.), Assn. Computing Machinery (coun. mem.-at-large 1966—70, Disting. Svc. award 1987, Allen Newell award 1994, Alan M. Turing award 1999), Am. Acad. Arts and Scis.; mem.: NAE, NAS, Royal Acad. Engring. (U.K.), Royal Netherland Acad. Arts and Scis. Methodist. Home: 413 Granville Rd Chapel Hill NC 27514-2723 Office: Univ NC Dept Computer Sci Sitterson Hall CB# 3175 Chapel Hill NC 27599-3175 E-mail: brooks@cs.unc.edu.

BROOKS, (TROYAL) GARTH, country music singer; b. Tulsa, Okla., Feb. 7, 1962; s. Troyal Raymond and Colleen Carroll Brooks; m. Sandy Mahl, 1986; children: Taylor Mayne Pearl, August Anna;1 child, Allie Colleen. BS in Avtg. and Journalism, Okla. St. Univ., 1984. Recording artist (albums) Garth Brooks, No Fences (Album of Yr. Acad. Country Music, 1991), Ropin' The Wind, 1991, Beyond the Season, The Chase, 1992, In Pieces, 1993 (Grammy nomination, Best Country Male Vocal for Ain't Goin' Down (Til the Sun Comes Up), The Hits, 1994, Fresh Horses, 1995, Sevens, 1997, The Limited Series, Double Live, 1998, In the Life of Chris Gaines, 1999, Scarecrow, 2001, (songs) The Dance (Video of Yr. award Country Music Assn., 1991, Song of Yr. and Video of Yr. awards Acad. Country Music, 1991), Friends in Low Places (Single Record of Yr. Acad. Country Music, 1991, Grammy award nomination), If Tomorrow Never Comes (Am. Music award for Country Song of Yr., 1991), The Thunder Rolls, We Shall Be Free (Video of Yr., Acad. Country Music), Somewhere Other Than The Night, Learning to Live Again, (TV spls.) This is Garth Brooks, 1992, This is Garth Brooks, Too, 1994, (TV Spls.) Garth Brooks: The Hits, 1995, Garth Brooks Live in Central Park, 1997. Named Best Male Country Music Performer, 1992, 1993, Best Male Musical Performer, People's Choice Awards, 1992, 1993, 1994, Artist of Decade, Acad. Country Music Awards, 1999; named to Grand Ole Opry; recipient Entertainer of Yr. award Acad. Country Music, 1991, 1992, 1993, 1994, Male Vocalist of Yr. award, 1991, Horizon award, Entertainer of Yr. award, Country Music Assn., 1991, 1992, Grammy award for Best Male Country Vocalist, 1992, Grammy award for Best County Collaboration with Vocals, 1998, Best Male Musical Performer, People's Choice Awards, 1995, Am. Music Awards, Favorite Country Artist & Favorit Country Album, 2000.

BROOKS, GARY, management consultant; BS in Biochem. Engring. and Ind. Mgmt., MIT, 1955; MSChemE and Ops. Rsch., U. Rochester, 1959. Cert. mgmt. cons., turnaround profl. With GE Co., 1955-56, Eastman Kodak Co., 1956-64; mgr. Technomic Cons. Inc., 1968-71; divsn. exec. Scott Paper Co., 1971-76; mng. prin. turnaround cons. firm New Eng., 1976-85; founder, chmn., CEO, Allomet Ptnrs., Inc., corp. restructuring, N.Y.C., 1985—. Also expert in interim crisis mgmt., family bus. issues; former nat. chmn. Inst. Mgmt. Cons.; lectr. in field, including U. Mass., Amherst, L.I. U., U. Rochester. Contbr. articles to profl. jours. Mem.: Family Firm Inst., Am. Bankruptcy Inst., Assn. Cert. Turnaround Profls. (1st pres.), Turnaround Mgmt. Assn. (founding mem., former bd. dirs., chair certification com.). Office: Allomet Ptnrs Ltd 370 Lexington Ave Rm 2010 New York NY 10017-6503 E-mail: gb@allomet.com.

BROOKS, GENE (LESLIE GENE BROOKS), cultural association administrator; b. Fletcher, Oklahoma, June 15, 1936; s. Frank and Ethel E. (Spears) B.; m. Nancy E. (Carman), Aug. 17, 1970; 1 child, Steven Frank. B of Music edn., Okla. Bapt. U., 1959; M of Music edn., U. Okla., 1962, D of Music edn., 1968; post grad., U. Colo. Chmn. music dept. Cameron Univ., Lawton, Okla., 1962-69, Midwestern State Univ., Wichita Falls, Tex., 1969-75, U. Ark., Little Rock, 1975-77; exec. dir. Am. Choral Dir. Assn., Okla. City, 1977—. Sec. gen. Internat. Fedn. Choral Music, 1982-85; dir. numerous choral festivals and conventions; guest conductor, clinician, adjudicator, and spkr.; mem. juries 25th Internat. Choir Competition, Varna, Bulgaria; 38th Internat. Choral Competition, Gorizia, Italy, 1999, 2000; Nat. Choir Competition, New Zealand, 2000; 6th Internat. Choral Competition, Riva del Garda, Italy, 2000; World Choir Olympics, 2000, 2002; Linz, Austria, World Choir Olypmics Busan, South Korea, and numerous others. Recipient Disting. Alumni Award, Okla. Bapt. U., 1985; in music, 1996; Disting. Alumni Award, U. North Okla., 1997. Mem. Music Tchr. Nat. Assn. (chmn. music in higher edn. 1975-77, nat. choral chmn. 1972-75); Music Educators Nat. Conf. (life); Coll. Music Soc. (life); Am. Choral Dir. Assn. (life). Southern Baptist. Avocations: travel, snow. Home: 18816 Woody Creek Dr Edmond OK 73003-4108 Office: Am Choral Dir Assn PO Box 2720 Oklahoma City OK 73101

BROOKS, GILBERT GIL, association development director; s. John T. and Inis V. Brooks; m. Helen Kuhn, Apr. 7, 1950; children: Katrina Stone, Maria Milner. Bd. mem. Mountain State Press, Charleston, W.Va. Mem.: St. Albans Writers, W.Va. Writers, Inc., W.Va. U. Alumni (assoc.). Lutheran. Personal E-mail: wvawriter@att.net.

BROOKS, GLENN ELLIS, political science educator, educational administrator; b. Kerrville, Tex., Aug. 6, 1931; s. Glenn Ellis and Ellen (Mason) B.; m. Ann Rankin, May 31, 1953 (div. Apr. 1992); children: Elizabeth Lee, Amy Mason, Celia Brooks Brown. BA magna cum laude, U. Tex., Austin, 1953, MA, 1956; PhD with distinction, Johns Hopkins U., 1960. Sales mgr. Univ. Tex. Press, Austin, 1953-55; research assoc. Com. on Govt. and Higher Edn., Balt., 1957-59; instr. to prof. polit. sci. Colo. Coll., Colorado Springs, 1960-96, prof. emeritus, faculty asst. to pres., 1968-70, chmn. dept. polit. sci., 1973-76, dean of coll. and faculty, 1979-87, dir. strategic planning, 1991-93. Rockefeller vis. lectr. U. Nairobi, Kenya, 1967-68; acad. visitor London Sch. Econs., 1972; NEH faculty fellow-in-residence Princeton (N.J.) U., 1978-79; bd. dirs. Am. Conf. Acad. Deans, 1982-85; cons. Nat. U. Lesotho, 1990, Am. Coun. Edn. Miver Program, 1992—; chief of party Fenix project Autonomous U. Puebla, Mex., 1994-96. Author: When Governors Convene: The Governors' Conference and National Politics, 1961; (with Frances E. Rourke) The Managerial Revolution in Higher Education, 1966. Contbr. chpts. to books, articles, essays to profl. publs. Bd. dirs. Colo. Humanities Program, Boulder, 1975-78, Citizens Goals for Colorado Springs, 1977—; mem. Chmn.'s Nat. Adv. Com. on Humanities in Primary and Secondary Schs. NEH, 1987—. Mem. Am. Conf. Acad. Deans (bd. dirs. 1982-86), Phi Beta Kappa, Phi Eta Sigma. Democrat. Home: 526 Observatory Dr Colorado Springs CO 80904-3970 E-mail: gbrooks@coloradocollege.edu.

BROOKS, H. ALLEN, architectural educator, author, lecturer; b. New Haven, Nov. 6, 1925; s. Harold Allen and Mildred (McNeill) B. BA, Dartmouth Coll., 1950; MA, Yale U., 1955; PhD, Northwestern U., 1957; D Engring. (hon.), Dalhousie U., 1984. Asst. prof. U. Ill., 1957-58; lectr. U. Toronto, 1958-61, asst. prof., 1961-64, assoc. prof., 1964-71, prof., 1971-86; vis. prof. Dartmouth Coll., 1969; Mellon chair Vassar Coll., 1970-71; vis. prof. Archtl. Assn., London, 1977-82. Author: The Prairie School: Frank Lloyd Wright and His Midwest Contemporaries, 1972 (recipient Alice Davis Hitchcock Book award 1973), Frank Lloyd Wright and the Prairie School, 1984, Le Corbusier's Formative Years: Charles-Edouard Jeanneret at La Chaux-de-Fonds, 1997 (Assn. Am. Pubs./Scholarly Pub. Divsn. Ann. award 1997); editor: Prairie School Architecture, 1975, Writings on Wright, 1981, The Le Corbusier Archive, 32 vols, 1982-85, Le Corbusier, 1987; editl. cons. Le Corbusier Sketchbooks, 1981-82; contbr. to numerous books and jours. With U.S. Army, 1946-47. Guggenheim Found. fellow, 1973-74; Can. Coun. fellow, 1975-76; Social Scis. and Humanities Rsch. Coun. Can. fellow, 1977-79, 83-85; Victoria U. fellow; receipent Wright Spirit award, Frank Llyod Wright Bldg. Conservency, 2002. Fellow Soc. Archtl. Historians; mem. Internat. Coun. Mus., Internat. Com. Monuments and Sites, Soc. Archtl. Historians U.S. (past pres., dir.), Soc. Archtl. Historians Gt. Britain, Soc. Study Architecture Can., Frank Lloyd Wright Bldg. Conservancy. Address: 9 River Ridge Rd Hanover NH 03755-1910

BROOKS, HARVEY, physics educator; b. Cleve., Aug. 5, 1915; married, 1945; 4 children. AB, Yale U., 1937; PhD, Harvard U., 1940; DSc (hon.), Yale U., 1962, Union Coll., 1962, Harvard U., 1963, Kenyon Coll., 1963, Brown U., 1964. Mem. staff underwater sound lab. Harvard U., 1942-45; asst. dir. ord rsch. lab. Pa. State U., 1945; rsch. assoc. rsch. lab., assoc. lab. head. Knolls Atomic Power Lab. Gen. Electric Co., 1946-50; prof. applied physics Harvard U., Cambridge, Mass., 1950-86, prof. tech. and pub. policy, 1975-86, dean divsn. engring. and applied physics, 1957-75, Benjamin Peirce emeritus prof. tech. and pub. policy, 1986—, Gordon McKay emeritus prof. applied physics, 1986—. Chmn. com. undersea warfare NRC, 1957-63, chmn. commn. soc. tech. sys., 1975-78; mem. adv. com. reactor safeguards, programs and policies AEC, 1958; chmn. solid state adv. panel Office Naval Rsch.; mem. Pres.'s Sci. Adv. Com., 1959-64, Nat. Sci. Bd., 1962-74; mem. adv. com. sci. and technol. devel. UN, 1987-91. Author one book and numerous tech. publs.; editor-in-chief Jour. Physics and Chem. Solids, 1956-80. Recipient E.O. Lawrence award Am. Engring. Soc., 1960; Guggenheim fellow, 1956-57. Fellow AAAS (Philip Hauge Abelson award 1993), Am. Phys. Soc. (Forum award 1993); mem. NAS (sr. mem. inst. medicine, chmn. com. sci. and pub. policy 1966-72), Nat. Acad. Engring., Am. Philos. Soc., Am. Acad. Arts and Sci. (pres. 1970-73). Achievements include research on solid state physics, underwater sound, nuclear reactors, and science policy. Office: Harvard U JFK Sch Govt 79 Jfk St Cambridge MA 02138-5801 Home: 46 Brewster St Cambridge MA 02138 E-mail: hbrooks@mediaone.net., harvey_brooks@harvard.edu.

BROOKS, JACK BASCOM, former congressman; b. Crowley, La., Dec. 18, 1922; s. Edward Chachere and Grace Marie (Pipes) B.; m. Charlotte Collins, Dec. 15, 1960; children: Jack Edward, Katherine Inez, Kimberly Grace. AA, Lamar Jr. Coll., Beaumont, Tex., 1939-41; BJ, U. Tex., 1943, JD, 1949. Bar: Tex. 1949. Mem. Tex. Legislature, 1946-50, 83rd-89th Congresses from 2nd Tex. dist., 1952-67, 90th-103rd Congresses from 9th Tex. dist., Washington, 1967-95. Author, Lamar Coll. bill, 1949. Lst lt. USMCR, 1942-46; col. Res. ret. Mem. ABA, State Bar Tex., Am. Legion, VFW, Sigma Delta Chi. Home: 1029 East Dr Beaumont TX 77706-4738 Office: 3535 Calder Ave Beaumont TX 77706-5025

BROOKS, JAMES ELWOOD, geologist, educator; b. Salem, Ind., May 31, 1925; s. Elwood Edwin and Helen Mary (May) B.; m. Eleanore June Nystrom, June 18, 1949 (dec.); children: Nancy, Kathryn, Carolyn. AB, DePauw U., 1948; MS, Northwestern U., 1950; PhD, U. Wash., 1954. Research assoc. Ill. Geol. Survey, 1950; geologist Gulf Oil Corp., Salt Lake City, summers 1951-53; instr. geol. scis. So. Meth. U., Dallas, 1952-55, asst. prof., 1955-59, assoc. prof., 1959-62, prof., 1962-95, chmn. dept., 1961-70, dean, assoc. provost univ., 1969-72, provost, v.p., 1972-80, interim pres., 1980-81, prof. emeritus, 1995—, provost emeritus, 1995—; pres., trustee Inst. for Study Earth and Man, Dallas, 1981-97, vice chmn., trustee, 1997—, pres. emeritus. Chmn., trustee ISEM Found., Dallas, 2000—; cons. geologist firm DeGolyer & MacNaughton, Dallas, 1954-59. Contbr. articles to profl. jours. Trustee Hockaday Sch., 1982-88, Dallas Mus. Natural History Assn., 1984—, v.p., 1986-88, pres., 1988-90, hon. life trustee, 1990—; mem. exec. bd., internat. rep. Circle Ten coun. Boy Scouts Am., 1982—, internat. com., chmn. 1984—; bd. vis. DePauw U., 1979-83, chmn., 1983; mem. Mayor's Task Force on Fair Park, 1992; chmn. Coun. Fair Park Instns., 1992-94. Fellow AAAS, Geol. Soc. Am., Tex. Acad. Sci., Explorers Club; mem. Am. Assn. Petroleum Geologists, Dallas Geol. Soc., Sigma Xi, Sigma Gamma Epsilon, Sigma Phi. Home: 7055 Arboreal Dr Dallas TX 75231-7315 Office: Inst Study Earth and Man PO Box 750274 Dallas TX 75275-0274 E-mail: jebrooks@mail.smu.edu.

BROOKS, JAMES L. writer, director, producer; b. Bklyn., May 9, 1940; s. Edward M. and Dorothy Helen (Sheinheit) B.; m. Marianne Catherine Morrissey, July 7, 1964 (div.); 1 dau., Amy Lorraine; m. Holly Beth Holmberg, July 23, 1978; children: Chloe, Cooper. Student, N.Y. U., 1958-60. Writer CBS News, N.Y.C., 1964-66; writer-producer documentaries Wolper Prodns., L.A., 1966-67; founder & owner Gracie Films, 1984. Guest lectr. Stanford Grad. Sch. Communications. Creator TV series Room 222, 1968-69 (Emmy award for outstanding new series 1969); co-creator, producer TV series Lou Grant (Peabody award 1978); exec. producer, co-creator TV series Mary Tyler Moore Show, 1970-77 (Emmy award for comedy writing 1971, 74-77, Outstanding Comedy Series 1975-77, Peabody award, 1977, Writers Guild Am. winner best teleplay The Last Show, nominated best teleplay in episodic comedy, 1972, 77, TV Critics Achievement in Comedy award 1977, Achievement in Series award 1977, Humanitas 1977); writer, producer TV series Paul Sand in Friends and Lovers, 1974; co-creator, co-exec. producer TV series Rhoda show, 1974-75 (Emmy awards for outstanding writing in drama 1978-80, outstanding drama 1979, 80, 2 Humanitas for 1977, 82); writer TV show The New Lorenzo Music Show, 1976; co-writer, co-producer TV film Thursday Game, from 1971; co-creator, exec. producer TV series Taxi, 1978-80 (Emmy award for best show, best writing, 1978-79, 79-80, 80-81, TV Film Critics Circle award for achievement in comedy and in a series, 1976-77, Golden Globe awards for best comedy series, 1978, 79, 80, Humanitas prize for episode entitled Blind Date, 1979); co-exec. producer, co-writer TV series Cindy, 1978 (Writers Guild nomination for outstanding script 1978); co-creator, exec. producer TV series The Associates, 1979; exec. producer, co-exec. producer, co-creator The Tracey Ullman Show, 1986-90 (Emmy awards Outstanding Variety or Comedy series 1987, 88, 90, winner Emmy awards Outstanding Writing Variety or Music Show 1988-89), The Simpsons, 1990— (winner Emmy awards Outstanding Animated Spl., Outstanding Animated Program, winner Outstanding Animated Program); writer, co-producer film Starting Over (Writers Guild nomination for Best Screen Comedy Adaption 1979); actor film Modern Romance, 1981; producer, writer, dir. film Terms of Endearment, 1983 (Gloden Globe Best Screenplay award 1983, Acad. awards for best film, best dir., best screenplay 1984, Best Dir. award Dirs. Guild Am. 1983, winner comedy based on material from another medium, 1983, Nat. Bd. Rev. Best Picture, 1983, Golden Globe award Best Picture 1983, N.Y. Film Critics Best Picture; writer, dir., producer film Broadcast News, 1987 (winner best picture, best. dir., best screenplay N.Y. Film Critics Awards, Dirs. Guild nomination for best dir., Acad. award nomination for Best Picture and Best Screenplay); exec. producer film Big, 1988 (Peoples Choice award for favorite comedy motion picture), The War of the Roses, 1989, Say Anything, 1989; exec. producer (TV series) The Critic, 1994, What About Joan, 2001; writer, co-prodr. I'll Do Anything, 1994; dir. (play) Bklyn. Laundry; prodr. Bottle Rocket, 1996, Jerry Maguire, 1996, As Good As It Gets, 1997, Riding in Cars with Boys, 2001. Mem. Dirs. Guild Am., Writers Guild Am., TV Acad. Arts and Scis., Screen Actors Guild, Acad. Motion Picture Arts and Scis. Office: Gracie Films/Columbia Pictures/Sony Pictures Ent Poitier Bldg 10202 Washington Blvd Culver City CA 90232-3119

BROOKS, JEAN EVELYN, social work educator; b. Bklyn., Nov. 29, 1947; d. Alexander G. and Ruth E. (Van Hise) Dingwall; m. James Brooks, Aug. 19, 1972; children: James, Anne, Carolyn. BA, Earlham Coll., 1969; MSW, U. Mich., 1971. Lic. cert. social worker, Miss. Fund raising asst. Planned Parenthood, Detroit, 1971-72, sr. counselor Washington, 1976-79; instr. social work Jackson (Miss.) State U., 1972-76, 79-80, asst. prof. social work, 1980—. Author curriculum Communicating Family Values, 1987. Bd. dirs. YWCA, Jackson, 1987-92; mem. cmty. adv. bd. Jackson Med. Mall, 1998-. Mem. NASW, Acad. Cert. Social Workers, Coun. Social Work Edn., Miss. Conf. on Social Welfare. Office: Jackson State Univ PO Box 18740 Jackson MS 39217

BROOKS, JEROME BERNARD, English and Afro-American literature educator; b. Houston, Mar. 20, 1932; s. Osburn Bernard and Agnes (Harrison) B. BA, Holy Cross Sem., Chgo., 1956, MA, 1960, Notre Dame U., 1962; PhD, U. Chgo., 1972. Instr. English Holy Cross Sem., 1962-66; lectr. English CCNY, 1968-72, asst. prof., 1972-75, assoc. prof., 1985-90, prof., 1991-95, chmn. dept. English, 1985-88, acting dean U. Affairs, 1988-89, dep. to the pres., 1991-95, prof. emeritus, 1996—. Cons. NEH, Washington, 1985, U. Mo. Press, Columbia, 1986; bd. dirs. N.Y. Alliance for Pub. Schs., Transp. Rsch. Consortium, Rice H.S.; vis. prof. English, Bard. Coll., Annandale-on-Hudson, N.Y. Author: Black Women Writers 1950-80, 1984; contbr. World Authors Encyclopedia, 1986, The Paris Review, 1994; co-editor Continuities mag., 1973-76. NEH grantee, 1979; named Fulbright Sr. Lectr. at U. Madagascar, USIA, 1976-78. Mem.: Princeton Club, Univ. Club of Chgo. Democrat. Roman Catholic. Avocation: play classical piano. Office: CUNY Dept English 138th St and Convent Ave New York NY 10031 E-mail: jbrooksx@msn.com.

BROOKS, JERRY CLAUDE, safety engineer, educator; b. College Park, Ga., Apr. 23, 1936; s. John Bennett and Mattie Mae (Timms) B.; m. Peggy Sue Thornton, Feb. 26, 1961; children: Apryll Denise, Jerry Claude, Susan Vereen. BS, Ga. Inst. Tech., 1958. Safety engr. Cotton Prodrs. Assn., Atlanta, 1959-64, dir. safety and loss control, 1964-70; dir. corp. protection Gold Kist, Inc., Atlanta, 1970-81; dir. corp. safety J.P. Stevens, 1981-84, dir. safety and security, 1984-86, dir. health and safety, 1986-88; dir. loss control Am. Yarn Spinners Assn., 1988-89; dir. safety Spring Industries, Inc., 1989-2000; cons. Occupational Safety Cons., 2000—. Instr., Ga. Safety Inst., Athens, Ga., 1971-78. Bd. dirs. Greater Lithonia (Ga.) Homeowners Assn., Ga. Soc. Prevention of Blindness, Ga. Safety Coun. Served with AUS, 1958-59. Mem. Am. Soc. Safety Engrs. (chpt. pres. 1968-69, regional v.p. 1974-76), Nat. Safety Coun. (gen. chmn. fertilizer sect. 1969-70, gen. chmn. textile sec. 1985-87, Disting. Svc. to Safety award 1989, Palmetto chpt. pres. 1994), So. Safety Conf. (v.p. bus. and

industry 1968-74, pres. 1974), Am. Textile Mfrs. Inst. (chmn. safety and health com. 1991-93, Donald B. Hayes lifetime achievement award 2000), Am. Soc. Indsl. Security, S.C. Occupl. Safety Coun. (bd. mem. 1994-99), Ga. Bus. and Industry Assn. (dir., named outstanding mem. 1981), Internat. Assn. Hazard Control Mgrs. (chpt. pres. 1979-80), Masons, Rosicrucians, Exch. Club (pres. 1969-70, Book of Golden Deeds award 1981) (Lithonia). Home: 100 Woodmere Ln Columbus NC 28722-4408 E-mail: jbrooks@aol.com.

BROOKS, JERRY ROBERT, small business owner; b. Gainesville, Tex., Dec. 28, 1925; s. Clay Younger and Mary Irene (Simmons) Brooks. BS in Econs., U. North Tex., 1948, MS in Econs., 1950. Lic. pvt. pilot 1946. Tool designer Nat. Supply divsn. ARMCO Stl., Inc., Gainesville, Tex., 1955—82; owner, mgr. Brooks Engring. Co., Gainesville, 1982—. Contbr. Mem. Gainesville Arts Coun., 1981—84. With USAAF, 1944—45. Recipient Internat. award merit, 1st Internat. Inventors Exhbns., 1965, 2d Internat. Inventors Exhbns., 1966, Gold Medal award, 3d Internat. Inventors Exhbns., 1967, Bronze medal, 20th Internat. Exhbn. New Inventions and Products, 1971. Mem.: AIAA, Planetary Soc., Nat. Space Soc. Achievements include nine patents in diverse fields. Avocation: musician (play trumpet). Home: 1716 Merrywood Way Gainesville TX 76240-5142 Office: Brooks Engring Co 921 N Grand Ave Gainesville TX 76240

BROOKS, JOAE GRAHAM, psychiatrist; b. Boston, June 14, 1926; d. Collins and Hannah Slade (Benton) Graham; m. Bernard Charles Brooks, Jan. 11, 1976; children by previous marriage: Anne Benton Millman, Jane Graham Selzer. Nursing degree, Mass. Gen. Hosp. Sch. Nursing, 1947; AB with distinction, U. Rochester, 1950, MD, 1954. Diplomate Am. Bd. Psychiatry and Neurology. Intern in medicine Duke Hosp., Durham, N.C., 1954-55; resident in psychiatry Mass. Mental Health Ctr., Boston, 1955-57; resident in child psychiatry Beth Israel Hosp., Boston, 1957-59, mem. staff, 1959-97; pvt. practice Brookline, Mass., 1959-97. Cons. New Eng. Home for Little Wanderers, Boston, 1959-75, Kimberly Clark Corp., 1983-97; asst. clin. prof. psychiatry Harvard U. Med. Sch., Boston, 1978-97; vol. psychiatrist Sr. Friendship Ctr. Health Clinic, Naples, Fla., 1998—; mem. Bd. Registration in Medicine of Mass., 1991-95. Author: No More Diapers! A Guide to Toilet Training, 1971, 2d edit., 1991, When Children Ask About Sex-A Guide for Parents, 1975, I'm A Big Kid Now! A Guide to Toilet Training for Children and Parents, 1989. Distinguished fellow APA (life), Acad. Child and Adolescent Psychiatry (life); mem. Mass. Psychiat. Soc., New Eng. Coun. Child Psychiatry (bd. dirs. 1979-82, pres. 1987-89). Home: 5950 Almaden Dr Naples FL 34119-4627

BROOKS, JOHN EDWARD, college president emeritus; b. Boston, July 13, 1923; s. John Edward and Mildred (McCoy) B. BS in Physics, Coll. Holy Cross, 1949; postgrad. in geophysics, Pa. State U., 1949-50; MA in Philosophy, Boston Coll., 1954, MS in Geophysics, 1959; S.T.D. in Dogmatic Theology, Gregorian U., Rome, Italy, 1963; H.H.D. (hon.), St. Ambrose Coll., 1976; D.Sc. (hon.), Worcester Poly. Inst., 1980; D Humanities, Assumption Coll., 1990; HHD (hon.), St. Anselm Coll., 1993; D Humanities (hon.), U. New England, 1994, Anna Maria Coll., 1994, Coll. of the Holy Cross, 1994. Joined Soc. of Jesus, 1950; ordained priest Roman Catholic Ch., 1959; instr. math. and physics Coll. of Holy Cross, Worcester, Mass., 1954-56, instr. theology, 1963-64, asst. prof., 1964-67, assoc. prof. religious studies, 1967-93, chmn. dept. theology, 1964-69, Loyola prof. humanities, 1993—, v.p., dean coll., 1968-70, pres., trustee, 1970-94, pres. emeritus, 1994—, sec. com. ednl. policy, 1968-70, chmn., 1970-94. Participant bibl. and archeol. consortium Jewish Inst. on Religion, Hebrew Union Coll., 1968; inst. acad. deans Am. Coun. Edn., St. Louis U., 1968; trustee St. Peter's Coll., Jersey City, 1969-75, Canisius Coll., Buffalo, 1974-80, Spring Hill Coll., Mobile, Ala., 1981-94, Anna Maria Coll., Paxton, Mass., 1998—; mem. Mass. Postsecondary Edn. Commn., Mass. 1202 Commn., 1974-77; mem. exec. com. New Eng. Colls. Fund, 1974, 78; mem. Mass. Pub./Pvt. Forum; mem. Worcester Downtown Devel. Corp., Mass. Biotech. Rsch. Inst., 1985—; bd. visitors Air U., 1978-86; bd. dirs. Worcester Mcpl. Rsch. Bur., Inc. Community trustee United Way Cen. Mass.; consortium dir. Social Svcs. Corp., Worcester; bd. dirs. Worcester Mechanics Hall Assn.; mem. commn. govtl. rels. Am. Coun. on Edn., 1989-92. With U.S. Army, 1942-46. Mem. Assn. Jesuit Colls. and Univs. (bd. dirs. 1970-94), Assn. Ind. Colls. and Univs. in Mass. (v.p. 1972-73, chmn. coms., exec. com.), New Eng. Assn. Schs. and Colls. (sec.-treas. 1985-92, pres.-elect 1993, pres. 1994), Econ. Club (pres. Worcester chpt. 1977-78, exec. com. 1978-86), Delta Epsilon Sigma, Alpha Sigma Nu. Office: Coll of Holy Cross Ciampi Hall Worcester MA 01610 E-mail: jbrooks@holycross.edu.

BROOKS, JOHN SAMUEL JOSEPH, pathologist, researcher; b. Phila., Feb. 2, 1948; BS in Biology, St. Joseph's Coll., Phila., 1970; MD, Thomas Jefferson U., 1974. Diplomate Am. Bd. Pathology. Resident in pathology U. Pa., Phila., 1974-78, chief resident, 1978, asst. prof., 1979-84, assoc. prof., 1984-88, prof., 1988-93; chmn. dept. pathology Roswell Pk. Cancer Inst., Buffalo, 1993—2002, chmn. dept. lab. medicine, 1997—2002, pres. med. staff, 1997-98; prof., vice chmn. pathology Med. Sch. SUNY, Buffalo, 1993—2002; prof. pathology U. Pa., 2002—. Vis. prof. Royal Marsden Hosp./Inst. Cancer Rsch., London, 1987; expert in immunohistochemistry. Author: Pathology, 1989; contbr. articles to New Eng. Jour. Medicine, Jour. of AMA, Jour. Urology, Internat. Jour. Ob.-Gyn. Pathology, Am. Jour. Pathology; editor Internat. Jour. Surg. Pathology, 1993-99; mem. bd. editors: Jour. Modern Pathology, Am. Jour. Surg. Pathology, and reviewer; contbr. over 140 articles to profl. jours. Fellow Royal Coll. Pathology; mem. AAAS, Am. Assn. Cancer Rsch., Pathology Soc. Phila. (pres. 1988-90), Ea. Coop. Oncology Group (chmn. sarcoma pathology com. Madison chpt. 1988-95), Internat. Acad. Pathology (edn. com. Atlanta chpt. 1989—), U.S.-Can. Acad. Pathology (coun. mem. 1993-96), Am. Soc. Clin. Pathologists (chair anat. pathology coun. 1995-97, dep. commr. 1997—, bd. dirs. 2000—), Arthur Purdy Stout Soc. for Surg. Pathologists (coun. mem. 1994), Am. Assn. Clin. Rsch., Fedn. Am. Soc. for Exptl. Biology, Medicine Coverage Adv. Com. Lab. Diagnostics Panel, Nat. Internat. Reputation in Diagnostic Surg. Pathology. Democrat. Roman Catholic. Achievements include research in significance of double phenotypes in sarcomas, growth factors in sarcomas, in immunohistochemistry; posthumous diagnosis of Pres. Cleveland's tumor. Home: 52 Mattson Rd Boothwyn PA 19061 Office: Surgical Pathology 6 Founders Hosp Univ Pa 34th and Spruce Sts Philadelphia PA 19104 E-mail: john.brooks@uphs.upenn.edu.

BROOKS, JOHN WHITE, lawyer; b. Long Beach, Calif., Sept. 3, 1936; s. John White and Florence Belle (O'Grady) B.; m. Elizabeth Ann Bellmore, June 21, 1958; children: Stephen Sanford, John Tinley. AB, Stanford U., 1958, LLB, 1966. Assoc. Luce, Forward, Hamilton and Scripps, San Diego, 1966-71, ptnr., 1971-81, sr. ptnr., 1981—; founding chmn. Internat. Svcs. Group, 1989—. Mem. Internat. Coun. Inst. Ams., Pacific Coun. Internat. Policy. 1996-98; panelist Ctr. for Internat. Comml. Arbitration, 1987—; bd. dirs. Union of Pan-Asian Communities, 1989-98, Ctr. for Dispute Resolution, 1986—; chmn. Pacific Rim Adv. Coun., 1984-91. Author: Passport Pal, The Pacific Rim, 1996—, The Heads Up Report; contbr. articles to profl. jours. Mem. Commn. of the Californias, 1977—79; chmn. San Diego Regional Yr. 2000 Working Group, 1998—2000; dir. Corp. Fin. Coun. of San Diego, 1977—82, chmn., 1980—81; bd. visitors Stanford Law Sch., 1978—80. With USN, 1958—63. Named Alfred P. Sloan scholar Stanford U., 1958, Rocky Mountain Mineral Law Found. Research scholar, 1966. Mem. ABA (bus. law sect., com. on internat. commercial transactions, subcom. on Asia-Pacific law and internat. bus. structures and agreements, com. on negotiated transactions, internat. law sect., subcom. on multinat. corps., com. on internat. comml. transactions), Calif. Bar Assn. (bus. law sect. com. on corps. 1977, vice chmn. com. on internat. practice 1986-87, exec. com. internat. law sect. 1987), San Diego County Bar Assn., Internat. Bar Assn. (com. on issues and trading in securities 1980-89, com. on procedures for settling disputes 1980—, com. on bus. orgns. 1989—), Inter-Pacific Bar Assn. (com. on internat. trade), Am. Arbitration Assn. (panel of arbitrators 1975-96), State Bar Calif. Avocations: greenhouse gardening, horse competitions, helicopters, wine, food. Office: Luce Forward Hamilton & Scripps 600 W Broadway Ste 2600 San Diego CA 92101-3372 E-mail: jwbrooks@luce.com.

BROOKS, JOSEPH FRANKLIN, real estate executive; b. Florala, Ala., Dec. 22, 1938; s. John William Brooks and Lattie Mae Kennedy Brooks Street; m. Annette D. Brooks, Feb. 25, 1967 (div. July 1996); children: William T., Robert D., Daniel J. BSBA, Auburn (Ala.) U., 1961. Realtor, 1966—; owner, pres. Joe Brooks Realty, Pensacola, Fla., 1972—; assoc. pastor Beulah Bapt. Ch., Pensacola, Fla. Adj. prof. real estate St. Leo Coll., Pensacola, 1970-72. Contbr. articles to profl. jour. V.p., trustee Tom Cox Evangelistic Assn., Inc., 2000-02. Lt. USN, 1961-66. Recipient Presdl. award of Honor Jaycee's, 1972, Cert. of Appreciation, 1980, Cert. of Appreciation Optimists Club, 1975-76, Disting. Svc. award United Way, 1977, Employee's Award of Excellence, 1977, 78, Cert. of Apreciation Children's Home Soc., 1981, Bellview Lion's Club, 1988, Boy Scouts Am, 1988, Cert. of Appreciation Scenic Hills Lion's Club, 1994, Internat. Mission Bd. So. Bapt. Conv., 2000—. Mem. Nat. Assn. of Realtos, Fla. Assn. of Realtors, Pensacola Assn. of Realtors (life, pres. 1976, Realtor of Yr. 1977, Golden R award 1996, Recognition as Mediation Chmn. 1989), Gulf Breeze Rotary, Pensacola Assn. of Realtors Found, Nat. Assn. of Home Builders, North Pensacola Optimist Club, Children's Home Soc. of Fla. (bd. dir., pres. western divsn.), Phi Beta Lambda (Lambda Cert. Appreciation). Republican. Baptist. Avocations: preaching, teaching bible, tennis. Home: 4054 Sandy Bluff Dr W Gulf Breeze FL 32563-2938 Office: 985 Rock Island Pl Pensacola FL 32505-2417

BROOKS, KARL BOYD, historian; b. Boise, Idaho, Aug. 23, 1956; s. Monte M. and Martha M. Brooks; m. Kathy Perkins, June 11, 1983 (div. Feb. 1, 2003); children: Jennifer, Dylan. PhD, Univ. of Kans., Lawrnece, Kans., 2000; JD, Harvard Law Sch., Cambridge, Mass., 1983; MS, London Sch. of Econ., London, Eng., 1980; BA, Yale Univ., New Haven, Conn., 1978. Bar: Idaho 1983, US Supreme Ct. 2001. Asst. prof. Univ. of Kans., Lawrence, Kans., 2000; program, exec. & Legis. dir. Idaho Conservation League, Boise, Idaho, 1993—96; assoc. Holland Chart, Boise, Idaho, 1990—93; assoc. gen. coun. Boise Cascade Corp., Boise, Idaho, 1983—90. Trustee Idaho Endowment Fund Invest. Bd., 1987—91, Boise State Univ. Found., 1990—94. Author: (articles) High Country News, 1998, Western Legal Hist., 1999, Idaho Yesterdays, 2001—02: Senator Idaho Senate, Boise, Idaho, 1986—92; pres. Meml. Stadium, Inc., Boise, Idaho, 1988—96; chair Prog. Lawrence Campaign, Lawrence, Kans., 2002—03. Recipient George C. Marshall Scholar, Marshall Commn./London, Eng., 1978—80; fellow Supreme Ct. Fellow, US Supreme Ct./ Wash., DC, 2001—02. Mem.: Idaho Conservation League (leader 1992), Am. Soc. for Environ. Hist., Org. of Am. Hist., Soc. of Self Fellows (pres. 2003—). Home: 440 Rock Fence Ct Lawrence KS 66049

BROOKS, KATHLEEN, journalist; b. Atlanta, Jan. 25, 1957; d. William Chesley and Sara (Brooks) Howton. BA, Stephens Coll., Columbia, Mo., 1978. Mktg. asst. The Laitram Corp., New Orleans, 1978-79; reporter Daily Home, Talladega, Ala., 1979-80, copy editor, 1980-81; asst. wire editor, reporter Gastonia (N.C.) Gazette, 1981, wire editor, 1981-84; asst. wire editor Comml. Appeal, Memphis, 1984-88, Washington editor, 1988-91, nat. editor, 1991—. Methodist. Office: The Comml Appeal 495 Union Ave Memphis TN 38103-3221 E-mail: brooks@gomemphis.com.

BROOKS, KEITH, retired speech communication educator; b. Tigerton, Wis., May 14, 1923; s. Oscar Derby and Henrietta (Mierswa) B.; m. Laquata Sue Walters, Dec. 29, 1951; children: Todd Randall, Craig William. BS, MS, U. Wis., 1949; PhD, Ohio State U., 1955. Mem. faculty Eastern Ky. State U., Richmond, 1949-53, Ohio State U., Columbus, 1953-87, prof. communication, 1968-87, prof. emeritus, 1987—, chmn. dept., 1968-75. Comms. cons. Procter & Gamble, Ohio Bd. Regents, Mead World Hdqs., U.S. Dept. Agr., Ohio Bell Telephone, Ea. R.R. Assn., Shaw U., Raleigh, N.C. Author: (with Bahn and Okey) Literature for Listening, 1968, The Communicative Act of Oral Interpretation, 1967, 2d edit., 1975, The Communicative Arts and Sciences of Speech, 1967, (with Dietrich) Practical Speaking, 1969. With USNR, 1945-46. Mem. Speech Communication Assn. (chmn. interpretation div., vice chmn., sec.), Internat. Communication Assn. (co-editor Newsletter 1979-80), Cen. States Speech Assn. (editor Jour. 1958-61), Am. Ednl. Theatre Assn. (bd. dir. 1958-60) Home: 364 Stonewall Ct Dublin OH 43017-1333 *The most important attribute of all is taking the time to care.*

BROOKS, KENNETH N. forestry educator; m. Pamela Naylor; children: Marianne, Robin, Cherie, Nicole. BS in Range Sci., Utah State U., 1966; MS in Watershed Mgmt., U. Ariz., 1969, PhD in Watershed Mgmt., 1970. Hydrologist North Pacific Divsn. Corps of Engrs., Portland, Oreg., 1971-73, Tng. and Methods br. Hydrologic Engring. Ctr., Davis, Calif., 1973-75; asst. prof. dept. forest resources U. Minn., St. Paul, 1975-79, assoc. prof., 1979-85, prof., 1985—, dir. grad. studies in nat. resources and mgmt., 1987—; fellow Environment and Policy Inst. East-West Ctr., Honolulu, 1983-84. Cons. nat. and internat. agencies and firms including Food and Agrl. Orgn. of UN, U.S. Agy. for Internat. Devel., World Bank; condr. workshops in field; Fulbright lectr., Taiwan, 1997-98. Co-author: Guidelines for Economic Appraisal of Watershed Management Projects, 1987, Watershed Management Project Planning, Monitoring and Evaluation: A Manual for the ASEAN Region, 1989, Hydrology and the Management of Watersheds, 1991, 3d edit. 2003, Challenges in Upland Conservation: Asia and the Pacific, 1993, Dryland Forestry, 1995; contbr. articles to profl. jours. Am. Inst. Hydrology (chmn. bd. registration 1995-2003, sec. 1992), Soc. Am. Foresters (chmn. water resources working group 1991-93), Am. Water Resources Assn. (dir. West North Ctrl. dist. 1987-90), Western Snow Conf., Internat. Soc. Tropical Foresters, Xi Sigma Pi, Sigma Xi, Phi Kappa Phi. E-mail: kbrooks@umn.edu.

BROOKS, KEVIN T. entrepreneur, educator; s. Paul N. Brooks, Jr. and Dynetta S. Brooks. BS, Mars Hill Coll., 1996—2000. Phys. edn. tchr. Westwood Mid. Sch., Danville, Va., 2000—; program supr. Danville Parks, Recreation & Tourism, Danville, Va., 2000—03. Personal trainer, Danville, Va., 2000—. Author: (book of poetry) Soul Of A Poet, 2003. Avocations: writing, weightlifting, track & field, football, basketball. Home: 384 Seminole Trail Danville VA 24540 Office: Aapecs 384 Seminole Trail Danville VA 24540 Personal E-mail: kpassion@gamewood.net.

BROOKS, LARRY ROGER, judge; b. Oklahoma City, Mar. 8, 1949; s. Stanley James and Dorothy Marguerite (Miller) B.; m. Rebecca Jean Nix, June 5, 1971. BS in Agronomy, Okla. State U., 1971, MS in Agronomy, 1973; JD, U. Okla., 1976. Bar: Okla. 1976. Pvt. practice law, Idabel, Okla., 1977; asst. dist. atty. Craig County Dist. Attys. Office, Vinita, Okla., 1978, Logan County Dist. Attys. Office, Guthrie, Okla., 1979-94; assoc. judge Dist. Ct., Logan County, Okla., 1995—. Ch. bd. mem. Guthrie (Okla.) Ch. of the Nazarene. Mem. Okla. Bar Assn., Guthrie Lions Club (pres. 1991-92), Train Collectors Assn., Nat. Ry. Hist. Soc. Avocations: toy train and railroad memorabilia, railroad history, riding trains. Home: 324 N Capitol St Guthrie OK 73044-3640 Office: Assoc Dist Judge Logan County Courthouse Guthrie OK 73044

BROOKS, LILLIAN DRILLING ASHTON (LILLIAN HAZEL CHURCH), adult education educator; b. Grand Rapids, Mich., May 27, 1921; d. Walter Brian and Lillian Church; m. Frederick Morris Drilling, 1942 (div. Apr. 1972); children: Frederick Walter, Stephen Charles, Lawrence Alan, Lynn Anne; m. Richard Moreton Ashton, Aug. 25, 1973 (dec. 1990); m. Ralph J. Brooks, May 21, 1994. Student, Grand Rapids Jr. Coll., 1939-41, Wayne State U., 1941-42, Grand Rapids Art Inst., 1945-49, UCLA, 1964-69, Loyola Marymount Coll., Westchester, Calif., 1970-73; life tchg. credential, U. So. Calif., Long Beach, 1973. Life teaching credential, Calif. Decorator John Widdicomb Furniture Co., 1945-49; tchr. art Inglewood (Calif.) Sch. Dist., 1965-73; tchr. adult edn. art Downey (Calif.) Unified Sch. Dist., 1973-95; tchr. art Assn. Retarded Citizens and Mentally Disadvantaged Students Downey Cmty. Health Ctr., 2001—02. Art tchr. institutionalized adults ages 18 to 60, 2000—; lectr. Downey Art League, 1990-92, Whittier (Calif.) Art Assn., 1991, h.s. and mid. sch. lectr., 1994-95; judge Children's Art Exhibit, Downey, 1992; participant Getty Found., San Francisco, 1993, Getty Found., Cranbrook, 1994, Getty Conf. on Aesthetics, 1995, Cin. U., 1992, El Segundo, 1994; mem. state accreditation com. Inglewood and Downey United Sch. Dists., 1966-70, 75-80, 85—; owner A & B Furniture Svc. Ctr., 1995—. One-woman shows include El Segundo Mcpl. Libr., 1965, Pico Rivera Art Gallery, 1978, Downey Art Mus., 1999; exhibited in group shows at Fairlane Show, Dearborn, Mich., 1959, Jane Lessing Art Gallery, 1966, Westchester Mcpl. Libr., 1971, Inglewood City Hall, 1973, Aegina Sch., Greece, 1973, Downey Mus. Art, 1992, 99-2000; represented in permanent collection U. Mich., Calif. Senate Bldg. Pres. bd. dirs. Downey Art Mus., 1996-2002, dir. Mus., 1998, vol. dir., 1999, bd. dirs. 1998-2000; art commr. City of Dearborn, Mich., 1954-59; former pres. Dearborn Art Inst., Pacific Art Guild; pres. Downey Art League, 1991-94, v.p., 1999-2000; pres. Exhbn. Ch., 1995, v.p. 1996-98; vol. dir. Art Mus., 1998-99; lectr. on art as a career local Downey high and mid. schs.; juried children's art shows; vol. tchr. basic art; judge art shows. Recipient Certs. of Appreciation for contbn. of leadership Coord. Coun. Downey, Downey Governing Bd., Downey Bd. Edn., 1997, 2002, Cmty. Svc. award for Outstanding Svc. Downey Rotary, 1994, Cert. of Recognition Calif. State Assembly, 1999, Downey Coord. Coun., 1998-99, award 2002; named Tchr. of Yr., Masons, Downey, 1986; painting chosen to represent dist. in state capital, 1999-2001. Mem. Calif. Coun. on Art Edn. (parliamentarian Downey 1990-92, Calco Excellence in Tchg. award 1991, various certs.). Avocations: reading, hiking, internat. travel, photography, painting. Home: 9318 Fostoria St Downey CA 90241-4020

BROOKS, LINTON FORRESTALL, federal agency administrator; b. Boston, Aug. 15, 1938; m. Barbara Julius; children: Julie, Kathryn. BS in Physics, Duke U., 1959; MA in Govt. and Politics, U. Md., 1972; disting. grad., USN War Coll., 1979. Commd. USN, advanced through grades to capt.; dir. arms control NSC, 1984—89; dep. head del., amb.; head U.S. del. on nuc. and space talks, chief strategic arms reductions negotiator State Dept.; asst. dir. strategic and nuc. affairs U.S. Arms Control and Disarmament Agy.; v.p., asst. to Pres. for policy analysis Ctr. Naval Analyses, Alexandria, Va., 1993—2001; dep. adminstr. def. nuc. nonproliferation Dept. Energy, Washington, 2001—02; acting under sec. of energy for nuclear security, acting adminstr. Nat. Nuclear Security Admin., Dept. of Energy, 2002—03, under sec. of energy for nuclear security, adminstr., 2003—. Cons. strategic arms reductions Clinton Adminstrn. Contbr. articles to profl. jours. Mem.: Phi Beta Kappa. Office: Forrestal Bldg 1000 Independence Ave SW Rm 7A-199 Washington DC 20585*

BROOKS, LITHIA ESTHER, finance executive; b. Troy, N.C., Nov. 2, 1951; d. Tom Stewart and Anne Grace (Ward) Brooks; 1 child, Leslie Grace Hahn. AS in Bus. Adminstrn. Acctg., Wingate U., 1972; BS in Bus. Adminstrn., Mt. Olive Coll., 1999. Cert. govtl. acctg. and fin. reporting, county adminstrn., acctg. and fiscal control, budgeting and fin. planning, effective mgmt.; cert. local govtl. fin. officer. Fin. officer Stanly County, Albemarle, N.C., 1972-86; dir. fiscal ops. Brunswick County, Bolivia, N.C., 1986—. Participant in numerous confs. Chmn. bd. dirs. Hope Harbor Home, Inc.; chmn. Criminal Justice Partnership Adv. Bd.; mem., budget officer Southeastern Mental Health Bd. Dirs. Named N.C. Outstanding Fin. Officer, 1991-92. Mem. Govt. Fin. Officers Assn., N.C. Assn. County Finance Officers (sec.-treas. 1988-89, 2nd v.p. 1989-90, 1st v.p. 1990-91, pres. 1991-92, chmn. legis. com. 1992-93, mem. nominating com. 1994—, mem. auditing com.), N.C. Cash Mgmt. Trust (chmn. adv. bd. 1987-88), NAFE, Nat. Assn. County Fin. Officers and Treasurers, Carolinas Assn. Govt. Purchasers. Home: PO Box 249 Bolivia NC 28422-0249

BROOKS, LORIMER PAGE, patent lawyer; b. Swampscott, Mass., May 11, 1917; s. William Lorimer and Maude (Page) B.; m. Arlene M. Cook, Nov. 9, 1941; children: Lorraine E. Brooks Phillips, Jr., Rosalind P. Brooks O'Malley. BS in elec. engring. with honors, Northeastern U., 1939; JD, Fordham U., 1948; postgrad., NYU Law Sch., 1951. Bar: N.Y. 1948, U.S. Dist. Ct. (so. dist.) N.Y. 1952, U.S. Dist. Ct. (ea. dist.) N.Y. 1957, U.S. Ct. Appeals (2d cir.) 1964, U.S. Dist. Ct. (we. dist.) N.Y. 1971, U.S. Supreme Ct. 1971, U.S. Ct. Appeals (fed. cir.) 1982. Patent agt. ITT, 1939-41, patent atty., 1945-50, Ward, Crosby, & Neal, N.Y.C., 1950-54; ptnr. firm Ward, McElhannon, Brooks & Fitzpartrick, N.Y.C., 1954-71, Brooks, Haidt, Haffner & Delahunty, N.Y.C., 1971-98; ptnr. Norris McLaughlin & Marcus, PA, N.Y.C., 1998—. Rep. Nat. Council Patent Law Assns., 1976-77. Patentee in field. Sec. Westchester Park Citizens Assn., 1950-52, pres., 1952-54; dir. Westchester County Cerebral Palsy Assn., 1962-64; mem. Young Men's Republican Club Eastchester, N.Y., 1952-56. Served with AUS, 1941-45. Mem. Westchester County Bar Assn. (ethics com. 1978-86), N.Y. Patent Law Assn. (bd. govs. 1961-64, 74-78, chmn. subcom. practice and procedure in cts. 1961-62, chmn. com. ethics and grievances 1973-74, 1st v.p. 1974-75, pres. 1975-76, past pres. com. 1976—), IEEE, Aircraft Owners and Pilots Assn., Tau Beta Pi. Home: 6 Hyatt Rd Briarcliff Manor NY 10510-2610 Office: Norris McLaughlin and Marcus 220 East 42nd St New York NY 10017

BROOKS, LORRAINE ELIZABETH, retired music educator; b. Port Chester, N.Y., Mar. 10, 1936; d. William Henry Brooks and Marion Elizabeth Brooks. BS in Music Edn., SUNY, Potsdam, 1958; M of Performance, Manhattan Sch. Music, 1970; cert. in Religion EPS, Trinity Coll., 2000. Dir. Camp Spruce-Mountain Lakes, North Salem, N.Y., 1964-73; youth adviser St. Peter's Episcopal Ch., Port Chester, N.Y., 1964-65, St. Andrew's-St. Peter's Ch., Yonkers, N.Y., 1970-73; v.p. South Yonkers Youth Council, 1970-76; assoc. Sisters Charity of N.Y., Scarsdale, 1978—; eucharistic minister, lector Our Lady of Victory Ch., Mt. Vernon, N.Y., 1981-93, eucharistic minister lector, 1981—93; asst. chaplain White Plains Hosp. Ctr., NY, 1981—2000; chaplain for renal patients St. Joseph's Med. Ctr., Yonkers, NY, 2000—. Cons. Quincy Tenants Assn., Mt. Vernon, 1986—; workshop presenter in kidney hemodialysis transplant; music educator cons., 2000—; chaplain for renal pts. St. Joseph Med. Ctr., Yonkers, NY, 2000—; choral dir. Elem. Middle Sch. Soloist Greenhaven Correctional Facility retreat, N.Y., 1994; recital St. Mary's Ch. Outreach Program, 1994. Vestrywoman St. Andrew's Episc. Ch., Yonkers, 1971-75; contralto soloist St. Peter's Episc. Ch., Port Chester, 1959-69, Cape Cod Roman Cath. Charismatic Conf., 1993; mem. Collegiate Chorale, N.Y.C., 1958-68; svc. team mem. Charismatic Cmty., Scarsdale, 1975-91; v.p. Willwood Tenant Assn., Mt. Vernon, 1981-82, pres., 1982-84; vol. speaker N.Y. Regional Transplant Program, 1992—; active Montefiore Med. Ctr. TRIO, 1991—, presenter kidney transplant program, 1995; active Teen/Twenty Encounter Christ, 1990-92; soloist concert Holy Spirit Episcopal Ch., Orleans, Mass.; facilitator Our Lady of the Cape, Brewster, Mass.; inspirational spkr. St. Joan of Arc, Orleans, Mass., 2002; lector, eucharistic min. St. Mary's Roman Cath. Ch., 1993—, facilitator RENEW program, 1994—, CORE team mem., 1996, coord. prayer group Day of Reflection, elected leader prayer group, 1998—, adviser young adults ministry, 1998-2002; asst. coord. RENEW, St. Mary's Ch., Mt. Vernon, N.Y., leader Charismatic Prayer Group, 1998-2000, cons. to Charismatic group, 2000—; coord. Life in the Spirit Program, 1997; trustee Edn. Parish Svc. Program, Trinity Coll., 2000; vol. chaplain for renal patients St. Joseph's M.C., Yonkers, N.Y., 2001—; team mem. Women's Cursillo-English, N.Y. Archdiocese; active Christopher Leadership course Gabriel Richard Inst., N.Y., 2000; vol. chaplain for renal patients St. Joseph's Med. Ctr., Yonkers, N.Y. Mem. Westchester County Sch. Music Assn. (exec. bd.), Scarsdale Tchrs. Assn. (exec. bd.), Music Educators Nat. Conf., West Cmty. Sch. Music Assn (exec. bd. 1967-70). Democrat. Roman Catholic. Avocations: swimming, reading, walking, organic cooking, concerts. E-mail: Brookhem@aol.com.

BROOKS, MARK HUNTER, information technology project administrator; b. Pinehurst, NC, Mar. 14, 1960; s. Brady Hunter and Mary Ann Brooks; m. Selina Malherbe, June 30, 1984; 1 child, Meredith. BS in Textile Mgmt., N.C. State U., 1982; MBA in Info. Systems, NYU, 1992. Cert. project mgmt. profl. Project Mgmt. Inst., 2001. Asst. dir. R & D Reliance Cons. Group, NYC, 1982-86; network planning analyst Sterling Drug Inc., NYC, 1986-90; sr. systems engr. Chase Manhattan Bank, N.A., NYC, 1990-91; sr. LAN specialist TIAA-CREF, NYC, 1991-96, tech. engring. cons., 1997-98, sr. tech. engring. cons. architecture group, 1998—, connectivity supr., 1998, environ. mgr. yr. 2000 testing team, 1998-2000, mgr. tech. svc. comm., 2000, participant tchr. info. Exch. program, 2000, mgr. projects team, 2001. Mem.-at-large bd. dir. N.Am. region NetWare Users Internat., 1991, v.p., pres.-elect, 1992, pres., 1993, advisor to bd. dir., 1994, chmn. leadership devel. and election com. 1995; pres., founding mem. Charlotte chpt. Microsoft Project Users Group, 2002--; founder, pres. NY LAN Assn., Inc., NYC, 1990-91; adv. bd. Networld Boston, 1993, Networld Dallas, 1993; readers adv. bd. LAN Times, 1993-96; corp. adv. bd. Tech. Mgr. Forum Internat., 1996—; program adv. bd. UNIX Expo, N.Y., 1996; coord. ann. conf. Conservative Bapt. Assn.-NY, 1998; judge PC Week/TMFI Best Practices Awards, 1999-2000, 02. Chmn. fin. com. Metro Bapt. Ch., NYC, 1986-88, trustee, 1988-90, vice chmn. bd. trustees, 1990; mem. missions com. Harmony Bapt. Ch., Middletown, NY, 1997-2000; Founding Bd. mem. NYU Stern Bus. Sch. Alumni of the Carolinas, Charlotte, NC, 2003 Recipient Disting. Recent Alumnus award NYU, 1994, Excellence in Fin. and Adminstrn. award Am. Soc. Assn. Execs., 1994, Computer World Mag. Premier 100 IT Leaders award, 2002. Democrat. Baptist. Avocations: aviation, rocketry, astronomy.

BROOKS, MATTHEW WAYNE, agrichemical regulatory chemist, consultant; b. Springfield, Mass., Oct. 13, 1961; s. Donald Wayne and Helen Brooks; m. Laura McKenna Kehoe, June 18, 1988; children: Sierra, Wyatt. BS, U.

Mass., 1983, MS, 1986, PhD, 1992. Chief chemist Mass. State Pesticide Analysis Lab., Amherst, 1986-88; sr. rsch. chemist FMC Co., Princeton, N.J., 1993-98; sr. chemistry cons. JSC, Inc., Arlington, Va., 1998—2001; dir. Ag-Chem. Consulting, LLC, 2002—. Author: (book chpt.) Encyclopedia of Agrichemicals, 2001; contbr. articles to profl. jours. Pres. Mercer County Literacy Vols., Princeton, 1995-98; treas. Montgomery Wood Homeowners Assn., Princeton, 1995-98; driver Meals on Wheels, Fairfax, Va., 2000-2001; grant reviewer United Way, Trenton, N.J., 1997-98. Mem. Am. Chem. Soc. Democrat. Office: Ag-Chem Cons LLC 12208 Quinque Ln Clifton VA 20124 Home Fax: 703-266-0128. E-mail: mwbrooks01@yahoo.com.

BROOKS, Mrs. MEL See BANCROFT, ANNE

BROOKS, MEL, producer, director, writer, actor; b. June 28, 1926; Author: sketch Of Fathers and Sons in New Faces of 1952, 1957, sketch Shinbone Alley; co-author: sketch All American, 1962; writer (for TV series) Your Show of Shows; also Caesar's Hour, The Sid Caesar, Imogene Coca, Carl Reiner, Howard Morris Special, 1967 (Emmy award for outstanding writing achievement in a comedy-variety); co-creator (TV series) Get Smart; recs. include 2000 Years, 2000 and One Years, 2000 and Thirteen Years, 2000 Year Old Man in the Year 2000, 1997 (Grammy award for Best Spoken Word Album Comedy 1998); writer, dir motion pictures including Producers, 1968 (Acad. award for Best Original Screenplay); writer, dir., star The Twelve Chairs, 1970; co-writer, dir., star Blazing Saddles, 1974; co-writer, dir. Young Frankenstein, 1974; co-writer, dir., prodr., star: Robin Hood: Men In Tights, 1993, Dracula: Dead and Loving It, 1995; co-writer, dir., star: Silent Movie, 1976; prodr., dir., co-writer and star: High Anxiety, 1977, Spaceballs, 1987, Life Stinks, 1991; writer, dir., prodr., star: History of the World Part I, 1981, writer, narrator: The Critic, 1964 (Acad. award for best animated short subject); actor, prodr. To Be or Not To Be, 1983; prodr.: 84 Charing Cross Road, 1987, The Elephant Man, 1980, Frances, 1982, My Favorite Year, 1982, Fly I, 1986, Fly II, 1989; guest actor (TV show) Mad About You (Emmy award for outstanding guest actor in a comedy series 1997, 98, 99); co-writer, composer, prodr. (Broadway musical) The Producers, 2001 (3 Tony awards). Office: c/o The Culver Studios 9336 Washington Blvd Culver City CA 90232-2628

BROOKS, MICHAEL PAUL, urban planning educator; b. Topeka, Kans., June 13, 1937; s. Paul Edward and Gladys Leora (Nansen) B.; m. Shirley Birdeen Rhoad, June 8, 1958 (div. Aug. 1983); children: David, Timothy, Susan.; m. Ann DeWitt Watts, Feb. 18, 1984. BA magna cum laude, Colgate U., 1959; M in City Planning, Harvard U., 1961; PhD, U. N.C., 1970. Dir. rsch. The N.C. Fund, Durham, 1963-66, dir. planning and program devel., 1966 67; lectr. dept. city and regional planning U. N.C., Chapel Hill, 1967-70, assoc. prof., 1970-71; prof. dept. urban and regional planning U. Ill., Urbana, 1971-78, head dept., 1971-78; dir. Bur. Urban and Regional Planning Rsch., 1971-77; dean Coll. Design, Iowa State U., Ames, 1978-84, Sch. Architecture and Environ. Design, SUNY, Buffalo, 1984-87, Sch. Community and Pub. Affairs, Va. Commonwealth U., Richmond, 1987-91, spl. asst. to provost for strategic planning, 1992—2003; prof. dept. urban studies and planning, 1993—. Cons. in field. Commr. Research Triangle Regional Planning Commn., Chapel Hill, N.C., 1969-71 Mem. Am. Planning Assn. (pres. 1979-80), Am. Inst. Cert. Planners, Assn. Collegiate Schs. Planning (pres. 1976-77) Democrat. E-mail: mpbrooks@saturn.vcu.edu.

BROOKS, PATRICIA SCOTT, principal; b. St. Louis, July 19, 1949; d. John Edward and Doris Louise (Webb) Scott; m. John Robert Brooks, May 22, 1986; 1 child, Ollie. BS, W.Va. State Coll., 1971; MA, Marshall U., 1974; adminstrv. cert., Ind. U., 1990. Cert. tchr., Ind. Tchr. spl. edn. Huntington (W.Va.) State Hosp., 1971; tchr. elem. edn. Kanawha County Sch., Charleston, W.Va., 1971-78, Washington Twp., Indpls., 1979-82, tchr. mid. sch., 1982-90, adminstrv. intern, 1989-90, asst. coord., 1990, 92, asst. prin., 1990-93; prin. Pike Twp., Indpls., 1993-2000, New Pike Twp. Sch.-Snacks Crossing Elem., 2001. Participant Ind. U. Tchr. as a Decision Maker Program, Bloomington, 1989; mem. Human Rels. Com., Indpls., 1996; presenter U.S. Dept. Edn. Panelist State PTA Conv. Recipient Tchr. Spotlight award Topics Newspaper, 1983; named one of 100 Outstanding Black Women in State of Ind., Nat. Coun. Negro Women, 1990, Ctr. for Leadership Devel. award, 2002; Danforth fellow Ind. U., 1989. Mem. Ind. Assn. for Elem. and Mid. Sch. Prins., Phi Delta Kappa, Delta Sigma Theta. Methodist. Avocations: tennis, cooking, reading, dancing. Home: 2432 Laurel Lake Blvd Carmel IN 46032-8902

BROOKS, PATRICK WILLIAM, lawyer; b. May 11, 1943; s. Mark Dana and Madge Ellen (Walker) B.; m. Mary Jane Davey, Dec. 17, 1966; children: Carolyn Walker, Mark William. BA, State Coll. Iowa, 1966; JD, U. Iowa, 1971. Bar: Iowa 1971, U.S. dist. Ct. (so. dist.) Iowa 1972, U.S. Sup. Ct. 1974, U.S. Ct. apls. (8th cir.) 1979. Tchr. Waterloo (Iowa) Cmty. Schs., 1966-68; mem. staff Donahue & Brooks, West Union, Iowa, 1971-72; ptnr. Mowry, Irvine, Brooks & Ward, Marshalltown, Iowa, 1972-84, 92—, Brooks, Ward & Trout, Marshalltown, Iowa, 1984-92. Mem. Fayette County (Iowa) Republican Ctrl. com., chmn. platform resolutions com., 1971-72; pres. Marshall County Young Reps., 1974; trustee Iowa Law Sch. Found., 1970-71; bd. dirs. Iowa Hist. Found., 1991-96. Mem. Am. Judicature Soc., Iowa Bar Assn., Marshall County Bar Assn. (pres. 1985-86), Iowa Trial Lawyers Assn., Iowa Def. Counsel Assn., Buick Am. Club (bd. dir. 2001—). Lutheran. Avocation: international road rally driver and mechanic. Office: Box 908 6 W Main St Marshalltown IA 50158-4941

BROOKS, PETER (PRESTON), French and comparative literature educator; b. N.Y.C., Apr. 19, 1938; s. Ernest and Mary Caroline (Schoyer) B.; m. Margaret Elisabeth Waters, July 18, 1959 (div. 1995); 3 children; m. Rosa Ehrenreich, May 15, 2001. BA, Harvard U., 1959, PhD, 1965; postgrad., U. Coll. London, 1959-60, U. Paris, 1962-63; MA (hon.), Yale U., 1975; Doctor (hon.), Ecole Normale Supérieure, 1997; MA (hon.), U. Oxford, 2001. Instr. French Yale U., 1965-67, asst. prof., 1967-72, assoc. prof., 1972-75, prof. French and comparative lit., 1975—, Chester D. Tripp prof. humanities, 1980-2001, dir. The Lit. Major, 1974-79, dir. Whitney Humanities Ctr., 1980-91, 96-01, chmn. dept. French, 1983-88, chmn. dept. comparative lit., 1991-97, Sterling prof. comparative lit. and French, 2001—. Vis. prof. Eastman U. Oxford, 2001—02. Author: The Novel of Worldliness, 1969, The Child's Part, 1972, The Melodramatic Imagination, 1976, Reading for the Plot, 1984, Body Work, 1993, Psychoanalysis and Storytelling, 1994, World Elsewhere, 1999, Troubling Confessions, 2000; co-editor: Law's Stories, 1996, Whose Freud?, 2000; contbg. editor Partisan Rev., 1972-88; mem. editl. bd. Yale French Studies, 1966—; chmn. Yale Jour. Criticism, 1987—. Acad. advisor Marlboro Co., 1975—; regional chmn. Mellon Fellowships in Humanities, 1982-84; trustee Hopkins Sch., New Haven, 1983-88; mem. adv. coun. West European program The Wilson Ctr.; mem. adv. bd. Stanford Humanities Ctr., 1996-2001; mem. humanities adv. coun. N.Y. Pub. Libr. Decorated Officier des Palmes Académiques, 1986; Marshall fellow, 1959, Morse fellow, 1967, Guggenheim fellow, 1973, Am. Coun. Learned Socs. fellow, 1980, NEH fellow, 1988. Fellow Am. Acad. Arts and Scis.; mem. MLA (exec. coun. 1993-97), Am. Phil. Soc., Yale Club, Elizabethan Club (New Haven), Century Assn. Democrat. Office: Yale U Dept Comparative Lit PO Box 208299 New Haven CT 06520-8299 E-mail: peter.brooks@yale.edu.

BROOKS, PETER STUYVESANT, real estate consultant; b. Newburgh, N.Y., June 23, 1942; s. Frank A. Brooks and Anne Corbin (Armstrong) Rice; m. Frances A. Camera, June 30, 1990. Instr. Duchess Community Coll., Poughkeepsie, N.Y., 1966-67, Mt. St. Mary Coll., Newburgh, 1969-70, Southampton (N.Y.) Coll., 1970-72; real estate broker Newburgh, 1972-77; from asst. sec. to sr. v.p. Chem. Bank, N.Y.C., 1977-91; ptnr. Austrian Roth & Ptnrs., N.Y.C., 1992-96; prin. Ernst & Young, N.Y.C., 1996—. Treas. N.Y.C. chpt. Appraisal Inst., 1989, sec., 1990, 1st v.p., 1991, pres. 1992; bd. dirs. N.Y. chpt. Counselors of Real Estate, 2002—. Bd. dirs. Grand Cen. Partnership, N.Y.C., 1988-92, Citizens Crime Commn., N.Y.C., 1989-2000. With U.S. Army, 1967-68. Mem. Real Estate Counselors, Appraisal Inst. Home: 40 Castle Heights Ave Tarrytown NY 10591-3702 Office: Ernst & Young 5 Times Sq 5th Fl New York NY 10036 E-mail: peter.brooks@ey.com.

BROOKS, PHILIP COOLIDGE, JR., archives, museum official; b. Dec. 1, 1940; s. Philip Coolidge and Dorothy Hamilton (Holland) Brooks; m. Susan Mary Fox, Dec. 21, 1965; 1 child, Anthony Franklin Coolidge. BA, U. Kans., 1962, MA, 1966; Exchange fellow, U. Reading, Eng., 1962—63, postgrad., 1964—65, Stanford U. Law Sch., 1963—64. Mus. specialist polit. history Smithsonian Instn., Washington, 1967—71; asst. to exec. dir. Nat. Archives, Washington, 1971—74, asst. to asst. archivist, pub. programs, 1974—83, also curator archives reception room, acting dir. edn. div., 1979—83, archives specialist, records centers, 1983—96, devel. officer, 1986—87, historian-archivist, 1989—93; ret., 1996. Pres. Inaugural Com., 1988—93. Contbr. articles on history to profl. jours. Mem. Gadsby's Tavern Acquisitions Commn., Alexandria, Va., 1974—78, Historic Records Adv. Com., Alexandria, 1975—77, Historic Alexandria Resources Com., 1983—97, Alexandria Libr. Co., 1989; vice chmn. Alexandria Assn., 1976—78; chmn. Alexandria Ad Hoc Lyceum Com., 1981—82, The Lyceum Co., 1983—87, vice chmn., 1987—91; mem., vice chmn. Alexandria Bicentennial Commn., 1972—83; chmn. Alexandria Mus. Task Force, 1979—80, Alexandria 250th Anniversary Com., 1997—2000; dir. RROC Found., 1984—92; pres. Rolls-Royce Found., 2000—03; mem. adv. Coun. Internat. Nontheatrical Events, 1989—97. Recipient Commendable Service award, Nat. Archives, 1976, Archivist's Achievement awards, 1985, Appreciation cert., City Alexandria, 1976, 1981, 1984, Va. Senate Joint Resolution of Commendation, 2000, Rolls-Royce Found. Commendation, 2003. Mem.: Nat. Trust Historic Preservation, Am. Assn. State and Local History, Am. Assn. Museums, Rolls Royce Owners Club (dir. 1978—84, editor The Flying Lady 1986—89, v.p. regions 1992—94), Bentley Drivers Club (rep. 1968—), Lambda Chi Alpha. Home: 3908 Col Ellis Ave Alexandria VA 22304-1704

BROOKS, PHILIP G. obstetrician-gynecologist; b. Chgo., July 19, 1933; MD, U. So. Calif., 1959. Intern L.A. County Gen. Hosp., 1959-60, resident in ob-gyn, 1960-64; fellow in endocrinology Free Hosp. Women, Harvard U., 1964-65; mem. staff Cedars-Sinai Med. Ctr., L.A., 1965—; clin. prof. UCLA Sch. Medicine, 1992—; pvt. practice Heldfond Brooks Margolin, L.A., 1965—. Mem. ACOG, Am. Assn. Gynecol. Laparoscopists, Am. Soc. Reproductive Medicine. Office: Heldfond Brooks Margolin 8631 W 3rd St Los Angeles CA 90048-5901

BROOKS, PHILIP RUSSELL, chemistry educator, researcher; b. Chgo., Dec. 31, 1938; s. John Russell and Louise Jane B.; children: Scott, Robin, Christopher, Steven. BS, Calif. Inst. Tech., 1960; PhD, U. Calif., Berkeley, 1964. Rsch. assoc. physics dept. U. Chgo., 1964; from asst. to assoc. prof. chemistry Rice U., Houston, 1964-75, prof., 1975—. Editor: State-to-State Chemistry, 1977. Vol. Boy Scouts Am., Houston, 1970—. Recipient Humboldt prize Alexander von Humboldt Found., 1985; predoctoral fellow NSF, 1960-63, postdoctoral fellow, 1963-64, Alfred P. Sloan fellow 1970-74, John Simon Guggenheim fellow, 1974-75, Vis. Erskine fellow U. Canterbury, 1991, JSPS fellow Japan Soc. Promotion Sci., 1992. Fellow Am. Phys. Soc.; mem. Am. Chem. Soc. Achievements include research on chemical reaction dynamics. Home: 1026 Glourie Cir Houston TX 77055-7504 Office: Rice U Chemistry Dept MS60 6100 Main St Houston TX 77005-1892 E-mail: brooks@python.rice.edu.

BROOKS, RICHARD C. electrical engineer, federal government executive; b. Philadelphia, Pa., Aug. 31, 1945; BEE with honors, U. Va., Charlottesville, 1967; MSE, Johns Hopkins U., 1970; PhD, U. Mo., Columbia, 1973; MBA, Va. Poly. Inst., 1978. Registered profl. engr., Va., 1972. Chief, integrated systems lab. Nat. Weather Svc./NOAA, Silver Spring, Md., 1989—96; dep. dir., systems acquisition office Nat. Oceanic & Atmospheric Adminstrn. (NOAA), Silver Spring, 1996—2002; dir., satellite & ground systems program NESDIS/Nat. Oceanic & Atmospheric Adminstrn. (NOAA), Suitland, Md., 2002—. Troop com. Boy Scouts Am., Arlington, Va., 1984—2003. Lcdr U.S. Pub. Health Svc., 1968—70, Baltimore, Maryland. Mem.: IEEE (sr.). Achievements include research in image processing and pattern recognition. Avocation: skiing. Office: NOAA Dept Commerce 4401 Silver Hill Rd FB4 Rm 3301 Suitland MD 20746 E-mail: richard.brooks@noaa.gov.

BROOKS, RICHARD DICKINSON, lawyer; b. Daytona Beach, Fla., Sept. 17, 1944; s. Richard D. Brooks and Violet (Hamilton) Christenson; m. Betty Jane Huba, Aug. 28, 1971; children: Hillary Ann, Richard Jason. BA, Marietta (Ohio) Coll., 1967; JD, Case Western Res. U., 1972. Bar: Ohio 1972, U.S. Dist. Ct. (so. dist.) Ohio 1975, U.S. Ct. Appeals (6th cir.) 1993. Assoc., ptnr. Bridgewater Robe Brooks & Keifer, Athens, Ohio, 1972-87; of counsel Arter & Hadden, Columbus, Ohio, 1987, ptnr., 1988—2003, Bailey Cavalieri LLC, Columbus, 2003—. Coach Upper Arlington Cub Scout Baseball, Columbus, 1989-90; pres. A.T.C.O. Inc. Sheltered Workshop, Athens, 1986; chmn. com. Athens Kiwanis, 1977-87; bd.d irs. Athens C. of C., 1984-87. Sgt. U.S. Army, 1968-70, Vietnam. Fellow Am. Bar Found., Ohio Bar Found. (pres. 1988); mem. ABA, Ohio Bar Assn. (exec. com. 1979-83), Columbus Bar Assn. (environ. law com.), Athens County Bar Assn. (pres. 1978-79), Ohio CLE Inst. (bd. dirs. 1989-90), Ohio State Legal Svcs. Assn. (bd. dirs. 1982—). Avocations: basketball, tennis, fishing, furniture restoration. Office: Bailey Cavalieri LLC 10 W Broad St Ste 2100 Columbus OH 43215-3422

BROOKS, ROBERT EUGENE, decision support software designer; b. Chgo., June 13, 1946; s. Robert Eugene and Shirley Mae (Kunkel) B.; m. Tonya Thompson, Aug. 19, 1969; children: Shannon, Gabriel, Cyrus, Aleisha, Aaron, Ethan, David. AB in Arts and Scis., U. Calif., Berkeley, 1968; MA in Physics, U. Tex., 1972; PhD in Mgmt., MIT, 1975. Asst. prof. bus. U. So. Calif., L.A., 1975—76; prin. Robert Brooks & Assocs., Norwalk, Calif., 1976-79; v.p. Transportation and Econ. Research Assocs., Washington, 1979-82; pres. RBAC, Inc., L.A., 1982—84; v.p. software devel. Profit Mgmt. Devel. Inc., L.A., 1984—87; ind. cons., 1987—. Cons. Arthur D. Little, Inc., Cambridge, Mass., 1972-75, Chase Econometrics, Bala Cynwyd, Pa., 1976, Mathematica, Inc., Princeton, N.J., 1977-78, 82, McDonnell-Douglas Corp., 1987-97, fed. and state govts., Washington, Sacramento, Austin, Tex., 1976-83, Logistic Solutions, 1990-95, Ventana Systems, 1987-97. Author: (computer models) GASNET, 1976, GASNET2, 1977, NETS, 1981, CMOTSIM, 1982; Profit Maker, 1986, GPCM, 1987. Mem. Inst. Mgmt. Scis. Mem. Ch. Scientology. Avocations: sports, music, new mathematics. Home: 2150 Micheltorena St Los Angeles CA 90039-3019

BROOKS, ROBERT FRANKLIN, SR., lawyer; b. Richmond, Va., July 13, 1939; s. Robert Noel Brooks and Annie Mae (Edwards) Miles; m. Patricia Wilson, May 6, 1972; children: Robert Franklin Jr., Thomas Noel, Courtenay M. Brooks Rainey. BA, U. Richmond, 1961, M of Humanities, 1993; JD, 1964. Bar: Va. 1964, N.Y. 1985, U.S. Dist. Ct. (ea. and we. dists.) Va. 1964, U.S. Ct. Appeals (4th cir.) 1965, U.S. Ct. Appeals (5th cir.) 1972, (2d cir.) 1979, (11th cir.) 1981, D.C. 1977, U.S. Supreme Ct. 1979. Assoc. Hunton & Williams, Richmond, 1964-71, ptnr., 1971—. Chmn. sect. II 3d Dist. Com., 1983; mem. rules evidence com. Supreme Ct. Va., 1984-85; mem. Fourth Cir. Judicial Conf. Trustee U. Richmond, chmn. exec. com., 1998-99, 99—. Fellow ABA, Am. Coll. Trial Lawyers (com. atty.-client relationships 1983-91, chmn. Va. state com. 1993-94), Am. Bar Found., Va. Law Found.; mem. N.Y. Bar Assn., D.C. Bar Assn., Va. State Bar (coun. 1986—, bd. govs. litigation sect. 1984-90, sec. 1985-86, chmn. 1986-87, com. lawyer fin. responsibility 1986-89, nominating com. 1990, spl. com. election methods 1989, chmn. bench-bar rels. com. 1987-88, faculty professionalism course 1988-90, governance com. 1990-91), Richmond Bar Assn. (chmn. judiciary com. 1985-87, chmn. com. on unprofl. conduct 1979-80, com. on improvement of adminstrn. of justice 1981-84), Va. Bar Assn. (profl. responsibility com. 1981-84). Home: 500 Kilmarnock Dr Richmond VA 23229-8102 Office: Hunton & Williams Riverfront Plz East Tower 951 E Byrd St Ste 200 Richmond VA 23219-4074

BROOKS, ROBERT LESLIE, bank executive; b. Kelvington, Sask., Can., June 2, 1944; s. Allan and Edith Brooks; m. Brenda Mary Griffin, Dec. 28, 1968; children: Derek, Keith, Ian. BSc, U. Man., Can., 1965; MBA, U. Western Ont., Can., 1968. Sys. comptr. Bank of N.S., Toronto, 1971—72, supr. sys. planning, 1972—73, chief acct., 1973—78, comptr., chief acct., 1978—80, gen. mgr. fin. and adminstr., 1980—83, sr. v.p. mgmt. and fin. info. sys., 1983—85, exec. v.p., gen. mgr. fin. and adminstrn., 1985—86, exec. v.p. investment banking, 1986—98, exec.v.p., group treas., 1998—2002, sr. exec. v.p. treasury and ops., 2002—. Bd. dirs. Scotia Realty Ltd., Scotia Capital Inc., Scotia Discount Brokerage Inc., Helix Investments Inc., Scotia McLeod Holdings Inc., Scotia Securities Inc., Scotia Properties Quebec Inc., Scotiabanc Inc., Scotia Holdings (US) Inc., Scotia Loan Co., Lawrence & Co. Inc., The Bank of Nova Scotia Asia Ltd., The Bank of Nova Scotia Internat. Ltd., The Bank of Nova Scotia Properties Inc., Scotia McLeod Corp., Scotia Merchant Capital Corp.; chmn. bd. dirs. Scotiabank (Ireland) Ltd.; bd. dirs. Heart & Stroke Found. Can., SSI Funding Co. BNS Investments Inc. Vol., past chair bd. Heart and Stroke Found. Ont. Mem.: Fin. Execs. Inst., Empire Club Can. (past pres.), Nat. Club. Home: 2061 Lakeshore Rd E Oakville ON Canada L6J 1M4 Office: Bank NS Exec Offices Scotia Plz 40 King St W Toronto ON Canada M5H 1H1

BROOKS, ROBERT MARK, civil engineer, educator; b. Kavali, India, Aug. 12, 1961; came to the U.S., 1986; s. Krishnamurthy and Vara Lakshmi (Kavaturu) Tangella. MS, U. Calif., Berkeley, 1988, PhD, 1989. Registered profl. engr., Pa. Asst. rsch. engr. inst. transp. studies U. Calif., Berkeley, 1989-90; dir. transp. engring. divsn. civil engring. dept. Temple U., Phila., 1991—. Mem. nat. roster on disaster svcs. and human resources ARC, Washington, 1994. Named Phila. Transp. Engr. of Yr., ASCE, 1994, Delaware Valley Young Engr. of Yr., Phila. Club Engrs., 1993, Outstanding Faculty of Coll. of Engring., Temple U. Coll. of Engring. Alumni Assn., 1995. Fellow ASCE; mem. NSPE (nat. com. on rsch. 1993-94), Pa. Soc. Profl. Engrs. (pres. Phila. chpt. 2001). Home: 1914 N Park Ave Apt C Philadelphia PA 19122 Office: Temple U Civil Engring Dept 12 and Norris St Philadelphia PA 19122

BROOKS, ROGER KAY, insurance company executive; b. Clarion, Iowa, Apr. 30, 1937; s. Edgar Sherman and Hazel (Whipple) B.; m. Marcia Rae Ramsay, Nov. 19, 1955 (div. Sept. 1989); children: Michael, Jeffrey, David; m. Saulene Richer, Mar. 17, 1990. BA magna cum laude, U. Iowa, 1959. With AmerUs Grp., Des Moines, 1964—; asst. sec. Central Life Assurance Co., 1964-68, v.p., 1968-70, exec. v.p., 1970-72, pres., 1972-92, chmn., 1992—. Mem. Des Moines Devel. Com. Fellow Soc. Actuaries; mem. Greater Des Moines C. of C. (past chmn.), Actuaries Club of Des Moines (past pres.), Iowa Ins. Hall of Fame, Iowa Bus. Hall of Fame, Phi Beta Kappa. Presbyterian (elder). Club: Des Moines (past pres.). Home: 5205 Woodland Des Moines IA 50312 Office: AmerUs Group PO Box 1555 Des Moines IA 50306-1555 E-mail: roger.brooks@amerus.com.

BROOKS, ROGER LEON, university president; b. El Dorado, Ark., Apr. 14, 1927; s. Roger Spurgeon and Lumae (Jackson) B.; m. Martha Edwina Withers, Aug. 25, 1950; children:Leslie, Roger, Geoffrey, Stephen, Douglas. BA, Baylor U., 1949; MA, U. Ill., 1950; PhD, U. Colo., 1959. Instr. English U. Colo., 1955-57, 58-60; prof. Tex. Tech U., Lubbock, 1960-64, assoc. dean Grad. Sch., 1964-67; dean Coll. Arts and Scis., East Tex. State U., Commerce, 1967-72; pres. Howard Payne U., Brownwood, Tex., 1972-79; v.p. adminstrv. affairs Houston Bapt. U., 1979-87; dir. Armstrong Browning Libr., Baylor U., 1987-96. Cons. Victorian Studies, 1967, Choice, 1970, Can. Coun., 1971 Editor: Studies in Browning and His Circle, 1987-96, Robert Browning and Victorian Culture, 1992, Elizabeth Barrett Browning and Victorian Culture, 1994; contbr. articles to profl. jours. Pres., bd. advs. Baylor U., 2000—. With USNR, 1945-51; lt. col. USMC, 1972-87, ret. Rsch. grantee U. Colo. at Oxford and Brit. Mus., 1957-58, Tex. Tech. U. at Bibliotheque Nationale, Paris, 1964, Am. Philos Soc. at N.Y. Public Libr., 1963, Brit. Mus., 1980, the Suratt-Lewis Libr. award, 1997. Mem. London Browning Soc., Manuscript Soc., Grolier Club (N.Y.C.), Westlake Club (Houston). Office: Baylor U Armstrong Browning Lib Waco TX 76798

BROOKS, SAM, publishing executive; b. Stamford, Conn. Sr. v.p. EBSCO Pub., Ipswich, Mass., 1991—. Contbr. articles to profl. jours. Mem.: ALA. Office: EBSCO Publishing 10 Estes St Ipswich MA 01938

BROOKS, SARAH, software developer, consultant, educator; b. Akron, Ohio, Sept. 12, 1920; d. Morris and Jennie (Teicher) Horowitz; m. Nathan Brooks, June 20, 1943; children: Arthur William, Joan Ellen, Marjory Bee. MS in Math., Syracuse U., 1965, PhD in Math. Edn., 1977; BS in Computer Sci., SUNY, Utica/Rome, 1983, MS in Computer Sci., 1990. Cert. secondary math., social studies tchr. Statis. clk. Utica Mutual Ins. Co., 1941-44; math. tchr. Utica Free Acad., 1957-66; prof. math., computer sci. Mohawk Valley Community Coll., Utica, 1967-86; cons. for Total Quality Mgmt., Rome, 1986—; owner SHB Stats., Utica, 1987—. Examiner Excelsior award N.Y. State, Albany, 1991—, Mohawk Valley Quality Improvement Coun. Quality award, Utica, 1990—. Examiner Excelsior award N.Y. State, Albany, 1991—, Mohawk Valley Quality Improvement Coun.. Quality award, Utica, 19906; adj. prof. Empire State Coll., 1992—. Mem. NOW, 1985—, Nat. Abortion Rights League, 1985—, Planned Parenthood, 1980—. Recipient grant N.Y. State Found. for Improvement of Undergrad. Instrn., 1980-81. Mem. Mohawk Valley Quality Improvement Coun. (sec. 1990-91), N.Y. State Math. Assn. 2 Yr. Colls. (sec. 1970-72), Assn. for Computer Machinery (chmn. 1985, vice chmn. 1986), Upstate Apple Users Group (sec. 1990, pres. 1991). Republican. Jewish. Avocations: computer programming, solving math problems, gardening. Home and Office: 117 Melrose Ave Utica NY 13502-5751

BROOKS, SONDRA, lawyer; b. Bklyn., Mar. 29, 1957; d. Frank Harry and Roslyn Louise Brooks; m. Lance Hillel Edwards, May 29, 1982; children: Devon Wesley, Alexandra Nell. BS, SUNY, Stony Brook, 1978; JD, Syracuse U., 1981. Bar: N.Y. 1982, U.S. Dist. Ct. (so. dist.) N.Y. 1982, U.S. Supreme Ct. 1985. Asst. dist. atty. Nassau County Dist. Attys. Office, Mineola, N.Y., 1981-87; asst. county atty. Suffolk County Attys. Office, Hauppauge, N.Y., 1987-88; ptnr. Boland & Brooks, Smithtown, N.Y., 1988—. Legal cons. Plaza Employment Agy., Lynbrook, N.Y., 1981—, Suffolk Ob-gyn. Assn., Pt. Jefferson, N.Y., 1981—. Editor Deviance and Delinquency, 1978, Syracuse Law Rev., 1980-81. Named Hon. Asst. Atty. Gen., State Ark., 1983, Outstanding Young Women of Am., 1986. Mem. NOW, Nassau County Bar Assn., Suffolk County Womens Bar Assn. (award 1995). Jewish. Avocations: skiing, tennis, reading, flying, travel. Home: 12 Crane Neck Rd East Setauket NY 11733-1628 Office: 222 E Main St Ste 212 Smithtown NY 11787-2814

BROOKS, SUSAN LOUISE, artist; b. Dayton, Ohio, Oct. 8, 1951; d. Ira Wilkenson and Harriet Louise (Hook) Armes; m. Edwin Paul Brooks, Apr. 7, 1979. BFA in Painting, Drawing and Graphics, Ohio State U., 1973, B of Art Edn., 1975. Tchr. art Columbus Pub. Schs., 1975-78, Sch. Dist. 211, Hoffman Estates, Ill., 1979-80; adminstrv. asst. NBI, Chgo., 1980-82, tng. ctr. coord. Detroit, 1982-84, office mgr. Chgo., 1984-86; software technician Advanced Systems, Inc., Chgo., 1986-89; inside sales Hitachi America Ltd., Schaumburg, Ill., 1990-94; pres. Chgo. chpt. Colored Pencil Soc. Am., 1994-97, nat. dir. exhbns., 1996—99, nat. pres., 1999—. Democrat. Presbyterian. Home: 4 Elmwood Dr Hawthorn Woods IL 60047-9043

BROOKS, TIMOTHY H. media executive; b. Exeter, N.H., Apr. 18, 1942; s. John W. R. and Olive P. (Bradbury) B. BA, Dartmouth Coll., 1964; MS, Syracuse U., 1969. Promotion asst. Sta. WTEN-TV, Albany, N.Y., 1966-68; sales promotion supr. Sta. WCBS-TV, N.Y.C., 1969-70; sr. rsch. analyst NBC Owned Stas. Div., N.Y.C., 1970-72; mgr. ratings rsch. NBC TV Network, N.Y.C., 1972-76, dir. TV network rsch., 1978-82, dir. program rsch., 1982-88; asst. dir rsch. and mktg. TV Advt. Reps., Inc., N.Y.C., 1976-77; sr. v.p., media rsch. dir. N.W. Ayer Inc., N.Y.C., 1989-90; v.p. rsch. USA Networks, N.Y.C., 1991-94, sr. v.p. rsch., 1994-99, Lifetime TV, N.Y.C., 2000—03, exec. v.p. rsch., 2003—. Adj. prof. communications L.I. Univ., Greenvale, N.Y., 1979-88. Author: The Complete Directory to Prime Time TV Stars, 1987; co-author: The Complete Directory to Prime Time Network and Cable TV Shows, 1946-present, 1979 (Am. Book award 1980, Broadcast Preceptor award San Francisco State U. 1981), TV's Greatest Hits, 1985, TV in the '60s, 1985, The Columbia Master Book Discography, 1999 (Assoc. Recorded Sound Collections award for Excellence, 2000); also numerous articles on history of TV and recording industry. Capt. U.S. Army, 1964-66, Vietnam, USAR, 1966-74. Mem. Assn. for Recorded Sound Collections (bd. dirs. 1979-97, pres. 1982-84, contbg. editor jour. 1986—, compiler Current Bibliography 1979—, founder ARSC awards for excellence in pub. rsch. on recs., chmn. awards com. 1989-97), Media Rating Coun. (exec. com., chmn. cable comm. 1993-96, chmn. 1997-99), Advt. Rsch. Found. (bd. dirs. 1995-2000, chmn. video electronic media coun. 1995—, chmn. 1998-99), Radio-TV Rsch. Coun., Cable and Telecomms. Assn. for Mktg. (chmn. rsch. com. 2003-), Cabletelevision Advt. Bur. (mem. rsch. com. 1991—), Record Rsch. Assocs., City of London Phonograph and Gramophone Soc., TV Assn. Progammers L.Am. (founding mem.). Avocations: hiking, camping. Office: Lifetime TV Worldwide Plaza 309 W 49th St New York NY 10019-7316 E-mail: brooks@lifetimetv.com.

BROOKS, TORREY DEXTER, real estate executive; b. N.Y.C., Dec. 9, 1954; s. B.V. and Audrey (Stephenson) B.; m. Lauren F. Faxon, Mar. 16, 1985; children: Brody, Brandon. AB, Dartmouth Coll., 1976; MBA, Stanford U., 1979; Cert. Property Mgr., Inst. Real Estate Mgmt., 1997. Product mgr. Progressive Casualty Ins. Co., Cleve., 1979-82; v.p. Western Lodging Group, Yountville, Calif., 1982-84; exec. v.p. Calif. Footwear, Redwood City, 1984-85; v.p. Brooks, Torrey & Scott, Inc., Norwalk, Conn., 1985—; founder, pres. Brody Realty Corp., Greenwich, Conn., 1986—; mem. Granite Nat. Realty, LLC, Norwalk, 1997—. Recipient awards Inst. Real Estate Mgmt., Chgo., 1998, Real Estate Cyberspace Soc., Boston, 1998. Mem. Greenwich Country Club (tennis club champion 1990-97). Avocations: golf, tennis. Office: Brooks Torrey & Scott Inc 542 Westport Ave Norwalk CT 06851-4434 Fax: 203-840-4848. E-mail: torrey@btsrealty.com.

BROOKS, WALTER S. dermatologist; b. Cleve., July 16, 1956; s. John R. and Christel W. (Plogsties) B.; m. Debra A. HArt, Aug. 29, 1981; children: Aaron S., David J.H., Arielle N. BA magna cum laude, U. Rochester, 1978, MD, 1982. Resident in internal medicine Rochester (N.Y.) Gen. Hosp., 1982-85; resident in dermatology U. Pitts., 1985-88; clin. instr. dermatology to clin. asst. prof. dermatology U. Rochester, 1989—; dermatologist pvt. practice, Rochester, 1988—. Trustee Rochester Acad. Medicine, 1996—99; vice-chair campaign Leadership Soc. Demratology Found., 1997, chair Upstate N.Y., 2002; amb., dermatology del. People to People, China, 2000; chmn. Upstate N.Y. Dermatology Found., 2001. Recipient Leadership award Dermatology Found. Soc., 1995. Fellow Am. Acad. Dermatology; mem. Nat. Bd. Med. Examiners, Buffalo-Rochester Dermatol. Assn. (pres. 1995-96), Rochester Dermatol. Soc. (pres. 1996-98). Avocation: photography. Home: 22 Silver Fox Dr Fairport NY 14450-8666 Office: 730 Weiland Rd Rochester NY 14626-3919

BROOKS, WILLIAM FERN, JR., lawyer; b. Kansas City, Mo., Sept. 2, 1926; s. William Fern and Gertrude Octavia (Kendig) B.; m. Jean A. Geggie, June 22, 1951; children— William Fern III, Elizabeth C. B.A., Union Coll., Schenectady, 1946; LL.B., U. Minn., 1961. Bar: Minn. 1961, U.S. Dist. Ct. Minn. 1961. Spl. asst. atty.-gen. State of Minn., 1961-64; ptnr. Chestnut, Jones, Brooks & Kennedy, Mpls., 1965-71; mem., officer Chestnut & Cambronne, P.A., Mpls., 1971—98, of counsel, 1998-2002, ret., 2002. Pres. Newspaper Guild of Twin Cities, AFL-CIO, Mpls., 1958-60, The Lawyers Credit Union, 1986—96, dir., vice chmn., 1997—, Minn. Tax Found., 1987—; chmn. Minn. Commn. on Alcohol Problems, St. Paul, 1971-75. With USNR, 1944-46, PTO. Mem. Minn. Bar Assn., ABA. Mem. Democratic Farm Labor Party. Episcopalian. Office: Chestnut & Cambronne PA 3700 Campbell Mithun Towers Minneapolis MN 55402

BROOKS, WILLIAM JAMES, III, lawyer; b. West Palm Beach, Fla., Aug. 5, 1953; s. William James and Mary Helen (Olson) B; m. Anna Marie Frances Bourgeois, Sept. 29, 1979; children: William James IV, James Andrew. BA, Mt. Union Coll., 1974; JD, U. Notre Dame, 1977; LLM in Taxation, Emory U., 1985. Bar: Minn. 1977, U.S. Dist. Ct. Minn. 1977. Asst. revisor Revisor of Statutes, St. Paul, 1977-78; assoc. counsel Investors Diversified, Inc., Mpls., 1978-80; ptnr. Brooks & Moehn, P.A., Mpls., 1981-84; asst. gen. counsel Farm Credit Services, St. Paul, 1985-86; ptnr. Brooks & Brooks, P.A., Bloomington, Minn., 1986-94. Mem. Minn. Bar Assn. Republican. Roman Catholic. Home and Office: 7712 Stonewood Ct Edina MN 55439-2641

BROOKS-GUNN, JEANNE, psychologist; b. Bethesda, Md., Dec. 9, 1946; d. Richard D. and Mary J. (Wood) Brooks; m. Robert W. Gunn, 1970. BA, Conn. Coll., 1969; EdM, Harvard U., 1970; PhD in Human Learning and Devel., U. Pa., 1975. Rsch. scientist, sr. rsch. scientist, dir. adolescent study program Ednl. Testing Svc. and St. Luke's-Roosevelt Hosp. Ctr., 1977—91. Asst. prof. pediatric psychology Coll. Physicians and Surgeons Columbia U., N.Y.C., 1978—85, prof. pediat., 1993—; Virginia and Leonard Marx prof. in child devel. and edn. Tchrs. Coll., Columbia U., N.Y.C., 1991—, founding dir., co-dir. Nat. Ctr. for Children and Families, 1992—; adj. assoc. prof. pediat. U. Pa., 1985—91; vis. scholar Russell Sage Found., 1989—90; founding dir., co-dir. Columbia U. Inst. for Child and Family Policy, 1998; vis. scholar Ctr. for Health and Wellness Woodrow Wilson Sch., Princeton U., 2002—. Author (with W. Matthews): He and She: How Children Develop Their Sex-Role Identity, 1979; author: (with M. Lewis) Social Cognition and the Acquisition of Self, 1979; author: (with A. Petersen) Girls at Puberty, 1983; author: (with G. Baruch) Women in Midlife, 1984; author: (with F. Furstenburg) Adolescent Mothers in Later Life, 1987; author: (with R. Lerner and A.C. Petersen) The Encyclopedia of Adolescence, 1991; author: (with L. Chase-Lansdale) Escape from Poverty, 1992; author: (with G. Duncan) Consequences of Growing Up Poor, 1997; author: (with G. Duncan and J.L. Aber) Neighborhood Poverty Context and Consequences for Children, 1997; author: (with M. Cox) Family Conflict and Cohesion, 1999; author: (with L. Berlin and A. Fuligni) Early Child Development in the 21st Century: Profiles of Current Research Initiatives, 2003; co-editor: (social policy reports) Society for Rsch. in Child Devel.; contbr. numerous articles on child devel. and social psychology to profl. jours. Trustee N.J. Neuropsychiat. Inst., 1979—85; pres. Soc. Rsch. in Adolescence. Recipient John Hill award, Soc. Rsch. on Adolescence, William Goode award, Am. Sociol. Assn.; grantee, NSF, Commonwealth Fund, NIH, Ford Found., Robert Wood Johnson Found., W.T. Grant Found. Fellow: AAAS, APA (Disting. award in pub. policy, Urie Bronfenbrenner award, William Caltue award, Urre Bronfenner award), Am. Psychol. Soc; mem.: N.Y. Acad. Scis. Office: Tchrs Coll Columbia U New York NY 10027

BROOKSHIRE, BRUCE G. retail grocery store executive; b. Dec. 1928; married. Grad., U. Tex., 1950. With Brookshire Grocery Co. Inc., Tyler, Tex., 1950—, now chmn., CEO. Office: 1600 SW Loop 323 PO Box 1411 Tyler TX 75710-1411*

BROOKSHIRE, MICHAEL L. forensic economist, economics educator; b. Erwin, Tenn., Sept. 11, 1950; s. Leo Arthur and Mary Francis Brookshire; m. Darranci W. Brookshire, May 22, 1988 (dec. Sept. 1994); m. Lynn Young, Aug. 3, 1998; children: Kristi, Nikki. BS in Econs., U. Tenn., 1971, PhD in Econs., 1975. Assoc. dir. placement U. Tenn., Knoxville, 1974-75; asst. prof. W.Va. Coll. Grad. Studies, Charleston, 1975-76; exec. officer U. Tenn., Knoxville, 1976-80; v.p. U. Cin., 1980-83; pres. forensic economist Michael Brookshire and Assocs., Charleston, 1975—; prof. econs. Marshall U., Charleston, 1983—. Author: Economic Damages: The Practice, 1987; contbr. articles to profl. jours. Mem. Nat. Assn. Forensic Econs. (pres. 1993-94, v.p. 1990—, exec. dir. 1999—, Outstanding Svc. award 2000, Past Pres. award 1995). Avocations: racquetball, reading, writing, research. Office: PO Box 546 Charleston WV 25322-0546 E-mail: mlboffice@aol.com.

BROOKS-KAYAL, AMY R. pediatrician, researcher, neurologist; b. Mich., 1962; d. Richard and Pat Brooks; m. Shuvashis R. Kayal; children: Anjali Kayal, Zachary Kayal. MD, Johns Hopkins U. Sch. of Medicine, 1988. Cert. ABPN 1996, ABP 1992. Asst. prof., neurology and pediat. U. of Pa. Sch. of Medicine, Phila., 1995—. Contbr. Recipient Alpha Omega Alpha, 1988; grantee Rsch. grants, NIH, 1997-2001, 1999-2004. Mem.: Soc. for Neuroscience, Child Neurology Soc. (Young Investigator award 1999, Rsch. award 2001), Am. Epilepsy Soc. (Jr. Investigator award 1998). Office: Children's Hospital of Philadelphia 3615 Civic Center Blvd ARC 502 Philadelphia PA 19104-4318

BROOKS-KORN, LYNNE VIVIAN, artist; b. Detroit, July 6, 1951; d. Loren Edward and Edith Zona (Gaub) Brooks; m. Howard Allen Korn, Apr. 17, 1977. BFA magna cum laude, U. Mich., 1973, MFA, 1976. Teaching fellow U. Mich. Sch. Art, Ann Arbor, 1976. Vis. lectr. various history of art depts.; over 280 solo and group shows since 1992. Numerous one-woman shows, including Grants Pass (Oreg.) Mus. Art, 1993, Red River Valley Mus., Vernon, Tex., 1993, Coll. Ea. Utah, 1994, Carlsbad (N.Mex.) Mus., 1994, Aberdeen (Scotland) Arts Ctr., 1995, Napa County Librs., 1996, MacLaurin Art Gallery, Ayr, Great Britain, 1996, Calif. State U., Chico, 1997, S.D. State U., 1998, Coll. Ea. Utah, 1999, Columbus Cultural Arts Ctr., 2000; group shows include Foster City (Calif.) Mus. Gallery, 1993, San Bernadino County Mus., Redlands, Calif., 1993, Ohio State U., 1994, Bryn Mawr (Pa.) Coll., 1995, Haggin Mus., Stockton, Calif., 1996, Smithsonian Instn., 1997, San Jose (Calif.) Inst. Contemporary Art, 1998, Lake Forest (Ill.) Coll., 1999, U. Bridgeport, Conn., 2000; represented in permanent collections San Bernadino County Mus., Longwell Mus., Downey Mus. Art, Red River Valley Mus., Yosemite Mus., Brit. Mus., Bryn Mawr Coll., others; work reviewed in numerous publs.; various commns. Recipient numerous awards for art, including Internat. Art Competition, 1987, 88, 89, Nepenthe Munki Soc., Wichita, Kans., 1989, Haggin Mus., Stockton, Calif., 1990, Menlo Park Civic Ctr., 1991, San Bernardino County Mus., 1992, Sweetwater County Art Guild, 1993, East Tex. State U., 1993, Breckenridge Fine Arts Ctr., 1993, Lake Worth Art League, Inc., 1993, 94, Amador County Arts Coun., 1993, Coastal Ctr. for Arts, St. Simons Island, Ga., 1993, Soc. We. Artists Signature Mem., 1994, Ea. Washington WC Soc., 1994, San Jacinto Coll., Pasadena, Tex., 1995, Peninsula Art Assn., Burlingame, Calif., 1996, San Jose Inst. Contemporary Art, 1998; Rackham grantee U. Mich., 1975. Mem. Coll. Art Assn., Soc. Western Artists (signature). Democrat. Avocations: classical choral singing, Karate. Studio: 700 Loma Vista Ter Pacifica CA 94044-2425

BROOKS SHOEMAKER, VIRGINIA LEE, librarian; b. Oklahoma City, Sept. 16, 1944; d. Leo B. and Eloise Gilreath; m. Phil Ashley Brooks, Aug. 10, 1972 (dec. Oct. 1982); 1 child, Philip Brooks; m. Gene Darrell Shoemaker, Feb. 16, 1986; children: Rob, Julie, Donna, Gary. Student, Oklahoma City C.C., 1980; BS, U. Ctrl. Okla., 1988, M in Sch. Media, 1991, postgrad., 2000—. With Dept. Human Svcs., Oklahoma City, 1970-75, State Dept. Librs., Oklahoma City, 1980-87; substitute tchr. Oklahoma City Schs., 1989-91; vol. libr. Children's Libr., Children's Hosp., Oklahoma City, 1992—; libr. vol. Corpus Christi Sch. Libr., 1998—; vol. children's sect. First Bapt. Libr.; vol. Libr. for Blind. Sponsor World Vision, Seattle, 1994—; active cub scouts Boy Scouts Am.; active, life mem. Meth. Ch. of the Servant, women mission groups, Wesley Meth.; vol. Habitat for Humanity, Vista Care Hospice; vol. childrens sect. First Bapt. Libr.; reading sch. libr. tutor, First Bapt. Good Shepherd Children's Dental Clinic. project transfer, vista care volunteer. Recipient Adopt-a-Park awards, Oklahoma City Beautiful, Omniplex Sci. Mus., Oklahoma City, 1986-89. Mem.: Omniplex Sci. Mus. Zool. Soc. (Adpot-a-Park award 1986—89), Internat. Reading Assn. (reading tutor), Coun. Exceptional Children, Classen Alumni Assn., U. Ctrl. Okla. Alumni Assn. Baptist. Avocations: piano, reading, creative writing, dogs, cats.

BROOKS-TURNER, MYRA, music educator; b. Knoxville, Tenn., Jan. 13, 1933; d. Paul David and Lilli Ray Brooks; m. Ronald J. Turner, June 11, 1960; children: Stacy Turner Steele, Cheryl Turner Walker, Teresa Turner Basler. Student of piano, voice and composition, Juilliard Sch. Music, 1945—51; BMus in Piano, So. Meth. U., 1955, MusM in Theory and Composition, 1956, postgrad. in Piano, 1957—58. Educator Dallas Indep. Schs., Tex., 1950—60, choral music specialist Knoxville City Schs., Tenn., 1960—65; composer-in-residence Birmingham Children's Theatre, Ala., 1965—68; music instr. Mercer U. Music Prep. Sch., Atlanta, 1975—77; instr. composition Maryville Coll. Pres. Sch. of the Arts, Tenn., 1978—80; music instr. U. Tenn., Knoxville, 1990—92; owner Myra Brooks Turner Studio of Music, Knoxville, Tenn., 1992—. Freelance writer, pub. MBT Productions, Knoxville, 1993—. Composer, producer : (musicals) Make Way for Love, 1955; Uh-Uh, 1956; Javaho Junction, 1958; composer, dir. The Green Dragon, 1965—68 (Seattle Nat. Playwriting First Place award); contbr. articles to profl. publs. and jours. Worship leader Epis. Ch. of Ascension, Knoxville, Tenn., 1992—93. Recipient Cultural Arts award, Tenn. Arts Commn., 1982. Mem.: Tenn. Fed. Music Clubs (state jr. counselor 1978—88, officer, state bd. 1978—89, Ea. Tenn. divisional v.p. 2002—, officer, state bd. 2002—, East Tenn. divsn. jr. counselor 2002—, editor State Piano Competition Book 2003, 2004—06), Nat. Fed. Music Clubs (jr. festivals bulletin advisor 1982—90), Knoxville Music Tchrs. Assn. (sec., bd. mem. 2000—01, Composer of Yr. 1978, 2001), Tenn. Music Tchrs. Assn., Nat. Music Tchrs. Assn., Ossoli Circle, Knoxville Writer's Group, Tuesday Morning Musical Club (pres. 1990—91), U. Tenn. Faculty Women's Club, Pi Kappa Lambda Nat. Music Honorary, Mu Phi Epsilon Internat. Frat. (pres. 1973—74, pres. Atlanta Alumnae, Music Therapy award 1974), Alpha Delta Pi. Republican. Episcopalian. Achievements include published 350 original piano solos, duets, art songs and anthems from 1993 to 2003. Avocations: study of French, study of Italian, lessons in computer graphics and finale, interior decorating, photography.

BROOME, BARRY DEAN, lawyer, estate and financial planning consultant; b. Gaffney, S.C., Jan. 24, 1942; s. Walter Dean and Virginia Mae (Moss) B.; BA, U. Cen. Fla., 1973, J.D., Atlanta Law Sch., 1987; m. Janis M. Black, Feb. 14, 1969; children— Gina Michelle, Tina Marie, Jana Malia, Barry Dean II. Pres., Barry Broome Co., estate and fin. planning, Jacksonville, Fla., 1963-78; dir. tng. and sales devel. Gulf Life Ins. Co., Jacksonville, 1978-81; adj. instr. fin. planning Ga. State U.; cons. to ins. cos. in so. states, Dunwoody, Ga., 1981—; advisor to securities industry in S.E. Mem. fin. com. North Fla. council Boy Scouts Am., 1978-81; fin. chmn. various Republican candidates on state and local level; mem. bishopric Ch. of Jesus Christ of Latter-day Saints, 1974-75, stake pres., 1976-80, mem. high council, 1975-76; bd. dirs. Housing Initiative of North Fulton Inc. Recipient spl. commendation Health Ins. Assn. Am., 1981; C.L.U.; chartered fin. cons. Mem. Am. Soc. C.L.U.s, Internat. Assn. Fin. Planning, Nat. Assn. Life Underwriters, Am. Arbitration Assn., Internat. Platform Assn. Contbr. articles on advanced underwriting to profl. publs. Home: 1125 Pinebloom Dr Roswell GA 30076-2633 Office: 9800 Old Dogwood Rd Roswell GA 30075-4612

BROOME, BURTON EDWARD, former insurance company executive; b. N.Y.C., July 10, 1935; s. Burton Edward and Ann Loretta (Wall) B.; m. Anne Curtis, June 21, 1974; 1 child, Chelsea Anne. BSc, Fordham U., 1963; MBA, U. Calif., Berkeley, 1964. Ins. examiner Crum & Forster, N.Y.C., 1956-60; audit mgr. Price Waterhouse, N.Y.C., 1960-74; v.p., contr. Transamerica Corp., San Francisco, 1974-99; mem. oper. com. ARC Reins. Corp., Honolulu, 1993-99; ret., 1999. Mem. profl. acctg. program U. Calif., Berkeley, 1982-99; bd. dirs. Transamerica HomeFirst Corp., San Francisco, 1994-98, River Thames Ins. Co., London, 1994-98. Chmn. adv. coun. SEC and Fin. Reporting Inst., U. So. Calif., L.A., 1982-99. With U.S. Army, 1954-55. Mem. Fin. Exec. Inst.

BROOME, JOHN WILLIAM, retired architect; b. Middle Haddam, Conn., Mar. 7, 1923; s. Bertram Clinton and Helen Millington (Connery) B.; m. Althea Pratt, May 31, 1980; children: Bertram Vedeler, Sheryl Lynn. B.Arch., U. Oreg., 1951. Archtl. work in, Oslo, Norway, 1951-54; planning technician Vancouver (Wash.) Housing Authority, 1954-56; archtl. designer Edmundson, Kochendoerfer & Kennedy, Portland, Oreg., 1956-58; ptnr. Broome, Oringdulph, O'Toole & Rudolf & Assos., Portland, 1958-85, ret., 1985. Mem. Gov. Oreg. Com. for Livable Oreg., 1967-71; commr. Oreg. Coastal Conservation and Devel. Commn., 1971-75; pres. The Wetlands Conservancy; trustee Meridian Park Hosp., Healthlink, Inc. Served with USMC, 1942-46. Decorated Air medal with 2 gold stars; recipient Regional Conservation award U.S. Fish & Wildlife Svc., 1990, Nat. Conservation award Environ. Law Inst., 1991, State Disting. Svc. award Oreg. Shores Conservation Coalition, 1992. Fellow AIA (pres. Portland 1966, Oreg. council 1967); mem. Phi Kappa Psi. Democrat. Address: PO Box 236 Tualatin OR 97062-0236

BROOME, OSCAR WHITFIELD, JR., accounting educator, administrator; b. Monroe, N.C., Feb. 3, 1940; s. Oscar Whitfield and Irma (Hinson) B.; m. Julia Carol Renegar, June 14, 1964; children: Christine Irma, Michael Whitfield. AB, Duke U., 1962; MS, U. Ill., 1964, PhD, 1971. Prof. acctg. U. Va., Charlottesville, 1967-91, prof. law, 1998—, Frank S. Kaulback Jr. prof. commerce, 1991—, assoc. dean, 1992-98, interim dean, 1997, dir. grad. studies, 1986-92, dir. Ernst & Young master's program, 1998—2001; exec. dir. Inst. Chartered Fin. Analysts, Charlottesville, 1978-84. Faculty fellow Price Waterhouse & Co., N.Y.C., 1964; vis. prof. U. Tex., Austin, 1975, Duke U., Durham, N.C., 1977-78, Tulane U., New Orleans, 2002; vis. rsch. scholar, Lancaster (Eng.) U., 1994; adminstr. exams. Inst. CFAs, 1973-77; bd. regents Coll. Fin. Planning, 1984-89, chmn., 1987-89; mem. CPA Exam. Rev. Bd., 1984-87, chmn., 1986-87; mem. exams. com. Nat. Assn. State Bds. Accountancy, 1995-2000; bd. dirs. Internat. Bd. Stds. and Practices for CFPs, 1989-91; mem. vis. adv. com. DePaul U. Sch. Accountancy, 1991-97. Named Outstanding Educator Va. Soc. C.P.A.'s, 1979; recipient Outstanding Faculty award Z Soc., 1988. Mem. AICPA (bd. examiners 1977-82), Assn. for Investment Mgmt. and Rsch. (investment analysis stds. bd. 1984-86), Nat. Assn. Accts. (pres. chpt. 1974), Phi Beta Kappa, Phi Kappa Phi, Beta Gamma Sigma, Beta Alpha Psi, Omicron Delta Kappa.

BROOMFIELD, ROBERT CAMERON, federal judge; b. Detroit, June 18, 1933; s. David Campbell and Mabel Margaret (Van Deventer) B.; m. Cuma Lorena Cecil, Aug. 3, 1958; children: Robert Cameron Jr., Alyson Paige, Scott McKinley. BS, Pa. State U., 1955; LLB, U. Ariz., 1961. Bar: Ariz. 1961, U.S. Dist. Ct. Ariz. 1961. Assoc. Carson, Messinger, Elliot, Laughlin & Ragan, Phoenix, 1962-65, ptnr., 1966-71; judge Ariz. Superior Ct., Phoenix, 1971-85, presiding judge, 1974-85; judge U.S. Dist. Ct. Ariz., Phoenix, 1985—, chief judge, 1994-99; judge Fgn. Intelligence Surveillance Ct., 2002—. Faculty Nat. Jud. Coll., Reno, 1975-82. Contbr. articles to profl. jours. Adv. bd. Boy Scouts Am., Phoenix, 1968-75; tng. com. Ariz. Acad., Phoenix, 1980—; pres. Paradise Valley Sch. Bd., Phoenix, 1969-70; bd. dirs. Phoenix Together, 1982—, Crisis Nursery, Phoenix, 1976-81; chmn. 9th Cir. Task Force on Ct. Reporting, 1988—; space and facilities com. U.S. Jud. Conf., 1987-93, chmn., 1989-93, chmn. security, space and facilities com., 1993-95, budget com., 1997—, chmn. economy subcom., 2003--; founding mem. Sandra Day O'Connor Inn of Ct., 1988-94. Recipient Faculty award Nat. Jud. Coll., 1979, Disting. Jurist award Miss. State U., 1986. Mem. ABA (chmn. Nat. Conf. State Trial Judges 1983-84, pres. Nat. Conf. Met. Cts. 1978-79, chmn. bd. dirs. 1980-82, Justice Tom Clark award 1980, bd. dirs. Nat. Ctr. for State Cts. 1980-85, Disting. Svc. award 1986), Ariz. Bar Assn., Maricopa County Bar Assn. (Disting. Pub. Svc. award 1980), Ariz. Judges Assn. (pres. 1981-82), Am. Judicature Soc. (spl. citation 1985), Maricopa County Med. Soc. (Disting. Svc. medal 1979). Lodges: Rotary. Office: US Dist Ct Sandra Day O'Connor Cthse 401 West Washington St #626 SPC 61 Phoenix AZ 85003-2158

BROOTEN, DOROTHY, nursing educator, former dean; b. Hazleton, Pa. married; two children. BSN, U. Pa., 1966, MSN, 1970, PhD in Ednl. Adminstrn., 1980. Assoc. prof. nursing Thomas Jefferson U., 1972-77; from asst. to assoc. prof. nursing U. Pa., 1977-88, prof. nursing, chair Health Care of Women & Childbearing, 1980-93, dir. Ctr. for Low Birthweight, Sch. Nursing, 1990-96, Overseers prof. perinatal nursing, 1990-96; dean, prof. Frances Payne Bolton Sch. Nursing Case Western Res. U., Cleve., 1998—2000; prof. Florida International Univ., 2001—. Cons. Sch. Medicine, U. Utrecht, The Netherlands, 1989, Ministry of Health, Malawi, Africa, 1991. Recipient Contbrn. to Nursing Sci. award ANA, 1988. Mem. Inst. Medicine-NAS, Am. Acad. Nursing (mem. gov. coun. 1988-91). Achievements include research on low birthweight prevention, postdischarge care of low birthweight infants, health care delivery. Office: Fl Internat U Rm ACII230 11200 SW 8th St Miami FL 33199

BROOTEN, KENNETH EDWARD, JR., retired lawyer, rancher, author, chief counsel United States Congress; b. Kirkland, Wash., Oct. 17, 1942; s. Kenneth Edward Sr. and Sadie Josephine (Assad) B.; m. Patricia Anne Folsom, Aug. 29, 1965 (div. Apr. 1986); children: Michelle Catherine, Justin Kenneth; m. Judy Diane Robinette, July 14, 2001. Diploma, Lewis Sch. Hotel, Restaurant and Club Mgmt., Washington, 1963; student, U. Md., 1964-66; AA with honors, Santa Fe C.C., Gainesville, Fla., 1969; BS in Journalism with highest honors, U. Fla., 1971, MA in Journalism and Communications with highest honors, 1972, JD with honors, 1975; law student, U. Idaho, 1972-73; diploma in internat. law, Polish Acad. Scis., Warsaw, 1974; postgrad. in Internat. Law, Trinity Coll.,Cambridge (Eng.) U., 1974. Bar: Fla., D.C., U.S. Dist. Ct. (no., mid. and so. dists.) Fla., U.S. Dist. Ct. D.C., U.S. Tax Ct., U.S. Ct. Appeals (5th, 9th, 11th and D.C. circs.), U.S. Supreme Ct., Trial Counsel Her Majesty's Govt. of United Kingdom. Asst. to several congressmen U.S. Ho. of Reps., Washington, 1962-67; adminstrv. asst. VA Cen. Office, Washington, 1967; adminstrv. officer VA Hosp., Gainesville, Fla., 1967-72; ptnr. Carter & Brooten, P.A., Gainesville, Fla., 1975-78, Brooten & Fleisher, Chartered, Washington and Gainesville, Fla., 1978-80; pvt. practice, Washington and Gainesville, 1980-86, Washington, 1987-88, Washington and Orlando, Fla., 1988-91, Washington and Winter Park, Fla., 1991-98; ret., 1998. Permanent spl. counsel, acting chief counsel, dir. Select Com. Assassinations U.S. Ho. of Reps., 1976-77; counsel Her Majesty's Govt. of U.K. (in U.S.). Author: Malpractice Guide to Avoidance and Treatment, 1987; episode writer TV series Simon and Simon; nat. columnist Pvt. Practice, 1988-90, Physicians Mgmt., 1991-93; commentator Med. News Network, 1993-94; contbr. more than 250 articles to profl. jours.; composer. Served with USCGR, 1960-68. Named one of Outstanding Young Men Am., U.S. Jaycees, 1977. Mem. Fla. Bar Assn., D.C. Bar Assn., Sigma Delta Chi. Episcopalian. Avocations: writing, marksmanship, dangerous game hunting. Address: The Oxbow Ranch Bascom FL 32423-9361

BROPHY, DENNIS RICHARD, psychology and philosophy educator, administrator, clergyman; b. Milw., Aug. 6, 1945; s. Floyd Herbert and Phyllis Marie (Ingram) B. BA, Washington U., 1967, MA, 1968; MDiv, Pacific Sch. Religion, 1971; PhD in Indsl. & Orgnl. Psychology, Tex. A&M U., 1995. Cert. coll. tchr., Calif. Ednl. rschr. IBM Corp., White Plains, NY, 1968—71; edn. minister Cmty. Congl. Ch., Port Huron, Mich., 1971—72, Bethlehem United Ch. Christ, Ann Arbor, Mich., 1972—73, Cmty. Congl. Ch., Chula Vista, Calif., 1974; philosophy instr. Southwestern Coll., Chula Vista, 1975; assoc. prof. psychology & philosophy Northwest Coll., Powell, Wyo., 1975—96, prof., 1996—, assessment testing coord., 1999—. Chmn. social sci. divsn., 1992-95; religious edn. cons. Mont.-No. Wyo. Conf. United Ch. of Christ. Mem. APA (Daniel Berlyne award 1996), Wyo. Coun. Humanities, Soc. Indsl. Orgnl. Psychology, Soc. Tchg. of Psychology, Yellowstone Assn. United Ch. Christ, Phi Beta Kappa, Phi Kappa Phi, Sigma Xi, Omicron Delta Kappa, Theta Xi, Golden Key Nat. Honor Soc. Faculty Outstanding Svc. award, 2003. Home: 533 Avenue C Powell WY 82435-2401 Office: Northwest Coll 231 W 6th St Powell WY 82435-1898 E-mail: brophyd@northwestcollege.edu.

BROPHY, JAMES DAVID, JR., humanities educator; b. Mt. Vernon, N.Y., Oct. 5, 1926; s. James David and Mildred (Stall) B.; m. Elizabeth Bergen, Mar. 26, 1951; children: Sheila, David, Katharine, Elizabeth, James Mark. Student, MIT, 1944-45; BA, Amherst Coll., 1949; MA, Columbia U., 1950, PhD, 1965; postgrad., U. Dijon, 1950-51. Instr. English Iona Coll., New Rochelle, N.Y., 1951-58, asst. prof., 1958-64, assoc. prof., 1964-68, prof., 1968—, chmn. dept., 1968-71, 80-82, emeritus prof., 1992—. Author: Edith Sitwell, 1968, W.H. Auden, 1970; Editor: The Achievement of Galileo, 1962, Modern Irish Literature, 1972, Contemporary Irish Writing, 1983, New Irish Writing, 1988. Served with USNR, 1945-46. Fulbright fellow France, 1950-51; N.Y. State scholar in internat. studies, 1965; recipient Pro Operis medal Iona Coll., 1971, Bene Merenti award, 1981, Pro Multis Annis award, 1991; Nat. Endowment for Humanities grantee, 1973; Wilton Park asso., 1979 Mem. Milton Soc. Am., English Inst., Columbia Club N.Y. Home: 39 Oceanview Dr Southampton NY 11968-4215 E-mail: j-ebrophy@worldnet.att.net.

BROPHY, JERE EDWARD, education educator, researcher; b. Chgo., June 11, 1940; s. Joseph Thomas and Eileen Marie (Sullivan) B.; m. Arlene Marie Pintozzi, Sept. 21, 1963; children: Cheryl, Joseph. BS in Psychology, Loyola U., Chgo., 1962; MA in Human Devel., U. Chgo., 1965, PhD in Human Devel., 1967. Rsch. assoc., asst. prof. U. Chgo., 1967-68; from asst. to assoc. prof. U. Tex., Austin, 1968-76; staff devel. coord. S.W. Ednl. Devel. Lab., Austin, 1970-72; prof. Mich. State U., East Lansing, 1976-92, co-dir. Inst. for Rsch. on Tchg., 1981-93, univ. disting. prof., 1993—. Co-author: Teacher-Student Relationships: Causes and Consequences, 1974; editor (book series) Advances in Research on Teaching, 1989—. Fellow Ctr. for Advanced Study in the Behavioral Scis., 1994. Fellow: APA, Internat. Acad. Edn., Am. Psychol. Soc.; mem.: Nat. Soc. for the Study of Edn., Nat. Coun. for the Social Studies, Nat. Acad. Edn., Am. Ednl. Rsch. Assn. (Palmer O. Johnson award 1983, Presdl. citation 1995). Office: Mich State U 213B Erickson Hall East Lansing MI 48824-1034

BROPHY, JERE HALL, manufacturing company executive; b. Schenectady, Mar. 11, 1934; s. Gerald Robert and Helen Dorothy (Hall) B.; m. Joyce Elaine Wright, Aug. 18, 1956; children: Jennifer, Carolyn, Jere. BS in Chem. Engring, BS in Metall. Engring, U. Mich., 1956, MS, 1957, PhD, 1958. Asst. prof. Mass. Inst. Tech., 1958-63; sect. supr. nickel alloys sect. Paul D. Merica Research Lab., Inco, Inc., Suffern, N.Y., 1963-67, research mgr. non-ferrous group, 1967-72, asst. mgr., 1972-73, mgr., 1973-77; dir. research and devel. and dir. Paul D. Merica Research Lab., Inco, Inc. (Inco Research and Devel. Center), 1978-80; dir. advanced tech. initiation INCO Ltd., N.Y.C., 1980-82; v.p., dir. Materials and Mfg. Tech. Ctr. TRW Inc., Cleve., 1982-86, v.p. mfg. and materials devel. automotive sect., 1986-88; v.p. technology Brush Wellman Inc., Cleve., 1988-96; cons., 1996—. Author: (with J. Wolff) Thermodynamics of Structure; Contbr. (with J. Wolff) tech. articles to profl. jours. Fellow Am. Soc. Metals, AAAS; mem. Am. Inst. Mining and Metall. Engrs. (dir. IMD div. 1973-76), Am. Mgmt. Assn. (research and devel. council 1975-87). Clubs: Edgewater Yacht. Episcopalian. Home and Office: 31905 Jackson Rd Chagrin Falls OH 44022-1707

BROPHY, JEREMIAH JOSEPH, former financial company official, former army officer; b. N.Y.C., Mar. 19, 1930; s. John Joseph and Mary Margaret (Moran) B.; m. Jane Guthrie, June 4, 1955; children: John, Sandy, Greg, Elizabeth, Diane, Stephen. Student, Manhattan Coll., 1947-48; BS, U.S. Mil. Acad., 1953; postgrad., Army Command and Gen. Staff Coll., 1963, Army War Coll., 1969, Monmouth Coll., 1981. Commd. 2d lt. U.S. Army, 1953; advanced through grades to brig. gen., 1976; advisor 12th Vietnamese Inf. Rgt., Vietnam, 1963-64; comdr. 1st Bn., 327th Inf. 101st Airborne Divsn., Vietnam, 1969-70; comdr. U.S. garrison Aschaffenburg, Germany; comdr. 3d Brigade, 3d Inf. divsn., 1973-75; comdr. U.S. garrison; asst. comdr. 8th Inf. div., 1976-78; dep. comdr. Combined Arms Tng. Devels. Agy., 1978-80; dep. comdr. U.S. Army Tng. Ctr. Ft. Dix, N.J., 1980-83; stockbroker Merrill, Lynch, Pierce, Fenner & Smith, Nashville; agt. Franklin Life Ins. Co.; exec. v.p. Gen. Trust Co.; divsn. mgr. Waddell & Reed Inc., Nashville, 1983-94; cert. fin. planner BMA Fin. Svcs. Inc., Nashville, 1995—2001. Decorated D.S.M., Bronze Star valor with oak leaf cluster, Purple Heart, Legion of Merit with oak leaf cluster, Vietnamese Cross of Gallantry (3 awards), Meritorious Svc. medal, Army Commendation medal with oak leaf cluster. Mem. Assn. Grad. U.S. Mil. Acad., West Point Soc. Mid. Tenn., Mil. Officers Assn. Am. (Mid Tenn. chpt. bd. dirs., pres. 1998). Roman Catholic. Home: 6071 Bethany Blvd Nashville TN 37221-4314

BROPHY, JOSEPH THOMAS, information company executive; b. N.Y.C., Oct. 25, 1933; s. Joseph R. and Mary (Mitchell) B.; m. Carole A. Johnson, June 8, 1957; children: Thomas J., David W., Patricia J., Maureen A., Kathleen M. BS cum laude, Fordham U., 1957; grad. sr. exec. program, MIT, 1987. Paramedic St. Clares Med. Ctr., N.Y.C., 1955-57; mathematician Vitro Labs., West Orange, N.J., 1957; dir. mgmt. info. systems Prudential Ins. Co., Newark, 1957-67; v.p. Huggins & Co. (cons. actuaries and mgmt. cons.), Phila., 1967-68; v.p., chief actuary Bankers Nat. Life Ins. Co., 1968-72; pres. Travelers Ins. Co., Hartford, Conn., 1972-93; chmn. Workgroup on Elect Data Interchange, Washington, 1992-95; cons. Actuarial Scis. Assocs., Somerset, N.J., 1993—; owner, dir. Solution Point, 1996—. Bd. dirs. Engineered Bus. Sys., Travtech, Inc., Travelers TPA, Inc., Ctr. Corp. Health, U.S. Behavioral Health, Travelers Health Sys., Conservco, Accent Color Scis.; cons. in field, 1967—; enrolled actuary Employee Retirement Income Security Act (ERISA). Author: A User's Guide to Project Management. Tech. editor: Actuarial Digest. Pres. St. Patrick's Pipe Band, Inc.; bd. dirs. Cath. Family Svcs., Conn. Opera, Conn. Acad. for Edn. in Math., Sci. and Tech., Hartford Grad. Ctr.; corporator St. Francis Hosp.; chmn. adv. bd. info. scis. Grad. Bus. Sch., Fordham U., Bronx, N.Y.; advisor Actuarial Studies, Hartford U., Sch. Pub. Health, Harvard U.; trustee St. Joseph Coll., Conn. With USMCR, 1949-50, AUS, 1952-54. Recipient Disting. Info. Sci. award Data Processing Mgmt. Assn., 1986. Fellow Soc. Actuaries; mem. Am. Acad. Actuaries, Acoustical Soc. Am., Hartford Actuaries Club, N.Y. Actuaries Club, Am. Arbitration Soc. (arbitrator), Greater Hartford C. of C. (bd. dirs.), Hartford Club, Internat. Brotherhood of Magicians, Telemedicine 200, Lake Sunapee Yacht Club. Home: 154 Garnet Hill Rd PO Box 701 Sunapee NH 03782-0701 Office: Actuarial Scis Assocs 270 Davidson Ave Somerset NJ 08873-4140

BROPHY, MARY O'REILLY, environmental scientist; b. N.Y.C., Aug. 3, 1948; d. Luke Edward and Regina (Mahoney) O'Reilly; children: Robert, Sara, Lena. Student, Fordham U., 1966-68; BS, U. Mich., 1970; MS, 1972, PhD, 1979. Rsch. asst. prof. Health Sci. Ctr., Syracuse, N.Y., 1979-84; environ. toxicologist Syracuse Rsch. Corp., 1984-86; pres. ARLS Cons., Inc., Syracuse, 1993—; sr. indsl. hygienist N.Y. State Dept. Labor, Syracuse, 1987-00; environ. specialist N.Y. State Dept. Transp., Binghamton, 2000—. Adj. asst. prof. SUNY Sch. Pub. Health, Albany, 1990—; adj. prof. chemistry LeMoyne Coll., 1998—; dir. Am. Bd. Indsl. Hygiene, Lansing, Mich., 1995—2001; mem. Z10 com. Am. Nat. Stds. Inst., 2001—; mem. adv. bd. N.Y. State Inst. for Health and the Environment, 2001—. Author: An Ergonomics Guide to VDTs, 1994, (with others) Occupational Ergonomics, 1996; contbr.: ILO's Encyclopedia of Occupational Health and Safety, 1998, Implications of Hormesis for Industrial Hygienists, 2003; contbr. articles to profl. jours. Mem. Am. Indsl. Hygiene Assn., Human Factors & Ergonomics Soc., N.Y. State Assn.Transp. Engrs. Avocations: Karate, fly-fishing, dance, folk harp. Home: 7705 Farley Ln Manlius NY 13104-9571 E-mail: mbrophy@gw.dot.state.ny.us.

BROPHY, SUSAN DOROTHY, adapted physical education educator; b. Waltham, Mass., Nov. 9, 1954; d. Lawrence A. and Dorothy M. (Furbush) B. BS, U. Mass., 1976; MS, U. Wis. La Crosse, 1981. Cert. tchr. phys. edn., adapted phys. edn. tchr., Mass. Substitute tchr. Waltham, Weston and Lexington (Mass.) Sch. Depts., 1976-77; supr. recreation, in-svc. trainer W. E. Fernald State Sch., Waltham, 1978-80; cons. adapted phys. edn. East Cen. Ohio Spl. Edn. Regional Resource Ctr., Dover, 1981-82; tchr. adapted phys. edn. Heartland Area Edn. Agy., Newton, Iowa, 1982-86, Lawrence (Mass.) Sch. Dept., 1986—2001, Andover Pub. Schs., Mass., 2001—. Co-chmn. Adapted Phys. Edn. State Com., Mass., 1986—, cert. com. phys. edn. Dept. Edn., Mass., 1989-92. Co-author: (assessment test) Heartland Gross Motor Evaluation, 1985. Coach Newton YMCA Swim Team, 1985-86, Waltham (Mass.) Youth Basketball Assn., 1993-2001; co-founder Stephanie's Toy Box, Newton, 1984. Fed. Govt. grantee, 1980-81, Horace Mann grantee, 1988-89 Mem. AAHPERD (mem. local arrangements com. 1998-99), Mass. Assn. Health, Phys. Edn., Recreation and Dance (co-chair com. adapted phys. edn. 1989—, Adapted Phys. Edn. Tchr. of the Yr. award 1997, mem. honor awards com. 2001—). Avocations: horticulture, antiques, bicycling, traveling. Home: 48 Marianne Rd Waltham MA 02452-6218 Office: Andover Pub Schs South Sch 55 Woburn St Andover MA 01810

BRORBY, WADE, federal judge; b. Omaha, 1934; BS, U. Wyo., 1956, JD with honor, 1958. Bar: Wyo. County and prosecuting atty. Campbell County, Wyo., 1963—70; ptnr. Morgan Brorby Price and Arp, Gillette, Wyo., 1961—88; judge U.S. Ct. Appeals (10th cir.), Cheyenne, Wyo., 1988—2001, sr. judge, 2001—. With USAF, 1958—61. Mem.: ABA, Wyo. Bar Assn. (commr. 1968—70), Def. Lawyers Wyo., Am. Judicature Soc., Campbell County Bar Assn. Office: US Ct Appeals 10th Cir O'Mahoney Fed Bldg Rm 2018 PO Box 1028 Cheyenne WY 82003-1028 also: Byron White US Courthouse 1823 Stout St Denver CO 80257*

BROSCOE, PETER A. mortgage banker, consultant; b. NYC, Sept. 6, 1963; s. Joseph Edward and Joan Broscoe; married, Aug. 24, 1984; children: Clark, Ashley, Prescott, McKenzie, Chase. BS in Music Bus. Adminstrn., St. Joseph's Coll., Rensselaer, Ind., 1985. Cert. direct endorsed underwriter Housing Urban Devel. Pres., CEO Mortgage Express, Inc., Greenwood, Ind., 1999—; mng. mem. Trinity Title Svcs., Greenwood, 1999—; mem. Broscoe Group Properties, Greenwood, 1999—, Express Mortgage LLC, Greenwood, 2003—. Bd. dirs. Premiere Credit of N.A., Indpls. Chmn. bd. Greenwood Christian Acad., 1999—2001; chmn. bd. Area Youth Ministry, Indpls., 1999—2000. Named one of Top 40 Most Influential People Under 40 in Ind., Indpls. Bus. Jour., 2003. Mem.: Ind. Assn. Mortgage Brokers, Nat. Assn. Mortgage Brokers. Republican. Office: Mortgage Express Inc Ste A 386 Meridian Parke Ln Greenwood IN 46143

BROSDA VON KUPFERBER, BARON ALEXANDER CHRISTIAN, investment banker; b. Huckeswagen, N. Rhine, Germany, Apr. 26, 1970; came to U.S., 1994; s. Christian-George and Emmi-Martina (Laugallies) B.; m. Katerina. Diploma, Humanistic-Classical and, Econ. Sch., Wuppertal, Germany, 1991. Investment banker various, Dusseldorf, Germany, 1991-92; exec. product mgr., sales trainer AWD, Hanover, Germany, 1992-93; chmn., CEO ABMK & Co. Internat. Ent., Inc., N.Y.C., 1994; v.p., mktg. dir. Lyon Mountain Spring Water, Inc., Stamford, N.Y., 1994—; shareholder, 1994; bd. dirs. The Maui Inst., Hawaii, 1994—; pres. Stamford Inst. for Rsch., Consulting and Internat. Comm., 1995—; CEO and chmn. bd. Stamford Fin. Theatrical Fund, Inc., 1995—. Exec. v.p., treas. European Mkt. Stamford Fin., Inc., N.Y., 1994-97; co-chmn. Taurus Internat. Investments, Inc., 1995. Chmn. ball com. Christmas Feeling Fund, Stamford, N.Y., vice chmn. of Fund. Recipient 20th Achievement award U.S. Libr. Congress, Degree of Merit for outstanding contribution to Finance and Industry, Melrose Press Ltd.; named Man of Yr., ABI, 1996, Hon. Dep. Gov., ABIRA, Hall of Fame of Internat. Bus. People. Mem. Club of Intellectuals, Cambridge, England, C. of C., Stamford, N.Y., Congressional Group, German-American C. of C., European-American C. of C., Rotary Internat., Police Benevolent Assn. (hon.), Comthur of Aragon Priory Order of St. John. Roman Catholic. Avocations: golf, reading, sailing, racing, diving. E-mail: alexbrosda@prodigy.net.

BROSELOW, LINDA LATT, medical office technician, aviculturist; b. Harrisburg, Pa., July 9, 1940; d. Herman and Ricci (Buch) Latt; m. Robert Joel Broselow, Nov. 26, 1966; children: Andrew M., Katherine, Jordan. BS, Pa. State U., 1962; MA, Columbia U., 1965. Vol. Peace Corps, Ankara, Turkey, 1962-64; office mgr. Robert J. Broselow, M.D., Lubbock, Tex., 1984-88, med. office technician, 1990-98. Vol. South Park Hosp., Lubbock, 1986-87, Ronald McDonald House, Lubbock, 1990-92. Mem. ASPCA, Am. Diabetes Assn., Am. Assn. Ret. Persons, Audubon Soc., Arkadashlar, Assn. of Univ. Women, Children Internat. Avocation: reading. Home: 4609 9th St Lubbock TX 79416-4710 Office: 4609 9th St Lubbock TX 79416 Fax: (806) 795-2005. E-mail: mamoollbb@sbcglobal.net.

BROSHAR, ROBERT CLARE, architect; b. Waterloo, Iowa, May 20, 1931; s. Clare McDanel and Stella Mae (Scott) B.; m. Joyce Elaine Lukes, June 27, 1953; children: Scott, Michael, Matthew, Patrick, Elizabeth. B.Arch., Iowa State U., 1954. Ptnr. Henry & Broshar, 1960-62, Thorson, Brom, Broshar, Snyder (architects), Waterloo, 1963-96. Bd. dirs., pres. Blackhawk County YMCA, 1972-75; chmn. bd. dirs. Goodwill Industries, 1995-96; mem. Gov.'s Com. Employment of Handicapped, 1975-79; bd. dirs. Central Gardens North Iowa, 2003 ; vice-chmn. Riverdity Soc. for Historic Preservation., 2003. 1st lt. AUS, 1954-56. Recipient Disting. Svc. award Iowa Easter Seal Soc., 1976, Leon Chatelain award Nat. Easter Seal Soc., 1983, Iowa State U. Alumni Achievement award, 1982, Arch. Excellence award Master Builders of Iowa, 2001; named Iowa State U. Parent of Yr., 1980. Fellow: AIA (Iowa pres. 1972, nat. dir. 1975—78, nat. v.p. 1979—81, 1982, nat. pres. 1983, Iowa Medal of Honor 1992), Royal Archtl. Inst. Can. (hon.); mem.: Soc. Archs. Guatemala (hon.), Soc. Archs. Mex. (hon.), Rotary (Paul Harris fellow), Phi Kappa Phi, Tau Sigma Delta, Delta Upsilon, Tau Beta Pi, Knight of St. Patrick Engring. Soc., Iowa State U. Order of Knoll. Republican. Methodist. Home: 15340 Dodge Ave Clear Lake IA 50428-8773 E-mail: rojobro@rconnect.com.

BROSILOW, COLEMAN BERNARD, chemical engineering educator; b. Phila., Nov. 14, 1934; s. Samuel and Ethel (Stein) B.; m. Rosalie Ziegleman, Feb. 18, 1962; children— Rachelle, Benjamin. BS, Drexel U., 1957; M.Ch.E., Poly. Inst. N.Y., 1959, PhD, 1962. Systems engr. Am. Cyanamid Co., Process Analysis Group, Wayne, N.J., 1962-63; asst. prof. chem. engring. Case Western Res. U., Cleve., 1963-67, assoc. prof., 1967-73, prof. chem. engring., 1973—2001, prof. emeritus, 2001—, chmn. dept. chem. engring., 1980-84. Chmn. bd. Control Soft Corp., 1985-2001, now bd. dirs.; vis. prof. chem. engring. The Technion, Haifa, Israel, 1971-72, Ben Gurion U., Israel, 2000; cons. in field. Contbr. articles to profl. jours.; editl. bd.: Am. Inst. Chem. Engrs. Jour, 1980-85, Techniques of Model-based Control, 2002; patentee in field. Founding mem. bd. trustees Solomon Schecter Day Sch. of Cleve., 1978—, pres., 1978-84. . Fellow AIChE (computing in chem. engring. award 1989); mem. Sigma Xi, Tau Beta Pi, Phi Lambda Upsilon. Jewish. Home: 25 Shoham St Rehovot 76227 Israel Office: Ben Gurion U of the Negev Dept Chem Engring PO Box 653 Beer Sheva 84105 Israel E-mail: cbb@po.cwru.edu.

BROSIUS, SCOTT DAVID, professional baseball player; b. Hillsboro, Oreg., Aug. 15, 1966; m. Jennifer Brosius; children: Allison, Megan, David. Student, Linfield Coll., Oreg. 3d baseman Oakland Athletics, Calif., 1987—97, N.Y. Yankees, 1998—. Office: c/o NY Yankees Yankee Stadium E 161st St and River Ave Bronx NY 10451

BROSKY, MARY ELIZABETH, dental educator, dentist; b. Pitts., Pa., Jan. 25, 1966; d. Joseph Paul Brosky and Mary Margaret Morgan; m. Paul Joseph Imdieke, Oct. 6, 2001. BA, Chatham Coll., Pitts., 1989; DMD, U. Pitts., 1994. Lic. prosthodontics U. of Pitts., maxillofacial prosthetics U. of Pitts. Med. Ctr. Asst. prof. prosthodontics U. of Minn., Mpls., 1998—; maxillofacial prosthodontist U. of Minn. Cancer Ctr., Mpls., 1998—. Prosthodontist U. of Minn. Faculty Practice, Mpls., 1998—. Contbr. articles to profl. jours. Dental Sch. sen. U. of Minn., Mpls., 2002—. Mem.: Internat. Assn. Dental Rsch. (assoc.), Am. Coll. of Prosthodontists (assoc.). Achievements include research in Dimensional change and strain during mandibular movement; The use of Ethyol woth or without Pilocarpine to provide relief of oral side effects in head and neck cancer patients undergoing radiation therapy; The Effect Of Chemotherapy And Radiotherapy On Saliva Quantity In Head And Neck Cancer Patients; The effect of Cevimeline on saliva quantity in head and neck cancer patients; Safety and efficacy of Benzydamine hydrochloride in head and neck cancer patients; The anterior cantilever length in the implant-supported screw retained mandibular prosthesis; A clinical study evaluating the compliance of resilient denture liners; Clinical evaluation resilient denture liner: Candida count and speciation; Determining the validity of new 3-D measuring devices. Office: U Minn 515 Delaware St SE Minneapolis MN 55455 E-mail: brosk001@tc.umn.edu.

BROSLOVSKY, LEWIS, physician; b. Lakewood, N.J., June 24, 1948; BA in Biology, Gettysburg Coll., 1970; MD, U. Bologna, Italy, 1977. Intern Brookdale Hosp. Medical Ctr., Bklyn., 1977-78, resident ob-gyn, 1978-81; attending ob-gyn Cmty. Gen. Hosp., Sullivan Co. Harris, N.Y., 1982-92; chmn. dept. ob-gyn. Horton Med. Ctr., Middletown, N.Y., 1992—. Fellow ACOG, Am. Soc. Colposcopy and Cervical Pathology; mem. Am. Assn. Gynecologic Laparoscopists. Office: 75 Crystal Run Rd Ste 200 Middletown NY 10941 also: 18 Old Monticello Rd Ferndale NY 12734-5201 also: 155 Crystal Run Rd Middletown NY 10941 also: 254 Route 17K Ste 201 Newburgh NY 12550-8300

BROSMAN, STANLEY ALLEN, urologist; b. Indpls., Nov. 11, 1934; s. Hyman Sam and Rose Mary (Korlin) B.; m. Victoria Brosman, July 11, 1983; children: Wayne, Michael, Gregory. BS, Ind. U., Bloomington, 1959; MD, Ind. U., Indpls., 1959. Diplomate Am. Bd. Urology. Commd. 1st lt. USAF, 1960, advanced through grades to lt. col., 1974; ret., 1975; intern Jackson Meml. Hosp., Miami, Fla., 1959—60; resident gen. surgery Wadsworth VA Hosp., LA, 1960—61; resident in urology UCLA, 1961—65; chief urology UCLA/Harbor Gen. Hosp., 1965—80; pvt. practice, Santa Monica, Calif., 1990—. Med. dir. Pacific Ctrs. for Clin. Rsch., 1996—; bd. dirs. Affiliated Rsch. Ctrs., 1993-2000, Prostate Cancer Rsch. Inst., 1998—, Ams. Doctor, Gurnee, Ill., 2000—. Contbr. over 200 articles to med. jours., chpt. to books. Recipient 0ver 250 rsch. grants from govtl. agys., including NIH, Nat. Cancer Inst. Mem. AMA, ACS, Am. Urol. Assn., Soc. Urologic Oncology, Soc. Surg. Oncology, Soc. Basic Urologic Rsch. Office: Pacific Urology Inst Ste 510 2021 Santa Monica Blvd Santa Monica CA 90404 E-mail: pacsm@aol.com.

BROSNAHAN, ROGER PAUL, lawyer; b. Kansas City, Mo., Aug. 9, 1935; s. Earl and Helen (Mottin) B.; m. Jill Farley, Aug. 2, 1958; children: Paul, Connor, Helen, Farley, Tracy, Hugh, Lee. BS, St. Louis U., 1956; LLB, Mich. U., 1959. Bar: Mo. 1959, Minn. 1959, U.S. Ct. Appeals (6th cir.) 1984, U.S. Ct. Appeals (10th cir.) 1999, U.S. Ct. Appeals (8th cir.) 1975, U.S. Supreme Ct. 1971. Ptnr. Streater, Murphy, Brosnahan & Langford, Winona, Minn., 1959-78, Kutak, Rock & Huie, Mpls., 1979-82, Robins, Kaplan, Miller & Ciresi, Mpls., 1982-93, Brosnahan, Joseph & Suggs P.A., Mpls., 1993-99; prin. Law Offices of Roger P. Brosnahan, Mpls., 1999—. Mem.: ATLA, ABA (state del. 1976—88), Nat. Conf. Bar Pres. (pres. 1980—81), Minn. Bar Assn. (pres. 1974—75), Minn. Trial Lawyers Assn., Am. Bd. Trial Advocates. Democrat. Roman Catholic. Office: Law Offices of Roger P Brosnahan 116 Center St Winona MN 55987 Mailing: 220 N Zapata Hwy #11A Laredo TX 78043 Fax: 507-457-3001. E-mail: rpbros@mwt.net.

BROSNAN, PETER LAWRENCE, documentary filmmaker; b. Bklyn., July 6, 1952; s. John Joseph and Audrey Barbara (Holran) B. BFA, NYU, N.Y.C., 1974; MA, U. So. Calif., 1979, Pepperdine U., 1995. Documentary filmmaker, writer, L.A., 1980—. Dir. DeMille Project, Hollywood Heritage, L.A., 1988—. Author: (screenplays) Heart of Darkness, 1992, The Ark, 1994, Perfect Target, 1996; co-author: (book) PML Report, 1989; writer: (documentary film) Ghosts of Cape Horn, 1980 (World Ship Trust award); prodr., dir.: (TV documentary) The Lost City, 1992; writer, segment prodr.: (PBS series) Faces of Culture, 1983-84 (Emmy award 1984), Writer Marketing, 1984 (Emmy award 1985); dir.: (documentary) Sand Castles, 1995. Democrat.

BROSS, IRWIN DUDLEY JACKSON, biostatistician; b. Halloway, Ohio, Nov. 13, 1921; s. Samuel and Mina (Jackson) B.; m. Rida Singer, Aug. 6, 1949; children: Dean, Valerie, Neal. BA in Math, UCLA, 1942; MA in Exptl. Stats, N.C. State U., 1948, PhD in Exptl. Stats, 1949. Research asso. dept. biostatistics Johns Hopkins U., 1949-52; asst. prof. public health and preventive medicine Cornell U., 1952-59; head research, design and analysis Sloan Kettering Inst., 1952-59; dir. biostatistics Roswell Park Meml. Inst., Buffalo, N.Y., 1959-83; pres. Biomed. Metatech., Inc., 1983—; research prof. biostatistics State U. N.Y. at Buffalo, 1961-83; asso. dept. epidemiology Johns Hopkins U., 1971-85. Author: Design for Decision, 1953, Scientific Strategies in Human Affairs: To Tell the Truth, 1975, Scientific Strategies to Save Your Life, 1981, Crimes of Official Science: A Casebook, 1988, Scientific Fraud vs. Scientific Truth, 1992, Fifty Years of Folly and Fraud in the Name of Science, 1994, (CD-ROM, 6 books) History of U.S. Science and Medicine in the Cold War, 1996; contbr. numerous articles in field to profl. jours. Served with U.S. Army, 1941-45. Mem. AAAS, Am. Statis. Assn., Biometric Soc., Am. Coll. Epidemiol. Home and Office: 109 Maynard Dr Buffalo NY 14226-3365 E-mail: idbross@pce.net.

BROSSMAN, MARK EDWARD, lawyer; b. N.Y.C., Aug. 13, 1953; s. Isadore Jack and Blanche Brossman. BS, Cornell U., 1975; JD, NYU, 1978, LLM in Labor Law, 1981. Bar: N.Y. 1979, U.S. Dist. Ct. (so. and ea. dists.) N.Y. 1979, U.S. Dist. Ct. (no. and we. dists.) N.Y. 1981, U.S. Ct. Appeals (6th cir.) 1981, U.S. Ct. Appeals (2d cir.) 1983, U.S. Supreme Ct. 1983, U.S. Ct. Appeals (11th cir.) 1989. Assoc. Morgan, Lewis and Bockius, N.Y.C., 1978-83, Grutman, Miller et al, N.Y.C., 1984-85, ptnr., 1985-86; counsel Chadbourne and Parke, N.Y.C., 1986-87, ptnr., 1987-98, Schulte, Roth & Zabel, N.Y.C., 1998—. Lectr. Cornell U., 1983—. Author: Social Investing for Pension Funds, 1982; contbr. articles to profl. jours. Mem. ABA, Assn. of Bar of City of N.Y., N.Y. State Bar Assn., Indsl. Rels. Research Assn., Phi Kappa Phi. Office: Schulte Roth & Zabel LLP 919 Third Ave New York NY 10022

BROSZ, MARGARET HEADLEY, pediatrics nurse; b. Dover, N.J., Dec. 31, 1951; d. Charles E. and Carolyn (Cobb) H.; m. Walter J. Brosz, May 28, 1978. Student, Douglass Coll., New Brunswick, N.J., 1970-72; BS in Nursing, Cornell U., 1974; MS, Boston Coll., Chestnut Hill, Mass., 1978. Cert. trainer medication adminstrs. Nurse Vis. Nurse Assn. Boston, 1974-76; pediatric nurse practitioner Wrentham (Mass.) State Sch., Boston Children's Hosp., 1978-80; staff nurse pediatrics ICU Thomas Jefferson U. Hosp., Phila., 1980-81; employee health clinician Children's Hosp. Phila., 1981-83; nurse mgr. The Woods Svcs., Langhorne, Pa., 1983—. Vol. interpreter Pennsbury Manor, Morrisville, Pa.; former bd. dirs. Pennsbury Soc. Mem. Devel. Disabilities, 1996—2001. Mem. Devel. Disabilities Nurses Assn.

BROTEN, ROBERT GARY, optician, writer; b. Seattle, Mar. 19, 1946; s. Fred T. Broten and Leona Broten (Howard); m. Fe Bondoc Bondoc, May 9, 1965 (div. June 10, 1996); 1 child, Robert Patrick. B.A., Mo. Valley Coll., Marshall, MO., 1976—78. Optician Am. Bd. of Opticianary, 2000. Optician Moreland Vision Ctr., Portland, Oreg., 2002—; optical lab tech/optician LensCrafters, Portland, Oreg., 1997—2002. Author: (novel) Cardinal Edict, (on-line article) How lenses are made. Founder/moderator Troutdale Fiction Writers Assn., Troutdale, Oreg., 1999—2000. E-4 USAF. Mem.: Opticians Assn. of Oreg., Am. Bd. of Opticianary. Personal E-mail: quest.bbisme@verizon.net.

BROTHERS, JOHN ALFRED, retired oil company executive; b. Huntington, W.Va., Nov. 10, 1940; s. John Luther and Genevieve (Monti) B.; m. Paula Sprague Benson, June 21, 1975. BS, Va. Poly. Inst., 1962, MS, 1965, PhD, 1966; postgrad advanced mgmt. program, Harvard U., 1981. With Internat. Nickel Co., 1962-64; with Ashland Oil, Inc., Ky., 1966—, sr. v.p., 1983-87; sr. v.p., group operating officer Ashland Oil Inc., 1987-97; with Ashland Chem. Co., Columbus, Ohio, 1974-88, pres., 1983-88; exec. v.p. Ashland, Inc., 1997-99; ret., 1999. Adj. prof. engring. Ohio State U., 1978—; pres. bus. adv. coun., 1981—. Bd. dirs. Columbus Mus. Art, Columbus Children's Hosp., Ohio Dominican Coll., 1984—. NSF fellow, 1965-66; named Outstanding Young Man U.S. C. of C., 1972 Mem. Am. Petroleum Inst., Chem. Mfrs. Assn., Columbus C. of C. (bd. dirs.), Tau Beta Pi, Phi Kappa Phi. Clubs: Scioto Country, Rolling Rock, Double Eagle Golf, Hole-in-the-Wall Golf, Mill Reef, Columbus. Republican. also: Ashland Inc PO Box 391 Covington KY 41015-0391

BROTHERS, JOYCE DIANE, television personality, psychologist; b. N.Y.C. d. Morris K. and Estelle (Rapoport) Bauer; m. Milton Brothers, July 4, 1949; 1 child, Lisa Robin. BS, Cornell U., 1947; MA, Columbia U., 1950, PhD, 1953; LHD (hon.), Franklin Pierce Coll., Gettysburg Coll., Lehigh U., 1994, Mt. St. Mary Coll., 1998. Asst. in psychology Columbia U., N.Y.C., 1948-52; instr. psychology Hunter Coll., N.Y.C., 1948-52; ind. psychologist, writer, 1952—. Co-host: TV program Sports Showcase, 1956; appearances: TV program Dr. Joyce Brothers, 1958-63, Consult Dr. Brothers, 1960-66, Ask Dr. Brothers, 1965-75; hostess (TV syndication) Living Easy with Dr. Joyce Brothers, 1972-75; columnist TV syndication, N.Am. Newspaper Alliance, 1961-71, Bell-McClure Syndicate, 1963-71, King Features Syndicate, 1972—, Good Housekeeping mag., 1962— ; appearances Sta. WNBC, 1966-70; radio program Emphasis, 1966-75, Monitor, 1967-75, Sta. WMCA, 1970-73, ABC Reports, 1966-67, NBC Radio Network Newsline, 1975— ; news analyst radio program, Metro Media-TV, 1975-76, news corr., TVN, Inc., 1975-76, Sta. KABC-TV, 1977-82, Sta. WABC-TV, 1980-82,, 86-88, Sta. WLS-TV, 1980-82, NIWS Syndicated News Service, 1982-84, The Dr. Joyce Brothers Program, The Disney Channel, 1985, Sta. KCBS-TV News, 1987—; spl. feature writer Hearst papers, UPI; current affairs spl. corr. Fox TV Syndication, 1990-97; featured on A&E's Biography, 1999; author: Ten Days to a Successful Memory, 1959, Woman, 1961, The Brothers System for Liberated Love and Marriage, 1975, How to Get Whatever You Want Out of Life, 1978, What Every Woman Should Know About Men, 1982, What Every Woman Ought to Know About Love and Marriage, 1988, The Successful Woman, 1989, Widowed, 1990, Positive Plus: The Practical Plan to Liking Yourself Better, 1994. Co-chmn. sports com. Lighthouse for Blind; door-to-door chmn. Fedn. Jewish Philanthropies, N.Y.C.; mem. fund raising com. Olympic Fund; mem. People-to-People Program. Winner $64,000 Question TV Program, 1956, $64,000 Challenge, 1957; recipient Mennen Baby Found. award, 1959, Newhouse Newspaper award, 1959, Am. Acad. Achievement award, Am. Parkinson Disease Assn. award, 1971, Deadline award Sigma Delta Chi, 1971, Pres.'s Cabinet award U. Detroit, 1975, Woman of Achievement award Women's City Club Cleve., 1981, award Calif. Home Econs. Assn., 1981, award Distrubutive Edn. Clubs Am., 1981, Golden Gavel Excellence in Comm. award Toastmasters, 1982, Pub. Svc. award Ridgewood Women's Club, 1987, Women Who Make a Difference award Sen. Bill Bradley, 1990, Gt. Am. award Bards of Bohemia, 1993, Diamond award, 1994, George M. and Mary Jane Leader Healthcare Achievement award, 1995, Nat. Cmty. Svc. award McQuade Children Svcs., 1998. Mem. Sigma Xi. Office: NBC Westwood One Radio Network 1700 Broadway New York NY 10019-5905

BROTHERSON, MARY LOU NELSON, education educator; b. N.Y.C., Oct. 9, 1933; d. Harry David and Estelle Molly (Cohen) Nelson; m. Donald E. Brotherson, July 19, 1959; children: Nancy, Elizabeth. B of Edn. magna cum laude, U. Miami, 1955; MEd, U. Ill., 1967, EdD, 1982. Tchr. elem. sch. Dade County Schs., Miami Beach, Fla., 1955-59, Champaign (Ill.) Unit 4, 1959-61; prof., dir. tchr. edn. Parkland Coll., Champaign, 1969-93; adj. prof. edn. St. Thomas U., North Miami, Fla., 1993 96; cons. in field, 1996—2003; adj. prof. grad. tchr. edn. Nova Southeastern U., 1996—2003; undergrad. adv. bd. Barry U., 2000—03. Interviewer and educator, Holocaust Documentation and Edn. Ctr., Miami, 1994-2003. Author: New Careers in Education: Teacher Aide Handbook, 1971; author/editor: Teacher Aide Manual for Special Education, 1982. Chair East Ctrl. Holocaust Edn. Com., 1989-93; bd. dirs. Sinai Temple, Champaign, 1983-86, Temple Sinai, North Miami Beach, 1996-03, Ctrl. Agy. Jewish Edn., Miami, 1994-97. Recipient Quality of Life award Champaign-Urbana Jewish Fedn.; U. Miami scholar, 1955; E.P.D.A. Nat. Leadership fellow U. Ill., 1977-80. Mem. Nat. Coun. Tchrs. English, Nat. Assn. Edn. Young Children (validator), Kappa Delta Pi (nat. Point of Excellence award), Delta Kappa Gamma. Independent. Jewish. Avocations: reading, music, art, storytelling. Home and Office: 3640 Yacht Club Dr Apt 810 Miami FL 33180-3571

BROTHERSTON, LEZ, set designer, costumer; Degree in Theatre Design, Ctrl. Sch. Art and Design, 1984. Set designer: Letter to Brezhnev, Highland Fling, Cinderella (1998 Olivier Award for outstanding achievement in dance), Swan Lake (Olivier Award), The Hunchback of Notre Dame, Giselle, Dracula, The Brontes, Strange Meeting, Romeo and Juliet, A Christmas Carol; other recent dance designs include: Just Scratchin' the Surface, Greymatter, David Copperfield, Northanger Abbey, The Last Romantics, Handling Bach, The Prisoner of Zenda, The Eleventh Commandment, Hindle Wakes (Manchester

Royal Exch., Manchester Evening News and Brit. Reg. Theatre award nominations), The Schoolmistress, Alarms and Excursions, Jane Eyre, The Sisters Rosenweig, Neville's Island (1995 Olivier Award nomination for best set design), Rosencrantz and Guildenstern Are Dead; opera designs include prodns. for Opera Zuld, Hong Kong Arts Festival, Opera North, Glyndebourne Touring Opera, Teatro Bellini, Royal Danish Opera and De Vlaamse Opera; musicals include: Side by Side by Sondheim, Maria Friedman by Special Arrangement. Winner 1999 Tony award for Swanlater for set and costume design, 1999 Barclays Theatre award for outstanding achievement in dance. Office: Mayer & Eden Ltd 34 Kingley Ct London W1R 5Le England

BROTHERTON, JONATHAN PAUL, music educator; b. Glennallen, Alaska, Oct. 11, 1961; s. Harley Alvin Brotherton and Mary Barbara Miller; m. Donna Faye Grubb, Dec. 13, 1986; children: Kayla, Matthew, Michael, Nicholas. BA, George Fox Coll., 1983; MusM, U. Cin., 1987, D in Music Adminstrn., 1998. Music instr. U. Alaska, Anchorage, 1988—92, Whitman Coll., Walla Walla, Wash., 1994—95; asst. prof. music Iowa Wesleyan Coll., Mt. Pleasant, Iowa, 1995—98; assoc. prof. music Greensboro (N.C.) Coll., 1998—. Summer dir. choral activities Brevard (N.C.) Music Ctr., 1994—98; guest lectr. in field. Mem.: Am. Choral Dirs. Assn., Music Educators Nat. Assn. Office: Greensboro Coll 815 West Market Street Greensboro NC 27401

BROTMAN, CAROL EILEEN, adult education educator, advocate; b. L.A., Feb. 17, 1955; d. Hyman and Beverly Joanne (Krause) B. AA, L.A. Pierce Coll., 1977; BA, U. So. Calif., L.A., 1984; postgrad., UCLA, 1990, cert. legal asst., 1991; grad. studies in spl. edn., Calif. State U., Northridge, 2000—. Cert. adult edn. tchr., Calif. Tchr. divsn. adult and career edn. L.A. Unified Sch. Dist., 1986—; tchr. adult edn. and ESL North Hollywood (Calif.) Adult Sch., 1987-94, dept. chair, 1990-91; pre-employment trainer Refugee Employment Tng. Project, 1995-99; tchr. ESL, Met. Skills Ctr., L.A., 1995-2000; tchr. ESL, spl. edn. Gardena (Calif.) Adult Sch. Coastal Asian Pacific Branch, 1999-2001; literacy tchr. Ctrl. Adult Sch., 2001; mem. adv. com. Jewish Programs for the Disabled, 2001—. Founder Families for Quality Care, San Fernando Valley, Calif., 1983-86; mem. com. L.A. Pub. Libr. Ctrl. Libr., internat. langs. dept. Langs. Enterprises and Resources Network, 1991; vol. paralegal Harriet Buhai Ctr. for Family Law, 1992-94; organizer adult-student cmty. group Thanksgiving dinner for new immigrants St. Patrick's Ch., North Hollywood, 1987-90; mem. Daily News Ednl. Adv. Bd., 1999—; literacy tchr. Ctr.Adult Sch., 2001; adv. com., ednl. adv. bd. Daily News, 1999-2001. Recipient Mayor's Commendation, 1984, Older Women's League, 1985, Cert. of Tribute, Harriet Buhai Ctr. for Family Law, 1992, 93, Cert. of Appreciation for Outstanding Vol. Work, Family Law Sect., L.A. County Bar Assn. and Superior Ct. of L.A., 1993, Cert. of Appreciation, Coastal Asian Pacific Mental Health Ctr., 2000, Autism Soc. L.A. Mem.: L.A. Film Tchrs. Assn., United Tchrs. of L.A., Rare Fruit Growers Assn., Calif. Coun. Adult Edn., Learning Disabilities Assn. Calif., Austism Soc. L.A. Home: 10921 Reseda Blvd Northridge CA 91326-2803 E-mail: CEBrotman@aol.com.

BROTMAN, DANIEL J. internist, researcher; b. Boston, Mass., Nov. 6, 1969; s. Carl J. and Sally C. Brotman; m. Edith Raphael, Apr. 12, 1997; children: Parker I., Naomi K. MD, U. Va., 1997. Diplomate Am. Bd. Internal Medicine. Resident in internal medicine Johns Hopkins Hosp., Balt., 1997—2000; assoc. staff in gen. internal medicine Cleve. Clinic Found., Cleve., 2000—. Asst. clin. prof. medicine Pa. State U., Hershey, 2001—. Contbr. articles to profl.jours. Mem.: Soc. Gen. Internal Medicine, ACP-Am. Soc. Internal Medicine, Nat. Assn. Inpatient Physicians, Alpha Omega Alpha. Office: Cleveland Clinic Found Desk E13 9500 Euclid Ave Cleveland OH 44195 Office Fax: 216-444-8530. E-mail: brotmad@ccf.org.

BROTMAN, DAVID JOEL, retired architectural firm executive, consultant; b. Balt., Jan. 21, 1945; BS in Architecture, U. Cin., 1968. Registered Ariz., Calif., Colo., D.C., Fla., Ga., Hawaii, La., Md., N.J., N.Y., Nev., Ohio, Oreg., Tex., Utah. Arch. Locke & Jackson, Balt., 1968, The Archtl. Affiliation, Towson, Md., 1968-75; joined RTKL, Balt., 1975-79, arch. Dallas, 1979-90, v.p., 1984—2000, exec. v.p., mng. dir. L.A., 1990-2000, vice chmn., 1994-2000; prin. Sunset Consultants, Manhattan Beach, Calif., 2000—. Tchr. U. Tex. Sch. Architecture, Arlington, Catonsville (Md.) C.C.; arbitrator Am. Stock Exch., N.Y. Stock Exch., Nat. Assn. Security Dealers. Prin. works include Galleria at South Bay, Redondo Beach, Calif., Eton Sq. (Design Tex. Soc. Archs., 1986), Computer Sci. Corp., Fairfax County, Va., AT&T Customer Tech. Ctr., Dallas (Honor award Dallas chpt. AIA 1988), Tysons Corner Ctr., McLean Va. (Design award Monitor Ctrs. and Stores of Excellence 1989, Design award Internat. Shopping Ctrs. 1989, Exceptional Design award Fairfax County, Va. 1990, Modernization Excellence award Bldgs., 1990, Excellence award Urban Land Inst. 1992), St. Andrews (Scotland) Old Course Hotel, Tower City Ctr., Cleve., Eastland Shopping Ctr., Melbourne, Australia, Morley City Shopping Ctr., Perth, Australia, Dong An Market, Beijing, China, Desert Passage at Alladin, Las Vegas, Sci. and Tech. Mus., Shanghi, 825 Market St., San Francisco, many others; contbr. articles to profl. jours. Mem.: AIA, Urban Land Inst., Nat. Coun. Archtl. Registration Bds., Internat. Coun. Shopping Ctrs. E-mail: sunset100@earthlink.net.

BROTMAN, RICHARD DENNIS, counselor; b. Detroit, Nov. 2, 1952; s. Alfred David and Dorothy G. (Mansfield) B.; m. Debra Louise Hobold, Sept. 9, 1979. AA, East L.A. Jr. Coll., 1972; AB, U. So. Calif., 1974, Ms, 1976. Lic. marriage, family and child counselor, Calif.; cert. counselor, Calif. Instructional media coord. Audiovisual divsn. Pub. Libr., City of Alhambra, Calif., 1971-78; clin. supr. Hollywood-Sunset Cmty. Clinic, L.A., 1976—; client program coord. North Los Angles County Regional Ctr. for Devel. Disabled, 1978-81; sr. counselor Eastern L.A. Regional Ctr. for Devel. Disabled, 1981-85; dir. cmty. svcs. Almansor Edn. Ctr., 1985-87; tng. and resource devel. Children's Home Soc. Calif., 1987-90; program supr. Pacific Clinics-East, 1990-94; assoc. dir. clin. svcs., dir. clin. svcs. Alma Family Svcs., 1994—2002; probable cause hearing officer Orange County (Calif.) Healthcare Agy., 1986—. Corp. dir. San Gabriel Mission Players, 1973-75. Mem. Am. Assn. for Marriage and Family Therapy (approved supr.), Calif. Pers. and Guidance Assn., Calif. Rehab. Counselors Assn. (officer), San Fernando Valley Consortium of Agys. Serving Devel. Disabled Citizens (chmn. recreation subcom), L.A. Aquarium Soc. Democrat. Home: 3515 Brandon St Pasadena CA 91107-4542 E-mail: brieftherapy@sbcglobal.net.

BROTMAN, STANLEY SEYMOUR, federal judge; b. Vineland, N.J., July 27, 1924; s. Herman Nathaniel and Fanny (Melletz) B.; m. Suzanne M. Simon, Sept. 9, 1951; children: Richard A., Alison B. BA, Yale U., 1947; LLB, Harvard U., 1950. Bar: N.J. 1950, D.C. 1951. Pvt. practice, Vineland, 1952-57; ptnr. Shapiro, Brotman, Eisenstat & Capizola, Vineland, 1957-75; judge U.S. Dist. Ct. N.J., Camden, 1975—; acting chief judge Dist. Ct. of V.I., 1989-92; judge U.S. Fgn. Intelligence Surveillance Ct., 1997—. Mem. N.J. Bd. Bar Examiners, 1970-74. Chmn. editl. bd. N.J. State Bar Jour, 1969-74; contbr. articles to profl. jours. Trustee Newcomb Hosp., Vineland, 1953-68. With U.S. Army, 1943-45, 51-52. Fellow Am. Bar Found., Jud. Conf. U.S. (space and facilities com. 1987-93); mem. ABA (ho. of dels. 1975-80, state del. 1982-93, mem. judicial immigration edn. project, chmn. adv. com. 1996—), Nat. Conf. Fed. Trial Judges (exec. com. 1984-87, chmn.-elect 1986-87, chmn. 1987-88, chmn. standing com. jud. selection, tenure and compensation 1988-92, chmn. steering com. of nominating com. 1992-93, standing com. Fed. Jud. Improvements 1992-2003), Am. Judicature Soc. (dir. 1995-2000), N.J. State Bar Assn. (pres. 1974-75), Cumberland County Bar Assn. (pres. 1969-70), Assn. of Fed. Bar of State of N.J., Harvard U. Law Sch. Assn. N.J. (pres. 1974-75), Fed. Judges Assn. (v.p. 1993-97), Yale U. Alumni Assn., Am. Legion, Jewish War Vets., Yale Club, B'nai B'rith, Masons, Shriners. Office: MH Cohen US Courthouse 6030 MH Cohen US Courthouse 4th and Cooper St Camden NJ 08102

BROTT, IRVING DEERIN, JR., lawyer, judge; b. Buffalo, June 28, 1930; s. Irving Deerin and Lillian May (Cooke) B.; m. Suzanne Hunt, July 11, 1959 (dec. Sept. 1979); children: Megan Cooke, Meryl Hunt, Gordon Alexander MacDonald; m. Donna Rey Kohl, Apr. 19, 1986. BS, Bowling Green State U., 1952; JD, U. Buffalo, 1955. Bar: N.Y. 1955. Assoc. Phillips, Lytle, Hitchcock, Blaine & Huber, Buffalo, 1957-68, ptnr., 1968-94; retired, 1995. Town justice Town of Aurora Ct., East Aurora, N.Y., 1966-94; asst. treas., treas., chmn. fin. com. Camp Fire Girls Buffalo and Erie County, 1966-79; bd. dirs. N.Y. Employee Benefits Conf., 1979-94, v.p., 1993-94. Mem. Erie County Bar Assn., N.Y. State Magistrates Assn., East Aurora Country Club, Myakka Pines Golf Club. Avocations: golf, tennis. Home: 950 Inlet Circle Rd Venice FL 34285

BROTTON, JOYCE DUPRAS, English language educator; m. Charles Michael Brotton, Oct. 26, 1968; children: Charles Michael, Ann Brotton Harvey. BA, George Mason U., 1992, MA, 1993, D in Arts, 2002. Intelligence processing U.S. Dept. of Def., Washington, 1963—68; prof. English No. Va. C.C., Annandale, Va., 1994—. Exec. sec. Adv. Bd., Cert. in Profl. Writing, Annandale, Va., 1999—; coord., cert. in profl. writing No. Va. C.C., Annandale, Va., 1999—; conf. chair Va. English Discipline Peer Group of C.C. English Tchrs., 2002. Prodr.(narrator): (televised video) The Theory of Editing, The Practice of Editing, Writing User Manuals; contbr. articles to profl. jours. Chair, scholarship awards Greenbriar Woman's Club, Fairfax, Va., 1995—2002; speaker-world lit. and profl. writing Speakers Bur., No. Va. C.C., Annandale, Va., 1998—2002. Mem.: Assn. Tchrs. of Tech. Writing (assoc.), Two-Year Coll. English (assoc.; presenter 1997—2001), Golden Key. Avocations: world travel, theater, reviewing books. Office: Northern Va Cmty Coll 8333 Little River Turnpike Annandale VA 22003 E-mail: jbrotton@nvcc.edu.

BROTZEN, FRANZ RICHARD, materials science educator; b. Berlin, July 4, 1915; came to U.S., 1941; s. Georg and Lena (Pacully) B.; m. Frances Burke Ridgway, Jan. 31, 1950; children: Franz Ridgway, Julie Ridgway. BS in Metall. Engring., Case Inst. Tech., 1950, MS, 1953, PhD, 1954. Salesman a Quimica Bayer Ltda., Rio de Janeiro, Brazil, 1934-41; mfrs. rep. R.G. Le Tourneau, Inc., Longview, Tex., 1947-48; sr. research assoc. Case Inst. Tech., Cleve., 1951-54; mem. faculty Rice U., Houston, 1954—, prof. materials sci., 1959-88, prof. emeritus, 1988—, dean engring., 1962-66, master Brown Coll., 1977-82. Vis. prof. Max Planck Inst., Stuttgart, W.Ger., 1960-61, 73-74, Fed. Poly. Inst., Zurich, Switzerland, 1966-67, U. Lausanne, (Switzerland), 1981 Author papers in field. Chmn. Houston Contemporary Arts Assn., 1964-65. Served to 1st lt. AUS, 1942-46. Recipient Sr. Scientist award W. German Govt., 1973-74; Guggenheim fellow, 1960-61 Fellow Am. Soc. Metals (chmn. Houston chpt. 1980-81); mem. AIME, Am. Phys. Soc., Soc. Engring. Sci., Sigma Xi, Tau Beta Pi Home: 2701 Bellefontaine St # H Houston TX 77025 Office: Rice U Dept Materials Sci PO Box 1892 Houston TX 77251-1892

BROTZMAN, DONALD GLENN, government official, lawyer; b. Logan County, Colo., June 28, 1922; s. Harry and Priscilla Ruth (Kittle) B.; m. Louise Love Reed, Apr. 9, 1944 (dec. Jan. 1995); children: Kathleen Love, Donald Glenn Jr.; m. Gwendolyn L. Davis, Aug. 3, 1996. BBS, JD, U. Colo., 1949. Bar: Colo. 1950, D.C., 1977. Since practiced in, Boulder; mem. Colo. Ho. of Reps., 1950-52, Colo. Senate, 1952-56; U.S. atty. Dist. Colo., 1959-61; mem. 88th, 90th-93d congresses from 2d Dist. Colo., Washington, mem. ways and means com.; asst. sec. army for manpower and res. affairs, 1975-77; of counsel Hopkins and Sutter (and predecessors), Chgo., Washington and Dallas, 1989—. Mem. Colo. Crime Commn., 1952-56; Colo. mem. Commn. Uniform State Laws, 1954-56. Colo. chmn. Easter Seal and Colo. Highlander Boys Club drives, 1958, Youth in Govt. program, YMCA, 1958-62; Republican candidate for gov. of Colo., 1954, 56; chmn. Indsl. Energy Users Forum, Washington; pres. Washington Indsl. Round Table; bd. visitors USAF Acad., 1966-72; mem. Golden Spike Commn., 1969-70. Served to lst lt., inf. AUS, 1942-46, PTO. Selected by Colo. press as Outstanding Freshman Mem. of House, 1951; as Outstanding Freshman Senator, 1953; recipient Disting. Svc. award Colo. Jaycees, 1954, Disting. Alumnus award Coll. Bus. and Adminstrn. U. Colo., 1975; named to U. Colo. Hall of Fame, 1976 Mem. ABA, Fed. Bar Assn., Colo. Bar Assn., Boulder County Bar Assn., Rubber Mfrs. Assn. (pres.), Natural Rubber Shippers Assn. (pres.), Tire Industry Safety Coun. (chmn.), Former Mems. of Congress Assn. (bd. dirs. 1993—), Am. Legion, VFW, Res. Officers Assn., Boulder C. of C., Masons (33 deg., medal of honor 1990), Rotary (bd. dirs. Boulder club), Beta Theta Pi, Phi Delta Phi (past magister). Republican. Methodist (Trustee). Home: 400 Madison St Apt 1604 Alexandria VA 22314-1727

BROUDE, RICHARD FREDERICK, lawyer, educator; b. L.A., June 6, 1936; s. Leo Martin and Frances (Goldman) B.; m. Paula Louise Galnick, June 8, 1958; children: Julie Sue, James Matthew, Mark Allen. BS, Washington U., St Louis, 1957; JD, U. Chgo., 1961. Bar: Ill. 1961, Calif. 1971, N.Y. 1989. Prof. law U. Nebr., Lincoln, 1966-69, Georgetown U., Washington, 1969-71; ptnr. Commons & Broude, L.A., 1974-77, Irell & Manella, L.A., 1977-80, Sidley & Austin, L.A., 1980-87, White & Case, L.A., 1987-90, Mayer, Brown & Platt, N.Y.C., 1990-99. Adj. prof. law U. So. Calif., L.A., 1978-90, St. Johns U., 2000—; adv. panel World Bank Insolvency Initiative; cons. OECD Forum for Asian Insolvency Reform. Author: Reorganizations Under Chapter 11, 1986—2003, Cases and Materials on Land Financing, 3rd, 1985; editor: Insolvency and Finance in the Transportation Industry, 1993, Collier Internat. Bus. Guide; mem. editl. bd.: Collier on Bankruptcy, contbg. editor: Collier Bankruptcy Practice Guide. Fellow Am. Bar Found., Am. Coll. Bankruptcy; mem. ABA (com. on bus. bankruptcy), Am. Law Inst. (advisor Transnat. Insolvency Project), Internat. Bar Assn. (chair insolvency and credit rights com. 1996-2000), Bar Assn. of City of N.Y., Calif. Bar Assn., Nat. Bankruptcy Conf. (conferee, chair com. on internat. aspects, vice chair legis. com.). Office: Law Offices of Richard Broude 400 E 84th St # 22A New York NY 10028-5611 E-mail: rfbroude@cs.com.

BROUDE, RONALD, music publisher; b. N.Y.C., Oct. 15, 1941; s. Irving and Anne Broude; m. Janyce Ingalls, Aug. 19, 1982. AB, Columbia Coll., 1962; MA, Columbia U., 1962, PhD, 1967. Pres., exec. editor Broude Bros. Ltd., N.Y.C. and Williamstown, Mass., 1973—; trustee Broude Trust for the publ. musicological editions, N.Y.C., 1981—. Mem. exec. bd. Soc. for Textual Scholarship, 1989—, Early Music Am., 1994-98.

BROUGH, BRUCE ALVIN, public relations and communications executive; b. Wayland, N.Y., Nov. 22, 1937; s. Alvin Elroy and Marjorie Huberta (McDowell) B.; m. Jane Virginia Koethen, Aug. 9, 1958; children: John David, Pamela Marjorie, Robert Bruce. BS in Pub. Rels., U. Md., 1960; MS in Mass Comm., Am. U., Washington, 1967. Comm. mgr. IBM Corp., various locations, 1965-74; owner, pres. Bruce Brough Assocs., Inc., Boca Raton, Fla., 1974-75; worldwide press rels. rep. Tex. Instruments Inc., 1975-76; v.p. pub. rels. Regis McKenna Inc., 1976-77; pres., prin. Pease/Brough Assocs., Inc., Palo Alto, Calif., 1978-80, Franson/Brough Assocs., Inc., San Jose, Calif., 1980-81; sr. v.p., dir. Advanced Tech. Network Hill and Knowlton, Inc., San Jose, Calif., 1981-86, sr. v.p., gen. mgr. Santa Clara, Calif., 1989; gen. corp. pub. rels. Signetics Corp., 1986-87; mktg. comm. mgr. Corp. Ctr. Philips Components divsn. Philips Internat., B.V., Eindhoven, The Netherlands, 1987-89; dir. corp. comm. Centigram Comm. Corp., San Jose, Calif., 1989-90; prin. Brough Comm., Santa Cruz, Calif., 1994—; dir. pub. rels. Acer Am. Corp., San Jose, 1998-99; v.p., dir. pub. rels. practice Cintara, Inc., San Jose, 2000—. Dir. corp. comm. Acer Am. Corp., San Jose, 1999-2000; v.p., pub. rels. practice dir. Cintera Corp., San Jose, 1999-2000; lectr. San Jose State U., 1977-83, 91—; cons. comm. and pub. rels., 1986—. Author: Publicity and Public Relations Guide for Business, 1984, revised edit., 1986, The Same Yesterday, Today and Forever, 1986; contbg. editor Family Bible Ency., 1973. Recipient Sustained Superior Performance award NASA, 1964, award Freedom's Found., 1963. Mem. Pub. Rels. Soc. Am. (accredited), Soc. Tech. Comm., Nat. Press Club, Sigma Delta Chi. Republican. Roman Catholic. Avocations: writing, fishing, skiing, boating, travel. Office: Brough Communications Inc 2035 Oak St A Napa CA 94559 Fax: 831-685-6159. E-mail: bruce@brough.com.

BROUGHTON, BARRY A. naturopathic physician; s. Raymond and Margaret Broughton; m. Angela M. Cousins; children: Joseph Baldwin, Ian. Cert. orthop. residency tng. program, U.S. Army, 1992; PhD in Health and Human Svcs., Columbia Pacific U., 1996; BS as Physician Assoc., U. Okla., 1990; D of Naturopathic Medicine, So. Coll. Naturopathic Medicine, Waldron, Arkansas, 2000. Cert. Am. Naturopathic Med. Cert. and Accreditation Bd., Fed. Intermediary Coun. on Alternative Medicine, lic. naturopath Washington, DC, Colo. Naturopathic Regulatory Bd. EMT/paramedic U.S. Army, Ft. Polk, La., 1983—88, family practice physician asst., 1990—92; orthop. physician asst. Evans Cmty. Hosp., Fort Carson, Colo., 1992—97; orthop. physician assoc. Orthopedics and Sports Medicine, Colorado Springs, Colo., 1996—2000; naturopathic physician Naturopathic & Sports Health, LLC, Colorado Springs, 2000—01, Naturopathic & Sports Health, Olean, NY, 2001—. Prof. Canyon Coll. Sch. Naturopathic Medicine and Healthcare, Caldwell, Idaho, 2001—. Contbr. articles to profl. jours. Served with med. corps U.S. Army, 1983—92. Fellow: Am. Bd. Naturopathic Physicians; mem.: Christian Med. & Dental Assn., N.Y. State Naturopathic Med. Assn., Am. Assn. Orthop. Medicine, Am. Naturopathic Med. Assn. Avocation: outdoor activities. Office: Naturopathic & Sports Health 757 E State St Olean NY 14760 Office Fax: 716-373-2257. E-mail: drbroughton@naturomd.com.

BROUGHTON, JAMES WALTER, real estate development executive, consultant; b. Atlantic City, Dec. 16, 1946; s. Walter Lennie and Janet Caroline (Mossman) B.; m. Sharon Carter, Mar. 10, 1980; children: Jennifer Christine, Matthew James. Student, U. Colo., Colorado Springs, 1967-68, U. Md., 1968-70, U. Colo., Denver, 1972-73. Asst. regional sales dir. Del E. Webb Corp., Denver, 1972-76; dir. mktg. Interval Internat., Miami, Fla., 1981-82; exec. dir. Time Sharing Inst., Miami, 1981-82; pres. J. Broughton, Inc., Miami, 1976-83, Spectrum Mktg. Group, Denver, 1983-84, Ocean Resourts Devel. Co., Ventura, Calif., 1984-85; sr. v.p. Fairfield Cmtys., Inc., Atlanta, 1985; chmn., pres., CEO, Lexes Enterprises, Inc., Las Vegas, Nev., 1985—. Bd. dirs. Consol. Resorts, Inc., PC Cons., Inc., Sea-Shore, Inc., Internat. Cruise and Excursion Gallery; pub. Time Sharing Ency., 1981, Time Sharing Ind. Rev., 1981. Contbr. articles to profl. jours. With USAF, 1964-71. Mem. Am. Resort Devel. Assn. (bd. dirs. 1985—, exec. com. 1988—, chmn. meetings coun. 1991—, resort devel. forum 1993—, treas. 1993—, recruitment award 1983, NTC svc. award 1987, Leader of Yr. award 1991, Industry Visionary Leader of Yr. award 1993), Nat. Time Sharing Coun. (chmn. 1984-86, bd. govs. 1984-92, recruitment award 1984), Interval Internat. (adv. bd. 1982-91), Urban Land Inst. (recreational devel. coun. 1993—). Republican. Office: 9593 Los Cotos Ct Las Vegas NV 89147-8205

BROUGHTON, PHILLIP CHARLES, lawyer, director; b. Findlay, Ohio, Sept. 21, 1930; s. Harold C. and Marian (Pierson) B.; children: Margaret Crockett, Phillip Charles, Anne Duvall, Elizabeth Cox. BA, Bowling Green U., 1953; JD, U. Mich., 1957; LLM, NYU, 1962. Bar: N.Y. 1957. Practiced in, N.Y.C., 1957—; mem. firm Thacher, Proffitt and Wood, 1957-93, of counsel, 1993—. Pres., bd. dirs. Midgard Found., N.Y.C.; pres., bd. trustees Asheville (N.C.) Art Mus.; trustee United Way Asheville, N.C. Mus. Art, Achilles Meml. Fund. Mem. ABA.

BROUGHTON, RAY MONROE, economic consultant; b. Seattle, Mar. 2, 1922; s. Arthur Charles and Elizabeth C. (Young) B.; BA, U. Wash., 1947, MBA, 1960; m. Margret Ellen Ryno, July 10, 1944 (dec.); children: Linda Rae Broughton Silk, Mary Catherine Broughton Boutin; m. Carole Jean Packer, 1980. Mgr. communications and managerial devel. Gen. Electric Co., Hanford Atomic Products Ops., Richland, Wash., 1948-59; mktg. mgr., asst. to pres. Smyth Enterprises, Seattle, 1960-62; dir. rsch. Seattle Area Indsl. Council, 1962-65; v.p., economist (mgr. econ. rsch. dept.) First Interstate Bank of Oreg., N.A., Portland, 1965-87; ind. economic cons., 1987—; mem. econ. adv. com. to Am. Bankers Assn., 1980-83; mem. Gov.'s Econ. Adv. Council, 1981-88; dir. Oregonians for Cost Effective Govt., 1989-90; instr. bus. communications U. Wash., Richland, 1956-57. Treas., dir. Oreg. affiliate Am. Heart Assn., 1972-78, chmn., 1980-81, dir., 1980-84. Served to 1st lt. U.S. Army, 1943-46; ETO. Mem. Western Econ. Assn., Pacific N.W. Regional Econ. Conf. (dir. 1967-94), Nat. Assn. Bus. Economists (co-founder chpt. 1971), Am. Mktg. Assn. (pres. chpt. 1971-72), Alpha Delta Sigma. Author: Trends and Forces of Change in the Payments System and the Impact on Commercial Banking, 1972; contbg. editor Pacific Banker and Bus. mag., 1974-80. Home and Office: 10127 SW Lancaster Rd Portland OR 97219-6302

BROUGHTON, ROBERT STEPHEN, irrigation and drainage engineering educator, consultant; b. Corbetton, Ont., Can., June 29, 1934; s. Arthur Stephen and Luella Margaret (Gray) B.; m. Ruth Mabel Smith, May 11, 1957; children: G. Anne, Sharon Mae, Heather Louise, Stephen Russell. BS in Agr., U. Toronto, 1956, B in Applied Sci., 1957; MCE, MIT, 1959; PhD in Drainage Engring., McGill U., Montreal, 1972; LLD (hon.), Dalhousie U., Halifax, N.S., Can., 1989. Cert. profl. engr., Ont., Que. Jr. engr. John Deere Plow Co., Welland, Ont., 1956; rsch. asst. MIT, Cambridge, 1957-59; hydraulic engr. conservation br. Ont. Govt., Toronto, 1959-61; lectr. in agrl. engring. McGill U., 1962-63, asst. prof. agrl. engring., 1963-66, assoc. prof., 1966-74, prof., 1974-98, prof. emeritus, 1998—. From v.p. to pres. Can. Soc. Agrl. Engring., 1968-75, chmn. drainage rsch. com.; speaker farmers' meetings. Author, editor book in field; contbr. over 130 articles to publs. Tchr. Sunday sch. Beaurepaire United Ch., Beaconsfield, Que., 1965-72, clk. of session, 1973-78. Recipient Internat. Achievement award Can. nat. com. Internat. Commn. Irrigation and Drainage, 1993, Genie award, 1994, Mastery for Svc. award Mc Gill U., 1995; named to Internat. Drainage Hall of Fame, 1994. Fellow Can. Soc. Agrl. Engring. (Maple Leaf award 1978, James Beamish award 1989), Am. Soc. Agrl. Engrs., Ordre des Ingénieurs du Que.; mem. Assn. Profl. Engrs. Ont., Corrugated Plastic Pipe Assn. (life). Mem. United Ch. Can. Achievements include research on design and construction of subsurface drainage systems for control of waterlogging and salinity of irrigated lands, assisted with irrigation and drainage projects in India, Pakistan, Egypt, Trinidad, El Salvador, Barbados, Canada, etc. Office: McGill U Macdonald Campus 21111 Lakeshore Rd Sainte-Anne-de-Bellevue QC Canada H9X 3V9

BROUILLETTE, DAN, federal agency administrator; b. Paincourtville, La. Grad., U. Md. Former ptnr. Alpine Group Inc.; legis. dir. to Congressman Billy Tallzin, 1989—97; sr. v.p. R. Duffy Wall & Assocs., 1997—2000; asst. sec. congl. and intergovtl. affairs Dept. Energy, Washington, 2001—. With U.S. Army. Office: Dept Energy Congl and Intergovtl Affairs 1000 Independence Ave SW Washington DC 20585-0001

BROUN, ELIZABETH, art historian, museum administrator; b. Kansas City, Mo., Dec. 15, 1946; d. Augustine Hughes and Roberta Catherine (Hayden) Gibson. BA, U. Kans., 1968, PhD, 1976; cert. advanced study, U. Bordeaux, France, 1967. Curator prints and drawings Spencer Mus. Art, Lawrence, Kans., 1976-83; asst. prof. U. Kans., Lawrence, 1978-83; asst. dir. chief curator Nat. Mus. Am. Art, Washington, 1983-88, acting dir., 1988-89; dir. Smithsonian Am. Art Mus. (formerly Nat. Mus. Am. Art), Washington, 1989—. Author: exhbn. catalogues Prints of Zorn, 1979, Prints and Drawings of Pat Steir, 1983, Patrick Ireland; Drawings 1965-85, 1986, Albert Pinkham Ryder, 1989; co-author: Benton's Bentons, 1980, Engravings of Marcantonio Raimondi, 1981. Woodrow Wilson fellow, 1968-69; Ford. Found. fellow, 1970-72 Mem. Phi Beta Kappa Office: Smithsonian Am Art Museum 750 Ninth St N W Ste 9550 Washington DC 20001-4505

BROUN, KENNETH STANLEY, lawyer, educator; b. Chgo., July 26, 1939; s. Fred G. and Helene (Smith) B.; m. Marjorie Enid Shagam, Jan. 29, 1961; children: Jonathan, Daniel. BS, U. Ill., 1960, JD, 1963. Bar: Ill. 1963, N.C. 1976. From assoc. prof. to prof. U. N.C. Law Sch., Chapel Hill, 1969—, hon. Brandis prof. law, 1990—; dir. Nat. Inst. Trial Advocacy, Chapel Hill, 1976-79; dean Sch. Law U.N.C., Chapel Hill, 1979-87; of counsel Petree & Stockton, Raleigh, N.C., 1988-94; mayor Town Chapel Hill, N.C., 1991-95. Co-dir. program in trial advocacy Black Lawyers Assn. South Africa; mem. Adv. Com. on Fed. Rules of Evidence, 1993-99, cons., 1999—. Author: Black Lawyers, White Courts, 2000; co-author (with R. Mosteller): Problems in Evidence, 4th edit., 2001; co-author: (with J. Strong et al) Handbook of Evidence, 5th edit., 1999; author: Brandis and Broun, North Carolina Evidence, 2003; co-author (with R. Mosteller et al): Cases and Materials in Evidence, 6th edit., 2002. Recipient award for teaching excellence U. N.C., 1978; fellow Internat. Soc. Barristers, 1978 Fellow Am. Bar Found., Internat. Soc. Barristers; mem. ABA, Nat. Inst. Trial Advocacy (chmn. 1993-94), N.C. Bar Assn. (v.p. 1991-92), Order of Coif. Home: 414 Whitehead Cir Chapel Hill NC 27514-4833 Office: U NC Sch Law Cb # 3380 Chapel Hill NC 27599-0001

BROUNTAS, PAUL PETER, lawyer; b. Bangor, Maine, Mar. 19, 1932; s. Peter Nicholas and Penelope (Spiropoulos) B.; m. Lynn Barrett Thurston, Sept. 7, 1963; children— Paul Peter, Jennifer VanWoert, Barrett Penelope AB summa cum laude, Bowdoin Coll., 1954; BA, Oxford (Eng.) U., 1956, MA, 1960; LLB, Harvard U., 1960. Bar: Mass. 1960. Assoc. Hale and Dorr LLP, Boston, 1960-64, jr. ptnr., 1964-68, sr. ptnr., 1968—2002, sr. counsel, 2003—. Guest presenter Harvard U. Bus. Sch., Cambridge, Mass., 1981-87; corp. sec. various corps.; panelist, lectr. corp., venture capital and securities law. Overseer Bowdoin Coll., Brunswick, Maine, 1974-82, pres. bd. overseers, 1979-82, trustee, 1983-96, chmn. bd. trustees, 1993-96; chmn. com. for Michael S.

Dukakis Gov. of Mass., 1976-88; chmn. Dukakis for Pres. Com., 1987-88; mem. corp. Children's Hosp. Med. Ctr., Boston, 1965-87, Boston Mus. Sci., 1966-91, Mass. Gen. Hosp., Boston, 1983-94; mem. bd. overseers Newton Wellesley Hosp., 1990-96; mem. Marshall Scholar Selection Com. N.E. Region, 1973-75, 88-92; mem. Weston Planning Bd., Mass., 1967-72, chmn., 1970-72; chmn. Met. Boston Citizen's Coalition for Cleaner Air, 1969-71; bd. dirs. Mass. Ctrs. of Excellence Corp., 1985-87. Served with U.S. Army, 1956-58. Marshall scholar, 1954 Mem. ABA, Mass. Bar Assn., Boston Bar Assn., Assn. Marshall Scholars and Alumni (treas. 1965-71, bd. dirs. 1988-90). Avocations: skiing, golf. Office: Hale and Dorr LLP 60 State St Boston MA 02109-1816 E-mail: paul.brountas@haledorr.com.

BROUS, THOMAS RICHARD, lawyer; b. Fulton, Mo., Jan. 7, 1943; s. Richard Pendleton and Augusta (Gilpin) B.; m. Patricia Catlin, Sept. 12, 1964; (dec. Sept. 1999); children: Anna Catlin Brous, Joel Pendleton Brous; m. Mary Lou McClelland Kroh, Sept. 8, 2001. BSBA, Northwestern U., 1965; JD cum laude, U. Mich., 1968. Bar: Mo. 1968, U.S. Dist. Ct. (we. dist.) Mo. 1968, U.S. Ct. Mil. Appeals 1968, U.S. Supreme Ct. 1971. Assoc. Watson & Marshall L.C., Kans. City, Mo., 1968-78, ptnr., 1978-96, mng. ptnr., 1992-94; shareholder Stinson, Mag & Fizzell, P.C., Kans. City, Mo., 1996—2002; ptnr. Stinson Morrison Hecker LLP, Kans. City, 2002—. Mem. steering com. U. Mo. Kansas City Law Sch. Employee Benefits Inst., 1990—2001, chmn. 1992-93; with Ctrl. Mtn. TE/GE Coun. IRS, 1997—. Author: Chapter 26, III Missouri Business Organizations, 1998; asst. editor Mich. Law Rev., 1966-68. Mem. vestry St. Andrews Episcopal Ch., Kansas City, 1974-77, Grace & Holy Trinity Cathedral, 1994—, chancellor, 1998—; trustee Mo. Repertory Theatre, Inc., Kansas City, 1990—, pres., 1995-98; v.p., treas. Barstow Sch., Kansas City, 1982-86; dir. Met. Orgn. to Counter Sexual Abuse, Kansas City, 1992-95. Capt. U.S. Army, 1968-72. Mem. ABA, Univ. Club (pres. 1988-89), Greater Kansas City Soc. Hosp. Attys., Kansas City Met. Bar Assn., Heart of Am. Employee Benefit Conf., The Mo. Bar Assn. (vice-chair employee benefits com. 1997-2000), Mo. Soc. Hosp. Attys., Delta Upsilon, Beta Gamma Sigma. Episcopalian. Avocations: reading, hiking, gardening. Office: Stinson Morrison Hecker LLP 1201 Walnut Ste 2800 Kansas City MO 64106 E-mail: tbrous@stinsonmoheck.com.

BROUSE, JOHN S. medical association administrator; Pres., CEO Highmark Inc., Camp Hill, Pa. Mem. bd. Blue Cross & Blue Shield Assoc.; chmn. bd. Inter-County Health Plan & Inter-County Hospitaliation; mem. bd. & exec. comm. Keystone Health Plan Central. Office: Highmark/Pa Blue Shield 1800 Center St Camp Hill PA 17089-0001

BROUSE, VIRGINIA MAY (GINNY BROUSE), retired rehabilitation nurse; b. Dowagiac, Mich., July 15, 1935; d. Fred. A. and Julia M. (Jordan) Culver; m. Robert E. Brouse, Aug. 26, 1955; children: Mark A., Gary S. BS, Western Mich. U., 1987; RN, Bronson Meth. Hosp. RN N.C., cert. case mgr., Commn. for Case Mgr., rehab. RN. Case mgr. Broward's Devel. Clinic, Ft. Lauderdale, Fla., 1987-89, IntraCorp, Ft. Lauderdale, Fla., 1989-90, Rehability, Ft. Lauderdale, Fla., 1990-93, Pinecrest Rehab. Hosp., Delray Bch., Fla., 1993-95, Thoms Rehab. Hosp., Ashville, NC, 1995-99; ret., 2000. Clinical fellow Nat. Rehab. Ctrs., 1993. Mem. Assn. Rehab. Nurses (cert. rehab. nurse). Avocation: basket making.

BROUSSARD, ANGELA G. (MILICENT MAXWELL), writer, poet, playwright; d. Morris and Mabel Hopkins Broussard; children: Rachael M., Jasmine L. Covmier. Student, Lamar U., Houston CC, Delta Coll. V.p. Black Women of Hope, Houston, Tex., 1999—2003. Author: In A Black Woman's Eyes, How To Save On Your Long Distance; playwright : Real Love from a Real Man. Achievements include first to to be an African American woman to tour a major production (stage play) playwright, producer, since the death of Lorraine Hansbury in 1965.

BROUSSARD, FRANCIS PETER, English educator; b. Lafayette, La., Aug. 27, 1941; s. Francis Peter and Florence Marie (Gladu) B.; m. Carmen Mary Lafosse, Sept. 18, 1964 (div. 1975). BA in English, U. Southwestern La., 1962; MA in English, Tulane U., 1970. Tchg. asst. Tulane U., New Orleans, 1971-75; glazer Ryder's Stained Glass Studio, Opelousas, La., 1976-77; asst. editor Internat. Cmty. of Christ, Reno, 1978-79; GED instr. Sierra Nev. Job Corps-Stead Facility, Reno, 1979-81; glazer, craftsman Beau Soleil Stained Glass Studio, Opelousas, 1981-83; pvt. practice Abita Springs, La., 1984-89; English instr. Delgado C.C., Slidell, La., 1989-96, Southeastern La. U., Hammond, 1996—. Chairperson GED dept. Sierra Nev. Job Corps, Stead Facility, Reno, 1980-81. Author of poetry. Narrator Creative Dance Ctr., Covington, La., 1985-99. With U.S. Army, 1965-69, Vietnam, 1967-68. Mem. La. Archaeol. Assn. Avocations: amateur archeologist, gardening. Home: 72562 Indian Trail Rd Abita Springs LA 70420-2444 Office: Southeastern La Univ PO Box 304 Hammond LA 70404-0304 E-mail: fbroussard@selu.edu., broussd@bellsouth.net.

BROUSSARD, THOMAS ROLLINS, lawyer; b. Houston, May 30, 1943; s. Charles Hugh and Ethel (Rollins) B.; m. Mollie Brewster, Jan. 13, 1968. BS cum laude in Econs., U. Pa., 1964; JD cum laude, Harvard U., 1967. Bar: N.Y. 1968, Calif. 1973. Tax atty. Esso Standard Eastern, Inc., N.Y.C., 1967-70; gen. tax counsel Atlantic Richfield Co., N.Y.C., Los Angeles, 1970-74; v.p. corp. affairs, sec., gen. counsel Technicolor, Inc., Los Angeles, 1974-80; mem. firm Nelson & Broussard, Los Angeles, 1980-81; pres. Thomas R. Broussard, Ltd., P.C., Los Angeles, 1981—; of counsel Law Offices of Joseph E. Bachelder, N.Y.C., 2002—. Mem. ABA, Calif., Los Angeles County bar assns., Assn. of the Bar of the City of N.Y. Office: 172 N Las Palmas Ave Los Angeles CA 90004

BROUSSEAU, CATHERINE DALTON, school health services director; b. Lowell, Mass., Oct. 24, 1942; d. Martin J. and Beatrice M. (Moynihan) Dalton; m. Richard C.J. Brousseau, Sept. 6, 1965; 1 child, Margaret E. Diploma, St. Josephs Hosp., Lowell, 1963; BA, New Eng. Coll., Henniker, N.H., 1977, MS, 1982. Cert. AIDS facilitator; cert. sch. nurse. Emergency rm. charge nurse St. Josephs Hosp., 1963-78; pub. health nurse City of Lowell, 1994—, school health svcs. program dir., 1994—. Author articles and manual. Mem. Mass. Pub. Health Assn., Mass. Sch. Nurses Assn., Am. Sch. Health Assn., Nat. Sch. Nurses Assn., Sigma Theta Tau. Home: 467 Arlington St Dracut MA 01826-5228 E-mail: cbrousseau@ci.lowell.ma.us.

BROUTHERS, LANCE ELIOT, finance educator; b. Cleve., Mar. 24, 1951; s. Jay M. and Carolyn Stern Brouthers; m. Xiaohong Mo Mo, July 4, 1999. BS, Ohio State U., 1973; MA, Memphis State U., 1977; PhD, Fla. State U., 1980, U. Fla., 1992. Asst. prof. Tex. Christian U., Ft. Worth, 1991—94; assoc. prof. U. Tex., San Antonio, 1994—2001; prof. U. Akron, Ohio, 2001—. Contbr. articles to profl. jours. Mem.: Acad. Mgmt., Acad. Internat. Bus. Avocations: comic book collector, comic book art collector, international travel. Home: 430 Dublin Ct Copley OH 44321 Office: U Akron Akron OH 44325 Personal E-mail: lance@uakron.edu.

BROWAR, LISA MURIEL, librarian; b. N.Y.C., Jan. 22, 1951; d. Elliott Andrew and Shirley (Kahn) B. B in English Lit., Ind. U., 1973, MLS, 1977; M in English Lit., U. Kans., 1976; postgrad., Ind. U.-Purdue. U., Indpls., 2001—. Cert. in fund raising mgmt., 2001. Asst. curator Beinecke Libr. Yale U., New Haven, 1979-81, archivist Sterling Meml. Libr., 1981-82; curator spl. collections Vassar Coll. Libr., Poughkeepsie, N.Y., 1982-87; asst. dir. rare books and manuscripts N.Y. Pub. Libr., N.Y.C., 1987-96; dir. The Lilly Libr., Ind. U., Bloomington, 1996-2001; libr. for English and Am. lit., philosophy and film studies Main Libr., Ind. U., Bloomington, 2001—02; univ. libr. New Sch. U., N.Y.C., 2002—. Editor RBM: A Jour. of Rare Books, Manuscripts, and Cultural Heritage, 1999-2003. Mem. ALA, Assn. Coll. and Rsch. Librs. (sec. rare books and manuscripts sect. 1987-89, chair, 1994-95, editor 1999—), Soc. Am. Archivists, Bibliog. Soc. Am., Grolier Club. Democrat. Avocations: opera, theatre, photography. Office: Fogelman Libr 65 Fifth Ave New York NY 10011

BROWDE, ANATOLE, electronics company executive, consultant; b. Berlin, June 10, 1925; came to U.S., 1940, naturalized, 1946; s. Alexander and Rebecca (Braude) Kutisker; m. Jacqueline Rousseau, Mar. 10, 1973; children: David, Elizabeth, Richard. BEE, Cornell U., 1948; postgrad., Northwestern U., 1948, Columbia U., 1951-52; MLA, Washington U., St. Louis, 1994, MA, 1996, PhD in History, 1999. Engr. Capehart-Farnsworth Corp., Ft. Wayne, Ind., 1948-51, Arma Corp., Bklyn., 1951-53; project engr. BOMARC, Westinghouse Electric Co., Balt., 1953-55; assoc. dir. missile dept. Avco Corp., Cin., 1955-59; with McDonnell Douglas Corp., 1959-90, v.p. engring. and mktg., 1979-81; v.p., gen. mgr. info. systems div. McDonnell Douglas Electronics Co., St. Charles, Mo., 1981-82, v.p. Microelectronics Ctr., 1982-87; v.p. ops. McDonnell Douglas Electronics Systems Co., 1987-89, dir. ops. integration, 1989-90; pres. Browde Cons. Inc., St. Louis, 1990—97. Adj. prof. Maryville U., St Louis, 1992—. Chmn. secondary schs. com. Cornell U., 1968-1976, mem. univ. council, 1971-77, 79—; trustee First Unitarian Ch., St. Louis, 1977-80, chmn., 1979-80, chmn. fin. com., 1985-1989. Mem.: Cornell (St. Louis), Cornell U. Coun. Republican. Unitarian Universalist. Achievements include development of Mercury, Gemini Spacecraft electronics, 1961-68, airborne collision avoidance system, 1968-72. Home: 12031 Carberry Pl Saint Louis MO 63131-3124

BROWDER, FELIX EARL, mathematician, educator; b. Moscow, July 31, 1927; s. Earl and Raissa (Berkmann) Browder; m. Eva Tislowitz, Oct. 5, 1949; children: Thomas, William. SB, MIT, 1946; PhD, Princeton U., 1948; MA (hon.), Yale U., 1962; D (hon.), U. Paris, 1990. C.L.E. Moore instr. math. MIT, 1948—51, vis. assoc. prof., 1961—62, vis. prof., 1977—78; instr. Boston U., 1951—53; asst. prof. Brandeis U., 1955—56; from asst. prof. to prof. Yale U., 1956—63; prof. math. U. Chgo., 1963—72, Louis Block prof. math., 1972—82, Max Mason disting. svc. prof., 1982—87, chmn. dept., 1972—77, 1980—85; v.p. rsch. Rutgers, The State U. NJ, 1986—91; univ. prof. Rutgers U., New Brunswick, 1986—. Vis. mem. Inst. Advanced Study, Princeton (N.J.) U., 1953—54, 1963—64; vis. prof. Princeton U., 1968, Inst. Pure and Applied Math., Rio de Janeiro, 1960, U. Paris, 1973, 1975, 1978, 1981, 1983, 1985; sr. rsch. fellow U. Sussex, 1970, 1976, England; Fairchild Disting. visitor Calif. Inst. Tech., Pasadena, 1975—76; spkr. Internat. Congress of Math., 1970, Sci. Bd. Santa Fe Inst., 1986—98, U.S. Nat. Med. Sci., 1999. Contbr. theorems to books, including Nonlinear Problems, 1966, Functional Analysis and Related Fields, 1970, Nonlinear Operators and Nonlinear Equations of Evolution in Banach Spaces, 1976, Nonlinear Functional Analysis and Its Applications, 1986. With U.S. Army, 1953—55. Fellow Guggenheim, 1953—54, 1966—67, Sloan Found., 1959—63, NSF sr. postdoctoral fellow, 1957—58. Fellow: AAAS (chmn. sect. A 1982—83); mem.: NAS (coun. mem. 1992—95), Math. Assn. Am., Am. Math. Soc. (editor bull. 1959—68, 1978—83, mem. coun. 1959—72, 1978—83, mng. editor 1964—68, 1980, exec. com. counl 1979—80, colloquium lectr. 1970, pres. 1999—2001), Am. Acad. Arts and Scis., Sigma Xi (pres. chpt. 1985—86). Achievements include development of linear and nonlinear partial differential equations; nonlinear functional analysis and fixed point and mapping theorems. E-mail: browder@math.rutgers.edu.

BROWDER, JOHN GLEN, former congressman, educator; b. Sumter, SC, Jan. 15, 1943; s. Archie Calvin and Ila (Frierson); m. Sara Rebecca Moore; 1 child, Jenny Rebecca. BA in History, Presbyn. Coll., 1965; MA in Polit. Sci., PhD in Polit. Sci., Emory U., 1971. Asst. in pub. relations Presbyn. Coll., Clinton, S.C., 1965; sportswriter The Atlanta Jour., 1966; investigator U.S. Civil Service Commn., Atlanta, 1966-68; prof. polit. sci. Jacksonville (Ala.) State U., 1971-87; mem. Ala. Ho. of Reps., Montgomery, 1982-86; sec. of state State of Ala., Montgomery, 1987-89; mem. 101st-104th Congresses from 3d Ala. dist., Washington, 1989-96; disting. vis. prof. nat. security affairs Naval Postgrad. Sch., Monterey, Calif., 1997—. Mem. Am. Polit. Sci. Assn., So. Polit. Sci. Assn. Democrat. Methodist. Office: Naval Postgrad Sch NS/BG Nat Security Affairs Dept Monterey CA 93943 E-mail: igbrowder@nps.navy.mil.

BROWDER, OLIN LORRAINE, legal educator; b. Urbana, Ill., Dec. 19, 1913; s. Olin Lorraine and Nellie (Taylor) B.; m. Edna Olive Forsythe, Sept. 9 1939 (dec. Nov. 1993); children: Ann Browder Sorensen, Catherine Browder Morris, John; m. Aleeta Swantner, May 17, 1997. AB, U. Ill., 1935, LL.B., 1937; S.JD, U. Mich., 1941. Bar: Ill. 1939. Practiced in Chgo., 1938-39; asst. prof. bus. law U. Ala., 1939-41; asst. prof. law U. Tenn., 1941-42; mem. legal dept. TVA, 1942-43; spl. agt. FBI, 1943-45; prof. law U. Okla., 1946-53, U. Mich., Ann Arbor, 1953-79, James V. Campbell prof. law, 1979-84, prof. emeritus, 1984—. Author: (with others) American Law of Property, 1953, (with L.W. Waggoner) Family Property Transactions, 1965, 3d edit., 1980, (with R. A. Cunningham, G.S. Nelson, W.B. Stoebuck, D.A. Whitman) Basic Property Law, 1966, 5th edit., 1989, (with L. W. Waggoner and R. V. Wellman) Palmer's Cases on Trusts and Succession, 4th edit., 1983. Mem. Order of Coif, Phi Beta Kappa, Beta Theta Phi, Phi Alpha Delta, Phi Kappa Phi. Home: 1520 Edinborough Rd Ann Arbor MI 48104-4128

BROWDER, WILLIAM BAYARD, corporation executive, lawyer; b. Urbana, Ill., Sept. 6, 1916; s. Olin Lorraine and Nellie Sheldon (Taylor) B.; m. Mary Bain Lehmann, Sept. 6, 1942 (dec. Feb. 1984); children: David Sheldon, Wendy Elisabeth, Amy Spence (dec.); m. Betty M. Kennedy, Jan. 5, 1985 AB, U. Ill., 1938, JD, 1941; LLD, MacMurray Coll., Jacksonville, Ill., 1979, Ill. Coll., 1990. Bar: Ill. 1941. Atty. I.C.R.R., 1941-47, Union Tank Car Co., Chgo., 1948-81, sec., 1952-77, dir., 1954-81, gen. counsel, 1956-79, v.p., 1965-74, sr. v.p., 1974-81; v.p., dir. Trans Union Corp., 1969-81, gen. counsel, 1969-79, sr. v.p., 1974-79, sr. v.p. law, 1979-81; v.p., dir. Ecodyne Corp., 1972-81. Dir. Procor, Ltd., 1952-81 Mem. Citizens Com. To Study Police-Community Relations in Chgo., 1966-67; chmn. Com. To Study Financing Community Colls. in Ill., 1974-75; pres. Chgo. Crime Commn., 1965-67; mem. adv. com. U. Ill. Coll. Commerce and Bus. Adminstrn., Champaign-Urbana, 1969-73; mem. Ill. Racing Bd., 1973-74; mem. Ill. Bd. Higher Edn., 1975-91, chmn., 1979-91; pres. Wilmette United Fund, 1962; life trustee YMCA-U Ill., 1966—, chmn., 1967-79; bd. dirs. Mid Am. chpt. ARC, 1963-65, Wilmette Pub. Libr., 1964-67, Northwestern Meml. Hosp., 1970-75; mem. U. Ill. Found., 1969—, bd. dirs., 1973-79, mem. pres.'s coun., 1974—; mem. Ill. Gov.'s Task Force on Pvt. Sector Initiatives, 1983-86, Ill. Gov.'s Commn. on Sci. and Tech., 1983-87; mem. Ill. Gaming Bd., 1993-99; bd. dirs. organized crime com. Chgo. Crime Commn.; trustee Trinity United Meth. Ch., chmn. bd. trustee, 1973-85. Mem. Am., Ill. bar assns., U. Ill. Law Alumni Assn. (pres. 1968-71), Chgo. Legal Club, Order of Coif, Union League Club (Chgo.) (dir. 1974-76), Westmoreland Country Club (Wilmette, Ill.) (sec., dir. 1979), Phi Beta Kappa, Phi Eta Sigma, Beta Theta Pi, Phi Alpha Delta. Methodist. Home: 1616 Sheridan Rd Unit 5F Wilmette IL 60091-1887 Home (Winter): 521 E Orange Grove Ave Sierra Madre CA 91024-2616

BROWDY, JOSEPH EUGENE, lawyer; b. Bklyn., July 23, 1937; s. Philip and Fannie (Asherowitz) B.; m. Anita Sue Rubenstein, June 18, 1958; childrenF: Jennifer, Daniel. BA, Oberlin Coll., 1958; LLB, NYU, 1961. Bar: N.Y. 1962, D.C. 1982. Assoc. Paul, Weiss, Rifkind, Wharton & Garrison, N.Y.C., 1962-71, ptnr., 1972-97, of counsel, 1998—. Adj. asst. prof. real estate NYU, 1976-86; lectr. in field. With U.S. Army Res., 1961-62. Mem. Assn. of Bar of City of N.Y. (com. real property law, chmn. subcom. on leasing 1989-92), Am. Coll. Real Estate Lawyers, Order of Coif, Phi Beta Kappa. Office: Paul Weiss Rifkind Wharton & Garrison 1285 Avenue of the Americas New York NY 10019-6065 E-mail: jbrowdy@paulweiss.com.

BROWER, CHARLES NELSON, lawyer, judge; b. Plainfield, N.J., June 5, 1935; s. Charles Hendrickson and Mary Elizabeth (Nelson) B.; children: Michael Claudio Joseph Hutchings, Carmen Désirée Ponti, Frederica Anne Amity, Jasmin Maria Plekavich, Charles Hendrickson II. BA cum laude, Harvard U., 1957, JD, 1961; cert. Parker Sch. Comp. & Internat. Law, Columbia U., 1962. Bar: N.Y. 1962, D.C. 1970, U.S. Supreme Ct. 1967, U.S. Ct. Appeals (D.C. cir., 2d, 5th, 6th, 7th, 8th, 9th, 11th and fed. cirs.), U.S. Ct. Internat. Trade, U.S. Dist. Ct. (so. and ea. dists.) N.Y., U.S. Dist. Ct. D.C. Assoc., then ptnr. White & Case LLP, N.Y.C., 1961-69; asst. legal adviser European affairs Dept. State, Washington, 1969-71, dep. legal adviser, 1971-73, acting legal adviser, 1973; ptnr. White & Case LLP, Washington, 1973-84, 88-00, spl. counsel, 2001—; mem. 20 Essex St. Chambers, London, 2001—. Judge Iran-U.S. Claims Tribunal, The Hague, 1984—88, 2001—, substitute judge, 1983—84, 1988—2000; dep. spl. counselor to the Pres., Washington, 1987; counsel and advocate for U.S., 92, Costa Rica, 98, Internat. Ct. Justice, The Hague; mem. Register of Experts UN Compensation Commn., 1991—; mem. sec. of state adv. com. on internat. law, 1996—; mem. panels of arbitrators and conciliators Internat. Ctr. for Settlement of Investment Disputes, 1998—; judge ad hoc Inter-Am. Ct. of Human Rights, 1999—. Fulbright scholar Rheinische Friedrich-Wilhelms-Universitaet, Bonn, and Hochschule fuer Politik, Berlin, 1957-78. Mem. ABA (chmn. sect. internat. law 1981-82, mem. ho. of dels. 1982, 84-98, bd. govs. 1985-88, mem. nominating com. 1992-94), Internat. Law Assn. (hon. v.p. Am. br.), Internat. Bar Assn., Am. Soc. Internat. Law (v.p. 1994-96, pres. 1996-98, hon. v.p. 1998—), Am. Law Inst., Assn. of Bar of City of N.Y., Coun. Fgn. Rels., Inst. Transnat. Arbitration (chmn. adv. bd. 1994-2000), Ctr. for Am. and Internat. Law (trustee 1996—), Met. Club, Chevy Chase Club. Episcopalian. Home and Office: Parkweg 13 2585 JH The Hague Netherlands E-mail: cbrower@20essexst.com., cbrower@whitecase.com.

BROWER, DANIEL ROBERTS, historian, educator, writer; b. Chgo., Jan. 9, 1936; s. Daniel Roberts and Edith May Brower; m. Francoise Lemenez de Kerdelleau, Aug. 13, 1959; children: Eric Stephan, Caroline Anne Wiehl, Valerie Elizabeth Pollock. BA, Carleton Coll., 1957; PhD, Columbia U., 1962. Asst. prof. Oberlin (Ohio) Coll., 1962—65; prof. dept. history U. Calif., Davis, 1968—, chmn. dept. history, 1999—. Author: The New Jacobins: The French Communist Party and the Popular Front, 1968, Training the Nihilists: Education and Radicalism in Tsarist Russia, 1985, The Russian City Between Tradition and Modernity 1850-1900, 1990; author: (co-editor) Russia's Orient: Imperial Borderlands and Peoples, 1700-1914, 1997; author: The World in the Twentieth Century: From Empires to Nations, 5th edit., 2002, Turkestan and the Fate of the Russian Empire, 2003. Mem.: Am. Assn. For The Advancement Slavic Studies. Avocations: travel, sea kayaking. Home: 1829 Tacoma Ave Berkeley CA 94707 Office: Dept History Univ Calif Davis CA 95616 Office Fax: 530-752-5301. E-mail: drbrower@ucdavis.edu.

BROWER, DAVID CHARLES, transportation executive; b. Glens Falls, N.Y., Oct. 3, 1945; s. Charles William and Doris Mae (Hubbell) B.; m. Eloise Mary O'Neil, Sept. 11, 1965 (div. 1986); children: Benjamin, Daniel; m. Jeanne M. Douglass, July 23, 1988. BBA, U. Vt., 1970. Indsl. engr. IBM Corp., Burlington, Vt., 1970-71, mktg. rep. Albany, N.Y., 1971-77; sr. sales rep. Digital Equipment Corp., Syracuse, N.Y., 1977-79, corp. order adminstrn. cons. Maynard, Mass., 1979-83, from sales ops. cons. to dist. ops. mgr. Marlborough, Mass., 1983-88, product ops. mgr., 1988-90; pres. Marlboro Transp., Marlborough, 1991—. Mem. Rotary (Marlboro pres., 1996-97), Marlboro C. of C. Office: Marlboro Transp 269 Mechanic St Marlborough MA 01752-1802 E-mail: marltrnspt@aol.com.

BROWER, DAVID JOHN, lawyer, urban planner, educator; b. Holland, Mich., Sept. 11, 1930; s. John J. and Helen (Olson) B.; m. Lou Ann Brown, Nov. 26, 1960; children: Timothy Seth, David John, II, Ann Lacey. BA, U. Mich., 1956, JD, 1960. Bar: Ill. 1960, Mich. 1961, Ind. 1961, U.S. Supreme Ct. 1971. Asst. dir. div. community planning Ind. U., Bloomington, 1960-70; rsch. prof. dept. city and regional planning U. N.C., Chapel Hill, 1970—, assoc. dir. Ctr. for Urban and Regional Studies, 1970-94; pres. Coastal Resources Collaborative, Ltd., Chapel Hill and Manteo, N.C., 1980—; counsel Robinson & Cole, Hartford, Conn., 1986—. Vis. prof., Vt. Law Sch., South Royalton, summers, 1994—. Author: (with others) Constitutional Issues of Growth Management, 1978; Growth Management, 1984, Managing Development in Small Towns, 1984, Special Area Management, 1985, Catastrophic Coastal Storms, 1989, Understanding Growth Management, 1989, Coastal Zone Management: An Evaluation, 1991, An Introduction to Coastal Zone Management, 1994, rev. edit. 2002, Natural Hazard Mitigation, 1999. Fellow Am. Inst. Cert. Planners (Coll. of Fellows); mem.Am. Planning Assn. (bd. dirs. 1982-85, chmn.-founder planning and law div. 1978, co-chmn. sustainable devel. group 1995—). Democrat. Episcopalian. Home: 612 Shady Lawn Rd Chapel Hill NC 27514-2009 Office: U NC CB # 3140 Chapel Hill NC 27599-0001 E-mail: brower@email.unc.edu.

BROWER, JAMES CALVIN, graphic artist, painter; b. Clarksburg, W.Va., Dec. 30, 1914; s. Leroy Cooper and Margaret Wood (Watkins) B.; m. Elsie Margaret Day, Sept. 19, 1936; children: James Lawrence, Sandra Joan, Margaret, Linda Ann, Beth. Grad. high sch., Charleston, W.Va., 1932. Pvt. practice, Huntington, W.Va., 1933-43, Toledo, 1952—; ptnr., art dir. Brower, Brownsberger and Burda, Toledo, 1944-51; dir. art and design Meeks Heit Pub. Co., 1992-99. Author, illustrator: Mood and Mode, 2003; illustrator: Education for Sexuality, 1970, Human Sexuality, 1982, Education for Sexuality and HIV/AIDS, 1993, Blowpipes, Northwest Ohio Glassmaking in the Gas Boom of the 1880s, 2002, Mood & Mode, A Selection of Transparent Watercolors, 2003; paintings featured in The Creative Artist, 1990, The Best of Watercolor 2, 1997, The Best of Watercolor Composition, 1997. Recipient Pres. award Okla. Watercolor Soc., 1987, Past Pres. award San Diego Watercolor Soc. Internat. Exhbn., 1989. Mem. Ohio Watercolor Soc. (hon.; signature mem., bd. dirs. 1986-92, publicity chmn. 1986-92, Gold medal 1984, Charles Burchfield Meml. award 1991, Exhbn. award 1992, made hon. mem. 2001), Northwestern Ohio Watercolor Soc. (pres. 1983-84), Nat. Water Color Soc. (signature mem., Artist's Mag./Liquitex award 1990, Mem.'s Exhbn. awards 1996, 98), Ky. Watercolor Soc. (artist mem.), Ga. Watercolor Soc. (signature mem., Gold award Nat. Exhbn. 1990), Midwest Watercolor Soc. (signature mem.), Toledo Fedn. Art Soc. (pres. 1987-88), Tile Club Toledo, Toledo Artists Club (gold medal 1998). Republican. Presbyterian. Avocations: chess, bridge. Home and Office: 2222 Grecourt Dr Toledo OH 43615-2918

BROWER, JANICE KATHLEEN, library technician; b. Chgo., July 29, 1952; d. Gerald B. (dec. Dec. 2000) and Emily (Kavicky) B. AA, Lincoln Coll., 1973; BS, Ill. State U., 1975; postgrad., U. Okla., 1984-86. Libr. assoc. Chgo. Pub. Libr., 1975-80, 81-83; libr. technician U. Okla. Biol. Sta., Norman, 1987; libr. technician III Jim E. Hamilton Correctional Ctr. Okla. Dept. of Corrections, Hodgen, 1987—. Lutheran. Avocations: reading, walking, visiting historical sites and museums, architecture. Office: Jim E Hamilton Correctional Ctr HC 63 Box 5390 Hodgen OK 74939-9712 E-mail: jkbrower@alltel.net., janice.brower@doc.state.ok.us.

BROWER, ROBERT CHARLES, rehabilitation counselor, small business owner; b. Allendale, NJ; s. William P. and Adele B.; m. Hilja Kristiansen, Dec. 21, 1963; children: Robert K., Kristine D. BA in Psychology, Rutgers U., 1963; MDiv, Luth. Theol. Sem., Phila., 1966; postgrad. in counselign, Princeton Theol. Sem., 1970-71; postgrad. in Bus. Adminstrn., N.Y. Inst. Tech., 1993—. Cert. rehab. counselor, disability mgmt. specialist, case mgr., N.Y., U.S. Dept. Labor; ordained to ministry Lutheran Ch., 1966. Pastor St. Paul Luth. Ch., E. Windsor, N.J., 1966-71; psychiatric rehab. counselor N.Y. State Office of Vocations., Cen. Islip, 1971-73; coord. Rehab. Inst., Mineola, St. James, N.Y., 1973-74; program dir. and mental health clinic adminstr. Skills Unlimited, Oakdale, N.Y., 1974-78; dist. mgr. Intracorp subs. CIGNA, Woodbury, White Plains, N.Y., 1978-83; mgr. disability mgmt. svcs. Nat. Ctr. Disability Svcs. (formerly Human Resources Ctr.), Albertson, N.Y., 1984-90; pres. Brower Rehab. Svcs., Inc., Medford, N.Y., 1990—. Adj. prof. Sch. Counseling, Rsch., Spl. Edn. and Rehab., Hofstra U., Uniondale, N.Y., 1988-2001; speaker in field. Cert. Disability Mgmt. Specialist Commn.,(bd. dirs., treas. 1993-94, vice chair 1994-95, chair 1995-96), rep. to Found. for Rehab. Cert., Edn. and Rsch., 1993-94, 99-2003, chair govt. affairs and pub. rels. com., treas. found., treas., vice chair, 1994-95, chair, 1995-96. Mem. AAUP, Nat. Rehab. Profls. in Pvt. Sector, Internat. Rehab. Assn. (chmn. commn. for certification of disability mgmt. specialists commn.), Nat. Rehab. Profls. in Pvt. Sector, Profl. Rehab. Assn. L.I. and N.Y.C. (Rehab. Profl. of Yr. in Ancillary Care 1994), Assn. Blauvelt Descendants (pres. 1998—), Delta Mu Delta. Avocations: sailing, photography. Home: 37 Crooked Pine Dr Medford NY 11763-4329 E-mail: rcbrower@optonline.net.

BROWMAN, DAVID L(UDVIG), archaeologist; b. Dec. 9, 1941; s. Ludvig G. and Audra (Arnold) B.; m. M. Jane Fox, Apr. 24, 1965; children: Lisa, Tina, Becky. BA, U. Mont., 1963; MA, U. Wash., 1966; PhD, Harvard U., 1970. Hwy. archaeologist Wash. State Hwy. Dept., Olympia, 1964-66; field dir. Yale U., New Haven, 1968-69; tutor Harvard U., 1969-70; mem. faculty Washington U., St. Louis, 1970—, prof. archeology, 1984—, chmn., 1986—. Dir. Cons. Survey Archeology, St. Louis, 1976—, Inst. Study of Plants, Food and Man, Kirkwood, Mo. 1979-84: cons. St. Louis Dept. Parks and Recreation, 1978—. Editor/author: Advances in Andean Archaeology, 1978, Economic Organization of Prehispanic Peru, 1984, Risk Management and Arid Land Use Strategies in the Andes, 1986, New Perspectives on Americanist Archaeology, 2002; editor: Cultural Continuity in Mesoamerica, 1979, Early Native Americans, 1980. Charter mem. Confluence St. Louis, 1983; mem. Gov.'s Adv. Coun. Hist. Preservation, 1982-89, sec. 1989-91. NSF fellow, 1967, grantee, 1974-75, 85—. Fellow AAAS; mem. Soc. Profl. Archaeologists (sec.-treas. 1981-83, grievance coord. 1997-98), AAUP (chpt. pres. 1980-82), Registry Profl. Archaeologists

(grievance coord. 1998-99), Mo. Assn. Profl. Archaeologists (v.p. 1981-82), Mo. Archaeology Soc. (trustee 1977—), Sigma Xi (chpt. pres. 1985-). Roman Catholic. Avocations: hiking, gardening. Office: Washington U PO Box 1114 Saint Louis MO 63188-1114

BROWN, A. PETER, music educator, researcher; b. Chgo., Apr. 30, 1943; s. Alfred Peter and Helen Christine (Jensen) Brown; m. Carol Vanderbilt, Mar. 23, 1968; 1 child, Heidi Elizabeth Vanderbilt. B of Music Edn., Northwestern U., Evanston, Ill., 1965, MMus, 1966, PhD, 1970; postgrad., NYU, 1970. Asst. prof. music U. Hawaii, Honolulu, 1969—74; from asst. prof. to assoc. prof. musicology Ind. U., Bloomington, 1974—81, prof. musicology, 1981—, chmn. musicology, 1997—. Faculty Aston Magna Acad., New Brunswick, NJ, 1989; vis. prof. U. Iowa, Iowa City, 1991. Author: Joseph Haydu's Keyboard Music, 1986, Performing Haydu's the Creation, 1986, The Symphonic Repertoire, 5 vols., 2002. Fellow, Am. Coun. Learned Soc., 1972—73, John Simon Guggenheim Found., 1978—79. Democrat. Avocation: collecting musical items. Office: Sch Music 1201 E 3d St Bloomington IN 47405 Business E-Mail: brownap@indiana.edu.

BROWN, ALAN ANTHONY, marketing executive; b. Winthrop, Mass., Feb. 6, 1936; s. Joseph Raymond and Harriet (Taylor) B.; m. Margret Egan, Aug. 8, 1961 (div. Feb. 1971); 1 child, Alan Jr.; m. Virginia A. Preno, Apr. 12, 1975; children: Linda, Diane, Michael, Sandra. BBA, Suffolk U., 1981, MBA, 1984. Test methods engr. RCA, Burlington, Mass., 1964-68; field svc. engr. BLH Electronics, Waltham, Mass., 1968; sales engr. AVCO Corp., Wilmington, Mass., 1968-71; sales rep. ITT Tech. Inst., Chelsea, Mass., 1971-75; dist. mgr. Continental Resources, Bedford, Mass., 1975-78; area mgr. Philips Test & Measurement, Woburn, Mass., 1978-81; distributor sales mgr. Hayes InstSer Inc., Billerica, Mass., 1981-85; sr. sales engr. Eaton Corp., Beverly, Mass., 1985-86; v.p. mktg. Hayes Instrument Svc. Inc., Billerica, Mass., 1986-92; svc. mgr. EIL Instruments Inc., Burlington, Mass., 1992-94; pres., CEO Viking Enterprise, Winthrop, Mass., 1994—. Del. Nat. Conf. of Standards Lab., Boulder, Colo., 1985—. Campaign worker Richard Deminto, Winthrop, 1988. Recipient Acad. Achievement award Sch. of Mgmt., 1983. Mem. Assn. MBAs, IEEE, Winthrop Lodge of Elks, VFW Post #6712,, Delta Mu Delta. Avocations: baseball cards, autographs. Home: 57 Central St Winthrop MA 02152-1633 Office: Viking Enterprise 57 Central St Winthrop MA 02152-1633 E-mail: alabro@msn.com.

BROWN, ALAN CHARLTON, retired aeronautical engineer; b. Whitley Bay, England, Dec. 5, 1929; came to U.S., 1956; s. Stanley and Dorothy (Charlton) B.; m. Gweneth Evelyn Bowler, July 26, 1952; children: Yvonne, Christine, Diane, Maureen. Diploma aeronautics, Hull (Eng.) Tech. Coll., 1950; MS, Cranfield (Eng.) Inst Tech., 1952, Stanford U., 1965; DSc (hon.), Cranfield (Eng.) U., 2001. Apprentice Blackburn Aircraft Ltd., Brough, Eng., 1945-50; aerodynamicist Bristol (Eng.) Aeroplane Co., 1952-56; rsch. scientist U. So. Calif., L.A., 1956-58, Wiancko Engrng. Co., Pasadena, Calif., 1958-60, Lockheed Missiles & Space Co., Palo Alto, Calif., 1960-66; group leader Lockheed Aero. Sys. Co., Burbank, Calif., 1966-69, dept. mgr., 1969-78; chief engr. F-117A Lockheed Aerospace Sys. Co., Burbank, Calif., 1978-82, dir. stealth tech., 1982-89; dir. engrng. Lockheed Corp., Calabasas, Calif., 1989-92. Fellow AIAA (Aircraft Design award 1990), NAE, Royal Aero. Soc. Democrat. Avocations: music, model aircraft. Home: 388 Aptos Ridge Cir Watsonville CA 95076-8518 E-mail: alnbrown@cruzio.com.

BROWN, ALAN CRAWFORD, lawyer; b. Rockford, Ill., May 12, 1956; s. Gerald Crawford and Jane Ella (Herzberger) B.; m. Dawn Lestrud, Apr. 16, 1998; children: Parker Crawford, Sydney Danielle, Sarah Kate, Drew Kristen, Connor Austin. BA magna cum laude, Miami U., Oxford, Ohio, 1978; JD with honors, U. Chgo., 1981. Bar: Ill. 1981, U.S. Dist. Ct. (no. dist.) Ill. 1981, U.S. Tax Ct. 1986. Assoc. Kirkland & Ellis, Chgo., 1981-87; sr. assoc. Coffield Ungaretti Harris & Slavin, Chgo., 1987-89; ptnr. McDermott, Will & Emery, Chgo., 1989—2001, Neal, Gerber & Eisenberg, Chgo., 2001—. Deacon Northminster Presbyn. Ch., Evanston, Ill., 1989-92; apiarist Chgo. Botanic Garden, Glencoe, Ill., 1988-97; active Kenilworth (Ill.) Union Ch. Mem. Order of Coif, Phi Beta Kappa. Office: Neal Gerber & Eisenberg Ste 2200 Two North LaSalle St Chicago IL 60602-3801 E-mail: acbrownesq@aol.com ., abrown@ngelaw.com.

BROWN, ALAN MARSHALL, JR., art dealer, curator, art appraiser; b. Mar. 15, 1947; s. Alan M. and Nancy (Derecktor) B.; m. Susan Sokol Brown. BS, Syracuse U., 1969. Owner, dir. Alan Brown Gallery, Naples, Fla., 1972—99. Adv. bd. Pelham Art Ctr., 1994—; exhibit designer, installer Ronald Feldman Fine Arts, NYC, Everson Mus., Syracuse, Arakawa exhibit Galerie Maeght, Paris, Alphonse Mucha exhibit Sindin Gallery, NY, Carol Anthony at Galerie d'Arte, Mexico City; curator, installer Andy Warhol print exhbn. Bond St. Gallery, Naples, Fla., 2002. Trustee Coun. for Arts in Westchester, 1983—95, sec., mem. exec. com., 1987—88; mem. art adv. bd. Pelham (N.Y.) Art Ctr., 1994—; bd. dirs. Westchester (N.Y) Pub. Art, 1986. Mem. Hartsdale C. of C. (v.p. 1987-88). Avocations: collecting american toys, native American art, peruvian textiles, African art. Address: 901 7th St S Naples FL 34102 E-mail: ambjr@aol.com.

BROWN, ALICE DALTON, artist; b. Danville, Pa., Apr. 17, 1939; d. Robert Hatcher and Elizabeth (Pond) Dalton; m. Eric Russell Brown, Aug. 20, 1960; children: Curtis, Colin, Eric. Student, Cornell U., 1958-59; BA, Oberlin Coll., 1962. One-woman shows include Fischbach Gallery, N.Y.C., 1985, 87, 89, 91, 93, 95, 98, 2000, 02, William Sawyer Gallery, San Francisco Calif., 1988, Springfield (Mo.) Art Mus., 1999; exhibited in group shows at McNay Mus., San Antonio, 1981, 89-90; represented in permanent collections Met. Mus. Art, N.Y., Maier Mus. Art, Va., Am. Express, N.Y.C., AT&T, N.Y.C., Gen. Electric Co., N.Y.C., Bank of N.Y., Southwestern Bell, St. Louis, Tampa Mus. of Art, Miami Mus. of Art, Springfield Art Mus. Office: 54 W 21st St Rm 707 New York NY 10010-6908

BROWN, ALICE ELSTE, artist; b. Balt., Nov. 5, 1922; d. Albert John and Anna Emily (Rosenbauer) Elste; m. Charles Hammond Brown, Nov. 30, 1946 (dec. Sept. 1994); children: Charles Hammond Jr., Barbara Brown Lander, Laurie Ellen. RN, U. Md., 1944; BS in Nursing Edn., Johns Hopkins U., 1949; BA in Art, Coll. Notre Dame, Balt., 1978; MA in Painting and Art Edn., Towson U., 1984. RN, Md. Nurse, head nurse U.S. Army Nurse Corps, U.S., Europe, 1944-46; pub. health nurse Balt. Health Dept., 1950-52; artist Balt., 1960—; artist-in-residence Pyramid-Atlantic Studios, Balt., 1987-92. Adj. instr. drawing and design Coll. Notre Dame, 1980. One-woman shows include Roland Park Libr., 1965, Greater Balt. Med. Ctr., 1964, exhibited in group shows at Md. Fedn. Art, 1970—79, Jewish Cmty. Ctr., 1970, Towson YMCA, 1960, Easton (Md.) Acad. Arts, 1977, Coll. of Notre Dame, 1980, Western Md. Coll., Westminster, 1990, Pyramid Atlantic, Washington, 1990, Rehoboth (Del.)Art League, 1996—. Home nursing tchr. ARC, Balt., 1950s; asst. leader, leader Girl Scouts Am., Balt., 1960s; vol. docent Balt. Mus. Art, 1970s. 1st lt., U.S. Army Nurse Corps, 1944-46. Recipient Pi Lambda Theta award Johns Hopkins U., 1949, Steinbugler award in art, Coll. Notre Dame, 1978. Mem. Nat. Mus. Women in the Arts (charter mem.), Md. Art Place, Rehoboth Art League (Thomas McFarland Skelly Meml. award 1998), Johns Hopkins U. Alumni Club. Democrat. Avocations: walking, biking, reading, archaeology, environmental concerns.

BROWN, ALTON RAYMOND, mathematician, researcher; b. Durham, N.C., July 15, 1944; s. Robert Lee Brown and Virginia Dare (Paschall) Williams; m. Becky Ann Popp, Aug. 16, 1996. BA in Math., North Tex. U., 1966; Cand. Phil. in Math., U. Calif., Berkeley, 1973, PhD in Math., 1990. Mem. tech. staff Data Dynamics, Sunnyvale, Calif., 1973-76, Litton, Sunnyvale, 1976-78, Lockheed, Sunnyvale, 1978-79; adv. engr. IBM, Gaithersburg, Md., 1979-83; mem. tech. staff MITRE, McLean, Va., 1983-90; pres. Applied Chaos, Arlington, Va., 1991-99; engring. fellow Raytheon, Falls Ch., Va., 1999—. Contbr. approx. 40 articles to profl. jours.; inventor chaos tng. method, design method, encryption method.

BROWN, ANDREAS LE, book store and art gallery executive; b. Coronado, Calif., Apr. 29, 1933; s. Harvey Clair and Helene Celeste (Kimball) B. AB, Calif. State U., San Diego, 1955; postgrad., Stanford U., 1955-57. Mem. faculty Calif. State U., 1960-63; staff rsch. fellow Humanities Rsch. Ctr., U. Tex., 1963-65; appraiser rare books, 1965-67; owner, pres. Gotham Book Mart & Gallery Inc., N.Y.C., 1967—, Sorer Realty Corp., N.Y.C., 1989—. Author: A Creative Century, 1970, (with Hal Morgan) Prairie Fires and Paper Moons, 1981; contbg. editor Antaeus; mem. adv. bd. Paris Rev. Trustee Edward Gorey Charitable Trust. With U.S. Army, 1958-59. Recipient Disting. Alumnus award, Calif. State U., San Diego, 2003. Mem. Manuscript Soc., Antiquarian Booksellers Assn. Am., Am. Booksellers Assn., Internat. League Antiquarian Booksellers, Sigma Chi, Grolier Club (N.Y.). Achievements include specializing in modern rare books and manuscripts. Home and Office: 41 W 47th St New York NY 10036-2838

BROWN, ANDREW M. otolaryngologist, allergist; b. Columbus, Ga., July 7, 1932; s. Leonard Franklin and Arizona Ruth (Embrey) Brown; m. Peggy Jean Inzer, 1956; children: Sarah Embrey Brown Hughes, Franklin Inzer; m. Renelda Joan Holcomb, June 23, 1985. BA cum laude, Baylor U., 1954; BS, U. Ala., 1958; MD, Med. Coll. Ala., 1962. Intern Lloyd Noland Found. Hosp., Fairfield, Ala., 1962-63; resident Barnes & Allied Hosp., Washington Hosp., St. Louis, 1963—67; pvt. practice Ear Nose & Throat Assocs. of Gadsden, P.A., Ala., 1970—; with Odess & Brown, Otolaryngologists, Birmingham, Ala., 1967-70. Office: 515 S 3rd St Gadsden AL 35901-5301 E-mail: ambrown@internetpro.net.

BROWN, ANN CATHERINE, investment company executive; b. St. Louis, Aug. 12, 1935; d. George Hay and Catherine Doratha (Smith) B. BA, Northwestern U., 1956; MBA, U. Mich., 1958. Copywriter Fred Gardner Advt. Co., N.Y.C., 1959-61, Batten, Barton, Durstine & Osborn, N.Y.C., 1961-63, Ogilvy & Mather Co., N.Y.C., 1963-64; copy group head Benton & Bowles Co., N.Y.C., 1964-66; pvt. investor, 1966-69; with Baker, Weeks & Co., Inc., N.Y.C., 1969-76, v.p., 1973-76; exec. v.p., dir. Melhado, Flynn & Assocs., Inc., N.Y.C., 1976-83; chmn., investment exec. A.C. Brown & Assocs. Inc., 1983—. Columnist Forbes mag., 1976-90. Home: 102 E Bay St Charleston SC 29401-2543

BROWN, ANN W. not-for-profit developer; m. Donald Brown, 1959; 2 children Student, Smith Coll., 1955-58; BA, George Washington U., 1959; LLD (hon.), Smith Coll., 2000. Past v.p. Consumer Fedn. Am.; chmn. bd. Pub. Voice, 1983-94; chmn. U.S. Consumer Product Safety Commn., 1994—2001, Safer Am. for Everyone, Palm Beach Gardens, Fla., 2001—. Nat. and local chmn. consumer affairs com. Ams. for Dem. Action; past chmn. adv. bd. Washington Consumer Protection Office. Named Washingtonian of Yr., Washingtonian Mag., 1989, Govt. Communicator of Yr., Nat. Assn. Govt. Communicators, 1995, Outstanding Alumna, George Washington U., 1996; recipient Champion of Safe Kids award, Nat. Safe Kids Campaign, 1994, Philip Hart Pub. Svc. award, Consumer Fedn. Am., 1999, Excellence in Pub. Svc. award, Am. Acad. Pediat., 2000, Nat. Working Parent award, Lokoff Found., 2000, Crystal Slipper award, 2002. Avocations: tennis, movies. Home and Office: SAFE Safer Am for Everyone 2734 Rhome Dr Palm Beach Gardens FL 33410 Office: SAFE Safer Am for Everyone 1776 I Street NW Ste 900 Washington DC 20006

BROWN, ANNE RHODA WIESEN, civic worker; b. Medford, N.J., Nov. 27, 1926; d. George William and Mary Rebecca (Hattman) W.; m. Richard C. Brown, Aug., 1995. BS, U. N.H., 1948; MRE, Andover Newton Theol. Sch., 1950. Cert. community coll. instr., Calif. Dir. Christian edn. Bapt. chs., Mass., R.I., 1950-54; tchr., recreator World Coun. Chs., France, 1955; dir. Christian edn. Bapt. chs., Norristown, Wayne, Pa., 1956-62; recreation worker U.S. mil. hosps. ARC, 1962-64, recreation supr. U.S. mil. hosps. and bases, 1964-1976, field dir., 1976-79, sta. dir. Osan AFB, Republic of Korea, 1979-80, asst. dist. dir. Camp Zama, Japan, 1981-83, March AFB, Calif., 1983-84, sta. mgr. Camp Pendleton, Calif., 1985-86, vol. resource assoc. Stuttgart, Germany, 1986-88. Sec. European Recreation Soc., Heidelberg, Germany, 1973-74. Author: Children Around the World, 1960. Bd. dirs. Project Pup, 1993-95. Recipient medal for civilian svcs. in Vietnam, U.S. Govt., 1968. Mem. AAUW (v.p. 1991-93), Tiger Bay Club (bd. dirs.). Democrat. Baptist. Avocations: handpainted eggs, animals, travel, hot air balloons.

BROWN, ANNE SHERWIN, speech pathologist, educator; b. Denver, Oct. 15, 1952; d. John Frederick and Barbara Toft Sherwin; m. Max Dennis Brown, June 15, 1985; children: Jack Steven, Michael Patrick. BA, Adams State Coll., 1974, MA, 1975. Tchr. Aurora (Colo.) Pub. Schs., 1978—. Author: Adopt-A-Cop, 1994. Bd. mgrs. YMCA, Aurora, 1996-98. Pub. Svc. Co. grantee, Denver, 1996-97, 98-99; Excel Energy Found. grantee, 2002-03. Mem. ASCD, Aurora Edn. Assn., Internat. Reading Assn. Avocations: reading, dancing, sewing, guitar, motorcycles. Home: 416 S Victor Way Aurora CO 80012-2447 Office: Aurora Pub Schs 395 S Troy St Aurora CO 80012-2472

BROWN, ANNIE MARIE VEDEL, real estate broker; b. Hellerup, Denmark, May 12, 1941; came to U.S., 1961; d. Tage Vedel and Karen Wium (Jensen) Taaning; m. Joseph Edward Brown III, Dec. 27, 1960; children: Christian, Eric, Lars. Student, U. Copenhagen, 1959-61; BS, Trenton State Coll., 1983. Lic. med. sec., Denmark, lic. in real estate, N.J.; lic. pvt. pilot. Med. sec. Burlington County Hosp., Mt. Holly, 1962-64; nursery sch. tchr. Cranberry House Sch., Medford, N.J., 1974-75; substitute tchr. Lenape Regional High Sch. System, Medford, 1978-84, Medford Twp. Schs., Medford, 1982-85; real estate assoc. B. Gary Scott Realtors, Etc., Medford, 1985-91; broker assoc. Briarwood Real Estate, Inc., Medford, 1991-96, Century 21, Medford, 1996—. Self-employed appraiser, Medford, 1987—; freelance writer, 1998—. Weekly columnist The Central Record, 1985-89. Exec. bd. Medford Home and Sch. Assn., 1981-89; cert. master gardener Burlington County, NJ. Mem. AOPA, AAUW (officer Medford chpt. 1989-95), Burlington County Bd. Realtors (edn. com. 1990—, by-laws com.), Nat. Residential Appraisers Inst., South Jersey Flyers, Pinelands Garden Club (pres. 1998-2000). Avocations: gardening, skiing, photography, travel, paddle sports. Home: 32 Friar Tuck Dr Medford NJ 08055-8542 Office: Century 21 Alliance 400 Stokes Rd Medford NJ 08055-8406 E-mail: Bbrownan@aol.com.

BROWN, APRIL SCHLEA, pharmacist; b. Lansing, Mich., Nov. 4, 1966; d. William Robert and Kathleen Louise Pederson; m. Steven James Brown, Sept. 26, 1991; children: Jordan Elizabeth, Stephanie Taylor, Ciera Nicole. Student, Palm Beach Atlantic U. Life Insurance Agent Dept. of Profl. Regulation, FL; Nuclear Technician Troxler Nuc. Electronics. Radiol. tech. cert. SW Fla. Regional Med. Ctr., Ft. Myers, 1986—87; owner Caravan Med./ Dental Supply, 1995—97, AS Brown Resource Group, 1998—2000, AS Brown Meteoritics, N.Y.C., 1999—2000; exec. prodr. New Park Pictures, 2003—. Creative cons. Young Punks Films, Tallahassee, 1994—97; editl. advisor Duchess Publications, Cape Coral, 1998—; creative cons. SMD studios, 2001—. Author: What About Hooters. America's Introduction to the Hilarious Reality of Hooters., The Publishing List; co-author: If.A book for people with way too much time on their hands. Legislative policy Fla. Pharmacy Assn., Tallahassee, 2001—02; nat. leadership inst. Wyeth-Pharmaceuticals, Washington, 2002—02. Recipient Nat. Leadership award, Nat. Assn. Chain Drug Stores; Marcus Family scholar, 2003. Mem.: Fla. Pharmacy Assn. (leadership award 2003), Union Concerned Scientists, Am. Assn. Publishers, Am. Assn. Pharm. Scientists, Am. Pharm. Assn. (chpt. pres. 2002—03), Phi Delta Chi. Avocations: piano, flute, writing, meteoritics & the cosmos (chondrites, stony-irons; unified theory, wave vs. particle), independent research (starlink cry9c gene; governmental rule/ illuminati), language/ religion (ancient hebrew, arabic, cuneiform; jewish, muslim). Personal E-mail: asbrowngroup@cs.com.

BROWN, ARLENE MEREDITH, family practice physician, educator; b. Los Alamos, N.Mex., July 29, 1953; d. Leon Joseph and Dorothy (Stern) B.; m. Paul Dennis Vordermann, Aug. 26, 1981; 1 child, Ryan David. AB, Washington U., St. Louis, 1975; MD, U. N.Mex., 1980. Diplomate Am. Bd. Family Practice, Nat. Bd. Med. Examiners. Resident in family practice Med. Coll. Wis., Milw., 1980-83, chief resident, 1982-83; pvt. practice, Ruidoso, N.Mex., 1983—. Asst. clin. prof. family and cmty. medicine U. N.Mex., Albuquerque, 1984—; pub. health officer Lincoln County (N.Mex.), 1994-2000; bd. dirs. N.Mex. Health Resources, Albuquerque, 1987-92, Inn Care Am., Tenn.; med. dir. Home Health/Hospice Lincoln County, 1985—. Founder, pres. Family Crisis Ctr., Lincoln County, 1983—; mem. Lincoln County Health and Wellness Bd., 1996-2000; bd. dirs. Cmty. Concerts, 1988-96. Named N.Mex. Family Doctor of Yr., 1994, Wyeth Ayerst award N.Mex. Med. Soc., 1994. Fellow: Am. Acad. Family Physicians (del. from N.Mex., bd. dirs. 2001—); mem.: N.Mex. Med. Soc. (coun. 1984—), Altrusa. Avocations: skiing, music, family. Office: Family Practice Assocs of Ruidoso 1401 Sudderth Dr Ruidoso NM 88345-6104

BROWN, ARNOLD, management consultant; b. Boston, Aug. 18, 1927; s. Frank and Frances B.; children: Pamela, Cynthia, Derek. BA with honors, UCLA, 1950. Asst. dir. sales promotion Mut. Benefit Life Ins. Co., Newark, 1957-61; v.p. Inst. Life Ins., N.Y.C., 1961-77; chmn. Weiner, Edrich, Brown, Inc., N.Y.C., 1977—; guest lectr. Harvard Bus. Sch., Duke U., Wharton Sch. Co-author: Supermanaging, 1984, Office Biology, 1993, Insider's Guide to the Future, 1997; mem. editl. bd. MacMillan Encyclopedia of the Future, On the Horizon mag.; contbr. articles to profl. jours. Served with USN, 1944-46. Office: 200 E 33rd St New York NY 10016-4874 E-mail: weinerbrown@earthlink.net.

BROWN, ARNOLD, physical therapy consultant; b. N.Y.C., Apr. 8, 1930; s. Murray and Tessie Brown; m. Alice L. Kahn, July 31, 1955; 1 child, Alan. BS in Edn., Panzer Coll., 1951; cert. in phys. therapy, Columbia U., 1952; MA in Psychology, Ball State U., 1972. Lic. phys. therapist, Ind. Staff phys. therapist VA Hosp., East Orange, N.J., 1954-55; sr. phys. therapist Cerebral Palsy Clinic, Union City, N.J., 1955-56; chief phys. therapist Mobility, Inc., New Rochelle, N.Y., 1956-57, Inland Steel Co. Hosp., East Chicago, Ind., 1957-67, Ball Meml. Hosp., Muncie, Ind., 1967-84; dir. phys. therapy Profl. Med. Svc., Clay County, Ind., 1984-86, St. Anthony Hosp., Michigan City, Ind., 1986-93; ret., 1993; cons. physical therapy, 1993-96. Cons. Lake County Assn. Retarded Children, Gary, Ind., 1963-67; insvc. instr. Ball Meml., St. Anthony Hosp., 1967-93; instr. Michigan City High Schs., Health Care Practicum, 1987-93; adj. clin. prof. phys. therapy Andrews U., Berrien Springs, Mich., 1987-93; clin. supr. student affiliations Ball State U., 1975-83, clin. instr. Ball State U., 1981-83; clin. supr. student affiliations Ind. U., 1975-83; mem. adv. bd. Vis. Nurse Assn., Muncie, 1972-78; tchr. health care practicum Michigan City H.S.'s, 1987-93. Author: Physiological and Psychological Considerations in Management of Stroke, 1976; author/instr.: Orientation to Physical Therapy, 1979, Body Mechanics, 1987(videotapes); contbr. to profl. jours. Bd. dirs. Nat. Multiple Sclerosis Soc., 1974-77, Easter Seal Soc., Muncie, 1976-78. With U.S. Army, 1952-54. Recipient Vocat. Dirs. award A.K. Smith Career Ctr., Michigan City, 1993. Mem. Am. Phys. Therapy Assn. (mgmt. sect.). Avocations: piano, walking, exercise, reading. Home: 2 Buckingham Ct Apt 2 Michigan City IN 46360-1588

BROWN, ARNOLD LANEHART, JR., pathologist, educator, university dean; b. Wooster, Ohio, Jan. 26, 1926; s. Arnold Lanehart and Wilda (Woods) B.; m. Betty Jane Simpson, Oct. 2, 1949; children— Arnold III, Anthony, Allen, Fletcher, Lisa. Student, U. Richmond, 1943-45; MD, Med. Coll. Va., 1949. Diplomate: Am. Bd. Pathology. Intern Presbyn.-St. Luke's Hosp., Chgo., 1949-50, resident, 1950-51, 53-56, asst. attending pathologist, 1957-59; practice medicine specializing in pathology Rochester, Minn., 1959-78; cons. exptl. pathology, anatomy Mayo Clinic, Rochester, 1959-78, also prof., chmn. dept., 1968-78; prof. pathology U. Wis., Madison, 1978—, dean Med. Sch., 1978-91. Mem. nat. cancer adv. council NIH, 1971-74, HEW, 1972-74; chmn. clearing house on environ. carcinogens Nat. Cancer Inst., 1976-80, chmn. com. to study carcinogenicity of cyclamate, 1975-76; mem. Nat. Com. on Heart Disease, Cancer and Stroke, 1975-79; mem. com. on safe drinking water NRC, 1976-77; mem. award assembly Gen. Motors Cancer Research Found., 1978-83, vice chmn., 1982-83; co-chmn. panel on geochemistry of fibrous materials related to health risks Nat. Acad. Scis.-NRC, 1978-80; chair working group Internat. Agy. for Research on Cancer, Lyon, France, 1979, 83, 87. Contbr. articles to profl. jours. Bd. sci. counselors Nat. Inst. Environ. Health Scis., NIH Nat. Toxicology Program, 1992—. With USNR, 1943-45, 51-53. Nat. Heart Inst. postdoctoral fellow, 1956-59 Mem. Am. Soc. Exptl. Pathology, Internat. Acad. Pathology, Assn. Am. Med. Colls. (chmn. council deans 1984-85). Home: 2822 Marshall Ct Madison WI 53705-2271 Office: 1300 University Ave Madison WI 53706-1510 E-mail: albrown1@facstaff.wisc.edu.

BROWN, ARNOLD M. state legislator; b. Sherman, S.D., Mar. 5, 1931; Mem. S.D. Ho. Reps. Dist. 7, Pierre, 1993-96; mem. health and human svc. and transp. coms. S.D. Ho. Reps.; mem. S.D. Senate from 7th dist., Pierre, 1997—, spkr., 2002—. Home: 1718 Teton Pass Brookings SD 57006-3626*

BROWN, ARTHUR EDMON, JR., retired army officer; b. Manila, Nov. 21, 1929; s. Arthur Edmon and Grace E. M. (Montgomery) B.; m. Jerry Deane Cook, June 6, 1953; children: Marian Brown Shope, Nan Brown Irick, Arthur Edmon III. BS, U.S. Mil. Acad., 1953; M.Public and Internat. Affairs, U. Pitts., 1965. Commd. 2d lt. U.S. Army, advanced through grades to gen.; mem. faculty U.S. Army War Coll., 1970-73; comdr. 1st Brigade, 1st Infantry Div. Fort Riley, Kans., 1973-75; mem. gen. staff Dept. Army, Washington, 1975-78; asst. div. comdr. 25th Infantry Div. Hawaii, 1978-80; dep. supt. U.S. Mil. Acad., West Point, 1980-81; comdr. U.S. Army Readiness and Moblzn., Region IV, Fort Gillem, Ga., 1981-83; dir. army staff Dept. Army, Washington, 1983-87; vice chief of staff U.S. Army, 1987-89, retired. Decorated Def. D.S.M., Army D.S.M. with oak leaf cluster, Bronze Star with 3 oak leaf clusters, Silver Star, Legion of Merit with 3 oak leaf clusters. Episcopalian. Home: 35 Fairway Winds Pl Hilton Head Island SC 29928-5547 also: 3302 N St NW Washington DC 20007-2807

BROWN, ARTHUR EDWARD, physician; b. Trenton, N.J., June 7, 1945; s. Milton Charles and Jeanne Ruth (Swern) B.; m. Jo Frances Meltzer, Nov. 24, 1985. BS, Bucknell U., 1967; MD, Jefferson Med. Coll., 1971. Intern, resident Roosevelt Hosp., N.Y.C., 1971-72, 74-76; trainee Nat. Cancer Inst., 1976-77; fellow infectious diseases Meml. Sloan-Kettering Cancer Ctr., N.Y.C., 1976-78, clin. asst. physician, 1978-82; asst. prof. medicine and pediatrics Cornell U. Med. Coll., N.Y.C., 1979-85, assoc. prof. clin. medicine and pediatrics, 1985-93, prof. clin. medicine and pediatrics, 1994—; asst. attending physician Meml. Hosp. for Cancer and Allied Diseases, N.Y.C., 1982-89, assoc. attending physician, 1989-93, attending physician, 1993—; assoc. attending pediatrician N.Y. Hosp., N.Y.C., 1985-94, attending pediatrician, 1994—. Vis. assoc. physician The Rockefeller U. Hosp., NYC, 1995—; cons, Anti-Infective Drugs adv. com FDA, USPHS, DHHS, 1997—; med. dir. Employee Health Svc. Meml. Sloan-Kettering Cancer Ctr., NYC, 2002—03, chief, 2003—. Editor: Infectious Complications of Neoplastic Diseases Controversies in Management, 1985, Infections in Oncology, 1993-2000; consulting editor Am. Jour. Medicine, 1984-86; mem. editl. bd. Antimicrobial Agts. and Chemotherapy, 1985-87, European Jour. Clin. Microbiology and Infectious Diseases, 1993—, Infections in Medicine, 1995—, Microbial Drug Resistance, 1996—; contbr. numerous articles to profl. jours. Trustee The Peddie Sch., Hightstown, N.J., 1999—. Surgeon, USPHS, 1972-74. Recipient 2d pl. HeSCA Print Festival, 1985, Bronze Plaque award Film Coun. Columbus, 1985, Bronze medal Internat. Film & TV Festival, N.Y.C., 1985, Semi-Finalist Am. Jour. Nursing Media Festival, 1986. Fellow ACP (councillor 2000-02, N.Y. chpt.), Infectious Diseases Soc. Am. (state and regional bd. dirs. 1995-98); mem. AAAS, Am. Fedn. for Med. Rsch., N.Y. County Soc. Internal Medicine (pres. 1994-96), N.Y. State Soc. Internal Medicine (dir. 1995—2000), N.Y. Soc. Infectious Diseases (sec., treas. 1993-97; v.p. 1997-98, pres.-elect 1998-99, pres. 1999-2000, immediate past-pres. 2000-01), Am. Soc. Microbiology, N.Y. Acad. Scis., Am. Soc. Clin. Oncology, Soc. Healthcare Epidemiology Am., Internat. Immunocompromised Host Soc., N.Y. Soc. Tropical Medicine, Multinat. Assn. of Supportive Care in Cancer. Achievements include research on AIDS, management of infectious complications of neoplastic diseases. Office: Meml Sloan-Kettering Cancer Ctr 222 East 70th St New York NY 10021 E-mail: brown2@mskcc.org.

BROWN, AUTRY, psychology educator, clergyman; b. Watson, Okla., May 1, 1924; s. Solon Lemley and Bessie Jane (Wilhelm) B.; m. Opal Irene Landers, Sept. 5, 1942 (dec.); children: Juanice, Rebecca, Steven, Deborah; m. Betty Parsons, Sept. 7, 2002. BA, Eastern N.M. U., 1950; M of Div., New Orleans Bapt. Theol. Sem., 1955, MRE, 1956, EdD, 1968; postgrad., Colo. State U., 1970, Southwest Mo. State U., 1985. Ordained to ministry Bapt. Ch., 1942. Pastor Bookcliff Bapt. Ch., Grand Junction, Colo., 1957-61, Carrollton Ave. Bapt. Ch., New Orleans, 1962-64, Immanuel Bapt. Ch., Ft. Collins, Colo., 1964-72; asst. prof. psychology Mo. Bapt. U., St. Louis, 1972-74, Southwest Bapt. U., Bolivar, Mo., 1974-76, prof. psychology, 1978-89, dir. counseling services, 1978-89; disting. prof. psychology, 1989—; cons. family ministry Colo. Bapt. Gen. Conv., Denver, 1976-78. Author: Church Family Life Conference Guidebook, 1973; contbr. books, profl. jour. Recipient Spl. Services award Bd. Trustees New Orleans Bapt. Theol. Sem., 1972. Mem. Am. Assn. Marriage and Family Therapy, Mo. Assn. Marriage and Family Therapy (Spl.

Service award 1984, treas. state exec. bd. 1979-83), Ozark Assn. Marriage and Family Therapy (pres. 1985-86), Mo. Assn. Counseling and Devel., Fellows Menniger Found. Avocation: collecting antique barbed wire. Home: 1526 W Laverne St Bolivar MO 65613 Office: Christian Tng Inst 1526 W Laverne St Bolivar MO 65613 E-mail: autrybrown@microcare.net., sabrown@sbuniv.edu.

BROWN, BARBARA SPROUL, retired librarian, consultant, writer; b. Salem, Mass., Jan. 12, 1934; d. Robert Hugh Sproul and Bernadette Elizabeth Marsolais; m. Bernard Peter Friesecke, Feb. 18, 1955 (div. Nov. 1975); children: Richardine, Rachel, Julie; m. Wallace Robert Brown, Jan. 16, 1988. AB magna cum laude, Boston U., 1967; MLS, Simmons Coll., 1971; cert. advanced grad. studies, Northeastern U., 1978. Cert. sch. libr. media specialist, instrnl. tech. specialist, Mass. Libr. Watertown (Mass.) Sch. Dept., 1969-97, profl. developer for faculty, 1990-96; instr. Watertown Adult Edn., 1983-87. Intern, cons. women's alcohol program CASPAR, Inc., Cambridge, Mass., 1977-79; cons. on database devel. Mindware Inc., Natick, Mass., 1982-83, Coleco Industries, Natick, 1983-84. Essay columnist Watertown Sun, 1990-02; author adult computer courses, 1983-96; contbr. short stories to lit. periodicals. Mem. Lexington (Mass.) Civil Rights Orgn., 1963-68; campaign worker Boston Dem. Com., 1985-93; bd. dirs. Coronado Unitarian Ch., 1999—. Mem. ACLU, Phi Beta Kappa, Beta Phi Mu. Democrat. Avocations: weight training, camping, motorclycling, competitive rifle shooting. Home: 1636 Donax Ave San Diego CA 92154-1003

BROWN, BARBARA JEAN, special and secondary education educator; b. Midland, Tex., Nov. 3, 1945; d. John Joseph and Sarah Beryl (Seely) Sury; m. Samuel Bradford Brown III, June 30, 1984. BA in English, U. Tex., Arlington, 1967, MAT in English and Humanities, 1979. Cert. gifted and English tchr., Tex., Fla. With Euless (Tex.) Jr. H.S./Hurst-Euless-Bedford Ind. Sch. Dist., 1967-84, Edgewater High Sch./Orange County Sch. Bd., Orlando, Fla., 1984-86; tchr. Lakeview Mid. Sch./Seminole County Sch. Bd., Sanford, Fla., 1986-98, Lake Mary (Fla.) H.S./ Seminole County Sch. Bd., 1998—. Curriculum writer Hurst-Euless-Bedford Ind. Sch. Dist., Hurst, mem. curriculum and dist. policy devel. com.; curriculum writer Seminole County Sch. Bd.; presenter Tex. Gifted Conf., Houston. Seminole County Sch. Bd. grantee, 1987-88, Svc. award, 1991, finalist, 1989-93; recipient Tchr. Merit award Walt Disney World Co., 1990-92; named Prominent Educator of Tex., 1983, Tchr. of the Yr., Coun. for Exceptional Children, 1991. Mem. NEA, PTA, Nat. Assn. Gifted Children, Seminole County Tchrs. English, Coun. Reading Tchrs., Fla. Scholastic Press Assn., Orlando Area City Panhellenic, Phi Mu (pres. Winter Park-Orlando chpt. 1988-91, nat. state day chmn. 1993-94), Sigma Tau Delta, Sigma Delta Phi. Roman Catholic. Home: 107 Hatfield Ct Longwood FL 32779-4606

BROWN, BARBARA JUNE, hospital and nursing administrator; b. Milw., Aug. 17, 1933; d. Carl W. and Nora Anne (Damrow) Rydberg; children: Deborah, Robert, Andrea, Michael, Steven, Jeffrey. BSN, Marquette U., Milw., 1955, MSN, 1960, EdD, 1970. RN, Wash., Wis.; cert. nurse adminstr. advanced. Adminstr. patient care Family Hosp., Milw., 1973-78; assoc. clin. prof. U. Wash., Seattle, 1980-87; assoc. adminstr. nursing Virginia Mason Hosp., Seattle, 1980-87; assoc. exec. dir. King Faisal Specialist Hosp., Riyadh, Saudi Arabia, 1987-91. Project dir. NIH, Sexual Assault Treatment Ctr., Milw., 1975-78; lectr., cons., 1974—. Founder, editor: Nursing Adminstrn. Quar., 1976—; editor-in-chief, regional v.p. Nurse Week, MountainWest, 2000—. Vol. ski instr. for disabled, Winter Park, Colo. Fellow: Nat. Acad. Practice, Am. Acad. Nursing (governing coun.); mem.: ANA, Grand County Pub. Health and Emergency Svcs. (chmn. health adv. com. 1994—96), Nat. League Nursing (bd. dirs., bd. govs. 2002—), Am. Orgn. Nurse Execs., Sigma Theta Tau.

BROWN, BARBARA S. environmental scientist; b. Newark, Aug. 5, 1951; d. Louis and Louise (Mumper) Stein; children: Kristin Leigh, Andrew Hayden. Student, Am. U., 1969-71; BS in Biology, U. Miami, 1976, postgrad. Staff scientist Environ. Sci. and Engring., Inc., Miami, 1978-86; dir. environ. crimes unit Dade County Environ. Resource Mgmt., 1986—2001, Dade County Police Dept., 2001—. Mem. Nat. Assn. Environ. Profls. E-mail: bsbrown@mdpd.com.

BROWN, BARRY STEPHEN, research psychologist; b. Bklyn., Sept. 26, 1937; s. Isidore Brook and Barbara (Drazin) B.; m. Ann J. Foley, Feb. 25, 1961; children: Rebecca, David, Mariam. AB, Bklyn. Coll., 1958; MS, Western Res. U., Cleve., 1959, PhD, 1963. Chief divsn. rsch. and stats. D.C. Dept. Human Resources, 1974-75; chief svcs. rsch. br. Nat. Inst. on Drug Abuse, Rockville, Md., 1975-82, dir. divsn. clin. rsch., 1982-85, dir. divsn. prevention and comms., 1985-86, chief treatment and early intervention rsch. br. Balt., 1986-88, chief cmty. rsch. br. Rockville, 1989-92; collaborating scientist Tex. Christian U., Ft. Worth, 1993—; adj. prof. U. N.C., Wilmington, 1993—; sr. investigator Friends Rsch. Inst., Balt., 1995—. Adv. bd. Ctr. for Therapeutic Cmty. Rsch., N.Y.C., 1993—; cons. Nat. Devel. and Rsch. Insts., N.Y.C., 1993—. Editor: Handbook on Risk of AIDS, 1993; mem. editl. bd. Substance Use and Misuse, 1989—, Jour. Substance Abuse Treatment, 1991—, Jour. Behavioral Health and Rsch., 1989—, Jour. of Drug Issues, 1997—; contbr. over 100 articles to sci. jours., chpts. to books. Recipient award Nat. Assn. State Alcohol and Drug Abuse Dirs., 1986, USPHS, 1979; grantee Nat. Inst. on Drug Abuse, 1994, 96, 99, 2001 Mem. Soc. Psychologists in Addictive Behaviors. Achievements include development of national research program to assess efficacy of outreach strategies designed to reduce risk of HIV infection to drug users and sexual partners; organizer technical assistance program to share successful outreach models leading to federal legislation institutionalizing and funding outreach. Home: PO Box 1695 Carolina Beach NC 28428-1695

BROWN, BENJAMIN A. investment advisor; b. N.Y.C., Feb. 13, 1943; s. Horace A. and Lillian A. (Hurwitz) B.; m. Elinore Carole Abravanel, Aug. 8, 1968; children— Adam Howard, Dina Lauren BBA in Acctg., Adelphi U., 1964; MBA in Fin. and Investments, Baruch Coll. CUNY, 1971. Registered investment advisor prin.-fin. mgmt. svcs. Acct. Samuel Greiff C.P.A., Atty., Forest Hills, N.Y., 1963-66; v.p. research dept. Walston & Co., N.Y.C., 1967-73; treas. ENSERCH Corp., Dallas, 1974-78, v.p. fin., 1978-82, v.p. fin. relations, 1982-96. V.p. Enserch Exploration, Inc., 1995-96; v.p. fin. and investor rels. EEX Corp., Houston, 1997-98; chief investment officer, mng. dir. Fin. Mgmt. Svcs., Dallas, 1999—. Mem. Am. Assn. Individual Investors, N.Y. Soc. Security Analysts, DAC Country Club, Univ. Club Houston. Avocations: walking, golf, numismatics, oenology. Home: 5200 Keller Springs Rd Apt 621 Dallas TX 75248-2744 Office: Candy & Schonwald Bldg 3116 Live Oak St Ste 201 Dallas TX 75204-6190 *I strive everyday to give more than I take and spend less than I make. My success and happiness are entirely attributable to a very loving and supportive family, including a perfect mate for more than 35 years, two children that reflect the best qualities parents could wish for, a mother and brother that are always there for me, in-laws that most can only dream about and one extraordinary granddaughter.*

BROWN, BENJAMIN ANDREW, journalist; b. Red House, W.Va., Apr. 30, 1933; s. Albert Miller and Mary Agnes (Donegan) B.; m. Joanne Gretchen Harder, May 22, 1956; children: Benjamin Andrew, Gretchen, Mark, Betsy Brown Larson. BS in Journalism, Fla. State U., 1955. Sportswriter Charleston (W.Va.) Daily Mail, 1955-57; with AP, 1957-93, gen. exec., 1976-78, 82-93, chief bur. Los Angeles, 1978-82; assoc. Am. Newspapers Cons., Ltd., Milw., 1993-95. Bd. dirs. Last Chance Press Club, Helena, Mont., 1969; v.p. Minn. Press Club, 1975 Office: PO Box 3012 Paso Robles CA 93447-3012 E-mail: babrown@charter.net.

BROWN, BENJAMIN THOMAS, urologist, educator; b. Beckley, W.Va., Sept. 30, 1948; s. Benjamin Porter Jr. and Nancy Jo (Ballengee) B.; m. Kimberlee Timbrook; children: Elizabeth Timbrook, James Schuyler. Student, Johns Hopkins U., 1966-69; MD, W.Va. U., 1973; MBA, U. S. Fla., 1997. Diplomate Am. Bd. Urology. Surg. intern W.Va. U., Morgantown, 1973-74, resident in medicine, 1974-75; resident in urology U. Miami (Fla.), 1975-78; pvt. practice Daytona Beach, Fla., 1978—; chief surgery Meml. Hosp, Ormond Beach, Fla., 1980-82, chief staff, 1986-87; chief urology Halifax Med. Ctr., Daytona Beach, 1982-84. Clin. asst. prof. family practice U. South Fla., Tampa, 1979—. Contbr. numerous articles to med. jours. Pres. I-Care, child abuse, Daytona Beach, 1988; vice chmn. adminstrv. bd. United Meth. Ch., 1990-91, pastor, mem. pastor-parish rels. com., 1990-94; unit bd. dirs. Am. Cancer Soc., 1993—, 2d v.p., 1994-97, pres.-elect, 1997-98, pres., 1998-99, mem. subcom. on prostate cancer, 1998-2001, chmn. 2001—, bd. dirs. Fla. divsn., 1998—, Fla. Divsn. Bd., ACS, 1996—; bd. dirs. Ptnrs. for Cmty. Health, 1993—, v.p., 1996-97; bd. dirs. Volusia County Coop. Health Group, 1991—, vice chmn., 1993-94, chmn., 1994-97, pres., 1998—. Fellow: ACS (chmn. com. on applicants ctrl. Fla. 1998—); mem.: AMA, Volusia County Med. Soc. (sec. 1990—91, pres.-elect 1991—92, pres. 1992—93, chmn. bd. govs. 1994—95, 1997—98), Fla. Med. Assn. (Volusia County del. 1990—96, 2d pl. Editl. award 1998), Underwater Med. Soc., Fla. Urol. Soc. (exec. com. 1990—2001, chmn. bylaws com. 1992—94, membership com. 1994—96, sec./treas. 1997—98, pres.-elect 1998—, pres. 1999—2000), Am. Urol. Assn. (bd. dirs. Southeastern sect. 1994—, bd. rep. to exec. com. 1996—99, treas. 1999, investment com. 1999—2002, treas. com. 1999—2002, jud. and ethics com. 2001—, pres.-elect 2002—), Volusia County (bd. dirs.), Univ. Club Volusia County (bd. dirs. 1986—89), Tiger Bay Club (2d v.p. 1995—97, pres. 1998—2000), Daytona Beach Quarterback Club (team physician 1987), Masons, Rotary. Republican. Home: 602 Riverside Dr Ormond Beach FL 32176-7714 Office: Atlantic Urol Assocs 545 Health Blvd Daytona Beach FL 32114-1493 E-mail: bbrown@atlanticurology.com.

BROWN, BERNICE LEONA BAYNES, foundation consultant, educator, consultant; b. Pitts., June 19, 1935; d. Howard Leon and Henrietta Lydia (Hodges) Baynes; m. James Brown, May 4, 1964; 1 child, Kiyeseni Anu. BFA, Carnegie Mellon U., 1957; MEd, U. Pitts., 1966. Tchr. Pitts. Pub. Schs., 1957-65; lectr. Carlow Coll., Pitts., 1964-67; edn. specialist Bay Area Urban League, San Francisco, 1967-68; asst. prof. San Francisco Coll. for Women, 1968-72; dean students Lone Mountain Coll., San Francisco, 1972-76; dir. San Francisco Pub. Schs. Commn., 1976; program exec. San Francisco Found., 1977-86, ednl. cons. San Francisco, 1987—; found. adminstr. Clorox Co. Found., 1989-91; dean of faculty and staff devel. City Coll. of San Francisco, 1991-98; dean Workforce Edn./Calworks Edn. and Tng., 1998—. Vis. scholar Stanford (Calif.) U., 1987-88. Mem. bd. of govs. Calif. Cmty. Colls., 1975-81, Calif. Post Secondary Edn. Commn., Sacramento, 1978-80, State Supt's Adv. Com. on Black Am. Affairs, Calif., 1985—; chair Found. Cmty. Svc. Cable T.V., San Francisco, 1982-84; trustee Schs. of Sacred Heart, San Francisco, 1982-87; bd. dirs. Urban Econ. Devel. Corp., 1988-2000, High/Scope Ednl. Rsch. Found., 1990-98, Network for Elders, 1997—, Cmty. Bds., Inc., 2000—; trustee Howard Thurman Ednl. Trust, 1989-94, Uprising Cmty. Credit Union, San Francisco, 2001—. Recipient Milestone award Citizen's Scholarship Found. of Am., 1995, Profl. Women of Yr. award, San Francisco Bus. & Profl. Women, Inc. Mem. San Francisco LWV (bd. mem. 2000—), Women and Founds. Corp. Philanthropy (bd. dirs. 1985-87), Assn. Black Found. Execs. (bd. dirs. 1978-82), Commonwealth Club of Calif. (bd. gov. 1988-91). Home: 1271 23d Ave San Francisco CA 94122-1605 Office: City Coll San Francisco Ocean Phelan 50 Phelan Ave San Francisco CA 94124-9411 E-mail: bbrown@ccsf.org.

BROWN, BETTY MARIE, government agency administrator; b. Siler City, N.C., June 11, 1952; d. Ardentries and Emma (Peoples) Mason; m. Tommy E. Brown, Aug. 8, 1968 (dec.); 1 child, Christopher T.; m. Roger L. Cook, June 10, 1973 (dec. Feb. 1981); 1 child, Felicia M. AAS, Phila. Community Coll., 1981; BS, Drexel U., 1986. Cert. early childhood edn. tchr., elem. edn. tchr., Pa. Mgr. Mr. Gourmet Deli, Phila., 1977-80; pres. Parents, Friends and Vols. Community Svc. Orgn., Phila., 1983—; tchr. Phila. Sch. Dist., 1988-89; remittance perfection clk. IRS, Phila., 1990-92; account analyst IRS-Automated Collection Sys., Phila., 1992—; with Censur Bur./Dept. Commerce, 1980. Tchr. Mid City YWCA, Phila., 1983-88. Sec. support community outreach project Dept. Human Svcs., Phila., 1990-91. Recipient Community Svc. award Dept. Human Svc., 1988. Baptist. Avocations: reading, swimming, dancing, flying, tennis. Home and Office: Parents of the 39th Dist 1132 Easton Rd Apt B Philadelphia PA 19150-2708 E-mail: BMBROWN52@go.com.

BROWN, BEULAH LOUISE, retired elementary educator; b. Warren County, Ohio, Feb. 21, 1917; d. Fred Austin and Roba E. (Doughman) Birmingham; m. William Dale Brown, Aug. 14, 1942 (dec. Apr. 1984). Student, Ohio U., 1937-39, BS in Edn. cum laude, 1957. Cert. tchr., Ohio. Tchr. 2d grade Bainbridge (Ohio) Village Sch., 1939-43; rsch. lab. asst. Mead Paper Corp., Chillicothe, Ohio, 1944-45; tchr. 2d grade Chillicothe City Schs., 1945-46, Marysville (Ohio) Schs., 1946-49; tchr. 1st grade Riley Twp. Sandusky County Schs., Fremont, Ohio, 1951-52; tchr. 2d grade Fremont City Schs., 1952-59, Lancaster (Ohio) City Schs., 1959-64, tchr. 1st grade, 1966-75; tchr. 2d grade Ashland (Ohio) City Schs., 1964-66. Supervising tchr. Bowling Green (Ohio) State U., 1955-59, Ohio U., Athens, 1960-64, 66-75, Ashland Coll., 1964-66. Mem. AAUW, Farifield County Ret. Tchrs., Ohio Ret. Tchrs., Clionian Literary Club, Kappa Delta Pi, Delta Kappa Gamma. Republican. Methodist. Avocations: reading, travel.

BROWN, BILLY CHARLIE, secondary school educator; b. Cookeville, Tenn., Feb. 20, 1947; s. Joe Homer and Sallie Mable (Hendrickson) B. BS in Forestry, BS in Edn., U. Tenn., 1969, EdD in Curriculum and Instruction, 1979; MA in Secondary Sci. Edn., Tenn. Tech. U., 1973, EdS in Secondary Sci. Edn., 1976. Cert. secondary sci. tchr., Ga., Tenn., Ky. Tchr., dept. chair Westwood Jr. High Sch., Manchester, Tenn., 1970-77; tchr., coach Feldwood High Sch., College Park, Ga., 1979-84; tchr., sci. Shiloh High Sch., Lithonia, Ga., 1984-87; coord. environ. energy sci. edn. ctr. U. Tenn., Knoxville, 1987-88; assoc. prof. Ky. Wesleyan Coll., Owensboro, 1990-93; with Cobb County Schs., Marietta, Ga., 1993—98; sci. edn. cons. Oak Ridge Nat. Lab., 1993-99; assoc. prof. edn., Insnl. EPSB Programs coord. Lindsey Wilson Coll., Columbia, Ky., 1999—. Vis. asst. prof. U. Tenn., Knoxville, 1988-90; co-dir. Ctr. for Environ./Energy/Sci. Edn., U. Tenn., Knoxville, 1988-90; sci. cons. area sch. dists. Ky. Wesleyan Coll., Owensboro, 1990-93; dir. Elem. Sci. Leadership Inst., Oak Ridge Nat. Lab., 1993—. Contbr. articles to profl. jours. Named Outstanding Classroom Tchr., Tenn. Edn. Assn., 1975. Mem. Nat. Sci. Tchr. Assn. (Outstanding Sci. Educator nominee 1991), Nat. Coun. Tchrs. Math., Mid-East Regional Assn. Educators Tchrs. Sci. Avocations: cultural music, sports coaching, writing, hiking. Home: 86 Edmonton Rd Columbia KY 42728-9422

BROWN, BILLYE JEAN, retired nursing educator; b. Damascus, Ark., Oct. 29, 1925; d. William A. and Dora (Megee) B. BSNEd, U. Tex. Med. Br., Galveston, 1953; MSNEd, St. Louis U., 1958; EdD, Baylor U., 1975. Asst. prof. U. Tex. Med. Br. Sch. Nursing, 1958-60; assoc. prof. U. Tex. Nursing Sch., Austin, 1960-67, assoc. dean, prof., 1968-72, dean, prof., 1972-89; prof. emeritus Sch. Nursing U. Tex., 1989—; mem. Nat. Adv. Council Nurse Tng., 1982-87. Nat. League for Nursing fellow, 1957-58; recipient Alumni Merit award St. Louis U., 1981; Am. Acad. Nursing fellow, 1984. Mem. ANA, Am. Assn. Colls. Nursing (pres. 1982-84, Sister Bernadette Armiger award 1990), Tex. League Nursing, Tex. Nurses Assn. (Nurse of Yr. 1980), Sigma Theta Tau (pres. 1989-91, Internat. Mary T. Wright Founders award 1999), Phi Kappa Phi (life).

BROWN, BLANCHE Y. secondary education educator, genealogy researcher; b. Saint Mary's, W.Va., Feb. 2, 1918; d. Lewis Frederick and Edna Clara (Walker) Yost; m. Vincent Robert Brown, June 1, 1946; children: Susan Elizabeth, Roberta Ann Brown Pugh. BA, Marietta Coll., 1939; postgrad., Columbia U., 1946, 47. Cert. secondary tchr. in sci. and English. Pers. supr. Packard Electric divsn. Gen. Motors Corp., Warren, Ohio, 1940-44; tchr. bus. edn. New Matamoras (Ohio) H.S., 1945-49; fin. sec. St. Paul's United Meth. Ch., Houston, 1949-50; pers. dept. Olin Chem. Corp., Pasadena, Tex., 1951-53; tchr. biology Pasadena H.S., 1958-78. Co-editor: Grandview Township's First Trustees Journal--1803-1843, 1991; editor Matamoras Area Hist. Soc. Newsletter, 1987-99. Recipient First Families of Ohio award Ohio Geneal. Soc., 1989, Award of Achievement Ohio Hist. Soc. for Matamoras Area Hist. Soc. Newsletter, 1992. Mem. Tex. Ret. Tchrs. Assn. (life), Nat. Soc. DAR (Marietta, Ohio chpt. schs. chmn. 1988-94, corr. sec. 1995-99, nat. Photography award 1989), Matamoras Area Hist. Soc. (genealogy and local history coord. for Sesquicentennial Celebration 1846-1996, Bicentennial Celebration 1797-1997), VFW Aux. (life), AAUW. Republican. Methodist. Avocations: photography, artwork with shells, writing. Home: 733 Main St New Matamoras OH 45767-6013

BROWN, BOB OLIVER, retired manufacturing company executive; b. Ft. Dodge, Iowa, June 5, 1929; s. Frank Arthur and Winona (Thietje) B.; m. JoAnn Louise Brown, Sept. 7, 1963 (div. Oct. 1989); children: Scott, Douglas. BSBA, U. Omaha, 1950; MS, U. Ill., 1951. CPA, Mo. Auditor Price Waterhouse, St. Louis, 1954-58, E A Rothaus, St. Louis, 1958-62; treas. Hazell Machine, St. Louis, 1962-64, Troug Nichols, Kansas City, Mo., 1964-66; v.p. Unitog Co., Kansas City, 1966-94; ret., 1994. Capt. USMC, 1951-54, Korea. Mem. AICPA, Mo. Soc. CPA, Tax Execs. Inst., Smithsonian Assocs., VFW, Am. Legion, Kansas City C. of C. Republican. Episcopalian. Home: Omaha, Nebr. Died Aug. 12, 2002.

BROWN, BRITT, retired publishing company executive; b. Long Beach, Calif., Apr. 23, 1927; s. Harry Britton and Victoria (Eaton) B.; m. Anne Louise McCarthy, June 19, 1948; children— Cathy Lynn, Cynthia Ann, Britt Murdock, Bruce McCarthy. Student, U. So. Calif., 1944-46; BA, U. Kans., 1947. Classified advt. salesman Wichita (Kans.) Eagle (now Wichita Eagle & Beacon Pub. Co.), 1947-50, classified mgr., 1952-55, advt. dir., 1956-62, v.p., sec., 1963-71, pub., pres., 1971-73, chmn., 1973-79. Served with USMCR, 1944-46, 50-51. Mem. Sigma Delta Chi, Kappa Alpha.

BROWN, BRUCE ANDREW, lawyer; b. Cleve., Oct. 16, 1959; s. Andrew and Ruby Louise (Bishop) B. BA, Brown U., 1981; JD, Columbia U., 1984. Bar: N.Y. 1985, Ohio 1990. Assoc. Proskaver Rose Goetz and Mendelsohn, N.Y.C., 1983-86, Finley, Kumble Wagner Heine Vnderberg Manley Myerson & Casey, N.Y.C., 1986-87; pvt. practice B. Andrew Brown & Assocs., Cleve., 1987—. Mem. NAACP, Urban League (bd. dirs. 1988—), Omega Psi Phi. Democrat. Moslem. Avocation: golf. Office: B Andrew Brown & Assocs 1300 Bank One Ctr 600 Superior Ave E Cleveland OH 44114-2611

BROWN, BRUCE BADEN, accountant; b. Seattle, Dec. 1, 1933; s. Charles Elric and Mabel Enid (Coleman) Brown; m. Lois Jean Bellemans-Brown, 1963 (div. 1979); 3 children; m. Teresita Grimarez Brown, 1981 (div. 1985); 1 child; m. Lois Jean Bellemans-Brown, 1991. BBA, U. Wash., 1960. Cert. enrolled agt. U.S. Treasury. Various to v.p. Weather Master of Wash., Lynnwood, 1975—77; sr. planning and programs analyst Saudi Aramco, Dhahran, Saudi Arabia, 1977—93; owner Lighthouse Tax Svc., Mukilteo, Wash., 1995—. Tax and bus. cons. Lighthouse Tax Svc., 1997—. Author: (novels) Desert Duel, 1999. Officer Mukilteo Hist. Soc., 1995—; coun. mem. City of Mukilteo, Wash., 1999—. Cpl. U.S. Army, 1951—54, Germany. Named Mukilteo Citizen of Yr., 2002. Home: 312 Cornelia Ave Mukilteo WA 98275 Office: Lighthouse Tax Svc 312 Cornelia Ave Mukilteo WA 98275

BROWN, BRUCE MAITLAND, philanthropy consultant; b. Bryn Mawr, Pa., Sept. 2, 1947; s. Charles Stuart and Margaret (Houston) B.; m. Elaine Eldredge, Sept. 3, 1983; 1 child, Carter Houston Brown. BA, Lawrence U., 1969; MA, U. Ky., 1973. Program analyst FDA, Rockville, Md., 1973-75, exec. secretariat, 1975-78, spl. asst., 1978-82, dep. dir., press ofc., 1982-86; v.p. communications Council for Responsible Nutrition, Washington, 1986-87; v.p. for charitable trusts CoreStates Trust and Investment Group, 1987-93; cons. Inst. for Non-profit Excellence, Radnor, Pa., 1993-95. Meteorologist Sta. WCAU-Radio, Phila., 1965; news dir., sports broadcaster Sta. WLFM-Radio, Appleton, Wis., 1965-69; aide U.S. Senator Hugh Scott, Washington, 1969; pub. rels. contr. Fellowship of Reconciliation, Nyack, N.Y., 1982; writer speeches FDA commrs., 1979-82; cons. Sewell C. Biggs Mus. Am. Art, 1994; bd. advisors Wayne Art Ctr., 1994—, chmn., 2002—; cons. Transworld Commerce Alliance, 1994-96; bd. dirs. PhilaPride, Inc., 1993-97; adv. bd. Resources for Human Devel., 1993-98; exec. bd. Am. Edn. Media Ctr., 1995—, v.p., 1998—. Trustee Lawrence U., 1994—97; bd. dirs. sec.-treas. Hoxie Harrison Smith Found., 1994—; rev. panelist cmty. devel. fund United Way Southeastern Pa., 1995—97; co-pres., bd. dirs. Brooke Valley Conservancy Assn., 1988—95; officer Paint Br. Farms Civic Assn., Coleville, Md., 1978—83; founder, trustee HBE Found., 1988—; mem. non-profit MBA adv. coun., bd, visitors Ea. Univ., 1990—; mem. adv. bd. Ctr. for Urban Resources, 1992—2000, Presbyn. Children's Village, 1997—2003, devel. com., 1994—, bd. dirs., 2003—; trustee Bryn Mawr Rehab. Found., 1997—98; mem. beneficiary adv. bd, Trusts and Estates Group, 1998—; mem. adv. coun. Esperanza Health Ctr., 1998; mem. devel. com. Camphill Village, Kimberton Hills, 1998—2003, Fellowship of Reconciliation, 1996—; mem. Phila. bd. World Vision's Love for Children, 1996—97; co-chmn. Kearsley Found., 2003—; trustee Resources Com. of Episc. Acad., Merion, Pa., 1995—98; sec. bd., mem. audit com., mem. ch. found. bd. Episcopal Diocese Pa., 1998—2003; bd. dirs. Resources for Better Families, 1994—97, Bermuda Artworks Found. Bd., 1992—96, Kearsley Bd., 1996—2000, Chester Rural Cemetery Assn., 1998; mem. adv. bd. Del. County Hist. Soc., 1999—. With U.S. Army, 1969—71. Mem.: Del. Valley Grantmakers (founding bd. dirs., v.p. 1989—91), The Philantrophy Roundtable, The Assemblies, Bay Head Yacht Club, Merion Cricket Club, Skytop Club. Episcopalian. Avocations: reading, gardening, meteorology, soccer, swimming.

BROWN, BRYAN D. career officer; b. Oct. 20, 1948; Commd. U.S. Army, advanced through grades to maj. gen., 1998; dir. requirements and strategic assessments U.S. Spl. Ops. Command, MacDill AFB, Fla., 1996-98; comdg. gen. Joint Spl. Ops. Command, Ft. Bragg, N.C., 1998—. Office: Joint Spl Ops Command PO Box 70239 Fort Bragg NC 28307-0239

BROWN, BYRON WILLIAM, JR., biostatistician, educator; b. Chgo., Apr. 21, 1930; s. Byron William and Ruth (Munson) Brown; m. Janet Louise Hyde, July 30, 1949; children: Byron William III, Eric Paul, Alan Thomas, Madeleine Magill, Mark Andrew, Lisa Anne. BA in Math., U. Minn., 1952, MS in Stats., 1955, PhD in Biostats., 1959. Asst. prof. biostats. Med. Sch. La. State U., New Orleans, 1956—57; from lectr. to prof. Sch. Pub. Health U. Minn., Mpls., 1957—65, prof., head biostats., 1965—68; prof., head divsn. biostats Stanford (Calif.) U., 1968—98, chmn. dept. health rsch. and policy, 1988—96, prof. emeritus, 1998—. Cons. govt. and industry. Author: books, books chpts. and articles in profl. jours. and encys.; co-author. With USAF, 1949. Fellow: AAAS, Am. Heart Assn., Am. Statis. Assn. (sect. pres., assoc. editor Jour.); mem.: Internat. Stats. Inst. (elected), Soc. for Clin. Trials (pres. 1988), Inst. Math. Stats., Biometrics Soc. (pres. Western N.Am. region 1978), Inst. Medicine (elected), Sigma Xi, Phi Beta Kappa. Home: 981 Cottrell Way Stanford CA 94305-1057

BROWN, C. HAROLD, lawyer; b. Mendenhall, Miss., July 28, 1931; m. Alicia Brown; children: Tracey Gwen, Terry Lynne, Allison Anne, Harold Allen. BA, Vanderbilt U., 1957; LLB, U. Tex., 1960. Bar: Tex. 1960. Sr. ptnr. Brown Pruitt Peterson & Wambsganss, P.C., Ft. Worth, 1960—. Pres. A.J. and Jessie Duncan Found. Past chmn. Ft. Worth Civil Svc. Commn.; past chmn. bd. dirs., past pres. Tarrant County Conv. Ctr., 1980; active Com. for Greater Tarrant County; past bd. dirs. Ft. Worth Camp Fire Girls; past bd. dirs. Nat. Com. for Adoption, Gladney Ctr., Adopt a Spl. Kid/Tex.; past bd. dirs. Tex. Assn. Licensed Children's Svcs.; mgr. campaign R.M. Stovall for Mayor of Ft. Worth, 1969, 71, 73, Richard T. Andersen for Tarrant County Commr., 1972, 76, 80, 84, Senator Al Gore for Pres., Tarrant County, Tex., 1988; past deacon U. Christian Ch., Ft. Worth. Sgt. U.S. Army, 1953-55. Recipient cert. Carnegie Hero Fund Commn., 1972; named Outstanding Young Texan, 1976; named to Gladney Ctr. Hall of Fame. Fellow Tex. Bar Found. (life), Southwestern Legal Found., Tarrant County Bar Found. (life), Ft. Worth-Tarrant County Bar Assn. (charter, life, bd. dirs. family law sect. 1978-80); mem. ABA, Tex. Bar Assn., Tarrant County Probate Bar, Ft. Worth Jr. Bar Assn. (pres. 1963), Am. Acad. Adoption Attys., Am. Acad. Hosp. Attys., Nat. Health Lawyers Assn., Pro Bono Coll. of State Bar of Tex., Badge and Shield, Vanderbilt U. Alumni Assn. (pres. 1966-67), Am. Brittany Club (Hall of Fame), Ridotto Club (pres. 1974), Petroleum Club, River Crest Country Club, Steeplechase Club, Nat. Commodore Club (adm.), Rotary, Masons, Shriners, Jesters, Alpha Tau Omega, Phi Delta Phi. Office: Brown Pruitt Peterson & Wambsganss PC 201 Main St Ste 801 Fort Worth TX 76102-3817 E-mail: brownpruittlaw@ad.com.

BROWN, CABOT, investment company executive; b. San Francisco, Aug. 24, 1961; s. Stephen Cabot and Caludine (Montgomery) B.; m. Mollie Ward, Aug. 6, 1988; children: Parker, Harrison, Madeline, Stuart. AB, Harvard U., 1983, MBA, 1987. Fin. analyst Lehman Bros., NYC, 1983-85; assoc. Volpe, Welty & Co., San Francisco, 1987-89, gen. ptnr., 1989-95; co-founder, mng. dir. Brown, McMillan & Co. LLC, San Francisco, 1996—2001; co-founder, mng. ptnr. Seven Hills Group LLC, 2001—. Bd. dir. Wham-O, Inc., Emeryville, Calif., Latin Axis, NYC, Mister Car Wash, Tucson, Apelon, Ridgefield, CT. Democrat. Home: 2744 Steiner St San Francisco CA 94123-4714 Office: Seven Hills Group 88 Kearny St San Francisco CA 94108 E-mail: cbrown@sevenhills.com.

BROWN, CAMPBELL, commentator; BA in Polit. Sci., Regis Coll. Polit. reporter KSNT-TV, Topeka, WWBT-TV, Richmond, Va., WBAL-TV, Balt., WRC-TV, Wash.; corr. NBC News, 1996—98, White Ho. corr., 1998—; co-anchor NBC Weekend Today, 2003—. Office: Weekend Today NBC News 30 Rockefeller Plz New York NY 10112*

BROWN, CARLTON E. college president; m. T. LaVerne Ricks-Brown; children: Kwame, Jamila. BA in English, U. Mass., 1971, EdD in Multicultural Edn., 1979. Faculty Sch. of Edn. Old Dominion U., Va., 1979-87; various to Dean Sch. Edn. Hampton U., 1987-90, dean Sch. Liberal Arts and Edn., 1990-96, v.p. for planning, dean Grad. Coll., 1996-97; pres. Savannah (Ga.) State U., 1997—. Mem. bd. Hampton City Sch. Bd., 1992-96, vice-chair 1995-97; bd. dirs. Savannah Econ. Devel. Coun., 1998—, Nat. Assn. for Equal Opportunity, 1999—; vice chair Savecon Devel. Authority, 2002—. Mem. Savannah C. of C. (bd. dirs. 1999—). Office: Savannah State Univ PO Box 20449 Savannah GA 31404-9707 E-mail: brownce@tigerpaw.savstate.edu.

BROWN, CAROL, artist; BFA, Cornell U. One woman shows include The Witkin Gallery, N.Y.C., 1987, Charles Lucien Gallery, N.Y.C., Rettig Y Martinez, Santa Fe, The Little Gallery, Ithaca, N.Y., Korn Gallery, Drew U., Madison, N.J.; exhibited in group shows at Etherton-Stern Gallery, Tucson, 1992, Missoula (Mont.) Mus. Fine Arts, Parrish Mus., Southampton, N.Y., Provincetown (Mass.) Art Assn. and Mus., 1993, Whitney Mus. at Stamford (Conn.), The Torrey (Utah) Gallery; represented in collections U.S. Embassy, Athens, Greece, Rabat, Morrocco, Ashgabat, Turkmenistan. Individual fellow Nat. Endowment for the Arts, 1994. E-mail: carolbrown9@earthlink.net.

BROWN, CAROL, make-up artist; b. Stockholm, Nov. 26, 1949; d. Julius C. and Violet (Moten) B. Student, Mt. St. Mary's Coll., 1968-72, European Exch. Program, 1972-74, L.A. Valley Coll., 1974-76. Cert. make-up artistry tchr., Calif. Makeup-artist Spelling Entertainment, Paramount, Disney, NBC, others, L.A., 1977—; CEO Natural to Knockout.com., L.A., 1996—; founder, CEO Carol Brown Natural Empowerment Found., L.A., 2000—. Aesthetic cons. C.B. Enterprises, 1990—; instr. Fred Segal Beauty, 1990—; spkr. in field; mem. adv. bd. Denise Roberts Found.; mem. speakerservices.com. Author: Natural to Knockout Makeup Application Beauty Guide, 2001. Vol. L.A. Mission, 1989—, Jenesee Ctr., L.a., 1996—, Sickle Cell Disease Assn. Am., L.A., 1996—. Recipient Outstanding Tech. Achievement award L.A. Black Media Coalition, 1989. Mem.: NATAS (mem. Emmy awards com. 1985—90, mem. show com. 1985—90, mem. exec. peer group com. 1985—93, 3 Emmy awards, 7 Emmy award nominations), NAACP, Assn. Image Cons. Internat., Colour Soc. Australia, Internat. Alliance Stage and Theatrical Emmployees, Aesthetics Internat. Assn. Office: Carol Brown Natural Empowerment Found PO Box 79083 Los Angeles CA 90079

BROWN, CAROLYN SMITH, communications educator, consultant; b. Salt Lake City, Aug. 12, 1946; d. Andrew Delbert and Olive (Crane) Smith; m. David Scott Brown, Sept. 10, 1982. BA magna cum laude, U. Utah, 1968, MA, 1972, PhD, 1974. Instr. Salt Lake Ctr., Brigham Young U., Salt Lake City, 1976-78, vis. asst. prof. Provo, 1978; asst. prof. Am. Inst. Banking, Salt Lake City, 1977—; prof., chmn. English, communication and gen. edn. depts. Latter Day Saints Bus. Coll., Salt Lake City, 1973—, dean acad. affairs, 1986-96, v.p. for acad. affairs, 1996—, acting v.p. for student affairs, 1999-2000. Founder Career Devel. Tng., Salt Lake City, 1979—, pres., 1979; cons. in-house seminars 1st Security REalty Svcs., USDA Natural Resource Conservation Svc., Utah Power & Light, Utah Soc. Svcs., Adminstrv. Office of Cts., HUD, Intermountain Health Care, Fidelity Investments, Am. Inst. Banking; mem. N.W. Assn. Schs. and Colls. Liaison, 1980—, Utah Bus. Coll. Dean's Com., 1990—. Author: (book) Writing Letters & Reports That Communicate, 8th edit., 1994, (poem) In Memory of the Baby Deers, 1996, Waiting (Editor's Choice award for Outstanding Achievement in Poetry), 1998. Demi-soloist Utah Civic Ballet (now Ballet West), Salt Lake City, 1964-68; active Mormon Ch.; C. of C. Bus. Edn. com., 1991-92. Named Tchr. of Month, Salt Lake City Kiwanis, 1981; NDEA fellow, U. Utah, 1972. Mem. Am. Bus. Communications Assn. (lectr. West/N.W. regional chpt. 1987), Delta Kappa Gamma (2d v.p. 1977-79), Lambda Delta Sigma (Outstanding Woman of Yr. 1983), Kappa Kappa Gamma (Outstanding Alumnus in Lit. 1974). Clubs: Alice Louise Reynolds Literary (Salt Lake City) (v.p. 1978-79, sec. 1985-86). Republican. Avocations: walking, hiking, slide lectures on Israel and literary topics. Office: LDS Bus Coll 411 E South Temple Salt Lake City UT 84111-1302

BROWN, CARROLL, diplomat, association executive, consultant; b. Selma, Ala., Oct. 5, 1928; s. Jack Crisman and Bessie (Bedsole) B.; m. Elvira DiMiceli, Apr. 2, 1953; children: David, Suzanne. AB, Columbia U., 1951, MA, 1953; postgrad., Johns Hopkins U., 1964-65. Joined Fgn. Service, 1957; posts include Yugoslavia, Poland, Washington, Austria; dep. dir. for Eastern European affairs Dept. State, Washington, 1974-76; dep. chief mission Am. embassy, Warsaw, 1976-79; consul gen. Düsseldorf, Fed. Republic Germany, 1979-81, Munich, Fed. Republic Germany, 1981-84; dir. Office Can. Affairs Dept. State, Washington, 1984-86, acting dep. asst. sec., 1986; mem. U.S. delegations to 41st and 42nd UN Gen. Assemblies, N.Y.C., 1986; pres., bd. dirs. Am. Council on Germany, 1988-99; owner ind. cons. firm, 1999—. Adv. bd. World Policy Inst. With USN, 1953-57. Decorated comdr.'s cross Order of Merit (Germany); recipient Meritorious Honor award and Superior Honor award U.S. Dept. State. Mem. Fgn. Svc. Assn., Diplomatic and Consular Officers, Ret., Coun. Fgn. Rels., Univ. Club. Home: 114 E 71st St # 3E 10021 E-mail: cbrown123@earthlink.net.

BROWN, CARROLL SMITH, anesthesiologist; b. Hartsville, S.C., Jan. 25, 1942; MD, Med. U. S.C., 1974. Diplomate Am. Bd. Anesthesiology. Resident Med. U. S.C., 1974-77; anesthesiologist Trident Regional Med. Ctr., Charleston, S.C., 1977—, Summerville Med. Ctr., 1977—, Trident Surg. Ctr., Charleston, 1977—. Fellow Am. Coll. Anesthesiology; mem. Am. Soc. Anesthesiologists, S.C. Med. Assn., S.C. Soc. Anesthesiologists, Charleston County Med. Assn., Dorchester County Med. Assn. Office: 9326 B Med Plaza Dr Charleston SC 29406-9198

BROWN, CHARLES D. lawyer; b. Honolulu, Hawaii, Sept. 10, 1960; s. Charles E. and Dolores M. (Danza) B. BS, Fordham U., 1982, JD, 1985. Bar: N.Y. 1986. Assoc. Dewey Ballantine, N.Y.C., 1985-94; v.p., asst. gen. counsel Beneficial Corp., Peapack, N.J., 1994-98, chmn. strategic planning counc. Wilmington, Del., 1996-98; mng. dir., gen. counsel Fitch Inc., N.Y.C., 1998—. Lectr. securities law Fordham U. Grad. Sch. Bus. Adminstrn., 1992-95; v.p., sec. and mem. of bd. of dirs. Harbour Island Inc., Tampa, Fla., 1995-98. Mem. ABA, Am. Assn. Corp. Counsels, N.Y. State Bar Assn., Assn. of the Bar of the City of N.Y., Fordham Coll. Alumni Assn. (class rep. 1986-97, class gift co-chair 1997, 2002), Fordham Law Sch. Alumni Assn., Holy Trinity Ch., Beta Gamma Sigma. Roman Catholic. Avocation: Travel. Office: Fitch Inc One State St Plaza New York NY 10004

BROWN, CHARLES DICKSON, not-for-profit fundraiser, consultant; b. Jacksonville, Fla., Jan. 23, 1953; s. Charles Dickson Brown and Margaret Alma Baines; m. Robin Gail Mamlet, Dec. 22, 1997; 1 child, Padgett Tift. BA, Princeton U., 1975. Assoc. dir. animal giving Princeton U., NJ, 1979—88; dir. devel. Pennington Sch., NJ, 1988—91, Lawrenville Sch., NJ, 1991—97; v.p., ptnr. A.T. Kearney Exec. Search, NY, 1997—98; dir. external affairs Solomon R. Guggenheim Mus., NY, 1998—99; exec. dir. devel. Johns Hopkins U., Balt., 1999—2000; dir. med. devel. Stanford U., Palo Alto, Calif., 2000—. Contbr. chapters to books. Trustee Trust Hidden Villa, Los Altos Hills, Calif., 2002—, Sequoia Fund, Visalia, Calif., 2003; advisor Raise the Frequency, San Francisco, 2003. Mem.: The Brook, Nassau Club. Independent. Episcopalian/Buddhist. Avocations: running, reading, cello, piano, fundraising. Home: 730 Josina Ave Palo Alto CA 94306 Office: Stanford Med Ctr 770 Welch Rd Ste 400 Palo Alto CA 94304 Fax: 650-723-8340. E-mail: cdbrown@stanford.edu.

BROWN, CHARLES DODGSON, lawyer; b. N.Y.C., Dec. 31, 1928; s. James Dodgson and Leonora Rose (Nichols) B.; m. Martha Lockhart Spindler, Apr. 5, 1963; children: Gregory Spindler, William Howard. BA, NYU, 1949, JD, 1952. Bar: N.Y. 1952, U.S. Dist. Ct. (so. and ea. dists.) N.Y. 1955, U.S. Supreme Ct. 1958, U.S. Ct. Appeals (2d cir.) 1988. Counsel, former ptnr. Thacher Proffitt & Wood, N.Y.C., 1954—. Co-author: Equipment Leasing, 1995—. Chmn. zoning bd. Asharoken, N.Y., 1965, alt. chmn. environ. bd., 1967, trustee, 1967, village justice, 1980—; chmn. Boy Scout Am., Northport, N.Y., 1989—; elder 1st Presbyn. Ch., Northport; mem. admiralty law inst. faculty Tulane U. Sch. Law, 1999. With U.S. Army, 1952-54. Mem. ABA, N.Y. Bar Assn., Maritime Law Assn. U.S. (proctor in Admiralty 1956, former chair to marine fin. com. 1996-2000), N.Y. State Magistrate Assn., Suffolk County Magistrate Assn., Northport Tennis Club. Republican. Avocations: scuba diving, wind surfing, tennis. E-mail: cbrown@tpwlaw.com., cbrown2@optonline.net.

BROWN, CHARLES EARL, lawyer; b. Columbus, Ohio, June 6, 1919; s. Anderson and Ruth (Keeran) B.; m. Mary Elizabeth Hiett, May 23, 1959; children: Douglas Charles, Rebecca Ruth. AB, Ohio Wesleyan U., 1941; JD, U. Mich., 1949. Bar: Ohio 1949. Pvt. practice, Toledo; assoc. Zachman, Boxell, Bebout & Torbet, 1950-53; ptnr. Brown, Baker, Schlageter & Craig (and predecessors), 1953-90, of counsel, 1990-95, Shindler, Neff, Holmes & Schlageter, 1996—. Chmn. steering and exec. coms. Auto Trim Wholesalers div. Automotive Service Industry Assn., 1960-68 Lucas County Rep. Exec. Com., 1968-92; trustee, sec. Joseph J. and Marie P. Schedel Found., 1963-93, pres., 1993—. Capt. AUS, 1941-46; col. Res. ret. Decorated Bronze Star; recipient John J. Pershing award U.S. Army Command and Gen. Staff Coll., 1963 Fellow Am. Bar Found. (state chmn. 1978-84), Ohio State Bar Found. (trustee 1987-92), Am. Coll. Trust and Estate Counsel; mem. ABA, Ohio Bar Assn. (bd. govs. real property sect. 1953-76, coun. of dels. 1973-84, exec. com. 1984-87), Toledo Bar Assn. (past mem. exec. com.), Sixth Cir. Jud. Conf. (life), Toledo Area C. of C. (past trustee, com. chmn.), Res. Officers Assn., Assn. U.S. Army, Phi Beta Kappa. Congregationalist (past chmn. trustees). Lodge: Masons (32 deg.). Home: 3758 Brookside Rd Toledo OH 43606-2614 Office: 1200 Edison Plaza 300 Madison Ave Toledo OH 43604-1561

BROWN, CHARLES ERIC, health facility administrator, biochemist; b. Nov. 23, 1946; s. Charles E. and Dorothy R. (Riddle) B.; m. Kathy Louise Houck, July 24, 1971; 1 child, Eric Nathaniel. BA in Chemistry, SUNY, Buffalo, 1968; PhD in Biochemistry, Northwestern U., 1973. Instr., fellow depts. chemistry, biochemistry, molec. biol. Northwestern U., Evanston, Ill., 1973-75; rsch. fellow Roche Inst. Molecular Biology, Nutley, N.J., 1975-77; from asst. prof. biochemistry to assoc. prof. Med. Coll. Wis., Milw., 1977-88; analytical bus. devel. coord. BP Rsch., 1988-92, analytical tech. mgr. BP Chems. Ltd., 1992-94; dir. Rsch. Resources Ctr. U. Ill., Chgo., 1994—. Adj. prof. chemistry U. Ill., Chgo., 1994—, adj. prof. mech. engring., 1998—; cons. Nicolet Instrument Corp., Metriflow, Inc., 1984-88. Contbr. articles in field to profl. jours., chpts. to books; developer biomedical and petrochemical equipment and techniques; patentee in field. Recipient Tech. Merit award Johnson Wax, 1987; NIH predoctoral fellow, 1968-72; Cottrell Rsch. grantee, 1979-82, Arthritis Found. grantee, 1984, Retirement Rsch. Found. grantee, 1987-88. Fellow Royal Soc. Chemistry; mem. AAAS, Internat. Soc. Magnetic Resonance, Soc. Neurosci., Am. Chem. Soc., Am. Soc. Pharmacology and Exptl. Therapeutics, Am. Soc. for Mass Spectrometry, Microscopy Soc. Am., Materials Rsch. Soc., Sigma Xi, Phi Lambda Upsilon. Office: Rsch Resources Ctr U Ill 901 S Wolcott Ave # E102 Msb Chicago IL 60612-7307 E-mail: charlieb@uic.edu.

BROWN, CHARLES EUGENE, retired electronics company executive; b. Huntingburg, Ind., Oct. 31, 1921; s. Lemuel C. and Bertha (McCormack) B.; m. Elizabeth Sherman McAllister, Aug. 16, 1952; children— Deborah, Judith, Robert, Sarah BS, Ind. U., 1948, MBA, 1950. Corp. staff Glidden Co., Cleve., 1949-59; dir. indsl. relations Cleve. Pneumatic Tool Co., 1959-62, Honeywell, Inc., Mpls., 1962—68; dir. employee relations Honneywell, 1968—73; v.p. employee relations Honeywell, Inc., Mpls., 1973—80, v.p. exec. human resources, 1980-85, sr. staff v.p., 1985-86. Bd. dirs. Family and Children's Services, Mpls., Honeywell Retiree Vol. Program. Served with U.S. Army, 1942-45. ETO Decorated Purple Heart Mem.: Minneapolis, Interlachen Country. Home: 5029 Bruce Pl Edina MN 55424-1321

BROWN, CHARLES FREEMAN, II, lawyer; b. Boston, Mar. 7, 1914; s. Arthur Harrison and Nellie Abigail (Kenney) B.; m. Caroline Gotzian Tighe, Nov. 12, 1949 (dec. Jan. 1951); m. Pamela Judith Wedd, Nov. 29, 1952; children— Penelope Susan, Nicholas Wedd. AB, Harvard U., 1936, LL.B., 1941. Bar: Mass. 1941. Assoc. atty. Sherburne, Powers & Needham, Boston, 1941-43; asst. gen. counsel, gen. counsel OSRD, Washington, 1943-47; counsel rsch. and devel. bd. and mil. liaison com. Office of Sec. of Def., patent advisor, mem. govt. patents bd., counsel Def. Prodn. Bd.; dep. asst. sec. gen. for prodn. and logistics NATO detailed from Office Sec. Def., Washington, London, Paris, 1947-53; asst. to pres. Hydrofoil Corp., Annapolis, Md., 1953-54; asso. gen. counsel CIA, Washington, 1954-60; v.p., treas. Sci. Engring. Inst., Waltham, Mass., 1960-66; dep. gen. counsel NSF, Washington, 1966-73, gen. counsel, 1973-76, chmn. interim compliance panel, 1970-71. Cons., 1976— Trustee Belmont (Mass.) Day Sch., 1963-66; bd. dirs. Hillcrest Children's Ctr., Washington, 1978-87, pres., 1980-83; pres. Cleveland Park Book Club, 1980-83, 91-94; bd. dirs. Cleveland Park Hist. Soc. Recipient Disting. Service award NSF. Mem. Fed. Bar Assn., Cosmos Club. Home and Office: 3500 Macomb St NW Washington DC 20016-3162

BROWN, CHARLOTTE, artist; d. Irving and Zella (Nathan) Marcus; m. Morton Brown (dec. July 1989); children: Alison, Jonathan David. BFA, Pratt Inst., Bklyn., 1956. Vis. artist Va. Commonwealth U., Richmond, 1983, Everson Mus. for Syracuse (N.Y.) Mus., 1979; adj. prof. C.W. Post Coll., L.I. U., Greenvale, N.Y., 1984—. Exhibited in solo shows at Nassau County Mus. Fine Arts, Roslyn, N.Y., 1976, 83, Hechscher Mus., Huntington, N.Y., 1984, Getler Pall Gallery, N.Y.C., 1980, 82, 84, Shippee Gallery, N.Y.C., 1987, Joy Horwich Gallery, Chgo., 1988, 92, Portals Ltd. Gallery, Chgo., 1999, others; group shows include Internt. Mus. Photography/George Eastman House, 1979, Cooper Hewitt Mus., 1980, So. Alleghenies Mus. Art, 1981, Caroline Corre Gallery, Paris, Pratt Graphics Ctr., 1984, Bergen Mus. Art and Sci., 1985; featured in art books and mags. Recipient Samual Mann Meml. prize Nat. Assn. Women Artists, 1975, Grand prize for painting, 1974, Graphics award Silvermine Guild of Artists, 1982, others; grantee Nat. Endowment for the Arts, Syracuse U., Va. Commonwealth U.; Creative Artist Pub. Svc. Printmaking fellow, 1976, 8282. Home: 425 E 58th St Apt 11B New York NY 10022-2300

BROWN, CHRISTOPHER PATRICK, health care administrator, educator; b. Phoenix, June 7, 1951; s. Charles Francis and R. Patricia (Quinn) B.; m. Tracey Ann Wallenberg, May 23, 1987; 1 child, Ryan Matthew. AA in Biol. Scis., Shasta Coll., Redding, Calif., 1976; AS in Liberal Arts, SUNY, Albany, 1977; grad. Primary Care Assoc. Program, Stanford U., 1978; BA in Community Svcs. Adminstrn., Calif. State U., Chico, 1982; M. in Health Svcs., U. Calif., Davis, 1984. Gen. mgr. Pacific Ambulance Svc., El Cajon, Calif., 1974; primary care assoc. Family Practice, Oregon-Calif., 1978-82; cons. Calif. Health Profls., Chico, 1982-84; bus. ops. mgr. Nature's Arts, Inc., Seattle, 1985-86; instr. North Seattle C.C., 1984-89, program dir., 1986-89; asst. dir. Pacific Med. Clinic North, Seattle, 1990-92; dir. Pacific Med. Clinic Renton (Wash.), Pacific Med. Ctr., 1992-95; dir. ops./physician svcs. St. Luke's Regional Med. Ctr., Boise, Idaho, 1995-97, adminstr. ambulatory care, 1997-98; adminstr. St. Luke's Meridian (Idaho) Med. Ctr., 1997-98; COO, sr. v.p. Medford (Oreg.) Clinic, 1998-2000; pres./cons. Integra Healthcare Solutions, 2000—. Mem. Butte County Adult Day Care Health Coun., Chico, 1982-84; bd. dirs., pres. Innovative Health Care Svcs., Chico, 1982-84; bd. dirs. Highline W. Seattle Mental Health Ctr., 1985-90, v.p. 1988-90; tech. adv. com. North Seattle C.C., 1992-93; bd. dirs. ARC, 1997-98. Mem. Internat. Platform Assn., Soc. Ambulatory Care Profls., Med. Group Mgmt. Assn., Multispecialty Group Exec. Soc., Accreditation Assn. for Ambulatory Health Care (accreditation surveyor 1996-97). Avocations: gardening, woodworking, church activities. Home: 345 Orth Dr Central Point OR 97502 E-mail: cbrown3394@aol.com.

BROWN, CINDY LYNN, family nurse practitioner, critical care nurse; b. Washington, July 11, 1956; d. Harry Carl and Betty (Gable) Sampson; m. Wayne Brown, 1998; children: Justin, Jesse. BSN, George Mason U., 1991; MSN, Marymount U., 1995. RN, Va.; CCRN; cert. family nurse practitioner; cert. clin. nurse specialist in critical care; cert. prescriptive authority; cert. ACLS, CPR instr./trainer, EMT; cert. chemotherapy adminstr. Coord. ARC, Honesdale, Pa., 1985-88; instr. CPR Fair Oaks Hosp., Fairfax, Va., 1988-97, extern critical care, 1990-91, trainer CPR instrn., 1991—; nurse critical care Washington Hosp. Ctr., 1991-94; flight nurse World Access Inc., 1993-94; emergency dept. nurse Mt. Vernon Hosp., Alexandria, Va., 1994-96; emergency nurse practitioner Potomac Hosp., Woodbridge, Va., 1996-97; family practice nurse practitioner Advanced Med. Ctr., Naples, Fla., 1997—. Lectr. in field; instr. sign lang. Fairfax County Schs., 1989-90; tissue and organ donation educator Nat. Student Nurses Assn., George Mason U., 1990-91, pres., 1990-91; 1st aid corps mem. ARC, Fairfax, 1988—. Active nat. disaster relief health svc. team for Hurricane Andrew, ARC, Homestead, Fla., 1992, Miss. River Flood, 1993, Hurricane Marilyn, St. Thomas, V.I., 1995, Tropical Storm Jerry, Bonita Springs, Fla., 1995, Hurricane Fran, N.C., 1996, Hurricane George, Naples, Fla., 1998. Named Nursing Student of Yr. Nursing Student Assn. Va., 1991, Student Leader of Yr. George Mason U., 1991. Mem. AACN (Essay award 1991), D.C. Nursing Assn., Va. Nurses Assn., Golden Key Honor Soc., Sigma Theta Tau (Leadership award Epsilon Zeta chpt. 1991), Alpha Chi, Delta Epsilon Sigma. Avocations: country western dancing, water sports. Home: 3231 60th St SW Naples FL 34116

BROWN, CLIFFORD BRYANT, financial consultant; b. Trenton, N.J., Dec. 7, 1970; s. Clifford and Dorothy Mae Brown; 1 child, Bryanna D. AA, So. Calif. Internat. Coll., 1995. Fin. cons. Ind. Capital Mgmt., Huntington Beach, Calif., 1994-95; fin. advisor Prudential, N.Y.C., 1996-98, Manhattan Planning Group, N.Y.C., 1998—. Vol., Hale Ho., N.Y.C. Sgt., USMC, 1989-95; mem. USMCR. Fellow Nat. Assn. Life Underwriters; mem. Harlem C. of C. Baptist. Avocations: travel, golf, basketball. Office: Manhattan Planning Group 60 E 42nd St Fl D49 New York NY 10165-0006

BROWN, COLIN, automotive executive; m. Cynthia Brown; 3 children. Grad., Williams Coll.; JD, Duke U. Gen. counsel Fuqua Industries, Atlanta, Cannon Mills, Kannapolis, NC, JM Family Enterprises, Deerfield Beach, Fla., 1992—97, COO, 1997—, pres., 2000—, CEO, 2000—. Office: JM Family Enterprises 100 Jim Moran Blvd Deerfield Beach FL 33442*

BROWN, CONNELL JEAN, retired animal science educator; b. Everton, Ark., Mar. 6, 1924; s. Clarence Jackson and Winnie Dee (Trammell) B.; m. Erma Dexter (Taylor), May 19, 1946; children— Craig Jay, Mark Allen BSA., U. Ark., 1948; MS, Okla. State U., 1950, PhD, 1956. Asst. prof. dept. animal sci. U. Ark., Fayetteville, 1950-57, assoc. prof., 1957-62, livestock sect. leader, 1978-81, prof., 1962-86, Univ. prof., 1986-90, prof. emeritus, 1990—; lectr. Internat. Stockman Show award, 1980. Contbr. articles to profl. jours. Served with USAAF, 1943-46; PTO. Recipient Rsch. award Performance Registry Internat., 1977, U. Ark. Coll. Agr. Rsch. award, 1981, Disting. Svc. award Ark. Cattlemans Assn., 1985; named to Am. Polled Hereford Assn. Hall of Merit, 1986, Ark. Agrl. Hall of Fame, 1994. Fellow AAAS, Am. Soc. Animal Sci. (pres. so. sect. 1975, leadership award so. sect. 1975); mem. Am. Genetics Assn., N.Y. Acad. Scis., So. Assn. Agrl. Scientists (bd. dirs.), Am. Registry Profl. Animal Scientists (pres. Ark. chpt. 1989), Kiwanis (dist. pres. 1984-85, lt. gov. 1992-93), Sigma Xi (pres. 1986-87), Gamma Sigma Delta (pres. 1967-68). Home: 188 Cydnee St Fayetteville AR 72703-3710 E-mail: cjb36@cox.internet.com.

BROWN, CORRINE, congresswoman; b. Jacksonville, Fla., Nov. 11, 1946; 1 child, Shantrel. BS, Fla. A&M U., 1969, MS, 1971; EdS, U. Fla., 1974. Mem. Fla. Ho. of Reps, 1982—92; del. Nat. Dem. Conv., 1988; mem. U.S. Congress from 3rd Fla. dist., 1993—; mem. transp. and infrastructure com., VA com. Mem. Sigma Gamma Rho. Democrat. Baptist. Home: 314 Palmetto St Jacksonville FL 32202-2619 Office: US Ho of Reps 2444 Rayburn Ho Office Bldg Washington DC 20515-0903*

BROWN, COURTNEY, political science educator, research institute administrator; b. Newark, July 26, 1952; s. John MacPherson Brown and Marian Courtney; m. Isabella Dorothy Brown; 1 child, Aziz MacPherson. PhD, Washington U., St. Louis, Mo., 1981. Assoc. prof. polit. sci. Emory U., Atlanta, 1986—2002. Dir. The Farsight Inst., Atlanta, 1995—2002. Author: (book) Serpents in the Sand, 1995, Ballots of Tumult, 1991, Chaos and Catastrophe Theories, 1995, Cosmic Voyage, 1996, Cosmic Explorers, 1999. Vol. U.S. Peace Corps, Kenya, 1981—83. Named Charles Grove Haines prof., UCLA, 1984—86; fellow Hewlett fellow, Carter Ctr., Emory U., 1990. Home: PO Box 49243 Atlanta GA 30359 Office: Emory U Dept Polit Sci Atlanta GA 30322 Home Fax: 404-289-3969; Office Fax: 404-289-3969. Personal E-mail: courtney@farsight.org. Business E-Mail: polscb@emory.edu.

BROWN, COURTNEY ALLISON, social worker; b. Kenner, La., Sept. 9, 1975; d. Charles and Yolanda Faye Brown; 1 adopted child, Benjamin Issac. BS in Psychology, Tulane U., 1997. Residential counselor Meth. Home for Children, New Orleans, 1997—98, case mgr., 1998—2000; mental health specialist Hope Haven Residential Treatment Ctr., Marrero, La., 2000; case mgr. Quality Ind. Svc. Coord. La., Chalmette, La., 2000—. Composer: (songs) Thank You Lord for Just Being There, 1995, By His Stripes, 1995, Lord You're Holy, 1999, United Saints Gospel Music, 2001; contbr. columns in newspapers; composer: (albums) Anointed Voices Strictly f For Praise & Worship, 1999; editor: Hullabaloo Viewpoint, 1994—95. Musical dir. Christian Fellowship, Violet, La., 2000—. Democrat. Baptist. Avocations: piano, drums, writing, basketball. Home: 2430 Dubrevil St New Orleans LA 70117 Office: Quality Independent 3016 B Jean Lafite Pkwy Chalmette LA 70043 E-mail: pudnin7@cs.com.

BROWN, CRAIG, advertising agency executive; b. 1951; BA in Acctg., Mich. State U., 1973. With Arthur Andersen & Co., Detroit, 1973-80, D'Arcy MacManus Masius, Inc., N.Y.C., 1980-85; exec. v.p., CFO D'Arcy Masius Benton & Bowles, N.Y.C., 1985-97; CFO DMB&B Comms. (formerly D'Arcy Masius Benton & Bowles), N.Y.C., 1997-98, exec. v.p., 1996-98; vice chmn., COO, CFO MacManus Group, N.Y.C., 1997—. Office: DMB&B Comms 1675 Broadway New York NY 10019-5820

BROWN, CRAIG WILLIAM, physical chemist; b. Denver, Aug. 3, 1953; s. Clarence William and Gail Margaret (Farthing) B.; 1 child, Russell Corey. BS in Chemistry, Colo. State U., 1975; MS, Fla. State U., 1977, PhD, 1980. Dep. dir. picosecond and quantum radiation lab. Tex. Tech. U., Lubbock, 1980-83; systems engr. Internat. Marine Systems, Inc., Seattle, 1983-87; freelance cons., 1987-88; staff scientist Heart Interface Corp., Kent, Wash., 1988-91, sr. project engr., 1991-93; cons. scientist Brooks Rand Ltd., Seattle, 1992-93, sr. scientist, 1993-99; cons. Environ. Protection Agy., Dept. Energy, 1995-97; mgr. rsch. N.W. Aluminum Techs., Seattle, 1999—. Mem. battery charger/inverter project tech. com. Am. Boat and Yacht Coun., Edgewater, Md., 1989-92; cons. on mercury speciation Environ. Protection and Dept. Energy, 1995-97; mgr. of inert anode aluminum prodn. rsch. project, 1996—. Contbr. articles to Phys. Rev. Letters, Jour. Chem. Physics, Jour. of the Minerals, Metals and Materials Soc., Light Metals; contbr. book revs. to Photochemistry and Photobiology; contbr. to conf. proceedings. Whiteford scholar Colo. State U., 1974-75, Honors scholar U. Denver, 1971-72, Gustavson fellow Colo. State U., 1974-75, Welch postdoctoral fellow Tex. Tech U., 1980-83; Dept. Energy rsch. grantee, 1994-96, innovative concepts program awardee, 1997-98; hon. prof. Albert Schweitzer U. Mem. AAAS, Am. Chem. Soc., N.Y. Acad. Scis., Minerals, Metals, and Materials Soc. Achievements include patents for switched multi-tapped transformer power conversion method and apparatus; patent for fluorescent spectrophotometer system with automatic calibration and improved optics block; numerous patents for low temperature aluminum smelting; design of power inverters and battery chargers; spectrophotometric instruments; research in chemical physics, atomic and molecular spectroscopy, chemical sensors, aluminum production. Avocations: guitar, songwriting. Office: Northwest Aluminum Techs 1080 W Ewing Pl Ste 202 Seattle WA 98119-1458 E-mail: cbrown@nwat.net.

BROWN, CRYSTAL JEANINE, writer; b. Bay Minette, Ala., Sept. 26, 1978; d. John M. Bolding and Kathy Lou Abbott; children: Megan Elizabeth Bryan, Ashland Victoria Bryan, Cassandra Jeanine Bryan. A in Social Sci., Faulkner State C.C., Bay Minette, 2000; student, Wash. State U., 2001—. Author: Embedded Dreams, 1997, A Prism of Thoughts; contbr. poetry to anthology. Vol. Deep South Coun. Girls Scouts of Am., Ala., 2001—02. Recipient Editors Choice award, Nat. Libr. Poetry, 1997. Avocations: poetry, genealogy, crafts, photography, sports. E-mail: tcbryan@earthlink.net.

BROWN, DALE, electronics executive; CEO Micro Electronics, Inc., Hilliard, Ohio. Office: Micro Electronics Inc 4119 Leap Rd Hilliard OH 43026-1117*

BROWN, DALE PATRICK, retired advertising executive; b. Richmond, Va., Aug. 11, 1947; d. Thomas Windom and Helen (Curtis) Patrick. BA in Journalism, U. Richmond, 1968, MA in English, 1978. Reporter city news sect. Richmond Times-Dispatch, 1968-71; free-lance writer, 1971-73; v.p., supr. pub. rels. account The Martin Agy., Richmond, 1973-77, account supr. advt., v.p., 1977-79, v.p., supr. advt. account, then group v.p. and sr. v.p., 1983-89; mgr. communications svcs. Mobil Chem. Co., Richmond, 1979-81; mgr. communications Whittaker Gen. Med., Richmond, 1981-83; exec. v.p. The Stenrich Group, Richmond, 1989 90; pres., chief exec. officer Sive/Young & Rubicam, Cin., 1990-98. Trustee U. Richmond, 1992—, mem. exec. com., 1999-2001, vice chair acad. program com.; mem. devel. bd. Good Samaritan Hosp., 1992-95, Leadership Cin.; bd. dirs. Met. Growth Alliance, 1997-99, Downtown Cin. Inc., 1995-98, Midwest Strategic Trust, 1993-97, Ohio Nat. Life Ins. (exec. com.), bd. dirs. Frisch's Inc., 1998—, Mercantile Libr., 2000—, Cin. C. of C., 1995-98; chair Acad. Career Women of Achievement, 1996-2001; bd. govs. Cin. chpt. Am. Assn. Advt. Agys., 1990-98. Recipient 2 AAF Silver medals, 1988, 96, Richmond Advt. Person of Yr. award Advt. Club Richmond, 1988, Woman of Achievement award Cin. YWCA, 1993, Human Rels. award Am. Jewish Com., Cin. chpt., 1996, various others including Addy, Effie, Clio awards N.Y. Art Dirs. Club. Mem. Pub. Rels. Soc. Am., Advt. Club Cin., Queen City Club (bd. dirs.), Comml. Club of Cin. Avocations: reading, travel, arts. Home: 1231 Martin Dr Cincinnati OH 45202-1737

BROWN, DALE SUSAN, government administrator, educational program director, writer; b. NYC, May 27, 1954; d. Bertram S. and Beatrice Joy (Gilman) Brown. BA, Antioch Coll., 1976. Rsch. asst. Am. Occupational Therapy Assn., Rockville, Md., 1976-79; writer Pres.' Com. on Employment of People with Disabilities, Washington, 1979-82, program mgr. handicapped concerns com., 1982—85, program mgr. labor com., 1985, 96-98, program mgr. work environment and tech. com., 1988-94, program mgr. com. on libr. and info. svcs., 1984-86, youth devel com., 1986-88, new products devel. team, 1987-90, agy. rep., 1991-93, with interagy. tech. assistance coordinating team, 1992-94; program mgr. Job Accomodation Network, 1997-99; mgr. Nat. Conf. of Youth with Disabilities, 2000; policy advisor Office Disability Employment Policy Dept. Labor, 2001—, mem. youth team, 2002—. Cons. in field, gen. assembly speaker nat. conv. Gen. Fedn. Women's Clubs, 1981, mem. Rehab Svcs. Adminstrn. Task Force on Learning Disabilities, 1981-83. Author: Steps to Independence for People with Learning Disabilities, 1980, Pathways to Employment for People with Learning Disabilities, 1991, Working Effectively with People Who Have Learning Disabilities and Attention Deficit Hyperactivity Disorder, 1995, I Know I Can Climb the Mountain, 1995, Learning Disabilities and Employment, 1997, Learning A Living Guide to Planning Your Career and Finding A Job for People with Learning Disabilities, Attention Deficit Disorder and Dyslexia, 2000, Job-Hunting Tips for the So-Called Handicapped, 2001, (films) They Could Have Saved Their Homes, 1982; dir.: (videotape) Part of the Team People with Disabilities in the Workforce, 1990; co-editor: Learning Disabilities Quar. Americans with Disabilities Act and Learning Disabilities, 1992; mem. editl. bd. Perceptions, 1981—83, Learning Disabilities Focus, 1988—90, In the Mainstream, 1994—98; guest editor: Learning Disabilities Rsch. and Practice, 1990—96; guest editor Learning Disability and Career Development, 2002; guest editor: Career Planning and Adult Devel. Jour., 2002. Bd. dirs. Closer Look Nat. Info. Ctr., Washington, 1980—83; bd. dir. Am. Coalition for Citizens with Disabilities, 1985—86; congrl. task force Rights and Empowerment of Ams. with Disabilities, 1988—90; profl. adv. bd. Nat. Attention Deficit Disorder Assn., 1996—99; bd. dir. Coun. on Quality and Leadership, 2000—; adv. bd. Internat. Ctr. for Disability Resources on the Internet, 2003—; chair conf. on Info. Tech. for User With Disabilities, 1989; spl. asst. for people with disabilities Federally Employed Women, 1991—92; blue ribbon panel Nat. Telecomm. Access for People with Disabilities, 1989—94; pres. Assn. Learning Disabled Adults, Washington, 1979—80; del. Nat. Writer's Union, 1999; rep. com. on fed. govt. as model employer, com. on youth with disabilities Presdl. Task Force on Employment of Adults with Disabilities, 1999—2002; judge, Ten Outstanding Young Ams. U.S. Jr. C. of C. Jaycees, 2003. Named one of Ten Outstanding Young Ams., U.S. Jr. C. of C. Jaycees, 1994; recipient, Margaret Byrd Rawson award, 1989, Personal Achievement award Women's Program USDOL, 1989, Individual Achievement award, Nat. Coun. on Communication Disorders, 1991, Spl. Achievement award, Pres.'s Com. on Employment of People with Disabilities, 1991, Gold Screen award, Nat. Assn. Gov. Communicators, 1991, Arthur S. Fleming award, 1992; grantee, Found. for Children with Learning Disabilities, 1982. Mem.: Inter Agency. Com. on Handicapped Employees (rep. 1989—91), Learning Disabilities Assn. Am. (bd. dirs. 1986—91), Nat. Assn. Govt. Communicators (Blue Pencil award 1986), Nat. Network of Learning Disabled Adults (founder, pres. 1980—81, rep. inter-agy. com. on comuter support handicapped employees 1998—99), ALA. Democrat. Office: Office Disability Employment Policy Dept Labor S1011 200 Constitution Ave NW Washington DC 20210

BROWN, DALE WEAVER, clergyman, theologian, educator; b. Wichita, Kansas, Jan. 12, 1926; s. Harlow J. and Cora Elisa (Weaver) B.; m. Lois D. Kauffman, Aug. 17, 1947; children: Deanna Gae, Dennis Dale, Kevin Ken. BA, McPherson Coll., 1946; BD, Bethany Theol. Sem., 1949; post grad., Drake U., 1954-56, Northwestern U. and Garrett Bibl. Inst., IL., 1956-58; PhD, Northwestern U., IL., 1962. Ordained to ministry Ch. of Brethren, 1946; pastor Stover Meml. Ch. of Brethren, Des Moines, 1949-56; dir. religious life, asst. prof. philosophy and religion McPherson Coll., 1958-62; assoc. prof. Christian theology Bethany Theol. Sem., Oak Brook, Ill., 1962-70; prof. Christian theology Bethany Theol. Sem., 1970-94. Del. standing com. Ch. of Brethren, 1954; moderator Middle Iowa Dist., 1952-53, mem. dist. and regional bds., gen. bd., 1960-62, moderator-elect. ann. conf., 1970-71, moderator, 1971-72. Author: In Christ Jesus: The Significance of Jesus as the Christ, 1965, Four Words for World, 1968, So Send I You, 1969, Brethren and Pacifism, 1970, The Christian Revolutionary, 1971, Flamed by the Spirit, 1978, Understanding Pietism, 1978, rev. edit., 1996, Berea College: Spiritual and Intellectual Roots, 1982, What About the Russians, 1984, Biblical Pacifism, 1986, Biblical Pacifism, new edit., 2003. Mem. Am. Acad. Religion, Internat. Bonhoeffer Soc., Fellowship of Reconciliation, Am. Theol. Soc. Home: 1101 College Ave Elizabethtown PA 17022-2236 E-mail: dwb1926b@aol.com.

BROWN, DALLAS COVERDALE, JR., retired army officer, retired history educator; b. New Orleans, Aug. 21, 1932; s. Dallas Coverdale and Rita Sydney (Taylor) B.; m. Joyce Regina Bush, July 26, 1955, (div. Aug. 1985); children: Dallas Coverdale, III, Leonard, Jan, Karen, Barbara; m. Elizabeth Taylor Vance, Sept. 3, 1985 BA in History and Polit. Sci. (Disting. Mil. Grad. 1954), W.Va. State Coll., 1954; MA in Govt., Ind. U., 1967, postgrad. in Def. Lang. Inst., 1966; grad., Command and Gen. Staff Coll., 1968, USA Russian Inst., 1970, Naval War Coll., 1974. Commd. 2d lt. U.S. Army, 1954, advanced through grades to brig. gen., 1978; service in Korea, W. Ger., Vietnam; dep. chief staff intelligence U.S. Army Forces Command, 1978-79; dep. vice dir. fgn. intelligence Def. Intelligence Agy., 1979-80; dep. comdr. U.S. Army War Coll., Carlisle Barracks, Pa., 1980-84; ret., 1984; assoc. prof. history W.Va. State Coll., Institute, 1984-96. Mem. bd. advisors W.Va. State Coll., 1990-91; mem. W.Va. Gov.'s Higher Edn. Advocacy Team, 1992-93, Hilton Head Fgn. Affairs Seminar, 1999—, Savannah (ga.) Coun. on World Affairs Inc., 2000-; bd. dirs. WPBY-TV (PBS), 1995-96. Constituent U.S. Army War Coll. Found.; mem. Mil. Adv. Coun., Ctr. for Def. Info. Decorated Def. Superior Service medal, Meritorious Service medal (2), Joint Service Commendation medal, Army Commendation medal, Meritorious Unit Commendation, Master Parachutist badge, Aircraft Crewman badge; named Alumnus of Yr. W.Va. State Coll., 1978; named to W.Va. State Coll. ROTC Hall of Fame, 1980 Mem. Assn. U.S. Army, Ret. Officers Assn., Nat. Eagle Scout Assn., Sun City Vets. Assn. (comdr. 1999-2000, trustee 2000—), W.Va. State Coll. Alumni Assn., Alpha Phi Alpha, Alpha Lambda Boule, Sigma Pi Phi, Pi Alpha Theta, Pi Sigma Alpha, Rocks Club. Unitarian Universalist. Home: Sun City Hilton Head 17 Devant Dr E Bluffton SC 29909-4537 E-mail: dallas17@hargray.com.

BROWN, DANIEL, art consultant; b. Cin., Nov. 4, 1946; s. Sidney H. and Genevieve Florence (Elbaum) B. AB cum laude, Middlebury Coll., 1968; AM, U. Mich., 1970; postgrad., Princeton U., 1971-72. Dir. cultural events U. Cin., 1972, spl. asst. to pres., 1973; v.p., corp. sec. Brockton Shoe Trimming Co., Cin., 1974—, sec. treas., 1997—; curator Maple Knoll Villag Retirement Cmty. Curator KZF Gallery, Cin., 1987-94, Katz and Dawgs Gallery, 1989-90, Antiques Design Ctr, 1998—, U. Clubs Ann. Art Exhibit, Antique & Design Studios, 1999—, Christ Hosp., 1999—, Regional Women Mid-Career Artists, 2000, art shows Design Studio, 1998-99; instr. Art Acad. Cin, 1980, 88—; prin. Daniel Brown, Inc., Cin. and Columbus, 1999—; panel leader Midwest Coll. Art Assn. Conv., 1995; curator, art adv. St. Joseph Orphanage, 2002—; art critic Cin. Mag., 1980-83, Cin. Herald, 1992-94, Cin. Art Acad. Newsletter, Provincetown Arts, 1988-90, USA Arts; editor, co-pub., co-owner The Blue Book of Cin., 1998—; commentator Sta. WKRC-TV, Cin.; art and music critic Sta. WCPO-TV, Cin., 1986-88; arts editor, essayist Cin. City Beat, 1994-95; guest curator New Art from Academe: An Overview The Cen. Exchange, Kansas City, Mo., 1988, Lyrical Abstractions, 1989, Design of the Future, 1989, Contemporary Landscape Kencabco Co., Cin., 1988, No. Ky. U., 1989, The Arts Consortium, 1991-94, Cuba Now Carnegie Arts Ctr., 1996; guest co-curator Tangeman Fine Arts Gallery, U. Cin., 1987, guest curator, 1988; permanent curator The KZF Art Gallery, Cin., 1987-95; guest co-curator The Artist at Mid-Career: A Dialogue Between Columbus and Cin., 1989-90; curator Liberties Restaurant, Cin., 1990-93, Fifth Third Bank, Cin., 1991-92, African-Am. Mus., 1992-93, African Am. Artists, 1994; guest spkr. Arts Consortium, 1994; guest critic dept. painting and drawing U. Cin., 1993—; corr. editor: Dialogue Mag., 1986-90, art reviewer, 1983—; lead editorialist: The Arts Consortium Newsletter, 1992; monthly editorialist Antenna Newspaper, 1995—; lectr.; curator, art exhbns., The Christ Hosp. and the Maple Knoll Retirement Cmty., 1999-; cons. in field. Author: David Bumbeck: The Romantic Classicist, 1989, Tom Bacher: High Tech American Impressionist, 1989, The Universe Watching: The Art of Nancy Fletcher Cassell, 1990, John Stewart: A Retrospective, 1991, Bukang Kim: Journey to the East, 1992, Hustlers, 1992-93, The Evolution of Form, Bukang Kim: A Retrospective, 1995, Robert Knipschid: Four Decades of Painting, 2002; columnist Art Acad. News, 1990-94, The Cin. Post, 1991, The Downtowner, 1991-95, Everybody's News, 1994; curator The 537 Gallery, 2000—, Maple Knoll Retirement Cmty., 2000; editor-in-chief Antenna Arts Mag., 1996-98. Mem. exhbns com. Contemporary Arts Ctr.; sec., bd. dirs. Mercantile Libr., 1985-91, treas., 1986, chmn. programs com., 1987—, Young Wing; trustee Contempory Arts Ctr., 1984-87, co-chmn. artists adv. bd., 1987, Vocal Arts Ensemble, 1984, Enjoy the Arts, 1985-88, v.p., 1986; mem. bd. advisors Cin. Artists Group Effort, 1986-88; guest curator Carnegie Arts Ctr., Covington, Ky., 1986—; juror art competitions, Cin. and Columbus, Ohio, 1986-87, Mansfield, Ohio, Kansas City, Mo.; mem. citizens' adv. com. Art Acad. of Cin., 1989—, trustee, 1991—; trustee Art Acad. Cin. Coop. Gallery, 1990; co-chmn. fine art com. The Arts Consortium, cin., 1990—, curator, 1991—; sole juror Art Acad. Alumni Juried Exhbn., 1992; trustee UMOJA Artists' Group, 1994. Recipient The Critic's Purse award Dialogue mag., 1985. Mem. Internat. Soc. Art Critics (N.Y. and Paris chpts.), Univ. Club (art com. 1990-91, guest curator 1992). Home: 2200 Victory Pkwy Apt 809 Cincinnati OH 45206-2823 Fax: 513-751-9616.

BROWN, DANIEL MORRIS, lens designer, consultant; b. Ft. Worth, Oct. 2, 1952; s. Morris Albert Brown and Juanita Joy Spaw; m. Mary Rose Wright, June 27, 1976; children: Jeremiah Daniel, Leah Rose, Nathaniel David. BS in Physics, Coast Guard Acad., New London, Conn., 1975; MS in Physics, Naval Postgraduate Sch., Monterey, Calif., 1979; MS in Computer Sci., Rensselaer Poly. Inst., 1987; MS in Physics, U. Ala., 1991. Engrng. physicist USCG Hdqs. (Optics & Acoustics), Washington, 1979—83; rsch. scientist USCG R&D Ctr., Groton, Conn., 1983—87; software engr. Vitro Corp., Groton, 1987—87; grad. rsch. asst. U. Ala., Huntsville, 1987—89; optical systems engr. Teledyne Brown Engrng., Huntsville, 1989—93, SY Tech., Inc, Huntsville, 1993—97; design mgr., chief lens designer MEMS Optical, Inc., Huntsville, 1997—2003. Cons. optical systems Brown & Assocs., Madison, Ala., 2002—03; pres., founder Optosensors Tech., Inc., Madison, Ala., 2003—. Contbr. chapters to books, articles to profl. jours. Ruling elder Redeemer Presbyn., Madison, 2000—; vol. instr. physics and computer sci. Life Christian Acad., Madison, 1998—2002. With USCG, 1975—87. Mem.: Internat. Soc. Optical Engring., Nat. Speleological Soc. Republican. Presbyterian. Achievements include patents in field; patents pending in field. Avocations: backpacking, hiking, bicycling, caving, banjo. Office: Optosensors Tech Inc 214 Wilson Hall Dr Madison AL 35757

BROWN, DARMAE JUDD, librarian; b. Sept. 14, 1952; d. William Robert and Dorothy Judd (Curtis) B. BA, W. Va. Wesleyan Coll., 1974; MA, U. Denver, 1975, M of Computer Info. Systems, 1992. Searching assoc. Bibliog. Ctr. for Rsch., Denver, 1975-76; libr. N.E. Colo. Regional Libr., Wray, 1976-81; head tech. svcs. Ector County Libr., Odessa, Tex., 1981-84, Waterloo (Iowa) Pub. Libr., 1984-89; sys. coord. Aurora (Colo.) Pub. Libr., 1989—2002. Vestry mem. St. Stephen's Episcopal Ch., 2001—. Mem.: ALA, Libr. and Info. Tech. Assn., Colo. Assn. Librs., Sigma Alpha Iota, Beta Phi Mu. Home: 12010 E Harvard Ave Aurora CO 80014-1808 E-mail: darmae@bemail.com.

BROWN, DARRELL JAMES, publishing executive; b. Abilene, Tex., Feb. 13, 1959; s. Don J. and Alma K. Brown; m. Patricia Lee Stevens, Apr. 2, 1983; children: Tova Lee, Devon Justice. BS in Psychology, U. Mo., 1981. Dir. retail dept. The May Cos., St. Louis, 1981; vice chmn., editor LEADERS Mag., N.Y.C., 1981—; v.p. Dormann Pub., Inc., N.Y.C., 1984—; v.p., sec. SIPA News Svc., N.Y.C., 1984—, Internat. Bd. Indsl. Advisors, N.Y.C., 1984—; pres. Global Change Inc., 1996—. Lectr., career guidance counselor in field. Mem. editl. bd. The Scottish Rite Jour. Founding exec. bd. mem., sec., treas. Acacia Frat., U. Mo., Columbia. Mem. The Young People's Leadership Found. (pres.), Scottish Rite Mason (33rd degree), Order of De Molay (Legion of Honor). Avocations: tennis, skiing. Office: Leaders Mag 59 E 54th St New York NY 10022-4211

BROWN, DAVID, motion picture producer, writer; b. N.Y.C., July 28, 1916; s. Edward Fisher and Lillian (Baren) B.; m. Liberty LeGacy, Apr. 15, 1940 (div. 1951); 1 son, Bruce LeGacy; m. Wayne Clark, May 25, 1951 (div. 1957); m. Helen Gurley, Sept. 25, 1959. AB, Stanford U., 1936; MS, Columbia U., 1937. Apprentice San Francisco News and Wall St. Jour., 1936; night editor, asst. drama critic Fairchild Publs., 1937-39; editorial dir. Milk Research Council, 1939-40; assoc. editor Street & Smith Publs., 1940-43; assoc. editor, exec. editor, editor-in-chief Liberty mag., 1943-49; editorial dir. Nat. Edn. Campaign, A.M.A., 1949; assoc. editor, mng. editor Cosmopolitan mag., 1949-52; mng. editor, story editor, head scenario dept. 20th Century-Fox Film Corp. Studios, Beverly Hills, Calif., 1952-56, mem. studio exec. com., 1956-60, producer, 1960-62; v.p., dir. story operation 20th Century Fox Film Corp., Beverly Hills, Calif., 1964-69, exec. v.p. creative operations, 1969-70, dir., 1968-70; exec. v.p. creative operations, dir. Warner Bros., 1971-72; ptnr. Zanuck/Brown Co., N.Y.C., 1972-87; owner Manhattan Project Ltd., 1987—; pres. Island World, 1990-92; exec. story editor, head scenario dept., editorial v.p. New Am. Library World Lit., Inc., 1963-64. Final judge for best short story pub. in mags. Benjamin Franklin Mag. ann. awards, 1955-58. Author: Brown's Guide ot Growing Gray, 1987, Let Me Entertain You, 1990, The Rest of Your Life is the Best of Your Life, 1991; contbr. Am. mag., Collier's, Harper's, Sat. Evening Post, Reader's Digest, Journalists in Action, 1963, others; editor: I Can Tell It Now, 1964, How I Got That Story, 1967; prodr.: (films) The Sting, 1973, The Sugarland Express, 1974, The Eiger Sanction, 1975, Jaws, 1977, MacArthur, 1977, Jaws II, 1978, The Island, 1980, Neighbors, 1981, The Verdict, 1982, Target, 1985, Cocoon, 1985; exec. prodr.: Driving Miss Daisy, HBO Women and Men, 1 and 2, 1990, 1991, The Player, 1992, A Few Good Men, 1992, Watch It, 1993, The Cemetery Club, 1993, Canadian Bacon, 1994, Kiss The Girls, 1997, The Saint, 1997, Deep Impact, 1998, Angela's Ashes, 1999, Chocolat, 2000, Along Came a Spider, 2001; prodr.: (plays) A Few Good Men, TRU, The Cemetery Club, The Shawl, Mr. Goldwyn, The Sweet Smell of Success, others. Trustee com. on film Mus. Modern Art, N.Y.C. Served as 1st lt., M.I. AUS, World War II. Mem. Acad. Motion Picture Arts and Scis. (recipient Irving G. Thalberg Meml. award 1991), Producers Guild Am. (David O. Selznick Lifetime Achievement award 1993), Nat. Press Club (Washington), Coffee Ho. Club (N.Y.C.), Bd. of Visitors Columbia U. Grad Sch. of Journalism, Players Club (N.Y.C.), Dutch Treat (N.Y.C.), Century Assn. (N.Y.C.), N.Y. Friars Club. Office: Manhattan Project Ltd 1775 Broadway Ste 410 New York NY 10019-1903 *Success, after all, is no more and no less than doing well what one wants to do most-regardless of where such an endeavor places one in the hierarchy of society.*

BROWN, DAVID G. academic administrator; AB in Econs. with honors, Denison U., 1958; PhD, MA in Econs., Princeton U., 1961. From asst. to assoc. prof. econs. U. N.C., Chapel Hill, 1961-66; Am. Coun. on Edn. fellow U. Minn., 1966-67; provost, v.p. for acad. affairs Drake U., 1967-70; provost, exec. v.p. for acad. affairs Miami U., 1970-82; pres. Transylvania U., 1982-83; spl. cons. Assn. Governing Bds., 1983-84; chancellor U. N.C., Asheville, 1984-90; provost Wake Forest U., Winston-Salem, NC, 1990-98, v.p., dean Internat. Ctr. for Computer Enhanced Learning, 1998—2003; interim pres. Ga. Coll. and State Univ., 2003—. Chair Asheville's Econ. Devel. Summit, 1986, Nat. Small Pub. Ivys Conf., 1988; leader numerous workshops. Author: The Market for College Teachers, 1965, The Mobile Professors, 1967, Leadership Vitality, 1979, Leadership Roles of Chief Academic Officers, 1984, (monograph) Economic Development: 1987 and Beyond, 1986, Electronically Enhanced Education, 1999, Always in Touch, 1999, Interactive Learning, 2000, Teaching with Technology, 2000, Ubiquitous Computing, 2003, Developing Faculty to Use Technology, 2003; contbr. articles and papers to profl. bulls. and jours., also book chpts. Recipient Big A award Asheville Area C. of C., 1990; named one of 100 Young Leaders of the Acad., Change Mag., 1978; rsch. grantee Carnegie, 1979, U.S. Dept. Edn., 1965, NSF, 1965. Mem. Nat. Assn. State Univs. and Land Grant Colls. (chair coun. on acad. affairs 1975-76), Nat. Coun. Chief Acad. Officers (chair ACE 1978-80), Nat. Am. Assn. for Higher Edn. (chair 1981-82), Nat. Higher Edn. Colloquium (chair 1984-86), Phi Beta Kappa, Omicron Delta Kappa. Office: Wake Forest U PO Box 7328 Winston Salem NC 27109-7328 Fax: 336-758-5012. E-mail: brown@wfu.edu.

BROWN, DAVID HARRY, speech educator; b. Cleve., Jan. 15, 1926; s. Joseph M. and Rose (Wolchok) Brown; m. Marilyn Nathan, Jan. 29, 1951 (dec. Dec. 1990); children: Holly, Mark; m. Rose Sanker, July 10, 1994. AB in Journalism/Speech, Cleve. Coll., 1950; MS in Pub. Rels., Am. U., 1980; grad., Montgomery Coll. Reporter Cleve. Press, 1950-51, 1959—67; sales correspondent Serbin, Inc., Miami, Fla., 1951-54; reporter Circleville (Ohio) Herald, 1954-56; state editor Columbus Citizen, 1956-59; asst. dir. pub. info. Dept. of Justice, Washington, 1967-69; pub. info. officer FAA, Washington, 1969-71, Dept. of Transp., Washington, 1971-74, Govt. Printing Office, Washington, 1974-91; adj. prof. speech Montgomery Coll., Rockville, Md., 1991-98; media columnist Montgomery Jour., 1998—. Pres. Brown Speak Comm., Rockville, 1994—; presenter at numerous conv. and confs.; cons./trainer verbal comms. and media rels. Author: I Would Rather Be Audited By the IRS Than Give a Speech, 1995; columnist Montgomery Jour., 1998—. Mem. planning commn., bd. zoning appeals, city councilman, University Heights, Ohio, 1962—67; chmn. bd. appeals Rockville, 1976—79; bd. dirs. Montgomery Coll. Found.; co-chair Montgomery County Citizens Polit. Action Com., 1999—2001; mem. adv. bd. Lifelong Learning Soc., Fla. Atlantic U., 2003—. With U.S. Army, WWII, lt. col. USAR, 1950—78. Decorated Meritorious Svc. medal, Combat Infantry Badge, Bronze star USAR; recipient Excellence award, Nat. Inst. for Staff and Orgnl. Devel., U. Tex., Dalton Pen award, 1997, Cmty. Hero award, Montgomery County Civic Fedn., 2002. Mem.: Nat. Assn. Govt. Comm. (founding pres.). Home and Office: Brown Speak Comm 5809 Nicholson Ln Apt 1116 Rockville MD 20852-5714 Home: 5152 Golf View Ct Apt 1825 Delray Beach FL 33484 E-mail: brownspeak@aol.com.

BROWN, DAVID HURST, lawyer, partner; b. Houston, May 11, 1950; BS, Northwestern U., 1972; JD, U. Tex., Austin, 1975. Bar: Tex. 1976. Briefing atty. U.S. Dist. Ct. (so. dist.) Tex., Houston, 1975-77; assoc. Vinson & Elkins, Houston, 1977-84, ptnr., 1984—. Mem. Maritime Law Assn. U.S., Tex. Assn. Def. Counsel, Tex. Bar Found., Houston Bar Assn. Episcopalian. Office: Vinson & Elkins LLP 1001 Fannin St Ste 2300 Houston TX 77002-6760

BROWN, DAVID MITCHELL, physician, educator, dean; b. Chgo., Nov. 11, 1935; m. Sandra Miriam Brown BS, U. Ill., Urban, 1956; MD, U. Ill., Chgo., 1960. Intern U. Ill. Research-Edn. Hosp., Chgo., 1960-61; resident in pediatrics U. Minn., Mpls., 1961-63, fellow in endocrinology and metabolism, 1963-65; attending staff pediatric eoncrinology USAF Hosp., San Antonio, 1965-67; asst. prof. pediatrics, lab. medicine and pathology U. Minn., Mpls., 1967-70, assoc. prof., 1970-73, dir. clin. labs., 1970-84, prof. pediatrics, lab. medicine and pathology, 1974—, dean. Med. Sch., 1984-93, dir. Gen. clin. Rsch. Ctr., med. dir. clin. trials unit, 1997—2002. Mem. adv. com. on rsch. on women's health NIH, 1995-99; co-chair orgainzing com. 7th Internat. Symposium on Basement Membranes, 1995; mem. planning com. NIH 3d Internat. Symposium on Kidney Disease of Diabetes Mellitus, 1991. With USAF, 1965-67. Recipient USPHS Research Career Devel. award, 1968-73 Mem. AAAS, Acad. Clin. Lab. Physicians and Scientists, Am. Diabetes Assn., Am. Pediatric Soc., Am. Physiol. Soc., Am. Soc. Clin. Pathology, Am. Soc. Nephrology, Am. Soc. Pediatric Nephrology, Central Soc. for Clin. Research, Endocrine Soc., Internat. Soc. Nephrology, Lawson Wilkins Soc. Pediatric Endocrinology, Mpls. Pediatric Soc., Orthopaedic Research Soc., Soc. Pediatric Nephrology, Soc. Pediatric Research, Am. Assn. Pathologists, Am. Soc. Bone and Mineral Research, Internat. Acad. Pathology, Assn. Am. Med. Colls. (chmn. council acad. Socs.), Am. Assn. Pathologists, Am. Soc. Cell Biology, Minn. Soc. Clin. Pathology, Alpha Omega Alpha. Home: 2571 Abbey Hill Dr Hopkins MN 55305-2332 Office: PO Box 404 516 Delaware St SE Minneapolis MN 55455-0356

BROWN, DAVID NELSON, lawyer; b. Harrodsburg, Ky, May 29, 1940; s. Irmel Nelson and Pauline (Harmon) Brown; m. Lois Aileen Everett, June 20, 1964; 1 child, Ian Richard. AB, Cornell U., 1963; JD, U. Chgo., 1966. Bar: DC 1967. Assoc. Covington & Burling, Washington, 1966—74, ptnr., 1974—, mgmt. com., 1989—93. Comment editor: U. Chgo. Law Rev. Mem.: ABA, Cosmos Club, Order of Coif. Episcopalian. Office: Covington & Burling 1201 Pennsylvania Ave NW Washington DC 20004-2401 E-mail: dbrown@cov.com.

BROWN, DAVID RANDOLPH, electrical engineer; b. L.A., Oct. 31, 1923; s. Gilbert and Blanche Mabel (Phillips) B.; m. Sally England, Dec. 17, 1944; children: Philip, Ellen, Polly, Ann. BSEE, U. Wash., 1944; SMEE, MIT, 1947. Group leader MIT Lincoln Lab., Lexington, Mass., 1951-58; assoc. tech. dir. MITRE Corp., Bedford, Mass., 1958-63; lab. dir. SRI Internat., Menlo Park, Calif., 1963-85, staff scientist, 1985-93. Fellow IEEE. Avocation: genealogy. Home: 1470 Sand Hill Rd Apt 309 Palo Alto CA 94304-2031

BROWN, DAVID RICHARD, school system administrator, minister; b. Manhattan, Kans., Oct. 22, 1929; s. Marion Arthur and Dorothy (Bailey) B.; m. Jeanette Christine Phoenix, July 28, 1962; children: David M., Mark, Thomas. BA, U. So. Calif., 1951; MDiv, U. Chgo., 1955; postgrad., U. So. Calif., 1956, 57. Ordained minister, Presbyn. Ch. Assoc. pastor Federated Community Ch., Flagstaff, Ariz., 1957-59; minister of edn. Lakeside Presbyn. Ch., San Francisco, 1959-62; pastor of edn. 1st Presbyn. Ch., Medford, Oreg., 1962-69, pastor Newark, Calif., 1969-75; founder, pastor Community Presbyn. Ch., Union City, Calif., 1975-89; founder, supt. Christian Heritage Acad., Fremont, Calif., 1984—2000; organizing pastor New Life Presbyn. Ch., Fremont, 1989—99; asst. prof. Chabot Coll., Hayward, Calif., 1975-80; pastor New Life Presbyn. Ch., Castro Valley, Calif., 1999—. Moderator Presbytery of No. Ariz., 1959, Presbytery of No. Calif., 2001—02; religion editor The Valley Citizen, Danville, Calif., 2000—. Dir.: (various Shakespearian theatrical prodns.), 1982—84 (Thesbian award, 1984). Pres. Boys Christian League, L.A., 1953-54, Coconino Assn. for Mental Health, Flagstaff, 1958-59; chaplain Mozumdar YMCA Camp, Crestline, Calif., 1952-56; chmn. Tri-City Citizens Action Com., 1986-90. Recipient plaque KC, 1989. Mem. Rotary (chpt. pres. 1988-89, Paul Harris fellow 1989). Avocations: skiing, stamps, choir, drama.

BROWN, DAVID RONALD, lawyer; b. Turtle Creek, Pa., Jan. 25, 1939; s. James R. and Mary A. (Barnes) Brown; m. Debra W. Brown; children: Michelle, Adrienne, Aaron, Eden, Jeremy. Student, Brown U., 1956-57; BS, U. Pitts., 1960; JD, Duquesne U., 1967. Bar: Penn. 1968, U.S. Dist. Ct. (we. dist.) Penn. 1967, U.S. Ct. Appeals (3d cir.) 1972, U.S. Tax Ct. 1986. Rschr. phys. chemistry Mellon Inst., Pitts., 1960-66; real estate lawyer Redevel. Authority of Allegheny County, Pitts., 1966-69; ptnr. Litman, Litman, Harris & Brown, Pitts., 1969-2000, Sherrard, German & Kelly, Pitts., 2000—. Lectr. Robert Morris Coll., 1978-84. Councilman Borough of Turtle Creek, Penn., 1963-67. Mem. ABA (real property and probate sect., bus. law sect.), Pa. Bar Assn., Allegheny County Bar Assn. (com. legal svcs. 1973-74, real property sect., probate and trust law sect.). Home: 1411 Grandview Ave Apt 202 Pittsburgh PA 15211-1157 Office: Sherrard German & Kelly 35th Fl Free Markets Ctr Pittsburgh PA 15222

BROWN, DAVID RUPERT, engineering executive; b. Chgo., Sept. 11, 1934; s. Hugh Stewart and Sara (Daniels) B.; m. Mary Heaton Nicolaus, Sept. 6, 1958; children: David R. Jr., Robert N., Sara D. BSME, Purdue U., 1956; MBA, U. Akron, 1968. V.p. engrng. Diamond Power Specialty Co., Lancaster, Ohio, 1974-77, v.p. ops., 1977-80, pres., 1980-82; sr. v.p., group exec. Babcock & Wilcox, Lancaster, 1982-85, Barberton, Ohio, 1985-87, v.p., gen. mgr., 1987;

with Worldwide Procurement Inc., Akron, Ohio, 1987-90; v.p. mktg. Stock Equipment Co., Chagrin Falls, Ohio, 1990-95. With U.S. Army, 1957-58. Mem. ASME, Pi Tau Sigma, Tau Beta Pi. Home: 1717 Brookwood Dr Akron OH 44313-5072 E-mail: DBrown2020@aol.com.

BROWN, DAVID T. manufacturing executive; m. Nancy Brown; 2 children. B in Econs., Purdue U., 1970. Salesman Procter & Gamble, Shearson Hammill, Eli Lilly; with Owens Corning, 1978—, v.p. roofing and asphalt divsn., pres. roofing and asphalt divsn., 1994—96, pres. bldg. materials sales and distrbn., 1996—97, v.p. then pres. insulating sys. bus., 1997—2001, COO, 2001—02, CEO, pres., 2002—. Office: 1 Owens Corning Pkwy Toledo OH 43659*

BROWN, DAVID WARFIELD, management educator; b. Evanston, Ill., Aug. 16, 1937; s. Lloyd Warfield and Nancy (Coleman) B.; m. Alice Bean, Feb. 29, 1964; children: Peter Bean, Sarah Alice. BA, Princeton U., 1959; JD, Harvard U., 1963. Bar: N.Y. 1966. Assoc. Patterson, Belknap & Webb, N.Y.C., 1966-69; chief-of-staff Congressman Edward I. Koch, Washington and N.Y.C., 1969-74; v.p. Rand Inst., N.Y.C., 1974-75; chmn. N.Y. State Commn. Investigation, N.Y.C., 1975-78; dep. mayor City of N.Y.C., 1978-79; commr. Met. Transp. Authority, N.Y.C., 1979-85; ptnr. Hawkins, Delafield & Wood, N.Y.C., 1980; pres. Blackburn Coll., Carlinville, Ill., 1989-91; prof. profl. practice (mgmt.) Milano Grad. Sch. Mgmt. and Urban Policy, New Sch. U., N.Y.C., 1996—. Lectr., adj. prof. pub. mgmt. Sch. Mgmt., Yale U., New Haven, 1979-89. Author: When Strangers Cooperate: Using Social Conventions to Govern Ourselves, 1995, Organization Smarts, 2002; co-editor: Higher Edn. Exch.; contbr. articles to profl. jours. Capt. USAR, 1963-65. English Speaking Union scholar, London, 1959-60. Mem. Assn. of Bar of City of N.Y., Kettering Found. (assoc., vis. scholar 1991-92). Home: 40 E 94th St Apt 19C New York NY 10128-0726

BROWN, DAVID WILLIAM, economist, educator, consultant; b. Meriden, Conn., Nov. 10, 1931; s. William Horace and Elsie Miriam (Lovett) B.; m. Jean Margaret Young, Dec. 27, 1956; children: Cheryl Maurine, Kevin William. BS with distinction and honors, U. Conn., 1953; MS, Cornell U., 1954; PhD, Iowa State U., 1956. Asst., assoc. prof. U. Tenn., Knoxville, 1956-58, internat. prof., 1968-82; vis. prof. U. Malaya, Singapore, 1958-60; extension economist, asst. to dean Texas A&M U., College Station, 1961-63; team leader, tech. adv. Iowa Iowa-USAID program, Puno and Lima, Peru, 1965-66, vis. prof. Iowa State U., Ames, 1967-68; chief situation, outlook svc. UN Food and Agriculture Orgn., Rome, 1982-87; sr. economist food crops project, Acad. Ednl. Devel. USAID, Jakarta, Indonesia, 1988-90; social scis. specialist, adj. prof. U. Ill.-USAID project, Peshawar, Pakistan, 1990-94. Adj. prof. econs., tech. and humanities Salve Regina U., 1999-01; vol. career counselor Peace Corps, 1967-82; vol. economist R.I. Ctr. for Comml. Agr., 1995—, R.I. Conservation Dists., 1995—, R.I. Dept. Transp. Watch, 1995—, mem. exec. bd. 2002—; mem. exec. bd. Dept. Transp. Watch, 2002—; mem. Naval Installation Restoration Adv. Bd., Newport, 1996—; counselor Interactivity Found., 1996—. Mem., programmer, spkr. Coun. Internat. Visitors, Newport, R.I., 1994—; mem. Planning Bd., City of Newport, 1996-2000; mem. Aquidneck Island Planning Commn., 1996-2000; mem. R.I. Tree Coun., 1996—; mem. Newport Tree Commn., 2002—, chmn., 2003—; mem. EPA/TAG Aquidneck Island Citizen's Adv. Bd., 1996—, founding mem. R.I. People's Energy Coun., 2002—. Mem. Am. Econ. Assn., Am. Agrl. Econs. Assn. Avocations: socio-economic history, folk music, urban forestrh. Home: 421 Bellevue Ave Apt 4C Newport RI 02840-6944 E-mail: djbrown2@prodigy.net.

BROWN, DEAN NAOMI, state official, geologist; b. Fairbanks, Alaska, Mar. 9, 1944; d. James Heuston and Betty (Jefford) Alexander; m. Jim McCaslin Brown, Sept. 1, 1963 (div. 1987); children: Robin Wendy, Shelly Reneé. BS in Geology, U. Wis., 1967. Lectr. geology U. Ind., Kokomo, 1971-72; geologist, landman Amax Coal Co., Indpls., 1974; asst. and field constrn. engr. Trans-Alaska pipeline Fluor Alaska, Inc., 1975-76; environ. geologist Civil Engr./AK, Wasilla, 1977; various positions to acting dir. agr. Alaska Dept. Natural Resources, 1978-87; office mgr. Northwind Aviation, Anchorage, 1987-88; geologist Placer Dome U.S., Inc., Nome, Alaska, 1988; journeyman carpenter Ensearch Corp., Bradley Lake, Alaska, 1989; from no. regional mgr. div. land and water mgmt. to Dep. State Forester AK Dept. Natural Resources, Anchorage, 1990—2003, acting dir. agr., 2003—. Adj. prof. natural resource econs. Alaska Pacific U., 1991, 93; vice-chair Alaskan-Chinese Timber Commn., 1993, Gov.'s Mktg. Alaska Forest Products Coun.; del. Coun. Western State Foresters, 1994-95, Nat. Assn. State Foresters, 1994; co-chair Dept. Nat. Resources Computer Group, 1996—; des. Statewide Emergency Response Commission, 1997—; mem. AK Wildland Fire Coord. Group, 1996—2000, chair, 1999—, Gov.'s Transition Team-Valley, 2002. Vol. Iditarod Trail Com. Recipient cert. of appreciation City of Valdez, Alaska, 1976, Anchorage Sch. Dist., 1983, 4-H Leaders, Palmer, Alaska, 1987, cert. of achievement Susitna coun. Girl Scouts U.S.A., 1982, Outstanding Achievement award Alaska Dept. Natural Resources, 1986. Mem. Aircraft Owners and Pilots Assn., Alaska Airman's Assn., Pacific Rim Arabian Horse Assn. (charter mem. 1997—), Alaska Horse Breeders Assn. (bd. dirs. 1984-90), Ninety-Nines. Avocations: flying, horse breeding and showing, painting, photography, gold mining. Home: PO Box 870366 Wasilla AK 99687-0366 Office: Alaska Dept Natural Resources 550 W 7th, Ste 1450 Anchorage AK 99501-5925

BROWN, DEBORAH A. social worker, therapist; b. Washington, May 13; BA, Va. State U., 1971; MSW, Howard U., 1974. Lic. ind. clin. social worker, Washington. Social worker Dept. Mental Health, Washington, 1977—. Utilization rev. coord. CHAMPUS, 1990-92, geriatric case mgr., 1993—. Active Ward Meml. AME Ch. Mem.: NASW, Nat. Assn. Black Social Workers, Acad. Cert. Social Workers. Republican.

BROWN, DENISE, poet; b. Chgo., Oct. 7, 1963; d. Earl L. and Dorothy Grier; married; 3 children. Author: (poetry) A Treasury of Great Poems, 1998, poems. Recipient Editor's Choice award, 1999, Cert. of Recognition, 2001, The Diamond Homer award, 1998.

BROWN, DENISE SCOTT, architect, urban planner; b. Nkana, Zambia, Oct. 3, 1931; arrived in U.S., 1958; d. Simon and Phyllis (Hepker) Lakofski; m. Robert Scott Brown, July 21, 1955 (dec. 1959); m. Robert Charles Venturi, July 23, 1967; 1 child, James C. Student, U. Witwatersrand, South Africa, 1948—51; diploma, Archtl. Assn., London, 1955; M of City Planning, U. Pa., 1960, MArch, 1965, DFA (hon.), 1994, Oberlin Coll., 1977, Phila. Coll. Art, 1985, Parsons Sch. Design, 1985; LHD (hon.), N.J. Inst. Tech., 1984, Phila. Coll. Textiles and Sci., 1992, Lehigh U., 2002; DEng (hon.), Tech. U. N.S., 1991; HHD (hon.), Pratt Inst., 1992; DFA (hon.), U. Pa., 1994; LittD (hon.), U. Nev., 1998; D. Arch. (hon.), U. Miami, 1997; DFA (hon.), Lehigh U., 2002. Registered architect, U.K. Asst. prof. U. Pa., Phila., 1960—65; assoc. prof., head urban design program UCLA, 1965—68; with Venturi, Rauch and Scott Brown, Phila., 1967—, ptnr., 1969—89; prin. Venturi, Scott Brown and Assocs. Inc., Phila., 1989—. Vis. prof. arch. U. Calif., Berkeley, 1965, Yale U., 1967—70; asst. prof. U. Pa., 1960—65, vis. prof. Sch. Fine Arts, 1982, 83; Eliot Noyes design critic in arch. Harvard U., Cambridge, Mass., 1989—90; mem. visitors com. MIT, 1973—83; mem. adv. com. dept. arch. Temple U., 1980—; cons. to dean search com. Sch. Arch. Washington U., St. Louis, 1992; mem. adv. bd. dept. arch. Carnegie Mellon U., 1992—96; mem. jury Prince of Wales Prize in Urban Design Grad. Sch. Design Harvard U., Cambridge, 1993; mem. bd. overseers U. Librs. U. Pa., 1995—. Author: Urban Concepts, 1990; co-author: Learning from Las Vegas, 1972, (rev. edit.), 1977, A View from the Campidoglio: Selected Essays, 1953-84, 1985, On Houses and Housing, 1992; contbr. ; prin. works include campus plans U. Mich., Dartmouth Coll., prin. works include city plans Miami Beach, Memphis, plans for Civic Ctr. Cultural Complex, Denver, Nat. Gallery, London, Hotel du Department de la Haute Garonne, Toulouse, France, Life Scis. Inst., U. Mich., exhibitions include retrospective on career and work at Phila. Mus. Art. Policy panelist design arts program NEA, 1981—83; mem. bd. adv. Architects, Designers and Planners for Social Responsibility, 1982—; mem. capitol preservation com. Commonwealth of Pa., Harrisburg, 1983—87; trustee Chestnut Hill Acad., Phila., 1985—89; mem. curriculum com. Phila. Jewish Children's Folkshul, 1980—86; bd. dirs. Ctrl. Phila. Devel. Corp., 1985—, Urban Affairs Partnership, Phila., 1987—91. Decorated chevalier de l'Ordre des Arts et des Lettres France, commendatore Order of Merit Italy; co-recipient The Phila. award, 1993; named to Germantown Hall of Fame, Germantown Hist. Soc., Pa., 2002; recipient Chgo. Architecture award, 1987, U.S. Presdl. award, Nat. Medal of Arts, 1992, Hall of Fame award, Interior Design mag., 1992, The Benjamin Franklin medal, Royal Soc. for Encouragement of Arts., Mfg. and Commerce, 1993, Topaz medal, Am. Coll. Schs. of Architecture/AIA, 1996, Giants of Design award, House Beautiful Mag., 2000, Joseph Pennell medal, Phila. Sketch Club, 2000, Vincent J. Scully Prize, Nat. Bldg. Mus., 2002, Edith Wharton Women of Achievement award for Urban Planning, 2002, Soc. for Environ. Graphic Design Fellow award, 2003. Mem.: Germantown Hist. Soc. of Phila. (Germantown Hall of Fame 2002, Soc. for Environ. Graphic Design Fellow award 2003), Royal Soc. Encouragement of Arts, Mfg. and Commerce, Soc. Archtl. Historians (bd. dirs. 1981—84), Soc. Coll. and Univ. Planning, Archtl. Assn. London, Am. Planning Assn., Archs. Designers and Planners for Social Responsibility, Am. Acad. Arts and Scis., Royal Inst. Brit. Archs., Athenaeum of Phila., Carpenters Co. of City and County of Phila., Internat. Women's Forum. Democrat. Jewish. Office: Venturi Scott Brown & Assocs Inc 4236 Main St Philadelphia PA 19127-1603

BROWN, DENNIS JAMES, industrial engineer, consultant; b. Omaha, Nebr., Oct. 24, 1942; s. Louis R. and Meta C. (Walters) B.; m. Carol Rivedal, May 12, 1962; children: Tracy L., Scott D. BSIE, U. Omaha, 1964. Dir. mfg. engring. Arctic Enterprises, Theif River Falls, Minn., 1970-80; v.p. engring. Mgmt. Sci., Inc., Appleton, Wis., 1980-86; dir. mfg. engring. UFE, Inc., Stillwater, Minn., 1986-90; gen. mgr. Dynasound, Inc., Grantsburg, Wis., 1990-93; tech. dir. Tulip Corp., Milw., 1993-95; gen. mgr. GreenMan Tech., Malvern, Ark., 1995-96; gen. mgr., prin. engr. Sienna Resources, Hot Springs, Ark., 1996-98; sr. cons. Grant Thornton, LLP, Alexandria, Va., 1998—. Bd. dirs. Trinity Luth. Ch., Hudson, Wis., 1986-93; dir. Family Svcs. of St. Croix, Stillwater, 1986-90; dist. chmn. Boy Scouts Am., Thief River Falls, 1973-80. Mem. Soc. Plastic Engrs. (chmn. 1965—), Am. Prodn. and Inventory Control Soc. Republican. Home and Office: 124 Corporate Terrace Unit 10B Hot Springs National Park AR 71913-7238

BROWN, DIANA L. elementary education educator; b. Bklyn., Oct. 9, 1946; d. Elva Jane Brown. AAS, N.Y.C. Community Coll., Bklyn.; BS, CCNY, 1980; postgrad., Nova U., Ft. Lauderdale, Fla. Cert. educator, Fla.; class cert. behavior analysis. Supr. outpatient clinics N.Y. Health and Hosps. Corp., N.Y.C.; asst. dir. Toddlers Country Club, Orlando, Fla.; tchr. Friends Sem., N.Y.C.; tchr. 3d grade Dover Shores Elem. Sch./Orange County Sch. Bd., Orlando, Fla.; 3d grade tchr. Shingle Creek Elem. Sch., 1993, 5th grade tchr., 1993-95, curriculum resource tchr., dean, 1995-97; alternative edn. tchr. Dover Shores Elem. Sch., 1997; 5th grade tchr. Tangelo Park Elem., 1997—2002, trainer for new tchrs., grant beginnings induction Orange County Sch. Bd., 2001—; tch. applied behavior analysis Rocklake Elem. Sch., 2002—, dean, 2002—. Sch.-based care team for students at risk; state sci. textbook adoption com., 1994-95; county sci. curriculum writing team, 1994-95. Author: Afro-Amercan Artists: A Bio-Bibliographical Directory. Named Tchr. of Yr. Dover Shores, 1990-91; Coun. of Black Faculty and Staff scholar. Mem.: NEA, Nat. Sci. Tchrs. Assn.

BROWN, DICK TERRELL, lawyer; b. Houston, Feb. 6, 1944; s. Archie Scales and Margaret Denman (Terrell) Brown; 1 child, Melissa Anne. BS in Mech. Engring., U. Tex.-Austin, 1965; JD, St. Mary's U., San Antonio, 1972. Bar: Tex. 1973, U.S. Dist. Ct. (we. dist.) Tex. 1977, U.S. Dist. Ct. D.C. 1984, U.S. Ct. Appeals (5th cir.) 1984. Assoc. Matthews, Nowlin, MacFarlane & Barrett, San Antonio, 1973-77; ptnr. McCamish, Martin, Brown and Loeffler, P.C., San Antonio, 1977-84, Austin, 1984-91, Brown & Lacallade, P.C., 1991—. Republican. Episcopalian. Home: Ste Ii300 1250 S Capital Of Texas Hwy Austin TX 78746-6495 Office: Brown & Lacallade PC Ste Ii300 1250 S Capital Of Texas Hwy Austin TX 78746-6495

BROWN, DONALD ARTHUR, lawyer; b. Washington, Feb. 1, 1929; s. Louis S. and Rose (Kliban) B.; m. Ann Winkelman, July 13, 1959; children: Cathy, Laura. BA in Econs., George Washington U., 1949, LL.B. (Case Club oral argument competition winner), 1952, LL.M., 1958. Bar: D.C. 1952. Sr. partner Brown, Gildenhorn & Jacobs (and predecessor), Washington, 1955—. Mem. faculty Practising Law Inst.; faculty Harvard U. Sch. Bus., Cambridge, Mass., 1984-93, Yale U. Sch. Mgmt., New Haven, 1986, George Washington U. Sch. Bus., Washington, 1994—; guest lectr. Am. U., Nat. Assn. Real Estate Counselors, Nat. Assn. Real Estate Investors; pres., sec. JBG Constrn., Inc.; partner JBG Assocs.; v.p., treas. JBG Properties, Inc.; trustee, gen. counsel Nat. Bank Rosslyn, Arlington, Va.; mem. minority enterprises com. SBA; finance com. Housing Devel. Corp.; mem. Model Cities Com. D.C.; apptd. by Pres. of U.S. commr. Internat. Cultural and Trade Ctr., 1988. Co-author: Understanding Real Estate Investments, 1967; contbr. articles to profl. jours. Exec. bd. Forest Hills Citizens Assn.; bd. dirs. D.C. Jr. C. of C.; mem. Friends Kennedy Center, Friends Corcoran Gallery, Big Bros. Orgn. D.C.; bd. dirs. Washington Area Tennis Patrons Found., 1964—, pres., 1973-75, Fed. city council; trustee Woodley House, psychiat. half-way house, Washington, 1973—, pres. bd. dirs., 1975—; trustee U. D.C., Sidwell Friends Sch., The Phillips Collection, 1984—; mem. art adv. council Washington Conv. Ctr. com. D.C. Conv. Ctr. Served as officer USNR, 1952-55. Named Washingtonian of Yr., Washingtonian mag., 1989. Mem. ABA, Fed. Bar Assn., D.C. Bar Assn., Washington Bd. Realtors (chmn. lawyer-realtor liaison com. 1972, chmn. investment property com. 1970), Economics Club of Washington, Burning Tree Club. Jewish (bd. mgrs. congregation 1962, treas. 1965). Club: Georgetown (Washington). Home: 2734 Rhone Dr Palm Beach Gardens FL 33410-1280 Office: Brown Gildenhorn & Jacobs 5301 Wise Ave NW Washington DC 20015

BROWN, DONALD CLYDE, surgeon; b. Pitts., May 17, 1936; MD, Case Western Res. U., 1961. Diplomate Am. Bd. Surgery. From intern to resident Allegheny Gen. Hosp., Pitts., 1961-64; resident Western Pa. Hosp., Pitts., 1964-67; med. staff Jeanette Hosp., Pa., 1969—; pvt. practice Irwin, Pa. With U.S. Army Med. Corps, 1967-69. Fellow ACS, Internat. Coll. Surgeons; mem. AMA. Office: Irwin Profl Ctr 100 Penna Ave Irwin PA 15642-3364

BROWN, DONALD DAVID, biology educator; b. Cin., Dec. 30, 1931; s. Albert Louis and Louise (Rauh) B.; m. Linda Jane Weil, July 2, 1957; children: Deborah Lin, Christopher Charles, Sharon Elizabeth. MS, MD, U. Chgo., 1956, D.Sc. (hon.), 1976, U. Md., 1983; DSc (hon.), U. Cin., 1992. Staff mem. dept. embryology Carnegie Instn. of Washington, Balt., 1963—, dir., 1976-94; prof. dept. biology Johns Hopkins U., 1968—. Pres. Life Scis. Research Found. Served with USPHS, 1957-59. Recipient U.S. Steel Found. award for molecular biology, 1973, V.D. Mattia award Roche Inst., 1975, Boris Pregel award for biology N.Y. Acad. Scis., 1976, Ross G. Harrison award Internat. Soc. Developmental Biology, 1981, Bertner Found. award, 1982, Rosenstiel award for biomed. sci., 1985, Louisa Gross Horwitz award, 1985, Feodor Lynen award U. Miami Winter Symposium, 1987. Fellow Am. Acad. Arts and Scis., AAAS; mem. Nat. Acad. Scis. (mem. coun. 1994-97), Soc. Devel. Biology (pres. 1975), Am. Soc. Biol. Chemists, Am. Soc. Cell Biology (pres. 1992, E.B. Wilson award 1996), Am. Philos. Soc. Home: 5721 Oakshire Rd Baltimore MD 21209-4217 Office: Carnegie Instn Washington 115 W University Pky Baltimore MD 21210-3301 E-mail: brown@ciwemb.edu.

BROWN, DONALD DOUGLAS, transportation company executive, retired air force officer, consultant; b. Montreal, Que., Can., Aug. 1, 1931; came to U.S., 1938; s. Donald Bannerman and Hilda Taylor (Noel) B.; m. Joan Teresa McAndrews, Aug. 7, 1954; children— Cathy J. Brown Peinhardt, James D., Nancy J. Brown May. BA, Columbia U., 1954; MBA, Syracuse U., 1965. Commd. officer U.S. Air Force, 1955, advanced through grades to maj. gen., 1979, ret., 1987, wing chief aircrew standardization, 1968-69, chief Weapon System Support div. in Directorate of Supply, then dir. logistics plans Scott AFB, Ill., 1973-75, asst. dep. chief of staff for logistics, 1975-76, from vice comdr. to comdr. McChord AFB, Wash., 1976-77, asst. dep. chief of staff for ops. Mil. Airlift Command Scott AFB, Ill., 1979-80, dep. chief of staff for plans, 1980-83, dep. chief of staff for ops. Mil. Airlift Command, 1983-84, comdr. 22d Air Force, Mil. Airlift Command Travis AFB, Calif., 1984-87, ret., 1987; chmn. bd. Evergreen Air Ctr. Inc. Cons. in aviation/logistics mgmt. Decorated Disting. Service medal with oak leaf cluster, Legion of Merit with oak leaf cluster, D.F.C. with oak leaf cluster, Bronze Star, Air medal with 4 oak leaf clusters, Republic of Vietnam Cross of Gallantry with palm Mem. Air Force Assn., Nat. Def. Transp. Assn. (appted. to bus. practices com.), Beta Gamma Sigma.

BROWN, DONALD JAMES, JR., lawyer; b. Chgo., Apr. 21, 1948; s. Donald James Sr. and Marian Constance (Scimeca) B.; m. Donna Bowen, Jan. 15, 1972; children: Megan, Maura. AB, John Carroll U., 1970; JD, Loyola U., Chgo., 1973. Bar: Ill. 1973, U.S. Dist. Ct. (no. dist.) Ill. 1973, U.S. Tax Ct. 1982. Asst. to state's atty. Cook County, Ill., 1973-75; assoc. Baker & McKenzie, Chgo., 1975-82, ptnr., 1982-95, Donohue, Brown, Mathewson & Smyth, Chgo., 1995—. Office: Donohue Brown et al 140 S Dearborn St Chicago IL 60603-5202

BROWN, DONALD JAMES, JR., insurance company executive; b. Inglewood, Calif., Sept. 30, 1955; s. Donald James and Kathleen Elizabeth (McKillips) B.; m. Joan Colleen Brewer, June 25, 1977 (div. May 1985); 1 child, Randy. BA, Calif. State U., Long Beach, 1979. Registered profl. adjuster. Estimator, supt. Home Improvement Builders, Santa Ana, Calif., 1979; asst. supt. Village Home of Calif., Santa Ana, 1980; claim rep. Aetna Life & Casualty, Orange, Calif., 1980-82, sr. claim rep., 1982-85, property specialist Woodland Hills, Calif., 1985-86; regional supr. United Pacific Ins. Co., Glendale, Calif., 1986-88; regional gen. adjuster Reliance Ins. Co., Glendale, 1988-90, regional property examiner Durham, N.C., 1990-92; property claim mgr. Home Ins. Co., Maitland, Fla., 1992-95; gen. adjuster Zurich U.S., Longwood, Fla., 1995—. Mem. membership com. Orange County Adjuster's Assn., Anaheim, Calif., 1983-84. Mem. Fla. Adv. Com. on Arson Prevention. Republican. Avocations: whitewater rafting, fishing, camping, sailing, motorcycle touring. Office: PO Box 915827 Longwood FL 32791-5827

BROWN, DONALD MALCOLM, plastic surgeon; b. Nelson, N.Z., May 28, 1945; came to U.S., 1947; s. Donald Roland and Edna M. (McPherson) B.; m. Susan E. Boeing, Sept. 3, 1989. MD, U. B.C., 1970. Diplomate Am. Bd. Otolaryngology and Plastic Surgery. Resident in otolarngology Manhattan Eye and Ear Hosp., N.Y.C., 1976; resident in plastic surgery Columbia U., N.Y.C., 1980; pvt. practice San Francisco, 1981—. Vis. prof. plastic surgery U. Liberia, Africa, 1980-81. Mem. AMA, Calif. Med. Assn., San Francisco Med. Assn., Am. Soc. Plastic and Reconstructive Surgery, Am. Soc. Aesthetic Surgery, Pacific Union Club, St. Francis Yacht Club. Avocations: flying helicopters, skiing, wind surfing. Office: 2100 Webster St Ste 429 San Francisco CA 94115-2380

BROWN, DONALD MCCARTY, economic development specialist; b. Elberton, Ga., Apr. 10, 1951; s. Donald McCarty Sr. and Joan Constantineau Brown; m. Jane Thornton, June 14, 1980; children: Laurie, Judson. B of Indsl. Engring., Ga. Tech., 1974, MS in Systems Engring., 1977. Mktg. specialist So. Co., Atlanta, 1977-90, Ga. Power Co., Atlanta, 1990-96; dir. econ. develop. Oconee County Govt., Watkinsville, Ga., 1996-98; econ. devel. specialist Ga. Dept. Industry, Trade and Tourism, Atlanta, 1998—2000; dir. office econ. devel. assistance U. Ga., Athens, 2000—. Bd. dirs. Oconee County Recreation Adv. Bd., Watkinsville, 1994—; vice chmn. Oconee County Wastewater Task Force, Watkinsville, 1992—; rsch. project advisor Elec. Power Rsch. Inst., Palo Alto, Calif., 1981-85, rsch. project advisor, 1991-95; soccer coach Oconee County Recreation Dept., Watkinsville, 1990-93, Athens United Soccer Assn., 1994-98, bd. dirs., 1997-98, in orgnl. devel., 1996—. Mem. Oconee Rotary Club (bd. dirs. 1996-98, com. chair 1996-98). Avocations: organic gardening, medicinal herbs, dulcimer playing, regional history.

BROWN, DONALD RICHARD, capacitor engineer; b. Milw., Sept. 25, 1925; s. Edwin Frances and Loretta Ethlyn (Howard) B.; m. Dorothy Jane (Carey), Sept. 5, 1947; children: Donald R. Jr., Kenneth Allen. BS in Physics and Math., Monmouth (Ill.) Coll., 1950. Dept. chief engring. Western Electric, Cicero, Ill., 1951-85; pres. D.R.B. Tech. Svcs. Ltd., Downers Grove, Ill., 1985—90. Patentee in field. Pres. Bruce Lake Home Owners Assn., 1960, Downer's Grove PTA, 1962. Served with USAF, 1944-45. Named one of top 100 technologists in western world by Tech. Mag., 1981. Avocations: fishing, personal computers, gardening, tennis, sports.

BROWN, DONALD VAUGHN, technical educator, engineering consultant; b. Fairfield, Maine, May 16, 1919; s. Walter C. and Hazel (Fogg) Brown; m. Christine R. Bishop, Mar. 14, 1945 (dec. Oct. 2000); 1 child, Donald V. Jr.; m. Wanda Jean Grant, June 1, 2002. BS, U. Maine, Orono, 1943; MS, Brigham Young U., 1963; EdD, Utah State U., 1965. Registered profl. engr., Maine. Apprentice engr. U.S. Steel Corp., Elwood City, Pa., 1943-47; works metallurgist Aluminum Co. of Am., Alcoa, Tenn., 1947-55; asst. v.p. Penobscot Fibre Co., Old Town, Maine, 1955-60; assoc. prof. Inst. Paper Chemistry, Appleton, Wis., 1960-62; instr. Brigham Young U., Provo, Utah, 1962-63, Utah State U., Logan, 1963-65; dean Fla. Keys C.C., Key West, 1965-66; dean, prof. Western Piedmont C.C., Morganton, N.C., 1966-68; prof. U. Tenn., Knoxville, 1968—. Cons. Assn. Am. States, Washington, 1976—, San Jose Costa Rica, S.A., Tenn. State Dept. Edn., Nashville, 1970—84, Maine State Libr., Augusta, 1970—; coord. Surname Index Project, 2001, Am. Adventure, Inc., Orlando, Fla., 1986—96, Thousand Trails Resorts, 1989—95, Coast to Coast Camping, Inc., Washington, 1986, Lincoln Acad., New Castle, Maine, 1994; cons. Capetown South Africa Mission, 2003—05; bd. dirs. Goodwill-Hinckley, Maine. Author: A Teaching Partnership, 1972, Metallurgy Basics, 1978; contbr. articles to profl. jours.; patentee 4 chemical processes. Scoutmaster Boy Scouts Am., Elwood City, Pa. and Alcoa, Tenn., 1946-52, scout commr., Massena, N.Y. and Orono, Maine, 1952-60; trustee Hinkley (Maine) Sch., 1978—. Lt. USN, 1944-46, 50-52, PTO, WW II, Korean War. Recipient Presdl. USN Unit citation, 1945. Mem. Am. Vocat. Assn., Am. Tech. Edn. Assn., Engring. Edn. Assn. (editing bd. 1968-79). Avocations: photography, sailing, hiking, camping. Home: 6423 Honeywood Knoxville TN 37918

BROWN, DONALD WESLEY, lawyer; b. Cleve., Jan. 2, 1953; s. Lloyd Elton Brown and Nancy Jeanne Hudson. AB summa cum laude, Ohio U., 1975; JD, Yale U., 1978. Bar: Calif. 1978, U.S. Dist. Ct. (no. dist.) Calif. 1978, U.S. Dist. Ct. (cen. dist.) Calif. 1990. Assoc. Brobeck, Phleger & Harrison, San Francisco, 1978-85, ptnr., 1985—2003, Covington & Burling, San Francisco, 2003—. Democrat. Home: 2419 Vallejo St San Francisco CA 94123-4638 Office: Covington & Burling One Front St San Francisco CA 94111

BROWN, DORIS JANE, nursing aide; b. Mo., Dec. 6, 1934; d. Lowell Emmitt and Lottie Nancy (Downing) Heinrich; m. Thomas B. Brown, Aug. 12, 1958 (div. 1967); 1 child, Doris Ann. AA, Penn Valley Met. C.C., 1982. Accredited nurse aide, Mo. Clk. Western Auto, Kansas City, Mo., 1952-55; acctg. sec. Allied Signal, Kansas City, 1955-58; various positions K.C. Paper Box Co., Kansas City, 1958-61, Winn-Senter Constrn. Co., Kansas City, 1961-90, exec. sec., 1990-92; adminstrv. asst. Miller & Assocs., Lee's Summit, Mo., 1992-93; nurse aide Nat. Health Care, West Plains, Mo., 1994-2001, Beverly Health Care, West Plains, 2001, Beautiful Savior Home, Belton, Mo., 2001—. Contbr. articles. Vol. Vista, Kansas City, Mo., 1961. Mem. nat. health care coms. Avocations: volunteer facilitator project literacy, sports. Home: 725 NE Tudor Rd #3 Lees Summit MO 64086-5789 Office: Beautiful Savior Home Y Hwy and Cambridge Belton MO 64012

BROWN, DOROTHY M. academic administrator; Prof. history Georgetown U., Washington, 1966—98, interim provost, 1998—99, provost, 1999—. Former chair history dept. Georgetown U. Office: Georgetown U Office of the Provost Box 571014/ ICC 650 Washington DC 20057-1014

BROWN, DUDLEY EARL, JR., psychiatrist, educator, health executive, former federal agency administrator, former naval officer; b. Berryville, Va., Apr. 10, 1928; s. Dudley Earl and Rosa Lee (Costello) B.; m. Lelia Adrienne Motley, June 22, 1953; children— Lelia Brown Farr, David, Kevin. BA, Washington and Lee U., 1949; MD, Med. Coll. Va., 1953. Diplomate: Am. Bd. Psychiatry and Neurology. Commd. lt. (j.g.) M.C. U.S. Navy, 1953, advanced through grades to rear adm., 1974; intern Naval Hosp., Portsmouth, Va., 1953-54, resident in neuropsychiatry Bethesda, Md., 1957-60; service in Vietnam; comdg. officer Nat. Naval Med. Center, Bethesda, 1975-76, Naval Regional Med. Center, San Diego, 1976-78; fleet surgeon U.S. Pacific Fleet and staff surgeon, comdr.-in-chief U.S. Forces, Pacific, 1978-80; ret., 1980; dep. asst. chief med. dir. for profl. services VA Central Office, Washington, 1980-82; assoc. dep. chief med. dir. VA, Washington, 1982-87; asst. prof. clin. psychiatry U. Pa. Med. Sch., 1967-70; prof. clin. psychiatry Uniformed Svcs. U. Health Scis., Bethesda, Md., 1981—, Med. Coll. Va., Va. Commonwealth U., Richmond, 1987—; dir. health policy studies, dir. Washington office Abt Assocs. Inc., 1987-93, v.p., 1992—, mng. v.p., 1993—2001. Sci. adv. bd. Ctr. Prisoner of War Studies, 1998—. Contbr. to med. jours. Decorated Legion of Merit; recipient Meritorious Svc. medal, Navy Commendation medal, VA Disting. Svc. medal, Disting. Alumnus Med. Coll. Va., 1993. Fellow ACP, Am. Psychiat.

Assn., Am. Coll. Psychiatrists; mem. Washington Psychiat. Soc., Nat. Health Coun. (bd. dirs. 1989-94), Assn. Mil. Surgeons U.S., Soc. Med. Cons. to Armed Forces (v.p. 1988-89, pres. 1989-90), Phi Gamma Delta, Alpha Epsilon Delta. Presbyterian. Home: 2415 Black Cap Ln Reston VA 20191-3027 Office: Abt Assocs Inc 4800 Montgomery Ln Ste 600 Bethesda MD 20814-3460 E-mail: dearlbown@aol.com.

BROWN, E. SHERWOOD, psychiatrist; b. Ft. Worth, Mar. 29, 1963; s. Edson Sherwood and Martha Anne (Dyer) B.; m. Sunhee Camille Hong, Apr. 26, 1997. BA, Tex. Christian U., 1985, PhD, 1989; MD, U. Tex., Houston, 1993. Diplomate Am. Coll. Psychiatry and Neurology. Rsch. fellow U. Tex. Southwestern Med. Ctr., Dallas, 1997-98, asst. prof. dept. psychiatry, 1998—. Adj. asst. prof. U. Tex. Coll. Pharmacy, Austin, 1999— Mem. editl. bd. Primary Care Companion, 2000—; mem. continuing med. edn. adv. bd. subcom. Jour. Clin. Psychiatry and Primary Care Companion, 2000-03; mem. editl. bd. Jour. Dual Diagnosis, 2003—; editor-in-chief Internet Jour. Mental Health; contbr. chpts. to books, articles to profl. publs. Faculty sponsor Sci. Tchr. Access to Resources at Southwestern, Dallas, 2001. Recipient Mentored Clin. Scientist Devel. award NIMH, 2000, Gerald L. Klerman award for clin. rsch. Nat. Alliance Rsch. on Schizophrenia and Depression, 2002; named Young Investigator Nat. Alliance Rsch. on Schizophrenia and Depression, 1996-98; travel fellow Am. Coll. Neuropsychopharmacology, 1999, Lilly travel fellow in biol. psychiatry, 1998; Exploration and Devel. grantee NIMH, 2001. Mem. AMA, Am. Psychiat. Assn., Tex. Soc. Psychiat. Physicians, Dallas County Med. Soc., Sigma Xi, Phi Beta Kappa. Avocations: travel, golf, studying Korean language. Office: U Tex Southwestern Med Ctr 5323 Harry Hines Blvd Dallas TX 75390 8849 E mail: sherwood.brown@utsouthwestern.edu.

BROWN, EARL KENT, historian, clergyman; b. Kent, Ohio, July 26, 1925; s. Earl Royal and Bernice Blanche (Howard) B. BA, Columbia U., 1948; S.T.B., Boston U., 1953, PhD (Howard fellow 1953-54, United Methodist Ch. Dempster fellow 1954-55), 1956. Ordained to ministry United Meth. Ch., 1957. Asst. prof. history Baldwin Wallace Coll., 1956-63, asso. prof., 1963; asso. prof. church history Boston U., 1963-70, prof., 1970-86, prof. emeritus, 1986—. Vis. prof. Case Western Res. U., 1961, Union Theol. Sem., Manila, 1970, United Theol. Coll., Bangalore, India, 1978, U. Manchester, Eng., 1979. Author: Women of Mr. Wesley's Methodism, 1983; Contbr. articles to acad. jours., religious periodicals. Fulbright fellow, 1962 Mem. Phi Beta Kappa. Home: Merrill Gardens #354 2261 Tuolumne Street Vallejo CA 94589

BROWN, EARLE PALMER, advertising agency executive; b. Manhasset, N.Y., Mar. 15, 1922; s. Palmer and Bessie (Twombley) B.; m. Barbara Mac Laughlin, July 1, 1946 (div. May 1984); children: Jeremy, Andrea (dec.), Scott, Alison, Gillian, Meredith; m. Joyce P. Baker, June 29, 1984. AB in Journalism, Washington and Lee U., 1944. Reporter News Leader, Richmond, Va., 1949; exec. sec. Soc. Indsl. Realtors, Washington, 1950-51; assoc. editor Archtl. Forum, N.Y.C., 1952; founder, pres. Earle Palmer Brown Assocs., Washington, 1953-73; chmn. bd. Earle Palmer Brown Co., Bethesda, Md., 1974—; columnist Gazette Papers, 1988—. Lectr. in field. Founder, 2d pres. Washington Area Tennis Patrons'; mem. bd. regents U. Md. System, 1989-99; mem. exec. com. The Univs. at Shady Grove; chmn. comms. adv. bd. Washington and Lee U. Sch. Bus.; campaign advisor, media cons. various pub. ofcls.; pres. Nat. Capital Area coun. Boy Scouts Am., 1991. Served with USN, WWII. Decorated Bronze Star with Combat V; recipient Silver Beaver and Disting. Eagle Scout award Boy Scouts Am., 1965, Citizen of Yr. award, 1990; citation USIA; named to Washington Bus. Hall of Fame, 1992. Mem. Am. Assn. Advt. Agys. (past chmn. Mid. Atlantic coun.), Am. Advt. Fedn. (Silver medal 1981), Nat. Fedn. Advt. Agys. (pres. 1967-68), Harness Tracks Am. (pres. 1978-80), Md. C. of C. (chmn. 1988-90), Met. Washington Tennis Assn. (past pres.), Congrl. Country Club (pres. 1994-95), Coral Beach Club, Capitol Hill Club, Omicron Delta Kappa. Avocation: tennis. Home: 9308 Mercy Hollow Ln Potomac MD 20854-4525 E-mail: ebrown@epb.com. *If I had my life to live over, I'd do almost everything the same way. Same college, same career, same branch of service. Only two changes--I'd learn to type and start playing tennis sooner.*

BROWN, EDGAR CARY, retired economics educator; b. Bakersfield, Calif., Apr. 14, 1916; s. Verne Brainard and Ruth (Cary) B.; m. Tomlin Edwards, May 28, 1937 (div.); children: Rebecca, Gretchen; m. Margaret Durham, June 6, 1969 (div.); children: Elizabeth, Robert. BS, U. Calif., Berkeley, 1937; PhD, Harvard U., 1948. Teaching fellow U. Calif. at Berkeley, 1937-39; economist U.S. WPB, 1940-41; teaching fellow Harvard U., 1941-42; economist U.S. Treasury Dept., 1942-47; prof. econs. MIT, Cambridge, 1947-86, head dept., 1965-83, 84-85, assoc. dean, head fgn. langs. and lits., 1985-86, prof. emeritus, 1986—. Vis. prof. econs. Yale U., 1953-54, U. Chgo., 1963-64; cons. various govt. agys., Brookings Instn., N.Y. State Regents Commn. on Higher Edn., 1992-93. Author: Financing Defense, 1951, Depreciation Adjustments for Price Changes, 1952, Studies in Economic Stabilization, 1967, Paul Samuelson and Modern Economic Theory, 1983; acting editor: Nat. Tax Jour, 1958-59; asso. editor: Jour. Pub. Econs, 1972-81. Guggenheim fellow, 1957; Ford Found. Faculty Research fellow, 1956-57 Mem. Nat. Tax Assn., Am. Econ. Assn., Am. Acad. Arts and Scis., Phi Beta Kappa, Beta Gamma Sigma. Home: Concord Park #313 68 Commonwealth Ave Concord MA 01742-2982 Office: MIT Dept Econs Cambridge MA 02139

BROWN, EDGAR HENRY, JR., mathematician, educator; b. Chgo., Dec. 27, 1926; s. Edgar Henry and Viola (Offen) B.; m. Gail Hamilton, June 13, 1954; children: Jessica, Nicholas. BS, U. Wis., 1949; MS, Wash. State U., 1951; PhD, MIT, 1954. Instr. Washington U., St. Louis, 1954-55, U. Chgo., 1955-57; Office Naval Res. fellow Brown U., 1957-58; faculty Brandeis U., 1958—, prof. math., 1963—. Vis. prof. Yale U., 1993, Math. Inst., Oxford, 1994. Served with USNR, 1944-46. NSF fellow, 1962-63; Guggenheim fellow, 1965-66; Brit. Sci. Research Council fellow, 1973-74, 82-83; sr. research fellow Jesus Coll., Oxford, 1986-87. Mem. Am. Math. Soc., Am. Acad. Arts and Sci. Home: 32 Fisher Ave Newton MA 02461-1117 Office: Brandeis U MS 050 Waltham MA 02454 E-mail: brown@brandeis.edu.

BROWN, EDMUND GERALD See BROWN, JERRY

BROWN, EDWARD JAMES, SR., utility executive; b. Ft. Wayne, Ind., Sept. 30, 1937; s. William Theodore and Jane Elizabeth (Dix) B.; m. Margaret Bessey, June 17, 1989; children: Edward James Jr., Elena Emily. BA, Yale U., 1959; MA, Fordham U., 1962. Chartered fin. analyst. Fin. writer E.F. Hutton & Co., N.Y.C., 1970-71; economist N.Y. Power Authority, N.Y.C., 1971-74, prin. economist, 1974-80, mgr., customer svcs., 1980-83, mgr. spl. projects, 1983-86, dir. strategic planning, 1986-93, dir. new bus., 1993-94. Mem. mgmt. com. Iroquois Gas Transmission System, 1989-94. Pres. Park Ave. Meth. Trust, N.Y.C., 1981—; pres. Friends of the Shakers, Inc., Sabathday Lake, Maine, 1982-84, dir., 1980—, treas., 1995—; trustee United Soc. of Shakers, Sabathday Lake, 1982-84, 95—, John St. Meth. Episcopal Trust Soc., N.Y.C., 1982—; bd. dirs. Meth. Ch. Home for Aged, Riverdale, N.Y., 1995-2001, 2003—, mem. investment com., 1983—, co-chmn., 1994-2003, treas., 1996-2001, pres., 2003—; pres. Meth. Ch. Home Fund, 1996-99; bd. dirs., treas. John Wesley Towers, 1999—; bd. dirs. Yorkville Emergency Alliance, N.Y.C., 1982-88; internat. adv. coun. Mus. of Am. Folk Art, N.Y.C., 1988-2001; dir., chmn. investment com. United Meth. City Soc., N.Y.C., 1999—. Mem. N.Y. Soc. Security Analysts, Assn. Investment Mgmt. and Rsch. Home: 500 E 85th St New York NY 10028-7405

BROWN, EDWARD MAURICE, retired lawyer, business executive; b. Watertown, NY, Aug. 22, 1909; s. Ernest E. and Eunice (Lewis) B.; m. Anne Amos, Oct. 2, 1937; children— Edward Dustin, Ernest Amos. AB magna cum laude, Miami U., 1931, LLD, 1972; JD, Harvard U., 1934. Bar: Ohio 1934, N.Y. 1948, U.S. Supreme Ct. 1941. Assoc. Nichols, Wood, Marx & Ginter, 1934-47; asst. to pres. McCall Corp., N.Y.C., 1947-49, v.p., asst. sec., 1949-51, v.p., sec., dir., 1951-57; treas. Sperry Gyroscope Co. div. Sperry Rand Corp., 1958-59, v.p., treas., 1959-60, v.p., adminstr., 1960-65; v.p. Sperry Group, 1965-68; asst. treas. Sperry Rand Corp., 1958-68; group exec. of Teledyne, Inc., 1968-80; chmn. bd. Teledyne Can. Ltd., 1971-81; ret., 1981. Trustee Village of Pelham Manor, N.Y., 1961-65, village mayor, 1965-67; bd. govs. Nat. Ctr. for Disability Svcs., 1965-93. Lt. comdr. USNR, 1942-45. Decorated Bronze Star with Combat "V" award for svc. Mem. ABA, Phi Beta Kappa, Phi Eta Sigma, Phi Sigma, Beta Theta Pi. Republican. Episcopalian. Home: 25 Ivywood Sq Oxford OH 45056-9494 E-mail: ebrown3@woh.rr.com.

BROWN, EDWIN WILSON, JR., physician, educator; b. Youngstown, Ohio, Mar. 6, 1926; s. Edwin Wilson and Doris (McClellan) B.; m. Patricia Ann Currier, Aug. 9, 1952; children: Edwin Wilson, John Currier, Wende Patricia. Student, Carnegie Inst. Tech., 1943, Houghton Coll., 1946-47, Amherst Coll., 1943-44; MD, Harvard U., 1953, M.P.H. (Nat. Found. fellow), 1957. Research fellow U. Buffalo, 1953-54; intern E.J. Meyer Meml. Hosp., Buffalo, 1954-55; resident pub. health Va. Dept. Health, 1955-56; tchr. medicine specializing in preventive medicine Boston, 1958-61, Hyderabad, India, 1961-63; assoc. med. dir. People-to-People Health Found., Washington, 1965-66; assoc. prof. medicine Ind. U.-Purdue U., Indpls., 1966-85, dir. div. internat. affairs, 1966-74, assoc. dean student services, dir. internat. services, 1979-85; pres. Global Health Svcs., Inc., Indpls., 1986—. Med. dir. Ind. Dept. Correction, 1974-76; sr. med. edn. advisor King Faisal U., Dammam, Saudi Arabia, 1977-78; field dir. Harvard Epidemiol. Project, Egedesminde, Greenland, 1956-57; asst. prof. preventive medicine Sch. Medicine Tufts U., 1958-61; dep. chief staff Boston Dispensary, 1961; vis. prof. preventive medicine Osmania Med. Coll., Hyderabad, India, 1961-63; asst. dir. div. internat. med. edn., dir. AAMC-AID project internat. med. edn. Assn. Am. Med. Colls., Evanston, 1963-65; exec. sec. Study Group on Childhood Accidents, Boston, 1959-61; research asso. Sch. Pub. Health, Harvard U., 1959-60; dir. Curtis Pub. Co., Inc.; cons. Boston City Health Dept., 1959-60, WHO, 1973-74; chmn. bd. dirs. Med. Assistance Programs, Inc. Contbr. articles to profl. jours. Bd. dirs. Paul Carlson Found., Campus Teams, Iran Found., CARE/MEDICO, Internat. Students Inc. Served with AUS, 1944-46, ETO. Recipient Pub. Svc. award Vets. Day Coun. Indpls., 1996, Patriarch of Antioch's award Knight Comdr. of Order of St. Mark, 1998. Fellow Am. Pub. Health Assn.; mem. Assn. Tchrs. Preventive Medicine, Indian Assn. Advancement Med. Edn., Mass. Med. Soc., Internat. Policy Forum (bd. govs.), Nat. Policy Coun., Rotary Internat., Sigma Xi. Home: 8153 Oakland Rd Indianapolis IN 46240-2747 Office: PO Box 40951 Indianapolis IN 46240-0951 E-mail: Ed@TheBrowns.com.

BROWN, ELI MATTHEW, anesthesiologist, department chairman; b. Balt., Apr. 24, 1923; s. Morris and Dora (Poliakoff) B.; m. Estelle Tamus Neidish, May 26, 1948; children: Otto, Morris, Jacqueline Brown Rosenblatt, Barbara Brown Smith. BS, U. Md., 1943; MD, U. Md., Balt., 1946. Diplomate Am. Bd. Anesthesiologists. Intern Jewish Hosp. Bklyn., 1946-47, resident, 1947-48, Valley Forge Gen. Hosp., Phoenixville, Pa., 1948-49; asst. prof. anesthesiology SUNY-Downstate, Bklyn., 1952-54; clin. asst. prof. Wayne State U., Detroit, 1957-61, clin. assoc. prof., 1961-73, prof., 1975-76, chmn., 1976-98, prof. emeritus, 1998—. Chmn. dept. anesthesia Sinai Hosp. Detroit, 1954-91. Contbr. articles to profl. jours. Maj. U.S. Army, 1948-51. Mem. AMA, Am. Soc. Anesthesiologists (pres. Ill. chpt. 1980-81), World Fedn. Soc. Anesthesiologists (del. 1978—), Am. Coll. Grad. Med. Edn., Assn. Univ. Anesthetists, Soc. Acad. Anesthesia Chmn. Avocations: golf, tennis. E-mail: ETMBrown@aol.com.

BROWN, ELIZABETH ANN, foreign service officer; b. Portland, Oreg., Aug. 15, 1918; d. Edwin Keith and Grace Viola (Foss) B. AB, Reed Coll., 1940; postgrad. (teaching fellow), Wash. State Coll., 1940-41; A.M., Columbia, 1943. Exec. asst. to chmn. 12th region WLB, Seattle, 1943-45; internat. affairs officer Dept. State, 1946-56; joined U.S. Fgn. Service, 1956; assigned Office UN Polit. Affairs, Dept. State, 1956-60; 1st sec. Am. embassy, Bonn, Germany, 1960-63; dep. dir. Office UN Polit. Affairs, 1963-65, dir., 1965-69; mem. State Dept. Sr. Seminar in Fgn. Policy, 1969-70; counselor for polit. affairs Am. embassy, Athens, Greece, 1970-75, dep. chief mission The Hague, Netherlands, 1975-78; sr. insp. Dept. State, 1978-79, cons., 1980—; ret., 1979. Adviser U.S. del. UN Gen. Assembly, 1946-50, 53, 55, 57-59, 64-65 Recipient 7th ann. Fed. Woman's award, 1967 Mem. Am. Fgn. Service Assn., Phi Beta Kappa. Home: 4848 Reservoir Rd NW Washington DC 20007-1561 Office: Dept State Washington DC 20007

BROWN, ELIZABETH ELEANOR, retired librarian; b. Charlotte, Mich., Aug. 29, 1921; d. Delbert Francis and Katherine Eleanor (Griffith) Brown. AB, Albion Coll., 1943; MLS, Pratt Inst., 1953. Info. specialist Enjay Co., N.Y.C., 1943-50; reports indexer Bakelite Co., Bound Brook, N.J., 1950-52; reference libr. IBM, Poughkeepsie, NY, 1953-69, Yorktown Heights, N.Y., 1953-69, info. retrieval specialist, libr. White Plains, N.Y., 1969-82, ret., 1982. Vol. Nat. Archives Rocky Mountain Region, 1986—; mem. del. spl. librs. to Russia and Czech Republic Citizen Amb. program People to People Internat., 1995. Mem.: DAR, ALA, Spl. Librs. Assn. (sec.-treas. engring. divsn. 1968—70, chmn. tech. sci. group N.Y.C. chpt 1970—71, archivist 1970—72, past pres. Hudson Valley chpt.), Am. Chem. Soc., Remsen-Steuben Hist. Soc., Eaton County Geneal. Soc., Kalamazoo Valley Geneal. Soc., Wales, Ireland, Scotland and Eng. Family Hist. Soc., Internat. Soc. Brit. Genealogy and Family History, Soc. Mayflower Descs., Pilgrim John Howland Soc., New Eng. Hist. Geneal. Soc., Colo. Geneal. Soc., Colo. Mayflower Soc., Gwynedd Family History Soc., Columbine Geneal. and Hist. Soc., Welsh-Am. Geneal. Soc., Colo. Welsh Soc., Grand Traverse Area Geneal. Soc., Rowe Hist. Soc., Mortar Bd., Phi Beta Kappa, Delta Zeta, Alpha Lambda Delta.

BROWN, ELIZABETH SCHMECK, fashion historian; b. Ancon, Panama, Sept. 7, 1918; d. Henry Penuel and Pansy Blossom (Logan) Schmeck; m. Walter Daniel Brown, July 29, 1944; children: David Henry, Walter Daniel Jr., Edward Logan, Kenneth Maclin. Student, U. Tex., 1935—37; BS, Cornell U., 1940, MS, 1945; student, Art Students League N.Y. Cert. family and consumer scis. AAFCS. Instr. textiles and clothing, curator costume collection Coll. Home Econs. Cornell U., Ithaca, NY, 1941—45; assoc. home economist McCall Pattern Co., N.Y.C., 1963—65; assoc. Uno Pattern Co., N.J. and Pa., 1972—74; lectr. on hist. dress, 1972—; appraiser of hist. dress, 1978—. Contbr. articles to profl. publs.; curated exhbns., NJ Divsn. on Women, Trenton, Kemmerer Mus., Bethelehem, Pa., Antiques at the Armory, Phila., Rutgers Inst. for Rsch. on Women, New Brunswick, N.J., N.J. Hist. Commn. Mem. Montgomery Twp. Bd. Edn., Skillman, NJ, 1969—81, various offices, including pres., 1975—77; legis. chmn., pres. Somerset County Sch. Bds. Assn., Somerville, NJ, 1977—80; testified to State Legis. and Bd. Edn. for mandate of Family Life Edn.; active N.J. Network Family Life, 1983—2002; mem. adv. coun. Family, Career, and Cmty. Leadership Am., 2001—; bd. dirs. Costume and Textile Group N.J., 2001—; bd. dir. (former treas.) Wesley Found., 1984—, Princeton U.; mem. PTA, Pitts.; pres. Whittier Sch., Park Ridge, Ill.; founding com. River-Ridge Council, Broomall, Pa. Fellow: Costume Soc. Am. (treas. 1980—86, bd. dirs. several terms 1982—, Bd. of Dir., several terms 1982—2004, corr. sec. 1986—92, pres. region II 1993—97, v.p. internal rels. 1998—2003, parliamentarian, bd. dirs.); mem.: AAUW (pres. Princeton br. 1973—75), N.J. Assn. Family and Consumer Scis. (state pres.'s unit nom. com., divsn. chair, apparel and textiles, archives and history), Am. Assn. Family and Consumer Scis. (nat. leader 1992), Van Harlingen Hist. Soc. (former trustee), Hist. Soc. Princeton (collections com.), Internat. Textile and Apparel Assn., N.J. Assn. Mus., PTA Pitts. (various offices), Internat. Sewing Machine Collectors Soc., Am. Assn. State and Local History, Cornell Alumni Assn., Princeton YWCA (vol. Friday Club 1968—2000), Y Canoe Club, Cornell Woman's Club (Pitts.) (pres., chair sec. sch. com.), Friday (com. mem. 2000—), Cornell Woman's Club (Chgo.), Cornell Woman's Club (Phila.), Phi Kappa Phi, Kappa Omicron Nu, Alpha Lambda Delta. Achievements include testified to State legislature and Bd. of Edn. for mandate of Family Life Edn; in process in 3-5 yrs. of giving my costume collection to the collection at the Coll. of Human Ecology there. Avocations: costume collection of over 2000 items, collecting antique paper patters, collecting antique sewing machines and other sewing items. Home and Office: 45 Whippoorwill Way Belle Mead NJ 08502 Fax: 908-874-7590 . E-mail: ebrown@nerc.com.

BROWN, EPHRAIM TAYLOR, JR., lawyer; b. Birmingham, Ala., Aug. 31, 1920; s. Ephraim Taylor and Lida (Otts) B.; m. Clara DeBardeleben Ebaugh, Oct. 21, 1949; children: Ephraim Taylor III, Clara DeBardeleben, Lida Otts. AB, Princeton U., 1941; LLB, Cornell U., 1943. Bar: Ala. 1943. Pvt. practice, Birmingham; assoc. Cabaniss, Johnston, Gardner, Dumas & O'Neal, 1943-52, ptnr., 1952-91; of counsel, 1992—. Chmn. spl. com. Revision Probate Laws Ala., 1967; chmn. bd. bar examiners Ala. State Bar, 1967-79. Bd. dirs. Childrens Fresh Air Farm; trustee, elder, deacon local Presbyn. ch. Fellow Am. Coll. Trust and Estate Counsel; mem. ABA, Ala. Bar Assn. (pres.), Birmingham Bar Assn., Ala. Law Inst. (mem. counsel), Birmingham Country Club, Sigma Alpha Epsilon. Home: 12 Cross Creek Park Birmingham AL 35213-2302 Office: PO Box 830612 2001 Park Pl Ste 700 Birmingham AL 35203-4804

BROWN, ERIC D. city planner, consultant, researcher; b. Akron, Ohio, June 13, 1976; s. Terrence E. and Denise Brown. BA, Ohio U., Athens, 1998; MBA, Frederick Taylor U., Moraga, Calif., 2001. Campaign cons. Dem. Nat. Com., Washington, 1998. Chmn. Zanesville Housing Adv. Com., 1999—; bd. dirs. Minority Bus. Resource Network, Zanesville, 1999—, Habitat for Humanity, Zanesville, 2000—; chmn. Muskegan County Dem. Club, Zanesville, 2000. Mem.: Ohio Conf. Cmty. Devel., Nat. Assn. Housing Redevelopment Ofcls., Am. Planning Assn., APSA. Democrat. Apostolic. Avocations: travel, golf, politics, theater, cultural arts. Home: 544 Brookover Ave Apt 7 Zanesville OH 43701 Office: City of Zanesville 401 Market St Zanesville OH 43701

BROWN, ERIC JOEL, biomedical researcher, researcher; b. Ann Arbor, Mich., Sept. 27, 1950; s. Bernard and Shirley (Mark) B.; m. Marion Glynn Peters, Apr. 2, 1983; 1 child, Abigail. AB, Harvard Coll., 1971; MD, Harvard Med. Sch., 1975. Intern, then resident Beth Israel Hosp., Boston, 1975-77; clin. assoc. LCI/NIAID/NIH, Bethesda, Md., 1977-79, expert, 1979-81, sr. investigator, 1981-85; assoc. prof. Washington U., St. Louis, 1985-90, co-dir. divsn. infectious diseases, 1989-99, prof., 1990-99; prof. medicine and immunology U. Calif., San Francisco, 1999—. With USPHS, 1981-85. Fellow Infectious Diseases Soc.; mem. Soc. for Clin. Investigation, Am. Assn. Physicians. Office: U Calif San Francisco PO Box 0654 San Francisco CA 94143-0001 E-mail: ebrown@medicine.ucsf.edu

BROWN, ERNEST CHRISTOPHER, lawyer, engineer; b. Reno, Nev., Dec. 12, 1953; 1 child, Christopher Sheridan. S.B., MIT, 1975; J.D., U. Calif.-Berkeley, 1978. Bar: Calif. 1978, U.S. Dist. Ct. (no. dist.) Calif. 1978, U.S. Dist. Ct. (cen. dist.) Calif. 1981. Trial lawyer Bronson, Bronson & McKinnon, San Francisco, 1978-81; corp. counsel Fluor Corp., Irvine, Calif., 1981-84; ptnr. Snodling, Yocca, Carlson & Routh, Newport Beach, Calif., 1984—; adj. faculty U. Calif.-Irvine Grad. Sch. Mgmt. Co-author: Architect-Engineer Malpractice, 1980. Recipient Karl T. Compton prize MIT, 1975; Harmon Legal Writing prize U. Calif.-Berkeley, 1977, Amjur award, 1978. Mem. ABA (forum com. constrn. industry), Calif. Bar Assn., Orange County Bar Assn. Office: 660 Newport Center Dr 16th Floor Newport Beach CA 92660

BROWN, FRANCES LOUISE (GRANDMA FRAN), artist, art gallery owner; b. Indpls., Oct. 19, 1925; d. Harley and Lenore (Spencer) Netherland; m. C.G. Clarkson, July 24, 1943 (div. Aug. 1967); children: James E. Clarkson, John B. Clarkson, Deborah L. Cromis. Thomas L. Currey, June 9, 1972 (dec. May 1978); m. George L. Brown, Jr., Mar. 3, 1982; 1 stepchild, Nancy Snow. BS in Edn., Miami U., 1968; MA in Edn., Ball State U., 1970. Elem. sch. tchr. Liberty (Ind.) Elem. Sch., 1968-71; tchr. Ball State U., Muncie, Ind., 1971-72; instr. Colby (Kans.) C.C., 1972-75; gallery owner, primitive artist Grandma Fran Art Gallery (formerly Currey Studio Gallery), Berryville, Ark., 1975—. Author: Now Hear This, 1974; works exhibited at Nat. Mus. Am. Art, Washington, Wichita (Kans.) Art Assn. Gallery, Ark. Coll., Batesville, South Ark. Art Ctr., El Dorado, Harding Coll., Searcy, Ark., U. Ark., Fayetteville, Eureka Springs (Ark.) Hist. Mus., Western State Coll. Colo., Gunnison, MacMurray Coll., Jacksonville, Ill., Colby (Kans.) Coll., Claremore (Okla.) Coll., Warren Hall Coutts, III, Meml. Art Gallery, Inc., El Dorado, Kans., Masur Mus. Art, Monroe, La., Nebr. State Hist. Soc. Mus., Lincoln, Ind. State Mus., Indpls., Ozark Folk Ctr., Mountain View, Ark., Ft. Smith (Ark.) Art Ctr., Ctr. for So. Folklore, Memphis, Rogers (Ark.) Hist. Mus., Albrecht Art Mus., St. Joseph, Mo., Shiloh Mus., Springdale, Ark., Internat. Ctr. Contemporary Art, Paris, John Judkyn Meml. Mus., Eng., Mykonos (Greece) Folklore Mus., Musees Royaux des Beaux-Arts de Belgique, Brussels, Setagaya Art Mus., Tokyo; represented in permanent collections Fukuoka City, Japan, Smithsonian Instn., Washington, Mus. Am. Folk Art, N.Y.C., Nebr. State Hist. Soc. Mus., Lincoln, Ind. State Mus., Indpls., Ozark Mountain Folk Ctr., Mountain View, Ctr. for So. Folklore, Memphis, others; paintings recognized in various books, newspapers and articles. Avocations: pilot, sewing, reading, fishing, cooking. Home and Office: Grandma Fran Art Gallery 3331 Highway 62 W Berryville AR 72616-8948

BROWN, FRANCIS WILLIAM, chemist, consultant; b. Mpls., Dec. 1, 1922; m. Lorraine Alice Wagner, Oct. 2, 1954; children: David Charles, James Francis. BSChemE, U. Minn., 1944. Chemist Minn. Mining and Mfg. Co., St. Paul, 1944-70, supr., 1970-73, sr. specialist, 1973-76, corp. scientist, 1976-89; ret., 1989. Cons. 3M, Minn. Mining and Mfg. Co., St. Paul, 1989-2001. Inventor in field. Recipient 3M Carlton award. Mem. Am. Chem. Soc. Home: 8924 Hunters Way Apple Valley MN 55124

BROWN, FRANK, social science educator; b. Gallian, Ala., May 1, 1935; s. Tom and Ora L. (Lomax) B.; m. Joan Drake, July 6, 1963; children: Frank G., Monica J. BS, Ala. State U., 1957; MS, Oreg. State U., 1962; MA, U. Calif., Berkeley, 1969, PhD, 1970. Sci. tchr. Oakland Pub. Schs. (Calif.), 1962-68; assoc. dir. N.Y. Com. on Edn., N.Y.C., 1970-72; dir. Urban Inst. CCNY, 1971-72; prof., coll. master SUNY, Buffalo, 1972-77; dean U. N.C., Chapel Hill, 1983-90, Cary C. Boshamer prof. edn., dir. ednl. rsch. and policy project studies for rsch. in social sci., 1990—. Vis. scholar U. Calif., Berkeley, 1990-91; project dir. Ford Found., N.Y.C., 1973-76, Spencer Found., Buffalo, 1976-78, NSF, Washington, 1979-80. Author: (with others) Fleischmann Commn. Report, 1973, Minority Enrollment in U.S. Institutions of Higher Education, 1977; contbr. articles to Ednl. Forum, Ednl. Researcher, Jour. Negro Edn., Jour. Black Studies, Am. Sch. Bd. Jour., numerous others; book series editor: Excellence Equity, Diversity, 1992—; editor: Emergent Leadership, 1976-80; guest editor: Edn. and Urban Soc., 1978, 89; editorial bds. Jour. Negro Edn., Jour. Ednl. Policy, Edn. and Urban Soc., Jour. Equity and Leadership, NABSE Jour., others. Bd. dirs. Buffalo Urban League, 1976-82; trustee White Rock Bapt. Ch., Durham, N.C., 1990—; chair Black Faculty/Staff caucus U. N.C., Chapel Hill, 1993-94. Grad. fellow Washington U., St. Louis, 1958, Oreg. State U., 1961, U. Calif.-Berkeley, 1968, fellow Rockefeller Found., 1979 Mem. Am. Ednl. Rsch. Assn. (sec. div. A 1980-82, v.p. 1986-88), Nat. Orgn. Legal Problems of Edn. (editorial bd. 1979-80, bd. dirs. 1990—), Assn. Social and Behavioral Scientists, Am. Assn. Colls. for Tchr. Edn. (bd. dirs. 1988—), Nat. Assn. Multicultural Edn., Assn. Sch. Bus. Ofcls. Internat., Am. Ednl. Fin. Assn., Am. Ednl. Rsch. Assn. (com. on minority affairs 1998—), Phi Delta Kappa, Alpha Phi Alpha (chpt. pres. 1977-78). Democrat. Baptist. Office: U NC Peabody Hall CB 3500 Chapel Hill NC 27599-3500

BROWN, FRANK EUGENE, JR., lawyer; b. Okemah, Okla., May 30, 1941; s. Frank Eugene and Mary Lois (Knie) B.; m. Gail Hart, Sept. 30, 1967; children— Christopher Matthew, Meredith Claire. B.A. in Physics Engring., Washington and Lee U., 1963. J.D. summa cum laude, 1965. Bar: Va. 1965, U.S. Dist. Ct. (ea. and we. dists.) Va. 1965, U.S. Supreme Ct. 1971, U.S. Ct. Appeals (4th cir.) 1976, U.S. Ct. Appeals (D.C. cir.) 1978. Law clk. to chief judge U.S. Dist. Ct. (we. dist.) Va., Roanoke, 1965-66; teaching asst. Washington and Lee Sch. Law, Lexington, Va., 1965-66; ptnr. Adams, Porter, Radigan & Mays, Arlington, Va., 1970-74, Barham, Radigan, Suiters & Brown, P.C., Arlington, 1974-86, ptnr. Tolbert, Smith, Fitzgerald & Stackhouse, 1986-87, Mays & Valentine (merged with Tolbert, Smith & Fitzerald), Arlington, 1987—; adj. prof. Potomac Sch. Law, Washington, 1974-75. Mem. Christian social relations com. St. Paul's Episc. Ch., Alexandria, Va., 1981-82; trustee Randolph-Macon Acad., Front Royal, Va., Served to capt. USAF, 1966-70. Mem. Va. State Bar (10th dist. grievance com. 1976-79), Va. Bar Assn. (profl. responsibility com. 1981—), Phi Beta Kappa, Order of Coif, Omicron Delta Kappa, Sigma Phi Epsilon, Phi Alpha Delta. Republican. Home: 504 Woodland Ter Alexandria VA 22302-3317 Office: Mays & Valentine 1660 International Dr # 600 Mc Lean VA 22102-4848

BROWN, FREDERIC JOSEPH, army officer; b. Fort Sill, Okla., July 18, 1934; s. Frederic Joseph and Kathryn (Richardson) B.; m. Harriette Anne Upham, July 7, 1956; children: Kathryn, Harriette, Judith. BS, U.S. Military Acad., 1956; MA, Grad. Inst. Internat. Studies, U. Geneva, Switzerland, 1963, PhD, 1967. Commd. officer U.S. Army, advanced through grades to lt. gen.; comdr. 1st squadron 4th cavalry, 1969-70; mem. staff Nat. Security Council, 1972-73; comdr. 1st Tiger brigade 2d Armored Divsn., Ft. Hood, Tex., 1975-76; comdr. U.S. Army Tng. Center Armor, Ft. Knox, Ky., 1977-78; asst. div. comdr. 8th Inf. Div. Baumholder, W. Ger., 1978-81; dep. chief of staff tng. U.S. Army Tng. and Doctrine Command, Ft. Monroe, Va., 1981-82; comdg. gen., chief armor U.S. Army Armor Ctr., Ft. Knox, Ky., 1983-86; comdr. 4th U.S. Army, Ft. Sheridan, Ill., 1986-89. Asst. prof. dept. polit. scis. U.S. Mil. Acad., West Point, N.Y.; mem. adj. rsch. staff Inst. for Def. Analyses; cons. in tng. tech. and devel.;

advisor to Dept. Def. tng. of fgn. armies, 1995—; advisor to Dept. of Army design of advanced learning for future Army, 1997—. Author: Chemical Warfare--A Study in Restraints, 1968 The United States Army in Transition II: Landpower in the Information Age, 1993; co-author: The United States Army in Transition, 1973; author numerous papers on info. age tng. for Inst. for Def. Analyses, 1989-2002; co-producer TV series on U.S. Army post-Vietnam All We Could Be, 1995-2002; developer advanced tng. policies and programs for U.S. Army Force XXI, 1996-98; designer Army R&D of advanced learning and leader devel., 2000—. Decorated D.S.M. with oak leaf cluster, Silver Star, Legion of Merit; Olmsted scholar, 1961-63 Mem. Coun. Fgn. Relas., Internat. Inst. Strategic Studies. Episcopalian. Home: 6317 Stoneham Ln Mc Lean VA 22101-2346 Office: Inst for Defense Analyses Simulation Lab 1801 N Beauregard St Alexandria VA 22311-1701 E-mail: fbrown@ida.org. *The essence of satisfaction is service to others. In my case, the opportunity to defend the values and wealth of our great nation.*

BROWN, FREDERICK CALVIN, physicist, educator; b. Seattle, July 6, 1924; s. Fred Charles and Rose (Mueller) B.; m. Joan Schauble, Aug. 9, 1952; children— Susan, Gail, Derek. BS, Harvard U., 1945, MS, 1947, PhD, 1950. Physicist Systems Research Lab., Harvard (NDRC), 1945-46; staff physicist Naval Research Lab., Washington, 1950; physicist Applied Physics Lab., U. Wash., 1950-51; asst. prof. Reed Coll., Portland, Oreg., 1951-55, U. Ill., Urbana, 1955-58, assoc. prof., 1958-61, prof., 1961-87, prof. emeritus, 1987—; assoc. Center for Advanced Study, 1969-70; prin. scientist, area mgr. Xerox Palo Alto (Calif.) Rsch. Ctr., 1973-74; prof. physics U. Wash., Seattle, 1987-99, prof. emeritus, 1999—. Vis. mem. St. Johns Coll., Oxford, Eng., 1964-65; cons. prof., applied physics dept. Stanford U., 1973-74 Author: The Physics of Solids-Ionic Crystals, Lattice Vibrations and Imperfections, 1967; Contbr. articles profl. jours. Recipient Alexander von Humboldt sr. scientist award U. Kiel, 1978; NSF sr. postdoctoral fellow Clarendon Lab., Oxford, 1964-65 Fellow Am. Phys. Soc. Achievements include being innovator in use of synchrotron radiation for spectroscopy; first observation of polaron mobility and mass in ionic crystals, luminescence and lifetime of point defects such as f-centers, charge density waves in layered crystals, and early photoemission experiments on high temperature superconductors. Home: 5915 25th Ave W Everett WA 98203-1468

BROWN, FREDERICK LEE, health care executive; b. Clarksburg, W.Va., Oct. 22, 1940; s. Claude Raymond and Anne Elizabeth (Kiddy) B.; m. Shirley Fiille Brown; children: Gregory Lee, Michael Owen-Price, Kyle Stephen, Kathryn Alexis. BA in Psychology, Northwestern U., 1962; MBA in Health Care Adminstrn., George Washington U., 1966; LHD (hon.), U. Mo., 1995. Vocat. counselor Cook County Dept. Pub. Aid, Chgo., 1962-64; from adminstrv. resident to v.p. ops. Meth. Hosp. Ind., Inc., Indpls., 1965—72, v.p. ops., 1972-74; exec. v.p., chief operating officer Meml. Hosp. DuPage County, Elmhurst, Ill., 1974-82, Meml. Health Svcs., Elmhurst, 1980-82; pres., CEO CH Health Techs., Inc., St. Louis, 1983-93; CEO Christian Health Svcs., St. Louis, 1986-93; pres., CEO CH Allied Svcs., Inc., St. Louis, 1988-93, Christian Health Svcs., St. Louis, 1986—93, BJC Health Sys., St. Louis, 1993—98, vice-chmn., 1999—2000; pres., CEO Christian Hosp. NE-NW, 1982—89, chmn., CEO, 1992—93. Adj. instr. Washington U. Sch. Medicine, St. Louis, 1982—2001; mem. chancellor's coun. U. Mo., 1990—94; mem. exec. com. HealthLink, Inc., 1986—92; pres., chief exec. officer Village North, Inc., 1986—93; chmn. shareholder comm. com. Am. Healthcare Systems, Inc., 1985—86, vice chmn., 1992; bd. dirs. Commerce Bank St. Louis, Am. Excess Inc. Ltd.; mem. corp. assembly Blue Cross Blue Shield Mo., 1991—95; vis. scholar, exec. in residence The George Washington U., 2001—02. Contbr. articles to profl. jours. Co-chmn. hosp. divsn. United Way Greater St. Louis, 1983, chmn., 1984, chmn. health svcs. divsn., 1985—86, vice chmn. region, 1988, bd. dirs., 1986—2001, exec. com., 1991—, chmn. audit com., 1992—2001; active Kammergild Chamber ORch., 1984—88, v.p., 1985—88, bd. dirs., 1987—91; active Mo. Heart Inst., 1988—92, Alton Meml. Hosp., 1987—91, bd. dirs., 1987—91; mem. exec. bd. St. Louis Area coun. Boy Scouts Am., 1989—2000, activities coun. chmn., 1993—95; chmn. Friends of Scouting Campaign, 1991—92; mem. medicaid budget trak force Mo. Dept. Social Svcs., 1990; mem. emergency rm. svcs. task force St. Louis Regional Med. Ctr., 1985; mem. corp. assembly Blue Cross Blue Shield of Mo., 1991; bd. dirs. Sold on St. Louis, 1991—93, St. Louis Reg. Commerce & Growth Assn., 1993—98; bd. trustees Webster Hills Math. Ch., 1990—92, commuunion steward, 1987. Fellow Am. Coll. Healthcare Execs. (chmn. credentials com. 1978, task force governance and constituencies 1986-87; mem. Gold Medal award com. 1985, chmn. task force on governance and constituencies 1986-87, com. on ethics 1989-91, chmn. awards & testimonials com., 1992-93, bd. regents 1991-93); gov. dist V, 1993-98; mem. Am. Acad. Med. Adminstrs. (life, state dir. 1988—, Health Care Exec. of Yr. 1990, Statesman in Healthcare, 1992), Hosp. Pres.'s Assn., Advt. Club Greater St. Louis, Am. Hosp. Assn. (coun. on mgmt. 1987, alt. del. for healthcare systems 1988-90, del. to ho. of dels. for health care systems 1991, fin. com. chair 1995, chair-elect 1998, chmn. 1999-2000), Am. Pub. Health Assn., George Washington U. Alumni Assn. for Health Svcs. Adminstrn. (preceptor 1975-93, Alumnus of Yr. award 1981, Frederick Gibbs award, 1993), Hosp. Assn. Met. St. Louis (bd. dirs. 1984-94, chmn. bd. 1988-89, sec. 1985-86, treas. 1987, chmn. coun. on pub. affairs and comms. 1985, vice chmn. 1987, various coms.), Greater St. Louis Health Care Alliance (co-chair 1992-96), Mo. Hosp. Assn. (mem. coun. on rsch. and policy devel. 1983-88, chmn. coun. on multi-instnl. hosps. 1986-88, mem. dist. coun. pres.'s 1986-89, bd. dirs. 1988-92, chmn. bd. trustees 1990), Cen. Ea. Profl. Rev. Orgn. (bd. dirs. 1982-85, various coms.), St. Louis Met. Med. Soc. (lay advisor 1990-92), Healthcare Execs. Study Soc., Internat. Health Policy and Mgmt. Inst. (bd. dirs. 1988—), Am. Protestant Health Assn. (bd. dirs. 1988-93, chmn. 1992-93), Pinnacle Peak Country Club, Forest Highlands Country Club. Republican. Home: 8409 E La Junta Rd Scottsdale AZ 85255-2859 also: 724 Forest Highlands Flagstaff AZ 86001 Office: Northern Ariz Healthcare 1200 North Beauer St Flagstaff AZ 86001 E-mail: fred.brown@nahealth.com.

BROWN, GARDNER RUSSELL, engineering executive; b. Sterling, Mass. m. Sondra Jupin Gillice, Jan. 12, 1980; children: Kevin, Stephen, Thomas. BS in Mech. and Nuclear Engring., USN, 1955. Project mgr U.S. AEC, Washington, 1953-71; mgr. Northeast Utilities Svc. Co., Berlin, Conn., 1971-73; dept. head Potomac Electric Power Co., Washington, 1971-88; CEO RusSon, Inc., Engrs. and Ind. Power Developers, Arlington, Va., 1981—. Asst. to chmn. Rep. Nat. Com. Conv., Dallas, 1984. Comdr. USN, 1945-70, PTO, Korea. Decorated Purple Hearts. Mem. Am. Nuclear Soc., U.S. Mex. C. of C., Explorers Club, Edgartown Yacht Club, Army Navy Club, Army Navy Country Club. Republican. Episcopalian. Achievements include patent in field. Office: RusSon Inc 1745 Jefferson Davis Hwy Arlington VA 22202-3402

BROWN, GARY SANDY, electrical engineering educator; b. Jackson, Miss., Apr. 13, 1940; s. John Leo and Welma (Kelley) B.; m. Mary Kathleen Connaughton, Mar. 16, 1970; children: Joshua John, Nathan Matthew. BSEE, U. Ill., 1963, MS, 1964, PhDEE, 1967. Grad. rsch. asst. Antenna Lab. U. Ill., Urbana, 1963-67; mem. tech. staff TRW Systems Group, Redondo Beach, Calif., 1969-70; sr. engr. Rsch. Triangle Inst., Durham, N.C., 1970-73; sr. scientist Applied Sci. Assocs., Apex, N.C., 1973-85; prof. elect. engring. Va. Poly. Inst. and State U., Blacksburg, 1985—, apptd. Bradley disting. prof. electromagnetics, 2002. With Wallops Flight Facility, NASA, Wallops Island, Va., 1974; cons. Naval Rsch. Lab., Washington, 1988-91, Decision Scis. Applications, Arlington, Va., 1988-91, DTI Inc., Torrance, Calif., 1987-91, Applied Physics Lab., Laurel, Md., 1987-88, Waste Policy Inst., Blacksburg, Va., 1991—, Motorola Corp., Chandler, Ariz., 1991-93; mem. NATO AGARD Electromagnetic Propogation Panel, 1993—; dir. Electromagnetic Interactions Lab. Contbr. chpts. to books, articles to profl. jours. Capt. U.S. Army, 1967-69. Recipient Best Paper awards R.W.P. King, 1978, Schelkunoff, 1999, Bradley Disting. Prof. Electromagnetics, 2002. Fellow IEEE (Third Millenium award 2000); mem. Antennas and Propagation Soc. of IEEE (pres. 1988), Am. Geophys. Union (editor's citation Radio Sci., Am. sects. 1986), Internat. Union of Radio Sci. (mem.-at-large 1987, sec. U.S. nat. com. 1997-99, chair U.S. nat. com. 2000-2002), NATO AGARD Sensors and Propagation Panel. Avocations: backpacking, jogging. Office: Va Poly Inst & State U Bradley Dept Elec Engr Blacksburg VA 24061

BROWN, GARY WAYNE, lawyer; b. Picher, Okla., Apr. 7, 1942; s. Andrew Ellis and Rosabell (Duree) Brown; m. Alice Jo Bell Brown, Feb. 15, 1969; children: Marc Andrew, Joshua Lawrence. AA, Norteastern Okla. A&M Jr. Coll., 1962; BS, U. Okla., 1964; JD, 1967. Bar: Okla. 1967, US Ct. Appeals for the Armed Forces 1968, DC 1970, US Dist. Ct./DC 1970, US Supreme Ct. 1974, US Ct. Fed. Claims 1976, Va. 1978, US Dist. Ct. (ea. dist.)/Va. 1978, US Ct. Appeals/DC, US Ct. Appeals (4th cir.). With Sachs, Greenebaum, Frohlich & Tayler, Washington, 1970—72; ptnr. Macleay, Lynch, bernhard, Gregg & Attridge, Washington, 1972—85, Bromley, Brown & Walsh, 1985—90; ptnr., mng. ptnr. Miles & Stockbridge, Fairfax, 1990—95; prin., chmn. bd. McClandish & Lillard, PC; adj. prof. law Georgetown U., 1970—74; adj. asst. prof. med. sch., 1994—97. Contbr. book. Lt. JAG USNR, 1967—70. Mem.: The Counsellors, Internat. Acad. Trial Lawyers, Intl. Assn. Def. Counsel, Am. Health Lawyers Assn., Va. Def. Lawyers, DC Def. Lawyers (pres. 1984, Lawyer of the Yr. 1996), Def. Rsch. Inst., Salvation Army (Fairfax County 1994—), Juvenile Diabetes Found. (co-pres., bd. dir., No. Va. chpt. 1980—81). Democrat. Episc. Home: 4909 Rock Spring Rd Arlington VA 22207-2705 Office: McLandlish & Lillard PC Fair Oaks Plaza 11350 Random Hills Rd Fairfax VA 22030-6044 E-mail: gwb@mclandlaw.com.

BROWN, GENE W. steel company executive; b. Warsaw, Ind., Feb. 16, 1936; s. Dean L. and Ilean (Clase) B.; m. Beverly A. Sink, Feb. 25, 1956; children: Lisa Jo, Scott Eugene. BSME, Purdue U., 1960; MBA, Northwestern U., 1967. Engr. Ill. Tool Works, Chgo., 1957-67; gen. mgr. Chgo. Gasket Co., 1967-69; ops. mgr. Maremont Corp., Harvey, Ill., 1969-74; gen. mgr. Marmon Group, Chgo., 1974-77; pres. Whittar Steel Strip, Detroit, 1977-88, Lisco Inc., Detroit, 1979—. Home: 6322 Palma Del Mar Blvd S # 9024 Saint Petersburg FL 33715-2700 also: 677 N 175 W Valparaiso IN 46385-8542 Office: Brownco Inc 277 Melton Rd Chesterton IN 46304-9746

BROWN, GEORGE E. judge, educator; b. Hammond, Ind., July 27, 1947; s. George E. and Violet M. (Matlon) B.; m. Patricia A. Schneider, June 6, 1970; children: Janet M., Elizabeth A. BS, Ball State U., 1969; JD, DePaul U., 1974; grad., Ind. Jud. Coll., 1996. Bar: Ind. 1974, Ill. 1974, U.S. Dist. Ct. (no. dist.) Ind. 1979, U.S. Supreme Ct. 1977, U.S. Tax Ct. 1977. Pvt. practice, LaGrange & Lake Counties, Ind., 1974-84; judge LaGrange County Ct., 1984-87, LaGrange Superior Ct., 1988—. Part-time chief dep. prosecutor LaGrange County, 1975—77; adj. faculty Tri-State U., Angola, Ind., 1991—. Vol. Jr. Achievement, 1997—. Mem.: ABA, Nat. Conf. State Trial Judges (criminal justice com.), Ind. Judges Assn. (com. protective orders), LaGrange County Bar Assn. (pres. 1978), Ind. State Bar Assn. (ho. of dels., com. on improvements in the jud. sys.), Rotary (past dir., v.p. 1999—2000, pres. 2000—01, bd. dirs. 2002—). Office: Lagrange Superior Ct Courthouse Lagrange IN 46761

BROWN, GEORGE LESLIE, legislative affairs and business development consultant, former manufacturing company executive, former lieutenant governor; b. Lawrence, Kans., July 1, 1926; s. George L. and Harriett Alberta (Watson) B.; m. Modeen; children: Gail Brown Chandler, Laura Nicole, Kim Doreen, Cynthia Renee; stepchildren: Ronnie, Carol, Angela, Sharolyn, Nyra. BJ, U. Kans., 1950; postgrad., U. Colo., 1950-51; A.M.P., Harvard Bus. Sch., 1980. Mem. writing staff Denver Post, 1950-65; asst. exec. dir. Denver Housing Authority, 1965-69; exec. dir. Met. Denver Urban Coalition, 1969-75; lt. gov. Colo. Denver, 1974-79; v.p. Grumman Corp., N.Y., 1979-90; assoc. Whitten & Diamond (formerly Lipsen, Whitten & Diamond), Washington, 1990-94; dir. Prudential Securities, 1994-97; of counsel Moser and Moser Law Firm, 1994—; v.p. L. Robert Kimball, Archtl. Engrs.; sr. v.p. Greenwich Ptnrs. Bd. dirs. Davis and Elkins Coll., Washington Trade Ctr., Joint Ctr. for Polit. Studies, Boys Choir of Harlem, Coll. Aeros., Air Force Meml. Found. Mem. Colo. Ho. of Reps., 1955, Colo. Senate, 1956-74. Served with USAAF, 1944-46. Recipient Adam Clayton Powell award for polit. achievement, 1975, Opportunities Industrialization Center Nat. Govt. award, 1975; George Brown Urban Journalism scholarship established at U. Kans. William Allen White Sch. Journalism, 1976 Mem. Kappa Alpha Psi. Office: Greenwich Partners 1090 Vermont Ave NW Ste 800 Washington DC 20005-4961

BROWN, SIR GEORGE NOEL, chief justice; b. Gales Point Village, Belize, June 13, 1942; s. Noel Todd and Elma Priscilla (O'Brien) B.; m. Eleanor Marie Williams, June 5, 1962 (div. May 1972); children: Georgia Yvette Marie, Aubrey Noel David, Marsha Elizabeth, Roxanne Patricia; m. Magdalene Elizabeth Bucknor, Aug. 24, 1974. Cert. in pub. adminstrn., Carlton U., Ottawa, Ont., Can., 1970; LLB with 2d class honors, U. W.I., Barbados, 1976; cert. in legal edn., Norman Manley Law Sch., Kingston, Jamaica, 1978; cert. in legis. drafting, Commonwealth Secretariat Law Sch., Nairobi, Kenya, 1979. Customs examiner Belize Customs and Excise Dept., Belize City, 1960-67; clk. of cts. Belize Magistrates Cts., Belize City, 1967-69; adminstrv. asst. Belize Ministry Trade and Industry, Belize City, 1970-72; lay magistrate, various cities, Belize, 1972-73; crown counsel Atty. Gen.'s Ministry, Belmopan, Belize, 1978-81, solicitor gen., 1981-84; puisne judge Belize Supreme Ct., Belize City, 1984-90, chief justice, 1990-98; law revsion commr. Law Revision Office, Belize City, 1998-99; legal cons., 2000—. Dep. gov. gen. Gov. Gen's. Office, Belize, 1986—95; mem. Belize Adv. Coun., 1986—88, sr. mem., 1988—2002; mem. prison parole bd., 1998—2000; chmn. bd. dir. Tubal Trade and Vocat. Inst., 2003—; chmn. Nat. Rehab. Com., 2003—. Mgr., coach primary and secondary sch. soccer teams, Belize City, 1986-99, 1st divsn. and semi-pro soccer club, Belmopan and Belize City, 1981-2000; sec., chmn. Belize Harbour Regatta Com., Belize City, 1958-85. Decorated Knight Order of Brit. Empire, 1991. Mem. Belize Bar Assn. (sec. 1979-81). Seventh Day Adventist. Avocations: yachting, soccer, drama, cricket. Home: 6203 Cor Park Ave Seashore Dr PO Box 236 Belize City Belize Office: Welch & Williams 76 Dean St PO Box 1117 Belize City Belize

BROWN, GEORGE STEPHEN, physics educator; b. Santa Monica, Calif., June 28, 1945; s. Paul Gordon and Frances Ruth (Moore) B.; m. Nohema Fernandez, Aug. 8, 1981 (div. 1992); 1 child, Sonya; m. Julie Claire Dryden, Mar. 22, 1997. BS, Calif. Inst. Tech., 1967; MS, Cornell U., 1968, PhD, 1973. Mem. tech. staff Bell Labs., Murray Hill, N.J., 1973-77; sr. research assoc. Stanford (Calif.) U., 1977-82, rsch. prof. applied physics, 1982-91; prof. physics U. Calif., Santa Cruz, 1991—, chair dept. physics, 1996-2000, vice provost, 2000—. Assoc. dir. Stanford Synchrotron Radiation Lab., Stanford, 1980-91. Mem. editorial bd. Rev. Sci. Instruments, 1983-86; contbr. articles to profl. jours. Fellow Am. Phys. Soc. Avocation: music performance. Home: 115 Wuarry Ct Santa Cruz CA 95060-2056 Office: U Calif Dept Physics Santa Cruz CA 95064

BROWN, GERALD CURTIS, retired army officer, engineering executive; b. Worcester, Mass., Aug. 10, 1942; s. Victor Curtis and Ethel (Dean) B.; m. Alelaide M. Forshey, June 28, 1964 (div.); children: Deborah Ann, Suzanne Marie; m. Jean Jennings, Aug. 1, 1998. BS, U.S. Mil. Acad., West Point, N.Y., 1964; MS, U. Ill., 1970. Registered profl. engr., Tex., Md., D.C., Fla., Ill. Commd. 2d. lt. U.S. Army, 1964, advanced through grades to brig. gen., 1988; capt. 18th Engr. Brigade, Vietnam, 1966-67; maj. 1st Air Cavalry Div., Vietnam, 1970-71; assoc. prof. history U.S. Mil. Acad., West Point, 1974-77; bn. comdr. 82d Combat Engr. Bn., Bamberg, Fed. Republic Germany, 1978-80; dist. engr. Balt. Dist., Corps Engrs., 1982-84; staff engr. U.S. Army Tng. and Doctrine Command, Ft. Monroe, Va., 1984-86; mil. exec. Office Undersec. Army, Washington, 1986-88; fellow Harvard U., Cambridge, 1988-89; comdg. gen. U.S. Army Corps Engrs., North Atlantic Div., N.Y.C., 1989-92; dir. Environ. programs Dept. of Army, The Pentagon, Washington, 1992-94; ret. U.S. Army, 1994; v.p. Sverdrup Civil, Inc., Falls Church, Va., 1994-95; v.p., mgr. Ea. Ops. Sverdrup Environ., Inc., Balt., 1995-98; v.p. Sverdrup Civil, Inc., Falls Church, 1998-99; program mgr. Parsons Brinckerhoff, London, 2000—01; assoc. dir. for ops. Fermi Nat. Accelerator Lab., Batavia, Ill., 2001—. Natl. Defense Exec. Reserve; Fed. Emerg. Mgmt. Agency, chmn. bd. of vis., fed. Emerg. Mgmt. Inst., Md., 1998-2000; founder, pres. Army Corps Engrs. Meml. Corp. Contbr. articles to mil. jours. Fellow Soc. Am. Mil. Engrs. (v.p. 1989-92, bd. dirs. 1993-96, founder, chmn. Acad. Fellows 1995-96); mem. ASCE, Army and Navy Club (Washington). Avocations: squash, golf. Office: Fermi Natl Accelerator Lab PO Box 500 MS 200 Batavia IL 60510-0500 E-mail: gcbrown@fnal.gov.

BROWN, GERALD EDWARD, physicist, educator; b. Brookings, S.D., July 22, 1926; BA, U. Wis., 1946; MS, Yale U., 1948, PhD, 1950; DSc, U. Birmingham, 1957; DSc (hon.), U. Helsinki, 1982, U. Birmingham, 1990, U. Copenhagen, 1998. Prof. physics U. Birmingham, 1959-60, Nordic Inst. Theoretic Atomic Physics, 1960-85, Princeton U., 1964-68, SUNY, Stony Brook, 1968-74, leading prof., 1974-88, dist. prof. physics, 1988—. Lectr. math physics, 1955-58; reader U. Birmingham, 1958-59; dir. nuclear astrophysics Inst. Theoretical Physics NSF, U. Calif., 1960. Recipient Boris Pregel award N.Y. Acad. Sci., 1976, Tom W. Bonner prize Nuclear Physics, 1982, Sr. Dist. Sci. award Alexander von Humboldt Found., 1987, John Price Wetherill medal Franklin Inst., Phila., 1992, Max-Planck medaille German Phys. Soc., 1997, Hans A. Bethe prize nuclear physics and astrophysics Am. Physics Soc., 2001. Office: SUNY Inst Theoretical Physics Stony Brook NY 11794-0001

BROWN, GERALDINE, nurse, freelance writer; b. Clemson, S.C. d. Isaac and Gladys (Patterson) B. AS in Nursing, U. D.C., Washington, 1973; real estate cert., Long and Foster Inst., College Park, Md., 1984; cert. in TV broadcasting, Columbia Sch., Bailey's Crossroads, Va., 1987; BSN, Bowie State U., 1989, MA in Comm., 1991, MSN, 1997; PhD, Howard U., 1994. RN, D.C., FCC Third Class License. Supr. staff nurse Walter Reed Hosp., Washington, 1970-76; supr. clin. nurse Dept. Human Svcs., Washington, 1976-78, cmty. health nurse, 1978-84; nursing instr. Phillips Bus. Sch., Alexandria, Va., 1984-85; pvt. nurse Washington, 1973—; faculty Howard U. Coll. Nursing, 1994—. Dir. pub. affairs Bible Way Chs. Worldwide, Inc., Washington, 1978-91; soc. columnist As It Happens, Charlotte (N.C.) Post, 1964-66; soc. editor Washington Cafe Soc. mag, 1971; contbr. feature stories Capital Spotlight newspaper, 1978—; mem. faculty Coll. Nursing, Howard U., 1994—. Asst. organizer DC Mayor's United Nations Day, 1980; vol. Met. Boys and Girls Clubs, Washington, 1980—; vol. Nursing Instr., The Washington Saturday Coll., 1982-84; Co. ARC, 1973—, Big Sisters of the Washington Met. Area, 1988—. Recipient certs. of excellence Govt. of D.C., 1978-84; cert. of appreciation Mayor of D.C., 1980, Meritorious Pub. Svc. award, 1980; svc. trophy Washington Saturday Coll., 1984. Mem. ANA, NAACP, Nat. Coun. Negro Women, Smithsonian Inst. (assoc.), Nat. Black Nurses Assn., Washington Urban League, Chi Eta Phi, Sigma Theta Tau. Democrat. Avocations: stamp collecting, traveling, writing poetry.

BROWN, GERALDINE REED, lawyer, consulting executive; b. L.A., Feb. 18, 1947; d. William Penn and Alberta Vernice (Coleman) Reed; m. Ronald Wellington Brown, Aug. 20, 1972; children: Kimberly Diana, Michael David. BA summa cum laude, Fisk U., 1968; JD, Harvard U., 1971, MBA, 1973. Bar: N.Y. 1974, U.S. Dist. Ct. (so. and ea. dists.) N.Y. 1974, U.S. Ct. Appeals (2d cir.) 1974, U.S. Supreme Ct. 1977, N.J. 1992, U.S. Dist. Ct. N.J. 1992, Pa. 1993. Assoc. White & Case, N.Y.C., 1973-78, atty. J.C. Penney Co., Inc., N.Y.C., 1978-88; pres. The Reed-Brown Cons. Group., Montclair, N.J., 1989—; counsel Spooner & Burnett, N.Y.C., 1993-98. Asst. prof. bus. law Montclair State Coll., 1990-92; adj. prof. bus. law Kean Coll. N.J., 1989-94; adj. prof. Law Sch. Seton Hall, 1995—; dir., sec., gen. counsel Renaissance Jr. Golf, Inc., Newark; instr. Hudson County C.C., Bergen C.C., Entrepreneurial Training Inst.; mem. com. on women and the cts. N.J. Supreme Ct. Bd. dirs. Coun. Concerned Black Execs., N.Y.C., 1977-88, Studio Mus. in Harlem, N.Y.C., 1980-81; mem. Montclair (N.J.) Devel. Bd., 1985-88, ad hoc com. on Montclair Econ. Devel. Corp., 1985-88; sec., bd. trustee Montclair YWCA, 1989-97, United Hosps. Med. Ctr., vice chmn., 1991-93, trustee, 1989-97, exec. com., chair bylaws com., chair strategic planning com., pers. com.; sec. bd. trustees, chair human resources com. Ramapo Coll.; chair bylaws com., N.J. United Minority Bus. Brain Trust; trustee Essex County Ct. Apptd. Spl. Advocates, 1989-93, Jr. League of Montclair, Newark Mental Health Resources Ctr., Montclair, N.J., 1991-96; trustee, sec. Montclair Early Childhood Corp., 1997-98; trustee, sec. St. Marks United Meth. Ch., Pineridge Brook Corp., United Meth. Homes. Mem. ABA (several coms. sect. corp., banking and bus. law, sect. internat. law and practice), N.J. Bar Assn. (mem. bus. orgns. com.), Essex County Bar Assn., N.Y. State Bar Assn. (continuing legal edn. com., legis. liason 1981-90, vice chmn. 1988-90, exec. com. of corp. counsel sect., chmn. com. on SEC, fin. corp. law and governance, chair com. atty. professionalism 1994-97, mem. task force on profession, com. rev. of cts. and professions), Assn. of Bar of City of N.Y. (corp. law com. 1978-81), N.Y. County Lawyers Assn. (corp. law com.), Exec. Women of N.J., Harvard Bus. Sch. Club, Harvard Law Sch. Assn. (trustee N.J. chpt.), Coalition 100 Black Women, Harvard Bus. Sch. Black Alumni Assn., Harvard Law Sch. Black Alumni Assn., Harvard Club (N.Y.C.), Phi Beta Kappa, Delta Sigma Theta (past chair social action com. Montclair alumnae chpt., past chair rules com., parlimentarian) Home and Office: The Reed-Brown Cons Group 180 Union St Montclair NJ 07042-2125 E-mail: rbcg1@aol.com.

BROWN, GERARD DANIEL, neonatologist, pediatrician; b. Norristown, Pa., Dec. 9, 1955; s. Edward B. and Mary J. Brown; m. Darlene F. Brown, July 30, 1983; children: Christopher, Gregory. BS, Elizabethtown Coll., 1977; DO, Phila. Coll. Osteo. Medicine, 1981. Diplomate Am. Bd. Pediats. Intern then resident Naval Hosp. San Diego; fellow U. Calif. San Diego Med. Ctr.; staff neonatologist Tri-City Med. Ctr., Oceanside, Calif., 1988-96; dir. NICU-TCCH Children's Hosp. Phila., 1996-98; dir. NICU The Reading (Pa.) Hosp. and Med. Ctr., 1998—. Wrestling coach Wyomissing (Pa.) Grapplers, 1998-99; religious instr. St. Ignatius Loyola, West Lawn, Pa., 1998—. Capt. USN, 1977-86; USNR, 1986—. Fellow Am. Acad. Pediats. Office: The Reading Hosp and Med Ctr 6th Avenue and Spruce St Reading PA 19612

BROWN, GERRI ANN, physical therapist; b. N.Y.C., May 1, 1948; d. S. Stanley and Corinne (Carlin) Schkurman; m. Michael Edward Brown, Oct. 2, 1971. BS in Phys. Therapy, Ithaca Coll., 1969. Registered phys. therapist, Colo., N.Y. Lectr. U. Colo. Med. Sch., Denver, 1970-81; dir. phys. therapy and team facilitator Wheatridge (Colo.) Regional Ctr., 1969-81; phys. therapist Ptnrs. Home Health Care, Lakewood, Colo., 1982-83, Mt. Evans Home Health Care, Evergreen, Colo., 1983-88, Western Home Health, Arvada, Colo., 1988-93, ICON Home Care, Lakewood, 1993-97, Vis. Nurse Assn., Denver, 1995—, 1995—. Lectr. U. Colo., Denver, 1970-81, U. No. Colo., Greeley, 1977-81; tchr., cons. ICON Home Care, Lakewood, 1993-97, Western Home Health Care, Arvada, 1988-93, Mt. Evans Health Care, 1983-88, Vis. Nurses Denver, 1996—; chairperson task force State of Colo., Denver, 1972-73. Mem. Citizens for Action, Idledale, Colo., 1975-76. Mem. Am. Phys. Therapy Assn. (sect. on geriatrics and home health care), Hiwan Golf Club. Avocations: golf, travel, music. Home: PO Box 88 Idledale CO 80453-0088 E-mail: bigboo49@aol.com.

BROWN, GILES TYLER, history educator, lecturer; b. Marshall, Mich., Apr. 21, 1916; s. A. Watson and Ettroile (Kent) B.; m. Crysta Beth Cosner, Nov. 21, 1951 (dec. July 1992). AB, San Diego State Coll., 1937; MA, U. Calif.-Berkeley, 1941; PhD, Claremont Grad. Sch., 1948; post-doctoral seminar, U. Edinburgh, Scotland, 1949. Tchr., counselor, Binet intelligence tester San Diego City Schs., 1937-46; chmn. social sci. div. Orange Coast Coll., Newport Beach, Calif., 1948-60; prof. history, chmn. social sci. div. Calif. State U., Fullerton, 1961-66, also chmn. history dept., dean grad. studies, 1967-83, assoc. v.p. acad. programs, 1979-83. Pub. lectr. nat., internat. affairs, 1951—; also cons. gerontology; participant Wilton Park Conf., Eng., 1976; mem. instl. rsch. bd. So. Calif. Coll. Optometry, 1980-97; past chmn. Hist. Landmarks Com. Orange County; mem. nat. task force Assessment Quality Masters' Degree, Coun. Grad. Schs., 1981-83. Author: Ships That Sail No More, 1966; Contbr. to: Help in Troubled Times, 1962; contbr. articles, book reviews to profl. jours. Trustee, past pres., past chmn. bd. World Affairs Coun. Orange County; past pres. U. Calif.-Irvine Friends Libr.; nat. bd. dirs., past nat. pres. Travelers Century Club; mem. Orange County Bd. The National Conf., 1984—; emeritus bd. dirs. Pacific Symphony Orch. Named Citizen of Yr., Orange Coast Coll., 1993; recipient hon. medal, DAR, 1977, Nat. Soc. Daus. Colonial Wars, 1984, Golden Orange award, World Affair Coun. of Orange County, 2002. Mem. AAAS, SAR, Am. Hist. Assn. (Pacific History award 1950), Western Assn. Grad. Schs. (exec. com. 1981-83), Phi Beta Kappa, Phi Delta Kappa, Phi Alpha Theta, Phi Beta Delta (hon. internat. scholar), Kappa Delta Pi, Explorers, Masons. Baptist. Home: 413 Catalina Dr Newport Beach CA 92663-4105

BROWN, GLENDA ANN WALTERS, ballet director; b. Buna, Tex., July 22, 1937; d. Jesse Olaf and Kathryn Jeanette (Rogers) Walters; m. David Dann Brown, Dec. 13, 1958 (div. 1995); children: Kathryn, Jean, Vanessa Lea. Grad. h.s., Beaumont, Tex. Mem. Melody Maids, Beaumont, 1950-60; asst. tchr. Widman Sch., Beaumont, 1952-55; owner, tchr. Walters Sch. of Dance, Jasper, Tex., 1955-59; assoc. tchr. Emmamae Horn Sch., 1964-81, artistic dir., 1981—; assoc. dir. Allegro Ballet Houston, 1974-81, artistic dir., 1981—; owner, dir. Allegro Acad. Dance, Houston, 1981—. Dir. Regional Dance Am., Nat. Craft Choreography Conf., 1987—2001; mem. adv. bd. Dance Tchr. Mag., 1998—; founder, dir. Glenda Brown Choreography Project, 2002—. Dance panel Cultural Arts Coun., Houston, 1979, Tex. Commn. on the Arts, 1988-90; sec. Riedel Estates Civic Club, Houston, 1975-78; Rep. poll worker, Houston,

1970-81; bd. dirs. Austrian Alps Performing Arts Festival, 1996-98; coord. First Nat. Regional Dance Am. Festival, 1997, bd. dirs. Tanzsommer/Austria, 1998—. Mem. Dance Masters Am. (exam. chair chpt. 3 1980-86), Regional Dance Am. S.W. (exec. v.p. 1981-2001), Dance Am., Nat. Assn. Regional Ballet (bd. dirs. 1985-88), Regional Dance Am. (nat. bd. dirs., v.p. 1988-95, pres. 1995-2001). Methodist. Avocations: camping, singing, golf, travel. Office: Allegro Ballet and Dance Acad 1570 S Dairy Ashford St Ste 200 Houston TX 77077-3870 E-mail: glendabrown@allegroballet.com.

BROWN, G(LENN) WILLIAM, JR., bank executive; b. Waynesville, N.C., June 9, 1955; s. Glenn William and Evelyn Myralyn (Davis) B.; m. Amy Margaret Moss, Apr. 14, 1984; children: Elizabeth Quinn, Lauren Alexandra. BS in Biology, BS in Polit. Sci., MIT, 1977; JD, Duke U., 1980. Bar: N.Y., 1980. Assoc. Donovan Leisure Newton & Irvine, N.Y.C., 1980-84, Sidley & Austin, N.Y.C., 1984-87, ptnr., 1988-89; v.p. Goldman Sachs & Co., N.Y.C., 1990-94; exec. dir. Goldman Sachs Internat. Fin., London, 1994-96; sr. v.p., global head sales AIG Internat. Inc., Greenwich, Conn., 1996-97; prin. Morgan Stanley & Co., Inc., N.Y.C., 1997, mng. dir., head FX sales for Am., 1997—. Editl. bd.: jour. Duke Law Jour., 1978—80. Mem. ABA, Am. Fin. Assn., Duke Law Sch. Alumni Assn. (bd. dirs. 2001-). Presbyterian. Home: Apt 38D One Central Park West New York NY 10023-7700 Office: Morgan Stanley Co 1585 Broadway Frnt 3 New York NY 10036-8200 E-mail: bill.brown@morganstanley.com.

BROWN, GLORIA VASQUEZ, central banker; b. Alice, Tex., Aug. 7, 1945; d. Mauro and Aurora (Canales) Vasquez; m. Larry R. Brown, July 5, 1986. BA in Math., Tex. Woman's U., 1967; postgrad., U. Tex., San Antonio, 1979. Tchr. math. Corpus Christi (Tex.) Ind. Sch. Dist., 1967-69, Columbus (Ohio) Ind. Sch. Dist., 1969-70; with Urban Mass Transp., Washington, 1971-77; owner/operator Derma Clinic, San Antonio, 1977-79; field svcs. officer Neighborhood Reinvestment Co., Dallas, 1979-89, spl. projects officer, 1989-91; cmty. affairs officer Fed. Res. Bank of Dallas, 1991-96, v.p. pub. affairs, 1997—. Lectr. in field; instr. So. Meth. U./Southwestern Grad. Sch. Banking. Creator: Breaking Ground, 1995 (Merit award 1995); creator/editor Banking and Cmty. Perspectives, 1992. Bd. dirs. Arts Dist. Friends, Dallas, 1991-94, Shared Housing Ctr., 1997—, Dallas Women's Found., 2000—, The Family Place, 2002—; mem. Region VI adv. coun. U.S. SBA, Dallas, 1992—; mem. program com. Dallas Nonprofit Capacity Bldg. Program, 1994-96; vice chair IMAGE de Dallas, 1993-94; mem. Hispanic 50, Dallas Friday Group. Recipient Women Making a Difference award Minority Bus. News, Dallas, 1995, Key to the City, City Coun. of Lafayette, La., 1980's; Leadership Tex. Found. for Women's Resources, Austin, 1996. Mem. Greater Dallas C. of C. (women's bus. issues adv. coun. 1994—, finalist Athena award 1998), Tex. Woman's U. Alumnae Assn., Hispanic Bankers Assn. Roman Catholic. Avocations: movies, travel, card games, walking. Home: 7107 Judi Ct Dallas TX 75252-6118 Office: Federal Reserve Bank Dallas 2200 N Pearl St Dallas TX 75201-2272 E-mail: Gloria.v.brown@dal.frb.org.

BROWN, GORDON STEWART, diplomat, business association administrator, writer; b. Rome, Feb. 24, 1936; s. George Stewart and Helen (Meyer) B.; m. Olivia Collins, Mar. 25, 1961; children: Marian E. Sprague, Louise M. Ingold, Stewart L. BA, Stanford U., 1957. Intelligence splst. U.S. Army, 1957-60; with fgn. svc. U.S. Dept. State, Tunisia, Saudi Arabia, Egypt, 1961-91, amb. to Mauritania, 1991-94; pres. U.S.-Qatar Bus. Coun., Washington, 1997-2000. Author: Coalition, Coercion & Compromise, 1997, The Norman Conquest of Southern Italy and Sicily, 2003. Served with U.S. Army, 1957-60. Recipient Meritorius Civilian Svc. award U.S. Sec. Def. Avocations: history, tennis. Home: 6225 32nd Pl NW Washington DC 20015-2427 E-mail: g.and.o.brown@erols.com.

BROWN, GREGORY K. lawyer; b. Warren, Ohio, Dec. 9, 1951; s. George K. and Dorothy H. (Gaynor) B.; m. Joy M. Feinberg, Apr. 10, 1976. BS in Bus. & Econs., U. Ky., 1973; JD, U. Ill., 1976. Bar: Ill. 1976. Assoc. atty. McDermott, Will & Emery, Chgo., 1976-80, Mayer, Brown & Platt, Chgo., 1980-84; ptnr. Keck, Mahin & Cate, Chgo., 1984-93, Oppenheimer Wolff & Donnelly, Chgo., 1994-97, Seyfarth, Shaw, Fairweather & Geraldson, Chgo., 1997-2000, Gardner, Carton & Douglas, Chgo., 2000—. Contbg. author: The Handbook of Employee Ownership Plans, 1989, Employee Stock Ownership Plans, 1989 Active Chgo. Coun. Fgn. Rels. Named One of the Top Benefits Lawyers Nat. Law Jour., 1998. Mem.: ABA (chair employee stock ownership plan com., tax law sect. Nat. Ctr. Employee Ownership, Employee Stock Ownership Plan Assn. chair legis. and regulatory adv. c 1997—99), Chgo. Bar Assn. (chmn. employee benefits com. 1988—89). Avocations: basketball, bicycling, golf, opera, theatre. Office: Gardner Carton & Douglas 191 N Wacker Dr Ste 3700 Chicago IL 60606-1698 E-mail: gkbrown@gcd.com.

BROWN, GREGORY MICHAEL, psychiatrist, educator, researcher; b. Toronto, Mar. 27, 1934; s. Norbert Joseph and Nellie Shaw (Diack) B.; m. Audrey Christina Shute, June 18, 1960; children: Jacqueline Anne Embleton, David Michael, Mary Catherine Brown Lutsch, Paul Douglas, Barbara Suzanne French, Joyce Christina, Patricia Elizabeth, Anne Marie; m. Elizabeth Mary East, July 14, 2000. BA, U. Toronto, 1955, MD, 1959, diploma in Psychiatry, 1964; PhD, U. Rochester, 1971. Intern St. Michael's Hosp., 1959-60; resident in medicine Shaughnessy Hosp., Vancouver, 1960-61; resident in psychiatry various hosps., Ont., 1961-64; ward physician Toronto Psychiat. Hosp., 1964-66; courtesy staff Peel Meml. Hosp., Brampton, Ont., 1964-66; fellow in clin. investigation dept. psychiatry U. Toronto, 1964-66, clin. tchr. in psychiatry, 1968-69, asst. prof. to assoc. prof., 1969-75, prof., 1975-77, prof. dept psychiatry, prof. dept. physiology, 1989-99, prof. Inst. Med. Sci., 1991-99, prof. emeritus, 1999—; prof. depts. neurosci. and psychiatry McMaster U., 1977-87, staff psychiatrist Med. Ctr., 1977—, chmn. dept. neurosci., 1977-87, prof. dept. neurosci., 1987-88, prof. dept. biomed. scis., 1988-89, prof. emeritus, 1989—; external examiner dept physiology U. Hong Kong, 1990-92; instr. medicine and psychiatry U. Rochester Sch. Medicine, N.Y., 1966-69; staff psychiatrist Clarke Inst. Psychiatry, Toronto, 1968-77, 90—, dir. rsch., 1990—, v.p. rsch., 1995-96, head neuroendocrinology rsch. sect., 1996-99; clin. scientist Ctr. Addiction and Mental Health, Toronto, 1999—. Pres., CEO CIDtech Rsch. Inc., Cambridge, Ont., Can., 1984—. Co-author: Frontiers in Neurology and Neuroscience Research, 1974, Clinical Neuroendocrinology, 1977, Neuroendocrinology and Psychiatric Disorder, 1984, The Pineal Gland: Endocrine Aspects, Advances in the Biosciences, 1985, Clinical Neuroendocrinology, 1988; assoc. editor Can. Jour. Physiology and Pharmacology, 1973-78; mem. editorial bd. Psychoneuroendocrinology, 1978-89, Jour. Pineal Rsch., 1981-89, Psychiatry Rsch., 1979—, Jour. Psychiatry and Neuroscience, 1990—; mem. exec. editorial bd. Progress in Neuro-Psychopharmacology and Biological Psychiatry, 1989—; mem. editorial bd. Biological Signals, 1991—; contbr. to books; contbr. articles to profl. jours. Named Rsch. assoc. Ont. Mental Health Found., 1968—, Traveling fellow Ont. Mental Health Found., 1966-68; recipient numerous rsch. awards, McNeil Lab. award, 1975, John Dewan award Ont. Mental Health Found., 1980, Heinz Lehmann award Can. Coll. Neuropsychopharmacology, 1983. Fellow APA, Royal Coll. Physicians; mem. Can. Psychiat. Assn., Ont. Psychiat. Assn., Am. Psychosomatic Soc. (councillor 1978-82), Can. Med. Assn., Ont. Med. Assn., Soc. Psychoneuroendocrinology (councillor 1981-87), Endocrine Soc., Can. Coll. Neuropsychopharmacology (chmn. publ. com. 1986-89), Can. Soc. Endocrinology and Metabolism (councillor 1981-83), Can. Soc. Clin. Investigation. Roman Catholic. Avocations: photography, music, theatre. Home: 100 Bronte Rd Unit 422 Oakville ON Canada L6L 6L5 Office: CIDtech Rsch Inc 1200 Franklin Blvd Cambridge ON Canada N1R 6T5

BROWN, GREGORY NEIL, university administrator, forest physiology educator; b. Detroit, Feb. 10, 1938; s. Robert Octavus and Dorothy Etta May (Kingsbury) B.; m. Patricia Lee Talbott, Dec. 16, 1961 (div. 1974); children: Kathryn Duket, Julie Ann, Deborah Louise; m. Janeth Christine Hartman, May 24, 1974 (dec. 1997); children: Kimberly Suzanne, Kevin Scott; m. Laura Jean Dale, June 27, 1998. BS, Iowa State U., 1959; MF, Yale U., 1960; DF, Duke U., 1963. Plant physiologist Oak Ridge Nat. Lab., 1963—66; asst. prof. forestry to prof. U. Mo.-Columbia, 1966—77, dir. grad. studies Sch. Forestry, 1969—74; prof. Iowa State U., Ames, 1977—78; dept. head, prof. U. Minn.-St. Paul, 1978—83; dean, prof. U. Maine-Orono, 1983—86, acting v.p. acad. affairs, 1986-87, 91-92, v.p. rsch. and pub. svc., 1987—92; dean, prof. Coll. Natural Resources, Va. Poly. Inst. and State U., Blacksburg, 1992—, interim dean Coll. Agrl. and Life Scis., 2003. Assoc. dir. Maine Agrl. Exptl. Sta., Orono, 1983-86, acting pres., 1992; assoc. dir. Va. Agrl. Exptl. Sta., Blacksburg, 1992—, interim provost, 1995; chair, bd. dirs. Powell River Project, 1996—; mem. sci. adv. bd. Nat. Ctr. Housing and the Environment, 2002—. Author-editor: Seedling Physiology and Reforestation Success, 1984; editor: International Directory of Woody Plant Physiologists, 1974-84, Jour. Forest Sci., 1979-82; editl. bd.: Renewable resources Jour., 2002—. Contbr. articles to profl. jours. Scoutmaster Boy Scouts Am., 1965-66; mem. Forestry Rsch. Adv. Coun., U.S. Sec. Agr., 2000-2002. Mem. Soc. Am. Foresters (chmn. physiology working group 1983-84), Nat. Assn. Profl. Forestry Schs. and Colls. (north Ctrl. rsch. chmn. 1981-82, nat. sec. treas. 1984-85, nat. pres. elect 1986-87, 94-95, pres. 1996-97), Internat. Union Forest Orgns. (chmn. working parties 1970-86), Nat. Assn. State Univs. and Land-Grant Colls. (chair bd. on natural resources 1997, chair U.S. geol. survey partnership com. 1997-2000), Soc. for Preservation and Encouragement of Barbershop Quartet Singing in Am. (pres. 1973-74), Sigma Xi, Xi Sigma Pi, Gamma Sigma Delta (jr. faculty award 1971). Lutheran. Home: 1810 Mountainside Dr Blacksburg VA 24060-9202 Office: Va Poly Inst and State U Coll Natural Resources 324 Cheatham Hall Blacksburg VA 24061 E-mail: browngn@vt.edu.

BROWN, H. WILLIAM, urban economist, private banker; b. L.A., Sept. 6, 1933; s. Homer William Brown and Carol Lee (Thompson) Weaver; m. Verlee Nelson, Aug. 1953 (div. 1955); 1 child, Shirlee Dawn; m. Shirley Rom, Jan. 18, 1955 (div. 1962). BA in Pub. Adminstrn., Calif. State U., 1956; MA in Bus. Adminstrn., Western States U., 1983, Phd in Urban Econs., 1984. Pres. Real Estate Econs., Sacramento, 1956-60; dir. spl. projects Resource Agy. Calif., Sacramento, 1960-65; program planning officer U.S. Dept. Housing and Urban Devel., Washington, 1965-66; asst. dir. regional planning U.S. Dept. Commerce, Washington, 1967-69; dir. internat. office Marshall and Stevens, Inc., L.A., 1970-72; vice chmn., CEO Investment Property Econ. Cons., 1972-97; chmn., CEO The Northpoint Investment Group, San Francisco, 1986-97; chmn. Global Adv. Resources, Palo Alto, Calif., 1997—. Chmn. Trade and Devel. Ctr. For UN, N.Y. 1983-88, pres. Ctr. for Habitat and Human Settlements, Washington 1977-90. Author: The Changing World of the Real Estate Market Analyst-Appraiser, 1988. Mem. MAI Appraisal Inst. (charge d'affaires), Le Groupe, Pvt. Bankers Assn. Avocation: worldwide people photography. Office: Global Adv Resources Stanford Ctr 130 Palo Alto CA 94306-1144

BROWN, HANK, foundation administrator, former university administrator, former senator; b. Denver, Feb. 12, 1940; s. Harry W. and Anna M. (Hanks) B.; m. Nana Morrison, Aug. 27, 1967; children: Harry, Christy, Lori. BS, U. Colo., 1961, JD, 1969; LLM, M in Tax Law, George Washington U., 1986. Bar: Colo. 1969; CPA, 1988. Asst. pres. Monfort of Colo., Inc., Greeley, 1969—70, corp. counsel, 1970—71; v.p. Monfort Food Distbg., 1971—72, v.p. corp. devel., 1973—75, v.p. internat. ops., 1975—78, v.p. lamb div., 1978—80; mem. Colo. State Senate, 1972—76, asst. majority leader, 1974—76; mem. 97th-101st Congresses from Colo. 4th dist., 1981—90; U.S senator from Colo. Washington, 1991—96; pres. U. No. Colo., Greeley, 1998—2002, Daniels Fund, 2002—. Chmn. Fgn. Rel. subcom. Near Ea. and South Asian affairs, Judicorp subcom. on constl. law. With USN, 1962-66. With USN, 1962—66. Decorated Air medal, Vietnam Svc. medal, Nat. Defense medal, Naval Unit citation. Republican. Congregationalist. Office: The Daniels Fund Ste 255 55 Madison St Denver CO 80206 E-mail: hbrown@mail.unco.edu.

BROWN, HARLEY MITCHELL, retired computer company executive, writer; b. Mt. Belvieu, Tex., Oct. 15, 1929; s. Hardy Mack and Eva Leandor (Warden) B.; m. Marjorie Rae Tuttle, Aug. 21, 1925; children: Deborah Diane Morel, Marjorie Joann Guin, Sallie Annette, Raylena Jean Ehlert. 9th grade, W. Columbia High Sch., Tex., 1946. Computer programmer U.S. Navy, 1947-58; chief systems and programming U.S. Bur. Customs, Washington, 1958-68; nat. systems mgr. Stromberg-Carlson, Houston, 1968-73; v.p. mktg. Compass Micromation, Houston, 1973-87; pres. Comtex Data Svcs., Inc., Houston, 1987-91; columnist The Kountze (Tex.) News, 1992—. Dir. Comtex Data Svcs., Inc., Houston, 1991—; guest lectr. Univ. Houston. Author: Hard Times in Hardin County, 1992, Pulpit Humor, 1995. With USN, 1946-58. Republican. Avocations: fishing, writing. Home: 25 Kings Ct Greenville TX 75401-4371

BROWN, HAROLD, former secretary of defense, corporate director; b. N.Y.C., Sept. 19, 1927; s. A.H. and Gertrude (Cohen) B.; m. Colene Dunning McDowell, Oct. 29, 1953; children: Deborah Ruth (Mrs. Eric Ploumis), Ellen Dunning (Mrs. Ray Merewether). AB, Columbia U., 1945, A.M., 1946, PhD in Physics (Lydig fellow 1948-49), 1949; 11 hon. degrees. Research scientist Columbia U., 1945-50, lectr. physics, 1947-48, Stevens Inst. Tech., 1949-50; divsn. leader E.O. Lawrence Radiation Lab. U. Calif., Berkeley, 1950-60, staff mem., group leader E.O. Lawrence Radiation Lab., 1952-60; dir. Lawrence Livermore (Calif.) Lab., 1960-61; dir. def. rsch. and engring. Dept. Def., Washington, 1961-65; sec. Dept. Air Force, Washington, 1965-69; pres. Calif. Inst. Tech., Pasadena, 1969-77; sec. def. Washington, 1977-81; disting. vis. prof. Sch. Advanced Internat. Studies Johns Hopkins U., Md., 1981-84, chmn. Fgn. Policy Inst., 1984-92, counselor Ctr. Strategic & Internat. Studies, 1992—; ptnr. Warburg, Pincus & Co., N.Y.C., 1990—. Bd. dirs. Philip Morris Inc., Cummins Engine Co., Mattel, Inc., Evergreen Holdings, Inc.; mem. Polaris Steering Com., 1956-58; mem. Pres.'s Sci. Adv. Com., 1960-61; sr. sci. advisor Conf. Discontinuance Nuclear Tests, 1958-59; U.S. del. SALT, Helsinki, Vienna and Geneva, 1969-77; chmn. Tech. Assessment Adv. Coun. to U.S. Congress, 1974-77; chmn. Commn. on Roles and Capabilities of U.S. Intelligence Comty., 1995-96; mem. exec. com. Trilateral Commn., 1973-76, trustee, 1992—; trustee Rand Corp., 1983-92, 93—. Author: Thinking About National Security: Defense and Foreign Policy in a Dangerous World, 1983. Trustee Beckman Found., 1982-95, chmn., 1993-95; trustee Rockefeller Found., 1983-93. Decorated Medal of Freedom; named One of 10 Outstanding Young Men U.S. Jaycees, 1961; recipient Medal of Excellence Columbia U., 1963; Joseph C. Wilson award in internat. affairs, 1976, Enrico Fermi award U.S. Dept. Energy, 1992. Mem. NAE, NAS, Am. Phys. Soc., Am. Acad. Arts and Scis., Bohemian Club, River Club, Met. Club, Phi Beta Kappa. Office: Ctr for Strategic & Intl Studies 1800 K St NW Ste 400 Washington DC 20006-2202

BROWN, HAROLD EUGENE, retired magistrate; b. Damascus, Ark., Jan. 6, 1935; s. Amos Eugene and Hazel Gladys (Thomas) B.; m. Carolyn Marie Sanders, Aug. 26, 1972; children: James Daryl, Deena Leigh, Cynthia Marie. Student, U. Md. Overseas Divsn., Verdun, France, 1962-64, Germanna C.C., 1978-84. Enlisted U.S. Army, 1954, advanced through grades to sgt. maj., 1977; White House liaison Chief of Staff Army, Washington, 1969—73; dep. dir. Def. Coop. Agy., New Delhi, 1973—77; post sgt. maj., co. comdr Fort A.P. Hill, Bowling Green, Va., 1977—81; magistrate 15th dist. Supreme Ct. Va., Fredericksburg, 1982—2002, apptd. chief magistrate, 1987—2000, apptd. magistrate VI, 2000—02; ret., 2002. Marriage commr. Commonwealth Va., 1984. Bd. dirs., former dir. Rappahannock Coun. Domestic Violence; bd. dirs. Rappahannock United Way. Decorated Cross of Gallantry (Republic of Vietnam). Mem. Am. Judges Assn., Va. Magistrates Assn., Va. Cmty. Criminal Justice Assn., Ret. Sgts. Maj. Assn. Avocations: golf, photography, computer programming. Home: 21 Rosewood Dr Fredericksburg VA 22408-1521 E-mail: hebrown5@aol.com.

BROWN, HAROLD MACVANE, lawyer; b. Colon, Panama, Oct. 2, 1940; s. Harold MacVane and Geraldine (Lynch) B.; m. Susan Murphy, June 20, 1970; children: Molly Curran, Katy Bradford. B.A., U. N.H., 1963; LL.M., Boston U., 1968. Bar: Mass. 1968, Alaska 1972, U.S. Dist. Ct. Mass. 1968, U.S. Dist. Ct. Alaska 1972. Assoc., Mahoney, McGrath, Atwood, Piper & Goldings, Boston, 1968-69; mem. atty.'s gen.'s office criminal div. Commonwealth of Mass., Boston, 1969-71; dist. atty. State of Alaska, 1971-73; ptnr. Ziegler, Cloudy, King, Brown & Peterson, Ketchikan, Alaska, 1974-85; atty. gen., State of Alaska, 1985-87; now ptnr. Heller, Ehrman, White & McAuliffe, Anchorage, Alaska. Mem. ABA, Alaska Bar Assn. (bd. govs. 1981—, pres., 1984). Mass. Bar Assn. Democrat. Episcopalian. Office: Heller Ehrman White & McAuliffe 1900 Enserch Ctr 550 W 7th Ave Ste 1900 Anchorage AK 99501-3578

BROWN, HARRY M. lawyer, consultant; b. Oradia-Mare, Romania, Oct. 9, 1947; came to U.S., 1951; s. Bernard and Lydia Brown; m. Perl Keller, Aug. 10, 1969; children: Michael, Elissa, Rochel, Bentzion, Shmuel. BA, Yeshiva Coll., 1969; JD, NYU, 1972. Bar: Ohio 1972. Atty., ptnr. Benesch, Friedlander, Coplan & Aronoff, Cleve., 1972—. Office: Benesch Friedlander Coplan 200 Public Sq Cleveland OH 44114-2301 E-mail: hbrown@bfca.com.

BROWN, HAZEL FAY NIXON, women's health nurse, educator, administrator; b. Columbus County, N.C., June 30, 1940; d. Roy A. and Lela M. (Watson) Nixon; m. Leonard L. Brown, May 3, 1964; children: Charles, Mona, Nadja, David. BSN, Berea (Ky.) Coll., 1962; MA in Edn., Wake Forest U., 1971; MSN, U. N.C., Greensboro, 1984, EdD, 1981. Cert. inpatient obstet. nurse, nursing adminstrn. advanced. Staff nurse Hoots Meml. Hosp., Yadkinville, N.C., 1962-66; instr., dir. Sch. Nursing Forsyth Meml. Hosp., Winston-Salem, N.C., 1967-74; prof. U. N.C., Greensboro, 1974—. Contbr. articles to profl. jours. Named Great 100 Nurses in N.C., 1990; recipient N.C. Nurse Educator of Yr., 1992, 2002, Award of Merit Internat. Congress on Women's Health Issues, 1998, Internat. Rsch. Utilization award Sigma Theta Tau Internat., Tchg. Excellence award Sch. of Nursing, 1999, Alumni Sr. Tchg. Excellence award U. N.C. Greensboro, 1999. Mem. ANA, NLN, AWHONN (Innovations in Teen Pregnancy award), Internat. Coun. Women's Health Issues, Sigma Theta Tau. Office: U NC Greensboro Sch Nursing Greensboro NC 27402-6172 E-mail: hazel_brown@uncg.edu.

BROWN, HELEN GURLEY, editor, writer; b. Green Forest, Ark., Feb. 18, 1922; d. Ira M. and Cleo (Sisco) Gurley; m. David Brown, Sept. 25, 1959. Student, Tex. State Coll. for Women, 1939—41, Woodbury Coll., 1942; LLD, Woodbury U., 1987; DLitt, L.I. U., 1993. Exec. sec. Music Corp. Am., 1942—45; exec. sec. William Morris Agy., 1945—47; copywriter Foote, Cone & Belding (advt. agy.), Los Angeles, 1948—58; advt. writer, account exec. Kenyon & Eckhardt (advt. agy.), Hollywood, Calif., 1958—62; editor-in-chief Cosmopolitan mag., 1965—97; editorial dir. Cosmopolitan Internat. Edits., 1972—; editor-in-chief Cosmopolitan Internat. Edits, 1997—. Named 1 of 25 most influential women in U.S., World Almanac, 1976—81; recipient Francis Holmes Achievement award for outstanding work in advt., 1956—59, Disting. Achievement award, U. So. Calif. Sch. Journalism, 1971, Spl. award for editl. leadership Am. Newspaper, Woman's Club, Washington, 1972, Disting. Achievement award in journalism, Stanford U., 1977, Matrix award in mag. category, N.Y. Women in Comm., 1985, Henry Johnson Fisher award, Mag. Pubs. of Am., 1995, Helen Gurley Brown Rshc. Professorship established name, Northwestern U. Medill Sch. Journalism, 1986, inducted into Pubs.' Hall of Fame, 1988. Mem.: AFTRA, Am. Soc. Mag. Editors (Hall of Fame award 1996), Authors League Am., Eta Upsilon Gamma. Office: Cosmopolitan The Hearst Corp 224 W 57th St New York NY 10019

BROWN, HELEN SAUER, fund raising executive; b. Findlay, Ohio, Feb. 7, 1923; d. Joseph Thomas and Mary Magdalene (Sweeney) Sauer; m. Thomas Francis Brown, June 10, 1944; children: Mary Helen Anne, Thomas F., Joachim J., Mary Christine, Mary Kathleen, Mary Elizabeth, Timothy J., Martin J., John Fitzgerald Kennedy. BA magna cum laude, Mundelein Coll. for Women, 1944, MA summa cum laude, 1970. V.p. T.F. Brown Co., Chgo., 1962-84; tchr. Nazareth Acad., La Grange Park, Ill., 1968-72; pastoral min. Ill., 1970—; dir. religious edn. Divine Savior Parish, Downers Grove, Ill., 1972-76; pres. Herself's Doings Ltd., La Grange, Ill., 1972—; retail store owner/mgr. Nettle Creek Shop, La Grange, 1976-85; dir. resource devel. Cmty. Family Svc. & Mental Health Assn., Lyons and Riverside Townships, Ill., 1986—. Cons., spkr. in field; pres. Religious Edn. Svcs., La Grange, 1972-86; adv. coun. U. Notre Dame Sch. of Theology, 1970-72. Author: Community and Social Justice, 1974. Trustee Mundelein Coll., Chgo., 1970-90; organizer ERA, Springfield, Ill., 1968—; peace activist, Washington, 1966—; commr. Lyons (Ill.) Mental Health Commn., 1978-80; commr. econ. devel. Village of La Grange, 1983-93; commr. program rev. Pvt. Industry Coun., Cook County, Ill., 1984-94; dir. Ill. Retirement Home Assn., Hinsdale, 1993—; chair Resident Coun., Bethlehem Woods. Named Woman of Century, West Suburban C. of C., 2002; recipient Welford award for disting. svc. to mental health, 1983; scholar Cardinal Meyer scholar, Archdiocese of Chgo., 1970. Mem. NAACP, AAUW, LWV, Nat. Soc. Fund Raising Execs. (cert. 1991), La Grange West Suburban C. of C. (chair pres.'s coun. 1985-96, pres. 1986-87, Woman of Yr. 1983), Women for Peace, Amnesty Internat., Bus. and Profl. Women/USA (Outstanding Working Woman Ill. chpt. 1993), Phoenix Soc., Women's Bd., Clergy and Laity Concerned for Justice and Peace, Gannon Ctr. Women and Leadership, Mundelein Coll. Alumnae, La Grange Cath. Women's Club, Kappa Gamma Pi. Democrat. Roman Catholic. Avocations: book reviewing, public opinion research, liturgical planning, philosophy, word puzzles. Home: 1571 W Ogden Ave Apt 2626 La Grange Park IL 60526-1769 E-mail: hsbtfb@msn.com.

BROWN, HENRY BEDINGER RUST, financial management company executive; b. Pitts., Feb. 13, 1926; s. Stanley Noel and Elizabeth Fitzhugh (Rust) B.; m. Betsey Jean Smith, Mar. 27, 1954; children— Peter, Alexander, Elizabeth, Harriet AB, Harvard U., 1948. Asst. v.p. Citibank, N.Y.C., 1954-63; 2d v.p. Tchrs. Ins. & Annunity Assn., N.Y.C., 1963-68; chmn. Res. Fund, N.Y.C., 1970-83; pres. Res. Mgmt. Co., Inc., N.Y.C., 1984-98, Transfer Solutions Inc., Leesburg, Va., 1998—. Councilman Town of Westfield, N.J., 1982-84. Served with USNR, 1944-46 Achievements include creating the first money mkt. fund.

BROWN, HENRY E., JR., congressman; b. Bishopville, S.C., Dec. 20, 1935; m. Billye Beaver; 3 children. D. Bus. Admin. (hon.), The Citadel, 1998. Ret. v.p. Piggly Wiggly Carolina Co.; mem. SC House Reps., 1985-2000, U.S. Congress from 1st S.C. Dist., 2001—. Mem. Congressional com. Transportation and Infrastructure, Budget, Veterans' Affairs; apptd. to Ways and Means com., 1989, chmn., 1995; chmn. Joint Tax Study Com.; mem. Budget and Control bd., Legislative Audit Coun., Joint Bond Review com.; served on Hanahan City Coun., 4 yrs., Hanahan Planning Com., 4 yrs. Mem. Cooper River Bapt. Ch. Served SC N.G., 9 yrs. Named Legislator Yr., SC Assn. Sch. Librs., 1998-99, Natl. Rep. Legislators Assn, 1999, SC Vocat. Dirs. Assn., 1999, Ind. Colls. of SC, 1995, SC Coll. Legislators, 1995, Outstanding Legislator, SC Sch. Bd. Assn., 1997. SC Legislator Yr., SC Assn. Realtors, 1997; named Servant Yr., SC Chamber, 1995, SC Taxpayers Watchdog, SC Treas. Office; awarded Order of Palmetto, State of SC, 2000; recipient Dir. award, SC Dept. Revenue, Guardian of Small Bus. award, SC Chap. NFIB, 1996. Past dir. Crime Stoppers, Berkeley Chamber of Commerce; Hammerton Lodge #332 A.F.M., North Charleston Rotary Club. Republican. Office: 2332 Rayburn House Office Bldg Washington DC 20515-3513*

BROWN, HERBERT CHARLES, chemistry educator; b. London, May 22, 1912; arrived in U.S., 1914; s. Charles and Pearl (Gorinstein) Brown; m. Sarah Baylen Brown, Feb. 6, 1937; 1 child, Charles Allan. AS, Wright Jr. Coll., Chgo., 1935; BS, U. Chgo., 1936, PhD, 1938, DSc (hon.), 1968; doctorate (hon.), Wayne State U., 1980, Lebanon Valley Coll., 1980, L.I. U., 1980, Hebrew U. Jerusalem, 1980, Pontificia Universidad de Chile, 1980, Purdue U., 1980; doctorates (hon.), U. Wales, 1981, U. Paris, 1982, Butler U., 1982, Ball State U., 1985, Nicolas Copernicus U., Torun, 1998. Asst. chemistry U. Chgo., 1936—38, Eli Lilly post-doctorate rsch. fellow, 1938—39, instr., 1939—43; asst. prof. chemistry Wayne U., 1943—46, assoc. prof., 1946—47; prof. inorganic chemistry Purdue U., 1947—59, Richard B. Wetherill prof. chemistry, 1959, Richard B. Wetherill rsch. prof., 1960—78, emeritus, 1978—. Vis. prof. UCLA, 1951, Ohio State U., 1952, U. Mex., 1954, U. Calif. at Berkeley, 1957, U. Colo., 1958, U. Heidelberg, 1963, SUNY, Stony Brook, 1966, U. Calif., Santa Barbara, 1967, Hebrew U., Jerusalem, 1969, U. Wales, Swansea, 1973, U. Cape Town, South Africa, 1974, U. Calif., San Diego, 1979; Harrison Howe lectr., 53; Friend E. Clark lectr., 53; Freud-McCormack lectr., 54; Centenary lectr., England, 55; Thomas W. Talley lectr., 56; Falk-Plaut lectr., 57; Julius Stieglitz lectr., 58; Max Tishler lectr., 58; Kekule-Couper Centenary lectr., 58; E.C. Franklin lectr., 60; Ira Remsen lectr., 61; Edgar Fahs Smith lectr., 62; Seydel-Wooley lectr., 66; Baker lectr., 69; Benjamin Rush lectr., 71; Chem. Soc. lectr., Australia, 72; Armes lectr., 73; Henry Gilman lectr., 75; others; hon. prof. Organomet Chem. Chinese Acad. Scis., 1994; chem. cons. to indsl. corps.; rschr. phys., organic and inorganic chemistry relating chem. behavior to molecular structure, selective reductions, hydroboration and chemistry of organoboranes. Author: Hydroboration, 1962, Boranes in Organic Chemistry, 1972, Organic Synthesis via Boranes, 1975, The Nonclassical Ion Problem, 1977; co-author (with A.W. Pelter and K. Smith): Borane Reagents, 1988; co-author: (with P.V. Ramachandran) Organoboranes for Syntheses, 2001; co-author: (with G. W. Kramer, A.B. Levy, and M. Mark Midland) Organic Syntheses via Boranes, Vol. 1, 2001; co-author: (with M. Zaidlewicz) Organic Syntheses via Boranes, Vol. 2, 2001; co-author: (with A. Suzuki) Organic Syntheses via Boranes, Vol. 3, 2003; contbr. articles to chem. jours. Bd. govs. Hebrew U., 1969—90; co-dir. war rsch. projects for U.S. Army, Nat. Def. Rsch. Com., Manhattan Project U. Chgo., 1940—43. Decorated Order of the Rising Sun, Gold and Silver Star

Japan; named one of Top 75 Disting. Contbrs. to Chem. Enterprise, Chem. & Engring. News, 1998; recipient Purdue Sigma Xi rsch. award, 1951, Nichols medal, 1959, award, Am. Chem. Soc., 1960, S.O.C.M.A. medal, 1960, H.N. McCoy award, 1965, Linus Pauling medal, 1968, Nat. medal of Sci., 1969, Roger Adams medal, 1971, Charles Frederick Chandler medal, 1973, Chem. Pioneer award, 1975, CUNY medal for sci. achievement, 1976, Elliott Cresson medal, 1978, C.K. Ingold medal, 1978, Nobel prize in Chemistry, 1979, Priestley medal, 1981, Perkin medal, 1982, Gold medal award, Am. Inst. Chemists, 1981, G.M. Kosolapoff medal, 1987, NAS award in chem. scis., 1987, Oesper award, Cin. sect. Am. Chem. Soc., 1990, Herbert C. Brown medal and award for creative rsch. in synthetic methods, Am. Chem. Soc., 1998; fellow (hon.) U. Wales Swansea, 1994. Fellow: AAAS, Indian Nat. Sci. Acad. (fgn.), Royal Soc. Chemistry (hon.); mem.: NAS, Chinese Acad. Sci. (hon. prof. 1994), Indian Acad. Sci., Chem. Soc. Japan, Pharm. Soc. Japan (hon.), Am. Chem. Soc. (chmn. Purdue sect. 1955—56), Am. Acad. Arts and Sci., Sigma Xi, Phi Beta Kappa, Alpha Chi Sigma, Phi Lambda Upsilon (hon.). Office: Purdue U Dept Chemistry Lafayette IN 47907

BROWN, HERBERT RUSSELL, lawyer, writer; b. Columbus, Ohio, Sept. 27, 1931; s. Thomas Newton and Irene (Hankinson) B.; m. Beverly Ann Jenkins, Dec. 2, 1967; children: David Herbert, Andrew Jenkins. BA, Denison U., 1953; JD, U. Mich., 1956. Assoc. Vorys, Sater, Seymour and Pease, Columbus, Ohio, 1956, 60-64, ptnr., 1965-82; treas. Sunday Creek Coal Co., Columbus, 1970-86; assoc. justice Ohio Supreme Ct., Columbus, 1987-93. Commr. Ohio Ethics Commn., 2002—, examiner Ohio Bar, 1967-72, Multi-State Bar, 1971-76, Dist. Ct. Bar, 1968-71; commr. Fed. Lands, Columbus, 1967-68, Lake Lands, Columbus, 1981; bd. dirs. Thurber House, 1992-94, Sunday Creek Coal Co.; adj. prof. Ohio State U. Coll. Law, 1997-2000; panelist Am. Arbitration Assn., 1993—. Author: (novels) Presumption of Guilt, 1991, Shadows of Doubt, 1994, (plays) You're My Boy, 1999, Peace with Honor, 2000, Mano A Mano, 2000, Power of God, 2002; mem. editl. bd. U. Mich. Law Rev., 1955-56. Trustee Columbus Bar Found., 1993—, pres., 2001—; candidate Ohio State Legis.; deacon, mem. governing bd. 1st Cmty. Ch., 1966—80; bd. dirs. Ctrl. Cmty. House Columbus, 1967—75. Capt. JAGC U.S. Army, 1956—57. Recipient Disting. Alumni citation, Denison U., 2003. Fellow Am. Coll. Trial Lawyers; mem. Ohio Bar Assn., Columbus Bar Assn. Democrat. Office: 5 E Long St Columbus OH 43215

BROWN, HERMIONE KOPP, lawyer; b. Syracuse, N.Y., Sept. 29, 1915; d. Harold H. and Frances (Burger) Kopp; m. Louis M. Brown, May 30, 1937 (dec. Sept. 1996); children— Lawrence D., Marshall J., Harold A. BA, Wellesley Coll., 1934; LLB, U. So. Calif., 1947. Bar: Calif. 1947. Story analyst 20th Century-Fox Film Corp., 1935-42; assoc. Gang, Kopp & Tyre, Los Angeles, 1947-52; ptnr. to sr. ptnr. Gang, Tyre, Ramer & Brown, Inc., Los Angeles, 1952—. Lectr. copyright and entertainment law U. So. Calif. Law Sch., 1974-77. Contbr. to profl. publs. Fellow Am. Coll. Trust and Estate Coun.; mem. Calif. Bar Assn. (chair probate law cons. group nd. legal specialization 1977-82, trust and probate law sect., exec. com. 1983-86, advisor 1986-89), L.A. Copyright Soc. (pres. 1979-80), Order of Coif, Phi Beta Kappa. Avocations: literature, theatre, music. Office: Gang Tyre Ramer & Brown Inc 132 S Rodeo Dr Beverly Hills CA 90212-2415

BROWN, HERSHEL M. retired newspaper publisher; b. Phila., Jan. 7, 1923; s. Paul and Sarah (Magil) B.; m. Lorraine Rose Blofson, Apr. 21, 1944; children: Susan R., Stephen J.(deceased), Adam L. Student, U. Pa., Phila., 1940-42; BS in Bus., Northwestern U., Evanston, Ill., 1944; MS in Journalism, Northwestern U., 1947. Reporter, editorial writer, music critic Globe Times, Bethlehem, Pa., 1947-48; rewrite, asst. to Sunday editor, music critic Post Gazette, Pitts., 1949-50; advt. copywriter, account exec., plans bd. chmn., v.p./exec. supr. Al Paul Lefton Co. Inc., Phila., Chgo., L.A., 1950-68; pub. Register News, Bordentown, N.J., 1968-96; pres. Lorraine Pub. Inc., Bordentown, N.J., 1968-96. V.p., trustee Jenkintown (Pa.) Music Sch.; pub. rels. dir. Co-Opera Co. Phila., 1950-57; bd. mem. Farnsworth Ave. Revitalization Project, Bordentown, N.J., 1984-90; mem. artists selection com. Cmty. Concerts Bordentown, Inc., 1982-96. Lt. USNR, 1944-46. Recipient 1st pl. awards Pa. Newspaper Pubs., 1948, N.J. Press Assn., 1971, 78. Mem.: Am. Newspaper Guild, Merchandising Execs. Club Chgo., Sigma Delta Chi. Jewish. Avocations: piano, cello, concerts, theater, record collecting, swimming. Home: 379 Landing St Lumberton NJ 08048-4525

BROWN, HILTON, visual arts educator, artist, writer; b. Momence, Ill., Sept. 22, 1938; s. Oswald E. and Maud M. (Shronts) B. Student, Goodman Theater/Art Inst. Chgo, 1956-58, U. Chgo., 1959-60, U. Ill., Chgo., 1961-62; cert. in fine arts, 1962; Diploma in Fine Arts, BFA in Painting, Sch. of Art Inst. Chgo., 1962, MFA in Painting, 1963. Instr. drawing/painting Sch. Art Inst. Chgo., 1962-65; asst. prof. fine art Sch. Fine Arts Washington U., St. Louis, 1965-68; asst. prof. fine arts Goucher Coll., Towson, Md., 1968-70, assoc. prof. fine arts, 1970-75, prof. and chair dept. visual arts, 1975-78; vis. assoc. prof. art history U. Del., 1974-78, prof. art conservation, 1978-84, Mayer prof. artists techniques, 1984-88, prof. art, art history and art conservation, 1988-92, Harriet T. Baily prof. art, art conservation, art history and mus. studies, 1992—. Cons., lectr. Nat. Tchr. Inst./Nat. Gallery of Art, Washington, 1990—. Author: (exhbn. catalog) The Art and Archives of Ralph Mayer, 1984; co-author (exhbn. catalog) Milk and Eggs: The American Revival of Tempera Painting, 1930-1950, 2002; co-curator (exhbn.) Brandywine River Mus., Akron Art Mus., Spencer Mus., U. Kans., 2002; one person show Susan Isaacs Gallery, Wilmington, Del., 1990, work in mus. collections Balt. Mus. of Art. Sec. bd. dirs. Gay and Lesbian Alliance of Del., Wilmington, 1991-93; co-chair Lesbian, Gay, Bisexual Caucus of Commn. to Promote Racial and Cultural Diversity, U. Del., 1992-99, chair faculty senate com. on diversity and affirmative action, 1993-95, 97-98. Democrat. Anglo-Catholic. Avocations: reading, gardening. Office: Univ of Delaware Mus Studies 301 Old College Hall Newark DE 19716 E-mail: hilton@udel.edu.

BROWN, HOLMES, public affairs executive; b. Prescott, Kans., Oct. 2, 1914; s. Frank Emerson and May Holmes Brown; m. Mary Ellen Lynch, Oct. 17, 1938; children: Holmes Cheney, Hamilton Frank, James Emerson. BS, Iowa State U., 1936; postgrad., GE Inst., 1936-39. Mgmt. technician GE, various locations, 1936-43; with pub. rels. Am. Locomotive, N.Y.C., 1945-50; pub. affairs exec. Colonial Williamsburg (Va.) Found., 1950; pub. rels. exec. Ford Motor Co., Dearborn, Mich., 1952-60; asst. to Sgt. Shriver War on Poverty, Washington, 1964-66; v.p. Am. Airlines, N.Y.C., 1966-68; pub. affairs officer Continental Group, N.Y.C., 1968-75; v.p. Continental Group Found., N.Y.C., 1975-79; pres., chmn. The Inst. for Applied Econs., N.Y.C., Va., 1979—. Prodr. nat. nutrition program GE Co., 1941-43; pres., chmn. N.Y. Bd. of Trade, 1979-85. Editor: How to Get the Most Our of the Food You Buy, 1942; prodr. Headstart Ednl. Guide Books, 1965; author: Can You Trust Network Evening News; author (newspaper article) Nixon's Enemy List, 1973. Pres. Fund for New Priorities, N.Y., 1977, bd. dirs., 1976-99. Recipient Outstanding Alumni award Iowa State U., 1957, Leadership award Fund for New Priorities, 1978, Silver Anvil award Am. Pub. Rels. Soc., 1959. Mem. Admirals Club (life), Nat. Press Club, Boars Head Sports Club, The Goodwin Soc. Colonial Williamsburg, The Nat. Hist. Soc., Va. Hist. Soc. Democrat. Episcopalian. Avocations: farming, tennis, sculpting, track, history. Home: High Mowing Farms 1894 Stillhouse Creek Rd Afton VA 22920-2043 Office: Inst for Applied Econs 1 Ednam Vlg Charlottesville VA 22903-4636

BROWN, HOWARD JORDAN, media executive; b. Chgo., July 31, 1923; s. Isidore and Gladys B.; m. Elizabeth Kassel, Mar. 2, 1960; children: Lucille Minn, Sarah Russ, Amy Tuchler. Ba, Princeton U., 1946; MS, Columbia U., 1948. Fgn. correspondent Chgo. Sun Times, 1948-49; with Cleve. Plain Dealer and Cleve. News, 1950-59, Ottaway Newspapers, Campbell Hall, N.Y., 1959-62, Kenosha (Wis.) News, 1962—; pres. United Comm. Corp., Kenosha, 1969—. Stockholder Kenosha News, Attleboro, Mass., Sun Chronicle, Watertown, S.D., Public Opinion, KEYC-TV12, Mankato, Minn., WWNY-TV7, Watertown, N.Y., also three weeklies and several shoppers. Bd. dirs. Kenosha Jewish Welfare Fund, YMCA; pres. Kenosha Christmas Charities, 1980—; trustee Carthage Coll., Kenosha, 1987—, Greater Kenosha Area Found., 1994—. With U.S. Army Infantry, 1943-46, ETO. Jewish. Avocation: tennis. Office: Kenosha News 5800 7th Ave Kenosha WI 53140-4136 E-mail: hjb@kenoshanews.com.

BROWN, HOWARD MARK, physician; b. Bronx, N.Y., July 3, 1961; s. Sheldon Alan and Frances (Krowitz) B.; m. Lenore Jay Ballen, July 5, 1997; children: Seth Maxwell Ballen, Nathan Michael Ballen. BA in Biology, Brandeis U., 1983; MD, Hahnemann U., 1990. Rsch. technologist Dana Farber Cancer Inst., Boston, 1984-86; physician Eldorado Internal Medicine, Tucson, 1993-95, New Pueblo Medicine, Tucson, 1995-96, Ariz. Cmty. Physicians, Tucson, 1996—. Mem. profl. adv. bd. Kelly Home Health, Tucson, 1999—2001; head sect. internal medicine Eldorado Hosp., Tucson, 1997—2000, pharmacy and therapeutics chmn., 2000—. Contbr. articlest to profl. jours. Mem. Ariz. Soc. Internal Medicine, Pima County Med. Soc., Maricopa County Med. Soc. Office: Ariz Cmty Physicians 1500 N Wilmot Rd Ste A-100 Tucson AZ 85712-4416

BROWN, HUGH AUCHINCLOSS, III, education educator; b. Orange, N.J., Feb. 5, 1945; s. Hugh Auchincloss Brown Jr. and Amanda Pope Brown; m. Jane Riley Brown, Aug. 18, 1988; children: Ben Jensen, Monica Jensen. BE, U. of Vt., 1969; MS in edn. psychology, U. of Utah, 1975, EdD, 1982. Dir. of didactic programs for veterans in cmty svc. Salt Lake City, 1975—76; instr., ednl. psychology and gen. studies U. of UT., 1978—93, coord. of vet. affairs, 1976—80, coord. of scholastic standards, 1980—83, asst. dir., acad. advising, 1981—83, athletic acad. adv., 1983—88, assoc. dir., acad. advising, 1988—97, asst. dean, curriculum adminstrn., 1998—99, assoc. dean of U. coll., 1999—2002, dir. of devel., 2002—. Mem. Undergrad Quality Com., 2003—, Bd. of Visitors for Student Initiatives, 2002—, New Student Adv. Team, 2002—. 1st. lt. U.S. Army, 1969—71, platton leader in Korea. Recipient Perlman award, 1988. Mem.: Nat. Assn. of Acad. Advisors, Nat. Acad. Advising Assn., Gt. Basin Rugby Union (pres. 1984—86, treas. 1982—84), Cottonwood Club. Avocations: golf, tennis, hiking, travel. Home: 1517 Spring Run Dr Salt Lake City UT 84117

BROWN, IFIGENIA THEODORE, lawyer; b. Syracuse, N.Y., Mar. 14, 1930; d. Gus and Christine Theodore; m. Paul Frederick Brown, Sept. 16, 1956; 1 child, Paul Darrow. BA, Syracuse U., 1951, LLB, JD, 1954. Bar: N.Y. 1956. Acting police justice Village of Ballston Spa, NY, 1960—62; sr. ptnr. Brown & Brown, Ballston Spa, 1958—95; ptnr. Brown Brown & Peterson Esqs, Ballston Spa, 1995—2000; of counsel Brown, Peterson and Craig, Ballston Spa, 2000—. Chmn. N.Y. State Bd. Real Property Svcs., Albany, 1996—. Mem. Charlton Sch. Bd., 1989-93, Ballston Spa Libr. Bd., 1991-94; founder pres. Saratoga County Women's Rep. Club; vice-chmn. Saratoga County Rep. Com., 1958-72. Mem. N.Y. State Bar Assn., Saratoga County Bar Assn. (treas. 1983-84, pres. 1984-85), Zonta (pres. Saratoga County 1962, 90), Order Ea. Star. Republican. Greek Orthodox. Avocations: church choir, piano. Home: 42 Hyde Blvd Ballston Spa NY 12020-1608 Office: Brown Peterson and Craig One E High St Ballston Spa NY 12020

BROWN, ILENE DE LOIS, special education educator; b. Wichita, Kans., Aug. 17, 1947; d. Homer DeWitt and Estella Lenora (Cleland) Rusco; m. Gale Robert Aaroe, Nov. 23, 1967 (div. July 1983); 1 child, Candice Yvonne. BEd in Elem. Edn., Washburn U., Topeka, 1969; MS, Nazareth Coll. Rochester, 1979. Cert. tchr. Idaho. Emotionally disturbed trainer Rochester Mental Health Ctr., Greece, N.Y., 1970-71, West Ridge, Greece, 1971-72; tutor kindergarten through grades 6 Craig Hill, Greece, 1978-79; resource rm. tchr. math. English Village, Greece, 1979-80; resource rm. tchr. grades 4-6 Lakeshore, Greece, 1980; tutor, translator Guadalajara, Mex., 1980-82; tchr. grade 1 English John F. Kennedy Sch., Guadalajara, 1982-83; tchr. various grades Greenleaf (Idaho) Friends Acad., 1983-89; resource tchr., high sch. spl. edn. community work coord. Middleton (Idaho) Primary Sch., 1989-91, tchr., 1991—, tchr. 2d grade, 1990—. Sunday sch. tchr. Mem. Coun. for Exceptional Children, Coun. for Children with Behavior Disorders and Learning Disabilities (officer, sec. state chpt. 1991-92), Middleton Profl. Devel. Com. (chairperson profl. devel. com. 1992-95—), Idaho Edn. Assn., Middleton Edn. Assn., Phi Delta Kappa. Avocations: bicycling, traveling, reading, birdwatching. Office: Mill Creek Elem Sch 500 N Middleton Rd Middleton ID 83644-5499 E-mail: ibrown@msd134.org.

BROWN, IRA HUGO, psychologist, educator; b. South Hill, Va., Aug. 25, 1935; s. Melvin Eugene and Mattie Pearl Brown; m. Alfreda Macklin Brown, Dec. 23, 1959; children: Tyira Anita McElhaney, Terrence Anthony Brown. BS in Biology, Cen. State U., 1956; MEd, Bowie State U., 1971; PhD, Union Inst., 1994. Advanced profl. cert. Md. State Dept. Edn.; lic. clin. profl. counselor. Classroom tchr. Mecklenburg County Bd. Edn., South Hill, Va., 1959-68; guidance counselor Prince George's County, Upper Marlboro, Md., 1968-99; counselor, psychologist Tri-County Youth Svcs. Bur., Charlotte Hall, Md., 1999—. Vestry mem. Trinity Episcopal Ch., S. Hilliva, Md., 1963-66, St. Christopher Ch., New Canoltor, Md., 1970-72, Trinity Episcopal Ch., Upper Marlboro, Md., 1995-98. Recipient Profl. Devel. Cert. ACA, 1992, Cert. of Recognition Edn., Prince George's County Bd. Edn., 1994. Mem. NEA, Am. Psychotherapy Assn., Md. State Tchrs. Assn., Md. Assn. for Counseling Devel., Prince George's Edn. Assn., Omega Psi Phi. Episcopalian. Avocations: swimming, reading, listening to classical and other music, team sports, travel. Office: Tri-County Youth Svcs Bur PO Box 400 Charlotte Hall MD 20622-0400 E-mail: tab490@earthlink.com.

BROWN, J. E. (BUSTER BROWN), lawyer, consultant; b. Dec. 10, 1940; BS, Tex. A&I U., 1963; JD, U. Tex., 1967. Mem. Tex. Senate, 1980—2002; chmn. natural resources com., sunset adv. com., natural resources interim com., water resources devel. com., Gulf States Marine Fisheries Commn., Tex. Water Found. Mem. Criminal Justice Com., So. Legis. Conf. Energy Commn., Am. legis. Exch. Coun. Telecom. Commn., Nat. Conf. State Legis. Comm. and Info. Policy, Legis. and Congl. Redistricting Com., Fin. Com., Nominations Com., Vets. Affairs and Mil. Installations Com., alt. Environ. com., Legal Com. Interstate Oil and Gas Compact Commn.; past chmn. Energy Coun.; adj. prof. U. Tex. Sch. Law.

BROWN, J'AMY MARONEY, journalist, media relations consultant, investor; b. Oct. 30, 1945; d. Roland Francis and Jeanne (Wilbur) Maroney; m. James Raphael Brown, Jr., Nov. 5, 1967 (dec. July 1982); children: James Roland Francis, Jeanne Raphael. Student, U. So. Calif., 1963-67. Reporter L.A. Herald Examiner, 1966-67, Lewisville Leader, Dallas, 1980-81; editor First Person Mag., Dallas, 1981-82; journalism dir. Pacific Palisades Sch., L.A., 1983-84; freelance writer, media cons., 1984-88; media dir., chief media strategist Tellem Inc., 1990-92, comm. cons., issues mgr., 1992—. Press liaison U.S. papal visit, L.A., 1987; pres., CEO and owner PRformance Group Comm., 1995—; auction chmn. Assn. Pub. Broadcasting, Houston, 1974, 75; vice chmn. Dallas Arts Coun., 1976-80; vice chmn. Met. March of Dimes, Dallas, 1980-82; del. Dallas Coun. PTAs, 1976-80; bd. dirs., pres. comtinuing edn. adv. bd. Santa Barbara City Coll.; bd. dirs. Montecito Assn., Women's Econ. Ventures, Santa Barbara Visual Arts Alliance; mem. core-coun. Santa Barbara Coun. on Self-Esteem; coord. specialist World Cup Soccer Organizing Com.; dir. J.M. Brown Charitable Found. Recipient UPI Editors award for investigative reporting, 1981. Mem. NAFE, Pub. Rels. Soc. Am. (accredited), Women Meeting Women, Women in Comm., Am. Bus. Women's Assn., Goleta Valley Art Assn., Santa Barbara C. of C. (media com.), Montecito Assn. (bd. dirs.). Republican. Roman Catholic. Home: 1143 High Rd Santa Barbara CA 93108-2430

BROWN, JACK D(ELBERT), chemist, researcher; b. Boise, Idaho, June 21, 1954; s. Robert and Shirley Fay (Piper) Brown; m. Leslie Anne Terry, June 21, 1981; children: Lauren Anne, Justin Andrew. Student, Boise State U., 1973-76; BS, Utah State U., 1983, PhD, 1987. Postdoctoral rschr. Colo. State U., Ft. Collins, 1986-88; sr. rsch. chemist Syntex Chems. Inc., Boulder, Colo., 1988-90, prin. rsch. chemist, Tech. Ctr., 1990—99, disting. scientist, 1999—2002, Tech. Ctr. Roche Colo. Corp., Boulder, 1998—; mgr. devel. Boehringer Ingelhem Chem., Inc., 2002—. Co-author: (book) Metabolism of Food Disaccarides, 1983; contbr. articles to profl. jours. Explorer scout advisor Boy Scouts Am., Boulder, 1991. Mem.: AAAS, N.Y. Acad. Scis., Am. Chem. Soc., Sigma Xi. Achievements include co-inventor. Home: 5731 FireLight Ter Moseley VA 23120 Office: Boehringer Ingelheim Chem 2820 N Normandy Dr Petersburg VA 23805 E-mail: jbrown@bichemicals.com.

BROWN, JACK H. supermarket company executive; b. L.A., June 14, 1939; Student, San Jose State U, UCLA. V.p. Sages Complete Marktes, San Bernardino, Calif., 1960-67, Marsh Supermarkets, Yorktown, Ind., 1971-77; pres. Pantry Supermarkets, Pasadena, Calif., 1977-79; pres. mid-west divsn. Cullum Cos., Dallas, 1979-81; pres., CEO Stater Bros. Markets, Colton, Calif., 1981—; also chmn. bd. dirs. Trustee U. Redlands, Calif.; bd. dirs. Goodwill Industries of inland Empire, San Bernardino; bd. councillors Calif. State U., San Bernardion. With USNR, 1956-62. Recipient Horation alger award Disting. Ams., 1992, Bus. Exec. of Yr. award U. so. Calif., 1993; Calif. State U., San Berardino Sch. Bus. named in his honor, 1992. Mem. Western Assn. Food Chains (v.p., bd. dirs., pres. 1987-88), Calif. Retailers Assn. (bd. dirs.), Food Mktg. Inst. (vice chmn.), So. Calif. Grocers Assn., Food Employers Coun. (bd. govs.), Life Savs. and Loan Assn. (dir.), Elks. Republican. Presbyterian. Office: Stater Bros Markets 21700 Barton Rd Colton CA 92324*

BROWN, JACK HAROLD UPTON, physiologist, biomedical engineer, academic administrator; b. Nixon, Tex., Nov. 16, 1918; s. Gilmer W. and Thelma (Patton) B.; m. Jessie Carolyn Schulz, Apr. 14, 1943. BS, S.W. Tex. State U., 1939; postgrad., U. Tex., 1939—41; PhD, Rutgers U., 1948. Lectr. physics Southwest Tex. State U., San Marcos, 1943—44; instr. phys. chemistry Rutgers U., New Brunswick, NJ, 1944—45, rsch. assoc., 1944—48; lectr. U. Pitts., 1948—50; head biol. scis. Mellon Inst., Pitts., 1948—50; asst. prof. physiology U. N.C., Chapel Hill, 1950—52; scientist Oak Ridge Inst. Nuclear Studies, 1952; assoc. prof. physiology Emory U. Med. Sch., Atlanta, 1952—58, prof., 1959—60, acting chmn. dept. physiology, 1958—60; lectr. physiology George Washington U. and Georgetown U. med. schs., Washington, 1960—65; exec. sec. biomed. engring. and physiology tng. coms. Nat. Inst. Gen. Med. Scis., NIH, Bethesda, Md., 1960—62; chief spl. rsch. br. div. Rsch. Facilities and Resources NIH, 1962—63, acting chief gen. clin. rsch. ctrs. br., 1963—64, asst. dir. ops. Div. Research Facilities and Resources, 1964—65; acting program dir. pharmacology/toxicology program Nat. Inst. Gen. Med. Scis., NIH, 1966—70, asst. dir. ops., 1965—66, assoc. dir. sci. programs, 1967—70, acting dir., 1970; spl. asst. to adminstr. Health Services and Mental Health Adminstrn., USPHS, Rockville, Md., 1971—72; assoc. dep. adminstr. for devel. Health Svcs. and Mental Health Adminstrn., USPHS, 1972—73; spl. asst. to adminstr. Health Resources Adminstrn., 1973—78; coord. Southwest Rsch. Consortium, San Antonio, 1974—78; prof. physiology U. Tex. Med. Sch., San Antonio, 1974—78; prof. environ. scis. U. Tex. at San Antonio, 1974—78; adj. prof. health svcs. adminstrn. Trinity U., 1975—78; assoc. provost rsch. and advanced edn. U. Houston, 1978—80, prof. biology, 1980—89, prof. emeritus, 1990—; adj. prof. U. Tex. Sch. Public Health, 1978—; prof. public adminstrn. Tex. Women's U., 1978—; adj. prof. community medicine Baylor Coll. Medicine, Houston, 1986—89; vice-chmn. SCORE (Svc. Corps of Retired Execs.), 1993—96; chmn., dist. dir., 1997—2003; regional editor Savant, 1996—2000, dist. mgr., 1997—2002; 69686. Fulbright lectr. U. Rangoon, 1950; cons. health systems WHO, Oak Ridge Inst. Nuclear Studies, Lockhead Aircraft Co., Drexel Inst. Tech., NASA, Vassar Coll., TelTech; mem. adv. bd. Ctr. for Cancer Therapy, San Antonio, 1974—, TelTech; bd. dirs. South Tex. Health Edn. Ctr.; cons. Univ. Tex. Health Sci. Ctr., Houston, Sumitomo Corp., Tokyo; rschr., instr. in radar U.S. Army, Scott Field, Ill. Author: Physiology of Man in Space, 1963, (with S.B. Barker) Basic Endocrinology, 1966, 2d edit., 1970, (with J.F. Dickson) Future Goals of Engineering in Biology and Medicine, 1968, Advances in Biomedical Engineering, vol. II, 1972, vols. III, IV, 1973, vol. V, 1974, vol. VI, 1976, Vol. VII, 1978, (with J.E. Jacobs and L.E. Stark) Biomedical Engineering, 1972, (with D.E. Gann) Engineering Principles in Physiology, vols. I, II, 1973, The Health Care Dilemma, 1977, Integration and Control of Biol. Processes, 1978, Politics and Health Care, 1978, Telecommunications in Health Care, 1981, Management in Health Care Systems, 1983, A Laboratory Manual in Animal Physiology, 1984, 3d edit., 1988, High Cost of Healing, 1985, (with J. Comolo) Productivity in Health Care Systems, 1987, Guide to Collecting Fine Prints, 1989, Educating for Excellence, 1991, Footsteps in Sci., 1993, Revisions of Starting and Running a Small Business, 1994, Starting a Small Nonprofit Business, 2002, Science and Society, 2002, Records for Small Business, 1995, Starting a Non Profit Business, 2001, Science and Society, 2002; editor: (with Ferguson) Blood and Body Functions, 1966, (with Miller) Exercise Physiology, 1966, Life Into Space, (Wunder), 1968; contbr. numerous articles on biomed. engring. to sci. jours. Mem. adv. bd. San Antonio Mus. Assn.; mem. spl. effects com. Tex. Sesquicentennial; bd. dirs. Inst. for Health Policy, U. Tex. Health Sci. Ctr. Served with USNR, 1941-42. With USN, 1941—42. Recipient cert. appreciation NIH, 1969, 1st pl. award Atlanta Internat. Film Festival, 1970, Achievement award NASA, 1977, spl. team award NASA, 1978, recognition award Emergency Med. Care, 1980, Best Tchr. award Nat. Mortar Bd., 1986, Most Disting. Alumni award S.W. Tex. State U., 1986; Gerard Swope fellow Gen. Electric Co., 1946-48; Fulbright grantee, 1950; Dept. of Def. grantee, 1950-52; NIH grantee, 1950-60; Cancer Soc. grantee, 1958; Damon Runyon Cancer award grantee, 1959; Dept. Energy grantee, 1980-81; NASA grantee, 1987-89. Fellow AAAS, Nat. Acad. Engring., IEEE (life, joint com. engring. in medicine and biology 1966—); mem. Am. Chem. Soc. (sr.), Biomed. Engring. Soc. (founder; pres. 1969-70, dir. 1968-69), Inst. Radio Engrs. (nat. sec. profl. group biomed. engring. 1962-64), N.Y. Acad. Scis., Endocrine Soc., Am. Physiol. Soc. (com. mem. 1959-63, nat. com. on animals in research 1985—), Tex. Print Soc. (founder, pres.), Soc. for Exptl. Biology and Medicine, Svc. Corps Ret. Execs. (vice chmn. 1994-95, chmn. 1995—), Sigma Xi (research award 1961, founder, pres. Alamo chpt. 1977-78), Council Biology Editors, Soc. Research Adminstrn., Pi Kappa Delta, Phi Lambda Upsilon, Alpha Chi. Clubs: Cosmos. Achievements include invention of of the capsule manometer; respirator for small animals and basal metabolic apparatus for small animals; dust sampler; apparatus for partitioning human lung volumes; laser credit card patient record system; Warburg apparatus calibrator. Home: 2908 Whisper View St San Antonio TX 78230-3743 Office: 8100 Cambridge St Apt 10 Houston TX 77054-3105

BROWN, JACK WYMAN, architect; b. Detroit, Oct. 17, 1922; s. Ernest E. and Mary Morse (Jones) B.; m. Joan M. Graham, Oct. 4, 1971; 1 dau., Elizabeth. BS, U. Mich., 1945. Designer Odell, Hewlett & Luckenbach, Inc., Birmingham, Mich., 1952-57; pres. Brown Assocs. Architects, Inc., Bloomfield Hills, Mich., 1957—; part-time instr. design Lawrence Inst. Tech., 1959. Mem. Mayor Detroit Task Force, 1969-70. Served with USNR, 1943-46. Co-recipient 1st prize nat. competition design Nat. Cowboy Hall Fame, 1967; recipient Institutions mag. award, 1980 Mem. AIA (chmn. working coms.), Am. Soc. Ch. Architecture (dir. 1960-64, 72—), Mich. Soc. Architects (design award St. Regis Ch. 1969, Fox Hills Elem. Sch. 1970, Andor Office Bldg. 1972, CAM Design award 1992). Home: 5980 Braemoor Rd Bloomfield Hills MI 48301-1419 Office: Brown Teefey Assocs Archs PC 4190 Telegraph Rd Bloomfield Hills MI 48302-2079 E-mail: jandjbrown@aol.com.

BROWN, JAMES CARRINGTON, III, (BING BROWN), public relations and communications executive; b. Wilmington, Del., May 17, 1939; s. James Carrington Jr. and Virginia Helen (Miller); m. Carol Osman, Nov. 3, 1961. Grad. security mgmt. group, Indsl. Coll. of the Armed Forces; BBS, Ariz. State U., 1984. Newsman, disc jockey, program dir. various radio stas., Ariz., 1955-60; morning news editor Sta. KOY, Phoenix, 1960-61; staff writer, photographer Prescott (Ariz.) Evening Courier, 1961; bus. editor, staff writer, photographer Phoenix Gazette, 1961-65; various communications positions Salt River Project, Phoenix, 1965-89; pres. Carrington Communications, Payson, Ariz., 1989—. Cons. comm., freelance writing, photography The Browns, Payson, 1965—; pub. info. officer Water Svc. Dept., City of Phoenix, 1991—2001; instr. Rio Salado C.C., Phoenix, 1989—93; guest lectr. various colls. and univs., 1975—; adj. prof. Walter Cronkite Sch. Journalism and Telecom., Ariz. State U., 1990—99; exec. prodr., prodr., asst. prodr. various ednl. videos. Bd. dirs. Grand Canyon coun. Boy Scouts Am., 1985-89, mem. adv. coun., 1990-2000; mem. exec. com. Cmty. Svc. Fund Drive, 1992-2001; mem. environment com. Phoenix Futures Forum, 1991-93; mem. project adv. com. for Am. Waterworks Assn. Rsch. Found. study of Pub. Involvement Strategies, Phase I, 1994-95, Phase II, 1998-2001; deacon Meml. Presbyn. Ch., 1980-82, elder, 1985-87; mem. spl. gifts com. United Way, Phoenix, 1986-89; mem. grant com. Beaver Valley Fire Dist., 2003—. Recipient Golden Eagle award Boy Scouts Am., 1992. Mem. Pub. Rels. Soc. Am. (accredited; Percy award Valley of the Sun chpt. 1999), Western Systems Coord. Coun. (chmn. pub. info. com. 1969-89), Ariz. Newspapers Assn. (Billy Goat award, Allied Mem. of Yr. 1985), Western Coalition Arid States (chmn. comm. subcom. 1991-93, chmn. com. and mem. com. 1993-2000, editor WESTCAS News 1991-2000, Disting. Performance award 1996, Founder's award 2000), Western Energy Supply and Transmission Assocs. (mem. pub. info. com. 1967-89), Phoenix Press Club (pres. 1982-83), Nat. Acad. TV Arts/Sci., (1968-1983), Heard Mus. Anthropology and Primitive Art, (1980-2001); Jazz in Ariz., World Affairs Coun., City, County Comms. and Mktg. Assn. (Savvy award for

outstanding video 1995-2001), Payson Choral Soc. Republican. Avocations: fly fishing, golf, photography, reading, cooking. Home and Office: Carrington Comm HC3 Box 670-I Payson AZ 85541

BROWN, JAMES CHANDLER, college administrator; b. Garden City, N.Y., Aug. 5, 1947; s. Harry Chandler and Lillian Marie (Cutter) B. BA, Susquehanna U., Selinsgrove, Pa., 1970; License es Lettres, Geneva U., 1978; postgrad., Stanford U., 1984. Rsch. asst. Geneva U., 1972—79; asst. Galerie Jan Krugier, Geneva, 1978—81; coord. pubs. So. Oreg. State Coll., Ashland, 1982-84; dir. pubs. So. Oreg. U., 1984—; resident dir. Oreg. Ctr., Oreg. Univ. Sys., Lyon, France, 2001. Cons. in field. Author: How to Sharpen Your Publications (brochure, Case award) 1985, College Viewbook (booklet), 1985. Sec. bd. dirs. Schneider Mus. Art, Ashland, 1985-94. Canton of Geneva grantee, 1974-79; awardee, Coun. for Advancement and Support of Edn., 1987-88, 95, 98, 2000, 01. Mem. Coun. for Advancement and Support of Edn., Omicron Delta Kappa Leadership Soc., Coun. of Mgrs. Methodist. Avocations: reading, hiking, cross country skiing, photography. Home: PO Box 187 Ashland OR 97520-0187 Office: Univ Lyon 2 18 Quai Claude Bernard 69007 Lyon France

BROWN, JAMES EARLE, lawyer; b. San Antonio, Aug. 13, 1945; s. Melville Marshall and Hazel Maurine (Bryan) B.; m. Camille Ashby Newsom, June 10, 1967; children: Kristen Bryan, Kasey Margaret. BBA, So. Meth. U., 1968, JD, 1972. Bar: U.S. Dist. Ct. (no. and ea. dists.) Tex. 1972. Assoc. Bean, Francis, Ford, Francis & Wills, Dallas, 1972-74; ptnr. Briggs, Brown & Berkley, Dallas, 1975-86, Baker, Brown & Dixon, Dallas, 1986—. Trustee Presby. Sch. Christian Edn., 1993-97, vice chair, 1996-97; trustee Union Theol. Sem. and Presbyn. Sch. Christian Edn., 1997-99, vice chair 1997 99; ruling elder Preston Hollow Presbyn. Ch., Dallas, 1981; v.p. Wilcox Endowment, Dallas, 1984. With U.S. Army, 1968-69. Mem. ATLA, Tex. Bar Assn., Dallas Bar Assn., Dallas Trial Lawyers Assn., Tex. Trial Lawyers Assn., Tex. Bd. Legal Specialization (cert.), Nat. Bd. Trial Advocacy (cert.), Coll. State Bar Tex., Dallas Athletic Club, Men's Golf Assn. (bd. dirs. 2002), So. Golf Assn. (assoc. bd. dirs. 2001-03, bd. dirs. 2003—), Vickery Meadow Learning Ctr. (bd. dirs. 2003—). Avocations: golf, snow skiing. Office: PO Box 12097 Dallas TX 75225-0097

BROWN, JAMES EDWARD, retired research scientist; b. Columbus, Ind., Jan. 9, 1945; s. Edward Alvin and Shirley Loraine (Hazelleaf) B.; widowed; children: Peter Corbin, Roger Wendell. BS in Chemistry, Iowa State U., 1967; PhD in Chemistry, Pa. State U., 1971. Postdoctoral fellow Worcester Found. for Exptl. Biology, Shrewsbury, Mass., 1971-73; rsch. biochemist U. Calif.-San Diego Sch. of Medicine, LJolla, 1973-82; rsch. mgr. hemostasis systems Helena Labs., Beaumont, Tex., 1982-84; sr. staff scientist Bayer Biotechnology, Inc., Berkeley, Calif., 1984 2002; ret., 2002. Contbr. articles to profl. jours. Landscape and trustee com. Lafayette United Meth. Ch., 1995. Mem. AAAS, Internat. Soc. on Thrombosis and Haemostasis, Am. Chem. Soc., Alpha Chi Sigma. Achievements include patents for immunoassay for cellular proteins, phospholipid afffinity purification of factor VIII:C; research in enhancement of the rate of activation of FVIII by non Willebrand factor. Home: 111 La Quinta St Moraga CA 94556-1024

BROWN, JAMES ELLIOTT, lawyer; b. Mt. Vernon, NY, Sept. 5, 1947; s. Gilbert E. and Doris (Elias) B.; m. Elizabeth Ferber, Nov. 16, 1970 (div. Jan. 1977); m. Virginia Linney Freeland, Nov. 26, 1977; children: Elias F., Benjamin J. BA, Cornell U., 1969; JD, U. Denver, 1974. Bar: Colo. 1974, U.S. Dist. Ct. Colo. 1974, U.S. Ct. Appeals (10th cir.) 1976. Assoc. Grant McHendrie Haines & Crouse, P.C., Denver, 1974-81, mng. ptnr. north office, 1984-89; pres. Brown & Harmon, Denver, 1993—. Bd. dirs. Turin Bicycles of Denver; guest lectr. U. Denver Coll. Law, 1980. Bd. govs. Adams County (Colo.) Econ. Devel., 1983-87; trustee Listen Found., Inc., 1988-91, v.p., 1991. Bd. govs. Adams County (Colo.) Econ. Devel., 1983-87. Mem. ABA, Colo. Bar Assn., Adams County Bar Assn., Denver Bar Assn., MetroNorth C. of C. (chmn. bd. dirs. 1986, bd. dirs. 1983-87, Econ. Developer of Yr. 1984), Rocky Mountain Rd. (pres. 1972-76), Rocky Mountain Radio League (Denver), MIle Hi DX Assn. (pres., v.p. 1990-93). Democrat. Jewish. Avocations: ham radio, running, bicycle riding, motor sports. Office: James E Brown & Assocs PC 1350 17th St Ste 306 Denver CO 80202-1525 E-mail: wy0j@aol.com.

BROWN, JAMES GASTON, retired obstetrician, gynecologist; b. Cypress, Ill., 1921; MD, U. Tenn., 1945. Diplomate Am. Bd. Obstetricians and Gynecologists. Intern St. Francis Hosp, Peoria, Ill., 1945, resident ob-gyn., 1948-49; resident gynecology Ill. Rsch. Hosps., Chgo., 1950-51; pvt. practice, 1951-86; ret. Mem. ACOG, AMA.

BROWN, JAMES JOSEPH, manufacturing company executive; b. N.Y.C., Apr. 4, 1928; s. Peter J. and Mary (O'Neil) B.; m. Mary E. McKeon, Dec. 30, 1961; children: Patricia, James, Carolyn, Denise, Erin. BS, Fordham U., 1952. C.P.A., N.Y. Acct. Touche, Ross, Bailey & Smart (C.P.A.s), N.Y.C., 1952-54; sr. acct. Price Waterhouse & Co. (C.P.A.s), Caracas, Venezuela and N.Y.C., 1954-63; mgr. internal audit Litton Industries, 1963-65; sr. v.p., chief fin. officer dir. Kidde, Inc., 1965-82; chmn. bd. Am. Desk Mfg. Co., 1982-97. Served with USA, 1946-48. Named Alumni Man of Year, Fordham U. Coll. Bus. Adminstrn., 1971 Mem. AICPA, N.Y. State Soc. CPAs, Econ. Club N.Y. Clubs: Treasurers of N.Y, Ridgewood Country, N.Y. Athletic. Office: 441 Weymouth Dr Wyckoff NJ 07481-1216 E-mail: jbrown9778@aol.com.

BROWN, JAMES JOSEPH, judge; b. Mineola, N.Y., Mar. 1, 1944; s. Thomas Patrick and Sally (Casey) B.; m. Alice May Manningham, Aug. 3, 1965; children: Thomas P., Scott L., Christine M., Daniel J. BA in History, U. Tex., 1968; JD, Boston Coll., 1971. Bar: Mass. 1971, U.S. Dist. Ct. Mass. 1971, U.S. Dist. Ct. Vt. 1972, U.S. Supreme Ct. 1973, U.S. Ct. Appeals (4th cir.) 1980, U.S. Ct. Appeals (5th cir.) 1983, U.S. Ct Appeals (10th cir.) 1984, Md. 1985, U.S. Dist. Ct. Md. 1985, U.S. Dist. Ct. D.C. 1986. Assoc. Levy & Winer PC, Greenfield, Mass., 1971-75; trial atty., dep. chief commercial litigation U.S. Dept. Justice, Washington, 1976-85, supervisory trial atty. environ. enforcement sec., 1987-90; supervisory trial atty. Asset Forfeiture Office Criminal div. U.S. Dept. Justice, 1990-95; U.S. adminstrv. law judge Office of Hearings and Appeals, Raleigh, N.C., 1995—. Sr. assoc. Saul, Ewing, Weinberg & Green, Balt., 1985-87; lectr., tchr. U.S. Dept. Justice, Washington, 1978-85, Russian Law Acad., Moscow and Samara, Russia, 1999. Author: Judgment Enforcement, 1994, pocket supplements, 1995-2003, 2d edit., 1999; editor: Scientific Evidence and Experts Handbook, 1999, pocket supplements, 2000-03. Sch. com. Town of Greenfield, 1973-75; bd. elders Forcey Meml. Ch., Silver Spring, Md., 1981-82, missions com. 1980-83, 88-90; bd. dirs. New Life Christian Camp, Raleigh, N.C., 2001—. With USNR, 1962-64. Recipient Outstanding Performance awards U.S. Dept. Justice, 1980-85, Spl. Achievement award, 1983, Disting. Svc. award, 1985. Mem. Mass. Bar Assn., Md. Bar Assn. Republican. Avocations: golf, poetry, writing. Office: US Administrative Law Judge Office of Hearings & Appeals 1305 Navaho Dr Raleigh NC 27609-7454 E-mail: james.j.brown@ssa.gov, jbrown358@nc.rr.com.

BROWN, JAMES JUSTIN, artist; b. Milton, Fla., June 28, 1973; s. Richard Brown. BArch, Va. Tech. Inst., 1996. Exhibited in group shows at COCA, Ureibo Gallery, exhibitions include Montserrat Coll. Art.

BROWN, JAMES KEVIN, professional baseball player; b. McIntyre, Ga., Mar. 14, 1965; Student, Ga. Tech. Inst. With Tex. Rangers, 1986-94, Balt. Orioles, 1995, Fla. Marlins, Miami, 1996-97, San Diego Padres, 1997-98; pitcher L.A. Dodgers, 1999—. Named Sporting News Coll. All-Am. Team, 1986, Am. League All-Star Game, 1992, Nat. League All-Star Team, 1996. Ranked 2nd in Am. League in victories, 1992. Office: LA dodgers 1000 Elysian Park Ave Los Angeles CA 90012-1112

BROWN, JAMES KNIGHT, lawyer; b. Rainelle, W.Va., Sept. 25, 1929; s. Hugh Allen and Florence Catherine (Knight) B.; m. Sarah Elizabeth Droste, June 21, 1952; children: Carolyn, Patricia, Julia. BS, W.Va. U., 1951, LLB, 1956. Bar: W.Va. 1956, U.S. Ct. Appeals (4th and 6th cir.), U.S. Supreme Ct. Assoc. Jackson & Kelly, Charleston, W.Va., 1956-62, ptnr., 1962-98; mem. Jackson & Kelly PLLC, Charleston, 1999—2001, of counsel, 2001—. Former W.Va. adv. bd. dirs. BB&T Corp. 1st lt. USAF, 1951-53. Fellow Am. Bar Found.; mem. ABA, W.Va. State Bar (pres. 1975-76), Order of Coif, Phi Beta Kappa. Democrat. Presbyterian. Avocations: woodworking, golf. Office: Jackson & Kelly PLLC 1600 Laidley Tower Charleston WV 25301-2189

BROWN, JAMES MILTON, law educator; b. Streator, Ill., July 16, 1921; BA, U. Ill., 1943; JD, U. Fla., 1963. Bar: Fla. 63, DC 68. Pres., gen. mgr. J.C. Ames Lumber Co., Streator, 1947—61, Brown-Vissering Constrn. Co., Streator, 1956—61; Sterling fellow Yale Law Sch., 1964—65; assoc. prof. law U. Miss., 1964—65; prof. law George Washington U., Washington, 1965—92, prof. emeritus, 1992—, dir. land use mgmt. and control program Nat. Law Ctr., 1965—92, sr. staff scientist Program of Policy Studies, 1965—82. Commr. Md. Nat. Capital Park and Planning Commn., 1991—2002; mem. various panels NAS; cons. in field. Contbr. articles to legal jours. Mem.: ABA, Fla. Bar Assn., DC Bar Assn., Order of Coif, Lambda Alpha, Phi Delta Phi. Home: 10035 Weeks Dr Brooksville FL 34601 Office: James Martin Brown 211 South Main St Brooksville FL 34601

BROWN, JAMES NELSON, JR., retired accountant; b. Bronx, N.Y., Apr. 17, 1929; s. James Nelson and Agnes Mary (Cummins) B.; m. Lila Barbara Watt, Dec. 12, 1950; children: Constance Ellen Brown Buttacavole, Nelson Arthur, Richard John. BSBA, Drake U., 1956. CPA; cert. internal auditor, fraud examiner. Sr. acct. Arthur Andersen & Co., N.Y.C., 1956-61; asst. v.p., dir. internal auditing Salomon Inc., N.Y.C., 1961-86, asst. v.p., dir. projects mgmt. dept., 1986-91, asst. v.p. environ. litigation dept., 1991-93, v.p., mgr. environ. litig. dept., 1994-97; cons. environ. litig. dept. Citigroup, Inc., N.Y.C., 1998—2002. Com. chmn. Cub Scouts, 1973-75; troop com. chmn. Boy Scouts Am., Carteret, N.J., 1976-77, 88-90, com. mem., 1978-87. Sgt. AUS, 1947-52. Mem. AICPA, VFW, Am. Mgmt. Assn., N.J. Soc. CPAs, Nat. Assn. Cert. Fraud Examiners, Inst. Internal Auditors, Am. Legion, Elks. Republican. Roman Catholic. E-mail: Jnbrownjr@aol.com.

BROWN, JAMES ROBERT, retired air force officer; b. Bozeman, Mont., June 17, 1930; s. Marley Robert and Ann Louise (Pace) B.; m. Sandra Shores, Dec. 19, 1964; children: James V., Brian R. BS, Mont. State U., 1953; grad., Squadron Officer Sch., 1962, Air Command and Staff Coll., 1964, Indsl. Coll. of Armed Forces, 1974. Commd. 2d lt. U.S. Air Force, 1953, advanced through grades to lt. gen., 1984, undergrad. pilot tng. program, 1954-54, bomb comdr., intelligence officer 20th Fighter-Bomber Wing Royal Air Force Station Wethersfield, England, 1955—58, fighter gunnery, instr. pilot, acad. instr. Nellis AFB, Nev., 1958—60, fighter weapons sch., rsch. and devel. project officer, instr. pilot, 1960—62, flight evaluator Tactical Air Command Langley AFB, Va., 1962-63, flight comdr., instr. pilot Davis-Monthan AFB, Ariz., 1964-66, tour duty, 1966-67, dir. tng. analysis and devel., 1967-71, staff action officer tactics br. chief, acting chief tactical div. for Directorate of Plans and ops. Washington, 1971-75, dir. ops. 388th Tactical Fighter Wing Korat Royal Thai AFB, Thailand, 1975-76, vice comdr. 3d Tactical Fighter Wing Clark Air Base, Philippines, 1976, comdr. 3d Tactical Fighter Wing, 1976-78, comdr. 313th Air div. and 18th Tactical Fighter Wing Kadena Air Base, Japan, 1978-81, dep. chief of staff for ops. Ramstein Air Base, Ger., 1981, asst. chief staff ops. Supreme Hdqrs. Allied Powers, Europe Mons, Belgium, 1981-84, comdr. Allied Air Forces So. Europe, dep. comdr. in chief U.S. Air Forces in Europe Naples, Italy, 1984-86; vice comdr. Langley AFB Tactical Air Command, Va., 1986-88; ret., 1988; dir. aviation programs East Inc., Chantilly, Va., 1991-94, 97—. Decorated D.D.S.M., D.S.S.M., Legion of Merit with oak leaf cluster, Bronze Star medal, Air Medal with four oak leaf clusters, Air Force Commendation medal with oak leaf cluster, Def. Superior Service medal Avocations: golf, bike riding, walking, horseback riding. Home: 1591 Stowe Rd Reston VA 20194-1602 E-mail: mpijrb@aol.com.

BROWN, JAMES RUSSELL, III, librarian; b. Charlottesville, Va., May 23, 1947; s. James Russell Jr. and Helen Irene (Elliott) B.; m. Ingrid Veltman (div.); 1 child, Ethan; m. Gail Bonnie Beskin, June 19, 1983. AB in Biology summa cum laude, Boston U., 1968; PhD in Sociology, Boston Coll., 1987; MS in LS, Long Island U., 1992. Cert. pub. libr., N.Y. Lab. technologist R.I.S.T. Labs., East Northport, N.Y., 1977-80, Dianetics Lab., Syosset, N.Y., 1980-87, St. Luke's Hosp., N.Y.C., 1987-90; libr. Glen Cove (N.Y.) Pub. Libr., 1990-95, Shelter Rock Pub. Libr., Albertson, N.Y., 1995—. Local 1199 shop steward St. Lukes Hosp., 1988-90; Teamsters Local 810 shop steward Glen Cove Pub. Libr., 1993-95. State com. mem. NY State Green Party, 2002—. Tufts U. Latin Am. teaching fellow, Guatemala and Mex., 1972-74. Mem. ALA, N.Y. Libr. Assn., Nassau County Libr. Assn., Beta Phi Mu (dir. 1994-98, archivist 1995-99). Avocations: hiking, backpacking. Home: 422 E Market St Long Beach NY 11561-2318 Office: Shelter Rock Pub Libr 165 Searingtown Rd Albertson NY 11507-1521 E-mail: jrb398@yahoo.com.

BROWN, JAMES SHELLY, lawyer; b. Trenton, N.J., May 5, 1945; s. Alexander Aloysius and Madlyn (Shelly) B.; m. Margaret Lee Martin, June 6, 1987; children: Elizabeth Paige, Kristen Blaire. BA, Hofstra u., 1968; JD, Fordham U., 1972. Bar: N.Y. 1973. Asst. dist. atty. County of N.Y., N.Y.C., 1972-78; ptnr. Wilson, Eiser, Moskowitz, Edelman and Dicker, N.Y.C., 1994—. Fellow Am. Coll. Trial Lawyers; mem. N.Y. State Bar Assn., Assn. of Bar of City of N.Y. Avocation: tennis. Home: 31 Old Parish Rd Darien CT 06820-4319 E-mail: brownj@wemed.com.

BROWN, JAMES SYLVESTER, JR., lawyer; b. May 7, 1932; BS, Georgetown U, 1954; LLB, St. John's U., 1959. Bar: NY 1959. Assoc. Willkie Farr & Gallagher, NYC, 1959—67, ptnr, 1968—. Mem.: NY Bar Assn., ABA (com. drafting wills and trusts, probate div.), Fellow Am. Coll. Probate Counsel, Phi Delta Phi. Home: 44 Milburn St Apt 2407 Bronxville NY 10708-3400 Office: One Citicorp Center 1 Citicorp Center 153 E New York NY 10022

BROWN, JAMES THOMPSON, JR., computer information scientist, logistics specialist; b. Orange, N.J., Jan. 3, 1935; s. James Thompson and Marjorie (Hale) B.; m. Alice Beasley, Oct. 3, 1959; children— Kathryn, James. B.M.E., Cornell U., 1957; M.S., Stanford U., 1964. Applied sci. rep. IBM Corp., Schenectady, N.Y., 1957-59, corp. staff mem., White Plains, N.Y., 1960-68; cons. Case & Co., Stamford, Conn., 1969-74, dir., 1975-83, pres., 1983-84; pres. Tom Brown & Co., Wilton, Conn., 1985—; advisor Russian Fedn. Customs Svc. Developer inventory mgmt. systems and svc. pricing techniques. Life mem. Rep. Inner Circle. Mem. Internat. Assn. Chain Stores (adviser, speaker 1971—), Nat. Grocers Assn. (adviser 1983—), Am. Inst. Indsl. Engrs. (sr. mem.), Inst. Ops. Rsch. and Mgmt. Scis., Landmark Club, Cornell Club (N.Y.), Capitol Hill Club. Republican. Home: 135 Middlebrook Farm Rd Wilton CT 06897-2019 Office: Tom Brown & Co PO Box 431 Wilton CT 06897-0431 *One of my guiding principles is not to try to solve a problem until I understand it. Understanding often means getting your hands dirty. And when I do understand, take the time to carefully think out the solution.*

BROWN, JAMES WARD, mathematician, educator, author; b. Phila., Jan. 15, 1934; s. George Harold and Julia Elizabeth (Ward) B.; m. Jacqueline Read, Sept. 3, 1957; children: Scott Cameron, Gordon Elliot. AB, Harvard U., 1955; AM, U. Mich., 1958, PhD (Inst. Sci and Tech. predoctoral fellow), 1964. Asst. prof. math. U. Mich., Dearborn, 1964-66, assoc. prof., 1968-71, prof., 1971—, acting chmn. dept., 1974, 85. Asst. prof. Oberlin Coll., 1966-68; editorial cons. Math. Rev., 1970-85; dir. NSF Grant, 1969 Author: (with R.V. Churchill) Complex Variables and Applications, 7th edit., 2003, Internat. Student edit., 1996, Japanese edit., 1995, Spanish edit., 1992, Chinese edit., 1985, Korean edit., 1992, Greek edit., 1993, Fourier Series and Boundary Value Problems, 6th edit., 2001, internat. student edit., 1993, Japanese edit., 1980; contbr. articles to U.S. and fgn. sci. jours. Recipient Disting. Faculty award U. Mich.-Dearborn, 1976, Disting. Faculty award Mich. Assn. Governing Bds. Colls. and Univs., 1983 Mem. Am. Math. Soc., Research Club of U. Mich., Sigma Xi. Home: 1710 Morton Ave Ann Arbor MI 48104-4522 Office: 4901 Evergreen Rd Dearborn MI 48128-1491

BROWN, JAN WHITNEY, small business owner; b. Roundup, Mont., Mar. 16, 1942; d. John Estes and Janet Lillian (Snyder) Dahl; m. William A. Brown III; children: Erik Lane, Kimberly Elise. BA in Sociology, Social Work, Carroll Coll., 1976. Sec. 1st Nat. Bank, Bozeman, Mont., 1962, Office of Gov., Helena, Mont., 1963—69; pub. info. coord. Helena Model City Program, 1969—73; pub. rels. and assn. mgmt. Mont. Bar Assn., Helena, 1973—76, Mont. Assn. Life Underwriters, Helena, 1973—76; legis. liaison Mont. Religious Legis. Coalition, Helena, 1975—81; exec. dir. Helena Food Share Inc., 1987; co-owner Jorud Photo and Gifts, Helena, 1971—2002; mem. state tax appeal bd., 1999—2001; mem. Mont. State Legislature, Helena, 1983—92; program specialist Mont. Dept. Environ. Quality, 2001—. Mem. legis. coun. Helena, 1989-92; bd. dirs. Helena Food Share, Inc., Bus. Improvement Dist.; chmn. state adminstrn. com. Mont. Ho. of Reps., 1989-92. Chmn. Mont. Medal of Valor Com., Helena, 1986-93; pres. United Way, Helena, 1982; bd. dirs. Mont. Area Health Edn. Ctr., Bozeman, 1988-93, Mont. Hunger Coalition, Helena, 1988-89, St. Peter's Hosp. Found. Bd., 1994-96, 97-2000, St. Peter's Hosp., 1994-2000, chair bd. dirs., 1997-99; Helena City Commr., 1993; vice chair Helena Citizens Coun., 1994-96; mem. cmty. adv. bd. U.S. Bank, 1994-99; sec.-treas. Mt. Soc. for Hosp. Governance, 1995-97; mem. visions com. United Way, 1997-98; mem. diocesan coun. Episcopal Diocese of Mont., 1997-99. Recipient Disting. Svc. award Mental Health Assn., 1976, Disting. Cmty. Svc. award Jaycees, 1982, Ann. Appreciation award Child Support Enforcement, 1985, United Way award, 1988, Cmty. Svc. award VFW, 1988. Mem. Nat. Assn. Hearing Officers, Nat. Assn. Adminstrv. Law Judges, Helena Unlimited. Democrat. Episcopalian. Avocations: symphony, choir. Office: 1520 E 6th Ave Helena MT 59601-4541

BROWN, JANE MARTIN THORNTON, educational administrator; b. Elberton, Ga., Mar. 6, 1951; d. Laurie William and Mary Frances (Martin) Thornton; m. Donald McCarty Brown Jr., June 14, 1980; children: Laurie Elizabeth, Judson McCarty. Student, U. Ala., 1969-70, Georgetown Coll., 1970-71; BS, Minot State Coll., 1973, MS, 1974. Speech-lang. pathologist Duval County Sch. System, Jacksonville, Fla., 1974-77, Newberry (S.C.) County Schs., 1977-78, Tri-County Spl. Edn. Coop., Murphysboro, Ill., 1978-79, Ga. Retardation Ctr., Atlanta, 1980-82, dir. speech-lang. pathology, 1982-87, coordinator of quality circles, 1983-86, coordinator of interdisciplinary habilitation, 1986—90, dir. programs, evaluation, research and tng., 1987-90, edn. coord. Athens, 1990-91; small bus. owner McCarty Enterprises, 1991—92; prof. Truett-McConnell Coll., Watkinsville, Ga., 1992-2000; coord. acad. support ctr. Athens Tech. Coll., 2000—. Chairperson Ga. Mental Retardation, Developmentally Disabled Network, Atlanta, 1987-89; expert panel mem. Speech Pathology Assessment Instrument Team, Athens, 1986-87, Ga. Dept. Edn., Atlanta, 1987. Presentor: (paper) Developmental Disabilities: Where do we go from Here? Pres. Citizen's Adv. Com., Atlanta, 1985-90; mem. Gainsboro Civic Assn., Atlanta, 1985-90, Gov.'s Edn. Com., N.D., 1972-74, Com. for Networking Conf., Atlanta, 1985-90; rep. Faculty Acad. Affairs, 1999-2000. Grantee Minot State Coll., 1973-74. Mem. Ga. Speech-Lang.-Hearing Assn., Retarded Citizens of Atlanta (Vital Svc. award 1987), Am. Assn. Mental Deficiency, Coun. for Exceptional Children, Mental Retardation Inst. (leadership dept. human resources 1989, finalist Mgr. of Yr. Ga. 1989). Democrat. Presbyterian. Avocations: soccer, collecting antiques. Office: Athens Tech Coll 800 US Hwy 29N Athens GA 30601

BROWN, JANET MCNALLEY, social worker; b. Denver, May 16, 1960; d. Michael Collins and Sharon Bess (Cook) McNalley. Student, Mt. Holyoke Coll., 1978-79; BA in Econs. with honors, Mills Coll., Oakland, Calif., 1982; MA in Social Scis., U. Calif., Irvine, 1987, elem. teaching credential, 1988; MSW, U. Tex., Arlington, 2001. Teaching asst. U. Calif., Irvine, 1986-88; employee benefits adminstr. Western Co. N.Am., Ft. Worth, 1988-89; trust officer Ameritrust Tex. N.A., Ft. Worth, 1989-90; thrift and profit sharing analyst Burlington No. R.R., Ft. Worth, 1990-93; assoc. human resources group Coopers & Lybrand, Dallas, 1993-94; pension coord. Bell Helicopter Textron, Inc., Ft. Worth, 1994-95; adminstr., cons. Rogers & Assocs., Ft. Worth, 1995-97; pvt. practice Ft. Worth, 1997—; social worker Vitas Hospice, 2001—. Owner Retirement Plan Mgmt., 1997—. Dem. del., Ft. Worth, 1990; mem. Network for Exec. Women, Bluebonnet Pl. Neighborhood Assn. Mem.: AAUW (membership v.p. 1990—92, charter Eleanor Roosevelt Found. 1990—92), Am. Soc. Pension Actuaries (qualified pension adminstr., cert. pension cons.), NASW. Avocations: dance, sewing, travel. Home and Office: 3408 Cockrell Ave Fort Worth TX 76109-3003

BROWN, JANET WITUCKI, nursing educator, geriatric researcher; b. Stevens Point, Wis., Nov. 27, 1946; d. Joseph John and Victoria Rose Tylka; m. Elmer Andrew Witucki, Aug. 19, 1967 (dec. Jan. 1999); 1 child, William James; m. J. Michael Brown, March 16, 2002. Diploma, St. Joseph's Sch. Nursing, 1967; BSN, Ball State U., 1991, MSN, 1994; PhD, U. Tenn., 2000. Staff nurse Meml. Hosp., Wausau, Wis., 1967-69; charge nurse, insvc. dir. Colonial Manor, Wausau, 1969-73, The Willows, Alexandria, Ind., 1979-81; allied health instr. North Ctrl. Tech. Inst., Wausau, 1973-79; staff nurse Cmty. Hosp., Anderson, Ind., 1981-85; instr., allied health coord. Ivy Tech. State Coll., Muncie, Ind., 1985-93, dir. practical nursing program, 1993-94; mem. nursing faculty Ball State U., Muncie, 1994-96; nursing instr. U. Tenn., Knoxville, 1998—2000; asst. prof. dept. adult health East Tenn. State U., 2000—01; asst. prof. U. Tenn. Coll. Nursing, 2001—. Bd. dirs. Day Star Alzheimer Adult Day Care Ctr., Muncie, 1993 96; mem. empathy rsch. team U. Tenn., Knoxville; adj. nursing faculty Walters State C.C., 1997; presenter in field. Contbr. articles to profl. jours. Bd. dirs. Sr. Citizen's Home Assistance Program, Knoxville, 2002—. Hilton A Smith grad. fellow, 1997-98. Mem. So. Nursing Rsch. Soc., Tenn. Nurses Assn., Ball State U. Nursing Alumni (bd. dirs. 1994-96), So. Gerontological Soc., Sigma Theta Tau, Phi Kappa Phi. Avocations: reading, travel. Home: 7320 Twin Creek Rd Knoxville TN 37920 E-mail: drjanw@aol.com.

BROWN, JANICE ROGERS, state supreme court justice; b. Laverne, AL, May 11, 1949; BA, Ca. St. U., Sacramento, 1974; JD, UCLA, 1977. Assoc. justice Calif. Supreme Ct., San Francisco, 1996—. Office: Calif Supreme Ct 350 Mcallister St Rm 1295 San Francisco CA 94102-4783*

BROWN, JANIECE ALFREIDA, pilot; b. Ellensburg, Wash., May 23, 1956; d. Don Elmer and LaRhee Deloris (Montgomery) Lewis; m. David E. Brown, Oct. 10, 1993. AA, Big Bend C.C., Moses Lake, Wash., 1980-82; BS, Ctrl. Wash. U., 1982-84. Pilot AAR Western Skyways, Troutdale, Oreg., 1984-87; airline capt. N.P.A., Inc., Pasco, Wash., 1987-89; flight engr. airline pilot Alaska Airlines, Seattle, 1989—, 1st officer Boeing 727 and MD-80, capt. MD-80, 1996—; bus. mgr. David Brown & Assocs., 1994-99; airline capt. MD-80 Alaska Airlines, Seattle, 1996—. Owner, bus. mgr. Champagne Creek Cellars, Roseburg, Oreg., 2001—. Lobbyist Save Our Watershed, Roslyn, Wash., 1978-80; pres. Interlachen, Inc., A Homeowners Assn., 1998-2002. Recipient Scholastic award CleElum (Wash.) High Sch., 1974. Mem. Airline Pilot Assn., 1990- (mem. dangerous goods com., 1991-2002), Alpha Eta Rho (pres. Ctrl. Wash. U. chpt. 1983-84). Avocations: skiing, sewing, backpacking, contractor, remodeler of own home and rental. Home: 20912 NE Interlachen Ln Troutdale OR 97060-8731 Office: Alaska Airlines PO Box 61900 Seattle WA 98178

BROWN, JARED, theater director, educator, writer; BFA, Ithaca Coll., 1960; MA Theatre, San Francisco State Coll., 1962; PhD Theatre, U. Minn., 1967. Instr. creative writing St. Paul Pub. Sch. System, 1962-63; teaching asst. U. Minn., 1963-64, instr. Communication Dept., 1964-65; from asst. prof. to prof. dept. theatre Western Ill. U., 1965-89, acad. dir. Semester in London, 1979-80; dir. Sch. Theatre Arts, Prof. Theatre Arts Ill. Wesleyan U., 1989—. Aided devel. (policies, curriculum), Theatre Dept. Western Ill. U., 1971; panel discussant Western Ill. U., 1973, 1974; chmn. panel Ill. Theatre Assn. Convention, 1976; panel discussant Assn. Theatre in Higher Edn. Convention, 1987; disting. faculty lectr. Western Ill. U., 1986, dir. grad. program dept. theatre, 1975-89, chmn. directing, theatre history and playwriting programs, dept. theatre, 1972-89; mem. panel judges to award NEH Summer Stipends, Ill., 1990; judge Am. Coll. Theatre Festival, 1973-74, 89-90; mem. various theatre coms. Ill. Wesleyan U.; mem. various coms. Univ., Coll. Fine Arts, Dept. Theatre Western Ill. U.; spkr., presenter in field. Author: The Fabulous Lunts, A Biography of Alfred Lunt and Lynn Fontanne, 1986, (Barnard Hewitt award 1987), Zero Mostel: A Biography, 1989, The Theatre in America During the Revolution, 1995; dir. plays including The Merchant of Venice, Hedda Gabler, Henry IV, La Ronde, Death of a Salesman, Cat on a Hot Tin Roof, A Streetcar Named Desire, Who's Afraid of Virginia Woolf, You Can't Take It With You, Brighton Beach Memoirs, Inherit the Wind, Peter Pan, Bye Bye Birdie, Guys and Dolls, Kiss Me Kate, 110 In The Shade, Annie, Funny Girl, Broadway Bound, Tartuffe, Antigone, She Loves Me, Noises Off, Sight Unseen, Bedroom Farce, Once in a Lifetime; appeared in My Fair Lady, Western Ill. U., 1978, On The Twentieth Century, 1986, various radio and TV programs; contbr. chpts. to texts, articles to profl. jours. Recipient stipend NEH, 1988, DuPont award for tchg. excellence, 1997; named Best Dir., The Pantagraph, 1991, 92, 94, 96; grantee Ill. Arts Coun., 1980, 81, 87, Western Ill. U., 1983-85, 86-87, 89, Cultural Arts Devel. Fund, 1980-89, Ill. Wesleyan U., 1990, Artistic/Scholarly Devel. grantee, 1999, 2002. Mem. Nat. Collegiate Players, Phi Kappa Phi, Theta Alpha Phi. Home: 18 Chatsford Ct Bloomington IL 61704-6220 Office: Sch Theatre Arts Ill Wesleyan U Bloomington IL 61702 E-mail: jbrown@iwu.edu.

BROWN, JASON WALTER, neurologist, educator, researcher; b. N.Y.C., Apr. 14, 1938; s. Samuel Robert and Sylvia (Brown) B.; children: Jonathan Schilder, Jovana Millay; m. Carine Hoeusler; 1 child, Ilya. BA, U. Calif.-Berkeley, 1959; MD, U.S.C., 1963. Intern St. Elizabeth's Hosp., Washington, 1963-64; resident in neurology UCLA, 1964-67; practice medicine specializing in neurology N.Y.C., 1970—; instr. Boston U. Med. Sch., 1969-70; asst. clin. prof. Columbia-Presbyn. Hosp., N.Y.C., 1970-75; vis. asst. prof. neurology Albert Einstein Coll. Medicine, N.Y.C., 1972-75; vis. assoc. prof. Rockefeller U., N.Y.C., 1978-79; clin. assoc. prof. neurology NYU, 1975-79, clin. prof., 1979—; pres. Inst. Research in Behavioral Neurosci. Vis. scholar N.Y. Psychoanalytic Inst., 1993—. Author: Aphasia, Apraxia and Agnosia, 1972, Mind, Brain and Consciousness, 1977, Life of the Mind, 1988; editor: Jargonaphasia, 1982; English Translation of Aphasie by Arnold Pick (Aphasia), 1973, Neuropsychology of Visual Perception, 1989, Classics in Neuropsychology; Apraxia and Agnosia, Self and Process, 1991, Time, Will and Mental Process, 1996, Mind and Nature, 2000, The Self-Embodying Mind, 2002; contbr. numerous articles on neurology to med. jours.; mem. editl. bd. Jour. Nervous and Mental Disease, Aphasiology, Advances in Neurolinguistics. Grantee NIH; fellow Alexander von Humboldt Found., 1979—, World Rehab. Fund, 1982, Founds. Fund for Research in Psychiatry, 1974-75. Jewish. Home and Office: 66 E 79th St New York NY 10021-0244 E-mail: drjbrown@hotmail.com.

BROWN, JAY MARSHALL, retired secondary school educator; b. Bklyn., July 26, 1933; s. Sidney and Bertha (Swirsky) Brown; m. Merle Thelma Kaminsky, Nov. 4, 1956; children: Sidney Matthew, Ellen Beth Factor. BS in Journalism, NYU, 1955, MA in Am. Civilization, 1960; postgrad., Yeshiva U., 1958-60, U. Conn., West Hartford, 1968-70; 6th yr. profl. diploma, So. Conn. State Coll., 1977. Pub. rels. dir, asst. credit mgr. Colonial Sand & Stone Co., N.Y.C., 1955-60; employment counselor N.Y.C. Dept. Welfare, 1960-63; attendance tchr. Bd. Edn., N.Y.C., 1963-65; youth dir. Jewish Community Ctr., Rochester, N.Y., 1965-67; exec. dir. Conn. Valley Regional B'nai B'rith Youth, New Haven, 1967-70; resource tchr. Sheridan Mid. Sch., Bd. Edn., New Haven, 1970-72; learning ctr. tchr. Bd. Edn., New Haven, 1972-74; social studies tchr. Troup Mid. Sch., Bd. Edn., New Haven, 1974-80; history tchr. Hillhouse HS, Bd. Edn., New Haven, 1980-93; ret., 1993. Tchr. U.S. history New Eng. Acad. Jewish Studies, New Haven, 1984—85; specialist audio-visual and media Quinnipiac Coll., Hamden, Conn., 1982. Contbr. Chmn. clear sch. mission com. Hillhouse HS, New Haven, 1984, mem. effective sch. steering com., 1984, mem. sch. planning and mgmt. team, 1988—91, coord. teenagers adv. program, 1989—91, mem. faculty senate, 1991—93; acting pres. Alliance Mentally Ill, 1993—94, pres., 1995—; mem. Commn. on Disabilities Town of Hamden, 2001—, chair Commn. on Disabilities, 2002—; corr. sec. Jewish Hist. Soc., New Haven, 1980—81; v.p. Regency Hills Condo Assn., 1994—95; active Mental Health Month Com., 1995—99; mem. Family resource Ctr. com. Consultation Ctr., 1994—98; coord. Mental Health Network Spkrs. Bur., 1996—97, 1998; facilitator Journey of Hope Ednl. Program, 2002—; vice chmn. Regional Mental Health Bd., Catchment Area 7, 1997—2002; mem. rev. and evaluation team State Regional Mental Health Bd. Dist. 2, 1996—2000, vice chmn., 1997—2000; bd. govs. Inst. Learning and Retirement, 1998—2000; coord. New Haven County's Mental Illness Awareness Week, 1998—, People Helping People Program, 1998—; mem. Hamden Commn. Disability Rights and Obligation, 2001—; chmn. Hamden Commn. Disability Rights, 2002—03; mem. Hamden Dem. Town Com., 1974—76; pres. Brotherhood Mishkan Israel, 1976—78, 1983—87, 1988—89, 2001—02, sec., 1997—98, treas., 1998—2001; asst. treas. Congregation Mishkan Israel, 1983—84, chmn. budget com., 1987—88, chmn. house and property com., 1979—84, trustee, 1978—84, 1986—92, 1994—2003, mem. pers. com., 1996—2002, mem. abatement com., 1997—98, libr., archivist, 1981—84, mem. ops. com., 1999—2002. Recipient Man of Yr. award of Merit, Congregation Mishkan Israel's Brotherhood, 1978, People Helping People award, Sears and NAMI, 2001. Mem.: New Haven County Ret. Tchrs. Assn. (v.p. 1994—95, sec. 1997—2003), Phi Delta Kappa. Democrat. Jewish. Avocations: philately, polit. items, sports items, cmty. svc.. Home: 25 Wright Ln Hamden CT 06517-2126 E-mail: jay_m_brown@sbcglobal.net., jmb25@juno.com.

BROWN, JEAN GAYLE, social worker; b. St. Joseph, Mo., May 22, 1953; d. Forrest Dale and Mildred M. (Benner) Paden; m. William G. Brown, Aug. 3, 1973; children: Abigail, Adam. BSW, Mo. Western State Coll., 1973; MSW, W.Va. U., 1976. Social worker Family Guidance Ctr., St. Joseph, Mo., 1973-77, family planning dir., 1977-83, adminstr., 1983-95; exec. dir. YWCA, St. Joseph, 1995—. Author: Parent-Child Sex Education: A Training Module, 1976, Sexuality Education: A Curriculum for Parent-Child Programs, 1982, (with others) Sexuality Education: A Resource Book, 1989. Pres. Midland Empire Girl Scout Coun., St. Joseph, 1986-90. Named one of Disting. Alumni Mo. Western State Coll., 1989. Mem. NASW, Acad. Cert. Social Workers, Am. Assn. Sex Educators, Counselors and Therapists (cert. sex educator). Mem. Christian Ch. Home: 5605 Pleasant Ave Saint Joseph MO 64503-2275 Office: YWCA St Joseph 304 N 8th St Saint Joseph MO 64501-1988

BROWN, JEANETTE GRASSELLI, retired university official; b. Cleve., Aug. 4, 1928; d. Nicholas W. and Veronica (Varga) Gecsy; m. Glenn R. Brown, Aug. 1, 1987. BS summa cum laude, Ohio U., 1950, DSc (hon.), 1978; MS, Western Res. U., 1958, DSc (hon.), 1995, Clarkson U., 1986; D Engring. (hon.), Mich. Tech. U., 1989; DSc (hon.), Wilson Coll., 1994, Notre Dame Coll., 1995, Kenyon Coll., 1995, Mt. Union Coll., 1996, Cleveland State U., 2000, Kent State U., 2000, Ursuline Coll., 2001; DSc (hon.), U. Pecs, Hungary, 2002. Project leader, assoc. Infrared Spectroscopist, Cleve., 1950-78; mgr. analytical sci. lab. Standard Oil (name changed to BP Am., Inc. 1985), Cleve., 1978-83, dir. technol. support dept., 1983-85, dir. corp. rsch. and analytical scis., 1985-88; disting. vis. prof., dir. rsch. enhancement Ohio U., Athens, 1989-95; ret., 1995. Bd. dirs. AGA Gas, Inc., USX Corp., McDonald Investments, BDM Internat., BF Goodrich Co., Nicolet Instrument Corp.; mem. bd. on chem. sci. and tech. NRC, 1986-91; chmn. U.S. Nat. Com. to Internat. Union of Pure and Applied Chemistry, 1992-94; mem. joint high level adv. panel U.S.-Japan Sci. and Tech., 1994-2001, Ohio Bd. Regents, 1995—, chmn., 2000-2002; vis. com. Nat. Inst. Stds. and Tech., 1988-91. Author, editor 8 books; editor: Vibrational Spectroscopy; contbr. numerous articles on molecular spectroscopy to profl. jours.; patentee naphthalene extraction process. Bd. dirs. N.E. Ohio Sci. and Engring. Fair, Cleve., Martha Holden Jennings Found., Cleve. Clinic Found.; chair bd. dirs. Cleve. Scholarship Programs, Inc., 1994-2000; trustee Holden Arboretum, Cleve., 1988—, Edison Biotech Ctr., Cleve., 1988-95, Cleve. Playhouse, 1990-96, Garden Ctr. Greater Cleve., 1990-93, Mus. Arts Assn., 1991—, Gt. Lakes Sci. Ctr., 1991—, Rainbow Babies and Children's Hosp., 1992-95, Nat. Inventors' Hall of Fame, 1993—, Ohio U., 1985-94, chmn. 1991-92; chair steering com. Mellen Ctr. Cleve. Clinic, 1996—. Recipient Disting. Svc. award Cleve. Tech. Soc. Coun., 1985; named Woman of Yr. YWCA, 1980; named to Ohio Women's Hall of Fame State of Ohio, 1989, Ohio Sci. & Tech. Hall of Fame, 1991, Humanitarian award Nat. Conf. Cmty. Justice, 2000, Medal of Honor, Ellis Island, 2002. Mem. Am. Chem. Soc. (chair analytical divsn. 1990-91, Garvan medal 1986, Analytical Chem. award 1993, Encouraging Women into Careers in Sci. award 1999), Soc. for Applied Spectroscopy (pres. 1970, Disting. Svc. award 1983), Coblentz Soc. (bd. govs. 1968-71, William Wright award 1980), Royal Soc. Chemistry (Theophilus Redwood lectr. 1994), Phi Beta Kappa, Iota Sigma Pi (pres. fluorine chpt. 1957-60, nat. hon. mem. 1987). Republican. Roman Catholic. Avocations: swimming, dance, music. Home: 150 Greentree Rd Chagrin Falls OH 44022-2424

BROWN, JEANNETTE ELIZABETH, retired science educator; d. Ada May Fox - Brown and Frederick Brown. BA, Hunter Coll., 1952—56; MSc, U. of Minn., 1956—58. Jr. chemist CIBA Pharm. Co., Summit, NJ, 1958—69; rsch. chemist Merck & Co. Inc., Rahway, NJ, 1969—95; vis. prof. of chemisty NJ. Inst. of Tech., Newark, 1993—95; N.J. Statewide Systemic Initiative coord. N.J. Inst. of Tech., Newark, 1995—98; N.J. statewide systemic initiative regional dir. NJ. Inst. of Tech., Newark, 1998—2002; ednl. cons. Self Employed, Hillsborough, NJ, 2002—. Chmn. Project SEED Com. Am. Chem. Soc., Washington, 1986—88; mem. of com. on equal opportunities in sci. NSF, Washington, 1991—98; mem. Black U. liason com. Merck & Co. Inc., Rahway, NJ, 1978—85. Mem. Cmty. Devel. Corp., Irvington, NJ, 2001—03; coun. mem. NJ. Assn. United Ch. of Christ, Montclair, NJ, 1998—2003; mem. Homesharing Bd., Bridgewater, NJ, 1998—2002. Recipient Women Chemist Com. Regional Award for Diversity, Am. Chem. Soc., 2002, Hunter Coll. Hall of Fame, Hunter Coll. Alumni Assn., 1991, Women in Sci. Videotape, Sch. of Dentistry U. of Mich., 1981; Tchg. Assistantship, U. of Minn., 1956—58, Dreyfus Chemistry Program, Camille and Henry Dreyfus Found., 2000—03. Mem.: AAAS, Am. Chem. Soc. (councilor North Jersey sect. 1982—), NY Acad. of Sci., Assn. for Women in Sci., Nat. Orgn. for Profl. Advancement of Black Chemists and Chem. Engineers, Iota Sigma PI (life). Protestant United Ch. Of Christ. Achievements include patents for synthesis of 12-Oxo-Trans (E) 10-Dodecanoic acid useful as a plant bioregulant; dipetidase inhibitors; use of pyrollidino ethano as a coccidiostat. Avocations: travel, gardening, fitness, swimming.

BROWN, JEFFREY DON, musician; b. Dallas, Tex., Apr. 18, 1970; s. Walter Don Brown; m. Sarah Marie Hibbard, June 24, 1995; 1 child, Alexandria Marie Hibbard-Brown. AA, Kilgore Coll., 1988—91; MusB, Stephen F. Austin State U., 1991—95, MusM, 1993—95; Dr. of Musical Arts, Mich. State U., 1997—2000. Cert. secondary edn./music Ill., Tex. Vocal music tchr. Dedham Country Day Sch., Dedham, Mass., 1996—97; grad. asst. Mich. State U., East Lansing, 1997—2000; dir. of music ministries First Christian Ch./Disciples of Christ, Lansing, Mich., 1997—2000; dir. of contemporary worship United Meth. Ch. of Libertyville, Ill., 2000—; dir. of choirs Adlai E. Stevenson H.S., Lincolnshire, Ill., 2000—01, Libertyville H.S., 2001—. Worship leader United Meth. Ch. of Libertyville, Ill., 2000—. Recipient Grad. Assistantship award, Mich. State U. Sch. of Music, 1997—2000, Outstanding Tchr. award, Ch. of Jesus Christ of Latter-Day Saints, Palllbo Grove, Ill., 2002. Mem.: Music Educators Nat. Conf. (corr.), Ill. Music Educators Assn. (corr.), Am. Choral Directors Assn. (corr.; none). Protestant. Home: 899 Fox Chase Dr Round Lake Beach IL 60073

BROWN, JENNIFER N. humanities educator; b. NYC, May 20, 1974; d. Francis Cabell and Nancy Leitow Brown; m. Jeffrey Robert Nemanick, Aug. 16, 2003. BA, Georgetown U., 1996, MA, 1997; PhD, CUNY, 2003. Instr. John Jay Coll., NYC, 1998—99, Hunter Coll., NYC, 1999—2001; writing fellow John Jay Coll., NYC, 2001—03; instr. NY U., NYC, 2001—03; asst. prof. Hartford (Conn.) U., 2003—. Contbr. articles to profl. jours. Mem.: MLA, Soc. Feminist Medieval Studies, Medieval Acad. Am. Avocation: fly fishing. E-mail: jennifernbrown@earthlink.net.

BROWN, JERROLD STANLEY lawyer; b. Little Falls, N.Y., Nov. 8, 1953; s. Stanley Clayton and Ruth Jane Brown; m. Catherine M. Agnello, Aug. 2, 1980. BA, SUNY, Albany, 1975; JD, Union U., 1979. Bar: N.Y. 1980, U.S. Dist. Ct. (no. dist.) N.Y. 1980, U.S. Dist. Ct. (we. dist.) N.Y. 1982, U.S. Ct. Appeals (2nd cir.) 1983, U.S. Supreme Ct. 1989. Law clk. to judge N.Y. Ct. Appeals, Albany, 1979-81; assoc. Hodgson Russ LLP, Buffalo, 1981-85; ptnr. Hodgson, Russ, Andrews, Woods & Goodyear, Buffalo, 1986—. Mem. adv. panel N.Y. Clean Air Act, 1996—. Note and comment editor Albany Law Rev., 1978-79. Mem. adv. bd. Salvation Army, Buffalo Area, 1999—; dir. Studio Arena Theatre, 1999—, v.p. bd. dirs., 2001—; ward leader Del. Dist. Rep. Party, 1992; Trustee Westminster Presbyn. Ch., Buffalo, 1986, pres., 1988, elder, 1992—93, 1997—2000. Mem. N.Y. State Bar Assn. (task force on commerce and industry 1998—). Office: Hodgson Russ LLP Ste 2000 One M & T Plz Buffalo NY 14203

BROWN, JERRY (EDMUND GERALD BROWN JR.), mayor, former governor; b. San Francisco, Apr. 7, 1938; s. Edmund Gerald and Bernice (Layne) B. BA in Latin/Greek, U. Calif., Berkeley, 1961; JD, Yale U., 1964. Bar: Calif. 1965. Research atty. Calif. Supreme Ct., 1964-65; atty. Tuttle & Taylor, Los Angeles, 1966-69; sec. state State Calif., Sacramento, Calif., 1970-74, gov., 1975-83; chmn. Calif. Dem. Party, 1989-90; Dem. candidate for Pres. of United States, 1992; mayor Oakland, Calif., 1999—. Author: (book) Dialogues, 1988. Trustee Los Angeles Community Colls., 1969. Democrat. Address: 1 Frank Ogawa Plz 3rd Fl Oakland CA 94612-1997*

BROWN, JERRY A. federal bankruptcy judge; b. Detroit, Jan. 31, 1932; m. Florence Freedman; three children. BA, Murray State Coll., 1954; LLB, Tulane U., 1959. Bar: La. 1959, Ky. 1959, U.S. Ct. Appeals (5th cir.) 1960, U.S. Ct. Appeals (11th cir.) 1981, U.S. Dist. Ct. (ea. dist.) La. 1960, U.S. Dist. Ct. (we. dist.) La. 1961, U.S. Dist. Ct. (mid. dist. La.) 1973, U.S. Dist. Ct. (we. dist.) Ky. 1981. Law clk. to Hon. John Minor Wisdom U.S. Ct. Appeals (5th cir.), 1959-60; assoc. Monroe & Lemann, New Orleans, 1960-63, ptnr., 1963-90; spl. counsel Bronfin & Heller, New Orleans, 1991-92; bankruptcy judge U.S. Bankruptcy (ea. dist.) La., New Orleans, 1992—. With U.S. Army, 1954-56. Office: US Bankruptcy Ea Dist 501 Magazine St Rm 741A New Orleans LA 70130-3319

BROWN, JERRY MILFORD, medical company executive; b. Anderson, S.C., Apr. 30, 1938; s. James Milford and Jane Elizabeth (McCord) B.; m. Alice Alberta Thompson, July 30, 1960; children: John Milford, Allen Thompson, James Milford II. BS, Furman U., 1960; MA in Biology, Wake Forest U., 1963, Temple U., 1967; PhD in Physiology, Dental Sch., U. Md., 1972. Commd. lt. U.S. Army, 1960, advanced through grades to lt. col., 1980; rsch. instr. Hahanemann Med. Coll., Phila., 1967-68; sect. leader, exptl. medicine divsn. Biomed. Lab., Edgewood Arsenal, Md., 1967-68; instr. anatomy Med. Sch., U. Md., Balt., 1970-77; sect. leader exptl. medicine divsn. U.S. Army Rsch. Inst. Environ. Medicine, Natick, Mass., 1973-76; dep. dir. U.S. Army Med. Intelligence and Info. Agy., Ft. Detrick, Md., 1976-80; dir. internat. health affairs Dept. Def., Washington, 1980-84; chief plans ops. security 2d Gen. Hosp., Germany, 1984-87; med. coord. Fed. Emer. Mgmt. Agy., Washington, 1987-90; nat. disaster med. system staff, bd. govs. Nat. Coun. Internat. Health, 1980-90; cons. and spl. asst. to the pres. Bio Tech. Gen. Corp., Iselin, N.J., 1991-99; pres., chief oper. officer NeuroSurg. Internat., 1995—; v.p., chief oper. officer M/D Frontiers, Springfield, Va., 1990—; pres. Automated Med. Products, Inc., Springfield, Va., 1990—; pres. CEO Automated Med. Products Corp., 1997—; mgr. Precision Med. Manufacturing L.L.C., Wheling, Ill., 2002—. V.p. Automated Systems, 1991—; assoc. dir. rsch. nat. study ctr. trauma and emer. medicine U. Md.; U.S. mem. Internat. Com. Mil. Medicine and Pharmacy, 1981-87, U.S. mil. mem. Joint Civil/Mil. Med. Working Group U.S., NATO, 1981—; mem. program planning com. Internat. Assembly Emer. Med. Svcs., Balt., 1984; congress lobbyist; cons. in field. Contbr. articles to med. jours.; pub. books in field of philately. Commr. Explorer Scouts, Natick, Mass., 1975-76; trustee Cardinal Spellman Philatlic Mus., Weston, Mass., 1980-97. Deocrated Meritorious Svc. medal with oak leaf clusters, Legion of Merit; recipient gold medal Res. Officers Assn., 1960. Mem. Electron Microscopy Soc. Am., Am. Stamp Dealers Assn., Ctrl. Atlantic Stamp Dealers Assn. (pres. 1977-81), Rsch. and Engring. Soc. Am., Balt. Philatelic Soc., Sigma Alpha Epsilon, Sigma Xi. Republican. Baptist. E-mail: jbrown@automatedmedproducts.com.

BROWN, JOAN PHILLIPS (ABENA JOAN BROWN), foundation administrator; b. Chgo. d. Lueola Reed; divorced. BA, Roosevelt U., 1954; MA, U. Chgo., 1963; honorary PhD, DHL (hon.), Chgo. State U. Dir. West Side YWCA, Chgo., 1963-65; cons. human relations YWCA of Met. Chgo., 1965-72, dir. program services, 1972-82; pres. ETA Creative Arts Found., Chgo., 1982—. Chmn. adv. bd., Dept. Cultural Affairs, Chgo.; sec. Dept. Cultural Affairs Bd., Chgo., 1983—; vice chairperson, vice chmn. bd. dirs., Muntu Dance Theatre, Chgo., 1985—; pres. emeritus African Am. Arts Alliance, Chgo.; mem. Woman's Bd. Chgo. Urban League; mem. League Chgo. Theaters. Recipient more than 75 awards for contbn. to the arts, from nat. and local civic grouups. Home: 7637 S Bennett Ave Chicago IL 60649-4007 Office: ETA Creative Arts Found 7558 S South Chicago Ave Chicago IL 60619-2644

BROWN, JOBETH GOODE, food products executive, lawyer; b. Oakdale, La., Sept. 15, 1950; d. Samuel C. Goode and Elizabeth E. (Twiner) Baker; m. H. William Brown, Aug. 4, 1973; 1 child, Kevin William. BA, Newcomb Coll. Tulane U., 1972; JD, Wash. U., 1979. Assoc. Coburn, Croft & Putzell, St. Louis, 1979-80; staff atty. Anheuser-Busch Cos. Inc., St. Louis, 1980-81, exec. asst. to v.p. sec., 1982-83, asst. sec., 1983-89, sec., v.p., 1989—. Trustee Anheuser-Busch Found., St. Louis, 1989—, St. Louis Sci. Ctr., Girls, Inc. of St. Louis; bd. dirs. St. Louis Zoo Friends, Met. Assn. Philanthropy. Mem. ABA, Mo. Women's Forum, Mo. Bar Assn., Bar Assn. Met. St. Louis, Am. Soc. Corp. Secs. (pres. 1992), Algonquin Golf Club, Order of Coif. Republican. Presbyterian. Office: Anheuser-Busch Cos Inc 1 Busch Pl 202-6 Saint Louis MO 63118-1852

BROWN, JOE BLACKBURN, judge; b. Louisville, Dec. 9, 1940; s. Knox and Miriam (Blackburn) B.; m. Marilyn McGowen, Aug. 10, 1963; children: Jennifer Knox, Michael McGowen. BA cum laude, Vanderbilt U., 1962, JD, 1965. Bar: Ky. 1965, Tenn. 1972, U.S. Supreme Ct. 1979. Asst. U.S. atty. Dept. Justice, Nashville, 1971-73, 1st asst. U.S. atty., 1974-81, U.S. atty., 1981-91, spl. asst. U.S. trustee, 1991-98; U.S. magistrate judge, U.S. Dist. Ct. (mid. dist.) Tenn., Nashville, 1998—. Lectr. law Atty. Gen.'s Advocacy Inst., 1982—; vice chmn. Atty. Gen.'s Adv. Com., 1986-87, chmn. subcom. on sentencing guidelines, mem. subcom. on budget and office mgmt., 1982-91; instr. math. and bus. law Augusta (Ga.) Coll., 1966-69; instr. law Nashville Sch. Law, 1999—. Contbr. articles to legal jours. Bd. dirs. Mid-Cumberland Drug Abuse Coun., Nashville, 1977-86; asst. scoutmastr Boy Scouts Am.; vestryman St. David's Episcopal Ch., sr. warden, 1982, 90; ch. atty. Episcopal Diocese of Tenn., 1995-98; lt. col. CAP, 1996—. Maj. U.S. Army, 1965-71; col. JAGC, USAR ret. Decorated Legion of Merit, Meritorious Svc. medal with 3 oak leaf clusters; recipient Disting. Svc. award Atty. Gen.'s Adv. Com., 1988. Fellow Tenn. Bar Assn., Nashville Bar Found.; mem. FBA (treas. 1978), Nashville Bar Assn. (bd. dirs. 1995-97, exec. com. 1996-97, v.p. 1997), Radio Amateur Transmitting Soc. (pres. 1997-98), Nat. Assn. Flight Instrs., Profl. Assn. Div Instrs., Ky. Bar Assn., NRA (life, Disting. Rifleman award), Harry Phillip Inn of Ct. (master of bench and bar 1994—), Order of Coif, Phi Beta Kappa. Republican. Home: 3427 Woodmont Blvd Nashville TN 37215-1421 Office: US Courthouse Rm 797 801 Broadway Nashville TN 37203-3816 E-mail: joe_b_brown@tnmd.uscourts.gov.

BROWN, JOHN B., III, federal agency administrator; B, SUNY, Brockport. Spl. agt. Bur. Narcotics and Dangerous Drugs, 1972—84, DEA, Mexico, 1984—88, group supr., group supr. Caribbean enforcement group, inspector and gen. inspector, deciding ofcl. for disciplinary matters, 1995—97; dor. El Paso Intelligence Ctr., Tex., 1997—2002; deputy adminstr. DEA, U.S. Dept. Justice, Alexandria, Va., 2002—. Office: US Dept Justice 2401 Jefferson Davis Hwy Alexandria VA 22301

BROWN, JOHN EUGENE, social science educator, minister; b. Ft. Wayne, Ind., July 3, 1931; s. Clifford Leo and Edith Eunice (Bolinger) B.; m. Edith Ann Beer, June 5, 1953 (div. May 1981); children: Beth Ann Brown-Reinsel, Lisa Suzanne, Christine Louise Brown St. Ours, John Jefferson; m. Gloria Margaret Limberg Hastings, Aug. 1, 1981; 3 stepchildren. BA, DePauw U., 1954; BDiv, San Francisco Theol. Sem., 1957; MA, Johns Hopkins U., 1959; PhD, Ball State U., 1970. Ordained min. Presbyn. Ch., 1961. Univ. chaplain's asst. Johns Hopkins U., Balt., 1958-60; asst. prof. religion Alma (Mich.) Coll., 1960-64; min. Christian edn. Grace Presbyn. Ch., Jenkintown, Pa., 1964-66; vis. asst. prof. history Centre Coll. of Ky., Danville, 1967; tchg. asst. in history Ball State U., Muncie, Ind., 1967-70; prof. history, philosophy and religion Harford C.C., Bel Air, Md., 1970-96; ret., 1996. Mem. Presbytery of Balt., 1970-96, honorably ret., 1996. Contbr. articles to profl. jours.; editor Harford Hist. Bull., 1982-85. Commr. Historic Preservation Commn., Harford County, Md., 1994-96; bd. dirs. Mus. Colquitt County History, Hist. Soc. Colquitt County, Ga., 1997-2001. Rsch. grantee on Havre de Grace Md., NEH and MD. Humanities Coun., Balt., 1985. Mem. Orgn. Am. Historians, Md. Hist. Soc., Ind. Hist. Soc., Hist. Soc. Harford County Md. (pres. 1986-88, George W. Archer lectr. 1994), St. Andrew's Soc. Balt., Balt. Fgn. Affairs Coun., Kiwanis Club Moultrie Ga. (bd. dirs., George F. Hixson fellow 1999) Bel Air Am. History Club (v.p. 1985-90). Presbyn. Avocations: history writing, civic service, opera, symphony, piano. Home: 3900 N Charles St Apt 411 Baltimore MD 21218

BROWN, JOHN LAWRENCE, JR., electrical engineering educator; b. Ellenville, N.Y., Mar. 6, 1925; s. John Lawrence and Grace Evelyn Brown; m. Marjorie Anne Schnelle, June 15, 1957 (div. Mar. 1969). BS, Ohio U., 1948; PhD, Brown U., 1953. Asst. prof. Pa. State U., State College, 1951-53, assoc. prof., 1953-60, prof. engring. rsch., 1960-69, prof. elec. engring., 1969-88, prof. emeritus, 1988—. Stocker vis. prof. Ohio U., Athens, Ohio, 1988-90. Author numerous papers in profl. jours. With U.S. Army, 1943-46, Prince vis. fellow Ariz. State U., Phoenix, 1982-83, Gen. Lew Allen Rsch. Chair Air Force Inst. Tech., Dayton, Ohio, 1984-85. Fellow IEEE (life); mem. Math. Assn. Am., Acoustical Soc. Am. Avocations: tennis, book collecting. Home: 1431 Curtin St State College PA 16803-3020 Office: Pa State Univ 121 Electrical Engineering E University Park PA 16802-2705 E-mail: jlb6@psu.edu.

BROWN, JOHN LEWIS, lawyer; b. Galesburg, Ill., July 2, 1955; s. Charles Lewis and Lois Maria (Nelson) B.; m. Cynthia Sue Bowen, Aug. 31, 1980; children: Whitney Rose, Vanessa Marie, Spencer Ross. BA, Northwestern U., 1977; JD, U. Iowa, 1980. Bar: Iowa 1980, Ill. 1980, Minn. 1984. Assoc. Lucas, Brown & McDonald, Galesburg, 1980-83; sr. atty., asst. v.p. ITT Consumer Fin. Corp., Mpls., 1983-93; asst. chief counsel John Deere Credit, Des Moines, 1993—. Mem. Iowa Bar Assn. Home: 804 57th Pl West Des Moines IA 50266-7235

BROWN, JOHN LOTT, educator; b. Phila., Dec. 3, 1924; s. John Lott and Carolyn Emma (Francis) B.; m. Catharine Hertfelder, June 11, 1948; children: Patricia Carolyn, Judith Elliott, Anderson Graham, Barbara Smith. BSEE, Worcester (Mass.) Poly. Inst., 1945, DSc (hon.), 1984; MA, Temple U., 1949; PhD, Columbia U., 1952. Personnel tng. and personnel mgr. Olney foundry Link-Belt Co., Phila., 1948-50; tech. dir. air force contract, dept. psychology Columbia U., 1952-54; head psychology div., aviation med. lab. Naval Air Devel. Center, Johnsville, Pa., 1954-59; dir. grad. tng. program physiology, 1962-65; asst., then asso. prof. physiology U. Pa. Med. Sch., 1955-65; prof. physiology and psychology Kans. State U., 1965-69; dean Grad. Sch., 1965-66, v.p. acad. affairs, 1966-69; prof. optics and psychology, dir. center visual sci. U. Rochester, N.Y., 1969-78; pres. U. South Fla., Tampa, 1978-88, prof. psychology, physiology and opthalmology, 1978-92, prof. indsl. engring., 1988-92, interim dir. Ctr. for Microelectronic Rsch., 1993-94, pres. emeritus, 1988—; interim pres. Worcester Poly. Inst., 1994-95. Chmn. com. vision NRC-Nat. Acad. Scis., 1965-70; chmn. vision rsch. program com. Nat. Eye Inst., 1975-78; trustee Worcester Poly. Inst., 1970-83, mem. alumni coun., 1975-76; trustee Illuminating Engring. Rsch. Inst., 1974-79; mem. U.S. nat. com. Internat. Commn. Optics, 1977. Author chpts. in books, also monographs, articles, 1953—; cons. editor: Perception and Psychophysics, 1972-90; editorial adv. bd.: Vision Research, 1971-77. Bd. dirs. Pub. Broadcasting Svc., 1980-83, Mid-Am. Inst. Profl. Devel., 1980-82, Fla. Gulf Symphony, 1979-81, Tampa Gen. Hosp. Found., 1980-81, Smith-Kettlewell Eye Rsch. Inst., 1991-97; mem. Fla. Council 100, 1978-88; mem. corp. bd. Tampa Performing Arts Hall, 1980-88; chmn. Tampa Bay Area R&D Authority, 1979-86, Tampa Bay Area Fgn. Affairs Com., 1979-92; chmn. bd. dirs. H. Lee Moffitt Cancer Ctr. and Rsch. Inst., 1984-88, Exec. Svc. Corp. of Tampa Bay, 1989-97, pres., 1994. With USNR, 1943-46, comdr., 1947-69. Recipient Research Career Devel. award NIH, 1961-62, Robert Goddard award Worcester Poly. Inst., 1969; sr. research fellow USPHS, 1959-61; grantee NIH; grantee NSF; grantee Office Naval Research; grantee Nat. Eye Inst.; grantee NIMH; grantee NASA. Fellow Optical Soc. Am. (exec. coun. Rochester chpt. 1975-76, assoc. editor jour. 1972-77), Am. Psychol. Assn., AAAS; mem. Assn. Rsch. Vision and Ophthalmology (pres. 1978), Soc. Neurosci., Psychonomic Soc., Fla. Assn. Colls. and Univs. (pres. 1988-89), Sigma Xi, Tau Beta Pi, Psi Chi, Phi Eta Sigma, Phi Kappa Phi, Omicron Delta Kappa, Phi Gamma Delta. Mem. Soc. Of Friends. Home: 105 Kendal Dr Oberlin OH 44074-1905 E-mail: jlottb@aol.com.

BROWN, JOHN PATRICK, newspaper executive, financial consultant; b. N.Y.C., Oct. 14, 1925; s. Patrick and Emma A (McCarrick) B.; m. Caroline T. Hopkins, Oct. 17, 1959 (dec. Nov. 2002); children: John Patrick, Anne B. Loftus. BBA, St. John's U., Jamaica, N.Y., 1949; MBA, N.Y.U., 1960. C.P.A., N.Y. Accountant Arthur Young & Co., C.P.A.s, N.Y.C., 1950-58; asst. treas. Paramount Pictures Corp., 1962-65; controller, treas. Washington Star, 1966-76; v.p. fin., treas. Bergen Evening Record Corp., N.J., 1976-82; dir. fin. and adminstrn. Washington Times, 1982-88. Adj. prof. acctg. Am. U., U. Va., Va. Tech. Served with AUS, 1944-46. Mem. AICPA, Fin. Execs. Inst., Internat. Newspaper Fin. Execs. Clubs: Metropolitan (Washington). Roman Catholic. Home and Office: 4230 Embassy Park Dr NW Washington DC 20016-3619

BROWN, JOHN ROBERT, lawyer; b. Muskogee, Okla., Apr. 22, 1948; s. John Robert and Betty Jane (Singleterry) B. BA, MA, Cambridge U., 1972; STB, Gen. Theol. Sem., 1973; STM, Union Theol. Sem., 1978, Harvard U., 1982; MA, STL, U. Louvain, Belgium, 1979; JD, Howard U., 1991. Bar: Ga. 1991, D.C. 1991, U.S. Supreme Ct. 1997; admitted Middle Temple, London,

2000; ordained priest Episcopal Ch., 1972, received into Roman Cath. Ch., 2001. Tchr., headmaster St. John's Sch., Oklahoma City, 1973-77; novice Soc. St. John the Evangelist, Cambridge, Mass., 1979-81; minor canon Pro-Cathedral of Holy Trinity, Brussels, 1981-83; assoc. rector St. James Ch., L.A., 1983-87; hon. assisting priest Ch. of the Ascension and St. Agnes, Washington, 1987-91; legis. aide U.S. Ho. of Reps., Washington, 1987-91; hon. asst. priest Ch. of Our Savior, Atlanta, 1991—2001; staff atty. Ga. Legal Svcs., Atlanta, 1991-1995; asst. gen. counsel State Bar Ga., Atlanta, 1996—. Reader Ecumenical Inst. World Coun. Ch., Geneva, 1978, Huntington Libr., San Marino, Calif., 1985-86, Coll. of Preachers, Nat. Cathedral, Washington, 1987, fellow, Center for Ethics in Public Policy and the Professions, Emory U., 1996-98. Contbr. articles to profl. jours. Vol. NIH, 1987—88, Fed. Charitable Campaign, Washington, 1988—89, Atlanta Project, 1991—96; spiritual adv. com. AIDS Project, L.A., 1984—86; mem. Mayor's Task Force on Family Diversity, 1984—86, Mcpl. Elections Com. L.A., 1984—86; governing bd. Robert Wood Johnson Homeless Health Care Project, L.A., 1985—87; trustees com. Opera Am., 1994—2001; co-trustee Freeman Found., 1994—97; adv. bd. Caring Hands Programs, 1983—87; mem. adv. bd. United Way of Metro Atlanta, 1993—97; adv. bd. Metro Atlanta Cmty. Found., 1994—97; chmn. social justice grants com. Threshold Found., 1994—96; capt. The Old Guard of The Gate City Guard, Atlanta, 1998—; bd. dirs. S.W. Assn. Episcopal Schs., 1974—77, Anglican Roman Cath. Commn. of Belgium, 1981—83; chaplain Most Venerable Order of St. John of Jerusalem, 1996—; bd. dirs. Cmty. Counseling Svc., L.A., 1983—86, Acad. Performing Arts, L.A., 1984—85, Right to Life League So. Calif., 1984—86, Cape Coast Outreach Found., 1984—86, Coun. Battered Women, Atlanta, 1991—94, AID Atlanta, 1993—2002, Atlanta Opera, 1993—2003, ACLU of Ga., 1994—2002, Fund for So. Cmtys., 1995—98, Funding Exch., 1997—99, Cathedral of St. Philip Bookstore, 1998 2003. Named one of Outstanding Young Men of Am., 1974; Yale U. rsch. fellow, 1983; recipient Mayor's Phoenix award, Atlanta, 1997. Fellow: Ga. Bar Found. (life); mem.: ABA (vice-chmn. fed. legis. com. gen. practice sect. 1989—91), Soc. Colonial Wars, Patrons of the Vatican Mus., Commerce Club (Atlanta), City Tavern Club, Harvard Club (Washington), United Oxford and Cambridge U. Club (London). Office: State Bar of Ga 104 Marietta St # 100 Atlanta GA 30303

BROWN, JOHN W. pediatric cardiothoracic surgeon; b. Martinsville, Ind., Feb. 18, 1945; s. Merle and Laverne Brown; m. Carol Ann Brighton, Jan. 25, 1969; children: Jason, Amy, Peter. BA, Ind. U., 1967, MD, 1970. Diplomate Am. Bd. Thoracic Surgery, 1979, Am. Bd. Surgery, 1977. Asst. prof. of surgery Ind. U. Sch. of Medicine, Indpls., 1978—83, assoc. prof. of surgery, 1983—88, prof. of surgery, 1988—, chief cardiothoracic surgery, 1990—. Co-dir. cardiovascular surgery Clarian Health Ptnrs., Indpls., 1998—. Lt. comdr. USPHS, 1972—74. Named Harris B Shumacker Prof. of Surgery, Ind. U. Sch. of Medicine, 1993. Mem.: AMA, Soc. of Thoracic Surgeons, Am. Assn. of Thoracic Surgeons. Avocations: bison ranching, hunting, fishing, travel. Office: Indiana University School of Medicine 545 Barnhill Dr # EH 215 Indianapolis IN 46202 Office Fax: 317-274-2940.

BROWN, JOHN WALTER, vocational education supervisor; b. Waverly, Va., Dec. 13, 1937; s. Wilburt Herman and Martha Ann (Holmes) B. BS in Vocat. Indsl. Edn., Va. State U., 1968; MEd in Vocat. Indsl. Edn., Pa. State U., 1970; cert. advanced study in edn., Johns Hopkins U., 1973; PhD in Vocat. Indsl. Edn., Pa. State U., 1976. Cert. tchr., advanced profl., prin., supr., supt., vocat. edn., Md. and Pa. Drafting instr. Peabody Sr. High Sch., Petersburg, Va., 1962-63; electronics instr. Hampstead Hill Jr. High Sch., Balt., 1965-66, Calverton Jr. High Sch., Balt., 1966-73, dep. prin., 1975-80; vice prin. Carver Vocat. Tech. Sr. High Sch., Balt., 1975; ednl. specialist Balt. City Pub. Schs., 1974, coord., 1980-84, div. specialist, 1984-89, curriculum specialist, 1989-93; prin. House One Rowland Intermediate Sch., Harrisburg, Pa., 1993-94; coord. profl. pers. devel. Pa. State Dept. of Edn., Harrisburg, 1994—2003, coord. profl. pers. devel. and acting mgr., divsn. product devel., 2001—. Instr. Va. State U., Petersburg, 1962-63, Coppin State Coll., Balt., 1972-73; mem. Balt. City Adv. Coun. on Vocat. Edn. and trade adv. subcoms. With U.S. Army, 1963-65. Named to Va. State U. Sports Hall of Fame. Mem. Am. Vocat. Edn. Assn., Nat. Assn. Indsl. and Tech. Edn., Pub. Schs. Adminstrs. and Suprs. Assn., Johns Hopkins Alumni Assn., Pa. State U. Alumni Assn., Va. State U. Alumni Assn., Iota Lambda Sigma, Phi Delta Kappa. Methodist. Avocations: sports, reading, travel, writing, gardening. Home: 5914 Charnwood Rd Baltimore MD 21228-1205 Office: Pa State Dept Edn Bur of Career and Tech Edn 333 Market St Harrisburg PA 17101-2210 E-mail: jobrown@state.pa.us.

BROWN, JOHN WAYNE, lawyer; b. East Orange, N.J., Nov. 17, 1949; s. John Edison and Margaret Patricia B.; m. Donna Potts, Nov. 18, 1978; children: Savannah Jane, Justin Taylor, Molly Ross. BA cum laude, Meth. Coll., 1971; JD, Wake Forest U., 1974; M in Law and Taxation, William and Mary Coll., 1980. Bar: Va. 1974, U.S. Dist. Ct. (ea. dist.) Va. 1975, U.S. Supreme Ct 1980, U.S. Tax Ct. 1980, U.S. Ct. Appeals (4th cir.) 1981. Pvt. practice, Chesapeake, Va., 1974-75; asst. dep. commonwealth atty. Commonwealth Atty's Office, Chesapeake, 1975-80; ptnr. Gordon & Brown, Chesapeake, 1980-86; pvt. practice Chesapeake, 1986—. Chmn. TowneBank (chmn. Chesapeake bd. dirs.). Co. chmn. Sch. Bond Referendum, Chesapeake; bd. dirs. Va. Sports Hall of Fame and Mus. Mem. Va. State Bar Assn., Va. Trial Lawyers Assn., Chesapeake Bar Assn., South Norfolk Ruritan Club. Republican. Methodist. Avocations: sailing, jogging, yard work, fishing, golf. Office: The 411 Bldg 411 Cedar Rd Chesapeake VA 23322-5566 also: 114 N Main St Suffolk VA 23434

BROWN, JOHN WILFORD, health products executive; b. Paris, Tenn., Sept. 15, 1934; s. Albert T. and Treva (Moody) B.; m. Rosemary Kopel, June 7, 1957; children: Sarah Beth, Janine. BSChemE, Auburn U., 1957. Process engr. Ormet Corp., Hannibal, Ohio, 1958-62; sr. engr. Thiokol Chem. Corp., Marshall, Tex., 1962-65; with Squibb Corp., Princeton, n.J., 1965-72, asst. to pros., 1970-72; pres. Edward Weck & Co. divsn. Squibb Corp., N.Y.C., 1972-77; chmn. bd. dirs., pres., CEO Stryker Corp., Kalamazoo, Mich., 1979—. Mem. Am. Chem. Soc., Health Industries Mfg. Assn. (bd. dirs.). Democrat. Mem. Ch. of Christ. Office: Stryker Corp 2725 Fairfield Ave Kalamazoo MI 49048-2605

BROWN, JOHN Y., III, state official; BA in History magna cum laude, Bellarmine Coll., Louisville, Ky., 1988; JD with distinction, U. Ky. Coll. Law, Lexington, 1992. Summer assoc. Stoll, Keenon & Park Law Firm, Lexington, Ky., 1990, Brown, Todd & Heyburn Law Firm, Louisville, Ky., 1991; dir. franchising Roasters Franchise Corp., Fort Lauderdale, Fla., 1992-94; sec. of state Commonwealth of Ky., Frankfort, 1996—. Grad. asst. Dale Carnegie Tng., 1987-92. Mem. ABA, Ky. Bar Assn. Democrat. Home: 7006 Foxcroft Pl Prospect KY 40059 Office: State Capitol Ste 152 Frankfort KY 40601-3493

BROWN, JONATHAN, art historian, fine arts educator; b. Springfield, Mass., July 15, 1939; s. Leonard Melvin and Jeanette (Levy) B.; m. Sandra Backer, July 22, 1966; children: Claire, Michael, Daniel. AB, Dartmouth Coll., 1960; M.F.A., Princeton U., 1963, PhD, 1964; MA (hon.), Oxford U., 1981. Mem. faculty Princeton, 1965-73, asso. prof. art and archaeology, 1971-73; asso. prof. art NYU, 1973-75, prof., 1976-84, Carroll and Milton Petrie prof., 1984—; dir. Inst. Fine Arts, 1973-78; Slade prof. fine arts Oxford (Eng.) U., 1981-82. Vis. mem. Inst. Advanced Study, Princeton, N.J., 1978-79; adv. com. dept. European paintings Met. Mus. Art, 1974-79; adv. bd. Master Drawings jour.; bd. dirs. Fundacion Duques de Soria, 1990—; curator Am. Philos. Soc., 1992-98, Velazquez in New York Museums, 1999, Los siglos de oro en los virreinatos de America, 1550-1700, 1999, Velazquez, Rubens, Van Dyck: Pintores Cortesanos del Siglo XVII, 1999, El Greco: Themes and Variations, 2001, (with Sir John Elliott) La almoneda del siglo, 2002, Princeton U. Art Mus., The Frick Collection; Andrew W. Mellon lectr. in fine arts Nat. Gallery of Art, 1994; mem. adv. com. Mus. del Prado. Author: Prints and Drawings by Jusepe de Ribera, 1973, Zurbaran, 1973, Murillo and His Drawings, 1976, Images and Ideas in Seventeenth Century Spanish Painting, 1978, A Palace for a King: The Buen Retiro and the Court of Philip IV, 1980; (with J.H. Elliott) also articles on Spanish art, (with others) El Greco of Toledo, 1982, Velazquez, Painter and Courtier, 1986, (with R.G. Mann) Spanish Paintings of the Fifteenth through Nineteenth Centuries, National Gallery of Art, 1990, The Golden Age of Painting in Spain, 1991, Kings and Connoisseurs: Collecting Art in 17th Century Europe, 1995, (with C. Garrido) Velázquez. The Technique of Genius, 1998, Painting in Spain, 1500-1700, 1998; editor: Picasso and the Spanish Tradition, 1996, Franklin and Condorcet: Two Portraits from the American Philosophical Society, 1997, Velázquez, Rubens y Van Dyck, 1999; co-editor: Sources and Documents in the History of Art: Italy and Spain 1600-1750, 1970, Los siglos de oro en los virreinatos de América, The Sale of the Century, 2002. Recipient Medalla de Oro de Bellas Artes, Gov. of Spain, 1986; Fulbright fellow, 1964-65; Am. Council Learned Socs. fellow, 1968-69; Nat. Endowment Humanities fellow, 1978-79; Guggenheim fellow, 1980-81; Order of Isabel la Catolica, 1986, Gran Cruz de Alfonso X el Sabio, 1996, Premio Elio Antonio Nebrija U. de Salamanca, 1997. Mem. AAAS, Coll. Art Assn. Am. (Arthur Kingsley Porter prize 1971), Hispanic Soc. Am. (corr.), Am. Philos. Soc., Real Academia de Bellas Artes (Madrid, corr., Valencia, corr.). Home: 71 Battle Rd Princeton NJ 08540-4945 Office: 1 E 78th St New York NY 10021-0119

BROWN, JONATHON ANDREW, healthcare executive; b. Bronx, N.Y., Feb. 11, 1966; s. Herbert and Caroline B. Diploma, Mt. Vernon Hosp., 1985; BSN, Barry U., 1991; MSN, U. Miami, 1994; MBA, Colo. State U., 2003. Cert. advancd nursing adminstrn., diplomate . Am. Bd. Healthcare Execs.; RN Fla. Asst. nurse coord. Mt. Vernon (N.Y.) Hosp., 1986-88; nurse Bapt. Hosp. of Miami, Fla., 1988-89, asst. nurse mgr., 1989-90; nurse mgr. Coral Gables (Fla.) Hosp., 1990-92; nursing systems analyst Homestead (Fla.) Hosp., 1992-93; chief nursing officer Coral Gables Hosp., 1993-97; v.p. patient care svcs. Episcopal Hosp., Phila., 1997-2000, Adirondack Med. Ctr., Saranac Lake, N.Y., 2000—. Contbr. articles to profl. jours. Mem. ANA, AACN, Am. Orgn. Nurse Execs., N.Y. Org. Nurse Execs. Republican. Avocations: bowling, swimming. Home: Apt A-18 85 N Middletown Rd Nanuet NY 10954-1944 Office: Adirondack Med Ctr PO Box 471 Lake Colby Dr Saranac Lake NY 12983 E-mail: jabrown1@aol.com.

BROWN, JOSEPH W., JR., (JAY BROWN), insurance company executive; Various positions to chief exec. Fireman's Fund Ins. Cos., 1975-92; chmn. Talegen Holdings, Inc., 1992-98; chmn., chief exec. MBIA Inc., 1998—, MBIA Ins. Cos., 1998—.

BROWN, JOSEPH WENTLING, lawyer; b. Norfolk, Va., July 31, 1941; s. Edwin Wallace and Nancy Jack (Wentling) B.; m. Pamela Jones, Aug. 18, 1966; children: Tyree, Palmer, Jeffrey, Hunter. BA, U. Va., 1965; LLB, Washington and Lee U., 1968. Bar: Nev. 1969, D.C. 1976, U.S. Dist. Ct. Nev. 1969. Pres. Jones Vargas Law Firm, Las Vegas, 1997—. Commr. Nev. Dept. of Wildlife, 1979-85; mem. U.S. Fgn. Claims Settlement Commn., 1981-87; bd. dirs. State Justice Inst., 1988-89, Wells Fargo Bank (Nev.); mem. Bd. of Litigation, Mountain States Legal Found., 1978-82. Editor: Washington and Lee Lawyer, 1967-68. Bd. dirs. Nev. Devel. Authority, Las Vegas C. of C., Nev. Cath. Cmty. Svcs., Wells Fargo Bnk, Nevv.; dep. counsel Rep. Nat. Conv., 1984; mem. Rep. Nat. Com., 2002—. Served with USMCR, 1963-69. Mem. ABA, ATLA, Nev. Bar Assn., Clark County Bar Assn., Spanish Trail Country Club, Rotary. Republican. Roman Catholic. Home: 17 Sawgrass Ct Las Vegas NV 89113-1326 Office: Jones Vargas 3773 Howard Hughes Pkwy Suite 300 S Las Vegas NV 89109

BROWN, JOSEPH WILLIAM, retired patent agent; b. Evanston, Wyo., Sept. 19, 1919; s. James Jr. and Mary (Duncombe) Brown. BS, U. Wyo., 1943, JD, 1947. Bar: (Patent) 1947. Patent agt. Shell Devel., Calif., 1946-54, mgr. polymer divsn., 1954-72, mgr. patents, 1972-80, ret., 1980. Capt. U.S. Army, 1944—46. Home: 698 E 2320 N Provo UT 84604-1749

BROWN, JOY ALICE, social services administrator; b. Redmesa, Colo., Mar. 19, 1917; d. Ezra E. and Alice M. (Pinkerton) Walker; m. Clayton Henry Brown, Apr. 9, 1941; children: Kimleigh Clayton, Loraleigh Joy. BA, Highlands U., 1958; MA, U. No. Colo., 1967, EdD, 1970. Tchr. La Plata County, Colo., 1936-41; prin. Bayfield (Colo.) pub. schs., 1942-46; tchr. Aztec (N.Mex.) pub. schs., 1946-63; spl. edn. coordinator primary schs. Palmer, Alaska, 1963-67; lab. sch. supr. U. No. Colo., 1967-70; assoc. prof. edn. N.Mex. State U., 1970-75; dir. Open Door Center, Las Cruces, N.Mex., 1975—. Cons. Tex. Edn. Service Center, Roswell (N.Mex.) schs.; sec. Dona Ana Human Services Consortium, 1977. Contbr. articles on edn. to profl. jours. Recipient Community Service award Las Cruces Eastside Center, 1972; Outstanding Contribution award N.Mex. Council of Exceptional Children, 1977. Mem. NEA, Council for Exceptional Children, Nat. Assn. Retarded Citizens, Phi Delta Kappa. Home: 34081 Country Rd M Mancos CO 81328

BROWN, JOYCE F. academic administrator; b. N.Y.C., July 7, 1946; d. Robert E. and Joyce Cappie Brown; m. H. Carl McCall, Aug. 13, 1983. BA, Marymount Coll., 1968; MA, NYU, 1970, PhD, 1980. Pres. Fashion Inst. Tech., 1998—; univ. dean Ctrl. Office CUNY, 1983—87, vice chancellor, 1987—90, prof. clin. psychology, 1994—, acting pres. Baruch Coll., 1990; pres. Fashion Inst. Tech., 1998—. Dep. mayor pub. and cmty. affairs, N.Y.C., 1990. Dir. N.Y.C. Outward Bound Ctrl. Pk. Conservancy; trustee Marymount Coll.; dir. Boys Harbor Inc., 1987—. Office: Fashion Inst Tech Seventh Ave at 27 St New York NY 10001-5992*

BROWN, JUDITH OLANS, lawyer, educator; b. Boston, May 29, 1941; d. Sidney and Evelyn R. (Lefkovitz) Olans; m. James K. Brown, Oct. 5, 1969. AB magna cum laude with distinction, Mt. Holyoke Coll., 1962; LL.B. cum laude, Boston Coll., 1965. Bar: Mass. 1965. Law clk. Supreme Jud. Ct., 1965-66; assoc. Foley, Hoag and Eliot, Boston, 1966-69; chief counsel Mass. Dept. Community Affairs, Boston, 1969-70; atty. adv. Office of Regional Counsel, HUD, Boston, 1970, asst. regional counsel, 1971, assoc. regional counsel, 1971-72; instr. Boston U. Law Sch., 1971, Northeastern U. Sch. Law, Boston, 1972, assoc. prof., 1972-75, prof., 1975-98, prof. emerita, 1998—. Vis. prof. Law Sch., Boston Coll., 1992. Contbr. articles to legal jours.; article and book rev. editor: Boston Coll. Indsl. and Comml. Law Rev., 1964-65. Mem. steering com. Lawyers Com. for Civil Rights under Law (emeritus); trustee Kimball Union Acad.1993-2003. Loeb fellow, 1972-73 Mem.: Order of Coif, Phi Beta Kappa. Home: PO Box 82 Plainfield NH 03781-0082 E-mail: jbrown@fcgnetworks.net.

BROWN, JULIE KATHARINE, social historian, photographic historian; d. Robert F. and Margaret (Hahn) McGraw; m. John Paul Brown, 1968; children: Margaret Ellen, Paul Francis. BA, Boston Coll., 1962; MA, U. Rochester, 1966; PhD, U. Queensland, Brisbane, Australia, 1985. Cert. tchr. NY. Post doctoral fellow dept art and art history U. Rochester, NY, 1989—90; resident scholar/visitor program/sr. rsch. fellow Smithsonian Instn., Washington, 1991—2003; fellow NEH, 1994—95; rsch. fellow Mo. Hist. Soc., St Louis, 2002; fellow Smithsonian Instn. Ctr. for Edn. and Mus. Studies, Washington, 2002—. Author: Making Culture Visible: The Public Display of Photography at Fairs, Expositions and Exhibitions in the United States, 1847-1900. Amsterdam: Gordon & Breach, 2001, Contesting Images: Photography and the World's Columbian Exposition, 1984, J. K. Brown and Margaret Maynard. Fine Art Exhibitions in Brisbane 1884-1916, 1980, Recovering Representations: Health Exhibits and Sites of Health at Internat. Expositions in the US, 1876-1904. Pisano scholar, NIH Mus., Bethesda, Md., 2002. Home Fax: 210-567-4587. Personal E-mail: jkbrown@aol.com.

BROWN, JUNE DYSON, elementary education educator, administrator; b. Petersburg, Va., July 28, 1949; d. James Elmer Sr. and Clara (Foster) Dyson; m. Robert Wendell Brown, Apr. 10, 1971; children: Jason, Joshua, James-Robert. BA in English, Emory & Henry Coll., 1971; MEd in Early Childhood Edn., U. Ga., 1993; EdS, U. Ga, 1998. Cert. elem. tchr., Ga. Tchr. DeKalb County Schs., Decatur, Ga., 1971-72, 76-78, Newton County Schs., Covington, Ga., 1972-74, 80-84, 85-88, Henry County Schs., McDonough, Ga., 1984-85; tchr., grade mgr. Gwinnett County Schs., Berkeley Lake, Ga., 1988-90; tchr., learner support strategist Cobb County Schs., Marietta, Ga., 1990-96, asst. adminstr., 1996—2000; Prin. Lamar County Elem. Sch., 2000—; prof. Piedmont Coll., 2000—. Active North Ga. Conf. Min.'s Wives, Atlanta, 1990-93; pres. Atlanta/Marietta Min.'s Wives, 1991-93 Mem. ASCD, DAR, Internat. Reading Assn., Profl. Assn. Ga. Educators, Kappa Delta Pi, Phi Kappa Phi. Methodist. Avocations: sewing, reading, beachcombing. Home: 811 Avalon Rd Thomaston GA 30286-4011

BROWN, JUNE EVELYN, librarian, documentalist; b. Ipswich, Suffolk, Eng., June 29, 1925; came to U.S., 1946; d. Frederick George and Evelyn Claudia (Barker) Laws; m. Ronald Martin Brown, Apr. 14, 1945 (dec. Aug. 1980); children: Erica Karen, Diane Rosemary. Nat. diploma design, Leicester (Eng.) Coll. Arts and Tech., 1944; BA, Alfred U., 1969; MLS, SUNY, Geneseo, 1970. Libr. asst. Herrick Libr. Alfred (N.Y.) U., 1960-69, acquisitions libr., 1969-77, univ. libr., 1977-87; Peace Corps vol., documentalist Ministry Econ. Devel., Tourism and Energy, St. John's, Antigua and Barbuda, 1987-89. Libr. trustee, So. Tier Libr. System, N.Y., 1989-96. Contbr. articles on libr. acquisitions, binding procedures and children's lit. to profl. jours. U.S. Dept. Edn. fellow, 1969. Mem. ALA, Nat. Libr. Assn., Libr. Assn. Antigua and Barbuda, N.Y. Libr. Assn., Antigua Artists Soc. (sec. 1987-89). Republican. Episcopalian. Avocations: painting, gardening, travel. Home: 30 Sayles St Alfred NY 14802-1324

BROWN, JUNE GIBBS, retired government official; b. Cleve., Oct. 5, 1933; d. Thomas D. and Lorna M. Gibbs; children: Ellen Rosenthal, Linda Windsor, Victor Janezic, Carol Janezic. BBA summa cum laude, Cleve. State U., 1971, MBA, 1972; postgrad., Cleve. Marshall Law Sch., 1973-74; JD, U. Denver, 1978; postgrad. Advanced Mgmt. Program, Harvard U., 1983. Cert. govt. fin. mgr., 1995; CPA, Ohio. Real estate broker, officer mgr. N.E. Realty, Cleve., 1963-68; staff acct. Frank T. Cicirelli, C.P.A., Cleve., 1970-71; asst. to comptr. S.M. Hexter Co., Cleve., 1971; grad. tchg. fellow Cleve. State U., 1971-72; dir. internal audit Navy Fin. Ctr., Cleve., 1972-75; dir. fin. sys. design Bur. of Land Mgmt., Denver, 1975-76; project mgr. Bur. of Reclamation, 1976-79; insp. gen. Dept. Interior, Washington, 1979-81, NASA, Washington, 1981-85; v.p. fin. and adminstrn. Sys. Devel. Corp., a Burroughs Co., 1985-86; assoc. adminstr. for mgmt. NASA, 1986-87; insp. gen. U.S. Dept. Def., Arlington, Va., 1987-90; dep. insp. gen. USN-CINCPACFLT, 1990; insp. gen. USN Pacific Fleet, Pearl Harbor, Hawaii, 1991-93, HHS, Washington, 1993-2001; inspector gen. HHS, SSA, Washington, 1995-96. Bd. dirs. Fed. Law Enforcement Tng. Ctr., 1984-85, Interagy. Auditor Tng. program Dept. Agr. Grad. Sch., 1983-85; chmn. interagy. com. on Info. Resource Mgmt., 1984-85; mem. bd. advisors Nat. Contract Mgmt. Assn., 1987-89, NIH Sci. Found., 2002—; mem. Pres.'s Coun. on Integrity and Efficiency, 1993-2001, vice chair, 1994-97, rep. Nat. Intergovtl. Audit Forum, 1994-98, (PCIE), 1998-2001, (HHS); mem. adv. coun. Govt. Auditing Stds., 1996-99; bd. dirs. Inspectors Gen. Auditor Tng. Inst. Mem. bd. advisors Howard U. Sch. Bus., 1987-89. Recipient award Am. Soc. Women Accts., 1969, 70, 71, Raulston award Cleve. State U., 1971, Pres.'s award Cleve. State U., 1971, Outstanding Achievement award U.S. Navy, 1973, Career Svc. award Chgo. region Fed. Exec. Bd., 1974, Outstanding Contbn. to Fin. Mgmt. award Denver region Fed. Exec. Bd., 1977, Donald L. Scantlebury award Joint Fin. Mgmt. Improvement Program, 1980, Outstanding Svc. award Nat. Assn. Minority CPA Firms, 1980, NASA Exceptional Svc. medal, 1985, Outstanding Achievement in Aerospace award, 1987, Woman of Yr. award, YWCA 1988, Bur. Land Mgmt., Dept. Interior, 1975, Disting. Pub. Svc. award Dept. Def., 1989, Meritorious Civilian Svc. award U.S. Navy, 1993, Nat. Capital Area chpt./Govt. Exec. Mag. award for leadership, 1994, George Washington U. Pi Alpha Alpha Pub. Svc. award, 1996; named Disting. Alumni Cleve. State U., 1990. Fellow Nat. Acad. Pub. Adminstrn. (standing panel exec. orgn. and mgmt., pub. svc. panel); mem. AICPAs, Assn. Govt. Accts. (nat. pres. 1985-86, nat. exec. com. 1977-87, vice chmn. nat. ethics com. 1978-80, 90, chmn. fin. mgmt. standards bd. 1981-82, service award 1973, 76, 93, outstanding achievement award 1979, Robert W. King Meml. award 1988, dir. Hawaii chpt. 1991-93, Nat. Pres.'s award 1999, Disting. Fed. Leadership award 1998), Hawaii Soc. CPAs (bd. dirs. 1991-93), Am. Accts. Assn., Nat. Contract Mgmt. Assn. (bd. advisors 1988-90), NASA Alumni Assn., Women in Aerospace, ASPA (at-large mem. nat. coun. 1994-98, Profl. Responsibility Exemplary Practice award 1990, pres.-nat. capital area chpt. 1989), Exec. Women in Govt., Beta Alpha Psi. E-mail: igjgb@yahoo.com.

BROWN, KAREN RIMA, orchestra manager, Spanish language educator; b. N.Y.C., Apr. 26, 1943; d. Alexander and Leona (Rosenfeld) Jaffe; m. Russell Vernon Brown, Aug. 13, 1966; children: Stephanie Leona and Gregory Russell. BA, Colby Coll., 1965; MA, U. Wis., 1966. Teaching asst. U. Wis., Madison, 1965-66, instr. Spanish Janesville, 1966-68, Baraboo, 1968-70, Eau Claire, 1970-71, Ohio U., Zanesville, 1978-98, assoc. prof., 1998—; mgr. Southeastern Ohio Symphony, New Concord, 1977-99. Lectr. Spanish Muskingum Coll., New Concord, 1984, 97-99; mem., music panelist Ohio Arts Coun., Columbus, 1979-83, 90-93; pres. S.E. Ohio Regional Arts Coun., Zanesville, 1978-80. Bd. dirs. Muskingum County Visitors and Conv. Bur., Zanesville, 1987-90, bd. sec., 1989-90; bd. dirs. Assn. of Two Toledos, 1984-87, Ohio Citizens Com. for Arts, Canton, 1979-84; mgr. emeritus Southestern Ohio Symphony Orch., 1999—. Mem. Am. Assn. Tchrs. Spanish and Portuguese, Ohio Valley Fgn. Lang. Assn., Bus. and Profl. Women, Phi Beta Kappa, Phi Sigma Iota, Sigma Delta Pi (hon.). Democrat. Avocations: travel, consultant to arts organizations, mentor for gifted high school students. Office: Ohio Univ-Zanesville 1425 Newark Rd Zanesville OH 43701-2695

BROWN, KARL BECK, civil engineer; b. Midland, Tex., July 29, 1968; s. Winfree L. and Emma L. (Seamans) B.; married; 1 child. BS in Ocean Engring., Tex. A&M U., 1991, M in Ocean Engring., 1997. Engr.-in-tng., Tex. Engring. technician Lummus Crest Inc., Houston, 1988-89, 92; civil engr. U.S. Army C.E., Galveston, Tex., 1992—. Pres. Krewe of Karl Mardi Gras Crew, Galveston, 1993—. Mem. Soc. Naval Architects and Marine Engrs., Tex. Soc. Profl. Engrs., Galveston County Tex. A&M Alumni Assn. Republican. Roman Catholic. Avocations: sand volleyball, world war i history. Office: US Army CE 2000 Ft Point Rd Galveston TX 77550-1229

BROWN, KATE, state legislator; b. Torrejon de Ardoth, Spain, 1960; BA, U. Colo.; JD, Lewis and Clark Coll. Mem. Oreg. Ho. of Reps., 1991-96, Oreg. Senate, 1997—; atty. Democrat. Office: State Capitol Bldg 900 Court St NE S-323 Salem OR 97301-4075 E-mail: sen.katebrown@state.or.us.

BROWN, KEITH, musician, educator; b. Colorado Springs, Colo., Oct. 21, 1933; s. Kenneth Vernon and Audrey Lucille (Nelson) B.; m. Leslee Joanne Scullin, June 13, 1954 (div. Jan. 1991); children: Robert Vernon, Lise Joanne, Kristin Patricia; m. Joann Alexander, May 14, 1994. B.Mus., U. So. Calif., 1957; M.Mus., Manhattan Sch. Music, 1964. Trombonist Indpls. Symphony Orch., 1957-58; mem. faculty, solo trombonist Aspen Festival, 1957-69; trombonist N.Y. Brass Quintet, 1958-59; prin. trombonist Casals Festival, San Juan, P.R., 1958-80; assoc. prin. trombonist Phila. Orch., 1959-62; prin. trombonist Met. Opera Orch., 1962-65; performed with Chamber Music Soc. of Lincoln Ctr., 1969-88; participant Marlboro Festival, 1970-73; dir. instrumental activities, prof. music, condr. univ. orch. Temple U., Phila., 1965-71; prof. emeritus, condr. Ind. U., Bloomington, 1971-97; condr., music dir. Bloomington Symphony Orch., 1975-80; chmn. brass dept., condr. Music Acad. of West, 1978-82, 85-87; co-founder Ensemble Mediation, 1998—. Artistic dir., condr. Camerata Orch., Bloomington, 1989-96; artistic/mus. dir. InterAm. Youth Orch. of the Festival Casals, San Juan, P.R., 1989-91. Regular guest condr. Orquesta Sinfonica Venezuela, coach, adv., guest condr, Orquesta Nacional Juvenil and Orquesta Sinfonica Simon Bolivar, Caracas, 1979—; coach, adviser Joven Orquesta Nacional de Espana, 1984-94; bd. advisers N.Y. Cornet and Sacbut Ensemble, 1984—; tchr. master classes, lectr., recitalist (1st western trombonist), conservatories in, Beijing and Shanghai, China, 1982, Beijing, 1988; guest condr. Sapporo (Japan) Symphony Orch., 1990, Orquesta del Principado de Asturias, Spain, 1991; author 10 vols. orchestral studies for trombone and tuba, numerous edits. of solos, brass ensembles, study materials, 1960—. Served with U.S. Army, 1953-56. Recipient spl. award Asociacion Musical, Caracas, Venezuela, 1979, Alumni award U. So. Calif. Sch. Music, 1957; Nat. Arts assoc. Sigma Alpha Iota, 1995. Mem. Internat. Trombone Assn., Phi Mu Alpha Sinfonia, Pi Kappa Lambda, Kappa Kappa Psi (hon.) Clubs: Rotary. Methodist. Avocations: tennis, sailing. Home: 2925 Olcott Blvd Bloomington IN 47401-2403 E-mail: brownk@indiana.edu.

BROWN, KEITH JOHN, computer applications analyst; b. Wedowee, Ala., Dec. 8, 1959; s. John Thomas and Jane Edmondson B.; m. Nancy Carol Hoerning, Apr. 27, 1991. BA, U. Ala., 1981; MA, U. N.C., 1983. Tchg. asst. U.N.C., Chapel Hill, 1983-84, 86-90, instr., 1984-85, data file cons., 1984-90, computer cons., 1990-94, applications analyst, 1994—. Contbg. author: (book) Challenges to Representative Democracy, 1999; contbr. articles to profl. jours. Vice-chmn. Dem. Party, Chatham County, N.C., 1995-99; mem. adv. bd. Cmty. Playhouse, Sanford, N.C., 1997-2000; mem. Census 2000 Complete Count Com., Chatham County, 1999-2000. Pogue fellow U. N.C., 1981-83. Mem. Phi Beta Kappa. Democrat. Mem. Ch. of Christ. Avocation: acting. Office: U NC Gen Adminstrn 910 Raleigh Rd Chapel Hill NC 27514-3916 E-mail: kjb@ga.unc.edu.

BROWN, KEITH LAPHAM, retired ambassador; b. Sterling, Ill., June 18, 1925; s. Lloyd Heman and Marguerite (Briggs) B.; m. Carol Louise Liebmann, Oct. 1, 1949; children: Susan, Briggs (dec.), Linda, Benjamin. Student, U. Ill., 1943-44, Northwestern U., 1946-47; LLB, U. Tex., 1949. Bar: Tex., Okla., Colo. Assoc. Lang, Byrd, Cross & Ladon, San Antonio, 1949-55; v.p., gen. counsel Caulkins Oil Co., Oklahoma City, 1955-70, Denver, 1955-70; founder, developer Vail Assocs., Colo., 1962; pres. Brown Investment Corp., Denver, 1970-87; developer Colo. State Bank Bldg., Denver, 1971; amb. to Lesotho Dept. State, 1982-84, amb. to Denmark, 1988-92; ret., 1992; chmn. Brown Investment Corp., Denver, 1993—. Mem. adv. bd. Ctr. for Strategic and Internat. Studies. Chmn. Rep. Nat. Fin. Com., 1985-88; hon. trustee, past pres. bd. Colo. Acad. Ensign USN, 1943-46. Mem. Coun. Am. Ambs. (pres.), San Antonio Country Club, Bohemian Club. Republican. Presbyterian. Address: PO Box 1172 Edwards CO 81632-1172 also: 11 Auburn Pl San Antonio TX 78209-4739 Office: 1490 Colo State Bank Bldg 1600 Broadway Denver CO 80202-4927

BROWN, KENNETH ANDREW, cardiologist, educator; b. N.Y.C., Jan. 16, 1951; s. Gerry and Rita (Alpert) B.; m. Suzanne R. Braun, Aug. 8, 1976 (div.); children: Daniel Everest, David Abraham. AB, Rutgers U., 1973; MD, Cornell U., 1977. Diplomate Am. Bd. Internal Medicine, Am. Bd. Cardiovascular Diseases; cert. nuclear cardiology Cert. Bd. Nuclear Cardiology. Intern Peter Bent Brigham Hosp.-Harvard U., Boston, 1977-78, resident, 1978-80; fellow in nuc. cardiology Mass. Gen. Hosp.-Harvard U., Boston, 1980-82; fellow in cardiology Beth Israel Hosp.-Harvard U., Boston, 1982-84; dir. nuclear cardiology, prof. medicine U. Vt. Coll. Medicine, Burlington, 1984—. Assoc. editor Jour. Nuclear Cardiology, 1993—; mem. editl. bd. Jour. Am. Coll. Cardiology 1994-98, Jour. Noninvasive Cardiology, 1996—; contbr. chpt. to book and articles to profl. jours. Mem. zoning bd. Town of Jericho, Vt., 1988-92. Recipient USPHS Nat. Rsch. award Mass. Gen. Hosp.-USPHS, Boston, 1980-82. Fellow Am. Coll. Cardiology, Am. Heart Assn., Soc. Nuclear Medicine; mem. Am. Soc. Nuclear Cardiology (founding mem., treas. 1992-96, v.p. 1996-97, pres. elect 1997, pres. 1998, bd. dirs. 1992—), Alpha Omega Alpha, Phi Beta Kappa. Avocations: mountain climbing, ice climbing, rock climbing, skiing. Office: Med Ctr Hosp Vt Cardiology Unit Colchester Ave Burlington VT 05401 E-mail: kenneth.brown@vtmednet.org.

BROWN, KENNETH LLOYD, lawyer; b. N.Y.C., Sept. 20, 1927; s. Edythe Schneider; m. Freya Dorothy Finkelstein, July 10, 1954; children: Ivy Hope Brown Hill, Patrice Shari Botting. BS, NYU, 1951; LLB, St. John's U., Bklyn., 1954. Bar: N.Y. 1955. Pvt. practice, Forest Hills, N.Y., 1955-61; asst. corp. counsel City of N.Y., 1962-78; ptnr. Rivkin, Radler & Kremer and predecessor firms, Uniondale, N.Y., 1977-98; pvt. practice Jamaica, N.Y., 1998—. Dem. dist. leader Queens County Dem. Orgn., Forest Hills, until 1982; mem. Forest Hills Jewish Ctr. With U.S. Army, 1945-47. Mem. Queens County Bar Assn. (various coms.), Am. Legion, Jewish War Vet. Post, Continental Regular Dem. Club (founder), Robert F. Kennedy, Jr. Dem. Club, B'nai B'rith, Masons, Knights of Pythias. Avocation: politics. Home: PO Box 457 Flushing NY 11375-0457 Office: 15049 Hillside Ave Jamaica NY 11432-3319 Fax: 718-297-5588.

BROWN, KENNETH RAY, banker; b. Cherokee, Okla., July 6, 1936; s. Tom Melton and Mary Elizabeth (Foster) B.; m. Elizabeth Kay Callahan, Oct. 17, 1964; children— Kathryn Sue, Elizabeth Ann, Angela Kay. BBA, U. Okla., 1957. Vice pres., then sr. v.p., sr. investment officer Bank One Okla., N.A., Oklahoma City, 1965-79, exec. v.p., 1979—. Mem. Inst. Chartered Fin. Analysts, Okla. Soc. Fin. Analysts, Econ. Club Okla. Presbyterian. Office: Bank One Okla NA 100 Broadway Cir Oklahoma City OK 73170-7220 E-mail: kbrown64@aol.com.

BROWN, KENT NEWVILLE, ambassador; b. Oakland, Calif., May 7, 1944; s. Victor B. and Mary E. (Shaver) B.; m. Norma Giorno, Dec. 29, 1995; children from previous marriage: Steven D., Karen E. BA, U. Calif., Davis, 1964, MA, 1966. 3rd sec. U.S. Embassy, Panama, 1967-69, 2nd sec. Prague, Czechoslovakia, 1970-73; watch officer to exec. secretariat U.S. Dept. of State, Washington, 1973-74; fellow Hoover Instn., Stanford, Calif., 1974-75; officer Soviet desk U.S. Dept. of State, Washington, 1976-80; 1st sec. U.S. Embassy, Moscow, 1980-83; sr. advisor U.S. Arms Control Del., Vienna, Austria, 1984-88; office dir. Strategic Nuc. Policy U.S. Dept. of State, Washington, 1989-90; polit. advisor Supreme Allied Comdr. Europe, Belgium, 1990-92; amb. U.S. Embassy, Tbilisi, Georgia, 1992-95; dir. pers. U.S. Dept. of State, Washington, 1995-96; v.p. govt. rels. Ea. Europe J.T. Internat., Geneva, 1996—. Bd. dirs. NATO workshop, Menlo Park, Calif. Bd. dirs. U.S.-Russia Bus. Coun. Mem. Internat. Inst. for Strategic Studies. Office: 12 Ch de Rieu Geneva 17 Switzerland E-mail: nbamron@online.ru.

BROWN, KEVIN JAMES, researcher, consultant; b. Sheboygan, Wis., July 12, 1952; s. Keith Hammond and Jean Lois (Van Ouwerkerk) B.; m. Ana Ligia Arevalo, Mar. 14, 1986 (div. Sept. 6, 1997). BA in English, Denison U., 1974; MBA in Mgmt., Pepperdine U., 1980; PhD, U. Pitts., 2003. Mgr. Flying Tiger Line, San Francisco, 1978-81; founder, pres. Angel Enterprises, Foster City, Calif., 1981-83; mgr. aerospace mktg. CF Airfreight, Inglewood, Calif., 1983-85; regional mgr. TNT Express divsn. Kwikasair, Inglewood, Calif., 1985; gen. mgr. Three Way Corp., Hawthorne, Calif., 1985-86; v.p. ops. Boardroom Bus. Products, Costa Mesa, Calif., 1986-88; dist. mgr. Nat. Inst. Bus. Mgmt., L.A., 1988; ind. contractor, realtor, broker Culver City, Calif., 1988-91; mng. broker. br. mgr. Vol. Realty Co., Knoxville, Tenn., 1991-93; franchise devel. sr. market analyst Coldwell Banker Residential Affiliates, Mission Viejo, Calif., 1993-96; grad. rsch. asst. U. Pitts., 1997-99; instr. polit. sci. Indiana U. of Pa., 1999-2001; exec. asst. to chancellor U. Wis.-River Falls, 2001—. Featured guest Sta. WIVK, 1992; contbr. articles to profl. jours. Named Hon. Ky. Col., 1993. Mem. ACLU, Am. Soc. Pub. Adminstrn., Assn. for Pub. Policy Analysts and Mgmt., Am. Polic. Sci. Assn., Acad. Polit. Sci., Soc. Study Social Problems, Acad. Mktg. Sci., Policy Studies Orgn., Pub. Citizen, World Future Soc., Wolf Edn. and Rsch. Ctr., Common Cause, People for Am. Way., Denison U. Alumni Assn., Pepperdine U. Alumni Assn., Silver Saddle Homeowners Assn., So. Poverty Law Ctr. Democrat. Avocations: reading, music, pets, computers, genealogy. Home: 181 Butternut Ct River Falls WI 54022

BROWN, LAMAR BEVAN, lawyer; b. Tooele, Utah, Apr. 26, 1951; s. John B. and Reva M. B.; children: Sean La Mar, Kyle Ross, Ian Lawrence. BA, Utah State U., 1974; JD, We. State U., 1980. Bar: Calif. 1980, U.S. Dist. Ct. (so. dist.) Calif. 1980, U.S. Ct. Appeals (9th cir.) 1986, U.S. Dist. Ct. (no. and ctrl. dist.) 1992. Assoc. Law Offices George Andrews, San Diego, 1980-82, Higgs, Fletcher & Mack, San Diego, 1982-90, Law Offices Craig McClellan, San Diego, 1990-95; mem. McClellan & Brown, San Diego, 1995—. Mem. Consumer Attys. Calif., Consumer Attys. San Diego, Western Trial Lawyers Assn., San Diego County Bar Assn. Democrat. Office: McClellan & Brown 1144 State St San Diego CA 92101-3529 E-mail: lamarbrown@aol.com.

BROWN, L(ARRY) EDDIE, tax practitioner, business accountant, real estate broker, financial planner; b. Aug. 31, 1941; s. Earl and Lois Ovoca (Norrod) B.; m. Lillian Virginia Edwards, Feb. 9, 1965; children: Clifford Bruce, Michael Dwayne, Jennifer Noelle. BBA, Ga. State U., 1974, MBA, 1976. Cert. tax profl.; accredited tax advisor; accredited bus. acct.; enrolled agt. Mgmt. trainee Citizens Bank, Cookeville, Tenn., 1963-65; office mgr. Redisco, Tampa, Fla., 1965-67; methods analyst Delta Air Lines, Atlanta, 1967-83; owner Brown Enterprises, College Park, Ga., 1971—, Fayetteville, Ga., 1995—. Pres. So. Heritage Properties, Inc., 1984—; instr. Ga. State U., 1976-80. Bd. dirs. Ga. Spl. Olympics, Atlanta, 1983-90; Ga. del. White House Conf. on Small Bus., 1995, Congl. Small Bus. Summit, 1998, 2000. With USAF, 1959-63. Mem. Nat. Soc. Tax Profls. (Ga. state com. 1994-99), Nat. Assn. Tax Practitioners (Ga. bd. dirs. 1994-98), Nat. Soc. Pub. Accts., Ga. Assn. Pub. Accts. (pres. So. Cres. chpt. 1993-95, bd. govs. 1994-2001, 1st v.p. 1996-97, pres. 1997-99), Fin. Planners Assn., Nat. Assn. Securities Dealers, Ga. Assn. Realtors, Civitan Club (pres. Airport-Southside, Atlanta 1982-83, treas. Airport Area, Atlanta 1979-81, Civilian of Yr. chpt. 1982, bd. dirs. Ga. dist. north 1984-86, trustee Ga. dist. North Found. 1985-88), Masons. Mem. Lds Ch. Office: Brown Enterprises 392 Glynn St N Fayetteville GA 30214-1191

BROWN, LAUREN EVANS, zoologist, researcher, zoologist, educator; b. Waukesha, Wis., Sept. 4, 1939; s. Winston Dever and Julianne Evelyn Brown; m. Jill Rae Hollingshead, Feb. 21, 1968; children: Lara Nell, Kara Anne Nash, Evan Saxon. BS, Carroll Coll., 1961; MS, So. Ill. U., Carbondale, 1963; PhD, U. Tex., Austin, 1967; postgrad., U. Melbourne, Australia, 1968. Rsch. asst. biochem. Dairyland Food Lab., Waukesha, 1960; tchg. asst. Mark Twain Inst., St. Louis, 1961; tchg. and rsch. asst. So. Ill. U., Carbondale, 1961—63; rsch. asst. Pine Hills Field Sta., Pine Hills Swamp, Ill., 1963; tchg. and rsch. asst. U. Tex., Austin, 1963—67; asst. prof. to assoc. prof. Ill. State U., Normal, 1967—77, prof., 1977—; chair sect. ecology, evolution, ethology and systematic biology Ill State. U., 1978—79, chair interdisciplinary studies, 1996—. Endangered species and environ. cons., 1966—; chair undergrad. and grad. curriculum coms. Ill. State U., 1974—83, athletic coun., rsch. grant evaluation com., 1992—95, curriculum infusion program mem., 1995—2002, libr. com., 1997—2002, chair libr. com., 1998—2002, hon. libr., 2002—; Houston Toad Recovery team US Fish and Wildlife Svc., 1978—84, 1998—; affiliate profl. scientist Ill. Natural History Survey, 1997—; presenter in field; interdisciplinary studies, 1996. Editor: Herpetologica, 1978—81, Coun. of Biology Editors, 1978—80, Alytes, 2000—; mem. editl. bd.: Ill. Natural History Survey, 1999—; contbr. chapters to books, articles to profl. jours. Grantee in field, 1962—, Rsch. Grant Evaluation Com., 1992—95. Mem.: Council of Biology Editors, numerous dissertation and thesis com., Internat. Soc. for the Study and Conservation of Amphibians (mem. editl. bd. 2000—), Am. Soc. Ichthyologists and Herpetologists, Declining Amphibian Populations Task Force, Soc. Study Amphibians & Reptiles (conservation com.), Herpetologists' League (bd. trustees 1979—80), Am. Rabbit Breeders Assn. (chair libr. com. 2001—02), US Fish and Wildlife Svc., Houston Toad Recovery Team. Achievements include rediscovery of the near extinct Houston Toad in Lost Pines. Avocations: swimming, hiking, breeding and rearing animals. Home: 15958 E 2550 North Rd Hudson IL 61748-9391 Office: Ill State Univ Dept Biological Sci Campus Box 4120 Normal IL 61790-4120

BROWN, LAURENCE DAVID, retired bishop; b. Fargo, N.D., Feb. 16, 1926; s. John Nicolai and Ada Amelia (Johnson) B.; m. Virginia Ann Allen, Sept. 6, 1950; children: Patricia Ann, Julia Louise, Claudia Ruth. BS, U. Minn., 1946; BA, Concordia Coll., 1948; M of Theology, Luther Theol. Sem., 1951. Ordained to ministry Evang. Luth. Ch., 1951. Pastor Our Savior's Luth. Ch., New Ulm, Minn., 1951-55; nat. assoc. youth dir. Evang. Luth. Ch., Mpls., 1955-60; nat. youth dir. Am. Luth. Ch., Mpls., 1960-68; instn. dir. Tchr. Tng., U. Minn., Mpls., 1968-69; exec. dir. Freedom from Hunger Found., Washington, 1969-73; sr. pastor St. Paul Luth. Ch., Waverly, Iowa, 1973-79; bishop Iowa Dist. Am. Luth. Ch., Des Moines, 1979-89, N.E. Iowa Synod, Evang. Luth. Ch. in Am., Waverly, 1989-92; prof. religion Wartburg Coll., Waverly, Iowa, 1992-93; interim sr. pastor Ctrl. Luth. Ch., Mpls., 1994-95, Calvary Luth. Ch., Mpls., 1996-97; ret. Bd. regents Luther Coll., Decorah, Iowa, 1989-92, Wartburg Coll., 1988-92, Wartburg Theol. Sem., Dubuque, Iowa, 1988-91, Self-Help, Inc., 1989-94. Author: Take Care: A Guide for Responsible Living, 1983; contbr. articles to profl. jours. Lt. USN, 1943-46. Lutheran. Avocation: reading. Home: 7201 York Ave S Apt 514 Edina MN 55435-4444

BROWN, LAWRENCE HAAS, banker; b. Evanston, Ill., July 29, 1934; s. Robert C. and Alice (Haas) B.; m. Ann Ferguson, June 23, 1956; children— Michael, Kenneth, Russell Student, Cornell U., Ithaca, N.Y., 1952-54; BBA, U. Mich., 1956. Sr. v.p. No. Trust Co., Chgo., 1958-89, ret., 1989. Chmn. Pub. Securities Assn., N.Y.C., 1980; vice chmn. Mcpl. Securities Rulemaking Bd., Washington, 1982; bd. dirs. Nuveen Funds. Pres. Highwood (Ill.) Pub. Libr., 1993—97; bd. dirs. United Way of Highland Park/Highwood. Lt. USN, 1956—58. Mem.: Exmoor Country (Highland Park, Ill.) (pres. 1984-85); Municipal Bond (pres. 1977). Republican. Presbyterian. Avocations: tennis, curling, golf. Home: 201 Michigan Ave Highwood IL 60040-1808 E-mail: ablbcurler@aol.com.

BROWN, LAWRENCE HARVEY (LARRY BROWN), professional basketball coach; b. Brooklyn, NY, Sept. 14, 1940; Student, U. North Carolina, Chapel Hill, NC, 1959-63. Amateur basketball player Akron Goodyears, Akron, OH, 1963-65; asst. coach U. North Carolina, Chapel Hill, NC, 1965-67; player New Orleans (ABA), New Orleans, 1967-68, Oakland (ABA), Oakland, CA, 1968-69, Washington (ABA), 1969-70, Virgina Squires (ABA) - Denver Nuggets (ABA), 1970-71, Denver Nuggets (ABA), Denver, 1971-73; head coach Carolina Cougars (ABA), 1972-74, Denver Nuggets (ABA), 1974-76, Denver Nuggets (NBA), Denver, 1976-79, UCLA, Los Angeles, CA, 1979-81, New Jersey Nets (NBA), Newark, 1981-83, U. Kansas, Lawrence, KS, 1983-88, San Antonio Spurs (NBA), San Antonio, 1988-92, Los Angeles Clippers (NBA), Los Angeles, CA, 1992-93, Indiana Pacers (NBA), Indpls., 1993-97, Phila. 76ers (NBA), 1997—2003, Detroit Pistons (NBA), 2003—. Mem. Am. Basketball Assn. All-Star Team, 1968—70, U.S. Olympic Team, 1964, Am. Basketball Assn. Championship Team, 1969; asst. coach U.S. Olympic Team, 2000; coach NBA Ea. Conf. All-STar Team, 2001; coached team to NBA Finals, 2001. Named Most Valuable Player, ABA All-Star Game, 1968, ABA Coach of Yr., 1973, 1975, 1976, IBM Coach of Yr., NBA, 2001. Office: Detroit Pistons Palace of Auburn Hills 2 Championship Dr Auburn Hills MI 48326*

BROWN, LEE P. mayor; m. Yvonne Brown (dec.); 4 children; m. Frances Young. BA in Criminology, Fresno State U., 1960; MA in Sociology, San Jose State U., 1964; MA in Criminology, U. Calif., Berkeley, 1968, PhD in Criminology, 1970. Patrolman San Jose (Calif.) Police Dept., 1960—68; sheriff Multnomah County, Portland, Oreg., 1975—78; commr. pub. safety City of Atlanta, 1978—82; chief Houston Police Dept., 1982—90; commr. N.Y.C. Police Dept., 1990—92; dir. Nat. Drug Control Policy, Washington, 1993—96; Radaslav A. Tsanoff Prof. pub. affairs dept. sociology Rice U., Houston, scholar James A. Baker III Inst. for Pub. Policy; mayor City of Houston, 1998—. Named Father of Yr., Nat. Father's Day Com., 1991, Politician of Yr., Libr. Jour., 1999. Office: City of Houston Office of Mayor PO Box 1562 Houston TX 77251*

BROWN, LEE PATRICK, mayor, city official, law enforcement educator; b. Wewoka, Okla., Oct. 4, 1937; s. Andrew and Zelma (Edwards) B.; m. Yvonne Carolyn Streets, July 14, 1958 (dec.); children: Patrick, Torri, Robyn, Jenna; m. Frances M. Young, Dec. 29, 1996. BA, Fresno State U., 1960; MA, San Jose State U., 1964; MS, U. Calif., 1968; PhD in Criminology, U. Calif., Berkeley, 1970; D of Pub. Affairs (hon.), Fla. Internat. U., 1982; LLD (hon.), John Jay Coll., 1985; HHD (hon.), Portland State U., 1990; LHD (hon.), Fresno State U., 1994; LLD (hon.), SUNY Brockport, 1995; doctorate (hon.), Howard U., Wiley Coll. Officer San Jose (Calif.) Police Dept., 1960-68; prof. Portland (Oreg.) State U., 1968-72; assoc. dir. Urban Affairs Inst. Howard Inst., Washington, 1972-75; sheriff Sheriff's Dept., Mulnomah County, Oreg., 1975-76; dir. Dept. Justice Services, Mulnomah County, 1976-78; commr. Dept. Pub. Safety, Atlanta, 1978-82; chief of police Houston Police Dept., 1982-90; police commr. N.Y.C., 1990-92; prof. Tex. So. Univ., 1992-93; dir. Nat. Drug Control Policy, Washington, 1993-96; mem. Pres. Cabinet, 1993-96; prof. Rice Univ., Houston, 1996-98; mayor City of Houston, 1998—. Adj. prof. U. Houston, U. Tex. Health Sci. Ctr., Houston, Tex. So. U., Houston; cons. U.S. Dept. Justice, Washington, Police Found., Washington, various state and local govts., Houston; chmn. Nat. Minority Adv. Council on Criminal Justice; mem. Nat. Adv. Commn. on Criminal Justice Standards and Goals, Washington, Nat. Commn. on Higher Edn. for Police, Washington, Commn. on Accreditation for Law Enforcement Agencies, Washington, Presdl. Task Force, 1993—. Co-author: Attitudes of Black Police Officers, 1976, Police and Society, 1981; editor: Neighborhood Team Policing, 1976, Violent Crime, 1981; author of numerous articles and book chpts. Bd. dirs. Boy Scouts Am., United Way, Urban League, Blue Bonnet Bowl, "Just Say No", Peoples Workshop for Visual and Performing Arts, Houston, 1987—, Nat. Black Child Devel. Inst., Washington, 1987—, Nat. Alliance Against Violence, N.Y., 1986—, Sheltering Arms, Houston, 1985—; task forcemem. Nat. Ctr. for Missing and Exploited Children, Washington, 1986—; adv. bd. Nat. Inst. Against Prejudice and Violence, Balt., 1987—; mem. Police Activities League, Houston, 1987—; mem. adv. policy bd. Nat. Incident Based Reporting System, 1988—; mem. adv. com. Fannie Mae, Washington, 1999; bd. dirs. Police Found., 2000; mem. U.S. Conf. of Mayors, Mayors and CEOs. Recipient Peace and Justice award Martin Luther King Jr., 1981, Nat. Law Enforcement award Nat. Black Police Assn., 1982, Disting. Alumnus award Fresno State U., 1983, Police Leadership award, Police Exec. Research Forum, 1987, Liberty Bell award Houston Young Lawyers Assn., 1987, August Vollmer award Am. Soc. Criminology, 1988, Cartier Pasha award Cartier Internat., 1992, Exemplary Leader award Am. Leadership Forum, 1994; named to Gallup Hall of Fame by Gallup, Inc., 1993; named Mgr. of Yr., Nat. Mgmt. Assn., Practitioner of Yr., Nat. Assn. of Blacks Criminal Justice, 1984, Communicator of Yr. Washington News Service, 1986, Father of Yr. Nat. Father's Day com., 1991, Politician of Yr. Libr. Jour., Technologist of Yr., Pub. Tech., Inc., 2002; named one of 100 Most Influential Black Ams., Ebony Mag., 2003; rsch. fellow Harvard U., 1988; Berkeley fellow, 2002. Mem. Internat. Assn. Chiefs of Police (past pres.), Nat. Orgn. of Black Law Enforcement Execs. (v.p. 1985, Robert Lamb Jr. Humanitarian award 1987), Police Exec. Research Forum, Internat. Narcotic Enforcement Officers Assn., Nat. Forum for Black Pub. Adminstrs., N.Y. Police Chiefs Assn., Tex. Police Assn., Tex. Criminal Justice Task Force, Nat. Police Athletic League, Mich. State U. (adv. council nat. neighborhood foot patrol ctr.), Nat. Research Council (com. on research on law enforcement and the adminstrn. of justice, com. on status of Black Ams.), Harvard U. (com. exec. session on community policing), Nat. Council on Crime and Delinquency (bd. dirs.), Nat. Acad. Pub. Adminstrn. (Nat. Pub. Svc. award 1988), Am. Soc. Pub. Adminstrn. (Nat. Pub. Svc. award 1988), Am. Leadership Forum, Forum Club of Houston (bd. dirs. 1987—), Calif. Alumni Club of Tex., Houston Bus. and Profl. Men's Club, Alpha Phi Alpha (Award of Merit 2000), Sigma Pi Phi. Democrat. Avocations: travel, reading. Office: City Hall 901 Bagby St Fl 3 Houston TX 77002-2526 E-mail: mayor@cityofhouston.net.

BROWN, LEON CARL, history educator; b. Mayfield, Ky., Apr. 22, 1928; s. Leon Carl and Gwendolyn (Travis) B.; m. Anne Winchester Stokes, Aug. 29, 1953; children: Elizabeth Boone, Joseph Winchester, Jefferson Travis. BA, Vanderbilt U., 1950; postgrad., U. Va., 1950-51, London Sch. Econs., 1951-52; PhD, Harvard, 1962. Fgn. Svc. officer., Beirut, 1954-55, Khartoum, Sudan, 1956-58; asst. prof. Mid. Ea. studies Harvard U., Cambridge, Mass., 1962-66; assoc. prof. Nr. Ea. history and civilization Princeton (N.J.) U., 1966-70, Garrett prof. fgn. affairs, 1970-93, Garrett prof. emeritus, 1993—, chmn. dept. Nr. Ea. studies, 1969-73, dir. program Nr. Ea. studies, 1969-73, 80-93. Author: (with C.A. Micaud and C.H. Moore) Tunisia: The Politics of Modernization, 1964, The Tunisia of Ahmad Bey, 1974, International Politics and the Middle East, 1984, Religion and State: The Muslim Approach to Politics, 2000; editor: State and Society in Independent North Africa, 1966, From Madina to Metropolis: Heritage and Change in the Near Eastern City, 1973, (with Norman Itzkowitz) Psychological Dimensions of Near Eastern Studies, 1977, Centerstage: American Diplomacy Since World War II, 1990, (with Cyril E. Black) Modernization in the Middle East, 1992, Imperial Legacy: The Ottoman Impact On The Balkans & The Middle East, (with Matthew Gordon) Franco-Arab Encounters, 1996, Diplomacy in the Middle East, 2001; translator with commentary: The Surest Path; The Political Treatise of a 19th Century Muslim Statesman, 1967. Served with USAAF, 1945-46. Mem. Middle East Studies Assn. (pres. 1975-76) Home and Office: 191 Hartley Ave Princeton NJ 08540-5613 E-mail: lcbrown@princeton.edu.

BROWN, LEONARD ASHLEIGH (SMOKEY), JR., lawyer; b. Newberry, S.C., July 24, 1969; s. Leonard Ashleigh and Sarah Gibson B.; m. Amy Durr, May 16, 1992; 1 child, Courtney. BA in History, Presbyn. Coll., 1991; JD, U. S.C. Sch. Law, 1997. Bar: S.C. Assoc. Welch Law Firm, Greenwood, SC, 1997—2001; owner, ptnr. Law Office of Smokey Brown, SC, 2001—; mcpl. judge Town of Chapin, SC, 2001—. Prosecutor City of Greenwood, 1998-2001, Lander U., Greenwood, 1999-2001; radio broadcaster Lander U. baseball, 1999-2000. Pres. Brown Ridge Homeowner's Assn., Greenwood, 1998-2000. Mem. ATLA, S.C. Assn. Criminal Def. Lawyers, S.C. Trial Lawyers Assn., Supreme Ct. Hist. Soc., Lake Murray-Irmo Rotary Club, Greater Irmo C. of C. Methodist. Avocations: baseball, historical traveling, hunting, reading, scuba diving. Office: Law Office Smokey Brown PC 7434 Forest Ct Irmo SC 29063-1545

BROWN, LES (LESTER LOUIS), journalist; b. Indiana Harbor, Ind., Dec. 20, 1928; s. Irving H. and Helen (Feigenbaum) B.; m. Jean Rosalie Slaymaker, June 12, 1959; children: Jessica, Joshua, Rebecca. BA in English, Roosevelt U., Chgo., 1950. Entertainment industry reporter, reviewer theatrical events Chgo. bur. Variety, 1953-55; asso. editor Downbeat mag., 1955; co-founder, operator folk music cabaret The Gate of Horn, Chgo., 1956; Chgo. bur. mgr. Variety, 1957-65; editor radio-TV dept. N.Y.C., 1965-73; asst. mng. editor, 1973; radio-TV corr. N.Y. Times, 1973-80; editor in chief Channels mag., 1980-87; sr. v.p. editorial devel. C.C. Pub., N.Y.C., 1987-91; pub. TV Bus. Internat. mag., 1988-91, editor in chief, 1990-91; columnist, 1992—; pub. World Guide, 1990. Cons. Revson Found., 1978, Ctr. for Comm., NYC, 1991-2003, World Alliance TV for Children, 1993-2001, Golden Rose Montreux TV Festival, 1994-2001, Monte Carlo TV Festival, 1994-2001; lectr. creative writing and entertainment industries Columbia Coll., Chgo., 1959-62, scholar-in-residence, 1985; lectr. comm. Hunter Coll., NYC, 1973-75, New Sch., NYC, 1977-83, Columbia U., 1994-96; lectr. Fordham U., 1995-2002, dir. TV Pantheon Oral History Project, 1996; Poynter fellow in modern journalism Yale U., 1977, lectr., 1978-80; assoc. fellow Morse Coll., 1978-86; Presdl. fellow Aspen Inst., 1978; bd. dirs. Dore Schary Awards, World TV and Radio Coun. UNESCO; sr. fellow Freedom Forum Media Studies Ctr. Columbia U., 1992-93. Author: lyrics Abilene, 1963, Television: The Business Behind The Box, 1971, Electric Media, 1973, New York Times Encyclopedia of Television, 1977, Keeping Your Eye on Television, 1979; Les Brown's Encyclopedia of Television, 1982, Fast Forward: The New Television and American Society, 1983, Les Brown's Encyclopedia of Television, 1992; also articles. Mem. Film-TV adv. bd. N.Y. State Coun. on Arts, 1975; pres. Media Commentary Coun. Inc. With AUS, 1951-53. Recipient Silver Cir. award N.Y. Chpt. Nat. Acad. TV Arts and Scis., 1996. E-mail: tvmaven@cloud9.net.

BROWN, LESTER B. social worker, educator; b. Whitmire, S.C., Jan. 11, 1943; s. William Barney and Minnie Eugenia (Vaughn) Brown. AB in Psychology, U. Chgo., 1969, AM in Social Work, 1971, PhD in Social Treatment, 1980. Sr. child care counselor, therapist Nicholas J. Pritzker Ctr. and Hosp., Chgo., 1964-68, 69; social worker I Ill. Dept. Children and Family Svcs., Chgo., 1967-70, social worker II, 1971; group homes social worker Jewish Children's Bur., Chgo., 1971-73; social worker, field instr. Jackson Park Hosp., Chgo., 1973, clin. dir., 1973-74, cons., 1975-77, SUNY, Albany, 1981, asst. prof. social work, chmn. undergrad. social welfare, 1981-86; prof. social worker Wayne State U., 1986-89; assoc. prof.. social work Calif. State U., Long Beach, 1989-95, prof. social work and Am. Indian studies, 1995—. Lectr. U. Wis., Milw., 1977—78, instr., 1978—80; lectr. U. Chgo., 1977—78; guest lectr. Boston Coll., 1981; cons., presenter in field. Author: (book) Two Spirit People: American Indian Lesbian Women and Gay Men, 1997, Aging Gay Men, 1997, Brief Treatment and a New Look at the Task Central Approach, 2003; contbr. articles to profl. jours., chapters to books; mem. editl. bd. Health Care Mgmt. Rev., 1981—84. Bd. dirs. Capital Dist. Travelers Aid Soc., 1983—86; condr. workshops ethnic sensitive work Pittsfield Sch. Dist., Mass., 1984; participant workshops mental health and child welfare; mem. com. Urban League. Grantee, SUNY, 1981, U.S. HHS, 1981, Sch. Social Welfare, 1982. Mem.: NASW, Coun. Social Work Edn., Acad. Cert. Social Workers. Democrat. Avocation: baking/cooking. Home: 810 Orizaba Ave Long Beach CA 90804-4926 Office: Calif State U Long Beach Am Indian Studies and Social Work 1250 N Bellflower Blvd Long Beach CA 90840-0006 Personal E-mail: res080mm@verizon.net. Business E-Mail: Lbrown2@csulb.edu.

BROWN, LESTER RUSSELL, research institute executive; b. Bridgeton, NJ, Mar. 28, 1934; s. Calvin C. and Delia (Smith) B.; m. Shirley Ann Woolington, June 12, 1960 (div.); children: Brian, Brenda. BS in Agrl. Sci., Rutgers U., 1955; MA in Agrl. Econs., U. Md., 1959; MPA, Harvard U., 1962; LHD (hon.), Dickinson Coll.; LLD (hon.), U. Md.; LHD (hon.), Franklin Coll.; LLD (hon.), Williams Coll., Rutgers U.; LHD (hon.), Glassboro State Coll., Tufts U.; LLD (hon.), Coll. of Wooster; LHD (hon.), Clark U., Ripon Coll., Otterbein Coll.; DSc (hon.), U. Pisa, McGill U.; LLD (hon.), U. Notre Dame; D of Pub. Svc. (hon.), Northland Coll.; LHD (hon.), St. Lawrence U.; DSc (hon.), Claremont Coll.; D of Social Sci. (hon.), Villanova U.; DSc (hon.), Westminster Coll., Utah, Westminster Coll., Pa., U. Conn., Ohio State U. With Dept. of Agr., 1958—69, adminstr. internat. agr. devel. service, 1966-69; adv. to sec. U.S. Dept. Agr., Washington, 1965—69; sr. fellow Overseas Devel. Council, 1969-74; pres., founder Worldwatch Inst., Washington, 1974-2000, Earth Policy Inst., Washington, 2001—. Faculty Salzburg Seminar in Am. Studies, 1971, 1974; guest scholar Aspen Inst., summers 1972-74; sr. adv. Japanese Ministry Agr., Forestry, & Fishery; vice chmn. Adv. Com. of the U.S. China Assoc. Environ. Edn.; bd. dirs. Worldwatch Norden. Author: Man, Land and Food, 1963, Increasing World Food Output, 1965, Seeds of Change, 1970, World Without Borders, 1972, In the Human Interest, 1974, (with Gail Finsterbusch)

Man and his Environment: Food, 1974, (with Erik Eckholm) By Bread Alone, 1974 (Christopher award), The Twenty-Ninth Day, 1978 (Ecologia Firenze award), (with Colin Norman and Christopher Flavin) Running on Empty, 1979, Building a Sustainable Society, 1981, State of the World, 1984-2001, (with others) Vital Signs, 1992-2001, (with Hal Kane) Full House, 1994, Who Will Feed China?, 1995, Tough Choices: Facing the Challenge of Global Food Scarcity, 1996; editor: (with Ed Ayres) World Watch Reader, 1998, (with Flavin and Sandra Postel) Saving the Planet, 1991, (with Gardner and Halweil) Beyond Malthus, 1999, Eco-Economy: Building an Economy for the Earth, 2001, (with Larsen and Fischlowitz-Roberts) The Earth Policy Reader, 2002, Plan B: Rescuing a Planet Under Stress and a Civiliaztion in Trouble, 2003, Worldwatch Issue Alert, 2000-01, Eco-Economy Updates, 2001—, others; contbr. articles to profl jours. Mem. adv. com. Inst. Internat. Econs.,UN Found., Eco-Policy Ctr./Rutgers U.; mem. bd. advisors Internat. Fund for China's Environment; bd. dirs. Inst. for Sustainable Devel., Poland; treas. and bd. mem. Fairview Found.; mem. adv. coun. Internat. Fund for Agrl. Rsch.; advisor Clean Up the World Project, Australia, Internat. Coun. Earth Day 2000; mem. adv. bd. Ctr. for a New Am. Dream; mem. nat. adv. bd. Population Connection (formerly Zero Population Growth); mem. adv. com. Internews; mem. adv. bd. Green House Network; bd. patrons Internat. Network Green Planners; mem. steering com. Ecol. Cities Project, U. Mass.; dir. Japan for Sustainability; mem. adv. coun. Ecology channel. Recipient Superior Svc. award Dept. Agr., 1965, Arthur S. Flemming award, 1965, A.H. Boerma award UN Food and Agrl. Orgn., 1981, UNEP Environ. Leadership medal, 1982, Lorax award Global Tomorrow Coalition, 1985, award World Wildlife Fund for Nature Internat., 1989, UN Environment prize, 1987, A Bizzozero award U. Parma, 1991, Humanist of Yr. award, 1991, Pro Mundo Habitabili award King Carl XVI Gustaf, Sweden, 1991, Delphi Internat. Cooperation award, 1991, Cervia Ambiente prize, Italy, 1992, Robert Rodale Lectr. award, 1992, Environmentalist of Yr. award Japan Jaycees, 1992, Cert. Spl. Recognition Assn. Am. Geographers, 1993, Blue Planet prize Asahi Glass Found., 1994, J. Sterling Morton Arbor Day award, 1995, Pub. Svc. award Fedn. Am. Scientists, 1995, Disting. Achievement award Heylar House Alumni Assn. Rutgers U., 1995; selected as 100 Who Made A Difference The Earth Times, 1995, 100 Champions of Conservation, Audubon Soc., 1998, Rachel Carson Environ. Achievement award Nat. Nutritional Foods Assn., 2000, Bruno H. Schubert Found. environment award, 2001, Natural Bus. Leadership award, 2002; named one of People of the Century, The Daily Jour., N.J., 2000, Excellence Adv. award Internat. Fund for China's Environment, 2002. Fellow World Bus. Acad.; mem. Coun. Fgn. Rels., World Future Soc., Cosmos Club, Sierra Club (adv. coun. for excellence in environ. engring.). Office: Earth Policy Inst Ste 403 1350 Connecticut Ave NW Washington DC 20036-1995 E-mail: lesterbrown@earth-policy.org.

BROWN, LILLIE HARRISON, music educator; b. Cin., July 7, 1937; d. James Albert and Lucille Elizabeth Harrison; m. Frederick Brown, Apr. 12, 1958 (dec. June 1996); children: Kevin Frederick(dec.), Gyll Renee Simpson, Carla Y. BS in Music Edn., U. Cin. Coll. Conservatory of Music, 1961. Music specialist Cin. Pub. Schs., 1961—91, 1999—2002; minister of music, ch. musician Bethel Bapt. Ch., Cin., 1956—. Nominating com. chmn. Coll. Conservatory Alumnae Bd., Cin., 1995—2001; music com. chmn. Hamilton County Ret. Tchrs., Cin., 1992—; mem. NAACP, 1994—. Mem.: Alpha Kappa Alpha (regional music chmn., dir., pres. 1972—76). Home: 1935 Crane Ave Cincinnati OH 45207

BROWN, LILLIE MCFALL, elementary school principal; b. Feb. 29, 1932; d. Clayton and Septertee (Dewberry) McFall; m. Charles Brown, Oct. 4, 1958; 1 child, Eric McFall. BA in Home Econ., Sci., Langston Univ., 1956; MA in Spl. Edn., Chgo. Tchrs. Coll., 1964; MA in Adminstrn., Seattle Univ., 1976. Home econ. tchr. Altue (Okla.) Separate Pub. Schs., 1955-56, first grade tchr., 1956-57, fourth grade tchr., 1957-60; middle sch. tchr. Chgo. Pub. Sch.s, 1960-64; spl. edn. primary tchr. Seattle Pub. Schs., 1966-67, spl. edn. intermediate tchr., 1967-68, program coord., 1968-71, elem. asst. prin., 1971-76, elem. prin., 1976—. Mem. Project READ, Seattle, 1968; chairperson Eighteenth Coll. Fair, Seattle, 2001. Contbr. articles to profl. jours. Treas. African Am. Alliance, 1980—; historian Wash. Alliance Black Sch. Educators, 1991—; vol. Olympic Games, Seattle, 1990; participant First African-African Am. Summit, Ibidijan, Cote d'Ivoire, 1991-92; mem. rsch. bd. advisors Am. Biog. Inst., 1995—; chair 18th Coll. Fair, Seattle, 2001. Sears Found. grantee, 1967; recipient Disting. Alumni award Nat. Assn. for Equal Opportunity in Higher Edn., 1997. Mem. NAACP, Nat. Assn. Elem. Sch. Prins., Assn. Wash. Sch. Prins., Elem. Prins. Assn. Seattle Pub. Schs., Prins. Assn. Wash. State, Prin. Assn. Seattle Pub. Schs., Ednl. Leadership, Phi Delta Kappa, Kappa Delta Pi, Delta Sigma Theta. Democrat. Baptist. Avocations: swimming, dance, bicycling, travel, reading.

BROWN, LLOYD DAVID, association executive, management educator; b. New Haven, Conn., Mar. 22, 1941; s. Lloyd and Laura Whitney (Dodge) B.; m. Jane Gibson Covey, June 14, 1969; children: Rachel Covey, Nathan Lloyd. BA in Social Rels., Harvard Coll., 1963; LLB, MPhil in Organizational Behavior, Yale U., 1969, PhD in Organizational Behavior, 1971. Community organizer Peace Corps, Dessie, Ethiopia, 1963-65; from asst. to assoc. prof. organizational behavior Case Western Res. U., Cleve., 1971-80; pres., chmn. Inst. Devel. Rsch., Boston, 1980—2001; from assoc. prof. to prof. Boston U. Sch. Mgmt., 1981-2001, chmn. organizational behavior, 1981-86, 97-99, faculty dir. doctoral program, 1993-95. Fulbright vis. lectr. Pub. Enterprise Ctr. for Continuing Edn., New Delhi, India, 1979-80; cons. Ford Found., WHO, World Bank, USAID, Asia and Africa, 1980—; vis. prof. pub. policy Kennedy Sch. Govt., Harvard U., 1999-2001, lectr., 2001—; dir. internat. programs Hauser Ctr. for Non-Profit Orgn., 1999—. Author: Learning From Changing, 1974, Managing Conflict at Organizational Interfaces, 1983, The Struggle for Accountability: NGO'S, Social Movements and the World Bank, 1998, Practice-Research Engagement for Civil Society in a Globalizing World, 2001; contbr. articles to profl. jours. Assoc. Synergos Inst., N.Y.C., 1987-99; mem. adv. coun. Vol. Fgn. Aid, Washington, 1997-2001; bd. dirs. World Edn. Inc., 2001—, Inst. for Devel. Rsch., 1980-2001, PRIA Internat., 1995—, Oxtam Am., 2002—, Consensus Bldg. Inst., 2002. Mem. Acad. Mgmt. (pres. organizational devel. div. 1984-85), Assn. for Rsch. on Nonprofit Orgn. and Vol. Action, Internat. Assn. for Third Sector Rsch. Democrat. Avocations: skiing, tennis, science fiction. Office: Harvard Univ Hauser Ctr Nonprofit Orgns 79 JFK St Cambridge MA 02138 E-mail: dave_brown@harvard.edu.

BROWN, LLOYD HARCOURT, JR., newspaper editor; b. Jacksonville, Fla., Sept. 28, 1939; s. Lloyd H. and Zada Elizabeth (Bentley) B.; m. Geraldine Raulerson (div. 1975); children: Lloyd H. III, Lori; m. Patricia Levine; 1 child, Amanda Dale. BA, U. North Fla., 1980. Copy boy Jacksonville Jour., 1957-59, reporter, 1959-79, editor, 1979-81, editorial writer, 1982-83, Fla. Times-Union, Jacksonville, 1983-93, editor editorial page, 1993—. Bd. dirs. Goodwill Industries, Jacksonville, 1994-2002; mem. Fla. Bar Grievance Com., Jacksonville, 1994-2002. With USAR and USMC, 1963-93. Avocation: golf. Home: 2833 Doric Ave Jacksonville FL 32210-4318 Office: Fla Times-Union 1 Riverside Ave Jacksonville FL 32202-4904

BROWN, LOIS HEFFINGTON, health facility administrator; b. Little Rock, Mar. 28, 1940; d. Carl Otis and Opal (Shock) Heffington; M. Ivy Roy Brown, June 21, 1984; children: Carletta Jo Rice, Roby Lynn Rice, Pherby Allison Graham, Phelan Missy Graham. Student, Guilford Tech. Community Coll., Jamestown, N.C., 1974-75, 77, 80. Cert. hearing aid specialist. Sec. Berger Enterprises, West Memphis, Ark., 1962-65; office mgr. Beltone Hearing Aid Ctr., Greensboro, N.C., 1975-81; owner Hearing Care Ctr., Cullman, Ala., 1982-85, Miracle-Ear Ctr., Cullman, Decatur, Fultondale, Jasper and Birmingham, Ala., 1985-87; pres. L&I Corp., Cullman, Decatur, Fultondale, Jasper and Birmingham, 1987-90, L & I Corp. Miracle Ear Ctr., Cullman, Decatur, Jasper, Ala., 1991-93; owner Conway (Ark.) Hearing Aid Ctr., 1994—, Beltone Hearing Aid Ctr., Conway, 1995-96. Distbr. Showcase Distbg. Co., Conway, North Little Rock, Ark. Gov.-appointed Ala. Bd. Hearing, chmn. of the bd., 1989-91. Mem. Nat. Hearing Aid Soc., Ark. Hearing Soc. (sec. 1996—), Ala. Hearing Aid Dealers Assn. (sec. 1984-86, 96-2002, v.p. 1986-88, bd. dirs. 1988-91), Ark. Hearing Aid Dealers Assn. (appt. by gov. to Ark. hearing aid bd. 2002—), Women of the Moose. Republican. Baptist. Avocations: music, swimming, gardening, tennis. Home: 77 Roden Mill Rd Conway AR 72032-9555

BROWN, LOREN DENNIS, internist, educator; b. Feb. 21, 1949; s. Wendell James and Vivian Rose (Young) B.; m. Debra Dee Winders, Feb. 27, 1971; children: Marcus Loren, Melissa Lynn, Katherine Megan. BA, U. Iowa, 1971; DO, Coll. Osteo Medicine Surgery, 1985. Diplomate Nat. Bd. Examiners for Osteo. Physicians and med. oncology. Intern Des Moines Gen. Hosp., 1974-75; resident in internal medicine Chgo. Osteo. Hosp., 1975-76, Youngstown Osteo. Hosp., 1976-77, fellow hematology/med. oncology Cleve. Clinic Found., 1977-79; practice medicine specializing in hematology/med. oncology Ctrl. Iowa Oncology & Hematology Assn. P.C., Des Moines, 1979—; assoc. prof. medicine U. Osteo. Medicine and Health Scis., Des Moines, 1979-96, prof. medicine, 1996—. Assoc. investigator North Central Cancer Treatment Group/Iowa Oncology Research Assn., Des Moines, 1980—; adj. prof. of medicine Des Moines U., 1996—. Mem. Am. Osteo Assn., Am. Coll. Osteo. Internists, Am. Soc. Clin. Oncology, Am. Soc. Hematology, Iowa Soc. Osteo. Physicians and Surgeons, Iowa Oncology Rsch. Assn. (co-prin. investigator 1984-90), Iowa Oncology Soc. Roman Catholic. Address: Med Oncology and Hematology Assocs 411 Laurel St Des Moines IA 50314-3005

BROWN, LORENE B(YRON), library educator, educational administrator; b. Plant City, Fla., Nov. 9, 1933; d. Benjamin and Sallie (Barton) Byron; m. Paul L. Brown, Aug. 1, 1974. BS, Fort Valley State Coll., 1955; MSL.S., Atlanta U., 1956; PhD, U. Wis., 1974. Cataloguer N.C. Central U., Durham, 1956-58, Gibbs Jr. Coll., St. Petersburg, Fla., 1958-60, Fort Valley State Coll., Ga., 1960-65, Norfolk State U., Va., 1965-70; assoc. prof., dean Atlanta U., 1970-89, prof., 1989—; dir. Info. Retrieval Workshops, Atlanta, 1976-78; evaluator Coop. Coll. Library Ctr., Atlanta, 1979-82; cons. United Bd. Coll. Devel., Atlanta, 1976-79. Mem. southeastern/Atlantic regional adv. coun. Nat. Network Librs. Medicine, 2001—03. Author: Subject Access for African American Material, 1995. Mem. Friends of Library, Atlanta, 1982. Recipient Rachel Schenk award Library Sch. U. Wis., Madison, 1971; So. Fellowship Found. fellow Atlanta, 1972-74 Mem. ALA, Am. Soc. for Info. Sci., Assn. Library and Info. Sci. Edn., Ga. Library Assn., Met Atlanta Library Assn., Beta Phi Mu. Democrat. Baptist. Home: 855 Flamingo Dr SW Atlanta GA 30311-2402 Office: Atlanta U Sch Libr and Info Studies 223 James P Brawley Dr SW Atlanta GA 30314-4358

BROWN, LORETTA ANN PORT, physician, geneticist; b. Kingston, N.Y., July 30, 1945; d. Frank and Sophie (Hormann) Port; m. Robert Don Brown, Aug. 22, 1970; 1 child, Adrian Robert. BS, SUNY, New Paltz, 1967; MS, U. Mich., 1968, postgrad., 1969; MD, Ea. Va. Med. Sch., Norfolk, 1981. Diplomate Am. Bd. Med. Examiners. Lab. tech. U. Mich., Ann Arbor, 1969-70; rsch. asst. M.D. Anderson Hosp. and Tumor Inst., Houston, 1970; rsch. instr. Baylor Coll. Medicine, Houston, 1971-76; instr. H.S. for Health Professions, Houston, 1974—75; adj. prof. biology Christopher Newport Coll., Newport News, Va., 1977; resident internal medicine Ea. Va. Med. Sch., Norfolk, 1981-84; asst. prof. medicine Med. Coll. Hampton Rd, Norfolk, 1984—; physician Health America, Hampton, Va., 1984-87, Tidewater Pulmonary Assocs., Newport News, Va., 1987-88; chief, admitting and screening VA Med Ctr., Hampton, 1988-92, staff physician, 1988—. Trainee genetics USPHS, Ann Arbor, Mich., 1967-69; rsch. participant NSF, Albion, Mich., 1966; cons. VA Med. Ctr., 1984-88. Contbr. articles to profl. jours. Recipient Achievement award Am. Med. Women's Assn., 1981, Am. Chem. Soc., 1966. Mem. Am. Morgan Horse Assn., Am. Horse Show Assn. (Morgan judge 1990—), Old Dominion Morgan Horse Assn. (v.p. 1987-89), Va. Carolina Morgan Horse Assn., Nu Pi Sigma. Roman Catholic. Avocations: horses, orchids. Office: VA Medical Ctr 590 170 Hampton VA 23667

BROWN, LORRAINE A. literature educator; b. Grand Rapids, Mich., Apr. 3, 1929; d. Benjamin Franklin Dundas and Eva Elizabeth Campbell; m. William Tiller; 1 child, Tamara Kay Tiller. BA in English and Edn., MA, U. Mich.; PhD, U. Md. From asst. prof. to prof. English George Mason U. Avocation: international theater. Home: 3125 Patrick Henry Dr Falls Church VA 22044

BROWN, LORRAINE ANN, event coordinator, minister, hypnotist; b. Providence, Mar. 15, 1947; d. Leonard Francis and Elaine Frances (Pettis) Millen; m. Jeffrey Schofield Brown, May 22, 1976 (div. 1983); 1 child, Kaneeta Sage; m. Dieter Paul Wuennenberg, July 14, 1965; 1 child, Desirée Jacqueline Wuennenberg. Student, Manhattan Sch. Printing, 1972, L.A. Trade Tech. Coll., 1981-83; BA in Bus., Antioch U., 1996; PhD, Universal Life Ch., 1999; hypnotist, Creative Learning Inst., 2000. Ordained minister Universal Life Ch., 1996; Reiki master. Comms. rep. TransAmerica Occidental, Los Angeles, 1973-77; owner, jewelry designer The Lorraine Brown Co., El Segundo, Calif., 1979-83; mgr. Silk Lingerie Outlet, Sherman Oaks, Calif., 1982-83; office mgr. Am. Silk Label, L.A., 1984; asst. prodn. coordinator Pacific Coast Mills, L.A., 1984-85; asst. designer jr. wear Judy Knapp Inc., L.A., 1986-87; sales exec. Integrated Aquatic Systems, Marina Del Rey, Calif., 1987-88; adminstrv. svcs. coord. GTE Govt. Svcs., El Segundo, Calif., 1988-94; event coord. Jackson Nat. Life Dist., Westwood, 1995-96; office mgr. Ind. Jour. Newspapers, 1996-97; project coord. Complex Legal Svcs., El Segundo, Calif., 1997-98; Reiki master, tchr., therapeutic touch instr. El Segundo, 1997—; owner, event coord. The Organizer, El Segundo, 1998—. Cert. master hypnotist; Reiki master; minister Universal Life Ch. Asst. leader Girl Scouts U.S., El Segundo, 1985-87; P.V.P. leader 4-H, 1991-94; vol. Tree Muskateers and Swift Project. Mem. Am. Bus. Women's Assn., Nurse Healers Internat., Svcs. Employees Assn. (pres.), Internat. Hypnosis Fedn., Young Exec. Singles, Advanced Degrees, Sierra Singles, Redbird, Art of Living Found. Avocations: gardening, decorating, floral designing, catering. Home and Office: 615 E Holly Ave #327 El Segundo CA 90245

BROWN, LOUIS, physicist, researcher; b. San Angelo, Tex., Jan. 7, 1929; s. Metz and Sadie (Johnson) Bishop; m. Lore Elisabeth Frick, July 24, 1952. BS, St. Mary's U., 1950; PhD, U. Tex., 1958. Teaching asst. dept. physics U. Tex. Austin, 1952-58; rsch. asst. dept. physics U. Basle, Switzerland, 1958-61; postdoctoral fellow dept. terrestrial magnetism Carnegie Instn., Washington, 1961-63, staff assoc., 1963-69, staff scientist, 1969-94; emeritus, 1994—. Electronics designer Mil. Physics Lab., Austin, 1955-57; acting dir. dept. terrestrial magnetism Carnegie Instn., 1991 92. Author: A Radar History of World War II, 1999; contbr. numerous articles to profl. jours. With U.S. Army, 1950-52. Recipient Amerbach prize U. Basle, 1963. Fellow Am. Phys. Soc.; mem. AAAS, Am. Geophysical Union. Achievements include collaboration on building of first operating source of polarized ions, on development of techniques for measuring the cosmogenic isotope 10Be in natural materials, on clarifying nature of threshold state in Be-8, and on demonstrating that lavas from island-arc volcanoes have a sedimentary component. Office: Carnegie Inst Washington Dept Terrestrial Magnetism 5241 Broad Branch Rd NW Washington DC 20015-1305

BROWN, LOWELL SEVERT, physicist, educator; b. Visalia, Calif., Feb. 15, 1934; s. Volney Clifford and Anna Marie Evelyn (Jacobson) B.; m. Shirley Isabel Mitchell, June 23, 1956; 1 son, Stephen Clifford. AB, U. Calif., Berkeley, 1956; PhD (NSF predoctoral fellow 1956-61), Harvard U., 1961; postgrad., U. Rome, 1961-62, Imperial Coll., London, 1962 63. From rsch. assoc. to assoc. prof. physics Yale U., 1963-68; mem. faculty U. Wash., Seattle, 1968—, prof. physics, 1970-2001, prof. emeritus, 2001—; mem. staff Los Alamos (N.Mex.) Sci. Lab., 2001—. Vis. prof. Imperial Coll., London, 1971-72, Columbia U., N.Y.C., 1990; vis. scientist Brookhaven Nat. Lab., summer, 1965-68, Lawrence Berkeley Lab., summer 1966, Stanford Accelerator Ctr., summer, 1967, CERN, Geneva, summer, 1979, Inst. for Theoretical Physics, U. Calif., Santa Barbara, winter 1999; mem. Inst. Advanced Study, Princeton, N.J., 1979-80; cons. Los Alamos Nat. Lab., spring 1999, vis. scientist, 1991; vis. physicist Deutches Elektronen-Synchrontron, Hamburg, 1986 Author: Quantum Field Theory, 1992; mem. editl. bd. Phys. Rev., 1978-81; editor Phys. Rev. D, 1987-95; contbr. articles to profl. publs. Trustee Seattle Youth Symphony Orch., 1986—95. Postdoctoral fellow NSF, 1961-63; sr. post-doctoral fellow, 1971-72; Guggenheim fellow, 1979-80 Mem. Ferrari Club of Am. (dir. Northwest region 1999—). Home: 621 Halona Santa Fe NM 87505 Office: X-7 MS F699 PO Box 1668 Los Alamos NM 87545 E-mail: lowellb@ferrariclub.com.

BROWN, LYNDA NELL, nursing educator; b. Humphreys County, Miss., Oct. 6, 1943; d. A. C. and Elizabeth (Holloway) Merchant; m. Walter U. Brown, Oct. 11, 1963; children: Rebecca E., Darren K., Sarah E. BSN, U. Miss., 1965; MS in Nursing, Boston U., 1974, EdD, 1977. Asst. prof. Boston Coll., Chestnut Hill, Mass., Vanderbilt U., Nashville; assoc. prof. U. Akron, Ohio, U. Ky., Lexington. Contbr. articles to profl. publs. Mem. ANA, Nat. League Nursing, ARN, Sigma Theta Tau (Excellence in Nursing award Delta Omega chpt., dist. lectr.).

BROWN, LYNETTE RALYA, journalist, publicist; b. Beloit, Wis., Dec. 15, 1926; d. Lynn Louis and Ethel Clara (Meeker) Ralya; m. Donald Adair Brown, Jr., Dec. 20, 1947; children: Donald Adair III, Alison Laura, Julia Carol. BA in Journalism, Mich. State U., 1948; MA in Journalism, Michigan State U., 1985; MA in Mass Comm., Wayne State U., 1983. Actress, publicist Grand Traverse Playhouse, Traverse City, Mich., 1946 (summer), N.Y. Summer Playhouse, Mackinac Island, Mich., 1947 (summer); writer WILS Radio, Lansing, Mich., 1947-48; writer, performer WJBK Radio, TV, Detroit, 1948-49; editor Denby Ctr. News, Detroit, 1949-51; freelance writer Oakland County, Mich., 1952-78; editor Henry Ford Mus., Dearborn, Mich., 1979-81; writer, reporter Legal Advertiser Newspaper, Detroit, 1983-85; publicist Bloomfield (Mich.) and Birmingham (Mich.) Pub. Librs., 1986-89; freelance writer, publicist Lynette Brown Comm., Birmingham, Mich., 1989—. Columnist: (newspaper) At the Libraries, 1986-89; solo performer Elizabeth Cady Stanton, 1995—. Probation sponsor Dist. Ct. Mich., 1960-70; publicist Oakland County Vol. Bur., 1979-82; leader sr. high/jr. high youth group Drayton Ave. Presbyn. Ch., Oakland County, 1952-54, 62-66, Pine Hill Congl. Ch., Oakland County, 1968-71, Northbrook Presbyn. Ch., Oakland County, 1976-77; polit. campaign worker Rep. candidates and non-partisan jud. candidates, 1952—; Cub Scout leader Royal Oak Emerson Sch., Oakland County, 1961-64; Girl Scout troop leader Bloomfield Twp. Meadow Lake Sch., Oakland County, 1966-71; dir. Martha Griffiths Project, 1989-. Grantee N.Y. State's Thanks Be To Grandmother Winifred Found., 1996, Elizabeth Kummer Award AAUW Mich., 2002. Mem. AAUW (chair women's issues, pub. info. dir. 1995-2000, state projects dir. 2000—), Oakland County C. of C. (Athena award 1995), Mich. Women's Studies Assn. (bd. dirs. 1999—). Home and Office: 6120 Westmoor Rd Bloomfield Township MI 48301

BROWN, MAHLON CARL, retired social science educator; b. Downsville, N.Y., Dec. 26, 1926; s. Carl and Sarah Elizabeth Brown; m. Thelma Marie D'Heedene, Oct. 22, 1949; children: William, Phillip, Scott. BA, Syracuse U., 1951, PhD in Social Sci., 1959. Dir. study abroad program Marshall U., Huntington, W.Va., 1974, developer, dir. W.Va. state social studies fair, 1978-82, prof., 1955-92; ret., 1992. Asst. dir. study abroad program SUNY, Buffalo, 1970. Staff sgt. U.S. Army, 1944-46. Mem. Kiwanis, USCG Auxiliary. Mem. United Ch. of Christ. Home: 132 Lancaster Dr Apt 711 Irvington VA 22480-9746 E-mail: melodee@crosslink.net.

BROWN, MARCIA JOAN, author, artist, photographer; b. Rochester, NY, July 13, 1918; d. Clarence Edward and Adelaide Elizabeth (Zimber) B. Student, Woodstock Sch. Painting, summers 1938, 39; student painting, New Sch. Social Research, Art Students League; BA, N.Y. State Coll. Tchrs., 1940; student Chinese calligraphy, painting, Zhejiang Acad. Fine Arts, Hangzhou, Peoples Republic China, 1985, 87; studied painting with Judson Smith, Stuart Davis, Yasuo Kuniyoshi, Julian Levi; LHD (hon.), SUNY, Albany, 1996. Tchr. English, dramatics Cornwall (N.Y.) High Sch., 1940-43; library asst. N.Y. Pub. Library, 1943-49; tchr. puppetry extra-mural dept. U. Coll. West Indies, Jamaica, B.W.I., 1953. Tchr. workshop on picture book U. Minn.-Split Rock Arts Program, Duluth, 1986, workshop on Chinese brush painting Brush Artists Guild, 1988; sponsor Chinese landscape painting workshops with Zhuo HeJun, 1988-89; sponsored workshops Chinese caligraphy with A. Wang Dong Ling, 1989-90, 92; invited speaker exhbn. illustrations, Japan, 1990, 94. Illustrator: The Trail of Courage (Virginia Watson), 1948, The Steadfast Tin Soldier (Hans Christian Andersen), 1953 (Caldecott Honor Book award), Anansi (Philip Sherlock), 1954, The Three Billy Goats Gruff (Asbjornsen and Moe), 1957, Peter Piper's Alphabet, 1959, The Wild Swans (Hans Christian Andersen), 1963, Giselle (Théophile Gautier), 1970, The Snow Queen (Hans Christian Andersen), 1972, Shadow (Blaise Cendrars), 1982 (Caldecott award 1983), How the Ostrich Got His Long Neck (Aardema, Mainichi Japan Picture Book award 1997, Tranlation Winner' prize Mainichi Newspapers and Sch. Libr. Assn. 1997), 1995, (with others) Sing a Song of Popcorn, 1988, Of Swans, Sugar Plums and Satin Slippers (Violette Verdy); author, illustrator: The Little Carousel, 1946, Stone Soup, 1947 (Caldecott Honor Book award), Henry Fisherman, 1949 (Caldecott Honor Book award), Dick Whittington and His Cat (retold), 1950 (Caldecott Honor Book award), Skipper John's Cook, 1951 (Caldecott Honor Book award), The Flying Carpet (retold), 1956, Felice, 1958, Tamarindo, 1960, Once a Mouse (retold), 1961 (Caldecott award), Backbone of the King, 1966, The Neighbors, 1967, The Bun (retold), 1972, All Butterflies, 1974 (Boston Globe Honor Book, Horn Book), The Blue Jackal (retold), 1977, Walk Through Your Eyes, 1979, (with photographs) Touch Will Tell, 1979; (with photographs) Listen to a Shape, 1979, Lotus Seeds; Children, Pictures and Books, 1985; (with others) From Sea to Shining Sea, 1993; translator, illustrator: Puss in Boots, 1952 (Caldecott Honor Book award), Cinderella (Charles Perrault), 1954 (Caldecott award 1955), How, Hippo!, 1969 (honor book Book World Spring Book Festival); author, photographer: film strip The Crystal Cavern, 1974; exhibited at Bklyn. Mus., Peridot Gallery, Hacker Gallery, Library Congress, Carnegie Inst., Phila. Print Club, Hammond Mus., North Salem, NY, 1988; one-woman show include: U. Albany, SUNY, 1997; represented in permanent collections Library of Congress, NY Pub. Library, Mazza Gallery Findlay (Ohio) Coll.; pvt. collections. Recipient Disting. Svc. to Children's Lit. award, U. So. Miss., 1972, Regina medal Cath. Libr. Assn., 1977, Disting. Alumnus medal SUNY, 1969, Laura Ingalls Wilder award, 1992; U.S. nominee Internat. Hans Andersen award illustration, 1966, 76; career rsch. material in spl. libr. collection, SUNY, Albany, de Grummond Collection, U. So. Miss., Hattiesburg, Kerlan Collection, U. Minn.; named Marcia Brown Rsch. Rm. in her honor SUNY, Albany, 2001. Fellow Internat. Inst. Arts and Letters (life); mem. Author's Guild, Print Coun. Am., Art Students League, Oriental Brush Artists Guild, Sumi-e Soc. Am, Am. Artists of Chinese Brush Painting.

BROWN, MARILYN SHULL, music educator; b. Takoma Park, Md., Jan. 11, 1937; Nat. cert. piano tchr. Founder Marilyn Brown Piano Studio, Raleigh, NC, 1963—86, founder and dir. Raleigh Conservatory Music, 1986—. Founder Raleigh Piano Tchrs. Performance Festival, 1968, Raleigh Symposium, N.C. Symposium Youth Concerto Competition; spkr. in field. Contbr. articles to mags. Founder and mem. Trinity Presbyn. Ch., 1968—. Mem.: RPTA (bd. dirs. 1968—), NCMTA, MTNA (cert. master tchr.). Republican. Avocations: reading, music. Home: 4609 Westminster Dr Raleigh NC 27604-5959 Office: Raleigh Conservatory Music 3636 Capital Blvd Raleigh NC 27604

BROWN, MARION LIPSCOMB, JR., publisher, photographer, writer, retired chemical company executive; b. Greenwood, Miss., Aug. 1, 1925; s. Marion Lipscomb and Martha Helen (Wheeler) B.; m. Dorothy Dell Tramel, Aug. 28, 1948; children: Paul Thomas, Marion Lipscomb III, Janet Marie, Jeffrey Robert. BSChemE, Miss. State U., 1950; cert in exec. devel., La. State U., 1969. Rsch. engr. Cities Service Corp., Lake Charles, La., 1951-53; with Miss. Chem. Corp., Yazoo City, 1953-87, v.p. rsch. and engring., 1972-74, v.p. research and devel., 1974-87; writer photography articles, 1990—. Exhibiting photographer in maj. mus. collections of world, tchr. photography; pub. Jour. Creative Photography, 1989-95. Author: Fertilizer Formulation Manual, 1967; contbr. articles to profl. jours.; patentee in fertilizer tech. Dir., coach Little Boys and Youth Baseball, 1958-68; engring. adviser Miss. State U., 1972-88, vice-chmn., chmn. adv. com. With USN, 1943-46, PTO. Named Photographer of Yr. award Miss. Inst. Arts and Letters, 1996. Mem. Am. Chem. Soc., Creative Edn. Found., Miss. State U. Dist. Alumni Assn. (pres. 1966). Methodist. Home: 315 E Nineteenth St Yazoo City MS 39194-2340 E-mail: marion@tecinfo.com.

BROWN, MARK MALLOCH, international organization official; Grad. in History, Cambridge (Eng.) U.; M in Polit. Sci., U. Mich. With UN High Commr. for Refugees, 1979-83; founder, editor The Economist Devel. Report, 1983-86; ptnr. internat. consulting firm; dir. external affairs World Bank, Washington, 1994-96, v.p. external affairs, 1996-99; admin. UN Devel. Program UN, Washington, 1999—. Dir. field ops. for Cambodian refugees, Thailand, 1979-81; dep. chief emergency unit, Geneva, 1981; vice-chmn. Bd. Refugees Internat., Washington; mem. Soros Adv. Com., Bosnia, 1993-94. Contbr. articles to profl. jours. Recipient (UN High Commr. for Refugees and staff) Nobel Peace prize, 1981. Office: UN Devel Program External Affairs 1 United Plaza New York NY 10017 Fax: 202-522-2644.

BROWN, MARK STEVEN, medical physicist; b. Denver, July 12, 1955; s. Clarence William and Gail Margaret (Farthing) B.; m. Mary Linda Avery, Oct. 9, 1988 (div. July 1995). Student, Northwestern U., 1973-74; BS, Colo. State U., 1977; PhD in Phys. Chemistry, U. Utah, 1984. GE postdoctoral fellow Yale U. Sch. Medicine, New Haven, 1984-86, assoc. rsch. scientist, 1986-87; rsch. asst. prof. U. N.Mex. Sch. Medicine, Albuquerque, 1987-89; med. physicist Swedish Med. Ctr. Porter Meml. Hosp., Englewood, Colo., 1989-92; instr. C.C. Denver, Denver, 1990, 91; asst. clin. prof. radiology U. Colo. Sch. Medicine, Denver, 1991-92, asst. prof. radiology, 1992-96; clin. physicist Elscint MR Inc., Ft. Collins, Colo., 1997-98; faculty dept. chemistry Met. State Coll. Denver, 1998—. Cons. InVivo Metrics, 1996-97, The Transinformics Group, 1996-97; MRI physics cons. advanced med. divsn., HEI, Inc., 1999—; peer rev. Jour. Magnetic Resonance Imaging, 1993—; rsch. assoc. U. Colo. Health Sci. Ctr., 2002—. Author: (with others) NMR Relaxation in Tissues, 1986; contbr. articles to profl. jours. Mem. Am. Chem. Soc., Internat. Soc. Magnetic Resonance In Medicine. Avocations: music, guitar, singing, skiing, swimming. Home: 4927 W 63d Ave Arvada CO 80003

BROWN, MARTIN HOWARD, physician; b. Bklyn., Feb. 21, 1953; s. Alan Aaron and Clarice (Steinberg) B.; m. Rebecca Jean Sarley; children: Meghan E., Elliott A. BS with honors, George Washington U., 1974, MD, 1978. Chief med. resident George Washington U. Hosp., Washington, 1981-82; staff physician Emergency Medicine Assocs., Bethesda, Md., 1982-83; asst. prof. medicine George Washington U. Med. Ctr., 1983—; aeromed. dir. Worldcare Travel Assistance Assn., Washington, 1985-88; vice chmn. dept. emergency medicine Nat. Hosp., Arlington, Va., 1985-87, chmn. dept., 1987-91; asst. prof. medicine Georgetown U. Hosp., Washington, 1988—; med. dir. USASSIST, Washington, 1988-98; chmn. dept. emergency medicine Washington Adventist Hosp., 1991-2000; med. dir. Md. Ambulance Svc., 1995-99, AXA Assistance, Chgo., 1995-99; chmn. dept. emergency medicine Inova Alexandria Hosp., 2000—. Trauma ctr. site reviewer State of Va.; mem. adv. com. Emergency Med. Svcs. Curriculum, No. Va. Community Coll., 1990-92; cons. in field. Trustee Nat. Hosp. Bd. Trustees, 1987-96; mem. adv. com. emergency med. svcs. Arlington County Bd., 1987-91, chmn. adv. com., 1991. Fellow Am. Coll. Emergency Physicians, Am. Coll. Physician Execs., Alpha Omega Alpha. Jewish. Home: 10901 Cripplegate Rd Potomac MD 20854-1628 Office: Emergency Medicine Assocs 1300 Picard Dr Rockville MD 20850-4008 E-mail: martin.brown@inova.com.

BROWN, MARY CATHLEEN, retired executive secretary, poet; b. McRae, Ga., June 8, 1956; d. Christine Yawn. A in Secretarial Sci., Crandall Jr. Coll., Macon, Ga., 1976; BA in Psychology, Augusta State Coll., 1991. Author poetry. Recipient Second prize 1999 Nat. Writers Assn. Poetry Contest, Nat. Writers Found., 1999, President's award for literary excellence, Nat. Author's Registry, 2002. Mem.: Pioneer Hist. Soc. Avocation: poetry. Home: Apt B-11 723 E Oak St Mc Rae GA 31055-1665 Personal E-mail: cathy4@planttel.net. E-mail: cthlnbrwn@netscape.net.

BROWN, MATTHEW, lawyer; b. N.Y.C., Mar. 26, 1905; s. Jack Goddard and Pauline B. (Roth) B.; m. Edna Goodrich, Nov. 8, 1932; 1 child, Patricia Brown Specter. BS, NYU, 1925; LLB, Harvard U., 1928; LLD (hon.), Suffolk U., 1983. Bar: Mass. 1928, U.S. Supreme Ct. 1935. Sr. ptnr. Brown, Rudnick, Freed & Gesmer, Boston, 1940-88, counsel, 1988—; spl. justice Boston Mcpl. Ct., 1962-72. Chmn. Boston Broadcasters, 1972-81. Selectman Town of Brookline, Mass., 1953-64; trustee New Eng. Aquarium, Boston, 1981-88; mem. Nat. Jewish Coalition, Boston, 1984, Holocaust Meml. Coun., Washington; bd. dirs. Palm Beach Fellowship of Christians and Jews, Palm Beach Civic League. Fellow Brandeis U., Waltham, Mass., 1985 (hon.). Mem. ABA, Mass. Bar Assn., Boston Bar Assn., Am. Jewish Com. (hon. v.p.), Combined Jewish Philanthropies (hon. trustee, life), Belmont Country Club. Home (Summer): Apt 8C 2 Commonwealth Ave Boston MA 02116-1408 Office: Brown Rudnick Bearach & Israeli One Fin Ctr Boston MA 02111 Home (Winter): 130 Sunrise Ave Palm Beach FL 33480-3961

BROWN, MELISSA M. ophthalmologist; b. Memphis, Oct. 11, 1950; d. Roy Seeley and Muriel Jean (Cobb) Moore; m. Gary C. Brown, Aug. 16, 1973; children: Heather, Heidi, Katie. BSN, Keuka Coll., 1972; MSN, Emory U., 1976; postgrad., U. Pa., 1980-82, St. Joseph's U., 1980-82; MD, Jefferson Med. Coll., 1986. RN, Pa. Staff nurse Mass. Gen. Hosp., Boston, 1972-73; nurse educator Crouse Irving Meml. Hosp., Syracuse, N.Y., 1973-75; nursing instr., asst. prof. U. Pa., Phila., 1976-80, Thomas Jefferson U., Phila., 1979-80; transitional resident Chestnut Hill Hosp., Phila., 1986-87; resident in ophthalmology Wills Eye Hosp., Phila., 1987-90; pvt. practice ophthalmology, Phila., 1990-99; pres./dir. Ctr. for Value Based Medicine, 2000—. Asst. surgeon Wills Eye Hosp., 1990—. Contbr. articles to profl. jours. Trustee Keuka Coll., Keuka Park, N.Y., 1991—; Rep. nominee U.S. Congress, 2002. Sr. fellow, Leonard Davis Inst. Pub. Policy, 2003—. Fellow Am. Acad. Ophthalmology; mem. AMA, Pa. Med. Soc. (mem. task force 1995—). Republican. Avocations: gardening, fishing, boating. Office: 1107 Bethlehem Pike Ste 210 Flourtown PA 19031-1919

BROWN, MELVIN HENRY, retired chemical engineer; b. Victor, Iowa, Dec. 6, 1919; s. Henry Nelson and Leita Katherine (Faas) B.; m. Mary Jane Stodgell, June 20, 1947; children: Marianne Louise, William Lee, Robert Nelson, Ellen Jeanne. BS in chemical engring., Iowa State U., 1942, MS in chemical engring., 1944, PhD in chemical engring., 1949. Rsch. assoc. Iowa Engring. Experiment Station, Ames, Iowa, 1942-49; rsch. engr. Alcoa Rsch. Lab., New Kensington, Pa., 1949-62, sr. scientist, 1962-72; scientific assoc. Alcoa Tech. Ctr., Alcoa Ctr., Pa., 1972-77, sr. scientific assoc., 1977-81, tech. cons., 1981-86; ret. Contbr. articles to profl. jours. Recipient IR100 awards for high strength aircraft alloy, 1987, 89, Profl. Achievment citation in engring., 1989. Mem. Am. Inst. Chem. Engrs., Am. Chem. Soc., Am. Assn. Advancement Sci., Rsch. Soc. Am. Republican. Lutheran. Achievements include 52 patents on corrosion, desalination, waste treatment, inhibitors, heat treatments and compositions of al alloys, sulfer removal from coal combustion and energy systems. Home: 1837 Shadyside Rd Lakewood NY 14750-9646 E-mail: perpetual@madbbs.com.

BROWN, MEREDITH M. lawyer; b. N.Y.C., Oct. 18, 1940; s. John Mason Brown and Catherine (Screven) Meredith; m. Sylvia Lawrence Barnard, July 17, 1965; 1 child, Mason Barnard. AB, Harvard U., 1961, JD, 1965. Bar: N.Y. 1965, U.S. Ct. Appeals (2d cir.) 1966, U.S. Dist. Ct. (so. dist.) N.Y. 1976. Law clk. to Hon. Leonard P. Moore U.S. Ct. Appeals (2d cir.), N.Y.C., 1965-66; assoc. Debevoise & Plimpton, N.Y.C., 1966-72, ptnr., 1973—, co-chair corp. dept., 1993—2001, chair or co-chair mergers and acquisitions group, 1985—. Author: (with others) Takeovers: A Strategic Guide to Mergers & Acquisitions, 2001, Global Offerings, 1994, Privatisations, 1994, Mechanics of Global Equity Offerings, 1995, International Mergers and Acquisitions: An Introduction, 1999; contbr. articles to profl. publs. Mem. ABA (fed. regulation of securities com., bus. law sect.), Assn. of Bar of City of N.Y. (chmn. profl. responsibility com. 1987-90), Internat. Bar Assn. (co-chmn. com. on issues and trading of securities, sect. on bus. law 1994-98, co-chmn. capital markets forum, sec. bus. law 1998-2002). Home: 1021 Park Ave New York NY 10028-0959 E-mail: mmbrown@debevoise.com.

BROWN, MICHAEL, information technology executive; b. Williamsport, Pa., Oct. 28, 1943; s. Irwin and Helen (Shuster) B.; m. Candance Carver, Apr. 8, 1967 (div. 1979); children: Kristin, Brett, Lee; m. Stephanie Barry, Apr. 21, 1984 BS, U.S. Naval Acad., 1966. Systems engr. Electronic Data Systems, Dallas, 1970-72; exec. v.p., chief info. officer New Eng. Life Ins. Co., Boston, 1972-93; exec. v.p. Fidelity Investments, Boston, 1993—2003; ret., 2003. With USN, 1966-70. Roman Catholic. Avocations: skiing, weight training.

BROWN, MICHAEL A. computer hardware company executive; b. 1958; BA in Econs., Harvard U.; MBA, Stanford U. Rsch. assoc. Braxton Assocs., 1982—84; from mktg. staff to COO Quantum Corp., Milpitas, Calif., 1984—93, CEO, 1995—2002, chmn., bd. dirs., 1998—; pres. DLT & Storage. Bd. mem. Digital Impact, Equal Logic, Nektar Therapeutics and Veritas. Office: Quantum Corp 501 Sycamore Dr Milpitas CA 95035-7485*

BROWN, MICHAEL DEWAYNE, federal agency administrator, lawyer; b. Guymon, Okla., Nov. 11, 1954; s. Wayne E. and R. Eloise B.; m. Tamara Ann Oxley, July 19, 1973; children: Jared Michael, Amy Aryann. Student, Southeastern State Coll., 1973-75; BA in Polit. Sci. and English, Cen. State U., Edmond, Okla., 1978; JD, Oklahoma City U., 1981. Bar: Okla. 1982, Colo. 1992, U.S. Dist. Ct. (no. and we. dists.) Okla. 1982, U.S. Ct. Appeals (10th cir.) 1982, U.S. Ct. Appeals (D.C. cir.) 1987. Assoc. Long, Ford, Lester & Brown, Enid, Okla., 1982-87; pvt. practice Enid, 1987—; gen. counsel & deputy dir. Fed. Emergency Mgmt. Agy., 2001—02; under secy. Preparedness & Response U.S. Dept. Homeland Security, Wash., DC, 2003—. Adj. prof. state and local govt. law legis. Oklahoma City U.; cons. No. Okla. Devel. Assn., Enid, 1983-91; gen. counsel Alpha Oil Co., Duncan, Okla., 1985—, Physicians Mgmt. Svc. Corps., 1985-90, Physicians of Okla., Inc., Physicians Med. Plan Okla., Inc., City Nat. Bank & Trust Co., 1987-88, Stanfield Printing Co., 1987—, Hammell Newspapers, Inc., 1987-90, Dillingham Ins., 1989-91, Suits Rig Corp., Suits Drilling Co., 1989-91; chmn. bd. dirs. Okla. Mcpl. Power Authority, Edmond, 1982-88, judges & stewards commr. Internat. Arabian Horse Assn., 1991—. Councilman City of Edmond, 1981; cons. Okla. Reps., Oklahoma City, 1983; bd. dirs. Okla. Christian Home, Edmond, 1985; Rep. nominee 6th Dist. U.S. Congress, 1988; co-chmn. Nat. Challengers Polit. Coalition, 1989-91; trustee, co-chair fin. com. Theodore Roosevelt Assn., 1994—. Michael D. Brown Hydroelectric Power Plant and Dam named in his honor, Kaw Reservoir, Okla., 1987. Mem. Okla. Bar Assn. (assoc. bar examiner 1984—), MD Physicians Okla., Ariz. and La., MD Physicians of Tulsa. Mem. Christian Ch. (Disciples Of Christ). Avocations: travel, photography, reading, wilderness adventures, swimming. Office: Dept Homeland Security Washington DC 20528*

BROWN, MICHAEL F. anthropologist, educator; b. N.Y., 1950; m. Sylvia Kennick Brown; 1 child, Emily C.L. AB, Princeton U., 1972; PhD, U. Mich., 1981. Lambert prof. anthropology and L.Am. studies Williams Coll., Williamstown, Mass., 1992—. Author: Tsewa's Gift, 1986, The Channeling Zone, 1997; co-author: War of Shadows, 1991, Who Owns Native Culture?, 2003. Smithsonian fellow, Smithsonian Instn., Washington, 1983, NEH fellow, Washington, 2001. Mem.: Inst. Advanced Study. Office: Williams Coll Dept Anthropology Stetson Hall Williamstown MA 01267

BROWN, MICHAEL JOHN, publishing executive; s. John William and Kathryn Ann B.; m. Regina Ann Hyatt, Aug. 19, 1967; children: Gregory (dec.), Alexander. BA, Marian Coll., 1965; MA, Niagara U., 1967. Instr. Coll. Mt. St. Joseph, Ohio, 1967-72; ednl. sales rep. W.B. Saunders Co., Phila., 1972-80; editor biology books Saunders Coll. Publ., Phila., 1980-84; from sr. editor to editor-in-chief nursing books W.B. Saunders Co., Phila., 1984-92; exec. editor medicine Lea & Febiger, Malvern, Pa., 1992-93; v.p., editor-in-chief Chapman & Hall, N.Y.C., 1994-95; exec. editor Mosby-Year Book, Inc., Phila., 1995-97; sr. editor Taylor & Francis, Phila., 1998; sr. v.p., publ. dir. Technomic Publ. Co., Inc., Lancaster, Pa., 1999—; exec. editor McGraw-Hill, N.Y.C., 2002—. Home: 1312 Grenox Rd Wynnewood PA 19096-2403 E-mail: brown.michael.j@att.net.

BROWN, MICHAEL JOHN, retired judge; b. Racine, Wis., Sept. 28, 1933; s. John Richard and Evelyn Mary Brown; m. Anna C. Nasiata, Jan. 21, 1966 (dec. Apr. 1975); children: Brian, Kevin, Michael L.; m. Nancy L. Patania, Oct. 14, 2000. LLB, U. Notre Dame, 1955; JD, U. Ariz., 1959. Bar: Ariz., U.S. Dist. Ct. Ariz., 1959, U.S. Ct. Appeals, 1965, U.S. Supreme Ct., 1974. Pvt. practice, Tucson, 1959-61; ptnr. Brown, Finn & Rosenberg, Tucson, 1962-66; chief city prosecutor City of Tucson, 1962-65; ptnr. Brown & Finn, Tucson, 1966-78; pvt. practice Michael J. Brown, P.C., Tucson, 1978-81; superior ct. judge Pima County Superior Ct. Ariz., Tucson, 1981-2001, presiding judge, 1991-99; ret., 2001. Mem. malpractice com. Supreme Ct. Ariz., 1982, mem. litigation com., 1983—, mem. jury utilization com., 1995—; nat. lectr. on jury reform and innovations. Pres., bd. dirs. La Frontera Ctr., Tucson, 1975-81. Fellow State Bar Ariz.; mem. Pima County Bar Assn. Avocations: rafting, scuba diving, racquetball. E-mail: judgemjb@aol.com.

BROWN, MICHAEL R. former defense industry executive; b. Kans. BEd, Ottawa U. Mktg. mgr. Singer; mktg. mgr. Amecom divsn. Litton Industries, Inc., College Park, Md., 1968-77, v.p. bus. devel. electronic warfare comm. sys., 1977-87, v.p. bus. devel. electronic warfare sys. group, 1987-89, corp. v.p., group exec. electronic warfare sys., 1989-92, corp. sr. v.p., 1992-95, exec. command., control, comm. sys. group, 1995, pres., 1995—, CEO, 1998—, chmn., 1999—2001. Mem. L.A. World Affairs Coun. Inducted into U. Ottawa Sports Hall of Fame. Mem. Navy League U.S., Assn. U.S. Army, Air Force Assn., Armed Forces Comm. Electronics Assn., Nat. Def. Indl. Assn., Aerospace Industries Assn., Assn. Old Crows. Office: Litton Industries Inc 21240 Burbank Blvd Woodland Hills CA 91367-6675

BROWN, MICHAEL ROBERT, lawyer; b. Worcester, Mass., Apr. 5, 1938; s. Walter David and Ethel Fay (Berman) B.; m. Susan Fay Lappin, July 8, 1962; children: Laura, Pamela. BA, Bowdoin Coll., 1959; JD, Columbia U., 1962. Bar: Mass. 1963, N.Y. 1968. Staff atty. NLRB, Washington, 1963-66; assoc. Simpson, Thacher & Bartlett, N.Y.C., 1966-70; ptnr. Herrick & Smith, Boston, 1970-84, Goldstein & Manello, Boston, 1984-90, Palmer & Dodge, Boston, 1990—2002, Seyfarth Shaw, Boston, 2002—. Adj. prof. employment law Sch. Law Suffolk U., Boston; Selectman, Wellesley, Mass., 1992-95. Fellow Coll. Labor and Employment Lawyers; mem. ABA, Mass. Bar Assn., Boston Bar Assn. Office: Seyfarth Shaw Two Seaport Ln Boston MA 02210-2028 E-mail: mrbrown@seyfarth.com.

BROWN, MICHAEL ROBERT, finance specialist; b. Joliet, Ill., Aug. 9, 1960; s. Robert Raymond and Virginia A. (Bianchi) B. AAS, Joliet Jr. Coll., 1980; BS, No. Ill. U., 1983, MBA, 1996. Acctg. supr. northern region DeKalb (Ill.) Genetics, 1982-85; fin. analyst Baxter Healthcare Corp., Deerfield, Ill., 1985, sr. fin. analyst, 1985-87, sr. consols. analyst, 1987-88, mgr. acctg. svcs., 1988-89, mgr. corp. acctg., 1989-93, dir. fin. planning McGaw Park, Ill., 1993-95, asst. contr. renal divsn., 1995-99, v.p. fin. renal divsn., 1999—. Vol. Jr. Achievement, United Way; bd. exec. advisors No. Ill. U. Mem. Inst. Mgmt. Accts., Chgo. Coun. Fgn. Rels., No. Ill. U. Alumni Assn., No. Ill. U. Exec. Club. Avocations: music, tennis. E-mail: mrbrown9@aol.com.

BROWN, MICHAEL STUART, geneticist, educator, administrator; b. N.Y.C., Apr. 13, 1941; s. Harvey and Evelyn (Katz) Brown; m. Alice Lapin, June 21, 1964; children: Jane Elizabeth, Ellen Sarah. BA, U. Pa., 1962, MD, 1966; DSc (hon.), Rensselaer Poly. Inst., 1982, U. Chgo., 1982, U. Pa., 1986, U. Buenos Aires, 1988, U. Paris, 1988, So. Meth. U., 1993, U. Miami, 1996; DSc (hon.), Rockefeller U., 2001. Intern, then resident in medicine Mass. Gen. Hosp., Boston, 1966-68; served with USPHS, 1968-70; clin. assoc. NIH, 1968-71; asst. prof. U. Tex. Southwestern Med. Sch., Dallas, 1971-74; Paul J. Thomas prof. genetics, dir. Ctr. for Molecular Genetics, U. Tex., 1977—, disting. chair in biomed. scis., 1989—. Mem. med. adv. bd. Scripps Inst.; bd. dirs. Pfizer Inc., 1996—, Regeneron, Inc., 1991—. Co-editor: The Metabolic Basis of Inherited Disease, 1983. Recipient Pfizer award, Am. Chemical Soc., 1976, Passano award, Passano Found., 1978, Lena Annenberg Hazen award, 1982, Albert Lasker Med. Rsch. award, 1985, Horwitz prize, 1985, Nobel prize in medicine or physiology, 1985, Nat. Med. Sci., U.S. Govt., 1988, Albany Med. Ctr. prize in medicine, 2003. Mem.: Albany Med. Ctr. (prize in Medicine 2003), Royal Acad. Scis. (fgn.), Harvey Soc., Assn. Am. Physicians, Am. Soc. Clin. Investigation, Nat. Acad. Scis. (Lounsbery award 1979). Office: U Tex Health Sci Ctr Dept Molecular Genetics 5323 Harry Hines Blvd Dallas TX 75390-9046 E-mail: mike.brown@utsouthwestern.edu.

BROWN, MIKE, professional sports team executive; Pres., chmn. & owner Cin. Bengals, 1966—. Address: 1 Paul Brown Stadium Cincinnati OH 45202-3418

BROWN, MORTON B. biostatistics educator; b. Montreal, Que., Can., Dec. 15, 1941; s. Israel I. and Leah (Shaikovitch) B.; m. Raya Sobol, Oct. 16, 1969; children— Danit, Alon B.Sc., McGill U., 1962; MA, Princeton U., 1964, PhD, 1965. Asst. research statistician UCLA, 1965-68, assoc. research statistician, 1975-77; vis. lectr. Tel Aviv U., 1968-69, sr. lectr., 1969-75, assoc. prof. stats., 1975-81; prof. biostatistics U. Mich., Ann Arbor, 1981—, chmn. dept., 1984-87; interim dir. biometrics core Ctr. for Clin. Investigation and Therapeutics, 1998—. Editor: BMDP Statistical Software, 1977 Fellow Royal Statis. Soc.; mem. Internat. Statis. Inst., Am. Statis. Assn., Biometric Soc., Inst. Math. Stats. Office: U Mich Dept Biostats Ann Arbor MI 48109-2029

BROWN, MYRA SUZANNE, librarian; b. Gainesville, Fla., Jan. 6, 1949; d. Samuel Jackson and Myra Frances (Whiddon) B.; m. Roman Jonas Yoder, Jan. 5, 1973; m. Jeremy Gallaudet Hole, May 3, 1986. Student European divsn., U. Md., West Berlin, 1967-69; BA, U. South Fla., 1971; MSLS, Fla. State U., 1972; postgrad., U. Cin., 1974. Libr. asst. Strozier Libr., Fla. State U., Tallahassee, 1973, libr. serials dept., 1973; libr. sci. and tech. dept. Pub. Libr. of Cin. and Hamilton County, 1973-74; libr. assoc. II Coll. Design, Architecture and Art Libr. U. Cin., 1975-77; assoc. univ. libr. State U. Sys. of Fla. Extension Libr., St. Petersburg, Fla., 1979-81, Edn. Libr. U. Fla. Librs., Gainesville, 1982-84, head and edn. bibliographer, 1984-90; asst. dept. chair humanities and social scis. svcs. dept. Smathers Librs. U. Fla., Gainesville, 1990-92, head and edn. bibliographer Edn. Libr., 1992—. Mem. reference liaisons discussion group Rsch. Librs. Group, Inc., 1990-92; reviewer Gale Rsch. Co., Inc., 1988—; participant rsch. panel Univ. Microfilms Internat., 1992; mem. nat. user group Libr. of Congress Cataloging Distbn. Svc., 1992-96; cons. Mus. Fine Arts Libr., St. Petersburg, Fla., 1981-82, Design, Architecture and Art Libr., U. Cin., 1975-77; participant focus group ISI, 1998, 99; participant rsch. panel, Libr. Supplies, 1999; cons. New Bus. Devel. Edn. titles Gale Rsch., 1998, 99. Contbr.: World Architecture Index: A Guide to Illustrations, 1991; contbr. articles to profl. jours. Aux. mem., vol. Shands Hops. of U. Fla., Gainesville, 1993-96, nominating com., 1995-96, sustaining mem., 1997—; advocate for homeless; mem. outreach com. Holy Trinity Episcopal Ch.; advocate for animal rights. Mem. ALA (chmn., planner, moderator preconf. and conf. program, reference svcs. in medium-sized rsch. librs. discussion group 1992—), Libr. Adminstrn. and Mgmt. Assn. (mem. econ. status and staff welfare com., 1993-95, staff devel. com. 1994-98, publs. com. 1999—), Spl. Librs. Assn. (info. tech. divsn., 1979-93, edn. divsn. Fla. chpt. 1979—, list svc. mgr. 1994—, presenter at ann. conf., 1999), Am. Ednl. Rsch. Assn. (divsn. E counseling and human devel. 1989-90, 92—, divsn. K. tchr. edn. 1994—), Fla. Ednl. Rsch. Assn., U. Fla. Librs. Assn. (v.p. 1983-84), Phi Delta Kappa (historian 1993-94). Democrat. Episcopalian. Avocations: church choir, hospital volunteering, animal welfare concerns, painting. Office: Smathers Librs of U Fla Edn Libr 1500 Norman Hall PO Box 117016 Gainesville FL 32611-7016

BROWN, NAN MARIE, clergywoman; b. Winton, N.C., Jan. 2, 1931; d. Richard and Aberdeen Elizebeth (Clanton) Watford; m. Joseph Linwood Blunt, June 9, 1947 (dec. Sept. 1970); children: Linette, Joseph Linwood Jr., Alvin; m. Frank Coolige Brown, Oct. 2, 1972; stepchildren: Ameedah Ali, Sami Nuridden. BS, D.C. Tchrs. Coll., 1972; MDiv magna cum laude, Va. Union U., 1982, D Ministry in Ch. Adminstrn., 1993; PhD in Pastoral Leadership (hon.), Va. U., 2003. Ordained to ministry Bapt. Ch., 1980. Clk., sec., adminstr. Dept. Commerce and AEC, Suitland, Germantown, Md., 1960-65; program analyst Job Corps, U.S. Office Econs., Washington, 1965-67; licensing asst. U.S. Nuclear Regulatory Commn., Bethesda, Md., 1967-72, pers. mgmt. analyst, 1972-74; mgr. nat. fed. women's program U.S. Dept. Energy, Germantown, 1974-76; nat. dir. fed. women's program U.S. Dept. Interior, Washington, 1979; asst. pastor Pleasant Grove Bapt. Ch., Columbia, Va., 1975-83; pastor Mt. Level Bapt. Ch., Dinwiddie, Va., 1983-87, New Hope Bapt. Ch., Esmont, Va., 1987-89; founder, pastor The Way of Cross Bapt. Ch., Palmyra, Va., 1989—; vice moderator, moderator Albemarle Bapt. Assn., 1996-98; moderator Slate River Bapt. Assn., 1997-99. Bd. dir. AIDS Svcs. Group, 1989-99, cons. Nan M. Brown Assocs., bus. cons.; vol. cons., reviewer AIDS proposals for funding Va. Health Dept., Richmond, 1979-89; founder, dir. Children's Saturday Enrichment Program, Palmyra, 1990—; mem. gen. bd. Bapt. Gen. Conv. Va., mem. social concerns com., 1990; vice moderator Slate River Bapt. Assn., 1995—; cert. AIDS trainer; adj. professor, Va. Union U., Samuel Dewitt Sch. of Theology, Evans-Smith Leadership Inst. 1982—; founder, CEO The Way of the Cross Comm. Devel. Corp., Inc., 1998—; bd. dirs. Women's Health, Va., Va. Bapt. Children's Home, Petersburg, 2001—; com. Va. State Health Dept., 1995-97. Author: (devotionals) The Word in Season, 1986, The Patience To Wait, Vol. I, 1988, Vol. II, 1992; contbg. author: Wise Women Bearing Gifts, 1988, Those Preachin' Women, 1988, Sister to Sister, 1995. Founder, pres. Black Women in Sisterhood for Action, Washington, 1979-82; vol. chaplain Martha Jefferson Hosp., Charlottesville, Va., 1993—; bd. dirs. AIDS Support Group, Charlottesville, 1990; mem. Fluvanna County Minority Health Coalition, 1993—; mem. Fluvanna County Commn. on Youth, 1999—; U.S. del. to Internat. Women's Yr. Conf. on Women, Mexico City, 1975; participant First All-Africa Theol. Conf./Bapt. World Alliance, Zimbabwe; selected by Women's Internat. Dem. Fedn. to represent U.S. as del. to World Congress on Women, Moscow, 1987, others; bd. dirs. Women's Health Va., 2000—. Named Disting. Black Woman, Black Women in Sisterhood for Action, 1982; recipient recognition for cmty. svc. Interfrat. Coun., Charlottesville, 1993, award for excellence Sister Care Internat., 1995, spl. achievement and cmty. svc. award Charlottesville Tribune, 1996. Mem. NAACP (pres. Fluvanna County chpt. 1979-81, cert. of appreciation 1994), Va. Women in Ministry (founder, pres. 1983-88, chaplain, Founder's award 1986, 90, 95). Avocations: reading, listening to music, sewing, travel, playing piano. Home: PO Box 39 18 Tabscott Rd Kents Store VA 23084-9731 Office: Way of Cross Bapt Ch State Rt 640 Palmyra VA 23084

BROWN, NANCY FIELD, editor; b. Troy, N.Y., Feb. 20, 1951; d. Robert Grant and Barbara Katherine (Field) B. BS in Journalism, Mich. State U., East Lansing, 1974. Asst. editor Mich. Am. Legion, Lansing, 1974-76, State Bar of Mich., Lansing, 1976-78, editor, 1976—, sr. dir. pubs., 1995-98, asst. exec. dir. publs., 1998—. Mem. Nat. Assn. Bar Execs. (cons. pubs. com. Chgo. chpt. 1989—), Mich. State U. Alumni Assn., Nat. Assn. Desktop Pubs., Am. Soc. Assn. Execs. Presbyterian. Avocations: reading, writing, photography, travel. Office: State Bar of Mich 306 Townsend St Lansing MI 48933-2012

BROWN, NANCY JANE, human resources specialist; b. Louisville, July 1, 1955; d. Charles Leonard and Melba Irene Brown. BA, Marshall U., 1977, MA, 1985, MS, 1988; postgrad., Va. Inst. Tech., 1998. Cert. nat. registered Safety Profls.; cert. tchr., W.Va., Ohio, first responder, Ohio. Human resources prof. Am. Elec. Power, Cheshire, Ohio, 1992-2000, safety and indsl. hygiene specialist, 1989-93, lab. tech., 1978-89; human resources and tng. specialist AKZO-Nobel Functional Chems. LLC, Gallipolis Ferry, W.Va., 2000—. Adj. prof. U. Rio Grande, Ohio, 1999—. EMT Pt. Pleasant Emergency Med. Svc., 1980-82; mem. adv. bd. U. Rio Grande, 1999-2000; pres. W.Va. chpt. Am. Soc. Safety Engrs., 1997-98; chair All-Ohio Safety Congress, Columbus, 1999-2001; hospitality com. Women's Internat. Network Utility Profls., Columbus, 1999-2001; mem. adv. bd. Gallipolis City Schs., 2001—. Named to Ohio Exemplary Women in Sci., 1985. Mem. DAR, ASSE, Am. Indsl. Hygiene Assn., Mid Ohio Valley Emergency Planning (pres. 1990), Soc. Human Resource Mgmt. Avocations: preventive medicine, nutrition, lapidary work, cultural activities, landscape gardening, dogs. Home: PO Box 939 Gallipolis OH 45631 Office: AKZO-Nobel Functional Chems LLC PO Box 1721 Gallipolis Ferry WV 25515-1721 E-mail: nancy.j.brown@akzo-nobel.com.

BROWN, NORMAN DONALD, history educator; b. Pitts., June 28, 1935; s. Donald Madden and Regina Deborah (Koehler) B.; m. Betty Jane Aldrich, Apr. 2, 1966; children: David, Tracy. BA summa cum laude, Ind. U., 1957; MA, U. N.C., 1959, PhD, 1963. Instr. history U. Tex., Austin, 1962-65, asst. prof., 1965-69, assoc. prof., 1969-83, prof., 1983-84, Barbara White Stuart Centennial prof. Tex. history, 1984—. Author: Daniel Webster and the Politics of Availability, 1969, Edward Stanly, 1974, Hood, Bonnet, and Little Brown Jug, 1984; editor: One of Cleburne's Command, 1980, Journey to Pleasant Hill, 1982. Woodrow Wilson fellow, 1957. Fellow: Tex. State Hist. Assn. (coun. 1989—93, 2d v.p. 1997—98, 1st v.p. 1998—99, pres. 1999—2000, coun. 2000—02); mem.: Civil War Preservation Trust, Civil War Round Table Assocs., Soc. Civil War Historians (adv. bd. 1986—), Soc. Historians Early Am. Republic, So. Hist. Assn., Orgn. Am. Historians, Sons of Union Vets. of the Civil War, Phi Kappa Phi, Phi Alpha Theta, Phi Beta Kappa. Democrat. United Methodist. Avocation: book and stamp collecting. Home: 2607 Barton Skyway Austin TX 78704-4602 Office: Univ Tex Dept History Austin TX 78712

BROWN, OLEN RAY, medical microbiology and toxicology expert witness, researcher, educator, consultant, writer; b. Hastings, Okla., Aug. 18, 1935; s. Willis Edward and Rosa Nell (Fulton) B.; m. Pollyana June King, Aug. 30, 1958; children: Barbara Kathryn, Diana Carol, David Gregory. BS in Lab. Tech., Okla. U., 1958, MS in Bacteriology, 1960, PhD in Microbiology, 1964. Diplomate Am. Bd. Toxicology. Instr. Sch. Medicine, U. Mo., Columbia, 1964-65, asst. prof., 1965-70, assoc. prof., 1970-77, prof. dept. molecular microbiology and immunology, 1981-96, rsch. prof., 1996—2001; joint ap-

pointments, prof. depts. microbiology and biomed. scis. Coll. Vet. Medicine, U. Mo., 1977-96, prof. biomed. scis., 1987-96. Guest lectr. Ross U., St. Kitts, W.I., 1984, 88; asst. dir. Dalton Rsch. Ctr., U. Mo., 1974-78, Dalton rsch. investigator grad. sch., 1968—; grant peer reviewer for program projects SCOR and Superfund grants NIH, 1979, Nat. Inst. Environ. Health Scis., Dept. Commerce, EPA, 1986, 90-99, Am. Inst. Biol. Scis. for Dept. Def., USAMRMC, Fund for Improvement of Secondary Edn., 2002; cons. drug abuse policy office White House, 1982, Immunol. Vaccines, Inc., Columbia, 1984—, Lab. Support, Inc., Chgo., 1988-89, Ea. Rsch. Group, Lexington, Mass., 1991—, Teltech, Mpls., 1992—, Scis. Internat., Inc., Alexandria, Va.; judge top 100 products for 1996, 99, Rsch. and Devel. Mag. Author: Laboratory Manual for Veterinary Microbiology, 1973, The Art and Science of Expert Witnessing, 2002; co-author: elem. and advanced lab. manuals for med. microbiology, 2 vols., 1978, 79; contbr. Progress in Clinical Research, Vol. 21, 1978, 79, Oxygen, 5th Internat. Hyperbaric Conf., Vols. I, II, 1974, 79, numerous articles to profl. jours.; book and film critic AAAS, Washington, 1986—; item preparer Am. Coll. Test, Med. Coll. Admissions Test, 1981—; mem. editorial staff Biomed. Letters, 1981—; responder Sci. and Math. Helpline for Mus. Sci. Discovery, Harrisburg, Pa., 1996—, reviewer profl. jours. Track and field ofcl. U. Mo. and Big Eight Conf., Columbia, 1979-86. Investigative rsch. grantee Office Naval Rsch., Dept. Def., 1968-81, NIH, 1976-88, NIEHS, 1981-94, 95—, USAID, 1983-86, Nat. Inst. Dental Health Scis., 1989-92. Fellow Am. Inst. Chemists (cert. chemistry and chem engring., profl. program bd. 1989-90, sd com. chemistry and environ. concerns); mem. Top One Percent Soc., Soc. Toxicology, Internat. Soc. Study Xenobiotics, Am. Chem. Soc., Am. Heart Assn., Internat. Soc. Exposure Analysts, Nat. Space Soc., Oxygen Soc., Columbia Track Club (sec.-treas. 1979-82). Avocations: long-distance running, oil painting. Office: U Mo Dalton Rsch Ctr Columbia MO 65211-0001

BROWN, OMER FORREST, II, lawyer; b. Somerville, NJ, Mar. 4, 1947; s. George Alvin and Frances (Schnitzler) B.; m. Sandra J. Cannon, Apr. 3, 1982. AB, Rutgers U., 1969; JD, Cornell U., 1972. Bar: NJ 1972, DC 1974, US Supreme Ct. 1976. Dept. atty. gen. dept. law and pub. safety State of NJ, Trenton, NJ, 1972-75; sr. trial atty. US Dept. Energy, Washington, 1979-83; ptnr. Davis Wright Tremaine, Washington, 1987-96, Harmon, Wilmot & Brown, LLP, Washington, 1997—. Bd. dir., sec. VideoTakes, Inc., Arlington, Va., 1986—; vis. lectr. Cornell U. Law Sch., 1993-95, 2002—; mem. OECD Contact Group on Nuc. Safety Assistance for Eastern Europe, 1994—; mem. G-7 Joint Task Force on Ukrainian Nuc. Legis., 1996—. Contbr. numerous articles on energy, enviro. and ins. law to legal jour. Capt. USAR, 1969-75. Recipient Class of 1931 award Rutgers U. Alumni Assn., 1979, Loyal Son of Rutgers award, 1980. Mem. ABA (various offices tort and ins. practice sect. 1981-96, coord. group on energy law 1995-99), Internat. Bar Assn., Fed. Bar Assn., DOE Contractor Atty. Assn., Univ. Club (Washington). Democrat. Roman Catholic. Address: PO Box 419 Saint Michaels MD 21663-0419 E-mail: omerb@aol.com.

BROWN, OTHA NATHANIEL, JR., political official, retired educator; b. DeQueen, Ark., July 19, 1931; s. Otha Brown and Elizabeth Gossitt; m. Marjorie Gay, June 19, 1956 (div. Feb. 1967); m. Lela Evelyn Brown, Dec. 30, 1975; children: Darrick O., Leland K. BS, Ctrl. State U., Wilberforce, Ohio, 1952; MA, U. Conn., 1956; 6th Yr. Profl. Diploma, U. Bridgeport, 1959. Cert. ednl. adminstr., sch. counselor, Conn. Tchr. Bd. Edn., Stratford, Conn., 1957-61, tchr., counselor Stamford, Conn., 1961-90; guidance dir., counselor J.M. Wright Tech. Sch., Stamford, Conn., 1990-92; coord. state program Dept. Human Resources, State of Conn., Hartford, 1992-93; dir., CEO regional campus U. Conn., Waterbury, 1994-98. Mem. State Jud. Task Force, Hartford, 1987-91; mem. internat. affairs com. Am. Waterworks Assn., Denver, 1992-99; mem. adv. bd. Patriot Nat. Bank, Stamford, 1994—. Author: (poetry) Remembering. . ., 1977; contbr. articles to profl. jours. Mem. Norwalk Common Coun., City of Norwalk, Conn., 1963-69, 77-81, majority leader, 1968, coun. pres., 1980-81; mem. Conn. Ho. of Reps., Hartford, 1966-72; trustee, sec. U. Conn., Storrs, 1975-93; commr. 2d Taxing Dist. and Water Dept., South Norwalk, Conn., 1982—, chmn., 1982—; charter mem. Action Housing, Inc., mem. exec. bd., 1970—. 1st lt. U.S. Army, 1952-54. Recipient The Univ. medal U. Conn., 1994; named Young Man of Yr., Jaycees, 1967; named to Hall of Fame, Ctrl. State U., Wilberforce, Ohio, 1996. Mem.: NAACP (v.p. 1967—69, F.D. Wharton, Jr. Lifetime Achievement award 2002), Norwalk Area Improvement League (founder, pres. 1976—), Masons, Elks, Alpha Phi Alpha (pres., dir.). Democrat. Avocations: writing, chorale singing, politics, jazz, travel. Home: 21 Shorefront Park Norwalk CT 06854-3752 Office: 2d Taxing Dist 164 Water St Norwalk CT 06854-3739 E-mail: o.brown719@aol.com.

BROWN, PAMELA WEDD, artist; b. Cauderan, Gironde, France, Nov. 21, 1928; came to U.S., 1953; d. William Basil and Nora Marsh (van Nostrand) Wedd; m. Charles Freeman Brown, Nov. 29, 1952; children: Penelope Susan, Nicholas Wedd. Student, Ecole des Beaux Arts, Paris, 1947-48, Academie Julian, 1946-51. Free lance fashion illustrator, Paris, 1947-48; dir. arts and crafts YWCA, Toronto, Ont., Can., 1951; dir. Washington Womens Arts Ctr., 1987-88; dir., pres. Washington Printmakers Gallery, 1990-91; co-pres. Studio Gallery, 1992-94. Artist in residence The Art Barn, Washington, 1986. Designer book plate Nat. Mus. Women in Arts Libr., 1985; represented in permanent collections Libr. of Congress, NIH, Nat. Mus. Am. History, Nat. Mus. Women in Arts. Precinct capt. Bd. of Elections and Ethics, Washington, 1970-80. Recipient First prize drawing, Academie Julian, Paris, 1947, Purchase award, The Jr. League, Newport News, Va., 1971, Equal awards, The Art League, Alexandria, Va., 1980, 1982, 1985, 1988, 2000, 2001. Mem. Studio Gallery D.C. (assoc.), The Art League, WPA/Corcoran, Woman's Nat. Dem. Club. Avocations: music, tennis, sailing, dance. Home: 3500 Macomb St NW Washington DC 20016-3162

BROWN, PATRICIA IRENE, retired law librarian, lawyer; b. Boston; d. Joseph Raymond and Harriet A. (Taylor) B. BA, Suffolk U., 1955, JD, 1965, MBA, 1970; MST, Gordon Conwell Theol. Sem., 1977. Bar: Mass. 1965. Libr. asst. Suffolk U., Boston, 1951-60, asst. libr., 1960-65, asst. law libr., 1965-85, assoc. law libr., 1985-92; ret.; human resources counselor Winthrop (Mass.) Sr. Ctr., 1993—. Author: A League of My Own: Memoir of a Pitcher for the All-American Girls Professional Baseball League, 2003. Dir. Referral/Resource Ctr., Union Congl. Ch., Winthrop, Mass.; vol. health benefits counselor Mass. Dept. Elder Affairs, 1994- . First Woman inducted into Nat. Baseball Hall of Fame, Cooperstown, N.Y., 1988, All- Am. Girls Profl. Baseball League, 1950-51. Mem. Assn. Am. Law Librs., Am. Congl. Assn. (bd. dirs. 1992—), Mass. Bar Assn. Avocations: television and movie history, walking, computers. Home: 1100 Governors Dr Apt 26 Winthrop MA 02152-3254 E-mail: pbrown@acad.suffolk.edu.

BROWN, PAUL EDMONDSON, lawyer; b. Van Buren County, Iowa, Dec. 24, 1915; s. William Allen and Margaret (Edmondson) B.; m. Lorraine Hill, Jan. 9, 1944; 1 child, Scott. BA, U. Iowa, 1938, JD with distinction, 1941. Bar: Iowa 1941, U.S. Supreme Ct. 1966. Ptnr. Mahoney, Brown, Mahoney, Boone, Iowa, 1946-52; v.p., counsel Bankers Life Co. (now Prin. Fin. Group), Des Moines, 1952-80; of counsel Grefe & Sidney, Des Moines, 1980-84, Davis, Hockensberg, Wine, Brown, Koehn, Shors, Des Moines, 1984-91; pvt. practice Des Moines, 1991—. Atty. County of Boone, Iowa, 1948-52; pres. Iowa Life Ins. Assn., Des Moines, 1980-85. With U.S. Army, 1942-46, col. USAR, 1946-70. Named Outstanding Young Man of Iowa, Iowa State Jr. C. of C., 1948; named to Iowa Ins. Hall of Fame, 2001. Mem. ABA, Iowa Bar Assn., Polk County Bar Assn., Assn. Life Ins. Counsel, U. Iowa Alumni Assn. (mem. Pres.' Club and various coms.), Civil War Roundtable, World War II State Monument Com., Downtown Des Moines Kiwanis Club (pres. 1961, Hixson fellow 1999). Republican. Congregationalist. Home and Office: 5804 Harwood Dr Des Moines IA 50312-1206 Fax: 515-255-7900. E-mail: peb200@aol.com.

BROWN, PAUL FREMONT, aerospace engineer, educator; b. Osage, Iowa, Mar. 10, 1921; s. Charles Fremont and Florence Alma (Olson) B.; m. Alice Marie Culver, Dec. 5, 1943; children: Diane, Darrell, Judith, Jana. BA in Edn. and Natural Sci., Dickinson State Coll., 1942; MS in Cybernetic Systems, San Jose State U., 1971. Profl. quality engr., Calif., 1978; cert. reliabilty engr., Am. Soc. Quality Control, 1976. Test engr., supr. Boeing Aircraft Corp., Seattle, 1948-56; design specialist, propulsion systems Lockheed Missiles and Space Co., Sunnyvale, Calif., 1956-59, supr. system effectiveness, 1959-66, staff engr., 1966-76, mgr. product assurance Hubble Space Telescope Program, 1976-83; v.p. rsch., devel. Gen. Agriponics Inc. of Hawaii, 1971-76; owner Diversatek Engrng. and Product Assurance Cons., 1983—. Instr., lectr. San Jose State U. Author: From Here to Retirement, 1988, The Winds of Hope, 2002; contbr. articles to profl. jours. Active in United Presbyn. Ch., 1965—; scoutmaster Boy Scouts Am., 1963-65. Served to 1st lt. USAF, 1943-46. Recipient awards for tech. papers, Lockheed Missiles and Space Co., 1973-75. Mem. Am. Soc. Quality Control, AIAA, Toastmasters Club (Sunnyvale, Calif.), Calif. Writers' Club (pres. South Bay br. 1993-94). Home and Office: 19608 Braemar Dr Saratoga CA 95070-5046 E-mail: anp3943@aol.com.

BROWN, PAUL M. lawyer; b. Jan. 10, 1938; s. I. Harry and Rose L. (Kresge) B.; m. Helga J. Fischer, Aug. 4, 1962 (div. 1977); children: Stephanie J., William A.; m. Ruth Reiter, June 28, 1986. Student, Williams Coll., 1955-57; BS in Econs., U. Pa., 1959; LLB, Columbia U., 1962. Bar: N.Y. 1963, U.S. Ct. Appeals (2d cir.) 1963, U.S. Dist. Ct. (so. and ea. dists.) N.Y. 1964, U.S. Dist. Ct. Mass. 1981, U.S. Ct. Appeals (3d cir.), U.S. Ct. Appeals (1st cir.) 1982, U.S. Dist. Ct. (we. dist.) N.Y. 1983, U.S. Ct. Appeals (6th cir.) 1983, U.S. Dist. Ct. R.I. 1985, U.S. Dist. Ct. (ea. dist.) Mich. 1986. Assoc. Berman & Frost, N.Y.C., 1963-66; ptnr. Havens, Wandless, Slitt and Tighe, N.Y.C., 1966-74, Whitman and Ransom, N.Y.C., 1975-94, Parson & Brown, N.Y.C., 1994-99, Satterlee Stephens Burke & Burke, N.Y.C., 1999—. Councilman Closter, N.J., 1970-74; police commr. Closter, 1970-73; trustee No. Valley Regional H.S., Demarest, N.J., 1972. With USAR, 1962-68. Mem. Assn. of Bar of City of N.Y., N.Y. State Bar Assn., Fed. Bar Coun., Am. Arbitration Assn. (panel of arbitrators), Univ. Club, Columbia Golf & Country Club, Las Campanas (N.Mex.) Club. Democrat. Office: Satterlee Stephens Burke & Burke 230 Park Ave New York NY 10169-0079 E-mail: pbrown@ssbb.com.

BROWN, PAUL NEELEY, federal judge; b. Denison, Tex., Oct. 4, 1926; s. Arthur Chester and Nora Frances (Hunter) B.; m. Frances Morehead, May 8, 1955; children: Paul Gregory, David H. II. JD, U. Tex., 1950. Assoc. Keith & Brown, Sherman, Tex., 1951-53, Brown & Brown, Sherman, 1953; asst. U.S. atty. for Ea. Dist. Tex. Texarkana and Tyler, Tex., 1953-59; U.S. atty. Ea. Dist. Tex., Tyler, 1959-61; ptnr. Brown & Brown and Brown Brothers & Perkins, Sherman, 1961-65, Brown and Perkins, Sherman, 1965; sole practice, Sherman, 1965-67; ptnr. Brown & Hill, Sherman, 1967, Brown Kennedy Hill & Minshew, Sherman, 1967-71, Brown & Hill, Sherman, 1971-76, Brown Hill Ellis & Brown, Sherman, 1976-85; U.S. dist. judge U.S. Dist. Ct. (ea. dist.) Tex., Sherman, 1985—, sr. US dist. judge, 2001. Served with USN, 1944-46, 50-51. Fellow Tex. Bar Found.; mem. Rotary. Presbyterian. Office: US Dist Ct Fed Bldg 101 E Pecan St Sherman TX 75090-5989

BROWN, PAUL SHERMAN, lawyer; b. June 26, 1921; s. Paul Michael and Norma (Sherman) Brown; m. Ann Wilson, Feb. 7, 1959; 1 child, Paul S. BS in Commerce, St. Louis U., 1943, JD cum laude, 1951. Bar: Mo. 51, U.S. Dist. Ct. (ea. dist.) Mo. 51, U.S. Ct. Appeals (8th cir.) 51, U.S. Supreme Ct. 66. Shareholder Brown & James, P.C., St. Louis, 1980—. Instr. St. Louis U. Night Law Sch., 1978—; lectr. in field; mem. com. on civil pattern jury instructions Mo. Supreme Ct. Contbr. articles to profl. jours. Fellow: Internat. Soc. Barristers, Internat. Acad. Trial Lawyers, Am. Coll. Trial Lawyers; mem.: ABA (vice-chmn. com. consumer products liability 1977—78), Am. Judicature Soc., Bar Assn. Met. St. Louis (pres. 1970—71), Lawyers Assn. St. Louis, Am. Bd. Trial Advocates, Mo. Bar Assn. (bd. govs. 1963—67), Order of Woolsack, St. Louis Amateur Athletic Assn. (bd. dirs. 1974—76, pres. 1976—78), Alpha Sigma Nu. Roman Catholic. Home: 7331 Kingsbury Blvd Saint Louis MO 63130-4143 Office: Brown & James 1010 Market St Ste 18 Saint Louis MO 63101-2270

BROWN, PEGGY ANN, artist; b. Ft. Wayne, Ind., Mar. 15, 1934; d. Nicholas Henry and Stella Jo (Meiners) Mattes; m. James Russel Brown, Oct. 4, 1958; children: Kurt R., James L., Nick W. BS in Journalism, Marquette U., 1956. Writer, prodr. WOWO Radio, Ft. Wayne, 1956-58; artist Nashville, Ind., 1970—. Mem. Am. Watercolor Soc. (bd. dirs. 1990-92, award 1980), Midwest Watercolor Soc. (bd. dirs. 1977-79), Nat. Watercolor Soc. (Best Show award 1993, Windsor-Newton award 2001), Watercolor USA Hon. Soc. (Merit award 1994, Coors Brewery award 2001), Allied Artists Am. (gold medal 1978), Rocky Mt. Watercolor Soc. (Merit award 1994), Watercolor Soc. Ind. (Best Show award 1992, 94, 2001). Avocations: camping, hiking, golfing, gardening, stitching. Home and Office: 1541 Clay Lick Rd Nashville IN 47448-8641 Home (Winter): 36743 E Eldorado Lake Rd Eustis FL 32736 E-mail: jpwestbreeze@aol.com.

BROWN, PERRY JOE, university dean; Student, Foothill Coll., Los Altos, Calif., 1962-63; BS in Forestry, Utah State U., 1967, MS in Forest Recreation, 1968, PhD in Outdoor Recreation & Social Psych, 1971; postgrad., U. Mich., 1968, 69-70. Lectr. forest sci. Utah State U., Logan, 1968-71, asst. prof. forest sci., 1971-73; asst. prof. recreatin resources Colo. State U., 1973-74, assoc. prof. recreation resources, 1974-79, prof., dept. head forest recreation resources, 1979-88, asst. dean Coll. Forestry, 1982-84; assoc. dean instrn., continuing edn. and internat. programs Oreg. State U., 1988-94; dean Sch. Forestry, prof. forest resources U. Mont., Missoula, 1994—, dir. Mont. Forest and Conservation Expt. Sta., 1994—. Social sci. project leader Oreg. State U.-Nat. Park Svc. Coop. Park Studies Unit, 1990-93; interim dir. Oreg. Tourism Inst., Oreg. State Sys. Higher Edn., 1987-89; mem. adv. bd. Va. Poly. Inst. and State U. Coll. Forestry and Wildlife; mem. numerous panels and task forces NAS, regional planning commns., fed. and state agys. and domestic and internat. profl. orgns.; profl. cons. to numerous fed., state and internat. land mgmt. agys., univs., cos. and the Forest Ecosystem Mgmt. Assessment Team social sci. team; leader Rocky Mountain Coop. Ecosys. Studies Unit; mem. nat. adv. bd. Nat. Forest Found., 2002—. Editor Utah Tourism and Recreation Rev., 1972-73; assoc. editor Jour. Leisure Rsch., 1977-79, Jour. Leisure Scis., 1982-85; mem. editl. bd. Jour. Forest and Landscape Rsch., 1993-99; author over 110 books, articles, papers and reports including 2 books and 16 book chpts. Recipient Cert. of Appreciation, USDA Forest Svc., 1988. Fellow Acad. Leisure Scis.; mem. Soc. Am. Foresters, Human Dimensions in Wildlife Study Group, Internat. Union Forestry Rsch. Orgns. (leader forest recreation, landscape planning and nature conservation sect. 1986-96, dep. coord. divsn. 6 1996—), Nat. Assn. Profl. Forestry Schs. and Colls. (western region chair, exec. bd. 1996-97, pres.-elect 1998-00, pres. 2000-02, past pres. 2002—). Office: U Mont Coll Forestry and Conservation Missoula MT 59812-0001

BROWN, PETER GILBERT, philosopher, educator, tree farmer; b. New Haven, Jan. 15, 1940; s. C. Victor and Margaret Elizabeth (Tullock) B.; children: David, Ethan, Margaret. BA, Haverford Coll., 1961; MA, Columbia U., 1964, PhD, 1969. Tutor St. John's Coll., Annapolis, Md., 1965-70; asst. v.p. for research Urban Inst., Washington, 1970-73; vis. fellow Battelle Seattle Research Center, 1973-74; fellow Acad. Contemporary Problems, Washington, 1974-76; dir. Ctr. Philosophy and Pub. Policy U. Md., 1976-81, acting dean/assoc. dean Sch. Pub. Affairs, 1980-84; asst. exec. v.p. U. Md. System, 1984-86; prof. pub. affairs U. Md., 1984-99, dir. environ. programs Sch. Pub. Affairs, 1989-97; prof. McGill U., 1998—. Vis. prof. Woodrow Wilson Sch., Princeton U., fall 1986, spring 1988, prof., dir. McGill Sch. Environment, 1998-2002; mem. sci. and tech. adv. bd. Environment Can., Ga. Tech. Sch. Pub. Policy; bd. dirs. Morgan Arboretum, Huntsman Marine Sci. Ctr. Author/editor: Restoring the Public Trust; The Commonwealth of Life; contbr. articles to profl. jours. Fellow: Inst. Soc. Ethics and Life Scis. Mem. Soc. Of Friends. Mailing: PO Box 268 Sargentville ME 04673-0268 Office: c/o McGill Sch Environment 3534 University Ave Montreal QC Canada H3A 2A7 E-mail: peter.g.brown@mcgill.ca. *Over the past thirty years I have endeavored to broaden and deepen our ideas about policy-oriented research. We need to examine our basic moral and scientific concepts as they apply to public policy. Without examining these concepts and the obligations they imply we are without standards to judge the legitimacy of our policies and the means to determine the ideals to which we should aspire together and as individuals. My most recent work has been on constructing a macro-economics compatible with our obligations to the commonwealth of life.*

BROWN, PETER MEGARGEE, lawyer, writer, lecturer; b. Cleve., Mar. 15, 1922; s. George Estabrook and Miriam (Megargee) B.; m. Alexandra Johns Stoddard, May 18, 1974; children: Peter, Blair Tillyer, Andree de Rapalyee, Nathaniel Holmes; stepchildren: Alexandra, Brooke Stoddard, Wallace Davis. Student, U. Calif., Berkeley, 1943-44; BA, Yale U., 1945, JD, 1948. Bar: N.Y. 1949. Spl. asst. atty. gen. State N.Y. and asst. counsel N.Y. State Crime Commn., 1951-53; asst. U.S. atty. So. Dist. N.Y., 1953-55, spl. asst., 1956; ptnr. firm Cadwalader, Wickersham & Taft, N.Y.C., 1959-82, head litigation and ethics coms.; ptnr. Brown & Seymour, N.Y.C., 1983-96; counsellor-at-law Peter Megargee Brown, N.Y.C., 1996—. Mem. Mayor's Com. on Judiciary, 1965-72, vice chmn., 1972-74 Author: The Art of Questioning: Thirty Maxims of Cross-Examination, 1987, Flights of Memory-Days Before Yesterday, 1989, Rascals: The Selling of the Legal Profession, 1989, One World at a Time: Tales of Murder, Joy and Love, 1991, Village: Where to Live and How to Live, 1997, Riot of the Century (Civil War Draft Riot 1863), 1999; author essays, articles on law profession, life and humor, pub. nationally. Mem. N.Y. County Rep. Com., 1958—; counsel on crime to Nelson Rockefeller, Campaign for Gov. N.Y.S., 1968; bd. dirs. Yale Alumni Fund, 1979-84; bd. dirs., pres. Episcopal Ch. Found., 1989-93; master of ceremonies Yale Class of 1944 50th Reunion, 1994, 55th reunion, 1999; chmn., co-founder Design and Art Soc., Ltd., N.Y.C.; pres. Trustees Riot Relief Fund; bd. regent Cath. St. John Divine; founding mem. Henry Morrison Flagler Mus., Palm Beach, Fla.; mediator, East Side N.Y. gang warfare, 1956-57; counsel Grand Jury Assn. N.Y. County, 1956-79; orientation specialist U.S. Army WWII, 1943-46; editor in ch. Camp Bowie Blade (commendation). Decorated knight Order St. John of Hosp. of Jerusalem, Soc. of Anchor Cross; recipient award for svc. to profession Fed. Bar Assn., N.Y., N.J. and Conn., 1962; recipient Trustees Gold medal for disting. svc., Fed. Bar Coun., 1971; Chmn.'s award Yale Alumni Fund, 1979, Disting. Svc. award Class of 1944, Yale U., 1983, Henry Knox Sherrill medal for outstanding svc. Episcopal Ch. Found., 1993, Speakers prize Browning Sch., Headmaster's medal for pub. svc. St. Andrew's Sch.; Named record scorer U.S. Army Phys. Efficiency Test 1943 (697 out of possible 700 a score still unbroken). Fellow Am. Bar Found., Am. Coll. Trial Lawyers, N.Y. State Bar Found.; mem. ABA, World Assn. Lawyers (founding), Soc. Colonial Wars, New England Soc., Sons of the Revolution, N.Y. State Bar Assn., Assn. of Bar of City of N.Y., Fed. Bar Coun. Found. (trustee, pres. 1961-62, chmn. bd. 1962-64, chmn. judiciary com. 1960-85), chmn. planning and program com. 2d cir. judicial conf. 1976-80), St. Nicholas Soc. (past pres.), Delta Kappa Epsilon (Phi chpt. Yale), Phi Delta Phi (magister Waite Inn 1947, pres. province I 1950-55). Episcopalian (vestryman, sr. warden 1961-77). Clubs: Union (N.Y.C.); Coral Beach (Bermuda). Office: 1125 Park Ave Ste 6A New York NY 10128-1243

BROWN, PETER OGDEN, lawyer; b. Ithaca, N.Y., Aug. 20, 1940; s. Frederick Shiras and Helen (Ogden) Brown; m. Nancy Tredwell Sunderland, Aug. 25, 1962; children: Jeffrey Scott, Douglas Henderson, Lori MacArthur. BA cum laude, Amherst Coll., 1962; LLD, Duke U., 1965. Assoc. Harter, Secrest & Emery, Rochester, N.Y., 1965-73, ptnr., 1973-80; sr. v.p., mgr. personal banking and trust group Chase Lincoln First Bank N.A., Rochester, 1981-90; exec. v.p., chief operating officer The Glenmede Trust Co., Phila., 1990-92; ptnr. Harter, Secrest & Emery, Rochester, 1993-2000, counsel, 2001—. Co-author: How to Live and Die with New York Probate, 1975, Proceedings of the 25th Univ. of Miami Institute on Estate Planning, 1991; contbr. articles to profl. jours. Overseer U. Mus. of U. Pa., Phila., 1991-93; bd. trustees Colgate Rochester Div. Sch., 1987-96, Capital Growth Mgmt. Funds, 1993—, TT Internat. Funds, 2000—, Healthcare Trustees of N.Y. State, 2000-03; mem. Acad. of Music Com., Phila.; mem. endowment com. Phila. Mus. Art, 1990-92; dir. Meml. Art Gallery of U. Rochester, 1992—, pres., chmn., 1980-84; bd. dirs., treas. Rochester Health Care, Inc., 1993-95; dir. Rocester Gen. Hosp., 1981-90, 93-2000, chmn. Rochester Gen. Hosp/The Genesee Hosp, 1999-2000; dir. Viahealth, Inc., 1999-2000; mem. bd. mgrs. Eastman Sch. Music, 1994—; chancellor Episcopal Diocese of Rochester, 1979-90, 98-2002; pres. Rochester Hist. Soc., 2001—. Fellow Am. Coll. Trust and Estate Counsel; mem. Am. Inst. ARchaeology (v.p. Rochester chpt.),Am. Bankers Assn. (mem. exec. com. trust divsn., chmn. personal svc. com. 1989-92), N.Y. State Bar Assn. (chmn. com. on taxation of trusts and estates 1988-89), Fla. Bar, Pa. Bar Assn., Rochester Hist. Soc. (trustee 2001—, pres. 2002—), Genessee Valley Club (treas. 1987-89). Republican. Avocations: archaeology, military history, painting, tennis, golf. E-mail: pbrown@hselaw.com.

BROWN, PHILIP HENRY, psychiatric social worker; b. N.Y.C., May 18, 1952; s. Max B. and Sylvia (Lippman) B.; m. Doreen O. Muller, Aug. 1, 1976; children: Caitlin, Matthew. BA, U. Conn., 1974, MSW, 1978. Bd. cer. diplomate in clin. social work. Mem. VISTA Conn. Dept. Corrections, Hartford, 1974-76; psychiat. social worker div. psychiatry Waterbury Hosp., Waterbury, Conn., 1978-85, Winchester Pub. Schs., Winsted, Conn., 1980-83; coord. emergency svc. Day Kimball Hosp., Putnam, Conn., 1985-87; pvt. practice psychiat. social work Plainfield, Conn., 1985-89; pvt. practice Canterbury, Conn., 1989—. Cons. New Milford (Conn.) Hospice, 1985-86; instr. psychology and sociology U. Conn., Torrington, Waterbury, Groton, Conn., 1981—, Northwestern Conn. Community Coll, Winsted, 1982-85, Plainfield (Conn.) Bd. Edn., 1997—. Instr. Conn. Emergency Med. Svcs., Hartford, 1981—; bd. dirs. Ea. Conn. Mental Health Bd., Norwich, Conn., 1986. Mem. Acad. Cert. Social Workers, Nat. Assn. Assn. Social Workers (Conn. bd. dirs. 1982-86), Washington Red Cross (bd. dirs. 1985). Home: 30 Major Dr Plainfield CT 06374-1720 Office: Canterbury Profl Bldg PO Box 266 39 S Canterbury Rd Canterbury CT 06331-1520

BROWN, PRESTON, lawyer; b. NYC, Oct. 6, 1936; s. John Mason and Catherine (Meredith) B.; m. Betsey G. Pinckney, Oct. 9, 1965 (div. Mar. 1982); children: Catherine St. George, John Preston; m. Eva N. Kasten, June 10, 2000. AB, Harvard U., 1958, LLB, 1961. Bar: N.Y. 1962, D.C. 1969, U.S. Supreme Ct. 1974. Assoc. Davis, Polk & Wardwell, N.Y.C., 1961-67; adminstrv. asst., del N.Y. State Constl. Conv., Albany, 1967; spl. asst. to under sec. HUD, Washington, 1967-69; resident counsel Curtis, Mallet-Prevost, Colt & Mosle, Washington, 1969-75, ptnr., 1975—. Contbr. articles to profl. jours. Bd. dirs. Goodwill Industries Am., Washington, 1969-75, Young Audiences of D.C., 1985-92, 93-99, 2000—, pres., 1989-92. Mem.: ABA, Knickerbocker Club NYC. Episcopalian. Home: 2231 48th St NW Washington DC 20007-1036 Office: Curtis Mallet-Prevost Colt & Mosle 1200 New Hampshire Ave NW Ste 430 Washington DC 20036 E-mail: pbrown@cm-p.com., PresBrown3@msn.com.

BROWN, RALPH SAWYER, JR., retired lawyer, business executive; b. Cohasset, Mass., July 21, 1931; s. Ralph Sawyer and Rosemary (Wyman) B.; m. Elizabeth Atkinson Rash, June 12, 1953; children— Lucy Victoria Phillips, Alexander Sawyer Batson. BA, Swarthmore Coll., 1954; LLB, Harvard U., 1957. Bar: Mass. bar 1957, N.Y. State bar 1963. Assoc. Hutchins & Wheeler, Boston, 1957-62, Carter, Ledyard & Milburn, N.Y.C., 1962-68; ptnr. Janklow & Traum, N.Y.C., 1968-71; sec., asst. gen. counsel Indian Head, Inc., N.Y.C., 1971-76, v.p., treas., 1976-79; v.p., gen. counsel, sec. Esquire, Inc., N.Y.C., 1979-83, sr. v.p., gen. counsel, sec., 1983-84; assoc. counsel Paramount Communications Inc., N.Y.C., 1984-93, sr. counsel, 1993-94. Mem. Phi Beta Kappa. Home: 160 W 86th St Ph 4 New York NY 10024-4074

BROWN, RAY KENT, biochemist, physician, educator; b. Columbus, Ohio, Apr. 7, 1924; s. Ray Stemen and Grace (Nunemaker) B.; m. Gertrude Lydia Harris, Jan. 25, 1947 (dec. Feb. 1998); children— Kimberly Brown, Kitene Kading, Kevin; m. Dorothy Skinner, Mar. 19, 1998. BA, Ohio State U., 1944, MD, 1947, MS, 1948; PhD, Harvard U., 1951. Intern Boston City Hosp., 1947-48; sr. asst. surgeon USPHS, Bethesda, Md., 1951-53; asst. dir. div. labs. and research N.Y. State Dept. Health, Albany, 1953-59, assoc. dir. div., 1959-63; asst. prof. biochemistry Albany Med. Coll., 1954-56, assoc. prof., 1956-61, prof., 1961-63, Wayne State U. Sch. Medicine, 1963-96, chmn. dept. biochemistry, 1963-87, prof. emeritus, 1996—. Mem. Highland Twp. (Mich.) Planning Commn., 1968-96. Served with U.S. Army, 1943-45, with USPHS, 1951-53. Mem. Am. Soc. Biol. Chemistry (Travel award 1958, 61, 64), Am. Assn. Immunologists, Biochem. Soc. Gt. Britain, Am. Chem. Soc. Home: 3820 Middle Rd Highland MI 48357-3044

BROWN, REGINALD JUDE, federal agency administrator; BS, U.S. Mil. Acad., 1961; MPA, Harvard U., 1965. Dir. adminstrn. Mitre Corp., McLean, Va., 1972-73; dep. adminstr. Office of Food, Cost of Living Coun., Washington, 1973-74; assoc. dir. Def. Manpower Commn., Washington, 1974-75; prin. analyst Congl. Budget Office, Washington, 1975-77; exec. dir. Pres.'s Commn. on Mil. Compensation, Washington, 1977-78; dir. Energy Div., Office of Price Monitoring, Coun.on Wage and Price Stability, Washington, 1979; exec. v.p. DECA Group Inc., Miami, Fla., 1979-81; sr. fellow Ctr. for Strategic and Internat. Studies, Washington, 1982-89; asst. adminstr. AID, Washington, 1989—; asst. secy. army manpower reserve affairs U.S. Dept. Defense,

Washington, 2001—. Co-author: The Lessons of Wage and Price Controls, 1977; contbr. articles to jours. in field. Decorated Meritorious Svc. medal, Bronze Star. Republican. Office: US Dept Defense Manpower Reserve Affairs 111 Army Pentagon Washington DC 20310-0111 Office Fax: 703-614-5975.

BROWN, RHONDA ROCHELLE, chemist, health facility administrator, lawyer; b. Shelbyville, Ky., July 13, 1956; d. Clifton Theophilus and Fannie Mae (Lawson) B. BA in Chemistry, U. Md., 1978; MA, Central Mich. U., 1983; JD, No. Va. Law Sch., 1992. Bar: Wash. 1998, D.C. 1994, U.S. Dist. Ct. D.C., U.S. Dist. Ct. Md. Analytical chemist Dept. Health and Mental Hygiene, Annapolis, Md., 1978-83, epidemiologist Balt., 1983-88; patent examiner U.S. Patent and Trademark Office, Xtal City, Va., 1989-90; freelance researcher New Carrollton, Md., 1990—; lawyer, pvt. practice Washington, 1998—. Mem. Am. Chem. Soc., Washington, 1978-82; mem., exec. bd. Nat. Lawyers Guild, Washington, 1987—; pres. Voucher Express, 1993—; mediator Superior Ct., Washington, 1993—; legal advt. mgr. Sentinel Newspaper. Subcommittee chmn. Anne Arundel County Task Force for Drug and Alcohol Abuse, 1979-80; pres., bd. mem. Md. Ornithological Soc., 1979-82; mem., exec. bd. Md. Condominium and Homeowners Assn., Rockville, Md., 1988-91. Named Outstanding Young Women of Am., 1983. Mem. ABA, ATLA (family divsn. 1999—), Nat. Assn. Criminal Def. Lawyers, Superior Ct. Trial Lawyers Assn. (criminal and family divsn.), Nat. Intellectual Propery Law Assn., Anne Arundel County Tennis Assn., Sigma Iota Epsilon.

BROWN, RICHARD CHRISTOPHER, retired epidemiologist; b. Gainesville, Fla., Jan. 16, 1932; s. Joseph P. and Mildred Smith Brown; m. Linda Dickinson, July 2, 1960 (div. Dec. 1984); children: Douglas R., Jennifer Brown Kirkham. AB, Western Res. U., 1953; MD, U. Fla., 1962; MPH, U. Calif., Berkeley, 1967. Diplomate Am. Bd. Preventive Medicine. Pub. health inspector Polk County Health Dept., Lakeland, Fla., 1956-57; rotating intern Va. Mason Hosp., Seattle, 1962-63; resident in preventive medicine Fla. Dept. Health, West Palm Beach, Fla., 1963-64; resident in internal medicine U.S. VA Hosp., Portland, Oreg., 1964-66; epidemiologist USPHS, Window Rock, Ariz., 1967-68; asst. prof. preventive medicine U. Okla. Med. Sch., Oklahoma City, 1967-68; staff physician Morton Plant Hosp., Clearwater, Fla., 1968-91, Bay Pines (Fla.) VA Med. Ctr., 1991—2001. Dir. Hernando County Health Dept., Brooksville, Fla., 1987-88; med. dir. Bay Pines VA Domicilary. Contbr. articles to profl. jours. Bd. dirs. ARC, Clearwater, Fla., 1970, spl. expert witness Agy. for Health Care Adminstrn., State of Fla. Bd. Medicine, Tallahassee, 1997-98. Asst. surgeon USPHS, 1962-67. Recipient Rsch. award Am. Geriatrics Soc., Lederle Lab., 1965, Physician Recognition award AMA, 1969. Fellow Am. Coll. Preventive Medicine; mem. Am. Coll. Epidemiology, Fla. Soc. Preventive Medicine (past pres.), Delta Tau Delta. Democrat. Episcopalian. Avocation: triathlon and marathon running. Home: 1157 Granada St Clearwater FL 33755-1054

BROWN, RICHARD DAVID, history educator; b. N.Y.C., Oct. 31, 1939; s. Alvyn Adolph and Dorothy (Kruskal) B.; m. Irene Quenzler, June 10, 1962; children: Josiah Henry, Nicholas Alvyn. AB, Oberlin Coll., 1961; AM, Harvard U., 1962, PhD, 1966. Fulbright lectr. U. Toulouse, France, 1965-66; asst. prof. history Oberlin (Ohio) Coll., 1966-71; assoc. prof. history U. Conn., Storrs, 1971-75, prof., 1975—, head dept., 1974-80, 94-95, dir. Humanities Inst., 2001—, Bd. Trustees Disting. prof., 2002—. Author: Revolutionary Politics, 1970, Modernization, 1976, Knowledge is Power, 1989, Strength of a People, 1996, Hanging of Ephraim Wheeler, 2003. Chair Hampton (Conn.) Bd. of Edn., 1983-85. Woodrow Wilson Found. fellow, 1961-62, 64-65; Charles Warren Ctr. fellow, 1970-71; Ind. Study and Rsch. fellow NEH, 1985; John Simon Guggenheim fellow, 1998-99. Mem. Am. Antiquarian Soc. (councillor 1994—, NEH fellow 1977-78, 92-93), Soc. Am. Historians, Inst. Early Am. History and Culture (councillor 1995-98), Soc. Historians of the Early Am. Republic (pres. 2001-02), Mass. Hist. Soc., Colonial Soc. Mass. Office: U Conn Dept of History U-2103 Storrs Mansfield CT 06269-2103 E-mail: Richard.D.Brown@UConn.edu.

BROWN, RICHARD E., III, military officer; BA in Psychology and History, Tex. Christian U., 1970; grad., Squadron Officer Sch., 1975; MA in Guidance and Counseling, U. Okla., 1977; disting. grad., Air Command and Staff Coll., 1983; nat. security mgmt. course, 1987; grad., Air War Coll., 1991, Armed Forces Staff Coll., 1993. Commd. 2d lt. USAF, 1970, advanced through grades to maj. gen., 1999; student pilot 3640th Flying Tng. Wing, Laredo AFB, Tex., 1970-71; A-1 skyraider pilot Nakon Phanom, RT AFB, Thailand, 1971-72; T-37 instr., flight examiner 80th Flying Tng. Wing, Sheppard AFB, Tex., 1973-77; A-7D fighter pilot 75th Tactical Flying Tng. Wing, England AFB, La., 1977-80; pers. staff officer Fighter Assignments Sect. Air Force Manpower and Pers. Ctr., Randolph AFB, Tex., 1980-82; F16 fighter pilot, ops. officer, squadron comdr. 50th Fighter Wing, Hahn Air Base, Germany, 1983-88; vice comdr. Warrior Prep. Ctr. USAF and U.S. Army Forces in Europe, Ramstein Air Base, West Germany, 1988-90; vice comdr. 56th Fighter Wing, MacDill AFB, Fla., 1991-92; chief air ops. sect., joint ops. and plans sect. Supreme Hdqs. Allied Powers Europe, NATO, Mons, Belgium, 1992-94; wing comdr. 24th Wing, comdr. U.S. So. Command Air Forces Forward, Howard AFB, Panama, 1994-95; wing comdr. 354th Fighter Wing, Eielson AFB, Ala., 1995-97; dir. logistics Hdqs. Pacific Air Forces, Hickam AFB, Hawaii, 1997-98; dir. joint matters Dep. Chief of Staff Air and Space Ops. Hdqs. USAF, Washington, 1998—. Decorated Silver Star with 2 oak leaf clusters, Legion of Merit, Def. Superior Svc. medal, D.F.C. with 7 oak leaf clusters, Meritorious Svc. medal with 3 oak leaf clusters. Office: HQ USAF/XOJ 1480 Air Force Pentagon Washington DC 20330-1480

BROWN, RICHARD ERIC, electrical engineer, consultant; b. Spokane, Wash., June 24, 1969; s. Richard Frank and Margaret Ann Brown; m. Christelle Marie Oeljen, Aug. 8, 1997; children: Colton children: Ashlyn. BSEE, U. Wash., 1991, MSEE, 1993, PhD, 1996; MBA, U. N.C., 2003. Registered profl. engr., NC. Dir. tech. ABB Inc., Raleigh, NC, 1996—2002; cons. KEMA, Chalfont, Pa., 2003—. Author: Electric Power Distribution Reliability, Reliability, 2002. Mem.: IEEE. Office: KEMA 4379 County Line Rd Chalfont PA 18914 E mail: rebrown@kema.us.

BROWN, RICHARD FRANCIS, command and control systems engineer, military officer; b. Newton, Mass., Sept. 17, 1945; s. Francis Healey and Kathryn Ellenor (Morrissey) B.; m. Mary Ellen Laird, June 12, 1972; 1 child, Patrick Aaron. BS, U. Mass., 1967. Field artillery officer U.S. Army, 1967-75; field artillery specialist tactical data systems U.S. Army Field Artillery Sch., Ft. Sill., Okla., 1975-87; telecomm. mgr. U.S. Army Combined Arms Command, Ft. Leavenworth, Kans., 1987—. Spl. staff asst. U.S. Army Sci. Bd., Washington, 1996-97. Contbr. articles to profl. jours. Lt. col. U.S. Army, 1967-97. Decorated Bronze Star with 2 oak leaf clusters, U.S. Army, Vietnam, 1969-70, Purple Heart, 1969-70, Army Commendation medal with V device, 1969-70; recipient Manprint Practitioner of Yr. award U.S. Army, 1998, Systems Analysis award for group achievement in ops. rsch. U.S. Army, 1985. Mem. Armed Forces Comm.-Electronics Assn. (pres. Kansas City chpt. 1988-91, v.p. 1992—), Leavenworth Bicycle Club (v.p. 1996-98). Avocations: bicycling, swimming, photography. Home: PO Box 3318 Fort Leavenworth KS 66027-0318 Office: Tradoc Program Integration Office-ABCS 415 Sheridan Ave Fort Leavenworth KS 66027 E-mail: brownr@leavenworth.army.mil.

BROWN, RICHARD HARRIS, information technology executive; b. New Brunswick, N.J., June 3, 1947; s. Harris Ransford and Winifred (Clelland) Brown; m. Christine Demier, Sept. 27, 1969; children: Ryan, Allison. BS in Communications, Ohio U., 1969. Comml. rep. Ohio Bell, Columbus, 1969—71, comml. mgr., 1971—74, dist. comml. mgr. Toledo and Cleve., 1974—80, div. mgr. Cleve., 1980—81; v.p. engring. & ops. United Telephone System, Inc. subs. United Telecommunications, Inc., Westwood, Kans., 1981—82; v.p. ops. United Telephone Co. of Midwest, Overland Park, Kans., 1982—83; v.p., COO United Telephone Co. of Fla., Apopka, 1983—87; sr. v.p. human resources & adminstrn. United Telecommunications, Inc., Shawnee Mission, Kans., 1987, sr. v.p. ops., 1987—89, exec. v.p., chief info. & planning officer, 1989; vice chmn., bd. dirs. Ameritech, 1993—95, 1993—95; pres., CEO H&R Block, Inc., Kansas City, Mo., 1995—96; CEO, bd. dirs. Cable and Wireless PLC, London, 1996—98; chmn., CEO EDS (Elec. Data Systems), Plano, Tex., 1998—2003. Bd. dirs. Vivendi Universal, Home Depot, Inc., DuPont; mem. Pres.'s adv. com. on trade and policy negotiations, Pres.'s nat. security telecom. adv. com. Trustee Ohio U. Found., Athens, 1989—, So. Meth. U.; vice chmn. Chgo. United Way Campaign, 1994. With USNG, 1969—74. Named Outstanding Alumnus, Coll. of Interpersonal Comms., Ohio U., 1988. Mem.: U.S.-Japan Bus. Coun., U.S.-France Bus. oun., Bus. Coun., The Bus. Roundtable, Execs. Club, Econ. Club, Comml. Club, Shoreacres Country Club, Chgo. Club.*

BROWN, RICHARD HARVEY, sociology, cultural studies and communications scholar, educator; b. N.Y.C., May 12, 1940; s. Samuel Robert and Sylvia B.; m. Nathalie Babel, April 5, 1967; 1 child, Ramiro Babel Brown. Cert., U. Lausanne, Switzerland, 1960; BA in Sociology and Social Instns., U. Calif., Berkeley, 1961; ed., Inst. East Asian Studies, 1963; MA in Sociology, Columbia U., 1965; PhD in Sociology, U. Calif., San Diego, 1973. Assoc. sociology U. Calif., San Diego, La Jolla, 1973; prof. sociology U. Md., College Park, 1975—, affiliate prof. program in comparative lit. Vis. instr. New Sch. for Social Rsch., N.Y.C., 1968; lectr. in sociology Calif. State U., 1971-72; guest prof. U. Ottawa, Can., 1979, U. Peking, U. Shanghai, U. Hangzhou, People's Republic of China, 1992; guest prof., sr. Fulbright lectr. U. Nacional, Bogota, Colombia, U. del Valle, Cali, Colombia, 1985, 93; guest prof. U. Catolica, Lima, Peru, 1995; mem. numerous coms. U. Md.; pres. Washington Inst. for Social Rsch. Author: A Poetic for Sociology, Toward a Logic of Discovery for the Human Sciences, 1977, 3d edit., 1989, Society as Text, Essays on Rhetoric, Reason and Reality, 1987, 2d edit., 1992, Social Science as Civic Discourse, Essays on the Invention, Uses and Legitimization of Social Theory, 1989, Toward a Democratic Science: Scientific Narration and Democratic Communication, 1995; editor, contbr.: Structure, Consciousness and History, 1978, Traditions and Transformations: Asian Indians in America, 1986, Migration and Modernization: The Indian Diaspora in Comparative Perspective, 1987, The Postmodern Turn in Sociological Theory, 1990, Modernization in East Asia: Economic, Political and Social Perspectives, 1992, Writing the Social Text: Poetics and Politics in Social Science Discourse, 1992, El Postmodernismo y la Sociologia, 1993, Cultural Perspectives on Modernization: Experiences of East Asia, 1993, Postmodern Representations, 1995; contbr. essays, reviews and articles to profl. jours., chpts. to books. Mem. Democratic Socialists of Am. Jewish. Home: 1601 16th St NW Apt 909 Washington DC 20011-1766 Office: U Md Dept Sociology College Park MD 20742-1315

BROWN, RICHARD HOLBROOK, library director, historian, researcher; b. Boston, Sept. 25, 1927; s. Joseph Richard and Sylvia (Cook) Brown. BA, Yale U., 1949, MA, 1952, PhD, 1955. Instr. history U. Mass., Amherst, 1955—59, asst. prof., 1959—62; assoc. prof. No. Ill. U., De Kalb, 1962—64; dir. Amherst Project, Amherst and Chgo., 1964—72; dir. rsch. and edn. Newberry Libr., Chgo., 1972—83, acad. v.p., 1983—94, sr. rsch. fellow, 1994—. Vis. prof. history and edn. Northwestern U., Evanston, Ill., 1971—84; cons. NEH, 1977—; bd. dirs. Chgo. Metro History Fair, 1977—, pres., 1984—91; cons. Ctr. Study So. Culture, U. Miss., 1979—; mem. Ill. Humanities Coun., 1980—86, chmn., 1982—83. Author: The Hero and the People, 1964, The Missouri Compromise: Political Statesmanship or Unwise Evasion?, 1964; gen. editor: Amherst Project Units in American History, 25 vols., 1964—75. Recipient George Washington Eggleston prize, Yale U., 1955; Andrew Mellon Postdoctoral fellow, U. Pitts., 1960—61. Mem.: Orgn. Am. Historians, Social Sci. Edn. Consortium (pres. 1975—77), Am. Antiquarian Soc. Democrat. Roman Catholic. Office: The Newberry Libr 60 W Walton St Chicago IL 60610-3380 E-mail: brownr@newberry.org.

BROWN, RICHARD L. lawyer; b. N.Y.C., Nov. 9, 1944; s. S. Robert and Frances S. B.; children: Jesselyn Alicia, Justin Alexander, Jeremy Brandon, Matthew Tyler, Garrett William. BA, Emory U., 1966; JD, NYU, 1969. Bar: N.Y. 1969, D.C. 1973, U.S. Ct. Appeals (D.C. cir.) 1974, U.S. Ct. of Claims 1980, U.S. Supreme Ct. 1980. Atty., advisor FCC, Washington, 1969-72; assoc. firm Farrow, Cahill, Kaswell & Schildhause, Washington, 1972-75; sr. ptnr. Brown Nietert & Kaufman, Chartered, Washington, 1975—. Gen. counsel Community Antenna TV Assn., 1972-75; pres. Alaskan Cable Network, Inc., Fairbanks, 1980-85; v.p., gen. counsel Soc. for Pvt. and Comml. Earth Stas., 1980-86; chmn. bd. trustees Rock Creek Internat. Sch., Washington, 2999-2002. Author: Low Power TV Handbook, 1981, licensing manual for land mobile radio-TV, 1980; co-author: The Satellite Earth Station Zoning Book, Questions & Answers About Satellite Earth Stations, The Business of Private Cable Television, The Low-Power TV Manual; contbr. articles to profl. jours. Mem. ABA, Fed. Communications Bar Assn. Office: Brown Nietert & Kaufman Chartered 2000 L St NW Ste 817 Washington DC 20036

BROWN, RICHARD LAWRENCE, lawyer; b. Evansville, Ind., Dec. 8, 1932; s. William S. and Mildred (Tenbarge) B.; m. Alice Rae Costello, June 14, 1957; children: Richard, Catherine, Vanessa, Mary, James. AA, Vincennes U., 1953; BA, Ind. State U., 1957; JD, Ind. U., 1960. Bar: Ind., 1960, U.S. dist. ct. (so. dist.) Ind., 1961, U.S. Ct. Apls. (7th cir.), 1972, U.S. Sup. Ct., 1972. Mng. ptnr. Butler, Brown, Hahn and Little, and predecessor firms, Indpls., 1961-85, Butler, Brown and Blythe, Indpls., 1985-92; city atty. City of Beech Grove, Ind., 1967—; pvt. practice, Beech Grove, 1992-2001; of counsel Blythe & Ost, Indpls., 1994-96, Holwager, Byers & Caughy, Beech Grove, 1996-2001. Sec., treas. Internat. Bus. Inst., Dayton, Ohio, 1987-2003, Internat. Pub. Inst., Dayton, 1987-96; bd. dirs. Vincennes U. Found. Editor: Indiana Municipal Lawyers Assn. Newsletter, 1985—. Chmn. bd. zoning appeals small cities and towns Marion County, Ind., 1965-66; gen. counsel Habitat for Humanity Greater Indpls., 1985-95; parish chmn. St. Jude's Ch. With U.S. Army, 1953-55. Fellow Indpls. Bar Assn.; mem. ABA, Ind. Bar Assn., Ind. Mcpls. Lawyers Assn. (co-editor newsletter, bd. dirs., pres. 1987-88), Vincennes U. Alumni Assn. (pres., bd. dirs. 1990-92), KC, Delta Theta Phi. Roman Catholic. Avocation: golf. Office: 1818 Main St Beech Grove IN 46107-1418 E-mail: rbrown080@comcast.net.

BROWN, RICHARD LEE, lawyer, director; b. Ft. Worth, Dec. 7, 1925; s. Marvin H. and Janie (McIntosh) B.; m. Elizabeth McPherson, Nov. 19, 1949; children: Beverly Elizabeth, Leigh Ann (dec.). Student, Rice U., 1942-43; LLB, U. Tex., 1949; LLM, George Washington U., 1954. Bar: Tex. 1949. Asst. dist. atty., Tarrant County, 1949- 50; spl. atty. Chief Counsel's Office, IRS, Washington, 1953-56; partner Friedman & Brown, 1956-60, Stone, Parker, Snakard & Brown, 1961-66, Law, Snakard, Brown & Gambill, 1967-81, 83-84; of counsel Bishop Payne Harvard & Kaitler, Ft. Worth, 1984-89, 91—; judge Ct. Appeals Tex. 2d Dist., 1981-83; chief civil div. Tarrant County Dist. Atty's Office, 1989-91. Former mem. bd. commrs. Pub. Housing Authority Ft. Worth, chmn., 1976-77; Chmn. bd., chmn. competition Van Cliburn Internat. Piano Competition, 1966-69. Served with AUS, 1944-46; Served with U.S. Army, 1950-53. Decorated Bronze Star medal, Combat Infantry badge and 3 battle stars. Fellow Tex. Bar Found. (life); mem. Tex. Bar Assn., Tarrant County Bar Assn. (pres. 1977-78) Office: 1800 Bank of Am Bldg 500 W 7th St Fort Worth TX 76102-4700

BROWN, RITA MAE, writer; b. Hanover, Pa., Nov. 28, 1944; d. Ralph and Julia Ellen B. AA, Broward Jr. Coll., 1965; BA, NYU, 1968; cinematography degree, Sch. Visual Arts, N.Y.C., 1968; PhD, Inst. Policy Studies, 1976; DLitt, Wilson Coll., 1992; LLD (hon.), William Woods U., Fulton, Mo., 2000; LLD (hon.), York (Pa.) Coll., 2003. Photo editor Sterling Pub., N.Y.C., 1969-70; lectr. Fed. City Coll., Washington, 1970-71; rsch. fellow Inst. Policy Studies, Washington, 1971-73; pres. Am. Artists Inc., Charlottesville, Va., 1980—. Vis. mem. faculty in feminist studies Goddard Coll., Plainfield, Vt., 1973—; mem. lit. panel NEA, 1978-81; Hemingway judge for 1st fiction PEN Internat., 1983; blue ribbon panelist Prime Time Emmy Awards, 1984, 86. Author: (translator) Hrotsvitra: Six Medieval Plays, 1971, (novels) The Hand That Cradles the Rock, 1971, Songs to a Handsome Woman, 1973, In Her Day, 1976, Southern Discomfort, 1982, Sudden Death, 1983, High Hearts, 1986, Bingo, 1988, Venus Envy, 1993, Dolley, 1994, Paydirt, 1995, Riding Shotgun, 1996, Murder, She Meowed, 1996, Mrs. Murphy Mysteries, 2001, Outfoxed, 2000, Alma Mater, 2001, The Plain Brown Rapper, 1972, Rubyfruit Jungle, 1974, Six of One, 1977, Starting from Scratch, 1987, Wish You Were Here, 1989, Rest in Pieces, 1991, Murder at Monticello, 1993, Mrs. Murphy Series, annual novels, 2002, Loose Lips, 1998, Outfoxed, 2000, Hotspur, 2002; (poetry) The Poems of Rita Mae Brown, 1987; TV series include I Love Liberty, 1982, Long Hot Summer, 1985, My Two Loves, 1986, The Alice Marble Story, 1986, Southern Exposure, 1990, Cat on th Scent, 1999, Loose Lips, 1999, Outfoxed, 2000, Pawing Through The Past, 2000; TV films include The Firls of Summer, 1989, Selma, Lord, Selma, 1989, Passing Through, 1993, A Family Again, 1994, others; (cable TV) The Mists of Avalon, 1986, The Nat Turner Story-African American Anthology, 1993, The Wall, K-9, 1993; (films) Slumber Party Massacre, 1982, Sweet Surrender, 20th Century Fox, 1986, Table Dancing, 1987, Mary Pickford, 1998. Former exec. officer NOW; bd. dirs. Human Rights Campaign Fund, N.Y.C., 1986; co-founder Radical Lesbians; founder Redstockings Radical Feminist Group, Nat. Gay Task Force, Nat. Women's Polit. Caucus. Recipient Award for Best Variety Show on TV Writers Guild Am., 1982, Outstanding Alumni, Am. Assn. Cmty. Colls., 1999, Outstanding Alumna, Broward Cmty. Coll., 1999, Literary Lion award N.Y. Pub. Library, 1986, Emmy award nomination for The Long Hot Summer, ABC mini-series, 1985; Emmy nomination for best variety show I Love Liberty, 1982; named Charlottesville favorite author The Observer, 1990, Athlete of the Week, The Observer, 1990. Mem. PEN Internat., Oak Ridge Foxhunt Club (Master of Foxhounds). Address: Tea-Time Farm 1295 Greenfield Rd Afton VA 22920-2937

BROWN, ROBERT ALAN, retired construction materials company executive; b. Mt. Vernon, Ill., July 20, 1930; s. Herbert E. and Opal (Clayborn) B.; m. Norma Jean Falz, June 16, 1953; children: Carla, Todd, Scott, David. BBA, U. Minn., 1953; postgrad., Harvard U. Bus. Sch., 1971. With Firestone Tire & Rubber Co., 1953-73, plant mgr., 1967-73, asst. to v.p. Akron, Ohio, 1973; dir. mfg. Firestone Internat. Co., Akron, 1973-75; exec. v.p. Firestone Can. Ltd., Hamilton, Ont., Can., 1975-78; pres. Carlisle Tire & Rubber Co., Pa., 1978-82, Carlisle Syntec Sys. (Pa.), 1982-94. Served with U.S. Navy, 1948-49. Presbyterian. Home: 1193 Peninsula Dr Central City PA 15926-9119

BROWN, ROBERT ALAN, atmospheric science educator, research scientist; b. LA, June 11, 1934; s. Carl Clayton and Olive (Hirst) B.; m. Marcia Louise Jobe, Dec. 12, 1957; children: Vanessa, Morgan, Tristin. BS, U. Calif., Berkeley, 1957, MS, 1963; PhD, U. Wash., 1969. Fellow U. Wash., Seattle, 1969-70, Nat. Ctr. Atmospheric Sci., Boulder, Colo., 1970-71; rsch. prin. investigator U. Wash. Polar Sci. Ctr., Seattle, 1971-73; prof. atmospheric sci. U. Wash., Seattle, 1983—. Adj. prof.: Naval Postgrad. Sch., 1983, Fraunhofer Inst., Garmish, Germany, 1991, U. Concepcíon, Chile, 1996, 2003, Ecole Poly., Paris, 1997. Author: Analytic Methods in Planetary Boundary Layer Models, 1973, Fluid Mechanics of the Atmosphere, 1991, The Tree, 2003; co-author: The Panzaic Principle, Microwave Remote Sensing for Ocean and Marine Weather Forecast Models, Ency. of Earth System Science, Surface Waves and Fluxes: Current Theory, Polar Oceanography, 1990; editor Pacific Ocean Remote Sensing Congress book series, 1992—, Remote Sensing of the Pacific Ocean with Satellites, 1998; contbr. over 80 articles to profl. jours. 1st lt. U.S. Army, 1957-59. Recipient Disting. Sci. award, Pan Ocean Remote Sensing Confs., 2000. Fellow Am. Meteorol. Soc.; mem. Am. Geophys. Union, Am. Oceanographic Soc., Sigma Xi, Phi Kappa Psi. Democrat. Office: U Wash Dept Atmospheric Sci PO Box 351640 Seattle WA 98195-0001

BROWN, ROBERT ARTHUR, chemical engineering educator; b. San Antonio, July 22, 1951; s. Ralph and Lillian (Rilling) B.; m. Beverly Ann Lamb, June 22, 1972; children: Ryan Arthur, Keith Andrew. BS, U. Tex., 1973, MS, 1975; PhD, U. Minn., 1979. Instr. U. Minn., Mpls., 1978; asst. prof. chem. engring. MIT, Cambridge, 1979-82, assoc. prof., 1982-84, prof., 1984—, Warren K. Lewis prof., 1992—, exec. officer dept. chem. engring., 1987-88, head dept. chem. engring., 1989-96, dean Sch. of Engring., 1996-98, co-dir. supercomputer facility, 1989-94, provost, 1998—. Cons. Lincoln Labs., Lexington, Mass., 1985-87, Mobil Solar Energy, Waltham, Mass., 1982-93. Contbr. over 160 articles to profl. jours. Recipient Outstanding Jr. Faculty award Amoco Oil Co., 1981, Camille and Henry Dreyfus Tchr.-Scholar award 1983; named one of Outstanding Young Texans-Execs. U. Tex., 1991. Mem. AAAS, NAE, NAS, AIChE (Allen P. Colburn award 1986, Profl. Progress award 1996), Soc. Indsl. and Applied Math., Am. Assn. Crystal Growth (Young Author award 1985), Am. Phys. Soc., Am. Acad. Arts and Scis. Office: MIT 3-208 Cambridge MA 02139 E-mail: rab@mit.edu.

BROWN, ROBERT CARROLL, lawyer; b. Ridley Park, Pa., June 24, 1948; s. Robert Carroll Sr. and Marjorie Elizabeth (Nowell) B.; m. Charlene M. Lipp, Oct. 4, 1986; children: Robert Charles, Gregory Scott, Michael Joseph. AB in Polit. Sci., Pa. State U., 1970; JD, Temple U., 1973. Bar: Pa.; U.S. Dist. Ct. (ea. dist.) Pa. 1977, Pa. Supreme Ct. 1973, U.S. Ct. Appeals (3d cir.) 1980. Judicial law clk. Ct. Common Pleas/Northampton County, Easton, Pa., 1973-74; assoc. Fox & Oldt, Easton, 1974-82; ptnr. Fox, Oldt & Brown, Easton, 1982—. Sec. Greater Easton Corp., 1977-82, Two Rivers Area Commerce Coun., Easton, 1983-85; officer Lehigh Valley Flying Club, Allentown, Pa., 1979-99. Mem. Northampton County Bar Assn. (sec. 1983-84), Pa. Bar Assn., Pa. Trial Lawyers Assn., Pa. Def. Inst. Republican. Presbyterian. Avocations: private pilot, sports cars, golf, spectator sports. Home: 420 Wedgewood Dr Easton PA 18045-5753 Office: Fox Oldt & Brown 6 S 3rd St Ste 508 Easton PA 18042-4591 E-mail: rcbjr2001@cs.com.

BROWN, ROBERT CHARLES, retired radiologist; b. Pottsville, Pa., Jan. 22, 1917; BS, Pa. State U., 1938; MD, Temple U., 1942. Diplomate Am. Bd. Radiology. Intern Nat. Naval Med. Ctr., Bethesda, Md., 1942-43; resident in radiology Phila. Gen. Hosp., 1951-54; chief dept. radiology Taylor Hosp., Ridley Park, Pa., 1954-55, St. Mary's Hosp., Phila., 1956-63, Riddle Meml. Hosp., Media, Pa., 1963-83, emeritus staff, 1983—.

BROWN, ROBERT CLARK, JR., county official; b. Akron, Ohio, Feb. 16, 1952; s. Robert Clark and Virginia Elizabeth (Raymont) B.; m. Patricia Ann Ream, Aug. 16, 1970; children: Stephen Clark, Melissa Kelly. BSBA, Bowling Green State U., 1974. Dist. scout exec. Boy Scouts Am., Ft. Wayne, Ind., 1974-76; agt. Res. Life Ins. Co., Ft. Wayne, Ind., 1976-77; v.p. Lehman Electric and Plbg., Inc., Huntington, Ind., 1977-88; sales exec. Felton Electronics, Inc., Huntington, Ind., 1986; agt. Landmark Ins. Agy., Huntington, Ind., 1989-92; mem. dealer rels. staff E.C.P. Inc., Huntington, Ind., 1992-96; sales exec. Sees Equipment & Supply Co., Inc., Huntington, Ind., 1996—2003; pres., CEO Huntington Co. C. of C., 2003—. Mem. common coun., City of Huntington, 1986—, pres. pro tempore, 1995-96, pres. bd. fin., 1986-87; chair Huntington County Solid Waste Mgmt. Dist., 1993, 97, vice chair, 1992, 96, sec., 1990-91, dir., 1990—; chair Rep. County Com. Huntington County, 1998-2003, precinct committeeman, 1983—; elder First Presbyn. Ch., Huntington, 1986—; bd. dirs. Samaritan Ctr., Huntington, 1982-84, pres., 1984; dir. Region IIIA Regional Econ. Devel. and Planning Agy., Kendallville, Ind., 1996-98; bd. dirs. Fed. Emergency Mgmt. Local Providers, Huntington, 1989—; com. on worship and theology, commr. to Presbytery of Wabash Valley, Presbyn. Ch. U.S.A., 1997-2003. Mem. Masons (past master 1986, Amity Lodge F&AM #483). Avocations: politics, electronics, golf, reading. Home: 2027 Camden Ct Huntington IN 46750-3994 Office: Huntington Co C of C 305 Warren St Huntington IN 46750 Fax: 260-356-5434. E-mail: rcbrownjr@fwi.com.

BROWN, ROBERT DALE, wildlife science educator, department head; b. Red Bluff, Calif., July 31, 1945; s. Charles Arthur and Carol Joyce (Dale) B.; m. Regan Mensch, June 30, 1981; children: Alex, Jason, Adam. Student, U. Calif., Davis, 1963-65; BS, Colo. State U., 1968; PhD, Pa. State U., 1975. From asst. prof. to assoc. prof. Tex. A&I U., Kingsville, 1975-81; from assoc. rsch. scientist to rsch. scientist C. Kleberg Wildlife Rsch. Inst., Kingsville, 1981-87; dept. head Miss. State U., Starkville, 1987-93, Tex. A&M U., College Station, 1993—, coord. Gulf Coast coop. ecosys. studies unit, 2002—. Dir. Inst. for Renewable Resources, College Station, 1995—. Editor: Antler Development in Cervidae, 1983, Translocation of Wild Animals, The Biology of Deer, 1991. Lt. col. USMCR, 1968-93. Mem. Am. Inst. Nutrition, Wildlife Soc. (v.p.), Am. Fisheries Soc., Nat. Assn. Univ. Fish and Wildlife Programs (past pres.), Soc. for Range Mgmt. Episcopalian. Avocations: scouting, hunting, fishing, scuba, sailing. Office: Tex A&M U # 2258 Dept Wildlife Fisheries Sci College Station TX 77843-2258 E-mail: rdbrown@tamu.edu.

BROWN, ROBERT E. retired transportation executive; b. Croydon, Eng., 1945; BS, Royal Mil. Coll., Kingston, Can.; postgrad., Harvard U., 1983. With Can. Armed Forces, Atomic Energy Can., Pub. Svc. Commn., Treasury Bd., Coun. Maritime Premiers, 1976-78; assoc. dep. minister Dept. Regional Indsl. Expansion; v.p. corp. devel. Bombardier, Inc., Montreal, Canada, 1987-89, sr. v.p. corp. devel. and strategic planning, 1989-90, pres., CEO, 1999—2002; pres. Canadair, 1990-92, Bombardier Aerospace Group-N.Am., 1992-96, pres., COO, 1996-99; ret., 2002; chmn. Air Can., 2003—. Bd. dirs. Nortel Networks Corp., Air Can.

BROWN, ROBERT FREEMAN, mathematics educator; b. Cambridge, Mass., Dec. 13, 1935; s. Irving and Charlotte (Frankel) B.; m. Brenda Webster, June 16, 1957; children: Geoffrey, Matthew. AB, Harvard Coll., 1957; postgrad., Am. U., 1959; PhD, U. Wis., 1963. Asst. prof. UCLA, 1963-68, assoc. prof., 1968-73, prof., 1973—. Author: Lefschetz Fixed Point Theorem, 1970, Applied Finite Math, 1977, Essentials of Finite Math, 1990, Finite Mathematics, 1992, A Topological Introduction to Nonlinear Analysis, 1993. Mem. Am. Math. Soc., Math. Assn. Am. (gov. 1986-89, Lester Ford award 1983). Democrat. Episcopalian. Avocations: singing, swimming, traveling. Office: Univ Calif Dept Math Los Angeles CA 90007

BROWN, ROBERT GROVER, engineering educator; b. Shenandoah, Iowa, Apr. 25, 1926; s. Grover Whitney and Irene (Frink) B. BS, Iowa State Coll., 1948, MS, 1951, PhD, 1956. Instr. Iowa State Coll., Ames, 1948-51, 53-55, asst. prof., 1955-56, assoc. prof., 1956-59, prof., 1959-76, Disting. prof., 1976-88, Disting. prof. emeritus, 1988—; research engr. N. Am. Aviation, Downey, Calif., 1951-53. Cons. various aerospace engring. firms., 1956— Author: (with R.A. Sharpe, W.L. Hughes) Lines, Waves and Antennas, 1961, (with J.W. Nilsson) Linear Systems Analysis, 1962, (with Patrick Y.C. Hwang) Introduction to Random Signals and Applied Kalman Filtering with MATLAB Exercises and Solutions, 3d edit., 1997. Fellow IEEE, Inst. Navigation (Burka award 1978, 84, Weems award 1994). Office: Iowa State U Dept Engring Ames IA 50011-0001

BROWN, ROBERT HORATIO, physician, neuromuscular research scientist; b. Boston, Aug. 18, 1947, s. Robert and Virginia (Lane) B.; m. Elaine V. Beilin, July 4, 1972; 2 children. BA, Amherst Coll., 1969; DPhil, Oxford U., 1973; MD, Harvard U., 1975. Assoc. neurologist Mass. Gen. Hosp., Boston, 1980—; assoc. prof. neurology Harvard Med. Sch., Boston, 1991—, prof. neurology; dir., neuromuscular unit Mass. Gen. Hosp; dir., founder Day Neuromuscular Research Lab., 1984—. Mem.: Inst. Medicine. Achievements include co-discovery of genes for Lou Gehrig's disease and hyperkalemic periodic paralysis. Office: Day Neuromuscular Rsch Lab Mass Genl Hosp E Bldg 149, Rm 6627, 13th St Charlestown MA 02129

BROWN, ROBERT J. (BOB BROWN), state official; b. Missoula, Mont., Dec. 11, 1947; s. Clifford Andrew and Jeanne M (Knox) Brown; m. Susan Kay Stoeckig, Sept. 20, 1975; children: Robin Sue, Kelly Charlynn. BS, Mont. State U, 1970, BS, 1974; MEd, U. Mont., 1988. Cert. secondary tchr. Tchr. govt., history Big Fork (Mont.) High Sch., 1979—86; tchr. history, econs. Flathead High Sch., Kalispell, Mont., 1986—; state rep. Mont. Ho. Reps., Helena, 1971—74; senator 2d dist. Mont. State Sen., Helena, 1974—96; sec. state State of Mont., 2001—. With USN, 1972—73. Mem.: Mont. Edn. Assn. (Golden Gavel award 1979), Moose, Am. Legion, Kiwanis, Phi Delta Kappa. Republican. Avocation: fishing. Home: 33 Cougar Trl Whitefish MT 59937 Office: Sec of State Room 260 Capitol PO Box 202801 Helena MT 59620*

BROWN, ROBERT LAIDLAW, state supreme court justice; b. Houston, June 30, 1941; s. Robert Raymond and Warwick (Rust) B.; m. Charlotte Banks, June 18, 1966; 1 child, Stuart Laidlaw. BA, U. of the South, 1963; MA in English and Comparative Lit., Columbia U., 1965; JD, U. Va., 1968. Bar: Ark. 1968, U.S. Dist. Ct. (ea. and we. divs.) Ark. 1968. Assoc. Chowning, Mitchell, Hamilton & Burrow, Little Rock, 1968-71; dep. prosecuting atty. 6th Jud. Dist., Prosecuting Atty. Office, Little Rock, 1971-72; legal aide Office Gov. Dale Bumpers, Little Rock, 1972-74; legis. asst. U.S. Senator Dale Bumpers, Washington, 1975-76; adminstrv. asst. Congressman Jim Guy Tucker, Washington, 1977-78; ptnr. Harrison & Brown, P.A., Little Rock, 1978-85; pvt. practice law, 1986-90; assoc. justice Ark. Supreme Ct., Little Rock, 1991—. Contbr. articles to profl. jours. Trustee U. of the South, Sewanee, Tenn., 1983-89, bd. regents, 1989-95. Fellow ABA, Ark. Bar Found (cert. of recognition 1981); mem. Ark. Bar Assn. Episcopalian. Fax: 501-683-4003. E-mail: Robert.Brown@mail.state.ar.us.

BROWN, ROBERT LORAN, music educator; b. Kingston, N.Y., June 21, 1944; s. Robert Loran and Margaret Lillian Brown; m. Mary Elizabeth Mathews, Nov. 25, 1966; 1 child, Kerry Louise. BS in Edn., SUNY, Fredonia, 1966; MusM, Ind. U., 1968; EdD in Coll. Tchg., Columbia U., N.Y.C., 1974. Cert. tchr. N.Y. Tchr. music West Seneca Mid. Sch., NY, 1966—67; arranger, copyist, pianist U.S. Mil. Acad., West Point, NY, 1969—71; prof. dept. music and fine arts divsn. chair Lincoln Meml. U., Harrogate, Tenn., 1972—85; prof., music dept. chair Lakeland C.C., Kirtland, Ohio, 1985—. Pianist, leader Bob Brown Trio/Quartet, 1962—96; pianist Harry Walters Quartet, Spl. Blend, 1960—99; ch. organist, pianist Painesville United Meth. Ch., Ohio, 1971—; adjudicator for scholarships Willoughby Sch. Fine Arts, Ohio, 1998; adjudicator student honors Cleve. Internat. Piano competition, 2003; clinician Nat. Assn. Jazz Educators, Dallas, 1978. Author: (book) Music in the Key of Life, 1995; contbr. ; composer: Now, 1976; prodr.(pianist): (video) Sites and Sounds, 1994. Pianist charitable fundraisers Lakeland C.C., 2000—01. With U.S. Army, 1968—71. Named Alumnus of the Yr., SUNY-Fredonia, 1999; grantee Summer Stipend, NEH, 1979. Mem.: NEA, Free Inquirers of N.E. Ohio, Lakeland Faculty Assn. Avocation: photography. Office: Lakeland Community Coll 7700 Clocktower Dr Kirtland OH 44094

BROWN, ROBERT LYLE, retired foreign affairs consultant; b. Dayton, Ohio, July 21, 1920; s. Joseph Sebastian and Elsie Lenore (Miller) B.; m. Marion Jean Jenkin, Nov. 14, 1947; 1 son, Garry Lyle. AB, Syracuse U., 1943; postgrad., Northwestern U., 1950-51, George Washington U., 1963-65. Corp. officer Evered, Inc., Camden, N.J., 1943-44; officer-in-charge consulate Noumea, 1944-48; vice consul, chief econ. sect., consulate gen. Casablanca, 1948-50; vice consul, chief econ. sect. Kobe and Osaka, 1951-54; consul, 2d sec., chief econ. sect., asst. comml. attache embassy Brussels, 1954-58; alt. U.S. observer Customs Coop. Council, 1954; acting U.S. commr. gen. Brussels World Fair, 1958; chief loan coordination br. econ. devel. div. Customs Coop. Council, 1959-62; dep. U.S. rep. Tripartite Gold Commn., Belgium; adviser U.S. dels. com. trade, com. industry and natural resources UN Econ. Commn. Asia and Far East, 18th Session, Bangkok; adviser U.S. del. Econ. Commn. Asia and Far East, Tokyo, 1962; mem. Sr. Seminar in Fgn. Policy, 1962-63; chief European personnel ops., 1963-65; counselor econ. affairs Am. embassy, Taipei, Republic China, 1965-68; dir. AID, Republic of China, 1966-67; dep. exec. sec. to 2 sec. State, 1968-71; dep. dir. Office Personnel Dept. State, 1972-75; minister, polit. adviser to Supreme Allied Comdr. Europe, 1975-79; sr. insp. Fgn. Service, 1979-80; insp. gen. Dept. State and Fgn. Service, 1981-83; assoc., cons. Worldwide Assn. Office of Gen. Alexander Haig, Hudson Inst., 1983-85. Cons. State Dept., 1983-88, Betac Corp., Washington, Mgmt. Logistics Internat., 1983-85, Worldwide Assocs., Hudson Inst.; treas. Com. for Am., 1986; adviser U.S. del. 24th Gen. Assembly UN, 1969; spl. asst. to sec. State for UN 25th Anniversary, 1970; observer N. Atlantic Assembly, 1976-79, Western European Union, 1979; mem. Pres.'s Council on Integrity and Efficiency, 1981-83; dep. U.S. negotiator U.S.-Belgium Friendship, Commerce and Navigation Treaty, 1960-62. Coord. Dept. State United Givers Fund campaign, 1960; bd. dirs. Internat. Sch., Brussels, Fulbright Com., Republic of China, 1965-68; v.p. Arlington dist. United Meth. Ch.; mem.-at-large adminstrv. bd. Walker Chapel, 1992-96. With USNR, 1943. Mem. U.S. Washington fgn. svc. assns., SHAPE Officers Assn., Delta Sigma Rho. Address: 3021 N Peary St Arlington VA 22207-5326

BROWN, ROBERT MUNRO, museum director; b. Riverside, N.J., Mar. 4, 1952; s. James Wendell and Janet Elizabeth (Munro) B.; m. Mary Ann Noel, June, 1973 (div. 1977); m. Claudia Leslie Haskell, Jan. 14, 1978. BA in Polit. Sci. cum laude, Ursinus Coll., 1973; MA in Social Scis., Rivier Coll., 1978; PhD in Early Am. History, U. N.H., 1983. Grad. asst. dept. history U. N.H., Durham, 1979-83, instr., 1983-84; site curator T.C. Steele State Hist. Site Ind. State Mus. System, Nashville, Ind., 1984-91; exec. dir. Hist. Mus. at Ft. Missoula, Mont., 1991—. Hist. interpreter Strawberry Banke, Portsmouth, N.H., 1980-83; instr. Rivier Coll., Nashua, N.H., 1986-91, N.H. Coll., Nashua and Salem, 1986-91; supr. pub. programs Mus. Am. Textile History, North Andover, Mass., 1985-91; sec.-treas. Western Mont. Heritage Ctr./No. Rockies Heritage Ctr., 1992-93; mem. grad. com. U. Mont., 1993; mem. steering com. Ft. Missoula, 1993; reviewer Inst. Mus. and Libr. Svcs., 1993—; reviewer Am. Assn. Mus.-Mus. Asessment Programs, 1997—; mem. Mont. Com. of the Humanities Spkrs. Bur., 1995—; lectr., presenter, chair panels in field. Contbr. articles to profl. jours. Trustee Historic Harrisville, N.H., 1989-91; bd. dirs. United Peoples Found., 1991-93, v.p., 1993; mem. planning com. Western Mont. Heritage Ctr., 1991, U. Mont. Centennial Celebration, 1992, Leadership Missoula, 1992; active open space, parks and resource planning and mgmt. project team City of Missoula, 1993; mem. blue ribbon task force Five Valleys Luth. Retirement Community Planning Com., 1994. Grantee, Mass. Coun. on Arts and Humanities, 1986, 1987, 1988, Int. Mus. Svcs., 1988, 1989, 1990, 1991, 1993, 1995, 1997, 1999, AT&T, 1988, Am. Wool Coun., 1988, BayBank, 1989, Am. Yarn Assn., 1989, North Andover Arts Lottery Coun., 1989, 1990, Mass. Cultural Coun., 1990, Greater Lawrence Cmty. Found., 1991, Mass. Arts Lottery Coun., 1991, Gallery Assn. for Greater Art, 1991, 1992, 1994, 1995, 1996, 1997, 1998, Mont. Comm. for Humanities, 1991, 1992, 1993, 1994, 1995, 1996, 1997, 1998, 1999, 2000, 2001, 2002, Sinclair Oil Co., 1991, Mont. Rail Link, 1992, 1998, 1999, 2001, 2002, 2003, U. Mont. Found., 1992, Pepsi-Cola Co., 1992, 1993, 1994, 1995, 1996, 1997, Coca-Cola Bottling Co., 1998, Cmty. Med. Ctr., 1999, St. Patrick Hosp., 1999, U.S. WEST Found., 1992, 1995, The Missoulian, 1992, 1995, Champion Internat., 1992, Mont. Cultural Trust, 1993, 1995, 1997, Missoula Rotary, 1993, Tex. Mus. Austin, 1993, Inst. Mus. Svcs., 1993, 1995, 1997, 1999, 2002, Zip Beverage Co., 1994, Bitterroot Motors, 1994, 1995, 1996, 1997, 1998, Grizzly Hackle, 1994, University Motors, 1995, 1996, Earl's Distbg., 1996, Norwest Bank, 1996, 1997, 1998, ALPS, 2001, 2002, Southgate Mall, 2002; scholar, U. N.H., 1979—83; rsch. grantee, 1982, Kellogg Found. fellow, 1987. Mem.: Greater Boston Mus. Educator's Roundtable (steering com. 1988—90), Mtn. Plains Mus. Assn. (Mont. state rep. 1995—97, ann. meeting local arrangements chair 1997, chmn. scholarship com. 1998, sec. 1998—2000, chmn. scholarship com. 1999, ann. meeting program co-chair 2000, treas. 2001—), Western Mont. Fundraisers Assn. (charter 1991, v.p. 1993—95, pres. 1995—97), Mus. Assn. Mont. (panelist 1994), Mont. Hist. Soc., Assn. Records Mgrs. and Adminstrs. (charter Big Sky chpt. 1992—94), Am. Hist. Assn., Am. Assn. State and Local History (state membership rep. 1996—98, state awards chair 2001—, program com. 2003), Am. Assn. Mus. (small mus. adminstrs. com., Mountain-Plains regional rep. 2000—), Kiwanis (Sentinel chpt.), Masons (Missoula chpt.), Phi Alpha Theta (Psi Pi chpt.). Democrat. Avocations: canoeing, cross-country skiing, snowshoeing. Home: 216 Woodworth Ave Missoula MT 59801-6050 Office: Hist Mus at Ft Missoula Ft Missoula Bldg 322 Missoula MT 59804 E-mail: ftmslamuseum@montana.com.

BROWN, ROBERT STEPHEN, physician, educator, health facility administrator; b. N.Y.C., May 21, 1938; s. Abraham J. Brown and Miriam (Margolies) Levy; m. Judith Elinor Kaufman, Dec. 18, 1960; children: Robert S. Jr., Debra Ann Brown Allen. AB magna cum laude, Harvard Coll., Cambridge, Mass., 1959; MD, Columbia Coll. Physicians and Surgeons, N.Y.C., 1963. Diplomate Am. Bd. Internal Medicine, Am. Bd. Nephrology. Intern and resident in medicine Bellevue Hosp., N.Y.C., 1963-65; clin. assoc. Nat. Cancer Inst., Bethesda, Md., 1965-67; resident in medicine, renal fellow New Haven Hosp. & Yale New Haven Hosp., 1967-69; dir. dialysis transplantation New Haven Hosp., 1969-72; dir. hemodialysis unit Boston City Hosp., 1972-73; clin. chief renal unit Beth Israel Hosp., Boston, 1973—; clin. chief nephrology Joslin Diabetes Clinic, Boston, 1999—; program dir. nephrology Beth Israel Deaconess Med. Ctr., 2001—. Asst. prof. medicine Sch. Medicine Yale U., New Haven, 1969-72, Sch. Medicine Harvard U., Cambridge, 1972-80, assoc. prof. medicine, 1980—; med. co-dir. Gambro Healthcare Dialysis, 1997—; mem. consulting staff Mt. Auburn Hosp., Cambridge, 1986—. Contbr. articles to profl. jours. Chmn. med. adv. bd., pres. Nat. Kidney Found. Mass. and R.I., N.H., Vt., Norwood, Mass., 1992—94, bd. dirs., 1992—; trustee, mem. bylaws and policy com. Nat. Kidney Found., N.Y.C., NY, 1994—99; bd. dirs. End State Renal Dis. Network of New Eng., New Haven, 2002—. Lt. comdr. USPHS, 1965—67. Regents scholar, 1959-63; recipient Outstanding Physician life award Nat. Kidney Found. Mass. and R.I., 1996. Mem. ACP, Am. Soc. Nephrology, Am. Heart Assn. Kidney Coun., Am. Soc. Transplant, Mass. Med. Soc., Renal Phys. Assoc., Alpha Omega Alpha, Newton Squash and Tennis Club (trustee, pres. 1985-86, Kontoff Merit 1982, Bronstein trophy 1988), Office: Beth Israel Deaconess Med Ctr 330 Brookline Ave Boston MA 02215-5400

BROWN, ROBERT STEPHEN, JR., physician; b. NY, NY, Sept. 14, 1963; s. Robert Stephen and Judith (Kaufman) B.; m. Susan M. Wilson, June 26, 1993; children: Jacqueline Rachel Wilson Brown, Robert Dylan, and Jake Thomas. AB, Harvard Univ., 1985; MD, N.Y.Univ., 1989; MPH, Univ. Calif., 1996. Attending physician Univ. Calif., San Francisco, 1995-96; med. dir. liver transplant Univ. NC, Chapel Hill, 1996-98; med. dir. for liver disease Columbia Univ., N.Y. Pres., NY, 1998—. Pres., bd. dir. Centerspan, Washington, 1999-2001. Contbr. articles to profl. jour. Recipient Young Investigator award Am. Soc. Transplantation, 1996. Fellow Am. Coll. Physicians, Am. Coll. Gastroenterology; mem. Am. Assn. Study Liver Disease, Am. Gastroenterological Assn., Am. Soc. Transplantation. Office: Ctr for Liver Disease N Y Presbyterian 622 W 168th St Fl 14 New York NY 10032-3720 E-mail: rb464@columbia.edu.

BROWN, ROBERT WALLACE, retired mathematics educator; b. Portland, Oreg., May 20, 1925; s. Bert and Stella (Conway) B.; m. Doris Arrilda Burroughs, Sept. 4, 1948; children: Robert Wallace, Janice Dianne. BS, Pacific U., 1950; MS, Oreg. State U., 1952, PhD, 1958. Mathematician, Nat. Bur. Standards, Corona, Calif., 1952-54; Mathematician Boeing Co., Seattle, 1958-66; vis. asso. prof. Oreg. State U., Corvallis, 1966-67; prof. math. U. Alaska, Fairbanks, 1967-82, head dept., 1967-77, 79-82; vis. prof. math. Lewis and Clark Coll., Portland, Oreg., 1982-85; ret., 1985. Contbg. author: Error in Digital Computation, 1965. With USNR, 1942—45. Mem. Math. Assn. Am., Am. Math Soc., AAAS, Sigma Xi, Pi Mu Epsilon, Sigma Pi Sigma. Home: 20755 SW Prindle Rd Tualatin OR 97062-9701

BROWN, ROBERT WAYNE, lawyer; b. Allentown, Pa., July 6, 1942; s. P.P. and Rose (Ferrara) B.; m. Rochelle Kaplan, Oct. 23, 1977; m. Shelley Sherman, Mar. 3, 1973; children: Courtney Sherman, Robin Thea, Ryan Palmer; m. Lupe Pearce, Nov. 22, 1996. AB, Franklin and Marshall Coll., 1964; JD, Cornell U., 1967. Bar: Ill. 1969, Pa. 1971. VISTA atty. Cmty. Legal Svcs., Detroit, 1967-68; asst. prof. law U. Ill., 1968-70; ct. adminstr., law clk. Lehigh County Ct. Common Pleas, 1971-72; ptnr. Gross & Brown, Allentown, 1972-76; pvt. practice law Allentown, 1976-77; sr. ptnr. Brown & Brown, Allentown, 1977-82, Brown, Brown & Solt, Allentown, 1982-85, Brown, Brown, Solt & Krouse, Allentown, 1985-89, Brown, Brown, Solt & Ferretti, Allentown, 1989—; city solicitor Allentown, 2002—. Instr. bus. law Muhlenburg Coll., 1973-76; pub. defender Lehigh County, 1973-74; mem. adv. bd. PNC Bank. Mem. Rape Crisis Coun. Lehigh Valley, 1978-84, Lehigh County Pre-trial Svcs., 1975-82; bd. dirs. Hispanic Am. Orgn., 1982-90, treas., 1983-86; bd. dirs. Lehigh County Sr. Citizens, 1980-88, pres., 1984-86; bd. dirs. Lehigh County Legal Svcs., 1973-77, Boys and Girls Club Allentown, 1994—, pres., 1998-2000; founding trustee Robert Clemente Charter Sch., 1998—. Recipient Cmty. Svc. award Hispanic Am. Orgn., 1985, Human Rels. Commn. award, Allentown, 1986; Lindback scholar Franklin and Marshall Coll., 1963-64. Mem. ABA, Pa. Bar Assn., Lehigh County Bar Assn., Order of Coif, Rotary (bd. dirs. Allentown 1998—). Democrat. Home: 225 Parkview Ave Allentown PA 18104-5323 Office: 1425 W Hamilton St Allentown PA 18102-4224 E-mail: rwbrown@onemain.com.

BROWN, ROBERT WILLIAM, physics educator, physicist; b. St. Paul, Oct. 3, 1941; s. William James and Florence Elizabeth B.; m. Janet Gans; children: Kimberly, Kyle, Kirsten. BS, U. Minn., 1963; PhD, MIT, 1968. Rsch. asst. MIT, Cambridge, Mass., 1963-68; rsch. assoc. Brookhaven Nat. Lab., Upton, N.Y., 1968-70; asst. prof. Case Western Res. U., Cleve., 1970-74, assoc. prof., 1974-82, prof., 1982-91, inst. prof., 1991—. Physics design advisor Cleve. and Ohio industry, 1981—; vis. prof. Fermi Nat. Lab., 1982; v.p. MRI Innovations in Biomed. Rsch., Detroit, 1995—; vis. prof. Washington U., St. Louis, 1995. Rsch. grantee NSF, NIH, 1972-2003; recipient Undergrad. Comp. Edn. award Dept. of Energy, 1997. Fellow Am. Phys. Soc. (chair Ohio sect. 2001-02); mem. Am. Assn. Physics Tchrs., Internat. Soc. Mag. Resonance in Medicine, Forum of Indsl. and Applied Physics (exec. bd. 1999-2003, Diekhoff grad. tchg. award 2003). Avocations: aerobics, music, sports physics, tutoring. Office: Case Western Res U Dept Physics 204 Rockefeller Bldg Cleveland OH 44106-7079 E-mail: rwb@cwru.edu.

BROWN, RONALD, retired stockbroker; b. Aug. 30, 1930; s. Arthur S. and Eleanor (Smith) B.; m. Patricia Joan Milner, Aug. 2, 1952; children: Mitchell Ronald, Valerie Patricia. BS, Purdue U., 1953; MBA, NYU, 1957. Security analyst E.W. Axe & Co., Tarrytown, N.Y., 1955-56, Stillman, Maynard, N.Y.C., 1956-61; instl. salesman Clark Dodge & Co., N.Y.C., 1961-67; gen. ptnr. Buttonwood Assocs., Jersey City, 1967-71; pres. Personal Investment Mgmt. Co., Mahwah, N.J., 1971-72; asst. v.p., account exec. E.F. Hutton N.Y.C., 1972-77; sr. v.p. Dean Witter Reynolds, Inc., 1979-97; ret., 1997. Contbr. articles to profl. jours. Rockland County Rep. committeeman, 1958-60. With U.S. Army, 1953-55. Mem. N.Y. Soc. Security Analysts Inst., Chartered Fin. Analysts, N.Y. Athletic Club, Assn. Investment Mgmt. and Rsch., Kappa Sigma, Scarsdale Golf Club. Home: 100 W 57th St New York NY 10019-3302 E-mail: dufferon@nyc.rr.com.

BROWN, RONALD, music educator; b. Aug. 18, 1951; s. Alphonso William Brown and Jimmie Mae Crisp. MusB, Cath. U. Am., 1992. Music tchr. Prince George's (Md.) County Pub. Schs., 1992—97, Howard County Pub. Schs., Columbia, Md., 1997—. Dir. music St. Martin's Cath. Ch., Washington, 1979—92, Simpson-Hamline United Meth. Ch., Washington, 1992—. Singer: Washington (D.C.) Cath. Choir, 1978—79, Paul Hill Corale, 1979—91, Washington (D.C.) Men's Camerata, 1986—89, Choir of the Nat. Shrine, 1987—92. Mem.: Music Educators Assn., Music Educators Nat. Conf. Avocations: reading, music. Home: Laurel MD 20724 Office: Atholton High School 6520 Freetown Rd Columbia MD 21044-4002

BROWN, RONALD DELANO, endocrinologist; b. Grosse Pointe, Mich., Dec. 28, 1936; s. Carroll Bradley and Alice Ruth (Chapper) B.; m. Marylee Ethel Lucas, July 27, 1957; children: Linda Diane, Kent William, Mark Steven. BS with distinction, U. Mich., 1959, MD with distinction, 1963. Diplomate Am. Bd. Internal Medicine, subspecialty in endocrinology and metabolism; lic. physician Mich. Intern Detroit Gen. Hosp., 1963-64; asst. resident in medicine U. Calif. Med. Ctr., San Francisco, 1966 68; chief resident in medicine San Francisco Gen. Hosp., 1968-69; fellow in endocrinology Vanderbilt U., Nashville, 1969-71, instr. medicine, 1969-71, asst. prof. medicine, 1971-73; assoc. prof. medicine Baylor Coll. Medicine, Houston, 1973-74, Mayo Med. Sch., Rochester, Minn., 1975-80; prof. medicine Health Scis. Ctr., U. Okla., Oklahoma City, 1980-93; clin. staff St. Joseph's Mercy Hosp., Clintown Twp., Mich., 1993—. Dir. U. Okla. Hypertension Ctr., 1986-93; chief clin. hypertension Health Scis. Ctr., U. Okla., 1980-93; chief hypertension VA Hosp., Oklahoma City, 1980-86; dir. multidisciplinary hypertension rsch. tng. program (NIH), Mayo Clinic, Rochester, 1977-80; chief endocrinology Ben Taub Hosp., Houston, 1973-74, assoc. dir. clin. rsch. ctr., 1973-74; coord. Tenn. Mid-South Regional Hyper-Control Program, Vanderbilt U., 1971-73; lectr. in field. Editl. bd. Jour. Clin. Endocrinology and Metabolism, 1987-91; reviewer for Life Scis., Annals of Internal Medicine, Jour. Lab. Clin. Medicine, Am. Jour. Medicine, Endocrinology, Mayo Clinic Proceedings, Steroids; contbr. 58 articles to profl. jours. Capt. USAF, 1964-66. Fellow ACP, Am. Coll. Endocrinologists; mem. Am. Soc. Hypertension, Am. Diabetes Assn., Am. Assn. Clin. Endocrinologists, Phi Kappa Phi, Phi Lambda Upsilon, Alpha Omega Alpha. Avocation: nursery. Office: 43171 Dalcoma Dr Ste 1 Clinton Township MI 48038-6307

BROWN, RONALD DELANO, scriptwriter, playwright, actor; b. Ft. Lewis, Wash., Nov. 11, 1948; s. Samuel Franklyn and Mabel (Nation) B.. BS, U. Md., 1972. Student advisor West L.A. Coll., L.A., 1986. Author: (TV series) Watercolors episode Spenser: for Hire, 1987, (plays) American Guerrilla, 1994, 1998, Victims, 1981; actor: Rush Hour, 1999; lyricist: Where Is It I Belong (The Supremes), voice-over actor: Booker T. Washington, NBC/WETA-PBS. Dir. L.A. Oral History Project United Way, L.A., 1980. Mem.: SAG, Writers Guild Am. (West). Democrat. Avocations: graphic arts, fine arts, history, antique guns.

BROWN, RONALD JAMES, lawyer, consultant; b. McKeesport, Pa., Nov. 4, 1951; s. James W. and Katherine V. (Amatangelo) Brown; m. Kathy E. Brown, July 6, 1996; children from previous marriage: Claudia Jean, Jocelyn Kaye. BA, U. Pitts., 1973, JD, 1976. Bar: Pa. 1976. Assoc. firm Lucchino, Gaitens & Hough, Pitts., 1976-79; asst. dep. contr. Allegheny County Contr.'s Office, Pitts., 1979-86; ptnr. Grogan, Graffam, Pitts., 1986—. Polit. cons. Brown-Giorgetti Cons., Pitts., 1990—; counsel Port of Pitts. Commn., 2003—. Del. Dem. Nat. Conv., 1978; Dem. candidate state senator North Hills, Pa., 1986; chmn. Nov. Caucus, Pitts., 1995—; mem. Dem. Forum Western Pa., Pitts., 1987—91; bd. dirs., treas. Dollar Energy Fund Western Pa. Recipient Commrs. award citation merit, Allegheny County Bd. Commrs., 1984. Mem.: Nat. Assn. Bond Lawyers, Allegheny County Bar Assn. Roman Catholic. Avocations: golf, reading, watching hockey, travel. Office: Grogan Graffam 4 Gateway Ctr Pittsburgh PA 15222-1000 E-mail: rbrown@grogangraffam.com.

BROWN, RONALD MALCOLM, engineering corporation executive; b. Hot Springs, S.D., Feb. 21, 1938; s. George Malcolm and Cleo Lavonne (Plumb) B.; m. Sharon Ida Brown, Nov. 14, 1964 (div. Apr. 1974); children: Michael, Troy, George, Curtis, Lisa, Brittney. AA, Southwestern Coll., 1970; BA, Chapman U., 1978. Commd. USN, 1956, advanced through grades to master chief, 1973, ret., 1978; engring. mgr. Beckman Inst., Fullerton, Calif., 1978-82; mfg. engring. br. mgr. Northrop Corp., Hawthorne, Calif., 1982-83; dir. of ops. Transco, Marina Del Rey, Calif., 1983-85; v.p. engring. and design Decor Concepts, Arcadia, Calif., 1985-87; design dir. Lockheed Aircraft Corp., Ontario, Calif., 1987-97; v.p. engring. and program mgmt. Ducommon Inc., Carson, Calif., 1997—2003; pres. BASIC Consulting Inc., Brea, Calif., 2003—. Mem. Rep. Nat. Com. and Pres.'s Club. Mem. Soc. Mfg. Engrs., Inst. Indsl. Engrs., Nat. Trust for Hist. Preservation, Fleet Res. Assn., Am. Film Inst., Nat. Mgmt. Assn. Avocations: golf, running, racquetball. Office: 101 W Central Brea CA 92821

BROWN, RONALD MILES, retired academic administrator; b. Riley, Kans., Mar. 19, 1931; s. James L. Brown, Margaret Beninga; m. Marilou Diemer, Dec. 29, 1959; children: Robert, Patrick. BA, U. Colo., Boulder, 1951; M.P.S., U. Colo., 1957; PhD, U. Mich., 1971. Sec. tchr. pub. schs., Boulder and Montrose, Colo., 1951—56; dir. student fin. aid U. Colo., Boulder, 1956—67; assoc. dir. Salzburg Seminar, Salzburg, Austria, 1964—65; dir. student fin. aid U. Mich., Ann Arbor, 1969—71; v.p., prof. U. Tex., Austin, 1971—2001. Mem.: Tarry House, Headliners Club. Episcopalian. Avocations: cooking, travel.

BROWN, RONALD OSBORNE, telecommunications and computer systems consultant; b. Winchester, Mass., Apr. 9, 1941; s. Herbert Walcott and Madeleine Louise (Osborne) B.; m. Annette L. Brown; children: Melinda E., Jeffrey J. BS with distinction, U. Maine, 1963; MS, Tufts U., 1965; PhD, Queens U., Kingston, Ont., 1972. Mem. tech. staff RCA Corp., Burlington, Mass., 1965-66; rsch. assoc. Queen's U., Kingston, Ont., 1966-71; mem. sci. staff BNR, Ottawa, Ont., 1971-72; sr. systems engr. GTE Corp., Needham, Mass., 1973-83; mgr. Coopers & Lybrand, Boston, 1983-87, nat. dir, 1987-88; pvt. practice cons. Melrose, Mass., 1988-91; pres. R.O. Brown Cons., Melrose, 1991—; COO Locatum LLC, 2001—, also bd. dirs. Bd. dirs. Coop. Comms. Contbg. editor: Networking Mgmt. Mag., 1988—93. Mem. IEEE, Assn. Profl. Engrs. Ont., Tau Beta Pi, Phi Kappa Phi, Eta Kappa Nu. Home: 864 Quaker Ridge Rd PO Box 470 South Casco ME 04077-0470 Office: 23 Baxter St Ste 2 Melrose MA 02176-3639 E-mail: brownro@aol.com.

BROWN, RONALD REA, software engineer, artist; b. Kansas City, Mo., Mar. 20, 1944; s. Stanton Rea and Agnes S. B.; m. Josette Adella Keenan, Aug. 14, 1977; children: Nathan William, Lisette Louise, Andrew Rea. BA in Math. magna cum laude, William Jewell Coll., 1966; MA in Math., U. Kans., 1968, MEd, Montclair State Coll., 1972. Cert. secondary sch. tchr., N.J., Pa. Vol. Peace Corps, Andhra Pradesh, India, 1969-70; tchr. Alternative West H.S., Lower Merion, Pa., 1973-79; software engr. Delta Data Syss., Trevose, Pa., 1979-83; sr. software engr. Unisys, Flemington, NJ, 1983-89, Thwing-Albert Instrument Co., Phila., 1990-94; sr. engr. Catalyst, Newtown, Pa., 1994-97, Thwing-Albert Instrument Co., Phila., 1997—. Presenter in field of art. Contbr. articles to profl. jours. Vol. Peace Corps, Andhra Pradesh, India, 1969-70. Mem. Internat. Soc. for Interdisciplinary Study of Symmetry, Lehigh (Pa.) Art Alliance (sculpture award 1992), YLEM, Internat. Sculpture Ctr., Art & Sci. Collaborations, Inc. Avocations: reading, fractals, virtual reality, robotics, 2d and 3d art based on the way a knight moves on a chessboard. Home: 569 Lake Warren Rd Upper Black Eddy PA 18972-9342 Office: Thwing-Albert Inst Co 10960 Dutton Rd Philadelphia PA 19154-3204 E-mail: rrbrown@epix.net.

BROWN, RONALD WELLINGTON, lawyer, educator, consultant, business executive, entrepreneur; b. Oct. 17, 1945; s. Leroy Harry and Mollie (Fitch) Brown; m. Geraldine Reed, Aug. 20, 1972; children: Kimberly Diana, Michael David. BA, Rutgers U., 1967; JD, Harvard U., 1971, MBA, 1973; postgrad., Columbia U., 1975. Bar: N.Y. 1975, U.S. Dist. Ct. (so. and ea. dists.) N.Y. 1975, U.S. Ct. Appeals (2d cir.) 1975, U.S. Supreme Ct. 1978. From atty. legal dept.

to staff counsel litigation ITT, N.Y.C., NY, 1973—84, staff counsel litigation, 1984—85; dir. N. Am. commonwealth antipiracy ops. Motion Picture Assn. Am., N.Y.C., 1986—87; real estate devel. and property mgmt. N.J. Transit Corp., Newark, 1988; exec. v.p. Reed, Brown Consulting Group, Montclair, NJ, 1991—; dir. bus. affairs Norjean Entertainment Mgmt., N.Y.C., 1997—2002; mng. dir. legis. regulatory and legal affairs Office Info. Tech., State of N.J., Trenton, 2003—. Vis. prof. Huston-tillotson Coll., Austin, Tex., 1978; of counsel Spooner & Burnett, N.Y.C., 1997—97; pres., CEO BRS & W Prodns., Inc., N.Y.C., 1992—94; adj. prof. law sch. Rutgers U., 1995; sec., dir., mem. exec. com. Studio Mus. in Harlem, N.Y.C., 1979—81. Author: (non-fiction) Economic and Trade Related Aspects of Transborder Flow: Elements of A Code for Transnational Commerce, 1986, Legal Aspects of Doing Business in the Middle East, 1975, Joint Ventures: A Tool for Small, Women, and Minority Owned Businesses, 2000; contbr. articles to profl. jours.; editor (mem. bd. editors): (law rev.) Harvard Civil Rights-Civil Liberties Law Rev., 1969—71; exec. prodr.(articles editor): (law rev.) Harvard Civil Rights-Civil Liberties Law Rev., 1970. Dir. Operation Crossroads Africa, Inc., N.Y.C., 1976—, v.p., 1981—86; pres., exec. dir., COO Sammy Davis Jr. Nat. Liver Inst., 1988—91; moderator White House Conf. Small Bus., 1995; mem. small bus. com. Prosperity N.J., 1996—; mem. N.J. Bd. Pub. Utilities Supplier Diversity Coun., 1997—; chmn. N.J. United Minority Bus. Brain Trust, 1997—2000, U.S. Small Bus. Adminstrn., 1999; CEO W.F. Golf Enterprises, Inc., 2000—; mem. environ. commn. Twp. of Monclair, 2002—03; chmn. staff parish rels. com. St. Marks United Meth. Ch., 1998—2000, vice chmn. Ch. coun., 2001—; mem. Bd. Edn., Montclair, NJ, 1986—, v.p., 1987, pres., 1988—; bd. dirs. One Hundred Black Men, N.Y.C., 1982—88, 1st v.p., 1985—87; bd. dir. Friends of the Davis Ctr. for the Performing Arts, 1987—88, Leonard Davis Ctr. for the Performing Arts, N.Y.C., 1984—89; mem. Planning bd. Twp. of Montclair, 1997—. Named Black Achiever in Industry, Harlem YMCA, 1984. Mem.: ABA (mem. coun., chmn. Euripean law com., sect. internat. law and practice 1984—86, assoc. editor Internat. Law News 1983—86), Union Internat. des Avocats, Am. Soc. Internat. Law, Internat. Law Assn., N.Y. State Bar Assn., Assn. Bar City N.Y. (chmn. subcom. on fed. legis. of com. on art law 1983—86), Am. Arbitration Assn., Omega Psi Phi. Methodist. Home: 180 Union St Montclair NJ 07042-2125 Office: PO Box 407 Montclair NJ 07042-0407 also: PO Box 212 300 Riverview Plaza Trenton NJ 08625

BROWN, ROWLAND CHAUNCEY WIDRIG, information systems, strategic planning and ethics consultant; b. Detroit, Oct. 11, 1923; s. Rowland Chauncey and Rhea (Widrig) B.; m. Kathleen Heather Sayre, May 18, 1946; children: Stephanie Anne Kugelman, Geoffrey Rowland Sayre (dec.), Kathleen Heather. BA cum laude, Harvard U., 1947, JD, 1950; sr. mgmt. Sloan Sch., MIT, 1969; D. Humane Letters (hon.), Ohio Dominican Coll., 1999. Bar: D.C. 1951. Counsel Econ. Sablzn. Agy., 1950-52; staff counsel SBA, 1954; counsel Machinery and Allied Products Inst., Washington, 1955-59; with Dorr Oliver, Stamford, Conn., 1959-70, pres., 1968-70; pres., chief exec. officer Buckeye Internat., Inc., Columbus, Ohio, 1970-80; chief exec. officer Online Computer Libr. Ctr., Columbus, 1980-89; with R. Brown & Assocs., Columbus. Adv. bd. tchg. and learning Ohio State U. Sr. internat. cons. Coun. for Ethics Econs. inter-profl. panel on tech. and ethics; hon. trustee Columbus Cmty. Cable Access; bd. dirs., visitor's bd. Ohio Dominican Coll.; trustee Coun. for Pub. Deliberation, Civic Life Inst. Decorated Air medal (3), Purple Heart, Korean Republic citation. Mem. ALA. Am. Soc. Info. Sci., Am. Assn. for Higher Edn., N.Y. Harvard Club, Columbus Club, Torch Club, Scioto Country Club, Rotary. Home and Office: R Brown & Assoc 2711 Edington Rd Columbus OH 43221-2502 E-mail: rcwbrow@columbus.rr.com.

BROWN, ROXANNE (JERENE ROXANNE BROWN), sales executive; b. L.A., July 5, 1947; d. John Phillip and Margaret Leona (Dalrymple) Ortiz; m. Terry Lee Wood, May 7, 1966 (div. Sept. 1969); 1 child, Tiffany Christine Wood Suraco; m. Christopher Corey Brown, July 17, 1984 (dec. Sept. 1984); children: Jason Michael and John Charles (twins); m. Richard L. Gibbs, Apr. 18, 1996 (dec. Feb. 2000). Student, Casper Coll., 1977. Info. operator Gen. Telephone, Baldwin Park, Calif., 1965-67, long distance operator Santa Maria, Calif., 1967-69; office mgr. Monroe Calculator, Las Vegas, Nev., 1972-74; mgr. Exch. Club, Salt Lake City, 1977-81, Pouches Inc., Salt Lake City, 1981-82; asst. producer KSTU TV 20, Salt Lake City, 1982-84; sec. ADVO - Sys., Inc., Orange, Calif., 1984-85, terr. sales rep., 1985-88, major account exec. Garden Grove, Calif., 1988-95; v.p. JRB & Assocs., Long Beach, Calif., 1995—. Cons. Rice - Urmana Advt., Huntington Beach, Calif., 1989-91. Bd. dirs. ACLU, Salt Lake City, 1977; precinct worker Voter Registrar, Huntington Beach, 1988, Long Beach, Calif., 1990; bd. dirs., sec. Alamitos Bay Beach Peninsula Preservation Group, 1996-98. Mem.: ACLU, SAG, Platform Speakers Assn., Alamitos Bay Garden Club (v.p., ways and means com. 1996—98). Avocations: sculpting, photography, sailing. Home: 77 Ximeno Ave Long Beach CA 90803-3056 E-mail: rocknsand@yahoo.com.

BROWN, RUSSELL JAY, nurse; b. Newfane, NY, May 30, 1961; s. Bennett Marion and Maryanne (Mikulec) B. AA, Niagara County C.C., 1982; diploma in nursing, Millard Fillmore Hosp., 1985; student, Tenn. Inst. Healing Arts, 2000. RN. Staff nurse Millard Fillmore Hosp., Buffalo, 1985-89, Meml. Med. Ctr., Savannah, Ga., 1989—98, Owensboro Mercy Health Sys., 1998-99, Tenn. Inst. Healing Arts Massage Sch., 1999—2000; massage therapist Health Pk./Owensboro Mercy Health Sys., 2000—; staff nurse Ohio County Hosp., ICU, 2001—. Rsch. nurse, Savannah, 1993-96; massage therapist, neuromuscular therapist, Owensboro Mercy Health System Health Park, 2000. Mem. AACN. Democrat. Avocations: reading, studying weather. Home: 844 Hoopee Hill Rd Hartford KY 42347-9666 E-mail: rbrown30@owensboro.net.

BROWN, RUTH GEISLER, engineering supervisor; b. Beaver Falls, Pa., Mar. 17, 1924; d. Carl Charles and Emily (Pletz) Geisler; m. Stuart Fife Brown, Apr. 13, 1944. Student, Johns Hopkins U., 1960—70. Svc. rep. Bell. Tel. of Pa., Pitts., 1942—43; draftsman to group engr. Martin Marietta Co., Middle River, Md., 1944—49, 1950—63; design draftsman Bendix Radio, Balt., 1949—50; engrng. staff assoc. missile programs and microelectronics Johns Hopkins U./Applied Physics Lab., Laurel, Md., 1963—75, sr. engrng. staff, supr. hybrid ops., 1975—79, divsn. staff, 1979—81, electronic design supr., 1981—83, engrng. design supr., 1983—90; ret., 1990. Mem.: NAFE, Internat. Electronic Packaging Soc., Internat. Soc. Hybrid Microelectronics. Republican. Home: 12628 W Parkwood Dr Sun City West AZ 85375-4626

BROWN, SAMUEL, retired corporate executive; b. Mobile, Ala., Mar. 2, 1908; s. Milton Leopold and Edna (Solomon) B.; m. Carolyn Elkan Greenfield, Nov. 2, 1930 (dec. Oct. 1989); children: Milton Leopold, Maxine Phyllis Brown Feibelman, Carol Lynn Brown Robinson. BS, U. Ala., 1929. Mng. ptnr. Brown & Brown, Mobile, 1935-42, owner, 1942-54; pres. Brown & Brown, Inc., Mobile, 1954-84, Brownfield Investment Corp., Mobile, 1954, also bd. dirs.; pres. Brown and Brown of Del., Inc., Wilmington, 1984—, also bd. dirs.; pres. Greenfield Lands, Inc., Atlanta, 1981—, also bd. dirs. Author: The Rotary Club of Mobile, Alabama, 1914-1986, Brown & Brown, May 1, 1877-Sept. 29, 1996 Events During 119 Years 5 Months; also articles. Pres. Rotary, Mobile, 1955-56, bd. trustees Mobile Pub. Libr., 1964. Recipient Disting. Svc. award Ala. Soc. for Crippled Children, 1973. Mem. Indsl. Fabrics Assn. (hon. life), Mobile Country Club. Republican. Jewish. Avocation: golf.

BROWN, SAMUEL JOSEPH, JR., engineer, scientist; b. New Orleans, May 6, 1941; s. Samuel Joseph and Camille (Trumbatory) B.; m. Josephine Monistere; children: Troy Joseph, Tricia Maria Brown Kenworthy, Kamryn Leigh Brown Johnson. BSME, U. La., Lafayette, 1966; MS in Applied Mechanics, U. Fla., 1968; PhD in Civil Engring. & Appl. Mechanics, U. Akron, 1982; MA, Sch. Theology, U. St. Thomas, Houston. Registered profl. engr., Ohio, Tex., La., Okla., Pa., Ala., Miss. New constrn. inspector New Orleans Port Authority, 1964; project mech. engr. Mid South Utilities, New Orleans, 1966; R&D cons. U. Fla., Gainesville, 1969-70; with design and devel. of prototype equipment Babcock & Wilcox McDermott Co., Akron, Ohio, 1970-78; cons. Sci. Mgt. Corp./O'Donnell & Assocs., Pitts., 1979-80, Quest Engring. Devel. Corp., Humble, Tex., 1980—; bd. dirs. Intertech Svcs. Inc., Houston, 1984—. Univ. faculty, vis. lectr., profl. devel. instr. in courses on computer simulation, failure analysis, fluid structure dynamics, component design and analysis, explosions and hazardous release protection, forensic engring. Author: Pressure Systems Energy Release Protection, 1986; co-author: Am. Soc. Metals Handbook of Engineering Mathematics, 1983, Handbook of Case Histories in Failure Analysis, 1993, 1994, Non-Linear Analysis of Light Water Reactor Components: Areas of Investigation/Benefits/Recommendations, 1980, Forensic Engineering: Part I, 1995; editor (and author): 20 tech. volumes; co-editor: Jour. Process Mech. Engring. (U.K.), 1990—92; contbr. Sponsor U. La. Alumni Assn., 1990, U. Akron Alumni Assn., U. Fla. Alumni Assn., 1991; pres. Lakeside Terrace Cmty. Assn., 1995-96. Fellow NASA, 1981, NDEA, 1966, Wisdom Soc., 1989; Personalities in Am. award ABI, 1990. Fellow: Am. Soc. Chem. Engrs. (tech. divsn. 1989—), AIChE, ASCE (tech. divsn. 1979—), ASME (codes and standards divsn. 1982—, chmn. subcom. on hazardous release protection, vice chmn. high pressure sys. com., pressure vessel and piping divsn. 1974—, edn. honors and awards subcom. OAC vice-chmn. 1974—83, chmn. OAC com. 1982—85, newsletter editor 1982—83, high pressure com. 1979—82, tech.. divsn., chmn. conf. tech. program com. 1985, Outstanding Tech. Paper award 1984, Bd. Govs. Svc. award 1992, Dedicated Svc. award 1995); mem.: Houston C. of C., Post Tng. Inst., Nat. Assn. Accident Reconstrn. Specialists, Human Factors and Ergonomics Soc., Soc. Mfg. Engrs., Am. Soc. Exptl. Mechanics (tech. divsn. 1978—), Am. Soc. Metals (tech. divsn. 1984—), Sigma Xi. Achievements include design of PWR, LWR, breeder, naval nuclear and geothermal power systems, and new mechanical-civil-aeronautical-chem. sys., equipment and structural concepts, redesign of systems, equipment and components following forensic anlaysis, and recognized as expert in forensic engineering and accident reconstruction. Office: Quest Engring Devel Corp 7500 Old North Belt Dr Humble TX 77396-2625

BROWN, SANDRA DEAN, counselor; b. Sept. 8, 1962; d. Joseph and Ozella Brown. BA, Am. Theology Coll., 1999, MA, 2000, PhD. Author: Virtuous Woman Unveiled, 1995, A Rise to Life, 1995, I Know My Name, 1995, Precious Stores for Children, 1996, Pleaase for the Children's Sake, 1996. Mem. Ruth K. Solomon Girls Vendor, Omaha, 1972—; pres. Your Positive Self Found., 2000—; minister Ministries of God, 2000—. Avocations: writing, clothing design, furniture design, singing, songwriting. Home: 4918 Ames Ave Apt 11 Omaha NE 68104

BROWN, SANDRA LEE, art association administrator, watercolorist; b. Chgo., July 9, 1943; d. Arthur Willard and Erma Emily (Lange) Boettcher; m. Ronald Gregory Brown, June 21, 1983; 1 child, Jon Michael. BA in Art and Edn., N.E. Ill. U., 1966; postgrad., No. Ill. U. Cert. K-9 tchr., Ill. Travel agt. Weiss Travel Bur., Chgo., 1959-66; tchr. Chgo. Sch. Sys., 1966-68, Schaumburg (Ill.) Sch. Dist. 54, 1968-94, creator coord. peer mentoring program for 1st-yr. tchrs., 1992-96; cons. Yardstick Ednl. Svcs., Monroe, Wis., 1994—2003; exec. dir. Monroe Arts Ctr., 1996—2001, Monroe Area Coun. for the Arts, Madisonville, Tenn., 2002—03; arts mgmt. cons. Helping Hands, Non-Profit Consulting, Knoxville, Tenn., 2003—. Mem. adv. bd. Peer Coaching and Mentoring Network, Chgo. suburban region, 1992-94; peer cons. Schaumburg Sch. Dist. 54, 1988-94. Exhibited in group shows Court House Gallery, Woodstock, Ill., Millburn (Ill.) Gallery, Gallerie Stefanie, Chgo., Monroe Arts Ctr., 1997. Campaign chmn. for mayoral candidate, Grayslake, Ill., 1989; campaign chmn. for trustee Citizens for Responsible Govt., Grayslake, 1991. Mem. Lakes Region Watercolor Guild, Delta Kappa Gamma (chmn. women in arts Gamma chpt. Ill. 1992-94, Alpha Mu chpt. 1995-97), Cmty. Arts League (Athens, Tenn.). Avocations: gardening, musician for barn dances, pre-war Appalachian, blues and cajun music, research collecting 78 rpm records. Home and Office: Helping Hands Non-Profit Consulting PO Box 1456 Athens TN 37371 *Life's greatest limitations are internal. Resolve those, and external experience transforms into opportunity.*

BROWN, SARAH M. artist, gallery owner, educator, publisher; b. Longview, Tex., Jan. 30, 1935; d. Phil Uhls and Fannie Belle (Keating) B. BFA with honors in figure drawing and figure painting, U. Chgo. and Art Inst. Chgo., 1957; student, Tulane U., 1960, Odyssey Studio, Atlanta, 1978, Nat. Watercolor Seminar, 1980. Tchr. ceramics Pensacola Fla. Jr. Coll., 1958; dir. art dept. Pensacola Fla. Adult Vocat. Sch., 1958-59; owner S. Brown Studio-Gallery, New Orleans, 1959-63, Atlanta, 1963-89, Roswell, Ga., 1986-89, Sarah Brown Studio-Gallery, Atlanta, 1989—. Founder Sarah Brown Art Tours, 1973—, The Little Brown Press, 1976—; conductor seminars in field. One-woman shows include Longview (Tex.) Art Assn., Pensacola Art Assn., Douglasville Cultural Arts Ctr., 1995, exhibited in group shows at Nat. We. Small Painting Exhbn., 1982 (Best of Show, 1st place), Palm Beach Galleries (3rd place show, 1st place We. category), NLAPW Ga. State Competition (1st place oils), Midwest Armory Art Exhibn., Chgo., Johnson Galleries, Three Arts Club, Southside Arts Festival, Delgado Mus., New Orleans, Pensacola Quadricentennial, Royal Orleans Hotel, New Orleans, Piedmont Art Festival, Berman Lipton Interiors, Atlanta Artists Group Show, Jr. C. of C., Am. Painters in Paris, Winter Park (Fla.) Outdoor Art Festival, Festival of the Masters, Lake Buena Vista, Fla., Knickerbocker Artists 31st Annual, N.Y.C., Catherine Lorillard Wolfe Art Club Exhibit, Nat. We. Small Painting Exhbn., Bosque Farms, N.Mex., Palm Beach Galleries, New Orleans, ABC Art and Frame Show, Atlanta, Wildlife Fedn., 1994, Safari Internat. Exhbn., Galleria Mall, Atlanta, 1995, Callawolde Cultural Arts Ctr., 2001, commns. include A.H. Stephens Meml., Crawfordville, State of Ga. Dept. Natural Resources, Warm Springs Lodge, Elijah Clarke Mus., New Echota Historic Site, Hofwyl Plantation, Savannah, Ga., Represented in permanent collections former Pres. Jimmy Carter, Sen. Geraldine Ferraro, Reynolds Plantation and Great Waters, Eatonton, Ga., St. Ives Country Club, featured art in mags., exhibitions include Cultural Art Ctr., Atlanta, 2001. Founder Mitzi Brown Drama Fund, Shamrock H.S., Atlanta, 1974. Mem. Nat. League Am. Pen Women, Nat. Mus. Women in the Arts (charter), Portrait Soc. Am., Inc., Atlanta High Mus., Atlanta Zool. Soc., Ga. Wildlife Fedn. Office: Sarah Brown Studio-Gallery 2947 Lookout Pl NE # 2 Atlanta GA 30305-3217 E-mail: sarahbrownstudio@aol.com.

BROWN, SEYMOUR R. lawyer, director; b. Cleve., Oct. 24, 1924; s. Leonard and Ella (Rubinstein) B.; m. Madeline Kusevich, July 8, 1956; children: Frederic M., Thomas R., Barbara L. N. Rybicki. BA, Case-Western Res. U., 1948; JD, Cleve. State U., 1953. Bar: Ohio 1953. Prin. Seymour R. Brown & Assocs., Cleve.; ptnr. Brown-McCallister Real Estate, Residential & Comml. Constrn., Melbourne, Fla., 1973-81. Spl. counsel to atty. gen. State of Ohio, 1963-70. Editor, pub.: Gt. Lakes Architecture, 1955-59. Chmn. CSC, University Heights, Ohio, 1978-82, 84-86, mem., 1976—; mem. exec. com. Cuyahoga County Rep. Orgn., 1966—; pres. Nat. Permanent Endowment Fund, Inc., 1988-92. With AUS, 1943-45. Decorated Purple Heart, Bronze Star; named to Ohio Mil. Hall of Fame, 2003. Mem. ABA, Ohio Bar Assn., Cleve. Bar Assn., Am. Arbitration Assn. (comml. arbitration panel), Zeta Beta Tau (nat. dir., nat. pres. 1978-80), Masons. Home: 3718 Meadowbrook Blvd Cleveland OH 44118-4422

BROWN, SHAUNA KIRSTI, music educator, researcher, composer; b. Santa Ana, Calif., Nov. 24, 1978; d. Gregory S. and Jan M. Pearson; m. Dennis B. Brown, Nov. 20, 1999. BA in Pub. Rels. and Spanish, Brigham Young U., 2000, cert. in TESOL, 2003. Dir. Project Read, Provo, Utah, 2000—. Sec. Mountainland Literacy Coalition, Provo, Utah, 2002—; pvt. piano tchr., 1993—. Composer: (songs) Epiphany, 2002; mng. editor: Lake Mountain Interactive, 2002—. Reporter Saratoga Springs (Utah) City Coun., 2002—. Grantee, City of Provo, Utah, 2000—02, City of Orem, Utah, 2000—02, Dept. of Workforce Svcs., 2002, Cmty. Literacy Mini grant, Utah Commn. on Vols., 2000, 2002. Mem.: ProLiteracy Worldwide, Utah Assn. of Adult, Cmty., and Continuing Edn., TESOL. Lds Ch. Achievements include research in the effect of native language literacy on second language acquisition for adults. Avocations: travel, reading, outdoor activities. Office: Project Read 550 North University Avenue Suite 215 Provo UT 84601 Office Fax: 801-852-7663. E-mail: projread@provo.lib.ut.us.

BROWN, SHEBA ANN, elementary education educator; b. Miss., 1951; married; 1 child, Joshua. BS in Elem. Edn., U. So. Miss., 1973. Tchr. 4th grade Biloxi (Miss.) Pub. Schs., 1973-74; tchr. 3d grade Ferncrest Acad., New Orleans, 1974-75, Cifton Ganus Pvt. Sch., New Orleans, 1975-78; tchr. 4th grade Putnam County Schs., Palatka, Fla., 1986-87; tchr. multi-age primary class Biloxi Pub. Schs., 1987—. Condr. workshops; presenter in field. Recipient Beverly Briscoe award Biloxi Schs., 1990, Enhancement award City of Biloxi, 1995, Leo Seal Tchr. Recognition award, 1999; named Miss. Tchr. of Yr., 1995, Women at the Top Coast Mag., 1996. Mem. Internat. Reading Assn., Nat. Coun. Tchrs. English, Jeff Davis PTA (treas.), Delta Kappa Gamma. Home: 135 Travia Ave Biloxi MS 39531-5328

BROWN, SHERI LYNN, artist, poet, educator; b. Bluefield, W.Va., Nov. 22, 1968; d. James H. and Rosa B. Wilkes. BA Comml. Art and Advt., Concord Coll., 1992. Owner T.J. Cool Advt., 1992—; writer Hill Top Records, Hollywood, Calif., 2001. Author numerous poems in anthologies. Mem. I Am His choir Scott St. Bapt. Ch., 1983—87. Mem.: Internat. Soc. Poets. Avocations: art, writing, trumpet, french horn, mellophone. Home: 120 Russell Terr Bluefield WV 24701-2932

BROWN, SHERROD, congressman, former state official; b. Mansfield, Ohio, Nov. 9, 1952; s. Charles G. and Emily (Campbell) B.; children: Emily, Elizabeth. BA, Yale U., 1974; MA in Edn., Ohio State U., 1979, MA in Pub. Adminstrn., 1981. Mem. Ohio Ho. of Reps., Mansfield, 1975-82; Sec. of State State of Ohio, Columbus, 1983-91; mem. U.S. Congress from 13th Ohio dist., Washington, 1993—; mem. energy and commerce com., internat. rels. com. Instr. Ohio State U., Mansfield, 1978-79 Author: Congress from the Inside, 1999. Active India Caucus. Recipient Eagle Scout Am. 1966, Friend of Edn. award, 1978 Mem. Nat. Assn. Secs. State Democrat. Lutheran. Office: US Ho of Reps 2332 Rayburn Ho Office Bldg Washington DC 20515-3513*

BROWN, SHIRLEY ANN, speech-language pathologist; b. Bklyn., Oct. 9, 1935; d. Hyman and Lillian (Fuhrer) Rubak; m. Ronald Wallace Brown, Sept. 29, 1956; children: Abbie Howard, Daniel Mark. BA, Bklyn. Coll., 1956, MA, 1961. Lic. speech/lang. pathologist, N.Y., N.J. Speech pathologist Richmond County CP Treatment Ctr., S.I., N.Y., 1956-59, Coney Island Hosp., Bklyn., 1959-61, Mendham Boro Schs. and Chatham Twp. Schs., 1962-67; pvt. practice home care speech pathologist various hosps. and med. facilities, 1967-79; dir. speech pathology dept. Englewood (N.J.) Hosp., 1974-92; speech pathologist Holy Name Hosp., Teaneck, N.J., 1992-96, chief speech-lang. pathology dept., 1996-2000; speech pathologist Home Health Care Agys., Bergen County, 1992—. Clin. supr. comm. disorders grad. program Kean Coll., NJ, 1993—2000, Montclair State U., 1996—2000; project leader speech-lang. pathology Multiple Sclerosis Consortium website editl. bd., 1999—2001; website project dir. Consortium of Multiple Sclerosis Ctrs., 2001—. Editl. bd. Internat. Jour. Multiple Sclerosis Care, 1999—. Chair svc. and rehab. Am. Cancer Soc., Hackensack, N.J. Recipient Nat. Honor citation for Profl. Edn., Am. Cancer Soc., 1985, Crimson Sword award Am. Cancer Soc., 1989. Mem.: Nat. Multiple Sclerosis Soc. (Greater North Jersey chpt., clin. chpt. programs, adv. com. 1998—), N.J. Speech, Lang. Hearing Assn. (Disting. Svc. award), Am. Speech., Lang. Hearing Assn. (cert., congl. action com., state chair career info., Continuing Edn. award 1983—, Outstanding Clin. Achievement award 1985). Avocation: cooking. Home and Office: 6 Sisson Ter Tenafly NJ 07670-1810

BROWN, SHIRLEY MARGARET KERN (PEGGY BROWN), interior designer; b. Ellensburg, Wash., Mar. 30, 1948; d. Philip Brooke and Shirley (Dickson) Kern; m. Ellery Kliess Brown, Jr., Aug. 7, 1970; children: Heather Nicole Coco, Rebecca Cherise, Andrea Shirley Serene, Ellery Philip. BA in Interior Design, Wash. State U., 1973. Apprentice then interior designer L.S. Higgins & Assocs., Bellevue, Wash., 1969-72; interior designer ColorsPlus Interiors, Inc., Bellevue, Wash., 1972, Strawns Office Furniture & Interiors, Inc., Boise, 1973-75, Empire Furniture, Inc., Tulsa; owner Inside-Out Design Co., Ltd., Boise, 1973-82; interior designer Architekton, Inc., Tulsa, 1984-86, Johnson Brand Design Group, Inc., 1986-87, Ellery Brown & Assocs. Arch., 1987—, Seattle Design Ctr.-Visions & Studio Programs, Scottsdale, Ariz., 1998—, Mehagian's Fine Furniture, Scottsdale, Ariz., ASID Designers' Showhouse, 2000. Lectr. in field. Contbr. articles to profl. jours.; featured designer Ariz. Lifestyle mag., 2002. Pres. PTA, co-chair capital bond prin. sel. com., enrollment rev. com., 1989-95; bd. dirs. Paradise Valley Young Life; designer West Valley Child Crises Ctr., Inc.; contributing designer West Valley Child Crisis Ctr. Recipient Seattle Design Ctr. Marjorie Siegel award, 1997, Phoenix Home and Garden Mag. ASID Showhouse, 2000. Mem.: AAUW, Nat. Soc. Interior Designers, Am. Soc. Interior Designers (dir. chpt. 1976—77, presdl. citation Oreg. chpt. 1977, chmn. Boise subchpt. 1977—79, sec. 1980—81, chmn. Wash. chpt. step workshop chmn. 1993—97, NCIDQ chmn. 1993—97, Wash. state presdl. citation 1995, presdl. citation Oreg. chpt. 1995—96, Wash. state presdl. citation 1996, 1997, Showhouse Mehagran's Designer award Phoenix Home and Garden Mag. 2000), Jr. League Phoenix, Wash. State U. Alumni Assn., Idaho Hist. Co., Jr. League Seattle, Zonta, Alpha Gamma Delta. Republican. Presbyterian. Office: Ladlows Fine Furniture 16000 Scottsdale Rd Scottsdale AZ 85254 E-mail: az-browns@hotmail.com.

BROWN, SHIRLEY MARK, retired science administrator; b. Phila., Apr. 25, 1924; d. Paul and Bertha Evelyn (Zucker) Mark; m. Bernard Beau, Sept. 1, 1947; children: Eric Joel, Aimee Susan. BA, Temple U., Phila., 1945, MA, 1947. Rsch. chemist U. Mich., Ann Arbor, 1947-50; instr. Upsala Coll., East Orange, 1960-74; acad. planner Rutgers U., New Brunswick, N.J., 1974-80, assoc. dir. Waksman Inst., 1980-88; exec. dir. Rutgers Rsch. and Ednl. Found., New Brunswick, 1980-94; assoc. dir. Office of Corp. Liaison and Technol. Transfer Rutgers U., 1988-91, adminstr. corp. contracts, 1991-94. Ct. mediator Union County, 2003. Sec. Joint Civic Com. Westfield 1962-66, Com. for Human Rights Westfield 1967-70; publicity chairperson. PTA Westfield 1963-67; counselor State Health Ins. Program, Union County, 2000-2003; vol. Zimmerli Art Mus., Rutgers U., 1994-2003, bd. dirs., 2003. Mem. LWV, Assn. Univ. Technol. Mgrs., Nat. Coun. Univ. Rsch. Adminstrs., Soc. Rsch. Adminstrs. Avocations: travel, theater, art history. Home: 146 Tudor Oval Westfield NJ 07090-2245 E-mail: smb146@msn.com.

BROWN, SIDNEY DEVERE, history educator; b. Douglass, Kans., Jan. 29, 1925; s. Leonard Reeves and Jessie Maybelle (Berger) B.; m. Ruth Esther Murray, Jan. 24, 1948; children: Margaret, Nancy, Russell, Frederick. AB, Southwestern Coll., Winfield, Kans., 1947; MA, U. Wis., 1950, PhD, 1952. Cert. in Japanese, U.S. Naval Oriental Langs. Sch. Tchr. history Protection (Kans.) High Sch., 1947-48; prof. history Okla. State U., Stillwater, 1952-71, U. Okla., Norman, 1971-95, dir. Asian studies, 1971-95, prof. emeritus history, 1995—; regents prof. history U. Sci. and Arts, Chickaska, Okla., 1996-2001. Vis. prof. U. Kans., Lawrence, summer 1958, U. Wis., Madison, summer 1960, U. Colo., Boulder, summer 1964, U. Nebr., Lincoln, summer 1965, U. Ill., Champaign, 1968-69, U. Mich., Ann Arbor, 2001-02. Author, translator: The Diary of Kido Takayoshi, 1986 (Japan Culture Translation prize 1986); contbr. chpts. to books. Dir. Okla. Symposium on East Asia, Norman, 1975-95; curator Okla. Mus. Natural History, Norman, 1974—; Dem. precinct chmn., Cleveland County, Okla., 1984-86; adv. bd. Okla. Jazz Hall of Fame, Tulsa, 1989-90. Lt. (j.g.) USNR, 1943-46. Decorated Order of Sacred Treasure with gold rays with neck ribbon (Japan); Japan Found. fellow, 1977-78, 84-85; Ford Found. fellow, 1956-57; inductee Okla. Higher Edn. Hall of Fame, 2000. Mem. AAUP (state sec.-treas. 1982-84), Assn. for Asian Studies (exec. com. 1983-84), Midwest Conf. on Asian Affairs, (pres. 1959-60), S.W. Conf. on Asian Studies (pres. 1977-78), Am. Hist. Assn. (exec. sec. conf. on Asian history 1970-75), Okla. Assn. Prof. Historians, Japan-Am. Soc. Okla. (life, pres. 1983), Asia Soc. Okla. (adv. bd. 1988—). Methodist. Avocations: jazz music, college basketball, foreign travel, political biographies. Home: 700 Nancy Lynn Ter Norman OK 73069-4222 E-mail: sdbrown4@juno.com.

BROWN, STANLEY MELVIN, lawyer; b. Derry, N.H., May 29, 1916; s. Norman Chandler and Ethel Violet (Hodgkins) B.; m. Thalia May Ryder, Nov. 10, 1942; 1 child, Kenneth Chad. AB, Dartmouth Coll., 1939; JD, Cornell U., 1942. Bar: N.Y. 1942, N.H. 1945, U.S. Ct. Appeals (1st cir.) 1947, U.S. Supreme Ct. 1948. Ptnr. McLane, Graf, Greene & Brown, Manchester, N.H., 1946-74, Brown & Nixon, P.A., Manchester, 1975-88; ptnr. Abramson Reis, Brown & Dugan (formerly Abramson Reis & Brown), 1988—. Chmn., mem. planning bd. Bradford, N.H., 1948-58, town counsel, 1953-65, selectman, 1986-89; mem. N.H. Senate, 1951-53; del. Republican nat. conv., 1952, 72. Served to lt. (s.g.) USNR, 1942-46, PTO. Mem. Manchester Bar Assn., Merrimack County Bar Assn., N.H. Bar Assn. (pres. 1968-69), ABA (ho. of dels. 1968—, chmn. ho. of dels. 1976-78, bd. govs. 1969-72), ATLA, Internat. Soc. Barristers, N.H. Bar Found. (treas. 1973-83). Office: Abramson Reis Brown & Dugan 1819 Elm St Manchester NH 03104-2910

BROWN, STEPHANIE CECILE, librarian, writer; b. Pasadena, Calif., Mar. 23, 1961; d. Harry Francis and Anne Catherine (Murray) B.; m. Derek Lawrence Christiansen, Dec. 1, 1991; children: Nathaniel, Thomas. BA, Boston U., 1984; MFA, U. Iowa, 1986; MLS, U. Calif., Berkeley, 1987. Libr. specialist Orange County Pub. Libr., 1989—. Author: Allegory of the Supermarket, 1998;

contbr. poetry to profl. publs. Recipient Jessica Maxwell Meml. Poetry prize Am. Poetry Rev., 1994. Roman Catholic. Office: San Juan Capistrano Regional Libr 31495 El Camino Real San Juan Capistrano CA 92675-2600

BROWN, STEPHEN D. lawyer; b. Boston, 1949; BA, Williams Coll., 1971; JD, Villanova U., 1976. Bar: Mass. 1976, Pa. 1978. Law clk. to Hon. Daniel H. Huyett, 3d U.S. Dist. Ct. (ea. dist.) Pa., 1976-78; ptnr. Dechert Price & Rhoads, Phila. Editor-in-chief Villanova U. Law Rev., 1976. Office: Dechert Price & Rhoads 1717 Arch St Ste 4000 Philadelphia PA 19103-2793 E-mail: stephen.brown@dechert.com.

BROWN, STEPHEN EDWARD, lawyer; b. Roanoke, Ala., Mar. 10, 1949; s. Edward E. and Jimmie (Dollar) B.; m. Kate Minor Eustis, Sept. 1, 1973; children: William Tucker, Kate Minor, Mary Cox. BA, Dartmouth Coll., 1971; JD, Tulane U., 1974. Bar: Ala, 1974, U.S. Dist. Ct. (no., mid. and so. dist.) Ala. 1974, U.S. Ct. Appeals (11th cir.) 1982, U.S. Supreme Ct. 1975. Ptnr. Bradley, Arant, Rose & White, Birmingham, Ala., 1974-89, Maynard, Cooper & Gale, Birmingham, Ala., 1989—. Co-chmn. Am. Heart Assn., Birmingham, 1987; co-chmn. legal div. United Way Ala., Birmingham, 1986; commr. Mountain Brook Athletics, Birmingham, 1988-91; chmn. Kid's Chance Scholarship Fund, 1994-95. Fellow Coll. of Labor and Employment Lawyers; mem. ABA (labor and employment sect. 1978—), Ala. Bar Assn. (exec. com., chmn. labor and employment law sect. 1981-86, exec. com., chmn. worker's compensation sect. 1991-95), Birmingham Bar Assn. (pres. young lawyers sect. 1982, exec. com. 1982, 88-90). Office: Maynard Cooper & Gale 2400 Am South/Harbert Plz 1901 6th Ave N Birmingham AL 35203-2618 E-mail: sbrown@mcglaw.com.

BROWN, STEPHEN HAYZE, JR., human services caseworker; b. Chgo., Sept. 7, 1954; s. Stephen Hayze Brown and Barbara Elizabeth Grandpré; m. Judith Eileen McCain, Mar. 5, 1997; 1 child, Javon. BS in Biology, Chgo. State U., 1981; diploma hematology and phlebotomy, Med. Careers Inst. Rsch. asst. Chgo. State U., 1980; instr. anatomy U. Ill. Coll. Dentistry, Chgo., 1982; ind. landscaping contractor, 1982-86, 87-89; tchr. Chgo. Bd. Edn., 1986-87; case mgr. Ill. Dept. Human Svcs., Chgo., 1999—. Assemblyman 44th Ward Assembly, Chgo., 1976-77. Ill. State scholar, 1972, Nat. Merit/Achievement scholar, 1972. Mem. Nat. Space Soc., The Planetary Soc. Roman Catholic. Avocations: music, science fiction, philosophy, comparative religion, astronomy.

BROWN, STEPHEN IRA, philosophy educator; b. Bklyn., July 14, 1938; s. Milton Frank and Ruth (Mittman) B.; m. Eileen Thaler, June 12, 1960; children: Jordan David, Sharon Jean. AB, Columbia Coll., 1960; MA in Teaching (Sloan fellow 1960-61), Harvard U., 1961, Ed.D., 1967. Instr. math. and edn. Simmons Coll., Boston, 1962-65; asst. prof. edn. Harvard U., 1966-72; vis. prof. Hebrew U., Jerusalem, 1970-71; asso. prof. Syracuse (N.Y.) U., 1972-73; mem. faculty SUNY, Buffalo, 1973-98, prof. math. edn., 1979-98, prof. philosophy of edn., 1982-98, prof. emeritus, 1998—. Vis. prof. U. Ga., Athens, 1979-80; vis. scholar Harvard U., Cambridge, Mass., 1993-94; participant ethics workshops Coll. Jewish Studies, Buffalo, 1974-76. Author: Some Prime Comparisions, 1978, Student Generations, 1987, Posing Mathematically, 1996, Reconstructing School Mathematics: Problems with Problems and the Real World, 2001; co-author: The Art of Problem Posing, 1983, rev. edit., 1990; co-author: Mathematics, Pedagogy and Secondary Teacher Education, 1996; co-editor: Progresssive Education: A Movement and Its Professional Journal, 1988, Problem Posing: Reflections and Applications, 1993; editor: Creative Problem Solving, 1989; mem. rev. bd. Ednl. Theory, 1983-87; mem. editl. bd. Math. Tchr., 1977-80, For Learning of Math., 1980-97; mem. adv. bd. Humanistic Math. Network Jour., 1995—; contbr. articles to profl. jours. Mem. adv. council Inst. Jewish Life, 1973-75. Grantee Dewey Found., 1979-80, NSF. 1983-86, 90-97; John Dewey sr. fellow, 1986-87. Fellow Philosophy Edn. Soc.; mem. John Dewey Soc. (bd. dirs. 1976-78), Math. Assn. Am., Nat. Council Tchrs. Math., Phi Beta Kappa, Phi Delta Kappa. Home: 86 Sherbrooke Ave Williamsville NY 14221-4606 E-mail: sibrown@acsu.buffalo.edu. *I attribute a large part of my success to lack of clarity and specificity with regard to goals, to ambiguity and vagueness with regard to principles, to a sense of humor which provides distance between a taken for granted reality and my personal world, and to a general disinclination to analyze what accounts for my success.*

BROWN, STEPHEN LEE, retired insurance company executive; b. Providence, July 6, 1937; AB, Middlebury Coll., 1958. CLU. With John Hancock Fin. Svcs. Inc. and John Hancock Life Ins. Co., Boston, 1958-2001, pres., chief ops. officer, vice chmn. bd., 1987-92, chmn., CEO, 1992-2000, chmn., 2000-2001. Bd. dirs. Ionics, Inc., Aspen Tech., Inc. Trustee emeritus Wang Ctr. for Performing Arts; bd. dirs. Alfred P. Sloan Found.; dir. Palm Beach Fla. Civic Assn. 1st lt. U.S. Army, 1956—59. Mem.: Comml. Club, Algonquin Club. Office: John Hancock Fin Svcs Inc John Hancock Place PO Box 111 Boston MA 02117-0111

BROWN, STEPHEN PHILLIP, judge; b. Birmingham, Ala., June 29, 1941; s. William P. and Milledge (Anderson) B.; m. Dorothy Louise Ogden, Aug. 6, 1967; children: Katherine, Phillip, Stephen. BSCE, Auburn U., 1963; LLB, Walter F. George Sch. Law, 1967. Bar: Ga. 1967, U.S. Dist. Ct. (mid. dist.) Ga. 1967, U.S. Ct. Appeals (11th cir.) Ga. 1967, U.S. Supreme Ct. 1967. Atty., regional counsel IRS, N.Y.C., 1967-69; ptnr. Brown, Katz, Flatau & Hasty, Macon, Ga., 1969-95; judge Superior Ct. Macon Judicial Cir., 1996—. *Judge Superior Court Macon Judicial Circuit since January 1994. Have since handled some of the most complex civil litigation in the history of the circuit, including complex family-stockholder fight of large corporation. This resulted in largest and most complex verdict in Circuit history. Also handled protracted fight highly public and emotionally charged fight between local hospitals over Certificate of Need to operate open-heart program. Initiator of legal ethics course that resulted in establishment of local American Inns of Court Chapter in Association with Walter F. George School of law at Mercer University.I have volunteered with local school reform in excess of twenty years.I was Chair of Committee that established a Mentoring Project that pairs children with adult mentors. This has been in existence 15 years.I also lead grant application that initiated Nurses in local schools as well as prevention drop out efforts. Also Chaired grant application that established a Medical magnet school at a local high school.I have worked 15 plus years and stlll work establishing and running an after school program in conjunction with Communities in Schools, which now serves more than 2,000 public school students.* Rep. Ga. House of Reps., Atlanta, 1971-74. Democrat. Methodist. Avocations: organic gardening, woodworking. Home: 2434 Wesleyan Dr N Macon GA 31210-6043 Office: Superior Ct Bibb City 310 Bibb County Courthouse Macon GA 31201

BROWN, STEPHEN THOMAS, judge; b. N.Y.C., Feb. 1, 1947; s. Albert and Ruth Hope (Kaff) B.; m. Yvonne Tobias Brown, Aug. 10, 1968. BS, Fla. State U., 1968; JD, U. Miami, Fla., 1972. Bar: Fla. 1972, U.S. Dist. Ct. (so. dist.) Fla. 1973, U.S. Dist. Ct. (mid. dist.) Fla. 1989, U.S. Ct. Appeals (11th cir.) 1973, U.S. Supreme Ct. 1976. Atty. Preddy, Kutner & Hardy, Miami, Fla., 1972-77, ptnr., 1977-86, Preddy, Kutner, Hardy, Rubinoff, Brown & Thompson, Miami, 1986-91; U.S. magistrate judge U.S. Dist. Ct. (so. dist.) Fla., Miami, 1991—. Adj. prof. U. Miami Sch. Law, 1983-84; vice chmn. auto ins. com. Fla. Bar, 1979-80, chmn. grievance com., 1981-84; mem. adv. com. on rules and procedures So. Dist. Fla., 1995--; mem. leadership coun. Fla. State U. Sch. of Arts & Scis. Mem. ABA, Acad. Fla. Trial Lawyers, Dade County Bar Assn., Fla. State U. Alumni Assn. (dist. v.p. 1993-99), Seminole Boosters Inc. (bd. dirs. 1988-93), Seminole Club Dade County (pres. 1984-87), U. Miami Law Sch. Alumni Assn. (bd. dirs. 1994—, v.p. 2000—). Avocations: snow skiing, golf. Office: US Dist Ct 300 NE 1st Ave Miami FL 33132-2126

BROWN, STEVEN BERNARD, counselor; b. Bklyn., Aug. 26, 1950; s. Louis Joseph and Helen (Rakoff) B. BS in Edn., L.I. U., 1972; MS in Edn., Bklyn. Coll., 1976, counseling, 1987. Advanced cert. counselor, N.Y., N.J. Tchr. Bd. Edn., N.Y.C., 1972-85, counselor, 1985—. Named Counselor of Yr., N.Y.C. Bd. Edn., 2001. Mem. ACA, UFT, NTA, Smoke Rise Club. Avocations: piano, sailing, skiing, tennis.

BROWN, STEVEN BRIEN, radiologist; b. Ft. Collins, Colo., Jan. 18, 1952; s. Allen Jenkins and Shirley Irene (O'Brien) B.; m. Susan Jane DiTomaso, Sept. 10, 1983; children: Allison Grace, Laura Anne. BS, Colo. State U., 1974; MD, U. Calif., San Diego, 1978. Diplomate Am. Bd. Radiology with cert. of added qualifications in Neuroradiology and Vascular and Interventional Radiology. Surg. intern U. Wash., Seattle, 1978-79; resident in radiology Stanford U., Calif., 1979-82, chief resident, 1981—82; fellow in interventional and neuroradiology Wilford Hall, USAF Med Ctr., San Antonio, 1982-83, staff radiologist, 1983-86, Luth. Med. Ctr., Wheat Ridge, Colo., 1986—, chief angiography and interventional radiology, 1987-96, v.p. med. staff, 2002—. Pres. Luth. Med. Ctr. Joint Venture, 1992-95; bd. mgrs. Primera HealthCare LLC, 1995-97; pres. HealthCare Select Inc., 1995—. Contbr. articles to profl. jours. Mem. Rep. Nat. Com., Washington, 1984—, Nat. Rep. Senatorial Com., 1985—, Rep. Presdl. Task Force, 1986—; grad. Rep. Leadership Program, 2000; bd. dirs. The Health Care Initiative. Maj. USAF, 1982-86. Fellow: Am. Coll. Radiology (exec. com. intersoc. commn. 1996—2000, counselor 2000—, managed care com. 2001—), Radiol. Soc. N.Am.; mem.: Colo. Preferred Physicians Orgn. (bd. dirs. 1987—, treas. 1998—), Soc. Cardiovasc. and Interventional Radiology, Western Neuroradiol. Soc. (sr.), Am. Soc. Neuroradiology (sr.), Rocky Mt. Radiol. Soc. (pres. 1994—95), Colo. Radiol. Soc. (pres. 1995—96), World Wildlife Orgn., Colo. Angio Club. Republican. Roman Catholic. Avocations: skiing, sailing, hiking, gardening. Office: Luth Med Center 8300 W 38th Ave Wheat Ridge CO 80033-6005

BROWN, STEVEN HARRY, engineering executive; b. Phila., Sept. 16, 1948; s. Robert Martin and Vera Ethel (Lipovsky) B.; m. Kathryn Helena Vassie, May 24, 1970; children: Chad, Joshua, Sean. ABS, Temple U., 1970, BS, 1971; MA, West Chester (Pa.) U., 1974. Diplomate Am. Acad. Health Physics (panel examiner 1988-91, appeals com. 1999-2001). Health physicist Temple U., Phila., 1969-71; tchr. phys. sci. Phila. Sch. Dist., 1971-76; mgr. radiation protection Westinghouse Electric Corp., Lakewood, Colo., 1976-80; mgr. western regional office Radiation Mgmt. Corp., Phila., 1980-82; prin. safety analysis engr. Rockwell Internat., Golden, Colo., 1982-83, program mgr. waste isolation pilot project, 1983-85; sr. project mgr. West Valley Demonstration Project Dames and Moore, West Valley, N.Y., 1985-87; dir. Radiol. Svcs., 1987-92; v.p. govt. svcs. Internat. Tech. Corp., Englewood, Colo., 1992—2002; v.p. DOE programs Shaw Group, Centennial, Colo. U.S. rep. Internat. Conf. on Radiation Hazards in Mining, Beijing, 1986. Mem. Nat. Health Physics Soc. (pres. Rocky Mountain chpt. 1982-83), Am. Nuclear Soc. Office: Shaw Group 9201 E Dry Creek Rd Centennial CO 80112

BROWN, STEVEN L. art educator; b. Chickasha, Okla., Nov. 26, 1951; s. Wendell Vinton and Beverly Jean (Holcombe) B.; divorced; children: Mat, Sean. BA, Okla. Coll. Liberal Arts, 1974; BFA, U. Okla., 1976; MFA, U. Ohio, 1978. Asst. prof. U. Americas, Puebla, Mex., 1978-79; instr. art U. Scis & Arts Okla., Chickasha, 1980-88, asst. prof. art, 1988-92, assoc. prof. art, 1992—2003, prof. art, 2003—. Adv. panelist Okla. State Arts Coun., Oklahoma City, 1988-94. One-man shows include Casa de la Cultura, Puebla, Mexico, 1979, Firehouse Art Ctr., Norman, Okla., 2001; group exhbns. include Emerson Mus. Art, Syracuse, N.Y., 1985, Sodarco Gallery, Quebec, Can., 1993, Reed Gallery, U. Maine, Resque Isle, 1994, Chautaugue (N.Y.) Art Assn. Gallery, 1996, Fine Art Ctr., Taos, N.Mex., 1997, Heuser Art Gallery, Bradley U., Peoria, Ill., 1998, Armory Art Ctr., West Palm Beach, Fla., 1999, Ridge Art Assn., Winter Haven, Fla., 2000. Recipient Okla. Visual Arts Coalition award of excellence, 2002. Mem. Individual Artists of Okla., Okla. Visual Arts Coalition. Avocations: art history, anthropology, philosophy. Home: 119 Skyline Dr Chickasha OK 73018-7265 Office: U Sci & Arts Okla PO Box 82345 Chickasha OK 73018 E-mail: facbrownsl@usao.edu.

BROWN, STEVEN SPENCER, lawyer; b. Manhattan, Kans., Feb. 26, 1948; s. Gerald James and Buelah Marie (Spencer) B. BBA, U. Mo., 1970, JD, 1973. Bar: Mo. 1973, U.S. Tax Ct. 1974, Ill. 1977, U.S. Dist. (no. dist.) Ill. 1979, U.S. Ct. Appeals (7th cir.) 1980, U.S. Ct. Claims 1986, Calif. 1989, U.S. Ct. Appeals (11th cir.) 1989, U.S. Ct. Appeals (5th cir.) 2000. Trial atty. IRS Regional Counsel, Chgo., 1973-78; sr. trial atty. IRS Dist. Counsel, Chgo., 1978-79; assoc. Silets & Martin Ltd., Chgo., 1979-85, ptnr., 1985-92, Martin, Brown & Sullivan Ltd., Chgo., 1992—. Adj. prof. John Marshall, Chgo., 1985—. Republican. Presbyterian. Avocations: golf, tennis. Home: 1030 N State St Apt 10H Chicago IL 60610-5485 Office: Martin Brown & Sullivan Ltd 10th Fl 321 S Plymouth Ct Chicago IL 60604-3912 E-mail: brown@mbslaw.com.

BROWN, STUART I. ophthalmologist, educator; b. Chgo., Mar. 1, 1933; s. Leonard and Ann (Gladin) B.; m. Isabel Bodor; children: Sarah, Emily BMS, U. Ill., Chgo., 1955, MD, 1957. Intern Jackson Meml. Hosp., Miami, Fla., 1957-58; resident in opthalmology, Eye, Ear, Nose and Throat Hosp., Tulane Med.Sch., New Orleans, 1961; fellow in cornea Mass. Eye and Ear Infirmary, Boston, 1962-66; clin. asst. prof. dept. opthalmology N.Y. Hosp.-Cornell Med. Ctr., N.Y.C., 1966, dir. cornea svcs. cornea rsch. lab., 1966-69, clin. assoc. prof., 1970-73; chmn., prof. dept. opthalmology U. Pitts. Sch. Medicine, 1974-82, U. Calif. Sch. Medicine, San Diego, 1983—. Bd. dirs. nat. adv. commn. Nat. Eye Bank, Inc. Recipient Heed Ophthalmic Found. award, 1976 Mem. Am. Acad. Ophthalmology, AMA, Assn. Rsch. in Vision and Ophthalmology, Assn. U. Profs. Ophthalmology, Internat. Soc. Eye Rsch. Office: U Calif San Diego Shiley Eye Ctr - Ophthalmol 9415 Campus Dr La Jolla CA 92093-0946 E-mail: sbrown@eyecenter.ucsd.edu.

BROWN, SUSAN ELIZABETH S. secondary school educator; b. Niagara Falls, NY, Feb. 25, 1940; d. Harold Marvin and Thelma A. (Lowenberg) Sonnichsen; m. Edward J. Hehre, Jr., June 22, 1963 (div. Apr. 1977); children: Nancy Elizabeth, Edward James III; m. Robert Goodell Brown, July 30, 1988 (div. Jan., 1999). BA, Cornell U., 1963; student, L.I. U., 1970-73; MALS, Dartmouth Coll., 1986; student, U. Geneva, Switzerland. Cert. profl. educator level II, Vt., libr./media specialist level I, Vt. Latin and French tchr. Pinkerton Acad., Derry, N.H., 1964-67; adminstrv. sec. New Eng. Bd. Higher Edn., New Eng. Coun. Higher Edn. Nurses, Durham, N.H., 1968; French tchr. Shelter Island (N.Y.) H.S., 1972; Latin, French, Journalism tchr. Woodsville (N.H.) H.S., 1974-88; Latin, French tchr. Thetford (Vt.) Acad., 1988—2003, telecomm. coord., 1993-94. Alternative cert. bds., N.H., Vt.; adj. prof. English Composition N.H. Comty. Tech. Coll., Claremont, 1998, 99, Littleton, 2000; adv. com. Nat. Latin Exam, 1999; mem. adv. coun. N.H. Coun. on Humanities, 1999. Contbr. articles to profl. jours. Trustee, chair Haverhill (N.H.) Libr. Assn., 1978-88, 2002--; moderator Haverhill U.C.C., 1985; treas. Latham Libr., Thetford, 1992-98. Mem. New Hampshire Classics Assn. (pres. 1966-68, hon. 1970, treas. 1977-87)), Classics Assn. New Eng. (exec. bd. 1981-87, 92-93, 2000-02, Matthew I. Wiencke award for excellence in secondary sch. tchrs. 2000), Sigma Tau Delta. Avocations: singing, library vol., sewing, reading, travel. Home and Office: 1260 Dartmouth Coll Hwy North Haverhill NH 03774 E-mail: roaringcreekfarm@valley.net.

BROWN, SUZANNE WILEY, museum director; b. Cheyenne, Wyo., Aug. 28, 1938; d. Robert James and Catharine Helen (Schroeder) Wiley; m. Ralph E. Brown, July 19, 1968; 1 child, Nina M. BS with honors, U. Wyo., 1960, MS, 1964; postgrad., U. Cin. Med. Sch., 1965-66, U. Ill., 1969-72. Rsch. asst. Harvard Med. Sch., 1962-63, U. Cin. Med. Sch., 1964-65; sr. lab. asst. U. Chgo., 1966-67; rsch. assoc. U. Colo. Med. Sch., 1968; tchg. asst. U. Ill., 1971-73; exec. asst. Chgo. Acad Scis., 1974-82, asst. dir., 1982-84, assoc. dir., 1984-90, ret. Mem. adv. bd. Mitchell Indian Mus., Evanston, Ill., Fechin Inst., Taos, N.Mex.; mem. collectors com. Field Mus., Chgo. NDEA fellow, 1960-62. Mem. Achievement Rewards Coll. Scis., Phi Beta Kappa, Sigma Xi, Phi Kappa Phi.

BROWN, SYLVIA, public relations executive, advertising executive; b. Watsonville, Calif., Nov. 28, 1946; BA, U. Calif., Berkeley, 1968; postgrad., Cen. Sch. Arts and Design, London, 1968-70. Asst. dir. Vorpal Gallery, San Francisco, 1972-73; editor, critic City Mag., San Francisco, 1973-75; dir. Braunstein/Quay Gallery, San Francisco, 1973-77; ptnr. Quay Ceramics Gallery, San Francisco, 1974-77; pub. relations dir. San Francisco Art Inst., 1977-79; ptnr. Brown and Collins, San Francisco, 1979—. Co-founder, editor Art Dealers Assn., San Francisco, 1973-79; co-founder, pres. bd. dirs. 80 Langton St., San Francisco, 1975-77; co-founder, bd. dirs. Zyzzyva, San Francisco, 1984-86. Contbg. editor: Images & Issues, 1979-81; critic: Art in America, 1974-78; author: (catalogue essay) Ron Nagle, 1978; exec. editor Art Wire, 1990-91. Recipient Addy award Advt. Fedn., 1986, Clarion award Women in Communications, Art Table No. Calif. Lifetime Achievement award, 1999; named in her honor Sylvia Brown Day, San Francisco, 1999. Mem.: Art Table (bd. dirs. San Francisco chpt. 1990—96, chair 1992—94, nat. bd. dirs. 2000—03, nat. v.p. 2001—03), Pub. Rels. Soc. Am. (publicity chmn. 1989—90, Eddy award 1987, Compass award 2001).

BROWN, SYLVIA G. law educator; BA in Ancient Greek magna cum laude, Vassar Coll., 1968; MA in Classical Studies, U. Mich., 1969, PhD in Classical Studies, 1972; JD, U. Pa., 1984. Bar: Pa., DC. Prof. internat. human rights law, hiwtory of Western polit. ideas Ryokoku U., Kyoto, 1996—. Home: 1-4-11 Akashia Dai Sanda City Hyogo-ken 669-1323 Japan

BROWN, TED LEON, JR., investment company executive; b. Lawrence, Kans., Jan. 14, 1956; s. Ted Leon and Simona (Garcia) B.; m. Cynthia Marie Fulmer, Jan. 26, 1974 (div. 1983); children: Chauntel M., Donald E.; m. Cynthia Jean Ford (div. 1993); children: Mark W. Kurta, Jennifer L. Kurta; m. Anne E. Scott, Aug. 19, 1995; 1 child, Amber Scott. Grad. high sch. Produce mgr. Pantry Pride, Lauderhill, Fla., 1971-77; asst. grocery mgr. Albertsons South Co., Plantation, Fla., 1977-79; pres. Brown & Brown Investments Inc., Ft. Lauderdale, Fla., 1980-91, Advent Investments Inc., Tamarac, 1990-92, Safeguard Investments Inc., Coral Springs, Fla., 1995-98; property mgr. Shaker Village, Tamarac, 1998-99, Cmty. Assn. Svcs., Boca Raton, Fla., 1999—2000, Castle Group Mgmt., Plantation, Fla., 2000—01, Fla. Cmty. Mgmt. Svcs., Inc., Coral Springs, Fla., 2001—. Chmn. adv. bd. Pinewood Elem. Sch., North Lauderdale, 1987-89; exec. dir. Fla. Lions Eye Bank, Miami, 1989-91; chmn. Boy Scouts Am., North Lauderdale, 1987. Recipient Landscape Excellence award,, City of Boca Raton, 1989, Landscape Maint. award, Tishman Speyer Properties, 1990, Gov.'s Achievement award, Lions, 1989. Mem. Lions (pres. Tamarac 1990-91). Home: 12162 NW 23rd Mnr Coral Springs FL 33065-3282 Office: Fla Cmty Mgmt Svcs Inc PO Box 9139 Coral Springs FL 33075

BROWN, TEION O'DELL, engineering executive; b. Chgo., Aug. 29, 1974; m. Sandra E. Brown; 1 child, McHale Campbell Brown. B in Engring., U. Ill., Chgo., 1997; M in Fin., Brown U., 1999. Pres., CEO Brown, Inc., Chgo., 2000—. Bd. dirs. Off-the-Street Club, Chgo., 1992, 93, 95, Spl. Olympics Ill.; chmn. bd. dirs., CEO ALU Found., N.Y.C., 1997-00. Avocations: reading, writing, baketball. Home and Office: 1520 S Hamlin Ave Chicago IL 60623

BROWN, TERRENCE CHARLES, art association executive, researcher, lecturer; b. N.Y.C., Oct. 2, 1949; s. Robert Carl and Ruth Carothers Johnson; m. Catherine Simms Citarella, Apr. 24, 1982; children: Peter Huston, Christopher Simms. BA, Vanderbilt U., Nashville, 1971. Curator Soc. Illustrators Mus. Am. Illustration, N.Y.C., 1972-83; dir. Soc. Illustrators, N.Y.C., 1983—. Instr. Sch. Visual Arts, N.Y.C., 1995—2000. Contbr.: 200 Years of American Illustration, 1976, The Illustrator in America: 1880-1980, 1984 Served to capt. USAR, 1971-79 Office: Soc of Illustrators 128 E 63rd St New York NY 10021-7303 E-mail: dir@societyillustrators.org.

BROWN, THEODORE LAWRENCE, chemistry educator; b. Green Bay, Wis., Oct. 15, 1928; s. Lawrence A. and Martha E. (Kedinger) B.; m. Audrey Catherine Brockman, Jan. 6, 1951; children: Mary Margaret, Karen Anne, Jennifer Gerarda, Philip Matthew (dec.), Andrew Lawrence. BS in Chemistry, Ill. Inst. Tech., 1950; PhD, Mich. State U., 1956. Mem. faculty U. Ill., Urbana, 1956—, prof. chemistry, 1965-93, prof. chemistry emeritus, 1993—, vice chancellor for rsch., dean Grad. Coll., 1980-86, dir.Beckman Inst. for Advanced Sci. and Tech., 1987-93. Vis. scientist Internat. Meteorol. Inst., Stockholm, 1972; Boomer lectr. U. Alta., Edmonton, Can., 1975; Firth vis. prof. U. Sheffield, Eng., 1977; mem. bd. govs. Argonne Nat. Lab., 1982-88, Mercy Hosp., Urbana, 1985-89, Chem. Abstracts Svc., 1991-96, Arnold and Mabel Beckman Found., 1994—, Am. Chem. Soc. Pub., 1996-2001. Author: (with R.S. Drago) Experiments in General Chemistry, 3d edit., 1970, General Chemistry, 2d edit., 1968, Energy and the Environment, 1971, (with H.E. LeMay and B.E. Bursten) Chemistry: The Central Science, 1977, 9th edit., 2003, Making Truth: Metaphor in Science, 2003; assoc. editor Inorganic Chemistry, 1969-78; contbr. articles to profl. publs. Mem. Govt.-Univ.-Industry Roundtable Coun., 1989-94; bd. dirs. Champaign County Opportunities Industrialization Ctr., 1970-79, chmn. bd. dirs., 1975-78. With USN, 1950-53. Sloan rsch. fellow, 1962-66, NSF sr. postdoctoral fellow, 1964-65, Guggenheim fellow, 1979. Fellow AAAS, Am. Acad. Arts and Scis.; mem. Am. Chem. Soc. (award in inorganic chemistry 1972, award for disting. svc. in advancement of inorganic chemistry 1993), Sigma Xi, Alpha Chi Sigma. Home: 10741 Crooked River Rd Unit 101 Bonita Springs FL 34135-1726

BROWN, THOMAS ANDREW, retired aircraft/weaponry manufacturing executive; b. Iowa City, Iowa, July 24, 1932; s. Charles Valentine and Mary Clementine (Proestler) B.; m. Louise Grafton Baggott, Aug. 31, 1957; children: James, Mary, Catherine. BA, State U. Iowa, 1953; BA with honors, Oxford U., 1955; MA, Harvard U., 1958, PhD, 1962. With Rand Corp., 1962-74, assoc. head info. sci., 1966-74, dir. strategic studies, 1983-85; asst. v.p. Sci. Applications, Inc., Los Angeles, 1974-77; dep. asst. sec. of def. program analysis and evaluation Dept. Def., Washington, 1977-81; ptnr. Booz, Allen & Hamilton, Bethesda, Md., 1981-83; mgr. strategic studies Northrop Corp., 1985-94. Served with USAF, 1955-57. Recipient Disting. Pub. Svc. medal Dept. Def., 1981; Rhodes scholar, 1953-55; NSF fellow, 1957-61 Home: 21912 234th Ave SE Maple Valley WA 98038-8423 E-mail: LittleTom@aol.com.

BROWN, THOMAS CARTMEL, JR., lawyer; b. Marion, Va., June 20, 1945; m. Sally Guy Lynch; children: Sarah Preston, Taylor Cardwell. AB, Davidson Coll., 1967; JD, U. Va., 1970. Bar: Va 1971. Assoc. Boothe, Prichard & Dudley, Alexandria, Va., 1971-76, ptnr., 1976-86, McGuireWoods LLP and predecessors, McLean, Va., 1986—. Mem. lawyers com. Nat. Ctr. State Cts., 1993—2003; sec., gen counsel Potomac KnowledgeWay, 1995—99. Mem. Va. Child-Day Coun., Richmond, 1987—91, No. Va. Roundtable, 1995—2001; pres. Alexandria Libr. Co., 2002—03; bd. dirs. Alexandria chpt. ARC, 1982—88; bd. dirs. Nat. Capital Area coun. Boy Scouts Am., 2002—. Fellow: Va. Law Found. (bd. dirs. 1997—, pres. 2003), Am. Bar Found.; mem.: Warren E. Burger Soc., Va. State Bar (chmn bus law sect 1987—88, bd govs health law sect 1998—, chair 2002—03), Va. Bar Assn. (pres. 1992), Omicron Delta Kappa. Office: McGuireWoods LLP 1750 Tysons Blvd Ste 1800 Mc Lean VA 22102-4231

BROWN, THOMAS HUNTINGTON, neuroscientist; b. N.Y.C., June 13, 1945; s. Thomas Huntington and Elvira R. (Crandall) B. BA in Molecular Biology, MA in Psychology, Calif. State U.-San Jose, 1972; PhD in Neurosci., Stanford U., 1977. Postdoctoral fellow Stanford U., Calif., 1977-79; asst. rsch. scientist Beckman Rsch. Inst., Duarte, Calif., 1979-82, assoc. rsch. scientist, 1982-86, rsch. scientist, 1986-88; prof. dept. psychology Yale U., New Haven, 1988—. Mem. joint appt. dept. cellular molecular physiology Yale U., 1992—, dir. Ctr. for Theoretical and Applied Neurosci., 1992-96; adviser NIH, NIMH study sects., 1982-83, 89-94, 94-98, mem. NIH-IFCN5 study sect., IFCN1 study sect., 1998—. Mem. editl. bd. Behavioral Neurosci. Jour., 1983-89, Network: Computation in Neural Systems, 1990-92, Synapse, 1990-2002, Hippocampus, 1990-93, Psychobiology, 1997-2000; contbr. articles to sci. jours., 1976—. Recipient Epilepsy Found. Am. award, 1980, McKnight Found. Scholar's award, 1981, McKnight Found. Career Devel. award 1984, Muscular Dystrophy Found. fellow, 1977, NIH fellow, 1978; grantee in field, 1980—. Mem. AAAS, Am. Psychol. Assn., Am. Psychol. Soc., Am. Physiol. Soc., N.Y. Acad. Sci., Conn. Acad. Sci. Engring., Soc. Neurosci., Internat. Neurol. Network Soc. Office: Yale U Dept Psychology PO Box 208205 New Haven CT 06520-8205

BROWN, THOMAS PHILIP, III, lawyer; b. Washington, Dec. 18, 1931; s. Raymond T. and Beatrice (Cullen) B.; m. Alicia A. Sexton, July 28, 1955; children: Thomas, Mark, Alicia, Maria, Beatrice. BS, Georgetown U., 1953, LL.B., 1956. Bar: D.C., Md. Pvt. practice law, 1958—. Author monograph and articles on legal malpractice. Pres. Cath. Youth Orgn. of Washington, 1972. Served to 1st lt. USMCR, 1955-58. Mem. Bar Assn. D.C. (pres. 1986, bd. dirs. 1987), Barristers Club, Columbia Country Club. Home: 5610 Wisconsin Ave Apt 208 Chevy Chase MD 20815 Office: Unit 2 5247 Wisconsin Ave NW Washington DC 20015

BROWN, TIMOTHY DONELL, professional football player; b. Dallas, July 22, 1966; BA, U. Notre Dame, 1988. Wide receiver L.A. Raiders, 1988—. Recipient Heisman trophy, 1987; named Wide Reciever on The Sporting News

Coll. All-Am. team, 1986, 87; Coll. Football Player of the Yr. The Sporting News, 1987, Kick Returner The Sporting News NFL All-Pro Team, 1988 Played in Pro Bowl, 1988, 91, 93-96. Office: Oakland Raiders 1220 Harbor Bay Pkwy Alameda CA 94502-6570

BROWN, TIMOTHY WILLIAM, writer; b. Rockford, Ill., Oct. 28, 1961; s. Lillian Carol Coryell and William Orla Brown; m. Audrey Beth Pass, Oct. 17, 1992; 1 child, Elena. BA, No. Ill. U., 1983. Author: Deconstruction Acres, 1997, Left of the Loop, 2001; editor: Tomorrow Mag., 1982—99. Com. chmn. Printers Row Book Fair, Chgo., 1998—2002. Grantee Cmty. Arts Assistance Program grant, City of Chgo., 1997, 2001, Spl. Assistance grant, Ill. Arts Coun., 2001. Personal E-mail: audrelv@speedsite.com.

BROWN, TINA, magazine editor; b. Maidenhead, Eng., Nov. 21, 1953; d. George Hambley and Bettina Iris May (Kohr) Brown; m. Harold Evans, Aug. 20, 1981; children: George Frederick, Isabel Harriet. MA, Oxford U.; D (hon.), The London Inst., 2001. Columnist Punch Mag., London, 1978; editor in chief Tatler Mag., London, 1979—83, Vanity Fair Mag., N.Y.C., 1984—92; editor New Yorker mag., N.Y.C., 1992—98; chmn., editor-in-chief Talk Media, 1998—2002. Author: (plays) Under the Bamboo Tree, 1973 (Sunday Times Drama award), Happy Yellow, 1977, (book) Loose Talk, 1979, Life As A Party, 1983. Named Most Promising Female Journalist, Young Journalist of Yr., 1978, Comdr. Brit. Empire, Her Royal Highness Queen Elizabeth, 2000; recipient Kathrine Pakenham prize, Sunday London Times, 1973, Mag. Editor of the Yr., Age Mag., 1988, USC Disting. Achievement in Journalism award, USC Journalism Alumni Assoc., 1994. Office: Attn Betty Greif 447 E 57th St New York NY 10022*

BROWN, TOD DAVID, bishop; b. San Francisco, Nov. 15, 1936; s. George Wilson and Edna Anne (Dunn) B.. BA, St. John's Coll., 1958; STB, Gregorian U., Rome, 1960; MA in Theology, U. San Francisco, 1970, MAT in Edn., 1976. Dir. edn. Diocese of Monterey, Calif., 1980—82, chancellor, 1982—89, vicar gen., chancellor, 1983—89; pastor St. Francis Xavier, Seaside, Calif., 1977—82; bishop Roman Catholic Diocese of Boise, Idaho, 1989—98; appointed and installed bishop Roman Cath. Diocese of Orange, Calif., 1998. Past mem. 3rd millenium com. U.S. Conf. Cath. Bishops, past chmn. com. on ecumenical and interreligious affairs, past mem. com. on mission, pastoral practices, past chair laity com.; chmn. subcom. interreligious affairs U.S. Conf. Cath. Bishop; past mem. episcopal bd. govs. N.Am. Coll. Named Papal Chaplain Pope Paul VI, 1975. Mem.: The Sovereign Mil. Hospitaller Order of St. John of Jerusalem of Rhodes and of Malta, The Equestrian Order of the Holy Sepulchre of Jerusalem, Canon Law Soc. Am. (past mem. Bishop's com. on liturgy, econ. concerns of the Holy See, Ea. Chs.), Cath. Biblical Assn., Cath. Theol. Soc. Am. Roman Catholic. Avocations: films, travel, reading, exercise. Office: Diocese of Orange Marywood Ctr 2811 E Villa Real Dr Orange CA 92867-1932

BROWN, TOM CHRISTIAN, newspaper publisher; b. Nampa, Idaho, July 24, 1947; s. Frank Thomas and Esther (Ulrich) B.; m. Carol Burroughs, May 31, 1969; children: Brian J., Maree C. BA in History with honors, Oreg. State U., 1969; MS in Journalism, Northwestern U., 1970. Reporter Corvallis (Oreg.) Gazette-Times, 1969; reporter, asst. city editor Billings (Mont.) Gazette, 1970-74; ops. mgr. Mont. Std., Butte, 1974-76; gen. mgr. Missoulian, Missoula, Mont., 1976-80, pub., 1980-86, Concord (N.H.) Monitor, 1987—. Bd. dirs., v.p. Newspapers of New Eng., Concord; pres. Page Buying Coop, Phila., 1994-96, chmn. bd., 1996-2001. Bd. dirs. United Way, Concord, 1989-96, 98—, Capital Ctr. for Arts, 1998—, Missoula YMCA, 1984-86; pres. Missoula Symphony, 1985, Mont. Press Assn., Helena, 1985; v.p. N.H. BBB, Concord, 1995-99; 2d v.p. Pacific N.W. Newspaper Assn., Portland, 1986; mem. Concord Task Force on Racism. Mem. Newspaper Assn. Am., New England Newspaper Assn. (com. chair 1994—), Merrimack C. of C. (bd. dirs. 1993-98, 99—), Missoula C. of C. (bd. dirs. 1977-84, v.p. 1983), Rotary (bd. dirs. Missoula chpt. 1976-79), Sigma Delta Chi. Avocations: running marathons, skiing, hiking, climbing, reading. Home: 15 Dwinell Dr Concord NH 03301-2542

BROWN, TRISHA, dancer; b. Aberdeen, Wash., Nov. 25, 1936; BA in Dance, Mills Coll., Calif.; D (hon.), Mills Coll., 1997; PhD in Fine Arts (hon.), Oberlin Coll. Founder, artistic dir. Trisha Brown Dance Co., N.Y.C., 1970—; founding mem. Judson Dance Theater; choreographer Grand Union Improvisation Group, 1970-76. Lectr. Mills Coll., Calif., Reed Coll., Oreg., NYU, N.Y.C., Goucher Coll., Md., Carnegie Mellon U., Pa.; condr. workshops and seminars throughout world. Choreographer Untitled, 1961, Trillium, 1961, Lightfall, 1963, Untitled Duet, 1963, Part of a Tango, 1963, Target, 1964, Rulegame Five, 1964, Motor, 1965, Homemade, 1965, Inside, 1966, Skunk Cabbage, 1967, Saltgrass and Waders, 1967, Medicine Dance, 1967, Snapshots, 1968, Ballet, 1968, Falling Duet, 1968, Sky Map, 1969, Dance with Duck's Head, 1968, Yellow Belly, 1969, Leaning Duets, 1970, The Stream, 1970, Man Walking Down the Side of a Building, 1970, Accumulation 4 1/2, 1971, Walking on the Wall, 1971, Leaning Duets II, 1971, Falling Duet II, 1971, Rummage Sale and the Floor of the Forest, 1971, Planes, 1968, Roof Piece, 1971, Primary Accumulation, 1972, Accumulating Pieces, 1973, Group Accumulation, 1973, Roof and Fire Piece, 1973, Spanish Dance, 1973, Structured Pieces, 1973, Figure 8, 1974, Drift, 1974, Spiral, 1974, Pamplona Stones, 1974, Locus, 1975, Line Up, 1976, Water Motor and Splang, 1978, Glacial Decoy, 1979, Opal Loop, 1980, Son of Gone Fishin', 1981, Set and Reset, 1983 (N.Y. Dance and Performance award, 1984), Lateral Pass, 1985 (N.Y. Dance and Performance award, 1986), Carmen, 1986, Newark, 1987, Astral Convertible, 1989, For M.G.: The Movie, 1991, Astral Converted, 1991, Another Story as in Falling, 1993, If you couldn't see me, 1994, Foray Forêt, 1990, You Can See Us, 1995, M.O., 1995, Twelve Ton Rose, 1996; featured (TV series) M.O., Sta. WNET-TV, N.Y.C., Dance in America, Sta. WGBH-TV, Boston, Dancing on the Edge, Making Dances; exhibitions include Venice Biennale, Toulon Mus., exhibited in group shows at Musée de Marseille, Numerals: Math. Concepts in Contemporary Art, The Pluralist Decade, New Notes for New Dance, Art and Dance: Images From the Modern Dialogue. Mem. Nat. Coun. on Arts, 1994. Decorated chevalier Ordre des Arts et des Lettres; recipient Creative Arts award, Brandeis U., 1982, Dance Mag. award, 1987, Samuel H. Scripps Am. Dance Festival award, 1994, Prix de la Danse la Société des Auteurs et Compositeurs Dramatiques award, 1996, Nat. medal of Art, 2003; fellow, Guggenheim Found., 1975, 1984, NEA Creative Artists Svc. Program, 1977, 1981—84; grantee, NEA, N.Y. State Coun. on Arts; MacArthur fellow, 1991. Mem.: Am. Acad. Arts and Letters (Nat. medal of Art 2003). Office: Trisha Brown Co care Rebecca Davis 625 W 55th St New York NY 10019-3560 Home Fax: 212-977-5347.

BROWN, TROY ANDERSON, JR., retired electrical distributing company executive; b. Tampa, Fla., July 7, 1934; s. Troy Anderson and Valerie Aldona (Mohler) B.; m. Jean Thompson, Aug. 22, 1962; children: Troy Anderson, III, George Albert, Douglas Alan. AB, Harvard U., 1956; JD, U. N.C., 1959. Bar: Fla. bar 1959. With Raybro Electric Supplies Inc., Tampa, 1960-99, exec. v.p., 1964-74, pres., 1974-99. Bd. dirs. Bay Cities Bank. Mem. exec. com. Tampa Com. 100, 1975, U. S.Fla. Found., 1974-75; chmn. bd. fellow U. Tampa, 1978; bd. dirs., vice chmn. Tampa Mus., 1977-79; bd. dirs. Tampa YMCA, 1977-79, Bay Cities Bank, 1999—, Tampa Marine Inst., 1976-77. With USAFR, 1959. Mem.: Tampa Mchts. Assn. (bd. dirs. 1980), Pres. Round Table Tampa (pres. 1971), Exch. Club Tampa (pres. 1970), Greater Tampa C. of C. (gov. 1968—74), Nat. Assn. Elec. Distbrs. (bd. dirs. 1989—91), Harvard Club N.Y.C., Harvard Club of Fla. (pres. 1984), Tampa Yacht and Country Club (bd. dirs. 1982—83), Ye Mystic Krewe Gasparilla, Jesters, Shriners. Episcopalian. Home: 1013 S Skokie St Tampa FL 33629-5237

BROWN, VALERIE ANNE, psychiatric social worker, educator; b. Elizabeth, N.J., Feb. 28, 1951; d. William John and Adelaide Elizabeth (Krasa) B. BA summa cum laude (fellow), C.W. Post Coll., 1972; MSW (Silberman scholar), Hunter Coll., 1975; PhD, Am. Internat. U., 1996. Diplomate Am. Bd. Examiners, Am. Bd. Clin. Social Work, Nat. Assn. Social Work; cert. addictions specialist; cert. master hypnotherapist; cert. psychophilogic integration therapist. Social work intern Greenwich House Counseling Ctr., N.Y.C., 1973-74, Metro Cons. Ctr., N.Y.C., 1974-75; sr. psychiat. social worker, co-adminstr. Essex County Guidance Ctr., East Orange, N.J., 1975-80; pvt. practice psychiat. social work, psychotherapy, 1979—. Sr. psychiat. social worker John E. Runnells Hosp., Berkeley Heights, N.J., 1980-86; dir. social work Northfield Manor, West Orange, N.J., 1987; clin. coord. Project Portals East Orange Gen. Hosp., 1987-88; asst. dir. ARS/Century House Riverview Med. Ctr., Red Bank, N.J., 1988-93; sr. clin. case mgmt. specialist Prudential Ins. Co., Woodbridge, N.J., 1993; clin. dir. Greenhouse-KMC, Lakewood, N.J., 1994-2000, Shoreline-KBH, Toms River, N.J., 1996-2000; tech. advisor Nat. Comm. Network, 1988—; mental health clinician III UMDNJ-UBHC, Edison, N.J., 2000—; instr. Brookdale Coll., 1991—; co-founder Women's Growth Ctr., Cedar Grove, N.J., 1979; counselor Passaic Drug Clinic, 1978-80; field instr. Fairleigh Dickinson U., Madison, N.J., 1981-86, Brookdale Coll., 1989-92; field supr. Union Coll., Cranford, N.J., 1986; instr. Sch. Social Work, NYU, N.Y.C., 1980-83, asst. prof., 1983-85; evaluator Intoxicated Driver Resource Ctr., Essex County, N.J., 1987-88. Alt. Monmouth County profl. adv. bd. Named Dist. Alumnae Mother Seton Regional H.S., Clark, N.J., 1997. Mem. NASW (Whittman Lifetime Achievement nominee 1997-98), Psi Chi, Pi Gamma Mu, Sigma Tau Delta. Avocations: reading, swimming, travel. Office: 20 Ellsworth Ct Red Bank NJ 07701-5403

BROWN, VALERIE SHARICE, venture capitalist; b. Silver Spring, Md., Aug. 26, 1967; d. Leroy Jr. and Rose Ann (Lanier) B. BS in Econs., U. Pa. Wharton, 1988; postgrad. in econs., U. Zimbabwe, Harare, 1989; MBA, Harvard Bus. Sch., 1994. Assoc. intern mgmt. Citibank N.A., Libreville, Gabon, 1988; rsch. asst. The World Bank, Washington, 1990; bus. analyst McKinsey & Co., N.Y.C., 1990-92; bus. devel. intern Merck & Co., West Point, Pa., 1993; coord. N.Am. region Women's World Banking, N.Y.C., 1994-95; dir. internat. ops.; mktg. mgr. Merck & Co., Inc., West Point, Pa. Dir. internat. ops. Ben & Jerry's Homemade, South Burlington, Vt., 1995; mktg. mgr. Merck & Co., West Point, Pa., 1997; prin. TL Ventures, LLC. Rotary Internat. fellow, 1989, Merck MBA fellow Merck & Co., 1992, AAUW fellow, 1992, George F. Baker scholar Harvard Bus. Sch., 1994. Mem. Harvard Bus. Sch. of Women Alumnae. Address: 533 E 6th St #5 New York NY 10009 E-mail: vbrown@mba1994.hbs.edu.

BROWN, VANDELLA, librarian; b. Senatobia, Miss., Apr. 23, 1952; d. Whitfield Sr. and Lue Walter (Heffner) Brown. BA, Memphis State U., 1977; MLS, U. Iowa, 1983. Libr. asst. Main Libr. Memphis/Shelby County, 1977-82; rschr. U. Iowa, Iowa City, 1982-83; libr. mgr. Memphis/Shelby County Pub. Libr., 1983-93, Columbus (Ohio) Met. Pub. Libr., 1993-98; libr. dir. E. St. Louis (Ill.) Pub. Libr., 1998-2000; network dir. Ill. State Libr., 2000—. Mem. adv. coun. Ill. State Libr., 1999. Author: (book) Celebrating the Family: Steps to Planning a Family Reunion, 1991, African-American Fiction: A Slamming Genre, 1997; rschr. Roots: The Second Generation, 1977. Pres. Reunion Ho. Family Reunion, Memphis, 1989—; regional OCLC network dir. adv. exec. com., 2001—; ex-official mem. users exec. bd. Ill. OCLC. Named Outstanding Supporter, Memphis State Black Student Assn., 1983; recipient letter of Recognition, City of Memphis Mayor, 1993. Mem.: ALA (mem. Black Caucus 1987), Ill. Libr. Assn. (chair diversity and racial com.). Democrat. Mem. Ch. Of Christ. Avocations: miniature book collecting, reading, gardening. Office: 300 S 2nd St # D Springfield IL 62701-1703 Fax: 217-557-2619. E-mail: vandellabrown@aol.com., vbrown@ilsos.net.

BROWN, VIVIAN ANDERSON, retired government agency administrator; b. Manor, Tex., Aug. 27, 1920; d. Carl Robert Anderson and Edna Belle Elizabeth Johnson Anderson; m. Karl Patrick Brown, Aug. 29, 1970 (dec. July 1976); stepchildren: Patrick Thomas, Peggy Ann, David Brian. Student, U. Tex., 1938—39, Mayfair Taylor Secretarial Sch., 1940—42. Purchasing clk. USAF, Bergstrom AFB, Tex., 4357, contracting officer, 1957—73; ret., 1973. Contbr. articles to profl. publs. (Outstanding award). Pres. women's orgn. Prince of Peace Luth. Ch., Austin, Tex. Recipient Vivian A. Brown Spl. Day honor, Mayor of Marshall, Tex., 1990, Gov. of Tex., 1990. Mem.: DAVA (state comdr. 1980—89), Nat. Assn. Ret. Fed. Employees (pres. 1979—81), Swedish Orgn. Carl-Widen Lodge (sec. 1998—2000). Democrat. Lutheran. Avocations: public speaking, reading, writing. Home: 7263 Creekside Dr Austin TX 78752

BROWN, W. MICHAEL, publishing company executive; Deputy chmn. Thomson Corp., Toronto, Ont., Can.

BROWN, WALTER REDVERS JOHN, physicist; b. Toronto, Ont., Can., Aug. 22, 1925; s. Ernest Redvers and Rita Mary (Brooks) B.; m. Anita Catherine Goggio, June 5, 1948 (div. 1972); children: Paul, Susan, Patricia, Judith; m. Beth Susan Southard, Oct. 12, 1974; 1 child, Amy. BS, U. Toronto, 1947; MS, U. Rochester, 1949. Sr. physicist Eastman Kodak Co., Rochester, N.Y., 1947-55; rsch. assoc. Boston U., 1955-57; asst. to dir. rsch. Itek Corp., Lexington, Mass., 1957-62; v.p. R & D United Carr Inc., Boston, 1962-69; exec. v.p. Ealing Corp., Cambridge, Mass., 1969-71; pres. Daedalon Corp., Salem, Mass., 1971—. Patentee in field. Fellow Optical Soc. Am. (Adolph Lomb medal 1956); mem. Eastern Yacht Club, St. Botolph Club. Roman Catholic. Home: 120 Atlantic Ave Marblehead MA 01945-3049 Office: Daedalon Corp PO Box 2028 Salem MA 01970-6228 E-mail: DAEDALON@COVE.COM.

BROWN, WAYNE J. former mayor; b. 1936; BS, Ariz. State U. Staff acct. Arthur Andersen & Co. CPA's, 1960-63; mng. ptnr. Wayne Brown & Co. CPA's, 1964-79; dir. acctg. Ariz. State Dept. Adminstrn., 1979-80; chmn. & CEO Brown Evans Distbg. Co., Mesa, Ariz., 1980—; mayor City of Mesa, 1996—2000. Office: 306 S Country Club Dr Mesa AZ 85211

BROWN, WENDY WEINSTOCK, nephrologist, educator; b. N.Y.C., Dec. 9, 1944; d. Irving and Pearl (Levack) Weinstock; m. Barry David Brown, May 2, 1971 (div. Sept. 1995); children: Jennifer Faye, Joshua Reuben, Julie Aviva, Rachel Ann. BA, U. Mass., 1966; MD, Med. Coll. of Pa., 1970; MPH, St. Louis U., 1999. Diplomate Am. Bd. Internal Medicine. Intern U. Ill. Affiliated Hosps., Chgo., 1970 71; resident in internal medicine The Med. Coll. Wis. Affiliated Hosps., Milw., 1971-74; gen. practitioner Vogelweh (W. Germany) Health Clinics, 1975-76; fellow in nephrology Med. Coll. of Wis. Milw. County Med. Complex, Milw., 1976-78; staff physician St. Louis VA Med Ctr., 1978—2003, acting chief, hemodialysis sect., 1983-85, chief dialysis/renal sect., 1985-90; dir. clin. nephrology, 1990—2003; staff physician St. Louis U. Hosps., 1978—2003, St. Louis City Hosp., 1982-85, St Mary's Health Ctr., St. Louis, 1994—2003; chief of staff VA Tenn. Valley Healthcare Sys., Nashville, 2003—. Assoc. prof. internal medicine St. Louis U. Health Sci. Ctr., 1985—98, prof. internal medicine, 1998—2003; prof. medicine Meharry Med. Coll.. Vanderbult Univ., 2003—. Reviewer Clin. Nephrology, Nephrology, Dialysis and Transplantation, Am. Jour. Nephrology, Am. Jour. Kidney Disease, Jour Am. Geriatric Soc., Jour. Am. Soc. Nephrology, Geriatric Nephrology and Urology, Kidney Internat.; med. editor NKF Family Focus; mem. editl. bd. Clin. Nephrology, Geriatric Nephrology, Internat. Urology and Nephrology; contbr. articles to profl. jours. Mem. adv. coun. Mo. Kidney Program, 1985-91, chmn., 1988-89; numerous positions Nat. Kidney Found., 1984—, nat. chmn., 1995-97; bd. dirs. United Way, St. Louis, 1994-2003, Nat. Kidney Found. Ea. Mo. and Metro East, Inc., 1980-94; bd. dirs. Combined Health Appeal Greater St. Louis, Inc., 1988, pres., 1989-92; bd. dirs. Combined Health Appeal Am., 1991-98, sec., 1992-96, vice chmn., 1996-98; editor-in-chief Advances in Replacement Theraoy, 2004—. Named Casual Corner Career Woman of Yr., 1986, Combine Health Appeal of Am. Vol. of Yr., 1991, Olympic Torch Bearer, 1996, St. Louis Health Profl. of Yr., 1997; recipient Upjohn Achievement award, Med. Coll. Wis. Affiliated HOsps., 1972, Cert. of Leadership, St. Louis YWCA, 1989, Chmn.'s award, Nat. Kidney Found. of Ea. Mo. and Metro East, 1990, award of excellence, 2002, Chmn.'s award, Nat. Kidney Found., Washington, 1990, Martin Wagner award, Nat. Kidney Found., 1999, award of excellence, Nat. Kidney Found. Ea. Mo. and Metro East, 2002. Fellow ACP; mem. Am. Soc. Nephrology, Internat. Soc. Nephrology, Coun. on Kidney in Cardiovascular Disease, Am. Heart Assn., St. Louis Soc. Am. Med. Women's Assn., St. Louis Internists (v.p. 1983-84, pres. 1984-85), Women in Nephrology (pres. 2000-02), Internat. Soc. for Peritoneal Dialysis, Am. Geriatrics Soc., Soc. for Exec. Leadership in Acad. Medicine (bd. dirs., program chair 1999—), Alpha Omega Alpha. Home: 100 Frontenac Frst Saint Louis MO 63131-3235 Office: VA Tenn Valley Healthcare Sys 1310 24th Ave S Nashville TN 37212-2637 E-mail: wendy.brown@med.va.gov.

BROWN, WESLEY ERNEST, federal judge; b. Hutchinson, Kans., June 22, 1907; s. Morrison H. H. and Julia (Wesley) B.; m. Mary A. Miller, Nov. 30, 1934 (dec.); children: Wesley Miller, Loy B. Wiley; m. Thadene N. Moore. Student, Kans. U., 1925-28; LLB, Kansas City Law Sch., 1933. Bar: Kans. 1933, Mo. 1933. Pvt. practice, Hutchinson, 1933-58; county atty. Reno County, Kans., 1935-39; referee in bankruptcy U.S. Dist. Ct. Kans., 1958-62, judge, 1962-79, sr. judge, 1979—. Apptd. Temporary Emergency Ct. of Appeals of U.S., 1980-93; dir. Nat. Assn. Referees in Bankruptcy, 1959-62; mem. bankruptcy divsn. Jud. Conf., 1963-70; mem. Jud. Conf., U.S., 1976-79. With USN, 1944-46. Mem. ABA, Kans. Bar Assn. (exec. council 1950-62, pres. 1964-65), Reno County Bar Assn. (pres. 1947), Wichita Bar Assn., S.W. Bar Kan., Delta Theta Phi. Office: US Dist Ct 414 US Courthouse 401 N Market St Wichita KS 67202-2089

BROWN, WILLIAM A. lawyer, mediator, arbitrator; b. Memphis, Nov. 6, 1957; s. Winn D. Sr. and Annie Ruth (Hurt) B.; m. Mary Lee Walker, Dec. 27, 1980. BBA, U. Miss., 1978, JD, 1981. Bar: Miss. 1981, U.S. Dist. Ct. (no. and so. dists.) Miss. 1981, U.S. Dist. Ct. (we. dist.) Tenn. 1987. Ptnr., pres. Walker, Brown & Brown, P.A., Hernando, Miss., 1981—. Pres. DeSoto Literacy Coun., Hernando, 1988, Am. Cancer Soc., Hernando, 1988, DeSoto County Econ. Devel. Coun., 1995—96; mem. Leadership 2000, 1990—91; chmn. Ch. Coun. Hernando United Meth. Ch.; vice-chmn. Hernando Preservation Commn., 1997—2000, chmn., 2001—; chmn. design com. Main St. Project, 1997—2000; allocations chmn. United Way of Mid-South DeSoto County. James O. Eastland scholar, 1978-81; Paul Harris fellow Rotary Internat., 1997. Mem. Miss. Bar Assn. (bd. dirs. young lawyers sect. 1988-89, Bd. Bar Commrs. 2002—), DeSoto County Bar Assn. (v.p. 1988-89, pres. 1996-98, bar commr. 2002—), Rotary (pres. Hernando chpt. 1989-90), Boy Scouts Am., N.W. Miss. (membership chmn. 1990, activities chmn. 1991). Methodist. Avocations: gardening, design and construction projects. Home and Office: Walker Brown & Brown PA PO Box 276 Hernando MS 38632-0276

BROWN, WILLIAM ALLEY, lawyer; b. La Grange, Tex., Sept. 5, 1921; s. Leon Dancy and Mary (Alley) B.; m. Ann Dyke Shafer, June 27, 1953; children: Ann Lenora, William Alley. B.B.A., U. Tex., 1942; Indsl. Adminstr., Harvard Bus. Sch., 1943; J.D., U. Tex., 1948. Bar: Tex. 1948, U.S. Dist. Ct. (we. dist.) Tex. 1950, U.S. Dist. Ct. (so. dist.) Tex. 1959, U.S. Ct. Appeals (5th cir.) 1950, U.S. Ct. Appeals (11th cir.) 1983. Assoc., ptnr. Powell, Wirtz Rauhut, Austin, Tex., 1950-58; ptnr. Powell, Rauhut, McGinnis, Reavley & Brown, Houston, 1958-61; assoc. gen. counsel Brown & Root, Inc., Houston, 1961-76, v.p., gen. atty., 1976-83; prof. constrn. law Tex. A&M U., College Station, 1983-91; ptnr. Brown & Brown Attys., Houston, 1991—. Served to 1st lt. U.S. Army, 1942-46, ETO. Mem. Sons of Rep. of Tex., Alpha Tau Omega. Republican. Episcopalian. Clubs: Frisch Auf Country (La Grange, Tex.), Plaza (Wichita Falls, Tex.). Home: 777 N Post Oak Rd Apt 609 Houston TX 77024-3806 Office: 6343 Skyline Dr Houston TX 77057-6901

BROWN, WILLIAM DOUGLAS, chemicals executive, lawyer; b. 1946; BA, Lafayette Coll., 1968; JD, U. Va., 1971. Bar: Pa. 1972. Various Air Products and Chems., Inc., Allentown, Pa., 1975—, v.p. adminstrn. air products gases and equipment group, 1997, v.p., gen. counsel, sec., 1999—. Mem. mgnt. com. Air Products and Chems., Inc., mem. corp. exec. com. Mem. ABA. Office: Air Products and Chems Inc 7201 Hamilton Blvd Allentown PA 18195-1526

BROWN, WILLIAM DOUGLAS, biology educator; b. Stillwater, Okla., July 26, 1965; s. Robert Charles and Patricia Anne Brown; m. Michelle Marie Kuns, May 29, 1999. BS, Simon Fraser U., 1987; MS, Ariz. State U., 1989; PhD, U. Toronto, Ont., Can., 1994. Postdoctoral fellow Simon Fraser U., Burnaby, Canada, 1994—95, U. Lausanne, Switzerland, 1996—98; postdoctoral rschr. Syracuse (N.Y.) U., 1998—2001; asst. prof. SUNY, Freedonia, NY, 2001—. Contbr. book chpts., articles to sci. jours. Fellow, Natural Scis. and Engring. Rsch. Coun. Can., 1994. Mem.: Animal Behavior Soc., Soc. for Study of Evolution, Am. Soc. Naturalists, Phi Kappa Phi. Office: SUNY Dept Biology Fredonia NY 14063 Fax: 716-673-3493. E-mail: william.brown@fredonia.edu.

BROWN, WILLIAM ERNEST, dentist; b. Benton Harbor, Mich., Aug. 29, 1922; s. William Ernest and Gertrude (Eliot) B.; m. T.N. McDonald, Oct. 21, 1944 (dec. July 1969); children: Judith M. Brown Smith, Wendy E. Brown Kerschbaum, Terrence N.; m. E.M. Tyree, Sept. 11, 1970 (dec. Jan. 2000). DDS, U. Mich., 1945, MS, 1947. Practice pediatric dentistry, Ann Arbor, Mich., 1947-62; part-time tchr. U. Mich., 1947-62; from asst. prof. to prof. dentistry, assoc. dir. W.K. Kellogg Found. Inst. Grad. and Postgrad. Dentistry, 1962-69; dean Coll. Dentistry, U. Okla., Oklahoma City, 1969-87; acting provost Health Scis. Ctr. U. Okla., 1973-75. Author: Oral Health, Dentistry and the American Public, 1974, Dental Education in the United States, 1976. Mem. City of Ann Arbor Human Rels. Commn., 1960-66, chmn., 1965-66; chmn. bd. dirs. ARC, Oklahoma County chpt., 1991-93; pres. Cmty. Coun. Ctrl. Okla., 1998-2000; bd. dirs. United Way of Metro Oklahoma City, 1998-2000; mem. Hall of Honor com. U. Mich. Dental Sch., 2003—. Recipient Gies Editorial award, 1965, 67 Mem. ADA, Am. Assn. Dental Schs. (pres. 1984-85), Am. Acad. Pediatric Dentistry, Am. Soc. Dentistry for Children. Home: 1666 Coburn Dr Ann Arbor MI 48108-9626 E-mail: driffil22@aol.com.

BROWN, WILLIAM FREDERICK, JR., protective services official; b. Montgomery, Ala., July 16, 1956; s. William F. and Joan M. Brown; m. Donna Marie Price, Mar. 1, 1980; children: William III, Alexandra, Nicholas. AA, L.A. Valley Coll., 1982; BA in Mgmt. with distinction, U. Redlands, 1987; MPA, U. So. Calif., 1995. Exec. cert. Calif. and Idaho Peace Officer Stds. and Tng. Commns. Paramedic Profl. Ambulance, Glendale, Calif., 1975-77; police officer Pacifica (Calif.) Police Dept., 1977-80; lt. Inglewood (Calif.) Police Dept., 1980-92; chief of police Moscow (Idaho) Police Dept., 1992-95, Lompoc (Calif.) Police Dept., 1995—. Grad. 169th session FBI Nat. Acad., Quantico, Va., 1992; 2nd v.p. Calif. Police Chiefs Assn.; bd. dirs. Domestic Violence Solutions, Santa Barbara County. Bd. dirs. North County Rape Crisis and Child Protection Ctr., Lompoc, 1996—; trustee Lompoc Dist. Hosp. Found., 1999-. Mem. Internat. Assn. Chiefs of Police (legis. com. 1994—), Calif. Res. Peace Officers Assn. (Res. Coord. of Yr. 1990), Police History Soc., Orders and Medals Soc. Am. (life, pres. So. Calif. affiliate 1982-92, bd. dirs.). Avocations: study of military and police history, medal collecting. Office: Lompoc Police Dept 107 Civic Center Plz Lompoc CA 93436-6968 E-mail: wbrown@impulse.net.

BROWN, WILLIAM FREDRICK, art educator; b. Evansville, Ind., June 21, 1947; s. Joseph Carl and Annette Elizabeth (Steinbach) B.; m. Laura Marie Nagy, June 29, 1969; children: Christopher Allen, Ryan Patrick. BS in art, Ind. State U., 1969; MFA, Sch. of the Art Inst. of Chgo., 1975. Instr. Henderson State U., Arkadelphia, Ark., 1975—77; asst. prof. Marshall U., Huntington, W.Va., 1977—80; prof. and chair dept. art U. Evansville (Ind.), 1980—. Roman Catholic. Avocation: travel. Home: 724 Hillcrest Dr Newburgh IN 47630-1359 Office: U Evansville 1800 Lincoln Ave Evansville IN 47714-1506 E-mail: BB32@evansville.edu.

BROWN, WILLIAM HILL, III, lawyer; b. Phila., Jan. 19, 1928; s. William H. Jr. and Ethel L. (Washington) B.; m. Sonya Morgan Brown, Aug. 29, 1952 (div. 1975); 1 child, Michele D.; m. D. June Hairston, July 29, 1975; 1 child, Jeanne-Marie. BS, Temple U., 1952; JD, U. Pa., 1955. Bar: Pa. 1956, D.C. 1972, U.S. Ct. Appeals (3d cir.) 1959, U.S. Ct. Appeals (4th cir.) 1978, U.S. Dist. Ct. (ea. dist.) Pa. 1957, U.S. Ct. Appeals (10th cir.) 1986, U.S. Ct. Appeals (5th cir.) 1988, U.S. Dist. Ct. D.C. 1994, U.S. Ct. Appeals (D.C. cir.) 1994, U.S. Ct. Appeals (fed. cir.) 1997, U.S. Ct. Appeals (8th cir.) 2002. Assoc. Norris, Schmidt, Phila., 1955-62; ptnr. Norris, Brown, Hall, Phila., 1962-68, Schnader, Harrison, Segal & Lewis, Phila., 1974—, mem. exec. com., 1983-87; chief of frauds Dist. Atty.'s Office, 1968, dep. dist. atty., 1968; commr. EEOC, Washington, 1968-69, chmn., 1969-73. Lectr. S.W. Legal Found., Practising Law Inst., Nat. Inst. Trial Advocacy; bd. dirs. United Parcel Svc., Inc., 1983—, Lawyers Com. Civil Rights Under Law; chmn. Phila. Spl. Investigation Commn. MOVE; pres. Nat. Black Child Devel., Inc., 1986-90; bd. dirs. Cmty. Legal Svcs., 1986—; mem. exec. com. Schnader, Harrison, Segal & Lewis, 1983-87; bd. dirs., mem. exec. com. Lawyers Com. Civil Rights Under law, 1977—, co-chair, 1991-93; mem. Commn. on Comml. Operation of U.S. Customs Svc., 1994-98. Contbr. articles to profl. jours. Bd. dirs. Mid. States Colls. and Secondary Schs., 1983-89, Main Line Acad., 1982—, Nat. Sr. Citizens Law Ctr., 1988-94; mem. nat. bd. govs. Am. Heart Assn., 1994-96, mem. audit com., mem. pub. affairs policy com., bd. dirs., 1986-94, mem. audit com., mem. pub. affairs policy com.; mem. adv. com. on appellate ct. rules Supreme Ct. Pa., 1989-95. With USAF, 1946-48. Recipient award of merit Fed. Bar Assn., Columbus, 1971, NAACP award, 1971, Dr. Edward S. Cooper award Am. Heart Assn., 1995, Whitney M. Young Jr. Leadership award Urban League, 1996, Whitney North Seymor award Lawyers Com. for Civil Rights Under Law,

1996, Champions for Social Justice and Equality award Black Law Students Assn. Rutgers-Camden, 1997, Earl G. Harrison Pro Bono award, 1998, law alumni award U. Pa., 2000. Fellow Internat. Acad. Trial Lawyers, Am. Law Inst.; mem. ABA, Phila. Bar Assn. (Fidelity award 1990), D.C. Bar Assn., Pa. Bar Assn., Fed. Bar Assn., Nat. Bar Assn., Inter-Am. Bar Assn., World Assn. Lawyers (founding mem.), Am. Arbitration Assn. (past bd. dirs.), Barrister's Assn. Phila., Inc. (J. Austin Norris award 1987), Citizens Commn. on Civil Rights, NAACP (bd. dirs legal def. and ednl. fund), Alpha Phi Alpha (Recognition award 1969). Republican. Episcopalian. Office: Schnader Harrison Segal & Lewis 1600 Market St Suite 3600 Philadelphia PA 19103-7286

BROWN, WILLIAM L. banker; b. Hendersonville, N.C., Feb. 1, 1922; s. William W. and Sarah (Maxwell) B.; m. Helen Presbrey, August, 1947; children: Kathryn H., Richard P., Steven J., Melissa M. Student, Mars Hill Coll., Newbury Coll.; MBA, Harvard, 1947. With First Nat. Bank Boston/Bank of Boston Corp., 1949-89, asst. v.p., 1949-59, v.p., 1959-66, sr. v.p., 1966-69, exec. v.p., 1969-71, bd. dirs., 1969-92, dir. of corp., 1970-92, pres., COO, 1971-83, chmn., CEO, 1983-87, ret., 1989. Bd. dirs. Gen. Cinema Corp., Chestnut Hill, Mass., Ionics, Inc., Watertown, Mass., N.Am. Mortgage Co., Santa Rosa, Calif.; trustee Bradley Real Estate Trust, Boston. Hon. life overseer Children's Hosp. Med. Ctr., Boston; trustee assoc. Boston Coll., Marine Biol. Lab., Woods Hole, Mass., trustee, mem. corp. Mus. Sci.; bd. dirs. Jobs for Mass., Inc., John F. Kennedy Libr. Found., Ret. Artery Bus. Com., Ret. Friends of Post Office Sq.; mem. corp. Northeastern U. Lt. USNR, World War II. Office: Bank of Boston MS/01-28-02 100 Federal St Fl 8 Boston MA 02110-1898

BROWN, WILLIAM MICHAEL, scientist, consultant, writer, editor, lawyer; b. Poole, Dorset, England, Nov. 17, 1965; came to US, 1991, naturalized, 1999; s. Michael C. and Shirley L. (Rowney) Brown. BSc in Biochemistry with chemistry summa cum laude, U. Southampton, Eng., 1988, PhD in Molecular Biology & Biochemistry, 1991; MBA, Fairleigh Dickinson U., 1997; JD magna cum laude, NY Law Sch., 1998. Bar: N.J. 1998, U.S. Dist. Ct. N.J. 1998, N.Y. 1999, U.S. Dist. Ct. (so. dist.) N.Y. 1999, U.S. Patent and Trademark Office 1999, U.S. Ct. Appeals (fed. cir.) 1999, D.C. 2002, Nebr. 2002, U.S. Dist. Ct. Nebr. 2002, U.S. Dist. Ct. D.C. 2002, U.S. Ct. Appeals (3d, 8th, 11th, D.C.) 2002, U.S. Ct. Fed. Claims 2002, U.S. Tax Ct. 2002, U.S. Supreme Ct. 2002; chartered chemist, European chemist, chartered biologist, European profl. biologist, cert. regulatory affairs. Rsch. fellow in neurology Ctr. Neurol. Diseases Brigham and Women's Hosp.-Harvard Med. Sch., Boston, 1991—93; postdoctoral. fellow Johnson & Johnson's Skin Biology Rsch. Ctr., Raritan, NJ, 1992—93; rsch. fellow Meml.-Sloan Kettering Cancer Ctr., NYC, 1993-94; sci. cons. Sills, Cummis, Zuckerman, Radin, Tischman, Epstein and Gross, Newark, 1994-96, Whitman, Breed, Abbott & Morgan, NYC, 1996-97; sci. advisor, then assoc. Kaye, Scholer, Fierman, Hays & Handler, NYC, 1997-99; patent counsel Taro Pharms., Hawthorne, NY and Haifa, Israel, 1999—2002; v.p.,chief intellectual property counsel Restoragen, Inc. (formerly BioNebraska, Inc.), Lincoln, Nebr., 2000—01, v.p., gen. counsel, 2001—02; sr. dir. legal affairs, co. sec. Pharmasset, Inc., 2002—. Vis. fellow NIH, Balt., 1991—92; freelance sci. cons., writer, editor, 1993—; hon. rsch. fellow dept. physiology and anatomy U. Tasmania, Hobart, Australia, 1995—2001; reviewer/evaluator Current Drugs, 1997—2002, Fin. Times Pharm. Publ., 1998—2001. Author: Alzheimer's Disease: Current Treatments and Future Prospects, 1999; co-author: Fetuin, 1995, Transcription, 2002; articles editor NY Law Sch. Law Rev., 1996-97; contbr. numerous articles to profl. jour. Recipient Brit. Assn. for Advancement of Sci. award, 1987, G. A. Kerkut biochemistry prize, 1988, Maxwell Found. award, 1987, Woodrow Wilson Constl. Law award, 1998, Otto L. Walter Disting. Legal Writing award, 1998; Wellcome Trust rsch. scholar, 1987, Irving Mariash scholar NY Law Sch., 1994-98; Vis. Rsch. fellow NIH, 1991-92. Fellow: Royal Soc. Encouragement of Arts, Mfg. and Commerce, Inst. Biology, Royal Soc. Chemistry; mem.: Regulatory Affairs Profl. Soc., NY Acad. Sci., Am. Assn. Pharm. Scientists, Federalist Soc., Delta Mu Delta, Epsilon Pi Tau, Sigma Xi. Achievements include (with Dr. A. Andreadis and Dr. K.S. Kosik) cloning of the human tau gene; (with Dr. K.M. Kziegielewska and Prof. N.R. Saunders) cloning of bovine, ovine and porcine fetuin cDNAs; research in Alzheimer's Disease. Office: Pharmasset Inc 1860 Montreal Rd Tucker GA 30084 Business E-Mail: wbrown@pharmasset.com.

BROWN, WILLIAM RANDALL, geology educator; b. Staunton, Va., Oct. 31, 1913; s. Thornton Lee and Ellen (Greer) B.; m. Elizabeth Blessing Whitmore, Aug. 20, 1942; children— Elizabeth Dudley, Denison Greer, Elaine Daingerfield. BS with final honors, U. Va., 1938, MA, 1939; PhD, Cornell U., 1942. Geologist Va. Geol. Survey, Charlottesville, 1942-45; mem. faculty dept. geology U. Ky., 1945—, assoc. prof., 1947-50, prof., 1950-84, prof. emeritus, 1984—; geologist U.S. Geol. Survey, 1965-76; rep. Am. Geol. Inst. to Internat. Field. Inst., Japan, 1967. Contbr. articles to profl. jours. Fellow Geol. Soc. Am. (chmn. S.E. sect. 1970-71); mem. Am. Assn. Petroleum Geologists, Sigma Xi. Home: 253 Shady Ln Lexington KY 40503-2034 Office: U Ky Dept Geol Scis Lexington KY 40506-0001

BROWN, WILLIAM ROBERT, association executive, consultant; b. Delaware, Ohio, Jan. 19, 1926; s. Omar Lloyd and Olive Ida (Johnson) B.; m. Dorothy Judd Curtis, Dec. 30, 1950; children— Darnae Judd, Ann Barlett Brown Nutt. BA, Ohio Wesleyan U., 1948; MA; research scholar, Ohio State U., 1949. Asst. Inst. Practical Politics, Ohio Wesleyan U., 1947-48; research dir. Mo. State C. of C., 1950-64; govtl. research dir. Del. State C. of C., 1964-65; assoc. research dir. Council of State Chambers of Commerce, Washington, 1965-78, pres., 1979-90, Commerce Service Ctr., Inc., 1986-90; cons., 1991—. Editor: State Tax Report, 1969-81, Jud. Report, 1969-81, Property Tax Report, 1979, State UC Report, 1984-90, State Chamber News, 1988-90. Trustee Nat. Found. for Unemployment Compensation and Workers Compensation; precinct chmn. Rep. Party, 1968-70; pres. Friends of the Railroad, 1980-89. Mem. Nat. Tax Assn., Estero (Fla.) C. of C. (exec. dir. 1998-2000), Bonita-Estero Rep. Club (pres. 1999-2001), Phi Beta Kappa, Pi Sigma Alpha, Kappa Delta Pi, Sigma Chi. Methodist. Home: 4160 Gunnison Ct # 821 Estero FL 33928 E-mail: aquilla@ix.netcom.com.

BROWN, WILLIAM SAMUEL, JR., communication sciences and disorders educator; b. Pottstown, Penn., Apr. 25, 1940; s. William Samuel and Elizabeth (Gallager) B.; m. Elaine Kay Whitehouse, Aug. 18, 1962; children: William Samuel III, Allen Reed. MA, SUNY, Buffalo, 1967, PhD, 1969. Speech therapist Crawford Cty. Schools, Meadville, Penn., 1962-65; rsch. asst. SUNY, Buffalo, N.Y., 1965-68; prof. U. Fla., Gainesville, Fla., 1970—. Contrib. numerous publications to scientific jours. Postdoctoral fellow U. Fla, Gainsville, 1968-70. Fellow Internat. Soc. Phonetic Sci. (coun. rep. 1980—), Am. Speech-Lang.-Hearing Assn., Acoustical Soc. Am.; mem. Am. Assn. Phonetic Sci. (exec. sec. 1980—). Republican. Presbyterian. Office: U Fla IASCP Dauer 63 Gainesville FL 32611

BROWN, WILLIAM VIRGIL, internal medicine educator; b. Royston, Ga., Sept. 25, 1938; m. Alice Brown; 2 children. BA in Physics and Chemistry, Emory U., 1960; MD, Yale U., 1964. Diplomate Am. Bd. Internal Medicine, Am. Bd. Endocrinology. Intern, asst. resident Osler Med. Svc. Johns Hopkins Hosp., Balt., 1964—66; clin. assoc. Nat. Heart and Lung Inst., Bethesda, Md., 1966—69; fellow in endocrinology and metabolism Yale-New Haven Hosp., 1969—70; asst. prof. medicine U. Calif. Dept. Medicine, San Diego, 1970—74, assoc. prof. medicine, 1974—78; dir. lipid rsch. clinic U. Calif., San Diego, 1972—78; prof. medicine Mt. Sinai Sch. Medicine, N.Y.C., 1978—87, dir. divsn. arteriosclerosis and metabolism, 1978—87; pres., CEO Medlantic Rsch. Found., Washington, 1987—91; Charles Howard Candler prof. internal medicine, dir. divsn. arteriosclerosis and lipid metabolism Emory U., Atlanta, 1991—, pres. faculty coun. and univ. senate, 1998—99; chief of medicine Atlanta VA Hosp., 1998—. Chmn. Gordon Conf. on Lipid Metabolism, 1984; metabolism study sect. NIH, 1985. Assoc. editor: Correct Controlled Clinical Trials, 2000—. Pres. faculty coun. and univ. senate Emory U., 1998—99. Fellow, Alexander von Humboldt. Fellow: ACP (master physician); mem.: Nat. Lipid Assn. (pres. 2002—), Am. Bd. Bioanalysis (high-complexity clin. lab. dir.), Southeastern Lipid Conf. (pres. 1997—99), Am. Soc. Exptl. Biology, Am. Soc. Clin. Investigation, Am. Fedn. Clin. Rsch., Am. Heart Assn. (mem. physiology study sect. 1978—80, mem. credentials com. aterioscleosis coun. 1978—80, chmn. credentials com. aterioscleosis coun. 1979—82, mem. nutrition com. 1981—86, mem. several rsch. con., chmn. nutrition com. 1982—86, bd. dirs. 1983, vice chmn. edn. and cmty. program com., pres. 1991—92, gold heart award 1996, R. Bruce Logue award 2000, fellow arteriosclerosis coun., fellow epidemiology and preventive cardiology coun., numerous others), Alpha Omega Alpha, Phi Beta Kappa. Achievements include research in study of the structure and metabolism of lipoproteins; study of the lipolytic enzymes, including their molecular and kinetic characteristics, diagnosis and treatment of the hyperlipoproteinemias; the relationship of lipoprotein metabolism to atheromatous vascular disorders. Office: Atlanta VA Hosp 1670 Clairmont Rd Decatur GA 30033-4004 Fax: (404) 235-3005. E-mail: w.virgil.brown@med.VA.gov.

BROWN, WILLIE LEWIS, JR., mayor, former state legislator, lawyer; b. Mineola, Tex., Mar. 20, 1934; s. Willie Lewis and Minnie (Boyd) B.; children: Susan, Robin, Michael. BA, San Francisco State Coll., 1955; LL.D., Hastings Coll. Law, 1958; postgrad. fellow, Crown Coll., 1970, U. Calif.-Santa Cruz, 1970. Bar: Calif. 1959. Mem. Calif. State Assembly, Sacramento, 1964-95, speaker, 1980-95, chmn. Ways and Means Com., 1971-74; chmn. revenue and taxation com., 1976-79; Democratic Whip Calif. State Assembly, 1969-70, majority floor leader, 1979-80, chmn. legis. black caucus, 1980, chmn. govtl. efficiency and economy com., 1968-84; mayor San Francisco, 1995—. Mem. U. Calif. bd. regents, 1972, Dem. Nat. Com., 1989-90; co-chmn. Calif. del. to Nat. Black Polit. Conv., 1972, Calif. del. to Nat. Dem. Conv., 1980; nat. campaign chmn. Jesse Jackson for Pres., 1988. Mem. State Legis. Leaders Found. (dir.), Nat. Conf. State Legislatures, NAACP, Black Am. Polit. Assn. Calif. (co-founder, past chmn.), Calif. Bar Assn., Alpha Phi Alpha, Phi Alpha Delta Democrat. Methodist. Office: Office of the Mayor City Hall Rm 200 1 Dr Carlton B Goodlett Pl San Francisco CA 94102-4603 also: US Conf Mayors Office of Exec Dir 1620 Eye St NW Washington DC 20006-4005*

BROWNBACK, LINDA MASON, health company executive; b. Columbus, Ohio, Mar. 31, 1947; d. Lloyd Walter and Ann Elizabeth (Seely) Mason; m. Clifford A. Bridges, Sept. 14, 1968 (div. Dec. 1982); 1 child, David Lloyd Bridges; m. Thomas S. Brownback, Oct. 28, 2001. BA summa cum laude, Ohio U., 1969; MA, Kutztown (Pa.) U., 1985. Diplomate Am. Psychotherapy Assn., Peak Performance-Neurotherapy Bd., cert. EEG biofeedback Biofeedback Cert. Inst. Am. Ptnr. Brownback, Masons & Assocs., Allentown, Pa., 1982—. Co-author: (novels) Neurotherapy in Dissociative Disorders, Introduction to Quantitative EEG and Neurofeedback, 1999. Bd. dirs. Lehigh Valley Nursing Mothers, 1993—98, Allentown Rescue Mission, 1996—99. Recipient Outstanding Alumni award, Kutztown U., 1995. Mem.: Assn. Applied Psychophysiology and Biofeedback (presenter 1992, 1998, 2000, 2001), Am. Bd. Forensic Examiners, Acad. Cert. Neurotherapists, Internat. Soc. for Study of Dissociation (co-presenter 1985, 1986, 1989), Mortar Bd., Phi Beta Kappa. Home: 1702 W Walnut St Allentown PA 18104-6741 Office: Brownback Mason & Assocs 1702 W Walnut St Allentown PA 18104-6741 E-mail: brownbackmason@enter.net.

BROWNBACK, SAM, senator, lawyer; b. Parker, Kans. m. Mary; children: Abby, Andy, Liz. BS in Agrl. Econs. with honors, Kan. State U.; JD, U. Kans. Farm broadcaster KKSU; ptnr. law firm, N.Y.C.; instr. law Kans. State U.; city atty. Ogden and Leonardville, Kans.; sec. agr., Washington; mem. 104th Congress from 2nd Kans. dist., Washington, 1994-96; U.S. Senator from Kans. Washington, 1996—. Mem. com., sci., and transp., fgn. rels., govtl. affairs, joint econ. coms.; fellow U.S. Trade Rep. Carla Hills, 1990-91, mem. intergovtl. adv. com.; spkr. on trade, agr., leadership, motivation, mem. com. health, edn., labor and pensions. Co-author: 2 books; contbr. numerous articles. Pres. Kans. Prayer Breakfast; developer Family Impact Statement; vice chmn. Riley County Rep. Com. Recipient Hon. Am. Farmer degree, FFA; named Outstanding Young Person, Osaka, Japan Jaycees, Kansan of Distinction, 1988. Republican. Office: US Senate 303 Hart Senate Office Bldg Washington DC 20510-0001*

BROWN-BANKS, JENNIFER ELAINE, writer, public relations administrator; b. Chgo., June 29, 1961; d. Major Harding and Arabella Brown Neal; m. Leandrew Banks; 1 child, Jaremy Dortch. AA, Robert Morris Coll., Chgo., 1994; postgrad., North Park U., Chgo., 1996-98, Chgo. State U., 1998—2002. Sr. analyst No. Trust Bank, Chgo., 1979-93; acctg. coord. St. Edmund's, Chgo., 1995-2000; feature writer Single Living Mag., Chgo., 1995—; office mgr. Schindler Comm., Chgo., 2000—. Contbg. author: Chocolate for a Woman's Heart, 1998, Chocolate for a Woman's Spirit, 1999. Recipient Vision award Brainerd Cmty. Devel., Chgo., 1994. Mem. Poets United to Advance the Arts (founder, pres.). Roman Catholic. Avocations: reading, writing poetry, music. E-mail: jenniferwriter@yahoo.com.

BROWN-BUCHANAN, DEBORAH ANN, financial consultant; b. Camden, N.J., Dec. 26, 1956; d. Robert James and Audrey Ann (Deso) Brown; m. Stephen Timothy Buchanan, April 25, 1987; children: Alexandria Deso, Ian Christian. AA, Gloucester County C.C., 1980; cert., Am. Inst. Paralegal Studies, Mahwah, N.J., 1983. Lic. series 65 registered rep.; cert. long term care specialist. Skip tracer W.T. Grants, Woodbury Heights, N.J., 1975-78; recovery supr. Princeton Bank (formerly Bank of N.J.), Moorestown, N.J., 1979-82; asst. sec. 1st People's Bank of N.J., Westmont, 1982-85; asst. v.p. Equibank, Pitts., 1985-86; asst. sec. Continental Bank of N.J., Haddonfield, 1986-88; ins. and investment prdr., registered rep. LUTCF Prudential Fin. Svcs., Marlton, N.J., 1989—. Lectr. Asst. to author/editor: Compliance Book on Banking Regulations, 1986. Sec. fin. com. St. Margaret Mary Cath. Ch., 1985-88. Fellow Life Underwriter Tng. Coun.; mem. NAFE, Nat. Assn. Life Underwriters, Nat. Assn. Securities Dealers, South Jersey C. of C. Avocations: free-lance writing and editing, travel, sports, lecturing, gardening. Home: 1151 Walnut Ave Woodbury Heights NJ 08097-1535 Office: Prudential Fin Svcs 5 Greentree Ctr Marlton NJ 08053-3422

BROWN-CHAPPELL, BETTY L. social worker, educator; b. San Francisco, Nov. 25, 1946; d. Benjamin Franklin and Clara Lucille (Williams) Brown; m. Michael James Chappell, Oct. 1, 1975; children: Michael Jahi, Aisha Ebony. BA, U. Mich., 1969, MSW, 1971; PhD, U. Chgo., 1991. Social caseworker Detroit Health Dept., 1971; cmty. svc. asst. Commn. on Cmty. Rels., Detroit, 1971-73; adminstrv. asst. Sr. Citizens Dept., Detroit, 1973-77; asst. dir. Walter Reuther Sr. Citizens Ctrs., Detroit, 1977-79; vis. instr., rsch. assoc. U. Ill. Chgo., 1979-80; coord. acad. adv., assoc. prof. Northeastern Ill. U., Chgo., 1980-84; asst. dean U. Chgo., 1984-89; field coord. Ill. State U., Normal, 1990-92; asst. prof. U. Mich., Ann Arbor, 1992-96; assoc. prof. Ea. Mich. U., Ypsilanti, 1996—, dir. BSW program, 2000—02. Mgmt. cons. United Tenants Speak, Detroit, 1994; ednl. cons. C.O.T.S., Detroit, 1994. Contbr. articles to profl. jours. Fellow U. Mich., 1991-92, Ill. Consortium on Edn. Opportunity, 1989-90, Delta Sigma Theta, 1988, Ctr. Urban Rsch. and Policy Studies, 1987; recipient Citation Acad. All-Am., 1988, Detroit Bd. Edn., 1975, Cert. Appreciation City Detroit Mayor's Office and Sr. Citizens Dept., 1976, Resolution of Merit Mich. State Rep., Jackie Vaughn, 1975. Mem. NASW (bd. dirs. Mich. 1999-2001, Mich. pres.-elect 2001-02, pres. 2002-, Mich. exec. coun. of pres. 2001-02), Nat. Assn. Black Social Workers (steering com. 1975-79, v.p. Detroit chpt. 1974-75). Avocations: tennis, embroidery, cycling, reading. Office: Eastern Mich U 351 Marshall Ypsilanti MI 48197-2239

BROWNE, ANN APRIL, purchasing manager; b. Washington, Apr. 9, 1945; d. Benjamin and Sarah (Barr) Mudrick. BA in Bus. Mgmt., Eckerd Coll., 1987. Cert. purchasing mgr.; accredited purchasing practitioner. Purchasing mgr. Gen. Kinetics, Rockville, Md., 1972-73; assoc. buyer Control Data Corp., Rockville, 1973-74; outside sales rep. Mid Atlantic Industries, Bladensburg, Md., 1974, U.S. C. of C., San Antonio, 1975; inside sales coord. Frabimore Equipment & Controls, Inc., Elk Grove Village, Ill., 1976-77; customer svc. rep. Viracon, Inc., Bensenville, Ill., 1977; purchasing mgr. Vectrol div. Westinghouse Elec. Corp., Oldsmar, Fla., 1978-83; purchasing agt. Helen Ellis Meml. Hosp., Tarpon Springs, Fla., 1987—2001; sr. purchasing specialist St. Petersburg Coll., Pinellas Park, Fla., 2001—. Mem. Material Mgmt. Assn. of Fla., Nat. Assn. Purchasing Mgmt. (cert.), Phi Theta Kappa. Avocations: photography, weight-lifting, reading, spectator sports.

BROWNE, ARTHUR, newspaper editor; Editorial page editor The Daily News, N.Y.C., mng. editor, 1995—, sr. mng. editor. Office: NY News Inc 450 W 33rd St New York NY 10001-2603

BROWNE, DALLAS, anthropology educator; b. Chgo., Oct. 9, 1944; s. William Eldridge and Ann (Sherman) B.; m. Imelda M. Siedentopf, Apr. 8, 1972; children— Eldridge, La Salle, Hubert, William. B.A., Northeastern U., 1966; M.A., U. Ill., 1971, Ph.D., 1983. Asst. prof. Wabash Coll., Crawfordsville, Ind., 1981-82, Colby Coll., Waterville, Maine, 1982-86, York Coll., Jamaica, N.Y., 1986-91; assoc. prof. anthropology So. Ill. U., Edwardsville, 1991—; cons. evaluation Kenya Govt., 1975; UNICEF; hon. consul for Tanzania. Ford Found. fellow, 1971, fellow Inst. Study Racism, 1980, Ctr. Polit. Studies and Inst. Social Research, 1984. Mem. Am. Anthropol. Assn., Soc. Urban Anthropology, Assn. Black Anthropologists (rep. east coast 1983—), New Eng. Black Studies (sec. 1984—), Midwest Assn. Latin Am. Studies, Eugene Redman Writers Assn.Am. Com. on Fgn. Rels., World Affairs Coun., Midwest African Studies Assn., Midwest Latin Am. Assn. Avocation: building models of famous inventions. Office: Dept Anthropology S Ill U Edwardsville Edwardsville IL 62026-0001

BROWNE, DIANA GAYLE, artist, social services; b. San Francisco, Aug. 31, 1924; d. Clarence Luther and Elsa Henrietta (Ericson) Sidelinger; m. Alfred B. Britton Jr., Sept. 2, 1942 (div. 1960); children: Alfred B. Britton III, Kathryn H. Lumbert, Patrick Luther Britton; m. James Stuart Browne M.D., May 19, 1963; children: Bruce Petter Browne, Julia Regina Browne. Student, Stanford U., 1947; BA with great distinction with honors, San Jose State U., 1949; MSW, U. Calif., 1958; BFA, San Francisco Art Inst., 1973. Lic. Clinical Social Worker, Calif. Clinical social worker Dept. of Mental Health, Sacramento, 1958-59; clin. social worker U. Calif. Med. Ctr., San Francisco, 1960-61, Langley Porter Neuropsych. Inst., San Francisco, 1961-65, Napa State Hosp., 1980-85; postgrad. Inst. for Clin. Social Work, Berkeley, 1981-83; freelance artist Mill Valley, Calif., 1966-80, 1985—. Mem. Acci Gallery, Berkeley, 1977-91, Alliance Women Artists, 1988-89. Recipient Merit award Calif. State Fair Fine Arts Div., 1989, Marin Arts Guild, Larkspur, Calif., 1977-79, Outdoor Art Club Mill Valley, AAUW, Art award Marin County Fair, 1977-78, 89-90. Mem. AAUW, DAR, Calif. Soc. Printmakers, Calif. Watercolor Assn. (signature mem., membership chmn. 1986-88, Merit award 1987), Marin Soc. Artists, Outdoor Art Club (Mill Valley), Alpha Chi Omega (pres. Santa Clara County alumnae 1949-51, Marin County alumnae 1966-68). Avocations: computer graphics, photography, geneology. E-mail: goldengate4@aol.com.

BROWNE, DONALD ROGER, speech communication educator; b. Detroit, Mar. 13, 1934; s. A. and L. Browne; m. Mary Jo Rowell, Aug. 23, 1958; children: Mary Kathleen, Stuart Roger, Steven Rowell. BA, U. Mich., 1955, MA, 1958, PhD, 1961. Corr. Voice of Am., fgn. service officer U.S. Info. Agy., Tunis, Tunisia and Conakry, Guinea, 1960-63; asst. prof. broadcasting Boston U., 1963-65; asst. prof. speech Purdue U., West Lafayette, Ind., 1965-66; assoc. prof. U. Minn., Mpls., 1966-70, prof., 1970—, dept. chair, 1989-93, 96-99. Fulbright lectr., Beirut, 1973-74; vis. lectr. Lund U., Sweden, spring 1993. Author: International Radio Broadcasting, 1982, Comparing Broadcast Systems, 1989 (BEA/NAB Electronic Media Book of Yr. award 1989, Outstanding Acad. Book in Comm. Category, Choice, 1990), Television/Radio News & Minorities, 1994, Electronic Media and Indigenous Peoples, 1996, Electronic Media and Industrialized Nations, 1999. Mem.Civic Orch. Mpls., 1966—. Served with U.S. Army, 1955-57. NATO fellow, Brussels, 1980. Mem. Broadcast Edn. Assn., Assn. for Edn. in Journalism and Mass Comm., Civic Orch. Mpls. Episcopalian. Avocation: playing trombone. Office: Univ of Minn 224 Church St SE Ford Hall Minneapolis MN 55455

BROWNE, FREDERICK DOUGLAS, physiologist, educator; b. Springfield, Ohio, June 3, 1929; s. Charles David and Ruth Noami Browne; m. Joyce Louise Burton, June 11, 1955; children: Fred, Sharon, Michael, Regina, Stephan, Monica. BS, U. Dayton, 1956; MS, Miami U., Ohio, 1958; postgrad., Case Western Res. U., 1963-66; EdD, Nova U., 1981. Ordained permanent deacon Maronite Cath. Ch., 1992. Rschr. artificial organs and exptl. heart surgery Cleve. Clinic, 1958-63; predoctoral fellow Coll. Medicine Case Western Res. U., Cleve., 1963-66; instr. sci. Cleve. Bd. Edn., 1966-69; asst. prof. St. John's Coll., Cleve., 1969-73; instr. Sch. Anesthesia Cleve. Clinic, 1973-74; prof. anatomy and physiology Cuyahoga C.C., Warrensville, Ohio, 1973-92; chair/CEO Ramesso, Inc., Copley, Ohio, 1993—. Contbr. articles to profl. jours. Pres., Bd. Cath. Edn., Diocese of Cleve., 1972-73; chmn. Civil Svc. Commn. Warrensville Heights, Ohio, 1970-72; councilman Warrensville Heights, 1982-85; bd. dirs. Summit County Cath. Social Svc.; mem. precinct com. Rep. Party, 2002, 2d lt. U.S. Army, 1952-54. NIH fellow, 1963-66. Mem. AAUP, Nat. Assn. Advancement Sci., N.Y. Acad. Scis., Ohio Coll. Biology Tchrs. Assn., Alpha Phi Alpha. Republican.

BROWNE, G.M. WALTER SHAWN, journalist, publisher, organizer; b. Sydney, Australia, Jan. 10, 1949; s. Walter Francis and Hilda Louise (Leahy) B.; m. Raquel Emilse Facal, Mar. 9, 1973; 1 stepson, Marcello Garcia. Grad. high sch. Chess player, 1957—; U.S. jr. champion, 1966; Australian champion, 1968-69; U.S. Open champion, 1971-73; Nat. Open champion, 1971-73, 75, 84, 86-87, 91, 94-95, 2002; U.S. champion, 1974-78, 80-83; Pan-Am. champion, 1974; Internat. German champion, 1975; mem. U.S. Olympic Team, 1974, 78, 82, 84; Nat. and U.S. Open Blitz chess champion, 1989; Pan-Pacific Blitz chess champion, 1991. Columnist Chess Life & Rev., Berkeley, Calif., 1973— ; lectr. in field; commentator at 1999 Fide World Championship, Las Vegas, Nev. Publisher: Strongest International Chess Tourneys, 1978-85. Named Internat. Master Fedn. Internat. des Eshecs, 1969, Internat. Grandmaster, 1969; winner German Open Championship, Mannheim, 1975; 1st pl. Venice, 1971; 1st pl. Rejkavik, Iceland, 1978; 1st pl. Wijk Am. Zee, Holland, 1974, 80; 1st pl. Indonesia, 1982, 2d-3d World Open, Phila., 1988; only 11 time winner Nat. Open, Can. Open champion, 1991, U.S. class champion, 1991, 7 time Am. Open champion; winner N.Am. Open 1991, 93, 94, 96; inducted into U.S. Hall of Fame, 2003. Mem. World Blitz Chess Assn. (pres., founder, pub., editor quar. mag. Blitz Chess 1988—). Achievements include performance of simultaneous chess exhibitions, including world record of 29-0 in 45 minutes, Adelaide, Australia, 1971. Played 106 competitors, including a computer, for a world record score of 94 wins, 9 draws, and 3 losses, and time of 7 hours, 20 minutes, N.Y.C., 1973, 1st pl., Gjovik, Norway, 1983, 1st pl., Naestved, Denmark, 1985; 1st pl. World Blitz Chess Assn.-Software Blitz Chess, Long Beach, Calif., 1988; defeated World Blitz champion, Mikhail Tal by a score of 2 1/2-1/2. 5-time Western Class champion, Concord and L.A.; 2-time Western States champion, Reno. Address: 8 Parnassus Rd Berkeley CA 94708-2011 Fax: 510-486-8078. E-mail: wbcablitz@aol.com.

BROWNE, JEFFREY FRANCIS, lawyer; b. Clare, South Australia, Australia, Mar. 1, 1944; came to U.S., 1975; s. Patrick Joseph and Irene Kathleen (Cormack) B.; m. Deborah Mary Christine West, Aug. 28, 1971; children: Veronique Namur Irene, Jeffrey James, Nicholas Patrick, Sophie Christina, Amy Elizabeth. LLB, Adelaide U., South Australia, 1966; LLM, Sydney U., Australia, 1968, Harvard U., 1976. Bar: South Australia 1969, Australian Capital Territory 1973, N.Y. 1978, Victoria 1982, New South Wales 1983, Western Australia 1983. Assoc. High Ct. Australia, Canberra, Australian Capital Territory, 1967-68; diplomat Dept. Fgn. Affairs, Canberra, 1969; 2d sec. Australian High Commn., London and Malaysia, 1970-71, acting high commr. Ghana, 1972; counsel nuclear tests case Internat. Ct. Justice, 1973-74; assoc. Sullivan & Cromwell, N.Y.C., 1976-81, ptnr., 1983—; gen. counsel Alcoa of Australia, Melbourne, 1981-82. Bd. dirs. Compinvest Pty. Ltd. Mem. Law Inst. Victoria, Australian Mining and Petroleum Law Assn., Law Coun. Australia (chmn. fin. and securities subcom., internat. trade and bus. law com.), Inst. Dirs. of Australia, Internat. Bar Assn. (sect. on energy and natural resources), Am. C. of C. in Australia (bd. dirs.), Am. Soc. Internat. Law, N.Y. Yacht Club, Melbourne Club. Office: Sullivan & Cromwell 125 Broad St Fl 28 New York NY 10004-2489 also: 101 Collins St Melbourne Victoria 3000 Australia E-mail: brownej@sullcrom.com.

BROWNE, JOHN CHARLES, physics researcher, former national research laboratory executive; b. Pottstown, Pa., July 29, 1942; s. Charles Ignatius and Mary Agnes (Titzer) B.; m. Susan Mary Mazzarella, Dec. 30, 1972 (div. Dec. 1984); children— Christopher Ryan, Adam Charles; m. Marti Moore, May 4, 1985; 1 child, Courtney Keese. BS, Drexel U., 1965; PhD, Duke U., 1969; DSc (hon.), Drexel U., 1998. Instr. Duke U., Durham, N.C., 1969-70; staff scientist Lawrence Livermore Lab., Calif., 1970-79; group leader Los Alamos Nat. Lab., 1979-81, div. leader, 1981-84, assoc. dir., 1984-93; dir. Los Alamos Neutron Sci. Ctr., Los Alamos, 1993—97; lab. dir. Los Alamos Nat. Lab., 1997—2003, sr. scientist, 2003—. Contbr. articles to profl. jours. NASA fellow, 1965-67 Fellow AAAS, Am. Phys. Soc. Roman Catholic. Avocations: skiing, tennis. Office: Los Alamos Nat Lab MS H 855 Los Alamos NM 87545-0001

BROWNE, (EDMUND) JOHN PHILLIP, oil company executive; b. Hamburg, Germany, Feb. 20, 1948; s. Edmund and Paula Browne. MA in Physics, Cambridge U., Eng., 1969; MS in Bus., Stanford (Calif.) U., 1980; DEng (hon.), Heriott Watt U.; DTech (hon.), Robert Gordon U.; DSc (hon.), Warwick U. Registered profl. engr., U.K. Petroleum engr. Brit. Petroleum Co., London, N.Y., Calif. and Alaska, 1969-79, regional petroleum engr., 1979-80, comml. mgr., 1981-83, group treas., 1984-86; chief exec. BP Finance Internat., 1984; mgr. forties field Brit. Petroleum Co., Aberdeen, Scotland, 1983-84; exec. v.p., CFO, CEO Standard Oil Co. of Ohio, Cleve., 1986-87; CEO Standard Oil Prodn. Co., 1987-89; chief fin. officer BP America, Inc., Cleve., 1987-89; mng. dir., chief exec. officer BP Exploration, London, 1989-95; mng. dir., bd. The Brit. Petroleum Co., PLC, 1991-98, group chief exec., 1995-98, BP Amoco (now BP p.l.c.), 1998—. Nonexec. dir. Redland PLC, 1992-96, Smithkine Beecham, 1995-99, Intel Corp., 1997-2001, Goldman Sachs; mem. supervisory bd. Daimler-Chrysler AG, 1997-2001. Emeritus chmn. adv. bd. Stanford Grad. Sch. Bus., 1997; trustee Brit. Mus., 1995—, Conf. Bd., Inc.; v.p. Prince of Wales Bus. Leaders Forum; hon. fellow St. John's Coll., Cambridge. Knighted, 1998; Trevelyan open scholar. Fellow Royal Acad. Engring., Inst. Mining and Metallurgy, Inst. Chem. Engrs. (hon.); mem. Athenaeum Club (London). Avocations: ballet, opera, photography, pre-columbian art.

BROWNE, JOHN ROBINSON, banker; b. Ft. Worth, Aug. 29, 1914; s. Virgil and Maimee Lee (Robinson) B.; m. Elizabeth Anne Hargett, Sept. 1, 1945 (dec. June 1990); children: John Robinson, Ann Browne (Mrs. John M. Dunker); stepchildren: Bob Allen Street, David H. Street; m. Christine H. Anthony, Mar. 20, 1992 (dec. May 1993); m. Barbara C. (Conner) Edwards, Nov. 18, 1994 (div. Apr. 2001). AB, Okla. U., 1938, JD, 1939; postgrad., Harvard Grad. Sch. Bus. Adminstrn., 1939-40; grad., Stonier Grad. Sch. Banking, Rutgers U., 1965. Bar: Okla. bar 1939. With Liberty Nat. Bank & Trust Co., Oklahoma City, 1945-46, 60-71, sr. v.p., 1960-71; gen. mgr. Coca-Cola Bottling Co., Colorado Springs and Pueblo, Colo., 1946-59; chief exec. officer Union Bancorp., Inc., Oklahoma City, 1971-89; chmn. bd. dirs. Sterling Sugars Co., Franklin, La., 1989-96, Cheyenne Propagation Co., Colo. Springs, Colo., 1989—. Mng. gen. ptnr. Glencoe-Vacherie Plantation Ltd., Okla., 1972—. Served from 2d lt. to lt. col., F.A. AUS, 1940-45. Mem. Okla. Bar Assn. Office: Colcord Bldg 15 N Robinson Ave Oklahoma City OK 73102-5405

BROWNE, JOSEPH PETER, retired librarian; b. June 12, 1929; s. George and Mary Bridget (Fahy) B. AB, U. Notre Dame, 1951; STL, Pontificum Athenaeum Angelicum, Rome, 1957, STD, 1960; MS in L.S., Cath. U. Am., 1965. Joined Congregation of Holy Cross, Roman Cath. Ch., 1947, ordained priest, 1955. Asst. pastor Holy Cross Ch., South Bend, Ind., 1955-56, libr., prof. moral theology Washington, 1959-64; mem. faculty U. Portland, Oreg., 1964-73, 75—, dir. libr., 1966-70, 76-94, dean Coll. Arts and Scis., 1970-73, assoc. prof. libr. sci., 1967-95, prof. emeritus, 1995—, regent, 1969-70, 77-81, chmn. acad. senate, 1968-70. Prof., head dept. libr. sci. Our Lady of Lake Coll., San Antonio, 1973-75; chmn. Interstate Libr. Planning Coun., 1977-79. Mem. Columbia River chpt. Huntington's Disease Soc. Am., 1975-90, pres., 1979-82; pastor St. Birgitta Ch., Portland, 1993—; chmn. Archdiocesan Presbyteral Coun., 1994-98, 2000-02; mem. coll. of cons. Archdiocese of Portland, 1995-2005. Recipient Culligan award U. Portland, 1979. Mem. ALA, Cath. Libr. Assn. (life, pres. 1971-73), Cath. Theol. Soc. Am., Pacific N.W. Libr. Assn. (pres. 1985-86), Oreg. Libr. Assn. (life, pres. 1967-68), Nat. Assn. Parliamentarians, Oreg. Assn. Parliamentarians (pres. 1985-87), Mensa Internat., All-Ireland Cultural Soc. Oreg. (pres. 1984-85), Ancient Order of Hibernians, KC. Democrat. Home: 11820 NW Saint Helens Rd Portland OR 97231-2319 E-mail: browne@up.edu.

BROWNE, LOVETIE W. special education educator, small business owner; b. Monrovia, Liberia, Jan. 12, 1965; arrived in U.S., 1993; d. Archibald J. Browne and Susannah B. Blackmon-Telewoda; m. Saye D. Gbalazeh, Sept. 15, 1984 (div. May 3, 2000); children: Saye M., Lovetie F. BS in Elem. Edn., Cuttington U. Coll., Suokoko, Liberia, 1988; MS in spl. edn., Coppin State Coll., Balt., 1995; cert. adv. study in edn., Coll. of Notre Dame, Balt., 2002. Cert. std. tchg. NJ, adv. profl. tchg. Md. Elem. sch. tchr. Archdiocese of Monrovia, Liberia, 1988—93; spl. edn. tchr. Balt. City Pub. Sch., 1994—. CEO My Heart's Appeal Inc., Balt., 1996—. Author: (book) A Sibling's Vow, 2001. Recipient Tchr. of Excellence award, Balt. City Coun. of PTAs Inc., 1997, Crystal award, Victor E. Ward Edn. Fund, 2002. Mem.: Nat. Edn. Assn., Coun. on Exceptional Children, Coppin State Coll. Alumni Assn. (parliamentarian 2002—). Democrat. Pentacostal. Achievements include founder, My Heart's Appeal, non-profit orgn. providing edn. and vocational assistance to mentally retarded children in West Africa. Avocations: reading, writing, humanitarian affairs, hearing people's stories, lifetime learning. Home: 1909 Greenberry Rd Baltimore MD 21209 Office Fax: 410-664-2174. E-mail: Blovetie@aol.com.

BROWNE, MALCOLM WILDE, journalist; b. N.Y.C., Apr. 17, 1931; s. Douglas Granzow and Dorothy Rutledge (Wilde) B.; m. Huynh thi Le Lieu, July 18, 1966. Student, Swarthmore Coll., 1948-50, N.Y.U., 1950-52. Cons. chemist, tech. writer, 1952-56; newsman, copy editor Middletown (N.Y.) Daily Record, 1958-60; with Balt. bur. A.P., 1960-61; chief Indochina corr., 1961-65; Saigon corr. ABC, 1965-66; freelance writer and corr. N.Y.C., 1966-68; corr. New York Times, in Buenos Aires, 1968-71, 1971-73, 1973-77, sci. corr., 1977-81; sr. editor Discover mag., 1981-84; sci writer N.Y. Times, 1985-00, retired, 2000; McGraw prof. writing Princeton (N.J.) U., 1995-96. Author: The New Face of War, 1965, Muddy Boots and Red Socks, 1993. Served with AUS, 1956-58. Recipient First prize World Press Photo award The Hague, 1963, Pulitzer prize fgn. corr., 1964, Overseas Press Club award, 1964, Sigma Delta Chi award, 1964, Louis M. Lyons award, 1964, Nat. Headliners Club award, 1964; A.P. Mng. Editors award, 1964, Grady-Stack medal Am. Chem. Soc., 1992; Edward R. Murrow Meml. fellow Coun. on Fgn. Rels., 1966-67. Mem.: Sigma Xi. Address: 36 E 36th St New York NY 10016-3463

BROWNE, RAY, congressman, insurance broker; b. Washington, Dec. 8, 1938; s. Woodrow Lee and Mary Isabelle (Manning) B.; m. Barbara Lee Andrus, May 17, 1979; children: Ray II, Molly Lee. Student, U. Md., 1959-62. CLU; ChFC. Life ins. agt., gen. agt. Aetna Life & Casualty, Washington, Cleve., Charleston, W.Va., 1964-82; ins. broker The Browne Co., Washington, 1982—; shadow rep. from D.C. U.S. Ho. of Reps., Washington, 2001—. Vis. lectr. John Carroll U., Cleve., 1972-77; speaker in field. Contbr. polit. and bus. commentary to newspapers, articles to profl. jours. Adv. neighborhood commr. Washington Govt., 1989-90; mem. drug strategy team Washington Govt., 1989-90; vice chair Hurt Home Bd., Washington, 1987-89; candidate for City Coun., Washington, 1990, Dem. Nat. Com., 1995—; mediator Washington Superior Ct., 1985-88; mem. parish coun. Holy Trinity Cath. Ch., Washington, 2001—. With USN, 1956-58. Mem. Nat. Assn. Life Underwriters (dir. No. Va. 1964-66), Greater Washington Chpt. CLU (bd. dirs., sec., treas., v.p., pres. 1982-91), Million Dollar Roundtable (life, Big Brothers and Big Sisters Merit award), Mensa, U. Md. M Club, Alpha Tau Omega (Silver Circle award 1984). Democrat. Roman Catholic. Office: The Browne Co 2621 O St NW Washington DC 20007*

BROWNE, RAY BROADUS, popular culture educator; b. Millport, Ala., Jan. 15, 1922; s. Garfield and Annie Nola (Trull) B.; m. Olwyn Orde, Aug. 21, 1952 (dec.); children— Glenn, Kevin; m. Alice Pat Matthews, Aug. 25, 1965; 1 child, Alicia. AB, U. Ala., 1943; A.M., Columbia U., 1947; PhD, UCLA, 1956. Instr. U. Nebr., Lincoln, 1947-50; instr. U. Md., College Park, 1956-60; asst. prof., assoc. prof. Purdue U., Lafayette, Ind., 1960-67; prof. popular culture Bowling Green (Ohio) State U., 1967—, Univ. disting. prof., 1975—. Author, editor over 50 books, including Melville's Drive to Humanism, 1971, Popular Culture and the Expanding Consciousness, 1973, The Constitution and Popular Culture, 1975, Dominant Symbols in Popular Culture, 1990, The Many Tongues of Literacy, 1992, Continuities in Popular Culture, 1993, The Cultures of Celebrations, 1994, Preview 2001: Popular Culture Studies in the Future, 1996, Lincoln-Lore: Lincoln in Contemporary Popular Culture, 1996, Pioneers in Popular Culture Studies, 1998, The Defining Guide to United States Popular Culture, 2000, The Detective as Historian, 2000, Mission Underway: The History of the Popular Culture Association/American Culture Association and Popular Culture Movement, 2002, Popular Culture of the Civil War and Reconstruction, 2003; creator, editor Jour. Popular Culture, 1967-82, Jour. Am. Culture, 1977-82. Served with U.S. Army, 1942—46. Mem. Popular Culture Assn. (founder, sec., treas. 1970—), Am. Culture Assn. (sec.-treas. 1977—). Democrat. Avocation: scholarly research. Home: 210 N Grove St Bowling Green OH 43402-2335 Office: Bowling Green U Jour Popular Culture Bowling Green OH 43403-0001 E-mail: rbrowne@bgnet.bgsu.edu.

BROWNE, RICHARD CULLEN, lawyer; b. Akron, Nov. 21, 1938; s. Francis Cedric and Elizabeth Ann (Cullen) Browne; m. Patricia Anne Winkler, Apr. 23, 1962; children: Richard Cullen, Catherine Anne, Paulette Elizabeth, Maureen Frances, Colleen Marie. BS in Econs., Holy Cross Coll., 1960; JD, Cath. U. Am., 1963. Bar: Va. 1963, U.S. Ct. Claims 1963, U.S. Ct. Customs and Patent Appeals 1963, D.C. 1964, U.S. Ct. Mil. Appeals 1963, U.S. Ct. Appeals (D.C. cir.) 1964, U.S. Supreme Ct. 1966, U.S. Ct. Appeals (fed. cir.) 1982, U.S. Ct. Appeals (9th cir.) 1983, U.S. Ct. Appeals (6th cir.) 1991, U.S. Ct. Appeals (7th cir.) 1998. Assoc. Browne, Beveridge, DeGrandi & Kline, Washington, 1963-68, ptnr., 1968-72, Schaffert, Miller & Browne, Washington, 1972-74; sr. counsel Office of Enforcement EPA, Washington, 1974-76; asst. chief hearing counsel U.S. Nuclear Regulatory Commn., Washington, 1976-78; sole practice Washington, 1978-79; ptnr. Winston & Strawn, Washington, 1980-2001, of counsel, 2001—. Lectr. U. R.I., 1975, Washburn U., 1978, Legal Ins., CSC, 1975—78, Hofstra U., 1987—, Nat. Inst. for Trial Advocacy, 1986—. Del. Montgomery County Civic Fedn., 1970—74; chmn. Citizens Adv. Com. on Rockville Corridor, 1972—77; mem. Montgomery County Potomac River Basin Adv. Com., 1972—74; chmn. Cath. U. Am. Fund, 1996—2001. Capt. JAGC USAF, 1963—66, capt. USAFR, 1966—69. Named Disting. Mil. Grad., Holy Cross Coll., 1960. Mem.: Cath. U. Gen. Alumni Assn. (bd. govs. 1992—, chair Gibbons medal com. 1995—2001, exec. com. 1995—2001), Cath. U. Law Sch. Alumni Soc. (bd. dirs. 1991—, pres. 1992—93, bd. visitors 1998—), Coll. Holy Cross General Alumni Assn. (bd. dirs. 1971—78, alumni senate 1978—97, nominations and elections com. 1995—, bd. dirs. 1997—, pres. 2002—03). Republican. Home: 7203 Old Stage Rd Rockville MD 20852-4438 Office: Winston & Strawn 1400 L St NW Ste 1000 Washington DC 20005-3508 E-mail: rbrowne@alumni.holycross.edu.

BROWNE, ROBERT SPAN, economist, researcher; b. Chgo., Aug. 17, 1924; s. William Henri and Julia Louise (Barksdale) B.; m. Huoi Nguyen, Apr. 6, 1956; children: Hoa Nguyen, Mai Julia, Ngo Alexi, Marshall Xuan. BA in Econs, U. Ill., 1944; MBA, U. Chgo., 1947; postgrad. in econs., CUNY. Economist U.S. Govt. Fgn. Aid Program Cambodia and Vietnam, 1955-61; project dir. Phelps-Stokes Fund, N.Y.C., 1963-65; asst. prof. econs. Fairleigh Dickinson U., Teaneck, N.J., 1965-71; dir. Black Econ. Research Center, N.Y.C., 1969-80; exec. dir. African Devel. Fund, 1980-82; sr. research fellow Howard U., 1982-85; staff dir. House Banking Subcom. on Internat. Devel., Fin., Trade and Monetary Policy., 1987-91. Internat. econ. cons., 1991—; mem. adv. com. Congl. Budget Office, 1976-80, Office Tech. Assessment, 1976-80; mem. Calvert adv. coun. on social investment, 1999--. Author: (with others) The Social Scene, 1972, The Lagos Plan vs. the Berg Report, 1984; Editor: Rev. Black Polit. Economy, 1970-71. Del. Nat. Dem. Conv., 1968, Black Polit. Conv., Gary, Ind., 1972; pres., bd. dirs. 21st Century Found.; bd. dirs. Africare, Calvert New Africa Fund, Aurora Assocs., Internat. Served with USAAF, 1944-46. Mem. Coun. Fgn. Rels. Home: 214 E Tryon Ave Teaneck NJ 07666-6132 E-mail: rbrowne306@aol.com.

BROWNE, ROGER MICHAEL, oral pathology educator, consultant; b. Birmingham, U.K., June 19, 1934; s. Arthur Leslie and Phyllis Maud (Baker) B.; m. Lilah Hilda Manning, May 31, 1958; children: Nicola Jane, Andrew Manning. BS, U. Birmingham, 1954, B of Dental Sci., 1957, PhD, 1960, DDS, 1974. Rsch. fellow U. Birmingham, 1958-60, lectr. in conservative dentistry, 1961-64, lectr. in dental pathology, 1964-67, sr. lectr. in oral pathology, 1967-77, prof. oral pathology, 1977-96, prof. emeritus, 1997—. Vis. prof. U. Lagos, Nigeria, 1969; postgrad. advisor in dentistry U. Birmingham, 1977-82, dir. Sch. Dentistry, 1986-89. Author: Colour Atlas of Oral Histopathology, 1975, Radiological Atlas of Diseases of the Teeth and Jaws, 1983, Atlas of Dental and Maxillofacial Radiology and Imaging, 1995; editor: The Investigative Pathology of Odontogenic Cysts, 1991, Self-assessment Picture Tests - Oral Radiology, 1997. Fellow Royal Coll. Pathologists, Dental Surgery Royal Coll. Surgeons (Charles Tomes medal 1995); mem. Internat. Assn. for Dental Rsch. (Disting. Scientist award in pulp biology 1991), Brit. Soc. Oral Pathology (pres. 1985-86, 91-94), Brit. Dental Assn. (pres. hosps. group 1986-87). Avocations: rugby football, tennis, walking. Office: Dental School St Chads Queensway B4 6NN Birmingham England

BROWNE, SPENCER IVAN, mortgage company executive, internet executive; b. 1949; married. BS, U. Pa., 1971; JD (cum laude), Villanova U., 1974. Spl. counsel SEC, 1974—79; ptnr. Brownstein Hyatt & Farber, Denver, 1983-84; pres., dir. MDC Holdings, Inc., 1984-96; pres., CEO, dir. Asset Investors Corp., 1988-96; pres., CEO & dir. Comml. Assets, Inc., 1994-96; with Strategic Asset Mgmt. LLC, Denver, 1996—. Bd. dirs. Annaly Mortgage Mgmt., Delta Fin. Corp., Nexus Resources Inc., Internet Commerce Group (chmn.). Office: Strategic Asset Mgmt LLC 650 S Cherry St Ste 420 Denver CO 80246-1806 E-mail: sibsam@aol.com., spencer@nexusresources.com.

BROWNE, STANHOPE STRYKER, lawyer; b. Colorado Springs, Colo., July 22, 1931; s. Samuel Stanhope Stryker and Florence Jeanette (Reynolds) B.; m. Elizabeth Whitney Sturges, Sept. 12, 1964; children: Katrina C., Whitney R. AB, Princeton U., 1953; LL.B., Harvard U., 1956. Bar: Pa. 1957. Assoc. Dechert LLP, Phila., 1956-65, ptnr., 1965-97, of counsel, 1998—, resident ptnr. Brussels, 1972—76. Lectr. internat. law. Contbr. articles to profl. jours. Chmn. Penn's Landing Corp., Phila., 1981-97, Com. to Preserve Am.'s Birthplace, 1965-72; vice chmn. World Affairs Council, 1978-90; bd. dirs. Phila. 1976 Bicentennial Corp., 1971-72, Greater Phila. Movement, 1970-71, Phila. Port Corp., 1984-90, Ecole Française Internationale de Philadelphie, 1991-99, The Ch. Found., 1998-2001, French Heritage Soc., Inc., 1999—; mem. exec. com. Cen. Phila. Devel. Corp., 1968-72, 77-99; mem. Phila. Dist. Export Council U.S. Dept. Commerce, 1983-96; vice pres. Pa. Prison Soc., 1962-69; pres. Greater Phila. Council of Chs., 1966-67; mem. Diocesan Coun. Episcopal Diocese of Pa., 1967-71; rector's warden St. Peter's Ch., 1983-90; chmn. Democrats Abroad, Belgium, 1975-76, Pa. Internat. Trade Conf., 1977-79; mem. adv. commn. Independence Nat. Hist. Park, Phila., 1969-72; hon. consul of France in Phila., 1986-96; mem. vestry Am. Cathedral in Paris, 2001-02. Recipient Pub. Service and Polit. Courage award Southeastern Pa. chpt. Ams. for Democratic Action, 1965; decorated Nat. Order of Merit, France, 1998. Mem. Phila. Bar Assn., French-Am. C. of C. (bd. dirs. Phila. chpt. 1989-2001), Independence Hall Assn. (bd. dirs. 1978-90, adv. com. 1990-99), Phila. Com. on Fgn. Rels., Brook Club (N.Y.C.), Phila. Club (bd. dirs. 1988-92), Phi Beta Kappa Democrat. Episcopalian. Office: Dechert LLP 4000 Bell Atlantic Tower 1717 Arch St Philadelphia PA 19103-2793 E-mail: stanhopesb@aol.com.

BROWNE, THOMAS REED, neurologist, researcher, educator; b. Lakewood, N.J., Aug. 10, 1943; s. Thomas Reed and Margaret (King) B.; m. Lynne Van Beuren, Mar. 27, 1969; children: Hilary Katherine, David Gerard. BA cum laude, Princeton U., 1965; MD with honors, U. Rochester, 1969. Diplomate Am. Bd. Psychiatry and Neurology, Am. Bd. Clin. Neurophysiology. Intern in medicine Cornell U. Med. Ctr., N.Y.C., 1969-70; staff assoc. epilepsy NIH, Bethesda, Md., 1970-72; resident in neurology Mass. Gen. Hosp., Boston, 1972-75; fellow in epilepsy Childrens Hosp., Boston, 1975-76; asst. prof. neurology Boston U. Sch. Medicine, Boston, 1976-80, assoc. prof. neurology, 1980-84, prof. neurology, 1984—, vice-chmn. dept. neurology, 1987—. Clin. instr. in neurology Harvard Med. Sch., 1976-86; lectr. neurology Harvard Med. Sch., Boston, 1987—; assoc. chief neurology svc. VA Med. Ctr., Boston, 1987-97, chief neurology svc., 1997-2000; med. info. dir. Grace Brain Ctr., 2000—; dir. Boston U. Comprehensive Epilepsy Ctr., 2002—. Editor: Epilepsy: Diagnosis and Management, 1983, 5th Frontiers of Pharmacology Symposium, Stable Isotopes in Pharm. Res., 1987, Handbook of Epilepsy, 1997, 3d edit. 2003, Stable Isotopes in Pharmaceutical Research, 1997; sect. editor Jour. Clin. Pharmacol., 1987—, Pharmacotherapy, 1982—, Am. Jour. Therapeutics, 1994—; contbr. 200 articles to profl. jours. Recipient Ciba Geigy award Internat. League Epilepsy, 1985. Fellow Am. Coll. Clin. Pharm. (regent 1985-90, McKeen Cattell award 1993), Am. Acad. Neurology, Am. EEG Soc.; mem. Am. soc. Clin. Pharmacol. Therapy, Mass. Epilepsy Soc. (profl. adv. bd.). Achievements includes development of stable isotope tracer methods for human pharmacology studies.

BROWNE, WILLIAM BITNER, lawyer; b. Springfield, Ohio, Nov. 23, 1914; s. John Franklin and Etta Blanche (Bitner) B.; m. Dorothy Ruth Gilbert, Aug. 31, 1939; children: Franklin G., Dale Ann Browne Compton. AB, Wittenberg U., 1935, LLD (hon.), 1970; postgrad., U. Bordeaux, 1935-36; JD cum laude, Harvard U., 1939. Bar: Ohio 1939, U.S. Dist. Ct. (so. dist.) Ohio 1941, U.S. Ct. Appeals (6th cir.) 1950, U.S. Supreme Ct. 1970. Assoc. Donovan, Leisure, Newton & Lumbard, N.Y.C., 1939-40; assoc. Corry, Durfey & Martin, Springfield, Ohio, 1940-48; ptnr. Corry, Durfey, Martin & Browne and successors, Springfield, Ohio, 1948-88; of counsel Martin, Browne, Hull & Harper, Springfield, 1988-94. Contbr. (articles to legal jours.). Bd. dirs. Wittenberg U., 1955-89; pres. Greater Springfield & Clark County Assn., 1948-49; vice chmn. Clark County Republican Central and Exec. coms., 1948-52; mem. Springfield City Bd. Edn., 1950-53; mem. exec. com. United Appeals Clark County, 1956-62. Capt. OSS Signal Corps, U.S. Army, 1942-46. Decorated Bronze Star; decorated Croix de Guerre with palm, Medaille de Reconnaissance Francaise; laureate Springfield Area Bus. Hall of Fame, 1993. Fellow Am. Coll. Trial Lawyers (ret.), Am. Bar Found., Am. Coll. Trust and Estate Counsel (ret.), Ohio Bar Found. (pres. 1979, Fellows rsch. and svc. award 1976); mem. ABA (del. 1971-76), Ohio Bar Assn. (pres. 1969-70, medal of honor 1973), Springfield Bar Assn. (pres. 1967), Springfield C. of C. (pres. 1961-62), Zanesfield Rod and Gun Club, Springfield Country Club, Rotary, Masons. Episcopalian. Office: Martin Browne Hull & Harper 1 S Limestone St PO Box 1488 Springfield OH 45501-1488

BROWNE, WILLIAM P. political science educator; b. Cherokee, Iowa, May 15, 1945; s. William Dale and Irene Etta Browne; m. Linda Sue Browne. BS, Iowa State U., 1967, MS, 1969; PhD, Washington U., St. Louis, 1971. Prof. polit. sci. Cen. Mich. U., Mt. Pleasant, Mich., 1971—. Mem. adv. bd. Henry A. Wallace Inst., Winrock, Ala., 1990-96; cons. agribus. orgn., non-profit instns., 1985—. Author: (books) Private Interests, Public Policy and American Agriculture, 1988 (Outstanding Scholarly Book award 1989), Cultivating Congress, 1995, Groups, Interests, and Public Policy, 1998 (Outstanding Scholarly Book award 1999), The Failure of National Rural Policy, 2001; mem. editl. bd. Agr. and Human Values, 1990-98, Policy Studies Jour., 1998-2001. Recipient Ford Found. Scholarly award for rural studies, 1992; vis. scholar USDA, 1985. Mem. Am. Polit. Sci. Assn., Am. Agrl. Econs. Assn. (Quality of Comm. award 1993), Rural Sociol. Soc., Am. Soc. Pub. Adminstrn., Midwest Polit. Sci. Assn., Mich. Assn. Polit. Scientists (pres. 1983-84), Policy Studies Orgn. (pres. 1999-2000). Republican. Roman Catholic. Avocations: fishing, shooting. Home: 320 Lakeshore Dr Manistee MI 49660 Office: Cen Mich U 313C Anspach Mount Pleasant MI 48859 Home (Winter): 234 Ria Terra Venice FL 34285 E-mail: lbbrowne@jackpine.com.

BROWNELL, BLAINE ALLISON, university administrator, history educator; b. Birmingham, Ala., Nov. 12, 1942; s. Blaine Jr. and Annette (Holmes) B.; m. Mardi Ann Taylor, Aug. 21, 1964; children— Blaine, Allison BA, Washington and Lee U., 1965; MA, U. N.C., 1967, PhD, 1969. Asst. prof. Purdue U., West Lafayette, Ind., 1969-74; assoc. prof., chmn. dept. U. Ala., Birmingham, 1974-78, prof., 1980-90, dean grad. sch., 1978-84, dean social and behavioral scis., 1984-90; provost, v.p. for acad. affairs U. North Tex., Denton, 1990-98; exec. dir. Ctr. Internat. Programs and Svcs. U. Memphis, 1998-2000; pres. Ball State U., Muncie, Ind., 2000—. Sr. fellow Johns Hopkins U., Balt., 1971-72; Fulbright lectr. Hiroshima U., Japan, 1977-78; dir. U. Ala. Ctr. Internat. Programs, 1980-90. Author: The Urban Ethos...., 1975, City in Southern History, 1977, Urban America, 1979, 2d edit., 1990, The Urban Nation 1920-80, 1981; editor Jour. Urban History, 1976-90, assoc. editor, 1990-95. Mem. Birmingham City Planning Commn., 1975-77, Jefferson County Planning Commn., 1975-77, Dallas Com. Fgn. Rels., 1990-98; chmn. Birmingham Coun. on Fgn. Rels., 1988-90. Mem. Am. Hist. Assn., Orgn. Am. Historians, So. Hist. Assn., Philos. Soc. Tex. Presbyterian. Office: Ball State U Office Of Pres Muncie IN 47306-0001

BROWNELL, EDWIN ROWLAND, banker, civil engineer, land surveyor; b. Tampa, Fla., Sept. 19, 1924; s. Clarence DeWolf and Helen Lucy (Hill) B.; m. Helen Marie Kegel, Jan. 22, 1948 (dec. Apr. 1967); 1 child, Nancy; m. Blanche Rosina Parisi, Dec. 26, 1967; children: Elizabeth, Elaine, Evelyn. BCE, U. Fla., 1947. Registered profl. surveyor, Fla., Ark., Ga., Miss., Nev., N.D., S.D., S.C., Tenn., W.Va. Cadastral engr. City of Miami, Fla., 1948-53; pres., CEO, chmn. E.R. Brownell & Assocs., Inc., Miami, 1953-93, real estate salesman, 1975—; founding dir. Total Bank, 1983—85, Am.'s Bank, 1980—83; pres., chief exec. officer, chmn. Brickellbanc Savs. Assn., Miami, 1985-89, also bd. dirs.; pres. Tri-County Engring. Co., 1983-89, Naples (Fla.) Title and Abstract Co., 1st Title and Abstract Co. Chmn. surveying com. U. Fla., Gainesville, 1974—, mem. pres.'s coun.; mem. nat. engring. degree accreditation team Nat. Coun. Engring. Examiners, Md., 1985-95, mem. team evaluating engring. readiness U.S. Armed Forces, 1980-81; chmn. engring. adv. com. Fla. Bd. Regents, Tallahassee, 1982-85; vice-chmn. legal grievance com. Fla. Bar, 1992-94. Elected county surveyor State of Fla., Dade County, 1956-60; chmn. Zoning Bd. Adjustment, Coral Gables, Fla., 1978-87; chmn. Coral Gables Planning and Zoning Bd., 1987-95; mem. Coral Gables Code Enforcement Bd., 1995-97, City of Coral Gables Historic Preservation Com., 1997, City of Coral Gables Constrn. Regulation Bd., 1997—; bd. dirs. Boys Club of Miami, 1980-83, Salvation Army South Fla., dir., 1990-94. Named Man of Yr., Dade County, Fla., 1989. Fellow Am. Congress Surveying and Mapping (hon. life, pres. 1980-81, Surveying Excellence award 1977, Miami Man Yr. 1990, Presdl. award 1994), NSPE, Nat. Soc. Profl. Surveyors (pres. 1978-79), Fla. Surveying and Mapping Soc. (hon., life), Profl. Surveyors and Mappers (pres. 1981), Fla. Soc. Profl. Land Surveyors (hon. life mem., Fla. Land Surveyor of Yr. 1973, pres. 1978-79, pres. Dade County chpt. 1965-69, hon., life mem. Dade County chpt. 1993); mem. AIA, NSF, Profl. Surveyors of Fla. (bd. dirs., chmn. 1993-94), Am. Soc. Photogrammetry and Remote Sensing (Presdl. citation 1982, 91, Merit award 1992), Am. Soc. Photogrammetry Found. (vice chmn. 1985-91), Am. Mil. Engrs., Am. Planning Assn., Internat. Geog. Info. Found. (vice-chmn.), Miami Bd. Realtors, Fla. Engring. Soc. (bd. dirs. 1992-94), Fla. Planning and Zoning Assn. (S. Fla. chpt.), Fla. Assn. Cadastral Mappers, Bus. Inc., Sierra Club (pres. 1977), Am. Contract Bridge Assn., Com. of 100, Bus. Inc., Granada Golf Assn., 10th Holers Golf Assn. (treas. 1995-96, pres. 1996-97, pres. 2003—), Coral Gables Country Club Fleet, Coral Gables 30 Yr. Club, Coral Gables Fin. Club (pres. 1998—2001), Century Club of Coral Gables (exec. sec., treas. 1993-96), Coral Gables Country Club (dir., pres. 1991-97, chmn., vice chmn. found. 1992-94, pres. fin. club 1998-02), Riviera Country Club, Holly Hills Country Club (N.C.), Computer Club Coral Gables (bd. dirs.), Kiwanis (pres. Southwest Miami chpt. 1979-81), Elks (Lodge #948), Lambda Alpha Internat., Kappa Alpha. Republican. Roman Catholic. Avocations: golf, bridge, traveling. Home: 1207 Sorolla Ave Coral Gables FL 33134-3515 Office: E R Brownell & Assocs Inc 3152 Coral Way Miami FL 33145-3210 E-mail: ebrow40862@aol.com.

BROWNELL, GORDON LEE, physicist, educator; b. Duncan, Okla., Apr. 8, 1922; s. Roscoe David and Mabel (Gourley) B.; m. Anna-Liisa Kairento; children: Wendy Silverman, Peter G., David L., James K., Piia Kairento, Janne Kairento. BS, Bucknell U., Lewisburg, Pa., 1944; PhD, Mass. Inst. Tech., 1950. Mem. faculty MIT, 1950—, prof., 1970-91, prof. emeritus, 1991—; dir. Physics Rsch. Lab., Mass. Gen. Hosp., Boston, 1950—. Bd. dirs. Neuroresearch Fund. Served to lt. (j.g.) USNR, 1944-46. Fellow Am. Phys. Soc., Am. Nuclear Soc., Am. Coll. Radiology (hon.); mem. Am. Assn. Physicists in Medicine (Coolidge award 1987), Soc. Nuclear Medicine (Paul C. Aebersold award 1975), European Soc. Nuclear Medicine (de Hevesy medal 1979, 2003) Clubs: Union Boat (Boston). Home: 45 Warren St Salem MA 01970-3132 Office: Mass Gen Hosp Physics Rsch Lab Boston MA 02114 also: MIT Cambridge MA 02139 E-mail: g.brownell@verizon.net.

BROWNELL, KELLY DAVID, psychologist, educator; b. Evansville, Ind., Oct. 31, 1951; s. Arnold Buffum and Margaret Elizabeth (Egly) Brownell; m. Mary Jo Gabriele, Aug. 20, 1977; children: Matthew Joseph, Kevin David, Kristy Elizabeth. BA, Purdue U., 1973; PhD, Rutgers U., 1977. Lic. clin. psychologist Conn. Postdoctoral fellow Brown U., Providence, 1977; from asst. prof. to assoc. prof. U. Pa., Phila., 1977—87, prof., 1987-90; prof. psychology Yale U., New Haven, 1991—, prof. epidemiology and pub. health, chair dept. psychology, 2003—, dir. Yale Ctr. Eating and Weight Disorders, 1994-2000, master of Silliman Coll. Author: (book) Handbook of Eating Disorders, 1986, Handbook of Behavioral Medicine, 1988, Eating Disorders in Athletes, 1991, Eating Disorders and Obesity, 1995, vol. 2, 2002, Behavioral Medicine and Women, 1998; contbr. articles to profl. jours. Recipient Cattell award, N.Y.

Acad. Scis., 1978, Choice award, ALA, 1989. Fellow: APA (pres. divsn. health psychology 1989—90), Acad. Behavioral Medicine Rsch., Soc. Behavioral Medicine (pres. 1988—89); mem.: Assn. Advancement Behavior Therapy (pres. 1988—89). Office: Yale U Dept Psychology Box 208205 Yale Sta New Haven CT 06520-8205

BROWNELL, NORA MEAD, federal agency administrator; b. Erie, Pa., May 18, 1947; d. George J. and Mary E. (Burke) Mead; m. Frederic M. Brownell, Sept. 9, 1972 (div.); children: Samantha, Peter, Alexa. Student, Manhattanville Coll., 1965-66, U. Syracuse, N.Y., 1966-69. Auction dir. channel 12 Stas. WHYY, Phila., 1980-81; inaugural dir., campaign cons. Re-election Campaign for Gov. Thornburgh, Harrisburg, 1981-82; dep. exec. asst. Gov. Richard Thornburgh, Harrisburg, Pa., 1982-87; v.p. corp. community rels. Meridian Bancorp, Inc., Phila., 1987-92; sr. v.p. corp. affairs Meridian Bancorp, Inc., Corestates Bancorp., 1992-96; acting exec. dir. Regional Performing Arts Ctr. Inc., 1997; apptd. commissioner Pa. Pub. Utility Commission, 1997—2001; commr. FERC, Washington, 2001—. Bd. dirs. NARUC, Times Pub. Co., Pa. Free Libr., Need Indeed, Please Touch Mus., Pa. Humanities Council, Susquehanna Art Mus., NRRI, Millennium Bank. Mem. Greater Phila. Cultural Alliance, Harmony House, Bus. Vols. for the Arts. Office: FERC 888 First St NE Washington DC 20426-4205 Office Fax: 202-208-0064.

BROWNELL, PATRICIA JANE, social worker, educator; b. Platteville, Wis., July 14, 1943; d. Richard and Thelma (Rowe) B.; m. James Gale Collins, Mar. 5, 1996. BA, U. Wis., 1967; MSW, Fordham U., 1978, PhD, 1994. Cert. social worker, N.Y. Caseworker dept. social svcs. Human Resources Adminstrn., N.Y.C., 1967-73, project coord. office spl. housing svcs., 1973-77, project mgr. office adminstrv. svcs., 1977-78, grants mgr., rsch. asst., sr. planner policy/program devel., 1978-83, exec. asst. to exec. dep. and dep. commr. home care svcs., 1983-90, dir. spl. projects office exec. dep. commr. family support, 1990-94, dep. dir. non-residential svcs. domestic violence program, 1994, adv. to exec. dep. commr. family support adminstrn., 1995—; from instr. to adj. prof. Fordham U. Grad. Sch. Social Svc., N.Y.C., 1990-94, asst. prof., 1995—. Vis. prof. behavioral sci. dept. Police Acad./N.Y.C. Police Dept., 2001—; adv. bd. Mary's House, 2000—; sec. DW Fin. Mgmt. Agy., 1995-97; cons. N.Y.C. Dept. for the Aging, 1998—; rsch. assoc. Ctr. for Hispanic Mental Health Rsch., 2000—; ad hoc coord. Fordham-St. James Field Placement and Cmty. Practice Project, 2000—; steering com. Interdisciplinary Ctr. for Family and Child Advocacy, 1997—; dir. profl. devel. Interdisciplinary Tng. for Pub. Child Welfare Workers and Supr. to Improve Child Welfare Svcs., 1997-2000; liaison Influencing State Policy, 1997— Co-author: Work with Older People: Challenges and Opportunities, 1994, Helping Battered Women: New Perspectives and Remedies, 1996, Social Work in Juvenile and Criminal Justice Settings, 2d edit., 1997, Multicultural Perspectives in Working with Families, 1997; (with E.P. Congress and I. Abelman) Battered Women and their Families: Intervention and Treatment Strategies, 1998; (with J. Berman) To Grandmother's House We Go and Stay: Perspectives on Custodial Grandparents, 2000; (with M. Moch) Social Work in the Era of Devolution: Toward a Just Practice, 2001; mem. editl. bd. (newsletter) Victimization of the Elderly and Disabled: Preventing Abuse, Mistreatment and Neglect, 1997—; contbr. articles to profl. jours. Bd. dirs. Fund for the Advancement Social Svcs., 1998—; steering com. N.Y.C. Elder Abuse Coalition, 1995—. Faculty Rsch. grantee Fordham U., 1996-97, 99—, N.Y.C. Dept. for the Aging grant, 1999—; Ravazzin scholar Ravazzin Ctr. for Social Work Rsch. in Aging, 1998—; Rational Emotive Inst. fellow, 1995; recipient Linda Mills Meml. award N.Y. State Divsn. Parole, 1993, Faculty Merit award, 1996-2000. Mem. NASW (welfare reform task force N.Y. chpt. 1994—, nominating com., del. assembly 2000—), State Soc. on Aging N.Y. (nominating com. 1999—, exec. com., co-chair social policy com. 2001—) Avocations: reading, yoga, drawing. Office: Fordham U Grad Sch Social Svc 113 W 60th St New York NY 10023 E-mail: brownell@fordham.edu.

BROWNER, CAROL M. former federal agency administrator; d. Michael Browner and Isabella Harty Hugues; m. Michael Podhorzer; 1 child, Zachary. Grad., U. Fla., 1977, JD, 1979. Gen. counsel govt. ops. com. Fla. Ho. of Reps., 1980; with Citizen Action, Washington; chief legis. aide environ. issues to Sen. Lawton Chiles, 1986—88; legis. dir. to Sen. Al Gore, Jr., 1988-91; sec. Dept. Environ. Regulation, Fla., 1991-93; administr. EPA, Washington, 1993—2000; principal The Albright Group L.L.C., 2001—. Mem. adv. coun. Harvard Med. Sch., Ctr. for Health and the Global Environment. Democrat. Office: The Albright Group 901 15th St NW Ste 1000 Washington DC 20005*

BROWNER, CAROLE HELEN, anthropologist, educator; b. NYC, May 23, 1947; d. Alfred H. and Shirley (Kapp) B.; m. Lawrence Howard Mintz, June 22, 1969 (div. Sept. 1976); m. Arthur Joseph Rubel, Jan. 1, 1986 (dec. Sept. 2001). BA, New Sch. Social Research, 1969; MA, U. Calif., Berkeley, 1972, PhD, 1976, MPH, 1977. Asst. prof. anthropology Wayne State U., Detroit, 1977-83, assoc. prof., 1983-84; asst. prof. psychiatry and biobehavioral scis. UCLA, 1983-87, assoc. prof., 1987-93, assoc. prof. anthropology, 1989-93, prof. psychiatry, behavioral scis., anthropology, 1993—. Cons. Xerox Corp., Palo Alto, Calif., 1977-78, Detroit Dept. Health, 1979-80, Nat. Inst. Edn., Washington, 1979, WHO, Geneva, 1980, Planned Parenthood, Tulsa, 1985, Social Sci. Rsch. Coun., N.Y.C., 1985, NSF, Washington, 1987, rev. panel cultural anthropology, 1987-89; mem. rev. panel NIH, 2002; mem. steering com. So. Calif. Applied Anthropology Network, L.A., 1983-85, mental retardation rsch. ctr. UCLA, 1983—, Sch. Medicine Universidad Nacional Autonoma de Mex., 1989-90; vis. scholar Russell Sage found., 1998-99; vis. prof. Univ. Rovirai Virgili, Spain, 1999. Editor Practicing Anthropology, 1983; mem. editl. bd. Med. Anthropology Quar., 1993-96, 99-2002, Ency. of Med. Anthropology, 2001-03; guest editor Social Sci. and Medicine, 2002-03; contbr. articles to profl. jours. Rsch. grantee Nat. Inst. Gen. Med. Scis, Washington, 1972-75, NSF, Washington, 1980-83, Wenner-Gren Found., N.Y.C., 1980-83, U. Calif. Mexus, Riverside, 1985-86, Nat. Inst. Child Health and Human Devel., 1989-94, MacArthur Found., Ford Found., 1995-96, Agy. for Health Care Policy Rsch., 1995-98, Ctrs. for Disease Control, 1994-96, Nat. Ctr. Human Genome Rsch., 1995-2002. Fellow Am. Anthrop. Assn. (exec. bd. 1995-96), Soc. Applied Anthropology (nominations and elections com. 1986-89, exec. bd. 1994-97); mem. Soc. Med. Anthropology (exec. bd. 1987-91, pres. 1995-97), Soc. Latin Am. Anthropology (councillor 1988-91), Pacific Inst for Women's Health (founding assoc.), Latin Am. Studies Assn., Sigma Xi. Office: Dept Psychiatry & Biobehavioral Scis Box 62 760 Westwood Plz Los Angeles CA 90024-1759 Office Fax: 310-794-6297. Business E-Mail: browner@ucla.edu.

BROWNFELD, ALLAN CHARLES, columnist; b. N.Y.C., Nov. 26, 1939; s. Benjamin and Estelle (Snyder) B.; m. Solveig Eggerz, June 2, 1970; children: Alexandra, Peter, Burke. BA, Coll. of William and Mary, 1961, JD, 1964; MA, U. Md., 1968. Faculty St. Stephen's Episcopal Sch., Alexandria, Va., 1964-65, U. Md., College Park, 1965-66; spl. asst. internal security com. U.S. Senate, Washington, 1967-69; asst. to rsch. dir. Rep. Conf. Ho. of Reps., Washington, 1970; spl. asst. Rep. Philip M. Crane, Washington, 1970-73; legis. asst. Rep. William Scherle, Washington, 1973-74; editor The New Guard, Washington, 1968-69; Washington editor Private Practice, 1970-75; assoc. editor The Lincoln Rev., Washington, 1984—; editor Issues, Washington, 1989—; cons. Accuracy in Media, Washington, 1984—. Mem. pres. Ronald Reagan's transition team EEOC, 1980. Author: Hung Up on Freedom, 1969, Dossier on Douglas, 1970, (U.S. Senate subcom. internal security study) The New Left, 1968; co-author: What the Negro Can Do About Crime, 1974, The Revolution Lobby, 1984. Bd. dirs. Coun. for Def. of Freedom, Washington, 1984—. Recipient Wall St. Jour. Found. award, 1963; decorated George Washington medal Freedoms Found., 1970, 71, 72, 73, 77, 84; named Disting. Lectr. U.S. Air Force Spl. Ops. Sch., 1970. Office: PO Box 9009 Alexandria VA 22304-0009

BROWNFIELD, WILLIAM R. ambassador; b. Fort Bragg, N.C., May 1952; m. Kristie A. Kenney. Grad., Cornell U., 1974; postgrad., U. Tex., 1976—78; grad., Nat. War Coll., 1993. Entered fgn. svc. U.S. Dept. State, 1979, polit. adviser to comdr.-in-chief U.S. So. Command, 1989—90, prin. dep. asst. sec. for internat. narcotics and law enforcement, 1998—99, dep. asst. sec. of state for Western Hemisphere, 1999—2002, U.S. amb. to Chile, 2002—, counselor for humanitarian affairs Geneva. Office: DOS Amb 3460 Santiago Pl Washington DC 20521

BROWNING, CHRISTOPHER R. historian, educator; b. Durham, N.C., May 22, 1944; s. Robert Willard and Eleanor (Oechsli) B.; m. Jennifer Jane Horn; children: Kathryn, Anne. BA, Oberlin Coll., 1967; MA, U. Wis., 1968, PhD, 1975. Instr. history Allegheny Coll., Meadville, Pa., 1969-71; asst. prof. history Pacific Luth. U., Tacoma, 1974-79, assoc. prof., 1979-84, prof., 1984-97, disting. univ. prof., 1997-99; Frank Porter Graham prof. history U. N.C., Chapel Hill, 1999—. J.B. and Maurice C. Shapiro sr. scholar in residence U.S. Holocaust Mus., 1996, Ina Levine scholar, 2002-03; George Macaulay Trevelyan lectr. Cambridge U., 1999. Author: The Final Solution and the German Foreign Office, 1978, Fateful Months, 1985, Ordinary Men, 1992 (Nat. Jewish Book award 1993), The Path to Genocide, 1992, Nazi Policy, Jewish Workers, German Killers, 2000, Collected Memories: Holocaust History and Post-War Testimony, 2003. Woodrow Wilson fellow, 1967-68, Alexander von Humboldt fellow, Germany, 1980-81, Fulbright rsch. fellow, Israel, 1989, Inst. for Advanced Studies fellow, Princeton, N.J., 1995; Ira Levine sr. scholar U.S. Holocaust Mus., 2003. Office: U NC Dept History Chapel Hill NC 27599-0001

BROWNING, COLIN ARROTT, retired banker; b. Jersey City, June 24, 1935; s. Colin John Herbert and Ellenor May (Coughlin) B.; m. Ellen Miriam McNeill, July 18, 1964; children: Colin Robertson, Paul William. BA, Cornell U., 1957; MBA, NYU, 1964. Trust adminstr. Chase Manhattan Bank, N.Y.C., 1960-64; v.p. Midlantic Bank, Newark, 1964-70, IBJ Schroder Bank and Trust Co., N.Y.C., 1970-71, sr. trust officer, 1971-72, sr. v.p., 1972-77, exec. v.p., mem. exec. com., 1977-93; chmn., pres. IBJ Schroder Internat. Bank and Trust Co., Miami, 1985-93, ret. Trustee Upper N.J. chpt. Multiple Sclerosis Soc., Newark, 1965-72, pres., 1969-70; trustee N.J. Shakespeare Festival, 1988-91; trustee Fla. Zool. Soc., 1995-99, pres. docent coun., 1997-99, dir., 1999—, bd. dirs., mem. exec. com. Mem. Corp. Fiduciaries Assn., Am. Lepidopterists Soc., Am. Orchid Soc., Xerces Soc., The Explorers Club, Pi Kappa Alpha, Beta Theta. Avocations: fly fishing, orchid growing.

BROWNING, DON SPENCER, religious educator; b. Trenton, Mo., Jan. 13, 1934; s. Robert Watson and Nelle Juanita Browning; m. Carol LaVeta Browning, Sept. 28, 1958; children: Elizabeth Dell, Christopher Robert. AB, Ctrl. Meth. Coll., Fayette, Mo., 1956; DDiv, Ctr. Meth. Coll., Fayette, Mo., 1984; BD, U. Chgo., 1959, PhD, 1964; DDiv, Christian Theol. Sem., Indpls., 1990; DDiv (hon.), U. Glasgow, Scotland, 1998. Asst. prof. Phillips U., Enid, Okla., 1963-65; instr. Div. Sch., U. Chgo., 1965-66, asst. prof., 1966-69, assoc. prof., 1969-77, prof., 1977-79, Alexander Campbell prof. ethics and social sci., 1979—; Woodruff prof. Emory U., 2001—02. Lectr. U. Birmingham, Birmingham, England, 1998. Author: Atonement and Psychotherapy, 1966, Generative Man: Society and Good Man in Philip Rieff, Norman Brown, Erich Fromm and Erik Erikson, 1973, The Moral Context of Pastoral Care, 1976, Pluralism and Personality: William James and Some Contemporary Cultures of Psychology, 1980, Religious Ethics and Pastoral Care, 1983, Religious Thought and the Modern Psychologies, 1987, A Fundamental Practical Theology, 1991; co-author: From Culture Wars to Common Ground: Religion and the American Family Debate, 1997, Reweaving the Social Tapestry: Toward a Public Philosophy and Policy of Families, 2001, Marriage and Modernization, 2003; sr. advisor (PBS documentary) Marriage--Just a Piece of Paper?. Recipient Oskar Pfister award Am. Psychiat. Assn., 1999; Guggenheim fellow, 1975-76, fellow Inst. Religion in Age of Sci., 2003; Lilly Endowment grantee, 1991-97, 97, 99. Home: 5513 S Kenwood Ave Chicago IL 60637-1713 Office: Univ of Chicago Divinity Sch Chicago IL 60637

BROWNING, JAMES ROBERT, federal judge; b. Great Falls, Mont., Oct. 1, 1918; s. Nicholas Henry and Minnie Sally (Foley) Browning; m. Marie Rose Chapell. BA, Mont. State U., Missoula, 1938; LLB with honors, U. Mont., 1941, LLD (hon.), 1978, Santa Clara U., 1989. Bar: Mont. 1941, D.C. 1953, U.S. Supreme Ct. 1952. Spl. atty. antitrust div. Dept. Justice, 1941—43, spl. atty. gen. litigation sect. antitrust div., 1946—48, chief antitrust dept. N.W. regional office, 1948—49; asst. chief gen. litigation sect. antitrust div. Dept. Justice (N.W. regional office), 1949—51, 1st asst. civil div., 1951—52; exec. asst. to atty. gen. U.S., 1952—53; chief U.S. (Exec. Office for U.S. Attys.), 1953; pvt. practice Washington, 1953—58; lectr. N.Y.U. Sch. Law, 1953, Georgetown U. Law Center, 1957—58; clk. Supreme Ct. U.S., 1958—61; judge U.S. Ct. Appeals 9th Circuit, 1961—76, chief judge, 1976—88, judge, 1988—. Reed justice com. on continuing edn., tng. and adminstrn. Jud. Conf. of U.S., 1967—68, com. on ct. adminstrn., 1969—71, chmn. subcom. on jud. stats., 1969—71, com. to study the illustrative rules of jud. misconduct, 1969, com. on the budget, 1971—77, adminstrn. office, subcom. on budget, 1974—76, mem., 1976—88, exec. com. of conf., 1978—87, com. to study the illustrative rules of jud. misconduct, 1985—87, com. to study U.S. jud. conf., 1986—88, com. on internat. conf. of appellate judges, 1987—90; David T. Lewis disting. judge-in-residence U. Utah, 1987; Blankenbaker lectr. U. Mont., 1987; Sibley lectr. U. Ga., 1987; lectr. Human Rights Inst., Santa Clara U. Sch. Law, Strasbourg. Editor-in-chief: Mont. Law Rev. Dir. Western Justice Found.; chmn. 9th Cir. Hist. Soc. 1st lt. U.S. Army, 1943—46. Decorated Bronze Star; named to, Order of the Grizzly, U. Mont., 1973; recipient Devitt Disting. Svc. to Justice award, 1990; scholar in residence, Santa Clara U., 1989, U. Mont., 1991. Mem.: FBA (bd. dirs. 1945—61, nat. coun. 1958—62), ABA (judge adv. com. to standing com. on Ethics and Profl. Responsibility 1973—75), Am. Soc. Legal History (adv. bd. jour.), Am. Judicature Soc. (chmn. com. on fed. judiciary 1973—74, bd. dirs. 1972—75, Herbert Harley award 1984), Inst. Jud. Adminstrn., Am. Law Inst., Mont. Bar Assn., D.C. Bar Assn., Nat. Lawyers Club (bd. govs. 1959—63). Office: US Ct Appeals 9th Cir PO Box 193939 San Francisco CA 94119-3939 *Notable cases include: pro bono case Bell vs. U.S., 349 U.S. 81, 1955.*

BROWNING, JESSE HARRISON, entrepreneur; b. Kingsville, Mo., July 27, 1935; s. Jesse Harrison and Anna Love (Swank) B.; m. Vicki Carol Thompson, Dec. 21, 1957; children: Caroline Kaye, Marcia Lynn, Nanci Ann, Susan Louise. MPA, U. So. Calif., 1988; PhD, U. Wash., 1995. Cert. mfg. engr. Field engr. The Boeing Co., Los Angeles, 1961-64; gen. mgr. SPI, Los Angeles, 1964-70; chmn. Browning Inc., Los Angeles, 1970-95; cons. global trade, transp. and logistic studies U. Wash., Seattle, 1995-2000, affiliate prof. civil and environ. engring.; ret., 2000; chmn. Vapor Engring., Los Angeles, 1979-87. U.S. del. Asia Pacific Econ. Cooperation; mem. transp. working group. Patentee in field. Mem. ASPA, World Coun. on Internat. Trade, World Affairs Coun., Am. Helicopter Soc., Am. Assn. Geographers, Soc. Mgr. Engrs., Propellor Club. Lutheran. Avocations: snow skiing, flying helicopters and airplanes, traveling, working out. Address: 4927 NE Tolo Rd Ste 1704 Bainbridge Island WA 98110

BROWNING, KATHRYN WHELCHEL, psychiatic nurse, corporate compliance officer; b. Gaffney, S.C., Aug. 20, 1942; d. Loyd Buel and Kathryn Marie (Mode) Whelchel; m. John Robert Browning, Sept. 23, 1962; children: Cynthia Rene, Robin Elaine. Diploma, Anderson (S.C.) Meml. Hosp., 1964; FNP, U. S.C., 1974; BSN, U. S.C., Spartanburg, 1981; M in Health Svcs. Adminstrn., Med. U. S.C., Charleston, 1989. RN, S.C.; cert. psychiat. and mental health nurse. Psychiat. nurse Anderson Meml. Hosp., 1964-65; nurse coord. Cherokee County Health Dept., Gaffney, 1966-75, family nurse practitioner, 1975-79; med.-surg. nurse Cherokee Meml. Hosp., Gaffney, 1965-66, family nurse practitioner, 1980-82, insvc. dir., 1982-83, quality assurance coord., 1983-87; program nurse specialist, quality assurance coord., corp. compliance officer Spartanburg Area Mental Health Ctr., 1987-2001, asst. dir., 2001—. Mem. adv. bd. Social and Heatlh Care Orgn. Coun., Gaffney, 1980-86, March of Dimes, Rock Hill, S.C., 1979-89, Community Long-Term Care, Gaffney, 1989-91; mem. Mental Health Assn., Gaffney, 1988—; mem. S.C. Lung Assn., Spartanburg, 1984-86. Mem. ANA, Piedmont Nurses Assn., Primary Care Nurse Practitioners (chair 1974-76), S.C. Employees Assn., S.C. Ednl. Consortium, S.C. Cmty. Mental Health Nursing coun., HIV/AIDS Consortium, Sigma Theta Tau. Democrat. Baptist. Avocations: cross-stitch, walking, skiing, foreign and home mission work. Home: 126 Foxfire Dr Gaffney SC 29340-5150 Office: Spartanburg Area Mental Health Ctr 250 Dewey St Spartanburg SC 29303-3028 E-mail: kwb30@spar.dmh.state.sc.us.

BROWNING, PETER CRANE, packaging company executive; b. Boston, Sept. 2, 1941; s. Ralph Leslie and Nancy (Crane) Browning; m. Carole Ann Shegog, Dec. 14, 1963 (div. 1974); children: Christina, Jennifer; m. Kathryn Anne Klucharich, July 27, 1974; children: Kimberley, Peter. AB in History, Colgate U., 1963; MBA, U. Chgo., 1976. Salesman, mktg. mgr. White Cap divsn. Continental Can, Northbrook, Ill., 1964-75; mgr. mktg. Conally Venture divsn. Continental Can, 1975-79; gen. mktg. and sales mgr. Bondware divsn. Continental Can, 1979-81, v.p., gen. mgr., 1981-84; v.p. gen. mgr. White Cap. div. Continental Can, 1984-86, exec. v.p., oper. officer, 1987-89; pres. Gold Bond Bldg. Products div. Nat. Gypsum Co., Charlotte, NC, 1989-90; pres., chmn., CEO Nat. Gypsum Co., Charlotte, 1990-93; exec. v.p. Sonoco Products Co., Hartsville, SC, 1993-96, pres., COO, 1996-98, pres., CEO, 1998-2000. Chmn. bd. dirs. Nucor corp., Wachovia Corp., Lowe's Cos., Inc., Phoenix Cos., Inc., Acuity Brands, Inc., ENPRO Industries; dean McColl Grad. Sch. Bus. Queens U., Charlotte, 2002. Life mem. coun. Grad. Sch./U. Chgo. Mem.: DeBordieu Country Club, Quail Hollow Country Club. Republican. Episcopalian. Avocations: mountain climbing, running, reading. Home: 2038 Providence Rd Charlotte NC 28211

BROWNING, ROBERT LYNN, educator, clergyman; b. Gallatin, Mo., June 19, 1924; s. Robert W. and Nelle J. (Trotter) B.; m. Jean Beatty, Dec. 27, 1947 (dec. 1977); children: Gregory, David, Peter, Lisa; m. Jackie L. Rogers, Aug. 26, 1979. BA, Mo. Valley Coll., 1945; MDiv, Union Theol. Sem., 1948; PhD, Ohio State U., 1960; postgrad., Columbia U., 1951-53, Oxford (Eng.) U., 1978-79, 84-85. Ordained to ministry Disciples of Christ Ch., 1947, transferred to United Meth. Ch., 1949. Minister edn. Old Stone Ch., Meadville, Pa., 1946-51, Cmty. Ch. at the Cir., Mt. Vernon, N.Y., 1951-53, North Broadway United Meth. Ch., Columbus, Ohio, 1953-59; prof. Christian edn. Meth. Theol. Sch., Delaware, Ohio, 1959-72, William A. Chryst prof. Christian edn., 1972-89, prof. emeritus, 1989—. Sr. counselor Coun. for Ethics in Econs., 1989—; pres. Meth. Conf. on Christian Edn., 1967-69; exec. dir. Commn. on Role of The Professions in Soc., Fellow Acad. for Contemporary Problems, 1974-76, commn. bd, 1976—; mem. Ohio Ethics Commn., 1999—. Author: Communicating with Junior Highs, 1968, Guidelines for Youth Ministry, 1970, What on Earth Are You Doing, 1966; (audiotape with Charles Foster) Communicating the Faith with Children, 1971, Ways the Bible Comes Alive, 1975, Ways Persons Become Christian, 1976 (with Charles Foster, Everett Tilson) Looking at Leadership with the Eyes of Biblical Faith, 1978, (with Roy Reed) The Sacraments in Religious Education and Liturgy: An Ecumenical Model, 1985, Models of Confirmation and Baptismal Affirmation: Liturgical and Educational Issues and Designs, 1995; contbg. author: An Introduction to Christian Education, 1966, Counseling and Psychotherapy: Classics on Theories and Issues, 1975, Foundations for Christian Education in an Era of Change, 1976, Preventing Adolescent Alienation: An Interprofessional Approach, 1983, Children, Parents and Change, 1984, Interprofessional Education, 1987, Congregations: Their Power to Form and Transform, 1988, Handbook for Families, 1998, Personal Narratives About the History of Methodist Christian Education in the Twentieth Century, 1999; editor: Integration: Objective Studies and Practical Theology, Proc. Assn. Profl. Edn. for Ministry, 1981, The Pastor as Religious Educator, 1989; contbr. articles on religious edn. to profl. jours. Bd. dirs. Southside Settlement, columbus, 1968-74, Tray-Lee Ctr., Columbus, 1955-59, Ohio State U. Wesleyan Found., 1960-78, vice chmn., 1976-78; bd. ministry ohio West Conf. United Meth. Ch., 1982-89. With USN, 1942-45. Recipient Paul Hinkhouse award Religious Pub. Rels. Coun. Am., 1971. Mem. Assn. for Profl. Edn. for Ministry (editor proc. 1980-82), Religious Edn. Assn., Assn. for Profs. and Rschrs. in Religious Edn. (pres. 1989), United Meth. Profs. Christian Edn. Home: 6613 Hawthorne St Worthington OH 43085-3071 Fax: 614-885-2059. E-mail: bobbrowni@cs.com.

BROWNING, SINCLAIR, writer; b. Long Beach, Calif., Nov. 17, 1946; d. George William Sinclair, Rowena Mae Morse; m. William Docker Browning, Dec. 17, 1974; 1 child, Benjamin Sinclair stepchildren: Christopher, Logan, Courtenay; m. Allyn D. Bates, Sept. 2, 1966 (div. Aug. 1974). BA in Lit. and Creative Writing, U. Ariz., 1970. Judge Shamus Awards Pvt. Eye Writers, 2001; judge Edgar Awards Mystery Writers of Am., N.Y.C., 2002; judge best 1st novel St. Martin's Press, 2000; judge best novel Edgaar, 2002, Shamus, 2002. Author: Enju, 1983, America's Best, 1995, The Last Song Dogs, 1999, The Sporting Club, 2000, Rode Hard, Put Away Dead, 2001, Crack Shot, 2002, Tragedy Ann, 2003; co-author: Lyons on Horses, 1991; editor: Feathers Brush My Heart, 2002; author: Hot and Sultry Night for Crime, 2003, Hit Biscuits, 2002. Nominee Ariz. Arts award, 2000. Mem.: Private Eye Writers of Am., Women Writing the West, Western Writers of Am., Internat. Assn. of Crime Writers, Sisters in Crime, Mystery Writers of Am., Authors Guild. Avocations: horseback riding, reading. Mailing: PO Box 8248 Tucson AZ 85738

BROWNING, TYSON R. operations research specialist; b. Arlington, Tex. s. Clint and Christina Browning; m. Meredith Browning. BS in Engring. Physics, Abilene Christian U., 1993; MS in Tech. and Policy, MS in Aeronautics and Astronautics (sys. engring.), MIT, 1996, Ph.D. in Tech. Mgmt. and Policy, 1998. Rsch. asst. Lean Aerospace Initiative, MIT, Cambridge, Mass., 1993—99; sr. project mgr. integrated co. ops. Lockheed Martin Aeronautics Co., Fort Worth, Tex., 1999—2003; asst. prof. enterprise ops. Neeley Sch. Bus. Tex. Christian U., Ft. Worth, 2003—. Contbr. articles to profl. jours. Deacon Altamesa Ch. of Christ, Fort Worth, Tex., 2000—03. Fellow, NSF, 1994—97; scholar, Barry M. Goldwater Found., 1991—93. Mem.: Inst. for Ops. Rsch. and Mgmt. Scis., Internat. Coun. Sys. Engring. Avocations: travel, scuba diving, soccer, football, running. Office: Tex Christian U Neeley Sch Bus Fort Worth TX 76129

BROWNING, VIVIAN BERNIECE, land developer; b. Damascus, Md., July 23, 1923; d. Herbert Day and Rosa May (Lewis) Barnes; m. Charles Hanford Browning, Dec. 10, 1941 (dec. June 1979); children: Charles Hanford Jr., Nancy Rosalie. Grad. h.s., Damascus. Bookkeeper Browning Constrn. Co., Inc., Germantown, Md., 1945; co-owner, mgr. Browning Pools, Inc., Germantown, 1945-79, cons., 1979-88; developer Hanford Estates, Monrovia, Md., 1986—. Contbr. poems to World of Poetry. Mem. United Meth. Women, Order Ea. Star. Republican. Avocation: singing.

BROWNING, WILLIAM DOCKER, federal judge; b. Tucson, May 19, 1931; s. Horace Benjamin and Mary Louise (Docker) B.; children: Christopher, Logan, Courtenay; m. Zerilda Sinclair, Dec. 17, 1974; 1 child, Benjamin. BBA, U. Ariz., 1954, LLB, 1960. Bar: Ariz. 1960, U.S. Dist. Ct. Ariz. 1960, U.S. Ct. Appeals (9th cir.) 1965, U.S. Supreme Ct. 1967. Pvt. practice, Tucson, 1960-84; judge U.S. Dist. Ct., Tucson, 1984—. Mem. jud. nominating com. appellate ct. appointments, 1975-79; mem. Commn. on Structural Alternatives, Fed. Ct. Appeals, 1997-99. Del. 9th Cir. Jud. Conf., 1968-77, 79-82; trustee Inst. for Ct. Mgmt., 1978-84; mem. Ctr. for Pub. Resources Legal Program. 1st lt. USAF, 1954-57, capt. USNG, 1958-61. Recipient Disting. Citizen award U. Ariz., 1995. Fellow Am. Coll. Trial Lawyers, Am. Bar Found.; mem. ABA (spl. com. housing and urban devel. law 1973-76, com. urban problems and human affairs 1978-80), Ariz. Bar Assn. (chmn. merit selection of judges com. 1973-76, bd. gove. 1968-74, pres. 1972-73, Outstanding Mem. 1980), Pima County Bar Assn. (exec. com. 1964-68, med. legal screening panel 1965-75, pres. 1967-68), Am. Bd. Trial Advocates, Am. Judicature Soc. (bd. dirs. 1975-77), Fed. Judges Assn. (bd. dirs.). Office: US Courthouse 405 W Congress St Ste 6160 Tucson AZ 85701-5061

BROWN-KUYKENDALL, DONITA, early childhood educator; b. Edmond, Okla., Dec. 23, 1953; d. Donald Gene and Juanita (Renner) Brown; children: Kristin Kuykendall, Kaitlin Kuykendall. BS in Elem. Edn., Southeastern Okla. State U., 1975; MEd, U. Ctrl. Okla., 1989. Tchr. Keystone Sch., Tulsa, 1975-76, Mid-Del Pub. Sch. Sys., Midwest City, Okla., 1976-78, 79-81, Bur. Indian Affairs, Albuquerque, 1978-79, Vietnamese Refugee Ctr., Oklahoma City, 1981-83, Yukon (Okla.) Pub. Sch. Sys., 1985-92; supr. early childhood practicums U. Ctrl. Okla., Edmond, 1992—2001; reading specialist Yukon Pub. Schs., 2001—. Adv. bd. Ea. Okla. County Vo-Tech. Child Devel. Ctr., Choctaw, 1994—; adv. bd. Okla. State Dept. Edn., Oklahoma City, 1992-95; curriculum adv. bd. Yukon Pub. Sch. Sys. Vol. Children's Def. Fund, Washington, 1991—. Mem. Nat. Assn. Educators of Young Children, AAUW, ASCD, Okla. Assn. Children Under Six, U. Ctrl. Okla. Alumni Assn., Okla. State Reading Assn., Kappa Delta Pi, Sigma Kappa, DAR. Methodist. Avocations: reading, quilting, spectator sports, theater, concerts. Home: 6512 N Grove Ave Oklahoma City OK 73132-7719

BROWN LEATHERBERRY, THOMAS HENRY, gospel music company executive, clergy member; b. Wilmington, Del., June 24, 1930; s. Glenn Ford and Rita (Leatherberry) Brown; m. Grace L. Wilson, Mar. 1, 1950 (div. 1978), m. Wendolyn M. King, Oct. 8, 2002; children: Linda Henry, Patricia Williams, Lucinda Brown, Martha Baccus, Tommy Jr. (dec.), Jason James. Student, Carnegie Hall Sr. Drama Sch., N.Y.C., 1961; A. in Engring. Comms., N.Y. Sch. Announcing, N.Y.C., 1968; BA in Behavioral Sci. and Bibl. Edn., U. Del.; M

Bibl. Theology, Ea. Bapt. U.; DD (hon.), Trinity Coll., Knoxville, Tenn., 1970. Artist, comedian Mantan Moreland, N.Y.C., 1959-62; road mgr., negotiator Langston Hughes Prodns., N.Y.C., 1963-66; dir. music Chs. of God in Christ, Bklyn., 1968-78; dir. arts Gospel Arts Coalition, Inc., Wilmington, 1978—; pastor Bible Way House of Prayer Worldwide Inc., Wilmington, 1989—; minister of music Bibleway Mid-Atlantic Diocese, Balt., 1990—. Dir. asst. Alvin Ailey Dancers, N.Y.C., 1963; disk jockey Sta. WWRL, N.Y.C., 1969, tchr. Christina Cultural Arts, Wilmington, 1983-89; music dir. World Christian Fellowship, 1989—. Dir. recs. Rite Enterprise Rec. Co., 1954; actor Prodigal Son, 1963, Black Nativity, 1964; asst. to producer (TV) MD, 1967; stage dir., program mgr. Gospel Music shows, CBS-TV, 1967; author (radio) America Calls, 1967, Israel Radio Calls, 1967; dir., engr. RCA Inst. TV, Sta. ABC-TV, 1968. Program dir. Y.M.C.A., Wilmington, 1978-81; entertainer for Gov. Dupont, State of Del., 1980; dir. gospel music coun. 6602, City of Wilmington, 1983. With U.S. Army, 1950-53. Named State Leader, African Am. Proclamation Inc., Phila., 1983; recipient Attestation Pilgrimage award, Minister of Courison, Jerusalem, 1983, award of Grand Performance, Jewish Community Rels. Com., Wilmington, 1988. Mem. BMI, Am. Guild Authors and Composers, Trinity Coll. Alumni Assn., Am. Legion (chaplain Brandywine, Del.), VFW (life), Masons (grand music dir. 1989—, past worshipful master, illustrious master, imperial dep. chaplain 1997—, past grand high priest, 33 degree, hon. past emperial potentate, 2002, royal select master thrice, Ill. master), Order Ea. Star (past worthy patron), Shriners, Elks (Appreciation award Paul Lawrence Dunbar lodge #106 1981), Heroines of Jericho (grand Joshua), Honor Guard Assn. (lt. col.), Del. Phylaxis Soc. (pres.), Epsilon Delta Psi (life). Democrat. Avocations: football, basketball, movies, playing organ and piano. Office: NOW Gospel Arts Singers PO Box 824 Wilmington DE 19899-0824

BROWNLEE, DELPHINE, actress, musician; b. Paris, July 19, 1930; d. John Donald and Carla (Oddone) B.; m. Dan Oluf Eriksen, Apr. 24,1954 (div. June 1958); 1 child, Lynn Michele; m. Theodore Robert Bashkow, Sept. 12, 1960. Grad., Neighborhood Playhouse, N.Y., 1949. Tchr. pvt. studio, 1977—; adj. prof. Montclair State U., 1981-84; faculty Conservatory Hackley Sch., 1985-90, Mt. Kisco Sch. Music. Several voice overs for TV and radio commercials, recitals at Carnegie Recital Hall, opera performances with Singers Theatre; original cast of Man of La Mancha, Fade-Out, Fade-In, Here's Love, Carnival, others. Mem. N.Y. Singing Tchrs. Assn., N.Y. State Music Tchrs. Assn., Nat. Coun. Jewish Women (past pres. No. Westchester sect. 1971-73), Actor's Equity Assn., Screen Actors Guild, Am. Federations TV and Radio Artists. Avocations: gardening, reading, birdwatching. Home: 92 Jay St Katonah NY 10536-3729

BROWNLEE, JUDITH MARILYN, priestess, psychotherapist, psychic; b. Beaumont, Tex., May 16, 1940; d. Alvin Maurice and Juanita M. (Whittington) B.; m. Theodore Blakey Peak, Apr. 12, 1974 (div. 1981); 1 child, Daniel David Brownlee Peak; m. Floyd S. Bond, Aug. 18, 1996. BA, Lamar U., Beaumont, Tex., 1962; postgrad., U. Denver, 1971; MA, Avalon Inst., Boulder, Colo., 1992; student, Our Lady Perpetual Responsibility, The Silent Cir., 1975-79. Wiccan priestess; cert. master tarot reader Am. Tarot Assn. Tchr. Deer Trail (Colo.) H.S., 1963-64, Lutcher Stark H.S., Orange, Tex., 1967-69; libr. technician Denver Pub. Libr., 1970-73; bus. exec. Weight Watchers Rocky Mtn., Denver, 1974; mail order divsn. mgr. Mile High Comics and Books, Denver, 1975-81; religious tchr. The Silent Cir., Denver, 1979-83; gov. employee Colo. Atty. Gen. Office, Denver, 1983-92; minister Fortress Temple, Denver, 1984-96; psychotherapist, 1992—; counselor Profl. Psychic Counselors Network, 1993-96, Morningstar Inc., 1997, Oracle Tree New Age Mall, 1997-2000, Astrological Health, 2001—03. Presenter, Am. Tarot Assn. Rocky Mountain Regional Conf., 1999; pub. spkr. Denver, 1988—, Spring Mysteries Festival, Seattle, 1988-92; workshop leader Spring Mysteries Festival, Seattle, 1988, 92, Dragonfest Pagan Festival, Denver, 1987-92; lectr. Isis Metaphys. Ctr., workshop leader, 1985—; lectr. Raven & Rose Bookstore, Ft. Collins Colo., 1992-93, Enchanted Chalice Bookstore, 1994-2000, Herbs & Arts Bookstore, 1996, Spirit Ways Bookstore, 1998; organizer Front Range Pagan Festival, 1995; guest spkr. Greeley (Colo.) Unitarian Fellowship, 1992, 1st Mennonite Ch., Denver, 2002; spkr. Rocky Mountain Fiction Writers Conv., 1993; creator, dir. Edn. for Pagan Youth com. Pagan Sch., 1990-94, 96-97; spkr. in field. Author: Pagan Parenting, 1987, The Wheel of the Year, 1988; contbr. articles to profl. jours.; participant Dedication to Faith, Images and Voices, 1999, Roundtable Discussions with Artist and Spiritual Leaders, 1999. Interviewee KOA Radio, 1984, 92, 95, 96, KNUS and KYBG, 1992, KUSA Channel 9, 1987, 90, Rocky Mountain News, Denver, 1992, Denver Post, 1996, 2000, 2001; cmty. prodr. Mile High Cablevision, 1987; tel. counselor Lifeline of Colo., Denver, 1988; field tng. supr. Iliff Sch. Theology, Denver, 1995-96; bd. dirs. Inst. for Interfaith/Intercultural Inst. U. Denver, 1999-2003. Recipient Hart and Crescent Disting. Youth Svc. award Covenant of the Goddess, 1995. Mem. Colo. Assn. Psychotherapists, Assn. Past Life Rsch. and Therapy, Daus. of New Moon (founder, facilitator), Soc. for Creative Anachronism (Colo. founder, CEO 1970-73, treas. 1981-83), Denver Area Sci. Fiction Assn. (editor 1969-70, dir. 1974-75, conf. chmn. 1970-75), Denver Area Interfaith Clergy Conf., Covenant Unitarian Universalist Pagans. Avocations: reading, theatre, films, science fiction, internet. Office: PO Box 172271 Denver CO 80217-2271 E-mail: judith1152@aol.com. *The two most important issues of this century will be the return of the Goddess (the feminine in Diety) and the re-imaging of our planet as Her Body (the Gaia Theory). We must give up our persona of "dominance over Nature" and remember again that we are part of Nature.*

BROWNLEE, JUNE MCGAUGH, health facility administrator; d. Louis V. and Maxine Burns McGaugh; m. Stephen Barry Brownlee, Aug. 30, 1969; children: Stephen Blake, Erin Brownlee Holloway. BBA, Tex. Woman's U., Denton, TX, 1985—87, MBA, 1999—2003. Cable tv sys. mgr. GRB Communication, Corinth, Tex., 1980—83; owner, mgr. JB Consulting, Denton, Tex., 1983—87; acctg. mgr. Budget Credit Corp., Carrollton, Tex., 1987—89; accounts payable mgr. HEA Mgmt. Group, Inc., Denton, Tex., 1989—93; pres./dir. Dance Elite, Inc., Denton, Plano, & The Colony, 1990—96; asst. dir. U. of North Tex. Student Health & Wellness Ctr., Denton, Tex. Exec. com. UNT HIPAA Steering Com., Denton, Tex., 2002—; program dir. South West Coll. Health Assn., Tex., 2002—; mem. Am. Coll. Health Assn., Balt. Author: (paper presentation) JC Penney, Case Study, 2001. Pres. Denton Dance Theatre, Denton, Tex., 1993—96; bd. mem. Denton Festival Found., Denton, Tex., 1998—2002; charter mem. Men Against Violence, Denton, Tex., 2001—03. Recipient Staff Contbn. Award, U. of North Tex., 1999, Soaring Eagle, 1999 & 2001, MBA All Star, Dallas Bus. Jour., 2003. Avocations: reading, geneology.

BROWNLEE, KARIN S. state legislator; m. Doug Brownlee; 4 children. BS in Microbiology, Kans. State U. Co-owner Patrons Mortgage Co.; mem. Kans. Senate, Topeka, 1996—, mem. commerce com., mem. fin. instns. and ins. com., 1996—, mem. utilities com., mem. claims against the state com., mem. arts and cultural resources com. Mem. steering com. Leadership Olathe, 1994—; mem. QPA issues com. Olathe Sch. Dist., 1993; mem. adv. com. Mahaffie Farmsted; women's ministry leader Olathe Bible Ch.; del. Rep. Nat. Conv., 1996; vice chair Johnston Rep. Party, 1994-96; chair Olathe Rep. Party, 1992-94. Mem. Olathe Area C. of C. Republican. Office: 300 SW 10th Ave Rm 143-n Topeka KS 66612-1504*

BROWNLEE, PAULA PIMLOTT, higher education consultant, former academic administrator; b. London, June 23, 1934; came to U.S., 1959; d. John Richard and Alice A. (Ajamian) Pimlott; m. Thomas H. Brownlee, Feb. 10, 1961; children: Kenneth Gainsford, Elizabeth Ann, Clare Louise. BA with honors, Somerville Coll., Oxford (Eng.) U., 1957, PhD in Organic Chemistry, 1959. Postdoctoral fellow U. Rochester, N.Y., 1959-61; rsch. chemist Am. Cyanamid Co., Stamford, Conn., 1961-62; lectr. U. Bridgeport, Conn., 1968-70; asst. prof., then assoc. prof. Rutgers U., N.J., 1970-76, assoc. dean, then acting dean Douglass Coll., 1972-76; dean faculty, prof. chemistry Union Coll., Schenectady, N.Y., 1976-81; pres., prof. chemistry Hollins U., Va., 1981-90; pres. Assn. Am. Colls. and Univs., Washington, 1990-98; prin. Pres.' Group, LLC, 1997—2003; founding prin. Nat. Acad. for Acad. Leadership. Bd. dirs. Acad. Search Consultation Svc. Author lab. manual; contbr. articles and chpts. to profl. publs. Sr. trustee U. Rochester; bd. dirs. Buena Vista U. Hon. fellow Somerville Coll., Oxford, Eng., 1996—. Mem. Am. Chem. Soc., Cosmos Club, Sigma Xi. Episcopalian.

BROWNLEE, R. L. federal agency administrator; Degree, U. Wyo.; MBA, U. Ala.; grad, U.S. Army War Coll. Commd. 2d lt. U.S. Army, advanced through grades to col.; mem. Rep. staf Senate Armed Svcs. Com., 1987—2001; prin. profl. staff mem. for Army and M.C. Corps program Spl. Ops. Forces and Drug Interdiction Policy and Support, 1987—96; nat. security advisor to Sen. John Warner, 1993—96; staff dir. Spl. Ops. Forces and Drug Interdiction Policy and Support, 1996—2001; under sec. of Army Dept. Def., Washington, 2001—. Decorated Silver Star, Bronze Star, Purple Heart. Office: Dept Def Under Sec 102 Army Pentagon Washington DC 20301-0102*

BROWNLEE, ROBERT CALVIN, pediatrician, educator; b. Due West, S.C., Mar. 13, 1922; s. Robert Calvin and Eleanor Louise (Pressly) B.; m. Judith Frances Irby; children: Eleanor Koets, Susan, Katherine Chambers, Jonathan, Robert Calvin. AB, Erskine Coll., 1943; MD, Vanderbilt U., 1945. Diplomate Am. Bd. Pediat. (pres. 1975), Am. Bd. Family Practice. Intern Vanderbilt U. Hosp., Nashville, 1945-46, resident, 1948-49, U. Va., Charlottesville, 1949-50; chief resident Vanderbilt U., Nashville, 1950-51; practice medicine, specializing in pediat. Christie Pediatric Group, Greenville, S.C., 1951-70; dir. pediat. Greenville Hosp. Sys., 1970-75; assoc. exec. sec. Am. Bd. Pediat., Chapel Hill, N.C., 1976, exec. sec., 1977-87, pres., 1987-92. Clin. prof. pediat. U. Pa., 1976-78; prof. Med. U. S.C., 1971-75; clin. prof. U. N.C., 1978-96. Contbr. articles to med. jours. With AUS, 1943-45; with M.C. USAF, 1946-48, 53. Mem. Am. Acad. Pediat., Ambulatory Pediat. Assn., So. Soc. Pediat. Rsch. Presbyterian. Home: 120 Sheffield Cir Chapel Hill NC 27517-6514

BROWNLEE, ROBERT HAMMEL, lawyer; b. Chester, Ill., Dec. 15, 1951; s. Robert Mathis and Geneva (Hammel) B.; m. Sue F., June 17, 1978. BS, So. Ill. U., Carbondale, 1973; JD, Vanderbilt U., Nashville, 1976. Bar: Mo. 1976, Ill. 1977, U.S. Dist. Ct. (ea. and we. dists.) Mo. 1976, U.S. Dist. Ct. (so. and cen. dists.) Ill. 1977, U.S. Ct. Appeals (8th cir.) 1979, Ky. 1999, U.S. Supreme Ct. 1999. Assoc. Thompson & Mitchell, St. Louis, 1976-82; ptnr. Thompson Coburn, St. Louis, 1982—. Mng. editor Vanderbilt Law Review, Nashville, 1975-76; mem. Bar Assn. of Met. St. Louis, 1976—, Ill. State Bar Assn., Springfield, Ill., 1977—, Am. Bankruptcy Inst., 1988—, Ky. Bar, 1999—. Co-author: Rights of Secured Creditors in Bankruptcy, 1987, Lender Liability in Missouri, 1988, Protection of Secured Interests in Bankruptcy, 1989, Litigation in Bankruptcy Proceedings, 1994, Interlocutory Appeal Issues Before the Bankruptcy Reform Commission, 1996; Author: Bankruptcy Impact on Commercial Leases, Advanced Missouri Real Estate Law, 1997, updated, 1999, 2001; Impact of the Bankruptcy Review Commissions Report on Creditor Issues, 1997, Vendor Protection in Maritime Bankruptcy Reorganizations, 2003, The Surbanes-Oxley Act of 2002: Potential Impacts on Future Administration of Large Chapter II Cases, 2003. Mem. Friends of the St. Louis Zoo., 1986—, St. Louis Bot. Garden Sponsors, 1987—; builder of the community United Way of Greater St. Louis, 1988—. Fellow Am. Coll. Bankruptcy Lawyers; mem. ABA (litigation sec. 1976—, co-chair jury instrn. subcom. of bankruptcy and insolvency com. 1994-99, bus. sec. 1976—, vice-chair claims trading subcom. bus. bankruptcy com. 1998-2001, chmn. subcom. adminstrn., U.S. trustee and jurisdiction and venue 2002-), Mo. Athletic Club, Mo. Bankers Assn. (chmn. legal adv. bd. 1997-98). Avocations: fishing, american art pottery, antiques, gardening. Office: Thompson Coburn LLP 1 US Bank Plz Ste 2600 Saint Louis MO 63101-1643 E-mail: rbrownlee@thompsoncoburn.com.

BROWNLEE, SARAH HALE, elementary special education educator; b. N.Y.C., Feb. 4, 1938; d. Ralph Cochran and Maud Catherine (Welfley) Hale; m. John Malcolm Brownlee Jr., Sept. 2, 1961; children: Hale Perry, John Malcolm. BArch., Va. Poly. Inst. and State U., 1960; MEd, State U. West Ga., 1993. Registered architect, Ga.; cert. tchr., N.C. Archtl. intern Baskervill & Son Architects, Richmond, Va., 1962-65, Rabun Hatch, Architects, Atlanta, 1984-86; ednl. missionary Presbyn. Ch. U.S.A., Yogyakarta, Indonesia, 1973-84; architect Spangler & Manley, Architects, Griffin, Ga., 1988-90; exceptional children's tchr. Pike County Elem. Sch., Zebulon, Ga., 1992-93, Harrisburg (N.C.) Elem. Sch., 1994-98; owner, mgr. tutoring svcs. Sarah's Study, Huntersville, 1998—2001, Beckley, W.Va., 2001—. Mem. presch. bd. Ramah Presbyn. Ch., Huntersville, N.C., 1995-99. Bright Ideas grantee Carolina Elec. Coops. & Union EMC, 1996. Mem. Coun. for Exceptional Children, Children and Adults with Attention Deficit Disorders, Nat. Trust for Hist. Preservation, Tau Sigma Delta, Phi Kappa Phi. Home and Office: 2012 S Kanawha St Beckley WV 25801

BROWNLEE, THOMAS MARSHALL, manufacturing executive; b. Omaha, Oct. 11, 1926; s. John Templeton and Reed (Marshall) B.; children: Linda Sue, Thomas John, Curtis Marshall, Reed Ann; m. Lenora A. Hollingsworth, Mar. 31, 1994. BSBA, U. Nebr., 1950. Asst. mgr. Daytona Beach (Fla.) C. of C., 1950, Tampa (Fla.) C. of C., 1952-53; exec. mgr. Tallahassee C. of C., 1953- 58; exec. v.p. Greater Columbia (S.C.) C. of C., 1959-63, Winston-Salem (N.C.) C. of C., 1963-64, Orlando Area (Fla.) C. of C., 1964-78; chmn. Brownlee Lighting Co., Orlando, 1978—. Mem. energy policy com. Orange County (Fla.) Schs.; mem. Fla. Energy Action Com.; mem. energy com. Nat. League Cities Contbr. articles to profl. jours. Bd. dirs. Loch Haven Art Mus.; bd. dirs. Chamber Inst., U. Ga.; mem. Orlando City Council.; pres. Christian Service Ctrs. Daily Bread. Served with USNR, 1944-46; as 1st lt. AUS, 1951-52. Mem. Fla. Energy Mgmt. Assn. (pres.), Illuminating Engring. Soc. (pres. Ctrl. Fla. chpt., bd. dirs., pres. internat. soc. 1996), Am. C. of C. Execs. Assn. (hon., pres. 1966), S.C. C. of C. Execs. Assn., Fla. C. of C. Execs. Assn. (pres. 1971), Better Bus. Bur. Ctrl. Fla. (chmn.), Knights Temple, Scottish-Am. Soc. Ctrl. Fla. (bd. dirs.), Orlando Scottish Games (exec. coun.), St. Andrews Soc. Ctrl. Fla. (pres.), Coun. Scottish Clans and Assn., Scottish Coalition, Caledonian Found., Country Club Orlando, Univ. Club, Tiger Bay Club (pres.), Clan Hamilton Soc. (Fla. commr.), Rotary, Phi Delta Theta. Episcopalian. Office: Brownlee Lighting 4600 Dardanelle Dr Orlando FL 32808-3832

BROWNLEE, WILSON ELLIOT, JR., history educator; b. Lacrosse, Wis., May 10, 1941; s. Wilson Elliot Sr. and Pearl (Woodings) B.; m. Mary Margaret Cochran, June 25, 1966; children: Charlotte Louise, Martin Elliot. BA, Harvard U., 1963; MA, U. Wis., 1965, PhD, 1969. Asst. prof. U. Calif., Santa Barbara, 1967-74, assoc. prof., 1974-80, prof. history, 1980—2002, spl. advisor to systemwide provost, 1995, assoc. systemwide provost, 1996, prof. emeritus, 2002—. Vis. prof. Princeton (N.J.) U., 1980-81; chmn. dept. history U. Calif., Santa Barbara, 1984-87, acad. senate, 1983-84, 88-90, systemwide acad. senate, 1992-93; dir. U. Calif.-Santa Barbara Ctr., Washington, 1990-91; chmn. exec. com. dels. Am. Coun. Learned Socs., N.Y.C., 1988-90, bd. dirs.; bd. dirs. Nat. Coun. on Pub. History, Boston; bicentennial lectr. U.S. Dept. Treasury, 1989; faculty rep. U. Calif. Bd. Regents, 1991-93; adj. prof. history Calif. State U., Sacto., 1997-99; mem. bd. control, U. Calif. Press, 1996-99; co-organizer Conf. On History of Reagan Presidency U. Calif., Santa Barbara and Vanderbilt U., 2002. Author: Dynamics of Ascent, 1974, 2nd edit., 1979, Progressivism and Economic Growth, 1974, Federal Taxation in America: A Short History, 1996; co-author: Essentials of American History, 1976, 4th edit., 1986, America's History, 1987, 3rd edit., 1997; editor: Women in the American Economy 1976, Funding the American State, 1996; co-editor: The Regan Presidency: Pragmatic Conservatism and Its Legacies, 2003; contbr. numerous articles to profl. jours., chpts. to books. Chmn. schs. com. Harvard Club, Santa Barbara, 1971-80, 85, 86; pres. Assn. for Retarded Citizens, Santa Barbara, 1982-84; 1st v.p. Assn. for Retarded Citizens Calif., Sacramento, 1983-84; pres. Santa Barbara Trust for Hist. Preservation, 1986-87, 95-97, 2002-03; trustee Las Trampas Inc., 1994-97, 2003, Calif. State Parks Found., 2002-03. Charles Warren fellow Harvard U., 1978-79, fellow Woodrow Wilson Ctr., Washington, 1987-88; recipient Spl. Commendation, Calif. Dept. Pks. and Recreation, 1988, Oliver Johnson award for Disting. Svc. U. Calif. Acad. Senate, 1998. Mem. Am. Hist. Assn., Orgn. Am. Historians, Econ. History Assn., Am. Tax Policy Inst. Office: U Calif Dept History Santa Barbara CA 93106 Business E-Mail: brownlee@history.ucsb.edu.

BROWNLOW, DONALD GREY, private school educator; b. Germantown, Pa., Jan. 17, 1923; s. John Charles Victor and Ruth (Hutchinson) B.; m. Sandra Barbara Dobbs, July 16, 1987; children: Kendall Hutchinson, Pamela Cooke, Douglas Grey, Priscilla Dobbs. Student, U. Zürich, 1946-47; BA, U. Pa., 1948, MA, 1949. Rsch. libr. Presbyn. Hist. Soc., Phila., 1949-50; master Am. history and inernat. rels. Haverford (Pa.) Sch., 1951—; dir. Haverford Tours, 1956-75, 81-95. Charter mem. World War II Meml. Soc.; mem. faculty grad. divsn. Pa. State U., 1966—; cons. Imperial War Mus., London. Author: Documentary History of the Paoli Massacre, 1952, Documentary History of the Battle of Germantown, 1955; The Battle of Brandywine, 1957, The Accused: The Ordeal of Rear Admiral Husband E. Kimmel, USN, 1968; Panzer Baron: The Military Exploits of General Hasso von Manteuffel, 1975, Checkmate at Ruweisat: Auchinleck's Finest Hour, 1977, Hell Was My Home, 1983, The Life and Times of Horst Wessel, 1995; author, producer Haverford School Faces the Cold War, Vol. 1, 1962, Vol. 2, 1963. Chmn. Planning Bd. West Nantmeal Twp., 1964-71; mem. Emergency Com. Chinese Refugees, 1962, Com. of One Million; chmn. Zoning Hearing Bd., Warwick Twp., 1976-84; bd. dirs. Gt. Valley Assn., 1959-62; mem. planning bd. Ctr. Teaching Ams., Immaculata Coll., 1961-69; eagle scout Boy Scouts Am., 1939, Quartermaster Sea Scout, 1943; active French and Pickering Creeks Conservation Trust; mem. U.S. Holocaust Meml. Coun.; charter mem. Air Force Meml. Found., WWII Nat. D-Day Mus., New Orleans. Maj. U.S. Army, 1942-84. Recipient Valley Forge Freedoms Found. medal 1962, Suez medal from gov. Suez, UAR, 1966, Diplôme of Appreciation, French Ministry of Def., 2001, Excellence medal US Army Inspector Gen., 2002; named Citizen of Honor of Utah Beach, Mayor of Sainte-Marie-du-Mont, France, 1975, name placed on Wall of Liberty by the Battle of Normandy Found., 1994; Cert. of Recognition (Cold War) signed by William J. Cohen, Sec. of Def, Letter of Appreciation and medal from Pres. Republic Korea for services in Korean War, 2003. Mem. VFW (life), Am. Hist. Assn. (life), Paoli Meml. Assn. (life), Germantown Hist. Soc., Chester County Hist. Soc., Smithsonian Assocs., Geneal. Soc. Pa., Pa. Soc., Am. Mus. Natural History, Res. Officers Assn. (life), Soc. Am. Magicians, Nat. Wildlife Fedn., Nat. Audubon Soc., Nat. Trust for Hist. Preservation, Libr. Congress Assocs., U.S. Holocaust Meml. Mus., Simon Wiesenthal Ctr., World Wildlife Fund, Pa. Sheriff's Assn., Zool. Soc. Phila., Am. Legion (life), Acad. Natural Scis. Phila., Nature Conservancy, Wilderness Soc., Franklin Inst., Charles Custis Harrison Soc., Reading Pub. Mus. Republican. Episcopalian. Home: PO Box 468 Elverson PA 19520-0468 Office: Haverford Sch Haverford PA 19041

BROWN-OLMSTEAD, AMANDA, public relations executive; b. Oct. 7, 1943; Office: A Brown-Olmstead Assocs Ste 312 75 John Wesley Dobbs Atlanta GA 30303-1800

BROWNRIGG, JOHN CLINTON, lawyer; b. Detroit, Aug. 7, 1948; s. John Arthur and Sheila Pauline (Taffe) B.; children: Brian M., Jennifer A., Katharine T. BA, Rockhurst Coll., 1970; JD cum laude, Creighton U., 1974. Bar: Nebr. 1974, U.S. Dist. Ct. Nebr. 1974, U.S. Tax Ct. 1977, U.S. Ct. Appeals (8th cir.) 1990. Ptnr. Eisenstatt, Higgins, Kinnamon, Okun & Brownrigg, P.C., Omaha, 1974-80, Erickson & Sederstrom, P.C., Omaha, 1980—. Lectr. law trial practice Creighton U. Sch. Law, Omaha, 1978-83; dir. Legal Aid Soc., Inc., Omaha, 1982-88, pres., 1987-88, devel. com., 1989—; dir. Nebr. Continuing Legal Edn., Inc., 1991-93. Chmn. law sect. Archbishop's Capital Campaign, Omaha, 1991; dir. Combined Health Agys. Drive, 2001-03. Sgt. USAR, 1970-76. Fellow ABA (commn. on lawyer assistance programs 1996-2000), Nebr. State Bar Found. (dir. 1991-93); mem. Nebr. State Bar Assn. (pres. 1992-93), Nebr. Assn. Trial Attys., Omaha Bar Assn. (pres. 1990-91). Avocations: golf, bicycling, hiking. Office: Erickson & Sederstrom PC Ste 100 10330 Regency Parkway Dr Omaha NE 68114-3761

BROWNRIGG, WALTER GRANT, cartoonist, corporate executive; b. Boston, Oct. 26, 1940; s. Philip Parker and Mary Jane (Grant) B.; children by previous marriage: Elizabeth Grant, Christopher Hertel; m. Judith Courtney Hamilton, Apr. 28, 1984; children: Carter Grant, Taylor Hamilton, Kelsey Anderson. AB in History cum laude, Princeton U., 1962; MBA, Columbia U., 1964. Asst. plant mgr. Berwick Weaving, Inc., Pa., 1964-72; asst. to v.p. Frank & Stessel, Inc., N.Y.C., 1972-73; sr. assoc. Drake Sheahan/Stewart Dougall, Inc., N.Y.C., 1973-76; exec. dir. Greater Hartford (Conn.) Arts Council, 1976-79; dir. Am. Council Arts, N.Y.C., 1979-83; cartoonist, creator Grantland, 1984—; pres. Grantland Enterprises, Inc., 1991. Spkr., cons. in field. Author: Effective Corporate Fundraising, Corporate Fundraising: A Practical Plan of Action. Mem. Charlottesville Rotary Club, Beta Gamma Sigma.

BROWNSBERGER, MARY GRACE, social services administrator, consultant; b. Spokane, Wash., Dec. 7, 1954; d. William Andrew and Delores Young (Irvine) Rinke; m. James Carl Welker, Mar. 10, 1973 (div. June 1985); children: Kelly Lee, Gregory Carl; m. Nicholas Mason Brownsberger, Apr. 27, 1991; stepchildren: Laura Christine, David Andrew. BA in Psychology summa cum laude, Marymount U., 1999; postgrad., LaSalle U., 2001—. Programmer, analyst City of Overland Park (Kans.), 1979-85; sr. programmer, analyst HDR Infrastructure, Inc., Alexandria, Va., 1985-86; sr. mgmt. analyst Inslaw, Inc., Washington, 1986-91; mgr. info. systems ICMA Retirement Corp., Washington, 1991-94, mgr. customer svcs., 1994-97; exec. dir. Project W.O.R.D., Arlington, Va., 1997—2001; per diem cons. Prentke Romich Co., 2001—. Family selection com. Habitat for Humanity, Washington, 1991—92, constrn. crew, 1987—92; vol. Spl. Equestrians, Warrington, Pa., 2001—; music, eucharistic and visitation ministries Our Lady Queen of Peace Ch., Arlington, Va., 1987—2001; membership chair Arlington Interfaith Coun., 2000—01. Recipient Edn. award, Pa. Psychol. Found. Mem.: AAUW, APA (student affiliate), Pa. Psychol. Assn. (Edn. award), Delta Epsilon Sigma, Psi Chi. Democrat. Roman Catholic. Avocations: crochet, spinning, reading, music.

BROWNSON, ANNA LOUISE HARSHMAN, publishing executive, editor; b. Indpls., May 4, 1926; d. Walter W. and Jennie Harshman; m. Charles B. Brownson (dec.); children: Dwight, Bruce, David, Catharine, Scott. BA, Butler U., 1949, postgrad., 1950-51. Asst. biochemistry lab. Ind. U. Med. Sch., Indpls., 1944-47; grad. asst. Butler U., Indpls., 1949-51; adminstrv. asst. to U.S. congressman from 11th Dist. Ind. Indpls., 1951-58; assoc. editor, treas. Congl. Staff Directory, Ltd., 1959-79, pres., 1980-96, pub. emeritus, 1996—. Pub. Advance Locator for Capitol Hill, 1963—82, owner, 1963—82, editor, 1963—82, Election Index Congl. Staff Directory, 1966—82, pub., 1966—82, owner, 1966—82; gen. ptnr. Brownson Partnership, 1976—; v.p. KnowWho.com, 1998—; corr. sec. Fusaliers; past pres. U.S. Cong. Aux.; exec. com. George C. Marshall Found., trustee. Bd. dirs. Madison Coun. The Libr. of Congress, Accokeek Found., Nat. Colonial Farm; v.p. Nat. Capitol area Boy Scouts Am. (silver Beaver award); active Mt. Vernon Life Guard, Gunston Hall, World Affairs Coun. Washington, Fairchild Gardens, Mount Vernon 100. Recipient Ann L. Brownson award Va. Assn. Museums, 1999. Mem. Internat. Palm Soc., Eisenhower World Affairs Inst., Potomac River Basin Consortium, Capitol Hill Club, U.S. Capitol Hist. Soc., Va. Assn. Mus. (sec., Professionalism in Mus. award 1999), Kappa Alpha Theta (treas. Zeta Iota House Corp.). Presbyterian. Home: 1261 S Alhambra Cir Coral Gables FL 33146-3104 Office: PO Box 17 Mount Vernon VA 22121-0017

BROWNSON, E. RAMONA LIDSTONE BRADY, retired secretary; b. Big Sandy, Mont., May 13, 1930; d. Elmer Gordon and Ethel Mercy (Kuhl) Lidstone; m. William Chauvin Brady, Oct. 10, 1949 (div. 1976); children: William Kim Brady, Colleen Kay Brady, Scott Patrick C. Brady; m. Elwyn James Brownson, Nov. 14, 1980 (dec. Aug. 1999). AS with honors, Mont. State U. No., 1976, BA with honors, 1977. Owner/operator Pep's Bar & Bowling Lanes, Big Sandy, 1954-76; guidance sec./registrar Havre (Mont.) High Sch., 1976-77; sec. to asst. supt. Havre Pub. Schs., 1977-78; sec./bookkeeper Bear Paw Devel. Corp., Havre, 1978-79; new accts./vault cash teller Great Am. Savings Bank, Havre, 1979-88; sec. to ombudsman U. Nebr., Lincoln, 1989-92, receptionist, sec. dept. human resources, 1992-97; records assoc. Nebraska Alumni, 2001—03; ret., 2003. Active Dems. Hill County, Mont., 1977-88, Nebr., 1988—; polit. precinct committeewoman Hill County, Mont., 1980-88; life mem. P.E.I. Hist. Soc., Can., Lidstone Soc., Plymouth, Eng.; charter mem. Big Sandy, Mont. Hist. Soc.; ctrl. com. mem. Lancaster County Dem., 2000—. Recipient Toastmasters' Internat. Speechcraft cert., 1979; named Dem. Vol. of Yr. Nebr. Dem. Party, 2003; No. Mont. Coll. scholar, 1949-50, 75-76. Mem. AAUW (internat. affairs chair 1986-88, booksale co-chair 1986), AARP, Nat. Assn. Edn. Office Pers., Cert. Ednl. Office Employee (cert. 1993), Nebr. Ednl. Office Pers., U. Nebr. Office Pers. (membership chair 1991-92), Mont. State U. No. Alumni, Lincoln Lancaster County Geneal. Soc., Assinboine Geneal. Soc. (charter), Irish/Scotch Soc., Eagles Aux. Lodge, VFW Aux. (life), Am. Legion Aux., The Westerners. Avocations: reading, dancing, genealogy/history, movies/theatre, travel, politics. Home: 2205 Southwood Pl Lincoln NE 68512-1375 Office: U Nebr Nebr Alumni Lincoln NE 68588

BROWNSON, JACQUES CALMON, architect; b. Aurora, Ill., Aug. 3, 1923; s. Clyde Arthur and Iva Kline (Felter) B.; m. Doris L. Curry, 1946; children—Joel C., Lorre J., Daniel J. BS in Architecture, Ill. Inst. Tech., 1948, MS, 1954. Instr., asst. prof. architecture Ill. Inst. Tech., 1949-59; prof. architecture, chmn. dept. U. Mich., 1966-68; chief design C.F. Murphy Assocs., Chgo., 1959-61; project architect, chief designer Chgo. Civic Ctr. Architects, 1961-68; dir. state bldg. div. State of Colo., Denver, 1986-88; pvt. practice Denver, 1988—. Former

mng. architect Chgo. Pub. Bldg. Commn.; past dir. planning and devel. Auraria Ctr. for Higher Edn., Denver; bd. dirs. Capital Constrn., Denver; guest lectr. architecture in U.S. and Europe. Prin. works include Chgo. Civic Ctr., Lake Denver, Colo., 1985, Chgo. Tribune/Cabrini Green Housing, 1993; author: History of Chicago Architects, 1996, Oral History of Jacuqes Calmon Brownson, 1996. Recipient award for Geneva House Archtl. Record mag., 1956; Design award for steel framed factory Progressive Architecture mag., 1957 Home and Office: 659 Josephine St Denver CO 80206-3722

BROWNSON, KENNETH C. university dean; b. Hazleton, Pa., Apr. 16, 1945; s. Kenneth George and Mary Louise (Dennion) B. AAS in Nursing, Del. Tech. and C.C., 1978; BS in Profl. Arts, St. Joseph's Coll., Standish, Maine, 1984; MS in Mgmt., The Am. Coll., 1986; MS in Psychology, Calif. Coast U., 1989; EdD in Adult and Nontraditional Edn., Newport U., 1991; Cert. in Cmty. Health Edn., Calif. Coll. Health Sci., 1999. RN, Del., Pa.; cert. psychiat. and mental health nurse; cert. allied health instr. Evening supr., asst. head nurse intensive/critical care unit Riverside Hosp., Wilmington, Del., 1980-83; staff RN, nurse/counselor crisis svc. unit Crozer-Chester Med. Ctr., Chester, Pa., 1983-94; pres. Adult Edn. Resource, New Castle, Del., 1987—; dean undergrad. studies Greenwich U., Australia, 1989—2001; prof. social studies Am. Pub. U. Sys. Mem. adv. bd. Insvc. Tng. Inst., 1991—99; v.p., bd. dirs. Brandywine Counseling, Inc., Wilmington. Mem. edit. bd. Health Care Mgr.; author: College at Home for Nurses and All Healthcare Professionals, 2002. With USN, 1965-69, Vietnam. Home and Office: 33 W 4th St New Castle DE 19720-5092 E-mail: kbrownson@comcast.net.

BROWNSON, ROGER JAMES, university official, photographer; b. Wayland, N.Y., Sept. 12, 1942; s. Wesley James and Alice Alberta Brownson; m. Judith Ray, Aug. 7, 1965; children: David James, Krista Lynn. BS, Kent State U., 1964, MS, 1966, postgrad., 1966-68, Bowling Green (Ohio) State U., 1967-68. Cert. history and social studies tchr., guidance counseling, spl. edn., Ohio. Tchr. Lorain (Ohio) City Schs., 1964-68; guidance counselor Lorain H.S., 1968-95, Admiral King H.S., Lorain, 1995-96; supr. student tchg. art dept. Bowling Green State U., 1996—. Vol. Naval ROTC program Lorain H.S. and Admiral King Naval Jr. ROTC, 1996—. Photographer: History of Lorain, Ohio, 1999. Vol. photographer Lorain County Visitors Bur., 1996—; photographer, vol. Vince Shipley polit. campaign for councilman, Lorain, 1998-99; vol., instr., photographer Sprit of Am. Program, Lorain, 1997—; photographer Friends Lorain County Metro Parks, 1996—; photographer Black River Hist. Soc., Lorain, 1996—, Ohio Scottish Games, 1997—. Recipient various awards for photography. Mem. Ohio Edn. Assn., Kappa Sigma. Republican. Methodist. Avocations: whitewater rafting, animal and outdoor photography, hiking, racquetball. Home: 2342 Lincoln Dr Lorain OH 44052-2723

BROWNSTEIN, BARBARA LAVIN, geneticist, educator, university official; b. Phila., Sept. 8, 1931; d. Edward A. and Rose (Silverstein) Lavin; m. Melvin Brownstein, June 1949 (div. 1955); children: Judith Brownstein Kaufmann, Dena. Asst. editor Biol. Abstracts, Phila., 1957-58; research fellow dept. microbial genetics Karolinska Inst., Stockholm, 1962-64; assoc. Wistar Inst., Phila., 1964-68; assoc. prof. molecular biology, dept. biology Temple U., Phila., 1968-74, prof., 1974-96, prof. emeritus, 1996—, chmn. dept., 1978-81, provost, 1983-90; sr. assoc. Ctr. Ednl. Rsch. U. Wash., Seattle, 1994—. Vis. scientist dept. tumor cell biology Imperial Cancer Rsch. Fund Labs., London, 1973-74; bd. dirs. Univ. City Sci. Ctr., Greater Phila. Econ. Devel. Coun., Forum Exec. Women; program officer NSF, 1992-93; sr. assoc. Inst. Ednl. Inquiry, Seattle, 1994—. Bd. dirs. Lopez Island Sch., 2001—. Recipient Liberal Arts Alumni award for excellence in teaching Temple U., 1980; recipient Outstanding Faculty Woman award Temple U., 1980 Fellow AAAS; mem. Am. Soc. Cell Biology, N.Y. Acad. Sci., Assn. Women in Sci., NSF (program officer 1992-93). Home: PO Box 835 Lopez Island WA 98261 Office: Inst Ednl Inquiry 124 E Edgar St Seattle WA 98102 E-mail: bbrownst@msn.com.

BROWNSTEIN, ELIZABETH SMITH, writer; d. Frank Edward and Grace Hanrahan Smith; m. Arnold Wallace Brownstein, Oct. 12, 1967 (div. 1973). BA in Polit. Sci., Wellesley Coll., 1952; MSc in Internat. Rels., London Sch. Econs. and Polit. Sci., 1967. Chief TV rschr. Meet the Press CBS, 1952—56; dir. The Experiment in Internat. Living, N.Y.C., 1960—66; assoc. prodr., writer Evening Edit. with Martin Agronsky, 1971—76; exec. prodr., program devel. mgr., asst. program mgr. WETA-TV, Washington, 1976—82. Dir. rsch. : (TV series) Smithsonian World, 1982—87; coord. prodr. : Smithsonian Video Collection, 1989—92; author: If This House Could Talk, 1999. Mem.: Soc. Women Geographers (sec. nat. exec. coun. 1990—96, Washington Group rep. 1996—2002), Alumni and Friends of London Sch. Econs. (exec. v.p. 1977—80, bd. dirs. 1977—, pres. 1980—82), Washington Press Club (bd. govs. 1979—83), Nat. Press Club. Democrat. Unitarian. Avocations: walking holidays, swimming, reading, films. Home: 4201 Cathedral Ave NW Washington DC 20016

BROWNSTEIN, MARTIN HERBERT, dermatopathologist; b. N.Y.C., Aug. 20, 1935; s. Samuel C. and Florence (Sturm) B.; m. Ann Lehman, June 23, 1964 (div. Aug. 1993); children: Sara Leah, Michael Ari. AB, Harvard U., 1956; MD, Albert Einstein Coll. Medicine, 1961. Intern Lenox Hill Hosp., N.Y.C., 1961-62; resident in internal medicine VA Hosps., N.Y.C., 1962-65; resident in dermatology NYU, N.Y.C., 1965-66; pvt. practice medicine specializing in dermatopathology N.Y.C., 1970-72, Great Neck, N.Y., 1972-84, Port Washington, N.Y., 1984—; Osborne fellow Armed Forces Inst. Pathology, Washington, 1968-69. Asst. clin. prof. dermatology N.Y. Med. Coll., N.Y.C., 1970-73, clin. assoc. prof. dermatology, 1973-78, clin. prof. dermatology, 1978-83; clin. prof. dermatology Mt. Sinai Med. Ctr., N.Y.C., 1983— . Chief editor Jour. Cutaneous Pathology, 1984; contbr. articles to profl. jours. Trustee North Shore Hebrew Acad., Great Neck, N.Y., 1979-80; hon. trustee Great Neck Synagogue, 1986-88; sec. Ramot Shapira World Youth Ctr., bd. dirs., chmn. Chabad, Port Washington, N.Y., bd. dirs. Nat. Com. Futherance Jewish Edn., Nassau County. With M.C. U.S. Army, 1966-68. Recipient Pres.'s award Union Orthodox Jewish Congregations of Am., 1983 Mem. ACP, AMA, Am. Soc. Dermatopathology (pres. 1983-84), N.Y. State Soc. Dermatology, Am. Acad. Dermatology (chmn. com. on pathology 1980-82), Med. Soc. N.Y. State, Med. Soc. N.Y. County, Dermatol. Soc. Greater N.Y. (pres. 1978-79), L.I. Dermatology Soc. (pres. 1992-94), N.Y. Acad. Medicine. Office: 2 N Plandome Rd Port Washington NY 11050 3443

BROWNSTEIN, RICHARD JOSEPH, lawyer; b. L.A., June 29, 1930; s. Alfred and Vera (Slifman) B.; m. Elisabeth B. Baer, July 15, 1955 (dec. Apr. 1973); children: J.B., Joyce A., Richard J., II; m. Shirley Jean Anderson, June 15, 1976 (div. Apr. 1983); m. Donna Oziel Sacks, Sept. 12, 1987. Student Reed Coll., 1948-50; LL.B., Willamette U., 1953. Bar: Oreg 1953, U.S Dist. Ct. Oreg. 1954. Assoc., then ptnr. White/Sutherland, Portland, Oreg., 1953-73; ptnr. Brownstein, Rask, Arenz, Sweeney, Kerr & Grim, Portland, 1973—; pres., bd dirs. Devel. Housing and Law Inst., Washington, 1984— . Mem., chmn. Met. Human Relations Commn., Portland, 1964-68, Oreg. adv. com. U.S. Civil Rights Commn., 1986-92, City of Portland Cable Regulatory Commn., 1986-93. Served to col. USAR, 1948-80. Mem. Oreg. Bar Assn. (corp. com. 1964-67, sec. civil rights com. 1967-70, group purchasing com. 1973-76, sec., chmn. legal secs. 1980-83, future of legal profession 1983-86, lawyers assistance com. 1986-89). Club: University (Portland). Lodge: B'nai B'rith (dist. pres. 1974-75). Home: 763 NW Powhatan Ter Portland OR 97210-2734 Office: Brownstein Rask Arenz Sweeney Kerr & Grim 1200 SW Main St Portland OR 97205-2040

BROWN-WAITE, VIRGINIA (GINNY BROWN-WAITE), congresswoman; b. Albany, N.Y., Oct. 5, 1943; m. Harvey Waite; children: Jeannien Roxby Waite, Danene Mitchell, Sue Meaders, Lorie Sue. BS, SUNY, 1976; MS, Russell Sage Coll., 1984. Former commr. Hernando County; former legis. dir. N.Y. State Senate; mem. Fla. State Senate, 1992—2002, U.S. Ho. of Reps. from 5th Fla. dist., 2003—. Active W Hernando GOP, United Way; bd. dirs. Hernando County Spouse Abuse Ctr. Mem. Bus. and Profl. Women's Club, Suncoast MG Club. Roman Catholic.*

BROWNWOOD, DAVID OWEN, lawyer; b. L.A., May 24, 1935; s. Robert Scott Osgood and Ruth Elizabeth (Bellamy) B.; m. Sigrid Carlson, Mar. 3, 1956 (div. 1972); children: Jeffrey Owen, Kirsten, Scott David, Daniel Stuart; m. Susan Sloane Jannicky, July 4, 1975; 1 child, Mary Ruth Bellamy; stepchildren: Bradbury, Stephanie Ellington. AB with distinction, Stanford U., 1956; LLB magna cum laude, Harvard U., 1964. Bar: Calif. 1965, N.Y. 1969. Law clk. Ropes & Gray, Boston, 1963; assoc. McCutchen, Doyle, Brown & Enersen, San Francisco, 1964-66; lectr. law U. Khartoum, Sudan, 1966-67, Kenya Inst. Adminstrn., Lower Kabete, 1967-68; assoc. Cravath, Swaine & Moore, N.Y.C., 1968-72, ptnr., 1973—2001, sr. counsel, 2003—, recruiting ptnr., 1978-82, mng. ptnr. for legal staff, 1983-86; ptnr. in charge London office, 1995—2001. Treas. N.Y. Law Inst., 1978-83, chmn. exec. com., 1983-88, pres., 1988-93. Mem. editorial bd. Harvard U. Law Rev., 1963-64. Nat. chair Harvard U. Law Sch. Fund, 1991—93; bd. dirs. Royal Oak Found., 2003—; pres. Benjamin Franklin House, 2002—; dir. Literacy Assistance Ctr., N.Y.C., 1983—94, co-chmn. bd. dirs., 1987—94; trustee Greenwich (Conn.) Country Day Sch., 1985—92, v.p., 1986—88, pres., chmn. bd. trustees, 1988—92; co-chmn. Harvard U. Law Sch. 25th Reunion Gift, 1988—89; N.Y. regional com. campaign Harvard Law Sch., 1991—95; com. on univ. resources Harvard U., 1991—, mem. Harvard law sch. vis. com., 1995—2001; keystone regional vice chair centennial campaign Stanford U., 1986—92; exec. com. Stanford U. N.Y. Coun., 1992—95; vice chmn. Stanford U. N.Y. Major Gifts Com., 1993—95; co-chair Stanford U. Ea. Coun., 1993; bd. govs. Stanford Assocs., 1993—95, pres., chmn. bd. govs., 1994—95; bd. advisors Stanford Trust (U.K.), 1995—2002; mem. Stanford U. UK/Western Europe Regional Adv. Bd., 2003—; mem. nat. bd. Outward Bound USA, 1993—96. 1st lt. USAF, 1956 61, fighter pilot Air Def. Command, capt. USAFR, Mass. Air N.G., 1961—66. Recipient Centennial medallion Stanford U., Stanford Assocs. award. Fellow Am. Bar Found., N.Y. State Bar Found.; mem. ABA, Internat. Bar Assn., N.Y. State Bar Assn., Assn. Bar City N.Y., The Pilgrims, Round Hill Club (Greenwich), Field Club (Greenwich), Sankaty Head Club (Nantucket), Siasconset Casino Assn. (Nantucket), Harvard Club (N.Y.C.). Home: 296 Old Church Rd Greenwich CT 06830 also: 61 Orange St Nantucket MA 02554 Office: Cravath Swaine & Moore 825 8th Ave New York NY 10015 also: Cravath Swaine & Moore 825 8th Ave Fl 46 New York NY 10019-7416 E-mail: dbrownwood@cravath.com.

BROWN-ZEKERI, LOLITA MOLANDA, elementary school educator; b. Stephens County, Mar. 15, 1963; d. James and Doris (Phillips) Brown; m. Austin Zekeri, Nov. 21, 1998; 1 child: Annabelle Lola. BS with honors, North Ga. Coll., 1985, MEd, 1989, EdS, 1994. Cert. tchr. Tchr., 2nd grade Jackson County Bd. Edn., Nicholson, Ga., 1985-87, chpt. 1 tchr., 1987—98, third grade tchr., 1998—. Chmn. grade level Jackson County Bd. Edn., 2002—03. Author: Exploring Blue Highways, 1995; co-author: Making Learning Funner, So People Want To Learn, A Longitudinal Study of Students' Perceptions About Schooling. Active Paradise AME Ch. trustee 1986-99, asst. Sun. Sch. sec. 1986-99, Sun. Sch. sec., 1999—, young adult choir mem. 1987-2001, Christian Edn. Youth Dept. 2d v.p. 1988—, Vacation Bible Sch. art coord. and tchr. 1986—. Mem. Ga. Edn. Assn., Assn. Childhood Educators Internat., North Ga. Coll. Union Bd. (chmn. decorations/hospitality com. 1983-84, sec. 1984-85), Benton Parent/Tchr. Orgn.

BROXMEYER, HAL EDWARD, medical educator; b. Bklyn., Nov. 27, 1944; s. David and Anna (Gurman) B.; m. C. Beth Biller, 1969; children: Eric Jay, Jeffrey Daniel. BS, Bklyn. Coll., 1966; MS, L.I. U., 1969; PhD, NYU, 1973. Postdoctoral student Queens U., Kingston, Ont., Can., 1973-75; assoc. researcher, rsch. assoc. Meml. Sloan Kettering Cancer Ctr., N.Y.C., 1975-78, assoc., 1978-83, assoc. mem., 1983; asst. prof. Cornell U. Grad. Sch., N.Y.C., 1980-83; assoc. prof. Ind. U. Sch. Medicine, Indpls., 1983-86, prof. medicine, microbiology and immunology, 1986—; sci. dir. Walther Oncology Ctr., Indpls., 1988—, chmn. microbiology and immunology, 1997—. Mem. hematology II study sect. NIH, Bethesda, Md., 1981-86, 95-2000, chair, 1997-2000; adv. com. NHLBI, NIH, Bethesda, 1991-94; chmn. bd. sci. counselors Nat. Space Biomed. Rsch. Inst., 1998—; mem. coun. Nat. Space Biomed. Rsch. Inst., 1999—, MSAB, Viacell Corp.; bd. dirs. Nat. Disease Rsch. Interchange. Assoc. editor Exptl. Hematology, 1981-90, Jour. Immunology, 1987-92, Stem Cells, 1996-97, Brit. Jour. Haematology, 1998—; editor Jour. LeuKocyte Biology, 1995—; sr. editor Jour. Hematotherapy and Stem Cell Rsch., 2000—; mem. editl. bd. Blood, 1983-87, Biotech. Therapeutics, 1988-95, Internat. Jour. Hematology, 1991—, Jour. Lab. Clin. Medicine, 1992—, Jour. Exptl. Medicine, 1992—, Annals Hematology, 1993—, Cell Transplantation, 1994—, Critical Rev. Oncology/Hematology, 1995—, Stem Cells, 1998—, Jour. Blood and Marrow Transplantations, 1998—, Cytokines, Cellular and Molecular Therapy, 1998—1 contbr. over 550 papers to profl. publs. Mem. ednl. com. Leukemia Soc. Am., Indpls., 1983—, nat. career devel. study sect., N.Y., 1991-95, 2000—. Recipient Founder's Day award NYU, 1973, Merit award Nat. Cancer Inst., 1987-95, Spl. Fellow award, 1976-78, and Scholar award, 1978-83, Gold medal City of Paris, 1993, World of Difference award Ind. Health Industry Forum, 1997, Leukemia Soc. Am., Landsteiner award Am. Assn. Blood Banks, 2002, Health Care Heroes award Indpls. Bus. Jour., 2002. Mem. AAAS, N.Y. Acad. Scis., Soc. for Leukocyte Biology, Am. Assn. Cancer Rsch., Am. Assn. Immunologists, Internat. Soc. Exptl. Hematology (pres. 1990-91), Am. Soc. Hematology (coun. mem. 2000—), Am. Fedn. Clin. Rsch., Am. Soc. Blood and Marrow Transplantation, Am. Soc. Hematology (coun. 2000—). Avocation: competitive Olympic-style weightlifting. Home: 1210 Chessington Rd Indianapolis IN 46260-1630 Office: Ind U Sch Medicine 950 W Walnut St Rm 302 Indianapolis IN 46202-5181 Fax: 317-274-7592. E-mail: hbroxmey@iupui.edu.

BROXTON, RANDALL, education educator, researcher; s. Joseph and Marie Rose Broxton. BS, U. of South Ala., 1968; MS, Troy State U., 1978. Cert. tchr. Fla. State Bd. Edn., 1968, Ala. State Bd. Edn., 1968. Tchr./dept. chair Escambia County Bd. of Pub. Instrn., Pensacola, Fla., 1968—77; history prof. Pensacola Jr. Coll., 1968—. Founder/bd. mem. Gulf South History & Humanities Conf., Pensacola, 1968—; founder/sponsor Jared Sparks Hist. Soc. of Pensacola Jr. Coll.; bd. mem. Pensacola History Coun., 2000—; bd. mem./officer Pensacola Hist. Soc., 1968—; chair-committee Learning Resources Ctr., Pensacola; com. chmn. Pensacola Alumni Chpt. of Kappa Delta Pi, pres., 1990—92. Author: (book) The History of the Gulf South History and Humanities Conf. 1968-2000; narrator : (film) The Pensacola Naval Aviation Mus.; The Greek Ch.; A Tour of St Michael's Cemetery; author: (walking tour) A Walking Tour of St Michael's Cemetery, A Walking Tour of St John's Cemetery, A Walking Tour of the Seville Square area, A Walking Tour of the Plaza Ferdinand area, A Walking Tour of the Jewish Cemetery, A Walking Tour of Upper North Hill, A Walking Tour of East Hill; editor: Lady Elizabeth Sewanee Rev., 1958, Occie Clubs: Her Role in Education and History, 1977, The Wife/The Other Woman, Emerald Coast Rev., 1988. Life-mem. Santa Rosa Hist. Soc., Milton, Fla. Recipient achievement, Kappa Delta Pi, 1978. Mem.: Bagdad Hist. Village Preservation Soc., White House Hist. Soc., Fla. Endowment for the Humanities, Fla. Trust for Hist. Preservation, Nat. Trust for Hist. Preservation, Fla. Hist. Soc., West Fla. Lit. Fedn. (Heritage Award -Lifetime Achievement 2001). Methodist. Avocations: writing, reading, gardening, travel. Home: PO Box 9101 Pensacola FL 32513-9101 Office: Pensacola Jr Coll 1000 Coll Blvd Pensacola FL 32504 Office Fax: 850-484-1563. E-mail: rbroxton@pjc.edu.

BROYLES, BONITA EILEEN, nursing educator; b. Ross County, Ohio, Sept. 29, 1948; d. Arthur Runnels and Mary Elizabeth (Page) Brookie; m. Roger F. Broyles, Dec. 29, 1984; children: Michael Richard Brown, Jeffrey Allen Brown. BSN, Ohio State U., 1970; MA with honors, N.C. Cen. U., Durham, 1988; EdD summa cum laude, LaSalle U., 1996. ADN instr., CPR instr. Piedmont C.C., Roxboro, N.C.; instr. nursing Watts Sch. Nursing, Durham; res. float staff nurse Durham County Gen. Hosp., Durham; dir. practical nursing edn., instr. Piedmont C.C., Roxboro, N.C.; maternity patient tchr. Mt. Carmel Med. Ctr., Columbus, Ohio. Second-level coord. assoc. degree nursing faculty Piedmont Community Coll., 1990—. Co-author: Test Manual for Bowden, Dickey, Greenberg Children and Their Families: The Continuum of Care, 1998; author: Clinical Companion for Ashwill and Droske Nursing of Children: Principles and Practice, 1997; author: (with Reiss and Evans) Pharmacological Aspects of Nursing Care, revised 6th edit., 2002; author: Dosage Calculation Practice for Nurses, 2003. Named ADN Educator of Yr. N.C. Assoc. Degree Nursing Coun., 1993; recipient nat. tchg. excellence award Nat. Inst. Staff Orgnl. Devel., U. Tex., Austin, 1998, Faculty Excellence award Piedmont Comty. Coll., 2001. Office: Piedmont CC Sch Nursing College St Roxboro NC 27573

BROYLES, MICHAEL E. music history educator, writer; s. William Kingsley Broyles and Margaret Louise Connally; m. Denise Von Glahn, Mar. 8, 2001; children: Eleanor Margaret Bloomquist, Tracy Katherine. BA, Austin Coll., 1967; PhD, U. Tex., 1967. Presdl. rsch. prof. U. Md. Baltimore County, 1993—94; disting. prof. music, prof. of am. history Pa. State U., University Park, 1994—. Trustee Soc. for Am. Music, Pitts., 2000—01. Author: The Emergence and Evolution of Beethoven's Heroic Style, 1987, Music of the Highest Class: Elitism and Populism in Antebellum Boston, 1992, A Yankee Musician in Europe, 1990, Mavericks and Other Traditions in American Music, 2003. Sr. fellow, NEH, 1989—90. Avocations: skiing, travel. Office: Pa State U 227 Music Bldg University Park PA 16802

BROYLES, STEPHEN DOUGLAS, public administrator; b. Columbus, Ohio, Sept. 7, 1947; s. Enoch Ernest and Georgina Marie (Weaver) B; m. Kay Lyn Porter, May 31, 1968; children: Paul Douglas, Leora Marie. BA, Ohio State U., 1969; MA, Webster Coll., 1978; DPA, U. Ala., 1995. Commd. 2d lt. U.S. Air Force, 1969, advanced through gades to lt. col., 1989; chief mgmt. support divsn. Def. Comms. Agy., Stuttgart, West Germany, 1983-87; dep. base comdr. USAFE, San Vito Air Base, Italy, 1987-89; chief seminar divsn. Air U., Maxwell AFB, Ala., 1989-92; ret. U.S. Air Force, 1992; asst. mgr. Pizza Hut Delivery, Montgomery, Ala., 1993-94; city adminstr. City of Muenster, Tex., 1995-2000; dean adminstrv. svcs. North Ctrl. Tex. Coll., 2000—. Mem. Am. Soc. Pub. Adminstrs., Kiwanis (pres. 1996-98). Avocations: reading, tai chi, swimming, hiking. Home: 407 W 9th St Muenster TX 76252-2241 Office: North Ctrl Tex Coll Gainesville TX 76240-4699 E-mail: eaglephant@ntin.net.

BROYTMAN, VLADISLAV I. hygenist; b. Moscow, Oct. 6, 1948; arrived in U.S., 1998; s. Iosif Broytman and Frida Tsvick; m. Nadezhda Broytman, Dec. 13, 1969; children: Natalya, Nick. Diploma, Med. Inst., Russia, 1973; PhD, Med. Inst., St. Petersburg, Russia, 1984; ScD, VAK, Moscow, 1994. Physician Sanitary Epidemiology Sta., Russia, 1973—85; chief Indsl. Hygiene Lab. Sci. Rsch. Indsl. Hygiene and Occupl. Diseases, Russia, 1985—90, pres., 1990—98; v.p. Art of Life, Inc. Ambulance, Phila., 2002—. Contbr. ; author: 4 monographs. Recipient Gold medal, Russia, 1989. Mem.: Hygienist Assn., N.Y. Acad. Sci. Achievements include patents in field. Home: 2375 Woodward St Apt 307ET Philadelphia PA 19115

BROZOVSKY, JOHN A. accounting educator; b. Spokane, Wash., Apr. 30, 1951; s. Victor Jerald and Orise (Watson) B.; m. Sue Ellen King, Apr. 14, 1984; 1 child, Joseph Victor. AAS, Spokane C.C., 1971; BBA, U. Tex., 1975, M in Profl. Acctg., 1978; PhD in Bus. Adminstrn., U. Colo., 1990. CPA, Tex.; cert. data processor; cert. computer programmer. Computer programmer U. Tex., Austin, 1974-77; computer programmer II Tex. State Health Dept., Austin, 1978-80; EDP auditor City of Austin, 1980-81; sr. internal auditor Enserch Corp., Dallas, 1981-83; lectr. Calif. State U., Fresno, 1983-86; rsch. and teaching asst U. Colo., Boulder, 1986-89; asst. prof. Va. Tech., Blacksburg, 1989-96, assoc. prof., 1996—. Presenter in field. Author: Advanced Accounting, 2000; contbr. articles to profl. jours. Am. Accctg. Assn. fellow, 1986, Gerald Hart fellow, 1987; grantee Calif. CPA Found., 1986-89, AICPA, 1988, Pamplin, 1992. Mem. Am. Acctg. Assn., Am. Econ. Assn., Am. Tax Assn., Nat. Tax Assn., Inst. Mgmt. Accts. (coach nat. championship team student case competition 1995, nat. finalists 1996, 1997, nat. semifinalists, 1998, 99, v.p. profl. edn. Roanoke chpt. 1997-98). Avocation: stamp collecting. Home: 9000 Newport Rd Catawba VA 24070-3018 Office: Va Tech Pamplin # 3007 Blacksburg VA 24061 E-mail: John.Brozovsky@vt.edu.

BROZOWSKI, LAURA ADRIENNE, mechanical engineer; b. Yokohama, Japan, May 12, 1960; arrived in U.S., 1961; d. John and Muriel Sydney (Jackson) Brozowski. BSME, U. Calif., 1982; MSME, Calif. State U., 1987; MBA, Pepperdine U., 1988. Registered profl. engr., Calif.; cert. profl. mgr. Inst. Cert. Profl. Mgrs. Engring. scientist Boeing Co., Canoga Park, Calif., 1982—. Author: in field. Recipient Space Achievement Mid Career award, Rotary Nat., Rotary Nat. Award for Space Achievement, 2003, Stellar award, 2003. Fellow: Inst. Advancement Engring.; mem.: NSPE, ASME, Nat. Mgmt. Assn. Avocations: music, continuing education, dance.

BROZZO, SHIRLEY A. language educator; b. Wakefield, Mich., Feb. 4, 1956; d. Maurice Clayton and Louise Marie (Arndt) Bachand; m. Joseph Edward Brozzo, Oct. 21, 1977 (div. Sept. 1989); children: Jamie Lynne, Brandi Jo, Steven Earl. BSBA, No. Mich. U., 1992, MA in English, 1994, MFA, 2003. Office asst. No. Mich. U., Marquette, 1990—93, tchg. asst. English, 1993—94; adj. instr. English Ctr. Native Am. Studies, Marquette, 1995—. Coord. GAP No. Mich. U., Marquette, 1994—; mem. adv. coun. Ctr. Native Am. Studies, Marquette, 1991—. Contbr. Avocations: knitting, crocheting, reading. Home: 6400 US 41 S #1 Marquette MI 49855 Office: No Mich Univ Interdisciplinary Programs 1401 Presque Isle Ave Marquette MI 49855-5301

BRUBAKER, CRAWFORD FRANCIS, JR., federal agency official, aerospace consultant; b. Fruitland, Idaho, Apr. 23, 1924; s. Crawford Francis and Cora Susan (Flora) B.; m. Lucile May Christensen, May 5, 1945; children: Eric Stephen, Alan Kenneth, Craig Martin, Paul David BA, Pomona Coll., 1946; MBA, U. Pa., 1948. Office mgr. Lockheed Calif. Co., Burbank, 1948-54, sales adminstr., 1954-57, with fighter contracts div., field office rep., 1959-65, asst. dir. fighter sales, 1965-69, dep. mgr. bid and proposals, 1969-74, mgr. govt. sales, 1974-76; dir. internat. mktg. devel. and policy Lockheed Corp., Burbank, 1976-83; dep. asst. sec. for aerospace U.S. Dept. Commerce, Washington, 1983-87; internat. aerospace cons., 1987—. Chair bd. trustees So. Calif. Presbyn. Homes; vice chmn. Industry Sector Adv. Com., Washington, 1979-83; mem. Aero. Policy Rev. Com., Washington, 1983-87; mem. bd. dirs. Life Svcs., Inc., 2003—. Vice chmn. So. Calif. Dist. Export Coun., L.A., 1980-83, 88-91, chmn., 1992-93. Lt. (j.g.) USN, 1943-45, PTO Mem. AIAA, Am. Defense Preparedness Assn., Kiwanis, Sigma Alpha Epsilon. Republican. Presbyterian. Avocations: numismatics, golf, fishing, photography. E-mail: dasbru@pacbell.net.

BRUBAKER, JAMES EDWARD, mechanical engineer; b. Chgo., Feb. 24, 1935; s. Samuel James and Mary Louise (Alward) B.; m. Phyllis Ann Evans, Aug. 18, 1956; children: David, Richard, Lisa, Mark. BS in Gen. Engring., U. Ill., 1956. Instr. engring. U. Ill., 1956-57; mgr. mechanism and core barrel devel. advanced submarine project Bettis Atomic Power Lab., Pitts., 1959-75; cog. engr. head access area and refueling equipment Clinch River Breeder Reactor, Pitts., 1975-83; project engr. Peacekeeper (MX) Missile Project, Advanced Reactor Divsn. Westinghouse Elec. Corp., Pitts., 1983—85, prin. engr. West Valley Nuc. Demonstration Project. Advanced Reactor Divsn., 1985-87, prin. engr. Tomahawk missile sys., naval environ. equipment, 1987-95, sr. project engr. advanced submarine reactor pumps Machinery Tech. Divsn., 1996—2000. Cons. USN, USAF and DOE. Patentee in field; editor Mechanism Design Manual and Mil. Specification for Naval Reactor CRDMs. Recipient Environ. Protection commendation U.S. Navy, 1995. Mem. Pleasant Hills Athletic Assn. (pres. 1976-77), Lions (pres. 1984-85, 2001-02, zone chair 2002—), Phi Kappa Tau. Republican. Avocations: tennis, golf, reading, travel.

BRUBAKER, KAREN SUE, small business owner; b. Ashland, Ohio, Feb. 5, 1953; d. Robert Eugene and Dora Louise (Camp) B. BSBA, Ashland U., 1975; MBA, Bowling Green State U., 1976. Supr. tire ctr. ops. B.F. Goodrich Co., Akron, Ohio, 1976-77, supr. tire ctr. acctg., 1977-79, asst. product mgr. radial passenger tires, 1979-80, product mgr. broadline passenger tires, 1980-81, group product mgr. broadline passenger and light truck tires, 1981-83, mktg. mgr. T/A high tech radials, 1983-86; product mktg. mgr. B.F. Goodrich T/A radials The Uniroyal Goodrich Tire Co., Akron, Ohio, 1986-91; product mktg. mgr. Michelin performance tires Michelin Americas Small Tires, Akron, Ohio, 1991-95; ind. EcoQuest Internat. distbr. DBA Indoor Air Repair, Fairlawn, Ohio, 1996—. Sect. chmn. indsl. divsn. United Way, Akron, 1983-86; mem. adv. coun. to trustees Coll. Bus. and Econs, Ashland U., 1990-92; vol. Hospice Vis. Nurses Svcs., 1995-; fund raiser Nat. Heart Assist and Transplant Fund/Judi Reali Transplant Fund, 1996. Recipient Alumni Disting. Service award Ashland Coll., 1986; Alpha Phi Clara Bradley Burdette scholar, 1975. Mem. Am. Mktg. Assn. (pres. Akron/Canton chpt. 1982-83, Highest Honors award 1983, nat. bd. dirs., v.p. bus. mktg. 1984-86, v.p. profl. chpts. 1987-89), Sales and Mktg. Execs. (v.p. membership, 1998-99), Akron Women's Network, Zonta Internat. (membership dir. 1987-94, 96—), Beta Gamma Sigma, Omicron Delta Epsilon. Home: 822 Village Pkwy Fairlawn OH 44333-3297 E-mail: airwaves@bigplanet.com.

BRUBAKER, LAUREN EDGAR, minister, educator; b. Birmingham, Ala., Oct. 8, 1914; s. Lauren Edgar and Nora (Drake) B.; m. Leonte Saye, June 6, 1944; children: Lauren Eugene, Edward Saye; m. Patricia Barnett, July 23, 1994. AB, Birmingham So. Coll., 1935; MDiv, Princeton Theol. Sem., 1938,

postdoctoral, 1946-47; STM, Union Theol. Sem., N.Y., 1942, ThD, 1944. Ordained to ministry Presbyn. Ch., 1938. Asst. pastor in, Parkersburg, W.Va., 1938-41; grad. asst. Union Theol. Sem., 1941-43; chaplain U.S. Army, 1943-46; grad. instr. Princeton Theol. Sem., 1946-47; prof. philosophy and religion, chaplain Parsons Coll., Fairfield, Iowa, 1947-49. Assoc. prof. U. S.C., Columbia, 1949-58, prof., 1958-79, Disting. prof., 1979-80, Disting. prof. emeritus, 1980—, univ. chaplain, 1949-94, chmn. dept. religious studies, 1949-80; adj. prof. Luth. Theol. So. Sem.; moderator Univ. Forum on S.C. Ednl. TV, 1965-73. Contbr. articles to profl. jours. Dir. S.C. Coun. Human Rels., 1966-69; exec. committeeman Columbia and Richland County Dem. party, 1950-60. Served to maj. AUS, 1943-46. Mem. AAUP (past officer), Inst. Religion (dir. 1960-63), S.C. Acad. Religion (founder 1968, pres. 1968), Am. Acad. Religion (pres. 1959), Presbyn. Edn. Assn. South, Columbia Ministers Assn. (pres. 1972), Assn. Coll. and Univ. Religious Affairs (bd. dirs. 1985-86), Columbia Forum Internat. Affairs (pres. 1971), Columbia Coun. for Internat. (bd. dirs., pres. 1986, 87), Nat. Assn. Coll. and Univ. Chaplains, Soc. Bibl. Lit. (past officer), Christian Jewish Congress S.C. (sec. 1982-90), Columbia CROP WALK (treas. 1983-98), Common Cause of S.C. (dir. 1988-2000, sec. 1989-96), Exec. Club Columbia (pres. 1960-61), Kiwanis (pres. 1986-87), Omicron Delta Kappa (faculty adviser 1968-71), Pi Gamma Mu, Phi Kappa Phi, Tau Kappa Alpha. Achievements include research on the teaching of religion in accredited colleges and universities. Home: 10450 Lottsford Rd Apt 4207 Mitchellville MD 20721-2752

BRUBAKER, ROBERT LORING, lawyer; b. Louisville, May 22, 1947; s. Robert Lee and Betty (Brock) B.; m Jeannette Marie Montgomery, Dec. 21, 1968; children: Benjamin Brock, Anne Montgomery. BA, Earlham Coll., 1969; JD, U. Chgo., 1972. Bar: Ohio 1972, U.S. Dist. Ct. (so. dist.) Ohio 1973, U.S. Ct. Appeals (6th cir.) 1975, U.S. Supreme Ct. 1978, U.S. Ct. Appeals (D.C. cir.) 1979, U.S. Ct. Appeals (3d, 4th and 7th cirs.) 1995. Asst. atty. gen. Atty. Gen.'s Office State of Ohio, Columbus, 1972-76; assoc. Porter Wright Morris & Arthur, Columbus, 1976-78, ptnr., 1979—. Editor: Ohio Environmental Law Handbook, 1990, 2d edit., 1992, 3d edit., 1994, Deposition Strategy, Law and Forms: Environmental Law. Mem. ABA (natural resources, energy and environ. law sect., pub. utility sect.), Ohio Bar Assn. (environ. law com.), Air and Waste Mgmt. Assn. (chmn. S.W. Ohio chpt. 1990-91, chmn. East Ctrl. sect. 1991-92), Columbus Bar Assn. (environ. law com.), Nat. Coal Coun. Home: 2661 Wexford Rd Columbus OH 43221-3217 Office: Porter Wright Morris & Arthur 41 S High St Ste 2800 Columbus OH 43215-6194 E-mail: rbrubaker@porterwright.com.

BRUBAKER, ROBERT PAUL, food products executive; b. Sturgis, Mich., Oct. 6, 1934; s. Leland C. and Ruth (Cunningham) Brubaker; m. Carol Cowart Highsmith, Nov. 14, 1998; children: Susan, Beverly, Thomas. BA, Mich. State U., 1956. With product mgmt. Gen. Foods Corp., White Plains, NY, 1959-67; exec. v.p. King Shrimp Co. Inc., Brunswick, Ga., 1967-80; pres. King & Prince Seafood Corp. (formerly King Shrimp Co. Inc.), Brunswick, Ga., 1980—2002, CEO, 1993—, chmn., 1995—. Bd. dirs. United Way, Brunswick, 1985—; organizing sponsor No is OK Youth Group, Brunswick, 1984—85. Lt. USAF, 1956—59. Mem.: Am. Frozen Food Inst. (bd. dirs., exec. com. 1998—2000, chmn. bd. dirs. 2002—), Nat. Fisheries Inst. (regional v.p. 1981—82, dir., sec. 1982—86, v.p., pres., chmn. 1986—89), Nat. Shrimp Breaders and Processors Assn. (pres., chmn. 1979—83), Soc. Internat. Bus. Fellows, Brunswick C. of C. (v.p. edn., dir. 1985—86, 1988—89, 1994—95), Ocean Forest Golf Club, Sea Island Golf Club, Rotary. Republican. Presbyterian. Avocations: golf, travel. Home: 206 Settlers Rd Saint Simons GA 31522-1925 Office: King & Prince Seafood Corp PO Box 899 1 King And Prince Blvd Brunswick GA 31520-8668

BRUBAKER, WILLIAM ROGERS, sociology educator; b. Evanston, Ill., June 8, 1956; s. Charles William and Elizabeth (Rogers) B. BA summa cum laude, Harvard U., 1979; MA, Sussex U., Eng., 1980; PhD, Columbia U., 1990. Prof. UCLA, 1994—, assoc. prof. sociology, 1991-94. Author: The Limits of Rationality, 1984, Citizenship and Nationhood in France and Germany, 1992, Nationalism Reframed, 1996; editor: Immigration and Politics of Citizenship in Europe and North America, 1989. Jr. fellow Soc. Fellows Harvard U., 1988-91; MacArthur fellow, 1994-99; NSF Young Investigator awardee; Guggenheim fellow, 1999-2000. Office: U Calif Dept Los Angeles Dept of Sociology 264 Haines Hall Los Angeles CA 90095

BRUBECK, DAVID WARREN, musician; b. Concord, Calif., Dec. 6, 1920; s. Howard and Elizabeth (Ivey) Brubeck; m. Iola Whitlock, Sept. 21, 1942; children: David Darius, Michael, Christopher, Catherine, Daniel, Matthew. MusB, U. Pacific, 1942; postgrad. study with Darius Milhaud, Mills Coll., 1946-49; PhD (hon.), U. Pacific, Fairfield U., U. Bridgeport, Mills Coll., Niagara U., Kalamazoo Coll., U. Duisburg, Germany, U. Nottingham, England, Cleve. Inst. Music. Leader Dave Brubeck Octet, Trio and Quartet, 1946—, 3 month tour Europe and Middle East for U.S. Dept. State, followed by tours Australia, Japan, and USSR, recordings with Atlantic Record Co., Columbia Record Co., Decca, Horizon, Concord Jazz, Fantasy Records, Music Masters, GRP, Telarc Records, Time Out (1st jazz LP to receive Gold Record); composer: (ballets) Points on Jazz, Glances, (orchestral) Elementals, They All Sang Yankee Doodle, (flute and guitar) Tritonis, (piano) Reminiscences of the Cattle Country, Four by Four, Chromatic Fantasy Sonata, (oratorios) Beloved Son, The Light in the Wilderness, Voice of the Holy Spirit, (cantatas) Gates of Justice, Truth Is Fallen, La Fiesta de la Posada, (chorus and orchestra) Pange Lingua, Mass: To Hope, I See, Satie, Four New England Pieces, Lenten Triptych, In Praise of Mary, Joy in the Morning, (choral) Earth Is Our Mother, and over 100 jazz compositions including Blue Rondo a la Turk, In Your Own Sweet Way, The Duke. Named to Hollywood Walk of Fame, 1994, Nat. Medal of the Arts, 1994, Am. Jazz Hall of Fame, 1995; recipient jazz polls conducted by Downbeat, Melody Maker, Cashbox, Billboard and Playboy mags., 1952—55, first jazz musician on cover of Time Mag., 1954, B.M.I. Jazz Pioneer award, 1985, Compostela Humanitarian award, 1986, Conn. Arts award, 1987, Am. Eagle award Nat. Music Coun., 1988, Ct. Bar Assn. award, 1992, Simon's Rock Disting. Achievement, 1992, Lifetime Achievement award NARAS, 1996, NEA Jazz Master award; Duke Ellington fellow Yale U., 1992. Mem.: Phi Mu Alpha. Office: Derry Music Co 1299 4th St Ste 409 San Rafael CA 94901-3030 also: care Sutton Artists Corp 20 W Park Ave Ste 305 Long Beach NY 11561-2019*

BRUCCOLI, MATTHEW JOSEPH, English educator, publisher; b. N.Y.C., Aug. 21, 1931; s. Joseph M. and Mary (Gervasi) B.; m. Arlyn Shuey Firkins, Oct. 5, 1957; children: Mary Firkins, Joseph Matthew, Josephine Arlyn, Arlyn Barbara. BA, Yale U., 1953; MA, U. Va., 1956, PhD, 1961. Prof. English U. S.C., Columbia, 1969—, Jefferies prof. English, 1976—. Dir. Ctr. for Edits. of Am. Authors, 1969-76; pres. Bruccoli Clark Layman, Pubs., 1976—, Manly Inc., 1981—. Author: The Composition of Tender Is the Night, 1963, The Last of the Novelists, 1977, The O'Hara Concern, 1975, Scott and Ernest, 1978, Some Sort of Epic Grandeur: The Life of F. Scott Fitzgerald, 1981, James Gould Cozzens, 1983, Ross Macdonald, 1984, The Fortunes of Mitchell Kennerley, Bookman, 1986, F. Scott Fitzgerald and Hemingway, 1994, Reader's Companion to Tender Is the Night, 1996; editor: Fitzgerald/Hemingway Annual, 1969-70; series editor Dictionary of Literary Biography, 1978—, Lost Am. Fiction, 1972-80, Pittsburgh Series in Bibliography, 1971—, Selected Letters of John O'Hara, 1978, Just Representations: A James Gould Cozzens Reader, 1978, Correspondence of F. Scott Fitzgerald, 1980, Understanding Contemporary American Literature, 1985—, Understanding Contemporary British Literature, 1989—, The Cambridge Edition of the Works of F. Scott Fitzgerald, 1991-93, Zelda Fitzgerald The Collected Writings, 1991, F. Scott Fitzgerald A Life in Letters, 1994, F. Scott Fitzgerald's Tender Is the Night, 1995, F. Scott Fitzgerald on Authorship, 1996, The Only Thing that Counts, 1996, American Expatriate Writers: Paris in the Twenties, 1997, (with A. Bruccoli) Thomas Wolfe's O Lost, 2000, (with P. Bucker) To Loot My Life Clean, 2000, Classes on F. Scott Fitzgerald, 2001, Classes on Ernest Hemingway, 2002. Recipient Thomas Cooper medal, 1999; fellow, Guggenheim Found., 1973. Mem.: S.C. Acad. Authors, Palmetto Club, Yale Club. Home: 31 Heathwood Cir Columbia SC 29205-1946 Office: U SC Dept English Columbia SC 29208-0001

BRUCE, BRENDA, pianist; b. Nov. 26, 1942; d. Leo Allen and Dorotha Mae (Russell) Bruce; m. Emmett W. Windham, Feb. 21, 1976 (div. Aug. 1988); m. Alvin Mark Fountain II, June, 2003. BMusic Edn., Ctrl. Meth. Coll., Fayette, Mo., 1964; MMus, New Eng. Conservatory, Boston, 1966; student piano master class, Claude Debussy Conservatory, St. Malo, France, 2000-01. Mem. faculty Dana Sch. Music, Wellesley, Mass., 1965-76, Campbell U., Buies Creek, N.C., 1977-79, Meredith Coll., Raleigh, N.C., 1979-90; pianist SAS Inst., Cary, NC, 1989—2001. Mem. adv. bd. Capitol Area Cmty. Chorus, Raleigh, 1999—; participant Master Class Pro Musica, St. Malo, France, 2000, 01. Performer, recitalist, 1964—, montage and piano, flute duo, 1992. Emerging Artists grantee City of Raleigh, 1992, Emerging Artists grantee United Arts, 1995, State Arts Coun. grnatee, 1995—, regional artists grantee, 1999-2001, NCMTA grantee. Mem. Nat. Music Tchrs. Assn., Nat. Guild of Piano, Raleigh Piano Tchrs. Assn., Cary-Apex Piano Tchrs. Assn.; Pi Kappa Lampda. Methodist. Avocations: bicycling, travel. Home: 101 Barbary Ct Cary NC 27511-5862 E-mail: brendabruce@mindspring.com.

BRUCE, DANA GLENN, lawyer; b. Peoria, Ill., June 16, 1958; s. Glenn D. and Kathleen M. Bruce; m. Jeanne L. Foster, July 9, 1994; children: Joey Wallish, Jami Wallish, Josh Wallish, Jeremy Wallish. BA, Oral Roberts U., 1980; MDiv, So. Meth. U., 1984, JD, 1987. Intern min. Trinity United Meth. Ch., San Antonio, 1983; min. White Rock United Meth. Ch., Dallas, 1983-84; law clk. Gibson, Dunn & Crutcher, Dallas, 1985-87, atty., 1987-93, Pryor & Bruce, Dallas, 1994—. Rancher, horse breeder Rising Star Ranch, Quinlan, Tex., 1995—. Notes and comment editor Jour. Air Law and Commerce, 1986-87; patentee solar Powered Christmas Lights, 1999. Republican. Methodist. Avocations: horseback riding, fishing, tennis. Home: Rising Star Ranch 6821 Dry Creek Rd Quinlan TX 75474 Office: Pryor & Bruce 302 N San Jacinto St Rockwall TX 75087-2555

BRUCE, DANIA GAYLE, interior decorator; b. Morristown, Tenn., Mar. 4, 1937; d. Fred W. and Katye (Jones) Hartman; m. Paul Love Bruce, 1961; children: Paula Ann Combs, John Richard, Ronald Powell. Student, Draughon's Bus. Coll., Knoxville, Tenn., 1957. Interior decorator, Morristown, Tenn., 1961—. Life mem. Witt PTA of Hemblen County, Morristown, 1981; pres. Jr. Reading Cir., Morristown, 1971-72; 2d v.p. Ladies Reading Cir., Morristown, 1989; bd. dirs., mem. exec. com. Holston Home for Children; trustee Morristown dist. United Meth. Ch.; mem. Hamblen County Election Commn., 2001-02. Mem. Beta Sigma Phi (first lady of Morristown 1972). Democrat. Methodist. Avocation: sports. Home: 865 Rouse Rd Morristown TN 37813-3952

BRUCE, DAVID LIONEL, retired anesthesiologist, educator; b. Champaign, Ill., Oct. 27, 1933; s. Lionel Harry and Freda Eleanor (Tipsword) B.; m. Geraldine Zawasky, Nov. 24, 1956 (div. 1967); children: Ellen Marie, Brian David; m. Sharon Jean Wells, Jan. 18, 1985. Student, U. Ill., 1951-54, MD, 1960. Diplomate Am. Bd. Anesthesiology. Intern Ill. Rsch. and Ednl. Hosp., Chgo., 1960-61; resident U. Pa., Phila., 1961-64; asst. prof. anesthesiology U. Ky. Med. Ctr., Lexington, 1964-66; from asst. prof. to prof. Northwestern U. Med. Sch., Chgo., 1966-77; prof. U. Calif., Irvine, 1977-81; prof. anesthesiology NYU Med. Sch., 1981-84; prof. U. Miss. Med. Ctr., Jackson, 1984-90, chmn. dept., 1985-90; dir. outpatient surgery Athens (Ga.) Regional Med. Cr., 1990-92; prof. anesthesiology U. South Fla., Tampa Gen. Hosp., 1992-93; med. dir. surg. svcs. Tampa Gen. Hosp., 1993; med. dir. outpatient surgery ctr. Athens (Ga.) Regional Med. Ctr., 1993-95. Cons. FDA, Rockville, Md., 1972-75, mem. adv. com., Bethesda, Md., 1973-77. Author: Klaus and Max: Their Friendship Defied Hitler, 2000; contbr. numerous articles to profl. jours. Cpl. U.S. Army, 1954-56. Recipient Rsch. Career Devel. award USPHS, 1967-72 Fellow Royal Soc. Medicine (Eng.) (travelling fellow 1975); mem. Am. Soc. Anesthesiologists. Avocations: music, writing.

BRUCE, DEBRA, poet, English language educator; b. Bristol, Conn., Apr. 4, 1951; d. Willard Arthur Bruce and Mary Elizabeth Conlin; m. Rick Kinnebrew, Aug. 21, 1981; 1 child, Kevin Kinnebrew. BA summa cum laude, U. Mass., 1974; MA, Brown U., 1976; MFA, U. Iowa, 1978. Instr. English Old Dominion U., Norfolk, Va., 1978-84; prof. English Northeastern Ill. U., Chgo., 1984—. Author: (books of poetry) Pure Daughter, 1983, Sudden Hunger, 1988, What Wind Will Do, 1997, (chapbook) Dissolves, 1977; contbr. poetry to anthologies including A Century in Two Decades, Naming the Daytime Moon, The Virago Book of Wicked Press, also mags. Creative writing fellow NEA, 1982, scriptwriting fellow, 1982, creative writing fellow Ill. Arts Coun., 1986, 99, Carl Sandburg Poetry award Chgo. Pub. Libr., 1989; recipient George Kent prize Poetry mag., 1999. Mem. Acad. Am. Poets, Associated Writing Programs, Poetry Soc. Am. (Gustave Davidson award 1989). E-mail: d-bruce-kinnebrew@neiu.edu.

BRUCE, DICKSON DAVIES, JR., history educator; b. Dallas, Apr. 11, 1946; s. Dickson Davies and Helen (Woodcock) B.; m. Mary Macreeda Watson, Sept. 28, 1967; 1 child, Emily Sarah. BA, U. Tex., 1967; MA, U. Pa., Phila., 1968, PhD, 1971. Prof. history U. Calif., Irvine, 1971—. Author: And They All Sang Hallelujah, 1974, Violence and Culture in the Antebellum South, 1979, The Rhetoric of Conservatism, 1982, Black Writing From the Nadir, 1989, Archibald Grimké, 1993, The Origins of African American Literature, 2001. Recipient James Mooney award So. Anthropol. Soc., 1973, Huntington Libr. Fellowship, San Marino, Calif., 1975, Fulbright Lectureship USIA, Szeged, Hungary, 1987-88. Mem. Orgn. Am. Historians, Soc. Historians of Early Am. Republic, So. Hist. Assn., Hist. Soc. Democrat.

BRUCE, DUNCAN ARCHIBALD, investor, writer; b. Pitts., Feb. 19, 1932; s. Archibald Duncan Bruce and Marian Colley; m. Tamara Bruce, Dec. 4, 1965; children: Jennifer, Elizabeth. BS in Econs., U. Pa., 1954. Pres. Edgewood Holdings, Inc., N.Y.C., 1989—2002, Normandie Holdings, Ltd., N.Y.C., 1996—. Author: (book) The Mark of the Scots, 1996, The Scottish 100, 2000, King Arthur Revisited, 2001. Hon. chieftan Bonnie Brae Scottish Games, Millington, NJ, 1990. Recipient Ellis Island medal of honor, Nat. Ethnic Coalition Orgns., 1998, Odom Heritage award, Scottish Weekend, 2002, Nat. Tartan Day award, Scottish Coalition, 2003. Fellow: Soc. Antiquaries Scotland; mem.: Caledonian Found., Burns Soc. City of N.Y. (trustee), Scottish Heritage USA (past bd. dirs.), St. Andrew's Soc. N.Y. (past historian, past bd. mgrs., 1st v.p., chmn. 250th ann. com., mem. exec. com.), Am. Scottish Found. (past bd. dirs., past treas., past v.p., hon. sponsoring com.), Mask and Wig Club, An Ceud Fear. Home: 185 E 85th St Apt 35D New York NY 10028-2150

BRUCE, ERIKA LYNN, lawyer; b. Dallas, Sept. 17, 1969; BA in Polit. Sci., Washington U., St. Louis, 1992; JD, St. Mary's U., San Antonio, 1995. Bar: Tex. 1995. Atty. Law Office of Helene S. Cohen, Dallas, 1995-97, Donohoe, Jameson & Carroll, P.C., Dallas, 1997—. Editor St. Mary's Law Jour., 1994-95. Bd. dirs. Hebrew Free Loan Assn., Dallas, 1995—. Mem. ABA, Tex. State Bar Assn., Dallas Bar Assn. (cmty. outreach program). Avocations: marathon running, music, hiking, movies, books. Office: Donohoe Jameson & Carroll PC 3400 Renaissance Tower 1201 Elm St Dallas TX 75270-2102

BRUCE, E(STEL) EDWARD, lawyer; b. Hutchinson, Kans., Nov. 23, 1938; s. Kenneth Dean and Josephine (Vigna) B.; m. Marnell Elaine Higley, Aug. 9, 1960; children: Anthony Dean, Caroline Bruce Macaulay. BA summa cum laude, Yale U., 1960, LLB magna cum laude, 1966. Bar: D.C. 1967, U.S. Ct. Appeals (1st, 2d, 3d, 4th, 5th, 6th, 8th, 9th, 10th, 11th, D.C. and Fed. cirs.), U.S. Supreme Ct. Law clk. U.S. Supreme Ct., Washington, 1966-67; assoc. Covington & Burling, Washington, 1967-73, ptnr., 1973—; adj. prof. constitutional law Georgetown U. Law Center, 1970-75. Mem. Appellate Judges Conf., Com. on Appellate Practice, 1993-2000; mem. faculty ABA Appellate Inst., 1992-2000. Mem. adminstrv. bd. Cornell Lab. Ornithology, 1998—; bd. dirs. Young Concert Artists, 2003—, Washington Area Lawyers for the Arts, 1993-99, Yale Law Sch. Fund, 1992-98, Audubon Nat. Soc., 1986-92. Lt. jg. USN, 1960—63. Mem.: ABA, Edward Coke Appellate Inn of Ct. (v.p. 2000—02, pres. 2002—03), D.C. Bar Assn., Am. Acad. Appellate, Am. Law Inst., Chevy Chase Club, Met. Club, Phi Beta Kappa, Order of Coif. Home: 2701 Foxhall Rd NW Washington DC 20007-1128 Office: Covington & Burling 1201 Pennsylvania Ave NW Washington DC 20004-2401

BRUCE, ISAAC ISIDORE, football player; b. Ft. Lauderdale, Florida, Nov. 10, 1972; Postgrad in phys. edn., Memphis State, 1992. Winner Super Bowl 35, 2000; wide receiver St. Louis Rams, 1995—, L.A. Rams, 1994—95. Bd. dirs. Childhaven; donator children orgn., homeless. Recipient Daniel F. Reeves Memorial award, 1996, Carroll Rosenbloom award, 1994. Achievements include first Rams receiver to earn consecutive Pro Bowl invitations; ranked fifth in NFL's all-time single season reception list; first player in history to record three consecutive games with at least 170 receiving yards. Office: 1 Rams Way Saint Louis MO 63045

BRUCE, JACKSON MARTIN, JR., lawyer; b. Milw., Apr. 10, 1931; s. Jackson Martin and Harriet (Edgell) B.; m. Lilias M. Morehouse, June 30, 1954; children: Lilias Stephanie, Andrew Edgell. AB magna cum laude, Harvard U., 1953, JD cum laude, 1957; MA with 1st class honors in Law, Cambridge U., 1955. Bar: Wis. 1957, Fla. 1973. Assoc. Quarles & Brady, Milw., 1957-64, ptnr., 1964-96; shareholder Dunwody, White & Landon, Naples, Fla., 1996—; counsel Michael Best & Friedrich, Milw., 1996—. Mem. joint editl. bd. Uniform Trusts and Estates Acts; contbr. articles to profl. jours. Bd. dirs. Living Ch. Found., Inc., 1965-98; trustee Univ. Sch. Milw., 1973-79. Fellow Am. Coll. Trust and Estate Counsel (bd. regents 1976-82, treas. 1990-91, sec. 1991-92, v.p. 1992-93, pres. 1994-95); mem. ABA (bd. govs. 1994-97, chmn. sect. real property, probate and trust law 1984-85, ho. dels. 1988-97, ethics com. 1998-2001), State Bar Wis. (chmn. bd. govs. 1979-80), Am. Bar Found., Am. Law Inst., Internat. Acad. Estate and Trust Law (mem. exec. coun. 1980-86), Nat. Conf. Bar Pres., Nat. Conf. Lawyers and Corp. Fiduciaries (chmn. 1984-90), Town Club, Milw. Club (bd. dirs. 1985-2001), The Club Pelican Bay. Home: 6101 Pelican Bay Blvd Apt 1201 Naples FL 34108-8183 also: 9008 N Bayside Dr Milwaukee WI 53217-1913 Office: Dunwody White & Landon 4001 Tamiami Trl N Ste 200 Naples FL 34103-3591 also: Michael Best & Friedrich 100 E Wisconsin Ave Ste 3300 Milwaukee WI 53202-4107 Business E-Mail: jbruce@dwl-law.com, jmbruce@mbf-law.com.

BRUCE, JAMES DONALD, academic administrator; b. Livingston, Tex., June 28, 1936; s. Vivian Eugene and Edna Lee (St. Clair) B.; m. Eleanor MacLaren, Nov. 25, 1959; children: David MacLaren, Heather MacLaren, Nathaniel MacLaren. BSEE, BS in Math., Lamar State Coll. Tech., Beaumont, Tex., 1958; SMEE, MIT, 1960, ScD, 1964. Mem. faculty MIT, Cambridge, 1964—, assoc. dean engring., 1971-78, dean, 1977-78, prof. elec. engring., 1973—, dir. indsl. liaison, 1979-82, dir. info. sys., 1983-86, v.p. for info. sys., chief info. officer, 1986—, program mgr. reengring adminstrv. process, 1994-98. Found. New Eng. Acad. and Rsch. Network (NEARnet), 1988—95, mem. steering com., 1988—95; bd. dirs. BBN Tech. Svcs., Inc., 1993—95; mem. network planning and policy adv. coun., Univ. Corp. for Advanced Internet Devel. (UCAID), 1998—2002, chmn. network planning and policy adv. coun., 1999—2002, mem. bd. trustees, 1999—; cons. to govt. and industry; mem. adv. com. elec. engring. Lamar U., 1993—; mem. tech. adv. com. Mass. Divsn. Capital Planning and Ops., 1993—95; mem. total quality edn. com. to sec. edn. Commonwealth of Mass., 1993—95; founder Marketplace Network, Inc., bd. dirs. Trustee Harvard Coop. Soc., 1974-84, 93-96; trustee Park St. Congrl. Ch., Boston, 1977-83, vice chmn. bd. trustees, 1979-81, chmn., 1981-83, deacon, 1985-96, elder, 1997-99, moderator-elect, 2003. Postdoctoral fellow, Ford Found., 1964—65. Sr. mem. IEEE; mem. Am. Soc. Engring. Edn., Consortium for Sci. Computing (trustee, mem. exec. com., 1984-90, vice chmn. 1986-88), Eta Kappa Nu, Tau Beta Pi. Home: 12 Woodpark Cir Lexington MA 02421-7208 Office: MIT 77 Massachusetts Ave Rm 10-219 Cambridge MA 02139-4307 E-mail: jdb@mit.edu.

BRUCE, JAMES EDMUND, retired utility company executive; b. Boise, Idaho, June 23, 1920; s. James E. and Bessie (Barcus) B.; m. Lois I. Stevens, Aug. 24, 1946; children: James E., IV, Steven, Robert, David. Student, Coll. Idaho, 1937-39; BA, Portland U., 1941; postgrad., Georgetown U., 1941-42; LLB, U. Idaho, 1949. Bar: Idaho 1948. Asst. atty. gen. State of Idaho, 1948-49; dep. pros. atty. Ada County, Idaho, 1949-51; with Idaho Power Co., Boise, 1951-87, v.p., 1968-74, pres., chief operating officer, 1974-76, pres., chief exec. officer, 1976-85, chmn., 1985-87, ret., 1987. Dir. Albertson's Inc., First Security Corp., 1981-93; chmn. Blue Cross of Idaho, 1988-90. Bd. dirs. Mountain States Legal Found., 1977-88; mem. St. Alphonsus Found., Boise State U. Found., Bishop Kelly Found., Boise Park Bd., 1958-78; chmn. Idaho State Lottery; Idaho chmn. U.S. Savs. Bonds, 1976-85; chmn. bd. trustees St. Alphonsus, 1985-2002; trustee Coll. Idaho, YMCA, Idaho Nature Conservancy; pres. Ada County Hwy. Dist. Commn. With U.S. Army, 1942-46. Mem. ABA, Boise Execs. Assn., Edison Electric Assn. (dir. 1978-85), N.W. Electric Light and Power Assn. (pres. 1982), Boise C. of C., Arid Club, Crane Creek Country Club, Rotary, Elks, K.C. Roman Catholic.

BRUCE, JEFFREY NEIL, neurosurgeon; b. Plainfield, N.J., July 18, 1956; s. Thomas Edward and Olga Mildred (Kmosko) B.; m. Rebecca Jo Hulshizer, Aug. 8, 1981; children: Zachary Thomas, Samuel Stanford, Rachel Anne, Eliza Mille. BA, U. Va., 1978; MD, Robert Wood Johnson Med. Sch., 1983. Diplomate Am. Bd. Neurol. Surgery. Resident in neurosurgery Columbia Presbyn. Med. Ctr., N.Y.C., 1985-90; med. staff fellow NIH, Bethesda, Md., 1984-85; asst. prof. Columbia U., N.Y.C., 1990-96, assoc. prof. neurosurgery, 1996—2002, prof. neurol. surgery, 2002—. Dir. Bartoli Brain Tumor Lab., Columbia U., N.Y.C., 1990—; dir. neuro-oncology Columbia Presbyn. Cancer Ctr., N.Y.C., 1992—; pres. N.Y. Soc. for Neurosurgery, 1998—2001. Mem. editl. bd.: Neurosurgery, 1997, Jour. Radiosurgery, 1997—, Current Surgery, 2000—. Brain Tumor Rsch. fellowship Assn. of Brain Tumor Rsch., 1990-92; recipient Nat. Brain Tumor Found. Rsch. award Nat. Brain Tumor Found., 1996. Fellow: ACS; mem.: Am. Assn. Neurol. Surgeons/Congress Neurol Surgeons (exec. bd. joint sect. on tumors 2000—), Am. Brain Tumor Assn. (sci. adv. coun. 2000—), The Pituitary Soc., Am. Assn. Neurol. Surgeons, N.Am. Skull Base Soc., Congress Neurol. Surgeons, Am. Soc. for Clin. Oncology, N.Am. Soc. for Neuro-oncology. Avocation: music. Office: Neurol Inst Columbia U Rm 434 710 W 168th St New York NY 10032-2603

BRUCE, JOHN ALLEN, foundation executive, educator; b. Kansas City, Mo., Sept. 17, 1934; BA, Wesleyan U., Middletown, Conn., 1956; MDiv., Gen. Theol. Sem., N.Y.C., 1959; PhD, U. Minn., 1972. Ordained to ministry Episcopal Ch., 1959. Clergyman, 1959-68; prof. U. Ala., Tuscaloosa, 1972-74; exec. dir. E.C. Brown Found., Portland, Oreg., 1974-98. Cons. to philanthropies and corp. programs; clin. prof. community medicine Sch. Medicine, Oreg. Health Scis. U., Portland, 1976-01. Author, editor various scholarly publs.; exec. prodr. ednl. films on family life, health and values. Bd. dirs., officer various cmty. orgns. Served to lt. USN, 1964-67. Recipient awards from med. orgns. and related groups. Mem. Cosmos Club. Republica. Home: 10678 SW Dogwood St Tualatin OR 97062

BRUCE, JUDITH ESTHER, retired music educator, elementary education educator; b. St. Louis, Oct. 16, 1945; d. Charles Edward and Helen Ruth (Yost) Poleos; m. Roy N. Bruce; children: Rory, Robert, Joshua. BS in Edn., Southeast Mo. State U., Cape Girardeau, 1967; MA in Theatre, Lindenwood U., 1992, MFA in Theatre, 1994. Vocal music tchr. Berkeley (Mo.) Elem. Schs., 1967-77, DeSmet Elem. Sch., Florissant, Mo., 1977-85; vocal and MIE Yamaha tchr. Walnut Grove Elem. Sch., Ferguson, Mo., 1985—2002. Talent cmn., benefit charity shows, Christian Hosp. Aux., St. Louis, 1977— Recipient Hall of Fame award, St. Louis Suburban Music Educators Assn., 2002—03. Mem.: St. Louis Suburban Music Educators Assn., Music Educators Nat. Conf., St. Louis Suburban Music Edc. Assn. (Hall of Fame award 2002—03, 2002—03), Ferguson-Florissant Cmty. Tchrs. Assn., Mo. State Tchrs. Assn. (treas. Ferguson-Florissant dist. chpt. 1967—2002), Raintree Arts Coun. of Lincoln and Pike Counties, White Shrine. Home: 17534 Highway NN Bowling Green MO 63334 E-mail: bruce12@accessus.net.

BRUCE, MELODY ANN, obstetrician-gynecologist; b. New Orleans, Apr. 26, 1953; d. John Markey and Irma Drusilla (Weisdorffer) B.; m. David Allan Ray, July 18, 1982; children: Isaac Michael Ray, Margaret Rose Ray, Arielle Elizabeth Ray. B.S., La. State U., Baton Rouge, 1975; M.D., La. State U.-New Orleans, 1978. Diplomate Am. Bd. Obstetrics and Gynecology. Intern, Albany (N.Y.) Med. Ctr., 1978-79, resident, 1979-81, chief resident, 1981-82; teaching cons. Kasturba Med. Coll., Manipal, Karnataka, India, 1982; practice medicine specializing in ob-gyn, Troy, N.Y., 1982—; asst. clin. instr. dept. ob-gyn Albany Med. Ctr., 1982-83; co-developer Capital Dist. Birthing Ctr., Troy, N.Y., 1983-84; mem. med. adv. bd. Planned Parenthood, Upper Hudson Valley, N.Y. State, 1994—; chief dept. ob/gyn Samaritan Hosp., 1996—, pres. med. staff, 1997; med. dir. women health svcs., Northeast Health, 1997—. Chmn. fund raising Saratoga County Teen Clinic, Clifton Park, N.Y., 1983; mem. adv. bd. Saratoga County Teen Clinic, Clifton Park, 1984; chmn. adult edn. B'nai Sholom Synagogue, Albany, 1984-85; bd. dirs. Albany Symphony Orch.,

1995—. Named Outstanding Young Woman of Am., Albany, 1980; Outstanding Woman Resident Am. Med. Women's Assn., Albany Med. Ctr., 1981. Fellow Am. Coll. Obstetricians/Gynecologists; mem. AMA, N.Y. State Med. Soc., Rensselaer County Med. Soc. Democrat. Home: 30 Brookside Ave Albany NY 12204-2217 Office: 2001 5th Ave Troy NY 12180-3340

BRUCE, PETER WAYNE, lawyer, insurance company executive; b. Rome, N.Y., July 12, 1945; s. G. Wayne and Helen A. (Hibling) B.; m. Joan M. McCabe, Sept. 20, 1969; children: Allison, Steven. BA, U. Wis., 1967; JD, U. Chgo., 1970; postgrad., Harvard Bus. Sch., 1986. Bar: Wis. 1970. Atty. Northwestern Mut. Life Ins. Co., Milw., 1970-74, asst. gen. counsel, 1974-80, gen. counsel, sec., 1980—, v.p., 1983-87, sr. v.p., gen. counsel, sec., 1987-90, sr. v.p. ins. ops., 1990-95, exec. v.p. ins. ops. & adminstrn., chief compliance officer, 1995-98, exec. v.p. accumulation products and long term care, 1998-2000, sr. exec. v.p. ins. ops. and long term care, 2000, sr. exec. v.p., 2000—. Bd. dirs. Northwestern Mut. Life Ins. Co., Milw., Northwestern Long-Term Care Ins. Co., Alverno Coll. Badger Meter Found., Growth Design Corp. Former chmn. Alverno Coll., Curative Rehab. Ctr., former mem. Shorewood Civic Improvement Found.; chair Milw. Archdiocese Resource Devel. Coun.; bd. dirs., chair Curative Found.; mem. Milw. Archdiocese Cath. Cmty. Found.; mem. Village of Shorewood (Wis.); mem. Village Shorewood Cmty. Devel. Assn., Wis. Equal Justice Fund; former mem. Planning and Devel. Commn. Mem. Wis. Bar Assn., Milw. Bar Assn., Am. Law Inst. Office: Northwestern Mut Life Ins Co 720 E Wisconsin Ave Milwaukee WI 53202-4703

BRUCE, RACHEL MARY CONDON, retired nurse practitioner; b. Bklyn., Dec. 18, 1940; d. Bernard Francis Sr. and Rachel Evelyn (Riggott) Condon; m. Donald Eugene Bruce, Sept. 27, 1966; children: Donald Eugene, Kevin Francis(dec.), Rachel Janine. BSN, Molloy Cath. Coll., 1962; MEd in Counselor Edn., U. Guam, Mangilao, 1975; cert. sch. nurse practitioner, U. Colo., 1984, cert. pediatric nurse practitioner, 1985. RN, Tex.; cert. pediatric nurse practitioner. Asst. head nurse med.-surg. unit Bklyn. Hosp., 1962-64; med.-surg. nurse Guam Meml. Hosp., Tamuning, 1971-72; sch. health counselor IV, Dededo Jr. H.S., Dept. Edn., Guam, 1973-76; asst. prof. nursing U. Guam, Mangilao, 1976-80; vis. nurse Indiana (Pa.) Vis. Nuses Assn., 1980-81; instr. first responder Police Acad. Guam C.C., Mangilao, 1981-84, prof., sch. health counselor, nurse practitioner Student Health Ctr., 1982-94; ednl. health cons. Mangilao, 1994-96; ret., 1996. Asst. prof. tng. project Peace Corps, Tumon, Guam, summer 1978; part-time pediatric nurse practitioner Family Med. Clinic, Tamuning, 1988-90; mem. adv. com. preparing Guam Nurse Practice Act, Nurse Practitioner Task Force, 1985-87, mem. revision com., 1993-96; mem. com. on family planning Guam Health Objectives for 1990, 1986-87; mem. grant writing com. Fipse (drug awareness) Guam C.C., 1989-91; Guam C.C. rep. to CEO's Task Force on Health Issues, 1989-90; lic. ednl. cons. sch. health, pediatrics, adolescent health and teen pregnancy. Co-author: (booklet) Growing Together, 1987, (revised) Growing Together, 1995. CPR instr. ARC, Guam, 1978-81; BCLS instr. Guam Heart Assn., 1981-84; vol. sexual assault counselor Counseling Advs. Reaching Out, Guam, 1982-84; founding bd. mem., co-vice chair Guam Arthritis Found., 1989; alto Guam Symphony Chorale, 1987-95, Montgomery County Chorale Soc., 2003—; sponsor Houston Symphony Soc., 1997—; vol. Cynthia Woods Mitchell Pavilion, Woodlands, Tex., 1997—. 1st lt. USAF Nurse Corps, 1964-66. Recipient proclomation for outstanding svc. in nursing Guam Legislature, 1988, award for outstanding profl. and cmty. svc., 1989, Governor's merit award for distinguished performance, 1987, 1992. Mem. ANA (nat. disting. svc. register 1988), AAUW (past pub. rels. officer, pub. pol. chair, 1998, v.p. programs 1999-2000, v.p. membership 2000-01), Tex. Nurses Assn., Nat. Assn. Sch. Nurses, Tex. Assn. Sch. Nurses, Am. Acad. Nurse Practitioners, Internat. Reading Assn. (grantee 1992), People to People Internat. (sch. health del. to Ea. Europe 1994), scuba diving team Kosrae Reef Preservation Project, 1998. Roman Catholic. Avocations: scuba diving, travel, gardening, reading. Home: 11 Timber Ln Conroe TX 77384-3159 E-mail: rachelbruce@txucom.net.

BRUCE, ROBERT DENTON, lawyer; b. Houston, Tex., Jan. 29, 1943; s. Simeon Kelley and Lucy Jane B.; m. Norma Gene Durant, June 5, 1965; children: Denton, Jennifer, Stuart. BBA, U. Tex., 1966; JD, St. Mary's U., San Antonio, 1972. Bar: Tex. 1972. Pvt. practice, Mineola, Tex., 1972—. City atty., Mineola, 1976—77, Alba, Tex., 1981—, Yantis, Tex., 2002—. Trustee sch. bd. Mineola Ind. Sch. Dist., 1976-82; pres. Mineola Indsl. Found., 1980-2000, adminstrv. bd. Meth. Ch., Mineola, 1978-80. With USNR, 1960-70. Avocations: tennis, reading, hunting. Office: PO Box 266 Mineola TX 75773-0266 E-mail: wctc@lcii.net.

BRUCE, ROBERT JAMES, retired academic administrator; b. Aug. 12, 1937; s. Andrew Carson and Ruth Lillian (Barr) B.; m. Judith Ann Garland, Aug. 29, 1959; children: Kimberley Bruce Campbell, Scott Garland. AB, Colby Coll., 1959; MA, U. Mass., Boston, 1964; postgrad., Boston U., 1964; LHD (hon.), Widener U., 1992, Wilkes U., 2001, Holy Family Coll., 2001. Devel. officer Colby Coll., Waterville, Maine, 1965-70; v.p. Bard Coll., Annandale-on-Hudson, N.Y., 1970-74, acting pres., 1974; v.p. univ. rels. Clark U., Worcester, Mass., 1975; v.p. devel. Widener U., Chester, Pa., 1975-81, pres., 1981—2001, pres. emeritus, 2002—, also trustee. Lectr. Queen Anne's Coll., U.K., Chorley Tchrs. Coll., U.K.; instr. Colby Coll.; chmn. Crozer-Keystone Health System; chmn. Univ. Tech. Park; trustee Episcopal Acad. Trustee Episcopal Acad. Recipient Bard Coll. medal, 1975, Disting. Alumnus award Colby Coll., 1985, Liberty Bell award; Fulbright grantee U.K., 1964-65. Mem.: Assn. Ind. Colls. and Univs. (past chmn.), Pa. Assn. Colls. and Univs., Am. Assn. Higher Edn., Nat. Assn. Ind. Colls. and Univs. (past chmn. bd.), Am. Assn. Colls., St. Andrew's Soc. Pa., Castine Golf Club (Maine), Winter Harbor (Maine) Yacht Club, Union League (Phila.), Phi Kappa Phi. Episcopalian. Home: 670 Heatherton Lane West Chester PA 19380 Office: Widener U Office Pres Emeritus Chester PA 19013

BRUCE, ROBERT VANCE, historian, educator; b. Malden, Mass., Dec. 19, 1923; s. Robert Gilbert and Bernice Irene (May) B. Student, MIT, 1941-43; BS, U. N.H., 1945; MA, Boston U., 1947, PhD, 1953. Instr. U. Bridgeport, Conn., 1947-48; master Lawrence Acad., Groton, Mass., 1948-51; rsch. asst. to Benjamin P. Thomas, Washington, 1953-54; mem. faculty Boston U., 1955—, assoc. prof. history, 1960-66, prof., 1966-84, prof. emeritus, 1984—. Vis. prof. U. Wis., Madison, 1962-63. Author: Lincoln and the Tools of War, 3d edit., 1989, 1877, Year of Violence, 3d edit., 1989, Bell: Alexander Graham Bell and the Conquest of Solitude, 3d edit., 1995, Brit. edit., 1973, Japanese edit., 1991, Lincoln and the Riddle of Death, 1982, The Launching of Modern Am. Sci., 2d edit., 1988 (Pulitzer prize 1988); contbg. author: Lincoln the War President, 1992, Feeding Mars, 1993, War Comes Again, 1995, The Lincoln Enigma, 2001; contbr. articles to profl. jour. With AUS, 1943-46. Guggenheim fellow, 1957-58; Henry E. Huntington fellow, 1966; recipient Pulitzer Prize in history, 1988. Fellow AAAS, Soc. Am. Historians; mem. Orgn. Am. Historians (life mem.), AAAS, Lincoln Group of Boston (pres. 1969-74), Phi Beta Kappa. Democrat. Home: 3923 Westpark Ct NW Olympia WA 98502

BRUCE, TAMMY, writer, columnist; d. Robert Benson Bruce and Vera Louise Cooper. BA, U. of So. Calif., L.A., 2001. Talk show host KFI Radio, L.A., 1993—98; contbg. editor www.FrontPageMagazine.com, L.A., 2002—; columnist www.NewsMax.com, L.A., 2002—. Author: (nonfiction book) The New Thought Police: Inside the Left's Assault on Free Speech and Free Minds, 2001, The Death of Right and Wrong: Exposing the Left's Assault on Our Culture and Values, 2003. Mem.: NOW (pres. L.A. chpt. 1990—96, bd. dirs. 1992—94), Author's Guild. Populist. Deist. Avocations: reading, politics, film, history, travel. Personal E-mail: heytammybruce@yahoo.com.

BRUCE, THOMAS ALLEN, physician, educator; b. Mountain Home, Ark., Dec. 22, 1930; s. Rex Floyd and Dora Madeline (Fee) B.; m. Dolores Fay Montgomery, May 28, 1960; children: T.K. Montgomery, Dana Fee Thomas. BSM., MD, U. Ark., 1955, DSc (hon.), 1995. Intern Duke Hosp., 1956-57; resident medicine Bellevue Hosp., N.Y.C., 1957, Meml. Center Cancer and Allied Diseases, N.Y.C., 1958, Parkland Meml. Hosp., Dallas, 1958-59; cardiopulmonary trainee Southwestern Med. Sch. of U. Tex., 1959-60; cardiac research fellow Hammersmith Hosp. and U. London Postgrad. Med. Sch., London, 1960-61, Harvard Bus. Sch., 1974. From instr. to prof. medicine Wayne State U., 1961—68, also asst. dean Sch. Medicine; prof. medicine, head cardiovascular sect. U. Okla. Med. Ctr., 1968—74; prof. medicine, dean Coll. Medicine U. Ark. Med. Scis., 1974—85, emeritus prof., 1997—, dean pro tem Coll. Pub. Health, 2001—02, prof. health policy and mgmt., 2001—; dean pro tem U. Ark. Clinton Sch. Pub. Svc., 2003—; med. dir. Barton Rsch. Inst., 1974—85; coord. Sino-am. Med. Exch. Program, 1979—85; rsch. support rev. com. NIH, 1983—85; program dir. in health W.K. Kellogg Found., 1985—97; co-chair session 312 Salzburg Seminar, Austria; mem. History of Medicine Assocs.; nat. adv. bd. cmty. health leadership program Robert Wood Johnson Found.; policy adv. bd. Ark. Ctr. for Health Improvement; founding mem. MidSouth Leadership Alliance; chmn. bd. trustees Watershed Found.; adj. staff Ark. Cmty. Found.; chmn. bd. dirs. Heifer Project Internat. Bruce Soc. Am. Rsch. and publs. on cardiovascular disease including left ventricular function in cardiac denervation, coronary heart disease, myocardial metabolism relating to phospholipids in graded cardiac ischmia, med. edn. with particular reference to rural health care, health promotion and disease prevention, primary health care, community-based pub. health. Master gardener, chmn. garden docents, adj. staff Wildwood Park Performing Arts; exec. bd. Ark. Com. on Fgn. Rels.; bd. dirs. Garvan Woodland Gardens. Recipient Ark. Gov. Meritorious Achievement award, Lugene Chilcote award, 1999, Double Helix award, U. Ark. Med. Sci., 2001, Lucy Lockett Cabe award, Wildwood Park for the Performing Arts, 2001, cons., Mid-So. Delta Initiative, Little Rock Ctrl. High Mus. Appreciation award, 2001, Ark. Ctr. for Health (improvement award, 2002, Giving Tree Soc. award, 2003. Fellow: ACP, Am. Coll. Cardiology; mem.: AMA, APHA, Assn. Am. Med. Colls., Leila Arboretum Soc. (pres. 1989—92), Am. Rhododentron Soc., Ark. Caduceus Club, Alpha Omega Alpha, Sigma Xi. Home: 6 Spy Glass Ln Little Rock AR 72212-4418 E-mail: abruce@vams.edu.

BRUCE, THOMAS ALLEN, financial consultant; b. Richland, Ga., Apr. 3, 1959; s. Thomas Clinton and Betty Moss Bruce; m. Judi Vogt, Oct. 25, 1998. BA, LaGrange Coll., 1981; MPA, Auburn U., 1990. Delinquent tax collector Ga. Dept. Revenue, Atlanta, 1992-97, chief spl. procedures, 1997-99; fin. cons. Chantilly, Va./Ga., 1999—. High commr. (rep. for family of Bruce Matters), 1995—, The Right Hon. The Earl of Elgin and Kincardine, Knight of the Thistle, Chief of the Name of Bruce; officer Order of St. John, 1995-2002, comdr., 2002. Fellow Soc. of Antiquaries of Scotland; mem. Bruce Internat. (life mem., nat. pres., U.S. br. 1994-2000), Royal Order Scotland. Home: 1345 Velvet Creek Way Marietta GA 30008 E-mail: tabruce@bellsouth.net.

BRUCE, THOMAS EDWARD, psychology educator, thanatologist; b. Vinton, Iowa, Dec. 3, 1937; s. George Robert and Lucille Etta (Aurner) B.; children: Scott Thomas and Suzanne Laura. BA, U. No. Iowa, 1961, MA, 1964; postgrad., U. Colo., 1968-71; MA, U. San Francisco, 1985. Lic. psychology educator, counselor, Calif. Tchr. various Iowa high schs., 1961-65; sociologist, counselor Office Econ. Opportunity, Denver, 1965-66; social sci. educator Arapahoe Coll., Littleton, Colo., 1966-69; lectr. U. Colo., Boulder, 1968-71; psychology educator Sacramento City Coll., Calif., 1972—. Thanatology cons. for hospices, survivor support groups, No. Calif., 1984—. Author: Grief Management: The Pain and the Promise, 1986, Thanatology: Through the Veil, 1992; contbr. articles to profl. publs. Co-founder, bd. dirs. Bereavement Resources Network, Sacramento, 1983-87; profl. dir. Children's Respite Ctr., Sacramento, 1985-88; pres.-elect., bd. dirs. Hospice Care of Sacramento, 1979-85. With U.S. Army, 1955-58. Recipient Pres.'s award Nat. Hospice Orgn., 1985. Mem. Sacramento Mental Health Assn. (Vol. Svc. award 1985, 87), Assn. for Death Edn. and Counseling, Thanatology Found., Am. Fedn. Tchrs., Faculty Assn. Calif. C.C.'s, Pi Gamma Mu, Phi Delta Kappa. Avocations: music, visual arts, travel, reading. Office: Sacramento City Coll 3835 Freeport Blvd Sacramento CA 95822-1318

BRUCE, WILLIAM A. airport executive; BS in Polit. Sci., UCLA, 1967; MPA, Calif. State U., L.A., 1971. Budget analyst, chief negotiator employee rels. City of L.A., 1969-80, various other positions, 1980-99; dir. airports adminstrn. L.A. World Airports, 1999—. Office: Los Angeles Dept Airports 1 World Way Los Angeles CA 90045-5803

BRUCE, WILLIAM ROBERT, physician, educator; b. Hamhung, Korea, May 26, 1929; s. George Findlay and Ellen (Tate) B.; m. Margaret MacFarlane, June 15, 1957; children: Graham Douglas, Lynda Jeanne, Kevin Robert. B.Sc., U. Alta., 1950; PhD, U. Sask., 1956; MD, U. Chgo., 1958. Intern Billings Hosp., Chgo., 1958-59; mem. faculty U. Toronto, Can., 1959, prof. biophysics, 1966—, prof. nutritional scis., 1985—. Mem. epidemiology sect. Ont. Cancer Inst., Toronto, 1959-81, sr. scientist epidemiology sect., 1989—; dir. Ludwig Inst. for Cancer Research, Toronto, 1981-88. Fellow Royal Coll. Physicians (Can.), Royal Soc. Can.; mem. Assn. Cancer Research. Research, publs. on X-ray and gamma ray penetration, control red blood cell prodn., action of anti-cancer agts. on normal and tumor cells, sperm prodn., computers in med. records, origins of human cancer. Home: 4 Marshfield Ct Don Mills ON Canada M3C 2E3 Office: U Toronto Dept Nutritional Scis 150 College St Toronto ON Canada M5X 3E2 E-mail: wr.bruce@utoronto.ca.

BRUCE, WILLIAM ROLAND, lawyer; b. Portsmouth, Va., July 13, 1935; s. William Roland Sr. and Elizabeth (Jack) B.; m. Katherine Martin, Sept. 1, 1956 (div. Apr. 1980); m. Rita Kay Glisson, Jan. 3, 1981; children: Kate, William, Elizabeth, Margaret, Andrew, Alexander. BA, U. Va., 1956, LLB, 1959. Bar: Va. 1959, Tenn. 1960, U.S. Supreme Ct. 1964. Assoc. Martin, Tate & Morrow, Memphis, 1959-62; sole practice Memphis, 1963-65; ptnr. Bruce & Southern, Memphis, 1965-72; chmn. Bruce, Brandon & Regan, P.C., Memphis, 1972-91; with Baker, Worthington, Crossley & Stansberry, Nashville, 1991-94, Stokes, Bartholomew, Evans & Petree, Nashville and Memphis, 1994—. Lectr. Vanderbilt U. Sch. Law, Nashville, 1972-79; mem. Tenn. Jud. Coun., 1997—; mem. Tenn. Housing devel. Agy., 1998—. Rep. Tenn. Ho. of Reps., Nashville, 1966-68; senator Tenn. Senate, Nashville, 1968-72; mem. Health Edn. and Housing Facility Bd. of Memphis, 1984—, chmn., 1984-87. Served to capt. U.S. Army, 1957-58. Named Tenn. Outstanding Young Man, Jaycees, 1969, Conservationist of Yr., Tenn. Conservation League, 1972. Fellow Nashville Bar Found., Tenn. Bar Found.; mem. ABA, Am. Bar Found. Democrat. Episcopalian. Avocation: sailing. Home: 4996 Sparta Hwy Smithville TN 37166-5156 Office: Stokes Bartholomew Evans & Petree 424 Church St Ste 2800 Nashville TN 37219-2386 E-mail: wbruce@stokesbartmoldhew.com.

BRUCH, BARBARA RAE, artist, educator; b. Seattle, Apr. 15, 1940; d. Willard Ray and Zephyr E. (Tull) B. BA, U. Wash., 1962, MFA, 1964. Children's art instr. Cornish Coll. Art, Seattle, 1965-67; artist-in-residence City of Seattle, 1967-78; lectr. art Seattle Pacific U., 1974-78; gallery dir. Husted Gallery, Seattle, 1978-94; art instr. Sev-Shoon Art Ctr., Seattle, 1994—; recording agt. Kappeler Inst., Seattle, 1995—. Art restorer Husted Gallery/Studio Tara, 1978 ; gallery coord. A New Space Gallery, Seattle, 1986-88; condr. art workshops. Illustrator: Stocks and Commodities mag., 1994—; one-woman shows include Seattle Pacific U., 1993, New Space Gallery, 1986, Husted Gallery, 1983, 85, Main Street Gallery, Duvall, Wash., 1998. Illustrator/mem. Friends of the Earth, Seattle, 1972-76, Wash. Wildlife Study Coun., Seattle, 1974-76. Recipient Editor's Choice award Nat. Libr. Poetry, 1995; Bank of Am. scholar, 1958. Mem. Seattle Women's Caucus for Art (pres. 1991-94, Kathe Kollwitz award 1996), No Limits for Women Artists. Avocations: reading, hiking, making jewelry. Office: Kappeler Inst PO Box 9229 Seattle WA 98109-0229

BRUCH, CAROL SOPHIE, lawyer, educator; b. Rockford, Ill., June 11, 1941; d. Ernest and Margarete (Willstätter) B.; m. Jack E. Myers, 1960 (div. 1973); children: Margarete Louise Myers Feinstein, Kurt Randall Myers. AB, Shimer Coll., 1960; JD, U. Calif.-Berkeley, 1972; Dr. honoris causa, U. Basel, 2000. Bar: Calif. 1973, U.S. Supreme Ct. 1980. Law clk. to Justice William O. Douglas U.S. Supreme Ct., 1972-73; acting prof. law U. Calif., Davis, 1973—78, prof., 1978—2001, rsch. prof., prof. emeritus, 2001—, chair doctoral program in human devel., 1996—2001. Acad. vis. law dept. U. Munich, 1978-79, 92, U. Cologne, 1990, U. Cambridge, 1990, London Sch. Econs. and Polit. Sci., 1991, Kings Coll., London, 1991; vis. prof. U. Calif., Berkeley, 1983, Columbia U., 1986, U. Basel, 1994, vis. Fulbright prof. Hebrew U., Jerusalem, 1996-97; vis. fellow Fitzwilliam Coll., Cambridge, Eng., 1990, U. Calif. Humanities Rsch. Inst., Irvine, 1999, vis. scholar Inst. for Advanced Legal Studies (Univ. London), 1991; cons. to Ctr. for Family in Transition, 1981, Calif. Law Revision Commn., 1979-82, NOW Legal Def. and Edn. Fund, 1980-81; lectr., legis. drafting and testimony, 1976—; mem. U.S. del. 4th Inter-Am. Specialized Conf. on Pvt. Internat. Law, OAS, 1989. Contbr. articles to legal jours. Editor Calif. Law Rev., 1971; editorial bd. Family Law Quar., 1980-87; Representing Children, 1995—, Am. Jour. of Comparative Law, 2001—; lectr. in field. Mem. adv. com. child support and child custody Calif. Commn. on Status of Women, 1981-83, child support adv. com. Calif. Jud. Coun., 1991-94, adv. com. on private internat. law U.S. Dept. State, 1989—, internat. child abduction steering com. Internat. Ctr. for Missing and Exploited Children (London), 1999—; host parent Am. Field Service, Davis, 1977-78. Max Rheinstein sr. rsch. fellow Alexander von Humboldt Found., Fed. Republic Germany, 1978-79, 92, Fulbright fellow, Western Europe, 1990, Fulbright Sr. Scholar, Israel, 1997, Disting. Pub. Svc. award U. Calif. Davis Acad. Senate, 1990. Mem. ABA, Calif. State Bar Assn., Am. Law Inst., Internat. Soc. Family Law (exec. coun. 1994-2000, 2002—), Order of Coif. Democrat. Jewish. Office: U Calif Sch Law 400 Mrak Hall Dr Davis CA 95616-5201

BRUCH, JOHN CLARENCE, JR., engineer, educator; b. Kenosha, Wis., Oct. 11, 1940; m. Susan Jane Tippett, Aug. 19, 1967. BCE, U. Notre Dame, 1962; MCE, Stanford U., 1963, PhD in Civil Engring., 1966. Acting instr. engring. Stanford (Calif.) U., 1966; asst. prof. engring. U. Calif., Santa Barbara, 1966-74, assoc. prof. engring., 1974-78, prof. engring., 1978—. Grantee, NSF, 1987—93, 1999—2003, NASA, 1997—2004. Mem. ASCE, Am. Sci. Affiliation, Sigma Xi, Tau Beta Pi. Avocations: golf, jogging. Office: U Calif Mech Engring Dept Santa Barbara CA 93106

BRUCH, VIRGINIA IRENE SULLIVAN, librarian, writer; b. Hickman, Ky., May 26, 1921; d. Thomas Terrell and Virginia Irene (Helm) Sullivan; BS, Murray U., 1943; m. Truman Elwood Bruch, Feb. 18, 1944; dau., Susan Irene (Mrs. Richard Lyons Rose). Librarian, Union City (Tenn.) High Sch., 1943-44; librarian, cataloger FTC Army Library, Washington, 1949-55; librarian, cataloger Army Library, Washington, 1955-65, chief catalog sect., 1965-71, chief tech. svcs. br., 1971-80; rsch. curator Boyhood Home of Robert E. Lee, Alexandria, Va., 1983—. Recipient prize Fed. Poet, 1956, first place essay category creative writing contest Va. Highlands Festival, 1976; Outstanding Performance award Army Library, 1979. Mem. Spl. Libraries Assn., A.L.A., Nat. Geneal. Soc., Va. Hist. Soc., Tenn. Hist. Soc., Ky. Hist. Soc., Louisville Hist. Soc., Filson Club. Mem. Christian Ch. (librarian 1960-72). Author: Proud Wanderers: My Mother's Family, 1981; Beneath the Oaks of Ivy Hill, 1982; contbr. to Am. Poetry mag., Poet Lore, Driftwood, Christian Herald, Fed. Poet, Badge of Honor, Family Heritage.

BRUCK, NICHOLAS, economist, educator; b. Yugoslavia, May 25, 1932; Austrian citizen, 1955-62; came to U.S., 1957; s. Nikolaus and Anna (Biebel) B.; divorced; children: Maria, Maya, Max, Thomas. BA, Vienna Sch. Econs., 1953, MBA, 1956, PhD, 1960; MA in Econs., Duke U., 1954. Econ. analyst Western Electric Co., N.Y.C., 1957-58, 1960-62, prof. econs. St. John's U., Jamaica, N.Y., 1962-66, Am. U., Washington, 1980-82; economist U.S. Bur. Labor Stats., Washington, 1966-67; chief fin. studies Inter-Am. Devel. Bank, Washington, 1968-79; sr. indsl. devel. officer UNIDO, Vienna, 1979-80; sr. fin. economist, seminar dir. Econ. Devel. Inst., World Bank, Washington, 1982-94; pres. Internat. Devel. Enterprise Assocs., Washington, 1994—; owner, operator Mimosa Farm, Potomac, Md., 1970—99. Instr. Hofstra U., L.I. U., Manhattan Coll., 1963—66, U. Colo., Boulder, Inst. Shipboard Edn., 1980; Fulbright vis. prof. San Carlos U., Guatemala, 1967—68; adj. prof. Johns Hopkins U., Balt., 1976—78, Georgetown U., Washington, 1977—78; professorial lectr. George Washington U., Washington, 1985—90; cons. in field. Editor: Capital Markets under Inflation, 1982, Banking and Investment Financing, in Russian, 2 vols., 1995; contbr. articles to profl. jours. Bd. dirs. Am. Coun. Voluntary Agys. for Fgn. Svc., 1963-73, German World Alliance, 2001—; chmn. World Assn. Trainers in Devel., 1992—; spl. advisor World Fedn. Devel. Banks, 1995—. With JAGC, U.S. Army, 1958-60. Fulbright scholar, 1953-54, grantee, 1967; Ford Found. fellow, 1965. Mem. Am. Econ. Assn., Soc. for Internat. Devel. (chmn. work group on financing devel. 1975-79, 80-81, bd. dirs. 1980-86, v.p. Washington chpt. 1981-82), Nat. Economists Club (founding, 1968-). Office: IDEA PO Box 57467 Washington DC 20037-0467 E-mail: ideas@attglobal.net.

BRUCK, PHOEBE ANN MASON, landscape architect; b. Highland Park, Ill., Nov. 26, 1928; d. George Allen and Louise Townsend (Barnard) Mason; m. F. Frederick Bruck, June 30, 1956 (dec. May 1997). Student Bard Coll., 1946-49; BS, Ill. Inst. Tech., 1954; MLA, Harvard U., 1963. Trainee, Nat. Gallery of Art, Washington, 1947, Mus. Modern Art, N.Y.C., 1948; head design dept. Design Research Inc., Cambridge, Mass., 1955-60; cons. The Architects Collaborative & Sert, Jackson Assocs., Inc., 1960-63; v.p. F. Frederick Bruck, Architect & Assoc., Inc., Cambridge, pres., 1993-96; vis. design critic dept. landscape architecture Harvard U. Grad. Sch. Design, 1971-79; v.p. The Buccaneers Co., 1989—, also bd. dirs; cons. The arts at Harvard and Radcliff, 1995—. Contbr. to New Landscapes for Living, 1980. Judge, New Eng. Flower Show, Mass. Hort. Soc., 1971-79, Thoreau Awards, Assn. Landscape Contractors, 1980; mem. Sci. Adv. Group for Edn., Cambridge Pub. Schs., 1981-82; chair Harvard Sq. Adv. Commn., 1986—; co-chair Quincy Sq. Design Com., 1991-97. Mem. Mass. Bd. Registration of Landscape Architects (chair 1992-95), Am. Arbitration Assn., Am. Soc. Landscape Architects, Boston Soc. Landscape Architects (pres. 1973-75, examining bd. 1978-81), Mass. Soc. Mayflower Descendants, Harvard Sq. Def. Fund (chmn. adv. ocm. 1987, bd. dirs. 1984-85, pres. 1985-86), Harvard U. Grad. Sch. Design Alumni Assn. (officer 1972-78), Soc. for Protection of New Eng. Antiquities (design adv. com). Episcopalian. Home and Office: 148 Coolidge Hl Cambridge MA 02138-5521

BRUCK, ROBERT IAN, education educator; b. New York, NY, June 25, 1952; s. Sidney Wolfgang and Sylvia Bruck; m. Debra Sue Schlessel, June 17, 1973; children: Isaac Samuel, Sarah Anne, Sonia Rose. BA, SUNY College, Buffalo; PhD, Syracuse U., 1974—78. Postdoctoral fellow Cornell U., 1977—79; asst./assoc prof. NC State U.; sci. advisor to the gov. of NC, 1990—92; prof. and dir. of environ. sci. NC State U., 1994—. Academic adv. bd. EPA, Washington, 1995—2002. Recipient Order Of The Longleaf Pine, State Of NC, 1992, The NC award For Sci., 1997, Outstanding achievement award, NC State U., 1997, Disting. alumnus award, SUNY Buffalo, 1997, Alumni Outstanding Tchr. award, NC State U., 1998. Mem.: Am. Phytopathological Soc. Democrat-Npl. Jewish. Avocations: mountain climbing, photography. Home: 1301 Larkhall Ct Cary NC 27511 Office: North Carolina State University Box 7106-Center For Earth Observation Raleigh NC 27695 Home Fax: 919-515-3439. Personal E mail: bob_bruck@ncsu.edu.

BRUCK, WILLIAM, business executive; b. Dayton, Ohio, Aug. 1, 1951; s. Emil J. and Lucy A. (Lombardi) B.; m. Jacqueline Youden, June 6, 1984 (div. Dec. 1987); m. Anita M. Brack, June 15, 1996; 1 child, Abby Elizabeth. AB, Brown U., 1973; MA, Duquesne U., 1974; PhD, U. Fla., 1977. Lic. clin. psychologist, Va.; nat. cert. counselor. Asst. prof. psychology Seattle U., 1978-79, West Ga. Coll., Carrollton, 1979-81; prin. Leadership Resources, Inc., Fairfax, Va., 1981-83; assoc. prof. psychology Marymount U., Arlington, Va., 1983-91, dir. instnl. rsch., 1986-91, prof. psychology, 1991-99; owner/operator Bill Bruck & Assocs., Falls Church, Va., 1986—; prin. Caucus Systems, Inc., Arlington, Va., 1999-2001; ptnr. Collaboration Archs., 2001—. Author: Special Edition Using WordPerfect Office, 1994, Special Edition Using PerfectOffice 3, 1995, Special Edition Using Novell GroupWise 4, 1995, Using Corel WordPerfect Suite 7, 1996, Using Corel WordPerfect Suite 8, 1997, The Essential Book for Microsoft Office 95, 1996, The Essential Book for Microsoft Office 97, 1997, The Essential Book for Microsoft Office 2000, 1999, Make Your Mouse Roar, 2001, Taming the Information Tsunami, 2002. Mem. APA, ASTD, Orgn. Devel. Network, Internat. Ctr. for Study of Psychiatry and Psychology (chmn. bd. dirs. 1993-2002). Avocations: martial arts (Black belt in karate 1972, 2d deg. black belt in Aikido 1992), racquetball, folk music, gardening. Office: 2686 Hillsman St Falls Church VA 22043 E-mail: bill@bruck.com.

BRUCKEN, LOIS GILBERT, volunteer; b. Parkersburg, W.Va., July 7, 1936; d. Rowland and Lula (Herdman) Gilbert; m. Robert Matthew Brucken, June 30, 1960; children: Nancy, Elizabeth, Rowland, Gilbert. BA, Marietta Coll., 1958. Bd. trustees Cleve. Internat. Program, 1978-84; pres. Shaker Heights (Ohio) PTA Coun., 1981-82; bds. trustees Cleve. Coun. on World Affairs, 1982-84; co-chmn. Shaker Heights Sch. Levy, 1983; pres. Shaker Heights Libr. Bd. Trustees, 1985-87, Plymouth Ch. Shaker Heights, 1989-90; v.p. Cleve. Bd. Edn. Adult Adv. Com., 1989-90; trustee, v.p. Cleve. Soc. for the Blind, 1979—; v.p. bd. trustees St. Luke's Hosp., Cleve., 1999—; pres. bd. trustees Shaker Family Ctr., 1999—2001; trustee St. Luke's Found., 1997—. Mem. Alpha Psi Omega, Pi Kappa Delta. Republican. Home: 18210 Fernway Rd Shaker Heights OH 44122-3434

BRUCKEN, ROBERT MATTHEW, lawyer; b. Akron, Ohio, Sept. 15, 1934; s. Harold M. and Eunice B. (Boesel) B.; m. Lois R. Gilbert, June 30, 1960; children: Nancy, Elizabeth, Rowland, Gilbert. AB, Marietta Coll., 1956; JD, U. Mich., 1959. Bar: Ohio 1960. Assoc. Baker & Hostetler, Cleve., 1960-69; ptnr., 1970—. Trustee Lakeside Assn., 1979-97, Marietta Coll., 1983—; sec., treas. Leader Shape, Inc., 1990—. Served with AUS, 1959-60. Mem. ABA, Ohio State Bar Assn. (chmn. probate and trust law sect. 1981-83), Cleve. Bar Assn. (chmn. probate ct. com. 1973-75), Am. Coll. Trust and Estate Counsel, Phi Beta Kappa. Congregationalist. Office: Baker & Hostetler 3200 Nat City Ctr 1900 E 9th St Ste 3200 Cleveland OH 44114-3475 E-mail: rbrucken@bakerlaw.com.

BRUCKENSTEIN, JOEL P. investment company executive, financial planner; b. N.Y.C., Jan. 18, 1956; s. Bernard and Anita B.; m. Viviana Srolovich, Sept. 18, 1990; children: Kevin, Alan, Eric. BA magna cum laude, SUNY, New Paltz, 1979. V.p. Kobayashi & Co., Tokyo, 1988-90, Bierbaum-Martin, Inc., N.Y.C., 1990-95; pres. Global Fin. Advisors, Inc., Pleasantville, N.Y., 1995-2000, Miramar, Fla., 2000—. Mem. adv. bd. Schwab Inst. Emerging Practices Adv. Coun., 1999. Mem.: Inst. Cert. Fin. Planners (pres.-elect 1999—, dir. tech. 1998—), Inst. Bus. and Fin., Internat. Assn. Fin. Planning, Fin. Planning Assn. (chmn. govt. rels. tax subcom. 2003, pres. Greater Hudson Valley chpt.), Nat. Assn. Personal Fin. Advisors. Avocations: scuba diving, reading. Office: Global Fin Advisors Inc PO Box 277930 Miramar FL 33027 E-mail: Joel@global-advisor.com.

BRUCKER, MARY C. nurse midwife; b. St. Louis, Mar. 26, 1948; d. Ted J. and Jane Estelle Morris Brucker. BSN, St. Louis U., 1970, MSN in Maternal Newborn Nursing, 1971; Nurse-Midwifery Cert., U. Miss., Jackson, 1973; D in Nursing Sci., Rush U., 1989. Cert. nurse-midwife U. Miss., Jackson, 1973—74, Cook County Hosp., Chgo., 1974—76, H. Hasson, MD, Chgo., 1976—82; dir., midwife at adolescent family ctr. Rush Presbyn. St. Lukes Med. Ctr., Chgo., 1983—85; cons. in midwifery practice and edn., 1986—2001; dir. Parkland Sch. Nurse-Midwifery, Dallas, 1989—. Vis. prof. So. Calif. Mar. Dimes, L.A., 1999—99. Named one of Gt. 100 Nurses in Dallas Ft. Worth, Gt. 100 Com., 1993; recipient Irwin Chabon award, ASPO Lamaze/Lamaze Internat., 1996, Nursing Excellence in Tchg. award, Nurse Week Nat. Mag., 2001. Fellow: Am. Coll. Nurse-Midwives (life; nat. chair continuing edn. 1979—81, nat. chair continuing competency 1990—93, mem. governing bd. 2000—03, cert., Regional award for excellence in midwifery practice 1995); mem.: Ctr. for Certification Preparation and Rev. (sec. 1995—2003), Nurses Adv. Coun. Mar. Dimes, Lamaze Internat. (pres., sec., treas., v.p., bd. advisor 1989—95). Office: Parkland Sch Nurse-Midwifery 5201 Harry Hines Blvd MS 6017A Dallas TX 75235 Personal E-mail: mbruck@parknet.pmh.org. E-mail: mbruck@parknet.pmh.org.

BRUCKER, PAUL C. academic administrator, physician; Pres. Thomas Jefferson U., Phila., 1990—. Office: Thomas Jefferson U Office of President 1020 Walnut St Philadelphia PA 19107-5567

BRUCKER, WILBER MARION, retired lawyer; b. Saginaw, Mich., Apr. 13, 1926; s. Wilber Marion and Clara (Hantel) B.; m. Doris Ann Shover, June 23, 1951; children: Barbara Ann, Wilber Marion, Paul Bradford. Student, Wayne State U., 1943; AB, Princeton U., 1949; JD, U. Mich., 1952. Bar: Mich. 1953. Assoc. Clark, Klein, Brucker & Waples, Detroit, 1952-58; pvt. practice Detroit, 1958-61; ptnr. Brucker & Brucker, Detroit, 1961-67, McInally, Rockwell & Brucker, Detroit, 1968-78, McInally, Brucker, Newcombe, Wilke and DeBona, Detroit, 1978-86; pres. Alliance Fin. Corp., 1986-89; sr. legal counsel Riley and Roumell, Detroit, 1990-96; dir. Bank of Dearborn, Mich., 1970-89, Alliance Fin. Corp., 1982-89; ret. Legal counsel Econ. Club Detroit, 1968-86; arbitrator Am. Arbitration Assn., 1965-79; bd. dirs. Cmty. Bank Dearborn. Bd. govs. Wayne State U., Detroit, 1967-78, chmn. bd. govs., 1972; pres. bd. trustees Arnold Home, 1968-96; mem. Witanagamote, 1956—, Centurions, 1977-96, Woodworkers, 1991—; mem. bd. canvassers City of Grosse Pointe Farms, Mich., 1972-74; pres. Grosse Pointe Sr. Mens Club, 1998-99. Mem. ABA, Mich. Bar Assn., Country Club of Detroit, Masons. Home: 253 Touraine Rd Grosse Pointe Farms MI 48236-3308

BRUCKHEIMER, JERRY, producer; b. Detroit, Sept. 21, 1945; Grad., U. Ariz. Former prodr., art dir. advt. agy.; co-founder Don Simpson/Jerry Bruckheimer Films, 1983. Assoc. prodr. (films) Culpepper Cattle Company, 1972, Rafferty and the Gold Dust Twins, 1975; prodr. (films) American Gigolo, 1980, Young Doctors in Love, 1982; (with George Pappas) Farewell My Lovely, 1975; (with Dick Richards) March or Die, 1977; (with William S. Gillmore) Defiance, 1980; (with Ronnie Caan) Thief, 1981, Cat People, 1982; (with Don Simpson) Flashdance, 1983, Beverly Hills Cop, 1984, Thief of Hearts, 1984, Top Gun, 1986, Beverly Hills Cop II, 1987, Days of Thunder, 1990, Bad Boys, 1995, Crimson Tide, 1995, Dangerous Minds, 1995; The Rock, 1996, Con Air, 1997, Enemy of the State, 1998, Armageddon, 1998, Gone in 60 Seconds, 2000, Coyote Ugly, 2000, Remember the Titans, 2000, Pearl Harbor, 2001, Black Hawk Down, 2001, Bad Company, 2002, Kangaroo Jack, 2003, Pirates of the Caribbean: The Curse of the Black Pearl, 2003, Bad Boys II, 2003; exec. prodr.: (with Don Simpson) The Ref, 1994, (TV) Soldier of Fortune, 1997, Dangerous Minds, 1996, Max Q, 1998, Swing Vote, 1999, C.S.I., The Amazing Race, CSI: Miami, Without a Trace, 2002, The Amazing Race III, 2002, Profiles From the Front Line, 2003, Skin, 2003, Fearless, Cold Case, 2003. Recipient ShoWest award Prodr. of Yr., 1999, David O. Selznick Lifetime Achievement award Prodrs. Guild of Am., 2000. Office: Jerry Bruckheimer Films 1631 10th St Santa Monica CA 90404-3705*

BRUCK LIEB PORT, LILLY, retired consumer advisor, broadcaster, columnist; b. Vienna, May 13, 1918; came to U.S., 1941, naturalized, 1944; d. Max and Sophie M. Hahn; m. Sandor Bruck, Mar. 7, 1943; 1 child, Sandra Lee (Mrs. John David Evans III); m. David L. Lieb, Dec. 7, 1985; m. Charles S. Port, Nov. 22, 1998. PhD in Econs., U. Vienna; postgrad., Sorbonne, Paris, Sch. of Econs., London, Sch. of Bus., Columbia U., 1941-42, Sch. of Social Work, NYU, 1964-66. Dir. consumer edn. Dept. Consumer Affairs, City of N.Y., 1969-78; project dir. Am. Coalition of Citizens with Disabilities, 1977-78; consumer advisor, broadcaster In Touch Networks, N.Y.C., 1978-90; consumer affairs commentator Nat. Pub. Radio, 1980-82; ret. Author: Access, The Guide to a Better Life for Disabled Americans, 1978; contbr. articles to disability and rehab. to books, ency. and mag. Presid. Scarsdale Hadassah, 1960-68. Chmn. Westchester county, Bonds for Israel, 1960-68; trustee Kol AMI-JCC, White Plains, N.Y.; assoc. Jewish Mus.; sponsor Lilly Bruck Lieb Creative Writing Program, Purchase Coll., SUNY; mem. pres.'s coun. White Plains (N.Y.) Hosp. Recipient Woman of Yr. award Anti Defamation League, 1972. Democrat. Home: 25 Murray Hill Rd Scarsdale NY 10583-2829 E-mail: lblone@aol.com.

BRUCKMAN, AMY SUSAN, computer scientist, educator; d. Cynthia May Zucker and Robert Zachary Bruckman, Bernard Zucker (Stepfather); m. Peter Andrew Weimann, Feb. 24, 2001. AB, Harvard U.; MSVS, MIT, 1991, PhD, 1997. Asst. prof. Coll. Computing, Ga. Inst. Tech., Atlanta, 1997—2003, assoc. prof., 2003—. Designer and developer (educational software) MOOSE Crossing, co-designer and developer (software) The Turing Game (award Arts and Culture, Global Info. Infrastructure awards, 1999). Named one of Leading Young Innovators Sci. and Tech. World, Tech. Rev. Mag., 1999; recipient Jan Hawkins award, AERA, 2003. Avocations: hiking, snorkeling, photography, video games, pinball. Office: Coll Computing Ga Inst Tech Atlanta GA 30332

BRUCKMAN, RICHARD R. aerospace engineer; Gen. mgr., sys. devel. dept. head Simulation Tech., Inc., 1979—81; owner, operator computer sys. devel. co., 1981—83; program mgr., chief sys. engr Naval Warfare Ctr. Weapons Divsn., 1983—89, carrier-based and vertical lift tactical aircraft sys. engring. divsn. head, 1994, weapon sys. support activity integrated product team leader, assoc. dept. head aircraft weapons integration dept., 1989—93; pres., owner RRB Assocs., Inc.; cons. Aerospace Safety Adv. Panel NASA, Washington. Office: Aerospace Safety Adv Panel NASA Hdqrs 300 E St SW Washington DC 20546

BRUCKNER, WILLA COHEN, lawyer; b. Paterson, N.J., Apr. 27, 1954; d. Seymour and Anita (Sax) Cohen. BS, U. Mich., 1975; MA, Yale U., 1976; JD, U. Pa., 1981. Bar: N.Y. 1982, N.J. 1983, U.S. Dist. Ct. (so. and ea. dists.) N.Y. 1986. Asst. analyst Congressional Budget Office, Washington, 1976-78; asst. counsel/atty. Mfrs. Hanover Trust Co., N.Y.C., 1981-85; dep. counsel, assoc. atty. Bank of Tokyo Trust Co./The Bank of Tokyo Mitsubishi, Ltd., N.Y.C., 1985-97; counsel Dresdner Kleinwort Benson N.Am. Svcs., N.Y.C., 1997-98, contract atty., 1998-2000; ptnr. Tannenbaum Helpern Syracuse & Hirschtritt LLP, N.Y.C., 2000—02; gen. counsel Hartz Trading, Inc., 2002—. Mem. ABA, N.Y. County Lawyers' Assn. Phi Beta Kappa. Office: Hartz Trading Inc 400 Plaza Dr PO Box 2353 Secaucus NJ 07096-2353 E-mail: willa.bruckner@canarycapital.com.

BRUCKSTEIN, ALEX HARRY, internist, gastroenterologist, geriatrician; b. Germany, Dec. 2, 1949; came to U.S., 1950; s. Jacob and Rose B., m. Dorothy Krausman, Mar. 23, 1973; children: Tammy, Sharon, Sarah, Michael. BS in Chemistry, CCNY, 1971; MD, Albert Einstein Coll. Medicine, 1975. Diplomate Am. Bd. Internal Medicine, Am. Bd. Gastroenterology, Am. Bd. Internal Medicine- Geriatrics. Intern in internal medicine Roosvelt Hosp., N.Y.C.; resident in internal medicine St. Luke's Hosp., N.Y.C.; resident in gastroenterology VA Hosp., N.Y.U., N.Y.C.; pvt. practice internal medicine, gastroenterology Staten Island, N.Y. Hosp. affiliations: Doctors' Hosp. Staten Island, N.Y., Staten Island U. Hosp. N., Staten Island U. Hosp. S., St. Vincent's Hosp., Staten Island; vis. clin. fellow Columbia U. Dept. Medicine, 1975-78, NYU Dept. Medicine, 1978-80; clin. asst. prof. medicine N.Y. Med. Coll., 1983-90, SUNY Health Sci. Ctr. at Bklyn., 1990—. Fellow ACP, Am. Coll. Gastroenterology; mem. AMA, Med. Soc. State N.Y., Richmond County Med. Soc., Am. Gastroent. Assn., N.Y. Soc. Gastrointestinal Endoscopy, N.Y. Acad. Gastroenterology, Am. Geriatrics Assn. Office: 2627 Hylan Blvd Staten Island NY 10306-4339

BRUDER, GEORGE FREDERICK, lawyer; b. Ann Arbor, Mich., June 4, 1938; s. George G. and Mary Louise (Pfisterer) Bruder; m. Jean Riley, July 10, 1965; children: Roxanne, Stephanie. AB, Dartmouth Coll., 1960; JD, U. Chgo., 1963. Bar: D.C. 1964. Counsel FPC, Washington, 1964—67; counsel Long Lines Dept. AT&T, Washington, 1967—68; assoc. Debevoise & Liberman, Washington, 1968—70, ptnr., 1971—75, Bruder, Gentile & Marcoux, Washington, 1976—97. Mem.: Fed. Energy Bar Assn. Democrat. Episcopalian. Home: 8 E Lenox St Chevy Chase MD 20815-4211 E-mail: gfbruder@erols.com.

BRUDER, HAROLD JACOB, artist, educator; b. N.Y.C., Aug. 31, 1930; s. Julius and Della (Wlodinger) B.; m. Anet Sirna, July 15, 1979; 1 child, Dellan; children from previous marriage: David, Shari. Cert., Cooper Union, 1951. Mem. faculty Kansas City Art Inst., 1963-65, Pratt Inst., 1965-66; prof. art Queens Coll., Flushing, N.Y., 1965-95, chmn. art dept., 1982-85, prof. emeritus, 1995—. Artist-in-residence, Aspen, Colo., 1967; One-man shows include, Robert Isaacson Gallery, N.Y.C., 1962, Forum Gallery, N.Y.C., 1968, 69, 72, 76, 79, Durlacher Bros., N.Y.C., 1964, 1967, William and Mary Coll., 1979, Queens Coll., N.Y.C., 1974, Queens Mus., N.Y.C., 1982, Armstrong Gallery, N.Y.C, 1984, 86, Contemporary Realist Gallery, San Francisco, 1988; group exhbns. include, Whitney Mus., 1970, Balt. Mus., 1970, Butler Inst., 1972, Cleve. Mus., 1974, Phila. Mus., 1976, represented in permanent collections, Hirshhorn Mus., Washington, Sheldon Meml. Gallery, Lincoln, Nebr., N.J. State Mus., Trenton; contbr. articles to profl. jours. NEA grantee, 1985 Home: 165 W End Ave Apt 3N New York NY 10023-5505 Studio: 200 W 72d St # 34 New York NY 10023 E-mail: dellan580257058@aol.com.

BRUDNER, HARVEY JEROME, physicist; b. N.Y.C., May 29, 1931; s. Joseph and Anna (Fiddelman) B.; m. Helen Gross, Dec. 18, 1963; children: Mae Ann, Terry Joseph, Jay Scott. BS in Engring. and Physics, NYU, 1952, MS, 1954, PhD, 1959; postgrad., U. Md., 1954-56, CCNY, 1958, Columbia U., 1959-61. Electronics engr. Bendix Corp., Teterboro, N.J., 1952; physicist U.S. Naval Ordnance Lab., White Oak, Md., 1953-54; sr. physicist Emerson Rsch. Labs., Washington, 1954-57; prin. physicist Emerson Radio, Jersey City, 1957-61; rsch. assoc. NYU Inst. Math. Scis., N.Y.C., 1957-60; guest scientist Rockefeller Inst. for Med. Rsch., N.Y.C., 1960-61; sr. rsch. assoc. Am. Can Co., Princeton (N.J.) Lab., 1964-67; v.p. R & D Westinghouse Learning Corp., N.Y.C., 1967-71, pres., 1971-76; also dir.; mem. adminstrv. com. Westinghouse Electric Corp., Pitts., 1971-76; pres. Westinghouse Electric Corp. (Westinghouse Learning Group), 1971-76, H.J.B. Enterprises, N.Y.C., 1961—, Med. Devel., Inc., N.Y.C., 1962; dir. Ideal Sch. Supply Corp., Ednl. Products, Inc., Document Reading Svcs., Ltd., Linguaphone Inst. Ltd., Info. Synergy, Inc., Cambridge Learning Connection, Inc.; chmn. new devels. com. Project Aristotle; acting dir. Gottscho Info. Center, Coll. Engring., Rutgers U.; prof. math., physics, dean sci. and tech. N.Y. Inst. Tech., 1962-64; instr. atomic physics N.Y. U., 1953-54. Cons. Nat. Inst. Edn., Mass. Inst. Tech., Rutgers U., Worcester Poly. Inst., Poly. Inst. N.Y., Nat. Inst. Community Devel., U.S. Ho. of Reps. Com. on Sci. and Tech.; mem. adv. com. Middlesex County Coll., 1966—, Paterson State Coll., 1975; mem. exec. planning com. tng. adv. sect. Nat. Security Indsl. Assn., 1966; nat. adv. bd. Am. Coll. in Jerusalem; dir. computers in edn. study Nat. Inst. Edn., 1979; bd. dirs. World Learning and Communications, 1978— Editl. commentator Another Opinion, Sta. WCBS, N.Y.C., N.Y. Power Authority; author: Semiconductor Physics, 1954, College Technical Mathematics, 1967, Algebra and Trigonometry-A Programmed Course with Applications, 1971, On Fermat's Last Theorem, 1979, Fermat and The Missing Numbers, 1994, How the Babylonians Solved Numbered Triangle Problems 3600 Years Ago, 1998; columnist Light-On Series: Ednl. Tech. Mag., Source Data: Datamation Mag.; chmn. editl. adv. bd. Tech. Horizons in Edn. Jour.; contbr. rsch. articles on atomic physics, radar, ednl., med., energy, electronic sys., biol. effects of radiation, laser tech., others, to novel publs. Mem. steering com. Project PROCEED, NSF, Mcpl. Alliance Com., Highland Park, 1990—; capt. long-range planning com. Highland Park Sch. Bd.; trustee Ross Hall Heights Assn., 1966; chmn., pres. Joyce Kilmer Authority, New Brunswick, NJ, 1985—; coord. WABC-TV News, N.Y.C., Joyce Kilmer Trees, 1994; coord. program Fermat and Babylonian Rectangles, Sta. WCTC, 1994; apprd. to Mcppl. Alliance Against Drugs and Alcohol, 1990—99; apptd. to Middlesex County Mcpl. Alliance Network, 1995—; coord. Project DATE (Drugs, Alcohol, Tobacco, Education), Rutgers U. N.J. Forum, 1995—, New Brunswick Cmty. Bridge Project, 2001, Vets. Day Project, 2001; pres. Highland Park Centennial Commn., 2002—; dir. cir. George Street Playhouse, New Brunswick, 2002—. Recipient Cert. Americanism Vets. Alliance of Raritan Valley, 1992, Kiwanis Internat. award 1993; Raritan-Millstone Heritage Alliance, 1998; named Knight, Order of the Swan, 1996, New Brunswick Historical Assn., 2003; 2 Nobel Laureates, Sta. WCTC, 2003, award Mayor Robert W. Johnson, Highland Park. Fellow IEEE (life, ednl. adminstrn. com., solar standards com., photovoltaic subcom.), mem., Am. Phys. Soc., Soc. Motion Picture and TV Engrs., Internat. Fedn. Med. Electronics, AAAS, Electronic Industries Assn. (edn. com.), Am. Ednl. Research Assn., Adult Edn. Assn. U.S.A., N.Y. Acad. Scis., Am. Mgmt. Assn. (ednl. adv. com.), Math. Assn. Am., Am. Soc. Tng. and Devel., Council Ams., Am. Judicature Soc., Am. Math. Soc., Am. Soc. Curriculum Devel., Knight, Order of the Swan, Sigma Xi, Sigma Pi Sigma, Tau Beta Pi. Clubs: Chemists (N.Y.C.); N.Y. Univ., The Midtown Exec. and Chemists' Club, N.Y.C., Toastmasters. Home: 812 Abbott St Highland Park NJ 08904-2909 E-mail: hjbe@aol.com. *I have tried to play a constructive part in permitting others to make a positive contribution to society; to achieve a proper mix of idealism, reason, and faith in my decision making; to apply science and technology for the betterment of humanity.*

BRUDNER, HELEN GROSS, social sciences educator; b. NYC; d. Nathan and Mae (Grichtman) Gross; m. Harvey Jerome Brudner, Dec. 18, 1963; children: Mae Ann, Terry Joseph, Jay Scott. BS, NYU, 1959, MA, 1960, PhD, 1973. Tchr. N.Y.C. Bd. Edn., 1959-60; instr. Pratt Inst., Bklyn., 1959-61; asst. prof. history N.Y. Inst. Tech., N.Y.C., 1961-63, dir. guidance, 1962-63; assoc. prof. Fairleigh Dickinson U., Rutherford, N.J., 1963-73, prof. history and polit. sci. Teaneck, N.J., 1974—, dir. Honors Coll. Rutherford, N.J., 1972-84, chmn. dept. social sci., 1980-88, pres. univ. senate, 1975-78, asst. provost, 1983—, dean, 1984, dir. grad. programs, assoc. dir. Sch. History, Polit. and Internat. Studies, 1995—, dir. lang. grad. studies, pres. acad. senate, 1996—; v.p. HJB Enterprises, Highland Park, N.J., 1970—. Vice chmn. bd. dirs. WLC Inc., Highland Park, 1990—; cons. auto ednl. systems, 1971—; participant bd. trustees F.D.U.; spkr. N.J. Com. for The Humanities. Contbr. articles to profl. jours. on constl. law, transfer of tech., futurism. Active women in politics project NSF, 1981; active consortium project women in Am. history NEH and Woodrow Wilson Found., 1980, Consortium on Global Interdependence, Princeton, 1984; bd. dirs. Options Spkrs. Bur., N.J. Credit Union League, N.J. Credit Union Shared Network, WLC Inc.; mem. Mcpl. Alliance Highland Park, Hist. Preservation Commn., Highland Park; chmn. bd. dirs. Fairleigh Dickinson U. Fed. Credit Union, 1987—; vice chmn. N.J. Adv. Com. on Women Vets., 1993—; design selection com. N.J. Korean Vets. Meml.; 2d v.p. bd. dirs. Casitas De Monte Corp., Calif. Recipient Woman of Yr. award Am. Businesswomen's Assn., 1980, Meritorious Svc. award N.J. Credit Union League, 1997, Cert. Spl. Congrl. Recognition, 2000. Mem. Am. Judicature Soc., Am. Hist. Soc., Acad. Polit. Sci., Phi Alpha Theta, Phi Sigma Alpha. Office: Fairleigh Dickinson U Sch History, Polit Internat Studies Teaneck NJ 07666

BRUDVIG, GLENN LOWELL, retired library director; b. Kenosha, Wis., Oct. 14, 1931; s. Lars L. Brudvig and Anna Elizabeth (Hillesland) B. Lovejoy; m. Myrna Winifred Michael, Oct. 1, 1953; children— Gary Wayne, Lee Anthony, James Lowell, Kristin Elizabeth BA in Edn., U. N.D., 1954, MA, 1956; MALS, U. Minn., 1962. Tchr. pub. schs. Mahnoman and Herman, Minn., 1954-55, 56-58; librarian, archivist U. N.D., Grand Forks, 1958-62, asst. librarian, 1962-63; supr. dept. libraries U. Minn., Mpls., 1964, dir. bio-med. libr., 1964-83; dir. librs. Calif. Inst. Tech., Pasadena, 1983-95, ret., 1995. Instr. library sci. U. N.D., Grand Forks, 1962-63; asst. dir. for research and devel. U. Minn., Mpls., 1968-79, instr. library sci., 1968-71, dir. Inst. Tech. Libraries, 1982-83; cons. Nat. Library of Medicine, Bethesda, Md., 1971-75. Contbr. articles to profl. jours. Served with U.S. Army, 1951-52 Nat. Library of Medicine grantee, 1967-79. Home: 15 Eagle Ridge Rd Saint Paul MN 55127-6411

BRUDVIG, JON LARSEN, history educator; b. Kenosha, Wis., Mar. 6, 1965; s. Manley Hale and Mary Ann Brudvig; m. Sandra Jean Swift, Oct. 10, 1987. BA, Marquette U., 1987, MA, 1989; PhD, Coll. of William and Mary, 1996. Instr. Thomas Nelson C.C., Hampton, Va., 1992-96; asst. prof. St. Leo Coll., Langley AFB, Va., 1994-96, U. Mary, Bismarck, N.D., 1996-2001, assoc. prof., 2001—. Contbr. articles and essays to profl. jours. Vol. ARC, Fort Eustis, Va., 1994-96, State Hist. Soc., Bismarck, N.D., 1996-98, Med Ctr. 1, Bismarck, 1999—. Va. Commonwealth fellow State Coun. of Higher Edn., 1993-94, rsch. fellowship Commonwealth Ctr., 1992-93; Bicknell scholarship Nat. Sons and Daus. of the Pilgrims, 1991-92. Mem. SAR, Hist. Soc., Nat. Social Sci. Assn., Pheasants Forever, Loyal Order of Moose, Elks, Freemasons, SSHA, Phi Beta Kappa. Democrat. Avocations: fishing, hunting. Office: U of Mary 7500 University Dr Bismarck ND 58504-9634 E-mail: jlbrud@umary.edu.

BRUECHERT, BEVERLY ANN, interior design consultant, recording artist, pianist; b. Oregon City, Oreg., May 3, 1960; d. Robert Wayne and Bonnie Helen (Troutner) B. BS in Applied Design with honors, Portland State U., 1986. Sales exec. in interior furnishing MW End Store, Portland, Oreg.; fabric designer Daisy Kingdom, Portland; sales exec. in design firm Chase Internat., Portland. Music dir. Calvary Presbyn. Ch., Portland, Waverly United Ch. of Christ; asst. music. dir. Sunset Presbyn. Ch., Oreg. Performer: (recordings) vocal and piano compositions, Twilight, a solo piano experience, 1994, Lights Out IV, Food Bank benefit, 1997, Daybreak, 2000; featured artist KINK Radio. Mem. ASCAP, Fashion Group Internat. Republican. Christian. Avocations: music, sports, travel. Home: 6645 W Burnside Rd Apt 524 Portland OR 97210-6646

BRUECKMANN, ROBIN M. riding instructor, horse show judge; b. Wilmington, Del., Jan. 4, 1958; d. James Edwin and Cynthia (Travis) Miller; m. William Robert Brueckmann, Aug. 1, 1986. BA, Averett Coll., Danville, Va.; 9. Cert. riding instr., cert. instr. educator. Riding instr. Los Saltadores, Belton, Tex., 1979, Stockton Farms Inc., Wilmington, 1979-83; stable mgr. Hueckeroth Stables, Southern Pines, N.C., 1983-85; riding instr. Thorncroft Therapeutic Horseback Riding Inc., Malvern, Pa., 1985-96; riding instr., author self employed, Summerfield, N.C., 1996—. Horse show judge USAEquestruian, 1984—. Author: Dressage in a Side Saddle, 1984, When Two Are One, 1998; editor, contbr. newsletters Thorncroft News, 1986-96, Centered Riding News, 1998-2001. Pres. bd. trustees Centered Riding Inc., Allentown, Pa., 1994-99. Recipient award for Horse of Yr., N.C. Dressage and Combined Tng. Assn., 1999, 2000, Gold, Silver and Bronze medals U.S. Dressage Fedn., 1987, 89, 93, Gold medal World Dressage Championships, 1999, freestyle Gold medal Individual (Denmark), 1999, rep. U.S. Paralympic Games (Sydney, Australia), 2000, others; named Instr. of Yr., Am. Riding Instr. Cert. Program, 1996. Mem. Internat. Side Saddle Orgn. (judge, instr.). Presbyterian. Avocations: riding horses, gardening, reading, training cats, yoga. Home: 6004 Lomond Dr Summerfield NC 27358-7801 Office: Namaste 6004 Lomond Dr Summerfield NC 27358-7801 Fax: 336-643-8491. E-mail: chiri302@aol.com.

BRUECKNER, JAN KEITH, economics educator; b. Berkeley, Calif., July 20, 1950; s. Keith Allan and Marjorie (Dumas) B.; m. Laura Trimarco, July 7, 1979; children: Eric, Claire. AB, U. Calif., Berkeley, 1972; PhD, Stanford U., 1976. Prof. econs. U. Ill., Urbana-Champaign, 1976—. Editor Jour. Urban Econs., 1991—; contbr. articles to profl. jours. Office: U Ill Dept Econs 1206 S 6th St Champaign IL 61820-6978

BRUEMMER, FRED, writer, photographer; b. Riga, Latvia, June 26, 1929; emigrated to Can., 1951, naturalized, 1956; s. Arist and Dorothea (Wahl) B.; m. Maud van den Berg, Mar. 31, 1962; children: Aurel, Rene. Student Fed. Republic Germany schs.; DLitt (hon.), U. N.B., Can., 1989. Self-employed writer-photographer specializing in arctic and antarctic regions, 1961—; books include The Long Hunt, 1969, Seasons of the Eskimo, 1971, Encounters with Arctic Animals, 1972, The Arctic, 1974, The Life of the Harp Seal, 1977, Children of the North, 1979, Summer at Bear River, 1980, The Arctic of the World, 1985, Arctic Animals, 1986, Seasons of the Seal, 1988, World of the Polar Bear, 1989, (with Eric S. Grace) Seals, 1991, The Narwhal, 1993, (with Angéle Delaunois), Les Animaux du Grand Nord, 1993, (with Karen Pandell) Land of Dark, Land of Light, 1993, Arctic Memoires: Living with the Inuit, 1993, (with Angéle Delaunois) Nanook and Naoya: The Polar Bear Cubs, 1995, Kotik: The Baby Seal, 1995, (with Thomas D. Mangelsen) Polar Dance, 1996, Seals in the Wild, 1998, Glimpses of Paradise: The Marvel of Massed Animals, 2002. Decorated Order of Can.; Recipient Queen Elizabeth II Silver Jubilee medal, 1978, Canadian Anniversary Commemorative medal, 1993. Fellow Arctic Inst. N.Am., Royal Can. Acad. Art, Travel Journalists Guild, N.Am. Nature Photography Assn. (Lifetime Achievement award 2003). Address: 2 Strathearn South Montreal West Montreal QC Canada H4X 1X4 E-mail: fredbruemmer@yahoo.ca.

BRUEN, JAMES A. lawyer; b. South Hampton, N.Y., Nov. 29, 1943; s. John Francis and Kathryn Jewell (Arthur) B.; m. Carol Lynn Heller, June 13, 1968; children: Jennifer Lynn, Garrett John. BA cum laude, Claremont Men's Coll., 1965; JD, Stanford U., 1968. Bar: Calif. 1968, U.S. Dist. Ct. (no., ea., so. and cen. dists.) Calif. 1970, U.S. Ct. Claims 1972, U.S. Tax Ct. 1972, U.S. Ct. Appeals (9th cir.) 1972, U.S. Supreme Ct. 1973, Ariz. 1993. Atty. FCC, Washington, 1968-70; asst. U.S. atty. criminal div. Office of U.S. Atty., San Francisco, 1970-73, asst. U.S. atty. civil div., 1973-75, chief of civil div., 1975-77; ptnr. Landels, Ripley & Diamond, San Francisco, 1977-2000, Farella Braun & Martel LLP, San Francisco, 2000—. Mem. faculty Nat. Jud. Coll. ABA; lectr. Am. Law Inst. Am. Bd. Trial Advocates, Practising Law Inst. Def. Rsch. Inst., others. Co-author: Pharmaceutical Products Liability, 1989; contbg. editor: Hazardous Waste and Toxic Torts Law and Strategy, 1987-92; contbr. numerous articles to profl. jours. Mem. ABA (vice chmn. environ. quality com. nat. resources sect. 1989-93, co-chmn. enforment litigation subcom. environ. litigation com. litigation sect. 1990-92), Am. Inn of Ct. (master-at-large), Internat. Soc. for Environ. Epidemiology. Avocations: scuba diving, travel. Office: Farella Braun & Martel Russ Bldg 30th Fl 235 Montgomery St San Francisco CA 94104 Fax: (415) 954-4480. E-mail: jbruen@fbm.com.

BRUEN, JOHN DERMOT, executive consultant; b. Glen Cove, N.Y., Oct. 19, 1930; s. John D. and Kathleen M. (Halferty) B.; m. Ann Theone Lee, June 22, 1957; children: Michael J., Kathleen A., Thomas L., Lisa M. BS, U. Md., 1959; MBA, U. Pitts., 1963; grad., Naval War Coll. Command and Staff Course, 1966, Army War Coll., 1972. Enlisted in U.S. Army, 1948, commd. 2d lt., 1953, advanced through grades to lt. gen., 1983; service in Korea, Germany, Azores, Thailand and Vietnam; dir. resources and mgmt. Office Dep. Chief Staff Logistics Hqrs., DA, 1977—79; comdr. Mil. Traffic Mgmt. Command, 1979-83; comdr. 21st Support Command, 1983-86; ret., 1986; pres. Bruen & Assocs., Springfield, Va., 1986—; vice chmn. internat. U.S. Computer-Aided Acquisition and Life-Cycle Support Industry Steering Group, 1991—95; hon. col. U.S. Army Transp. Corps Regt., 1997—2001. Contbr. articles on leadership, mgmt. to profl. jours. Decorated Def. D.S.M., Army D.S.M., Legion of Merit with two oak leaf clusters, Bronze Star with one oak leaf cluster, Meritorious Svc. medal

with one oak leaf cluster, Army Commendation medal with one oak leaf cluster; named to U.S. Inf. Officer Candidate Sch. Hall of Fame, 1979, U.S. Army Transp. Corps Hall of Fame, 2000; named Grand Officer of the Order of the Crown, Belgium, 1986; recipient Computer-Aided Acquisition and Life-Cycle Support Meritorious Svc. award, 1996. Mem. U.S. Army Transp. Corps Regiment Assn. (pres. 1997-2001), Nat. Def. Transp. Assn., Assn. U.S. Army, Mil. Officers Assn. Am. (bd. dirs. 1986-94). Roman Catholic. Office: 6104 Greenlawn Ct Springfield VA 22152-1314

BRUENE, WARREN BENZ, electronic engineer; b. Beaman, Iowa, Nov. 1, 1916; s. Fred Karl and Luella Lydia (Benz) B.; m. Mildred Clare Meyer, July 13, 1941; children: Julia Beth Bruene James, Jo Carol Bruene Lilley. BSEE, Iowa State U., 1938. Registered profl. engr., Tex. Design engr. Collins Radio Co., Cedar Rapids, Iowa, 1939-46, project engr., 1946-54, group head, 1954-57, dept. staff, 1957-60, dept. head, 1960-61, div. staff, Richardson, Tex., 1961-73; div. staff Rockwell Internat., Richardson, 1973-84; sr. engr. Electrospace Systems, Inc., Richardson, 1984-90; pvt. practice radio engring. cons. Dallas, 1990—. Vis. com. U. Tex., Austin, 1966-72. Co-author 7 tech. books; contbr. articles to profl. jours. Inventor 22 patents. Named Engr. of Yr., Preston Trail chpt. Tex. Soc. Profl. Engrs., 1975, profl. achievement citation in engring. Iowa State U., 1993. Fellow IEEE (sect. chmn. 1958-59, region dir. 1962-63), Toastmasters (Richardson) (area gov. 1969). Republican. Methodist. Avocations: economics, amateur radio, technical writing. Home: 7805 Chattington Dr Dallas TX 75248-5307

BRUENER, JAMES WILLIAM, fundraiser; b. Port Edwards, Wis., July 4, 1950; s. William John and Dorothy Anne (Lobner) B.; life ptnr. Clifford Goltz, Aug. 1, 1992. BA, U. Minn., 1972. Fundraiser Friends for a Non-Violent World, Mpls., 1992—. Mem. Soc. Of Friends. Avocations: theater, symphonic performances, opera, art museums. Home: 1179 Edmund Ave Saint Paul MN 55104-2523

BRUESCHKE, ERICH EDWARD, physician, researcher, educator; b. nr. Eagle Butte, S.D., July 17, 1933; s. Erich Herman and Eva Johanna (Joens) B.; m. Frances Marie Bryan, Mar. 25, 1967; children: Erich Raymond, Jason Douglas, Tina Marie, Patricia Frances, Susan Eva. BS in Elec. Engring, S.D. Sch. Mines and Tech., 1956; postgrad., U. So. Calif., 1960-61; MD, Temple U., 1965. Diplomate Am. Bd. Family Practice, also cert. in geriatrics. Intern Germantown Dispensary and Hosp., Phila., 1965-66; mem. tech. staff Hughes Research and Devel. Labs., Culver City, Calif., 1956-61; practiced gen. medicine Fullerton, Calif., 1968-69; dir. research Ill. Inst. Tech. Research Inst., Chgo., 1970-76; research asst. prof. Temple U. Sch. Medicine, 1965-69; mem. staff Mercy Hosp. and Med. Center, Chgo., 1970-76; vis. prof. Rush Med. Coll., Chgo., 1974-76, prof., chmn. dept. family practice, 1976—, program dir. Rush. Christ family practice residency, 1978-93, vice dean, 1992—, acting dean, 1993-94, dean, 1994-2000, v.p. univ. affairs, 2000—02; trustee Anchor HMO, 1976-81, v.p. med. and acad. affairs, 1981—; trustee Synergon Health Systems, 1993-98; vice chmn., bd. dirs. Rush Presbyn. St. Lukes Health Assocs., disting. prof. medicine, 2002—, Rush Med. Coll. of Rush U., 2002—. Sr. attending Presbyn.-St. Luke's Hosp., Chgo., 1976—; med. dir. Chgo. Bd. of Health West Side Hypertension Ctr., 1974—78; bd. dirs. Comprehensive Health Planning Met. Chgo., 1971—74, Fedn. of Ind. Ill. Colls. and Univs., West Suburban Higher Edn. Consortium; adv. com. Edn. to Careers, Health and Medicine/Chgo. Bd. Edn. Editor-in-chief Disease-a-Month, 1998—; assoc. editor Primary Cardiology, 1979-85; cons. editor for family practice Hosp. Medicine, 1986—; med. editor World Book/Rush Presbyn. St. Lukes/Med. Ency., 1987—; contbr. articles to profl. jours. Served with USAF, 1966-68. Named Physician Tchr. of Yr. Ill. Acad. Family Physicians, 1988, alumni of yr. Temple U. Sch. Medicine, 1996. Fellow Am. Acad. Family Physicians, Inst. of Medicine of Chgo.; mem. IEEE (chmn. Chgo. sect. Engring. in Medicine and Biology group 1974-75), Internat. Soc. for Artificial Internal Organs, Am. Fertility Soc., Am. Occupational Med. Assn. (recipient Physician's recognition award 1969, 72, 75), Chgo. Med. Soc., Am. Heart Assn., Assn. for Advancement Med. Instrumentation, N.Y. Acad. Scis., Sigma Xi, Phi Rho Sigma, Eta Kappa Nu, Alpha Omega Alpha. Home: 319 N Lincoln St Hinsdale IL 60521-3442 *It is important to be courageous and do what you really want to do rather than what is expected or what seems to be currently popular. If life is approached with a spirit of goodwill and one is strong enough to follow one's own desires, then the contribution made and the success achieved can be a credit to humanity and also a source of endless enjoyment. The real secret of life is self-discipline; this allows the tempering of short-term needs with the necessary long-term planning to achieve a stable life and a meaningful contribution to humankind.*

BRUESEKE, HAROLD EDWARD, magistrate; b. Sandusky, Ohio, Mar. 19, 1943; s. Edward W. and Jolanda (Sommer) B.; m. Bonnie A. Beaver, Aug. 12, 1967; children: Matthew E., Michael A. BA with honors, Elmhurst Coll., 1965; JD, Ind. U., 1968; grad., Ind. Judicial Coll., 2000. Bar: Ind., 1968, U.S. Dist. Ct. (no. and so. dists.) 1968, U.S. Supreme Ct. 1978; lic. real estate broker, Ind. Staff atty. Legal Svcs./Legal Edn., South Bend, Ind., 1968-70; pvt. practice South Bend, 1971-92; dep. pros. atty. St. Joseph County, South Bend, 1971-73; juvenile referee St. Joseph Probate Ct., South Bend, 1973-92, judge pro tem, 1993, magistrate, 1993—. Instr. Ivy Tech. State Coll., South Bend, Ind., 2003—. Contbg. author: Juvenile Benchbook, 1980-92. Bd. dirs. Eden Theol. Sem., St. Louis, 1989-2001, various other civic orgns., South Bend, 1968—; bd. dirs., elder Zion United Ch. of Christ, South Bend, 1994-96. Mem. ABA, Ind. State Bar Assn., St. Joseph County Bar Assn., Nat. Coun. Juvenile and Family Ct. Judges, Ind. Coun. Juvenile and Family Ct. Judges (bd. dirs., sec., v.p. pres. 1980-2000), Jud. Conf. Ind. (dir. 1998-2000). Avocations: amateur radio, recreational vehicles, computers. Home: 52741 Arbor Dr South Bend IN 46635-1205 Office: Juvenile Justice Ctr 1000 S Michigan St South Bend IN 46601-3426 E-mail: bhbruese@comcast.net., hbrueseke@jjconline.org.

BRUESKE, CHARLOTTE, poet, composer; b. Plainview Township, Minn., Jan. 1, 1934; d. Layton Floyd and Berneta Dallas (Thompson) B. AA, Pasadena City Coll., 1976; BA, Calif. State U., Fullerton, 1984; postgrad., Fuller Theol. Sem. Author: Once in a Coon's Age, 1989, The Ancestors of Gottlob August Bruss and Bertha Pauline Goede, 1989, A Search for the Records of the Orphans of Dannan, 1990; composer, lyricist numerous works, including Evergreen, 1990, Every New Day, 1991, Lift Up One Another, 1991, Where the Red Ferns Abound, 1995, To Touch This World by Love, 1996, Because of Love, 1997, Poems of the Seasons, To Every Life, 1998; co-author: (with J'hana Brueske) I Heard a Robin Sing Today, 1997, Consider the Lilies, 1997, Life Friend, 1998, Where Love Abides, 1998, The Bells in the Steeple, 1999, Anthology of Love: Morning Light, The Hug of Heaven, Break Not The Morn At Dawning, 2001, Anthology: Still I See the Dawn, Healing Hands, Sunset, 2002, Seasons of the Heart, 2003. Recipient Cert. of Merit Virginia Baldwin/Talent Assocs., 1977. Democrat. Mem. Reformed Ch. Am. Home: PO Box 134-321 Big Bear Lake CA 92315 E-mail: charlottebrueske@juno.com.

BRUESS, CHARLES EDWARD, lawyer; b. St. Paul, Oct. 15, 1938; s. Edward Charles and Eleanor Mabel (Hammersten) B.; m. Jean Ellen Gustafson, Aug. 26, 1962; children: Steven Charles, Karen Jean. BA, U. Minn., 1959; student, Ohio U., 1959-60; JD, Ind. U., 1963. Bar: Ind. 1963, U.S. Dist. Ct. (so. dist.) Ind. 1968, U.S. Supreme Ct. 1966. Assoc. Barnes, Hickam, Pantzer & Boyd, Indpls., 1967-71; ptnr. Barnes & Thornburg (formerly Barnes, Hickam, Pantzer & Boyd), Indpls., 1972-94, of counsel, 1995-96, ret., 1996; dep. clk. U.S. Dist. Ct. (so. dist.) Ind., 1999—. Trustee Eagle-Union Community Sch. Corp., Zionsville, Ind., 1978-90; dir. Tri-County Ctr. Inc., 1991-94, dir., sec. Zionsville Pub. Libr., Leasing Corp., 1992—; bd. dirs. Hussey-Mayfield Meml. Pub. Libr. Found., 1999—. Fellow Ind. Bar Found.; Lawyers Club (Indpls.). Republican. Methodist. Home: 3517 Inverness Blvd Carmel IN 46032

BRUETT, KAREN DIESL, sales and fundraising consultant; b. N.Y.C., May 15, 1945; d. Francis J. and Dorothy (Peterson) Diesl; m. William H. Bruett, Jr., Mar. 18, 1967; 1 child, Lindsey Diesl. BA in English, St. Lawrence U., 1966; MA, Hunter Coll., 1971. Tchr. English Freeport (N.Y.) pub. schs., 1966-70; exec. interviewer, researcher Louis Harris & Assocs., N.Y.C., 1970-72; dir. adult edn. West Side YMCA, 1972-76, mem. bd. mgrs., 1978-83; v.p. new bus. devel. Gaylord Adams & Assocs., Inc., N.Y.C., 1976-81; account exec. John Blair Mktg., N.Y.C., 1981-83, v.p. sales, 1983-84, sr. v.p., gen. sales mgr., 1984-86; ind. sales and fundraising cons. Bd. dirs. Resolution, Inc., S. Burlington, Vt., HMI, Inc., Norwood, Mass. Trustee St. Lawrence U., 1978—, vice chair trustees, 1995-2001, chair alumni fund, 1983-84, chair annual giving, 1984-88, chair planning com., 1987-88, chair pressl. search com., 1994-95, mem. exec. com., 1987—, chair devel. com., 1988-95, chair nominating com., 1999—; trustee Vt. Coun. on Arts, 1986-91, vice chair bd. trustees, chair devel. com., 1988-91; bd. advisors Somerset Hills Edn. Found., 1997—; del. Am.-Soviet Youth Forum, Baku, USSR, 1974. Mem. Internat. Women's Forum. Home and Office: 110 Mosle Rd Far Hills NJ 07931-2229

BRUGGEMAN, TERRANCE JOHN, financial corporate executive; b. Mandan, N.D., Oct. 20, 1946; s. George Edward and Marcella Merle (Gray) B.; m. Nancy Ellen Hohman, June 28, 1969 (div. 1997); children: Todd M., Megan P. BA, U. Notre Dame, 1968; postgrad. bus. adminstrn., U. Chgo., 1968-70. Div. mgr., v.p. Continental Ill. Nat. Bank, Chgo., 1968-77; asst. treas. Gould Inc., Rolling Meadows, Ill., 1977-78, treas., 1978-80, v.p., treas., 1980-81; chmn. Gould Fin. Inc., Rolling Meadows, 1978-81; v.p. fin. and adminstrn. AM Internat., Inc., Chgo., 1981-85; mng. dir. Dean Witter Reynolds, Inc., 1985-86; sr. mng. dir. Bear, Stearns and Co., Inc., N.Y.C., 1986-89; sr. v.p., bd. mem., chief ops. officer Lear Siegler Inc., Livingston, N.J., 1989-90; sr. v.p., bd. dirs., chief fin. officer chief ops. officer Grimes Aerospace and FL Industries, Livingston, 1989-90; mng. ptnr. Three Cities Rsch., Inc., N.Y.C., 1990-93; chmn., pres. and CEO Network Mgmt. Inc., Fairfax, Va., 1993-97, chmn., CEO Piatl Holdings Inc., Mt. Laurel, N.J., 1993-99; chmn., pres., CEO Syscon Corp., Falls Church, Va., 1995-96; chmn., CEO Norcross Safety Products, Oak Brook, Ill., 1996, Red Ball Inc., Louisville, 1996, So. Cross O'Fallon Bldg. Products, St. Louis, 1996, Red Giraffe, Louisville, 1996; chmn., CEO, pres. Diversa Corp., San Diego, 1996-99; chmn., pres., CEO Provasis Theraputics, Inc., San Diego, 1999—. Bd. dirs. Yulex Corp., Harnifschfeger Industries, Inc., SGI, Inc., Silver Eagle Transport, Inc., Stationers Distbg., Inc., Alpha Wire Inc., Miss Erika Inc., Garden Ridge Pottery Corp., Pameco Holding Inc., Curtis Industries Inc., Gulf Coast Lubrication. Bd. dirs. Lincoln Park Zool. Soc., 1972—, pres., CEO, 1984-87; bd. dirs. North Shore Youth Health Svc., 1979-80, N.Y. Zool. Soc./The Wildlife Conservation Soc., 1987-96, Biocom, 1999—, Chmn.'s Roundtable, 1999—. Mem. Fin. Execs. Inst., Am. Assn. Zool. Parks and Aquariums, Chgo. Club, Notre Dame Club. Home: 7553 High Ave La Jolla CA 92037-5214 E-mail: tbruggeman@san.rr.com.

BRUGGER, DAVID JOHN, media consultant; b. Bethlehem, Pa., Feb. 5, 1943; s. Vincent Francis and Frances Stephanie (Miller) Brugger; m. Joanne Kay Strouf, Oct. 26, 1973. BA in Journalism, Duquesne U., 1965; MS in Theater, CUNY, 1968; postgrad., Drake U., 1973-74, Harvard U., 1980. Exec. prodr. Sta. KDIN-TV, Des Moines, 1968-70; prodn., ops. mgr. Iowa Pub. Broadcasting Network, Des Moines, 1970-71, network ops. mgr., 1971-73, dir. adminstrn., 1973-77; gen. mgr. Sta. WUFT-TV-FM, Gainesville, Fla., 1977-81; dir. Broadcast Svc. Corp. Pub. Broadcasting, Washington, 1981-83; v.p. Telecomm Corp. Pub. Broadcasting, Washington, 1983-87; sr. v.p. Corp. Pub. Broadcasting, Washington, 1987; pres., bd. dirs. Assn. Am.'s Pub. TV Stas., Washington, 1988-2000; pres. Global Media Consulting, Washington, 2000—. Cons. Republic of China, Taipei, Taiwan, 1983, Va. Dept. Info. Tech., Richmond, 1989, Fla. Postsecondary Edn. Planning Commn., Tallahassee, 1990, Internat. Found. Electoral Sys., 2001, Nat. Telecom. Info. Agy., 2003, Meridian Internat. Ctr., Indonesia Internat. Found. Election Sys., Nat. Ednl. Telcom. Assn., BMR Assocs., Taiwan Pub. Broadcasting Found., Iowa Pub. TV Network, Bar Assocs.; cons., lectr. Fundacion Agnel Ramos, Hato Rey, PR, 1990; mem. consumer adv. com. FCC, 2003—05. Prodr.: (TV program) Interracial Dating and Marriage, 1967 (N.E.T. award, 1968); exec. prodr. (TV program) The Bicycle, 1968 (Ohio State award, 1968). Named to Hall of Fame, Boys and Girls Clubs Am., 1992; recipient Disting. Svc. award, Ea. Pub. Radio Network, 1984, Lowell award, Pub. Broadcasting, 2000; Bklyn. Coll. TV Ctr. scholar, 1965. Mem.: Soc. Profl. Journalists, Greater Washington Soc. Assn. Execs., Am. Soc. Assn. Execs. (Excellence in Govt. Rels. award 1992), USIA Pvt. Sector Ctr., Nat. Boys Club Alumni Assn. (award 1988), Cosmos Club. Roman Catholic. Avocations: golf, swimming, photography.

BRUGGER, GEORGE ALBERT, lawyer; b. Erie, Pa., Jan. 19, 1941; s. Albert F. and Georgia V. (Bach) B.; children from previous marriage: Laura, Linda, Mark; m. Ann Rosenberg. BA, Gannon Coll., 1963; JD, Georgetown U., 1967. Bar: Md. 1968, D.C. 2002, U.S. Dist. Ct. Md. 1972, U.S. Supreme Ct. 1972. Law clk. to U.S. asst. atty. gen. U.S. Dept. of Justice, Washington, 1963-66; mgr. pub. affairs Air Transport Assn. of Am., Washington, 1966-68; ptnr. Beatty & McNamee, Hyattsville, Md., 1968-75; sr. ptnr., pres. Fossett & Brugger, Chartered, Greenbelt, Md., 1975—. Bd. dirs. Prince George's County Fin. Svcs. Corp. Chmn. bd. dirs. Prince George's Econ. Devel. Corp.; pres. Laurel Regional Hosp. Found. Recipient Disting. Alumni award Gannon Coll. Fellow Md. Bar Found.; mem. ABA (chmn. land use regulation com.), Md. Bar Assn. (bd. dirs.), Prince George's County Bar Assn. (pres. 1982), Prince George's Law Found., (bd. dirs.), Prince George's County C. of C. (Disting. Svc. award 1980, 83, 85), Fed. Bar Assn. (dir.). Roman Catholic. Avocations: collecting watches, marine tropical fish. Home: The Colonnade 2801 New Mexico Ave NW Washington DC 20007 also: 5546 N Harbor Village Dr Vero Beach FL 32967 Office: Fossett & Brugger Chartered 6404 Ivy Ln Ste 720 Greenbelt MD 20770-1425

BRUGIONI, DAVID MICHAEL, graphic designer, illustrator, artist; b. Gary, Ind., Sept. 21, 1956; s. Dominic and Delores Brugioni; m. Nancy Tarr, Nov. 2, 1985 (dec. Feb. 2001); children: Heather, Catherine. Student, W.Va. No. C.C., Wheeling, 1986, 87. Percussionist various club bands, Wheeling, 1980—; digital photo editor The Times Leader News, Martins Ferry, Ohio, 1990—2002. Illustrator: editl. cartoons, 1993, 94, 97, 98, 99, 2000, 2001, 2002. Recipient 2nd pl. award of merit for editl. cartoon AP Ohio, 1999. Avocations: art, playing drums. Home: 1203 Wolfe Avenue Louisville KY 40213

BRUGIONI, DINO ANTHONY, writer, lecturer, consultant; b. Bevier, Mo., Dec. 16, 1921; s. John and Frances (Fraulini) B.; m. Theresa Harich, Jan. 29, 1949; children: Theresa, John. BA, George Washington U., 1947, MA, 1948. Liaison officer Tenn. Valley Authority, Washington, 1945—48; officer CIA, Washington, 1948—55; sr. officer, aerial reconnaissance, photo interpretation expert Nat. Photog. Interpretation Ctr., Washington, 1955—82. Cons. CIA, 1982—, Nat. Imagery and Mapping Agy., Washington, 1995-97; lectr. in field, Harvard, MIT, U. Calif., Berkeley, Nat. War Coll., Def. Intelligence Coll., State Dept. Fgn. Svc. Sch., Smithsonian Instn. Author: The Holocaust Revisited: A Retrospective Analysis of the Auschwitz-Birkenau Extermination Complex, 1979, The Civil War in Missouri: As Seen from the Capital City, 1987, Eyeball to Eyeball: The Inside Story of the Cuban Missile Crisis, 1991, From Balloons to Blackbirds, 1993, Photo Fakery: The History and Techniques of Photographic Deception and Manipulation, 1999; contbr. over 80 articles to profl. jours.; appeared on numerous TV shows, U.S., Germany, France, Japan. Recipient commendation for performance during Cuban Missile Crisis, Pres. Kennedy, 1962, award for best scholarly article Nat. Intelligence Study Ctr., 1970, Sherman Kent award for outstanding contbns. to lit. of intelligence, 1973, 79, CIA Career Intelligence medal, CIA Intelligence medal of Merit, 1982, Disting. Alumnus award Jefferson City Pub. Schs. Alumni Assn., 1980, Pioneer in Space medal, 1986. Mem.: DAV, VFW, Purple Heart Assn., Medmenham Club. Roman Catholic. Avocations: writing, travel. Home and Office: 301 Storck Rd Hartwood VA 22406-4731

BRUGMAN, JACQUELYN JOY, physician assistant; b. Albion, Nebr., Nov. 6, 1957; d. John George and Adrene Joy Noble; m. Thomas Wayne Brugman; children: Andrew, Carissa, Brianna. BS, U. of Nebr. Med. Ctr., 1988. Cert. P.A.-C by NCCPA NE, 1988. LPN Luth. Hosp., Norfolk, Nebr., 1977—78, Albion Hosp., Nebr., 1978—81, Wolf Meml. Good Samaritan Ctr., Albion, Nebr., 1981—84, Hillhaven Nursing Home, Lincoln, Nebr., 1984—86; physician asst. Primus Clinic, Papillion, Nebr., 1988—90, Phillip Meyer, M.D., Council Bluffs, Iowa, 1990—91, Boone County Health Ctr., Albion, Nebr., 1991—2002. Bd. mem. Wolf Meml. Good Samaritan Ctr., Albion, 1994—96; bd. of edn. mem. St. Michael's Cath. Sch., Albion, 1999—2001, bd. of edn. pres., 2001—02. Recipient Outstanding Svc. award, Nebr. Acad. of Physician Assistants, 1999, Physician Asst. of the Yr., 2001. Fellow: Nebr. Acad. of Physician Assistants (continuing edn. chmn. 1995—2000), Am. Acad. of Physician Assistants. R-Consevative. Roman Catholic. Avocations: writing, reading, music, gardening. Office: Boone County Medical Clinic 405 Broadway Fulerton NE 68638 Office Fax: 308-536-2727.

BRUKBAKER, LINDA, obstetrician, gynecologist; b. Oak Park, Ill., Oct. 30, 1955; d. George Albert and Marian Constance Tetzlaff; m. Warren Earl Brubaker, June 25, 1983; children: Aleah, Anita, Keene. BA with honors, Univ. Ill., Chgo., 1977; MD, Rush Univ., Chgo., 1984. Cert. Am. Bd. of Ob/Gyn., lic. DEA, physician and surgeon Ill., controlled substance Ill. House staff Rush Presbyn. St. Luke's Med. Ctr., Chgo., 1984—88, adj. attending, 1988—90; asst. attending Rush Presbyn. St. Luke's Hosp., Chgo., 1990—98, sr. attending, 1998—2000, Loyola Univ. Med. Ctr., 2000—. Fellowship Rush Univ. Rush Med. Coll., Chgo., 1982—83; residency Rush Presbyn. St. Luke's Med. Ctr., Chgo., 1984—88, chief resident, 1987—88, fellowship, 1988—90; prof. Loyola Univ. Med. Ctr., Maywood, 2000—. Author: Operative Gynecology, 2000, The Female Pelvic: A Multidisciplinary Approach, 1996; contbr. over 52 articles to profl. jour., chapters to books. Recipient Urogynecologist of the Yr., Nat. Assn. for Continence, 2002, Faculty Tchg. award, Othro Pharm./CREOG, 1998, Outstanding Svc. on the Edn. Commn. of ACOG, 1998, Faculty Tchg. award, 1992. Fellow: ACOG; mem.: Rush Surgical Soc. (pres. 2001—02, pres.-elect 2000—01), Internat. Urogynecological Assn., Internat. Continence Soc., Chgo. Gynecological Soc. (pres.-elect 2002—), Ctrl. Assn. of OB/GYN, Am. Found. for Urologic Disease, ACS, Soc. of Gynecologic Surgeons (program com. chair 2000—01, chmn., bylaws com. 2001, bylaws com. chair 2002—), Am. Urogynecologic Soc. (sec.-treas. 1997—2000, v.p., program co-chair 2000—01, pres. elect, program co-chair 2001—02, pres. 2002—). Avocations: reading, orchids, sports. Office: Loyola Univ Med Ctr 2160 S First Ave Maywood IL 60153

BRULEY, DUANE FREDERICK, academic administrator, consultant, engineer; b. Chippewa Falls, Wis., Aug. 3, 1933; s. Casper Sepharald and Hazel Ella (Kuehn) B.; m. Suzanne Bigler, June 14, 1959; children: Scott, Randall, Mark. Student, Eau Clare (Wis.) State U., 1951-53; BSChemE, U. Wis., 1956; student, Oak Ridge (Tenn.) Sch. of Reactor Tech., 1957; M in Mech. Engring., Stanford U., 1959; PhD in Chem. Engring., U. Tenn., 1962. Registered profl. engr., S.C. Nuclear engr. Union Carbide Nuclear Co., Oak Ridge, Tenn., 1956-59; head tennis coach U. Tenn., 1961; prof. chem. engring., head tennis coach Clemson (S.C.) U., 1962-73; head chem. engring., head tennis coach Tulane U., New Orleans, 1973-77; head tennis profl. Timberlane Country Club, Gretna, La., 1973-76; v.p. acad. affairs, asst. tennis coach Rose Hulman Inst. Tech., Terre Haute, Ind., 1977-81; head biomed. engring., dir. rehab. engring. ctr. La. Tech. U., Ruston, 1981-84; dean sch. of engring., prof. engring. sci. Calif. Poly U., San Luis Obispo, 1984-91; program dir. biochem. and biomass engring. NSF, Washington, 1987-90, sect. head bioengring. and environ. systems, 1989-90; pres. Synthesizer, Inc., 1988—; dean engring. U. Md., Baltimore County, 1991-94, dir. bioengring., rsch. prof., 1994—. Vis. prof. Princeton (NJ) U., 1970, U. Yamagata (Japan), U. Hokkido, 1975, U. Minn., 1997; adj. prof. dept. chem. engring. U. Louisville, 2002—; cons. Westvaco, Charleston, S.C., 1964-67, DuPont, Ponchartrain, La., 1974-79, Am. Enka Corp., 1970-71, Milliken and Co., 1978-79, Exxon, Baton Rouge, La., 1978-79, El Paso Products Co., 1980-82, Electronics Assocs., Inc., Long Branch, NJ, 1984-88, CRAY Rsch., 1986, EDS, 1995; varsity football and tennis U. Wis., Eau Claire, football adv. coun., 2003—; semi profl. football Chippewa Marines, 1953-54; co-program dir. Nat. Heat Transfer Conf., Balt., 1997, chmn. conf. coord. com., 1998; chmn. nat. heat transfer coord. com. AIChE/ASME, 1998, Nat. Heat Transfer Ann. Conf., 1999; dir. ann. Biodownstream Processing Symposium ASME/AIChE, 2003. Author: (chpt.) Mathematics of Microcirculation, 1980; editor: Oxygen Supply, 1973, Oxygen Transport to Tissue, 1973, 83, 88, 91, 92, 94, 98, Hyperthermia, 1988, Protein C and Related Anticoagulants, 1990; rsch. editorial bd.: Biomedical Instrumentation and Technology, 1993-97; contbr. articles to profl. jours.; co-developer BWK Technique for high speed numerical integration. Cons. ARC; narrator five part TV series on biomed. engring., 1982, TV Biomed. Engring. Sta. WEAU, Eau Clare, Wis., 1982; keynote spkr. First Cray Acd., Rsch. Louisville, 2001; recorded for Wis. Pub. TV Network Biotechnology/Bioengring.; head tennis profl. Montebello Tennis Club, 1989-90; referee Sunshine Cup Internat. Jr. Tennis Tournament, Miami, 1966-69. Recipient Ann. Rsch. award La. Tech. U., 1983, Gold medal downhill skiing Nat. Standard Race, 1987, Alumni Disting. Svc. award U. Wis., Eau Claire, 1992, Spl. Opportunity award in Bioengring. The Whitaker Found., 1994—; named 2d Winningest Tennis Coach in Atlantic Coast Conf. history, 1990, one of Outstanding Educators of Am., 1972; NSF Goalie grantee with ARC-Protein C, 2001-2004. Fellow AIChE (chmn. heat transfer energy conversion divsn., chmn. com. for Donald Q. Kern award 1997, chmn. com. for Max Jakob Meml. award 1997, Disting. spkr.), Am. Inst. Med. and Biol. Engring. (founding fellow acad. coun.), ämemä ASME (exec. bd., bioprocess engring. program, chmn. bioprocess engring. subdivsn., Disting. spkr.); mem. Internat. Soc. on Oxygen Transport Tissue (co-founder 1973, pres. 1983, exec. com., founder, chmn. com. Melvin H. Knisely award 1983—, keynote spkr. 25th anniversary 1997, 26th ann. meeting, Budapest, Hungary 1998), N.Y. Acad. Scis., Calif. Soc. Profl. Engrs. (hon.), Soc. Automotive Engrs. (Ralph R. Teetor Ednl. award 1986), Nat. Soc. Profl. Engrs., Am. Soc. Engring. Edn. (1st Pl. Rsch. award 1967, Biomed. Instrumentation and Tech. Outstanding Rsch. Paper award 1966, 97), La. Engring. Soc. (Charles M. Kerr Pub. Rels. award 1983), U.S. Profl. Tennis Assn., U.S. Tennis Assn. (hon. life), Sigma Xi, Tau Beta Pi. Avocation: tennis (#1 mens 35 doubles and #3 mens 35 singles in SC). Home: 7345 Swan Point Way Columbia MD 21045-5010

BRULTE, JAMES L. state legislator; b. Glen Cove, N.Y., Apr. 13, 1956; BA, Calif. State Poly. U. Mem. staff U.S. Senator S.I. Hayakawa, Rep. Nat. Com., 1981; asst. to asst. sec. for res. affairs Dept. Def., from 1984; later White House advance rep. for Vice Pres. of U.S.; mem. Calif. State Assembly, 1990-96, Calif. State Senate, 1996—, vice chair budget and fiscal rev. com., mem. fin., investment and internat. trade com., vice chair energy, utilities and comms. com. Served with Calif. Air N.G., 1974. Republican. Office: State Capitol Rm 5087 Sacramento CA 95814 also: 10861 Foothill Blvd Ste 325 Rancho Cucamonga CA 91730-3859*

BRUMBACK, CHARLES TIEDTKE, retired newspaper executive; b. Toledo, Sept. 27, 1928; s. John Sanford and Frances Henrietta (Tiedtke) B.; m. Mary Louise Howe, July 7, 1951; children: Charles Tiedtke Jr., Anne Meyer, Wesley W., Ellen Allen. BA in Econs., Princeton U., 1950; postgrad., U. Toledo, 1953-54. CPA, Ohio, Fla. With Arthur Young & Co., CPAs, 1950-57; bus. mgr., v.p., treas., pres., CEO Sentinel Star Co. subs. Tribune Co., Orlando, Fla., 1957-81; pres., CEO Chgo. Tribune subs. Tribune Co., 1981-88, pres., COO, 1988-90, CEO, 1990-95, chmn., 1993-95, bd. dirs., 1981-96. Bd. dirs. Avid Tech., Inc. Bd. dirs. Robert R. McCormick Tribune Found.; life trustee Northwestern U., Chgo. Hist. Soc.; trustee Culver Ednl. Found.; trustee Northwestern Meml. Hosp., chmn., 1987-90. 1st lt. U.S. Army, 1951-53. Decorated Bronze star. Mem. AICPA, Fla. Press Assn. (treas. 1969-76, pres. 1980, bd. dirs.), Am. Newspaper Pubs. Assn. (bd. dirs., treas. 1991-92), Newspaper Assn. Am. (bd. dirs., sec., 1992-93, vice chmn. 1993-94, chmn. 1994-95), Comml. Club Chgo., Chgo. Club, Tavern Club. Home: 1500 N Lake Shore Dr Chicago IL 60610-6657 Office: Tribune Co 435 N Michigan Ave Chicago IL 60611-4066 E-mail: cbrumback@tribune.com, charlie435@aol.com.

BRUMBACK, CLARENCE LANDEN, physician; b. Denver, Apr. 19, 1914; s. Carl Alvin and Hildur Athelia (Landen) B.; m. Lucile Leslie Gillie, June 17, 1943; children— Richard, Carl. AB, U. Kans., 1936, MD, 1943; MPH, U. Mich., 1948. Diplomate Am. Bd. Preventive Medicine. Intern U.S. Marine Hosp., San Francisco, 1943-44; dir. pub. health Laclede County, Mo., 1947, AEC, Oak Ridge, 1948-50; dir. Palm Beach County (Fla.) Health Dept., 1950-86; coord. grad. edn. Palm Beach County Health Dept., 1986-2000. Clin. prof. U. Miami; adj. prof. Fla. Atlantic U., Boca Raton, Fla.; trustee Am. Bd. Preventive Medicine, 1969-78. Mem. editl. bd. Jour. Public Health Policy, 1981-88; contbr. articles to profl. jours. Bd. dirs. Palm Beach County chpt. A.R.C., Am. Lung Assn. S.E. Fla., Heart Assn. Palm Beach County, Community Mental Health Center Palm Beach County, Palm Beach County unit Am. Cancer Soc., Palm Beach County Mental Health Assn., Palm Beach County Health Dept., 1950-86; pres. YMCA of Palm Beaches, 1970. With AUS, 1944-47. Recipient Meritorious Svc. award Fla. Public Health Assn., 1968; Merit award State of Fla., 1972; Physician of Yr. award Am. Assn. Public Health Physicians, 1975, Lifetime Achievement award, 2000. Fellow APHA (Sedgwick Meml. medal 1989, mem. exec. bd. 1964-70), Am. Coll. Preventive Medicine, Royal Soc. Health; mem. AMA (Dr. Nathan Davis award 1993), Fla. Med. Assn. (cert. of Merit award 1995), Palm Beach County Med. Soc., Rotary, Elks. Democrat. Lutheran. Home: 1242 Devonshire Way Palm Beach Gardens FL 33418-6864 Office: 826 Evernia St West Palm Beach FL 33401-5708

BRUMBACK, GARY BRUCE, industrial and organizational psychologist; b. New Castle, Ind., July 23, 1935; s. Donald Clair and Doris Lydia (Utterberg) B.; m. Doris Anne Ast, June 15, 1958; children: Babette Anne, Lyndia Claire. BA, Ind. U., 1958; MA, Ohio State U., 1960, PhD, 1963. Rsch. asst. Ohio State U., Columbus, 1958-62; rsch. scientist N.Am. Aviation, Columbus, 1962-63; rsch. psychologist U.S. Dept. HEW, Washington, 1964-73; sr. rsch. scientist Am. Inst. for Rsch., Washington, 1973-79; psychologist pers. mgr. U.S. HHS, Washington, 1979-94. Author: Tall Performance from Short Organizations through We/Me Power, 2002; mem. editl. bd. Pub. Pers. Mgmt. Jour., 1986, 91, 93; reviewer in field; rev. adv. com. Pers. Psychology; contbr. chpts. to books, articles to profl. jours. Sec. Banana Beach Assn., Ocean City, Md., 1978-84. Fellow APA, Am. Psychol. Soc. (charter); mem. Acad. Mgmt., Soc. for Bus. Ethics, Sigma Xi, Phi Beta Kappa. Home and Office: 10 Cottonwood Ct Palm Coast FL 32137-4307 E-mail: GBrumback@aol.com.

BRUMBACK, ROGER ALAN, neuropathologist, researcher; b. Washington, Feb. 15, 1948; s. Oscar Benjamin and Frances Elaine (Neufeld) B.; m. Mary Helen Skinner, Apr. 26, 1969; children: Darryl Wyatt, Audrey Christine, Owen Eliot. BS, Pa. State U., 1967; MD, Pa. State U., Hershey, 1971. Diplomate Nat. Bd. Med. Examiners, Am. Bd. Pediatrics, Am. Bd. Psychiatry and Neurology, Am. Bd. Pathology; cert. clin. electroencephalography. Pediatric intern Johns Hopkins Hosp., Balt., 1971-72, pediatric asst. resident, 1972-73; fellow in pediatrics Johns Hopkins U. Sch. Medicine, Balt., 1971-73; asst. resident neurology Barnes Hosp., St. Louis, 1973-74; fellow in pediatric neurology Washington U., St. Louis Children's Hosp., 1973-75; clin. assoc. neurology and exptl. neuropathology med. neurology br. Nat. Inst. Neurol. and Communicative Disorders and Stroke, Nat. Insts. of Health, Bethesda, Md., 1975-77; clin. instr. neurology and pediatrics U. Pitts., 1977-78; asst. prof. neurology U. N.D., Fargo, 1978-79, asst. prof. pediatrics, 1978-82, assoc. prof. neurology, 1980-82; resident/fellow anatomic pathology and neuropathology svcs. Strong Meml. Hosp., U. Rochester (N.Y.), 1982-86; assoc. prof. pathology U. Okla., Oklahoma City, 1986-89, chief neuropathology sect. Health Scis. Ctr., 1987-2000, prof. pathology, 1989-2000; interim chmn., dept. pathology Okla. U., Oklahoma City, 1999-2000; prof. pathology, chmn., dept. pathology Creighton U. Med. Ctr., St. Joseph Hosp., Omaha, 2001—, prof. psychiatry, 2003—. Chief neurology svc. V.A. Med. Ctr., Fargo, 1978-82, dir. Muscular Dystrophy Assn. Clinic, Fargo, 1978-82, co-dir., Oklahoma City, 1988-91; adj. assoc. prof. pediatrics U. Okla., 1986-90, adj. assoc. prof. psychiatry and behavioral scis., 1986-91, adj. prof. pediatrics, 1990-2000, adj. prof. psychiatry and behavioral sci., 1991-2000, adj. prof. neurology 1991-2000, adj. prof. orthopaedic surgery, 1996-2000, David Ross Boyd prof. pathology, 1997-2000, adj. prof. geriatric medicine, 1998-2000; clin. care cons. dermatology br. Nat. Cancer Inst., 1987-2000; chief pathology and lab. med. svc. VHA Nebr.-Western Iowa Health Care Sys., Omaha, 2001—. Author (with W.H. Olson, G. Gascon, L.A.Christoferson): Practical Neurology for the Primary Care Physician, 1981; author: (with J.W. Gerst) The Neuromuscular Junction, 1984; author: (with R.M. Herndon) The Cerebrospinal Fluid, 1989; author: (with M.H. Brumback) The Dietary Fiber Weight Control Handbook, 1989; author: (with R.W. Leech) Hydrocephalus: Current Clinical Concepts, 1991; author: Neurology and Clinical Neuroscience, 1993; author: (with W.H. Olson, G. Gascon, V. Iyer) Handbook of Symptom-Oriented Neurology, 2nd edit., 1994; author: (with R.W. Leech) Neuropathology and Basic Neuroscience, 1995; author: (with C.E. Coffey) Textbook of Pediatric Neuropsychiatry, 1998; author: (with W.A. Weinberg, C.R. Harper) Attention, Behaviour, and Learning Problems in Children: Protocols for Diagnosis and Treatment, 2001; chief editor: Jour. Child Neurology, 1986—, mem. editl. bd.: Jour. Geriatric Psychiatry and Neurology, 1994—. With USPHS, 1975-77. Mem. Am. Acad. Neurology, Am. Assn. Electrodiagnostic Medicine, Am. Assn. Neuropathologists, Am. Acad. Pediats., Am. Neurol. Assn., Child Neurology Soc., Coun. Biology Editors, Coll. Am. Pathologists, Internat. Child Neurology Assn., Soc. for Exptl. Neuropathology (sec.-treas. 1988-93, pres. 1995-97), Behavioral Neurology Soc. (councillor 1990-91, sec.-treas. 1991-93, pres. 1993-95). Republican. Lutheran. Home: 11421 Shirley St Omaha NE 68144 Office: Creighton U Med Ctr Dept Pathology Pathology Dept 601 N 30th St Omaha NE 68131 E-mail: rbrumback@pathology.creighton.edu.

BRUMBAUGH, JOHN A., JR., electrical engineer; b. Pittsburg, Kans., Aug. 23, 1927; s. John A. and Leona G. (Finley) B.; m. Shirley Jean Ellis, July 8, 1950; children: Mark Alan, Steven Thomas, Scott Andrew. Design engr. McNally Pitts. Mfg. Co., Pittsburg, 1949-55; plant engr. Morton Salt Co., Hutchinson, Kans., 1955-59, asst. plant mgr. Port Huron, Mich., 1959-65, plant mgr. Grand Saline, Tex., 1965-70, facility mgr. Hutchinson, Kans., 1970-84, Morton Salt div. Morton Internat., Inc., Rittman, Ohio, 1984-89; ret. Lt. USNR, 1945-46. Recipient Boss of Yr. award Bus. and Profl. Women, 1979 Mem. Kans. Assn. Commerce, Assn. Commerce and Industry (dir. 1974-84), Tex. Mfs. Assn., (dir. Dallas chpt. 1966-70), East Tex. C. of C. (dir. 1968-70), Am. Legion, Lions (pres. local club 1964-65). Avocations: golfing, hunting, fishing, boating, hiking. Home: 431 Allen Dr Wadsworth OH 44281-2120 E-mail: brumbaughj@aol.com.

BRUMBAUGH, JOHN MOORE, lawyer; b. Lima, Peru, Aug. 3, 1945; s. John Granville and Annie Lee (Moore) B.; m. Caroline Patterson, Aug. 12, 1967; children: John Patterson, David Elliott, Katherine Anne, Caroline Moore. BA, Wabash Coll., 1967; JD, U. Fla., 1970. Bar: Fla. 1970, U.S. Ct. Appeals (5th and 11th cirs.), U.S. Dist. Ct. (so. dist.) Fla., U.S. Supreme Ct. Law clk. to judge U.S. Dist. Ct. (so. dist.) Fla., Miami, Fla., 1970-72; assoc. Frates, Floyd, Pearson, Miami, 1972-76; ptnr. Richman, Greer, Weil Brumbaugh Mirabito & Christensen, PA, Miami, Fla., 1976—, mng. ptnr., 1990—. Trustee Trinity Episcopal Sch., Miami, 1985-89, chmn. bd. trustees, 1987-90; trustee St. Thomas Episc. Day Sch., 1988-90, Palmer Trinity Sch., 1996—, vice-chmn., 1999-2001, chair, 2001—; bd. dirs. Miami City Club, 1998-2002. Fellow Am. Coll. Trial Lawyers, Internat. Soc. Barristers; mem. ABA (standing com. on specialization 1997—, chair 2000—), Am. Bar Found., Fla. Bar (mem. bd. legal specialization and edn. 1984-85, 87-2001, chmn. 1993-94, cert. civil trial lawyer), Blue Key, Phi Delta Phi.

BRUMBY, JAMES REMLEY, III, (KNOX BRUMBY), retired priest; b. Marietta, Ga., Apr. 24, 1921; s. James Remley and Martha Louise Brumby; m. Vesta Frances Palmer, Aug. 20, 1971; m. Ferrell Louise West, Dec. 24, 1944; children: Ferrell Lynora, Martha Suzanne. At, U. Fla., 1940—42; BA, U. of the South, Sewanee, Tenn., 1948, MDiv, 1951. Priest-in-charge St. Johns Episcopal Ch., Brooksville, Fla., 1951—53, St. Margarets Episcopal Ch., Inverness, Fla., 1951—53; asst. Holy Trinity Episcopal Ch., West Palm Beach, Fla., 1953—54; vicar Holy Spirit Ch., West Palm Beach, 1953—55, rector, 1955—60, St. Mary's Ch., Daytona Beach, Fla., 1960—66; canon missioner Diocese S. Fla., Ft. Lauderdale, 1966—70; chmn. dept. of missions Diocese Fla., Ft. Lauderdale, 1966—70, supply priest Tallahassee, 1970—88; founder, priest Ch. Atonement, Ft. Lauderdale, 1966—70; priest-in-charge Ch. Ascension, Carrabelle, Fla., 1988—2003. Dept. Christian edn. Diocese S. Fla., Orlando, 1952—58, dept. promotions, 1954—56, chair dept. young people, 1954—56, dept. mission and ch. ext., 1957, chair dept. camps and conf., 1958—66, mem. exec. bd., 1960—66; mem. Youth Bd. Provence IV, 1956—59; pres. Palm Beach Ministerial Assn., 1957—58, Volusia County Ministerial Assn., Daytona Beach, 1962—63; trustee Univ. South, Sewanee, Tenn., 1963—69, chair trustees com. to make student body co-ed, 1969, acting dir. ch. rels., 1984—90; founder, chmn. bd. Louttit Manor for Elderly, Daytona Beach, 1964—66; hon. canon St. Lukes Cathedral, Orlando, 1966; dep. to Gen. Conv., 69; mem. diocesan coun. Diocese Fla., 1996—2000, canon Apalachee regional coun. ministry, 1996—2000, exec. bd., 1996—2000. Author: (book) I Am a Part of All I Have Met, 1999. Lt. col. USAAF, 1942—45 USAR, 1946—58. Democrat. Avocations: painting, sailing, flying. Home: Village of Shell Point 67 Connie Dr Crawfordville FL 32327

BRUMELLE, KENNETH COY, retail store owner; b. Odessa, Tex., Mar. 18, 1945; s. Clarence Lee and Leota (Jones) B.; m. Sharon Jean Suther, Dec. 21, 1967; 1 child Jenni Rebecca. AS, Odessa Coll., 1966; BBA, Tex. Tech U., 1968. Buyer trainee Sanger Harris, Dallas, 1969-71, buyer, 1971-73, White House Dept. Stores, Beaumont, Tex., 1973-74, mdse. mgr., 1974-77; owner Outlaw Jean Store, Odessa, Tex., 1977-97; pres. COLAM, Inc. Bd. dirs. Better Bus. Bur., 1991—. With U.S. Army, 1968-69, Tex. N.G., 1969-74. Mem. Nat. Fedn. Ind. Bus., Tex. Retail Mchts. Assn. (bd. dirs. 1987—), Tex. Retail Assn. (state chmn. membership com. 1991—), Odessa C. of C., Optimist (v.p. Odessa club), Masons. Republican. Methodist. Home: 1809 E 52nd St Odessa TX 79762-4547 Office: COLAM Inc 4526 E University Blvd Bldg 5 Odessa TX 79762-8138

BRUMER, MIRIAM, artist, educator; BA, U. Miami; MFA, Boston U. Mem. faculty N.Y. Inst. Tech., Five Towns Music and Art Found., 1977—, Hunter Coll., 1976-81, Marymount Manhattan Coll., 1976-86, NYU, 1983—, Queens Mus. Art, 1987—. Artist-in-residence N.Y. Found. for Arts, 1985. One-woman shows include Hankook Gallery, N.Y.C., 1982, Payne Gallery, Moravian Coll., Pa., 2001, Conant Hall Gallery, Princeton, NJ, 2002; exhibited in group shows Fordham U., 1980, Boston City Hall Gallery, 1983, AIR Gallery Invitationals, N.Y., 1983-95, 22 Wooster St. Gallery, N.Y., 1984, Leonardo di Mauro Gallery, 1987, Schneyer & Shen, 1987, Broadway Mall Gallery, N.Y., 1989, 90, Sally Hawkins Gallery, N.Y., 1993, Barnard-Biderman Gallery, N.Y., 1994, Massman Gallery, Kansas City, Mo., 1995, Mus. Stony Brook, N.Y., 1996, Hunterdon Mus. Art, N.J., 1997, 98, Polo Gallery, N.J., 1998, City Without Walls Gallery, Newark, 2000, 2002, Ceres Gallery, N.Y., 2002, Nat. Arts Club, N.Y., 2003, others; represented in permanent collections Chase Manhattan Bank, Bell Labs., N.Y. Bank for Savs., Payne Gallery Moravian Coll. Collection, Payne Gallery Moravian Coll., also pvt. collections. Ludwig Vogelstein Found. grantee; Com. Visual Arts grantee, 1979, 80. Home: 250 W 94th St New York NY 10025-6954

BRUMFIELD, WILLIAM CRAFT, Slavic studies educator; b. Charlotte, N.C., June 28, 1944; s. Lewis F. and Pauline Elizabeth (Craft) B. BA, Tulane U., 1966; PhD in Slavic langs., U. Calif., Berkeley, 1973. Vis. lectr. U. Wis., Madison, 1973-74; asst. prof. Harvard U., Cambridge, Mass., 1974-80; assoc. prof. Tulane U., New Orleans, 1984-91, prof. Slavic langs., 1992—. Resident dir. Am. Coun. Tchrs. of Russian Pushkin Inst. Program, Moscow, 1979-80; co-dir. Summer Inst. for Coll. Faculty, NEH, 1994; lectr. on architecture, photography and lit. at museums and univs throughout U.S. and Europe. Author: Gold in Azure: One Thousand Years of Russian Architecture, 1983, The Origins of Modernism in Russian Architecture, 1991, A History of Russian Architecture, 1993, An Archtl. Survey of St. Petersburg: 1840-1916, 1994, Lost Russia: Photographing the Ruins of Russian Architecture, 1995, Landmarks of Russian Architecture: A Photographic Survey, 1997; editor, contbr.: Reshaping Russian Architecture: Western Technology, Utopian Dreams, 1990, Christianity and the Arts in Russia, 1991, Russian Housing in the Modern Age: Design and Social History, 1993, Commerce in Russian Urban Culture: 1861-1914, 2001, Zhilishche V Rossii: vek XX, 2001, Predprinimatelstrov i gorodskaia kultura V Rossii, 2002; contbr. articles to profl. jour.; represented in permanent collections at Photographic Archives, Nat. Gallery Art, Washington; elected to Russian Acad. of Architecture, 2002. Woodrow Wilson fellow, 1966, NEH fellow Nat. Humanities Ctr., 1992-93, fellow Harvard Russian Rsch. Ctr., 1980-81, Guggenheim fellow, 2000-2001; NEH Collaborative Fellowship Am. Coun. for Internat. Edn., 2001-02; sr. exch. scholar Internat. Rsch. Exchs. Bd./Am. Coun. Learned Socs. U.S.-USSR Exch., Moscow, 1983-84, rsch. scholar Kennan Inst., Washington, 1989; grantee Samuel H. Kress Found., 1996-97, grantee Nat. Coun. for Eurasian and East European Rsch., 1999-2000; elected to Russian Acad. Architecture, 2002. Mem. Am. Assn. Advancement Slavic Studies, Soc. Archtl. Historians, Inst. Modern Russian Culture (head photography sect.), Am. Coun. Tchrs. of Russian, Soc. of Historians of East European and Russian Art and Architecture, Russian Acad. Architecture. Office: Tulane U Slavic Dept New Orleans LA 70118 E-mail: brumFiel@tulane.edu.

BRUMIT, LAWRENCE EDWARD, III, oil field service company executive; b. Brunswick, Ga., Feb. 5, 1950; s. Lawrence Edward Jr. and Felicite (Smith) B.; m. Leila Ann Parker, Feb. 21, 1976; children: Mary Louise, Lawrence Edward IV. BS in Petroleum Engring., Mont. Tech., 1974. Field engr. Dowell, Farmington, N. Mex., 1974; service engr. Dowell Schlumberger, Warri, Nigeria, 1975, mgr., Cork, Ireland, 1976, tech. engr., Galeota, Trinidad, 1977, mgr., San Fernando, Trinidad, 1978-79, tng. ctr. mgr., Pau, France, 1980, div. mgr. S.W. Africa, Luanda, Angola, 1981-82, tech. mktg. mgr., Paris, 1983-84, v.p., region mgr., Paris, 1984-86, pres. compagnie de services, 1985—, mgr., v.p. Europe Africa, 1986-88; dir. personnel Schlumberger Ltd. Drilling and Pumping Svcs., Paris, 1988-90; v.p., gen. mgr. Dowell Schumberger North Am., Houston, 1991-95, rancher Flying "B" Ranch, 1995—; bd. dirs. Mont. Tech. Found., 1993-96. Recipient All Conf. Baseball Outstanding Coll. Athlete of Am. award Frontier Conf., 1969-71, 72, No. 1 Player and Capt. award, 1971. Mem. Soc. Petroleum Engrs. Romann Catholic. Avocations: flying; golf. Home: 4425 Sundown Rd Missoula MT 59804-7109

BRUMLEY, LARRY GENE, music educator; b. Ada, Okla., Jan. 23, 1946; s. Joe Bailey and Margie Maurine Brumley; m. Elizabeth Ann Aldrich, Dec. 30, 1967; children: Michael, Gary, Philip. B.Music Edn., Tex. Christian U., 1972; MA with distinction, Calif. State U., Fresno, 1977. Tchr. choir and band Terra Bella Elem. Sch., Calif., 1972—73; tchr. choir and orch. Porterville HS, Calif., 1973—81; percussionist Bakersfield Philharmonic, Calif., 1962—64, Riverside Symphony, Calif., 1964—66, U.S. 4th Army Band, San Antonio, 1967—69, Tulare County Symphony, Tulare, Calif., 1972—81, Marshall Symphony, Tex., 1981—; prof., dir. choirs and voice Panola Coll., Carthage, Tex., 1981. Bd. dirs. Shreveport Chamber Singers, 1986—; drummer in "light jazz" combo; asst. dir. 1st Presbyn. Ch., Ft. Worth, 1970—72; music dir. First United Meth. Ch., Porterville, Calif., 1972—81, North Highlands United Meth. Ch., Shreveport, La., 1986—98, First United Meth. Ch., Carthage, Tex., 1998—; chorus master Shreveport Opera, 1986—88; condr. Shreveport Chamber Singers, 1986—; choral adjudicator Heritage Festivals, Inc., Salt Lake City, 1986—. Ad hoc mem. curriculum revision com. Tex. Coord. Bd. of Colls. and Univs.; county chmn. Rep. Party of Panola County, 1995—; bd. dirs. Shreveport Summer Music Festival, 1981—, Marshall Symphony, 1984 . With U.S. Army, 1966—69. Mem.: Tex. Jr. Coll. Tchrs. Assn., Tex. Music Educators Assn., Am. Choral Dirs. Assn., Am. Fedn. Musicians, Tex. Two-Year Coll. Choral Dirs. Assn. (pres. 1982—83, regional rep. 1990—93), Lions (past bd. dirs.). Republican. Methodist. Avocations: golf, travel, reading, cuisine dining. Home: 1128 Oakwood Carthage TX 75633 Office: Panola College 1109 W Panola St Carthage TX 75633-2341

BRUMM, JAMES EARL, lawyer, trading company executive; b. San Antonio, Dec. 19, 1942; s. John Edward and Marie Oletha (Gault) B.; m. Alicia Joan Pine, Aug. 17, 1968 (div. Mar. 1991); children: Christopher Kenji, Jennifer Kimiko, Laurie Kiyoko; m. Yuko Tsuchida, Apr. 17, 1991. AB, Calif. State U., Fresno, 1965; LLB, Columbia U., 1968. Bar: N.Y. 1969. Assoc. Reid & Priest, N.Y.C., 1968-72, Logan, Takashima & Nemoto, Tokyo, 1973-76; exec. v.p., gen. counsel, dir. Mitsubishi Internat. Corp., N.Y.C., 1977—; pres. Mitsubishi Internat. Corp. Found., N.Y.C., 1992—. Bd. dirs. Brunei LNG, Tembec, Inc., Mitsubishi Corp., Japan, 1995—2002. Trustee Spuyten Duyvil Nursery Sch., Bronx, NY, 1991—95; bd. dirs. Sanctuary for Families, 2000—; bd. visitors Columbia Law Sch., 1998—; mem. corp. adv. coun. Earthwatch; mem. adv. bd. Global Forest Trade Network; bd. dirs. Jr. Achievement Internat., 1997—2000, Internat. Sch. Svcs., 1997—99, Forest Trends, 2003—, Am. Bird Conservancy, 2003—. Mem. ABA, bd. dirs. Forest Trends, 2003-, Internat. Bar Assn., Assn. Bar City N.Y. (chmn. com. on internat. trade 1990-93, chmn. task force on internat. legal svcs. 1998-2001, rep. to Internat. Bar Assn. 2001--), Univ. Club, Nippon Club. Home: 255 W 84th St Apt 6C New York NY 10024-4327 Office: Mitsubishi Internat Corp 520 Madison Ave New York NY 10022-4213

BRUMMEL, LISA, information technology executive; BA in Sociology, Yale U.; MBA, U. Calif., L.A. Sales mgmt. Prentice Hall Inc.; from mgr. to corp. v.p. home products divsn. Microsoft, Redmond, Wash., 1989, corp. v.p. home products divsn. Active Hopelink cmty.svc. programs; vol. U. Wash. Med. Ctr.; bd. dir. Wash. Acad. Performing Arts. Office: One Microsoft Way Redmond WA 98052-6399

BRUMMEL, MARK JOSEPH, magazine editor; b. Chgo., Oct. 28, 1933; s. Anthony William and Mary (Helmreich) B. BA, Cath. U. Am., 1956, STL, 1961, MSLS, 1964. Joined Order of Claretians, Roman Cath. Ch., 1952; ordained priest Order of Caretians, Roman Cath. Ch., 1960; librarian, tchr. St. Jude Sem., Momence, Ill., 1961-70; asso. editor U.S. Cath. mag., Chgo., 1971-72; editor U.S. Cath. Mag., 1970—2002; dir. St. Jude League, Chgo., 1970—2002. Treas. Eastern Province Claretians, 1998—, also bd. dirs.; bd. dirs Chgo. Family Health Ctr. Editor Today mag., 1970-71; contbr. article to publ. Chmn. bd. Eighth Day Ctr. for Justice, Chgo., 1988-92; bd. dirs. Assn. of Chgo. Priests, 1994-96; mem. Ill. Cath. Conf., 1993-96. Mem. Cath. Press Assn. (St. Francis De Sales award 1996), Associated Ch. Press. (v.p. 1985-87). Avocation: photography. Home: 205 W Monroe St Chicago IL 60606- Office: US Cath 205 W Monroe St Fl 7 Chicago IL 60606-5033 E-mail: markbrummel@claret.org.

BRUMMER, JAMES J. adult education educator, writer; b. Buffalo, July 21, 1946; s. George J. and Helen Olivia (Beste) Brummer; 1 child, Julia Maria. BA, U. Wis., Eau Claire, 1969; MA, Boston U., 1972, PhD, 1980. Lectr. U. Wis. Stout, Menomonie, 1980—86; prof. U. Wis., Eau Claire, 1991—, chair dept. philosophy, 1997—. Author: Corporate Responsibilities and Legitimacy, 1991; contbr. articles to profl. jours. Recipient Hall of Honor Alumni award, U. Wis., Eau Claire, 2002, Max Schoenfeld award for humanities tchg., 2003. Avocation: tennis. Home: 3613 South Anita Dr Eau Claire WI 54701 Office: U Wis Dept Philosophy/Religious Studies Eau Claire WI 54701

BRUN, HENRY, publishing executive; b. N.Y.C., Feb. 11, 1940; BA, Bklyn. Coll., 1958-62; MS, Pace U., 1975. Supr. N.Y.C. Sch. Sys., 1962-90; prin. John Jay H.S., Bklyn., 1990-94; COO Amsco Sch. Pubs. Inc., N.Y.C., 1994-95, pres., 1995—. Author: Women of the Ancient World, The Retreat from Imperialism, Global Studies: Civilizations of the Past and Present, The World Today, America Today, Global History: The Growth of Civilizations. Mem. Am. Archeol. Assn., Soc. Antiquaries Newcastle upon Tyne, Soc. Promotion Roman Studies. Office: Amsco Sch Pubs Inc 315 Hudson St New York NY 10013-1009

BRUNACINI, ALAN VINCENT, protective services official; b. Jamestown, N.Y., Apr. 18, 1937; s. John N. and Mary T. Brunacini; m. Rita McDaugh, Feb. 14, 1959; children: Robert Nicholas, John Nicholas, Mary Candice. BSA=, Ariz. State U., 1970, MPA, 1975. Mem. Phoenix (Ariz.) Fire Dept., 1959—, bn. chief then asst. fire chief, 1971—78, fire chief, 1978—. Condr. nat. seminar on fire dept. mgmt., 1970—. Author: Fireground Command; contbr. articles to profl. jours. Scholar Redford scholarship, 1968. Mem.: Soc. Fire Svc. Instrs., Internat. Assn. Fire Chiefs, Nat. Fire Protection Assn. (chmn. fire svc. section 1974—78, dir. 1978), Am. Soc. Pub. Adminstrn. (Superior Svc. award 1980). Office: Office of Fire Chief 150 S 12th St Phoenix AZ 85034-2301

BRUNALE, VITO JOHN, aerospace engineer; b. Mt. Vernon, N.Y., July 2, 1925; s. Donato and Antoinette (Wool) B.; m. Joan Florence Montuori, Apr. 23, 1949; 1 child, Stephen. AAS, Stewart Aero. Inst., 1948; BSAE, Tri-State U., 1958; MSME, U. Bridgeport, 1966; DSc, Nev. Inst. Tech., 1973; PhD (hon.), Internat. U., Spain, 1987; DSc, Pacific Western U., 1984. Rsch. engr. Norden Labs., White Plains, N.Y., 1948-55; instr. Tri-State U., Angola, Ind., 1955-58; engring. cons. Norden Div. United Aircraft, Norwalk, Conn., 1958-67; chief engring. cons. Singer-Kearfott Corp., Pleasantville, N.Y., 1967-73; chief engr. Diagnostic/Retrieval Systems, Mt. Vernon, N.Y., 1973-76; tech. problem mgr. Fairchild Republic Co., Farmingdale, N.Y., 1977-87; sr. tech. expert Sikorsky Aircraft, 1987—. Cons. in field; engring. tutor to coll. students; v.p. Lithoway, Inc., 1969-73; lectr. in field; tech. guest speaker numerous tech. soc. meetings.; participant engring. exchange program, USSR, People's Republic China. Contbr. articles to profl. jours. including Product Engring., Aviation Week, Environ. Scis. Participant U.S.A. Citizen Amb. Program. Served with USAAF, 1943-45. Decorated Purple Heart (3), Air medals, D.F.C. Tri-State U. tcht. fellow, 1955-58; NSF grantee; recipient Aircraft Design award, 1948, Inst. Aero. Sci. Lecture award, 1948, Norden Rsch. award, 1963, Cost Reduction award, 1965, Singer Engring. award, 1970, 72, Fairchild outstanding achievement award, 1985, 86, 87, Fairchild award of excellence, 1984, Am. Biographical Inst. and Research Assn. Outstanding Performance award, 1989, Aircraft Recognition award, 1986, citation N.Y. State Assembly, 1988, Conspicuous Service Cross N.Y. State, 1988, Prisoner of War medal, 1988, others; honoree Nat. Air and Space Mus.; named to Wisdom Hall of Fame, 1998. Mem. AIAA (award 1973, Aviation award 1994, Sr. Mem. award 1994, Merit award 1998, membership award 1998, award 1998), VFW, DAV, K.C., U.S. Naval Inst., Air Force Assn., Am. Ordnance Asssn., Inst. Environ. Sci., Nat Space Inst., Newman Club, Internat. Students Assn., Internat. Platform Assn., World Inst. of Achievement. Roman Catholic. Achievements include patent (with others) for Bearing Spin Rail Test; development of method of discriminate displacement for equilibrium of structures, of the position point vibration isolation technique, of the vapress vibration system, of advanced techniques for structural and vibration analyses, of the Doppler-Inertial-Loran system, of state of the art mathematical and structural analyses techniques, of Mars Doppler Lander system, computer time studies, anti-corrosion methods; resolution of 140 technical problems on the Fairchild A-10 aircraft, of more than 30 technical problems with the Saab-Fairchild 340; solution of Grumman A-6A radar tracking problem in Vietnam; elimination of technical problems on LEM inertial guidance; rsch. in mfg. productivity, co-planer structural analyses. Home: 459 Bronxville Rd Bronxville NY 10708-1102 Office: Main St Bronxville NY 10708-1102

BRUNCK, TERRI LEE, journalist; b. Atlanta, Mar. 26, 1977; d. Robert Cornell and Barbara Lee Brunck. AA, Fla. Coll., 1997; BA, U. Ala., 1999. Reporter Northport (Ala.) Gazelle, 1998—99, Comml.-Dispatch, Columbus, Miss., 2000, Cullman (Ala.) News, 2000—. Named to Ala. Edn. Media Honor Roll, Ala. Assn. Sch. Bds., Tuscaloosa, 1999. Mem.: Soc. Profl. Journalists. Office: Cullman Times 300 4th Ave SE Cullman AL 35055

BRUNDA, DANIEL DONALD, retired aerospace engineer, consultant, inventor; b. Lansford, Pa., Oct. 22, 1930; s. Michael Theodore and Ella (Jurba) B. BSME, Lehigh U., 1952, MSME, 1953; postgrad., Johns Hopkins U., 1955, Princeton U., 1958-65, Drexel U., 1983. Registered profl. engr., N.J.; cert. expert witness and cons. Engr. Bell Aircraft aerodynamicist Glenn L. Martin, Balt.; devel., test, evaluation and performance propulsion engr. Bell Aircraft Glenn L. Martin & Curtiss Wright, Princeton, N.J., 1953-57; aerospace engr. rsch. U.S. Naval Air Propulsion Ctr., Ewing, N.J., 1957-72, local mgr. ind. R&D, 1972-83; powerline radiation energy engring. cons. Ewing, N.J., 1978—. Dep. dir. gen. Internat. Biog. Inst. in the Americas, 2000; founder Electromagnetic Powerline Radiation Engrs., Am. Biog. Inst., 2000. Author: Powerline Radiation, Your Genes, Hereditary Diseases, The Unified Nature of Electromagnetic Radiation Energy and Control, and the Radiation Limits of Human Beings, 2003, Design of Safe Electric Transmission and Distribution Lines, 2003; contbr. more than 20 articles to profl. jours. Recipient Lifetime Achievement award, IBC, 2002, World Lifetime Achievement award, API, 2002. Fellow Bioelectromagnetic Soc. (assoc.); mem. ASME (life), AIAA, Am. Biographical Inst. Rsch. Assn. (lifetime dep. gov., named Amb. of Grand Eminence 2002, World Lifetime Achievement award 2002). Achievements include research, patents, and copyrights on powerline radiation, which determined the molecular weight, radiation limits, inductive impedance of average adult human beings; proved that powerline radiation is a cause of cancer; explained mathematically Volta's electrophonic effect 1800 A.D.; discovered Brunda's Absorbance Law and the Absorbance of DNA. Home and Office: Powerline Radiation Energy Engring Cons 106 W Upper Ferry Rd Ewing NJ 08628-2724

BRUNDAGE, BRUCE HOWARD, cardiologist; b. Blakely, Pa., Sept. 19, 1938; MD, N.J. Coll. Medicine/Dentistry, 1965. Diplomate Am. Bd. Internal Medicine. Intern Tripler Army Hosp., Honolulu, 1965-66; resident Fitzsimmons Gen. Hosp., Denver, 1966-69; cardiology fellow Letterman Gen. Hosp., San Francisco, 1969-71; chief cardiac catheterization U. Calif., San Francisco, 1976-83; chief cardiology U. Ill., Chgo., 1983-89, acting head of medicine, 1989-90; mem. faculty Harbor-UCLA Med. Ctr., Torrance, Calif., 1990-98, chief cardiology, 1990-98; cons. in cardiology Bend (Oreg.) Meml. Clinic, 1998—; med. dir. heart svcs. St. Charles Med. Ctr., 1998—; med. dir. Heart Inst. of the Cascades. Master Am. Coll. Cardiologists; fellow ACP, Am. Coll. Chest Physicians; mem. AHA, Pulmonary Hypertension Assn. (pres. 2002-). Office: Bend Meml Clinic 1501 NE Med Ctr Dr Bend OR 97701 E-mail: bbrundag@scmc.org.

BRUNDAGE, RUSSELL ARCHIBALD, retired data processing executive; b. N.Y.C., Feb. 16, 1929; s. Eugene Columbus and Sophia Catherine (Gillies) B.; m. Barbara Jane Nelson, May 18, 1958; children: Russell Archibald, Nelson David, Beth Ellen, Paul Winston. BA, Washington Sq. Coll., NYU, 1957. With U.S. Fgn. Service, State Dept., 1950-55; applied sci. writer IBM Corp., N.Y.C. and White Plains, N.Y., 1957-60; with Colonial Penn Group, Phila., 1960-81, v.p., 1972-81; pres. Colonial Penn Group Data Corp., 1970-77; v.p. Nat. Assn. Plans, Inc., 1971-81; v.p. data processing SAI Group, Inc., 1982; pres. SAI Data Services Div., 1983-86; v.p. MIS Mut. Assurance Co., Phila., 1989-94; v.p. Green Tree Ins. Co., Phila., 1989-94; v.p., bd. dirs. Valley Ins. Co., Phila.,

1990-92, Green Tree Ins. Co., Phila., 1992-94. V.p. Am. Loyalty Ins. Co., Gahanna, Ohio, 1989-94, also bd. dirs.; v.p., sec. Mut. Assurance Co., Green Tree Ins. Co., Am. Loyalty Ins. Co., 1991-94. Chmn. Lee Magisterial Dist. Republican Com., Fairfax County, Va., 1966; bd. dirs. S.E. Pa. chpt. Am. Heart Assn., 1993-96. Served with USAF, 1947-50. Mem. Vets. 7th Regt. N.Y. Republican. Presbyterian (Ret. Elder, Active Deacon). Home: 23 Wincrest Dr Phoenixville PA 19460-5735

BRUNDAGE, WILLIAM FITZHUGH, historian, educator; b. Lancaster, Pa., Nov. 5, 1959; s. Robert Vernier Brundage and Mary Elizabeth Lee Rust; m. Heidi Ann Wulczyn, Mar. 27, 1962. BA, U. Chgo., 1981; PhD, Harvard U., 1988. Asst. prof. Queen's U., Kingston, Ont., Can., 1989-97; assoc. prof. U. Fla., Gainesville, 1997-99, prof., chair, 1999—2002; William B. Umstead prof. U. N.C., Chapel Hill, 2002—. Author: Lynching in the New South, 1993 (Merle Curti award 1994), A Socialist Utopia in the New South, 1996; editor: Under Sentence of Death, 1997, Where These Memories Grow, 2000. Mem. Am. Hist. Assn., So. Hist. Assn. (co-chair program com. 2000—), Orgn. Am. Historians, Am. Studies Assn. Office: U NC Dept History CB 3195 Chapel Hill NC 27514-3195

BRUNDIGE, ROBERT WILLIAM, JR., lawyer; b. Dayton, Ohio, Feb. 4, 1944; s. Robert W. and Elizabeth (Marquardt) B.; m. Katherine D. Muller, Dec. 18, 1971; children: Elizabeth, Allyson. BA, Yale U., 1966; JD, Vanderbilt U., 1969. Bar: N.Y. 1970, U.S. Dist. Ct. (so. and ea. dists.) N.Y. 1972, U.S. Tax Ct. 1973, U.S. Ct. Appeals (2d cir.) 1975, U.S. Ct. Appeals (11th cir.) 1983, U.S. Ct. Appeals (5th cir.) 1985, U.S. Supreme Ct. 1996, N.J. 1997, U.S. Dist. Ct. N.J. 1997, U.S. Ct. Appeals (3rd cir.) 2000. Assoc. Sage, Gray, Todd & Sims, N.Y.C., 1969-75, ptnr., 1976-86, Hughes, Hubbard & Reed, LLP, N.Y.C., 1987—. Mem. Vanderbilt Law Sch. Nat. Alumni Bd., Nashville, 1993-98; del. Yale U. Assn. of Yale Alumni, 1994-98; mem. Yale Alumni Fund, 1971—; mem. Yale Club of Bergen County and Vicinity, 1977—; presenter in field. Author: (with others) The McGraw-Hill Construction Business Handbook, 2d edit., 1985; mem. adv. bd. Vanderbilt Jour. Transnational Law, 2000—; contbr. article to profl. jours. Trustee Ridgewood Pub. Edn. Found., 1990-97, pres., 1990-93; pres. dean's coun. Vanderbilt U. Law Sch., Nashville, 1996—. Recipient Disting. Svc. award Vanderbilt Law Sch., 1995. Mem. ABA (sect. litigation, chmn. subcom. on commodities 1984-86). Episcopalian. Avocations: tennis, fly fishing, gardening. Home: 251 Palmer Ct Ridgewood NJ 07450-2316 Office: Hughes Hubbard & Reed 1 Battery Park Plz Fl 17 New York NY 10004-1405

BRUNDTLAND, GRO HARLEM, international organization executive; b. Oslo, Apr. 20, 1939; d. Gudmund and Inga (Brynolf) Harlem; m. Arne Olav Brundtland, 1960; children: Knut, Kaja, Ivar, Jorgen. MD, Oslo U., 1963; M.P.H., Harvard Sch. Pub. Health, 1965. Med. officer Nat. Directorate of Pub. Health, Oslo, 1965-67; asst. med. dir. Sch. Health Services, Oslo, 1968-74; minister of environment Norwegian Govt., 1974-79, M.P. from Oslo, 1977-79, mem. standing com. on fin., chmn. standing com. on fgn. and constitutional affairs, 1979-81, dep. leader Labour Party's parliamentary group, 1979-81, leader Labour Party and parliamentary group, 1981-92, standing com. on fgn. and constl. affairs, 1981-86; chmn. standing com. on fgn. and constnl. affairs; prime minister of Norway Norwegian Govt., 1981, 86-89, 90-96; dir.-gen. WHO, Geneva, 1998—. Contbr. scientific work in child growth and devel. Mem. Ind. Commn. on Disarmament and Security Issues, UN, 1980; chmn. World Commn. on Environment and Devel., 1983; bd. dirs. Better World Soc., 1985. Recipient Third World prize Third World Found., 1989, Indira Gandhi prize, 1990, Onassis Found. award, 1992, World Ecology award, Internat. Ctr. for Tropical Ecology, 2001.

BRUNE, EVA, fundraiser; b. Bklyn., Apr. 20, 1952; d. Paul Mass and Edythe Siegel; m. David H. Brune, Oct. 30, 1988; children: Jared Alexander, Isaac Nicolai. BFA, Calif. Coll. Arts and Crafts, Oakland, 1978. Visual arts dir. Sonoma (Calif.) County Arts Commn., 1980-82; assoc. dir. Visual Arts Ctr. of Alaska, Anchorage, 1982-83; program dir. Internat. Sculpture Ctr., Washington, 1983; dir. Pro Arts, Oakland, 1983-85; devel. dir. A Traveling Jewish Theater, San Francisco, 1985-88; mng. dir. INTAR Hispanic Arts. Ctr., N.Y.C., 1988-94; dir. ann. fund The Big Apple Circus, N.Y.C., 1994-96; exec. dir. CityKids Found., N.Y.C., 1996-98; nat. dir. instnl. advancement Young Audiences, Inc., N.Y.C., 1998-2001; dir. devel. Dance Theatre of Harlem, 2001—03; dir. instn. adv. Eldridge St. Project, N.Y.C., 2003—. Instr. Calif. Coll. Arts and Crafts, Oakland, 1978-79. Past bd. dirs. Alliance Resident Theaters, N.Y.C., Citiarts, N.Y.C.; former panelist theater program Nat. Endowment for Arts, Washington, OPERA Am., Fla. State Coun. on Arts, Westchester County Coun. on Arts, N.Y.; panelist N.J. State Coun. on Arts. Recipient fellowships Nat. Endowment for the Arts, Washington, 1980, 82. Jewish. Avocations: piano, furniture building, writing. E-mail: evabrune@hotmail.com.

BRUNE, KENNETH LEONARD, lawyer; b. Fort Madison, Iowa, Aug. 23, 1945; s. Bernard John and Colette Mary (Steffensmeier) B.; m. Judith Ann Sears, Oct. 17, 1970; children— James Bernard, Adrian Margaret, Sarah Anne. B.A., St. Ambrose Coll., 1967; M.A., U. Iowa, 1972; J.D., U. Tulsa, 1974. Bar: Iowa 1975, Okla. 1975, U.S. Dist. Ct. (we. and no. dist.) Okla. 1976, U.S. Ct. Appeals (10th cir.) 1976, U.S. Supreme Ct. 1980. Law clk. U.S. Dist. Ct. (no. dist.) Okla., Tulsa, 1975-77; asst. dist. atty., Tulsa County, Okla., 1977-78; judge dist. ct., Tulsa County, 1978-79; assoc. Holliman, Langholz, Runnels & Dorwart, Tulsa, 1980-81, ptnr., 1981—; gen. counsel Make Today Count, Tulsa, 1979-83, Okla. Oncology Nursing Soc., Tulsa, 1980-83; chmn. bd. Legal Services Eastern Okla., Tulsa, 1981, bd. mem., 1980—; judge temp. ct. appeals Okla. Supreme Ct., Tulsa, 1981; asst. prof. U. Tulsa Law Sch., 1984. Div. chmn. United Way, Tulsa, 1980-83. Served to 1st lt. U.S. Army, 1969-71, Vietnam. Decorated Bronze Star; St. Ambrose Coll. presdl. scholar, 1965-67. Mem. Okla. Bar Assn., Tulsa County Bar Assn. (speakers com. 1980-83), Delta Epsilon Sigma. Democrat. Roman Catholic. Home: 3519 S Florence Ave Tulsa OK 74105-2909 Office: Holliman Langholz Runnels & Dorwart 10 E 3d St 700 Holarud Bldg Tulsa OK 74103

BRUNELL, JERRY ALBERT, insurance executive; b. Cologne, Fed. Republic of Germany, Jan. 31, 1926; s. Otto Moritz and Paula (Gutman) B.; m. Anne Cahn, Dec. 25, 1954; children: Ronald Marc, Janet Felice. Student, Bklyn. Poly. Inst., 1944-47, CCNY, 1947-50. Pres. Brunell Assocs., Inc., Kew Gardens, N.Y., 1950-80; exec. v.p., treas. Nussbaum Brunell Assoc., Inc., Valley Stream, N.Y., 1981—. Pres., pub. Aufbau newspaper, 1975—. Hon. commr. Commn. for Protocol, N.Y.C., 1981-91, Dept. Spl. Events, 1973-77; chmn. peer review panel. N.Y. State Auto Ins. Plan, 1993—. Mem. Ind. Ins. Agts. Assn. (presdl. citation N.Y. 1982, chmn. downstate ann. meeting 1980-92), Ind. Ins. Agts. Assn. Queens County (past pres.), Profl. Ins. Agts., Ins. Square Club (pres. 1986). Democrat. Jewish. Club: New World (pres.). Lodge: Masons (master 1968, treas. 1979-93). Home: 7350 Kinghurst Dr Bldg 44 Delray Beach FL 33446-2985 also: 84-51 Beverly Rd Kew Gardens NY 11415-2123 Office: 10 5th St Valley Stream NY 11581-1245 also: 68 Winnebago Rd Putnam Valley NY 10579-1543

BRUNELL, MARK ALLEN, professional football player; b. L.A., July 17, 1970; m. Stacy Brunell; children: Caitlin, Jacob. BA in History, 1992. 2nd quarterback Green Bay Packers, 1994—95; quarterback Jacksonville Jaguars, 1995—. Staged inaugural Mark Brunell Charity Golf Tournament to benefit Wolfson Children's Hosp.; spokesman Leukemia Soc. Am., 1996; active Fellowship Christian Athletes. Named Most Valuable Player Rose Bowl, 1991, NFL Offensive Player of Week, 1996, AFC Offensive Player of Week, 1996, Pro Ball AFC, 1997. Avocations: hunting, fishing, golf. Office: Jacksonville Jaguars 1 Alltel Stadium Pl Jacksonville FL 32202-1917

BRUNELL, PHILIP ALFRED, physician, educator; b. N.Y.C., Feb. 1, 1931; s. Irving and Rose Brunell; children: Wayne, Robert, Rhonda. BS, CCNY, 1950; postgrad., N.Y. U., 1950-51; MS in Physiology, U. Ill., 1952; MD, U. Buffalo, 1957. Diplomate in pediatrics and pediatric infectious diseases Am. Bd. Pediatrics. Research asst. physiology U. Ill., 1951-52, teaching asst., 1952-53; intern E.J. Meyer Meml. Hosp., Buffalo, 1957-58; resident in pediatrics Children's Hosp., Buffalo, 1958-60; asst. in pediatrics Cornell U., 1960-61; instr. pediatrics Emory U., 1961-64; asst. prof. pediatrics N.Y. U. Sch. Medicine, 1964-71, assoc. prof., 1971-75; prof., chmn. dept. pediatrics U. Tex. Health Sci. Center, San Antonio, 1975-81, prof., head div. infectious diseases dept. pediatrics, 1981-87; attending physician Santa Rosa Children's Hosp., San Antonio, 1975-81; prof. pediatrics UCLA; chief pediatrics Bexar County Hosp. Dist. Teaching Hosps., San Antonio, 1975-81; vice chmn. Cedars Sinai Med. Ctr., L.A., 1987-96, cons. in pediat., 1997-98. Cons. Brooke Army Med. Ctr., Wilford Hall USAF Med. Ctr., 1977-81; mem. cons. group on vaccine devel., 1991-94; cons. FDA, 1994-96; vis. rschr. Nat. Inst. Allergy and Infectious Diseases, 1995; spl. expert Lab. Clin. Investigation Nat. Inst. Allergy and Infectious Dis., NIH, 1997-99, Gt. Ormund St. Childrens Hosp, London, 2000. Chief med. editor Infectious Diseases of Children, 1987—; contbr. chpts. to books; contbr. articles to med. jours. Chmn. Internat. Year of Child, San Antonio, 1979-80; bd. dirs. Santa Rosa Children's Hosp. Found. Served with USPHS, 1961-64. USPHS fellow, 1971-72 Fellow Infectious Diseases Soc. Am. (awards com. 1979, chmn. 1982); mem. Am. Acad. Pediatrics (chmn. com. pediatric research 1977-78, chmn. com. infectious diseases 1978-85), Am. Soc. Microbiology, Am. Acad. Microbiology, Am. Pediatric Soc., Soc. Pediatric Infectious Diseases (council 1984, pres. 1987-89), World Pediatric Infectious Diseases Soc. (sec. 1996-2003, pres. 2d internat. conf.), Soc. Pediatric Research, San Antonio Pediatric Soc., Tex. Pediatrics Soc. (awards com.), Coun. Tex. Pediatric Dept. Chmn. (chmn. 1978-81), Tex. Med. Assn. (sec. treas. pediatric sect. 1979-80, pres. 1980-81), Bexar County Med. Soc., Tex. Infectious Disease Soc., Western Soc. Pediatric Rsch., L.A. Pediatric Soc. Home: 7111 Woodmont Ave Apt 713 Bethesda MD 20815-6235 Office: NIAID NIH Lab of Clin Investigation Rm 11n229 Bldg 10 Bethesda MD 20892-0001 E-mail: pbrunell@niaid.nih.gov.

BRUNELLE, ROBERT L. retired state education director; b. Somersworth, N.H., Sept. 19, 1924; s. Lorenzo A. and Laomie (Carter) B.; m. Diane P. Gagnon, June 14, 1947; children— Roberta, Marc B.Edn., U. N.H., M.Edn., 1958; Ed.D., Boston U., 1972. Prin. Elem. Schs., Somersworth, N.H., 1952-58; supt. schs. Somersworth Schs., Somersworth, N.H., 1958-68; dep. commr. edn. State Dept. Edn., Concord, N.H., 1968-76, commr. edn., 1976-86, exec. dir. Gov.'s Excellence in Edn. Program, 1986-88; ret., 1988. Trustee U. N.H., 1976-86. Chmn. state employees div. United Way Fund of Greater Concord, 1971-72; v.p. Daniel Webster coun. Boy Scouts Am., 1978-88; awards chmn. Philbrook Children's Found., 1991-95, Ch. Coun., 1992-93; mem. programs and svcs. com. Crotched Mountain Found., 2001—. With USN, 1944-53 Recipient Award of Excellence, Pa. Sch. Bds. Assn.; Sears Found. scholar Mem. Am. Assn. Sch. Adminstrs., N.E. Regional Exch. (chmn. 1984-85), Am. Automobile Assn. (chmn. 1984-87), Ret. Adminstrs. (chmn. 1992-94, 2002—), Am. Legion, Phi Delta Kappa, Kiwanis (v.p. 1958-59, pres. 1959-60). Roman Catholic. Home: 83 Rockingham St Concord NH 03301-2649

BRUNELL-JOINER, KARLEA, academic administrator, educator; b. Burlington, Vt., Dec. 21, 1970; d. Donald Raymond and Elveta Ceclia Brunelle; m. Gregory Joiner, June 20, 1998; 1 child, Jack Joiner. BA, St. Michael's Coll., Colchester, Vt., 1992; MEd, Rutgers Univ., New Brunswick, N.J., 1993; PhD, Fla. State Univ., Tallahassee, Fla., 1999. Monitor Rutgers Univ., Piscataway, NJ, 1993, career counseling asst., 1993; counselor Kilgore Jr. CC, Kilgore, Tex., 1994; acad. advisor Fla. State Univ., Tallahassee, 1994—97, peer adv. coord., 1996—98, acad. support svc. coord., 1998—99; dir. of first yr. student devel. Western New Eng. Coll., Springfield, Mass., 1999—2002; asst. dean of studies Assumption Coll., Worchester, Mass., 2002—. Adj. faculty Springfield Coll., Mass., 2000—01, Western New Eng. Coll., Springfield, Mass. Vol. adv. Cath. student union Fla. State Univ., Tallahassee, 1996; dir. Cath. student ctr. Kilgore Jr. CC, Tex., 1996. Mem.: Nat. Orientation Dir. Assn., Nat. Acad. Advt. Assn., Nat. Assn. Student Personnel Adminstr., Am. Coll. Personnel Assn. Avocations: golf, skiing, scrapbooks. Office: Assumption Coll 500 Salisbury St Worcester MA 01609

BRUNELLO-MCCAY, ROSANNE, sales executive; b. Cleve., Aug. 26, 1960; d. Carl Carmello and Vivan Lucille (Caranna) B.; m. Walter B. McCay, Feb. 26, 1994; children: Angela Breanna, Mikala Bell. Student, U. Cin., 1978-81, Cleve. State U., 1981-82. Indsl. sales engr. Alta Machine Tool, Denver, 1982; mem. sales./purchases Ford Tool & Machine, Denver, 1982-84; sales/ptnr. Mountain Rep. Enterprises, Denver, 1984-86; pres., owner Mountain Rep. Ariz., Phoenix, 1986—; pres. Mountain Rep. Oreg., Portland, 1990—, Mountain Rep. Wash., 1991—, Mountain Rep. Calif., Sunnyvale, 1997—, San Clemente, 1998—, Port Clinton, Ohio, 1999—; we. regional sales mgr. Offshore Internat., Inc., Tucson, 2002—. Sec. Computer & Automated Systems Assoc., 1987, vice chmn., 1988, chmn., 1989. Active mem. Rep. Party, 1985—; mem. Phoenix Art Mus., Grand Canyon Minority Coun., 1994; vol. Make-A-Wish Found. fund raiser, 1995—. Named Mrs. Chandler Internat., Mrs. Ariz. Internat. Orgn., 1996, Mrs. East Valley U.S., 1997; finalist Mrs. Ariz. Internat., 1996, Ms. Ariz. 2000, Ms. U.S. Continental Pageant. Mem. NAFE, Soc. Mfg. Engrs. (pres. award 1988), Computer Automated Assn. (sec. 1987, vice chmn. 1988 chmn. 1989), Nat. Hist. Soc., Italian Cultural Soc., Tempe C. of C., Vocat. Ednl. Club Am. (mem. exec. bd., pres. 1987—). Roman Catholic. Avocations: sports, aerobics, dancing, skiing, golfing, tennis. Office: Mountain Rep Ariz 410 S Jay St Chandler AZ 85225-6253 E-mail: rosanne@mtnrep.com.

BRUNENKANT, JON LODWICK, lawyer; b. Washington, June 17, 1950; s. Edward James and Jeanette (Lodwick) B. BA with honors, Northwestern U., 1972; JD with honors, George Washington U., 1975; MBA with honors, Iran Ctr. for Mgmt. Studies, 1977. Bar: D.C. 1978, Va. 1975, U.S. Supreme Ct. 1978, U.S. Ct. Appeals (3d, 5th, 6th, 7th, 8th, 10th, 11th and D.C. cirs.) 1978. Assoc. Grove, Jaskiewicz, Gilliam & Cobert, Washington, 1978-83, ptnr., 1983-89; ptnr. Travis & Gooch, Washington, 1990—. Mem. ABA, Fed. Energy Bar Assn. Office: Travis & Gooch 1100 15th St NW Washington DC 20005-1707

BRUNER, EDWARD M. anthropology educator; b. N.Y.C., Sept. 28, 1924; s. Milton J. and Bessie (Hinds) B.; m. Elaine C. Hauptman, Mar. 21, 1948; children— Jane R., Dan M. BA, Ohio State U., 1948, MA, 1950; PhD, U. Chgo., 1954. Instr. dept. anthropology U. Chgo., 1953-54; asst. prof. dept. anthropology Yale U., 1954-60; assoc. prof. dept. anthropology U. Ill., Urbana, 1961-65, prof., 1965-94, prof. emeritus, 1994—, head dept., 1966-70. Dir. Doris Duke Am. Indian Oral History Project, 1967-73; cons. Ford Found., Nat. Assessment Edn. in Indonesia, 1969-70; chmn. test com. in anthropology Ednl. Testing Service, Princeton, N.J., 1967-69; cons. cultural anthropology rev. com. NIMH, 1966; mem. grants com. Social Sci. Research Council, N.Y.C., 1966. Contbr., editor Conf. Procs. Am. Ethnol. Soc., 1984, (with Victor Turner) Anthropology of Experience, 1986. Contbr. articles to profl. jours. Ctr. for Advanced Study in Behavioral Sci. fellow, 1960-61; sr. scholar East West Ctr. Inst. Advanced Projects, Honolulu, 1963, summer scholar Sch. of Am. Rsch., Santa Fe, 1992; rsch. grantee NIMH, NSF, Wenner Gren Found., Ford Found., Social Sci. Rsch. Coun. Fellow Am. Anthrop. Assn. (rep. to AAAS 1979-81, bd. dirs. 1989-91); mem. Am. Ethnol. Soc. (pres. 1981-82), Assn. for Asian Studies (mem. Indonesian studies com. 1973—, chmn. 1976-78), Soc. Humanistic Anthropology (pres. 1989-91). Field research Am. Indians, Indonesia, Africa. Home: 2022 Cureton Dr Urbana IL 61801-6226

BRUNER, JANET M. neuropathologist; b. East Liverpool, Ohio, Oct. 2, 1949; d. Russell Edward and Hazel Isabel (Pride) Roof; m. Charles Thomas Bruner, July 8, 1972. BS in Pharmacy, U. Toledo, 1972, MS in Pharm. Sci., 1974; MD, Med. Coll. of Ohio, 1979. Resident in pathology Med. Coll. of Ohio, Toledo, 1979-82; fellow neuropathology Baylor Coll. Medicine, Houston, 1982-84; chief neuropathologist M.D. Anderson Cancer Ctr., Houston, 1984-99, chair dept. pathology, 1998—, Ferenc and Phyllis Gyorkey endowed chair rsch. edn. path., 1998—. Test com neuropathology Am. Bd. Pathology, Tampa, Fla., 1988-93. Author: Pathology of Tumors of the Nervous System, 1998; contbr. articles to profl. jours. Grantee NIH, 1992—. Mem. AMA, Houston Soc. of Clin. Pathologists (pres. 1990-91), Am. Assn. of Neuropathologists, Am. Soc. of Clin. Pathologists, U.S./Can. Acad. of Pathology, Tex. Med. Assn. Achievements include research on brain tumor biologic behavior, glial cell transformation, tumor suppressor genes, cell proliferation kinetics, and gene therapy of brain tumors. Home: 5115 S Braeswood Blvd Houston TX 77096-4147 Office: MD Anderson Cancer Ctr Pathology 1515 Holcombe Blvd Houston TX 77030-4009

BRUNER, JEFFREY BENHAM, foreign language educator; b. Holdenville, Okla., Mar. 20, 1961; s. Eugene and Billye Jo B.; m. Deborah Elaine Wilkinson, June 16, 1984 (div. Feb. 1995); m. Twyla Anne Meding, Dec. 22, 1995. BA in Spanish, Okla. Bapt. U., 1983; MA in Spanish, Rutgers U., 1986, PhD in Spanish, 1990. Asst. prof. Trenton (N.J.) State Coll., 1988-90, W.Va. U., Morgantown, 1990-96, assoc. prof., 1996—, chair dept. fgn. langs., 2002—. Mem. adv. bd. W.Va. U. Phil. Papers, 1994—. Contbr. articles to profl. jours. V.p., bd. dirs. Maintain People's Coop., Morgantown, 1996-2000. Recipient Radiol. Cons. Assn. award, Morgantown, 1992; Riggle fellow, W.Va. U., 1992. Mem. ACLU, MLA (del. assembly 2003—), N.E. MLA, So. Comparative Lit. Assn., 20th Century Spanish Soc. Avocations: cross country skiing, cycling, hiking, travel. Office: WVa U Dept Fgn Langs Chitwood Hall Morgantown WV 26506-6298

BRUNER, MICHAEL LANE, communications educator; b. Kans. City, Mo., July 25, 1958; s. Lee Roy and Vivian Bruner(Stepmother); m. Meryl C. Perl, Oct. 21, 1984. PhD, U. of Wash., 1997; BA in Speech Comm., U. Calif., Northridge, 1991. Asst. prof. of communication Babson Coll., Wellesley, Mass., 1997—2002; asst. prof. of pub. communication Ga. State U., Atlanta, 2002—. Co-founder Carma Bums, L.A., 1985. Author: Twisted Cadillac, 1996, Outlaw Bible of American Poetry, 1999, After the Break In/Evergreen Review, 2001, Strategies of Remembrance, 2002; assoc. editor: Quar. Jour. of Speech, 1999, 2001; contbr. articles to profl. jours. Recipient Wilma Grimes Meml. Tchg. award, U. of Wash., 1996; fellow Glavin Ctr. for Entrepreneurial Studies fellow, Babson Coll., 1999—2000; scholar MacFarlane scholarship, U. of Wash., 1996. Mem.: Am. Soc. for the History of Rhetoric, Rhetoric Soc. of Am., Assn. for the Study of Nationalities, Internat. Soc. for the History of Rhetoric, Nat. Comm. Assn. Office: Georgia State University 1052 One Park Place Atlanta GA 30303-3083 Office Fax: 440-651-1409. E-mail: joumib@langate.gsu.edu.

BRUNER, PHILIP LANE, lawyer; b. Chgo., Sept. 26, 1939; s. Henry Pfeiffer and Mary Marjorie (Williamson) B.; m. Ellen Carole Germann, Mar. 21, 1964; children: Philip Richard, Stephen Reed, Carolyn Anne. AB, Princeton U., 1961; JD, U. Mich., 1964; MBA, Syracuse U., 1967. Bar: Wis. 1964, Minn. 1968. Mem. Briggs and Morgan P.A., Mpls., St. Paul, 1967-83; founding shareholder Hart and Bruner P.A., Mpls., 1983-90; ptnr. Faegre & Benson, Mpls., 1991—, head constrn. law group, 1991—2001. Adj. prof. William Mitchell Coll. Law, St. Paul, 1970-76, U. Minn. Law Sch., 2003-; lectr. law seminars, univs., bar assns. and industry; chmn. Supreme Ct. Minn. Bd. Continuing Legal Edn., 1994-98. Co-author: Bruner and O'Conner on Construction Law, 7 vols., 2002; contbr. articles to profl. jours. Mem. Bd. Edn., Mahtomedi Ind. Sch. Dist. 832, 1978-86; bd. dirs. Mahtomedi Area Ednl. Found., 1988-94, 2002—, pres., 1988-91, 2002—; bd. dirs. Minn. Ch. Found., 1975—, pres., 1989-97; chmn. constrn. industry adv. bd. West Group, 1991—. Served to capt. USAF, 1964-67. Decorated Air Force Commendation Medal; recipient Disting. Service award St. Paul Jaycees, 1974; named One of Ten Outstanding Young Minnesotans, Minn. Jaycees, 1975. Fellow Am. Coll. Constrn. Lawyers (founding mem., bd. govs. 1999-2002, sec. 2003—), Nat. Contract Mgmt. Assn., Am. Bar Found.; mem. ABA (chmn. internat. constrn. divsn. forum com. on constrn. industry 1989-91, chmn. fidelity and surety law com. 1994-95, regional chmn. pub. contract law sect. 1990-96), Internat. Bar Assn., Inter-Pacific Bar Assn. (vice chmn. internat. constrn. com. 1995-97), Fed. Bar Assn., Minn. Bar Assn. (vice chmn. litigation sect. 1979-81), Wis. Bar Assn., Hennepin Bar Assn., Am. Arbitration Assn. (nat. panel arbitrators), Mpls. Club. Presbyterian. Home: 8432 80th St N Stillwater MN 55082-9331 Office: Faegre & Benson 2200 Wells Fargo Ctr 90 S 7th St Minneapolis MN 55402-3901 E-mail: pbruner@faegre.com., Philipbruner@hotmail.com.

BRUNER, WILLIAM EVANS, II, ophthalmologist, educator, researcher; b. Cleve., Oct. 10, 1949; s. Clark Evans and Pauline (Schrenk) B.; m. Susan Lee Fraser, June 7, 1975; children: Amanda Lee, Andrew Evans. BA, Wesleyan U., 1971; MD, Case Western Res. U., 1975. Diplomate Am. Bd. Ophthalmology. Intern in surgery Univ. Hosps., Cleve., 1975-76, resident in ophthalmology, 1976-79; fellow in cornea and anterior segment surgery Johns Hopkins Hosp., Balt., 1979-81; asst. prof. ophthalmology Case Western Res. U., Cleve., 1981-89, assoc., 1989-93, assoc. clin. prof., 1993-96, clin. prof., 1996—. Sr. editor; manual of Corneal Surgery, 1987; contbr. chpts. to med. textbooks and articles to profl. jours. Trustee Case Western Res. U, Cleve., Hawken Sch., Gates Mills, Ohio. Recipient Alfred S. Maschke award Case Western Res. U. Sch. Medicine, 1975. Fellow Am. Acad. Ophthalmology; mem. ARVO, Wilmer Residents Assn., cleve. Acad. Medicine, Alpha Omega Alpha, Tavern Club, Cleve. Skating club, The Kirtland Club. Avocations: snow skiing, boating, sailing, golf, music. Home: 2906 Weybridge Rd Shaker Heights OH 44120-1874 Office: 1611 S Green Rd Cleveland OH 44121-4128

BRUNER, WILLIAM GWATHMEY, III, lawyer; b. Gadsden, Ala., Nov. 29, 1951; s. William G. and Nicolette A. (Diprima) B.; m. Eloisa Fernandez, Aug. 7, 1976; children: Nicolette, Virginia, William, Weston. BSE, U. Mich., 1973; JD, U. Va., 1976. Bar: Ind., Pa. Assoc. Bingham, Summers, Indpls., 1976-78; corp. counsel Scott Paper Co., Phila., 1978-86; group counsel Emhart Corp., Farmington, Conn., 1986-89; corp. counsel Black & Decker, Towson, Md., 1989-93, sr. corp. counsel, 1994—. Mem. ABA (EEO com. labor and employment law sect., taxation sect.). Republican. Roman Catholic. Office: Black & Decker Corp 701 E Joppa Rd Baltimore MD 21286-5502

BRUNER-WELCH, ANN S. physician assistant; b. Boulder, Colo., Oct. 10, 1962; d. Elmo Cody Jr. and Ruth Bruner; m. Donald M. Bruner-Welch, Mar. 23, 1985; children: Kyle, Elaine. AS, Santa Rosa Jr. Coll., 1993, Mission Coll., 1983; cert. physicians asst., U. Calif., 1995. Firefighter City of Santa Rosa, 1982-93; physician asst. Family Practice Ctr., Santa Rosa, 1993—2001, Chase-Dennis Team Health, Santa Rosa, Calif., 1996-2001, S.W. Cmty. Health Ctr., Santa Rosa, Calif., 1997—2000, Steven Smith, MD, Santa Rosa, Calif., 1999—2002, Ketah Mehta, MD, 2001—02, Sutter of Santa Rosa Emergency Dept., 2002—. CPR inst. Am. Heart Assn., Santa Rosa, 1983—; first aid instr., disaster svcs. ARC, Palo Alto, Calif., Boulder, Colo., 1967-85; medic Sports Car Club of Am., Sonoma, Calif., 1987-95; pres., charter mem. Redwood Empire, Live Steamers, 2002—; founding mem. Trueworthy Live Steam Co., LLC. Contbr. articles to profl. jour. PTAG bd. dir. Merryhill Sch., 2002—04. Fellow Am. Acad. of Physician Assts., Calif. Acad. of Physician Assts.; mem. Nat. Coun. for Cardiopulmonary and Critical Care, Calif. Profl. Firefighters, Calif. State Firefighters Assn., Santa Rosa Firefighters, Calif. State Railroad Mus. Avocations: ice skating, teaching, writing, railroading, embroidery. Home: PO Box 134 Santa Rosa CA 95402-0134

BRUNET, JAMES ROBERT, public administration educator; b. Queens, N.Y., Nov. 6, 1966; s. Joseph Robert Brunet and Margaret Delabo; m. Greta C. Larkin, Sept. 19, 1992. BA, Siena Coll., 1988; MPA, U. Conn., 1990; PhD, N.C. State U., 2003. Asst. project mgr. Gov.'s Mgmt. and Productivity Office, Albany, N.Y., 1990-92; budget examiner N.Y. State Divsn. Budget, Albany, 1992-93; asst. dir. Cmty. Justice Resource Ctr. Guilford Coll., Greensboro, N.C., 1994-96; asst. prof. N.C. State U., Raleigh, 2000—. Mem. ASPA, Am. Soc. Criminology. Roman Catholic. Avocations: civil war history, bass guitar. Home: 3614 Mandavilla Way Apex NC 27539 E-mail: jim_brunet@ncsu.edu.

BRUNETTI, MELVIN T. federal judge; b. Reno, 1933; m. Gail Dian Buchanan; children: Nancy, Bradley, Melvin Jr. Attended, U. Nev., 1951-53, 1956-57, 1960; JD, U. Calif., San Francisco, 1964. Mem. firm Vargas, Bartlett & Dixon, 1964-69, Laxalt, Bell, Allison & Lebaron, 1970-78, Allison, Brunetti, MacKenzie, Hartman, Soumbeniotis & Russell, 1978-85; judge U.S. Ct. Appeals (9th cir.), Reno, 1985-99, sr. judge, 1999—. Mem. Council of Legal Advisors, Rep. Nat. Com., 1982-85. Served with U.S. Army N.G., 1954-56. Mem. ABA, State Bar of Nev. (pres. 1984-85, bd. govs. 1975-84). Office: US Ct Appeals US Courthouse 400 S Virginia St Ste 506 Reno NV 89501-2194*

BRUNETTI, WAYNE H. utility company executive; BSBA, U. Fla.; grad. degree, Harvard U. With treasury dept. Fla. Power & Light, from 1964; pres., CEO Mgmt. Sys. Internat. Inc., 1991-94; pres., COO Pub. Svc. Co. Colo., Denver, 1994-2000; pres., CEO Xcel Energy Inc, Mpls., 2000—. Bd. dirs. Sun Bank Miami. Bd. dirs. Fla. Power & Light, United Way, Assoc. Industries Fla., Fla. C. of C., South Miami Hosp., Dade Found.; pres. bd. dirs. Haven Ctr. for Mentally Retarded; mem. various coms. Elec. Power Rsch. Inst., Edison Elec. Inst. Office: Xcel Energy Inc 414 Nicollet Mall Minneapolis MN 55401

BRUNETTI, WAYNE HENRY, utilities executive; b. Cleve., Oct. 13, 1942; s. Henry Joseph and Lillian (Lupo) B.; m. Mary Kelly, Aug. 17, 1963; children: Kelly Christine, Andrew Wayne. BSBA in Acctg., U. Fla., 1964; program for mgmt. devel., Harvard U., 1974. Acct. Fla. Power and Light Co., Miami, Fla., 1964-68, systems analyst, 1968-69, project coordinator, 1969-72, mgr. property acctg., 1972-73, mgr. corp. acctg., asst. comptroller, 1973-77, asst. to v.p. pub.

affairs, 1977-80, dir. energy mgmt., 1980, v.p. energy mgmt., 1980-83, v.p. divs., 1983-84, group v.p., 1984-87, exec. v.p., 1987-91; pres., CEO Mgmnt. Systems Internat., Fla., 1991-94; pres., COO Public Svc. Co. of Colo., 1994-96, pres., CEO, 1996—; chmn., pres., CEO New Century Energies, Inc., Denver, 2000—; pres., CEO Xcel Energy, 2001—. Bd. dirs. Sun Bank Miami, Fla. Power & Light Co. United Way of Dade County, Miami (bd. dirs. 1986—). Mem. Associated Industries Fla. (bd. dirs. 1986—), Dade Found. (bd. gov. 1988—), Fla. C. of C. (bd. dirs. 1989—), Edison Electric Inst. Democrat. Roman Catholic. Office: Xcel Energy 800 Nicollet Mall Minneapolis MN 55402

BRUNETTO, FRANK, electrical engineer; b. Graniti, Messina, Italy; came to U.S., 1930:; s. Rosario Brunetto and Maria (Mannino) B.; m. Bella Forman, Apr. 13, 1942; children: Russ, Theodore. BEE, Blky. Poly. U., 1953. Elec. engr. USN Applied Sci. Lab., Bklyn., 1953-69; mem. atomic and hydrogen bomb testing staff USN, Johnston Island, Pacific Ocean, 1962; revenue officer IRS, N.Y.C., 1970-72; maintenance engr. Dept. HUD, N.Y.C., 1972-95, ret., 1995. Author: Reforming Selenium Rectifiers, 1966, Introducing The Gate Turn-Off Switch, 1963; patentee in field; contbr. articles to sci. and profl. jours. With U.S. Army, 1942-45, ETO. Mem. AIAA, Sci. Rsch. Soc. Roman Catholic. Achievements include patents on dynamic testing of silicon control rectifiers and of gate turn-off switches. Home: Apt 1525 16445 Collins Ave Sunny Isles Beach FL 33160-4560

BRUNGARD, DANIEL V. small business owner, city official; b. St. Louis, Feb. 28, 1964; s. Edward G. Jr. and Virginia V. Brungard; m. Helen L. Juniewicz, Oct. 20, 1990; children: Mitchell E., Matthew D. BA in Polit. Sci., Webster U., St. Louis, 1995, MA in Internat. Rels., 1996. Rsch. analyst Anheuser-Busch Cos., Inc., St. Louis, 1984-98; dir. devel. Bridgeway Counseling Svcs., St. Charles, Mo., 1998-99, Lindenwood U., St. Charles, 1999-2001; alderman City of O'Fallon, Mo., 1997—; prin. The Brungard Group, LLC, 2001—. Mem. O'Fallon Planning and Zoning Commn., 1998-2000; bd. dirs. Urban Choice Coalition. Mem. Mo. Mcpl. League (bd. dirs.), Leadership Mo. Alumni Assn. (bd. dirs.). Republican. Roman Catholic. Avocation: golf. Office: City of O Fallon 100 N Main St O Fallon MO 63366-2200 Fax: 636-379-5617. E-mail: dbrungard@ofallon.mo.us.

BRUNGARDT, PETE, state legislator; m. Rosie Brungardt. Mem. Kans. State Senate, 2001—, vice chair fed. and state affairs com., mem. commerce com., mem. corrections and juvenile justice oversight com., mem. fin. instns. and ins. com., mem. pub. health and welfare com. Home: 522 Fairdale Rd Salina KS 67401 Office: 436 S Ohio St Salina KS 67401 E-mail: peterose@midusa.net., brungardt@senate.state.ks.us.*

BRUNGER, AXEL THOMAS, biophysicist, researcher, educator; b. Leipzig, Germany, Nov. 25, 1956; came to U.S., 1982; s. Hans and Hildegard (Müller) B. Diploma, U. Hamburg (Germany), 1980; PhD, Tech. U. Munich, 1982. Postdoctoral fellow Max-Planck Inst., Martinsried, Germany, 1984; rsch. assoc. Harvard U., Cambridge, Mass., 1982-83, 85-87; asst. investigator Howard Hughes Med. Inst., New Haven, 1987-92, assoc. investigator, 1992-95, investigator, 1995—; asst. prof. Yale U., New Haven, 1987-91, assoc. prof., 1991-93, prof., 1993-2000, Stanford U., Calif., 2000—. Recipient Röntgen prize for bioscis. Würzburg U., 1995, Gregori Aminoff prize Royal Swedish Acad. Scis., 2003; NATO postdoctoral fellow Deutscher Akademischer Austauschdienst, Bonn, Germany, 1982-83. Mem. AAAS, Am. Crystallographic Assn., Am. Chem. Soc., Protein Soc. Achievements include studies of protein structure and function, developments in macromolecular x-ray crystallography and solution NMR spectroscopy. Office: Stanford U James H Clark Ctr Rm E300-C Stanford CA 94305-5432

BRUNGRABER, ROBERT J. civil engineer, educator; b. Dec. 20, 1929; s. Louis Rudolph and Beatrice Emogene B.; m. Ruth Ann Rupp, June 13, 1951; children: Robert Lyman, Margaret Ruth. BSCE, U. Mich., 1951; MS, Cornell U., 1956; PhD, Carnegie Inst. Tech., 1963. Field engr. Porter-Urquhart-Skidmore, Owings & Merrill, cons. engrs., Casablanca, Morocco, 1951—53; instr. Cornell U., Ithaca, NY, 1953—56; rsch. engr. Alcoa Rsch. Labs., New Kensington, Pa., 1956—60; asst. prof. civil engring. Princeton U., 1962—66; assoc. prof. civil engring. Union Coll., Schenectady, NY, 1966—68; prof. civil engring. Bucknell U., Lewisburg, Pa., 1968—, presdl. prof., 1979—92, prof. emeritus, 1992—. Founder, pres. Slip-Test, Inc., 1976; structural cons. Borough Hall, Princeton, NJ, 1966; Intergovtl. Pers. Act appointee Nat. Bur. Stds., 1974—76; dir., treas., mem. nat. exec. com. Nat. Inst. Bldg. Scis., 1976—81. Contbr. articles to profl. publs. Mem.: ASTM (Charles H. Irvine award, Merit award), ASCE (chmn. com. lightweight alloys of metals structural divsn. 1969—73), Moles, Cosmos Club, Nassau Club, Phi Kappa Phi, Sigma Xi, Phi Gamma Delta, Chi Epsilon, Tau Beta Pi. Achievements include patents for in field; research in structural applications of aluminum, particularly welded applications, pile foundations, and slip resistance of footwear and/or walkway surfaces; supr. design and constrn. of Stephen J. Potter Meml. Lab., Union Coll., 1967; stuctural test facility at Bucknell U., 1985 (now named R.J. Brungraber Structural Test Facility); design of original system for reinforcing obsolete steel truss bridges; invention of NBS-Brungraber device for measuring the slip-resistance of footwear and/or walkway surfaces. E-mail: sliptestinc@aol.com.

BRUNGS, ROBERT ANTHONY, theology educator, institute director; b. Cin., July 7, 1931; s. Adolph and Helen (Klosterman) B. AB, Bellarmine Coll., Plattsburgh, N.Y., 1955; Licentiate in Philosophy, Fordham U., 1956; PhD in Physics, St. Louis U., 1962; Sacred Theology Licentiae, Woodstock (Md.) Coll., 1965. Asst. prof. physics St. Louis U., 1970-75, assoc. prof. physics, 1975-83; dir. Inst. for Theol. Encounter with Sci. and Tech., St. Louis, 1968—. Cons. Vatican, Rome, 1973-84, Council Cath. Bishops, Washington, 1973-92; mem. adv. bd. Zygon Mag., Chgo., 1975-96. Exec. producer video program DECISION, 1987, Lights Breaking, 1985; author: Building the City,1 967, A Priestly People, 1968, You See Lights Breaking Upon Us: Doctrinal Perspectives on Biological Advance, 1989; contbr. 60 articles to mags., newspapers, profl. jours. Mem. AAAS, Am. Phys. Soc., Sigma Xi, Phi Beta Kappa. Office: Inst for Theol Encounter with Sci and Tech 221 N Grand Blvd Saint Louis MO 63103-2006 Fax: 314-977-7211. E-mail: brungsr@slu.edu.

BRUNIE, CHARLES HENRY, investment manager; b. N.Y.C., July 17, 1930; s. Charles Henry and Olivia (Swanston) B.; m. Jean Isbell Corley, June 23, 1965; stepchildren: William Corley, Jean Corley Yankus, Ellen Corley. BA, Amherst Coll., 1952; MBA, Columbia, 1956. Analyst N.Y. Life Ins. Co., N.Y.C., 1956-60, Faulkner, Dawkins & Sullivan, 1960-63, Oppenheimer & Co., N.Y.C., 1963-65, gen. ptnr., 1965-82, mem. exec. com., 1969-82; chmn. Oppenheimer Capital, 1969-96, chmn. emeritus, 1996-2000; trustee Manhattan Inst., 1978—, chmn. bd., 1980-1990, chmn. emeritus, 1990—; chmn. Brunie Assocs., N.Y.C., 2001—. Served with AUS, 1952-54. Mem. N.Y. Soc. Security Analysts, Chartered Financial Analysts, Mont Pelerin Soc., Delta Upsilon. Clubs: Knickerbocker (N.Y.C.), Doubles (N.Y.C.), Annabell's (London), Bronxville Field, Siwanoy Country (Bronxville). Home: 21 Elm Rock Rd Bronxville NY 10708-4202 Office: Brunie Assocs 600 3d Ave 17th Fl New York NY 10016

BRUNING, ANTHONY STEVEN, lawyer; b. St. Louis, Oct. 24, 1955; s. Frederick Charles Jr. and Pauline (Shrum) B.; m. Cynthia Louise Leonard, Nov. 2, 1979; children: Anthony Steven Jr., Ryan Leonard, Michele Louise, Joseph Alexander. BA, U. Mo., 1977; JD, St. Louis U., 1980. Bar: Mo. 1980, U.S. Ct Appeals (8th cir.) 1980, U.S. Dist. Ct. (ea. dist.) Mo. 1980. Assoc. Leritz, Reinert & Duree PC, St. Louis, 1980-86, ptnr., 1986-90, Leritz, Plunkert and Bruning PC, St. Louis, 1990—. Speaker in field. Mem. Mo. Bar Assn. (rep. exec. com., young lawyers sect. coun. 1982-86), St. Louis Met. Bar Assn., ABA, Ill. Bar Assn., Mo. Assn. Trial Attys., Assn. Trial Lawyers Am., Mo. Athletic Club. Democrat. Avocations: fishing, hunting. Office: Leritz Plunkert & Bruning PC 1 City Ctr Ste 2001 Saint Louis MO 63101-2402 E-mail: abruning@leritzlaw.com.

BRUNING, JAMES LEON, academic administrator, educator; b. Bruning, Nebr., Apr. 1, 1938; s. Leon G. and Delma Dorothy (Middendorf) Bruning; m. E. Marlene Schaff, Aug. 24, 1958; children: Michael, Stephen, Kathleen. BA, Doane Coll., 1959; MA, U. Iowa, 1961, PhD, 1962. Chmn. dept psychology Ohio U., Athens, 1972-76, acting dean arts and scis., 1976-77, assoc. dean, 1977-78, vice provost, 1978-81, provost, 1981-93, trustee prof., 1993—, v.p. regional higher edn., 1998—99, dir. Enterprise project, 2002—03. Planning cons. NCHEMS, Boulder, Colo., 1979—80; provost Shawnee (Ohio) State U., 1996. Author: (book) Computational Handbook of Statistics, 1997, Research in Psychology, 1970; contbr. articles to profl. jours. Chair task force Ohio Bd. Regents, 1994—95. Grantee, Esso, 1963—64, NIMH, 1963—66, EPDA, 1974—75, OBOR, 1989—91. Mem.: APA (vis. scientist), AAAS, Midwestern Psychol. Assn., Sigma Xi. Democrat. Lutheran. Home: 6148 Melnor Dr Athens OH 45701-3577 Office: Ohio U Psychology Dept Athens OH 45701 E-mail: bruningj@ohio.edu.

BRUNING, JON CUMBERLAND, state attorney general; b. Lincoln, Nebr., Apr. 30, 1969; s. Roger Howard and Mary Genevieve (Cumberland) B.; m. Deonne Leigh Niemack, July 8, 1995, two children, Lauren Caroline, Jon Cumberland Jr. BA with high distinction, U. Nebr., 1990, JD with distinction, 1994. Bar: Nebr. 1994, U.S. Dist. Ct. Nebr. 1994, U.S. Ct. Appeals (8th cir.) 1994. Pvt. practice, Papillion, Nebr., 1993-97; mem. Nebr. Legislature from 3rd dist., Lincoln, 1997—2002; atty. gen. State of Nebr., 2003—. Mem., Gretna United Methodist Church, Nebr. State Bar Assoc., Phi Beta Kappa. Republican. Methodist. Home: 17501 Riviera Dr Omaha NE 68136-1951 Office: State Capitol PO Box 98920 Lincoln NE 68509

BRUNK, SAMUEL FREDERICK, oncologist; b. Harrisonburg, Va., Dec. 21, 1932; s. Harry Anthony and Lena Gertrude (Burkholder) B.; m. Mary Priscilla Bauman, June 24, 1976; children: Samuel, Jill, Geoffrey, Heather, Kirsten, Peter, Christopher, Andrew, Paul, Barbara BS, Ea. Mennonite Coll., 1955; MD, U. Va., 1959; MS in Pharmacology, U. Iowa, 1967. Diplomate Am. Bd. Internal Medicine, Am. Bd. Internal Medicine in Med. Oncology. Straight med. intern U. Va., Charlottesville, 1959-60; resident in chest diseases Blue Ridge Sanatorium, Charlottesville, 1960-61; resident in internal medicine U. Iowa, Iowa City, 1962-64, fellow in clin. pharmacology (oncology), 1964-65, 66-67, asst. prof. internal medicine, 1967-72; assoc. prof. internal medicine, 1972-76; fellow in medicine (oncology) Johns Hopkins U., Balt., 1965-66; clin. assoc. prof. med. Okla. State U. Coll. Osteo; vis. physician bone marrow transplantation unit Fred Hutchinson Cancer Treatment Ctr., U. Wash., Seattle, 1975; practice medicine specializing in med. oncology Des Moines, 1976-94; attending physician Iowa Luth. Hosp., 1976-94, Iowa Meth. Med. Ctr., 1976-94, Charter Hosp., 1976-94, Mercy Hosp. Med. Ctr., 1976-94; dir. med. oncology Hahne Regional Cancer Ctr., DuBois, Pa., 1994; attending physician DuBois Regional Med. Ctr., 1994; dir. Pa. Cmty. Cancer Care, 1995; attending physician St. Mary's Regional Med. Ctr., 1994; med. oncologist cancer treatment ctrs. Am. Southwestern Regional Med. Ctr., Tulsa, Okla., 1995—2001, chief med. oncology cancer treatment ctrs. Am., 2002—; attending physician Meml. Med. Ctr., Tulsa, Okla., 1995—. Chief of staff Iowa Luth. Hosp., 1990, chmn. dept. internal medicine, 1988; cons. physician Des Moines Gen. Osteo. Hosp., 1976-94; prin. investigator Iowa Oncology Rsch. Assn. in assn. with N. Cen. Cancer Treatment Group and Ea. Coop. Oncology Group, 1978-83; prin. investigator Iowa Oncology Rsch. Assn. Comty. Clin. Oncology Program, 1983-84; mem. cancer care com. St, Mary's, Pa., 1995. Contbr. articles to profl. jours. Bd. dirs. Iowa div. Am. Cancer Soc., 1971-89, Johnson County chpt., 1968-72. Mosby scholar, U. Va., 1959 Fellow ACP, Am. Coll. Clin. Pharmacology; mem. AMA, Okla. Medical Soc., Tulsa County Medical Soc., Am. Soc. Clin. Oncology, Raven Soc., Alpha Omega Alpha. Roman Catholic. Home: 2929 E 69th St Tulsa OK 74136-4541

BRUNK, SARA J. music educator; b. Shawano, WI, Apr. 5, 1977; d. Stephen Kenneth and Virginia Mae (Krull) Boenmke; m. Eric Ryan Brunk, June 24, 2000; 1 child, Clara Mae. BA, Luther Coll., Deborah, Iowa, 1995—99. Piano tchr., Minnetonka, Minn., 2000—03. Mem.: Minn. Music Tchr. Assoc. (mem. 2001—03). Avocations: hiking, painting, gardening, travel. Home: 16612 Seymour Dr Minnetonka MN 55345

BRUNK, THOMAS WALTER, art historian; b. Romeo, Mich., Nov. 25, 1949; s. Norman Brunk and Margie Velma Smith. MA in Art and Arch. History, Norwich U., 1992; PhD in Art History, The Union Inst., 1997. Clk. coord. Rouge Steel Co., Dearborn, Mich., 1971—, UAW Local 600, 1971—; founder, pres. The Indian Village Hist. Collections, Inc., Detroit, 1973—92; pres. The Stapleton Found. for Health Edn., Wayne State U., Detroit, 1980—95, Detroit Masonic Temple Libr. and Mus., Detroit, 2001; prof. archtl. history Coll. for Creative Studies, Detroit, 2001. Guest curator Mich. State U., Detroit, 1976, Detroit Inst. Arts, 1976, Detroit Hist. Mus., 1978, 79, 81, 84, U. Mich. Mus. Art, Ann Arbor, 1995—96; pres. The Pewabic Soc., Inc., Detroit, 1988—89. Author: Arts and Craft in Detroit 1906-1976: The Movement, The Society, The School, 1976, Pewabic Pottery: Marks and Labels, 1978, Pewabic in Architecture, 1979, Dichotomy, 1980, 1981, 1999, Bulletin of the Detroit Institute of Arts, 1981, The Acanthus Club, 1981, Leonard B. Willeke: Excellence in Architecture and Design, 1986, A Tribute to Edgar Louis Yaeger, 1988, American Craft, 1989, Selected Works By Contemporary Hispanic Artists in Michigan, 1989, The Grosse Pointe Artists Association, 1992, The Grand American Avenue 1850-1920, 1994, Tonnancour, 1994, 1997, Painting with Fire, 1995. Mem.: Mich. Archival Assn., Detroit Inst. Arts Founders Soc., Alliance Francaise Detroit, Soc. Archtl. Historians (pres. The Saarinen (Mich.) chpt. 1989—93, 1998—), The Players, Acanthus Club, Witenagemote Club, The Scarab Club (pres. 1990—92), Algonquin Club Detroit and Windsor, Prismatic Club, Masons, Scottish Rite. Avocations: historic preservation, ceramics, photography, genealogy, travel. Home: 1479 Seminole Ave Detroit MI 48214-2708 Office: Detroit Masonic Temple Libr and Mus 500 Temple Ave Detroit MI 48201-2659 E-mail: brunk@spamcop.net.

BRUNK, ULF TJELVAR, pathology educator, consultant; b. Lund, Sweden, Oct. 26, 1937; s. Sture W. and Ruth A.E. (Lindgren) B.; m. Kristina M. Nyström, 1973 (div. 1985); children: Malin, Sofia. MD, U. Lund, 1964; PhD, U. Uppsala, Sweden, 1973. Intern and resident depts. ob-gyn., cytology and pathology Lund, Karlstad, Stockholm and Uppsala; asst. prof. U. Uppsala, 1970-73, assoc. prof., 1973-81; prof. pathology U. Linköping, Sweden, 1981—; adj. prof. USC, Los Angeles. Mem. Swedish Med. Res. Coun., 1982-92, v.p., 1992-95. Contbr. over 250 articles on free radical rsch. to med. jours., chpts. to books. Mem. Swedish Assn. Physicians, Internat. Soc. for Free Radical Rsch. Office: U Linköping Dept Pathology S-581 85 Linköping Sweden E-mail: ulf.brunk@inr.liu.se.

BRUNK, WILLIAM EDWARD, astronomer; b. Cleve., Nov. 24, 1928; s. Edgar Rea and Mabel Mowbray (Pearson) B.; 1 dau., Anna Kathryn. BS, Case Inst. Tech., 1952, MS, 1954, PhD, 1963. Aero. research scientist Lewis Flight Propulsion Lab., NACA, Cleve., 1954-58; aerospace engr. Lewis Research Center, NASA, Cleve., 1958-64; staff scientist for planetary astronomy NASA Hdqrs., Washington, 1964-65, program chief planetary astronomy, 1965-77, discipline scientist planetary astronomy, 1977-82, chief planetary sci. br., 1982-85; mgr. solar system sci. Univ. Space Rsch. Assn., Washington, 1985-94; ret., 1994. Recipient Exceptional Service medal NASA, 1985. Fellow AAAS; mem. Am. Astron. Soc. (Harold Mazursky Meritorious Svc. award 1995), Internat. Astron. Union; Mem. Sigma Xi. Home: PO Box 3466 Annapolis MD 21403-0466 E-mail: wbrunk@erols.com.

BRUNKE, DAWN BAUMANN, writer, editor; b. Madison, Wis., Nov. 6, 1959; d. Richard Joseph and Carol Edler Baumann; m. Bob Brunke, May 25, 1991; 1 child, Alyeska Isabela. BA, Lawrence U., 1977—81. Massage Therapist AMTA, Wash. D.C., 1985. Instr. Potomac Inst. of Myotherapy, Washington, 1986—88; massage therapist Gaithersburg, Md., 1986—88; editor Alaska Wellness Mag., Anchorage, 1995—; massage therapist Alaska Club, Wasilla, 2001—. Author: (short stories) In God's Garden (Grand Prize; Anchorage Daily News/ U. of Alaska Creative Writing Contest, 1997), Before She Was the Queen of Syrup (Editors Choice, Anchorage Daily News/ U. of Alaska Creative Writing Contest, 1998), (nonfiction book) Animal Voices [] Telepathic Communication in the Web of Life, (children's books) Who Lives Here?. Home: P O Box 877229 Wasilla AK 99687

BRUNKEN, GERALD WALTER, SR., manufacturing company executive; b. Oak Park, Ill., May 31, 1938; s. Walter Richard and Elenore (Troost) B.; m. Louise Nunziato, June 29, 1968; children: Gerald Jr., Patrick. BS, Lincoln Coll., 1958; BA in Econs., Baker U., 1961. Br. coord. A.M. Castle, Franklin Park, Ill., 1961-62; sales rep. Proviso West Realty, Berkley, Ill., 1962-65; CEO Addison (Ill.) Machine Engring., 1965—, CEO, pres., 1995—; pres. Sci. Tube Inc., Addison, 1971-95. One man show, Addison, 1971; contbr. articles to profl. jours. Cub master Boy Scouts Am., Addison, 1976-78; athletic dir. St. Philip the Apostle Sch., Addison, 1982-84; pres. Driscoll Cath. High Booster Club, 1985-86. Mem. Fabricating Mfrs. Assn. (speaker, panelist), Am. Tube Assn. (speaker, panelist), Ducks Unlimited (treas. Salt Creek chpt. 1982-90, zone chmn. State of Ill. 1990—, Spl. Projects awards 1987, 88, 89, 90), KC. Roman Catholic. Avocations: painting, writing, hunting, fishing. Home: 5N029 Honey Hill Dr Wayne IL 60184

BRUNKHURST, WILLIAM LEE, JR., music educator; b. Atlanta, July 5, 1936; s. William Lee Brunkhurst and Grace Mina (Applegate) Honour; 1 child, David James Jeffryes. BFA, U. Ga., 1958; Tchr.'s Cert., Davidson Coll., Charlotte, N.C., 1969; postgrad., Davidson Coll., 1972. Supply tech. VA Hosps., Tucson, N.Y.C., Fresno, Calif., 1960—68; tchr. Peace Corps, Andhra Pradesh, India, 1965—67; draft counsellor Am. Friends Svc. Com., 1967—72. Pvt. piano instr., N.Y.C., 1960—80; tchr. Blakney H.S., Waynesboro, Ga., 1968—72. Author: (autobiography) The Long Journey Home, 2001, poems, plays. Buddy vol. AIDS patients Gay Mens' Health Crisis, N.Y.C., 1985—87. With U.S. Army, 1959—64. State of Ga. grantee, 1969, State of Ga. scholar, 1972. Mem.: Phi Mu Alpha, Phi Beta Kappa. Democrat. Quaker. Avocations: jogging, writing, studying Sanskrit, swimming. Home: 317 2d Ave Apt 1 New York NY 10003

BRUNN, THOMAS LEO, SR., lawyer; b. Ionia, Mich., Mar. 14, 1937; s. Walter W. and Catherine M. (Fox) B.; m. Constance P. Perz, Sept. 28, 1963; children: Thomas Leo, Timothy J., Maribeth, Heather. BS, John Carroll U., 1959; JD, Cleve. Marshall Law Sch., 1967. Bar: ohio 1967. Pres. The Brunn Law Firm Co., L.P.A. Cleve. Served to 1st lt. U.S. Army, 1959-62. Mem. ABA, Ohio Bar Assn., Cleve. Assn. Civil Trial Attys. (pres. 1982-83), Fedn. Ins. Counsel (vice chmn. product liability com.), Chagrin Valley Country Club (Chagrin Falls, Ohio). Office: 208 Hoyt 700 W St Clair Ave Cleveland OH 44113 E-mail: brunn@core.com.

BRUNNER, ELLEN MARGARET, not-for-profit fundraiser; d. Carl David Prohaska and Ellen Melinda Engelking; m. Bryan Keith Brunner, May 9, 1998; 1 child, William Edward. BA, Franklin (Ind.)Coll., 1994; M in Pub. Affairs, Ind. U., Indpls., 1997. Asst. devel. Sigma Theta Tau Internat., Indpls., 1994—96; assoc. dir. Miami U., Oxford, Ohio, 1997—2000; pres. Columbus Regional Hosp. Found., Columbus, 2000—03, officer planned maj. gifts, 2003—. Mem. com. Mayor's Adv. Coun., Columbus, 2000—02. Mem.: Columbus C. of C. (assoc.; women's profl. conf. com. 2002—03), Nat. Com. Planned Giving (assoc.), Rotary (assoc.; chair club svc. 2003—). Office: Columbus Regional Hospital Foundation 2400 East 17th Street Columbus IN 47201

BRUNNER, GEORGE MATTHEW, management consultant, former business executive; b. Newark, Jan. 17, 1925; s. Mathias J. and Mary E. (Fuith) B.; m. Ruth E. Owens, Nov. 16, 1953. AB in Chemistry, Columbia U., 1949, MChemE, 1950. Devel. engr. J.T. Baker Chem. Co., Phillipsburg, N.J., 1950-53; plant mgr. Internat. Minerals & Chem. Corp., Niagara Falls, N.Y. and Houston, 1953-62; mfg. engring. mgr. Gen. Foods Corp., Hoboken, N.J., Houston and Lafayette, Ind., 1962-71; v.p. mfg. W.R. Grace & Co., St. Simons Islands, Ga., 1971-73; pres., chief exec. officer S.A. Schonbrunn & Co., Inc., Palisades Park, N.J., 1973-82; v.p. ops. Am. Maize Products Co., Stamford, Conn., 1982-84; mgmt. cons., 1984—. Served with AUS, 1943-45. Decorated Purple Heart. Mem. Nat. Coffee Assn. (dir.), Pres.'s Assn., Am. Chem. Soc., Am. Inst. Chem. Engrs., Electrochem. Soc., 5th Armored Div. Assn. (pres. 1980-81). Patentee in field. Home and Office: 1221 Clays Trl Oldsmar FL 34677-4866

BRUNNER, JAMES EDWIN, lawyer; b. Kalamazoo, June 11, 1952; m. Rosemary C. Brunner; children: Matthew, Jacob, Seth. BS in Engring. magna cum laude, U. Mich., 1974, JD cum laude, 1977. Assoc. Consumers Energy Co., Jackson, Mich., 1977-93, asst. gen. counsel, 1993—. Mem. ABA. Office: Consumers Energy Co One Energy Plz Jackson MI 49201-2276

BRUNNER, JOHN HARRY, surgeon; b. Kansas City, Mo., 1939; MD, Washington U., St. Louis, 1965. Diplomate Am. Bd. Surgery. Intern, resident surgery Barnes Hosp.-Washington U., St. Louis, 1965-71; surgeon Bulton-Eisele Clinic, Hot Springs, Ark., 1971—. Surgeon St. Joseph's Med. Ctr., Hot Springs. Fellow ACS, SW Surg. Congress; mem. Alpha Omega Alpha. Office: Bulton-Eisele Clinic 1 Mercy Ln Ste 201 Hot Springs National Park AR 71913-6457

BRUNNER, KATHLEEN MARIE, humanities educator; b. Torrance, Calif., Nov. 5, 1953; d. Earl Allen and Patricia Nellie Brunner; life ptnr. Michael Foote, 1991. MA in Comparative Lit., U. Wash., Seattle, 1990—92, PhD in Comparative Lit., 1990—97, MA in Romance Langs. & Lit., 1993—94. Reader U. Wash., Seattle, 1991—94, tchg. asst., 1994—96; lectr. Alliance Francaise de Seattle, 1999—; instr. Highline C.C., Des Moines, Wash., 2001—02. Bd. mem., past pres., past v.p., past sec. Alliance Francaise de Seattle, 1998—; bd. mem., sec. French-American C. of C. Pacific-Northwest, Seattle, 1999—; adv. bd. mem., French Studies Dept. U. Wash., Seattle, 2003—. Contbr. articles to profl. jours. Recipient Vignernon d'honneur du Beaujolais, Union Interprofessionel des vins du Beaujolais, 2002; Study Grant, French Govt., 2000. Mem.: Wash. Assn. For Lang. Tchrs., Soc. French Profs. et Francophones d'Amerique, Groupe D'Etudes Sartriennes. Avocations: swimming, travel, photography. Office Fax: 206-223-6258. E-mail: brunnerk@lanepowell.com.

BRUNNER, LILLIAN SHOLTIS, nurse, writer; b. Freeland, Pa. d. Andrew J. and Anna (Tomasko) Sholtis; m. Mathias J. Brunner, Sept. 8, 1951; children: Janet Brunner Cramer, Carol Ann Brunner Burns, Douglas Mathias. RN, diploma, U. Pa., 1940, BS, 1945, LittD (hon.), 1985; MS in Nursing, Case-Western Res. U., 1947; ScD (hon.), Cedar Crest Coll., 1978. RN, Pa. Head nurse U. Pa. Hosp., Phila., 1940-42, operating room supr., 1942-44, head, fundamentals of nursing dept., 1944-46; asst. prof. surgical nursing Yale U. Sch. Nursing, New Haven, Conn., 1947-51; surgical supr. Yale-New Haven Hosp., 1947-51; Lillian Sholtis Brunner chair med.-surg. nursing U. Pa., 2001. Rsch. project dir. Sch. Nursing Bryn Mawr (Pa.) Hosp., 1973-77; co-founder History of Nursing Mus., Pa. Hosp., Phila., 1974; mem. bd. overseers Sch. Nursing U. Pa., 1982-88; bd. overseers emeritus, 1988—; chmn. nursing adv. Presbyn.-U. Pa. Med. Ctr., Phila., 1970-88, 90-93, trustee, 1976-88, 90-95, vice chmn. bd. trustees, 1985-88; mem. com. profl. advisory Vis. Nurse Assn., Lancaster, Pa., 1996-99; sec. Glen Coun., Willow Valley Manor North, 1997-2000. Author: Manual of Operating Room Technology, 1966, (with others) Lippincott Manual of Nursing Practice, 1974, 4th edit., 1986, Textbook of Medical and Surgical Nursing, 1964, 6th edit., 1988; editl. bd. Jour. Nursing and Health Care, Nursing 1999, Nursing Photobook Series, 1978-90. Bd. dirs. Presbyn. Found. for Phila., 1995-99. Recipient Disting. Alumnus award Frances Payne Bolton Sch. Nursing, Case Western Res. U., 1980, Alumni award for merit Soc. Alumni Assns., U. Pa., and Am. Dream Achievement award Class of '45, U. Pa., 1995. Fellow: Am. Acad. Nursing (Living Legend award 2002); mem.: Nurses Alumni Assn. U. Pa. Hosp., Philanthropic Ednl. Orgn., Nat. League for Nursing (judge nat. writing contest 1982—84, Disting. Svc. award 1979), ANA, Acad. U. Pa., Ben Franklin Soc., Internat. Old Lacers Soc., Nat. League Am. Pen Women (sec. Phila. chpt. 1972—76, nat. sec. 1984—86), Pi Lambda Theta, Pi Gamma Mu, Sigma Theta Tau. Home and Office: Apt J-411 645 Willow Valley Sq Lancaster PA 17602-4871 E-mail: LilalmaB@aol.com.

BRUNNER-MARTINEZ, KIRSTIN ELLEN, pediatrician, psychiatrist; b. Allentown, Pa., July 26, 1959; d. John Wilson and Ulla Brita (Arvide) Brunner; m. Fred F. Martinez. BS, Muhlenberg Coll., Allentown, Pa., 1981; DO, Phila. Coll. Osteo. Medicine, 1986. Diplomate Am. Bd. Pediatrics, Am. Bd. Psychiatry and Neurology in child and adolescent psychiatry and adult psychiatry. Resident U. Ky., 1992; dept. dir. Integra Health Family Devel. Ctr., Cedar Rapids, Iowa, 1993-98; with Hamot Inst. for Behavioral Health, Erie, Pa., 1998-2001; med. dir. Hamot Child and Adolescent Psychiat. Unit, Erie, 1999-2001, Sarah Reed Children's Ctr., Erie, 2001—. Fellow Am. Acad. Pediatrics; mem. AMA, Am. Acad. Child and Adolescent Psychiatry, Am. Psychiat. Assn. Avocations: cross country skiing, soccer (outdoor and indoor). Office: Sarah Reed Children's Ctr 1020 E 10th St Erie PA 16503

BRUNO, ANDREW FELIX, ophthalmologist; b. Pitts., Jan. 6, 1942; s. Joseph Anthony and Rose Marie (Petraglia) B.; m. Frances Ann Mayni, Aug. 14, 1965; children: Andrew Francis, Kimberly Susan. BS in Biology, Georgetown U., 1963; MD, U. Pitts., 1967. Intern Health Ctr. Hosp. U. Pitts., 1967-68, resident Eye and Ear Hosp., 1970-73; pvt. practice in ophthalmology Deerfield Beach, Fla., 1973—. Chief of surgery North Broward (Fla.) Med. Ctr., 1996—. Sr. asst. surgeon USPHS, 1968-70. Office: 1609 SE 3rd Ct Deerfield Beach Fl 33441-4418

BRUNO, ANTHONY D. lawyer; b. Newark, N.J., May 3, 1956; s. Frank and Delores (Fleming) B.; m. Gina Mabey, Aug. 1982; children: Chris, Dan, Will. BA in Polit. Sci., Syracuse U., 1978; JD, George Washington U., 1981. Bar: N.Y. 1981, N.J. 1981. Atty. Shearman & Sterling, N.Y.C., 1981-84; assoc. gen. counsel Warner-Lambert, Morris Plains, NJ, 1984-2000; exec. v.p., gen. counsel Galen Holdings Plc, Rockaway, NJ, 2001—. Office: 100 Enterprise Dr Ste 280 Rockaway NJ 07866 E-mail: tbruno@wclabs.com.

BRUNO, BARBARA ALTMAN, social worker; b. N.Y.C., May 26, 1947; m. Joseph Peter Bruno, Oct. 2, 1977. AB in English, Cornell U., 1969; MSW in Psychiat. Social Work, Calif. State U., Sacramento, 1974; PhD in Psychology, Columbia Pacific U., 1987. Diplomate clin. social work; cert. social worker, N.Y. Group facilitator San Francisco DWI Sch., 1975-76; social svc. coord. Kosher Nutrition Project, San Francisco, 1975-76; counselor SUNY, Purchase, 1980-81, Pace U. Counseling Ctr., N.Y.C., 1981-84; group leader No. Westchester YMHA/YWHA, Pleasantville, N.Y., 1981-91; pvt. practice psychotherapy Pleasantville, 1984—. Adj. faculty Westchester Community Coll., Valhalla, N.Y., 1990—, COED program, Pleasantville, 1988-92; founder Weight Release Svcs., Pleasantville, 1989—, Thinside Out, Pleasantville, 1985-90. Author: Quakers, 1985, Worth Your Weight, 1996, (with Curtis Jones) From Segregation to Sobriety, 2000; editor Roundup, 1990-98; well being columnist Dimensions mag.; contbr. articles to profl. jours., chpt. to book. Fellow Soc. Clin. Social Work Psychotherapists (cert.), Nat. Assn. to Advance Fat Acceptance (chair Westchester-Rockland chpt. 1989-91, nat. bd. dirs. 1991-97, mental health advisor 1991—); mem. Acad. Cert. Social Workers.

BRUNO, CATHY EILEEN, educator, management consultant, former state official; b. Binghamton, N.Y. d. Martin Frank and Beverly Carolyn (Hamlin) Piza; m. Frank L. Delaney (div.); m. Paul R. Bruno, May 5, 1990. BA, SUNY, Binghamton; MSW, Syracuse U. Psychiat. social worker Broome Devel. Ctr., Binghamton, 1973-74, 76, congl. legis. aide, 1975; asst. dir. Bur. Program and Fiscal audits N.Y. State Office Mental Retardation and Devel. Disabilities, Albany, 1976-80; statewide coord. Intermediate Care Facilities for Developmentally Disabled, 1980; cert. coord. Western County Svc. Group, 1980-83, Upstate unit dir. Bur. Cert. Control, 1983-85; dir. ICF/DD Survey and Rev., 1985-89; area dir. Bur. Program Cert., 1989-95; dir. Bur. Transitional Svcs., 1995-97, mgmt. cons., 1997—. Adj. instr. SUNY Sch. Social Welfare, Albany, 1982-83; adj. faculty C.C. of Southern Nev., Las Vegas, 1998. Vol. U. Nev. Coop. Ext. Master Gardener program, 1997—; bd. dirs. Worldwide AIDS Movement, 2000—01. Mem. Am. Mgmt. Assn. Home and Office: 293 Canyon Spirit Dr Henderson NV 89012-3472

BRUNO, DAVID JOSEPH, JR., chemical engineer, researcher; b. Martins Ferry, Ohio, Sept. 6, 1951; s. David Joseph Bruno, Sr. and Betty Katherine (Krotky) Bruno; m. Margaret Karen Conditt, Feb. 13, 1988; children: Joshua-Nathan, Holly Noelle. BS in chem. engring., Case Western Res. U., 1973; MS in chem. engring., U. Cin., 1979. Rsch. engr. Procter & Gamble, Cin., 1973—75, tech. leader, 1975—79, sect. head, 1979—87, assoc. dir., 1987—98, rsch. fellow, 1998—. Food sci. adv. bd. U. Ill., Champaign, Ill., 1983—97; adv. bd. Case Western U., Chem. Engr. Dept., Cleve., 2001—. Author: (paper) Olestra Process Technology, 1988. Named Scoutmaster of Year, Dan Beard Boy Scout Coun., 1997; recipient Outstanding Svc. award, 1998, Nat. Jamboree Scoutmaster, 1997, 2001. Fellow: Am. Inst. of Chem. Engr. Republican. Roman Catholic. Achievements include patents in field of soy protein analogs; Olestra fat free processing. Avocations: backpacking, Boy Scouts, hiking. Home: 6959 Rock Springs Dr Liberty Twp OH 45011 Office: Procter & Gamble 6071 Ctr Hill Rd Cincinnati OH 45224 Home Fax: 513-779-7528. E-mail: bruno.dj@pg.com.

BRUNO, GRACE ANGELIA, accountant, retired educator; b. St. Louis, Oct. 11, 1935; d. John E. and Rose (Goodwin) B. BA, Notre Dame Coll., 1966; MEd, So. Ill. U., 1972; MAS, Johns Hopkins U., 1983; PhD, Walden U., 1985. CPA, Mo., Md., N.J. Tchr. Sch. Sisters of Notre Dame (SSND) of St. Louis, 1962-80; pres. Bruno-Potter, Inc., Avon By The Sea, N.J., 1981—. Asst. treas., instr. acctg. Coll. of Notre Dame of Md., Balt., 1978-80, treas., 1979-80; asst. prof. acctg. Georgian Ct. Coll., Lakewood, N.J., 1985-91; fin. advisor James Harry Potter gold medal award ASME, N.Y.C., 1980—. Elected to Internat. Platform Assn., 1987. Mem. AICPA, N.J. Soc. CPAs, St. Louis Bus. Educators (treas. 1972-73), Inst. Bus. Appraisers, Inc., Johns Hopkins Univ. Faculty Club. Democrat. Roman Catholic. Home and Office: 419 3rd Ave Avon By The Sea NJ 07717 E-mail: gbruno4u@monmouth.com.

BRUNO, HAROLD ROBINSON, JR., retired journalist, writer; b. Chgo., Oct. 25, 1928; s. Harold R. and Tallulah H. (Kandel) B.; m. Margaret E. Christian, Nov. 12, 1959; children: Harold, Daniel. BS in Journalism, U. Ill., 1950. Reporter Advt. Age, Chgo., 1950; sports editor DeKalb (Ill.) Chronicle, 1950-51; reporter City News Bur., Chgo., 1953-54, Chgo. American, 1954-60, Newsweek mag., 1960-63, bur. chief, 1963-66, news editor N.Y.C., 1966-71, chief polit. corr. Washington, 1971-78; polit. dir. ABC News, Washington, 1978-97, polit. analyst, 1997-98; ret., 1998; sr. polit. analyst Politics.com, 1999-2000. Adv. bd. Internat. Programs and Studies, pres.'s coun., U. Ill.; adv. bd. Washington Ctr. for Politics and Journalism; moderator Vice Presdl., 1992. Columnist Firehouse mag; Contbr. articles to various publs. Bd. dirs. Chevy Chase Fire Dept.; adv. bd. Presdl. Classroom for Young Ams.; mem. Port Chester (N.Y.) Vol. Fire Dept.; dir., chmn. Fallen Firefighters Found., Nat. Fire Acad. With U.S. Army, 1951-53. Recipient Lowell Thomas award Internat. Platform Assn., 1984, Pres. award Internat. Assn. Fire Chiefs, 1999; Fulbright scholar, 1956-57; named Fire Svc. Person of Yr. Cong. Fire Svc. Inst., 1995. Mem. Nat. Fire Protection Assn., Nat. Vol. Fire Coun., AFTRA, Chgo. Newspaper Reporters Assn., Friendship Fire Assn., U. Ill. Alumni Assn. (bd. dirs., Illini achievement award 1984), Bethesda-Chevy Chase Rescue Squad Alumni, Soc. Profl. Journalists, Chgo. Press Vets. Assn. (Press Vet. of Yr. award 1999), Internat. Assn. Fire Fighters (hon.), Tau Delta Phi. Jewish. Home: 3414 Cummings Ln Chevy Chase MD 20815-3238

BRUNO, JOSEPH L. state legislator, senate majority leader; BSBA, Skidmore Coll. Mem. N.Y. State Senate, Albany, 1976—, chmn. senate elections com., 1989-93, chmn. senate ins. com., 1985-89, vice chmn. legis. commn. on solid waste mgmt., 1985-89, chmn. senate com. on consumer protection, 1979-84, pres., 1995—. State senate majority leader, 1995—; asst. majority leader for conf. ops., 1989-95; chmn. senate commerce, econ. devel. and small bus. com., 1993 95; chmn. legis. com. on pub.-pvt. cooperation, 1989-95 Mem., chmn. Rensselaer County Rep. Com., 1974-77; past pres. N.Y. State Assn. Young Reps.; mem. Italian Cmty. Ctr., Troy, N.Y., Troy Boy's Club, Troy Music Hall Assn. Mem. N.Y. State Sheriffs Assn. (hon.), St. Mary's Acad. Alumni Assn. (past pres), N.Y. State Jaycees (past v.p.), Soc. ofthe Friends of St. Patrick (bd. dirs.), VFW (Brunswick Post 831), Elks. Office: NY State Senate State Capitol 909 Legislative Office Bldg Albany NY 12247*

BRUNO, LISA, law librarian; b. N.Y.C., Apr. 1, 1951; d. Dominic A. and Earline H. (Reed) B. BA, U. South Fla., 1973; MLS, Fla. State U., 1976. Cert. libr., N.Y. Law libr. Carlton, Fields, Ward, Emmanuel, Tampa, Fla., 1986-88; info. specialist Consumers Union, Yonkers, N.Y., 1991; law libr. Libr. of U.S. Cts., 11th Cir., Atlanta, 1992; sales rep. Lawyers Coop. Pub., Rochester, N.Y., 1994-95; cons. Info. Brokers, Atlantic Beach, Fla., 1995—; sr. account exec. Questel Orbit Telecom grp., France, 1999—. Lectr./guest spkr. in field. Contbr. articles to profl. jours. Avocations: ballet, art appreciation, travel. Office: Information Brokers 377 Plaza St Atlantic Beach FL 32233-5441 also: 377 Plaza St Atlantic Beach FL 32233-5441

BRUNO, LOUIS VINCENT, special education educator; b. Allegheny County, Pa., Feb. 10, 1959; s. Thomas E. and Anna Marie (Lavra) B. BS in Elem. Edn., U. Pitts., 1981, MEd in Mentally/Physically Handicapped, 1982, cert. secondary prins., 1990. Cert. tchr. expectations and student achievement/gender/ethnic expectations and student achievement coord., learning potential assessment device instr., instrumental enrichment trainer. Tchr. Steel Valley Sch. Dist., Munhall, Pa., 1981-82; adult living program instr. United Cerebral Palsy Assn., Pitts., 1982; from learning disabilities tchr. to asst. prin. Wilkinsburg (Pa.) Sch. Dist., 1982—98, asst. prin. Wilkinsburg (Pa.) Mid. Sch., 1998—; prin. 8th Linton Mid. Sch., Pitts., 1999—. Mem. adv. bd. TV and Video Tchrs. Assn. of Western Pa. Home: 301 Mcgregor Dr Verona PA 15147-3433 E-mail: loubruno@aol.com., lbruno@phsd.k12.pa.us.

BRUNO, MICHAEL STEPHEN, ocean engineering educator, researcher; b. Nutley, N.J., Apr. 16, 1958; s. Frank Joseph and Annie Marie (Golden) B. BS, N.J. Inst. Tech., 1980; MS, U. Calif., Berkeley, 1981; PhD, MIT, 1986. Registered profl. engr., N.J. Prin. engr. N.J. Dept. Environ. Protection, Toms River, 1981-82; rsch. asst. MIT, Cambridge, 1982-86; asst. prof. N.J. Inst. Tech., Newark, 1986-89; assoc. prof., dir. Davidson Lab. Stevens Inst. Tech., Hoboken, N.J., 1989-98; prof. Stevens Inst. Tech, Hoboken, NJ, 1998—. Young investigator Office of Naval Rsch., Washington, 1991. Editor-in-chief Jour. Marine Environ. Engring., 1991—; contbr. articles to profl. jours. Mem. Planning Bd., West Caldwell, N.J., 1990-93. Recipient Fulbright Scholar, 1996. Mem. ASCE (Outstanding Svc. award 1987), ASME, Am. Geophys. Union, Pan Am. Fedn. Ocean Engrs. (sec.-gen. 1990—), Soc. Naval Architects and Marine Engrs., Tau Beta Pi. Office: Stevens Institute of Technology Castle Point Sta Hoboken NJ 07030-5907

BRUNO, PETER JACKSON, pastor, counselor, consultant; b. White Plains, N.Y., Dec. 27, 1945; s. Charles Fredrick and Barbara B.; m. Barbara Suesens; 1 child, Linda; 2d m. Corky Jean Brown, July 3, 1976; children: Benjamin, Elizabeth. BA in Psychology, Brown U., 1968; MEd in Counseling, Mont. State U., 1978. Ordained min. Wesleyan Ch.; nat. cert. counselor. Addictive disease counselor Mont. State Hosp., Galen, 1973-76; tchg. asst. Mont. State U., Bozeman, 1977-78; psychologist V Ea. Mont. Mental Health, Miles City, 1979-92; pvt. practice counselor Glendive, Mont., 1992-98; sr. pastor New Hope Wesleyan Ch., Terry, Mont., 1998—; nat. marriage and family cons., 1996—. Clin. cons. Dept. Family Svcs., Miles City, Home on the Range, Sentinel Butte, N.D., Pine Hills Sch., Miles City, all 1992-94; clin. dir. Big Sky Ranch, Glendive, 1992-97. Author: New Ways Workbook, 1992, The Miracles of Marriage, 1996, What Every Couple Should Know, 1999, Maximizing Your Marriage, 2002, Complete Marriages, 2003. Pres. Montanans for Children, Youth and Families, Inc. Named Mont.'s Outstanding Direct Svc. Provider, Mental Health Assn. Mont., 1982. Mem. Great Plains Counseling Assocs. (dir.), Toastmasters Internat. (Disting. Leadership award 1995), Nat. Spkrs. Assn., Internat. Platform Assn. Office: New Hope Wesleyan Ch PO Box 520 501 Garfield Ave Terry MT 59349-0520

BRUNS, BILLY LEE, electrical engineer, consultant; b. St. Louis, Nov. 21, 1925; s. Henry Lee and Violet Jean (Williams) Bruns; m. Lillian Colleen Mobley, Sept. 6, 1947; children: Holly Renee, Kerry Alan, Barry Lee, Terrence William. BA, Washington U., St. Louis, 1949; postgrad., Sch. Engring., St. Louis, 1959-62; EE, ICS, Scranton, Pa., 1954. Registered profl. engr., Mo., Ill., Wash., Fla., La., Wis., Minn., N.Y., N.C., Iowa, Pa., Miss., Ind., Ala., Ga., Va., R.I., Wyo. Supt., engr., estimator Schneider Electric Co., St. Louis, 1950-54, Ledbetter Electric Co., St. Louis, 1954-57; tchr. indsl. electricity St. Louis Bd. Edn., 1957-71; pres. B.L. Bruns & assocs. Cons. Engrs. Inc., St. Louis, 1963-72; v.p., chief engr. Hosp. Bldg. & Equipment Co., St. Louis, 1972-76; pres., prin. B.L. Bruns & Assocs. Cons. Engrs., St. Louis, 1976—. Tchr. elec. engring. U. Mo. St. Louis extension, 1975-76. Tech. editor The National Electrical Code and Blueprint Reading, Am. Tech. Soc., 1959-65. Mem. Mo. Adv. Coun. on Vocat. Edn., 1969-76, chmn., 1975-76; leader Explorer post Boy Scouts Am., 1950-57. Served with AUS, 1944-46, PTO, Okinawa. Decorated Purple Heart. Mem. NSPE, Mo. Soc. Profl. Engrs., Profl. Engrs. in Pvt. Practice, Am. Soc. Heating, Refrigeration and Air Conditioning Engrs., Illuminating Engrs. Soc., Am. Mgmt. Assn., Nat. Fire Protection Assn. (health care divsn., archtl./engr. divsn.), Masons. Baptist. Home: 1243 Hobson Dr Ferguson MO 63135-1422

BRUNS, DAVID EUGENE, medical educator, researcher; b. St. Louis, Dec. 12, 1941; s. Eugene H. and Ellen E. (Johnson) B.; m. M. Elizabeth Hirst; children: Elizabeth, David. BSChemE, Washington U., 1963, AB, 1965; MD, St. Louis U., 1973. Diplomate Nat. Bd. Med. Examiners. Instr. pathology Sch. Medicine Washington U., St. Louis, 1973-77, vis. prof. pathology, 1985-86; asst. prof. U. Va., Charlottesville, 1977-81, assoc. dir. of clin. chem. and toxicology, 1977—, assoc. prof. dept. pathology, 1981-90, prof. pathology Sch. Medicine, 1990—. Exec. coun. Acad. of Clin. Lab. Physicians and Scientists, Salt Lake City, 1990-93; pres. Assn. Clin. Scientists, 1985-86; Richard Gadsden Meml. lectr. U. SC, 2002. Author, editor (with Bruns, Lo and Wittmer) Molecular Testing in Laboratory Medicine, 2002; editor Clin. Chemistry, Washington, 1990—, Yearbook of Pathology and Laboratory Medicine, Molecular Testing in Laboratory Medicine, 2002; contbr. articles to profl. jours., 1975—; co-editor: Yearbook of Pathology and Laboratory Medicine, 1995-97; inventor Immunochemical Assays for Human Amylase Isoenzymes and Related Monoclonal Antibodies, 1993. Recipient Israel Diamond Lecture award Brown U. Sch. of Med., 1990, Sunderman award Clin. Scientist of the Year, Assn. of Clin. Scientists, 1987, Outstanding Contbns. to Rsch. award Am. Assn. for Clin. Chemistry, 1987, Outstanding Contbns. Clin. Chemistry award, Am. Assn. Clin. Chemistry, 1998, Bernard Gerulat award, 2001, Norman Kubasik award, 2001; Presdl. Citation, Am. Assn. Clin. Chemistry, 2001. Office: U Va Med Sch PO Box 214 Charlottesville VA 22908-0001 E-mail: dbruns@virginia.edu.

BRUNS, NICOLAUS, JR., retired agricultural chemicals company executive, lawyer; b. N.Y.C., Sept. 27, 1926; s. Nicolaus and Emily Marie (Hawkins) B.; m. Joan-Carol Littleton, Aug. 29, 1959; children: Nicolaus III, Gregory. BS, U. Miami, Fla., 1947; JD, Georgetown U., 1949, LL.M., 1952. Bar: D.C. 1950, Ill. 1965, U.S. Supreme Ct. 1965, N.Y. 1980. Spl. asst. U.S. Navy Dept., Washington, 1950-57; sr. trial atty. U.S. Dept. Justice, Washington, 1957-65; sr. atty. Internat. Minerals and Chem. Corp., Skokie, Ill., 1965-70, asst. gen. counsel, 1970-74, gen. counsel ops., 1974-79, v.p., sec., assoc. gen. counsel Northbrook, Ill., 1979-87; sr. v.p., sec., gen. counsel IMC Fertilizer Group Inc., Northbrook, Ill., 1987-90; antitrust policy coun. U.S. C. of C., Washington, 1981-90. Adj. prof. Loyola U., Chgo., 1980-81, Lake Forest Grad. Sch. Mgmt., Ill., 1981—; cert. arbitrator Am. Arbitration Assn., Nat. Assn. Securities Dealers, 1990-2003. Adminstrv. asst. to v.p. Boy Scouts Am., N.E. Ill. area, 1967, 80; pres. Fund for Perceptually Handicapped, Skokie, Ill., 1976, Concerned Help in Learning Devel., Highland Park, Ill., 1974-75. With U.S. Army, 1945-46. Mem. ABA (antitrust and securities com.), Chgo. Bar Assn., Fed. Bar Assn., Am. Soc. Corp. Secs. (bd. dirs. 1985-87, pres. Midwest region 1984), K.C. (past grand knight Washington coun.), Mich. Shore Club (Wilmette, Ill.), Harbour Ridge Club (Stuart, Fla.). Republican. Roman Catholic. Home: 8 Regentwood Rd Northfield IL 60093-2728 also: 2532 NW Seagrass Dr Palm City FL 34990-4884

BRUNS, WILLIAM JOHN, JR., business administration educator; b. Pasadena, Calif., July 13, 1935; s. William John and Carol Jane (Stalder) B.; m. Barbara Jean Dodge, Apr. 12, 1957 (div. 1980); children: Robert William, John Richard, David James, Michael Alan.; m. Sharon Merle McKinnon, July 16, 1982; 1 child, Anastasia Catherine. BA, U. Redlands, Calif., 1957, D.BA (hon.), 1976; MBA, Harvard U., 1959; PhD, U. Calif. at Berkeley, 1963. Asst. prof. econs., then asst. prof. econs. and indsl. adminstrn. Yale U., 1962-66; asso. prof., then prof. accounting U. Wash., 1966-72; prof. bus. adminstrn. Harvard U., 1972-93, Henry R. Byers prof. bus. adminstrn., 1993—2001, emeritus, 2001—; vis. prof. bus. adminstrn. Northeastern U., 2001—. Cons. to industry. Author: Accounting for Decisions: A Business Game, 1966, Accounting and Its Behavioral Implications, 1969, Introduction to Accounting: Economic Measurement for Decisions, 1971, A Primer on Replacement Cost Accounting, 1976, Cases in Management Accounting, 1981, 85, Accounting and Management: Field Study Perspectives, 1987, Performance Measurement, Evaluation, and Incentives, 1992, The Information Mosaic, 1992, Accounting for Managers: Text and Cases, 1994, 99; book rev. editor: Accounting Rev, 1967-69; mem. editorial bd., 1969-72, 76-78; advisory editor: Addison-Wesley Pub. Co; mem. editorial bd.: Accounting, Orgns., and Soc, 1975-79, Jour. of Managerial Issues, 1993—. Mem. Quinnipiac council Boy Scouts Am., 1964-66; Chief Seattle council, 1966-72, Algonquin council, 1972-81. Danforth grad. fellow, 1957-62; Danforth assoc., 1967-89. Mem. Am. Acctg. Assn., Inst. Mgmt. Accts. Home: 46 Garden Rd Wellesley MA 02481-3015 Office: Harvard Bus Sch Soldiers Fld Boston MA 02163-1317 E-mail: wbruns@hbs.edu.

BRUNSON, BURLIE ALLEN, aerospace transportation executive; b. Bakersfield, Calif., Apr. 28, 1945; s. Burlie B. and Mary Helen (Self) Brunson; m. Lois L. Corbett, Apr. 25, 1968; children: Marci L., Meredith L. BS, U.S. Naval Acad., 1967; MS, Oreg. State U., 1972, PhD, 1983; MBA, George Washington U., 1995. Commd. officer USN, Pensacola, Fla., 1968-70; rsch. asst. Oreg. State U., Corvallis, 1970-72; rsch. oceanographer Naval Ocean Sys. Ctr., San Diego, 1972-78; rsch. physicist Naval Ocean R & D Activity, Bay St. Louis, 1978-81; prin. scientist Planning Sys. Inc., McLean, Va., 1981-86, v.p., 1986-88, sr. v.p., tech. dir., 1988-89, exec. v.p., COO, 1989-91; v.p., ASW Lockheed Sanders Inc., Nashua, NH, 1991-92; dir. Maritime Systems Lockheed Corp., Calabasas, Calif., 1992-94; v.p. Washington ops. Lockheed Martin Corp., Bethesda, Md., 1995-99, v.p. programs, plans and analysis, 1999—. Contbr. articles to profl. jours. Fulbright scholar, Ctrl. U., Quito, Ecuador, 1968. Mem.: Am. Mgmt. Assn., Nat. Def. Indsl. Assn., Am. Geophys. Union, Acoustical Soc. Am. (tech. reviewer 1980—), Sigma Xi, Beta Gamma Sigma, Phi Kappa Phi. Republican. Presbyterian. Achievements include patents in field. E-mail: burlie.a.brunson@lmco.com.

BRUNSON, JOHN SOLES, lawyer, investor; b. Houston, Jan. 8, 1934; s. Nathan Bryant and Jonnie E. (McMillian) B.; m. Joan Erwin, Dec. 26, 1953; children: W. Mark, Dana Ruth. BBA, Baylor U., 1956, LLB, 1958, JD, 1965. Bar: Tex., 1958, U.S. Supreme Ct., 1961. Assoc. Dillingham, Schleider & Lewis, Houston, 1958-64; ptnr. Brunson & Brill, Houston, 1964-70, Baker, Heard & Brunson, Houston, 1970—72, Brunson & Erwin, Houston, 1972-84. Pres. New Asia Products, Inc., 1984-92; chmn. Clavis Investment Co., 1984—; bd. dirs. Ridgewood Devel. Mem. Harris County (Tex.) Dem. Exec. Com., 1959-65, Tex. Dem. Exec. Com., 1963-74; mem. exec. bd. Bapt. Gen. Conv. Tex., 1988-94; trustee First Bapt. Acad., 1996-2002, chmn., 2000-2002; trustee Houston Christian H.S., 1997—, Macedonian Call Found., 1991—. Mem. ABA, State Bar Tex. Office: 7555 Katy Fwy Apt 70 Houston TX 77024-2119 E-mail: onejsb@swbell.net.

BRUNSON, KENNETH WAYNE, cancer biologist; b. Chico, Tex., Sept. 18, 1936; s. George Starr and Gwendolyn Laverne (Mount) B.; m. Myrna Marquerite Lapré, Jan. 26, 1963; children: Gregory Sean, Geoffrey Gordon. BA in Biology, Chemistry, U. N. Tex., 1964, MA in Biology, Chemistry, 1966; PhD in Microbiology, Biochemistry, U. Minn., 1973; postdoctoral Tumor Biology, The Salk Inst., San Diego, Calif., 1974-77. Lectr. U. Calif., Riverside, 1974-75; rsch. assoc. The Salk Inst., La Jolla, Calif., 1974-77; asst. specialist U. Calif., Irvine, 1977-79; asst. prof. Sch. Medicine Ind. U., Indpls., Gary, 1979-84, assoc. mem. grad. sch. Bloomington, 1979-84; sr. rsch scientist Pfizer Inc, Groton, Conn., 1984-91; assoc. prof. Sch. Medicine U. Pitts., 1991-99; affiliate mem. U. Pitts. Cancer Inst., 1991-94, mem., 1994-99, dir. Tumor Model Lab., 1995-99, dir. in vivo preclin. rsch. for health scis., 1996-99, sect. head cancer metastasis biology program, 1991—95; dep. dir. Inst. for Cancer Rsch. U. North Tex. Health Sci. Ctr., Ft. Worth, 1999—2002, dir., 2002—03, adj. prof. dept. molecular biology and immunology, 2000—01, mem. grad. faculty microbiology and immunology program, 2001, rsch. prof. dept. molecular biology and immunology, 2001—03; sr. dir. Sopherion Therapeutics, Inc., New Haven, 2003—. Mem. expert panel workshop Exptl. Metastasis: Designing New Strategies, 1988; founding mem. sci. edn. com. Pfizer, Inc., Groton, Conn., 1987—91. Mem. editl. bd.: In Vivo, 2002—, sci. advisor: 10-vol. treatise Cancer Growth and Progression, 1986—89; contbr. Mem. planning com. Regional Health Adminstrn. Conf., Ind., 1984; mem. exec. bd. Shadyside Action Coalition, Pitts., 1993—96, chmn. parking and transp. com., 1993—95; mem. Lake Country Place Assn., 2001—; bd. dirs. Tarrant County unit Am. Cancer Soc., 2002—03, bd. dirs.Lake County unit, 1981—84; bd. dirs. Pa. Soc. Biomed. Rsch., 1997—99. With U.S. Army, 1958—61. Recipient XVI Internat. Cancer Congress award Internat. Union Against Cancer, New Delhi, India, 1994. Mem. Am. Assn. for Cancer Rsch., Am. Assn. Immunologists, Am. Soc. Cell Biology, Metastasis Rsch. Soc., Am. Soc. for Microbiology, (chmn. edn. com., Ind. br.), Am. Inst. Biol. Scis., Pa. Soc. Biomed. Rsch. (bd. dirs. 1997-99). Achievements include pioneering research in cancer metastasis models, some of which has been described in Sci. Am., Mar., 1979, Proceedings of Nat. Acad. of Sci., 1980, Cancer Growth and Progression, 1989, and Biologic Therapy of Cancer, 1995. Home: 49 Hampton Rd Hamden CT 06518 Office: Sopherion Therapeutics Inc 300 George St New Haven CT 06511

BRUNSON, MABEL (MABEL DIPPER), researcher; b. Oshoto, Wyo., Mar. 24, 1934; d. Robert Emmett and Gennevieve Mae (Irwin) Brislawn; m. Donald George Brunson, Jan. 1, 1959; children: Daniel F., David G. Student, Nieman's Bus. Coll., 1956. Rschr., sec. Bob Brislawn, Spanish Mustang Registry Inc., Oshoto, 1943-79; legal sec. Scotty Gladstone/Richard Macy law offices, Sundance, Wyo., 1957-58; cons. Bob Brislawn, Spanish Mustang Registry Inc., 1957-79; sec., clk. Farmers Home Adminstrn., Sundance, 1958-59, Soil Conservation Svc., Sundance, 1975-82. Co-author: Spanish Mustang Registry, Inc., 1996; author: Mr. Mustang and the Spanish Horses, Life of Bob Brislawn, 2002; also author brochures. Sec., treas. Homemaker's Clubs, Wyo., 1959-76; religious tchr. Cath. Chs., Upton and Sundance, Wyo., 1965-80, eucharistic min., Sundance, 1984-2002; cub scout leader Boy Scouts Am., Sundance, 1972-79. Recipient Svc. award Boy Scouts Am., 1979; named Centennial Woman of Yr. St. Paul's Cath. Ch., 1990. Avocations: history, genealogy, western art, writing. Office: Brunson Enterprises 1310 Oak Creek Rd Aladdin WY 82710-9729

BRUNSTEIN, JOHN DAVID, biochemist, researcher; b. Denver, Jan. 2, 1970; s. Karl Avrum and Marion O'Meara Brunstein. BSc with honors, Simon Fraser U., Vancouver, Can., 1992; PhD, U. B.C., Vancouver, Can., 1997. Lab. technician dept. chemistry Simon Fraser U., Burnaby, B.C., 1992; postdoctoral fellow Haartman Inst., U. Helsinki, Helsinki, Finland, 1998—2000; instr., rsch. assoc. U. B.C., Vancouver, 2000—. Contbr. articles to profl. jours. Recipient Gov. Gen.'s Bronze medal Gov.-Gen. of Can., 1988; Postgrad. fellow PGS-A and PGS-B, Nat. Scis. and Engring. Rsch. Coun. Can., 1993-96, Postdoctoral fellow Ctr. Internat. Mobility Finland, 1998, 99. Mem. Am. Soc. for Virology (assoc.). Avocations: backpacking, fishing, photography, sailing. Home: 2168 W 2d Ave #303 Vancouver BC Canada V6K 1H6 Office: UBC Dept Biochemistry 2146 Health Sci Mall Vancouver BC Canada V6T 1Z3 Office Fax: 604-822-5227. E-mail: brunstei@interchange.ubc.ca.

BRUNSVOLD, BRIAN GARRETT, lawyer, educator; b. Mason City, Iowa, Apr. 10, 1938; s. P.O. and Arlene J. (Garrett) B.; m. Mary Sue Willey, Nov. 28, 1963; 1 child, Laura Ann. BS in Chem.Engring., Iowa State U., 1960; JD, George Washington U., 1967. Bar: Va. 1967, D.C. 1967. Law clk. U.S. Ct. Claims, Washington, 1966-67; atty. firm Finnegan, Henderson, Farabow, Garrett & Dunner, Washington, 1967—. Professorial lectr. in law George Washington U., Washington, 1975-96. Co-author: Drafting Patent License Agreements, 1984, 91, 98. 1st lt. C.E., U.S. Army, 1961-63, Korea. Mem. Licensing Execs. Soc. (trustee 1987-89, counsel 2000—, Cert. of Merit 1988). Avocations: tennis, hunting, fishing. Office: Finnegan Henderson Farabow Garrett & Dunner 1300 I St NW Fl 6-8 Washington DC 20005-3315 E-mail: brunsvob@finnegan.com.

BRUNT, HARRY HERMAN, JR., psychiatrist; b. Phila., Jan. 22, 1921; s. Harry Herman and Ann (Zurbrugg) B.; m. Zoe M. Bower, July 2, 1944; children: Marianne Brunt Tallman, Margaret B. Griffin, Jane, Mary Lazar. BS with honors, Va. Poly. Inst., 1942; MD, U. Pa., 1945. Diplomate: Am. Bd. Psychiatry and Neurology. Intern, Lankenau Hosp., 1946; resident psychiatry Trenton (N.J.) State Hosp., VA Hosp., Coatesville, 1948-52; practice medicine specializing in psychiatry Trenton, 1952, Princeton, N.J., 1952-54, Hammonton, N.J., 1954-69, Long Branch, N.J., 1969-74; acting asst. clin. dir. Trenton State Hosp., 1952; asst. supt. N.J. Neuropsychiat. Inst. Princeton, 1952-54; med. dir. Ancora State Hosp., 1954-69; dir. dept. psychiatry Monmouth Med. Center and Pollak Clinic, Long Branch, 1969-74, Jersey Shore Med. Ctr., 1980; pvt. practice, 1974—. Assoc. prof. psychiatry Jefferson Med. Coll., 1952-66; instr. psychiatry U. Pa., 1953-65; adj. asso. prof. psychiatry Temple Med. Sch., 1968-70; prof. psychiatry Hahneman Med. Coll., 1970-74; clin. prof. psychiatry Robert Wood Johnson Med. Sch., New Brunswick, N.J., 1971-96. Cons. bur. family services Dept. Health, Edn. and Welfare Dept., 1960-68. Served to capt. M.C. AUS, 1946-48. Fellow ACP, AAAS, Am. Psychiat. Assn. (dist. life, chmn. future planning com. assembly dist. brs., mem. policy com. area III 1968,

recorder 1969, speaker 1971-72, trustee 1972-73, 74-75), Am. Geriatric Soc., Am. Coll. Psychiatrists (founding); mem. AMA, Monmouth County Med. Soc. (exec. com.), N.J. Neuropsychiat. Assn. (past pres.), Med. Soc. N.J. (chmn. coun. mental health), Beach Haven Yacht Club (commodore 1992-93), Alpha Kappa Kappa, Phi Kappa Phi. E-mail: hhbmd@webtv.net. *I have obtained a great deal of satisfaction from helping others throughout my life but little of this would have been possible without my family's backing and sacrifice. The family is still what makes life worth living.*

BRUNT, MANLY YATES, JR., psychiatrist; b. Winston-Salem, N.C., Nov. 7, 1926; s. Manly Yates and Jessie Corina (Evans) B.; M.D., Wake Forest U., 1948; m. Jacklyn Beatrice Bray, Dec. 2, 1961; children— Diane Strachan, William Bray, Douglas Evans, Kenneth Sherman. Intern, Grad. Hosp. U. Pa., 1949-50; exec. med. officer Inst. of Pa. Hosp., Phila., 1952-62, mem. sr. attending staff, 1968—, prin. investigator Behavior Research Lab., 1957-61; mem. faculty U. Pa., 1953-68; dir. emeritus dept. psychiatry Bryn Mawr (Pa.) Hosp., past pres. staff and chmn. exec. com. Pres. Community Nursing Bur. Met. Phila., 1961-64; bd. dirs. Main Line Health Care Group, Inc. Served with M.C., AUS, 1950-52. Diplomate Am. Bd. Psychiatry and Neurology. Mem. AMA, Am. Psychiat. Assn., Am. Psychoanalytic Assn., Phila. Coll. Physicians and Surgeons, Wake Forest U. Med. Alumni Assn. (pres. 1985), Alpha Omega Alpha. Republican. Presbyterian. Clubs: Merion Cricket, Phila. Skating and Humane Soc., Little Egg Harbor Yacht. Mailing: 1084 E Lancaster Ave Rosemont PA 19010

BRUNTON, DANIEL WILLIAM, mechanical engineer; b. Ft. Wayne, Ind., Sept. 25, 1956; s. Paul Edward and Margaret Alice (Rice) B.; m. Carol Marie Pryor, Feb. 19, 1994; children: Edward Daniel, Ann Marie. BS, UCLA, 1978, MS in Engring., 1980, M of Engring., 1986. Mem. tech. staff Hughes Missiles Group, Canoga Park, Calif., 1978-89, dept. mgr., 1989-93; mech. engr. dept. mgr. Litton Itek, Lexington, Mass., 1993-94; sr. engr. Raytheon Missile Sys., Tucson, 1994-97, engring. fellow, 1997—. Mem. Soc. Photonic Instrumentation Engrs., Tau Beta Pi. Achievements include 3 patents on optical design, optical material testing, and mechanisms. Office: Raytheon Missile Sys PO Box 11337 Tucson AZ 85734-1337

BRUSCA, RICHARD CHARLES, biologist, researcher, educator; b. L.A., Jan. 25, 1945; s. Finny John and Ellenora C. (McDonald) B.; m. Caren Irene Spencer, 1964 (div. 1971); children: Alec Matthew, Carlene Anne; m. Anna Mary Mackey, 1980 (div. 1987); m. Wendy Moore, 1998. BS, Calif. Poly. State U., 1967; MS, Calif. State U., L.A., 1969; PhD, U. Ariz., 1975. Curator, rschr. Aquatic Insects Lab., Calif. State U., L.A., 1969—70; resident dir. U. Ariz. and U. Sonora (Mex.) Coop. Marine Lab., 1970—71; prof. biology U. So. Calif., L.A., 1975—86; head Invertebrate Zoology sect. Los Angeles County Mus. Natural Hist., 1984—87; Joshua L. Baily curator, chmn. dept. invertebrate zoology San Diego Natural History Mus., 1987—93; prof., dir. grad. program in marine biology U. Charleston, SC, 1993—98, assoc. dir. Grice Marine Lab., 1993—98; rsch. prof. dept. ecology and evolutionary biology U. Ariz., 1998—; exec. dir. Ariz.-Sonora Desert Mus., Tucson, 2001—. Dir. acad. program Catalina Marine Sci. Ctr., U. So. Calif., 1978—82; field rschr. No., Ctrl. and So. Ams., Polynesia, Australia, New Zealand, Antarctica, Saharan and Sub-Saharan Africa, Europe; bd. dirs. Orgn. for Tropical Studies, Slocum-Lunz Found., Intercultural Ctr. for the Study of Deserts and Oceans, Sonoran Sea Aquarium, Tucson; mem. panels NAS/NSF; chairperson adv. com. Smithsonian Instn., Systematics Agenda 2000; chairperson adv. com., inland waters crustacea specialist Internat. Union for Conservation of Nature Species Survival Commn.; mem. adv. bd. All Species Found., 2001; mem. adv. bd. Sch. Renewable Natural Resources U. Ariz., 2003—. Author: Common Intertidal Invertebrates of the Gulf of California, 1980; co-author: A Naturalist's Seashore Guide, 1978, Invertebrates, 1990, 2d edit., 2003, Isopod Systematics and Evolution, 2001; contbr. over 100 articles to sci. jours. Recipient U.S. Antarctic Svc. medal, 1965, numerous rsch. awards; grantee NSF, Nat. Geog. Soc., Charles Lindberg Found, NOAA, Nat. Park Svc., Dept. Def., Am. Philos. Assn., others. Fellow: AAAS, Linnean Soc. London; mem.: Wallace Rsch. Fedn., Assn. Sea of Cortez Rschrs. (hon.; life), Soc. for Systematic Biology, Crustacean Soc. (pres.), U. Edinburgh Biogeography Study Group, Willi Hennig Soc., S.Am. Explorers Club, Sigma Xi. Avocations: photography, mexican and mesoamerican indigenous art and culture, latin american politics. Office: Ariz-Sonora Desert Mus 2021 N Kinney Rd Tucson AZ 85743 E-mail: rbrusca@desertmuseum.org.

BRUSCH, JOHN LYNCH, physician, educator, hospital administrator; b. Boston, Nov. 3, 1943; s. Charles and Margaret Agnes (Lynch) Brusch; m. Patricia Gahan, May 12, 1973; children: Amy Claire, Meaghan, Patrick. BS, Tufts U., 1965, MD, 1969. Diplomate Am. Bd. Internal Medicine, Am. Bd. Infectious Disease, Am. Bd. Geriatrics. Intern New Eng. Med. Ctr., Boston, 1969-70, resident in medicine, 1970-71; resident in infectious disease, 1971-74; asst. chief medicine Brighton Pub. Health Svc. Hosp., Boston, 1974-76; pvt. practice physician Cambridge, Mass., 1976—; chief medicine Youville Hosp., Cambridge, 1991—, dir. cmty. medicine, 1995—; clin. assoc. medicine Mass. Gen. Hosp., Boston, 1996—; med. dir. transitional care unit, chief medicine Somerville Hosp., 1999—. Assoc. chief medicine Cambridge Health Alliance, 1999—, dir. hosp. bd., 2003—; asst. prof. medicine Harvard Med. Sch., 2001—; bd. dirs. North Cambridge Coop Bank. Co-author: (book) Infective Endocarditis; assoc. editor: Infectious Disease Practice, 1984—, mng. editor: Emedicine, 2001—; contbr. articles to profl. jours. With USPHS, 1974—76. Decorated knight of the Holy Sepulchre. Fellow: ACP; mem.: Am. Soc. Microbiology, Longwood Cricket Club. Home: 52 Radcliffe Rd Belmont MA 02478-3340 Office: Cambridge Hosp 1493 Cambridge St Cambridge MA 02139-1099 E-mail: jbruschmd@aol.com.

BRUSEWITZ, GERALD HENRY, agricultural engineering educator, researcher; b. Green Bay, Wis., June 1, 1942; s. Henry Jackson and Wardeen Mae (Thiel) B.; m. Glenna Sue Williams, May 12, 1990; children: Kelly K., Nicole J. BS in Agr., U. Wis., 1964, BSME, 1965, MSAE, 1966; PhDAE, Mich. State U., 1969. Registered profl. engr., Okla. Rsch. asst. U. Wis., Madison, 1965-66; asst. prof. Okla. State U., Stillwater, 1969-75, assoc. prof., 1975-80, prof., 1980-92, interim dept. head, 1985, regents prof., 1992—2002, emeritus regents prof., 2002—. Sabbatical leave U. Calif., Davis, 1979, Cornell U., 1988; vis. engr. solar energy dept. Kuwait Inst. for Sci. Rsch., 1980; cons. Cen. Machine & Tool Co., Enid, Okla., 1986, Clements Food Co., Oklahoma City, 1986-87, Omnidata Internat. of Logan, 1990. Recipient Dist. Svc. to Students award Alpha Epsilon, Outstanding Engring. Faculty award Halliburton, 1991, Outstanding Agriculture Faculty award, 1994. Fellow Am. Soc. Agrl. Engrs. (Paper awards 1990, 97, 2000); mem. Inst. Food Technologists, Alpha Zeta. Methodist. Avocations: racquetball, cycling, hiking. Office: Okla State U Biosystems and Agrl Engring 216 Ag Hl Stillwater OK 74078-0001 E-mail: jbrusew@okstate.edu.

BRUSH, CRAIG BALCOMBE, retired French language and computer educator; b. N.Y.C., May 28, 1930; s. John Mitchell and Josephine (Marple) B. BA, Princeton U., 1951; MA, Columbia U., 1955, PhD, 1966. Tchr. English, French Choate Sch., Wallingford, Conn., 1951-54; instr. French Columbia Coll., N.Y.C., 1955-63, asst. prof., 1963-67, City Coll., CUNY, 1967-70; assoc. prof. Fordham U., N.Y.C., 1970-73, prof. French, computers, 1973-95, ret., 1995. Author: Montaigne and Bayle, 1966, Selected Writings of Pierre Gassendi, 1972, From the Perspective of the Self, 1994. With NYNG, 1948-56. Fulbright fellowship, Paris, 1957-59. Mem. MLA, Société des Amis de Montaigne, Assn. for Computers and the Humanities, N.E. for Computers and the Humanities, Soc. Sr. Scholars (Columbia U.). Democrat. Avocations: music, theater, scuba diving. Home: 411 W 115th St New York NY 10025-1741

BRUSH, GEORGE W. college president; b. Boonton, N.J., Sept. 4, 1921; s. George W. and Adele (Tillotson) B.; m. Dorothy E. Mackallor, Sept. 24, 1942; children: Elithe, Lawrence, Kathleen, Sharon, George III, Charles, Nancy, Elizabeth. BS, Fairleigh-Dickinson U., 1960; MA, NYU, 1964, EdD, 1969. Cert. airframe and powerplant tech. FAA. Dir. tng. Teterboro (N.J.) Sch., 1947-50; dir. admissions Coll. Aeros. (formerly Acad. Aero.), Flushing, N.Y., 1950-66, exec. dean, 1966-80, v.p., 1980-83, pres., 1984-90, pres. emeritus, 1990, trustee, 1990-94. Cons. cmty. colls., N.Y. and N.J., 1965—, N.Y. State Bd. Regents, 1971-85; visitor Middle States Assn. Colls. and Schs., 1975—; faculty cons. Excelsior Coll., Albany, N.Y.; chair bd. trustees Plaza Coll., N.Y.C. Chmn. Maywood Planning Bd., N.J.; arbitrator Better Bus. Bur., Bergen County, N.J., 1976—; trustee, edn. chair N.J. Aviation Hall of Fame and Mus. Staff sgt. U.S. Army, 1944-46. Recipient disting. alumni award Coll. Aeros., adminstrs. award FAA, 1990, Disting. Svcs. award U. of State of N.Y.; named vol. of yr. Bergen County, 1992; elected to N.J. Aviation Hall of Fame, 2002. Mem. AIAA, FAA (Frank Taylor award 1995), Aviation Writers Assn., Am. Legion, Wings (bd. govs. 1986-89, chmn. edn. com.), K of C, HOAI (pres. Estero chpt.). Home and Office: 21030 Butchers Holler Estero FL 33928-2201

BRUSH, STEPHEN GEORGE, history of science educator; b. Bangor, Maine; s. Edward Newcomb and Lillian Maynard (Hatfield) B.; m. Phyllis Egbert; children: Denise, Nicholas. AB in Physics, Harvard U., 1955; DPhil in Physics, Oxford (Eng.) U., 1958. Postdoctoral fellow Imperial Coll., London, 1958-59; physicist Lawrence Radiation Lab., Livermore, Calif., 1959-65; rsch. assoc. Harvard Project Physics, Cambridge, Mass., 1965-68; lectr. Harvard U., Cambridge, Mass., 1966-68; assoc. prof. U. Md., College Park, 1968-71, prof., 1971—, Disting. univ. prof. History of Sci., 1995—. Author: The Kind of Motion We Call Heat, 1976, Statistical Physics and the Atomic Theory of Matter, 1983, History of Modern Science, 1988, History of Modern Planetary Physics, 1996; co-author: Physics, The Human Adventure: From Copernicus to Einstein and Beyond, 2001; co-author: Introduction to Concepts and Theories in Physical Science, 1973, 2d rev. edit.; author, editor: Kinetic Theory, 1965, vol. II, 1966, Vol. III, 1972. Rhodes scholar, Oxford U., 1955-58; NSF grantee, 1965—; Guggenheim fellow, 1999-2000. Fellow AAAS, Am. Phys. Soc. (councillor 1987-90); mem. History of Sci. Soc. (pres. 1990-91, Pfizer award 1977, Hazen Edn. prize 2001). Achievements include theoretical research calculation showing that a system of charged particles (plasma) will condense from gas to solid under conditions of high pressure and low temperature. Office: U Md Dept History Inst Phys Sci and Tech College Park MD 20742-0001

BRUSHABER, GEORGE KARL, college-theological seminary president, minister; b. Milw., Dec. 15, 1938; s. Ralph E. and Marie C. (Meister) B.; m. N. Darleen Dugar, Jan. 27, 1962; children: Deanna Lyn Dalberg, Donald Paul. BA, Wheaton Coll., 1959, MA, 1962; MDiv, Gordon-Conwell Theol. Sem., 1963; PhD, Boston U., 1967. Ordained to ministry Bapt. Gen. Conf., 1966. Prof. philosophy, chair dept. Gordon Coll., Wenham, Mass., 1963-72; dir. admissions and registration Gordon-Conwell Theol. Sem., 1970-72; v.p., acad. dean Westmont Coll., Santa Barbara, Calif., 1972-75; v.p., dean of coll. Bethel. Coll., St. Paul, 1975-82; pres. Bethel Coll. & Theol. Sem., St. Paul and San Diego, 1982—. Staley Found. lectr. Anderson U., Sioux Falls Coll., sec. for higher edn. Bapt. Gen. Conf., Arlington Heights, Ill., 1982—; cons., evaluator Minn. Humanities Commn., St. Paul. Editor Gordon Rev., 1965-70; pub., founding editor Christian Scholar's Rev., 1970-79; exec. editor Christianity Today, 1985-90, chmn. sr. editors, 1990-2000; contbr. articles to religious jours. Bd. dirs. Youth Leadership, Mpls., 1982—, Fairview Elders' Enterprises Found., 1989—, Scripture Press Ministries Found., 1994—; adv. bd. Mpls./St. Paul Salvation Army, 1992--; chair bd. Scripture Press Ministries, 1994—; adv. coun. Evang. Environ. Network, 1994—; mem. Commn. on Minorities in Higher Edn. Am. Coun. Edn., 1995-99. Mem. Christian Environ. Assn., Christian Coll. Consortium (bd. dirs.), Nat. Assn. Evangs. (trustee 1982—), Minn. Pvt. Coll. Coun. (bd. dirs. 1982—), Minn. Consortium Theol. Sems. (bd. dirs. 1982—), Cook Comm. Internat. (bd. dirs. 1998—), Coun. Ind. Colls. (bd. dirs. 1984-89), Am. Philos. Assn., Evang. Theol. Soc., Am. Assn. Higher Edn., Swedish Coun. Am. (bd. dirs. 2000—), Soc. Christian Philosophers, Fellowship Evang. Sem. Pres., Minn. Club, North Oaks Country Club. Home and Office: Bethel Coll and Theol Sem 3900 Bethel Dr Saint Paul MN 55112-6902

BRUSHART, THOMAS MARSHALL, hand surgeon, neuroscience researcher; b. Washington, D.C., June 16, 1949; s. Marshall Earl Brushart and Ruthanna Maxwell Weber; m. Sandra Thornhill, June 12, 1971; children: Suzanne Thornhill, Elizabeth Maxwell. BA, Harvard U., 1971, MD, 1976. Diplomate Am. Bd. of Orthopaedic Surgery, cert. added qualifications in hand surgery Am. Bd. of Orthopaedic Surgery. Surg. intern Beth Israel Hosp., Boston, 1976—77; surg. resident Harvard Combined Orthopaedic Surgery Program, Boston, 1977—81; fellow in hand surgery Curtis Hand Ctr., Balt., 1982—83, attending surgeon, head of rsch., 1983—94; assoc. prof. of orthopaedic surgery, plastic surgery, and neurology Johns Hopkins U., Balt., 1994—97, prof. of orthopaedic surgery, plastic surgery, and neurology, 1997—; vice-chairman for rsch. Johns Hopkins Orthopaedics, Balt., 2001—. Pres. Sunderland Peripheral Nerve Soc., Balt., 2001—; sec. treas. The Sunderland Peripheral Nerve Soc., Balt., 1995—2001. Recipient L. W. Freeman award, Nat. Spinal Cord Injury Found., 1979, Emmanuel Kaplan Anatomy prize, N.Y. Hand Soc., 0002, Thomas M. Brushart Professorship in Hand Surgery, Johns Hopkins U., 2000—; grantee, NIH, 1997—. Mem.: Peripheral Nerve Soc., Sunderland Soc., Am. Soc. for Surgery of the Hand (chmn. rsch. com. 1991—97, chmn. residents' and fellows' com. 1995—96, Bunnell Traveling fellow 1990—91, Joseph Boyes award 1994, 1995), Am. Acad. of Orthopaedic Surgeons, Orthopaedic Rsch. Soc., Brit. Soc. for Surgery of the Hand, Cosmos Club. Achievements include research in elucidation of the mechanisms involved in regenerating appropriate connections after nerve injury. Avocations: photography, mountaineering, fly fishing. Office: Johns Hopkins Orthopaedics 601 North Caroline St Baltimore MD 21287

BRUSHWOOD, DAVID BENSON, pharmacy educator, lawyer; b. Columbia, Mo., Sept. 26, 1948; s. John Stubbs and Carolyn (Norton) B.; m. Mary Christine Parks; children: Charles, Paul, John, Julie. BA, U. Kans., 1970, BS in Pharmacy, 1975, JD, 1981. Bar: Kans. 1981, U.S. Dist. Ct. Kans. 1981. Pharmacist Gessler Drug Co., Wichita, Kans., 1975-78; atty. Fisher, Patterson, Sayler & Smith, Topeka, 1981-82; asst. prof. Phila. Coll. Pharmacy, 1982-85; assoc. prof. W.Va. U., Morgantown, 1985-90; prof. U. Fla., Gainesville, 1990—. Named Kanehl scholar, 1979; recipient Nat. Assn. Retail Druggists award, 1975, Outstanding Tchr. award, Sch. of Pharmacy, W. Va. U., 1986, James Hartley Beal award, 1981, 1983, Larry M. Simonsmeier Paper award, 1998, Mayday Scholar award, 1999, 2001. Mem. Am. Soc. for Pharmacy Law (pres. 1986-88, editor Pharmacy Law Ann. 1987-91). Home: 5704 NW 42nd Rd Gainesville FL 32606-4376 Office: U Fla Coll Pharmacy PO Box 100496 Gainesville FL 32610-0496 E-mail: brushwood@cop.ufl.edu.

BRUSILOW, SAUL, pediatrics researcher; b. Bklyn., June 7, 1927; s. Samuel Michael and Marie (Arenson) B.; m. Sallie Evans (dec.); children: William, Susan, Alexander (dec.). AB, Princeton U., 1950; MD, Yale U., 1954. Diplomate: Am. Bd. Pediatrics, Am. Bd. Pediatric Nephrology. Intern, asst. resident Grace-New Haven Hosp., 1954-56; asst. resident Johns Hopkins Hosp., Balt., 1956-57; research fellow Johns Hopkins U., Balt., 1957-59, instr., 1959-60, asst. prof., 1960-64, assoc. prof., 1964-74, prof., 1974-98, prof. emeritus, 1998—. Pres. Nutritional Resources, Balt., 1994—96; dir. med. affairs Ucyclyd Pharma, Glen Burnie, Md., 1996—98. Contbr. articles on pediatrics to profl. jours.; patentee in field; author: Inborn Errors of Metabolism. Served with USNR, 1945-46. Recipient Sci. Rsch. award Joseph P. Kennedy Jr. Found., 1995, Achievement award Nat. Urea Cycle Disorders Found., 1995; grantee NIH, 1959-97. Mem. Soc. Pediatric Research, Am. Fedn. Clin. Research, Am. Physiol. Soc., Am. Pediatric Soc. Democrat. Jewish. Home: 4804 Keswick Rd Baltimore MD 21210-2325 Office: Johns Hopkins U Sch Medicine Park 334 600 N Wolfe St Baltimore MD 21287-0005 E-mail: sbrusilo@jhmi.edu.

BRUSKEWITZ, FABIAN W. bishop; b. Milw., Sept. 6, 1935; Ordained priest Roman Catholic Ch. 1960. Bishop Diocese of Lincoln, Nebr., 1992—. Office: Chancery Office PO Box 80328 Lincoln NE 68501-0328*

BRUSO, ARTHUR, artist; b. Albany, N.Y. s. George Kenneth and Thomasine Marie (Calvanese) Bruso; life ptnr. Raymond Mingst. BS, SUNY, New Paltz, 1978; MFA, U. Pa., 1988. Cert. tchg. N.Y. Artist in residence Dorland Mountain Arts Gallery, Dorland, Calif., 2002; co-founder Gallery Studios, Curious Matter. Exhibitions include Alchemist Garden, 2000—, Assn. Sublimation, 1993—, Different Kinds of Project Stares, 1988—95. Roman Catholic. Home: Lachesis 272 Fifth St Jersey City NJ 07302

BRUST, DAVID, physicist; b. Chgo., Aug. 24, 1935; s. Clifford and Ruth (Klapman) B. BS, Calif. Inst. Tech., 1957; MS, U. Chgo., 1958, PhD, 1964. Rsch. assoc. Purdue U., Lafayette, Ind., 1963-64, Northwestern U., Evanston, Ill., 1964-65, asst. prof. physics, 1965-68; theoretical rsch. physicist U. Calif. Lawrence Radiation Lab., Livermore, 1968-73. Cons. Bell Telephone Lab., Murray Hill, N.J., 1966. Campaign coord. No. Calif. Scientists and Engrs. for McGovern, 1972. NSF travel grantee, 1964; NSF rsch. grantee, 1966-68. Mem. Am. Phys. Soc., Am. Assn. Coll. Profs., Internat. Solar Energy Soc., Astron. Soc. of Pacific, Nature Conservancy, Calif. Acad. Sci., Commonwealth Club. of Calif., World Affairs Coun. No. Calif., Commonwealth Club Anza Borrego Desert, Natural History Assn., Planetary Soc., Sierra Club, Sigma Xi. Office: PO Box 13130 Oakland CA 94661-0130

BRUST, JOHN CALVIN MORRISON, neurology educator; b. Syracuse, N.Y., Aug. 20, 1936; s. John C.M. and Constance (Cook) B.; m. Mary Duncan, Oct. 23, 1965; chldren: Mary Duncan, Frederick Eliot Noyes, James Charles Morrison. AB, Harvard U., 1958; MD, Columbia U., 1962. Diplomate Am. Bd. Psychiatry and Neurology. Intern Presbytn. Hosp., N.Y.C., 1962-63, resident in neurology, 1966-69, attending in neurology, 1969—, Harlem Hosp. Ctr., N.Y.C., 1969-75, dir. dept. neurology, 1975—; prof. clin. neurology Columbia U., N.Y.C., 1975—. Author: Neurological Aspects of Substance Abuse, 1993, The Practice of Neural Science, 1999; contbr. over 200 articles to profl. jours. and textbooks. Lt. USNR, 1962-65. Fellow Am. Acad. Neurology; mem. Am. Neurol. Assn., Am. Clin. and Climatological Assn., Century Assn., N.Y. Practitioners Soc., Alpha Omega Alpha. Office: Harlem Hosp Ctr Dept Neurology 506 Lenox Ave Dept New York NY 10037-1802

BRUSTAD, ORIN DANIEL, lawyer; b. Chgo., Nov. 11, 1941; s. Marvin D. and Sylvia Evelyn (Peterson) B.; m. Ilona M. Fox, July 16, 1966; children: Caroline E., Katherine L., Mark D. BA in History, Yale U., 1963, MA, 1964; JD, Harvard U., 1968. Bar: Mich. 1968, U.S. Dist. Ct. (so. dist.) Mich. 1968. Assoc. Miller, Canfield, Paddock and Stone, Detroit, 1968-74, sr. ptnr., 1975—, chmn. employee benefits practice group, 1989-96, dep. chmn. tax dept., 1989-93. Bd. dirs. Electrocon Internat., Inc., Ann Arbor, Mich. Mem. editl. adv. bd. Benefits Law Jour.; contbr. articles to profl. jours. Fellow Am. Coun. Employee Benefits Counsel (charter); mem. ABA, Mich. Bar Assn., Detroit Bar Assn., Mich. Employee Benefits Conf. Avocations: sailing, skiing, reading, piano. Home: 1422 Macgregor Ln Ann Arbor MI 48105-2836 Office: Miller Canfield Paddock & Stone 150 W Jefferson Ave Fl 25th Detroit MI 48226-4432 E-mail: odbrusta@aol.com., brustad@millercanfield.com.

BRUSTEIN, ABRAM ISAAC, insurance company executive; b. Bridgeport, Conn., Jan. 14, 1946; s. Louis and Flora (Forman) B.; m. Barbara Bederick Rudman, July 3, 1969; children: Asher Jeremey, Darrah Bethany, Garrett Michael. BA, U. Conn., 1968; MS in Mgmt., Am. Coll., 1985. CLU, CLF, chartered fin. cons. Agt. N.Y. Life Ins. Co., Stamford, Conn., 1968-70, sales mgr., 1970-75, gen. mgr. Amherst, N.Y., 1975-79, Bala Cynwyd, Pa., 1979-87; gen. agt. Penn Mut. Life Ins. Co., Phila., 1987-94; exec. dir. Prudential Ins. Co. Am., Lutherville, Md., 1994-95; v.p. Phoenix Home Life Ins. Co., Hartford, Conn., 1995-98; mng. dir. Mut. N.Y., Towson, Md., 1998—; mng. dir. nat. recruiting MONY Group, N.Y.C., 1999—. Mem. rev. panel Am. Coll., Bryn Mawr, Pa., 1984—, focus group mem. Masters Degree com., 1986; lectr. local univs., 1985—. Served with USAR, 1969-75. Named to, NAIFA-G.P. Hall of Fame, 2002. Mem. Gen. Agts. and Mgrs. Assn. (pres. 1986-87, Nat. Mgmt. award 1978-91), Am. Soc. CLUs and Chartered Fin. Cons., Phila. Assn. Life Underwriters (pres. 1988-89), Penn Mut. Agy. Assn. (pres. 1990-91), Germantown Cricket Club (Phila.), Chestnut Ridge Country Club (Lutherville, Md.). Jewish. Avocations: tennis, golf, aerobics, skiing, bicycling. Home: 313 W Timonium Rd Lutherville Timonium MD 21093-2930 E-mail: abrustein@mony.com.

BRUSTEIN, LAWRENCE, financial executive; b. Liberty, N.Y., Oct. 11, 1936; s. Leo and Rae (Smoller) B.; m. Ellen Gloria Sheppard, June 20, 1965; children: Jacqueline, Michael. BS, U. Buffalo, 1958. CPA, N.Y. With Irving Handel & Co., CPAs, N.Y.C., 1959-62, Robert Simons & Co., CPAs, N.Y.C., 1962-64, E&L Distbrs., Inc., 1964-66, Barney's, N.Y.C., 1966-68; controller Holly Stores div. K-Mart, North Bergen, N.J., 1968-70; v.p., treas. Marcade, Jersey City, 1970-86; exec. v.p. Modells, N.Y.C., 1987—. Editl. adv. bd. Retail Tech mag. Exec. v.p. Reform Temple of East Brunswick, 1977— . Mem. AICPA, N.Y. State Soc. CPAs, Internat. Mass Retail Assn. (chmn. fin.). Home: 15 Rolling Meadows Blvd S Ocean NJ 07712 Office: Modells 498 7th Ave Fl 20 New York NY 10018-6704 E-mail: brustein@aol.com.

BRUSTEIN, MARTIN, financial adviser; b. N.Y.C., Feb. 4, 1924; s. Max and Blanche (Haft) B.; m. Guenne Rabin (div. 1975); children: Jamie Abrams, Richard; m. Millicent Stein Cooper, June 29, 1976. Student, Swarthmore Coll., 1942-43; BS in Bus., Lehigh U., 1947. Lic. life ins., N.Y.; registered rep. N.Y. Stock Exchange. Sales mgr. S. Brustein Inc., N.Y.C., 1947-49; pres. Walter Marshall Spinning Corp., Thornton, R.I., 1949-69, Glenn Brustein Yarn Corp., N.Y.C., 1969-73; sec.-treas. Glenn of Am. Spinning Corp., Thornton, 1969-73, Jaymee Industries Inc., N.Y.C., 1971-74; pres. M. Brustein Textile Corp., N.Y.C., 1974-81; account exec. Philips Appel & Walden, N.Y.C., 1981-88; sr. investment exec. Raymond James Fin. Corp., N.Y.C., 1988—. Chmn. yarn div. United Jewish Appeal, N.Y.C., 1965. Commdg. officer USN, 1942-46. Mem. Am. Arbitration Assn., Nuveen Adv. Coun. (charter), Century Club Oppenheimer Mgmt. Corp., Fresh Meadow Country Club, Shelter Rock Tennis Club (Manhasset, N.Y.), Westhampton Sport and Tennis Club, Sigma Alpha Mu. Home: 206 Melbourne Rd Great Neck NY 11021-4913 also: Box 978-37 Halsey Rd Remsenburg NY 11960 Office: Raymond James Financial Eab Plz West Tower Uniondale NY 11556-0001 E-mail: mart485@aol.com.

BRUSTEIN, MICHAEL LABE, lawyer; b. May 13, 1949; s. Louis and Flora Eva (Forman) B.; m. Joan Lorraine Goldfrank; 1 child, Tess. BA cum laude, NYU, 1971; MD, U. Conn., 1974. Bar: Conn. 1974. Chief adult and vocat. edn. br. Office Gen. Counsel HEW, Washington, 1974-79; legal cons. Dept. Edn. Transition Team, Washington, 1980; ptnr. Brustein & Manasevit, Washington, 1980—. Legal cons. Nat. Assn. Workforce Bds., Nat. Inst. Edn., State Edn. Agencies of N.Y., Calif., N.Mex., Tenn., Fla., R.I., Wyo., Ga., La., N.C., Mich., W.Va., Ark., P.R.; lawyers com. Civil Rights Under Law; gen. counsel Nat. Assn. Partnerships in Equity. Author: School-to-Work User's Guide: Understanding Federal Cost Principles and Avoiding Audit Liability, 1997, The AVA Guide to the School-to-Work Opportunities Act, 1994, The AVA Guide to Federal Funding for Tech-Prep, 1993, The AVA Audit Handbook: Avoiding Liability Under the 1990 Perkins Act, rev. edit., 1992; contbr. articles to profl. jours. Mem. Nat. Assn. Fed. Fin. Adminstrs. (gen. counsel), Nat. Assn. State Couns. Vocat. Edn. (gen. counsel), Nat. Coordinating Coun. Vocat. Student Orgns. (gen. counsel), D.C. Bar Assn., Conn. Bar Assn., N.Y. Bar Assn., Phi Beta Kappa, Phi Sigma Alpha. Home: 3726 Van Ness St NW Washington DC 20016-2226 Office: 3105 South St NW Washington DC 20007-4419 E-mail: mbrustein@bruman.com.

BRUSTEIN, ROBERT SANFORD, English language educator, theatre director, author; b. N.Y.C., N.Y., Apr. 21, 1927; s. Max and Blanche (Haft) B.; m. Norma Ofstrock, Mar. 25, 1962 (dec.); children: Phillip Cates (stepson), Daniel Anton; m. Doreen Beinart, Dec. 20, 1996; stepchildren: Jean Beinart, Peter Beinart. BA, Amherst Coll., 1948, LittD; postgrad., Yale Drama Sch., 1948-49, U. Nottingham, Eng., 1953-55; MA, Columbia U., 1950, PhD, 1957; LittD, Lawrence U.; LLD, Beloit Coll., 1975; ArtsD, Bard Coll., 1981; LHD, Emory U., 1983; Arts D, Marlboro Coll., 1995, Middlebury Coll., 1996, Hebrew Coll., 1997. Instr. English Cornell U., 1955-56; instr. drama Vassar Coll., 1956-57; faculty Columbia, 1957-66, prof. English and comparative lit., 1965-66; prof. English Yale U., New Haven; dean Yale U. (Sch. Drama); founder, artistic dir. Yale Repertory Theatre, 1966-79; dir. Loeb Drama Centre; also founder, artistic dir. Am. Repertory Theatre Co.; prof. English Harvard U., 1979—. Drama critic New Republic, 1959-67, 78—, contbg. editor, 1959-79; guest theatre critic London Observer, 1972-73; contbr. to N.Y. Times, 1972—; directed and adapted plays including: Ghosts, 1982, Six Characters in Search of an Author, 1984, The Changeling, 1985, Tonight We Improvise, 1986, Right You Are, 1987, The Father, 1990, When We Dead Awaken, 1992, The Seagull, 1994, The Cherry Orchard, 1995, The Wild Duck, 1996, The Master Builder, 1999, Enrico IV, 2001, Lysistrata, 2002; panel mem. Nat. Endowment for Arts, 1969-72, 81-84; created, adapted Shlemiel the First, 1994. Author: The Theatre of Revolt: Studies in the Modern Drama, 1964, Seasons of Discontent: Dramatic Opinions 1959-1965, 1965, The Third Theatre, 1969, Revolution as Theatre: Notes on the New Radical Style, 1971, The Culture Watch, 1975, Critical Moments, 1980, Making Scenes, 1981, Who Needs Theatre, 1987, Reimagining American Theatre, 1991, Dimbocracy in America, 1994, Culturak Calisthenics, 1998, The Siege of the Arts, 2001, (plays) Demons, 1995, Nobody Dies on Friday, 1996, Poker Face, 1999, The Face Lift, 1999, Chekhov on Ice, 2000, Three Farces and A Funeral, 2000, Divestiture, 2001; editor: The Plays and Prose of Strindberg, 1964; contbr. articles to profl. jours. Trustee Sarah Lawrence Coll., 1973-77.

Served with U.S. Mcht. Marine, 1945-47. Recipient George Jean Nathan award dramatic criticism, 1962, 87, George Polk Meml. award outstanding criticism, 1965, Eliot Norton award, 1984, award in criticism Jersey City Jour., 1967, award Outstanding Achievement in Am. Theater, New Eng. Theater Coun., 1985, Tiffany award for excellence in theatre Internat. Soc. Performing Arts Adminstrs., 1987, Thomas De Gaetan award UITT, 1991, Disting. Svc. to Arts award Am. Acad. Arts and Letters, 1995, ATHE award for lifetime achievement in the theatre, 2000, named to Theater Hall of Fame, 2002; Fulbright fellow, 1953-55; Guggenheim fellow, 1961-62; Ford Found. fellow, 1964-65, Nat. Arts Journalism Program sr. fellow Columbia U., 2003. Mem. Am. Acad. Arts and Scis., Am. Acad. Arts and Letters. Office: Harvard U Loeb Drama Center Cambridge MA 02138

BRUSTEIN, WILLIAM IRVING, sociology educator; b. Fairfield, Conn., July 13, 1947; s. Louis I. and Flora Eva Brustein; m. Yvonne Christine Ramey, Feb. 14, 1981; children: Arielle Lauren, Maximilian Samuel. BA, U. Conn., 1969; MA, John Hopkins U., 1971; PhD, U. Wash., 1981. Asst., then assoc. prof. sociology U. Utah, Salt Lake City, 1981-88; assoc. prof. sociology U. Minn., Mpls., 1989-94, prof., Morse alumni disting. tchg. prof. sociology, 1994-2000, adj. prof. polit. sci., 1994-2000, dir. Ctr. for European studies, 1992-95, chair dept. sociology, 1995-98, disting. McKnight univ. prof., 2000—01; prof. sociology, history and polit. sci. U. Pitts., 2001—, UCIS prof. internat. studies, 2001—, dir. Univ. Ctr. Internat. Studies, 2001—. Panelist sociology program NSF, Washington, 1998-2000; vis. scholar London Sch. Econs. and Polit. Sci., 1999. Author: The Social Origins of Political Regionalism: France, 1849 to 1981, 1988, The Logic of Evil: The Social Origins of the Nazi Party, 1925-1933, 1996 (James S. Coleman Disting. Contbn. to Rational-Choice scholarship 1997); editor: Nazism as a Social Phenomenon, 1998; cons. editor Am. Jour. Sociology, 1998-2000. Bd. dirs. Jewish Family Svc., St. Paul, 1991-95, Hillel, Mpls., 1998-2000; exec. bd. Student Project for Amity Among Nations, Mpls., 1998-2000. Grantee NSF, Washington, 1999. Mem. Am. Sociol. Assn. (coun. mem. polit. sociology and comparative hist. sociology 1987-90, 88-91, sec.-treas. rational choice sect. 1995-97, chair PhD granting depts. 1996-98), Am. Polit. Sci. Assn., Assn. Internat. Edn. Adminstrs. (bd. dirs. 2003—), Nat. Assn. State Univs. Land-Grant Colls. (task force internat. edn. 2003—), Phi Beta Kappa. Democrat. Avocations: coaching boys soccer, reading, international travel, skiing. Home: 5 Old Timber Trail Pittsburgh PA 15238 Office: Office of Dir U Pitts Univ Ctr Internat Studies 4G40 Wesley W Posvar Hall Pittsburgh PA 15260 Fax: 412-624-4672. E-mail: brustein@ucis.pitt.edu.

BRUSTMAN, RICHARD D. civil engineer, consultant; b. N.Y.C., Nov. 21, 1942; s. Mark C. Brustman and Martha A. Fower; m. Loretta Louise DeMartini, July 20, 1968; children: Daniel L., Caroline M. BCE, Cornell Univ., Ithaca, N.Y., 1963, MCE, 1966. Surveyor N.Y. Transit Authority, Brooklyn, NY, 1963; engr. N.Y. State Dept of Pub. Works, Albany, NY, 1966—68; highway planner N.Y. State Dept of Transp., Albany, NY, 1968—71, traffic safety analyst, 1971—79, statewide trans. planner, 1979—86, policy and mgmt. advisor, 1986—99; bd. mem. N.Y. Bicycling Coalition, Albany, NY, 2001—. Panels on transp. issues Nat. Acad. Sci., Washington, 1975—92. Contbr. articles to profl. jour. Vol. officer United Way, Boy Scouts, Albany, NY, 1970—. Mem.: State Acad. of Pub. Admintsrn., ASCE.

BRUTON, CAROLE DIANE, music educator; b. Dayton, Ohio, Oct. 17, 1945; d. Walter Andrews and Helen Irene (Brecht) Buchanan; m. David Gray Hoover Jr., Mar. 21, 1970 (dec. Aug. 1986); children: Sarah Elizabeth, David Edward; m. Thomas Davis Bruton, Sept. 12, 1987. MusB, Otterbein Coll., 1967; MusM, S.W. Bapt. Theol. Sem., 1992, D of Musical Arts, 1996. Piano tchr., Dayton, 1966-78, Arlington, Tex., 1978-92. Coord. instrumental music Pantego Christian Acad., Arlington, Tex., 1985-89; tchg. fellow S.W. Bapt. Theol. Sem., Ft. Worth, 1990-96, piano tutor, 1996-98, adj. prof. piano, 1998-2000; adj. prof. piano Grayson County Coll., Denison, Tex., 1995-98, Mountain View Coll., Dallas, 1996—. Mem. Nat. Coll. Musicians, Van Cliburn Found., Music Tchrs. Nat. Assn., Creative Motion Alliance (membership chair 1997-98, sec. 1998-2000), S.W. Music Tchrs. Assn., Ft. Worth Piano Tchrs. Forum, Tex. Music Tchrs. Assn., Ft. Worth Music Tchrs. Assn. (chair original composition contest 1993—, v.p. membership 1999-2001, 1st v.p. 2003—). Republican. Avocations: reading, interior decorating. Home: 6108 Fannin Dr Arlington TX 76001-5692 E-mail: tom-carolebruton@sbcglobal.net.

BRUTON, HENRY JACKSON, educator, economist; b. Dallas, Aug. 30, 1921; s. Guss and Mary (Clark) B.; m. Mary Frances Barnes, Apr. 21, 1959. AB, U. Tex., 1943; PhD, Harvard, 1952. Prof. econs. Yale, 1952-58; prof. econs. Williams Coll., Williamstown, Mass., 1962—; econ. cons. in Iran, 1958-60, 1960-61, 1970-71, 1975-76. Vis. prof. econs. U. Bombay, 1961-62, U. Chile, 1965-66 Author: Inflation in a Growing Economy, 1963, Principles of Development Economics, 1965, Productividad en America Latina, 1968, On the Search for Well-Being, 1997; contbr. articles to profl. jours. Served with AUS, 1943-46, ETO. Home: 300 Syndicate Rd Williamstown MA 01267-2121 Office: Williams Coll Dept Econs Williamstown MA 01267

BRUTON, JOHN MACAULAY, trade association executive, consultant; b. Mexico City, Nov. 13, 1937; s. Edmund Macaulay and Byrd (Grant) B.; m. Frances McMillan Marks, Nov. 25, 1960; children: Alexander, Macaulay, Brinley. BA, Duke U., 1959. Pres., gen. mgr. Grant Advt. de Panama, Panama City, 1970-72, Mexico City, 1972; comm. dir. Am. C. of C. of Mex., Mexico City, 1972-74, gen. mgr., 1974-77, exec. v.p., CEO, 1977—2002, councillor, 2002—; sr. mng. dir. Marratt Jones Global Stratagem, Mexico City, 2003—. V.p. exec. mgmt. Assn. Am. C. of C. in Latin Am., L.A., Washington, 1985-88, v.p. membership svc., 1988—. Bd. dirs. Am. Benevolent Soc., Mex., 1964-68, Am. Soc. Mex., 1975-78, 80-84; adv. bd. Jr. League Mexico City, 1978—; bd. trustees Fomento Educacional A.C., 1988—, treas., 1993—. Mem. Univ. Mex. (bd. dirs. 1979-83, pres. 1981-82). Episcopalian. Home: Ameyalcalli Ocotepec 80 10200 Mexico City Mexico Office: Edificio Omega Campos Eliseo 5 345-5 Mexico City Mexico E-mail: jbruton@manattjones.com.

BRUTON, REBECCA ANN, mayor, commissioner; b. Arkansas City, Kans., Dec. 12, 1949; d. Robert Thomas and Gloria JoAnn (Jackson) Bush; m. Ronald Dean Bruton, Sept. 23, 1973. BS, Southwestern Coll., Winfield, Kans., 1975; grad. Inst. Mcpl. Leadership, Wichita State U., 2001. Elem. tchr. USD #471, Dexter, Kans., 1977—88; owner, sec. Bruton's Towing and Salvage, Arkansas City, 1988—; mayor, city commr. City of Arkansas City, 1999—2003; founder A Piece of the Garden Ministries, 1989—. Bd. trustees S. Ctrl. Kans. Regional Med. Ctr., Arkansas City, 2000—03; bd. dirs. Strother Field Commn., Arkansas City, 2000—03. Preacher Medicalodge East, Arkansas City, 1992—2001. Named Vol. of Yr., Medicalodge East, 1999—2000. Mem.: Kans. Sunshine Coalition Open Govt. (charter mem.), Kans. Taxpayers Assn. Avocations: Bible study, reading. Office: Bruton's Towing and Salvage 1800 South Fourth Arkansas City KS 67005 Fax: 620-442-4798. E-mail: actycomm@ArkCity.org.

BRUUN, PER MOLLER, civil engineer, consultant; b. Skagen, Denmark, Feb. 28, 1917; arrived in U.S., 1952; s. Niels Bruun and Marie Moller; m. Elizabeth Bruun, Sept. 29, 1943; children: Brita, Niels. MSCE, Tech. U. Denmark, 1941, DSc, 1954; D (hon.), U. Santander, 1978, U. Iceland, 1996. Coastal engr. Ministry of Pub. Works, Denmark, 1941—49, Ministry Edn., Denmark, 1949—54; chmn. coastal engrs. U. Fla., Gainesville, 1954—66; chmn. port engrs. Tech. U. Norway, Trondheim, 1966—78; cons. Hilton Head, SC, 1978—. Asst. prof. Tech. U. Denmark, 1954—66. Author: Coast Stability, 1954, Port Engineering, 1973, Port Engineering, 2d edit., 1976, Port Engineering, 3d edit., 1983, Port Engineering, 4th edit., 1990, Design and Construction of Mounds for Breakwaters and Coastal Protection, 1985, Tidal Inlets and Littoral Drift, 1960, Tidal Inlets and Littoral Drift, 2d edit., 1968, Tidal Inlets and Littoral Drift, 3d edit., 1978; contbr. Artilleryman Danish Armed Forces, 1941—42, artilleryman Danish Armed Forces, 1945—46. Named Knight of Icelandic Falcon, 1994; recipient Coastal award, Internat. Orgn. Coastal Dynamics, 2001, Internat. Coastal Conf. award, ASCE, 2002, Medal of Honor, Fla. Shore and Beach Preservation Assn., 1992. Fellow: ASCE (life); mem.: Norwegian Acad. Tech. Scis., Danish Acad. Tech. Scis., Danish Assn. Hydraulic Rsch. (hon.), Fla. Shore Protection Assn. (hon.). Avocation: writing. Home: 34 Baynard Cove Hilton Head Island SC 29928

BRUVOLD, KATHLEEN PARKER, lawyer; BS in Math., U. Denver, 1965; MS in Math., Purdue U., 1967; JD, U. Cin., 1978. Bar: Ohio 1978, U.S. Dist. Ct. (so. dist.) Ohio 1978, U.S. Dist. Ct. (ea. dist.) Ky. 1979. Mathematician bur. rsch. and engring. U.S. Post Office, 1967; instr. math. Purdue U., West Lafayette, Ind., 1967-68, asst. to dir., tng. coord., programmer Administrv. Data Processing Ctr., 1968-71; instr. math. Ind. U., Kokomo, 1969-70; pvt. practice Cin., 1978-80; asst. dir. Legal Adv. Svcs. U. Cin., 1980-89, assoc. gen. counsel, 1989—2002; asst. atty. gen. State of Ohio, 1983—2002. Chair Ohio pub. records com. Inter-univ. Coun. Legal Advisors, 1980-84; presenter various confs. and symposiums. Active com. group svcs. allocation United Way and Community Chest; v.p. Clifton Recreation Ctr. Adv. Coun., 1983-84; vice chair Cin. Bilingual Acad. PTA, 1989-90. U. Denver scholar, Jewel Tea Co. scholar; Nat. Merit finalist. Mem. ABA, Nat. Assn. Coll. and Univ. Attys. (bd. dirs., co-chair taxation sect., com. ann. meeting arrangements, program com., publs. com., bd. ops. com., JCUL editl. bd. nominations com., honors and award com., intellectual property sect., com. continuing legal edn. 1992-2002), Cin. Bar Assn. (com. taxation, program chmn. 1985-86, sec. 1986-87, com. computer law). Home: 536 Evanswood Pl Cincinnati OH 45220-1527

BRUYA, JOHN ROBERT, art educator; b. Oakland, Calif., Aug. 17, 1941; s. William Clement and Margurite Alene (Giesa) B.; m. Marilyn Catherine Rosera; children: Sara Allison, Kirsten Catherine. BA in Edn., Eastern Wash. U., 1963; MFA, U. Wash., 1970. Tchr. art Wendler Jr. High Sch., Anchorage, 1964-67; instr. U. Wash., Seattle, 1970-71; prof. art Slippery Rock (Pa.) U., 1971—. Mem. craft adv. com. Pa. Coun. Arts; sabbatical rschr., France, 1999-2000. Recipient Top Ten Sr. Yr. Eastern Wash. U., Cheney, 1963; named Artist of Yr. Butler County (Pa.)/Music & Arts Festival, 1985. Mem. Am. Craft Coun., Soc. N.Am. Goldsmiths, Pa. Art Edn. Assn. (Outstanding Pa. Higher Edn. Art Educator 1994), Associated Artists Pitts. (bd. dirs. 1972-75), Pitts. Craftsmen's Guild (bd. dirs. 1971-75). Democrat. Roman Catholic. Avocations: gourmet cooking, raising Bonsai. Home: 326 State St Grove City PA 16127-1629 Office: Slippery Rock U Art Dept Slippery Rock PA 16057 E-mail: robert.bruya@sru.edu.

BRUYN, HENRY BICKER, physician; b. Bklyn., Jan. 24, 1918; s. Henry Bicker and Mary Janet (Retter) B.; m. Marion Helen Burkhardt, Sept. 19, 1942; children: Martha Elizabeth, Barbara Jane, Charles DeWitt, Jonathan Henry; m. Harriet Hall Brainerd, Apr. 22, 1973; m. Jennie Low, Jan. 7, 1994. BA, Amherst Coll., 1940; MD, Yale, 1943. Intern pediatrics New Haven Hosp., 1943-44; resident Buffalo Children's Hosp., 1944-45; fellow infectious disease U. Calif. Med. Sch., San Francisco, 1946-47, mem. faculty, 1948-98, clin. prof. medicine and pediatrics, 1969-98, ret., 1998. Chief isolation svc. San Francisco Gen. Hosp., 1950-59, chief pediatrics, 1954-59; lectr. Sch. Pub. Health, U. Calif., Berkeley, 1960-98, dir. student health svc., 1959-72; cons. City of San Francisco, 1974-91, U.S. Naval Hosp., U.S. Army Hosp., Children's Hosp. East Bay, Calif. Viral and Rickettsial Disease Lab.; mem. med. svc. com. Alameda County Coun. Social Planning, 1962-64; med. cons. Morrisonnn Ctr. Rehab., 1954-58, Medic-Alert Found., Elizabeth Kenney Found., San Francisco, 1950-52; med. dir. Drug Abuse Rehab. New Bridge Inc.; pres. Berkeley Med. Instrument Co., 1960-68. Co-author: Handbook of Pediatrics, 1st-15th edit, 1979-86, Handbook of Medical Treatment, 1972, Current Diagnosis and Therapy, 1972, Practice of Pediatrics, 1963, Drinking Among Collegians, 1970, Parents Guide to Child Raising, 1978, Parents Medical Manual, 1978; contbr. articles to profl. jours. Bd. dirs. Alameda County Council Alcoholism, 1960-70, Alameda County Suicide Prevention, 1962-70, Ronoh Sch., 1966-70, New Bridge Found., 1968-98, Carmel Valley Manor, 1969-98, Goodwill Industries, 1972-92, Com. Children's TV, 1977-79, Jack B. Goldberg Found., 1978-98, Am. Found. for Traditional Chinese Medicine, 1990-98; trustee, mem. ch. council Arlington Community Ch., 1954-72. Served to lt. comdr. M.C. USNR, 1945-46, 53-54. Mem. AMA, APHA, Royal Soc. Health, Am. Coll. Health Assns. (pres. 1965-66), Pacific Coast Coll. Health Assn. (pres. 1968-69), Am. Fedn. Clin. Rsch., Western Soc. Clin. Rsch., Am. Acad. Pediatrics (chmn. cmty. svcs. com. No. Calif. sect. 1962-94), Calif. Acad. Medicine, Order Golden Bear, Delta Tau Delta, Nu Sigma Nu. Home: 432 Woodland Rd Kentfield CA 94904-2636

BRUZELIUS, NILS JOHAN AXEL, journalist; b. Stockholm, Feb. 27, 1947; came to U.S., 1958; s. Axel Sture and Constance (Brickett) B.; m. Lynne A. Weil, Aug. 10, 2002. BA in History, Amherst Coll., 1968. Reporter, bur. chief Middlesex News, Framingham, Mass., 1968-70; reporter, state house corr. AP, Boston, 1970-73; med./mental health writer Boston Globe, 1973-79, investigative reporter, 1979-81, asst. met. editor, 1981-86, health and sci. editor, 1986-99, fgn. editor, 1999—2001; sr. editor sci. desk Nat. Pub. Radio, Washington, 2002—; dep. nat. editor sci. Washington Post, 2002—. Mem. Boston Globe investigative team receiving Disting. Investigative Reporting award Investigative Reporters and Editors Assn., 1979, Disting. Journalism citation Scripps-Howard Found., 1979, Pulitzer prize for spl. local reporting, 1980; Knight Sci. Journalism fellow MIT, 1992-93. Mem.: Investigative Reporters and Editors, Nat. Assn. Sci. Writers, Ocean Cruising Club. Home: 133 D Street SE Washington DC 20003

BRUZS, BORIS OLGERD, retired management consultant; b. Riga, Latvia, July 11, 1933; s. Boris and Zelia (Neumanis) B.; m. Anne Quoniam de Schompre, Feb. 10, 1988. Lic. es Sc., U. Paris, Paris; BA, Bowdoin Coll.; MPC, U. Strasbourg, France. Tech. svc. mgr. Union Carbide Internat., Geneva, 1959-62; gen. mgr. Profile Steel Co., Detroit, 1962-64; cons. Booz, Allen & Hamilton, Zurich, Switzerland, 1964-66, ptnr. Dusseldorf, Germany, 1966-69, mng. ptnr. Paris, 1969-79, pres. internat. affairs N.Y.C., 1979-94; ret., 1994. Mem. Inst. Mgmt. Cons., Polo Club. Home: 16 Rue Maitre Albert 75005 Paris France Office: Booz Allen & Hamilton 101 Park Ave 21st Fl New York NY 10178-0002

BRYAN, A(LONZO) J(AY), retired service club official; b. Washington, N.J., Sept. 17, 1917; s. Alonzo J. and Anna Belle (Babcock) B.; m. Elizabeth Elfreida Koehler, June 25, 1941 (div. 1961); children: Donna Elizabeth, Alonzo Jay, Nadine; m. Janet Dorothy Onstad, Mar. 15, 1962 (div. 1977); children: Brenda Joyce, Marlowe Francis, Marilyn Janet. Student. Retail florist, Washington, N.J., 1941-64. Active WalMart Corp., 1989—2003. Fund drive chmn. ARC, 1952; bd. dirs. Washington YMCA, 1945-55, N.J. Taxpayers Assn., 1947-52; mem. Washington Bd. Edn., 1948-55. Mem. Washington Grange, Sons and Daus. of Liberty, Soc. Am. Florists, Nat. Fedn. Ind. Businessmen, Florists Telegraph Delivery Assn., C. of C., Masons, Tall Cedars of Lebanon Club, Jr. Order United Am. Mechanics, Kiwanis (pres. Washington N.J. 1952, lt. gov. internat. 1953-54, gov. N.J. dist. 1955, sec. 1957-64, sec. S.E. area Chgo. 1965-74, editor The Jersey Kiwanian 1958-64, internat. staff 1964-85, sec.-treas. Rocky Mountain dist. 1989, pres. South Denver 1990-91, editor Rocky Mountain Kiwanian 1990-96), Breakfast Club (Chgo., pres. 1981-82). Methodist. Home: 8115 S Poplar Way B 203 Centennial CO 80112-3174

BRYAN, ARTHUR LEE, music educator; b. Berkeley County, SC, Feb. 6, 1951; s. Robert Marion and Alnetha McKelvey Bryan; children: Shay'La Yvonne Bryan-Harris, Arthur Lee Bryan,II, Jonathan Lamont. BA in Music Edn., Tex. Coll., 1975. Texas Teacher Certificate (Provisional - All - Level - Music) Tex. Edn. Agy., 1975. Instr. music Tex. Coll., Tyler, Tex., 1978—81, dir. choir, 1978—81, admissions counselor, 1978—81; staff sgt. U.S. Army, Fort Hood, Tex., 1981—2001; bandsmen, trumpet player 2nd Infantry Divsn. Band, Eighth Army Band, Camp Casey, 1982—2001; bandsmen, trumpet player 1st Cavalry Divsn. Band, Fort Hood, Tex., 1982—2001; bandsmen, trumpet player Eighth Army Band, Seoul, 1982—2001; dir. bands Fairway Middle Sch., Killeen, Tex., 2001—; ret. U.S. Army, 2001. Mem. Ancient Egyptian Arabic Order Nobles Mystic Shrine, Killeen, Tex., 1985—2002. Decorated Meritorious Svc. Medal Dept. of the Army, NATO Metal NATO; recipient Coined For Excellence, Commdg. Gen. for UNC; CFC; US Forces Korea, 1998, Commdg. Gen. For III CORPS and Ft. Hood, 1997, Command Sgt. Maj. of the Army, 1996, Coined for Excellence, Commanding Gen. for III CORPS and Fort Hood, 1998, 1999. Mem.: VFW, NEA (assoc.), Tex. Bandmasters Assn. (assoc.), Music Educators Nat. Conf. (assoc.), World Kido Fedn., Korea Kido Assn., N.G. Assn. Tex. (life), 1st Cavalry Divsn. Assn. (life), US Taekwondo Union, Masons, Alpha Kappa Mu, Phi Mu Alpha Sinfonia (assoc.), Omega Psi Phi (life; past basileus 1986—2002, past chaplain, keeper of records and seal). Democrat. Episcopalian. Home: 2404 Edgefield Street Killeen TX 76549 Office: Fairway Middle School 701 Whitlow Avenue Killeen TX 76541 Home Fax: 254-519-5599; Office Fax: 254-519-5599. Personal E-mail: arthurbryan@earthlink.net. E-mail: arthurbryan@hotmail.com.

BRYAN, BARBARA DAY, retired librarian; b. Livermore Falls, Maine, May 20, 1927; d. Lorey Clifford and Olga Elvira (Bergquist) Day; m. Robert S. Bryan, June 24, 1950. BA in Psychology, U. Maine, 1948; MS in Library Sci., So. Conn. State U., 1964. Catalog dept. asst. Yale U. Library, New Haven, 1948-49; departmental library cataloger Harvard U., Cambridge, Mass., 1949-51; descriptive cataloger Yale U. Library, New Haven, 1951-52; cataloger Fairfield (Conn.) Pub. Library, 1952-54, reference librarian, 1954-57, asst. librarian, order librarian, 1957-65; asst. dir. libraries Fairfield U., 1965-74, university librarian, 1974-96, u. libr. emerita, 1996—. Mem. Conn. State Libr. Bd., Hartford, 1978—92, chair, 1987—92; bd. dirs. Bibliomation, Inc., Stratford, Conn., 1987—91. Pres. Friends Nyselius Libr., Fairfield U., 1998—2000, mem. exec. bd., 2001—; commr. Fairfield Hist. Dist. Commn., 2003—. Recipient Disting. Alumnus award So. Conn. State U. Sch. of Libr. Sci., 1979; named Conn. Libr. Assn. Libr. of Yr., 1988. Mem. ALA (life, Conn. chpt. councilor 1977-80), Assn. Coll. and Rsch. Librs. (constn. and by laws com. 1986-90, mem. coll. libr. sect. stds. com. 1991-95), New Eng. Libr. Assn. (mem. com. 1981-85, coun. mem. 1975-77), Conn. Libr Assn., Fairfield Hist. Soc. (libr. vol.), Conn. Audubon Soc., Oak Lawn Cemetery Assn. (bd. dirs. 1994—), Assn. Conn. Libr. Bds. (bd. dirs., chair legis. com. 1996—), Inst. Ret. Profl. (adv. bd. 1998-2001), Fairfield U. Retirees Assn. (pres. 2003—), Phi Beta Kappa, Phi Kappa Phi. Democrat. Avocations: reading, walking. Home: 999 Merwins Ln Fairfield CT 06824-1919

BRYAN, BARRY RICHARD, lawyer; b. Orange, N.J., Sept. 5, 1930; s. Lloyd Thomas and Amy Rufe (Swank) B.; m. Margaret Susannah Elliot, July 24, 1953; children— Elliot Christopher, Peter George (dec.), Susannah Margaret, Sallie Catharine. BA, Yale U., 1952, JD cum laude, 1955; diploma in comparative legal studies, Cambridge U., Eng., 1956. Bar: N.Y. 1959. Legal advisor to gen. counsel Sec. of U.S. Air Force, Washington, 1956-58; assoc. Debevoise & Plimpton, N.Y.C., 1958-62, ptnr., 1963-93, presiding ptnr., 1993-98, of counsel, 1999—2001. Served to 1st lt. USAF, 1956-58. Fulbright scholar Trinity Coll., Cambridge U., 1956. Mem. ABA, Assn. of Bar of City of N.Y., Union Internationale des Avocats, Country Club of New Canaan, Fishers Island Club, Order of Coif, Phi Beta Kappa. Episcopalian. Home: PO Box 197 Isabella Beach Rd Fishers Island NY 06390 Office: Debevoise & Plimpton 919 3rd Ave Fl 43 New York NY 10022

BRYAN, CAROLYN J. music educator, saxophonist; b. Dubois, Pa., Dec. 7, 1963; d. Frank H. and Elizabeth J. (Moyer) Bryan. BME, Baldwin-Wallace Coll., Berea, Ohio, 1985; MMusic, Ind. U., 1987, DMus, 1997. Cert. K-12 music tchr., Ohio, Minn. Band dir., area coord. Musicl Youth, Inc., Cleve., 1987-92; lectr. music theory and edn. Baldwin-Wallace Coll., 1990-92; dir. bands Dakota Meadows Middle Sch./ISD 77, Mankato, Minn., 1995-97; assoc. prof. music Ga. So. U., Statesboro, 1997—. Performing artist Yamaha Corp., 1997—; vis. prof. saxophone Youngstown (Ohio) State U., 1991; vis. instr. music Gustavus Adolphus Coll., St. Peter, Minn., 1993-94; presenter in field. Author lit. and rec. revs.; performer audio rec. Winds of Ind., 1995. Spl. Initiatives grantee Coll. Liberal Arts and Social Scis., Ga. So. U., 1999, 2001, Faculty Rsch. grantee Ga. So. U., 1999. Mem. Music Educators Nat. Conf., N.Am. Saxophone Alliance, Nat. Assn. Coll. Wind and Percussion Instrs., Internat. Alliance Women in Music, Pi Kappa Lambda, Mu Phi Epsilon, Phi Kappa Phi. Avocations: reading, music, travel. Office: Ga So U PO Box 8052 Statesboro GA 30460-8052 E-mail: cbryan@gasou.edu.

BRYAN, CHARLES STONE, internal medicine educator; b. Columbia, S.C., Jan. 15, 1942; s. Leon Stone and Mary Morrill (Leadbeater) B.; m. Donna Hennesee, Oct. 30, 1982; children: Eleanor Chandlee, Emily Singleton. Student, Harvard U., 1960-62; BA, Johns Hopkins U., 1964, MD, 1967. Diplomate Am. Bd. Internal Medicine, Am. Bd. Infectious Diseases. Intern in pathology Johns Hopkins Hosp., Balt., 1967-68; intern in medicine Vanderbilt U. Hosp., Nashville, 1968-69, resident, fellow, 1971-74; pvt. practice Columbia, S.C., 1974-77; dir. infectious diseases U. S.C. Sch. Medicine, Columbia, 1977-93, Heyward Gibbes disting. prof. medicine, chmn. dept., 1992-2000; dir. Ctr. Bioethics and Med. Humanities, 2000—. Author: A Most Satisfactory Man, 1996, Osler: Inspirations from a Great Physician, 1997, Infectious Diseases in Primary Care, 2002; editor Jour. S.C. Med. Assn., 1977—; contbr. articles to profl. jours. Chmn. Midlands Care Consortium, Columbia, 1993—. Surgeon USPHS, 1969-71. Master ACP (Laureate award 1993); fellow Royal Coll. Physicians (Edinburgh), Infectious Diseases Soc. Am.; mem. Am. Clin. and Climatological Assn., Am. Assn. for History Medicine (William Osler medal 1967), Am. Osler Soc. (sec.-treas. 2000-), S.C. Infectious Diseases Soc. (pres. 1994), Columbia Med. Soc. (pres. 1992), Waring Libr. Soc. (pres. 1988). Avocations: medical history, golf. Office: U SC Sch Medicine 2 Richland Medical Park Dr Columbia SC 29203-6864

BRYAN, COLGAN HOBSON, aerospace engineering educator; b. Trenton, S.C., Oct. 7, 1909; s. John William and Mary (Hobson) B.; m. Sara Lucille Turbeville, June 18, 1938 (dec. Nov. 17, 1975); 1 son, Colgan Hobson; m. Carol Lindsay Smelley, July 14, 1979 (dec. Sept. 20, 1993). BS in Elec. Engring, U. S.C., 1932; M.Ed., Duke U., 1940; MS in Aero. Engring, Ga. Inst. Tech., 1948. Registered profl. engr., Ala. Faculty U. Ala., 1942—, prof. aerospace engring., 1948—, chmn. dept., 1952—; research scientist NASA, 1962; on leave with U. Tenn. Space Inst., 1968-69. Cons. to industry, 1941— Mem. Ala. Aero. Commn., 1944-48. Recipient Charles Henry Ratcliff award for excellence in teaching, 1976, Outstanding Faculty award Delta Tau Delta, 1976, George H. Denny Outstanding Faculty award Sigma Chi, 1976, Disting. Engring. fellow, 2002; established Colgan H. Bryan Aerospace Engring. Scholarship, 1991. Fellow AIAA (assoc., Disting. Svc. award 1980, Disting. fellow 2002); mem. NSPE, ASME, AAUP, NEA, Am. Soc. Engring. Edn., Am. Ordnance Assn., Ala. Soc. Profl. Engrs. (Engr. of Yr. award Tuscaloosa chpt. 1990), Ala. Edn. Assn., Acacia (life), Pi Tau Chi (faculty adviser). Clubs: Kiwanian (pres. Tuscaloosa 1966, recipient Service award 1966, Distinguished Service award 1977). Episcopalian. Achievements include research projects in theoretical and applied aerodynamics, energy (solar and wind). Home: 12 Lakeshore Dr Tuscaloosa AL 35404-4982 Office: U Ala PO Box 861461 Tuscaloosa AL 35486-0013 Fax: 205-348-7240.

BRYAN, GEORGE THOMAS, pediatrician, academic administrator; b. Sewanee, Tenn., Nov. 19, 1930; s. Lawton P. and Velma (Courtney) B.; m. Peggy Marie Graham, Dec. 19, 1952; children: Ralph T., Janice M. Student, Vanderbilt U., 1949-51; MD, U. Tenn., 1955. Intern D.C. Gen. Hosp., 1955-56; resident in pediatrics U. Iowa Hosp., Iowa City, 1956-58, fellow in pediatric endocrinology, 1958-59; clin. assoc. pediatrics, Lab. Clin. Investigation NIH, USPHS, Bethesda, Md., 1959-60, acting head pediatric svc., 1960-61, pediatrician clin. endocrinology br. Nat Heart Inst., 1961-63; asst. prof. pediatrics U. Tex. Med. Br., Galveston, 1963-67, assoc. prof., 1967-73, prof., 1973—, asst. dir. clin. study ctr., 1963-72, assoc. dir., 1972-75, assoc. dean curricular affairs, 1974-77, dean Sch. Medicine, 1977-95, dean emeritus Sch. Medicine, 1995—. Contbr. articles to profl. jours. Lt. USNR, 1956-59. Markle scholar, 1967-72. Mem. Am. Pediatric Soc., Soc. Pediatric Rsch., Am. Acad. Pediatrics, Lawson Wilkins Soc. Pediatric Endocrinology, Endocrine Soc., Am. Fedn. Clin. Rsch., So. Soc. Pediatric Rsch., AMA, Tex. Med. Assn., Galveston County Med. Soc., Am. Assn. Med. Colls., Sigma Xi. Mem. Christian Ch. Office: U Tex Med Br 301 University Blvd Galveston TX 77555-1011 E-mail: gtbryan@utmb.edu.

BRYAN, HENRY C(LARK), JR., retired lawyer; b. St. Louis, Dec. 8, 1930; s. Henry Clark and Faith (Young) B.; m. Sarah Ann McCarthy, July 28, 1956; children— Mark Pendleton, Thomas Clark, Sarah Christy Nussbaum. AB, Washington U., St. Louis, 1952, LL.B., 1956. Bar: Mo. 1956. Law clk. to fed. judge, 1956; assoc. McDonald & Wright, St. Louis, 1956-60; ptnr. McDonald, Bernard, Wright & Timm, St. Louis, 1961-64, McDonald, Wright & Bryan, St. Louis, 1964-81, Wright, Bryan & Walsh, St. Louis, 1981-84; pvt. practice law, 1984-96; ret., 1996. V.p., dir. Harbor Point Boat & Dock Co., St. Charles, Mo., 1966-80, Merrell Ins. Agy., 1966-80. Served to 1st lt. AUS, 1952-54 Mem. ABA, Mo. Bar Assn., St. Louis Bar Assn. (past chmn. probate and trust sect., marriage and div. law com.), Kappa Sigma, Phi Delta Phi Lodges: Elks. Republican. Episcopalian. Home: 41 Ladue Ter Saint Louis MO 63124-2047

BRYAN, HENRY COLLIER, clergyman, retired secondary school educator; b. Atlanta, Apr. 10, 1941; s. Thomas Harper and Rubye (Collier) B. Student, Temple U., 1959-63, 64, 70; BEd, Cheyney U., 1962; postgrad., Va. Union U., 1965-66; MDiv, Ea. Bapt. Theol. Sem., 1968; postgrad., Howard Law Sch., 1962-63, U. Alaska, Juneau, 1990. Cert. math. tchr., Phila.; ordained to ministry Am. Bapt. Ch., 1968. Tchr. math. Masterman Demonstration Sch., Phila., 1968-71, Phila. High Sch. for Girls, 1971-97; ret., 1997. Chaplain Alpha Phi Alpha Fraternity, Phila, 1968—. Assoc. min. Zion Bapt. Ch., 1967-68; asst. min. Wynnefield United Presbyn. Ch., 1969-72; Charter mem. North br. Y's Men Assn., Phila., 1972—; bd. dirs. Cherry Hill (N.J.) Civic Assn., 1992—. Recipient Outstanding Young Men Am. award Wynnefield Presbyn. Ch., Phila., 1971. Mem.: ASCD, NAACP (life), NSTA (life), Pa. Coun. Tchrs. Math., Pa. Coun. Suprs. Math., Nat. Coun. Suprs. Math., Math. Assn. Am., Phila. Fedn. Tchrs. (bldg. rep. Girls' H.S. 1996—97), Phila. Health Computer Users Group (life), Am. Baptist Mins. Coun. (life), Nat. Coun. Tchrs. Math. (life), Assn. Tchrs. Math. Phila. (life), Alpha Phi Alpha (life), Phi Delta Kappa (life). Avocations: computers, electronics, sports, chess, world travel. Home: 17 W Brook Dr Cherry Hill NJ 08003-1109

BRYAN, JAMES LEE, oil field service company executive; b. Waco, Tex., Aug. 18, 1936; s. Andrew Walton and Thelma Lee (Clements) B.; m. Joretta Griffin, Nov. 28, 1958; children— Deborah Lee, Catherine Ann, Rebecca Kaye, Cynthia Jean. BS in Geology, Baylor U., 1958. Drilling fluids engr. Dresser Industries, La., 1959-61, dist. engr., 1961-62, dist. mgr., 1962-65, gen. mgr., 1965-67, mng. dir., 1967-69, area mgr. Middle and Far East, 1969-72, 1972-74, v.p. Western ops., 1974-77, exec. v.p. Magcobar div., 1977-79; pres. Magcobar Group, 1980-86; pres., CEO M-I Drilling Fluids Co., 1986-90; v.p. ops. Dresser Industries, 1990-94, sr. v.p. ops., 1994-98; exec. v.p. Newpark Drilling Fluids, Inc., Houston, 1999—. Mem. Inst. Mech. Engrs., Am. Petroleum Inst., Soc. Petroleum Engrs., Petroleum Equipment Supply Assn., Nomads, Pi Epsilon Tau. Clubs: Champions, Lochinvar, Petroleum. Republican. Baptist. Office: 1311 Broadfield Blvd Ste 600 Houston TX 77084-5126

BRYAN, J(AMES) P(ERRY), JR., energy company executive; b. Houston, Jan. 17, 1940; s. James Perry Bryan Sr. and Gretchen (Smith) Josey; m. Mary Jon Lewis, Jan. 21, 1961; children: Alicia and John Bracken. BA, U. Tex., 1962; LLB, 1965; BFT, Am. Inst. Foreign Trade, 1966. V.p. Morgan Guaranty Trust Co., N.Y.C., 1966-69; v.p. dir. investment banking Dominick & Dominick, N.Y.C, Houston, 1969-74; pres., CEO The MortgageBanque, Inc., Houston, 1974-78; v.p, regional dir. corp. fin. dept. E.F. Hutton & Co., Inc., Houston, 1978-81; chmn., CEO Torch Energy Advisors, Inc., Houston, 1981—; Neuvo Energy Energy Assets Internat. Corp., Houston, 1987—95; chmn. & CEO Bellwether Exploration Co., Houston. Bd. dirs. Torch Energy Advisors, Inc., Bellwether Exploration Co., Neuvo Energy Co., Park Nat. Bank, Torchmark Corp., Republic Waste Inds. Founder, editor Internat. Law Jour.; contbr. reviews and articles on Tex. history to mags. and jours. Chmn. endowment fund, other offices Tex. State Hist. Assn.; chmn. fund raising com., past. chmn., pres. Tex. Hist. Found.; chmn. devel., adv. bd. Inst. Texan Cultures; trustee Nita Stewart Haley Meml. Libr.; past trustee, chmn. nominating com. Harris County Heritage Soc; mem. adv. bd. Bazoria County Hist. Mus.; founding chmn., past bd. dirs. South Main Ctr. Assn.; founder, bd. dirs. Collector's Inst.; bd. dirs. The Book Club of Tex.; chmn., dir. fund raising River Oaks Bapt. Sch., others. Mem. ABA, Tex. Bar Assn., Houston Bar Assn., Univ. Tex. Ex-Students Assn. (life), Philos. Soc. Tex., Houston Country Club, Tex. Breakfast Club (treas. Houston), Tejas Club, Argyle Club, Nat. golf Links Am., Phi Delta, Delta Phi Epsilon. Office: Torch Energy Advisors Inc 1221 Lamar St Ste 1600 Houston TX 77010-3039

BRYAN, JAMES SPENCER, lawyer; b. Pitts., Oct. 26, 1944; s. Joseph and Zella Mae (Spencer) B.; m. Karen Smith, May 27, 1972. B.A., Harvard U., 1966; J.D., U. Pa., 1971; postgrad. Stanford U., 1967-68. Bar: Calif. 1972, U.S. Dist. Ct. (cen. dist.) Calif. 1973, U.S. Dist. Ct. (ea. and so. dists.) Calif. 1981. Jud. clk. U.S. Dist. Ct. (so. dist.) N.Y., N.Y.C., 1971-72; assoc. O'Melveny & Myers, Los Angeles, 1972-79, Seyfarth, Shaw, Fairweather & Geraldson, Los Angeles, 1979-82; ptnr. Dretzin & Kauff, Los Angeles, 1982-87, Lawler, Felix & Hall, L.A., 1987-90, Arter & Hadden, L.A., 1990—; judge pro tem Los Angeles Mcpl. Ct., 1983-84. Contbr. to Vanderbilt Law Rev., 1974, Loyola Law Rev., Los Angeles, 1981. NDEA fellow Stanford U., 1967. Mem. ABA, Calif. Bar Assn., Order of Coif. Democrat. Office: Arter & Hadden 700 S Flower St Los Angeles CA 90017-4101

BRYAN, JEAN MARIE WEHMUELLER, nurse; b. St. Louis, Aug. 10, 1964; d. Harold Leroy and Rose Marie (Maurer) Wehmuelle; m. Michael Thomas Bryan; children: Emily, Dennis. ADN, St. Louis C.C., 1984; BSN cum laude, U. Mo., St. Louis, 1986; MBA, Fontbonne U., 2001. RN, Mo. Libr. asst. St. Louis County Libr., 1980-86; charge/staff nurse Incarnate World Hosp., St. Louis, 1986-88, Alexian Bros. Hosp., St. Louis, 1988-89, Compre Health, Inc., St. Louis, 1989-91; office nurse to pvt. practice physician St. Louis, 1991-97; owner Stained Glass Classics Studio, 1992—; billing ctr. processor Am. Home Patient, Inc., 1997-98; med. cost analyst ESSE Health, 1998-2000; data analyst United Healthcare of the Midwest, 2001; case mgr./outcomes mgr. St. Anthony's Med. Ctr., St. Louis, 2001—. Republican. Lutheran. Home: 200 Martigney Dr Saint Louis MO 63129-3412

BRYAN, JOHN HENRY, food and consumer products company executive; b. West Point, Miss., 1936; BA in Econs. and Bus. Adminstrn., Rhodes Coll., Memphis, 1958. Joined Bryan Foods, 1960; with Sara Lee Corp. (formerly known as Consol. Food Corp.), Chgo., 1960—; from exec. v.p. to pres. Sara Lee Corp. (formerly known as Consol Food Corp.), Chgo., 1974, CFO, 1975—, chmn. bd., 1976—, also bd. dirs. Bd. dirs. GM Corp., BP Amoco Corp., Bank One. Chmn. bus. adv. coun. Chgo. Urban League; bd. govs. Nat. Women's Econ. Alliance, Chgo.; trustee, vice chmn., exec. com. U. Chgo., Rush-Presbyn.-St. Luke's Med. Ctr.; trustee Com. Econ. Devel.; trustee, treas. Art Inst., Chgo.; chmn. Catalyst, Chgo. com. Chgo. Coun. on Fgn. Rels.; mem. trustee's coun. Nat. Gallery Art, Washington; mem. Pres.'s com. on the arts and humanities; bd. dirs. Bus. Com. for Arts. Decorated Legion of Honor France, Order of Orange Nassau The Netherlands, Order of Lincoln medallion; named Man of Yr., Harvard Bus. Sch. Club Chgo., Exec. Yr., Crain's Chgo. Bus., 1992; named to Jr. Achievement Chgo. Bus. Hall of Fame, 1992, Miss. Hall of Fame, 1992; recipient Nat. Humanitarian award, NCCJ, William H. Albers award, Food Mktg. Inst. Mem.: Bus. Roundtable, Bus. Coun., Grocery Mfrs. Assn. (sr.; past chmn. bd.). Office: Sara Lee Corp 3 1st Nat Plz 70 W Madison St Ste 4500 Chicago IL 60602-4260

BRYAN, JOHN JOSEPH, physician; b. Bisbee, Ariz., Aug. 9, 1921; s. Wirt Gold and Viola Catherine (Snarr) B.; m. Annie Dee Pickens, Aug. 28, 1948; children: Celia Keath, Dee Alice Brentlinger, Susan Paige Chastain. BS in Chemistry, Baylor U., 1946, MD, 1954. Diplomate Am. Bd. Pathology, Clin. Pathology, 1970. Clin. pathologist Bluefield (W.Va.) Sanitarium Hosp., 1959-79, Clinch Valley Clin. Hosp., Richland, Va., 1959-79, Stevens Clin. Hosp., Welch, W.Va., 1959-79, 82-87, Bluefield Comm. Hosp., 1979-82; staff phys. VAMC, Waco, Tex., 1987-92, chief of staff, 1993-95; chief, environ. medicine VA Ctrl. Tex. Health Care Sys., Marlin, Temple and Waco, 1996-97; ret., 1997. Instr. chemistry Tex. A & M Univ., Coll. Sta., Tex., 1948—50; clin. asst. prof. Pathology and Lab. Medicine Tex. A & M Univ. Health Sci. Ctr. Va Med. Ctr., Waco, Tex., 1994—96. Pres. Bapt. Gen. Assn. of Va., Richmond, 1971; trustee Bapt. Sunday Sch. Bd., Nashville, 1977-87, chmn., 1985-86. Lt. med. corp. USN Res., 1944-46, 54-55. Fellow Coll. Am. Pathologists, Am. Soc. Clin. Pathologists, Assn. Clin. Scientists; mem. Am. Chem. Soc., AMA, So. Med. Assn., Tex. Med. Assn., Tex. Soc. Pathologists. Republican. Avocations: gardening, houseplants, photography, softball. Home: 9923 Sandalwood Dr Waco TX 76712-3139 E-mail: jjb_i@msn.com.

BRYAN, JOHN LELAND, retired engineering educator; b. Washington, Nov. 15, 1926; s. George W. and Buena (Youe) B.; m. Sarah Emily Barton, June 7, 1950; children: Joan Marie, Steven Leland. AA, Okla. State U., 1950, BS, 1953, MS, 1954; D.Ed., Am. U., 1965. Field rep. Grain Dealers Mut. Ins. Co., Indpls., 1950, Jackson, Miss., 1950-52; sr. instr. U. Md., 1954-56, prof., 1956-93; ret., 1993. Fire prevention engr., civil engring. div. U.S. Coast Guard, Washington, summers 1960-64 Author: Fire Detection and Suppression Systems, 1973, 3d edit., 1993, Automatic Sprinkler and Standpipe Systems, 1976, 3d rev. edit., 1997. Mem. Soc. Fire Protection Engrs., Nat. Fire Protection Assn., ASTM, Iota Lambda Sigma, Psi Chi, Kappa Delta Pi, Phi Kappa Phi. Home: 2399 Bear Den Rd Frederick MD 21701-9328

BRYAN, JOHN RODNEY, management consultant; b. Berkeley, Calif., Dec. 29, 1953; s. Robert Richard and Eloise (Anderson) Putz; m. Karen Nelson, Jan. 20, 1990. BA in Chemistry, U. Calif., San Diego, 1975; MBA, Rutgers U., 1985. Agt. Prudential, San Diego, 1975-79; sales mgr. Herman Schlorman Showrooms, L.A., 1980-83; pvt. practice mgmt. cons. Basking Ridge, N.J., 1983-85; mgmt. cons. The Brooks Group, Hollywood, Fla., 1985-99; pvt. practice San Diego, 1988—. With Western Productivity Group, 1990-95; pres. eProcesses Consulting, Inc., 1999—. Elder La Jolla Presbyn. Ch., 1991—. Mem. Inst. Indsl. Engring., Rutgers Club So. Calif., Beta Gamma Sigma. Avocations: singing, golf. Address: 6265 Hurd Ct San Diego CA 92122-2917 Office: 1025 Prospect St Ste 330 La Jolla CA 92037 E-mail: jbryan@eprocessesconsulting.com.

BRYAN, JOHN STEWART, III, newspaper publisher; b. Richmond, Va., May 4, 1938; s. David Tennant and Mary Davidson Bryan; m. Alice Pyle Zimmer, 1963 (div. 1985); children: Elizabeth Talbott, Anna Saulsbury; m. Lisa-Margaret Stevenson, 1993. BA, U. Va., 1960; LHD (hon.), Hampden-Sydney Coll., 1997, Emory and Henry Coll., 1999, Coll. of William and Mary, 2001. Former advt. salesman Burlington (Vt.) Free Press; former reporter The Tampa (Fla.) Times; pub. The Tampa Tribune and Times, 1976—77, Richmond Times-Dispatch, Richmond News Leader, 1978—. Bd. dirs. Media Gen., Inc., Richmond, vice-chmn., exec. v.p., 1985—, chmn., pres., CEO, 1990—; bd. dirs. Mut. Ins. Co., Bermuda. Past pres. or chmn. Tampa Bay Art Ctr., Tampa Citizens Safety Coun., Tampa United Way, Gulf Coast Symphony, Jr. Achievement Richmond, Goodwill Industries Richmond, United Way Greater Richmond; trustee Va. Found. Ind. Coll., chmn., 1993—95; trustee Thomas Jefferson Found., George C. Marshall Found., World Affairs Coun. Richmond; overseer Hoover Inst. With USMC, 1960—62. Mem.: S.R., SAR, Va. Bus. Coun., World Bus. Coun., Soc. Profl. Journalists, Newspaper Assn. Am. (dir. 1990—93, 1997—), Newspaper Advt. Bur. (chmn. 1991—92), Va. Press Assn. (bd. dirs. 1980—86), So. Newspapers Pub. Assn. (found. chmn. 1978—79, pres. 1981—82), Fla. Press Assn. (life; pres. 1971—72; Disting. Svc. award 1975), Fla. Soc. Newspapers Editors (life), Fla. Coun. of 100, Farmington Country Club, Tampa Yacht and Country Club, Commonwealth Club, Country Club Va., Bohemian Club. Home: 4608 Sulgrave Rd Richmond VA 23221-3119 Office: Media Gen Inc PO Box 85333C Richmond VA 23293-5333

BRYAN, JOSEPH SHEPARD, JR., lawyer; b. Wilson, N.C., Nov. 8, 1922; married; five children. BS, U.S. Naval Acad., 1944; JD, Harvard U., 1950. Bar: Fla., N.C. Asst. prof. pub. law and govt. U. N.C., 1950-54; counsel Winn-Dixie Stores, Inc., Jacksonville, Fla., 1954-61; gen. counsel Winn-Dixie Stores Inc., Jacksonville, Fla., 1961-66, sec., 1961-66, v.p., gen. counsel, sec., 1966-91, also bd. dirs.; of counsel Holland & Knight, Jacksonville, 1991—. Mem. adv. bd. 1st Union Nat. Bank of Fla., Inc.; bd. dirs. Shands Tchg. Hosp. Clins., Inc., Gainesville, Fla., Jacksonville Cmty. Found., Bok Tower Gardens Found., Jacksonville Symphony Assn., Cultural Coun. Greater Jacksonville, Inc.; exec. com., bd. dirs. Baptist St. Vincent's Health Sys., Jacksonville; bd. govs. The Nat. Conf. Chmn. Westminster Retirement Cmtys., 1998—. With USN, 1944-47, 51-52. Recipient Individual award Arts Assembly of Jacksonville, Inc., Humanitarian award Nat. Conf. Christians and Jews. Mem. ABA, Am. Arbitration Assn., Am. Corp. Counsel Assn., Riverside Presbyn. Ch. Home: 1651 Beach Ave Jacksonville FL 32233-5840 Office: Holland & Knight LLP PO Box 52687 50 N Laura St Jacksonville FL 32202-3664

BRYAN, KAY MARIE, minister; b. Independence, Mo., Oct. 16, 1936; d. Joseph Price and Naoma Muriel (Upham) Scott; m. William Burgess (div. Nov. 1976); children: Deborah Tinker, William Burgess, Phillip Burgess; m. Travis Johnson; 1 child, Steve Johnson; m. Marlan William Bryan, July 28, 1984. BA in Health Care Mgmt., Park U., 1978. Accredited records technician; cert. profl. healthcare quality. Records technician St. Luke's Hosp., Kansas City, Mo., 1973-76; asst. dir. med. records U. Health Sci., Kansas City, Mo., 1976-78; dir. med. records Toledo (Ohio) Hosp., 1978-84; dir. med. records and quality assurance Gateway Rehab. Ctr., Aliquippa, Pa., 1985-97, ret., 1997; min. Cmty. of Christ, 1999—. Officiating coord. Aaronic Mins., Aaronic priesthood; field instr. U. Pitts., 1985-97, Allegheny C.C., Pitts., 1994-97; cons. Pa. Health Info. Mgmt., 1987-97. Mem. Am. Assn. Healthcare Quality, Western Pa. Assn. Healthcare Quality, Am. Health Info. Mgmt. Assn., Western Pa. Health Info. Mgmt. Assn., Beaver Valley Piecemakers, Ohio Assn. Health. Avocations: organ, piano, quilting, dollmaking, crocheting. Home and Office: 17800 Bolger Rd Apt 408B Independence MO 64055-6775

BRYAN, LAWRENCE DOW, college president; b. Barberton, Ohio, Jan. 30, 1945; s. W. Richard and Celia A. (Evans) B.; m. Marjorie Napier, June 15, 1968; children: Mark Evans, Alexa Marie. BA, Muskingum Coll., 1967; MDiv., Garrett Theol. Sem., 1970; PhD, Northwestern U., 1973. Tchg. asst. Nat. Coll. Edn., Evanston, Ill., 1969-71; biog. rsch. fellow Garrett Theol. Sem., Evanston, 1972-73; asst. prof. religious studies, chaplain McKendree Coll., Lebanon, Ill., 1973-77, asst. v.p. acad. affairs, 1977-78, dean, 1978-79, assoc. prof., 1978-79; prof. philosophy and religion, v.p., dean Franklin (Ind.) Coll., 1979-90; pres. Kalamazoo Coll., 1990-96, MacMurray Coll., Jacksonville, Ill., 1997—. Trustee Parkstone Group of Funds, 1994-98. Mem. Forum for Kalamazoo County, 1990-94, Kalamazoo Symphony Orch. Bd., 1990-96; pres. Heyl Found., Kalamazoo, 1990-96; bd. dirs. Bronson Hosp., 1991-96; trustee Interlochen Ctr. for Arts, 1994-97; pres. Jacksonville Main St. Bd. Dirs. Mem. Internat. Bonhoeffer Soc., Fed. Ind. Ill. Colls. and Univs., Rotary, Phi Sigma Tau, Delta Sigma Rho-Tau Kappa Alpha, Alpha Psi Omega, Theta Alpha Phi. Methodist.

BRYAN, LISA MARGARET STEVENSON, volunteer; b. N.Y.C., July 25, 1949; d. Walker Woods, Jr. and Virginia Vogt Stevenson; m. Alexander Campbell Sanger, Oct. 31, 1970 (div. 1977); m. John Stewart Bryan III, July 2, 1993; stepchildren: Talbott Bryan Maxey, Anna S. Bryan Sullivan. BA, Columbia U., 1972. Buyer Saks Fifth Ave., N.Y.C., 1976-82; msde. mgr. Laura Ashley Ltd., N.Y.C., 1982-83; v.p. mktg. Nat. Audubon Soc., N.Y.C., 1983-86; dir. product devel. & licensing Smithsonian Instn., Washington, 1986-92. Chmn. Richmond (Va.) Better Housing Coalition, 1999—; vice pres. Va. League Planned Parenthood, 1994—; pres. Downtown Presents, 2001—. Office: 4608 Sulgrave Rd Richmond VA 23221 E-mail: Lissyland@att.net.

BRYAN, MARY ANN, interior designer; b. Dallas, Nov. 16, 1929; d. William C. and Harriet E. (Carter) Green; m. Frank Wingfield Bryan, Aug. 31, 1957; children: Frank Wingfield, Elizabeth F. BS in Interior Design, U. Tex., 1950. Head of stock Foleys Dept. Store, Houston, 1952-53, asst. buyer, 1953-54, buyer, 1955-60; exec. tng. dir. Foleys Dept Store, Houston; owner, pres. The Bryan Design Assocs., Inc., Houston, 1961—2003. Mem. Tex. Bd. Archtl. Examiners, 1993—99. Mem. interior design adv. bd. Art Inst. of Houston, Houston C.C.; U.S. del. Friendship Among Women. Fellow Am. Soc. Interior Designers (nat. bd. dirs. 1984-86, 91-92; pres. Gulf Coast chpt. 1975), Chi Omega. Office: 5120 Woodway Dr Ste 8009 Houston TX 77056-1788 E-mail: maryannb@bryandesigns.com.

BRYAN, NORMAN E. dentist; b. South Bend, Ind., Jan. 20, 1947; s. Norman E. and Frances (Kuhn) B.; m. Constance C. Cook, Feb. 23, 1974 (div. Apr. 1985); m. Linda Markley, Dec. 31, 1986; 1 child, Noelle. AB, Ind. U., 1969; DDS, Ind. U. Purdue U., Indpls., 1973. Sr. dentist Downtown Dental Svcs., Elkhart, Ind., 1973—. Specialist Temporomandibular Joint Disfunction. Author: Canine Endodontics, 1982. Mem. ADA, Ind. Dental Assn., Elkhart Dental Assn. (pres. 1976-77, 84-86), Am. Acad. Head, Neck and Facial Pain, Great Lakes Cruising Club (Chgo.). Republican. Avocations: sailor, photography, painter. Office: 505 Vistula St Elkhart IN 46516-2809

BRYAN, PAUL EDWARD, pharmacist; b. Winfield, Kans., July 23, 1944; s. Brooks Cecil and Sarah Elizabeth (Miller) B.; m. Yvonne Catherine Ritz, Dec. 4, 1971; children: Rose Marie, Joan Renae. BS in Pharmacy, N.Mex. U., 1967. Pres. Valley Drug, Inc., Valley Center, Kans., 1973—. Bd. dirs. Wichita Acad. Pharm., v.p., 1996—2001, pres., 1998—99. Treas. Valley Center Libr., 1984. Named Citizen of Yr., Interclub Coun., 1983. Mem. Valley Center Lions (sec. 1996-2000), Valley Center C. of C. (bd. dirs. 1994-97, 2002-). Republican. Home: 301 S Dexter Ave Valley Center KS 67147-2020 Office: Valley Drug Inc PO Box 255 126 W Main St Valley Center KS 67147-2214 E-mail: paulb723@aol.com.

BRYAN, RICHARD H. lawyer, educator, former senator; b. Washington, July 16, 1937; m. Bonnie Fairchild; 3 children. BA, U. Nev., 1959; LLB, U. Calif., San Francisco, 1963. Bar: Nev. 1963, DC 2002. Dep. dist. atty., Clark County, Nev., 1964—66; pub. defender, 1966—68; counsel Clark County Juvenile Ct., 1968—69; mem. Nev. Assembly, 1969—73, Nev. Senate, 1973—79; atty. gen. State Nev., 1979—83, gov., 1983—89; senator from Nev. U.S. Senate, 1989—2001; ptnr., mem. exec. com. Lionel, Sawyer & Collins, 2001—. Former mem. U.S. Senate coms. on commerce, sci. and transp., Dem. Policy Com., Fin. Com., Banking, Housing and Urban Affairs Com., Senate Nominating Steering and Coord. Com., Select Com. on Intelligence; adj. prof. polit. sci. U. Nev., Las Vegas, 2001—. Former pres. Clark County Legal Aid Soc.; bd. dirs. Las Vegas C. of C.; bd. trustees Nev. Devel. Authority, 2001—. 2d lt. U.S. Army, 1959—60. Recipient Disting. Svc. award, Vegas Valley Jaycees. Mem.: ABA, Coun. of State Govts. (past pres.), Am. Judicature Soc., Clark County Bar Assn., Elks, Masons, Lions, Phi Alpha Theta, Phi Alpha Delta. Democrat. Office: Lionel Sawyer & Collins 1700 Bank Am Plaza 300 S 4th St Las Vegas NV 89101

BRYAN, ROBERT ARMISTEAD, university administrator, educator; b. Lebanon, Pa., Apr. 26, 1926; s. Morris Armistead and Katherine (Maulfair) B.; m. Kathryn Elizabeth Williams, Feb. 3, 1953; children: Lyla, Matthew. BA, U. Miami, 1950; MA, U. Ky., 1951, PhD, 1956. Teaching asst. U. Ky. at Lexington, 1950-54, instr., 1956-57; lectr. extension div. U. Calif., Tokyo, Japan, 1955-56; dean advanced studies, dir. sponsored rsch. Fla. Atlantic U., 1969-70; mem. faculty, adminstrn. U. Fla., Gainsville, 1957-90, prof. English, 1968-90, dean faculties, 1970-71, assoc. v.p. acad. affairs, 1971-75, v.p. acad. affairs, 1975-85, provost, 1985-89, interim pres., 1989-90, ret., 1990; interim pres. U. Cen. Fla., 1991-92, U. South Fla., 1993-94. Reader Coll. Bd. Exams., Ednl. Testing Svc., 1958-61; cons. So. Assn. Schs. and Colls., 1965-73, also chmn. visitation com., 1966-67; cons. HEW, Nat. Assn. of State Univs. and Land Grant Colls., 1990-91; cons. Fla. Bd. Regents, 1994-95; trustee Bethune-Cookman Coll., 1994-2001; mem. Fla. Postsecondary Edn. Planning Commn., 1996-2000. Bibliographer: Twentieth Century Literature, 1958-61. Served with U.S. Mcht. Marine, 1944-47, with AUS, 1954-56. Decorated Royal Order North Star (Sweden) Mem. MLA, Southeastern Renaissance Conf., S. Atlantic Mod. Lang. Assn., Sigma Chi. Episcopalian. Home: 9518 SW 56th Pl Gainesville FL 32608-4332

BRYAN, ROBERT FESSLER, former investment analyst; b. New Castle, Pa., Jan. 19, 1913; s. Harry A. and Nell (Fessler) B.; m. Elaine A. Norwood, Sept. 7, 1940; children: Diane Elaine Bryan Lyon, Barbara Norwood Bryan Bardo; m. Dorothy Darr MacKenzie, Aug. 11, 1961; m. Gertrude B. Bruneau, Feb. 10, 1978. AB summa cum laude, Oberlin Coll., 1934; PhD, Yale, 1939. Instr. econs. Yale U., 1935-36, 37-39, Princeton U., 1936-37; economist Lionel D. Edie & Co., Inc., N.Y.C., 1939-40, asst. v.p., 1943-45, v.p., 1946-48; price exec., rubber br. OPA, 1941-42; economist Goodyear Aircraft Corp., Akron, Ohio, 1943; with J.H. Whitney & Co., N.Y.C., 1948-50, partner, 1951-59; financial v.p., treas., dir. Whitney Communications Corp., 1959-69; ret., 1969. Ptnr. Whitcom Investment Co., 1967-69. Mem. exec. com. Yale Grad. Sch. Council, 1969-73; trustee Oberlin Coll., 1960-70. Mem. Am. Mgmt. Assn. (fin. coun. 1952-55), Gulfstream Golf Club, Gulfstream Bath and Tennis Club, Ocean Club, Ekwanok Country Club, Phi Beta Kappa. Home: Delray Beach, Fla. Died May 16, 2002.

BRYAN, ROBERT J. federal judge; b. Bremerton, Wash., Oct. 29, 1934; s. James W. and Vena Gladys (Jensen) B.; m. Cathy Ann Welander, June 14, 1958; children: Robert James, Ted Lorin, Ronald Terence. BA, U. Wash., 1956, JD, 1958. Bar: Wash. 1959, U.S. Dist. Ct. (we. dist.) Wash. 1959, U.S. Tax Ct. 1965, U.S. Ct. Appeals (9th cir.) 1985. Assoc., then ptnr. Bryan & Bryan, Bremerton, 1959-67; judge Superior Ct., Port Orchard, Wash., 1967-84; ptnr. Riddell, Williams, Bullitt & Walkinshaw, Seattle, 1984-86; judge U.S. Dist. Ct. (we. dist.) Wash., Tacoma, 1986—. Mem. State Jail Comm., Olympia, Wash., 1974-76, Criminal Justice Tng. Com., Olympia, 1978-81, State Bd. on Continuing Legal Edn., Seattle, 1984-86; mem., sec. Jud. Qualifications Commn., Olympia, 1982-83; chair Wash. Fed.-State Jud. Coun., 1997-98. Author: (with others) Washington Pattern Jury Instructions (civil and criminal vols. and supplements), 1970-85, Manual of Model Criminal Jury Instructions for the Ninth Circuit, 1992, Manual of Model Civil Jury Instruction for the Ninth Circuit, 1993. Chmn. 9th Ct. Jury Com., 1991-92; bd. dirs. Fed. Jud. Ctr., 2000—. Served to maj. USAR. Mem.: 9th Cir. Dist. Judges Assn. (sec.-treas. 1997—99, v.p. 1999—2001, pres. 2001—03). Office: US Dist Ct 1717 Pacific Ave Rm 4427 Tacoma WA 98402-3234

BRYAN, ROSEMARIE LUISE, lawyer; b. Erlangen, Germany, May 20, 1951; arrived in U.S., 1956; d. Rudolf and Elise (Lindner) Schöfer; m. Bates William Bryan Jr., Jan. 6, 1990. BA in English, George Mason U., Fairfax, Va., 1981; JD, U. Va., 1984. Bar: Tenn. 1985, U.S. Dist. Ct. (ea., mid. and we. dists.) Tenn., U.S. Ct. Appeals (6th cir.), U.S. Supreme Ct. Mng. shareholder Shumacker Witt Gaither & Whitaker, Chattanooga, 1984—. Bd. dirs., sec., treas. Families, Inc., Chattanooga, 1989-94; bd. dirs. Family and Children's Svcs., Inc., Chattanooga, 1986-93; dir., v.p. pers. Girls Inc., 1995-97, pres., 1997-2000; bd. dirs. Tenn. River Gorge Trust, 2001—03, Boys Club/Girls Club, 2003—,Ballet Tenn., 2003—. Fellow Tenn. Bar Found., Chattanooga Bar Found., Internat. Soc. Barristers; mem. Tenn. Bar Assn. (dir. litigation sect. 1987-88), Chattanooga Bar Assn. (dir. 1988-90). Roman Catholic. Avocation: fishing. Office: ShumackerWitt Gaither&Whitaker 736 Market St Ste 1100 Chattanooga TN 37402-4856 Fax: 423-266-4138. E-mail: rbryan@swgwlaw.com.

BRYAN, SHARON ANN, lawyer; b. Kansas City, Mo., Dec. 18; d. George William and Dorothy Joan (Henn) Goll; children: Lisa Ann, Holly Renee. BJ, U. Mo., 1963; diploma, Stanford Radio and TV Inst., 1961; postgrad., NYU Sch. Arts and Sci., 1963-64; cert. personal fin. planning profl., UCLA, 1986; JD, U. So. Calif., 1989. Cert. specialist in family law. Proofreader, copy editor Cadwalader, Wickersham and Taft, N.Y.C., 1963-64; manuscript editor, writer nonsci. sects. N.Y. State Jour. Medicine, Med. Soc. State N.Y., N.Y.C., also mng. editor Staffoscope, 1965-66; manuscript editor Transactions, editor Perceiver Am. Acad. Ophthalmology and Otolaryngology, Rochester, Minn., 1969-72, hist. writer, 1972-82; atty. Burkley, Moore, Greenberg & Lyman, Torrance, Calif., 1989-91; with Christopher M. Moore & Assocs., 1991-99, Moore, Bryan & Schroff, 1999—. Writer publicity articles Ft. Lee (Va.) Cmty. Theatre; mediator Dept. 2 Superior Ct. of Calif., Ctrl. Dist. and Dept SWJ, S.W. Dist. Author: Pioneering Specialists: History of the American Academy of Ophthalmology and Otolaryngology, 1982. Vol. honor roll soc. Meml. Sloan-Kettering Cancer Ctr.; active N.Y. Hosp. Women's League, 1965-67; docent L.A. County Mus. Natural History, 1982-86; vol. Harriet Buhai Ctr., 1990-97; pres. Malaga Cove Homeowners Assn., 1999-2000. Mem.: NOW, ATLA, ABA, Assn. Cert. Family Law Specialists (bd. dirs. 2003—), South Bay Women Lawyers Assn. (rec. sec. 1994—95, pres. 1996—97), Los Angeles County Bar Assn. (exec. com. 1996—98, family law sect. exec. com. 2001—, del. to State Bar Calif.), Women's Lawyers Assn. L.A (bd. govs. 1991—97, chmn. family law sect. 1993—97), N.Y. Acad. Scis., Am. Med. Writers Assn. (editor conv. bull. 1966), Kappa Alpha Theta (chmn. membership com. N.Y. chpt. 1966), Kappa Tau Alpha. Home: 533 Via Del Monte Palos Verdes Estates CA 90274-1205 Office: 21515 Hawthorne Blvd Ste 490 Torrance CA 90503 E-mail: sharon@mbslawcorp.com.

BRYAN, THOMAS LYNN, lawyer, educator; b. Wichita, Kans., June 10, 1935; s. Herbert Thomas and Ruth Marjorie (Williams) B.; m. Virginia Alice Cooper, June 13, 1981; children from previous marriage— Victoria Lynne Hague, Douglas Edward BA, U. Kans., 1957; LLB, Columbia U., 1960. Bar: N.Y. Assoc. Willkie Farr & Gallagher, N.Y.C., 1960-66, ptnr., 1967-92; adj. prof. Stetson U. Coll. Law, 1993-97. Co-author: Business Acquisitions, 1971, 2d edit. 1981 Mem. Longboat Key Club, Upper Ridgewood Tennis Club, Phi Beta Kappa Republican. Avocations: tennis, sports, golf, theatre. Home: 77 Lakewood Ave Ho Ho Kus NJ 07423-1507 also: 3448 Mistletoe Ln Longboat Key FL 34228-4146

BRYAN, WENDELL HOBDY, II, (HOB BRYAN), state senator; b. Amory, Miss., Dec. 5, 1952; s. Wendell Hobdy and Nadine (Morgan) B. BA, Miss. State U., 1974; JD, U. Va., 1977. Bar: Miss. 1977. Pvt. practice, Amory, 1977—; senator Miss. Senate, 1984—; chmn. Senate Fin. Com., 1996-99, Senate Elections Com., 2000—. Democrat. Baptist. Office: PO Box 75 205 Main St Amory MS 38821-0075

BRYANT, ARTHUR H. lawyer; b. Harrisburg, Pa., Aug. 11, 1954; s. Albert Irwin and Marjorie (Weinrib) B.; m. Nancy Kaye Johnson, Aug. 17, 1991; 1 stepchild, Vinnie Johnson; 1 child, Wallace Johnson Bryant. AB with hons., Swarthmore Coll., 1976; JD, Harvard U., 1979; D (hon.), Ripon Coll., 1998. Bar: Pa. 1981, U.S. Dist. Ct. (ea. dist.) Pa. 1981, U.S. Ct. Appeals (3d cir.) Pa. 1981, U.S. Ct. Appeals (11th cir.) Ga. 1985, U.S. Ct. Appeals (6th cir.) Ohio 1986, U.S. Ct. appeals (D.C. cir.) 1986, U.S. Ct. Appeals (9th cir.) Calif. 1987, U.S. Ct. Appeals (7th cir.) Ill. 1988, U.S. Ct. Appeals (5th cir.) Tex. 1988, D.C., 1989, U.S. Supreme Ct. 1989, U.S. Ct. Appeals (1st cir.) 1996. Intern Rosenman, Colin & Freund, N.Y.C., 1978, N.Y. Civil Liberties Union, N.Y.C., 1978, Cambridge & Somerville Legal Svcs., Cambridge, Pa., 1979; law clk. U.S. Dist. Ct. (so. dist.), Tex., 1979-80; atty. Kohn, Savett, Marion & Graf., Phila., 1980-84; staff atty. Trial Lawyers for Pub. Justice, Washington, 1984-87, exec. cir., 1987—. Recipient George Moscone Meml. award Consumer Atty. Assn. L.A., 2003; named one of 20 young lawyers making a difference in the world ABA Barrister mag., 1991, one of 50 most influential people in coll. sports Coll. Sports Mag., 1994, one of 45 lawyers whose vision and commitment are changing lives The Am. Lawyer, 1997, one of 100 most influential lawyers in Am. Nat. Law Jour., 2000; recipient Wasserstein Pub. Interest law fellowship, 1996. Mem. ABA (Pursuit of Justice award 2003), ATLA. Office: Trial Lawyers Pub Justice Ste 275 One Kaiser Plaza Oakland CA 94612

BRYANT, BARBARA EVERITT, academic researcher, market research consultant, former federal agency administrator; b. Ann Arbor, Mich., Apr. 5, 1926; d. William Littell and Dorothy (Wallace) Everitt; m. John H. Bryant, Aug. 14, 1948; children: Linda Bryant Valentine, Randal F., Lois. AB, Cornell U., 1947; MA, Mich. State U., 1967, PhD, 1970; HonD, U. Ill., 1993. Editor art Chem. Engring. mag. McGraw-Hill Pub. Co., N.Y.C., 1947-48; editl. rsch. asst. U. Ill., Urbana, 1948-49, free-lance editor, writer, 1950-61; with continuing edn. adminstrn. dept. Oakland Univ., Rochester, Mich., 1961-66; grad. rsch. asst. Mich. State U., East Lansing, 1966-70; sr. analyst to v.p. Market Opinion Rsch., Detroit, 1970-77, sr. v.p., 1977-89; dir. Bur. of the Census, U.S. Dept. Commerce, 1989-93; rsch. scientist Sch. Bus. Adminstrn., U. Mich., 1993—. Author: High School Students Look at Their World, 1970, American Women Today & Tomorrow, 1977, Moving Power and Money: The Politics of Census Taking, 1995; contbr. articles to profl. jours. Mem. U.S. Census Adv. Com., Washington, 1980—86, Mich. Job Devel. Authority, Lansing, 1980—85; state editor LWV of Mich., 1959—61; bd. dirs. Roper Ctr. for Pub. Opinion Rsch., 1993—; mem. nat. adv. com. Inst. for Social Rsch., U. Mich., 1993—. Fellow: Am. Statis. Assn.; mem.: Am. Assn. Pub. Opinion Rsch., Am. Mktg. Assn. (pres. Detroit 1976—77, midwestern v.p. 1978—80, v.p. mktg. rsch. 1982—84, found. trustee 1993—2001), Rotary, Cosmos Club. Republican. Presbyterian. Avocation: swimming. Home: 1505 Sheridan Dr Ann Arbor MI 48104-4051 Office: U Mich Sch Bus Ann Arbor MI 48109-1234 E-mail: bryantb@umich.edu.

BRYANT, BERTHA ESTELLE, retired nurse; b. Va., Jan. 11, 1927; d. E.F. and Julia B. Diploma, Sibley Meml. Hosp., Washington, 1947; BS, Am. U., 1948; MA, Tchrs. Coll., Columbia U., 1962. Staff nurse, head nurse NIH, Bethesda, Md., 1954-59; asst. dir. nursing USPHS Alaska Native Hosp., Mt. Edgecumbe, 1959-61; instr. Sch. Nursing, U. Mich., 1962-64; chief div. clin. nursing Bur. Nursing, D.C. Dept. Public Health, Washington, 1964-65; commd. Nurse Corps, USPHS, 1965, nurse dir., capt., 1974—. Nurse cons., hosp. facilities services br., div. hosps. and med. facilities Bur. Health Services, HEW, Silver Spring; nurse cons., social analysis br., div. health services research and analysis Nat. Center Health Services Research, Health Resources Adminstrn., HEW, Rockville, Md.; nurse cons. div. extramural research Nat. Center Health Services Research, Office Asst. Sec. Health, HHS, Hyattsville, Md., 1977-81 Contbr. articles to profl. jours. Mem. AAUW, Assn. Mil. Surgeons U.S., Commd. Officers Assn. USPHS

BRYANT, CARMEN JULIA, missionary, educator; b. Redding, Calif., Apr. 25, 1943; d. Ray Kenneth Michaels and Nettie Pearl Bradley; m. Donald Roy Bryant, June 1, 1963; children: Julia Lynn Webster, Brenda Sue Dodd, James Robert. BA in Spanish, Pacific U., Forest Grove, Oreg., 1964; MA in Exegetical Theology, Western Sem., Portland, 1992, ThM, 2000. Lic. Oreg., 2000. Tchr. Forest Grove (Oreg.) Pub. Sch., 1964—65; missionary, Bible translator CB Internat., Indonesia, 1969—92, missionary educator, 1992—97; missionary Mission to the Ams., Portland, 1997—; adj. prof. theol. writing Western Sem., Portland, 1998—2000; adj. prof. writing and Spanish Multnomah Bible Coll., Portland, 1999—. Mem.: Evang. Theol. Soc. Conservative. Baptist. Achievements include first to reduce two Dayak tribal languages to writing and developed dictionaries for the languages (Borneo). Avocation: piano. Home: 1285 SE Maple St Hillsboro OR 97123 Office: Multnomah Bible Coll 8435 NE Glisan St Portland OR 97220 Office Fax: 503-254-1268. Personal E-mail: carmenhills@earthlink.net. E-mail: cjbryant@multnomah.edu.

BRYANT, CLIFTON DOW, sociologist, educator; b. Jackson, Miss., Dec. 25, 1932; s. Clifton Edward and Helen (Dow) B.; m. Nancy Ann Arrington, Sept. 13, 1953; m. Patty Maurine Watts, Feb. 1, 1957; children: Melinda Dow, Deborah Carol, Karen Diane, Clifton Dow II. Student, U. Miss., 1950-53, BA, 1956, MA, 1957; postgrad., U. N.C., Chapel Hill, 1957-58, La. State U., 1958-60, PhD, 1964. Vis. instr. dept. sociology and anthropology Pa. State U., summer, 1958; instr., rsch. assoc. dept. sociology and anthropology U. Ga., 1960-63; asst. prof., assoc. prof., chmn. dept. sociology and anthropology Millsaps Coll., Jackson, Miss., 1963-67; summer research participant, tng. and tech. project Oak Ridge Asso. Univs., summer 1967; prof., head dept. sociology and anthropology Western Ky. U., Bowling Green, Ky., 1967-72; prof. sociology Va. Poly. Inst. and State U., Blacksburg, 1972—; head dept. Va Poly. Inst. and State U., Blacksburg, 1972-82. Vis. prof. Xavier U., Philippines, 1984-85, vis. prof., vis. rsch. scholar Miss. Alcohol Safety Edn. Program, Miss. State U., (summer), 1985; vis. Fulbright prof. dept. grad. inst. sociology Nat. Taiwan U., Taipei, Republic of China, 1987-88; vis. scientist U.S. Army summer faculty rsch. and engring. program, 1993; participant Fulbright-Hays Seminar Abroad program, Hungary, 1993, China, 1998. Author: Khaki-Collar Crime: Deviant Behavior in Military Context, 1979, Sexual Deviancy and Social Proscription, 1982; editor and contbr.: Deviant Behavior: Occupational and Organizational Bases, 1974, The Social Dimensions of Work, 1972, Sexual Deviancy in Social Context, 1977, Deviant Behavior: Readings in the Sociology of Norm Violations, 1990; editor-in-chief: The Encyclopedia of Criminology and deviant Behavior, 4 vols., 2001, Death and Dying: A Reference Handbook, 2 vols., 2003; co-editor, contbr.: Deviancy and the Family, 1973, The Rural Work Force: Nonagricultural Occupations in America, 1985; compiler: Handbook of Audio-Visual Resources to Accompany Social Problems Today, 1971; editor: Social Problems Today: Dilemmas and Dissensus, 1971; co-editor: Introductory Sociology: Selected Readings for the College Scene, 1970; editor in chief Deviant Behavior: An Interdisciplinary Jour., 1978-91; editor So. Sociologist, 1970-74; mem. editorial bd. Criminology: An Interdisciplinary Jour, 1978-91; chmn. editorial policy bd., founding editor-in-Chief Deviant Behavior: An Interdisciplinary Journal, 1992—; chmn. editorial bd. Sociol. Symposium, 1968-80; assoc. editor Sociol. Forum, 1979-80, Sociol. Spectrum, 1981-85; mem. bd. adv. editors Sociol. Inquiry, 1981-85, assoc. editor, 1997—; bd. editors Society and Animals, 1997—; assoc. editor spl. issue Marriage and Family Relations, fall 1982, Sociological Inquiry, 1997—; contbr. chpts. to books, articles, book reviews to profl. publs. Served to 1st lt., M.P. U.S. Army, 1953-55. Recipient E. Gordon Ericksen Outstanding Grad. Faculty award sociology dept. Va. Poly. Inst. and State U., 1992, 93, spl. award for continuing contbn. to undergrad. tchg. enterprise, 1992, Undergraduate Tchg. Excellence award, 1995-96, 2001. Mem. Am. Sociol. Assn., Am. Soc. Criminology, So. Sociol. Soc. (pres. 1978-79, Disting. Book award 2001), Mid-South Sociol. Assn. (pres. 1981-82, Disting. Career award 1991), Rural Sociol. Soc., Soc. Anthropology of Work, Internat. Sociol. Assn., Inter-Univ. Seminar on Armed Forces and Society, So. Assn. Agr. Scientists, Omicron Delta Kappa, Phi Kappa Phi, Alpha Phi Omega, Alpha Kappa Delta, Pi Kappa Alpha, Phi Beta Delta. Presbyterian. Home: 1724 E Ridge Dr Blacksburg VA 24060-8568 Office: Va Poly Inst State U Dept Sociology Blacksburg VA 24061 E-mail: cbryant@vt.edu.

BRYANT, DANIEL J. federal agency administrator; married; 2 children. Bachelor Degree, JD, Am. U.; Masters Degree, Oxford (Eng.) U. Law clk., spl. asst. U.S. Dept. Justice, 1987—92; mem. permanent subcom. on investigatiosn U.S. Senate Gov. Affairs Com.; speech writer former Atty. Gen. William Barr; policy dir. First Freedom Coalition, 1994—95; majority counsel Crime Subcom., 1995—99; majority chief counsel House Judicary Com. Crime Subcom., 1999—2001; asst. atty. gen. legis. affairs U.S. Dept. Justice, Washington, 2001—. Office: US Dept Justice Office Legis Affairs 950 Pennsylvania Ave NW Washington DC 20530

BRYANT, DENNIS MICHAEL, publisher, educator; b. Austin, Tex., June 30, 1947; s. L.D. and Mildred (Perkins) B.; m. Nancy Louthan, Apr. 17, 1976; children: Michael, Sarah. BS, Trinity U., 1970. Sales mgr. Southland Equipment Co., Houston, 1973-74; mgr., equipment specialist Briggs Weaver Co., San Antonio, 1974-81; life ins. specialist N.Y. Life Ins. Co., San Antonio, 1981-85; territorial ins. specialist Merrill Lynch Life Agy., San Antonio, 1985-86; life and group ins. mgr. Cen. Fin. Ins. Svcs., San Antonio, 1986—, owner Bryant Agy./Trinity Fin. Concepts, San Antonio, 1988-92; chmn. Focus on Growth, Inc., 1993—. Chmn. Focus on Growth, Inc. Active Project Any Baby Can, San Antonio, 1983-88, pres. 1984-85. 1st lt. U.S. Army, 1971-73. Republican. Avocations: skiing, running, flying. Home: 110 Skyvue Ave New Braunfels TX 78132 4635

BRYANT, DON ESTES, economist, scientist; b. Truman, Ark., May 18, 1917; s. James Monroe and Olivia (Mayfield) B.; m. Jess Ann Chailer, Jan. 27, 1956; children: Stephen Williamson (dec.), Patrice Ann. Student, Cass Tech. Trade Coll., 1938-41. Pres., founder Consol. Aircraft Products, El Segundo, Calif., 1949-57, Trilan Corp., El Segundo, 1957-62, The Am. Inventor, Palos Verdes Estates, Calif., 1962-68; chmn., founder Message Control Crop., Palos Verdes Estates, 1968-70; scientist Econ. Rsch., Palos Verdes Estates and Lake Arrowhead, Calif., 1970—. Cons. Svc. Corps. Ret. Execs. Assn.-SBA, L.A., 1965-67; founder Bryant Inst. and Club U.S.A. (United to Save Am.), 1991, J. Ayn Bryant and Assocs., 1991. Inventor missle and satellite count-down systems for USAF; formulator sci. of human econs.; host TV talk show World Peace Through Free Enterprise, 1985; author: 10-book children's series The 1, 2, 3's of Freedom and Economics, 1988. Served with USN, 1935-37. Republican. Roman Catholic. Avocations: sailing, woodworking. Home: 329 Greenview Ln Fallbrook CA 92028-1864

BRYANT, DONALD ASHLEY, molecular biologist; b. LaGrange, Ky., Mar. 12, 1950; s. Roger William Jr. and Wanda Lillian (Partin) B.; m. Rita Jean Corio, July 20, 1974 (div. Aug. 1988); m. Veronica Lynne Stirewalt, Aug. 24, 1991. BSc in Chemistry, MIT, 1972; PhD in Molecular Biology, UCLA, 1977. Postdoctoral assoc. Pasteur Inst., Paris, 1977-79, Cornell U., Ithaca, N.Y., 1979-81; prof. biochemistry and molecular biology Pa. State U., University Park, 1981—, Ernest C. Pollard prof. biotech., 1992. Vis. prof. Swiss Fed. Tech. U., Zurich, 1989-90, Australian Nat. U., Canberra, 1996-97. Assoc. editor Archives of Mircobiology, 1988-98, Photosynthesis Rsch., 1988-98; mem. editl. bd. Jour. Bacteriology, 1986-91; editor 3 books in field; contbr. articles to profl. jours., chpts. to books. Mem. AAAS, Am. Acad. Microbiology, Am. Soc. Microbiology, Am. Soc. Plant Physiology, Am. Soc. Biochemistry and Molecular Biology, Internat. Soc. Plant Molecular Biology, Internat. Soc. Photosynthesis Rsch. Democrat. E-mail: dab14@psu.edu.

BRYANT, DONALD LOYD, insurance company executive; b. Orchard, Iowa, Jan. 30, 1919; s. Lester E. and Bessie (Farless) B.; m. Eileen Galloway, May 11, 1941; children: Donald Loyd, Hedy E. Bryant Garlock, Brenda K., Becky Bryant Hubert. B.Ed., So. Ill. U., 1940. With War Manpower Commn., Mt. Vernon, Ill., 1940; agt., dist. mgr. Equitable Life Assurance Soc. U.S., Elgin and Carbondale, Ill., 1946-54, agy. mgr. St. Louis, 1954-69, v.p., chief agy. staff ops. N.Y.C., 1969-71, v.p. corp. relations, 1971-72, sr. v.p. corp. relations, 1972-74, exec. v.p., spl. asst. to pres., 1974-78, exec. v.p., 1978-81. Bus exec.-in-residence Tex. Christian U., Ft. Worth, 1980— ; cons. Nat. Exec. Services Corp.; bus. exec.-in-residence So. Ill. U. Served to lt. USN, 1942-46. Recipient Alumni Achievement award So. Ill. U., 1964, 88. Mem.: Quail Ridge Golf and Tennis (Boynton Beach, Fla.). Presbyterian. Home and Office: 1489 Partridge Pl N Boynton Beach FL 33436-5409 *On each job, behave as though you will be on that job for the remainder of your working life. In this way you avoid mistakes because you'd have to live with those mistakes. You are careful to pick good associates because you will have to live with them forever. You give security to your subordinates, command their loyalty, because they sense you'll be there forever. Ironically you'll then do such a superior job that you'll be promoted over and over while behaving as though you'll be on your job forever.*

BRYANT, DOUGLAS E. public health service official; BS in Health Edn., U. S.C., 1976, MPH, 1981. Communicable disease investigator S.C. Dept. Health & Environ. Control, 1976—78, dist. dir. Upper Savannah Health Dist., 1982—85, dir. office primary care, 1986—87, asst. to commr., 1987—93, commr., 1993—; dir. specialized health care svcs. S.C. Dept. Corrections, 1978—81; asst. adminstr. State Pk. Health Ctr., 1981—82; interim exec. dir. Orangeburg Family Health Ctrs., Inc., 1985—86. Adv. bd., bd. visitors Lander Coll.; adj. prof. dept. health adminstrn. U. S.C.; adv. bd. AHEC Rural Physician, Athletic Trainers. Mem.: So. Health Assn., S.C. Pub. Health Assn., Am. Coll. Hosp. Adminstrs., Delta Omega. Office: Dept Health & Environ Control 2600 Bull St Columbia SC 29201-1708

BRYANT, EDWARD, former congressman, lawyer; b. Jackson, Tenn., Sept. 7, 1948; m. Cyndi Lemons; 3 children. BA, U. Miss., 1970, JD, 1972. With U.S. Army Judge Advocate Gen.'s Corps, 1972-78; army prosecutor Ft. Carlson, 1975-77; legal instr. U.S. Mil. Acad., 1977-78; ptnr. Waldrop & Hall, 1978-91, 93-95; U.S. atty. Western Dist. of Tenn., 1991-93; mem. U.S. Congress from 7th Tenn. dist., 1995—2002; mem. energy and commerce com. Republican.

BRYANT, EDWARD CURTIS, college admissions consultant; b. Albany, N.Y., Oct. 23, 1925; s. Wilbur Curtis and Hilda Elizabeth (Lauritzen) B.; m. Mary Lou Ellis, Dec. 1, 1972; children: Ellen Bryant Aulson, Diane Bryant (dec. 1968), Curt Bryant, Kim Bryant Watson, Daron Jacobs, Carrie Burns. BS, Boston U., 1950, MS, 1951, Cert. Advanced Grad. Specialization, 1953; EdD, U. Palm Beach, 1970; HHD (hon.), Sussex (Eng.) Coll. Tech., 1970. Nat. cert. counselor and career counselor. Tchr., coach Weston (Mass.) Pub. Schs., 1951-52, Melrose (Mass.) Pub. Schs., 1952-53; counselor Boston U., 1953-58, sailing coach, asst. dean men, 1958-62; guidance dir. Masconomet Regional H.S., Boxford, Mass., 1962-66; pres. Bryant-McIntosh Jr. Coll., Lawrence, Mass., 1966-69; guidance dir. Rockport H.S., 1970-82; edn. specialist USN, Boston, 1982-88; past exec. dir. Mass. Sch. Counselors Assn., Ipswich, 1988-94; interim dean of students Newburyport H.S., Mass., 1998-99. Admissions counselor USCG Acad., Norwich U.; past mem. Nat. Def. Exec. Res., Washington, 1988-94, area coord. U.S. Naval Acad. Admissions, 1990—; vice chmn. mil. affairs com. bd. fellows Norwich U., Northfield, Vt., 1983-99. Monthly columnist Ed's View (several leadership awards 1970—), MSCA. Chmn. Winthrop (Mass.) Sch. Bd., 1956-62; mem. Masconomet Sch. Bd., 1967-71, Employer Support Guard and Res., 1998—; pres. Parents Assn. Norwich U., 1979-82, North Shore Guidance Dirs., 1990—2002; pres. New Eng. Safe Boating Coun., 1982—, exec. dir., 1982-98, Mass. Career Devel. Assn., 1996—, pres., 1996—; mem. recruiting dist. adv. coun. USN, 1973—, admissions coun., 1977—; Mass. Exec. Com. Capt. USCG, USN, 1943-46, USCGR, 1958 82. Recipient Tchr.'s medal Freedoms Found., 1962, Educator's medal, 1981, commendation medal, 1973, USCG, 1982, Achievement medal USCG, 1982, Recruiting ribbon, 1997, Brotherhood citation NCCJ, 1962, leadership award Navy Recruiting Dist. Assistance Coun., 1988, U.S. Naval Acad. Commandants award, 1994, U.S. Naval Acad. Alumni award, New Eng., 1997, Admissions award U.S. Coast Guard, 1999, WWII Asiatic-Pacific medal, WWII Am. Campaign medal, Cold War certificate. Mem. Mass. Sch. Counselors Assn. (hon. trustee 1999), New Eng. Conf. Counseling and Devel. (bd. dirs. 1983-93, Leadership award 1999), Mass. Coll. Pers. Assn. (Leadership award 1986), Mass. Career Devel. Assn. (pres. 1998—), Mass. Sch. Counselors Assn. (Leadership award 1988), Northeast Counselors Assn. (pres. 1998-99, 2002-03), North Shore Guidance Dirs. (pres. 1966, 93-02, Hall of Fame award 1985), Res. Officers Assn. (life, Mass. chpt. pres. 1974-75, Leadership award 1975), USCG Aux. (flotilla comdr. Mass. 1984-99, Recruiting award 1990), Navy League (bd. dirs. Mass. Bay Coun., pres. 1983-84, cert. of merit 1986), Am. Legion (post comdr. Boxford 1971, 88, 90, 91), Rotary (pres. Ipswich 1990-91, Paul Harris fellow), VFW (life, judge adv. 1999—). Republican. Avocations: golf, boating, walking, travel, grandchildren. Home and Office: 90 Topsfield Rd Ipswich MA 01938-1648 E-mail: captecb29@aol.com.

BRYANT, GEORGE MCEWAN, lawyer; b. NYC, Nov. 24, 1941; s. Sydney James and Ruth Cutter (McEwan) B.; m. Barbara Ann Phyfe, Sept. 10, 1966; children: Meredith Lee, Scott McEwan. BA, Brown U., 1963; LLB, Columbia U., 1966. Bar: N.J. 1966, N.Y. 1969, U.S. Dist. Ct. N.J. 1966. Assoc. Cravath Swaine & Moore, NYC, 1968-72, Marshall Brattner Greene Allison & Tucker, NYC, 1972-74, Davies Hardy Ives & Lawther, NYC, 1974-77; asst. gen. counsel NY Life Ins. Co., NYC, 1977-96, Met. Life Ins. Co., NYC, 1996—. Bd. dirs., v.p. United Way of Ridgewood, Glen Rock and Ho-Ho-Kus, 1978-80; vice chmn. Ridgewood Republican Mcpl. Com., 1979-82; bd. dirs., treas. Ramapo Hunt and Polo Club Estates, 1983-90. Mem. ABA, Bergen County Bar Assn., The Moorings Country Club. Republican. Mem. Ref. Ch. in Am. Home: 207 Phelps Rd Ridgewood NJ 07450-1420 Office: Met Life Ins Co 10 Park Ave Morristown NJ 07962-1902 E-mail: gbryant@metlife.com.

BRYANT, HUBERT HALE, lawyer; b. Tulsa, Jan. 4, 1931; s. Roscoe Conkling and Curlie Beatrice (Marshall) B.; m. Elnora Geraldine Roberson, Oct. 25, 1952; children— Cheryl Denise, Tara Kay. BA, Fisk U., 1952; LL.B., Howard U., 1956. Bar: Okla. bar 1956, U.S. Dist. Ct. bar for No. Dist. Okla 1956, U.S. Ct. Appeals (10th cir.) 1967, U.S. Supreme Ct. bar 1980. Individual practice law, Tulsa, 1956-67, 81-84, 86—. Asst. city prosecutor, City of Tulsa, 1961-63, chief city prosecutor, 1963-67, asst. U.S. atty., No. Dist. Okla., 1967-77, U.S. atty., 1977-81; mcpl. ct. judge City of Tulsa, 1984-86. Trustee 1st Bapt. Ch., Tulsa, 1970-75, 96-2002; bd. dirs. Tulsa Urban League, 1962-64. Recipient Outstanding Alumni award Howard U. Sch. Law, 1981, 30 Yr. Outstanding African Am. Lawyer award Met. Tulsa Urban League, 1997 Mem. NAACP, Nat. Bar Assn. (Named to Hall of Fame), Okla. Bar Assn., Tulsa County Bar Assn., Okla. Trial Lawyers Assn., Nat. Set, Masons (named Mason of Yr. local chpt. 1963, Outstanding Citizen award 1978), Sigma Pi Phi, Alpha Theta Boule, Alpha Phi Alpha. Democrat. Home: 1818 N Boston St Tulsa OK 74106 Office: 2623 N Peoria Ave Tulsa OK 74106-2512

BRYANT, JAMES, pathologist; b. Chgo., Feb. 18, 1950; s. Harold and Esther (Gooder) B.; m. Joy Ann Cwirla, Sept. 3, 1983; children: Peter, Kristy, Michael. BS, U. Ill., Chgo., 1971; MD, Loyola U., Chgo., 1974. Diplomate Am. Bd. Pathology. Resident Rush-Presbyn. St. Luke's Med. Ctr., Chgo., 1975-78; attending pathologist Edgewater Hosp., Chgo., 1978-80, Meth. Hosp. Gary, Ind., 1980; chief pathologist Glendale Heights (Ill.) Community Hosp., 1980-85; chmn. pathology Provident Med. ctr., Chgo., 1985-86; pvt. practice Chgo., 1986—. Cons. Cir. Ct. Cook County, Chgo., 1982—, U.S. Dist. Ct., Chgo., 1989—. Contbr. articles to sci. publs. Recipient Physician's Recognition award AMA, 1979. Fellow Am. Soc. Clin. Pathologists; mem. AAAS, Am. Soc. Cytology, N.Y. Acad. Scis. Republican. Achievements include invention of rapid tissue processing for histopathology, original description selective deficiency Immunoglobulin G in serum, herpes simplex hepatitis, induction malignant skin neoplasm by long-standing benign neoplasm; correlation between tissue levels of thromboxane synthetase and patterns of cancer metastases. Office: 105 W Adams St # 3900 Chicago IL 60603-4109

BRYANT, J(AMES) BRUCE, lawyer; b. Dettlebach, Fed. Republic Germany, Jan. 23, 1961; came to U.S., 1964; s. John Thomas and Doris Jean (Hazenbuahler) B.; 1 child, James Bruce II. BA, Northwestern State U., Natchitoches, La., 1984; MJ, La. State, 1986; JD, Miss. Coll., 1989. Bar: Miss., Tex. 1995, U.S. Dist. Ct. (no. and so. dists.) Miss., U.S. Ct. Appeals (5th cir.) La. 1991, U.S. Dist. Ct. (we. dist.) La. 1994. With residential life La. State U., Baton Rouge, 1985-86; law libr. worker Miss. Coll. Sch. Law, Jackson, 1986-87; clk. Brunini Law Firm, Jackson, 1987-88; ptnr. Cook & Bryant, Bay St. Louis, Miss., 1989-90; assoc. Cook, Yancey, King & Galloway, Shreveport, La., 1990-93; prof. bus. law La. State U., 1991-92, prof. paralegal sci., 1994-96; staff atty. State of La. Office of Support Enforcement, Shreveport, 1993-95; atty. Storm Operating Co. Inc. of La., 1994-98; sr. regional atty. State of La. Dept. Health and Hosps., Shreveport-Bossier City, La., 1995—; prof. comms. law, pub. rels and advt. Northwestern State U., 1996—; spl. asst. dist. atty. 1st Jud. Dist., Caddo Parish, La., 1998—. Bd. dirs. Extra Mile; cons. Wyman Fed. Credit Union, Geismar, La., 1989-90, Comml. Nat. Bank, Shreveport, 1990-93; owner, pres. SHOWBIZZ Entertainment Agys., Shreveport, 1992—; v.p. Godfather Prodns., Inc., Shreveport-Bossier City, La., 1994—; owner La. Ctr. for Law and Justice, 1995—; spl. asst. dist. atty. Caddo Parish, 1998—; owner, pres. Dreamworks Internat., 1999—. Editor, author (with others): Art & Bylaws for Moot Court, 1989; contbr. to The Silence Within, 2000. Del. Republican Dist. IV, 1994—; bd. dirs. Shreveport Little Theatre, 1995-2000, Extra Mile, 1996—; vol. N.W. La. Coalition for Mentally Ill, 1995—, pres., 2002-; vol. Shreveport/Bossier Svc. Connection, 2001—; mem. L.A. Pro Bono Project, Tex. Bar Assn. Pro Bono Project (Outstanding Svc. Award 2002). Recipient Outstanding Svc. award, Tex. State Bar Pro Bono Project, 2002. Mem. ABA, La. Bar Assn. (mem. health law sect.), Pro Bono Project, Miss. Bar Assn., Assn. Trial Lawyers Am., La. Trial Lawyers Assn., Hancock County Bar Assn. (social chmn.), Shreveport Bar Assn. (comml. litigation sect., editor newsletter), TKE Alumni Assn. (pres.), Univ. Club (mem. com. 1994—). Roman Catholic. Avocations: martial arts, weightlifting, skiing, shooting. Home: PO Box 444 Shreveport LA 71162-0444 Office: La Ctr for Law and Justice 711 Texas Advocates Bldg Shreveport LA 71120

BRYANT, JANICE ANN, special education department administrator; b. Ada, OK, Mar. 11, 1955; d. Virgil and Corine Townsend; m. Larry Paul Bryant, Mar. 16, 1985; children: Samuel Paul, Mark Nathaniel. BS in Edn, E Ctrl Univ, Ada, OK, 1973—77, MEd, 1978—80. Cert. tchr. mental retardation OK, elem. edn. OK, 7th/8th gr. Social Studies OK, learning disabilities tchr. OK, reading specialist OK. Mem.: Oklahoma Dirs. Spl. Svcs. Baptist. Avocations: gardening, needlecrafts, cooking.

BRYANT, JANNIE, accountant; b. Corpus Christi, Tex., Aug. 10, 1956; d. Robert Hall Finn and Laura Frances Passmore; m. Bill Bryant, July 4, 1997; children: Cynthia Katherine, Charles Robert Sadler, Julie Marie Moeller, Susan Patricia Moeller. Acct., Hondo, Tex., 1991—99; exec. v.p. Ever Change, Hondo, 2000—. Vocat. Grant, Trull Found., 2002. Mem.: Rotary (assoc.). R-Liberal. Methodist. Avocations: horseback riding, travel. Home: 3040 Fm 2676 Hondo TX 78861 Office: Ever Change PO Box 61 Hondo TX 78861 Home Fax: 830-741-3799; Office Fax: 830-741-3799. Personal E-mail: cjbstar@hotmail.com.

BRYANT, JOHN, author, publisher; b. Washington, Oct. 26, 1943; Student, Antioch Coll., 1963; BA in Math., Am. U., 1968; postgrad. in philosophy of logic, Union Grad. Sch., Yellow Springs, Ohio, 1978-79. Founder, mgr. Socratic Press, St. Petersburg, Fla., 1986—, 701 Advt., St. Petersburg, 1986—. Author: The Mortal Works of J.B.R. Yant and Other Irritations, 1987, The Most Powerful Idea Ever Discovered, 1987, Success in Marriage Guaranteed, 1987, Bryant's Law and Other Broadsides, 1989, Systems Theory and Scientific Philosophy, 1991, Mortal Words Special Topics Series, 25 vols., 1994-97, others; creator Mortal Words Birds cartoon feature; columnist and cartoonist, Nationalist Times, 1994-98; editor, pub. Birdman's Weekly Internet Letter, 1998—; contbr. articles to profl. jours. Founder, dir. extended family program Unitarian Soc. Germantown, Phila. Mem. Mensa. Avocations: computers, tennis, futures trading, pigeons. E-mail: john@thebirdman.org. *It is nice to be loved, but it is better to be feared.*

BRYANT, JOHN BRADBURY, economics educator, consultant; b. July 7, 1947; s. Royal Calvin and Martha Preble (Jones) B.; m. Evelyn Sandra Seltzer, June 24, 1973; 1 child, Aryn Royale. BA, Oberlin Coll., 1969; MS, Carnegie-Mellon U., 1973, PhD, 1975. Economist, bd. govs. FRS, Washington, 1974-77; sr. economist Fed. Res. Bank, Mpls., 1977-81; assoc. prof. U. Fla., Gainesville, 1980-81; cons. Fed. Res. Bank, Dallas, 1983-86, 91-92; Fox assoc. prof. Rice U., Houston, 1981-84, Fox prof. econs., 1984—, prof. mgmt., 1987—. Vis. scholar Hoover Inst., Stanford U., 1988-89; vis. fellow Center, Tilburg U., Netherlands, 1998-99. Contbr. articles to profl. jours., books. Office: Rice U Dept Econs MS22 6100 Main St Houston TX 77005-1892

BRYANT, JOHN HOWARD, writer; b. Indpls., Ind., Aug. 24, 1938; s. Howard Gustav Bryant, Ruth Irene (Dunkin) Bryant; m. Kathe Bryant, Apr. 8, 1961; 1 child, Jeffrey Conan. BA in Philosophy, Marian Coll., 1991. Lectr. philosophy Ind. State U., Ind. Sch. Medicine, Internat. Soc. for value Inquiry, 2003, Ind. Sch. Medicine, World Congress of Phil., 2003, World Congress Philosophy, Istanbul, Turkey; presenter in field. Author: The Internat. Mag. of Electronics Technology, 1977, Proc. of Nat. Conf. on Ethics in Am., 1994—95; contbr. articles to profl. jours.; author: Korean Jour. of Thinking and Problem Solving, 1997—2000, (jour.) Sophia: A jour. for Philos. Theology and Cross-Cultural Philosophy of Religion and Ethics, 2000, New Horizons in Edn., 2000, (jour.) Sophia: A jour. for Philos. Theology and Cross-Cultural Philosophy of Religion and Ethics, 2002—03, Australian Friend, 2002, Korean Jour. of Thinking and Problem Solving, 2003. Mem.: Nat. Coun. Excellence in Critical Thinking, Viktor Frankl Inst. Logotherapy. Mem. Soc. Of Friends. Home: 1323 Almond Ct Plainfield IN 46168

BRYANT, JOHN WILEY, former congressman; b. Lake Jackson, Tex., Feb. 22, 1947; s. Robert Link and Billie Ray (Wiley) B.; m. Janet Elizabeth Watts, Dec. 28, 1968; children: Amy, John Wiley Jr., Jordan. BA, So. Meth. U., 1969; JD, So. Meth U., 1972. Bar: Tex. 1972. Chief counsel Tex. Senate Subcom. on Consumer Protection, Austin, 1973; adminstrv. asst. Tex. Senate, Austin, Dallas, 1972-73; mem. Tex. Ho. of Reps., 1973-83, 98th-103rd Congresses from 5th Tex. dist., Washington, D.C., 1983-96; former majority whip for Tex. U.S. House; mem. Glast, Phillips & Murray, Dallas. Mem. Ho. Com. on Energy and Commerce, Ho. Com. on Judiciary, Ho. Com. on Budget; chmn. The Bryant-Link Co.; U.S. amb. World Radiocomm. Conf., 1997. Chmn. World Affairs Coun. Greater Dallas. Named Hardest Working Legislator, Tex. Capital Press Corps, 1977, Outstanding Legislator, Tex. Monthly Mag., 1977, 1979; named one of Five Outstanding Young Texans, Tex. Jaycees, 1979. Mem. Hist. Preservation Soc., Lions Eye Bank (Dallas) (life). Democrat. United Methodist. Office: Glast Philips & Murray 13355 Noel Rd Ste 2200 Dallas TX 75240-1518

BRYANT, JOSEPHINE HARRIET, library executive; b. Oshawa, Ontario, Canada, Dec. 3, 1947; d. Donald Joseph and Margaret Mary (Quilty) B.; children: David Joseph, Michael Andrew. BA, U. Toronto, Ont., 1969, BLS, 1970, MLS, 1974; diploma in Pub. Adminstrn., U. Western Ont., London, 1988. Libr. Ont. Hydro, Toronto, 1970-74; libr. supr. Brampton Pub. Libr. and Art Gallery, Canada, 1974-77, br. head, 1977-79; regional dir. Fairview North York Pub. Libr., Canada, 1983-85, mgr. century libr., 1986, dep. dir., 1986-88, CEO, 1988-98; city libr. Toronto Pub. Libr., Canada, 1998—. Co-chair faculty info. sci. fundraising com. and dean's adv. com. U. Toronto. Co-chair U. Toronto Faculty Info. Sci. Fundraising com.; mem. U. Toronto Dean's Adv. com. Mem. ALA, Can. Libr. Assn., Ont. Libr. Assn., Inst. Pub. Adminstrn., Urban Libr. Coun., Bertelsmann Found., Can. Inst. for Hist. Micro-reprodns. Avocation: golf. Office: Toronto Pub Libr 789 Yonge St Toronto ON Canada M4W 2G8

BRYANT, KAREN WORSTELL, financial advisor, investment company executive; b. Cadillac, Mich., Sept. 7, 1942; d. Harley Orville and Rose Edith (Bell) Worstell; children: Lynda Jean Bashoor, Tracey Jo Taylor, Cynthia Jill Warren, Troy Thomas; m. Robert Melvin Bryant, Nov. 29, 1968. Student, Cen. Mich. U., 1963-67, Mich. State U., 1966, Johns Hopkins U., 1982-83, Loyola U., 1983. Sales rep. Xerox Corp., Southfield, Mich., 1972-74; cons. and employment contracts IBM World Trade Asia, The Policy Study Grp., Johnson & Johnson Internat., Tokyo, Japan, 1974-79; area sales mgr. Universal Plastics, McLean, Va., 1979-81; exec. product mgr. The Western Union Telegraph Co., Upper Saddle River, N.J., 1981-86; dir. mktg. and sales support The Nat. Guardian Corp., Greenwich, Conn., 1986-88; v.p., fin. cons. Salomon Smith Barney, Paramus, N.J., 1988-97; sr. v.p., fin. advisor Morgan Stanley, Pearl River, NY, 1997—. Guest lectr. for orgns.; guest on TV documentaries. Mem.: Bus. Network Internat., Nature Conservancy, Am. Lung Assn., World Wildlife Fedn., NY State Horse Coun., Haverstraw Marina. Avocations: horseback riding, power boating, decorating, horticulture. Home: Clermont on the Hudson One Main St 1301 Nyack NY 10960-3251 Office: Morgan Stanley Box 1726 One Blue Hill Plz 1st Fl Pearl River NY 10965-2535

BRYANT, KEITH LYNN, JR., history educator; b. Oklahoma City, Nov. 6, 1937; s. Keith Lynn and Elsie L. (Furman) B.; m. Margaret A. Burum, Aug. 14, 1962; children: Jennifer Lynne, Craig Warne. BS, U. Okla., 1959, MEd, 1961; PhD, U. Mo., 1965. From asst. prof. to prof., assoc. dean U. Wis., Milw., 1965-76; prof. Coll. Liberal Arts Tex. A&M U., College Station, 1976-88, head dept. history Coll. Liberal Arts, 1976-80, dean, 1980-84; prof. history U. Akron, Ohio, 1988-2000, head dept., 1988-95, prof. emeritus, 2000—. Cons. So. Ry., NEH. Author: Alfalfa Bill Murray, 1968, Arthur E. Stilwell, Promoter with a Hunch, 1971, History of the Atchison, Topeka and Santa Fe Railway, 1974, William Merritt Chase: A Genteel Bohemian, 1991, Culture in the American Southwest, 2001; co-author: A History of American Business, 1983; bd. editors Western Hist. Quar., 1984-87, Southwestern Hist. Quar., 1980-87; editor Railroads in the Age of Regulation, 1900-1980, 1988. Various offices local Rep. Party, Okla., Tex.; chmn. Bush for Pres., Brazos County, 1979-80. Served to 1st lt. U.S. Army, 1959-60. Recipient William H. Kiekhofer award U. Wis., 1968, George W. and Constance M. Hilton book award Ry. and Locomotive Hist. Soc., 1990, David P. Morgan Article award Ry. and Locomotive Hist. Soc., 1998; grantee Am. Philos. Soc., 1968, NEH, 1984. Mem. So. Hist. Assn. (chmn. Frank Owsley book award com. 1988), Western History Assn., Tex. Hist. Assn., Lexington Group, S.W. Conf. Humanities Consortium (pres. 1982-83). Presbyterian. Home: PO Box 5366 Bryan TX 77805-5366

BRYANT, KOBE, professional basketball player; b. Aug. 23, 1978; Student, Lower Merion (Pa.) High Sch. Player L.A. Lakers, 1996—. Named to NBA All-Rookie 2nd Team, 1996—97. Office: 555 N Nash St El Segundo CA 90245-2818

BRYANT, L. GERALD, management consultant; b. Norman, Okla., July 27, 1942; s. Lewis Cullen and Ludie A. (Skacel) B.; m. Linda Sue Farris, June 12, 1964; children: David Graham, Heather Leigh. BBA, U. Okla., 1964; MHA, Washington U., St. Louis, 1968. Acct. Pan-Am. Petroleum Corp., Tulsa, 1964-66; adminstrv. asst. Baylor U. Med. Ctr., Dallas, 1968-70, adminstr. C.P.C.H., 1970-72, assoc. dir., 1972-75, assoc. dir. planning and budget, 1975-80, sr. v.p., 1980-81, Baylor Health Care System, Dallas, 1981-84, COO, exec. v.p., 1984-92, exec. v.p. strategy devel., 1992—2000; pres. Bryant Consulting Group, 2000—. Bd. dirs. Regional Health Planning Agy., Irving, Tex., 1979—83; adj. faculty Wahington U. Sch. Med., St. Louis, 1983—2000, U. Ala., Birmingham, 1992—2000, Trinity U., San Antonio, 1996—2000; active Blue Ribbin Task Force on Health Care Reform, Tex. Hosp. Assn., 1992—93; devel. bd. dirs. Allied Bank, Dallas. Contbr. chpts. to books. Bd. dirs. Arthritis Found. Dallas, 1980-84; bd. dirs. Preservation Dallas, 1995—; deacon Wilshire Bapt. Ch., Dallas, 1976—; bd. dirs. Dallas Sci. Pl., 1995—. Fellow Am. Coll. Health Care Execs.; mem. Am. Hosp. Assn. (coun. regents 1994—, ho. of dels. 1996—, region 7 policy bd. 1994—), Tex. Hosp. Assn. (coun. on health planning 1981-84, coun. on pre-paid health plans 1984—), Am. Soc. Hosp. Planning, Am. Mgmt. Assn. Lodges: Rotary. Republican. Baptist. Avocations: antique furniture collecting, travel, gardening. Home and Office: 9622 Hillview Dr Dallas TX 75231

BRYANT, MARIA ISABEL, social sciences educator; d. Tomas Serrano Garcia and Antonia Mercado Rodriguez; m. Brian A. Bryant; 1 child, Ashley L. D in Arts, George Mason U.; postgrad. in PhD program, Am. U., 1995. Rsch. asst. U. of PR, Rio Piedras, PR, 1981—83; student asst. Old Dominion U., Norfolk, Va., 1985—86. Contbr. chapters to books. Mem.: Am. Sociol. Assn. (mem. tchg. sociology task force), Alpha Kappa Delta (founding mem. 1990). Office: Coll Southern Md PO Box 910 La Plata MD 20646 E-mail: mariab@csmd.edu.

BRYANT, MATTHEW SCOTT, research scientist; s. Vivian Milton and Joyce Bryant; m. Jennifer Chao, May 7, 1995. BS, Rochester Inst. Tech., 1982; PhD, MIT, 1987. FDA sr. staff fellow Nat. Ctr. for Toxicological Rsch., Jefferson, Ark., 1987—90; rsch. chemist Chem. Industry Inst. Toxicology, Research Triangle Park, NC, 1990—92; sr. prin. scientist Schering-Plough Rsch. Inst., Kenilworth, NJ, 1992—2000; dep. dir. Bayer, West Haven, Conn., 2000—. Mem.: Am. Assn. For Cancer Rsch. Office: Bayer 400 Morgan Ln West Haven CT 06516 Personal E-mail: matthew.bryant@alum.mit.edu. E-mail: matthew.bryant.b@bayer.com.

BRYANT, PAUL T. electronics engineering manager; b. Washington; s. Herbert Arnold and Lucy Mae Bryant; m. Sharon Lynn Wilson; children: Matthew Paul, Andrew Paul. BS in Elec. Engring., U. Md., 1964; Program Mgmt. Cert., Def. Sys. Mgmt. Coll., 1981. Engr. Value Engring., Alexandria, Va., 1964-66; electronic design engr. White Electromagnetics Inc., Rockville, Md., 1966-68; sys. engring. dept. head Litton Industries, College Park, Md., 1968-76; electronic warfare program mgr. Naval Electronic Sys. Command, Washington, 1976-84; advanced concepts sect. head Naval Rsch. Lab., Washington, 1984-91; engring. sect. head NASA, Greenbelt, Md., 1991-97, engring. br. head, 1997—. Patentee in field. Chmn. Bowie Postal Customer Adv. Coun., Md., 1994-98; bd. mem. Takoma Park Cmty. Svc. Ctr., Md., 1994-98. Recipient letter of appreciation U.S. Postal Svc., 1994, Joint Spl. Ops. Com., 1988. Home: 16306 Alderwood Ln Bowie MD 20716-1511 Office: NASA-Goddard Space Flight Ctr Code 565 Greenbelt MD 20771-0001

BRYANT, PAUL THOMPSON, English language educator; b. Oklahoma City, Aug. 24, 1928; s. Paul Dewey and Lynnis (Thompson) B.; m. Genevieve Dale Bryant, Aug. 27, 1949; children: Elaine Lynette Bryant Smyth, Christopher Dale. BS, U. Okla., 1950, MS, 1952, MA, 1956; PhD, U. Ill., 1965. Editor Inst. of Tech., Wash. State U., Pullman, 1954-56, Am. Soc. Engring. Edn., Urban, Ill., 1958-64; dir engring. pubs. U. Ill., Urban, 1958-64; chmn. Dept. English Colo. State U., Ft. Collins, 1969-75, faculty English, 1964-84, assoc. dean grad. sch., 1980-84; prof. English, dean Grad. Coll. Radford (Va.) U., 1984-93; ind. scholar, writer, cons., 1993—. Author essays, poems, short stories; author: H.L. Davis, 1978; editor, compiler essay collection: Geography to Geotechnics, 1969; co-editor essay collection: Frontier Experience and the American Dream, 1989. Bd. dirs. NRV Cmty. Sentencing, Christiansburg, Va., 1985-91; bd. dirs. Buncombe County Friends of Libr., 1999—, v.p., 2000-2002, pres., 2002—; trustee Sci. Mus. of Western Va., Roanoke, 1989-92; adv. coun. Assn. for the Study of Lit. and the Environment, 1994-2000. With U.S. Army, 1946-47. Mem. MLA, Coll. English Assn. (pres. 1982-83), Western Lit. Assn. (exec. com. 1989-91), conf. of So. Grad. Schs. (pres. 1991-92). E-mail: ptbryant@ioa.com.

BRYANT, RUTH ALYNE, banker; b. Memphis, Jan. 12, 1924; d. James Walter and Leola (Edgar) B. Student, Rhodes Coll. (formerly Southwestern Coll.), Memphis, 1941-43; LHD (hon.), U. Mo., St. Louis, 1990. Clk. Fed. Res. Bank of St. Louis (Memphis Br.), 1943-47, exec. sec., 1947-60, asst. cashier, 1968-69, asst. v.p., 1969-73, v.p., 1973-90. Trustee chancellor's coun. U. Mo., St. Louis, 1979—, chmn., 1985-88; pres. Premiere Performances, 1990-96, vice chmn., 1996-98, bd. dirs., 1998; mem. adv. bd. Salvation Army, St. Louis, 1983-91, DePaul Health Ctr., St. Louis, 1984-87; adv. coun. Hope Ctr., St. Louis, 1987, chmn., 1990-91; chmn. adv. coun. Riverway Sch., 1989-95; bd. dirs. Assocs. of St. Louis U. Librs., 1977—, pres., 1983-85; bd. dirs. The Vanderschmidt's Sch., 1980-86, Internat. Edn. Consortium, 1988-92; bd. dirs. St. Louis Merc. Libr., 1989—, sec., 1990-92, v.p., 1992-94, pres., 1994-2000; trustee Mo. Coun. on Econ. Edn., 1989-93; bd. dirs. Dance St. Louis, 1992—, v.p., 1993-94, English Lang. Sch., 1993-97; mem. devel. bd. U. Mo. Press, 2002—. Fellow: Winston Churchill Meml.; mem.: Bank Mktg. Assn. (dir. Mo.-Ill. chpt. 1976—79), English Speaking Union (bd. dirs. 1989—, 1989—, v.p. 1992—96, nat. bd. dirs. 1995—96, pres. 1997—, nat. bd. dirs. 1998—), Nat. Assn. Bank Women (editor Woman Banker 1959—62, v.p. so. region 1967—68, pres. 1970—71, trustee ednl. found. 1974—75), Mo. Bankers Assn. (mktg. and pub. rels. com. 1974—76), Am. Inst. Banking (nat. women's com. 1962—63, pres. Memphis chpt. 1968—69), Alliance Francaise of St. Louis (exec. v.p. 2001—03, pres. 2003—), Am. Soc. Arts and Letters, Rhodes Coll. Internat. Alumni Assn. (exec. bd. 1999—2000), Univ. Club, St. Louis, The Venerable Order of St. John in Jerusalem (comdr.). Home: 625 S Skinker Blvd Apt 202 Saint Louis MO 63105-2301

BRYANT, THOMAS EDWARD, physician, lawyer; b. Bellamy, Ala., Jan. 17, 1936; s. Howard Edward and Alibel (Nettles) B.; m. Lucie Elizabeth Thrasher, July 9, 1961; children: Thomas Edward, Evelyn Thaxton. AB, Emory U., 1958, MD, 1962, JD, 1967. Bar: Ga. 1967. Intern Grady Meml. Hosp., Atlanta, 1962-63; dir. health affairs OEO, Washington, 1969-71; pres. Nat. Drug Abuse Council, 1971-79; chmn., dir. Pres.'s Commn. Mental Health, 1977-79; chmn. Aspirin Found. of Am., 1987—, Nonprofit Mgmt. Assocs., Inc., 1989—. Pres. Friends of Nat. Library of Medicine, 1985— ; exec. dir. County Behavioral Health Inst., 1997—. Served with USAF, 1963-65. Recipient Exceptional Service award OEO, 1971 Mem. Ga. Bar Assn., D.C. Bar Assn., Nat. Acad. Scis., Inst. Medicine. Clubs: Cosmos (Washington); Century Assn. (N.Y.C.). Democrat. Office: Non Profit Mgmt Assocs Inc 1555 Connecticut Ave NW Ste 200 Washington DC 20036-1126

BRYANT, THOMAS LEE, magazine editor; b. Daytona Beach, Fla., June 15, 1943; s. Stanley Elson and G. Bernice (Burgess) B.; m. Patricia Jean Bryant, June 30, 1979. BA in Polit. Sci., U. Calif., Santa Barbara, 1965, MA in Polit. Sci., 1966. Fgn. svc. officer U.S. Dept. State, Washington, Buenos Aires, 1967-69; radio broadcaster KDB Sta., Santa Barbara, Calif., 1969-72; magazine editor, now editor-in-chief Road & Track, Newport Beach, Calif., 1972—. Mem. Internat. Motor Press Assn., Motor Press Guild, Sports Car Club of Am. Avocations: golf, trap and skeet shooting. Office: c/o Hachette Filipacchi Mags Inc 1499 Monrovia Ave Newport Beach CA 92663-2752*

BRYANT, TIMOTHY CLARK, investment brokerage executive; b. Akron, Ohio, Apr. 11, 1943; s. Alan Willard and Clara Sherman (Clark) B.; m. Mary Esther Snell, Jan. 17, 1981. AB, Dartmouth Coll., 1967; MBA, U. Chgo., 1971; MS in Taxation, DePaul U., 1975. CPA, Ill. Dir. fin. and adminstrn. Fibre Box Assn., Chgo., 1975-77, Akers Packaging Co., Middletown, Ohio, 1977-78; dir., sec., treas. CompuShop, Inc., Dallas, 1978-80, dir., 1980-85; v.p. fin., dir. Rubicon Corp., Richardson, Tex., 1980-82, Automated Mgmt. Inc., Dallas, 1982-83, Avian Corp., Clearwater, Fla., 1983-85, pres., bd. dirs., 1985-87; v.p. investments A.G. Edwards and Sons, 1990—. Chmn. bd. dirs. Adventures Away, Inc., Chgo., 1983-87; pres., treas., bd. dirs. Talk2 Corp., Clearwater, 1987-90; cons. Nevada Brake Corp., 1985-91, So. Conf. Bur., Inc., 1987-90, Innovative Products Group, Inc., 1987-90. With U.S. Army, 1965-66, Korea. Mem. AICPA, Chgo. Yacht Club, Vinoy Club. Home: 307 Brightwaters Blvd NE Saint Petersburg FL 33704-3709 Office: A G Edwards & Sons 3170 3rd Ave N Saint Petersburg FL 33713-7684

BRYANT, VERONICA MARIA, hospital administrator, writer; b. Washington, Aug. 1, 1967; d. Gilliam Peter and Ariminta DeWara Nelson; m. Joseph Gerard Bryant, May 4, 1991. At, No. Va. CC, Woodbridge, 1996. Cashier Giant Food, Washington; loans control asst. US Dept. of Agrl., Washington; mgr. Pizza Hut, Dale City, Va.; lic. daycare provider Veronica's Learning Ctr., Dumfries, Va.; found. asst. Potomac Hosp., Woodbridge, Va.; exec. asst. Children's Hosp. Found., Washington. Author: (book) True Happiness, 2003, poetry. Avocations: writing, movies, entertaining, socializing, dancing.

BRYANT, WALTER, secondary school educator; b. Phila., Pa., June 20, 1952; s. Walter and Mary Bryant. BA, Rutgers U., 1975. Cert. Secondary English Edn. 1975. Tchr. of english Maple Shade H.S., Maple Shade, NJ, 1975—. Mem.: Nat. Coun. of Tchrs. of Eng. Avocations: exercise, reading, travel, good food. Home: 1803 Wharton Road Mount Laurel NJ 08054 Office: Maple Shade High School 180 Frederick Ave Maple Shade NJ 08052 Personal E-mail: wbryant27@comcast.net.

BRYANT, WARREN F. retail executive; Sr. v.p. supermarket divsn. Dillon Co. Inc., pres., CEO, 1995—99; sr. v.p. Kroger Co., 1999—2002; CEO, pres. Long Drug Stores Corp., 2002—, acting COO, 2003—. Office: 141 N Civic Dr Walnut Creek CA 94596*

BRYANT, WAYNE RICHARD, state legislator; b. Camden, N.J., Nov. 7, 1947; s. Isaac Rutledge Sr. and Anna Mae (Jones) B.; 1 child, Wayne Richard Jr. BA, Howard U., 1969; JD, Rutgers U., 1972; LLD, Howard D., 1991. Bar: U.S. Supreme Ct. Freeholder Camden County, N.J., 1979-82; dist. 5 N.J. State Assembly, 1982-95; mem. N.J. Senate, Dist. 5, Trenton, 1995—. Vice-chmn. transportation & comms. com., N.J. State Assembly, 1982—, ind. authorities & commn. coms., 1982—, majority leader, 1990-91; staff atty. Camden Regional Legal Svc., Inc., 1972-74; ptnr., Zeller & Bryant, 1974—. Recipient legis. achievement award N.J. Fedn. Dem. Women, 1988, equal justice award Legal Svc. N.J., 1990, Arthur Armitage disting. alumni award Rutgers U. Sch. Law, 1992. Mem. Nat. Black Caucus, ABA, N.J. Bar Assn., Camden County Bar Assn. Address: 501 Cooper St Camden NJ 08102-1210*

BRYANT, WINSTON, former state attorney general; b. Donaldson, Ark., Oct. 3, 1938; BBA, Ouachita Bapt. U., 1960; LLB, U. Ark., 1963; LLM in Adminstrv. Law, George Washington U., 1970. Bar: Ark. 1963. Pvt. practice, Malvern, Ark., 1964—66, 1971—75; atty. Ark. Ins. Commn., 1966; asst. U.S. atty. Eastern Dist. Ark., 1967; legis. asst. to Senator from Ark., 1968—71; dep. pros. atty. Hot Spring County, Ark., 1971—75; mem. Ark. Ho. of Reps., 1973—76; sec. of state State of Ark., Little Rock, 1976—80, lt. gov., 1981—91, atty. gen., 1991—98. Instr. polit. sci. Ouachita Bapt. U., 1971—73, Henderson (Ark.) State U., 1973—. Active Ark. Youth Svcs. Planning Adv. Coun., 1974, Ark. Gov.'s Ad Hoc Com. on Workmen's Compensation, 1975. With inf. U.S. Army, 1963—64. Mem.: ABA, Ark. Bar Assn. (ho. of dels.), Ark. Farm Bur., Malvern C. of C. (pres. 1972), Am. Legion. Baptist.

BRYANT-SALA, KAREN, music educator; d. William D. Bryant and Rosemary Oshel; m. John C. Sala (div.); 1 child, John Douglas Sala. B in Music Edn., Murray State U., 1967; MusM, North Tex. State U., 1968. Music tchr. Gibson City (Ill.) Unit Schs., 1969; prof. music John A. Logan Coll., Carterville, Ill., 1970—. Mem.: NEA, Am. Assn. for Women in C.C. (pres. 2002—03), Am. Choral Dirs. Assn., Music Educators Nat. Conf., Ill. Music Edn. Assn., Sigma Alpha Iota. Baptist. Office: John A Logan Coll 700 College Rd Carterville IL 62918

BRYCE, MARGUERITE MAHER, social worker, educator; b. Pitts., Mar. 18, 1928; d. Raphael R. and Grace Margaret Connors Maher; m. John B. Bryce, Jr., Oct. 20, 1951; children: Anita, Lauren, Rita, Jerry. BA in Psychology, U. Pitts., 1949, MSW, 1951; family therapy cert., Smith Coll., 1988. Lic. social worker and clin. social worker, Pa.; diplomate Am. Bd. Examiners in Clin. Social Work, NASW (nat. del. 1990, chmn. mental health com., Social Worker of the Yr. for State of Pa. 1993). Psychiat. social worker N.J. State Hosp., Trenton, 1951-52; supr. med. and surg. svcs. dept. social work U. Ala., Birmingham, 1963-69; clin. social worker Cystic Fibrosis Ctr., Children's Hosp. Pitts., 1969-85, outpatient psychiatry clin. social worker, 1985-90; clin. social worker dept. orthopaedics Children's Hosp., Pitts., 1990-93; pvt. practice Pitts., 1993—. Preceptor in field, 1975—; field instr. U. Ala. Grad. Sch. Social Work, 1962-69, field instr., 1980—; instr. sociology Allegheny C.C., 1978-88; field instr. U. Pitts., 1980-90. Contbr. articles to profl. jours. Mem. ctr. com. Cystic Fibrosis Found., mem. edn. com., young adult com., editor team newsletter, mem. State of Art Conf. on Cystic Fibrosis, 1985. Recipient Disting. Alumni award U. Pitts. Grad. Sch. Social Work, 1994. Mem. Acad. Cert. Social Workers, U. Pitts. Sch. Social Work Alumnae Soc. (pres. 2000—). Home: 209 Sunridge Dr Pittsburgh PA 15234-1022 Office: Village Sq 201 414-416 Allegheny River Blvd Oakmont PA 15139

BRYCE, WILLIAM DELF, lawyer; b. Georgetown, Tex., Aug. 7, 1932; s. D.A. Bryce and Frances Maxine (Wilson) Bryce Bakke; m. Sarah Alice Riley, Dec. 20, 1954; children: Douglas Delf, David Dickson. BA, U. Tex., 1955; LLB, Yale U., 1960. Bar: Tex. 1960, U.S. Dist. Ct. (we. dist.) Tex. 1963, U.S. Ct. Claims 1964, U.S. Supreme Ct. 1971. Briefing atty. Tex. Supreme Ct., Austin, 1960-61; sole practice, 1961—. Lectr. U. Tex., 1965-66. Editor, Tex. Supreme Ct. Jour. Served to 1st lt. USAF, 1955-57. Fellow Tex. Bar Found. (sustaining; life); mem. ABA, State Bar Tex., Travis County Bar Assn., Williamson County Bar Assn., Rotary Internat. (dist. 5870 gov. 1999-2000). Home: 308 E University Ave Georgetown TX 78626-6813 also: 511 S Main St Georgetown TX 78626-5609

BRYCHTOVA, JAROSLAVA, sculptor; b. Semily, Czechoslovakia, 1924; m. S. Libensky. Student, Acad. Applied Arts, Prague, Czechoslovakia, 1945—51, Acad. Fine Arts, Prague, 1947—50. Designer Zeleznobrodské sklo, Zelezny Brod, Czech Republic, 1950—84. Guest lectr. Pilchuck Summer Sch., Stanwood, Wash., Ctr. Creative Studies, Detroit, others; presenter in field. Office: 7 N Saginaw St Pontiac MI 48342-2148 also: Heller Gallery 420 W 14th St New York NY 10014-1064

BRYDEN, RODERICK M. professional sports team executive; b. Port Elgin, N.B., Can. Degree in law, Mt. Allison U., U. Mich. Former prof. law U. Saskatchewan; founder Systemhouse, Paperboard Industries; chmn., CEO SC Stormont Corp.; co-chmn., gov., CEO Ottawa Senators Hockey Club. Former spl. asst. to fed. govt. cabinet min. Office: SHL Systemhouse Inc 50 O'Connor St Ottawa ON Canada K1P 6L2 also: Ottawa Senators 1000 Palladium Dr Kanata ON Canada K2V 1A5

BRYDEN, WILLIAM DONALD, JR., retired manufacturing executive, retired military officer; b. Phila., May 6, 1935; s. William Donald and Georgia Elizabeth (Sherry) B.; m. Mary Lou Pursell, Aug. 5, 1959; children: Donald Christopher, William Scott. BS in Metall. Engring., U. Pa., 1962. Cert. Master Navigator, USAF. Commd. 2nd lt. USAF, 1959, advanced through grades to lt. col., 1977, ret., 1985, instr. navigator, 1959—65, chief materials tech. Space and Missiles Systems L.A., 1966-69, weapons system officer 18th spl. ops. squadron Udorn, Thailand, 1970-71, chief navigator, flight test wing Wright Patterson, Ohio, 1971-74, chief engr. A-10 flight test program Edwards AFB, Calif., 1974-78, dir. test policy Andrews AFB, Md., 1978-81, comdr. Ascension Aux Air Field Ascension Island, 1981-83, dep. program mgr. data system modernization Sunnyvale, Calif., 1983-85; mgr., FAA Tower Systems IBM Advanced Automation Systems, Rockville, Md., 1985-96, Lockheed Martin Internat. Air Traffic Mgmt., London and Swanwick, Eng., 1997-2000. Bd. dirs. Signal Hill Home Assn., Burke, Va., 1979-81, Flints Grove Homeowners' Assn., North Potomac, Md., 1986-90, Landfalls Property Owners Assn., Wilmington, N.C., 2003—; mem. KWV, Ascension Island, 1981-83; instr. U.S. Power Squadron, Rockville, Md., 1988-98, mem. adv. bd. New Hanover County Transp.Commn. Decorated Air medal with one silver, three bronze clusters, DFC, Legion of Merit. Mem.: UNCW Adult Scholars (bd. dirs.), Landfall Found. (web and data mgr.), Air Force Assn. Republican. Episcopalian. Avocations: boating, model railroads, stained and etched glass, woodworking. Address: 805 Gull Point Rd Wilmington NC 28405-5264

BRYDGES, THOMAS EUGENE, lawyer; b. Niagara Falls, N.Y., June 1, 1942; s. Earl W. and Eleanor M. (Mahoney) B.; m. Melissa May, May 26, 1990; children: Andrew MacLeod, Elizabeth Hendricks. BA in History, Syracuse U., 1971, JD, 1973. Bar: N.Y. 1974, U.S. Dist. (we. dist.) N.Y. 1974, U.S. Ct. Appeals (2d cir.) 1978. Assoc. Jaeckle, Fleischmann & Mugel, Buffalo, 1973-78, ptnr., 1979—. Bd. dirs., sec. Theodore Roosevelt Inagural site, 1999—. Author: (with others) Employment Discrimination Law, 1980—. Trustee Daemen Coll., Amherst, N.Y., 1988—; bd. dirs., v.p. Art Park & Co., Lewiston, N.Y., 1976—. Capt. U.S. Army, 1962-68, Vietnam. Decorated Bronze Star, Air medal, Army Commendation (2). Mem. ABA (labor sect.), Erie County Bar Assn. (bd. dirs. 2002--), N.Y. Bar Assn. (labor law com.). Office: Jaeckle Fleischmann & Mugel 700 Fleet Bldg Buffalo NY 14202 E-mail: tbrydges@jaeckle.com.

BRYDON, RUTH VICKERY, history educator; b. San Jose, Calif., June 2, 1930; d. Robert Kingston and Ruth (Bacon) Vickery; m. Harold Wesley Brydon, Mar. 28, 1951 (div.); children: Carol Ruth Brydon Koford, Marilyn Brydon Belove, Kenneth Wesley. BA, Stanford U., 1952; postgrad., San Jose State Coll., 1964-65; MA, Calif. State Coll., Chico, 1987. Cert. tchr., Calif.; cert. sch. adminstr. Tchr. Lincoln Sch., Kathmandu, Nepal, 1959-60, Am. Sch. Port-au-Prince, Haiti, 1962-63; tchr. social studies Norte Vista H.S., Riverside, Calif., 1965-67, chmn. social studies dept., 1966-67; tchr. home econs., social studies Westwood (Calif.) H.S., 1967-90, mentor tchr., 1984-85; media specialist Lake Havasu H.S., 1990-91; history instr. Mohave C.C., Lake Havasu Campus, 1990—. Instr. Elderhostel, 1992—; coord. extended day classes Lassen Coll., 1977-84. Author: Westwood, California: A Company Town in Comparative Perspective, 1990-1930, 1995. Co-chairperson Alamanor Art Show, 1980-84; curator Lake Havasu Mus. of History, 1999—; bd. dirs. Lake Havasu Mus. History. NDEA grantee, 1967. Mem. Archeol. Soc. Ariz. Episcopalian. Home: 2681 N Cisco Dr Lake Havasu City AZ 86403-5020 E-mail: rvbrydon@redrivernet.com.

BRYJA, FRANK JOSEPH, food distribution executive; b. East Chicago, Ind., Feb. 13, 1942; s. Frank Max and Lillian Bryja; m. Sharon Chandler Bryja, Aug. 29, 1963; children: Cynthia, Elizabeth, F. Michael, Catherine, Mary Kay. BS in Mgmt. and Adminstrn., Ind. U., 1965; postgrad., Ball State U., 1965-67. Dept. head store mgr. Nat. Tea Co., East Chicago, Ind., 1958-65; tng. supr., various positions Marsh Supermarkets, Yorktown, Ind., 1965-72, dir. R&D, 1972-74, buyer pvt. label brands, 1974-76, dir. grocery merchandising, 1976-85, exec. dir. mktg., 1985-86, asst. v.p., 1986-89, v.p. merchandising, 1989-96, pres., COO Indpls., 1996—. Mem. Marsh Employees Fed. Credit Union, Yorktown, 1965-90, pres., 1981-90, treas., 1975-81; mem. retail adv. panel Howard Marlboro Group, Chgo., 1969-80, DDB Needham Retail Adv. Bd., 1974-88, C.I.E.S., Paris, 1989-96; mem. Ind. State Egg Bd., pres., 1988-90. Named to Order Ky. Cols. Mem. Elks. Roman Catholic. Avocations: fishing, hunting, reading, travel. Office: Marsh Supermarkets LLC 9800 Crosspoint Blvd Indianapolis IN 46256-3350

BRYNES, RUSSELL KERMIT, pathologist, educator; b. NYC, May 7, 1945; s. Kermit and Lore (Brunn) B.; m. Angelita Sales Cordero, May 31, 1970; children: Barbara, Erica. BA, U. Mass., 1967; MD, Tufts U., 1971. Diplomate Am. Bd. Pathology, Nat. Bd. Med. Examiners; lic. physician, Calif. Intern then resident U. Chgo. Hosps. and Clinics, 1971-73, USPHS fellow, 1973 75; resident U. Minn. Hosps., 1975-77; dir. clin. hematology lab. Emory U. Hosp., Atlanta, 1979-86; from asst. to assoc. prof. pathology Emory U., Atlanta, 1979-86; assoc. prof. pathology U. So. Calif., L.A., 1986-91, clin. prof. pathology, 1993-98, prof. clin. path., 1998—; dir. dept. clin. pathology City of Hope Nat. Med. Ctr., Duarte, Calif., 1991-98. Dir. clin. hematology LA County U. So. Calif. Med. Ctr., LA, 1986-91, dir. spl. hematology lab., 1998—. Editor, assoc.: Hematology: Clinical and Laboratory Practice, 1993; contbr. over 100 articles to profl. jours. Maj. U.S. Army Med. Corp, 1977-79. Mem. Am. Soc. Clin. Pathologists (dep. commr. 1991-99, bd. dirs. 1998—), Am. Soc. Hematology, U.S. and Can. Acad. Pathology, L.A. Soc. Pathologists (v.p. 1994, pres. 1995), Soc. Hematopathology. Avocations: bicycling, traveling. Office: 2011 Zonal Ave # HMR209 Los Angeles CA 90089-0110

BRYNJOLFSSON, ARI, nuclear physicist; b. Akureyri, Iceland, Dec. 7, 1926; arrived in U.S., 1965, naturalized, 1970; s. Brynjolfur and Gudrun (Rosinkarsdottir) Sigtryggsson; m. Marguerite Reman, Dec. 22, 1950; children: Ariane, Olaf, Erik, John, Alan Cand. Phil., U. Copenhagen, 1949, Cand. Mag., Mag. Scien., U. Copenhagen, 1954; Dr.Phil., Niels Bohr Inst., U. Copenhagen, 1973; post grad., Advanced Mgmt. Program, Harvard U., 1971. Dir. radiation rsch. Danish Atomic Energy Rsch. Establishment, Roskilde, Denmark, 1957-65; chief radiation rsch. U.S. Army Natick (Mass.) Lab., 1965—72, dir. U.S. food irradiation program, 1972—80, spl. asst. for physics, 1980—88; project dir. Facility for Food Irradiation Tech. UN Joint FAO/IAEA Divsn., Wageningen, Netherlands, 1988-90; project dir. internat. tng. ctr. joint FAO/IAEA divsn. Internat. Atomic Energy Agy., Vienna, 1990-92; pres. Applied Radiation Industries, Wayland, Mass., 1992—. Contbr. articles to profl. jours. Subspecialties: Nuclear physics; radiation biology. Current work: Astrophysics, theoretical physics, general theory of relativity. Biological effects of radiation. Spl. scholar NRC and U. Iceland, 1954-55, Alexander von Humboldt scholar U. Göttingen, Fed. Republic Germany, 1955-57; recipient Mollers Found. award for exceptional svc. to Danish industry, 1965, Tech. award Am. Nuc. Soc. Radiation Sci., 1988. Mem.: Am. Phys. Soc. Home and Office: Applied Radiation Industries 7 Bridle Path Wayland MA 01778-3206 E-mail: aribrynjolfsson@comcast.net.

BRYNJOLFSSON, ERIK, management educator, researcher; b. Roskilde, Denmark, Apr. 14, 1962; m. Martha Pavlakis. AB, SM, Harvard U., 1984; PhD, MIT, 1991. Ptnr., co. founder Foundation Technologies, Cambridge, Mass., 1986-90; instr. Harvard U.; asst. prof. MIT Sloan Sch., Cambridge, Mass., 1990-95, assoc. prof., Douglas Drane chair, 1995-2000, George and Sandi Schussel chair, prof., 2001—; dir. Ctr. for e-Bus. MIT, 1999—. Vis. prof. Stanford (Calif.) U., 1996-98. Contbr. numerous articles to profl. jours. Office: MIT Sloan Sch 50 Memorial Dr Rm E53-313 Cambridge MA 02142-1347

BRYNN, EDWARD PAUL, former ambassador; b. Pitts., Aug. 1, 1942; s. Walter Bruggeman and Mary Margaret (Callahan) B.; m. Jane Cooke, Apr. 1, 1967; children: Sarah, Edward, Kiernan, Anne-Elizabeth, Justin-Oliver. BS in Fgn. Svc., Georgetown U., 1964; MA in History, Stanford U., 1965, Phd in History, 1968; MLitt, Trinity Coll., Dublin, Ireland, 1968, PhD in Politics, 1977. Prof. history USAF Acad., Colorado Springs, Colo., 1968-72, 76-78; polit. officer Am. Embassy, Colombo, Sri Lanka, 1973-75, Bamako, Mali, 1978-80; staff mem. Senate Select Com. on Intelligence, Washington, 1981-82; dep. chief of mission Am. Embassy, Nouakchott, Mauritania, 1982-85, charge d'affaires Moroni, Comoros, 1985-87, dep. chief of mission Yaounde, Cameroon, 1987-89, amb. Ouagadougou, Burkina Faso, 1990-93; prin. dep. asst. sec. Bur. of African Affairs, 1993-95; amb. Am. Embassy, Accra, Ghana, 1995—98; internat. affairs advisor Nat. War Coll., Washington, 1998-99; assoc. provost internat. programs U. N.C., Charlotte, 1999—. Chmn. Charlotte World Affairs Coun., 2002—. Author: Crown and Castle, 1979, Church of Ireland, 1980. Lt. col. USAFR, 1990. Mem. Am. Fgn. Svc. Assn. Home: 3306 Lakewood Edge Dr Charlotte NC 28269 E-mail: ebrynn@email.uncc.edu.

BRYSON, ARTHUR EARL, JR., retired aerospace engineering educator; b. Evanston, Ill., Oct. 7, 1925; s. Arthur Earl and Helen Elizabeth (Decker) B.; m. Helen Marie Layton, Aug. 31, 1946; children: Thomas Layton, Stephen Decker, Janet Elizabeth, Susan Mary. Student, Haverford Coll., 1942-44; BS, Iowa State U., 1946; MS, Calif. Inst. Tech., 1949, PhD in Aeronautics, 1951; MA (hon.), Harvard., 1956. With Container Corp. Am., 1947-48, United Aircraft Corp., 1948; research asst. aero. Calif. Inst. Tech., 1949-50; mem. tech. staff Hughes Research & Devel. Labs., 1950-53; mem. faculty Harvard, 1953-68, Gordon McKay prof. mech. engring., 1961-68; mem. faculty Stanford, 1968-93, chmn. dept. applied mechanics, 1969-71, chmn. dept. aero. and astronautics, 1971-79, Paul Pigott prof. engring., 1972-93; Hunsaker prof. Mass. Inst. Tech., 1965-66. Mem. nat. com. Fluid Mechanics Films, 1961-68 Author: (with Y.C. Ho) Applied Optimal Control, 1969, Control of Spacecraft and Aircraft, 1994, Dynamic Optimization, 1998, Applied Linear Optimal Control, 2002. Served as ensign USNR, 1944-46. Recipient Rufus Oldenberger medal ASME, 1980, Control Systems Sci. and Engring. award IEEE, 1984, Bellman Heritage award Am. Auto Control Coun., 1990. Fellow AIAA (hon., assoc. editor jour. 1963-65, bd. dirs. 1965-68, Pendray Award 1968, mechanics and control of flight award 1980, Dryden lectr. 1984, Von Karman lectr. 1994); mem. NAS, NAE (aero. and space engring. bd. 1970-79), Am. Acad. Arts and Scis., Am. Soc. Engring. Edn. (Westinghouse award 1969), Sigma Xi, Tau Beta Pi. Congregationalist. Office: Stanford U Durand Building Stanford CA 94305 E-mail: brysonae@stanford.edu.

BRYSON, ARTHUR JOSEPH, lawyer; b. Ashland, Ky., Sept. 17, 1946; s. Arthur T. Jr. and Albertina Peña; m. Kathleen Connor May 15, 1971. AB, Ea. Ky. U., 1969; JD, U. Ky., 1972. Accredited estate planner Nat. Assn. Estate Planners and Couns. Trust officer Second Nat. Bank, Lexington, Ky., 1972-80, v.p., 1980-85, Commerce Nat. Bank, Lexington, 1985-86; prin. Arthur J. Bryson, Lexington, 1986—. Bd. dirs. Bluegrass R.R. Mus., Inc., Lexington, 1977-81, So. Ry. Hist. Assn., 1994—, sec., 1994-2003. Mem. Ky. Bar Assn., Bluegrass Estate Planning Coun. (bd. dirs. 1982-89, sec. 1986, treas. 1987, v.p. 1988, pres. 1989). Avocation: railway history. Office: 376 S Broadway St Lexington KY 40508-2512 E-mail: joebryson@hotmail.com.

BRYSON, GARY SPATH, cable television and telephone company executive; b. Longview, Wash., Nov. 8, 1943; s. Roy Griffin and Marguerite Elizabeth (Spath) B.; m. Bobbi Bryson; children: Kelly Suzanne, Lisa Christine. AB, Dartmouth Coll., 1966; MBA, Tuck Sch., 1967. With Bell & Howell Co., Chgo., 1967-79, pres. consumer and audio-visual group, 1977-79; chmn. bd., CEO Bell & Howell Mamiya Co., Chgo., 1979-81; exec. v.p. Am. TV & Communications Corp., subs. Time, Inc., Englewood, Colo., 1981-88; v.p. diversified group US West, Englewood, 1988-89, pres. cable communications div., 1989-92; pres., CEO TeleWest Internat., 1992-93; pres. SkyConnect, Boulder, 1994-96. Comm. cons., 1996—. Mem. Phi Beta Kappa, Sigma Alpha Epsilon. Republican. Lutheran. Home: PO Box 2097 Edwards CO 81632 E-mail: gsbryson@earthlink.net.

BRYSON, JOHN E. utilities company executive; b. N.Y.C., July 24, 1943; m. Louise Henry BA with great distinction, Stanford U., 1965; student, Freie U. Berlin, Federal Republic Germany, 1965-66; JD, Yale U., 1969. Bar: Calif., Oreg., D.C. Asst. in instrn. Law Sch., Yale U., New Haven, Conn., 1968-69; law clk. U.S. Dist. Ct., San Francisco, 1969-70; co-founder, atty. Natural Resources Def. Council, 1970-74; vice chmn. Oreg. Energy Facility Siting Council, 1975-76; assoc. Davies, Biggs, Strayer, Stoel & Boley, Portland, Oreg., 1975-76; chmn. Calif. State Water Resources Control Bd., 1976-79; vis. faculty Stanford U. Law Sch., Calif., 1977-79; pres. Calif. Pub. Utilities Commn., 1979-82; ptnr. Morrison & Foerster, San Francisco, 1983-84; sr. v.p. law and fin. So. Calif. Edison Co., Rosemead, 1984; exec. v.p., chief fin. officer Edison Internat. and So. Calif. Edison Co., 1985-90, chmn. of bd., CEO, 1990-99; chmn., pres., CEO Edison Internat., 2000—. Lectr. on pub. utility, energy, communications law.; former mem. exec. com. Nat. Assn. Regulatory Utility Commrs., Calif. Water Rights Law Rev. Commn., Calif. Pollution Control Financing Authority; former mem. adv. bd. Solar Energy Research Inst., Electric Power Research Inst., Stanford Law Sch.; bd. dirs. Pacific Am. Income Shares Inc., The Boeing Co., Walt Disney Co. Mem. bd. editors, assoc. editor: Yale U. Law Jour. Past bd. dirs. World Resources Inst., Washington, Calif. Environ. Trust, Claremont U. Ctr., Grad. Sch., Stanford U. Alumni Assn.; bd. dirs. The Keck Found.; former trustee Stanford U., 1991. Woodrow Wilson fellow Mem. Calif. Bar Assn., Oreg. Bar Assn., D.C. Bar Assn., Nat. Assn. Regulatory Utility Commrs. (exec. com. 1980-82), Stanford U. Alumni Assn. (bd. dirs. 1983-86), Phi Beta Kappa. Office: Edison Internat 2244 Walnut Grove Ave Rosemead CA 91770-3714

BRYSON, MELVIN JOSEPH, retired biochemist; b. Providence, Utah, June 7, 1916; s. Charles Melvin and Martha Jane Bryson; m. Devona Smart, May 11, 1942; children: Melvin Joseph Bryson, Jr., Betty Sue. BS, Utah State Univ., Logan, UT, 1946; MS, Univ. Utah, Salt Lake City, UT, 1948; PhD, Tex. A&M Univ., College Station, TX, 1952. Asst. dir. Eaton Lab of Norwich, Norwich, NY, 1952—57; rsch. asst. Univ. Utah Sch. of Medicine, Salt Lake City, 1957—59, rsch. asst. prof., 1959—83; lab dir. Inter West Endocrine Lab, Salt Lake City, 1984—94. Maj. US Army, 1941—45, Europe. Home: 5262 Woodcrest Drive Salt Lake City UT 84117-7435

BRYSON, NANCY S. federal agency administrator; BA in History, Boston U.; JD, Georgetown U. Staff atty., asst. counsel for appellate litig. U.S. Dept. of Labor, Occupl. Safety and Health Divsn. Solicitor's Office, 1975—79; trial atty., asst. chief land and natural resources divsn. environ. def. sect. U.S. Dept. of Justice, 1979—84; ptnr. Crowell & Moring, Washington, 1998—2001; gen. counsel USDA, Washington, 2001—. Vol. mediator D.C. Bar. Office: USDA Gen Counsel 1400 Independence Ave SW Washington DC 20250

BRYSON, VERN ELRICK, nuclear engineer; b. Woodruff, Utah, May 28, 1920; s. David Hyrum and Luella May (Eastman) B.; m. Esther Sybil de St Jeor, Oct. 14, 1942; children: Britt William, Forrest Lee, Craig Lewis, Nadine, Elaine. Commd. 2d lt. USAAF, 1941; advanced through grades to lt. col. USAF, 1960, ret., 1961; pilot, safety engr., civil engr., electronic engr., nuclear engr., chief Aeronaut. Systems div., Aircraft Nuclear Propulsion Program, Wright-Patterson AFB, Ohio, 1960-61; chief Radiation Effects Lab., also chief Radiation Effects Group Boeing Airplane Co., Seattle, 1961-65; nuclear engr. Aerospace Corp., San Bernardino, Calif., 1965-68; service engr., also head instrumentation lab., Sacramento Air Logistic Ctr. USAF, McClellan AFB, Calif., 1968-77; owner, mgr. Sylvern Valley Ranch, Calif., 1977—. Mem. panel Transient Radiation Effects on Electronics, Weapon Effects Bd., 1959-61. Contbr. research articles on radiation problems to profl. pubs. Decorated D.F.C. with oak leaf cluster, Air medal with 12 oak leaf clusters. Mem. IEEE. Mem. Ch. Jesus Christ of Latter-day Saints. Home: 1426 Caperton Ct Penryn CA 95663-9515 E-mail: esybil@earthlink.net.

BRYSON, WILLIAM CURTIS, federal judge; b. Houston, Aug. 19, 1945; m. Julia Penny Clark; 2 children. BA magna cum laude, Harvard Coll., 1969; JD, U. of Tex. Sch. of Law, 1973. Law clk. to Justice Henry Friendly U.S. Ct. of Appeals, 2d Cir., 1973—74; law clk. to Justice Thurgood Marshall U.S. Supreme Ct., 1974—75; atty. Miller, Cassidy, Larroca & Lewin, 1975—78; asst. to the Solicitor Gen. U.S. Dept. of Justice, 1978—79; chief Appellate Sect., Criminal Divsn., 1979—82; spl. counsel Organized Crime & Racketeering Sect., Criminal Divsn., 1982—86; dep. solicitor gen., 1986—94; dep. assoc. atty. & acting assoc. atty. gen., 1994; cir. judge Fed. Cir., Washington, 1994—. Office: US Ct of Appeals for the Fed Cir 717 Madison Pl NW Washington DC 20439*

BRZEZANSKI, JAY MARIAN, financial executive; b. Washington, Jan. 24, 1947; BS, U.S. Mil. Acad., 1968; MBA, U. Va., 1970; MMAS, Command and Gen. Staff Coll., 1982. Internal audit mgr. IBM, Armonk, N.Y., 1970-73; loss prevention mgr./dir. systems Abraham & Straus, Bklyn., 1977-81; spl. asst. to treas., sr. v.p. fin. Gimbels-N.Y., Batus, N.Y.C., 1981-83, group fin. mgr., 1983; CFO D.B. Brown, Perth Amboy, N.J., 1984-86; v.p., CFO, treas., corp. sec. Tangent Internat., N.Y.C., 1986-90; CFO, v.p. fin. and adminstr. D.A.M. Operating, Inc., Long Island City, N.Y., 1991-95; sr. v.p. RBC, Inc., Long Island City, N.Y., 1995-96, BDC, Inc., Randolph, N.J., 1997-2000; CFO Coop. Holdings, Inc., Lyndhurst, N.J., 2000—. Commr. Boy Scouts Am., 1970-74, explorer advisor, 1971-75; mem. City Coun. Clifton, 1978-80, mem. Planning Bd., 1979; chmn. Mt. Arlington Planning Bd., 1996-2003, land use bd., 1996-03; councilman for muncipality, 2003; ; founding charter mem. Rep. Nat. Task Force, 1984—. Served with U.S. Army, 1966-69; lt. col. USAR, 1966—; col. 1990-91, U.S. Army, Desert Storm, Saudi Arabia; col. USAR, 1996—. Decorated Order of St. George, Order of Merit, Italy, Legion of Merit; comdr. Order Brit. Empire; recipient DAR Citizens award, 1970, CD award, 1974, Disting. Svc. Order, 1985; named to Knight Comdr. St. John's Knights of Malta. Mem. VFW (comdr.), Inst. Internal Auditors (cert.), Assn. U.S. Army, Am. Legion, Systems Mgmt. Assn., Res. Officers Assn., Am. Mgmt. Assn., KC (4th deg.), Knights of Malta (Comdr. 1988). Roman Catholic. Address: c/o Cooperative Comm Inc 210 Clay Ave Lyndhurst NJ 07071

BRZEZINSKI, ZBIGNIEW, political science educator, author; b. Warsaw, Mar. 28, 1928; came to U.S., 1953, naturalized, 1958; s. Tadeusz and Leonia (Roman) B.; m. Emilie Anna Benes, June 11, 1955; children: Ian, Mark, Mika. BA with 1st class honors in Econs. and Polit. Sci., McGill U., 1949, MA in Polit. Sci., 1950; PhD, Harvard U., 1953. Inst. govt. and research fellow Russian Research Center, Harvard U., 1953-56; asst. prof. govt., research assoc. Russian Research Center and Center Internat. Affairs, Harvard U., 1956-60; assoc. prof. public law and govt. Columbia U., 1960-62, prof., 1981-89. Dir. Rsch. Inst. Internat. Change, 1962-77; mem. faculty Russian Inst., 1960-77; dir. Trilateral Commn., 1973-76; asst. to pres. U.S. for nat security affairs, 1977-81; ofcl. Nat. Security Coun., 1977-81; counselor Ctr. Strategic and Internat. Studies, 1981—; prof. Nitze Sch. Advanced Internat. Studies, Johns Hopkins U., 1989—; mem. policy planning coun. U.S. Dept. State, 1966-68, Pres.'s Fgn. Intelligence Adv. Bd., 1987-91; mem. Joint Com. Contemporary China, Social Sci. Rsch. Coun., 1961-62; guest lectr. numerous pvt. and govt. instns. 1953—, participant internat. confs., 1955—. Author: The Permanent Purge-Politics in Soviet Totalitarianism, 1956, The Soviet Bloc— Unity and Conflict, 1960, Ideology and Power in Soviet Politics, 1962, Alternative to Partition, 1965, Between Two Ages, 1970, The Fragile Blossom, 1971, Power and Principle, 1983, Game Plan, 1986, The Grand Failure: The Birth and Death of Communism in the Twentieth Century, 1989, Out of Control, 1993, The Grand Chessboard, 1997; co-author: Totalitarian Dictatorship and Autocracy, 1957, Political Power: USA/USSR, 1964 (German edit. 1966), also numerous articles.; editor, co-author, contbr.: Political Controls in the Soviet Army, 1954; Editor, co-author, contbr.: Africa and the Communist World, 1963, Dilemmas Of Change In Soviet Politics, 1969, Dilemmi Internationazionali In Un-epoca Teconetronica, 1969; columnist: Newsweek, 1970-72; co-editor: Russia and the Commonwealth of Independent States: Documents, Data and Analysis, 1997. Mem. hon. steering com. Young Citizens for Johnson, 1964. Recipient Presdl. Medal of Freedom, 1981, U Thant award, 1995, Order of White Eagle, Poland, 1995. Fellow AAAS; mem. Coun. Fgn. Relations. Clubs: Metropolitan (Washington). Office: Ctr Strategic & Internat Studies 1800 K St NW Washington DC 20006-2202

BRZOZOWSKY, KEITH WILLIAM, software consultant; b. Scranton, Pa., Dec. 6, 1967; s. William John and Jeannette Mihok Brzozowsky. BS in Aerospace Engring., U.S. Naval Acad., 1989; MBA, U. Hawaii, 1997. Cert. nuclear engr. officer, U.S. Dept. Energy, 93. Commd. ensign USN, 1989, advanced through grades to lt., resigned, 1997; product mktg. mgr. Applied Materials, Inc., Santa Clara, Calif., 1997—2000; project mgr. ECnet, Inc., Mountain View, Calif., 2000—01; dir. profl. svcs. Corticon Techs., Inc., San Mateo, Calif., 2001—. Mem.: U.S. Naval Acad. Alumni Assn., Beta Gamma Sigma. Republican. Lutheran. Avocations: baseball, military history, guitar, weight training, golf. Home: 1000 Escalon Ave Apt 2124 Sunnyvale CA 94085 Office: Corticon Techs Inc 400 S El Camino Real Ste 1275 San Mateo CA 94402 E-mail: keithbz@yahoo.com.

BRZUSTOWICZ, JOHN CINQ-MARS, lawyer; b. Rochester, N.Y., Feb. 1, 1957; s. Richard J. and Alice (Cinq-Mars) B.; m. Diane Day, Aug. 22, 1981; children: Richard Reed, Megan Day, Emily Day-Hanson. BA, Coll. Wooster, 1979; JD, Case Western Res. U., 1985; cert., Cornell Inst. Labor Rels., 1982. Bar: Pa. 1985, U.S. Dist. Ct. (we. dist.) Pa. 1985, U.S. Ct. Appeals (3d cir.) 1986, U.S. Supreme Ct. 1990. Asst. to dir. Inst. Am. Music U. Rochester, Rochester, 1979-82; assoc. Peacock, Keller, Yohe, Day & Ecker, Washington, Pa., 1985-88, Sable, Makoroff & Libenson, Pitts., 1988-90; pvt. practice Brzustowicz Law Offices, McMurray, Washington, Pa., 1990-94; shareholder Day, Brzustowicz & Malkin, P.C., McMurray, Pa., 1995—. Chmn. bd. dirs. Inst. for Am. Music of Eastman Sch. Music, 1997—; chmn. law libr. Washington County (Pa.) Bar, 1992; mem. com. Jud. Inquiry Bd., Pa., 1991-94; dir. Hanson Inst. of Am. Music of the Eastman Sch. of Music, U. Rochester, 1995. Co-author: Pennsylvania School Law, 1992, Pennsylvania Adminstrative Law, 1987; editor: So You Want to Be A Lawyer, 1990; advisor on PBC documentary: Life of Howard Hanson, An American Masterpiece, 1987. Pres. Newman Club, Coll. Wooster, 1976-79; v.p. Young Reps., Wooster, Ohio, 1977-79; co-founder, officer Wooster Polo and Hunt Club, 1976-79, bd. dirs. Hanson Inst. Am. Music of Eastman Sch. Music, 1996, Washington County Fund, 1998-2000, Pyramid Gallery, Rochester, N.Y., 1997—; mem. fin. com. JFK Sch., 1998—. Recipient Merit award Inst. Am. Music, 1981, Outstanding Scholar award Rotary, Albert H. Robbins award for Meritorious Svc. in Advancement of Am. Art, 2000. Mem.: KC, ATLA, ABA, Pa. Young Lawyers for Washington County (state rep. 1988), Washington County Bar Assn. (legis. com. 2001—), Allegheny County Bar Assn., Pa. Bar Assn. (del. 1992), Wash. C. of C., Peters Twp. C. of C. Roman Catholic. Avocations: reading, woodworking, biology. Home: 56 Mckennan Ave Washington PA 15301-3531 Office: 3821 Washington Rd Mc Murray PA 15317-2964 E-mail: dexterdawg@aol.com.

BRZUSTOWICZ, STANISLAW HENRY, clinical dentistry educator; b. Bklyn., Apr. 30, 1919; s. John Stanislaw and Victoria (Szutarski) B.; m. Wanda Frances Seglow, July 3, 1949; children: Robert, Thomas, Michael, Linda. BS, St. John's U., 1940; DDS, Columbia U., 1943. Pvt. practice, Bklyn., 1947-74, New Hyde Park, NY, 1963-93; prof. clin. dentistry Columbia U. Sch. Dental and Oral Surgery, N.Y.C., 1946-87, prof. emeritus clin. dentistry (operative), 1987—; course dir. preclin. operative dentistry, attending dentist Presbyn. Hosp., N.Y.C., 1974—89; spl. lectr. in dentistry, 1990—. Bd. dirs., v.p. Prospect Pattern & Machine Works, Inc., Bklyn., 1962-72; bd dirs., sec. to bd. Atlas Savs. & Loan Assn., Bklyn., 1962-94. Contg. author Differential Diagnosis of Mouth Diseases, 1943 Served to capt. U.S. Army, 1943-46 Mem. ADA, N.Y. State Dental Soc., 2d Dist. Dental Soc., Nat. Med. and Dental Soc., Cath. Dentist Guild (joint program dental care for indigent children with Cath. Guardian Soc. 1949-54), Roger Bacon Sci. Soc., Kosciuszko Found., Holy Name Soc., Omicron Kappa Upsilon. Republican. Roman Catholic. Home: 58 Executive Dr New Hyde Park NY 11040-1014 Office: Columbia U Sch of Dental and Oral Surgery 630 W 168th St New York NY 10032-3795

BSOUL, SAMER A. dentist, educator; b. Irbid, Jordan, Jan. 1, 1971; arrived in U.S., 1998; s. Abdel-Rahman M. and Najieh M. Bsoul. BDS, Jordan U. Sci. and Tech., 1993. Oral and maxillofacial radiology U. Tex. Health Sci. Ctr., San Antonio, 2003. Rsch. fellow U. Tex. Health Sci. Ctr., San Antonio, 1998—2000, tchg. asst., 2000—. Scholar, Ministry Health, Jordan, 1989—93. Home: Apt #335 8100 Huebner Rd San Antonio TX 78240 Office: Univ Tex Health Sci Ctr 7703 Floyd Curl Dr Mail Code 7919 San Antonio TX 78229-3900 Office Fax: 210-567-3333. Personal E-mail: bsoul@uthscsa.edu. E-mail: bsoul@uthscsa.edu.

BU, RULEI, artist, educator; b. Shanghai, July 23, 1970; arrived in U.S., 1998; s. Xinnong Bu and Grace Gao. BFA, Shanghai U., 1993. Tchr. Shanghai U., 1993—98; artist Rockville, Md., 1998—2000; pres. A A Studio, Inc., Germantown, Md., 2001—. One-man shows include Rockville City Hall, 1999, Gaithersburg (Md.) City Hall Gallery, 2000, Strathmore Hall Arts Ctr., Md., 2000, NIH, 2000, Dumbarton Concerts Gallery, Washington, 2000, Rockville (Md.) Arts Pl., 2000, Glenview Mansion Art Gallery, Md., 2001, Kensington Art Gallery, 2002, Framer's Choice Gallery, 2001, 2002, Weinberg Ctr. Arts, 2002, Gaithersburg Arts Barn, 2003. Recipient Clemente Family award, The Art League, Alexandria, Va., 2000, JoAnn Rose award, League of Reston (Va.) Artists, 2001, 1st pl. award, The Delaplaine Visual Arts Edn. Ctr., Frederick, Md., 2001. Mem.: Montgomery County Art Assn. (1st pl. 1999, 2001), Rockville Art League (1st pl. 1999, 2000), Gaithersburg Fine Arts Assn. (1st pl. 1999, 2000, 2001). Office: A A Studio Inc 18109 Coachmans Rd Germantown MD 20874

BUATTA, MARIO, interior designer; b. N.Y.C., Oct. 20, 1935; s. Felix and Olive B.; student Wagner Coll., 1953-54, Cooper Union, 1958-59, Parsons Sch. Design, Europe, 1961; Ph.D. (hon.), Wagner Coll. Asst. decorator B. Altman & Co., N.Y.C., 1959-61, Elisabeth Draper Inc., N.Y.C., 1961, Keith Irvine and Co., N.Y.C., 1962; pvt. practice interior decorating, N.Y.C., 1963—, works include: Protocol Offices of 1964 World's Fair, exec. offices Met. Opera House at Lincoln Center, N.Y.C.; dean of design Chgo. Merchandise Mart Design Community. Bd. dirs. East Side House Settlement, N.Y.C.; past bd. dirs. Kips Bay Boys Club, N.Y.C., Fashion Inst. Tech., N.Y.C.; work in process includes: redecoration of Blair House, the White House Guest House. Bd. dirs. Royal Oak, Nat. Trust Gt. Britain, The Hist. House Trust, N.Y.C.; chmn. Winter Antiques Show, East Side House Settlement benefit; hon. chmn. Cooper Hewitt Mus., Decorative Arts Soc. Mem. Am. Soc. Interior Designers. Designs included in numerous publs. Inducted into Interior Design Hall of Fame; Giant of Design award Ho. Beautiful Mag., 2002, Pratt Legend award Pratt Inst., 2003. Office: 120 E 80th St New York NY 10021-0306

BUB, ALEXANDER DAVID, acoustical engineer; b. Milw., Oct. 19, 1949; s. Alex Robert and Rose (Monafo) B.; m. Kay Lynn Johannes, Jan. 5, 1982; 1 child, David. AAS in Electronic Communications, Milw. Sch. Engring., 1969, MS in Engring. Mgmt., 2000; BA in Econs., History and Anthropology, U. Wis., Milw., 1976. Nuclear weapons specialist USAF, 1969-73; with Harley Davidson, Inc., Milw., 1977—, project mgr., 1997—, with powertrain devel. group, 1993—, sect. lead power generation, 1999—, project mgr. tech. devel., 2000—03, program staff engr. tech. devel., 2003—. U.S. nat. champion 410 Superbike, 1979, Mexican champion 750 Prodn. and Open Superbike, 1980, Midwest champion Supertwins and Formula Twins, 1985, 86, 87, Sport Supermotard Superbikers2 Champion, 2002. Mem. Acoustical Soc. Am. (guest speaker conf. 1990, 92), Soc. Automotive Engrs., Western/Eastern Roadracing Assn., Am. Motorcyclist Assn. Avocations: motorcycle rr, mx, trials riding, mountain bikes, skiing, amateur radio WA9OLH. Home: W4802 Knuth Rd Random Lake WI 53075-1355 Office: Harley Davidson Inc 11800 W Capitol Dr Wauwatosa WI 53222 1007

BUBARIS, GUS JOHN, real estate analyst; b. N.Y.C., Feb. 3, 1952; s. Gus and Athena (Chandris) B. BA, C.W. Post Coll., L.I. U., 1974; MA, SUNY, Binghamton, 1976. Real estate dir. OPM Leasing Services, inc., N.Y.C., 1976-80; real estate mgr. Bell System, East Orange, N.J., 1980-86; asst. treas. Chase Manhattan Bank, N.Y.C., 1986-89; account officer Fed. Deposit Ins. Corp., N.Y.C., 1989-92; sr. asset mgr. Sterling Equities, Great Neck, N.Y., 1993-98; asst. v.p. Green Point Fin. Svcs., Bklyn., 1998—; instr. Port Washington Sch. Continuing Edn., 2000—. Bd. dirs. Bubaris Enterprises, Astoria, N.Y. Bd. dirs., Elytis Chair Fund Rutgers U.; computer instr. Port Washington (N.Y.) H.S., 1993—. Mem. Hellenic Univ. Club (treas. 1986-87), computer cons. 1984-90), Hellenic Am. C. of C., Hellenic Am. Bankers Assn. Republican. Greek Orthodox. Avocations: sailing, downhill skiing, cycling. Home: 6 Birchwood Ave Port Washington NY 11050-3904 Office: 807 Manhattan Ave Brooklyn NY 11222-2710

BUBASH, PATRICIA JANE, special education educator; b. St. Louis; d. Emil John and Anne Marie (Candrl) B. BA in Deaf Edn., Fontbonne U., 1974; postgrad., St. Louis U., 1975-76, U. Mo., Columbia, 1982-84, U. Mo., St. Louis, 1984; MA in Edn., Washington U., 1996. Life cert. K-12 tchr. of deaf, learning

disabilities, emotional and behavior disorders, K-8 elem. tchr., Mo. Tchr. of deaf Spl. Sch. Dist. St. Louis County, 1974—. Mem. curriculum devel. action com. Drug Free Schs.; character plus com., profl. devel. com. bldg. rep. Drug Edn. Task Force. Mem. Jr. League St. Louis, 1989—; mem. bd. jr. divsn. St. Louis Symphony Soc., co-chmn. membership, 1991-92, 92-93; co-chmn. Gypsy Caravan Vols., St. Louis, 1991, 92-93; leader Boy Scouts Am., 1984—, Explorer Scouts, 1990, Girl Scouts U.S.A., 1984—, Just Say No Club, 1987—; mem. The Troupe of Dance St. Louis, 1991—; mem. Step Up St. Louis, 1991—; active Alliance Francaise; mem. bd. dir. St. Louis-Lyon Sister Cities, Inc., 2002. Named Tchr. of Month, Spl. Sch. Dist. St. Louis County, 1987, 2000-01; recipient Spl. Needs Tchr. award Boy Scouts Am., 1989, 96, Classroom Scouting, 2002, Outstanding Leader of Yr., 2002, Commitment to Kids award Spl. Sch. Dist. St. Louis County, 2001, Spl Amb. award, 2003; Fulbright scholar Tchr. Exch., U.S./U.K., 2002-03. Mem. Coun. for Exceptional Children, Mo. Edn. Assn., Alexander Graham Bell Assn. for Deaf, Coun. Edn. of Deaf, St. Louis Ski Club, St. Louis Skating Club. Roman Catholic. Avocations: french, dancing, swimming, tennis, snow skiing. Office: Spl Sch Dist St Louis County 12110 Clayton Rd Saint Louis MO 63131-2516

BUBE, RICHARD HOWARD, materials scientist, educator; b. Providence, Aug. 10, 1927; s. Edward Neser and Ella Elvira (Baltteim) B.; m. Betty Jane Meeker, Oct. 9, 1948 (dec. Apr. 2, 1997); children: Mark Timothy, Kenneth Paul, Sharon Elizabeth, Meryl Lee; m. Mary Anne Harman, Sept. 9, 2000. Sc.B., Brown U., 1946; MA, Princeton U., 1948, PhD, 1950. Mem. sr. research staff RCA Labs., Princeton, N.J., 1948-62; prof. materials sci. and elec. engring. Stanford U., 1962-92, prof. emeritus, 1992—, chmn. dept., 1975-86, assoc. chmn. dept., 1990-91. Cons. to industry and govt. Author: A Textbook of Christian Doctrine, 1955, Photoconductivity of Solids, 1960, The Encounter between Christianity and Science, 1968, The Human Quest: A New Look at Science and Christian Faith, 1971, Electronic Properties of Crystalline Solids, 1974, Electrons in Solids, 1981, 3d edit., 1992, Fundamentals of Solar Cells, 1983, Science and the Whole Person, 1985, Photoelectronic Properties of Semiconductors, 1992, Putting It All Together: Seven Patterns for Relating Science and Christian Faith, 1995, One Whole Life: Personal Memoirs of Richard H. Bube, 1995, Photoinduced Defects in Semiconductors, 1996, Photovoltaic Materials, 1998; also articles; editor Jour. Am. Sci. Affiliation, 1969-83; mem. editl. bd. Solid State Electronics, 1975-94, Christians in [illegible] assoc. editor Ann. Rev. Materials Sci., 1969-83. Fellow Am. Phys. Soc., AAAS, Am. Sci. Affiliation; mem. Am. Soc. Engring. Edn. (life), Internat. Solar Energy Soc., Sigma Xi. Evangelical. Home: 753 Mayfield Ave Stanford CA 94305-1043 *I find no contradiction or conflict between science and Christian faith, but rather a marvelous compatibility that touches all aspects of life.*

BUBENIK, JAN, cancer researcher, biology educator; b. Brno, Czech Republic, Apr. 23, 1940; s. Jan and Terezie (Klimentová) B. MD, Charles U., Prague, Czechoslovakia, 1962; PhD, Acad. Scis., Prague, 1965, DSc, 1973. Sr. investigator Acad. Scis., Prague, 1965-72, chief dept., 1972—; dep. dir. Inst. Molecular Genetics, Prague, 1990—; assoc. prof. Charles U., 1992-95, Komenius U., Bratislava, Slovakia, 1993—. Vis. scientist Stockholm U., 1969-70, Cancer Ctr., Houston, 1992-93; vis. prof. Fibiger Inst., Copenhagen, 1985, 92; prof. cellular and molecular biology Charles U., 1995—. Contbr. over 230 articles to profl. jours.; mem. editl. bd. Internat. Jour. Oncology, Neoplasma, Gene Therapy, Jour. Cancer Rsch. and Clin. Oncology, Microbiologica, Jour. Exptl. and Clin. Cancer Rsch., others. Recipient State prize in medicine Czechoslovakia, 1985, Yamagiwa-Yoshida award Internat. Union Against Cancer, 1991, E. Nuti prize for cancer rsch. Assn. Promozione Study Immunology of Tumor, Rome, 1992. Mem. European Cytokine Soc., Internat. Endotoxin Soc. (charter mem.), N.Y. Acad. Scis., European Assn. for Cancer Rsch. (exec. com.). Roman Catholic. Avocations: sport fishing, scuba diving. Office: Czech Acad Sci Flemingovo nám 2 166 37 Prague 6 Czech Republic E-mail: bubenik@img.cas.cz.

BUBENIK, OLDRICH VENCESLAS, surgeon, oncologist; b. Czech Republic, Sept. 16, 1943; came to U.S., 1980; MD, Queens U., 1972. Diplomate Am. Bd. Surgery. From intern to resident in surgery Royal Victoria Hosp.-McGill U., Montreal, 1972-78; fellow in surg. oncology Ellis Fischel State Cancer Hosp., Columbia, Mo., 1980-82; surg. staff Brookings (S.D.) Med. Clinic, 1999—. Mem. ACS, AMA, S.D. State Med. Assn., Am. Soc. of Gen. Surgeons. Address: 12005 Pike 9162 Louisiana MO 63353

BUBLITZ, DEBORAH KEIRSTEAD, pediatrician; b. Boston, Feb. 28, 1933; d. George and Dorothy (Kingsbury) Keirstead; m. Clark Bublitz, June 1, 1958; children: Nancy B. Dyer, Susan B. Schooleman, Philip K. Bublitz, Caroline D. Bublitz, Elizabeth E. Bublitz. BS, Bates Coll., 1955; MD, Johns Hopkins U., 1959. Resident St. Louis Children's Hosp., 1959-60, U. Colo. Health Sci. Ctr. and Dept. Health and Hosps., Denver, 1968-74; pvt. practice Littleton, Colo., 1974—; asst. clin. prof. pediatrics U. Colo. Health Sci. Ctr. and Children's Hosp., 1975-87, assoc. clin. prof. pediatrics, 1987—. Creditials com. Swedish/Porter Hosp., Englewood, Colo., 1985-87, chief dept. pediatrics, 1985-87; med. assoc., advisor LaLeche League, 1975—. Author: (with others) Clinical Pediatric Otolaryngology, 1986. Fellow Am. Acad. Pediatrics; mem. AMA, Colo. Med. Soc. (women's governing coun. 1990-96, asst. chair women's governing coun. 1993-94, chair, 1994-95), Arapahoe Med. Soc., Am. Women's Med. Assn. Episcopalian. Avocations: painting, gardening, bird watching, grandchildren. Home: 5621 Blue Sage Dr Littleton CO 80123-2713 Office: Littleton Pediatric Med Ctr 206 W County Line Rd Ste 110 Highlands Ranch CO 80129-2319 E-mail: littletonpeds@uswest.net.

BUBNIAK, SHARON MARGARET, retired elementary education educator; b. Worcester, Mass., Aug. 9, 1945; d. William Raymond and Mildred Marion (Whalen) (dec.) Stanton; m. Robert Martin Bubniak, July 27, 1968 (div. 2001); children: Gregory Mitchell, Jesse Monroe. BS in Edn., SUNY, Brockport, 1967; MS in Edn., Syracuse (N.Y.) U., 1971; vocat. cert., Cen. Tech., Syracuse, 1978. Cert. tchr. Tchr. grade 4 Park View Elem. Sch., Kings Park, N.Y., 1967-68; sci./math. tchr. Fillmore Elem. Sch., Cedar Rapids, Iowa, 1968-69; classroom tech. Dr. King. Elem. Sch., Syracuse, 1969-72; math. lab. specialist Clinton/Dr. King Elem. Schs., Syracuse, 1972-73, Sumner/Cathedral/Seymour Elem. Schs., Syracuse, 1974-75, Seymour Elem. Sch., Syracuse, 1975-78, Our Lady of Solace/Holy Cross/Percy Hughes, Syracuse, 1980-81, Percy Hughes/Bishop Ludden High/Holy Trinity, Syracuse, 1981-82, St. Daniels/St. John the Bapt./Blessed Sacrament, Syracuse, 1982-83, Meachen Elem. Sch., 1982-88, Roberts Elem. Sch., 1983-88, Danforth Magnet Elem. Sch., 1988-95, 2d grade tchr., 1995—2000; ret., 2000; tax profl. H&R Block, Syracuse, NY, 2001—. Tchr. religious edn. Vacation Bible Sch., St. Augustine's Ch., Baldwinsville, N.Y., 1981-89, dir. folk singing group, 1987-88, mem. choir, 1974-96, Eucharistic min., 1996-2000, greeter, 1997-2000, pastoral visitor, 1997-2000; mem. math contest com. Syracuse City Sch. Dist., 1992-93; mem. Danforth Intermediate Task Force, 1992-93, peer coaching program, 1993-94, acad. intervention com., 1993-94; St. Margaret's Ch., Mattydale, N.Y., 2000; GED tchr., 2000-2002; homebound tchr. SCSD, Baldwinsville, 2001—. Den leader pack 189 Boy Scouts Am., Seneca Knolls, N.Y., 1981-88, dir. arts/crafts cub day camp, 1984, mem. roundtable Hiawatha coun. Cub Scouts, Syracuse, 1986-87, com. person troop 119, Baldwinsville, 1988—, mem. retreat weekend, 1990-91, 93-94, mem. adult leadership tng., 1989, mem. Order of the Arrow, 1991—, mem. ordeal induction, 1991, mem. brotherhood induction, 1992, treas., 1994-97, asst. advisor camping promotions, 1997-2000, mem. Vigil Honor induction, 1996; rescue mission vol. monthly meals and holidays, 1996-; mem. choir St. Margaret's Ch., Mattydale, N.Y., 2001-; mem. Nature Conservancy, N.Y. State Right to Life. Mem. AARP, N.Y. State Tchrs. Retirement Sys., Onondaga County Ret. Tchrs. Assn., N.Y. State Ret. Tchrs. Assn., N.Y. State United Tchrs., Assn. Math. Tchrs. N.Y. State, Syracuse Edn. Assn. (treas. 1977-78), Nat. Coun. Tchrs. Math., Beaver Lake Nature Ctr., Elks, Sierra Club. Democrat. Roman Catholic. Avocations: singing, camping, reading, decorating, weight training, healthy eating. Home: 904 Darlington Rd Syracuse NY 13208-2429 E-mail: smbubniak@juno.com .

BUC, NANCY LILLIAN, lawyer; b. Orange, N.J., July 27, 1944; d. George L. and Ethel Buc. AB, Brown U., 1965, LLD (hon.), 1994; LLB, U. Va., 1969. Bar: Va. 1969, N.Y. 1977, D.C. 1978. Atty. Fed. Trade Commn., Washington, 1969-72; assoc. Weil, Gotshal & Manges, N.Y., 1972-77, ptnr., 1977-78, Washington, 1978-80, 81-94, Buc & Beardsley, Washington, 1994—; chief counsel FDA, Rockville, Md., 1980-81. Mem. recombinant DNA adv. com. NIH, 1990-94; consensus panelist NIH Consensus Devel. Conf. on Effective Med. Treatment of Heroin Addiction, 1997; adj. prof. law Georgetown U. Law Ctr., 2000-2002. Mem. editl. bd. Food Drug and Cosmetic Law Jour., 1981-87, 94-97, Jour. of Products Liability, 1981-92, Health Span: The Jour. of Health, Bus. & Law, 1984-95. Mem. adv. com. on new devels. in biotech. 1986-89, mem. adv. com. on govt. policies and pharm. R & D, 1989-93, Office of Tech. Assessment, Washington, mem. com. to study drug abuse medications devel. and rsch., 1993-95; mem. com. on contraceptive R & D, Inst. Medicine, Washington, 1994-96; trustee Brown U., 1973-78, 1998—; fellow, 1980-92. Recipient Disting. Svc. award Fed. Trade Commn., Washington, 1972, Award of Merit FDA, Rockville, 1981, Sec.'s Spl. citation HHS, Washington, 1981, Ind. award Associated. Alumni of Brown U., 1991. Mem. ABA (mem. spl. com. to study FTC 1988-89), Com. of 200, Nat. Partnership for Women and Families (bd. dirs.). Office: Buc & Beardsley 919 18th St NW Ste 600 Washington DC 20006-5507

BUCCELLA, WILLIAM VICTOR, lawyer; b. Seattle, Oct. 23, 1943; s. Fred J. and Adeline J. (Carriero) Buccella; m. Mary A. O'Shea, Aug. 26, 1967; children: Mark Brendon, Jennifer Ball, Peter James. BS, Canisius Coll., 1965; JD, Cornell U., 1968. Bar: NY 1968, US Dist. Ct. (we. dist.)/NY 1972. Law clk. US Dist. Ct. (we. dist.), NY, 1972—74; assoc. Diebold & Millonzi, Buffalo, 1974—77; assoc. gen. counsel Wheelabrator-Frye, Inc., Hampton, NH, 1977—81, gen. counsel, 1981—83; v.p., asst. gen. counsel the Signal Co., Inc., La Jolla, Calif., 1983—86; mng. dir., gen. counsel The Henley Group, Inc., La Jolla, Calif., 1986—90; ptnr. Hinckley, Allen, Snyder & Comen, Boston, 1990—92, Goodwin, Proctor & Hoar, Boston, 1992—; dir. New Eng. Legal Found., Boston; chief counsel Rep. Nat. Conv., 1996. Lt. JAGC USN, 1969—72. Mem.: NY State Bar Assn., ABA.

BUCCHERI, ELIZABETH C. musician, educator; b. Chester, S.C., Sept. 26, 1942; d. James Boyce Bankhead and Johng'y R. Bankhead McCaskill; m. John Stephen Buccheri, June 15, 1968; children: Mark Robert, Sarah Elizabeth. BS, Winthrop U., Rock Hill, S.C., 1964; MMus, Eastman Sch. Music, Rochester, N.Y., 1966, DMusArts, 1978. Disting. vis. prof. North Park U., Chgo., 1969—; pianist Chgo. Symphony Chorus, 1969-99; asst. condr. Lyric Opera Chgo., 1987—; music dir. Chamber Music at North Park, Chgo., 1981—. Sr. lectr. Northwestern U. Musician (rec. for) CRI, Sony, Cedille, Boston, Albany and Spectrum labels. Mem. trustees coun. U. Rochester; mem. alumni coun. Eastman Sch. Music.; active Books on Wheels, Evanston (Ill.) Pub. Libr., 1988—. Mem. Chgo. Fedn. Musicians, Soc. Am. Musicians. Democrat. Avocations: gardening, needlework, cooking, reading, crossword puzzles. E-mail: e-buccheri@northwestern.edu.

BUCCI, THOMAS VINCENT, music educator, pianist, composer; b. Providence, Sept. 7, 1926; s. Vincent Anthony and Anna Bucci; m. Catherine Elizabeth Conway; children: Thomas, Anne Cignoli, Vincent, Kathleen Ball, David. Bachelor's degree, New England Conservatory of Music, 1951, Master's degree, 1961. Cert. tchr. Maine. Instrumental music supr. Portland Maine Sch. Dept., 1952—81; mem. piano faculty U. So. Maine, Gorham, 1971—. Organist St. Joseph's, Portland, 1965—. Composer: (work for viola and piano) Concertante, 1976, (chorus and piano composition) Three Sketches, 1978, (work for chorus and orch.) Four Longfellow Pieces, 1996, (orch. piece) Italian Folk Fantasy, 1987, (trumpet trio) Trio for Trumpets, 1979, (work for chorus and orch.) MASS, 1978. Accompanist Maine All-State Chorus; music adjudicator Music Educators Assns., 1965—90; mus. dir. Portland Lyric Theater, 1952—65; guest condr. Portland Youth Orch., 1965—75; piano soloist Portland Symphony, 1965—80. Staff Sgt. U.S. Army. Recipient commn. for chorus and organ piece, 1st Congl. Ch. on Meeting House Hill, 1978, commn. for brass quintent, R.I. Philharm. Orch., woodwind quintet premier, Kennedy Ctr. Mem.: Nat. Educators Assn., Maine Music Educators, Music Educators Nat. Conf., Italian Heritage Club. Home: 140 Abby Ln Portland ME 04103 Personal E-mail: tbucci@maine.edu.

BUCCIERO, JOSEPH MARIO, JR., executive consultant; b. Phila., Mar. 27, 1948; s. Joseph Mario Sr. and Carmela (Biscari) B.; m. Nancy Louise Arnquist, Aug. 19, 1972; children: Paul Joseph, Mark Benjamin. BS, Villanova U., 1969. Software programmer, project software engr. Leeds and Northrup Co., North Wales, Pa., 1969-72, applications engr., 1972-74; systems cons. Macro Corp., Horsham, Pa., 1974-76, consulting engr., 1976-82, sr. consulting engr., 1982-89; strategic bus. unit mgr. Alstom ESCA, Bellevue, Wash., 1989-90; prin. cons. KEMA-ECC, Fairfax, Va., 1990—; bus. area mgr. KEMA Consulting, Fairfax, 1991—; v.p. KEMA Consulting, Inc., Fairfax, 1992-98; sr. v.p. KEMA Cons., Horsham, Pa., 1999—, KEMA, Inc., Chalfont, Pa., 2001—. Contbr. articles to profl. jours. Ch. coun. pres. Little Zion Luth. Ch., Telford, Pa., 1980-85. Mem. IEEE (sr. mem.). Avocations: bowling, down hill skiing, traveling.

BUCCINO, ALPHONSE, university dean emeritus, consultant; b. N.Y.C., Mar. 14, 1931; s. Aniello and Anna (Tino) B.; m. Estelle Marie Ambrose, Mar. 22, 1953; 1 child, Daniel Laurence. BS, U. Chgo., 1958, MS, 1959, PhD, 1967. Head math dept. DePaul U., Chgo., 1963-70; sci. edn. adminstr. NSF, Washington, 1970-84; dean edn., prof. U. Ga., Athens, 1984-94; edn. advisor Office of Sci. and Tech. Policy, Exec. Office of Pres., Washington, 1992-93; pres. Contemporary Comm. Inc., Bethesda, Md., 1994—. Cons. innovation mgmt. Author, editor conception and design numerous planning and policy documents, official org. pubs. Capt. USMC, 1951-54, Korea. Woodrow Wilson Found. fellow, 1958, NSF fellow, 1959-61. Fellow AAAS; mem. Am. Math. Soc., Nat. Coun. Tchrs. of Math., Am. Ednl. Rsch. Assn. (mem. fin. com. 1976-79). Roman Catholic. Avocations: bicycling, cooking. Home and Office: 5615 Glenwood Rd Bethesda MD 20817-6727 E-mail: abuccino@earthlink.net.

BUCCINO, DANIEL L. psychotherapist, consultant; BA, MA, Johns Hopkins U., 1987; MSW, Smith Coll., 1989. Diplomate NASW, Am. Bd. Examiners in Clin. Social Work. Clin. supr./student coord. cmty. psychiatry, psychotherapist Johns Hopkins Bayview Med. Ctr., Balt., 1989—; pvt. practice psychotherapy Balt., 1992—; co-founder, co-dir. Balt.-Washington Brief Therapy Inst., Inc., Balt., 1994—. Asst. prof. psychiatry Johns Hopkins U. Sch. Medicine, Balt., 2000—; clin. asst. prof. U. Md. Sch. Social Work, Balt., 1996—; clin. asst. prof., faculty field instr. Smith Coll. Sch. Social Work, Northampton, Mass., 1998—; presenter and cons. in field. Editor: Maryland Social Work Legal Handbook, Vol. 1, 1994, Vol. 2, 1996; contbr. articles to profl. jours., books, and newspapers. Mem. IPFE, Clin. Social Work Fedn. and Guild, Johns Hopkins Civility Initiative. Office: 711 W 40th St Ste 456 Baltimore MD 21211-2199

BUCCINO, ERNEST JOHN, JR., lawyer; b. Oct. 29, 1945; s. Ernest J. and Rachel (Talarico) B.; m. Martha Mollinedo, Dec. 27, 1968; 1 child, Anastasia. BS, Temple U., 1967, MEd, 1969, JD, 1973. Bar: Pa. 1973, N.J. 1974, U.S. Dist. Ct. (ea. dist.) Pa. 1973, U.S. Ct. Appeals (3d cir.) 1973, U.S. Supreme Ct. 1978. Officer, counsel Blue Cross Greater Phila., 1973-74; law clk. Supreme Ct. Pa., Phila., 1974; mem. Gross & Buccino, P.A., Phila., 1975-96; pvt. practice Phila., 1996-97; prin. Buccino Law Office, Phila., 1997—. Lectr. Roscoe Pound, 1986, Trial Advocacy Found. Pa., Phila., 1984; mem. civil procedure rules com. Supreme Ct. Pa., 1994—. Author: The Barrister Vol. XVI, #3, 1985. Chmn. eastern dist. LAWPAC, Harrisburg, Pa., 1983—. Mem. ABA, ATLA, Pa. Bar Assn., Pa. Trial Lawyers Assn. (bd. dirs. 1982—), Phila. Trial Lawyers Assn. (bd. dirs. 1982—, lectr. luncheon series 1986), Justinian Soc. (bd. dirs. 1982—), Phila. Bar Assn. (chmn. econs. of law practice 1983, nominating com. 1982-83), Sons of Italy. Office: 2112 Walnut St Philadelphia PA 19103-4808 E-mail: EJB@buccino.com.

BUCCO, ANTHONY MARK, lawyer; b. Passaic, N.J., Apr. 12, 1962; s. Anthony Rocco and Helen Bucco; children: Anthony, Lauren, Jenna. BA in Bus. Mgmt./Econs. magna cum laude, Lycoming Coll., 1984; JD cum laude, Seton Hall U., 1987. Bar: N.J. 1987, D.C. 1989. Legal asst. Morris County Prosecutor's Office, Morristown, N.J., 1986; assoc. Villoresi, Edwards & Jansen, Boonton, N.J., 1986-90, Mudge, Rose, Guthrie, Alexander & Ferdon, Parsippany, N.J., 1990-93; ptnr. Jansen, Bucco, DeBona & Semrau, Boonton, 1994—2002. Mem. adv. bd. DAYTOP at Mendham, N.J., 1992—; dep. commr. Morris County Crime Stoppers, Morristown, 1996—; bd. dirs. Angel Connection Inc., Rockaway, N.J. Active Boonton Fire Dept., 1980—, Boonton Bd. Edn., 1987-93; county com. mem. Boonton Twp. Rep. Com., 1998—; coun. mem. Govs. Coun. on Alcoholism and Drug Abuse, Trenton, N.J., 1998—. Mem. ABA, N.J. State Bar Assn., Morris County Bar Assn., N.J. Inst. for Mcpl. Attys., Boonton Rotary (pres.-elect 1999-00). Republican. Roman Catholic. Office: Jansen Bucco DeBona & Semrau 413 W Main St Boonton NJ 07005-1149

BUCCO, ANTHONY R. state legislator; b. Boonton, N.J., Feb. 24, 1938; m. Helen Jayne Bucco; 1 child, Anthony M., Community Coll of N.Y., Hume Inst. Dist. mgr. United Resin Products, Inc.; exec. v.p. Thomas W. Dunn Corp.; mem. Morris County Bd. Freeholders, 1989-92; chair. Boonton Municipal Republican Comm., 1993-95; mayor Town of Boonton, N.J., 1984-89; assemblyman N.J. Gen. Assembly, 1995-98; mem. N.J. Senate, Dist. 25, Trenton, 1998—. Mem. solid and hazardous waste and state govt. coms. N.J. State Assembly. Mem. Boonton Bd. Adjustment, 1976, Bd. Aldermen, 1978, former pres.; mayor City of Boonton; mem. Morris County Bd. Chosen Freeholders, 1989-92, Morris County Econ. Commn., Pvt. Indsl. Coun., Human Svc. Adv. Commn., Morris County Mcpl. Utilities Authority. Mem., Elks, Boonton Bd. of Aldermen, So. Boonton Field Club, Morris County Human Srvs., Morris County Bd. Social Srvs., Morris County Municipal Utility Authority. Office: 60 Broadway Ste 21 Denville NJ 07834-2706 Address: NJ Senate State House Sec Gen Assembly CN-098 Trenton NJ 08625*

BUCEY, CONSTANCE VIRGINIA RUSSELL, retired elementary school educator, education educator; b. Miami, Aug. 22, 1936; d. Mose and Lillian (Jones) Russell; m. Henry Lee Bucey. BS Virginia State Coll., 1959, postgrad. U. Miami, 1961—63; postgrad. Fla. A&M U., Tallahassee, 1962—63; postgrad. UCLA, 1970; MA and Reading Specialist Credential, Pepperdine U., 1976. Tchr. J.R.E. Lee Elem. Sch., South Miami, Fla., 1959—67, Margaret Duff Elem. Sch., Rosemead, Calif., 1974—82, Hillcrest Elem. Sch., Monterey Park, Calif., 1982—95; ret., 1995; part-time prof. Calif. State U. Charter Sch. Edn., L.A., 1998—, univ. supr. in divsn. curriculum and instrn., 1998—. Bd. pres., v.p., dir. First Fin. Fed. Credit Union, 1973—82, dir., 1985—. Los Angeles Ct. juror docent. Recipient Vol. Achievement Filene award, 1997, awards for oil paintings, various exhbns. Mem.: AAUW, NEA, Nat. Assn. Credit Union Presidents, Ret. Tchrs. Calif., Garvery Sch. Tchrs., Calif. Tchrs. Assn., Reading Specialists of Calif., Women Aware, Southland Art Assn., Bus. and Profl. Womens Club, Am. Legion Aux., Alpha Kappa Alpha. Home: 871 Ashiya Rd Montebello CA 90640

BUCHALTER, MARTIN, pharmaceutical medical device company executive; b. N.Y.C., Feb. 28, 1932; s. Samuel David and Esther (Springer) B.; m. Carol C. Schechter, Aug. 11, 1963; children: Vida Harband, Neal, Rona Buchalter Popkin. BS, Phila. Coll. Pharmacy and Sci., 1955; MS, L.I. U., 1965. Pres. Parker Labs., Inc., Orange, N.J., 1958—; pharm. cons. N.J. Divsn. Instn. and Agys., Trenton, 1962-73. Adj. prof. U. R.I., 1965-70; trustee Phila. Coll. Pharmacy and Sci., dir. Alumni Assn.; chmn. exhibitor adv. coun. Am. Inst. Ultrasound in Medicine. Trustee Orange Meml. Hosp., N.J. Mem. Am. Pharm. Assn., N.J. Pharm. Assn., Am. Phys. Therapy Assn., Assn. for Advancement of Med. Instrumentation, N.J. State C. of C., Health Industry Mfrs. Assn., World Trade Assn. of N.J., Rho Chi. Achievements include pioneer work in ultrasound field. Office: Parker Labs Inc 286 Eldridge Rd Fairfield NJ 07004-2509

BUCHAN, ALAN BRADLEY, rail transportation executive, consultant; b. N.Y.C., Mar. 1, 1936; s. Harold Bradley and Grace Viola (Lahrs) B.; m. Janet Lucille Riemersma, Feb. 20, 1960; children: Robert Michael, Richard Steven, Kathleen Ann. BCE, Norwich U., 1957; MLA, cert. in Hist. Preservation, U. Pa., 1992. Track supr. The Pa. R.R., various locations, 1964-66, indsl. engr. Phila., 1966-68; tng. supr. Penn Cen. Transp. Co., Phila., 1968-69; dir. tng. and safety Franklin Mint, Inc., Franklin Center, Pa., 1969-71; dir. mgmt. devel. N.Y.C. Transit Authority, Bklyn., 1971-72; sr. cons. Cole, Warren and Long, Phila., 1972-74, Transp. and Distbn. Assocs., Media, Pa., 1974-77, v.p., 1977-86, pres., 1986-89, TSD, Inc., Phila., 1986-89; v.p. transp. Day & Zimmermann, Inc., Phila., 1986-89; prin. Alan Buchan & Assocs., Mount Laurel, N.J., 1989—. Vis. lectr. U. Pa., 1993; open space program adminstr. County Burlington, N.J., 1992-98. V.p., trustee Whitesbog Preservation Trust, 1993-97; chmn. adv. bd. N.J. Historic Sites Coun., bd. dirs., chair bldg. and grounds com. YMCA Camp Ockanickon, pres., 2003; bd. dirs. Pa. RR Tech. and Hist. Soc. Mem. Chi Epsilon. Republican. Episcopalian. Avocation: model making. Home: 785 Cornwallis Dr Mount Laurel NJ 08054-3209 E-mail: abbuchan1@comcast.net.

BUCHAN, DOUGLAS CHARLES, petroleum company executive, government official; b. Bklyn., Aug. 4, 1936; s. Charles J. and Amelia P. (Petraca) B.; 1 son, Paul Douglas. Student, U. Fla., 1954-56. Pres. Buchan Gas Co., St.Petersburg, Fla., 1955-86, Buchan Oil Co., St.Petersburg, 1966-89, Grill Parts Distbrs., 1982-86, Site Mgmt., 1983—; dep. asst. sec. energy U.S. Dept. Energy, Washington, 1989—. Mem. U.S. SEanate Bus. Adv. Com., 1984—. Pres. Pinellas County Rep. Ivory Club; chmn. Pinellas campaign Reagan-Bush, Fla. campaign George Bus for Pres. 1st lt. U.S. Army, 1958-65. Mem. Nat. Oil Jobbers Coun., Nat. Liquified Petroleum Gas Assn., Fla. Petroleum Marketers Assn. (v.p.), Oil Fuel Inst. Fla (pres., chmn. bd.), St. Petersburg Yacht. Episcopalian. Home: 1067 42nd Ave NE Saint Petersburg FL 33703-5235 Office: US Dept Energy 1000 Independence Ave SW Washington DC 20585-0001 E-mail: buchandoug@msn.com.

BUCHAN, JONATHAN EDWARD, JR., lawyer; b. Mullins, S.C., Sept. 1, 1950; s. Jonathan Edward and Margaret Alice (Liles) B.; m. Suzette Rogers Phillips, Nov. 22, 1986; 1 stepchild, Geoffrey Eliot Eloge; 1 child, Caroline Phillips. AB magna cum laude, Princeton U., 1972; JD, Duke U., 1978. Bar: N.C. 1978. Co-founder, sr. editor, Osceola News Weekly, Columbia, SC, 1973—74; govt. reporter Charlotte Observer, Columbia, SC, 1974—75; govt. editor Charlotte (NC) Observer, 1983—84; ptnr. Helms Mulliss & Wicker and predecessor firms, Charlotte, 1984—. Mem. adj. faculty dept. mass media law Wake Forest Law Sch., 1992—; bd. dirs. Legal Svcs. for So. Piedmont, Inc., 1993-98. Co-author: 50-State Survey of Libel Law, N.C. Sect., 1981—; contbg. author: North Carolina Media Law Handbook, 2001. Pres., bd. dirs. Hospice at Charlotte, Inc., 1982-88; adv. bd. Trust for Pub. Land, Carolinas. 2001—. Avocations: fly fishing, tennis, reading. Home: 2342 Thetford Ct Charlotte NC 28211-3268 Office: Helms Mulliss & Wicker PO Box 31247 201 N Tryon St Ste 3000 Charlotte NC 28202-1157 E-mail: Buchan247@aol.com, jon.buchan@hmw.com.

BUCHAN, RONALD FORBES, internal and preventive medicine physician; b. Concord, N.H., Sept. 24, 1915; s. Robert and Mary Jean (Forbes) B.; m. Maureen O'Regan, June 17, 1940; children: Robert Bruce, Joan Dallas (Mrs. Fleming), Ian Forbes Morgan. AB, U. N.H., 1936; MD, C.M., McGill U., 1942; postgrad., Princeton U., 1958. Diplomate Nat. Bd. Med. Examiners, Am. Bd. Preventive Medicine. Reporter Concord Daily Monitor, 1936; asst. exec. sec. Unemployment Compensation Commn., N.H. Dept. Labor, 1937; sanitarian City of Concord and Eastern Health Dist. N.H., 1938; chief, med. unit Bur. Indsl. Hygiene, Conn. Dept. Health, 1943-46; dir. Hartford Small Plant Indsl. Med. Svcs., 1946; clin. dir., asst. prof. indsl. medicine Yale U. Inst. Occupational Medicine and Hygiene, 1946-48; assoc. clin. prof. indsl. medicine N.Y.U. Bellevue Post Grad. Med. Sch., 1948-57; assoc. med. dir. Prudential Ins. Co. Am., 1948-49, dir. employee health, 1949-57, med. dir., v.p. med. svcs., 1957-74, cons. occupational medicine, environ. medicine, toxicology, 1974—. Chief med. dir., v.p. Mediscreen, 1974-87; propr. Portsmouth (N.H.) Athenaeum; assoc. clin. prof. preventive medicine Tufts U. Sch. Medicine, 1958-74; vis. lectr. numerous med. schs., 1948-89. Narrator (audio hist. tour) The Freedom Trail, Boston, (audio visual hist. survey) Shipbuilding on the Kennebec-Maine Maritime Mus.; author: Industrial Toxicology; contbr. Oxford Medicine, Current Therapy, Occupational Medicine, Encyclopedia-Medico-Chirurgicale (Paris); also numerous articles to profl. and lit. jours. Chmn. rsch. adv. com. Brattleboro (Vt.) Retreat, 1960-70; mem. sci. adv. bd. Office Chief Staff USAF, chmn. life scis. human factors facilities, 1960-65, protocol rank, lt. gen.; cons. R.I. Group Health Assn., 1973-75, Harvard Community Health Plan, 1972-75; bd. dirs. Met. Boston chpt. ARC, 1971-73, chmn. com. on safety, 1972-74; founding mem. Challenger Space Ctr., 1987; trustee Miles Meml. Hosp., Damariscotta, Maine, 1988-91. Sr. asst. surg., USPHS, 1943-46; surgeon-lt. York (Maine) Militia-Gov.'s Footguard, 1971— Recipient Honor award Wisdom Soc., 1970. Fellow Am. Coll. Occupl. and Environ. Medicine (past pres.), Am. Coll. Preventive Medicine (chmn. com. on clin. procedures 1972-74), Am. Acad. Occupl. Medicine (past pres.), Acad. Medicine N.J. (past pres.); mem. AAAS, Am. Indsl. Hygiene Assn., Am. Acad. Ins. Medicine, AMA

(assoc. editor Archives Environ. Health), Assn. Internationale Pour La Medicine Du Travail (permanent commn. 1965-74), Mass. Med. Soc., Ramazzini Soc., Academie Europeene des Arts, Sciences et des Lettres, Am. Assn. Sr. Physicians, N.Y. Acad. Scis., Nat. Trust Hist. Preservation, Soc. for Preservation of New Eng. Antiquities, John Buchan Soc. (Edinburgh), Osler Libr. (patron McGill U., Montreal), Soc. for Protection of N.H. Forests, North Country Authors and Scientists League (past pres.), Newcomen Soc. N.Am., St. Andrew's Soc. of Maine, Can. Hist. Soc., N.H. Hist. Soc., Clan Buchan U.S.A., Clan Forbes U.S.A., U.N.H. Alumni Assn. (gen. awards com. 1987-90, sec. U.N.H. class of '36, 1981—, Pres.'s Coun. 2000—), McGill U. Alumni Assn., Friends of Bowdoin Coll., Friends of Mt. Holyoke Coll., Friends of Middlebury Coll., Strawberry Bange Mus. (patron), Black Heritage Tr. Portsmouth, N.H. (patron). Home: Mount St Mary # 308 1701 Hooksett Rd Hooksett NH 03106-1644 *Where three physicians foregather there are two skeptics.*

BUCHAN, RUSSELL PAUL, publisher, gas company executive, entrepreneur; b. St. Petersburg, Fla., May 24, 1947; s. Charles Joseph and Amelia (Petraca) B. BS in Econs. magna cum laude, Stetson U., 1969; MA, Vanderbilt U., 1975. Asst. to pub. Trend Publs., Tampa, Fla., 1971-74; book editor South Mag., Tampa, 1973-74; owner Buchan Gas Co., St. Petersburg, 1968—. Pub. Buchan Publs., St. Petersburg, 1980—96; pres. Buchan Gas Co., Grills Parts Dist., 1986—. Host Radio Sta. WTAN, Clearwater, Fla.; co-author: Florida: A Guide to the Best Restaurants, Resorts, Hotels, 1992, Florida Weekends, 1991, rev. edit., 1994; pub.: Florida's Best Beach Vacations, Florida County Inns, 1993. Mem. Pinellas County Gas Adv. Bd., 1979-88, vice-chmn., 1982-83, chmn. 1986-87; bd. dirs. Eckerd Coll. Library Friends, 1971-85, 91-95, chmn., 1982. Named Res. Grand champion Fla. State Barbecue Championship, 1995; Woodrow Wilson fellow, 1969. Mem. Pinellas County Gas Assn. (sec.-treas. 1977-78, pres. 1979-80), Fla. Young Gassers (dist. dir. 1979-81), Nat. LP Gas Assn., Fla. LP Gas Assn. (dir. 1979-81), Fla. Mag. Assn. (treas. 1974-75), Tampa Bay Econs. Forum, Kansas City Barbecue Soc., Internat. Wine and Food Soc. (br. chmn. St. Petersburg 1979-80), Wine Friends, WineBuffs, Brotherhood Knights of Vine, Order of Dali. Republican. Roman Catholic. Office: Buchan Gas Co 6150 49th St N Saint Petersburg FL 33709-2116

BUCHANAN, ANDREW SIMPSON, writer; b. Glasgow, Scotland, Aug. 21, 1965; came to U.S., 1998; s. Andrew Livingston and Catherine Cameron B.; m. Patricia Ann Cignarella, Aug. 12, 1994; children: Aimee, Katerina. MA with honors, U. Glasgow, Scotland, 1990; PhD, U. St. Andrews, Scotland, 2000. Lic. referee U.S. Soccer Fedn. Mgmt. trainee Std. Life Assurance. Co., Edinburgh, Scotland, 1990-92; freelance writer Summit, N.Y., 1998—; tchr. Randolph H.S., NJ. Soccer coach, trainer Summit Soccer Club, 1999—. Author: Peace With Justice, 2000. Mem. Nat. Soccer Coaches Assn. Am. Avocations: soccer, scottish politics. Home: 12 Aubrey St Summit NJ 07901

BUCHANAN, BOB BRANCH, education educator; b. Richmond, Va., Aug. 7, 1937; s. Ben Keys Buchanan and Hazel Weisiger; m. Melinda Baab Speas, June 12, 1965; children: Anne, Alice, Elizabeth Buchanan Fretz, Catherine Buchanan Chang. BA, Emory & Henry Coll., Va., 1958; PhD, Duke U., N.C., 1962. Lectr. U. of Calif., Berkeley, 1963—68, assoc. prof., 1968—74, prof., 1974—, dept. chair, 1982—86, 1996—99. Project mgr. U.S. Dept. of Agr., Washington, 1980; adv. coms. NSF, Washington, 1980—84; pres. Am. Soc. of Plant Biologists, Rockville, Md., 1995—96. Editor: (book) Biochemistry and Molecular Biology of Plants (Silver award and Book award, 2001); author: (rsch. article) Procs. of the Nat. Acad. of Scis., Ann. Rev. of Plant Physiology (Citation Classic, 1980). Pres.parent's group Women's Rowing Team, Berkeley, Calif., 1989—90; mem. Neighborhood Preservation Group, Berkeley, Calif., 2000; home used as polling pl. for elections Berkeley, Calif. Recipient Bessenyei medal, Hungarian Ministry of Edn., 1987, Charles F. Kettering award, Am. Soc. of Plant Biologists, 1998. Fellow: Guggenheim Found., Am. Acad. for the Advancement of Sci., Am. Acad. of Arts & Scis.; mem.: NAS. Achievements include discovery of Redox regulation and the reverse citric acid cycle in studies on photosynthesis, role of a key protein in germination and biotechnology in studies on seeds; patents for Inventor on six patents. Avocations: swimming, reading, farming. Home: 19 Tamalpais Rd Berkeley CA 94708 Office: U of Calif 111 Koshland Hall Berkeley CA 94720 Office Fax: 510-642-7356. E-mail: view@nature.berkeley.edu.

BUCHANAN, BRUCE, II, political science educator; b. Shelby, Mont., July 28, 1945; s. Neil and Dorothy Jean (Gallup) B.; m. Susan Safford Bright, June 10, 1964 (div. June 1976); m. Stephanie Ann Sokolewicz, Jan. 3, 1981; children: Kathryn Elaine, Douglas Neil, Jacqueline May. BA, Stanford U., 1967; MA, Yale U., 1969; MPhil, 1970, PhD, 1972. Prof. U. Ga., Athens, 1973-74, U. Tex., Austin, 1974—. Author: The Presidential Experience, 1978, The Citizens Presidency, 1987,Electing A President, 1991, Renewing Presidential Politics, 1996. Exec. dir. Markle Commn. on Media and Electorate, 1988-90; rsch. dir. Markle Found. Presdl. Election Study, 1992, dir. Markle Presdl. Watch, 1996. Mem. Am. Polit. Sci. Assn. (award for best paper on presidency 1997), Presidency Rsch. Group. Avocations: cello, sports, gardening. Home: 1304 Wilshire Blvd Austin TX 78722-1127 Office: U Tex Dept Govt Austin TX 78712-1087 E-mail: bruceb@mail.la.utexas.edu.

BUCHANAN, BRUCE, functional metal artist, photographer; b. Washington, Sept. 10, 1947; s. Lloyd and Marguerite Belva (Smith) B. Student, Long Beach C.C., U. New Orleans. Artist. Former deep-sea diver, pipe welder nationwide and P.R.; tchr. diving for Mexican govt., Veracruz, 1982. Bd. dirs. Unitarian Universalist Ch., chmn. social action com., literacy vol.; founder Free Meal Kitchen; bd. dirs. Buxton (Maine) Land Trust; active Unity Ch. With U.S. Army, 1974. Mem.: Cast Iron Seat Collectors Assn. Avocations: taking care of abused and abandoned animals, helping disadvantaged and oppressed people, creating unique, outrageous things of beauty. Office: Big City Enterprises PO Box 556 Bar Mills ME 04004-0556 Address: PO Box 556 Bar Mills ME 04004-0556 E-mail: bbuchananbigcity@sacoriver.net.

BUCHANAN, DEBRA ANNETTE, artist, jeweler; b. Toledo, Ohio, Feb. 10, 1957; d. Charles Sylvester and Caroline Belle B. BFA, Columbus Coll. Art and Design, 1993. Cert. diamontology, gemology. Exhibited in shows at Toledo Mus. Art, 20 North Gallery, Toledo, Lourdes Coll., Sylvania, Ohio, Seagate Gallery, Toledo, Midwestern Mus. Art, Elkhart, Ind., Turning Point Gallery, Washington, Lexington (Ky.) Art League, 2001, Harrisburg (Pa.) 72d Ann. Exhbn, The Mus. Store Gallery. Bd. dirs. Spectrum Friends of Fine Art, Toledo, 1996-99. Home: 2009 Idaho Toledo OH 43605

BUCHANAN, EDWARD A. education educator; b. Newark, Aug. 28, 1937; s. Osborne B. and Edna Dorothy (Weber) B.; m. Gladys J. Buchanan, Aug. 28, 1965; children Roger, Becky. AB, Rutgers U., 1959; MRE, N.Y. Theol. Sem., 1962; PhD, So. Bapt. Theol. Sem., 1970. Tchr. Cen. Sch., Middlesex, N.J.; assoc. prof. psychology and edn. Grand Rapids (Mich.) Bapt. Coll.; dean of acad. affairs, prof. Lancaster (Pa.) Bible Coll.; prof. edn., dir. continuing edn. Bethel Theol. Sem., St. Paul; sr. prof. edn. Southeastern Bapt. Theol. Sem., Wake Forest, N.C. Contbr. articles to profl. jours. Mem. bd. dirs. Trinity Acad., Raleigh, N.C. Mem. APA, ASCD, Am. Edni. Rsch. Assn., Nat. Soc. Study of Edn. Home: 1113 Silent Brook Rd Wake Forest NC 27587-7145 E-mail: gedbue@earthlink.net.

BUCHANAN, GLORIA JEAN, sales executive; b. Bowling Green, Ky., Nov. 3, 1950; d. Albert M. and Lenora (Hayes)Paschal; m. Michael C. Moonan (div.); 1 child, Shelly; m. Andrew George. Mgr. Alexander Wallcovering, Falls Church, Va., 1976-81; decorator Duron Paints and Wallvocering, Beltsville, Md., 1982-84, sales rep., 1984-85, archtl. rep., 1985-86, dir., 1986-91; dir. archtl. sales dept. McCormick Paint Works Co., Rockville, Md., 1991-96; area sales mgr. PPG Industries Archtl. Finishes, Pitts., 1997—, sr. cons., 1999—. Bd. govs. Washington Bldg. Congress, 1994—. Mem. NAFE, Constrn. Specification Inst. (industry dir. 1993-94, membership chmn. 1993-94, v.p. 1995-97, pres. 1997-98, dir. region inst. 2000—, inst. dir. 2000), Interior Design Soc., Washington Sales and Mktg. Council. Republican. Episcopalian. Home: 5227 Blossom Hill Dr Haymarket VA 20169 Office: PPG Industries Inc 1 PPG Plaza Pittsburgh PA 15272-0001 E-mail: gbuchanan@ppg.com.

BUCHANAN, JAMES JUNKIN, classics educator; b. Pitts., Mar. 7, 1925; s. James Junkin and Charity (Packer) Buchanan; m. Joanne Harriett Cherrington, Mar. 31, 1951 (dec. May 26, 2002); children: Susan Grier, Edison Cherrington, Constance P. Leyden, James Junkin, Charles Sturm. AB, Princeton U., 1946, PhD, 1954; MBA, Harvard U., 1948. Investment advisor First Boston Corp, Pitts., 1948-51; asst. prof. classics Princeton U., N.J., 1953-60, dir. tchr. placement, 1957-60, sec. schs. com., 1957-60; dean Coll. Arts and Scis. So. Meth. U., Dallas, 1960-63; chmn. dept. classics Trinity U., San Antonio, 1963-64; prof. classical langs. Tulane U., New Orleans, 1964-87, prof. emeritus, 1987—. Author: Theorika, 1962; translator: Zosimus: Historia Nova, 1967; editor Ency. Americana, 1954-60; editor and translator: Boethius: Consolation of Philosophy, 1957; contbr. articles to profl. jours. Trustee, Trinity Sch., New Orleans, 1967-76. Served with USNR, 1942-43 Page fellow in classics, 1953-54 Mem. Classical Assn. Eng., Classical Assn. of Middle West and South, Archaeol. Inst. Am., Am. Philos. Assn., Colonial Club (gov. 1956-61) (Princeton), Harvard-Yale-Princeton Club (Pitts.), Princeton Club (N.Y.C.), Univ. Club (Pitts.), Boston Club (New Orleans), Phi Beta Kappa (pres. La. Alpha chpt. 1974-75, 85-87). Democrat. Episcopalian. Avocations: travel; tennis; horseback riding; music. Home: Canterbury Pl 310 Fisk St Apt 501 Pittsburgh PA 15201

BUCHANAN, JAMES MCGILL, economist, educator; b. Murfreesboro, Tenn., Oct. 2, 1919; s. James McGill and Lila (Scott) Buchanan; m. Anne Bakke, Oct. 5, 1945. BS, Middle Tenn. State Coll., 1940; MA, U. Tenn., 1941; PhD, U. Chgo., 1948; D honoris causa (hon.), U. Giessen, 1982, U. Zurich, 1984, George Mason U., U. Valencia, New U. Lisbon, 1987, Ball State U., 1988, City U., London, 1988, Lycoming Coll., 1992, Free U., Rome, 1993, U. Bucharest, 1994, Acad. Econ. Studies, Romania, 1994, U. Catania, 1994, U. Porto, 1995, U. Valladolid (Spain), 1996, Fuanceso Marroquin U., Guatemala, 2001. Assoc. prof. U. Tenn., 1948—50, prof. econs., 1950—51; prof. Fla. State U., 1951—56, U. Va., 1956—62, Paul G. McIntyre prof. econs., 1962—68, chmn. dept., 1956—62; prof. UCLA, 1968—69; Univ. Disting. prof. Va. Poly. Inst., 1969—83, prof. emeritus, 2000—; Univ. Disting. prof. George Mason U., 1983—99, prof. emeritus, 1999—; adv. dir. Ctr. for Pub. Choice, 1969—; assoc. prof. Francesco Marroquin U., Guatemala, 2001. Fulbright rsch. scholar, Italy; Ford Faculty rsch. fellow, 1959—60; Fulbright vis. prof. Cambridge U., 1961—62. Author (with C.L. Allen and M.R. Colberg): Prices, Income and Public Policy, 1954; author: Public Principles of Public Debt, 1958, The Public Finances, 1960, Fiscal Theory and Political Economy, 1960; author: (with G. Tullock) The Calculus of Consent, 1962; author: Public Finance in Democratic Process, 1966, The Demand and Supply of Public Goods, 1968, Cost and Choice, 1969; author: (with N. Devletoglou) Academia in Anarchy, 1970; editor (with R. Tollison): Theory of Public Choice, 1972; editor: (with G.F. Thirlby) LSE Essays on Cost, 1973; author: The Limits of Liberty, 1975; author: (with R. Wagner) Democracy in Deficit, 1977; author: Freedom in Constitutional Contract, 1978, What Should Economists Do?, 1979; author: (with G. Brennan) The Power to Tax, 1980, The Reason of Rules, 1985; author: Liberty Market and State, 1985, Economics: Between Predictive Science and Moral Philosophy, 1987, Explorations in Constitutional Economics, 1989; editor: Economics and Ethics of Constitutional Order, 1991, Better than Plowing, 1992, Ethics and Economic Progress, 1994; editor: (with Yong Yoon) Return to Increasing Returns, 1994; author: Post-Socialist Political Economy, 1997; author: (with R. Congleton) Politics By Principle, Not Interest, 1998; author: Collected Works of James Buchanan, Vols. I-XIII, 2000; editor: Collected Works of James Buchanan, Vols. XIV-XIX, 2001, Collected Works of James Buchanan, Vol. XX, 2002. Lt. USNR, 1941—46. Decorated Bronze Star; recipient Seidman award, 1984, Nobel Prize in Econs., 1986. Fellow: Am. Acad. Arts and Scis.; mem.: Mt. Pelerin Soc. (pres. 1984—86), Western Econ. Assn. (pres. 1983), So. Econ. Assn. (pres. 1963), Am. Econ. Assn. (exec. com. 1966—69, v.p. 1971, dist. fellow 1983—). Home: PO Box G Blacksburg VA 24063-1021 Office: George Mason U Buchanan House Mail Stop 1 E6 Fairfax VA 22030-4443

BUCHANAN, JOHN DONALD, retired health physicist, radiochemist; b. Mesa, Ariz., Oct. 1, 1927; s. John Freeborn and Marguerite (Brimhall) B.; m. Donna Marie Smith, Aug. 27, 1955; children— Margaret MacNeil, John Michael, Andrew Tierney, David Brimhall. BS in Chemistry, U. Ariz., 1949. Diplomate Am. Bd. Health Physics. Sr. chemist Tracerlab, Inc., Richmond, Calif., 1950-59; staff asso. Gen. Atomic div. Gen. Dynamics Corp., San Diego, 1959-62; mgr. nuclear applications and measurements Teledyne-Isotopes Inc., Palo Alto, Calif., 1962-71; mgr. applied research Internat. Nutronics Inc., Palo Alto, 1971-73; supr. radiol. monitoring programs NUS Corp., Rockville, Md., 1973-75; sr. health physicist, radiochemist U.S. Nuclear Regulatory Commn., Washington, 1975-94. Author papers on radiation protection, radioanalytical chemistry, radioactivity measurements, radioisotope applications. Served with USNR, 1945-46. Recipient Meritorious Service award U.S. Nuclear Regulatory Commn., 1981 Fellow AAAS, Am. Inst. Chemists, Health Physics Soc.; mem. Am. Nuclear Soc., Am. Chem. Soc., Am. Acad. Health Physics, Phi Lambda Upsilon, Phi Delta Theta. Home: 7508 Dew Wood Dr Rockville MD 20855-1007

BUCHANAN, JOHN LYNN, retired broadcast executive; b. Garland, Tex., Aug. 19, 1920; s. William Irl and Kathryn Raney Buchanan; m. Stella West, Oct. 31, 1947; children: John Lynn II, Elizabeth Ann Ashurst. Grad., Ryan Sch. Aeronautics, San Diego, 1941; student in engring., North Tex. State U.; student, U. Minn., NYU. Autopilot, radio-compass test engr. Sperry Gyroscope Co., N.Y.C.; B-29 aircraft field engr. aero. divsn. Honeywell, 1943—46; assigned Pacific Air Svc. Command, Manila, 2d A.F. Hdqrs., B-29 XX A.F. Hdqrs., Colorado Springs, Guam, Tinian; indsl. sales engr. Honeywell, N.Y.C. and Phila., 1947—50; with Alf Landon Radio Corp.; mgr. Sta. KTLN, Denver, 1950—55; founder Sta. KWBY, Colorado Springs, 1954, Sta. KSSS, Colo. Springs, 1955, Sta. KDAB, Denver, 1959, Sta. KKSN, Dallas-Ft. Worth, 1960; v.p. mktg. Ameco, Cable-TV, Inc., Phoenix, 1959—65; v.p. acquisitions Am. Cable TV (subs. Ameco, Inc.); founder Diversified Media Brokers, Dallas, 1966; ret., 1985; instr. 313th, 314th, 315th, 73d, 58th & 509th wings in high level precision bombing Honeywell autopilot & Norden bombsights. Founding mem. U.S. Air Mus., Duxford, England; docent Pima Air and Space Mus., Tucson; mem. Rep. Nat. Com. Pilot, bombardier, flight engr. USAF, 1941—46. Mem.: USAF Assn., Nat. Cable TV Assn., Nat. Assn. Broadcasters, Sigma Chi (life).

BUCHANAN, JOHN MACHLIN, biochemistry educator; b. Winamac, Ind., Sept. 29, 1917; s. Harry James and Eunice Blanche (Miller) B.; m. Elsa Nilsby, Dec. 11, 1948; children: Claire Louise, Stephen James, Lisa Renee, Peter Nilsson. AB, De Pauw U., 1938, D.Sc., 1975; MS, U. Mich., 1939, D.Sc., 1961; PhD, Harvard, 1943. Instr. dept. physiol. chemistry Sch. Medicine U. Pa., 1943-46, asst. prof., 1946 49, asso. prof., 1949-50, prof., 1950-53; NRC fellow Med. Nobel Inst., Stockholm, 1946-48; prof., head div. biochemistry dept. biology Mass. Inst. Tech., 1953-67, Wilson prof. biochemistry, 1967-88, Wilson prof. emeritus, 1988—. Lectr. Harvey Soc., 1958 Mem. editorial bd.: Jour. Biol. Chemistry, 1961-67, Jour. Am. Chemistry Soc, 1961-72, Physiol. Revs, 1957-60, 65-71. Civilian with Nat. Def. Research Com., 1943; mem. subcom. blood and related substances NRC, 1951-55, mem. med. fellowship bd., 1954—; mem. sci. adv. bd. Boston Biomed. Rsch. Inst., 1975-93, Papanicoulaou Cancer Research Inst., 1975-81. Fellow Guggenheim Meml. Found., 1964-65; leave of absence to Salk Inst. Biol. Studies LaJolla, Calif. Mem. Am. Soc. Biol. Chemists (sec. 1969-72), Am. Chem. Soc. (Eli Lilly award in biol. chemistry 1951), Internat. Union Biochemists (mem. nat. com.), Nat. Acad. Scis., Am. Acad. Arts and Scis., Sigma Xi. Home: 56 Meriam St Lexington MA 02420-3622

BUCHANAN, JOHN MACLENNAN, Canadian provincial official; b. Sydney, N.S., Can., Apr. 22, 1931; s. Murdoch William and Flora Isabel (Campbell) B.; m. Mavis Forsyth, Sept. 1, 1954; children: Murdoch, Travis, Nichola, Natalie, Natasha. BSc, Mt. Allison U., cert. engring., 1954; LLB, Dalhousie U., Halifax, N.S., 1958; DEng (hon.), N.S. Tech. Coll., 1979; LLD (hon.), St. Mary's U., 1982; DCL, Mt. Allison U., 1981; LLD (hon.), St. Francis Xavier U., 1986; D Polit. Sci. (hon.), U. de St. Anne, 1989. Bar: Called to bar, created queen's counsel 1972. Pvt. practice, Halifax, 1958-71; mem. N.S. Legislative Assembly, Halifax, from 1967; min. public works, then fisheries; premier of N.S., 1978-90. Created Queen's Counsel, 1972; leader Progressive Conservative Party in N.S., from 1971; elected mem. legis. assembly for Halifax-Atlantic provinces gen. election, 1967, 70, 74, 78, 81, 84, 88, apptd. Privy Coun., 1972; apptd. to Senate of Can., 1990, bd. dirs. Legal Aid for N.S. Barristers Assn. Active Boy Scouts Am., pres. exec. oun., chmn. policy bd., 1978-90. Mem. Can. Bar Assn., N.S. Barristers Assn., Can.-U.S. Parliamentary Assn. (bd. dirs.), Royal Can. Legion, Buchanan Soc. of Glasgow, Scotland (bd. dirs.), Halifax Club, City Club, Lions, Masons, Shriners, Odd Fellows. Progressive Conservative. Mem. Progressive Ch. Can. Office: The Senate Ottawa ON K1A OA4 Canada

BUCHANAN, L A, band director, music educator; b. Texarkana, Tex., Apr. 23, 1944; d. Frank Boyd and Hazel Mae Buchanan. MusB, Arkansas Tech., Russellville, Ark., 1966, MusM. Band dir. Norman Jr. High, Crossett, Ark., 1966—68, Van Buren Jr. High, Van Buren, Ark., 1968—69, Chaffin Jr. High, Ft. Smith, Ark., 1969—95; part-time band dir. Van Buren Sch., Van Buren, Ark., 1996—2003; instr. Univ. of Ark.-Ft. Smith, Ft. Smith, Ark., 2000—03. Exec. dir. Ft. Smith Chorale, Ft. Smith, Ark. Recipient Ark. Bandmaster of the Yr., Ark. Bandmaster Assoc., 1993. Mem.: Ark. Sch. Band & Orch. Assoc. (pres.), Ark. Bandmasters Assoc. (pres. adm. adv.), Phi Beta Mu (state chmn.). Presbyterian. Avocations: golf, fishing. Office: Univ of Ark- Ft Smith PO Box 3649 Fort Smith AR 72913-3649

BUCHANAN, LEWIS VICTOR, research scientist; b. Ithaca, N.Y., Nov. 13, 1957; s. Lewis V. and Virginia L. Buchanan; m. Julia Lynn Carpenter, Oct. 16, 1982; children: Andrew J., Anthony J. MA, Western Mich. U., 1983. Cert. surg. rsch. specialist Acad. Surg. Rsch./Minn., 2002. Rsch. assoc. The Upjohn Co., Kalamazoo, 1982—86, biologist, 1986—89; rsch. biologist Pharmacia & Upjohn, Kalamazoo, 1989—95; rsch. scientist Pharmacia Corp., Kalamazoo, 1995—. Contbr. articles to profl. jours. Orgnl. leader Boy Scouts Am., Kalamazoo, 1994—2002. Mem.: Am. Soc. Microbiology (assoc.). Achievements include research in FDA approvals of drugs for treatment of cardiac arrhythmias, and bacterial infections. Office: Pharmacia Corp 301 Henrietta St 7250-209-314 Kalamazoo MI 49001 Personal E-mail: lewis.v.buchanan@pharmacia.com. E-mail: lewis.v.buchanan@pharmacia.com.

BUCHANAN, LOVELL, entertainer; b. Ephrata, Pa., Mar. 22, 1949; s. Virginia (Eidemiller) Windham; m. Marie Veronica Sheetz. BS cum laude, Millersville (Pa.) U., 1977. Cert. tchr., Pa. Machinist Alcoa Corp., Lancaster, Pa., 1973-74; tchr. Manheim Twp. Sch. Dist., Lancaster, 1978-81, Downingtown (Pa.) Sch. Dist., 1982-83; tech. trainer Hamilton Tech. Co., Lancaster, 1984-88; pres. FunFoolery Prodns. Creator Dimmer the Million Dollar Robot, Prof. Funfoolery character, Chuckles the Clown (permanent collection Clown Hall of Fame, Delevan, Wis.), Whistling Willie, Chef Percy Produce, Juan D. Waiter, Monsieur Von Juggle; sculptor: It's Magic, 1978, Optical Illusions, 1998 (permanent collections Ripley's Believe It or Not Mus., Atlantic City, N.J.); author: The Fun Foolery Book of Magic, 2002. With USN, 1968-72, Vietnam. Decorated Gallantry Cross. Mem. Internat. Brotherhood Magicians, Soc. Am. Magicians, Internat. Jugglers Assn., World Clown Assn., Humane League (Appreciation award, 1985), Epsilon Pi Tau. Republican. Home: 2726 Chapel Rd Lancaster PA 17603-5917

BUCHANAN, MARY ESTILL, education trustee; b. San Francisco, Colo., Nov. 15, 1934; d. Carl Albert Henlein and Elizabeth Yager; m. Dodds Buchanan (dec.); m. David Grozier (dec.); children: David, Stephen, Helen, Eugene, Catharine, Bruce. BA, Wellesley Coll., 1956; MBA with distinction, Harvard U., 1962. Dir. Nat. State Bank, Colo., 1966—74; trustee Colo. Bd. Agr., Colo. Land Grant Univs., 1970—74; Women in Govt. chmn. Colo. Commn. States Women, 1970—74; sec. of state Colo., 1974—82; Rep. nominee U.S. Senate, Colo., 1980; trustee Naropa U., Boulder, Colo., 1993—. Mem. bioethics com. Metro-Denver Cmty., Colo., 1993—, Kaiser-Permanente, Colo., 2000—. Fellow: Denver U. Ctr. for Pub. Health Policy; mem.: Am. Soc. for Bioethics and Humanities. Avocations: skiing, canoeing, bicycling. Address: 1153 Cascade Ave Boulder CO 80302-7568

BUCHANAN, RAY ALLEN, clergyman; b. Houston, Jan. 8, 1947; s. Wilbur Allen and Louise (Zwahr) B.; children: Peter Andrew, Amy Krysteen. BA, U. N.C., Wilmington, 1972; MDiv, Southeastern Bapt. Theol. Seminary, 1976; DD, Shenandoah Coll., 1990. Ordained to ministry United Meth. Ch., 1977. Pastor North Mecklenburg United Meth. Ch., Union Level, Va., 1973-77, Oak Hall (Va.) United Meth. Ch., 1977-79, Bedford (Va.) Cir. United Meth. Ch., 1979-81; co-founder, co-dir. Soc. St. Andrew, Big Island, Va., 1979-97; founder, pres., CEO Stop Hunger Now, 1998—. Mem. Va. ann. conf. United Meth. Ch. Co-editor Gleanings, 1986; co-author: Prepare the Way of the Lord!, 1986; author: Pass the Potatoes, 1987, Bones Will Not Suffice: Poems for the Dead of Night, 1997; contbr. articles, poems to various publs. Mem. nat. com. for World Food Day; co-organizer Va. Congress on Hunger; bd. dirs. Internat. Food Banking Assn., Faithnet, Child Rescue Ctr., Sierra Leone; past pres. Clan Buchanan Soc. Internat. Recipient Disting. Alumnus award U. N.C.-Wilmington, 1985, Real Am. Hero award Maxwell House, 1992, Lynchburg Humanitarian award NCCJ Assn. Christians and Jews, 1998, Nat. Humanitarian award Caring Inst., 1998. Avocations: writing, photography, horses, hunting, bonsai. Office: Stop Hunger Now 2501 Clark Ave Raleigh NC 27607-7213 E-mail: r.buchanan@stophungernow.org., StopHunberNow1@yahoo.com. *Of all the obscenity spawned by an immoral society, nothing compares to the vulgarity of hunger. Erasing this moral outrage is the greatest challenge of our age.*

BUCHANAN, RICHARD KENT, electronics company executive; b. Schenectady, Sept. 10, 1951; s. Richard Linton and Jeanette (Dunn) B.; m. Diane Carolyn Laffler, Oct. 14, 1984; 1 child, Lindsay Sarah. BSEE, USAF Acad., 1973; MBA, Harvard U., 1980. Commd. 2d lt. USAF, 1973, advanced through grades to capt., 1976; resigned, 1978; mgmt. cons. Bain and Co., Boston, 1979-82; corp. dir. strategy Gen. Instrument Corp., N.Y.C., 1982-84; mgr. strategic planning GE Med. Systems Group, Milw., 1984-86, mgr. mktg. magnetic resonance, 1986-87, product gen. mgr. magnetic resonance bus. unit, 1987-89; dir. strategic mktg. Motorola Communications Sector, Schaumburg, Ill., 1989-91; dir. internat. networks svcs. Motorola Land Mobile Sector, Schaumburg, Ill., 1991-94; v.p., gen. mgr. Am. Parts Divsn., Motorola, Schaumburg, Ill., 1994-97, Radio Products Group, N.Am. Divsn., Motorola, Rolling Meadows, Ill., 1997-2000; v.p., gen. mgr. Global eBusiness, Motorola, Deer Park, Ill., 2000—. Contbr. numerous articles on time div. multiple access comm. systems to profl. jours. Scholar NSF, 1968. Mem. IEEE, N.Y. Acad. Scis. Republican. Avocations: skiing, travel, art, swimming. Home: 1076 Aberdeen Rd Palatine IL 60067-4313 Office: Motorola 21440 W Lake Cook Rd Deer Park IL 60010 Personal E-mail: rkentb333@aol.com.

BUCHANAN, ROBERT AUGUSTUS, JR., cardiologist; b. Greensboro, N.C., May 23, 1943; s. Robert Augustus and Marie Simpson Buchanan; m. Ruth Smitherman, Aug. 24, 1968; children: Robert Jed, Elizabeth Brooke, Virginia Ruth. BA, U. N.C., 1965; MD, Wake Forest U., 1969. Diplomate Am. Bd. Internal Medicine in internal medicine and cardiovasc. medicine. Intern in internal medicine Vanderbilt U., Nashville, 1969-72; resident in cardiology U. Ala., Birmingham, 1972-74; chief cardiology Durham (N.C.) Regional Hosp., 1982—; pres. Triangle Heart Assocs., Durham, 1998—. Instr. cardiology U. Ala., Birmingham, 1972-74; clin. assoc. Duke U., Durham, 1976—. Pres. med. staff Durham Regional Hosp., 1997-98. Fellow Am. Coll. Cardiology; mem. Phi Beta Kappa, Alpha Omega Alpha. Republican. Presbyterian. Home: 8 Surrey Ln Durham NC 27707 Office: Triangle Heart Assocs 2609 N Duke St Durham NC 27704 Fax: (919) 220-5563.

BUCHANAN, ROBERT MCLEOD, lawyer; b. N.Y.C., Oct. 4, 1932; s. Albert William and Elizabeth (McLeod) B.; m. Jane Vidaud Britton, July 6, 1957; children: Robert M. Jr., Jamy B. Buchanan Madeja, Stephen S., Genevra V. Buchanan Casais. BA, Dartmouth Coll., 1954; JD, Harvard U., 1959. Bar: N.Y. 1960, Mass. 1969, U.S. Supreme Ct. 1973. Assoc. Debevoise & Plimpton, N.Y.C., 1959-68; ptnr. Sullivan & Worcester LLP, Boston, 1968-2000, of counsel, 2000—. Contbr. articles on antitrust law to profl. jours. Moderator Town of Weston, Mass., 1980—, mem., chmn. fin. com., 1975-80; chmn. weston Hist. Dist. Study Com., 1973. With U.S. Army, 1954-56. Mem. Mass. Bar Assn. (ethics com. 1986—), Boston Bar Assn. (chmn. antitrust com. 1980-86), Harvard Faculty Club. Unitarian Universalist. Avocations: reading, guitar playing, sailing. Office: Sullivan & Worcester LLP 1 Post Office Sq Ste 2300 Boston MA 02109-2129 E-mail: RMB@SANDW.COM.

BUCHANAN, SCOTT EUGENE, political science educator; b. Columbus, Ga., Feb. 8, 1970; s. Luther Edward and Marie Ammons Buchanan; m. Kelea L. Poole, Dec. 12, 1992; children: Eugenia, Mary. BA, U. Ga., 1992; MA,

Auburn U., 1995; PhD, U. Okla., 1999. Asst. prof. polit. sci. Gordon Coll., Barnesville, Ga., 1999—2002, Columbus State U., 2002—. Contbr. chpts. to books and articles to profl. jours. Mem. So. Polit. Sci. Assn., Ga. Polit. Sci. Assn. (mem. exec. com.). Presbyterian. Avocations: traveling, reading, research, family activities.

BUCHANAN, WALTER WOOLWINE, electrical engineer, educator, academic administrator; b. Lebanon, Ind., Oct. 6, 1941; s. Eugene Neptune and Amy Malvina (Woolwine) B.; m. Carol Ann Saunders, Dec. 28, 1968 (div. 1978); children: William Saunders, John Douglas; m. Charlotte Jane Drake, 1985. BA, Ind. U., 1963, JD, 1973, PhD, 1993; BS in Engring., Purdue U., 1982, MS in Elec. Engring., 1984. Bar: Ind.; registered profl. engr., Ind., Fla., Tenn., Oreg., Mass. Aerospace engr. Martin Co., Denver, 1963-64, Boeing Co., New Orleans, 1964-65; audit coord. Ind. Tax Bd., Indpls., 1970-73; atty. VA, Indpls., 1973-79; electronics engr. Naval Avionics, Indpls., 1979-86; asst. prof. Ind. U.-Purdue U., Indpls., 1986-93, U. Ctrl. Fla., Orlando, 1993-95; assoc. prof., chair Mid. Tenn. State U., Murfreesboro, 1995-96; prof., dean Oreg. Inst. Tech., Klamath Falls, 1996-99; prof., dir. Northeastern U., Boston, 1999—. Cons. Benjamin/Cummings Pubs., Menlo Park, Calif., Holt, Rinehart & Winston, N.Y.C., Houghton Mifflin Co., Boston, MacMillan Pub. Co., Columbus, Delmar Pub. Co., Albany, Prentice Hall, Simon & Schuster, Columbus, Oxford U. Press, N.Y.C., Discovery Press, L.A., Inst. for Sci. Info., Phila., Microsoft Corp., Redmond, Wash., Utah Bd. Regents, Pa. State U., Altoona, Excelsior Coll., Albany, NY; evaluator Accreditation Bd. for Engring. and Tech., Balt.; mem. Tech. Accreditation Commn., 1998—2003; grants reviewer NSF, Washington; mem. editl. bd. Internat. Jour. of Modern Engring. Mem. editl. bd. Jour. Engring. Tech.; contbr. over 90 articles to profl. jours. Past chmn. theater adv. bd. Ind. U.-Purdue U., Indpls., faculty coun., 1989-92, exec. com., 1991-92; fundraiser Ind. U. Found., Indpls.; tech. com. Ind. Bus. Modernization Corp., Indpls., 1990-93; vestry St. Paul's Ch., Klamath Falls, Oreg., 1998-99. Lt. comdr. USN, 1965-69, Vietnam. Recipient Glenn W. Irwin award, Peter Marbaugh award Ind. U.-Purdue U. Indpls., 1988; Wright scholar Ind. U., 1961; Rsch. grantee Ctr. on Philanthropy, 1992, Fla. Engring. and Indsl. Experimentation Sta., 1993. Fellow: Am. Soc. for Engring. Edn. (exec. bd. ednl. rsch. and methods divsn. 1986—92, exec. com. engring. tech. divsn. 1994—, past chair, internat. engring. tech. Listserv adminstr., Centennial award 1993, Frederick J. Berger award 2000—03, James H. McGraw award 2003, rsch. grantee); mem.: NSPE (educator, exec. bd., past chair, Profl. Engrs. in Edn. award 1992, 1997), IEEE (sr.; com. tech. accreditation activities, past chair, press electronics tech. editl. bd.), Indpls. Sci. and Engring. Found. (bd. dirs. 1988—92), Profl. Engrs. in Oreg. (chair engring. edn. 1997—99, pres. elect 1999), Tenn. Soc. Profl. Engrs. (chair engring. edn. 1996), Soc. Mfg. Engrs. (sr.), Fla. Engring. Soc. (chair engring. edn. 1993—95), Ind. Soc. Profl. Engrs. (chair engring. edn. 1988—92), Engring Tech. Leadership Inst. (exec. coun., past chair), Univ. Faculty Club (bd. dirs. 1988—93), Scientech Club (bd. dirs. 1990—92), Order of Engr., Engring. and Sci. Hall of Fame, Phi Beta Delta, Delta Phi Alpha, Tau Alpha Pi (pres.). Republican. Episcopalian. Achievements include systems test evaluation on the Apollo booster rocket. Office: Northeastern U Sch Engring Tech 120 Snell Engring Ctr Boston MA 02115-5000 Fax: 617-373-2501. E-mail: buchanan@coe.neu.edu.

BUCHANAN, WILLIAM H., JR., retired lawyer, venture capitalist; b. Summit, N.J., July 2, 1937; s. William Hobart and Margaret R. B.; m. Eleanor A. Lincoln, June 18, 1966; children: Diana A., Jessica R. AB, Princeton U., 1959; LL.B., Harvard U., 1963. Bar: N.Y. 1964. Assoc. firm Shearman & Sterling, N.Y.C., 1963-70; v.p., sec., gen. counsel Reuben H. Donnelley Corp., N.Y.C., 1970-91, sr. v.p., chief legal counsel, 1991-97; asst. sec., assoc. gen. counsel Dun & Bradstreet Corp., N.Y.C., 1976-79, v.p., sec., assoc. gen. counsel, 1979-91, v.p. law, 1991-96, v.p. law, sec., 1996-97; pres. Spencer Trask Spin-Off Group LLC, 1998—2001; exec. v.p. Spencer Trask Intellectual Capital Co. LLC, 1999—2001; ret., 2001. Served with USMCR, 1959-60. Mem. Am. Soc. Corp. Secs. (pres. N.Y. regional group 1979-80, nat. treas. 1979-83, bd. dirs. 1983-86). Clubs: Princeton (N.Y.C.); New Canaan Field, Port Royal Club, Naples, Fl., Grey Oaks County Club, Naples, Fl. Republican. Presbyterian.

BUCHANAN, WILLIAM JENNINGS, lawyer, judge; b. Newberry, S.C., Oct. 2, 1948; s. James Willie and Martha Morton (Jennings) B.; m. Phyllis Kaye Brunson, June 3, 1978; children: Ashley, Whitney. BS in Mktg., U. S.C., 1983, JD, 1987. Bar: S.C. 1987, U.S. Dist. Ct. S.C. 1988. Assoc. Setzler, Chewning & Scott, West Columbia, S.C., 1988-93; pvt. practice Columbia, S.C., 1993—. Assoc. judge City of Cayce, S.C., 1988-93; instr. Midlands Tech. Coll., Columbia, S.C., 1989-96. Mem. Sertoma Internat., Columbia, 1987-89, real propert, probate and trust sect. Mem. ABA, S.C. Bar Assn., Richland County Bar Assn., Lexington County Law Enforcement Ofcls. Assn. Baptist. Avocations: golf, fishing, hunting, snow skiing, boating. Home: 1728 Shadowood Dr Columbia SC 29212-1318 Office: Korn Law Firm PA 1611 Hampton St Columbia SC 29201

BUCHBERG, AKIVA, product designer, inventor, consultant; b. Tel Aviv, Jan. 3, 1953; s. Mordechai Marcus and Rachel (Resnick) Buchberg; m. Dominique Batsheva Dolo, Sept. 15, 1977; 1 child, Thomas M. Pres. Akido Ltd., Tel Aviv, 1977—86; pres. & COO Abaco S.A., Paris, 1986—91; chmn. & CEO Wrapco Internat. N.V., Curacao, Netherlands Antilles, 1992—2000; pres. & CEO B.I.H. Inc., Miami, Fla., 1993—2003. Active cons. M.G.A. Tech. Group, France, International Paper, United States, Israeli Aircraft Industries, Israel, Burger King Corp., United States, RayKay Inc., Japan, Cartier, Paris, Kabbalah Center Internat., many others, 1986—2003. Achievements include more than 250 U.S. and international patents; inventor products, new technologies for high speed machines. Home and Office: 1717 Ferrari Dr Beverly Hills CA 90210

BUCHBINDER, DARRELL BRUCE, lawyer; b. N.Y.C., Oct. 17, 1946; s. Julian and Bernice (Levy) Buchbinder; m. Janet Grey McLean, Jan. 22, 1977; children: Julian Bradford, Andrew Grey, Ian Jeffress. BA in Politics with honors, NYU, 1968, JD, 1971. Bar: N.Y. 1972, U.S. Dist. Ct. (so. and ea. dists.) N.Y. 1973. Sole practice, N.Y.C., 1972-79; atty. Port Authority of N.Y. and N.J., N.Y.C., 1979-83, prin. atty., 1983-86, dep. chief fin. divsn. Law Dept., 1986-92, chief pub. securities law divsn. law dept., 1992-2001, asst. gen. counsel, 2001—02, dep. gen. counsel, 2002—03, 1st dep. gen. counsel, 2003—. With USNR, 1968—70. Mem.: Nat. Assn. Bond Lawyers, Pi Sigma Alpha. Republican. Business E-Mail: dbuchbin@panynj.gov.

BUCHBINDER, SHARON BELL, health care management educator; b. Washington, Nov. 27, 1951; d. James Wright and Effie Naomi (Rhodes) Bell; m. Dale Buchbinder, May 9, 1976; 1 child, Joshua Harlow. BA in Psychology, U. Conn., 1973; MA in Psychology, U. Hartford, 1976; AAS in Nursing, SUNY, Albany, 1981; PhD iin Pub. Health Scis., U. Ill., Chgo., 1992. RN, Md. Intravenous technician dept. intravenous therapy Hartford (Conn.) Hosp., 1974-76; supr. dept. intravenous therapy Albany Med. Ctr. Hosp., N.Y., 1976-80; asst. rsch. scientist N.Y. Dept. Mental Hygiene, Albany, 1980-81; staff specialist Nat. Commn. on Nursing, Chgo., 1982-83; staff specialist divsn. nursing Am. Hosp. Assn., Chgo., 1983-84; sr. rsch. assoc. divsn. evaluation and nomenclature med. terminology and nomenclature AMA, Chgo., 1984-86, exec. asst., 1986-88, mktg. exec., 1988-89, asst. dept. dir. dept. preventive medicine, 1989-90; dir. devel. Norbel Sch., 1990-91; postdoctoral fellow in children's mental health svcs. Sch. Hygiene and Pub. Health Johns Hopkins U., Balt., 1993-94, sr. staff rsch. coord. dept. pediats. Sch. Medicine, 1994-95, rsch. assoc. dept. pediats. Sch. Medicine, 1995-96; assoc. prof. dept. health scis. Towson U., Md., 1996—, coord. healthcare mgmt. program, 2000—. Contbr. articles to profl. jours., chpts. to books; spkr. in field. Rsch. grantee Mut. Life Ins. Co. of N.Y., 1986, Faculty Devel. grantee Towson U., 1997, AHCPR, 1995, Shriver Ctr. grantee, 1999, Curative Health Svcs. grantee, 2000; CIAT Tech. fellow, 1999. Mem.: APA, AAUW, NAFE, Internat. Soc. Rsch. Healthcare Fin. Mgmt. (sr. editor jour. Rsch. in Healthcare Fin. Mgmt.), AcadamyHealth, Acad. Mgmt., Upsilon Phi Delta, Eta Sigma Gamma (Beta Zeta chpt.), Delta Omega (mem. Lambda chpt.), Phi Kappa Phi. Democrat. Jewish. Avocation: fishing.

BUCHEISTER, PATRICIA LOUISE (PATT PARRISH), author, artist; b. Waterloo, Iowa, Mar. 27, 1942; d. David Melvin and Elaine Rebecca Fluharty; m. Raymond Cecil Bucheister, Jan. 14, 1961; children: Scott Raymond, Todd David. Author: Make the Angel Weep, 1979, Summer of Silence, 1980, Feather in the Wind, 1981, The Sheltered Haven, 1981, The Amberley Affair, 1983, Lifetime Affair, 1985, The Dragon Slayer, 1986, Night and Day, 1986, Two Roads, 1987, The Luck of the Irish, 1988, Flynn's Fate, 1988, Touch the Stars, 1988, Time Out, 1988, Fire and Ice, 1989, Near the Edge, 1989, Elusive Gypsy, 1989, Once Burned, Twice as Hot, 1990, Relentless, 1990, The Rogue, 1990, Tropical Heat, 1990, Tropical Storm, 1991, Hot Pursuit, 1991, Island Lover, 1992, Mischief and Magic, 1992, Struck By Lightning, 1992, Tilt at Windmills, 1992, Island Lover, 1992, Stroke by Stroke, 1992, Tame a Wildcat, 1993, Unpredictable, 1995, Strange Bedfellows, 1994, Instant Family, 1995, Hot Southern Nights, 1995, Instant Family, 1995, Wild in the Night, 1994, Gypsy Dance, 1997, Below the Salt, 1999, others. Recipient Silver Palette award, 1986. Mem. Romance Writers Am., Published Authors Network, Nat. Soc. of Tole and Decorative Painters. Mailing: care Ray Bucheister/Gen Dynamics US Naval Support Activity PSC 810 Box 217 Fpo AE 09619 E-mail: raypatt@mindspring.com.

BUCHELE, WESLEY FISHER, retired agricultural engineering educator; b. Cedar Vale, Kans., Mar. 18, 1920; s. Charles John and Bessie (Fisher) B.; m. Mary Jagger, June 12, 1945 (dec. 2000); children: Rod, Marybeth, Sheron, Steven. BS, Kans. State U., 1943; MS, U. Ark., 1951; PhD, Iowa State U., 1954. Registered profl. engr., Iowa, Calif. Jr. engr. John Deere Tractor Works, Waterloo, Iowa, 1946-48; asst. prof. U. Ark., Fayetteville, 1948-51; agrl. engr. USDA, Ames, Iowa, 1954-56; assoc. prof. Mich. State U., East Lansing, 1956-63; prof. Iowa State U., Ames, 1963-89, prof. emeritus, 1989—. Vis. prof. U. Ghana, Legon, 1968-69, Beijing Agrl. Engring. U., 1983-84; vis. scientist Commonwealth Sci. and Indsl. Rsch. Orgn., Australia, Internat. Inst., Tropical Agr., Ibadan, Nigeria, 1979-80, Internat. Rice Rsch. Inst., Manila, 1991-92; cons. engr. Detroit Arsenal, Ordnance Corps, Waterways Exptl. Sta., Corps of Engrs., U.S. Steel Corp., GM, Detroit, 1974-76; bd. dirs. Farm Safety 4 Just Kids, Earlham, Iowa, Self-Help, Inc., Waverly, Iowa, JAC Tractor Co. Author 18 books; inventor 23 patents. Mem. Ames Energy Com., 1974-75; advisor Living History Farm, Urbandale, Iowa, 1965—, bd. govs., 1984—. Maj. U.S. Army, 1943-46, PTO; maj. Ordnance Corps, USAR, 1946-69, ret. Named Eminent Engineer Iowa Engring. Soc., 1989 Fellow Am. Soc. Agrl. Engrs. (bd. dirs. 1978-80, McCormick-Case award 1988, Henry A. Wallace award for significant contbn. to agr. 2003), Nat. Inst. Agrl. Engrs.; mem. AAAS, Soc. Automotive Engrs., Am. Soc. Agronomy (mem. com. 1961-65), Steel Ring, Internat. Assn. Mechanization of Field Experiments (v.p. 1964-93), Internat. Platform Assn., Osborne Club, Toastmasters. Avocations: photography, travel, golf, inventing, writing. Home and Office: 239 Parkridge Cir Ames IA 50014-3645 E-mail: wbuchele@mns.com

BUCHENAU, JURGEN, historian; b. Warleberg, Germany, Mar. 31, 1964; came to U.S., 1986; s. Helmut Buchenau and Sabine Marianne Louise Prange; m. Ana-Isabel Aliaga Buchenau, July 31, 1993; children: Nicolas, Julia. MA, U. N.C., 1988, PhD, 1993. Asst. prof. Wingate (N.C.) U., 1993-97, U. So. Miss., Hattiesburg, 1997-99, U. N.C., Charlotte, 1999—2002, assoc. prof., 2002—. Author: In the Shadow of the Giant, 1996, Werkzeuge des Fortschrits, 2002; contbr. articles to profl. jours. Recipient Sturgis Leavitt award, S.E. Coun. Latin Am. Studies, 1998, Harvey L. Johnson award, 2002. Office: U NC Dept History Charlotte NC 28223

BUCHENROTH, STEPHEN RICHARD, lawyer; b. Bellefontaine, Ohio, Feb. 8, 1948; s. Richard G. and Patricia (Muller) B.; m. Vicki Anderson, June 6, 1974; children: Matthew Brian, Sarah Elizabeth. BA, Wittenburg U., Springfield, Ohio, 1970; JD, U. Chgo., 1974. Bar: Ohio 1974, U.S. Dist. Ct. (so. and no. dists.) Ohio 1974, U.S. Ct. Appeals (6th cir.) 1974. Ptnr. Vorys, Sater, Seymour & Pease, Columbus, Ohio, 1974—. Author: Ohio Mortgage Foreclosures, 1986, Ohio Franchising Law, 1990, also chpts. in books. Trustee, v.p. Godman Guild Assn., Columbus, 1977-83; trustee, sec. Neighborhood Homes, Inc., Columbus, 1977-85; mem. bd. rev. Worthington Pers., 1981—; pres. Worthington Alliance for Quality Edn., 1989-91; chmn. bd. advisors paralegal program Capitol U. Law Sch., 1991; pres. bd. trustees Worthington Edn. Found., 1997-98; mem. Ohio Supreme Ct. Commn. on CLE, 1994-2000, chmn., 1999; bd. advisors C.H.A.D.D. of Ctrl. Ohio, 1993-97; bd. trustees Wittenberg U., 2000—. Recipient Cmty. Svc. award Legal Assts. Ctrl. Ohio, 1987. Mem.: ABA (forum com. franchising), Am. Coll. Real Estate Lawyers, Columbus Bar Assn. (pres. 1992—93, bd. govs., Bar Svc. medal 2000), Ohio State Bar Assn. (coun. dels., chmn. legal assts. com., bd.govs. real property sect., chmn. 2003). Republican. Lutheran. Home: 2342 Collins Dr Columbus OH 43085-2810 Office: Vorys Sater Seymore & Pease 52 E Gay St PO Box 1008 Columbus OH 43215-3161 E-mail: SRBuchenroth@vssp.com.

BUCHER, KATHERINE TOTH, education educator, librarian; b. Shickshinny, Pa., July 30, 1947; d. George Washington and Edith May (Laidacker) Toth; m. Glenn Allen Bucher, June 10, 1970. BS, Millersville State Coll., 1969; MLS, Rutgers U., 1970; EdD, Auburn U., 1976. Elem. libr. Benton (Pa.) Area Schs., 1969; curriculum materials libr. Radford (Va.) Coll., 1970-71; head libr. Macon County-Tuskegee (Ala.) Pub. Libr., 1971-74; tchg. asst. Auburn (Ala.) U., 1974-75; adj. faculty Cath. U., Washington, 1979-84, U. N.C., Chapel Hill, 1979-82; prof. graduate program, dir. of elementary and middle sch. edn. Old Dominion U., Norfolk, Va., 1975—. Author: Computers and Technology in School Library Media Centers, 1994, 2d rev. edit., 1998, (with M. Lee Manning) Teaching in the Middle School, 2001, (with M. Lee Manning) Classroom Manangement, 2003; children's lit. cons. WAVY-TV, Norfolk, 1992—, WVEC-TV, Norfolk, 1992—; contbr. articles to profl. jours. Mem. adv. com. Norfolk Pub. Libr., 1990—; mem. Va. Auctioneers Assn., Richmond, Va., 1992—. Mem. Am. Libr. Assn., Am. Assn. Sch. Librs., Va. Ednl. Media Assn. Avocations: needlework, antiques and collectibles, rail fan. Office: Old Dominion Univ Dept Edn Curriculum Norfolk VA 23529-0161 E-mail: kbucher@odu.edu.

BUCHER, RICHARD DAVID, sociology educator; b. New Haven, Connecticut, Apr. 13, 1949; s. Charles Augustus and Jacqueline (Dubois) B.; m. Patricia Lawrence, July 28, 1973; children: James, Kathryn, Suzette. BA in Sociology, Colgate U., 1971; MA in Sociology, NYU, 1974; PhD in Sociology, Howard U., 1983. Instr. sociology Rock Valley Coll., Rockford, Ill., 1972-73; prof. sociology Balt. City C.C., Md., 1974—, coord. sociology, 1982-89, dir. Inst. Intercultural Understanding, 1991-96. Campus liaison Am. Assn. C.Cs./Kellogg Beacon Coll. project Promoting Intercultural Awareness and Understanding in Md. Cmty. Coll., 1992-94. Co-author: Recreation for Today's Society, 1974, 2d edit., 1984; author: Diversity Consciousness: Opening Our Minds to People, Cultures, and Opportunities, 2000. Chair Carroll County Cmty. Rels. Commn. Westminster, Md., 1990-91; chair pers. parish rels. com. Wesley-Freedom Ch., Eldersburg, Md., 1982-84. Grantee Fund for Improvement Post-Secondary Edn., Washington, 1989-90; recipient tchg. excellence award Nat. Inst. Staff and Orgnl. Devel., 1994, Ann. award Carroll County Human Rels. Commn., 2002; named Carnegie Found. for Advancement of Tchg./Case Md. Prof. of Yr., 2000. Mem. Am. Sociol. Assn., So. Sociol. Soc., Soc. for Disability Studies. Democrat. Methodist. Avocations: walking, swimming, family recreation. Home: 2538 Vance Dr Mount Airy MD 21771-8814 Office: Balt City C C 2901 Liberty Heights Ave Baltimore MD 21215-7807 E-mail: rdbucher@aol.com.

BUCHERT, STEPHANIE NICOLE, music educator; b. Seaford, Del., Sept. 2, 1976; d. John George and Connie Lee Chapis; m. Todd Michael Buchert; 1 child, Colby Skyler. student, BS in Music Edn., West Chester U., 1998. Cert. music tchr. Choir dir., asst. band dir. Cape Henlopen H.S., Lewes, Del., 1998—2002; choir dir., music tchr. Lewes Mid. Sch., 2002—. Mem. Delaware Jr. All State Chours Com., 2002—03. Mem.: Del. State Educators Assn., Del. Music Educators Assn. Avocations: singing, reading, drawing. Home: 18547 Whaleys Corner Road Georgetown DE 19947 Office: Lewes Mid Sch 820 Savannah Rd Lewes DE 19958

BUCHHOLZ, DONALD ALDEN, stock brokerage company executive; b. LaPorte, Tex., Mar. 10, 1929; s. Fred T. and Chrystine (McCombs) B.; m. Ruth Vernon, May 17, 1958; children: Robert, Chrystine Louise. BBA, North Tex. U., 1952. C.P.A., Tex. Acct., staff auditor Peat, Marwick & Mitchell, Dallas, 1952-54; asst. sec.-treas., chief acct. ICT Discount Corp., 1954-56; comptr. Eppler-Guerin & Turner, Inc., 1956-59; ptnr. Cheshier-Buchholz, pub. accts., 1959-60; comptroller, sec. Parker Ford, Inc., stock brokers, Dallas, 1960-63, also dir., 1962-63; v.p., chief adminstrv. officer, sec. Weber, Hall, Cobb & Caudle, Inc., Dallas, 1963-72, also bd. dirs.; ptnr., chmn. bd. S.W. Securities Group, 1972—; chmn. bd. Buckley Oil Co., Dallas, 1994-99, 1st Savs. Bank, Arlington, Tex., 1994—. Bd. govs. N.Y. Stock Exch., 1969-71; assoc. mem. Am. Stock Exch.; mem. Chgo. Bd. Trade, Midwest Stock Exch.; bd. dirs. Security Bank N.A., Garland, Tex., 1987—; mem. found. bd. U. North Tex., 1998—; dir. Nat. Ctr. for Policy Advisors, 2003—. Trustee Garland Ind. Sch. Bd., 1971-74, pres., 1973-74; trustee Dallas County C.C. Dist., 1978-97, pres., 1982-84, 90-92; bd. dirs. Garland Meml. Hosp., 1981-85, Garland Meml. Hosp. Found., 1981, Alliance of Higher Edn., 1994-96, Coun. for Higher Edn. Accreditation, 1996-97, Dallas Citizens Coun., Old Red Found. 1997-2002, U. North Tex. Found., Dallas County C.C. Dist. Found.; mem. bus. adv. bd. Baylor U., 1991-94, pres. adv. bd. Hankamer Sch. Bus., 1995-97; bd. dirs. Nat. Ctr. Policy Analysis, 2003—. Recipient U. North Tex. Outstanding Alumnus Svc. award, 1999, U. North Tex. Disting. Alumnus award, 2001. Mem. Nat. Security Dealers Assn. (chmn. bus. conduct com. dist. 6 1985-87, bd. govs. 1988-91), Securities Industry Assn. (exec. com. south cen. dist. 1986—, exec. bd. 1990-93), Dallas Security Dealers Assn. (sec. 1961), Tex. Stock and Bond Dealers Assn. (treas. 1982, v.p. 1986-87, pres. 1987-88), Chief Execs. Round Table, Lakewood Country Club, Eastern Hills Country Club, City Club Dallas, Kiwanis (pres. 1957-58). Baptist. Home: 7712 Glenshannon Cir Dallas TX 75225- Office: SWS Group Inc 1201 Elm St Ste 3500 Dallas TX 75270-2180

BUCHHOLZ, ESTER SCHALER SCHALER, psychologist; b. Buffalo, Buffalo, Oct. 4, 1933; d. Harry Snow and Rose (Hoffman) Schaler; m. Bernard Buchholz (div. 1987); children: Gary Feinman, David Buchholz, Philip Buchholz; m. Leonard Wolf, Sept. 20, 1987. BA, Hunter Coll., 1962; PhD, NYU, 1969. Lic. psychologist. Clin. asst. NYU Psychology Clinic, 1962-63; clin. intern Met. Hosp., 1964-65; NIMH rsch. fellow Manhattan and Bklyn. Vet. Adminstrn. Hosps., 1966-68; staff psychotherapist, supr. Washington Square Inst., N.Y.C., 1967-75; asst. prof. sch. psychology Sch. of Edn. Health Nursing and Arts Professions, NYU, 1975-82; assoc. prof. NYU, 1983—; cons. psychologist Manhattan, 1970-82, 1977-82; dir. psychology of parenthood program Dept. of Applied Psychology, NYU, 1981—; dir. sch. psychology programs SEHNAP, NYU, 1986-92; pvt. practice, 1969—. Adj. asst. prof. NYU, 1972-75, Yeshiva U., summer 1973; supr. child analytic program, post-grad. Ctr. for Mental Health, 1982-91; dir. psychoanalytic tng. Inst. Child, Adolescent and Family Studies, N.Y.C., 1991—; presenter, spkr. in field. Author: Ego and Self Psychology Group Women, Children, Parents and Adolescents, 1983 (reprinted as Group Interventions with Children, Adolescents and Parents 1994), The Call of Solitude: Alone Time in a World of Attachment, 1997; cons. editor Psychoanalytic Psychology; contbg. editor Am. Jour. of Orthopsychiatry; contbr. numerous articles to profl. jours. Cons. community elem. schs. and high schs. bd. dirs. Summit Sch. for Children with Disabilities Queens, N.Y.; coord. child and adolescent snalytic tng. bd. mem. Inst. for Child, Adolescent and Family Studies; mem. jr. sci. rsch. tng. program, N.Y. Acad. Scis. Fellow Am. Orthopsychiat. Assn.; mem. Am. Psychol. Assn., Coun. for Exceptional Children, Fedn. of Am. Scientists, Internat. Assn. Applied Psychology, Nat. Accreditation Assn. for Psychoanalysis, Nat. Assn. of Sch. Psychology, Nat. Register of Health Svc. Providers in Psychology, N.Y. Acad. of Scis., N.Y. State Psychol. Assn., Regional Psychol. Assn., Sch. Psychology Eductors Coun. of N.Y. State, Soc. for Quantitative Study of Psychoanalysis. Achievements include research in the field of psychoanalytic psychology, adolescence, and the development need for alone-time. Office: 1 University Pl New York NY 10003-4516

BUCHHOLZ, RONALD LEWIS, architect; b. Milw., Jan. 14, 1951; s. Raymond LeRoy and Della (Krause) B.; m. Mary Lou Stockhausen, May 20, 1972; children; Lauren Robert, Geoffrey Alan. BS in Architecture, U. Wis., Milw., 1973, cert. pub. mgr., 1995. Registered architect, Wis. Archtl. appraiser Am. Appraisal Co., Milw., 1973; plan examiner, bur. bldgs., structures Wis. Dept. Industry, Labor & Human Rels., Madison, 1973-76, staff architect, 1976, architect, adminstrv. code cons., bur. code devel., 1976-80, dep. dir., 1980-83, asst. dir., 1983-87, asst. office divsn. codes & applications, 1987-89, dep. divsn. adminstr. divsn. safety & bldgs., 1989-96, Wis. Dept. Commerce, Madison, 1996—. Instr. U. Wis., Madison Ext., also. state cert. courses for bldg. and dwelling insps.; mem. Wis. Bldg Code Adv. Rev. Bd., 1976-89, Fire Prevention Coun., 1978-89, adv. com. Alternative Energy Tax Credits, 1978, 80, Dept. Devel. Permit Ctr., 1984-89; mem. Interagy. Com. on Spills of Hazardous Materials, 1981-82, Flood Hazard Interagy. Coord. Coun., 1985-90; mem. adv. com. Wis. Elec. Supply, 1984-86; state rep. U.S. EPA Study Group for Underground Storage Tank Regulations, 1987-90. Author tech. reports. Vol. leader Boy Scouts Am.; coach Madison Area Youth Soccer Assn., 1984-87; basketball coach Madison Parochal Sch. League, 1984-95. With U.S. Army N.G., 1970-76. Mem. Resdl. Facilities Coun. (exec. sec. 1976-78), Bldg. Ofcls. and Code Adminstrs. Internat., Inc., Internat. Conf. Bldg. Ofcls., Inc., Wis. Soc. Cert. Pub. Mgrs. (pres. 2000-01, cert. mgr. program policy bd., sec. 19-2001, chair 2002—), So. Bldg. Code Congress Internat., Am. Acad. Cert. Pub. Mgrs. (pres.-elect 2003), Nat. Eagle Scout Assn., KC. Roman Catholic. Home: 2587 Monument Ct Fitchburg WI 53711-5470 Office: 4th Fl 201 W Washington Ave Madison WI 53703-2760 Fax: 608-266-9946. E-mail: rbuchholz@commerce.state.wi.us.

BUCHHOLZ, WILLIAM JAMES, communications executive, educator; b. Ladysmith, Wis., July 17, 1945; s. James Fossegard and Hazel Winnefred (Crandell) B.; m. Dorothy Ann Kostka, June 17, 1967; children: Christopher, Jeffrey. BA, U. Wis., Eau Claire, 1967; MA, Ohio U., 1968; PhD, U. Ill., 1976. Grad. asst. U. Ill., Urbana, 1972-76; asst. prof. English, bus. communication, info. design Bentley Coll., Waltham, Mass., 1976-83, assoc. prof., 1983-91, prof., 1991—, dir. undergrad./grad. bus. communication programs, 1988-95, co-chmn. dept. English, 1993; chmn. dept. English, 1995-2000; cons. in corp. comm. and internet, 1978—; chmn. dept. info. design and corp. comm., 2001—. Mgr. pubs. Scholastech Inc., Cambridge, Mass., 1983-9; cons. in field. Author: (with others) Truth and Taste: Revisiting High Ethical Standards, 1994, Writing in Business and Manufacturing, 1998; editor, author: Communication Training and Consulting in Business, Industry and Government, 1983; co-editor, contbr.: The Challenge of Change, Managing Communications and Building Corporate Image in the 1990s, 1989, Global Communications: Applying Resources Strategically, 1990; co-editor: New Corporate Relationships, 1991; contbr. articles to profl. jours., chpts. to books. With USN, 1968-72. Grantee FIPSE, 1986, 87; fellow NDEA-IV, 1967-68, inst. fellow Bentley Coll., 1991-92, Mem.: Boston IA, Phi Sigma Epsilon. Roman Catholic. Avocations: personal computing, swimming, cross-country skiing, reading, travel. Home: 44 Raffaele Dr Waltham MA 02452-0313 Office: Bentley Coll Grad Ctr 175 Forest St Waltham MA 02452-4713 E-mail: wbuchholz@bentley.edu.

BUCHIN, JACQUELINE CHASE, clinical psychologist; b. Providence, Nov. 27, 1935; d. Leslie Thurber and Mary Hillyer (Lyon) Chase; m. Stanley Ira Buchin, Sept. 14, 1957; children: Linda Chase Sullivan, David Lyon, Gordon Tomlinson. BA, Wellesley Coll., 1957; MEd in Counseling Psychology, Antioch U., 1979; PsyD, Mass. Sch. Profl. Psychology, Boston, 1990. Lic. clin. psychologist Mass. Dir., coord. emergency housing program Multi-Svc. Ctr., Newton, Mass., 1978-81; family therapy intern Newtom Guidance Clinic, 1981-82, Framingham (Mass.) Youth Guidance, 1982-84; psychology intern The Arbour Hosp., Boston, 1984-85, Solomon Carter Fuller Hosp., Boston, 1985-86, Behavior Assocs., Boston, 1986-90; staff psychologist Biobehavioral Treatment Ctr., Brookline, Mass., 1990—; fellow in clin. cognitive therapy program Mass. Gen. Hosp., Boston, 1993-95, clin. assoc., 1995—, rsch. clinician, 1995—. Clin. instr. Psychology Dept. Harvard Med. Sch., Boston, 1995—; faculty mem. Inst. Cognitive Therapy Mass. Gen. Hosp., Boston, 1996—99; founding mem. Acad. Cognitive Therapy, Boston, 2000. Pres. Wellesley Jr. Svc. League, 1972—73; mem., bd. dirs. Jr. League of Boston, 1975—77; bd. dirs. Wellesley Cmty. Chest and Coun., 1972—73, Wellesley Friendly Assoc., 1972—73, Family Counseling Region W, 1969; bd. dirs. Wellesley chpt. ARC; bd. dirs. Wellesley Cmty. Child Care, 1976, Human Rels. Svc.; trustee Mass. Sch. Profl. Psychology, chmn. human resources com., 1991—99. Mem.: APA, Mass. Psychol. Assn., Assn. for Advancement of Behavior Therapy. Episcopalian. Home: Union Wharf Boston MA 02109-1206 Office: Biobehavioral Treatment Ctr 1051 Beacon St Brookline MA 02446-3282

BUCHIN, JEAN, psychologist, educator; b. N.Y.C., Aug. 15; d. Mac and Celia Jacobs; children: Peter J., John D. BA, CUNY; MA, Columbia U.; PhD, NYU. Tchr. N.Y.C. Pub. Schs.; counselor, asst. prof. CUNY. Mem. Nat. Bd. Cert. Counselors, Nat. Bd. Cert. Career Counselors; asst. prof. coord. Which Way With Women program Baruch Coll.; vis. asst. prof. NYU; cons. N.Y.C. Tchrs. Consortium; mem. Spkrs. Bur., Child Abuse Ctr.; mgmt. tng. cons. Met. Life Ins. Co., N.Y.C.; cons. assessment programs N.Y.C. Divsn. Pers., Sci. and Tech. Adv. Bd.; cons. N.J. Human Resources Divsn.; career cons. AARP; lectr., leader

workshops 53d St. Y., NYU, Queens Coll., A.W.E.D., leader workshops Marymount Coll.; mediator ABA; cons. Child Abuse Ctr. Author: Singular Parent, Noah's Ark Minus One. Washington Sq. Coll. fellow. Mem. AAUP, ACA, APA (pres. Tri State chpt. divsn. 35), Ea. Psychol. Assn., Met. N.Y. Assn. for Applied Psychology, Bus. and Profl. Women, Career Devel. Specialists Network.

BUCHIN, STANLEY IRA, management consultant, finance educator; b. N.Y.C., Sept. 7, 1931; s. K. and Bertha (Handman) B.; m. Jacqueline Thurber Chase, Sept. 14, 1957; children: Linda C., David L., Gordon T. SB, MIT, 1952; MBA, Harvard U., 1956, DBA, 1962. Asst. to treas. Bay State Abrasives, 1956-58; rsch. asst. Harvard Bus. Sch., 1958-59, rsch. assoc., 1959-60, instr., 1960-61, lectr., 1961-62, asst. prof., 1962-66, assoc. prof., 1966-69; pres. Applied Decision Sys., Wellesley, Mass., 1969-78; v.p. Temple, Barker & Sloane, Inc., Lexington, Mass., 1975-80, sr. v.p., 1980-90; prin. Arthur D. Little, 1991-99. Pres. Boston-Bermuda Cruising Ltd., 1992-97, Gen. Ship Cruising Corp., 1994-97; vis. lectr. Templeton Coll. Oxford (Eng.), 1991-93; prof. Arthur D. Little Sch. Mgmt., 1992—; assoc. prof. Boston U., 1997—; chmn. acad. policy com. Met. Coll., long-range planning com. Mass. Sch. Profl. Psychology. Author: E-Book about Business Strategy, 2000, E-Book about Marketing, 2001. Trustee, chmn. long range planning com. Mass. Sch. Profl. Psychology. With Chem. Corps, U.S. Army, 1952-54. IBM fellow, 1962-63; George F. Baker scholar, 1956. Mem. Am. Mktg. Assn., Inst. Mgmt. Sci., Fin. Mgmt. Assn., Harvard Club Boston, Tau Beta Pi. Republican. Congregationalist. Home: Union Wharf # 304 Boston MA 02109-1206 Office: 808 Commonwealth Ave Boston MA 02215-1206 Business E-Mail: sbuchin@bu.edu.

BUCHKO, AARON ANTHONY, management educator; b. Lakewood, Ohio, June 7, 1956; s. Walter B. and Blanche Martha (Vaida) B.; m. Kathleen Jo Hughbanks, May 23, 1981. AAS, Grand Rapids (Mich.) Jr. Coll., 1975; BS, Ferris State U., 1977; MBA, Bradley U., 1983; PhD, Mich. State U., 1990. Sales rep. ABC Records & Tapes, Grand Rapids, 1977-78, Lieberman Enterprises, Peoria, Ill., 1978-79; mktg. rep. Johnson & Johnson, Inc., Peoria, 1979; asst. mktg. mgr. Foster & Gallagher, Inc., Peoria, 1979-83; mktg. dir. PJS Publ., Peoria, 1983-84; grad. asst. Mich. State U., East Lansing, 1984-89; assoc. prof. mgmt. Bradley U., Peoria, 1989—2002, prof. mgmt., 2002—. Cons. in field. Co-author: Field Casework: Methods for Consulting to Small and Startup Businesses, 1996; contbr. articles to profl. jours., textbooks. Mem. Canton Country Club, River City Athletic Club, Beta Gamma Sigma, Sigma Iota Epsilon, Delta Tau Delta. Lutheran. Avocations: running, fly fishing, golf, reading. Home: 1719 W Tiffany Ct Peoria IL 61614 1721 Office: Bradley University 326 Baker Hl Peoria IL 61625-0001

BUCHMAN, ELWOOD, internist, pharmaceutical company medical director; b. Ottumwa, Iowa, June 10, 1923; s. Abe and Sarah (Redman) B.; m. Kathleen Field, June 8, 1945 (deceased); children— Elizabeth Anne, Bernard Kip; m. Eloise Marolf Schooley Buchman, June 30, 1989. BA, U. Iowa, 1940, MD, 1943. diplomate Am. Bd. Internal Medicine. Intern D.C. Gen. Hosp.; resident in internal medicine Wayne State U., VA Hosp., Detroit; fellow U. Pa., 1956; mem. staff Wayne State U. Med. Sch., VA Hosp., Detroit, 1946-52; assoc. prof. U. Iowa, Iowa City, from 1952; chief med. service VA Hosp., Des Moines, 1969-73; med. dir. Cintest Inc., Cin., 1980-86; former assoc. dir. Norwich Eaton Pharm. Co.; and div. dir. Merrell Pharm. Rsch. Ctr., Cin. Sr. examiner numerous ins. cos. Contbr. numerous articles to med. jours. Served to capt. M.C., U.S. Army; lt. col. USAR. Fellow ACP, Am. Coll. Gastroenterology, Am. Soc. Clin. Pharmacology and Therapeutics; mem. Am. Profl. Practice Assn., Acad. Medicine Cin., Sigma Xi, Alpha Omega Alpha. Home: 15456 N Boswell Blvd Sun City AZ 85351 E-mail: buck-eloise@iopener.net.

BUCHMAN, KENNETH WILLIAM, lawyer; b. Plant City, Fla., Nov. 20, 1956; s. Paul Sidney and Beryle (Solomon) B.; m. MarDee H. Buchman, May 9, 1985; 1 child, Katherine Elizabeth. AA, U. Fla., 1976, BBA, 1978, JD, 1981. Bar: Fla. 1981; U.S. Dist. Ct. (Mid. dist.) Fla. 1981; U.S. Ct. Appeals (11th cir.) 1986; U.S. Supreme Ct. 1988; bd. cert. city, county, local govt. law. Ptnr. Buchman and Buchman, Plant City, 1981-85, Buchman and Buchman, PA, Plant City, 1985-91; pvt. practice Plant City, 1991-2000; asst. city atty. City of Plant City, 1982-91, city atty., 1991—. City atty. San Antonio, Fla., 1995-2000; mem. exec. coun. city, county and local govt. law sect. Fla. Bar., 1997—. Mem.: Plant City Bar Assn., Fla. Mcpl. Attys. Assn. (steering com. 1999—2002, exec. bd. 2002—), Masons. Jewish. Office: 302 W Reynolds St Plant City FL 33566-3314

BUCHMAN, M. ABRAHAM, lawyer; b. Bklyn., Oct. 25, 1916; s. Judah Louis and Augusta Buchman; m. Ann P. Buchman, July 25, 1950; 1 child, Amy. BA cum laude, NYU, 1935; LLB cum laude, St. Lawrence U., 1938, JSD summa cum laude, 1939. Bar: N.Y. 1939, U.S. Dist. Ct. (so. dist.) N.Y. 1946, U.S. Ct. Appeals 1949, Supreme Ct. U.S. 1964. Plant mgr., contr. Atlas Import & Export Co., 1931-39; ptnr. Buchman & O'Brien, N.Y.C., Washington, 1940—, San Francisco. Cons. to sec. USAF, 1946-52; cons. to State Dept. at various meetings Coun. of Europe on prep. of conv. for wines and spirits; cons. Am. Wine Assn., 1993—, Vermouth Inst., Inc., 1943-64, Internat. Vermouth Inst., 1964—, Fedn. Italiana Industriali, Produttori ed Esportatori di Vini, Acquavit, Liquori, Sciroppi, Aceti ed Affini, 1962—; Am. Beverage Alcohol Assn., 1963—. Maj. USAF, 1942-46. Fellowship in adminstrv. law named in his honor Columbia U. Law Sch., 1985—. Mem. ABA, FBA (pres. Empire State chpt. 1995-97), Assn. ICC Practitioners, Fed. Bar Coun., Internat. Bar Assn., Phi Beta Kappa. Home: 5301 Woodlands Blvd Tamarac FL 33319-3025 Office: Buchman & O'Brien LLP 10 E 40th St Rm 708 New York NY 10016-0200 also: 1331 Pennsylvania Ave NW Washington DC 20004-1710 also: 505 Sansome St San Francisco CA 94111-3106

BUCHMAN, MARK EDWARD, banker; b. Caldwell, N.J., June 19, 1937; s. Samuel Joseph and Dorothy Eunice (Friedland) B.; m. Mary Angela Dolan, June 6, 1964 (div. 1991); children: Jennifer Ann, Romy Ellen; m. Arletta Martin, Mar. 18, 2002. BS, U. Pa., 1959; AMP, Harvard U., 1977. Sr. v.p., dep. gen. mgr. Mfrs. Hanover Trust Co., N.Y.C., 1962-82; exec. v.p. Union Bank, Los Angeles, 1982-88; pres. Govt. Nat. Mortgage Assn., Washington, 1988-89; prin. Buchman & Assocs., 1989-90; pres., CEO Bank of L.A., 1990-92, Liberty Bank, Honolulu, 1993-94. Mem. pres.'s council U. Pa., 1984—; Pacific Asia Mus., Pasadena, Calif., 1983-85. Served to lt. (j.g.) USN, 1959-62. Mem. Coun. on Fgn. Rels., Asia Soc., Japan-Am. Soc. So. Calif. (pres.), Calif. Bankers Assn. (pres. 1986-87), Assn. Res. City Bankers, Calif. Club, Riviera Country Country Club (L.A.), Vintage Club (Indian Wells, Calif.). Republican. Avocations: tennis, skiing, golf, bridge. Home: 225 Delfern Dr Los Angeles CA 90077-3544 E-mail: shibuihito@aol.com.

BUCHMAN, STEVEN RICHARD, plastic surgeon, medical association administrator, director; s. Nathan and Lillian Ann Buchman; m. Cynthia Marie Boufford, July 12, 1997; children: Brevin Chase, Alexandra Tate children: Lauren Kendall. MD, Med. Coll. of Va., 1985. Plastic Surgery U. Pa., 1992. Cheif pediatric plastic surgeon CS Mott Children's Hosp., Ann Arbor, Mich., 1993—; dir., craniofacial anomalies program U. Mich. Med. Ctr., Ann Arbor, 1993—. Sci. program chair Plastic Surgery Rsch. Coun. Contbr. Learning Channel episode. Recipient Bernd Spiessel Rsch. award, Am. Soc. of Maxillofacial Surgeons, 1998. Achievements include development of rodent model of distraction osteogenesis. Office: U Mich Med Ctr 1500 E Med Ctr Dr Ann Arbor MI 48109-0219

BUCHMANN, ALAN PAUL, lawyer; b. Yonkers, N.Y., Sept. 5, 1934; s. Paul John and Jessie Gow (Perkins) B.; m. Lizabeth Ann Moody, Sept. 5, 1959. BA summa cum laude, Yale U., 1956; postgrad, U. Munich, 1956-57; LLB, Yale U., 1960. Bar: Ohio 1960, U.S. Dist. Ct. (no. dist.) Ohio 1963, U.S. Ct. Appeals (6th cir.) 1968, U.S. Supreme Ct. 1977, Fla. 1996. Assoc. Squire, Sanders & Dempsey, Cleve., 1960-70, ptnr., 1970-96; pvt. practice St. Petersburg, Fla. Contbr. articles to profl. jours. State chmn. Ohio Young reps., 1970-71, nat. committeeman, 1971-74; mem. exec. com. Cuyahoga County Reps., 1969-95, fin. com., 1987-94; mem. Selective svc. Bd., 1967-75; trustee Cleve. Internat. Program, 1979-82, 94-95; pres. English Speaking Union, 1981-83. Recipient Robert A. Taft award Young Reps., 1969, Outstanding State Chmn. award, 1971, James A. Rhodes award, 1974; Fulbright fellow U. Munich, 1956-57. Mem. ABA (chmn. pub. utility law sect. 1989-90, sect. del. 1996—, mem. coord. com. on legal edn. 1991-97, mem. nominating com. 2003—), Fla. Bar Assn., Ohio State Bar Assn., St. Petersburg Bar Assn., Hillsborough County Bar Assn. E-mail: bbuchmann1@aol.com.

BUCHNESS, MICHAEL PATRICK, cardiothoracic surgeon; b. Balt., Sept. 19, 1939; s. John Adam and Catherine (Horn) B.; m. Margaret A. Struble, June 11, 1966; children: Michael John, Eleanor Ann. BS, Loyola Coll., Balt., 1962; MD, U. Md., 1966. Diplomate Am. Bd. Surgeons, Am. Bd. Thoracic Surgery. Intern USPHS, Staten Island, N.Y., 1966-67, resident in medicine, 1967-68, chief outpatient clinic Cleve., 1968-69; resident in surgery U. Md., Balt., 1969-73, asst. prof. vascular surgery, 1973-74, resident thoracic surgery, 1974-76; cardiac surgeon Peninsula Regional Med. Ctr., Salisbury, Md., 1976—, chief of surgery, 1988-90. Mem. ACS, Am. Coll. Cardiology, Soc. for Thoracic Surgery, Ea. Vascular Soc., Chesapeake Vascular Soc. Republican. Roman Catholic. Avocations: running, skiing, bird watching. Office: Cardiovascular Surg Assocs PA 201 Pine Bluff Rd Salisbury MD 21801-7163

BUCHOLTZ, HAROLD RONALD, lawyer; b. Newark, Jan. 24, 1952; s. Samuel and Dorothy (Sorren) B. BBA, Rutgers U., 1973; JD, U. Va., 1976; LLM in Taxation, Georgetown U., 1980. Bar: Va. 1976, D.C. 1980, U.S. Tax Ct. 1980, U.S. Supreme Ct. 1980, U.S. Ct. Appeals (fed. cir.) 1981, U.S. Ct. Appeals (D.C. cir.) 1982, U.S. Ct. Appeals (11th cir.) 1983. Atty. office of the chief counsel IRS, Washington, 1976-81; assoc. Pope, Ballard & Loos, Washington, 1981, Holland & Knight, Washington, 1982-84; ptnr. Holland & Knight LLP, Washington, 1985—. Contbr. articles to profl. jours. Mem. ABA (taxation sect.), Am. Law Inst., Va. Bar Assn., D.C. Bar Assn. Home: 1901F N Adams St Arlington VA 22201-3609 Office: Holland & Knight LLP 2099 Pennsylvania Ave NW Washington DC 20006 E-mail: hbucholt@hklaw.com.

BUCHOLZ, ARDEN, historian, educator; b. Chgo., May 14, 1936; s. Arden Kingsbury and Betty (Lutz) B.; m. Sue Ann Tally, July 7, 1962; children: Merritt, Mark. AB, Dartmouth Coll., 1958; diploma, U. Vienna, Austria, 1960; AM, U. Chgo., 1965, PhD, 1972. Tchr. English Amerikan Orta Okulu, Talas-Kayseri, Turkey, 1958-60; tchr. history Latin Sch Chgo., 1965-70; disting. tchg. prof. history SUNY, Brockport, 1970—, dir. grad. program in history, 1990-97; dir. SUNY program Brunel U., Uxbridge, Eng., 1987-88. Cons. NEH, Washington, 1988, WXXI TV, Rochester, N.Y., 1990-92, Houghton Mifflin Co., Boston, 1982-84, Harper & Row, N.Y.C., 1983-86; rsch. assoc. U.S. Army Mil. History Inst., Carlisle Barracks, Pa., 1985. Author: Hans Delbrueck and German Military Establishment, 1985, Moltke, Schlieffen and Prussian War Planning, 1991, Delbrück's Modern Military History, 1997, Moltke and the German Wars, 1864-1871, 2001. Pres. bd. edn. Lyndonville (N.Y.) Ctrl. Sch., 1980-87. With U.S. Army, 1961-64. Recipient Chancellor's award SUNY, 1977; Rodney Dennis fellow Harvard U., 2001. Mem. Phi Alpha Theta. Home: 13510 Roosevelt Hwy Waterport NY 14571-9712 Office: SUNY Dept History Brockport NY 14420 E-mail: abucholz@brockport.edu.

BUCHOWSKI, MICHAL JANUSZ, anthropologist; b. Poznan, Poland, Dec. 20, 1955; s. Bogumil Janusz and Cecylia Anna (Koczorowska) B.; m. Stanislava Maria Rechtorisova, Aug. 21, 1981 (div. 1998); children: Jan, Zuzanna; m. Izabela Kolbon, June 30, 2001. MA, Adam Mickiewicz U., 1979, PhD, 1983, dr. habilitatus, 1990. Univ. asst. Adam Mickiewicz U., Poznan, 1979-84, asst. prof., 1984-90, assoc. prof., 1990-98, prof., 1998—; prof. Comparative Ctrl. European Studies European U.-Viadrina, Frankfurt/Oder, Germany, 1998—. Vis. prof. U. Kans., Lawrence, 1993, Rutgers U., New Brunswick, N.J., 2001—; rsch. assoc. Ctr. Nat. de la Recherche Scientifique, Paris and Ctr. Marc Bloch-Berlin, 1994-95. Author: Magic: Its Functions and Structure, 1986, Rationality, Translation, Interpretation, 1990, Magic & Ritual, 1993, Reluctant Capitalists, 1997, The Rational Order, 1997, Rethinking Transformation, 2001; co-author: On Fundamentals of Anthropological Interpretation, 1992. Fulbright rsch. scholar, 1990-91; Kosciuszko Found. fellow, 1993, 2001—, postdoctoral fellow Commonwealth Ctr. for Lit. and Cultural Change U. Va., 1992, Humboldt Found. fellow, 1996-97. Mem. European Assn. Social Anthropologists, Polish Ethnological Soc., Polish Sociol. Soc. Avocations: bicycling, music. Office: Adam Mickiewicz U ul sw Marcin 78 61-809 Poznan Poland also: Rutgers Univ 172 College Ave PO Box 5062 New Brunswick NJ 08903 E-mail: mbuch@amu.edu.pl.

BUCHSBAUM, KAREN FUSON, public relations executive, consultant; b. New Bern, N.C., Dec. 26, 1953; d. Robert Henderson and Amelia Carmen Fuson; m. Frederick Joel Buchsbaum, Nov. 23, 1979; 1 child, Ashley. BS in Comms., U. Tenn., Knoxville, 1975. Asst. dir., pub. info. dir. Greater Tampa (Fla.) Bicentennial Coun., 1975-76; dir. pub. rels. St. Francis Hosp., Miami Beach, Fla., 1977-79; dir. advt., comms. and pub. rels. Cedars Med. Ctr., Miami, Fla., 1979-84; prin., co-owner Comms. Strategies, Inc., Coral Gables, Fla., 1984—2002; comm. cons., 2002—. Bd. visitors U. Tenn. Coll. Comms., Knoxville, 1987—; mem. pub. rels. adv. coun. U. Miami, Coral Gables, 1997-2002. Advisor Crime Watch Am., 1994-95; pres. Epilepsy Found. South Fla., Miami, 2000-2002; pres. Carver Elem. Sch. PTA, Coral Gables, 1992-93; participant Leadership Miami, 1984; pub. rels. chair spl. events Gulliver Schs. Parents Assn., 2001-03; pub. rels. chair charity golf tournament Kidney Found. South Fla., 2002. Recipient award Nat. Health Info. Coun., 1999,2000, Pub. Rels. award, 1988-94, 98—, Fla. Hosp. Assn., 1978, 80, 81, 82, 83, 84, 86, 88, 89, 91, 92, 93, 96, 97, 98, 99, 2000, touchstone award Am. Soc. Hosp. Mktg. and Pub. Rels., 1986, Health and Medicine award for direct mktg. videos Telly Awards, 2000, Cardiovascular Comms. award Am. Heart Assn., 1998, 99, Healthcare Mktg. Report awards 1988, 89, 90, 91, 92, 93, 94, 98, 99, 2000, 2001. Fellow Pub. Rels. Soc. Am. (accredited, chmn. Sunshine dist. 1989, pres. Miami chpt. 1983, MacEachern award 1986), South Fla. Hosp. Pub. Rels. and Mktg. Assn. (pres. 1979), Fla. Soc. for Healthcare Pub. Rels. and Mktg. (bd. dirs. 1979-84). Avocations: travel, reading, antiques, golf, dancing. Home: 13627 Deering Bay Dr # 804 Coral Gables FL 33158

BUCHSBAUM, PETER A. lawyer; b. Bklyn., Dec. 27, 1945; s. Arnold and Rose (Chanes) B.; m. Elaine Frey, Dec. 24, 1967; children: Matthew, Andrew, Aaron. AB, Cornell U., 1967; JD, Harvard U., 1970. Law sec. to Chief Justice Hon. Joseph Weintraub, Trenton, 1970-71; lawyer N.J. State Tax Policy Commn., Trenton, 1971-72; staff counsel ACLU, Newark, 1972-74; asst. dep. pub. adv. N.J. Dept. Pub. Adv., Trenton, 1974-79; lawyer Warren, Goldberg, & Berman, Princeton, N.J., 1979-84; ptnr. Hannoch Weisman, Princeton, 1984-91, Greenbaum, Rowe, Smith, Ravin & Davis, Woodbridge, N.J., 1991—. Spl. counsel N.J. State League Mcpl., Trenton, 1988—94; counsel Borough Flemington, NJ; commr. N.J. Law Rev. Commn., Newark; adj. faculty Rutgers-Camden (N.J.) Law Sch.; cons. APA Growing Smart Project. Columnist: N.J. Reporter Mag., Princeton, 1982—2000, State and Local Law News ABA, 1996—; co-editor: State and Regional Comprehensive Planning, 1993; reporter: Land Use Law and Zoning Digest Mag.; contbr. articles to profl. jours. Bd. dirs. Hunterdon County United Way, Hunterdon County Housing Corp., Flemington, N.J., Best Lawyers in Am.; mayor West Amwell Twp., N.J.; mem. N.J. State Dem. Com. Named one of Best Lawyers in Am. Mem. ABA (coun. sect. on state and local govt. land), Am. Coll. Real Estate Lawyers, N.J. State Bar Assn. (chmn. land use law sect. 1986-87, sect. trustee 1983-96, appellate practices com. 1999-2002, media award 1987). Democrat. Jewish. Avocations: hiking, writing. Home: 126 Bowne Station Rd Stockton NJ 08559-1907 Office: Greenbaum Rowe Smith Ravin Davis & Himmel Metro Corp Campus I PO Box 5600 Woodbridge NJ 07095-0988 E-mail: pbuchsbaum@greenbaumlaw.com.

BUCHSIEB, WALTER CHARLES, orthodontist, director; b. Columbus, Ohio, Aug. 30, 1929; s. Walter William and Emma Marie (Held) b.; m. Betty Lou Risch, June 19, 1955; children: Walter Charles II, christine Ann. BA, Ohio State U., 1951, DDS, 1955, MS, 1960. Pvt. practice dentistry specializing in orthodontics, Dayton, Ohio, 1959-93. Cons. orthodontist Miami Valley Hosp., Children's Med. Ctr., Dayton; orthodontic cons. Columbus Children's Hosp.; assoc. prof. dept. orthodontics Ohio State U. Coll. Dentistry, 1984—, clinic dir., 1993—98, mem. dean's adv. com.; mem. fin. and program com. United Health Found., 1971—73. Bd. dirs. Hearing and Speech Ctr., 1968-82, 2d v.p., 1976-78, pres., 1978-79; orthodontic advisor State of Ohio Dept. Health, Bur. Crippled Children's Svcs., 1983-84; elder Luth. ch., 1965-68, v.p. 1974. Capt. AUS, 1955-58. Fellow Am. Coll. Dentists (pres. Ohio sect. 1988); mem. ADA (alt. del. 1968, del. 1991, coun. on ann. sessions and internat. rels. 1984-88), Am. Assn. Dental Schs., Am. Cleft Palate Assn., Am. Assn. Dental Schs., Internat. Assn. Dental Rsch., Ohio Dental Assn. (sec. coun. legis. 1969-78, v.p. 1978-79, pres.-elect 1979-80, pres. 1980-81, polit. action com. 1987-95, Coun. on constn. and By- Laws 1988-92, Achievement award 1989), Dayton Dental Soc. (pres. 1970-71), Am. Bd. Orthodontics, Gt. Lakes Soc. Orthodontists (sec.-treas. 1972-75, pres. 1977-78), Internat. Coll. Dentists,Am. Assn. Orthodontists (chmn. coun. legis. 1976, speaker of house 1982-85, ad hoc com. to revise by-laws, coun. on govtl. affairs 1988-96, recipient James E. Brophy Dist. Svc. award 1992, bd. mem. polit. action com.), Pierre Fauchard Acad., Coll. of Diplomats Am. Bd. Orthodontics (pres. 1990-91), Ohio State U. Alumni Assn. (advocates group), Delta Upsilon (pres. Ohio State U. alumni chpt. 1997-99, alumni advisor 2000—), Psi Omega, Masons, Rotary (pres. 1973-74, Paul Harris fellow). Republican. Lutheran. Home: 1212 Harrison Pond Dr New Albany OH 43054-9553 Office: Ohio State U Orthodontics Dept 305 W 12th Ave Columbus OH 43210-1267 E-mail: buchsieb.1@osu.edu.

BUCHTEL, MICHAEL EUGENE, optical mechanical engineer; b. Denver, Jan. 29, 1939; s. William Paxton and Lorraine Edith (Hammond) B.; m. Gloria Jean Guerrero, Sept. 29, 1967. BS, West Coast U., Compton, Calif., 1972. Sr. engr. Ford Aerospace Corp., Newport Beach, Calif., 1972-92; pres. The Techtel Co., Costa Mesa, Calif., 1992—. Cons. Internat. Orgn. for Standards, Pforzheim, Switzerland, 1993—. Patentee for optical scanner in U.S. and Japan. With U.S. Army, 1962-64. Mem. Internat. Soc. for Optical Engrs., Am. Soc. Design Engrs. Republican. Roman Catholic. Office: The Techtel Co 1666 Newport Blvd Costa Mesa CA 92627-3717

BUCHWALD, DON DAVID, lawyer; b. Bklyn., May 10, 1944; BA, Cornell U., 1965, JD, 1968. Assoc. Marshall, Bratter, Greene, Allison & Tucker, N.Y.C., 1970-73; asst. U.S. atty. So. Dist. of N.Y., N.Y.C., 1973-80, dep. chief criminal, 1977-80; ptnr. Buchwald & Kaufman, N.Y.C., 1980-99; pvt. practice Don Buchwald, LLP, N.Y.C., 1999—. Served to sgt. U.S. Army, 1968-70. Mem. ABA, Fed. Bar Council, Assn. of the Bar of the City of N.Y., N.Y. State Bar Assn. Office: 100 Park Ave New York NY 10017-5516

BUCHWALD, HENRY, surgeon, educator, researcher; b. Vienna, June 21, 1932; came to U.S., 1939; naturalized; s. Andor and Renee (Franzos) B.; m. Emilie D. Bix, June 6, 1954; children: Jane Nicole, Amy Elizabeth, Claire Gretchen, Dana Alexandra. BA summa cum laude, Columbia U., 1954, MD, 1957; MS in Biochemistry, PhD in Surgery, U. Minn., 1967. Diplomate Am. Bd. Surgery. Intern Columbia/Presbyn. Med. Ctr., N.Y.C., 1957-58; resident fellow in surgery U. Minn., Mpls., 1960-67; asst. prof. surgery U. Minn. Med. Sch., Mpls., 1967-70, assoc. prof., 1970-77, prof. surgery, prof. biomed. engring., 1977—, dir. grad. surg. tng., resident tng. program, in-tng. exam.; chmn. credentials com. Pres. Minn. Inventors Hall of Fame, 1989-92, chmn. bd. dirs. 1992-94; vis. prof., lectr. McLaren Gen. Hosp., Flint., Mich., 1979, Buffalo Surg. Soc., Mpls., 1980, G.P. Wratten Surg. Symposium, Washington, 1980, Frontiers of Medicine Series, Chgo., 1980, Minn. Endocrine Club, Mpls., 1980, Symposium on Surgery, Tokyo, 1980, Northwestern Med. Assn., Sun Valley, Idaho, 1981, Mayo Clinic, Rochester, Minn., 1981, BSG/Glaxo Internat. Teaching Day, Norwich, Eng., 1982, Mass. Gen. Hosp., Boston, 1983, SUNY Stony Brook, 1984, D.C. Gen. Hosp., Washington, 1984, L.A. Surg. Soc., 1987, Sch. Dentistry, Dept. Continuing Edn., U. Minn., 1988, others; Alfred Strauss vis. lectr., Chgo., 1989; dir. postgrad. course Bariatric Surgery Primer, ACS; spkr., cons. in field.; presenter numerous confs. and symposia. Author: (with others) Hepatic, Biliary and Pancreatic Surgery, 1980, Lipoproteins and Coronary Atherosclerosis, 1982, Atherosclerosis: Clinical Evaluation and Therapy, 1982, Nutrition and Heart Disease, 1982, Advances in Vascular Surgery, 1983, Advances in Surgery, 1984, others; contbr. Gibbon's Surgery of the Chest, 4th edit., 1983, Hardy's Textbook of Surgery, 1983, Implantable Pumps: ASAIO Primers in Artificial Organs, 1987; contbr. over 250 articles to profl. jours., trans.; mem. editorial bd. Chirurgia Generale, Jour. Clin. Surgery, Infu-Systems Internat., Diabetes, Nutrition and Metabolism, Obesity Surgery Jour. Am. Soc. Artificial Int. Orgn., Jour. Bacteriol. Surgery, Online Jour. Current Clin. Trials, also guest editor other jours. Capt. SAC, USAF, 1958-60. Recipient Inventor of Yr. award Minn. Inventors Hall of Fame, 1988, 90, Clin. Scholar award U. Minn., 1991, Diehl award U. Minn.; recipient numerous rsch. grants univs., Nat. Heart and Lung Inst., Nat. Cancer Inst., Nat. Inst. Arthritis, Metabolism and Digestive Diseases, NIH, med. founds., pharm. cos., corps., 1956—. Fellow ACS (gov., 1999—, Samuel D. Gross award 1969), Am. Surg. Assn., Soc. Univ. Surgeons, Cen. Surg. Assn. (program com. 1982-85, chmn. 1984-85, treas. 1992-94, pres. 1997-98), Assn. Acad. Surgery (Disting. Svc. award 1976), Epidemiology Coun. and Cardiovascular Coun. Am. Heart Assn. (established investigator), Am. Coll. Cardiology, Soc. Surgery Alimentary Tract, Soc. Clin. Trials (program com. 1984-85); mem. AAAS, Minn. Surg. Assn. (First Clin. Rsch. award 1965), Mpls. Surg. Assn., Minn. Heart Assn., Am. Assn. History Medicine, Am. Soc. Artificial Internal Organs (program com. 1984-87, sect. editor Trans.), Internat. Study Group Diabetes Treatment with Implantable Insulin Delivery Devices (sec.-gen. 1984-88, chmn. 1989-94), St. Paul Surg. Soc. (hon.), Am. Coll. Nutrition (mem. editorial bd.), Am. Soc. Bariatric Soc. (pres. 1998-99), Guerner Am. Coll. Surg., 1988—, dir, course in Bariatric Surgery, Am. Coll. Surgery, 2003—, Internat. Soc. Obesity Surgery (pres. 2003—), Paleopathology Club, Alpha Omega Alpha. Avocations: running, riding, tennis, reading, chess. Home: 6808 Margarets Ln Minneapolis MN 55439-1019

BUCHWALD, JED ZACHARY, environmental health researcher, science history educator; b. N.Y.C., June 25, 1949; BA, Princeton U., 1971; MA, Harvard, 1973, PhD, 1974. Instr., dir. Inst. History Philosophy Sci. and Tech. U. Toronto, 1974—92; prof., dir. Dibner Inst. for History of Sci. and Tech. MIT, 1992—. Author: (book) The Creation of Scientific Effects, 1994. Named MacArthur fellow, John D. and Katherine T. MacArthur Found., 1995; recipient award for excellence in environ. health rsch., Lovelace Inst., Albuquerque, 1995. Office: MIT Dibner Inst History/Sci MIT-E56-100 38 Memorial Dr Cambridge MA 02142-1347

BUCHWALD, NAOMI REICE, judge; b. Kingston, N.Y., Feb. 14, 1944; BA cum laude, Brandeis U., 1965; LLB cum laude, Columbia U., 1968. Bar: N.Y. 1968, U.S. Ct. Appeals (2d cir.) 1969, U.S. Dist. Ct. (so. and ea. dists.) N.Y. 1970, U.S. Supreme Ct. 1978. Litigation assoc. Marshall, Bratter, Greene, Allison & Tucker, N.Y.C., 1968-73; asst. U.S. atty. So. Dist. N.Y., N.Y.C., 1973 80, dep. chief civil divsn., 1976-79, chief civil divsn., 1979-80; U.S. magistrate judge U.S. Dist. Ct. (so. dist.) N.Y., N.Y.C., 1980-99, chief magistrate judge, 1994-96, U.S. dist. judge, 1999—. Editor Columbia Jour. Law and Social Problems, 1967-68. Recipient spl. citation FDA Commrs., 1978, Robert B. Fiske Jr. Assn. William B. Tendy award, Outstanding Pub. Svc. award Seymour Assn., Columbia Law Sch. Class of 1968 Excellence in Pub. Svc. award, 1998. Mem. Fed. Bar Coun. (trustee 1976-82, 97-2000, v.p. 1982-84), N.Y. State Bar Assn., Assn. of the Bar of the City of N.Y. (trademarks and unfair competition com. 1988-89, mem. long range planning com. 1993-95, litigation com. 1994-96, ad hoc com. on jud. conduct 1996-99; prof., jud. ethics com. 2002-2003), Phi Beta Kappa, Omicron Delta Epsilon. Office: US Ct House Foley Square New York NY 10007-1316

BUCHWALD, PETER SANDOR, research scientist; b. Kolozsvar, Transylvania, Romania, Feb. 27, 1963; arrived in U.S., 1992; s. Péter Szilard and Margit (Török) Buchwald; m. Amy Formanek, May 16, 1986; children: Zoltan, Zsuzsa. BS, U. Babes-Bolyai, Kolozsvar, Romania, 1986; PhD, U. Fla., 1997. Tchr. Petru Maior Lyceum, Gherla, Romania, 1986—90, Brassai Samuel Lyceum, Cluj, Romania, 1990; computerized info. mgr. RMDSz, Cluj, 1990—92; rsch. assoc. U. Fla., Gainesville, 1992—97, post doctoral rsch. assoc., 1998—2000; sr. rsch. scientist IVAX Rsch., Inc., Miami, 2000—. Contbr. over 40 articles to profl. jours., chapters to books; author: (software program) QLOGP, Soft Drug Design, 1999. Mem.: AAAS, Am. Assn. Pharm. Sci., Am. Chem. Soc., Phi Kappa Phi. Achievements include development of simple molecular size-based model for organic liquids and water. Office: IVAX Rsch Inc 4400 Biscayne Blvd Miami FL 33137

BUCK, CAROLYN J. federal official; BA, U. Minn.; JD with honors, George Washington U. Chief counsel Office of Thrift Supervision, Washington, 1992—. Office: Office Thrift Supervision 1700 G St NW Washington DC 20552-0003

BUCK, DANIEL MICHAEL, engineering executive; b. Allentown, Pa., Nov. 16, 1955; s. Melvin Michael Buck, Rosemarie Elizabeth Buck; m. Marla Treckelo Buck; children: Brian, Marissa. BSMetE, U. Notre Dame, 1977, MBA, 1979. EIT. Various engring., sales, mktg., and bus. mgmt. positions Air

Products & Chems., Allentown, 1979—97, comml. mgr., 1997—. Contbr. articles to profl. jours. Coach Children's Basketball, Volleyball and Baseball, Orefield, 1992—2002; chmn. devel. com. St. Joseph the Worker Parish, Orefield, 1999—2002, Eucharistic minister, 1996—2002; bd. dirs. Nat. Football Found. & Coll. Hall of Fame, Lehigh Valley, 1990—2002. Mem.: Alumni Assn. - Notre Dame (treas., pres. 1990—96). Roman Catholic. Avocations: baseball, football, basketball, golf, reading. Home: 2784 Rickenbacker Ct Orefield PA 18069 Office: Air Products & Chems Inc 7201 Hamilton Blvd Allentown PA 18195 Office Fax: 610-481-8647. Business E-Mail: buckdm@apci.com.

BUCK, DONALD TIRRELL, retired finance educator; b. Manchester, N.H., Nov. 17, 1931; s. Harry Forrest and Gladys (Tirrell) B.; m. Marion Gilmour, Aug. 2, 1969; children: Marianne Elizabeth, Elizabeth Allison Tirrell Buck Rizzo. BS, U. N.H., 1955, MA, 1961. Analyst New England Mut. Life Ins. Co., Boston, 1957-59; instr. fin. U. Pa. Wharton Sch. Bus., Phila., 1961-65; asst. prof. econs. and fin. So. Conn. State Coll., New Haven, 1965-74; assoc. prof. So. Conn. State U., New Haven, 1975-80, prof., 1981-97, emeritus prof., 1998—, mem. faculty senate, 1968-76, chmn. dept. acctg. fin., 1984-85. Pub. mem. investment adv. coun. to treas. State of Conn., Hartford, 1983-92. Contbr. articles to profl. publs. Mem. adv. coun. Bd. Higher Edn. State of Conn., 1983-85; participant econ. workshop hearings legis. fin. com. Gen. Assembly, Conn., 1978-83. With U.S. Army, 1955-57. Mem. AAUP (pres. So. Conn. State U. chpt. 1981-83), SAR (pres. Nathan Hale chpt. 1993-96, auditor Conn. State chpt. 1993-99), Am. Econ. Assn., Soc. Colonial Wars in State of Conn., Boston Athenaeum (life mem.). Congregationalist. Home: Old Town St Hadlyme CT 06439-0129 Office: So Conn State U 501 Crescent St New Haven CT 06515-1330

BUCK, EARL WAYNE, insurance investigator, motel owner; b. La Porte City, Iowa, Jan. 15, 1939; s. Edwin Earl and Uleta Pearl (Purdy) B.; m. Maxine E. Parker, Oct. 19, 1969; children: Brian, Douglas, Stuart, Teresa. LLB, La Salle U., 1969. Asst. mgr. Chgo. br. Atwell, Vogel & Sterling, Scarsdale, N.Y., 1965-70; pvt. detective, Sioux City, Iowa, 1968-74; mgr. Milw. br. Atwell, Vogel & Sterling, Scarsdale, N.Y., 1970; sr. auditor Comml. Union Ins. Co., Chgo., 1970-74; police chief McHenry Shores (Ill.) Police Dept., 1973-79; self-employed ins. investigator McHenry, Ill., 1980-88, Rapid City, S.D., 1988—; owner Corral Motel, Rapid City, 1988—. Liquor liability investigator for various ins. cos., 1980-88; farm owner, 1986-96; owner High Plaines Detective Agy., 1990-. Chmn. McHenry Shores (Ill.) Zoning Commn., 1972, Police Support Subcom., C. of C. Pub. Safety Com.; key contact Help Abolish Legal Tyranny; active Rapid City Police Res., 1989-90, North Rapid Civic Assn., 1991—, pres., chmn. bd., 1993-94; active Pennington County Air Quality Bd., 1990-93, chmn., 1992-93. With U.S. Army, 1957-61. Recipient Police Meritorius Service award Vill. of McHenry Shores, 1979. Mem. Midwest Ins. Auditors Assn., McHenry County Police Chief's Assn., Rapid City Police Officers Assn., Rapid City Area Hospitality Assn. (bd. dirs.), Rapid City Area C. of C. (safety com. 1989-91), Am. Legion, Fed. Weed and Seed Program Rapid City (steering com.), NRA, Moose. Republican. Lutheran. Avocations: flying, amateur archaeology, photography, fishing, hunting.

BUCK, FRANCIS SCOTT, pathologist, educator; b. Eskridge, Kans., Oct. 6, 1921; s. Robert Willard Buck and Helen Miriam Dill; m. Dorothy Irene Hollenbeck, Sept. 10, 1948; children: Ronald Scott, Richard Allen, Robert Grant, Dottiann Irene Buck Pino. Student, Fresno State Coll., 1939-43, 45-47; DO, Coll. Osteo. Physicans/Surgeon, L.A., 1951; MD, Calif. Coll. Medicine, 1962. Cert. anatomic and clin. pathology Am. Bd. Pathology. Dir. pathology L.A. County Hosp., 1955-68; chief physician, pathologist L.A. County/U. So. Calif. Med. Ctr., L.A., 1968-85, attending physician, 1985—. Mem. profl. staff assn. L.A. County/U. So. Calif. Med. Ctr., L.A., 1968-85; v.p., bd. govs. Am. Osteopathic Coll. Pathology, 1961-62. Contbr. articles to med. jours. Mem. donor recruitment com. L.A./Orange County ARC Blood Bank, 1980-81; bd. trustees Reformed Presbyn. Ch. N.Am., 1972-79; elder Reformed Presbyn. Ch. L.A., 1971—. Capt. U.S. Army Air Force, 1942-45. Mem. AMA, Calif. Med. Assn., Calif. Soc. Pathologists, L.A. Soc. Pathologists, Grad. Soc. Pathologists, L.A. County/U. So. Calif. Med. Ctr. (sec., pres. 1979-85). Republican. Avocations: theology, teaching bible, fishing, hiking, gem cutting. Home: 240 Cherry Dr Pasadena CA 91105-1325

BUCK, GENE, graphics company executive, satirist, historian; b. Seattle, July 4, 1946; s. Gene Cecil and Theodosia Ann (Burr) B. Student, U. Hawaii, 1975-76, U. Wash., 1976-79, Kingswork Inst., Honolulu, 1979-80. Owner Cypress Fine Arts, Monterey, 1981-87, Gene Buck, Publicist, Monterey, 1983-87; dir. Aaron Burr Accord, Seattle, 1987—; chmn. Aaron Burr Commemorative Stamp Com., Seattle, 1981—; owner Storyville Graphics, Seattle, 1990—. Cons. Spencer Prodns., Inc., N.Y.C., 1975-98, Bing Crosby Hist. Soc., Tacoma, 1975-94; dir. Brotherhood for Respect, Elevation, and Advancement of Dishwaters, Monterey, 1983-85, founder Empire of Burravia, 1985—. Author: Wayward Souls adaption of Outward Bound: The Movie, 1999, ABC Color and Learn Book, 1997, (with Gerald E. Mowery) Who's Who in the Slow-Lane, 1997, The Great D.B. Cooper Hoax, 1989, Aaron Burr, My Burr Book, 1999, Betty Oops, 1999. Chmn. Rose St. Commons, Seattle, 1992-98, Stop the Train!, Seattle, 1993-98; dir. Soc. of Disenfranchised, Seattle, 1987-96, dir., 1980-98; chmn. Goldwater Alliance, 1998—; founder, pres. Leo Lassen Legacy Project, 1999—; co-founder TV Audience Screen Extra Guild, 2003—; founder, pres. Aaron Burr Legacy Project, 1999—. With USNR, 1974-78. Avocation: collecting betty boop memorabilia. Home: Solarium Penthouse LaFong Twr 8311 54th Ave S Seattle WA 98118-4702

BUCK, GURDON HALL, lawyer, urban planner; b. Hartford, Conn., Apr. 10, 1936; s. Richard Saltonstall and Aloha Frances (Hall) B.; children: Keith Saltonstall, Frances Josephine, Daniel Winthrop; m. Martha Finder, 1996. BA in English, Lehigh U., 1958; JD, U. Pa., 1965. Bar: Conn. 1965, U.S. Dist. Ct. 1966, U.S. Ct. Appeals (2d cir.) 1966. Assoc. Shipman & Goodwin, Hartford, 1965-67; v.p., counsel R. F. Broderick & Assocs., Hartford, 1968-69; ptnr. Pelgrift, Byrne, Buck & Connolly, Hartford and Farmington, Conn., 1969—78, Byrne, Buck & Steiner and predecessor Byrne & Buck, Farmington, 1975-78; sr. ptnr. real estate and land use sects., chmn. common interest group Robinson & Cole, Farmington and Hartford, 1979—. Author: Condominium Development, Forms with Commentary, 1990, 2d edit., 1992; prin. co-author: The Connecticut Condominium Manual, 1972, 2d edit., 2003, Real Estate Brokers Community Associations Handbook, rev. edit., 1982, Connecticut Common Interest Ownership Manual, 1984, 2d edit., 2003, The Alaska Common Interest Ownership Manual, 1985, Attorney's and Lenders Guide to Common Interest Communities, 1989, 2nd edit., 1999; contbr. articles on zoning, condominiums, planned unit devels. to profl. jours.; columnist various newspapers. Lt. USCGR, 1958-62. Recipient Disting. Svc. award Glastonbury (Conn.) Jaycees, 1968. Mem. ABA (common interest com. law com., real property and probate, joint editl. bd. real property laws, adv. Uniform Planned Cmty. Act, Model Real Estate Coop. Act, Uniform Common Interest Ownership Act), Am. Law Inst. (advisor, Restatement on Property 3d Servitudes), Am. Coll. Real Estate Lawyers (bd. dirs. 1986-92, common ownership com.), Anglo-Am. Real Property Inst. (bd. govs. 1994—), Cmty. Assns. Inst. (nat. trustee 1982-88, pres. Conn. chpt. 1980-83, sec. 1986-89, bd. dirs. 1992-98, pres. rsch. found. 1980-83, Century Club, Byron Hanke Disting. Svc. award, Acad. of Authors), Am. Planning Assn., Am. Inst. Cert. Planners, Internat. Bar Assn. (panelist common ownership consumer protection 1987), Conn. Bar Assn. (chmn. com. opinions, vice chmn. real estate sect., pro bono com., chair cmty. svc. com., ed. Conn. Bar Jour.), Statewide Legal Svcs. (bd. dirs., pres.), Hartford County Bar Assn., Conn. Assn. Homebuilders Orgn. (developer's coun., pres. statewide legal svcs. 1998—). Office: 1 Commercial Plz Hartford CT 06103-3509 *The common interest community is the mutual sharing of resources and lives through the land. It is as old as civilization itself and as modern as the latest marketing techniques.*

BUCK, HENRY WILLIAM, JR., obstetrician-gynecologist; b. Kansas City, June 4, 1934; s. Henry William Sr. and Nina Irene (Krebs) B.; m. Barbara Laviece Mallory, Sept. 6, 1963; children: Mallory Renee, Andrew William. BA, U. Kans., 1956, MD, 1960. Cert. Am. Bd. Ob.-Gyn. Gynecologist Student Health Svc. U. Kans., Lawrence, head gynecology dept. Student Health Svc., 1987—; pvt. practice Lawrence, 1967—87. Pres. bd. dirs. Douglas County Citizens' Com. on Alcoholism, Lawrence, 1983—; chmn. task force HPV disease Am. Coll. Health Assn. Capt. USAF, 1965-67. Fellow ACS, Am. Coll. Ob-Gyns.; mem. AMA, Kans. Med. Soc., Kans. Ob-Gyn. Soc. (pres. 1980-81), Kappa Sigma, Omicron Delta Kappa. Republican. Lutheran. Avocations: photography, music, writing, travel. Home: 306 Homestead Dr Lawrence KS 66049-2000 Office: U Kans Watkins Meml Health Ctr Student Health Svc Ctr Lawrence KS 66045-7559

BUCK, JAMES E. financial exchange executive; Sr. v.p. & corp. sec. N.Y. Stock Exch., N.Y.C., 1993—.

BUCK, JAMES MAHLON, JR., venture capital executive; b. Bryn Mawr, Pa., Apr. 27, 1925; s. J. Mahlon and Grace Irene (Knapp) B.; m. Elia Garrett Durr, Sept. 15, 1953; children: Caroline Buck Rogers, James M. III. AB in Econs., Princeton U., 1946. Ops. mgr. Smith, Kline and French, Inc., Phila., 1948-56, v.p. ops., 1956-65; chmn., chief exec. officer The Drug House, Inc., Phila., 1965-77; chmn. Alco Health Services Group, Valley Forge, Pa., 1977-83; pres., CEO TDH Capital Ptnrs., Radnor, Pa., 1977—. Adv. bd. mem. Phila. Phillies, 1981—. Bd. dirs. The Bryn Mawr (Pa.) Hosp. Found., 1978—. With U.S. Army, 1943-45, ETO. Mem.: Merion Golf (Ardmore, Pa.); Merion Cricket (Haverford, Pa.). Republican. Presbyterian. Avocations: tennis, golf, music, spectator sports. Home: 121 Rose Ln Haverford PA 19041-1724 Office: TDH Capital Corp PO Box 8234/Radnor Ct 259 N Radnor Chester Rd Ste 210 Radnor PA 19087-5259 also: Phila Phillies PO Box 7575 Philadelphia PA 19101-7575

BUCK, JANE LOUISE, psychology educator; b. Reading, Pa., Mar. 10, 1933; d. C. Robert and Viola Louise (Berger) B.; m. Leo Laskaris, Oct. 7, 1954 (div. Aug. 1978); 1 child, Julie. BA, U. Del., 1953, MA, 1959, MEd, 1966, PhD, 1971. Instr. U. Del., Newark, 1964-66; rsch. assoc. Rsch. for Better Schs., Phila., 1967-68; asst. prof. Del. State U., Dover, 1969-73, assoc. prof., 1973-77, prof. psychology, 1977-98. Cons. in stats. E.I. duPont de Nemours, Wilmington, Del., 1983-93; vis. prof. Ctr. for Sci. and Culture, U. Del., 1986; bd. dirs. The Blvd. and Beyond, Wilmington. Author: Specifying the Risk, 1985; contbr. articles to profl. jours. Speaker, evaluator Del. Humanities Forum, 1980-88; pres. Del. Gerontol. Soc., Newark, 1987-88; mem. town coun. Chesapeake City, Md., 1998-2000; commr. parks and recreation, Chesapeake City, Md., 1998-99; bd. dirs. Friends of Cecil County Libr., 2000. Mem. AAAS (mem. sr. scientists and engrs.), AAUP (nat. coun. 1987-90, 93-99, pres. Del. State U. chpt. 1976-80, 95-98, chief negotiator 1982-98, mem. nat. com. on historically Black colls. and univs. and status of minorities in the profession 1988-91, 1998-2000, interim sec. Del. Conf 1991-92, pres. Del. conf. 1993-2000, mem. nat. com. govtl. rels. 1994-97, Sternberg award for collective bargaining 1994, nat. pres. 2000—), Am. Psychol. Soc., Coun. Tchrs. Undergrad. Psychology, Humanities and Tech. Assn., Am. Statis. Assn. (v.p. Del. chpt. 1999-2000), Danforth Assocs., Kappa Delta Pi, Psi Chi, Alpha Chi Omega. Avocations: classical music, reading, gardening, sewing, computer graphics. E-mail: buck@count.com.

BUCK, JOHN E. sculptor, print maker, educator; b. Ames, Iowa, Feb. 14, 1946; m. Deborah Butterfield; 2 children. BFA, Kans. City Art Inst., 1968; MFA, U. Calif., Davis, 1972. Instr. in sculpture Mont. State U., Bozeman, 1976-90. Sculptor and print maker: solo exhibitions include: Kans. City (Mo.) Art Inst., John Buck, 1988, Fine Arts Mus. San Francisco, John Buck: Woodblock Prints, 1993— (travels), Palm Springs Desert Mus., 1994, John Buck: Sculpture, 1994, The Contemporary Mus., Honolulu, John Buck: A Survey Exhibition, 1995; group exhibits Seattle Art Mus., Seattle, Calif. Permanent Collection, 1992, Newport Harbor Art Mus., Newport Beach, Calif., Beyond the Bay, 1993, Laguna Gloria Art Mus., Austin, Human Nature, Human Form, 1993, The Oakland (Calif.) Mus., Here and Now, 1994; commissions include: Ahmanson Commercial Devel., Chgo., 1991, Prin. Fin. Group, Des Moines, Iowa, 1989, Lewis and Clark Coll., Portland, Oreg., 1999, Swedish Hosp., Seattle, 1999, Meridian Plz., Sacramento, 2001; represented by Zolla/Lieberman Gallery, Chgo., Greg Kucera Gallery, Seattle, DC Moore Gallery, N.Y.C., Imago Galleries, Palm Desert, Calif. Recipient Individual Artist's award NEA, 1980, awards in the visual arts, Nat. Artists Award, 1984. Fax: (406) 585-9757.

BUCK, LAWRENCE PAUL, academic administrator, educator; b. Pittsburg, Kans., Oct. 6, 1944; m. Judy L.; children: David L., Laura T. BA, Wichita State U., 1966; MA, Ohio State U., 1967, PhD in History, 1971. Asst. prof. Widener U., Chester, Pa., 1971-77, assoc. prof. history, 1977-85, prof. history, 1985—, dean Coll. Arts and Scis., 1981-84, acad. v.p., provost, 1984—, acting pres., 1994, 2001—02. Author: Die Haltung der Nurnberger Bauernschaft im Bauernkrieg, 1970, Opposition to Tithes in the Peasants' Revolt, 1973, Civil Insurrection in a Reformation City, 1976, Demands for Reform by Urban Dissidents During the German Peasants' Revolt, 1977, The Reformation, Purgatory, and Perpetual Rents in the Revolt of 1525 at Frankfurt am Main, 1985; translator: Monemvasia: The Town and Its History, 1981; co-editor: The Social History of the Reformation; contbr. articles to profl. jours., book chpts. Rsch. grantee Am. Philos. Soc., 1973, NEH, 1974. Mem. Am. Soc. Reformation Rsch., 16th Century Study Conf. Office: Widener U Office of the Provost One University Pl Chester PA 19013 E-mail: lawrence.p.buck@widener.edu.

BUCK, LEE ALBERT, retired insurance company executive, evangelist; b. Jonesboro, Ark., July 28, 1923; s. Lee A. and Annie (Ballew) B.; m. Audrey Ruth McMurphy, Feb. 26, 1945; children— Melody Anne, Merrilee Ruth, Bonnie Sue, Lisa Carol. BA with honors, U. Mich., 1947, MA in Colonial Am. History, 1948; C.L.U., 1960. With N.Y. Life Ins. Co., 1949—, dir. agys., 1962-63, 2d v.p., 1963-64, v.p. agys., 1964-66, regional v.p. charge Southeastern U.S., 1964-67, v.p. mktg., 1967-74, sr. v.p. group mktg., 1974-78, sr. v.p. mktg., 1978-83; lay evangelist St. Paul's Episcopal Ch., Darien, Conn., 1983—; chmn. Com. for Freedom (polit. action com.), Washington. Bd. dirs. N.Y.C. Relief Inc., Singapore Cons. Inc.; internat. speaker and tchr. leadership principles speaker, tchr. bus. principles and practices to aid Ea. European nations. Author: Tapping Your Secret Source of Power. Past bd. dirs. Greater N.Y. councils Boy Scouts Am.; formerly bd. dirs. Ams. for Indian Opportunity; bd. dirs. Walter Hoving Home; former chmn. bd. Life Underwriter Tng. Council; trustee Regent U., Va. Beach, Va.; past trustee Barrington (R.I.) Coll.; bd. dirs. Faith Alive, Episcopal Renewal Ministries; lay evangelist Episcopal Ch. U.S.A.; nat. v.p., chmn. evangelism commn. Brotherhood of St. Andrew; bd. dirs. Washington for Jesus, Episc. Renewal Ministries; trustee Regent U.; active St. Judes Episc. Ch., Marietta, Ga. Served to lt. USNR, 1942-46, 50-52. Named Disting. Fellow Flint No. High School, 1993. Mem. Nat. Assn. Life Underwriters, Am. Soc. CLUs, Life Ins. Mktg. and Research Assn. (dir.), Agy. Mgmt. Tng. Council. Episcopalian. Home: 3416 PAces Ferry Cir SE Smyrna GA 30080

BUCK, LINDA DEE, executive recruiting company executive; b. San Francisco, Nov. 8, 1946; d. Sol and Shirley D. (Setterberg) Press. Student, Coll. of San Mateo, Calif., 1969-70. Head hearing and appeals br. Dept. Navy Employee Rels. Svc., The Philippines, 1974-75; dir. human resources Homestead Savs. & Loan Assn., Burlingame, Calif., 1976-77; mgr. VIP Agy., Inc., Palo Alto, Calif., 1977-78; exec. v.p., dir. Sequent Pers. Svcs., Inc., Mountain View, Calif., 1978-83; founder, pres. Buck & Co., San Mateo, 1983-91. Publicity mgr. for No. Calif., Osteogenesis Imperfecta Found. Inc., 1970-72; cons. Am. Brittle Bone Soc., 1979-88; mem. Florence (Oreg.) Area Humane Soc., 1994—, Friends of Libr., Florence, 1994—; bd. dirs. Florence Festival Arts, 1995; bd. dirs., dir. women Rhododendron Scholarship Program, Florence, 1995. Jewish.

BUCK, LOUISE ZIERDT, psychologist; b. Edgewood, Pa., Nov. 21, 1919; d. Conrad Henry and Nancy Leora (Harshberger) Zierdt; div. 1954; children: David Randall, Susan Buck Sutton. BS, Pa. State U., 1940; MEd, U. Pitts., 1954; EdD, Columbia U., 1978; advanced cert., Bklyn. Coll., 1984. Lic. sch. psychologist, clin. psychologist, N.Y. Tchr., dir. Chatham Village Nursery Sch., Pitts., 1953-55; tchr., dir. Yellow Springs (Ohio) Community Nursery Sch., 1955-58; tchr. Oak Lane Country Day Sch., Phila., 1958-59, Walden Sch., N.Y.C., 1959-60, Bank St. Sch. for Children, N.Y.C., 1960-61; early childhood tchr., coord. sch. psychology Bd. Edn., City of N.Y., 1961-87; asst. prof. Bklyn. Coll., 1978-80; rsch. fellow Albert Einstein Coll. Medicine, Bronx, N.Y., 1988-89; psychotherapist Fifth Ave Ctr. for Psychotherapy, N.Y.C., 1989, Met. Ctr. for Mental Health, N.Y.C., 1990—. Psychologist cons. Bd. Edn. City of N.Y., 1987-88; pvt. practice, N.Y.C. Contbr. articles to profl. jours. Mem. APA, N.Y. State Psychol. Assn., Soc. for Psychoanalytic Psychotherapy. Democrat. Avocations: traveling, swimming, the arts. Home: 444 E 86th St Apt 34C New York NY 10028-6459 Office: 27 W 96th St Ste 1A New York NY 10025-6515 E-mail: louisebuck@webtv.net.

BUCK, MATTHIAS, science educator; b. Hamburg, Germany, Nov. 30, 1967; arrived in U.S., 1995; s. Henneke and Christa Buck. BA, George Watsons Coll., 1987; MA, U. Cambridge, 1990; DPhil, U. Oxford, 1995. Rsch. assoc. Sloan Kettering Cancer Ctr., N.Y.C., 1999—2002; asst. prof. Case Western Res. U., Cleve., 2002—. Fellow, Harvard U., Cambridge, Mass., 1995—99, NIH, 2001—02; grantee, Am. Cancer Soc., 2003, Am. Heart Assn., 2003—. Mem.: Ireland Cancer Ctr., Cleve. Mus. Art, City Club Cleve. Avocations: dancing, poetry, photography, travel. Office: Case Western Res U Med Sch Dept Physiology & Biophysics 10900 Euclid Ave SOM E 646 Cleveland OH 44106 E-mail: mxb1500@po.cwru.edu.

BUCK, PITMAN AUGUST, JR., writer; b. Houston, Aug. 1, 1929; s. Pitman August, Sr. and Katherine W. Kaule B.; m. Nellwyn Angela Foster, Dec. 21, 1957; children: Kevin Dwayne, Phillip Warren, Eric David. Student, Stephen F. Austin State Coll., 1951-52, U. Houston, 1955-57. Chem. technician; ret., 1984. Author: American Freedom and Zionist Power, 1977, The Colossal Fraud of Involuntary Perjury, 1996; editor: Torah, Zionism and Palestine, 1983; contbr. numerous articles to publs. Del. Nat. Conf. Great Decisions in U.S. Fgn. Policy, 1975, testified before U.S. Senate Com. on Fgn. Affairs; pres. Ams. for Middle East Peace, Houston, 1982-83; v.p. Gulf Coast Coun. Fgn. Affairs, Texas City, Tex., 1976-77. Home and Office: 2525 Sunnycrest Dr Texas City TX 77590-5018

BUCK, ROBERT TREAT, JR., gallery director, former museum director, educator; b. Fall River, Mass., Feb. 16, 1939; s. Robert Treat and Hazel B.; m. Nicole Challamel, July 2, 1966; children: Thomas, Philip. BA, Williams Coll., 1961; student, Mus. Tng. Program Met. Mus. Art, 1963-64; MA, NYU, 1965. Lectr., researcher Toledo Mus. Art, 1964-65; asst. curator, instr. art and archaeology Washington U., St. Louis, 1965-67, dir. art gallery, 1968-70; asst. dir. Albright-Knox Art Gallery, Buffalo, 1970-73, dir., 1973-83, Bklyn. Mus., 1983-96, Marlborough Gallery, N.Y.C., 1997—2001; exec. dir. Exhbns. Internat., N.Y.C., 2002—. Adj. prof. dept. art SUNY, Buffalo, 1972-73; mem. N.Y. Coun. for Humanities, 1976-82; mem. art adv. panel IRS, 1978-82; bd. rep. Pratt Inst. Arts, 1984-96, Hirshhorn Mus., 1987-97, Am. Fedn. Arts, 1987-97, Internat. Coun. Mus. Modern Art, 1987-95. Author: Sam Francis: Paintings, 1947-1972, 1972, Diebenkorn: The Ocean Park Paintings, 1976, Sonia Delaunay: A Retrospective, 1980, Ferdinand Leger Retrospective, 1982, Leon Polk Smith: Selected Works, 1943-1992, Promised Gift to Brooklyn Museum, 1993, Reinhardt: Early Works, 1941-52, 1998, Keith Sonnier: Sculpture, 1966-98, 1998, Monte Carlo Internat. Sculpture Festival, Contemporary Am. Sculpture, 2000. Mem. Assn. Art Mus. Dirs. (trustee, sect., treas., v.p., pres. 1995-96).

BUCK, THOMAS RANDOLPH, retired lawyer, financial services executive; b. Washington, Feb. 5, 1930; s. James Charles Francis and Mary Elizabeth (Marshall) B.; m. Alice Armistead James, June 20, 1953; children: Kathryn James, Thomas Randolph, Douglas Marshall, David Andrew; m. Sunny Clark, Sept. 15, 1971; 1 child, Carey Virginia; m. Yvonne Brackett, Nov. 27, 1981. BA summa cum laude, Am. U., 1951; JD, U. Va., 1954. Bar: Va. 1954, Ky. 1964, Fla. 1974. Asst. gen. atty. Seaboard Air Line R.R. Co., 1958-63; sec., gen. counsel Am. Comml. Lines. Inc., Houston, 1963-68; asst. gen. counsel Tex. Gas Transmission Corp., 1968-72; sec., gen. counsel Leadership Housing Inc., 1972-77; pres. law firm Buck and Golden, P.A., 1975-92; exec. v.p., gen. counsel Buck Fin. Svcs., Inc., Ft. Lauderdale, Fla., 1992-99. Chmn. Hanover Bank Fla.; adj. prof. bus. law Broward C.C., Fla. Bd. dirs. Sheridan House for Youth; trustee Fla. Bapt. Found. Served to capt. USMCR, 1954-58. Mem. Assn. ICC Practitioners (nat. v.p., mem. exec. com.), Maritime Law Assn. U.S., Am. Judicature Soc., Omicron Delta Kappa, Alpha Sigma Phi, Delta Theta Phi. Clubs: Kiwanian, Propeller of U.S. Home: 2873 SW 13th Dr Deerfield Beach FL 33442

BUCK, TOM, journalist; b. Star City, Ind., Mar. 18, 1917; s. Grover Felix and Maud Kauffman B.; m. Ruth Moss, June 16, 1953; children: Mary Buck Young, Thomas Luscombe. BA, Ind. U., 1939. Reporter Chgo. City News Bur., 1939-40; reporter, writer Chgo. Tribune, 1940-73; pub. affairs mgr. Chgo. Transit Authority, 1973-80; press sec. Chgo. Mayor Jane Byrne, 1983; cons. editor Blue Cross/Blue Shield, Chgo., 1989—2002; publicity cons. Chgo., 1983—2002. Adj. prof. Loyola U., Chgo., 1981—93. Author: Buck, Buck, What's Up? Tales of 60 Years in Journalism, 2003. With Evanston (Ill.) Sch. Dist. 65 Bd., 1968—74. Capt. U.S. Army, 1941—46. Mem.: Chgo. Press Vets. Assn., The Cliff Dwellers, Saddle and Cycle Club. Home: 2655 Sheridan Rd Evanston IL 60201

BUCK, WILLIAM JOSEPH, theatrical designer, educator; b. Newark, Jan. 22, 1954; s. Paul and Amelia Buck; m. Susan Conaty. BA, Glassboro State Coll., 1975; MFA, Yale U., 1984. Dir. design dept. theatre U. S.C., Columbia, 1984-88; asst. prof. Mt. Holyoke Coll., South Hadley, Mass., 1988-92; artistic dir. Children's Playshop, Harrisonburg, Va., 1994—; prof., sch. dir. Sch. Theatre and Dance, James Madison U., Harrisonburg, 1992—. Cons. in theatre Chapin (S.C.) pub. schs., Harrison Found. for the Arts, Glassboro pub. schs. Pub.: stage adaptation Velveteen Rabbit for New Plays Inc.; designer : over 175 prodns. at univs., theater works, theatre-in-the-works, changing stages; pub. (plays) Jacky's Magical Bean Stalk for New Plays Inc. Carolina Venture Fund grantee. Mem.: Dramatists Guild, Puppeteers of Am., Southeastern Theatre Conf., United Scenic Artists (local 829), Union Internat. de La Marionnette. E mail: buckwj@jmu.edu.

BUCKALEW, MARTHA HARTER, music educator, musician; b. Raleigh, N.C., Oct. 14, 1941; d. William Bryan and Helen Wheat (Coffman) Nesbit; m. Edward Arthur Harter III, Feb. 24, 1966 (div. 1983); 1 child, Edward Arthur IV; m. Louis Clair Buckalew, Aug. 22, 1984. BA in Music and Piano cum laude, U. S.C., 1965. Pvt. tchr., Columbia, S.C., 1965-66, New Orleans, 1966-68, Columbus, Ohio, 1975-97; founder, dir., pianist Chamber Theatre Consort, Columbus, Ohio, 1983-97. Tchg. asst., libr. U. S.C., Columbia, 1965-66; dir. sr. citizens music program Jewish Ctr., New Orleans, 1966-68; catalogue audio visual dept. Grandview Pub. Libr., Columbus, 1972-73; publicity coord. Prestige Concerts, Columbus, 1974-75; founder, dir. Clavier Concerts, Columbus, 1976-77; lectr., recitalist Capital Conservatory Music, Columbus, 1981, 92. Author: Whatever Happened to Nannerl Mozart and Fanny Mendelesohn?, 1983, A Portrait of Clara Schumann, 1988, The Song of Alma Mahler, 1997; contbr. articles to profl. jours. Vol. Citizens Against Glen Echo Rezoning, Columbus, 1978; pianist Summit United Meth. Ch., Columbus, 1982-83; vol., fund raiser sch. bd., Columbus, 1995; rschr. Glen Echo Hist. Dist., 1995-97. Mem. Music Tchrs. Nat. Assn. (cert.), Nat. Guild Piano Tchrs., World Wildlife Fund, Ohio Music Tchrs. Assn. (dist. chmn. 1976-78), Ohio Hist. Soc., Delta Omicron, Phi Beta Kappa (Alumna of the Year 1996). Avocations: sewing, knitting, crocheting, gardening, cooking.

BUCKAWAY, WILLIAM ALLEN, JR., lawyer; b. Bowling Green, Ky., Dec. 3, 1934; s. William Allen and Kathryn Anne (Scoggin) B.; m. Bette Joan Cross, July 27, 1963; 1 child, William Allen III. AB, Centre Coll. of Ky., 1956; JD, U. Louisville, 1961. Bar: Ky. 1961, U.S. Dist Ct. (we. dist.) Ky. 1961, U.S. Dist. Ct. (ea. dist.) Ky. 1986, U.S. Supreme Ct. 1975. Assoc. Tilford, Dobbins, Caye & Alexander, Louisville, 1961-78; ptnr. Tilford, Dobbins, Alexander, Buckaway & Black, Louisville, 1978—; gen. counsel, corp. sec. Clean Coal Power Resources, 2003—. Atty. Masonic Homes of Ky., Louisville, 1985—; gen. counsel Kosair Charities. Elder 2d Presbyn. Ch., Louisville, 1975; emeritus mem. bd. govs. Lexington (Ky.) unit Shriners Hosp. for Crippled Children, 1986, sec., 1989-94; mem. children's oper. bd. Kosair Children's Hosp., 1986-99; mem. bd. govs. Norton Health Care, Louisville, 1999—. With USNR, 1956-58. Named Disting. Alumnus U. Louisville Sch. Law, 1986, Centre Coll., 1986. Mem. SAR (pres. Ky. soc. 1999-2000, pres. Louisville-Thrusion chpt. 2002-03), Nat. Eagle Scout Assn., Soc. of the Cin. in State of Va., Sons Confederate Vets. (adj. John Hunt Morgan Camp 1993-96), Masons (33 deg., past master Crescent Hill lodge 1967, chmn. jurisprudence and law com. imperial coun. Shrine of N.Am. 1989-91), Kosair Shrine Temple (potentate 1986), Rotary, Soc. Colonial Wars (Ky. coun.), Soc. War of 1812 (pres. Ky. soc.

1998-2000, judge advocate gen., gen. soc.2003—), Sigma Chi, Phi Alpha Delta. Home: 1761 Sulgrave Rd Louisville KY 40205-1643 Personal E-mail: bbuckaway@aol.com. E-mail: wbuckaway@tilfordlaw.com.

BUCKBERG, ALBERT, retired economist; b. Bklyn., Aug. 25, 1922; s. Isidor Paul and Anna (Litwack) Buckberg; m. Gloria Lois Bean, Feb. 26, 1967; 1 child, Elaine Karen. BA in Econs., George Washington U., 1947; MA, U. Mich., 1954, PhD, 1960. Instr. econs. U. Mich., 1955—57, Iowa State U., 1957—60, asst. prof., 1960—62; fiscal economist Bur. Budget, 1962—66; economist joint com. taxation US Congress, 1966—77, sr. economist, 1977—91; ret., 1991. With U.S. Army, 1943—46. Decorated Bronze Star. Mem.: Nat. Tax Assn., Am. Econ. Assn. Address: 4224 45th St NW Washington DC 20016-2468

BUCKELEW, ROBIN BROWNE, aerospace engineer; b. York, Pa., Mar. 14, 1947; d. Grant Hugh and Frances (Coleman) Browne; m. William Paul Buckelew, June 5, 1971; children: Leon, Christina. BS in Aerospace Engring., U. Ala., 1970; MS in Engring., U. Ala., Huntsville, 1977, PhD in Engring., 1994. Registered profl. engr., Ala. Aerospace engr. U.S. Army Missile Command, Redstone Arsenal, Ala., 1970-74; sys. engr. U.S. Army Missile Intelligence Agy., Huntsville, Ala., 1974-81; group leader air vehicle Sentry U.S. Army Ballistics Missile Def. Sys. Command, Huntsville, 1981-83; interceptor engr. High Endoatmospheric Def. Interceptor U.S. Army Ballistics Missile Def. System Command, Huntsville, 1983-85; chief air vehicle divsn. HEDI project U.S. Army Strategic Def. Command, Huntsville, 1985-88, chief Ground Based Interceptor Experiment Office, 1988-91, chief engr. HEDI project, 1991 92; dir. Sys. Directorate, U.S. Army Space and Strategic Def. Command, Huntsville, 1993 91, dir. Engring. and Sys. Directorate, 1994-95; dir. Missile Def. Battle Integration Ctr., 1995-97; dir. Ctr. for Land Warfare Office of the Chief of Staff of the Army, Washington, D.C., 1997-2000; spl. asst. for sys. Dep. Undersec. for Army Ops. Rsch., Washington, 2000-01; dir. for Applied Sensors Guidance and Electronics Directorate, Rsch., Devel. & Engring. Ctr. U.S. Army Aviation and Missile Command, Redstone Arsenal, 2001—. Contbr. articles to AIAA conf. proceedings. Bd. dirs. Trinity Personal Growth Ctr., Huntsville, 1990-92. Named Strategic Def. Engr. of Yr., NSPE, 1990, Disting. Engring. fellow, U. Ala., 1993, Alumni of Achievement, U. Ala., Huntsville, 2002; named to, State of Ala. Engring. Hall of Fame, 1995; recipient Superior Civilian Svc. award, U.S. Army, 1991, Outstanding Alumna award, U. Ala., Huntsville, 1996, Meritorious Civil Svc. award, U.S. Army, 1997, Presdl. Rank award, U.S. Govt., 1998, Disting. Engring. Alumni Acad. award, U. Ala., 2003. Fellow AIAA (assoc.); mem. Capstone Engring. Soc. (bd. dirs. 1990-98), Ancient Order St. Barbara, Sigma Xi. Methodist. Home: 117 Bel Air Rd SE Huntsville AL 35802-3107 E-mail: robin.buckelew@rdec.redstone.army.mil.

BUCKELS, MARVIN WAYNE, savings and loan executive; b. Sterling, Colo., Feb. 11, 1929; s. Harvey and Myrl (Tarr) B.; m. Doris Torrance, Aug. 1, 1959; children: Lisa K., Devon Carol. BA, U. Denver, 1951; MS, U. Wis., 1952. With Beatrice Foods, Denver, 1952-55; loan counselor Midland Fed. Savs. and Loan Assn., Denver, 1955-56, treas., 1956-62, exec. v.p., 1962-85, Western Capital Investment Corp., Denver, 1985-91. Vice-chmn. Colo. Bd. Vocat. Edn., 1967; pres. Adult Edn. Coun. Met. Denver, 1970; bd. dirs. Auraria Higher Edn. Ctr., 1975-79, vice chmn. bd., 1977-78; bd. dirs. Auraria Found., 1992—, treas., 1997—; bd. dirs. Rocky Mountain Hosp., 1979, pres., 1980; chmn. Colo. Postsecondary Edn. Facilities Authority, 1981—; bd. dirs. Denver Civic Ventures, Inc., 1986, chmn., 1987-90; legis. policy com. Colo. Assn. Commerce and Industry, 1986-89; treas. Colo. Pub. Affairs Coun., 1987-89; bd. dirs. Colo. Symphony Orch., 1990-2000, treas., 1990-96; chmn. The Downtown Denver Partnership, 1991-92. With U.S. Army, 1946-48. Mem. U.S. Savs. and Loan League, Colo. Savs. and Loan League (legis com.), Am. Savs. and Loan Inst. (past pres. Denver chpt.), Contrs. Soc. (past pres. Denver chpt., nat. bd. govs.), Sys. and Procedures Assn. (past pres. Denver chpt.), Adminstrv. Mgmt. Soc. (past pres. Denver chpt.), Denver Metro C. of C. (past chmn. spl. task force studying sch. bond issue, mem. pub. affairs coun. 1991-93, loaned exec. Nat. Alliance Businessmen's program), Phi Beta Kappa. Democrat.

BUCKHOLTZ, THOMAS JOEL, computer and telecommunications executive; b. L.A., Sept. 19, 1945; s. Joel and Sylvia Lee (Joseph) B.; m. Helen Chu, Nov. 22, 1973; 1 child, Catheryne M. BS in Math., Calif. Inst. Technology, 1967; PhD in Physics, U. Calif., Berkeley, 1971. Scientist, engr. aerospace, def. and rsch. orgns., 1963-72; physicist Lawrence Livermore (Calif.) Nat. Lab., 1972-77; v.p. Ins. Tech. Co., 1976-78, Berkeley (Calif.) Tech. Assocs., 1978-81; software mgr. Friends Amis, 1981-82; sr. analyst Pacific Gas & Electric Co., San Francisco, 1982-89; commr. GSA, Washington, 1989-93; lectr. George Washington U., Washington, 1993; sr. prin. cons. Oracle Corp., 1997-98; exec. v.p. Beyond Insight Corp., 1998—2002; founder, prin., owner T.J. Buckholtz & Assoc., Calif., 1974—. Mem. working group Pres.'s Coun. on Competitiveness, 1990-91; mem. Mil. Comm. Electronics Bd., 1991-93, Interagency Com. for Fed. Lab. Tech. Transfer, 1991-93, Computer Sys. Tech. Adv. Bd., U.S. Dept. Commerce, Washington, 1989; mem. Calif. Info. Tech. Commn., 1996-99; mem. telecom. program adv. bd. U. San Francisco, 1994—; mem. adv. bd. Goldman Sch. Pub. Policy, U. Calif., Berkeley, 1999—; mem. corp. rels. com. World Affairs Coun. No. Calif., 1999-2000; chmn. web tech. adv. bd. Rep. Nat. Com., 2000; mem adv. bd. Sch. Bus. and Mgmt., Notre Dame de Namur U., 2001—. Author: Information Proficiency: Your Key to the Information Age, 1995; contbr. various articles on computer sci., physics and math. to profl. jours.; co-host TV program Issues Today, 2001—. Bd. dirs. Tech. Network, 2000-01; life mem. The Assocs. of the Calif. Inst. Technology, Pasadena, 1979—; regional chmn. Caltech Alumni Fund, 1988-89, class chair, 1999; county co-chmn. Bush-Quayle '88, Piedmont, Calif., 1988; mem. Wilson coun. Woodrow Wilson Internat. Ctr. for Scholars, Smithsonian Instn., 2000-02; trustee Com. Econ. Devel., 2000—; mem. info. tech. nat. steering com. George W. Bush for Pres., 2000. Recipient Grad. fellowship NSF, 1967-71, Senate Cert. of Recognition, State of Calif., 2002. Mem. Am. Phys. Soc. Republican. E-mail: tjb@alumni.caltech.edu.

BUCKI, CARL LEO, judge; b. Buffalo, July 11, 1953; s. John Ferdinand and Adeline (Graczyk) B.; m. Deborah Colleen Bruch, July 22, 1978; 1 child, Craig R. BA magna cum laude, Cornell U., 1974, JD cum laude, 1976. Bar: N.Y. 1977, U.S. Dist. Ct. (we. dist.) N.Y. 1978. Confidential clk. N.Y. Ct. Appeals, Buffalo, 1976-77; assoc. Moot & Sprague, Buffalo, 1977-83, ptnr., 1983-90, Cohen, Swados, Wright, Hanifin, Bradford & Brett, 1990-93; judge U.S. Bankruptcy Ct. we. dist. N.Y., 1993—. Editor: The American Constitution From a Polish Ethnic Perspective, 1990; contbr. articles to profl. jours. Pres. Polish Cmty. Ctr., Buffalo, 1978—80, St. Gregory the Great Sch. Bd., Amherst, NY, 1991—96, chair, 1992—95; v.p. Parents Anonymous of Buffalo, 1981; bd. mgrs. Buffalo and Erie Hist. Soc., 1993—, vice-chair, 1995—96, chair, 1996—2001; nat. bd. dirs. Polish Union Am., Buffalo, 1982—86, nat. atty., 1986—93; bd. dirs. Polish Arts Club, 1997—99. Named citizen of yr. Ampol Eagle Newspaper, Buffalo, 1977, 98. Mem. ABA (exec. com. young lawyers divsn. 1987-89), N.Y. State Bar Assn. (mem. exec. com. young lawyers sect. 1984-91, chmn. 1988-89, mem. Ho. of Dels. 1989-91, nominations com. 1990-94), Erie County Bar Assn. (chmn. comml. and bankruptcy law com. 1987-90), Nat. Conf. Bankruptcy Judges (cir. rep. to bd. govs. 2001—), Profl. and Businessmen's Assn. (pres. 1981), Chopin Singing Soc. Home: 225 Halston Pky East Amherst NY 14051-1856 Office: U S Bankruptcy Ct 300 Pearl St Buffalo NY 14202-2510 Business E-Mail: clb@nywb.uscourts.gov.

BUCKINGHAM, AMYAND DAVID, chemistry educator; b. Sydney, NSW, Australia, Jan. 28, 1930; s. Reginald Joslin and Florence Grace (Elliot) B.; m. Jillian Bowles, July 24, 1965; children: Lucy Elliot, Mark Vincent, Alice Susan. BSc with honors, Sydney U., 1951, MSc, 1953; PhD, Cambridge U., Eng., 1956, ScD, 1985. Cert. chemist; cert. physicist. Lectr., tutor Christ Ch., Oxford, Eng., 1955-65; lectr. Oxford U., 1958-65; prof. theoretical chemistry Bristol (Eng.) U., 1965-69; prof. chemistry Cambridge (Eng.) U., 1969-97, prof. emeritus, 1997—; fellow Pembroke Coll., Cambridge, 1970-97, emeritus fellow, 1997—. Author: Laws and Applications of Thermodynamics, 1964; editor: Organic Liquids, 1978, Principles of Molecular Recognition, 1993; editor Molecular Physics, 1968-72, Internat. Revs. in Phys. Chemistry, 1981-89, Chem. Physics Letters, 1978-99. Trustee Henry Fund, 1976—. Decorated comdr. Brit. Empire. Fellow Royal Soc. (coun. 2000-01, Hughes medal 1996), Royal Soc. Chemistry (Faraday medal, 1998), Inst. of Physics (Harrie Massey medal, 1995), Optical Soc. Am. (Townes Award 2001), Am. Phys. Soc., Royal Australian Chem. Inst.; mem. AAAS (hon.), NAS (fgn. assoc.), Am. Chem. Soc., Internat. Acad. Quantum Molecular Sci., Internat. Union Pure and Applied Chemistry (com. phys. chemistry and biophys. chemistry divsn., v.p. 2001-03), Royal Swedish Acad. Scis. (fgn.). Avocations: cricket, tennis, travel. Office: Univ Chem Lab Lensfield Rd Cambridge CB2 1EW England E-mail: adb1000@cam.ac.uk.

BUCKINGHAM, BARBARA RAE, educator; b. Union City, Ind., Jan. 27, 1932; d. Ray E. and Edith A. (Wagner) B. BA cum laude, Hanover Coll., 1954; MA, Ind. Univ., 1956. Tchr. City Sch. Dist., Marion, Ohio, 1956-64, social studies educator Rochester, NY, 1966—. Editor: Revonah, 1954; art work Aldelphean, 1959. Vol. Peace Corps, Ethiopia, 1964-66, Mary Cariola Children's Ctr., Christian Heritage Homes, Hope Hall, Congresswomen Louise Slaughter Campaign, 1996-97, 96-98; gov. bd. Rochester Returned Peace Corps Vols., 1968-76; election com. mem. Councilwoman Letvin, Gates, N.Y., 1980; steering com. Pub. Affairs Forum, Hanover, 1952, DAR. Mem. AAUW (pres. 1958-59), DAR, Nat. Peace Corps Assn., Friends of Ethiopia, Rochester Tchr. Assn., Pi Gamma Mu (Outstanding Grad. award 1954), Gamma Sigma Pi, Alpha Phi Gamma. Democrat. Presbyterian. Avocations: travel, art work. Home: 64 Lyellwood Pkwy Rochester NY 14606-4532

BUCKINGHAM, BETTY JO, library media consultant; b. Aug. 6, 1927; d. Irvin Amos and E(lsie) Dean (Webb) B. BA, Iowa State Tchrs. Coll., 1948; MS in Libr. Sci., U. Ill., Urbana, 1953; PhD, U. Minn., 1978. Tchr. English Earlham (Iowa) Cmty. Sch., 1948-50; tchr., libr. Harlan (Iowa) Cmty. Sch., 1950-54; libr. Ft. Madison (Iowa) Cmty. H.S., 1954-60, Kurtz Jr. H.S., Des Moines, 1960-64; cons. Iowa Dept. Edn., Des Moines, 1964—94. Lectr. U. Minn.-Mpls., 1970. Author, editor: Growth Notes for School Media Specialists, New Iowa Standards for Library Media Programs, 1989, Selection of Instructional Materials, A Model Policy and Rules, 1980, 1994; author: Weeding the Library Media Center Collections, 1984, Weeding the Library Media Center Collections, 1994, Planning the School Library Media Center Budget, 1984, Planning the School Library Media Center Budget, 1994; editor: Iowa and some Iowans, 1995, Women at the Well, 1987, Plan for Progress in the Library Media Center, P-K12, 1991; joint compiler in field: ; contbr. ; author: History of Local Church, 1994, Church District, 2002, Lenten and Advent Dramas, 1996. Mem. steering com. women's caucus Ch. of the Brethren, 1977-80, editor Cistern periodical, 1980-87, Femailings periodical, 1994-97, bd. dirs. No. Plains dist., 1984, pres., 1985-89, conf. moderator, 1990-91, 2002—. Mem. ALA, NEA, Am. Assn. Sch. Librs. (past sec., pres., councillor 1984-85), Iowa Ednl. Media Assn. (cons. 1973-83), Iowa Libr. Assn., Intellectual Freedom Found., Women's Fellowship Prairie City (past pres.), Beta Phi Mu, Kappa Delta Pi. Democrat. Avocations: reading, classical music, writing. Home: 10048 Highway F70 W Prairie City IA 50228-8471

BUCKINGHAM, DAVID COWAN, judge; b. Murray, Ky., Oct. 29, 1951; s. Robert Ray and Betty Sue (Hutson) B.; m. Dianne Lee Armstrong, July 10, 1982; 1 child, Tyler Daniel. BA, Murray State U., 1974; JD, U. Louisville, 1977. Bar: Ky. 1977. Asst. county atty. Calloway County, Murray, 1978-81; sole practice Murray, 1978-81; dist. judge 42nd Judicial Dist., Murray, 1982-86; circuit judge 42nd Judicial Cir., Murray, 1987-96; judge Ct. of Appeals, 1997—. Mem. Ky. Bar Assn., Calloway County Bar Assn. Democrat. Mem. Ch. of Christ. Avocations: golf, baseball card collecting. Office: 312 S 8th St Murray KY 42071-2428

BUCKINGHAM, EDWIN JOHN, III, lawyer; b. Grand Forks, N.D., Sept. 15, 1947; s. Edwin John Jr. and Kathryn Ruth (Aird) B.; m. Cheryl Ann Pantalone, 1971; 1 child, Emma Nicole. AB, Yale U., 1969, JD, 1972. Bar: N.Y. 1973, Tex. 1978. Assoc. Shea Gould Climenko & Kramer, N.Y.C., 1972-74; assoc. gen. counsel Celanese Corp., N.Y.C., 1974-77; mgr. legal affairs Solvay Polymers, Inc., Houston, 1977-79, dir. legal affairs, 1979-81, gen. counsel, v.p., 1981—, Solvay Am., Inc., Houston, 1984—. Sec. Wessex Civic Assn., Houston, 1986-88. Named Chevalier de l'Ordre de Leopold, Belgium. Mem. ABA, Am. Corp. Counsel Assn., Tex. Bar Assn., Tex.-Mex. Bar Assn. Avocations: fencing, birding. Office: Solvay Am 3333 Richmond Ave Houston TX 77098-3007

BUCKINGHAM, MICHAEL JOHN, oceanography educator; b. Oxford, Eng., Oct. 9, 1943; s. Sidney George and Mary Agnes (Walsh) B.; m. Margaret Penelope Rose Barrowcliff, July 15, 1967. BSc with hons., U. Reading (Eng.), 1967, PhD, 1971. Postdoctoral rsch. fellow U. Reading, 1971-74; sr. sci. officer Royal Aircraft Establishment, Farnborough, Eng., 1974-76, prin. sci. officer, 1976-82; exchange scientist Naval Rsch. Lab., Washington, 1982-84; vis. prof. MIT, Cambridge, 1986-87; sr. prin. sci. officer Royal Aircraft Establishment, 1983-86, 1987-90; prof. oceanography Scripps Instn. of Oceanography, La Jolla, Calif., 1990—. Vis. prof. Inst. Sound and Vibration rsch., Southampton, Eng., 1990—; UK nat. rep. Commn. of European Communities, Brussels, Belgium, 1989-92; dir. Arctic rsch. Royal Aerospace Establishment, Farnborough, 1990-94; Lansdowne visitor U. Victoria, B.C., Can., 2000; chair Scripps Faculty, 2000-01. Author: Noise in Electronic Devices and Systems, 1983; editor: Sea Surface Sound '94, Proceedings of the III Internat. Mtg. on Natural Phys. Processes Related to Sea Surface Sound; editor-in-chief Jour. Computational Acoustics; editor Phys. Acoustics; contbr. articles to profl. jours.; patentee in field. Recipient Clerk Maxwell Premium, Inst. Electronic and Radio Engrs. London, 1972, A.B. Wood Medal, Inst. Acoustics, Bath, Eng., 1982, Alan Burman Pub. award, Naval Rsch. Lab., 1988, Commendation for Disting. Contbns. to ocean acoustics Naval Rsch. Lab., 1986. Fellow Inst. Acoustics (U.K.), Inst. Elec. Engrs. (U.K.), Acoustical Soc. Am. (chmn. acoustical oceanography tech. com. 1991-95, Sci. Writing award for profls. in acoustics 1997), Explorers Club; mem. Am. Geophys. Union, N.Y. Acad. Scis., Sigma Xi. Avocations: photography, squash, private pilot. Home: 7956 Caminito Del Cid La Jolla CA 92037-3404 Office: Scripps Inst Oceanography Marine Phys Lab La Jolla CA 92093-0238 E-mail: mjb@mpl.ucsd.edu.

BUCKINGHAM, VIRGINIA, editor; m. David Lowy; 1 child, Jack. B in Comms., Boston Coll., 1987. Dep. press sec., asst. press sec. to Gov. Weld and Lt. Gov.; press. sec. to Gov. Weld and Lt. Gov. Cellucci, 1994-95; campaign mgr. Gov. Weld's bid for U.S. Senate; chief of staff to Gov. Cellucci and Lt. Gov. Swift, 1997-2000; exec. dir., CEO Mass. Port Authority (Massport), East Boston, 2000—01; dep. editl. page editor Boston (Mass.) Herald, 2003—. Office: Boston Herald One Herald Square PO Box 2096 Boston MA 02106*

BUCKLAND, BARRY CHRISTOPHER, chemical engineer; b. London, Jan. 6, 1948; BSc, Manchester (Eng.) U., 1970; MSc, U. Coll. London, 1971, PhD in Biochem. Engring., 1974. Biochem. engr. Abbott Lab., Chgo., 1974-77; sr. engr. Lederle Lab., Pearl River, N.Y., 1977-80; dir. Fermentation Pilot Plant, Merck & Co. Inc., Rahway, N.J., 1980-86, biochem. process R&D, 1986-90, sr. dir., 1990-93, exec. dir., 1993-96; v.p. Bio Process R&D, Merck & Co. Inc., 1996—. Vis. prof. Univ. Coll., London, 1989—, Rutgers U., 1990—. Fellow Am. Inst. Med. & Biol. Engring., Internat. Inst. Biotechnology (lectr. 1995); mem. AICE (dir. Food, Pharm. & Bioentring. Divsn. 1993-95), Am. Chem. Soc. (lectr. 1994), Nat. Acad. Engring. Office: PO Box 4 West Point PA 19486-0900 E-mail: barry_buckland@merck.com.

BUCKLAND, MICHAEL KEEBLE, librarian, educator; b. Wantage, Eng., Nov. 23, 1941; came to U.S., 1972; s. Walter Basil and Norah Elaine (Rudd) B.; m. Waltraud Leeb, July 11, 1964; children: Anne Margaret, Anthony Francis. BA, Oxford U., 1963; postgrad. diploma in librarianship, Sheffield U., 1965, PhD, 1972. Grad. trainee Bodleian Library, Oxford, Eng., 1963-64; asst. librarian U. Lancaster (Eng.) Library, 1965-72; asst. dir. for tech. svcs. Purdue U. Libraries, West Lafayette, Ind., 1972-75; assoc. prof. Sch. of Info. Mgmt. and Sys. U. Calif., Berkeley, 1976-79, dean, 1976-84, prof., 1979—, assoc. v.p. library plans and policies, 1983-87; v.p. Ind. Coop. Library Svcs. Auth., 1974-75. Co-dir. Electronic Cultural Atlas Initiative, 2000—; vis. scholar Western Mich. U., 1979; vis. prof. U. Klagenfurt, Austria, 1980, U. New South Wales, Australia, 1988. Author: Book Availability and the Library User, 1975, (with others) The Use of Gaming in Education for Library Management, 1976, Reader in Operations Research for Libraries, 1976, Library Services in Theory and Context, 1983, 2d edit., 1988, Information and Information Systems, 1991, Redesigning Library Services, 1992; editor: Historical Studies in Information Science, 1998, Robert Gitler and the Japan Library School, 1999. Fulbright Rsch. scholar U. Tech., Graz, Austria, 1989. Mem. ALA, Am. Soc. Info. Sci. (pres. 1998), Assn. Libr. and Info. Sci. Edn., Calif. Libr. Assn. Office: U Calif Sch Info Mgmt And Sys Berkeley CA 94720-0001

BUCKLER, MARILYN LEBOW, school psychologist, educational consultant; b. N.Y.C., Mar. 18, 1933; d. Herman and Gertrude (Abolitz) Lebow; m. Sheldon A. Buckler, June 1, 1952 (div. 1978); children: Julie, Eve, Sarah Buckler Welcome. BS cum laude, NYU, 1954; MEd in Counseling, Northeastern U., 1970. Cert. ednl. psychologist, Mass.; sch. guidance counselor, Mass., sch. psychologist, Mass. Kindergarten tchr. Washington Pub. Schs., 1955-56, Stamford (Conn.) Pub. Schs., 1956-58; guidance counselor Framingham (Mass.) Pub. Schs., 1969-70; sch. psychologist, guidance counselor Carlisle (Mass.) Pub. Schs., 1970-95; parent program cons. Reach out to Schs. program Wellesley Coll.-Stone Ctr., 1993—. Tchr. parenting course Middlesex C.C., Bedford, Mass., 1990—, cons. LEAP program, 1992-93; workshop leader, creator parenting courses, various pvt. schs. and orgns., Mass., 1990—; spl. project cons., workshop specialist "Families First" Wheelock Coll., 1995—. Mem. ACA, Mass. Sch. Counselor Assn., Mass. Sch. Psychologists Assn., Pi Lambda Theta. Avocations: films, cooking, traveling, reading.

BUCKLER, SHELDON A. technology company executive; b. N.Y.C., May 18, 1931; s. Morris H. and Mollie M. (Smith) B.; m. Dorothea J. Chandler, June 30, 1978; children: Julie, Eve, Sarah. BA, NYU, 1951; PhD, Columbia U., 1954. Rsch. assoc. U. Md., 1954-56; rsch. group leader Am. Cyanamid Co., Stamford, Conn., 1956-62; mgr. organic unit AMF, Springdale, Conn., 1962-64; with Polaroid Corp., Cambridge, Mass., 1964-94, vice-chmn. bd., 1990-94; chmn. bd. Commonwealth Energy Sys., Cambridge, 1995-99. Chmn. bd. Lord Corp., 2000—; bd. dirs. Parlex Corp., MCT Corp. Contbr. articles to profl. jours.; patentee in field. Trustee Va. Union U., 1973-75; chmn. bd. Mass. Eye and Ear Infirmary, 1996-2002. With U.S. Army, 1954-56. Recipient Maurice Holland award Indsl. Rsch. Inst., 1998. Mem. Am. Chem. Soc., Phi Beta Kappa. Office: Lord Corp 111 Lord Dr Cary NC 27511-7923 E-mail: sheldonbuckler@comcast.net.

BUCKLES, JUDITH ANN, dental educator, program administrator; b. Franscisville, Ind., Feb. 15, 1940; d. Lawrence Melvin and Mary Rosella Johnston; m. Edward Donald Buckles, Jan. 27, 1962; children: Dawn Marie, Erica Danielle, Erin Nichole. Cert. dental nurse, Elkhart (Ind.) U. Medicine and Dentistry, 1959; AAS, Purdue U., 1986, BS with honors, 1991. Cert. dental asst. Dental asst. Francis A Jones, DDS, Lafayette, Ind., 1959-69, Raymond Price, DDS, Lafayette, 1969-73; program supr., sr. instr. Ivy Tech. State Coll., Lafayette, 1973—. Religious instr. St. Ann Ch. and Shrine, Lafayette, 1980-95; asst. with fund raising St. Ann Rosary Soc., Lafayette, 1979—, St. Ann Social Club, Lafayette, 1994—, St. Ann Parish Coun., 2000-. Fellow Am. Dental Assts. Assn., Nat. Assn. Dental Assts., Ind. Dental Assocs. Assn., Lafayette Dental Assts. Assn., German-Am. Club, Phi Kappa Phi. Avocations: collecting antique depression glass ware, collecting cookbooks, collecting boyd bears and angels, collecting porcelain dolls, collecting german dishes. Office: Ivy Tech State Coll 3101 S Cressy Ln Lafayette IN 47905-6299

BUCKLES, ROBERT HOWARD, retired investment company executive; b. Champaign, Ill., June 30, 1932; s. Renick Hull and Ethel Maxine Buckles; m. Linda Carol Porter, Dec. 27, 1958; children: Meredith Ann, Christopher John. BA, Stanford U., 1953; MBA, Harvard U., 1957. Security analyst Lehman Corp., N.Y.C., 1957-65, v.p., 1965-69, exec. v.p., 1969-73, pres., 1973-84, also bd. dirs.; pres. Gas Properties, Inc., 1973-84; exec. v.p., dir. Lehman Mgmt. Co., 1973-84; pres., chief investment officer Rothschild Asset Mgmt. Inc., 1984-87; mng. dir. Rothschild, Inc., 1984-87; chief investment officer, sr. mng. dir. Furman Selz Capital Mgmt., 1987-97. Dir. One William St. Fund.; bd. dirs. Assn. Publicly Traded Investment Funds. Contbr. articles to profl. publs. With security agy. AUS, 1954-56. Mem. N.Y. Soc. Securities Analysts. Home: 425 E 58th St Apt 35C New York NY 10022-2300

BUCKLES, STEPHEN GARY, economist, educator; b. Kansas City, Mo., June 11, 1943; s. Orland and Leighfern (Emry) B.; m. Mary Parker Harmon, Nov. 28, 1970. AB, Grinnell Coll., 1965; PhD, Vanderbilt U., 1976. Economist Joint Coun. Econ. Edn., N.Y.C., 1970-74; prof. U. Mo., Columbia, 1976-88; pres. Nat Coun. Econ. Edn., N.Y.C., 1989-94; prof. econs., sr. lectr. Vanderbilt U., Nashville, 1994—. Vis. prof. Vanderbilt U., 1983; tchr. NYU, 1972-74; past chair individual investors adv. com. N.Y. Stock Exch.; mem. mgmt. team, standing com. 2006 Econs. Nat. Assessment. Recipient tchg. awards U. Mo., 1986-87, John Scotram Leadership award Nat. Assn. Econ. Educators, 1989, Student's Choice award Vanderbilt, 1996, William Forbes award for Pub. Awareness, 1998, Marvin Bower award in econ. edn., 2002. Mem. Nat. Coun. Econ. Edn. Home: 24 Great Is Darien CT 06820-5932 Office: Vanderbilt U Dept Econs Nashville TN 37235 E-mail: stephen.buckles@vanderbilt.edu.

BUCKLEW, NEIL S. educator, past university president; b. Morgantown, W.Va., Oct. 23, 1940; s. Douglas Earl and Lanah L. (Martin) B.; children—Elizabeth, Jennifer, Jeffrey. AB, U. Mo.; MS, U. N.C.; PhD (grad. fellow), U. Wis. Dir. personnel Duke U., 1964-66; dir. employee relations U. Wis., 1966-70; prof., v.p. Central Mich. U., Mt. Pleasant, 1970-76; prof., provost Ohio U., Athens, 1976-80; pres. U. Mont., Missoula, 1981-86, W.Va. U., 1986-95, prof., 1995—. Vis. rsch. fellow Pa. State U.; arbitrator in field. Author: Public Sector Collective Bargaining, Planning in Higher Education. Mem. Nat. Assn. State Univs. and Land Grant Colls. Office: West Va U PO Box 6025 Morgantown WV 26506-6025 E-mail: nbucklew@wvu.edu.

BUCKLEY, CHARLES ROBINSON, III, lawyer; b. Richmond, Va., Oct. 9, 1942; s. Charles Robinson and Eleanor (Small) B.; m. Virginia Lee, Apr. 17, 1971; children: Richard, Rebecca. BS, U. N.C., 1965, JD, 1969. Bar: N.C. 1969, U.S. Supreme Ct. 1979. Asst. city atty. City of Charlotte, N.C., 1969-78; ptnr. Constagny, Goines, Buckley & Boyd, 1978-81, Taylor & Buckley, Charlotte, 1981-85, Buckley McMullen & Buie, P.A., Charlotte, 1994—. Town atty. Town of Matthew (N.C.), 1978—; faculty Ctrl. Piedmont C.C., 1970. Bd. dirs. Charlotte City Employees Credit Union, 1974-78; pre. PTA, 1980-82; bd. visitors Luth. Theol. So. Sem., 1989-93. Recipient Cert. of Merit, City of charlotte, 1982. Mem.: N.C. Assn. Mcpl. Lawyers (bd. dirs. 1979—81, v.p. 1995—96, 1st v.p. 1996—97, pres. 1997—98), N.C. Bar Assn., Optimist Club (pres. 1982—83), Rotary Club (pres. Charlotte South Rotary Found. 2003—), Phi Alpha Delta. Democrat. Lutheran. Home: 6813 Linda Lake Dr Charlotte NC 28215-4019 E-mail: CRB3@bellsouth.net.

BUCKLEY, CLAUDE LANGFORD, artist; b. Madrid, May 15, 1959; came to U.S., 1972; s. Fergus Reid and Elizabeth Hanna (Howell) B.; divorced; children: Ian Howell, Aidan Michael. BFA, U. of the South, 1980. Aartist, 1980—. Works include portrait of H.R.M. Juan Carlos de Borbon, King of Spain. Mem Springdale Hall. Roman Catholic. Avocations: photography, outdoor activities. Home: PO Box 1421 Camden SC 29020-1421

BUCKLEY, CORNELIUS MICHAEL, priest, educator, chaplain; b. L.A., Nov. 2, 1925; s. Cornelius Buckley and Mary Ellen Breen. BA, Santa Clara U., 1950; MA in Philosophy, Gonzaga U., 1956, MA in History, 1958; Doctorate, Sorbonne U., Paris, 1967. Entered Soc. Jesus, ordained Jesuit priest Saint-Leu-d'Essarant, France, 1962. Asst. prof. Santa Clara (Calif.) U., 1967—69; pres. St. Ignatius Coll. Preparatory, San Francisco, 1970—73; dean Arts and Scis. U. San Francisco, 1972—73, 1972—73, prof. history, 1976—2000, prof. emeritus, 2000—; hosp. chaplain Santa Teresita Hosp., Duarte, Calif., 2000—. Trustee U. Santa Clara, 1975—80, U. San Francisco, 1970—76; pres. senate of priests Archdiocese San Francisco, 1972—75. Author: A Frenchman, A Chaplain, A Rebel..Hyppolite Gache, 1980, Nicolas Point, His Life Northwest Chronicles, 1988, When Jesuits Were Giants, 1998; transl.: works from French and Spanish into English. Chaplain San Francisco City and County Jail, 1994—99. With USN, 1944—46, PTO. Named Disting. Citizen, Mayor San Francisco, 1971, a day in honor, Bd. Suprs. San Francisco, 1998. Mem.: Fellowship Cath. Scholars (trustee 1989—99). Avocations: translating, history, writing. Home and Office: Santa Teresita Hosp 819 Buena Vista St Duarte CA 91010-1703 Fax: 626-357-7166. E-mail: cmbsj62@hotmail.com.

BUCKLEY, EDWARD JOSEPH, retired academic dean; b. Belleville, Ont., Can., Aug. 28, 1920; s. William John and Mary Jane (Conlin) B. BA, U. Ottawa, Ont., 1952, MA, 1958. Tchg. master Ont. Coll. Edn., Toronto; treas. Famous Players Can. Corp., Belleville, 1940-60; dir. Fed. Govt. Adult Tng. Program, Belleville, 1960-70; dir. tech. divsn. Loyalist Coll. Applied Arts and Scis., Belleville, 1970-75, dean continuing edn., 1976-85. Author: History of St. Michael's Paris: 1829-1979, 1983. Mem., chmn. Belleville Separate Sch. Bd.,

1943-60; bd. dirs. Belleville Dept. Health, 1949-56; mem. Belleville Retarded Children's Authority, 1952-59. Decorated Knight Equestrian Order Holy Sepulchre, Knight Sovereign, M.I. Order Malta. Mem. K.C. (state dept. Ont. 1978-80, dir. New Haven 1983-90). Liberal. Roman Catholic. Home: 153 Dundas St W Belleville ON Canada K8P 1A7

BUCKLEY, EDWARD T., JR., career officer; b. Chippewa Falls, Wis., Aug. 16, 1945; Commd. U.S. Army, advanced through grades to brig. gen., 1997, dep. chief staff doctrine tng. and doctrine command, 1997-99, asst. divsn. comdr. 7th infantry divsn. Ft. Carson, Colo., 1999—.

BUCKLEY, EUGENE KENYON, lawyer; b. St. Louis, Dec. 30, 1928; s. Eugene Patrick and Berenice (Kenyon) B.; m. Rosalie Kohl, Oct. 25, 1952; children: Ann, Daniel, Thomas, Stephen, Martin. AB, JD, St. Louis U., 1952. Bar: Mo. 1952, U.S. Dist. Ct. (ea. dist.) Mo. 1954, U.S. Supreme Ct. 1956, U.S. Ct. Appeals (8th cir.) 1964. Assoc. Mark D. Eagleton, Atty., St. Louis, 1954-60, Evans & Dixon, St. Louis, 1960-62, ptnr., 1962-98; of counsel Noce & Buckley, St. Louis, 1998—. Mem. 22d Cir. Jud. Commn., St. Louis, 1970-75; co-chmn. fed. practice com. U.S. Dist. Ct. (ea. dist.) Mo., 1983-92; chair CJA adv. group, 1991-95. 1st lt. USAF, 1952-54. Recipient award of Honor, Lawyers Assn. St. Louis, 1989, Disting. Svc. award St. Louis County Bar Assn., 1995, Purcell Professionalism award Mo. Bar Found., 1996. Fellow Am. Coll. Trial Lawyers; mem. Bar. Assn. St. Louis (chmn. trial sect. 1979-80), Assn. Def. Counsel St. Louis (pres. 1971-72), Mo. Orgn. Def. Lawyers (bd. dirs. 1984-90). Roman Catholic. Avocations: fly fishing, travel. Office: Noce & Buckley 1139 Olive St #800 Saint Louis MO 63101-1928

BUCKLEY, F.H. economist, educator; b. Saskatoon, Sask., Canada, Aug. 4, 1948; s. F.J. and H.B. Buckley; m. Esther Goldberg; 1 child, Sarah. BA, McGill U., Montreal, Canada, 1969, LLB, 1974; LLM, Harvard U., 1975. Prof., dir. George Mason Law and Econs. Ctr., Arlington, Va. Author: The Morality of Laughter, 2003; editor: The Fall and Rise of Freedom of Contract, 1999. Office: George Mason Law and Econs Ctr 3301 N Fairfax Dr Arlington VA 22201

BUCKLEY, FREDERICK JEAN, lawyer; b. Wilmington, Ohio, Nov. 5, 1923; s. William Millard and Martha (Bright) B.; m. Josephine K. Buckley, Dec. 4, 1945; children: Daniel J., Fredrica Buckley Elder, Matthew J. Student, Wilmington Coll., 1941-42, Ohio State U., 1942-43; AB, U. Mich., 1948, LLB, 1949. Bar: Ohio 1950, U.S. Dist. Ct. (so. dist.) Ohio 1952, U.S. Supreme Ct. 1978, U.S. Ct. Appeals (6th cir.) 1981, Fla. 1982, U.S. Dist. Ct. (mid. dist.) Fla. 1991; cert. cir. ct. mediator, Fla.; cert. arbitrator Fla. state and fed. cts. Assoc. G.L. Schilling, Sr., Wilmington, 1951-52; ptnr. Schilling & Buckley, Wilmington, 1953-56; sole practice Wilmington, 1956-62; sr. ptnr. Buckley, Miller & Wright, Wilmington, 1962—2002. Chmn. The Wilmington Savs. Bank, 1971—; solicitor City of Wilmington, 1954-63. Contbr. articles in field. With AUS, 1943-46, ETO. Joint program Mich. Inst. Pub. Adminstrn. fellow, 1948. Fellow Am. Coll. Trial Lawyers; mem. ABA, Am. Arbitration Assn. (comml. panel), Ohio State Bar Assn., Clinton County Bar Assn., Fla. Bar, Fla. Acad. Profl. Mediators, Collier County Bar Assn., Ohio State Bar Found. Republican. Methodist. Home and Office: # 95 4031 Gulf Shore Blvd N Naples FL 34103

BUCKLEY, GEORGE W. sporting goods executive; PhD in Engring., U. Southhampton (Eng.). Various mgmt. positions Brit. Railways Bd., GEC Turbine Generators Ltd., Detroit Edison Co.; past pres. elec. motors divsn. Emerson Elec. Co.; pres. Mercury Marine unit Brunswick Corp., Fond du Lac, Wis., 1997-2000, chmn. & CEO Lake Forest, Ill., 2000—. Office: Brunswick Corp 1 N Field Ct Lake Forest IL 60045-4811*

BUCKLEY, J. STEPHEN, newspaper publisher; b. Pasadena, Calif., Mar. 22, 1942; s. John Stephen and Jane (Oliver) B.; m. Susannah Marie Smith, Aug. 27, 1965; children: Melissa Lynn, Amy Marie. Student, Dartmouth Coll., 1959-61; BA with high honors, Rutgers U., 1966; postgrad., Pa. State U., 1967—68. Gen. mgr. Press Enterprise, Inc., Bloomsburg, Pa., 1987-88; pub. The Courier Tribune, Asheboro, N.C., 1989-90, The Times-Reporter, New Phila., Ohio, 1990-92, The Record, Troy, N.Y., 1992-96, The Times-News, Burlington, N.C., 1996—. Prof. Bloomsburg U., 1987-88; v.p. cmty. newspaper divsn. Freedom Comm., Inc., 1999—; bd. visitors Elon U. Pres. Indsl. Devel. Authority, Bloomsburg, 1987; commr. N.Y. State Commn. on the Capital Region. Mem. Alamance County C. of C. (vice-chmn. 1999—), Anglers' Club of N.Y., Confrerie de Chevalier de Taste du Vin. Avocations: fishing, hunting, skiing, hockey, golf. Office: Times News 707 S Main St Burlington NC 27215-5844

BUCKLEY, JAMES LANE, retired judge; b. N.Y.C., Mar. 9, 1923; s. William Frank and Aloise Josephine (Steiner) Buckley; m. Ann Frances Cooley, May 22, 1953; children: Peter P., James F., Priscilla L., William F., David L., Andrew T. BA, Yale U., 1943, LLB, 1949. Bar: Conn. 1950, D.C. 1953. Assoc. Wiggin & Dana, New Haven, 1949—53, Reasoner & Davis, Washington, 1953—57; v.p. Catawba Corp., N.Y.C., 1956—70; mem. U.S. Senate from N.Y. State, 1971—77; mem. firm Donaldson, Lufkin & Jenrette, N.Y.C., 1977—78; bus. cons., 1978—80; undersec. for security assistance U.S. Dept. State, Washington, 1981—82; pres. Radio Free Europe/Radio Liberty, Munich, 1982—85; cir. judge U.S. Ct. Appeals for D.C. Cir., 1985—96, sr. judge, 1996—, retired, 2000. Co-chmn. U.S. Del. to UN Conf. on Environ., Nairobi, 1982; chmn. U.S. Del. UN Conf. on Population, Mexico City, 1984. Author: If Men Were Angels, 1975. Rep. candidate for U.S. Senate, Conn., 1980. Lt. j.g. USNR, 1943—46.

BUCKLEY, JEREMIAH STEPHEN, lawyer; b. San Francisco, Oct. 12, 1944; s. Jeremiah Stephen and Flora (Saur) Buckley; m. Deborah Stanley, Nov. 5, 1983. AB, Fairfield U., 1966; JD, U. Va., 1969. Bar: Conn. 1969, D.C. 1972, U.S. Supreme Ct 1980. VISTA vol. Wayne County Legal Svcs., Detroit, 1969-70; asst. counsel govt. ops. com. U.S. Ho. of Reps., Washington, 1971-73; minority counsel housing subcom. U.S. Senate, Washington, 1973-77, minority staff dir. banking com., 1977-79; ptnr. Leighton, Lemov, Jacobs & Buckley, Washington, 1979-84, Thacher Proffitt & Wood, Washington, 1984-93, Goodwin Procter LLP, 1994—. Mem.: ABA, Fed. Bar Assn., Electronic Fin. Svcs. Coun., Millwood Golf Club, Kenwood Golf Club. Office: 1717 Pennsylvania Ave NW Washington DC 20006-4614 E-mail: jbuckley@goodwinprocter.com.

BUCKLEY, JOAN N. English educator; b. Mpls., Jan. 27; d. Carl J. and Helene (Groth) Naglestad; m. Wendell D. Buckley, June 7, 1957; children: David, Julie. BA, St. Olaf Coll., Northfield, Minn., 1952; MA, U. Chgo., 1956; PhD, U. Iowa, 1976. Instr. English Concordia Coll., Moorhead, Minn., 1956-63, asst. prof., 1963-69, assoc. prof., 1969-76, prof. English, 1976—. Named Flaat Disting. Prof., Concordia Coll., Glydenvand Prof.; NEH grantee 1977, 1980, 1983. Mem.: Norwegian-Am. Hist. Assn. (bd. dirs.), Delta Kappa Gamma (Tau State 1st v.p., U.S. forum chair, Woman of Achievement 2001). Home: 2317 Rivershore Dr Moorhead MN 56560 Office: Concordia College Dept English Moorhead MN 56562 E-mail: buckley@cord.edu.

BUCKLEY, JOHN JOSEPH, JR., health care executive; b. Evanston, Ill., Oct. 5, 1944; s. John Joseph and Mary Ruth (Smith) B.; m. Sarah Amelia Puceloski, May 16, 1970; children— Ruth Mary, Patricia Kimberly, John Joseph III AB, Kenyon Coll., 1966; MBA, George Washington U., 1969. Asst. adminstr. Maricopa County Gen. Hosp., Phoenix, 1969-71, St. Joseph's Hosp. and Med. Ctr., Phoenix, 1971-74, assoc. adminstr., 1974-76, v.p., 1976-79, pres., 1984-88, St. Anthony's Hosp., Amarillo, Tex., 1979-84, St. Anthony's Devel. Corp., Amarillo, 1982-84; chief operating officer Harrington Cancer Ctr., Amarillo, 1982-84; sr. v.p. Mercy Health System, Cin., 1988-91; pres. So. Ill. Healthcare Enterprises, Carbondale, Ill., 1992—2001, Jack Buckley & Assocs., Herrin, Ill., 2001—; interim pres., CEO St. Mary's Hosp. of East St. Louis, Ill., 2002; interim COO, St. Joseph Campus of Via Christi Med. Ctr., Wichita, Kans., 2003—; interim CEO St. Joseph Regional Ctr., Tex., 2003—. Pres. So. Ill. Hosp. Svcs., Health Svcs. of So. Ill., Regional Health Plan, 1992-2001. Active Amarillo Alliance of Cmty. Svc. Execs., Amarillo Area Acad. Health Ctr. Corp., Amarillo Area Hosp. Home Care, Amarillo Found. Health and Sci., Panhandle chpt. Tex. Soc. to Prevent Blindness, Amarillo Jr. League, Children's Oncology Svcs. of Tex. Panhandle; Amarillo diocesan coord. health affairs; mem. adminstrv. com. Amarillo; pres. Mercy Svcs. Corp., 1984-88; bd. dirs. Greater Phoenix Affordable Health Care Found., 1984-88; trustee Kenyon Coll., Gambier, Ohio, 1991-95, mem. alumni coun., 1998-2003, pres., 2001-02; mem. SI Edge, 1995—. Fellow: Am. Coll. Healthcare Execs. (regent Ariz. 1984—88, regent So. Ill. 1998—2002); mem.: Ariz. Hosp. Assn., Ariz. Kidney Found., Cath. Health Assn. U.S., Ill. Hosp. and Health Sys. Assn. (trustee 1995—2001, chmn. 2000), Tex. Hosp. Assn. (trustee 1983—84), Alumni Assn. of George Washington U. Health Svcs. Mgmt. and Policy (pres. 1995—97), Delta Phi (pres. alumni assn. 1988—2000). Republican. Roman Catholic. Office: Jack Buckley & Assocs 1907 S 27th St Herrin IL 62948 E-mail: jackbuckleyjr@earthlink.net.

BUCKLEY, JOHN JOSEPH, obstetrician, gynecologist; b. Youngstown, Ohio, Jan. 21, 1930; s. John Joseph and Rosalie Catherine (Singler) B.; m. Anne Theresa Finnerty, Apr. 24, 1954; children: John, Joy, Colleen, Mollie. BS in Biology cum laude, Holy Cross Coll., 1952; MD, Ohio State U., 1959. Staff St. Elizabeth Med. Ctr., Youngstown, Ohio, 1963—, chief ob-gyn., 1977-80, chief of staff, 1986—; practice medicine specializing in ob-gyn. Youngstown, Ohio, 1963—. Asst. prof. Northeastern Ohio Coll. Medicine, Rootstown, 1980—. Co-founder Right to Life, Youngstown, 1970. Served to lt. USN, 1952-55, with res. MC, 1959-63. Fellow ACOG; mem. AMA, Ohio Med. Assn., Mahoning County Med. Assn., Youngstown Soc. Ob-Gyns., Alpha Omega Alpha (Physician of Yr. 2002), Youngstown Country Club, Cotillion Club. Democrat. Roman Catholic. Avocations: skiing, water sports, stamps, travel. Home: 1337 Stonington Dr Youngstown OH 44505-1657 Office: 935 Trailwood Dr Youngstown OH 44512-5008

BUCKLEY, JOHN JOSEPH, JR., lawyer; b. N.Y.C., May 18, 1947; m. Jane Emily Genster, Jan. 12, 1980; children: Emily, Darcy, Claire, Connor. AB, Georgetown U., 1969; JD, U. Chgo., 1972. Bar: N.Y. 1973, D.C. 1977. Law clk. to judge John Minor Wisdom U.S. Ct. Appeals, New Orleans, 1972-73; law clk. to justice Lewis F. Powell Jr. U.S. Supreme Ct., Washington, 1973-74; spl. asst. to atty. gen. Edward H. Levi U.S. Dept. Justice, Washington, 1975-77; assoc. Williams & Connolly, Washington, 1977-80, ptnr., 1981—. Fellow: Am. Coll. Trial Lawyers; mem.: ABA, Phi Beta Kappa, Order of Coif. Home: 2955 Newark St NW Washington DC 20008-3339 Office: Williams & Connolly 725 12th St NW Washington DC 20005-5901 E-mail: JBuckley@wc.com.

BUCKLEY, JOSEPH PAUL, III, polygraph specialist; b. Chgo., July 6, 1949; s. Joseph Paul and Helen (Lavelle) B.; m. Patricia Nemeth, June 17, 1972; children: Megan, Michael, Patrick, Thomas. BA, Loyola U., Chgo., 1971; MS in Detection of Deception, Reid Coll. Detection of Deception, Chgo., 1973. Lic., Ill. Detection of deception examiner John E. Reid & Assocs., Inc., Chgo., 1971—, chief polygraph examiner, 1978-80, dir. Chgo. office, 1980-82, pres. corp. Chgo., Milw., 1982—. Chmn. Ill. Detection of Deception Examiner Com., 1978-82; mem. adv. com. Office of Tech. Assessment, 1983 Co-author: Criminal Interrogation and Confessions, 1st edit., 1962, 4th edit., 2001, The Investigator Anthology, 1999; contbr. articles to profl. jours. Mem. Am. Polygraph Assn. (v.p. 1979-80, chmn. pub. rels. com. 1979-80, 84-95, awards), Ill. Polygraph Soc. (v.p. 1981, pres. 1982-83), Am. Acad. Forensic Scis., Am. Mgmt. Assn., Am. Soc. Indsl. Security (investigations com. 1983-89), Spl. Agts. Assn., Internat. Pers. Mgmt. Assn., Internat. Assn. Chiefs Policy, Chgo. Crime Commn. Office: 250 S Wacker Dr Ste 1200 Chicago IL 60606-5841 E-mail: jbuckley@reid.com.

BUCKLEY, MICHAEL EDWARD, lawyer; b. L.A., June 13, 1950; s. Robert and Barbara Ann (Johansing) B.; m. Catherine Delores Busch, Oct. 14, 1978; children: Robert Timothy, Mara Busch, Jeffrey Johansing, Thomas Elliot. BA, UCLA, 1972; JD, Santa Clara U., 1975. Bar: Nev. 1975, Calif. 1976, D.C. 1982, U.S. Dist. Ct. Nev. 1975. Shareholder Jones Vargas, Las Vegas, Nev., 1975—. Instr. dept. fin. U. Nev. Las Vegas, spring 1987, fall 1989; mem. Block Grant Com., State of Nev. Dept. Human Resources, 1996—, chair, 1998-99. Author: (with others) Nevada Real Estate Transactions, 1988. Bd. trustees HELP of So. Nev., Las Vegas, 1985-91, adv. bd., 1991—, pres. 1987-89; mem. City of Las Vegas Planning Commn., 1994-2002, chmn., 1999-2000. Mem. ABA, Cmty. Assn. Inst. (legis. action com.), State Bar Nev. (chair real estate com., bus. law com.), Am. Coll. Real Estate Lawyers, State Bar Calif., D.C. Bar. Democrat. Roman Catholic. Avocations: reading, writing, travel. Office: Jones Vargas 3rd Fl S 3773 Howard Hughes Pkwy Las Vegas NV 89109-0949 E-mail: meb@jonesvargas.com.

BUCKLEY, MICHAEL FRANCIS, lawyer; b. Saranac Lake, N.Y., Nov. 1, 1943; s. Francis Edward and Marjorie (Mooney) B.; m. Mary Thornton, June 26, 1965; children: Sean, Kathleen. BA, Dartmouth Coll., 1965; JD, Cornell U., 1968. Bar: N.Y. 1969, Fla. 1982, U.S. Dist. Ct. (we. dist.) N.Y. 1970. Assoc. Harter, Secrest & Emery, Rochester, N.Y., 1968-75, ptnr., 1976—. Contbg. author: Estate Planning and Probate in New York, 1985; co-editor: Administration of New York Estates, 1990. Bd. dirs. Highland Hosp. Found., Rochester, 1981-95, pres., 1984-87; bd. dirs. Highland Hosp., 1987—, pres., 1992-94; bd. dirs. Highland Health Sys., Inc., 1995-97, Strong Ptnrs. Health System, Inc., 1997—, YMCA of Greater Rochester, 1997—, Highland Cmty. Devel. Corp., 1998-2002, Highland Living Ctr., Inc., 1998-2002, Rochester Area Cmty. Found., 1999—, James B. Wilmot Found., Inc., 2000—, U. Rochester Med. Ctr., 2000—. Fellow Am. Coll. Trusts and Estates Counsel; mem. N.Y. State Bar Assn. (exec. com. trusts and estates law sect. 1988-92), Monroe County Bar Assn. (chmn. trusts and estates sect. 1984-85, banking liaison com. 1985-86), Fla. Bar Assn., Estate Planing Coun. Rochester, Internat. Assn. Fin. Planners. Roman Catholic. Avocations: basketball, platform tennis. Home: 571 Thomas Ave Rochester NY 14617-1432 Office: Harter Secrest & Emery 1600 Bausch & Lomb Pl Rochester NY 14604-2711 E-mail: mbuckley@hselaw.com.

BUCKLEY, MICHAEL J. theology educator; b. San Francisco, Calif., Oct. 12, 1931; s. Michael T. and Eleanor (Fletcher) B. BA in Philosophy, Gonzaga U., Spokane, 1955, MA in Philosophy, 1956; STM in Theology, U. Santa Clara, Calif., 1963; PhD, U. Chgo., 1967; STD (hon.), Spring Hill Coll., 1989; DD (hon.), Jesuit Sch. of Theology at Berkley, 1994. Asst. prof. philosophy Gonzaga U., Spokane, 1968 69; from asst. to assoc. prof. theology Jesuit Sch. Theology, Berkley, 1969-86; rector Jesuit Sch. of Theology, Berkley, 1969-73; vis. prof. Pontificial Gregorian U., Rome, 1973-75; vis. scholar Santa Clara, Calif., 1981-83; exec. dir. coms. on doctrine, pastoral rsch. and practices Nat. Conf. of Catholic Bishops, Washington, 1986-89; prof. theology U. Notre Dame, South Bend, Ind., 1989-92, Boston Coll., 1992—, dir. Jesuit Inst., 1992—. Del. gen. congregations Soc. Jesus, Rome, 1974-75, 83, 95; pres. Catholic Theol. Soc. Am., 1991-92; mem. bd. trustees various univs.; mem. bd. dirs. (jour.) Theol. Studies, 1990—; mem. adv. com. Ctr. for Theol. Inquiry. Author: (books) Motion and Motion's God, 1971, At the Origins of Modern Atheism, 1990. Named Cosmos and Creation lectr. Cosmos and Creation Soc., 1988, Hanley lectr. U. Manitoba, 1991, Bowles lectr. Catholic Chaplaincy, Harvard, 1994. Mem. Am. Acad. Religion, Am. Theological Soc., Catholic Theol. Soc. Am., Metaphysics Soc. Am., Alpha Sigma Nu. Roman Catholic.

BUCKLEY, MIKE CLIFFORD, lawyer; b. Atlanta, Sept. 1, 1944; s. Clifford Robert Buckley and Winifred Davis (Clayton) Coleman; m. Elizabeth Trimble, June 17, 1967. AB, U. Calif., Berkeley, 1966; JD, U. Calif., 1969. Bar: Calif. 1969. Assoc. Lawler, Felix & Hall, L.A., 1969-72; asst. West Coast counsel ITT, L.A., 1972-74; ptnr. Crosby, Heafey, Roach & May, Oakland, Calif., 1974—. Pres. TeleNetwork, Inc., Oakland, 1984-92; treas. Salem Luth. Home of the East Bay Inc., 1992-98; lectr. Calif. Continuing Edn. of Bar, Berkeley, 1978—; workshop leader Hastings Coll. Advocacy, San Francisco, 1981-85; adv. com. U.S. Bankruptcy Ct., San Francisco, 1984-89. Mem. ABA, Calif. Bar Assn., Alameda Bar Assn., San Francisco Bar Assn. Democrat. Home: 246 Pershing Dr Oakland CA 94611-3235 Office: Reed Smith Crosby Heafey LLP PO Box 2084 Oakland CA 94604-2084 E-mail: mbuckley@chrm.com.

BUCKLEY, PAUL RICHARD, insurance executive; b. Brownfield, Maine, Jan. 8, 1935; s. John Joseph and Ruth Ann B.; m. Anita Lucia Lebel, Oct. 11, 1958; children: Lisa, Paul Jr., Scott, Julie. BA, U. Maine, 1957; LLB, U. Maine, Portland, 1961. Bar: Maine 1961. Ptnr. Longley Assocs., Lewiston, Maine, 1958-80; prin. The Buckley Group, Lewiston, 1980—. Contbr. articles to profl. jours. Pres., bd. dirs. St. Mary Hosp., Lewiston, Maine, 1970-77; bd. dirs, Maine Dental Svcs., Portland, 1975-80, Recipient J. Putnham Stephens award, Maine Life Assn., 1987. Mem. ABA, Maine Bar Assn. (bd. dirs. ins. trust 1975-80), Androscoggin Bar Assn., New Eng. Life Leaders Assn. (pres. 1974-75), Am. Coll. Life Ins. Underwriters, Advanced Underwriters, Million Dollar Round Table (pres. 1984-85). Avocations: hunting, fishing, tennis, reading. Home: 10 Amy Ln Cumberland ME 04021 Office: The Buckley Group Ste 401 95 Market St Portland ME 04101

BUCKLEY, PETER JOHN, psychiatrist; b. Dunedin, New Zealand, Apr. 2, 1943; s. William Charles and Anne Agnes (Campbell) B.; m. Denise Joan Almao, Dec. 11, 1968 (div. Feb. 1977); m. Maxine Joan Antell, July 7, 1977; 1 child, Eric. MD, U. Otago, Dunedin, 1966. Diplomate Am. Bd. Psychiatry and Neurology. Intern Dunedin Pub. Hosp., New Zealand, 1967; resident in psychiatry Albert Einstein Coll. Medicine, N.Y.C., 1968-70, fellow in child and adolescent psychiatry, 1970-72, assoc. prof. psychiatry, 1980-87, prof. psychiatry, 1987—; dir. psychiat out-patient svcs. Jacobi, N.Y.C., 1976-93. Dir. residency tng. in psychiatry Albert Einstein Coll. Medicine, N.Y.C., 1993—; tng. and supr. psychoanalyst Columbia U. Ctr. for Psychoanalytic Tng. and Rsch., N.Y.C., 1996—. Editor: Essential Papers on Object Relations, 1986. Fellow Am. Psychiat. Assn.; mem. Am. Psychoanalytic Assn. Office: Montefiore Med Ctr Office Residency Tng 3331 Bainbridge Ave Bronx NY 10467 E-mail: pbuckley@montefiore.org.

BUCKLEY, PRISCILLA LANGFORD, magazine editor; b. N.Y.C., Oct. 17, 1921; d. William Frank and Aloise (Steiner) B. BA, Smith Coll., 1943. Copy girl, sports writer UP, N.Y.C., 1944; radio rewrite staff mem. U.P., 1944-47, Paris corr., 1953—56; news editor Sta. WACA, Camden, S.C., 1947-48; reports officer CIA, Washington, 1951-53; with Nat. Rev. Mag., N.Y.C., 1956—, mng. editor, 1959-86, sr. editor, 1986-99. Mem. U.S. Adv. Commn. Pub. Diplomacy, 1984-91. Editor: The Joys of National Review, 1995; columnist One Woman's Voice Syndicate, 1976-80; author: String of Pearls, On the Newsbeat in New York and Paris, 2001. Mem. Sharon Country Club (Conn., sec. 1973-77, pres. 1978-80, 94-95). Home: Great Elm Sharon CT 06069 Office: Nat Review 215 Lexington Ave New York NY 10016-6023 E-mail: pbuckley@mohawk.net.

BUCKLEY, RALF CHRISTOPHER, research scientist; b. Bishop's Castle, England, Apr. 13, 1954; arrived in Australia, 1975; s. Franklin Barry and Jane Patience Poole (Allsebrook) B. BA with honors, Cambridge U., 1973, MA, 1975; PhD, Australian Nat. U., 1978. Chief environ. scientist Australian Mineral Devel. Labs., Adelaide, 1982-86; prof. environ. mgmt. Bond U., Gold Coast, Australia, 1989-90; prof. engring. & applied sci. Griffith U., Gold Coast, Australia, 1991-95, chair ecotourism, 1995—. Dir. Wet Tropics Queensland World Heritage Mgmt. Authority, 1990, Ctr. Environ. Mgmt., Gold Coast, 1989—, Internat. Ctr. Ecotourism Rsch., Australia, 1993—, Nature and Adventure Tourism, CRC Tourism, Australia, 1997—; adj. prof. bus. Bond U., 1990—, dean engring. and applied sci. Griffith U., 1996-97, rsch. program leader Coop. Rsch. Ctr. Sustainable Tourism, 1996—. Author: Handbook for Environmental Audit, 1980, Environmental Planning Techniques, 1987, Perspectives in Environmental Management, 1993, Case Studies in Ecotourism, 2003 others; editor: Ant-Plant Interactions in Australia, 1982, International Trade, Investment & Environment, 1994, Tourism Ecolabelling, 2000, Nature-based Tourism, Environment and Land Management, 2003; contbr. over 200 articles to profl. jours. Australian Inst. Marine Sci. fellow, Townsville, 1979, Waite Inst. fellow Adelaide U., 1979, Rothmans rsch. fellow Australian Nat. U., Canberra, 1980-81, U. New England fellow, Armidale, Australia, 1987, sr. rsch. fellow Australian Nat. U., 1988, sr. Fulbright fellow, 1994. Mem. Ecol. Soc. Australia, Ecotourism Assn. Australia, Internat. Assn. Impact Assessment, Inst. Arid-Zone Rsch., Internat. Ecol. Assn., The Ecotourism Soc., Nat. Environ. Law Assn., Worldwide Fund Nature, Environ. Inst. Australia, Australian Conservation Found. Avocations: surfing, sailboarding, kayaking, snowboarding, kiteboarding. Office: Griffith U Parklands Dr Southport 4217 Australia E-mail: r.buckley@griffith.edu.au.

BUCKLEY, REBECCA HATCHER, physician, educator; b. Hamlet, N.C., Apr. 1, 1933; d. Martin Armstead and Nora (Langston) Hatcher; m. Charles Edward Buckley III, July 9, 1955; children: Charles Edward IV, Elizabeth Ann, Rebecca Kathryn, Sarah Margaret. BA, Duke U., 1954; MD, U. N.C., 1958. Intern Duke U. Med. Ctr., Durham, N.C., 1958-59, resident, 1959-61, pediat. allergist and immnologist, 1961—. Dir. Am. Bd. Allergy and Immunology, Phila., 1971-73, chair exam. com., 1971-73, co-chair bd. dirs., 1982-84; chair Diagnostic Lab. Immunology, 1984-88; mem. staff Duke U. Med. Ctr.; asst. prof. pediat. and immunology, 1968-72, assoc. prof. pediat., 1972-76, prof. pediat., 1976-79, assoc. prof. immunology, 1972-79, prof. immunology, 1979—, J. Buren Sidbury prof. pediat., 1979—. Contbr. articles to profl. jours. Recipient Allergic Diseases Acad. award Nat. Inst. Allergy and Infectious Diseases, 1974-79, Merit Rsch. award NIH, 1987-97, Nat. Bd. award Med. Coll. Pa., 1991, Clemons von Pirquet award Georgetown, 1993, Disting. Tchr. award Duke U. Med. Alumni Assn., 1993, Lifetime Achievement award Immune Deficiency Found., 1994, Disting. Svc. award Am. Acad. Allergy and Immunology, 1996, Disting. Faculty award Duke U. Med. Alumni Assn., 1998. Fellow AAAS (chair med. scis. sect. 2001-03), Am. Acad. Allergy and Immunology (exec. com. 1975-82, pres. 1979-80, hon. fellow award 1999); mem. Am. Assn. Immunologists, Soc. Pediatric Rsch., Am. Acad. Pediatrics (Bret Ratner award 1992), Southeastern Allergy Assn. (pres. 1978-79), Am. Pediatric Soc. (coun. mem. 1991—, pres. 1999-2000, chmn. immune deficiency found. med. adv. com. 2003—). Republican. Episcopalian. Home: 3621 Westover Rd Durham NC 27707-5032 Office: Duke U Med Ctr PO Box 2898 Durham NC 27710-2898 E-mail: BUCKL003@mc.duke.edu.

BUCKLEY, RICHARD BENNETT, asset management company executive; b. Providence, Nov. 7, 1942; s. Alfred and Helen (Searles) B.; m. Karen Owen, May, 1982; 1 child, Owen Searles. BA, Denison U., 1965; JD, Syracuse U., 1968; Exec. MBA, U. New Haven, 1982. Bar: U.S. Supreme Ct. 2001. Successively asst. dean, dir. placement, dean admissions, lectr. ins. law, assoc. dean, dir. placement, dir. admissions, asst. prof. law Syracuse (N.Y.) U., 1968-74, assoc. prof., 1974-77; pres. Schiavone Tire & Rubber Reclamation Corp., New Haven, Conn., 1978-80, Schiavone Sports, New Haven, 1978-80; v.p. Cowen Asset Mgmt., N.Y.C., 1980-87, spl. ltd. ptnr., 1986-92, sr. v.p., 1987—, exec. v.p., 1990—; dir., 1992-98; also bd. dirs.; dir. S.G. Cowen, N.Y.C., 1999-00; sr. v.p. Prudential Securities Inc., New Haven, Conn., 2000—. Chmn. bd. dirs. Founders Bank, New Haven, 1984-95; mentor Sch. Orgn. and Mgmt. Yale U., New Haven, 1987-89; bd. dirs. Saab Fin. Auto Receivables Corp., Saab Fin. Auto Receivables Corp. II, Saab Fin. Auto Receivables Corp. III, Saab Fin. Svcs. Corp., adv. New Oxford Dictionary of Am. English. Author: Handbook on Profl. Ethics and Responsibility, 1973; mng. editor Ins. Counsel Jour., 1971-87; spl. subject advisor New Oxford Dictionary of American English; contbr. legal articles to profl. jours. Trustee First Congl. Ch., Guilford, Conn., 1996, chmn. of trustees, 2003, Hamden Hall Country Day Sch. Assoc. fellow, Berkeley Coll. Yale U., 2002—. Mem. ABA, Order of Coif, Quinnipiack Club (pres. 1992-93), Rotary (pres. 1987-88, Spl. Pers. award 1982-83, Rotarian of Yr. 1985-86). Avocations: sailing, skiing, tennis, fly fishing. Home: 34 Grove Hill Rd Guilford CT 06437-3126 Office: Wachovia Securities LLC 157 Church St New Haven CT 06510-2100

BUCKLEY, ROBERT JOHN, academic research administrator; b. N.Y.C., Jan. 12, 1949; s. John Patrick and Mary Elizabeth (Carroll) B.; m. Lillian Perez, Apr. 28, 1973. BA, Fordham U., 1970; MBA, NYU, 1976. Asst. dir. devel. Hunter Coll. CUNY, 1970-72, asst. to dean programs in edn., 1972-77, dir. office research adminstrn., 1977—. Chair coun. grants officers CUNY, 1984-86, 88—. Mem. Nat. Coun. Univ. Rsch. Adminstrs., Soc. Rsch. Adminstrs., Assn. Univ. Tech. Mgrs. Office: CUNY Hunter Coll 695 Park Ave New York NY 10021-5024

BUCKLEY, ROBERT MATTHEW, electrical engineer; b. Bklyn., Nov. 14, 1947; s. Matthew Louis and Catherine Sienna Buckley; m. Linda Susan Montagne, May 16, 1971; children: Christopher, Kevin, Michael. BSc, N.Y. Inst. Tech., 1972; postgrad., Embry Riddle U., Nova Southeastern U. Engring. asst. N.Y. Telephone, Bklyn., 1972-74; project engr. PRD, Syosset, N.Y., 1974-77; engr. Citibank, Melville, N.Y., 1977-81; engring. specialist ILS Divsn. Grumman Aerospace, Bethpage, N.Y., 1981-84; engring. mgr. AIL, Deer Park, N.Y., 1984-85; v.p. engring. TTI, Ronkonkama, N.Y., 1985-90; v.p. ATTI, Hauppauge, N.Y., 1990—. Contbr. articles to profl. jours. Leader Boy Scouts Am., Medford, N.Y., 1985; pres. NYPMAC, Medford, 1987-89. With USMCR, 1969-71. Mem. IEEE. Roman Catholic. Achievements include patent for video display and analyzer, new phase noise measurement technique, new use for phase noise measurement, and patent for generating programmable spectrally pure doppler signals. Office: ATTI 110 Ricefield Ln Hauppauge NY 11788-2008

BUCKLEY, ROBERT PAUL, aerospace company executive; b. Portsmouth, N.H., Aug. 18, 1947; s. Paul John and Margaret Mary (Bennett) B.; m. Evelyn L. Levesque, Jan. 12, 1985; children: Mark Robert, Maeghan Margaret, Caitlin

Evelyn. AB with honors, Providence Coll., 1969; MBA with honors, Harvard Bus. Sch., 1975. Bus. analyst Lockheed, Sunnyvale, Calif., 1975-76, asst. to v.p., 1976-77; bus. devel. mgr. Textron Sys. Corp. (formerly Avco), Wilmington, Mass., 1977-78, mgr. bus. planning, 1978-80, bus. line contr., 1980-82, dir. bus. devel., 1982-83, dep., tactical systems, 1983-85, dir. R & D programs, 1985-89, asst. to pres., 1989-90, v.p., 1990—. Contbr. articles to profl. jours. Mem. local Rep. election campaign staffs, Providence, 1969, N.H. 1980, 1984. Served to capt. U.S. Army, 1969-73, Vietnam. Decorated two Bronze Stars, 16 Air medals. Mem. Am. Mgmt. Assn., Am. Defense Preparedness, USAF Assn. Republican. Roman Catholic. Avocations: family, reading, golf. Office: Textron Sys Corp 201 Lowell St Wilmington MA 01887-4113

BUCKLEY, SHERYL LEA, physician, anesthesiologist; b. Cleve., Aug. 20, 1946; d. William Faulkner and Marjorie (Kitchen) B. BA, Hiram (Ohio) Coll., 1968; MD, Med. Coll. Pa., 1972; MS in Adminstrv. Medicine, U. Wis., 1999. Diplomate Am. Bd. Anesthesiology. Anesthesiologist Cleve. Clinic, 1976-82; assoc. dir. anesthesia St. Luke's Hosp., Cleve., 1982-89; dir. anesthesia MetroHealth St. Luke's Med. Ctr., Cleve., 1989-93; med. dir. Rockside Surgery Ctr., 1993-99; anesthesiologist Anesthesia Care of Ohio, 1999—2002; vice chmn. anesthesiology Barberton Citizens Hosp., 2002—. Trustee Hiram Coll., 1990—. Home: 18827 Cliff Cir Cleveland OH 44126-1707 Office: Barberton Citizens Hosp Anes 155 Fifth St NE Barberton OH 44203

BUCKLEY, SUSAN, lawyer; b. Rockville Center, N.Y., Dec. 24, 1951; BA, Mt. Holyoke Coll., 1973; JD, Fordham U., 1977. Bar: N.Y. 1978, D.C. 1980. Ptnr. Cahill Gordon & Reindel, N.Y.C., 1985—. Mem. ABA, N.Y. State Bar Assn. (com. on media law 1992-95), Bar Assn. N.Y.C. (com. comm. law 1986-89). Office: Cahill Gordon & Reindel 80 Pine St Fl 17 New York NY 10005-1790

BUCKLEY, TERRENCE PATRICK, lawyer; b. N.Y.C., May 7, 1945; s. Cornelius and Catherine (Sheehan) B.; m. Patricia Ann McComb, Oct. 7, 1976; children: Shannondoah, Heather. BA, Iona Coll., 1967; JD, Bklyn. Law Sch., 1972. Bar: N.Y. 1972, U.S. Dist. Ct. (so. and ea. dists.) N.Y. 1977, U.S. Supreme Ct. 1993. Asst. dist. atty. Dist. Atty.'s Office, N.Y.C., 1972-74; law instr. Western State U., Fullerton, Calif., 1975; assoc. McDonald, Pulaski & Harlan, San Diego, 1975-77; atty.-in-charge Nassau-Suffolk Law Svcs., Riverhead, N.Y., 1977-78; spl. asst. atty. gen. N.Y. State Atty. Gen. Office, N.Y.C., 1978-86; trial counsel Pelletreau & Pelletreau, Patchogue, N.Y., 1986-87; pvt. practice Islandia, N.Y., 1988—. Instr. health law SUNY, Stony Brook, 1988, 90; adminstrv. law judge Divsn. Parole, L.I. City, N.Y., 1987-88. With U.S. Army, 1969-71. Recipient Excellence award Am. Jurisprudence, 1972. Mem. ATLA, NACDL, Suffolk County Bar Assn., Am. Inns of Ct. (Alexander Hamilton Inn), Brehon Law Soc., Frank Hogan Assocs. Roman Catholic. Avocations: skiing, running, sailing, hiking, kayaking. Office: 1 Suffolk Sq Ste 520 Islandia NY 11749-1528

BUCKLEY, THOMAS HUGH, historian, educator; b. Elkhart, Ind., Sept. 11, 1932; s. Bernard Leroy and Martha B. (Swoveland) B.; m. Julie Griffith; children: Christopher, Kathryn, Elizabeth, Thomas, Barbara. Student, Northwestern U., 1950-53; AB, Ind. U., 1955, MA, 1956, PhD (grad. fellow), 1961. From instr. to prof. U. S.D., 1960-69; vis. prof. Ind. U., 1969-71; prof., chmn. dept. U. Tulsa, 1971-81, chmn. humanistic studies, 1975-81, Jay Walker research chair Am. History, 1981—, assoc. dean Grad. Sch., 1995-2000; cons. on overseas edn. to Nat. Edn. Corp. Author: The United States and the Washington Conference, 1921-1922, 1970 (award as best first book by an historian 1971); co-author: American Foreign and National Security Policies, 1914-1945, 1987; editor: Research and Roster Guide of Soc. Historians of Am. Fgn. Relations, 1980-86; contbr. chpts. in books. Postdoctoral fellow Stanford U., 1968, U. Wis., 1983, Brown U., 1986, U. Tex., 1991; Fulbright fellow, U. Western Australia, 1986. Mem. Orgn. Am. Historians, Soc. Historians of Am. Fgn. Relations, Tulsa Com. Fgn. Relations, Phi Alpha Theta, Lambda Chi Alpha. Republican. Methodist. Home: 1301 Terrace Dr Tulsa OK 74104-4409 Office: Univ Tulsa Dept History Tulsa OK 74104 *Success comes in the race of life not always to the swiftest but to those who keep on running.*

BUCKLEY, TODD CHARLES, psychologist; b. Freeport, N.Y., Aug. 8, 1970; s. John and Maryann Buckley. BA in Psychology, SUNY, Albany, 1992, PhD in Clinical Psychology, 1999. Rsch. scientist Boston VA Med. Ctr., 1999—; asst. prof. Boston U. Sch. Medicine, 1999—. Conf. submission reviewer Internat. Soc. for Traumatic Stress Studies, 1997; grant reviewer Nat. Swiss Sci. Found., 1998. Ad hoc reviewer Jour. Clinical Psychology, 1999—; contbr. articles to profl. jours. Recipient Rsch. grant, Sigma Xi, 1998. Mem.: APA, Assn. for Advancement of Behavior Therapy. Republican. Avocations: hunting, fishing, harpsichord, automotive restoration. Home: 50 Jewett St Roslindale MA 02131 Office: Boston VAMC 116B2 150 S Huntington Ave Boston MA 02130

BUCKLEY, VIRGINIA LAURA, editor; b. N.Y.C., May 11, 1929; d. Alfred and Josephine Marie (Manetti) Iacuzzi; m. David Patrick Buckley, July 30, 1960; children: Laura Joyce, Brian Thomas. BA, Wellesley Coll., 1950; MA, Columbia U., 1952. Tchr. English Bennett Coll., Millbrook, N.Y., 1954-56, Berkeley Inst., Bklyn., 1956-58; copy editor World Pub. Co., N.Y.C., 1959-69; children's book editor Thomas Y. Crowell, N.Y.C., 1971-80; editl. dir. Lodestar Books, N.Y.C., 1980-97; contbg. editor Clarion Books, N.Y.C., 1997—. Author: State Birds, 1986; contbr. articles to profl. jours. Mem. ALA Home: 33 Brook Ter Leonia NJ 07605-1504 Office: Clarion Books 215 Park Ave S New York NY 10003-1603 E-mail: vbuckley@worldnet.att.net.

BUCKLEY, WILLIAM FRANK, JR., magazine editor, writer; b. N.Y.C., Nov. 24, 1925; s. William Frank and Aloise (Steiner) B.; m. Patricia Taylor, July 6, 1950; 1 child, Christopher T. Student, U. Mexico, 1943; BA, Yale U., 1950; LHD (hon.), Seton Hall U., 1966, Niagara U., 1967, Mt. St. Mary's Coll., 1969, U. S.C., 1985, Converse Coll., 1988, U. South Fla., 1992, Adelphi U., 1995; LLD (hon.), St. Peter's Coll., Syracuse U., Ursinus Coll., 1969, Lehigh U., 1970, Lafayette Coll., 1972, St. Anselm's Coll., 1973, St. Bonaventure U., 1974, U. Notre Dame, 1978, N.Y. Law Sch., 1981, Colby Coll., 1985; DScO (hon.), Curry Coll, 1970; LittD (hon.), St. Vincent Coll., 1971, Fairleigh Dickinson U., 1973, Alfred U., 1974, Coll. William and Mary, 1981, William Jewell Coll., 1982, Albertus Magnus Coll., Coll. St. Thomas, Bowling Green State U., 1987, Coe Coll., 1989, St. John's U., Minn., 1989, Grove City Coll., 1991. Instr. Spanish lang. Yale U., New Haven, 1947-51; assoc. editor Am. Mercury, N.Y.C., 1952; founder, pres., editor-in-chief Nat. Rev., N.Y.C., 1955-90, editor-at-large, 1991—; syndicated columnist, 1962—; host weekly TV show Firing Line, 1966-99; Froman disting. prof. Russell Sage Coll., 1973. Lectr. New Sch. Social Rsch., 1967-68. Author: God and Man at Yale, 1951, (with L. Brent Bozell) McCarthy and His Enemies, 1954, Up from Liberalism, 1959, Rumbles Left and Right, 1963, The Unmaking of a Mayor, 1966, The Jeweler's Eye, 1968, The Governor Listeth, 1970, Cruising Speed, 1971, Inveighing We Will Go, 1972, Four Reforms, 1973, United Nations Journal, 1974, Execution Eve, 1975, Saving the Queen, 1976, Airborne, 1976, Stained Glass, 1978 (Am. Book award best mystery 1980), A Hymnal, 1978, Who's On First, 1980, Marco Polo, If You Can, 1982, Atlantic High, 1982, Overdrive, 1983, The Story of Henri Tod, 1984, The Temptation of Wilfred Malachey, 1985, See You Later Alligator, 1985, Right Reason, 1985, High Jinx, 1986, Racing Through Paradise, 1987, Mongoose, R.I.P., 1988, On The Firing Line, 1989, Gratitude, 1990, Tucker's Last Stand, 1991, WindFall, 1992, In Search of Anti-Semitism, 1992, Happy Days Were Here Again, 1993, A Very Private Plot, 1994, The Blackford Oakes Reader, 1995, Brothers No More, 1995, Buckley: The Right Word, 1996, Nearer, My God, 1997, The Lexicon, 1998; editor: The Committee and Its Critics, 1962, Odyssey of a Friend: Whittaker Chambers' Letters to William F. Buckley, Jr., 1954-1961, 1970, American Conservative Thought in the Twentieth Century, 1970, (with Charles Kesler) Keeping the Tablets, 1988; contbr. to Racing at Sea, 1959, The Intellectuals, 1960, What is Conservatism?, 1964, Dialogues in Americanism, 1964, Violence in The Streets, 1968, The Beatles Book, 1968, Spectrum of Catholic Attitudes, 1969, Great Ideas Today Annual, 1970, Essays on Hayek, 1976; also periodicals. Conservative Party candidate for mayor, N.Y.C., 1965; mem. USIA Adv. Commn., 1969-72; pub. mem. U.S. del. to 28th Gen. Assembly UN, 1973. Served to 2d lt., inf. AUS, 1944-46. Recipient Best Columnist of Yr. award, 1967, Disting. Achievement award in journalism U. So. Calif., 1968, Emmy award for outstanding program achievement NATAS, 1969, Cleveland Amory award for best interviewer/interviewee TV Guide, 1974, Bellarime medal, 1977, Americanism award Young Rep. Nat. Fedn., 1979, Carmel award Am. Friends of Haifa U., 1980, Creative Leadership award NYU, 1981, Lincoln Lit. award Union League, 1985, Shelby Cullom Davis award, 1986, Lowell Thomas Travel Journalism award, 1989, Julius award for outstanding pub. svc. U. So. Calif. Sch. Pub. Adminstrn., 1990, Gold medal award Nat. Inst. Social Scis., 1992, Presdl. Medal of Freedom, 1991, Adam Smith award Hillsdale Coll., 1996. Fellow Soc. Profl. Journalists, Sigma Delta Chi; mem. Council on Fgn. Relations, Mont Pelerin Soc. Clubs: New York Yacht, Century, Phila. Soc., Bohemian. Republican. Roman Catholic. Office: Nat Rev 215 Lexington Ave New York NY 10016-6023

BUCKLIN, DONALD THOMAS, lawyer; b. Providence, July 11, 1938; s. Elmer F. and Anne (Scott) B.; m. Kathryn L. Alfera, Nov. 30, 1963; children: Donald R., Heather Anne. BS in Acctg., Providence Coll., 1960; JD cum laude, Am. U., 1967. Bar: Va. 1968, D.C. 1968. Supervisory acct. GAO, 1960-67; law clk. to judge U.S. Dist. Ct. D.C., 1967-68; asst. U.S. atty. for D.C. Dept. Justice, Washington, 1968-71; ptnr. Rowley & Scott, Washington, 1971-74, Truitt, Fabrikant, Bucklin & Lenzner, Washington, 1974-76, Wald, Harkrader & Ross, Washington, 1977-85, Squire, Sanders & Dempsey, 1986—. Contbg. author: Antitrust Counseling and Litigation Techniques, 1984. Served to 1st lt. USAR, 1960-68. Fellow Am. Coll. Trial Lawyers; mem. ABA (criminal law sect. white collar crimes and offenders 1976-77, litigation sect. com. on liaison with state and local bar assns.), D.C. Bar Assn. (treas. Criminal Practice Inst. 1972-73, exec. coun. young lawyers sect. 1973-75, Young Lawyer of Yr.), D.C. Bar (litigation sect. steering com., treas. 1985, bd. govs. 1986-89, bd. dirs., exec. com. 1989—, pres. 1995-96). Office: Squire Sanders & Dempsey 1201 Pennsylvania Ave NW PO Box 407 Washington DC 20044-0407

BUCKLIN, LEONARD HERBERT, lawyer; b. Mpls., Apr. 17, 1933; s. Leonard A. and Lilah B. (Nordland) B.; m. Charla Lee; children: Karen, Anne, David, Douglas, Lea, Gregory. BS in Law, U. Minn., 1955, JD, 1957. Bar: Minn. 1957, U.S. Dist. Ct. Minn. 1957, N.D. 1960, U.S. Dist. Ct. N.D. 1960, U.S. Ct. Appeals (8th cir.) 1971, U.S. Supreme Ct. 1973, Colo. 1989, U.S. Dist. Ct. Colo. 1989, Tex. 1992, U.S. Dist. Ct. Tex. 1993. Ptnr. Larson, Loevinger, Lindquist, Freeman & Fraser, Mpls., 1957-60, Zuger & Bucklin, Bismark, N.D., 1960-87; gen. counsel Provident Life Ins. Co., 1965-85; pres. Bucklin Trial Lawyers P.C., 1988-95; of counsel Bucklin and Klemin, Bismark, 1992—, Allison and Huerta, Corpus Christi, 1992-97; owner Bucklin of Counsel Attys., 1997—. Lectr. legal, med. and bus. ethics; cons. on ethics to attys. and bus.; mem. trial procedures com. N.D. Supreme Ct., 1977-92. Author: Civil Practice of North Dakota, 1975, 2d edit., 2002. Fellow Internat. Acad. Trial Lawyers (bd. dirs.); mem. ABA (litigation and bus. law sects., Ctr. Profl. Responsibility), United Network for Organ Sharing (patient affairs, ethics, profl. stds. com., bd. dirs.), ATLA, Tex. Trial Lawyers Assn., Winthrop Soc., Joseph Bucklin Soc. (exec. dir.), Chopin Soc. Tex., Tex. Ctr. for Legal Ethics, Million Dollar Advocates Forum, Rotary (Paul Harris fellow Corpus Christi), Order of Coif, Phi Delta Phi, Delta Sigma Rho. Methodist. Home and Office: 8063 S Michele Ln Tempe AZ 85284-1362 E-mail: ofcounsel@bigfoot.com.

BUCKLIN, LOUIS PIERRE, business educator, consultant; b. N.Y.C., Sept. 20, 1928; s. Louis Lapham and Elja (Barricklow) B.; m. Weylene Edwards, June 11, 1956; children: Randolph E., Rhonda W. Student, Dartmouth Coll., 1950; MBA, Harvard U., 1954; PhD, Northwestern U., 1960; PhD with honors (hon.), Stockholm Sch. Econs., 2001. Asst. prof. bus. U. Colo., Boulder, 1954-56; instr. in bus. Northwestern U., Evanston, 1958-59, assoc. dean Grad. Sch. Bus. Adminstrn., 1981-83; prof. bus. adminstrn. U. Calif., Berkeley, 1960-93, prof. emeritus, 1993—. Mem. ASUC Aux. Enterprise Bd., 1999—, chmn., 2000-2001; vis. prof. Stockholm Sch. Econs., 1983, INSEAD, Fontainebleau, France, 1984, Erasmus U., Rotterdam, Netherlands, 1993-94, Cath. U. Leuven, Belgium, 1994; prin. Bucklin Assocs., Lafayette, Calif., 1975—; adv. bd. Gemini Cons., San Francisco, 1987-94. Author: (books) A Theory of Distribution Channel Structure, 1966, Competition Evolution in the Distrubutive Trades, 1972, Productivity in Marketing, 1979; editor: Vertical Marketing Systems, 1971, (books) Channels and Channel Institutions, 1986, (journal) Jour. of Retailing, 1996—2001. Mem. City of Lafayette Planning Commn., 1990-93. Capt. USMC, 1951-53, Korea. Recipient Alpha Kappa Psi Found. award for best paper in Jour. Mktg., 1993, Lifetime Recognition for scholarly contbns. to retailing Soc. for Mktg. Advances, 2001. Mem. Inst. for Ops. Rsch. Mgmt. Scis., Am. Mktg. Assn. (Paul D. Converse award 1986), Soc. for Mktg. Advances (Lifetime Achievement award 2001). Democrat. Avocations: travel, microcomputers, photography. Office: U Calif Haas Sch Bus Berkeley CA 94720-0001 E-mail: pbucklin@haas.berkeley.edu.

BUCKLO, ELAINE EDWARDS, United States district court judge; b. Boston, Oct. 1, 1944; married. AB, St. Louis U., 1966; JD, Northwestern U., 1972. Bar: Calif. 1973, U.S. Dist. Ct. (no. dist.) Calif. 1973, Ill. 1974, U.S. Dist. ct. (no. dist.) Ill. 1974, U.S. Ct. Appeals (7th cir.) 1983. Law clk. U.S. Ct. Appeals (7th cir.), Chgo.; pvt. practice, 1973-85; U.S. magistrate judge U.S. Dist. Ct. (no. dist.) Ill., Chgo., 1985-94, judge, 1994—. Spkr. in field. Contbr. articles to profl. jours. Mem. jud. conf. com. on adminstrn. Magistrate Judge Sys., 1998—; mem. vis. com. No. Ill. U. Sch. Law, 1994—; mem. Northwestern U. Law Bd., 1996-99. Mem. ABA (standing com. law and literacy 1995-98), FBA (v.p. 1990-92, pres. Chgo. chpt. 1992-93), Women's Bar Assn. Ill. (bd. dirs. 1994-96), Chgo. Coun. Lawyers (pres. 1977-78). Office: US Dist Ct No Dist Everett McKinley Dirksen Bldg 219 S Dearborn St Ste 1988 Chicago IL 60604-1794

BUCKMAN, JAMES EDWARD, lawyer; b. N.Y.C., Oct. 2, 1944; s. John Burr and Mary Dolores (Ullery) B.; m. Nancy Lee McLaughlin, Aug. 23, 1969; children: Elizabeth Ahern, Anne Tracy, Julia Walsh. AB, Fordham U., 1966; JD, Yale U., 1969. Bar: N.Y. 1969, Ga. 1974, U.S. Dist. Ct. (no. dist.) Ga. 1974. Assoc. Dewey, Ballantine, Bushby, Palmer & Wood, N.Y.C., 1969-72; asst. gen. counsel Gable Industries, Inc., Atlanta, 1972-74; assoc. then ptnr. Troutman, Sanders, Lockerman & Ashmore, Atlanta, 1974-85, ptnr., 1990-92; exec. v.p., gen. counsel Days Inns of Am., Inc., Atlanta, 1985-89, HFS Inc., Parsippany, N.J., 1992-96; now vice chmn., gen. counsel Cendant Corp, Parsippany, 1996—. 1st lt. USAFR, 1969-75. Mem. ABA, Atlanta Bar Assn., State Bar Ga. Roman Catholic. Avocation: running. Office: Cendant Corp 9 W 57th St 37th Fl New York NY 10019

BUCKMAN, THOMAS RICHARD, foundation executive, educator; b. Reno, May 3, 1923; s. Thomas Eli and Georgia Christina (Damm) B.; m. Gunhild Margareta Malmkjell, May 1, 1948; children: Anne Christina, Carol Erica. BA, U. Pacific, 1947; MA, U. Minn., 1951, B.L.S. (H.W. Wilson scholar), 1953. Clk., Permit Office for Germany, Allied High Commn., Stockholm, 1949-50; sr. clk. U. Minn. Libr., 1952-53; asst. reference libr. Oreg. State U. Libr., 1953-54; King Gustav V fellow in Sweden, Am. Scandinavia Found., 1954-55; asst. libr. Modesto (Calif.) Jr. Coll. Libr., 1955-56; head acquisitions dept. U. Kans. Libr., 1956-60, assoc. dir., 1960-61, dir. libraries, 1961-68, lectr. in Scandinavian, 1958-61; prof. bibliography, univ. libr. Northwestern U., Evanston, Ill., 1968-71; pres. Found. Ctr., N.Y.C., 1971-91, sr. advisor, 1991-93; pres., chmn. Engring. Info. Found., 1995—. Past chairperson bd. dirs. Telecom. Coop. Network, E.S.T.C., N.A., Engring. Info., Inc. Editor, translator: Modern Theatre: Seven Plays and an Essay (by Pär Lagerkvist), 1966; editor: Bibliography and Natural History, 1966, University and Research Libraries in Japan and the United States, 1972; contbr. articles to profl. jours. With USNR, 1943-46. Guggenheim fellow, 1964-65, Scandinavian studies fellow U. Minn., 1952, H.W. Wilson scholar, 1953. Mem. ALA (chmn. internat. rels. adv. com. for liaison with Japanese librs. 1967-71, dir. internat. rels. office 1966-67), Soc. for Advancement of Scandinavian Study (sec.-treas. 1959-69), Am. Scandinavian Found. (bd. dirs. 1978-82). Home: 30 Lincoln Plz Apt 30S New York NY 10023-7126 Office: Engring Info Found 180 W 80th St Ste 207 New York NY 10024-6301

BUCKMORE, ALVAH CLARENCE, JR., computer scientist, ballistician; b. Lewiston, Maine, Sept. 11, 1944; s. Alvah Clarence and Mary (Begin) B. Student, Holyoke C.C., Nat. Radio Inst., Famous Writers Sch., U. Mass. Cert. firearms instr.; lic. amateur radio operator. CEO, chief scientist Buckmore Enterprises, Westfield, Mass., 1974—; developer math./engring. software database for microcomputer Calculated Solutions (formerly SC Applied Tech. Inc.), Columbia, S.C. Mgmt. cons. firearms industry; instr. Mass. Mil. NCO Acad., 1976; mem. Mass. State Rifle and Pistol Team, 1976. Contbr. Collier's Ency., articles to profl. jours. Mem. Mass. Rep. Party, Rep. Presdl. Task Force, Mass. Rep. Senate Com., at-large del., 1992—; comm. officer, dir. RACES for Mass. Emergency Mgmt. Agy., Area III, 1996—. Recipient Internat. Recognition award, 1979; NSF fellow, 1978—. Mem. AAAS, Computer Soc. of IEEE, NRA (life), DAV (life), Am. Def. Preparedness Assn., Nat. Assn. Federally Lic. Firearms Dealers (mem. sr. coalition), Assn. for Computer Tng. and Support, Math. Assn. Am., Am. Radio Relay League, Soc. Amateur Radio Astronomers, Amateur Radio Satellite Corp., Vietnam Vets. Am. (mem. vets. coun. Liberty chpt. 219), Am. Fedn. Police, Am. Legion, N.Y. Acad. Scis., Mount Tom Amateur Repeater Assn. Achievements include development of amateur radio satellite communications, of parallel processing techniques, algorithms, and code for ballistic applications; over 38 major discoveries made in ballistics, including the discovery of 3 new sciences: time physics, the study of the physical properties of time; force-fields, the study of the absorption, displacement, projection, or reflection of kinetic energy; and ballistic signatures, the study of the physical characteristics of a bullet in terminal flight. Address: 18 Tannery Rd Westfield MA 01085-4822 E-mail: K1TMA@arrl.net., K1TMA@amsat.org. *Since the age of 15 years it has been my consistent objective in life to develop a genuine ability to think, talk and use information properly and, over these years—which include the experience of my serving as an illegal POW with only partial official recognition—I have wavered very little, if at all.*

BUCKNAM, MARY OLIVIA CASWELL, artist, educator; b. Modesto, Calif., Feb. 6, 1914; d. Charles Henry and Helen Anne (Cross) Caswell; m. William Nelson Bucknam, June 22, 1946 (dec. 1966); children: William Nelson Jr., Charles Henry. BA, Calif. State U., San Jose, 1936; postgrad., U. Calif., Berkeley, 1938, Calif. State U., Stanislaus, 1968-75, U. San Francisco, 1968-75. Tchr. Stanislaus County (Calif.), 1936-38, Modesto (Calif.) Schs., 1938-43, San Bernardino (Calif.) City, 1943-46; art tchr. Klamath Union Schs., Klamath River, Calif., 1960-61; co-owner Bigfoot Ranch and Resort, Klamath River, 1960-66; art tchr., tchr. Riverbank (Calif.) City Schs., 1966-79; art cons. Riverbank Elem., 1986; gallery artist Cen. Calif. Art League, Modesto, 1986—. One-person show C.C.A. Ctr., 1998; exhibited in group shows at Siskiyow Artists Assn., 1961-66 (Best of show, First award, others), Stanislaus County Shows, 1975-90 (Best of show, First award, others), Caswell Park Remembered, 2000, Great Valley Mus., Modesto, 2002; Three Sisters Show Gallery, 1991-93, Travels with my Paintbrush, 1991-2003; represented in permenant collections. Donor with Caswell family of land for Caswell State Park, San Joaquin County, Calif., 1995; pres. Caswell Sch. PTA, Ceres, Calif., 1956-57, Ceres Study Club, 1952-53; v.p. Siskiyou Artists Assn., Yreka, Calif., 1963-65; pres. Modesto Tchrs. Assn., 1940-41; vol. tchr. adult watercolor classes; active Trinity Singers Choirm 1990—. Named Woman of Distinction Soroptimist Internat., Ceres, Calif., 1992, Outstanding Woman of Stanislaus County Stanislaus County Commn. for Women, 1994; recipient Outstanding Achievement in Visual Arts, Stanislaus Arts Coun., 2000. Mem. AAUW (Modesto br., fellowships chair 1959-60, historian 1956), Ctrl. Calif. Art League (chmn. bank shows Modesto 1988-94, co-chair young artists show Modesto 1986, 88, 89, 90, head art gallery docent 1994-99), Calif. Ret. Tchrs. Assn., Stanislaus County Hist. Soc., Sierra Club, Tuolumne River Lodge, Delta Kappa Gamma (hist.-photography 1985-94, v.p. chpt. 1969-71), Kappa Delta Pi. Republican. Presbyterian. Avocations: painting, world travel, art gallery docent, church service. Home: 2704 La Palma Dr Modesto CA 95354-3229

BUCKNER, ELMER LA MAR, insurance executive; b. Provo, Utah, Apr. 27, 1922; s. Elmer R. and Altis LaVern (Maxfield) B.; m. Melba Hale, Oct. 3, 1945; children: Lynda, Brent, Terry, Kathy, David. BS, Brigham Young U., 1946; HHD (hon.), Weber State U., 1994. CLU. Ptnr. Buckner-Radmall Ins. Counselors, Ogden, Utah, 1947-62, co. inc. pres., 1962-85. Mem. Utah Ho. of Reps., 1965-67, Utah Senate, 1967-75, asst. majority leader, 1971-75. Bd. govs. ARC, 1956-62, mem. exec. com., 1961-62; mem. gen. bd. Young Men's Mut. Improvement Assn., LDS Ch., 1957-58, young men's gen. bd., 1980, regional rep., 1981-87; bishop Ogden 55th Ward, 1958-63, pres. Ogden LDS Temple, 1987-90; 2d counselor Weber Heights Stake presidency, 1963-68; pres. Weber State Coll. Stake, 1968-73, Sacramento mission, 1975-78; former dir. Citizens Com. for Hoover Report; mem. Com. on Religion in Am. Life Inc.; former mem. adv. com. FOA; v.p. Lake Bonneville coun. Boy Scouts Am., 1968-69, pres., 1970, program chmn. Western region, 1973-75; mem. alumni bd. Brigham Young U., 1959-63, pres., 1961-62; v.p. Ogden Area United Fund, 1962, pres. No. Utah, 1963; chmn. Utah Cancer Crusade, 1970; v.p. Utah Cancer Soc., 1971, Utah div. Am. Cancer Soc.; del. Rep. Nat. Conv., Chgo., 1960, chmn. Weber County Reps., 1960-64; elector Utah State Reps., 1964; mem. Utah Bd. Regents Higher Edn., 1981-85; bd. dirs. western region bd. Boy Scouts Am., 1986-2002, pres. area II coun., 1985-87. 1st lt. USAAF, World War II; 23 missions. Recipient Silver Beaver award Boy Scouts Am., 1967, Silver Antelope award, 1983; Disting. Alumni award Weber State Coll., 1983, Alexis de Tocqueville award United Way Am., 1987, Alumni Disting. Svc. award Brigham Young U., 1991; named Utah Ins. Agt. of Yr., 1973. Mem. U.S. C. of C. (bd. dirs. 1955-56), U.S. Jaycees (pres. 1954-55), Utah Jaycees (pres. 1952-53), Ogden C. of C. (bd. dirs. 1980, pres. 1982, Utah Hall of Fame award 1989), Ogden Jaycees (pres. 1950), Jr. Chamber Internat. (treas. 1956), Weber Coll. Alumni Assn. (pres. 1958-59), Kiwanis (pres. Ogden club 1967), Sigma Gamma Chi (internat. pres. 1967-69). Home: 1550 Country Hills Dr Ogden UT 84403-2512

BUCKNER, JENNIE, newspaper editor; m. Steven Landers; 1 child Katie. BS in Journalism with honors, Ohio State Univ. Mng. editor San Jose Mercury News, Calif.; v.p. news Knight-Ridder, Inc., 1989-93; v.p., editor The Charlotte Observer, N.C., 1993—. Bd. visitors Davidson Coll., 1994—. Mem. Am. Soc. Newspaper Editors (bd. dirs. 1998—). Office: The Charlotte Observer PO Box 30308 Charlotte NC 28230-0308 E-mail: jbuckner@charlotteserver.com.

BUCKNER, JOANN, special education educator, consultant; b. Youngstown, Ohio, Mar. 1, 1948; d. Raymond Chester and Edna Ruby (Hood) B. MusB, Youngstown State U., 1970; MEd, Northeastern State U., 1986. Cert. std., music, learning disabilities, autism, traumatic brain injured, other health impairement. Music tchr. Austintown (Ohio) Fitch, 1970-71, Ctrl.-Hover Sch., Akron, Ohio, 1971-74, Berkshire Schs., Burton, Ohio, 1974-79; learning disabilities tchr. Cleveland (Okla.) Pub. Schs., 1980-81; learning disabilities specialist Sallisaw (Okla.) Schs., 1981-2001, Van Buren Schs., 2001—. Instr. Carl Albert Jr. Coll., Sallisaw, 1990-2001; adv. bd. mem. Indian Capital-Vo Tech, Sallisaw, 1994—. Vol. Cystic Fibrosis, Tulsa, Okla., 1985; chpt. pres. Am. Diabetes Assn., Sallisaw, 1986. Named Pledge of Yr., Sigma Alpha Iota, Youngstown, 1968. Mem. Alpha Delta Kappa. Avocations: raising lhaso apos, swimming, arts and crafts, collecting father christmas. Home: RR 2 Box 259A Sallisaw OK 74955-9683

BUCKNER, JOHN KENDRICK, aerospace engineer; b. Indpls., June 13, 1936; s. Roland Kendrick and Lucille (Cave) B.; children: James Kendrick, Bari Kay, Kendrick Ann. BA in Math., DePauw U., 1958; MS in Aero-Engring., Stanford U., 1960. Aerodynamics sr. engr. Gen. Dynamics, Ft. Worth, 1960-69, supr. aerodyns., 1969-75, aircraft project engr., 1975-77, mgr. flight controls, 1977-80, dir. advanced programs, 1980-89, v.p. spl. programs, 1989-95; cons. tech. and strategic aerospace mgmt. Ft. Worth, 1996—. Com. mem. Nat. Rsch. Coun./Naval Studies Bd., Washington, 1990, Aeronautics and Space Engring. Bd., 1992-96; mem. aerospace rsch. and tech. subcom. aeronautics adv. com. NASA, Washington, 1988-93. Bd. dirs. Am. Heart Assn., Ft. Worth, 1990—, chmn., 1995-97. Fellow AIAA (chmn. aircraft design tech. com. 1990-92, pub. policy com. 1988—). Achievements include design of high performance jet fighters F-111 and F-16, management of new business strategy, technology development, new aircraft, and special programs including new aircraft, National Aerospace Plane and many advanced technology development projects. Home: # 527 3080 Bellaire Ranch Dr Fort Worth TX 76109-1823 E-mail: jkbuckner@aol.com.

BUCKNER, JOHN KNOWLES, investor; b. Springfield, Mo., Sept. 8, 1936; s. Ernest Godfrey and Mary Helen (Knowles) B.; m. Lorraine Catherine Anderson, Sept. 22, 1962; children: John Knowles, Allison. BA, Williams Coll., 1958; MS, Mass. Inst. Tech., 1960; PhD, nuclear engring., Stanford U., 1965; grad., Advanced Mgmt. Program, Harvard, 1974. Mgr. analysis dept. EG&G Inc., Bedford, Mass., 1966-70; dir. electronic data processing, controller, v.p. financial ops. Eastern Gas & Fuel Assos., Boston, 1970-77; exec. v.p., chief operating officer, dir. Waters Assos., Inc., Milford, Mass., 1977-80; v.p., chief fin. officer Prime Computer, Inc., Natick, Mass., 1980-83; sr. v.p., chief fin. officer EG & G, Inc., Wellesley, Mass., 1983-86; vice chmn., chief fin. officer

Control Data Corp., Mpls., 1986-89; chmn. Pensco Pension Svcs. Inc., San Francisco, 1989-98, Bohdan Automation, Inc., Mundelein, Ill., 1994-98. Contbr. articles on engring., data analysis and systems to profl. jours. AEC spl. fellow nuclear sci. and engring., 1959, 62-65 Mem.: Assn. Univs. for Rsch. in Astronomy (bd.d ir. 2003—), Sigma Xi, Phi Beta Kappa, Chi Psi. Home: 1824 Green St San Francisco CA 94123-4922 Office: Pensco Pension Svcs Inc 250 Montgomery St San Francisco CA 94104-3406 *My present success, such as it is, has resulted from a willingness and ability to work hard, motivate others, and apply my own training and ideas to the particular task at hand, irrespective of the nature of the field of endeavor. My approach has always been to attain a level of technical and managerial competence necessary to bring about change. Generally, my goal is to make a contribution in as many areas of human conduct as my diligence and native ability will allow.*

BUCKNER, NATHAN ANDREW, music educator, musician; b. Eugene, Oreg., July 29, 1964; s. Paul Eugene and Kay Lamoreux Buckner. MusB, Juilliard Sch., 1987; MusM, Ind. U., 1989; D in Musical Arts, U. Md., 1996. Assoc. prof. piano U. Nebr., Kearney, 1997—. Pianist Sandhill Trio, Kearney, 1998—; founding mem. Delmarva Piano Festival, Rehoboth Beach, Del., 1992—. Editor: Philip Antony Corri: Complete Piano Music, 1997. Mem.: Music Tchrs. Nat. Assn., Phi Kappa Phi. Home: 409 W 32d St Kearney NE 68845 Office: U Nebr at Kearney Kearney NE 68849 Business E-Mail: bucknern@unk.edu.

BUCKNER, PHILIP FRANKLIN, newspaper publisher; b. Worcester, Mass., Aug. 25, 1930; s. Orello Simmons and Emily Virginia (Siler) B.; m. Ann Haswell Smith, Dec. 21, 1956 (div. Nov. 1993); children: John C., Frederick S., Catherine A.; m. Mary Emily Aird, Dec. 15, 1995 (div. Sept. 1997). AB, Harvard U., 1952; MA, Columbia U., 1954. With Bay State Abrasive Products Co., 1954-59; Reporter Lowell (Mass.) Sun, 1959-60; pub. East Providence (R.I.) Post, 1960-62; asst. to treas. Scripps League Newspapers, Seattle, 1964-66, divsn. mgr., 1966-71; pres. Buckner News Alliance, Seattle, 1971—. Pub. daily newspaper group including Carlsbad (N.Mex.) Current-Argus, 1971-90, Pecos (Tex.) Enterprise, 1971—, Fontana (Calif.) Herald-News, 1971-89, Banning and Beaumont (Calif.) Gazette, 1971-74, Lewistown (Pa.) Sentinel, 1971-93, Tiffin (Ohio) Advertiser-Tribune, 1973-93, York (Pa.) Daily Record, 1978—, Winsted (Conn.) Citizen, 1979, Excelsior Springs (Mo.) Standard, 1978, Oroville (Calif.) Mercury-Register, 1983-89, Corona (Calif.) Independent, 1984-89, Minot (N.D.) News, 1989-93. Avocation: mountain climbing. Office: Buckner News Alliance 2101 4th Ave Ste 2300 Seattle WA 98121-2317

BUCKNER, SALLY BEAVER, English educator, writer; b. Statesville, N.C., Nov. 3, 1931; d. Henry George and Foda Leigh (Stack) Beaver; m. Robert Lynn Buckner, Aug. 21, 1954; children: George Robert, Sally Lynn, Theodore Warren. AB in English, U.N.C., Greensboro, 1953; MA in English, N.C. State U., 1970; PhD in Curriculum and Instrn., U. N.C., Chapel Hill, 1980. Tchr. Arlington Jr. H.S., Gastonia, N.C., 1953-54, Protestant Sch., Goldsboro, N.C., 1962-65; journalist Raleigh Times, N.C., 1966-68; tchg. asst. N.C. State U., Raleigh, 1968-70; prof. English Peace Coll., Raleigh, 1970-98. Mem. scholar's adv. bd. MotheRead; chair N.C. Writers' Conf., 1988-89. Author: (poetry collection) Strawberry Harvest, 1986; editor: (anthology) Our Words, Our Ways, 1991, 95, Word and Witness: 100 Years of North Carolina Poetry, 1999. Mem. Legis. Study Commn. for Emotionally Disturbed Children, N.C., 1970-71, Women's Good Will Com., Goldsboro, N.C., 1963-65; co-chair arts edn. panel Dept. Cultural Resources, Raleigh, 1977-81; bd. dirs. N.C. Autism Soc., 1969-73, N.C. Lit. and Hist. Soc., 1981-86. Recipient Ragan-Rubin award N.C. English Tchr.'s Assn., 1993, Sam Ragan award, St. Andrew's Coll, Laurinburg, N.C., 1993, R. Hunt Parker award N.C. Lit. and Hist. Soc., 1999; named Alumnae Disting. Prof., Peace Coll., 1991. Mem. N.C. Poetry Soc. (poet laureate festival chair 1988-89), N.C. Lit. Hall of Fame (mem. selection com.). Democrat. Baptist. Avocations: music, gardening, reading. E-mail: quenell@mindspring.com.

BUCKNER-BROWN, JOYCE, allied health instructor; b. Greenwood, Miss. BS, Tougaloo Coll., 1977; M in Health Sci., Miss. Coll., 1991; PhD, Miss. State U., 1995. Registered respiratory therapist. Asst. prof. U. So. Miss., Hattiesburg, 1995-97; interim chair Jackson (Miss.) State U., 1997-98, asst. prof., 1998—. Cons. Joyce Buckner-Brown & Assocs., Ridgeland, Miss., 1999—. Seminar leader on health and wellness comm. chs., 1998-99. Grantee Ctrs. Disease Control, 1998, Miss. Tobacco Pilot Program, 1998-2000. Mem. APHA, ASPA, Nat. Assn. African Am. Studies (bd. dirs. 1997, leadership award 1999, 2000), Miss. Soc. Respiratory Care, Nat. Rural Health Assn., Nat. Minority Health Assn. Avocations: reading, travel. Office: Jackson State U Sch Allied Health Scis 350 W Woodrow Wilson Ave Jackson MS 39213-7681 E-mail: joyce.buckner-brown@jsums.edu.

BUCKNER-REITMAN, JOYCE, psychologist, educator; b. Benton, Ark., Sept. 25, 1937; d. Waymond Floyd Pannell and Willie Evelyn (Wright) Whitley; m. John W. Buckner, Aug. 29, 1958 (div. 1970); children: Cheryl, John, Chris; m. Sanford Reitman, Aug. 13, 1994. BA, Ouachita Bapt. Coll., 1959; MS in Edn., Henderson State U., 1964; PhD, North Tex. State U., 1970. Lic. psychologist, Tex., marriage and family therapist; cert. Nat. Registry Health Svc. Providers in Psychology; master trainer in imago relationship therapy. Assoc. prof. U. Tex., Arlington, 1970-80, chmn. dept. edn., 1976-78; pvt. practice psychology, Arlington, 1974—. Dir., chief profl. officer Southwest Inst. Relationship Devel., Weatherford, Tex.; author, profl. speaker; appeared on internat. TV shows, including Oprah Winfrey Show. Mem. APA, Nat. Assn. for Imago Relationship Therapy (pres.), Nat. Speakers Assn., Am. Assn. Marital and Family Therapy. Avocations: dancing, travel, art. Home: 2208 Farmer Rd Weatherford TX 76087-6964 E-mail: JoyBuckner@aol.com.

BUCKNUM, MICHAEL JOHN, research scientist, crystallographer, educator; b. Trenton, N.J., Apr. 23, 1963; s. Walter Frederick and Barbara Dockter B.; m. Hsi-cheng Shen, July 7, 1995. BA, Ind. U. Pa., 1985; MS, U. Ky., 1988; PhD, Cornell U., 1996. Staff editor Chem. Abstracts Svc., Columbus, Ohio, 1988-89; patent examiner U.S. Patent and Trademark Office, Crystal City, Va., 1996-97; rschr. Hard Materials Corp., Ithaca, NY, 1997-2000; instr., rschr. Ill. East C.C., Olney, 2000-2001, Ga. Coll. & State U., Milledgeville, 2001—03, Fullerton Coll., Calif., 2003—. Contbr. 20 articles to profl. jours. Grad. fellow U. Ky., 1985-86, NIH fellow Cornell U., 1994-96. Mem. Am. Chem. Soc. Democrat. Roman Catholic. Achievements include contributions to the theory of spiroconjugation, theory of elasticity, crystallography, and applied geometric topology.

BUCKSBAUM, MATTHEW, real estate investment trust company executive; b. Marshalltown, Iowa, Feb. 20, 1926; s. Louis and Ida (Gerwin) B.; m. Carolyn Swartz, Aug. 3, 1952; children: Ann B. Friedman, John. BA in Econ., U. Iowa, 1949. Owner, operator Regional Supermarket Chain, Marshalltown, 1949-54; owner, developer Pvt. Real Estate, Iowa, 1954-64; chmn. Gen. Growth Properties, Chgo., 1964—. Trustee, past chmn. Aspen (Colo.) Music Festival & Sch. Sgt. USAF, 1944-46, PTO. Mem. Internat. Coun. Shopping Ctrs. (past chmn.), Urban Land Inst., Nat. Assn. Real Estate Investment Trusts. Jewish. Office: General Growth Properties Inc 110 N Wacker Dr Chicago IL 60606-1511 Fax: (312) 960-5463.

BUCKSTEIN, CARYL SUE, writer; b. Denver, Aug. 10, 1954; d. Henry Martin and Hedvig (Neulander) B. BS in Journalism, U. Colo., 1976. Editor Rifle (Colo.) Telegram, 1976; corr. So. Colo. Pueblo (Colo.) Star-Jour. and Chieftain, 1977-84; corr. The Denver Post, 1985; staff editor Nat. Over-the-Counter Stock Jour., Denver, 1985-89; writer Rocky Mountain News, Denver, 1990-92; editor Urban Spectrum, Denver, 1993; contbg. writer Boulder (Colo.) County Bus. Report, 1992—. Bd. mem. Holiday Project, Denver, 1996; mem. exec. bd. Denver Newspaper Guild, 1998. Recipient 1st Place Gen. Assignment Bus. Articles, Colo. Press Women, Denver, 1985, 90, 91. Mem. Colo. Soc. Profl. Journalists (sec.-treas. 1988), Denver Newspaper Guild (bd. dirs. 1998). Avocations: inventing, writing. E-mail: dowrite@earthlink.net.

BUCKSTEIN, MARK AARON, lawyer, mediator, educator; b. N.Y.C., July 1, 1939; s. Henry Al and Minnie Sarah (Russ) B.; children: Robin Beth, Michael Alan. BS in Math., CCNY, 1960; JD, NYU, 1963. Bar: N.Y. 1963, U.S. Dist. Ct. (so. and ea. dists.) N.Y. 1965, U.S. Supreme Ct. 1981. Assoc. Russ & Weyl, Massapequa, N.Y., 1963-64; assoc. counsel Mut. Life Ins. Co. N.Y., N.Y.C., 1964-65; assoc. Moses & Singer, N.Y.C., 1965-67, Leinwand, Maron & Hendler, N.Y.C., 1967-68; sr. ptnr. Baer Marks & Upham, N.Y.C., 1968-86; sr. v.p. external affairs, gen. counsel TWA, Inc., N.Y.C., 1986-92; exec. v.p. Am. Arbitration Assn., N.Y.C., N.J., 1992-93; exec. v.p., gen. counsel GAF Corp. and Internat. Specialty Products, Wayne, NJ, 1993-96; counsel Greenberg Traurig, Ft. Lauderdale, Fla., 1996-99, Profl. Dispute Resolution, Inc., Boca Raton, Fla., 1999—. Spl. prof. law Hofstra U. Law Sch., Hempstead, N.Y., 1981-93; adj. prof. law Rutgers U. Law Sch., Newark, 1994-96; bd. dirs. Bayswater Realty & Capital Corp., N.Y.C., Travel Channel Inc., N.Y.C., TWA, GAF Corp., Internat. Specialty Products, Consultis; mem. exec. com. Herzfeld & Stern, N.Y.C., 1981-84; mem. nat. arbitration and mediation com. NASD, 1998-2001. Trustee Bronx H.S. Found., 1984-96. Mem. ABA, N.Y. Bar Assn., Assn. of Bar of City of N.Y., KP (past dep. grand chancellor 1978). Jewish. Avocations: tennis, music, theater, puzzles. Office: Profl Dispute Resolution 2424 N Federal Hwy Boca Raton FL 33431 E-mail: mabresolve@aol.com.

BUCKWALTER, JOSEPH ADDISON, orthopedic surgeon, educator; b. Ottumwa, Iowa, June 21, 1947; s. Joseph Addison and Carole Ann (Kelly) B.; m. Kathleen Coen, May 31, 1975; children: Jody, Andrea, Abigail. BS with high distinction, U. Iowa, 1969, MS, 1972, MD, 1974. Diplomate Am. Bd. Orthopaedic Surgery (recert., oral examiner 1988—, dir. 1990—, mem. examinations com. 1992—, chmn. examinations com. 1992-93, chmn. cert. renewal com. 1992—); lic. surgeon Iowa. Intern in internal medicine U. Iowa, Iowa City, 1974-75, resident in orthopaedics, 1975-77, 78-79, Nat. Rsch. Svc. Award rsch. fellow, 1977-78, from asst. prof. to assoc. prof. orthopaedic surgery, 1979-85, prof. orthopaedic surgery, 1985—. Mem. R&D devel. com. VA Med. Ctr. Com., 1985-88; mem. orthopaedic tumor therapy group U. Iowa Cancer Ctr., 1981—, cancer edn. subcom., 1982-90; mem. grants and fellowships adv. com. Iowa City Vets. Med. Ctr., 1983-86, chief orthopaedic surgery, 1987-91; mem. Arthritis Found. Rsch. Com., 1985-86; mem. panel NIH Consensus Devel. Confs., Bethesda, Md., 1984, 88; mem. rheumatology rsch. adv. bd. Syntex Corp., 1987-94; mem. adv. bd. WHO Multinational Collaborative Study on Predictors of Osteoarthritis, 1992; mem. sci. adv. com. Specialised Ctr. Rsch. on Osteoarthritis Rush-Presbyn.-St. Luke's Med. Ctr., Chgo., 1993—; mem. Nat. Arthritis and Musculoskeletal and Skin Diseases Adv. Coun., NIH, 1993—; disting. lectr. Hosp. Spl. Surgery, N.Y.C., 1982, Coll. Physicians and Surgeons-N.Y. Orthopaedic Hosp., 1988, U. N.Mex., 1989; guest lectr. Wilford Hall Med. Ctr., San Antonio, 1983, vis. prof., 1984; vis. prof. U. Miami, Fla., 1986, Cath. Med. Colls., Seoul, Republic of Korea, 1989, U. Pitts., 1993, Ohio State U., Columbus, 1994; vis. orthopaedic prof. U. So. Calif., L.A., 1990; Am. Orthopaedic Assn. 1991 Internat. vis. prof. Nuffield Orthopaedic Ctr., Oxford (Eng.) U., 1991, vis. prof. orthopaedics, 1991; vis. prof. orthopaedics, U. N.C., 1991; OREF Hark lectr. and vis. prof. U. Wash., Seattle, 1992; Watson Jones lectr. Royal Coll. Surgeons (Gt. Britain), 1992; A.M. Rechtman lectr. Phila. Orthopaedic Soc., 1993; Predl. guest spkr. 1993 Japanese Orthopaedic Assn. Rsch. Meeting, Matsumoto, Japan, 1993; Kelly Rsch. Award vis. prof. Mayo Clinic, Rochester, Minn., 1993; participant numerous workshops and confs. Cons. reviewer: Jour. Bone and Joint Surgery, 1979—, cons. editor for rsch., 1989—; bd. assoc. editors: Jour. Orthopaedic Rsch., 1982-85, mem. editl. adv. bd., 1985-88, co-editor-in-chief, 1993—; mem. editl. adv. bd. Orthopaedics, 1986-90; reviewer: The Lancet, 1993—; contbr. articles to profl. jours. Student rsch. fellow U. Iowa Coll. Medicine, 1970. Fellow Am. Inst. Med. and Biol. Engring. (founding), Am. Acad. Orthopaedic Surgeons (mem. com. basic scis. 1983-85, chmn. com. evaulation 1985-90, mem. at large, bd. dirs. 1988-89, mem. steering com. for devel. Musculoskeletal Conditions in U.S. 1990-92, chmn. coun. for rsch. and sci. affairs 1990-93, 94—, sec. 1993-94); mem. AAAS, Internat. Soc. Limb Salvage, Brit. Orthopaedic Assn. (companion mem.), Orthopaedic Rsch. Soc. (sec.-treas. 1985-88, bd. dirs. 1985-91, pres. 1989-90), Am. Orthopaedic Assn. (exch. fellowship com. 1989-90, chmn. internat. vis. prof. com. 1993—), Am. Orthopaedic Soc. for Sports Medicine (chmn. rsch. awards com. 1988-90, rsch. com. 1989-91), Internat. Skeletal Soc., Iowa Orthopaedic Soc., Johnson County Med. Soc., Musculoskeletal Tumor Soc., 20th Century Orthopaedic Assn., Girdlestone Orthopaedic Soc., Phi Beta Kappa, Alpha Omega Alpha. Office: U Iowa Hosps Dept Orthopaedics 200 Hawkins Dr Iowa City IA 52242-1009

BUCKWALTER, KATHLEEN C. academic administrator, educator; BSN, U. Iowa; MA in Psychiatric/Mental Health Nursing, PhD in Nursing, U. Ill., Chgo. Assoc. dir. Gerontological Nursing Interventions Rsch. Ctr., dir. Ctr. on Aging U. Iowa, Found. disting. Prof., assoc. provost health scis., 1997—. Contbr. over 200 articles to profl. jours., 75 chpts. to books; editor: Nursing Diagnosis and Intervention for the Elderly (Maas, M., Buckwalter, K.C., Hardy, M.A.), 1991, Geriatric Mental Health: Current and Future Challenges, 1992, others. Mem.: IOM. Office: U Iowa Coll Nursing 101 Nursing Bldg 234 CMAB Iowa City IA 52242

BUCKWALTER, ROGER JEROME, editor, columnist, TV interviewer; b. New Britain, Conn., Aug. 14, 1946; s. Benjamin Irving and Harriet Hoskins Buckwalter; m. Karen Ruth Adelson, June 8, 1974. BS in Broadcasting, U. Fla., 1968, MA in Journalism, Comm., 1969. Columnist The Jupiter (Fla.) Courier, 1978—, editl. page editor, 1982-2001, sr. writer, 2000-01. Guest lectr. Palm Beach C.C., Lake Worth, Fla., 1992, 98, Fla. Atlantic U. Jupiter, Fla., 2000; guest interviewer WPTV, Channel 5, W. Palm Beach, Fla., 1994-99; polit. forum moderator Jupiter (Fla.)-Tequesta-Juno Beach C. of C., 1995—; mem. Fla. Atlantic U. Honors Coll. Adv. Bd., 1999—, com. chair 2001—; mem. Wal-mart Scholarship Selection bd., 2000-2001; mem. adv. bd. Palm Beach Atlantic Nat. Vocal Competition, 2001-, Smoke Free Workplaces Campaign, Fla., 2002; bd. dir. Cancer Alliance Help and Hope. Vice chmn. Charter Rev. Com., Juno Beach, Fla., 1973-74; pres. Jupiter-Tequesta (Fla.) Unit Am. Cancer Soc., 1997-2000, com. chair, 2000—; mem. Friends of Jupiter Theatre, 2001; bd. dirs. Loxahatchee River Hist. Soc., 2003—, v.p. for strategic planning, 2003—; bd. dirs Peolpe Helping People with Cancer, 2003—; mem. Cancer Assoc. Network, 2003—. 1st lt. U.S. Army, 1969-71, Vietnam. Recipient 36 journalism awards including Best News Story award Surburban Newspapers Am., 1976. Mem. Nat. Conf. Editl. Writers, Fla. Press Assn. (Best Serious Column awards 1987, 96, Best Editl. awards 1989, 90, 93, 96), Fla. Press Club (Opinion and feature writing awards 1997). Avocations: painting, theater, writing. E-mail: rogekar@aol.com.

BUCKWALTER, RONALD LAWRENCE, federal judge; b. Lancaster, Pa., Dec. 11, 1936; s. Noah Denlinger and Carolyn Marie (Lawrence) B.; m. Dollie May Fitting, May 9, 1963; children: Stephen Matthew, Wendy Susan. AB, Franklin and Marshall Coll., 1958; JD, Coll. William and Mary, 1962. Prin. Ronald L. Buckwalter, Esquire, Lancaster, 1963-71; ptnr. Shirk, Reist and Buckwalter, Lancaster, 1971-80; dist. atty. Lancaster County, Lancaster, 1978-80; judge 2nd Jud. Dist. Commonwealth Pa., 1980-90, U.S. Dist. Ct., Phila., 1990—. Sec. City Lancaster Authority, 1970; bd. dirs. Am. Cancer Soc., Lancaster, 1982, Boy Scouts Am., Lancaster, 1984, YMCA, Lancaster, 1990. 1st lt. U.S. Army NG, 1962-68. Recipient Pub. Life and Letter award Phi Sigma Alpha, 1990. Mem. Am. Judicature Soc., Fed. Bar Assn., Fed. Judges Assn., Pa. Bar Assn., Lancaster Bar Assn. (pres. 1988). Office: US Dist Ct 14614 US Courthouse 601 Market St Philadelphia PA 19106-1713*

BUCOLO, GAIL ANN, biotechnologist; b. Port Chester, N.Y., July 27, 1954; d. Joseph Anthony and Jenne (Tomassetti) B. BS in French, Oneonta State Coll., 1976; MA in French, Middlebury Coll., 1977; postgrad., Columbia U., 1981-82; MS in Biotechnology, Manhattan Coll., 1995. Technician N.Y. Hosp., N.Y.C., 1983-86; rsch. technician NYU Hosp., N.Y.C., 1986; sr. rsch. technician Meml. Sloan Kettering, N.Y.C., 1986-88, Columbia U., N.Y.C., 1988-2001; tchr. Cathedral H.S., N.Y.C., 2001—. Corr. Scienceport, Rye, N.Y., 1994-96; adj. prof. Mercy Coll., Dobbs Ferry, N.Y., 1996—. Mem. AAAS, N.Y. Acad. Scis., Sigma Xi. Roman Catholic. Achievements include work on the factor VIII inhibitor and discovery that it inhibited reverse transcriptase of HIV; work on spinal cord injury and neuronal regeneration which was implemented at the Miami Project in Fla. Home: 288 W 238th St Apt 4F Bronx NY 10463-2319 Office: 350 E 56th St New York NY 10022

BUCOVE, ARNOLD DAVID, psychiatrist; b. Toronto, Sept. 22, 1934; BA, Columbia U., 1956; MD, NYU, 1961. Diplomate Am. Bd. Psychiatry and Neurology. Intern Lenox Hill Hosp., N.Y.C., 1961-62; resident in psychiatry Bellevue Hosp., N.Y.C., 1962-63, St. Luke's Hosp., N.Y.C., 1963-65; chief psychiatry 36th Tactical Hosp., Bitburg, Germany, 1965-67; pvt. practice psychiatry Pleasant Valley, NY, 1967—93, Poughkeepsie, N.Y., 1992-93; pvt. practice Oneonta, N.Y., 1993-99; attending staff Craig House, Beacon, N.Y., 1977-93; asst. dir. Dutchess County Mental Health Clinic, Poughkeepsie, N.Y., 1967-68; chief psychiatry Fox Meml. Hosp., Oneonta, 1993-99, sec.-treas. med. staff, 1997-98, pres.-elect, 1998-99, pres., 1999; pvt. practice Millbrook, NY, 1967—; staff psychiatrist St. Francis Hosp. Counseling Ctr., Poughkeepsie, NY, 1999—. Cons. psychiatrist Greer Children's Cmty., Millbrook, N.Y., 1968-77; mem. courtesy staff Sharon (Conn.) Hosp., 1967-90; cons. IBM, Poughkeepsie, 1968. Contbr. articles to profl. jours. Bd. dirs. Town of Washing Civic Assn., Millbrook, 1986-93, Millbrook Music Assn., 1986-92; mem. vestry Grace Ch., Millbrook, 1971-74, mem. vestry St. Peter's Ch., Millbrook, 1989-92. Capt. USAF, 1965-67. Fellow Am. Psychiat. Assn. (pres. Mid-Hudson chpt. 1977-79); mem. Millbrook Hunt (bd. govs. 1968-71), Millbrook Golf and Tennis Club, Poughkeepsie Tennis Club. Avocations: riding, skiing, tennis.

BUCUR, JOHN CHARLES, neurological surgeon; b. Youngstown, Ohio, Mar. 5, 1925; s. John and Victoria (Marginean) B.; m. Emily Leanne Elmore; children: John Ellsworth, Dean Charles, Victoria Ann, Michael Paul, Teri Leanne. BS, Ohio U., 1947; postgrad., U. Biarritz, France, 1946; MD, U. Pitts., 1951, M of Surgery, 1952. Diplomate Am. Bd. Neurol. Surgery. Intern Western Pa. Hosp., Pitts., 1951-52; resident in neurosurgery Long Beach (Calif.) VA Hosp., 1953-56, staff neurosurgeon, 1956-57; neurosurg. cons. Harbor Gen. Hosp., Torrance, Calif., 1956-57; pvt. practice Falls Church, Va., 1957—; chief of staff Nat. Orthop. and Rehab. Hosp., Arlington, Va., 1973; chief neurol. surgery Fairfax Hosp., Falls Church, 1961-75, Nat. Orthop. and Rehab. Hosp., 1957-79, No. Va. Drs. Hosp., Arlington, 1963—, Arlington Hosp., 1977—; attending neurosurgeon Alexandria Hosp., 1959—, Circle Terrace Hosp., Alexandria, Va., 1962—. Sec., dir. 7 Corners Med. Bldgs., Inc., Falls Church, 1958—; bd. trustees Goodwin House, Inc., Alexandria, Va. Mem. Va. Gov.'s Com. for Regional Med. Program, 1969-77; chmn. bd. dirs. Network Health Plan, 1984-87; bd. dirs. Nat. Hosp. for Orthop. and Rehab., Goodwin House, Inc. With U.S. Army, 1943-45; ETO. Fellow ACS; mem. Am. Assn. Neurol. Surgery, Mid-Atlantic Neurosurgery Soc., Washington Acad. Neurosurgery, Neurosurg. Soc. Vas., No. Va. Acad. Surgery, Congress Neurol. Surgeons, Pan Am. Med. Assn., So. Med. Assn., Arlington County Med. Soc., Va. Health Assn. (pres.), Fairfax County Med. Soc., Am. Legion, Army-Navy Country Club, Masons. Episcopalian. Office: 6305 Castle Pl Falls Church VA 22044-1905

BUCY, J. FRED, JR., retired electronics company executive; b. Tahoka, Tex., July 29, 1928; s. J. Fred and Ethel (Montgomery) Bucy; m. Odetta Greer, Jan. 25, 1947 (dec. Dec. 2000); children: J. Fred III, Roxanne, Diane. B.Physics, Tex. Tech. U., 1951; M.Physics, U. Tex., 1953; DSc (hon.), Tex. Tech U., 1994. With Tex. Instruments, Inc., Dallas, 1953-85, engr. 53-63, corp. v.p. mil. sys., 1963-67, corp. group v.p. microchips, 1967-72, exec. v.p., 1972-75, exec. v.p., chief operating officer, dir., 1974-76, pres., chief operating officer, dir., 1976-84, pres., chief exec. officer, dir., 1984-85, cons., 1985-97. Bd. dirs. Thomas Group, Inc., Optical Data Sys., Inc., Hypres, Inc., S.W. Rsch. Inst., Rectractable Tech. Inc., Intrusion Inc., Sanders Assocs., Inc., Alliant Techsystems, Inc.; cons., chmn. Tex. Nat. Rsch. Lab. Com. Patentee in field. Mem. Tech. Assessment of U.S. Congress; mem. Comptroller Gen's Panel, Pres.'s Commn. for Nat. Agenda for 80's,; comm. chmn. Nat. Rsch. Coun., Washington, Def. Sci. Bd. Dept. Def.; mem. bd. regents Tex. Tech U., Health Sci. Ctr. Tex. Tech U., 1973-91; chmn. bd. regents Tex. Tech U. and Health Sci. Ctr., 1980-82, 89-90; mem. adv. com. rsch. Tex.Higher Edn. Coordinating Bd.; external adv com. Arnold O. and Mabel M. Beckman Inst. Advanced Sci. Tech., U. Ill.; adv. coun. Woodrow Wilson Internat. Ctr. for Scholars, Washington; chmn. Tex. Sci. Adv. Coun.; nat. chmn. Enterprise Campaign Tex. Tech U.; mem. vis. com. Russian Rsch. Ctr., Harvard U.; mem. physics vis. com. MIT; mem. marine sci. adv. coun. U. Tex., 2002. Recipient Disting. Engr. award Tex. Tech U., 1972, Disting. Alumnus award, 1991. Fellow IEEE; mem. NAE, Am. Inst. Physics, Soc. Exploration Geophysicists, Conf. Bd., Cosmos Club (Washington), Dallas Petroleum Club, Tau Beta Pi, Sigma Pi Sigma, Eta Kappa Nu (Eminent Mem.). Address: PO Box 780929 Dallas TX 75378-0929 E-mail: jfbuce@aol.com.

BUDAEV, BAIR V. mathematician, researcher; b. Tsolga, USSR, May 20, 1954; came to U.S., 1995; s. Vladimir Sh. and Margarita L. (Khazankina) B.; m. Ludmila J. Budaeva, Oct. 20, 1989; 1 child, Nina. Diploma, Leningrad (USSR) U., 1976, cand. of scis., 1979; DSc, Russian Acad. Sci., St. Petersburg, 1995. Instr. Leningrad Mil. Sch. Constrn. Engring., 1979-84; rschr. Steklov Math. Inst., Leningrad, 1984-95, U. Calif., Berkeley, 1995—. Avocations: camping, cross-country skiing. Office: Univ Calif Dept Mech Engring Etcheverry Hall Berkeley CA 94720 E-mail: budaev@cml.me.berkeley.edu.

BUDAI, WILLIAM H. music educator; s. James W. and Diane K. Budai. B.Mus.Edn., Ctrl. Mich. U., 1992; MusM, Bowling Green State U., 1995; PhD in Piano Pedagogy, U. Okla. Accompanist/faculty Interlochen (Mich.) Arts Camp, 1991—; faculty Ind. U.-Purdue U., Indpls., dir. Music Acad. Pianist Beres/Budai Piano Duo, Bowling Green, 1995—. Mem. Phi Mu Alpha (pres. 1991-92, treas. 1990-91), Kappa Delta Pi (treas. 1991-92), Phi Kappa Phi, Phi Eta Sigma, Pi Kappa Lambda, Golden Key. Home: 3606 N Three Rivers Rd Gladwin MI 48624-8345

BUDALUR, THYAGARAJAN SUBBANARAYAN, chemistry educator; b. India, July 14, 1929; came to U.S., 1969, naturalized, 1977; s. Subbanarayan Subbuswamy and Parvatham (Gopalakrishnan) B.; children: Chitra, Poorna, Kartik. MA, U. Madras, 1951, M.Sc., 1954, PhD, 1956. Reader organic chemistry U. Madras, 1960-68; prof. chemistry U. Idaho, Moscow, 1968-74; prof. chemistry, dir. div. earth phys. sci. U. Tex., San Antonio, 1974-2000, emeritus prof., 2000—. Lectr. in field. Author: Mechanisms of Molecular Migrations; Selective Organic Transformations; Editorial bd. chem. jours.; contbr. articles to profl. jours.; 3 patents in field. Recipient Intra Sci. Research award, 1966 Fellow Am. Chem. Soc.; mem. Chem. Soc. London, Soc. Cosmetic Chemistry N.Y. Acad. Sci., Am. Inst. Chemists, Sigma Xi, Phi Kappa Phi. Clubs: Lions. Home: 6119 Amble Trl San Antonio TX 78249-2108

BUDANITSKY, SANDER, lawyer; b. Riga, Latvia, Feb. 9, 1972; came to the U.S., 1979; s. Grigory and Miriam Budanitsky; m. Kimberly Anne Rudolph, Nov. 16, 1997. BA, Dickinson Coll., 1993; JD, Widener U., 1996. Bar: N.J. 1996, Pa. 1996. Legal intern U.S. Dept. Justice, Office of the U.S. Trustee, Phila., 1995-96; assoc. Seigel & Mongiardo, P.C., Ridgewood, N.J., 1997-98, Robert C. Diorio, Elizabeth, N.J., 1998—. Avocation: rugby. Office: Law Offices Robert C Diorio 431 Morris Ave Elizabeth NJ 07208-3612

BUDD, BERNADETTE SMITH, lawyer, newspaper executive, public relations consultant; b. N.Y.C., Feb. 23, 1948; d. Stanley Allen and Toby (Percak) Smith; m. Thomas Witbeck Budd, July 4, 1988; children: Amanda Rose Kronin Castel, Karen Wendy Kronia Campisi, Paige Elizabeth Glickman, Kelly Lynn Budd Tinsley. BA in History and English, Bucknell U., 1964; MA in Liberal Studies, SUNY, Stony Brook, 1971; EdM, Columbia U., 1982; JD, Jacob D. Fuchsberg Law Ctr., 1998. Tchr. history N.Y., 1964-69; innovator pre-sch. programs, 1975-79; editor, pub. Cmty. Jour., Wading River, N.Y., 1978—, advt. mgr., 1978—; editor Shoreham-Wading River Newsletter, 1978-88; editor-in-chief Restatement Touro Law Ctr., 1997-98. Profl. breeder, shower A.K.C. golden retriever dogs; cons., workshop leader, 1979—; exec. dir. Suffolk County chpt. NYCLU, 1998-2000. Editor: C. of C. Directory, Shoreham, 1983, 84; contbr. articles N.Y. Times, Reader's Digest, Psychology Today Mag.om., 1979-82. Advisor Teen Recreation Adv. Com., Shoreham-Wading River, 1979-82; mem. Nuclear Emergency Evacuation Com., 1979-82; pres. PTA, Wading River, 1980-83; v.p. Spl. Edn. PTA, Wading River, 1979-80, Am. Civil Liberties Union Student Chpt. Touro Law Ctr.; active Com. Gifted and Talented Children, Wading River, 1979-80, Occupational Edn. Commn., 1979-80; mem. Suffolk County Human Rights Commn. Recipient Disting. Service award Am. Cancer Soc., 1982-83; award of merit N.Y. State Pub. Relations Assn., 1982-83; award of honor Nat. Sch. Pub. Relations Assn., 1981. Mem. Wading River C. of C. (bd. dirs. 1979-80), Suffolk County Bus. and Profl. Women's Assn., Women's Equal Rights Congress, East End Women's Network, N.Y.C. Press Assn., Rocky Point C. of C. (bd. dirs.), Soc. Profl. Journalists, L.I. Press Club, Sigma Delta Chi, Kappa Kappa Gamma. Roman Catholic. Home and Office: Cmty Jour PO Box 619 Wading River NY 11792-0619 E-mail: bernadettesbudd@aol.com.

BUDD, DAVID GLENN, lawyer; b. Dayton, Ohio, May 19, 1934; s. Glenn E. and Anna Elizabeth (Purdy) B.; m. Barbarann Dumbaugh, Apr. 4, 1964; children: Anne Elizabeth, David Glenn II. AB with honors, Ohio U., 1959; JD

with honors, U. Cin., 1962. Bar: Ohio 1962, U.S. Dist. Ct. (so. dist.) Ohio 1963, U.S. Dist. Ct. (no. dist.) Ohio 1967, U.S. Supreme Ct. 1967, Fla. 1980, U.S. Dist. Ct. (mid. dist.) Fla. 1981, U.S. Tax Ct. 1989. Assoc. Young, Pryor, Lynn, Strickland & Falke, Dayton, 1962-65; trial atty. U.S. Dept. Justice, Cleve., 1965-67; chief antitrust sect. Atty. Gen. Ohio, Columbus, Ohio, 1967-69; ptnr., sr. corp. atty. Cox & Brandabur Attys., Xenia, Ohio, 1969-74; asst. v.p., asst. sec. law Jim Walter Corp., Tampa, Fla., 1974-76; sec., gen. counsel, asst. treas. Gardinier Big River, Inc., Gardinier, Inc., Tampa, 1976-80; assoc. Young, Van Assenderp, Varnadoe & Benton, P.A., Naples, Fla., 1981-84; ptnr. Van Koughnet & Budd, Naples, 1984-85; sr. ptnr. Budd, Hines & Thompson, Naples, 1985-88, Budd & Thompson, Naples, 1989-92, Budd, Thompson & Zuccaro, Naples, 1993-95, Budd & Zuccaro, Naples, 1996-97, Budd and Bennett, Naples, 1998—. Legal counsel to bd. dirs. of numerous corps. Vol. Legal Aid Soc., Xenia, 1972; active Newcomen Soc. N.Am. With USN, 1952-54. Mem. ABA (bus. law sect.), Fla. Bar Assn., Collier County Bar Assn., Blue Key Club, Omicron Delta Kappa, Pi Gamma Mu, Phi Kappa Tau. Republican. Presbyterian. Avocations: health fitness club, tennis, golf, boating. Home: 3757 Fountainhead Ln Naples FL 34103-2734 Office: Budd and Bennett 3033 Riviera Dr Ste 201 Naples FL 34103-2750 E-mail: buddbennett@aol.com.

BUDD, ELAINE, social worker; b. Pitts., Dec. 26, 1923; d. Jacob and Bessie (Cohen) L.; children: Jonathan, Sandra. BS in Social Sci. with highest honors, Carnegie Mellon U., 1944; postgrad., Wayne State U., 1944; MSW, U. Pitts., 1948. Lic. ind. clin. social worker, Minn. Social worker various orgns. and agys., 1948-58; rsch. asst. NIMH, Bethesda, Md., 1959-60; dir. Camp Chi Jewish Cmty. Ctr., Chgo., 1949-56; with dept. selection and evaluation U.S. Peace Corps, Washington, 1961-62; dir. social work careers Dept. Human Svcs., State Minn., St. Paul, 1964-65, dir. adoption recruitment, dir. human svcs., 1965-69; faculty Sch. Social Work, Univ. Minn., Mpls., 1971-73; mgmt. analyst Hennepin County Affirmative Action, Mpls., 1973-74; developer and dir. family life edn. svcs. Jewish Family and Children's Svc., Mpls., 1974-78; sr. social worker Hennepin County Dept. Community Svcs., Mpls., 1982—; pvt. practice Mpls., 1990—. Counselor and group facilitator Chrysalis Ctr. for Women, Mpls., 1979-82; presenter at internat. conf.; invited to teach in Israel. Activist Kennedy for Pres., Washington, 1960, Peace Corps, Washington, 1960, Anti-Nuclear Movement, Minn., 1965—; union grievance chairperson, Chgo., 1950; mem. Simon Wiesenthal Ctr., CARE; mem. Elaine Budd Spl. Family Life Ednl. Fund, Jewish Family and Children's Svc., Mpls. CARE Legacy Soc., Hadassah Founders Group. Recipient Outstanding and Innovative Svc. award Nat. Assn. County Orgns., 1988, Spl. Honors Citation County Commrs. Hennepin County, 1992. Mem. Minn. Bd. Social Work, Amnesty Internat., Mus. of Tolerance, Walker Art Ctr., Hadassah, Holocaust Mus., Doctors without Borders, Physicians for Social Responsiblity, Alzheimer's Assn., Simon Wiesenthaler Ctr., Southern Poverty Ctr., Phi Kappa Phi, Pi Delta Epsilon. Avocations: reading, walking, social action, discussion groups, music. Home: 111 Marquette Ave Apt 2102 Minneapolis MN 55401-2032 Address: The Kenwood 825 Summit Ave Unit #1402 Minneapolis MN 55403

BUDD, ISABELLE AMELIA, research economist; b. Granite City, Ill., Feb. 8, 1923; d. Floyd Harry and Amelia Frederica (Bradvogel) Marx; BS, U. Mo., 1944; postgrad. U. Wis., 1946; m. Louis John Budd, Mar. 3, 1945; children: Catherine Lou, David Harry. Research economist Ralston Purina Co., St. Louis, 1945-46; govtl. legislator, Durham, N.C., 1975-79; fin. and govtl. cons., Durham, 1972-88. Troop leader Girl Scouts U.S.A., 1955-61; mem. environ. concerns com. Duke U., Durham, 1972-77, co-chmn., 1974-75; mem. Durham City Council, 1975-79; Durham del. Council Govts., 1976-78; mem. exec. com. regional govt. criminal justice com., 1976-78; chmn. personnel policy com. regional govt., 1977-78; bd. dirs. Durham County Sr. Citizens Coordinating Council, 1982-85, Raleigh-Durham Internat. Airport Authority, 1983-85; chmn. bd. trustees Raleigh-Durham Firemen's Relief Fund, 1983-89. Mem. AAUW (life), N.C. Center for Public Policy Research, Greater Durham C. of C., S.W. Durham Assn. (charter mem., treas. 1973-76), Mark Twain Circle of Am. (founding mem. 1986, govt. advisor), Nat. Trust for Historic Preservation, Historic Preservation Soc. Durham (charter mem.), N.C. Mus. Life and Sci., Friends of Duke U. Library (life), Ind. Scholars Assn. (life). Author articles on estates. Home: 2753 Mcdowell Rd Durham NC 27705-5715

BUDD, JIM, communications manager; b. Austin, Minn. s. Stanley James and Margaret (Deutschman) B. Student, Austin State Jr. Coll. Head of CCTV dept. Northwest Camera Svc., Mpls., 1971-72; head of video svc. dept., engring., TV studio and video svc. dept. ops. Internat. Communications Svcs., Mpls., 1972-73; talent scout coord. and video cons. Wag Arts Prodns.-Talent Agy., Mpls., 1972-75; electronics dept. svc. mgr. Gordon Electric Co., Austin, 1975-78; operational ptnr. in design and mfr. of projection TV consoles with McAllister Trading Co. and ABC Electronics, Austin, 1979-84; video systems specialist The Electronics Warehouse, Inc., Rochester, Minn., 1984-85; engr., video dir., mgr. ABC Electronics & Video, Austin, 1985—; producer, dir. N.W. TV-Prodns., Austin, 1986—; mem. broadcast video staff KAAL-TV, Austin, 1997-98. Video sys. design cons. Script author, narrator of documentary videofilm: "Celebration of Hmong New Year"--Laos, 1991; producer: (video) Big Isl. Rendezvous, 1995, (video film) Olympic Torch Relay Festival, 1996. Videographer Summerset Theatre of Austin Cmty. Coll., 1987; prodn. fund vol. PBS Sta. KSMQ-TV, Austin, 1988-2002. Mem. Am. Film Inst., Am. Legion. Roman Catholic. Office: ABC Electronics Svcs 1008 5th Ave NW Austin MN 55912-2114 E-mail: jim2@smig.net.

BUDD, LOUIS JOHN, English language educator; b. St. Louis, Aug. 26, 1921; s. Vincent and Sophia (Kajszo) Budrewicz; m. Isabelle Amelia Marx, Mar. 3, 1945; children: Catherine Lou, David Harry. BA, U. Mo., 1941, MA, 1942; PhD, U. Wis., 1949; DLitt, U. Mo., 1988, Elmira Coll., 1995. Instr. U. Mo., Columbia, 1942, 46, U. Ky., Lexington, 1949-52; asst. prof. Duke U., Durham, N.C., 1952-60, assoc. prof., 1960-66, prof., 1966-83, James B. Duke prof., 1983-91, chmn. dept. English, 1973-79. Mem. vis. faculty Washington U., St. Louis, summer 1954, Northwestern U., Evanston, Ill., summer 1961; lectr. seminar Kraft div. Internat. Paper Co., summer 1959; Fulbright lectr., India, 1967, 72; vis. lectr. U. Damascus, Syria, 1978; chmn. Jay B. Hubbell Ctr. for Am. Lit. Historiography, 1976-87. Author: Mark Twain: Social Philosopher, 1962, Robert Herrick, 1971, Newspaper and Magazine Interviews with Samuel L. Clemens, 1874-1910, 1977, Our Mark Twain: The Making of His Public Personality, 1983; editor: Robert Herrick's The Web of Life and Clark's Field, 1970; (with others) Toward a New American Literary History, 1980, Critical Essays on Mark Twain, 1867-1910, 1982, 1910-80, 1983, New Essays on Adventures of Huckleberry Finn, 1985, On Mark Twain: The Best from American Literature, 1987, Mark Twain's Collected Tales, Sketches, Speeches and Essays (2 vols.), 1992, Mark Twain: The Contemporary Reviews, 1999; mem. editl. bd. A Selected Edition of W.D. Howells, South Atlantic Rev, 1978-81, U. Miss. Studies in English, 1979-95, South Atlantic Quar., 1980-87; mng. editor Am. Lit, 1979-86, chmn. editl. bd., 1986-91, Am. Lit. Realism 1870-1910, 1986—, Studies in Am. Humor, 1974—; contbr. numerous articles to profl. jours. Hon. trustee Mark Twain Meml., 1992—. 2d lt. USAAF, 1942-45. Guggenheim fellow, 1965-66; Am. Philos. Soc. grant, 1956, 70, 73; Nat. Endowment for Humanities sr. fellow, 1979-80; recipient J.H. Fisher award South Atlantic Depts. of English, 1997. Mem. MLA (Hubbell medal 1998), Am. Humor Studies Assn. (pres. 1979, 93), AAUP (pres. Duke chpt. 1971-72), Internat. Humor Studies Assn., Mark Twain Circle of Am. (founding pres. 1986-87, hon. life mem.), Phi Beta Kappa (pres. Duke Chpt. 1963-64). Home: 2753 Mcdowell Rd Durham NC 27705-5715 Office: Duke U Dept English Durham NC 27708-0015

BUDD, PATRICIA JEAN, counselor; b. Phillipsburg, N.J., May 6, 1947; d. Joseph Lewis and Josephine (Lesko) B. BS, Bloomsburg U., 1969; MEd, Lehigh U., 1974, PhD, 1991. Lic. psychologist, Pa. Secondary English tchr. Phillipsburg High Sch., 1969-73; secondary sch. counselor Whitehall (Pa.) High Sch., 1974—; psychologist, part-time pvt. practice, 2000—. Psychotherapist Alliance for Creative Devel., Allentown, Pa., 1987-2000; adj. asst. prof. Lehigh Univ. Dept. of Coun. Psych., 1994—; workshop presenter Kutztown U., 1997, Pa. State Counselors Conv., Hershey, 1986, 94, Pa. State Assn. Student Couns., Allentown, 1986, 88, NEA N.E. Regional Leadership Conf., Portland, Maine, 1988, Pa. Student Assistance Profls. Conv., 1994, 96, 98, Am. Coun. Assn., 1993, Kutztown U. Art Conf., 1997; mem. allied health staff/ dept. psychiatry Quakertown (Pa.) Community Hosp., 1987-91; part-time instr. Carbon-Lehigh Intermediate Unit, 1989—, Colonial-Northampton Intermediate Unit, 1990-98, Schuylkill Intermediate Unit, 1997-98. Guest spkr. Whitehall Exch. Club, 1986, 95; mem. adv. bd. Northampton County Children, Youth and Families Divsn.; mem. Pa. Atty. Gen.'s Family Violence Task Force, 1998-99. Mem. ACA, NEA, APA, Pa. Sch. Counselors Assn., Chi Sigma Iota (pres. Alpha Tau chpt. 1988-90, William W. Purkey Profl. Devel. award 1992), Lehigh Univ. Alumni Coun. (exec. bd. 1997-99, pres. 2002-), Pa. Assn. Student Assistance Profls., Phi Delta Kappa. Avocations: photography, writing, music, reading. Office: Whitehall H S 3800 Mechanicsville Rd Whitehall PA 18052-3348

BUDD, RICHARD WADE, university official, communications scientist, priest; b. Henderson, Md., Aug. 24, 1934; s. Bryan William and Dorothea Marie (Fouvy) B.; m. Claudia L. Wolff; children: Kimberly, Richard Wade, Janna, Eric, Gary, Stephanie. BA, Bowling Green U., 1956; MA, U. Iowa, 1962, PhD, 1964. Ordained preist 2002. Reporter, staff writer Dayton (Ohio) Daily News, 1956-57; rsch. assoc., instr., asst. prof., dir. Inst. Comm. Studies, U. Iowa, Iowa City, 1960-71; prof., disting. prof., assoc. dean Rutgers Coll. Rutgers U., New Brunswick, N.J., chmn. dept. human comm., 1971-80, dir. Sch. Comm. Studies, 1980-83, dean. Sch. Comm., Info. and Libr. Studies, 1983-97; v.p. for info. and technology Regent U., Virginia Beach, Va., 1997—2000, disting. scholar, 2000—; chmn. bd. Newstatements Comm. Cons., 1973-80; cons. in field.; rector Ch. of the Good Shepherd, Richmond, Va., 2002. Author: Introduction to Content Analysis, 1964, Content Analysis of Communication, 1967, Approaches to Human Communication, 1972, Human Communication Handbook Simulations and Games, 1975, Mass Communication: Dialogue and Alternatives, 1976, Interdisciplinary Approaches to Communication, 1979, Beyond Media, 1988; assoc. editor Human Communication Research, 1974-83, Communication Quar, 1975-83; mem. editorial bd. Jour. Communication, 1976-82, Communication Yearbook, 1977-86, Mass Communications Yearbook, 1979—. Mem. Cmty. Arts Coun. East Brunswick, 1973—80; exec. coun. East Brunswick Youth Baseball Program, 1974; active Boy Scouts Am.; priest Episcopal Diocese of So. Va., 2001; chmn. bd. dirs. Anglican Ctr. for Theology and Spirituality, Diocese of So. Va., 2003—. Lt. USNR, 1957—60. Mem. Internat. Comm. Assn. (pres. 1976-77), AAAS, Nat. Comm. Assn., Am. Assn. Public Opinion Rsch., Assn. Edn. in Journalism, ALA (com. on accrediting 1995-99), Assn. Libr. Info. Edn. Episcopalian. Home: 120 Cypress Crk Williamsburg VA 23188-7804 Office: Ch of the Good Shepherd 4206 Springhill Ave Richmond VA 23225 E-mail: rwbudd@regent.edu.

BUDD, THOMAS WITBECK, lawyer; b. Phila., Nov. 1, 1939; s. Reginald Masten and Elizabeth (Charlton) B.; divorced; children: Kelly Budd Tinsley, Paige Budd Glickman; m. Bernadette Smith Budd, July 4, 1988; stepchildren: Amanda Kronin. BA, Washington and Lee U., 1961, LLB, 1964. Bar: Va. 1964, N.Y. 1965, U.S. Supreme Ct. 1982. Assoc. Buell Clifton & Turner, N.Y.C., 1964-69, ptnr., 1969-70, Clifton Budd & Burke, N.Y.C., 1970-76, Clifton Budd Burke & Demaria, N.Y.C., 1976-88, Clifton, Budd & Demaria, N.Y.C., 1988—. Contbr. ; editor (newsletter): Labor and Employment Law; co-author: (Labor and Employment Aspects of Bankruptcy Re-organization) Jour. of Bankruptcy Law and Practice, 2002. Mem. law coun. Washington and Lee U., 1978-81, 84-85. Mem. ABA (labor and employment law sect.), N.Y. Bar Assn. (labor law sect.), N.Y.C. Bar Assn. (labor law sect.), Washington Soc. Washington and Lee U., Princeton Club (N.Y.C.), St. George's Golf and Country Club (Stony Brook, N.Y.). Home: 3 Colgate Ct Shoreham NY 11786-1221 Office: Clifton Budd & Demaria 420 Lexington Ave New York NY 10170-0002 E-mail: twbudd@cbdm.com.

BUDDE, NEIL FREDERICK, publishing company executive, editor, publisher; b. Elmhurst, Ill., June 19, 1956; s. Robert Earl and Phyllis Jean (Plummer) Budde; m. Virginia Bowman Edwards, May 22, 1982. BA, Western Ky. U., 1977; MBA, U. Louisville, 1982. Copy editor Richmond (Va.) Times Dispatch, 1977—78, The Courier-Jour., Louisville, 1978—81, asst. bus. editor, 1984—86; assoc. editor Courier-Jour. Mag., Louisville, 1981—84; reporter, editor USA Today, Rosslyn, Va., 1986—87; assoc. editor Dow Jones Info. Systems, Princeton, NJ, 1987—88, dep. editl. dir., 1988—93; editor The Wall Street Jour. Interactive Edition, N.Y.C., 1993—, editor, exec. dir., 1996—98, v.p., editor, 1998—99, v.p., editor, pub., 1999—. Avocations: golf, tennis, photography. Home: 6 Round Top Rd PO Box 75 Oldwick NJ 08858-0075 Office: Dow Jones & Co 200 Liberty St Fl 11 New York NY 10281-1099

BUDDEN, FREDERICK RICHARD, music educator; b. Topeka, Kans., Aug. 3, 1952; s. Frederick Herbert Budden Jr. and Jean Ann Budden; m. Katherine Diane Bowers, Jan. 11, 1986; children: Rebecca Nicole, Richard Lawrence, Regina Marie, Russell Frederick. BS in Music Edn., Kans. State U., 1974, MusM, 1984. Music tchr. Caney (Kans.) Valley Unified Sch. Dist., 1974—76, Phillipsburg (Kans.) Unified Sch. Dist., 1976—77, Kaw Valley Unified Sch. Dist., St. Marys, Kans., 1977—. Mem.: Nat. Edn. Assn., Music Educators Nat. Conf., Kans. Choral Dirs. Assn. (sec., treas.). Avocations: music, photography, woodcarving, fishing, hunting, tennis. Home: 29185 Delia Road Saint Marys KS 66536 Office: Rossville High School 800 S Main Rossville KS 66536

BUDDENBAUM, JUDITH M. communications educator, writer; b. Indpls., Jan. 5, 1941; d. Donald LeRoy and Lydia Elizabeth (Kruge) Mitchell; m. Warren E. Buddenbaum, Jan. 28, 1961; children: Donald, Katherine, David. AB, Ind. U., 1962, MA, 1979, PhD, 1962. Reporter, photographer Valley Times, Beaverton, Oreg., 1971—74; instr. St. Mary-of-the-Woods (Ind.) Coll., 1982—84; prof. journalism and tech. comm. Colo. State U., Ft. Collins, 1984—. Freelance writer, 1974—; founder, co-editor Jour. Media and Religion. Author: Reporting Religion News, 1998; co-author: Applied Communication Research, 2001; co-editor: Religion and Popular Culture, 2001. Bd. dirs. The Luth. Mag., Chgo., 1999—. Rsch. grantee, Ctr. Middletown Studies, Ball State U., 1992, 1996, 2000. Mem.: Assn. Edn. in Journalism and Mass Comm. (founder, past chair Religion and the Media Interest Group, Lifetime Rsch. award), Soc. Scientific Study of Religion, Am. Acad. Religion (pub. understanding of religion bd. 2001—). Office: Colo State U Dept Journalism and Tech Comm Fort Collins CO 80523 Office Fax: 970-491-2908. E-mail: Judith.Buddenbaum@colostate.edu.

BUDDIE, AMY M. psychologist, researcher; b. Fairview Park, Ohio, Mar. 1, 1974; d. Ronald Joseph Budddie and Mary Eileen Buddie. BA, Ohio U., Athens, 1996; MA, Miami U., Oxford, Ohio, 1998; PhD, Miami U, Oxford, Ohio, 2001. Tchg. asst. Miami U., Oxford, Ohio, 1996—2001; postdoctoral rschr. Rsch. Inst. on Addictions, Buffalo, 2001—. Contbr. articles to profl. jours., chpt. to book. Named Psi Chi Grad. Student of Yr., Miami U.., 2001; recipient Grad. Student Achievement award. Mem.: Soc. for Personality and Social Psychology, Am. Psychol. Soc., Am. Psychol. Assn. Avocations: Ju Jitsu, Karate, running. Office: Rsch Inst on Addictions SUNY Buffalo 1021 Main St Buffalo NY 14203 E-mail: abuddie@ria.buffalo.edu.

BUDE, RONALD OTTOMAR, radiologist; b. Alton, Ill., Nov. 23, 1951; s. Ottomar Edward and Lenora Marie Bude; m. Lois Helene Otte, June 7, 1979; children: Tekla Lenore, Thea Helena. BSChemE, U. of Missouri-Rolla, 1973; MD, U. of Ill., Chgo., 1977. Diplomate Am. Bd. of Radiology, 1981. Staff radiologist U. of Mich. Hosps., Ann Arbor, Mich., 1989—. Fellow: Am. Inst. Ultrasound in Medicine, Soc. of Radiologists in Ultrasound, Am. Coll. Radiology; mem.: Assn. of U. Radiologists, Radiol. Soc. of N.Am. Lutheran. Office: Univ Mich Hosp Dept Radiology B1D 502 1500 E Medical Center Dr Ann Arbor MI 48109-0030 Office Fax: 734-647-9339. Personal E-mail: ronbude@umich.edu. E-mail: ronbude@umich.edu.

BUDEIR, MOHAMMED HASSAN, surgeon; b. Syria, 1951; MD, Aleppo Med. Sch., 1974. Diplomate Am. Bd. Surgery, Am. Bd. Surg. Critical Care. Intern Monmouth Med. Ctr., Long Branch, N.J., 1977-78; resident in surgery St. Agnes Hosp., Balt., 1978-82; fellow in cardiovascular surgery Tex. Heart Inst., Houston, 1982-84; chief gen. surgery svc. Brandywine Hosp., Coatesville, Pa., 1993—95, chmn. Dept. Surgery, 2002—; ptnr. Brandywine Surg. Group, Coatesville. Fellow ACS; mem. Internat. Soc. Endovascular Specialists, Denton Cooley Cardiovascular Surg. Soc., Chester County Med. Soc., Pa. Med. Soc., Soc. Critical Care Medicine, Ea. Assn. Surg. Trauma. Office: Brandywine Surg Group Brandywine Profl Bldg 213 Reeceville Rd Ste 36 Coatesville PA 19320-1540 Fax: 610-384-6630.

BUDELMANN, BERND ULRICH, zoologist, educator; b. Hamburg, Germany, Apr. 1, 1942; came to the U.S., 1987; s. Gunther and Minna (Siemssen) B. PhD, U. Munich, 1970; degree, U. Regensburg, 1975. Asst. prof. U. Regensburg, Germany, 1973-78, assoc. prof., 1978-87, Heisenberg fellow, 1979-84; assoc. prof. U. Tex., Galveston, 1987-93, prof., 1993—, chief div. biol. marine resources, 1996-2000. Mem. sci. adv. bd. Stazione Zoologica Anton Dohrn, Naples, Italy, 1992-2000; exec. sec. Cephalopod Internat. Adv. Coun., 1994-2000. Contbr. articles to Nature, Philos. Transactions of Royal Soc., Jour. Comparative Physiology. Bd. dirs. Galveston Symphony Orch., 1994—. Grantee Deutsche Forschungsgemeinschaft, 1979-85, NIH, 1989—, Wellcome Trust, 1991, NSF, 1997—. Mem. Am. Soc. Gravitational and Space Biology, Assn. for Rsch. on Otolaryngology, Barany Soc., Deutsche Zoologische Gesellschaft, Gesellschaft Deutscher Naturforscher und Arzte, Internat. Soc. Neuroethology, J.B. Johnson Club, Neurotological and Equilibriometric Soc., Soc. for Exptl. Biology, Soc. for Neurosci., Verband Deutscher Biologen, Rotary Club Galveston (bd. dirs. 1999-2001, officer 2002--), Sigma Xi (sec. chpt. 1988—). Lutheran. Home: 1823 Bayou Shore Dr Galveston TX 77551-4336 Office: U Tex Med Br Marine Biomed Inst Galveston TX 77555-1069 E-mail: bubudelm@utmb.edu.

BUDIG, GENE ARTHUR, former chancellor, professional sports executive; b. McCook, Nebr., May 25, 1939; s. Arthur G. and Angela (Schaaf) B.; m. Gretchen VanBloom, Nov. 30, 1963; children: Christopher, Mary Frances, Kathryn Angela. BS, U. Nebr., 1962, MEd, 1963, EdD, 1967; LLD, Ill. State U., 1982; LHD, U. Nebr., 1989, Baker U., 1995. Exec. asst. to gov. Nebr., Lincoln, 1964-67; adminstrv. asst. to chancellor, asst. prof. ednl. adminstrn. U. Nebr., Lincoln, 1967-70, asst. vice chancellor acad. affairs, prof. ednl. adminstrn., 1970, asst. v.p., dir. pub. affairs, 1971; v.p., dean univ. Ill. State U., Normal, 1972, pres., 1973-77, W.Va. U., Morgantown, 1977-81; chancellor U. Kans., Lawrence, 1981-94; pres. Am. Baseball League, N.Y.C., 1994—. Author: (with Dr. Stanley G. Rives) Academic Quicksand: Expectations of the Administrator, 1973; editor, contbr. chpts. to Perceptions in Public Higher Education, 1970, Dollars and Sense: Budgeting for Today's Campus, 1972, Higher Education - Surviving the 1980s, 1981, A Higher Education Map for the 1990s, 1992; editorial cons. chpts. in Phi Delta Kappan, 1976—; contbr. articles to profl. jours. Mem. Intergovtl. Coun. on Edn., 1980-84; trustee Nelson-Atkins Mus. Art, Kansas City, Mo.; bd. dirs. Truman Libr. Inst., Midwest Rsch. Inst., Univ. Field Staff Internat. Maj. gen. Air N.G., 1985-92; asst. to chief of staff N.G. Bur., 1990-92. Named One of 10 Outstanding Young Persons, Ill. Jaycees, 1975, One of Top 100 Leaders in Am. Higher Edn., Change mag. and Am. Coun. on Edn., 1979, One of 75 Outstanding Young Men and Women Educators Am., Phi Delta Kappa, 1981; recipient Disting. Svc. award Baker U., 1990. Office: Am Baseball League 245 Park Ave Fl 28 New York NY 10167-0002

BUDINGER, THOMAS FRANCIS, radiologist, educator; b. Evanston, Ill., Oct. 25, 1932; married, 1965; 3 children. BS, Regis Coll., 1954; MS, U. Wash., 1957; MD, U. Calif. Berkeley, 1964, PhD, 1971. Asst. chemist Regis Coll., Colo., 1953—54; analytical chemist Indsl. Labs., 1954; sr. oceanographer U. Wash., 1961—66; physicist Lawrence Livermore Lab., U. Calif., 1966—67; resident physician Donner Lab. and Lawrence Berkeley Lab., 1967—76; H. Miller Prof. med. rsch. and group leader rsch. medicine Donner lab., prof. elec. engring. and computer sci. Donner Lab., U. Calif. Berkeley, 1976—. With Peter Bent Brigham Hosp., Boston, 1964; dir. med. svc. Lawrence Berkeley Lab., 1968—76, sr. staff scientist, 1980—; chmn. study sect. NIH, 1981—84; prof. radiology U. Calif. San Francisco, 1984—. Recipient Spl. award, Am. Nuc. Soc., 1984. Mem.: AAAS, Soc. Magnetic Rsch. Medicine (pres. 1984—85), Soc. Nuc. Medicine, N.Y. Acad. Scis., Am. Geophys. Union. Achievements include research in imaging body functions, electrical, magnetic, sound and photon radiation fields, electron microscopy, polar oceanography; nuclear magnetic resonance, reconstruction tomography and instrument development, and cardiology. Office: Lawrence Berkeley Lab Ctr for Functional Imaging 1 Cyclotron Rd Mail Stop 55-121 Berkeley CA 94720-0001

BUDINGTON, WILLIAM STONE, retired librarian; b. Oberlin, Ohio, July 3, 1919; s. Robert Allyn and Mabel (Stone) B.; m. Irma Johnson BA, Williams Coll., 1940, L.H.D., 1975; BS in L.S, Columbia U., 1941, MS, 1951; BS in Elec. Engring, Va. Poly. Inst., 1946. Reference librarian Norwich U., 1941-42; librarian, engring. and phys. scis. Columbia, 1947-52; asso. librarian John Crerar Library, Chgo., 1952-65, librarian, 1965-69, exec. dir., librarian, 1969-84. Mem. U.S.-USSR Spl. Libraries Exchange, 1966; bd. dirs. Center for Research Libraries, 1970-72, chmn., 1972; mem. vis. com. on libraries Mass. Inst. Tech., 1972-77 Served with AUS, 1942-46. Fellow AAAS, Med Library Assn.; mem. ALA, Am. Soc. Info. Sci., Spl. Libraries Assn. (pres. 1964-65, Hall of Fame 1984), Am. Soc. Engring. Edn., Assn. Research Libraries (dir. 1970-74, pres. 1973), Assn. Coll. and Research Libraries (Acad. Research Librarian of Year 1982), Phi Beta Kappa, Tau Beta Pi, Eta Kappa Nu. Clubs: Caxton, Arts. Home: 211 Wood Terrace Dr Colorado Springs CO 80903-2337

BUDMAN, ALAN DAVID, lawyer, law educator; b. Phila., Feb. 18, 1953; s. Harry and Ida G. B.; m. Susan Arlene Schwartz, Apr. 4, 1981; children: Heather Jana Budman, Traci A. Budman. BS, Penn State U., 1974; JD, Del. Law Sch., 1977. Bar: Pa. 1977, U.S. Dist. Ct. (ea. dist.) Pa. 1977, U.S. Supreme Ct. 1997. Corp. tax atty. Penn Ctrl. Corp., Phila., 1977-79; grad. sch. instr. Villanova U., Phila., 1980; law instr. Penn State U., Abington, 1979—; pvt. practice Phila., Abington, 1979—. Co-author: Comparative Negligence, 1984. Vol. Big Brother, Phila., 1978—84; chmn. devel. com. Am. Heart Assn., Phila., 1990—92; committeeman Dem. City Com., Phila., 1983—87; v.p. Melrose B'Nai Israel, Cheltenham, Pa., 1985—88; bd. dirs. Temple Sinai, Dresher, Pa., 1997—; pres. Temple Sinai Men's Club, Dresher, Pa., 2003—, Ctrl. H.S. Alumni Assn., Phila., 1988—91. Mem. Comml. Law League, Pa. Bar Assn., Phila. Bar Assn., Montgomery Bar Assn. Democrat. Jewish. Avocations: skiing, golf, the internet. Office: 1150 Old York Rd Ste 2 Abington PA 19001-3712

BUDNER, RUTH STERN, social worker; b. Milw., June 6, 1937; d. Morris and Anita B. (Tarnofsky) Stern; m. Harvey Morton Budner, June 23, 1957; children: Ann, Jonathan, Beth. AB, Goucher Coll., 1958; MS, Simmons Coll., 1960. Lic. social worker, Mass. Social worker Vista del Mar Childcare Svc., L.A., 1960-61, James Jackson Putnam Children's Ctr., Boston, 1962-63, Boston State Hosp. Psychiat. Home Treatment Svc., Boston, 1963, St. Ann's Home, Methuen, Mass., 1969-71; pvt. practice clin. social worker Wayland, Mass., 1972—. Mem. NASW, Mass. Soc. Clin. Social Work. Home and Office: 8 Hobbs Rd Wayland MA 01778-3710

BUDNIAKIEWICZ, THERESE, writer; b. Mons, Belgium, Sept. 28, 1948; came to U.S., 1961; naturalized, 1967; d. Tadeusz Eugeniusz and Janina Antonina (Więckowska) B.; m. Bart S. Ng, July 6, 1972. BA in Math., U. Chgo., 1971; MA in Comparative Lit., U. Mich., 1972, PhD in Comparative Lit., 1986. Lectr. English, Ind. U.-Purdue U., Indpls., 1987-92. Author: Fundamentals of Story Logic, 1992; contbr. Ency. of Semiotics, 1998. Named Internat. Writer of the Yr., Internat. Biog. Ctr., Cambridge, Eng., 2003. Mem. MLA, Semiotic Soc. Am., Can. Semiotic Assn., Internat. Assn. for Semiotics of Law, Internat. Assn. for Semiotic Studies. Avocation: publishing technologies. Home and Office: 5823 Dapple Trace Indianapolis IN 46228-1698 E-mail: tbudniakiewicz@math.upui.edu.

BUDNICK, ERNEST JOSEPH, music industry executive; b. N.Y.C., 1948; s. Louis and Caroline (Probert) B.; m. Susan Swingle, Sept. 8, 1984. Cert. Data Processing, Comml. Programming Unltd., N.Y.C., 1968; grad., Dale Carnegie Inst., 1988; cert. in pub. rels., NYU, 1991, cert. in real estate sales, 1998. Lic. real estate sales, N.Y. IBM computer operator Seamen's Bank for Savs., 1966-68; programmer/analyst W.T. Grant and Co., 1969-73; owner Underground Records, N.Y.C., 1970; systems analyst Ins. Svcs., N.Y.C., 1973-77; pres., owner Bernard Friedman Video Prodns., N.Y.C., 1973-85, Nat. Digital Diagnostics, N.Y.C., 1973-75; systems analyst Mfrs. Hanover, N.Y.C., 1977-80; mgr. corp. video/media Salomon Bros., Inc., N.Y.C., 1980-92; pres., CEO Consol. Mgmt., Tech. & Comm., N.Y.C., 1993-99; pres. UMO.com Music, N.Y.C., 1995—; owner, record prodr. UMO Underground Records, N.Y.C., 2003—. Pres. UMO Music, 1995—. Author: Effectively Leveraging Business Technology, 1993; creator, writer: (TV series) The Observers, 1986; composer, singer, engr. (single) Keep on Playing, 1980. Conservator N.Y. Pub. Libr., 1990—; mem. Mus. of Moving Image, 1990—. Fellow Mus. of Broadcasting; mem. Am. Film Inst. (mem. coun. 1984—), Nat. Assn. Rec. Arts and Scis., Pub. Rels. Soc. Am., Internat. Assn. Bus. Communicators, Nat. Assn. TV Arts and Scis., Am. Mgmt. Assn., Toastmasters. Avocations: video effects, computer engring., chess, music engring. Office: EJ Budnick & Co 10 W 15th St Ste 313 New York NY 10011-6819 E-mail: ejbudnick@mindspring.com.

BUDNICK, LAWRENCE DAVID, physician, medical educator; b. Nov. 17, 1953; BS, CUNY Bklyn. Coll., 1974; MPH, Harvard U., Boston, 1977; MD, SUNY, Bklyn., 1977. Intern Georgetown VA Hosps., Washington, 1977-78; resident Brookdale Hosp., Bklyn., 1978-80; resident in pub. health N.Y.C. Dept. of Health, 1980-81; epidemic intelligence svc. officer Ctrs. for Disease Control, 1982-84; physician, advisor Exxon Corp., East Millstone, N.J., 1989-94; dir. occupl. medicine N.J. Med. Sch., Newark, 1995—, assoc. prof. clin. medicine, 1994-98, assoc. prof. medicine, 1998—. With USPHS, 1982-86. E-mail: budnicla@umdnj.edu.

BUDNIK, PATRICIA MCNULTY, retired elementary education educator; b. Riverside, N.J., July 2, 1936; d. Norbert E. and Mabel E. (Seifert) McNulty; divorced; children: Barry J., Scott D. BEd, U. Miami, Coral Gables, Fla., 1967, MEd, 1972; EdD, Nova U., 1991. Elem. tchr. Dade County Pub. Schs., Miami, Fla., 1967-2001; ret., 2001. English prof. Hunan Edn. Coll., Changsha, China, summer terms, 1994, 95, 96, 97, 99, 2000, 2001, Hunan Normal U., summer 2002; adj. faculty Nova Southeastern U., Ft. Lauderdale, Fla. Contbr. articles to profl. jours. Mem. choir, Evangelism Explosion Team St. Andrews Presbyn. Ch., Sunday sch. supt. With U.S. Army. Grantee Found. Excellence Pub. Edn., 1986, 87, Broward Community Found., 1990. Mem. Nat. Assn. Edn. Young Children, Assn. Childhood Edn. Internat., Internat. Reading Assn., Fla. Reading Assn., United Tchrs. Dade (bldg. steward). Home: 1820 N 45th Ave Hollywood FL 33021-4104

BUDNY, JAMES CHARLES, federal agency administrator; b. Dearborn, Mich., Aug. 11, 1948; s. William B. and Marion Catherine (Jazdzewski) B.; m. Maureen Anne Taylor, July 9, 1970; 1 child, Andrea. BBA, Ea. Mich. U., 1970; JD, Detroit Coll. Law, 1981. Revenue agent IRS, Dearborn, 1972-75, employee plans specialist Detroit, 1975-79, appeals officer, 1979-87, assoc. chief, 1987-97, sr. assoc. chief, 1997-98, regional appeals employee plans coord., 1990-95, acting chief Cleve. Appeals Office, 1995, chief Mich. appeals, 1999-2000, dep. area dir., 2000—01, appeals mgr. internat. specialists, 2002—; sec. Cass Plaza Corp., Grosse Ile, Mich., 1980—, v.p., 1983-90, pres., 1990—, also bd. dirs. Sec. Indsl. Park Promotion Com., Grosse Ile, 1986-91; asst. registrar Grosse Ile Youth Recreation Assn. for Football, 1991-92; bd. dirs. Waters Edge C.C., Grosse Ile, 1999—; bd. dirs. tax clinic Mich. State U.-Detroit Coll. Law; mem. adv. bd. to dean Coll. Bus., Eastern Mich. U., 2001—. Mem. Inst. Mgmt. Accts., Ea. Mich. U. Alumni Assn., Detroit Coll. Law Alumni Assn., Metro Detroit Alumni (Senate bd. govs. 1994-2000), Delta Theta Phi. Roman Catholic. Avocations: racquetball, jogging, walking, music, golf. Office: Mich Appeals Office IRS 477 Michigan Ave Rm 470 Detroit MI 48226-2544 also: Cass Plz Corp PO Box 412 Grosse Ile MI 48138-0412 *Personal philosophy: Work hard-play hard....expect to give more than you will receive in any endeavor and enjoy and be proud of what you've attained and don't worry about what you have not attained!*

BUDOFF, PENNY WISE, retired physician, author, researcher; b. Albany, N.Y., July 7, 1939; d. Louis and Goldene Wise. BA, Syracuse U., 1959; MD, SUNY-Upstate Med. Sch., 1963. Intern St. Luke's Meml. Hosp., Utica, N.Y., 1963-64; practice medicine specializing in family practice, women's health, Woodbury, N.Y., 1964-85; clin. assoc. prof. family medicine SUNY, Stony Brook, 1980—97. Founder, dir. emeritus North Shore U. Hosp. Women's Healthcare (formerly Penny Wise Budoff, MD Women's Health Svcs.), 1985-97, Bethpage, N.Y., 1985, ground-breaking women's health care facility; attending dept. ob/gyn. North Shore U. Hosp., 1992-97; asst. prof. ob/gyn. Cornell U. Med. Coll., 1993-96, pres. Bonne Forme Vitamins and Skin Care, divsn. Vitamins for Women, Farmingdale, N.Y., 1983—; TV guest on women's medicine and health issues; mem. spl. menopause NIH, 1993; clin. rsch. on menstrual pain, premenstrual syndrome, menopause, breast cancer and osteoporosis. Author: No More Menstrual Cramps and Other Good News, 1980, No More Hot Flashes and Other Good News, 1983, No More Hot Flashes and Even More Good News, 1998, World Book Health and Medical Annual, 1994; med. reviewer Jour. JAMA; contbr. articles to profl. jours. Bd. dirs. Coalition Against Domestic Violence. Named Woman of Yr. C.W. Post Coll., 1981; recipient Nat. Consumers League award, 1983, Max Cheplove award Erie chpt. N.Y. State Acad. Family Physicians, 1983, Women of Distinction award Soroptimist Internat. of Nassau County, L.I., 1990, award for promoting better understanding of menopause N.Am. Menopause Soc., 1999; honoree Nassau County Coalition Against Domestic Violence, 1992. Fellow Nassau County Med. Soc., Am. Acad. Family Physicians (nat. com. on pub. rels.); mem. NOW (Equality award in Health 1988, Unsung Heroine award), Am. Med. Women's Assn. (co-chmn. nat. women's health com., liaison), Nassau Acad. Family Physicians (past pres.). E-mail: pennybudoff@bonneforme.com., pennybudoff@aol.com.

BUDREVICS, ALEXANDER, landscape architect; b. Riga, Latvia, Jan. 3, 1925; arrived in Can., 1952; s. Alfred and Adele (Martinous) B.; m. Milija Vite, Apr. 8, 1948; children: Valdis, Dace, Arnis. Grad. hort. sch., Latvia, 1944; grad. landscape architect, St. Alban's (Eng.) Sch. Art, 1949, London Coll. Art, 1951. Registered landscape architect, Ont., Can. Practice landscape architecture, Latvia, Germany, Belgium, Eng., until 1952; staff various firms, 1952-65; pres. Alexander Budrevics & Assocs. Ltd., Don Mills, Ont., 1965—. Ptnr. Golf Course Devel. Assn., 1969—. Designer over 3000 projects including Nat. Home Show, 1958—, CNE hort. shows, Century Sq.; contbr. articles to profl. jours. Trustee Helen M. Kippax Meml. Scholarship Fund.; chmn. exec. bd. Latvian Boy Scouts Assn.; pres. gen. assembly Latvian Nat. Fedn. Can., 1992—2000, hon. mem., 2000—; pres. Kristus Darz Home for the Aged, 1989—92, Ont. Swimming Pool Assn., Toronto, 1964; pres. cultural and edn. fund Latvian Nat. Fedn. Can., 2002—. Fellow Can. Soc. Landscape Architects (life), Am. Landscape Architects Soc., Am. Inst. Landscape Architects (internat. pres. 1969-71), Ont. Assn. Landscape Architects (emeritus, pres. 1977-78, Disting. Achievement award 1987), Latvian Nat. Fedn. Can. (pres. 2002-2003), Can. Latvian Bus. and Profl. Assn. (pres. 1971—), Latvian Nat. Fedn. Can., (pres. 2003), Bd. of Trade Club, Empire Club of Can. Mem. Progressive Conservative Party. Lutheran. Avocations: gardening, travel, golf. Office: Alexander Budrevics & Assoc 895 Don Mills Rd Ste 212 Toronto ON Canada M3C 1W3 Fax: 416-444-5208. E-mail: alex@budrevics.com.

BUDZINSKI, JAMES EDWARD, interior designer; b. Jan. 4, 1953; s. Edward Michael and Virginia (Caliman) B. Student, U. Cin., 1971-76. Mem. design staff Perkins & Wills Archs., Inc., Chgo., 1973-75, Med. Architectonics, Inc., Chgo., 1975-76; v.p. interior design Interior Environs., Inc., Chgo., 1976-78; pres. Jim Budzinski Design, Inc., Chgo., 1978-80; dir. interior design Robinson, Mills & Williams, San Francisco, 1980-87; dir. design, interior arch. Whisler Patri, San Francisco, 1987-90; v.p. design sales and mktg. Deepa Textiles, 1990-95; v.p. Workplace Studio One Workplace L. Ferrari, San Jose, Calif., 1997-2000, Strategic Envisioner, 2000—. Instr. design Harrington Inst. Design, Chgo.; cons. Chgo. Art Inst., Storwal Internat., Inc.; spkr. profl. confs. Designs include 1st Chgo. Corp. Pvt. Banking Ctr., 1st Nat. Bank Chgo. Monroe and Wabash Banking Ctr., 1978, IBM Corp., San Jose, Deutsche Bank, Frankfort, Crowley Maritime Corp., San Francisco, office for Brobeck, Phleger and Harrison, offices for chmn. bd. Fireman's Fund Ins. Cos., Nob Hill Club, Fairmont Hotel, San Francisco, offices for Cooley, Goodword, Castro, Huddleson, and Tatum, Palo Alto, Calif., offices for Pacific Bell Acctg. divsn., San Francisco, showroom for Knoll Internat., San Francisco, lobby, lounge TransAm. Corp. Hdqs., San Francisco, offices for EDAW, San Francisco, showroom for Steelcase, Inc., Bally of Switzerland, N.Am. Flagship store, San Francisco; corp. Hdqs. Next Inc., Redwood City, Calif., Schafer Furniture Design, Lobby Renovation 601 California, San Francisco, Bennedetti Furniture Inc. Furniture Design. Pres. No. Calif. chpt. Design Industries Found. for AIDS. E-mail: jbudzinski@oneworkplace.com.

BUDZINSKY, ARMIN ALEXANDER, investment banker; b. Steyr, Austria, Nov. 25, 1942; arrived in US, 1951, naturalized, 1957; s. Alexander Wladimir and Maria Gisella B.; m. Pamela Plimmer, Oct. 29, 1978 (div. 1992); children: Andrea, Natalie; m. Laura Martin, Mar. 11, 2000. AB, John Carroll U., 1964; MA. (NDEA fellow) Fulbright fellow, Rutgers U., 1969. Instr. in English Cleve. State U., 1969-72; corp. fin. cons. Citibank NA, N.Y.C., 1974-76, Dean Witter & Co., N.Y.C., 1976-77, Merrill Lynch Pierce Fenner & Smith, N.Y.C., 1977-83; v.p. corp. fin. Dunoco Corp., Houston, 1983; pres. Porcari Fearnow Capital Markets Group, Inc., Houston, 1985-86, Itec Securities Corp., Houston, 1985-86; v.p., dir. project fin., prin. Eppler, Guerin & Turner, Inc., Dallas, 1987—92; ptnr. Garland Group, 1992-93; sr. v.p., CFO Heard Energy Corp., 1993-98; pres. Archangel Diamond Corp., Vancouver, B.C., 1996-97, pres, CEO, 1997-98, chmn., 1997-98; exec. v.p., dir. United Am. eHealth Techs. Inc., Cambridge, Mass., 1998-2001; exec. v.p., CFO Decorize Inc., Springfield, Mo., 2002—. Mem. industry adv. com. N.Am. Security Administrs. Assn, Oil Investment Inst.; dirs. U. Chgo. Grad Sch. Bus. Alumni Assn. Home: 1413 S St Marys Ave Springfield MO 65804 E-mail: aab@albud.com.

BUE, CARL OLAF, JR., retired federal judge; b. Chgo., Mar. 27, 1922; s. Carl Olaf and Mabel Port (Shollar) B.; m. Mary Kathryn Waring, Dec. 27, 1948; children: Kathryn Anne, Richard Charles. AA, U. Chgo., 1942; student, U. Rome, Italy, 1945; PhB, Northwestern U., 1951; D of Jurisprudence, U. Tex., 1954. Bar: Tex. 1954. Assoc. firm Royston, Rayzor & Cook, Houston, 1954-58, mem. firm, 1958-70; U.S. dist. judge So. Dist. Tex. (Houston div.), 1970-87. Lectr. various law schs. and admiralty seminars in Tex. and other states. Contbr. articles to profl. jours. Served to capt., Adj. Gen. Dept. AUS, 1942-46, MTO. Recipient Good Citizenship medal Houston chpt. SAR, 1975, Tex. Supreme Ct. Justice Joe R. Greenhill award as outstanding jurist Mcpl. Cts. Assn., 1977, Northwestern U. Alumni Merit award for disting. profl. svc. in law, 1997; establishment at U. Tex. Sch. of Law of the Judge Carl. O. Bue Jr. Endowed Presdl. scholarship in law, 1988. Mem. Am., Fed., Tex., Houston Bar Assns., Maritime Law Assn. of U.S., Houston Philos. Soc. at Rice U., Alpha Delta Phi, Phi Alpha Delta. Republican. Lutheran. Home: 338 Knipp Rd Houston TX 77024-5044

BUECHE, WENDELL FRANCIS, agricultural products company executive; b. Flushing, Mich., Nov. 7, 1930; s. Paul D. and Catherine (McGraw) B.; m. Virginia M. Smith, June 14, 1952 (dec. May 12, 1992); children: Denise, Barbara, Daniel, Brian; m. Nancy Bird Jacobson, June 24, 1994; children: Meredith, Stuart, Julia. BSM.E., U. Notre Dame, 1952. With Allis-Chalmers Corp., 1952-88, dist. mgr., 1961-64, sales and mktg. mgr., 1964-69, group exec. v.p West Allis, Wis., 1973-76, exec. v.p. elec. groups, 1976-77, exec. v.p., chief adminstrv. and fin. officer, 1977-80, exec. v.p., head solids process equipment sector and fluids processing group, chief fin. officer, 1980-81, pres., chief operating officer, dir., 1981-83, pres., CEO, dir., 1984-86, chmn., 1986-88, ret., 1988; CEO IMC Global, Northbrook, Ill., 1993-97, chmn. bd. dirs., 1994-98, bd. dirs. Bd. dir. M&I Marshall Illsley Bank, M&I Corp.; advisor Am. Indsl. Ptnrs., LPP, Windpoint Ptnrs. Fund III, IV and V LP, K-B Ptnrs. I & II LP. Mem. council Med. Coll. Wis. 1987—, ongoing adv. coun., past chmn., U. Notre Dame. Mem.: TFI (past chmn.), Nat. Assn. Mfrs. (past dir.), The Chgo. Racquet Club, Longboat Key Club. Office: IMC Global 919 N Michigan Ave Ste 520 Chicago IL 60611-1602 E-mail: wfbueche@aol.com.

BUECHEL, WILLIAM BENJAMIN, lawyer; b. Wichita, Kans., July 27, 1926; s. Donald William and Bonnie S. (Priddy) B.; m. Theresa Marie Girard, Nov. 3, 1955; children: Sarah Ann, Julia Elaine. Student, U. Wichita, 1947-49; BS, U. Kans., 1951; LLB, 1954. Sole practice, Concordia, Kans., 1954-56; stockholder Paulsen, Buechel, Swenson, Uri & Brewer Chartered, Concordia, 1971-75; sec.-treas., 1975-77; pres., 1977-92; of counsel, 1993-95; ret. Bd. dirs. County Bank & Trust, Concordia, 1971-92, mem. trust and adminstrn. com. Citizens Nat. Bank, 1992—. Bd. dirs. Cloud County C.C. Found., 1983-89. Mem. ABA, Kans. Bar Assn. (mem. exec. coun. 1966-68, chmn. adv. sect. profl. ethics com. 1974-76), Cloud County Bar Assn. (pres. 1984-86), Elks, Moose, Rotary. Republican. Methodist.

BUECHLEIN, DANIEL MARK, archbishop; b. Jasper, Ind., Apr. 20, 1938; s. Carl and Rose (Blessinger) Buechlein. BA, St. Meinrad Coll., 1961; student, St. Meinrad Sch. Theology, 1961—64; Lic. Sacred Theology, Benedictine U. Sant' Anselmo, Rome, 1966. Ordained priest Roman Cath. Ch., 1964, consecrated bishop 1987, archbishop 1992. Asst. dean students St. Meinrad Coll., 1966—68, dir. spiritual formation, 1968—71; pres., rector St. Meinrad Sch. Theology, 1971—82, St. Meinrad Sch. Theology and St. Meinrad Coll., 1982—87; bishop Diocese of Memphis, 1987—92; archbishop Indpls., 1992—. Chmn. divsn. religion St. Meinrad Coll., 1967—71; mem. Archabbey Coun., 1967—87; formation com. Conf. of Major Superiors of Men USA, 1971—78; nat. steering com. for follow-up of Nat. Assembly Sem. Rectors and Ordinaries, 1983; com. on priestly formation Nat. Conf. Cath. Bishops, 1987—89, chmn., 1990—93, com. on marriage and family life, 1987—89, advisor doctrine com., com. on doctrine, 1989—93, adminstrv. com., 1990—93, budget com., bishop's emergency relief com., 1990—92, chmn. ad hoc com. to oversee use of Catechism of Cath. Ch., subcom. on pastoral message in abortion, 1994—, bd. dirs.; peritus Internat. Synod on Priestly Formation, Rome, 1990; bd. dirs. S.E. Regional Office for Hispanics Affairs, S.E. Pastoral Inst.; co-pres. Disciples of Christ-Roman Cath. Internat. Dialogue, 1995—. Co-author (with Bleichner and Leavitt): Preparing a Diocesan Priest: The Holistic Experience, 1987, Celibacy for the Kingdom, 1990, Commentary on a Survey of Priests Ordained Five to Nine Years, 1991; contbr. articles to profl. jours. Named Hon. chaplain, KC, Tenn., 1987. Mem.: Nat. Cath. Edn. Assn. (chmn. exec. com. sem. divsn. 1984—86), Theol. Edn. Assn. Mid-Am. (sec. 1972—74, 1980—82, v.p. 1974—76, pres. 1976—78, 1982—84), Midwest Assn. Theol. Schs. (sec.-treas. 1972—74, ptrd. 1974—75), Midwest Assn. Sem. Spiritual Dirs. (founding coord. 1971), Nat. Assn. Sem. Spiritual Dirs. (founding coord. 1972). Office: Archdiocese Indpls PO Box 1410 Indianapolis IN 46206*

BUECHLER, ELIZABETH JEAN, obstetrician-gynecologist; b. Derby, Conn., Dec. 5, 1954; d. Peter Robert and Mary Frances (Hartman) B.; m. Thomas O. Sagui, Mar. 3, 1979; children: Patrick, Samantha, Allison. BS, Pa. State U., 1974; MD, Jefferson Med. Coll., 1976. Diplomate Am. Bd. Ob-Gyn. Intern Presbyn. U. Pa. Med. Ctr., Phila., 1976-77; resident Beth Israel Hosp., Boston, 1977-80; pvt. practice Boston, 1981-85; chief dept. ob-gyn. Harvard Community Health Plan, Medford, Mass., 1986-91; dir. ob-gyn. Harvard Vanguard Med. Assocs., Boston, 1991—. Clin. instr. Harvard U. Med. Sch., Boston, 1981—. Fellow Am. Coll. Ob-Gyn.; mem. Am. Med. Women's Assn., Am. Soc. for Colposcopy and Cervical Pathology. Office: Harvard Vanguard Med Assocs 185 Dartmouth St Boston MA 02116 E-mail: elizabeth_buechler@vmed.org.

BUECHNER, CARL FREDERICK, minister, author; b. N.Y.C., July 11, 1926; s. Carl Frederick and Katherine (Kuhn) B.; m. Judith Friedrike Merck, Apr. 7, 1956; children: Katherine, Dinah, Sharman. Grad., Lawrenceville Sch., 1943; AB, Princeton U., 1947; BD, Union Theol. Sem., 1958; DD, Va. Episc. Sem., 1982, Lafayette U., 1984; LittD, Lehigh U., 1987, Cornell Coll., 1989; DD, Yale U., 1990, Sewanee U., 1993; LittD, Susquehanna U., Wake Forest U., 1998, Wake Forest U., 2000. Ordained minister United Presbyn. Ch. U.S.A., 1958. Tchr. English Lawrenceville Sch., 1948-53; tchr. creative writing, summer sessions N.Y.U., 1954-55; chmn. dept. religion Phillips Exeter Acad., 1958-67, sch. minister, 1960-67; William Belden Noble lectr. Harvard, 1969; Russell lectr. Tufts, 1971; Lyman Beecher lectr. Yale U., 1977; Harris lector Bangor Sem., 1979; Smyth lectr. Columbia Sem., 1981. Lectr. Trinity Inst., 1990. Author: A Long Day's Dying, 1950, The Seasons' Difference, 1952, The Return of Ansel Gibbs, 1958, The Final Beast, 1965, The Magnificent Defeat, 1966, The Hungering Dark, 1969, The Entrance to Porlock, 1970, The Alphabet of Grace, 1970, Lion Country, 1971, Open Heart, 1972, Wishful Thinking, 1973, Love Feast, 1974, The Faces of Jesus, 1974, Treasure Hunt, 1977, Telling the Truth, 1977, Peculiar Treasures, 1979, The Book of Bebb, 1979, Godric, 1980 (Pulitzer Prize finalist), The Sacred Journey, 1982, Now and Then, 1983, A Room Called Remember, 1984, Brendan, 1987, Whistling in the Dark, 1988, The Wizard's Tide, 1990, Telling Secrets, 1991, The Clown in the Belfry, 1992, Listening to Your Life, 1992, The Son of Laughter, 1993, The Longing for Home, 1996, On the Road with the Archangel, 1997, The Storm, 1998, The Eyes of the Heart, 1999, Speak What We Feel, 2001. Trustee Barlow Sch., 1965-71. With AUS, 1944-46. Recipient Irene Glascock Meml. intercollegiate poetry award, 1947; O'Henry prize for story The Tiger, 1955; Richard and Hinda Rosenthal award for the Return of Ansel Gibbs, 1958 Mem. Nat. Coun. Churches (com. on lit. 1954-57), Coun. Religion in Ind. Schs. (regional chmn. 1958-63), Presbytery No. New Eng., Century Assn., Univ. Club (N.Y.C.). Presbyterian. Home and Office: 3572 State Rt 315 Pawlet VT 05761-9753

BUECHNER, JACK W(ILLIAM), lawyer, government affairs consultant, educational association administrator; b. St. Louis, June 4, 1940; s. John Edward and Gertrude Emily (Richardson) B.; children from previous marriage: Patrick John, Terrence J.; m. Nancy Chanitz; 1 child, Charles Chanitz. BA, Benedictine Coll., 1962; JD, St. Louis U., 1965. Bar: Mo. 1965, U.S. Dist. Ct. (ea. dist.) Mo. 1965, D.C., 1998, U.S. Ct. Appeals (8th cir.) 1965, U.S. Ct. Appeals (D.C. cir.) 1998. Ptnr. Buechner, McCarthy, Leonard, Kaemmerer, Owen & Laderman, Chesterfield, Mo., 1965-93; mem. 100th-102d U.S. Congresses from 2d Mo. dist., 1987-91; dep. minority whip, 1989-90; vice-chmn. Rep. study group, pres. Internat. Rep. Inst., Washington, 1991-93; prin., dir. internat. svcs. The Hawthorn Group, Arlington, Va., 1993-95; ptnr. Manatt Phelps & Phillips, Washington, 1995—2001; pres., CEO, A Presdl. Classroom for Young Americans, 2002—; of counsel Schmeltzer, Aptaker and Shepard. State rep. 94th dist. Mo. Gen. Assembly, 1972-82, minority leader, 1974-78; mem. state adv. com. U.S. Commn. on Civil Rights, 1975-82; bd. dirs. Coun. Cmty. Democracies. Lay advisor St. Louis Med. Soc., 1989-92; Mo. Tourism Commn., 1976, 82-85; prin. Coun. for Excellence in Govt.; bd. dirs. Presdl. Classroom, 2000-. Recipient Meritorious Svc. award St. Louis Globe-Democrat, 1973, Legis. Achievement award St. Louis Police Officers, 1982, Pub. Svc. award Women's Polit. Caucus, Mo., Disting. Svc. award Cardinal Glennon Hosp., Mo., 1982, Nat. Security Leadership award Am. Security Coun. Found., 1988, 89, Family and Freedom award, Golden Bulldog award, 1987, 88, Guardian of Small Bus. award Nat. Fedn. Ind. Bus., 1987, 88, 90, 91, Enterprise award U.S. C. of C., 1988, 89, 90, Sound Dollar award, 1988, Eagle of Freedom award Am. Security Coun. Foun., 1990. Mem. Mo. Bar Assn., D.C. Bar Assn., Mo. Soc. Washington (pres.), Nat. Conf. State Socs. (1st v.p.), Ctr. Nat. Policy (bd. dirs. 1997—, bd. dirs. Alliance for responsible Cuba policy), Assn. Former Mems. of Congress (bd. dirs., v.p.), The Pericles Inst. (pres. 2001-), The Zorig Found., John Marshall Club (Outstanding Atty. award 1986), Lions, Phi Delta Phi. Republican. Episcopalian. Avocations: golf, reading, travel. Home: 1303 Altamira Ct Mc Lean VA 22102-2201 Office: Presdl Classroom 119 Oronoco Alexandria VA 22314-2015 also: Schmeltzer Aptaker and Shepard 2600 Virginia Ave NW Washington DC 20037 E-mail: jackb@presidentialclassroom.org.

BUECHNER, JOHN C. academic administrator; Dir. govtl. rels., then dir. pub. affairs U. Colo. System Ofice, Denver, until 1989; chancellor U. Colo., Denver, 1988-96, pres., 1996—2000, pres. emeritus, 2000—. Office: U Colo-Denver Office of Pres Campus Box 35 Boulder CO 80309-0035

BUECHNER, ROBERT WILLIAM, lawyer, educator; b. Syracuse, N.Y., Oct. 29, 1947; s. Donald F. and Barbara (Northrup) B.; m. Angela Marian Hustler, May 28, 1978; children: Julia Maria, Robert William Jr., Leslie Ann, James Bradley. BSE, Princeton U., 1969; JD, U. Mich., 1974. Bar: Ohio, 1974, Fla. 1974, U.S. Dist. Ct. (so. dist.) Ohio 1974, U.S. Tax Ct. 1974. Assoc. Frost & Jacobs, Cin., 1974-79; pres. Buechner, Haffer, O'Connell, Meyers & Healey Co., L.P.A., Cin., 1979—. Adj. prof. Salmon P. Chase Coll. Law, No. Ky., 1975-82; instr. Cin. chpt. Chartered Life Underwriters, 1976-96; lectr. Million Dollar Roundtable, Atlanta, 1981; prodr., host TV show Greater Cin. Bus. Rev., 1993—. Author: (with others) Why Universal Life, 1982, Prosper Through Tax Planning, 1982, Living Gangbusters, 1986, The 8 Pathways to Financial Success, 1987, 93, 98. Mem. planning divsn. Cin. Cmty. Chest, 1978-84; trustee Cin. Venture Assn., 1994-99, pres., 1997-98; trustee Cin. Country Day Sch., 1979-93, pres., 1990-93. Recipient Alumnus of Yr. award Cin. Country Day Sch., 1985, First winner of John Warrington Cmty. Svc. award, 1997. Mem. Cin. Bar Assn. (chmn. taxation sect. 1984-85), S.W. Ohio Tax Inst. (chmn. 1981-82), Cin. Assn. (trustee 1999—, pres. 2002—), Gyro Club (sec. 1982-83, v.p. 1999-2000), Princeton Club (pres. 1982-84). Republican. Methodist. Avocations: golf, tennis, bridge. Office: Buechner Haffer O'Connell Meyers Healey Co LPA 105 E 4th St Ste 300 Cincinnati OH 45202-4023 E-mail: rhuechner@bhomh.com.

BUECHNER, THOMAS SCHARMAN, artist, retired glass manufacturing company executive, museum director; b. Sept. 25, 1926; s. Thomas Scharman and Anne Evans (Lines) B.; m. Mary C. Hawkins, Sept. 15, 1949; children: Barbara Lines, Thomas Scharman, Matthew. Student, Princeton U., 1945, Ecole des Beaux Arts, Fontainebleau, 1946, Paris, 1947, Arts Students League, N.Y.C., 1946, 48, Institut voor Pictologie, Amsterdam, 1947. Designer Compañía de Fomento, San Juan, P.R., 1946; asst. display mgr. Met. Mus. Art, N.Y.C., 1949-51, tchr., 1949-51; dir. Corning Mus. Glass, N.Y., 1951-60, 75-80, pres., 1971-87; v.p., dir. cultural affairs Corning Glass Works, 1985-87, ret., 1987, cons., 1987—; faculty art sch. Bild-Werk, Fravenau, Germany, 1988—. Head dept. art Corning Community Coll., 1958-60; bd. dir. Bklyn. Mus.; chmn. Corning Glass Works Found., 1971-87; v.p. Steuben Glass, Corning, 1971-73, pres., 1973-82, chmn., 1982-85. Author: Glass Vessels in Dutch Painting of the 17th Century, 1952, Life and Work of Frederick Carder, 1952, Guide to the Collections of the Corning Museum of Glass, 1955, Guide to the Collections of the Brooklyn Museum, 1967, Norman Rockwell, Artist Illustrator, 1970, Arts of David Levine, 1979, Ogden Pleissner, 1984, How I Paint, 2000; portrait and landscape painter; one-man shows: Adler Gallery, N.Y.C., 1982, 84, Arnot Art Mus., 1985, 95, Heller Gallery, N.Y.C., 1989, Gallery M, Lindau, Germany, 1989, Gallery Nakama, Tokyo, 1990, 93, 96, O.K. Harris Gallery, N.Y.C., Schloss Weissenstein, Regen, Germany, 1996, Melberg Gallery, Charlotte, N.C., 2002, Principle Gallery, Alexandria, Va., 2002, West End Gallery, Corning, N.Y., 2002; represented in permanent collections Met. Mus. Art, Nat. Mus. Am. Art, Smithsonian Inst., Bklyn. Mus., Lincoln Ctr., Herbert F. Johnson Mus. Cornell U., Musée des Arts Decoratifs, Lausanne, Switzerland, Renwick Mus., Smithsonian, Washington, Corning Mus. of Glass, Corning, N.Y. Trustee Tiffany Found., Pilchuck Sch., Corning Mus. Glass, Corning Glass Works Found., Rockwell Mus., Arnot Art Mus. Arts of the Southern Finger Lakes; pres. Rockwell Mus. 1982-87, trustee 1987—. Recipient Forsythia award Bklyn. Bot. Garden, 1971, Gari Melchers medal Am. Artist fellows, 1971. Mem. Bklyn. Inst. Arts and Sci. (trustee 1971-72, pres. 1971-72), Nat. Collection Fine Arts. (commr. 1972-91). Clubs: Century Assn. Episcopalian. Studio: 10503B North Rd Corning NY 14830-3264

BUECKER, THOMAS ROBERT, museum curator; b. Lincoln, Nebr., Nov. 14, 1948; s. Robert Walter and Jeanette Lucille Buecker; m. Colleen Kay Buecker, Aug. 17, 1974; children: Michael, Anne. BA, U. Nebr., Kearney, 1973; MA, Chadron (Nebr.) State Coll., 1992. Curator Neligh Mills Hist. Site, Nebr. State Hist. Soc., Neligh, 1977-85, curator Ft. Robinson Mus. Crawford, 1985—. Author: Water-Powered Flour Mills of Nebraska, 1984, Fort Robinson and the American West, 1999, Fort Robinson and the American Century, 2002; co-author: The Crazy Horse Surrender Ledger, 1993. Recipient Herbert S. Schell award S.D. State Hist. Soc., 1996. Mem. Custer Battlefield Hist. and Mus. Assn., Pine Ridge Corral of Westerners, Coun. on Am.'s Mil. Past. Democrat. Methodist. Avocation: reading books on custer and little bighorn. Office: Ft Robinson Mus PO Box 304 Crawford NE 69339-0304

BUEHLER, EVELYN JUDY, poet; b. Chgo. d. Marzell William and Ida Mae Rubbia (Fields) Regulus; m. Henry Eric Buehler, Aug. 23, 1985; children: Ashley Leonard, Evelyn Judy. Student, Harold Washington Coll., Chgo. Author: Tales of Summer, 1998, Sunshine and Shadows, 2003; contbr. short stories to Daring to Dream, 1995, Tears of Fire, 1995, A Moment to Remember, Wisdom of the Ages, 1997, Mortal Thoughts, 1997, Calm Winds, 1997, To Have and to Hold, 1997, A Writer's Season, 1995, The Best Writers of 1995, Wordly Thoughts and Lyrics of Poetry, 1995, Millennium The Alpha The Omega, Silver Words and Golden Thoughts, Where Words Haven't Spoken; contbr. poetry to Today's Greatest Poems, Our Twentieth Century's Greatest Poems, Our World's Best Loved Poems, Our World's Most Beloved Poems, Night Skies in Winter, Worldly Thoughts, Lyrics of Poetry, Am. Poetry Anthology, Best New Poets of 1987, Poems That Will Live Forever, The Best Poems of the 90's, Whispers in the Wind, Outstanding Poets of 1994, The Songs of Poetry, At Day's End, Calm Fires, 1995, Mortal Words, 1995, Words of the Soul, 1996, Beginning of a New Dawn, 1996, A Time to Remember, 1996, The Best Writers of 1996, Tears of a Soul, 1997, The Isle of View, 1997, The Other Side of Midnight, 1997, Diamonds and Pearls, 1997, Today, Tomorrow and Beyond, 1997, Masquerade of Words, 1997, The Best Writers of 1997, Endless Skies of Blue, 1998, The Best Poems of 1998, 2000 Outstanding People of the 20th Century, 1998, Outstanding Poets of 1998, 1998, The Silence Within, 2002, God Bless America, 2002, Letters From The Soul, 2002, (e-book) Sunshine and Shadows, 2002, others; contbr. chpts. to books, poetry to books and articles to profl. publs., photographs to books. Named to Internat. Poetry Hall of Fame. Mem.: Internat. Soc. Poets (life). Democrat. Baptist. Avocations: gardening, bicycle riding, hiking, art. Home: 5658 S Normal Blvd Chicago IL 60621-2966 E-mail: Evelyn_Judy_Buehler@yahoo.com.

BUEHLER, JOHN WILSON, lawyer; b. Fresno, Calif., Aug. 16, 1950; s. John A. and Elizabeth (Wilson) B.; children: Nathaniel J., Christopher J. BA, U. Calif., Santa Cruz, 1973; JD magna cum laude, Willamette U., 1977. Bar: Oreg. 1977, U.S. Dist. Ct. Oreg. 1978, U.S. Ct. Appeals (9th. cir.) 1981. Law clk. to presiding justice U.S. Dist. Ct., Portland, Oreg., 1977-79; assoc. Bullivant, Wright et al, Portland, 1979-83; ptnr. Bullivant, Houser, Bailey, Pendergrass & Hoffman, Portland, 1984-95, Buehler & Buehler, Lake Oswego, 1995—. Bar examiner Bd. of Bar Examiners, Portland, Oreg., 1985-88 (chmn. 1987-88); mem. Oreg. Bd. Investigators, 2002—, vice chmn., 2003. Vol. atty. sr. law project City of Portland, 1980—. Mem. ABA, Oreg. Bar Assn., Multnomah Bar Assn, Def. Research Inst., Oreg. Assn. Def. Counsel., Internat. Assn. Spl. Investigation Units (counsel Oreg. chpt). Democrat. E-mail: buehlerjw@aol.com.

BUEHLER, MARTIN, hotel executive; b. Berne, Switzerland, May 24, 1947; s. Ernst Jakob and Marie (Studer) B.; m. Rosemarie Eugster, Feb. 29, 1968 (div.); children: Christiane, Mark. BBA, U. Berne, Switzerland, 1967; postgrad., Tufts U., 1978. Cert. travel agt., internat. mktg. auditor. Mgr. Tourist Info., Berne, 1972-75; exec. v.p. Inter-Europe-Hotels, Berne, 1979-84; pres. Dial Europe Inc., Miami, Fla., 1984-85; v.p. Europe Choice Hotels, Berne, 1985-88; exec. v.p. Hotel & Touristik Expert Inc., Berne, 1988-91; area pres., CEO Europe and Mid. East Park Plz. Hotels & Resorts Internat., Montreux, Switzerland, 1991-98; chmn. Boutique Hotels & Resorts Internat., Miami, 1999—, First Capital Hosp. Fin. Group, Miami, 1999—. Guest prof. Hosta, Lexsin, Switzerland, 1988-91, Ritz Hotel Sch., Switzerland, 1993, Fairleigh Dickinson U., 1994; adminstr. Internat. Jazz Festival, Berne, 1976-85. Author textbook: Hotel Marketing, 1989. Fellow Internat. Mktg. Audit Assn. Office: 1220 Washington Ave Miami FL 33139 E-mail: mbuehler@boutiquemair.com.

BUEHLER, THOMAS, psychotherapist, expressive therapist, artist; b. Zurich, Switzerland, Aug. 9, 1943; came to U.S 1989. s. Adolf and Margrit (Gredig) B.; m. Rosemarie Schiller, Apr. 19, 1995. MS, Med. Sch. U. Zurich, 1970. Cert. psychotherapist, Switzerland. Intern Accredited Swiss Hosp., 1969-75; multimedia artist Switzerland, 1973—. Psychotherapist and expressive therapist, 1979—; co-founding, training therapist Internat. Sch. of Interdisciplinary Studies, 1982-85, advisory bd. Swiss Assocs. of Psychotherapists, 1984-85; founding chmn. Cardon Found., 1991—, Cirio Found., N.Y., 1993— Author: Der Vulkan ist aufgebrochen, 1976; one man performance Roter Stadtkriecher, 1985, Red Broadway Crawler, 1985, one-man shows, New World Art Ctr., N.Y.C., 1999, The Depot Gallery, Montauk, N.Y., 1999, The Office Gallery, N.Y.C., 2001, 03. Mem. Internat. Assoc. of Artist Therapists, Nat. Expressive Therapy Assn., Swiss Assoc. of Psychotherapists. Avocations: piano, guitar, travel, wilderness, foreign cultures. Home: 140 Grand St #3WR New York NY 10013-3127 Office: Cirio Found Ste 1004 80 8th Ave New York NY 10011

BUEHLER, THOMAS LEE, lawyer, educator; b. Highland, Ill., Jan. 9, 1948; s. Leo Thomas and Jeanne H. Buehler; m. Marsha Anne Centner, June 12, 1970; children: Jennifer Lee, Camilla Jeanne. AB, Xavier U., 1970; JD, U. Ky., 1975. Bar: Ohio 1975, U.S. Dist. Ct. (so. dist.) Ohio 1975. Atty. U.S. Shoe Corp., Cin., 1975-77, asst. sec., 1977-83, asst. sec., assoc. gen. counsel, 1983-87, deputy gen. counsel, 1987-95; pres. Thomas Food Equipment, Inc., Traverse City, Mich., 1996—. Adj. assoc. prof. econs. and indsl. rels. Xavier U., Cin., 1975-86; adj. prof. law Salmon P. Chase Coll. Law No. Ky. U., 1995. Author: Selected Cases on Labor Problems, 1986, Selected Cases on Business Regulation, 1982, Selected Cases on Collective Bargaining, 1983. Served to 1st lt., U.S. Army, 1971-73. Mem. Ohio Bar Assn., Cin. Bar Assn., Am. Corp. Counsel Assn. (bd. dirs., sec. Cin. chpt. 1983—. pres. 1985), Am Soc. Corp. Secs. (treas. Cin. chpt. 1988—), Antique and Classic Boat Soc. (vice comdr. Cin. chpt. 1990—). Republican. Roman Catholic. Home: PO Box 196 Omena MI 49674-0182 also: 4100 Omena Point Rd Omena MI 49670 Office: Thomas Food Equipment Inc 1767 Barlow St Traverse City MI 49686-4722

BUEHLMEIER, HARRY SCOTT See GORDON, SCOTT

BUEHRLE, MARK, baseball player; b. St. Charles, Mo., Mar. 23, 1979; Pitcher Chgo. White Sox, 2000—. Office: Chgo White Sox 333 W 35th St Chicago IL 60616

BUEL, RICHARD VAN WYCK, JR., history educator, writer, editor; b. Morristown, NJ, July 22, 1933; s. Richard Van Wyck Sr. and Frances Worthington (Thompson) B.; m. Joy Evelyn Margaret Day, June 5, 1964 (dec. Apr. 1987); m. Marilyn Ellman Frankel, July 18, 1992; 1 child, Margaret Alexandra. AB, Amherst Coll., 1955; A.M., Harvard U., 1957, PhD in Am. History, 1962. Tchg. fellow in history Harvard U., Cambridge, Mass., 1958-62; asst. prof. history Wesleyan U., Middletown, Conn., 1962-69, assoc. prof., 1969-75, prof., 1975—2002, emeritus prof., 2002—, chmn. history dept., 1978-81. Ray A. Billington vis. prof. U.S. history Occidental Coll., 1999-00. Author: Securing the Revolution, 1972, Dear Liberty, 1980 (Round Table of Am. Revolution award 1981), (with Joy D. Buel) The Way of Duty, 1984 (Colonial Dames of Am. Book award 1985), In Irons, 1998 (Fraunces Tavern Mus. Book award 1999) assoc. editor History and Theory, 1970-91; contbr. articles to profl. jours., chpts. to books. Bd. dirs. No. Middlesex United Fund, Middletown, Conn., 1965-68; mem. Bd. Fin., Haddam, Conn., 1972-74 Fellow Charles Warren Ctr., Harvard U., 1966-67, Am. Coun. Learned Socs., 1966-67, 74-75, NEH, 1985; Guggenheim Found., 1986; jr. humanist fellow NEH, 1971-72; John Carter Brown fellow, 1986. Mem. Conn. Acad. Arts and Scis. (v.p. 1975-81), Am. Hist. Assn., Inst. Early Am. History and Culture, Soc. History Early Republic, Orgn. Am. Historians, Am. Antiquarian Soc., New Eng. Hist. Assn. (v.p. 1991, pres. 1992), Assn. Study Conn. History, Conn. Coord. Com. for Promotion History (pres. 2001—), Pettipaug Yacht Club (rear commodore 1984-86, vice-commodore 1986-88, commodore 1988-90), Conn. Hist. Commn., Conn. Humanities Coun., Acorn Club, Phi Beta Kappa. Avocation: dinghy racing. Home: 55 N Main St Essex CT 06426-1073 Office: Wesleyan Univ Dept History Middletown CT 06459-0002

BUELL, BRUCE TEMPLE, lawyer; b. Pueblo, Colo., Mar. 18, 1932; s. Jewett C. and Eva Lorraine (Allen) B.; m. Joan Carol Souders, June 20, 1953; children: Alan D., Susan L. Buell, Bonnie L. Iten. AB, Princeton U., 1953; postgrad., Harvard Law Sch., 1953-54, George Washington U. Law Sch., 1955-57; LLB, U. Denver, 1958. Bar: Colo. Asst. trust dept. Cen. Bank & Trust Co., Denver, 1957-58; assoc. Holland & Hart, Denver, 1958-64, ptnr. Colorado Springs and Denver, Colo., 1964-96; atty. pvt. practice, Colorado Springs, Colo., 1996—. Bd. dirs., counsel Jefferson Bank & Trust, Lakewood, Colo., 1971-76; counsel, sec. Colo. Bus. Devel. Corp., Denver, 1965-83; gen. counsel Colo. Bankers Assn., Denver, 1961-85. Pres. Colo. Lawyer Trust Account Found., Denver, 1982-85, 88-89, Arvada (Colo.) Hist. Soc., 1974-75; chmn. adv. coun. Arvada Ctr. for Arts, 1978-79; dir. North Jeffco Recreation and Pk. Dist., Arvada, 1976-80; trustee, chmn. Presbytery of Denver Trust Fund, 1983-85; trustee, sec.-treas. Viola Vestal Coulter Found., 1964—, pres., 1998—; trustee Edmondson Found., 1996—, v.p., 2000—; trustee Pikes Peak Cmty. Found., 1998—; bd. dirs., v.p. Samaritan Counseling Ctr., Colorado Springs, 1991-96; mem. Colo. Forum, Denver, 1989-93. Served to capt. USNR, 1954-76. Recipient Vol. of Yr. award Denver Bar Assn., 1982, Man of Yr. award Arvada C. of C., 1983, Bruce T. Buell award Colo. Lawyer Trust Acct. Found., 1991, U. Denver Law Sch. Professionalism award, 1995. Fellow Colo. Bar Found.; mem. ABA, Colo. Bar Assn., El Paso County Bar Assn. (treas. 2000-2002), Colorado Springs Estate Planning Coun., Winter Night Club (pres. 1996-97). Presbyterian. Avocations: tennis, music, prison ministry, church work. Home: 2512 Rigel Dr Colorado Springs CO 80906-1031 Office: Buell & Ezell LLP 118 S Wahsatch Ave Ste 210 Colorado Springs CO 80903-3679 E-mail: buell-law@msm.com.

BUELL, DEXTER, artist, sculptor; b. Seattle, 1960; BS in Art magna cum laude, U. Wash., 1984; MFA in Sculpture, Yale U., 1984. Asst. prof. sculpture Coll. of Charleston, S.C., 1989-91; asst. to artists Alice Aycock, Mel Kendrick and Antony Gormley, 1991-93; asst. to artist Chuck Close, 1996-97. Artist-in-residence Summer Sch. Music and Art Yale U., Norfolk, Conn., 1988; vis. critic art, architecture and ecology Sch. Art Yale U., New Haven, 1990; lectr. Arch. Ctr. Clemson (S.C.) U., 1991; resident Ucross (Wyo.) Found., 1995; adj. instr. photography Raritan Valley C.C., Somerville, NJ, 1997; vis. critic Cooper Union, N.Y.C., 1997, adj. instr. photography, 98; lectr. Maine Coll. Art, Portland, 1997, queens Coll. Grad. Fine Arts CUNY, 1998. One-woman shows include William Halsey Gallery Coll. Charleston, 1990, Nexus Contemporary Art Ctr., Atlanta, 1992, A.R.T. inc., N.Y.C., 1998, exhibited in group shows at Yale U., 1989, S.C. State U., Columbia, 1992, U. Tenn., Knoxville, 1992, Artists Space, N.Y.C., 1992, Ohio Theater, 1998, A.R.T. inc., 1999, Ex-Teresa Mus., Mexico City, 1999, Art & Idea, 1999, Represented in permanent collections Denver Art Mus., work reviewed in various publs. Recipient award, Louis Comfort Tiffany Found., 1997; fellow in visual arts, S.C. Arts Commn., 1991—92, fellow in video art, N.Y. Found. Arts, 1998, faculty R & D grantee, Coll. Charleston, 1990—91. Mem.: Phi Beta Kappa.

BUELL, EDWARD RICK, II, lawyer; b. Des Moines, Jan. 28, 1948; s. Edward Rick and Betty-Jo (Heffron) B.; B.S. with high honors, Mich. State U., 1969; J.D. magna cum laude, U. Mich., 1972; children— Erica Colleen, Edward Rick III. Bar: D.C. 1973, Calif. 1975; cert. specialist in taxation law, Calif. Assoc. firm Arent, Fox, Kintner, Plotkin & Kahn, Washington, 1972-74, Brobeck, Phlegher & Harrison, San Francisco, 1974-77; ptnr. Winokur, Schoenberg, Maier & Zang, San Francisco, 1977-81; ptnr. Buell & Berner, San Francisco, 1981— . Mem. ABA, San Francisco Bar Assn., Order of Coif. Contbr. articles to legal jours. Home: 50 Stewart Dr Belvedere Tiburon CA 94920-1323

BUELL, MARK PAUL, lawyer; b. St. Petersburg, Fla., Mar. 9, 1951; s. Harold E. and Jeane Charlotte (Russell) B.; m. Ellen Courtney Rendall, Apr. 28, 1984; children: Mary Ellen, Johnston Rodd, Rendall Jeane. BS, U. Fla., 1973, JD, 1976. Bar: Fla. 1976, U.S. Ct. Appeals (5th and 11th cirs.), U.S. Dist. Ct. (mid., so. and no. dists.) Fla. Assoc. Shackleford, Farrior, Stallings & Evans, P.A., Tampa, Fla., 1976-82, shareholder, 1982-90, Schropp, Buell & Elligett, P.A., Tampa, 1990—. Mem. Hillsborough County Bar Assn. (pres. young lawyers sect. 1981-82, pres. 1992-93, chmn. eminent domain com. 1993-94), Fla. Bar (young lawyers bd. govs. 1981-87, vice chmn. eminent domain com. 1995-97, bd. govs. 1997-2001, bd. cert. civil trial lawyer and bus. litigation law), Am. Bd. Trail Advocates (pres. 2003 Tampa Bay chpt.) Office: Schropp Buell & Elligett PA 3003 Azeele St Ste 100 Tampa FL 33609

BUELOW, GEORGE JOHN, musicologist, educator; b. Chgo., Mar. 31, 1929; s. George J. and Florence (Cook) B. Mus.B., Chgo. Mus. Coll., 1950, Mus.M., 1951; postgrad., U. Hamburg, Germany, 1953-54; PhD, N.Y. U., 1961. Instr. music history Chgo. Conservatory, 1959-61; from asst. prof. to asso. prof. musicology U. Calif., Riverside, 1961-68; prof., chmn. dept. music U. Ky., 1968-69; prof., dir. grad. program in music Rutgers U., New Brunswick, N.J., 1969-77; prof. musicology Ind. U., 1977-98. Mem. Commn. Mixte Internat. Inventory Musical Sources; co-chmn. Internat. Johann Mattheson Symposium, Wolfenbüttel, Fed. Republic Germany, 1981 Author: Thorough-bass Accompaniment According to J.D. Heinichen, 1966, 3d edit., 1992, Johann Mattheson's Opera, Cleopatra, in Das Erbe deutscher Musik, vol. 69, 1975, The Ariadne auf Naxos by Hofmannsthal and Strauss, 1975, Man and Music: The Late Baroque, vol. 4, 1993; Am. editor: ACTA Musicologica, 1967-86; editor: Coll. Music Soc.'s Symposium, 1970-71; mem. exec. com. The New Grove Dictionary of Music and Musicians, 1971-80; editor: UMI Research Press Studies in Musicology, 1977-89; mem. nat. adv. bd. Die Musik in Geschichte und Gegenwart, 1990-98; contbr. articles profl. jours; co-editor: New Mattheson Studies, 1983, Musicology and Performance Paul Henry Lang, 1997. Mem. German nat. screening com. Fulbright-Hays Program, 1993-97. Guggenheim fellow, 1967, Rutgers Rsch. Coun. fellow, 1974-75; Fulbright scholar Germany, 1954-55; Festa musicologica: Essays in Honor of George J. Buelow, 1995. Mem. Am. Musicol. Soc., Internt. Musicol. Socs. (mem. direktorium 1987-97), Royal Mus. Assn., Am. Bach Soc. (pres. bd. dirs. 1987—), Am. Handel Soc. (v.p., bd. dirs. 1989-94). Home: 2935 N Bankers Dr Bloomington IN 47408-1021 E-mail: Buelow@indiana.edu.

BUENDIA, IMELDA BERNARDO, clinical director, physician; b. Iloilo City, The Philippines, Nov. 12, 1944; d. Carlos P. and Coleta (De la Cruz) Bernardo; m. Arsenio G. Buendia, June 5, 1971; children: Mary Elaine, Joseph Carlo, Adrian Cesar. BS, U. The Philippines, 1964, MD, 1969. Diplomate Am. Bd. Family Practice. Resident in pediats. Philippine Gen. Hosp., Manila, 1969-71; resident in family practice St. Michael's Hosp., Milw., 1971-75; med. officer Talihina (Okla.) Hosp., 1975-78, Wewoka (Okla.) Indian Clinic, 1978-92, clin. dir., 1992-96; med. officer El Reno Indian Clinic, 1996—, clin. dir., 1997—. Active Phil-Am. Civic Orgn., Oklahoma City, 1978—. Recipient Dir. Excellence award USPHS, 1993. Fellow: Am. Acad. Family Physicians; mem.: Philippine Med. Assn. Okla. (treas. 1989, sec. 1990, 2000, pres.-elect 1994, pres. 1995). Home: 2105 Wyckham Pl Norman OK 73072-3042 Office: 1621A E Highway 66 El Reno OK 73036-5769

BUENO, OTAVIO AUGUSTO, philosopher, educator; b. Santos, São Paulo, São Paulo, Brazil, Feb. 27, 1970; s. Luiz Fernando and Lais Graci Bueno; m. Patricia Reis Maragliano, June 22, 1996. BA in Philosophy, U. São Paulo, 1993, MA in Philosophy, 1996; PhD, U. Leeds, Eng., 1999. Tchg. asst. dept. philosophy U. São Paulo, 1990-94; tutor, rsch. fellow U. Leeds, 1996-99, lectr. sch. philosophy, rsch. fellow, 1999-2000; lectr. dept. philosophy York (Eng.) U., 1999-2000; asst. prof. dept. philosophy Calif. State U., Fresno, 2000—02, U. SC, Columbia, 2002—. Reviewer Mathematical Reviews, 1995—. Contbr. articles to profl. jours. Scholar Com. of Vice-Chancellors and Principals of the Universities of the United Kingdom, 1996-99, rsch. grant Nat. Sci. Found., 2002—; Tetley-Lupton scholar U. Leeds, 1996-99. Mem. Philosophy of Sci. Assn., Brit. Soc. Philosophy of Sci., Can. Philos. Assn. Avocations: contemporary literature, history of art. Office: Dept Philosophy Univ South Carolina Columbia SC 29208

BUENO, PABLO CESAR, aeronautical engineer, educator; b. Bogota, D.C., Colombia, May 25, 1977; s. Jaime Otoniel Bueno and Lorena Restrepo. BS in Aero. Engring., The USAF Acad., Colorado Springs, Colo., 1998; MS in Engring., U. Tex., 2002. Cert. aero. engr., Consejo Profesional Nacional de Ingenierías Eléctrica, Mecánica, 1998; glider instruction pilot Colombian Civil Aero. Authority, 1999, lic. glider pilot Colombian Civil Aero. Authority, 1999, cert. tech. specialist flight instr. Colombian Civil Aero. Authority, 1999. Quality assurance dir. Aeroindustrias Leaver y Cia. S.A., Bogota, Colombia, 1998—99; lectr. dept. aero. engring. Universidad de San Buenaventura, Bogota, Colombia, 1998—99; rsch. asst. Ctr. for Aeromechanics Rsch., U. Tex.tin, Austin, Tex., 2000—; tchg. asst. dept. aeromechanics rsch. U. Tex., Austin, Tex., 2001, asst. instr. dept. aerospace engring., 2003—. Univ. liaison with Colombian Air Force and Nat. Police Universidad de San Buenaventura, Bogota, D.C., Colombia, 1999; contbg editor AIAA Student Jour., Austin, Tex., 2001—02; soaring instr. pilot - competition aerobatics team 94 Flying Tng. Squadron, USAF, Colo., 1996—98. Contbr. Pres. and founder Colombian Student Assn. - The U. of Tex. at Austin, Austin, Tex., 2001. Cadet 1st class USAF, 1994—98. Decorated numerous mil. awards USAF. Mem.: Am. Soc. Engring. Edn. (membership coord. 2001—02, treas. 2002), Asociacion Pro-Agencia Espacial Colombiana, Am. Phys. Soc., AIAA. Avocations: flying, motorsports, soccer.

BUENO DE MESQUITA, BRUCE JAMES, political science educator; b. N.Y., Nov. 24, 1946; s. Abraham and Clara (Pieniek) B.; m. Arlene Carol Steiner, Aug. 11, 1968; children: Erin, Ethan, Gwen. BA, Queens Coll., 1967; MA, Univ. Mich., 1968, PhD, 1971; DHL, U. Groningen, 1999. Asst. prof. Mich. State Univ., East Lansing, 1971-73; from asst. prof. to prof. Univ. Rochester, Rochester, N.Y., 1973-86; sr. fellow, prof. Stanford Univ., Stanford, Calif., 1986—; dir. Policon, Washington, 1981-89, Decision Insight Inc., N.Y., 1989—; Silver prof. NYU, NYC, 2002—. Author: The Wartrap, 1981, War and Reason, 1992, Principles of International Politics, 2000, 2d edit., 2003, Trial of Ebenezer Scrooge, 2001, Logic of Political Survival, 2003. Bd. advisors James Baker Inst. Rice Univ., 1997—. Recipient Guggenheim fellow, Guggenheim Found., 1978, Karl Deutsch award Internat. Studies Assn., 1985, Alumni star award Queens Coll., 1998. Mem. AAAS, Internat. Studies Assn. (pres. 2002-03), Am. Polit. Sci. Assn. (coun. mem. 2002-03), Peace Sci. Soc. Avocations: squash, border war ballads. Office: Hoover Institution Stanford Univ Stanford CA 94305

BUERGENTHAL, THOMAS, international judge, educator; b. Lubochna, Slovakia, May 11, 1934; came to U.S., 1951, naturalized, 1957; s. Mundek and Gerda (Silbergleit) B.; children: Robert, John, Alan; m. Marjorie J. Bell, 1983; stepchildren: Sebastian, Cristina. BA, Bethany Coll., 1957, LLD, 1981; JD, NYU, 1960; LLM, Harvard U., 1961, SJD, 1968; dr.jur. (hon.), U. Heidelberg, 1986; dr. jur. (hon.), Free U. of Brussels, 1997; LLD, SUNY, Buffalo, 2000, Am. U., 2002, U. Minn., 2003. Bar: N.Y. 1961, D.C. 1983, U.S. Supreme Ct. 1982. Instr. law U. Pa., 1961-62; from asst. prof. to prof. SUNY, Buffalo, 1962-75; vis. prof. U. Tex., Austin, 1975-76, prof., 1976-77, Fulbright and Jaworski prof., 1977-80; judge Inter-Am. Ct. Human Rights, 1979-91, pres., 1985-87; dean, prof. law Am. U., Washington, 1980-85; disting. prof. law and human rights Emory U. Sch. Law, 1985-86, I.T. Cohen prof. of human rights, 1987-89; Lobingier prof. comparative law and jurisprudence George Washington U., Washington, 1989-2000, Lobingier prof. emeritus, 2000—; judge Adminstrv. Tribunal, Inter-Am. Devel. Bank, 1989-94, pres., 1993-94. Mem. UN Human Rights Commn., 1995—99, Claims Resolution Tribunal for Dormant Accounts in Switzerland, 1998—2002, vice-chmn., 1999—2000; judge Internat. Ct. of Justice, 2000—; adv. com. Restatement (3d) of the Fgn. Rels. Law of U.S.; chmn. human rights com. U.S. Nat. Commn. for UNESCO, 1976—79; U.S. rep. UNESCO Human Rights Working Group, 1977—78; U.S. expert UN Interregional Expert Meeting on Crime Prevention and Control, 1978; mem. adv. bd. Pres. Holocaust Commn., 1978—80; v.p. UNESCO Congress on Tchg. of Human Rights, 1978; mem. UN Truth Commn. for El Salvador, 1992—93, U.S. Holocaust Meml. Coun., 1996—2001, chmn. com. on conscience, 1997—2000. Author: Law-Making in the International Civil Aviation Organization, 1969; (with L.B. Sohn) International Protection of Human Rights, 1973; (with J.V. Torney) International Human Rights and International Education, 1976, International Law and the Helsinki Accord, 1977; (with R.E. Norris) Human Rights: The Inter-Am. System, 1982; (with D. Shelton) Protecting Human Rights in the Americas, 1982, 4th edit., 1995; (with S. Murphy) Public International Law in a Nutshell, 3d edit., 2002, (with D. Shelton and D. Stewart)International Human Rights in a Nutshell, 3d edit., 2002; (with Grossman and Nikken) Manual Internacional de Derechos Humanos, 1990; (with Kiss) La Protection Internationale des Droits de l'Homme, 1991; contbr. articles to profl. jours. Recipient Pro-Humanitas Ring, West-Ost Kulturwerk, Fed. Republic of Germany, 1978, Disting. Svc. in Legal Edn. award NYU Law Sch. Assn., 1987, Wolfgang Friedmann Meml. award Columbia U. Law Sch., 1989. Mem. Am. Law Inst., Am. Soc. Internat. Law (v.p. 1980-82, hon. pres. 2001—, Goler T. Butcher medal for excellence in internat. human rights 1997, Manley Hudson medal 2002), Coun. Fgn. Rels., Inter-Am. Inst. Human Rights (pres. 1980-92, hon. pres. 1992—). Office: Internat Ct Justice Peace Palace 2517 KJ The Hague Netherlands Fax: (31-70) 302-2464. E-mail: t.buergenthal@icj-cij.org.

BUERKLE, JACK VINCENT, sociologist, educator; b. West Frankfort, Ill., Aug. 9, 1923; s. Henry Adam and Clemence (Henderson) B.; m. Martha Louise Edwards; children: Stephen Vincent, Melanie Lake. BA, U. Ill., 1948, MA, 1949; PhD, U. Ia., 1954. Asst. prof. Lake Forest Coll., 1954-55; asst. prof. Yale, 1955-60; mem. faculty Temple U., 1960—, prof. sociology, 1963—, chmn. dept., 1963-71; sr. v.p. The French Riviera, Inc., Phila., 1994—. Vis. prof. Der Wirtschaftshochschule, Mannheim, West Germany, 1966-67; host Jazz Encounters, Sta. WRTI, Phila., 1987—, Jazz Encounters Today, 1992—; co-host Crossover, 1998—. Author: Bourbon Street Black, 1973; assoc. editor: Jour. Marriage and the Family, 1982— ; Contbr. articles to profl. publs. Served with AUS, 1943-46. Mem. Am. Sociol. Assn., Am. Psychol. Assn., Eastern Sociol. Soc., Institut International de Sociologie, Sigma Xi. Presbyn. (ruling elder). Club: Corinthian Yacht of Cape May (N.J.) (commodore). Home: 526 Revere Rd Merion Station PA 19066-1033 Office: Temple Univ Dept Sociology Philadelphia PA 19122

BUERMANN, PETER BRUCE, psychologist, program administrator; b. Mineola, N.Y., July 3, 1938; s. Ralph and Marjorie Elizabeth (Peters) Buermann; m. Dorothy Richardson, June 15, 1963; children: Jennifer Beth, Amy Marie, Andrea Lee. BS in Edn., Upsala Coll., 1959; EdM, Rutgers U., 1961, EdS, 1969; EdD, Temple U., 1984. Tchr. Atlantic Highlands (N.J.) High Sch., 1959-60, Clinton Place Jr. High Sch., Newark, 1961-62; psychologist South River (N.J.) Schs., 1963-64; dir. spl. svcs. Ewing Twp. Schs., Trenton, N.J., 1964-78; exec. dir. Project Child Infant & Presch. Program, Trenton, 1973-93; dir. student personnel svcs. Mercer County Spl. Svcs., Trenton, 1978-93; project mgr. Phila. Child Guidance Ctr., 1993-95; program adminstr. Children's Home Soc. of N.J., 1995—98; ptnr. Buermann Assocs., Newtown, 1998—2002; pvt. practice, 2003—. Fellow: Acad. for Cerebral Palsy and Devel. Medicine; mem.: Assn. for Child Psychology and Psychiatry, Soc. for Pediat. Psychology. Avocation: travel. Home: 19 S Chancellor St Newtown PA 18940-2107

BUESCHEN, ANTON JOSLYN, physician, educator; b. Toledo, June 7, 1940; s. Robert F. and Mary J. (Joslyn) B.; m. Norma Jean McClanahan, Sept. 5, 1964; children— Anton, Elaine. Student, Va. Mil. Inst., 1958-61; MD, U. Va., 1965. Diplomate: Am. Bd. Urology. Intern in surgery Vanderbilt U., 1965-66, asst. resident in surgery, 1966-67; resident in urology Ind. U., Indpls., 1969-72; practice medicine specializing in urology Birmingham, Ala., 1973—; instr. urology Tulane U. Sch. Medicine, 1972-73; asst. prof. div. urology dept. surgery U. Ala., Birmingham, 1973-75, assoc. prof., 1975-79, prof., 1979—, dir. div. urology, 1975-95, 99—; chief urology sect. Children's Hosp., Birmingham, 1978-86. Pres. U. Ala. Health Svcs. Found., 2001—. Contbr. numerous articles on urology to profl. jours. Served with M.C. U.S. Army, 1967-69. Mem. ACS, AMA (Billings Gold medal 1978), AAUP, Am. Urol. Assn. (bd. dirs., 2003—), Am. Urol. Assn. Southeastern Sect. (sec. 1997-2000, pres.-elect 2000-01, pres. 2001-2002, bd. dirs. 1994-2003), Am. Found. Urologic Disease (bd. dirs. 2000—), Am. Assn. Clin. Urologists, Soc. Univ. Urologists, Birmingham Urology Club, Jefferson County Med. Soc., Soc. for Pediatric Urology, Soc. Urologic Oncology, So. Med. Assn. (chmn. urology sect. 1987), Med. Assn. Ala. Office: U Ala Div Urology University Sta Birmingham AL 35294-0001

BUESCHER, THOMAS PAUL, labor market analyst; b. Cleve., May 16, 1949; s. Victor Paul and Geraldine Juel (Durkin) B.; m. Pamela Ann Pisciotta, Jan. 29, 1977; 1 child, Brittany Beth. BBA, Kent State U., 1975. Guest instr. for exec. MBA program Cleve. State U.; trustee IAPES Found. Corp. Author: (analysis report for nat. league of cities) Demographic Analysis of the Targeted Job Tax Credit program for Cleve., 1985. Mem. allocations panel Fedn. of Cath. Cmty. Svcs., 1987-92; mem. Local Welfare Reform Panel for Congress, 1987, Cleve. area Gov.'s Regional Econ. Adv. Bd., 1992—, Cleve. Area Devel. Corp. Bd., 1994—; mem. consortium to develop a nat. inst. Labor Market Info.; chmn. Initiative V task force, mem. adv. com. Cleve. Pub. Schs., 1988-93; mem. Am.'s Labor Market Info. Sys. Tng. Inst. Consortium. Mem. Internat. Assn. Pers. in Employment Security (Ohio pres. 1988, internat. v.p. 1993-94, award of merit 1989, inducted into Hall of Fame 1990, internat. pres.-elect 1994-95, internat. pres. 1995—), Am. Labor Market Info. Sys. Tng. Inst. Consortium, I.A.P.E.S-.(Internat. Assn. of Personnel in Employmet Security.), (mem. profl. devel. program revision team). Democrat. Avocations: volleyball, softball, golf, tennis. Home: 464 Calverton Pl Brunswick OH 44212-1820 Office: Ohio Dept job and family services 5739 Chevrolet Blvd Cleveland OH 44130-1414

BUESSELER, JOHN AURE, ophthalmologist, management consultant; b. Madison, Wis., Sept. 30, 1919; s. John Xavier and Gerda Pernille (Aure) B.; m. Cathryn Anne Hansen, Dec. 26, 1959; 1 child, John McGlone. PhB, U. Wis., 1941, MD, 1944; MBA, U. Mo., 1965. Intern Cleve. City Hosp., 1944-45; resident U. Pa. Hosp., 1948-51; practice medicine specializing in ophthalmology Madison, 1953-59; prof., founding chief ophthalmology U. Mo., Columbia, 1959-66, chmn. dept. surgery, 1960-61; exec. officer Mo. Crippled Children's Service, 1967-70; exec. dir. Kansas City Gen. Hosp. and Med. Ctr., 1969-70; founding dean Tex. Tech U. Sch. Medicine, Lubbock, 1970-73, founding v.p. health affairs Univ. Complex, 1970-75, prof. dept. ophthalmology, prof. health orgn. mgmt., 1971-98, founding chmn. dept. health orgn. mgmt., 1971—75, prof. grad. sch. faculty, 1972-80, chmn. dept. ophthalmology, 1973-75; adj. prof. bus. adminstrn. Coll. Bus. Tex. Tech., Lubbock, 1992-98. Univ. prof. (disting. and multidisciplinary) Univ. Complex, 1973-98; founding v.p. health scis., founding CEO Tex. Tech. Univ. Health Scis. Ctr., 1971-74; pres. Radiol. Testing Lab., Inc., Madison, 1956-59; dir. House of Vision, Inc., Chgo., 1973-82; v.p. Madison Radiation Ctr., Inc., 1956-59; cons. NASA, mem. space medicine adv. group on devel. Orbiting Space Lab., Washington, 1963-66; cons. AEC, mem. Assn. Midwestern Univs.-Argonne (Ill.) Nat. Lab. biology com., 1965-69; cons. to pres. Argonne Univs. Assn., Chgo., 1967-68; comdr. 94th Gen. Hosp., U.S. Army Res., Mesquite, Tex., 1973-75; co-founder, incorporator, bd. dirs., past pres. Joint Commn. on Allied Health Pers. in Ophthalmology, Inc.; mem. Residency Rev. Com. for Ophthalmology, 1974-80, chmn., 1978-80; sr. cons., CEO, founder Health Orgn. Mgmt. Sys. Internat., 1978—; co-founder, founding chmn., chmn. bd. dirs. Tex. Aviation Heritage Found., Inc., 1997-99; co-founder, founding chmn., chmn. com. on regional bus., econ. and environ. devel. Lubbock Econs. Coun., 1996-99. Contbr. articles to profl. jours. Served to capt. AUS, World War II, ETO; to maj. USAF, Korea; to col. USAR, Vietnam. Decorated Air medal with cluster, Legion of Merit; recipient Gold

Medallion award for disting. achievement in ophthalmology Mo. Ophthal. Soc., 1967, Tex. Tech. U. Bd. Regents Resolution of Congratulations, 1973, Cert. of Citation Tex. Ho. of Reps., 1973, 87, Disting. Alumnus citation U. Wis. Sch. Medicine, 1987. Fellow ACS, Am. Acad. Ophthamology (Disting. Svc. in Edn. award 1969); mem. AMA, Tex. Med. Assn., Mo. Ophthal. Soc. (founder, past sec.-treas., pres., dir.), Alpha Omega Alpha. Home: 3305 59th St Lubbock TX 79413-5517

BUESSER, ANTHONY CARPENTER, lawyer; b. Detroit, Oct. 15, 1929; s. Frederick Gustavis and Lela (Carpenter) B.; m. Carolyn Sue Pickle, Mar. 13, 1954; children: Kent Anderson, Anthony Carpenter, Andrew Clayton; m. Bettina Rieveschl, Dec. 14, 1973. BA in English with honors, U. Mich., 1952, MA, 1953, JD, 1960. Bar: Mich. 1961. Assoc. Chase, Goodenough & Buesser, Detroit, 1961-66; ptnr. Buesser, Buesser, Snyder & Blank, Detroit and Bloomfield Hills, Mich., 1966-81; sole practice Birmingham, Mich., 1981—. Trustee Detroit Country Day Sch., Beverly Hills, Mich., 1970-94, chmn. bd., 1977-82, 84-87, bd. chmn. emeritus, 1987—, chmn. nominating com., 1987-94. Served with AUS, 1953-55. Recipient Avery Hopwood award major fiction U. Mich., 1953, Outstanding Alumnus award Detroit Country Day Sch., 1988. Mem. ABA, State Bar Mich., Detroit Bar Assn. (pres. 1976-77), Oakland County Bar Assn., Am. Judicature Soc., Thomas M. Cooley Club (pres. 1974-76), Alpha Delta Phi, Phi Delta Phi. Home: 756 Honey Creek Dr Ann Arbor MI 48103-1638

BUETENS, ERIC D. lawyer; b. Rochester, N.Y., Jan. 30, 1953; s. Melvin and Shirley Doris (Gerber) B.; m. Carol Rebecca Osborn, Feb. 7, 1986; children: Rachel Catherine, Sarah Louise. BFA, U. N.Mex., 1976; JD magna cum laude, Syracuse U., 1986. Bar: Fla. 1986. Ptnr. Buetens & Buetens, Hobe Sound, Fla., 1986—. Chmn. Martin County Law Libr. Com., 2001—; mem. strategic planning com. Martin County Sch. Dist., 2000—; chmn. com. Martin County Law Libr., 2001—; pres. Friends of the Mid-County Libr., Inc., 1995—2001; chmn. Sch. Improvement Plan, 1995—96. Mem. Fla. Bar Assn. (vice-chmn. individual rights com. 1988, legis. com. pub. interest sect. 1990-91). Democrat. Home: 381 SW Timber Trl Stuart FL 34997-6289 Office: 8965 SE Bridge Rd Hobe Sound FL 33455-5327

BUETOW, DENNIS EDWARD, physiologist, educator; b. Chgo., Ill., June 20, 1932; s. Earl Frank and Helen Anna (Roeske) Buetow; m. Mary Kathleen Carney, Oct. 29, 1960; children: Katherine, Thomas(dec.), Michael, Ellen. BA, UCLA, 1954, MS, 1957, PhD, 1959. Biologist NIH, Bethesda, Md., 1959-65; biochemist Balt. City Hosps., 1959-65; assoc. prof. physiology U. Ill., Urbana, 1965-70, prof., 1970—, head dept. physiology and biophysics, 1983-88. Cons. in field. Contbr. articles to profl. jours. Grantee, NIH, NSF, Life Ins. Med. Rsch. Fund, Am. Heart Assn., USDA. Fellow: AAAS, Gerontol. Soc.; mem.: Am. Soc. Plant Biology, Am. Fedn. Aging Rsch., Soc. Protozoologists, Am. Physiol. Soc., Am. Soc. Cell Biology. Home: 2 Eton Ct Champaign IL 61820-7602 Office: Univ Ill 524 Burrill Hall Urbana IL 61801 E-mail: d-buetow@uiuc.edu.

BUETTNER, ANNE YU RAMONA WING-MUI, psychologist; b. Apr. 9, 1948; came to U.S., 1968; d. Hing-wan and Sin-wah (Yau) Yu; m. Dennis Vanosdall, Apr. 8, 1989 (div. 1990); m. Patrick E. Buettner, Dec. 1992; 1 child, James. BA in Psychology with honors, Ohio U., 1971; MA, So. Ill. U., 1975. Psychol. examiner Delta Counseling and Guidance Ctr., Monticello, Ark., 1975—76; psychologist assoc. Mid-Nebr. Cmty. Mental Health Ctr., Grand Island, 1977—. Supr. satellite clinic Loup Valley Mental Health Ctr., Loup City, Nebr., 1978-79; project dir. Protection from Domestic Abuse, 1978-79; pres. Taskforce on Domestic Violence and Sexual Assault, Grand Island, 1980-82; bd. dirs. Ctrl. Mediation Ctr. of Ctrl. Nebr., chmn., 1997-98, Nebr. Ctrl. Dist. Dept. Health. Mem. Mental Health Bd. Hall County, 1979; mem. fellows Menninger found., 1983-84; commr. Nebr. Commn. on Status of Women, 1990-95, vice chair, 1990-91, sec., 1991-92; bd. dirs. YWCA, Nebr.,1984-89; bd. examiners Mental Health Practice, 1993—, sec., 1994-98; mem. adv. coun. Office of Dispute Resolution, Nebr., 1997—, vice-chmn., 1998-99, coun. mem., 1996—; bd. dirs. Voices for Children, 1997—. Ohio U. Psi Chi scholar, 1968-71 Mem.: AAUW (pres. Grand Island chpt. 1984—86, v.p. Nebr. divsn. 1986—90), Ctrl. Dist. of Nebr. Dept. of Health (bd. dirs. 2002—), Am. Assn. for Marriage and Family Therapy (bd. dirs. 2002—), Am. Assn. Marital and Family Therapy Regulatory Bds. (del. Nebr. 1994—2001, treas. 1997—2001), Asian-Am. Psychol. Assn., Internat. Platform Assn., Northam Assn. Masters in Psychology (pres. Nebr. chpt. 1995—), Am. Assn. Sex Educators, Counselors and Therapists, Nebr. Assn. for Marriage and Family Therapy (v.p. 1981—84, pres. 1986—87, legis. chmn. 1988—, pres. 1998—99), Grand Island Assn. for Child Abuse Prevention (v.p. 1988—90, bd. dirs. 1993—, pres. 1994—95). Home: 714 S Broadwell Ave Grand Island NE 68803-6243 Office: Mid-Plains Ctr 914 Baumann Dr Grand Island NE 68803-4401 E-mail: buettnerp@aol.com.

BUFANO, RALPH A. museum director; Dir. Museum of Flight, Seattle. Office: Museum of Flight 904 E Marginal S Seattle WA 98108-4097

BUFE, CHARLES GLENN, geophysicist, researcher; s. Bancroft Washington and Margaret Elizabeth Bufe; life ptnr. Jacquelyn Claire Abbott, Nov. 18, 1967; children: Sierra Noel children: Glennica Joy Magee, Nathaniel Renfield. BS in Geophys. Engring., Mich. Technol. Univ., 1960, MS in Geophysics, 1962; PhD in Geology, The U. of Mich., 1969. Rsch. geophysicist U. of Mich., Ann Arbor, 1967—69, Nat. Oceanic and Atmospheric Adminstrn., San Francisco, 1969—73; vis. prof. U. of Wis., Milw., 1973; geophysicist U.S. Geol. Survey, Menlo Pk., Calif., 1973—80, liaison to DOE and FEMA Washington, 1980—85, rsch. geophysicist Denver, 1986—; sci. advisor to U.S. govt. Joint Commn. on Econ. Cooperation, Riyadh, Saudi Arabia, 1985—86. Lt. NOAA Officer Corps, 1964—66. Fellow, NSF, 1960—62, Grove Karl Gilbert Fellowship, U.S. Geol. Survey, 1993; scholar, Nat. Merit Scholarship Corp., 1956—60. Mem.: Soc. of Exploration Geophysicists, Seismol. Soc. of Am., Am. Geophys. Union. Liberal. Achievements include research in plate tectonics and earthquake recurrence and prediction; discovery of a precise, time-predictable earthquake recurrence model; first to use time-to-failure analysis in predictive earthquake models. Avocations: photography, sailing, scuba diving, high country hiking, fly fishing. Home: 901 Miami Way Boulder CO 80305 Office: U S Geological Survey MS 966 Box 25046 DFC Denver CO 80225 Personal E-mail: cgbufe@yahoo.com. E-mail: cbufe@usgs.gov.

BUFF, EUGENE, geneticist, researcher; b. Moscow, Apr. 16, 1967; naturalized U.S. citizen, 2000; s. Michail Z. and Noemi B. (Shkundina) B.; m. Katerina Y. Sherman, Jan. 6, 1996; children: Adel Malka, Yehuda Zelig. MD, MS in Biochemistry, Pirogov Moscow State Med. Inst, 1989; postgrad., Vavilov Inst. Gen. Genetics, Moscow, 1989-90; PhD in Genetics, Russian Acad. Scis., Moscow, 1993. Rsch. asst. Inst. Gene Biology, Moscow, 1990-92, rsch. assoc., 1992-94; assoc. Howard Hughes Med. Inst., Brigham and Women's Hosp., Boston, 1994-97; rsch. fellow MGM Cancer Ctr., Charlestown, Mass., 1997-99; v.p. prodn., chief scientist Foresight Sci. & Tech., Inc., New Bedford, Mass., 1999—. Biology tchr. Migdal Ohr Jewish H.S., Moscow, 1991-94; rsch. fellow Harvard Med. Sch., Boston, 1994-99. Contbr. articles to profl. jours. Mem. AUTM. Jewish. Avocations: coin collecting, literature. Office: Foresight Sci & Tech Inc PO Box 6815 New Bedford MA 02742-6815 E-mail: emb@myself.com.

BUFF, GAYLE HELENE, financial advisor; b. Utica, N.Y., Sept. 6, 1951; d. Henry Morris and Evelyn Rose (Maistelman) B. BS, Northeastern U., 1974; MS, Boston U., 1975; MBA in Fin., Northeastern U., 1985. Cert. Fin. Planner, Chart. Fin. Analyst. Mem. adj. faculty Northeastern U., Boston, 1988—95; adj. faculty Boston U., Boston, 1990-96; acct. mgr. The Acacia Group, Waltham, 1988-89; fin. advisor, prin. BUFF Capital Mgmt., Newton, Mass., 1989—; adj. faculty Bentley Coll., 1996—. Bd. dirs. Boston Security Analysts Soc., Am. Lung Assn. of Middlesex; chair N.E. Region Bd. Nat. Assn. Personal Fin. Adv.; mem. Boston Estate Planning Coun., Assn. of Investment Mgmt. and Rsch. Avocations: cycling, hiking. Address: 111 Hyde St Newton MA 02461-1237 Office: 111 Hyde St Newton MA 02461-1237 Fax: 617-332-6326. E-mail: gayle@buffcapital.com.

BUFF, IVA MOORE, librarian, musicologist; b. Port Arthur, Tex., Aug. 28, 1932; d. Thomas Richard and Iva Catherine (Smith) Moore; m. Frank P. Buff, Dec. 21, 1956; children: Susan Kathleen, Marjorie Anne. BA, MusB, U. Rochester, 1953, PhD, 1973; MA, Smith Coll., Northampton, Mass., 1954. Tchr. math. Brearley Sch., N.Y.C., 1954-55; research assoc. in musicology U. Rochester (N.Y.), 1973-75, head dept. acquisition and collection devel., 1979-91. Reader-cons. AAUW, 1989—. Author: The Chamber Duets & Trios of Carissimi, 1973, A Thematic Catalog of the Sacred Works of Giacomo Carissimi, 1979; articles Modern Music Librarianship, 1989, reviewer; asst. music rev. editor NOTES, 1986-87; assoc. editor: Am. Choral Rev., 1990-91. Fellow AAUW, 1973-75. Mem. Am. Musicol. Soc., Music Libr. Assn., Internat. Assn. Music Librs., Genesee Early Music Soc. (bd. dirs. 1990—), Mu Phi Epsilon. Avocation: photography. Home: 90 Roby Dr Rochester NY 14618-2112

BUFF, MARGARET ANNE, psychiatric nurse practitioner; b. Hanover, N.H., Nov. 2, 1955; d. Kenneth Andrew and M. Irene (Pender) Le Clair; m. James Steve Buff, Jan. 2, 1982; children: Jennifer, Steven, J. Thomas. BSN, BA in Psychology, RN, U. N.H., 1979; MA in Counselor Edn., U. N.Mex., 1985; MSN in Psychiat./Mental Health Nursing, Rivier Coll., 1997. RN, N.H., Mass.; ARNP, 1998. Staff nurse Vista Sandia Hosp., Albuquerque, 1980-81; charge nurse Los Lunas (N.Mex.) Hosp. and Tng. Sch., 1981-82; child devel. specialist Pueblo Infant Parent Edn. Project, Bernalillo, N.Mex., 1985-86; nurse, therapist Heights Psychiat. Hosp., Albuquerque, 1986-87; charge nurse Meml. Hosp., Albuquerque, 1987-88; staff nurse So. N.H. Regional Med. Ctr., Nashua, N.H., 1990-98; with Greater Lawrence (Mass.) Mental Health Ctr., 1998-2000; psychiatric nurse practioner Behavioral Health Care Svcs., Worcester, Mass., 2002—. Roman Catholic. Avocations: swimming, tennis. Home: 28 Hillside Dr Brookline NH 03033-2123 Office: Amherst Psychiat Svcs 135 Rte 101A Amherst NH 03031

BUFFENBARGER, R. THOMAS, labor union administrator; s. Bob and Betty Buffenbarger; m. Linda Buffenbarger; children: Amy, Andrew. With Internat. Assn. Machinists and Aerospace Workers, 1986-87, exec. asst. to internat. pres., 1987-91, gen. v.p., 1991-97, internat. pres., 1997—. Co-chair Machinists Non-Partisan Polit. League. Office: Internat Assn Machinists and Aerospace Workers 9000 Machinists Pl Upper Marlboro MD 20772-2675

BUFFENSTEIN, ALLAN S. lawyer; b. Richmond, Va., Sept. 21, 1940; m. Frona Buffenstein. BA, U. Richmond, 1962, LLB, 1965. Bar: Va. 1965. Ptnr. McCandlish Holton, Richmond. Lectr. Continuing Legal Edn. The Troubled Project, The Troubled Condominium Va. Law Found. Pres., chmn. bd. Richmond Jewish Community Ctr., 1982-84. Mem. ABA, Va. Bar Assn., Am. Bankruptcy Inst., Richmond Bar Assn. Office: McCandlish Holton 1111 E Main St PO Box 796 Richmond VA 23218-0796

BUFFETT, SUSAN THOMPSON, investment company executive; m. Warren Buffett, Apr. 1952. Dir. Berkshire Hathaway, Omaha. Office: Berkshire Hathaway 1440 Kiewit Plz Omaha NE 68131

BUFFETT, WARREN EDWARD, entrepreneur; b. Omaha, Aug. 30, 1930; s. Howard Homan and Leila (Stahl) B.; m. Susan Thompson, Apr. 19, 1952; children: Susan, Howard, Peter. Student, U. Pa., 1947-49; BS, U. Nebr., 1950; MS, Columbia, 1951. Investment salesman Buffett-Falk & Co., Omaha, 1951-54; security analyst Graham-Newman Corp., N.Y.C., 1954-56; gen. partner Buffett Partnership, Ltd., Omaha, 1956-69; now chmn. Berkshire Hathaway Inc., Omaha, 1970—, also CEO. Chmn. bd. Berkshire Hathaway, Inc., Nat. Indemnity Co., Nat. Fire & Marine Ins. Co., See's Candy Shops, Inc., Columbia Ins. Co., Buffalo Evening News; bd. dirs. Capital Cities/ABC, Salomon, Inc., Coca-Cola Co., Fechheimer Bros. Co., Associated Retail Stores, Scott and Fetzer Co., Home & Auto Ins. Co., Omaha World Herald, Precision Steel Warehouse, Inc. Life trustee Grinnell Coll., 1968—, Urban Inst. Office: Berkshire Hathaway Inc 1440 Kiewit Plz Omaha NE 68131

BUFFINGTON, GARY LEE ROY, safety engineer, construction executive; b. Custer, SD, Dec. 6, 1946; s. Donald L. B. and Madge Irene (Selby) Lampert; m. Kathleen R. Treloar, Aug. 3, 1965; children: Katherine, Lowell, Gary Jr. BS in Bus. Edn., Black Hill State Coll., 1971; AA in Criminal Justice, U. S.D., 1972, MS, 1974. Cert. safety profl., EMT, law enforcement officer, mine safety and health adminstrn. instr., OSHA instr., safety exec., safety mgr., safety specialist; Canadian registered safety profl.; lic. pvt. investigator; cert. safety and health mgr. Contract miner Homestake Mining Co., Lead, S.D., 1966-72; dep. sheriff, criminal investigator Pennington County Sheriff's Dept., Rapid City, S.D., 1972-77; fed. mine inspector U.S. Dept. of Labor, Mine Safety and Health Adminstrn., Birmingham, Ala., 1977-79, supr., spl. investigator, 1979-81, supr., mine inspector Grand Junction, Colo., 1981-83; safety and security mgr. Black & Veatch Engrs. Stanton Energy Ctr., Orlando, Fla., 1983-87; loss control mgr. Black & Veatch Engrs. AES Thames Cogeneration Plant, Uncasville, Conn., 1987-90; loss control mgr. Trans-Mo. River Tunnel project Black & Veatch, Engrs.-Architects, Kansas City, Mo., 1990-92; mgr. safety and security. metro rail constrn. mgr. Parsons-Dillingham, L.A., 1992-95; asst. dir. constrn. safety L.A. Metro Rail Project Met. Transp. Authority, 1995-99; owner Safety Expert Witness Am. Safety Cons., L.A., 1990—; constrn. safety mgr. Parsons Constructors Inc., Pasadena, Calif., 1999—2002. Mem. ANSI A-10 Accredited Standards Com., Washington, 1984—, Mine Safety and Health Adminstrn. Standards Com., Arlington, Va., 1981-83. Named Police Officer of the Year, Sundown Optimist Club, Rapid City, 1975; recipient Meritorious Achievement award, U.S. Dept. of Labor, Arlington, 1979, Monetary Spl. Achievement award, U.S. Dept. Labor, Arlington, 1980. Mem. Am. Soc. Safety Engrs. (adminstr. mining divsn. 1998—, Safety Profl. of Yr. constrn. specialty 2000-2001, named Safety Profl. of Yr. mining specialty 2002-03), World Safety Orgn., Am. Indsl. Hygiene Assn., Am. Soc. for Indsl. Security, Nat. Safety Coun., Inst. for Safety and Health Mgmt., Nat. Fire Protection Assn., Assn. for Can. Registered Safety Profls., Moose Lodge. Republican. Lutheran. Avocations: photography, sports. Home: 20025 W Jacana Ct Santa Clarita CA 91351-5562 Office: PO Box 71017 Los Angeles CA 90071-0017 E-mail: gbuff46@yahoo.com.

BUFFINGTON, LINDA BRICE, interior designer; b. Long Beach, Calif., June 21, 1936; d. Harry Bryce and Marguerite Leonora (Tucciarone) Van Bellehem; children: Lisa Ann, Phillip Lynn. Student, El Camino Jr. Coll., 1955-58, U. Calif., Irvine, 1973-75. Cert. interior designer, Calif.; lic. gen. contractor, Calif., home improvement contractor, Calif. With Pub. Fin., Torrance, Calif., 1954-55, Beneficial Fin., Torrance and Hollywood, Calif., 1955-61; interior designer Vee Nisley Interiors, Newport Beach, Calif., 1964-65, Leon's Interiors, Newport Beach, Calif., 1965-69; ptnr. Marlind Interiors, Tustin, Calif., 1969-70; owner, designer Linda Buffington Interiors, Villa Park, Calif., 1970—. Cons. in field. Mem. Bldg. Industry Assn. (past pres. Orange County chpt. 1989, 90), Internat. Soc. Interior Designers, Nat. Assn. Home Builders. Republican. Office: Linda Buffington Interiors PO Box 362 17853 Santiago Blvd Ste 107 Villa Park CA 92861-4199

BUFFKINS, ARCHIE LEE, television executive; b. Memphis, Mar. 30, 1934; s. John and Ada (Stittiams) B.; div.; 1 child, LeRachel Harombe. BS, Jackson State U., 1956; MA, Columbia, 1961, EdD, 1963; postgrad. research, Harvard U., summer 1972; postgrad. study, July 1994; postgrad. research, Oxford U., summer 1972, U. Amsterdam, summer 1972, Tel-Aviv U., 1973-74, U. Maine, 1970-71, Chgo. Conservatory, summer 1956. Instr. div. band music Ft. Ord (Calif.) Mil. Band Sch., 1957-58; instr., chmn. div. humanities Morristown (Tenn.) Coll., 1958-59; asst. prof., dir. freshman studies, div. fine arts Jackson (Miss.) State U., 1960-61; assoc. prof., head dept. music Ky. State U., Frankfort, 1963-66; prof., dir. grad. research in music, dept. music and fine arts Tex. So. U., Houston, 1966-68; prof., chmn. dept. music R.I. Coll., Providence, 1968-70; exec. asst. to chancellor U. Maine Eight-Campus System, Portland, 1970-71; chancellor U. Md., Eastern Shore, Princess Anne, 1971-75; asst. dean grad. studies U. Md. (College Park Campus), 1975-79; pres. Nat. Commn. on Cultural Diversity, Kennedy Center, 1979-85, dir. Office Cultural Diversity, 1985-93; cons. prodr. Kennedy Ctr., 1992-93; sr. v.p. broadcasting Md. Pub. TV, Owings Mills, 1993—, interim pres., CEO, 1995-97, sr. v.p. strategic devel., rsch., 1997-99; v.p. corp. affairs Sinclair Broadcast Group, Inc., Cockeysville, MD, 1999-2001; pres. Legacy of LearningCorp., Baltimore, 2001—. Commr. higher edn. Afro-Am. Edn. Assn. in R.I., 1968-71; dir. Conf. on Black Students and Higher Edn. in R.I., R.I. Coll., 1969, Conf. on Higher Edn. and Urban Setting, Boston, 1969, Md. Pub. Broadcasting Commn., 1986-93; coordinator Conf. on Afro-Am. Studies and High Sch. Curriculum, U. Maine, 1971; chmn. Nat. Black Think Tank, 1976; pres. John F. Kennedy Center Nat. Commn. on Blacks in the Arts; Chief adminstr. Free Urban Edn. Center, Houston, 1966-68; dir. Acad. Tutorial Inst. in Black Community of Houston, 1966-68, Black Fine Arts Festival, 1966; exec. dir. Eastern div. Council on Afro-Am. Studies, Boston, 1968-71; chmn. exptl. curriculum com. Gov.'s Sch. for Gifted in Arts, Providence, 1968, bd. dirs., 1969-70; chmn. edn. policy com., bd. dirs. Nat. Sch. Vol. Program, Inc., N.Y.C., 1968-70; chmn. edn. task force (Portland Model Cities Project), 1970-71; founder, dir. Center for Exptl. Studies in Higher Edn. Adminstrn., Portland, 1970-71; sr. adviser Nat. Accrediting Assn. for Afro-Am. Programs, N.Y.C., 1968-71; mem. U.S. Nat. Adv. Council on Adult Edn., 1974-79; chmn. Nat. Task Force on Adult Edn. and Urban Policy, 1977, Nat. Black Music Colloquium and Competition, 1978, Md. Black Congress on Higher Edn.; coordinator Black Higher Edn. Caucus of U. Md. System; chmn. Nat. Task Force on Urban Policy and Adult Edn.; chmn. exec. council Regional Research and Clearinghouse Network on Minorities and Grad. Edn.; chmn. Inter-Instnl. Task Force on Pluralism, 1990-95; mem. Gov. Info. Tech. Bd., Md., 1995—; appt. by Md. Gov. to Md. Commn. for Celebration 2000, 1997, bd. dirs. Safe Waterways in Md. Foundn. (SWIM), 2000—. Producer: Tribute to Historically Black Colls. and Univs, 1980, White House/Kennedy Center Jazz Salute to Lionel Hampton, White House Phase I, Kennedy Center Concert Hall Phase II, 1981; appeared with, Monterey Symphony Orch., Bach Festival Orch., Columbia U. Orch., Riverside Symphony Orch., Waukegan Community Orch., Tchrs. Coll. Concert Wind Ensemble, Ft. Ord Symphonic Concert Band, San Jose Woodwind Ensemble, Memphis String and Woodwind Chamber Ensemble.; co-producer: television series Tell It Like It Is, Community Service Television Project, Houston, 1967; Author: An Intellectual Approach to Musical Understanding, 1965, Philosophical Thoughts of a University Scholar, 1973, Arts Advocacy: The Economic Impact of the Arts in an Age of Austerity, Parts I and II; mem. bd. advisers, bd. dirs.: Urban Concerns mag; contbr. articles to profl. jours.; Composer: The Night Is Dark, 1967, Trio in A Minor, 1967, Mass, 1967, Integrity: Tone Poem for String Orchestra, 1968, Symphony For Tomorrow, 1969, Melodies For A Soprano, 1969, String Quartet No. 2, 1972, Sonata For Violin and Piano, 1972, Suite For Violin and Piano, 1972, Sonatina for Violin and Piano (for Sanford Allen), 1980, others. Bd. dirs. Eastern Shore Heart Assn., Salisbury, Md., R.I. Council on Arts, R.I. Philharmonic Orch., Internat. Econ. Devel. Corp., 1969-70, Afro-Art Center, Inc., 1968-70, Maine Savs. Bank, Center for Experiments in Higher Edn., Houston, 1967-70; trustee Peninsula Gen. Hosp., Salisbury, Md., 1970-76, Portland Symphony Orch., 1968-70; mem. exec. bd. Afro-Am. Soc., N.Y.C., 1966-70, New Eng. States Coll. Assn. Music Faculties, Plymouth, N.H., 1968-70, Delmarva council Boy Scouts Am., Wilmington, Del., 1970-76; mem. corp. bd. Edn. Devel. Center, Inc., Newton, Mass., 1970-72, Peoples Savs. Bank & Trust, Providence, 1968-70; mem. exec. bd. Nat. Christian Leadership Conf. for Israel, 1970-75; mem. Nat. Arts Evaluation Panel for Minority Programs, 1970-80; bd. dirs. Afro-Am. Museums Assn., Washington, 1980-95; mem. adv. bd. D.C. Youth Chorale Assn., 1981—, Prince George's Performing Arts, 1987-95; mem. nat. task force on anti-Semitic incidents Anti-Defamation League, N.Y.C., 1980-81; mem. nat. steering com. Martin Luther King Holiday, Washington, 1980-95; mem. planning com. Nat. Black Coll. Day, 1981—; mem. Com. for a Free World, N.Y.C., 1981—, The Jazz Philharmonic Orch., 1987—; mem. exec. com. Coalition for Strategic Stability in Middle East, Washington, 1981—; Am. chmn. FUBA: South African Sch. of the Arts, 1986; bd. trustees Md. Citizens for Arts, 1995; bd. dirs. Gordon Ctr. for Performing Arts at Jewish Cmty. Ctr., 1994—; dist. chmn. Balt. Trailblazers-Boy Scouts Am., 1994-99, bd. dirs. Balt. coun., 2000—; trustee St. Mary's Coll. Md., 2000—. Served with U.S. Army, 1956-58. Recipient Young Classical Musician award Memphis Music Soc., 1952; Black Intellectual Leadership award Houston, 1967; Disting. Alumni award Jackson State U., 1973; Nat. Cultural Recognition award Tuskegee, Ala., 1981; named to Mid-Eastern Athletic Conf. Hall of Fame Durham, N.C., 1981 Mem. Md. Assn. for Higher Edn. (chmn. panel adminstrv. affairs 1973), Mid. States Assn. Colls. and Secondary Schs. (evaluation bd. 1972-96), Am. Coun. on Edn., Nat. Assn. State Univs. and Land-Grant Colls., NAACP (exec. bd. Prince George's chpt. 1979-86, chmn. edn. com. 1980-86, Md. edn. com. 1985-87). Fax: (410) 539-0404. E-mail: abuffkins@starpower.net.

BUFFLER, PATRICIA ANN, epidemiologist, educator, retired dean; b. Doylestown, Pa., Aug. 1, 1938; d. Edward M. and Evelyn G. (Axenroth) Happ; m. Richard T. Buffler, Jan. 20, 1962; children: Martyn R., Monique L. BSN, Cath. U. Am., 1960; MPH, U. Calif., Berkeley, 1965, PhD in Epidemiology, 1973. Prof. epidemiology sch. pub. health U. Tex. Health Sci. Ctr., Houston, 1979—91; prof. U. Calif., Berkeley, 1991—, dean sch. pub. health, 1991—98, dean emerita, 1998—. Mem. expert adv. panel on occupl. health WHO, 1985—; mem. environment, safety and health adv. com. U.S. DOE, 1992—95; mem. bd. on water sci. and tech. NRC, 1992—94; chair, bd. dirs. Mickey Leland Nat. Urban Air Toxics Rsch. Ctr., 1994—97, Societal Inst. of Math. Scis.; mem. Nat. Commn. on Superfund, Keystone Ctr., 1992—94; mem. adv. panel on mng. nuc. materials from warheads U.S. Congress Office Tech. Assessment, 1992—93; bd. sci. counselors Nat. Inst. for Occupl. Safety and Health, 1991—93; mem. sci. adv. bd. radiation adv. com. subcom. on cancer risks associated with electric and magnetic fields U.S. EPA, 1990—93, mem. sci. adv. bd., 1996—; mem. Nat. Adv. Coun. on Environ. Health Scis., 1995—98, NAS, Nat. Coun. Radiation Protection. Contbr. articles to profl. jours. Fellow: AAS, Inst. Medicine, Am. Coll. Epidemiology (pres.-elect 1990—91, pres. 1991—92); mem.: APHA (epidemiology sect. 1964—), Internat. Soc. for Environ. Epidemiology (pres.-elect 1989—91, pres. 1992—94), Soc. of Toxicology, Internat. Commn. on Occupl. Health, Internat. Soc. for Exposure Assessment (charter, bd. internat. councillors 1993—), Internat. Epidemiol. Assn., Soc. for Occupl. and Environ. Health, Am. Epidemiol. Soc., Soc. for Epidemiol. Rsch. (pres.-elect, pres., past pres. 1984—88), Collegium Ramazzini. Office: U Calif Sch Pub Health 714-F University Hall 140 Earl Warren Hl Berkeley CA 94720-0001

BUFFMIRE, DONALD K. internist; b. Grand Rapids, Minn., Aug. 18, 1922; m. Jane Enkema, June 11, 1945; 3 children. BS, BM in Zoology, Northwestern U., 1944, MD, 1948. Diplomate Am. Bd. Internal Medicine. Intern Evanston (Ill.) Hosp., 1947-48; resident in internal medicine Mayo Found., Rochester, Minn., 1948-51, U. Minn., Mpls., 1950; founder, past chmn. Phoenix Med. Assocs.-Mayo Health Sys., 1954—; now ret. Elder Orangewood Presbyn. Ch.; Trustee, past chmn. Blood Sys., Inc., Scottsdale, Ariz.; former mem. coord. devel. adv. bd. U. Ariz. Coll. Medicine; trustee Flinn Found., Phoenix, 1965—, pres. bd. trustees 1982-98, chmn., 1984-98, chmn. emeritus, 1998—. Capt. Med. Corps U.S. Army, 1951-53. Recipient Dr. Joseph E. Ehrlich medal Maricopa County Med. Soc., 1992, Dr. Clarence Salsbury award Maricipa County Med. Soc., 1987, Disting. Svc. to Society award Northwestern U., 1998, The Spirit of Philanthropy award, Nat. Soc. Fund Raising Execs., 1999; Donald K. Buffmire Vis. Lectureship in medicine established at U. Ariz. by Flinn Found., 1998; named as one of 25 leaders who helped shape modern-day Phoenix, Phoenix mag., 1991; inducted into Grand Rapids, Minn. Sports Hall of Fame, 1990. Fellow ACP (Laureate award 1991), Am. Coll. Chest Physicians, Royal Soc. Medicine; mem. AMA, Am. Soc. Internal Medicine, Ariz. Med. Assn. (Pres.' Disting. Svc. award 1998), Ariz. Heart Assn. (pres. 1958-59), Sigma Chi (Significant Sig award 2001). Home: 3311 E Valley Vista Ln Paradise Valley AZ 85253-3739 Office: Mayo Cmty Int Med Mayo Health Sys 3600 N 3rd Ave Phoenix AZ 85013-3904 E-mail: enkie@aol.com.

BUFFON, CHARLES EDWARD, lawyer; b. Topeka, Sept. 8, 1939; s. Merritt Woodbridge and Clare Marie (Waterfall) B.; m. Kathleen Craig Vreeland, June 6, 1964; children: Alexandra, Nathaniel Edward. AB in Internat. Rels. magna cum laude, Dartmouth Coll., 1961; LLB cum laude, Harvard U., 1964. Bar: D.C. 1965, U.S. Ct. Appeals (D.C. cir.) 1965, U.S. Ct. Appeals (6th cir.) 1966, U.S. Supreme Ct. 1971, U.S. Ct. Appeals (9th cir.) 1975, U.S. Ct. Appeals (2d cir.) 1980, U.S. Ct. Appeals (4th cir.) 1980, U.S. Ct. Appeals (3d cir.) 1981, U.S. Ct. Appeals (fed. cir.) 1982, U.S. Dist. Ct. Md. 1992, U.S. Ct. Appeals (11th cir.) 2000. Assoc. Covington & Burling, Washington, 1964-73, ptnr., 1973—. Adj. faculty U. Va. Law Sch., 1968-86, Am. U. 1988-92; lectr. in field. Contbr. articles to profl. jours. Fellow Am. Bar Found.; mem. ABA (litigation, intellectual property and antitrust sects.), D.C. Bar Assn. (past chmn. legal ethics com., spl. com. legal specialization, past mem. steering com. sect. cts., lawyers and adminstrn. justice, D.C. rules profl. conduct edn. com., spl. com. model rules profl. conduct, long range planning com., chmn. com. on multidisciplinary practice, Cert. Appreciation 1987), Phi Beta Kappa. Office: Covington & Burling 1201 Pennsylvania Ave NW Washington DC 20004-2401 E-mail: cbuffon@rov.com.

BUFFORD, SAMUEL LAWRENCE, federal judge; b. Phoenix, Ariz., Nov. 19, 1943; s. John Samuel and Evelyn Amelia (Rude) B.; m. Julia Marie Metzger, May 13, 1978. BA in Philosophy, Wheaton Coll., 1964; PhD, U. Tex., 1969; JD magna cum laude, U. Mich., 1973. Bar: Calif., N.Y., Ohio. Instr. philosophy La. State U., Baton Rouge, 1967-68; asst. prof. Ea. Mich. U., Ypsilanti, 1968-74; asst. prof. law Ohio State U., Columbus, 1975-77; assoc. Gendel, Raskoff, Shapiro & Quittner, L.A., 1982-85; atty. Paul, Weiss, Rifkind, Wharton & Garrison, N.Y.C., 1974-75, Sullivan Jones & Archer, San Francisco, 1977-79, Musick, Peeler & Garrett, L.A., 1979-81, Rifkind & Sterling, Beverly Hills, Calif., 1981-82, Gendel, Raskoff, Shapiro & Quittner, L.A., 1982-85; U.S. bankruptcy judge Ctrl. Dist. Calif., 1985—. Bd. dirs. Fin. Lawyers Conf., L.A., 1987-90, Bankruptcy Forum, L.A., 1986-88; lectr. U.S.-Romanian Jud. Delegation, 1991, Internat. Tng. Ctr. for Bankers, Budapest, 1993, Bankruptcy Technical Legal Assistance Workshop, Romania, 1994, Comml. Law Project for Ukraine, 1995-96, 99, Ea. Europe Enterprise Restructuring and Privitization Project, U.S. AID, 1995-96, World Bank Global Judges Forum, 2003, Morocco Jud. Tng.Program; cons. World Bank Project, 2002; cons. Calif. State Bar Bd. Examiners, 1989-90; bd. trustees Endowment for Edn.; bd. dirs. Nat. Conf. Bankruptcy Judges, 1994-2000; bd. dirs. San Pedro Enterprise Community, 1997—. Sr. author: International Insolvency, 2001, editor-in-chief: Am. Bankruptcy Law Jour., 1990—94; contbr. articles to profl. jours. Younger Humanist fellowship NEH. Mem. ABA, L.A. County Bar Assn. (mem. profl. responsibility and ethics com. 1979—, chair profl. responsibility and ethics com. 1985-86, chair ethics 2000 liaison com. 1997-2002), Order of Coif. Office: US Bankruptcy Ct 255 E Temple St Ste 1582 Los Angeles CA 90012-3332

BUFFUM, KATHLEEN D. artist; b. Abington, Pa., Dec. 5, 1925; d. Leroy Adolph Frederick and Julia Elizabeth (Suwall) Droescher; m. John McEntee Bowman Jr., Dec. 17, 1961 (dec. Dec. 1970); 1 child, (dec.) Alexandra Kip Bowman; m. (dec.) George Allen Buffum, Oct. 2, 1972; stepchildren: George Allen, Price. Grad., Harcum Coll., Bryn Mawr, Pa., 1944; student, Pa. Acad. Fine Arts, Phila., 1957-59, Barnes Found. Pvt. Mus. Sch., Merion, Pa., 1971-72. Solo shows include Phila. C.C., 1998; exhibited in juried shows at Pa. Acad. Fine Arts, The Art Alliance, Smithsonian Inst., The Sketch Club, Woodmere Mus., Am. Coll., Bryn Mawr, Art Studnets League, Rehoboth Beach, Del., Villanova (Pa.) U., others; more than 160 paintings in pvt. collections. Mem. maternity com. Thomas Jefferson U. Hosp. Womans Bd.; active Phila. Antiques Show Com. U. Pa. Hosp. Recipient Violet Oakely prize, 1972. Mem. Wayne Art Ctr., Pa. Acad. Fine Arts (womans bd.), Phila. Acad. Fine Arts, Woodmere Mus. Republican. Episcopalian. Address: 200 N Wynnewood Ave Wynnewood PA 19096-1433

BUFFUM, WILLIAM ERWIN, social worker, educator; b. Grand Rapids, Mich., Dec. 11, 1944; s. Erwin Clair and Sena (Lucas) B.; m. Valerie Jane Regetz, Feb. 20, 1973; 1 child, Lindsay Louise. BA, Calvin Coll., 1966; MSW, U. Mich., 1970; PhD, Case Western Reserve U., 1981. Prof. U. Houston Sch. Social Work, 1999—2002; assoc. dean Barry U. Sch. Social Work, 1999—2003; dir. Aurora U. Sch. of Social Work, Ill., 2003—. Mem. editorial bd. Jour. Sociology and Social Welfare, Jour. Community Practice. Bd. dirs. Refugee Svc. Alliance, Houston, 1988-99. Mem. NASW, Coun. on Social Work Edn., Assn. Community Orgn. and Social Adminstrn. Democrat. Avocations: running, sailing. Home: 231 Abington Ln North Aurora IL 60542 Office: Aurora U Sch Social Work 347 S Gladstone Ave Aurora IL 60506-4892 E-mail: wbuffum@aurora.edu.

BUFORD, BARBARA FEST, retired state agency employee; b. Camden, N.J., Mar. 26, 1941; d. Robert Eugene Fest and Helen Agnes Besso; m. Jefferson R. Taylor (div. 1972); children: Patricia A., Laurie B., Jeff Jr.; m. Rivers Henderson Buford Jr., July 15, 1976. BA in History & Criticism Art cum laude, Fla. State U., 1992. Clk. Divsn. Corrections and Sec. of State State of Fla. Govt., Tallahassee, 1962—66; clk. Fla. Legis., 1967, clk., 1970, 1972—82. Mem. Phi Beta Kappa. Episcopalian. Avocations: art, birding, calligraphy. Home: 3224 Independence Ct Tallahassee FL 32312 E-mail: barive@aol.com.

BUFORD, EVELYN CLAUDENE SHILLING, retired consumer products company executive; b. Ft. Worth, Sept. 21, 1940; d. Claude and Winnie Evelyn (Mote) Hodges; m. William J. Buford, Mar. 1982; children by previous marriage: Vincent Shilling, Kathryn Lynn Shilling LA Chapelle. Student, Hill Jr. Coll., 1975-76, Tarrant County (Tex.) Jr. Coll., 1992-93. With Imperial Printing Co., Inc., Ft. Worth, 1964-70, corp. sec., 1977-79, gen. sales mgr. coml. divsn., 1982—89; with Tarrant County Hosp. Dist., Ft. Worth, 1973-77, asst. to asst. adminstr., 1981-84; merch. asst. J.C. Penney Co., Hurst, Tex., 1989—96; ret., 1996. Mem. Exec. Women Internat. (life, dir., publs. chair, v.p. 1984, pres. 1985, chair adv. com. 1986-87, scholarship dir. 1988-93, corp. publ. com. 1988-89, dir. South ctrl. region 1993-94). Republican. Methodist. Home: 1025 Kenneth Ln Burleson TX 76028-2246

BUFORD, ROBERT PEGRAM, lawyer; b. Roanoke Rapids, N.C., Sept. 7, 1925; s. Robert Pegram and Edith (Rawlings) Buford; m. Anne Bliss Whitehead, June 26, 1948; children: Robert, Bliss, Peyton. LLB, U. Va., 1950. Bar: Va. 1949. Sr. counsel Hunton & Williams, Richmond, Va. Bd. visitors U. Va., Charlottesville, 1972—80; chmn. Met. Richmond C. of C., 1973; bd. trustees St. Paul's Coll., Lawrenceville, Va., 1977—85. Recipient Disting. Svc. award, Jr. C. of C., 1961, Va. Profl. Assn., 1965, Good Govt. award, Richmond First Club, 1967. Fellow: Va. Law Found., Am. Bar Found.; mem.: ABA, Va. Bar (assoc.), Commonwealth Club, Country Club of Va. Home: 506 Kilmarnock Dr Richmond VA 23229-8102 Office: Hunton & Williams Riverfront Pla E Tower PO Box 1535 Richmond VA 23218-1535 E-mail: rbuford@hunton.com.

BUFORD, RONETTA MARIE, music educator; b. Kansas City, Mo., Sept. 17, 1946; d. Joseph Ronald and Violet Katheryne (Jennison) Coursey; 1 child, Frederick Kenyatta. Bachelor of Music Edn., Lincoln U. of Mo., 1968; M in Liberal Arts, Baker U., 1996. Cert. vocal and instrumental music tchr., Mo. Chmn. vocal music M.L. King Jr. High Sch., Kansas City, 1968-71; chmn. music dept. Southeast Jr. High Sch., Kansas City, 1971-75; chmn. fine arts Paseo High Sch., Kansas City, 1975-90; vocal music specialist Met. Advanced Tech. H.S., Kansas City, 1990-98, asst. girls basketball coach, asst. cross country coach, 1992-98; owner Buford's Day Care, 1996-97, Buford's Mini Univ.; TRAC music instr. Crispus Attucks Elem. Sch., 2001—. Summer music specialist Horace Mann Elem. Sch., Kansas City, 1972; mentor Students at Risk, Kansas City, 1988; vis. lectr. Lincoln U., Jefferson City, Mo., 1980, 85, 87, NE Mo. State U., Kirksville, 1986; panelist Sta. KPRS, Kansas City, 1987; Title One mentor K.C. Mo. Sch. Dist.; min. music N.W. Mo. Conf. A.M.E. Ch., Kansas City, 1984-91, choir dir., 1985—; dir. sr. choir Ward Chapel A.M.E. Ch., KAnsas City, 1985-87; instr. of choir, band and orch. N.E. Law, Pub. Svc. and Mil. Sci. H.S., 1998-99; girl's varsity asst. basketball coach, girl's jr. varsity basketball coach, drill mistress N.E. Lady Vikings Drill Team, fine arts dept. chairperson. Author: (curricula) Junior High Learning Task, 1972, Motivating the Unmotivated, 1986. Asst. troop scoutmaster Boy Scouts Am.; spl. cons. music United Meth. Ch. Women; active NAACP; parent chaperone Kansas City Marching Cobras Drill Team, 1993—. Recipient Meritorious Service award Lincoln U. Vocal Ensemble, 1985, Outstanding Tchr. award Black Archives Mid-Am., 1987; named one of Outstanding Young Women of Am., 1983. Mem. NAACP, AAUW, MADD, Am. Choral Dirs. Assn., Am. Fedn. Tchrs., Am. Assn. Retired Persons, Music Educators Nat. Conf., Nat. Assn. Negro Women, Order Eastern Star, Order Cyrenes, Heroines of Jericho, Daus. of Isis, Tri-M Music Honor Soc., Order Golden Circle, Nat. Coaches Assn., Bethel A.M.E. Ch. (life), Bethel Missionary Soc., Mass Choir and Parsonage Club, Licoln U. Mo. Alumni Assn., Vocat. Indsl. Clubs Am., "C" Scholarship Club, Alpha Kappa Alpha, Phi Delta Kappa, Sigma Alpha Iota. Avocation: photography. Home: 3610 E 26th St Kansas City MO 64127-4321 Office: Kansas City Sch Dist 1211 Mcgee St Kansas City MO 64106-2416

BUFORD-BAILEY, TONJA YEVETTE, Olympic athlete; b. Dayton, Ohio, Dec. 13, 1970; d. Georgianna Buford; m. Victor Bailey, Oct. 28, 1995. Grad., U. Ill., 1993. Mem. U.S. Olympic Team, Barcelona, 1992, Atlanta, 1996. Named winner 16 individual Big Ten Championships, U. Ill., winner 9 relay Big Ten Championships; recipient conf. title indoor awards for 55 and 200 dashes, 55 hurdles, conf. title outdoor awards for 100, 200, 400 and both hurdles, Bronze medal, Pan Am. Games, Havana, Cuba, 1991, Silver medal, Pam Am. Games, Argentina, 1995, Silver award, World Championships, Gothenburg, 1995, Bronze medal 400 meter hurdles, Olympic Games, Atlanta, 1996. Achievements include ranked 7th in world for 400 meter hurdles, 1992; ranked 5tj in the world 400 meter hurdles, 1993; ranked 2d in the world 400 meter hurdles, 1995; ranked 3d in the world 400 meter hurdles, 1996; ranked 6th in the world 400 meter hurdles, 1997. Office: USA Track and Field PO Box 120 Indianapolis IN 46206-0120

BUGBEE, JOAN BARTHELME, retired corporate communications executive; b. Galveston, Tex., Dec. 31, 1932; d. Donald and Helen (Bechtold) Barthelme; m. George A. Bugbee, Apr. 2, 1966; children: Richard, John. BA in Journalism, U. Colo., 1955. Pub. rels. rep. Philco Corp., Phila., 1957-60; account exec. Jacobs Keeper Newell Assoc., Houston, 1960-63; pub. rels. rep. Tex. Ea. Corp., Houston, 1963-66; assoc. editor Oil and Gas Digest Mag., Houston, 1978-79; mgr. corp. comms. Pennzoil Co., Houston, 1980-87, dir. corp. comms., 1987-90, v.p. corp. comm., 1990-96; ret., 1996; pub. rels. cons. Bd. dir., mem. bd. exec. com. Blue Ridge Pub. TV., mem. and publicity person, alternatives to War; book reviewer for The Roanoke Times. Mem. Radio Reading Svc., Sta. WVTF; publicity chmn. Roanoke chpt. Brady/Million Mom Mar. Recipient Outstanding Presentation award, Phila. chpt. Pub. Rels. Soc. Am., 1959. Mem.: Red Hat Soc., Phi Beta Kappa. Maronite Catholic.

BUGEJA, MICHAEL JOSEPH, educator, writer; b. Hackensack, N.J., May 24, 1952; s. Michael Carl and Josephine (Apap) B.; m. Diane Faye Sears, Sept. 16, 1979; children: Shane Michael, Erin Marie. BA in German, St. Peter's Coll., 1974; MS in Comms., S.D. State U., 1976; PhD in English, Okla. State U., 1985. State editor UPI, Sioux Falls, S.D., 1976-79; prof. Okla. State U., Stillwater, 1979-86, Ohio U., Athens, 1986—, spl. asst. to pres., 1996—. Hon. chancellor Nat. Fed. of State Poetry Soc. Author: Art and Craft of Poetry, 1994, Living Ethics, 1996, Guide to Writing Magazine Nonfiction, 1997, Millennium's End, 1999, Living Without Fear, 2001; mem. adv. bd. Writer's Digest, Cin., 1999, Coll. Values, 2000. Fellow Nat. Endowment for Arts, 1990, Ohio Arts Coun., 1997; NEH grantee, 1984; recipient Outstanding Tchr. award Amoco, 1985. Lutheran. Office: Ohio Univ EW Scripps Sch Athens OH 45701

BUGEN, DAVID HENRY, financial advisor; b. Easton, PA, Mar. 7, 1948; s. Phil and Hanna (Goldsmith) B.; m. Barbara Gasparri, May 19, 1991; children: Sarah, Marta. BA, Rutgers U., 1970, MBA, 1972. Cert. fin. planner. Mkt. rsch. analyst Supermkts. Gen. Corp., Woodbridge, NJ, 1972—74; budget & fin. analyst Dept. Human Svcs., Trenton, NJ, 1974—76; assoc. dir. Greystone Park Hosp., Morris Plains, NJ, 1976—79; executive Fin. Blue Prints, Florham Park, NJ, 1979—83, Individual Asset Planning, Morristown, NJ, 1983—96, Bugen Stuart Korn & Cordaro, Chatham, NJ, 1996—2001; ptnr. Regent Atlantic Capital, Chatham, 2001—. Adj. faculty County Coll. of Morris, Randolph, NJ, 1982—99; adj. prof. Coll. for Fin. Planning, Denver, 1985—87. Bd. dirs. Farleigh Dickinson U. Fin. Adv. Bd. Madison, N.J., 1988-92. Named 1 of Top 200 Fin. Planners in U.S., Money Mag., 1987, Worth Mag., 1996—2002, 1 of Top 250 Fin. Advisors, 2001—02, 1 of top 100 fin. planners, Mutual Fund Mag. Mem. Internat. Assn. for Fin. Planning (bd. dirs. 1980-85, chmn. 1984-85), Park Ave. Club. Avocations: reading, tennis, skiing. Office: Regent Atlantic Capital LLC 1 Main St Chatham NJ 07928-2407 E-mail: dbugen@regentatlantic.com.

BUGENTAL, JAMES FREDERICK THOMAS, retired psychologist, educator; b. Fort Wayne, Ind., Dec. 25, 1915; s. Richard Francis and Hazel Jeanette (Veness) B.; m. Mary Edith Smith, Feb. 11, 1939 (div. 1967); children: James Owen, Jane Pattie Eum; m. Elizabeth Catherine Keber, June 23, 1968; 1 child, Karen Marie. BS in Edn., West Tex. State Coll., 1940; MA in Sociology, George Peabody Coll., 1941; PhD in Psychology, Ohio State U., 1948; LHD (hon.), Saybrook Inst., 1993. Diplomate Am. Bd. Examiners in Psychology. Asst. prof. psychology, counselor Ga. Sch. of Tech., 1944-45; asst. prof. psychology UCLA, 1948-54; ptnr., psychologist Psychol. Svc. Assocs., L.A., 1947-67; cons. project on future of edn. Stanford Rsch. Inst., Palo Alto, Calif., 1967-69; psychologist Palo Alto, Santa Rosa, Calif., 1967-69, San Rafael, Calif., 1967-88; cons., lectr. Disting. clinician-educator, J.F. Kennedy U., 1988, vis. scholar, U. Mont., 1988, disting. vis. prof., Calif. Sch. Profl. Psychology, Alameda, 1989-90. Author: Psychotherapy Isn't What You Think, 1999, Intimate Journeys: Stories from Life-Changing Therapy, 1990, The Art of the Psychotherapist, 1987, Psychotherapy and Process: The Fundamentals of an Existential-Humanistic Approach, 1978, The Search for Existential Identity: Patient-Therapist Dialogues in Humanistic Psychotherapy, 1976, The Search for Authenticity: An Existential Analytic Approach to Psychotherapy, 1965; editor: Challenges of Humanistic Psychology, 1967; contbr. articles to profl. jours.; editl. bd. 11 jours. Lt. USNR, 1945-46. Rockefeller scholar Calif. Inst. of Integral Studies; recipient Pathfinder award Assn. for Humanistic Psychology, 1991; fellow USPHS, Ohio State U., 1946-48. Fellow Am. Psychol. Assn. (divsn. humanistic psychology, First Rollo May award 1996; divsn. clin. psychology, cert. disting. contbn. 1986, honored career divsn. psychotherapy, 2002); mem. Assn. for Humanistic Psychology (pres. 1962-63), Calif. Psychol. Assn. (pres. 1960-61), So. Calif. Psychol. Assn. (pres. 1955-56), L.A. Soc. of Clin. Psychologists (pres. 1952-53). Democrat. Episcopalian. Avocations: friends, concerts, writing. Home: 24 Elegant Tern Rd Novato CA 94949-6619 Office: 24 Elegant Tern Rd Novato CA 94949-6619

BUGG, CAROL DONAYRE, interior designer; b. N.Y.C., June 8, 1937; d. Carlos G. and Frances M. (Burkhart) Donayre; m. James S. Bugg, Dec. 24, 1968; step-children: Karen, Ken, Darlene, Jim, Whitney. AA, Georgetown Visitation Coll., Washington D.C., 1957; student in Spanish, Georgetown U., Washington D.C., 1960; student interior design, Internat. Inst. of Interior Design, Washington, 1967; interior decorator, Parsons Sch. Design, Paris, 1984. Design asst. W&J Sloane, Washington D.C., 1967-68, The H. Chambers Co., Washington D.C., 1968-69; dir. design Internat. Cosmetic Co., Washington D.C., 1970-72; interior decorator Stix, Baer & Fuller, St. Louis, 1972-73, Burklew Design Assocs., Md., 1973-76; pres. Carol Donayre Bugg & Assocs., 1976-85; v.p., dir. design Decorating Den Systems, Inc., Bethesda, Md., 1984—. Author: (book) Dream Rooms For Real People, 1990, Divine Design, 1994, Smart & Simple Decorating, 1999; lectr. in field. Mem. decorating com. Congl. Women's Club, Washington D.C.; sponsor Leader Dogs For the Blind, Rochester, Mich.; active gourmet gala March of Dimes, Washington D.C. Mem. Am. Soc. Interior Design (Washington D.C. chpt. chmn. ways and means com. 1979), Color Mktg. Group. Home: 3717 Bradley Ln Chevy Chase MD 20815-4256 Office: Decorating Den Systems Inc 19100 Montgomery Village Ave Gaithersburg MD 20886-3701

BUGG, JACE, golfer; b. Henderson, Ky., Sept. 6, 1976; married. Student, Rend Lake Jr. Coll. Mem. Can. Profl. Golf Tour, 1997—. Named winner, SC Challenge, 2001. Avocations: fishing, hunting. Office: c/o Canadian Tour 212 King St W Ste 203 Toronto ON Canada M5H 1K5

BUGGE, LAWRENCE JOHN, lawyer, educator; b. Milw., June 1, 1936; s. Lawrence Anthony and Anita (Westenberg) B.; m. Mary Daly, Nov. 28, 1959 (div.); m. Elaine Andersen, Jan. 29, 1977; children: Kristin, Laura, Jill, David, Carol. AB, Marquette U., 1958; JD, Harvard U., 1963. Bar: Wis. 1963. Assoc. Foley and Lardner, Milw., Madison, Wis., 1963-70, ptnr., 1970-96, of counsel, 1996—. Pres. Nat. Conf. Commrs. on Uniform State Laws, 1989-91; adj. prof. law U. Wis. Law Sch., Madison, 1997—. Mem. Wis. Bar Assn. (pres. 1980-81), Mil. Bar Assn. (pres. 1974-75), Milw. Young Lawyers Assn. (pres. 1969-70). Home: 313 Walnut Grove Dr Madison WI 53717-1228 Office: Foley & Lardner PO Box 1497 150 E Gilman St Madison WI 53701-1497 E-mail: ljbugge@itis.com.

BUGGEY, LESLEY JOANNE, education educator, consultant; b. Mpls., July 25, 1938; d. Leslie Francis and Blanche (Moore) B. BS, Macalester Coll., 1960; MEd, U. Wash., Seattle, 1968; PhD, U. Wash., 1971. Cert. elem. tchr., Minn. Tchr. elem. Mpls. Pub. Schs., 1960-71; co-dir. Social Studies Svc. Ctr., St. Paul, 1971-73; lectr. in edn. Stanford (Calif.) U., 1973-74; edml. cons., author, tchr., lectr. in edn. U. Minn., Mpls., 1974—. Cons. in field. Speaker various orgns. Mem. ASCD, Nat. Coun. Geographic Edn. (past bd. dirs.), Nat. Coun. Social Studies (nat. com. mem.), Minn. Coun. for Social Studies. Presbyterian. Avocations: sewing, reading, travel. Office: Univ Minn Room 125 PeikH 159 Pillsbury Dr SE Minneapolis MN 55455

BUGHER, ROBERT DEAN, professional society administrator; b. Lafayette, Ind., Oct. 17, 1925; s. Walter Earl and Lillie Victoria (Feldner) B.; m. Patricia Jean McConnell, Sept. 7, 1945; children: Vickie Leigh, Robert James. Student, Millsaps Coll., 1943, Miami U., Oxford, Ohio, 1944; BS in Civil Engring, Purdue U., 1948; MPA, U. Mich., 1951. Staff engr. Mich. Mcpl. League, 1948-53; mgr. Mcpl. Purchasing Svc., 1951-53; sec.-treas. Mich. Mcpl. Utilities Assn., 1951-53; asst. dir. Am. Pub. Works Assn., 1953-58, exec. dir., 1958-89, exec. dir. emeritus, 1990—. Lectr. Internat. Seminar on Ekistics, Athens, Greece, 1970; chmn. nat. adv. coun. Keep Am. Beautiful, Inc., 1974-75; chmn. Nat. Conf. on Solid Waste Disposal Sites, Washington, 1971; advisor pub. mgmt. program Northwestern U., 1977-82; bd. dirs. Pub. Adminstrn. Svc., Chgo., 1958-73; trustee Nat. Acad. Code Adminstrs.; chmn. Coun. Internat. Urban Liaison, 1982-84; trustee Nat. Tng. and Devel. Svc., Am. Consortium for Internat. Pub. Adminstrn.; adv. com. internat. divsn. GAO, 1979-80. Editor: pub. works sect. Municipal Yearbook Internat. City Mgmt. Assn., 1953-58, People Making Public Works History-A Century of Progress 1894-1994, 1998 ; cons. editor pub. works sect., Mcpl. Pub. Works Adminstrn., 1957; chmn. adv. bd. Internat. Ctr. Acad. State and Local Govts., 1985-87. Served to 1st lt. USMCR, 1943-45. Mem. ASCE (life), Am. Pub. Works Assn. (hon.), Internat. Pub. Works Fedn. (treas. 1985-89, sec.-gen. 1990), Am. Soc. Assn. Execs., Am. Soc. Pub. Adminstrn., Internat. Union Local Authorities (pres. U.S. sect. 1977-79, v.p. 1968-70, 75-77), Internat. Solid Wastes and Pub. Cleansing Assn. (v.p. 1968-70), Internat. Fedn. Mcpl. Engrs. (treas. 1976-79), Pub. Works Hist. Soc. (hon., treas. 1975-89), Sigma Alpha Epsilon. Baptist. Home: 8238 E Del Cadena Dr Scottsdale AZ 85258-2319 Office: 2345 Grand Blvd Ste 500 Kansas City MO 64108-2641 E-mail: rdpjbugher@msn.com.

BUGIELSKI, ROBERT JOSEPH, state legislator; b. Chgo., June 5, 1947; s. Edward Leon and Lottie Regina (Ptak) B.; m. Dona Rosalie Obrzut, Aug. 2, 1980. BS in Bus. Edn., Chgo. State U., 1971. Tchr. Weber High Sch., Chgo., 1971-83; asst. athletic dir., 1973-78; dir. devel. Weber High Sch., Chgo., 1974-83, adminstrv. bd. dirs., 1975-83; rep. Ill. Gen. Assembly, Chgo., 1987—. Named Legislator of Yr. Am. Legis. Exch. Coun., 1991. Democrat. Roman Catholic. Office: 6839 W Belmont Ave Chicago IL 60634-4646

BUGLI, DAVID, conductor, arranger, composer; b. N.Y.C., Apr. 2, 1950; BMus, Ithaca Coll., 1972; MMus, U. Mass., 1978. Founder, musical dir., condr. Carson City Symphony (formerly Carson City Chamber Orch.), Nev., 1984—. Tchr. music Pub. Sch., 1972—77; computer programmer/analyst, 1979—; 1st pres. Carson Access TV Found., 1991. Office: Carson City Symphony PO Box 2001 Carson City NV 89702-2001 E-mail: dbugli@aol.com.

BUGLI, NEVILLE JIMMY, mechanical engineer; b. Bombay, Oct. 13, 1961; came to U.S., 1983; s. Jimmy Burjorji and Gool Jimmy (Udachia) B.; m. Binaifer Neville Mehta, Jan. 8, 1991. BSME, Shivaji U., 1983; MSME, U. Minn., 1986. Rsch. asst. particle tech. U. Minn., Mpls., 1984-86; rsch. engr., coord. Am. Filtrona Corp., Richmond, Va., 1986-91; engr. product design, tech. specialist Ford Motor Co., Dearborn, Mich., 1991-97; sr tech. specialist Visteon Corp., Energy Transformation Systems, Dearborn, 1997—2002; tech. fellow Visteon, Powertrain Sys., 2002—. Patentee in field; contbr. articles to profl. jours. Mem. ASME, Am. Assn. Aerosol Rsch., Am. Filtration Soc. (bd. dirs.), Soc. Automotive Engrs. (com. 1990—). Zorastrian. Avocations: music and hi-fi equipment, martial arts, hiking, wines. Office: Visteon Corp Energy Mgmt Applications 15200 Commerce Dr Dearborn MI 48120 E-mail: nbugli@visteon.com.

BUGLIANI, ANN C. international studies educator; b. N.Y.C., Aug. 4, 1942; d. Caesar A. and Ana C. Gonzalez; m. Americo Bugliani, Jan. 1, 1961. BA, DePaul U., 1964; MA, Northwestern U., Evanston, Ill., 1966, PhD, 1973. Asst. prof. Loyola U. Chgo., 1978-82, assoc. prof., 1982-99, prof. modern lang. and lit., 1999—, chair dept. lang. and lit., 1986-92, dir. Loyola Rome Ctr. of Liberal Arts, 2001—03. Author: Women and the Feminine Principle in the Works of Paul Claudel, 1977, The Instruction of Philosophy and Psychoanalysis by Tragedy, 1998; editor: Chairing the Foreign Language and Literature Department. Decorated Order of Les Palmes Académiques, French Republic, 1997. Mem. MLA, Assn. Depts. Fgn. Langs. (pres. 1992), Paul Claudel Soc. (pres. 1979-80), Am. Assn. Tchrs. French, Am. Assn. Tchrs. Italian, Association des Membres de L'Ordre des Palmes Academiques. Address: Via Mazzini 3 Pietrasanta Lu 55045 Italy E-mail: abuglia@luc.edu.

BUGLIARELLO, GEORGE, academic administrator, educator; b. Trieste, Italy, May 20, 1927; arrived in U.S., 1951, naturalized, 1964; s. Federico and Spera (Gefter-Wondrich) B.; m. Virginia Upton Harding, 1960; children: Federico David, Nicholas Luigi. DEng summa cum laude, U. Padua, Italy, 1951; MSCE, U. Minn., 1954; DSc, MIT, 1959; LLD (hon.), Carnegie-Mellon U., 1986, Trinity Coll., 1997; MD (hon.), U. Trieste, 1989; EngD (hon.), Milw. Sch. Engring., 1991; LLD (hon.), Ill. Inst. Tech., 1993, EngD (hon.); LLD (hon.), Pace U., 1994, LHD (hon.). Rsch. engr. U. Padua, 1951; from rsch. asst. to rsch. assoc. MIT, 1956-59; mem. faculty Carnegie-Mellon U., 1959-69, prof. biotech. and civil engring., 1956-69, chmn. biotechnology program, 1964-69; dean engring. U. Ill. Chgo. Cir., 1969-73; pres. Poly. U., Bklyn., 1973-94, chancellor, 1994—2003, pres. emeritus, Univ. prof., 2003—. Bd. hydraulic cons. U.S. Waterways Exptl. Sta., 1968—74; mem. sci. adv. panel Armed Forces Explosive Safety Bd., 1968—69; mem. biomed tng. engring. com. NIH, 1966—70; mem. commn. edn. Nat. Acad. Engring., 1970—73, chmn. com. ednl. sys., 1970—73, mem. tech. edn. stds. com.; chmn. bd. sci. and tech. for internat. devel. NAS, 1979—83; sci. policy reviewer Portugal OECD, 1982—83, others; U.S. rep. steering com. on sci. for stability program NATO, 1984—97, mem. steering com. on sci. for peace, 1997—2000; chair engring. adv .com. Lawrence Livermore Nat. Lab.; mem. U. Chgo. rev. com. for the decision and info. scis. divsn. Argonne Nat. Lab.; trustee William R. Kenan Jr. Inst. Engring. Tech. and Sci., Paul and Daisy Soros Fellowship for New Ams.; mem. Found. Future Bd. Advisors; bd. dirs. Lord Corp., Comtech. Corp., Keyspan Energy, Symbol Techs., Inc., Jura Corp. Co-author: (book) Computer Systems and Water Resources, 1974, The Impact of Noise Pollution, 1976, Technology, The Community and the University, 1976; editor: Bioengineering--An Engineering View, 1967, Women in Engineering, 1972, The History and Philosophy of Technology, 1979; co-editor: East-West Technology Transfer, 1996, Technology in Society; interim editor-in-chief: The Bridge; contbr. articles. Trustee ANSER, 1974-2000, Teagle Found., Greenwall Found., 1984-2000, Lord Found. N.C., Commn. Ind. Colls. and Universities, 1993-96; bd. visitors Duke U. Sch. Engring., 1975-2000; mem. N.Y. Partnership, 1980 , High Tech. Task Force, 1985-90, chmn., 1988-90, Mayor's Commn. Sci. and Tech., 1984-90, chmn., 1987-90; exec. com. Bd. Trustees Commn. Ind. Colls. and Univs., N.Y., 1986-89; alumni rep. MIT vis. com. for Civil Engring., 1985-91; chair, N.Y.C. Mayor's Task Force on Gramercy Park Steam Pipe Explosion, 1989-90, N.Y.C. Mayor's Adv. Coun. on Devel. of Recycling Markets and Businesses; active Nat. Medal Tech. Nomination Evaluation Com., 1987-92, chmn. 1991-92; chair Nat. Acads. Megacities Project Habitat II Conf.; mem. Nat. Acad. Sci. Com. Human Rights; mem. U.S. Nat. Acads.-Russian Acad. Sci. Com. on Terrorism Confronting the U.S. and Russia. Recipient Alza prize Biomed. Engring. Soc.; NATO sr. fellow Tech. U. Berlin, 1968; N.Y. Mayor's Awd. Excellence Sci. and Tech., 1994, N.Y. Acad. of Scis. Fellow AAAS (chair com. sci., engring. and pub. policy, 1986-89, chair panel on phys. scis. and engring. 1987-89, project 2061 1985-89), Am. Soc. Engring. Edn., ASCE (chmn. exec. com. engring. mechanics divsn. 1971-72, chmn. interdivisional task com. civil engring. in medicine and health care delivery 1969-73, Huber rsch. prize 1967), Am. Inst. Med. and Biol. Engring. (founding fellow); mem. NAE (coun. 1989-93, adv. com. tech. and the environ. 1989-92, internat. affairs adv. com. 1988-92), Internat. Assn. Hydraulic Rsch. (chmn. task com. computer langs. 1969-72), N.Y. Acad. Medicine, Nat. Assn. for Sci., Tech. and Soc. (trustee 1988—, pres. 1989-90, hon. lifetime mem.), Nat. Rsch. Coun. (bd. engring. edn. 1991-96, chair bd. on infrastructure and constructed environ. 1994-97, chair com. on alt. techs. to replace anti-pers. landmines 1999-2000, vice chair com. on army sci. and tech. for homeland def. 2002--, others), N.Y. Acad. Scis. (pres'. coun. 1990—, mem. com. human rights 1996—), Italian Soc. Advancement Sci. (hon. mem.), Sigma Xi (disting. lectr. 1996—, past pres., bd. dirs.), Nat. Acad. Engring. (chair steering com.on megacities 1999--, Russ prize com. 2000, fgn. sec. 2003-). Home: 5 Terrace Dr Port Washington NY 11050-3419 Office: Polytechnic U 6 Metrotech Ctr Brooklyn NY 11201-3840

BUGNO, WALTER THOMAS, civil engineer; b. Scranton, Pa., Oct. 11, 1942; s. Walter A. and Elizabeth (Phillips) B.; m. Helen N. Steltzner, Nov. 30, 1963; children:Melia A., Dawn A., Janelle A., Timothy A., Peter W. BSCE, MSCE, U. Minn., 1967. Registered profl. engr., Calif., Alaska. Project mgr. Chevron Texaco, San Francisco, 1968—. Adviser Pres.'s Arctic Rsch. Commn., Wash-

ington, 1992, Can.'s Nat. Energy Bd., Dartmouth Coll. Sch. Engring., 1990. Contbr. articles on developing petroleum res. using tunnelling, other petroleum drilling topics to profl. publs. Corp. chmn. Ch. of Christ, Pleasant Hill, 1986—. Fellow ASCE. Republican.

BUHAC, IVO, gastroenterologist; b. Dubrovnik, Croatia, Sept. 4, 1926; s. Ivan and Blazenka (Dulcic) B.; m. Susanne Rossband, Sept. 14, 1963; 1 child, John. MD, U. Med. Sch., Zagreb, Croatia, 1952, ScD, 1963; MD, U. Med. Sch., Erlangen, Germany, 1962. Staff physician Hosp. O. Novosel, Zagreb, 1957-68; resident in gastroenterology VA Hosp., Richmond, Va., 1968-70; asst. prof. medicine Albany (N.Y.) Med. Coll., 1970-74, assoc. prof. medicine, 1974-82, prof. medicine, 1982-88, chief of gastroenterology, 1970-88. Contbr. articles to Gastroenterology, Hepatology, N.Y. State Jour. Medicine, Deutsche Medizinische Wochenschrift. Mem. Am. Gastroenterology Assn., Am. Assn. for Study of Liver Diseases, N.Y. Acad. Scis. Achievements include research on the pathophysiology of ascites formation in liver cirrhosis, diagnosis of disease causing death of Herod the Great. Home: 82 Robinwood Dr Clifton Park NY 12065-2737 E-mail: ibuhac@nycap.rr.com.

BUHAGIAR, MARION, editor, author; b. N.Y.C., Oct. 27, 1932; d. George and Mae (Pietrzak) B.; 1 child, Alexa Ragozin. BA cum laude, Hunter Coll., 1953; postgrad., Mt. Holyoke Coll., 1954. Economist U.S. Dept. Commerce, 1954-57; bus. reporter Time mag., 1957-59; assoc. editor Fortune mag., 1960-73, story devel. editor, 1970-73; text editor Time-Life Books, N.Y.C., 1973-76; v.p. Boardroom Inc., 1977-84; editor Boardroom Reports, 1977-84; exec. editor Bottom Line/Personal, 1980-84; pres. Expert Connections, N.Y.C., 1994—2002; editor Street Smart Investing, 1987-89; ret., 2003. Author: How to Build a College Fund for Your Child, 1989, Battle Plan for American Business, 1992, I-Power, 1992; editor: The Book of Secrets, 1989. Adv. bd. Scientists Inst. for Pub. Info., N.Y.C. E-mail: dorset2@aol.com.

BUHAIN, WILFRIDO JAVIER, medical educator; b. Bacoor, Cavite, Philippines, Oct. 12, 1940; m. Carlota Torres; children: Ronald, Edgar. AA, BS, U. Philippines, 1959, MD, 1964. Diplomate Am. Bd. Internal Medicine, Am. Bd. Pulmonary Diseases. Rsch. fellow in cardiology U. Philippines, Philippine Gen. Hosp., 1964-65; rotating intern Queens Hosp. Ctr., N.Y.C., 1965-66, resident in internal medicine, 1965-68; clin. fellow in pulmonary diseases Hosp. of U. Pa., 1968-69, chief pulmonary function lab. dept. medicine, 1971-72, rsch. fellow in pulmonary diseases Hosp. of U. Pa., VA Hosp., Phila., 1969-71; assoc. in medicine, cardiovascular-pulmonary div. med. dept. U. Pa. Sch. Medicine, 1971-72; assoc. in medicine, dept. medicine Mt. Sinai Sch. Medicine, CUNY, 1972-74; clin. instr. medicine Georgetown U., 1976-95. Chief pulmonary function lab. dept. medicine Mt. Sinai Hosp. Svcs./City Hosp. Ctr. at Elmhurst, 1973-74; med. dir. respiratory therapy dept. Mt. Vernon Hosp., 1978—, chmn. dept. medicine, 1987-88, pres. med. staff, 1996-98; mem. exec. com. Alexandria Hosp., 1983; trustee, chmn. med. affairs coun. Inova Health Sys., 1998-99. Contbr. articles to profl. jours. Queensborough Soc. grantee; Pa. Thoracic Soc. grantee. Fellow ACP, Am. Coll. Chest Physicians; mem. Am. Soc. Internal Medicine, Alexandria Med. Soc., Va. Med. Soc., Philippine Med. Assn. (exec. dir., past pres. Metro-Washington), Assn. Philippine Physicians in Am. (v.p.). Avocations: tennis, golf, ballroom dancing. Office: 6300 Stevenson Ave Ste B Alexandria VA 22304-3554

BUHITE, THOMAS JESSE, SR., employee benefits consultant; b. Balt., Aug. 26, 1946; s. Jesse Paul and Bernice June (Dixon) B.; m. Janet Lynn Fields, oct. 6, 1968; children: Thomas Jesse Jr., John Michael. BS, U. Md., 1977; postgrad., Loyola Coll. Md., 1981-83, Potomac Sch. Law, Washington, 1980-82. Lic. life, health, property and casualty ins. advisor, Md.; lic. life, health, property and casualty ins. broker-agt. Claims mgr. Hardester Corp., Balt., 1975-76; claims mgr./asst. to gen. counsel Johns Hopkins Hosp., Balt., 1977-81; dir. risk mgmt. Johns Hopkins U., Balt., 1981-86; asst. v.p. Med. Mut. Liability Ins. of Md., Balt., 1986-87; sr. v.p. Coastal Group, Inc./Century Am. Ins. Co., Durham, N.C., 1987-88; pres., chief exec. officer Risk Mgmt., Inc., Columbia, Md., 1988-90, Health Claims Adminstrs., Inc., Columbia, Md., 1988-90; pres., chief exec. officer, chmn. bd. dirs. Health Benefits Adminstrs. Inc., Forest Hill, Md., 1990—2001; pres. Chesapeake Marine Svc. Group, Md., 2002—. Bd. dirs. Genesis Ltd., Hamilton, Bermuda, 1981-86, chmn. bd. ops. com., sr. claims officer; bd. dirs. Risk Mgmt., Inc.; faculty adminstrv. tng. program Johns Hopkins U., Balt., 1981-86, guest lectr. exec. small bus. program, 1989—. Co-author: Employer's Workers' Compensation Handbook, 1981, The Physician's Guide to the Worker's Compensation System, 1982; contbr. articles to profl. jours. Chmn. bd. trustees Jarrettsville United Meth. Ch., 1989-90; coord., organizer Tiger Cub Scouts, Madonna, Md., 1988-89; com. chmn. Cub Scouts, Jarrettsville, 1989-90, asst. cub master, 1990-91, cub master, 1992-93; vice commodore Sea Scouts/Boy Scouts Am., Balt. Area Coun., 1999—; pres. Jarrettsville Recreation Coun., 1993-94, Jarrettsville Youth Football and Cheerleading, 1993-94; pres. com. Harford County Recreation Coun., 1993-94; skipper BSA Sea Explorer Ship, 1994—. Recipient award of merit Balt. Area coun. Boy Scouts Am., 1998. Mem. Am. Soc. Healthcare Risk Mgmt. of Am. Hosp. Assn., Practising Law Inst., Risk and Ins. Mgmt. Soc. (chpt. pres. 1989-90), Md. Self-Insurers & Employers Compensation Assn. (treas. 1981-82), Balt. Yacht Club, Masons. Republican. Methodist. Avocations: boating, fishing, camping, hunting, golf. Home: 4160 Norrisville Rd White Hall MD 21161-9309 E-mail: buhitesr@aol.com.

BUHL, CYNTHIA MAUREEN, foreign policy educator and advocate; b. Los Angeles, Apr. 14, 1952; d. Albert Buhl and Dorothy Jane (Loth) Henry. BA, Lewis & Clark Coll., 1974. Dir. Resource and Counseling Ctr., Portland Youth Advs., Oreg., 1971-72; resource coordinator S.E. Youth Service Ctr., Portland Action Coms. Together, 1975-77; sec., asst. Human Rights Office Nat. Council Chs. Christ, N.Y.C., 1977-78; human rights coordinator Coalition for a New Fgn. and Mil. Policy, Washington, 1978-85; cons. Fgn. Policy Edn. Fund, Washington, 1986; nat. adv. bd. Caribbean Basin Info. Project, 1983-85; bd. dirs., legis. dir. Pax Am.'s/Priorities-PAC, 1986-90; legis. dir. Ctrl. Am. Working Group, 1990-93; dir. Indigenous Peoples Program, Bank Info. Ctr., 1994-96; legis. dir. U.S. Rep. James A. McGovern, 1997—. Author: Citizen's Guide to the Multilateral Development Banks and Indigenous Peoples: The World Bank, 1994, Spanish transl., 1995, Bahasa transl., 1996, Russian transl., 1996; co-editor: Central America 1985: Basic Information and Legislative History on U.S.-Central American Relations, 1985. Contbr. articles to various jours., mags. Co-chmn. Human Rights Working Group, Washington, 1978-81, chmn., 1982-85; chmn. Central Am. Lobby Group, 1983-85; mem. Commn. on U.S.-Central Am. Relations, 1983-85.

BUHLER, GREGORY WALLACE, lawyer; b. Englewood, N.J., Oct. 17, 1949; s. Wallace and Mary Jane (Burton) B.; m. Jan Clark, Sept. 7, 1968; children— Jennifer, Casey. B.A., C.W. Post Coll., 1971, J.D., Hofstra Law Sch., 1974. Bar: N.Y. 1975, U.S. Dist. Ct. (so. and ea. dists.) N.Y. 1975, U.S. Ct. Claims 1979, U.S. Ct. Appeals (2d cir.) 1984, U.S. Supreme Ct. 1985, U.S. Ct. Appeals (5th cir.) 1989. Assoc. Whitman & Ransom, N.Y.C., 1974-76; from atty. to v.p. legal Pan Am. World Airways, Inc., N.Y.C., 1976—p; v.p., gen. coun. and sec. Kiwi Internat. Airlines, Inc., Newark, N.J., 1996—. Home: 633 Cardinal Rd Cortlandt Manor NY 10567-5201

BUHLER, JILL LORIE, editor, writer; b. Seattle, Dec. 7, 1945; d. Oscar John and Marcella Jane (Hearing) Younce; 1 child, Lori Jill Moody; m. John Buhler, 1990; stepchildren: Christie Reynolds, Cathie Zatarian, Mike. AA in Gen. Edn., Am. River Coll., 1969; BA in Journalism with honors, Sacramento State U., 1973. Reporter Carmichael (Calif.) Courier, 1968-70; mng. editor Quarter Horse of the Pacific Coast, Sacramento, 1970-75, editor, 1975-84, Golden State Program Jour., 1978, Nat. Reined Cow Horse Assn. News, Sacramento, 1983-88, Pacific Coast Jour., Sacramento, 1984-88, Nat. Snaffle Bit Assn. News, Sacramento, 1988; pres., chief exec. officer Communications Plus, Port Townsend, Wash., 1988—; bd. sec. N.W. Maritime Ctr., 2001—, 2001—. Mag. cons., 1975—. Interviewer Pres. Ronald Regan, Washington, 1983; mng. editor Wash. Thoroughbred, 1989-90. Mem. 1st profl. communicators mission to USSR, 1988; bd. dirs. Carmichael Winding Way, Pasadena Homeowners Assn., 1985-87; mem. scholarship com. Thoroughbred Horse Racing's United Scholarship Trust; mem. governing bd. Wash. State Hosp. Assn., 1996-2000, mem. legis. policy com., 1999—, hosp. commr. Jefferson Gen. Hosp., 1995—, chair bd. dirs. 1997-2000; mem. Jefferson County Bd. Health, 1997—, vice chmn., 1998, chmn. 2001. Recipient 1st pl. feature award, 1970, 1st pl. editorial award Jour. Assn. Jr. Colls., 1971, 1st pl. design award WCHB Yuba-Sutter Counties, Marysville, Calif., 1985, Photography awards, 1994, 95, 96. Mem. Am. River Jaycees (Speaking award 1982), Am. Horse Publs. (1st Pl. Editl. award 1983, 86), Port Townsend C. of C. (trustee, v.p. 1993, pres. 1994, officer 1996, 97, 98), Mensa (bd. dirs., asst. local sec., activities dir. 1987-88, membership chair 1988-90), Kiwanis Internat. (chair maj. emphasis program com., treas. 1992—), 5th Wheel Touring Soc. (v.p. 1970). Republican. Roman Catholic. Avocations: sailing, photography. Home: 440 Adelma Beach Rd Port Townsend WA 98368-9280 E-mail: jillb@olypen.com.

BUHLER, LESLIE LYNN, museum director; BA with honors in History and Art History, Syracuse U., 1969; postgrad., New Sch. for Social Rsch., 1971, Am. U., 1980. Asst. for cmty. programs Met. Mus. Art, N.Y.C., 1970-72; program coord. resident assoc. program Smithsonian Instn., Washington, 1972-75; instnl. devel. officer Nat. Archives and Records Svc., Washington, 1975-78; ind. cons., 1977—85; dir. devel., membership and mktg. Alban Inst., Inc., Bethesda, Md., 1985-88, dir. ops., 1988-89, exec. v.p., 1989-99, acting pres., 1994-95; exec. dir. Tudor Place Historic House and Garden, Washington, 2000—. Grant reviewer Office of Mus. Programs, NEH, Washington, 1973-74. Bd. dirs. Mus. of City of Washington, 1980-84; vol. advisor Nat. Mus. for Bldg. Arts, Washington, 1977-79. Recipient cert. of appreciation Am. Revolution Bicentennial Adminstrn., 1976. Office: Tudor Place Found 1644 31st St NW Washington DC 20007

BÜHNEMANN, GUDRUN, social studies educator; PhD, U. Vienna, Austria, 1980. Sr. rsch. fellow Bhandarkar Oriental Rsch. Inst., Pune, India, 1980—89; rsch. fellow Nagoya (Japan) U., 1989—91; vis. rsch. scholar Kyoto (Japan) U., 1991—92; Spalding vis. fellow U. Oxford, England, 1992; asst. prof. U. Wis., Madison, 1992—94, assoc. prof., 1994—99, prof., 1999—. Fellow, Numata Found., 1991—92, NEH, 1997—98; postdoctoral rsch. fellow, Deutscher Akademischer Austauschdienst, 1980—82, Deutsche Forschungsgemeinschaft, 1983—95, postdoctoral fellow, Japan Soc. Promotion of Sci., 1983—85, rsch. fellow, Am. Coun. Learned Societies, 1998. Office: U Wis-Madison 1240 Van Hise Hall 1220 Linden Drive Madison WI 55370

BUHNER, BYRON BEVIS, health science facility administrator; b. Hammond, Ind., Feb. 19, 1950; s. John Colin and Betty (Bevis) B.; children: Zachery Aaron, Rebecca Bevis. AB in Comm., Ind. U., 1976, MS in Human Resource Devel., 1981. Adminstr. Ind. U., Indpls., 1976-77, instr. evaluator sch. nursing, 1981-82; tng. specialist Ayr-Way, Target Stores, Indpls., 1977-81; assoc. exec. dir. Cen. Ind. Regional Blood Ctr., Indpls., 1984-88, pres., chief exec. officer, 1988—; founding mem. Blood Ctrs. Ins. Exch., Risk Retention Group, 1993, chmn. bd. dirs., 1993-96, dir., 1996—; adminstr. Blood Rsch. and Edn. Foundn. of Ind., Inc., Indpls., 1985-89, bd. mem., 1989-94. Mem. dean's adv. coun. Ind. U. Sch. Liberal Arts, 1999—; bd. dirs. Irwin Union Bank & Trust, Hamilton County, 2000—. Producer: Multi-Image film, Focus on Transition, 1981, A Manager's Perspective, 1981; photographer: Sound, Slide program, Wearable - Arts '81. Trustee Coun. Cmty. Blood Ctrs., 1986-97, chmn. purchasing com., 1988-92, chmn. fin. com., treas., 1992-94, v.p., 1994-96, pres., 1997-99, chmn. exec. com., chmn. group svcs. com., chmn. long-range planning com. Mem. Am. Acad. Healthcare Execs. (diplomate), Ind. U. Alumni Assn. (bd. dirs. 1983-88), Am. Assn. Blood Banks, Ind. Assn. Blood Banks (bd. dirs. 1988-91), Kiwanis. Avocations: sailing, jogging, hockey, photography, coaching youth sports. Home: 14051 Stone Key Way Fortville IN 46040-9675 Office: Cen Ind Regional Blood Ctr 3450 N Meridian St Indianapolis IN 46208-4437 E-mail: bbuhner@cirbc.org.

BUHNER, JAY CAMPBELL, former professional baseball player; b. Louisville, Ky., Aug. 13, 1964; m. Leah Buhner; children: Brielle, Chase, Gunnar. Student, McClennan C.C., Waco, Tex. Outfielder N.Y. Yankees, N.Y.C., 1987—88, Seattle Mariners, 1988—2001. Active Cystic Fibrosis Found., Seattle, Juvenile Diabetes Assn. Named Houston Area Player of Yr., Houston chpt. Baseball Writers Assn. Am., 1993, 1995; recipient Gold Glove award, 1996, Breath of Life award, Cystic Fibrosis Found., 1997. Office: c/o Seattle Mariners PO Box 4100 1st Ave S and Atlantic Seattle WA 98104

BUHOLTE, AGNESE, library director; b. Līgatne, Cēsis, Latvia, June 5, 1952; d. Jānis Dancis and Rasma (Timermane) Dance; m. Jānis Buholts, Sept. 7, 1974; children: Jānis, Inese. Diploma in lib. scis., U. Latvia, Riga, 1974. Diplomated librarian and bibliographer. Librarian Patent and Tech. Lib. of Latvia, Riga, 1974—75, chief librarian, 1975—76, head methodics dept., 1976—85, dir., 1985—. Mem. Lib. Assn. Latvia (bd. dirs. 1990—), Latvian Academic Lib. Assn. (v.p. 1998—2001, bd.dir. 2002—). Avocations: gardening, sewing, knitting, travel, music. Home: 14 Upes St Apt 11 Riga Latvia LV-1013 Office: Patent and Tech Libr of Latvia Skunu Iela 17 1974 Riga Latvia Fax: (371) 7210767. E-mail: agnese.buholte@patbib.lv.

BUHR, WALTER HEINRICH WILHELM, economics educator; b. Bremen, Germany, Aug. 27, 1938; s. Hans and Elisabeth (Gloatz) B.; m. Inge Elfriede Kaden, Apr. 12, 1967; children: Kerstin, Jan, Henning. Diploma, U. Freiburg/Br., Fed. Republic Germany, 1961, Dr. rer. pol., 1965; privatdozent, U. Kiel, Fed. Republic Germany, 1972, Sci. asst. U. Kiel, 1966-72, docent of econs., 1972-73; rsch. assoc. U. Calif., Berkeley, 1968-70; prof. econs. U. Siegen, Germany, 1973—2003, prof. emeritus, 2003—. Co-author: Urban Development Models (in German) 1981; co-editor: Competition among Small Regions, 1978; contbr. articles to profl. jours. Mem. Regional Sci. Assn. Internat., Am. Econ. Assn. Home: Am Schieferberg 9 57074 Siegen Germany Office: U of Siegen Holderlinstr 3 57068 Siegen Germany E-mail: buhr@vwl.wiwi.uni-siegen.de.

BUHROW, WILLIAM CARL, religious organization administrator; b. Cleve., Jan. 18, 1934; s. Philip John and Edith Rose (Leutz) B.; m. Carole Corinne Craven, Feb. 14, 1959; children: William Carl Jr., David Paul, Peter John, Carole Lynn. Diploma, Phila. Coll. Bible, 1954; BA, Wheaton (Ill.) Coll., 1956, MA, 1959. Ordained to ministry Gen. Assn. Regular Bapt. Chs., 1958. Asst. pastor (Hydewood Park Bapt. Ch.), N. Plainfield, N.J., 1959-63; with Continental Fed. Savs. & Loan Assn., Cleve., 1963-81, sr. v.p., 1971-75, pres., chief exec. officer, dir., 1975-81; chmn. bd. Security Savs. Mortgage Corp., Citizens Service Corp., New Market Corp., CFS Service Corp., 1975-81; trustee Credit Bur. Cleve., 1975-81, Bldg. Expositions, Inc., 1974-84; registered rep. IDS/Am. Express, Cleve., 1982-83; gen. credit mgr. Forest City Enterprises, Inc., Cleve., 1983-85; pres. Forest City Ins. Agy., Inc., Cleve., 1983-85; asst. v.p. Mellon Fin. Services Corp., Cleve., 1985-87; exec. adminstr. The Gospel Ho. Ch. and Evangelistic Ctr., Walton Hills, Ohio, 1988—. Trustee Bapt. Bible Coll. and Theol. Sem., Clarks Summit, Pa., 1977-90; vice chmn. bd. deacons Cedar Hill Bapt. Ch., Cleveland Heights, Ohio, 1981-87; trustee, sec. and treas. Gospel House Prison Ministry Found., 1992—. Mem. Christian Bus. Men's Com. Internat., Nat. Assn. Ch. Bus. Adminstrn. Baptist. Home: 1044 Linden Ln Lyndhurst OH 44124-1051 Office: 14707 Alexander Rd Cleveland OH 44146-4924 *The supreme goal of my life is to please and honor the Lord Jesus Christ in all that I say and do. The standards, goals, and ideals outlined in the Bible, God's Holy Word, are the ones which I have adopted for my life. True happiness for me lies in the accomplishment of God's perfect will in my life and that of my family and in introducing others to Christ so they may know Him as their own personal Saviour, too. Herein lies the key to my success as a Christian administrator.*

BUI, KHOI TIEN, college counselor; b. Binh Dinh, Vietnam, Dec. 23, 1937; came to U.S., 1975; naturalized, 1982; s. Luu and Quang Thi (Tran) B.; m. Yen Kim Nguyen, Dec. 7, 1962; children: Khanh, Huy, Huan. BS in Agri., Agrl. Coll., Vietnam, 1962; BS, Law U., Vietnam, 1965; MS, Polit. and Bus. Mgmt. U., Vietnam, 1972, PhD; DLitt (hon.), London Inst. for Applied Rsch., 1991; DE (hon.), World Acad., 1997; PhD (hon.), Inst. Affairs Internat., 1997. With Ministry Agri., Republic of Vietnam, 1962-75; counselor Houston C.C., 1976—, chmn. Indochinese Culture and Refugee Info. Ctr., 1981—. Nat. Planner Tng., Taiwan, 1963, Philippines, 1965, Australia, 1968, Japan, 1970, Thailand, 1971. Author: (poetry books) America My First Feelings, 1981, 20 Poems and 1000 Thoughts, 1994; contbr. to other poetry books, novel and textbook in Vietnamese. Founder, moderator radio sta. The Voice of Free Vietnam, Houston, 1980—; chmn. Indochinese and Refugee Info. Ctr., Houston Community Coll. Decorated knight Order of Templars, officer de l'ordre des Arts et des Lettres; recipient Nat. Lit. prize Republic Vietnam, 1966, Houston's Poet Laureate award, 1984, Golden Poet award World of Poetry, 1985, Edn. award, 1985, Men of Achievement award, 1989, Medal of Honor, 1990, One-in-a-Million Medal, 1991, Most Admired Man of the Decade award, 1992, Twentieth Century award for Achievement, 1992, various medals Govt. of the Republic of Vietnam; named Man of Yr., 1990, Internat. Man of Yr., 1992, Albert Einstein medal, 1996, Literature medal, 1996. Fellow Royal Soc. Lit.; mem. Leadership Houston Assn., Pen Am. Ctr. Avocations: writing poetry, reading, swimming. Home: 13715 Towne Way Dr Sugar Land TX 77478-1652 Office: Houston CC 1300 Holman St Houston TX 77004-3834 E-mail: buihuyluc@hotmail.com.

BUICE, BONNIE CARL, lawyer, priest; b. East Point, Ga., May 20, 1932; s. Bonnie Carl and Mahalia Elizabeth (Ramsey) B.; m. Patterson Nall, Dec. 14, 1957 (div. Apr. 1982); children: Merrianne, Shannon, Samuel, William, Christopher; m. Hulane E. George, Feb. 18, 1984. AB, Mercer U., 1954, JD, 1957; MA in Theology, U. Notre Dame, 1975. Bar: Ga. 1954, U.S. Dist. Ct. (no. dist.) Ga. 1957, U.S. Dist. Ct. (mid. dist.) Ga. 1983, U.S. Ct. Appeals (11th cir.) 1991; ordained priest Episcopal Ch., 1975. Assoc. Nall, Miller, Cadenhead & Dennis, Atlanta, 1957-61; ptnr. Robinson, Buice, Harben & Strickland, Gainesville, Ga., 1961-74; curate Holy Trinity Parish, Decatur, Ga., 1975-79; rector St. Francis Ch., Macon, Ga., 1979-84; ptnr. George & Buice, Milledgeville, Ga., 1984-86, Waddell, Emerson, George & Buice, Milledgeville, 1986-94, Waddell, Emerson & Buice, Milledgeville, 1994-2000; of counsel Waddell & Assoc., 2000—; assoc. priest St. Stephens Episcopal Ch., Milledgeville, 1986-91; rector St. James Episcopal Ch, Macon, 1992—; of counsel Waldell & Assocs., 2000—. Mem. Ocmulgee Bar Assn. (pres. 1991-92), Baldwin County Bar Assn. (treas. 1991-92). Home: 115 Maplewood Ave SW Milledgeville GA 31061-3646 Office: PO Box 630 Milledgeville GA 31059-0630

BUILDER, J. LINDSAY, JR., lawyer; b. Miami, Fla., Feb. 6, 1943; s. John Lindsay and Majorie (Merrell) L.; m. Jean Fern, Aug. 3, 1968; children Margaret Merrell, John Lindsay III. BE, Vanderbilt U., 1965, JD, 1970. Bar: Fla. 1970, U.S. Dist Ct. (mid. dist.) Fla. 1971, U.S. Supreme Ct. 1976. Assoc., ptnr. Maguire, Voorhis & Wells P.A, Orlando, Fla., 1970-84; ptnr. Godbold, Allen, Brown & Builder P.A., Winter Park, Fla., 1984-88, Allen, Brown & Builder P.A., Winter Park, 1988-90, Honigman, Detroit, Orlando, 1991-96, Graham, Builder, Jones, Pratt and Marks, Winter Park, Fla., 1996—. Mem. bd. trust Vanderbilt U., Nashville, 1990-92, Winter Park Mem. Hosp., chmn. 1994-96. Lt. (j.g.) USN, 1965-67. Mem. Orange County Bar Assn. (pres. 1983-84), Vanderbilt U. Law Sch. Alumni (bd. dirs. 1985, pres.), Vanderbilt U. Alumni (pres. bd. dirs. 1989-90). Republican. Episcopalian. Avocations: golf, running. Office: Graham Builder Jones Pratt & Marks 369 N New York Ave Winter Park FL 32789-3124 E-mail: lbuilder@grahambuilder.com.

BUILER, DOROTHY MARION, business owner; b. Athens, Wis., Apr. 20, 1925; d. Edwin Herman and Katherine Dorothy (Dick) Mueller; m. Donald J. Builer, May 24, 1947; 1 child, Thomas Edwin. Grad. h.s., Athens. Owner, ptnr. Builer's Sport Shop, Wausau, Wis., 1959—, Campers Haven, Heafford Junction, Wis., 1967—. Mem. Internat. Platform Assn., Bus. and Profl. Women Club (pres. Marathon county 1968-69, pres. Northwood dist. 1973-74), Wausau Womans Club (pres.-elect 1988-90, pres. 1990-91), Am. Legion Aux. (pres. local unit 1958-59, pres. 8th dist. 1963-64, chmn. State of Wis. aux. conv. 1964), Valley Garden Club, Wausau Wheelers Bike Club (organizer). Home: 3919 Pine Cone Ln Wausau WI 54403-2384

BUIST, HENRY, economist; b. Charleston, Sc, June 28, 1962; s. Henry and Anne Kennedy Buist; m. Angelique Marie-eve Williams, July 22, 1989; children: Madeleine Reichel, Suzanne Kennedy. BA Economics, Vassar Coll., Poughkeepsie, NY, 1980—84; PhD Economics, U. Of Pa, Phila., PA, 1984—91. Sr. rsch. assoc. Wharton Sch. of Bus., Phila., 1988—91; economist U.S. Dept. of Agr., Washington, 1991—93; dir. fannie Mae, Washington, 1993—. Author: (journal articles (3) Real Estate Economics, (journal article) Jour. of Managerial Fin., Jour. of Housing Rsch., (book article) Ency. of Agr. Sci., (research report) Agr. Economics Rsch. Report. Recipient Chairman's Award, Fannie Mae, 1997, Charles M. Tiebout Prize, Western Regional Sci. Assn., 1992; grantee Office of the Provost, U. of Pa, 1990. Mem.: Am. Econ. Assn. Home: 6608 Tina Lane McLean VA 22101 Office: Fannie Mae 3900 Wisconsin Ave Washington DC 20016 Personal E-mail: henrybuist@cox.net. E-mail: henry_buist@fanniemae.com.

BUIST, RICHARDSON, retired corporate executive, retired banker; b. Bklyn., Aug. 8, 1921; s. George Lamb and Adelaide (Richardson) B.; m. Jean Mackerley, Oct. 2, 1948; children: Peter Richardson, Jean Morford Buist Earle, Mary Elizabeth Buist Lueth. Student, Yale U. Advt. copywriter Ecloss Co., Sparta, N.J., 1946-48; advt. mgr. Sussex County Ind., Newton, N.J., 1948-50, Dover (N.J.) Advance, 1950-53; bus. mgr. N.J. Herald, Inc., Newton, 1953-70, dir., v.p., 1958-70, pub., 1967-70; dir. N.J. Press Assn., 1966-70; asst. sec., asst. treas. Morford Conservation Co., Hamburg, 1965-72, pres., 1986-95, v.p., 1995-2000, dir. emeritus, 2000—. Trust officer Midlantic Nat. Bank/Sussex & Mchts., Newton, 1971-88, 2002—, Midlantic Nat. Bank, Edison, N.J., 1972-86, cons. 1986-90, dir. Newton Cemetary Co., 1989-2000, v.p., 1998-2000. Pres. Sussex County chpt. Am. Cancer Soc., 1956-58, Sussex County Music Found., 1959-61; mem. Morris-Sussex Area Health Facilities Planning Coun., 1965-68; v.p. Sussex County Coun. Arts, 1971-73; chmn. pub. rels. Morris-Sussex Area Coun. Boy Scouts Am., 1986-88; trustee Sussex County Music Found., 1955-75; v.p., chmn. fin. devel. com. Newton Meml. Hosp., 1966-68, bd. govs. 1962-88, 93-95, emeritus 1995—, pres. bd. govs., 1968-71, chmn., 1971-73; founding incorporator, trustee NW Jersey Health Care, 1971-76; trustee, mem. exec. com. regional health planning coun. Health Systems Agy., 1976-83, 1984-87, v.p., 1978-79; trustee United Way of Sussex County, 1984-90, spl. gifts chmn., 1984-88, mem. allocations com. 1990-93; dir. North Jersey Health Care Corp., 1988-95, dir. emeritus, 1995—, asst. treas., 1991-93; dir. Prime Care, Inc., 1989-95, chmn. bd. trustees, 1989-92; mem. Sussex County Arts and Heritage Coun., chmn. hist. house tour, 1993-95; steering com. N.J. Highlands Coalition, 1993—. Mem. N.J. Vet. Med. Soc. Aux. (del. 1979-82, 88-91, 2d v.p. 1990-91), Am. Vet. Med. Soc. Aux. (nat. chmn. legis. com. 1986-88, long-range planning com. 1990-95, chmn. 1992, mem. constitution, by-laws coms. 1993-95), Rotary (pres. 1967-68, Paul Harris fellow 1988, Svc. Above Self award 1993, Meritorious Svc. award 1998), Vernon Civic Assn. (dir. 1996-2000, v.p. 1997-98). Home: 4123 Fellowship Rd Basking Ridge NJ 07920

BUITENHUIS, PETER MARTINUS, language professional, educator; b. London, Eng., Dec. 8, 1925; s. John A. and Irene (Cotton) B. BA with honors, Jesus Coll. Oxford (Eng.) U., 1949, MA, 1954; PhD, Yale, 1955. Instr. U. Okla., Norman, 1949-51; instr. Am. studies Yale, 1954-59; assoc. prof. English Victoria Coll. U. Toronto, Ont., Can., 1959-66; vis. prof. U. Calif.-Berkeley, 1966-67; prof. McGill U., Montreal, Que., Can., 1967-75; prof., chmn. dept. English Simon Fraser U., Burnaby, B.C., Can., 1975-82; prof. emeritus English Simon Fraser U., Burnaby, B.C., Can., 1992. Author: Hugh MacLennan, 1968, The Grasping Imagination: the American Writings of Henry James, 1970, The Great War of Words: British, American and Canadian Propaganda and Fiction, 1914-1933, 1987, The House of the Seven Gables: Severing Family and Colonial Ties, 1991; editor: Selected Poems of E. J. Pratt, 1968, (with I. Nadel) George Orwell: A Reassessment, 1988, (with D. Staines) The Canadian Imagination; contbr. articles to profl. jours., popular press. Served to sub-lt. Royal Navy, 1943-46, Eng. Can. Coun. fellow, 1962-63; Am. Coun. Learned Socs. fellow, 1972-73; Social Scis. and Humanities Rsch. Coun. fellow, 1982-83, 91-94. Mem.: Assn. Can. Studies, Can. Assn. Am. Studies (pres. 1968—70), Am. Studies Assn. Home: 7019 Marine Dr West Vancouver BC Canada V7W 2T4 Office: Simon Fraser U Dept English Burnaby BC Canada V5A 1S6 E-mail: buitenhu@sfu.ca.

BUJANOVICH, WILLIAM MATTHEW, marketing professional; b. Milw., Oct. 5, 1965; s. Nicolas Bujanovich Daniel, Leone Bujanovich Judith; m. Cynthia Therese Jarzembinski. BA, U. Wis., 1988; M Internat. Mgmt., Am. Grad. Sch. Internat. Mgmt., 1990. Small bus. advisor U.S. Peace Corps, Santiago, Chile, 1992—94; dir. internat. mktg. & sales Alto-Shaam Internat., Menomonee Falls, Wash., 1994—. Commr. Landmarks Commn., New Berlin, Wis., 1991—92, cons., 1994—2002. Mem.: Milw. World Trade Assn. Home: 195 Aqua View Dr Cedarburg WI 53012 Office: Alto-Shaam Internat W164 N9221 Water St Menomonee Falls WI 53051 Office Fax: 262 251 1907. Personal E-mail: bbujanovich@yahoo.com. Business E-mail: billb@alto-shaam.com.

BUJOLD, LOIS MCMASTER, writer; b. Columbus, Ohio, Nov. 2, 1949; d. Robert Charles and Laura Elizabeth (Gerould) McMaster; m. John Fredric Bujold, Oct. 9, 1971 (div. Dec. 1992); children: Anne Elizabeth, Paul Andre. Author: (novels) Shards of Honor, 1986, The Warrior's Apprentice, 1986, Ethan of Athos, 1986, Falling Free, 1988 (Nebula award, 1989), Brothers in Arms, 1989, Borders of Infinity, 1989, The Vor Game, 1990 (Hugo award, 1991), Barrayar, 1991 (Hugo award, 1992, 1st place Locus poll, 1992), Mirror Dance, 1994 (Hugo & Locus awards, 1995), Cetaganda, 1996, Memory, 1996, Komarr, 1998 (Minn. book award, 1999), A Civil Campaign, 1999, The Curse of Chalion, 2001 (Mythopoeic award, 2002), Diplomatic Immunity, 2002, Paladin of Souls, 2003, (novellas) The Borders of Infinity, 1987, The Mountains of Mourning, 1989 (Nebula and Hugo awards, 1990), Labyrinth, 1989 (Best Novella/Novelette Analytical Lab., 1990), Weatherman, 1990 (Best Novella Analytical Lab., 1991); contbr. short stories to sci. fiction mags., articles to profl. jours. Mem.: Novelists, Inc., Sci. Fiction and Fantasy Writers Am. Office: Spectrum Literary Agency 320 Central Park W Ste 1D New York NY 10025-7659 E-mail: lois@dendarii.com.

BUJON DE L'ESTANG, FRANCOIS, diplomat; b. Neuilly sur Seine, France, 1940; m. Anne de Margerie; four children. Grad., Inst. Politique Paris, Ecole Nat. Adminstrn., Harvard U. Joined Ministry Fgn. Affairs, 1966, staff mem. office of the permanent sec., 1966-69, spl. advisor, dep. to pres. diplomatic advisor, 1969-73, from second to first sec. French Embassy in the U.S., 1973-75, first sec., second counselor French Embassy in London, 1975-78; advisor on internat. affairs to del. gen. for energy Ministry Industry, Paris, 1978-80; dir. internat. rels. Atomic Energy Commissariat, 1980-81; chief of staff Min. Industry, 1981-86; creator, pres., CEO COGEMA, Inc., Washington, 1986-88; sr. advisor for diplomatic affairs, def. and cooperation French Govt., 1989-91, amb. of France to Can., 1991-92; sr. v.p. Compagnie de Navigation Mixte and Via Banque, Paris, 1992-95; chmn., CEO S.F.I.M., 1992-95; founder FBE Internat. Cons., 1992-95; amb. of France to the U.S. Washington, 1995—. French rep. bd. govs. Internat. Atomic Energy Agy., 1979—; bd. dirs. SOFRATOME, TECHNICATOME, EURODIF, Inst. Francais des Rels. Internat. Mem. editl. bd. Revue des Deux Mondes. Pres. Harvard Bus. Sch. Club France. Named Knight of the Order of the Legion of Honor, Officer of the Nat. Order of Merit. Office: 4101 Reservoir Rd NW Washington DC 20007-2186

BUKALA, PHYLLIS, social worker; b. Galion, Ohio, Mar. 12, 1947; d. Joseph and Virginia (Rower) Sidwell; m. Chris Bukala, Jan. 15, 1983; 1 child, Mark. ADN, Bronx Community Coll., 1971; BA in Psychology, Marymount Manhattan Hosp., 1974; MSW, Worden Coll., 1978; MBA, Webster U., 1988. Registered social worker, S.C. Asst. clin. svcs. HSA Coastal Carolina, Myrtle Beach, S.C.; dir. discharge planning Georgetown (S.C.) Hosp. Maj. USAF, 1975-83. Mem. NASW. Home: 109 Ashford Cir Summerville SC 29485-8127

BUKANTZ, SAMUEL CHARLES, physician, educator; b. N.Y.C., Sept. 12, 1911; s. Barnett and Bertha (Stelson) B.; m. A. Jewell Williams, Apr. 5, 1941; children: Jessica, Dorothy. BS, Washington Sq. Coll., N.Y. U., 1930; MD, NYU, 1934. Intern in pathology Mt. Sinai Hosp., N.Y.C., 1934-35, intern in medicine, 1935-36, house physician, resident, 1936-38; assoc. prof. medicine Washington U., St. Louis, 1946-58, fellow in allergy, 1946-47; assoc. prof. medicine U. Colo., 1958-63; dir. medicine and research Children's Asthma Research Inst. and Hosp., 1958-63; assoc. prof. clin. medicine N.Y. U., 1963-72; prof. medicine U. South Fla., 1972—, head div. allergy and immunology, 1972-82, emeritus dir., 1982—, prof. med. microbiology and immunology, 1996—; pvt. practice medicine specializing in allergy and immunology N.Y.C., 1938-40, 66-72, St. Louis, 1954-58, Tampa, Fla., 1972-82; chief sect. allergy and clin. immunology VA Hosp., Tampa, 1972-82. Editor: Hosp. Practice, 1968— ; Contbr. numerous articles on allergy and immunology to profl. jours. Served with AUS, 1941-46. Lucius Littauer and Parmelee fellow in pneumonia research, 1938-41; NIH grantee, 1947-63 Fellow ACP, AAAS; mem. Am. Coll. Chest Physicians, Am. Soc. Clin. Investigation, Cen. Soc. Clin. Rsch., Am. Acad. Allergy, Am. Coll. Allergy, Alpha Omega Alpha. Democrat. Jewish. Home: 4940 W San Rafael St Tampa FL 33629-5404 Office: U South Fla Coll of Medicine Box MDC 19 12901 Bruce B Downs Blvd Tampa FL 33612-4742 E-mail: sbukantz@hsc.usf.edu.

BUKER, ROBERT HUTCHINSON, SR., army officer, thoracic surgeon; b. Loi Mwe, Kengtung, Burma, Dec. 6, 1928; came to U.S., 1940; s. Richard S. and Minola (Hutchinson) B.; m. Ethel Hunt, Sept. 25, 1949; children: Robert Hutchinson, Traci, Nina Ruth. AB, Boston U., 1949; MS, U. Maine, 1952; MD, Columbia U., 1956; postgrad., Indsl. Coll. of Armed Forces, 1978-79. Diplomate: Am. Bd. Surgery, Am. Bd. Thoracic Surgeons. Intern Gorgas Hosp, C.Z., 1956-57; gen. surg. residency Gorgas Hosp., C.Z., 1957-60; resident in thoracic surgery Kennedy V.A. Hosp., 1962-64, Tenn. Med. Ctr., 1962-64; capt. U.S. Army, 1964, advanced through grades to maj. gen.; chief surg. cons. Pentagon, Washington, 1973-76; comdr. U.S. Army Hosp., Wuerzburg, Germany, 1976-78; dep. chief staff opns. Health Services Command, Fort Sam Houston, Tex., 1979-80; comdr. Gen. Leonard Wood Army Hosp., Ft. Leonard Wood, Mo., 1980-81; commdr. Acad. Health Scis., Ft. Sam Houston, 1981-83; commdg. gen. Brooke Army Med. Center, Ft. Sam Houston, 1983-85; dep. Surgeon Gen. U.S. Army, Washington, 1985-89; chief surg. svcs. S.E. Kaiser-Permanente Med. Group, Atlanta, 1989-91. Chief legal medicine and risk mgmt. Kaiser-Permanente Med. Group, Atlanta, 1991-94; clin. prof. surgery Uniform U. Health Scis., Bethesda, Md., 1981—. Fellow ACS (bd. govs. 1987-89), Am. Coll. Chest Physicians, Am. Coll. Physician Execs.; mem. AMA, Soc. Thoracic Surgeons, So. Thoracic Surg. Assn., Am. Acad. Med. Dirs. Baptist. E-mail: mgrbuker@att.net.

BUKONDA, NGOYI K. ZACHARIE, health care management educator; b. Lubumbashi, Shaba, Zaire, Feb. 14, 1951; came to U.S., 1987; s. Munyuka Kalambayi and Tumba (Tshileo) Marie; m. Muyumba Kapinga Agnes, Aug. 29, 1975; children: Munyuka Ngoyi, Muyumba Ngoyi, Kalambayi Ngoyi, Tshileo Ngoyi, Kashala Ngoyi, Ntumba Gloria Ngoyi. BS in Health Systems Mgmt., U. Kinshasa, Zaire, 1981; Diploma in Teaching, U. Zaire, 1983; MPH, U. Minn. Sch. Pub. Health, 1989; PhD, U. Minn., 1994. Hosp. adminstr. Gen. Hosp., Bukavu, Zaire, 1975-76; dep. chmn. Med. Tech. Inst., Kindu, 1976-78; chief of bur. Ministry of Health Zaire, Kinshasa, 1981-83, chief div., 1983-87; health planner Sanru B.P. 3355 Kinshasa, Kinshasa, 1987; asst. prof. Inst. Superieur de Techniques Medicales, Kinshasa, 1981-87; grad. fellow African Am. Inst., N.Y.C., 1987-94; grad. tchg. asst. Grad. Program in Social and Adminstrv. Pharmacy, Mpls., 1991-94; asst. prof. health care mgmt. So. Ill. U., Carbondale, 1994-97; asst. prof. pub. and cmty. health No. Ill. U. Sch. Allied Health Professions, DeKalb, 1997—2003, assoc. prof., 2003—. Acad. sec. Inst. Superieur de Techniques Medicales, Kinshasa, 1983—86; cons. Joint Commn. Worldwide Consulting, 1999—; prin. investigator Zambia Hosp. Accreditation Descriptive Study; rsch. cons. Botswana-Harvard Partnership Inst. for HIV Rsch. and Edn., 2000—; co-investigator Male Involvement in Prevention of Mother to Child Transmission of HIV/AIDS in Botswana, 2001; mem. Press Bd., No. Ill. U., 2001—, mem. adv. bd. Ctr. for Black Studies, 2002—, mem. faculty senate, 2002—, chair faculty rights and responsibilities com., 2003—, mem. undergrad. acad. environ. com., 2003—, mem. responsible conduct of scholarship com., 2003—; rsch. cons. Peters Inst. for Pharm. Care, U. Minn. Coll. Pharmacy, 2002—; mem. dean award com. Coll. Health & Human Scis., No. Ill. U., 2002—; cons. HIV care Divsn. of Netcare Group, South Africa, 2003—; cons. NIMH-MRISP faculty devel. project in mental health rsch. Morehouse Coll., 2003—. Reviewer: Pub. Health Nursing, 1996—, mem. editl. bd.: Selected Health Sys. of Africa, 1999—; editor: Leja Bulela Newsletter. Mem. health and human scis. curriculum com. No. Ill. U., 2000—02; fed. pres. Union for Democracy and Social Progress, 1999—2003. Named Hon. Citizen of Louisville, 1986; recipient Plaque for Outstanding Work for Mems. of Leja Bulela, 2000—01, Recognition plaque, Internat. African Students Assn. and Yale African Students Assn., 2001; grantee, Mac Arthur Interdisciplinary Program on Peace Internat., 1991; Afgrad fellow, African Am. Inst., 1987, Melendy Grad. fellow Coll. of Pharmacy, 1991, Lilian Cobb Faculty Internat. Travel fellow, No. Ill. U., 2003, Grad. Sch. Summer fellow, 2003. Mem. APHA, Internat. Assn. HIV/AIDS, Am. Pharmacy Assn., Assn. des Adminstrs. Gestionnaires (pres. 1981-87). Roman Catholic. Home: 956 Quail Run Dekalb IL 60115-6116 Office: No Ill U Sch Allied Health Profs Dekalb IL 60115 E-mail: nbukonda@niu.edu., ngoyizacharie@juno.com.

BUKOSKI, KIKA G. state representative; b. Hawaii, Sept. 14, 1965; s. Samuel K. Bukoski and Jacqueline K. Campbell; children: Deven-Hannah Keonaona, Duke Issac Kaimana. BS in bus. adminstrn., U. of Phoenix-Hawaii Campus. V.p. Horizon Waste Industries, Inc., Maui Disposal Co., Inc. Mem. Maui C. of C., Maui Contractors Assn., Maui Hotel Assn., C. of C. of Hawaii. Past appointee Maui County Bd. of Ethics; past vol. Hula Bowl Maui; past bd. mem. Big Bros. Big Sisters; mem. Kula Sch. PTA, Pukalani Cmty. Assn., Kula Cmty. Assn.; past vol. Maui Marathon, Maui County Fair. Mem.: Kamehameha Alumni Assn., Imua Na Opio O Maui, Hawaiian Canoe Club (past bd. mem.), Rotary Club of Maui. Republican. Office: State Capitol Rm 317 S Beretania St Honolulu HI 96813 Fax: 808-586-6331. E-mail: repbukoski@Capitol.hawaii.gov.*

BUKOVAC, MARTIN JOHN, horticulturist, educator; b. Johnston City, Ill., Nov. 12, 1929; s. John and Sadie (Fak) B.; m. Judith Ann Kelley, Sept. 5, 1956; 1 dau., Janice Louise. BS with honors, Mich. State U., 1951, MS, 1954, PhD, 1957; D honoris causa, U. Bonn, Germany, 1995. Asst. prof. horticulture Mich. State U., East Lansing, 1957-61, assoc. prof., 1961-63, prof., 1963; NSF sr. postdoctoral fellow Oxford U., U. Bristol, Eng., 1965-66; univ. disting. prof., 1992—. Vis. lectr. Japan Atomic Energy Rsch. Inst., 1958; adviser IAEA, Vienna, 1961; NAS exch. lectr. Coun. Acads., Yugoslavia, 1971; vis. scholar Va. Poly. Inst., Blacksburg, 1973; guest lectr. Polish Acad. Scis., 1974; disting. vis. prof. N.Mex. State U., 1976; vis. prof. Japan Soc. Promotion Sci., Osaka Prefecture U., 1977; guest lectr. Serbian Sci. Coun., Fruit Rsch. Inst., Cacak, Yugoslavia, 1979; John A. Hannah Disting. lectr. Mich. State Hort. Soc., 1980; vis. prof. U. Guelph, Ont., Can., 1982, Ohio State U., 1982, U. Zagreb, Yugoslavia, 1983, Ohio State U., 1990; collaborator Agrl. Rsch. Svc. USDA, 1982—; guest rschr. Hort. Rsch. Inst., Budapest, Hungary, 1983, Inst. Obstbau und Gemusebau U. Bonn, Fed. Republic Germany, 1986; Batjer Meml. lectr. Wash. State Hort. Soc., 1985; mem. agrl. rsch. adv. com. Eli Lilly Co., Indpls., 1971-88; cons. Dept. Agr.; disting. lectr. Dept. Sci. and Tech. Peoples Republic China, 1984; commencement spkr. Mich. State U., 1986; mem. internat. adv. bd. divsn. life scis. Ctr. for Nuclear Studies, Atomic Energy Commn., Grenoble, France, 1993-2000; Monselise Meml. lectr. Hebrew U., 1994; Agrl. Rsch. Svc. B.Y. Morrison Meml. lectr., 1994, Kermit Olson Meml. lectr. Univ. Minn., 1997; pres. Martin J. Bukovac Inc., 1996-2001; Donald L. Reichard Meml. lectr., Ohio State U., 1999; sci. exch. lectr. Nara (Japan) Inst. Sci. and Tech., 2000. Mem. exec. adv. bd. Ency. of Agrl. Scis., 1991-96; mem. editl. adv. bd. Ctr. for Agr. and Bioscis. Internat., 1989—; internat. editl. bd. Horticultural Sci., Budapest; mem. editl. bd. Ency. of Agrl. Sci., 1991-96. Pres. Okemos Music Patrons, Mich., 1973-74; bd. dirs. Mich. State U. Press, 1983-92. 1st lt. U.S. Army, 1951-53. Recipient citation meritorious rsch. Am. Hort. Soc., 1970, Disting. Faculty award Mich. State U., 1971, Disting. Svc. award Mich. Hort. Soc., 1974, Disting. Faculty award Mich. Assn. Governing Bds., 1986, Hatch Meml. Medallion award USDA, 1987, Industry Man of Yr. award Nat. Cherry Festival, 1987, Alexander von Humboldt Rsch. prize, 1995, Am. Soc. Agrl. Engring. Outstanding Paper award, 1995, Gold Veitch Meml. medal Royal Hort. Soc., 2003; Bukovac Disting. Lectr. established in his honor Mich. State Hort. Soc., 1995. Fellow AAAS, Am. Soc. Hort. Sci. (hon. life, pres. 1974-75, Joseph Harvey Gourley award 1969, 76, Marion Meadows award 1975, citation of appreciation 1975, Carroll R. Miller award 1980, Outstanding Rschr. award 1988, M.A. Blake award for disting. grad. tchg. 1975, Hall of Fame inductee 2001); mem. NAS, Am. Chem. Soc., Am. Soc. Plant Biologists (Dennis R. Hoagland award 1988), Bot. Soc. Am., Scandinavian Soc. Plant Physiologists, Japanese Soc. Plant Physiologists, Internat. Soc. Hort. Sci., Soc. Exptl. Biology, Mich. State U. Faculty Club, Sigma Xi (pres. 1978-79 rsch. award Kedzie chpt.), Phi Kappa Phi, Gamma Sigma Delta. Home: 4428 Seneca Dr Okemos MI 48864-2946 Office: Mich State U Dept Horticulture East Lansing MI 48824 E-mail: bukovacm@msu.edu.

BUKOVEC, JOSEPH ALOYSIUS, special education educator; b. Hoboken, N.J., Nov. 9, 1929; s. Alois and Sophie (Draksler) B.; m. Adeline Nicole Cinotti, Aug. 17, 1964 (dec. Jan. 9, 1985); m. Linda Lee Torrisi, Apr. 14, 1991. BA, Seton Hall U., 1951; MA, Jersey City State Coll., 1967; EdD, Columbia U., 1971. Cert. secondary English, reading, Latin, handicapped tchr., prin./supr., N.J. Tchr. Bd. Edn., Teaneck, NJ, 1962-97, co-project dir./project coord. The Comm. Workshop, 1978-97; adj. prof. Jersey City State Coll., Jersey City, 1972-75, Fairleigh Dickinson U., Teaneck, 1981-84, 98-99, Felician Coll., Rutherford, NJ, 1998-99. Author: Monitoring Student Activities, 1978, Monitoring Student Programs, 1979; co-author: Annotated Bibliography on Professional Education of Teachers, 1969; contbr. articles to profl. jours.; appeared in passion play Park Theatre, Union City. With U.S. Army, 1954-56. Recipient William A. Liggitt award for ednl. excellence Phi Delta Kappa, 1978, Exemplary Project award N.J. State Dept. Edn., 1978. Mem. NEA, Internat. Reading Assn., N.J. Edn. Assn., Teaneck Tchrs. Edn. Assn., Bergen County Edn. Assn. Avocations: acting, photography. Home and Office: 11 Hampton Pl Nutley NJ 07110-2813

BUKOWSKI, ELAINE LOUISE, physical therapist, educator; b. Phila., Feb. 18, 1949; d. Edward Eugene and Melanja Josephine (Przyborowski) B. BS in Phys. Therapy, St. Louis U., 1972; MS, U. Nebr., 1977. Lic. phys. therapist, N.J.; diplomate Am. Bd. Disabilities Analysts (sr. analyst, prof. adv. coun. 1995—). Clk. City of Phila., 1967; staff phys. therapist St. Louis Chronic Hosp., 1973, Cardinal Ritter Inst., St. Louis, 1973-74; dir. campus ministry musicals Creighton U., Omaha, 1974-75; tchg. asst. U. Nebr. Med. Ctr., Omaha, 1975-76; lectr. in anatomy U. Sci. and Tech., Kumasi, Ghana, 1977-78; chief phys. therapist Holy Family Hosp., Berekum, Ghana, 1978-79; coord. info. & guidance The Am. Cancer Soc., Phila., 1979-81; staff phys. therapist Holy Redeemer Vis. Nurse Assn., Phila., 1981-83, rehab. supr. Swainton, N.J., 1983-87; asst. prof. phys. therapy Richard Stockton Coll. N.J., Pomona, 1987-96, assoc. prof., 1996—2002, prof., 2002—03. Bd. dirs. The Bridge, Phila., 1979-80; vacation relief phys. therapist, N.J., summer 1988—; mem. profl. adv. coun. Holy Redeemer VNA, Swainton, N.J., 1982-93, chmn., 1985-91, mem. pers. com., cons. hospice program, 1985-87, rehab. cons., 1987-88; legis. adv. coun. subcom. on edn. and health care Cape May & Cumberland Counties, 1988-90; utilization rev. cons. rehab. svcs., 1990; mem. fitness screening team N.J. State Legislature, 1990, mem. geriatric rehab. del. Citizen Amb. Program, China, 1992; middle states accreditation team evaluator, 1997-98. Co-author slide study program, (video) Going My Way? The Low Back Syndrome, 1976; author: Muscular Analysis of Everyday Activities, 2000. Vol. Am. Cancer Soc., Phila., 1979-82, Walk-a-Day-in-My Shoes prog. Girl Scouts Am., Cape May County, N.J., 1983-86; task force phys. therapy prog. Stockton State Coll., Pomona, N.J., 1985-88. U.S. Govt. trainee, 1971, 72; Physical Therapy Fund grantee, 1975, 76; recipient Vol. Achievement award Am. Cancer Soc., 1981. Mem. Am. Phys. Therapy Assn. (edn. sect., orthop. sect., vice chmn. so. dist. 1993-96, 99-2001, chmn. 1996-98, bd. dirs., ho. of dels. 1994-97, key contact voting dist. 2, mem. N.J. legis. network 1989-96, 1999-2002, mems. mentoring program 1998—, chair nominating com. 2002—, key act voting dist., Phys. Therapy Club (sec. 1971-72), N.J. Phys. Therapy Assn. (rsch. com. 1995-97). Avocations: gardening, music, reading, poetry. Office: Richard Stockton Coll NJ Phys Therapy Program Jim Leeds Rd Pomona NJ 08240 E-mail: elaine.bukowski@stockton.edu.

BUKOWSKI, EUGENE RAYMOND, electrical engineer; b. Hammond, Ind., Apr. 24, 1960; s. Eugene Raymond and Jacqueline Marie Bukowski; m. Susan Jean Thalmann, June 4, 1983; children: Elizabeth, Caroline. BSEE, Purdue U., 1983; MSEE, Duke U., 1987; MS Mfg. Mgmt., Kettering U., 1997. Cert. Shainin, LLC Red X Master, 2002; Am. Soc. for Quality Six Sigma Black Belt 2003. Purdue industry coop. edn. engr. IBM, Rsch. Triangle Park, NC, 1979—82, integrated circuit design engr., product devel., 1983—87, account engr., mktg., svcs. South Bend, Ind., 1987—90; integrated circuit design engr., product devel. GM, Kokomo, Ind., 1990—94, bus. analyst, strategy mgmt., 1994—97, fin. analyst, capital mgmt., 1997—99; statis. engr., quality Delphi Corp., Kokomo, 1999—. Author: (patent for) Method and Apparatus for the Generation of Long Time Constants Using Switched Capacitors (Patent 5,552,648), 1996. Vol. Nat. Leukemia and Lymphoma Soc., Indpls., 2001—03. Mem.: Am. Soc. Quality, Am. Statis. Assn., Eta Kappa Nu. Achievements include patents in field of Method and apparatus for the generation of long time constants using switched capacitors; A static method to negate offset voltages in CMOS operational amplifiers; CMOS signal threshold detector; CMOS precision gain amplifier; CMOS reference voltage generator; Single ended reciever circuit with hystersis. Avocation: 2000 U.S. Tennis Assn. NTRP champion, midwest sect.. Home: 7000 Oakbay Dr Noblesville IN 46060 Office: Delphi Corp PO Box 9005 Kokomo IN 46904-9005 Office Fax: 765-451-3325. Personal E-mail: erbukjr@aol.com. E-mail: eugene.r.bukowski@delphi.com.

BUKRY, JOHN DAVID, geologist; b. Balt., May 17, 1941; s. Howard Leroy and Irene Evelyn (Davis) Snyder Student, Colo. Sch. Mines, 1959-60; BA, Johns Hopkins U., 1963; MA, Princeton U., 1965, PhD, 1967; postgrad., U. Ill., 1965-66, De Anza Coll., 1995-96. Geologist U.S. Army Corp Engrs., Balt., 1963; research asst. Mobil Oil Co., Dallas, 1965; geologist U.S. Geol. Survey, La Jolla, Calif., 1967-84, U.S. Minerals Mgmt. Svc., La Jolla, 1984-86, U.S. Geol. Survey, Menlo Park, Calif., 1986-96, scientist emeritus La Jolla, 1996-98, Menlo Park, 1998—; rsch. assoc. Geol. Rsch. Divsn. Scripps Instn. Oceanography-U. Calif., San Diego, 1970—2003. Cons. Deep Sea Drilling Project, La Jolla, 1967-87; lectr. Vetlesen Symposium, Columbia U., N.Y.C., 1968, 3d Internat. Planktonic Conf., Kiel, Fed. Republic Germany, 1974, Brit. Petroleum Exploration Seminar on nannoplankton biostratigraphy, Houston, 1989; shipboard micropaleontologist on D/V Glomar Challenger, 5 Deep Sea Drilling Project cruises, 1968-78; mem. stratigraphic correlations bd. NSF/Joint Oceanographic Instns. for Deep Earth Sampling, 1976-79. Author: Leg I of the Cruises of the Drilling Vessel Glomar Challenger, 1969, Coccoliths from Texas and Europe, 1969, Leg LXIII of the Cruises of the Drilling Vessel Glomar Challenger, 1981; editor: Marine Micropaleontology, 1976-83, mem. edtl. bd. Micropaleontology, 1985-90. Mobil Oil, Princeton U. fellow, 1965-67; Am. Chem. Soc., Princeton U. fellow, 1966-67; vis. scholar U. Calif., 2003—. Fellow AAAS, Geol. Soc. Am., Explorers Club, mem. NSTA, Hawaiian Malacological Soc., Paleontol. Rsch. Inst., Am. Assn. Petroleum Geologists, Mars Soc., Planetary Soc., Soc. Econ. Paleontologists and Mineralogists, Internat. Nannoplankton Assn., Ecol. Soc. Am., European Union Geoscis., Oceanography Soc., U. Calif.-San Diego Ida and Cecil Green Faculty Club, San Diego Shell Club, Princeton Club No. Calif., Sigma Xi. Achievements include research in stratigraphy, paleoecology and taxonomy for 300 new species of marine nannoplankton used in ocean history studies; new study of Holocene global climate change showing Medieval Warm and Little Ice Age in nannoplankton cored in the Gulf of California. Avocations: basketball, photography, shell and mineral collecting. Office: US Geol Survey MS-910 345 Middlefield Rd Menlo Park CA 94025-3591 E-mail: dbukry@usgs.gov.

BULA, RAYMOND J. agronomist; b. Antigo, Wis., Aug. 3, 1927; s. Stanley and Mary (Klamerus) B.; m. Mary G. Wipperfurth, Aug. 9, 1952; children— R. Gregory, William J., Margaret A., Joseph M., Michael S., Catherine M., Julie C., Carol P. BS, U. Wis., 1949, MS, 1950, PhD, 1952. Asst. prof. N.Y. State Agr. Exptl. Sta., Geneva, N.Y., 1952-53; agronomist Alaska Agr. Expt. Sta., Palmer, 1953-56; agronomist, prof. Purdue U., West Lafayette, Inc., 1956-79; area dir. U.S. Dept. Agr., 1974-79; dir. U.S. Dairy Forage Rsch. Ctr., Madison, Wis., 1979-84; dir. rsch. Phytofarms Am., Inc., De Kalb, Ill., 1984-86; exec. dir. Wis. Ctr. for Space Automation and Robotics, U. Wis., Madison, 1986-94; dir. Wis. Ctr. for Space Automation and Robotics U. Wis., Madison, 1994-98; prin. Ag Space Tech., LLC, Madison, 1999—. Tech. editor: Agronomy Jour, 1980-83. With AUS, 1945-47. Fellow AAAS, Am. Soc. Agronomy; mem. Am. Soc. Gravity and Space Biology, Crop Sci. Soc. Am., Am. Soc. Plant Physiologists, Sigma Xi, Phi Kappa Phi. Roman Catholic.

BULAN, LIANA, dentist; b. Bucharest, Romania, Mar. 7, 1971; arrived in U.S., 1998; d. Sergiu and Stephanie Bulan; m. Petru Groza, Apr. 5, 1997. DDS, U. Toronto, Can., 1995. Postgrad. intern Toronto Hosp., Canada, 1995—96; gen. practice dentistry Toronto, Canada, 1996—98, Walterboro, SC, 1998—. Founder, exec. editor: Jour. Non-Locality and Remote Mental Interactions; contbr. articles to profl. jours. Mem.: Nat. Qigong Inst., Soc. for Sci. Exploration, Omicron Kappa Upsilon.

BULGER, BRIAN WEGG, lawyer; b. Chgo., May 27, 1951; s. John Burton and Mary Jane (Wegg) B.; m. Laura Ellen McErlean, Sept. 12, 1981; children: Burton, Kevin. AB cum laude, Georgetown U., 1972, JD, 1977. Bar: Ill. 1977, U.S. Dist. Ct. (no. dist.) Ill. 1977, U.S. Ct. Appeals (4th, 7th and 8th cirs.) 1977, U.S. Supreme Ct. 1980. From assoc. to ptnr. Pope Ballard Shepard & Fowle, Chgo., 1977-87; ptnr., dept. head Katten Muchin & Zavis, Chgo., 1987-94; founding ptnr. Meckler, Bulger & Tilson, Chgo., 1994—. Adj. prof. U. Wis. Mgmt. Inst., Milw., 1980-2000, U. Chgo. Grad. Sch. Bus., 2000— Contbr. articles to profl. jours. Mem. ABA (former chair pub. employer labor rels. com. sect. on urban state and govt. law), Ill. State Bar Assn., Georgetown Law Alumni (bd. dirs. 1984-93). Roman Catholic. Avocations: baseball, reading, boating, skeet shooting. Office: Meckler Bulger Tilson Ste 1800 123 N Wacker Dr Chicago IL 60606

BULGER, CARRIE ANN, science educator; b. St. Paul, Minn., Oct. 26, 1971; d. Michael William and Kim Ann Bulger; life ptnr. William C. Coleman. PhD, U. of Conn., 2000. Asst. prof. Quinnipiac U., Hamden, Conn., 2000—. Contbr. articles to profl. jours. First v.p. Quinnipiac Faculty Fedn., Hamden, Conn., 2001—03. Mem.: Internat. Assn. Applied Psychologists, Acad. of Mgmt., Soc. for the Psychol. Study of Social Issues, Soc. for Indsl.-Orgnl. Psychology. Achievements include research in issues faced by women in various types of workplaces. Avocations: yoga, reading, travel. Office: Quinnipiac U CL-AC1 275 Mount Carmel Ave Hamden CT 06518

BULGER, ROGER JAMES, academic health center executive; b. Bklyn., May 18, 1933; s. William Joseph and Florence Dorothy (Poggi) B.; m. Ruth Ellen Grouse, June 8, 1960; children: Faith Anne, Grace Ellen. AB, Harvard U., 1955, MD, 1960; postgrad., Emmanuel Coll., Cambridge (Eng.) U., 1955—56; hon. degree, Thomas Jefferson U., 1995, U. Md., Western U. Health Scis., 1998, Kirkesville U. Osteo. Medicine, 1999, Rush U., 2001. Intern, then resident in internal medicine U. Wash. Hosps., 1960—62; trainee in infectious disease and microbiology U. Wash., 1962—63; renal and metabolic diseases Boston U., 1963—64; from asst. prof. to assoc. prof. medicine U. Wash. Med. Sch., Seattle, 1966—70; med. dir. Univ. Hosp., Seattle, 1967—70; prof. cmty. health scis., assoc. dean allied health Duke U. Med. Ctr., 1970—72; exec. officer Inst. Medicine, Nat. Acad. Scis., 1972—76; prof. internal medicine George Washington U. Sch. Medicine, 1972—76; prof. internal medicine, family and community medicine, dean Med. Sch., chancellor Worcester campus U. Mass., 1976—78; pres. U. Tex. Health Sci. Ctr., Houston, 1978—88; pres., CEO Assn. Acad. Health Ctrs., 1988—. Bd. dirs. Georgetown U., Rsch. Am. Author: Hippocrates Revisited, 1973, In Search of Modern Hippocrates, 1987, Technology, Bureaucracy and Healing, 1988, The Quest for Mercy, 1998; also articles, chpts. in books; mem. editl. bd. various jours. Bd. dirs. Georgetown U., Rsch. Am.! Lionel de Jersey Harvard fellow, 1955-56. Fellow ACP, Acad. for Health Svcs. Rsch. (disting.); mem. Inst. Medicine, Infectious Disease Soc. Am., Nat. Acad. Social Ins. Office: Assoc Acad Health Ctrs 1400 16th St NW Ste 720 Washington DC 20036-2230 E-mail: rbulger@acadhlthctrs.org.

BULL, BERGEN IRA, retired equipment manufacturing company executive; b. Lansing, Mich., Feb. 28, 1940; s. W. Ira and Thelma (Roof) B.; m. Janet Mary Blachford, Sept. 22, 1961; children: Damon, Lauren. BA, Mich. State U., 1962; MA, Middle Tenn. State U., 1965; JD, Lewis and Clark Coll., 1969. Bar: Oreg. 1969. Acct. Hyster Co., Portland, Oreg., 1965-66, mem. credit dept., 1966-67, asst. to sec., 1967-71, asst. sec., 1971-72, sec., 1972-78, v.p., legal officer, sec., 1978-86, v.p., gen. counsel, sec., 1986-87, v.p. corp. adminstrn., gen. counsel, sec., 1987-89; v.p., gen. counsel, sec. NACCO Materials Handling Group, Inc., 1989-95, ret., 1995. Instr. bus. law Portland State U., 1971-72 Loaned exec. United Fund, 1968; mem. Diocesan Coun. and vice chancelor Episcopal Diocese of Eastern Oreg., 2000—; bd. dirs. Assoc. Oreg. Industries, 1981—96, Jr. Achievement, 1980—2001, vice-chmn., 1993, chmn., 1994; bd. dirs. Modern Group, Ltd., 1995—, Sunriver Music Festival, 1997—, treas., 1997—99, pres., 2000; bd. dirs. Sunriver Nature Ctr., 1998—, v.p., 2000, pres., 1999—2000. Mem. Oreg. Bar Assn. (inactive), Multnomah Athletic Club, Sage Springs Club & Spa, Bend Golf and Country Club, Crosswater Club. Episcopalian.

BULL, BEVERLY JANE, piano and voice educator; b. Ogdensburg, N.Y., Apr. 18, 1927; d. David William and Mary (Coe) Cheney; m. George H. Bull, Jr., Nov. 4, 1961; 1 child, Melanie Jane Bull Byers. Student, Daynes Bus. Sch., Bath, N.Y., 1948; BA in Music, Piano and Voice, Elmira Coll., 1952; postgrad. in Voice, Cornell U., 1952-55. Sec.-receptionist Cornell U., Ithaca, N.Y., 1952-55; exec. sec. to pres. Gt. Western, Hammondsport, N.Y., 1956-58; tchr. music Avoca (N.Y.) Ctrl. Sch., 1960-61; pvt. tchr. piano, voice and oral interpretation, Homer, N.Y. Dir. adult ch. choirs and children's choirs, 1944—;

tchr. music Day Care Ctr., Syracuse, N.Y., pvt. sch., Liverpool, N.Y., 1997—99. Appeared in numerous programs including poetry readings, playing and singing of sacred, classical and popular songs; soprano soloist. Vol. pianist and singer various hosps., including VA Hosp. Mem. Order Ea. Star (former dir. choir Steuben chpt.). Republican. Avocations: sewing, writing, poetry, gardening. Home: 1642 White Bridge Cir Homer NY 13077-9707

BULL, BRIAN STANLEY, pathology educator, medical consultant, business executive; b. Watford, Hertfordshire, Eng., Sept. 14, 1937; came to U.S., 1954, naturalized, 1960; s. Stanley and Agnes Mary (Murdoch) B.; m. Maureen Hannah Huse, June 3, 1963; children: Beverly Velda, Beryl Heather. BS in Zoology, Walla Walla Coll., 1957; MD, Loma Linda (Calif.) U., 1961. Diplomate: Am. Bd. Pathology. Intern Yale U., 1961-62, resident in anat. pathology, 1962-63; resident in clin. pathology NIH, Bethesda, Md., 1963-65, fellow in hematology and electron microscopy, 1965-66, staff hematologist, 1966-67; research asst. dept. anatomy Loma Linda U., 1958, dept. microbiology, 1959, asst. prof. pathology, 1968-71, assoc. prof., 1971-73, prof., 1973—, chmn. dept. pathology, 1973—, chmn. dept. pathology and human anatomy, 1993—, assoc. dean for acad. affairs sch. medicine, 1993-94, dean sch. medicine, 1994—2003. Cons. to mfrs. of med. testing devices; mem. Internat. Commn. for Standardization in Hematology, pres., 1997-99. Mem. bd. editors Blood Cells, Molecules and Diseases, 1995—; contbr. chpts. to books, articles to med. jours.; patentee in field; editor-in-chief Blood Cells N.Y. Heidelberg, 1985-94. Served with USPHS, 1963-67. Nat. Inst. Arthritis and Metabolic Diseases fellow, 1967-68; recipient Daniel D. Comstock Meml. award Loma Linda U., 1961, Merck Manual award, 1961, Mosby Scholarship Book award, 1961; Ernest B. Cotlove Meml. lectr. Acad. Clin. Lab. Physicians and Scientists, 1972; named Alumnus of Yr., Walla Walla Coll., 1984, Honored Alumnus, Loma Linda U. Sch. Medicine, 1987, Humanitarian award, 1991, Citizen of Yr., C. of C. of Loma Linda, 1997. Fellow Am. Soc. Clin. Pathologists, Am. Soc. Hematology, Coll. Am. Pathologists, FDA Panel on Hematology and Pathology Devices, Nat. Com. on Clin. Lab. Standards, N.Y. Acad. Scis.; mem. AMA, Calif. Soc. Pathologists, San Bernadino County Med. Soc. (William C. Cover Outstanding Contbn. to Medicine award 1994), Acad. Clin. Lab. Physicians and Scientists, Am. Assn. Pathologists, Sigma Xi, Alpha Omega Alpha. Seventh-day Adventist. Achievements include patents in field of blood analysis instrumentation; development of quality control algorithms for blood analyzer calibration; origination of techniques and instrumentation for the measurement of thrombosis risk and for regulation of anti-coagulation during cardiopulmonary bypass. Office: Loma Linda U Sch Medicine 11234 Anderson St Loma Linda CA 92354-2871 E-mail: bbull@som.llu.edu.

BULL, DAVID, fine art conservator; b. Bristol, Eng., Mar. 5, 1934; came to U.S., 1978; s. Andrew John Michael and Betty (Horler) B.; m. Janette Christine Brewer, July 26, 1955 (div. Nov. 1986); children: Victoria, Stephen, Matthew, Nicholas, Sebastian; m. Teresa Jarvis Longyear, June 3, 1989; 1 child, David Douglas John. Nat. diploma, city and guilds diploma, West of Eng. Coll. Art, 1955. Restorer of paintings City Art Gallery, Bristol, 1957-60; restorer Nat. Gallery, London, 1960-65; ptnr. David Bull and Robert Shepherd (art restorers), London, 1965-78; head painting conservation J. Paul Getty Mus., Malibu, Calif., 1978-80; dir. Norton Simon Mus., Pasadena, Calif., 1980-81; pres. Fine Art Conservation and Restoration Inc., 1981—; head of painting conservation Nat. Gallery Art, Washington, 1984-89, chmn. of painting conservation, 1990-99, sr. cons., 1999—. Bd. dirs. Save Venice, Inc. Fellow Internat. Inst. Conservation. Home and Office: 173 E 80th St New York NY 10021-0438 E-mail: fineartcons@erols.com

BULL, FRANK JAMES, architect; b. Chattanooga, June 25, 1922; s. Louis H. and Augusta (Clausius) B.; m. Betty Frances Graham, May 7, 1949; 1 child, Birney O'Brian. BS in Architecture, Ga. Inst. Tech., 1948, BArch, 1949. Registered architect, Ga., Fla., Ala.; cert. Nat. Coun. Archtl. Registration Bds. Pilot Pan Am. World Airways, N.Y., Fla., 1942-46; architect Aeck Assocs. Architects, Atlanta, 1948-57; ptnr. Bull & Kenney Architects, Atlanta, 1957-88, Bull, Brown & Kilgo, Architects, Atlanta, 1988—. Bd. dirs. Compass Environ. Inc.; cons. Fed. Republic of Germany Embassy, Washington, 1986-93; archtl. cons. for golf clubhouse Quinta do Peru, Sesimbra, Portugal and Palheiro Golfe, Funchal, Madeira Island, Portugal, 1991; lectr. in field. Co-author: Asbestos Abatement: Vol. 5 The Sourcebook on Asbestos Diseases, 1991; contbr. articles to profl. jours.; prin. works include Sanctuary for Holy Innocents Episc. Ch., Atlanta, Atlanta Speech Sch. and Clin., Hummel Hall Episc. H.S., Alexandria, Va., Jekyll Island Golf Clubhouse, McLarty Hall, Tull Hall, Turner Gymnasium, Westminster Schs., Atlanta, Dunwoody Country Club, Atlanta, East Lake Golf Clubhouse Restoration, Atlanta, others. Charter trustee Holy Innocents Episcopal Sch., Atlanta, 1962-68, chmn., 1966; founder Galloway Schs., Atlanta, 1969-75. Recipient Rambusch prize Ecole de Beaux Arts, 1940. Mem. AIA (treas. Atlanta chpt. 1976-78, bd. dirs. Ga. assn. 1971-74), Am. Arbitration Assn. (mem. nat. panel constrn. industry arbitrators 1977—), Nat. Asbestos Coun. (founder, charter v.p., bd. dirs. 1983-86, 89-90, treas. 1987, exec. com. 1983-87), Cherokee Town and Country Club (charter, bd. govs. 1976-79, chmn. capital appropriations com., chmn. green com.), Omicron Delta Kappa, Tau Beta Pi, Phi Kappa Phi, Phi Eta Sigma, ANAK, Beta Theta Pi. Republican. Episcopalian. Avocations: golf, writing, lecturing. Home: 34 Willow Gln NE Atlanta GA 30342-1341 Office: Bull Brown & Kilgo Architects AIA 2815 Clearview Pl Ste 100 Atlanta GA 30340-2131

BULL, GEORGE ALBERT, retired banker; b. Red Lion, Pa., May 28, 1927; s. Mervin E. and Edna May (Gohn) B.; m. Grace Kathryn Rudolph, Nov. 13, 1949; children: Donna Carol, Diana Sue, David Alan. Student, Grad. Sch. Banking, Rutgers U., 1961. From teller to cashier Citizens Nat. Bank, Front Royal, Va., 1947-64; asst. vp., cashier Monticello Nat. Bank, Charlottesville, Va., 1964; asst. cashier Nat. Bank & Trust Co., Charlottesville, 1964-80, asst. to pres., 1985-88, sr. exec. v.p., asst. to pres., 1988-89; exec. v.p., treas. Jefferson Bankshares Inc., Charlottesville, 1979-89. With U.S. Army, 1945-46. Mem. Masons. Home: 2315 Wakefield Rd Charlottesville VA 22901-1843

BULL, HELEN MAY, artist, writer; b. Sweet Springs, Mo., Apr. 20, 1920; d. John Theodore Langewisch and Ethel Henrietta (Von Berkelo) Butemeyer; widowed; children: Jan Emerson Bull, Guy William Bull. BFA, Otis Art Inst., L.A., 1971; advanced certification Indsl. Rels., UCLA, 1983. Dir. Brazilian Primitive Painting Exhbn., L.A., 1972; pres. Bay West Assn. of Comty Assistance to Homeless Youngsters, L.A., 1973-74; artist, represented by Agora Art Gallery, N.Y.C. Panelist Inst. for Study of Women in Transition, 1976; nursing career devel. con., San. Antonio, Tex., 1978-80. Artist: Spl exhbn. of canvasses in Vista Rm., Faculty Ctr. UCLA, 1973, Art in Permanent Collections includes KTSC-TV, Pueblo, Colo, and framed mural of St. Luke, St. Luke's Luth. Ch., (Gold award 1993); one-person show Agora Gallery, 1999; exhibited group show at Agora Gallery, 1998. Recipient Cert. of merit, UCLA Juried Faculty Exhibit, 1960. Lutheran. Avocations: travel, hiking, numismatics. Office: Agora Art Gallery 560 Broadway New York NY 10012-3938

BULL, HENRIK HELKAND, architect; b. N.Y.C., July 13, 1929; s. Johan and Sonja (Geelmuyden) B.; m. Barbara Alpaugh, June 9, 1956; children: Peter, Nina. B.Arch., Mass. Inst. Tech., 1952. With Mario Corbett, San Francisco, 1954-55; pvt. practice, 1956-68; ptnr. Bull, Field, Volkmann, Stockwell, Calif., 1968-82, Bull, Volkmann, Stockwell, Calif., 1982-90, Bull Stockwell and Allen, Calif., 1990-93, Bull, Stockwell, Allen & Ripley, San Francisco, 1993-96, BSA Architects, San Francisco, 1996—. Vis. lectr. Syracuse U., 1963; Mem. adv. com. San Francisco Urban Design Study, 1970-71 Works include Sunset mag. Discovery House, Tahoe Tavern Condominiums, Lake Tahoe, Calif., Snowmass Villas Condominiums, Aspen, Colo., Northstar Master Plan Village and Condominiums, Moraga Valley Presbyn. Ch., Calif., Spruce Saddle Restaurant and Poste-Montane Hotel, Beaver Creek, Colo., Bear Valley visitor ctr., Point Reyes, Calif., The Inn at Spanish Bay, Pebble Beach, Calif., Taluswood Cmty., Whistler, B.C., Jackson Gore Village, Okemo, Vt. Served as 1st lt. USAF, 1952-54. Fellow AIA (pres. N. Calif. chpt. 1968, Firm award Calif. chpt. 1989) Democrat. Office: BSA Architects 350 Pacific Ave San Francisco CA 94111-1708

BULL, HOWARD LIVINGSTON, lawyer; b. Binghamton, N.Y., Oct. 7, 1942; s. Glen Chapel Bull and Martha Gertrade (Mott) Skinner; m. Sheila Kay Settle, Apr. 22, 1977; children: John Keese, Jason Howard, Justin Thomas. AB, DePauw U., 1964; JD, U. Va., 1967. Bar: Calif. 1973, U.S. Dist. Ct. (no. dist.) Calif. 1973, U.S. Ct. Appeals (9th cir.) 1973. Assoc. Owen, Melbye & Rohlff, Redwood City, Calif., 1973-74; corp. atty. Varian Assocs., Inc., Palo Alto, Calif., 1974-99; pvt. practice Mountain View, Calif., 1999—. Pres. Midpeninsula chpt. UN Assn.-USA, 1985, Northern Calif. div., Palo Alto, 1987; trustee Ben Lomond (Calif.) Quaker Ctr., 1975-80. Served to capt. USAF, 1968-72. Mem. ABA, Am. Corp. Counsel Assn., Santa Clara County Bar Assn. (steering com. corp. counsel sect. 1984-86), Palo Alto Area Bar Assn., DePauw Alumni Club (pres. 1975). Republican. Mem. Soc. of Friends. Avocations: sports, camping, bicycling, woodworking. Home: 1457 Isabelle Ave Mountain View CA 94040-3039 Office: Counsel to Bus in Comml Law 1457 Isabelle Ave Mountain View CA 94040 E-mail: howardbull@earthlink.net.

BULL, INEZ STEWART, special education, gifted music educator, coloratura soprano, pianist, editor, author, curator; b. Newark, Apr. 13, 1920; d. Johan Randulf and Aurora (Stewart) B. Diploma in piano, Juilliard, 1946; cert., Chautauqua Inst. Sch. Music, 1940-46; diploma, U. Oslo Grad. Sch., Norway, 1955; MusB, N.Y. Coll. Music, 1965; MA, NYU, 1972, EdD, 1979. Piano tchr. Juilliard Inst. Musical Art, NY, NY, 1942-43; chmn. music dept. Casement's Coll., Ormond Beach, Fla., 1949-50; dir. music Essex County Girls Vocat. & Tech. HS, Newark, 1953-57; dir. music, organist State of N.J. Institution for Retarded Girls North Jersey Tng. Sch., Totowa, NJ, 1953-68; spl. edn. gifted coord. Jefferson Magnet Sch. Pub. Sch. Sys., Union City, NJ, 1956-95; dir. Upper Montclair Music Sch., Montclair, NJ, 1945—, Ole Bull Music Sch., Potter County, Pa., 1952-68. Adjudicator Lycoming Coll., Williamsport, Pa., 1948—; conductor Whippany Symphony Orch., 1951-52; curator, builder Ole Bull Mus., Carter Camp, Pa., 1968—; dir. youth chorus Jefferson Sch., Union City, 1956-95; dir. Hudson County Elem. Choral Festival, 1971—; artist-in-residence, Union City; guest lectr. Columbia U., N.Y.C., Yale U. Grad. Sch. Music, Hartford, Conn., NYU, Lycoming Coll., Williamsport, Pa., Mansfield U., Pa., Princeton U., NJ, U. Scranton, Pa., Jersey City State Coll. Author: 27 books; editor: various newsletters and mag.; author: (song) Evening Prayer, 1934, I Will Bow and Be Humble, 1954, Voice of Am., 1952; recording artist Educo Records, soloist WFMB radio sta., Daytona Beach, Fla., 1949—50, NBC, Hartford, Conn., WNJR, Union, N.J., 1952—68, WNBT-ABC, Wellsboro, Pa., 1997—2002, Norsk Rikskringkasting, Oslo, Radio and TV Franchise, Paris, recitals, France, Norway, Eng., Switzerland, S. Am., US. Choir dir. First Congl. Ch., 1940-43, Holy Trinity Luth. Ch., Nutley Luth. Ch., 1953-55; organist, choir dir. North Jersey Tng. Sch. Chapel, 1952-68; founder, dir. Ole Bull Music Festival, 1952—; dep. gov. and mem. rsch. bd. advisors Am. Biog. Inst., Raleigh; US State Dept amb. of goodwill to Norway by order of Pres. Dwight D. Eisenhower, 1953, Norwegian Goodwill amb. to US by order of King Haakon VII, 1953. Recipient Freedom medal-Eisenhower medal, 1953, Sterling Silver plaque King Olav V of Norway, 1966, NJEA award, 1970, Performing Arts Prestige award in Edn., 1976, Olympic Gold medal Norwegian Govt., 1992, Silver medal of Honor, 1991, Gold medal of Honor, 1992, Pa. Senate Legis. citation, 1992, Outstanding Tchr. of the Handicapped in the U.S. Nat. Rsch. Coun., 1970, Woman of Distinction honorable mention award Girl Scout Coun. of Greater Essex County, 1996, Artisan award Oakeside Bloomfield Cultural Ctr., 1996, 50 Women You Should Know award Internat. YWCA, 1996, inducted into Millenium Hall of Fame, Am. Biog. Inst., 1998; named Am. Biog. Inst. World Laureate, 1999, St. Olav medal King Harald V (Norway), 1999, Outstanding Woman in Arts award World History Project/Twp. of Montclair, 2000, key to the City Renovo award, Pa., 2000, 2002, Am. Medal of Honor award Pres. of U.S., 2001, Nobel Peace prize, 2002, Congl. Medal of Merit, 2003, World Laureate Am. Biog. Inst., 1999, Congl. Medal of Excellence, Am. Biog. Inst., 2003; Fulbright scholar U. Oslo (Norway) Grad. Sch., 1955; film made in her honor A Child is Waiting, 1963. Mem. Ole Bull Hist. Soc. (pres. 1972—), Phi Delta Kappa (pres. 1984-86, newsletter editor 1984-92), Kappa Delta Pi (pres. 1984—, newsletter editor 1984—, counselor NYU Beta Pi chpt. 1996), Pen & Brush Club, Internat. Percy Grainger Soc. (v.p.), NYU Alumnae Club Inc. (bd. dirs., rec. sec., newsletter editor, 1979—). Republican. Avocations: concert pianist, soprano, writer. Home: 172 Watchung Ave Montclair NJ 07043-1737 Home (Summer): 79 S Cherry Springs Rd Galeton PA 16922 Office: Robert Waters Sch 2800 Summit Ave Union City NJ 07087-2329

BULL, JAMES C. poet; b. Blaine, Tenn., Mar. 20, 1945; s. James Conley and Esther F. (Hensley) Bull; m. Maret Delavallade, June 15, 1965 (div. Dec. 1967); 1 child, Maarja Esther. Author: (poetry) Spirit of Earth, 1999, Voices of Quiet, 2001, Braids of Fire, 2001, Western the Big Red, 2002, A Photographic History of Fort Ringgold Texas and the Men Who Patroled the Military Trail, Circa 1900, 2002. Home: 2455 Indian Ridge Rd Blaine TN 37709-5927

BULL, KENNETH WINSON, retired rancher; b. Bangs, Tex., Dec. 4, 1930; s. Malta Willis Bull and Lessie D. Conklin; m. Barbara Louise Bell, June 28, 1952; children: Karen Camille, Kenneth Lewis. BSME, Okla. State U., 1958; M in Nuclear Physics, Tex. A&M, 1965; M in Radiol. Physics, U. Tex. Health Sci. Ctr., Dallas, 1973. Self-employed McCulloch County, Tex., 1974—; radiation cons. Brady, Tex., 1974—; asst. prof. U. Tex. Health Sci. Ctr., Dallas, 1973-74; physicist USAF, Washington, 1965-71, engr. Dayton, 1958-63, radar observer Eglin AFB, Fla., 1952-61, control tower operator Almagordo, N.Mex., 1951-52. Contbr. articles to profl. jours. County Chmn., McCulloch County Rep. Party, 1976—; dir. Richland Spl. Utility Dist., Tex., 1988—; pres. Cen. Tex. Taxpayers Assn., Brady, 1990—; mayor pro tem City of Brady, 1978-82. Lt. col. USAF, 1951-71. Decorated Legion of Merit, USAF. Mem. McCulloch County Crime Stoppers (pres. 1988-92), Nat. Cattlemens Assn., McCulloch County Ind. Cattlemens Assn. (pres. 1976-77), Civil Def. for Emergency mgmt. (bd. dirs., dept. 1982-84). Republican. Methodist. Avocations: golf, fishing, poetry, crafts. Office: 151 PR 827 Rochelle TX 76872-9715

BULL, MARGARET JANE, nurse educator; Diploma, Milwaukee County Hosp., 1969; PhD, U. Wis., Milw., 1986. Postdoctoral fellow Clin. Nurse Scholars program Robert Wood Johnson Found., Rochester, N.Y., 1986-88; assoc. prof. U. Minn., Mpls., 1988-97, U. Md., Balt., 1997—2000; prof. Marquette U., Milw., 2000—. Author more than 39 articles on continuity of care and healthcare for elders. Fulbright scholar King's Coll., London, 1999. Fellow Am. Acad. Nursing; mem. Sigma Theta Tau. Mailing: 5998 Sycamore St Greendale WI 53129

BULL, SANDY (ALEXANDER BENJAMIN BULL), musician, composer; b. N.Y.C., Feb. 25, 1941; s. Harry and Daphne (Bayne) B.; m. Candice Ann Marks, June 20, 1979; children: Cassandra, Jesse, Jackson. Studied banjo with Eric Darling, 1955-57; student in music, Boston U., 1959-61; studied percussion with Billy Higgins, 1961-64, studied oud with Hamza El Din, 1963-68, studied sarod with Ali Akbar Khan, 1976-77. Multi-instrumentalist on guitar, keyboards, bass, banjo, pedal steel, percussion, oud and sarod, also engr., composer, arranger, prodr.; host/prodr. The Music of Man/WNCN-FM, N.Y.C., 1963; compositions include Blend, Gospel Tune, No Deposit No Return Blues, Carnival Jump, Moodswing Salsa, Serious City, Alligator Wrestler, Rain Forest, Sanctified Steel, Love is Forever; recordings include The Samplers in Person, 1960, The Folksingers of Washington Square, 1962, Fantasias, 1963, Inventions, 1965, E. Pluribus Unum, 1969, Demolition Derby, 1972, Jukebox Sch. of Music, 1988 (Best Liner Notes award Nat. Assn. Ind. Record distbr. 1989, 20 Best Albums of 1988 Nat. Pub. Radio), Vehicles, 1991, Steel Tears, 1996 (nominated best folk album Nashville Music Awards 1997), Sandy Bull: Re-inventions: The Best of the Vanguard Yrs., 1999; arrangements include L. Bonfa's Manha de Carnival for oud, two movements of Carl Orff's Carmina Burana for 5 string banjo, excerpt from J.S. Bach's Brandenburg Concerto # 5 for Fender guitar, strings and Fender Rhodes; instrumental arrangement of C. Berry's Memphis. Mem. NARAS, ASCAP, Audio Engring. Soc. Avocations: learning bach chorales on keyboard, skiing. Office: Timeless Rec Soc PO Box 1177 Franklin TN 37065-1177

BULL, VIVIAN ANN, college president; b. Ironwood, Mich., Dec. 11, 1934; d. Edwin Russell and Lydia (West) Johnson; m. Robert J. Bull, Jan. 31, 1959; children: R. Camper, W. Carlson. BA, Albion (Mich.) Coll., 1956; postgrad., London Sch. Econs., 1957; PhD, NYU, 1974. Economist Nat. Bank Detroit, 1955-59; with Bell Telephone Labs., Murray Hill, N.J., 1960-62; dept. econs. Drew U., Madison, N.J., 1960-92, assoc. dean, 1978-86; pres. Linfield Coll., McMinnville, Oreg., 1992—. Bd. dirs. Chem. Bank N.J., Morristown; trustee Africa U., Zimbabwe; treas. Joint Expedition to Caesareu Maritima Archaeology, 1971—. Author: Economic Study The West Bank: Is It Viable?, 1975. Trustee, assoc. Am. Schs. Oriental Rsch., 1982-90; trustee Colonial Symphony Soc., 1984-92, The Albright Inst. of Archaeol. Record; commr. Downtown Devel. Commn., Madison, 1986-92; mem. Univ. Sen. United Meth. Ch., 1989-96, gen. bd. higher edn., 1988-92; mem. planning bd. Coll. Bus. Adminstrn., Africa U., Zimbabwe, 1990-91; exec. com. Nat. Assn. Commns. on Salaries, United Meth. Ch., 1986-92. Fulbright scholar, 1956, Paul Harris fellow Rotary Internat., 1988; named Disting. Alumna Albion Coll., 1979; recipient Salute to Policy Makers award Exec. Women in N.J., 1986, John Woolman Peacemaking award George Fox Coll., 1994, Equal Opportunity award Urban League of Portland, 1995. Mem. Nat. Assn. Bank Women, Phi Beta Kappa. Avocations: archaeology, traveling, music. Address: Linfield Coll Office of the Pres 900 S Baker St Mcminnville OR 97128-6808

BULL, WALTER STEPHEN, police officer; b. Collingswood, N.J., May 17, 1933; s. Walter Stephen and Mabelle (Miller) B.; m. Dolores Ruth Kinkade, June 19, 1954; children: Douglas, Donald, Diana, Daniel, David, Dwayne. AAS, Amarillo Coll., 1977, AS, 1978; BS, Wayland Bapt. U., 1978; MA, West Tex. State U., 1982. Advanced cert. Tex. Commn. Law Enforcement Tng. and Edn. Lt. Amarillo (Tex.) Police Dept., 1957-91; ret. Active Boy Scouts Am. Staff sgt. USAF, 1952-56. Mem. Internat. Assn. Chiefs Police (life), Tex. Police Assn., Air Force Assn., Law Enforcement Lions Club, Am Legion (life, post, dis. and div. comdr.), Gideons Internat., Soc. Mayflower Descs. (mem. coun.). Home: 1915 Manhattan St Amarillo TX 79103-4222

BULLA, CLYDE ROBERT, writer; b. King City, Mo., Jan. 9, 1914; s. Julian W. and Sarah Ann (Henson) B. Columnist Tri-County News, King City, Mo., 1942-47. Author 70 books for young people including White Bird, 1966, Shoeshine Girl, 1975, A Lion to Guard Us, 1981, A Place for Angels, 1995, The Paint Brush Kid, 1999. Recipient Commonwealth Children's Book award Commonwealth Club, Calif., 1970; recipient Christopher award The Christophers, 1972, Sequoyah Book award Okla. Sch. Children, 1978, Charlie May Simon award Ark. Sch. Children, 1976, book award S.C. Sch. Children, 1980, Focal award L.A. Pub. Libr., 1991. Mem. Soc. Children's Book Writers, Authors Guild

BULLARD, EDGAR JOHN, III, museum director; b. L.A., Sept. 15, 1942; s. Edgar John and Katherine Elizabeth (Dreisbach) B. BA, UCLA, 1965, MA, 1968; LHD (hon.), Loyola U., New Orleans, 1987. Asst. to dir., curator spl. projects Nat. Gallery Art, Washington, 1968-73; dir. New Orleans Mus. Art, 1973—. Alternate mem. Citizens Stamp Adv. Com., 1969-71, mem. mus. adv. panel Nat. Endowment for Arts, 1974-77. Author: Edgar Degas, 1971, John Sloan 1871-1951, 1971, Mary Cassatt: Oils and Pastels, 1972, A Panorama of American Painting, 1975. Nerdrum: The Drawings, 1994, Henry Casselli: Master of the American Watercolor, 2000. Bd. dirs. La. Cultural Alliance, 1988-91, New Orleans Jazz and Heritage Found., 1974-78; trustee New Orleans Opera Assn., 2001—, Ga. Mus. Art, U. Ga., Athens, 1975-80, Kneisel Hall Chamber Music Sch., Blue Hill, Maine, 1986-02, La. Soc. for Prevention Cruelty to Animals, 1986-93, New Orleans Jazz Orch., 2003—, Haystack Mountain Sch. of Crafts, Deer Isle, Maine, 2003—; mem. adv. bd. Tulane Univ. Coll., 1999-2001; trustee Amistad Rsch. Ctr., Tulane U., 2001—. Decorated Order of Republic of Egypt, officer Am. Soc. Venerable Order St. John Jerusalem, chevalier Order of Arts and Lettres of France; Samuel H. Kress Found. fellow, 1967-68; recipient New Orleans Mayor's Art award, 1993. Mem.: Am. Assn. Mus. (bd. dirs. 1996—98), Assn. Art Mus. Dirs. Democrat. Episcopalian. Home: 1805 Milan St New Orleans LA 70115-5443 also: Greenlea Reach Rd Deer Isle ME 04627 Office: New Orleans Mus Art PO Box 19123 New Orleans LA 70179-0123 E-mail: jbullard@noma.org.

BULLARD, ERVIN TROWBRIDGE, horticulturist; b. New York, Ny, May 25, 1920; s. Frank Marcus and Elizabeth Trowbridge Bullard; m. Marie Jump Groo Bullard, Apr. 20, 1995; m. Madonna Jean Bullard, Sept. 4, 1948 (dec. Dec. 1, 1993); children: John Marcus, Carol Ann Rice, Ellen Sue Schedin. PhD, Purdue U., West Lafayette, IN, 1950; MS, Cornell U., Ithica, NY, 1946; BS, NC State, Raleigh, NC, 1943. Pres. Bullard Consulting, Palm Coast, Fla., 1986—; chief of party Ohio State U. in Burma, 1984—86; agr. advisor US AID, Washington, 1954—79; assoc. educator U. of Idaho, Parma, Idaho, 1950—54. Contbr. to various books on tropical horticulture. Pfc Marine Corps, 1942—44, United States. Recipient Fulbright Award, US Govt., 1951. Mem.: Interamerican Soc. for Tropical Horticulture. Presbyterian. Avocations: fishing, stamp collecting. Home: 135 Cimmaron Drive Palm Coast FL 32137

BULLARD, JOHN KILBURN, educational association administrator; b. New Bedford, Mass., Aug. 21, 1947; s. John Crapo and Katharine (Kilburn) B.; m. Anne Dunbar, June 27, 1981; children: Elizabeth, Anthony, Matthew. BA magna cum laude, Harvard U., 1969; MArch, M in City Planning, MIT, 1974. Agt. Waterfront Hist. Area League (WHALE), New Bedford, 1974-85; mayor City of New Bedford, 1986-92; dir. fisheries representation New Bedford (Mass.) Seafood Co-op, 1992-93; dir. Office of Sustainable Devel. NOAA, Dept. Commerce, Washington, 1993-98; fellow Harvard Inst. Politics, 1998; dir. Family Bus. Ctr. U. Mass., Dartmouth, 1998—2002; pres. Sea Edn. Assn., 2002—. Chmn. urban econ. policy com. U.S. Conf. of Mayors, 1988-92. Photographer 3 covers for Sail mag., 1970-71. Recipient Honor Award Nat. Trust for Hist. Preservation, 1981, Preservation award Mass. Hist. Commn., 1983, Design award Mass. Gov. Michael Dukakis, 1987. Democrat. Unitarian Universalist. Avocations: sailing, tennis. Home: 19 Irving St New Bedford MA 02740-3426

BULLARD, JOHN MOORE, religion educator, church musician; b. Winston-Salem, N.C., May 6, 1932; s. Hoke Vogler and May Evangeline (Moore) B. AB, U. N.C., 1953; AM, 1955; MDiv, Yale U., 1957; PhD, 1962. Ordained to ministry United Meth. Ch., 1955. Asst. in instrn. Yale U., New Haven, 1957-61; asst. prof. religion Wofford Coll., Spartanburg, S.C., 1961-65, assoc. prof., 1965-70, Albert C. Outler prof. religion, 1970—, chmn. dept., 1962—, faculty sec., 1988—. Minister music (organist-choirmaster) Ctrl. United Meth. Ch., Spartanburg, 1961-72, Bethel United Meth. Ch., 1972-88, Second Presbyn. Ch., Spartanburg, 1994, Palmetto Moravian Fellowship, 1994—; lectr. Eureka Coll., 1967, Furman U., 1982, Barton Coll., 1992; vis. prof. Biblical Lit. U. N.C., Chapel Hill, 1966, 67, U. N.C. at Charlotte, summer 1974; vis. prof. comparative religion Converse Coll., Spartanburg, S.C., 1984. Contbr. numerous signed articles to Dictionary of Bibl. Interpretation, Encyclopedia of the Ancient World, and profl. jours. With Naval ROTC, 1950-52. Grantee NEH summer seminar Harvard U., 1982, U. Pa., 1986, Yale U., 1987; Fulbright-Hays grantee, Pakistan 1973, Fund for the Study of Gt. Religions in Asia, 1970-71; James fellow Yale U.; NEH/Wofford rsch. grantee U. London, 1975; named to Ky. Cols.; Dana Fellow Emory Univ's. Grad. Inst. Liberal Arts, 1989-90. Mem. Soc. Bibl. Lit. (pres. so. sect. 1968-69), Am. Acad. Religion, Am. Guild Organists (dean chpt. 1965-67), Organ Hist. Soc., S.C. Acad. Religion (pres. 1974-75), Southeastern Hist. Keyboard Soc., New Bach Soc. (Leipzig), Moravian Music Found. (bd. trustees), Phi Mu Alpha Sinfonia. Avocation: early keyboard music. Home: 104 Hickman Ct Hillbrook Forest Spartanburg SC 29307 Office: Wofford Coll Dept Religion 429 N Church St Spartanburg SC 29303-3612 E-mail: bullardjm@wofford.edu.

BULLARD, JUDITH EVE, psychologist, systems engineer; b. Oneonta, N.Y., Oct. 5, 1945; d. Kurt and Herta (Deutsch) Leeds; divorced; children: Nicholas A., Elizabeth A. BA in Polit. Sci., Spanish U., Oreg., 1966, MA in Psychology, 1973; MBA, George Washington U., 1994. Cert. Project Mgr. 1993, lic. realtor N.J. Supr. residential program Skipworth Juvenile Home, Eugene, Oreg., 1966-68; research asst. Oreg. Research Inst., Eugene, 1968-69, 83-85; supr. residential program Ky. Correctional Facility, Lexington, 1969-70; research asst. U. Oreg., Eugene, 1970-73; asst. dir. Regional Mental Health Clinic, Frankfort, Ind., 1974-76; dir. mental health Lane County Mental Health, Eugene, 1977-80; cons. Managerial Communications, Eugene, 1980-83; sys. engr. AT&T Bell Labs., Holmdel, N.J., 1985-91, mgr. strategic/tech. planning, 1992-95, mgr. reliability, customer satisfaction, process engring., 1996—; dir Lucent/Bus. Comm. Sys., 1998—2000; tech. mgr. Sys. Test Quality Configuration Processed, Alameda, Calif., 1999—2001; ret., 2001; cons., 2002. Mem. strategic task force Globa Bus. Comm. Sys., chairperson customer based panels edn. forum, 1991-95, mgr. forward looking work/tech. coord. tech. ptnr. program, 1994—, chairperson 2-day software symposium, tech. chmn. strategy conf., 1995, chmn. Breakthru Tech. project, 1996, software design project, 1999-2000, coord. planned and executed Rsch. Tech. Exch. Symposium, mem. leadership team Cultural Change project; exec. prodr. 13TV Broadcast Solutions, 1996, Art Tchr., St. Agnes, 2002- Prodr. (video) The World is Our Work Place, 1991. Bd. dirs. Asbury Park 10K, Jersey Shore 1/2 Marathon, 1985—,

Women's Resource and Survival Ctr., Keyport, N.J., 1986—; chairperson Area Affirmative Action Com., 1990—; pres. Affirmative Action Diversity Coun.; active Alliance Neighborrs 9/11 Support Group, 2002—. Mem. Women's Profl. Network (trustee Holmdel br. 1987—), N.J. Bd. Realtors, Nat. Bd. Realtors, Nat. Art Collectors Assn., Partnership in Edn. & Bus., Corrections in Mental Health, Human Factors Soc. Avocations: running, biking, swimming, tennis, cooking.

BULLARD, MARCIA, publishing executive; b. Springfield, Ill., Aug. 28, 1952; d. Clark Wesley and Eileen (Kloppenburg) B. AA, Springfield (Ill.) Coll., 1972; BS, So. Ill. U., 1974; MBA, George Washington U. Reporter Democrat and Chronicle newspaper, Rochester, N.Y., 1974-79, mag. editor, 1979-82; dep. mng. editor Life sect. USA Today, Washington, 1982-85; mng. editor USA WEEKEND mag., Washington, 1985-89, editor, 1989—, pres., CEO, 1996. Tutor 2 schs. D.C., 1984-89, Literacy Vols., Washington, 1987. Mem. AP Mng. Editors, Newspaper Assn. Am., Am. Soc. Newspaper Editors. Office: USA WEEKEND 7950 Jones Branch Dr Mc Lean VA 22107*

BULLARD, RAY ELVA, JR., retired psychiatrist, hospital administrator; b. Dallas, Jan. 25, 1927; s. Ray Elva and Beatrice (Taylor) B.; children by previous marriage: Suzanne, Ray Elva. BS, U. Wash., 1948; MD (Mead Johnson scholar), U. Tex. Med. Br., Galveston, 1953, BA, U. Tex., 1957. Diplomate Am. Bd. Psychiatry and Neurology. Intern Houston VA Hosp., 1953-54; resident in gen. practice U. Iowa, summer 1954, Nan Travis Meml. Hosp., Jacksonville, Tex., 1954-55; gen. practice medicine Normangee, Blanco and Austin, Tex., 1955-63; resident in psychiatry VA Hosp., Topeka, 1963-66, chief sect. psychiatry, 1966-71, chief svc., 1971-73; asso. prof. psychiatry U. Okla., 1971-73; supt. Hollidaysburg (Pa.) State Hosp., 1973-76, Torrance (Pa.) State Hosp., 1976-94. Cons. Allegheny Valley Counseling Ctrs., 1994—; guest lectr. Pa. State U., U. Pitts.; adj. asst. prof. psychiatry U. Pitts. Sch. Medicine, 1978—; adj. asst. prof. St. Francis Coll., 1983-94. Served with U.S. Army, 1944-46. Menninger Found. fellow, 1963-66 Fellow APA (life); mem. AMA (Physicians Recognition award 2000), Am. Psychiat. Assn., Pa. Psychiat. Assn., Pa. Med. Assn., Masons. Episcopalian. Home: RR 1 Box 82A Vandergrift PA 15690-9801 E-mail: jbullard@kiski.net.

BULLARD, ROCKWOOD WILDE, III, lawyer; b. Chgo., May 20, 1944; BA, Wayne State U., 1971; JD with honors, New Eng. Sch. Law, 1974. Bar: D.C. 1974, Mich. 1976, U.S. Dist. Ct. (ea. dist.) Mich. 1976, U.S. Dist. Ct. (we. dist.) Mich. 1977, U.S. Ct. Appeals (6th cir.) 1978, U.S. Supreme Ct. 1979; panel chmn. Atty. Discipline Bd. State Bar Mich., 1984—; Mem. Bullard Anderson PLC, Served as spl. agt. M.I., U.S. Army, 1967-69. Mem. Mich. Bar. Assn., Oakland County Bar Assn., D.C. Bar Assn. Office: 6060 Dixie Hwy Ste H Clarkston MI 48346 E-mail: rwb@bullardanderson.com.

BULLARD, ROGER PERRIN, artist; b. N.Y.C., July 2, 1913; s. Roger Harrington and Annie Adams (Sturges) B.; m. Georgie Genevieve Hosford, Nov. 15, 1944; 1 child, Virginia Anne. Student, Art Students League, N.Y.C., 1934-37, Universal Photographers Inc., The Bullard Haven Tech. Sch., Bridgeport, Conn., 1946. Freelance artist, Fairfield, Conn., 1937-40; machinist Heime Co., Fairfield, 1947-50, Exide Battery, Fairfield, 1950 52, Dictaphone, Bridgeport, Conn., 1952-55; draftsman Aircraft Drafting, Bridgeport, 1955-57, Sikorski Aircraft and Valve Corp., Bridgeport, 1955-56; airbrush artist Poly Photo, Bridgeport, 1957; freelance photographer Fairfield, 1958-77. Contbr. pen and ink drawings to Prof. Henry Fairfield Osborn's book, Probosidea Memoirs Mus. Natural History, N.Y.C., 1933-35. With U.S. Army, 1940-45, WWII. Republican. Episcopalian. Avocations: photography, art research, tennis, writing. Home: c/o Mary Rouseau 449 Mill Plain Rd Fairfield CT 06430-5047

BULLARD, SHARON WELCH, librarian; b. San Diego, Nov. 4, 1943; d. Dale L. and Myrtle (Sampson) Welch; m. Donald H. Bullard, Aug. 1, 1969. BS in Edn., U. Ctrl. Ark., 1965; MA, U. Denver, 1967. Tchr. libr. Humphrey pub. schs., Ark., 1965-66, libr., 1969-70; media splst. Adams County Sch. Dist. 12, Denver, 1967-69; catalog libr. Ark. State U., Jonesboro, 1970-75; head documents cataloging Wash. State U., Pullman, 1979-83; head serials cataloging Davidson Libr. U. Calif., Santa Barbara, 1984-88; head ACCESS svcs. Davidson Libr., 1988-98; head adminstrv. svcs., personnel U. N.C., Greensboro, 1998—. Cons. Ctr. Robotic Sys. Microelectronics Rsch. Libr., Santa Barbara, 1986, retrospective conversion project Calif. State Libr., 1987, ombudsman's office U. Calif., Santa Barbara, 1988; distributor Amway, 1985-91. Canvasser Citizens for Goleta Valley, 1985-86; adv. bd. Total Interlibr. Exch., 1994-96. Mem.: NAFE, ALA (chmn. heads circulation U. Calif. 1997—98, bldgs. for colls. and univs. com. 1998—2000, publs. com. 1998—2001, chair publs. com. 2000, program com. 2001—, bldg. cons. list com. 2002—, subcom. on advancement and promotion 1987—91, 1995—96, chmn. subcom. advancement and promotion 1996—97), Libr. Adminstrn. and Mgmt. Assn. (circulation/access svcs. com., equipment com. 1993—97), Assn. Col. and Rsch. Librs. (intern membership com. 1993—94, extended campus libr. sect. guidelines com. 1995—96), So. Calif. Tech. Processes Group (membership com. 1987), Libr. Assn. U. Calif. Santa Barbara, Calif. Libr. Assn. (tech. svcs. chpt. so. Calif. sect.), N.C. Libr. Assn. (planning commn. annual conf. 1998—99), Notis Users Circulation Interest Group (presenter meeting 1992, moderator meeting 1993—95, CIRC SIG steering com. 1993—97, chair elect 1994—95, chair 1995—96, program com. 1996—97), Pi Lambda Theta (sec. Santa Barbara chpt. 1990—91, hospitality com. 1991—92, exec. bd.). Avocations: walking, camping, white-water rafting, swimming. E-mail: sharon_bullard@uncg.edu., swbullard@aol.com.

BULLARD, WILLIS CLARE, JR., lawyer; b. Detroit, July 12, 1943; s. Willis C. and Virginia Katherine (Gilmore) B.; children: Willis C. III, Melissa Ann, Kaila Michelle. AB, U. Mich., 1965; JD, Detroit Coll. Law, 1971. Bar: Mich. 1971. Practice of law, Detroit, 1971-77, Troy, Mich., 1977-80, Milford, Mich., 1983—; supr. Highland Twp., Mich., 1980-82; mem. Mich. Ho. of Reps., 1983-96, Mich. Senate from 15th dist., Lansing, 1996—2002; county commr. from 2d dist., 2003—. Asst. Rep. caucus chmn., 1983-84, asst. Rep. floor leader, 1985-88, chmn. House Rep. campaign, 1987-90; chmn. House taxation com., 1993-96; chmn. task force Midwestern Legis. Conf. Coun. State Govts., 1985-86; mediator cir. and dist. cts., 1988—. Bd. dirs. Dunham Lake Property Owners Assn., 1975-78, treas., 1975-76, pres., 1976-78; mem. Dunham Lake Civic Com., 1982-87; trustee Highland Twp., 1978-80, mem. zoning bd. appeals, 1979. Named Legislator of Yr. Mich. Twp. Assn., 1984, Nat. Rep. Legislator of Yr., 2000. Mem. Oakland County Bar Assn., State Bar Mich., Oakland County Assn. Twp. Suprs. (sec.-treas. 1981), Michigamua. Clubs: U. Mich. of Greater Detroit, Highland Republican, Highland Men's (sec. 1979, pres. 1980). Republican. Home: 1849 Lakeview Dr Highland MI 48357-4817

BULLARD-DILLARD, REBECCA, biochemist, educator; b. Sylacauga, Ala., Sept. 20, 1959; d. George Edgar Chambers and Catherine Hentz; m. Ted Dillard. PhD, U. S.C., 1996. Grad. tchg. asst. dept. chemistry U. S.C., Columbia, 1990—91, grad. rsch. asst., 1991—96, postdoctoral supr. undergrad. rschrs. Children's Cancer Rsch. Ctr., 1996—96; adj. instr. chemistry Midland's Tech. Coll., Columbia, 1995; asst. prof. biology Claflin U., Orangeburg, SC, 1996—99, assoc. prof., chair, dept. biology, 1999—. Dir. rsch. devel. Claflin U., 2000—; mem. state steering com. S.C. Biomed. Rsch. Infrastructure Network, Columbia, 2001—. Contbr. articles to profl. jours.; assoc. editor Jour. Environ. Monitoring and Restoration, 2002—. Named Disting. Prof. of the Yr. for Claflin U., Gov.'s Office State of SC., 2002; recipient Extramural Associates Rsch. Devel. award, NIH, 2000—03; grantee Girls Emulating Maturity and Strength (GEMS) Program, Sunshine Ladies Found., 2001—02; Gina Fenzi Meml. Grad. Rsch. fellow, Lupus Found. of Am., 1989. Mem.: AAAS, AAUP, NSTA, AAUW, S.C. Cancer Alliance, Am. Soc. Microbiology, Am. Chem. Soc., So. Poverty Law Ctr. Libertarian. Office: Claflin U 400 Magnolia St Orangeburg SC 29115 Office Fax: 803-535-5776. E-mail: rdillard@claflin.edu.

BULLARO, GRACE RUSSO, literature, film and foreign language educator, speaker, book reviewer; b. Salerno, Italy, July 11, 1949; arrived in U.S., 1958; d. Salvatore and Carmela (Paciello) Russo; m. Frank John Bullaro, Sept. 19, 1971; children: Christian, Adrian Alexander. BA magna cum laude, CCNY, 1971; MA, SUNY, Stony Brook, 1989, PhD in Comparative Lit., 1993. Grad. tchg. asst. SUNY, Stony Brook, 1988-92; adj. asst. prof. SUNY-Nassau C.C., Garden City, N.Y., 1990—, CUNY-Lehman Coll., Bronx, N.Y., 1991-2000, adj. assoc. prof., 2000—02, asst. prof., 2002—; with Lincoln Ctr., N.Y.C., 1998; collaborative educator; asst. prof. CUNY-Lehman Coll., Bronx, 2002—. Mem. libr. com. CUNY, 1998, mem. acad. senate, 1997—; mem. faculty exec. com. Lehman Coll., Bronx, NY, 1999—, English dept. libr. acquisitions liaison, 2000—; mem. Tchr. of Yr. selection com.; mem. profl. adv. bd. Am. Biograph. Inst., 2002—; fgn. langs. acquisitions cons. Syosset (N.Y.) Pub. Libr., 2002—; book reviewer in field. Contbr. chpts. to books and articles to profl. jours. Acad. senate CUNY, Lehman Coll., 1997-99, 2001—, CUNY, 1998—, mem. Faculty Exec. Com., 1999—; liaison English Dept. Libr. Acquistions, 2000—; cons. Pub. Libr. Fgn. Lang. Acquisitions, Syosset, N.Y., 2002—. Recipient Chancellor and Pres.'s award for Excellence in Tchg., SUNY-Stony Brook, 1992, Adj. Tchr. of Yr. award, CUNY-Lehman Coll., 2001. Mem. MLA, Nat. Coun. Tchrs. English, Assn. Italian-Am. Educators, Inst. Français, Soc. Profs. Français, Phi Beta Kappa. Avocations: fitness trainer, tennis, travel, swimming, horseback riding. Office: CUNY Lehman Coll English Dept Bedford Park Blvd W Bronx NY 10468 E-mail: gracerbullaro@msn.com.

BULLEN, DANIEL BERNARD, mechanical engineering educator; b. Iowa City, July 20, 1956; s. John Bernard and Helen May (Ferguson) B.; m. Elizabeth Ann Clark, Aug. 17, 1979; children: Katherine Andrea, Mark Bernard, Sarah Elizabeth, Rachel Suzanne. BS in Engring. Sci., Iowa State U., 1978; MS in Nuclear Engring., U. Wis., 1979, MS in Material Sci., 1981, PhD in Nuclear Engring., 1984. Registered profl. engr., Calif., N.C., Ga., Iowa. Engr. Lawrence Livermore (Calif.) Nat. Lab., 1984-86; sr. engr. Sci. and Engring. Assocs., Inc., Pleasanton, Calif., 1986-88; pres. DG Engring., Inc., Livermore, 1988-89; asst. prof. nuclear engr. N.C. State U., Raleigh, 1989-90, Ga. Inst. Tech., Atlanta, 1990-92; assoc. prof. mech. engring. Iowa State U., Ames, 1992—, dir. nuclear reactor lab., 1993-2000, coord. nuclear engring. program, 1993-96. Cons. Lawrence Livermore Nat. Lab., 1988-91, Electric Power Rsch. Inst., Palo Alto, Calif., 1989-96, Internat. Lead Zinc Rsch. Orgn., Research Triangle Park, N.C., 1990-98, HDR Engring., Inc., Omaha, 1991—, APA, Inc., Omaha, 1996-97; mem. U.S. Nuclear Waste Tech. Rev. Bd., 1997—. Contbr. articles 60 to profl. jours. Mem. NSPE, ASME, ASM Internat., Mineral, Metals and Materials Soc. AIME, Am. Nuclear Soc., Am. Ceramic Soc. (tech. reviewer 1986—), Materials Rsch. Soc., Am. Soc. Engring. Edn. Roman Catholic. Home: PO Box 1768 Ames IA 50010-1768 Office: Iowa State U 3034 Black Engring Ames IA 50011-0001 E-mail: dbullen@iastate.edu.

BULLERDICK, KIM H. petroleum executive; b. 1953; BA, Wittenberg U.; JD, U. Va. Gen. coun. Giant Industries, Inc., Scottsdale, Ariz., v.p., sec., subs. officer. Office: Giant Industries Inc 23733 N Scottsdale Rd Scottsdale AZ 85255-3466 Fax: 480-585-8893.

BULLETT, VICKY, basketball player; b. Oct. 4, 1967; Grad., U. Md., 1989. Forward-center, Italy, 1990—93, 1993—97, WNBA - Charlotte (N.C.) Sting, 1997—99, Washington Mystics, 1999—. Named to, Italian League All-Star Teams, 1992, 1995, 1996, 1997, Goodwill Games Team, 1989, World Championship Qualifying Team & USA Select Team, 1986, All-ACC Tournament Team, 1989, Kodak All-Am. Team, 1989; recipient U.S. Olympic gold medal, 1988, Bronze medal, 1992. Avocations: softball, tennis, tap dancing, keyboards, reading. Office: Washington Mystics MCI Ctr 601 F St NW Washington DC 20004-1605

BULLIET, RICHARD WILLIAMS, history educator, novelist; b. Rockford, Ill., Oct. 30, 1940; s. Leander Jackson and Mildred Idell (Williams) B.; m. Lucianne Cherry, June 24, 1962; 1 child, Mark Paul BA, Harvard U., 1962, MA, 1964, PhD, 1967. Instr. Harvard U., Cambridge, Mass., 1967-70, asst. prof., 1970-73; lectr. U. Calif.-Berkeley, 1973-75; assoc. prof. history Columbia U., N.Y.C., 1976-79, prof., 1979—. Author: The Patricians of Nishapur, 1972, The Camel and the Wheel, 1977 (Dexter prize), Conversion to Islam in the Medieval Period, 1979, Islam: The View from the Edge, 1993; (novels) Kicked to Death by a Camel, 1973; The Tomb of the Twelfth Imam, 1979, The Gulf Scenario, 1984, The Sufi Fiddle, 1991; co-author: The Earth and Its Peoples, 1997; co-editor: The Encyclopedia of the Modern Middle East, 1996; editor: The Columbia History of the Twentieth Century, 1998; host-narrator: (documentary TV series) The Middle East, 1985; editor Jour. Iranian Studies, 1987-90. Guggenheim fellow, 1975-76 Mem. Mid. East Studies Assn. (exec. sec. 1977-81), Phi Beta Kappa. Avocation: painting. Home: 90 Morningside Dr New York NY 10027-7124 Office: Columbia U Mid East Inst New York NY 10027 E-mail: rwb3@columbia.edu.

BULLINGTON, GAYLE ROGERS, writer, researcher; b. Watsonville, Calif., May 17, 1923; d. Manley Duane and Gladyce Thelma (Horton) Rogers; m. Keith Charles Brown, Nov. 26, 1944 (div. Feb.4, 1963); children: Kendall Keith, Kevin Doran; m. Jack William Bullington, Dec. 23, 1978. BA, UCLA, 1946, secondary sch. cert., 1947; postgrad. studies, Calif. Luth. U., Northridge U., 1962—65; MA, Calif. Luth. U., 1974. Cert. tchr., Calif. Tchr. Southgate (Calif.) Jr. H.S., 1947-48, Virgil Jr. H.S., L.A., 1948-50, North Hollywood (Calif.) H.S., 1950-52, Van Nuys (Calif.) H.S., 1953-54, Thousand Oaks (Calif.) H.S., 1963-79. Author: The Second Kiss, 1972, NAKOA's Woman, 1975—81, Gladyce With a C, 2000, Dark Corners, 2002, My Name Was Mary, 2003. Mem. ACLU, Pub. Citizen, Common Cause, Nation Assocs. Home: 23119 19th Ave NE Arlington WA 98223-7631 E-mail: gaylerogers@verizon.net.

BULLITT, JILL HAMILTON, artist, educator; b. Seattle, Wash., Aug. 21, 1951; d. Stimson Bullitt and Carolyn Ashley Kizer; m. David Earl Rigsbee, July 28, 1995; 1 child, Makaiya. AB with distinction, Stanford (Calif.) U., 1973; MFA, U. N.C., 1999. Exec. dir. Dieu Donné Papermill, Inc., NYC, 1989-90; tchg. fellow in art U. NC, Chapel Hill, NC, 1997-99; vis. lectr. in art Duke U., Durham, NC, 1998; asst. prof. art Mount Olive Coll., NC, 1999—; prof. Savannah Coll. of Art and Design, 2000; vis. lectr. in art Univ. of Wash., Seattle, 2003. Scholar-in-residence Hamilton Coll., 1995-96; dir. Harbor Properties, Inc., Seattle, 1977-87; cons. The Stern Fund, NYC; vis. lectr., U. Wash., 2003. Exhibited in group shows at Am. Acad. Arts and Letters Invitational, NYC, 2003, Lee Hansley Gallery, 2003, Bickett Gallery, 2002, Am. Acad. in Rome, 1999, Ackland Mus., UNC., 1999; one-person shows include Bickett Gallery, Raleigh, NC, 2002, Elon U., 2002, Alcott Gallery, UNC, 1998, St. Andrews Coll., 1997, Mt. Olive Coll., 1996, 99. Pres. Friends of the Internat. Sch. of Art, Monte Castello di Vibio, Italy, NYC, 1993—2001; co-founder El Salvador Media Edn. Project, Washington, 1986; mem. fin. com. Countdown '87, Washington, 1987—88; exec. dir. Boca Lupo Fund, NYC, 1987—95; co-dir. The Energy Project, Corp. Data Exch., NYC, 1979—80; co-founder, bd. dirs. Ctrl. Am. Media Edn. Project, Washington, 1986—87; bd. dir. Threshold Found., San Francisco, 1986. Recipient David R. Hunter Founder's award A Territory Resource Found., Seattle, 1993; finalist award in painting, Am. Acad. Arts and Letters, 2003, honorable mention, Icarus award, 2002. Mem. Coll. Art Assn. Democrat. Episcopalian. Avocations: travel, skiing, music. Home: 315 Oakwood Ave Raleigh NC 27601-1062

BULLOCH, KATHLEEN LOUISE, educational professional; b. Teaneck, N.J., Feb. 20, 1949; d. Thomas Joseph and Daisy Loretta Oates; m. Clifford Allen Bulloch, June 17, 1972; 1 child, Sean Andrew. BA, William Patterson Coll., 1971; MA, Montclair State Coll., 1972. Cert. speech pathologist Am. Speech/Lang./Hearing Assn. Chief speech pathologist Barnert Speech Clin., Paterson, N.J., 1971-73; speech/lang. pathologist Brick Town, N.J., 1973 79, Riverside (Calif.) County Office of Edn., 1979-98; mentor tchr. Riverside County Office of Edn., 1992-98, curriculum specialist, 1998-99; intern program supr. Calif. State U., San Bernardino, 1998-99. Ednl. cons. Creative Children's Group, N.Y.C., 1995—; C-FASST Sr. Trainer Calif. State Dept. Edn., Sacramento, 1998; book reviewer Am. Speech/Lang. Assn., Washington, 1996—. Scriptwriter: (children's TV) Bloopy's Buddies, 1997; author: Phantom Tollbooth Unit, 1994, Adventures in Space, 1992; co-author: Adult Aphasia Program, 1977. Named to Outstanding Young Women of Am., 1983. Mem. ASCD, Am. Speech/Lang./Hearing Assn., Calif. Speech/Lang./Hearing Assn., Am. Ednl. Rsch. Assn., Coun. for Exceptional Children. Anglican Catholic. Avocations: reading, writing, exercise, music. Home: 466 S Westridge Cir Anaheim CA 92807-3732 Office: Riverside County Office Edn 3939 13th St Riverside CA 92501-3505 E-mail: bulloch@earthlink.net.

BULLOCK, ANNA MAE **See TURNER, TINA**

BULLOCK, BRUCE STANLEY, lawyer; b. Kissimmee, Fla., Oct. 29, 1933; s. Arthur Stanley and Athalia (Griffin) B.; m. Lydia Austill, July 8, 1960; children: Bruce Stanley Jr., Margaret Bullock Martin. BA, U. Fla., 1955, JB, 1967. Bar: Fla. 1962, U.S. Dist. Ct. (mid. and no. dists.), U.S. Supreme Ct., U.S. Ct. Appeals (11th crct.); diplomate Am. Bd. Trial Advocates; cert. crct. ct. mediator. Atty. assoc. Marks Gray Conroy & Gibbs, Jacksonville, Fla., 1962-66, atty., ptnr., 1966-73; atty., pres. Bullock & Alexander, Jacksonville, 1973-74, Bullock, Childs, Pendley & Reed, Jacksonville, 1974-95; ptnr. Bullock, Childs, Pendley & Reed, PA, Jacksonville, 1995—. Pres. N.E. Fla. Med. Malpractice Claims Coun. Dir., committeeman, gen. counsel Duval County (Fla.) Rep. Party. Lt. USAF, 1955-59. Mem. Jacksonville Bar Assn., Jacksonville Assn. Def. Counsel (pres.), Fla. Def. Lawyers Assn., Def. Trial Lawyers Assn., Def. Rsch. Inst., U. Fla. Alumni Club (pres.), Rotary Club (v.p. S. Jacksonville chpt.), Am. Bd. Trial Advocates (pres. local chpt. 1999). Republican. Episcopalian. Avocations: fishing, boating, nature. Home: 2510 Hickory Bluff Ln Jacksonville FL 32223-6503 Office: Bullock Childs Pendley Reed 1551 Atlantic Blvd 2d Fl Jacksonville FL 32207 E-mail: bbullock@bcprlaw.com.

BULLOCK, C. HASSELL, religious studies educator, minister; b. Bessemer, Ala., Apr. 20, 1939; s. Erbie Laura and Agnes Cordelia (Farr) Bullock; m. Rhonda Rebecca Nichols, July 2, 1965; children: Scott Brian, Rebecca Cordelia. BA, Samford U., 1961; BD, Columba Theol. Sem., 1964; PhD, Hebrew Union Coll., 1970. Asst. prof. Lee U., Cleveland, Tenn., 1968—72; pastor First Presbyn. Ch., Trusville, Ala., 1972—73; prof. Wheaton Coll., Ill., 1973—. Tchr. Chgo. Sunday Evening Club, 1976. Author: An Introduction to the OT Prophetic Books, 1986, An Introduction to the OT Poetic Books, 2d edit., 1988, Encountering the Book of Psalms, 2001. Bd. dirs. Wheaton Christian Grammar Sch., 1978—81. Mem.: Soc. Bibl. Lit., Evangelical Theol. Soc. Presbyterian. Home: 1111 N Wshington St Wheaton IL 60187 Office: Wheaton Coll 500 College Ave Wheaton IL 60187 Office Fax: 630-752-5296. E-mail: c.h.bullock@wheaton.edu.

BULLOCK, ELLIS WAY, JR., architect; b. Birmingham, Ala., Sept. 11, 1928; s. Ellis Way Sr. Bullock and Martha (Foute) Alexander; m. Ann Ardelia Pope, Nov. 28, 1950; children: Ellis Way III, Elbert Pope, John Howard Keith, William Frank. BArch, Auburn U., 1954. Registered architect, Fla., Ala., Ga., Miss., S.C., N.C. Apprentice architect Yonge, Look & Morrison, Pensacola, Fla., 1954-58; owner Ellis Bullock Architect, Pensacola, 1958-73; pres., CEO Bullock-Tice and Assocs. Arch., Inc., Pensacola, 1973—96. Pres. Fla. AIA, 1977, treas. AIA Rsch. Corp., Washington, 1980-81; chmn. Energy in Arch., Washington, 1980-82; mem. faculty adv. com. Auburn U. Sch. Architecture, 1980—, chmn., 1988-89; mem. Nat. Architecture Accrediting Bd., Washington, 1982-86; mem. adv. coun. U. Fla. Coll. Architecture, 1986—. Contbr. articles to profl. jours. Chmn. Pensacola Hist. Commn., 1967; chmn. City of Pensacola Archtl. Review Bd., 1968, Pensacola Bldg. Bd. of Appeals, 1970—; bd. dirs. Pensacola Symphony, 1998-2000, Fla. Bd. Architecture and Interior Design, 2002—; exec. bd. Auburn U. Coll. Architecture, Design and Constrn., 2000—; mem. Blue Ribbon Task Force on Edn., Escambia County, Fla., 1985-86; mem. adv. coun. U. Fla., 1986—; mem. sesquicentennial commn. State of Fla. 1st lt. U.S. Army, 1950-54. Recipient 1st Honor AIA-Navy, 1977, 78, Award of Merit, 1976; recipient Outstanding Design award for Air Force Systems Command Hdqrs., 1980, Gov.'s Design award, 1982, 84, Merit award for U.S. Air Force Design, 1983, Design Excellence award Air Force Regional Civil Engrs., 1984, award of merit Navy Youth Ctr., 1990, award of merit Navy Bowling Ctr. Complex, 1990; named Profl. of Yr., Pensacola News Jour., 1977. Fellow AIA (bd. dirs. 1979-82, v.p. 1981-82, jury coll. of fellows 1988-91, exec. com. coll. of fellows 1993—, bursar 1993—, vice chancellor 1994-95, chancellor 1995-96, regional rep. Fla. Caribbean 1990—, numerous awards N.W. chpt. 1974—, award of excellence Fla. N.W. chpt. 1980, 82, 86, 89, 90, Gold medal Fla. chpt. 1988, Millennium award of honor Fla. chpt. 2000), Am. Archtl. Found. (regent 1995-96, EXCOM 1995-96, task force account and reason 1988, program chmn. nat. conv. com. 1986); mem. Fla. Assn. AIA (pres. 1977, govtl. liaison com. 1984—, Gold medal 1988, gold medal noiminating com. 1990-91, balanced curriculum task force 1990, chmn. design awards jur. Ctrl. Fla. chpt. 1980, speaker ann. conf. 1997-98), Fla. Archtl. Found. (trustee 1988—, chmn. 1993), Inst. Bus. Designers (award for contractual interiors 1977), NRA, St. Andrews Soc., Rotary (Paul Harris fellow 1994). Home: 2 Hyde Park Rd Pensacola FL 32503-5830 Office: Bullock Tice Assocs 909 E Cervantes St Ste B Pensacola FL 32501-3281

BULLOCK, FRANK WILLIAM, JR., federal judge; b. Oxford, N.C., Nov. 3, 1938; s. Frank William and Wilma Jackson (Long) B.; m. Frances Dockery Haywood, May 5, 1984; 1 child, Frank William III BSBA, U. N.C., 1961, LLB, 1963. Bar: N.C. 1963. Assoc. Maupin, Taylor & Ellis, Raleigh, N.C., 1964-68; asst. dir. Adminstrv. Office of Cts. of N.C., Raleigh, 1968-73; ptnr. Douglas, Ravenel, Hardy, Crihfield & Bullock, Greensboro, N.C., 1973-82; judge U.S. Dist. Ct. N.C., Greensboro, 1982—, chief judge, 1992-99. Mem. bd. editors N.C. Law Rev., 1962-63; contbr. articles to profl. jours. Mem. N.C. Bar Assn., Greensboro Bar Assn., N.C. Soc. of Cin., Fla. Soc. Colonial Wars, Greensboro Country Club. Republican. Presbyterian. Avocations: golf, tennis, running, history. Office: US Dist Ct PO Box 3223 Greensboro NC 27402-3223*

BULLOCK, JERRY MCKEE, retired military officer, consultant, educator; b. Ralls, Tex., June 2, 1932; s. Arthur Vaughn and Lillian McKee B.; m. Velma Lucille Young, Aug. 30, 1954; children: Ronnie Jay, Randy Ross, Roddy McKee, Kathy L. Bullock Chiero, Kevin L., Kelly L. Bullock Wheeler, Kristie E. Bullock Tumlinson. BA, East Tex. State U., 1954; grad., Indsl. Coll. Armed Forces, 1978, Air War Coll., 1977; MA, Webster U., 1981. Lic. profl. counselor, Tex. Commd. 2d lt. USAF, 1954, advanced through grades to col., 1974, dep. chief security police, ret., 1981; exec. dir. Family and Marriage Counseling, San Marcos, Tex., 1981-83; dir. human resources Tracor Aerospace, Austin, Tex., 1983-90; cons., owner Creative Edn. Inst., San Marcos, 1990-95. Exec. dir. Global Strategies Internat., Inc., 1999-2001; del. Conf. to Write Stockholm Accords on Reverence and Reconciliation to Eliminate Ethnic Cleansing, 2000. Author: Short History of the Air Force Security Police, 1997, SP History, Vol. II, 1999; editor: The Mexican War Jour.; staff writer San Marcos Daily Record; contbr. articles toprofl. jours. Active Industry, Edn. Task Force, Austin, 1989—, State Human Resources Com., 1989-91, Bicycle Advocacy Coalition, 1991; pastor, CEO Hill Country Faith Ministries, 1992-98; exec. dir. Global Strategies for Religious Liberty, 1999-2001; del. Conf. on Reverence & Reconciliation, Stockholm. Decorated Legion of Merit with 3 oak leaf clusters, Bronze Star. Mem. Air Force Security Police Assn. (chmn. bd. dirs. 1986-92, exec. dir. 1992—), Tex. Assn. Bus. (bd. dirs. 1990-92, state exec. com. 1991), Barons of Magna Charta, SCV, SAR, Descendents of Mex. War Vets., Sons of Rep. Tex. Republican. Baptist. Avocation: bicycling. Home: 818 Willow Creek Cir San Marcos TX 78666-5060 E-mail: JBullock@corridor.net.

BULLOCK, KURT EVAN, humanities educator; b. Muncie, Ind., July 21, 1959; s. Ray Edward and Jeanne Louise Bullock. BA, Taylor U., 1981, BS, 1982; MA, Ball State U., 1993, PhD, 2001. Sports writer Chronicle-Tribune, Marion, Ind., 1979—81; tchr., coach South Putnam H.S., Greencastle, Ind., 1983—84, East Noble H.S., Kendallville, Ind., 1984—85; mag. editor Taylor U., Upland, Ind., 1985—89; publs. dir. Ball State U., Muncie, 1989—93; publs. designer Ohio State U., Columbus, 1993—95; vis. asst. prof. English Grand Valley State U., Allendale, Mich., 2000—02, asst. prof. English, 2002—. Author (short story collection): Margin of Balance, 1993; author, editor, designer A Sense of Place: Ball State University, 1993. Mem.: NCTE, MLA, Conf. on Coll. Composition and Comm. Office: Grand Valley State U Dept English Allendale MI 49401

BULLOCK, MOLLY, retired elementary school educator; d. Wiley and Annie M. Jordan; m. George Bullock; children: Myra A. Bauman, Dawn M. BS in Edn., No. Ariz. U., 1955, postgrad., 1958, LaVerne U., 1962, Claremont Grad. Sch., 1963, Calif. State U. L.A., 1966. Tchr. Bur. Indian Affairs, Kaibeto, Ariz., 1955-56, Crystal, N.Mex., 1956-59, Covina (Calif.) Valley Unified Sch. Dist., 1961-95, supervising master tchr. trainees LaVerne U. and Calif. State U. - L.A., 1961-71, mem. curriculum devel. adv. bd., 1977-79; ret., 1995. Cons. Bauman Curry Co., PR; mem. voting com. Excellence in Edn. awards Lawry's Foods; attendee reading conf. Claremont (Calif.) Grad. Sch. Author: (poems) A Tree (Golden Poet, 1991), What is Love (Golden medal of honor), The Change of Seasons (Dimond Homer trophy, 1999, Poet of the Yr. medallion). Vol. visitor area convalescent hosps.; mentor to former students. Mini grantee, Hughes/Rotary Club/Foothill Ind. Bank, 1986—90. Mem.: NAFE, Covina Unified Edn. Assn., Internat. Platform Assn., Internat. Soc. Poets (hon.). Avocations: poetry, collecting jewelry, dolls, paintings.

BULLOCK, SANDRA, actress; b. Washington, July 26, 1964; d. John and Helga B. Grad., Washington-Lee H.S., Arlington, Va., 1982. Appearances include (TV movies) Bionic Showdown: The Six-Million Dollar Man and the Bionic Woman, 1989, (TV series) Working Girl, 1990, (feature films) Fire on the Amazon, 1991, Love Potion #9, 1992, The Vanishing, 1993, Demolition Man, 1993, The Thing Called Love, 1993, Wrestling Ernest Hemingway, 1993, Speed, 1994 (Best Female Performance, Most Desirable Female MTV Movie awards), While You Were Sleeping, 1995 (Favorite Actress in a Motion Picture award People Choice Awards 1996), The Net, 1995, Two if by Sea, 1996, A Time to Kill, 1996, In Love and War, 1996, Practical Magic, 1998, Gun Shy, 1999, Forces of Nature, 1999, Exactly 3:30, 1999, 28 Days, 2000, Famous, 2000, Divine Secrets of the Ya-Ya Sisterhood, 2002; actor, prodr. Kate and Leopold, 1996, Murder By Numbers, 2002, Two Weeks Notice, 2002; actor, writer Making Sandwiches, 1996, Speed II, 1997; actor, exec. prodr. Hope Floats, 1998; voice Prince of Egypt, 1998. Recipient Best Actress MTV's Big Picture, 1994-95, Best Actress US Mag., 1995, Favorite Actress in a Comedy/Drama Theatrical and Favorite Actress-Comedy Video awards Block-Buster Entertainment Awards, 1996, Favorite Actress People's Choice award, 1997, 1999, ShoWest Female Star of the Year, 2001, Am. Comedy Award for Funniest Female Performer in a Motion Picture, 2001.*

BULLOCK, STEPHEN C. lawyer; b. Miami, Fla., May 9, 1949; BS, NYU, 1973; JD cum laude, Harvard U., 1989. Bar: Conn. 1989, Pa. 1989. Asst. counsel Pratt & Whitney; staff atty. United Tech. Corp.; asst. gen. counsel Carrier Corp., Syracuse, NY; v.p., counsel Carrier Sales and Distbn., LLC, Syracuse, NY. Mem. ABA (mem. business law and antitrust sects.). Office: Carrier Corp Carrier Pkwy PO Box 4800 Syracuse NY 13221-4800

BULLOCK, STEVEN CARL, lawyer; b. Anderson, Ind., Jan. 19, 1949; s. Carl Pearson and Dorothy Mae (Colle) B.; m. Debra Bullock; children: Bradford, Christine, Justin, Evan. BA, Purdue U., 1971; JD, Detroit Coll., 1985. Bar: Mich. 1985, U.S. Dist. Ct. (ea. dist.) 1985, Ct. of Appeals (6th cir.) 1993, U.S. Supreme Ct. 1993. Pvt. pracitce, Inkster, Mich., 1985—. With USAF, 1971-75. Mem. Mich. Bar Assn. (criminal law sect.), Detroit Bar Assn., Detroit Funder's Soc., Recorder's Ct. Bar Assn., Suburban Bar Assn., Criminal Def. Lawyers of Mich. Avocations: golf, travel. Office: 2228 Inkster Rd Inkster MI 48141-1811 E-mail: lawone123@aol.com.

BULLOCK, THEODORE HOLMES, biologist, educator; b. Nanking, China, May 16, 1915; s. Amasa Archibald and Ruth (Beckwith) B.; m. Martha Runquist, May 30, 1937; children: Elsie Christine, Stephen Holmes. Student, Pasadena Jr. Coll., 1932-34; AB, U. Calif. at Berkeley, 1936, PhD, 1940, U. Frankfurt, 1988, Loyola U., Chgo., 2000. Research assoc. Yale U. Sch. Medicine, 1942-43, instr. neuroanatomy, 1943-44; instr. Marine Biol. Lab., Woods Hole, Mass., 1944-46, head invertebrate zoology, 1955-57, trustee, 1955-57; asst. prof. anatomy U. Mo., 1944-46; asst. prof. zoology U. Calif. at Los Angeles, 1946, assoc. prof., 1948, prof., 1955-66; Brain Research Inst., U. Calif. at Los Angeles, 1960-66; prof. neurosci. Med. Sch., U. Calif. at San Diego, 1966-82, prof. emeritus, 1982—. Mem. AEC 2d Resurvey of Bikini Expdn., 1948. Author: (with G.A. Horridge) Structure and Function in the Nervous Systems of Invertebrates, 2 vols., 1965; (with others) Introduction to Nervous Systems, 1977; (with W. Heiligenberg) Electroreception, 1986 (with E. Basar) Brain Dynamics, 1989, (with E. Basar) Induced Rhythms in the Brain, 1992, How Do Brains Work?, 1993. Fellow, Ctr. Advanced Study in Behavioral Scis., Palo Alto, 1959—60; Sterling fellow zoology, Yale U., 1940—41, Rockefeller fellow exptl. neurology, 1941—42, Fulbright scholar, Stazione Zoologica, Naples, 1950—51. Fellow AAAS; mem. NAS, Am. Soc. Zoologists (chmn. comparative physiology div. 1961, pres. 1965), Soc. Neurosci. (pres. 1973-74), Internat. Soc. Neuroethology (pres. 1984-86), Am. Physiol. Soc., Soc. Gen. Physiologists, Am. Acad. Arts and Scis., Am. Philos. Soc., Internat. Brain Research Orgn., Phi Beta Kappa, Sigma Xi. E-mail: tbullock@ucsd.edu.

BULLOCK, WELDON KIMBALL, health facility administrator, pathologist, pathology educator; b. Vernal, Utah, Jan. 6, 1908; s. John Kimball and Adelaide (Arnold) B.; m. Dosia Opal Newton, Dec. 26, 1931; children: John, Jim. BA, U. Utah, 1930; MD, Northwestern U., 1934, MSc in Pathology, 1942. Diplomate Am. Bd. Pathology; lic. MD, Calif., Idaho, Utah. Intern Alameda County Hosp., 1933-34; resident in medicine Cook County Hosp., 1940-41; resident in pathology L.A. County-U. So. Calif. Med. Ctr., 1946-47; head surg. pathology LAC-U. So. Calif. Med. Ctr., 1949-69; instr. pathology Sch. Medicine U. So. Calif., 1947-48, asst. prof., 1955-62, clin. prof., 1963-74, clin. prof. emeritus, 1974—; exec. dir. Calif. Tumor Tissue Registry, various locations, 1955-95, dir. emeritus, 1995—; chief pathology svc. Orthop. Hosp., 1956-63; assoc. pathologist St. Luke Hosp., 1963-70, chief pathologist, 1970-77, assoc. pathologist, 1977-81; clin. prof. pathology Sch. Medicine Loma Linda U., 1992—. James Ewing fellow in pathology Meml. Hosp. for Cancer and Allied Disease, 1948-49; cons. Calif. Assn. Cytotechnologists, 1962—, So. Calif. Acad. Oral Pathology, 1963—, Orthop. Hosp., 1963—; mem. Am. Joint Com. Cancer Staging and End Result Reporting, 1963-69, chmn. audio-visual task force, 1966-69, mem. exec. com., 1969; mem. rev. com. clin. cancer tng. grants Nat. Cancer Inst., 1965-68; mem. cancer planning com. Calif. Regional Med. Program, Area V, U. So. Calif., 1967-69; mem. pub. health svc. spl. project rev. com. HEW, State of Calif., 1967-69; meml. lectr. Arthur Purdy Stout Soc. Surg. Pathologists, 1979. Author: Oral Cancer & Tumors of the Jaws, 1956; contbr. articles to profl. jours. Lt. Col. U.S. Army Res., 1941-45, PTO. Decorated Bronze Star. Mem. AMA, Coll. Am. Pathologists (mem. com. cancer 1965-70), Am. Soc. Clin. Pathologists, Soc. Surg. Oncology, Calif. Med. Assn., Calif. Soc. Pathologists (mem. exec. com. 1960-62, sec.-treas. 1962-65, pres.-elect 1965-66, pres. 1966-67), L.A. County Med. Assn. (chmn. com. med. examiner 1968-72), L.A. Soc. Pathologists (past pres. exec. com. 1961-62), Soc. Grad. Pathologists-L.A. County-U. So. Calif. Med. Ctr., Soc. Grad. Surgeons-L.A. County-U. So. Calif. Med. Ctr. Home: 525 N Curtis Ave # 113 Alhambra CA 91801 Office: Calif Tumor Tissue Registry 11021 Campus St # 335 Loma Linda CA 92354 E-mail: cttr@linkline.com.

BULLOCK, WILLIAM CLAPP, JR., banker; b. Bronxville, N.Y., June 28, 1936; s. William and Elizabeth (Van Wagnen) B.; m. Edith Swain, June 21, 1958; children: Wendy, Martha, Sarah, Bill. BA, Yale U., 1958; postgrad., NYU, 1958-60. Asst. treas., asst. v.p. nat. divsn. Morgan Guaranty Trust Co., N.Y.C., 1958-69; v.p., sr. loan officer Merrill Trust Co., Bangor, Maine, 1969-71, exec. v.p., 1971-73, pres., 1973—, CEO, 1980-82, also chmn. bd. dirs.; pres. Merrill Bankshares Co., 1973—, CEO, 1980-82; exec. v.p., dir. Fleet Fin. Group, 1986-88; also chmn. bd. dirs. Merrill Bankshares Co.; pvt. practice as fin. cons., 1989—. Dir. Fed. Res. Bank of Boston, 1985-88; chmn. Merrill Mchts. Bank, 1992—; bd. dirs. Maine Health Care. Chmn. Maine Gov.'s Task Force on Indian Land Claims, 1979-80; bd. dirs. Assoc. Industries Maine, 1978-81, Atlantic Salmon Fedn., Miramichi Salmon Assn.; bd. dirs. New England Coun., 1981—, past pres.; past treas., past trustee Maine Maritime Acad.; past trustee Maine Cmty. Found., Bangor Theol. Sem., Maine State Retirement Sys.. Mem. Maine Bankers Assn. (bd. dirs., past pres.), Am. Bankers Assn., Maine C. of C. (past bd. dirs.), Yale Club, N.Y. Anglers Club. Home: 44 Bald Hill Reach Rd Orrington ME 04474-3630 Office: 201 Main St Bangor ME 04401-6402

BULLOFF, JACK JOHN, physical chemist, consultant; b. N.Y.C., Dec. 9, 1914; s. John Stevens and Selma (Lyadova) B.; m. Gertrude Scher, Nov. 11, 1942 (dec. Oct. 1951); 1 child, Eric Douglas (dec.); m. Florence Gutin, Oct. 4, 1952 (dec. May 1996); children: Dorie Lee, Aaron Harley, Steven Marc. BS in Chemistry, CUNY, 1939; PhD in Phys. Chemistry, Rensselaer Poly. Inst., 1953. Asst. prof. chemistry Associated Colls. Upper N.Y., Ovid/Plattsburgh, 1946-50; teaching fellow Rensselaer Poly. Inst., Troy, N.Y., 1950-52; project supr. Commonwealth Engring. Co., Dayton, Ohio, 1953-56; rsch. assoc. Battelle Meml. Inst., Columbus, Ohio, 1956-68; prof., dir. sci. and tech. studies SUNY, Albany, 1968-76; adj. prof.-in-residence Fla. State U., Tallahassee, 1977-78; cons. safety and wastes J.T. Baker Chem. Co., Phillipsburg, N.J., 1978-84; chief cons. scientist N.Y. State Legis. Commn. on Sci. Tech., Albany, 1985-92; prin. J. Bulloff Chem. and Environ. Cons., Schenectady, N.Y., 1968—. Jr. scientist Los Alamos Nat. Lab., N.M., 1946; vis. lectr. NSF, 1960-66; Kimberley Clark ann. lectr., 1963; cons., expert witness, Schenectady, N.Y., 1968—. Co-author 18 books in field; co-editor: Semiconductor Abstracts, 1959-62, Foundations of Mathematics, 1969; contbr. over 100 articles to profl. jours. With U.S. Army chem. corps. 1942-44, med. corps. 1944-46, ETOUSA. Recipient Best Paper award Tech. Assn. Graphic Arts, 1961. Fellow AAAS (emeritus), Am. Inst. Chemists (emeritus, chair safety in the chemists' workplace com., 1993-94, co-chair coms. in chemistry and environ. concerns, govt. activities and safety in the chemists' workplace 1995-96, govt. activities com. 1995—), Am. Chem. Soc. (emeritus 1989—, various positions 1953-78); mem. N.Y. Acad. Scis. (emeritus 1993—), Ohio Acad. Sci. (v.p. 1966). Achievements include 29 patents for volatile compound metals deposition, air odor control, metallic soaps, and dextran chemistry, others; innovation in xerography and lithography, image-wise photopolymerization, technological forecasting and environmental impact and technology assessment. Home and Office: Ste 5220 8140 Township Line Rd Indianapolis IN 46260-5866 E-mail: bulloff@indy.net. *Once you realize that longevity offers opportunity for more than one career and that everything in the universe has been related to every other thing therein for many billions of years, being a polymath is finding that relation.*

BULLOUGH, JOHN FRANK, organist, music educator; b. Washington, Oct. 15, 1928; s. John and Mabel Jean (McCalip) B.; m. Dorothy Baines, Apr. 10, 1950; children: John Frank, Lynn Diane Lazar, Patricia Ann Gibbs. BA, George Washington U., 1954; MCh choirmaster cert., Am. Guild Organists, 1956; SMM, Union Theol. Sem., 1958. Organist, asst. prof. music Hartford Theol. Sem. Found., Conn., 1958-64; from asst. prof. music to assoc. prof. to prof. Fairleigh Dickinson U., Teaneck, NJ, 1964-93, chmn. dept. fine arts, 1974-79. Music dir. Hartford Ctr. Ch., 1960-64; organist, choirmaster St. Paul's Episcopal Ch., Englewood, NJ, 1973-95; music dir., conductor The Bergen Chorale, Tenafly, NJ, 1987-91. Contbr. articles to profl. jour. V.p. bd. trustees Bergen Philharm. Orch., NJ, 1973—80; bd. dir., auditions com. Rodland Found., 2002—. Mem. AAUP, Am. Guild Organists (dean Hartford chpt. 1963-64, No. Valley NJ chpt. 1975-77, chmn. region II 1984-88, convener No. NJ dist. 1991-92, dean No. NJ cpth. 1995-97), Coll. Music Soc. Episcopalian. Home: 488 Fairidge Ter Teaneck NJ 07666-2617 E-mail: jbmadrigal@aol.com.

BULLOUGH, ROBERT VERNON, JR., educator; b. Salt Lake City, Feb. 12, 1949; s. Robert Vernon and Dolores Elaine (Clarke) B.; m. Dawn Ann Mortensen, June 18, 1976; children: Joshua Benjamin, Seth Thomas, Adam Neve, Rachel Elizabeth. BS in History, U. Utah, 1971, MEd, 1973; PhD, Ohio State U., 1976. Tchr. East High Sch., Salt Lake City, 1971-73; teaching assoc., then fellow Ohio State U., Columbus, 1973-76; asst. prof., then assoc. prof. U. Utah, Salt Lake City, 1976-89, prof. ednl. studies, 1989—99, emeritus prof., 1999—; dir. rsch. Ctr. Improvement Tchr. Edn. and Schooling and prof. tchr. edn. Brigham Young U., 1999—. Mem. Holmes Group Writing Com., 1984-86. Author: Democracy in Education: Boyd H. Bode, 1981, Human Interests in the Curriculum: Teaching and Learning in a Technological Society, 1984, The Forgotten Dream of American Education, 1988, First Year Teacher: A Case Study, 1989, Emerging as a Teacher, 1992, First Year Teacher--Eight Years Later, 1997, Becoming a Student of Teaching, 2d edit., 2001, Uncertain Lives: Children of Promise, Teachers of Hope, 2001; co-author: Becoming a Student of Teaching, 1995; mem. editl. bds.; contbr. articles to profl. jours. Recipient Outstanding Writing award, AACTE, 1997. Mem. Am. Ednl. Rsch. Assn. (Outstanding Book award divsn. B 2003), Soc. for Study of Curriculum History, Profs. of Curriculum, Phi Beta Kappa, Phi Eta Sigma, Phi Kappa Phi, Phi Delta Kappa. Mem. Lds Ch. Avocations: book collecting, house restoration, furniture restoration, family history. Office: Brigham Young U 149 McKay Bldg Provo UT 84602

BULLOUGH, VERN LEROY, sexologist, historian, nursing educator, researcher; b. Salt Lake City, July 24, 1928; s. D. Vernon Bullough and Augusta Rueckert; m. Bonnie Uckerman, Aug. 2, 1947 (dec. 1996); children: David-(dec.), James, Steven, Susan, Michael; m. Gwen Brewer, Aug. 15, 1998. BSN, Calif. State U., Long Beach, 1981; BS, U. Utah, 1951; MA, U. Chgo., 1951, PhD, 1954. Assoc. prof. Youngstown (Ohio) U., 1954-59; from asst. prof. to prof. Calif. State U., Northridge, 1959—79; dean faculty natural and social scis. SUNY Coll., Buffalo, 1980-89, disting. prof., 1988-93, disting. prof. emeritus, 1993—. Adj. prof. U. So. Calif., 1994—2003, Ctr. for Sex Rsch., Calif. State U., Northridge, 1994—; fellow Ctr. for Medieval-Renaissance Studies UCLA, 1995—. Author, co-author: more than 50 books; editor (sr. editor): Free Inquiry; mem. editl. bds.: 8 jours., 2003—; contbr. more than 200 articles to profl. jours. Active in civil liberties and civil rights orgns.; founding mem. first fair housing group in U.S., 1959. With Security Agency U.S. Army, 1946—48. Named Oustanding Prof, Calif Stat Univ sys, Disting Prof, SUNY; recipient Kinsey award, numerous other awards for rsch. into sexuality, history, medicine, nursing and cmty. svcs. Fellow: Coun. for Sci. Medicine and Mental Health, Com. for Sci. Investigation of Claims to the Paranormal, Acad. Humanism (laureate), Am. Acad. Nursing, Soc. Sci. Study Sex (past pres.); mem.: Internat. Humanist and Ethical Union (past pres.). E-mail: vbullough@csun.edu.

BULMAHN, T. PAUL, oil and gas company executive; Counsel Tenneco, 1978—84; v.p., gen. counsel Plumb Oil Co., 1984—88; pres. Harbert Oil & Gas Corp., 1988—91; pres., chmn. ATP Oil & Gas Corp., Houston, 1991—. Office: ATP Oil & Gas Corp 4600 Post Oak Pl Ste 200 Houston TX 77027

BULMAN, WILLIAM PATRICK, data processing executive; b. Corona, N.Y., Jan. 11, 1925; s. William T. and Bridget A. (Gibbons) B.; m. Jane G. Jones, June 30, 1952. BS, U. Upper N.Y., 1947; BBA, Syracuse (N.Y.) U., 1949, MBA, 1977. In systems/programming Mohawk Airlines, Utica, N.Y., 1951-55; data processing mgr. Gold Medal Packing, Utica, 1956-59, West End Brewing, Utica, 1960-73; coord. on-line data processing systems Sperry-Univac, Unica, 1973-76, data processing mgr., 1976-77; programmer/analyst MDS, Herkimer, N.Y., 1977-86; sr. programmer, analyst Momentum Techs., Herkimer, 1986-89; ret., 1989. Cons. Bilb-Tech, 1989—. Mem. Data Processing Mgmt. Assn. (v.p., treas.), Assn. Systems Mgmt. Address: 35 Ashwood Ave Whitesboro NY 13492-1701 E-mail: bilb-t@msn.com.

BULMER, MARTIN, sociologist, educator; b. Newcastle-on-Tyne, England, Aug. 25, 1943; s. Charles Philips Trevelyan and Edith Bulmer; m. Joan Boer, Aug., 1966; children: Michael, Georgina. BSc in Sociology, London Sch. Econs., 1967; PhD, U. London, Eng., 1981. Lectr. U. Durham, Eng., 1970-74; statistician Brit. Govt., London, 1975; from lectr. to reader London Sch. Econs., 1975-93; vis. prof. U. Chgo., 1987; prof. sociology Southampton (Eng.) U., 1993-95; Found. Fund prof. U. Surrey, Guildford, Eng., 1995—. Vice-chair Rsch. Resources and Methods Com. Econ. and Social Rsch. Coun., 1985-87; editor Ethnic and Racial Studies, Acad. Jour., 1992—. Author: The Chicago School of Sociology, 1984; co-editor: (essays) The Social Survey in Historical Perspective, 1991, (lectures) Citizenship Today, 1996; (reader) Social Research in Developing Countries, 1993, Racism, 1999. Mem. Brit. Sociol. Assn., Am. Sociol. Assn., Internat. Sociol. Assn. Mem. Soc. Of Friends. Avocations: cinema, walking. Office: U Surrey Dept Sociology Guildford GU2 7XH England E-mail: m.bulmer@soc.surrey.ac.uk.

BULOW, GEORGE MITCHELL, entrepreneur; b. New Rochelle, N.Y., May 26, 1949; s. Harry N. Bulow and Ruth (Silverman) Kaufman; m. Lucienne Carasso, June 22, 1975; children: Harris, Alessandra. BA, Clark U., 1971; MBA, Columbia U., 1974. Asst. v.p. Chase Manhattan Bank, NA, N.Y.C., 1974-87; pres. Interactive Internat. Inc., N.Y.C., 1987—. Pres. Bohlen Industries N.Am., Inc., N.Y.C., 1980—, Beaumont Farms, Inc., N.Y.C., 1994—. Office: Interactive Internat Inc 290 West End Ave New York NY 10023-8106 E-mail: ivie@erols.com.

BULOW, HARRY TIMOTHY, music educator; b. Des Moines, Iowa, Feb. 19, 1951; s. Harry and Thelma Vera Bulow; m. Ellen Leung, June 18, 1992; children: Timothy Christian, Hannah Kathleen. PhD, UCLA, 1983; BA in Music with distinction, San Diego State U., 1975. Asst. prof. music Santa Barbara (Calif.) City Coll., 1982—88; assitant prof. music U. Hawaii, Hilo, 1988—92; assoc. prof. music Univ. NC, Charlotte, 1992—. Composer: (musical composition) Textures for Wind Ensemble, 2002 (Nat. Band Association's Award in Composition, 1980), Pillars for Large Orchestra (Internat. Composer's Competition award, 1978, Oscar Esla Internat. Composers Award, Alicante, Spain, 1986), Movements for Chamber Orchestra (New Music Award, Omaha Symphony Orch., 1985), Sonata for Piano (Tampa Bay Composers Forum Award for Chamber Music Composition, 1998), (musical compositon) Mutations for Flute (Tucson Flute Club's Award for Musical Composition, 1978). Fellow Composer fellow, Nat. Endowment Arts, 1985, NC Artist fellow, NC Arts Coun., 1995—96, 2001—02. Mem.: ASCAP (22 musical composition awards 1980—2002), Composers Forum, Coll. Music Soc., Soc. Composers, Inc., Southeastern Composers League. Home: P O Box 806 Cornelius NC 28031 Office: Univ NC at Charlotte 9201 University City Blvd Charlotte NC 28223

BULOW, JACK FAYE, retired library director; b. Elmira, N.Y., June 7, 1942; m. June Burwell, May 22, 1971. Associates degree, Corning (N.Y.) C.C., 1968; BA, U. Ala., Birmingham, 1971; MLS, U. Ala., Tuscaloosa, 1973. Community svcs. libr. Birmingham Pub. Libr., 1973-77, assoc. dir., 1977-93, dir., 1993—2002, ret., 2002. Developer Books-by-Mail program, Birmingham and Jefferson County, 1976; participant exec. in residence program Birmingham-So. Coll., 1987, Leadership Birmingham, 1992; elected as del. White House Conf. on Libr. and Info. Svc., Washington, 1991; elected as regional rep. White House Conf. on Libr. and Info. Svcs. Task Force, Washington, 1992; bd. dirs. Literacy Coun. Ctrl. Ala., Birmingham, 1993-2000; mem. Nat. League Cities, Washington, 1993—; mem. long range planning com. Birmingham Mus. Art, 1993-99; mem. cultural affairs com. Operation New Birmingham, 1988—; sec. Birmingham Pub. Libr. Found.; patron Cahaba River Soc. Birmingham, 1992—. With USCG, 1960-64. Recipient Forestry Recognition award Ala. Forestry Commn., 1977. Mem. ALA (chair fundraising and fin. devel. sect. 1997), Am. Hist. Print Collectors Soc., Am. Mgmt. Assn., Nat. Soc. Fund Raising Execs., Southeastern Libr. Assn., Ala. Libr. Assn. (pres. 1995, Eminent Libr. award 2000), Birmingham-So. Coll. Fine Arts Soc. Avocations: reading, golf, travel, fishing.

BULTAN, AYKUT, communications systems engineer; came to U.S., 1997; BSEE, Middle East Tech. U., Ankara, Turkey, 1986, MSEE, 1989, PhD in Elec. Engring., 1995. Rsch. and design engr. Comm. Lab. ASELSAN Corp., Ankara, 1986-89; rsch./tchg. asst. dept. elec. engring. Middle East Tech. U., Ankara, 1990—95; asst. prof. computer engring. dept. Ea. Mediterranean U., Famagusta, Cyprus, 1996-97; vis. scholar elec. and computer engring. dept. N.J. Ctr. for Multimedia Rsch., N.J. Inst. Tech., Newark, 1997-99; comms. sys. engr. Interdigital Comm. Corp., Melville, NY, 2000—. Contbr. articles to profl. jours. Undergrad. student fellow Turkish Sci. and Tech. Rsch. Assn., 1982-86. Achievements include research in time-frequency signal analysis and its applications in wireless communications; design of algorithms for third generation wireless systems; patents in field. Avocations: skiing, scuba and skin diving, reading. Office: Interdigital Comm Corp 2 Huntington Quadrangle Melville NY 11747-4508 Fax: 631-622-0100. E-mail: aykut.bultan@interdigital.com.

BULTMANN, WILLIAM ARNOLD, historian, educator; b. Apr. 10, 1922; s. Paul Gerhardt and Elsa (Johnson) B.; m. Phyllis Jane Wetherell, Dec. 28, 1949; 1 child, Janice Jane. BA, UCLA, 1943, PhD, 1950. Assoc. prof. history Ctrl. Ark. U., Conway, 1949—52, prof., 1954—57; assoc. prof. Ohio Wesleyan U., Del., 1957—61, prof., 1961—65, We. Wash. U., Bellingham, 1965—87, chmn. dept., 1968—70, dean arts and scis., 1970—72, provost, 1971—73. Vis. assoc. prof. U. Tex., Austin, 1952—53; vis. prof. U. N.H., 1965, 66; acad. cons. Wash. Commn. Humanities, 1973—87, NEA, 1976—87; reader Ednl. Testing Svc., Princeton, 1973—85; Fulbright sr. lectr. Dacca (Bangladesh) U., 1960—61; rsch. fellow Ohio Wesleyan U., 1964; feature writer, columnist Sea mag., 1974—93; feature writer Venture mag., 1981—85, Poole Publs., 1988—92. Co-author: Border Boating, 1978; co-founder, mem. editl. bd. Albion, 1968—84, mng. editor Brit. Studies Intelligencer, 1973—80; co-editor: Current Research in British Studies, 1975; editor: Jib Sheet, 1981—86. Adminstrv. officer Bellingham Power Squadron, 1981—82, comdr., 1982—84; bd. dirs. Bellingham Maritime Heritage Found., 1980—85; mem. Wash. Arboretum Found., 1992—97. Recipient rsch. award, Social Sci. Rsch. Coun., 1957; fellow for fgn. study, Fund for Advancement Edn., 1953—54. Mem.: AAUP, Mystery Writers Am., Pacific and Pacific N.W. Conf. Brit. Studies, Conf. Brit. Studies, Ch. History Soc., Nat. Tropical Botanical Garden Soc., Am. Hist. Assn., Interclub Boating Assn., Nat. Boating Fedn., Wash. Athletic, Park Athletic Recreation, Bellingham Yacht (chmn. pub. rels. com. 1981—86), Birch Bay Yacht, Squalicum Yacht (trustee 1979—82), Pi Gamma Mu, Phi Delta Kappa, Phi Beta Kappa. Episcopalian. Home: 1600 43rd Ave E Apt 101 Seattle WA 98112-3245

BUMANN, SHARON ANN, sculptor; b. Syracuse, N.Y., June 28, 1953; d. G. Bruce and Erma Jean (Gibbs) Stallknecht; m. George Charles BuMann, Aug. 26, 1972; children: George Bruce, Amy Beth. AAS in Graphic Arts with honors, Onondaga C.C., Syracuse, N.Y., 1975; BFA in Sculpture magna cum laude, Syracuse U., 1984; postgrad., U. Hartford, 1990, Lyme Acad., 2001. Owner, operator BuMann Sculpture Studio, Central Square, N.Y., 1977—. Adj. prof. Onondaga C.C.; lectr., juror and artist-in-residence, award winning sculptor; bronze conservator. Creator, bronze monuments, lifesize butter sculptures, exhibitions include of butter sculptures N.Y. State Fair, 1996—2002, State Fair of Tex., 1997—2002, Tulsa State Fair, 1998—2002, Erie County Fair, 1997—2001, Kans. State Fair, 2000—02. Bd. dirs., chair Fort Brewerton (N.Y.) Hist. Expansion, 1997—. Mem. Nat. Sculpture Soc., Internat. Sculpture Ctr., Onondaga C.C. Alumni Assn. (pres., 1992-94). Avocations: equestrian activities, boating. Office: BuMann Sculpture Studio 90 Kellar Rd Central Square NY 13036-2122

BUMBAUGH, DAVID EDWARD, religious studies educator, minister; b. Chambersburg, Pa., Nov. 1, 1936; s. David Edward and Julia Watson Bumbaugh; m. Beverly Ann Keplinger, June 7, 1956; children: Mark David, Geoffrey Douglas, Stephen Drew, Julia Anna Shah. BA, Wilmington Coll., 1958; BD, Meadville Theol. Sch., 1964. Min. Unitarian Universalist Cmty. Ch., Chicago Heights, Ill., 1964—69, Mt. Vernon Unitarian Ch., Alexandria, Va., 1969—84, First Universalist Ch., Syracuse, NY, 1984—88, Unitarian Ch. in Summit, NJ, 1988—98; assoc. prof. ministry Meadville Lombard Theol. Sch., Chgo., 1999—. Pres. Unitarian Universalist Hist. Soc., Boston, 2000—. Author: (theology) The Education of God, 1994, (history) Unitarian Universalism: A Narrative History, 2000; contbr. articles to profl. jours. Chair Unitarian Universalists for the Chgo. Freedom Movement, 1966—69; bd. mem. Diversity Task Force, Summit, 1995—98, St. Lawrence Unitarian Universalist Dist., Buffalo, 1986—88; pres. Metro N.Y. Unitarian Universalist Mins. Assn., Summit, 1993—95. Independent. Unitarian Universalist. Home: 5530 S Shore Dr #21C Chicago IL 60637 Office: Meadville Lombard Theological School 5701 S Woodlawn Ave Chicago IL 60637 Office Fax: 773-256-3006. Personal E-mail: revbev@aol.com. E-mail: dbumbaugh@meadville.edu.

BUMBERY, JOSEPH LAWRENCE, diversified telecommunications company executive; b. St. Louis, May 30, 1929; s. John Andrew and Lillian Belle (DeVinney) B. BS, St. Louis U., 1951. Asst. comptroller Magic Chef, Inc., St. Louis, 1955-57; dir. audits and systems Bemis Corp., St. Louis, 1957-62; asst. comptroller Studebaker Corp., South Bend, Ind., 1962-65; with ITT, N.Y.C., 1965-86, v.p., 1979—, asst. comptroller, 1969—. Served to 1st lt. USAF, 1951-53. Decorated Knight Order St. John of Jerusalem; named Mem. Augustinian Order Gen. Curia of Order Rome, 1988, Governor Am. Soc. Order of St. John of Jerusalem, 1990.

BUMBLEBURG, JOSEPH THEODORE, lawyer; b. Lafayette, Ind., Jan. 5, 1937; s. Theodore Joseph and Elizabeth Mary (Delaney) B.; m. Constance J. Peterson, Dec. 26, 1966; children: Theodore William, Amy Ann. BA, U. Notre Dame, 1958; JD, Ind. U., 1961. Bar: Ind. 1961, U.S. Ct. Mil. Appeals 1962, U.S. Dist. Ct. (no. dist.) Ind. 1964, U.S. Ct. Appeals (7th cir.) 1970, U.S. Supreme Ct. 1970, U.S. Ct. Appeals (fed. cir.) 1985. Capt., judge adv. U.S. Army, Ft. Gordon, Ga., 1961-64; ptnr. Ball, Eggleston, Bumbleburg, McBride, Walkey & Stapleton PC, Lafayette, 1964—. Commr. City of Lafayette Police Civil Svc. Commn., 1971-75, v.p., 1971-72, pres., 1972-75; sec. Tippecanoe County Sheriff's Merit Bd., 1968—; mem. Lafayette Bd. Zoning Appeals, 1970-71; advisor to registrants SSS, 1967-69, 72-75; mem. pastoral coun. St. Mary's Cathedral, 1968-70, 74-78; mem. nat. bd. govs. ARC, 1975-81; bd. dirs. United Way, Lafayette, 1972-75; mem. cmty. adv. coun. Sch. Nursing, Purdue U., 1979-85; state trustee Ivy Tech. State Coll., vice-chmn., 1998-00, chmn., 2000-02; elected Acad. of Law Sch. Alumni Fellows, Ind. U. Law Sch., Bloomington, 2002. Recipient Cert. appreciation Chief Naval Edn., 1978, Gold award United Way, 1978, Pres. U.S. Citation for Community Achievement, 1979, Cert. appreciation ARC, 1972, 81, Harriman award ARC, 1992. Fellow Ind. Bar Found. (master); mem. Ind. Bar Assn., Greater Lafayette C. of C. (bd. dirs. 1986-91, chmn. 1988-89), Am. Legion (nat. security coun. 1970-83, Ind. judge advocate, 1999—, Post II Legionnaire of Yr. 1982-83, Dept. Ind. Disting.

Svc. award 2001), K.C., Phi Theta Kappa (hon.). Home: 726 Owen St Lafayette IN 47905-1878 Office: Ball Eggleston Bumbleburg McBride Walkey & Stapleton PC PO Box 1535 Lafayette IN 47902-1535 E-mail: jbumbleburg@ball-law.com.

BUMGARDNER, JOEL DAVID, biomedical engineer, educator; b. Huntsville, Ala., Apr. 18, 1961; s. Carl L. and Ann (Adams) B. BS in Biology, Fla. State U., 1984; BS in Materials Engring., MS in Biomed. Engring., U. Ala., Birmingham, 1989, PhD in Biomed. Engring., 1994. Rsch. fellow U. Ala., Birmingham, 1988-93; J. William Fulbright fellow U.S., Sweden, 1993-94; assoc. prof. dept. agrl. and biol. engring. and biomed. engring program Miss. State U., Starkville, 1994—. Dir. 16th So. Biomed. Engring. Conf., Biloxi, Miss., 1996-97. Reviewer Dental Materials Jour., Dallas, 1994—, Jour. Biomedical Materials Rsch.; mem. editl. bd., Jour. Prosthetic Dentistry, Jour. Biomed. Materials Rsch.; contbr. articles to profl. jours.; contbr. chpt. to ency., 1995. Co-chmn. Decorative Arts and Preservation Forum-Columbus (Miss.) Historic Found., 1997, mem. steering com., 1995-99; mem. com. Health Choice Am. Heart Walk, Columbus, 1995-2001. Recipient young biomed. engr. investigator grant Whitaker Found., 1999-2001, Hearin Faculty Excellence award Miss. State U. Coll. Engring., 2001, 02; Biomed. rsch. grantee NIH, Washington, 1992-94, 2002—, biomed. equipment grantee NSF, Washington, 1995, 2002; named Outstanding Faculty Advisor, Gold Key Soc., 1999; Japan Soc. for Promotion of Sci. fellow, 2000. Mem. ASTM, Soc. Biomaterials (chmn. membership com. 1995-96, mem.-at-large 2002-2003), Internat. and Am. Assn. Dental Rsch. (mem. constn. com. 1995-98), Biomed. Engring. Soc., Inst. Biol. Engring. Avocations: biking, tennis, reading, antiques. Office: Miss State U Box 9632 Mississippi State MS 39762-9632

BUMGARDNER, KATHRYN H. retired librarian; b. Nashville, Nov. 10, 1922; d. Max and Aline (Farrar) Hamrick; m. Walter Gaynor Bumgardner, July 21, 1948; children: Linda Browning, Donna Carol, Larry Gaynor; B.A., George Peabody Coll., Nashville, 1943; BS in Library Sci., Peabody Library Sch., 1944. Cert. librarian, Va., Ga. Librarian, White County High Sch., Sparta, Tenn., 1944-45; asst. librarian Abilene (Tex.) Christian Coll., 1946-48; catalog librarian Va. Commonwealth U., Richmond, 1966-69; assoc. librarian U. West Fla., Pensacola, 1970-74; asst. dir. Watauga Regional Library, Johnson City, Tenn., 1975-83; asst. dir. Lake Blackshear Regional Library, Americus, Ga., 1983-84. Mary Mildred Sullivan scholar, 1943. Republican. Mem. Ch. of Christ. Home: 4120 April Rd Pensacola FL 32504-7706

BUMGARNER, JAMES MCNABB, judge; b. Peru, Ill., Sept. 13, 1919; s. Joshua Mills and Ethel (McNabb) Bumgarner; m. Helen D Welker, Feb. 7, 1942 (dec. May 1981); children: Barbara Malany, Sally Guth; m. Elizabeth L Miller, Feb. 12, 1983; stepchildren: Tad Miller, Brian Miller, Mathew Miller. BS in Psychology with honors, U. Ill., 1941, JD, 1946. Commd. 2nd lt. USAAF, 1942; advanced through grades to col. USAF, 1967, ret., 1974; pvt. practice Rantoul, Ill., 1947, Hannah, Mattoon, Ill.; cir. judge 10th Jud. Cir. of Ill., 1979—. Mem. pres. coun. U. Ill. Named Disting. Grad. of, U. Ill. Coll. Law; named to, Sr. Illinoisians Hall of Fame. Mem.: VFW, Air War Col Alumni Asn, Judge Advs Asn, Timber Growers Asn, Putnam County Hist Soc, Putnam County Bar Asn, Univ Ill Alumni Asn, Ill Bar Asn, Vietnam Vets Bar Asn, Ret Judge Advs Asn, Ret Officers Asn, Vietnam Vets Ill, Am Legion, Ill Col Law Deans Club, Rotary, Phi Alpha Delta. Home: 1010 Market St PO Box 225 Hennepin IL 61327-0225 E-mail: jimbum@bumgarner.org.

BUMGARNER, MARLENE ANNE, writer, editor, educator; b. Yorkshire, Eng., Nov. 6, 1947; arrived in U.S., 1949, naturalized, 1965; d. Rowland and May (Whittaker) Skirrow; m. John Owen Bumgarner, June 17, 1967 (div. 1982); children: Dona Ana, John Rowland; m. Robert Eltgroth, Feb. 19, 1983 (div. 1992); children: Deborah Ruth, Jamie Lynn. AA, Coll. San Mateo, 1967; BA, San Diego State Coll., 1970; MA, San Jose (Calif.) State Coll., 1982; EdD, Nova Southwestern U., 1992. Tech. editor electronics firms, 1967—70; coordinator Peer Counseling Center, Las Cruces, N.Mex., 1970—72; tchr. elem. sch., 1974—76, 1982—84; owner, mgr. Morgan Hill (Calif.) Trading Post natural food store, 1976—80; editor Natural Living Newsline, 1979—81; mgr. Natural Living Assocs., 1979—82; dir. Morgan Hill Country Day Sch., 1980—82; prof. child devel., chair social sci. Gavilan Coll., 1979—85, coord. child devel. programs, 1985—99, chair social sci. dept., 1999—2001, dir. & grant mgr. Tchr. & Reading Develop Partnership, 2001—. New products editor Classroom Computer Learning mag., 1980-82. Author: Book of Whole Grains, 1976, (contbr.) The People's Cookbook, 1977, Organic Cooking for (not-so-organic) Mothers, 1980, (contbr.) Real Food Places to Eat, 1981, Working With School-Aged Children, 1999; food columnist San Jose Mercury, 1977-80, Gilroy Dispatch, 1984-86; sr. tech. writer Boole and Babbage, Inc., 1983-85; contbg. editor Mothering mag., 1981-87; contbr. articles to Mother's Manual, Baby Talk, Am. Baby, McCalls, Family Computing and others. Bd. dirs. Calif. Sch. Age Consortium, 1998—; apptd. mem. Morgan Hill Libr. Commn., 1999; supt. Sunday sch. St. John's Episc. Ch., 1985—85, sr. warden, 1992—94; leader, founder La Leche League of Morgan Hill, 1977—85; coord. Morgan Hill Cmty. Garden, 1982—84; participant C.C. Leaders for the 80's, 1987. Named Woman of Achievement, Santa Clara County, 1987, Educator of Yr., Morgan Hill C of C, 2001. Mem.: AAUW, Nat. Sch. Age Care Alliance, Nat. Assn. Edn. Young Children. E-mail: mbumgarner@gavilan.edu.

BUMGARNER, ROBERT LINVILLE, pathologist, retired military officer; b. Long Branch, Calif., Oct. 15, 1944; BS in Physics, Mich. State U., 1967, MD, 1974. Diplomate Am. Bd. in Anatomic and Clin. Pathology. Commd. ensign USN, 1967, advanced through grades to capt., 1987; intern, resident Naval Med. Ctr., Portsmouth, Va., 1975-79; chief of lab. Naval Submarine Med. Ctr., Groton, 1979-83; dir. Navy Drug Screening Lab., Jacksonville, 1983; force med. officer, commdr. submarine force U.S. Pacific Fleet, 1984-86; dir. for undersea medicine and radiation health USN, Washington, 1986-91; dir., commdg. officer Armed Forces Radiobiology Rsch. Inst., Bethesda, Md., 1991-95; dir. ancillary svcs. Naval Med. Ctr., San Diego, 1995-99; fleet surgeon U.S. Pacific Fleet, 1999—2001; prin. scientist Springfield Rsch. Facility, Alexandria, Va., 2002—. Expert in toxicology, radiobiology, biol. agts., 2002--. Fellow Coll. of Am. Pathologists (lead lab. accreditation inspector 1999-2001). Office: Springfield Rsch Facility 6350 Walker Ln Ste 400 Alexandria VA 22310-3243 Fax: 703-440-9595. E-mail: bummerbob@attglobal.net

BUMPAS, STUART MARYMAN, lawyer; b. Little Rock, Oct. 7, 1944; s. Hubert Wayne Bumpas and Martha Conway (Maryman) Gaylord; m. Diane Ellen DeWare, Oct. 1, 1977. BA, Brown U., 1966; JD, U. Tex., 1969; LLM, George Washington U., 1973. Bar: Tex. 1969, D.C. 1972. Atty.-advisor Office of Chief Counsel, Washington, 1969-72; asst. to commr. IRS, Washington, 1973-74; ptnr. Locke, Purnell, Rain, Harrell, Dallas, 1974-98, Locke, Liddell & Sapp, Dallas, 1999—. Adj. prof. employee benefits So. Meth. U., Dallas, 1975; lectr. Washington Non-Profit Tax Conf., Am. Law Inst., Ann. Non-Profit Orgns. Inst. Contbr. articles to profl. jours. Exec. com. Meadows Sch. of Arts, So. Meth. U., Dallas; bd. dirs. Callier Ctr. for Comm. Disorders, Dallas, 1984—, Friends of Alzheimer's Dis. Ctr., Southwestern Med. Sch., Goodwill Industries, Dallas; bd. dirs., v.p. Dallas Grand Opera Assn., 1984; mem. Mayor's Commn. on Internat. Devel. Task Force on Arts and Culture, Dallas, 1988; nat. counsel Am. Heart Assn., Dallas, 1979—; trustee The Lamplighter Sch.; gen. counsel The Hockaday Sch.; gen. counsel, bd. trustees, exec. com. Dallas Mus. Art; bd. trustees Southwestern Med. Found. Mem. ABA (mem. exempt orgns. com.), Tex. Bar Assn. (former chmn. legal aspects of arts com.), Dallas Bar Assn., Bus. Adv. Com., Am. Coun. on Germany, Coun. on Fgn. Rels. Clubs: Dallas Petroleum, Brook Hollow Golf, Idlewild (Dallas); Soc. Cin. (Washington), Coral Beach and Tennis (Bermuda). Episcopalian. Home: 5306 Surrey Cir Dallas TX 75209-2427 Office: Locke Liddell & Sapp 2200 Ross Ave Ste 2200 Dallas TX 75201-6776 E-mail: sbumpas@lockeliddell.com.

BUMPASS, LARRY LEE, sociologist, educator; b. Detroit, Feb. 16, 1942; s. Yancey Washington and Emma Lee (Moore) B.; m. Janet Arlene Angles, Aug. 3, 1962; children— Shauna Lynn, Carri Noelle. BA, Wheaton Coll., 1963; MA, U. Mich., 1965, PhD, 1968. Research assoc. Office of Population, Princeton U., 1967-70; mem. faculty dept. sociology U. Wis., Madison, 1970—, prof., 1973—; dir. Center for Demography and Ecology, 1977-80. Fellow Econ. Commn. for Europe, UN, Geneva, Switzerland, 1974; chmn. population and social sci. study sect. NIH, 1978-80; chmn. internat. research awards program on determinants of fertility in developing countries Population Council, 1981-85; bd. overseers Mich. Panel Study of Income Dynamics, 1984-87 ; dir. Nat. Survey Families and Households, 1986—; mem. NIH Population Rsch. Com., 1989-93, Bd. Overseers Gen. Soc. Survey, 1990-95, MacArthur Found. Rsch. Network on Successful Mid-life Adjustment; mem. Bd. Children Youth Families, NTL Acad. Scis., 1993—; Nat. Acad. Of Arts & Scientists, 1997. Author: The Later Years of Childbearing, 1970, Social Demography, 1978, Am. Families and Households, 1988; Editor: Demography, 1978-81. Mem. Population Assn. Am. (bd. dirs. 1973-77, 2d v.p. 1986, 1st v.p. 1986, pres.1990), Am. Sociol. Assn. (chmn. population sect. 1982), Internat. Union for Sci. Study of Population, AAAS, ACLU. Home: 5821 Barton Rd Madison WI 53711-3432 Office: 3224 Social Sci 1180 Observatory Dr Madison WI 53706-1320 E-mail: Bumpass@ssc.wisc.edu.

BUMPERS, DALE L. former senator, former governor, lawyer; b. Charleston, Ark., Aug. 12, 1925; s. William Rufus and Lattie (Jones) B.; m. Betty Lou Flanagan, Sept. 4, 1949; children: Dale Brent, William Mark, Margaret Brooke. Student, U. Ark., 1943, 46-48; JD, Northwestern U., 1951. Bar: Ark. 1952. Pres. Charleston Hardware and Furniture Co., 1951—66; pvt. practice Charleston, 1952-70; operator Angus cattle farm, 1966-70; gov. of Ark., 1971—75; U.S. senator from Ark., 1975-98; atty. Arent Fox Kintner Plotkin & Kahn, Washington, 2000—03; dir. Ctr. for Def. Info., 1999. Mem. appropriations com., energy and natural resources com., small bus. com., senate Dem. policy com. Pres. Charleston Sch. Bd., 1969-70. Sgt. USMC, 1943-46. Mem. Charleston C. of C. (pres.) Democrat. Methodist. Address: Arent Fox Kintner Plotkin & Kahn 1050 Connecticut Ave NWNW Washington DC 20036-5339

BUNCH, FRANKLIN SWOPE, retired architect; b. Madison, Ind., Jan. 4, 1913; s. Walker Franklin and Susan Beatrice (Swope) B.; m. Virginia Aurelia Boggs, June 8, 1937; children: Franklin Swope, Dean Boggs. BS in Arch, U. Fla., 1934. Draftsman, designer, architect and constrn. supr. various Fla. architects, 1934-41; archtl. engr. U.S. Engrs. Dist. Office, Jacksonville, Fla., 1942-43, Jacksonville Naval Air Sta., 1944-45; partner Kemp, Bunch & Jackson Architects, Inc., Jacksonville, 1946-69, sr. v.p., 1970-82. Pres. Fla. Bd. Architecture, 1959-61; mem. com. on exams. Nat. Council Archtl. Registration Bds., 1961-62; pres. bldg. code adv. bd., Jacksonville, 1949-68, mem. examining com., from 1949; chmn. bldg. codes adjustment bd. Jacksonville Consol. Govt.; mem. housing com. Jacksonville Council on Aging, 1962 Projects include S. Central Home Office Prudential Ins. Co. Am., gen. offices Seaboard Coast Line R.R., Fla. State Prison, Starke, Hdqrs. Bldg. State Rd. Dept., Tallahassee. Pres. Little Theatre of Jacksonville, 1952-53. Fellow AIA (emeritus); mem. Fla. Assn. Architects (pres. 1947-48, now emeritus), Jacksonville Jr. C. of C. (chmn. luncheon club 1938), Jacksonville Area C. of C. (chmn. city, county, state affairs com. 1963, chmn. fed. assistance 1949 68), Phi Kappa Tau. Baptist.

BUNCH, JAMES RAYMOND, mathematician, educator; b. Globe, Ariz., Sept. 23, 1940; s. Raymond Eugene and Mary Genevieve (Cull) Bunch. BS, U. Ariz., 1962; MA, U. Calif., Berkeley, 1965, PhD, 1969. Asst. in math. Argonne Nat. Lab., 1969—70; instr. dept. math. U. Chgo., 1970—71; asst. prof. dept. computer sci. Cornell U., Ithaca, NY, 1971—74; assoc. prof. dept. math. U. Calif. San Diego, La Jolla, 1974—80, prof., 1980—2002, chair dept. math., 2002—. Co-author: LINPACK Users' Guide, 1979; editor: Sparse Matrix Computations, 1976. Fulbright fellow, 1962, Woodrow Wilson fellow, 1962. Mem.: Am. Math. Soc., Soc. for Indsl. and Applied Math. Office: UCSD Dept of Math 9500 Gilman Dr La Jolla CA 92093-0112

BUNCH, JENNINGS BRYAN, JR., electrical engineer; b. Richmond, Va., Feb. 9, 1929; s. Jennings Bryan and Cora Irving (Wilson) B.; m. Dale Metcalf, Feb. 2, 1952 (dec. Nov. 1996); children: Jennifer, Pamela; m. Harriet Walton, Jan. 2, 1999. BSEE with distinction, Va. Mil. Inst., 1950; MSEE, U. Pitts., 1969. Engr. in tng. Va. Electric & Power Co., Alexandria, Richmond, 1950, 53; test engr. and mktg. assignments GE, Schenectady, N.Y., 1956-63, application engr., 1956-63, regional application engr. Pitts., Phila., 1963-73, sr. application engr., project mgr. Phila. and Schenectady, 1973-82, Malvern, Pa., 1982-91; cons. Star Design, Moorestown, N.J., 1992-96. Contbr. articles on electric utility distbn. automation systems to profl. publs. Exec. dir. Sending Experienced Ret. Vols. Everywhere (SERVE), 1993-2003. 1st lt. U.S. Army, 1950-52. Fellow: IEEE; mem.: Tau Beta Pi. Republican. Presbyterian. Avocations: hiking, astronomy.

BUNCH, RICHARD ALAN, writer, educator; b. Honolulu, June 1, 1945; s. Thornton Carlisle and DeLores (Veal) B.; m. Rita Anne Glazar, Aug. 11, 1990; children: Katharine, Richard Jr. AA in Liberal Arts, Napa Coll., 1965; student, Stanford -in-Britain, Grantham, Lincolnshire, Eng., 1966; BA in Comms., Stanford U., 1967; MA in History, U. Ariz., 1969, MDiv, 1970, DD, 1971; postgrad., Vanderbilt U., 1972—75, Temple U., 1975—76; JD, U. Memphis, 1980. Tchg. asst. philosophy Vanderbilt U., Nashville, 1973-74; instr. philosophy Belmont U., 1973-74; law clk. Cir. Ct. Shelby County, Tenn., 1979-81; atty. Horne and Peppel, Memphis, 1981-83; law clk. Tenn. Ct. Appeals, 1983; instr. philosophy Chapman U., 1986-87; instr. law Sonoma State U., 1986-87, instr. philosophy, 1990-91. Lectr. U. Calif., Berkeley, 1995; adj. humanities faculty Napa Valley Coll., 1985—; instr. history and humanities Diablo Valley Coll., 1991-94, 97. Author: Summer Hawk, 1991, Night Blooms, 1992, Wading the Russian River, 1993, Santa Rosa Plums, 1996, A Foggy Morning, 1996, South By Southwest, 1997, Sacred Space, 1998, Rivers of the Sea, 1998, Greatest Hits: 1970-2000, 2001; (play) The Russian River Returns, 1999; contbr. Hawai'i Rev., Black Mt. Rev., The Plaza, Black Moon, Red Cedar Rev., Xavier Rev., Cold Mountain Rev., Poetry New Zealand, Orbis, European Judaism, The Windsor Rev., Fugue, Poetry Nottingham, Oreg. Rev., others; assoc. news editor, reporter, feature writer Napa Valley Times, 1985. Staff Nashville Human Rights Forum, 1974-75; chmn. housing authority-bldg. authority bd. City of Napa, 1985-89. Recipient Grand prize Ina Coolbrith Nat. Poetry Day Contest, 1989, Jessamyn West prize in creative writing, 1990. Mem. Ina Coolbrith Cir. Home: 248 Sandpiper Dr Davis CA 95616-7546

BUNCH, ROBERT CRAIG, librarian; b. Houston, Mar. 31, 1954; s. Robert Kern and Gretchen Ann (Schopps) B.; m. Delana Ann Roberts, Oct. 30, 1986. BA in Philosophy, U. Houston, 1979, MA in Philosophy, BS in Psychology, 1982, MEd, 1986; MLS, Sam Houston State U., Huntsville, 1992; MLIS, U. Tex., 1994. Cert. tchr., Tex. Psychiat. technician Meth. Hosp., Houston, 1979-83, 84-89, tchg. asst. U. Houston, 1981 82; acad. asst. U. Tex., Austin, 1983-84; tchr. Houston Ind. Sch. Dist., 1986-89, Coldspring-Oakhurst (Tex.) pub. schs., 1989-90; student libr. asst. Sam Houston State U., Huntsville, 1991; dist. libr. Coldspring-Oakhurst Consolidated Ind. Sch. Dist., 1991—. Editl. bd. Ref. Books Bull., Chgo., 1994-98; rev. editor Popular Culture in Librs., 1991-96. Mem. adv. bd. Humanities Exhibits Interactive, Tex. Com. for Humanities, Austin, 1996-99; bd. dirs. Libr., Helicon Pub., Oxford, Eng., 1997-2001. NEH fellow, 1992, 95, 97, Coun. for Basic Edn. fellow, 1996; Fulbright Meml. Fund scholar, 2000. Mem. ALA, Am. Assn. Sch. Librs. (Frances Henne award 1994), Tex. Libr. Assn., Tex. Assn. Sch. Librs. Home: PO Box 117 Oakhurst TX 77359-0117 Office: Coldspring-Oakhurst H S Libr PO Box 39 Coldspring TX 77331-0039 E-mail: cbunch@esc6.net.

BUNCHER, CHARLES RALPH, epidemiologist, educator; b. Dover, N.J., Jan. 18, 1938; BS, MIT, 1960; MS, Harvard U., 1964, ScD, 1967. Statistician Atomic Bomb Casualty Comsn., NAS, 1967-70; chief biostatistician Merrell-Nat. Labs., 1970-73, asst. prof. stats., 1970-73; prof. and dir. divsn. epidemiology and biostats. Med. Coll., U. Cin., 1973-96, prof. biostats. and epidemiology, 1973—, dir. grad. edn., 2001—. Fellow Am. Stats. Assn., Am. Coll. Epidemiology; mem. APHA, Biometrical Assn., Soc. Epidemiol. Rsch., Soc. Med. Decision Making, Soc. Clin. Trials, Tau Beta Pi. Achievements include research in cancer epidemiology; screening, diagnosis and treatment, as well as occupational and environmental epidemiology; risk analysis; statistical research; clinical trials; design of experiments; pharmaceutical research; biostatistical analysis, pharmaceutical statistics, ALS epidemiology. Office: U Cincinnati Div of Epidemiology & Biostatistics PO Box 670183 Cincinnati OH 45267-0183 E-mail: charles.buncher@uc.edu.

BUNCHMAN, HERBERT HARRY, II, plastic surgeon; b. Washington, Feb. 23, 1942; s. Herbert H. and Mary (Halleran) B.; m. Marguerite Fransioli, Mar. 21, 1963 (div. Jan. 1987); children: Herbert H. III., Angela K., Christopher; m. Janet C. Quinlan, Oct. 4, 1998. BA, Vanderbilt U., 1964; MD, U. Tenn., 1967. Diplomate Am. Bd. Surgery, Am. bd. Plastic Surgery. Resident in surgery U. Tex., Galveston, 1967-72, resident in plastic surgery, 1972-75; practice medicine specializing in plastic surgery Mesa, Ariz., 1975—; chief surgery Desert Samaritan Hosp., 1978-80. Contbr. articles to profl. jours. Eaton Clin. fellow, 1975. Mem. AMA, Am. Soc. Plastic Surgery, Am. Soc. Aesthetic Plastic Surgery, Singleton Surgical Soc., Tex. Med. Assn., So. Med. Assn. (grantee 1974), Ariz. Med. Assn. Office: Plastic Surgery Cons PC 1520 S Dobson Rd Ste 314 Mesa AZ 85202-4727 Fax: 480-833-2967. E-mail: office@bunchman.com.

BUNCHMAN, TIMOTHY EDWARD, nephrologist, educator; b. Mt. Vernon, Ill., May 19, 1956; s. Harry John and Patricia June Bunchman; m. Norma Jean Maxvold, May 21, 1982; children: Nicole Jean, Erik Christian, Meghan Anne, Shannon Ester, Maria Murphy. BA, St. Louis U., 1978; MD, Loyola Stritch Sch. Medicine, 1981. Prof. pediatric nephrology and transplantation U. Mich., Ann Arbor, 1991—2000, U. Ala., Birmingham, 2000—. Conservative. Roman Catholic. Achievements include first to initial studies in solid organ transplantation in children and continuous renal replacement therapies in children with renal failure. Avocations: hiking, scuba diving. Home: 709 Crested Fern Ln Birmingham AL 35244 Office: University of Alabama @ Birmingham ACC 516 1600 7th St Sth Birmingham AL 35233 Office Fax: 205-975-7051. Personal E-mail: tbunchman@peds.uab.edu. E-mail: tbunchman@peds.uab.edu.

BUNDA, ROBERT, state legislator; b. Waialua, Hawaii, Apr. 25, 1947; m. Gail Bunda; children: Rachel, Ryan, Ashley, Robson, James Robert. BS, Tex. Wesleyan Coll., 1974; postgrad., U. Dallas, 1975. Ind. businessman; ins. broker, 1979—; banking exec., 1973-79; mem. Hawaii Ho. of Reps., Honolulu, 1983-94, Hawaii Senate, Dist. 22, Honolulu, 1994—, senate pres. Creator Hawaii's first ocean mgmt. plan; co-creator Hawaii Hurricane Relief Fund. Mem. Wahiawa Cmty. and Bus. Assn.; dir. West Oahu YMCA; mem. Wahiawa Gen. Hosp., Eames Kumiai Assn. With USAF, with Tex. NG, with Hawaii NG. Mem.: Lions (Wahiwa club). Democrat. Office: State Capitol 415 S Beretania St Honolulu HI 96813-2407

BUNDA, STEPHEN MYRON, political advisor, counselor, lawyer, classical philosopher; b. Jersey City, N.J., Oct. 5, 1949; s. Stephen and Anna (Yaschak) B. BA summa cum laude, St. Peter's Coll., Jersey City, 1971; MA with honors, New Sch. Grad. Faculty, N.Y.C., 1976; JD, Rutgers Law Sch., Newark, N.J., 1987. Bar: N.J. Pol. cons. Democratic Party, N.J., 1977-92; pol. adv. Govt. of Ukraine, 1991—; counsellor-at-law Bunda & Co., Lyndhurst, N.J., 1994—. Advisor on Ukraine to U.S. Congress, Office of the Pres., Nat. Security Coun., Washington, 1991—. Mem. Nat. Honor Soc., Am. Hist. Assn., Am. Philos. Assn., Ukrainian-Am. Bar Assn., N.J. Bar Assn., Soc. for Ukrainian-Jewish Rels., Ukrainian Nat. Assn., Lawyers Com. for Human Rights. Democrat. Mem. Ukrainian Catholic Ch. Avocations: reading philosophy and history, educational travel and sight-seeing, music, art, literature, theatre. Home: 691 Union Ave Lyndhurst NJ 07071-2815 Office: Stephen Myron Bunda Esquire PO Box 461 Lyndhurst NJ 07071

BUNDI, RENEE, art director, graphic designer; b. Elmont, NY, Apr. 20, 1962; d. Anthony Joseph and Marion Rose (Graziano) B. Student, St. John's U., 1980-84. Creative dir. Coastal Comm., NYC, 1985-86; art and prodn. coord. Cahner's Pub. Co./Datamation mag., NYC, 1986-87; sr. prodn. editor CMP Publ./Var Bus. Computer Sys. News, Manhasset, NY, 1987-89, asst. art dir., 1989-91; assoc. art dir. Varbus. CMP Publ., 1991-94; sr. art dir. Info. Week Mag., 1994-2000; instr. graphic design and media arts The Gibbs Sch., 2000-01; chair web design, digital media and animation, program dir. The Gibbs Sch., Design and Animation Ctr., 2001—02; program dir. Gibbs Design and Animation Center. Recipient Print Design award Print mag., 1988, 91, 92, 93, 94, 95, 98, Ozzie Design award Mag. Design and Prodn., 1988, 89, 90, 91, 98. Mem. Graphic Artist Guild, Soc. Publ. Designers (Excellence in Design award 1987, 88, 89, 92, 93, 94), ASBPE (Excellence of Design 1997, 98), MacIntosh User's Group, Soc. Illustrators (Best Spot Illustration). Roman Catholic. Avocations: theatre, bowling, painting, photography.

BUNDROS, THOMAS ANTHONY, utilities executive; b. Toledo, Aug. 7, 1956; s. Anthony Thomas and Thalia (Collins) B.; m. Lara Sue Seifert, May 7, 1994; children: Anthony, Anna Grace. BS in Econs. & Bus. Adminstrn., U. N.C., Greensboro, 1978, MBA in Fin., 1980. Fin. analyst Conoco. Inc., Greensboro, N.C., Houston, 1981-84; with The So. Co., Atlanta & N.Y.C., 1984-97; CFO Dalton (Ga.) Utilities, 1997—. Mem. Rotary, Sigma Tau Gamma. Republican. Greek Orthodox. Avocations: travel, investments, theatre, tennis, gardening. Home: 1918 Chadwell Dalton GA 30720-7126 Office: Dalton Utilities 1200 Parrott Pky Dalton GA 30722-0869 E-mail: tbundros@dutil.com.

BUNDY, ANNALEE MARSHALL, library director; b. Chgo., Feb. 11, 1938; d. Warren Elmer and Marie Thresa (Madden) Marshall; m. John Willard Bundy, Mar. 11, 1961. B.A. U. N.H., 1960; MLS, Simmons Coll., 1961. Assoc. head libr. Coll. Guam Libr., Agana, 1961-62, head libr., 1962-63; tech. libr. E.I. duPont de Nemours & Co., Maydown Works, Londonderry, No. Ireland, 1963-65; head libr. children's rm. Schenectady County (N.Y.) Libr., 1965-66; documents and periodicals libr. Grad. Sch. Pub. Affairs, SUNY, Albany, 1966-67; asst. dir. Medford (Mass.) Pub. Libr., 1967-73; dir. librs. Somerville (Mass.) Pub. Libr., 1973-78; dir. Providence Pub. Libr., 1978-88; program dir. EPA Librs. and Records Ctrs., 1990-91; exec. dir. Ames Free Libr., Easton, Mass., 1992—. Adj. faculty U. R.I. Grad. Libr. Sch.; cons. libr. bldgs., automation, govt. rels.; mem. adv. com. R.I. Sch. Design; mem. accreditation vis. team New Eng. Bd. Higher Edn.; challenge grant panelist NEH. Compiler: Alternatives in Print, II, 1972; mem. editl. bd. The Bottom Line: A Fin. Mag. for Librs.; contbr. articles to profl. jours. Mem. Mass. Cable TV Commn., 1975-79; bd. corporators Butler Hosp., 1983—; bd. dirs. Leadership R.I., 1984-88, R.I. Film and Video Competition. Recipient David E. Sweet award Leadership R.I., 1987, Disting. Leadership Alumni award Nat. Assn. Cmty. Leadership Orgns., 1987; Brown Humanities Inst. fellow, 1985-87. Mem. ALA (PLA/MLS sect. pres. 1981-82, chmn. Allie Beth Martin award com. 1986), New Eng. Libr. Assn., Agawam Hunt Club, Providence Art Club. Office: 53 Main St North Easton MA 02356-1496

BUNDY, BLAKELY FETRIDGE, early childhood educator, advocate; b. Chgo., Aug. 31, 1944; d. William Harrison and Bonnie Jean (Clark) Fetridge; m. Harvey Hollister Bundy III, Aug. 20, 1966; children: Harvey Hollister Bundy IV, Elizabeth Lowell, Reed Fetridge. BA cum laude, Wheaton Coll., Mass., 1966; MEd, Nat.-Louis U., 1985. Tchr. Norwich (Vt.) Kindergarten, 1966-67, Willow Wood Pre-Sch., Winnetka, Ill., 1983-93, bd. dirs., 1972-81, adv. bd., 1981-83, 93—. Bd. dirs. North Ave. Day Nursery, Chgo., 1970-76; exec. dir. Winnetka Alliance for Early Childhood, 1989—; accreditation system validator, mentor Nat. Acad. Early Childhood Programs, Washington, 1986—; mem. pres.'s commn. Wheaton Coll., Norton, Mass., 1987-99; trustee Brooks Sch., North Andover, Mass., 1993—; mem. adv. bd. Ctr. for Early Childhood Leadership, 2002—, Filene Ctr. for Work and Learning, Wheaton Coll., 1999—; cons. editor Nat. Assn. Edn. Young Children, 1991-94. Editor: Early Childhood; contbr. articles to Chgo. Tribune, Redbook, Glamour mags., Early Childhood News, Child Care Ctr. Mag., Chgo. Sun-Times, Day Care and Early Education, Young Children, other publs. Mem. Ill. Shore Coun. Girl Scouts U.S., 1981-89, World Found. for Girls Guides and Girl Scouts Friends of Our Cabana Com., Cuernavaca, Mexico, 1986-94. Mem.: Olive Baden-Powell Soc. (London), Chgo. Metro Assn. Edn. Young Children (steering com. Near North Suburban chpt. 1986—2001, commn. on salaries and working conditions 1988—92, co-chair pub. rels. com. 1992—2000, bd. dirs. 1992—, photography editor Connections 1992—, chair accreditation project mgmt. com. 1994—98, coeditor News & Views: The Accreditation Project Newsletter 1996—98, pres. 2003—), Ill. Soc. Early Childhood Profls. (bd. dirs. 1993—96, editor newsletter), World Assn. Girl Guides and Girl Scouts, Nat. Assn. for the Edn. Young Children (pres. 2003—, photographer publs.), Ocean Reef Club (Key Largo, Fla.), Yacht Club, Stevensville Club (Mich.), Indian Hill Club (Winnetka). Episcopalian. Avocations: golf, boating. Office: Winnetka Alliance for Early Childhood 1235 Oak St Winnetka IL 60093-2168

BUNDY, CHARLES ALAN, foundation executive; b. Cheraw, S.C., Jan. 5, 1930; s. Jackson Corbett and Ruby Jones (Hughes) B.; m. Margaret Ellen Jackson, Feb. 27, 1954; children: Charles Alan, Robert Jackson, Dan Hughes. AB, Wofford Coll., 1951; DH (hon.), Charleston So. U. Mgr. prodn. planning J.P. Stevens & Co., Inc., Rockingham, N.C., 1951-54; mgr. Jesup (Ga.) C. of C., 1954-56, Lancaster (S.C.) C. of C., 1956-61; dist. mgr. U.S. C. of C., Birmingham, Ala., 1961-65; exec. v.p. Macon (Ga.) C. of C., 1965-71, Greg Enterprises, Lancaster, 1971-72; pres. Springs Found., Inc. and Close Found., Inc., Lancaster, 1972-97, ret., 1997; pvt. practice cons., 1997—. Chmn. SC

Parks, Recreation and Tourism Commn., 1983—89; mem. SC Coordinating Coun. for Econ. Devel., 1986—89; mem., past chmn. S. E. Coun. on Founds.; trustee Columbia Coll., 1976—88, SC Found. Ind. Colls., 1982—93; chmn. Gov.'s Freshwater Wetlands Forum, 1989, Lancaster County Strategic Plan, 1990; trustee J. Marion Sims Found., Inc.; mem. State Govt. Reorgn. Commn., 1991; chmn. bd. 1st Meth. Ch., 1978, 1979; bd. dir. Springs Meml. Hosp. Mem. Lancaster County Higher Edn. Commn., Lancaster County C. of C. (past pres.), Rotary (past pres.). Home: 518 Briarwood Rd Lancaster SC 29720-1802 Office: Springs Found Inc 201 W Gay St Lancaster SC 29720 E-mail: mjbundy@comporium.net.

BUNDY, CHERYL LASOTA, non-profit executive, consultant; b. Kansas City, Feb. 21, 1967; d. Thomas Richard and Barbara (Miller) LaSota; m. William Paul Bundy, May 30, 1992; children: Katherine Taylor, William Paul Jr. BA, Smith Coll., 1988; MPA, NYU, 1997. Registered rep. Morgan Stanley, N.Y.C.; assoc. dir. bus. devel. OFFITBANK, N.Y.C., 1990-96, west coast rep., 1996-98; dir. centennial planning Assn. Jr. Leagues Internat., N.Y.C., 1998—2001; dir. devel. and gift planning St. James Ch., 2002—. Vol. Jr. League, N.Y.C., 1989-01, bd. dirs., 1994-96; bd. dirs. Alumnae Fund of Smith Coll., Northampton, Mass., 1993-96. Jr. League L.A., 1997-98; v.p. YWCA, N.Y.C., 2001—; vice chmn. St. Mary's Found. for Children, 2001, Bayside, N.Y., 2001—. Home Fax: 212-706-1459. E-mail: bundy_cheryl@hotmail.com., clb@stjames.org.

BUNDY, DAVID JOHN, civilian military employee; b. Elmhurst, Ill., Jan. 20, 1953; s. David John and Betty Jean (Newgent) B. BSME, Rose Hulman Inst. Tech., 1975; MS in Adminstrn., George Washington U., 1980. Test dir. Materiel Test Directorate, Aberdeen Proving Ground, Md., 1975-79, sr. test dir., 1982-83; chief Test and Evaluation Office U.S. Army Ordnance Ctr. and Sch., Aberdeen Proving Ground, Md., 1983-91; sr. test dir. Materiel Test Directorate, Yuma Proving Ground, Ariz., 1980-81; asst. project mgr. Project Mgr. for Instrumentation Targets and Threat Simul., Orlando, Fla., 1991-99; acquisition mgmt. specialist, mem. competitive devel. group U.S. Army Acquisition Corps, Orlando, 1999—2002, project dir., 2002. Vol. Make A Wish Found., Ctrl. Fla., 1996-97, Leukemia Soc., Orlando, Fla., 1995-96. Mem. Soc. Automotive Engrs. (chmn. Balt. sect. 1985-86, Outstanding Young Mem. award 1988). Presbyterian. Avocations: golf, walking, stamp collecting, bowling. Home: 1211 Flowers Pointe Ln Orlando FL 32825-5520 Office: PEO STRI Digitized Tng 12350 Research Pkwy Orlando FL 32826-3276

BUNDY, JANE BOWDEN, artist, educator; b. Jersey City, N.J., Mar. 14, 1922; d. John Stanley and Caroline (White) Bowden; m. Wendell Stimpson Brown Jr., June 20, 1942 (dec. Aug. 1992); children: Wendell S. Brown, Caroline E. Calbos, Barbara J. Valentine, Jeffrey L. Brown, Cynthia J. Brown; m. Donald Lawson Bundy, Oct. 15, 1999 (dec. Sept. 2000). BS in Phys. Edn., Douglass Coll., 1942; studies with Betty Abel, Little Silver, N.J., 1962; studies with John Terelak, Marblehead, Mass., 1968-70; studies with Amelia James, Atlanta, 1975-82, studies with Ouida Canaday, 1982-94, studies with Joseph Perrin, 1994. Cert. tchr. phys. edn. and sci. K-12. Substitute tchr. Elem. Sch., Little Silver, N.J., 1965-68, Title I tchr., 1967-68; substitute tchr. Marblehead and Lynn, Mass., 1968-70, DeKalb County, Decatur, Ga., 1970—2002. Publicity chmn., sec., v.p. DeKalb County Art Ctr., Atlanta, 1976—; sec., v.p. Artists Atelier of Atlanta, 1993—. Exhibitions include acrylics, watercolors, collages and drawings, animal portraits; contbr. articles to profl. jours. V.p., sec., bd. dirs. PTA, Little Silver, 1958-70; bd. dirs. AAUW, Little Silver, 1960-70. Mem. Callanwolde Guild (bd. dirs. 1976—), Atlanta Artists Club (Merit award 1995). Republican. Presbyterian. Avocations: tennis, bridge, reading, gardening, bowling. Home: 2110 Gunstock Dr Stone Mountain GA 30087-1621 Studio: Artists Atelier Atlanta 800 Miami Cir NE Ste 200 Atlanta GA 30324-3048 E-mail: janebundy@prodigy.net.

BUNDY, MARY LOTHROP, retired clinical social worker; b. Boston, Apr. 9, 1925; d. Francis B. and Eleanor (Abbott) Lothrop; m. McGeorge Bundy, June 10, 1950 (dec. Sept. 1996); children: Stephen M., Andrew L., William L., James A. AB magna cum laude, Radcliffe Coll., 1946; MSW, Hunter Coll., 1980. Assoc. dir. admissions Radcliffe Coll., Cambridge, Mass., 1949-50; clin. social worker Jewish Bd. of Family and Children's Svcs., Bklyn., 1980-84; pvt. practice N.Y.C., 1984-95; ret., 1995. Vice-chmn. and trustee Radcliffe Coll., Cambridge, 1962-80, acting v.p., 1978-79 ; overseer Harvard U., Cambridge, 1971-77; bd. dirs. Corning (N.Y.) Inc., 1973-97, Levi Strauss & Co., 1973-85; trustee and chair Edward W. Hazen Found., N.Y.C., 1985-95; bd. dirs. Found. for Child Devel., N.Y.C., 1985-98. Trustee Metropolitan Museum of Art, N.Y.C., 1968-78. Mem. NASW, Acad. Cert. Social Workers, Phi Beta Kappa.

BUNDY, WAYNE M. retired geologist, consultant; b. Anderson, Ind., Jan. 10, 1924; s. Ernest Frank and Flossie (Miley) B.; m. Lorraine Vivian Jerabek, May 7, 1945; children: Mark, Janet, Michael. AB, Ind. U., 1950, MA, 1954, PhD, 1957. Geol. technician N. Mex. Bur. of Mines, Socorro, 1951-53; petrographer Ind. Geol. Survey, Bloomington, 1953-57; rsch. dir. Georgia Kaolin Co., Elizabeth, N.J., 1957-75, v.p. tech. Springfield, N.J., 1975-91; cons. Contbr. articles to profl. jours.; author: The Art of Discovery: Fueling Innovation for Company Growth, Innovation, Creativity and Discovery in Modern Organizations; numerous patents in indsl. minerals, including Kaolin Modified for use in various applications. Sgt. USMC, 1943-45. Fellow Tech. Pulpaper 12 Industry; mem. Clay Minerals Soc. (pres. 1985). Home: PO Box 614 Tesuque NM 87574

BUNDY-DESOTO, TERESA MARI, language educator, vocalist; d. Jose Jesus Avila-Carrillo and Maria del Pilar Lozano Avila; m. Glendon B. Bundy, Oct. 15, 1972 (div. May 20, 1987); children: Pete Hernandez Bundy, Angelita Dianne Bundy, Crystal Lorraine Bundy-Schwabenland, Ivan Glen Bundy; m. John B. Soto, Mar. 31, 1996. AA magna cum laude, Fresno City Coll., 1976; BA summa cum laude, Calif. State U., Fresno, 1978; Spanish and bilingual tchg. credential, 1979. Master tchr., trainer Proteus Adult Edn., Visalia, Calif., 1967—73; tchr. trainer Fresno City-County Manpower Commn., Calif., 1973—76; tchr. Spanish, mentor tchr. Ctrl. Unified Sch. Dist., Fresno, 1979—86; dept. chairperson Madera Unified Sch. Dist., Calif., 1986—89; tchr. Spanish, English Hoover HS/Fresno Unified Sch. Dist., 1989—. Rschr., trainer Office of Edn., Washington, 1968—74; adult edn. tchr. Chavez Adult Edn. Ctr.; alt. chief examiner ofcl. GED testing ctr. Gen. Ednl. Devel. Testing Svc., 1999—; spkr. in field. Singer: recorded 2 CDs and mus. videos under stage name Luz De Luna. Profl. radio announcer Spanish Radio Stas., Fresno, 1978—96; TV model Spanish TV Univision, Fresno, 1980; judge Miss Laverkin, Utah, 1982. Recipient Miss El Futuro C.U., 1967, 1972. Mem.: Am. Coun. on Edn., Calif. Tchr. Assn. Democrat. Mem. Lds Ch. Home: 1149 E San Bruno Ave Fresno CA 93710 E-mail: luzdeluna@comcast.net.

BUNE, KAREN LOUISE, criminal justice official; b. Washington, Mar. 6, 1954; d. Harry and Eleanor Mary (White) B. BA in Am. Studies cum laude, Am. U., 1976, MS in Adminstrn. of Justice with distinction, 1978. Case mgr. Arlington (Va.) Alcohol Safety Action Program, 1979-94; victim specialist Office of Commonwealth's Atty., Arlington, Va., 1994—; cons. victim issues Dept. Justice/Office for Victims, 2001—. Case mgr. regional rep. of case mgmt. com. of Dirs. Assn. Commn. on Va. Alcohol Safety Action Program, Richmond, 1980-81, 84-85, 88-89, mem. subcom. studying treatment issues, 1988-94; chair career guidance subcom. alumni adv. com. Sch. Pub. Affairs Am. U., Washington, 1991-94; participant IACP Summit on Victims of Crime, 1999, nat. forum on terrorism, NCJA, 2002; adj. prof. George Mason U., Fairfax, Va., Marymount U., Arlington, Va. Recipient spl. achievement award Dept. Navy, 1973, merit award Arlington County, 1986, 97, Woman of the Yr. Am. Biog. Inst., 1990, Carl T. Earles meml. cmty. svc. award No. Va. Crime Prevention Assn., 1999, 2001, cert. of recognition for svc. to crime victims 3d Ann. Neighborhood Day, 1999, cert. of appreciation U.S. Dept. Justice, 2000; inducted into Hall of Fame for outstanding achievement in case mgmt. Mem.: AAUW (nat. and Arlington, Va. chpt.), APHA, NAFE, ASPA (pres. No. Va. chpt. 2003—), Internat. Assn. Forensic Mental Health Svcs., Am. Acad. Experts in Traumatic Stress, Assn. Traumatic Stress Specialists, Am. Sociol. Assn., Am. Pub. Human Svcs. Assn., Am. Profl. Soc. on Abuse of Children, Nat. Ctr. Women in Policing, Am. Probation and Parole Assn., Soc. for Study of Social Problems, Va. Assn. Female Execs., No. Va. Fraternal Order Police, No. Va. Crime Prevention Assn., Soc. Profl. Journalists, Va. Crime Prevention Assn., Internat. Narcotic Enforcement Officers Assn., Va. Sheriffs Inst., Am. Soc. Criminology, So. Criminal Justice Assn., Acad. Criminal Justice Scis., Am. Police Hall of Fame (cert. of appreciation 1985), Nat. Assn. Women Law Enforcement Execs., Nat. Ctr. Victims of Crime, Nat. Orgn. Victim Assistance, Nat. Criminal Justice Assn., Nat. Assn. Chiefs Police (award of merit 1986), Internat. Assn. Chiefs of Police (nat. adv. bd. on police-based victim response 2000—), Nat. Air Disaster Alliance Found., Washington Ind. Writers, World Affairs Coun., Am. U. Alumni Assn. (immediate past pres. sch. pub. affairs chpt. 1994—96), Nat. Press Club, Phi Delta Gamma (1st v.p. 1981—82), Phi Alpha Alpha, Phi Kappa Phi. Avocations: concerts, dancing, travel, theatre, writing. Home: 926 16th St S Arlington VA 22202-2606 Office: Office of Commonwealth's Atty Ste 5200 1425 N Court House Rd Arlington VA 22201-2659

BUNGAARD, ERNEST See GRAY, ALLEN

BUNGARZ, WILLIAM ROBERT, pediatrician; b. N.Y.C., June 21, 1951; s. Robert Charles and Evelyn Mae (Marshall) B.; m. Beverly Ann Blaine, Sept. 30, 1984; children: Katherine, Rebecca. BS, SUNY, Stony Brook, 1974; MD, Autonomous U. Guadalajara, Mexico, 1982. Fifth pathway intern New Rochelle (N.Y.) Hosp. Med. Ctr., 1983; resident North Shore U. Hosp., Manhasset, NY, 1984—86, chief resident pediatrics, 1986—87; pediatrician, ptnr. Gould, Elice, Hyman & Bungarz, Great Neck, NY, 1987—. Mem. choir St. Mary's Roman Cath. Ch., Manhasset, NY. Fellow Am. Acad. Pediat.; mem. Great Neck Choral Soc. (pres. 1995-99). Republican. Roman Catholic. Avocations: choral singing, skiing. Home: 178 Rockwood Rd Manhasset NY 11030-2027 Office: Gould Elice Hyman & Bungarz 15 Barstow Rd Great Neck NY 11021-2229 Fax: (516) 829-2713. E-mail: wbungarz@aol.com.

BUNGE, CHARLES ALBERT, library science educator; b. Kimball, Nebr., Mar. 18, 1936; s. Louis Herman and Leona Hazel (Cromwell) B.; m. Joanne C. VonStoeser, Aug. 20, 1960; children: Lorraine A., Jeffrey C. Stephen L. AB, U. Mo., 1959; MSLS, U. Ill., 1960, PhD, 1967. Reference libr. Daniel Boone Regional Libr., Columbia, Mo., 1960-62; Ball State Tchrs. Coll., Muncie, Ind., 1962-64; rsch. assoc. Libr. Rsch. Ctr., U. Ill., 1964-67; mem. faculty Sch. Libr. and Info. Studies U. Wis., Madison, 1967—97, prof. emeritus, 1997—. Author: Professional Education and Reference Efficiency, 1967; columnist: Wilson Library Bull, 1972-81. Mem. ALA (pres. ref. and adult svcs. divsn. 1987-88, chair com. on accreditation 1990-92, Mudge award 1983, mem. coun. 1993-96, Beta Phi Mu award 1997), Assn. Libr. and Info. Sci. Edn. (pres. 1980-81, Prof. Contribution award 1997), Wis. Libr. Assn. (pres. 1972-73, Libr. of Yr. 1983), Phi Beta Kappa, Beta Phi Mu. Home: 509 Orchard Dr Madison WI 53711-1318

BUNGE, RUSSELL KENNETH, writer, poet, editor; b. Long Beach, Calif., Apr. 28, 1947; s. Kenneth Duncan Bunge and Mona Irene (Deleree) Coker; ptnr. Mr. Kelly A. Quiros. BA in Creative Writing, Calif. State U., Long Beach, 1972; MA in Humanities, Calif. State U., Dominguez Hills, 1985. Cert. C.C. tchr., Calif. Spl. svcs. cons. AT&T Comms., San Luis Obispo, Calif., 1973-90; info. cons. Obispo Info. Group, San Luis Obispo, 1990-95; pub. deleree com, San Luis Obispo, Calif., 1996—. Mem. adv. bd. Calif. Online Resources for Edn., Long Beach, 1993-94; edn. coord. SLONET Info. Network, 1993-95, dir., 1997-98. Author: Double Lives: Poems 1984-1985, 1985, Junction, 2001; editor: Obispo Web Digest: on the World Wide Web, 1994-96; contbr. poems to profl. publs. Founding mem. AIDS Support Network, San Luis Obispo, 1984. Mem. MLA, Assn. Study Lit. & Environ. Office: Wirewove Web Solutions PO Box 771 San Luis Obispo CA 93406-0771 E-mail: rkbunge@pacbell.net.

BUNGEY, MICHAEL, advertising executive; b. 1941; With Nestle, London, 1961-65, Crawford Advt., London, 1965-69, SH Benson, London, 1969-71; founder Michael Bungey & Ptnrs. (sold to Dancer, Fitzgerald & Sample, then Saatchi & Saatchi, then merged into DFS Dorland), 1971; CEO DFS Dorland (name changed to BSB Dorland), 1987-88; regional dir. Europe Backer Spielvogel Bates Worldwide, Inc. (now Bates Worldwide, Inc.), 1988-92; chmn., CEO Cordiant Comm. Group (subs., holding co.) Bates Worldwide Inc., 1993—. Bd. dirs. Cordiant plc. Office: Bates Worldwide Inc Chrysler Bldg 498 7th Ave New York NY 10018-6798

BUNGO, MICHAEL WILLIAM, physician, educator, science administrator; b. Passaic, N.J., July 18, 1950; s. John C. and Mary Bungo; children: Elise Nicole, Jonathan Michael. BS in Chemistry, Rensselaer Poly. Inst., 1971; MD, N.J. Med. Sch., 1975. Diplomate Am. Bd. Internal Medicine, Subsplty. Bd. Cardiovasc. Diseases. Intern in internal medicine New England Deaconess Hosp., Boston, 1975-76, resident, 1976-78; asst. in medicine Peter Bent Brigham Hosp., Boston, 1976-77; cardiology fellow New England Deaconess Hosp., Harvard Med. Sch., Boston, 1978-80; head cardiovascular lab. NASA, Johnson Space Ctr., Houston, 1980-85; mem. Aerospace Medicine Bd., Houston, 1980-91; dir. Space Biomed. Rsch. Inst. NASA, Johnson Space Ctr., Houston, 1986-90; chief scientist med. scis. divsn. NASA, 1990-91; prof. medicine U. Tex., Galveston, med. dir. heart sta. divsn. cardiology, 1995—2002, vice chmn. dept. internal medicine, 1999—2002; assoc. dean U. Tex. Med. Sch., Houston, 2002—; chief of staff LBJ Gen. Hosp., Houston, 2002—. Chmn. dept. medicine St. John Hosp., Houston, 1987—89; fellowship advisor NRC, Washington, 1984—89. Editor: Results of Life Sciences Aboard the Space Shuttle, 1987; contbr. abstracts and articles to jours., chpts. to books; tech. reviewer Circulation, Aviation, Space and environ. Medicine, 1989—; mem. editl. bd. Aviation, Space and Environ. Medicine, 1997-2000. Recipient medal NASA, 1986. Fellow ACP, Am. Coll. Cardiology; mem. Am. Heart Assn., Aerospace Med. Assn. (Louis H. Bauer Founders award 1987), Tex. Med. Assn., Phi Lambda Upsilon. Office: U Tex Houston Med Sch Chief of Staff LBJ Hosp 5656 Kelley St Houston TX 77026

BUNIM, MARY-ELLIS, television producer; b. Northampton, Mass., July 9, 1946; d. Frank Roberts and Roslyn Dena (LaMontagne) Paxton; m. Robert Eric Bunim, Jan. 31, 1971 (div. 2000); 1 dau., Juliana. Pres. Bunim-Murray Prodns., L.A., 1988—. Exec. prodr. series Search for Tomorrow, CBS-TV, 1976-81, As the World Turns, CBS-TV, 1981-84, Santa Barbara, NBC-TV, 1984-86, syndicated Crime Diaries, ABC-TV series Loving, 1989-90, FBC series American Families, 1990; co-creator, exec. prodr. MTV series The Real World, 1992—, Road Rules, 1995—, Real World, Road Rates Challence, 1999—, Making the Band, 2000—, NBC spl. Friends and Lovers, 1994, NBC spl. High School Reunion: Class of '86, 1996, (ABC pilot) Catch Me If You Can, 1998, (ABC pilot) Detroit Receiving, 1999, (CBS movie) Personally Yours, 2000, Fox's Love Cruise, 2001, Fox's Girl Next Door: The Search For A Playboy Playmate, 2002, syndicated series Starting Over, 2003—, (feature film) The REal Cancun, 2003, (VH1 series) Born to Diva, 2003.

BUNIN, JEFFREY HOWARD, management consultant; b. N.Y.C., July 15, 1948; s. Herbert Bunin and Ruth Bunin Lefkowitz. BS in Engring., CUNY, 1971; MBA, Rutgers U., 1976. Engr. Airco Carbon Graphite, Niagrara Falls, N.Y., 1971-72, Airco Indsl. Gases, Murray Hill, N.J., 1972-76; fin. analyst Great A&P Tea Co., Montvale, N.J., 1976-78; mgr. fin. analysis MRI Div., Am. Can, Clark, N.J., 1978-80; dir. planning Matheson Gas Products Inc., Secaucus, N.J., 1980-99, Matheson Tri-Gas, Inc., 1999-2000; CEO Bunin Mgmt. Advisors, LLC, 2000—. Adj. prof. Rutgers Bus. Sch., 2001—. Mem.: Inst. Mgmt. Accts., Alumni Assn. Rutgers U. Sch. Bus. Mgmt. (pres. 1997—2000, trustee, officer 1995—), Masons. Home: 159 Franklin St Bloomfield NJ 07003-4978 E-mail: jbunin@alumni.rutgers.edu.

BUNJUN, SEEWOONUNDUN, economics educator; b. Lalmatie, Flacq, Mauritius, Sept. 25, 1943; came to U.S., 1973; s. Anauth and Deeneswarry Bunjun; children: Deepika, Shipra. BA in Econs. with honors, U. Delhi, 1968; MA in Econs., Delhi Sch. Econs., 1970; PhD in Econs., Pa. State U., 1978. Sr. lectr. econs. U. Mauritius, Reduit, 1970-74; grad. teaching asst. Pa. State U., 1973-78; rsch. asst. Internat. Food Policy Rsch. Inst., Washington, 1978-79; from asst. to prof. econs. East Stroudsburg (Pa.) U., 1979—. Adviser Ministry of Fin., Govt. of Mauritius, Port-Louis, 1985-86; vis. prof. Faculty Law and Mgmt., Faculty Social Studies and Humanities, U. Mauritius, 1995, 2000. Home: RR 2 Box 72 Bushkill PA 18324-9621 Office: East Stroudsburg U Dept Bus Mgmt and Econs East Stroudsburg PA 18301

BUNKER, BERYL H. retired insurance executive, community volunteer; b. Chelsea, Mass., Aug. 18, 1919; d. Albert Crocker and Eva Agnes (Norris) Hardacker; m. John Wadsworth Bunker, Oct. 31, 1942. Student, Simmons Coll., 1936-38, Boston Coll. Law, 1948-49; grad., Bentley Sch. Acctg., Boston, 1958; BBA with highest honors, Northeastern U., 1962, MBA, 1967; D of Humane Svc. (hon.), Simmons Coll., 2001. CFA. Legal rsch. clerk Frank Shepard Co., N.Y.C., 1938-43; cost acct. Johns Manville Corp., Pittsburg, Calif., 1943-46; studio mgr. Wheelan Studios, Boston, 1946; clerical supr. Columbian Purchasing Group, Boston, 1946-48; office mgr. Wellesley (Mass.) Coll., 1948-51; statistician Eastman Kodak Co., Rochester, N.Y., 1951-53; investment officer John Hancock Mut. Life, Boston, 1953-74; sr. v.p. John Hancock Advisers, Boston, 1974-84. Nat. bd. dirs. YWCA of the U.S.A., 1988-94, hon. bd. dirs., 1998—, mem. World Svc. Coun., 1992—; pres. bd. dirs. Boston YWCA, 1985-87, active 1977-96; chair bd. Vis. Nurses Assn. Cape Cod Found., South Dennis, Mass., 1995; bd. dirs. Old South Meeting House Mus., Boston, 1989-92; trustee Simmons Coll., 1994-2000, chair centennial com. 1999-2000, corporator, 2000—; mem. women's coun. exec. com. Pine St. Inn, 1992—; bd. visitors Women's Edn. and Ind. Union, 2000—; adv. com. Boston Women's Fund, 2001—; mem. adv. com. On The Rise, 1997—; mem. Ct. for Women in Politics and Public Policy, Assocs. of the Boston Pub. Libr. Bd., The Coll. Club of Boston, 1998—, Cambridge YWCA, Neighborhood Assn. of the Back Bay; honoree Pine St. Inn Women's Coun., 2000. Recipient Philanthropy award Women in Devel., 1990, Disting. Alumni award Bentley Coll., 1994; named Woman of Achievement, Cambridge YWCA, 1991, Lifetime Service to Women award, On The Rise, 1998, Lifetime Achievement award, College Club, 1998, Outstanding Alumna North Eastern U., 2000. Mem. AARP, LWV, NOW, AAUW, Assn. Investment Mgmt. Rsch., Mass. Action for Women, Mass. Women Polit. Caucus, Boston Security Analysts Soc. (treas. 1973-76), Mass. Women's State Wide Legis. Network (dir. 1987), Simmons Coll. Alumnae Assn. (pres. 1989-91, Alumnae Svc. award 1984, Planned Giving award 1993), Older Women's League, The Internat. Alliance, Harwich Hist. Soc., Project Vote Smart, Women's Ednl. and Indsl. Union, Friday Forum, Eire Soc., Wellesley Ctrs. for Women. Avocations: fundraising, theater, reading. Home: 790 Boylston St Apt 22F Boston MA 02199-7921

BUNKER, DUSTY, writer; b. Newport, R.I., Nov. 5, 1937; d. Lloyd Coby and Marjorie Louise Brown; m. A. Reid Bunker, Jr., July 1, 1958; children: April, Melanie, Matthew, Sarah. Student, U. N.H., 1955—58; Art Cert., Famous Artists' Sch., Westport, Conn., 1971. Columnist Manchester Union Leader, NH, 1972—77, Mademoiselle Mag., N.Y.C., 1994, Seacoast Scene, Hampton, 1979—80. Cons. writer Time-Life Books, Alexandria, Va., 1988; cartoonist Tree Line, 1978; lectr. in field; condr. workshops in field. Co-author (with Faith Javane): Numerology and the Divine Triangle, 1979; co-author: (with Victoria Knowles) Birthday Numerology, 1982; author: Numerology and Your Future, 1980, Numerology, Astrology and Dreams, 1987, [illegible]: The Geometry of the Goddess, 1989, Dream Cycles, 1981, 2000, The Number Mysteries: One Deadly Rhyme, 2001, The Number Mysteries: The Two-Timing Corpse, 2002. Mem.: Sisters in Crime, Mystery Writers of Am. Avocations: reading, movies, writing humorous skits. Home: 236 Middle Rd Brentwood NH 03833

BUNKER, JOHN BIRKBECK, cattle rancher, retired sugar company executive; b. Yonkers, N.Y., Mar. 28, 1926; s. Ellsworth and Harriet (Butler) B.; m. Emma Cadwalader, Feb. 27, 1954. BA, Yale U., 1950. With Nat. Sugar Refining Co., 1953-62; pres. Gt. Western Sugar Co., Denver, 1966; pres., CEO Holly Sugar Co., Colorado Springs, Colo., 1967-81, chmn., CEO, 1971-81; pres., CEO Calif. and Hawaiian Sugar Co., San Francisco, 1981-88, vice chmn., 1988-89, ret., 1989; gen. ptnr. Bunker Ranch Co., 1989—; chmn. Wheatland Bankshares and First State Bank of Wheatland, 1992-99, dir. emeritus. Trustee Colo. Coll., 1973-94; trustee emeritus Asia Found., 1985-94. Mem. Wyo. Nature Conservancy, Wyo. Stockgrowers Assn., Wyo. Heritage Found. Home: 1451 Cottonwood Ave Wheatland WY 82201-3412

BUNKER, MATTHEW D. humanities educator; b. Junction City, Kans., July 14, 1957; s. Herbert L. and Eudora J. Bunker; m. Lois A. Graham, Dec. 26, 1979. BS, Kans. State U., 1979, MS, 1989; JD, U. Kans., 1985; PhD, U. Fla., 1993. Atty. Hampton, Royce, Engleman & Nelson, Salina, Kans., 1985—86; journalist Manhattan Mercury, Manhattan, Kans., 1989—90; Reese Phifer profe. journalism U. Ala., Tuscaloosa, 1997—. Author: Justice and the Media: Reconciling Fair Trials and a Free Press, 1997, Critiquing Free Speech: First Amendment Theory and the Challenge of Interdisciplinarity, 2001. Mem.: Assn. Edn. in Journalism and Mass Comm/ (head Law Divsn. 1999—2000). Avocation: golf. Office: U Ala 478 Phifer Hall Box 870172 Tuscaloosa AL 35487-0172

BUNKER, ROBERT JOSEPH, national security consultant, educator; b. Pasadena, Calif., Mar. 9, 1962; s. Joseph L. and Eleanor B. (Marrone) B.; m. Pamela J. Ligouri, Sept. 9, 1989; children: Khirin, Kaden, Kreffan. BA in History, Calif. State Poly. U., 1983, BS in Anthropology and Geography, BS in Social Sci., BA in Behavioral Sci., Calif. State Poly. U., 1985; MA in Govt., Claremont Grad. Sch., 1987, PhD in Polit. Sci., 1993. Adj. prof. nat. securities studies program Calif. State U., San Bernardino, 1995—2002; cons. Nat. Law Enforcement and Corrections Tech. Ctr. West, El Segundo, Calif., 2000—. Prof. unconventional warfare Am. Mil. U., Manassass Park, Va., 1993-96. Editor: Less-Than-Lethal Weapons: Reference Guide Book, 2000, Non-State Threats and Future Wars, 2003. Founding mem. L.A. County Terrorism Early Warning Group, 1996. Fellow Inst. Land Warfare, assn. of U.S. Army, Arlington, Va., 1999-2000. Mem. Soc. Mil. History. Republican. E-mail: bunker@law-west.org.

BUNKOWSKE, EUGENE WALTER, religious studies educator; b. Wecota, S.D., July 3, 1935; s. Walter Adolph and Ottilie Sophie (Richter) B.; m. Bernice Bock; children: Barbara, Nancy, Walter, Joel. AA, Concordia Acad. and Jr. Coll., St. Paul, 1955; BA, Concordia Seminary, 1958, BD, MDiv, 1960; MA in Linguistics, UCLA, 1964, C Phil in Linguistics, 1968, PhD in Linguistics, 1976; LittD, Concordia Coll., 1983; DD, Christ Coll., 1991; DLitt, Concordia U., St. Paul, 1997. Missionary Luth. Ch.-Mo. Synod, Africa, 1960-82, congl. pastor, pioneer ch. planter, 1960-74, chmn. Nung Udoe dist., 1960-61, builder chs., schs., hosp., 1960-67, medical worker Ogoja Province, 1961-66, justice of peace Ogoja Province, 1962-74, chmn. Ogoja dist., 1964-69, chmn. Evang. Luth. Mission in Nigeria, 1965-67, analyzer Yala lang., orthography devel. & Bible translator, 1967-71, counselor to Yala Paramount Chief, 1969-74, fourth v.p., 1989-92, 95-98, third v.p., 1992-95; dir. mission Concordia Theol. Seminary, Ft. Wayne, Ind., 1982-88, mission prof., 1982—, mission chair prof., 1986—, grad. prof. mission, 1990—, chmn. dept. pastoral ministries, 1985-88; chmn. mission dept., 1988-90; supr. D Missiology program, chmn. Mission and Comm. Congress Concordia Theol. Seminary, Ft. Wayne, Ind., 1984—. Ling. cons. and adminstr. Luth. Bible Translators, Liberia, Sierra Leone, 1970-74; dir. Vacation Inst. for Tng. in Applied Linguistics and Bible Translation, U. Liberia, Monrovia, 1971-74; cons. United Bible Soc., 1974-80, regional translations coord., 1980-82; cons. Near West Side Cleve. Cluster, St. Paul Internat. Mission Bd. Author: Orede, 1973, Woka yi Ijona, 1974, Topics in Yala Grammar, 1976, God's Mission in Action, 1986, The Body of Christ in Mission, 1987, God's Communicators in Mission, 1988, Receptor Oriented Gospel Communication, 1989, The State of Gospel Communication Today, 1990, Church Growth: A Biblical Perspective, 1991, The Role of the Laity in Gospel Communications, 1992, The Christian Family: Nurture and Outreach, 1993, Multicultural Outreach: Bridging Cultures - Theirs and Ours, 1995, Struggling with Change: Reaching the Lost in Changing Times, 1999, The Lutherans in Mission, 2000; translator Yala Bible, 1967-74; contbr. articles to religious and profl. publs., chpts. to books. Mem. God's Word to Nations Bible Soc. (bd. dirs., trans. and tech. cons.), World Mission Prayer League (bd. dirs.), All Nations Mission (bd. dirs., cons.), Luth. Soc. for Missiology (founding organizer). Republican. Lutheran. Avocations: travel, reading, hiking. Home: 5724 Lancashire Ct Fort Wayne IN 46825-5910 Office: Concordia Theol Seminary 6600 N Clinton St Fort Wayne IN 46825-4916

BUNKŠE, EDMUNDS VALDEMĀRS, geographer, educator, consultant; b. Liepāja, Latvia, July 29, 1935; came to U.S., 1950; s. Jēkabs Bunkše and Anna Leontine Bucholcs Birznieks; m. Moira Daly (div.); Elizabeth Murray Sutherland, Feb. 9, 1988 (div.); m. Grizelda Astrida Liepins, Oct. 15, 1995; children: Andrejs, Margarita. AB, Syracuse U., 1962; MA, U. Calif., Berkeley, 1966, PhD, 1973; D honoris causa, U. Latvia, 1991. Tchg. asst. U. Calif., Berkeley, 1963-65; instr. Coll. Holy Names, Oakland, Calif., 1965-67; cartographer Assn. Bay Area Govts., Berkeley, 1965; instr. U. Del., Newark, 1969-73, asst. prof., 1973-80, assoc. prof. dept. geography, 1980—, dir. London program, 1991. Adj. prof. U. Latvia, Riga, 1995—; assoc. prof. Latvian TV, Riga, 1992-95. Editor GeoJour. Baltic Peoples, 1994; contbr. articles to profl. jours. and book. Mem. com. CIES-Fulbright Selection, Washington, 1992-95, Danish-Latvian Coop.,

1990-95; in edn. reform U. Latvia, Riga, 1992—; mem. promotion and Dr. Habilis com. U. Latvia. Fulbright awardee, Lund U., Sweden and U. Coll. London, 1983-84, U. Latvia, 1990. Mem. Latvian Acad. Sci. (fgn.), Fulbright Alumni Assn., Assn. Am. Geographers, Assn. Latvian Geographers, Lidums. Mem. Evang. Luth. Ch. Achievements include development of geography as a literary-artistic field of study and research. Avocations: sailing, skiing, sketching, chess. Office: U Del Dept Geography Newark DE 19716 E-mail: ebunkse@udel.edu.

BUNN, CHARLES NIXON, management consultant; b. Springfield, Ill., Feb. 8, 1926; s. Joseph Forman and Helen Anna Frieda (Link) Bunn; m. Cecine Cole, Dec. 26, 1951 (div. 1987); children: Sisene, Charles; m. Marjorie Fitzmaurice, Apr. 5, 1988. Student, U. Ill., 1943-44; BS in Engring., U.S. Mil. Acad., 1949; MBA, Xavier U., Cin., 1958. Flight test engr. GE, Cin., Also Edwards AFB, Calif., 1953-59, strategic bus. planner advanced reactor sys. dept. Sunnyvale, Calif., 1979-84; sr. missile test engr., space sys. divsn. Lockheed Aircraft Corp., USAF Satellite Test Ctr., Sunnyvale, Calif., 1959-60, 63-70, economist, advanced planning dept., 1961-63; econ. and long-range planning cons. Los Altos, Calif., 1970-73; head sys. planning, economist, strategic bus. planning Western Regional hdqrs. U.S. Postal Svc., San Bruno, Calif., 1973-78; strategic bus. planning cons., investment analysis cons., 1978-79, strategic planning cons., 1984—. With inf. paratroops U.S. Army, 1944—45, with inf. and rangers U.S. Army, 1949—53, Korea. Decorated Battle Star (5). Mem.: Sigma Nu. Episcopalian. Home and Office: 7387 Via Laguna San Jose CA 95135-1345 E-mail: FitzBunn@hotmail.com.

BUNN, PAUL A., JR., oncologist, educator; b. N.Y.C., Mar. 16, 1945; s. Paul A. Bunn; m. Camille Ruoff, Aug. 17, 1968; children: Rebecca, Kristen, Paul H. BA cum laude, Amherst Coll., 1967; MD, Cornell U., 1971. Diplomate Nat. Bd. Med. Examiners, Am. Bd. Internal Medicine, Am. Bd. Med. Oncology. Intern U. Calif., H.C. Moffitt Hosp., San Francisco, 1971-72, resident, 1972-73; clin. assoc. medicine br. Nat. Cancer Inst., NIH, Bethesda, Md., 1973-76; sr. investigator med. oncology br. Nat. Cancer Inst., Washington VA Hosp., 1976-81; asst. prof. medicine med. sch. Georgetown U., 1978-81; head cell kinetic sect., Navy med. oncology br. Nat. Cancer Inst., Bethesda, 1981-84; assoc. prof. medicine uniformed svcs. Univ. Health Scis., Bethesda, 1981-84; prof. medicine health scis. ctr. U. Colo., Denver, 1984—, head divsn. med. oncology, 1984-94, dir. cancer ctr., 1987—. Instl. rev. bd. NIH, Nat. Cancer Inst., 1982-84; intramural support contract rev. com. Nat. Cancer Inst., 1982-84; cancer com. U. Colo., 1984—, faculty senate health scis. ctr., 1985—, exec. com. sch. medicine, 1987—; med. bd. Univ. Hosp., 1987—; external sci. advisor cancer ctr. U. Miami, 1988-92, U. Ark., 1989-94, U. Va., 1991-94, others; oncology drug adv. com. FDA, 1992-96; sci. secretariat 7th World Conf. Lung Cancer, 1994; bd. dirs. Univ. Hosp. Resource Coun.; oncology drug adv. com. FDA, 1992-96. Author: Carboplatin (JM-8) Current Perspectives and Future Directions, 1990, Clinical Experiences With Platinum and Etoposide Therapy in Lung Cancer, 1992, (with M.E. Wood) Hematology/Oncology Secrets, 1994; assoc. editor Med. and Pediatric Oncology, 1984—, Jour. Clin. Oncology, 1991—, Cancer Rsch., 1992—, others; contbr. chpts. to books and articles to profl. jours. Bd. dirs. Colo. divsn. Am. Cancer Soc., 1989—, Leukemia Soc. Am., 1991—; bd. dirs. The Cancer Venture, 1993-94, Fair Share Colo., 1993-94; chmn. Solid Tumor Oncology Edn. Found., 1996—. With USPHS, 1973-84. Decorated Medal of Commendation; recipient Sci. of Yr. award Denver chpt. ARCS, 1992; named one of 400 Best Drs. in Am., Good Housekeeping Mag., 1991, 92; grantee Schering Plough, 1988-89, Burroughs Wellcome, 1991—, Bristol-Myers Squibb, 1993—, others. Fellow ACP; mem. AAAS, Am. Soc. Hematology (mem. sci. subcom. neoplasia 1989-92), Am. Assn. Cancer Rsch., Am. Soc. Clin. Oncology (chair program subcom. 1985-86, 90, pres.-elect 2001—), Am. Fedn. Clin. Rsch., Am. Assn. Cancer Insts. (bd. dirs. 1992—), Internat. Assn. Study Lung Cancer (bd. dirs. 1988—, pres. 1994-97), Western Assn. Physicians, S.W. Oncology Group, Lung Cancer Study Group, Alpha Omega Alpha. Office: U Colo Cancer Ctr Box B188 4200 E 9th Ave Denver CO 80220-3706

BUNN, ROBERT BURGESS, lawyer; b. Boise, Idaho, May 31, 1933; s. Marion Roy and Lois Lucile B.; m. Frances Patten Bull, Sept. 12, 1959; children: Carolyn B., F. Robin, Andrew R., Kathryn B. AB cum laude, Harvard U., 1955, LLB, 1961. Bar: Hawaii 1961, U.S. Dist. Ct. Hawaii 1961, U.S. Ct. Appeals (9th cir.) 1963, U.S. Supreme Ct. 1973. Ptnr. Cades, Schutte, Fleming & Wright, Honolulu, 1961—. Counsel Honolulu Symphony Soc., 1974-80, Hawaii Opera Theatre, Honolulu, 1980-82, 86—, pres., 1982-86, bd. dirs., 1980—. Lt. USN, 1958-61. Mem. ABA, Am. Coll. Real Estate Lawyers, Hawaii Bar Assn., Pacific Club. Avocations: tennis, wine, investments. Home: 2493 Makiki Heights Dr Honolulu HI 96822-2547 Office: Cades Schutte Fleming & Wright PO Box 939 Honolulu HI 96808-0939 E-mail: rbunn@cades.com.

BUNN, RONALD FREEZE, lawyer, academic administrator; b. Jonesboro, Ark., Aug. 1, 1929; s. S. Neal and Velma (Freeze) B.; m. Rita E. Hess, Mar. 29, 1955; children: Robin Gail, Katharine Sue, Lisabeth Joann. BA, Rhodes Coll., 1951; LLD, Southwestern at Memphis, 1973; MA, Duke U., 1953, PhD, 1956; postgrad., U. Cologne, Fed. Republic Germany, 1954-55; JD, U. Mo., 1989. Bar: Mo. 1990. Instr. U. Tex., Austin, 1956-59, asst. prof., 1960-64; asso. prof. La. State U., Baton Rouge, 1964-67, U Houston, 1967-69; prof., dean U Houston (Grad. Sch.), 1969-74, interim dean arts and scis., 1972-74, asso. dean faculties, 1974-75, acting v.p., dean faculties, 1975-76; v.p. acad. affairs State U. N.Y. at Buffalo, 1976-80; provost U. Mo., Columbia, 1980-86, prof. polit. sci., 1986—2000; ptnr. Shurtleff, Froeschner, Bunn and Hoffman, Columbia, 1992—; adj. prof. law, 2001. Vis. lectr. Ind. U., 1962; cons. Coun. Grad. Schs. Author: Politics and Civil Liberties in Europe, 1967, German Politics and the Spiegel Affair: A Case Study of the Bonn System, 1968; Contbr. articles profl. jours. Bd. dirs. S.W. Center for Urban Research, Houston, chmn. bd., 1975-76. Fulbright predoctoral scholar, 1954-55, Fulbright rsch. scholar, 1963; NATO sr. fellow in sci., 1973. Mem. Mo. Bar Assn. (labor law com.), So. Polit. Sci. Assn. (past mem. exec. coun.), Nat. Employment Lawyers Assn., Southwestern Polit. Sci. Assn. (past v.p.), Am. Coun. on Germany, Phi Beta Kappa (pres. Mo. Alpha chpt. 1986-88), Omicron Delta Kappa. also: 25 N 9th St Columbia MO 65201-4845

BUNN, TIMOTHY DAVID, newspaper editor; b. Syracuse, N.Y., Sept. 29, 1946; s. John Stewart and Katherine (Smolnycki) B.; m. Nancy Grady, May 27, 1968 BS in Journalism, Syracuse U., 1972. Pub. info. officer Central N.Y. Regional Planning Bd., Syracuse, 1972-74; met. editor Rochester Democrat & Chronicle, N.Y., 1974-79; asst. city editor Miami Herald, Fla., 1979-81; mng. editor Syracuse Post-Standard, 1981-82; exec. editor Syracuse Herald Jour., 1982-95; dep. exec. editor Syracuse Post-Std., 1995—. Served to capt. U.S. Army, 1967-71. Recipient Cmty. Svc. award NAACP, 1984, Cmty. Appreciation award Am.-Arab Anti-Discrimination Com. Mem. Am. Soc. Newspaper Editors Office: The Post-Standard Clinton Sq PO Box 4915 Syracuse NY 13221-4915

BUNN, WILLIAM BERNICE, III, physician, lawyer, epidemiologist; b. Raleigh, N.C., June 28, 1952; s. William Bernice Jr. and Clara Eva (Ray) B.; m. Shirley Welch, July 31, 1982; children: Ashley Howell, Elizabeth Jordan. AB, Duke U., 1974, MD, JD, 1979; MPH, U. N.C., 1983. Diplomate Am. Bd. Internal and Occupational Medicine. Intern, then resident in internal medicine Duke U. Med. Ctr., 1981-83, fellow in occupational medicine dept. community medicine, 1983; asst. prof. Sch. of Medicine Duke U., Durham, N.C., 1984-86, dir. rsch. in occupational medicine Sch. of Medicine, 1985-86; dir. occupational health and environmental affairs Bristol Myers Co., Wallingford, Conn., 1986-87, sr. dir. occupational health and environ. affairs, 1987-88; asst. clin. prof. Yale U., New Haven, 1986—; clin. asst. prof. U. Colo., Boulder, 1989; assoc. clin. prof. U. Cin., 1989—; corp. med. dir. Manville Sales Corp., Denver, 1988, v.p., corp. med. dir., 1988-89, sr. dir. for health safety and environ., v.p., 1989-92; dir. internat. med. affairs Mobil Corp., Princeton, N.J., 1992—; med. dir., dir. health, workers compensation, health benefits & safety Navistar Internat. Corp., Chgo., v.p. health safety and productivity, 1998—, v.p. health safety security and productivity, 2003—. Cons. author, co-editor Dellacorte Publs., N.Y.C., 1984-87; sci. adv. bd. U.S. EPA, Washington, 1991—; chmn. radiation epidemiology com. NAS, Washington, 1991-95; assoc. prof. clin. preventive medicine Northwestern Sch. Medicine; bd. sci. counselors Nat. Inst. Occupl. Safety and Health. Author: (with others) Effects of Exposure to Toxic Gases, 1986; author, editor: Poisoning, 1986, Occupational Problems in Clinical Practice; editor: Occupational and Environmental Medicine; editor, author: Issues in International Occupational and Environmental Medicine, 1997, International Occupational and Environmental Medicine, 1998. Bd. dirs. Colo. Safety Assn., Denver, 1988-90, Gaylord Hosp., Wallingford, 1987-88, Meriden-Wallingford Hosp., 1986-88, Chem. Industry Inst. Toxicology, 1989-91, Am. Coll. Occupational and Environ. Medicine, 1993—. NIOSH scholar, 1980; NIH fellow, 1982-83, Nat. Inst. Occupational Safety and Health fellow, 1983-84. Fellow Am. Occupl. Medicine Assn. (co-chmn. acad. affairs com. and publs. com. 1985-90, nat. affairs com. 1985-86, chmn. pubs. com. 1990, bd. dirs. 1993—, chair internat. coun. 1994, sec. 1995, mem. exec. com. 1995), Am. Coll. Occupl. and Environ. Medicine; mem. ACP, AMA, APHA, Occupl. Medicine Assn. Conn. (sec., pres.-elect 1986-88), Internat. Coll. Occupl. Health, Phi Beta Kappa, Phi Eta Sigma. Office: 455 N Cityfront Plaza Dr Chicago IL 60611-5503 also: Yale U Dept Epidemiology & Pub Health New Haven CT 06520 also: U Colo Sch Pharmacy Dept Toxicology Boulder CO 80309-0001 also: U Cin Dept Occupational Med Cincinnati OH 45267-0001

BUNNELL, GEORGE ELI, lawyer; b. Miami, Fla., Apr. 28, 1938; s. George A. and Lillian E. (Hurley) B.; Dianne Railton, Dec. 1, 1990; children: Kelley, Courtney. BA, U. Fla., 1960, LLB, 1962. Bar: Fla. 1963, U.S. Dist. Ct. (so. dist.) Fla. 1963, U.S. Supreme Ct. 1970, U.S. Ct. Appeals (11th cir.) 1982. Assoc. Nicholson, Howard & Brawner, Miami, 1963-64, Dean, Adams, George & Wood, Miami, 1964-67, ptnr., 1968-71; officer, dir. Huebner, Shaw & Bunnell, P.A., Ft. Lauderdale, Fla., 1972-77; pres., dir. Bunnell, Woulfe, Kirschbeum, Keller, McIntyre & Gregoire, Ft. Lauderdale, 1977—. Mem. advance staff White House, 1974-76; mem. City of Ft. Lauderdale Marine Adv. Bd., 1974-76, City of Ft. Lauderdale Civil Svc. Bd., 1977-79; bd. dirs., sec. Ft. Lauderdale Mus. Art, 1990—. Fellow Am. Coll. Trial Lawyers; mem. Internat. Assn. of Def. Counsel, Am. Bd. Trial Advs. (pres. Ft. Lauderdale chpt. 1992), Def. Rsch. inst., Fla. Def. Lawyers Assn., Broward County Bar Assn., Fla. Acad. of Hosp. Attys., Am. Health Lawyers Assn., Lauderdale Yacht Club. Republican. Office: Bunnell Woulfe Kirschbaum Keller McIntyre Gregoire 888 E Las Olas Blvd Fl 4 Fort Lauderdale FL 33301-2272 E-mail: geb@bunnellwoulfe.com.

BUNNELL, JOHN BLAKE, lawyer; b. Nashville, Apr. 20, 1958; s. James Crusman Jr. and Virginia Claire (Cross) B.; m. Candace Diane Tucker, Oct. 1, 1982. BS, Austin Peay State U., 1979; MS in Planning, U. Tenn., 1988, JD, 1990. Bar: Tenn. 1991, U.S. Dist. Ct. (mid. dist.) Tenn. 1992, U.S. Dist. Ct. (ea. dist.) Tenn. 1995. Editl. editor, editorialist The All State, Austin Peay State U. Student Newspaper, Clarksville, Tenn., 1975-78; planning intern/adminstrn. Hopkinsville (Ky.)-Christian County Planning Commn., 1978-79; energy tech. analyst Tenn. Energy Authority, Nashville, 1979-80; rsch. asst. U. Tenn. Planning Rsch. Ctr., Knoxville, 1980-83; legal noncommissioned officer 844th Engr. Battalion, Knoxville, 1986-94; asst. dist. atty. gen. Office of Dist. Atty. 21st Dist., Franklin, Tenn., 1991-92; pvt. practice Nashville, 1992; asst. pub. defender Office of Pub. Defender 4th Jud., Newport, Tenn., 1992-96; legal assistance officer U.S. Army Operation Joint Endeavor, Ft. Benning, Ga., 1996-97. Sec., dir. Cumberland Cmtys. Commn., Knoxville, 1991-94, 96—; trial def. counsel Team II, 213th Legal Spt. Orgn., Louisville, 1996-2000; legal assistance atty. 1077th RTU, Oak Ridge, Tenn., 2001—; city atty., Parrottsville, Tenn., 1999—; civil mediator under Rule 31, Tenn. Supreme Ct., 1999—. Author: The Impact of Industrial Revenue Bonds on Job Creation in Tennessee: A Longitudinal Approach. Exec. com. Cocke County ptnrship., 1998-99; pres. Newport/Cocke County C. of C., 1998; mem. Newport Cocke County Econ. Devel. Bd., 1998-99. Sgt. U.S. Army, 1990-91. Mem. Tenn. Assn. Criminal Def. Lawyers, Sevier County Bar Assn., Cocke County Bar Assn., Newport (Tenn.) Kiwanis Club (chmn. retention subcom. 1993-94), Nat. Trust for Hist. Preservation, Order Ky. Cols., Phi Kappa Phi, Pi Kappa Alpha. Methodist. Avocations: archaeology, camping, running, swimming. Office: PO Box 286 124 McSween Ave Newport TN 37822

BUNNELL, PETER CURTIS, photography and art educator, museum curator; b. Poughkeepsie, N.Y., Oct. 25, 1937; s. Harold Curtis and Ruth (Buckhout) B. BFA, Rochester Inst. Tech., 1959; MFA, Ohio U., 1961; MA, Yale U., 1965. Curator of photography Mus. Modern Art, N.Y.C., 1966-72; prof. history of photography and modern art Princeton (N.J.) U., 1972—2002, prof. emeritus, 2002—. Curator of photography Art Mus. Princeton U., 1972-02, dir., 1973-78, 98-2000. Author; Clarence H. White, 1987, Minor White: The Eye That Shapes, 1989, Degrees of Guidance, 1993, Thomas Joshua Cooper, 1995, Ruth Bernhard: Photographs, 1996, Aaron Siskind: The Bond and The Free, 1997, Walter Chappell: Time Lived, 2000, Remembering Limelight, 2001, Edward Ranney: The Character of the Place, 2003; editor: A Photographic Vision, 1980, The Art of Pictorial Photography, 1992, Photography at Princeton, 1998. Guggenheim fellow, 1979, Asian Cultural Coun. Rsch. fellow, 1984. Fellow Royal Photographic Soc. (hon.); mem. Soc. for Photog. Edn. (chmn. 1973-76), The Friends of Photography (pres. 1978-87, chmn. 1987-92), Century Assocs. Club. Office: Princeton U Dept Art And Archaelogy Princeton NJ 08544-1018

BUNNELL, WILLIAM PAUL, orthopaedic surgery educator; b. Montrose, Pa., Sept. 2, 1942; m. Marcia Bunnell; children: Jennifer, Christine. BS, Houghton Coll., 1964; MD, Temple U., 1968. Diplomate Nat. Bd. of Med. Examiners, Am. Bd. of Orthopaedic Surgery. Intern Temple U., Phila., 1968-69; resident orthopaedic surgery State Univ. Hosp. of the Upstate Med. Ctr., Syracuse, 1971-73; resident in gen. surgery USPHS Hosp., S.I., 1969-71; asst. prof. pediatrics and orthopaedic surgery Upstate Med. Ctr., Syracuse, 1975-79; fellow in pediatric orthopaedics A.I. duPont Inst., Wilmington, Del., 1974; dir. orthopaedics Alfred I. duPont Inst., Wilmington, Del., 1979-87, asst. med. dir., 1983-86, surgeon in chief, 1985-87, assoc. med. dir., 1986-87; assoc. prof. orthopaedic surgery Thomas Jefferson U. Sch. of Medicine, Phila., 1979-87, prof. orthopaedic surgery, 1987; prof. dept. pediatrics and orthpaedic surgery Loma Linda (Calif.) U. Med. Ctr., 1987-2000, chmn. dept. orthopaedic surgery, 1987-2000; fellow in foot and ankle surgery Loma Linda U. Med. Ctr., 1996—. Hosp. staff Loma Linda Cmty. Hosp., 1987—, Loma Linda U. Med. Ctr., 1987—, VA Hosp., Loma Linda, 1987—, San Bernardino County Med. Ctr., 1987—, others. Author: (with others) Surgery of Musculoskeletal System, 1983, 2d edit., 1990, The Pediatric Spine, 1985, Pediatric Orthopaedics, 1986, The Hip, 1992; contbr. numerous articles to profl. publs. Mem.: Am. Orthopaedic Foot and Ankle Soc., Pediatric Orthopaedic Soc. N.Am., Scoliosis Rsch. Soc., San Bernardino County Med. Soc., Christian Med. and Dental Assn., Am. Orthopaedic Assn., Am. Acad. Orthopaedic Surgeons, Am. Acad. of Cerebral Palsy and Devel. Medicine. Office: Loma Linda Orthopaedics 11234 Anderson St # A517 Loma Linda CA 92354-2804

BUNNER, WILLIAM KECK, lawyer; b. Fairmont, W.Va., Sept. 2, 1949; s. Scott Randolph and Virginia Lenore (Keck) B. BS in Secondary Edn. magna cum laude, W.Va. U., 1970, MA in History, 1973, ABD in History, 1975, JD, 1978, postgrad., 1998—. Bar: W.Va. 1978, U.S. Dist. Ct. (so. dist.) W.Va. 1978, U.S. Dist. Ct. (no. dist.) W.Va. 1985. Tchr. Monongalia County Bd. Edn., Morgantown, W.Va., 1970-78; contract lawyer dept. fin. and adminstrn. State of W.Va., Charleston, 1978-79; pvt. practice law Fairview, W.Va., 1979-84; pres. Farm Home Svc., Inc., 1983—; ptnr. Bunner & Bunner, Morgantown and Fairview, 1984-92. Pres. Climates, 1988—; presenter History of Barn Dance in U.S.A., Rush D. Holt History Conf., W. Va. U., 1999. Author: Planting Churches: A Case Study of Western Monongalia County, West Virginia, 2000, Anxiety, Alienation and Adjustment: Filmnoir and the Returning Warriorfrom WWII, 2000. Pres. Monongalia County Young Dems., 1974; parliamentarian Monongalia County Dem. Exec. Com., 1982-94; counsel, parliamentarian Young Dem. Clubs W.Va., 1974-77; bd. dirs., supr. Monongahela Soil Conservation Dist., 1982—; advisor West Run Watershed Improvement Dist., 1983—; mem. W.Va. Commn. on Rural Abandoned Mines, Rural Alliance, Monongalia County Solid Waste Auth., 1989—, also chmn., 1990-92. Mem. ABA, Monongalia County Bar Assn., Assn. Rural Conservation, Soil Conservation Soc. Am., United Taxpayers' Assn. (counsel), Monongalia County Hist. Soc., Marion County Hist. Soc., Marion County Bar Assn., W.Va. Trial Lawyers Assn, Phi Alpha Delta, Phi Alpha Theta. Democrat. Avocations: music, politics, farming, videos, regional history and genealogy. Home and Office: 15 Devine Rd Fairview WV 26570-8711

BUNNETT, JOSEPH FREDERICK, chemist, educator; b. Portland, Oreg., Nov. 26, 1921; s. Joseph and Louise Helen (Boulan) B.; m. Sara Anne Telfer, Aug. 22, 1942; children: Alfred Boulan, David Telfer, Peter Sylvester (dec. Sept. 1972). BA, Reed Coll., 1942; PhD, U. Rochester, 1945. Mem. faculty Reed Coll., 1946-52, U. N.C., 1952-58; mem. faculty Brown U., 1958-66, prof. chemistry, 1959-66, chmn. dept., 1961-64; prof. chemistry U. Calif., Santa Cruz, 1966-91, prof. emeritus, 1991—. Erskine vis. fellow U. Canterbury, N.Z., 1967; vis. prof. U. Wash., 1956, U. Wurzburg, Germany, 1974, U. Bologna, Italy, 1988; rsch. fellow Japan Soc. for Promotion of Sci., 1979; Lady Davis vis. prof. Hebrew U., Jerusalem, Israel, 1981; mem. adv. coun. dept. chemistry Princeton (N.J.) U., 1985-89; mem. NRC com. on alternative chem. demilitarization techs., 1992-93; mem. Dept. Def. panel on Gulf War Health Effects, 1993-94; co-chmn. peer rev. com. Russian-Am. Joint Evaluation Program, 1995-96; co-chmn. NATO Advanced Rsch. Workshop on Chem. Problems Associated with Old Arsenical and Mustard Munitions, Lodz, Poland, 1996; working group chem. weapons destruction, scientific adv. bd. Orgn. Prohibition Chem. Weapons, 1999—. Co-editor: Arsenic and Old Mustard: Chemical Problems in the Destruction of Old Arsenical and Mustard Munitions, 1998; contbr. articles to profl. jours. Trustee Reed Coll., 1970-97, trustee emeritus, 1997—. Fulbright scholar U. Coll., London, 1949-50, U. Munich, 1960-61; Guggenheim fellow U. Munich, 1960-61; recipient James Flack Norris award in phys. organic chemistry Am. Chem. Soc., 1992; named hon. mem. Societa Chimica Italiana. Fellow AAAS, Internat. Union Pure and Applied Chemistry (chmn. commn. phys. organic chemistry 1978-83, sec. organic chemistry divsn. 1981-83, v.p. 1983-85, pres. 1985-87, chmn. task force on sci. aspects of destruction of chem. warfare agts. 1991-95, chmn. com. on chem. weapon destruction 1995-2001, fellow, 2002.); mem. Am. Acad. Arts. and Scis., Am. Chem. Soc. (editor jour. Accounts of Chem. Rsch. 1966-86), Royal Soc. Chemistry (London), Pharm. Soc. Japan (hon.), Acad. Gioenia (U. Catania, hon.), Soc. Argentina de Investigaciones en Quimica Organica (hon.). Home: 608 Arroyo Seco Santa Cruz CA 95060-3148 Office: U Calif Dept Chemistry Santa Cruz CA 95064 Fax: 831-459-2935. E-mail: bunnett@chemistry.ucsc.edu.

BUNNING, JIM, senator, former professional baseball player; b. Southgate, KY, Oct. 23, 1931; BS, Xavier U., 1953. Profl. baseball player, 1955-71; with Detroit Tigers, 1955-63, Phila. Phillies, 1964-67, Pitts. Pirates, 1968-69, L.A. Dodgers, 1969, Phila. Phillies, 1970-71; ret. profl. baseball, 1971; congressman Ky. State Senate, Frankfort, 1979-83; mem. 100th-104th Congresses from 4th Ky. dist., 1987-98; mem. budget com.; mem. ways and means com.; U.S. senator from Ky., 1999—. Mem. Spl. Com. on Aging, Com. on Energy and Natural Resources, Com. on Banking, Com. Housing and Urban Affairs. Played in eight All-Star Baseball games during career. Republican. Office: US Senate 316 Hart Senate Office Bldg Washington DC 20510-0001*

BUNSHAFT, MARILYN JANOSY, community services specialist; b. N.Y.C., July 27, 1935; d. Albert and Fay Janosy; m. Warren Owen Bunshaft, Aug. 28, 1955; children: Albert J., Jess A., Charles E. BA, Queens Coll., 1957; MS, Hofstra U., 1961. Treas. Crawford Pharmacy, Inc., Roslyn, N.Y., 1978-94; tax preparer pvt. practice, East Meadow, N.Y., 1982-90; cmty. info. specialist East Meadow Pub. Libr., 1988—. Mem. adv. bd. Ctr. for Gerontology, Hofstra U., 2000—. Mem. Adv. Com. on Environ., Hempstead, N.Y., 1980-84; bd. dirs. Nassau Suffolk Lung Assn., N.Y., 1987-96, N.Y. State Lung Assn., 1991-94; mem. allocations com. United Way of Long Island, N.Y., 1991—. Mem. LWV (bd. dirs. Hempstead E., 1961—, pres. 69-70, 76-78); East Meadow C. of C. (bd. dirs. 1992—), Am. Libr. Assn., Pub. Libr. Assn. Avocations: reading, designing clothes, travel, gardening. Office: East Meadow Pub Libr 1886 Front St East Meadow NY 11554-1700 E-mail: mbunshaft@yahoo.com.

BUNT, RANDOLPH CEDRIC, mechanical engineer; b. Pascagoula, Miss., Dec. 3, 1958; s. Cedric and Linda Lou (McGuire) B.; m. Raechel Amy Ellis, May 15, 1982; children: Ashley Michele, Ryan Christian, Raechel Victoria, Savannah Marie. BME, Auburn U., 1979, MS, 1982. Registered profl. engr., Ala., Ga. Asst. engr. So. Co. Svcs., Birmingham, Ala., 1982-84, engr. II, 1984-86, engr. I, 1986-87, sr. engr., 1987-88, Ga. Power Co., Birmingham, 1988-89; project engr. So. Nuclear Oper. Co., Birmingham, 1989—. Project mgr. Ga. Power Co., Atlanta and Birmingham, 1987-89; chmn. GE Nuclear Turbine Conf., 1993-95, 2001, vice-chmn. GE turbine outage optimization com., 1997-99, chmn., 1999—. Capt. Birmingham Amateur Hockey Assn., 1985; stewardship chmn. Moody United Meth. Ch., 1995—96; pres. United Meth. Men, mem. fin. com., 2001—02; trustee Friends of Moody Schs., 1994—97; chmn., co-founder GE Nuclear Turbine Users Group; vice chmn. Fairbanks Morse Owners Group, 1994—96, chmn., 1996—2003, EPRI Turbine-Generator Users Group, 2000—02. Mem.: NSPE, ASME, Terry Turbine Users Group (vice chmn. 1993—99, chmn. 1999—2001, EPRI Tech. Transfer award 2002), So. Nuclear Nat. Mgmt. Assn. (treas. 1991—92, bd. dirs. 1994—95, chmn. BWROG generator equipment reliability group 2001), Birmingham Engring. Coun. (chmn. Discover E 1993—95, treas. 1995—96, sec. 1996—97, v.p. 1997—98, pres. 1998—99), Ala. Soc. Profl. Engrs. (chmn. student engring. yr. com. 1987—92, chmn. Math Counts program 1990—95, sec. 1992—93, v.p. 1993—95, pres. 1995—97, state pres.-elect 1998—99, state pres. 1999—2001, co. chmn. 1993 conf., Young Engr. of Yr. award 1991, Engr. of Yr. 1992, Profl. Engr. in Industry award), Toastmasters. Republican. Methodist. Home: 1005 Muscadine Cir Leeds AL 35094-1027 Office: So Nuclear Oper Co 42 Inverness Center Pky Birmingham AL 35242-4809

BUNTEN, BRENDA ARLENE, geriatrics nurse; b. Paris, Ill., May 7, 1947; d. Arthur Ray Sr. and Maxine L. (Bacon) B. A in Arts and Scis., Lakeland Coll., Mattoon, Ill., 1968; ADN, Kapiolani C.C., Honolulu, 1992. Charge nurse Meml. Med. Ctr., Springfield, Ill., 1968-76, Mattoon Health Care Ctr., 1977-79; agy. nurse Kahu Malama, Inc., Honolulu, 1983; charge nurse, staff devel. coord., infection control officer Hale Nani Health Ctr., Honolulu, 1979-93, also nursing staff scheduler, supr., 1979-93; unit mgr. Randal Mill Manor, Arlington, Tex., 1994—; supr. Heritage Oaks, Arlington, Tex., 1994—; dir. nursing Patriot Heights Health Care Ctr., 1998—; asst. dir. nursing Covenant Care Ctr., San Antonio, 1998—; staff nurse Warm Springs Rehab. Hosp., 1999—, Univ. Health Systems, San Antonio, 2002—. Fundraiser Challenger Run Hawaii, Honolulu, 1986—; co-owner, cons. retail sales Sunset Enterprises, Honolulu, 1982—. Named Am. Biog. Inst. Woman of the Year, 1997, dep. gov., 1997. Mem. USS Lancelot, Citizens Police Acad. Alumni Assn., Citizens Fire Acad. Alumni Assn. Avocations: marathon running, biking, baseball, football, circuit training. Home: PO Box 680743 San Antonio TX 78268-0743

BUNTEN, WILLIAM DANIEL, retired banker; b. Goodland, Kans., Sept. 18, 1931; s. William Livingston and Nelle Elizabeth (Boyle) B.; m. Charlene Sue Riemen, May 23, 1954; children: Jane Denise Bunten Hanisch, Barbara Sue Bunten DeVoe, Patricia Joann Bunten Buckner. AB, Baker U., 1953; LLB, Washburn U., 1956; MBA, U. Pa., 1958. Bar: Kans. 1956, Mich. 1959. From asst. cashier to v.p. Nat. Bank Detroit, 1957-67; from v.p. to pres. Mchts. Nat. Bank, Topeka, 1967-79; sr. exec. v.p. United Cen. Bank, Des Moines, 1979-81; from sr. v.p. to exec. v.p. United Cen. Bancshares, Des Moines, 1979-82; pres. INTRUST Bank and predecessor firm 1st Nat. Bank, Wichita, Kans., 1982-96, also bd. dirs. Vice chmn. bd. dir. INTRUST Fin. Corp. and predecessor firm 1st Fin. Corp., Wichita, Kans., 1982—96; bd. dir. Lakeway Airpark, Inc., pres., 2000—01. Bd. dirs., v.p. Jayhawk coun. Boy. Scouts Am., Topeka, 1968-78, Mid-Iowa coun., 1980-2; bd. dirs. United Way, Topeka, 1969-77, pres. 1977; bd. dirs. United Way, Des Moines, 1980-82, United Way Wichita, 1983-88, pres. 1987; bd. dirs. Topeka C. of C., 1969-74, pres. 1973; bd. dirs. Wichita C. of C., 1986-88, Greater Downtown Wichita, 1986-88, pres. 1987; bd. dirs. Downtown Action Corp., Wichita, 1988-91; bd. dirs. YMCA, Wichita, 1988-96, pres. 1992-94, sec. bd. dirs. Boys/Girls Clubs S. Cen. Kans., 1990-96; trustee Quivira coun. Boy Scouts Am., 1983-96; trustee Stormont Vail Hosp., Topeka, 1974-79, treas. 1978-79; trustee Baker U., Baldwin City, Kans., 1987-90; bd. dirs. Hospice, Wichita, 1983-84, Wichita State U. Endowment Assn., Wichita, 1984-95, dir. Health Affiliates Inc., Wichita, 1992-96. Mem. Washburn U. Alumni Assn. (bd. dirs. 1989-92, pres. 1991-92), Washburn U. Endowment Assn. (trustee 1990—), Rotary (bd. dirs. Topeka club 1977-78, treas. Wichita club 1988-89, trustee Lakeway 1999, Topeka 2003, Rotary Club Found.), Masons, Blue Lodge, Shriners, Washburn U. Law Sch. Alumni Assn. (trustee 2002—). Republican. Ecumenical. Avocations: flying, golf, reading, running. Home: 4000 SW Clarion Place Topeka KS 66610 E-mail: bbunten@3r9.org.

BUNTEN, WILLIAM WALLACE, state senator; b. Topeka, Apr. 5, 1930; m. Jo Ann Bunten, 1962. B in Bus. Adminstrn., U. Kans., 1952. V.p. Kaw Dehydrating Co., 1954—84; mem. Kans. Ho. of Reps., 1963—90; pres. Bunten Co., 1990—; mem. Kans. Senate, 2003—. Capt. USMC, 1952—54. Republican. Office: 460-E State Capitol 300 SW 10th Ave Topeka KS 66612 Address: 1701 SW 30th Topeka KS 66611 Office: 800 SW Jackson 66612*

BUNTING, ANNE EVELYN (EVE BUNTING), author; b. Maghera, Ireland, Dec. 19, 1928; came to U.S., 1958, naturalized, 1969; d. Sloan Edmund and Mary (Canning) Bolton; m. Edward Davison Bunting, Mar. 26, 1951; children— Christine Ann, Sloan Edward, Glenn Davison. Student, Meth. Coll., Belfast, Ireland, 1935-45, Queen's U., 1945-47. Lectr. UCLA, 1978-79, Chautauqua Writer's Conf.; bd. dirs. The Writer Mag., Soc. Book Writers and Illustrators. Author: over 100 children's books, including One More Flight, 1976 (Golden Kite award, Outstanding Sci. Book award), Ghost of Summer, 1977 (Jr. Lit. Guild selection), The Big Cheese, 1977, Winter's Coming, 1977, (with Glenn Bunting) Skateboards, How to Make Them, How to Ride Them, 1977, If I Asked You Would You Stay? (ALA best book award 1985), The Man Who Could Call Down Owls, 1985, Sixth Grade Sleepover, 1986, Ghost's Hour, Spook's Hour, 1987 (Booklist Best Book of Yr., Sch. Library Jour. best book award), The Wednesday Surprise, 1989 (ALA notable, Sch. Libr. Jour. best book award), Smoky Knight, 1990, The Wall, 1990, Someone is Hiding on Alcatraz Island, 1990, A Sudden Silence, 1990, (novel) The Two Giants, 1972. Recipient Edgar Allen Poe award, Mystery Writers of Am., Literacy award, PEN, Mark Twain award, State of Mo., Kerlan award, U. Minn., Regina medal, Cath. Libr. Am., Golden Kite award, Simon Weisenthal and Holocaust Mus. award, Commonwwealth Club Calif. award, 25 state awards voted by children of each state. Mem. Author's Guild, Soc. Children's Book Writers (bd. dirs.), So. Calif. Council on Writing for Children and Young People. Democrat. Home: 1512 Rose Villa St Pasadena CA 91106-3525 *My life divides rather neatly into two parts, Pre-American and American— the first part spent in Ireland, the second in the United States. In the first period I was young, I got married I had babies. In the second I'm growing older, I'm still married, my babies have grown, I'm writing books. Writing books is like having babies: after the work and pain comes the joy and fulfillment. Better 200 books and 3 children than the other way around.*

BUNTING, CAROLYN ANNE, writer; b. Waltham, Mass., Sept. 17, 1949; d. Lawrence Earl and Josephine Ann (MacPherson) Rogers; m. Richard Dennis Bunting, Sept. 27, 1975; children: Dennis Richard, Christine Marie. Grad. high sch., Waltham, Mass. Author: (anthology books) Poem, 1986, 89, 90, 92, Poetic Song, 1989. Roman Catholic. Avocation: poetry. Home: 49 Nelson St # 3 Quincy MA 02169-4806

BUNTING, DAVID CUYP, economics educator, consultant; b. Chgo., Sept. 22, 1940; s. Van Asmus and Jane (Whittemore) B.; m. Susan Jean Wilkins, Oct. 28, 1978; children: Maxwell C., Henri N. BS, Ohio State U., 1962, MA, 1964; MS, U. Wis., 1966; PhD, U. Oreg., 1972. Asst. prof. Ea. Wash. U., Cheney, 1971-76, assoc. prof., 1976-80, prof., 1980—. Cons. Bonneville Power Adminstrn., Spokane, Wash., 1985-99. Author: Rise of Large American Corporations, 1987; contbr. articles to profl. jours. Soccer coach Spokane Youth Sports Assn., 1985-94. Mem. Am. Econ. Assn., Royal Econ. Soc., Internat. Health Economists Assn., Soc. for Advancement of Socio-Econs. Democrat. Home: 2311 E 17th Ave Spokane WA 99223-5121 Office: Ea Wash U PAT 300 Dept Economics Cheney WA 99004 E-mail: dbunting@ewu.edu.

BUNTING, JOHN L. counseling administrator, insurance agent; b. Philadelphia, Pennsylvania, Dec. 11, 1955; s. Leola Torrence; m. Darlene Carter; children: Donaven, Darla, Danielle. BA, Glassboro St. Coll., Glassboro, N.J., 1978; MA, Rowan U., Glassboro, N.J., 1997. Cert. tchr. of the handicapped, and guidance counselor st. of NJ. Guidance counselor Millville Bd. of Edn., Millville, NJ, 1997—, Bridgeton Bd. of Edn., Bridgeton, NJ, 1991—97; regulatory ofcl. N.J. Casino Control Commn., 1982—91. Alumni bd. of dir. Rowan U., Glassboro, NJ, 1984—; task force on minority recruitment retention Glassboro St. Coll, NJ, 1986; adv. bd. Glassboro, Rowan Edn. Opportunity Program, NJ, 1986—; subcommittee on edn. FMR, assemblyman E. Salmon, 1st Legis. Dist., NJ, 1988—90; coll. transition team Glassboro, Rowan Coll., 1993; job tng. partnership act, NJ, 95; evaluation com. Middle States B.H.S. Guidance Dept., NJ, 1995. Zoning bd. City of Bridgeton, NJ, 1986—91, asst. bd., 1985—88; bd. of dir. N.J. Pub. Employees Ret. Sys. Fed. Credit Union, 1988—89; alt. Cumberland County Planning Bd., 1992—94; bd. Cumco Fed. Credit Union, 1997—. Recipient John Wesley Good Citizenship Award, 1974, Yr. for Action Valuable Svc. Award, Glassboro St. Coll., 1977, Outstanding Young Men of Am., 1981, 1988, Appreciation Award, Rowan Univ. Edn. Opportunity Program, 1988, 1994. Avocations: music, running. Home: 8 Glenview Ter Bridgeton NJ 08302 Office: Lakeside Middle Sch 2 No Sharp St Millville NJ 08332-1999

BUNTON, PHIL, editor-in-chief; Editor-in-chief Star Mag., Tarrytown, NY. Office: Star Magazine Ste 218 505 White Plains Rd Tarrytown NY 10591-5108

BUNTROCK, ROBERT EDWARD, information consultant, organic chemist; b. Mpls., Nov. 19, 1940; s. Eric Frank and Louise Ada (Intorf) B.; m. Gloria Carolyn Kral, June 24, 1961; children: Stephen Robert, Christine Louise Selby. BS in Chemistry, U. Minn., 1962; MA, Princeton U., 1964, PhD, 1967. Rsch. chemist Air Products & Chem., Allentown, Pa., 1967-70, Amoco Oil Co., Whiting, Ind., 1970-71; rsch. info. scientist Amoco Corp., Naperville, Ill., 1971-80, sr. rsch. info. scientist, 1980-85, rsch. assoc., 1985-95; pres. Buntrock Assocs., Inc., Princeton, Minn., 1995—. Mem. adv. bd. Derwent Ltd., London, 1980-86, Chem. Abstracts Svc., Columbus, Ohio, 1985-2000, Questel Orbit, McLean, Va., 1989-93. Contbr. articles to Searcher, Database, Online, Jour. Chem. Info. and Computer Sci., 1975—; patentee in field. Bd. dirs. Naperville Area Transcribing for the Blind, 1973-80. Mem. Am. Chem. Soc. (chmn. divsn. chem. info. 1981, bd. dirs. Chgo. sect. 1985-2000), Assn. Ind. Info. Profls., Sigma Xi. Lutheran. Avocations: reading, recorders, cross-country skiing, bicycling, choir. Office: Buntrock Assocs Inc 11335 300th Ave NW Princeton MN 55371-3349

BUNTS, FRANK EMORY, artist; b. Cleve., Mar. 2, 1932; s. Alexander Taylor and Mary (Corbin) B.; m. Norah Jean Grassle, Aug. 1, 1964. Student, Yale U., Cleve. Inst. Art; MA, Case Western Res. U., 1964. Instr. Cleve. Inst. Art, 1963-64, Ark. State U., 1965-67; mem. faculty U. Md., 1967-77, prof., 1973-77, dir. grad. art studio program, 1972-77; pres. VIA Art. One-person shows include Comara Gallery, L.A., 1967, 68, Franz Bader Gallery, Washington, 1969, 73, 75, St. John's Coll., Annapolis, Md., 1972, Deson Zaks Gallery, Chgo., 1972, Gallery 118, Mpls., 1974, Nat. Acad. Scis., Washington, 1976, Cath. U. Am., Washington, 1978, Plum Gallery, Washington, 1979, Flatiron Studio, N.Y.C., 1987, Maryanne McCarthy Fine Art, N.Y.C., 1988-89, Limelight Club, N.Y.C., 1988, Loft Lawyers, N.Y.C., 1990, 91, Roberta Wood Gallery, Syracuse, N.Y., 1993, Effect/Cause Mail Project, 1993-95, others; group shows: San Francisco Mus. Art, 1965, Cleve. Mus. Art, 1961, 62, 63, 65, 66 (2), 67, 68, Cleve. Inst. Art, 1964, Purdue U., Lafayette, Ind., 1964-69, El Paso (Tex.) Mus. Art, 1965, Nat. Arts Club, N.Y.C., 1965, Wittenberg U., Springfield, Ohio, 1966, Pacific Luth. U., Tacoma, Wash., 1966, Scripps Coll., Clairmont, Calif., 1967, U. Detroit, 1967, U. Calif., Long Beach, 1967, Palm Springs Desert Mus., Calif., 1967, Loyola U., L.A., 1968, Salt Lake City Art Ctr., 1968, U. N.H., 1968, Brigham Young U., Provo, Utah, 1968, Ind. State U., Terre Haute, 1968, Brooks Meml. Art Gallery, Memphis, 1968, 73, Cath. U., Washington, 1969, U. Md., 1969, 70, 72, Traveling Show, 1975-76, Fine Arts Gallery San Diego, 1971, Henri Gallery, Washington, 1971, Reicher Gallery, Barat Coll., Lake Forest, Ill., 1972, Corcoran Gallery Art, 1972, Va. Poly. Inst., Blacksburg, 1973, Birmingham (Ala.) Mus. Art, 1973, Indpls. Mus. Art, 1976, Gallery K, Washington, 1978, Studio Gallery, Washington, 1976-77, Modern Mus. Art, Rijeka, Yugoslavia, 1978, Baak Gallery, Cambridge, Mass., 1978, 79, Maryanne McCarthy Fine Art, N.Y.C., 1987, 88, 89, and Southampton, N.Y., 1989, Christie's N.Y.C. Preview and Auction, 1990, Univ. Sch., Cleve., 1990, Guild Hall, East Hampton, N.Y., 1991, 92, Lillian Heidenberg Gallery, N.Y.C., 1991-92, Roberta Wood Gallery, Syracuse, 1993-96, Angel Art Pacific Design Ctr., L.A., 1993, Divine Design 95, L.A., Black and Herron Gallery, N.Y.C., 1996; Intercommunication Ctr., Tokyo Opera City, Tokyo, Japan, 1998, VIA Art Found., New York (one person exhibition), 1999—, Roberta Wood Gall., Chapel Hill, NC, 2001, represented in collections Mus. Art, Cleve. Mus. Art, Fine Arts Gallery, San Diego, Library of Congress, Corcoran Gallery Art, Washington, Cooperstown Art Assn., N.Y., Chinese Artists Assn., Beijing; artwork in the following videos: The Man from U.N.C.L.E., episode The Pop Art Affair, 1966, Callanetics, M.C.A., 1986, Portrait of an Artist by Konrad Gylfason, 1986, music video Always and Forever, Whistle C.C. Prodns., 1990, documentary video San Francisco Ctr. for Visual Studies, 1990, Breaking Some Eggs-A Wisconsin Breakfast, 2003; work reproduced in Cleve. Mus. Art. Bull., May 1962, May 1968, Md. Art Gallery Catalog, 1969, 72, Indpl. Mus. Art catalog Painting and Sculpture Today, June 1976, Internat. Exhibition catalog Modern Mus. Art, Rijeka, Yugoslavia, 1978, The Catalog of Am. Drawings, Watercolors, Pastels and Collages Corcoran Gallery Art, Washington, 1983, N.Y. Art Rev., 1988, Millenium Art Collection, 2002. Office: VIA Art Inc 15 W 24th St New York NY 10010-3214 E-mail: bunts@earthlink.net.

BUNT SMITH, HELEN MARGUERITE, lawyer; b. LA, Oct. 8, 1942; d. Alan Verbanks and Nettie Virginia (Crandall) Bunt; m. Charles Robert Smith, Jan. 12, 1974; children: John, Sharon. BS, U. Calif., L.A., 1964; JD, Southwestern U., 1972. Bar: Calif. 1972; cert. secondary tchr., Calif. Tchr. L.A. City Schs., 1965-72; pvt. practice Pasadena, Calif., 1973—. Law Day chmn. Pasadena Bar Assn., 1980, sec., 1981. Editor (newsletter) Lawyer's Club, 1984-85. Sunday sch. tchr. Lake Ave. Ch., Pasadena, 1977-1998, church choir 1999-2003; mem. Pasadena Sister Cities Com., 1994-96. Mem. San Gabriel Bar Assn. (bd. dirs., sec. 1999—, pres.). Avocations: jogging, singing, stained glass. Office: 465 E Union St Ste 102 Pasadena CA 91101-1783

BUNUAN, JOSEFINA SANTIAGO, early childhood education educator, graduate program coordinator; b. Cabanatuan, Nueva Ecija, The Philippines, Sept. 11, 1935; came to U.S., 1963; d. Jose Villanueva and Ignacia (Santiago) B. AB in Psychology, U. Philippines, 1958; diploma, Melbourne (Australia) Coll. of Early Childhood Edn.; MEd in Psychometrics, Boston U., 1965, EdD in Psychometrics, 1969; postgrad. in devel. psychology, Harvard U., 1985-86. Instr. U. Philippines, Quezon City, 1960-62; grad. asst. Boston Coll., 1963-64; elem. sch. tchr. St. ColumbKille's Sch., Brighton, Mass., 1964-65; resident counselor Boston U., 1965-67; prof. edn. Worcester (Mass.) State Coll., 1969—99, grad. coord., 1985—. Mem. adv. bd. Worcester State Coll. Child Ctr., 1975—, dir. Piaget Inst., 1980; ednl. cons. Filipino Assn. of Greater Boston, 1986-90; presenter, speaker 20th World Congress Orgn. for Early Childhood Edn. No. Ariz. U., Flagstaff, 1992; sec. Restoring Sight Internat., Inc. Found., 2003—; spkr. and presenter in field. Contbr. articles to profl. jours. Recipient UN scholarship Melbourne Dept. Edn., 1959-61, Colombo Plan scholarship, 1959-61; fellow U. Philippines, 1965-69. Mem. Nat. Assn. Early Childhood Tchr. Educators, Nat. Assn. for Edn. Young Children, Orgn. Mondiale pour l'Edn. Prescolaire, Mass. Assn. Early Childhood Edn., Mass. State Coll. Assn., Early Childhood Ednl. Exch., Phi Delta Kappa. Democrat. Roman Catholic. Office: Worcester State Coll 486 Chandler St Worcester MA 01602-2832

BUNYAN, ELLEN LACKEY SPOTZ, retired chemist; b. Clark Mills, Pa., Aug. 14, 1921; d. Scott Richard and Mary Ellen (Beal) Lackey; children: Mark Stephen Spotz, Leslie Claire Spotz, Elizabeth Grace O'Rourke. BS, U. Pitts., 1942; PhD, U. Wis., 1950. Sr. technologist Eastman Kodak Co., Kingsport, Tenn., 1942-44; instr. chemistry U. Wis., Milw., 1946-47, rsch. assoc. dept. chemistry Madison, 1950-52; instr. physics St. Agnes Acad., Houston, 1965; Welch fellow chemistry Rice U, Houston, 1968-69; lectr. Montgomery Coll., Rockville, Md., 1970-72; asst. prof. chem. tech. U. D.C., Washington, 1972-78, assoc. prof., 1978-91; ret., 1991. Guest worker Nat. Bur. Stds., 1976; adj. prof. continuing edn. Walter Reed Army Med. Ctr. U. D.C., Washington, 1991—94, adj. prof., 1995—2000, mem. adv. coun. mortuary sci. program, 2002; curriculum developer Allied Health Chemistry. Contbr. articles to profl. jours. Bd. dirs. Takoma Pk. Symphony, 1988—2001; mem. adv. bd. Cambodian Children's Assn., Inc. Fellow, Nat. Urban League Eastman Kodak Co., 1976. Mem.: Am. Chem. Soc., Sigma Delta Epsilon, Sigma Xi. Methodist.

BUNYAN, S. WYANNE, arbitrator, mediator, realtor; b. St. Petersburg, Fla., 1945; BA, Calif. State U., San Francisco, 1967; JD, Georgetown U., 1971; LLM, London Sch. Econs., London, 1997. Bar: Calif. 1971, D.C. 1972, Alaska 1976, U.S. Ct. Claims, U.S. Supreme Ct. Faculty, asst. dean Hastings Coll. Law U. Calif., San Francisco, 1971-76; chief coun. to Calif. Sec. State Calif. State Govt., Sacramento, 1976-77; asst. atty. gen. State Alaska, Juneau, Anchorage, 1978-83; gen. coun. Bering Straits Native Corp., Nome, Anchorage, 1983—84, U.S. Merchant Marines, 1991—93, U.S. Small Bus. Adminstrn., 1993—94; expdn. historian Antarctica, Palmyra, Howland Islands, 1994—95; realtor Kauai, Hawaii, 1999—. Office: PO Box 445 Hanalei HI 96714-0445

BUNYI, MILAGROS CALDERON, economics and marketing research executive; b. Manila, Mar. 20, 1942; d. Feliciano and Marie (Veloria) Calderon; m. Bernardo Aguila Bunyi, Oct. 27, 1963 (dec. Aug. 1980); children: Maria Aurora, Baron. A in Commerce, Philippine Coll. of Commerce, Manila, 1962; AB in Econs., Far Ea. U., Manila, 1967; MS in Econs., U. of St. Tomas, Manila, 1973; MPA, U. of The Philippines, Quezon City, 1997. Hearing stenographer Presdl. Anti-Graft Com., Manila, 1962-63; sec. legal and tax affairs Ysmael Steel Mfg. Co., Quezon City, 1963-68; instr. econs. U. of the East, Manila, 1968-70; auditing examiner Commn. on Audit Nat. Electrification Adminstrn., Quezon City, 1975-78; sr. economist Philippine Sugar Commn., Quezon City, 1978-81, supervising economist, 1981-88; econ. and mktg. rsch. div. chief Sugar Regulatory Adminstrn., Quezon City, 1986—. Sec. bd. dirs. Sugar Employees' Credit Coop., Quezon City. Contbr. articles to profl. publs. Active with local homeowners' assn.; mem. Evnag. Apologetics Ministries Team. Recipient lit. award Nat. Electrification Adminstrn., 1978, Gawad Saka award Sec. Dept. Agr. Mem. Philippine Econ. Soc. Orthodox Christianity. Avocations: reading, teaching, cooking, aerobics. Office: care/SRA PO Box 70, UP, Diliman Quezon City 1101 Philippines

BUNZA, LINDA HATHAWAY, editor, writer, composer, institution director; b. Hartford, Conn., Feb. 23, 1946; d. Richard Collins and Alma C. Forest Hathaway, John Hennion Fisher and Eleanor Williston Chase; m. Geoffrey J. Bunza; children: Stephen, Matthew. BA, Bates Coll., 1968; MA, The Hartford Sem. Found., 1971; PhD, Syracuse U., 1974. Editl. asst. The Harvard Ednl. Rev., Cambridge, Mass., 1974—76; mng. editor The Andover Rev., Andover, Mass., 1976—79; dir. Columbia Rsch. Inst. Arts and Humanities, Portland, Oreg., 1998—2002. Editor Renaissance Mag., Hartford, 1963—64; editl. asst. Symposium Mag., Syracuse, NY, 1973—74; editor Soc. Arts, Religion, and Contemporary Culture, N.Y., NY, 1974—78; lectr. in field. Composer: (Classical Music Composition) There is Something Still Floating, 1999, Report From A Spiral, 1998, Snow Mountain, 2000, RiverMusic, 1995, Mythology of Clouds, 1993, Sphere, 1992, Cascadia, 1989, Widmanstatten Lines, 1987, View from a Mobius Strip, 1986, Sounds from the Olympic Peninsula, 1998, Electric Night, 1984, Odalisque, 1982, Awakening Night, 1981; editor: (Book) Adventures and Misadventures of Dr. Sonjee by Dr. Prasanna Pati, Snehalata Press, 2001, (Novel) Against Parched Winds by Kanta Luthra, (Book) Art of Literary Criticism, 2000; author: Theories of Modern Art-I, 1972, Theories of Modern Art-II, 1973, Theories of Modern Art-III, 1973; author: (catalog) Blue Note: The Art of Bruce Warner, 2000, Air, 2001, Where Art Reveals Itself in Symbols, Words are Hard to Find, 2001; mem. editl. bd. Anima Mag., 1973—95. Bd. dirs. Fear No Music 20th Century Ensemble, 2000—02, Third Angle New Music Ensemble, Portland, 2000—03, Contemporary Art Coun., Portland Art Mus., 2001—03, Portland Baroque Orch., 2000—03; arts and culture com. City Club of Portland, 2000—03, arch. com., 1999—2002. Recipient Pres.'s award, Beaverton Arts Commn., 2000. Mem.: Portland Inst. Contemporary Art, European and Am. Art Coun., Portland Art Mus., Northwest Bookfest (program com.), Ancient Egypt Studies Assn., The Coll. Music Soc., Soc. Composers Internat., Friends William Stafford Assn. (life). Office: Columbia Rsch Inst Arts and Humanities PO Box 25316 Portland OR 97298 Home Fax: 503-297-0520. Personal E-mail: bunza@teleport.com. Business E-Mail: columbiaarts@aol.com.

BUNZEL, JOHN HARVEY, political science educator, researcher; b. N.Y.C., Apr. 15, 1924; s. Ernest Everett and Harriett (Harvey) B.; m. Barbara Bovyer, May 11, 1963; children— Cameron, Reed AB, Princeton U., 1948; MA, Columbia U., 1949; PhD, U. Calif.-Berkeley, 1954; LL.D., U. Santa Clara, 1976. Mem. faculty San Francisco State U., 1953-56, 63-70, vis. scholar Ctr. Advanced Study in Behavioral Scis., 1969-70; mem. faculty Mich. State U., East Lansing, 1956-57, Stanford U., Calif., 1957-63; pres. San Jose State U., Calif., 1970-78; sr. research fellow Hoover Inst. Stanford U., Calif., 1978—. Mem. U.S. Commn. on Civil Rights, 1983-86. Author: The American Small Businessman, 1962; Anti-Politics in America, 1967; Issues of American Public Policy, 1968; New Force on the Left, 1983, Challenge to American Schools: The Case For Standards and Values, 1985, Political Passages: Journeys of Change Through Two Decades 1968-1988, 1988, Race Relations on Campus: Stanford Students Speak, 1992; contbr. articles to profl. jours., popular mags., newspapers. Weekly columnist San Jose Mercury-News. Bd. dirs. No. Calif. Citizenship Clearing House, 1959-61; mem. Calif. Atty. Gen.'s Adv. Com., 1960-61; del. Calif. Democratic Conv., 1968; del. Dem. Nat. Conv., 1968 Recipient Presdl. award No. Calif. Polit. Sci. Assn., 1969, cert. of Honor San Francisco Bd. Suprs., 1974, Hubert Humprey Pub. Policy award Policy Studies Orgn., 1990; grantee Ford Found., Rockefeller Found., Rabinowitz Found. Mem. Am. Polit. Sci. Assn. Home: 1519 Escondido Way Belmont CA 94002-3634 Office: Stanford U Hoover Inst Stanford CA 94305

BUNZL, RUDOLPH HANS, retired manufacturing executive; b. Vienna, July 20, 1922; arrived in U.S., 1940, naturalized, 1944; s. Robert Max and Nellie Margaret (Burian) Bunzl; m. Rema R. Templeton, Apr. 6, 1947 (div.); children: Ann Mary Bunzl Kamoe, Carol Elizabeth Bunzl Showker; m. Esther R. Mendelsohn, Nov. 14, 1970. BSChemE, Ga. Inst. Tech., 1943; MA in History, U. Richmond, 1994. With Shell Chem. Co., Calif., 1943-54; v.p. Am. Filtrona Corp., Richmond, Va., 1954-59, pres., 1959-83, CEO, 1983-87, chmn. bd., 1987-95. Pres. R.E.B. Found.; trustee Richmond Symphony Found. With U.S. Army, 1944—46. Mem.: AICE. Office: 5516 Falmouth St Ste 205 Richmond VA 23230-1819

BUONGIORNO, JACOPO, research scientist; b. Milan, June 1, 1971; arrived in U.S., 1997; s. Cesare Buongiorno and Norma Brigata; m. Hannele T. Jarva, Aug. 24, 1971; 1 child, Nicolas J. PhD in Nuc. Engring., MIT, 2000; BS in Nuc. Engring., Poly. Milan, 1996. Rsch. scientist Idaho Nat. Engring. and Environ. Lab., Idaho Falls, Idaho, 2000—01, rsch. program dir., 2001—. Sec. Internat. Assn. Hydraulic Engring. and Rsch., Madrid, 2002—. Mem.: ASME (Best Tech. Paper award 8th Internat. Conf. on Nuc. Engring. 2000), Am. Nuc. Soc. (Mark Mills award 2001). Achievements include design of innovative nuclear reactor designs. Office: INEEL PO Box 1625 Idaho Falls ID 83415-3860 Office Fax: 1(208)526-2930. Personal E-mail: jbuong@msn.com. E-mail: buonj@inel.gov.

BUONO, ANTHONY FRANCIS, business educator; b. Bronx, N.Y., Sept. 13, 1947; s. Frank Dominic and Jeannette (Gehl) B.; BS, U. Md., 1975; MA, Boston Coll., 1977, PhD, 1981; m. Mary Alice Keyl, Jan. 11, 1970; 1 child, Christopher Keyl. Rsch. assoc. Lab. Psychosocial Studies, Boston Coll., 1976-78, lectr. dept. orgnl. studies, 1977-79; instr. Nat. Assn. Bank Women Inst., Simmons Coll., summers 1979-85; asst. prof. dept. mgmt. Bentley Coll., Waltham, Mass., 1979-84, assoc. prof., 1985-89, prof., 1990—, dept. chair, 1989-94, rsch. fellow ctr. for bus. ethics, 1992—; orgn. devel. cons. in field. With USAF, 1969-75. NIMH grantee, 1976-78. Mem. Acad. Mgmt., Eastern Acad. Mgmt., Am. Sociol. Assn., Roman Catholic. Author: (with James L. Bowditch) Quality of Work Life Assessment: A Survey Based Approach, 1982; A Primer on Organizational Behavior, 1985, 5th edit., 2001, The Human Side of Mergers and Acquisitions: Managing Collisions Between People, Culture and Organizations, 1989; (with Lawrence T. Nichols) Corporate Policy, Values and Social Responsibility, 1985; editor: Current Trends in Management Consulting, 2001; Developing Knowledge and Value in Manangement Consulting, 2002, Enhancing Inter-Firm Networks and Interorganizational Strategies, 2003; asst. editor Bus. and the Contemporary World, 1987-96; contbr. articles to profl. jours. Home: 15 Virginia Ridge Rd Sudbury MA 01776-1053 E-mail: abuono@bentley.edu.

BUONO, BARBARA, state legislator; b. July 28, 1953; JD, Rutgers Univ. Dem. Minority Parliamentarian assembly appropiatioans com., N.J., 1994—. COuncilwoman Metuchen, 1993-94, police comm., 1993-94., co-chair McGreevey for Gov. Office: 1967 State Route 27 Ste 20 Edison NJ 08817-3262*

BUONO, FRANK LOUIS, orthopedic surgeon; b. New Haven, Feb. 17, 1934; s. Louis Paul and Anna (Basilicata) B.; m. Edythe Ann Sliz, June 20, 1960 (dec. 1987); children: Elisa Beth, Julienne Marie, Lauren Anne, Frank Louis Jr., Jon Andrew; m. Susan R. Houchens, Dec. 31, 1999. BA, U. Conn., 1956, MA, 1958; MD, Hahnemann Med. Coll., Phila., 1962. Diplomate Am. Bd. Orthop. Surgeons. Intern USAF Med. Ctr., Royster, Ohio, 1962-63; resident Phila. Naval Hosp., 1964-67, Santa Rosa Med. Ctr., San Antonio, 1967-68; orthop. surgeon USAF Med. Svc., 1962-70, Western Ky. Orthop. Assocs., Bowling Green, 1970—. Contbr. articles to profl. jours. Lt. col. USAF, 1962-70, lt. col. USAR, 1990—. Fellow AMA, Am. Acad. Orthop. Surgeons; mem. So. Med. Assn., So. Orthop. Assn. (councillor 1996—), Ky. Orthop. Soc., Mid-Am. Orthop. Soc. Avocations: flying, stone carving, wood working, gardening. Home: 2069 Mccubbin Dr Bowling Green KY 42104-3864 Office: Western Ky Orthop Assocs 1777 Ashley Cir Bowling Green KY 42104-3339

BUONO, KATHLEEN ANN CLEARY, nursing specialist; b. Bklyn., Dec. 9, 1964; d. Sarah Murphy; m. James Gerard Buono, Jan. 9, 1988; children: James Gerard, Rebecca Rose. Diploma, Albany (N.Y.) Med. Ctr. Sch. Nursing, 1985; BSN, SUNY, New Paltz, 1988; MS, Russell Sage Coll., 1997. RN, N.Y.; cert. FNP. Staff nurse oper. rm. Albany Med. Ctr.; staff nurse Benedictine Hosp., Kingston, NY; clin. instr. Meml. Sch. Nursing, 1994-99; staff nurse/clin. nurse specialist obstetrics Albany Med. Ctr., 1999—. Adj. faculty The Sage Colls., 2002—. Mem.: Sigma Theta Tau (v.p. Delta Pi chpt. 1999—2001). Home: PO Box 272 New Baltimore NY 12124-0272

BUOTE, ROSEMARIE BOSCHEN, retired special education educator; b. Jamaica, NY, Nov. 13, 1939; d. George Frederick and Mary (Bernadick) Boschen; m. Victor Roy Buote, June 27, 1964; children: Kristine Enos, Alissa Cassidy. BA, Barrington (R.I.) Coll., 1962; MEd, R.I. Coll., Providence, 1985, Fitchburg (Mass.) State Coll., 1991. Cert. spl. edn. and elem. tchr. Elem. tchr. Town of Barrington, 1962-68, 69-70; resource rm. instructional aide Town of Rehoboth, Mass., 1983-84; spl. edn. tchr., behavior mgmt. specialist Dept. of Edn. Tri-County Dist., Ednl. Svcs. in Instnl. Schs., Taunton, Mass., 1985—2002; ret., 2002. Sec. Conservation Commn., Town of Dighton, 1971—74, Friends of the Taunton Libr. B d.; lay eucharistic minister Pastoral Outreach Commn., Episcopal Diocese Mass.; bd. dirs. Gordon Coll. Alumni Bd., Wenham, Mass., 1989—92, Am. Cancer Soc. S.E. Mass. Mem.: AAUW (Mass. state v.p. for membership 2003—, sec., Taunton area br. past pres.), Mass. Computer Using Educators, Coun. for Children with Learning Disabilities, Coun. Children with Behavioral Disorders, Coun. Exceptional Children, Southeastern New Eng. Marine Educators, Nat. Marine Educators Assn., Red Hat Soc., Dighton Garden Club (pres. 1979—82), Delta Kappa Gamma (pres. 2002—). Avocations: reading, writing, gardening, theater. Home: 1690 Wellington St Dighton MA 02715-1000 Fax: (508) 669-5894. E-mail: Rosemariebuote@aol.com.

BURACK, ELMER HOWARD, management educator; b. Chgo., Oct. 21, 1927; s. Charles and Rose (Taerbaum) B.; m. Ruth Goldsmith, Mar. 18, 1930; children— Charles Michael, Robert Jay, Alan Jeffrey BS, U. Ill., 1950; MS, Ill. Inst. Tech., 1956; PhD, Northwestern U., 1964. Prodn. supt. Richardson Co., Melrose Park, Ill., 1953-55; prodn. control mgr. Fed. Tool Corp., Lincolnwood, Ill., 1955-59; mgmt. cons. Booz, Allen & Hamilton, Chgo, 1959-60; mem. faculty Ill. Inst. Tech., Chgo, 1960-78, prof. mgmt., 1978; prof. mgmt., chair U. Ill.-Chgo., 1978—, head dept., dir. doctoral studies CBA, 1990-96, prof. mgmt. emeritus, 1997. Pres. Ill. Mgmt. Tng. Inst., 1975-77; mem. Ill. Gov. Adv. Coun. Employment and Tng., 1976-83, vice chmn., 1980-83; mem. NSF mission to Russia, 1979. Author: Manpower Planning, 1972, Personnel Management, 1982, Growing-Careers for Women, 1980, Introduction to Management, 1983, Career planning and Management, 1983, Planning for Human Resources, 1983, Creative Human Resource Planning, 1988, Career Management, 1990, Corporate Resurgence and the New Employment Relationships, 1993, Human Resource Planning, 4th edit., 2001, Retiring Retirement, 2002; contbr. articles to profl. jours. With USAAF, 1945-47 Research grantee Dept. Labor, 1965-68; recipient Alumni award for disting. svc. Coll. Bus. U. Ill., Chgo., 1996. Mem. Nat. Acad. Mgmt. (chmn. pers./human resource divsn. 1974-75, health divsn. 1978-79), Human Resource Mgmt. Assn. Chgo. (pres. 1974-75), Soc. Human Resource Mgmt., Pers. Accreditation Inst. (bd. dirs. 1978-89), Midwest Human Resource Planners Group (founding mem., bd. dirs. 1984-95), B'nai B'rith. Office: U Ill MC243 601 S Morgan St Rm 718 Chicago IL 60607-7100

BURACK, MICHAEL LEONARD, lawyer; b. Willimantic, Conn., Oct. 10, 1942; s. Meyer and Rose Ann (Kravitz) B.; m. Maria Gallego, Oct. 20, 1978; children: Victoria Luisa, Cristina Maria. BA summa cum laude, Wesleyan U., Middletown, Conn., 1964; postgrad. in physics, Calif. Inst. Tech., 1965; MS in

Applied Physics, Stanford U., 1967, JD, 1970. Bar: Calif. 1971, D.C. 1972. Law clk. to judge U.S. Ct. Appeals for 9th Cir., San Francisco, 1970-71; assoc. Wilmer, Cutler & Pickering, Washington, 1971-77, ptnr., 1978-2000, of counsel, 2001—. Mem. staff D.C. Jud. conf. Com. on Adminstrn. of Justice under Emergency Condition, 1972-73; mem. adv. com. govt. applications of ADR of Ctr. for Pub. Resources, 1988; mem. jud. evaluation com. D.C. Bar, 1991-94. Assoc. editor Jour. Pub. Contract Law, 1988-94. Mem. ABA, Order of the Coif, Phi Beta Kappa, Sigma Xi. Office: Wilmer Cutler & Pickering 2445 M St NW Washington DC 20037-1487 E-mail: mburack@wilmer.com.

BURAK, ERIC STEVEN, pharmaceutical researcher; s. Robert B and Claire Burak; m. Dennie M Shaffron, Oct. 29, 1989; 1 child, Casey Rachel. BS, Drexel U., 1983—88; PhD, Temple U., 1988—92. Rsch. scientist, drug metabolism and pharmacokinetics Ciba Pharmaceuticals, Summit, NJ, 1992—94; group leader, pharmacokinetics ProCyte Corp., Kirkland, Wash., 1994—95; dir., drug metabolism and pharmacokinetics Guilford Pharmaceuticals Inc., Balt., 1996—2002; dir., preclinical devel. Rib-X Pharmaceuticals Inc., New Haven, 2002—. Mem.: Am. Assn. of Pharmaceuticals Scientists (assoc.). Achievements include patents for N-Oxides of Heterocyclic Esters, Amides, Thioesters, and Ketones. U.S. Patent No. US 6, 251, 892 B1. Issued: Jun. 26, 2001. Home: 51 Bone Mill Rd East Haddam CT 06423 Office: Rib-X Pharmaceuticals Inc 300 George St New Haven CT 06511

BURAK, H(OWARD) PAUL, lawyer; b. N.Y.C., July 9, 1934; s. Harry and Bette (Hauer) B.; m. Edna K. Goodman, Oct. 18, 1970; children: Hally Ann., Jason Lewis. BS, Cornell U., 1954; LLB, Columbia U., 1957. Bar: N.Y. 1958, D.C. 1967, U.S. Dist. Ct. (so. and ea. dists.) N.Y. 1967, U.S. Ct. Appeals (2d cir.) 1960, U.S. Supreme Ct. 1964. Assoc. Cadwalader, Wickersham & Taft, N.Y.C., 1957-63; dep. asst., asst. gen. counsel Agy. for Internat. Devel. U.S. State Dept., Washington, 1963-67; assoc. Rosenman Colin Kay Petschek & Freund, N.Y.C., 1967-69; ptnr. Rosenman & Colin, N.Y.C., 1969—2002, Katten Muchin Zavis Rosenman, N.Y.C., 2002—. Bd. dirs. Sony Corp. Am., N.Y.C., Sony Music Entertainment, Inc., N.Y.C., Sony Pictures Entertainment, Inc., Culver City, Calif., Sony USA Found., N.Y.C. Rev. editor Columbia Law Rev., 1956-57; author pamphlets. Mem. adv. bd. N.Y.C. Ballet. Mem. ABA, Assn. of Bar of City of N.Y., Fed. Bar Coun., N.Y. Bar Assn., Internat. Bar Assn., Univ. Club. Office: Katten Muchin Zavis Rosenman 575 Madison Ave New York NY 10022-2585 Business E-Mail: hpburak@kmzr.com.

BURAKOFF, STEVEN JAMES, immunologist, educator; b. N.Y.C., Oct. 13, 1942; s. Jack and Adelene (Van Praag) B.; m. Suzanne Weindling, Sept. 3, 1965; 1 child, Alexis. BA, Lehigh U., 1964; MA, Queens Coll., Flushing, N.Y., 1965; MD, Albany Med. Coll. Union U., 1970; MA (hon.), Harvard U., 1984; DHL hon., Spertus Inst., Chgo., 2002. Diplomate Am. Bd. Internal Medicine. Intern, resident N.Y. Hosp., Cornell Med. Ctr., 1970-73.; instr. Harvard Med. Sch., Boston, 1976-77, asst. prof., 1977-80, assoc. prof., 1980-83, prof., 1983—2000; chief pediat. oncology Dana Farber Cancer Inst., Boston, 1985-2000; Margaret M. Dyson prof. pediat. Harvard Med. Sch., Boston, 1998-2000; Laura and Isaac Perlmutter prof. NYU Sch. Medicine, 2000—. Ted Williams sr. investigator, Dana Farber Cancer Inst., 1995-2000; dir. Skirball Inst. for Biomolecular Medicine, 2000—, NYU Cancer Inst., 2000—; bd. dirs. The Med. Found. Contbr. over 300 articles to profl. jours. Recipient Sr. Faculty award Am. Cancer Soc., 1980-85. Mem. Am. Soc. Clin. Investigation, Am. Assn. Immunologists (head program com. 1985-86), Assn. Am. Physicians, Transplantation Soc.

BURAN, DAVID RUNYON, fundraiser; b. Endicott, NY, Sept. 26, 1940; s. Stephen Runyon and Helen (Tinus) B.; m. Delores Baldwin, Feb. 22, 1942; children: David Stephen, Natalie Buran Granger, Sally Buran Dickinson. BA, Colgate U., Hamilton, N.Y., 1962, MA, 1964. Tchr. Cazenovia (N.Y.) H.S., 1963-65; tchr., head football coach Holland Patent (N.Y.) Ctrl. Sch., 1965-67; asst. prof. Trinity Coll., Hartford, Conn., 1967-71; dir. athletics Shady Side Acad., Pitts., 1971-82; headmaster Shadyside Acad. jr. Sch., Pitts., 1982-86, Hebron (Maine) Acad., 1986-92; dir. major gifts Mass. Gen. Hosp., Boston, 1992-99; dir. devel. Albany Med. Ctr. Found., NY, 1999—2002, supr. external rels., 2002—. Bd. dirs. Doane Stuart Sch., Albany, Outdoor Explorations, Medford, Mass., 1995-98, Hebron Cmty. Bapt. Ch., 1986-92; mem. alumni bd. Colgate U., Hamilton, N.Y., 1989-92; pres. Maine Assn. Ind. Schs., 1992; sr. v.p. external rels. Albany Med. Ctr. Found., 2002—; sec. Albancy Med. Prize in Biomed. Rsch., 2003—. Mem. Nat. Soc. Fundraising Execs. Republican. Roman Catholic. Avocations: golf, fishing, photography, reading, gardening. Office: Albany Med Ctr Found 43 New Scotland Ave Albany NY 12208 E-mail: burand@mail.amc.edu.

BURANELLI, VINCENT JOHN, writer; b. N.Y.C., Jan. 16, 1919; m. Agnes Wallace Gillespie, Oct. 31, 1952. BA, Nat. U. Ireland, Dublin, 1947, MA, 1948; PhD, Cambridge (Eng.) U., 1951. Writer Lowell Thomas News, N.Y.C., 1952-64, Am. Heritage, N.Y.C., 1965-66; writer, editor Gen. Learning, Time-Life Inc., N.Y.C., 1966-67; freelance writer, editor, book reviewer, 1967—. Lectr. U.S. lit. Author: (biographies) Edgar Allan Poe, 1961, 2nd edit., 1977, The King and the Quaker: A Study of William Penn and James II, 1962, Josiah Royce, 1964 (Best Biography of 1964, N.J. Authors), Louis XIV, 1966, The Wizard from Vienna: Franz Anton Mesmer, 1975; (history) Gold: An Illustrated History, 1979, The Eighth Amendment, 1991; author: (with Nan Buranelli) Spy/Counterspy: An Encyclopedia of Espionage, 1982 (Best History of 1983, N.J. Authors); editor: The Trial of Peter Zenger, 1957. With U.S. Army, 1941-45. Kaltenborn fellow in journalism, N.Y.C., 1952-53. Mem. Authors Guild, Cambridge Union, Royal Dublin Soc. Home: Apt 413 866 Denbigh Blvd Newport News VA 23608-4480

BURAS, NATHAN, hydrology and water resources educator; b. Barlad, Romania, Aug. 23, 1921; came to U.S., 1947; s. Boris and Ethel (Weiser) B.; m. Netty Stivel, Apr. 13, 1951; 1 child, Nir H. BS with highest honors, U. Calif., Berkeley, 1949; MS, Technion, Haifa, Israel, 1957; PhD, UCLA, 1962. Registered profl. engr., Israel. Prof. hydrology and water resources Technion, 1962-80, dean, 1966-68; vis. prof. Stanford (Calif.) U., 1976-81; prof., head of dept. hydrology and water resources U. Ariz., Tucson, 1981-89, prof. hydrology and water resources, 1989—. Vis. prof. Technical U. Valencia, Spain, 1998; cons. Tahal, Ltd., Tel Aviv, 1963-73, World Bank, Washington, 1972-76, 79-82, Regional Municipality of Waterloo, Ont., Can., 1991-93, U.S. AID, Washington, 1992-93, Great No. Paper Co., 1992-2001, Inner Mongolia Assn. for Sci. and Tech., China, 1993-99; apptd. mem. standing com. on terminology Internat. Glossary of Hydrology UNESCO, 1996. Author: Scientific Allocation of Water Resources, 1972; editor: Control of Water Resources Systems, 1976, Management of Water Resources in North America, 1995, Reflections on Hydrology, 1997. Mem. Israel-Mex. Mixed Commn. on Sci. Cooperation, 1976, So. Ariz. Water Resource Assn., 1982-2002; active Pugwash Workshops, 1991, 92, 93. Named Laureat du Congres, Internat. Assn. Agrl. Engring., 1964; recipient Cert. of Appreciation, USDA., 1970, award for Edn. and Pub. Svc. in Water Resources U. Coun. on Water Resources, 1994, award for Excellence Gov. of Ariz., 1995. Fellow ASCE (life), Ariz.-Nev. Acad. Sci., Internat. Water Resources Assn.; mem. Am. Geophys. Union, Am. Water Resources Assn. (charter). Jewish. Avocations: music, hiking. Home: 5541 E Circulo Terra Tucson AZ 85750-1003 Office: U Ariz Dept Hydrology And Water Res Tucson AZ 85721-0001 E-mail: buras@hwr.arizona.edu.

BURAS-ELSEN, BRENDA ALLYNN, retired public affairs executive; b. New Orleans, May 1, 1954; d. Allen Anthony and Gloria Violet (Short) B. BA in Commerce, Loyola U., New Orleans, 1976, MBA, 1984. Stenographer Texaco Inc., New Orleans, 1974-76, engr.'s asst., 1976-78, natural gas contracts analyst, 1978-80, pub. affairs asst., 1980-83, pub. and govt. affairs coord. S.E. region, 1983-89; banking officer, mgr. pub. rels. and mktg. promotion Alerion Bank, New Orleans, 1990, asst. v.p., cmty. reinvestment act officer, 1990; pub. affairs advisor Mobil Oil Corp., Chalmette, La., 1990-92; rep. western region Multi-Quest Internat., Inc., 1992. Cert. lectr. Silva Method Mind Devel. and Stress Control. Prodr. Bringing Out the Best Awards Show, 1988. Loaned exec. United Way Greater New Orleans, 1978, mem. speakers bur., 1979-83, vol. leadership devel. program, 1987; voting commr. St. Bernard Parish, 1976-80; chmn. subcom. United Way Corp. Recognition/Thank-You, 1988-89; vice chair yr.-round comm. com. United Way, 1989-90, external comm. com., 1990; mem. ctrl. svc. budget com., 1990; host media com. Rep. Conv., 1988; chair pub. rels. com., mem. grants and membership coms., bd. dirs. New Orleans Food Bank for Emergencies, 1989, bd. dirs., vice chair comm. com., mem. edn. svcs. com.; bd. dirs. Met. Area Com., 1991, Jefferson Performing Arts Soc., 1992, Friend of 4-H, St. Bernard Parish, 1992; mem. St. Bernard adv. coun. United Way Greater New Orleans, 1991-92, prodr. Saints Pre-game show, 1991; mem. adv. coun. Family Svc., 1991-92. Named Outstanding Comm. Com. Vol., United Way, 1988. Mem. Assistance League. Republican. E-mail: nolalac@ez2.net.

BURATOVICH, MICHAEL ANTHONY, geneticist; b. Fresno, Calif., Apr. 18, 1961; s. Mike Thomas and Lucy Ann (Jurica) Buratovich; m. Carolyn Elizabeth Oskam, June 25, 1994; children: Rachel Ann, Anastasia Jenny, Emily Elizabeth. BS, U. Calif., Davis, 1984, MA, 1986; PhD, U. Calif., Irvine, 1994. Lectr. Golden West Coll., Huntington Beach, Calif., 1992-94; postdoctoral fellow Sussex U., Falmer, Eng., 1994-97, U. Pa., 1997-99; asst. prof. biochemistry Spring Arbor (Mich.) Coll., 1999—. Lectr. Student Spkrs. Assn., Irvine, 1988-94. Contbr. articles to profl. jours. Mem. AAAS, Genetics Soc. of Am., Nat. Ctr. for Sci. Edn. Republican. Baptist. Avocations: preaching, historical research, walking, philosophy and history of science, singing. Office: Spring Arbor U Dept Biochemistry 106 E Main St Spring Arbor MI 49283 E-mail: michaelb@arbor.edu.

BURATTI, DENNIS P. lawyer; b. Madison, Wis., 1949; JD, U. Wis., 1973. Bar: Wis. 1973, Minn. 1973. Gen. counsel Ryan Cos., Mpls. Office: Ryan Companies Ste 300 50 S 10th St Minneapolis MN 55403

BURAU, KEITH DEAN, science educator, researcher; m. Monika R. Burau, 1975; children: Heidi M., Keith M. BA in Biometry/Health, S.W. State U., 1973; MS in Biometry/Health Info. Systems, U. Minn., 1975, PhD in Biometry/Health Info. Systems, 1980. Analyst/programmer dept. phys. medicine and rehab. Spinal Cord Injury Ctr. U. Minn., Mpls., 1978—79, applications programmer Health Sci. Computer Svc. Ctr., 1979—80; programmer analyst II U. Tex., Sch. Pub. Health, Houston, 1980—83, asst. prof. biometry, 1983—2002, assoc. prof. biometry, 2002—. Office: Univ Tex Sch Pub Health PO Box 20186 Houston TX 77225-0186

BURBANK, DANIEL C. astronaut; b. Manchester, Conn., July 27, 1961; s. Dan and Joan Burbank; married; 2 children. BSEE, USCG Acad., 1985; MSc in Aero. Sci., Embry-Riddle Aero. U., 1990. Commd. 2d lt. USCG, 1985, advanced through grades to comdr., various assignments, 1985—88; assigned to Coast Guard Air Sta., Elizabeth City, NC, 1988—92, Cape Cod, Mass., 1992—95, Sitka, Alaska, 1995—96; astronaut NASA, Houston, 1996—. Astronaut Space Shuttle Atlantis, 2000. Decorated Defense Superior Svc. meda USCG, Nat. Def. Svc. medal, Humanitarian Svc. medal; recipient Achievement award, Tex. Soc. Daughters of Am. Revolution, 1988. Mem.: Nat. Space Soc., USCG Acad. Alumni Assn., USCG Pterodactyls, Order of Daedalians (Orville Wright Achievement award 1988). Avocations: running, skiing, hiking, sailing, amateur astronomy. Office: Astronaut office CB NASA Johnson Space Ctr Houston TX 77058

BURBANK, JANE RICHARDSON, language educator; b. Hartford, Conn., June 11, 1946; d. John and Helen Lee (West) B.; m. Frederick Cooper, Sept. 3, 1985. BA, Reed Coll., 1967; MLS, Simmons Coll., 1969; MA, Harvard U., 1971, PhD, 1981. Asst. prof. Harvard U., Cambridge, Mass., 1981-85, U. Calif., Santa Barbara, 1985-86, assoc. prof., 1986-87, U. Mich., Ann Arbor, 1987-95, prof., 1995—2002, NYU, 2002—. Reviewer Kritika, 1983, Russian Rev., 1984, 98, Am. Hist. Rev., 1988, 91, 96, Jour. Modern History, 1989, 92, 94, Slavic Rev., 1990, Harvard Ukrainian Studies, 1991; presenter in field; dir. ctr. Russian E. European studies U. Mich., 1992-95, 98. Author: Intelligentsia and Revolution: Russian Views of Bolshevism, 1917-1922, 1986; editor: Perestroika and Soviet Culture, 1989, Imperial Russia, New Histories for the Empire, 1998; editor Kritika, 1978-80; mem. editl. bd. Ind.-Mich. Series in Russian and East European Studies, Kritika, 1999—; contbr. articles to profl. jours. Fulbright-Hayes Rsch. award, 1991, Krupp Found. fellow, Ctr. for European Studies, Harvard U., 1977-78, Whiting fellow, 1980-81, Am. Coun. Learned Socs. fellow, 1983-84, Hoover Inst. Postdoctoral fellow, 1990-91; grantee NEH, 1984, 97, Harvard U., 1982-84, Internat. Rsch. and Exchs. Bd., Acad. Exch. with the USSR, 1987-88, 91, U. Mich., 1990, 91, 93, 94, 97; fellow Ctr. for Advanced Study in the Behavioral Scis., 2002-03. Mem. Am. Hist. Assn., Am. Assn. for the Advancement of Slavic Studies, Social Sci. Rsch. Coun. (joint com. on Soviet studies 1988-93), Nat. Coun. for Eurasia and East European Rsch., Phi Beta Kappa. Office: NYU 53 Washington Sq South New York NY 10012 E-mail: jane.burbank@nyu.edu.

BURBANK, JOHN THORN, cleaning industry executive; b. St. Paul, Sept. 18, 1939; s. Richard Hart and Rae (Parkins) B.; divorced; children: Jennifer, Leslie, Betsy. Student, U. Minn., 1957-62. V.p. Burbank Burns, Mpls., 1963-65, Twin City Index, Mpls., 1965-68, Pentagon Corp., Mpls., 1968-72, AS Industries, Mpls., 1972-78; pres. Minn. Graphics, Mpls., 1978-84; v.p. Graphics Unltd., Mpls., 1984-87, Perfection Graphics, Mpls., 1987-90; pres. Burbank Svcs., Inc., Edina, Minn., 1990—. Mem. adv. bd. Dakota County Votech, Rosemount, Minn., 1982-91. Nation officer YMCA Indian Princess, Bloomington, Minn., 1975; pres. PTA, Bloomington, 1970; coach Traveling Youth Hockey, Bloomington, 1970-84. With USNR, 1961-63. Mem. Internat. Typesetting Assn. (regional pres. 1976-77, program chmn. 1975, 76). Episcopalian. Avocations: tennis, walking, reading, computers, music. Home and Office: 5101 W 70th St Apt 316 Edina MN 55439 E-mail: johnyba555@aol.com.

BURBANK, NELSON STONE, investment banker; b. Winchester, Mass., Sept. 16, 1920; s. Willis H. and Vivian (Casson) B.; m. Rita B. Healey, Feb. 12, 1950; children: Peter N., Nelson Stone, Jane Vivian. Student, Boston U., 1946-47. Registered rep. Vance, Sanders & Co., Inc., Boston, 1946-53; pres. Burbank & Co., Inc., Boston, 1953-83; dir., registered rep. A.G. Edwards and Sons, Inc., 1982-83; pres., bd. dirs. Colonial Investment Services, Inc., 1983-85. Bd. dirs. MassBank for Savs., Reading, ret., 1994; bd. govs. Boston Stock Exch., 1965-73, vice chmn., 1968-71, chmn., 1971-73; bd. dirs. Ag Edwards & Sons, Inc. Vice chmn. ARC, 1963-82; chmn. bd. dirs., sponsor Burbank YMCA, Reading, 2001-02; sponsor Burbank Ice Arena, Reading. With AUS, 1942-45. Decorated D.F.C., Air medals. Mem. Nat. Assn. Securities Dealers (mem. bus. conduct com. 1971-73, gov. 1974-77, cons 1985-88) Home and Office: 24 Juniper Cir Reading MA 01867-1836

BURBANK, ROBINSON DERRY, crystallographer; b. Berlin, N.H., Oct. 3, 1921; s. Paul William and Hazel Louise (Robinson) B.; m. Jeannette Murielle Bisson, July 14, 1945 (div. 1975); children: Paul Robinson, Claudia Olive. BA, Colby Coll., 1942; PhD, MIT, 1950. Rsch. asst. Manhattan Project, MIT, Cambridge, 1942-45, Lab. Insulation Rsch., MIT, 1945-50; sr. physicist Gaseous Diffusion Plant, Oak Ridge, Tenn., 1950-53; group leader, crystallography Olin Industries, New Haven, Conn., 1953-55; tech. staff Bell Telephone Labs., Murray Hill, N.J., 1955-86. U.S. del. Internat. Union Crystallography, Stony Brook, L.I., N.Y., 1969, Amsterdam, 1975; mem. U.S.A. Nat. Com. Crystallography, 1968-76. Contbr. technical papers to profl. jours. Bd. dirs. Chester Twp. Taxpayers Assn., N.J., 1961-65, 70-74, pres. 1973. Mem. Am. Crystallographic Assn. (charter mem., treas. 1965-68, v.p. 1974, pres. 1975), Com. Sci. Soc. Presidents, Phi Beta Kappa, Sigma Xi. Achievements include X-ray crystallography of inorganic compounds, interhalogen compounds, noble gas compounds, phase transformations, thin films. Home: 45 Woodland Ave Summit NJ 07901-2141

BURBANK, STEPHEN BRADNER, law educator; b. NYC, Jan. 8, 1947; s. John Howard and Jean (Gedney) B.; m. Ellen Randolph Coolidge, June 13, 1970; 1 child, Peter Jefferson. AB, Harvard U., 1968, JD, 1973. Bar: Mass. 1973, Pa. 1976, U.S. Supreme Ct. 1977. Law clk. Supreme Jud. Ct. of Mass., Boston, 1973-74, Chief Justice Warren Burger, Washington, 1974-75; gen. counsel U. Pa., Phila., 1975-80, asst. prof. law, 1979-83, assoc. prof. law, 1983-86, prof. law, 1986—, Fuller prof. law, 1991-95; Berger prof. law, 1995—. Reporter 3rd Cir. Jud. Discipline Rules, Phila., 1981-82, 84, 3rd Cir. Task Force on Rule 11, Phila., 1987-89; mem. Nat. Commn. on Jud. Discipline and Removal, 1991-93; mediator, arbitrator Ctr. for Pub. Resources, NY, 1986—; cons. Dechert, Price & Rhoads, Phila., 1986—; mem. CPR Arbitration Commn., 1997-2000; spl. master NFL, 2002—. Mem. Com. to Visit Harvard and Radcliffe Coll., Cambridge, Mass., 1979-85; mem. adv. bd. Inst. Contemporary Art, Phila., 1982-99; charter trustee Phillips Acad., Andover, Mass., 1980-97. Mem. Am. Law Inst. (life, adviser transnational rules of civil procedure 1997—, adviser internat. jurisdiction and judgments 1999—), Am. Arbitration Assn. (mem. panel of arbitrators 1985—), Century Assn., Am. Jud. Soc. (mem. exec. com. 1997-2002, v.p. 1997-99), Phi Beta Kappa. Avocations: swimming, travel, tennis. Office: U Pa Sch Law 3400 Chestnut St Philadelphia PA 19104-6204 E-mail: sburbank@law.upenn.edu.

BURBELO, PETER DENIS, molecular cell biologist; s. Gregory Miroslav and Elsa Burbelo; m. Helen Lynsey Thompson, Aug. 9, 1995; children: Hugo Julian, Alexander Gergory. PhD, U.of RI, 1980—86. Post-doctoral fellow/staff fellow Nat. Inst. of Dental Rsch., NIH, Bethesda, Md., 1986—94; rsch. fellow MRC, U. Coll. London, London, 1994—96; rsch. asst. prof. Dept of Biochemistry, Georgetown U. Med. Ctr., 1996—98; asst. prof. of oncology Lombardi Cancer Ctr., Georgetown U. Med. Ctr., 1998—. Rsch. grants, Nat. Inst. of Health, Dept. of Def. Breast Cancer Program, 1998—2002. Achievements include research in understanding the molecular details of signal transduction pathways that regulate cytoskeletal organization and cell motility. Office: Georgetown U Med Ctr 3970 Reservoir Rd NW Rm W210 NRB Washington DC 20057 E-mail: burbelpd@georgetown.edu.

BURBICK, JOAN, English educator; b. Chgo., June 20, 1946; d. Michael and Eileen Burbick; 1 child, Claire Burbick Huntsberry. BA, Boston Coll., 1968; MA, Brandeis U., 1969, PhD, 1974; MA, Wesleyan U., Middletown, Conn., 1976. Asst. prof. Wash. State U., Pullman, 1978-83, assoc. prof., 1983-88, prof. English, 1988—, Edward R. Meyer prof., 1996-99, Lewis Buchanan prof., 1999—2002. Vis. prof. U. Colo., Boulder, 1988-89. Author: Thoreau's Alternative History, 1987, Healing the Republic, 1994, Rodeo Queens and the American Dream, 2002; adv. bd. Legacy jour., 1985—; mem. editl. bd. ESQ jour., 1978—; contbr. articles to profl. jours. (Foerster award Am. Lit. 1986). Andrew Mellon fellow Ctr. for Humanities, Wesleyan U., 1976-77, Martha Sutton Weeks fellow Stanford U. Humanities Ctr., 1987-88; recipient Norman Foerster award MLA/Am. Lit. assn., 1986. Mem. Pacific N.W. Am. Studies Assn. (v.p., pres. 1980's). Avocation: photography. Office: Wash State U English Dept Pullman WA 99164-5020 E-mail: burbick@wsu.edu.

BURBIDGE, E. MARGARET, astronomer, educator; b. Davenport, Eng. d. Stanley John and Marjorie (Stott) Peachey; m. Geoffrey Burbidge, Apr. 2, 1948; 1 child, Sarah. BS, PhD, U. London; Sc.D. hon., Smith Coll., 1963, U. Sussex, 1970, U. Bristol, 1972, U. Leicester, 1972, City U., 1973, U. Mich., 1978, U. Mass., 1978, Williams Coll., 1979, SUNY, Stony Brook, 1985, Rensselaer Poly. Inst., 1986, U. Notre Dame, 1986, U. Chgo., 1991. Mem. staff U. London Obs., 1948-51; rsch. fellow Yerkes Obs. U. Chgo., 1951-53, Shirley Farr fellow Yerkes obs., 1957-59, assoc. prof. Yerkes Obs., 1959-62, rsch. fellow Calif. Inst. Tech., Pasadena, 1955-57; mem. Enrico Fermi Inst. for Nuclear Studies, 1957-62; prof. astronomy dept. physics U. Calif. San Diego, 1964—89; dir. Royal Greenwich Obs. (Herstmonceux Castle), Hailsham, Eng., 1971-73; univ. prof. U. Calif., San Diego, 1984-91, prof. emeritus, 1991—, rsch. prof. dept. physics, 1990—. Lindsay Meml. lectr. Goddard Space Flight Ctr., NASA; Abby Rockefeller Mauze prof. MIT, 1968; David Elder lectr. U. Strathclyde, 1972; V. Gildersleeve lectr. Barnard Coll., 1974; Jansky lectr. Nat. Radio Astronomy Observatory, 1977; Brode lectr. Whitman Coll., 1986; Hitchcock lectr. U. Calif., Berkeley, 2001. Author (with G. Burbidge): Quasi-Stellar Objects, 1967; editor: Observatory mag., 1948—51; mem. editl. bd.: Astronomy and Astrophysics, 1969—85. Co-recipient Warner prize in Astronomy, 1959; recipient Bruce Gold medal, Astronomy Soc. Pacific, 1982, U.S. Nat. medal of Sci., 1984, Sesquicentennial medal, Mt. Holyoke Coll., 1987, Einstein medal, World Cultural Coun., 1988; fellow hon. fellow, Univ. Coll., London, Girton Coll., Lucy Cavendish Coll., Cambridge. Fellow: Royal Astron. Soc., Am. Acad. Arts and Scis., Nat. Acad. Scis. (chmn. sect.12 astronomy 1986), Royal Soc.; mem.: Internat. Astron. Union (pres. commn. 28 1970—73), Am. Astron. Soc. (v.p. 1972—74, pres. 1976—78, Henry Norris Russell lectr. 1984), Grad. Women Sci. (hon.). Office: U Calif-San Diego Ctr Astrophysics Space Scis Mail Code # 0424 La Jolla CA 92093 E-mail: mburbidge@ucsd.edu.

BURBRIDGE, ANN ARNOLD, music educator, choir director; b. Galesburg, Ill., Sept. 13, 1947; d. Adis Michael and Janet Louise (Frymire) Arnold; m. Robert Arthur Burbridge, June 27, 1970; children: Britt, Michael, Mark. BMEd, Augustana Coll., 1969; MMEd, Tex. Tech. U., 1987, postgrad.; Kodaly cert. levels 1, 2 and 3, Silver Lake Coll., 1990; advanced Kodaly cert., U. North Tex., 1993; postgrad., Tex. Tech U.; Choral Music Experience level I cert., London; Choral Music Experience level II cert., No. Ill. U., 1995, Choral Music Experience level III cert., 1996, Choral Music Experience level IV cert., 1997, Choral Music Experience artist-tchr., 1998. Tchr. Washington Jr. High Sch., Chicago Heights, Ill., 1969-70, Magnolia Sch., Valdosta, Ga., 1970-71; music tchr. Mountain Home AFB (Idaho) Presch. and Kindergarten, 1971-82, Christ the King Cathedral Sch., Lubbock, Tex., 1982-84; tchr. music Nat Williams Elem. Sch. Lubbock Ind. Sch. Dist., 1985-99; music instr. Lubbock Christian U., 1997-99; dir. choir Madison H.S., San Antonio, 1999—2001, Brackenridge H.S., San Antonio, 2001—02; fine arts adminstr. for elem. music and secondary choral San Antonio Ind. Sch. Dist., 2002—. Mem. campus performance objectives com., author curriculum materials for elem. music; dist. mentor; scorer Tex. Master Tchr. Exam; validator Nat. Bd. Profl. Tchg. Stds., 2002; fine arts team writer Tex. Edn. Agy.; fine arts team writer Tex. Essential Knowledge and Skills: Web Resources and Tex. Curriculum Tex. Edn. Network; founder, past artistic dir. Lubbock Children's Choir; clinician, presenter in field; author, cons. Glencoe McGraw Hill Pub. Co., Macmillan Publ. Co.; mem. team writing guidelines and models of integrated arts and interdisciplinary studies Nat. Consortium Arts. Author: Fundamentals of Music, 1987; author, cons. Silver Burdett Ginn Publ. Co. Bd. mem. Llano Estacado Friends of Piano Found.; mem. Nat. Integrated Arts and Interdisciplinary Studies com. Nat. Consortium of Arts; clinician, cons. TEA Fine Arts Cadre, 2002—. Recipient Disting. Svc. award Lubbock Jaycees, Innovative Teaching Strategy award, LISD. Mem. Am. Choral Dirs. Assn., Orgn. Am. Kodaly Educators, Music Educators Nat. Conf. (nat. registered and cert.), Kodaly Educators Tex., Tex. Music Educators Assn. (state chair elem. music 1995-97, past region XVI chair), Tex. Classroom Tchrs. Assn. (rep.), Lubbock Elem. Music Tchrs. Assn. (treas.), Tex. Music Educators Conf. (state pres. 2000-02), Tex. Coalition Music Advocacy (past state pres.), Phi Delta Kappa (past v.p. programs and del. Llano Estacado chpt.). E-mail: Ann@SATX.RR.com., aburbridge@SAISD.net.

BURCAT, JOEL ROBIN, lawyer; b. Phila., Oct. 28, 1954; s. David Sidney and Jessie (Goldberg) B.; m. Gail Rene Hartman, May 30, 1982; children: Dina Michelle, Shira Elizabeth. Student, Temple U., 1972-73; BS, Pa. State U., 1976; JD, Vt. Law Sch., 1980. Bar: Pa. 1980, U.S. Dist. Ct. (mid. dist.) Pa. 1980, U.S. Dist. Ct. (we. dist.) Pa. 1988, U.S. Dist. Ct. (ea. dist.) Pa. 1993, U.S. Ct. Appeals (3d cir.) 1981, U.S. Ct. Appeals (fed. cir.) 2001, U.S. Supreme Ct. 1984, U.S. Ct. Fed. Claims 2001. Asst. atty. gen. Pa. Dept. Environ. Resources, Harrisburg, 1980—83; assoc. Rhoads & Sinon, Harrisburg, 1983—88, Kirkpatrick & Lockhart, Harrisburg, 1988—91, ptnr., 1992—2002, Saul Ewing LLP, Harrisburg, 2002—, vice chair environ. dept., 2003—. Spl. counsel Pa. Senate Com. on Environ. Resources and Energy, Harrisburg, 1986—87; gen. counsel Nat. Wilderness Inst., Washington, 1991—93; mem. rules com. Pa. Environ. Hearing Bd., 1984—88. Author, editor: Pennsylvania Environmental Law and Practice, 1994, 2002. Trustee United Jewish Cmty., Harrisburg, 1991—94, v.p., 1996—97, Yeshiva Acad., Harrisburg, 1986, pres., 1996—97; dir. Friends of State of Pa. Mus., 1999—2002. Recipient Best Publ. award Assn. Continuing Legal Edn., 1999. Mem. ABA (standing com. environ. law 1979-80, law student liaison), Pa. Bar Assn. (sec. environ. mineral and natural resource law sect. 1990-91, vice-chmn. 1991-92, chmn. 1992-93, ethics com. 1984-97, chmn. pro bono com. 1999—, Spl. Achievement award 1993, cert. of recognition 1994). Republican. Jewish. Avocations: guitar playing, classical music, jogging, hiking, gardening. Office: Saul Ewing LLP Two N Second St 7th Flr Harrisburg PA 17101 E-mail: jburcat@saul.com.

BURCH, ANNETTA JANE, writer; b. Valdosta, Ga., Feb. 10, 1947; d. James Louie and Ethel Lucille (Padgett) B. Student, N. Fla. Jr. Coll., Madison, Cen. Fla. C.C., Lecanto. Activity dir. Concordia Manor, Inc., St. Petersburg, Fla., 1983-84; rsch. clk. St. Petersburg Times, 1987; columnist Tampa Tribune, Citrus County, Fla., 1994-96; activity dir. Sugarmill Manor, Inc., Homosassa, Fla., 1990-92; dir. resident svcs. Barrington Place, Lecanto, Fla., 1992-94; office mgr. Boys and Girls Club, Crystal River, Fla., 1995-96; dir. pub. rels. Nature Coast Tourism Devel., Inc., Crystal River, 1999—2001. Former mem. Citrus County Code Enforcment Bd., vice chmn., 1998, chmn., 1999; corr. The Newscaster. Published in Fla. Living Mag., 1999, 00. Former amb. Citrus County C. of C.; former bd. dirs. Homosassa Springs Area C of C.; former

officer Friends of Beverly Hills Libr., 1994; former mem. com. Ctrl. Fla. Symphony, 1994; vol. writer for various clubs and orgns. for local newspapers, correspondent, The Newscaster weekly newspaper; sec. Nature Coast Rep. Club, 1996, pres. 1997, 99; chmn. Citrus County Ad Hoc Fla. WWII Meml. Com.; mem. Citrus County Federated Rep. Women; mem. Rep. Nat. Com., Fla. State Rep. Party; numerous other activities. Recipient Disting. Svc. award Fla. Rep. Party, 1998. Mem.: Fla. State Assn. Pen Women (historian), Nature Coast Br. Nat. Orgn. Am. Pen Women (pres.), Citrus County Rep. Women, Old Courthouse Restoration Hist. Soc., Humane Soc. Citrus County (life). Avocations: travel, writing, reading. Home: PO Box 1095 Homosassa Springs FL 34447-1095 E-mail: gritsrus@hotmail.com.

BURCH, DONALD VICTOR, lawyer; b. Niagara Falls, N.Y., Feb. 18, 1944; s. Victor James and Marva (Bogardus) B.; m. Sharron Burch, Aug. 27, 1966; children: Elizabeth Katherine, Craig Donald. BA, Vanderbilt U., 1966; JD, U. Ala., 1969. Bar: Miss. 1970. Assoc. Daniel, Coker, Horton & Bell, Jackson, Miss., 1970-76, ptnr., 1977—, shareholder. Dir. Gulf Coast Law Inst., Gulfport, Miss., 1977-81. Mem. ABA (mem. appellate practice subcom. 1981—), Miss. Bar Assn. (mem. workers compensation com. 1985-87), Hinds County Bar Assn., Def. Research Inst., So. Assn. Workers Compensation Adminstrs. Clubs: Reservoir Area Exchange (Jackson) (pres. 1987-88). Lodges: Optimists. Republican. Episcopalian. Home: 784 Benwick Dr Brandon MS 39047-8112 Office: 4400 Old Canton Rd Jackson MS 39211-5982 E-mail: dburch@danielcoker.com.

BURCH, FRANCIS BOUCHER, JR., lawyer; b. Balt., Feb. 27, 1948; s. Francis Boucher and Mary Patricia (Howe) B.; children: Sara E., Francis B. III, Michael F.; m. Elisabeth J. Harper, Sept. 29, 2002. Student, U. Fribourg, Switzerland, 1968-69; BA, Georgetown U., 1970; JD with honors, U. Md., 1974. Bar: Md. 1974, U.S. Ct. Appeals (4th cir.) 1975, U.S. Supreme Ct. 1994. Assoc. litigation dept. Piper & Marbury LLP, Balt., 1974-81, ptnr. litigation dept., 1981—, chmn. litigation dept., 1991-94, chmn., 1994-99; co-chmn. Piper Rudnick LLP, Balt., 1999—. Contbr. articles to profl. jours. Bd. dirs. Greater Balt. Com., 1996—, vice-chmn., 1998—2001, chmn., 2001—03; mem. Leadership Program, 1990—, bd. dirs., 1993—98, vice-chmn., 1994—96, chmn., 1996—98, chmn. selection com., 1994—95; trustee Calvert Sch., 1989—2000, chmn. com., 1991—2000, chmn., 1991—95, sec., 1991—95; trustee Western Md. Coll., 1996—2001, Johns Hopkins Health Sys. Corp., 1994—96, Johns Hopkins Hosp., 1994—96, Johns Hopkins Medicine, 1996—, Balt. Mus. Art., 1990—96, 1998—2000, mem. exec. com., 1991—96, chmn. ann. giving com., 1991—93, treas., 1992—94, v.p., 1994—96, co-chmn. devel., 1994—96; bd. visitors U. Md. Sch. Law, Balt., 1993—, U. Md., 1995—; campaign cabinet, chmn. emerging markets United Way Ctrl., Md., 1994; chmn. Leadership Giving, 1999. With U.S. Army N.G., 1970—76. Fellow Am. Bar Found., Am. Coll. Trial Lawyers, Md. Bar Found.; mem. ABA, Am. Law Inst., Md. Bar Assn. (Disting. Svc. award litigation sect. 1981), Balt. City Bar Assn. (chmn. jud. appts. com. 1990-91, exec. coun. 1990-91), 4th Cir. Jud. Conf., Rule Day Club, Lawyers' Round Table Balt., Center Club, River Bend Club. Democrat. Roman Catholic. Avocations: skiing, surfing. Office: Piper Rudnick LLP 6225 Smith Ave Baltimore MD 21209-3600

BURCH, FRANCIS FLOYD, clergyman; b. Balt., May 15, 1932; s. Thaddeus Joseph and Francis Fidelis (Greenwell) B. BA, Fordham U., 1956, MA, 1958; PhL, Woodstock Coll., 1957, STL, 1964; postgrad., Tronchinnes, Belgium, 1964-65; Docteur, U. Paris, Sorbonne, 1967. Joined Soc. of Jesus, 1950, ordained priest Roman Catholic Ch., 1963. Tchr. Gonzaga H.S., Washington, 1957-60; asst. prof. English St. Joseph's U., Phila., 1967-71, assoc. prof., 1971-76, prof., 1976—, asst. acad. dean, 1972-74, bd. dirs., 1971-76, sec. bd. dirs., 1971-75. Artist-scholar-in-residence Millersville U., Pa., 1978. Author: Tristan Corbiere: l'originalite des "Amours jaunes" et leur influence sur T.S. Eliot, 1970; editor: (with P.O. Walzer) Tristan Corbiere: Oeuvres completes, 1970, Sur Tristan Corbiere: lettres inedites adressees au poete et premieres critiques le concernant, 1975; translator: The Path to Transcendence: From Philosophy to Mysticism in Saint Augustine (Paul Henry), 1981, 2d edit., 2000, The Personalist Challenge: Intersubjectivity and Ontology (Maurice Nedoncelle), 1984; contbr. articles to profl. jours. Recipient Merit award St. Joseph's U., 1980, 83. Mem. MLA, Internat. Soc. Neoplatonic Studies, Alpha Epsilon Delta, Alpha Sigma Nu. Home and Office: 5600 City Ave Philadelphia PA 19131-1308 E-mail: fburch@sju.edu.

BURCH, G. DAVID, sculptor; b. Charlottesville, Va., Oct. 31, 1925; s. Paul Randolph Burch and Doris Katherine Fisher; m. Mary Alma Crawford, Mar. 29, 1947 (div. Sept. 1976); children: Tina Marie, David Randolph, Anthony Bayard. Grad., Radford H.S., 1943. With Thiokol Corp.; now ret. Instr. photography Cecil C.C., North East, Md., 1974-84; guest lectr. Cecil County Arts Coun.; artist-in-residence Prince George's C.C. One-person shows at Cecil County Arts Coun., Elkton, Md., 1990, Arnold & Porter, Washington, 1992, Art Gallery, Essex (Md.) C.C., 1993, Cecil County C.C., 1993, Md. Fedn. Art, Annapolis, 1995, Sullivan County Mus. Art, Hurleyville, N.Y., 1997, INSA Gallery, Seoul, Korea, 1997, Gallery B.A.I., N.Y.C., 1997, 98; exhibited in group shows at Haltzman Gallery, Towson (Md.) State U., 1991, 92, Md. Fedn. Art, Annapolis, 1991, Washington Sq., 1992, Greensboro (N.C.) Artist League Gallery, 1992, CAA Galleries, Chautauqua (N.Y.) Instn., 1992, Artshowcase Gallery, Balt., 1992, Dundalk (Md.) C.C., 1992, Internat. Sculpture Ctr., Washington, 1993, Fairfax County Coun. of Arts, Annandale, Va., 1993, Isospin Two South, Balt., 1993, Art Gallery, Essex C.C., Md., 1992, 94, Ward-Nasse, N.Y.C., 1992-94, 2000, Epilepsy Soc. N.Y., N.Y.C., 1994, AAAS, Washington, 1993, 95, Am. Ctr. Physics, College Park, Md., 1994, 95, Marlboro Gallery, Prince George's County C.C., Largo, Md., 1992, 93, 96, Perry House Galleries, Alexandria, Va., 1993, 96, Columbia (Md.) Art Ctr., 1996, 2000, Mill River Art Ctr. Gallery, Ellicott City, Md., 1996, 2000, Liriodendron Mansion, Bel Air, Md., 1995, 97, Pa. State U., Media, 1994, 96, 97, Gallery Art Club 21, Seoul, 1995, Lancashire U., Preston, Eng., 1995, St. Helens (Eng.) Coll. Art and Design, 1996, Gallery B.A.I., Barcelona, Spain, 1996, Pratt Libr., Falls Point, Balt., 1996, Sharjah (United Arab Emirates) Internat. Art Biennial, 1997, Forum Artis Mus., Modena, Italy, 1997, Cecil County Arts Coun., Elkton, Md., 1998, Md. Ho. Dels., Annapolis, 1997-2001, Acad. of Arts, Easton, Md., 1998, Cecil C.C., Md., 1999, West Md. Coll., Westminster, 1999, Towson (Md.) U., 1999, Grounds for Sculpture, Hamilton, N.J., 2000, Hood Coll. Fredrick, Md., 2001, Md. Fedn. Art Balt. Gallery, 2001, Creative Alliance, Balt., 2001, Del. Ctr. Contemporary Arts, Wilmington, Del., 2001. With USMC, WWII. Recipient Sculpture award Towson State U., 1992, 1st Pl. Sculpture award Epilepsy Soc., 1994, Perry House Galleries, Alexandria, 1996, cert. of merit, Sharjah Biennial mgmt. Com., UAE, 1977, Gov's. Individual Artist Arts nomination award, 2000; decorated Purple Heart, USMC, WWII. Home: 1585 Tome Hwy Port Deposit MD 21904

BURCH, HAMLIN DOUGHTY, III, retired sheet metal professional; b. Oakland, Calif., June 14, 1939; s. Hamlin D. Burch II and Bernice I. (Ingerski) Bortscheller; m. Zettie A. Honeycutt, Nov. 16, 1957 (div. 1974); children: Paula Christine Grothaus, Victoria Jaylee Alberti, Hamlin D. IV. Grad., Modesto (Calif.) High Sch. Sheet metal worker Fred L. Hill., Modesto, 1960-62, Olson's Plumbing, Turlock, 1962-64, Hansen's Inc., Modesto, 1964-74; Lang's Engerprises, Modesto, 1974-87; sheet metal worker Mendenhall, Sacramento, 1987, South Valley Mech., San Juan Baptiste, 1987-88, Brott Mech., Tulare, 1988, ret. Mem.: NRA, Sheet Metal Workers Internat. Assn., Sierra Club. Democrat. Roman Catholic. Avocations: metal working, wood working, gardening.

BURCH, JAMES LEO, science research institute executive; b. San Antonio, Nov. 28, 1942; s. Joseph Leo Jr. and Doris Babette (Hagy) B.; m. Kathleen Marie Dowdy, Dec. 30, 1965; children: Angela Marie, Charles Joseph, Kenneth James. BS in Physics, St. Mary's U., San Antonio, 1964; PhD, Rice U., 1968; MS in Adminstrn., George Washington U., 1973. Space physicist Goddard Space Flight Ctr. NASA, Greenbelt, Md., 1971-74, space physicist Marshall Space Flight Ctr. Huntsville, Ala., 1974-77; sr. rsch. physicist S.W. Rsch. Inst., San Antonio, 1977-78, sect. mgr., 1978-80, dept. dir., 1980-85, v.p., 1985—. Prin. investigator NASA Dynamics Explorer Mission, 1978-92, Nasa Atlas Shuttle Mission, 1989-93, ESA Rosetta Comet orbiter, 1996—, NASA Image Midex mission, 1996—; mem. space sci. and applications adv. com. NASA, 1990-93; mem. NAS Space Studies Bd., 2000—; chair NAS com. Solar and Space Physics, 2000—. Assoc. editor Jour. Geophys. Rsch., 1977-79, 94-96, Geophys. Rsch. Letters, 1978-82, editor, 1989-90, editor-in-chief, 1990-93; contbr. numerous articles to profl. jours. Capt. U.S. Army, 1968-71. Recipient Disting. Alumnus award St. Mary's U., 1987. Fellow Am. Geophys. Union (pres. space physics and aeronomy sect. 1996-98), Internat. Acad. Astronautics. Roman Catholic. Avocation: running. Office: SW Rsch Inst 6220 Culebra Rd San Antonio TX 78238-5100 E-mail: jburch@swri.edu.

BURCH, JOHN CHRISTOPHER, JR., investment banker; b. Nashville, Jan. 18, 1940; s. John Christopher and Frances Vivian (Harris) B.; m. Susan Marie Klein, Sept. 13, 1969; children: Frances Marie, Christina Polk, John Christopher III. BA, Vanderbilt U., 1966. Credit analyst Bank N.Y., N.Y.C., 1966-70; v.p. instl. sales Loeb Rhoades & Co., N.Y.C., 1970-75, J.C. Bradford & Co., Nashville, 1976-82; mng. dir. SunTrust Equitable Securities Corp., Nashville, 1982-2001; pres. Capital Markets Advisors LLC, Nashville, 2001—. Co-author: Capital Markets Handbook, 1999, 4th edit., 2003. With U.S. Army, 1962-65. Mem. Nashville Security Dealers Assn., Assn. Investment Mgmt. and Rsch., Securities Industry Assn., (chmn. syndicate com. 1998-2000, bd. dirs. chair so. dist. 2001), Nat. Assn. Security Dealers (arbitrator), Belle Meade Country Club (Nashville). Episcopalian. Home: 705 Hillwood Blvd Nashville TN 37205-1315 Office: Capital Markets Advisors LLC Ste 228 2200 Twenty First Ave S Nashville TN 37212 Fax: 615-292-6757. E-mail: jburch@capitalmarketsadvisors.com.

BURCH, JOHN RUSSELL, JR., library director; b. Peoria, Ill., Mar. 22, 1968; s. John Russell and Idalia Amparo (Murgas) B.; m. Samantha Jo Bailey, July 1, 1989; children: Morgan Lourrae, Alexandra Christine, Christopher Simpson, Kayleigh Jo. BA in History, Berea (Ky.) Coll., 1990; MS in Libr. Sci., U. Ky., 1992, MA in History, postgrad., U. Ky., 2003—. Grad. asst. U. Ky. Agrl. Libr., Lexington, 1991-92; govt. documents libr. So. Ark. U., Magnolia, 1992-93; reference libr. Cumberland Coll., Williamsburg, Ky., 1993-95, pub. svcs. libr., 1995, tech. svcs. libr., 1995-2000; dir. libr. svcs. Campbellsville (Ky.) U., 2000—. Book reviewer Libr. Jour., Am. Ref. Books Ann., Choice Mag. Mem.: Phi Alpha Theta. Republican. Office: Campbellsville U Montgomery Libr 1 University Dr Campbellsville KY 42718-2799 E-mail: jburch@campbellsvil.edu.

BURCH, JOHN THOMAS, JR., lawyer; b. Balt., Feb. 22, 1942; s. John T and Katheryn Estella (Peregoy) Burch; m. Linda Anne Shearer, Nov. 1, 1969; children: John Thomas, Richard James. BA, U. Richmond, 1964, JD, 1966; LLM, George Washington U., 1971. Bar: Va 1966, US Supreme Ct 1969, DC 1974, Mich 1983, Md 1993. Pvt. practice, Richmond, 1966, Washington, 1974-77; pres. Burch, Kerns and Klimek, 1977-82, Burch & Assocs., Washington, 1982-95, Burch & Bennett, P.C., Washington, 1983-85; ptnr. Alagia, Day, Marshall, Mintmire & Chauvin, Washington, 1985-90, Maloney & Burch, Washington, 1990-96; pres. Burch & Cronauer, P.C., Washington, 1995—2001, Burch & Assocs., Washington, 1982-95; with office of gen. counsel Dept. of Vets Affiars, 2001—. Rep committeeman City of Alexandria, Va., 1975—92; aide-de-camp brigadier gen to gov State of Va, 1976—; alt del Rep Nat Conv, 1988, 1994. Decorated Bronze Star, Meritorious Serv Medal. Mem.: VFW (dep comdr 1986—87), ABA (secy pub contract law sect 1976—77), Va War Meml Found (trustee), Nat Vietnam and Gulf War Vets Coalition (nat chmn 1983—2001), Spec Forces Asn, Fed Bar Asn (nat coun, dep secy 1982—83), Knights of Malta (cheveliar sovereing mil. order St. John Jerusalem), Cheveliar, Sons of Confederate Vets, Am Legion, Va Soc SAR (pres 1975—76, Patriots Medal 1978, Good Citizenship Award 1970), Soc of War 1812, Order St Constantine Magna, Scabbard and Blade, Phi Sigma Alpha, Phi Alpha Delta. Republican. Episcopalian. Home and Office: Burch & Cronauer PC 1015 N Pelham St Alexandria VA 22304

BURCH, JOHN WALTER, mining equipment company executive; b. Balt., July 14, 1925; s. Louis Claude and Constance (Boucher) B. m. Robin Neely Sinkler, Apr. 19, 1952; children: John C., Robert L., Charles C., Anne N. BS in Commerce, U. Va., 1951; postgrad., U.S. Coast Guard Acad., 1951. With Procter & Gamble Co., Phila., 1953-65, sales mgr., 1960-65; v.p. Warner Co., Phila., 1965-73; chmn. bd., CEO S.S. Keely Co., Phila., 1973-75; pres., chmn. bd., CEO Burch Materials Co., Inc., Wayne, Pa., 1975—; ptnr., mgr. Integrated MRO, LLC, 1998—. Dir. Eagle's Eye, Inc., Wayne; bd. dirs. Nat. Multiple Sclerosis Soc., 1970-81, v.p., exec. com., 1974-77; bd. dirs. Pa. Sports Hall of Fame, 1974—, v.p., exec. com., 1974-79; chmn. Am. Legion Tennis Tournaments for State of Pa., 1975-82; mem. U.S. Congl. Adv. Bd., 1982, bd. dirs. Eagle's Eye Lacrosse Club, 1982-87. With USN, 1943-46, USCG, 1951-53. Named All-Am. in lacrosse, 1949, Archdiocese of Phila. gymnasium named in honor of John Burch family, 2003. Mem. Merion Cricket Club, Merion Golf Club, Willoughby Golf Club. Republican. Roman Catholic. Home: 6 Ringneck Ln Wayne PA 19087 Office: Burch Materials Co Inc 685 Kromer Ave Berwyn PA 19312-1317 E-mail: burchmatls@prodigy.net.

BURCH, MARY SEELYE QUINN, law librarian, consultant; b. Worcester, Mass., Oct. 16, 1925; d. James Henry and Mary Seelye (O'Donnell) Quinn; m. Walter Douglas Burch, Aug. 18, 1972; children: Cathi, Andrew, David, John, Joan. BS, Suny, 1976; MLS, Pratt Inst., 1979. Law libr. N.Y. Supreme Ct., Troy, 1969-82; chief law libr. Office Ct. Adminstrn., Albany, N.Y., 1982-86; libr. N.Y. State Libr., 1986-89, ret., 1989; owner Mary S. Burch Law Libr. Svc., 1983—2003. Instr. legal rsch. SUNY, 1981; selected to meet with deans of law schs. in China for improvement of legal reference materials in China. Mem. N.Y. State Bar Assn. (lectr. 1980), Ulster County Bar Assn. (cons. 1980), Am. Assn. Law Librs., Assn. Law Librs. Upstate N.Y. (pres. 1971, v.p. 1981). Roman Catholic. Avocations: pilot, swimming, sewing. Home: 312 Diamond Rock Cir Troy NY 12182

BURCH, MICHAEL IRA, public relations executive, former government official; b. St. Louis, Jan. 20, 1941; s. Horatio and Iona (Anderson) B.; m. Sherilynn J. Hummel, Dec. 26, 1987; children: Paige Anne Engelson, Michelle Hummel. BA, U. Mo., 1963; postgrad., Boston U., 1965, Am. U., 1972-75. Commd. 2d lt. U.S. Air Force, 1963, advanced through grades to lt. col., 1979, served in tactical air command units, 1963-72, served at Pentagon in offices Air Force and Def. secs., 1972-83, ret., 1983; pres. Washington Communications Corp., 1983; asst. sec. for pub. affairs U.S. Dept. Def., Washington, 1983-85; v.p. communications Aerospace group McDonnell Douglas Corp., Washington, 1985-88, v.p. pub. relations St. Louis, 1988-92; sr. v.p. Burson-Marsteller, Washington, 1992-95; pres. Civitas Comm. Group, Alexandria, Va., 1995—, Nature Works, Inc., 1997—. Bd. advisors MIT Enterprise Forum. Recipient Disting. Service medal Dept. Def., 1983, Disting. Pub. Service medal Dept. Def., 1985 Mem. Nat. Aviation Club, Def. Orientation Conf. Assn. (bd. dirs.), Air Commando Assn., Am. Legion. Republican. Episcopalian. Avocation: sailing. Office: Civitas Comm Grp PO Box 639 Burgess VA 22432-0639 E-mail: civitas@his.com.

BURCH, ROBERT DALE, lawyer; b. Washington, Jan. 30, 1928; s. Dallas Stockwell and Hepsy (Berry) B.; m. Joann D. Hansen, Dec. 9, 1966; children: Berkeley, Robert Brett, Barrett Bradley. Student, Va. Mil. Inst., 1945-46; BS, U. Calif. at Berkeley, 1950, JD, 1953. Bar: Calif. bar 1954. Since practiced in, Los Angeles and Beverly Hills; ptnr. Gibson, Dunn & Crutcher, 1961—. Lectr. U. So. Calif. Inst. Fed. Taxation, 1960, 62, 65, 75; guest lectr. U. Calif.-L.A. Law Sch., 1959; lectr. C.E.B. seminars U. Calif.; founder Robert D. Burch Ctr. for Tax Policy and Pub. Fin., U. Calif., Berkeley. Author: Federal Tax Procedures for General Practitioners; Contbr. profl. jours., textbooks. Bd. dirs. charitable funds. With AUS, 1945-47. Mem. Beverly Hills Bar Assn. (bd. govs., chmn. probate and trust com.), Law Trust, Tax and Ins. Council (past czar), Los Angeles World Affairs Council. Home: 1301 Delresto Dr Beverly Hills CA 90210-2100 Office: Gibson Dunn & Crutcher 2029 Century Park E Ste 4000 Los Angeles CA 90067-3032 also: 333 S Grand Ave Los Angeles CA 90071-1504

BURCH, STEPHEN KENNETH, financial services company executive, real estate investor; b. Fairmont, W.Va., Feb. 1, 1945; s. Kenneth Edward and Gloria Lorraine (Wilson) B.; m. Juliana Yuan Yuan, June 17, 1972 (div. Feb. 1985); children: Emily, Adrien. AB in Econs., Washington U., St. Louis, 1969. V.p. TSI Mgmt., Los Angeles, 1970-71; pres. Investors Choice Cattle Co., Los Angeles, 1972-76; v.p. Clayton Brokerage Co., St. Louis, 1976-84; pres. Yuan Med. Lab., St. Louis, 1976-78; v.p. Restaurant Assocs., St. Louis, 1982-83, Am. Capital Equities, St. Louis, 1984-89; pres. Burch Properties, Inc., St. Louis, 1984—; owner Clayton-Hanley, Inc., St. Louis, 1987-88; pres., owner Clayton Securities Services, Inc., St. Louis, 1988—; CEO Huntleigh Securities Corp., 2000—, also bd. dirs. Mng. ptnr. 600 S. Ptnrs., St. Louis, 1976-87, Midvale Ptnrs., St. Louis, 1979—; mng. mem. Del Coronado Investment Co., LLC, 1997—. Bd. dirs. AMC Cancer Rsch. Ctr., 1989-91. Mem. Sigma Phi Epsilon (pres. alumni bd. 1981-87). Avocations: wine, movies. Office: Huntleigh Securities Corp 7800 Forsyth Blvd 5th Fl Saint Louis MO 63105 E-mail: sburch@hntlgh.com.

BURCH, SUSAN ANN, human resource developer, educator; b. DeKalb, Ill., Sept. 18, 1946; d. Leon David and Dorothy Rose (Schade) Larson; m. Thomas Lee Burch, Oct. 10, 1970; children: Lee Thomas, Shannon Joy. BA, No. Ill. U., 1968, MS in Edn., 1982, ABD, 1993. English tchr. Dist. 129, Aurora, Ill., 1968-72; adminstrv. asst. Dean's Grant, Dekalb, 1981-82; instr. psychology, coord. gifted Waubonsee C.C., Sugar Grove, Ill., 1982-97, mgr. children's programs, 1984-97, grant writer, 1989—; program dir. fashion merchandising Internat. Acad. Merchandising and Design, chgo., 1997-98; human resource developer Acxion Corp., Chgo., 1998—. Freelance cons., Sugar Grove, 1986-97, corp. trainer, 1990—; field reader U.S. Dept. Edn., 1993-95. Advisor ednl. Found., Plano, Ill. 1989-90. Mem.: Ill. Assn. for Gifted Children, Am. Soc. Tng. and Devel., Assn. for Applied and Therapeutic Humor, Am. Assn. Adult Continuing Edn., Internat. Soc. Performance Improvement (Chgo. chpt.), Kappa Delta Pi. Avocations: writing, reading, dancing, music, sewing. Home: 3S 515 Marion Cir Sugar Grove IL 60554

BURCH, THADDEUS JOSEPH, JR., physics educator, clergyman; b. Balt., June 4, 1930; s. Thaddeus and Francis Fidelis (Greenwell) B. AB, Bellarmine Coll., 1954; MA, Fordham U., 1956, MS, 1966, PhD, 1968; S.T.B., Woodstock Coll., 1960, S.T.L., 1962. Ordained priest, Roman Catholic Ch., 1961. Joined S.J. Roman Catholic Ch., 1948; asst. prof. St. Joseph's Coll., Phila., 1969-72, Fordham U., N.Y.C., 1972-74; vis. assoc. prof. U. Conn., Storrs, 1974-76; assoc. prof. Marquette U., Milw., 1976-80, prof., 1980—, chmn. dept. physics, 1977-86, acting dean grad. sch., 1985-87, dean grad. sch., 1987—2003. Univ. del. Argonne (Ill.) Univs. Assn., 1977-82 Contbr. articles on physics to profl. jours. Mem. Am. Phys. Soc., Am. Assn. Physics Tchrs., Sigma Xi Home: 230 Jefferson St Leonardtown MD 20650-4800 Office: 1404 W Wisconsin Milwaukee WI 53233

BURCH, THOMAS JOSEPH, state representative; b. Louisville, July 19, 1931; 5 children. AB, Bellermine Coll., 1959. Prodn. control mgr. GE, Appliance Park, Ky., 1952—91; mem. Ky. Ho. of Reps., 1972—74, 1978—; ret. GE, Appliance Park, Ky., 1991. Mem. Ky. Organ Donation Coun., Ky. Welfare Reform Coun., Kosair Children's Hosp. Lions Found. With USN, 1948—52, with USNR, 1952—56. Mem.: NOW, Ky. Domestic Violence Assn. Democrat. Roman Catholic. Office: Capitol Annex Rm 332 E Frankfort KY 40601

BURCH, VORIS REAGAN, retired lawyer, mediator, arbitrator; b. Liberty, Tex., Feb. 10, 1930; s. Voris Reagan and Jessamae (Coffey) B.; m. Claudia Ramsland, Dec. 30, 1978; children: Melissa Burch Lively, Voris Reagan III. BBA, Tex. A&M U., 1952; JD, U. Tex., 1957. Bar: Tex. 1957. Assoc. Baker & Botts, Houston, 1957-69, ptnr., 1969-95, ret., 1995. Served to 1st lt. USAF, 1952-54. Mem. State Bar Tex. (chmn. labor law sect. 1970-71), Houston Bar Assn., Phi Delta Phi. Home and Office: 5761 Indian Cir Houston TX 77057-1302 E-mail: reaganburch@houston.rr.com.

BURCH, WILLIAM MARK, II, retired lawyer; b. Peabody, Mass., Oct. 28, 1917; s. Charles Bell and Jane Montgomery (Bell) B.; m. Irene Ethel Miller, June 5, 1954; children: Barbara, Elizabeth. JD, Detroit Coll. of Law, 1949; LLM, George Washington U., 1967. Bar: Mich. 1949, U.S. Ct. Mil. Appeals 1955, U.S. Supreme Ct. 1955. Commd. 2d. lt. USAF, 1942, advanced through grades to col., 1966; navigator instr. various assignments, 1943-45, staff judge, 1950-72, dir. USAF Judiciary, 1972-77; claims adjustor Mich. Unemployment Commn., Detroit, 1945-49; chmn. pers. coun. Brevard County, Melbourne, Fla., 1972-99; ret., 1999. Bd. dirs. Snug Harbor Homeowners Assn. Mem. ABA, FBA, Mich. Bar Assn. Home: 2 W Point Dr Cocoa Beach FL 32931-5304 E-mail: wburch2@earthlink.net.

BURCHAM, EVA HELEN (PAT BURCHAM), retired electronics technician; b. Bloomfield, Ind., Apr. 11, 1941; d. Paul Harold and Hazel Helen (Buzan) B. Grad., Blackstone Sch. of Law, 1988, Paralegal Inst., Phoenix, 1991; grad. paralegal, So. Career Inst., Boca Raton, Fla., 1991. With Naval Weapons Support Ctr./Crane Div. Naval Surface Warfare, Crane, Ind., 1967-76, 78-80; electronics technician Naval Weapons Support Ctr., Crane, Ind., 1980-97. With U.S. Army, 1976-77, with Res. 1977-81. Named to Am. Women's Hall of Fame. Mem. NAFE (exec. bd. chair), NOW, Am. Soc. Naval Engrs., Soc. Logistics Engrs., Am. Legion, Federally Employed Women, Fed. Women's Program, Profl. Women's Network (pres. 1993, bd. dirs.), Blacks in Govt., Nat. Paralegal Assn. (registered paralegal), Nat. Fedn. Paralegal Assn., Inc., Toastmasters (gov.). Roman Catholic. Home: 200 W Washington St Loogootee IN 47553-2324

BURCHARD, JOHN KENNETH, retired chemical engineer; b. St. Louis, May 12, 1936; s. Kenneth Reginald and Vernora Emma (Angell) B.; m. Elizabeth Lee Suesserott, Aug. 23, 1958; children— John Christopher, Gregory Charles. BS, Carnegie Mellon U., 1957, MS, 1959, PhD, 1962. Head systems analysis group United Tech. Ctr., Sunnyvale, Calif., 1961-68; chief scientist Combustion Power Co., Menlo Park, Calif., 1968-70; lab. dir. EPA, Research Triangle Park, N.C., 1970-80; dir. chem. engring. div. Research Triangle Inst., Research Triangle Park, 1980-83; pres. Search Assocs., Inc., Chapel Hill, N.C., 1983-85; dir. Office of Research Adminstrn. U. Cen. Ark., Conway, 1985-87; asst. dir. Office Research Devel. Ariz. State U., Tempe, 1987-90; mgr. spl. projects Ariz. Dept. Environ. Quality, Phoenix, 1990-98, sr. sci. advisor, 1998-2001. Mem. bd. sci. advisors N.C. Energy Inst. Contbr. articles to profl. jours. Served with AUS, 1963-64. Shell Oil fellow, 1958-59; NSF fellow, 1960-61 Mem. Am. Inst. Chem. Engrs., Soc. Rsch. Adminstrs., Sigma Xi, Tau Beta Pi.

BURCHELL, HOWARD BERTRAM, retired physician, educator; b. Athens, Ont., Can., Nov. 28, 1907; s. James Edward and Edith (Milligan) B.; m. Margaret Helmholz, Aug. 14, 1942; children: Susan Burchell Profeta, Judith Burchell Bush, Cynthia Burchell Patterson, Rebecca Burchell Wilbur. MD, U. Toronto, Can., 1932; PhD., U. Minn., 1939. Intern Toronto Gen. Hosp., 1932-34; rsch. fellow U. Pitts., 1934-36; fellow in medicine Mayo Clinic, Rochester, Minn., 1936-39, cons. in medicine, 1946-68; spl. student London Hosp., 1939-40; prof. medicine U. Minn., Mpls., 1968-85, prof. emeritus, 1985—. Mem. adv. com. USAAF, 1947-40, Nat. Heart Coun., NIH, 1955-60; lectr. U.S., Can., The Netherlands, Israel. Contbr. more than 350 articles to profl. jours. Maj. USAAF, 1941-46. Fellow Am. Coll. Cardiology (master tchr. 1969, 74); mem. Am. Heart Assn. (Herrick award 1972), Assn. Am. Physicians, Am. Physiol. Soc. Mem. Unitarian-Universalist Ch. Avocation: history of medicine. Home: 3701 Bryant Ave S #412 Minneapolis MN 55409 Fax: 612-824-1911.

BURCHENAL, JOAN RILEY, science educator; b. N.Y.C., Dec. 11, 1925; d. Wells Littlefield and Bertha Barclay (Fahys) Riley; m. Joseph Holland Burchenal, Mar. 20, 1948; children: Elizabeth Payne Burchenal Paul (dec.), Joan Littlefield Burchenal Nycum, Barbara Fahys Burchenal Landers, Caleb Wells, David Holland, Joseph Emory Barclay; 1 stepchild, Mary Holland Burchenal Nottebohm. BA, Vassar Coll., 1946; MAT, Yale U., 1971; MA, Fairfield U., 1981. Sci. tchr. New Canaan (Conn.) Country Sch., 1968-69, Low Heywood Sch., Stamford, Conn., 1968-69, The Thomas Sch., Rowayton, Conn., 1972-73, Darien Bd. Edn., Conn., 1973-91, ret. Mem. panel on grants for tchrs. enhancement program NSF, 1987, 92; K-12 sci. curriculum com., 1994-2000. Hon. chmn. Darien Sci. Fair, 1986; mem. steering com. Holly Pond Saltmarsh Conservation Com., 1968—71; mem. acad. courses com. Darien Cmty. Assn., 1964—71, chmn., 1971; trustee Garrison Forest Sch., 1959—62; rep. Town Meeting of Darien, 1993—, mem. edn. com., 1993—, chair edn. com., 1995—97, rules com., 2000—; cmty. rep. K-12 Sci. Curriculum Com., 1994—2000; elder First Presbyn. Ch. of New Canaan, 1994—97, Stephen min., 1994—; bd. dir., chmn. standards com. A Better Chance, Darien, Conn., 1985—99; bd. dir. Darien Nature Ctr., 1975—91, Darien Audubon Soc., 1978—86, Darien LWV, 1951—62, Alumnae and Alumni Vassar Coll. Recipient Presdl. award for excellence in sci. teaching Nat. Sci. Tchrs. Assn., NSF, Washington, 1985. Mem. AAAS, N.Y. Acad. Sci., Nat. Assn. Biology Tchrs., Nat. Sci. Tchrs. Assn., Assn. Presdl. Awardees in Sci. Teaching (nominating

com. 1987-90), Cosmopolitan Club, Ausable Club, Noroton Yacht Club, Phi Beta Kappa. Republican. Presbyterian. Avocations: reading, travel, trekking, birding. Home: 18 Juniper Rd Darien CT 06820-5707 E-mail: jhbjrb@aol.com.

BURCHETT, MICHAEL HENRY, education educator; b. Knoxville, Tenn., July 11, 1965; s. Jean Sizemore Burchett; m. Jennifer Dawn James, June 24, 1994. BA, U. of Va., 1991; MA, Clemson U., S.C., 1994. Adj. prof. history Limestone Coll., Gaffney, SC, 1996—; pres. Terraplane Pubs., Greenville, SC, 1996—. Author: (monograph) The Health of A New South, 1996; contbr. ; editor: (web site) The New Terraplane. Rsch. Grant, State of S.C., 1993—94, C. Bascom Slemp Scholar, U. of Va., 1990—91. Mem.: Orgn. of Am. Historians, So. Hist. Assn.

BURCHFIEL, BURRELL CLARK, geology educator; b. Stockton, Calif., Mar. 21, 1934; s. Beryl Edward and Agnes (Clark) B.; children: Brian Edward, Brook Evans, Banjamin Clark, Halsey Royden. BS, Stanford U., 1957, MS, 1958; PhD, Yale U., 1961. Prof. geology Rice U., 1961-76, MIT, 1977-84, Schlumberger prof. geology, 1984—. Served with U.S. Army, 1958-59. Fellow Geol. Soc. Am., Am. Acad. Arts and Scis., Nat. Acad. Scis., Am. Geophys. Union, European Union Geoscis. (hon. fgn.); mem. Geol. Soc. Australia, Am. Assn. Petroleum Geologists, Chinese Acad. Scis. (fgn.). Home: 9 Robinson Park Winchester MA 01890-3717 Office: MIT 77 Massachusetts Ave # 54-1010 Cambridge MA 02139-4307 E-mail: bchurch@mit.edu.

BURCHFIELD, BOBBY ROY, lawyer; b. Middlesboro, Ky., Oct. 23, 1954; s. Roy and Anna Lee (McCreary) B.; m. Teresa J. Miller, Apr. 6, 1996; 1 child, Taylor Nicole. BA, Wake Forest U., 1976; JD, George Washington U., 1979. Bar: D.C. 1980, U.S. Ct. Appeals (3rd cir.) 1981, U.S. Dist. Ct. D.C. 1982, U.S. Dist. Ct. Md. 1982, U.S. Ct. Appeals (D.C. cir.) 1982, U.S. Ct. Appeals (9th cir.) 1985, U.S. Supreme Ct. 1986, U.S. Ct. Appeals (5th cir.) 1989, U.S. Ct. Appeals (6th cir.) 1993. Law clk. to Judge Ruggero J. Aldisert U.S. Ct. Appeals (3rd cir.), Pitts., 1979-81; assoc. Covington & Burling, Washington, 1981-87, ptnr., 1987—. Gen. counsel Bush-Quayle '92, 1992. Editor-in-chief George Washington U. Law Rev., 1978-79. Gen. counsel Rep. Nat. Lawyers Assn., 1991—92; nat. chmn. George Washington U. Nat. Law Ctr. Ann. Fund, 1990—91, Wake Forest U. Coll. Fund, 1999—2000; mem. Wake Forest U. Alumni Coun., 1990—93, chmn., 1997—2001; vol. George Bush for Pres., Washington, 1986—88. Mem.: ABA. Republican. Office: Covington & Burling 1201 Pennsylvania Ave NW PO Box 7566 Washington DC 20044-7566 E-mail: BBurchfield@cov.com.

BURCHFIELD, BRUCE ALLEN, entrepreneur; b. Ft. Dodge, Iowa, Apr. 3, 1947; s. Stanley H. and Bertha (Sampson) B.; m. Mary Ellen Porter, Dec. 15, 1971; children: Shawn, Stewart, Jennifer. BS in Engring., Iowa State U., 1970; MBA, Loyola U., Chgo., 1973. Engr. Reynolds Aluminum, Brookfield, Ill., 1970-73; v.p. First Nat. Bank Chgo., 1973-82; pres. CIRRUS System, Inc. subs. Mastercard Internat., 1982-88; exec. v.p. Mastercard Internat., 1988. Mem. Electronic Funds Transfer Assn. (chmn. 1986-87, bd. dirs.), Medinah Country Club, Bonita Bay Club. Republican. Methodist. Avocations: golf, skiing. Home: 320 E Chicago Ave Naperville IL 60540-5406

BURCHILL, WILLIAM ROBERTS, JR., lawyer; b. N.Y.C., Dec. 6, 1947; s. William Roberts and Marion (Eisenhower) B. BA, U. Pa., 1969; JD, George Washington U., 1972. Bar: D.C. 1973, U.S. Dist. Ct. D.C. 1976, U.S. Ct. Appeals (D.C. cir.) 1976, U.S. Supreme Ct. 1978. Atty. magistrates div. Adminstrv. Office U.S. Cts., Washington, 1973-74, atty. office gen. counsel, 1974-76, assoc. gen. counsel, 1976-82, dep. gen. counsel, 1982-85, gen. counsel, 1985-94, assoc. dir., gen. counsel, 1994—. Mem. ABA, Fed. Bar Assn., Penn Club N.Y., Phi Delta Phi. Office: Adminstrv Ofc US Cts 1 Columbus Cir NE Washington DC 20544-0001

BURCHMAN, LEONARD, government official; b. N.Y.C., Jan. 30, 1925; s. Hyman John-Hood and Edith (Speedady-Cohen) B.; m. Marilyn F. Burchman, June 11, 1950; children— Marc Harris, Corey Andrew BA, U. Denver, 1949; MA, Columbia U., 1950. Dir. press affairs N.Y. State Eisenhower presdl. campaign, 1951-52; info. officer-advance sec. labor Dept. Labor, Washington and N.Y.C., 1953-60; pres. Medigard Chem. Corp., N.Y.C., 1961; dir. integovtl. rels. Dept. Labor, Washington, 1971-78; acting asst. sec., gen. dep. asst. sect. pub. affairs HUD, Washington, 1981—. Dir. labor rels. to U.S. Senator Kenneth Keating, N.Y., 1964; pub. affairs cons. to Gov. John Lodge of Conn., 1952; sr. advisor to Coretta Scott King; chmn. Martin Luther King Jr. Fed. Holiday Commn., 1985—, commr., 1989—, treas., 1989-92. Producer Office Mgmt. Budget/NSF film: Strengthening Intergovernmental Relations between Federal and State and Local Governments, 1976. Chmn. bd. Am. Heart Assn., Washington, 1981-83; pres. Found. for Study U.S. Cabinet, 1985-89; pres. J.R.L.W., Leisure World, Md., 1994-96; chmn. FIIND, Found. to Interrupt Illegal Narcotics and Drugs To Children, 1989—; founding pres. VOTE, Voice of the Elderly, 1997—; founder nat. Consumer Watch-Out, to protect sr. citizens against Scams and Frauds, 1988—; mem. Montgomery County (Md.) Commn. on Aging, 1997—, States Attys. Task Force on Elder Abuse. Recipient Disting. Svc. award Sec. HUD. Mem.: DAV (comdr. U.S. Dept. Labor Post), Am. Legion (comdr. U.S. Dept. Labor Post).

BURCH-MARTINEZ, BERKELEY ALISON, primary education educator; b. Santa Monica, Calif., Nov. 20, 1967; d. Robert Dale and Joann Hansen B.; m. Gilbert Jesse Martinez, June 24, 1998; children, Sterling Alexander, Carsen Aren. BA, U. Calif., Irvine, 1992; MA, Pepperdine U., 1993. Tchr. spl. edn. King City (Calif.) Union Sch. Dist., 1997-98; tchr. kindergarten, 1st grade Ocean View Sch. Dist., Oxnard, Calif., 1998—. Mem. NEA, Calif. Tchrs. Assn., Internat. Reading Assn. Avocations: writing, education.

BURCHMORE, DAVID WEGNER, lawyer; b. Evanston, Ill., Mar. 5, 1952; s. Robert Norris and Margaret Rose (Wegner) B.; children: Jonathan, Katherine, Elizabeth, Claire; m. Ellen Siebenschuh, May 28, 2000. AB, Princeton U., 1973; MA, U. Va., 1975, PhD, 1979, JD, 1986. Bar: Ohio 1986, U.S. Dist. Ct. (no. dist.) Ohio 1986, U.S. Ct. Appeals (6th cir.) 1986, U.S. Ct. Appeals (4th cir.) 1998, U.S. Ct. Appeals (9th cir.) 1999. Vis. asst. prof. Calif. Inst. Tech., Pasadena, 1978-81; asst. prof. SUNY, Binghamton, 1981-83; ptnr. Squire, Sanders & Dempsey, Cleve., 1986—. Sec. med. lit. sect. Phililogical Assn. Pacific Coast, 1981-82. Editor: Text and Image, 1986; articles editor Va. Law Rev., 1985-86. Princeton U. scholar, 1972-73, Robert D. Saltz Meml. fellow U. Va., 1977, Dillard fellow, 1984-85. Mem. Medieval Acad. Am., Cleve. Bar Assn. (exec. coun. environ. law com. 1993-96), Water Environment Fedn., Ohio Water Environment Assn. (chair govt. affairs com.). Republican. Methodist. Office: 4900 Key Tower Cleveland OH 44114 Home: 2963 Kingsley Rd Shaker Heights OH 44122-2813

BURCH-PESSES, THOMAS MICHAEL, music educator; b. Oxnard, Calif., Jan. 31, 1945; s. Albert J. and Doris V. Pesses(Stepmother); m. R. Jane Burch-Pesses, Nov. 16, 1988. BS, SUNY, Albany, 1989; MusM, Cath. U. Am., Washington, 1992, D in Musical Arts, 1995. Cert. adjudicator Oreg., 1995. Enlisted musician USN, Washington, 1962—71, bandmaster, 1971—95; prof. music Pacific U., Forest Grove, Oreg., 1995—, co-condr. Oreg. Symphonic Band, Portland, Oreg. Asst. leader US Naval Acad. Band, Annapolis, Md., 1974—77, Washington, 1984—86; musical dir. Midshipmen Drum and Bugle Corps, Annapolis, Md., 1989—93; leader U.S. Naval Acad. Band, Annapolis, 1989—93; head USN Music Program, Washington, 1993—95. Editor: Overture in C by Simon Catel, 1995; contbr. articles to profl. jours. Recipient George S. Howard citation of Musical Excellence, John Philip Sousa Found., 1992; Wye fellow, Aspen Inst., 1999. Mem.: Oreg. Music Educators Assn. (coll. chair 1989—2002, 2d v.p. 2002—), Nat. Band Assn. (mil. liaison 1992—95, Oreg. state chair 1997—), Oreg. Band Dirs. Assn., Coll. Band Dirs. Nat. Assn., Music Educators Nat. Conf. Avocations: running, travel, comic book collecting. Home: 5598 SE Sierra Ct Hillsboro OR 97123 Office: Pacific U 2043 College Way Forest Grove OR 97116 Office Fax: 503-352-2910. Personal E-mail: embeepee@aol.com. E-mail: burchpem@pacificu.edu.

BURCHUM, JACQUELINE ROSENJACK, family nurse practitioner; b. Corona, Calif., Apr. 17, 1955; d. Richard C. and Jo Ann (Hicks) Rosenjack; m. Charles Tony Burchum, Apr. 17, 1976; 1 child, Charles O. Assoc.'s degree in Nursing, U. Tenn., Martin, 1981; BS in Nursing, Union U., 1985; MSN, U. Tenn., Memphis, 1996, DNSc, 2002. Cert. advanced cardiac life support instr., basic cardiac life support instr., EMT, emergency nurse; cert. family nurse practitioner. Mem. faculty U. Memphis. Mem. ANA, Emergency Nurses Assn., Tenn. Nurses Assn., Transcultural Nursing Soc. Migrant Clinicians Network, Internat. Consortium Parse Scholars, Sigma Theta Tau. Home: 410 Sand Pit Loop Camden TN 38320-6426 E-mail: jburchum@memphis.edu.

BURCK, JOSEPH RUSSELL, medical educator, consultant, minister; b. Roswell, N.Mex., Dec. 28, 1937; s. William Joseph and Leta Gladys (Menefee) Burck; m. Dorothy Antoinette Pilc, Aug. 6, 1960; children: Peter Warren, Elisabeth Varner. AB, Princeton U., 1959; BD, Princeton Theol. Sem., 1964, PhD, 1976. Ordained Presbytery of Phila., 1970, cert. pastoral counselor Am. Assn. Pastoral Counseling, 1977, chaplain supr. Assn. Clin. Pastoral Edn., 1981, chaplain Assn. Profl. Chaplains, 1998. Assoc. editor bibliography in polit. sci. Princeton Info. Tech., 1967—69; educator in pastoral care in Germany, seminaries in Lueckendorff near Zittau, Herborn, Stuttgart, Tuebingen U., Innere Mission, Berlin, 1972—74; dir. chaplaincy svcs. Larned (Kans.) State Hosp., 1976—78; asst. prof of religion and health Rush-Presbyn.-St. Luke's Med. Ctr., Chgo., 1978—85, assoc. prof. religion, health, and human values, 1985—, dir. program in ethics and ethics consultation svc., 1988—. Peer reviewer of articles Critical Care Medicine, Des Plaines, Ill., 1999—; chairperson ethics adv. com. Inst. of Medicine of Chgo., 1990—91; project dir. Clergy Ethics Study Group, 1988—90; interpreter Internat. Congress on Pastoral Care and Counseling, Arnoldshain, Germany, 1973, mem., U.S. del., Edinburgh, Scotland, 79, San Francisco, 83; outside mem. animal care and use com. U. of Ill. at Chgo., 1988—93; mem. nat. task force to prepare a brief course in ethics Assn. of Profl. Chaplains, 1993—95; chairperson com. on sr. faculty appointments and promotions, Coll. Health Scis. Rush U., 1988—92; editor, Rush ethics reporter Rush-Presbyn. St. Luke's Med. Ctr., 1991—94; bd. of dirs. representing Rush Coll. of Health Scis. Rush Geriatric Interdisciplinary Team Tng. Program, Chgo., 1997—; co-course dir. ethics in medicine Rush Med. Coll., Chgo., 1998—, course dir., clerkship, med. ethics, 1993—; vice-chair work group on governance and adminstrn. NCA accreditation rev. Rush U., Chgo., 1997; chair ethics grand rounds Rush-Presbyn.-St. Luke's, 1980—99; cons. to author of book, ethical issues, and patient rights Joint Commn. on the Accreditation of Health Care Orgns., Chgo., 1997—98; course dir. spiritual dimensions of health care Teleconference Network of Tex., Austin, 1992—97; pres. Chgo. Clin. Ethics Programs, 1994—95; lay mem., nat. ethics and peer rev. com. Am. Assn. of Electrodiagnostic Medicine, 1993—2000. Co-editor: Clergy Ethics in a Changing Society: Mapping the Terrain (10 Best Books in Ministry of the &r., 1991); author: (e-book) Is it OK to have money and still go to church?; contbr. articles, columns, essays to profl. jours., chapters to books. Adult Christian educator, instr. courses in adult Christian edn., faith and illness, theology of genetics, med. ethics, faith and money, various chs., Chgo., 1980—. Recipient Profl. Svc. award, Teleconf. Network of Tex., 1993, Rsch. award, Joint Coun. on Rsch. in Pastoral Counseling, 1988, World Coun. of Chs. fellowship, 1971—72, doctoral fellowship in theology and personality, Princeton Theol. Sem., 1964—67; grantee, Greenwall Found., 1999—2000. Mem.: Presbytery of Chgo., Assn. for Clin. Pastoral Edn., Assn. of Profl. Chaplains (nominated to White Ho. bioethics adv. commn. 1999), Inst. of Medicine of Chgo. (bd. of govs. 1990—91), Assn. for Bioethics and the Humanities. Presbyterian. Achievements include One of the first Americans teaching pastoral care in Germany, when pastoral care paradigm changed from communicating messages to listening to people; development of one of the early professionalized ethics consultation services in U.S. hospitals; Only American involved in founding of German Society for Pastoral Psychology; First online certificate of graduate study in bioethics in the U.S; development of Innovative Language For Education In Health Care Ethics; Intensive use of clinical working rounds for teaching clinical ethics. Avocations: travel, photography, hiking, opera, films. Home: 1138 Clinton Ave Oak Park IL 60304-1826 Office: Rush-Presbyn-St Luke's Med Ctr 1653 W Congress Pkwy Chicago IL 60612 Office Fax: 312-942-6464. Personal E-mail: russell_burck@rush.edu.

BURCKEL, NICHOLAS C. historian, educator, school librarian, dean; b. Evansville, Ind., Aug. 15, 1943; s. Arthur J. and Anna Irene Burckel; m. Lenore M. Herriges, June 21, 1969. BA in History, Georgetown U., 1965; MA, U. Wis., 1967, PhD in History, 1971; MLS, U. Wis., Milw., 1983. Cert. archivist Acad. Cert. Archivists, 1989. Asst. archivist U. Wis., Madison, 1971—72; dir. archives and area rsch. ctr. U. Wis. Parkside, 1972—82, exec. asst. to chancellor, 1975—82, assoc. dir. libr./learning ctr., 1982—85, asst. vice chancellor, 1985; assoc. dean libr. Wash. U., St. Louis, 1986—95; dean libr. Marquette U., Milw., 1995—. Pres. Midwest Archives Conf., Chgo., 1979—81; acad. libr. mgmt. intern U. Chgo., 1984—85; presdl. apppointee to commn. Nat. Hist. Publications and Records Commn., Washington, 1996—; bd. dirs. Ctr. Rsch. Libr., Chgo., 1998—; corp. coun. U. Wis. Sch. of Info. Studies, Milw., 2002—; chmn. Wis. Libr. Svcs. Bd., Madison, 2001—02. Editor: Immigration and Ethnicity, Racine: Growth and Change in a Wisconsin County (First place Coun. for Wis. Writers Scholarly Book award, 1977), Progressive Reform, Kenosha Retrospective: A Biographical Approach (State Hist. Soc. of Wis. Award of Merit, 1982); co-author: Wis. Yesterday and Today; mem. editl. bd.: Portal: Libraries and the Acad., 2000—. Recipient Disting. Alumnus, U. Wis., Milw., 2002; fellow, Ford Found., 1968—69, Palmer Sch. of Libr. and Info. Sci., 1995; scholar, Georgetown U., 1961—65. Fellow: Soc. Am. Archivists (life; pres. 1996—97). Home: 7012 N Braeburn Ln Milwaukee WI 53209 Office: Marquette Univ 1355 W Wisconsin Ave Milwaukee WI 53201 Home Fax: 414-247-0960; Office Fax: 414-288-7813. E-mail: nicholas.burckel@marquette.edu.

BURCKHALTER, JOSEPH HAROLD, chemistry educator; b. Columbia, S.C., Oct. 9, 1912; s. Edward Wilson Burckhalter and Elizabeth Belle Strain; m. Virginia Ruth Feikert, July 10, 1943 (div. Mar. 1989); children: David Liggett, Robert Edward, Jane Ellen; m. Julia Riddick Johnston, Oct. 7, 1989. BS in Chemistry, U. S.C., 1934; MS in Chemistry, U. Ill., 1938; PhD in Chemistry, U. Mich., 1942. Sr. rsch. chemist Parke, Davis & Co., Detroit, 1942-47; assoc. prof., pharm. chemistry U. Kans., Lawrence, 1947-50, prof., chmn. pharm. chemistry, 1950-60; Fulbright prof. Tuebingen U., Germany, 1955-56; prof., chmn. medicinal chemistry U. Mich., Ann Arbor, 1960-83; prof. pharm. chemistry Nat. Def. Med. Ctr., Taiwan, 1974-75; rsch. prof., med. chemistry Fla. Inst. Technology, Melbourne, 1983—; ret., 1983. Cons. NIH, Bethesda, Md., 1956-82, Parke, Davis & Co., Detroit, 1947-60, The Upjohn Co., Kalamazoo, 1960-70. Author: (book) Essentials of Medicinal Chemistry, 1976; patentee in field. Inducted into Nat. Inventors Hall of Fame, Akron, Ohio, 1995; recipient Am. Innovator award U.S. Patent and Trademark Office, Washington, 1995, Disting. Alumni awards U. S.C., U. Ill., 1997, 99; decorated Order of Palmetto, S.C., 1996. Mem. Am. Pharm. Assn. Found. (recipient First Rsch. Achievement award med. chemistry 1962), Am. Chem. Soc. Avocations: reading, tennis, bridge, dancing, crossword puzzles. Achievements include patent for fluorescent antibody labeling agents, FITC and RITC; research in field of marketing synthetic drugs made with formaldehyde. Home: 734 Green Valley Ln Melbourne FL 32940-1713 Office: Fla Inst Technology Life Scis Rsch Complex 3325 W New Haven Ave Melbourne FL 32904-3537

BURCROFF, RICHARD TOMKINSON, II, economist; b. Ticonderoga, N.Y., Nov. 10, 1939; s. Richard Tomkinson and Anna (Gonyea) Burcroff; m. Maria-Clara Soberano Roldan, June 9, 1974; children: Kevin, Ana;children: Kirsten, Trevor. BS in Econs., Rensselaer Polytechnic Inst., 1961; PhD in Econs., U. Wash., 1972; postgrad. in Law & Econs., Yale U., 1973. Asst. prof. U. Hawaii, Honolulu, 1968-73; visiting prof. U. Philippines, Quezon City, 1973-74; sr. economist Asian Devel. Bank, Manila, 1974-79; prin. economist World Bank, Washington, 1979-97; pres. Crown Point Cons., Inc., 1997—. Cons. State of Hawaii Legal Svcs. Office, Honolulu, 1969—71, U. Hawaii Sch. Edn., 1970, U.S. AID, Washington, 1970—72; vis. rsch. assoc. Inst. Philippine Culture Ateneo da Manila, Quezon City, 1973—75; advisor Rsch. Ctr. Rural Devel., Beijing, 1987—89; dir. transition in socialist agr. project World Bank, 1994—97, cons., acting sector mgr., 2002—03; rsch. advisor Rural Asian update Asian Devel. Bank, Manila, 1997. Author: Turkey-Opportunities for Agricultural Growth with Exports, 1982, China-Managing an Agricultural Transformation, 1991; author: (with others) Options for Food Policy and Agricultural Sector Reform in the former USSR, 1992, Rural Asia: Challenge and Opportunity, 1988; contbr. Active Lincolnia Park Civic Assn., Annandale, Va., 1981—96, Burgundy Farms Country Day Sch., Alexandria, Va., 1985—92; fin. advisor Lincolnia Park Recreation Assn., Annandale, 1989—90. ;t/ USN, 1961—65. Rsch. grant, Yale U. Found., 1973, Asia Found., 1973, Rockefeller Found., 1973—74, Ford Found., 1994. Mem.: Soc. Internat. Devel., Am. Econs. Assn. Democrat. Office: 1400 East-West Hwy #1724 Silver Spring MD 20910

BURD, JOHN STEPHEN, academic administrator, music educator; b. Lock Haven, Pa., Apr. 6, 1939; s. John Wilson and Lily (Fye) B.; m. Patricia Ayers, June 3, 1961; children: Catherine Elizabeth, Emily Susanne. B in Music Edn., Greenville Coll., 1961; MS in Sacred Music, Butler U./Christian Theo. Sem., 1964; PhD, Ind. State U., 1971. Adj. music instr. Rose Hulman Inst. Tech., Terre Haute, Ind., 1969-71; assoc. prof. Greenville (Ill.) Coll., 1971-76; prof. edn. Lindenwood Coll., St. Charles, Mo., 1976 80; v.p. acad. affairs Maryville U., St. Louis, Mo., 1980-85; pres. Brenau U., Gainesville, Ga., 1985—. Team evaluator Nat. Coun. Accreditation Tchr. Edn., 1979-84; mem. exec. coun. Women's Coll. Coalition, 1989-92, NAICU Commn. on State Rels. Bd., 1991—; adv. bd. Wachovia Bank, Gainesville. Editor: New Voices in Education, 1969-71; contbr. articles to profl. jours. Choir dir. Ctr. Presbyn. Ch., St. Louis, 1984-85, Maryville U., St. Louis, 1983-85; v.p. Christian Arts, Inc., N.J., 1965—; adv. bd. N.E. Ga. Med. Ctr.; bd. dirs. Gainesville Symphony, 1991-94, Crawford W. Long Mus.; chair Gainesville Redevel. Authority, Chicopee Park Commn. Recipient Outstanding Young Alumnus award Greenville Coll., 1982, Disting. Alumnus award, 1991. Mem. Am. Assn. Tchr. Edn., Am. Assn. Higher Edn., So. Assn. Women's Colls. (pres. 1988-89), Ga. Found. Ind. Colls. (exec. bd. 1986—, vice chmn. 1993), Ga. Assn. Colls. (pres. 1989-90, 2003—), Gainesville C. of C. (bd. dirs.), Ga. Found. Ind. Colls. (vice chmn. 1993, 2003). Methodist. Avocations: tennis, travel, art. Office: Brenau U 1 Centennial Cir Gainesville GA 30501-3697 E-mail: jburd@lib.brenau.edu.

BURD, LAURENCE I. obstetrician-gynecologist; b. N.Y.C., 1940; BA, U. Rochester, 1962; MD, U. Health Scis., 1966. Diplomate Am. Bd. Ob-Gyn. Intern Michael Reese Hosp., Chgo., 1966-67, resident ob-gyn., 1967-71, obstetrician-gynecologist; fellow perinatal medicine U. Colo., 1973-75; instr. U. Ill., assoc. prof. Mem. ACOG, Perinatal Rsch. Soc., Soc. Gynecol. Investigation, Soc. Maternal-Fetal Medicine. Office: U Ill at Chgo Dept Ob-Gyn Chicago IL 60612

BURD, ROBERT MEYER, hematologist, oncologist, educator; b. N.Y.C., Aug. 25, 1937; s. David and Anne (Popkin) B.; m. Alice Stoller, May 30, 1964; children: Russell J., Stephen J. AB, Columbia U., 1959, MD, 1963. Diplomate Am. Bd. Internal Medicine, Am. Bd. Hematology and Oncology. Intern Albert Einstein Med. Sch., N.Y.C., 1963-64, resident in internal medicine, 1964-66; hematology fellow Montefiore Hosp., N.Y.C., 1966-67; specializing in hematology and oncology pvt. practice medicne, Fairfield, Conn., 1969—; assoc. prof. medicine Yale U., New Haven, 1975, assoc. clin. prof. of medicine, 1975—; chief of hematology/oncology St. Vincent's Med. Ctr., 1980—; asst. prof. clin. medicine Columbia U. Coll. Physicians & Surgeons, 1998—. Chmn. hosp. com. on cancer, mng. ptnr. Med. Specialists of Fairfield, LLC, 1995—; attending physician Yale Hosp., New Haven; mem. staff Bridgeport (Conn.) Hosp.; adj. prof. medicine N.Y. Med. Coll.; med. cons. U.S. News and World Report, 1990; dir. oncology fellowship Yale-St. Vincent Hosp., 1991—96, N.Y. Med. Coll., St. Vincent's Med. Ctr., Bridgeport; adv. bd. rituxan Genentech; adv. bd. taxoten Aventis. Mem. editl. bd. (exhibitions), 1974—78. Active Lukemia Soc. Am., Hemophilia Found.; chmn. profl. edn. com. Am. Cancer Soc. Lt. comdr. USN, 1967-69. Ettinger Meml. fellow Am. Cancer Soc., 1982. Fellow ACP; mem. AMA, AAAS, Am. Soc. Hematology, Am. Soc. Internat. Medicine, Am. Soc. Clin. Oncology, N.Y. Acad. of Scis., Internat. Soc. Thrombosis and Hemostasis, Conn. Oncology Assn., Soc. Columbia Grads., Columbia U. Alumni Fedn. Coun., Columbia U. Alumni Club (pres. Fairfield Co. 1983-85, editor newsletter 1982-91), Bridgeport Med. Sco. (Physician of Yr. 1993). Office: 425 Post Rd Fairfield CT 06430-6232

BURD, STEVE, food service executive; b. 1949; BS, Carroll Coll., 1971; MA in Econs., U. Wis., 1973. With fin. and mktg. So. Pacific Transp. Co., San Francisco; with Arthur D. Little, N.Y.C., 1982-87; mgmt. cons., 1986-91; cons. Stop & Shop Cos., Boston, 1988-89, Fred Meyer Inc., Portland, Oreg., 1989-90, Safeway Inc., Oakland, Calif., 1986-87, 91—, pres., CEO, 1992—, chmn. bd. dirs. Office: Safeway Inc 5918 Stoneridge Mall Rd Pleasanton CA 94588-3229

BURDELIK, THOMAS L. lawyer; b. Chgo., June 4, 1959; s. Thomas L. and Roberta P. (Raber) B.; m. Mary Kathleen Igyarto; children: Clayton Thomas, Dylan Patrick. BA, North Cen. Coll., 1981; JD, John Marshall Sch. Law, 1984. Bar: Ill. 1984. Assoc. Parrillo, Weiss & Moss, Chgo., 1984-87; sr. assoc. McSherry & Gray, Chgo., 1987; Parillo, Weiss & Moss, Chgo., 1987-89; prin. Thomas L. Burdelik & Assocs., Chgo., 1989—. Past guest lectr. on legal argument U. Ill. at Chgo. and St. Xavier Coll., Chgo.; co-mgr. Sheffield Garden Walk, 1997; instr. in fed. trial bar tng. Chgo. Bar Assn.; mock trial judge Northwestern U. Law Sch., 2001. Featured spkr. Chgo. Bar Assn. Seminars on Trial Practice, Cross Exam., Uninsured/Underinsured Motorist Claims, Role of Accident Reconstructionists and Jury Consultants in Trials in Cook County, spkr. sem. spon. by IL Trial Lawyers Assoc on Damages. Mem. Nat. Handgun Control, 1990-95, Nat. Abortion Rights Action League, 1990-95, Internat. CARE, 1991-95; vol. Northwestern Hosp., Chgo., 1991-95; mem. Ranch Triangle Comm. Orgn.; vol. fundraiser Off the Street Club of Chgo., 1991—. Mem. Chgo. Bar Assn. (instr. Fed. Trial Bar Tng. Course), Amnesty Internat., Randolph Athletic Club. Democrat. Roman Catholic. Office: 123 W Madison St Ste 19 Chicago IL 60602-4511 E-mail: burdelik@univcas.com.

BURDEN, CEDRIC JEROME, SR., English educator; b. Mobile, Ala., Nov. 6, 1969; s. Andrew O'Neal and Juanita (Coleman) B.; m. Teresa Ballard, Mar. 26, 1995; children: Jasmine Renee, Cedric Jerome Jr. AS, S.D. Bishop State Coll., 1989; BA, Univ. Montevallo, 1991, M, 1992. English prof. Lawson State Cmty. Coll., Birmingham, Ala., 1993—. Editing cons. Writing Voyage, 1996, Fictions, 1997, 98; author companion website Progressions, 5th edit. Sec. Alabaster Parks and Recreation Adv. Bd., 1997-98; mem. Alabaster Planning and Zoning Bd.; grad. Ala. C.C. Leadership Acad.; mem. young adv. bd. Big Bros Big Sisters Birmingham. Mem. Ala. Assn. for Developmental Edn., Nat. Assn. for Devel. Edn., Nat. Coun. of Tchrs. of Eng., Alabaster Lions Club (sec.-treas. 1997-98), Alpha Phi Alpha. Avocations: model car building, pets, playing saxophone. Home: 620 Park Forest Ln Montevallo AL 35115-8994 Office: Lawson State Cmty Coll 3060 Wilson Rd SW Birmingham AL 35221-1717 E-mail: cburden@lawsonstate.edu., ced2342@aol.com.

BURDEN, JAMES EWERS, lawyer; b. Sacramento, Oct. 24, 1939; s. Herbert Spencer and Ida Elizabeth (Brosemer) B.; m. Kathryn Lee Gardner, Aug. 21, 1965; children: Kara Elizabeth Crabtree, Justin Gardner. BS, U. Calif., Berkeley, 1961; JD, U. Calif., Hastings, 1964; postgrad., U. So. Calif., 1964-65. Bar: Calif. 1965, Tax Ct. U.S. 1969, U.S. Supreme Ct. 1970. Assoc. Elliott and Aune, Santa Ana, Calif., 1965, White, Harbor, Fort & Schei, Sacramento, 1965-67, Miller, Starr & Regalia, Oakland, Calif., 1967-69, ptnr., 1969-73, Burden, Aiken, Mansuy & Stein, San Francisco, 1973-82, James E. Burden, Inc., San Francisco, 1982—; founder, dir., COO KineMed, Inc., Emeryville, Calif., 2001—, sec., 2001—, bd. dirs., 2001—. Bd. dirs. IP Floor Products, Inc., San Leandro, Calif., Denver; founder Gloucestershire Innovation Centre, Gloucester, Eng., EuroGen Pharmas. Ltd., Gloucester; underwriting mem. Lloyds of London, 1986-93; instr. U. Calif., Berkeley, Merritt Coll. 1968-74; pres., prin. Dorset Capital LLC; founder Info4cars.com., Inc., Asheville, N.C. Contbr. articles to profl. jours. Mem.: ABA, Inst. of Dirs. (London), St. Andrews Golf Club (Fife, Scotland), Faculty Club U. Calif. Berkeley, The Univ. Club, Commonwealth Club of Calif., Claremont Country Club. Office: One Maritime Plz 4th Fl San Francisco CA 94111-3407 E-mail: jeburden@compuserve.com.

BURDEN, JEAN PRUSSING, poet, writer, editor; b. Waukegan, Ill., Sept. 01; d. Harry Frederick and Miriam (Biddlecom) Prussing; m. David Charles Burden, 1940 (div. 1949). BA, U. Chgo., 1936. Sec. John Hancock Mutual Life Ins. Co., Chgo., 1937-39, Young & Rubicam, Inc., Chgo., 1939-41; editor, copywriter Domestic Industries, Inc., Chgo., 1941-45; office mgr. O'Brion Russell & Co., Los Angeles, 1948-55; adminstr. pub. relations Meals for Millions Found., Los Angeles, 1955-65; editor Stanford Research Inst., South Pasadena, Calif., 1965-66; propr. Jean Burden & Assocs., Altadena, Calif., 1966-82. Lectr. poetry to numerous colls. and univs., U.S., 1963—; supr. poetry workshop Pasadena City Coll., Calif., 1960-62, 66, U. Calif. at Irvine, 1975; also pvt. poetry workshops. Author: Naked as the Glass, 1963, Journey Toward Poetry, 1966, The Cat You Care For, 1968, The Dog You Care For, 1968, The Bird You Care For, 1970, The Fish You Care For, 1971, A Celebration of Cats, 1974, The Classic Cats, 1975, The Woman's Day Book of Hints for Cat Owners, 1980, 84, Taking Light from Each Other, 1992; poetry editor: Yankee Mag, 1955—2002; pet editor: Woman's Day Mag, 1973-82; contbr. numerous articles to various jours. and mags. MacDowell Colony fellow, 1973, 74, 76;

Recipient Silver Anvil award Pub. Relations Soc. of Am., 1969, 1st prize Borestone Mountain Poetry award, 1963, Gold Crown award for lit. achievement, 1989. Mem. Poetry Soc. Am., Acad. Am. Poets, Authors Guild. Address: 1129 Beverly Way Altadena CA 91001-2517 *I think that man is constantly trying to bring down into the world of time the essences of what he dimly but intuitively feels is timeless. One of the ways in which he tries is through poetry. Without poetry, a certain kind of Reality is speechless. Or to put it a slightly different way, I believe that we inhabit two worlds at once, the world of time and the world of timelessness, and that poetry is a bridge that lets us cross over.*

BURDEN, ORDWAY PARTRIDGE, investment banker; b. N.Y.C., N.Y., Nov. 20, 1944; s. William A. M. and Margaret L. (Partridge) B.; m. Jean Poor Lynch, October 5, 1991. AB magna cum laude, Harvard U., 1966, MBA, 1968; postgrad., Harvard Law Sch., 1969-71. Gen. ptnr. William A.M. Burden Co., N.Y.C., 1968-86, dir., 1986—. Cons. on police functions Nat. Commn. for Rev. Fed. and State Laws Relating to Wiretapping and Electronic Surveillance; cons. Commn. on Rev. Nat. Policy Toward Gambling. Former mem. adv. bd. Bur. Justice Stats., Dept. of Justice; mem. nat. sponsoring com. Nat. Law Enforcement Officers Meml. Fund; v.p. Florence V. Burden Found., N.Y.C., 1990—. Mem. Internat. Assn. Chiefs Police (past mem. 5 coms.), Nat. Sheriffs Assn. (former mem. standards-ethics-edn.-devel. com.), Nat. Crime Prevention Coun. (bd. dirs.), Law Enforcement Assistance Found. (founder, pres. 1977—), Nat. Law Enforcement Coun. (founder, chmn. 1979—), Capitol Hill Club, Metropolitan Club.

BURDESHAW, WILLIAM BROOKSBANK, engineering executive; b. East Orange, N.J., Nov. 20, 1930; s. Thomas Anderson and Margaret (Villecco) B.; m. Monica Dorr, Sept. 27, 1957; children: Leath, Thomas, Anne, Alison. BS, U.S. Mil. Acad., 1953; MSEE, Ga. Inst. of Tech., 1961. Commd. 2d lt. U.S. Army, 1953, advanced through grades to brig. gen., 1975, ret., 1979; CEO, chmn. Burdeshaw Assocs., Ltd., 1979—. Cons. Def. Sci. Bd., 1985-87. Engring. mgmt. cons. co. named by INC. mag. as 121st of 500 fastest growing pvt. cos., 1985. Mem. Burning Tree Club, Congl. Country Club, George Town Club (Washington), Cripple Creek Club (Bethany Beach, Del.). Republican. Episcopalian. Office: Burdeshaw Assoc Ltd 4701 Sangamore Rd Bethesda MD 20816-2500

BURDETT, JAMES RICHARD, treasurer; b. Oak Park, Ill., Jan. 4, 1934; s. Paul Eswald and Ruth (Woodward) B.; m. Marilyn Carole Stoker, Aug. 29, 1959; children: Deborah Lyn, Daniel James, Donna Carole. Student, Grinnell Coll., 1953-54; BS in Econs., U. Ill., 1956. Owner James R. Burdett, Lombard, 1983-92; pres. Burdett's Inc., 1993-99, Master of the Links, Lombard, 1988-99. Speaker conf. Golf Course Superintendent Assn., Anaheim, Calif., 1993. Treas. YMCA, 2001—. Mem. Midwest Assn. Golf Course Supts., Ill. Turfgrass Found. (pres. 1965-66). Mem. Christian Sci. Ch.

BURDETTE, ROBERT BRUCE, retired lawyer; b. Cin., Oct. 8, 1945; s. Lumas Carter and Myrtle Margaret (Diesel) B. AB, Columbia Coll., 1967; JD, U. Cin., 1973. Bar: Ohio 1973, U.S. Supreme Ct. 1978. Legis. atty. Libr. Congress, Washington, 1973—2003. Author: A Step Beyond The Graetz Prepayment Analysis, 1992. Mem. Mensa, St. Andrew Club, W.A.R. Goodwin Soc. Colonial Williamsburg. Methodist. Avocation: gilding and rum collecting. Home: 323 Dogleg Dr Williamsburg VA 23188

BURDGE, RABEL JAMES, sociology educator; b. Columbus, Ohio, Dec. 14, 1937; s. Alonzo Marshall and Mariam Francis (Prentice) B.; m. Sharon Sue Payne, June 30, 1962 (dec. June 1975); children— Stephanie, Amy, Jill; m. Joyce Loretta Piggush, Aug. 2, 1977. BS, Ohio State U., 1959, MS, 1961; PhD, Pa. State U., 1965. Asst. prof. sociology U.S. Air Force Acad., Colo., 1966-68; lectr. U. Colo., Colorado Springs, 1966-68; asst. prof. sociology U. Ky., Lexington, 1968-72, assoc. prof., 1972-76; assoc. prof. environ. sociology, rural sociology, urban and regional planning and leisure studies; dept. agrl. econs. and leisure studies U. Ill. Inst. Environ. Studies, Urbana, 1976-80, prof., 1980—96; prof. emeritus U. Ill., 1996—; prof. sociology and environ. studies Western Wash. U., Bellingham, 1996—. Vis. scholar Sch. of Australian Environ. Studies, Griffith U., Brisbane, 1982, 86, hon. prof., 1991—; vis. prof. Sch. Planning and Landscape, U. Manchester, Eng., 2002. Author (books): (with N. Cheek and D. Field) Leisure and Recreation Places, 1976, (with Paul Opryszek) Coping with Change: An Interdisciplinary Assessment of the Lake Shelbyville Reservoir, 1981, (with E.M. Rogers) Social Change in Rural Societies, A Rural Sociology Textbook, 3d edit., 1988, A Community Guide to Social Impact Assessment, 1998, 2d edit., 1999, A Conceptual Approach to Social Impact Assessment, 1994, 2d edit., 1998; editor Jour. Leisure Rsch., 1971-74; co-editor, founder: Leisure Scis., an Interdisciplinary Jour., 1977-82, Society and Nat. Resources: An Internat. Jour., 1988-98; co-editor Longman-Cheshire Internat. Environ. Studies Series, 1990—; contbr. articles to profl. publs. Served to capt. arty. U.S. Army, 1965-68. Recipient George B. Hartzog Jr. award for environ. rsch. Clemson U., 1995. Mem. AAAS, Am. Sociol. Assn., Rural Sociol. Soc. (v.p. 1982-83, treas. 1994-2000, editor The Rural Sociologist, 1994-2000, named Disting. Rural Sociologist, 1996), Nat. Recreation and Park Assn. (Theodore/Franklin D. Roosevelt award for outstanding rsch. 1982), Internat. Assn. for Impact Assessment (pres. 1990-91, treas. 1993-96, Rose-Hulman Inst. Tech. award for contbns. to impact assessment), Acad. Leisure Scis., Sigma Xi, Phi Kappa Phi, Gamma Sigma Delta, Alpha Kappa Delta. Democrat. Methodist. Home: PO Box 4056 Bellingham WA 98227-4056 Office: Western Wash U Dept Sociology Bellingham WA 98225-9081 E-mail: burdge@cc.wwu.edu.

BURDI, ALPHONSE ROCCO, anatomist; b. Chgo., Aug. 28, 1935; s. Alphonse Rocco and Anna (Basilo) B.; m. Sandra Shaw, Mar. 22, 1968; children— Elizabeth Anne, Sarah Lynne. BS, No. Ill. U., DeKalb, 1957; MS, U. Ill., 1959, U. Mich., 1961, PhD, 1963; Doctorate (hon.), U. Athens, Greece, 2000. Predoctoral fellow physiology U. Ill., 1957-59; NSF summer fellow U. Mich., 1960, NIH trainee, 1960-61, NIH predoctoral research fellow, 1962, mem. faculty, 1962—, prof. cell and devel. biology, 1974—; rsch. scientist Center for Human Growth and Devel. Dir. integrated pre-med.-med. program U. Mich. Mem. editorial bd.: Cleft Palate Jour. 1972-88, Am. Jour. Phys. Anthropology, 1971-75, C.C. Thomas Am. Lectr. Series in Anatomy, 1971-88, Jour. Dental Research, 1977-87 . Grantee NIH. Mem. Internat. Assn. Dental Research, Am. Assn. Dental Research, Am. Cleft Palate Assn., Teratology Soc., Am. Assn. Anatomists, Am. Assn. Phys. Anthropology, Sigma Xi. Home: 2600 Page Ct Ann Arbor MI 48104-6249 Office: U Mich Dept Cell & Devel Biology Med Sci Bldg 2 Ann Arbor MI 48109-0616

BURDICK, GEORGE HAROLD, investment company executive; b. Bridgton, Maine, Mar. 5, 1958; s. Lewis Avery and Nancy J. (Conant) B.; 1 child, Armin Lewis. BA in Journalism, U. Maine, 1980; postgrad., Golden Gate U., 1984-85; attended, NYU, Albany, 1989. CFP. Account exec. Dean Witter, Alexandria, Va., 1985-88; sr. fin. cons. Merrill Lynch, Wellesley, Mass., 1992-98; first v.p. Morgan Stanley Dean Witter, Westborough, 1998—. Capt. U.S. Army, 1980-88; capt. N.Y. Army Nat. Guard, 1988-91. Mem. Internat. Bd. CFP, Am. Soc. CLU and ChFC, Mensa Soc., Audubon Soc. Avocations: martial arts, running, reading. Office: Morgan Stanley One Technology Dr Westborough MA 01581 Address: 24 Wheeler Rd Westborough MA 01581-3533 E-mail: george.burdick@morganstanley.com.

BURDICK, GLENN ARTHUR, physicist, engineering educator; b. Pavilion, Wyo., Sept. 9, 1932; s. Stephen Arthur and Mary Elizabeth (McClerg) B.; m. Joyce Mae Huggett, July 14, 1951; children: Stephen Arthur, Randy Glenn. BS, Ga. Inst. Tech., 1958, MS, 1959; PhD, MIT, 1961. Registered profl. engr., Fla. Office mgr. Statewide Contractors, Las Vegas, Nev., 1955-56; spl. tool designer Ga. Inst. Tech., Atlanta, 1954-55, instr., 1956-59; sr. mem. rsch. staff Sperry Microwave, Oldsmar, Fla., 1961-65; prof. elec. engring. U. So. Fla., Tampa, 1965—, dean Coll. Engring., 1979-86, prof. elec. engring., 1965-86, disting. prof. engring., 1986—, dean emeritus, 1986—; pres. Burdick Engring. and Sci., Inc., 1983—. Invented underground pipeline leak detector, 1956, sail boat mast insulation, 1981. Mem. Tampa Bay Fgn. Affairs Com., 1981-88, Pinellas County (Fla.) High Speed Rail Task Force, 1992-91, Gov. of State of Fla. Energy Task Force, 1980-85; vice chmn. Fla. Task Force for Sci. Energy and Tech. Svc. to Industry, 1981-82. Tex. Gulf scholar, 1957-58; NSF fellow, 1958-61, Woodrow Wilson fellow, 1958-59; named Engring. Faculty Mem. of Yr. State of Fla., 1986. Fellow Am. Assn. Forensic Sci., Nat. Fire Protection Agy., Am. Bd. Forensic Examiners, Nat. Acad. Forensic Engrs.; mem. Fla. Engring. Soc. (Engr. of Yr. award 1981), Internat. Soc. Hybrid Microelectronics (nat. pres. 1974), IEEE (sr. mem., Engr. of Yr. award 1980), Nat. Acad. Forensic Engring., N.Y. Acad. Sci., U.S. Profl. Engrs. Edn. (vice-chmn. SE region, 1986-88), Clearwater Tennis Club (pres. Fla. chpt. 1965, 69), Downtown Club. Home: 18728 Lake Iola Rd Dade City FL 33523-6117 Office: Burdick Engring and Sci Inc 18530 Lake Iola Rd Dade City FL 33523-6149

BURDICK, KIM ROGERS, historic preservation consultant; b. Binghamton, N.Y., Nov. 10, 1948; d. Philip Mather and Martha Elizabeth (Wooster) Rogers; m. Ralph Edward Burdick, Aug. 21, 1971; children: Robert, Elizabeth, Edward. Cert. French, U. Neuchatel, Switzerland, 1969; BA, SUNY, Cortland, 1970; MA, SUNY, Cooperstown, 1971; MPA, U. Del., 1990; Diplome langue francaise, French Ministry Edn. Libr. Wm. Jeanes Libr., Plymouth Meeting, Pa., 1972-79; pres. Del. Folklife Project, Wilmington, 1981-88; legis. fellow Del. Ho. Rep., Dover, 1988, 89; ho.-senate laision Del. Gen. Assembly, Dover, 1989-98; pres. Burdick Assocs., Rockland, Del., 1998—; mem. Washington-Rochambeau Trail Com., 2002, chmn., 2003. Working group mem. Nat. Ednl. Goals Panel, Washington, 1995-97; mem. Del. Art Mus. Coun., bd. dirs. 1993-95. Contbr. articles to profl. jours. Bd. dirs. Old Swedes Found., 2002—, World Trade Ctr. Ins., Del., 2003. Hagley/Winterthur Rsch. fellow, 2000, Coun. State Govt. Toll fellow, 1994, Patricia Harris Pub. Svc. fellow, 1988, 89, Del. Humanities Forum fellow, 1986, N.Y. State Coun. of Arts fellow, 1970-71. Mem. Nat. Trust for Hist. Preservation (bd. advisors 1991-2001), Art Mus. Coun. (pres. 1993-95), Del. Civil War Soc. (bd. dirs. 1997-2000), Del. Soc. Mayflower Descs. (bd. v.p., pres. 2002), Del. Huguenot Soc. (v.p. 1996-98, pres. 1998—), Preservation Del. (founding mem., bd. dirs. 1993-99), Col. Dames. Episcopalian. Avocations: history, art, french. Home: 2420 Dorval Rd Wilmington DE 19810-3529 Office: Burdick Assn PO Box 40 Rockland DE 19732-0040 E-mail: RBurd2420@aol.com.

BURDICK, LARRY G. school system administrator; Supt. Pryor (Okla.) Pub. Schs. State finalist Nat. Supt. Yr., 1992. Office: Pryor Pub Schs 521 SE 1st St Pryor OK 74361-4600 E-mail: burdickl@pryor.k12.ok.us.

BURDICK, LOU BRUM, public relations executive; b. Bloomer, Wis., Nov. 4, 1943; s. Francis Albert and Lucille May (Gorton) Peil; m. Robert P. Brum, Dec. 26, 1971 (div. 1977); m. Allan L. Burdick, Feb. 12, 1981; 1 child, Matthew Francis. Adminstr. Bozell & Jacobs, Mpls., 1965-67; pub. rels. mgr. Apache Corp., Mpls., 1967-76; v.p., dir. fin. rels. Edwin Neuger & Assocs., Mpls., 1976-78; chmn. bd., chief exec. officer Brum & Anderson Pub. Relations, Inc., Mpls., 1978-86; pres. Padilla, Speer, Burdick & Beardsley, Inc., Mpls., 1987, Lou Burdick and Assocs., Mpls., 1988—; dir. communications Office of Gov., St. Paul, 1989-91. Bd. dirs. Hennepin County Libr. Found., 1991-97, Minn. Coun. on Founds., 1998-2000, Courage Found., 2002—, Nami-MN, 2002—; campaign mgr. Printy for Gov., 1990. Recipient Outstanding Achievement award for entrepreneurship Mpls. YWCA, 1985. Mem. Pub. Rels. Soc. Am. (pub. rels. recognition award 1985), Minn. Women's Econ. Roundtable (bd. dirs.), Minnekahda Country Club. Home: 6609 Sally Ln Edina MN 55439-1042

BURDICK, ROBERT W. newspaper editor; b. Feb. 11, 1948; m. Patty Burnett; 1 child, David. B in Polit. Sci., Fla. Atl. U., 1969. Reporter Miami Herald, Fla. Today; night city editor Palm Beach (Fla.) Post; mng. editor Palm Beach Daily News; asst. mng. editor Wichita (Kans.) Eagle; city editor/metro editor/asst. to exec. editor San Jose (Calif.) Mercury News, 1978-82; asst. mng. editor Denver Post, 1982-84; asst. mng. editor/mng. editor/editor L.A. Daily News, 1984-94; mng. editor, gen. mgr. Rocky Mountain News, Denver, 1994-98, pres., 1998—2000; exec. v.p., gen. mgr. Naples (Fla.) Daily News, 2000—02, pres., pub., 2002—. Mem. Am. Soc. Newspaper Editors, Soc. Profl. Journalists, AP News Execs. Coun. (past bd. mem., past pres. Calif., Nev. chpt., past editor AP Mng. Editors News), Metro Denver C. of C. (bd. dirs.), NCCJ (bd. dirs. Denver chpt.). Avocations: skiing, hiking. Office: Naples Daily News 1075 Central Ave Naples FL 34102

BURDICK, WILLIAM MACDONALD, biomedical engineer; b. Providence, R.I., Apr. 24, 1952; s. Franklin Pierce and Lola Alice (Cook) B. BS, Ind. U. Pa., 1975; M of Engring., Tex. A&M U., 1981; postgrad., U. Tex., 1982-86. Engring. analyst FDA, Winchester, Mass., 1988-90, reviewer neurological devices Rockville, Md., 1990-94, reviewer, gen. hosp. and personal use devices, 1994—. Inventor in field; contbr. articles to profl. jours.; contbr. poem to: Dance on the Horizon (Editor's Choice award Nat. Libr. Poetry), America at the Millennium. With USAF, 1976-78. Mem. Biomed. Engring. Soc., Humane Soc. U.S., Am. Assn. Med. Instrumentation, Nat. Multiple Sclerosis Soc. Congregationalist. Avocations: reading, writing (poetry, songs, fiction), gardening, sports. Office: 9200 Corporate Blvd Rockville MD 20850-3229 E-mail: wmb@fda.cdrh.gov.

BURE, PAVEL, hockey player; b. Moscow, Mar. 31, 1971; Wing Fla. Panthers, Sunrise, 1998—2002; player NY Rangers, NY, 2002—. Named Regular Season and Playoff Top Goal Scorer, NHL, 1993—94, Top Goal Scorer, 1999—2000, 2000—01; recipient Calder Meml. Trophy, 1991—92. Office: NY Rangers 2 Penn Plz New York NY 10121

BURES, FRANK ADOLPH, journalist, writer; b. Iowa City, Nov. 3, 1971; s. Frank Allen and Ruth Anfinson Bures; m. Bridgit Kaye Jordan, Nov. 24, 1972. BA, St. Olaf Coll., 1995. Tutor Immigrant & Refugee Cmty. Orgn., Portland, Oreg., 1998—2002. Avocation: languages, travel, literature. Home: 224 Lake Dr Winona MN 55987

BURFORD, ANNE MCGILL, lawyer; b. Casper, Wyo., Apr. 21, 1942; d. Joseph John and Dorothy Jean (O'Grady) McGill; m. David Gorsuch, June 4, 1964 (div. 1982); children: Neil, Stephanie, J.J.; m. Robert Fitzpatrick Burford, Feb. 20, 1983 (dec. 1993). Student, Nat. U. Mex., 1955-56, 58, Regis Coll., Denver, 1959; BA, U. Colo., 1961, LLB, 1964. Bar: Colo. 1964, D.C. 1985. Asst. trust adminstr. 1st Nat. Bank of Denver, 1966-67; instr. Metro State Coll., 1966-67; asst. dist. atty. Jefferson County, 1968-71; dep. dist. atty. City and County of Denver, 1971—73; hearing officer Real Estate Commn., State Bds. Cosmetology, State Bd. Vet. Medicine, State Bd. Optemetric Examiners and Profl. Nursing, 1974-75; corp. counsel Mountain Bell Telephone Co., Denver, 1975-81; mem. Colo. Ho. of Reps., 1977-81, chmn. state affairs com., 1979-80, chmn. legal svcs. com., 1980; adminstr. EPA, Washington, 1981—83; lectr., author Washington, 1983—89; pvt. practice Denver, 1993—. Author: Are You Tough Enough, 1986. Del. Nat. Conf. State Legislators; mem. Nat. Conf. Commrs. on Uniform State Law, 1979, 80; presdl. del. to Kenya's Independence, 1983; loaned exec. mgmt. and efficiency task force Colo. Dept. Regulatory Agys., 1976; adminstr. EPA, Washington, 1981-83; former bd. dirs. YMCA. Fulbright scholar, Jaipur, India, 1964-65. Mem. Mortar Bd., Phi Alpha Delta, Delta Delta Delta. Republican. Roman Catholic. Home and Office: 3853 S Hudson St Denver CO 80237-1050

BURG, BRENT LAWRENCE, lawyer; b. Houston, Mar. 2, 1940; s. Abner Danford and Bess (Levin) B.; m. Patricia S. Petitt, 1980; 1 child, Brook Lawrence. BA, U. Tex., 1962; JD, 1966. Bar: Tex. 1966, U.S. Dist. Ct. (so. dist.) Tex. 1966, U.S. Ct. Appeals (5th cir.) 1966, U.S. Supreme Ct. 1970, U.S. Ct. Appeals (4th cir.) 1976, U.S. Dist. Ct. Md. 1976, U.S. Ct. Appeals (11th cir.) 1981. Dist. judge 309th Dist. Ct., Harris County, Tex., 1981-82; assoc. mcpl. judge City of Piney Point Village, 1990-98, City of Bunker Hill Village, 1991-98; ptnr. Rentz, Burg and Assocs., Houston, 1983-95; pvt. practice Brent Burg, Houston, 1995-98; assoc. judge 312th Dist. Ct., Houston, 1999—; of counsel Fouts & Moore, L.L.P., 1996-98. Chairperson Houston Vol. Lawyers Program, Inc., 1988-89, 89-90. Fellow Tex. Bar Found.; mem. Houston Bar Found., State Bar Tex. (grievance com.), Houston Bar Assn. (family law sect. treas. 1978-79, chairperson elect 1980-81, dir. 1982-83, chairperson 1984-85; mem. Supreme Ct. of Tex. child support and visitation guidelines adv. com. 1986-87, 96-97), Phi Alpha Delta. Office: 312th District Ct 1115 Congress St Houston TX 77002-1927

BURG, FREDRIC DAVID, physician, university dean; b. Chgo., May 23, 1940; s. Paul S. and Muriel C. (Buchsbaum) B.; m. Nancy Green, Oct. 5, 1997; children: Benjamin, Bethanny, David, Kathryn, Paul James, Jennifer Margaret. BA cum laude, Miami U., 1961; MD with distinction, Northwestern U., 1965. Diplomate Am. Bd. Pediatrics. Intern, resident, chief resident in pediatrics Northwestern U. Med. Sch., Chgo., 1965-68; cons., sr. surgeon Bur. Community Environ. Mgmt., USPHS, 1968-70; Kellogg fellow Ctr. for Teaching in Higher Edn. Northwestern U., 1970-71; assoc. exec. sec., dir. evaluation and research Am. Bd. Pediatrics, Chgo. and Phila., 1971-77; adj. assoc. prof. U. Pa., 1976-80, assoc. prof., 1980-82, prof. pediatrics, 1982-97, prof. emeritus, 1997—, assoc. dean for acad. programs, 1980-89, vice dean for edn., dir. office acad. programs, 1989-95; prof., assoc. dean U. Ala. Sch. medicine, Huntsville, 1996—; exec. dir. U. Ala. Huntsville Health Ctr. Pres., CEO, Valley Found., Huntsville, Ala., 2003—; trustee, bd. overseers U. Pa. Sch. Medicine, 1992-95; assoc. dir. Nat. Bd. Med. Examiners, Phila, 1971-78, v.p., dir. dept. grad. and continuing med. evaluation, 1976-80, mem. Part III com., 1981-87, cons., 1988-89, also mem. NBME task force computer based testing; cons. ACP, 1983-92, chmn. MKSAP/PMP com.; mem. Fgn. Med. Sch. Panel, State of N.J., 1983-90, State of N.Y.; bd. dirs. Children's Sea Shore House. Phila., Martha Lloyd Cmty. Svcs., Troy, Pa.; v.p., pres. & chief exec. officer Valley Found., Huntsville, Ala.; nat. chair Orgn. Regional Med. Campuses, 2001. Sr. editor Current Pediatric Therapy, 1992—, Pediatrics-A Problem Based Review; mem. editl. bd., publs. com. Joint Commn. Accreditation of Hosps., 1983-87; contbr. articles to med. jours. Served with USPHS, 1968-70. Sr. fellow Inst. for Rsch. in Higher Edn., 1996-99. Fellow Am. Acad. Pediat.; mem. Ambulatory Pediatrics Assn. (sec.-treas. 1977-80, pres. 1983-84), Assn. Am. Med. Colls. (chmn. N.E. group on med. edn., nat. steering group med. edn., nat. chmn. 1989-90, project dir. Robert Wood Johnson Commn. on Sci. and Med. Edn., 1990-92, chair group on regional med. campuses 2003—), Internat. Pediat. Assn. (steering com. 1985-97), Am. Edn. Rsch. Assn., Pa. Med. Soc. (chmn. coun. on accreditation 1986-87), Phila. Pediat. Soc. (treas. 1980-82) Office: U Ala Sch Medicine 301 Governors Dr Huntsville AL 35801 E-mail: burgf@uasomh.uab.edu.

BURG, H. PETER, financial executive; b. Akron; BS, MBA, U. Akron; postgrad., Harvard U. Fin. analyst trainee Ohio Edison, assoc. fin. analyst, econ. analyst, dir. fin. studies, treas., 1974, v.p., 1985, sr. v.p., CFO, 1989, FirstEnergy Corp., pres., COO, 1998-99, pres. & CEO, 1999-00; chmn. & CEO FirstEnergy Corp, Akron, OH, 2000—. Interim pres. Pa. Power, 1994-95; pres. Ohio Edison, The Illuminating Co., Toledo Edison Co.; mem. fin. com. Edison Elec. Inst.; bd. dirs. Energy Ins. Mutual, Key Bank. Bd. dirs. Summit County chpt. ARC; past pres. U. Akron Alumni Assn.; past bd. dirs. Akron Child Guidance Ctr.; active various coms. United Way. Office: FirstEnergy Corp 18th Fl 76 S Main St Fl 18 Akron OH 44308-1812

BURG, JOHN PARKER, signal processing executive; b. Great Bend, Kans., Dec. 17, 1931; s. Kenneth Edwin and Viola Mae (Parker) B.; m. Ida Elizabeth Groome; children Ida Elizabeth, Clarence Oscar Edwin; m. Shirley Joan Steele, Apr. 10, 1976; children: Nathan Parker, Emily Diane, Paul Andrew. BS in Physics, BA in Math., U. Tex., 1953; MS in Physics, MIT, 1960; PhD in Geophysics, Stanford U., 1975. Asst. engr. Tex. Instruments, Inc., 1956-57, engr., 1960; sr. rsch. geophysicist Geophys. Svc., Inc., Dallas, 1960-73; chmn. bd. dirs. Time and Space Processing, Inc., Santa Clara, Calif., 1973-83; pres. Entropic Processing, Inc., Cupertino, Calif., 1983—, also chmn. bd. dirs. Cons. oil cos., ESL, Inc., Naval Undersea Ctr., 1969-75; cons. Digicon, Inc., Houston, 1982-83; chmn. bd. dirs. Entropic Rsch. Lab., Washington, 1984-98, Entropic Geophysical, Inc., 1984-91, Entropic Speech Inc., 1984-02, Affordable Bldg. Sys., 2000—. Inventor patent predictive seismic deconvolution, multi-channel filtering. Recipient Rsch. Publication award Naval Rsch. Lab., 1984; named Life Master Am. Contract Bridge League. Fellow IEEE (contbr. to jour.). Avocation: bridge theory. Office: Entropic Processing Inc 20990 Valley Green Dr Apt 703 Cupertino CA 95014-1846 E-mail: john.parker.burg@att.net.

BURG, MAURICE BENJAMIN, physiologist, internist; b. Boston, Apr. 9, 1931; s. Charles and Augusta (Green) Burg; m. Judith Anne Braverman (dec.); m. Ruth Cooper, Dec. 30, 1967; children: Elizabeth, Laurence, Joan, Robert. AB, Harvard U., 1952, MD, 1955. Investigator Lab. Kidney/Electrolyte Metabolism Nat. Heart Lung and Blood Inst., NIH, Bethesda, Md., 1956—, chief Lab. Kidney/Electrolyte Metabolism, 1975—. Contbr. articles to profl. jours. Mem.: NAS. Office: Nat Heart Lung Blood Inst 10 Center Dr Msc 1603 Bethesda MD 20892-0001

BURG, RALPH, art association executive; b. Malden, Mass., Jan. 2, 1914; s. Joseph and Bessie (Meyer) B.; m. Fay E. Pristaw, Jan. 10, 1937; children: Stephen, Harvey. BA, Boston U., 19366. V.p. Beacon Musical Inst. Co., Boston, 1939-70; pres., owner Quisisana Lodge, Center Lovell, Maine, 1946-76; chmnn. Edna Hibel Soc., Coral Springs, Fla., 1979-99. Editor: Hibeletter newsletter, 1979-2002. Mem. Friends for Life, B'Nai B'rith. Recipient Cultural award Minister of Culture, Flanders, Belgium, 1983. Mem. Kiwanis (various coms. Boston chpt. 1946-70), Synergistic Assn. (pres. Boston chpt. 1962-70), Edna Hibel Soc. (chmn. 1979-2002), Woodlands Country Club. Avocations: golf, tennis, writing, bridge, saxophone. Home: 4604 King Palm Dr Tamarac FL 33319-6121 Office: Edna Hibel Soc PO Box 9721 Coral Springs FL 33075-9721 E-mail: maestroralph@cs.com.

BURGARD, RALPH, cultural and education planner; b. Buffalo, June 22, 1927; s. Willard Henry and Elise (Waite) Burgard; m. Elaine Johansen Hawk, Apr. 8, 1989 (div. Dec. 1994); m. Marjorie Dean Martin, Aug. 8, 1998; children: Christopher, Timothy, Nadia; m. Cecily Ward, Mar. 17, 1956 (div. Apr. 1985). BA in Philosophy, Dartmouth Coll., 1949. Mgr. R.I. Philharm. Orch., Providence, 1952—54; assoc. mgr. Buffalo Philharm. Orch., 1954—55; dir. Winston-Salem (N.C.) Arts Coun., 1955—57, St. Paul Coun. Arts and Scis., 1957—65; exec. dir. Am. Coun. Arts, N.Y.C., 1965—70; pres. Burgard Assocs., 1970—, Beaufort, 1994—. Author: (book) Arts in the City, 1968. Founder St. Paul Chamber Orch., 1958, A+ Schs. Program, 1987, Spectra Schs., 1998, A3 Schs., 2000; former sec. N.Am. Assembly State and Provincial Arts Agys.; former mem. adv. panel Nat. Endowments Arts, N.Y. State Coun. Arts, N.Y.C. Cultural Coun.; mem. Nat. Coun. Amenity Planners. Named Ralph Burgard Day, City of St. Paul, 1986; recipient 10th Yr. Tribute, Hartford Arts Coun., 1981, Merit award, Assn. Coll. Univ., Cmty. Art Adminstrs., 1982, Tribute, Nat. Assembly Cmty. Arts, 1987, Chancellor's award, N.C. Sch. Arts, 1997, Selina Roberts Ottum award, Ams. for Arts, 2000. Mem.: Century Assn. Avocations: rowing, books, nature. Office: Burgard Assocs PO Box 156 Beaufort NC 28516

BURGDOERFER, JERRY, lawyer; b. Jeffersonville, Ind, May 3, 1958; s. Jerry Jack and Barbara Jean Burgdoerfer. BS, Ind. U., 1980, MBA, JD cum laude, Ind. U., 1983. Bar: Ill. 1984, U.S. Dist. Ct. (no. dist.) Ill. 1984, U.S. Tax Ct. 1984. Assoc. Adams, Fox, Adelstein, Rosen & Bell, Chgo., 1983-88, ptnr., 1988-89; assoc. Jenner & Block, Chgo., 1989-90, ptnr., 1991—; with Mori Hamada Matsumoto, Tokyo, 1991—93; co-chair corp. dept. Jenner & Block, Chgo., 1999—2002, co-chair securities practice group, 2000—, mem. mgmt. com., 2002—. Author: (book) Director and Officers Liability: Prevention, Insurance and Indemnification, 2000, Securities Law, 2003; contbr. articles to profl. jours. Vol. United Cerebral Palsy Assn., 1995—, dir., 1999—; mem. exec. com. Northwestern U. Sch. Law Ann. Garrett Corp. and Securities Law Inst. Named 2d Benton, Nat. Moot Ct. Competition, 1982. Mem.: ABA, Chgo. Coun. Fgn. Rels., Chgo. Bar Assn. (chairperson '34 Act Com. 1996—98, reporter securities com. 1997—98, vice chair 1998—99, chair 1999—2000), Ill. Bar Assn., Inter Pacific Bar Assn., Internat. Bar Assn., Japan Am. Soc. Chgo., Exec. Club Chgo., Ind. U. Alumni Club Chgo. (vol. 1988—89), Econ. Club Chgo., Phi Delta Theta (sec. chpt. 1977—78, co-founder, mem. steering com. Chgo. alumni club 1988—89), Phi Delta Phi, Phi Eta Sigma. Avocations: bicycling, water-skiing, Japanese language. Office: Jenner & Block 1 E Ibm Plz Fl 4000 Chicago IL 60611-7603

BURGDOERFER, JERRY J. marketing and distribution executive; b. Connersville, Ind., Nov. 20, 1935; s. Louis M. and Edna (Seele) B.; m. Barbara Jean Hofherr, Aug. 15, 1954; children: Steven, Jerry, Jeffrey, Stuart. BS, Ind. U., 1957. Indsl. engr. Colgate Palmolive Co., Jeffersonville, Ind., 1958-59, mktg. mgr. N.Y.C., 1959-63, Am. Can Co., Green Bay, Wis., 1963-65, dir. sales, 1966-67, v.p., 1968-70; pres., dir. Am. Garden Products, Inc., Boston, 1970-71; exec. v.p. Facelle Co. div. Internat. Paper Co., N.Y.C., 1971-73; v.p. worldwide mktg. Hertz Corp., N.Y.C., 1973-77, exec. v.p., dir., from 1977; pres., chief exec. officer Berkey Inc., N.Y.C., 1979-86, Carysfort Enterprises Inc., Key Largo, Fla., 1987—; v.p. corp. mktg. AT Cross Co., Lincoln, R.I., 1991—, also bd. dirs.; prin. JJB Assocs., Bristol, R.I., 1996—. Bd. dirs. Avis Inc. Served with arty. U.S. Army, 1957-58. Recipient Torch of Liberty-Man of Yr. award B'nai B'rith Mem. Acad. Alumni Fellows (Ind. U.), Phi Delta Theta, Barrington Yacht Club (bd. govs.).

BURGE, CATHERINE ALICE, musician, educator; b. Ann Arbor, Mich., Oct. 27, 1956; d. Furman Horace and Dorothy Louise (Anderson) Burge; m. Paul J. Schorsch, May 8, 1999. BFA, Ohio U., 1978; MusM in Piano, Clarinet, U. Idaho, 1980; postgrad., San Francisco Conservatory of Music, 1981; D in Musical Arts, U. Colo., 2003. Clarinetist, solo pianist Wash./Idaho Symphony, Pullman, Wash., 1978-80; clarinetist Spokane (Wash.) Wind Symphony, 1980; pianist Spokane Ballet, 1980; entertainer Sweet Talk, W.Va., 1981-83; with sales dept., keyboardist Roberts Music Co., Pitts., 1983-84; music therapist, coord. activities Regency Hall Nursing, Pitts., 1984-85; minister of music Cranberry Christian Ctr., Pitts., 1986-87; clarinetist, solo pianist U.S. Army Band Europe, pianist U.S. Army Jazz Combo, pianist, keyboardist U.S. Army Europe Chorus, U.S. Army Europe Quintet Heidelberg, Fed. Republic of Germany, 1987-90; vocalist, keyboardist U.S. Army Field Band, 1990-98; asst. prof. music CC Denver, 1999-2000, music dept. coord., 2000-01; music instr., choral accompanist U. Colo., Boulder, 2001—; pianist, keyboardist Colo. Wind Ensemble, 2002—; mem. piano faculty Front Range C.C., 2003—; performer New Orleans Piano Inst., 2003. Keyboardist N. Star Players, Pitts., 1985—86; instr. Abundant Life Sch., 1995—99; keyboardist, arranger Abundant Life Ch., 1999; Carnegie Hall debut with Soldier's Chorus, U.S. Army Field Band, Erich Kunzel and Pops Orch, 1997; pianist, vocalist Orchard Rd. Christian Ctr., Denver, 2000—01. Singer: Orchard Rd. Christian Ctr., 2000—01; performer: New Orleans Piano Inst., 2003. Dir. music. Camp Wohelo-Theater, Pa., 1985; pianist North Hills Civic Chorus, Wexford, 1985, North Star Kids, Pitts., 1986; keyboardist North Way Christian Cmty., Wexford, Pa., 1983—86; pianist Christian Servicemen's Ctr., Eppleheim, Germany, 1987—, Tompkins Chapel, U.S. Army Europe; vocalist New Life Ch. Worship, Colorado Springs, 2003—. Recipient Silver medal, Internat. Piano Rec. Competition Am. Music divsn.; fellow, U. Idaho, Doctoral Rsch. grantee, U. Colo., 2002. Mem.: Music Tchrs. Nat. Assn. (professionally cert.). Avocations: skiing, bicycling, outdoor activities. Office: Coll Music Univ Colo Boulder Campus Box 301 Boulder CO 80309-0301 E-mail: catburge@aol.com.

BURGE, DAVID ALAN, patent lawyer, writer; b. Anderson, Ind., July 22, 1943; s. James Swisher and Esther M. (Sheppard) B.; m. Carolyn J. Alter, Nov. 24, 1966; children: Benjamin, Thomas. BS in Gen. Engring. with highest honors, U. Ill., 1966; JD, U. Louisville, 1970. Registered patent atty. Pres. David A. Burge Co LPA, Cleve., 1975—. Author: Patent and Trademark Tactics and Practice, 1980, 3rd edition, 1999; contbr. chpts. in books. Pres. Gen. Engring. Constituent Alumni Assn., 1984, 85. Mem.: ABA, Sigma Delta Kappa, Gamma Epsilon, Associated Locksmiths of Am., Am. Intellectual Property Law Assn., Cleve. Bar Assn., Phi Eta Sigma, Sigma Tau, Phi Kappa Phi. Avocations: antique tools, woodworking. Office: David A Burge Co LPA 2901 S Park Blvd Cleveland OH 44120-1842

BURGE, DAVID RUSSELL, concert pianist, composer, piano educator; b. Evanston, Ill., Mar. 25, 1930; s. Russell David and Sylvia (Swensen) B.; m. Liliane Choney, 1993; 1 child, Russell David. MusB, Northwestern U., 1951, MusM, 1952; DMus Arts, Eastman Sch. Music, 1956; postgrad., Cherubini Conservatory, Florence, Italy, 1956-57; DFA, Bucknell U., 1980. Instr. piano Northwestern U., 1949-52; assoc. prof. music, composer-pianist in resident Whitman Coll., 1957-62; dir. MacDowell Hall Concert Series at coll., 1959-62; organist Ch. of Christ Scientist, Walla Walla, 1958-62; from asst. prof. music to prof. U. Colo., 1962-75; chmn. piano dept. Eastman Sch. Music, U. Rochester, N.Y., 1975-87, prof., 1975-93, Kilbourn prof., 1978-79; artist-in-residence U. Calif., Davis, 1975; guest prof. piano U. Stockholm, Sweden, 1981, 92, Banff Ctr., Can., 1983-84, 86, U. Auckland, New Zealand, 1988; composer-in-residence San Diego Ballet Co., 1997—. Guest prof. Odense, Denmark, 1997; guest prof. composition U. Pa., 1977; guest prof. music history U. Gothenberg, Sweden, 1980, 92; feature writer San Diego Reader; guest prof. composition San Diego State U., 2000. Rec. artist, Mercury, Advance, Candide, Nonesuch (grammy nomination 1974), CRI Records, Mus. Heritage Soc. Records, Vox Records, Proviva Records, Wergo, Albany, Capstone Records, Classico Records, Fleur de Son Classics; composer: opera Intervals, 1961; trio for violin, cello, piano, 1962; work for piano Eclipse, 1963; for flute-piano Sources I, 1964; for violin-celeste-piano Sources II, 1965; for piano Eclipse II, 1966, Sources IV, 1969; for clarinet-percussion Sources III, 1967; for soprano-piano A Song of Sixpence, 1967, Life Begins at 40, 1998; for flute-clarinet-violin-cello-piano-tape Aeolian Music, 1968; String Quartet, 1969, Twone in Sunshine, an Entertainment for Theater, 1969; for violin-orch. that no one knew, 1969, Songs of Love and Sorrow, 1989, for solo piano Go-Hyang, 1994, Sonata for Violin and Piano, 1994, Liana's Song: A Ballet in Six Parts, 1995, The Dark Journey, 12 Pieces for Dance, 1995, 24 Preludes for Piano, 1996, Luna Lunera, a Ballet in 12 Parts, 1996, Moku (Island) for three percussionists, 1998; La Loteria Ballet, 1998, The Thousand Paper Cranes, 2001, Kaleidoscope (ballet), 2001; for piano and orch. Dances of Love and Laughter, 1998, When Love Prevails for solo vibraphone, 2001, Dibujos (sketches) for violin and piano, 2003; also songs, anthems.; contbr. over 200 articles to periodicals; columnist: Keyboard Mag., Clavier Mag., Piano Quar.; music reviewer: Music Library Assn. Notes; first major postarmistice concert, Seoul, Korea, 1953, New York debut playing all-modern program, 1961; toured, Korea, 1953-54, Europe, 1956-57, U.S.A., annually, 1960—, Eastern Europe, 1974, Far East, Australia, N.Z., 1984, 88; author: Twentieth-Century Piano Music, 1990; Vanishing Spring, 1998. Served with AUS, 1952-54, Korea. Decorated by U.S. Army for cultural relations work in Korea, 1954; recipient Alumni Merit award Northwestern U., 1974, Colo. Gov.'s award, 1975, Distinguished Alumni award Eastman Sch. Music, 1975, Deems Taylor award for mus. journalism ASCAP, 1978-79; Fulbright fellow in Italy, 1956-57; Faculty Research lectr. U. Colo., 1972 Mem. ASCAP, Internat. Webern Soc. (charter), Am. Soc. Univ. Composers (founder, nat. chmn. 1970-74), Pi Kappa Lambda. Address: 5243 Caminito Apartado San Diego CA 92108-4204 E-mail: music@davidburge.net.

BURGE, JOHN WESLEY, JR., management consultant, consultant; b. Mobile, Ala., Sept. 11, 1932; s. John Wesley and Mary Jo (Guest) B.; m. Shirley Paulette Roberts, Mar. 29, 1958; children: John, Delene, Eric, Kurt, Karen. Student, Centenary Coll., San Antonio Coll., UCLA. Engring. and mgmt. staff ITT Gilfillan, 1954-69; pres., gen. mgr. Rantec, Calabasas, Calif., 1969-71, chmn. bd., 1971-89; pres., gen. mgr. electronics and space divsn. Emerson Electric Co., St. Louis, 1971-80, corp. group v.p. govt., def., 1977-89; ret., 1989; pvt. practice, 1975— With USAF, 1950-54. Decorated Grand Cordon of Order Al-Istiqlal (Jordan). Presbyterian. E-mail: jburge@cox.net.

BURGE, STEVEN DONALD, city administrator; b. Omaha, Mar. 14, 1950; s. Melvin Lloyd and Mary Ann Burge. Cert. EMT, Western Iowa Tech. Coll., Sioux City, 1985; BS in Polit. Sci., BS in Sociology, Wayne (Nebr.) State Coll., 1992; MPA, U. Nebr., Omaha, 1997; postgrad., S.D. State U., 1999—. Cert. emergency med. technician. Mgr. housing devel., Norfolk, Nebr., 1994; city adminstr. City of Creighton (Nebr.), 1995, City of Dakota City, Nebr., 1998-2000. Bd. dirs. Cardinal Devel.; pres. Northeast Nebr. Devel. Network, 1997; pres. retail Ccom. Nebr. Public Power Dist., 1997; active Overall Econ. Devel. Plan, 1998. Active Knox County 911 Sys., 1995—98, Creighton Devel. Corp., 1995—98, Temporary Housing Action Team, 1994—95, Sgt Bluff Planning and Zoning, 1985—86; Sunday sch. tchr. Dakota City United Meth. Ch., 1998—2000; bd. dirs. N.E. Loess Hills Resource and Conservation and Devel., West Point, Nebr., 1998—2000; pres. Hwy. 35 Expy. Com., 1998—2000; active Pioneer Valley Days Com., 1986—87. Mem.: Nebr. Econ. Devel. Assn., Nebr. Planning and Zoning Assn., Midwest Sociol. Soc., Great Plains Sociol. Soc., Am. Sociol. Assn., Assn. Humanist Sociology, Jaycees (bd. dirs. Kimball County 1977—78, v.p. Kimball County 1979, v.p. Lyons 1980, regional dir. Nebr. 1981, pres. Council Bluffs 1982, pres. Sgt. Bluff 1985—87, regional dir. Iowa 1988, chmn. bd. Sgt. Bluff 1988, Iowa Hawkeye Corps 1989—2003), Alpha Kappa Delta (pres. 2000). Avocation: motorcycles/motorcycle riding. Home: 303 Spring Ave N Lake Preston SD 57249 Office: SD State U Scobey Hall #208 Brookings SD 57007

BURGE, WILLARD, JR., software company executive; b. Johnson City, N.Y., Oct. 2, 1938; s. Willard Sr. and Catherine Bernice (Matthews) B.; m. Carol Crockenberg, June 16, 1961; children: Willard III, Pennie Lynn. Registered profl. engr., Ohio. Indsl. engr. Harnischfeger Corp., Escanaba, Mich., 1966-67; sr. indsl. engr. Gen. Electric, Ladson, S.C., 1968-74, advanced mfg. engr. Mentor, Ohio, 1971-74; corp. staff engr. Eaton Corp., Willoughby Hills, Ohio, 1974-79, supr. N/C programming, 1979-80, supr. mfg. engring., 1980-82, mgr. mfg. systems engring., 1982-87; bus. unit mgr. MSC Products, Eaton Corp., Costa Mesa, Calif., 1987-91; pres., CEO CAM Software, Inc., Provo, Utah, 1991-93; chief exec. officer Key Svcs., Cypress, Calif., 1993—. Bd. dirs. CAM Software, Inc.; presenter in field. With U.S. Army, 1957. Mem. Soc. Mfg. Engrs. Republican. Avocations: photography, computers, start-up businesses. Home and Office: 6150 Geanie Ct Chino Hills CA 91709-6364 E-mail: wburgejr@msn.com.

BURGEE, JOHN HENRY, architect; b. Chgo., Aug. 28, 1933; s. Joseph Zeno and Helen (Dooley) B.; m. Gwendolyn Mary Henson, June 30, 1956; 1 son, John Gerard. BArch, U. Notre Dame, 1956, DEngr (hon.), 1983. Supt. constrn. Holabird & Root & Burgee, Chgo., 1955-56; project mgr. Naess & Murphy, Chgo., 1958-61; adminstr. design, project architect C. F. Murphy Assos., Chgo., 1961-65; assoc. ptnr. C. F. Murphy Assocs., 1965-67, ptnr., 1967; assoc. Philip Johnson (Architects), N.Y.C., 1967-68; ptnr. Johnson/Burgee, N.Y.C., 1968-82, John Burgee Architects, N.Y.C., 1982-98, Santa Barbara, Calif., 1998—. Chmn. Archtl. Rev. Bd., Bronxville, N.Y., 1974-75; chmn. Bronxville Planning Commn., 1975-77 Works include, I.D.S. Center, Mpls., Niagara Falls Conv. Center, Pennzoil Place, Houston, Crystal Cathedral, Los Angeles, AT&T Hdqrs., N.Y.C., PPG Hdqrs., Pitts., Transco Tower, Houston, Republic Bank, Houston, Nat. Center for Performing Arts, Bombay, 101 California Street, San Francisco, International Place, Boston, 190 South LaSalle Street, Chicago, IBM Headquarters, Atlanta, Mus. of Broadcasting, New York Canadian Broadcast Ctr., Toronto, Takashamya Dept. Store, N.Y., Capital Holding Ctr., Louisville, Puerto de Europa, Madrid, One Detroit Ctr., Marina Hotel and Shopping Ctr., Singapore, Ch. St. Mary, Lakeville, Conn. Pres. German-Am. Club, Bad Kreuznach, Germany, 1957-58, chmn. bldg. material sect. Met. Crusade of Mercy, Chgo., 1966-67; pres. Chgo. Br. North Montessori Sch. Bd., 1962-63, Lawrence Park Hilltop Assn., 1974-75; chmn. architecture com. Statue of Liberty/Ellis Island Centennial Commn.; mem. adv. coun. Coll. Engring. U. Notre Dame, 1982-88; bd. dirs. Lenox Hill Hosp., 1982-91, Parsons Sch. of Design, 1985-92, U. Notre Dame, 1988—, Chgo. Athenaeum, 1989-92, Music Acad. of the West, 2002-, 1st vice chmn., 2003. With U.S. Army, 1956—58. Recipient Reynolds Aluminum prize, 1978, honor award U. Notre Dame, 1981, Chgo. Architecture award. Fellow AIA, Urban Design Inst.; mem. Archtl. League N.Y. (dir.), Inst. Architecture and Urban Studies (dir. 1983, chmn., pres. 1984) Clubs: Saddle Cycle (Chgo.), Arts (Chgo.), University (Chgo.), Shenarock Shore (Rye, N.Y), Am. Yacht, Century Assn. Home: 639 Hot Springs Rd Santa Barbara CA 93108-2030 E-mail: burgeearchitect@cox.net.

BURGER, AMBROSE WILLIAM, agronomy educator; b. Jasper, Ind., Nov. 27, 1923; s. August and Katherine (Lechner) B.; m. Janice Fay Brandenburg, Aug. 24, 1946; children— Katherine, Marie, Patricia, Carol; m. Phyllis J. Voorhees Jacob, Oct. 25, 1967; stepchildren— Judy, Paul BS in Agronomy, Purdue U., 1947; MS in Agronomy, U. Wis., 1948, PhD, 1950. Asst. prof. agronomy U. Md., College Park, 1950-53; assoc. prof., then prof. agronomy U. Ill., Urbana, 1953-86, prof. agronomy emeritus, 1987—. Researcher in field crop sci.; developer color photographs and descriptions of crop and weed plants Served with U.S. Army, World War II Decorated Purple Heart with oak leaf cluster; recipient Paul A. Funk award U. Ill., 1972, Outstanding Freshman Tchr. award Alpha Lambda Delta, 1980, Campus award for excellence in teaching U. Ill., 1980, 82, Sr. Faculty award Coll. Agr., 1986 Fellow Am. Soc. Agronomy (Agronomic Edn. award 1964); mem. Crop Sci. Soc. Am., Nat. Assn. Colls. and Tchrs. Agr. (book rev. editor, Disting. Educator award 1984, Outstanding Tchr. Advisor award 1984, Ensminger-Interstate Disting. Tchr. award 1986), K.C., Moose, Elks, Delta Tau Alpha. Roman Catholic. Home: 2010B Eagle Ridge Ct Urbana IL 61802-8617 also: 638 Bird Bay Dr E Apt 112 Venice FL 34292-1222 E-mail: a-burger@uiuc.edu., awpjburger@aol.com.

BURGER, CHESTER, retired management consultant; b. Bklyn., Jan. 10, 1921; s. Benjamin W. and Terese (Felleman) B.; m. Hannah Kaufman, Jan. 30, 1948; children: Jeffrey Allen, Todd Oliver, Amy Louise; m. Ninki Hart, Jan. 9, 1959 (dec. Jan. 1969); m. Elisabeth Miller Owen, Sept. 2, 1971. BA, Bklyn. Coll., 1946. With CBS Radio, 1941-42; 1st U.S. TV reporter, visualizer CBS TV News, 1946-48; asst. news editor CBS-TV, 1948-50, news editor, 1950-52, film assignment editor, 1952-53, nat. mgr., 1953; writer-prodr. Omnibus program Ford Found., 1954-55; cons. Life mag., 1955; with pub. rels. dept. AT&T Co. and assoc. cos., 1955-88; pub. rels. counsel, asst. to pres. Ruder and Finn, Inc., 1955-57, v.p. plans, 1957-60; pres. Comm. Counselors (pub. rels. divsn. Interpublic, Inc.), N.Y.C., 1960-62, Echelons Office Temporaries, Inc. (and assoc. cos.), 1963-65, Chester Burger & Co., Inc. (mgmt. cons.), 1964-88, sr. cons., 1988-90; counsel James E. Arnold, Inc., N.Y.C., 1991-2000; cons. Coca-Cola Export Corp., 1964 65; guest lectr. New Sch. for Social Rsch., 1967, U. Mich. Grad. Sch. Bus. Adminstrn., 1969-72, NYU Divsn. Bus. and Mgmt., 1970-76, Dalhousie U., 1970; cons. Am. Bankers Assn., 1973-85, Alyeska Pipeline Svc. Co., 1974, AARP, 1986, Am. Cancer Soc., 1986-88, ret., 1988. Cons. The Carter Ctr., Atlanta, 1994; lectr. pub. rels. role in mgmt. Author: Survival in the Executive Jungle, 1964, Executives Under Fire, 1966, Executive Etiquette, 1969, Walking the Executive Plank (also pub. as Creative Firing), 1972, The Chief Executive, 1978, Inside Public Relations, 1984, 1988, also articles; editor: Mike and Screen Press Directory, 1953, 1954, 1955; contbg. editor: Quar. Rev. Pub. Rels. (now Pub. Rels. Quar.), 1959—2002, Popular Photography mag., 1967—68; editor: (monthly newsletter) Persuasion, 1972—74; mem. editl. adv. bd.: Pub. Rels. Jour., 1975—79. Bd. dirs. N.Y. Interracial Coun. for Bus. Opportunity, 1965-68, N.Y. Diabetes Assn., 1964-67, Nat. Comm. Coun. for Human Svcs., 1973-76; dir. Choice in Dying, Inc., 1993-96, treas. 1996, nat. chmn., 1999; bd. dirs. Union Theol. Sem., N.Y.C., 1990-94; sec., exec. com., trustee Nat. Urban League, 1967-76; pub. rels. chmn. Young Pres.' Orgn., 1962-63; adv. com. Black Exec. Exch. Program, 1969-85; 1st v.p. Nat. Urban League Devel. Found., Inc.; mem. pvt. sector adv. commn. U.S. Info. Agy., 1981-86; nat. adv. coun. Conn. Coll., 1982-88; adv. coun. Project Orbis, 1989-94; pres. bd. trustees, elder Ctrl. Presbyn. Ch. City of N.Y., 1984—; mem. White House Health Project Task Force, 1992; adv. bd. Population Commn. Internat., 1993—; bd. advisors Medicare Rights Ctr., 1996-98; bd. dirs. Ctr. for Cmty. Leadership, 1996-98; adv. bd. dirs. U.S. Sec. of Air Force Office of Pub. Affairs, 1998—; mem. pres.'s commn. of 125 U. Tex., Austin, 2003—. With AUS, 1942-46. Recipient Disting. Svc. citation United Negro Coll. Fund, 1974, award for Outstanding Svc., USIA, 1982, 1st Drew Middleton Pub. Affairs award USMC, 1991, medal for Outstanding Svc. to U.S., Govt. of U.S., 1995; named Counselors Counselor and life mem. Counselors Acad., 1988; named to Hall of Fame for Lifetime Contbns. to Profession, Arthur W. Page Soc., 1992. Mem. Telephone Pioneers Am. (hon.), Am. Pub. Rels. Assn. (dir. N.Y. chpt., nat. dir. 1959-60, v.p. ea. chpt. 1960-61), Pub. Rels. Soc. Am. (accredited; dir. 1961-63, John W. Hill award N.Y. chpt. 1980, Gold Anvil award for unusually significant contbns. 1987, chmn. Coll. Fellows 1989-90), Internat. Assn. Bus. Communicators (Spl. award 1995), Am. Arbitration Assn. (nat. panel arbitrators 1972-94), Nat. Assn. Securities Dealers (nat. panel arbitrators 1993—), Assn. Former Intelligence Officers, Century Club. Home: 33 W 67th St New York NY 10023-6224 E-mail: chetburger@aol.com.

BURGER, DAVID MARK, composer, educator, multimedia designer; b. NYC, 1950; s. Rev. Alfred and Bertie Burger; m. Sasha Spielvogel; 1 child, Silkie;children from previous marriage: Yael, Ariel. BA in classical lang. magna cum laude, Queens Coll., NYC, 1970, MA in classical lang. magna cum laude, 1971. Songwriter and copyrighter Richie Havens; designer multimedia prodns., 1976—95; composer choral and ensemble music, 1975—. Mem. TAYKU modern Hebrew ensemble, 1971—76. Composer: (songs) Windblown, Tree of Jade, Stories of Glory, One Thirty; copyrighter: choral works Freedom; composer: The Israel Trilogy: Prayer for the Peace of Israel, 1975, The Ancient Hope, 1978, The Declaration of Independence of Israel, 1998, Songs to Jerusalem, 1977, When I am Dead, My Dearest, 1979, Abundant Peace (Shalom Rav), 1980, Blessed is the Eternal God (Baruch El Elyon), 1984, Grant Peace (Sim Shalom), 1985, We Came to Sing in Jerusalem, 1988, A Kaddish for Spain (Kaddish Sepharad), 1992, From the Dead Sea Scrolls: Psalms 151 and 154-155 (Shirat Halev), 1993, A Prayer for Healing (Mi Shebeirach), 2000, Variations on a Theme by David Crosby, 2001, Sky Split, 2002, Peace Blessing (Brachah L'shalom), 2003, (films) Dark Angel, 2001, (dance) T'filah, 1995, Birthright, 2002; author: (scholarly work) First Vocalization of Texts of Psalms 151, 154 and 155 from the Dead Sea Scrolls. Recipient Alter Machlis award, Queens Coll., 1971, ASCAP Spl. awards, 1990—2003; grantee grad. asst. in music, Queens Coll., 1973. Mem.: Phi Beta Kappa. E-mail: DavidMarkBurger@msn.com.

BURGER, EDMUND GANES, architect; b. Yerington, Nev., Mar. 28, 1930; s. Edmund Ganes and Rose Catherine (Kobe) B.; m. Shirley May Pratini, Jan. 21, 1968; 1 dau., Jane Lee. B.M.E., U. Santa Clara, 1951; B.Arch., U. Pa., 1959. Engr. Gen. Electric Co., 1951-52; design engr. U. Calif. Radiation Lab., 1952-57; John Stewardson fellow in architecture, 1959; architect Wurster, Bernardi & Emmons, San Francisco, 1960-63, founder Burger & Coplans, Inc. (Architects), San Francisco, 1964, pres., 1964-79; owner Edmund Burger (Architect), 1979—. Guest lectr. U. Calif., Berkeley. Important works include Acorn Housing Project, Oakland, Calif., Crescent Village Housing Project, Suisun City, Calif., Coplans residence, San Francisco, Betel Housing Project, San Francisco, Grand View Housing Project, San Francisco, Albany (Calif.) Oaks Housing, Grow Homes, San Pablo, Calif., Mariposa Housing, Dunleavy Plaza Housing, Potrero Ct. Housing, San Francisco, Lee residence, Kentfield, Calif., Burger residences, Lafayette, Calif., Oceanside, Oreg., and El Cerrito, Calif., Yamhill Valley Vineyards Winery, McMinneville, Oreg., Portico De Mar, shop and restaurant complex, Barcelona, Spain, Hendrickson residence, Newport Beach, Calif., Hamilton residence, Winters, Calif., Sanders residence, Yuba City, Calif., Strack/Villars residence, Kentfield, Calif., Breton residence, Oakland, Visitor's Facilities Yosemite Nat. Park, Calif.; author: Geomorphic Architecture, 1986. Recipient citation for excellence in community architecture AIA, 1969, award of merit AIA, award of merit Homes for Better Living, 1970, 79, 1st Honor award, 1973, 81, Holiday award for a beautiful Am., 1970, Honor award 4th Biennial HUD awards for design excellence, 1970, Bay Area awards for design excellence, 1969, 74, 78, Apts. of Year award Archtl. Record, 1972, Houses of Year award, 1973, Calif. Affordable Housing Competition award, 1981, HUD Building Value into Housing award, 1981, Community Design award Calif. Council AIA, 1986; design grant Nat. Endowment for Arts, 1980, HUD, 1980; constrn. grant HUD, 1981. Office: PO Box 10193 Berkeley CA 94709-5193

BURGER, EDWARD JAMES, JR., health care policy executive; b. Cleve., Feb. 23, 1933; s. Edward James Burger and Edith Marie Archias; m. Sarah Greene, June 17, 1960; children: Heidi, Hilary. BSc, McGill U., 1954, MD, MChir, 1958; M Indsl. Health, Harvard U., 1960, DSc, 1966. Diplomate Nat. Bd. Med. Examiners, cert. Med. Coun. Can., lic. physician D.C., Vt. Mem. faculty Harvard Sch. Pub. Health, Boston, 1966-69; assoc. J.F. Kennedy Sch. Govt. Harvard U., Cambridge, Mass., 1967-69; mem. staff Office Sci. and Tech. Exec. Office of the Pres., Washington, 1969-76; prof. medicine Georgetown U. Med. Ctr., Washington, 1974-89, dir. Inst. Health Policy Analysis, 1981-89, pres., 1989—. Pres. E.J. Burger Assocs., Washington, 1976—; cons. Carnegie Commn. on Sci., Tech. and Govt., N.Y.C., 1989; mem. Nat. Inst. Chem. Studies, Charleston, W.Va., 1986—, Nat. Cancer Adv. Bd., Washington, 1973—76. Author: Protecting the Nation's Health, 1976, Science at the White House, 1981; editor: Risk, 1990. Bd. dirs. Coun. Ct. Excellence, Washington, Washington Internat. Sch., 1979—83; mem. legal adv. bd. Nat. Legal Ctr. for Pub. Interest, Washington, 1984—. Lt. comdr. USN, 1961—64. Guggenheim fellow, 1960—61. Fellow: ACP; mem.: AAAS, Am. Coll. Preventive Medicine, Cosmos Club, Harvard Club Boston. Avocations: tennis, piano. Office: Inst Health Policy Analysis 1150 18th St NW Ste 275 Washington DC 20036

BURGER, HAROLD ALAN, virologist; b. N.Y.C., Aug. 29, 1947; s. Aaron and Vera (Barmasel) B.; m. Barbara Weiser, July 15, 1973. BS, U. Chgo., 1969; PhD, Rockefeller U., 1976; MD, Albert Einstein Coll. Medicine, 1978. Diplomate Am. Bd. Internal Medicine. Intern, resident dept. medicine Montefiore Hosp., N.Y.C., 1978-80; sr. resident dept. medicine Stanford U. Med. Ctr., Calif., 1980-81; fellow Divsn. Infectious Diseases, 1981-85; co-dir. HIV rsch. Wadsworth Ctr., N.Y. State Dept. Health; prof. medicine Albany Med. Coll. Office: NY State Dept Health Wadsworth Ctr 120 New Scotland Ave Albany NY 12208-3425 E-mail: burger@wadsworth.org.

BURGER, HENRY G. vocabulary scientist, anthropologist, publisher; b. N.Y.C., June 27, 1923; s. B. William and Terese R. (Felleman) B.; m. Barbara G. Smith, Nov. 29, 1991. BA with honors (Pulitzer scholar), Columbia Coll., 1947; MA, Columbia U., 1965, PhD in Cultural Anthropology (State Doctoral fellow), 1967. Indsl. engr. various orgns., 1947-51; Midwest mfrs. rep., 1952-55; social sci. cons., 1956-67; anthropologist Southwestern Coop. Ednl. Lab., Albuquerque, 1967-69; assoc. prof. anthropology and edn. U. Mo., Kansas City, 1969-73, prof., 1973-93, prof. emeritus, 1993—, founding mem. univ. wide doctoral faculty, 1974-93; founder, pub. The Wordtree, Overland Park, Kans., 1984—. Lectr. CUNY; adj. prof. ednl. anthropology U. N.Mex., 1969; anthrop. cons. U.S. VA Hosp., Kansas City, 1971—72; spkr. in field; columnist linguistic column New Times, New Verbs, 1988—. Author: Ethno-Pedagogy, 1968, 2nd edit., 1968; editor, compiler: The Wordtree, a Branching Dictionary for Solving Phys. and Social Problems, 1984, selected for exhibit at 3 insts., selected as topic Cambridge Ency. of the English Lang., 1995—, 7 time citee Oxford English Dictionary, —, mem. editl. bd. Coun. Anthropology and Edn., 1975—80; contbr., articles; interviewee Voice of America, 2002. Capt. AUS, 1943-46. NSF Instl. grantee, 1970. Fellow World Acad. Art and Sci., Am. Anthrop. Assn. (life), Royal Anthrop. Inst. Gt. Britain (life); mem. European Assn. for Lexicography, Internat. Assn. Semiotic Studies, English-Speaking Union (v.p. Kansas City chpt. 1995-96), Dictionary Soc. N.Am. (life, terminology com.), Kans. Acad. Sci. (life), Assn. Internationale de Terminologie, Academie Europeenne des Scis., Arts et Lettres (corr.), Columbia U. Club, Phi Beta Kappa. Achievements include discovery of the branchability of processes (corresponding, for materials, to the periodic table of elements); research on computerized causality and reasoning. Office: The Wordtree 10876 Bradshaw St Overland Park KS 66210-1148 E-mail: burger@cctr.umkc.edu. *The computer analyzes prose information into tabulation, whence it can be re-formed diversely. Therefore computerization has revolutionized my authorship from textbooks to reference books.*

BURGER, HERBERT FRANCIS, advertising agency executive; b. Ligonier, Pa., Mar. 5, 1930; s. Adolph G. and Elizabeth (Johannsen) Burger; m. Jane Coulter, Oct. 1, 1966; children: Matthew F., Jennifer. BS in Econs, Thiel Coll., Greenville, Pa., 1952; MA in Journalism, Syracuse (N.Y.) U., 1955. C. Mgmt. trainee Joy Mfg. Co., 1955-56; account exec. Ketchum, MacLeod & Grove, Pitts., 1956-58, Marsteller Inc., Pitts., 1958-65; with Creamer Inc., Pitts., 1965-76; pres. Creamer Inc. (Pitts. divsn.), 1976-86; chmn., ptnr. St. George Group, Inc., Pitts., 1986-98. Bd. dirs. Overly Mft. Co., Pitts., Offices of Promotion; chmn. Pitts. Media Group, Pitts. Downtown Partnership; pres. Speedwell Enterprises, 1986—. Chmn. Pitts. Downtown Plan. With U.S. Army, 1953—55. Mem.: Pitts. Press Club, Pitts. Advt. Club (dir.), Grove City Country Club, Longue Vue Country Club, Duquesne Club. Republican. Lutheran. Home: 301 Wildburry Rd Pittsburgh PA 15238

BURGER, JOAN M. judge; b. Chgo., Mar. 15, 1944; d. Willaim James Herrmann and Cecile Dolores Malooly; m. Gary K. Burger, Mar. 19,1 966; children: Gary K. Jr., Christine M. Mattson, Eric W. BS, Loyola U., 1966; JD cum laude, St. Louis U., 1976. Legal officer Juvenile Ct., St. Louis, 1976-78; asst. circuit atty. 22nd Jud. Cir., St. Louis, 1978-80; cir. judge, 1995—; assoc. Law Offices Terry Flanagan, St. Louis, 1980-87; sole practice St. Louis, 1987-95. Bd. dirs. Monsanto YMCA, St. Louis, 1983-94; mem. Leadership St. Louis, 1990-91; mem. venture grant United Way, St. Louis, 1991-95; mem. Aid to Victims of Crimes, St. Louis, 1992-94. Mem. Women Lawyers Assn. (pres. 1982-83, Pres.'s award 1988, chairperson women in profession com. 1983-85, sec. solo and small firm sect. 1993). Home: 3512 Crittenden St Saint Louis MO 63118-1108 Office: 22nd Jud Cir 10 N Tucker Blvd Saint Louis MO 63101-2044

BURGER, MICHAEL, humanities educator; s. Robert Henry Burger and Burden Susan Lundgren; m. Miriam Carrol Davis, July 30, 1993. BA in History, Mich. State U., 1984; MA in History, U. Calif., Santa Barbara, 1986, PhD, 1991. Asst. prof. history Miss. U. for Women, Columbus, 1992—97, assoc. prof. history, 1997—2000, prof. history, 2000—. Author: Commentaries on Sources for the History of Western Civilization, 2003; editor: Sources for the History of Western Civilization, 2 vols., 2003. Named Miss. Humanities Tchr. of Yr., Miss. Humanities Coun. Mem.: Medieval Acad. Am., Hist. Soc., Am. Hist. Assn., Phi Alpha Theta, Phi Beta Kappa. Office: Miss Univ for Women Divsn Humanities Columbus MS 39701 Office Fax: 662-329-7348. Business E-Mail: mburger@muw.edu.

BURGER, RICHARD L. museum director; BA in Archaeology cum laude, Yale Coll., 1972; MA in Anthropology, U. Calif., Berkeley, 1975, PhD in Anthropology, 1978. Joined faculty Yale U., New Haven, 1981—, chmn. dept. anthropology, dir. Peabody Mus. Natural History. Cons. U.S. Justice Dept. and Customs Svc., Washington, N.Y.C., 1980-83; vis. prof. archaeology program U. Nat. Mayor de San Marcos, Lima, 1987; sr. fellow pre-Columbian studies program Dumbarton Oaks, 1991-96, chmn. fellows' adv. bd., 1994-96; panel mem. Archaeometry sect. NSF, 1995-97; docent social sci. faculty U. Nat. Mayor de San Marcos, 1998—. Author: The Prehistoric Occupation of Chavin de Huantar, Peru, 1984, Social and Economic Organization in the Prehistoric Andes, 1984, Chavin and the Origins of Peruvian Civilization, 1992, Emergencia de la Civilizacion en los Andes: Ensayos de Interpretacion, 1993, Excavaciones en Chavin de Huantar, 1998; asst. editor Current Rsch. Am. Antiquity, 1987-93; mem. editl. bd. Inst. Francais D'Etudes Andines, 1986—, Jour. World Prehistory, 1987—, Andean Past, 1987—, Boletin de Arqueologia PUCP, 1998—; contbr. articles to profl. jours. Fulbright-Hays doctoral disseration rsch. abroad fellow, 1975-76, postgrad. fellow Orgn. Am. States, 1978-79, fellow pre-Columbian studies Dumbarton Oaks, Trustees for Harvard U., Washington, 1980-81, Jr. Faculty fellow social scis. Yale U., 1984-85, Fulbright Hays fellow for rsch. Lecturing Coun. for Internat. Exch. Scholars, Pontificia U. Cath., Lima, 1985, 1993. Mem. Inst. Andean Rsch. (exec. bd. mem., 1991—, treas. 1994—), Phi Beta Kappa, Sigma Xi. Office: Peabody Mus Yale Univ 170 Whitney Ave New Haven CT 06511-8902

BURGES, STEPHEN JOHN, civil engineer, hydrologist; b. Newcastle, Australia, Aug. 26, 1944; s. William Charles and Iris Cavell May (Evans) B.; m. Sylvia Ellen Tregidga, Aug. 29, 1970. BSc, BE with honors, U. Newcastle, Australia, 1967; MS, Stanford U., 1968, PhD, 1970. Registered profl. engr., Wash.; registered profl. hydrologist. Asst. prof. U. Wash., Seattle, 1970-75, assoc. prof., 1975-79, prof. civil engring., 1979—. Mem. water sci. tech. bd. NRC, 1985-89, chmn. com. on climate change and water resources mgmt., 1990-92, mem. com. on basic rsch. opportunities in the earth scis., 1998-2000; mem. peer rev. com. water sci. tech. bd. Corps. of Engrs., 2001-02; Kisiel lectr. U. Ariz., 1997; Langbein lectr. Am. Geophys. Union, 2001. Contbr. articles to profl. jours. Fulbright-Hays Travel grantee, 1967. Fellow ASCE, AAAS, Am. Geophys. Union (editor Water Resources Rsch. jours. 1981-84, Water Resources Monographs 1984-86, exec. com. hydrology sect. 1980—, pres.-elect sect. 1992-94, pres. hydrology sect. 1994—, chmn. Horton award com. 1988-92, mem. com. on fellows 1990-92, mem. publs. com. 1996-98, chmn. bd. jour. editors 1996-98, chmn. devel. com. 2002—); mem. Am. Water Resources Assn., Internat. Assn. Hydraulic Rsch., Internat. Assn. Hydrology Scis., Sigma Xi. Achievements include research in hydrology, hydrologic processes, hydrologic engineering, water resource systems, stochastic hydrology. Home: 4306 54th Ave NE Seattle WA 98105-4941 Office: U Wash Box 352700 Dept Civil Engring Seattle WA 98195

BURGESON, JOYCE ANN, travel agency official; b. Jamestown, N.Y., Sept. 10, 1936; d. Walter Edward and Marion (Cree) Van Horn; m. David G. Burgeson, Sept. 10, 1955; children: Kathalene, Donna, Jeffrey, Karen, Christine. AS, Empire State Coll., SUNY, Saratoga Springs, 1990. Bookkeeper Burgeson Wholesale, Jamestown, 1962-88; realtor assoc. Kote Realty, Jamestown, 1982-89; real estate appraiser Goldome Bank, Jamestown, 1986-89; travel saleswoman, tour escort Cert. Travel Tours, Jamestown, 1983-90, 96—, Travelhost of Jamestown, 1990-95; payroll mgr. The Resource Ctr., Jamestown, 1988-95. Prin. Burgeson Bus. Seminars, Jamestown, N.Y., 1990—. Vol. Alamanda Elem. Sch.; mem. adminstrv. bd. 1st United Meth. Ch., Jamestown, NY, 1985—95; cert. lay spkr. United Meth. Ch., 1987—; mem. bd. Maple Grove HS, Bemus Point, NY, 1979—82. Mem. Toastmasters, Order of Vikings. Avocations: travel, lay speaking, camping. Home and Office: PO Box 923 Frewsburg NY 14738-0923 Address: 622 Monet Acres St West Palm Beach FL 33410-3339 E-mail: dgb622@yahoo.com.

BURGESON, MARILYN See SIEMON-BURGESON, MARILYN

BURGESS, ANN WOLBERT, nursing educator; Van Ameringen prof. nursing U. Pa., Phila., prof. of psychiat. and mental health nursing. Mem.: NAS. Office: Boston College School of Nursing, Cushing Hall 140 Commonwealth Ave Chestnut Hill MA 02467

BURGESS, CHARLES ORVILLE, history educator; b. Portland, Oreg., Jan. 18, 1932; s. Rex Orville and Glendora Almanda (Sundrud) B.; m. Cora Cloepfil, June 22, 1952; children: Donna Claire Majer, Jo Dell Nicholls, Robert Charles; m. Patricia Stewart Anderson, Apr. 22, 1976; children: Marc Richard Anderson, Brian Stewart Anderson, Tricia Louise Crozier, Kristen Anne Klein. BA, U. Oreg., 1957; MS (Danforth fellow), U. Wis., 1958, PhD, 1962; Nat. Postdoctoral fellow, Harvard U., 1967-68. Asst. prof. U. Calif., Riverside, 1962-64; asst. prof. history edn. U. Wash., Seattle, 1964-66, assoc. prof., 1966-70, prof., 1970—, chmn. area ednl. policy studies, 1970-92; prof. emeritus, 1992. V.p. divsn. F Am. Ednl. Rsch. Assn., 1977-79; fgn. expert Peoples Republic of China, 1984-85. Author: The Origins of American Thought (published in China as Meiguo Sixiang Yuanyuan); 1988, (with M.L. Borrowman) What Doctrines to Embrace, 1969, Profile of an American Philanthropist (Nettie Fowler McCormick), 1962; co-editor: (with Charles Strickland) G. Stanley Hall on Natural Education, 1965; co-author: (with Y. Yang and G. Zhu) Cultivating the World of Selfhood (published in China as Kaituo Zi Wode Shijie), 1997. Wash. com. civil rights ACLU, 1965-67; bd. dirs. Seattle Folklore Soc., 1966—; pres. History Edn. Soc., 1971-72. With USAF, 1950-54. Mem.: History of Edn. Soc. (pres. 1971—72), Phi Beta Kappa. Home: 14350 22nd Ave SW Burien WA 98166

BURGESS, CHARLOTTE GAYLORD, academic administrator; b. San Diego, Sept. 9, 1947; d. Charles Reid and Virginia (Huck) Gaylord; m. Larry Eugene Burgess, Oct. 7, 1973. BA in Psychology, U. Redlands, 1969, MA in Higher Edn. Adminstrn. & Counseling, 1970; postgrad., U. Calif., Riverside, 1978-79. Asst. to v.p. for student affairs U. Redlands, Calif., 1970-71, asst. dean, dir. student activities, 1971-79, dean of admissions, 1979-80, dean of students, 1980—2003, v.p., dean of student life, 2003—. Contbr. articles and essays to profl. publs. Mem. citizens adv. com. LWV, 1981-86; corp. body Redlands Comty. Hosp., 1981-92; bd. dirs. Family Svc. Assn., 1975-81, 82-95, 2002-, chair nominating com., 1987, counseling com., 1985-89, chair long-range planning com., 1986-95, strategic change com., 1997-98, exec. com., 1994-96, chair capital compaign, 2001; bd. dirs. Redlands YWCA, 1974-98, pres., 1990-92, 94-96, chair women's resource com., 1981-82, chair personnel commn., 1976-77, chair program commn. 1978-81, mem. equip com., 1985-88, exec. evalation commr., 1987, chair Hometour Selection Com., 1994—, Y Alliance, 1998—, chair 2002—; bd. dirs. YMCA, 1998—; gala food chair A. K. Smiley Pub. Libr., 1994,98, 2002; mem. Redlands Area Hist. Soc., 1972—; mem. citizens adv. com. City of Redlands Open Space, 1986-98; mem. Redlands Street Tree Com., 1987-96, 2001—; co-chair ann. campaign Redlands United Way, 1979, mem. admissions and allocations com., 1983-86; bd. dirs. Inland Empire World Affairs Coun., 1978-82. Recipient 2d Mile award Redlands Rotary Club, 1996 Mem. Nat. Assn. Student Pers. Adminstrs. (mem.-at-large So. Calif. exec. com. 1994—, Region VI award 1996), Redlands C. of C. (dir. 1998—, chair tourism com. 2003—),, So. Calif. Hist. Soc., Delta Kappa Psi (Redlands Alumni chpt., patroness 1972-89, Woman of Yr. Alumnae award 1978, U. Redlands Cmty. Svc. award 2001). Episcopalian. Avocations: reading, decorating, antiques, traveling. Home: 923 W Fern Ave Redlands CA 92373-5877 Office: U of Redlands PO Box 3080 Redlands CA 92373-0999 E-mail: char_burgess@redlands.edu.

BURGESS, DAVID, lawyer; b. Detroit, Nov. 30, 1948; s. Roger Edward and Claire Theresa (Sullivan) B.; m. Rebecca Culbertson Stuart, 1985 (dec. 1988); m. Catherine Mounteer, 1993; children: Jalil Riahi, Leila Riahi, Bryan Valentine, Grace Catherine. BS in Fgn. Svc., Georgetown U., 1970, MS in Fgn. Svc., JD, Georgetown U., 1978. Bar: D.C. 1978, U.S. Dist. Ct. D.C. 1979, U.S. Ct. Appeals (D.C. cir.) 1979, U.S. Ct. Appeals (fed. cir.) 1988, U.S. Ct. Internat. Trade 1988. Rsch. asst. Georgetown U. Sch. Bus. Adminstrn., Washington, 1975, asst. to dean, 1975-76; rsch. assoc., prof. Acad. in the Pub. Svc., Washington, 1976-79; asst. editor Securities Regulation Law Report, Washington; legal editor Internat. Trade Reporter Bur. Nat. Affairs, Washington, 1978-79; atty. Cadwalader, Wickersham & Taft, Washington, 1979-81; mng. editor Bur. Nat. Affairs, Washington, 1981-82; dir. U.S. Peace Corps, Niamey, Niger, 1982-84, Rabat, Morocco, 1984-85; dir. policy planning, mgmt. Peace Corps, Washington, 1985-87; dir. Bur. Human Rights and Humanitarian Affairs U.S. Dept. State, Washington, 1987-92; regional dir. Lawyers for Bush-Quayle Re-Election Campaign, 1992; chief party Rwanda Dem. and Governance Project, 1994, Russia NGO Sector Project, Moscow, 1994. Dir. democracy and civil soc. program, sr. advisor World Learning, Washington, 1995, dir. U.S. Democracy Fellows program, Washington, 1995-2002, dir. bus. devel., 2002-03; exec. v.p. Am.'s Devel. Found., Alexandria, Va., 2003—; spkr. workshops Minority Legis. Edn. Program, Ind. Assn. Cities and Towns, Georgetown U. Continuing Edn. Program, Comms. Workers Am., Colo. State U., U. Wis. Alumni rep. Internat. Sch. Bangkok, 1972-74; adj. prof. Inst. of World Politics, Washington, 2002—. Author: Financing Local Government, 1977, 2d edit., 1978, Preparation of the Local Budget, 2 vols., 1976, 2d edit., 1978, Local Government Accounting Fundamentals, 2d edit., 1977, Understanding Federal Assistance Programs, 2d edit., 1978, The POW/MIA Issue: Perspectives on the National League of Families, 1978; contbr. articles to publs. Mem. adv. com. Arlington County Fiscal Affairs, 1993-94; mem. pres. coun. Mary Washington Coll.; mem. Rep. Nat. Com.; vol. G.W. Bush Campaign, 1999-2000; bd. mem. U.S. Selective Svc. Sys., Region II Va., 2002-. Mem. D.C. Bar Assn., Washington Fgn. Law Soc., Hoyas Unltd. (pres. 1992-94), Federalist Soc., Georgetown U. Alumni Assn. (bd. govs. 1975-00, class rep. 1971-91, mem. alumni senate 2000—), Rep. Nat. Lawyers Assn., Pachyderm Club No. Va. (pres. 1992-93), Pres.'s Club. Republican. Roman Catholic. Home: 3115 1st Pl N Arlington VA 22201-1037 Office: 101 N Union St Ste 200 Alexandria VA 22314 E-mail: dburgess@adfusa.org.

BURGESS, DAVID LOWRY, artist; b. Phila., Apr. 27, 1940; s. Eric Turner and Ruth Elizabeth (McNees) Burgess; m. Janet Levengood, Mar. 25, 1960; children: Kirsten Deidre, Audrey Veronica, Vashti Gabrielle. Grad., Pa. Acad. of Fine Art, U. Pa., 1961. Lectr. Phila. Coll. Art, 1964-66; arts advisor Edn. Devel. Center, 1966-68; mem. faculty Harvard U. Sch. Edn., Cambridge, Mass., 1967-68; instr. Boston U., 1969; prof. Mass. Coll. Art, 1969-89; fellow Ctr. Advanced Visual Studies M.I.T., 1971-89; dean Carnegie-Mellon U. Coll. Fine Arts, Pitts., 1989-92, A.W. Mellon prof. art, 1992—; dir. SIMLAB, 1995-97; Koopman disting. chair in art Hartford (Conn.) U. Sch. Art, 2000. Mem. Nat. Humanities faculty, 1968—80; disting. artist ECHO-UQAM, Montreal, Canada; fellow Studio Creative Inquiry, CMU. Author: (book) Fragments, 1967, Looking and Listening, 1969, Memory, Environment, Utopia, 1973, Burgess: The Quiet Axis Trecarre, Montreal, Canada, 1987, one man shows include Inst. Contemporary Art, Boston, 1971, Carpetner Ctr., Harvard U., 1975, MIT, 1978, U. Que., Montreal, 1984, De Cordova Mus., Mass., 1985, 1988, Pewna Acad. Fin Arts Mus., 1987—88, exhibited in group shows at Boston Mus. Fine Arts Elements Exhbn., 1971, Multiple Interaction Team, 1972—74, CAYAC, Spain and Latin Am., 1972—74, Documenta 6, Kassel, Germany, 1977, Vienna Bienal, 1979, Sky Arts Conf, MIT, 1981—83, 1986, Ars Electronica, Austria, 1982, 1986, Kunst Acad., Germany, 1982, Artists Earthwatch, N.Mex., 1984, Monocle, Hamburg, Kunsthalle, Germany, 1985, De Cordova Mus., 1985, Pa. Acad. Fine Arts, 1987—88, Herning Kunst Mus., Denmark, 1989, Kunstverein, Karlsrahe, Germany, 1989, Contemporary Mus., Helsinki, Finland, 1989, Art Transition, 1991, Differentiel, Aix en Provence, France, 1992, Mu Gallery, Boston, 1993, MIT Mus., Cambridge, 1994, Tufts U., Mass., 1995, Pitts. Biennal, 1996, Nagoya City Mus., 1997, Fed. Res. Bank, Boston, 1998, Common Light, Cambridge, 2000, Joselott Mus. Hartford Sch. Art, 2000, Represented in permanent collections Boston Mus. Fine Arts, Houghton Libr., Harvard U., Nat. Collection Fine Arts, Washington, Smithsonian Collection, Pa. Acad. Fine Arts, Herning Kunstmuseum, Denmark, De Cordova Mus., Lincoln, Mass., SkyArt, Delphi, Greece, Mandala Pitts. Ctr. Arts, Lincoln Ctr. Galleries, NYC; appearances : (TV series) Nova, Artists in the Lab, 1982; Artists Earthwatch, KNME, 1985; Smithsonian World, 1987; New VR Techs. MSNBC, 1997; Seed of the Infinite Absolute, 2001; appearances Hartford Museum of Political Life, Hartford, Conn., 2002, Pitts. Ctr. for the Arts, 2002. Mem. First Night Internat. Bd., 2003—; founding mem. exec. bd. Cambridge Arts Coun.; mem. adv. bd. Art, Edn. and Ams. Recipient Am. Acad. Arts and Letters, Nat. Inst. Arts and Letters award, 1972, Gold award, Le Devoir, Montreal, 1989; fellow Guggenheim, 1973—74; grantee Nat. Endowment Arts, 1977—78, 1984, 1986, Rockefeller Found., 1979—80, 1985—87, Mass. Coun. Arts and Humanities, 1982, Mass. Artists Found., 1983, Mass. Coun. Arts and Humanities, 1987—88, Kellogg Found., 2001, Cambridge Arts Coun., 2000. Address: 1375 Cordova Rd Pittsburgh PA 15206-1430 E-mail: ib30@andrew.cmu.edu.

BURGESS, DON R. judge; b. Beaumont, Tex., Oct. 28, 1946; m. Barbara Grossman, Aug. 14, 1976; 3 children. BA, U. Tex., Austin, 1968; JD, U. Houston, 1971; LLM, U. Va., 1992. Bar. Tex., U.S. Dist. Ct. (ea. dist.) Tex., U.S. Ct. Mil. Appeals, U.S. Ct. Appeals (5th & 11th cirs.), U.S. Supreme Ct. Prosecutor Orange County (Tex.) County Dist. Attys. Office, 1973-74; atty. pvt. practice, Orange, Tex., 1974; ptnr. Pate & Burgess, Bridge City, Tex., 1975-77; judge 260th Dist. Ct., Bridge City, Tex., 1978-84, Tex. Ct. Appeals (9th dist.), Beaumont, 1984—. Col. USAR, 1968—2001. Decorated Meritorious Svc. medal, Army Commendation medal with 2 oak leaf clusters. Mem. Chi Phi, Phi Alpha Delta (pres. student Bar Assn.) Office: Tex Ct Appeals 1001 Pearl St Ste 333 Beaumont TX 77701-3549 E-mail: burgess@ih2000.net.

BURGESS, GARY THOMAS, social studies educator, consultant; b. San Rafael, Calif., Aug. 5, 1965; s. Bruce Miles Burgess and Marilyn Sheard; m. Tamara Natasha Spence, Sept. 13, 1997 (div. June 5, 2002). BA, Brigham Young U., 1990; MA, Ind. U., 1992, PhD, 2001. Adj. prof. Brigham Young U., Provo, Utah, 1996—2000; asst. prof. Hampton (Va.) U., 2000—. Founder Oral History Rsch. Ctr. Hampton (Va.) U., 2002—, dir. Oral History Rsch. Ctr., 2002—; cons. Nat. Intelligence Coun., Washington, 2002—; dir. Tanzania field studies Brigham Young U., 1996—2000. Author: Mambo: Swahili Lessons I, 2001, World Societies Since 1500, 2001; contbr. articles to profl. jours. Vol. Am. Red Cross, Hampton, 2001; forum organizer African Voices in the 21st Century Hampton (Va.) U., 2001—03; founder Students for Internat. Devel., Provo, 1990. Fellow, Fulbright-Hays U.S. Dept. Edn., 1995, NEH, 2002. Mem.: Tanzania Studies Assn., Am. Hist. Assn., African Studies Assn. Mem. Lds Ch. Avocations: kayaking, sailing, travel, hiking. Home: 232 C Dockside Drive Hampton VA 23669 Office: Hampton University Dept Political Science and History Hampton VA 23668

BURGESS, HAYDEN FERN (POKA LAENNI), lawyer; b. Honolulu, May 5, 1946; s. Ned E. and Nora (Lee) B.; m. Puanani Sonoda, Aug. 28, 1968. B in Polit. Sci., U. Hawaii, JD, 1976. Bar: Hawaii 1976, U.S. Tax Ct., U.S. Ct. Appeals (9th cir.). Pvt. practice, Waianae, Hawaii, 1976—; pres. Hawaii Coun. for 1993 and Beyond, Honolulu, 1991—; exec. dir. Waianae Coast Cmty. Mental Health Ctr., 1997—. V.p. World Coun. Indigenous Peoples before UN, 1984-90; human rights adv., writer, speaker in field; pres. Pacific and Asia Coun. Indigenous Peoples; cons. on indigenous affairs, 1984; indigenous expert to ILO Conv.; expert UN seminar on effects of racism and racial discriminations on social and econ. rels. between indigenous peoples and states, 1989—; del. Native Hawaiian Convention, chmn. Trustee Office Hawaiian Affairs, Honolulu, 1982-86; mem. Swedish Nat. Commn. on Mus., 1986; leader Hawaiian Independence Movement; mem. Hawaiian Sovereignty Elections Coun. E-mail: plaenui@pixi.com.

BURGESS, J. WESLEY, neuropsychiatrist; b. Mar. 5, 1952; BS, Purdue U., 1974; PhD, N.C. State U., 1979; MD, U. Miami, 1987. Diplomate Am. Bd. Med. Examiners. Rsch. assoc. N.C. Mental Health Dept., 1975-79; with Caribbean Primate Rsch., La Parquera, P.R., 1976-79; faculty psychology U. Calif., Davis, 1979-81; faculty UCLA, 1981-84, Western Grad. Sch. Psychology, 1989-90; intern Stanford U., 1987-88, resident in psychiatry, 1988-91, staff psychiatrist Alzheimer's Rsch. Inst., 1989-90; dir. psychiat. emergency svc. Palo Alto Veterans Med. Ctr., 1989-90; chief resident Stanford U. Med. Ctr., 1990-91; faculty Pacific Grad. Sch. Psychology, 1990-92; dir. adolescent div. Ctr. Mood Disorders, L.A., 1991-93; faculty Calif. Sch. Profl. Psychology, 1991-92. Expert panel Superior Ct., Juvenile Ct., Mcpl. Ct. Calif., L.A.; chief investigator SmithKline Beecham/Chemtrials, 1992-94; clin. cons. Fox Network, Warner Bros., others. Contbr. articles to profl. jours. UCLA neuropsychiat. Inst. fellow, 1981-83, Stanford NIMH fellow, 1990-91; recipient Mead Johnson award Psychiatry, 1991, Physician of Yr. award Physicians Adv. Bd., 2003. Mem. AMA (Physicians Recognition award), No. Calif. Psychiat. Soc. (Rsch. award 1991), Los Angeles County Med. Assn., So. Calif. Pediatric Assn., Am. Psychiat. Asns., Calif. Psychiat. Assn., So. Calif. Psychiat. Soc., Am. Assn. Advancement Psychotherapy, Internat. Soc. Adolescent Psychiatry, Am. Soc. Adolescent Psychiatry, Am. Soc. Clin. Psychopharmacology, Calif. Med. Assn., Acad. Magical Arts. Avocations: slide guitar, growing orchids. Office: 11980 San Vicente Blvd Ste 620 Los Angeles CA 90049-6604 E-mail: zatochi@aol.com.

BURGESS, JAMES HARLAND, physics educator, researcher; b. Portland, Oreg., May 11, 1929; s. Harland F. B. and Marion U. (Burgess); m. Dorothy R. Crosby, June 10, 1951; children: Karen, Donald, Joanne. BS, Wash. State U., 1949, MS, 1951; PhD, Washington U., St. Louis, 1955. Sr. engr. Sylvania Electric Products, Mountain View, Calif., 1955-56; research assoc. Stanford U., Palo Al to, Calif., 1956-57, asst. prof. physics Palo Alto, Calif., 1958-62; assoc. prof. Washington U., St. Louis, 1962-73, prof., 1973-98, prof. emeritus, 1998—. Cons. in field, 1956-66. Mem. Am. Phys. Soc., Am. Assn. Physics Tchrs., Phi Beta Kappa, Sigma Xi Office: Washington U Physics Dept 1 Brookings Dr Saint Louis MO 63130-4899

BURGESS, JOHN FRANK, management consultant, former utility executive, former army officer; b. Lanett, Ala., Nov. 18, 1917; s. John Frank and Mary Catherine (Heard) B.; m. Helen Hamby, Aug. 26, 1939; children: Beverly, Barbara, Frank. BS, Auburn U.; MA, George Washington U. Commd. 2d lt. U.S. Army, 1941, advanced through grades to col., ret., 1969; regional v.p. Consol. Edison Co. of N.Y., Inc., N.Y.C., 1969-83; cons. mgmt. Melville, N.Y., 1983-85; assoc. cons. Power Mgmt. Assocs., Inc., Groton, Conn., 1985-87; Columbia, Md., 1985-89. Active bds. various civic and profl. orgns., Queens, N.Y., 1969-83. Decorated Legion of Merit with 2 oak leaf clusters; named Man of Yr. Queens County Bldg and Contractors Assn., 1977 Episcopalian. Home: 9860 Terrace Lake Pt Roswell GA 30076-3742

BURGESS, JOHN H. ergonomist, consultant; b. Niagara Falls, Aug. 9, 1923; s. John Hersha and Mary Ann (Crandell) B.; m. Sylvia Marie Johnson, June 30, 1965. BS, Kent State U., 1948; MA, U. Miami, 1950. Engring. psychologist Bell Aerosystems, Buffalo, 1955-66; ops. rschr. Adolf Meyer Ctr., Decatur, Ill., 1966-74; engring. psychologist Dept. of Army, Champaign, Ill., 1974-76; ergonomist Syracuse, N.Y., 1976—. Instr. in psychology Western Coll., Oxford, Ohio, 1951-52; adj. prof. Syracuse U., 1983-84. Author: Systems Approaches to Public Services, 1978, Designing For Humans, 1986, Human Factors in Industrial Design, 1988, Managing Stress for a Healthier Life, 2000; contbr. articles to jours. in field. Sgt. AUS, 1943-46. Recipient award for design of auditory warning Nat. Safety Coun., 1980. Mem. APA, Human Factor & Ergonomics Soc. Home: 3412 Midland Ave Syracuse NY 13205-2033

BURGESS, JOHN HERBERT, physician, educator; b. Montreal, Que., Can., May 24, 1933; s. John Frederick and Willa Reta (McGinness) B.; m. Andrea Clouston Rutherford, May 30, 1958; children: Willa, Cynthia, Lynn, John. BSc, McGill U., Montreal, 1954, MD, CM, 1958. Med. resident Montreal Gen. Hosp., 1958-60, 62-64, dir. div. cardiology, 1973-94; Nuffield rsch. fellow U. Birmingham, Eng., 1960-62; McLaughlin rsch. fellow Cardiovascular Rsch. Inst., San Francisco, 1964-66; asst. prof. medicine McGill U., 1966-69, assoc. prof., 1969-75, prof., 1975—. Contbr. articles to profl. jours. Decorated Order of Can.; hon. fellow Coll. Medicine, South Africa. Master ACP; fellow Am. Coll. Cardiology, Royal Coll. Physicians and Surgeons Can. (pres. 1990-92), Royal Coll. Physicians (Edinburgh), Royal Australasian Coll. Physicians (hon.), Royal Coll. Physicians (London); mem. Can. Soc. Clin. Investigation. Avocations: cross country skiing, photography. Home: 639 Murray Hill Westmount QC Canada H3Y 2W8 Office: Montreal Gen Hospital 1650 Cedar Ave Montreal QC Canada H3G 1A4

BURGESS, JOHN PAUL, minister, religion educator; b. Denver, Dec. 18, 1954; s. Charles Samuel and Elizabeth Ann (Bulger) B.; m. Deborah Lynn Shoemaker, July 9, 1988; children: Hannah Ruth, Luisa Katherine, Rachel Elizabeth. BA, Colo. Coll., 1976; MA, U. Chgo., 1980; MDiv, McCormick Sem., 1983; PhD, U. Chgo., 1986. Ordained to ministry Presbyn. Ch. (U.S.A.), 1984. Asst. prof. religion, campus minister Doane Coll., Crete, Nebr., 1986-91; parish assoc. Westminster Presbyn. Ch., Lincoln, Nebr., 1989-91; assoc. for theol. studies Presbyn. Ch. (U.S.A.), Louisville, 1991—98; assoc. prof. theology Pitts. Theol. Sem., 1998—. Contbr. articles to profl. publs.; author: The East German Church and the End of Communism, Why Scripture Matters. NEH grantee, 1990-91. Mem. Am. Acad. Religion, Soc. Christian Ethics. Office: 616 N Highland Ave Pittsburgh PA 15206

BURGESS, JOHN RICHARD, engineer; b. Leeds, England, Sept. 5, 1947; s. Richard and Margaret B.; m. Christine Farr, Aug. 2, 1969 (div. 1984). BSc, Leeds Polytechnic, 1976; MBA, Durham (Eng.) U., 1997. Chartered engr.; register European engr.; state registered clin. scientist. Head med. electronics Airedale Dist. Health Authority, Kieghley, England, 1971—79; head med. engring. Devonshire Area Health Authority, Exeter, 1979—90; dir. ops. Med. and Tech. Adv. Svcs., Birmingham, 1990—91; cons., clin. dir. No. Lincolnshire and Goole NHS Trust, Grimsby, 1992—; divisional dir. N.E. Lincs NMS Trust, Grimsby, 2001—. Bd. dirs. IPEM Engring., London. Capt. Air Tng. Corps., Eng., 1984. Fellow Chartered Inst. of Mgmt.; mem. Nat. Health Svc. Confedn. (quality com. 1999), Inst. Physics in Engring. Medicine, Royal Coll. Medicine (assoc.), Windermere Cruising Assn. (commodore 2002). Avocations: sailing, badminton, walking. Home: 9 Iona Dr DN36 4XU Grimsby England Office: No Lincolnshire & Goole NHS Scartho Rd DN332BA Grimsby England Fax: 01472875340. E-mail: john.burgess@nlg.nhs.uk.

BURGESS, LARRY EUGENE, library director, history educator; b. Montrose, Colorado, July 18, 1945; s. Eugene Floyd and Edyth Eleanor (Faussone) B.; m. Charlotte Reid (Gaylord), Oct. 7, 1973. BA, U. Redlands, Calif., 1967; MA, Claremont Grad. Sch., 1969, PhD, 1972. Archivist A.K. Smiley Pub. Libr., Redlands, Calif., 1972-85, libr. dir., 1986—. Adj. prof. history, U. Redlands, 1972—, U. Calif., Riverside, 1979—; book reviewer Lincoln Herald, 1988—. Author: Mohonk: Its People and Spirit, 1980; (with others) A Day with Mr. Lincoln, (with others), 1994; co-author: The Hunt for Willie Boy, 1994. Vice-chmn. Calif. Heritage Preservation Commn., 1977-84; Hist. Soc. So. Calif., L.A., pres., 2003—; bd. dirs. U. Redlands, 1987-2001. Recipient Archival Award of Excellence Calif. Heritage Preservation Commn., 1991; Preservation Merit Award Calif. Hist. Soc., 1992, Cmty. Enrichment Award Hist. Soc. So. Calif., 1994. Mem. Soc. Am. Archivists, So. Calif. Archivists (past pres.), Zamorano Club (bd. dir. 1994—, pres. 1999-2002), Rotary Club Relands (pres. 1999-2000). Avocations: travel, gardening, book collecting. Home: 923 W Fern Ave Redlands CA 92373-5877 Office: A K Smiley Pub Libr 125 W Vine St Redlands CA 92373-4728 E-mail: admin@aksmiley.org.

BURGESS, LARRY LEE, commercial investment executive; b. Phoenix, May 13, 1942; s. Byron Howard and Betty Eileen (Schook) B.; m. Mary Jane Ruble, Mar. 9, 1985; children: Christopher, Patrick; children from previous marriage: Byron, Damian. BSEE, Naval Postgrad. Sch., 1972; MSEE, Naval Postgrad. Sch. Officer USN, 1973; MS in Civil Engring., U. Colo., 2002. Officer USN, Washington, 1964-85; corp. exec. Lockheed-Martin, Denver, 1985-98; pres. L & M Capital Investments, LLC, Denver, 1987—; CEO L&M Property Mgmt. Co., LLC, 1988—; pres. L&M Constrn., LLC, 1998, Dreams LLC, 2001—. Presenter in field; pres. 3515 Brighton Blvd. LLC, 2002—, 3198 Blake St., LLC, 2002—. V.p. Denargo Market Neighborhood Assn.; co-pres. Upper Larimer Neighborhood Assn.; pres. Elyria Swansia Bus. Assn.; coach Youth Activities, Corpus Christi, 1976-78; coach youth basketball Littleton (Colo.) YMCA, 1992-2000, Chatfield Competitive Basketball, 1996-2000, Jefferson County Recreational Basketball, 1997-98; spkr. in local schs., Littleton, 1987-90; bd. dirs. Elyria/Swanson Bus. Orgn. Named to Kans. Basketball Hall of Fame, 1993. Mem. AIAA (dir.), SASA, Armed Forces Comm. Navy League, Kiwanis. Republican. Home: 3 Red Fox Ln Littleton CO 80127-5710 E-mail: lbur238057@aol.com.

BURGESS, MARILYN K. science educator; b. Yale, Mich., Dec. 12, 1960; d. Elton Leroy and Virginia Lee Burgess; m. William E. Shadley, Dec. 27, 1981 (div. June 1991); m. Craig L. Forgaard, May 30, 1993. BS in Liberal Arts, BS in Edn., Ctrl. Mich. U., 1987; postgrad., U. Alaska, Calif. State U., U. Hawaii, Hilo, Mich. Tech. U. Adult edn. tchr. Brown City (Mich.) Schs., 1987-88; sci. tchr. Poughkeepsie (N.Y.) City Schs., 1988-89; naturalist Glacier Bay Nat. Park, Gustavus, Alaska, 1991—; mgr., framer Fireweed Gallery, Gustavus, Alaska, 1996-98; sci. and math. tchr. Gustavus Sch., 1989—. Participant Gustavus Emergency Response, 1992; health fair student coord. Bartlett Meml. Hosp.,

Gustavus, 1999—. Grantee NSF, 1995-2002, Alaska Sea, 1995; state finalist for Excellence in Sci. Tchg. award 2002.. Mem.: NSTA, AAAS, NEA (bldg. rep. 1994—), Alaska Sci. Tchrs. Assn., NCSM, Nat. Coun. Tchrs. Math. Avocations: dogs, reading, singing. Office: Gustavus Sch 1 School Street PO Box 120 Gustavus AK 99826 E-mail: marilynb@gustavus.ak.us.

BURGESS, MARJORIE LAURA, retired protective services official; b. Whitakers, N.C., Nov. 24, 1928; d. Benjamin and Laura Lenora (Ford) Harrison; m. Bonus David Dixon, July 24, 1948 (div. Apr. 1970); children: David Kingsley (dec.), Terence David, Michael Jerome; m. William A. Burgess, June 6, 1970 (div. July 1976). AS in Correction Adminstrn., John Jay Coll. Criminal, Justice, N.Y.C., 1971; BA in Social Scis., John Jay Coll Criminal Justice, N.Y.C., 1972, postgrad., 1973-75. Correction officer N.Y. State Dept. Correction, Bedford Hills, N.Y., 1959-67, correction sgt., 1967-73, correction lt., 1973-82, 86-90, capt., 1982-86; ret., 1990. Adv. coun. divsn. sr. svcs. Bergen County, 1997. Author: (poetry) Walking on the Road of Life, 1997, Life! It's More Than A Notion, libr. of congress Watermark press, 2000. Vol. intergenerational program Martin Luther King Srs. Ctr. Mem. AAUW, Am. Correctional Assn., Alumni Assn. John Jay Coll., The Smithsonian Assocs., Retired Pub. Employees Assn., AARP. Democrat. Baptist. Avocations: writing, singing, playing scrabble, reading.

BURGESS, MARY ALICE (MARY ALICE WICKIZER), publisher; b. San Bernardino, Calif., June 21, 1938; d. Russell Alger and Wilma Evelyn (Swisher) Wickizer; m. Michael Roy Burgess, Oct. 15, 1976; children from previous marriage: Richard Albert Rogers, Mary Louise Rogers Reynnells. AA, Valley Coll., San Bernardino, 1967; BA, Calif. State U., San Bernardino, 1975, postgrad., 1976-79, U. Calif., Riverside, 1976-79. Lic. real estate salesman, Calif.; real estate broker, Calif. Sec.-treas. Lynwyck Realty & Investment, San Bernardino, 1963-75; libr. asst. Calif. State U., San Bernardino, 1974-76, purchasing agt., 1976-81; co-pub. The Borgo Press, San Bernardino, 1975-99; owner MilleFleurs Info. Svcs., 2000—. Co-pub: (with Robert Reginald) Science Fiction and Fantasy Book Review, 1979-80; co-author (with M.R. Burgess) The Wickizer Annals: The Descendents of Conrad Wickizer of Luzerne County, Pennsylvania, 1983, (with Douglas Menville and Robert Reginald) Futurevisions: The New Golden Age of the Science Fiction Film, 1985, (with Jeffrey M. Elliot and Robert Reginald) The Arms Control, Disarmament and Military Science Dictionary, 1989, (with Michael Burgess) The House of the Burgesses, 2d edit., 1994; author: The Campbell Chronicles: A Genealogical History of the Descendants of Samuel Campbell of Chester County, Pennsylvania, 1989, (with Boden Clarke) The Work of Katherine Kurtz, 1992-93, (with Michael Burgess and Daryl F. Mallett) State and Province Vital Records Guide; editor: Cranberry Tea Room Cookbook, Still The Frame Holds, Defying the Holocaust, Risen from the Ashes: A Story of the Jewish Displaced Persons in the Aftermath of World War II, Being a Sequel to Survivors (Jacob Biber), 1989, Ray Bradbury: Dramatist (Ben P. Indick), 1989, Across the Wide Missouri: The Diary of a Journey from Virginia to Missouri in 1819 and Back Again in 1821, with a Description of the City of Cincinnati, (James Brown Campbell), Italian Theatre in San Francisco, Into the Flames: The Life Story of a Righteous Gentile, Jerzy Kosinski: The Literature of Violation, The Little Kitchen Cookbook, Victorian Criticism of American Writers, 1990, The Magic That Works: John W. Campbell and The American Response to Technology, 1993, Libido into Literature: The "Priméra Época" of Benito Pérez Galdós, 1993, A Triumph of the Spirit: Stories of Holocaust Survivors, 1994, A Way Farer in a World in Upheaval, 1993, William Eastlake: High Desert Interlocutor, 1993, The Price of Paradise: The Magazine Career of F. Scott Fitgerald, 1993, The Little Kitchen Cookbook, rev. edit., 1994, An Irony of Fate: William March, 1994, Hard-Boiled Heretic: Ross Macdonald, 1994, We The People!, 1994, The Chinese Economy, 1995, Voices of the River Plate, 1995, Chaos Burning on My Brow, 1995; co-editor and pub. (with Robert Reginald) of all Borgo Press publs.; also reviewer, indexer, researcher and editor of scholarly manuscripts. Chmn. new citizens Rep. Women, San Bernardino, 1967; libr. San Bernardino Geneal. Soc., 1965-67; vol. Boy Scout Am., Girl Scouts U.S., Camp Fire Girls, 1960s. Recipient Real Estate Proficiency award Calif. Dept. Real Estate, San Bernardino, 1966. Mem. City of San Bernardino Hist. and Pioneer Soc., Calif. State U. Alumni Assn., Cecil County (Md.) Hist. Soc., Gallia County (Ohio) Hist. and Geneal. Soc., DAR (membership and geneal. records chmn. 1964-66, registrar and vice regent San Bernardino chpt. 1965-67). Avocations: genealogy, films, travel. Office: MilleFleurs PO Box 2845 Box 2845 San Bernardino CA 92406-2845

BURGESS, MEREDITH NANCY STRANG, advertising agency executive; b. Rockland, Maine, Apr. 27, 1956; d. Walter P. and Charlene M. (Perkins) Strang; m. James L. Burgess, June 24, 1978 (div. Sept. 1999); children: Christopher James, Matthew Strang, Andrew Charles. BS, U. Maine, 1978. Store activities rep. McDonald's Corp., Boston, 1978-79; account exec. Arnold & Co., Inc., Portland, Maine, 1979-80, field account supr., 1980-81, account supr. for McDonald's advt. in Maine, 1981-83, account svc. mgr., 1984, v.p., 1985-86; pres., co-owner Burgess, Brewer, Stanyon & Payne Inc., Portland, 1986-90; owner, pres. Burgess Advt. & Assocs., Inc., Portland, 1990—. Mem. Camden (Maine) Rep. Town Com., 1974-80, Cumberland (Maine) Rep. Town Com., 1980—; officer Cumberland County Rep. Com., 1990-94; del. Maine Rep. Conv., 1974, 76, 78, 80, 88, 90, 92, 94, 96, 98, 2000, 1st alt. to Rep. Nat. Conv., 1976; committeewoman from Knox County, Maine Rep. Com., 1980-81; bd. dirs. Ronald McDonald House, 1982-89, U. Maine Alumni Coun., 1986-92, Greater Portland C. of C., 1992-93, Maine Chamber and Bus. Alliance, 1994-98; bd. dirs. Ronald McDonald House of Portland, 1988—, pres., 1995-99; mem. bd. visitors U. Maine, 2002—, vice chair 2003—. Recipient Conwell award, 1992, Tribute of Women in Industry (TWIN) award, 1993, Star awards Vols. of Am., 1996, Edward Bernays award Maine Pub. Rels. Coun., 1996, Block M Alumni Activities award U. Maine, 1993, Adult Good Samaritan award ARC, 2001, Jefferson award for pub. svc., 2003. Mem. Am. Assn. Advt. Agys. (bd. dirs. N.E. chpt. 1993—, govt. rels. com. 1994—), Greater Portland Advt. Club (bd. dirs. 1984-91), Maine Geneal Soc., Maine Hist. Soc. (bd. dirs. 1993-2002), Soc. Mayflower Desc (bd. dirs. 1991-95), U. Maine Alumni Assn. (bd. dirs. Cumberland County chpt. 1995—, pres. 1996-99), Alpha Phi. Home: 12 Country Charm Rd Cumberland Center ME 04021-9580 Office: Burgess Advt & Assocs Inc 1290 Congress St Portland ME 04102-2113

BURGESS, MICHAEL, library director, writer; b. Fukuoka, Kyushu, Japan, Feb. 11, 1948; came to U.S., 1949; s. Roy Walter and Betty Jane (Kapel) B.; m. Mary Alice Wickizer, Oct. 15, 1976; stepchildren: Richard Albert Rogers, Mary Louise Reynnells AB with honors, Gonzaga U., 1969; MLS, U. So. Calif., 1970. Periodicals librarian Calif. State U., San Bernardino, 1970-81, chief cataloger, 1981-94, prof., 1984—, head tech. svcs. and collection devel., 1994—. Editor Newcastle Pub. Co., North Hollywood, Calif., 1971—92; pub. Borgo Press, San Bernardino, 1975—91, Brownstone Books, San Bernardino, 1991—99, Sidewinder Press, San Bernardino, 1991—99, Unicorn & Son, San Bernardino, 1991—99, Burgess & Wickizer, San Bernardino, 1991—99, Emeritus Enterprises, 1993—99, Starmont House, 1993—99; assoc. editor SFRA Rev., 1993—94, Millefleurs Info. Svcs., San Bernardino, 2000—. Author 92 books and short works under pen names Michael Burgess, R(obert) Reginald, Boden Clarke, and others, with occasional co-authors, including: Stella Nova, 1970, Cumulative Paperback Index, 1939-1959, 1973, Contemporary Science Fiction Authors, 1975, The Attempted Assassination of John F. Kennedy, 1976, Things to Come, 1977, Up Your Asteroid!, 1977, Science Fiction and Fantasy Literature, a Checklist, 1700-1974, 1979, The Paperback Price Guide, 1980, 2nd edit., 1983, Science Fiction & Fantasy Awards, 1981, If J.F.K. Had Lived, 1982, The House of Burgesses, 1983, 2nd edit., 1994, The Wickizer Annals, 1983, Tempest in a Teapot, 1983, A Guide to Science Fiction & Fantasy in the Library of Congress Classification Scheme, 1984, 2nd edit., 1988, The Work of Jeffrey M. Elliot, 1984, Futurevisions, 1985, Lords Temperal & Lords Spiritual, 1985, 2nd edit., 1995, The Work of Julian May, 1985, The Work of R. Reginald, 1985, The Work of George Zebrowski, 1986, 2nd edit., 1990, 3rd edit., 1996, Mystery and Detective Fiction in the Library of Congress Classification Scheme, 1988, The Work of William F. Nolan, 1988, 2nd edit., 1998, The Arms Control, Disarmament, and Military Security Dictionary, 1989, Hancer's Price Guide to Paperback Books, 3d edit., 1990, Reginald's Science Fiction and Fantasy Awards, 2nd edit., 1991, 3d edit., 1993, Reference Guide to Science Fiction, Fantasy, and Horror, 1992, Science Fiction and Fantasy Literature, 1975-1991, 1992, The Work of Robert Reginald, 2nd edit., 1992, The State and Province Vital Records Guide, 1993, The Work of Katherine Kurtz, 1993, St. James Guide to Science Fiction Writers, 1996, CSUSB Faculty Authors, Composers and Playwrights, 1996, rev. edit., 1996, BP 250, 1996, Xenograffiti, 1996, Codex Derynianus, 1998, Katydid and other Critters, 2001; editor: Ancestral Voices, 1975, Alistair MacLean, 1976, Ancient Hauntings, 1976, Phantasmagoria, 1976, R.I.P., 1976, The Spectre Bridegroom and Other Horrors, 1976, John D. MacDonald and the Colorful World of Travis McGee, 1977, Dreamers of Dreams, 1978, King Solomon's Children, 1978, They, 1978, Worlds of Never, 1978, Science Fiction & Fantasy Book Review, 1980, Candle for Poland, 1982, The Holy Grail Revealed, 1982, The Work of Bruce McAllister, 1985, rev. edit., 1986, George Orwell's Guide Through Hell, 1986, 2nd edit., 1994, The Work of Charles Beaumont, 1986, 2nd edit., 1990, California Ranchos, 1988, The Work of Chad Oliver, 1989, The Work of Colin Wilson, 1989, The Work of Ian Watson, The Work of Reginald Bretnor, 1989, The Work of Ross Rocklynne, 1989, To Kill or Not To Kill, 1990, The Work of Dean Ing, 1990, The Work of Jack Dann, 1990, The Work of Pamela Sargent, 1990, 2nd edit., 1996, The Trilemma of World Oil Politics, 1991, The Work of Louis L'Amour, 1991, The Work of Brian W. Aldiss, 1992, Geo. Alec Effinger, 1993, Polemical Pulps, 1993, Sermons in Science Fiction, 1994, The Work of Elizabeth Chater, 1994, The Work of Jack Vance, 1994, The Work of William Eastlake, 1994, The Work of William F. Temple, 1994, The Work of Gary Brandner, 1995, The Work of Stephen King, 1996, Running From The Hunter, 1996; author of 11,500 essays, 17 short stories; editor of 1,250 books. Recipient MPPP award, 1987, Lifetime Collectors award for Contbn. to Bibliography, 1993, Pilgrim award, 1993; named title II fellow U. So. Calif., 1969-70. Mem. NEA, AAUP, ALA, ACLU, Sci. Fiction and Fantasy Writers Am., Mystery Writers Am., Calif. Tchrs. Assn., Calif. Faculty Assn. (statewide librs. task force 1986-89, 93—, editor newsletter 1987-89), Calif. Libr. Assn., San Bernardino Hist. and Pioneer Soc., Internat. Assn. for Fantastic in Arts, Internat. PEN, U.S.A. Ctr. West, Nat. Geneal. Soc., Sci. Fiction Rsch. Assn., Horror Writers Am. Office: Millefleurs PO Box 2845 San Bernardino CA 92406-2845 also: Calif State U Libr 5500 University Pkwy San Bernardino CA 92407-2318

BURGESS, MICHAEL, congressman; b. Denton, Tex., Dec. 23, 1950; m. Laura Burgess; 3 children. BS, MS, North Tex. State U.; MD, U. Tex., Houston; M in Med. Mgmt., U. Tex., Dallas. Resident Parkland Hosp., Dallas; pvt. practice Ob-Gyn. Assocs., Lewisville, Tex.; chief of staff Lewisville Med. Ctr., chief obs.; mem.26th Dist. Tex. U.S. Ho. Reps. from 26th Tex. dist., 2003—; mem. transp. and infrastructure com. U.S. Ho. Reps., mem. sci. com. Mem.: Denton County Med. Soc. (pres.). Office: 1721 Longworth HOB Washington DC 20515 also: Ste 230 1660 S Stemmons Fwy Lewisville TX 75067*

BURGESS, MICHAEL H. management consultant; b. Jacksonville, Fla., Aug. 25, 1956; s. Robert H. and Margaret (Raulerson) B.; m. Patricia Ferguson, Sept. 8, 1979; children: Daniel H., Thomas B. BSBA, Samford U., 1978; MBA, Ga. State U., 1989. Credit mgr. GE Capital, Gainesville, Fla., 1978-79, br. mgr. Tallahassee, 1979-91, mktg. svcs. rep. Jacksonville, 1981-82, mgr. mktg. svcs., 1982-85, mgr. inventory financing, 1985-86, new bus. devel. mgr. Atlanta, 1986-94, dir. of mktg./Mexico Mexico City, 1994-95, client svc. mgr., 1995-97; pres. Burgess Cons., Inc., Atlanta, 1997-2000; pres., gen. mgr. Crown Internat. Cons., Atlanta, 2000—. Republican. Presbyterian. Avocations: water skiing, camping, hunting.

BURGESS, PAULA LASHENSKE, health facility administrator; b. Athol, Mass., Mar. 22, 1955; d. John Joseph and Lotta Catherine (Maroni) Lashenske; m. Jack Leland Burgess Jr., May 15, 1982; children: Jack Leland III, Brian Lane. AAS in Paralegal Studies, Durham (N.C.) Tech. C.C., 1988; Assoc. Risk Mgmt., Ins. Inst. Am., 1990; BSN, St. Anselm's Coll., 1977; MHA, Duke U., 1983. RN, N.C.; lic. real estate agt., N.C. Staff nurse Morton Plant Hosp., Clearwater, Fla., 1977-78, Duke U. Med. Ctr., Durham, 1978-86, risk mgr., 1984—; adminstrv. intern Durham County Gen. Hosp., 1982; dir. utilization rev. High Point (N.C.) Meml. Hosp., 1983-84. Co-author: Mapping Your Risk Management Course in Stand-Alone Hospitals, 1996; co-contbr.: Liability Issues in Perinatal Nursing, 1997; co-author newsletter N.C. Soc. for Healthcare, 1990. Mem. Durham County Rep. Women's Club, 1996—; vol. Duke Children's Classic, Durham; mem. N-Vestment Inc., Durham, 1996—. Mem. Am. Soc. Healthcare Risk Mgmt. (spl. projects com. 1994, nominating com. 1996, hist. com. 1998—), Risk and Ins. Mgmt. Soc. (Piedmont chpt. society dir. 1994-96, pres. 1990-91, Southeastern regional conf. com. 1990, 94, co-chair golf tournament 1992-93). Republican. Roman Catholic. Avocations: golf, tennis, basketball, investments, croquet. Home: 2013 Sprunt Ave Durham NC 27705-3251 Office: Duke U Med Ctr PO Box 3811 Durham NC 27702-3811

BURGESS, RICHARD RAY, oncology educator, molecular biology researcher, biotechnology consultant; b. Mt. Vernon, Wash., Sept. 8, 1942; s. Robert Carl and Irene Marjorie (Wegner) B.; m. Ann Baker, June 17, 1967; children— Kristin, Andreas BS in Chemistry, Calif. Inst. Tech., 1964; PhD in Biochemistry and Molecular Biology, Harvard U., 1969. Helen Hay Whitney fellow Inst. Molecular Biology, Geneva, 1969-71; asst. prof. oncology McArdle Lab. Cancer Research U. Wis., Madison, 1971-77, assoc. prof., 1977-82, prof., 1982—, dir. Biotech. Ctr., 1984-96, James D. Watson Prof. Oncology, 2001—. Cons. in field; mem. NSF study sect. in biochemistry, 1979-84; chmn. bd. Consortium for Plant Biotech. Rsch., Inc., 1992-96. Series editor U. Wis. Biotech. Ctr. Resource Manuals; editor-in chief Jour. Protein Expression and Purification, 1990—; contbr. articles to profl. jours. Bd. dirs. Coun. Biotech. Ctrs., 1991-93; mem. Gov.'s Coun. on Biotech. Grantee NSF, 1978-80, 85-90, NIH, 1980—, Nat. Cancer Inst., 1971—; Guggenheim fellow, 1983-84; recipient medal Waksman Inst., 1999. Fellow Am. Acad. Microbiology; mem. Am. Soc. Biochemistry and Molecular Biology, Am. Chem. Soc. (Pfizer award 1982), Am. Assn. Cancer Research, Am. Soc. Microbiology, Protein Soc. Home: 10 Knollwood Ct Madison WI 53713-3479 Office: U Wis McArdle Lab Cancer Rsch 1400 University Ave Madison WI 53706-1526

BURGESS, ROBERT KINGSLEY, aeronautical engineer; b. Englewood, NJ, May 27, 1929; s. Charles Leon Burgess and Nina Doris King; m. Arlene Doris Killian, June 25, 1960; children: Holly Robaczynski, Kristin Hummel. BS in Aero. Engring., Purdue U., 1951; postgrad., NYU, 1953—55, New Haven Coll., 1956—57. Registered profl. engr., Conn. Flight test engr. Sikorsky Aircraft, Stanford, Conn., 1951—62, project engr., 1962—70, chief sys. engring. ABC helicopter, 1970—74, tech. dir. internat. mktg., 1974—77, chief test ABC helicopter, 1977—78, chief competitive evaluation, 1978—79, chief engring. changes UH-60A, 1979—83, H-60 derivative engring. mgr., 1983—85; sr. project engr. AH-64A McDonnell Douglas, Mesa, Ariz., 1985—86, project mgr. engring. change control, 1986—90, dept. mgr. product sustainment, 1990—91, dept. mgr. AH-64B, 1991—92, engring. project mgr. AH-64A/B/D, 1991—. Test pilot, cons. engr. Bridgeport (Conn.) Flight Svc., 1959; design engr. Auto Parts Mfg., Inc., Branford, Conn., 1979—81; cons. engr. Newport (RI) Offshore, Ltd., 1981—82. Contbr. articles to profl. jours. Mem.: AHS, AIAA, Aircraft Owners and Pilots Assn. Achievements include patents for electrically heated windshield wiper blade for ground vehicles. Avocation: flying. Home: 8120 E Appaloosa Tr Scottsdale AZ 85258 Office: Boeing Co 5000 E McDowell Rd Mesa AZ 85215 Fax: 480-891-6433. E-mail: bob.burgess@boeing.com.

BURGESS, ROBERT RONALD, human resources executive; b. Memphis, Dec. 2, 1943; s. Doyle Eugene Burgess and Mildred Burgess (Sparks) Hamill; m. Suzie Strong, June 28, 1985; 1 child, Mary Weldon. BS in Psychology, Memphis State U., 1967, MEd, 1975, EdD (ABD), 1979. Dir. Teen Challenge, Vienna, Austria, 1971-73; religious affairs coord. Memphis State U., 1973-80; dir. human resources The Peabody, Memphis, 1980-81, GE/RCA, Memphis, N.Y.C., 1981-86; exec. dir. The Promus Companies, Memphis, 1986-99; v.p. human resources Argosy Gaming Co., Alton, Ill., 1999—. Chmn. coord. coun. Profl. Religious Assn. in Higher Edn., N.Y.C., 1978-79. Editor: Dialogue on Campus, 1978. Fund raiser WKNO Edn. T.V., Memphis, 1989, United Way, Memphis, 1988. With U.S. Army, 1969-71. Recipient Disting. Svc. award U.S. Army, Berlin, 1971. Mem. Human Resources Assn., Human Resources Planning Soc. (corp. sponsor 1989—), St. Louis Club. Avocations: antique restoration, gardening, fatherhood. Home: 50 Berkshire Dr Saint Louis MO 63117-1046 Office: Argosy 219 Piasa St Alton IL 62002-6232

BURGESS, ROBERT SARGENT, retired human services consultant; b. Providence, Oct. 19, 1916; s. Alexander Manlius and Abby (bullock) B.; m. Ruth Elizabeth Carter, Sept. 21, 1940 (dec.); children: Joan Chesebro, Marjorie Waite, Robert S. Jr., David Dyer; m. Mary Lou Hemmerling, June 4, 1999. BA, Brown U., 1938; MA, U. Chgo., 1943. Cert. social worker. Field sec. Am. Friends Svc. Com., midwest area, 1938-41; asst. dir. Ill. Bd. Welfare Commrs., Chgo., 1942-43; asst. warden R.I. Correctional Instns., Cranston, RI, 1943-46; sr. supr. R.I. Divsn. Pub. assistance, Providence, 1946-50; exec. dir. R.I. Heart Assn., Providence, 1950-57; planning dir. Health & Welfare Assn., Pitts., 1964-78; exec. dir. R.I. Coun. Cmty. svcs., Providence, 1964-74. Spl. del. Internat. Conf. Social Welfare, The Hague, Nairobi and San Juan, 1972-75; cons. Conservation Commn., Hanover, N.H., 1991-99. Author: (book) "To Try the Bloody Law" the story of Mary Dyer. Pres. R.I. Consumers Coop., Providence, 1947-51; 1st male mem., bd. dirs. Planned Parenthood of R.I., Providence, 1968-71; chmn. R.I. State Coun. on Aging, Providence, 1969-71, Mass. Bd. Pub. Welfare, Boston, 1973-78, chmn., 1975-78; chmn. Providence Model Cities Coun., 1973. Mem. NASW (nat. bd. dirs. 1971-74, Robert S. Burgess Comty Svc. award), Am. Friends Svc. Com., Democratic Socialist Am., Conservation Law Found., Adult Chamber Music Players, Assn. for Statewide Health and Welfare (nat. pres. 1972-73). Socialist. Avocations: tennis, squash, square dance calling, writing, orchestra and quartet playing. Home: 80 Lyme Rd Apt 167 Hanover NH 03755-1230

BURGESS, RUTH LENORA VASSAR, speech and language educator; b. Pune, India, Aug. 6, 1939; d. Theodore R. and F. Estelle (Barnett) Vassar; m. Stanley Milton Burgess, Feb. 26, 1960; children: John Bradley, Stanley Matthew, Scott Vassar, Heidi Amanda Elizabeth, Justin David. BS in Edn., Tex. Tech. U., 1960; MA, U. Mo., 1968, PhD, 1979. Speech therapist Inkster (Mich.) Pub. Schs., 1961-62; mid. sch. tchr. Strafford (Mo.) Pub. Schs., 1962-63; speech therapist Fulton (Mo.) Pub. Schs., 1967-68; speech-lang. clinician Springfield (Mo.) Pub. Schs., 1963-66; asst. prof. Evangel Coll., Springfield, 1968-76; prof. Sch. Tchr. Edn. S.W. Mo. State U., Springfield, 1976—, dir. Ctr. Rsch. and Svc., 1990 97. Mem. sci. adv. bd. Internat. Ctr. Enhancement of Jerusalem, Israel, 1993—; field reviewer Dept. Edn., Washington, 1993-96, U.S. Vocat. Rehab., Washington, 1993, 94, 96,99; mem. evaluation team Title I Springfield Schs., 1994. Author: The Status of the Educational Resource Teacher, 1981; editor The Learner in the Process, 1978-80; contbr. articles to profl. jours. Ex-officio bd. dirs. Orphanage Assn., Pune, 1968—; mem. Kodaikanal-Woodstock Alumni Assn., Atlanta, 1956—; mem. Women Issues Network, Springfield, 1993—. Grantee Dept. Edn., 1978-83, 90-92, Dept. Elem. and Secondary Edn., 96, Mellon Found., 1988-90. Mem. AAUW, ASCD, Am. Speech, Lang. and Hearing Assn. (cert.), Internat. Assn. for Cognitive Edn. (field editor 1990-94). Avocations: literary group, hiking, creative writing, travel, advocacy. Office: SW Mo State U 901 S National Ave Springfield MO 65804-0088 E-mail: rvb649f@smsu.edu.

BURGESS, SAMUEL BULLOCK, pathologist, consultant; b. Providence, May 3, 1915; s. Alexander Manlius and Abby (Bullock) B.; m. Jane Clapp, June 28, 1941; children: Martha, John M. AB, Brown U., 1939, ScM, 1941; MD, Boston U., 1950. Diplomate Am. Bd. Pathology. Pathologist Windham Cmty. Meml. Hosp., Willimantic, Conn., 1955-56; assoc. pathologist Lemuel Shattuck Hosp., Boston, 1956-57; chief lab. svc. U.S. VA Hosp., Providence, 1957-59; dir. labs. Cambridge (Mass.) Hosp., 1959-61, Glover Meml. Hosp., Needham, Mass., 1961-80; pvt. practice Medford, N.J., 1980—. Asst. prof. pathology Boston U. Sch. Medicine, 1956-80; assoc. prof. pathology Temple U. Sch. Medicine, Phila., 1980-81, U. Medicine and Dentistry N.J., Stratford, 1990—. Author: Understanding the Autopsy, 1993; contbr. articles to profl. jours. Active Am. Friends Svc. Com., Phila., 1976-92. Fellow Coll. Am. Pathologists; mem. AAAS, Friends Med. Soc. (chmn. 1990-99). Mem. Soc. Of Friends. Home and Office: 108 Medford Leas Medford NJ 08055-2226 E-mail: burgess@medleas.com.

BURGESS FLORES, ELSA MARIE, counselor, health educator, advocate; b. Douglas, Ariz., Dec. 21, 1927; d. Ysabel Burgess; m. Benjamin Flores, Jan. 1, 1955; children: Margaret Ann, Michael Martin, Matthew Maurice. AAS, Lamson Bus. Coll., Tucson, 1955. Cert. HIV/AIDS educator. Founder, counselor Faro de Amor, Douglas and Sonora, Mexico, 1970—. Vol. health educator, Gay rights and issues advocate, Douglas and Sonora, 1991—. Author: (autobiography) Autumn Farewell, 1999 Despedida en Otoño, 2002. Recipient award for love, support and guidance Kansas City AIDS Coun., 1990, Vol. of Yr. award Ariz. Rural Health Office, 1997. Office: Faro de Amor 1624 11th St Douglas AZ 85607 E-mail: elsa@cybertrails.com.

BURGET, DEAN EDWIN, JR., plastic surgeon; b. Toledo, June 29, 1936; s. Dean E. Sr. and Marie E. (Alwine) B.; m. A. Undine Ehrman, Mar. 16, 1957 (div. Mar. 1993); children: Mark A.E., Kevin Phillips, Undine Peeples; m. Gabriella Morocz, May 14, 1993. BS, U. Toledo, 1958; MD, Yale U., 1962. Diplomate Am. Bd. Plastic Surgery. Intern surgery U. Hosps., Cleve., 1962, resident in anesthesiology, 1963; resident in gen. surg. Hahnemann Med. Coll. and Hosp., Phila., 1966-68; resident in plastic surg. Temple U. Hosp., Phila., 1968-70, U.S. Govt. fellow in rehab. surgery, 1970-71, instr. plastic surgery, 1970-71, Med. Coll. Pa., Phila., 1970-71, assoc. clin. prof., 1979-81; asst. prof., dir. divsn. plastic surgery Hahnemann Med. Coll. and Hosp., Phila., 1972-75; staff surgeon, cons. surgeon various cmty. hosps., 1975-85; pvt. practice Devon, Pa., 1985—. Fellow ACS; mem. Am. Soc. Plastic and Reconstructive Surgeons, Pickering Hunt Club (Phila.), Ausable Club/Adirondack Mountain Res. (St. Huberts, N.Y.), Yale Club (N.Y.C.), Rittenhouse Club (Phila.), Penn Club, St. Nicholas Soc. City N.Y., Pa. Soc. Sons Revolution, Colonial Soc. Pa., Soc. Colonial Wars Pa., Nat. Huguenot Soc., Soc. War 1812, Phila. Soc. Promoting Agr. Office: 500 Chesterbrook Blvd Wayne PA 19087

BURGGRAF, FRANK BERNARD, JR., landscape architect, retired educator; b. N.Y.C., Nov. 13, 1932; s. Frank Bernard and Johanna (Verbaan) B.; m. Jane Martin Rannenberg, June 25, 1955 (div. 1997); children: Helen Marguerite, Frank Bernard, John Christian; m. Margaret Goff, Oct. 31, 1998. BS, SUNY-Syracuse, 1954; MLA, U. Pa., 1958. Registered landscape architect, N.Y. Asst. prof. U. Ga., Athens, 1958-63; assoc. prof., dir. regional planning grad. program Pa. State U., University Park, 1963-70; chief planning analyst N.Y. State Pub. Service Commn., Albany, 1970-80; cons. landscape architect, planner Delmar, N.Y., 1980-84; prof. landscape architecture U. Ark., Fayetteville, 1984-97, dir. program in landscape architecture, 1984-87, emeritus prof. landscape architecture, 1997—. Mem. N.Y. State Bd. Landscape Architecture, 1977-84, chmn., 1979-81 Contbr. articles to profl. jours. Bd. dirs. Fayetteville Mcpl. Airport, 1997—. Served to lt. col. USAF, 1954—81. Fellow Am. Soc. Landscape Architects; mem. Am. Planning Assn., Elks (exalted ruler local lodge, 1990). Democrat. Home: 18665 Brentwood Mountain Rd Winslow AR 72959-9755 E-mail: fburggraf@hotmail.com.

BURGHARDT, RAYMOND FRANCIS, JR., ambassador; b. NYC, May 27, 1945; s. Raymond Francis and Marguerite (Schroeder) B.; m. Susan Day, Aug. 2, 1969; children: Helen, Caroline. BA, Columbia Coll., 1967; postgrad., Columbia Sch. Internat. Affrs., 1967-68. With U.S. Fgn. Svc., 1969—; dep. dir. Office of Vietnam, Laos and Cambodia Dept. of State, Washington, 1980-82; polit. counselor U.S. Embassy, Tegucigalpa, Honduras, 1982-84; dir. Latin Am. affairs Nat. Security Coun., Washington, 1984-85, spl. asst. to pres., sr. dir. Latin Am., 1985-87; polit. counselor U.S. Embassy, Beijing, 1987-89, dep. chief of mission Seoul, Korea, 1990-93, charge d'affaires, 1993, dep. chief of mission Manila, 1994-96, U.S. consul gen. Shanghai, 1997—99; dir. Am. Inst., Taiwan, 1999—2001; amb. to Vietnam Dept. of State, 2001—. Mem. Am. Fgn. Svc. Assn., Asia Soc., Manila Yacht Club, Wianno Club. Avocations: cross-country skiing, hiking, music. Office: US Embassy Ba Dinh Dist 7 Lang Ha Hanoi -0200 Vietnam*

BURGHARDT, WALTER FRANCIS, JR., veterinarian; b. Columbus, Ohio, Sept. 18, 1952; s. Walter Francis and Helen Wanda (Watrobinski) B.; m. Charleen S. Horkott, July 24, 1993; stepchildren: Joel Webster, Christopher Webster; 1 child, Kurt. BA, Fla. Atlantic U., 1974, MA, 1975; DVM, U. Fla., 1980; PhD in Biopsychology, U. Md., 1988. Diplomate Am. Coll. Vet. Behaviorists. Prin. investigator, dept. exec. officer Armed Forces Radiobiology Research Inst., Bethesda, Md., 1980-84; animal behavior cons. Behavior Clin. for Animals, Washington, 1985-95; assoc. veterinarian Colonial Animal Hosp., Boynton Beach, Fla., 1985; chief mil. pub. health 482d Med. Squadron, Homestead AFB, Fla., 1984-95; hosp. dir. Abacus Animal Hosp., Coral Springs, Fla., 1985-95; chief pub. health 433 Med. Squadron, Kelly AFB, Tex., 1995-97, hosp. admin., 1998—; chief behavioral medicine and mil. working dog studies Mil. Working Dog Vet. Svc., Lackland AFB, Tex., 1995—. Cons. Whittle Communications (Purina), Am. Vet. Med. Assn., Reader's Digest. Contbg. writer Pet Supplies Mktg.; contbr. articles and papers in field. Capt. USAF, 1980-84, Res. maj. 1989-97, Lt.C. 1997—. Research fellow U. Fla. Coll. Vet.

Medicine, 1977. Mem. AVMA, Am. Vet. Soc. Animal Behavior (sec.-treas. 1984-88, pres. 1989-92), Bexar County Vet. Med. Assn., Assn. Mil. Surgeons U.S., Res. Officers Assn., Blue Key. Republican. Presbyterian. Avocations: bicycling, boating, scuba diving. Office: 341 TRS/SGV 1219 Knight St Lackland A F B TX 78236

BURGHART, JAMES HENRY, electrical engineer, educator; b. Erie, Pa., July 18, 1938; s. Chester Albert and Mary Virginia (Burke) B.; m. Judith Ann Hoff, July 8, 1961; children— Jill Kathryn, Mark Alan. BS in Elec. Engring, Case Inst. Tech., 1960, MS (U.S. Steel Found. fellow 1961-63), 1962, PhD, 1965. Asst. prof., then assoc. prof. elec. engring. SUNY, Buffalo, 1969-75; prof. elec. engring. Cleve. State U., 1975—, chmn. dept., 1975-85, 89-97. Served as officer USAF, 1965-68. Mem. IEEE (chmn. Cleve. sect. 1980-81, sec. region 2 1989-96, profl. activities coord. region 2 1997-2000, Ohio area chair region 2 2001—2002, awards and recognition chair, 2003-), Am. Soc. Engring. Edn., Sigma Xi, Eta Kappa Nu. Home: 5501 Strathaven Dr Cleveland OH 44143-1970 Office: 1983 E 24th St Cleveland OH 44115-2403 E-mail: j.burghart@ieee.org.

BURGHDUFF, JOHN BRIAN, mathematics educator; b. Augusta, Ga., July 16, 1958; s. Richard Dean and Betty Kay (Hebeler) B. BS in Applied Maths., Tex. A&M U., 1980; MS in Maths., Ohio State U., 1982; PhD in Math., U. Houston, 1994. Teaching asst. Tex. A&M U., College Station, 1978-80, Ohio State U., Columbus, 1980-82; instr. San Jacinto Coll., Houston, 1982-88, U. Houston, 1988-92; prof. Kingwood Coll., 1992—2003; chair dept. math and philosophy Cypress-Fairbanks Coll., Tex., 2003—. Vol. youth dir. League City (Tex.) Ch. of Christ, 1982-86; faculty sponsor San Jacinto Coll. Bapt. Student Union, Houston, 1982-86; vol. Magnificat House Homeless Shelter, Houston, 1989—. Mem. Math. Assn. Am., Am. Math. Soc., Inst. for Combinatorics and its Applications. Democrat. Episcopalian. Achievements include research in spectra of graphs and permanents of matrices. Home: 4122 O'Meara Dr Houston TX 77025-5423 Office: Cypress-Fairbanks Coll Dept Math and Philosophy Cypress TX 77433 E-mail: john.burghduff@nhmccd.edu.

BURGHEIM, RICHARD, magazine editor; b. St. Louis, July 5, 1933; s. Nathaniel H. and Mary (Rudman) B. BA, Harvard U., 1955. Writer Time Mag., N.Y.C., 1960-71; dir. cable TV programming Time Inc., N.Y.C., 1972-73; editor People Mag., N.Y.C., 1974-81, 89-92; mng. editor TV-Cable Week, White Plains, N.Y., 1982-83; editor Life Mag., N.Y.C., 1984—85, Money Mag., N.Y.C., 1986-89; cons. editor Time Inc., N.Y.C., 1993—, N.Y. Times Upfront, 1999—. Cons. cable programming Ford Found., N.Y.C., 1972; lectr. Harvard Inst. Telecomm. and Pub. Policy, Cambridge, 1972. Contbg. editor mags., including Harper's. Bd. dirs. Children's Express, N.Y.C., 1994-97, Doe Fund, N.Y.C., 1999—, Goddard Riverside Comty. Ctr., N.Y.C., 1999—. USCG, 1956-59. Home: 230 Central Park W Apt 16D New York NY 10024-6040 Office: Time Inc Time And Life Bldg New York NY 10020

BURGIN, CHARLES EDWARD, lawyer; b. Marion, N.C., Dec. 16, 1938; m. Ellen Salsbury Burgin; children: Ellen, Lucy. BA, U. N.C., 1961; LLB, Duke U., 1964. Bar: N.C.; U.S. Supreme Ct. Law clk. to Hon. J. Braxton Craven Jr. U.S. Dist. Ct., U.S. Ct. Appeals, 1964-66; prosecuting atty. McDowell County Criminal Ct., 1966-68; sr. ptnr. Dameron, Burgin & Parker, P.A., Marion, N.C., 1968—. Bd. dirs. Shadowline, Inc.; lectr. in field. Contbr. articles to profl. jours. Bd. dirs. McDowell County Recreation Commn. 1977-87, First Union Nat. Bank 1975—; McDowell County Mountain Rescue Team 1980—; McDowell Arts and Crafts Assn. 1980—. Fellow Am. Coll. Trial Lawyers (state chmn. 1996-98, named Best Lawyers in Am. 1993—), Internat. Soc. Barristers, Am. Bar Found.; mem. ABA, N.C. Bar Assn. (pres. 1993-94), Defense Rsch. Inst., Am. Soc. Hosp. Attys., N.C. Assn. Defense Lawyers, U.S. Supreme Ct. Bar Assn. Office: Dameron Burgin & Parker PA PO Drawer 1049 26 W Court St Marion NC 28752-3906 E-mail: cburgin@dameronburginlaw.com.

BURGIN, GEORGE HANS, computer scientist, educator; b. Liestal, Switzerland, Feb. 13, 1930; s. Jakob and Fanny B.; m. Ulrike Franziska, July 8, 1960; children: Bernard, Claudia, Paul. Diplom ingenieur, Swiss Fed. Inst. Tech., Zurich, 1953, PhD, 1961. Registered profl. engr., Calif. Design specialist Gen. Dynamics Corp., San Diego, 1962-64; sr. scientist Decision Sci., San Diego, 1964-82; chief scientist Titan Systems, San Diego, 1982-94; prin. staff engr. Titan Info. Systems, 1994-96, chief engr., 1996-98; staff engr. Comm-Quest Techs., 1998-99, IBM/Encinitas, 1999-2000, Triton Newtork Systems, 2000—01; sr. staff scientist Natural Selection, Inc., La Jolla, Calif., 2002—. Lectr. San Diego State U., 1979-89. Contbg. author: Simulation, 1968, 2d edit., 1989; author, inventor air combat simulation program Adaptive Maneuvering Logic; contbr. articles to profl. jours. Served to 1st lt. Swiss Army. Mem. IEEE. Achievements include invention of adaptive maneuvering logic air combat simulation program. Home: 6284 Avenida Cresta La Jolla CA 92037-6505 Office: Natural Selection Inc 3333 N Torrey Pines Ct La Jolla CA 92037 E-mail: gburgin@natural-selection.com., gburgin@incom.net.

BURGIN, MARK SEMJONOVICH, mathematician, computer scientist, philosopher; b. Kiev, Ukraine, Jan. 9, 1946; s. Simon R. and Raya A. (Feldman) B.; 1 child, Anatole M. MS in Math., Moscow State U., 1968, PhD in Math., 1971; ScD in Logic and Philosophy, Inst. Philosophy, Acad. Sci., Kiev, 1989. Jr. sci. researcher Rsch. Inst. of Computer Systems, Moscow, 1971-78; sr. sci. researcher All Union Rsch. Inst. of Fishery and Oceanography, Moscow, 1978-80; vice-head dept. computer aided design Inst. for Design of Machinery Factories, Kiev, 1981-82; lectr. Kiev State U., 1982-85; sr. sci. researcher Rsch. Inst. Pedagogy, Kiev, 1985-90; leading scientist dept. artificial intelligence Inst. Applied Info. Sci., Kiev, 1990-92; leading scientist Inst. Sci. of Sci., Kiev, 1992-94, head Assessment Lab., 1994-98; chief scientist Inst. Psychology, Kiev, 1995-98; prof. Inst. Content and Methodology Edn., Kiev, 1996-97, Kiev State U., 1997-98, Internat. Solomon U., 1993-98; vis. scholar U. Calif., L.A., 1998—, vis. prof., 2002—. Cons. Inst. Econs., Kiev, 1987-90, mem. sci. bd. Inst. Philosophy of Acad. Sci., Kiev, 1991—; mem acad. coun. Inst. Sci. of Sci., 1991-98, Inst. of Stats., 1996-98; cons. Sci. Centre Ecology, Kiev, 1991-93; hon. prof. Aerospace Acad. Ukraine. Contbr. more than 500 sci. articles to profl. jours.; author: more than 30 monographs and booklets, including, Proving and Understanding, 1986, Informatics as a Science and Problems of Its Teaching, 1987, Methodological Conciousness in Modern Science, 1989, Problem of Choice Based on Efficiency Estimation, 1990, Expert Evaluation in Sociological Studies, 1990, Axiological Aspects of Scientific Theories, 1991, World of Theories and Power of Mind, 1992, The Structure-Nominative Analysis of Theoretical Knowledge, 1992, Nomological Structures in Scientific Theories, 1993, Communication and Interaction in Teachers Activities, 1993, Measurement and Evaluation in Science, 1995, The Structural Level of Nature, 1996, Mathematical Modeling of Classifications in Statistics, 1997, Fundamental Structures of Knowledge and Information, 1997, Non-Diophantine Arithmetics, 1997, Intellectual Components of Creativity, 1998, On the Nature and Essence of Mathematics, 1998, Entertainment and Information, 2001, Bible Through the Prism of Science, 2001. Mem.: AAAS, Soc. for Judgment and Decision-Making, Cognitive Tech. Soc., Assn. Computing Machinery, Internat. Assn. Fuzzy-Set Mgmt. and Econs., European Assn. Logic, Lang. and Info., Gesellschaft für Angewandte Math. and Mechanik, Internat. Acad. Man in Aerospace Sys., Aerospace Acad. Ukraine, Ukrainian Acad. Info. Scis., N.Y. Acad. Scis., Internat. Assn. Founds. Scis., Lang. and Cognition, Internat. Acad. of Original Ideas, Psychol. Soc. Ukraine, Internat. Assn. Artificial Intelligence, Pedagogical Soc. Ukraine, Philos. Soc. of the Ukraine, Am. Math. Soc., Moscow Math. Soc., Math. Assn. Am., IEEE Computer Soc., Math. Assn. Am., Soc. Indsl. Applications Math., Assn. Computing Machinery. Achievements include development of theory of non-Diophantine arithmetics, theory of named sets (fundamental triads), general theory of properties, theory of logical varieties, the structure-nominative approach in methodology of science, theory of hypernumbers and hyperintegration, neoclassical analysis; discovery of general information theory, mathematical theory of technology, discontinuous topology, system theory of time; contributions to theory of superrecursive algorithms, theory of computational complexity, theory of linear algebras and omega-algebras. Home: 1635 N Martel Ave Apt 308 Los Angeles CA 90046-3540 Office: Dept Math Univ Calif Los Angeles CA 90095-0001 E-mail: mburgin@math.ucla.edu.

BURGIN, WALTER HOTCHKISS, JR., educational administrator; b. Harrisburg, Pa., Apr. 14, 1935; s. Walter Hotchkiss and Wilhelmina (Buntin) B.; m. Barbara Isabelle Waddell, June 15, 1957; children: Christine, Jennifer. AB, Dartmouth Coll., 1957; postgrad., Princeton U., 1957-59; EdM, Harvard U., 1964. Tchr. math. Phillips Exeter (N.H.) Acad., 1964-72, Mercersburg (Pa.) Acad., 1959-64, chmn. dept., 1961-64, headmaster, 1972-97; tchr. math. Sidwell Friends Sch., Washington, 1997-98; exec. dir. Edward E. Ford Found., Washington, 1998—2002; tchr. math. Maret Sch., Washington, 2002—. Mem. Pa. Bd. for Pvt. Acad. Schs., 1973-94. NSF fellow, 1957-59, Shell fellow, 1964. Mem. Math. Assn. Am., Nat. Assn. Prins. Sch. for Girls, Headmasters Assn. (treas. 1993-96, v.p. 1996-97), Nat. Coun. Tchrs. Math., Nat. Assn. Ind. Schs. (bd. dirs. 1989-96, sec. 1992-96), Pa. Assn. Ind. Schs. (exec. com. 1980-90). Democrat. Mem. United Ch. of Christ. Home: 2153 California St NW Apt 402 Washington DC 20008-1845 E-mail: whburgin@aol.com.

BURGIN, WILLIAM LYLE, architect; b. Colorado Springs, Colo., Apr. 30, 1946; m. Virginia Margaret Wojtul, Sept. 23, 1967; 1 child, Desdemona. BA, R.I. Sch. Design, 1972, BArch, 1973. Ptnr. Estes/Burgin Partnership, Providence, 1980-89; pres. William L. Burgin Architects, Newport, R.I., 1989—. V.p. Jamestown Hist. Soc., 1994. Recipient Preservation award Nat. Trust for Hist. Preservation, 1986, Custom Housing Selection award Builder mag., Nat. Assn. Home Builders, 1989, Design and Planning Merit award Builder's Choice, 1993, Mayor's award City of Newport, 1988-90, People's Choice award for affordable housing design R.I. Housing and Fin. Corp., 1990, AIA honor award, 1995-96, Gold medal for best new house, 1995, Housing award Fine Home-building mag., 1997; Rhode Island AIA Honor award Capt. Roger Wheeler Stage Beach Pavilion, 1998, Custom Home Mag. merit award Black Point House, 1999, New England AIA Honor award, 1999. Mem. AIA (citation 1993, Spl. citation for care 1987, honor award 1988, 93), Conanicut Yacht Club (commodore 1996-98), Nat. Tennis Club (v.p. Newport, R.I.), Jamestown Hist. Soc. (pres.). Avocations: court tennis, skiing, yachting, astronomy. Office: William L Burgin Architects Inc 150 Bellevue Ave Newport RI 02840-3230 E-mail: wburgin@williamburgin.com.

BURGIO, MICHAEL, medical researcher; b. Bklyn., N.Y., Sept. 20, 1942; s. John Duffy and Diega Burgio; m. Roberta Somersetin, Aug. 28, 1966 (div. July 31, 1990); children: Todd, Andera Lyn. Student, Fairleigh Dickinson U., 1963. Med. rschr. Siemens Cardiac Pacemaker, Yardley, Pa., 1985—94, Home Infusion Therapy, Bklyn., 1994—97, Burgio Enterprises, Bronx, 1995—. Author: (book) Rehabilitation of Chronic Pulmonary Diseases, 1989, Rehabilitation of Chronic Cardiac Diseases, 1989, Training Manual/Cardiac and Pulmonary Rehabilitation, 1989. Roman Catholic. Achievements include development of new method to start heart after surgery. Home: 2440 Pearsall Ave Bronx NY 10469 Fax: 718-655-1888. E-mail: burmkb@aol.com.

BURGMAN, DIERDRE ANN, lawyer; b. Logansport, Ind., Mar. 25, 1948; d. Ferdinand William Jr. and Doreen Walsh Burgman. BA, Valparaiso U., 1970, JD, 1979; LLM, Yale U., 1985. Bar: Ind. 1979, U.S. Dist. Ct. (so. dist.) Ind. 1979, N.Y. 1982, U.S. Dist. Ct. (so. dist.) N.Y. 1982, U.S. Ct. Appeals (7th cir.) 1982, U.S. Ct. Appeals (D.C. and 2d cirs.) 1984, U.S. Supreme Ct. 1985, D.C. 1988, U.S. Dist. Ct. (ea. dist.) N.Y. 1992. Law clk. to chief judge Ind. Ct. Appeals, Indpls., 1979-80; prof. law Valparaiso (Ind.) U., 1980-81; assoc. Dewey, Ballantine, Bushby, Palmer & Wood, N.Y.C., 1981-84, Cahill Gordon & Reindel, N.Y.C., 1985-92; v.p., gen. counsel N.Y. State Urban Devel. Corp., N.Y.C., 1992-95; dep. insp. gen. State N.Y., 1992-95; of counsel Vandenberg & Felieu, N.Y.C., 1995-99; cons. Salans, N.Y.C., 1999—2000, counsel, 2000. Note editor Valparaiso U. law rev., 1978-79; contbr. articles to law jours. Mem. bd. visitors Valparaiso U. Sch. Law, 1986—95, chmn., 1989—92, mem. nat. coun., 2001—. Ind. Bar Found. scholar, 1978. Mem. ABA (trial evidence com. 1983-86, profl. liability com. 1986-89, ins. coverage litigation com. 1990-92), Assn. Bar City N.Y. (com. profl. responsibility 1988-91, com. profl. and jud. ethics 1991-95, mem. coun. jud. adminstrn. 1997-99), New York County Lawyers Assn. (com. Supreme Ct. 1987-94, chmn. 1990-93, bd. dirs. 1991-97, 2002—, exec. com. bd. dirs. 1992-95, fin. and pers. com. 2003,mem. found.,2003), N.Y. State Bar Assn. (mem. Ho. Dels. 1994-98, mem. com. on profl. stds. for atty. conduct 2002—). Home: 345 E 56th St Apt 5C New York NY 10022-3744

BURGMAN, DOUG, information technology executive; b. Arthur, N.C. Bachelor, N.D. State U.; MBA, Stanford U.; Doctor (hon.), N.D. State U. With McKinsey and Co., Chgo.; investor Gt. Plains divns. Microsoft, Redmond, Wash., 1983—84, pres., chmn., CEO Gt. Plains divsn., 1984, sr. v.p. Bus. Solutions. Named one of Top 100 Most Influential People in Acctg., Acctg. Today mag. Office: Microsoft Way One Microsoft Way Redmond WA 98052-6399

BURGOON, MARK P. science educator; s. Elmer C. and Lynn M. Burgoon. PhD, Rockefeller U., 1991. Rsch. assoc. U. Colo. Health Scis. Ctr., Denver, 1997—98, asst. prof., 1998—. Mem.: N.Y. Acad. of Scis. Independent. Roman Catholic. Office: U Colo Health Scis Ctr Box B182 4200 E 9th Ave Denver CO 80220

BURGOS, HECTOR HUGO, trading company executive; b. Mexico City, D.F., Dec. 1, 1954; came to U.S., 1989; s. Jose H. and Luz Maria (Esparza) B.; m. Myrna O. Marten, Oct. 25, 1979; children: Myrna, Hugo, Hector, Mariel. BBA, U. Iberoamericana, Mexico City, 1976; MBA, U. Tex., 1979; postgrad., Harvard U., 1987. Strategic planning mgr. IEM Westinghouse, Mexico City, 1974-77; mng. dir., capital markets dir. Operadora De Bolsa, Mexico City, 1980-88; CEO, mng. dir. Aigle Internat., Laredo, Tex., 1989-90; ptnr., CEO Agronegocios SA de CV, San Antonio, 1990-92; chmn. Buosa SA de CV, Santa Fe, Mex., 1992—. Ptnr., bd. dirs. Bursamex S.A. de CV, Operadora de Financiamiento SA, Banca Quadrum SA de C.V., Bursamex S.A. de C.V., Promotora Hidalguense S.A., Buosa S.A. de C.V., Video Prima S.A. de C.V., TV Azteca, Ferrioni SA. Mem. Young Pres.'s Orgn., Harvard Club. Avocations: tennis, skiing, golf, sailing. Home: 7 Morning Downs San Antonio TX 78257-1228 Office: 1284 Monte Caucaso Mexico City 11000 Mexico

BURGOS-SASSCER, RUTH, chancellor emeritus; b. N.Y.C., Sept. 5, 1931; m. Donald Sasscer, June 14, 1958; children: Timothy, James, Julie, David. BA, Maryville (Tenn.) Coll., 1953; MA, Columbia U., 1956; PhD, Fla. State U., 1987. Mem. faculty Inter-Am. U., P.R., 1968-71; dept. chair U. P.R., Aguadilla, 1972-76, dir. non-traditional programs Cen. Adminstrn. Regional Coll., 1976-81, dir., dean, chief exec. officer, 1981-85; v.p. faculty and instrn. Harry S. Truman Coll., Chgo., 1988-93; pres. San Antonio Coll., 1993-96; chancellor Houston C.C. Sys., 1996-2000; sr. fellow U. Houston Law Ctr. Inst. of Higher Edn Law and Goverance, 2001—. Bd. dirs. Nat. Hispanic Coun. C.C.s. Bd. dirs. Greater Houston Partnership, Houston Read Commn., City of Houston Ethics Com., Am. Assn. C.C., Internat. Consortium for Ednl. and Econ. Devel., Laredo Nat. Bank, Houston. Mem. Am. Assn. C.C., Internat. Consortium for Ednl. and Econ. Devel. Presbyterian. Home: 530 Bolton Pl Houston TX 77024-4601 E-mail: ruthburgossas@hotmail.com.

BURGSTAHLER, ROBERT, manufacturing executive; BS, Duke U., 1966; MBA, U. Mich., 1967. Pres. 3M Canada; v.p. fin. and adminstrv. svs. 3M Co, 2000—02, sr. v.p. business development, 2002—. Bd. dirs. Clarcor Inc., Rockford, Ill., 2001—. With U.S. Army, 1968—70. Office: 3M Company 3M Ctr Saint Paul MN 55144*

BURGWEGER, FRANCIS JOSEPH DEWES, JR., lawyer; b. Evanston, Ill., July 5, 1942; s. Francis Dewes and Helen Theodosia (Chancellor) B.; m. Kathleen Marie Wessel, Sept. 3, 1978; children: Lauren Elizabeth, Francis Joseph Dewes III, Sherman Ward Chancellor. BA, Yale U., 1964; JD, U. Pa., 1970. Bar: Calif. 1971, N.Y. 1988, U.S. Ct. Appeals (9th cir.) 1971, U.S. Dist. Ct. (cen. dist.) Calif. 1971. Law clk. to Hon. Shirley M. Hufstedler U.S. Ct. Appeals 9th Cir., L.A., 1970-71; assoc. O'Melveny & Myers, L.A., 1971-78, ptnr., 1978-85, O'Melveny & Myers LLP, N.Y.C., 1985-97, sr. counsel, 1997—2003. Contbr. articles on environ. law. Capt. U.S. Army, 1964-67, Vietnam. Mem. Assn. of Bar of City of N.Y., N.Y. State Bar Assn., L.A. County Bar Assn. (exec. com. R.P. sect.). Avocations: books, wine, agriculture. Office: O'Melveny & Myers LLP 153 E 53rd St Fl 54 New York NY 10022-4611

BURHANS, FRANK MALCOLM, mechanical engineer; b. Hagerstown, Md., Dec. 11, 1920; s. William Humphrey Sr. and Ethel Adella (Forthman) B.; m. Jean Maria Dermott, Oct. 10, 1943; children: Stephen William, Douglas Allan, jeffrey Malcolm; m. Dorothy Olson Mutchler, July 29, 1995. BE in Mech. Engring., Johns Hopkins U., 1942; postgrad., U. Conn., 1942-43. Registered profl. engr., Wash. Design engr. Pratt & Whitney, East Hartford, Conn., 1942-55, Ford Motor Co., Dearborn, Mich., 1955-58; sr. design engr. Fairchild Engine Divsn., Deer Park, N.Y., 1958-59; sr. specialist engr. Turbine Divsn. Boeing Co., Seattle, 1959-66; prin. engr. Boeing Aircraft Engine Installations, 1967-86. Active Boy Scouts Am. Served with AC, U.S. Army, 1945-47. Recipient Silver Beaver award Boy Scouts Am. Mem. AIAA, ASME, Masons (past master/Bellevue), Lions (pres. 1996-97, zone chair 2001-02). Presbyterian (elder). Achievements include pioneering designer gas turbines and gas turbine installations.

BURHOE, BRIAN WALTER, automotive service executive; b. Worcester, Mass., Apr. 9, 1941; s. Walter De Forest and Dorothy Merrium (Gould) B.; m. Lynda Clayton, May 28, 1960 (div. May 1972); children: Mark S., Ty C., Scott M.; m. Joan Elaine Bredenberg, Oct. 21, 1989. Arts Baccalaureate, Clark U., Worcester, 1963, MA in History, Internat. Relations, 1971; cert. advanced mgmt. program, Northwestern U., 1985. Tchr. Orleans (Mass.) Sch. System, 1965-67; mgr. labor rels. Ill. Central R.R., Chgo., 1967-74, exec. asst., 1974-77; dir. human resources Midas Internat. Corp., Chgo., 1977-79, v.p. human resources, 1979-89, sr. v.p. human resources, 1989-98; pres. The Old Bookseller, Inc., 1998—. Mem.: Ill. Safety Coun. (chmn. 1992—94). Avocation: collecting out of print books. Home: 325 Nebraska St Frankfort IL 60423 Office: The Old Bookseller Inc 11 S White St Frankfort IL 60423

BURI, PHILIP JAMES, lawyer; b. Spokane, Wash., Dec. 27, 1960; s. Earl James and Bonnie Jean B.; m. Darcie Ann Donegan, May 29, 1993; children: Abraham, Elena, Isabel. AB, Princeton U., 1983; JD, Harvard U., 1987. Bar: Wash. 1988, U.S. Dist. Ct. (we. dist.) Wash. 1998, U.S. Dist. Ct. (ea. dist.) Wash. 1998, U.S. Ct. Appeals (9th cir.) 1998. Law clk. to Hon. Barbara Rothstein U.S. Dist. Ct., Seattle, 1987-89; trial lawyer Antitrust Divsn. U.S. Dept. Justice, Washington, 1989-93; law clk. to Hon. Richard Guy Wash. Supreme Ct., Olympia, 1993-95; atty. Brett & Daugert, Bellingham, Wash., 1995—. Bd. dirs. Bellingham Cmty. Food Co-op, 1996—. Mem. Wash. State Bar Assn. (ct. rules com. 1996—). Avocations: bicycling, skiing. Office: Brett & Daugert 300 N Commercial St Ste 5008 Bellingham WA 98225-4002

BURIAN, JARKA MARSANO, performing arts educator; b. Passaic, N.J., Mar. 10, 1927; s. Jaroslav Valerian and Olga Marsano Burian; m. Grayce Susan DeLeo, June 15, 1951. BA, Rutgers U., 1949; MA, Columbia U., 1950; PhD, Cornell U., 1955. From asst. prof. to prof. SUNY, Albany, 1559, chair theatre dept., 1971—74, 1977—78, prof. emeritus, 1993—; theatre dir.-prodr. Arena Summer Theatre, Albany, 1959, 1963—64, 1966—68, 1972—73. Assoc. editor Theatre Jour., 1981—90; contbg. editor: Theatre Design and Tech., 1989—; author: (book) The Scenography of Josef Svoboda, 1971—, Svoboda: Wagner, 1983—, Modern Czech Theatre, 2000—, Leading Creators of Twentieth-Century Czech Theater, 2002—; editor: The Secret of Theatrical Space, 1993— (Golden Pen award, 1995). Sgt. U.S. Army, 1946—47, sgt. U.S. Army, 1950—51. Recipient Regional Arts award, Albany-Schenectady League of Arts, 1998; fellow Rsch. fellow, NEH, 1974; grantee Lectr. grantee, U.S. State Dept. to Czechoslovakia, 1965, Rsch. grantee, Internat. Rsch. Exch. Bd., 1969, 1974—75, 1993—94, Fulbright Found., 1982, 1988. Mem.: AAUP, U.S. Inst. for Theatre Tech., Internat. Fedn. for Theatre Rsch., Am. Soc. for Theatre Rsch., Theatre in Higher Edn., Phi Beta Kappa. Avocations: travel, competitive swimming. Home: 71 Berkshire Blvd Albany NY 12203

BURICK, LAWRENCE T. lawyer; b. Dayton, Ohio, May 15, 1943; s. Lee and Doris (Brenner) B.; m. Cynthia Joy Rosen, Aug. 31, 1969; children: Carrie R., Samuel J. BA, Miami U., 1965; JD, Northwestern U., 1968. Bar: Ohio 1968. Assoc. Smith & Schnacke, Dayton, 1969-78, ptnr., 1978-89, Thompson Hine LLP, Dayton, 1989—. Chmn. Dayton Jewish Ctr., Ohio, 1982—83, Jewish Cmty. Rels. Coun., 1980—81; pres. Jewish Fedn. Greater Dayton, Ohio, 1989—93, bd. dir., 1977—; chmn. United Jewish Campaign, 1997—99, Nat. Conf. Cmty. and Justice, 2002—; bd. dir. Jewish Edn. in Svc. to N.Am., 1994—99, v.p., 1997—99; chmn. Dayton region Nat. Conf. Cmty. and Justice, 1997—, v.p., 1999—2002, chair, 2002—; bd. dir. Beth Abraham Synagogue, 1997—. Recipient Wasserman Leadership award, Jewish Fedn. Greater Dayton, 1978. Mem. Ohio State Bar Assn., Dayton Bar Assn., Am. Bankruptcy Law Forum, Am. Bankruptcy Inst. Office: Thompson Hine LLP PO Box 8801 2000 Courthouse Plz NE Dayton OH 45401-8801 E-mail: larry.burick@thompsonhine.com.

BURINI, SONIA MONTES DE OCA, apparel manufacturing and public relations executive; b. Havana, Cuba, Apr. 28, 1935; d. Francisco and Nilda (Diaz) Montes de Oca; m. Franco Burini, Apr. 5, 1959. Student, U. Havana, 1954-57, Georgetown U., 1958; BA in History cum laude, U. Miami, Coral Gables, Fla., 1971. Adminstr. Roma Fashions, Inc. D/B/A Franco B., Coral Gables, 1976-95; entrepreneur, pub. rels. exec., 1995—. Founder Nat. Parkinson Found., 1986—; v.p. Vizcayans Fund Raising Orgn., 1990—, chmn. fine arts events, 1993-95; co-chmn. 1st annual fund raising event Am. Cancer Soc. Winn-Dixie Hope Lodge Ctr.; mem. women with heart group Heart Assn. Greater Miami, Fla., 1981—; founder, bd. dirs. Cancer Link program U. Miami Comprehensive Cancer Ctr., 1987; chmn. spring fantasy luncheon Am. Cancer Soc., 1988; founding chmn. Rose Group, Am. Lung Assn., chmn. Rose Ball, 1989; amb. Mercy Hosp. Found., 1987-95; bd. dirs. Newborn program U. Miami, 1978, bd. dirs., 1982-87, amb. category years; vol. guide Viscaya Mus., Dade County, Fla., 1972-79, chmn. various coms., 1979—, found. bd. dirs., steering com., mem. com. of 100; bd. dir., Young Patroness of the Opera, 1979-87; grand patron Greater Miami Opera, 1986-95, bd. dirs., 1978—, chmn. opera gala, 1987, mem. opera guild, 1988; founding bd. mem. Ears Dears U. Miami, 1986—, chmn. 1990 gala; mem. Dade County Performing Art Ctr. Trust, 1993—; spl. chmn. fine arts events Vizcayans, 1993—; mem. sister cities com. Cities of Miami, Fla. and Nice, France, 1994—, Nat. Trust Hist. Preservation, 1997—. Named Oustanding Woman of Yr. Mayor of Dade County, 1986, Woman of Yr. Heart Assn. Greater Miami, 1986, named to Miss Charity Biscayne Bay Marriott Hotel and Marina, 1987, One of the Leading Ladies for the March of Dimes, 1998. Mem. Nat. Trust Historic Preservation, Ballet Soc. Miami (bd. dirs. 1979-80, named one of Miami's Oustanding Women 1986), Confrerie de la Chaine des Rotisseurs, NAFF, Nat. Found. Peace (bd. adv. 2001—), Opera Guild Fla. Grand Opera (bd. dirs. 2003—). Home: 5401 Collins Ave Apt 1016 Miami Beach FL 33140 Office: Roma Fashions Inc 3311 Ponce De Leon Blvd Coral Gables FL 33134-7210 also: Corregidor Aguirre 21 Las Palmas de Canaria Spain also: Burini Enterprises, Inc PO Box 347558 Coral Gables FL 33234-7374

BURISH, THOMAS GERARD, academic administrator; b. Peshtigo, Wis., May 4, 1950; s. Bennie Charles and Donna Mae (Willkom) B.; m. Pamela Jean Zebrasky, June 19, 1976; children: Mark Joseph, Brent Christopher. AB summa cum laude, U. Notre Dame, 1972; MA, U. Kans., 1975, PhD, 1976. Lic. psychologist, Tenn. Asst. prof. psychology Vanderbilt U., Nashville, 1976-80, assoc. prof., 1980-86, prof., 1986—2002, dir. clin. tng., 1980-84, chair dept. psychology, 1984-86, assoc. provost, 1986—92, provost, 1992—2002; pres. Washington and Lee U., Lexington, Va., 2002—. Mem. cancer rsch. manpower rev. com. Nat. Cancer Inst., 1991-96; co-chair Bridge task force com. Am. Cancer Soc., 1994-96; mem. breast cancer rsch. panel US Army Med. Rsch., 1995-2001. Co-editor: Coping with Chronic Disease, 1983, Cancer, Nutrition and Eating Behavior, 1985; co-author: Behavior Therapy, 1987, Health Psychology, 1991. Chmn. St. Mary's Sch. Bd., Nashville, 1982-83; participant Leadership Nashville, 1989-90; vice chair, bd. dir. Am. Cancer Soc. Fellow Am. Psychol. Assn., Am. Psychol. Soc.; mem. Acad. Behavioral Medicine Rsch., Phi Beta Kappa. Roman Catholic. Office: Washington and Lee U Washington Hall Lexington VA 24450

BURK, JAMES STEVEN, sociologist; b. Balt., Oct. 9, 1948; s. John Franklin and Peggy Gladys B.; m. Patricia Andrea Garcia, Oct. 21, 1967; children: Jacqualine Lee, Theodore Michael. BS, Towson U., 1975; AM, U. Chgo., 1978, PhD, 1982. Lectr. U. Chgo., 1980-81; asst. prof. Tex. A&M U., College Station, 1984-90, assoc. prof., 1990-97, prof., 1997—. Vis. asst. prof. McGill U., Montreal, Que., Can., 1981-83, Tex. A&M U., 1983-84. Author: Values in the Marketplace, 1988; editor: On Social Organization and Social Control, 1991, The Military in New Times, 1994, The Adaptive Military, 1998. Exec. coun. Inter-Univ. Sem. Armed Forces & Soc., 1981—. NSF grantee, 1980-81; Nat. Inst. Mental Health fellow, 1978-79. Mem. Am. Sociol. Assn. Democrat. Presbyterian. Avocations: racquetball, watercolors. Office: Tex A&M U Dept Sociology College Station TX 77843-0001

BURK, NORMAN, retired oral surgeon; b. Dallas, Sept. 28, 1937; s. Rubin and Lena (Shodnisky) B.; m. Beverly Rae Hyken, Aug. 27, 1961; children: Ronald S., Steven J. BS, U. Okla., 1959; DDS, U. Mo., Kansas City, 1962. Diplomate Am. Bd. Oral and Maxillofacial Surgery. Resident in oral surgery Kansas City (Mo.) Gen. Hosp., 1965; practice dentistry specializing in oral surgery Kansas City, Mo., 1965—; mem. staff Truman Med. Ctr., Independence Sanitarium and Hosp.; chief staff Bapt. Meml. Hosp., 1976-77, Menorah Med. Ctr., 1975-85; sec. med. staff St. Joseph Health Ctr., Kansas City, Mo., 1992-93; ret. Clin. assoc. prof. U. Mo., Kansas City, 1965-85; appointed to Blue Cross/Blue Shield peer review com. for Greater Kansas City Oral Surgeons. Contbr. articles to profl. jours. Bd. dirs. Kehilath Israel Synagogue. Recipient Ralph Ringo Coffey MD award Truman Med. Ctr., 1997. Fellow Am. Coll. Oral and Maxillofacial Surgeons, Am. Assn. Oral and Maxillofacial Surgeons, Internat. Congress of Oral Implantologists, Acad. Osseointegration, Am. Coll. Oral and Maxillofacial Surgeons (founder); mem. Kansas City Soc. Oral Surgeons (pres. 1974), Mo. Soc. Oral Surgeons (pres. 1979), ADA, Midwestern Mo. and Kansas City Soc. Oral and Maxillofacial Surgeons, Delta Sigma Delta (advisor 1966-74), Univ. Study Club (pres. 1970), B'nai Brith Lodge. Avocations: cycling, photography, travel. Home: 8400 Delmar Ln Shawnee Mission KS 66207-1824 Office: Burk Ennis & Allen 1010 Carondelet Dr Kansas City MO 64114-4859

BURK, RAYMOND FRANKLIN, JR., physician, educator, researcher; b. Kosciusko, Miss., Dec. 9, 1942; s. Raymond Franklin and Florence Annie (Davis) B.; m. Enikoe Vikor, June 17, 1967; children: Teresa Marie, Stephen Morrison. BA, U. Miss., 1963; MD, Vanderbilt U., 1968. Diplomate Am. Bd. Internal Medicine. Intern Vanderbilt Hosp., Nashville, 1968—69; resident in medicine Vanderbilt Hosp., Nashville, 1969—70; asst. prof. medicine and biochemistry U. Tex. S.W. Med. Sch., Dallas, 1975—78; assoc. prof. medicine and biochemistry La. State U. Sch. Medicine, Shreveport, 1978—80; assoc. prof. medicine U. Tex. Health Sci. Ctr., San Antonio, 1980—82, prof., 1982—87; prof. medicine Vanderbilt U., 1987—. Rschr. in field; mem. staff Vanderbilt U. Hosp., Nashville. Contbr. articles to med. jours. Maj. M.C., U.S. Army, 1970-73. Grantee NIH, 1974—. Mem. Am. Soc. Biol. Chemists, Am. Soc. Clin. Investigation, Am. Inst. Nutrition. Office: Vanderbilt U Med Sch Div Gastroenterology Med Ctr N Nashville TN 37232-2279 E-mail: raymond.burk@vanderbilt.edu.

BURK, ROBERT S. lawyer; b. Mpls., Jan. 13, 1937; s. Harvey and Mayme (Cottle) B.; m. Eunice L. Silverman, Mar. 22, 1959; children: Bryan, Pam, Matt. BBA in Indsl. Rels., U. Minn., 1959; LLB, William Mitchell Coll. Law, 1965. Bar: Minn. 1966; qualified neutral under Rule 114 of the Minn. Gen. Rules of Practice, 1995—. Labor rels. cons. St. Paul Employers Assn., 1959-66; labor rels. mgr. Koch Refining Co., St. Paul, 1966-72, mgr. indsl. rels., 1972-75, mgr. indsl. rels., environ. affairs, 1975-77; sr. atty. Popham, Haik, Schnobrich & Kaufman, Ltd., Mpls., 1977-95, pres., CEO, 1986-90; ptnr. Burk & Seaton, P.A., Edina, Minn., 1995-2001, Burk & Landrum, P.A., Edina, 2001—. Chair bd. trustees William Mitchell Coll. Law, St. Paul, 1994-96, sec. 1991. Recipient Hon. Ronald E. Hachey Outstanding Alumnus award William Mitchell Coll. Law Alumni Assn., 1993. Mem. ABA (labor sect.), Minn. Bar Assn. (labor sect.). Office: Burk & Landrum PA 7400 Metro Blvd Ste 100 Edina MN 55439 Office Fax: 952-835-1867. E-mail: rburk@burklandrum.com. *Credibility is the only trait that marks your existence.*

BURK, ROGER CHAPMAN, engineering educator; b. Oakland, Calif., Nov. 10, 1953; s. Chapman and Ann Burk; m. Robin Kowalchuk, May 25, 1974; 1 child, Charity Jane Elisabeth. BA, St. John's Coll., Annapolis, Md., 1974; MS, Air Force Inst. Tech., Wright-Patterson AFB, Ohio, 1985; PhD, U. N.C., 1993. Commd. 2d lt. USAF, 1978, advanced through grades to maj., 1989, ret., 1995; sr. scientist SAIC, Chantilly, Va., 1995—98; sr. project engr. The Aerospace Corp., Chantilly, 1998—2000; asst. prof. sys. engring. U.S. Mil. Acad., West Point, NY, 2000—. Cons. Toffler Assocs., Manchester, Mass., 2001—. Contbr. Mem.: Assn. for Unmanned Vehicle Sys. Internat., Mil. Ops. Rsch. Soc., Inst. for Ops. Rsch. and Mgmt. Sci. Episcopalian. Avocations: target shooting, bicycling. Office: US Military Acad Dept Systems Engring West Point NY 10996

BURKA, ROBERT ALAN, lawyer; b. Washington, Dec. 25, 1944; s. Fred and Louise S. (Lehmann) B.; m. Maria Eva Karpati, Dec. 22, 1968; children: Jacqueline A., Michael S., Jennifer L. AB, Dartmouth Coll., 1966; MSc in Econs., U. London, 1967; JD, Harvard U., 1970. Bar: N.Y. 1971, D.C. 1975, U.S. Supreme Ct. 1978. Law clk. to Hon. Judge Milton Pollack U.S. Dist. Ct. (so. dist.) N.Y., N.Y.C., 1971; assoc. Kaye Scholer Fierman Hays & Handler, N.Y.C., 1971-74, Bergson, Borkland, Morgolis & Adler, Washington, 1974-79; dep., then acting asst. dir. Bur. of Competition FTC, Washington, 1979-82; ptnr. LaRoe Winn & Moerman, Washington, 1982-84; pvt. practice Washington, 1984-87; ptnr. Knopf & Burka, Washington, 1987-92, Foley & Lardner, Washington, 1992—. Fulbright and Reynolds scholars, 1966-67. Mem. Phi Beta Kappa. Office: Foley & Lardner 3000 K St NW Ste 500 Washington DC 20007-5143 E-mail: rburka@foleylaw.com.

BURKARD, THOMAS ROBERT, publishing executive, writer; b. South Amboy, NJ, Dec. 15, 1950; s. Frank Joseph and Victoria Veronica (Lytkowski) Burkard; m. Nancy Leonia Baumgartner, Sept. 29, 1986; 1 child, Sarah Susan Raymond. BA in Urban/Outdoor Recreation, Kean U., Union, N.J., 1980; courses, Middlesex County Coll., Edison, N.J., 1975—77. Sheriff's officer Middlesex County Sheriff's Dept., New Brunswick, NJ, 1973—75; phys. edn. tchr. Sacred Heart Sch., South Amboy, NJ, 1977—78; owner/operator Tom Burkard Lawn & Landscaping, South Amboy, NJ, 1979—94; phys. ed. tchr. Sacred Heart Sch., South Amboy, NJ, 1984—85; rec. asst. City of South Amboy, South Amboy, NJ, 1987—; pub. South Amboy-Sayreville Times, South Amboy, NJ, 1991—. Author: The Ultimate Mickey Mantle Trivia Book, 1997. Named Recognition as Hon. mem., South Amboy First Aid & Safety Squad, 1999; recipient Sayreville Comm., Ladies Aux. to the Veterans of Fgn. War, 1994, Cert. of Appreciation, Elks Lodge 2555/ South Amboy, 1998—99, Citation, State of NJ Senate & Gen. Assembly, 1999, Cert. of Appreciation, Morgan First Aid Squad, 1999, Joint Legis. Resolution, Chamber of Commerce / Trenton, NJ, 2001, NJ Senate, Gen. Assembly/ Trenton, NJ, 2001, Gen. Assembly, 2001, Resolution, City of South Amboy/ NJ, 2001, Middlesex County Bd. of Freeholders/ NJ, 2001, proclamation, Office of the Mayor/ South Amboy, NJ, 2001, Bus. Leader of Yr. award, Old Bridge-Sayreville-South Amboy C. of C., 2001. Mem.: NJ Press Assoc., NJ Sportswriters Assoc., Knights of Columbus #426. Roman Catholic. Avocations: music, baseball, walking, travel, photography, researching. Office: South Amboy-Sayreville Times PO Box 3027 South Amboy NJ 08879-1216

BURKART, JEFFREY EDWARD, communications educator; b. Chgo., Sept. 12, 1948; s. Irwin John and Florence Henrietta (Drzich) B.; m. Martha Louise Gaertner, Aug. 13, 1972; children: Jonathan, David, Andrew. BA, Concordia Tchrs. Coll., 1971; MA, U. Nebr., 1977; PhD, U. Minn., 1988. Cert. elem. and secondary sch. tchr., Ind., Mo. Wis., Nebr. Organist, choral dir., youth dir. St. John's Luth. Ch., Bingen, Ind., 1969-70; tchr. Wyneken Meml. Luth. Sch., Decatur, Ind., 1969-70; residence counselor Concordia Coll., River Forest, Ill., 1970-71; instr. Luth. High Sch. North, St. Louis, 1971-72, Martin Luther High Sch., Greendale, Wis., 1972-75; tchr. St. John's Luth. Sch., Seward, Nebr., 1975-77; prof. ednl. communications/media, dir. audiovisual svcs. Concordia U., St. Paul, 1977-97, media cons., 1997—, assoc. dean for Christian ministry, 1999—, assoc. dean Coll. Vocation and Ministry, 1999—. Cons. Luth. Ch.-Mo. Synod, St. Louis; ednl. cons. St. Paul Pub. Schs., 1989, Elk River (Minn.) Sch. Dist., 1988-89; dir. European study Am. Inst. Fgn. Study, Greenwich, Conn.; editor-at-large and Christian edn. specialist Concordia Pub. Ho., 1996. Author: The Sonday School Book, 1995, Sure You Can Use a Little Good News!, 1996, Creative Worship, 1996, The Seeds That Grew and Grew, 1997, The Man Who Couldn't Speak, 1998, A Surprise in Disguise, 1999, Down Through the Roof, 1999, Don't Get Burned (musical), 1999, (video tape) The Hospital Zone, 2000, Camel's Hair and Honey, 2000; composer contemporary ch. music; author articles on children's lit. and early childhood edn., also drama and music articles; author religious video, filmstrip series; presenter in field; author, composer: (musical) Man Overboard, 1995; composer, lyricist In League with Our Lord, 1999, Jesus Cares for China's Children, 2000, We're In Jesus' Company, 1999, Anyone Who Welcomes, 2000, (children's book) The Hidden Prince, 2002; (CDs) Oh, Come, Lord Jesus, 2001, Oh, Come, Emmanuel, 2002, Oh, Come Risen One, 2003. Mem. Assn. for Supervision and Curriculum Devel., Luth. Edn. Assn., Assn. of Luth. Ch. Musicians, Phi Delta Kappa. Avocations: music, photography, reading, astronomy, travel. Office: Concordia Univ 275 Syndicate St N Saint Paul MN 55104-5494 E-mail: jburkart@csp.edu.

BURKE, ALEXANDER JAMES, JR., publishing company executive; b. NYC, Apr. 24, 1931; s. Alexander James and Josephine Eleanor (McGrath) B.; m. Suzanne Jeanne Gatti, June 25, 1955; children: James, Brian, Christopher, Nancy, Thomas, Matthew, Alexander John. BA cum laude, Holy Cross Coll., 1953; MA, Fordham U., 1956; MA in Scripture, Immaculate Conception Sem., 1997; PhD in Scripture, Fordham U., 2002. Prof. English Fordham U., 1953-56, 59-60; editor W.H. Sadlier Co., N.Y.C., 1959-60; mgr. Doubleday Bookstore, Manhasset, N.Y., 1952; with McGraw-Hill Book Co., N.Y.C., 1960—, gen. mgr., 1969-70, v.p., 1970-73, exec. v.p., 1973-74, pres., 1974-82, McGraw-Hill Internat. Book Co., N.Y.C., 1983-85, exec. v.p., 1985-87; pres. Phoenix Learning Resources, 1987—; prof. English, dir. pub. studies program Hofstra U., N.Y.C., 1994—. Bd. dirs. Adult Edn. Council St. Louis, 1965, Commn. on Radio and TV, Cath. Archdiocese St. Louis, 1968-72. With USAF, 1956-59. Mem. Assn. Am. Pubs. (exec. com., dir., chmn. 1978-85), Book Industry Study Group (exec. com., dir. 1976—), Am. Soc. Curriculum Devel., Nat. Coun. Tchrs. English, Cath. Bibl. Assn., Alpha Sigma Nu Roman Catholic. Home: 455 Ryder Rd Manhasset NY 11030-2761 Office: Phoenix Learning Resources 12 W 31st St New York NY 10001-4415 E-mail: ajburkejr@aol.com.

BURKE, BRUCE LOWELL, consumer products company executive; b. Bklyn., May 13, 1936; s. Jack and Gertrude (Gardner) B.; children: Abby Muhlfelder, Jeffrey Allen, Florie Michelle; m. Susan Majosi-Bass, June 15, 2003. BS, Fairleigh Dickinson U., 1960, MBA (cum laude), 1965. Packaging exec., Chgo., 1959-74; food svc. exec. N.Y.C., 1974-87; priv. practice cons. Clifton, N.J., 1987—; sales and mgmt. exec. Tourneau, Inc., N.Y.C., 1993-2001; sales assoc. Neiman Marcus, Paramus, N.J., 2001—. Judge Am. Inst. at the City of N.Y., 1962. With N.J. Nat. Guard, 1957-60. Jewish. Avocation: computers and technology. Home and Office: 45 Sycamore Rd Apt C Clifton NJ 07012-1375 E-mail: bburke18@optonline.net.

BURKE, CAMERON S. legal administration; b. Nov. 23, 1953; m. Barbara; 3 children. BA in History, U. Oreg., 1976; MS in Judicial Adminstrn., U. Denver, 1980. Calendar & courtroom clk. U.S. Dist. Ct., Idaho, 1976-79; trial court adminstr. Lincoln County Cir. & Dist. Cts., 1981-85; chief deputy clk. U.S. Dist. Ct., Ariz., 1985-89; court exec. U.S. Dist. & Bankruptcy Cts., Idaho, 1989—. Contbr. articles to profl. jours. Chi Psi Ednl. scholar. Mem. Am. Judicature Soc., Nat. Ctr. State Cts., Nat. Assn. Ct. Mgmt., Oreg. Assn. Ct. Adminstrn. (past pres.), Fed. Ct. Clks. Assn. (past pres., Bob Christ award 1996, Angie award 2000), Ariz. Cts. Assn. (past pres.). Office: US Dist & Bankruptcy Cts Fed Bldg & US Courthouse 550 W Fort St # 39 Boise ID 83724-0101

BURKE, DANIEL J. state legislator; b. Chgo., Dec. 17, 1951; Student, Loyola U., Berlitz Sch. Lang., DePaul U. Dep. city clk., Chgo, 1979—; Ill. state rep. Dist. 23, 1991—. Mem Edn. Appropriations, Election Law, Elem. & Secondary Edn., Labor and Commerce, Transp. & Vehicles Coms., Ill. Ho. of Reps. Mem. Internat. Mcpl. Clks. Assn. (legis. co-chmn.), Gov. Fin. Officers Assn. Address: 2650 W 51st St Chicago IL 60632-1560*

BURKE, DANIEL MARTIN, lawyer; b. Casper, Wyo., Sept. 9, 1946; s. Michael Joseph and Mary Josephine (Sirridge) Burke; m. Ellen Arden, July 3, 1970; children: Daniel Martin III, Kathleen Ellen, Brendan Arden, Anne Mary, Susan Theresa. BA, U. Wyo., 1968, JD, 1970. Law clk. to judge U.S. Ct. Appeals (10th cir.), Cheyenne, 1970; spl. asst. atty. gen. State of Wyo., Cheyenne, 1970—71; instr. Casper Coll., 1971—75; county and pros. atty. Natrona County, Casper, Wyo., 1975—79; mem. Burke, Horn & Lewis, Casper, 1975—79; pres. Burke & Horn, P.C., Casper, 1979—82, Burke & Brown, P.C., Casper, 1983—86; pvt. practice Casper, 1986—. Chmn. bd., pres. Rocky Mountain Comms. Network, Inc., 1982—87; v.p., dir. Evco, Inc., 1982—86; dir. Guaranty Fed. Bank, First Nat. Bank Evanston, Wyo., 1981—86, Wyo. Fin. Svcs., Inc., 1981—86; gen ptnr. Bantry Bay Co., 1974—88; pres. The Chrysostom Corp.; sec. Shamrock Ranch Co., Casper, 1969—. Bd. arbitrators Am. Arbitration Assn.; asst. city atty. City of Casper, 1971—74; mem. coun. St. Anthony Parish; mem. St. Anthony Parochial Sch. Bd. Mem.: ABA, Wyo. Assn. County Attys. (pres. 1977—78), Nat. Assn. Dist. Attys. (dir. 1977—78), Am. Judicature Soc., Natrona County Bar Assn., Casper C. of C., Casper Country Club, KC. Republican. Roman Cath. Home: 1048 S Lincoln St Casper WY 82601-3331 Office: 231 E 10th St Casper WY 82601-3744

BURKE, DAVID, corporate chef, executive chef; b. Bklyn., Feb. 27, 1962; divorced; three children. Student, The Culinary Inst. Am. Recipient Meilleurs Ouvriers de France diploma Internat. Food Festival, Tokyo, 1988, Robert Mondavi Culinary Award of Excellence, 1996, Auggie Award Culinary Inst. Am., 1996, Five Diamond Award of Excellence, AM. Acad. Hospitality Scis., 1997; named Nat. Adv. Com. of Chefs in Am., Chef of Yr., 1991. Avocations: pinball, travel, skiing, antiquing. Office: Park Ave Cafe 100 E 63rd St New York NY 10021-7303

BURKE, GEORGE WILLIAM, III, surgery educator; b. Boston, Jan. 25, 1953; s. Donna Theresa Rosa, Apr. 5, 1986; children: George Mitchell, Elisabeth Rosa, Renee Julia. BA in Biochemistry magna cum laude, Harvard Coll., 1974; MD, U. Mass., 1978. Diplomate Am. Bd. Surgery; lic. physician, Fla., Mass. Resident New Eng. Deaconess Hosp., Boston, 1978-81, 83-85, Bapt. Hosp., Boston, 1981-82, Dana-Farber Cancer Inst., Boston, 1982-83; fellow in surg. endoscopy Mass. Gen. Hosp., Boston, 1986; fellow in surg. transplant U. Minn., Mpls., 1986-87; asst. prof. U. Miami, Fla., 1987-92, assoc. prof. assoc. dir. divsn. transplantation, 1992-98, prof. surgery, 1998—. Lectr. and presenter in field. Referee jours.; contbr. abstracts to publs. Grantee Kidney Found. South Fla., 1988-92, faculty U. Miami, 1987, Immunological Monitoring in Vascularized Pancreas Transplants, 1990—. Mem. Am. Soc. Transplant Surgeons, Cell Transplantation Soc., Soc. Laparoendoscopic Surgeons, Soc. Critical Care Medicine, Soc. Univ. Surgeons. Avocations: running, rowing, sailing. Office: U Miami Transplantation Dept Miami FL 33136

BURKE, GRACE DORA REYNOLDS, medical/surgical nurse; b. Lakewood, Pa., Mar. 24, 1925; d. Carroll George and Esther Lena (Lloyd) Reynolds; m. C. Grafton Burke Jr., Nov. 22, 1956; children: Daniel, David. Diploma in nursing, Wilson Meml. Hosp. Sch. Nursing, Johnson City, N.Y., 1948; BA, Roberts Wesleyan Coll., 1952. RN, Pa.; cert. tchr., correctional health profl., HIV/AIDS edn. instr., Pa. Instr. med./surg. nursing Pottstown (Pa.) Meml. Ctr. Sch. Nursing, 1964-71; tchr. Western Montgomery Vocat. Tech. Sch., Limerick, Pa., 1977-81; staff nurse Correctional Med. Systems, Graterford, Pa., 1984-90; AIDS edn. nurse State Correctional Instn., Graterford, 1990-95; ret., 1995. Dir. health svcs. Valley Forge Christian Coll., Phoenixville, Pa., 1987—88; PRN nurse in family practitioners office; substitute sch. nurse Greenville County Sch. Sys. Vol. ARC Disaster Nursing Svc., Greenville, S.C., 1998—. Mem. C.S. Wilson Nursing Alumnae. Avocations: swimming, crocheting, travel. E-mail: gandgburke@juno.com.

BURKE, HENRY PATRICK, lawyer; b. Scranton, Pa., May 12, 1942; s. Thomas and Dorothy Maria (McCloskey) B.; m. Alyce Louise McCrone, July 5, 1975; children: Henry Patrick, Daniel. BS, U. Scranton, 1964; JD, Villanova U., 1967. Bar: Pa. 1968, U.S. Dist. Ct. (mid. dist.) Pa. 1968, U.S. Ct. Appeals (3d cir.) 1994, U.S. Ct. Appeals (fed. cir.) 2001, U.S. Ct. Internat. Trade 2001; lic. real estate broker, Pa. Law clk. Ct. Common Pleas, Lackawanna County, Pa., 1968-69; lectr. bus. law U. Scranton, 1968-69; assoc. Haggerty & McDonnell, Scranton, 1969-75; assoc. counsel Scranton Redevel. Authority, 1969-70; spl. atty. gen. and legal opinion writer Pa. State Workers' Compensation Bd., 1972-97, legal opinion writer, 1972-97; sec., gen. counsel Opportunity Products Today, Inc., 1998; assoc. Burke and Douglass, Scranton, Pa., 1975-80; co-owner Directel Inc. Wireless, 1999-2000; pvt. practice law Scranton, 1969—. Author: The Burke-Duggan Family, From Opporession to Freedom, 1981. Mem. exec. com. Pa. unit Am. Heart Assn., 1973-74, asst. treas. Keystone chpt., 1972; del. Dem. Nat. Conv., 1972, chmn. econ. com. Dem. Nat. Platform Com., 1972; trustee Lackawanna Jr. Coll., 1977-79, solicitor, 1979-83; mem. alumni bd. govs. U. Scranton, 1969-75, pres. Nat. Alumni Soc., 1983-85; solicitor Cath. Social Svcs., 1978-95, bd. dirs., 1978-97; pres., owner Scranton-Wilkes Barre Twins, Inc., 1993-94; pres. Atlantic Collegiate Baseball League, 1995-97. Bd. dirs. Pennsylvanians for Human Life, 2001—, Secular Franciscan Order, 2002—; bd. dirs. Lackawanna br. Pa. Assn. for Blind, 1988—, chmn., 2003—, pres., 2003—. Mem. ABA, Pa. Bar Assn., Lackawanna Bar Assn., Greater Scranton Bd. Realtors, Pa. Assn. Realtors, Nat. Assn. Realtors, Intertel, Internat. Soc. Philos. Enquiry, Mensa, Alpha Sigma Nu. Democrat. Roman Catholic. Home: 319 Church St Dunmore PA 18512-1911 Office: 527 Linden St Scranton PA 18503

BURKE, JACQUELINE YVONNE, telecommunications executive; b. Newark, Apr. 10, 1949; d. Trim and Viola (Smith) Russell; m. Harry Clifford Burke Jr., Aug. 20, 1968 (div. 1977); 1 child, Terence Christopher. Student, Howard U., Washington, 1966-67; HHD, London Inst. Applied Rsch., 1993; Cert. of License for Gospel Ministry, Annointed Tabernacle, Greensboro, N.C., 1994; DD, Shiloh Theol. Sem., Stafford, Va., 1997. Ordained to ministry Covent Ministries Internat., 1994, Faith Tabernacle Outreach Ministries, 1995. Teaching asst. Barringer High Sch., Newark, 1967; course developer Prudential Property and Casualty Ins., Newark, 1968-74; exec. Ad-A-System, Avenel, N.J., 1974-77; staff mgr. AT&T, Basking Ridge, N.J., 1977-83; quality assurance mgr. ops. and engring. Bell Communications Rsch., Morristown, NJ, 1984-86, dir. traffic routing adminstr., mem. tech. staff, 1986-91, tng./devel. specialist, 1991-93, performance technologist, 1993—2002, pastor Faith Tabernacle Ch., 1999; apptd. dean Charles Reid Bible Coll., Plainfield, NJ, 1998—2000. Instr. Summer Tech. Edn. Program, Morristown, 1987; pres. Jacqueline Burke Enterprises, 1991—; pres., founder Liberation By Edn. Ministries, South Plainfield, N.J., 1995—; dean Divine Healing Temple Bible Tng. Outreach Ctr., Plainfield, 1994-95; sr. performance cons. ASCI, N.J., 1998. Am. del. to Africa Africa -Am. Summit, 1993; cons., instr. Black Achievers/YMCA, Newark, 1985; pres. Archway Pregnancy Ctr., Elizabeth, NJ, 1985—89; mem. adv. bd. Bros. and Sisters, Inc., 1989—; exec. dir. Internat. Ministries, 1997—2000; instr. Youth for Christ, Fanwood, NJ, 1984—86; exec. dir. edn. and tng. Faith Tabernacle Ch., 1996—, chair bd. elders, assoc. pastor, 1997—98, pastor, 1999—2000; tchr. Neighborhood Bible Study, 1989—; dean Divine Healing Temple Bible Tng. Outreach Ctr., 1994—95; bd. dirs. Faith Tabernacle Outreach Ministries, 1997, Bright Cmty. Ministry, 1997—2000; appt. to bd. advisors Am Biog Inst. Rsch., 1989; sec. Women Aglow, 1991—92. Recipient Tribute to Woman in Industry award YWCA, 1985, Black Achiever award, 1985, Sojourner Truth award Nat. Assn. Negro Bus. and Profl. Women, 1989, Bellcore Synergy III cert., 1989, Recognition award YWCA, 1986, Cert. of Recognition Urban Women's Ctr., 1990, Bellcore Software Devel. and Software Com. Quality award, 1991, Recognition award Woman Aglow Fellowship, Plainfield chpt., 1993; named Outstanding Young Woman Am., 1985; Proclamation from City Mayor of Plainfield, 1990. Mem. NAFE, Nat. Assn. Negro Bus. and Profl. Women's Club, Inc., Career Options/YWCA, Am. Mgmt. Assn., Am. Soc. Training Devel., Tribute to Women and Industry (speaker, mem. mgmt. forum 1985—), Internat. Platform Assn., Am. Biog. Inst. (rsch. bd. advisors 1989—). Democrat. Home: 229 West Ave South Plainfield NJ 07080-1924

BURKE, JAMES DONALD, museum administrator; b. Salem, Oreg., Feb. 22, 1939; s. Donald J. and Ellin (Adams) B.; m. Diane E. Davies, May 17, 1980 BA, Brown U., 1961; MA, U. Pa., 1966; PhD, Harvard U., 1972. Curator Yale U. Art Gallery, New Haven, 1972-78; asst. dir. St. Louis Art Mus., 1978-80, dir., chief exec. officer, 1980-99, dir. emeritus, 1999—. Cons., panel mem. IRS, Washington, 1980—; scholar-in-residence Washington U., St. Louis, 1999—, Mercantile Libr., U. Mo., St. Louis, 1999—. Author: Jan Both, 1974, Charles Meyron, 1974; contbr. articles to profl. jours.; organizer in field. Pres. St. Louis Art Mus. Found., 1985—99, Gateway Found., 1986—. Fulbright fellow, 1968-69 Mem. Coll. Art Assn., Print Council Am., Am. Assn. Mus., Assn. Art Mus. Dirs. Office: Saint Louis Art Mus One Fine Arts Dr Forest Park Saint Louis MO 63110

BURKE, JAMES EDWARD, consumer products company executive; b. Feb. 28, 1925; s. James Francis and Mary (Barnett) B.; m. Alice Eubank, Apr. 27, 1957 (dec.); children: Mary Clotilde, James Charles; m. Diane W. Burke, Nov. 7, 1981. BS in Econs., Holy Cross Coll., 1947; MBA, Harvard U., 1949. Sales rep., then asst. brand mgr., brand mgr. Procter & Gamble, 1949-52; product dir. Johnson & Johnson, 1953-54, dir. new products, 1954-57, dir. advt. and merchandising, 1958-62, gen. mgr. Baby Products Co. divsn., 1962-64, exec. v.p. mktg., 1964-65, gen. mgr. Johnson & Johnson Products Co. divsn., 1965-66, pres., 1966-70, chmn. bd., 1970-71, corp. dir., mem. exec. com., 1973-76, dir., mem. exec. com. parent co., 1965-89, former vice-chmn. exec. com., from 1971, CEO, chmn. bd. parent co., 1976-89. Chmn. emeritus Partnership for Drug-Free Am., 1989-2002. Ensign USN, WWII, PTO. Office: Johnson & Johnson 100 Albany St Ste 200 New Brunswick NJ 08901-1227

BURKE, JAMES JOSEPH, JR., investment banker; b. Wilmington, Del., Dec. 19, 1951; s. James Joseph and Kathleen Gertrude (Nauss) B.; m. Jeanne Elizabeth Burke, Aug. 6, 1977; children: James III, Jennifer, Brian. AB in Psychology, Brown U., 1973; MBA with distinction, Harvard U., 1979. 2d v.p. Chase Manhattan Bank, N.Y.C., 1973-77; assoc. Merrill Lynch, N.Y.C., 1979-83, v.p., 1983-85, mng. dir., 1985-94; pres., CEO Merrill Lynch Capital Ptnrs., N.Y.C., 1987-94; mng. ptnr. First Capital Ptnrs., N.Y.C., 1994—, Stonington Ptnrs., Inc. (formerly First Capital Ptnrs.), N.Y.C., 1995—. Bd. dirs. Ann Taylor Stores Corp., N.Y.C., Lincoln Tech. Inst., Inc., West Orange, NJ, Edn. Mgmt. Corp., Pitts. Pres. In-Sch. Divsn. Boy Scouts Am., N.Y.C.; trustee Seton Hall Prep. Sch., West Orange, N.J.; bd. overseers Seton Hall U. Sch. Diplomacy and Internat. Rels., Brown U. Sports Found. Office: Stonington Ptnrs 767 5th Ave New York NY 10153-0023 E-mail: JBurke@stonington.com.

BURKE, JOHN, priest; b. Washington, Sept. 15, 1928; s. William Francis and Grace Allison (Logan) B. AB, Cath. U. Am., 1950, MA, 1965, STD, 1969. Joined Order Preachers, ordained priest Roman Cath. Ch., 1960. Prof. homiletics St. Stephen's Coll., Dover, Mass., 1961-64, Immaculate Conception faculty, 1964-67, 90, asst. prof., summers 1964-69, asst. prof. drama, 1968-72, dir. Preaching Workshop, 1965-67, dir. Preachers Inst., 1967-72; mem. faculty Washington Theol. Coalition, 1968-69; coord. Nat. Congress for the Word of God, 1972; founder, exec. dir. Nat. Inst. for the Word of God, Washington, 1972—, prof. Dominican House of Studies, Washington, 1990—. Author: Bible Sharing Youth Retreat Manual, 1983, Beginners' Guide to Bible Sharing, Vol. I, II, 1984, The Homilist's Guide to Scripture, Theology and Canon Law, 1987; editor: Gospel Power: Toward the Revitalization of Preaching, 1978, Bible Sharing: How to Grow in the Mystery of Christ, 1979, A New Look at Preaching, 1983,A Good News Spirituality, 2000; contbr. articles to profl. jours.; producer TV film Chimbote, 1964. Mem. Radio-TV Dirs. Guild of AFTRA, Phi Beta Kappa. Roman Catholic. Address: 487 Michigan Ave NE Washington DC 20017-1584 E-mail: burkeop@aol.com. *For lasting happiness in life, one needs to experience the active presence of God.*

BURKE, JOHN PATRICK, internist, educator; b. Marshalltown, Iowa, Jan. 19, 1940; s. Raphael Eggleston and Marjorie N. (Busch) B.; m. Andrea Marie Keane, May 9, 1970; children: Paul, Matthew, Edward, Erin. BA, summa cum laude, U. Iowa, 1961, MD, 1964. Diplomate Am. Bd. Internal Medicine, Am. Bd. Infectious Disease. Intern Yale-New Haven Hosp., 1964-65, resident in medicine, 1965-67; rsch. fellow Harvard med. unit Boston City Hosp., 1968-70; chief infectious disease sect. LDS Hosp., Salt Lake City, 1970—; epidemic intelligence svc. officer Ctr. for Disease Control and Prevention, 1967—70. Asst. prof. medicine U. Utah, Salt Lake City, 1970-75, assoc. prof., 1975-83, prof., 1983—, Mark Presdl. endowed chair in medicine, 1999—; spl. reviewer NIH, Bethesda, Md., 1978, 80; mem. tech. panel on infections within hosps. Am. Hosp. Assn., 1996; cons. Inst. Medicine, NAS, 1998—, Ctrs. for Disease Control and Prevention, 1994, 99, Nat. Patient Safety Found., 1999, Lewin Group, 1999-2000; mem. scientific adv. coun. HEart and Lung Inst. LDS Hosp. Found., 1990—; co-founder, bd. dirs. TheraDoc, Inc., 1999. Mem. editl. bd. Am. Jour. Infection Control, 1981-97, Infection Control and Hosp. Epidemiology, 1979-88, 2003-; contbr. numerous articles to med. jours., chpts. to books. Surgeon USPHS, 1967-70. NIH-Nat. Inst. Allergy and Infectious Disease grantee, 1974-79, 79-82, 83-85, 86-89, FDA, 1999. Fellow Infectious Disease Soc. Am., ACP; mem. Soc. for Healthcare Epidemiology Am. (councillor 1981-82, treas. 1985-88, v.p. 1991, mem. bd. dirs. 1991-93, pres. 1992), Am. Med. Info. Assn., Utah Med. Assn. (del. 1975-77), Am. Epidemiol. Soc., Alpha Omega Alpha, Phi Beta Kappa. Mem. Christian Ch. Home: 1966 Yale Ave Salt Lake City UT 84108-1827 Office: LDS Hosp Med Office Bldg Ste 204 370 9th Ave Salt Lake City UT 84103 E-mail: john.burke@hsc.utah.edu.

BURKE, JOHN EDWARD, communications editor; b. Huntington, W.Va., Aug. 10, 1942; s. Charles Joseph and Eloise Marie (Sang) B.; m. Mary Catherine Enright; children: John Lindsey, Elizabeth Ann, Caroline Catherine. BA, Marshall U., 1965; MFA, Ohio U., 1966; PhD, Ohio State U., 1971. Intern U.S. Ho. Reps., 1960-61; news writer, editor Sta. WSAZ-TV, Huntington, 1962-65; instr. Kent State U., 1966-69; dir. TV Arts dept. Cleve. Summer Sch. for Arts, 1967-68; asst. to dir. Ohio State U. Telecomms. Ctr., 1969-71; project dir. Ohio Valley Med. Microwave TV System, Columbus, 1971-73; dir., assoc. prof. biomed. comms. Ohio State U. Coll. Medicine; assoc. prof. comms. Coll. Social and Behavioral Scis., 1972-84; assoc. dean acad. affairs, prof. U. Ill. Coll. Associated Health Professions, Chgo., 1984-87; sr. mgr. sci. rels. Pharm. Products divsn. Abbott Labs., 1987-97; exec. dir., CEO Accreditation Assn. Ambulatory Health Care Inc. Adj. prof. Ohio State U., Columbus, 1989—; cons. univs., bus., industry, including U. Tenn., Nat. Med. Audio-Visual Center, Upjohn Co., N. Central Assn. Colls. and Univs., WHO, AMA. Author: History of Public Broadcasting Act of 1967, 1979; contbr. articles to profl. jours.; editor Jour. Allied Health, 1978-87; editor emeritus Jour. Allied Health, 1987—. USPHS grantee, 1972-77. Fellow Am. Soc. Allied Health Professions; mem. Health Scis. Comms. Assn., Coun. of Biology Editors, Am. Med. Writers Assn., Am. Soc. Assn. Execs., Alpha Psi Omega, Alpha Epsilon Rho. Democrat. Roman Catholic. Home: 567 Maple St Winnetka IL 60093-2335

BURKE, JOHN JAMES, utility executive; b. Butte, Mont., July 25, 1928; m. Nancy M. Calvert, July 12, 1952; children: Cheryl Burke Harris, Mary Burke Orizotti, Kathleen Novak, John James, III, Elisabeth Orizotti. BS in Bus., BA in Law, U. Mont., 1950, JD, 1952. Bar: Mont. 1952, U.S. Supreme Ct. 1957. Ptnr. Weir, Gough, Booth and Burke, Helena, 1954-59; atty. Mont. Power Co., Butte, 1959-67, v.p., 1967-78, exec. v.p., 1979-84, vice chmn. bd. dirs., 1984-93. Dir. Lazard Funds Inc., Pacific Steel & Recycling, Sletten Constrn. Co. Trustee U. Mont. Found., Carroll Coll., Mont., Mont. Hist. Soc., 1988-2000, B.K. Wheeler Found.; co-chmn. Mont. Renaissance Fund Bus. Coun.; past pres. City County Planning Bd., 1966-78; past dir. Vigilante coun. Boy Scouts Am., Shining Mountains coun. Girl Scouts U.S.A.; vice chmn. Gov. Task Force/Renew Mont. Govt. Capt. JAGC, USAF, 1952-54, with Res., 1954-61. Mem. ABA (mem. coun. pub. utility law sect.), State Bar Mont., Silver Bow County Bar Assn., Mountain States Legal Found. (past bd. dirs.), Nat. Assn. Mfrs. (past bd. dirs.), Edison Electric Inst. (exec. adv. com. on planning), Butte C. of C. (v.p. 1965-72), U. Mont. Alumni Assn. (past bd. dirs.), Montana Club, Butte Country Club, Elks, Rotary (sec. Helena 1955-58), 116 Club (Washington), Phi Delta Phi. Roman Catholic. Home and Office: 50 Burning Tree Ln Butte MT 59701-3904 E-mail: jjburke@in-tch.com.

BURKE, JOHN K(IRKLAND), JR., lawyer; b. Richmond, Va., Jan. 26, 1952; s. John Kirkland and Archer (Christian) B.; m. Miriam Smith, July 23, 1977; children: John K. III, Ruth H., B. Smith. BA in History with distinction, U. Va., 1974, JD, 1977. Bar: Va. 1977, U.S. Dist. Ct. (ea. and we. dists.) Va. 1977, U.S. Ct. Appeals (4th cir.) 1977. Law clk. to Justice George M. Cochran Supreme Ct. Va., Staunton, 1977-78; assoc. Mays and Valentine, L.L.P., Richmond, Va., 1978-84; ptnr. Mays and Valentine, Richmond, Va., 1984-2000, chmn. bus. and comml. litigation practice group; ptnr. Troutman Sanders LLP, Richmond, 2001—. Mem. City of Richmond's Human Rels. Comm., 1991-97. Mem. Va. Bar Assn., Bar Assn. of City of Richmond (bd. dirs. 1994-98), Soc. of the Cin. for State of Va. (asst. treas.), Va. State Bar, Country Club Va. (bd. dirs. 1999-2001). Avocations: sports, reading, music. Office: Troutman Sanders LLP PO Box 1122 Richmond VA 23218-1122 E-mail: john.burke@troutmansanders.com.

BURKE, JOHN MICHAEL, lawyer; b. Chgo., Oct. 9, 1941; s. John and Catherine Mary (Barrett) B.; m. Maureen Kay Fox, Oct. 5, 1968; children: Brian, Timothy, Michael. BBA, Loyola U., 1964, JD, 1965. Bar: Ill. 1965, U.S. Dist. Ct. (no. dist.) Ill. 1965, U.S. Ct. Appeals (7th cir.) 1968, U.S. Dist. Ct. (no.dist.) Ind. 1986. Assoc. Pretzel & Stouffer, Chgo., 1965-69, Shaheen, Lundberg & Callahan, Chgo., 1969-70; ptnr. Burke & Burke, Ltd., Chgo., 1970—. Sgt. U.S. Army, 1965-68. Mem. ATLA, CBA, Ill. State Bar Assn. (chmn. tort coun., svc. award 1984, mem. civil practice com. 1997—, mem. jud. evaluation com. 2002—), Ill. Trial Lawyers (bd. mgrs. 1988—), Appellate Lawyers Ill., Westmoreland Country Club (Wilmette, Ill.). Home: 2241 Kenilworth Ave Wilmette IL 60091-1523 Office: Burke & Burke Ltd 30 N LaSalle St Ste 2800 Chicago IL 60602 E-mail: jburke@burke-burke.com.

BURKE, JOSEPH C. former university official; b. New Albany, Ind., Mar. 20, 1932; s. Dennis F. and Beatrice V. (McDevitt) B.; m. Joan Thompson, Sept. 1, 1956; children: Maura, Colleen. BA, Bellarmine Coll., Louisville, 1954; MA, Ind. U., 1958, PhD, 1965. Instr. Ohio Wesleyan U., Delaware, 1960-62; asst. prof. to prof. history Duquesne U., Pitts., 1962-70; prof. history Loyola of Montreal, 1970-73, acad. v.p., 1970-73, SUNY Coll., Plattsburgh, 1973-74, pres., 1974-85; provost, vice chancellor for acad. affairs SUNY Sys., Albany, 1985-95; pres. Rsch. Found. SUNY, Albany, 1990-95, interim chancellor, 1994; sr. fellow, dir. higher edn. prog. Nelson A. Rockefeller Inst. Govt., Albany, 1956. Cons. leadership adn planning for colls. and univs. Contbr. books, monographs, chpts. and articles to profl. jours., chpts. to books on higher edn. Trustee Miner Found. Rsch.; chmn. bd. Miner Agrl. Inst. Grantee Pew Charitable Trusts Luce Found., 1996—, Ford Found., 1996—. E-mail: burkejo@rockinst.org.

BURKE, KATHLEEN B. lawyer; b. Bklyn., Sept. 2, 1948; BA, St. John's U., 1969, JD, 1973. Bar: Ohio 1973. Ptnr. Jones, Day, Reavis & Pogue, Cleve. Chair Notre Dame Coll. of Ohio, 2002—. Pres. Cleve. Skating Club, 2000-2002. Fellow Ohio State Bar Found. (pres. 2000); mem. Ohio State Bar Assn. (pres. 1993-94). Office: Jones Day Reavis & Pogue North Point 901 Lakeside Ave E Cleveland OH 44114-1190

BURKE, KATHLEEN J. foundation administrator; Exec. v.p., pers. rels. officer BankAmerica Corp., San Francisco, now vice chmn., pers. rel. officer; exec. dir. Stupski Family Found., Mill Valley, Calif., 2000—. Office: # 110 2 Belvedere Dr Mill Valley CA 94941-2418 E-mail: kathleen@stupski.com.

BURKE, KATHLEEN J. music director, writer; b. Detroit, Mich. d. Arthur Reginald and Lois Genevieve Brooks; married, Apr. 17, 1982; children: Sean Patrick, Conor Timothy. A in History, Butte Jr. Coll., Calif., 1975; BS in History, Calif. State U., Fullerton, 1977. Pub. rels. sports Burke Sports Mktg., Eugene, Oreg., 1977—79, Burke Comms., Irvine, Calif., 1983—90, pub. rels. gen. Mission Viejo, Calif., 1991—98, pub. rels. music, 1999—2002, Parodudes Inc., Pitts., 1999—2002, mgr. booking, 2001—02. Author, editor: PSA for Project Independence, 1988 (2d pl., Calif. Press Women, 1988). Vol. Rep. Party, Calif., 1991—92; vol. meals ministry S.V.C.C., Calif., 1991—2002, vol. christian missions, 2000—. Mem.: Recording Acad., Women in Comms., Nat. Mus. of Women in Arts, Nat. Assn. Rock Radio, Gospel Music Assn. Avocations: distance running, biking, hiking, triathlons. Office: Burke Comms 24161 Saiero Ln Mission Viejo CA 92691-4131 E-mail: music4filmbiz@cox.net.

BURKE, KELLY HOWARD, former air force officer, business executive, investor; b. Mobile, Ala., June 7, 1929; s. Kelly Howard and Vesta (Trussell) B.; m. Denny Ray Hosey, Dec. 30, 1951; children: Bethany, Patricia, Kelly Howard, III. BS in History, Auburn U., 1952; MS in Internat. Rels., George Washington U., 1968; postgrad., Naval War Coll., 1967-68, RAF Staff Coll., 1969-71, Indsl. Coll. Armed Forces, 1964-65. Commd. 2d lt. U.S. Air Force, 1953, advanced through grades to lt. gen., 1979; comdr. 379th Bomb Wing Wurtsmith AFB, Mich., 1973-74; comdr. 2d Bomb Wing Barksdale AFB, La., 1974-75; dep. chief of staff/plans SAC, 1975-78; dir. operational requirements Hdqrs. U.S. Air Force, Washington, 1978-79, dep. chief of staff/research, devel. and acquisition, 1979-82; ret., 1982; chmn. bd. Stafford, Burke and Hecker, Inc., Alexandria, VA, 1982. Bd. dirs. Singer Co., Tiger Internat. Inc., Flying Tigers Line Inc., Orbital Scis. Corp., OWCC Found., Children's Advocacy Ctr.; cons. White House Sci. Office, NRC, Def. Sci. Bd., Sci. Adv. Bd., others; frequent lectr. Chmn. editl. bd. Aerospace Am.; contbg. editor Armed Forces Jour.; contbr. numerous articles on nat. security issues to publd. Decorated D.S.M. with oak leaf cluster, Legion of Merit, D.F.C., Meritorious Svc. medal, Air medal with oak leaf clusters; established Burke Scholarship Endowment for 15 4-yr. coll. scholarships annually to needy students; named Fla. Benefactor of Yr. for this and other charitable activities, 1995. Mem. Nat. Space Club, Nat. Aviation Club Episcopalian. Home: 803 Choctaw Ln Shalimar FL 32579-2248 Office: Stafford Burke and Hecker 1006 Cameron St Alexandria VA 22314-2427 E-mail: kbxel@aol.com.

BURKE, KENNETH ANDREW, advertising executive; b. Sept. 9, 1941; s. Frank Flory and Margret Anne (Tomè) B.; m. Karen Lee Burley, July 1, 1968; children: Allison Leigh, Aric Jason. BSBA in Mktg., Bowling Green (Ohio) State U., 1965. Mem. Green Bay Packers Nat. Football League, Sask. Roughriders, Can. Football League; acct. exec. lang, Fisher, Stashower, Cleve., 1967-69; v.p., acct. supr. Tracy-Locke, Dallas, 1969-72; v.p. Grey Advt., N.Y.C., 1972-76, Griswold Eshleman, Cleve., 1976-79; sr. v.p., gen. mgr. Simpson Mktg., Columbus, Ohio, 1979-81; pres., CEO, chmn. Martcom Inc., Columbus, Ohio, 1981-91; chmn. ret. Ad Factory, Inc., Advt. and Mktg., Ad Factory Outlets, Columbus, Ohio, 1991-98; exec. v.p. Berkshire Product Inc., Tampa, Fla., 1983-89. Author: Bordini and the Black Knight, 1975. Mem. adv. bd. columbus chpt. Am. Cancer Soc., 1980-88. Recipient USN Achievement award, 1975. Mem. Am. Mktg. Assn., Columbus Advt. Fedn., NFL Alumni Assn., Cleve. Advt. Club (Merit award 1968), Columbus C. of C., Upper Arlington C. of C., Theta chi. Republican. Roman Catholic. Home: 1753 Bedford Rd Columbus OH 43212-2004 Office: Ad Factory Corp Offices 22 Gay Street Columbus OH 43215 E-mail: kenburke@adfactoryinc.com.

BURKE, KEVIN CHARLES ANTONY, geologist; b. London, Nov. 13, 1929; came to U.S., 1973; s. Charles Henry and Kathleen (Daly) B.; m. Angela Marion Phipps, Jan. 23, 1960; children: Nicholas, Matthew, Jane. BSc, Univ. Coll., London, 1951, PhD, 1953. Lectr. U. Ghana, 1953-56; geologist Brit. Geol. Survey, 1956-61; head geology dept. U. West Indies, Kingston, Jamaica, 1961-65; prof. geology U. Ibadan, Nigeria, 1963-71, SUNY-Albany, 1973-83; prof. U. Houston, 1983—; dir. Lunar and Planetary Inst., 1983-88; scholar in residence NRC, Washington, 1989-92. Vis. prof. U. Toronto, 1971-73, Calif. Inst. Tech., 1976, U. Minn., 1977, U. Calgary, 1979; cons. in field. NSF grantee, 1976— Fellow Geol. Soc. Am.; mem. AAAS, Am. Geophys. Union, Nigerian Mining, Geol. and Metall. Soc. (pres. internat. com. on the lithosphere 1992-95, Du Toit meml. lectr. 1995). Achievements include research in plate tectonics. Office: U Houston Dept Geoscis Houston TX 77204-0007 *There is much luck in a scientific career. I could not have known when I chose to become a geologist in 1948 that understanding of the problems I studied would be revolutionized by Plate Tectonics in 1965. To make the most of such an opportunity in geology a breadth of experience, both geographically and in different branches of geology, has proved vital.*

BURKE, LAWRENCE J. editor-in-chief; Founder, chmn., editor-in-chief Outside Mag. (now called Mariah Media Inc.), 1976—. Office: Outside Mag 400 Market St Santa Fe NM 87501*

BURKE, LILLIAN WALKER, retired judge; b. Thomaston, Ga., Aug. 2, 1917; d. George P. and Ozella (Daviston) Walker; m. Ralph Livingston Burke, July 8, 1948 (dec.); 1 son, R. Bruce. BS, Ohio State U., 1947; LLB, Cleve. State U., 1951, postgrad., 1963-64; grad., Nat. Coll. State Judiciary, U. Nev., 1974. Bar: Ohio 1951. Gen. practice law, Cleve., 1952-62; asst. atty. gen., 1962-66; mem., vice chmn. Ohio Indsl. Commn., 1966-69; judge Cleve. Mcpl. Ct., 1969-87, chief judge, 1981, 85, vis. judge, 1988-97; ret., 1997. Guest lectr. Heidelburg Coll., Tiffin, Ohio, 1971; cons. Bur. Higher Edn., HEW, 1972. Pres. Cleve. chpt. Nat. Council Negro Women, 1955-57, recipient certificate of award, 1969; sec. East dist. Family Service Assn., 1959-60; mem. council human relations Cleve. Citizens League, 1959-79; mem. Gov.'s Com. on Status of Women, 1966-67; pres. Cleve. chpt. Jack and Jill of Am., Inc., 1960-61; v.p.-at-large Greater Cleve. Safety Council, 1969-79; mem. Cleve. Landmarks Commn., 1990-97; woman ward leader 24th Ward Republican Club, 1957-67; mem. Cuyahoga County Central Com., 1958-68; sec. Cuyahoga County Exec. Com., 1962-63; alt. del. Rep. Nat. Conv., Chgo., 1960; bd. dirs., chmn. minority div. Nat. Fedn. Rep. Women, 1966-68; life mem., past bd. dirs. Cleve. chpt. NAACP; bd. dirs. Greater Cleve. Neighborhood Centers Assn., Catholic Youth Counselling Services; trustee Ohio Commn. on Status of Women, 1966-70, Consumers League Ohio, 1969-75, Cleve. Music Sch. Settlement; bd. mgmt. Glenville YWCA, 1960-70; mem. project com. Cleve. Orch.; apptd. mem. City Planning Comm. Cleve., 1997-2002. Recipient achievement award Parkwood Christian Meth. Episcopal Ch., 1968, Martin Luther King Citizen's award, 1969, outstanding achievement award Ta-Wa-Si Scholarship Club, 1969, Outstanding Svc. award Morning Star Grand chpt., Cleve., 1970, award of honor Cleve. Bus. League, 1970, svc. award St. Paul AME Ch., Lima, Ohio, 1972, Woman of Achievement award Inner Club Coun., Cleve., 1973, cert. of award Nat. Coun. Negro Women, 1969, Cleve. Found. Goff Philanthropic Leadership award, 1997; named Career Woman of Yr., Cleve. Women's Career Clubs, 1969, Jewel of Yr., Women's City Club, 2002, award for hist. preservation So. African Hist. Soc., 2002, Woman of Achievement award YWCA, 2003. Mem. ABA, Nat. Assn. Investment Clubs (pres. Dynasty Investors Club 1992-96, bd. dirs. N.E. Ohio Coun. 1993—), Nat. Bar Assn., Ohio Bar Assn., Cuyahoga County Bar Assn., Cleve. Bar Assn., Am. Judicature Soc., Am. Judges Assn. (bd. govs. 1982-86, chmn. conv. agenda com. 1981-83), Phillis Wheatley Assn., Women Lawyers Assn. (hon. adviser), Ohio State U. Alumni Assn. (life), Cleve. Marshall Law Sch. (life), Am. Bridge Assn. (life), Women's City Club (Cleve.), Altrusa, Alpha Kappa Alpha. Mem. Ch. Of Christ. Home: 1357 East Blvd Cleveland OH 44106-4018

BURKE, LOUIS, gynecologist, educator, researcher; b. Boston, Mar. 6, 1920; s. Charles and Bella (Dekelbaum) B.; m. Dorothy Julia Robinson, May 30, 1945; children: Steven, Jeffrey; m. Martha Russin, Mar. 1, 1998. BS, Tufts Coll., 1941, MD, 1944. Diplomate Am. Bd. Ob-Gyn. Intern in surgery Beth Israel Hosp., Boston, 1944-45, resident in obstetrics, 1951-52, ob-gyn., 1960-85, acting ob-gyn. chief, 1989-90, chief colposcopy, laser clinic, 1980—, sr. obstetrician, 1985—; resident in surgery Mt. Sinai Hosp., N.Y.C., 1947-49, resident in gynecology, 1949-50; resident in obstetrics Booth Meml. Hosp., Brookline, Mass., 1950-51; pvt. practice Boston, 1952; instr. ob-gyn Med. Sch. Harvard U., Boston, 1964-69, asst. clin. prof., 1969-73, asst. prof., 1973-80, assoc. prof. ob-gyn., 1980-2000, prof., 2000—. Author: Colposcopy in Clinical Practice, 1977, Colposcopy: Text and Atlas, 1990; assoc. editor: Colposcopy and Gynecologic Laser Surgery, 1983; mem. editl. bd.: The Female Patient, 1982, Intelligence Reports in Ob-Gyn., 1984, Jour. of Gynecologic Surgery, 1984. Capt. USMC, 1945-47. Recipient Frank Sinatra award Pan Am. Cancer Cytology Congress, 1978, Gold Medal award U. Autonoma de Barcelona. Fellow Am. Coll. Ob-Gyn.; mem. Am. Soc. For Colposcopy and Cervical Pathology (Disting. svc. award 1994), Internat. Fedn. for Cervical Pathology and Colposcopy (treas.), Boston Obstetric. Soc. (mem. Prudential com.), Gtr. Boston Med. Soc. (pres.). Office: Beth Israel Deaconess Hosp 330 Brookline Ave Boston MA 02215-5400 E-mail: LBurke1@caregroup.Harvard.Edu.

BURKE, MARGARET ANN, computer and communications company specialist; b. N.Y.C., Feb. 25, 1961; d. David Joseph and Eileen Theresa (Falvey) B. BS in Computer Sci., St. John's U., Jamaica, N.Y., 1982; MBA, U. Md., 1994. Cert. data processor. Software specialist Bell Atlantic Corp., Washington, 1983—. Active Friends of Hillwood Mus., Washington. Mem. NAFE, Alliance Francaise, Nat. Fedn. Rep. Women, Am. Film Inst. Roman Catholic. Home: 6652 Hillandale Rd Unit A Bethesda MD 20815-6406 Office: Bell Atlantic 13100 Columbia Pike Silver Spring MD 20904-5296

BURKE, MARGUERITE JODI LARCOMBE, writer, executive services professional; b. Pasadena, Calif. d. Richard Albert and Marguerite (Colella) L.; m. Theodore Jockers; children: Richard Larcombe, Sir Blair; m. Roger Eugene Burke, PhD, Columbia U. Photographers model Ford Agy., N.Y.C.; freelance writer Savannah, Ga.; pres. Jodi Larcombe Assocs., Murfreesboro, N.C., 1970—; freelance computer programmer Murfreesboro, 1981—. Exec. asst. Resinall Corp., Severn, N.C., 1981—, computer programmer, 1981-89. Author: Sailing Cookbook, 1979, others; contbr. numerous articles to mags.; dir. Shotgun Theater Prodns., 1995. Chmn. bd. dirs. Shotgun Theater Prodns., N.Y., 1996—; patron Avery Fischer Hall, N.Y.C., 1979—; mem. Mus. Art N.Y.C., 1979—. Mem. Met. Opera Oncore Soc., Am. Film Soc., Met Opera Patron Assn. (2d century cir.), Met. Opera Nat. Coun., N.Y.C. Opera, Murfreesboro Hist. Soc. Avocations: sailing, reading, sewing, traveling, classical music. Home and Office: Jodi Larcombe Assocs 12 Gale Ln Ormond Beach FL 32174 Office Fax: 386-586-3725.

BURKE, MARIANNE KING, state agency administrator, financial executive, consultant; b. Douglasville, Ga., May 30, 1938; d. William Horace and Evora (Morris) King; divorced; 1 child, Kelly Page. Student, Ga. Inst. Tech., 1956-59, Anchorage C.C., 1964-66, Portland State U., 1968-69; BBA, U. Alaska, 1976. CPA, Alaska. Sr. audit mgr. Price Waterhouse, 1982-90; v.p. fin., asst. sec. NANA Regional Corp., Inc., Anchorage, 1990-95; v.p. fin. NANA Devel. Corp., Inc., Anchorage, 1990-95; sec.-treas. Vanguard Industries, J.V., Anchorage, 1990-95, Alaska United Drilling, Inc., Anchorage, 1990-95; treas. NANA/Marriott Joint Venture, Anchorage, 1990-95; v.p. fin. Arctic Utilities, Inc., Anchorage, 1990-95, Tour Arctic, Inc., Anchorage, 1990-95, Purcell Svcs., Ltd., Anchorage, 1990-95, Arctic Caribou Inn, Anchorage, 1990-95, NANA Oilfield Svcs., Inc., Anchorage, 1990-95, NANA Corp. Svcs., Inc., Anchorage, 1992-95; dir. divsn. ins. State of Alaska, 1995-99; pres. Marianne K. Burke Cons., 1999—. Cons. to Ins. Regulatory and Deve. Authority of India, 2002—; mem. State of Alaska Medicaid Rate Commn., 1985—88, State of Alaska Bd. Accountancy, 1984—87; bd. dirs. Nat. Assn. Ins. Commrs. Edn. and Rsch. Found.; cons. internat. ins. domicile. Bd. dirs. Alaska Treatment Ctr., Anchorage, 1978, Alaska Hwy. Cruises; treas. Alaska Feminist Credit Union, Anchorage, 1979-80; mem. fund raising com. Anchorage Symphony, 1981. Mem. AICPA, Internat. Assn. Ins. Suprs. (funded mem.), Alaska Soc. CPAs, Govtl. Fin. Officers U.S. and Can., Fin. Execs. Inst. (bd. dirs.), Nat. Assn. Ins. Commrs. (bd. dirs.). Avocations: travel, reading. Home: 3818 Helvetia Dr Anchorage AK 99508-5016 E-mail: mkburke@gci.net.

BURKE, MARJORIE TISDALE, retired special education educator; b. Chase City, Va., May 27, 1926; d. Henry and Sallie Keene; m. Willie Tisdale, 1948; children: Michael S., Carita F., Lydia R.; m. William C. Vaughn, 1966 (div. 1976); m. Faxie Burke, May 22, 1993. BS, Va. State Coll., 1956. Tchr. elem. edn. Newark (N.J.) Bd. Edn., 1951-53, tchr. spl. edn., 1954-64, Elizabeth (N.J.) Bd. Edn., 1964—92, Fauquier Bd. Edn., Warrenton, Va., 1992—; tutor, subs. tchr. Va.; ret., 1992. Cmty. parent advocate in spl. edn.; Mary Kay beauty cons., 1973—. Mem. Mt. Pleasant Bapt. Ch., Gainesville, Va., also choir mem., usher, sec., v.p. women's aux., pres. scholarship fund, asst. supt. Sunday sch., chairperson of greeters. Mem. AAUW, AARP, NAACP (chmn. edn. com. Prince William County 1994—), Nat. Coun. Negro Women (sr. caretaker), Garden Club Va., Nat. Congress Black Women, Inc. (Prince William chpt.), Housekeepers Club of Aldie (v.p.). Avocations: yoga, poetry, singing, volunteer work at hospital and church. Home: PO Box 3 Gainesville VA 20156-0005

BURKE, MICHAEL DESMOND, pathologist, educator; b. Galway, Ireland, May 25, 1935; came to U.S., 1959; s. James and Margaret (McKee) B.; m. Joan Long, June, 1960 (div. Apr. 1966); children: James Niall, Richard Joseph; m. Maria Sperazi, June 19, 1966: children: Marina, Claudia. MB, BCh., BAO, Nat. U. of Ireland, Galway, 1959. Diplomate Am. Bd. of Pathology in Clin., Chem. and Anatomical Pathology. Assoc. pathologist Mt. Sinai Hosp., Mpls., 1969-81; from asst. prof. to prof. pathology U. Minn., Mpls., 1971-81; prof. pathology and dir. clin. pathology U. Hosp. SUNY, Stony Brook, N.Y., 1981-95; prof. pathology, vice chmn. lab. medicine, dir. clin. labs. N.Y. Presbyn. Hosp./Weill Cornell Med. Ctr., N.Y.C., 1996—. Faculty of Pathology fellow Royal Coll. Physicians of Ireland, 1993; trustee Am. Bd. Pathology, Tampa, Fla., 1997, sec., 2002; edtl. cons. clin. pathology Stedman's Med. Dictionary 25th edit., 1990. Editor Clinical Decisions and Laboratory Use, U. Minn. Press, 1982; adv. editor Lab. Medicine, 1985; assoc. editor Am. Jour. of Clin. Pathology, 1990-2000. Capt. USAR, 1961-63. Fellow Am. Soc. Clin. Pathologists (pres. 1995-96, Disting. Svc. award 1984, Ward Burdick award 1998), Coll. of Am. Pathologists; mem. AMA, Am. Assn, for Clin. Chemistry (Outstanding Speaker award 1991), Acad. Clin. Lab. Physicians and Scientists (pres. 1993-94, Gerald T. Evans award 1997, Cotlove Lectureship award 1998). Office: NY Presbyn Hosp Cornell Med Ctr 525 E 68th St New York NY 10021-4870 E-mail: dburke@rcn.com., dburke@mail.med.cornell.edu.

BURKE, MICHAEL HENRY, lawyer; b. Washington, Oct. 28, 1952; s. John Joseph and Mary Catherine (Gaul) B.; m. Ann McFarland, Jan. 31, 1981; children: Allison M., Andrew M. BA magna cum laude, Tufts U., 1974; JD, Georgetown U., 1977. Bar: Mass. 1977, U.S. Dist. Ct. Mass. 1979. Assoc. Bulkley, Richardson and Gelinas L.L.P., Springfield, Mass., 1977-83, ptnr., 1983—. Pub. adminstr. Commonwealth of Mass., 1980-90. Mem. ABA, Mass. Bar Assn., Hampden County Bar Assn. Roman Catholic. Home: 50 Meadowbrook Rd Longmeadow MA 01106-1341 Office: Bulkley Richardson and Gelinas LLP 1500 Main St Springfield MA 01115-0001 E-mail: mburke@bulkley.com.

BURKE, PAUL E., JR., governmental relations consultant; b. Kansas City, Mo., Jan. 4, 1934; s. Paul E. and Virgnia (Moling) B.; m. Debbie Weihe; children: Anne Elizabeth, Kelly Patricia, A. Catherine, Jennifer Marie. BSBA, U. Kans., 1956. Mem. Kans. Ho. of Reps., 1972-74, Kans. Senate, 1975-97, majority leader, 1985-89, pres., 1992—96; pres., chairman/CEO Issues Mgmt. Group, Inc., Lawrence, Kans., 1996—. Chmn. Legis. Coordinating Coun., 1995; pres.-elect Nat. Conf. State Legislatures, 1990-91, pres., 1992; pres. Nat. Conf. State Legislatures Found., 1994; mem. Fed. Adv. Commn. Intergovtl. Rels., 1993-96. Councilman City of Prairie Village, Kans., 1959-63; mem. Kans. Turnpike Authority, 1965-69, chmn., 1969; mem. adv. bd. Sect. Corrections, 1973-78; mem. Gov.'s Mil. Adv. Coordinating Coun., 2002--. Capt. USAF, 1956-59; Capt. USNR, 1963-88. Mem. Kans. Assn. Commerce and Industry, Masons, Shriners, Rotary. Republican. Episcopalian. Address: 2009 Camelback Dr Lawrence KS 66047 *Personal philosophy: The reponsibility for serving in an elected capacity is one of the greatest privileges extended by one's constituents. Understanding how to convert that responsibility to the highest level of benefit for them is our greatest challenge. Service to others--rather than self--is the key.*

BURKE, PEGGY HUDGINS (MARGARET HUDGINS BURKE), auditor; b. Aug. 30, 1951; BA, U. of the South, 1973; BS, Med. Coll. Va., 1974; MBA, U. N.C., Charlotte, 1995. CPA N.C., 2003. Practice mgr. MedCorp Health Sys., Columbia, SC, 1986-91; med. technologist V.A. Hosp., Columbia, SC, 1991-92, Presbyn. Hosp., Charlotte, 1992-95, fin. dir. lab., 1997-98, corp. compliance dir., 1998-2000; practice adminstr. Shelby (N.C.) Med. Assoc., 1996-97; dir. internal audit and compliance Novant Health, Inc., Charlotte, 2000—. Vestry St. Andrews Episcopal Ch., Mt. Holly, NC, 1998—99. Home: 201 Timberlane Dr Belmont NC 28012-7726 Office: 200 Hawthorne Ln Charlotte NC 28204-2515 E-mail: burkespd@aol.com.

BURKE, RICHARD A. manufacturing executive; CEO Trek Corp., Waterloo, Wis., chmn. Office: Trek Corp 801 W Madison St Waterloo WI 53594-1243

BURKE, RICHARD KITCHENS, lawyer, educator; b. Helena, Ark., Aug. 21, 1922; s. James Graham and Myrtie May (Kitchens) B.; m. Bonnie Beth Byler, Jan. 21, 1946; children: Charles, Bonnie Louise. Student, U. Va., 1939-40; BA, U. Ark., 1942, LLB, 1947; PhD, Vanderbilt U., 1957. Bar: Ark. 1947, Ariz. 1959, S.D. 1974. Ptnr. Burke, Moore & Burke, Helena, 1947-52; asst. prof. polit. sci. U. Ariz., 1957-60; ptnr. Robertson, Childers, Burke & Drachman, Tucson, 1960-67; prof. polit. sci. U. Southwestern La., 1967-69; U.S. atty. Dist. Ariz., Dept. Justice, 1969-72; dep. asst. atty. gen. U.S. Dept. Justice, Washington, 1972-73; prof. law U. S.D. Sch. Law, 1973-84, dean, 1974-80; prof. law U. Ark., 1984-86, prof. emeritus, 1986—. Mem. Ariz. Rep. State Com., 1963-67; Rep. congl. candidate So. Dist. Ariz., 1962; chmn. citizen's adv. com. Ampitheater Sch. Dist., Tucson, 1964-66. With USN, 1942-45, 53-54. Decorated Air medal; Ford fellow Vanderbilt U., 1957. Mem. Am. Bar Assn., State Bar S.D., State Bar Ariz., Ark. Bar Assn. Republican. Mem. Christian Ch. Home: 13 Minentonka Dr Cherokee Village AR 72529

BURKE, ROBERT BERTRAM, lawyer, political consultant, lobbyist; b. Cleve., July 9, 1942; s. Max and Eve (Miller) B.; m. Helen Choate Hall, May 5, 1979 (div. Oct. 1983). BA, UCLA, 1963, JD, 1966; LLM, London Sch. Econs., 1967. Bar: D.C. 1972, U.S. Supreme Ct. 1977, Calif. 1978. Exec. dir. Lawyer's Com. Civil Rights Under Law, Washington, 1968-69; ptnr. Fisk, Wolfe & Burke, Paris, 1969-71; assoc. O'Connor & Hannan, Washington, 1972-74; pvt. practice Washington, 1974-79, L.A., 1978-93; contract lobbyist Rose & Kindel, L.A., Sacramento, Washington, 1993—. Cons. Commonwealth Pa., Harrisburg, 1973. Chmn. So. Calif. Hollings for Pres., 1984; pres. Bldg. and

Appeals Bd. City of L.A.; bd. dirs. Vols. of Am.; mem. exec. com. State Bar of Calif. pub. law sect. Mem. ABA UCLA Law Alumni Assn. (pres.). Jewish. Home: 277 S Irving Blvd Los Angeles CA 90004-3809 E-mail: bburke@rosekindel.com.

BURKE, ROBERT HARRY, surgeon, educator; b. Cambridge, Mass., Dec. 22, 1945; s. Harry Clearfield and Joan Rosalyn (Spire) B.; m. Margaret Cauldwell Fisher, May 4, 1968; children: Christopher David, Catherine Cauldwell. Student, U. Mich. Coll. Pharmacy, 1964—67; DDS, U. Mich., 1971, MS, 1976; MD, Mich. State U., 1980. Diplomate Am. Bd. Oral and Maxillofacial Surgery, Am. Bd. Cosmetic Surgery. Pvt. practice cosmetic and reconstructive surgery, Ann Arbor, Mich. House officer oral and maxillofacial surgery U. Mich. Sch. Dentistry, U. Mich. Hosp., Ann Arbor, 1973-76; clin. asst. prof. dept. oral surgery U. Detroit Sch. Dentistry, 1976-77; adj. asst. rsch. scientist Ctr. Human Growth and Devel. U. Mich., 1976-77, adj. rsch. investigator, 1982-85; clin. asst. prof. Mich. State U., East Lansing, 1978-80, 1987—; house officer surg. emphasis St. Joseph Mercy Hosp., Ann Arbor, 1980-81; adj. rsch. investigator dept. anatomy U. Mich. Med. Sch., 1982-85; adj. clin. asst. prof. oral and maxillofacial surgery U. Mich., 1984-86, 2002-2003, adj. clin. assoc. prof. maxillofacial surgery, 2003—; lectr. U. Detroit Sch. Dentistry, 1986, assoc. clin. prof. oral and maxillofacial surgery, 1987-90; cons., lectr. dept. occlusion U. Mich. Sch. Dentistry, 1986, asst. clin. prof. dept. maxillofacial sugery, 2002, assoc. adj. clin. prof., 2002—; head sect. dentistry and oral surgery dept. gen. surgery St. Joseph Mercy Hosp., 1982-87, mem. exec. com. dept. gen. surgery, 1984-87; chmn. com. emergency care rev. Beyer Meml. Hosp., Ypsilanti, Mich., 1986, also active, 1987, 1990-2000; active staff St. Joseph Meml. Hosp.; courtesy staff Saline (Mich.) Cmty. Hosp., 1978-88; Chelsea (Mich.) Med. Ctr., 1978-88, 90-92, McPherson Cmty. Hosp., Howell, Mich., 1984-87, Herrick Meml. Hosp., 1998—, Bixby Hosp., 1998—, Annapolis Hosp., 2000-2002, Oakwood Hosp., 2000-2002; dir. Mich. Ctr. Cosmetic Surgery. Mem. editl. bd. Topics in Pain Mgmt., 1985—; contbg. editor Am. Jours. Cosmetic surgery, 1990-91; sect. editor Internat. Jour. Aesthetic and Restorative Surgery, 1992-95, 96-2000, Internat. Jour. Cosmetic Surgery and Aesthetic Dermatology, 2000—. Campaign chmn. med. and dental sects. United Way Washtenaw County, Ann Arbor, 1982, dental sect. 1983; profl. adv. com. March of Dimes Genesee County Valley Chpt., Flint, 1979; pres. Huron Pkwy. Pla. Condominium, 1984—. Fellow: Am. Acad. Aesthetic and Restorative Surgery, Am. Coll. Oral and Maxillofacial Surgeons, ACS, Internat. Coll. Surgeons; mem.: Inst. Study Profl. Risk, Washtenaw County Med. Soc., European Assn. for Cranio-Maxillofacial Surgery, Chalmers Lyons Acad. oral Surgery, European Soc. Aesthetic Surgery and Liposuction, Internat. Soc. Cosmetic Laser Surgeons, Am. Assn. Craniomaxillofacial Surgeons, Am. Assn. Cosmetic Maxillofacial Surgeons, AMA, Pres.'s Club, Victor's Club, Omicron Kappa Upsilon. Congregationalist. Office: 2260 S Huron Pky Ann Arbor MI 48104-5151 E-mail: info@robertburke.com.

BURKE, ROBERT LAWRENCE, consultant; b. Elmira, N.Y., Dec. 30, 1928; s. Edmund and Gertrude Landin B.; m. Dorothy Ann Halvorsen, June 4, 1952; children: Randi Ann, Karen, Robert L. Jr., Elizabeth. BS, U.S. Mil. Acad., 1952; MA in Journalism, U. Ala., 1964. Commd. 2d lt. U.S. Army, 1952, advanced through grades to col., 1972, retired, 1977; mgr. Am. Newspaper Pubs. Assn., 1977-82, sr. v.p., 1982-91; cons. Orange, Va., 1991—. Lectr. in field. Contbr. articles to profl. jours. Pres. Civic Assn., Fairfax, Va., 1979-80; chmn. Orange County (Va.) Rep. Party, 1997-2002; chmn. 30th Legis. Dist. Rep. Com., Va., 2001—; mem. Piedmont Environ. Coun., Va., 1998—. Decorated Vietnam Cross of Gallantry with gold palm, Army Commendation medal, Joint Svc. Commendation medal, Legion of Merit with (2) oak leaf clusters, Def. Superior Svc. medal; recipient Disting. Grad. award Def. Lang. Inst., 1966, Outstanding Alumnus Journalism award U. Ala., 1980. Mem. Nat. Press Club, Nat. War Coll. Alumni Assn., U.S. Mil. Acad. Assn. Grads., U. Ala. Alumni Assn. Home: 13506 Conway Ln Orange VA 22960-2542

BURKE, ROBERT THOMAS, lawyer; b. Phila, Pa, May 8, 1943; BA, U. Santa Clara, 1965; MA, UCLA, 1966; JD, 1972. Bar: Calif. 1972. Ptnr. Pettit & Martin, San Francisco, 1972—; chief article editor UCLA Law Rev., 1971—72. Lt. USAR, 1967—69. Mem.: Bar Assn. San Francisco, State Bar Calif., ABA (mem. com. proprietary rights in software compute law divsn. 1982). Address: Pettit And Martin Ste 208 60 E Sir Francis Drake Blvd Larkspur CA 94939-1713

BURKE, RUTH, writer; b. LA, Jan. 16, 1933; d. Thomas Arthur and Bertha Morgan King; children: D. Julian Montelbano, Alan D., Carol Burke Ward, Michael L. (dec.), Laurel Perry, Abram D. AA, East L.A. Coll., 1957; AB, San Diego State U., 1967; postgrad., Western N.Mex. U., 1996—. Cert. tchr. Ariz. English instr. Reed Christian Coll., Compton, Calif., 1985; writing instr. Cochise Coll., Benson, Ariz., 1996. Reviewer Interrace Mag., Atlanta, 1993, Lambda Book Report, Washington, 1996—, Cath. Libr. World. Mem. editl. bd. True Romance, True Experience; columnist Ariz. Range News, Willcox, 1995-99; contbr. articles to profl. jours. including Arizona Highways. Libertarian. Avocations: study of the desert, black history, study of the great depression. Home: PO Box 128 San Simon AZ 85632-0128 E-mail: bowiedesertrat@yahoo.com.

BURKE, SEAN, professional hockey player; b. Windsor, Ontario, Canada, Jan. 29, 1967; With New Jersey Devils, 1987—91; with Hartford Whalers/Carolina Hurricanes, 1992—98, Phoenix Coyotes, 1999—. Played in 1989 NHL All Star Game. Achievements include Silver Medalist with Canadian Olympic Hockey team in 1992. Office: America West Arena/Cellular One Ice Den 9375 E Bell Rd Scottsdale AZ 85260

BURKE, SHEILA P. federal administrator; b. San Francisco, Jan. 10, 1951; d. George Abbott and Mary Joan (Winfield) B.; m. David Chew, Jan. 1983; children: Daniel, Kathleen, Sarah. BSN, U. San Francisco, 1973; MA in Pub. Adminstrn., Harvard U., 1982. Staff nurse Alta Bates Hosp., Berkeley, Calif., 1973-74; dir. student affairs Nat. Student Nurses Assn., N.Y., 1974-75, dir. program and field svcs., 1975-77; legis. asst. Senator Bob Dole, 1977-78; profl. staff mem. Senate Com. Fin., U.S. Senate, 1979-82, dep. staff dir., 1982-85; dep. chief of staff Senate Majority Leader Bob Dole, U.S. Senate, 1985-86; chief of staff Senator Bob Dole, 1986-96; sec. U.S. Senate, Washington, 1995; undersec. Am. Mus. and nat. programs Smithsonian Instn., Washington, 2000—. Adj. nursing faculty Georgetown U.; rsch. asst J.F. Kennedy Sch. Govt., Harvard U., 1980-81, advisor to dean, 1996, exec. dean, lectr. pub. policy, 1996-2000; adj. lectr. J.F. Kennedy Sch. Govt., Harvard U., 2000—. Republican. Address: 1323 Merrie Ridge Rd Mc Lean VA 22101-1826

BURKE, STEVEN CHARLES, healthcare administration executive; b. May 23, 1951; s. Charles Hulett and Carole Ruth (Mason) B.; m. Margaret Hudgins, Aug. 9, 1975; 1 child, David. BA, U. So. Sewanee, 1973; MHA, Duke U., 1975. Planning analyst Greenville Hosp., S.C., 1975-78, asst. dir. facility devel. and constrn., 1978-79, asst. v.p. planning, 1979-83; dir. planning and mktg. Youngstown Hosp. Assn., Ohio, 1983 84; v.p. planning and mktg. Western Res. Care Sys., Youngstown, 1984-86; v.p. mktg. Richland Meml. Hosp., Columbia, S.C., 1986-91; v.p. corp. svcs. Gaston Health Care, 1992-98; exec. dir. Preferred Care Network, Charlotte, N.C., 1998-99; sr. v.p. physician and bus. devel. Presbyn. Healthcare, Charlotte, 1999-2001, v.p. ancillary svcs., 2001—. Fellow Am. Coll. Healthcare Adminstrs., Arts and Sci. Coun. Episcopalian. Avocations: choral singing, woodworking, bicycling. Home: 201 Timberlane Dr Belmont NC 28012-7726 Office: Presbyn Healthcare 200 Hawthorne Ln Charlotte NC 28204-2515 E-mail: scburke@novanthealth.org.

BURKE, STEVEN FRANCIS, organization executive; b. St. Paul, May 23, 1952; s. Paul Stanley and Irene Marie (Wagner) B.; m. Kathleen Mary Frost, Mar. 23, 1974; children: Susan, Kathleen, Elizabeth, Michael, Thomas. BS, U. Minn., 1974; owner pres. mgmt. program, Harvard U., 1991. V.p. N.Am. Outdoor Group Inc., Minnetonka, Minn., 1978-84, exec. v.p., 1984-88, pres., 1988-90, pres., CEO, 1990—99; pres. N.Am. World Travel Inc., Minnetonka, Minn., 1989-91, also bd. dirs., 1989-91. Mgr. Bur Oak Properties LLC; bd. dirs. Larson and Burke Inc., Hopkins, Minn., Comml. Banl Chaska, Minn. Mem. pastoral coun. St. Hubert Cath. Ch., Chanhassen, Minn., 1984-85; pres. Wildlife Forever Inc., Hopkins, 1987—; bd. dirs. Holy Family Cath. H.S., Victoria, 1999—. Capt. USMC, 1974-78. Mem. NRA, N.Am. Hunting Club (pres. 1978—), N.Am. Fishing Club (pres. 1988—). Avocations: hunting, fishing, golf, scuba diving, flying. Office: Comml Bank Chaska 609 N Walnut St Chaska MN 55318-2075

BURKE, THOMAS JOHN, communications executive; b. Appleton, Wis., Jan. 23, 1947; s. John George and Rosella Sally (Vanderlois) B.; m. Barbara Jean Koth, June 13, 1970; children: Bradley John, Michael James. BSME, Purdue U., 1970; MBA, Fairleigh Dickinson U., 1979. Registered profl. engr., N.J. Salesman Am. Air Filter, Louisville, 1970-72; product mgr. Polycon, Ramsey, N.J., 1972-74; sales engr. Joy Mfg., N.Y.C., 1974-75, sr. sales engr. Chgo., 1975-88; publ. Node News, 1988; pres. Burke Ventures Ltd./Burke Communication Systems (now Burke Telecom), Oak Park, Ill., 1988—; publ. Node News, 1996; pres. Phone Svcs. Internat., Chgo., 1998—2000; CEO, chmn. bd. dirs. ProCom Network Svc. Inc., 2000—01. Jaycee trainer Life Dynamics, Chgo., 1983-86; lectr. Leadership Tng., Chgo., 1983-87; cons. Time Mgmt., Chgo., 1983-87; co-owner Minou Cafe & Bakery, Oak Park, Ill., 1986-92; chmn. bd. ProCom Network Services, 2000. Author: Dream Genesis, 1986, History of Imperial Hotel and Frank Lloyd Wright, 1987; co-pub. Chic Menu Guide. Pres. Oak Park Austin Coun. for Cmty. Rels., 1983 87; mem. edn. com., pub. spkr. Frank Lloyd Wright Home and Studio, 1986—; officer Oak Park Mall Mchts. Assn., 1988—92; cub master Boy Scouts Am., Oak Park, 1985—89; docent Chgo. Arch. Found., 2003—. Mem. Oak Park C. of C. (Athena judge Best Bus. Women of Yr. 1988—), Friends of Small Bus., Entrepreneurial Coun., Jaycees (v.p. 1983-86, Oak Park Jaycee of Yr. 1983), TLC Book Club (co-counder). Achievements include development of whole new generation of telecommunication services under the product name Magi Call, the first two-way prepaid phone card; one call voice mail with auto call back. Avocations: sailing, reading, bicycling, art. Home: 742 N Taylor Ave Oak Park IL 60302-1750 E-mail: tburke@burkecommsystems.com.

BURKE, THOMAS JOSEPH, JR., lawyer; b. Oct. 23, 1941; s. Thomas Joseph and Violet (Green) B.; m. Sharon Lynne Forke, Aug. 29, 1964; children: Lisa Lynne, Heather Ann. BA, Elmhurst Coll., 1963; JD, Chgo.-Kent Coll. Law, 1966. Bar: Ill. 1966, U.S. Dist. Ct. (no. dist.) Ill. 1967, U.S. Ct. Appeals (7th cir.) 1972, U.S. Supreme Ct. 1972, U.S. Ct. Appeals (11th cir.) 1994, U.S. Ct. Appeals (6th cir.) 1995. Assoc. Lord, Bissell & Brook, Chgo., 1966-74, ptnr., 1974—. Fellow: Am. Coll. Trial Lawyers; mem.: Assn. Advancement Automotive Medicine, Soc. Automotive Engrs., Product Liability Adv. Coun., Ill. Assn. Def. Trial Counsel, Def. Rsch. Inst., Soc. Trial Lawyers, Chgo. Bar Assn., Mid-Day Club, Phi Delta Phi, Pi Kappa Delta. Republican. Roman Catholic. Office: Lord Bissell & Brook 115 S La Salle St Ste 3300 Chicago IL 60603-3801 E-mail: tburke@lordbissell.com.

BURKE, THOMAS JOSEPH, civil engineer; b. Grosse Pointe Park, Mich., Sept. 1, 1927; s. Cyril Joseph and Marie Estelle (Sullivan) B.; BCE, Villanova U., 1949; m. Elaine Kiefer, Nov. 10, 1951; children: Judy Lee Burke Brooks, Kathleen Marie Harness, Maureen Elaine Beck, Thomas P. Chmn., Burke Rental Service, Sterling Heights, Mich., 1949—, Cyril J. Burke, Inc., Sterling Heights, Mich., 1949— . Trustee Villanova U., 1980— . Served to lt. USAF, Korea. Mem. ASCE, Detroit Builders Exchange (v.p. 1976-78, dir. 1975-78), Associated Equipment Distbrs. (dir. 1955-58, 75-78), Associated Underground Contractors (dir. 1965-68), Mich. Ready Mix Concrete Assn. (dir. 1960-65), Villanova U. Alumni Assn. (nat. v.p. 1978-79, nat. pres. 1980), Detroit Engring. Soc., Grosse Pointe Yacht Club, Otsego Ski Club, Ocean Reef Club, Detroit Athletic Club, Huron Shores Golf Club, Villanova U. of Detroit Club (pres. 1955-65). Roman Catholic. Home: 578 Shelden Rd Grosse Pointe Shores MI 48236-2640 also: 688 N Lakeshore Rd Port Sanilac MI 48469-9713 Office: PO Box 8010 36000 Mound Rd Sterling Heights MI 48311-8010

BURKE, THOMAS MICHAEL, lawyer; b. Summit, N.J., Feb. 10, 1956; s. Robert William and Eleanor Mary (Kelley) B.; m. Nancy Robin Mogab, Sept. 24, 1983; children: Colleen Margaret, Michael Thomas, Brendan Robert. BA, Notre Dame U., 1978; JD, St. Louis U., 1981. Bar: Mo. 1981, Ill. 1982, U.S. Dist. Ct. (ea. dist.) 1981. Assoc. Moser, Marsalek, Carpenter, Cleary & Jaeckel, St. Louis, 1981-86; ptnr. Noonan & Burke, St. Louis, 1986-92; prin. Thomas M. Burke, PC, St. Louis, 1992—. Bd. dirs. Legal Svcs. Ea. Mo., 1995-97. Active Vol. Lawyers program, St. Louis, St. Louis Hills Homeowner's Assn., 1984-94. Mem. Mo. Bar Assn. (bd. govs., 1998—, chair fin. com. 2002--), Ill. Bar Assn., Interest On Lawyers' Trust Accounts (bd. dirs. 1997-2002, pres. 2000-01), Bar Assn. Met. St. Louis (treas. 1992-93, sec. 1993-94, v.p. 1994-95, pres.-elect 1995-96, pres. 1996-97), St. Louis Bar Found. (sec. 1993-94, treas. 1995-96), Lawyers Assn. St. Louis (exec. com. 1987-92, sec. 1992-93, treas. 1992-93, v.p. 1993-94). Office: 701 Market St Ste 1075 Saint Louis MO 63101-1886 E-mail: tburke@burkelawfirm.com.

BURKE, THOMAS RAYMOND, lawyer; b. Lincoln, Nebr., Apr. 15, 1928; s. Raymond C. and Florine (Kost) B.; children from previous marriage: Thomas R., Timothy J. (dec. 1998), Melanie A., Pamela (dec. 1963), Laura M., Lisa M., Daniel C.; m. Barbara Schafer, Apr. 17, 1993; stepchildren: Robyn, Stephen, Holly, Jamie. JD, Creighton U., 1951. Bar: Nebr. 1951. Assoc. Kennedy, Holland, DeLacy & Svoboda, Omaha, 1956-62, ptnr., 1963—, sr. ptnr., 1970-98; of counsel Lamson Dugan & Murray LLP, 1998—. Lect. Coll. St. Mary, 1960-80. Past pres. adv. bd. Archbishop Bergan Mercy Hosp., past chmn. fin. com.; co-chmn. NCCJ, 1969-77, nat. trustee, 1972-78, bd. dirs., 1969-95, bd. govs., 1995—; mem. Archbishop's Com. for Ednl. Devel., 1975-98, chmn., 1975-78, 87-95; founding trustee, pres., gen. counsel Omaha Archdiocesan Ednl. Found.; co-chair Archbishop's $25 Million Campaign for Ednl. Excellence, 1991; adv. bd. Mercy HS; mem. pres.'s coun. U. Nebr., 1979-85, Coll. St. Mary, 1979-85; bd. dirs. Duchesne Acad., 1979-82, trustee, 1982-87, pres., trustee, 1985-87; bd. dirs. Christian Urban Edn. Svc., 1982-97, United Arts Omaha, 1983-98; trustee Nat. Jewish Hosp. (humanitarian award 1983), Denver, 1983; bd. dirs., exec. com., fin. com. United Way of Midlands, 1984-90, ann. campaign chmn., 1986; mem. st. Joseph High Devel. Bd., 1983-88; diocesan rep., trustee Nat. Cath. Ednl. Assn., 1984-87; chmn. bd. dirs. Bergan Mercy Found., 1992-98, bd. dirs. 1992—; founding chmn. bd. dirs. New Cassel Found., 2000-01, bd. dirs., 2001-; mem. com. Stephen Ctr. Devel., 2000-, hon. chair ann. campaign, 2002. Named Citizen of Yr., United Way of Midlands, 1992; named to Aksarben Ct. of Honor, 1998, Face on Barroom Floor Press Club, 2001; recipient Brotherhood award, 1991, Humanitarian award, 1991, Spirit of Francis award, New Cassel Fedn., 2002. Fellow Am. Bar Found.; mem. Omaha Bar Assn. (pres. 1971), Am. Coll. of Trust and Estate Counsel, Nebr. Bar Assn. (pres. 1978-79, exec. coun. 1966-72, 78-87, pres.'s adv. coun. 2000—), Omaha Bus. Men's Assn. (pres. 1962, Man of Yr. 1970), Rotary Found. (trustee), Omaha Rotary Club (pres. 1992-93), Nat. Lawyers Assn., Omaha Press Club. Office: 10306 Regency Parkway Dr Omaha NE 68114-3708 E-mail: Tburke@ldmlaw.com.

BURKE, THOMAS SEBASTIAN, JR., educator, writer; s. Colonel Thomas Burke Bishop and Anne Holderread; m. Michele Leonard, May 7, 2000; 1 child, Simone. MFA in Writing and Poetics, Naropa U., Boulder, Colo., 1996. Program dir. MRA creative writing Naropa U., Boulder, Colo., instr. summer writing program; instr. U. Denver, Tenn. State U., Nashville, 1997—98. Exec. com. AAUP, Colo. Author (composer): (feature film) American Reel, author: (musical drama) Soft Trumpet, Slow Guitar: The Ballad of Sonny Liston. Recipient Essay award, New Millenium Writing, 1997. Mem.: Broadcast Music, Inc., Writers Guild of Am. Office: Naropa U 2130 Arapahoe Boulder CO 80302 E-mail: jrburke@naropa.edu.

BURKE, THOMAS WILLIAM, executive benefits consulting company official; b. Harmon, Ill., Aug. 1, 1947; s. John William and Mary Eileen (Long) B.; m. Mary Ellen Bosau, Nov. 27, 1970; children: Kelly, Colleen, Shannon, Tommy, Michael. BS, St. Joseph's Coll., Collegeville, Ind., 1969. CLU; ChFC; CFP; lic. ins. counselor. Asst. mgr. Conn. Gen., Chgo., 1970-77; v.p. Fin. Industries, Austin, Tex., 1977; pres. T.W. Burke Assocs., Austin, 1978-87; dir. advanced underwriting SunLife, Dallas, 1988-92; pres. Hefner Assocs., Richardson, Tex., 1992—. Tchr. continuing edn. ABA, Tex. Soc. for CPA's and Atty. CPA's, U. Tex., 1986—. Coach Little League, 1991—; bd. advisor St. Joseph's Coll. Mem. Nat. Assn. Life Underwriters, Nat. Assn. Securities Dealers, Assn. Advanced Life Underwriters, Soc. CLU's, Dallas C. of C. (govt. affairs com. 1993-94), Million Dollar Round Table. Roman Catholic. Avocations: golf, coaching baseball. Office: Hefner & Assocs 600 W Campbell Rd Ste 7 Richardson TX 75080-3388

BURKE, TIMOTHY JOHN, lawyer; b. Syracuse, N.Y., June 5, 1946; s. Francis Joseph and Alice Marie Burke; m. Denise Kay Blied, Mar. 18, 1978; 1 child, Aimee Noel; 1 child from a previous marriage, Ryan Alexander. BA with distinction, Ariz. State U., 1967, JD cum laude, 1970. Bar: Ariz. 1970, U.S. Dist. Ct. Ariz. 1970, U.S. Ct. Appeals (9th cir.) 1974. Trial atty. Antitrust divsn. U.S. Dept. Justice, Washington, 1970-72, asst. to dir. ops., 1972-74; assoc. Fennemore Craig, Phoenix, 1974—, dir., 1978—. Part-time instr. legal writing Ariz. State U., 1974-75, adj. faculty assoc. profl. responsibility Coll. of Law, 2001-03. Mem. panel rev. bd. Phoenix United Way, 1975-76; bd. dirs. Florence Crittenton Svcs., Phoenix, 1980-88, pres., 1985-87; bd. dirs. Law Soc. Ariz. State U. Coll. Law, 1991-97, 99—, pres., 2000—; bd. dirs. Valley of Sun Cmtys. in Schs., 1995-2001. Recipient spl. commendation U.s. Dept. Justice, 1973. Fellow Am. Bar Found., Ariz. Bar Found.; mem. ABA (antitrust and litigation sects., vice chmn. bus. torts and unfair competition com. 1996-98, chair 1998-2001, vice chmn. state enforcement com., 2001-, editor Bus. Torts and Unfair Competition Newsletter 1996-98), FBA, Assn. Profl. Responsibility Lawyers (bd. dirs. 1993-98, pres. 1996-97), State Bar Ariz. (coun. antitrust sect., chmn. 1985-88, chmn. advt. com. 1992-94, ethics com. 1994-2001, chmn. 1995-2001, mem. task force on future of profession 2000, mem. case conflicts com. 2001—), Maricopa County Bar Assn. Office: Fennemore Craig 3003 N Central Ave Ste 2600 Phoenix AZ 85012-2913

BURKE, TIMOTHY MICHAEL, lawyer, educator; b. Cleve., Feb. 10, 1948; s. Ralph and Frances (Dilley) B.; m. Patricia Kathleen LaGrange, June 6, 1970; children: Nora Frances, Tara Kathleen, Michael Ralph. AB, Xavier U., Cin., 1970; JD, U. Cin., 1973. Bar: Ohio 1973, U.S. Dist. Ct. (so. dist.) Ohio 1979, U.S. Ct. Appeals (6th cir.) 1978, U.S. Supreme Ct. 1979. Legis. asst. to coun. mem. Cin. City Coun., 1971-74; spl. asst. to Congressman Tom Luken Cin., 1974, 76-77; exec. dir. Little Miami, Inc., Cin., 1975-76; prin. Manley Burke and predecessor firm, Cin., 1977—; spl. counsel to atty. gen. State of Ohio, 1978-95; law dir. Village of Lockland, Ohio, 1982—2003, Village of Evendale, Ohio, 2003—. Lectr. Xavier U., 1975-78, 81, 82-83, adj. asst. prof., 1983-85; adj. assoc. prof. U. Cin., 1977-78, 79, dir. law enforcement tech. program, 1977-78. Bd. dirs. Tri State Air Com., 1972-80, chmn., 1976-78; chmn. land use subcom. water quality adv. com. Ohio-Ky.-Ind. Regional Coun. Govts., 1975-76; bd. dirs. Lower Coun. Little Miami, Inc., 1976-82; mem. alumni bd. govs. Xavier U., 1970-76, 78-79, v.p., 1980-81, pres., 1981-82; candidate for U.S. Ho. of Reps. from 1st dist. Ohio, 1978; chmn. legal com. Cin. Zoo, bd. dirs., 1980-91; co-chmn. Zoo Tax Levy Campaign, 1982, 86; commr. Cin. Park Bd., 1991-94; participant Fgn. Policy Conf. for Young Am. Polit. Leaders, U.S. Dept. State, 1980; chmn. Hamilton County Bd. Elections, 1993—; exec. co-chmn. Hamilton County Dem. Party, 1982-86, 88-89, chmn., 1993-99, co-chmn., 1999-; co-chmn. Cin. Dem. Com., 1983-89, chmn., 1989-97; 1st v.p. Ohio Dem. County Chairs Assn., 1995-99; internat. supr. Bosnia Mcpl. Elections, 1997, Elections Tng. Slovakia, 2002; team leader Law Enforcement and Justice Team, Cinti, Can. Served to 1st lt. U.S. Army, 1974. Recipient svc. award Ohio River Valley Com. for Occupational Safety and Health, 1983, Leadership award Xavier U., 1984; named Ohio Dem. of Yr. Ohio Dem. Party, 1995. Mem. ABA, Am. Planning Assn. (legal sect.). Roman Catholic. Home: 3560 Mcguffey Ave Cincinnati OH 45226-1919

BURKE, WILLIAM ROMNEY, urologist; b. Safford, Ariz., May 31, 1943; s. Ernest William and Hannah (Romney) B.; m. Mary Susan Wilkinson, June 11, 1969; children: Caroline, Kimberly, Suzanne, Brendan, Juliana, Kevin, Christopher, Kathleen, Brynn, David. AB, Stanford U., 1964; MD, Yale U., 1970. Diplomate Am. Bd. Urology. Surg. intern U. UT Med. Ctr., Salt Lake City, 1970-71, resident in surgery, 1971-72; resident in urology Yale-New Haven (Conn.) Hosp., 1972-76; instr. surgery Yale Med. Sch., New Haven, 1975-76; urologist Denver Clinic, 1976-78, Clackamas Urol. Clinic, Oreg. City, Oreg., 1978-95, The Urology Clinic, Portland, 1995-99; pvt. practice Oreg. City, Oreg., 1999—. Asst. clin. prof. urology U. Colo. Med. Ctr., Denver, 1978; chmn. dept. of surgery Willamette Falls Hosp., Oregon City, 1987-89; bd. dirs. Williamette Falls Hosp., Oregon City, Oreg. Contbr. articles to profl. jours. Mem. City of West Linn (Oreg.) Planning Commn., 1985-86; chmn. long range com. West Linn Sch. Dist., 1984, 89, mem. budget com. 1987-93. Mem.: Am. Urol. Assn. (We. sect.), N.W. Urol. Soc., Oreg. Urol. Soc., Oreg. Med. Assoc. (del. 1986—2002, trustee 2002—), Clackamas County Med. Soc. (pres. 1989, bd. dirs. 1992—). Democrat. Mem. Ch. LDS. Office: 1510 Division St Ste 1 Oregon City OR 97045-1527 E-mail: wrburkefamily@hotmail.com.

BURKE, WILLIAM TEMPLE, JR., lawyer; b. San Antonio, Oct. 30, 1935; s. William Temple and Adelaide H. (Raba) B.; m. Mary Sue Johnson, June 8, 1957; children: William Patrick, Michael Edmond, Karen Elizabeth. BBA, St. Mary's U., San Antonio, JD, 1961. Bar: Tex. 1961. Practice law, Dallas; founder, pres. Burke Wright & Keiffer, PC, 1985-98; of counsel Hance/Scarborough/Wright, Dallas, 1998-2000, Hance, Scarborough, Wright Ginsberg and Brusilow, Dallas, 2000—. Co-founder, v.p., dir. Tex. Cath. Cmty. Credit Union, 1966-69, vice-chmn. bd. dirs., 1990-91; v.p. Dallas County Hist. Survey Com., 1966; pres. Dallas Mil. Govt. Assn., 1962-63; pres. men's club St. Patrick's Parish Roman Cath. Ch., 1963, prin. jr. H.S. Christian devel. program, 1970, chmn. scout troop com., 1976-78, chmn. fin. com., 1984-87, bldg. com., 1978-87, chmn. bd. consultors, 1978-81; bd. dirs. Dallas County War on Poverty, 1965-66; trustee Montserrat Jesuit Retreat House, 1995-2000, treas., 1996-97; bd. dirs. Montserrat Found., 1999-2000; vice-chmn. Cath. Commn. Appeal Diocese of Dallas, 1993-97. 1st lt. U.S. Army, 1958-60; capt. USAR ret. Fellow Tex. Bar Found. (life), Coll. of State Bar Tex., Dallas Bar Found. (sr. life); mem. ABA, Tex. Bar Assn., Dallas Bar Assn. (co-founder, chmn. bankruptcy and comml. law sect. 1976-77, 86-87, courthouse liaison com. 1985—, lectr. 1985—, chmn. spkrs. com. 2001—02), Am. Bankruptcy Inst., John C. Ford Am. Inn Ct. (co-founder, pres. 2000—, Serjeant of the Inn (Hon.), 2003), Dallas Safari Club, Serra Internat. Met. Club (pres. Met. Dallas 1997-98, dist. gov.-elect 2003—. Outstanding Mem. award 1995), Internat. Order Alhambra (exemplar 1978-95), KC (co-founder Greater Dallas chpt., council 799 grand knight, trustee 1964-69, dist. examplar 4th degree 1968-69, Man of Yr. award 1970), Optimists (v.p., bd. dirs. Dallas 1965-66, Man of Yr. award 1966, Pres.'s award 1968), Phi Delta Phi (life), Tau Delta Sigma (pres., 1957). Home: 9751 Larchcrest Dr Dallas TX 75238-2112 Office: 1401 Elm St Ste 4750 Dallas TX 75202 E-mail: wburke@hswgb.com.

BURKE, WILLIAM THOMAS, law educator, lawyer; b. Brazil, Ind., Aug. 17, 1926; JD, U. Ind., 1953; JSD, Yale U., 1959. Bar: Ind. 1953. Rsch. assoc. and lectr. Yale U., 1956-62; assoc. prof. Ohio State U., 1962-64, prof., 1964-68, U. Wash. Sch. Law, Seattle, 1968-99, emeritus, 1999. Mem. adv. com. Law of Sea Task Force, Dept. State; mem. A217 Ocean Policy Com., Nat. Acad. Scis. Author: (with M. S. McDougal) The Public Order of the Oceans, 1962, Contemporary Legal Problems in Ocean Development, 1969, (with Legatski and Woodhead) National and International Law Enforcement in the Ocean, 1975, The New International Law of Fisheries, 1994, International Law of the Sea-Documents and Notes, 1997, 99. Office: U Wash Sch Law Gates Hall Seattle WA 98105 E-mail: sealaw1@comcast.net., burke@u.washington.edu.

BURKEE, IRVIN, artist; b. Kenosha, Wis., Feb. 6, 1918; s. Omar Lars and Emily (Quardokas) B.; m. Bonnie May Ness, Apr. 12, 1945; children: Brynn, Jill, Peter (dec.), Ian (dec.). Diploma, Sch. Art Inst. Chgo., 1943, postgrad., 1944-45. Owner, silversmith, goldsmith Burkee Jewelry, Blackhawk, Colo., 1950-57; painter, sculptor, Aspen, Colo., 1957-78, Cottonwood, Ariz., 1978—, Pietrasanta, Italy, 1978—. Instr. art U. Colo., 1946, 50-53, Stephens Coll., Columbia, Mo., 1947-49. Researched and created copper, silver, and bronze mural of Human History of Colorado, Colorado Historical Museum, Denver, 2002, copper, bronze and silver mural of Rocky Mountain wild birds for Aspen Ctr. Environ. Studies, Aspen, 2000; exhibited in group shows Art Inst. Chgo., Smithsonian Instn. (award 1957), Milw. Art Inst., Krannert Mus., William Rockhill Nelson Gallery, St. Louis Art Mus., Denver Art Mus., Frederik Meijer Sculpture Gardens, Grand Rapids, Mich.; represented in southwestern galleries, also pvt. collections throughout U.S.; work illustrated in books Design and Creation of Jewelry, Design through Discovery, Walls. John Quincy Adams Travel fellow Sch. Art Inst. Chgo., 1945; Rocky Mountain Coll. Sculpture grantee, 1972. Mem. Nat. Sculpture Soc., Sedona Chamber Music Soc. (painter yearly festival poster 1989—). Address: PO Box 5361 Lake Montezuma AZ 86342-5361 E-mail: ibburkee@hotmail.com.

BURKE-FANNING, MADELEINE, artist; b. New Orleans, Feb. 12, 1941; d. Henry Raymond Burke Sr. and Ella Mae Falgout-Burke; children: Denise Angele Duizend-Hargis, Michele Renee Duizend-Meyer, Jeanne Monet Duizend-Fillman; m. Joel Cornell Fanning, Mar. 28, 1981. Student, Pensacola (Fla.) Jr. Coll., 1988-96. Coord. New Orleans World Trade Ctr., Pensacola Cultural Ctr.; adj. prof. advanced watercolor Pensacola Jr. Coll.; tchr. nat. and internat. workshops; instr. advanced watercolor City of Pensacola, Vickrey Ctr., Fla. One-woman shows include Michele Dion Gallery, 1994, Soho Gallery, 1994, Wise Choice Gallery, 1996, The Wright Place, 1997, Awakenings, Gulf Breeze, Fla., 1997—98, The Shoppe Gallery, 1998, Pensacola Mus. Art, 1998—2003, Adams Street Gallery, 1998, Ducks Unltd., Pensacola, 1998, Right Angles Gallery, 1999, Kate Holmes-Branton Gallery, 1999—2002, The Art Market, Gulf Breeze, Fla., 2000, Art and Design Soc., Ft. Walton Beach, Fla., 2000, White Cloud Gallery and Gifts, Pensacola, 2000, Sam Houston Racetrack, Houston, 2001, Corner Copia, Orange Beach, Ala., 2000—03, N.W. Fla. Laser and Skincare Inst., Laurie Grizzard Gallery, 2001—, The MANE Event Expressions Gallery, Pensacola, 2001—, Laurie Grizzard Gallery, 2001—03, Kotlarz Gallery, Pensacola, 2002—, Stockamp Gallery, 2002—03, Woodcock Interiors and Gallery, Pensacola, Fla., 2003—, exhibited in group shows at Pensacola Jr. Coll., 1988—96, Gnu Zoo, 1995—96, Eastern Shore Mus. Art, Fairhope, Ala., 1994—96, Pensacola Regional Airport, 1996, World Trade Ctr., 1996, Schmidt's Gallery, 1996, Pensacola Cultural Ctr., 1997, Adams Street Gallery, 1998, Artel Gallery, 1999—2002, Vickney Ctr., 1999—2003, Visual Art Ctr. of N.W. Fla., Panama City, 2001, The Avenue, St. Paul's Roman Cath. Ch., Pensacola, Fla., 2001—03, Woodcock Interior and Gallery, 2003; host (TV show) Art and Healing, 1997, (TV feature) Inside Scope, New Orleans, 1993, (TV show) Art Vision, 1994, Culture Center BLAB TV, 1996; host : (TV show) Everything Old is New Again, Pensacola Heritage Assn., 2002; TV appearance N.W. Fla. Arts Coun. Art Auction, Sanger Theatre, Pensacola, 2001; exhibitions include Sanger Theatre, 2003, exhibited in group shows at Woodcock Gallery, Pensacola, Fla., 2003. Art judge Just Say No Program, 1996—97, PTA Reflective Program, 1997—98; art chairwoman Pensacola chpt. Ducks Unltd., 1998; instr. Ctr. Ind. Living, Pensacola, 1998—2000, Vickrey Ctr., Pensacola, 2000—03, Pensacola Jr. Coll., 2000—03. Recipient Rockport Pubs. award of distinction for inclusion in Best of Watercolor: Painting Texture, 1997, Collected Best of Watercolor, 2002. Mem.: Artel.Art with an Edge, Bay Cliff Watercolor Soc. (founder), Woodbine Figure Painters, Pensacola Mus. Art, N.W. Fla. Arts Coun., Tallahassee Watercolor Soc., La. Watercolor Soc., Fla. Watercolor Soc., Nat. Mus. Women in Arts, Am. Soc. Portrait Artists. Avocations: gardening, reading, traveling, sailing, photography. Home: Palm Cottage Studio 4160 Rommitch Ln Pensacola FL 32504-4490

BURKEN, RUTH MARIE, utility company executive; b. Kenosha, Wis., Sept. 25, 1956; d. Richard Stanley and Anne Theresa (Steplyk) Wojtak; m. James H. Burken, Oct. 15, 1988. AAS, Gateway Tech. Inst., 1976; BA, U. Wis., Parkside, 1980; AAS, Coll. of DuPage, 1995. Transp. aide Kenosha Achievement Ctr., 1977; libr. clk. U. Wis.-Parkside, Kenosha, 1978-80, lifeguard, 1980; asst. mgr. K Mart Corp., Troy, Mich., 1980-88, regional office supr., 1988, internal auditor, 1989-92, sr. field auditor, 1992-98; gen. auditor Nicor Gas, Naperville, Ill., 1998-2000, billing splist., 2000—. Mem. VFW, NAFE, Distributive Edn. Clubs Am. (parliamentarian 1976), U. Wis.-Parkside Alumni Assn., Am. Gas Assn. Roman Catholic. Office: Nicor Gas 1844 W Ferry Rd Naperville IL 60563-9600 E-mail: rburken@nicor.com.

BURKERT, ROBERT RANDALL, artist; b. Racine, Wis., Aug. 20, 1930; s. Clarence George and Margaret Ann (Sorenson) B.; m. Nancy Ekholm, Aug. 29, 1953; children: Claire, Rand. BS, U. Wis., 1952, MS, 1955. Instr. art Denison U., 1955-56; prof. drawing, printmaking, painting U. Wis., Milw., 1956-92, prof. emeritus, 1993—. One-man shows include Bradley Galleries, Milw. (8 shows), 1972-86, Rubiner Galleries, Detroit (6 shows), 1973-85, Posner Galler, Milw., 1990, 93, Retrospective, U. of Wis., Milw., 1994, Myhelan Cultural Ctr., Long Valley, Pa., 2001, others; group shows include Pratt Graphic Ctr., 1972, U.S. Cultural Ctr., Tel Aviv, 1973, Milw. Art Mus., 1975, 30 Yr. Retrospective, Wustum Mus., Racine, Wis., 1985; represented in permanent collections Tate Gallery, London, Boston Mus. Fine Arts, Met. Mus. Art, Phila. Mus., numerous others; wall mural Road to Country, 1972, wall mural Butterflies, 1986; work reproduced in Artist Proof, 1971, Compleat Printmaker, 1973, Art of the Print, 1976, 100 Years of American Printmaking, 1983, 150 Years of Wis. Printmaking, 1998; directed and produces "Colors of Change" documentary video, 1994. Former trustee Milw. Art Mus. Recipient numerous awards for prints, drawings and paintings; U. Wis. research grantee, 1969, 71, 73, 75, 77; Knapp grantee for ednl. research, 1973, Wis. Arts grantee, 1977; Fromkin grantee, 1980; recipient Gov.'s Print Commn., 1985. Home: PO Box 858 East Orleans MA 02643-0858

BURKERT, WALTER, Greek language educator, historian; b. Neuendettelsau, Germany, Feb. 2, 1931; arrived in Switzerland, 1969; s. Adolf and Luise (Grossmann) B.; m. Maria Bosch, Aug. 1, 1957; children: Reinhard, Andrea, Cornelius. PhD, U. Erlangen, Fed. Republic Germany, 1955; LLD, U. Toronto, 1988; PhD (hon.), U. Fribourg, Switzerland, 1989, Oxford (Eng.) U., 1996, U. Chgo., 2001. Dozent U. Erlangen, 1961-65; jr. fellow Ctr. Hellenic Studies, Washington, 1965-66; prof. Tech. U. Berlin, 1966-69, U. Zürich, Switzerland, 1969-96. Sather prof. U. Calif., Berkeley, 1977. Author: Lore and Science in Ancient Pythagoreanism, 1972, Homo Necans, 1983, Greek Religion, 1985, Greek Mystery Cults, 1987, The Orientalizing Revolution, 1992, Creation of the Sacred, 1996; contbr. numerous articles to scholarly pubs. Decorated Orden Pour le Mérite; recipient C.F. Gauss medal Braunschweigische Wissenschaftliche Gesellschaft, 1982, Balzan prize, 1990, Ingersoll prize, 1992. Mem. Heidelberger Akademie der Wissenschaften, Bayerische Akademie der Wissenschaften, Oesterreichische Akademie der Wissenschaften, Berlin-Brandenburgische Akademie der Wissenschaften, Brit. Acad., Am. Philos. Soc., Am. Acad. Arts and Scis. Home: Wildsbergstrasse 8 CH-8610 Uster Switzerland Office: Klassisch-Philologisches Seminar Rämistrasse 68 CH-8001 Zurich Switzerland E-mail: walter_burkert@bluewin.ch.

BURKES, LIONEL SEATON, science educator, writer, researcher; b. Hindsville, Ark., Mar. 25, 1933; s. Elmo C. and Bernie Ethel (Cook) B.; m. Pansy Lenora Hobbs Burkes, Dec. 24, 1961; children: Geoffrey Dion (dec.), Eric Kevin, Cynthia Michele, Aaron Shane, Mark Alan. BSE, U. Ark., 1960; MA in Biol. Sci., U. Mont., 1964. Cert. adminstrn. and sci., Ark., Iowa; sci. N. Mex. Instr. sci. and sociology Corona (N. Mex.) Municipal Schs., 1960-62; instr. sci. Albuquerque (N. Mex.) Pub. Schs., 1964-66; instr. biology and zoology U. Wis., Whitewater, 1966-69; asst. prof. edn. Mo. We. State Coll., St. Joseph, 1970-71; asst. campus dir. Southeastern Cmty. Coll., West Burlington, Iowa, 1971-75; dir. Inst. Mgmt. and Continuing Edn. Iowa Wesleyan Coll., Mt. Pleasant, 1977-78, 83-84; instr. scis. Fort Smith (Ark.) Pub. Schs., 1985-94; retired, 1995; researcher, writer, 1995—. Spl. rschr. Sandia Nat. Labs., Albuquerque, summers 1985-87. Contbr. articles to profl. jours. Leader U.S. delegation People to People Youth Sci. Exchange, Russia, Ukraine, 1990, China, Hong Kong, 1991, New Zealand, Australia, 1992; judge sci. fair pub. schs. N. Mex. and Ark., 1984-95; spkr. Career Days Westark C. C., Fort Smith, Ark., 1991-93. Nat. Sci. Found. Fellow U. Mont., 1961-64; recipient Nat. Security Clearance U.S. Dept. Energy, 1986, Outstanding Tchr. Proclamation Mayor of Fort Smith, Ark., 1995. Avocations: writing, reading, research, traveling abroad, hiking.

BURKES-RAWLINS, SARAH, nutritional elementary school educator, counselor; d. Henry and Eldora (Abshaw) Burkes. BA, Jackson State U. and Tex. Coll.; MA, East Tex. State U., 1982. Tchr. Chgo. Bd. Edn.; with Blue Cross-Blue Shield, Chgo., 1972—75; comm. counselor Malcolm X Coll., Chgo., 1977—80; instr. reading and English Accounters Cmty. Ctr., Chgo., 1977—80; agt. Equitable Life Ins., Chgo., 1980—82; rep. World Book-Childcraft Ency., 1981—, HerbaLife, 1986—. Mem.: MLA, United Ednl. Employees Assn., Nat. Life Underwriters Assn., Chgo. Reading Assn., Nat. Coun. Tchrs. English, Internat. Reading Assn., Alpha Kappa Alpha. Home and Office: 15759 Clifton Park Ave Markham IL 60426-3918 Address: PO Box 12051 Chicago IL 60612-0051

BURKET, GEORGE EDWARD, JR., retired family physician; b. Kingman, Kans., Dec. 10, 1912; s. George Edward and Jessie May (Talbert) Burket; m. Mary Elizabeth Wallace, Nov. 12, 1938; children: George Edward III, Carol Sue, Elizabeth Christine. Student, Wichita State U., 1930—33; MD, U. Kans., 1937. Diplomate Am. Bd. Family Practice (pres. 1975-1977). Intern Santa Barbara (Calif.) Gen. Hosp., 1937—38, resident, 1938—39; grad. asst. in surgery Mass. Gen. Hosp., Boston, 1955—56; practice medicine Kingman, 1939—73; preceptor in medicine U. Kans. Med. Sch., 1950—73, assoc. prof., 1973—78, clin. prof., 1978—84. Bd. dirs. Kingman Savings and Loan Assn. Contbr. articles to profl. jours. Mem. Kingman Bd. Edn., 1946—58, Kans. State Bd. Health, 1960—66. Mem.: AMA, Soc. Tchrs. Family Medicine, Assn. Am. Med. Colls., Am. Acad. Family Physicians (pres. 1967—68, John Walsh Founders award 1979), Kans. Med. Soc. (pres. 1966—67), Inst. Medicine NAS (sr.), Wichita Country Club, Garden of Gods Club (Colorado Springs, Colo.), Shriners, Masons, Alpha Omega Alpha. Republican. Episcopalian. Home: Larksfield Pl V-208 7373 E 29th St N Wichita KS 67226-3405

BURKET, JOHN MCVEY, retired dermatologist; b. Des Moines, Iowa, Oct. 4, 1935; s. George Austin and Elma (McVey) B.; m. Janice Lee Feilmeyer, Dec. 29, 1956; children: Denise, Bradley, Brent, Diana, Dawn, Brian. BA, U. Iowa, 1957, MD, 1960. Diplomate Am. Bd. Dermatology, Am. Bd. Dermopathology. Resident in dermatology U. Iowa Hosp., Iowa City, 1964; chief dermatology USAF, March AFB, 1964-66; pvt. practice dermatology Medford, Oreg., 1966—. Contbr. articles to profl. jours., chpts. to books. Avocations: hunting, fishing.

BURKETT, BRADFORD CHARLES, lawyer; b. Phila., Aug. 29, 1960; s. Frederick R. and Barbara E. Burkett; m. Marcia P. Borggaard, Aug. 17, 1985; children: Gillian, Brady, Kate. BA, Rutgers U., New Brunswick, N.J., 1982; JD, Rutgers U., Camden, N.J., 1985. Bar: N.Y. 1985, N.J. 1985. Assoc. Kaye Scholer Fierman Hays & Handler, N.Y.C., 1985-94; sr. v.p., gen. counsel The Multicare Cos., Inc., Hackensack, N.J., 1994-97; sr. v.p., gen. counsel, bus. devel. Telesis Med. Mgmt., Inc., White Plains, NY, 1997-2000; CEO Physician Weblink, Inc., Englewood Cliffs, NJ, 2000—02; CEO, bd. dirs. deNovis, Inc., Lexington, Mass., 2002—. Mem. bd. dir. CareMatrix, Inc., Newton, Mass., Vitality Beverage, Inc., Tampa, Fla. Mem. ABA, Nat. Health Lawyers Assn., Assn. Bar City N.Y. Office: deNovis Inc One Cranberry Hill Rd Lexington MA E-mail: b.burkett@att.net.

BURKETT, JOHN PHILIP, economics educator; b. 1950; BA, Cornell U., 1971; PhD in Econs., U. Calif., Berkeley, 1981. Staff economist Lawrence Berkeley Lab. U. Calif., 1978; rsch. asst. SSRC programme U. London, 1979, rsch. officer SSRC programme, 1980-81; asst. prof. dept. econs. U. R.I., 1981-86, assoc. prof. dept. econs. 1986-92, prof. dept. econs. 1992— Adj. assoc. prof. dept. econs. Brown U., 1986; vis. scholar Russian Rsch. Ctr. Harvard U., 1988-89; vis. assoc. prof. dept. econs. U. Calif., Berkeley, 1990-91; rsch. assoc. Inst. Internat. Studies, U. Calif., Berkeley, 1992-93; rsch. contract, Nat. Coun. for Soviet and E. European Rsch., 1988-89; mem. selection com. for spl. projects with Eurasia, Internat. Rsch. and Exchs. Bd., 1993-94; rep. U. R.I. to Inter-Univ. Consortium for Polit. and Social Rsch., 1984-85, 86-87; exec. dir. Inst. for the Study of Internat. Aspects of Competition, 1995—. Mem. editorial bd. Economics of Planning, 1990—; Author: The Effects of Economic Reform in Yugoslavia: Investment and Foreign Trade Policy, 1959-76, 1983; contbr. articles, book revs. to profl. jours. Summer Faculty fellow, U. R.I., 1985, grant-in-aid U. R.I., 1982, 85, Am. Coun. of Learned Societies fellow, 1985-86, Nat. Coun. for Soviet and East European Rsch. grant, 1985-86, Mellon fellow in Soviet and East European Econs., Brookings Instn., 1985-86, Nat. Acad. Scis. grant for rsch. in Yugoslavia, 1987, Internat. Rsch. and Exch. Bd. fellow for rsch. in Yugoslavia, 1987-88; Rsch. scholar Kennan Inst. for Advanced Russian Studies, 1988-89. Mem. Am. Economic Assn., Am. Statistical Assn., Decision Analysis Soc., Econometric Soc., Internat. Health Econs. Assn., Internat. Soc. for Bayesian Analysis, Phi Beta Kappa. Office: Univ R I Dept Econs 10 Chaffee Rd Ste 3 Kingston RI 02881-2017 E-mail: burkett@uri.edu.

BURKETT, LLOYD A. secondary education educator and administrator, automotive engineer; b. N.Y.C. s. Lloyd A. and Edith Burkett. BS, CCNY; MA, Brooklyn Coll., 1992; PhD, Walden U., Mpls., 1998. Cert. high sch. tech. tchr., N.Y. Design engr. Gibbs and Cox, Inc., N.Y.C.; technical, investigator City of N.Y.; tchr. tech. Bronx (N.Y.) H.S. Sci., 1996—2003, Freeport H.S., 2003—. Mem. Tennessee River Band, Chickamauga Cherokee Indians. Mem. AIAA, Soc. Automotive Engrs. Office: Freeport HS 50 S Brookside Ave115 Freeport NY 11520

BURKETT, ROSEMARY L. artist; b. Milw., June 12, 1935; d. Edward Charles Earl and Mary Catherine (Gresh) Lange; m. Lawrence Earl Burkett, Feb. 11, 1956; children: Russell Lawrence, Roy Edward, Randell Earl. Student, Milw. Sch. Design and Tech., 1953-55. Comml. artist Am. Lace Paper Co., Milw., 1953-55; drafter Ken Cook Pub. Co., Milw., 1955-56; layout artist Wis. Graphic Lithographers, Milw., 1956; freelance portrait artist St. Petersburg, Fla., 1973—. Exhibited in numerous art shows in Fla., Tenn., Pa., Ill. and Wis., 1970-93; painted over 400 animal portraits, 1973-93. Former sec. Pinellas Park (Fla.) Art Soc. Avocations: pets, animal welfare organizations.

BURKETT, TRENTON SHANE, music educator; b. Pensacola, Fla., Aug. 5, 1969; s. Carrie B. and Mary Lois Burkett. MS in Edn., Troy State U., 1996, MusB Edn., 1993; AA, Pensacola Jr. Coll., 1989. Assoc. dir. bands Marianna Mid. Sch., Marianna, Fla., 1993—95, chmn. music dept., 1995—96; assoc. dir. bands Daleville H.S., Daleville, Ala., 1996—98, dir. bands, 1999—. Bd. dirs. SE U.S. Concert Band Clinic and Honor Bands, Troy, 2002—; cons. h.s. block-scheduling Auburn U., Auburn, Ala., 1995. Conductor (symphonic band performance) Exhibition, Alabama Music Educator's Association Conference (Citation of Excellence, 2002), Exhibition, Southeastern United States Concert Band Clinic (Cert. of Appreciation, 2002). Recipient Enrollment Award, Fla. Music Educator's Assn., 1996, Tchr. of the Yr., Marianna Mid. Sch., 1993, Oustanding Young Man of Am., Outstanding Young Am., 1996, Cert. of Appreciation, Ala. Army Nat. Guard, 1146th, 1998. Mem.: NEA, Ala. Edn. Assn., Internat. Assn. of Jazz Educators, Music Educator's Nat. Conf., Nat. Band Assn. (Citation of Excellence 2002), Modern Music Masters Honor Soc. (hon.; sponsor), Ala. Bandmaster's Assn. (assoc.; vice chmn. dist. VIII 1999—2001, bd. dirs., chmn. dist. VIII 2002—, Citaiton of Excellence 2002), Ala. Music Educator's Assn. (assoc.), Kappa Delta Pi (assoc.), Delta Chi (life; lettered officer 1991—93). Home: 35 Magnolia Dr Daleville AL 36322 Office: Daleville High School Band 626 N Daleville Ave Daleville AL 36322 Home Fax: 334-598-3850; Office Fax: 334-598-3850. Personal E-mail: trentonburkett@msn.com. E-mail: burkett@daleville.k12.al.us.

BURKEY, LEE MELVILLE, lawyer; b. Beach, N.D., Mar. 21, 1914; s. Levi Melville and Mina Lou (Horner) B.; m. Lorraine Lillian Burghardt, June 11, 1938; 1 child, Lee Melville, III BA, U. Ill., 1936, MA, 1938; JD with honor, John Marshall Law Sch., 1943. Bar: Ill., 1944, U.S. Dist. Ct., 1947, U.S. Ct. Appeals, 1954, U.S. Supreme Ct.; 1983; cert. secondary tchr., Ill. Tchr. Princeton Twp. High Sch., Princeton, Ill., 1937-38, Thornton Twp. High Sch., Harvey, Ill., 1938-43; atty. Office of Solicitor, U.S. Dept. Labor, Chgo., 1944-51; ptnr. Asher, Gubbins & Segall and successor firms, Chgo., 1951-94; of counsel, 1995—. Lectr. bus. law Roosvelt Coll., Chgo., 1949—52. Contbr. numerous articles on lie detector evidence. Trustee, Village of La Grange, Ill., 1962-68, mayor, 1968-73, village atty., 1973-87; commr., pres. Northeastern Ill. Planning Commn., Chgo., 1969-73; mem. bd. dirs. United Ch. Christ, Bd. of Homeland Ministries, 1981-87; mem. exec. com. Cook County Coun. Govts., 1968-70; life mem. La Grange Area Hist. Soc.; bd. dirs. Better Bus. Bur. Met. Chgo., Inc., 1975-82, Plymouth Place, Inc., 1973-82; mem. exec. bd., v.p. S.W. Suburban Ctr. on Aging, 1993—. Brevet 2nd Lt. Ill. Nat. Guard, 1932. Recipient Disting. Alumnus award John Marshall Law Sch., 1973, Meritorious Svc. award Am. Legion Post 1941, 1974, Honor award LaGrange Area Hist. Soc., 1987, Cmty. Svc. award S.W. Suburban Ctr. on Aging, 2000. Fellow: Coll. Labor and Employment Lawyers. (charter); mem.: SAR (state pres. 1977, Good citizenshp medal 1973, Patriot medal 1977), ABA (coun. sect. labor and employment law 1982—86, governance officer 1986—96), Chgo. Bar Assn., Ill. Bar Assn. (sr. counsellor 1994), United Empire Loyalists Assn. Can., La Grange Country Club, Masons, Theta Delta Chi, Order John Marshall. Mem. First Congl. Ch.

BURKHALTER, SUSAN SHIVELY, music educator, organist; b. Washington, Apr. 16, 1946; d. William Mays and Thelma Louise (Kanatzer) B.; m. Curtis Allen Shively, Feb. 5, 1977; children: Rachel Mirabel, Stuart William. MusB, Coll. Wooster, 1970. Organist, choir dir. Olivet Episcopal Ch., Springfield, Va., 1976-77; children's choir dir. Our Savior Lutheran Ch. and Sch., Arlington, Va., 1997-1998; pvt. piano tchr., freelance organist, 1976-2001; organist, choir dir. Grace Reformed United Ch. of Christ, Washington, 2001; interim organist Kirkwood Presbyn. Ch., Springfield, 2001—02. Advisor music majs. Coll. Wooster, Ohio, 1995—. Contbr. mags. and newspapers including Washington Post, American Organist, Psychology Today, and more; performer in various concerts. Vol. Carderock Springs Elem. Sch., Bethesda, Md., 1988-95, Pyle Middle Sch., 1994-2000, Walt Whitman High Sch., 1997—; mem. Sierra Club, ASPCA, World Wildlife Fund, African Wildlife Fund; mem. Gen. Fedn. Women's Clubs, Suburban Women's Club of Montgomery County, Md., 1999—. Mem. Music Tchrs. Nat. Assn., Am. Guild Organists, Carderock Springs Swim and Tennis Club. Democrat. Avocations: cats, sewing, gardening, art, writing poetry. Home: 7504 Hamilton Spring Rd Bethesda MD 20817-4542 E-mail: scastlekep@aol.com.

BURKHARDT, DOLORES ANN, library consultant; b. July 28, 1932; d. Frederick Christian and Emily (Detels) Burkhardt. BA, U. Conn., 1955; MS, So. Conn. State Coll., 1960; postgrad., Cen. Wash. State Coll., 1962, Columbia, 1964—; 6th yr. diploma, U. Conn., 1972. Asst. librarian So. Conn. State Coll. Libr., summers 1960,62; sch. libr. tchr. Farmington High Sch., Unionville, Conn., 1955-65; libr. cons., media specialist East Farms Sch., Farmington, Conn., 1967-70; sch. libr. coord. K-12 Durham-Middlefield, Conn., 1970-72; media specialist Regional Dist. 10, Burlington-Harwinton, Conn., 1972-78, ednl. media cons., 1978—. Instr. Boston U. Media Inst. Spl. cons. Conn. Dept. Edn., 1965— . Mem. AAUW (sec. 1956-58), NEA, Conn. Edn. Assn., New Eng. (pres. 1969-70), Conn. (2d v.p. 1965—, chmn. sch. libr. devel., chmn. standards com. 1970-72, chmn. instructional materials selection policy com. Region 10), Sch. Libr. Assns., Am. Assn. Sch. Librarians, New Eng. Sch. Devel. Coun., Phi Delta Kappa. Lutheran. Home and Office: 812 Savage St Southington CT 06489-4629 E-mail: daburkhardt@msn.com.

BURKHARDT, DONALD MALCOLM, retired lawyer; b. N.Y.C., Jan. 21, 1936; s. Seymour and Ruby Victoria (Brownrigg) B.; m. Gail Lee Burkhardt; children: Susan Lynn McIlhenny, Steven Lee. BA, Dartmouth Coll., 1957; LLB, U. Mich., 1961. Bar: Colo. 1961, U.S. Dist. Ct. Colo. 1961, U.S. Ct. Appeals (10th cir.) 1962, U.S. Supreme Ct. 1988. Assoc. Grant, Shafroth, Toll & McHendrie, Denver, 1961-66; ptnr. Grant McHendrie, P.C., Denver, 1967-93; spl. counsel Inman Flynn & Biesterfeld, P.C., Denver, 1993-2001. Scoutmaster Boy Scouts Am., Denver, 1962-64; pres. Rangers Club, Young Am. League, Denver, 1972-76; ski patroller Nat. Ski Patrol System, Winter Park, Colo., 1967—. Republican. Presbyterian. Avocations: sports, outdoors. Home: 2833 E 8th Ave Denver CO 80206-3827 *Notable cases include: Burak vs. Gen. Am. Life Ins. Co. 836 F. 2d 1287, 10th cir., 1988; 1st Nat. Bank in Alamosa vs. Ford Motor Credit Co., 748 F Supp. 1464 Colo., 1990.*

BURKHARDT, EDWARD ARNOLD, railway executive; b. N.Y.C., July 23, 1938; s. Edward Arnold Burkhardt Sr. and Kathryn C. (Pfister) Dow; m. Sandra Kay Schwaegel, June 9, 1967; 1 child, Cythia Kay. BS Indsl. Adminstrn., Yale U., 1960. Various operating positions Wabash R.R., St. Louis, 1960-64, Norfolk and Western Rlwy., St. Louis, 1964-67; asst. to gen. mgr. Chgo. Northwestern Transp. Co., 1967-68, gen. supt. transp., 1968-70, asst. v.p. transp., 1970-76, v.p. mktg., 1976-79, v.p. transp., 1979-87; bd. dirs., pres., CEO Wis. Ctrl. Transp. Corp., Chgo., 1987-99; chmn. Tranz Rail Ltd., 1993-99; bd. dirs., pres. Algoma Ctrl. Rlwy. Inc., 1995-99; bd. dirs., chmn., CEO English, Welsh and Scottish Ry. Ltd., 1995-99; bd. dirs., chmn. Australian Transport Network, 1997-99; pres./CEO Rail World, Inc., 1999—; pres. RailPolska, 1999—. Pres. CargoCentral Europe, 2000—; chmn. Baltic Rail Svc., 2000—. Trustee Village of Kenilworth, Ill., 1984—93; bd. dirs. John W. Barringer R.R. Libr., St. Louis, Wheeling & Lake Erie Rlwy. Co., Nat. Railway Mus., York, England, England, Lake Superior Mus. Transp., Duluth, Minn., Nat. Railroad Mus., Green Bay, Wis. Recipient Hon. consul New Zealand, Chgo. Mem.: Am. Assn. R.R. Supts. (bd. dirs.), Union League Club, Kenilworth Club, Western Ry. Club. Republican. Episcopalian. Office: Rail World Inc Ste 500N 8600 W Bryn Mawr Ave Chicago IL 60631-3579 E-mail: eaburkhardt@railworld-inc.com.

BURKHARDT, FREDERICK HENRY, editor; b. Bklyn., Sept. 13, 1912; BA, Columbia U., 1933; LittB, Oxford U., 1935; PhD, Columbia U., 1940, LLD (hon.), 1974, Mich. U., 1968, Ball State U., 1976. Instr., asst. prof. philosophy U. Wis., Madison, 1937-43, assoc. prof. philosophy, 1946-47; pres. Bennington (Vt.) Coll., 1947-57, Am. Coun. Learned Socs., N.Y.C., 1957-74; gen. editor The Works of William James, 19 vols. Harvard Press, 1975-88; founder, editor The Correspondence of Charles Darwin, 13 vols. sponsored by ACLS and Cambridge U. Libr., 1985—. Rsch. analyst Office of Strategic Svcs., 1943-45; acting chief Divsn. Rsch. for Europe, Dept. State, 1945-46; dep. dir. Office Pub. Affairs, U.S. High Commr. for Germany, 1950-51; mem. N.Y.C. Bd. Higher Edn., 1966-73, chmn., 1969-71; trustee N.Y. Pub. Libr., 1970-71, chmn., 1974; chmn. Nat. Commn. on Librs. and Info. Sci., 1971-78. Editor, translator: J.G. Herder: God, Some Conversations On Spinoza's System, 1940, 62; editor: Cleavage in Our Culture, 1952; contbr. The Comparative Reception of Darwinism, 1975. Lt. USNR, 1944-46. Recipient Alumni award for excellence Columbia U., 1987, Morton N. Cohen award for disting. edition of letters MLA, 1991; Queen's Univ. prize Cambridge U., 2002. Mem. Am. Philos. Soc. (Thomas Jefferson Gold medal, 2003), Am. Acad. Arts and Scis., Century Assn. Home and Office: PO Box 1067 Bennington VT 05201-1067 E-mail: fhb@sover.net.

BURKHARDT, RONALD ROBERT, advertising executive; b. Jackson, Mich., July 25, 1948; s. Robert Edward and Lois Jeane (Ordway) B. AA, Jackson C.C., 1968; BBA in Advt., Western Mich. U., 1970. Copywriter, producer Campbell-Ewald Co., Detroit, 1973-75; sr. writer Cargill-Wilson & Acree/DDB, Atlanta, 1976-78; sr. v.p., creative dir. Flemister & Burkhardt, Atlanta, 1978-80; sr. writer Bozell & Jacobs, N.Y.C., 1980-81; creative supr. Young & Rubicam, N.Y.C., 1981-84; v.p., creative group head Lowe-Marschalk, N.Y.C., 1984-86; chmn., CEO, exec. creative dir., ptnr. and founder Burkhardt & Christy Advt. Inc., N.Y.C., 1986-95; CEO, creative dir., ptnr. and founder Burkhardt & Ptnrs. Ltd., N.Y.C., 1996—; co-founder, CEO, creative dir. Pillow Vision, Inc., 2001—. Pro bono cons. mayor's office, N.Y.C., Save Am. Forests, Washington; judge Clios, Internat. TV and Film Festival N.Y., CEBA Awards, Andy Awards, Stephen Kelly Awards, Addy Awards, Mercury Radio Awards, N.Y. Festivals. Contbr. articles to profl. jours. including Adweek, AdAge; exec. prodr.: (short film) Red, 2001, The Mark, 2003; one-man shows include The Soho, 2001, Forbes Gallery, N.Y.C., 2002, Star Gallery, 2003, Trump Towers Art Release Galleries, NYC, 2003. Exec. com. N.Y. Korean Vets. Meml. Commn.; pro-bono Riverkeeper. Recipient over 200 awards including Andy award Advt. Club, 1978-93, Clio award, 1983, 85, 87-88, 90-93, award Art Dirs. Club, 1983, 85, 87-89, 94, N.Y. Internat. Festivals, 1989-95, Gold Addy award, 1983, 89, 91, Creativity award 1988-94, 96-99, Graphics Ann. award, 1992, Mobius Gold, 1991, 95-96, Black Book award, 1993, Telly Gold statues, 1990-95, 97-99. Mem. One Club for Art and Copy (award 1976, 78, 80, 82, 84, 86, 89, 93, Comm. Arts Advt. Ann. award 1995, Effie Silver award 1997, Effie Gold award 1998, Cannes Internat. Film Festival (France) (del.). Republican. Avocations: skiing, tennis, motorcycling, baseball, Karate. Office: Burkhardt & Ptnrs Ltd 225 E 48th St New York NY 10017 *Intensity of purpose fuels energy, and makes life a relentless series of powerful achievements.*

BURKHART, CRAIG GARRETT, dermatologist; b. Toledo, Ohio, Apr. 15, 1951; s. Garrett Giles B. and Mary Katherine (Egarius) B.; m. Anna Kristiina Jutila, Apr. 12, 1975; children: Kristiina Maria, Craig Nathaniel, Heidi Rebecca. BA, U. Pa., 1972; MD, Med. Coll. Ohio, 1975; MSc in Pub. Health, U. Toledo, 1983. Diplomate Am. Bd. Dermatology. Intern, resident, fellow U. Mich. Hosps., 1976-79; dermatologist in pvt. practice, 1979—; pres. Gar-Nat Lab., Inc., 1997—. Clin. prof. medicine Med. Coll. Ohio; clin asst. prof. dermatology Ohio U. Coll. Osteo. Medicine. Editor Jour. Dermatology and Allergy, 1980—; mem. editl. bd. Jour. Current Adolescent Medicine, 1980—; mem. editl. adv. bd. Ohio State Med. Jour., 1982—, Cortlandt Forum, 1999—; contbr. chpts. to books, articles to profl. jours.; patentee in field. Mem. Toledo Zoo, Toledo Mus. Art. F.M. Douglass Found. rsch. grantee, 1998, 2000, 01. Mem. AMA, Acad. Dermatology, Ohio State Med. Assn., Mich. Dermatologic Assn., Toledo Acad. Medicine, Med. Coll. Ohio Alumni Assn., Phi Beta Kappa (pres. N.W. Ohio 1984-86). Home: 4556 Crossfields Rd Toledo OH 43623-2628 Office: 5600 Monroe St Ste 106B Sylvania OH 43560-2728 E-mail: cgbakb@aol.com.

BURKHART, HAROLD EUGENE, forestry educator; b. Wellington, Kans., Feb. 29, 1944; s. Walter F. and Zelma (Lutz) B.; m. Katherine West, June 12, 1971; 1 child, Anna Katherine. BS, Okla. State U., 1965; MS, U. Ga., 1967, PhD, 1969. Asst. prof. Va. Poly. Inst. and State U., Blacksburg, 1969-73, assoc. prof., 1973-78, prof., 1978-81, Thomas M. Brooks prof., 1981-99, univ. disting.

prof., 1999—. Author: Forest Measurements, 1983, 94, 2002; contbr. sci. articles to profl. jours. Sr. Rsch. fellow NRC, 1976-77; recipient Sci. Achievement award Internat. Union Forestry Rsch. Orgns., 1981, J. Shelton Horsley Rsch. award Va. Acad. Sci., 1983, Outstanding Faculty award State Coun. for Higher Edn. in Va., 1988, Disting. Agr. Alumnus award Okla. State U., 1993. Fellow AAAS, Soc. Am. Foresters (Barrington Moore Meml. award 1991); mem. Biometric Soc., Am. Forestry Assn., Sigma Xi, Phi Kappa Phi, Xi Sigma Pi. Presbyterian. Avocations: gardening, running. Office: Va Poly Inst and State U Dept Forestry Blacksburg VA 24061 E-mail: burkhart@vt.edu.

BURKHART, JENNIFER ELLEN, business psychologist; b. Marietta, Ohio; BA, Ohio State U., 1978, MA, 1980, PhD, 1987. Psychology intern Ohio State U., Columbus, 1979-81, Profl. Counseling Svc., Columbus, 1981-82, Franklin County Bd., Columbus, 1982; staff psychologist Western Psychiat. Inst. & Clinic, Pitts., 1983-87; pres. J.E. Burkhart, P.C., Pitts., 1988—. Author: (chpt.) Advances in Development Disorders, 1987; co-author: (chpt.) Advances in Mental Retardation and Developmental Disabilities, 1983, Current Issues and Practices in Special Education, 1987, Advances in Developmental Disorders, 1987, Treating Childhood and Adolescent Psychopathology: A Handbook, 1988; contbr. articles to profl. jours. Mem. Greater Washington Bd. Trade, Cystic Fibrosis Met. Washington D.C. chpt. Golf Com., Leadership Washington Affiliate program; affiliate mem. Leadership Fairfax; mem. Suburban Md. Tech. Coun.; mem. Dingman Ctr. for Entrepreneurship, U. Md., Women of Washington; mem. corp. sponsorship and Gala coms. Washington Performing Arts Soc. Mem. APA. Home and Office: 2538A Fairfax Dr Arlington VA 22201-2863 E-mail: JEB3806@aol.com.

BURKHART, JOHN ERNEST, minister, religion educator; b. Riverside, Calif., Oct. 25, 1927; s. Joseph Ernest and Lockie Louisa (Dryden) B.; m. Virginia Bell French, Sept. 16, 1951; children: David Aaron, Audrey Elizabeth, Deborah Ann. BA, Occidental Coll., 1949; BD, Union Theol. Sem., 1952; PhD, U. So. Calif., 1959; DD, Occidental Coll., 1964. Ordained to ministry United Presbyn. Ch., 1952. Pastor Presbyn. U. U. So. Calif., L.A., 1953-59, from instr. to prof. of Theology, 1959-1990; prof. Systematic Theology McCormick Theol. Sem., Chgo., 1990-93, prof. emeritus, 1993—. Vis. prof. Garrett Theol. Sem. Evanston, Ill., 1966, DePaul U., Chgo., 1970. Author: Kingdom, Church, and Baptism, 1959, Understanding the Word of God, 1964, Worship, 1982; contbr. articles to profl. jours. 1st lt., chaplain USAF, 1952-53. Fellow Royal Anthrop. Inst., Soc. for Values in Higher Edn.; mem. Am. Acad. Religion, Cath. Theol. Soc. of Am., N.Am. Acad. Liturgy, Am. Theol. Soc. (pres. 1969-70), Midwest Alumni Club (v.p. 1985-90), Quadrangle Club, Blue Key, Rotary, Phi Beta Kappa. Democrat. Presbyterian. Home: 569 Woodland Ridge Dubuque IA 52003 E-mail: burkhart@mchsi.com.

BURKHART, JOHN HENRY, retired physician; b. Knoxville, Tenn., May 14, 1920; s. Fred McKinley and Stella Bogle (Henry) B.; m. Marjorie Nell Blaylock, Nov. 20, 1943; children: John McLain, Patrick Henry, William Lindsey. BA, U. Tenn., Knoxville, 1941; MD, U. Tenn., Memphis, 1945. Diplomate Am. Bd. Family Practice. Intern Knoxville Gen. Hosp., 1945-46, resident internal medicine, 1948-49; pvt. practice, Knoxville, 1949-94; chief staff St. Mary's Hosp., Knoxville, 1965; retired, 1994. Mem. Knoxville Bd. edn., 1958-59, chmn., 1959-65; ruling elder Presbyn. Ch. Capt. M.C., USAAF, 1946-48. Recipient Outstanding Alumnus award U. Tenn. Coll. Medicine, 1990, Gen. Practitioner of Yr. award Tenn. Acad. Gen. Practice, 1964. Mem. AMA (Disting. Svc. award 1991), Tenn. Med. Assn. (pres. 1965, Disting. Svc. award 1975, Outstanding Physician of Yr. award 1984), Knoxville Acad. Medicine (pres. 1964), Kiwanis (pres. Knoxville 1959), Omicron Delta Kappa, Alpha Omega Alpha, Kappa Sigma, Phi Chi. Home: 1905 Emoriland Blvd Knoxville TN 37917-3115

BURKHART, KEITH KARL, emergency medicine physician, medical toxicologist; b. Reading, Pa., May 5, 1956; BS Biology, Ursinus Coll., 1978; MD, Med. Coll. Pa., 1982. Diplomate Am. Bd. Emergency Medicine, Am. Bd. Med. Toxicology. Resident in emergency medicine U. Cin. Hosps., 1982-85; fellow in toxicology Rocky Mountain Poison Drug Ctr., Denver, 1988-90; asst. prof. medicine Pa. State U. Hershey Med. Ctr., 1990-95, assoc. prof. medicine and pharmacology, 1995-2000, prof. medicine, emergency medicine and pharmacology, 2000—. Mem. Am. Coll. Emergency Physicians, Am. Acad. Clin. Toxicology, Am. Coll. Med. Toxicology, European Assn. Poisons Ctrs. and Clin. Toxicologists, Am. Assn. Poison Control Ctrs. Office: Dept of Emergency Medicine Milton S Hershey Med Ctr PO Box 850 Hershey PA 17033-0850 E-mail: kburkhart@psu.edu.

BURKHART, SANDRA MARIE, art dealer; b. Cleve., Dec. 29, 1942; d. John Joseph Norris and Audrey Eleanor Kegg McGuire Marshall; m. Thomas Henry Burkhart, Oct. 29, 1960 (div. Sept. 26, 1979); children: Bryan, Brad, Lisa, Michelle. Student, Evergreen Valley Coll., San Jose, 1978-80, San Jose City Coll., 1978-80, West Valley Coll., Saratoga, Calif., 1978-79. Med. technician Eye Med. Clinic, San Jose, 1980-83; ind. corp. art salesperson San Jose, 1983-92; corp. sales dir. Phoenix Gallery, San Jose, 1986-88; v.p. mktg. Whittlers Mother, San Francisco, 1989-90; dir. Martin Lawrence Galleries, Santa Clara, Calif., 1990-97. Avocations: watercolors, crafts, tennis, skiing, horses. Home and Office: 1353 Greenwich Ct San Jose CA 95125-5964

BURKHART, STEPHANIE GLORIA, protective services official, writer; d. Paul Rosaire Cardin and Stephanie Arlene Chase; m. Brent Donald Burkhart, Nov. 14, 1991; 1 child, Andrew Michael. AA in Liberal Arts, U. of Md., 1991; BS in Polit. Sci., Calif. Bapt. U., 1995. 911 dispatcher LA Police Dept., 2000—. Author: (novel) Destination: Berlin, All That Remains, Are Your Dirty Little Secrets. Staff sgt. U.S. Army, 1986—97. Decorated Army Svc. Ribbon U.S. Army, Overseas Svc. Ribbon, Good Conduct medal, German Marksmanship, Gold German Army, Nat. Def. Svc. medal U.S. Army, NCO Profl. Devel., Army Commendation medal, Army Commedation medal, Army Achievement medal, Nato medal, Army Superior Unit award, Armed Forces Svcs. medal. Roman Catholic. Avocation: reading. Home: 30519 Cannes Pl Castaic CA 91384 Personal E-mail: botrina@pacbell.net.

BURKHOLDER, DONALD LYMAN, mathematician, educator; b. Octavia, Nebr., Jan. 19, 1927; s. Elmer and Susie (Rothrock) B.; m. Jean Annette Fox, June 17, 1950; children: Kathleen, Peter, William. BA, Earlham Coll., 1950; MS, U. Wis., 1953; PhD, U. N.C., 1955. Asst. prof. math. U. Ill., Urbana, 1955-60, assoc. prof., 1960-64, prof., 1964-98, prof. Ctr. for Advanced Study, 1978-98, prof. emeritus, 1998—. Sabbatical leaves U. Calif., Berkeley, 1961-62, Westfield Coll., U. London, 1969-70; vis. prof. Rutgers U., 1972-73; researcher Stanford U., 1961, Hebrew U., 1969, Mittag-Leffler Inst., Sweden, 1971, 82, U. Paris, 1975, Institut des Hautes Études Scientifiques, 1986, U. Edinburgh, 1986, Tel Aviv U., 1989, U. New South Wales, 1991; Mordell lectr. Cambridge U., 1986; Zygmund lectr. U. Chgo., 1988; trustee Math. Scis. Rsch. Inst., 1981-84; bd. govs. Inst. Math. and Its Applications, 1983-85, chmn., 1985. Editor: Annals Math. Statistics, 1964-67. Fellow Inst. Math. Statistics (Wald lectr. 1971, pres. 1975-76); mem. NAS, Am. Math. Soc. (mem. editorial bd. Trans. 1983-85), London Math. Soc., Am. Acad. Arts and Scis. Achievements include research in probability theory and its applications to other branches of analysis. Home: 506 W Oregon St Urbana IL 61801-4044

BURKHOLDER, JO ELLEN, anthropologist, educator; b. Huntington Beach, Calif., Oct. 10, 1968; d. Warren Stanford Burkholder, Jr. and Janice Ellen Lateana; m. Peter E. Killoran, May 24, 1997; 1 child, Ian Stanford Killoran. BA, Wellesley Coll., Wellesley, Massachusetts, 1986—90; MA, U. Calif., Santa Barbara, 1993; PhD, SUNY, Binghamton, 1997. Adj. prof. Indiana U. of Pa., 1998—99; asst. prof. No. Ky. U., Highland Heights, 1999—. Project dir. Pub. Archaeology Facility, Binghamton, 1997, Ecoscience, Moscow, 1996; ceramic analyst Iwawi Archaeological Project, Bolivia, 1993—; bd. dirs. Ky. Humanities Coun., Lexington. Author: Andeau Past, 2002; contbr. articles to profl. jours. Mem. Christ Ch. Cathedral, Cincinnati, Ohio, 1999—2003, Ky. Humanities Coun., Lexington, Ky., 2000—03. Recipient Nat. Wall of Tolerance award, So. Poverty Law Ctr., 2001; fellow, Binghamton U., 1993; grantee, Indiana U. of Pa., 1999. Fellow: Inst. for Andean Studies; mem.: NOW, Bolivian Studies Assn., Assn. for Feminist Anthropology, Soc. for Latin Am. Anthropoogy, Ky. Orgn. for Profl. Archaeology, Soc. for Am. Archaeology (Women in Archaeology interest group), Am. Anthrop. Assn. Democrat. Episcopalian. Achievements include research in Tiwanaku culture of South America; underground railroad. Avocations: yoga, reading, travel, cooking. Office: No Ky U Nunn Dr Highland Heights KY 41099 E-mail: burkholderj@nku.edu.

BURKHOLDER, JOYCE LYNN, clinical social worker; b. Phila., Oct. 28, 1951; d. J. Edward and Mae Elizabeth (Wood) B.; m. Dirk Denier Vandergon, May 31, 1983; children: Austin Edward, Alexandra Mae. BSW, Temple U., 1975; MSW, Calif. State U., Sacramento, 1985. Lic. clin. social worker, Nev. Caseworker Silver Springs Martin Luther Sch., Plymouth Meeting, Pa., 1974-76; counselor Turning Point Youth Svc., Ambler, Pa., 1976-77; dir., counselor Aquarian Effort Alternative House, Sacramento, Calif., 1978-81; dir. social svcs., case mgr. Truckee Meadows Hosp., Reno, 1983-84; clin. social worker U. Calif. Davis Med. Ctr., Sacramento, 1985-86; cons. Greater Nev. Home Health Care, Revo, 1988-90; sec., bd. dirs. Pathways, Reno, 1990—; pvt. practice, 1993-99. Instr. U. Nev., Reno, 1991. Bd. dirs. Aux. to Washoe County Med. Soc., Reno, 1989-90; founder/co-chair Washoe County Domestic Violence Fatality Rev. Team, 1994-2002; chair food and beverage "Race for the Cure" Susan B. Komen Found., No. Nev. affiliate, 1999-2002. Mem. Nat. Assn. Social Workers. Avocations: skiing, walking, piano, scuba diving. Home: 4288 Bitterroot Rd Reno NV 89509-0617

BURKHOLDER, MARK ALAN, historian, educator; b. Chgo., Sept. 3, 1943; s. M.M. Burkholder and Agnes V. Neuenschwander; children: Kristen, Jennifer; m. Carol D. Burkholder. BA, Muskingum Coll., 1965; MA, U. Oreg., 1967; PhD, Duke U., 1970. Asst. prof. history U. Mo., St. Louis, 1970-76, 1976-81, prof. history, 1981—, asst. dean arts and scis., 1977-80, assoc. dean arts and scis., 1980-83, chair dept. history, 1995-2001, dean arts and scis., 2001—; acad. assoc. to v.p. acad. affairs U. Mo. Sys., Columbia, 1983-84, assoc. v.p. acad. affairs, 1989-91. Author: Biographical Dictionary of Councilors of the Indies, 1717-1808, 1986, Politics of a Colonial Career, 1982; co-author: Biographical Dictionary of Audiencia Ministers in the Americas, 1687-1821, 1982, From Impotence to Authority: The Spanish Crown and the American Audiencias, 1687-1808, 1977, Colonial Latin America, 1990, 4th edit., 2001 (Edwin Lieuwin award for promotion of excellence in tchg. of Latin Am. History 1994). Bd. dirs. Citizens for Modern Transit, St. Louis, 1997—. Home: 400 S 14th St Apt 1016 Saint Louis MO 63103 Office: U Mo 8001 Natural Bridge Rd Saint Louis MO 63121-4401 Fax: (314) 516-5700. E-mail: burkholder@umsl.edu.

BURKHOLDER, OWEN EUGENE, religious organization administrator; b. Bluesky, Alta., Can., Oct. 28, 1949; s. Paul and Doris Burkholder; m. Ruth Ann Augsburger; children: Minnette, Marla, Michelle. Grad., Ont. Mennonite Bible Inst., Kitchener, 1967; BA, U. Alta., Edmonton, 1970; MDiv, Eastern Mennonite Sem., Harrisonburg, Va., 1975. Assoc. pastor Bluesky Mennonite Ch., summer 1972; congl. coord., pastor Cmty. Mennonite Ch., Harrisonburg, Va., 1972-80; Campus Life Club dir. Shenandoah Valley Youth for Christ, Harrisonburg, 1973-80; pastor Park View Mennonite Ch., Harrisonburg, 1981-95; moderator Va. Mennonite Conf., Harrisonburg, 1982-84, conf. min., 1996—; rep. Va. Mennonite Conf. Mennonite Ch. Gen. Bd., Elkhart, Ind., 1985-93, moderator, 1995-97. Chair bd. Crossing Creeks, 1998-2001. Mem. Harrisonburg-Rockingham Assn. Chs. & Congregations (pres. 1994-95). Mennonite. Office: Va Mennonite Conf 901 Parkwood Dr Harrisonburg VA 22802-2418

BURKHOLDER, PETER MILLER, physician, educator; b. Cambridge, Mass., May 7, 1933; s. Paul Rufus and Lillian Maud (Miller) B.; m. Barbara Beers, June 3, 1956; children: Kristen Ryner, Lisanne Ryner. BS, Yale U., 1955; MD, Cornell U., N.Y.C., 1959; degree in naturopathy (hon.), S.W. Coll. Naturopathic Medicine, 2001. Intern pathology N.Y. Hosp.-Cornell Med. Ctr., 1959-60; NIH trainee in pathology Cornell U., 1960-63, instr., 1963-64, asst. prof., 1964-65, Duke U., 1965-69, asso. prof., 1969-70, U. Wis.-Madison, 1970-72, acting chmn. dept. pathology, 1971-72, prof., 1972-79, chmn. dept. pathology, 1972-74; dir. Kidney Disease Inst., N.Y. State Dept. Health, 1979-80; dep. dir. div. labs. and research N.Y. State Dept. Health, 1980-81, dir. Ctr. Lab. Scis., 1981-82; chief of staff VA Med. Ctr., Ann Arbor, Mich., 1982-84, staff pathologist, 1984-89; prof. pathology U. Mich., Ann Arbor, 1982-89; chmn. dept. pathology Maricopa Med. Ctr., Phoenix, 1989-95, asst. med. dir., 1995; clin. prof. dept. pathology U. Ariz., Tucson, 1989—. Prof. pathology Southwest Coll. Naturopathic Medicine, 1996-2000, chief acad. officer, 2000. Author: Atlas of Human Glomerular Pathology, 1974; contbg. author: Structural Basis of Renal Diseases, 1968, Pathobiology Annual, 1971, Tissue Typing and Transplantation, 1973, Glomerulonephritis Morphology Natural History and Treatment, 1973, Cornell Seminars in Nephrology, 1975; mem. editorial bd. Kidney Internat, 1970-76, Lab. Investigation, 1972-83, Exptl. Pathology, 1984-86, Clin. Nephrology, 1989-92; contbr. numerous articles to profl. jours. NIH grantee, 1961-78 Mem. AMA, Am. Soc. Exptl. Pathology, Am. Assn. Pathology, Am. Soc. Immunology, Am. Soc. Nephrology, Internat. Acad. Pathology, Internat. Soc. Nephrology, Coll. Am. Pathology, Am. Soc. Clin. Pathologist, Am. Coll. Physician Execs., Renal Path. Soc., Pluto Soc. Home: 7248 N Red Ledge Dr Paradise Valley AZ 85253-2849

BURKHOLDER, ROGER GLENN, artist, author; b. Omaha, Feb. 5, 1944; s. Christian Kenneth and Beverley Pierce (Manning) B. BA, Harvard U., 1967. Owner Mosaic, Denver, 1977, Formers' Understandings, Omaha, 1997—. Exhibitions include Mass. Mental Health Ctr., Boston, 1968, Maple Crest Care Ctr., Omaha, 1999, Dale Clark Libr., 2002, Lauritzen Gardens, 2003; author: How Did That Sun Get Out, 2000. Mem. Lawyers' Com. Nuclear Policy, N.Y.C., 1997—, Peace Action, Washington, 1997—, War Resisters League, 2002—, U.S. Pacifist Party, 2002. Mem.: War Resisters League. Mem. Internat. Soc. for Krishna Consciousness. Avocation: guitar. Home: 5624 Burdette St Omaha NE 68104-4902 Office: Formers' Understandings PO Box 4406 Omaha NE 68104-0406 E-mail: formersund@hotmail.com.

BURKHOLDER, STEVE, mayor; Owner A&S Group; sr. cons. CI Internat.; mayor City of Lakewood, Colo., 1999—. Office: City Hall 480 S Allison Pkwy Lakewood CO 80226-3123 E-mail: sburkholder@lakewood.org.*

BURKHOLDER, TIMOTHY JAMES, insurance company executive; b. Athabasca, Alta., Can., Aug. 25, 1948; arrived in U.S., 1993; s. Paul Leonard and Doris Wilma (Stalter) Burkholder; m. Sharon Rose Sitler, Aug. 2, 1969; 3 children. B in Commerce, U. Alta., 1970. Computer project mgr. Govt. of Alta., Edmonton, Canada, 1970—80; gen. mgr. Burkholder Bldg. Supplies Ltd., Bluesky, Canada, 1980-84; exec. sec. N.W. Conf. Mennonite Ch., Edmonton, 1984-93; v.p. Mennonite Bd. Edn., Elkhart, Ind., 1993—2002; dir. ch. rels. Sharing Svcs. Agy., Goshen, Ind., 2003—. Ind. travel agt. Global Travel Internat., Maitland, Fla., 1990—. Editor: N.W. Conf. newsletter, 1984—93. Bd. dirs. Mennonite Reporter, Waterloo, Canada, 1988—93, Mennonite Ch. Gen. Bd., Elkhart, 1985—93; mem. Mennonite Ch. USA Design Team, 1999—2001; bd. dirs. Hesston (Kans.) Coll., 1977—85. Recipient medal of bravery, Gov. Gen. of Can., 1983. Mem.: Mennonite Econ. Devel. Assn., Am. Mktg. Assn. Office: Sharing Svcs Agy 1013 Division St PO Box 773 Goshen IN 46527 E-mail: timjh@juno.com.

BURKHOLDER, WENDELL EUGENE, retired entomology educator, researcher; b. Octavia, Nebr., June 24, 1928; s. Elmer and Susie Burkholder; m. Leona Rose Flory, Aug. 18, 1951; children: Paul Charles, Anne Carolyn, Joseph Kern, Stephen James. AB, McPherson Coll., 1950; M.Sc., U. Nebr., 1956; PhD, U. Wis., 1967. Rsch. entomologist U.S. Dept. Agr., 1956-96, 1965-96; asst. prof. U. Wis.-Madison, 1967-70, asso. prof., 1970-75, prof. entomology, 1975-96; prof. emeritus, 1996—. Lectr. in field. Mem. editorial bd.: Jour. Chem. Ecology, 1980-96, Jour. Stored Products Rsch., 1992-98; contbr. chpts. to books and articles to profl. jours. Served with U.S. Army, 1951-53. NSF grantee, 1972-75, 79; Rockefeller Found. grantee, 1974-77; Nat. Inst. Occupational Safety and Health grantee, 1977-79 Mem. AAAS, Entomol. Soc. Am., Wis. Entomol. Soc., Wis. Acad. Sci. Arts, and Letters, Internat. Soc. Chem. Ecology, Sigma Xi. Achievements include patents in field. Home: 1726 Chadbourne Ave Madison WI 53726-4108 Office: U Wis Entomology Dept 237 Russell Lab Madison WI 53706-1598

BURKI, FRED ALBERT, labor union official; b. Chgo., Apr. 8, 1926; s. John and Helen (Kramer) B.; children— Bill, Ken, Scott. Student, Northwestern U., U.Ill. Started as grocery clk., 1947; pres. local 470 United Retail Workers Union, Westchester, Ill., 1951-53, rep., 1953-62, field supr., 1963-65, nat. v.p., 1966-71, nat. exec. dir., 1971-81; internat. v.p. United Food and Comml. Workers Union, AFL-CIO, 1981—; pres. local 881, 1981—. Guest lectr. labor edn., advisor U. Ill. Circle Campus, Chgo.; labor edn. adv. U. Ind., 1967—, Loyola U., 1978—; mem. Midwest Com. Labor Study in Europe; labor adv. com. Senator Charles Percy, 1977—; chmn. Westchester Bldg. Corp., 1971-83. Bd. dirs. Chgo. Regional Blood Bank/Blood Services, Blood Ctr. of No. Ill., 1983—, Midwest Assn. for Sickle Cell Anemia, 1986—; trustee United Retail Workers Union-Super-Valu Trust Fund.; mem. Ill. Detection of Deception Com., 1982— ; pres. Human Services Ltd., 1984— . Served with AUS, 1943-47; battalion exec. officer, maj. Res., 1947-67, ret. Decorated Bronze Star medal; named Man of Year Combined Counties Police Assn., 1977 Mem. V.F.W. (past officer), Mil. Police Assn., Res. Officers Assn. E-mail: FBurki@aol.com.

BURKI, NAUSHERWAN, pulmonologist; b. Shillong, India, Sept. 25, 1946; children: Shamyl, Zareefa, Taimur, Menelle. MBBS, Punjab U., 1962; PhD, London U., 1969. Diplomate Am. Bd. Internal Medicine. From asst. prof. to prof. U. Ky. Med. Ctr., Lexington, 1974—. Fellow Am. Coll. Chest Physicians, Am. Coll. Physicians; mem. Am. Thoracic Soc., Am. Med. Rsch. Soc., Am. Physiol. Soc. Avocations: skiing, scuba, mountaineering, archaeology. Office: U Ky Med Ctr 800 Rose St # Mn614 Lexington KY 40536-0001

BURKLE, RONALD W. former food service executive, business investor; b. 1953; Pvt. practice, 1975-88; pres. Jurgensen's, Pasadena, Calif., 1986-88; prin. Yucaipa Mgmt. Co., Claremont, Calif., 1986—; chmn. Food 4 Less Supermarkets, La Habra, Calif., 1989—, Dominick's Finer Foods, Northlake, Ill., until 1998; chmn., mem. exec. com. Kroger's Foods, Inc.; CEO Smith's Food & Drug Ctrs., Inc., Salt Lake City; chmn. Fred Meyer. Office: Yucaipa Co 5th Fl 10000 Santa Monica Blvd Fl 5 Los Angeles CA 90067-7007

BURKLIN, FREDERICK O. minister, educator; b. Changshu, Jianxi, China, May 22, 1929; arrived in U.S., 1955; s. Gustav Heinrich and Lina Minna Marie (Pfeifferling) B.; m. Joyce M. Austin; children: Walter G., Ruth A. Fox, Arnold W., Alice G. BA, Grace Coll., Winona Lake, Ind., 1956; BD, MDiv, Grace Theol. Sem., Winona Lake, 1959; ThM, Westminster Theol. Sem., Phila., 1979. Registrar Bibelschule Bergstrasse, Seeheim, Germany, 1962—65, acad. dean, 1966—83, bus. mgr., 1983—90; prof. Greater Europe Mission, Monument, 1961—97, assoc. missionary, 1997—. Contbr. book. Gen. Assembly Of Reg. Bapt. Ch. Avocation: philately. Home: 3973 Elmscourt Dr Stone Mountain GA 30083

BURKLOW, KATHLEEN ANN, psychologist; b. Evansville, Ind., Oct. 23, 1964; d. Donald Ray and Kyung Ai Burklow; m. John Michael Berlier, May 1999; 1 child, Grace Berlier. BA, Vanderbilt U., 1987; MA, U. Cin., 1990, PhD, 1994. Lic. psychologist Ohio, 1997. Intern Children's Hosp., Columbus, 1993—94; postdoctoral fellow Cin. Children's Hosp. Med. Ctr., 1994—97, asst. prof. psychology, 1997—. Contbr. Recipient K23 Career Devel. award, NIH/Nat. Ctr. for Rsch. Resources, 2000. Mem.: APA. Office: Cincinnati Children's Hosp Med Ctr Divsn of Psychology ML3015 3333 Burnet Ave Cincinnati OH 45229-3026

BURKLOW, THOMAS RAY, pediatric cardiologist; b. Seoul, South Korea, Mar. 26, 1961; came to U.S., 1962; m. Carolyn Ann Sullivan. AB, Wash. U., St. Louis, 1983, MD, 1987. Diplomate Am. Bd. Pediats. Commd. 2d. lt. U.S. Army, 1987, advanced through grades to lt. col., 1999; resident Walter Reed Army Med. Ctr., Washington, 1987-90, mem. staff, 1992-93, asst. chief pediat. cardiology, 1996—, asst. chief pediats, 2001—; mem. staff Heidelberg (Germany) Army Cmty. Hosp., 1990-92; fellow pediat. cardiology Children's Nat. Med. Ctr., Washington, 1993-96. Fellow Am. Acad. Pediats., Am. Coll. Cardiology; mem. Alpha Omega Alpha. Office: Walter Reed Army Medical Ctr Dept Pediatrics Washington DC 20307-0001

BURKMAN, ERNEST, JR., education educator; b. Detroit, Oct. 4, 1929; s. Ernest and Rose (Emmehizer) B.; m. Nancy Barron, Mar. 11, 1953; children: Laura, Linda, Jan, Patricia. BS, Ea. Mich U., 1952; MS, U. Mich., 1955, MA, 1958, EdD, 1961. Sci. tchr. Edsel Ford High Sch., Dearborn, Mich., 1955-60; from asst. prof. to prof. Fla. State U., Tallahassee, 1960—. Co-dir. Turkish Nat. Sci. Lise Project, Ankara, 1961-66; dir. Intermediate Sci. Curriculum Study, 1966-72, U.S. and nationwide, Individualized Sci. Instruction System Project, U.S. and nationwide, 1972-81; cons. over 35 agys., U.S. and 15 countries, 1961—. Author: Current Trends in Science Education, 1966, The Natural World, 1975-88; co-author, editor: Individualized Science Instructional System, (25 vol. book series), 1981-88; contbr. articles to profl. jours. Fellow AAAS; mem. Nat. Sci. Tchr. Assn., Am. Ednl. Rsch. Assn. Office: Fla State U Coll Edn Tallahassee FL 32306

BURKMAN, RONALD THOMAS, JR., physician administrator, medical educator; b. Potsdam, N.Y., June 24, 1943; s. Ronald Thomas Burkman and Alma Evelyn Tunnison; m. Mildred Hoyhtya Burkman, July 25, 1970; children: Jason Theodore, Marnie Anne. BS, St. Lawrence U., 1965; MD, Albany (N.Y.) Med. Coll., 1969. Diplomate Am. Bd. Ob-Gyn. Rotating intern U. Wash., Seattle, 1969-70; resident in ob-gyn. Albany (N.Y.) Med. Ctr., 1970-73; faculty, prof. dept. ob-gyn. Johns Hopkins Med. Sch., Balt., 1973-87; prof., chair dept. ob-gyn. Henry Ford Health System, Detroit, 1987-95, Bay State Med. Ctr., Ann Tufts U. Sch. Medicine, Springfield, Mass., 1995—. Advisor NIH, Bethesda, 1985—. Author: Handbook of Contraception and Abortion, 1989; co-author: LaprocatorTM: Preventive Care and Maintenance, 1980, Prevention Care and Maintenance of Advanced Laparoscopic Systems, 1980, Reproductive Health Education in the Developing World, 1982, Family Planning Methods and Practice: Africa, Reproductive Health in Africa, 1984; editor: International Dictionary of Biology and Medicine, 1986, Churchill's Illustrated Medical Dictionary, 1989; co-editor: Surgical Equipment and Training in Reproductive Health, 1980, Reproductive Health Education and Technology: Issues and Future Direction, 1988; reviewer 12 jours.; editor The Female Patient, 1998—; author, editor 15 textbooks; contbr. numerous articles to profl. publs. Mem. Alpha Omega Alpha. Office: Baystate Med Ctr 759 Chestnut St Springfield MA 01197 E-mail: RTB@BHS.org.

BURKS, BRENDA ROUNSAVILLE, retired music educator, city council; b. Summerville, Ga., Nov. 7, 1944; d. Clifford and Louise McCutchins Rounsaville. BA in Music Edn., Spelman Coll., 1966; M in Music Edn., Ga. State U., 1974; postgrad., Fisk U., 1975, Emory U., 1976. Lifetime cert. music tchr. K-12. Choir dir. ladies singing ensemble W. 5th St. Ch. of Christ, Summerville, Ga., 1960-81; pvt. music tchr. Atlanta, 1966-84; music tchr. adult night sch., 1966-84; city coun. mem. City of Summerville, 1997—. Mentor Summerville Mentoring Com., 1997—. Mem. Adminstrv. Headstart Bd., Summerville, 1995—99, Literacy Bd. of Chattanooga County, Summerville, 1995—97; career advisor Consolidated Base Personnel Office (CBPO), Dobbins AFB, Marietta, 1983—84; sec. Martin Luther King Jr. Commn., Summerville, 1998—99, Ladies Bible Study; bd. dirs. Downtown Devel. Authority, Summerville, 1999- . Recipient Tng. Award, Univ. of Ga. & the Ga. Municipal Assoc., 2003. Mem.: Chattooge County Libr. Bd. (Bd. of Trustees 2002—05). Democrat. Mem. Ch. of Christ. Avocations: sewing, making preserves, baking pies and cakes, watching videos, bicycling.

BURKS, BRIAN SCOTT, veterinarian; b. Fresno, Calif., Aug. 12, 1968; s. Marlton Maurice and Cynthia Gail (Dick) Burks; m. Amy Beth Harrison. Student, Calif. State U., Fresno, 1986-90, U. Liverpool, Eng., 1990-92; DVM, Okla. State U., 1995. Intern Equine Med. Assocs., Glencoe, Mo., 1995-96; resident in equine internal medicine U. Ga., Athens, 1996-97; veterinarian Reed Equine Assocs., Grantville, Pa., 1997-98; assoc. veterinarian Fox Run Equine Ctr., Apollo, Pa., 1998—. Contbr. articles to profl. jours. Mem. Am. Vet. Med. Assn., Am. Assn. Equine Practitioners, Alpha Psi. Republican. Bapt. Avocations: piano, hiking, leathercraft, tennis, country music. Home: 119 Kenneth Dr Delmont PA 15626 Office: Fox Run Equine Ctr 798 Fox Rd Apollo PA 15613-9641 E-mail: BrianBurksDVM@att.net.

BURKS, ROCKY ALAN, independent living center executive, consultant; b. San Bernardino, Calif., June 12, 1952; s. Lloyd Jackson and Vivian Elnora B.; m. Nikki Ann Stone (div. 1974); 1 child, Gannon Leroy; m. Lydia Ann Deatherage, Aug. 20, 1983. BA in Social Welfare, BA in Sociology, Calif. State U., Chico, 1979. Instrument flight instr. USAF, Del Rio, Tex., 1971—75; dir.

outreach and recruitment, Office of Vets. Affairs Calif. State U., Chico, 1976—81; exec. dir. Easter Seal Soc. of Butte County, Chico, 1981—82, No. Calif. Ind. Living Program, Chico, 1982—85; soc. worker Butte County (Calif.) Welfare Dept., 1985—87; exec. dir. Ind. Living Svcs. of N. Calif., Inc., Chico, 1988—. Bd. dirs. Calif. Coalition of Ind. Living Ctrs., Sacramento, Calif., pres., 1991-94; bd. dirs. Pub. Interest Ctr. on Long-term Care, Sacramento, treas., 1994-98; mem. disability access adv. bd. Divsn. of the State Arch., Sacramento, 1995-99, Disabled Access Bd. of Appeals, Butte County Building Divsn., Oroville, 1994—; disability access code adv. com. Calif. Bldg. Stds. Commn., 1999—, bldg., fire and other codes adv. com., 2002—; mem. DRA fund, advisory and distbn. com. The San Francisco Found., 1999—; bd. dirs. Nonprofits' Ins. Alliance of Calif., Santa Cruz, 1999—; universal design adv. bd., Divsn. State Architect, 2002-03; mem. ADA adv. com. Butte County Bd. Suprs. 2002-2003. Editor (newsletter) Independent Life, 1988—, Voice, 1976-81. Transp. adv. commn. Butte County Assn. Govts., Oroville, 1992—; mem. Californians for Disability Rights. Recipient Cert. of Congl. Recognition, Congressman Wally Herger, Chico, 1993, 96, Disability Advocate award Calif. Assn. Persons with Handicaps, 1994, Region IX Disability Advocate award Nat. Coun. Ind. Living, 1998, Master Instr. award Air Tng. Command, USAF, 1975; named citizen Chickasaw Indian Nation. Mem. Am. Legion, Vietnam Vets. Am., Masons, Shriners, Scottish Rite, Chico Breakfast Lions (pres. 1991-92, Lion of Yr. award 1990, Melvin Jones fellow), Lions Eye Found. Calif. and Nev. (life). Avocations: scuba diving, boating, reading, art. Home: 4135 Keefer Rd Chico CA 95973-8956 Office: Ind Living Svcs No Calif 1161 East Ave Chico CA 95926-1018 E-mail: ilsnc@sunset.com.

BURLAND, J(OHN) ALEXIS, psychoanalyst; b. N.Y.C., Sept. 17, 1931; s. Elmer Granville and Catherine Alexander (Dobrushina) B.; m. Patricia Ruth Millar, Mar. 30, 1963. BA, Colgate U., 1952; MD, Columbia U., 1956; MSc, Temple U., 1962. Intern Mary Hitchcock Meml. Hosp., Hanover, N.H., 1956-57; resident in psychiatry Temple U. Hosp., Phila., 1957-58, 60-61; resident in child psychiatry St. Christopher's Hosp., Phila., 1961-63; candidate in gen. and child adolescent psychoanalysis Phila. Psychoanalytic Inst., 1963-72; pvt. practice Bala Cynwyd, Pa., 1963—. Assoc. prof. psychiatry Temple U. Hosp., St. Christopehrs Hosp., Phila., 1963-79; clin. prof. Jefferson Med. Coll., Thomas Jefferson U., Phila., 1979—; tng.-supervising psychoanalyst Inst. Psychoanalytic Ctr. of Phila., 1983—, pres., 1991-97. Editor: Rapprochement: Critical Phase of Separation-Individuation, 1980, Self & Object Constancy, 1985. Lt. comdr. USNR, 1958-60. Fellow Am. Psychiat. Assn. (disting. life); mem. Am. Psychoanalytic Assn., Internat. Psychoanalytic Assn., Assn. Child Psychoanalysis, Psychoanalytic Ctr. of Phila. (pres. 1977-80), Union League, Phi Beta Kappa, Delta Upsilon Avocations: classical music, theater, ballet, writing, scuba diving. Home and Office: 15 Colwyn Ln Bala Cynwyd PA 19004-2308 E-mail: AlexBurland@aol.com.

BURLEIGH, A. PETER, ambassador; b. L.A., Mar. 7, 1942; s. Ralph Wendell and Margaret (McKenney) B. AB, Colgate U., 1963; postgrad., U. Pa., 1965-66. Vol. Peace Corps, Nepal, 1963-65; joined Fgn. Svc., 1967; various positions Dept. State, Washington, 1967-85, dir. No. Gulf Affairs, 1985-87, dep. asst. sec. for Near Eastern and South Asian Affairs, 1987-89, dep. asst. sec. for intelligence and rsch., 1989-91, coord. for counter-terrorism, amb., 1991-92, dep. asst. sec. for pers., 1992-95; amb. Dem. Socialist Republic Sri Lanka, Republic Maldives, 1995-97; dep. U.S. rep. to UN, 1997-99; ret. Recipient Presdl. Svc. award U.S. Govt., 1990, 93, Disting. Svc. award Sec. of State, Washington, 2000, Presdl. Disting. Svc. award, 2000. Office: 2300 Riverlane Ter Fort Lauderdale FL 33312-4762 E-mail: apburl@bellsouth.net.

BURLEIGH, LEWIS ALBERT, lawyer; b. Augusta, Maine, May 15, 1940; s. Lewis A. and Ursula (Maher) B.; m. Rinda H. Burleigh, June 22, 1963; children: Lewis A. IV, Jennifer, Erica. AB cum laude, Harvard U., 1962, JD, 1965. Bar: N.Y. 1966, Mass. 1973,Calif. 1982, Pa. 1985. Assoc. Dewey Ballantine Bushby Palmer & Wood, N.Y.C., 1965-72; ptnr. Csaplar & Bok (name changed to Gaston & Snow), Boston and San Francisco, 1973-91, Day Berry & Howard, Boston, 1991—2001, Dechert LLP, Boston, 2001—. Fellow Am. Coll. Investment Counsel; mem. ABA, N.Y. State Bar Assn., Calif. Bar Assn., Am. Soc. Internat. Law, Harvard Club. Avocation: flying. Office: Dechert LLP 200 Clarendon St Fl 27 Boston MA 02116 E-mail: lewis.burleigh@dechert.com.

BURLEIGH, WILLIAM ROBERT, newspaper executive; b. Evansville, Ind., Sept. 6, 1935; s. Joseph Charles and Emma Bertha (Wittgen) B.; m. Catherine Anne Husted, Nov. 28, 1964; children: David William, Catherine Anne, Margaret Walden. BS, Marquette U., Milw., 1957; LLD (hon.), U. So. Ind., 1979. From reporter to editor, pres. Evansville Press, 1951-77; editor Cin. Post, 1977-83; v.p., gen. editl. mgr. Scripps-Howard Newspapers, Cin., 1984-86, sr. v.p. newspapers and publs., 1986-90, exec. v.p., 1990-94, pres., COO, 1994-96, pres., CEO, 1996-99; chmn., CEO E.W. Scripps Co., Cin., 1999-2000, chmn., 2000—. With AUS, 1957-58. Mem. Queen City Club, Cin. Lit. Club, Cin. Country Club, Cin. Comml. Club, Alpha Sigma Nu. Roman Catholic. Office: E W Scripps 312 Walnut St Cincinnati OH 45202-4024

BURLESKI, JOSEPH ANTHONY, JR., information technology executive; b. Poughkeepsie, N.Y., June 30, 1960; s. Joseph Anthony Burleski Sr. and Fredeline Cyr; m. Judith Ann Lezon, June 10, 1989; children: Joseph Anthony III, Jessica Ann. BSBA, Marist Coll., 1982; MBA Mktg., U. Phoenix, 1992; grad. in human rels. and effective speaking, Dale Carnegie, 1990. Cert. project mgmt. profl. Project Mgmt. Inst.; IBM cert. exec. project mgr. Computer operator IBM, Poughkeepsie, 1982-83, lead/sr. computer operator, 1983-84, systems programmer, 1984-85, assoc. systems programmer, 1985-86, mgr. offshift computer ops., 1986-87, mgr. info. processing Boulder, Colo., 1987-88, mgr. MVS systems programming, 1988-91; mgr. location and field svcs. devel. Integrated Systems Solutions Corp. subs. IBM, Boulder, 1991-93, mgr. location and field svc. devel. ind. test, 1992-93; mgr. VM/VSE svcs. Integrated Sys. Solutions Corp. subs. IBM, Boulder, 1993-94, account mgr., 1994-96; delivery project exec. IBM Global Svcs., Boulder, 1997-98, delivery exec. St. Louis, 1998—2000, sr. delivery project exec., 2001—; cert. exec. project mgr. IBM, 1999—; chair IBM Cert. Bd., 2000—. Mentor IBM, 1987—; mem. IBM Data Processing Ops. Coun., Poughkeepsie, 1983-92, Project Mgmt. Inst., 1995 ; grad. asst. Dale Carnegie Inst., Boulder, 1990-98. Coach Spl. Olympics, 1987-98; mem. Order of the Arrow Hon. Soc., chpt. sec., editor, 1976-77, chpt. pres. 1977-78, chpt. treas. 1980-81; asst. cubmaster Boy Scouts Am., 2002-03, cubmaster, 2003—. Mem. Am. Mgmt. Assn., Am. Assn. Individual Investors, Marist Coll. Alumni Assn. (contbr.), Vigil Nat. Honor Soc.; clubs K.of C. Roman Catholic. Avocations: running, reading, camping, hiking, raising tropical fish. Office: Bldg 302-3E MD S306-2182 325 JS McDonnell Blvd Hazelwood MO 63042 E-mail: burleski@us.ibm.com.

BURLING, WILLIAM JOHN, literature educator; b. Ladysmith, Wis., Jan. 27, 1949; s. Wesley and Patricia Burling; m. Brenda Jean Gunnes, Dec. 20, 1968 (div. Mar. 1, 1976); m. Debra Kay Drake, July 11, 1980; children: Amanda Nicole, Andrew Wayne. BS in Psychology, U. Wis., Eau Claire, 1972, MA in English, 1974; PhD, Pa. State U., 1985. Asst. prof. English Auburn (Ala.) U., 1985—89; prof. English S.W. Mo. State U., Springfield, 1989—. Author: The Colonial American Stage 1665-1774: A Documentary Calendar, Summer Theatre in London 1661-1820, and the Rise of the Haymarket Theatre, A Checklist of New Plays and Entertainments on the London Stage, 1700-1737; editor: The Plays of Colley Cibber. Mem.: Midwestern Am Soc. 18th Century Studies (pres. 2002), Springfield Astron. Soc. (pres. 2000—03). Home: 2658 E Corona Cir Springfield MO 65804 Office: SW Mo State U 901 S National Springfield MO 65804 Personal E-mail: wjb692f@smsu.edu.

BURLINGAME, ALMA LYMAN, chemist, educator; b. Cranston, R.I., Apr. 29, 1937; s. Herman Follett Jr. and Rose Irene (Kohler) B.; children: Mark, Walter; m. Marilyn F. Schwartz, Feb. 14, 1993; 1 stepchild, Corey Schwartz. BS, U. R.I., 1959; PhD, MIT, 1962. Asst. prof. U. Calif., Berkeley, 1963-68, assoc. chemist, 1968-72, rsch. chemist, 1972-78, prof. San Francisco, 1978—, Univ. Coll., London, 1996—2002. Vis. prof. Ludwig Inst. for Cancer Rsch., London, 1993-94. Editor: Topics in Organic Mass Spectrometry, 1970, Mass Spectrometry in Health and Life Science, 1985, Biological Mass Spectrometry, 1990, Mass Spectrometry in the Biological Sciences, 1995, Mass Spectrometry in Biology and Medicine, 2000; dep. editor Molecular and Cellular Proteomics, 2002—; contbr. With USAR, 1954-62. Guggenheim Found. fellow, 1970. Fellow AAAS. Office: U Calif Dept Pharm Chemistry San Francisco CA 94143-0001 E-mail: alb@itsa.ucsf.edu.

BURLINGAME, EDWARD LIVERMORE, book publisher; b. N.Y.C., Jan. 21, 1935; s. Anson and Elizabeth Harlow (Hussey) B.; m. Perdita Remony Plowden, May 18, 1963; children: Remony Elizabeth, Phyllida Anne, Roger Anson. BA, Harvard U., 1957; AMP, Harvard Bus. Sch., 1982. Editor MacGibbon & Kee, Ltd., London, 1959-61; sr. editor New Am. Library, N.Y.C., 1961-65; v.p., editor in chief Walker & Co., N.Y.C., 1965-68; sr. v.p., editor-in-chief trade div. J.B. Lippincott Co., Phila. and N.Y.C., 1968-78, dir., 1970-78; v.p., pub. Lippincott & Crowell, N.Y.C., 1979-80; v.p., editor-in-chief, pub. trade group Harper & Row, Pubs., Inc., N.Y.C., 1980-87; pub. Edward Burlingame Books (an imprint of HarperCollins Pubs.), 1987-93; pres. The Adventure Libr., 1993—. Mem. Eastern regional panel Pres.'s Commn. on White House Fellowships, 1982-84; mem. vis. com. New Sch. for Social Rsch., 1991-95. Served to lt. (j.g.) USNR, 1957-59. Mem. Assn. Am. Pubs. (copyright com. 1976-77, internat. freedom to publish com. 1977-80, exec. council gen. pub. div. 1981-88, vice chmn. 1984-85, chmn. 1985-86), PEN (treas., exec. bd. 1970-73). Clubs: Century Assn. Home: 79 Nash Rd North Salem NY 10560-3710 E-mail: edwardb@pobox.com.

BURLINGAME, MICHAEL ASHTON, historian, retired educator; b. Washington, Sept. 13, 1941; s. Harry Lamson and Estelle Boughton (Embry) B.; m. S.L. Silberman, Aug. 22, 1968 (div. Mar. 15, 1980); children: Rebecca, Jessica. Student, Phillips Acad., Andover, Mass., 1956-60; BA, Princeton (N.J.) U., 1964; PhD, Johns Hopkins U., Balt., 1971. May Buckley Sadowski prof. history Conn. Coll., New London, 1968-2001. Author: The Inner World of Abraham Lincoln, 1994; editor: An Oral History of Abraham Lincoln, 1996, Inside Lincoln's White House, 1997, Lincoln Observed, 1998, A Reporter's Lincoln, 1998, Lincoln's Journalist, 1998, Inside the White House in War Times, 2000, At Lincoln's Side, 2000, With Lincoln in the White House, 2000, "Lincoln's Humor" and Other Essays by Benjamin P. Thomas, 2002, Dispatches from Lincoln's White House, 2002, The Real Lincoln by Jesse W. Weik, 2002. Recipient prize Abraham Lincoln Assn., Springfield, Ill., 1995, Lincoln Diploma of Honor, Lincoln Meml. U., Harrogate, Tenn., 1998, hon. mention Lincoln prize Gettysburg Coll., 2001. Mem. Orgn. Am. Historians, Am. Hist. Assn., Abraham Lincoln Assn., Nat. Assn. Scholars, The Historical Soc., Abraham Lincoln Inst. Avocations: concerts, opera, hockey, tennis, lacrosse. Home: 2 Chippechaug Trail Mystic CT 06355 E-mail: mabur@conncell.edu.

BURLINGAME-SMITH, JUNE, English language educator, administrator; b. Barrington, N.J., June 1, 1935; d. Leslie Grant and Esther (Bellini) Burlingame; m. Gregory Lloyd Smith, July 6, 1963 (dec. July 1997); children: Gilia Cobb Smith, Cyrus Comstock Smith. BA, Reed Coll., 1956; MS, Ind. U., 1959; MA, Calif. State U., Dominguez Hills, 1986. Prof. English L.A. C.C.-Harbor Coll., Wilmington, 1986—, pres. acad. senate, 1997-2000, staff devel. coord., 2001—. Mem. exec. bd. Harbor Interfaith Shelter, San Pedro, Calif., 1993—, Harbor Area YWCA, 2001—; mem. task force Recreation and Pks. L.A., San Pedro, 1999; mem. Cabrillo Marine Aquarium Vol. Neighborhood Oversight Com., 2000—; pres. Pt. Formin Residents Assn., 2000—; chair coordinated plan subcom. Port of L.A. Citizens Adv. Parliamentarian Com., 2002—. Mem. AAUW (legis. chair 1988—), Nat. Coun. Tchrs. of English. Office: Harbor Coll 1111 Figueroa Pl Wilmington CA 90744-2311 E-mail: burling102@aol.com.

BURMAN, DIANE BERGER, career management and organization development consultant; b. Pitts., Dec. 7, 1936; d. Morris Milton and Dorothy June (Barkin) Berger; m. Sheldon Oscar Burman, Dec. 15, 1926; children: Allison Beth, Jocelyn Holly, Harrison Emory Guy. BA, Vassar Coll., 1958; MA, Middlebury Coll., 1961. Tchr. of French Allderdice High Sch., Pitts., 1960-61, Mamaroneck (N.Y.) High Sch., 1961-64; personnel specialist G.D. Searle & Co., Skokie, Ill., 1972-77, orgn. devel. tng. cons., 1977-78; personnel and orgn. devel. cons. Abbott Labs., North Chgo., 1978-82; orgn. devel. cons., v.p., mgr. career devel. Harris Bank, Chgo., 1982-97; ind. mgmt. cons. in orgn. devel., career devel., 1997—; pres. Dee Burman & Assoc., Highland Park, Ill., 1997—. Mem. edit. bd. Orgn. Devel. Jour., 1987. Bd. advisors Grad. Sch. Bus. No. Ill. U. Mem. ASTD (bd. dirs. Chgo. career devel. profl. practice area 1987—), Internat. Quality Leadership Inst. (sec., bd. dirs. 2000), Orgn. Devel. Network (founder, exec. dir. Chgo. chpt. 1986-89), Assn. Psychol. Type-Nat. Conf., Orgn. Devel. Inst. (adv. bd. 1987-91, chmn. nat. conf. 1990), Nat. Assn. Bank Women, Internat. Assn. Career Mgmt. Profls. (bd. dirs. Chgo. chpt. 1999-2001, co-chair pub. com. 1999), Am. Counseling Assn., Vassar Club (bd. dirs. 1975-80, 95—, chair career assistance com. 1997—, co-sec. 2000-2001, co-chmn. ann. scholarship benefit, 2002). Jewish. Avocations: biking, playing flute, traveling. Home and Office: 247 Prospect Ave Highland Park IL 60035-3357 E-mail: deeburman@aol.com.

BURMAN, SHEILA FLEXER ZOLA, special education educator; b. N.Y.C., May 1, 1935; d. Jack and Edna (Eagle) Flexer; m. Eugene Lee Zola, July 7, 1957 (div. Aug. 1973); children: Leslie Sheldon, Sharon Joanne; m. Milton Burman, Mar. 19, 1978 (dec. Apr. 1999). Student, Hunter Coll., 1952-55; BA in Edn., BS, UCLA, 1957, 85, spl. edn. cert. for learning handicapped, 1985; and severely handicapped; MS in Counseling, U. LaVerne, 1983; resource specialist cert., Calif. Luth. U., 1988. Cert. tchr., spl. edn. tchr., resource specialist, pupil pers. credential. Tchr. L.A. Unified Sch. Dist., 1957-62, tchr. 3rd grade gifted, 1977-81, spl. edn. tchr., 1981-88, mid. sch. resource tchr., 1987—89, elem. resource tchr., 1989—96, spl. edn. coord., 1997—. Cert. tchr., spl. edn. tchr., resource specialist, pupil pers. credential. Pres. L.A. chpt. Brandeis U. Nat. Women's Com., 2000-02, western region v.p. membership, 2000—; bd. dirs. U. Women, U. of Judaism. Grantee CTIP 1988, Computer 1989. Mem. Coun. for Exceptional Children, Assn. Ednl. Therapists, United Tchrs. L.A., Calif. Tchrs. Assn., UCLA Alumni Assn., UCLA Grad. Sch. Edn. Alumni Assn., Hunter Coll. Alumni Assn., Pi Lambda Theta. Avocations: swimming, reading, needlepoint. Home: 15455 Hamner Dr Los Angeles CA 90077-1802 Office: 4525 Irvine Ave North Hollywood CA 91602-1915

BURMEISTER, EDWIN, economics educator; b. Chgo., Nov. 30, 1939; s. Edwin Carl and Dorothy (Braithwaite) B. BA, Cornell U., 1961, MA, 1962; PhD, MIT, 1965. Asst. prof. econs. Wharton Sch., U. Pa., Phila., 1965-68, assoc. prof., 1968-71; vis. prof. econs. Duke U., 1971-72, vis. prof. econs. Fuqua Sch. Bus. and dept. econs., 1981-82; vis. prof. econs. Sch. Gen. Studies and vis. fellow dept. econs. Research Sch. Social Sci. Australian Nat. U., 1974-75; prof. econs. U. Pa., Phila., 1972-76; prof. econs., mem. Ctr. for Advanced Studies U. Va., Charlottesville, 1976-79, Commonwealth prof. econs., 1979-90; rsch. prof. econs. Duke U., 1990—. Vis. prof. econs. U. Chgo., 1980; prof. econs. and fin. U. Ill., 1982 Author: (with A. Rodney Dobell) Mathematical Theories of Economic Growth, 1970, Capital Theory and Dynamics, 1980, (others); contbr. articles to profl. jours. NSF grantee, 1964-81, 83-89; FTC contractee, 1979-80; Guggenheim fellow, 1974-76, NSF grad. fellow, 1962-65, NSF summer fellow, 1962, hon. Woodrow Wilson fellow, 1961-62. Fellow Econometric Soc. Address: Duke University Dept Econs DPC 90097 Durham NC 27708-0097

BURMEISTER, JOHN LUTHER, chemistry educator, consultant; b. Fountain Springs, Pa., Feb. 20, 1938; s. Luther John and Frieda May (Tielmann) B.; m. Doris Aileen Crawford, June 25, 1960; children: Lisa Anne, Jeffrey Scott. BS in Chemistry, Franklin and Marshall Coll., 1959; PhD in Chemistry, Northwestern U., 1964. Instr. chemistry U. Ill., Urbana, 1963-64; asst. prof. chemistry U. Del., Newark, 1964-69, assoc. prof., 1969-73, prof., 1973-93, alumni disting. prof., 1993—, assoc. chmn. dept., 1974—, NCAA faculty athletic rep., 1982—. Pres. Covered Bridge Farms Maintenance Corp., Newark, 1977-79; chmn. chemistry edit. rev. bd. Control Data Corp., Mpls., 1981-85. Mem. editl. bd. Inorganica Chimica Acta, Padua, Italy, 1967-88, Synthesis and Reactivity in Inorganic and Metal-Organic Chemistry, N.Y.C., 1970-98; contbr. numerous articles to profl. jours. Ruling elder Head of Christiana Presbyn. Ch., Newark, 1969—. Recipient Excellence in Tchg. award Lindback Found. Del. Alumni Assn., 1968, 79, award for Excellence in chemistry Tchr., Chem. Mfrs. Assn., Washington, 1981, faculty recognition award Mortar Bd., 1984, Prof. of Yr. award Coll. Arts and Sci., 1985, Del. Prof. of Yr. award Carnegie found. for Advancement Tchr. and Cun. for Acvancement and Support Edn., 1994, Disting. Del. Scientist award, 1994, Excellence in Tchg. award Alpha Lambda Delta, 1997, Coll. Arts and Sci. Disting. Alumni Prof. award, 1997. Mem. Am. Chem. Soc. (sec.-treas. inorganic divsn. 1975-77, alt. councillor, 1977-79, assoc. nat. com. on chem. edn. 1983-84, councillor Del. sect. 1987-89), Sigma Xi, Phi Lambda Upsilon, Phi Kappa Phi (v.p. Del. chpt. 1979-80, pres. 1980-81), Omicron Delta Kappa. Republican. Office: U Del Dept Chemistry-Biochemistry Newark DE 19716 E-mail: jlburm@chem.udel.edu.

BURMEISTER, PAUL FREDERICK, farmer; b. Great Bend, Kans., June 11, 1938; s. Ferdinand Frederick Adam and Gertrude Nellie (Hanson) B. BA in Chemistry and Agr., Ft. Hays State U., 1960; postgrad., U. Kans., 1961. Farmer, Claflin, Kans., 1952-61, 64—. Farmer coop. Kans. Agrl. Experiment Sta., Ft. Hays Br. Sta., Hays, Kans., 1970, Kans. Rural Ctr., Whiting, 1991, 92; panel mem. Kans. Sustainable Agr. Conf., Great Bend and Salina, 1991, 92; mem. Kans. Natural Resource Coun., Topeka, 1975—, Nat. Resources Def. Coun., N.Y.C., 1975—; participant, U. Akron Nat. Energy Forum, 1976, Nat. Low-Level Radioactive Waste Mgmt. Strategy Rev. Workshop, Washington, 1981; participant pub. forum on radioactive wastes Office Radiation Programs, EPA, Denver, 1978; guest spkr., Rapid City, S.D., 1993; mem. Kans.-Okla. Conf. Coun., 1999—; mem. farmer adv. com. Sunshine Farm Project, The Land Inst., Salina, 1995-2001. Contbr. articles to environ. and agrl. jours. Vol. Am. Peace Corps, Ludhiana, India, 1961-63; local organizer campaign Union of Concerned Scientists, Cambridge, Mass.; lobbyist on environ. protection and conservation issues, Topeka, 1976-80; mem. Renew Am., Washington, 1980—; mem. The Menninger Found., Topeka, 1989—, Environ. Action, 1982—; lay mem. ad hoc task force on ecology Christian lifestyle United Ch. of Christ, 1977-78, commn. on outreach Kans.-Okla. conf., 1988-96, 98-99, network environ. and econ. responsibility; del. to 23rd Gen. Synod meeting of United Ch. of Christ, Kansas City, Mo., 2001; mem. Kans.-Okla. Conf. Coun. United Ch. Christ, 1999-2003; participant Kans. Citizens Forum Com. for Humanities, Topeka, 1987; mem. farmer adv. com. Sunshine Farm Project, Land Inst., Salina, Kans., 1995-2001. With USNG, 1963-69. Recipient Bankers award Banks of Barton County, Kans. and U.S. Soil Conservation Svc., 1990. Mem. Nat. Wildlife Fedn. (life), Nat. Coun. Returned Peace Corps Vols., Nat. Arbor Day Found., World Wildlife Fund (charter), Am. Wind Energy Assn., Am. Solar Energy Soc. (life), Midwest Renewable Energy Assn., 1998—, Kans. Assn. Wheat Growers, Kans. Farmers Union, Kans. Organic Prodrs., Inc., Friends of the Earth, Cousteau Soc. (founding yr. mem.), Kans. State Hist. Soc. (life), Kans. Wildlife Fedn., Sierra Club (life), Native Forest Coun., Ducks Unlimited Inc., Environ. Def., Wilderness Soc., Friends of India, Rainforest Alliance, Nat. Parks Conservation Assn., Tau Kappa Epsilon (sec. 1958-59, scholar 1959), Nature Conservancy, Phi Eta Sigma (historian 1958-59), Phi Kappa Phi, Delta Epsilon. Avocations: photography, hiking, exploring. Address: 1332 NE 180th Rd Claflin KS 67525-9219

BURNAMAN, STEPHEN PAUL, music educator; b. Lubbock, Tex., Oct. 8, 1964; s. Jerry Lynn and Nancy Kate Burnaman. MusB, Stephen F. Austin U., 1988; MusM, New Eng. Conservatory, 1990; D in Musical Arts, U. Tex., 1997. Lectr. U. Tex., Austin, 1998—99; asst. prof. Huston-Tillotson Coll., Austin, 1999—. Organist Hillcrest Bapt. Ch., Austin, 1994—. Recipient Coulter award, Brazos Valley Symphony, 1991. Mem.: Austin Dist. Music Tchrs. Assn. (v.p. 1999—2001, pres. 2001—02), Nat. Guild Piano Tchrs., Tex. Music Tchrs. Assn. Republican. Home: 9500 Jollyville Rd # 124 Austin TX 78759 Office: Huston_Tillotson Coll Dept Music 900 Chicon St Austin TX 78702 Personal E-mail: StephenDMA@aol.com.

BURNELL, ELVIN WALLACE, industrial engineer, security specialist; b. Edison, Ohio, Aug. 4, 1938; s. Lester E. and Ilo S. (Sherman) B.; m. Dorothy Cameron, June 27, 1958 (div. Nov. 1967); children: Natalie, Valerie, Nathan, Vanessa; m. Linda E. Fritz, Jan. 5, 1974; children: Brigette A., Tanya N. BS, U. Akron, Ohio, 1972, MBA, 1977. Statis. analyst State of Ohio, Mansfield, 1959-65; indsl. engr. Borg-Warner Co., Mansfield, 1966; mgr. engring. dept. Pioneer Rubber Co., Willard, Ohio, 1966-73; indsl. engring. mgr. Eagle Rubber Co., Ashland, Ohio, 1973-80; quality assurance profl. U.S. Dept. Def., Cleve., 1980-95; security speciaist State of Ohio, Mansfield, 1996—. Lectr. level IV U. Akron, 1977-82. Patentee in field. Master sgt. Air Nat. Guard, 1955-67, 72-98. Decorated USAF Meritorious Svc. medal. Mem. Inst. Indsl. Engrs. (sr., chpt. pres. 1978, award of excellence 1978), Am. Soc. Quality Control (auditor 1997), Internat. Assn. Counterterrorism and Security Profls. (Reid Inst.-Trained Investigator), Gardners of Am. (nat. pres. 1992-93, bd. dirs. 1993—), Men's Garden Club Am. (pres. Ctr. Great region 1992, disting. svc. award 1993), Mansfield Men's Garden Club (pres. 1988, Ohio Master Gardener 1995). Avocations: gardening, reading, backpacking. Home: 1220 Sheier Rd Mansfield OH 44903-8644 E-mail: elvin.burnell@ohmans.ang.af.mil.

BURNER, CLARA MILLER, librarian; b. Gettysburg, Pa., May 27, 1943; d. Herbert and Ruth (Myers) Miller; m. Emory C. Bogle, March 21, 1970 (div. March 1991); 1 child, Andrew Miller Ibrahim Bogle; m. Robert Henry Burner, Aug. 20, 1995 (dec.). BA in Spanish, Pa. State U., 1965; MLS, Pratt Inst., 1968. Reference libr. Richmond (Va.) Pub. Libr., 1970-76, branch libr., 1977-85, deputy city libr., 1985—, acting city libr., 1996-97. Mem. Am. Libr. Assn. (Va. chapt.). Methodist. Office: Richmond Public Library 101 E Franklin St Richmond VA 23219-2107

BURNER, DAVID L. aerospace services company executive; b. Lodi, Ohio; m. Rosemary Burner; 3 children. BS in Commerce, Ohio U., 1962. Various postions aerospace industry; with B.F. Goodrich Co., Richfield, Ohio, 1983—, pres. aerospace divsn., 1987, pres., 1995—, CEO, chmn. and pres., 1996—. Bd. dirs. B.F. Goodrich Co., bd. govs. Aerospace Inst. Am., Washington. Bd. dirs. The Greater Cleve. Growth Assn.; active Cleve. Scholarship Programs Inc., Summit Edn. Initiative, Salvation Army Greater Cleve., Ohio U. Found., Cleve. Orch. Office: The BF Goodrich Co Four Coliseum Ctr 2730 W Tyvola Rd Ste 600 Charlotte NC 28217-4578

BURNETT, ARTHUR LOUIS, SR., judge; b. Spotsylvania County, Va., Mar. 15, 1935; s. Robert Louis and Lena Victoria (Bumbry) B.; m. Ann Lloyd, May 14, 1960; children: Darnellena, Arthur Louis II, Darryl, Darlisa, Dionne. BA summa cum laude, Howard U., 1957; LLB, NYU, 1958; grad., Fed. Exec. Inst., 1978. Bar: D.C. 1958, U.S. Dist. Ct. Md. 1963, U.S. Supreme Ct. 1964. Atty. Gen.'s Honor Program atty. fraud sect. criminal divsn. U.S. Dept. Justice, Washington, 1958, atty. to acting dep. chief gen. crimes sect., 1960-65; spl. asst. U.S. atty., Balt. and East St. Louis, Ill., 1961-63; asst. U.S. atty. D.C., 1965-68; legal adviser, gen. counsel D.C. Dept. Met. Police, 1968-69; U.S. magistrate U.S. Dist. Ct., Washington, 1969-75; asst. gen. counsel legal adv. divsn. U.S. CSC, 1975-78; assoc. gen. counsel Office of Personnel Mgmt., 1979-80; U.S. magistrate U.S. Dist. Ct. D.C., 1980-87; judge Superior Ct. D.C., 1987-98, sr. judge, 1998—; faculty Fed. Jud. Center, 1970—, Nat. Jud. Coll., 1974—. Judge-in-residence Children's Def. Fund, 1998—; program chmn. ann. meeting Nat. Conf. Spl. Ct. Judges, Washington, 1973, chmn. elect, acting chmn., 1974-75, chmn., 1975; program chmn. ann. meeting Nat. Council U.S. Magistrates, Williamsburg, Va., 1974, pres., 1983-84; program participant D.C. Circuit Jud. Conf., 1974, U.S. Ct. Claims Jud. Conf., 1979; adj. prof. Columbus Sch. Law, Cath. U. Am., 1997—, Cath. U., 1997—, Sch. Law Howard U., 1998—. Mem. NYU Law Rev., 1957-58 Bd. dirs. Fellowship of Christian Athletes, Washington, Nat. Assn. for Children of Alcoholics, 2000—. Recipient Founders Day award NYU, 1958, Sustained Superior Performance award U.S. Atty. Gen., 1963, Disting. Service award CSC, 1978, Meritorious Service award U.S. Office of Personnel Mgmt., 1980, Jud. award of excellence Washington Met. Trial Lawyers Assn., 1999, award of excellence Nat. Conf. State Trial Judges, 1999, Outstanding Disting. Service award Fed. Bar Assn., 1983. Mem. ABA (Franklin N. Flashner jud. award as outstanding judge on ct. of spl. jurisdiction 1985, coun. adminstrv. law and regulatory practice sect. 1987-90, liaison rep. of adminstrv. law and regulatory practice sect. to adminstrv. conf. of U.S. 1990-94, mem. JAD task force on improving opportunities for minorities 1988-97, 98—, judge Edward R. Finch Law Day USA speech award 1991, asst. sec. 1991-93, chair civil right and employment discrimination com. 1992-95, sec. adminstrv. law and regulatory practice 1993-95, chmn. CJS com. on criminal rules and evidence 1993-97, standing com. on substance abuse 1995-99, co-chmn. editl. bd. Criminal Justice Mag. 1997-2000, adv. com. and standing com. on pro bono and pub. svc. 2001-, State Justice Initiatives award, 2002), FBA (sect. coord. 1987-88, chmn. fed. litigation sect. 1984-85, chmn. standing com. on U.S. magistrates, dep. chmn. sect. adminstrn. of justice 1983-84, chmn. standing com. on U.S. magistrate, chmn. sect. adminstrn. of justice 1983-84, 95-97, pres. D.C. chpt. 1984-85, chmn. profl. ethics com. 1991-93, chmn. audit com. 1999—, standing com. unmet leagl needs of children, 2003—, Disting. Svc. award 1978, The Pres.'s award 1994, Earl Kintner award, 2002), Washington Bar Assn. (chmn. jud. coun. 2000-01, Ollie Mae Cooper award 1997), Nat. Bar Assn. (chmn. cmty. and youth action com. jud. coun. 1995—, chmn. profl. ethics com., jud. coun. asst. sec., The Pres.'s award 1996), Bar Assn. D.C., D.C. Unified Bar, Am. Judicature Soc., Am. Judges Assn. (sec-treas. Prettyman-Leventhal Inn of Ct. Washington 1991-94,

pres. 1994-95), Phi Beta Kappa, Omega Psi Phi. Office: Superior Ct DC Chambers JM-680 500 Indiana Ave NW Washington DC 20001-2131 E-mail: albsr2alb@aol.com., burnetta@dcsc.gov.

BURNETT, BARBARA DIANE, social worker; b. Charleston, W.Va., Aug. 20, 1928; d. LeRoy Sparks and Hallie Catherine (Walker) Montague; m. Clyde Ray Burnett, Sept. 20, 1947 (div. Nov. 1972); children: Beverly O'Reilly, Pamela Van Scotter, Marcia Montague(dec.), Janet Summers, Craig. BS, U. Wis., 1949; MS, Pa. State U., 1963; MSW, Va. Commonwealth U., 1977. LCSW Fla. Spl. edn. tchr. Palm Beach County Sch. Bd., various locations, 1964-75; social worker Project Peace Elizabeth Falk Found., Boca Raton, Fla., 1977-78; social worker Cmty. Home Health, Boynton Beach, Fla., 1978-90, Hospice Care Broward Inc., Ft. Lauderdale, Fla., 1986-91; pvt. practice supr. MSW profls. Broward County, Fla., 1991—. Instr. social work Barry U., Fla. Internat. U., Fla. Atlantic U. Active Dem. Party, Broward County, 1977—, crucible jr. hon., U. Wisc., 1948, mortar bd. sr. hon., 1949. Named Fla. Renal Social Worker of the Yr., Nat. Kidney Found., Tampa, 1998. Mem.: LWV, Common Cause, Nat. Kidney Found. (coun. nephrology social workers), Am. Assn. Kidney Patients (bd. mem.), Omicron Nu, Phi Lambda Theta. Democrat. Episcopalian. Avocations: reading, walking, swimming, attending grandchildrens special events, traveling. Home: 104 SE 10th St Apt G101 Deerfield Beach FL 33441-5352 Office: Fresenius Med Care Plantation Artificial Kidney Ctr 849 Nob Hill Rd Plantation FL 33324

BURNETT, CAROL, actress, comedienne, singer; b. San Antonio, Apr. 26, 1933; d. Jody and Louise (Creighton) B.; m. Joseph Hamilton, 1963 (div.); children: Carrie Louise, Jody Ann, Erin Kate; m. Brian Miller, 2001. Student, UCLA, 1952-54. Introduced comedy song I Made a Fool of Myself Over John Foster Dulles, 1957; Broadway debut in Once Upon a Mattress, 1959; regular performer in Garry Moore TV show, 1959-62; appeared several CBS-TV spls., 1962-63; star Carol Burnett Show, CBS-TV, 1966-77, Carol & Co., 1990-91; appeared on Broadway, Once Upon a Mattress, 1960, Plaza Suite, 1970, I Do, I Do, (musical) 1973, Same Time Next Year, 1977, Moon Over Buffalo, 1995 (Tony nomination), co-wrote play (with Carrie Hamilton), Hollywood Arms, 2001; films include Who's Been Sleeping in My Bed, 1963, Pete 'n' Tillie, 1972, Front Page, 1974, A Wedding, 1977, Health, 1979, Four Seasons, 1981, Chu Chu and the Philly Flash, 1981, Annie, 1982, Noises Off, 1992, Moon Over Broadway, 1997, Get Bruce, 1999, The Trumpet of the Swan (voice), 2001; TV movies Friendly Fire, 1978, The Grass is Always Greener Over the Septic Tank, 1979, The Tenth Month, 1979, Life of the Party, 1982, Between Friends, 1983, Hostage, 1988, Men, Movies, and Carol, 1994, Seasons of the Heart, 1994, The Marriage Fool, 1998 (American Comedy award, 1998), Grace, 1998; club engagements, Harrah's Club, The Sands, Caesar's Palace, MGM Grand; TV specials Julie and Carol: Together Again, 1989, Happy Birthday Elizabeth: A Celebration of Life, 1997, Putting it Together, 2000, Carol Burnett: Show Stoppers, 2001; TV series Mad About You, 1996-1998; TV miniseries Fresno, 1986, A Century of Women, 1994; dir., writer The Universal Story, 1995, also prodr. Southern Star: Portrait of Atlanta, 1996; prodr. Fred Astaire: Puttin' On His Top Hat, 1980, Fred Astaire: Change Partners and Dance, 1980, Bacall on Bogart, 1988, Fred Astaire Songbook, 1991, Southern Star: A Portrait of Atlanta, 1996, others. Recipient outstanding comedienne award Am. Guild Variety Artists, 5 times; Emmy award for outstanding variety performance Acad. TV Arts and Scis., 5 times; Emmy award for best supporting actress in a comedy series for Mad About You, 1997; TV Guide award for outstanding female performer, 1961, 62, 63; Peabody award, 1963; Golden Globe award for outstanding comedienne of year Fgn. Press Assn., 8 times; Woman of Year award Acad. TV Arts and Scis.; 12 People's Choice awards; 1st ann. Nat. TV Critics Circle award for outstanding performance, 1977; San Sebastian Film Festival award for best actress for A Wedding, 1978; 1st Ace award Best Actress Between Friends, 1983, Horatio Alger award Horatio Alger Assn. Disting. Ams., 1988; named One of 20 Most Admired Women Gallup Poll, 1977. Address: ICM 8942 Wilshire Blvd Fl 2 Beverly Hills CA 90211-1934

BURNETT, CLARENCE AUBREY (RUSTY BURNETT), personnel services company executive; b. Seagraves, Tex., May 29, 1941; s. Raymond Otis and Mae Adeline (Pollock) B.; m. Dinah Kay Castle, June 7, 1961 (div. Mar. 1973); children: Barbara Ann, Sara Kathryn; m. Susan Elaine Walk, Dec. 27, 1973. BBA, U. Tex., 1963. From analyst to mgr. Ea. ops. Continental Pipeline Co., Houston, 1963—75; pres. The Burnett Cos., Houston, 1975-95, exec. v.p., CFO, 1995—. Mem. Nat. Assn. Temporary Services (bd. dirs. 1986-91), Tex. Assn. Temproary Services (bd. dirs. 1985-86). Republican. Avocations: flying, scuba diving, golf, tennis, running. Home: 201 Vanderpool Ln Apt 34 Houston TX 77024-6124 Office: The Burnett Cos Inc 9800 Richmond Ave Ste 800 Houston TX 77042-4548 E-mail: rusty@burnettps.com.

BURNETT, CRYSTAL BLYTHE, marketing professional; b. Moundridge, Kans., Nov. 12, 1965; d. John Milford and Judy Carlene (Stucky) S.; married, 1993. Student, Wichita State U., 1984-87; BS in Journalism, U. Kans., 1989. Cert. mktg. dir. Dispatcher, sec. Digital Computing Ctr., Wichita, Kans., 1985-86; production asst. Stephan Advt. Agy., Wichita, 1986-87; asst. to exec. sec. Kans. Scholastic Press Assn., Lawrence, 1987-89; recreation leader Boston Recreation Ctr., Wichita, 1987; profl. intern The Clay Ctr. Dispatch, Clay Center, Kans., 1988; photography stringer AP, 1988; profl. intern Stephan Advt. Agy., Wichita, 1989; retail exec. trainee Dillard Dept. Stores, Inc., Wichita, 1989-90, area sales mgr., 1990-91; asst. mktg. dir. West Ridge Mall, Topeka, 1991-92, The Forum Shops at Caesers, Las Vegas, Nev., 1992; mktg. dir. Machesney Park (Ill.) Mall, 1992-94, West Ridge Mall, Topeka, Kans., 1994-98; regional mktg. dir. Simon Property Group, Little Rock, Ark., 1998-99, Independence, Mo., 1999—. Mem. steering com. Topeka Breast Cancer Coalition; bd. dirs. Honor A Student Incentive Program, 1995-98. Recipient U.S. Nat. Leadership Merit award, 1984; Frances E. Taylor scholar, U. Kans., 1988. Mem. Am. Mktg. Assn. (Nat. and Kansas City chpts.), Internat. Coun. Shopping Ctrs. (Cert. Mktg. Dir. 2000), Topeka C. of C. (Honor A bd. dirs.), Order of Omega, Alpha Phi (promotions chmn. and philanthropy chmn. Gamma Xi chpt. 1984—). Office: Simon Property Group Kansas City Regional Office 14825 E 42d St Ste 240 Independence MO 64055 E-mail: cburnett@simon.com.

BURNETT, E. C., III, state supreme court justice; b. Spartanburg, S.C., Jan. 26, 1942; s. E.C. Jr. and Lucy (Byars) B.; m. Jami Grant, 1963; children: Curry, Sharon, Jeffrey. AB, Wofford Coll., 1964; JD, U. S.C., 1969. Bar: S.C. 1969. Mem. S.C. Ho. of Reps., 1973-74; probate judge Spartanburg County, 1976-80; judge family ct., 1980-81, Seventh Jud. Cir., 1981-95; assoc. justice S.C. Supreme Ct., 1995—. Elder Mt. Calvary Presbyn. Ch. Mem. ABA, S.C. Bar Assn. Home: 200 Burnett Rd Pauline SC 29374-2610 Office: State Supreme Court PO Box 11330 Columbia SC 29211*

BURNETT, ELIZABETH (BETSY BURNETT), counselor; b. Ohio; m. Gilbert C. Burnett, Jan. 2, 1973; children: Jeffrey, Stephanie. BS in Med. Tech. with honors, Rutgers U., 1976; MA in Counseling with honors, Denver Sem., 1992. Lic. prof. counselor, Colo.; nat. cert. counselor; master addictions counselor. Med. technologist various hosps., Denver and Plainfield, N.J., 1976-92; missions dir. Bear Creek Ch. and Family of Faith Ch., Denver, 1985-89; dir. Providence Counseling Ministry and Providence Homes, Denver, 1989-99; ind. counselor, psychology instr. C.C. Aurora, 1999—. Program cons. various urban counseling svcs. and rehabs., Denver, Colorado Springs, Mich., Calif., Australia, 1992—; urban ministry cons. Denver Sem., 1991-99; contract counselor So. Gables Ch., Littleton, Colo., 1992-96, presenter divorce recovery workshops, 1992-96; ministry ptnr. Mosaic Ch., 2002—; spkr. in field. Author: Handbook of Urban Christian Counseling, 1992. Children's dir. mothers of preschoolers, vacation Bible sch., and missions edn. program Bear Creek Ch., Denver, 1982-85; deaconess, lay leader So. Gables Ch., Littleton, 1992-96. Recipient med. tech. award Muhlenberg Hosp., 1976. Mem. Am. Assn. Christian Counselors, Am. Soc. Clin. Pathologists. Avocations: reading, needlework, painting, hiking. Office: 7475 W 5th Ave Lakewood CO 80226

BURNETT, GARY MAIN, social work administrator, crisis counselor; b. Pontiac, Mich., Sept. 14, 1951; s. Kenneth Almeron Burnett and Thalia Ann (Main) Cather; m. Gail Susan Hewitt, Sept. 21, 1974; children: Alexander Main, Adam Tyler. BS in Psychology, No. Mich. U., Marquette, 1973; MA in Counseling, Oakland U., Rochester, Mich., 1977. Lic. profl. counselor, Mich.; cert. social worker, Mich. Asst. mgr. K-Mart Corp., Mt. Morris, Mich., 1974-75; coord. residence hall Oakland U., Rochester, 1975-78, adminstrv. asst., 1978-80, asst. dir. student affairs, 1980; exec. dir. Threshold Counseling Svcs., Royal Oak, Mich., 1980-84; client svcs. mgr. Cmty. Placement Program, Mt. Clemens, Mich., 1984-86; dir. Macomb County Crisis Ctr., Mt. Clemens, 1986—. Mem. adv. bd. Sq. Lake Mental Health, Pontiac, Mich., 1988-89; chmn. adv. coun. Macomb County Substance Abuse Svcs., Mt. Clemens, 1990—; clin. coord. Macomb Emergency Response Group, Mt. Clemens, 1991—. Chmn. bd. dirs. Common Ground, Birmingham, Mich., 1978-81; supr. Milestones Crisis Residential Svcs., Macomb County, 1996-98, Homeless Assistance Program, Macomb County, 1997-2002; bd. dirs. Macomb Homeless Coalition, 1999-2002. Recipient Vol. Svc. award Gov. William Milliken, Birmingham, 1977, Plaque of Appreciation, Common Ground Bd. Dirs., Birmingham, 1981. Mem. Mich. Crisis Response Assn., Internat. Critical Incident Stress Found., Warren Hist. Soc., The Planetary Soc., Maple Leaf Club, House of Burnett, Inc. Avocations: piano, genealogy, astronomy. Home: 3829 Dawson Ave Warren MI 48092-3209 Office: Macomb County Crisis Ctr 46360 Gratiot Ave Chesterfield MI 48051-2800 E-mail: gburnett18@comcast.net.

BURNETT, GEORGE JOHN, internist; b. Buffalo, Oct. 25, 1943; s. Joseph and Margaret (Palkawsky) B.; m. Maria-Antoinette Garuti; children: George Joseph Jr., Jeffrey, Lisa. BA, SUNY, Buffalo, 1961-65; MD, U. Bologna, Italy, 1971. Intern Millard Fillmore Hosp., Buffalo, 1971-72, resident, 1972-74, chief med. resident, 1974-75, attending, staff physician, 1975—; clin. asst. prof. SUNY Sch. Medicine, Buffalo, 1975—, preceptor in cmty. acad. practice, 1993; pvt. practice, Williamsville, N.Y., 1975—. Maj. USAR, 1972-80. Fellow ACP; mem. N.Y. State Soc. Internal Medicine, Erie County Med. Soc. Republican. Roman Catholic. Home: 22 Summit Ave Buffalo NY 14214-2306 Office: 8600 Sheridan Dr Williamsville NY 14221-6233

BURNETT, HENRY, lawyer; b. N.Y.C., Feb. 24, 1927; s. Lucien Dallam and Ruth (Hinkle) B.; m. Florence Stewart, July 19, 1952; children: Marian Starr, Betsy Callaway, Henry Stewart. BA, U. Va., 1947, LLB, 1950. Bar: Va. bar 1950, Fla. bar 1951. Ptnr. Fowler, White, Burnett, Hurley, Banick & Strickroot, Miami, Fla., 1957-93, pres., 1957-93; ptnr. Fowler, White, Burnett and predecessor firm, Miami, Fla., 1993—. Bd. dirs. Dade County Citizens Safety Council, Travelers Aid, United Family and Children's Services. Served with USNR, 1945-46. Fellow Am. Coll. Trial Lawyers; mem. Am., Fla., Dade County bar assns., Fla. Def. Lawyers Assn. (pres. 1967-68), Dade County Def. Bar Assn. (pres. 1966-67), Internat. Assn. Def. Counsel (exec. com. 1972-74, pres. 1976-77). Clubs: Riviera Country. Episcopalian. Home: 8871 SW 68th Ave Miami FL 33156 Office: Nations Bank Tower 100 SE 2nd St Fl 18 Miami FL 33131-2195

BURNETT, HOWARD JEROME, academic administrator emeritus; b. Holyoke, Mass., Oct. 14, 1929; s. William and Bridget (Breck) B.; m. Barbara J. Ransohoff, June 12, 1954 (dec. Mar. 1991); children: Lee Ann, Sue Allison, Mark Howard; m. Maryann de Palma, May 28, 1994. BA, Amherst Coll., 1952, Oxford U., 1954, MA (Rhodes scholar), 1958; LL.D., Ithaca Coll., 1965; PhD, N.Y. U., 1965; DHL, Washington and Jefferson Coll., 1998. Cons. Booz, Allen & Hamilton, 1958; sec. A.L. Ransohoff Co., Inc., N.Y.C., 1958-60; mem. internatl. econs. staff Texaco, Inc., N.Y.C., 1960-62; asst. to pres. Corning (N.Y.) Community Coll., 1962-64; pres. Coll. Center of the Finger Lakes, Corning, 1964-70, Washington and Jefferson Coll., Washington, Pa., 1970-99, pres. emeritus, 1999—. Civilian aide to Sec. of the Army for Western Pa., 1978-80; mem. Nat. Adv. Bd. on Internat. Edn. Programs, U.S. Dept. Edn., 1987-88. Served to lt. USNR, 1955-58. Mem. Assn. Am. Rhodes Scholars, Duquesne Club, Rolling Rock Club, Phi Beta Kappa, Delta Kappa Epsilon.

BURNETT, JEAN BULLARD (MRS. JAMES R. BURNETT), biochemist; b. Flint, Mich., Feb. 19, 1924; d. Chester M. and Katheryn (Krasser) Bullard; B.S., Mich. State U., 1944, M.S., 1945, Ph.D. (Council fellow), 1952; m. James R. Burnett, June 8, 1947. Research assoc. dept. zoology Mich. State U., East Lansing, 1954-59, dept. biochemistry, 1959-61, acting dir. research biochem. genetics, dept. biochemistry, 1961-62, assoc. prof., asst. chmn. dept. biomechanics, 1973-82, prof. dept. anatomy, 1982-84, prof. dept. zoology, Coll. Natural Sci. and Coll. Osteo. Medicine, 1984— ; assoc. biochemist Mass. Gen. Hosp., Boston, 1964-73; prin. research assoc. dermatology Harvard, 1962-73, faculty medicine, 1964-73, also spl. lectr., cons., tutor Med. Sch.; vis. prof. dept. biology U. Ariz., 1979-80. USPHS, NIH grantee, 1965-68; Gen. Research Support grantee Mass. Gen. Hosp., 1968-72; Ford Found. travel grantee, 1973; Am. Cancer Soc. grantee, 1971-73; Internat. Pigment Cell Conf. travel grantee, 1980; recipient Med. Found. award, 1970. Mem. AAAS, Am. Chem. Soc., Am. Inst. Biol. Sci., Genetics Soc. Am., Soc. Investigative Dermatology, N.Y. Acad. Scis., Sigma Xi (Research award 1971), Pi Kappa Delta, Kappa Delta Pi, Pi Mu Epsilon, Sigma Delta Epsilon. Home: PO Box 805 Okemos MI 48805-0805 Office: Mich State Univ Dept Zoology Natural Sci Bldg East Lansing MI 48824

BURNETT, KATHARINE PERSIS, art historian, educator; b. Stoughton, Wis., Dec. 5, 1955; d. Peter Paul Alexander and Doret M. Burnett; m. Robert H. Moustakas, Aug. 27, 1988; children: Sacha B. Moustakas, Misha B. Moustakas. BA, Wellesly Coll., 1978; MA, U. Mich., 1986, cert. grad. studies, 1989, PhD, 1995. Vis. instr. art history Kalamazoo (Mich.) Coll., 1990; vis. asst. prof. art history U. Mich., Dearborn, 1990—91, Ohio State U., Columbus, 1996—97; postdoctoral fellow, lectr. art history U. So. Calif., L.A., 1997—98; asst. prof. art history program and East Asian langs. and cultures U. Calif., Davis, 1998—2000, asst. prof. art history program, 1998—. Art cons. Tao Xin Zhai; vol. Taipei Art Guild, Taibei, Taiwan, 1980, dir., 81; curatorial intern Indpls. Mus. Art, 1988—89; cons. Chinese Ceramics Collection Domino's Pizza Inc., Ann Arbor, Mich., 1989—90; curatorial asst. U. Mich. Mus. Art, 1991; presenter in field. Contbr. articles to profl. jours. Recipient Summer stipend, NEH, 2000; postdoctoral fellow, Andrew W. Mellon Found., U. So. Calif., 1997—98. Mem.: AAUW, AAUP, Fulbright Assn., Lee Inst. for Japanese Art, Oriental Ceramic Soc., Assn. for Asian Studies, Coll. Art Assn. Office: Univ Calif Dept Art and Art History 1 Shields Ave Davis CA 95616

BURNETT, LONNIE SHELDON, obstetrics and gynecology educator; b. Saratoga, Tex., Aug. 2, 1927; s. Lonnie and Lois (Swift) B.; m. Betty Pearle Scruggs, Dec. 22, 1950; children: Anne Julian, Michael Julian. BS, U. Tex., 1948; MD, U. Tex., Galveston, 1953. Diplomate Am. Coll. Obstetricians and Gynecologists (chmn. Tenn. sect. 1988-91, mem. com. on sci. program, 1988-91). Intern Henry Ford Hosp., Detroit, 1953-54; resident in internal medicine Mayo Clinic, Rochester, Minn., 1954-55; resident in ob-gyn Johns Hopkins Hosp., Balt., 1957-62, fellow in microbiology, 1962-64; asst. prof. microbiology Johns Hopkins U., Balt., 1964-67, asst. prof. ob-gyn., 1964-70, assoc. prof., 1970-76; chmn. dept. ob-gyn. Vanderbilt U., Nashville, 1976-95, prof. ob-gyn., 1976—, Frances and John C. Burch prof. ob-gyn., 1995—. Mem. ob-gyn. text com. Nat. Bd. Med. Examiners, 1988-91. Co-author: Novak's Textbook of Gynecology, 11th edit., 1988; contbr. articles to profl. jours. Capt. USAF, 1955-57. Macy scholar Josiah Macy Jr. Found., 1965-70. Mem.: Nashville Acad. Medicine (pres. 1999—2000), Tenn. Ob-Gyn. Soc. (pres. 1988—90). Republican. Episcopalian. Avocation: photography. Home: 78 Concord Park W Nashville TN 37205-4707 Office: Vanderbilt Med Ctr N Dept Ob-Gyn 1611 21st Ave S Nashville TN 37212-3103 E-mail: lsburnett@comcast.net.

BURNETT, MARY PARHAM, lawyer, airline captain; b. Jacksonville, Fla., Feb. 19, 1956; d. William Harold and Mary (Copeland) P.; m. Lane Thomas Burnett, Jan. 12, 1985. BA, Western State Coll., Colo., 1976; BS in Hotel-Restaurant Adminstrs., Fla. State U., 1977, JD, 1984. Bar: Fla. 1985, Colo. 1999, U.S. Dist. Ct. (mid. dist.) Fla. 1985; cert. arbitrator/mediator. Capt. Am. Airlines, 1985—; expert witness, legal cons. Prof. aviation law Jacksonville U. Recipient Order of the Daedalians, Civil Airmanship award, 1998, Am. Airlines Spirit of Am. award, 1998. Mem. Aircraft Owners and Pilots Assn. (panel atty. legal svcs. plan), Fla. Bar (cert. aviation lawyer 1997—, aviation law cert. com. 1998-2002), Jacksonville Bar Assn., The Ninety-Nines Inc., Fla. Real Estate Brokers, Jacksonville Airport Authority (inagural bd. mem., 2001-05). Republican. Methodist. Avocations: water/snow skiing, racquetball, bicycling, boating, fishing. Home: 3745 Beauclerc Circle N Jacksonville FL 32257-4923 Office: Lane Burnett PA 331 E Union St Jacksonville FL 32202-2787 E-mail: mpburnett@attbi.com.

BURNETT, PATRICIA HILL, portrait artist, author, sculptor, lecturer; b. Bklyn. d. William Burr and Mimi (Uline) Hill; m. William Anding Lange, 1944 (div. 1947); 1 child, William Hill; m. Harry Albert Burnett III,, Oct. 9, 1948 (dec. 1979); children: Harry Burnett III, Terrill Hill, Hillary Hill; m. Robert L. Siler, 1989. Student, U. Toledo, 1937-38, Goucher Coll., 1939-41, MA program Inst. D'Allende, Mex., 1967, Wayne State U., 1972; pvt. studies with, John Carroll, Detroit, 1941-44, Sarkis Sarkisian, 1956-60, Wallace Bassford, Provincetown, Mass., 1968-72, Walter Midener, Detroit, 1960-63. Actress Long Ranger and Green Hornet prgrams, Radio Blue Network, 1941-46; tchr. painting and sculpture U. Mich. Extension, Ann Arbor, 1965—. Lectr. N.Y. Speakers Bur., 1971—; propr. Burnett Studios, Detroit, 1962-88, mgr., 1962—; appt. to Mich. Quarter Commn. by gov. Engler, 2002. Numerous one-woman shows of paintings and sculptures include Scarab Club, Detroit, 1971, Midland (Mich.) Art Ctr., Wayne State U., Detroit, The Gallery, Ft. Lauderdale, Fla., Agra Gallery, Washington, Salon des Artes, Paris; numerous group shows include: Palazzo Pruili Gallery, Venice, 1971, Detroit Inst. of Arts, 1967, Butler Mus., Cleveland, 1972, Windsor (Ont., Can.) Art Ctr., 1973, Weisbaden (Germany) Gallery, 1976, Retrospective Show: Birmingham Bloomfield Art Assn., 1997; represented in permanent collections: Detroit Inst. Arts, Wayne State U., Wooster (Ohio) Coll., Ford Motor Co., Detroit, Bloomfield Art Assn., Bloomfield Hills, Mich., Henry Ford Hosp. Collection, Fed. Ct. Appeals in Washington, City-County Bldg., Detroit, Mich. State Capitol Bldg., Royal Acad. of Art, London, Moscow Mus., Moscow, Russia, Mich. State Capital, Lansing, Mich., Royal Palace of India, New Delhi, Palace of The Philippines, Manila, Mansion of Prime Minister, Greece; also pvt. collections: numerous portrait paintings including Indira Ghandi, Benson Ford, Joyce Carol Oates, Mrs. Edsel Ford, Betty Ford, Mayor Roman Gribbs, Princess Olga Mrivani, Lord John Mackintosh, Marlo Thomas, Viveca Lindfois, Betty Freidan, Gloria Steinem, Congresswoman Martha Griffiths, Margaret Papandreou, Valentina Tereshkova, Barbara Walters, Margaret Thatcher, Corazon Aquino, Violetta Chamarra, Jackie Joyner Kersee, Mayor Dennis Archer, Wayne U. pres. David Adamany, author Kate Millett, Michele Engler and triplets, Patricia Ireland, Rosa Parks, others; mem. editl. bd. Am. Portrait Soc.; author: True Colors: An Artist's Journey from Beauty Queen to Feminist. Chairwoman of Mich. Women's Commn., 1972—; pres. Detroit House of Correction Commn., 1975—; treas. Rep. Dist. I of Mich., 1973—; mem. Issues com., Rep. State Ctrl. Com., 1975-76; sec. Rep. State Ways and Means com., 1975—, Detroit Libr. Commn., 1980-85, Detroit Human Rights Commn., 1976-80, Detroit City Planning Commn., 1985-90; mem. Mich. State Adv. Coun. vocat. Edn.; mem. Mich. Arts in Edn. Coun., 1978—; mem. New Detroit Arts Com., 1979—; chmn. World Feminist Commn., 1974—; life mem. NAACP. Recipient Silver Salute award Mich. State U., 1976, Most Popular award San Diego Sculpture Show, 1971, First prize award Cape Cod Artists Show, 1968, State of Mich. award for creativity Gov. John Engler, 1999, Life Accomplishment award Mich. Women's Found., 2001; named Disting. Woman of Mich., Bus. and Profl. Women's Orgn., 1974, Disting. Woman Northwood Inst., 1977, Artist of Yr., Mich. Art Train, 1989, Disting. Woman award Mich. Bus. and Profl. Women Internat.; named to Ohio Hall of Fame, 1987, Mich. Women's Hall of Fame, 1988, one of Most Outstanding Women in Mich., Women in Advt., 1998, one of 10 People with Most Clout Outside of County, Detroit Free Press, 1998, one of 95 Most Powerful Women in Mich., Corp. Mag., 2002; elected to Internat. Hall of Fame, 2002. Mem. Mich. Women's Forum (founder 1989, bd. dirs. 1989-99, Internat. Women's Forum, bd. dirs. 1989-99), Detroit Inst. Arts (dir. membership com. 1958—), Nat. Assn. Commns. for Women (pres. 1976-78), Mich. Acad. of Arts, Detroit Soc. Women Painters and Sculptprs, Women in the Arts, Scrab Club (dir. 1962-63), Ibex Club (pres. 1951), NOW (nat. bd. 1971-75, del. UN conf. Mex., 1975, Feminist of Yr.), Coun. Leading portrait Painters (elect), Women's Econ. Club, N.Y. Portrait Club (nat. adv. bd. 1977—), French-Am. C.of C. (v.p.), Alpha Phi, Zonta, Detroit Econ. Club (bd. dirs.) Episcopalian. Home: 13 Oaks Ct Bloomfield Hills MI 48304-2120

BURNETT, SUSAN WALK, personnel service company owner; b. Galveston, Tex., Aug. 21, 1946; d. Joe Decker and Ruth Corinne (Lowe) Walk; m. Rusty Burnett, Dec. 27, 1973; stepchildren: Barbara, Sara. BA in Journalism, U. Ark., Fayetteville, 1968. Asst. pub. rels. mgr. Sta. KATV, Little Rock, 1968-69; speech writer Assoc. Milk Producers, Inc., Little Rock, 1969-70; mgr. Allied Personnel, Houston, 1970-74; owner, pres. Burnett Pers. Svcs., Houston, 1974—. Exec. bd. dirs. Arthritis Found.; bd. dirs. Goodwill, Better Bus. Bur. Recipient Appreciation awards Lyndon Johnson Space Ctr., NASA, 1983, State of Tex., 1984, Top Houston Woman Bus. Owner award Nat. Assn. Women Bus. Owners, 1996, Blue Chip award U.S. C. of C., Philanthrophy award Houston Bus. Jour.; named one of 10 Women on the Move in Houston, Houston Chronicle, 1996, Most Outstanding Woman in Bus. YWCA, 1997, Entrepreneur of Yr., 1998; named 2001 Woman Bus. Entrepreneur, Women's Bus. Enterprise Alliance; named to 2000 Women of Excellence, Women's Enterprise. Mem.: Am. Staffing Assn. (bd. dirs.), Houston Assn. Pers. Cons. (v.p. 1985, pres. 1986, Outstanding Contbn. to Placement Industry and Cmty. award 1995), Tex. Assn. Pers. Cons. (v.p. 1985), Nat. Assn. Pers. Cons., Chi Omega Alumnae. Avocations: reading, golf, travel. Office: Burnett Staffing Specialists Inc 9800 Richmond Ave Ste 800 Houston TX 77042-4548

BURNETTE, ADA M. PURYEAR, educational administrator; b. Darlington, S.C. d. Theodore and Floia (King) Peoples; m. Paul Lionel Puryear, March 27, 1954 (div. 1975); children: Paul Lionel, Jr., Paula Lynn. BA in Math., Talladega Coll., 1953; postgrad., Chgo. State U., 1954-56; MA in Reading, U. Chgo., 1958; PhD, Fla. State U., 1986; postgrad., Fla. A&M U., 1994. High sch. math tchr., Winston-Salem, N.C., 1953-54; elem. tchr. Chgo. Pub. Schs., 1954-58; reading clinician U. Chgo., 1958; dir. reading clinic, asst. prof. Norfolk State U., 1958-61, Tuskegee Inst., 1961-66; coord. freshman math., asst. prof. math. Fisk U., 1966-70; adminstr. early childhood basic skills and elem. edn. State of Fla. Dept. Edn., Tallahassee, 1973-88; assoc. prof., program dir., grad. studies dir. Bethune-Cookman Coll., Daytona Beach, Fla., 1988-90; dir., supt. Fla. A&M Univ. Devel. Rsch. Pub. Sch. Dist., Tallahassee, 1990-93; coord., prof., dept. chmn., dir. PhD program devel. Fla. A&M Univ., 1993-98, coord., prof., 1998—, prof., dir. Robert H. Anderson Ednl. Leadership Libr., 1998—. Pres. Faculty Senate Fla. A&M U., 1999—; hostess radio talk show, 1977—79; sec.-treas. Afro-Am. Rsch. Assocs., 1968—74; tutor, diagnostician, lectr., cons., planner, 1958—; cons. Job Corps, N.C. Advancement Sch., pub. co.; lectr. univ. classes. Regular columnist profl. jours., 1974—; writer grants proposals; weekly columnist Capital Outlook, 1991-97, contbr. articles to profl. publs. Pres. PTA, 1975—76, v.p., 1983—84; edn. commentator Sta. WFSU, 1993—94; mem. NAACP, United Fund com., Leon County 4C Bd., Urban League; pres. Norfolk Women's Interracial Coun., 1960; trustee Fla. A&M U., 2003—; del. state dem. women's meeting, Fla., 1978, 1979; mem. Dem. Exec. Com. Leon County, 1981—88, 1991—93. Mem.: Fla. Soc. Cert. Pub. Mgrs. (newsletter bd.), Am. Assn. Sch. Adminstrs., Socs. Docta Inc. (sec. 1987—93), So. Assn. Colls. and Schs. (elem. and mid. sch. commn.), Assn. Childhood Edn. Internat., Leon Assn. Children Under Six (pres. 1977), So. Assn. Children Under Six, Fla. Assn. Children Under Six, Nat. Assn. Edn. Young Children, Nat. Assn. Elem. Sch. Prins., Internat. Reading Assn. (nat. early childhood com., nat. textbook com., nat. awards com., nat. media com., pres. Concerned Educators Black Students 1983—86, nat. med. com., libr./media com.), Fla. ASCD (regional dir. policy rev. jour. editl. bd. 1995—), Alliance of Black Sch. Educators, Assn. State Cons. on Early Childhood Edn., Fla. State Reading Assn., Fla. Coun. Elem. Edn., Fla. Assn. Suprs. and Adminstrs., The Holidays (pres., v.p., nat. sec. fin. 1993—97, nat. v.p. 1997—2001, nat. pres. 2001—), Drifters (pres., nat. membership chmn. 1977—79, historian, reporter 1992—94, pres. 1994—, Nat. Now Black Woman 1984), FAMU Ladies Art and Social Club (pres.), Alpha Kappa Alpha (treas., summer sch. dir., undergrad. adv., parliamentarian sec.), Pi Lambda Theta, Phi Kappa Phi (pres. 1985—86, v.p. pub. rels. chair), Phi Delta Kappa. Presbyterian (deacon). Home: PO Box 38543 Tallahassee FL 32315-8543 Office: Fla A&M U Gore Edn Ctr C-204A Tallahassee FL 32307 *Never do anything illegal or immoral as you strive for excellence and do your best in all you do in your journey to make this world a better place.*

BURNETTE, CHARLES GALYON, protective services official; b. Tampa, Fla., Nov. 20, 1958; s. Charles Galyon Burnette and Eugenia Sue Fowler; m. Pamela Lea Cannon, Sept. 5, 1981; children: Autumn Lea, Heather Miranda. AA in Criminal Justice, Okaloosa-Walton Jr. Coll., 1978, BA in Criminal Justice with honors, 1980. Patrol officer St. Petersburg Police Dept., 1982-85, burglary detective, 1985-88, acting sgt., 1988-89, sgt. patrol divsn., 1989-90, 92-99, sgt. field tng., 1990-92, detective sgt. divsn. vice and narcotics, 1999—. Mem. task force St. Petersburg's Crime Prevention through Environ. Design, 1998—. Loaned exec. United Way, St. Petersburg, 1998, mem. Keel Club, 1998-2000, 2002. Recipient Herman Goldstein Internat. award for Individual Problem

Solving in Policing, 1996. Mem. NRA, Fla. Narcotics Officer's Assn., Alpha Phi Sigma, Lambda Alpha Epsilon, Phi Kappa Phi. Avocation: reading. Home: 8273-101 Court N Seminole FL 33777 Office: St Petersburg Police Dept 1300-1 Ave N Saint Petersburg FL 33705

BURNETTE, MARIE (HELEN MARIE BURNETTE), music educator; b. Eden, N.C., Feb. 9, 1940; d. Herbert H. and Helen E. (Short) B. BA, MusB, U. N.C., Greensboro, 1962, MusM, 1964. Dir. choir, organist Friendly Ave. Bapt. Ch., Greensboro, 1962-63; minister of music, edn. First Bapt. Ch., Kernersville, NC, 1963-64; pvt. practice piano instrn. High Point, NC, 1964—. Contbr. articles to profl. jours. Organist Green St. Bapt. Ch., High Point, 1964-67; music asst., organist Emerywood Bapt. Ch., 1989—; sec. Friends HP Libr., 1992-94; bd. dirs. High Point Cmty. Chorus, 1998—, Musical Art Guild U. N.C., 2000-02. Recipient Svc. award Emerywood Bapt. Ch., 2000. Mem. Am. Guild Organists, Music Tchrs. Nat. Assn. (sec., treas. Southern div. 1979-81, nat. sec. 1987-89), Ind. Music Tchrs. of Music Tchrs. Nat. Assn. (chmn. 1981-83), N.C. Music Tchrs. Assn. (pres. 1977-79, Svc. award 1984), High Point Piano Tchrs. (pres. 1975-76, 90-92, 99—, svc. award 1997), Music for Great Space (bd. dirs. 1995—), Piedmont Artists (v.p. 1989-90), N.C. Organ Festival, Mu Phi Epsilon, Pi Kappa Lambda. Republican. Avocations: reading, travel. Home and Office: 401 Nathan Hunt Dr High Point NC 27260-7824

BURNETTE, OLLEN LAWRENCE, JR., historian; b. Bethel, N.C., Sept. 30, 1927; s. Ollen Lawrence and Eva E. (Highsmith) B.; m. M. Elizabeth Tull, Aug. 25, 1951; children: Ollen L. III, Elizabeth B. Newsome-Cousins, Graham T., John H., William N.; m. Susan B. Spencer, Oct. 27, 1995; m. Jeanne A. MacRitchie, June 10, 2000. BA in History, U. Richmond, 1945; MA in History, U. Va., Charlottesville, 1948, PhD in History, 1952; LLD, Southwestern Adventist Coll., 1989. Instr. of history Petersburg (Va.) H.S., 1948-49, VMI, Lexington, 1951-53; editor Charles Scribner's Sons, N.Y.C., 1953-57; dir. publs. State Hist. Soc. Wis., Madison, 1957-63; rsch. prof. history, dept. chmn. Birmingham (Ala.)-So. Coll., 1963-72; dean of faculty, rsch. prof. history Stratford Coll., Danville, Va., 1972-74; vis. prof. history N.C. State A&T U., Greensboro, 1974-75; exec. dir. West Piedmont Planning Commn., Martinsville, Va., 1975-80; pres. Timber Ridge Enterprises, Ltd., Lynchburg, 1980—, Around Again, LLC, Cons., Lillian, 1996—. Asst. to supt. VMI, Lexington, 1981-86. Author: Beneath the Footnote: A Guide to the Use of American Historical Documentation, 1970, A Syllabus of American History, 1959, Wisconsin Witness to F. J. Turner, 1958; editor: Life in America, 1972, A Soviet View of the American Past, 1962, Coastal Kingdom: A History of Baldwin County, Alabama, 2001. Bd. dirs. Stonewall Jackson Hosp., Lexington, 1980-83; elder Timber Ridge Presbyn. Ch., Lexington, 1980—; moderator Shenandoah Presbytery, 1988. Mem. Am. Inst. Cert. Planners, Nat. Assn. Rev. Appraisers (sr.), Am. Hist. Assn., Orgn. Am. Historians, Va. Highlands Scottish Soc. (bd. dirs. 1989—), Omicron Delta Kappa, Phi Beta Kappa. Avocations: photography, hiking, travel. Home and Office: 34231 Kathryn Dr Lillian AL 36549-5105

BURNETTE, RALPH EDWIN, JR., judge; b. Lynchburg, Va., Sept. 25, 1953; s. Ralph Edwin and Carlease (Samuels) B. BA, Coll. William & Mary, 1975, JD, 1978. Bar: Va. 1978. Assoc. Edmunds & Williams, Lynchburg, 1978-83, ptnr., 1983-2001; gen. dist. ct. judge 24th Jud. Dist. Ct. Va., 2001—. Adj. prof. law Coll. William and Mary, 1996-2002, Washington & Lee U. Deacon Peakland Bapt. Ch., Lynchburg, 1983-86; pres. Kaleidoscope Festival, Lynchburg, 1985, Lynchburg Symphony Orch., 1989-91; bd. dirs. Centra Health, Inc., 1987-97, United Way Cen. Va., 1989-90, Amazement Sq. Children's Mus. Mem. Va. Bar Assn., Va. State Bar (pres. 1993-94, pres. young lawyers conf. 1985, chmn. com. on alternative dispute resolution 1985-89, mem. bar coun., 1986-95, vice chmn. standing com. on legal ethics 1986-88, chmn. com. on long range planning 1988-91, mem. exec. com. 1990-95), Lynchburg Bar Assn. (pres. 1991-92), Avocations: golf, music, boating. Office: Lynchburg Gen Dist Ct 905 Court St Lynchburg VA 24504

BURNETTE, THOMAS N. career officer; b. Oct. 23, 1944; Commd. U.S. Army, advanced through grades to lt. gen., 1997; now dep. comdr. Joint Forces Command, Norfolk, Va. Office: US Joint Forces Command 1562 Mitscher Ave #200 Norfolk VA 23551-2488

BURNEY, DEREK, information technology executive; BS in Computer Sci., Carleton U. V.p., mgr. IMSI, Ottawa, Canada; chief tech. officer Corel Corp., Ottawa, 1993—, pres., CEO, 2000—. Bd. dirs. Snowsuit Fund. Office: Corel Corp 1600 Carling Ave Ottawa ON Canada K1Z 8R7

BURNHAM, BRYSON PAINE, retired lawyer; b. Chgo., Oct. 11, 1917; s. Raymond and Patti (Paine) B.; m. Frances Katherine Burns, Feb. 8, 1941; children: Janice Young, Stephanie Paine. BA, U. Chgo., 1938, JD, 1940. Bar: Ill. 1940, Colo. 1983. Assoc., then ptnr. Mayer, Brown & Platt, Chgo., 1940-83; of counsel Shand, McLachlan and Newbold, Durango, Colo., 1985-93. Bd. dirs. Fort Lewis Coll. Found., 1986-2002. Home: 315 Highland Hill Dr Timberline View Estates Durango CO 81301

BURNHAM, CHRISTOPHER BANCROFT, federal agency administrator; b. N.Y.C., Sept. 28, 1956; s. Alexander O. and Joan B.; m. Courtney Burnham; 1 child, George Emerson. BA, Washington & Lee, 1980; MPA, Harvard U., 1992. Mem. N.Y. Futures Exch., N.Y.C., 1983-85; rep. Conn. Gen. Assembly, Hartford, 1987-92; banker First Boston, N.Y.C., 1990-93, Advest Corp. Fin., Hartford, 1993-95; former state treas. State of Conn., Hartford; chief fin. officer, asst. sec. for resource mgt. U.S. Dept. State, Washington, 2001—. Maj. USMCR, Persian Gulf War. Republican. Episcopalian. Office: US Dept State Bureau Fin Mgt & Policy 2201 C St NW Washington DC 20520 Office Fax: 202-647-8174.

BURNHAM, DANIEL PATRICK, aerospace transportation executive; b. Birmingham, Mich., Nov. 28, 1946; s. Edward Francis and Helen Cecilia (Keane) B.; m. Mary Margaret Cavanaugh, June 8, 1968; children: Daniel, Amy, Peter, Ellen. BS in Econs., Xavier U., 1968; MBA in Fin., U. N.H., 1970. Corp. controller Carborundum Corp., Niagara Falls, N.Y., 1976-78, dir. strategy devel., 1979-80, dir. abrasives mktg., 1980-81, gen. mgr. insulation div., 1981-82; v.p., controller Allied Corp., Morristown, N.J., 1982-84, v.p., gen. mgr. engineered plastics, 1984-86; pres. Plastics and Performance Matls. div. Allied-Signal Inc., Morristown, N.J., 1986-88, pres. fibers div., 1988-90; pres. AiResearch Group, Torrance, Calif., 1990-92, Allied-Signal Aerospace Co., Torrance, Calif., 1992-97; vice chmn., bd. dirs. Allied Signal, Lexington, Mass., 1997-98; COO, pres. Raytheon Co., Lexington, Mass., 1998, pres., 1998—99, chmn., pres., 1999—2000, chmn., CEO, 2000—03, chmn., 2003—. Bd. dirs. FleetBoston Fin. Corp.; chmn. Nat. Minority Supplier Development Coun.; mem., past chmn. exec. com Aerospace Industries Assn.; mem., past chmn. Pres. Nat. Security Telecomm. Adv. Coun. Trustee Xavier U.; mem. Congl. Medal of Honor Found. Bd. Served to capt. U.S. Army, 1970. Republican. Roman Catholic. Office: Raytheon Co 141 Spring St Lexington MA 02421-7899

BURNHAM, DAVID BRIGHT, writer, educator; b. Boston, Jan. 24, 1933; s. Addison Center and Dorothy (Moore) B.; m. Sophy Tayloe Doub, Mar. 12, 1960 (div. 1984); children: Sarah Tayloe, Molly Bright; m. Joanne Omang, 1985. BA, Harvard, 1955; DHL (hon.), John Jay Coll., CUNY, 2003. Reporter UPI, Washington, 1959-61, Newsweek mag., Washington, 1961-63; writer CBS, N.Y.C., 1963-65; asst. dir. Pres.'s Commn. Law Enforcement and Adminstrn. of Justice, Washington, 1965-67; reporter N.Y. Times, 1967-86; journalist/writer Aspen Inst. Humanistic Studies, 1980-82. Co-dir., co-founder Transactional Records Access Clearinghouse, 1989—; assoc. rsch. prof. S.I. Newhouse Sch. Pub. Communications, Syracuse U.; mem. adv. bd. EPIC. Author: The Rise of the Computer State, 1983, A Law Unto Itself: Power, Politics and the IRS, 1989 (Best Investigative Book Investigative Editors and Reporters 1990), Above The Law: Secret Deals, Political Fixes, and other Misadventures of the U.S. Dept. of Justice, 1996, Recipient George K. Polk award, L.I. U., 1968, Silurians award, 1968; N.Y. New spaper Guild award, 1968; Gold Typewriter award for investigative reporting N.Y. Reporters Assn., 1972; named fellow Alicia Patterson Found., 1987, Rockefeller Found. scholar, Bellagio, Italy, 1992. Home: 524 6th St SE Washington DC 20003-2705 E-mail: burnham@epic.org.

BURNHAM, DAVID HENDERSON, management consultant; b. Quincy, Mass., Mar. 4, 1942; s. Roger Appleton and Phyllis Katherine (Kline) B.; m. Frances Margarita Parry, Feb. 15, 1964; children: Amery Appleton, Hugh Tebault Ramseyer. BA, Northeastern U., 1964; MBA, Harvard U., 1969. With U.S. Peace Corps, Ethiopia, 1964—66; assoc. Sterling Inst., Boston, 1969; v.p., treas. McBer & Co., Boston, 1970-72, pres., 1972-77, David H. Burnham and Assocs., orgn. devel. cons., Boston, Singapore, Sydney, London, 1977-91; dir. strategic planning Interaction Assocs., Cambridge, Mass., 1992-94; ptnr. Burnham Rosen Group, Boston, 1994—. Proprietor Boston Athaeneum, 2000—. Producer film Motives Moving Business (Am. Film Festival award 1975); contbr. articles to profl. jours. Treas., v.p. Children's Mus., Boston, 1972-81, pres., CEO, 1981-83, chmn., 1984-86, hon. trustee, 1988—; pres. Cavalier King Charles Spaniel Club, Louisville, 1972-78; bd. dirs. Children's Mus., London, 1984-86, Mental Health Found., U.K., 1987-88, Drive for Youth Programme, U.K., 1986-91; mem. com. Derby Acad. Coun., Hingham, Mass., 1974-81; mem. vestry St. Stephen's Episcopal Ch., Cohasset. Honoree Boston Coun. for Arts for svc. to Boston Pub. Libr., 2000; recipient McKinsey award Harvard Bus. Rev., 1976. Mem.: ASTD, OD Network, Greater Boston Assn. Tng. and Devel. (dir. 1997—2000), New England Hist. and Genealogical Soc. (dir. 1999—), Assn. Mgmt. Edn. and Devel. (Eng.), Harvard Bus. Sch. Assn., Bostonian Soc. (life), Colonial Soc. Mass. (life), Cohasset Yacht Club, Cohasset Golf Club, Harvard Club (Boston), Somerset Club (Boston). Home: 30 Atlantic Ave Cohasset MA 02025-1803 Office: Burnham Rosen Group 199 State St Boston MA 02109-2648 E-mail: dburnham@burnrose.com.

BURNHAM, DONALD CLEMENS, manufacturing company executive; b. Athol, Mass., Jan. 28, 1915; s. Charles Richardson and Freda (Clemens) B.; m. Virginia Gobble, May 29, 1937 (dec. 2002); children: David Charles, Joan (Mrs. Robert Graham), John Carl, William Lawrence (dec.), Mary Barbara (Mrs. F. David Throop). BS in Mech. Engring, Purdue U., 1936, D.Eng. (hon.), 1959, Ind. Inst. Tech., 1963, Drexel Inst. Tech., 1964, Poly. Inst. Bklyn., 1967. With Gen. Motors Corp., 1936-54, asst. chief engr. Oldsmobile div., 1953-54; with Westinghouse Electric Corp., 1954-80, group v.p., 1962-63, pres., chief exec. officer, 1963-68, chmn., chief exec. officer, 1969-75, dir.-officer, 1975-80. Emeritus trustee Carnegie Inst., Am. Wind Symphony Orch., Pitts. Theol. Sem. Maj. AUS, WWII. Recipient Outstanding Achievement in Mgmt. award Am. Inst. Indsl. Engrs., 1964 Mem. ASME, Soc. Mfg. Engr. (Hoover Medal award 1978), Soc. Automotive Engrs., IEEE, Nat. Acad. Engring., Am. Assn. Engring. Socs. (Nat. Engring. award 1981). Home: 1290 Boyce Rd Apt C233 Pittsburgh PA 15241-3950

BURNHAM, HAROLD ARTHUR, pharmaceutical company executive, physician; b. Boston, Nov. 6, 1929; s. Howard Rowland and Edna Adelaide (Teachout) B.; m. Lucienne Jeanne Seas, June 28, 1952; children: Philippe Henri, Isabelle Jeanne BS, Union Coll., 1951; MA, Middlebury Coll., 1952; postgrad., Albany State Tchrs. Coll., 1953-54, Adelphi U., 1958-59, Nassau Community Coll., 1961-62; MD, U. Md., 1966. Diplomate Am. Bd. Med. Examiners, Am. Bd. Family Practice (charter). Tchr. sci., French and track team coach South Glens Falls Cen. High Sch., N.Y., 1952-54; med. rep., hosp. salesman Upjohn Co., Bklyn., 1956-62; intern South Baltimore Gen. Hosp., 1966-67; resident in family practice Glen Cove Community Hosp., N.Y., 1967-69; practice family medicine Glen Cove, 1969-75; assoc. med. dir. Winthrop Labs. div. Sterling Drug Inc., N.Y.C., 1975-76, med. dir. Glenbrook Labs. div., 1977, v.p. med. affairs, sr. v.p. Winthrop Product Inc., 1977-80, 1977-80, Sydney Ross Co. and Sterling Products Internat., N.Y.C., 1977-80; v.p., med. dir. Glenbrook Labs. div. Sterling Drugs, Inc., N.Y.C., 1980; med. dir. Choay Labs. Inc., N.Y.C., 1980-82; asst. med. dir. L.I. State Vets. Home, Stony Brook, 1993-94; primary care physician ambulatory care clinics Nassau County Dept. Health, Mineola, N.Y., 1995-96; physician, English transl. cons. hematology dept. Hotel Dieu Hosp., Paris, 2001—. Spl. cons. Labs. Choay, S.A., Paris, 1982—; asst. med dir. United Presbyn. Residence, Woodbury, N.Y., 1983-93; instr. Sch. Practical Nursing, Glen Cove Community Hosp., 1970-75; instr. geriatrics in coop. with Glen Cove Community Hosp. Family Practice Residency Program, 1983-93; cons., clinician in medicine Nassau County Pub. Health Dept., 1975-76, mem. long term health care com., 1989-96; med. cons. Webb Inst. Naval Architecture and Marine Design, Glen Cove, N.Y., 1970-96; clin. asst. prof., SUNY, 1993-94; attending physician infectious diseases HIV Clinic, Nassau County Med. Ctr., East Meadow, N.Y., 1995-96; preceptor family practice program North Shore U. Hosp. at Glen Cove, 1999—. N.Am. corr. weekly Internet French med. publ. Expression Médicale, 1998—. Scoutmaster Boy Scouts Am., Glens Falls, N.Y., 1953-54, com. mem., 1968—, merit badge counsellor for first aid, pub. health emergency care, chemistry and mammals for Sagamore dist., 1968—; mem. Clan Gordon, 1983—, bagpiper Highlanders Pipes and Drums Band, Locust Valley, N.Y., 1982—, chmn., 1986—; lay reader St. John's of Lattingtown Episcopal Ch., N.Y., 1968—, vestryman, 1983—, clk. of vestry, 1986—; 7-8th gr. Sunday Sch. tchr., 1967—; mem. search com. for new rector, 1993—, jr. high Sunday sch. tchr., 1967-; trustee Hawley Found., 1984—, v.p. bd., 1991-99, v.p. emeritus, 1999—; Rep. election site inspector Nassau County, 1997—; del. to 120th conf. Episcopal Diocese of L.I.; vol. primary care physician Project U.S.A., Rural Indian Health Svc. Ctrs., Oneida (N.Y.) Iroquois Reservation and Owyhee (Nev.) Indian Hosp., 1995—. Recipient Alvin H. Toffler award, North Shore U. Hosp. Class of 2002. Fellow Am. Acad. Family Physicians (charter); mem. AMA (life; 14 continuing edn. awards), Pan Am. Med. Soc., N.Y. State Med. Soc. (life), Nassau County Med. Soc. (life), L.I. Scottish Clans Assn. (trustee 1984—, piper to chief 1986—), Nu Sigma Nu. Episcopalian. Office: 18 Purdue Rd Glen Cove NY 11542-2009 E-mail: scorpio-6@erols.com.

BURNHAM, J. V. retired sales executive; b. Pascagoula, Miss., May 23, 1923; s. George Luther and Eli Vashti (Hough) B.; m. Patti Lauri Latham, May 18, 1946; children: James Steven, Jon Douglas, Richard Scott, Bruce Edward, Vernon Alan. AA, Jones County (Miss.) Jr. Coll., 1946; AS, Rochester Inst. Tech., 1948; BS, U. Houston, 1951, MEd, 1963. Mgr. The Progress-Item, Ellisville, Miss., 1948-50; asst. prof., asst. mgr. U. Houston Journalism and Printing Plant, 1950-57; estimator, product supt. purchasing Chas. P. Young Co., Houston, 1957-67, asst. sec.-treas., 1967-69, v.p. sales, 1969-91, sr. v.p., 1991—2001, ret., 2001. Assoc. editor Am. Oceanography, 1968-71; southwest corr. Inland Printer and Nat. Lithographer, 1952-60. Founding mem. Am. Air Mus.; pres. Printing Industries of Gulf Coast, Houston, 1971—73; chmn. emeritus, bd. dirs. Tex. Printing Edn. Found., Houston; active The Heritage Found., The Concord Coalition, Adm. Nimitz Found., Am. Air Mus., Hist. Mt. Vernon, Young America's Found., Rep. Presdl. Task Force, Nat. Rep. Senatorial Com. Order of Merit, Nat. Rep. Congl. Com.; life, chmns. adv. bd. Rep. Nat. Com.; active Rep. Party of Tex., Rep. Nat. Candidate Trust, George Bush Pres. Libr. & Mus., Reagan Pres. Found., Young Am. Found., Judicial Watch. Lt. USNR, 1943—46. Recipient Scouters award Boy Scouts Am., 1960, Scouters Key award, 1965, Wood Badge award, 1964; named Man of Yr., Houston Graphics Soc., 1968, Printing Industry of Gulf Coast, 1970. Mem.: BAMPAC, Rochester Inst. tech. Alumni Assn., Tex. Police Officers Assn., Pres's. Club of Chas. P. Young Co. (charter, Outstanding Sales Achivement award), Mt. Vernon Ladies Assn., Juvenile Diabetes Found., Am. Diabetes Assn., Am. Kidney Found., High Frontier, Hummel Collectors Club (Houston), Crime Stoppers of Houston (gold cir. member), Ducks Unltd., U.S. Navy Meml. Found., Naval Aviation Mus. Found., Houston Public TV, United Srs. Assn., WWII Meml. Found., Claremont Inst., Nat. Eagle Scout Assn. (life), Tex. State Rifle Assn. (life), Naval Airship Assn. (life), Am. Legion (life), U. Houston Alumni (life), Jones County Jr. Coll. Alumni (life), U.S. Navy Pub. Affairs Alumni Assn. (life), VFW (life), PGA Ptnrs. Club (life; charter), NRA (life), U.S. Hist. Soc. (life), Am. Fedn. Police, Gun Owners Am., Second Amendment Found. (charter), Second Amend Task Force, USS Constitution Mus. Found., Houston Lithographic Club, Rep.-Presdl. Legion of Merit, U.S. Golf Assn., Houston Golf Assn., Citizens Against Govt. Waste, NRA Whittington Ctr. Founders Club, Braeburn Country Club, 100 Club Houston, Houston Craftsmens Club (hon.; life, past pres., Ben Franklin award 1971), Nat. Home Gardening Club (life), Santa Fe Trail Gun Club (life). Republican. Methodist.

BURNHAM, JOHN LUDWIG, agent; b. L.A., Mar. 1, 1953; s. Jerome Ludwig and Linda (Benjamin) B.; m. Andrea Buckland Feldstein, Aug. 12, 1989; 1 child, Daisy. BA, UCLA, 1976, JD, 1980. Agt. Kohnner Levy, L.A., 1979-81, ICM, L.A., 1981-84, William Morris Agy., Beverly Hills, Calif., 1984—, co-head, sr. v.p. movie dept., 1991—. Office: William Morris Agy Inc 151 S El Camino Dr Beverly Hills CA 90212-2775

BURNHAM, PATRICIA WHITE, consultant, advocate, writer, business executive; b. Omaha, July 30, 1933; d. William Max and Berniece Irene (Shockey) Orr; m. William L. White, June 18, 1955 (div. Nov. 1979); children: Lucinda, Christopher, Duncan; m. Robert A. Burnham, Feb. 23, 1980. BA in English, DePauw U., Greencastle, Ind., 1955; MA in English, Ill. State U., 1966, PhD in Adminstrn., 1977. Tchr. Morton Grove (Ill.) and Evansville (Ind.) pub. schs., 1955-60; instr. Ill. State U., Normal, 1963-71, dir. Nat. Student Exchange, 1971-74, acad. advisor and continuing edn. coord., 1974-76, asst. dean, 1976-79; assoc. dir. Ill. Bd. Higher Edn., Springfield, 1979-80; assoc. vice provost Ohio State U., Columbus, 1980-81; specialist bus. ins. Nationwide Ins. Co., Columbus, 1981-83; v.p. pvt. banking Chase Manhattan Bank, N.A., N.Y.C., 1983-88; pres. Transitions Group, Inc., East Burke, Vt., 1986—. Adj. prof. U. Vt., 1997—. Author: Life's Third Act, 1994; contbr. articles to publs. and seminars on successful aging, adult policies and programs. Pres. Cmty. Vt. Elders, 1994—99; bd. dirs. Northeastern Vt. Hosp., St. Johnsbury, 1997—, bd. chair, 2000—; bd. dirs. Vt. Cmty. Loan Fund, Vt. Coun. on Humanities, Vt. Assn. Non-Profit Orgns., 1998—2000. Mem. Gerontol. Assn., Phi Beta Kappa, Phi Delta Kappa. Congregationalist. Avocations: hiking, literature, computers. Office: Transitions Assocs PO Box 43 Lower Waterford VT 05848 Home: 391 Copenhagen Road Waterford VT 05819 E-mail: pat.burnham@together.net.

BURNHAM, ROBERT ALAN, academic administrator, educator; b. Rochester, N.Y., July 4, 1928; s. J. Robert and Susan (Mason) Burnham; m. Shirley Semingson, Feb. 12, 1953 (div.); m. Patricia Orr White, Feb. 23, 1980. BA magna cum laude, U. Wash., 1955; PhD, Stanford U., 1972. Assoc. prof., assoc. dean Coll. Edn. U. Ill., Urbana, 1969-76; rsch. dir. Ill. Sch. Problems Commn., Springfield, 1974-77; prof., dean. Coll. Edn. Ill. State U., Normal, 1976-79, Ohio State U., Columbus, 1979-83, acting v.p. comm. and devel., 1982-83; prof., dean Sch. Edn., Health, Nursing and Arts Professions NYU, N.Y.C., 1983-89, prof., dir. Ctr. Ednl. Tech. and Econ. Productivity, 1989-96, prof. emeritus, 1996—; v.p. Transitions Assocs., Waterford, Vt., 1989—; interim pres. Lyndon State Coll., 1997-98; cons. Vt. State Colls., 1998-2000. Coord. N.Y. Ednl. Policy Fellowship Program Inst. Ednl. Leadership, N.Y.C., 1986—94; pres. Educator's Distance Learning Consortium, Inc., 1990—93; resident cons. Belarus Ministry of Edn., Minsk, 1995; workshop presenter, lectr. Contbr. articles to profl. jours. Bd. dirs. reparative bd. Vt. Dept. Corrections, 1997—2000. With U.S. Army, 1948—52. Grantee, U.S. Office Edn., 1966. Mem. Tchr. Edn. Conf. Bd. (pres. Albany, N.Y. chpt. 1984—89), Am. Assn. Colls. Tchr. Edn. (instnl. rep. bd. dirs. 1981—85), Nulhegan Gateway Assn. (pres., bd. dirs. 2000—), Kingdom Trail Assn., Inc. (bd. dirs. 1996—2000), N.E. Kingdom Travel and Tourism Assn. (pres. 2000—02), Phi Beta Kappa. Congregationalist. Avocations: hiking, skiing, technology. Home: PO Box 43 391 Copenhagen Rd Lower Waterford VT 05848-0043

BURNHAM, STEPHEN JOHN, civil engineer; b. Springfield, Mass., June 13, 1948; s. Orvis Samuel, Jr. and Shirley Nairne (Turnwall) B.; m. Marjorie Elizabeth Viken, Feb. 14, 1970; children: Sandra Janice, Lisa Jennifer, Todsaporn Soonthorn. BSCE, U. Calif., Davis, 1970. Registered profl. engr., Minn., Ariz. With Fed. Hwy. Adminstrn., Washington, 1970—, planning and rsch. engr. Lincoln, Nebr., 1986—. Fin. officer CAP, Phoenix, 1983, Fairfax, Va., 1984-86, Lincoln, 1986-89, squadron comdr., 1991-92; treas. SDA Ch., Fairfax, 1986; life master Am. Contract Bridge League (sec. treas. unit 184, 1994-2000). Life mem. Am. Mensa (pres. Lincoln chpt. 1992-93, regional vice chair 1997—). Democrat. Office: Fed Hwy Adminstrn 100 Centennial Mall N Rm 220 Lincoln NE 68508-3803

BURNHAM, VAN ROBINSON, JR., general practice physician; b. Marks, Miss., Feb. 20, 1920; s. Van Robinson Burnham and Nettie Lee Robinson; m. Barbara Jeanne Braswell, July 28, 1948; children: Barbara Jeanne, Van Robinson III, Robert Conner. BS, U. Miss., 1941; MD, Northwestern U., 1943. Intern Pa. Hosp., Phila., 1944, resident in pathology, 1945—46; gen. practice medicine Vaiden, Miss., 1947—48; family practice medicine Clarksdale, Miss., 1948—; chief of staff Coahoma County Hosp., Clarksdale, Miss., 1970-75; staff N.W. Miss. Regional Med. Ctr., Clarksdale, Miss., 1980—. Dir. Valley Bank, Greenwood, Miss., 1997—. Pres. North Delta Mus., Friars Point, Miss., 1985—; trustee Miss. Dept. Archives and History, Jackson, 1988—. Lt. comdr., USNR, 1945-46, 1953-55. Fellow Am. Assn. Family Physicians; mem. Rotary (Paul Harris fellow 1995), Mensa, Intertel. Republican. Methodist. Avocations: genealogy, archaeology, history, painting. Home: 931 Carr Ave Clarksdale MS 38614-3048 Office: 266 Yazoo Ave Clarksdale MS 38614-4330

BURNHAM, WALTER DEAN, political science educator; b. Columbus, Ohio, June 15, 1930; s. Alfred Huntington Jr. and Gertrude Elinor (Hamburger) B.; m. Patricia Ann Mullan, June 7, 1958; children: John Patrick, Anne More. BA, Johns Hopkins U., 1951; AM, Harvard U., 1958, PhD, 1962; LittD (hon.), Rutgers U., 1982. Instr. polit. sci. Boston Coll., 1958-61; asst. prof. Kenyon Coll., Gambier, Ohio, 1961-64, Haverford (Pa.) Coll., 1964-66; from assoc. to full prof. Washington U., St. Louis, 1966-71; prof. MIT, Cambridge, Mass., 1971-88, Ruth and Arthur Sloan prof. polit. sci., 1984-88; Frank C. Erwin Jr. Centennial prof. govt. U. Tex., Austin, 1988—. Vis. scholar Phi Beta Kappa, 1995—. Author: Presidential Ballots, 1955, 2d. edit., 1976, Critical Elections, 1970, The Current Crisis in Am. Politics, 1982, Democracy in the Making, 1983, 2d edit., 1986. With U.S. Army, 1953-56. Fellow Social Sci. Rsch. Coun., 1963, Guggenheim Found., 1974, Ctr. Advanced Study in Behavioral Sci., 1979. Fellow Am. Acad. Arts and Scis.; mem. Am. Polit. Sci. Assn. (mem. coun. 1984-86, pres. organized sect. on politics and history 1993-94), Phi Beta Kappa (vis. scholar 1995-96). Avocation: opera. Home: 4207 N Hills Dr Austin TX 78731-2827 Office: U Tex Dept Govt Burdine Hall # 536 Austin TX 78712

BURNIM, KALMAN AARON, theatre educator emeritus; b. Malden, Mass., Mar. 7, 1928; s. Jack K. and Sadie (Levy) B.; m. Verna Ruth Lesser, June 6, 1928; children: Ira, Judith, Esther Burnim Ouray. BA in Drama magna cum laude, Tufts U., 1950; MA in Theater, Ind. U., 1951; PhD, Yale U., 1958. Mng. exec. New England Adding Machine Co., Boston, 1951-55; asst. prof. Valparaiso (Ind.) U., 1958-59, U. Pitts., 1959-60, Tufts U., Medford, Mass., 1960-61, assoc. prof., dir. theater, 1961-65, prof. drama, 1965, chmn. dept. drama, exec. dir. theater, 1966-75, Fletcher prof. oratory and drama, 1971-87, emeritus prof., 1987—. Rsch. prof. English George Washington U., Washington, 1975-76, 85-86; mem. nat. screening com. for theater Fulbright Commn., Washington, 1985-89; mem. exec. com. Internat. Fedn. for Theatre Rsch., 1979-83, 91-95; panelist, del. various confs. Author: David Garrick, Director, 1961; co-author: The Prompter, An Eighteenth Century Theatrical Paper, 1966, The Biographical Dictionary of Actors, Actresses, Dancers, Managers, and Other Stage Personnel in London Stage, 1660-1800, 16 vols., 1973-93, (George Freedley Meml. award Theatre Library Assn. 1979, 94), Pictures in the Garrick Club. A Catalogue, 1997, (with P.H. Highfill Jr.) John Bell, Patron of Theatrical Portraiture, 1998, (with Andrew Wilton) The Richard Bebb Collection in the Garrick Club, 2001; editor (anthology) The Complete Plays of George Colman the Elder, 6 vols., 1983, (monograph) The Letters of Sarah and William Siddons to Hester Lynch Thrale Piozzi, 1969; assoc. editor Ednl. Theatre Jour., 1968-70; contbr. articles to profl. jours. Guggenheim fellow, 1964-65, Folger Library fellow, 1957-58, 69, 71; Sterling fellow Yale U., 1957-58; Am. Council for Learned Socs. grantee, 1966, 71; NEH grantee, 1967-68, 70, 74-76, 85-86; Tufts faculty research grantee, 1960-81. Mem. Am. Soc. for Theatre Rsch. (pres. 1985-91, mem. exec. com. 1960-63, 64-69, 72-75, 83-86, program chmn. 1963-65, 76, chmn. publs. com. 1975-76, 79-82, del. to Am. Coun. Learned Socs. 1976-82, spl. citation 1994), Brit. Soc. for Theatre Rsch., Am. Soc. for Eighteenth-Century Studies, IREX (chmn. commn. on Am.-Soviet theatre exchs. 1988-91), Coll. Fellows Am. Theatre, Phi Beta Kappa (pres. Tufts chpt, 1983-85), Garrick Club. Home: 2633 Imperial Pine Dr Spring Hill FL 34606-3417 also: 22 Cranmore Ln Melrose MA 02176-1507 E-mail: kburnim@aya.yale.edu.

BURNINGHAM, KIM RICHARD, former state legislator; b. Salt Lake City, Sept. 14, 1936; s. Rulon and Margie (Stringham) Burningham; m. Susan Ball Clarke, Dec. 19, 1968; children: Christian, Tyler David. BS, U. Utah, 1960; MA, U. Ariz., 1967; MFA, U. So. Calif., 1977. Cert. secondary tchr., Utah. Tchr. Bountiful (Utah) High Sch., 1960-88; mem. Utah Ho. of Reps., Salt Lake City, 1979-94; cons. Shipley Assocs., Bountiful, 1989-94, Franklin Covey, 1994—. Gubernatorial appointee as exec. dir. Utah Statehood Centennial Commn., 1994-96; mem. Utah State Bd. Edn., 1999-2000, vice chmn., 2000-01, chmn., 2001—; bd. dirs. Nat. Assn. State Bds. Edn., 2000-2001 (pres. 2003-). Author dramas for stage and film, also articles; columnist, Davis County Clipper,

2000—. Mem. state strategic planning com. Utah Tomorrow, 1989—. Recipient Carl Perkins Humanitarian of Yr. award, ACTE, 2002. Mem. NEA, PTA (life), Utah Edn. Assn., Davis Edn. Assn., Nat. Forensic League. Mem. Lds Ch. Avocations: gardening, history. Home: 932 Canyon Crest Dr Bountiful UT 84010-2002 E-mail: krb84010@aol.com.

BURNISON, BOYD EDWARD, lawyer; b. Arnolds Park, Iowa, Dec. 12, 1934; s. Boyd WIlliam and Lucile (Harnden) B.; m. Mari Amaral; children: Erica Lafore, Alison Katherine. BS, Iowa State U., 1957; JD, U. Calif., Berkeley, 1961. Bar: Calif. 1962, U.S. Supreme Ct. 1971, U.S. Dist. Ct. (no. dist.) Calif. 1962, U.S. Ct. Appeals (9th cir.) 1962, U.S. Dist. Ct. (ea. dist.) Calif. 1970, U.S. Dist. Ct. (ctrl. dist.) Calif. 1992. Dep. counsel Yolo County, Calif., 1962-65; assoc. Steel & Arostegui, Marysville, Calif., 1965-66, St. Sure, Moore & Hoyt, Oakland, Calif., 1966-70; ptnr. St. Sure, Moore, Hoyt & Sizoo, Oakland and San Francisco, 1970-75; v.p. Crosby, Heafey, Roach & May, P.C., Oakland, 1975-2000, also bd. dirs.; pres. Boyd E Burnison A Profl. Law Corp., Walnut Creek, Calif., 2001—. Advisor Berkeley YMCA, 1971—, Yolo County YMCA, 1962—65, bd. dirs., 1965; trustee, sec., legal counsel Easter Seal Found., Alameda County, 1974—79, hon. trustee, 1979—; trustee Alameda County Law Libr., 2001—; bd. dirs. Easter Seal Soc. Crippled Children and Adults of Alameda County Calif., 1972—75, Moot Ct. Bd., U. Calif., 1960—61, East Bay Conservation Corps, 1997—2000, treas., 2000. Named Vol. of Yr., Berkeley YMCA, 1999. Fellow: ABA Found. (life); mem.: ABA (labor rels. and employment law sect., equal employment law com. 1972—), Sproul Assoc. Boalt Hall Law Sch. U. Calif. Berkeley, Indsl. Rels. Rsch. Assn., Contra Costa County Bar Assn. (labor law sect.), Bar Assn. San Francisco (labor law sect.), Yuba Sutter Bar Assn., Yolo County Bar Assn. (sec. 1965), Alameda County Bar Found. (bd. dirs. 1993—95), Alameda County Bar Assn. (chmn. memberships and directory com. 1973—74, 1980, chmn. law office econs. com. 1975—77, assn. dir. 1981—85, pres. 1984, vice chmn. bench bar liaison com. 1983, chmn. 1984, Disting. Svc. award 1987), State Bar Calif. (spl. labor counsel 1981—84, labor and employment law sect. 1982—), Nat. Conf. Bar Pres.'s, Rotary (Paul Harris fellow), Round Hill Country Club, Iowa State Alumni Assn., Order Knoll, Phi Delta Phi, Pi Kappa Alpha. Democrat. Home: PO Box 743 2500 Caballo Ranchero Dr Diablo CA 94528 Office: Boyd E Burnison A Profl Law Corp 1600 South Main Plz Ste 130 Walnut Creek CA 94596 Fax: (925) 817-2411. E-mail: boyd@bburnison.com.

BURNLEY, JUNE WILLIAMS, secondary school educator; b. St. Augustine, Fla., Mar. 13, 1936; d. Marcellus Henry Gilford and Ella (Broadus) Williams. BS, N.C. Agrl. and Tech. U., 1958; MA, Villanova U., 1975, St. John's Coll., Annapolis, Md., 1995; student, Oxford U., London, 1995. Cert. English tchr., counseling psychologist. Grade sch. tchr., 1958-59; lang. arts supr. Wharton Ctr., Phila., 1967-68; English/French lang. tchr. Hatch. Jr. H.S., Camden, N.J., 1962-68; English tchr. George Washington H.S., Phila., 1968-93, secondary counseling intern, 1975. Mem. Pa. State Coun. English Tchrs., 1968-93, Educators to Africa, Phila., 1993-97; tutor Temple-New Career Ladders, 1975-76. Mem. Germantown Civic League, Phila., 1993, West Mt. Airy Neighbors, Phila., 1968—, Social Action Com., Phila., 1993-95, Germantown Hist. Soc., Unitarian Soc. Germantown; vol. guide in tng. Phila. Mus. Art, 1996—. Pa. State Bd. Edn. fellow, 1985, Arco & Exxon fellow, 1991, St. John's Coll. fellow, 1992-93. Fellow Commonwealth Partnership; mem. Nat. Coun. English Tchrs. (Svc. award 1972), Eleanor Trailor Readers (co-founder), Literary Group (founder), Literati (founder), Amnesty Internat., Phi Delta Kappa, Delta Sigma Theta. Avocations: reading, travel, knitting, sewing, word games. Home: 700 Elkins Ave Apt E3 Elkins Park PA 19027-2315

BURNLEY, KENNETH STEPHEN, school system administrator; m. Eileen Burnley; children: Traci, Trevor. BS, MA, PhD, U. Mich. Tchr. various schs., Mich.; asst. track coach U. Mich.; tchr., coord., asst. prin., prin., dir. Ypsilanti Bd. Edn.; instr. Ea. Mich. U.; asst. supt. instrn. Waverly Bd. Edn.; supt./CEO Fairbanks (Alaska) North Star Borough Sch. Dist.; supt. schs. Colorado Springs (Colo.) Sch. Dist. 11, 1987—. Speaker in field. Bd. dirs. Colo. Nat. Bank Exch. Named Supt. of Year, Am. Assn. Sch. Adminstrs., 1993. Mem. Colo. Springs C. of C. (bd. dirs.). Avocations: exercising, weight training, boxing, reading, chess.

BURNS, ARTHUR LEE, architect; b. Indpls., July 5, 1924; s. Charles Raymond and Dorothy Frances (Young) B.; m. Dorothy Maxine Kingsland, Oct. 26, 1946 (dec.); children— Stephen Robert (dec.), Melody Lee; m. Frances C. Mathers, Jan. 12, 1988. BS in Architecture, U. Cin., 1949. Archtl. draftsman Foster Engring. Co., Ltd., Indpls., 1941-42; archtl. draftsman Albert V. Walters (Architect), Cin., 1946-48; chief draftsman Arend & Arend (Architects), Cin., 1948-49; architect The McGuire & Shook Corp., Indpls., 1949-84, v.p., 1964-71, sec.-treas., 1972-73, pres., 1974-75, exec. v.p., 1976-77, v.p., 1978-79, sec.-treas., 1980-84; archtl. cons., 1984—. Bd. dirs. Friends of Winter Haven Pub. Libr., 1995—2001, 2002—, pres., 1997—98. Served with USAF, 1943—46. Fellow AIA (sec.-treas. Indpls. chpt. 1965-66, v.p. 1967, pres. 1968, mem. documents bd. 1973-85, chmn. 1978-79); mem. Ind. Soc. Architects (bd. dirs. 1968-69, v.p. 1971, pres. 1972, Edward D. Pierre medal 1972), Constrn. Specifications Inst. (v.p. Indpls. chpt. 1966-67, pres. 1967-68), Broad Ripple Sertoma Club Indpls. (v.p. 1973-74, pres. 1974-75, Gold Honor Club), Cypress Gardens Sertoma Club Winter Haven (bd. dirs. 1991-99, 2000-02). Republican. Methodist. Home: 2987 Plantation Rd Winter Haven FL 33884-1235

BURNS, B. DARREN, lawyer; b. Balt., Mar. 8, 1964; s. Bruce C. and Barbara (Merson) B.; m. Jennifer Duffy, July 2, 1994; children: Callie Elizabeth, Duffy Patrick. BA in English, Hampden Sydney Coll., 1986; JD, Coll. William & Mary, 1990. Bar: Md. 1991, U.S. Dist. Ct. Md., 1991, U.S. Cir. Ct. (4th cir.) 1992. Law clerk Cir. Ct. Anne Arundel County, Md., 1990-91; assoc. atty. Shapiro and Olander, Balt., Annapolis, Md., 1992-94; staff atty. Anne Arundel County Pub. Schs., Annapolis, 1994—2001; atty. Reese & Carney, LLP, Annapolis, 2001—. Class agent Severn Sch., Severna Park, Md., 1983—. Mem. Md. State Bar Assn., Md. Sch. Bd. Attys. Assn., Edn. Law Assn., Anne Arundel Bar Assn., Annapolis Touchdown Club (pres. 1999-2000). Home: 612 Pin Oak Rd Severna Park MD 21146-3607 Office: Reese & Carney LLP 170 Jennifer Rd Ste 245 Annapolis MD 21401

BURNS, B. THOMAS, broadcasting executive; b. East St. Louis, Ill., Jan. 10, 1936; s. Thomas Stephen Burns and Anita Marguerite (Sale) Piot; m. Mary Ellen Christgau, Dec. 29, 1957; children: Anna Lee Burns Fine, Jeannine Charlotte Burns Dvorak. BS in Broadcast Journalism, U. Ill., 1957; MBA, U. Chgo., 1974; postgrad., Harvard U., 1980. News dir. Sta. WSDR Radio, Sterling, Ill., 1957; news editor Sta. WLS Radio, Chgo., 1958; mktg. writer ITT, Chgo., 1959-61; pub. rels. mgr. GTE, Northlake, Ill., 1961-69; pres., gen. mgr. Sta. WEFM Radio, Michigan City, Ind., 1969—. Pres., gen. mgr. Sta. WLLT Radio, Sterling-Rock Falls-Dixon, Ill., 1989—; prin., gen. mgr. Sta. WDKR Radio, Decatur, Ill., 1989-2002; cons. Sta. WDKR, WXFM Radio and others, Mt. Zion, Ill., 1984—; assoc. prof. Valparaiso (Ind.) U. Coll. Bus., 1974-77. Ind. dir. Nat. Assn. FM Broadcasters, 1972-73; bd. dirs. Blackhawk Waterways Conv. and Vis. Bur., Polo, Ill., 1993—, Michigan City (Ind.) Main St. Assn., 1992-96, Sterling (Ill.) Main St. Assn., 2003—; bd. dirs. Downtowns of Ill. Associated, 1996—, v.p., 1997-98, pres. 1999-2001; pres. N.W. Ill. MBA Roundtable, Sterling, 1997—99; active Downtown Econ. Devel. Com., Decatur, 1997; bd. dirs. Decatur Small Bus. Coun., 1986-87; mem. Sterling Sister City Com., 1995—. Mem. U. Chgo. Mgmt. Roundtable, Mt. Zion C. of C. (bd. dirs. 1987-88), Rock Falls C. of C. (bd. dirs. 1996-2002), Rotary. Lutheran. Avocations: sailing, amateur radio, travel, photography, motorcycling. Home: 602 Woodland Ct Mount Zion IL 62549-1440

BURNS, BARBARA BELTON, investment company executive; b. Fredericktown, Mo., Dec. 10, 1944; d. Clyde Monroe and Mary Celestial (Anderson) Belton; m. Larry J. Bohannon; Mar. 27, 1963 (div.); 1 child, Timothy Joseph; m. Donald Edward Burns, Nov. 1, 1980; stepchildren: Brian Edward, David Keone (dec.). Student, Ohio State U., 1970-75. Dir. nat. sales Am. Way, Chgo., 1976-77; recruiter Bell & Howell Schs., Columbus, Ohio, 1978-80; pres., founder Bardon Investment Corp., Naples, Fla., 1980-90; founder Cambridge Mgmt. Co., Columbus, 1983-86; pres., CEO Charter's Total Wardrobe Care, Columbus, 1984-89; founder, exec. Phoenix Bus. Group, Inc., 1990—; founder, pres. Celestial Group Inc., Las Vegas, 1999—; pres., Bondtech Direct Nutraceuticals, 2002—. Treas. Vicace-Columbus Symphony, 1981—82; fundraiser Grant Hosp., Columbus, 1986; chmn. Impresarios/Opera Columbus, 1986—87; founding mem. Columbus Women's Bd., 1986—87; mem. devel. com. Babe Zaharias/Am. Cancer Soc.; auction chmn. Opera Ball-Opera/Columbus, 1989; tennis tournament chmn. NABOR Scholarship Fund, 1990—91; mem. Philharm. Chorale, Naples, Fla., 1992, First Presbyn. of Las Vegas Chancel Choir, 1998—; spokesman Diabetes Found. Collier County, Fla., 1992—, pres., 1994, Diabetes Found., 1994—; elder Vanderbilt Presbyn. Ch., 1994. Named Entrepreneur of Yr. Arthur Young/Venture mag., 1988, Outstanding Vol. Opera Columbus, 1986, Vol. of Yr. Diabetes Found., 1994; recipient Design award Reynoldsburg C. of C., 1988. Mem. Naples C. of C. (new bus. com. 1990—), Las Vegas C. of C. Republican. Avocations: tennis, boating, travel, music.

BURNS, BEBE LYN, journalist; b. Baytown, Tex., Nov. 2, 1952; d. L.L. and Edith Elizabeth B.; m. George Frederick Rhodes Jr., Nov. 30, 1980; 1 child, Elizabeth Kathleen. BA, U. Houston, 1974; MS in Journalism, Northwestern U., 1975. Reporter, anchor Sta. WSPA-TV, Spartanburg, S.C., 1975-76, Sta. KHOU-TV, Houston, 1976-79; reporter Sta. KTVI-TV, St. Louis, 1979-82; bus. reporter Sta. KPRC-TV, Houston, 1982-95; prin. Burns Kopatic, Houston, 1996-97, Bebe Burns Comm., Houston, 1997—. Adj. prof. U. Houston Sch. Comm., 1998—. Bd. dirs. Presbyn. Sch., 1996—2002, Houston Area Parkinson's Soc., 1991—95, CanCare of Houston, Inc., 1995—97; founding mem. Greater Houston Women's Found.; active Friends of Fleming Pk., Blvd. Oaks Civic Assn. Recipient awards Headliners Club Tex. 1988, Tex. AP Broadcasters, 1988, Am. Women in Radio & TV, 1988, Press Club Houston, 1987, 88, Press Club Dallas, 1981, 93, Employee award for help to jobless Tex. Employment Commn., 1993, Bus. Advocacy award North Harris-Montgomery C.C. Dist. & Bus. & Industry Coun., 1993; named one of Women on the Move Houston Post and Tex. Exec. Women, 1988, Small Bus. Media Adv. of Yr. SBA, 1992. Mem. Soc. Profl. Journalists. E-mail: bebeburns@bebeburns.com.

BURNS, BERNARD JOHN, III, public defender; b. Alexandria, Va., Apr. 28, 1956; s. Bernard John and Mary Theresa (O'Malley) B.; m. Pamela Sue Endres, June 9, 1990; 1 child, Kristie Keener. BA in Journalism, U. Iowa, 1982, JD with distinction, 1984. Bar: Iowa 1985, U.S. Dist. Ct. (so. dist.) Iowa 1987, U.S. Supreme Ct. 1989, U.S. Ct. Appeals (8th cir.) 1992. Asst. appellate defender Iowa Appellate Defender, Des Moines, 1985-94; asst. pub. defender Des Moines Adult Pub. Defender, 1994-99; asst. fed. defender Office of Fed. Defender, Des Moines, 1999—. Author: 4A Iowa Practice: Criminal Procedure. Bd. dirs. Met. Arts Alliance Greater Des Moines, 1996-2003, pres., 2000; mem. Iowa Criminal and Juvenile Justice Planning Commn., 1993-99; chmn. Jazz in July Planning Com., Des Moines, 1997—; keyboard player Goodnight Dallas. Named Outstanding Sr., Iowa Sch. Journalism, 1982. Mem. Nat. Assn. Fed. Defenders, Iowa Pub. Defenders Assn. (pres. 1991-99), Chopin Soc. (v.p. 1982), Blackstone Inn of Ct., Am. Mock Trial Assn., Judges Hall of Fame, Friends of Iowa Civil Rights, Inc. (Spl. Recognition award), Phi Beta Kappa. Avocations: composer, actor, writer, tae kwon do instructor, musician. Office: Fed Defender 300 Walnut St Ste 295 Des Moines IA 50309-2258

BURNS, BETTY X. music educator; b. St. Louis, Sept. 16, 1926; d. James Arnest and Elizabeth Levina (Allen) Delvas; m. Douglas Corzine Burns, Sept. 8, 1945 (dec. 1974); children: Cynthia Burns Benavides, Stephen, Clark, Nathan; m. Valdis Kibens, No.v 27, 1988. Student, Washington U., St. Louis, 1951, Sherwood Conservatory of Music, Chgo., 1960; studies with Carl Benseik, St. Louis, 1940-56; studies with Harold Zabrack, N.Y.C., 1970-73; student, U. Mo., St. Louis, 1979. Jazz singer, 1965-75; dir. New Music Acad., St. Louis, Mo., 1968—. Clinician Nat. Piano Found., St. Louis, 1962-73; mem. faculty Webster Coll., St. Louis, 1969-73; adjudicator profl. assns.; dir. workshops Kjos Pub., San Diego, 1972-75; specialist jazz improvization and group teaching, 1968—. Author: (with others) You Do It Books, 1972-75; contbr. articles to mags. Mem. Piano Tchrs. Forum (pres.), Nat. Music Tchrs. Assn., Mo. Music Tchrs. Assn. (judge), Piano Tchrs. Guild (chmn.), St. Louis Music Tchrs. Assn. (pres. 1994-98). Avocations: trading stock market, psychic healing. Home and Office: 172 Hastings Way Saint Charles MO 63301-5506

BURNS, BRENDA, state senator; b. LaGrange, Ga., Nov. 22, 1950; 3 children. Mem. Ariz. Senate, Dist. 17, Phoenix, 1994—; pres. Ariz. Senate, 1996—2000. Nat. chair Am. Leg. Exch. Coun., 1999; exec. bd. Am. Legis. Exch. Coun. Republican. Office: State Capitol Legis Dist 17 1700 W Washington St Phoenix AZ 85007-2812

BURNS, BRENDA CAROLYN, retired special education administrator, chemical dependence counselor; b. Scalf, Ky., July 22, 1947; d. Lindberg and Ina Jean (Mills) Bingham; m. Michael Burns (div. 1985). BA in English, Wright State U., Dayton, OH, 1968, BA in Spanish, 1971, MEd in Spanish, English and Edn., 1973; MEd in Counseling, Cleve. State U., Cleve., 1985; MAEd in Sch. Psychology, U. Akron, 1985. Cert. in Spanish, English, counseling, sch. psychology, sch. social work, pupil pers., Ohio; cert. chem. dependence counselor. Tchr. Spanish Centerville (Ohio) City Sch., 1971-73; tchr. Spanish and English Rocky River (Ohio) City Sch., 1973-78; sch. counselor Brooklyn (Ohio) City Sch., 1978-84; intern sch. psychologist Westlake (Ohio) City Sch., 1984-85; sch. psychologist Brooklyn City Sch., 1985-87, sch. psychologist, coord. student svcs., 1987-97, dir. pupil svcs., 1997-99; ret., 1999. Adv. coun., chair Cuyahoga Spl. Edn. Svc. Ctr., Cleve., 1991-92; chem. dependency counselor Oakview at S.W. Gen. Health Ctr. Avocations: reading, raising dogs, walking, movies.

BURNS, BRIAN PATRICK, lawyer, business executive; b. Cambridge, Mass., July 12, 1936; s. John Joseph and Alice (Blake) B.; m. Sheila Ann O'Connor, June 23, 1962; children: Sheila Ann, Brian Patrick, Sean Richard, Roderick O'Connor. BA, Holy Cross Coll., 1957; LLB, Harvard U., 1960. Bar: Mass. 1960, N.Y. 1961, Calif. 1965. Law clk., spl. asst. to regional adminstr. New York Regional Office, SEC, 1958-59; assoc. Webster, Sheffield, Fleischmann, Hitchcock & Brookfield, N.Y.C., 1960-64; ptnr. Cullinan, Hancock, Rothert & Burns, San Francisco, 1965-74; sr. ptnr. Cullinan, Burns & Helmer, San Francisco, 1975-78; firm Burns & Whitehead, San Francisco, 1978-86; chmn., chief exec. officer, chmn. exec. com. Boothe Fin. Corp., San Francisco, 1981-87, also bd. dirs.; chmn. Robert Half Internat. Inc., 1987-88; chmn., CEO BF Enterprises Inc., 1987—. Dir. U.S. Banknote Corp., N.Y.C., from 1967, chmn. exec. and fin. coms., 1973-76; dir. Coca Cola Bottling Co., N.Y., 1974-86, chmn. exec. com., 1979-86; dir. Kellogg Co., 1979-89, chmn. fin. com. 1984-89; dir. Calif. Jockey, 1980-89; dir., chmn. audit com. Flexi-Van Corp., N.Y.C., 1984-85; dir., chmn. exec. com. Pinnacle Petroleum Corp., The Woodlands, Tex., 1983-85; dir., chmn. ops. review com. Brink's Inc., Chgo., 1976-78; dir., chmn. acquisition com. Pacific Holding Corp., Los Angeles, 1972-78; dir., mem. exec. com. Beverly Wilshire Hotel, Beverly Hills, Calif., Calif., 1967-86; dir., chmn. exec. com. USR Industries, The Woodlands, 1980-83; dir., chmn. audit com. ROCOR Internat., Palo Alto, Calif., 1976-82; underwriting mem. Lloyds of London, 1978-89; lectr. continuing edn. of bar U. Calif., 1969, 74, 76, advanced bus. seminar, 1971; seminar on investment opportunities in wine industry McGraw Hill Coll., N.Y., 1973, Legal Edn. Inst., 1976. Bd. dirs. Boys Club of San Francisco, 1971-80, Am. Irish Found., 1978-87, Am. Ireland Fund, 1987—; trustee Holy Cross Coll., 1978-89. Mem. ABA (mem. small bus. com. corp. bus. and banking sect. 1972-76), State Bar Cal. (vice chmn. com. on corps. 1971-75), Bar Assn. San Francisco (chmn. com. on corp. banking and bus. law 1968-69), Calif. Jockey Club (dir. San Mateo, Calif. 1988-89). Clubs. Royal Dublin Soc.; Bohemian, Burlingame Country, Family, Olympic, Sky, N.Y. Athletic, Les Ambassadeurs, Mil. and Hospitaller Order St. Lazarus of Jerusalem (comdr. companion). Roman Catholic. Office: BF Enterprises Inc 100 Bush St Ste 1250 San Francisco CA 94104-3914

BURNS, CAROL J. architect, educator; b. Cedar Rapids, Iowa, Nov. 24, 1954; d. Robert Joseph and Alice T. (Neuhaus) B. Student, Bryn Mawr Coll., 1973-75; BA, Yale Coll., 1980, MArch, 1983. Assoc. prof., asst. chair archtl. dept. Harvard U., Cambridge, Mass., 1987-99; dir. Harvard Inst. Affordable Housing, 1989—2002; prin. Taylor & Burns Architects, Boston, 1993—. Vis. prof. U. Va., Yale U., MIT, 2000—; mem. exec. bd. Boston Soc. Archs. Author: (with others) Drawing/Building/Text, 1990; author, editor (with others): Thinking the Present, 1990; editor Yale Sch. Architecture Perspecta 21, 1984; designer Founders' Hall (Kans. AIA, Masonry Inst., Faith and Forum awards 2000), Greybirch House (Conn. AIA award 1992, Worcester AIA award 1992), Harrington Performing Arts Ctr. (Boston AIA award 2000), Casa Nueva Vida (Opening Doors award 1999); group shows include AIA Nat. Hdqrs., 1999, Robert Lehman Gallery, N.Y.C., 1996, Norfolk 4 Plus 4, 1983; contbr. articles to profl. and acad. jours. Mem. Boston Art Commn., 2003—. Recipient Edn. Honors award AIA, 1996, Jour. of Architecture Edn. design award, 2000.

BURNS, CARROLL DEAN, insurance company executive; b. Chattanooga, Dec. 22, 1932; s. William Thomas and Lillis (Gill) B.; m. Jean Baird, Aug. 29, 1954; children: Randy, Lori. BS, U. Tenn., 1954. C.P.A., Tenn., Ohio. With Provident Life and Accident Ins. Co., Chattanooga, 1957-63, mgr. data processing, 1960-63; with Union Central Life Ins. Co., Cin., 1963-79, exec. v.p., comptr., bd. dirs., 1974-79; pres., CEO Life Ins. Co. Ga., Atlanta, 1979-94; exec. v.p. Georgia US Corp., Atlanta, 1989-94; ret., 1995. Pres., COO Southland Life Ins. Co.; bd. dirs. Union Cen. Life Assurance Corp., Life Ins. Co. Ga., First of Ga. Ins. Group, Assoc. Drs. Ins. Co., Southland Ins. Co.; former chmn. Civil Svc. Bd., Fairfield, Ohio. Former trustee Better Bus. Bur. Cin. Served with USAF, 1955-57. Mem. BEta Alpha Psi, Atlanta Country Club, Georgian Club, Sugarloaf Country Club. Baptist. Home: 2075 Sugarloaf Club Dr Duluth GA 30097-4098 E-mail: cdburns@charter.net.

BURNS, CATHERINE ELIZABETH, art dealer; b. Winnipeg, Man., Can., June 21, 1953; came to U.S., 1955; d. Robert Franklin and Claire Margaret (Lillington) B. BA, U. Calif., Davis, 1975; MA in Museology, U. Minn., 1978. Adj. prof., curator univ. gallery U. Mass., Amherst, 1978-80; curator gallery of art Washington U., St. Louis, 1981-82; dealer in 19th and early 20th century prints and drawings Catherine E. Burns Fine Prints, Oakland, Calif., 1982—, also appraiser. Mem. Nat. Trust for Hist. Preservation, Oakland Heritage Alliance. Grantee Nat. Endowment for Arts, 1981-82. Mem. Graphic Arts Coun., Alliance Francaise. Avocations: architectural history, music, french culture and language. Office: PO Box 11201 Oakland CA 94611-0201

BURNS, C(HARLES) PATRICK, hematologist-oncologist; b. Kansas City, Mo., Oct. 8, 1937; s. Charles Edgar and Ruth (Eastham) B.; m. Janet Sue Walsh, June 15, 1968; children— Charles Geoffrey, Scott Patrick. BA, U. Kans., 1959, MD, 1963. Diplomate Am. Bd. Internal Medicine, subsplty. bds. hematology, med. oncology. Intern Cleve. Met. Gen. Hosp., 1963-64; asst. resident in internal medicine Univ. Hosps., Cleve., 1966-68, sr. resident in hematology, 1968-69; instr. medicine Case Western Res. U., Cleve., 1970-71; asst. chief hematology Cleve. VA Hosp., 1970-71; asst. prof. medicine U. Iowa Hosps., Iowa City, 1971-75, assoc. prof. medicine, 1975-80, prof., 1980—, dir. sect. med. oncology, co-dir. divsn. hematatol./oncology, 1980-85, dir. div. hematology, oncology, blood marrow transplantation, 1985-99. Vis. scientist Imperial Cancer Rsch. Fund Labs., London, 1982-83; cons. U.S. VA Hosp.; mem. study sect. on exptl. therapeutics NIH, Cancer Ctr. Support Rev. Commn. Nat. Cancer Inst., NIH, NIH Cancer Clin. Investigation Rev. Com., Com. H Nat. Cancer Inst., VA Med. Rsch. Svc. Career Devel. Com.; mem. external adv. com. U. Oreg. Cancer Ctr., 1994-2000. Mem. bd. assoc. editors Cancer Rsch., 1988-2000, rsch. and publs. on hematologic malignancies, tumor lipid biochemistry, leukemia and oncology, role of oxidation in cancer treatment, mem. Am. Bd. of Internal Medicine Cmty., recent advances in hematology, 2002—; cons. Irish Rsch. Bd., Dublin, 2000—. Served to capt. M.C., AUS, 1964-66. Am. Cancer Soc. fellow in hematology-oncology, 1968-69, USPHS fellow in medicine, 1969-70; USPHS career awardee, 1978 Fellow ACP; mem. AAAS, Am. Bd. Internal Medicine (Subsplty. bd. hematology 1992-98), Am. Soc. Hematology, Am. Assn. Cancer Rsch., Internat. Soc. Hematology, Ctrl. Soc. Clin. Rsch., Am. Soc. Clin. Oncology, Soc. Exptl. Biology and Medicine, Oxygen Soc., Royal Soc. Medicine, Am. Fedn. Clin. Rsch., Internat. Soc. for the Study of Fatty Acids and Lipids, Phi Beta Pi, Lambda Chi Alpha, Alpha Omega Alpha. Home: 2046 Rochester Ct Iowa City IA 52245-3246 Office: U Iowa Univ Hosps Dept Medicine Iowa City IA 52242 E-mail: c-burns@uiowa.edu.

BURNS, CHESTER RAY, medical history educator; b. Nashville, Dec. 5, 1937; s. Leslie Andrew and Margaret (Drake) B.; m. Ann Christine Griffey, Aug. 31, 1962; children: Christine, Derek. BA, Vanderbilt U., 1959, MD, 1963; PhD, Johns Hopkins U., 1969. Asst. prof. history medicine U. Tex. Med. Br., Galveston, 1969-71, James Wade Rockwell asst. prof. history medicine, 1971-75, James Wade Rockwell assoc. prof., 1975-79, James Wade Rockwell prof., 1979—. Cons. Nat. Ctr. for Health Svcs. Rsch., Washington, 1976-78; mem. nat. bd. cons. NEH, Washington, 1978-83. Editor: Humanism in Medicine, 1973, Legacies in Ethics and Medicine, 1977; Legacies in Law and Medicine, 1977; co-editor: Philosophy of Medicine and Bioethics: A Twenty Year Retrospective and Critical Appraisal, 1997; co-editor: Proceedings of the 37th International Congress on the History of Medicine, 2002, Saving Lives, Training Caregivers, Making Discoveries A Centennial History of the University of Texas Medical Branch at Galveston, 2003; author numerous essays. Bd. dirs. The Grand 1894 Opera House, Galveston, 1986-88. Mem. Am. Assn. for History of Medicine (exec. coun. 1972-75), Soc. for Health and Human Values (pres. 1975-76), Am. Osler Soc. (bd. govs. 1984-87, 2002—, 1st v.p. 2003—), Internat. Soc. for History of Medicine (treas. 1991—), Tex. State Hist. Assn. (exec. coun. 1993-97), Rotary (pres. Galveston club 1980-81, gov. Dist. 5910, 1993-94). Democrat. Methodist. Avocations: swimming, photography. Office: U Tex Med Br Ashbel Smith Bldg Rm 2 Galveston TX 77555-1311 E-mail: cburns@utmb.edu.

BURNS, CONRAD RAY, senator; b. Gallatin, Mo., Jan. 25, 1935; s. Russell and Mary Frances (Knight) B.; m. Phyllis Jean Kuhlmann; children: Keely Lynn, Garrett Russell. Student, U. Mo., 1952-54. Field rep. Polled Hereford World Mag., Kansas City, Mo., 1963-69; pub. rels. Billings (Mont.) Livestock Com., 1969-73; farm dir. KULR TV, Billings, 1974; pres., founder No. Ag-Network, Billings, 1975-86; commissioner Yellowstone County, Billings, 1987-89; senator from Montana U.S. Senate, 1989—. Mem. Aging Com., Small Bus. Com., chmn. Appropriations Subcom. of Mil. Constrn., chmn. Com. Sci. and Transp. Subcom. of Comms., chmn. Energy and Nat. Resources With USMC, 1955-57. Mem. Nat. Assn. Farm Broadcasters, Am. Legion, Rotary, Masons, Shriners. Republican. Lutheran. Avocation: football officiating. Office: US Senate 187 Dirksen Senate Off Bldg Washington DC 20510-0001*

BURNS, DAN W. manufacturing company executive; b. Auburn, Calif., Sept. 10, 1925; s. William and Edith Lynn (Johnston) B.; 1 child, Dan Jr. Dir. materials Menasco Mfg. Co., 1951-56; v.p., gen. mgr. Hufford Corp., 1956-58; pres. Hufford div. Siegler Corp., 1958-61; v.p. Siegler Corp., 1961-62, Lear Siegler, Inc., 1962-64; pres., dir. Electrada Corp., Culver City, Calif., 1964; pres., chief exec. officer Sargent Industries, Inc., L.A., 1964-85, chmn. bd. dirs., 1985-88. Now chmn. bd. dirs., CEO Arlington Industries, Inc.; bd. dirs. Gen. Automotive Corp., Dover Tech. Internat., Inc., Kistler Aerospace Corp.; overseer Hoover Instn., Stanford U. Bd. dirs. San Diego Aerospace Mus., Smithsonian Inst., The Pres.'s Cir., Nat. Acad. Scis., Atlantic Coun. of U.S., George C. Marshall Found.; bd. overseers Hoover Instn., Stanford U. Capt. U.S. Army, 1941-47; prisoner of war Japan; asst. mil. attache 1946, China; adc to Gen. George C. Marshall 1946-47. Mem. OAS Sports Com. (dir.), L.A. Country Club, St. Francis Yacht Club, Calif. Club, Conquistador del Cielo, Cosmos Club Washington. Home: 7400 Bryan Canyon Rd Carson City NV 89704-9588

BURNS, DANIEL HOBART, management consultant; b. Atlanta, Jan. 26, 1928; s. Hobart H. and Florence (Kuhn) B.; B.A., U. Ala., 1949; grad. Armed Forces Staff Coll., 1966, Air Command and Staff Coll., 1969, Air War Coll., 1972; postgrad. U. S.C., 1975, Regent Coll., U. B.C., 1978-79, Trinity Episcopal Sch. for Ministry, 1979-80; m. Barbara Ann Grimsley, Jan. 15, 1949 (div. July 1974); children: Eric Grimsley, Daniel Hobart, Barbara Bennett, Arlene Chester; m. Ann Lyn Horrell, Sept. 28, 1979 (div. Mar. 1997); children: Jessica Florence, Stephen John. Account exec. Sta. WCOS, Columbia, S.C., 1949-51; sales mgr. sta. WIS, Columbia, 1951-57; ins. agt. Aetna Life Ins. Co., Columbia, 1957-60; propr. Daniel H. Burns Co., mgmt. cons., broker, Columbia, 1960—; pres., dir. Nat. Search, Inc., 1966—, Indsl. Surveys, Inc., 1968—; Alliance Bldg. Industries, 1971-84; cons., Ednl. TV Network, govts. of Israel, Greece, W. Ger., Fed. Grants Projects, S.C. Ednl. TV Network; guest lectr. U. S.C.; cons. sales mgmt. and market analysis, analytical and conceptual problem solving; owner Western Rare Books-Fine Art, 1983—, Internat. Galleries, Empire Gallery, Empire Pub. Co.; bd. dir. Boulder Sch. of Massage Therapy. Pres., Schneider Sch. PTA, 1963-66; supr. registration City of Columbia, 1962-69; asst. project dir., statewide law enforcement edn. through TV, 1966-69; cons. Pitts. Leadership Found., 1980-81; dist. commr. Boy Scouts Am.; pres., committeeperson Boulder County Rep. Party; pres., bd. dirs. Internat. Communications Resources Found.; bd. dirs. Travelers Aid Assn. Am., Nat. Council USO; Columbia Sch. Theology for Laity; bd. dirs., exec. com. Consol. Agys. of United Funds; Richland County chpt. Nat. Found. Served with USAAF, 1943-46; lt. col. USAF ret. Mem. S.C. Football Ofcls. Assn., Columbia Real Estate Bd., Air Force Assn., Am. Y-Flyer Yacht Racing Assn., AAUP, Am. Mgmt. Assn., Nat. Assn. Ednl. Broadcasters, Soc. for Advancement Mgmt., Am.

Soc. Real Estate Appraisers, Interprofl. Cons. Council, Nat. Assn. Security Dealers, Soc. Am. Archivists, Nat. Hist. Soc., Internat. Platform Assn., Hist. Columbia Found., S.C. Press Assn., Columbia C. of C., Am. Soc. Personal Adminstrn., Sierra Club, Columbia Lyric Opera, Internat. Christian Leaders, Fellowship Christian Athletes, English Speaking Union, N. Am. Yacht Racing Union, Sigma Phi Epsilon. Episcopalian/Anglican. Clubs: Charleston (S.C.) Yacht; Yachting of Am., Workshop Theatre, First Nighters, Columbia Squash Racquets, Town Theatre, Masons (Shriner), Rotary. Author publs. in field. Home: 7425 Empire Dr Boulder CO 80303-5007 Office: 7425 Empire Dr Boulder CO 80303-5007 E-mail: empgal@earthlink.net.

BURNS, DAVID MITCHELL, writer, musician, former diplomat; b. Pineville, Ky., Dec. 1, 1928; s. Judge and Louise (Cooke) B.; m. Sandra Dunlop, June 8, 1955; children: David A., Patrick C. BA, Princeton U., 1953; student, Sch. Advanced Internat. Studies, Johns Hopkins U., 1957, 60, Howard U., 1957, 60, Fgn. Service Inst., Tangier, Morocco, 1967-69. Advt. trainee Gen. Electric Co., 1953; instr. English U. Kans., 1954-55; asst. cultural affairs officer Am. embassy, Damascus, Syria, 1955-56, Beirut, 1956; dir. Iran-Am. Soc., Isfahan, 1957; information officer Am. consulate general Salisbury, Fedn. Rhodesia and Nyasaland, 1957-59; pub. affairs officer Am. embassy, Bamako, Mali, 1960-62; cultural affairs officer Tunis, Tunisia, 1962-63; cultural policy officer Africa, USIA, 1963-67, Am. embassy, Tunis, Tunisia; pub. affairs officer Am. interests sect. embassy of Switzerland, Algiers, Algeria, 1969-72; dir. sci. and tech. programs USIA, 1972-77; dir. climate project AAAS, Washington, 1978-90. Author: Gateway: Dr. Thomas Walker and the Opening of Kentucky, 2000, Quests; CD's as leader of Hot Mustard Quintet include Swing Song, Don't Postpone Joy, Nothing Loved Is Ever Lost, Rainbow Room, 1975—; contbr. articles to newspapers and mags., 1953—. Fulbright grant l'Universite de Lille and Salzburg Seminar in Am. Studies, 1953-54; recipient award of merit Ky. Hist. Soc., 2001. Mem. Nat. Assn. Sci. Writers, Nat. Book Critics Cir., Jazz Journalists Assn. Clubs: Cosmos, Dacor (Washington). Office: 1712 19th St NW Washington DC 20009-1606 E-mail: davesand@starpower.net. *Constant course correction.*

BURNS, DENVER P. forestry research administrator; b. Bryan, Ohio, Oct. 27, 1940; married; 1 child. BS, Ohio State U., 1962, MS, 1964, PhD in Entomology, 1967; MPA, Harvard U., 1981. Asst. entomologist So. Forest Experiment Sta., 1962-68, rsch. entomologist, 1968-72, asst. dir., 1972-74; staff asst. to dep. chief for rsch. U.S. Forest Svc., 1974-76; dep. dir. North Ctrl. Experiment Sta., 1976-81; dir. Northeastern Forest Experiment Sta., Radnor, Pa., 1981-92, Rocky Mountain Sta., 1992—. Mem. AAAS.

BURNS, DONALD SNOW, registered investment advisor, financial and business consultant; b. Cambridge, Mass., July 31, 1925; s. Jules Ian and Ruth (Snow) B.; m. Lucy Lee Keating, July 15, 1947 (div.); childen: Julie Ann Wrigley, Patti B. Boyd, Laurie Bidegain, Wendi Collins, Loni Monahan, Robin Alden; m. Bettye Geurin, July 31, 1997. Student, Williams Coll., 1943-44; M in Baking, Am. Inst. of Baking, 1947. Baker O'Rourke Baking Co., Buffalo, 1946-49; gen. mgr. Glaco Co. of So. Calif., L.A., 1949-51; regional mgr. Glaco Div. of Ekco Prodn. Co., Chgo., 1951-53, gen. mgr., 1953-56; pres. McClintock Mfg. Div. Ekco Prodn. Co., Chgo., 1956-61; v.p. Ekco Products Co., Chgo., 1961-67; pres., chmn. Prestige Automotive Group, Garden Grove, Calif., 1967-78; chmn. Prestige Holdings Ltd., Newport Beach, Calif., 1978—. Chmn. bd. Newport Nat. Bank, Newport Beach, 1961-67; bd. dir. Securitas Trust, Monte Carlo, Monaco, Am. Safety Equipment Co., Glendale, Calif., Internat. Tech. Corp., Torrance, Calif., Escorp, San Luis Obispo, Calif.; dir. Internat. Rectifier, El Segundo. Author: (short story) The Goose that Neighed, 1967, (books) Two and a Half Nickels, 1970, Light My Fire, 1979. Mem. Calif. State U. Adv. Bd., Fullerton, 1973-76; bd. dirs. Santiago Coll. Found., Santa Ana, Calif., 1989-90, Orange County Sheriff's Adv. Coun., Calif., 1978—, pres., 1987-88; chmn. bd. trustees Orme Sch. Mayer Ariz., 1976-78. With USNR, 1943-46. Mem. Jonathan Club. Avocations: sailing, scuba diving, flying, auto racing, fishing. E-mail: dburns00@yahoo.com.

BURNS, EDWARD CHARLES, infosystems specialist; b. Newark, Sept. 22, 1942; s. Edward Joseph and Anna Marie (Grim) B.; m. (div.); children: Anneliese, Edward. BS, St. Peter's Coll., 1964; MBA cum laude, Fairleigh Dickinson U., 1973. Assoc. programmer IBM, Cranford, N.J., 1969-70; tech. support mgr. Beneficial Data Processing Corp., Morristown, N.J., 1970-75; mgr. computer performance planning group Warner-Lambert Co., Morris Plains, N.J., 1975-82; mgr. tech. devel. Internat. Paper Co., Denville, N.J., 1982-83; sr. v.p. global infrastructure svcs. The CIT Group, Livingston, NJ, 1983—. Adj. assoc. prof. computer tech. County Coll. of Morris, Randolph, N.J., 1973-87; assessment cons. Thomas Edison State Coll., Trenton, N.J., 1978—, mem. bus. degree adv. com., 1979-94; evaluator Am. Coun. on Edn., Washington, 1980—. Mentor Distance Independent Adult Learning, 1995—. Capt AUS, 1960-68. Decorated Bronze Star. Mem. Civil Air Patrol, Am. Assn. Collegiate Independent Study. Roman Catholic. Avocation: flying. Home: 23 Molly Stark Dr Morristown NJ 07960-5140 Office: The CIT Group Inc 1 CIT Drive Livingston NJ 07039-5703 E-mail: mentor@prodigy.net., ed.burns@cit.com.

BURNS, EDWARD J., JR., actor, film director; b. Valley Stream, N.Y., Jan. 29, 1968; s. Edward Sr. and Molly Burns; m. Christy Turlington, 2003. BA, Hunter Coll. Motion picture dir., writer, prodr.; motion picture actor; entrepreneur Irish Twin Prodn. Co. Actor, dir., writer (films) The Brothers McMullen, 1995 (Jury Spl. prize Deauville Film Festival, 1995, Ind. Spirit award, 1995, Nova award, 1995, Grand Jury prize Sundance Film Festival, 1995), She's the One, 1996, No Looking Back, 1998, Sidewalks of New York, 2001; actor: (films) Saving Private Ryan, 1998, 15 Minutes, 2001, Any Given Sunday, 1999, Life or Something Like It, 2002, Confidence, 2003; writer, actor, prodr., dir. (films) Ash Wednesday, 2002, writer, prodr. (TV series) The Fighting Fitzgeralds, 2001. Recipient ShowWest award for Screenwriter of Yr., 1996. Office: c/o ICM 8942 Wilshire Blvd Beverly Hills CA 90211-1934

BURNS, SISTER ELIZABETH MARY, hospital administrator; b. Estherville, Iowa, Mar. 3, 1927; d. Bernard Aloysius and Viola Caroline (Brennan) B. Diploma in Nursing, St. Joseph Mercy Sch. Nursing, Sioux City, Iowa, 1952; BS in Nursing Edn, Mercy Coll., Detroit, 1957; M.Sc. in Nursing, Wayne State U., 1958; Ed.D., Columbia U., 1969. Joined Sisters of Mercy, Roman Cath. Ch., 1946; nursing supr. Mercy Med. Center, Dubuque, Iowa, 1952-55; supr. orthopedics and urology St. Joseph Mercy Hosp., Sioux City, 1955-56; dir. Sch. Nursing, 1958-63; chmn. dept. nursing Mercy Coll. of Detroit, 1963-73; dir. health services Sisters of Mercy, Province of Detroit, 1973-77; pres., chief exec. officer Marian Health Center, Sioux City, 1977-87; sabbatical leave, 1988. Coord. life planning Sisters of Mercy, 1989-90, mem. province adminstrv. team, 1990-98; cons. Trinity Health, 2001—. Bd. dirs. Mercy Sch. Nursing of Detroit, 1968-77, Mercy H.S., Farmington Hills, Mich., 2000—; mem. exec. com. Greater Detroit Area Hosp. Coun., 1973-77; trustee St. Mary Coll., Omaha, 1981-82, Briar Cliff Coll., Sioux City, 1981-87, Battle Creek Health Sys., 2002—, Mercy Med. Ctr., Sioux City, Iowa, 2001—; chmn. Mercy Health Adv. Coun., 1978-80. Mem. Western Iowa League for Nursing (pres. 1960-62), Nat. League for Nursing, Sisters of Mercy Shared Svcs. Coordinating Com., Cath. Hosp. Assn. (trustee 1977-80), Sisters of Mercy Health Corp. (trustee 1988-90, governance coord. 1998-2001), Mercy Health Svcs. (chair bd. 1990-95, membership bd. 1995-98, historian 1998-2001). Address: 28554 Eleven Mile Farmington MI 48336-1507 E-mail: eburns@mercydetroit.org., burnse@trinity-health.org.

BURNS, ELLEN BREE, federal judge; b. New Haven, Conn., Dec. 13, 1923; d. Vincent Thomas and Mildred Bridget (Bannon) Bree; m. Joseph Patrick Burns, Oct. 8, 1955 (dec.); children: Mary Ellen, Joseph Bree, Kevin James. BA, Albertus Magnus Coll., 1944, LLD (hon.), 1974; LLB, Yale U., 1947; LLD (hon.), U. New Haven, 1981, Sacred Heart U., 1986, Fairfield U., 1991. Bar: Conn. 1947. Dir. legis. legal svcs. State of Conn., 1949-73; judge Conn. Cir. Ct., 1973-74, Conn. Ct. of Common Pleas, 1974-76, Conn. Superior Ct., 1976-78, U.S. Dist. Ct. Conn., New Haven, 1978—, chief judge, 1988-92, sr. judge, 1992—. Trustee Fairfield U., 1978-85, Albertus Magnus Coll., 1985—. Recipient John Carroll of Carrollton award John Barry Council K.C., 1973, Judiciary award Conn. Trial Lawyers Assn., 1978, Cross Pro Ecclesia et Pontifice, 1981, Law Rev. award U. Conn. Law Rev., 1987, Judiciary award Conn. Bar Assn., 1987, Raymond E. Baldwin Pub. Svc. award Bridgeport Law Sch., 1992. Mem.: ABA, Conn. Bar Found., Conn. Bar Assn., New Haven County Bar Assn., Am. Bar Found. Roman Catholic. Office: US Dist Ct 141 Church St New Haven CT 06510-2030

BURNS, EUGENE HUGH, JR., biology educator; b. Knoxville, Tenn., July 23, 1965; s. Eugene Hugh and Edith Marlene Burns. BA, U. Tenn., 1987, PhD, 1995. Rsch. assoc. Baylor Coll. Medicine, Houston, 1995—97; asst. prof. Drew U., Madison, NJ, 1997—99, Shawnee State U., Portsmouth, Ohio, 1999—2002, assoc. prof., 2002—. Spkr. on anthrax Rotary Club, Shawnee State U., 2002. Contbr. articles to profl. jours. Recipient Instructional Materials grant, Shawnee State U., 1999. Mem.: Nat. Assn. Biology Tchrs., Ohio Acad. Scis., N.Y. Acad. Scis., Am. Soc. for Microbiology, Phi Beta Kappa. Roman Catholic. Achievements include research in Bordetella bronchiseptica and group A streptococcus. Office: Shawnee State U Dept Natural Sci 940 2d St Portsmouth OH 45662

BURNS, FRANCIS RAYMOND, medical facility administrator, researcher; b. Ogden, Utah, Oct. 13, 1935; s. Gerald Eugene and Lucy Marie (Sargent) B.; m. Marilyn McDonald, Feb. 15, 1959 (div. Sept. 1968); children: Lawrence R., John W.; m. Lucia Esperanza Gaitan, Sept. 19, 1993; 1 child, Francis Leonard. AA, San Francisco City Coll., 1961; BA, San Francisco State U., 1968, postgrad., 1968-72; MA, Calif. State U., 2001. Dir. Biofeedback Clinic Noogenesis Inc., San Francisco, 1968—, dir. clinic, head R&D, 1968—, dir., pres., 1968—. Inventor in field. Vol. coord. San Francisco Neighborhood Renovation Group, 1972-74. With USN, 1953-56. Nominated Fulbright fellow, 2001. Avocations: gardening, camping, travel, innovative research, reading. Office: Noogenesis Inc Ste 102 1301 Ignacio Valley Rd Walnut Creek CA 94598

BURNS, GEORGE FRANKLIN, archivist, retired language educator; b. Milan, Aug. 17, 1921; s. George Franklin Burns and Pearle Barbee Katherine; m. Mary John Wade, Aug. 24, 1968 (dec. 1999); 1 stepchild, Scott Lockwood II. BA, Cumberland U., 1942, JD, 1944; MA, George Peabody Coll., 1967; PhD, Vanderbilt U., 1973. Reporter Wilson County News, Lebanon, Tenn., 1942—43; assoc. editor Lebanon Dem., 1943—66; staff corr. Nashville Banner, 1948—65; reviewer lit. page The Tennessean, Nashville, 1962—77, columnist, 1980—81; prof. English and pub. rels. dir. Cumberland U., Lebanon, 1959—63, 1966—74; faculty Tenn. Technol. U., Cookeville, 1974—90; emeritus prof. Cumberland U., Lebanon, 1989—, English archivist, 1991—. Historian, editor Tenn. Commn. for Commemoration of 50th Anniversary of 2d Army Tenn. Maneuvers, 1993—95; founder Vol. State Athletic Conf., 1947. Author: (critical book) Mr. Faulkner in Tennessee, 1986, 5 books on Tenn. history; contbr. Cir. Dem. Nat. Com., 1999—; chair Wilson County Libr. Bd., 1956; sec. Regional Planning Commn., 1950—60. Recipient Disting. Svc. award, Jaycees, 1952, C. of C., 1958. Mem.: MLA (life), History Assocs. (past pres.), Rotary (Paul Harris award), Sigma Alpha Epsilon. Democrat. Presbyterian. Avocations: photography, travel. Home: 1809 Andover Dr Garland TX 75041 Office: Cumberland U Archives PO Box 1415 Lebanon TN 37088

BURNS, H(ERBERT) MICHAEL, corporate director; b. Toronto, Ont., Can., June 19, 1937; s. Charles Folwer Williams and Janet Mary (Wilson) B.; m. Susan P. Cathers, Dec. 23, 1980; children: Charles F.M., Janet Michelle. Student, Cornell U., Trinity Coll. Sch., Port Hope, Can. With Nesbitt Burns (and predecessor cos.), 1958-77; dep. chmn., bd. dirs. Extendicare Inc. Pres., treas. Kingfield Investments Ltd. and assoc. subs.; bd. dirs. Algoma Ctrl. Corp., Landmark Global Fin. Inc., Phoenix Can. Oil Ltd. Bd. dirs., past pres. Royal Agrl. Winter Fair; bd. govs. Trinity Coll. Sch., Olympic Trust Can.; chancellor Rennison Coll., U. Waterloo, Can.; bd. dirs. Can. Fedn. for AIDS Rsch. Mem. Toronto Club, Kappa Alpha. Avocations: recreation, farming. Home: Kingswood 1314 King Vaughan Rd Maple ON Canada L6A 2A5 Office: Extendicare Inc 3000 Steeles Ave E Ste 300 Markham ON Canada L3R 9W2

BURNS, HUGH L. priest, writer; b. Derby, Conn., June 27, 1953; s. Hugh L. Burns and Elizabeth Ann Griffin. MA STL, Dominican House of Studies, Wash., D.C., 1983, MDiv STB, 1980; BA, Boston Coll., 1975. Preacher, pub. spkr. Dominican Fathers, Jersey City, 1989—, dir., founder Bayamón, PR, 1987—89, Wash. Inst. Ethics & Spirituality, DC, 1985—87, St. Catherine Siena Symposium, Wash., DC, 1980—87; assoc. pastor Our Lady of Sorrows, Takoma Park, Md., 1983—87; commdntator Nat. Pub. Radio, Newark Pub. Radio. Trustee U. Ctrl., Bayamóm, PR, 1988—89. Commentator: Nat. Pub. Radio, N.Y. Pub. Radio; contbr. articles to jours. Mem. Dem. Town Com., Needham, Mass., 1971—75. Roman Catholic. Avocations: painting, photography. Office: Dominican Preaching 525 Bergen Ave A 45 Jersey City NJ 07304 Fax: 201-432-2987.

BURNS, IVAN ALFRED, grocery products and industrial company executive; b. Leamington Spa, England, Jan. 18, 1935; s. Cecil Ivan and Dorothy Constance (Mote) B.; m. Angela Loeffel, May 16, 1959; children: Pauline Cecile, Charla Cheyney, Claudine. BS, Coventry Coll., 1958. Various positions Deere & Co., Moline, Ill., 1969-73; dir. internat. ACF Industries Inc., N.Y.C., 1973-75, v.p., 1975-81, pres., COO, 1981-84, chmn., CEO, 1983-90; dir. CPC Internat. Inc., Englewood Cliffs, NJ, 1985-87, pres. corn refining divsn., 1987-90, exec. v.p. adminstrn., 1987—; pres., dir. Picca Enterprises, Inc., New Canaan, Conn., 1984-96. Bd. dirs. Continental Corp., N.Y.C. Patentee valve, 1980. Bd. dirs. United Way, New York, 1984-85; mem. bus. adv. bd. Northwestern U., 1983-92. Mem. Conf. Bd. Republican. Mem. Ch. of England. Avocations: horse breeding, collecting netsukes. Home and Office: 57 Deer Park Rd New Canaan CT 06840

BURNS, J. ROBERT, physician; b. Norristown, Pa., July 7, 1937; s. Jess Evans and Ruth Holt B.; m. Janet Marie Kirchhof, Aug. 12, 1961; 1 child, Bryan Douglas. BS, Ursinus Coll., 1959; MD, Hahneman U., 1963. Intern Hahneman U., Phila., 1963-64; resident Lahey Clin., Boston, 1964-67; rsch. fellow, thoracic disease Mayo Clin., Rochester, Minn., 1969-70, clin. fellow, thoracic disease, 1970-71; physician Geisinger Med. Ctr., Danville, Pa., 1971—. Clin. prof. medicine Jefferson Med. Coll., Phila., 1990—; dir. pulmonary and critical care medicine, chmn. bioethics com., med. advisor, respiratory svcs., mem. tech. assessment com., Geisinger Med. Ctr. Capt. USAF, 1969-71. Fellow Am. Coll. Physicians, Am. Coll. Chest Physicians; mem. Am. Thoracic Soc., Am. Soc. Law, Medicine, and Ethics, Am. Coll. Hyperbaric Medicine, Undersea & Hyperbaric Medicine Soc., Pa. Thoracic Soc., Soc. Crit. Care Medicine, Kennedy Inst. Ethics. Avocations: skiing, windsurfing, golf, bicycling, photography. Office: Geisinger Med Ctr 20-37 Pulmonary and Critical Care Medicine Danville PA 17822

BURNS, JAMES MILTON, retired educator; b. Coal City, Ind., Feb. 22, 1922; s. Ray L. and N. Eugenie (Pickett) B.; m. Thomasina Ciofalo, Aug. 22, 1970. MusB, Manhattan Sch. Music, 1949, MusM, 1953; EdD, Fairleigh Dickinson U., 1984. Tchr. music Atlantic City Bd. Edn., 1968-92. Researcher acoustics of band instruments. With USAAF, 1942-46. Mem. over 20 profl. assns.

BURNS, JAMES SCOTTE, II, secondary school educator; b. Wichita, Kans., Sept. 1, 1962; s. James Scott Burns and Jeane Marie Rhodes; m. Anastasia M.S. Wright, July 4, 1983; children: Sonia, James. BA in English, Regis U., 2000. Cert. tchr. Colo. Tchr. Jefferson Acad. Charter Sch., Broomfield, Colo., 1994—; musician Denver, 1980—97. Cons., writer JA Core Knowledge Assessment Team, Broomfield, 1999—; instr., dir. JA Student Debate Project, Broomfield, 2000—. Author: (nonfiction/humor) Homedad: The Wit and Wisdom of Hunter/Gatherer Homemaking, 1997; composer: (musical composition) Antfarm, 1987 (Hon. Mention - Colo. Composers Classic, 1987); author: (nonfiction essay) The Department of Customer Service, 1997, (book) The Armageddon Reader. Judge Odyssey of the Mind, Denver, 1996—97; registered agt., copy cons. Coloradans for Charter Schs., Arvada, 1999—2002. Mem.: Nat. Sci. Tchrs. Assn., Am. Assn. of Educators, Alpha Sigma Nu. Libertarian. Unitarian Universalist. Avocations: literature, music, history, humor. Home: 9340 Estes Ln Broomfield CO 80021 Office: Jefferson AcadCharter Sch 9955 Yarrow St Broomfield CO 80021 Office Fax: 303-438-1049. Personal E-mail: musetramp@attbi.com.

BURNS, JAMES W. education educator; b. New Haven, Jan. 24, 1937; s. James W. and Helen M. (Wieliesz) B.; children: Amy, Kristin, Katherine. BS, Ctrl. Conn. State U., 1958; MEd, Pa. State U., 1964, EdD, 1969. Tchr. Greenwich (Conn.) Pub. Schs., 1958-64; dir. Curriculum Ctr. Pa. State U., University Park, 1964-68; prof. edn., reading recovery tchr. and leader trainer Western Mich. U., Kalamazoo, 1968—. Mem. Internat. Reading Assn., Nat. Coun. of Tchrs. of English, Mich. Reading Assn., NGA. Home: 5093 Century Ave Kalamazoo MI 49006-5713 Office: 3414 Sangren Hall Kalamazoo MI 49007

BURNS, JAMES WILLIAM, business executive; b. Winnipeg, Man., Can., Dec. 27, 1929; s. Charles William and Helen Gladys (Mackay) B.; m. Barbara Mary Copeland ; children: James F.C., Martha J., Alan W. B in Commerce, U. Man., 1951; MBA, Harvard U., 1953, LLD (hon.), 1988. With Great-West Life Assurance Co., 1953—, dir., 1970, pres., CEO, 1971-79; pres. Power Corp. Can., 1979-86, dep. chmn., 1986—2002; chmn., CEO Power Fin. Corp., 1986-90. Bd. dirs. Investors Group Gt.-West Life Assurance Co., Gt.-West Lifeco, Inc., Gt.-West Life and Annuity Ins. Co., London Life Ins. Co., London Ins. Group, Inc.; dir. emeritus Power Corp. Can., Power Fin. Corp. Founding dir. Man. Mus. Man and Nature; past chmn. Conf. Bd. Can.; mem. Gov.'s Coun., Shaw Festival. Named Officer of the Order of Can.; Hon. col. Queen's Own Cameron Highlanders of Can. Mem. St. Charles Country Club, Man. Club, Toronto Club, Mount-Royal Club. Office: Power Corp Can 2600 One Lombard Pl Winnipeg MB Canada R3BOX5

BURNS, JOHN FRANCIS, state official, educator; b. Joliet, Ill., Sept. 13, 1945; s. Francis J. and Agnes A. (Vidmar) B.; m. Melinda A. Peak, 1995; 1 child, Alyssa Marie. BA in History, Lewis Coll., 1967; MA in History, Wash. State U., 1972; cert., Western Wash. U., 1977, Acad. Cert. Archivists, 1989. Cert. tchr. Calif. Instr. Skagit Valley Coll., Mt. Vernon, Wash., 1972-75; Pace prof. Chapman Coll., Orange, Calif., 1975-76; instr. Western Wash. U., Bellingham, 1976; project adminstr. Wash. State Records Bd., Olympia, 1977-81; chief of archives State of Calif., Sacramento, 1981-95; dir. Calif. State Archives and Golden State Mus., 1995-97; history and social sci. cons., online course models project dir. Calif. Dept. Edn., 1997—. Cons. and lectr. in field; adj. prof. history Calif. State U., Sacramento, 1987—; adj. prof. libr. sci. San Jose State U., 1999--. Author: Approaching the Millenium: Prospects and Perils in California's Archival Future, 1992; editor: Historical Records of Washington State, 3 vols., 1980-81, Guide to the Los Angeles Police Department Records of the Robert F. Kennedy Assassination Investigation, 1993, Social Studies Review, 1999, History of Sacramento, 1999, Capital Dreams: The Transformation of Sacramento, 2003; co-editor Washington State Guide to Governor's Papers, 1977, Taming the Elephant: Politics, Government and Law in Pioneer California, 2003; contbr. chpts. to books, articles to profl. jours. Sec. Calif. Heritage Preservation Commn., Sacramento, 1981-97; coord. Calif. Hist. Records Adv. Bd., Sacramento, 1981-97; chmn. Nat. Steering Com. of State Records Coord., Sacramento, 1983-85; mem. Calif. Hist. State Capitol Commn., Sacramento, 1984-97, exec. dir. Calif. State Archives Found., 1987-97; mem. Sacramento Commn. History and Sci., 1993-99; mem. adv. bd. Calif. Internat. Studies Project, 1998--. Lt. USN, 1967-70, Vietnam. Recipient Calif. State Govt. Mgmt. award, 1986, 89, Calif. Mil. History Medal award, 1997, Publs. award Sacramento County Hist. Soc., 1999, Spl. Achievement award Sacramento County Hist. Soc., 2000, Resolution of Hon. award Sacramento County Bd. Suprs., 1999-2000, Presdl. award Calif. Coun. Soc. Studies, 2001-02, Diane Brooks award, 2003; grantee Nat. Hist. Publ. and Records Commn., Washington, 1977-86, U.S. Dept. Edn., 1998-2001. Mem. Nat. Assn. Govt. Archives and Records Adminstrs. (v.p. 1986-88, bd. dirs. 1983-85, pres. 1988-90), Soc. Am. Archivists (chmn. com. goals and priorities 1987-90), Calif. Com. for Promotion of History (steering com. 1984-87, award of merit 1989), Spindex Users Network (chmn. 1979-81), Orgn. Am. Historians, Soc. Calif. Archivists (cert. recognition 1989), Calif. Coun. for the Social Studies (dept. rep. 1998—), Nat. Coun. for the Social Studies, Am. Assn. for State and Local History (host com. chair 1998), Nat. Coun. for History Edn. (host com. chair 2000). Office: Calif Dept Edn Stds and Assessment 1430 N St Ste 5408 Sacramento CA 95814 E-mail: jburns@cde.ca.gov.

BURNS, JOHN JOSEPH, JR., financial and insurance holding company executive; b. Cambridge, Mass., June 27, 1931; s. John Joseph and Alice (Blake) Burns; m. Barbara Ann Miller, Oct. 18, 1958; children: John J. Burns III, Christine, Gregory, Timothy, Jennifer. BS in Fin., Boston Coll., 1953; MBA, Harvard U., 1955. Asso. buying dept. and arbitrage dept. Goldman Sachs & Co., N.Y.C., 1957-63; assoc. N.Y. Securities, N.Y.C., 1963-67, gen. ptnr., 1968; v.p. fin., dir. Alleghany Corp., N.Y.C., 1968-77, pres., dir., 1977—, mem. exec. com., 1977—, CEO, 1992—. Bd. dirs. Burlington No. Santa Fe Corp., Dallas, Fidelity Nat. Fin. Corp., Santa Barbara, Calif. With USN, 1955—57. Mem.: Links Club. Roman Catholic. Office: Alleghany Corp 375 Park Ave Ste 3201 New York NY 10152-3297

BURNS, JOHN JOSEPH, pharmacology educator; b. Flushing, N.Y., Oct. 8, 1920; s. Thomas F. and Katherine (Kane) B. BS, Queens Coll., 1942; MA, Columbia U., 1948, PhD, 1950. With lab. chem. pharmacology Nat. Heart Inst., 1950-60, dep. chief lab., 1957-60; head sec. clin. pharmacology, also adj. asst. prof. biochemistry NYU research service Goldwater Meml. Hosp., Welfare Island, N.Y., 1950-57; dir. research pharmacodynamics div. Wellcome Research Labs., Burroughs Wellcome & Co. (U.S.A.) Inc., Tuckahoe, N.Y., 1960-66; v.p. for research Hoffmann-LaRoche Inc., Nutley, N.J., 1967-84. Vis. prof. pharmacology Albert Einstein Coll. Medicine, 1960-68, Cornell U. Med. Coll., 1996—; adj. prof. Cornell U. Med. Coll., 1969-84, Rockefeller U., 1984-94; adj. mem. Roche Inst. Molecular Biology, 1984-96; cons. pharmacology and toxicology programs NIH; chmn. com. problems drug safety Drug Rsch. Bd., 1965-72. Author articles metabolism drugs, vitamins and carbohydrates. Served with AUS, 1944-46. Fellow Am. Inst. Chemists; mem. Inst. Medicine, Nat. Acad. Scis., N.Y. Acad. Scis. (v.p. 1964-65), Am. Soc. Pharmacology and Exptl. Therapeutics (pres. 1972-73), Am. Soc. Biol. Chemists, Am. Inst. Nutrition, Am. Coll. Neuropsychopharmacology, Internat. Union Pharmacology (pres. 1975-78) Home: 331 Lansdowne Westport CT 06880-5651

BURNS, JOHN MITCHELL, academic administrator; BS in Edn. and Chemistry, N.Mex. State U., 1963, MS in Biology and Microbiology, 1966; PhD in Zoology and Endocrinology, Ind. U., 1969. Endocrinology rsch. fellow Mayo Med. Sch., Rochester, Minn., 1976-77; chmn. dept. biol. scis. Tex. Tech U., Lubbock, 1987-95, vice provost acad. affairs, 1995-97, interim provost, 1996-97, provost, 1997—. Spkr. in field. Contbr. articles to profl. jours. Recipient Disting. Tchg. award Amoco, 1977, Outstanding Tchg. and Svc. award Arts and Scis. Coun., 1980, Omicron Delta Kappa, 1991, Outstanding Tchg. award Jr. Panhellenic Assn., 1975, Mortar Bd., 1981, Pres.' Excellence in Tchg. award, 1986; named Outstanding Centennial Alumnus Coll. Arts and Scis. N.Mex. State U., 1988. Fellow Endocrine Soc. Address: PO Box 42019 Lubbock TX 79409-2019

BURNS, JOHN RICHARD, chiropractor, educator; b. Champaign, Ill., Sept. 30, 1951; s. Dale Eugene and Martha Ellen Burns; m. Vickie Lynn Rockwell, Mar. 9, 1974; children: Kelly, Keith. D of Chiropractic, Palmer Coll. of Chiropractic, 1973. Instr. Palmer Coll. Chiropractic, Davenport, Iowa, 1973-77, asst. prof., 1977-80, assoc. prof., 1980-85, prof., 1985—, chmn. technique, 1977-99, spl. asst. to pres., 1999—2003, spl. adv. to chancellor, 2003—. Practice chiropractic East Moline Chiropractic Clinic. Author: Extremities: Adjusting and Evaluation, 1983. Dir. Palmer Rugby Team, 1975-76. Fellow Internat. Chiropractors Assn. (bd. dirs.), Gonstead Clin. Study Soc., Ill. Prairie State Chiropractic Assn. (bd. dirs., Chiropractor of Yr. 1989, Lifetime Achievement award 2002). Office: East Moline Chiropractic 379 Avenue of the Cities East Moline IL 61244

BURNS, JOSEPH ARTHUR, planetary science educator; b. N.Y.C., Mar. 22, 1941; s. John Driscoll and Genevieve Mary (McCarthy) B.; m. Judith Ann Klein, July 1, 1967; children: Patrick M., Caitlin M. BS, Webb Inst., Glen Cove, N.Y., 1962; PhD, Cornell U., 1966. Asst. prof. Cornell U., Ithaca, NY, 1966-67, 68-74, assoc. prof., 1974-81, prof., 1981-94; Irving Porter Church prof. engring. and astronomy, 1994—; chmn. theoretical and applied mechs. Cornell U., Ithaca, NY, 1987-93, vice provost phys. scis. and engring., 2003—; NRC rsch. assoc. NASA Goddard Space Ctr., Greenbelt, Md., 1967-68; NAS exch. fellow Inst. Geophysics, Moscow, 1973; sr. scientist NASA Ames Rsch. Ctr., Mountain View, Calif., 1975-76, 82-83. Astronome titulaire Observatoire de Paris, France, 1979, 84; vis. prof. astronomy U. Calif., Berkeley, 1982-83; vis. prof. planetary sci. U. Ariz., Tucson, 1989-90; mem. space and earth scis. adv. com. NASA, 1983-87, solar sys. exploration com., 1988-92, NAS space studies bd., 1989-95, chair NAS com. planet exploration, 1992-95, mem. solar sys. decadal panel

NRC, 2001-02. Author 160 rsch. articles, 1966—; editor: Planetary Satellites, 1977, Satellites, 1986; editor Icarus-Internat. Jour. of Solar Sys. Studies, 1979-97; bd. rev. editors Sci., 2000—. Recipient various rsch. awards and grants NSF, 1976-86, 97, NASA, 1976—, NATO, 1998-2000, N.Y. Coun. Arts, 1972, NASA Sci. Achievement awards, 1997, 98, 2000. Fellow AAAS, Am. Geophys. Union; mem. Internat. Acad. Astronautics, Russian Acad. Sci., Am. Astron. Soc. (chmn. planetary scis. 1983-84, chmn. dynamical astronomy 2000-2001, v.p. 2001—, Masursky Prize 1994), Internat. Astron. Union (mem. solar sys. com. 1986-89, v.p. solar system 1996-99, v.p. celestial mechanics 2003—). Office: Cornell U Kimball Hall Dept Astronomy Ithaca NY 14853 E-mail: jab16@cornell.edu.

BURNS, JOSEPH M. economist; b. N.Y.C., Aug. 2, 1938; s. Arthur F. and Helen (Bernstein) B.; m. Ellen N. Herbst, Sept. 3, 1992; children: Stephen Juran, Rebecca Anne. AB, Swarthmore Coll., 1960; MA, U. Chgo., 1961, PhD, 1967. Economist rsch. dept. Fed. Reserve Bank N.Y., N.Y.C., 1961-62; asst. prof. dept. econs. UCLA, 1966-71; assoc. prof. dept. econs. Rice U., Houston, 1971-74; sr. economist, dep. dir. monetary rsch. office asst. sec. for internat. affairs U.S. Dept. Treasury, Washington, 1974-76; sr. economist, assoc. dir. rsch. div. econs. and edn. Commodity Futures Trading Commn., Washington, 1976-79; sr. economist antitrust div. U.S. Dept. Justice, Washington, 1979-2000. Vis. assoc. prof. dept. econs. Stanford (Calif.) U., 1973-74; professorial lectr. fin. dept. Georgetown U. Sch. Bus., Washington, 1979, 84. Author: Accounting Standards and International Finance, 1976, A Treatise on Markets, 1979; contbr. articles to profl. jours. Earhart Found. fellow, 1963-65; Ford Found. fellow, 1965-66; Hoover Instn. fellow, 1973-74. Mem. Am. Econ. Assn. (census adv. com. 1972-75).

BURNS, JOSEPHINE DORA, artist; b. Llandudno, Wales, July 2, 1917; came to U.S., 1926; d. Vincent Leo and Harriet Matilda (Williams) Lazzaro; m. Jerome Burns, Nov. 17, 1943. Cert., Cooper Union Art Sch., N.Y.C., 1939; BFA, Cooper Union Art Sch., 1976. Draftsman George Sharp, Marine Architect, N.Y.C., 1941-45; co-dir. Hicks St. Gallery, Bklyn., 1958-63; assoc. dir. Brownstone Gallery, Bklyn., 1969-76. Exhibited in group shows at C.W. Post Coll. Mus., Bklyn. Mus., Nat. Arts Club, Nat. Acad., Audubon Artists Exhibit, Alonzo Gallery, N.Y.C., Okla. Mus. Art, Salena Gallery L.I. U., 1984, Thompson's Gallery, London, 1999, 2000; solo exhibit Auld Alliance Gallery, Nashville, 1994; exhibit of 32-page color catalogue for exhibit Gallery Ynys Môn, Anglesey, North Wales, 1998. Fellow MacDowell Colony, 1960, 62, 64, 65, 68, Yaddo, 1961. Home: 248 Garfield Pl Brooklyn NY 11215-2207 also: 47 Church Walks Llandudno Conway LL30 2HL Wales

BURNS, KENNETH JONES, JR., lawyer, consultant; b. Cleve., Oct. 3, 1926; s. Kenneth Jones and Isabel (Nanson) B.; m. Edith Louise Mitten, June 23, 1949; children: Deborah, Kenneth Jones III, Sarah, Elizabeth, Nancy, Andrew. BS, Northwestern U., 1948, JD, 1951. Bar: Ill. 1951, Ohio 1972. Asso. Jenner & Block, Chgo., 1951-60, partner, 1961-72; sr. v.p., gen. counsel, sec. Anchor Hocking Corp., Lancaster, Ohio, 1972-79; v.p., gen. counsel, sec. Internat. Minerals & Chem. Corp. (later Mallinkrodt Inc.), Northbrook, Ill., 1979-93; exec. legal cons. Mallinckrodt Inc., Northbrook, 1993-98. Legal counsel Chgo. Jr. Assn. Commerce and Industry, 1955-58; lectr. Northwestern U. Sch. Law, 1955. Pres. Wilmette Civic Improvement Assn., 1958-62; v.p., dir. Citizens of Greater Chgo., 1961-64; bd. dirs. Am. Bar Endowment, 1975-90, v.p., 1981-83, pres., 1983-85. With USNR, 1945-46, 51-52. Recipient Key award Chgo. Jr. Assn. Commerce, 1956 Fellow Am. Bar Found. (dir. 1983-85, 90-2000, treas. 1993-96, v.p. 1996-98, pres. 1998-2000); mem. ABA (chmn. jr. bar conf. 1961-62, ho. of dels. 1962-64, 71—, asst. sec. 1967-71, sec., gov. 1971-75), Ill. Bar Assn., Chgo. Bar Assn. (bd. mgrs. 1961-63), Am. Bar Retirement Assn. (bd. dirs. 1982-86), Assn. Gen. Counsel, Am. Law Inst., Ill. Bar Found., Chgo. Barrister Inn (pres. 1966-67), Legal Club Chgo. (exec. com. 1981-82), Law Club Chgo., Order of Coif, Sigma Chi, Phi Delta Phi. Clubs: Skokie (Ill.) Country. Home and Office: 15 Warrington Dr Lake Bluff IL 60044-1322

BURNS, KENNETH LAUREN, filmmaker, historian; b. Bklyn., July 29, 1953; s. Robert Kyle and Lyla Smith (Tupper) B.; children: Sarah, Lilly. BA, Hampshire Coll., 1975; LHD (hon.), Bowdoin Coll., 1991; LittD (hon.), Amherst Coll., 1991; LHD (hon.), U. N.H.; DFA, Franklin Pierce Coll.; LittD (hon.), Notre Dame Coll., Manchester, N.H.; HHD (hon.), Coll. of St. Joseph, Rutland, Vt.; LHD (hon.), Springfield Coll. Ill., Pace U.; PhD (hon.), CUNY. Pres., owner Florentine Films, Walpole, N.H., 1975—. Films include Brooklyn Bridge, 1981 Christopher award 1963, Erik Barnouw prize Hist. Films), The Shakers: Hands to Work, Hearts to God, 1984 (CINE Golden Eagle award 1984), Huey Long, 1985 (Silver Baton award Dupont-Columbia Journalism 1988), The Statue of Liberty, 1985 (Christopher award 1987, CINE Golden Eagle award, Acad. award nomination 1986), Thomas Hart Benton, 1988 (CINE Golden Eagle award 1988, Golden Apple award Nat. Ednl. Film Festival 1989), The Congress, 1988 (CINE Golden Eagle award 1989, Red Ribbon Am. Film Festival 1989), The Civil War, 1990 (Emmy award for outstanding information series 1991, for outstanding individual achievement, writing 1991, CINE Gold Eagle award, Lincoln prize Gettysburg Coll. 1991, Dartmouth Film award 1990, Bell I. Wiley award Civil War Round Table, N.Y., 1991, D.W. Griffiths award, Christopher award, Peabody award 1990, Gabriel award 1991, People's Choice award 1991, Humanitas award 1991, Charles Frankel prize NEH 1991, Grammy award (2) 1992, numerous others), Radio Pioneers, 1981, Baseball (Outstanding Informational Series Emmy award), The West, 1996 (Erik Barnouw prize 1997), Thomas Jefferson, 1997, Lewis and Clark: The Journey of the Corps of Discovery, 1997, Frank Lloyd Wright, 1998, Not for Ourselves Alone: The Story of Elizabeth Cady Stanton & Susan B. Anthony, 1999, Jazz, 2000, Mark Twain, 2001; author: (with others) Centennial, 1986, (with Amy Stechler Burns) The Shakers: Hands to Work, Hearts to God, 1987, (with Geoffrey Ward and Ric Burns) The Civil War: An Illustrated History, 1990, Empire of the Air, 1992: retrospectives Smithsonian Instn., 1991, Walker Arts Ctr., Mpls., 1991, Pub. Broadcasting Svc., 1991-92, (with Geoffrey C. Ward) Baseball, 1994, (with Dayton Funcan) Lewis & Clark: The Journey of the Corps of Discovery, 1998. Trustee Hampshire Coll., Amherst, Mass., 1992—, N.H. Humanities Coun.; bd. dirs. MacDowell Colony, Peterborough, N.H. Mem. Acad. Motion Picture, Arts and Scis., Soc. Am. Historians, N.H. Humanities Coun. (trustee), Mass. Hist. Soc. (corr.). Home and Office: Maple Grove Rd P O Box 613 Walpole NH 03608*

BURNS, KEVIN MICHAEL, editor; b. Boston; s. William Leslie and Frances Mary Burns; m. Marie Kashan, Nov. 15, 1991 (div.);1 child, M. Reneé; stepchild, Catherine Ann Taylor; life ptnr. Isabel Taylor. AS in Surg. Tech., Baylor U., 1969; BA, Bridgewater State Tchrs. Coll., 1976; MS (hon.), Yale U., 1977. Sr. employment interviewer Mass. Divsn. Employment Security, Quincy, 1978; owner Trackside Restaurant, ME; vocat. rehab. counselor Mass. Rehab. Commn., Hyannis, Mass., 1978-79; mktg. cons. Stephi-Volt Corp., Chambersburg, PA, 1989-1996; local dir. Save Children Found., Louisville, 1999-2000; assignment editor Sta. WHAS-TV, Louisville, 2000—. Mem. U.S. Civil Def. Org., Hull, Mass., 1976-79. Sgt. USMC, 1969-70. Decorated Purple Heart, Bronze Star; recipient Emmy, 1999. Mem. Ky. Cols. (hon.). Democrat. Roman Catholic. Avocations: biking, swimming, sailing. E-mail: marine01usa@hotmail.com.

BURNS, KITTY, playwright; b. Chgo., Feb. 1, 1951; d. Joseph Lewis and Evelyn Marian (Smith) B. Author: (plays) Terminal Terror, 1991 (Silver award San Mateo Playwriting Contest 1991), Psycho Night at the Paradise Lounge, 1994, If God Wanted Us to Fly He Would Have Given Us Wings!, 1996; pub. Samuel French, Inc.; creator, performer The Vampire Tour of San Francisco; creator/author The Vampire Tour of New York. Mem.: Dramatists Guild. Avocations: writing children's books, poetry, short stories, acting, horseback riding.

BURNS, LARRY ALAN, judge; b. Pasadena, Calif., June 29, 1954; m. Kristi Francis, 1980; 2 children. BA in Speech and English, Point Loma Coll., 1976; JD, U. San Diego, 1979. Bar: Calif. 1979. Deputy dist. atty., San Diego, 1979-85; asst. U.S. atty., 1985-97; dir., corp. sec. Bank Commerce, San Diego, 1994-97; magistrate judge U.S. Dist. Ct., San Diego, 1997—. Fellow Am. Coll. Trial Lawyers; mem. Am. Bd. Trial Advocates (assoc.). Avocation: gardening. Office: Edward J Schwartz US Courthouse 940 Front St Rm D San Diego CA 92101-8994

BURNS, LESLIE KAYE, artist; b. Columbus, Miss., Sept. 21, 1953; d. Fayette Charles Jr. and Mary Theo (Wright) B. BFA in Printmaking/Advt. Art cum laude, Miss. U. for Women, 1975; MFA in Photography/Printmaking, U. Ala., 1978. Multi-image prodr., photographer Pitluk Group Advt. Agy., San Antonio, 1981-87; dir. media prodn. Inst. Texan Cultures U. Tex., San Antonio, 1987-2001. Artist: From a Girl to a Woman: Necole's Fifteenth Birthday, 1999 (47th Ann. Columbus Internat. Film and Video Festival honoree, Assn. Women in Comms. San Antonio Profl. chpt. award of merit for outstanding achievement in field of comms. 1999), Tex. Folklife Festival: 30 Pub. Svc. Announcement (Tex. Festivals and Events Assn. Mktg. award for pub. svc. ad or ad 2000). Recipient mktg. award Tex. Festivals and Events Assn., 1998. Mem. Am. Assn. Museums. Avocation: collecting folk and fine art.

BURNS, M. ANTHONY, transportation services company executive; b. Las Vegas, Nev., Nov. 1, 1942; s. Mitchel and Zella (Pulsipher) B.; m. Joyce Jordan, Nov. 14, 1962; children: Jill, Mitchel, Shauna. BS in Bus. Mgmt, Brigham Young U., 1964; MBA in Fin., U. Calif., Berkeley, 1965; hon. doctorate, Fla. Internat. U., 1989. With Mobil Oil Corp., N.Y.C., 1965-74, controller, 1970-72, cost-of-living coordinator, 1973, fin. analysis mgr., 1973-74; with Ryder System, Inc., Miami, Fla., 1974—, exec. v.p., chief fin. officer, 1978 79, pres., chief ops. officer, 1979-83, pres., chief exec. officer, 1983-85, chmn., pres., chief exec. officer, 1985—, also bd. dirs. Exec. v.p., CFO, pres. Ryder Truck Rental, Inc., 1980-81; bd. dirs. J.C. Penney Co., Inc., Pfizer Inc., The Chase Manhattan Corp., The Chase Manhattan Bank, N.A.; mem. nat. adv. coun. sch. mgmt. Brigham Young U., 1981—. Mem. bd. visitors Grad. Sch. Bus. Adminstrn., U. N.C., Chapel Hill, 1988-93; mem. bd. overseers Wharton Sch., 1989-94, assoc. trustee U. Pa., 1989-94; bd. dirs., trustee United Way Dade County, Fla., 1981—, chmn., 1991-93, Dade County campaign, 1988, bd. govs., 1989-92, chmn. S.E. region United Way of Am., 1989-92; trustee Nat. Urban League, 1984-94, chmn., 1987-89, vice chmn., 1989-94, hon. trustee, 1994—. Named Marketer of Yr. Acad. Mktg. Sci., 1983, Americanism award Anti-Defamation League, 1984, Bus. Leader of Yr. The Miami News, 1985, Ricks Coll. Bus. Leader of the Century, 1989, Fin. World CEO of Decade in Transp., Freight & Leasing, 1989, CEO of Yr., 1984, 85, 87, Bus. Leadership Hall of Fame, 1987; recipient Boneh Yisroel award Greater Miami Jewish Fedn., 1989, Silver medallion award Nat. Conf. Christians & Jews, 1988, Community Svc. award Advt. Fedn. Gt. Miami, 1987, Joseph Wharton Bus. Statesman award Wharton Sch. Club, 1987, Jesse Knight Indsl. Citizenship award Brigham Young U., 1988, Robert W. Laidlaw Humanitarian award Epilepsy Found. South Fla., 1989, Good Scout award Boy Scouts Am., 1990., Sand in my Shoes award Greater Miami C. of C., 1991, Equal Opportunity award Nat. Urban League, 1992, Humanitarian of Yr. award ARC, 1993. Mem. Bus. Coun., Bus. Roundtable (policy com.), Bus.-Higher Edn. Forum. Office: Ryder System Inc 3600 NW 82nd Ave Miami FL 33166-6623

BURNS, MARCELLINE, psychologist, researcher; BA in Psychology, San Diego State U., 1955; MA, Calif. State U., L.A., 1969; PhD, U. Calif., Irvine, 1972. Co-founder So. Calif. Rsch. Inst., L.A., 1973—. Cons., expert witness alcohol and drug effects on performance, FSTs, HGN, and drug recognition; lectr. in field. Contbr. articles to profl. jours. Recipient Public Svc. award U.S. Dept. Trans., 1993. Achievements include research on alcohol and drug effects, field sobriety tests and drug recognition. Office: So Calif Rsch Inst 11914 W Washington Blvd Los Angeles CA 90066-5816

BURNS, MARIE T. retired secondary education educator; b. Nashua, N.H. d. Charles Henry and Eleanor Agnes (Martin) O'Neil; m. Thomas M. Burns; children: Ann Burns Pelletier, Mary Burns Powlowsky, Catherine Burns Patten. BA, Regis Coll.; postgrad., Rivier Coll. Cert. tchr., N.H. Tchr. English Pelham (N.H.) Sch. Dept., City of Nashua. Former trustee, chmn. of house com., sec. bd. dirs. Mary A. Sweeney Home; judge, participant River Coll. Literacy Festival. Mem. Nashua Tchrs. Union (mem. secondary grouping practices com. Nashua Sch. Dist.), N.H. Ret. Tchrs., Nashua Ret. Tchrs.

BURNS, MARVIN GERALD, lawyer; b. Los Angeles, July 3, 1930; s. Milton and Belle (Cytron) B.; m. Barbara Irene Fisher, Aug. 23, 1953; children: Scott Douglas, Jody Lynn, Bradley Frederick. BA, U. Ariz., 1951; JD, Harvard U., 1954. Bar: Calif. 1955. Bd. dirs. Inner City Arts for Inner City Children. With AUS, 1955-56. Mem.: Beverly Hills Tennis, Sycamore Park Tennis. Home: 10350 Wilshire Blvd Ph 4 Los Angeles CA 90024-4734 Office: 9107 Wilshire Blvd Ste 800 Beverly Hills CA 90210-5533 E-mail: mburns@lurie-zepeda.com. *I believe that hard work in its time and place, play in its time and place, love, understanding and practice of the golden rule at all times, in all places, a firm belief in truth and honesty and that there is no better land, no better system, no better life than our imperfect, necessary to improve, America, leads to personal fulfillment and a better life for all.*

BURNS, MATTHEW LYNWOOD, surgeon; b. Lake City, Fla., Dec. 25, 1934; s. William James and Annie L. (Hyatt) B.; m. Patricia B. Brusky, Oct. 16, 1965; children: Jennifer A., Matthew L. Jr., Julie L. BS, La. State U., 1957; MD, Emory U., 1961. Diplomate Am. Bd. Surgery. Intern Tripler Gen. Hosp., Honolulu, 1961-62; resident surgery Emory U. Affiliated Hosp., Atlanta, 1962-68; med. dir. Fayette Cmty. Hosp., Peach Tree City, Ga., 1996-98 (ret. 1998); pres., med. cons. PAMB, Inc., Newnan, Ga., 1989—. Fellow ACS, Am. Coll. Angiology. Office: PAMB Inc 16 Dogwood Rd Newnan GA 30263-3106

BURNS, MAX, congressman; b. Millen, Ga., Nov. 8, 1948; m. Lora Dean Black, 1972; children: Andrew, Nathan. B in Indsl. Engring., Ga. Tech. U., 1973; M in Bus. Info. Sys., Ga. State U., 1977, PhD in Bus. Adminstrn., 1987. Mgr. Oxford Industries, N.Am. Mission Bd. So. Bapt. Conv.; prof. info. sys. Ga. So. U. Coll. Bus. Adminstrn., Statesboro; congressman 12 Dist. Ga. U.S. Ho. Reps., 2003—. Instr., Australia, New Zealand, Republic of Korea; cons. Gulfstream Aerospace and Grinnell Corp. Mem. CSRA Regional Devel. Ctr.; former chmn. regional 1 adv. coun. Ga. Dept. Industry, Trade, and Tourism; mem. Screven County Commn., 1993—98, chmn., 1997—98; deacon Jackson Bapt. Ch.; bd. dirs. Screven County Livestock Assn., Cmty. Christian Sch. Bd., Ga. Limousin Assn. 1st It. USAR. Office: 512 Cannon HOB Washington DC 20515-1012*

BURNS, MICHAEL JOSEPH, operations and sales-marketing executive; b. Passaic, N.J., Feb. 18, 1943; s. Michael Joseph and Ellen Kathryn (Warman) B.; m. Emma Anne, Dec. 19, 1964; children: Michael, Jeffrey, Tricia, Stephen. BA in English, William Paterson Univ., Wayne, N.J., 1964; JD, Seton Hall U., Newark, 1975. Bar: N.J. 1975. Purchasing analyst Am. Brands Co., 1972-75; div. purchasing mgr. Dutch Boy Paints, NL Industries, 1975-76; v.p. purchasing Dutch Boy, Inc., 1977-78; pres., gen. mgr. Dutch Boy, Inc. (Dutch Boy coatings div.), 1978-80; pres., CEO Kroehler Mfg. Co., Naperville, Ill., 1980-88; pres., COO Rymer Co., Rolling Meadows, Ill., 1983-88; pres. Emerald Group, Lake Forest, Ill., 1989-90; pres., CEO Designer Foods, Inc., Wilmington, Del., 1990-91; chmn., pres., CEO SeaWatch Internat., Ltd., Easton, Md., 1991-99; pres., CEO Pioneer Human Svcs., Seattle, 1999—. Served to capt. USMCR, 1964-67, Vietnam. N.J. State scholar; recipient Disting. Alumni award Wm. Paterson Univ. Mem. ABA, Am. Arbitration Assn. Presbyterian. Office: 7440 W Marginal Way S Seattle WA 98108-4141 E-mail: mike.burns@p-h-s.com.

BURNS, MICHAEL THORNTON, historian, educator, farmer; b. N.Y.C., Dec. 30, 1947; s. Frank Xavier Burns and Mary Lou DeWeese; m. Elizabeth Topham Kennan, June 8, 1986; 1 stepchild: Frank Alexander Kennan. BA summa cum laude, UCLA, 1976, MA, 1977; PhD, Yale U., 1981. Tchg. fellow Yale U., New Haven, 1978-79; vis. dir. d'etudes Ecole des Hautes Etudes, Paris, 1991; from asst. to assoc. prof. Mt. Holyoke Coll., South Hadley, Mass., 1981-93, prof. of modern European history, Dana faculty fellow, 1993—2002, prof. emeritus, 2002—; affiliate scholar Centre Coll., Danville, Ky.; owner, operator Cambus-Kenneth Cattle and Thoroughbred Horse Farm, Danville, Ky., 2000—. Adv. editor Blackwell's New Perspectives, Oxford, Eng., 1995-2001, Ency. of French-Am. Rels., 2001-; cons. WGBH Western Traditions, Boston, 1986-87, The Jewish Mus., Dreyfus Affair, N.Y.C., 1987; awards panel mem. Phi Beta Kappa, Washington, 1994-95. Author: (books) Rural Society and French Politics, 1984, Main Trends in History (rev. of G. Barraclough) 1991, Dreyfus: A Family Affair, 1992 (Phi Alpha Theta Best Book award 1993, Prix Bernard LeCache 1994), France and the Dreyfus Affair 1999. Vol. Holyoke Therapeutic Riding, Holyoke, Mass., 1992-93; bd. dirs. Five Coll. Pub. Sch. Ptnrship, Amherst, Mass., 1988-92, Bluegrass Conservancy, Lexington, Ky., 2002-. Fellow Woodrow Wilson Internat. Ctr. for Scholars, Washington, 1992-93, Rockefeller Found. Humanities, N.Y., 1983-84, Tocqueville award French-Am. Found., N.Y.C., 1979-80, Fulbright award, 1979-80. Mem. Thoroughbred Club of Am., Thoroughbred Owners and Breeders, Phi Beta Kappa, Phi Alpha Theta. Episcopalian. Avocations: horseback riding, gardening, hist. architl. restoration. Office: Mt Holyoke Coll 50 College St South Hadley MA 01075

BURNS, MICHAEL WILLIAM, lawyer former state legislator; b. Balt., Feb. 16, 1958; s. William Charles and Helen Kearns Burns. BS magna cum laude, U. Md., Towson, 1980; JD with honors, U. Md., 1983. Clk. Circuit Ct. Judge, 1983-84; atty. Balt., 1984—; Rep. state del. State of Md., 1995-99. Mem., ranking Rep. house jud. com. 1997-99, mem. subcom. on civil law and procedure, 1995-99; devel. and comm. cons. Mem. Md. State Rep. Ctrl. Com., 1978-81, 86-90, 94-97, 98-2001; legal counsel Md. State Rep. Party, 1987-88; exec. dir. Dole for Pres. Com., Md., 1987-88, Md. State Rep. Party, 1988-89; bd. dirs. Md. Underage Drinking Prevention Coalition, 1995-2002, Chesapeake Ctr. for Creative Arts, 1996-2002; del. Rep. Nat. Conv., 1988, 96; past pres. adv. bd. Salvation Army of Glen Burnie, Md., 1999; mem. Mothers Against Drunk Drivers. Mem.: KC. Home: 201 Homewood Rd Linthicum MD 21090-2605

BURNS, NED HAMILTON, civil engineering educator; b. Magnolia, Ark., Nov. 25, 1932; s. Andrew Louis and Ila Mae (Martin) B.; m. Martha Ann Fontaine, June 11, 1955; children: Kathryn Jane, Stephanie Ann, Michael Everett. BS, U. Tex., 1954, MS, 1958; PhD, U. Ill., 1962. Registered profl. engr., Tex. Instr. U. Tex., Austin, 1957-59, asst. prof., 1962-65, assoc. prof., 1965-70, prof. civil engring., 1970 83, Zarrow Centennial prof. engring., 1983—; assoc. dean engring. for acad. affairs, 1989-93; dir. Ferguson Structural Engring. Lab., 1994-97. Rsch. asst. U. Ill., Urbana, 1959-62. Author: (with T. Y. Lin) Design of Prestressed Concrete Structures, 1981 (McGraw Hill Book of Month 1982), S.I. Version-Design of Prestressed Concrete Structures, 1982; contbr. articles to profl. jours. With U.S. Army, 1955—57. Recipient Gen. Dynamics Tchg. award U. Tex. Coll. Engring., 1965, AMOCO Tchg. award, 1983, Martin P. Korn award for outstanding jour. paper, 1993, Blunk Meml. Professorship Tchg. award U. Tex., 1996-97. Fellow Prestressed Concrete Inst. (com. mem. 1968—, Martin Korn award for best paper 1993, Disting. Educator award 2000); mem. NSPE (chpt. pres. 1970), ASCE (com. chmn. 1975—, T. Y. Lin award 1994), Am. Concrete Inst. (bd. dirs. 1983-87, Joe Kelley award for contbns. to engring. edn. 1990), Post-Tensioning Inst. (bd. dirs. 1975), Tex. Soc. Profl. Engring. (Young Engr. of Yr. award 1970, Travis chpt. Engr. of Yr. award 1987). Democrat. Baptist. Home: 3917 Rockledge Dr Austin TX 78731-2921 Office: U Tex Dept Civil Engring Austin TX 78712

BURNS, PAT, professional hockey coach; b. Montreal, Que., Can., Apr. 4, 1952; Coach Les Olympiques de Hull, Montreal, 1983-87; head coach affiliate club Montreal Canadiens, Sherbrooke, Que., Can., 1987-88, head coach, 1988-92, Toronto Maple Leafs, 1992-97, Boston Bruins, 1997—2000, New Jersey Devils, 2002—. Asst. coach Can. Jr. Team, 1986. Named Coach of Yr. NHL's Broadcasters Assn., 1989, Sporting News, 1989 Hockey News, 1989. Office: NJ Devils Continental Airlines Arena 50 Rte 120 N East Rutherford NJ 07073

BURNS, PATRICK OWEN, venture capital company executive; b. Yonkers, N.Y., Aug. 6, 1937; s. Edward Dermott and Anne L. (Gallagher) B.; m. Barbara Hope Van Riper, Nov. 4, 1967; children: Patrick Owen, Elizabeth Willett. AB, Dartmouth Coll., 1959; LLB cum laude, Harvard U., 1962. Bar: N.Y. 1964, U.S. Dist. Ct. (so. dist.) N.Y. 1965. Legal advisor Dept. Coops., Lesotho, 1962-63; assoc. Milbank, Tweed, Hadley & McCloy, N.Y.C., 1963-69; nat. dep. dir. Interracial Coun. for Bus. Opportunity, N.Y.C., 1969-75; acting nat. exec. dir., 1972-74; exec. v.p. Minority Equity Capital Co., Inc., N.Y.C., 1971-78, dir., 1974-85, pres., 1978-85; ptnr. Consumer Venture Group, 1985; v.p. R&D Funding Corp., 1986-97; v.p., 1st v.p., sr. v.p. Prudential Securities, 1986-97; sr. advisor Early Stage Enterprises, 1997—2002, AcrossFrontiers Internat., Inc., 1999—2002. Bd. dirs., vice chmn. Euclid Sys. Corp.; bd. dirs. Progen Inds., Ltd.; chmn. StablEyes, Inc.; cons. Warren Commn., 1964; mem. exec. com. SEC Govt. Bus. Forum on Small Bus. Capital Formation, 1983—85; chmn. Task Force State Capital Formation, 1984. Contbr. articles to profl. jours. Regent L.I. Coll. Hosp., 1976—, vice chmn. bd., 1981—97; trustee Continuum Health Ptnrs., Inc., 2001—, St. Luke's-Roosevelt Hosp. Ctr., 2001—, Beth Israel Med. Ctr., 2001—, Beth Israel Found., 2001—, New Cmty. Found., 1998—, Continuum Hospice Care, 2003—; pres. Friends of Bushnell-Sage Libr., Sheffield, Mass., 2002—; candidate N.Y.C. City Coun., 1969; bd. dirs. Resources for Children with Spl. Needs., Inc., 1990—, pres., 1994—; bd. dirs. Cobble Hill Health Ctr., 1976—, Nat. Ctr. Social Entrepreneurs, 1985—2002, Heights & Hill Cmty. Coun., Inc., 1992—, pres., 1999—2002; dir. New Cmty. Devel. Loan Corp., 2002—. Class of '26 fellow Dartmouth Coll. Mem. Am. Assn. Minority Enterprise Small Bus. Investment Cos. (dir. 1979-85, chmn. bd. 1983-85), Coun. Fgn. Rels., N.Y. Venture Capital Forum, Nat. Assn. Small Bus. Investment Cos. (gov. 1983-85), Sheffield (Mass.) Hist. Soc. (fin. com. 1999—). Democrat. Home: 22 Sidney Pl Brooklyn NY 11201-4607 Office: 2810 Towerview Rd Herndon VA 20171 Office Fax: 718-246-5964. Business E-Mail: pburns64@aol.com.

BURNS, PAUL YODER, forester, educator; b. Tulsa, Okla., July 4, 1920; s. Paul Patchin and Mary Emily (Knowles) B.; m. Kathleen Iola Chase, Dec. 4, 1942; children: Virginia B. Belland, Margaret B. Feierabend, Nancy B. McNeill. BS, U. Tulsa, 1941; M in Forestry, Yale U., 1946, PhD, 1949. Asst., assoc. prof. U. Mo., Columbia, 1948-55; prof. forestry La. State U., Baton Rouge, 1955-86, prof. emeritus of forestry, 1986-96. Dir. sch. forestry La. State U., Baton Rouge, 1955-76; commr. La. Forestry Commn., Baton Rouge, 1955-76. Editor: Forest Management in Plan & Practice, 1956, Southern Forest Soils, 1959; co-editor: Southern Forestry in Practice, 1977, Christmas Tree Production & Marketing, 1983. Pres. bd. dirs. La. State U. YMCA-YWCA, Baton Rouge, 1957-59; mem. La. Conf. Ch. Bd., Baton Rouge, 1967-73; pres. La. Coun. Human Rels., Baton Rouge, 1987-89; chair bd. dirs. The FISH Good Samaritans, Baton Rouge, 1996. Recipient Disting. Alumnus award U. Tulsa, 1974, Humanitarian award Baton Rouge Coun. Human Rels., 1984, Peacemaking award, Bienville House Ctr. for Peace, Baton Rouge, 1991, Brotherhood award Baton Rouge chpt. NCCJ, 1995. Fellow Soc. Am. Foresters, La. Soc. Am. Foresters (chmn. 1990, Disting Svc. to Forestry 1989), Phi Kappa Phi, Sigma Xi, Xi Sigma Pi. Presbyterian. Avocations: tennis, piano. Home: 2137 Cedardale Ave Baton Rouge LA 70808-2810 Office: La State Univ Sch Renewable Natural Resources Baton Rouge LA 70803-0001 E-mail: pyburns@lycos.com.

BURNS, PETER CARMAN, geologist, educator; b. Fredericton, New Brunswick, Can., Oct. 17, 1966; s. Carman George Burns and Ruth Joyce Linden; m. Tammy Elizabeth Chesley, Aug. 29, 1992; 1 child, Kelson Owen. PhD, U. Manitoba, Winnipeg, 1994. From asst. to Massman assoc. prof. U. Notre Dame, Ind., 1997—2002, Massman chair and prof., 2002—. Contbr. articles to profl. jours. Recipient Donath medal, Geol. Soc. Am., 1999. Fellow: Mineral. Soc. Am. (life MSA award 2001); mem.: Am. Chem. Soc., Mineral. Assn. Can. (councillor 1997—2002, Young Scientist medal 1998, Hawley medal 1997). Home: 309 N Merrifield Ave Mishawaka IN 46544 Office: University of Notre Dame 156 Fitzpatrick Notre Dame IN 46556 Office Fax: 574-631-9236. Personal E-mail: pburns@nd.edu. Business E-Mail: pburns@nd.edu.

BURNS, R. NICHOLAS, federal official; b. Buffalo, Jan. 28, 1956; BA in European History summa cum laude, Boston Coll., 1978; MA in Internat. Econs. and Am. Fgn. Policy with distinction, Johns Hopkins Sch. Advanced Internat. Studies, 1980. Intern U.S. Embassy Nouakchott, Mauritania, 1980-81; program officer A.T. Internat., 1981-82; vice consul and staff asst. to the Amb. in Cairo, Egypt, 1983-85; polit. officer Am. Consulate Gen., Jerusalem, 1985-87; staff officer dept. ops. ctr. and secretariat Dept. of State, 1987-88, spl. asst. to the counselor of the dept. for Soviet and Ea. European Affairs, 1989-90, dir. Soviet affairs, 1990-93, sr. dir. for Russian, Ukraine and Eurasia affairs and spl. asst. to the pres., 1993-95, sr. fgn. svc. officer, nat. security coun. staff at the White House, 1991—; spokesman for Sec. of State, acting asst. sec. pub. affairs Dept. State, 1995-97; U.S. amb. to Greece, 1997-2001; U.S. permanent rep. (designate) US Mission to NATO, 2001—. Mem. Phi Beta Kappa. Office: 91 Vasilissis Sophias Blvd 10160 Athens Greece

BURNS, REBECCA ANN, educator, librarian; b. Waynesboro, Pa., Dec. 28, 1946; d. John Albert and Betty Jane (Mason) Castelluccio; m. Terry Lee Burns, 1966; children: Todd Darin, Derick Jason. BS, Shippensburg U., 1968, postgrad., 1969, 70, 75, Pa. State U., 1973-74, 87, 89, U. Wyo., 1989. Cert. elem. tchr., library sci. tchr., Pa. Migrant educator Waynesboro (Pa.) Sch. Dist., 1971-72, elem. tchr., 1968-71, 74-79, Mifflin County Sch. Dist., Lewistown, Pa., 1972-74; test examiner Office Personnel Mgmt. U.S. Govt., State College, Pa., 1982-83; instr. Adult Basic Edn.- Gen. Edn. Devel. and Career Tng. Mifflin County Job Tng. Partnership Act, Lewistown, 1985-86; libr. State Correctional Inst.-Rockview, Bellefonte, Pa., 1983-85, Midd-West Sch. Dist., Middleburg, Pa., 1986-89; edn. adminstrn. assoc., pupil transp. specialist Pa. Dept. Edn., Harrisburg, 1989-90, edn. adminstrn. specialist, coord. non pub. sch. svcs., 1990-93, basic edn. assoc., youth edn. and employment coord., 1993-97, basic edn. assoc., work-based learning coord., 1997—2002; pvt. practice Harrisburg, 2002—. Lobbyist for stamp commemorating adult edn.; educator for women's rights, devel. and implementation of regis. apprenticeships for youth in Penn. Mem. AARP, Nat. Assn. State and Territorial Apprenticeship Dirs., Ea. Seaboard Apprenticeship Conf., Pa. Fedn. Tchrs., Apprenticeship Assn., Fedn. State Cultural and Ednl. Profl., Aux. to Pa. Ret. State Police. Roman Catholic. Avocations: reading, collecting antique prints, travel. Home and Office: 4422 Saybrook Ln Harrisburg PA 17110-3477 E-mail: racb1228@aol.com.

BURNS, RED, academic administrator; Master tchr. comms. interactive telecomms. program Tisch Sch. Arts NYU. Chair Tokyo Broadcasting Sys. Chair; bd. dirs. Media Lab Europe, The Visual Media Task Force, The Convergent Media Group; mem. adv. bd. The N.Y. Times Digital Company; juror On-Line Journalism Awards, Nat. Mag. Awards, Webby Awards; prin. investigator three on-going rsch. programs funded by Interval Rsch., Intel and Microsoft. Creator CD-ROM on chaos theory, Electronic Neighborhood. Bd. dirs. The Charles H. Revson Found.; ProBono.net; Ivrae Inst.; mentor The Ross Sch. Named one of 100 top leaders of N.Y.'s economy, Crain's N.Y., top 100 most infulential women in bus., Top 25 Influential People on the Net, Newsweek's 50 for the Future, N.Y. Cyber Sixty, N.Y. Mag.; named to Silicon Alley's 100; recipient Matrix award, 1997, All-Star Educator award, Crain's, Award of Excellence in Sci. and Tech., Mayor of N.Y.C., Spl. Educator award, Art Dir. Club. Mem.: N.Y. New Media Assn. (founding mem.). Office: NYU Tisch Sch Arts 721 Broadway 4th Fl New York NY 10003-6807

BURNS, RICHARD DEAN, history educator, publisher, writer; b. Des Moines, June 16, 1929; s. Richard B. and Luella (Everling) B.; m. Frances R. Sullivan, Jan. 14, 1950 (dec. July 1993); 1 son, Richard Dean; m. Glenda F. Burns, Sept. 21, 1996; stepchildren: Scott E. Burns, Kent C. Burns, Dana Burns Mayadag. BS with honors, U. Ill., 1957, MA, 1958, PhD, 1960. Prof. emeritus Calif. State U., L.A., 1960-92, prof., 1970-92, chmn. dept., 1969-72, 86-92. Pubr./pres. Regina Books, 1980—; vis. lectr. L.A. City Coll., Whittier Coll., U. Minn., Mpls., 1964-65, UCLA, U. So. Calif.; program cons., lectr. Western Ctr., NEH, 1973-75. Author: (with W. Fisher) Armament and Disarmament, 1964, (with D. Urquidi) Disarmament in Historical Perspective, 4 vols, 1969, (with E. Bennett) Diplomats in Crisis, 1975; editor: An Arms Control and Disarmament Bibliography, 1977, Guide to American Foreign Relations Since 1770, 1982, (with M. Leitenberg) The Wars in Vietnam, Cambodia, and Laos, 1945-82, 1984, Harry S. Truman: A Bibliography of His Times and Presidency, 1984, Herbert Hoover: A Bibliography of His Times and Presidency, 1991, Encyclopedia of Arms Control and Disarmament, 3 vols., 1993, (with A. DeConde, F. Logevall) Encyclopedia of American Foreign Policy, 3 vols., 2002, (with Lester Brune) Chronological History of U.S. Foreign Relations, 3 vols., 2002; bibliographer, series editor: War/Peace Bibliographies, 1973—; pub. Regina Books, 1981—; contbr. articles to profl. jours. Served with USAF, 1947-56. Named Univ. Outstanding Prof., 1978-79; Social Sci. Rsch. Coun. fellow, 1959-60; grantee NEH, 1978-79, U.S. Inst. Peace, 1991-92. Mem. Conf. on Peace Rsch. (nat. coun. 1970-72), Soc. Historians Am. Fgn. Rels. (nat. coun. 1986-89), Phi Kappa Phi, Phi Alpha Theta. Office: Regina Books PO Box 280 Claremont CA 91711-0280

BURNS, RICHARD FRANCIS, mechanical engineer; b. Detroit, May 21, 1931; s. John Adgidius and Mary Teresa (Lockman) B.; m. Mary Kathryn McAlister, May 23, 1959; children: Richard Francis Jr., Christopher Joseph, Moira Elizabeth, Colleen Siobhan. BS, U.S. Naval Acad., 1954; MS in Marine Engrng., MIT, 1962. Registered profl. engr., Va. Commd. ens. USN, 1954, advanced through grades to comdr.; ops. officer, navigator USS Shark, Norfolk, Va., 1962-64; submarine repair supt. Norfolk Naval Shipyard, Portsmouth, Va.; project officer Planning, Estimating, Repairs and Alterations to Submarines, Portsmouth, N.H., 1967-69; sr. advisor Joint U.S. Mil. Mission Aid to Turkey, Gö, Turkey, 1970-72; navigation project officer Trident Strategic System project Office, Washington, 1973-76; sr. engr. Vitro Corp., Silver Spring, Md., 1976-88, Scientex Corp., Washington, 1989-90; assoc. editor Sea Tech. Mag., Compass Publs., Arlington, Va., 1990—. Mem. Nat. Def. Indsl. Assn. Avocations: triathletics, biathletics, skiing.

BURNS, RICHARD GORDON, retired lawyer, writer, consultant; b. Stockton, Calif., May 15, 1925; s. Earl Gordon and Alberta Viola (Whale) B.; m. Eloise Estelle Beil, June 23, 1951 (div. May 25, 1985); children: Kenneth Charles, Donald Gordon. AA with honors, U. Calif., Berkeley, 1948; AB, Stanford U., 1949, JD, 1951. Atty. Clausen & Burns, San Francisco, 1951—61; cons. Wyo. Pacific Oil Co., L.A., 1956—; pvt. practice Corte Madera, Calif., 1961—86; pub. Good Book Pub., Kihei, Hawaii, 1991—. Bd. dirs. Clean Fuels Hawaii. Co-author (with Bill Pittman): Courage To Change, 1998; author (as Dick B.): New Light on Alcoholism: God, Sam Shoemaker and A.A., 1999; author: The Akron Genesis of Alcoholics Anonymous, 1998, Anne Smith's Journal, 1998, Dr. Bob and His Library, 1998, The Good Book and The Big Book: AA's Roots in the Bible, 1998, The Oxford Group and Alcoholics Anonymous, 1998, That Amazing Grace, 1996, The Books Early AAs Read for Spiritual Growth, 1999, Good Morning!Quiet Time, Morning Watch, Meditation, and Early A.A., 1998, Turning Point: A History of Early A.A.'s Spiritual Roots and Successes, 1997, Utilizing A.A.'s Spiritual Roots for Recovery Today, 1999, The Golden Text of A.A., 1999, By the Power of God, 2000, Why Early A.A. Succeeded: The Good Book in Alcoholics Anonymous Yesterday and today, 2001, An 11 Year Project, 2001, Making Known the Biblical Roots of A.A., 2002, God and Alcoholism: A Growing Opportunity in the 21st Century, 2002, Hope!: The Story of Geraldine Owen Delaney, Alina Lodge and Recovery, 2002, Cured! A Proven Solution for Alcoholics and Addicts, 2003, Comments at First Nationwide AA History Conference, 2003; : Twelve Steps for You, 2003, When Early AAs Were Cured and Why, 2003; editor: Stanford Law Rev., 1950. Dir. Almonte Sanitary Bd., Marin County, Calif., 1962-64; v.p./sec. Lions Club, Corte Madera, 1961-64; pres. Almonte Improvement Club, Mill Valley, Calif., 1960, Cmty. Ch., Mill Valley, 1971, C. of C., Corte Madera, 1972, Corte Madera Ctr. Merchant Co., 1975, Redwoods Retirement Ctr., Mill Valley, 1980. Sgt. U.S. Army, 1943-46. Mem. Am. Hist. Assn., Alcohol and Temperance History Group, Authors Guild, Maui Writers Guild, Christian Assn. for Psychol. Studies, Assn. Med. Edn. and Rsch. in Substance Abuse, Stanford Alumni Assn., Phi Beta Kappa, Delta Tau Delta, Phi Delta Phi. Avocations: travel, bible study, swimming, walking. Office: PO Box 837 Kihei HI 96753-0837 E-mail: dickb@dickb.com.

BURNS, RICHARD OWEN, lawyer; b. Bklyn., Nov. 16, 1942; s. James I. and Ida (Shore) B.; m. Lynda Gail Birnbaum, Dec. 24, 1967; children: Marc Adam, Lisa Ann, Susan Danielle. BS, Wilkes Coll., 1964; JD, Bklyn. Law Sch., 1967. Bar: N.Y. 1967, U.S. Dist. Ct. (so. dist.) N.Y. 1969, U.S. Dist. Ct. (ea. dist.) N.Y. 1979. Assoc. Clune & O'Brien, Mineola, N.Y., 1967-73, Clune, Burns, White & Nelson, Harrison, N.Y., 1973-78; ptnr. Schurr & Burns, P.C., Spring Valley, N.Y., 1978-98; pvt. practice, Chestnut Ridge, N.Y., 1998—. Bd. dirs. Rockland County unit Am. Cancer Soc., West Nyack, N.Y., 1979-85, 86-92, pres., 1981-83; bd. dirs. Hudson Valley Health System Agy., Sterling Park, N.Y., 1979, Vets. Meml. Assn., Congers, N.Y., 1980-86; mem. Wilkes U. Coun., Wilkes-Barre, Pa., 1995—. Recipient Reese D. Jones award Wilkes Coll. Jr. C. of C., 1964. Mem. Rockland County Bar Assn., N.Y. State Bar Assn., N.Y. State Trial Lawyers Assn. Democrat. Jewish. Home: 140 Waters Edge Congers NY 10920-2622 Office: 500 Chestnut Ridge Rd Chestnut Ridge NY 10977-5646

BURNS, RICHARD RAMSEY, lawyer; b. Duluth, Minn., May 3, 1946; s. Herbert Morgan and Janet (Strobel) B.; Jennifer, Brian; m. Elizabeth Murphy, June 15, 1984. BA with distinction, U. Mich., 1968, JD magna cum laude, 1971. Bar: Calif. 1972, U.S. Dist. Ct. (no. dist.) Calif. 1972, U.S. Ct. Appeals (9th cir.) 1972, Minn. 1976, U.S. Dist. Ct. Minn. 1976, Wis. 1983, U.S. Tax. Ct. 1983. Assoc. Orrick, Herrington, Rowley & Sutcliffe, San Francisco, 1971-76; ptnr. Hanft, Fride, P.A., Duluth, 1976—. Gen. counsel Murphy, McGinnis Media, Duluth, Minn., 1982—, Murphy TV Stas., Madison, Wis., 1982—. Chmn. Duluth-Superior Area Comty. Found., 1988-90; chair United Way of Greater Duluth, Inc., 1998-99; bd. dirs. Miller Dwan Found., Northland Coll., Ashland, Wis. Fellow Am. Coll. Trust and Estate Counsel; mem. Calif. Bar Assn., Wis. Bar Assn., Minn. Bar Assn. (past. exec. com., past chmn. probate and trust coun.), 11th Dist. Bar Assn. (past pres., past chmn. ethics com.), Arrowhead Estate Planning Coun. (pres. 1980), Northland Country Club (pres. 1982), Boulders Club, Kitchi Gammi Club (bd. dirs.). Republican. Avocations: travel, golf, reading, fishing. Home: 180 Paine Farm Rd Duluth MN 55804-2609 Office: Hanft Fride PA 1000 First Bank Pl 130 W Superior St Ste 1000 Duluth MN 55802-2056 E-mail: rrb@hanftlaw.com.

BURNS, RICHARD ROBERT, chemicals executive; b. Litchfield, Ill., July 7, 1947; s. Martin E. and Virginia M. (Prange) B.; m. Sandra R. Meadows, Oct. 13, 1973; children: Kevin M., Sean T., Paul A., Lara M. BSChE, U. Tex., 1970. Prodn. engr. Union Carbide Corp., Tex., W.Va, 1970-78, dept. head, 1978-85, asst. plant mgr., 1986-97, corp. process cons., lic. profl. engr., 1997-01; corp. process cons. Dow Chem. Co., 2001; chief cons. Börn Solutions, League City, Tex., 2001—. Lutheran. Avocations: golf, family activities. Home: 4502 Masters Dr League City TX 77573-5805 E-mail: burnsrr@net.com.

BURNS, ROBERT, JR., architect, freelance writer, artist; b. Jackson, Miss., Jan. 29, 1936; s. Robert Sr. and Grace Hortense (Inmon) B. BS in Architecture, Ga. Inst. Tech., 1959, BArch, 1960. Registered architect emeritus, Miss. Architect Overstreet, Ware, Ware & Lewis, Jackson, 1961-70, Ware, Lewis & Eaton, Jackson, 1970-71, Jones & Haas, Jackson, 1971-74, Leon Burton & Assocs., Jackson, 1974-75, Glenn Albritton Designer, Jackson, 1975-83, Breland & Farmer, Jackson, 1983-84, The Plan House, Jackson, 1984-86; part-time tchr. art dept. Miss. Coll., 1987; architect Johnny Wynne & Assocs., Ltd., Jackson, 1995-96. Tenor soloist 1st Bapt. Ch., Jackson, 1967-68, 1st Christian Ch., Jackson, 1968-71, Covenant Presbyn. Ch., Jackson, 1971-74, Galloway Meml. United Meth. Ch., 1989-91, Northminster Bapt. Ch., Jackson, 1995-97, St. Luke's United Meth. Ch., Jackson, 1991-94, song leader, 1991-94; tenor soloist Woodland Hills Bapt. Ch., Jackson, 98-00; mem. Friends of the Gallery, Meml. Art Gallery, Jackson, 1981-93; mem. rev. panel Arts Alliance of Miss., 1989. Sgt. USAR, 1961-67. Mem. Am. Hemerocallis Soc., Inc. Republican. Baptist. Avocations: art, writing, music, growing daylilies and flowers. Home: 609 Broadway Ave Jackson MS 39216-3206

BURNS, ROBERT ALAN, economic developer, educator; b. Parson, W.Va., Jan. 25, 1973; s. Robert Lee and Sharon Burns. BA in Econs., Davis & Elkins Coll., 1995; MA in Econs., W.Va. U., 1997. Computer cons. Tucker County Emergency Ambulance Authority, Parsons, W.Va., 1997-98, Town of Davis, W.Va., 1997-98; instr. W.Va. Wesleyan Coll., Buchannon, W.Va., 1998—; exec. dir. Tucker County Devel. Authority, Parsons, 1998—. Tchg. asst. W.Va. U., Morgantown, 1995-97, cmty. fellow, 1998-99. City councilman City of Parsons, 1998-2000; team mem. Tucker County Regional Jail Com., Parsons, 1998—. Mem. W.Va. Econ. Devel. Coun., Tucker County C. of C. Republican. Baptist. Home: 405 Walnut St Parsons WV 26287-1050 Office: Tucker County Devel Authority 215 1st St Parsons WV 26287-1235 Fax: (304) 478-3455. E-mail: rburns@meer.net.

BURNS, ROBERT ARTHUR, lawyer; b. Independence, Iowa, 1944; BS, Iowa State U., 1966; JD, U. Iowa, 1972. Bar: Minn. 1972, Iowa 1972. Ptnr. Dorsey & Whitney L.L.P., Mpls., 1978—. Office: Dorsey & Whitney LLP Ste 1500 50 S Sixth St Minneapolis MN 55402-1498 E-mail: burns.bob@dorseylaw.com.

BURNS, ROBERT E. bank executive; BS in Acctg., Fairleigh Dickinson U., 1972. CPA Eisner Lubin, N.Y.C., 1972-73; auditor Auburn Savs. (N.Y.) Bank, 1974-75, v.p., controller, 1976-83; sr. v.p. Norstar Bank, Syracuse, N.Y., 1983-90; sr. v.p., treas., controller Fleet Bank New Hampshire, N.H., 1990-92; sr. v.p., controller Fleet Bank of Maine, Portland, Maine, 1992-94; dir. corp. fin. ops. Fleet Nat. Bank, Providence, 1994—. Office: Fleet Nat Bank 125 Dupont Dr Providence RI 02907-3105

BURNS, ROBERT EDGAR, retired protective services official, writer; b. Dunedin, Fla., Feb. 14, 1953; s. Clarence Edgar and Beverly Ann (Tuttle) Burns; m. Kathie Lynn Loomis, Nov. 3, 1950; children: Roger, Amy Creighbaum. Student, U. Md., Aberdeen Proving Grounds, 1981—83. Cert. state law enforcement officer, state corrections officer, state pvt. investigator, state law enforcement officer. Dep. sheriff Pasco County Sheriff's Office, New Port Richey, Fla., 1986—89, Pinellas County Sheriff's Office, Largo, Fla., 1983—86, 1998—2001. Polit. campaign mgr. Bill Rowan for Sheriff campaign, New Port Richey, 1990—92. Author: (book) It's Me Loving You!, 2001 (Poet of Yr., 2002, Poet of Month of Dec., 2000, Poet of Month of Jan., 2002, Internat. Poet of Merit, 2002). With M.P. U.S. Army. Recipient 1st Pl. Pub. Spkg. award, State of Fla. Dept. Edn., 1969. Mem.: Pinellas County Sheriff's Office, Internat. Soc. Poets, Am. Songwriters Assn. (life). Republican. Baptist. Avocations: writing poetry, writing songs, oil canvas painting, playing harmonica and guitar, singing. Personal E-mail: robertburns2@mac.com. Business E-Mail: robertburns2@mac.com.

BURNS, ROBERT IGNATIUS, historian, educator, clergyman; b. San Francisco, Aug. 16, 1921; s. Harry and Viola Marie (Whearty) B. BA, Gonzaga U., 1945, MA, 1947, Fordham U., 1949; Phil.B., Jesuit Pontifical Faculty, Spokane, Wash., 1946, Phil.Lic., 1947; S.Th.B., Jesuit Pontifical Faculty, Alma, Calif., 1951, S.Th.Lic., 1953; postgrad., Columbia U., 1949, Oxford (Eng.) U., 1956-57; PhD summa cum laude, Johns Hopkins U., 1958; Doc.ès Sc.Hist., Fribourg (Switzerland) U. (double summa cum laude), 1961; hon. doctorates, Gonzaga U., 1968, Marquette U., 1977, Loyola U., Chgo., 1978, Boston Coll., 1982, Georgetown U., 1982, U. San Francisco, 1983, Fordham U., 1984, U. Valencia, 1985. Mem. Jesuit order; ordained priest Roman Catholic Ch., 1952. Asst. archivist Jesuit and Indian Archives Pacific N.W., Province, Spokane, 1945-47; instr. history dept. U. San Francisco, 1947-48, asst. prof., 1958-62, assoc. prof., 1963-66, prof., 1967-76; sr. prof. dept. history UCLA, 1976—, named overscale (chair), 1987—; dir. Inst. Medieval Mediterranean Spain, 1976—; prof. methodology, faculty history Gregorian U., Rome, 1955-56. Guest lectr. humanities honors program Stanford U., 1960; vis. prof. Coll. of Notre Dame, Belmont, Calif., 1963; James chair Brown U., Providence, 1970; faculty mem. Inst. Advanced Study, Princeton, N.J., 1972; Levi della Vida lectr. UCLA, 1973; vis. prof., Hispanic lectr. U. Calif. at Santa Barbara, 1976; staff UCLA Near Eastern Center, 1979—, UCLA Center Medieval-Renaissance Studies, 1977—; Humanities Coun. lectr. NYU, 1992; Columbus Quincentennial Commn. of Calif. State Legislature, 1992. Author: The Jesuits and the Indian Wars of the Northwest, 1966, reprinted 1985, The Crusader Kingdom of Valencia: Reconstruction on a Thirteenth-Century Frontier, 1967, Islam Under the Crusaders: Colonial Survival in the Thirteenth-Century Kingdom of Valencia, 1973, Medieval Colonialism: Post-Crusade Exploitation of Islamic Valencia, 1975, Moors and Crusaders in Mediterranean Spain, 1978, Jaume I i els Valencians del segle XIII, 1981, Muslims, Christians and Jews in the Crusader Kingdom of Valencia, 1983, El reino de Valencia en el siglo XIII, 1983, Society and Documentation in Crusader Valencia, 1985, The Worlds of Alfonso the Learned and James the Conqueror, 1985, Emperor of Culture: Alfonso X, 1990, Foundations of Crusader Valencia, 1991, rev. transl. Els fonaments del regne croat de València, 1995, El Regne Croat de València, 1994, Jews in the Notarial Culture, 1996, Negotiating Cultures: Bilingual Surrender Treaties in Muslim Crusader Spain, 1999, El papel de Játvia, 1999, Las Siete partidas of Alfonso X, 5 vols., 2000; bd. editors: Trends in History, 1979—, Anuario de Estudios Medievales (Spain), 1985—, Bull. of the Cantigueiros, 1986—, Catalan Rev., 1986—, Medieval Encounters, 1998—; co-editor: Viator, 1980-93; assoc. editor Ency. of Medieval Iberia; mem. editl. bd. U. Calif. Press, 1985-88, chair, 1987-88, mem. bd. of control, 1987-88; contbr. articles to profl. jours. Trustee Hill Monastic Manuscript Library, 1977-81; mem. adv. bd. Am. Bibliog. Center, 1982— . Recipient Book award Am. Hist. Assn. Pacific Coast Br., 1968, Am. Assn. State Local History, 1967, Am. Cath. Hist. Assn., 1967, 68, Book award Inst. Mission Studies, 1966, Am. Cath. Press Assn., 1975, Phi Alpha Theta, 1976; Haskins medal Medieval Acad. Am., 1976; Premi de la Critica, 1982; Premi Catalonia, 1982, Premi Internacional Llull, 1988; Cross of St. George Catalan Govt., 1989; Guggenheim fellow, 1963-64; Ford Found. and Guggenheim grantee, 1980; NEH fellow, 1971, 73, 75-83, 88, Am. Coun. Learned Socs. fellow, 1972; travel grantee, 1975; Robb Publ. Grantee, 1974; Darrow Publ. grantee, 1975; Consejo Superior de Investigaciones Cientificas (Spain) travel grantee, 1975, 82; Valencia province and Catalan region publ. grantee, 1981; Del Amo Grantee, 1983; U.S.-Spain treaty grantee, 1983-85; grantee Consejo Superior de Investigaciones Cientificas (Spain), 1985; Mellon Publ. grantee, 1985, U.S.-Spain Treaty grantee, 1999. Fellow Medieval Acad. Am. (trustee 1975-77, prize com. 1980, scribe 1987—), Accio Cultural del Pais Valencia; mem. Hispanic Soc. Am. (hon.), Am. Cath. Hist. Assn. (pres. 1975, coun. 1976—), Soc. Spanish Portuguese Hist. Studies (exec. coun. 1974-77), Am. Hist. Assn. (del. Internat. Congress Hist. Scis. 1975, 80, pres. Pacific Coast br. 1979-80, exec. coun. 1981-83), Medieval Assn. Pacific (exec. coun. 1975-77), Acad. Rsch. Historians Medieval Spain (pres. 1976), N.Am. Catalan Soc., Tex. Medieval, Inst. Catalan Studies, Barcelona (elected). Office: UCLA History Dept Los Angeles CA 90095-0001

BURNS, ROBERT WILLIAM, lawyer; b. Lewiston, Idaho, Aug. 26, 1943; s. William Harry and Mary Jane (Stephenson) B.; m. Sherry Lyn Ogle, Nov. 1963 (dec. Nov. 1964); m. Suzanne Loretta Cherry, Oct. 2, 1965; children— Rebecca Lyn, William Hardin. B.A. in Bus., U. Wash., 1966; J.D. Magna cum laude, Gonzaga U., 1973. Bar: Wash. 1973, U.S. Dist. Ct. (ea. and we. dists.) Wash. 1973, U.S. Ct. Appeals (9th cir.) 1981, U.S. Supreme Ct. 1982. Law clk., bailiff U.S. Dist. Ct. (ea. dist.) Wash., Spokane, 1971-74; assoc. Paine Lowe Coffin Herman & Okelly, Spokane, 1974-77; adj. prof. Gonzaga Law Sch., 1977; prin. Foulds Felker Burns & Johnson, P.S., Seattle, 1977-82; founder, pres. Burns & Ricketts, P.S., Seattle, 1982— . Served to capt. U.S. Army, 1966-68; Vietnam. Mem. Wash. State Bar Assn. (chmn. young lawyers sect. 1976-77), ABA, Def. Research Inst., Wash. Trial Lawyers Assn., Assn. Trial Lawyers Am. Republican. Presbyterian. Office: Burns & Ricketts PS PO Box 21926 Seattle WA 98111-3926

BURNS, RONALD C. music educator; m. Laurilee Kerr, May 29, 1988; children: Travis Carl, Brianna Lee. B of Gen. Studies, La. Coll., Pineville, 1992; MusM, Northwestern State U., Natchitoches, La., 1994, EdD, 2002. Cert. tchr. K-12 La., 1992. Band dir. Dry Prong Jr. High, La., 1991—96, Grant H.S., Dry Prong, La., 1991—96; adj. prof. music La. Coll., Alexandria, 1994—; dir. of bands Alexandria Sr. High, La., 1996—; orch. dir. Calvary Conservatory of Music, Alexandria, La., 1996—. Mem.: La. Music Educator's Assn., Music Educator's Nat. Conf., Kappa Delta Pi. Office: Alexandria Sr High 000 Ola Ln Alexandria LA 71303

BURNS, SANDRA, lawyer, educator; b. Bryan, Tex., Aug. 9, 1949; d. Clyde W. and Bert (Rychlik) B.; 1 son, Scott. BS, U. Houston, 1970; MA, U. Tex., 1972, PhD, 1975; JD, St. Mary's U., 1978. Bar: Tex. 1978; cert. tchr., adminstr., supr. instrn., Tex. Tchr. Austin (Tex.) Ind. Sch. Dist., 1970-71; prof. child devel./family life and home econs. edn. Coll. Nutrition, Textiles and Human Devel. Tex. Women's U., Denton, 1974-75; instrnl. devel. asst. Office of Ednl. Resources divsn. instr U. Tex. Health Sci., San Antonio, 1976-77; legis. aide William T. Moore Tex. Senate, Austin, fall 1978, com. clk.-counsel, spring 1979; legal cons. Colombotti & Assocs., Aberdeen, Scotland, 1980; corp. counsel 1st Internat. Oil and Gas, Inc., 1983; contracted atty. Humble Exploration Co., Inc., Dallas, 1984; assoc. Smith, Underwood, Dallas, 1986-88; pvt. practice Dallas, 1988—; mem. grad. faculty Tex.A&M U., Commerce. Atty. contracted to Republic Energy Inc., Bryan, Tex., 1981-82, ARCO, Dallas, 1985; vis. lectr. Tex. A&M U., fall 1981, summer, 1981; lectr. home econs. Our Lady of the Lake Coll., San Antonio, fall, 1975. Contbr. articles on law and edn. to profl. jours. Mem. Coll. of the State Bar of Tex., Phi Delta Kappa. Office: Preston Commons West 300 8117 Preston Rd Dallas TX 75225 E-mail: burns@attorney-mediator.com.

BURNS, SCOTT, columnist; b. Cambridge, Mass., Nov. 9, 1940; s. Robert Milton Clark Burns and Joanne (Mahoney) Blasius; m. Allegra Wendy Eames, Dec. 11, 1965 (div. Sept. 1990); children: Jasper Bayard (dec.), Oliver Byron; m. Carolyn Jo Schroeder, Jan. 2, 1995. BS, MIT, 1962. Columnist, editor Boston (Mass.) Herald Am., 1977-83; columnist Dallas (Tex.) Morning News, 1985—; syndicated columnist, 1980—. Author: Squeeze It Til The Eagle Grins, 1972, Home, Inc., 1975. Office: Dallas Morning News Communications Ctr PO Box 655237 Dallas TX 75265-5237

BURNS, SHIRLEY M. artist, educator; b. Kingsport, Tenn., Oct. 1, 1934; d. Kenneth MacDonald and Louise Gwendolyn (Cox) Cross; m. Richard Carroll Burns, Dec. 15, 1960; children: Jay Bradford, Kurt MacDonald. BS, East Tenn. State U., 1957, postgrad., 1957-86. Cert. tchr., Tenn., Va., Wash. Tchr. 3d grade Kempsville (Va.) Elem. Sch., 1955-56; tchr. art Princess Anne (Va.) H.S., 1957-58, Mt. Vernon Elem. Sch., Alexandria, Va., 1959-60, Harrisburg (Pa.) Jr. H.S., 1961; tchr. 6th grade art and social studies Silverdale (Wash.) Elem. Sch., 1967-70; tchr. art North Kitsap H.S., Poulsbo, Wash., 1978-84. Drawing instr. Harrisburg YMCA, 1961, pvt. lessons, Hawaii, 1964-65; docent Hall of Indians/Mus. Natural History, Smithsonian Instn., Washington, 1970-71; ptnr. The Art Cellar, Silverdale, 1971-75; instr. adult craft classes Olympic Coll., Bremerton, 1975-77; instr. pottery Bainbridge Island Park and Recreation Dist., 1984—, also adult sculpture classes, 1995—. Exhibited works in Bainbridge Arts and Crafts Gallery and Christmas Shows, 1991—, Studio Tour, Bainbridge Island, 1991-99, Bainbridge in Bloom, 1997-99; two-person show Collective Visions, 2001, 02; group show Collective Visions Gallery, Bremerton, Wash., 2001; permanent disply of sculptural works at Seattle Aquarium, 1995—. Fundraiser, Friends of the Libr., Bremerton, Wash. Recipient awards for art. Mem. AAUW, PEO, Bainbridge Island Music and Arts, The Clay People, Bainbridge Arts and Crafts, Bainbridge Island Arts and Humanities, Seattle Art Mus. Methodist. Avocations: music appreciation, tennis, reading. Home: 8270 NE Meadowmeer Rd Bainbridge Island WA 98110-1241 E-mail: shrburns@aol.com.

BURNS, STEPHEN GILBERT, lawyer; b. N.Y.C., Apr. 29, 1953; s. Gilbert Leo and Ellen (Scully) B.; m. Joan Louise Wallace, Aug. 6, 1977; children: Christopher, Allison. Student, U. Vienna, Austria, 1974; BA, Colgate U., 1975; JD, George Washington U., 1978. Bar: D.C. 1978, U.S. Ct. Appeals (D.C. cir.) 1980. Atty. Nuclear Regulatory Commn., Washington, 1978-83, dep. chief counsel regional ops. and enforcement, 1983-86, legal asst. to commr., 1986-89, exec. asst. to chmn., 1989-91, dir. Office of Commn. Appellate Adjudication, 1991-94, assoc. gen. counsel, 1994-98, dep. gen. counsel, 1998—. Recipient Disting. Svc. medal, Nuclear Regulatory Commn., 2001. Mem. ABA. Presbyterian. Office: US Nuclear Regulatory Commn Office Of Gen Counsel Ms 15B21 Washington DC 20555-0001

BURNS, TERRENCE MICHAEL, lawyer; b. Evergreen Park, Ill., Mar. 2, 1954; s. Jerome Joseph Burns and Eileen Beatrice (Collins) Neary; m. Therese Porucznik, Mar. 24, 1979; children: David, Steven, Theresa, Daniel. BA, Loyola U., Chgo., 1975; JD, DePaul U., 1978. Bar: Ill. 1978, U.S. Dist. Ct. (no. dist.) Ill. 1978, U.S. Ct. Appeals (7th cir.) 1979, U.S. Supreme Ct. 1985, U.S. Dist. Ct. (no. dist.) Ind. 1989. Asst. state's atty. Cook County, Chgo., 1979-85; ptnr. Rooks, Pitts & Poust, Chgo., 1985—. Mem. inquiry bd. Ill. Supreme Ct. Atty. Registration and Disciplinary Commn., Chgo., 1986-90, chair hearing bd., 1990—. Mem. ABA (ann. meeting adv. com.), Chgo. Bar Assn. (treas. 1997-99, 2d v.p. 1999-2000, 1st v.p. 2000-01, pres. 2001—, bd. mgrs. 1995-97, chair fin. com. 1997-99, criminal law com. 1979-83, jud. candidate evaluation com. 1981-86, 87-95, chmn. investigation divsn. evaluation com. 1991-92, chmn. hearing divsn. evaluation com. 1992-93, gen. chmn. 1993-95, ct. liaison com. 1993-95, tort reform subcom. 1997), Chgo. Bar Found. (bd. dirs. 1999-2000). Roman Catholic. Office: Rooks Pitts & Poust 10 S Wacker Dr Ste 2300 Chicago IL 60606-7407

BURNS, THAGRUS ASHER, manufacturing company executive, former life insurance company executive; b. Columbia City, Ind., Feb. 19, 1917; s. Harlow A. and Hazlette (Wise) B.; m. Dorothy Kimble, May 1, 1942; children: Steven L., Gerald A. AB, Wabash Coll., 1939. With Lincoln Nat. Life Ins. Co., Ft. Wayne, Ind., 1939-80, treas., 1967-80, Lincoln Nat. Life Co., 1967-80, Lincoln Nat. Corp., 1968-80; pres. Burns Mfg. Inc., Ft. Wayne, 1980—. Treas., dir. Lincoln Nat. Life Found. Served to lt. USNR, 1942- 45. Mem. Financial Execs. Inst., Phi Beta Kappa. Achievements include inventor automatic feeder for typewriter, inserting machine and clipping catcher for hedge trimmer. Home and Office: 2118 Heritage Park Dr Fort Wayne IN 46805-5802

BURNS, THOMAS DAVID, lawyer; b. Andover, Mass., Apr. 4, 1921; s. Joseph Lawrence and Catherine (Horne) B.; m. Sylvia Lansing, Sept. 14, 1946 (div. 1982); children— Wendy Tilghman, Lansing, Diane Longley, Lisa; m. Marjorie Andrew Brown, Mar. 12, 1983 Student, Phillips Andover Acad., 1938, Brown U., 1938-41; LLB, Boston U., 1943. Bar: Mass. 1944, U.S. Dist. Ct. 1948, U.S. Ct. Appeals 1951, U.S. Supreme Ct. 1957. Assoc. Friedman, Atherton, King & Turner, Boston, 1946-50, ptnr., 1950-60; sr. and founding ptnr. Burns & Levinson, Boston, 1960—. Mem. Jud. Coun. Com. of Mass., 1973-77, mem. Mass. Jud. Nominating Commn., 1979-83; mem. Mass. Spl. Legis. Commn. on Malpractice, 1975—; chmn. Joint Com. Boston and Mass. Bar Com. on Jud. Selection, 1970-75; spl. counsel to Boston City Coun., 1981. Co-editor: Recollections of World War II Phillips Andover, 1938; contbr. articles to profl. jours Chmn. Planning Bd. Appeals, Andover, 1956-57; trustee Stratton Mountain Vt. Civic Assn., Mus. Am. Textile History, 1992—; v.p., bd. dirs. Birch Hill Corp., Stratton, Vt.; chmn. Andover Rep. Fin. Com., 1953-57; trustee, clk. Pike Sch., Andover; mem. alumni coun. and devel. com. Phillips Andover Acad., Boston U. Law Sch.; mem. Mass. Hist. Soc., Western Front Assn.; mem. adv. bd. PBS channel II WGBH, Boston. Lt. USNR, 1943-46, PTO, ETO. Fellow Am. Coll. Trial Lawyers, (state chmn. 1968, bd. regents 1970-76, treas. 1974-77), Am. Coll. Trial Lawyers Found. (dir.), Mass. Bar Found (trustee), Mass. Bar Assn. (mem. exec. com.), Am. Bar Found., ABA, Boston Bar Assn. (exec. coun.), Boston Vis. Nurse Assn., Boston Bar Found., Fed. Ins. and Corp. Counsel, Internat. Assn. Def. Counsel, Nat. Assn. R.R. Trial Counsel, Mass. Def. Lawyers Assn. (dir.), Delta Kappa Epsilon, North Andover Country Club, The Country Club (Brookline), Coral Beach Club (Bermuda), Duxbury Yacht Club, Boston City Club, Boston U. Law Sch. (alumni award, Disting. profl. svc. award 1996). Republican. Home: 5 Union Wharf Boston MA 02109-1202 Office: Burns & Levinson 125 Summer St Ste 602 Boston MA 02110-1616 E-mail: tburns@b-l.com.

BURNS, THOMAS SAMUEL, history educator; b. Michigan City, Ind., June 7, 1945; m. Carol Ann Morris, June 29, 1968; 1 child, Catherine Elizabeth. AB, Wabash Coll., 1967; postgrad., Am. Sch. Classical Studies, Athens, summer 1967; MA, U. Mich., 1968, PhD, 1974. Asst. prof. history Emory U., Atlanta, 1974-80, assoc. prof., 1980-85, Samuel Candler Dobbs prof. history, 1985—, chmn. dept. history, 1989-92. Dir. summer seminar for sch. tchrs. NEH, 1985, 88; adj. prof. U. Windsor, Ont., summer 1978, 79; vis. research prof. Kommission für alte Geschichte und Epigraphik des deutschen archäologischen Instituts in München, spring 1982; vis. research prof. Römisch-Germanische Kommission des deut. arch. Instituts, Frankfurt, spring 1982; Gastprof. Universität Augsburg, 1986. Author: The Ostrogoths: Kingship and Society, 1980, A History of the Ostrogoths, 1984, (with B.H. Overbeck) Rome and the Germans as Seen in Coinage, 1987, Barbarians within the Gates of Rome, 1994, (with J.W. Eadie) Urban Centers and Rural Realities, 2000, Rome and the Barbarians 100 B.C.-A.D. 400, 2003; co-dir. of Archaeological excavations in Passau, Germany, 1978-79, Manching, Germany, 1985, Pecs, Hungary, 1998; contbr. articles to profl. jours. With U.S. Army, 1969-71. Recipient Emory Williams Disting. Teaching award Emory U., 1982; Fulbright fellow Fed. Republic Germany, 1986, Boak fellow in ancient history U. Mich., 1971-74; Disting. Vis. scholar-in-residence U. Adelaide, Australia. Mem. Medieval Acad. Am. (nominating com. 1987-88), Ga. Classical Assn., AAUP (pres. Emory U. chpt. 1983-84), Am. Canoeing Assn., Phi Beta Kappa, Omicron Delta Kappa. Avocations: camping, fishing, wilderness canoeing, travel. Home: 268 Woodview Dr Decatur GA 30030-1037 Office: Emory U Dept History Atlanta GA 30322-0001

BURNS, TONI ANTHONY, artist; b. L.A., Sept. 6, 1937; d. Earle Francis and LaVerne Myrtle (Holmberg) Anthony; m. George Orin Burns, May 14, 1965; children: Robert Anthony, James Randolph. BA in Fine Arts, Calif. State U., Long Beach, 1959, postgrad., 1960. Cert. secondary tchr., Calif. Interior decorator Ruth Connor Interiors, Downey, Calif., 1960-62; tech. illustrator N.Am. Rockwell Corp., Downey, 1962-64, McDonnell-Douglas Aircraft, Long Beach, Calif., 1964-65; graphic layout artist Beckman Instruments, Fullerton, Calif., 1968-70; owner, creator Original Art Rock Owls, San Juan Capistrano, Calif., 1970-78; custom jewelry designer Jewelry by Toni Burns, San Juan Capistrano, 1979-98; jewelry designer, ptnr. SuperNatural Art, San Juan Capistrano, 1999—; prin., owner Silver Dolls, San Juan Capistrano, 2003—. Wholesale exhibitor L.A. Gift Show, 1971-78, Beckman Handcrafts, L.A., 1982. Juried shows include Village West Gallery, Laguna Beach, Calif., summers 1971-75, Art-A-Fair Festival, Laguna Beach, 1984-86, Downey Art Mus., 1992, Fine Arts Pavillion, 1993. Recipient 1st pl. San Clemente Art Gallery, 1984, 99. Mem. Am. Craft Coun., Metal Arts Soc. So. Calif. Avocations: family genealogy, travel, photography. Office: SuperNatural Art 31412 Windsong Dr San Juan Capistrano CA 92675-2788 E-mail: info@supernaturalart.com.

BURNS, VIRGINIA, social worker; b. Boston, June 10, 1925; d. Thomas Patrick and Katherine Louise (Dempsey) Burns. AB in Sociology, Boston U., 1946, MSW, 1951; EDd honors, Wheelock Coll., 1994. Group work specialist Boston Children's Svc. Assn., 1951-58; group work cons. East London Family Svc. Units, 1958-59; assoc. exec. sec. group work coun. Welfare Fedn. Cleve., 1959-62; sr. staff mem. Office Juvenile Delinquency & Youth Devel. U.S. Dept. Health, Edn. and Welfare, Washington, 1962-67, asst. to asst. sec. cmty. svcs., 1967-69; sr. assoc. youth involvement study New Transcentury Found., Washington, 1969-70; assoc. prof., dir. social svc. project U. Chgo., Sch. Social Svc. Adminstrn., 1970-73; dir. cmty. svc., divsn. drug rehab. Dept. Mental Health, Boston, 1973-76; dir. cons. & edn. program Mass. Mental Health Ctr., Boston, 1976-82; lectr. mental health Harvard Med. Sch., Boston, 1978-82; dir. advocacy, Boston Children Svc. Assn. Mass. Soc. Prevention of Cruelty Children, Boston, 1983-94; instr. social welfare, coord. cmty. projects Smith Coll. Sch. Social Work, Northampton, Mass., 1994-99; instr. social welfare policy Salem (Mass.) State Coll. Sch. Social Work, 1993-99. Cons. in field. Contbr. . Founding chair Children's Advocacy Network Mass., 1984—93, Latchkey Children's Coalition Mass., 1988—92; v.p. Mass. Human Svc. Coalition, 1984—99; legis. liaison Mass. Working Group on Women in Prison, 2000—; bd. dirs. Hispanic Office Planning and Evaluation, 1990—97, Here House, 1989—90, Parents Helping Parents, 2001—02; bd. advisors Aid to Incarcerated Mothers, 2002—; active United Fair Economy, Boston, 1994—99, Tax Equity Alliance Mass., 1990—99. Named Alumna of Yr., Boston U. Sch. Social Work, 1968; scholar, Fulbright, 1958—58. Mem.: NASW (chair polit. action com. Mass. chpt. 1984—2001, award for greatest contbn. to social policy and change 1990), Boston U. Alumni Assn. (Disting.). Avocations: gardening, bicycling, cooking, flower arranging. Home: 41A Cushing St Cambridge MA 02138-4581 E-mail: Burns472@aol.com.

BURNS, WARD, textile company executive; b. New Bedford, Mass., May 31, 1928; s. Frederick Lloyd and Pauline (Ward) B.; m. Cynthia A. Butterworth, Dec. 19, 1964; children: Helen Abby, David Ward, Walton Lloyd. BA, Amherst Coll., 1950; MBA, Harvard U., 1952; spl. student, NYU, 1955-57; LLD (hon.), Phila. Coll. Textiles and Sci., 1984. CPA, N.Y. Mgr. Price Waterhouse & Co. (C.P.A.s), N.Y.C., 1954-62; assoc. Laurence S. and David Rockefeller, Brussels, Belgium, 1962 65; with J.P. Stevens & Co., Inc., N.Y.C., 1965-88, controller, 1969-78, group v.p., 1978-80, pres., 1980-86, vice chmn., 1987-88. Also dir. mem. exec. com.; bd. dirs. Stevens Graphics, Inc., Atlanta, 1972-92; cons. ARS, Milan, Italy, HVL, Brussels, ARCO, Florence and Milan, 1963-65 Mem. editorial adv. bd.: Jour. Accountancy, 1969-72. Treas., dir. Internat. Sch. Brussels, 1963-65; bd. dirs. Internat. Sch. Brussels Found., N.Y.C., 1965—, pres. 1967-97; pres. Friends New Cavell Hosp. Inc.; bd. dirs., 1972-78; trustee Daniel Webster Coll., Nashua, N.H., 1995—, chmn., bd. trustees, 1997-99; vice chmn. Friends of the Amherst Coll. Libr., 1978—. Served as capt. USAF, 1952-53. Mem. AICPA, N.Y. State Soc. CPAs, Fin. Execs. Inst., St. Andrews Soc., Univ. Club, Links Club, Econs. Club N.Y.C., The Pilgrims, Sky Club, Chappaquiddick Beach Club, Edgartown Yacht Club, Clove Valley Rod and Gun Club, Amherst Club (N.Y.), Harvard Club (Boston), Phi Alpha Psi, Phi Kappa Psi. Office: 104 W 40th St Fl 10 New York NY 10018-3617

BURNS, WILLIAM JOSEPH, audiologist, speech-language pathologist; b. Providence, Mar. 23, 1958; s. William Joseph and Janice Louise (Rzeczkowski) B.; m. Tyonia Sue Legg, Sept. 18, 1981; children: Kevin William, Dennis Christopher, Ryan James, Colleen Veronica. BA, John Carroll U., University Heights, Ohio, 1981; MS, Lamar U., Beaumont, Tex., 1988. Cert. clin. competence in audiology and speech-lang. pathology. Audiologist, speech pathologist Nova Care, Pensacola, Fla., 1988, 94; pvt. practice audiology/speech pathology Keflavik, Iceland, 1991-94; program mgr. Health Tech, Dallas, 1994; area mgr. Mariner, Inc., Pensacola, 1995-96; audiology dir. Profl. Hearing, Pensacola, 1996—; area mgr. Theracor Rehab., 1997-98; staff audiologist Omni Healthcare, 1999-2000. Staff audiologist Omni Healthcare, 1999—; cons. audiology, Pensacola, 1994-2000. Contbr. articles to profl. jours. Instr., trainer ARC, 1984—; usher Navy Meml. Chapel, Pensacola, 1995-97. Lt. USN, 1983-84, USNR, 1984—. Named Instr.-Trainer of Yr., ARC, Pensacola, 1996. Mem. Am. Speech and Hearing Assn. (ACE award 1996, 2000), Naval Res. Assn. (life), Res. Officers Assn. (life, chpt. pres. 1983—), Am. Legion (life). Republican. Roman Catholic. Avocations: photography, genealogy, travel. Home: 1028A Mitscher Dr Key West FL 33040

BURNS, WILLIAM JOSEPH, federal agency administrator; m. Lisa Carty. BA in History, LaSalle U., 1978; M Internat. Rels., Oxford U., PhD, 1981. With U.S. Fgn. Svc., 1982—, polit. officer, staff mem. Bur. Near East Affairs, staff mem. Office of Dep. Sec. State; spl. asst. to Pres., sr. dir. Near East, South Asian Affairs Nat. Security Coun.; acting dir., prin. dep. dir. policy planning staff Dept. of State; minister-counselor for polit. affairs U.S. Fgn. Svc., Moscow; exec. sec. and spl. asst. to sec. Dept. of State; amb. U.S. Fgn. Svc., Amman, 1998—2001; asst. sec. for the Near East U.S. Dept. State, Washington, 2001—. Author: Economic Aid and American Policy Toward Egypt, 1955-1981. Recipient Disting. Honor award State Dept., James Clement Dunn award, others; Marshall scholar, 1978-81. Office: US Dept State Near Eastern Affairs 2201 C St NW Washington DC 20520-6243

BURNSHAW, STANLEY, writer; b. N.Y.C., June 20, 1906; s. Ludwig Behr and Sophia (Klevmann) B.; m. Lydia Powsner (dec.); children: Sandra Bonnie, Valerie, Amy, David. BA, U. Pitts., 1925; MA, Cornell U., 1933; L.H.D. honoris causa, Hebrew Union Coll.-Jewish Inst. Religion, 1983; DL, CUNY, 1996. Advt. bus., Pitts., 1925-27, N.Y.C., 1928-32; drama critic, co-editor New Masses, N.Y.C., 1933-36; pubs. The Cordon Co., Inc., N.Y.C., 1936-38; pres., gen. mgr. Dryden Press, Inc., N.Y.C., 1939-58; v.p. Holt, Rinehart & Winston, Inc., N.Y.C., 1958-65, adviser to pres., 1965-67; Regents lectr. U. Calif., winter 1980; disting. vis. prof. English U. Miami, 1989. Mem. organizing group, then lectr., dir. studies in World lit. Grad. Inst. of Book Publishing, N.Y. U., 1958-62; Bd. judges Nat. Book Award, 1967, 72; awards adv. com. Nat. Book Com., 1967— ; Mem. organizing bd. editors, then cons. editor Adult Leadership (mag. supported by Fund for Adult Edn., Ford Found.), 1953-55; bd. dirs. Nat. Translation Ctr., Columbia U. Author: The Wheel Age, 1928, André Spire and His Poetry, 1933, The Iron Land, 1936, The Bridge, 1945, The Revolt of the Cats in Paradise, 1945, The Sunless Sea, 1947, Early and Late Testament, 1952, Caged in an Animal's Mind, 1963, The Seamless Web, 1970, 2d edit., 1991, In the Terrified Radiance, 1972, Mirages: Travel Notes in the Promised Land, 1977, The Refusers, 1981, My Friend, My Father, 1986, Robert Frost Himself, 1986, A Stanley Burnshaw Reader, 1990; editor: Two New Yorkers, 1938, The Poem Itself, 1960, 1995, Varieties of Literary Experience, 1962, The Modern Hebrew Poem Itself, 1965, rev. edit., 1989; editor Poetry Folio mag., 1926-28; contbg. editor Modern Quar., 1932-33, Theatre Workshop, 1935-38; contbr. to Columbia U. Dictionary Modern European Literature, 1947, Dictionary World Literature; L'Approdo Letterario, Italy, Delphica Tetradia, Greece, Nouvelle Revue Francaise, N.Y. Times Book Rev., Poetry, Atlantic Monthly, Sewanee Rev., Saturday Rev.; Stanley Burnshaw Spl. Issue pub. by Agenda, Brit. mag., 1984. Recipient award for lit. Nat. Inst. Arts and Letters, 1971; ann. Stanley Burnshaw Lectr. in Poetics established in his name at U. Tex., Austin, 1997, CUNY, 1998. Mem. Am. Inst. Graphic Arts (dir. 1960-61), Coll. Pubs. Group. Home: 250 W 89th St New York NY 10024

BURNSIDE, MARY BETH, biology educator, researcher; b. San Antonio, Apr. 23, 1943; d. Neil Delmont and Luella Nixon (Kenley) B. BA, U. Tex., 1965, MA, 1967, PhD in Zoology, 1968. Instr. med. sch. Harvard U., Boston, 1970-73; asst. prof. U. Pa., Phila., 1973-76, U. Calif., Berkeley, 1976-77, assoc. prof., 1977-82, prof., 1982—, dean biol. scis., 1984-90, chancellor prof., 1996-99, vice chancellor rsch., 2000—. Mem. nat. adv. eye coun. NIH, 1990-94; mem. sci. adv. bd. Lawrence Hall of Sci., Berkeley, 1983—, Whitney Labs., St. Augustine, Fla., 1993-97; mem. bd. sci. councillors Nat. Eye Inst., 1994—. Mem. editl. bd. Invest. Ophthalmol. Vis. Sci., 1992-94; contbr. numerous articles to profl. jours. Mem. sci. adv. bd. Mills Coll., Oakland, Calif., 1986-90; trustee Bermuda Biol. Sta., St. George's, 1978-83; dir. Miller Inst., Berkeley, Calif., 1995-98. Recipient Merit award NIH, 1989-99, Outstanding Alumna award U. Tex., 1999; rsch. grantee, NIH, 1972—, NSF. Fellow AAAS; mem. Am. Soc. Cell Biology (coun. 1980-84). Avocations: hiking, deserts, mountains, great danes. Office: U Calif MC # 3200 335 Life Scis Addn # 3200 Berkeley CA 94720-0001

BURNSIDE, ORVIN CHARLES, agronomy educator, researcher; b. Hawley, Minn., June 9, 1932; s. John J. and Sena (Dwyre) B.; m. Delores Schattschneider, Dec. 22, 1954 (dec. 1990); 2 children; m. B.D. Clarice Hanson, Aug. 10, 1991. BS, N.D. State U., 1954; MS, U. Minn., 1958, PhD, 1959. Rsch. asst. U. Minn., St. Paul, 1956-59; prof. dept. agronomy U. Nebr., Lincoln, 1959-85; prof. weed sci., dept. agronomy and plant genetics U. Minn., St. Paul, 1985-98, ret., 1998. Cons. weed sci. Contbr. chpts. to textbooks, articles to jours.; patentee. 1st lt. M.I., Counter Intelligence Corp, U.S. Army, 1954-56. Named Outstanding Spokesman for Agr., Nebr. Agrl. Chem. Assn., 1970; recipient CIBA-Geigy award, 1979, Rsch. award Gamma Sigma Delta, 1980, 97. Fellow Am. Soc. Agronomy, Weed Sci. Soc. Am. (rsch. award 1979); mem. Internat. Weed Sci. Soc., North Cen. Weed Sci. Soc. (hon.), Am. Legion, Toastmasters, Kiwanis. Republican. Lutheran.

BURNS III, MATTHEW J. diplomat; b. Mass., Feb. 17, 1955; s. Matthew J. Burns, Jr., Barbara J. Burns; m. Beatriz Q. Burns, Jan. 28, 1981; 1 child, Matthew A. Burns. BA with indiviual concentration, U. Mass., 1977; M in Pub. Affairs, U. Tex., Austin, 1993. Adminstrv. officer Embassy Rome U.S. Dept. State, Washington, 1995—97, adminstrv. counselor Embassy Tel Aviv, 1997—99, sr. advisor to CFO, 1999—2001, dir. Ctr. for Adminstrv. Innovation, 2001—. Cubmaster Pack 1113, Fairfax, 2001—02. Named Eagle Scout, Boy Scouts Am., 1973; recipient award for Acad. Excellence, The Lyndon Baines Johnson Found., 1993. Mem.: ASPA, Am. Fgn. Svc. Assn. Office: US Dept State 2201 C St NW Washington DC 20520 Office Fax: 202-663-3212. Business E-Mail: burnsmj2@state.gov.

BURR, BROOKS MILO, zoology educator; b. Toledo, Aug. 15, 1949; s. Lawrence E. and Beverly Joy (Herald) B.; m. Patti Ann Grubb, Mar. 5, 1977 (div. July 1987); 1 child, Jordan Brooks. BA, Greenville Coll., 1971; MS, U. Ill., 1974, PhD, 1977. Cert. scuba diver Nat. Assn. Underwater Instrs. Lab. instr. dept. biology Greenville (Ill.) Coll., 1971-72; rsch. asst. Ill. Natural History Survey, Champaign, 1972-77, affiliate scientist Ctr. for Biodiversity Urbana, 1989—; from asst. prof. to prof. dept. zoology So. Ill. U., Carbondale, 1977—. Mem. adv. panel U.S. Fish and Wildlife Svc., 1990—; adj. prof. dept. biology U. N.Mex., Albuquerque, 1991—; adj. prof. dept. ecology, ethology and evolution U. Ill., 1993—. Co-author: A Distributional Atlas of Kentucky Fishes, 1986, A Field Guide to Fishes, North America North of Mexico, 1991 (selected as one of Outstanding Acad. Books of 1992 by Choice Mag.); contbr. more than 120 articles to profl. jours. Recipient Paper of Yr. award Ohio Jour. Sci., 1986, Coll. Sci. Rsch. award, So. Ill. Univ., 2001; Phi Kappa Phi Outstanding scholar So. Ill. U., 2002. Mem. AAAS, Am. Soc. Ichthyologists and Herpetologists (sec., mem. exec. com. 1990-94, pres.-elect 2000, pres. 2001—), Soc. Systematic Zoology, Biol. Soc. Washington, Assn. Systematic Collections, Sigma Xi (Leo M. Kaplan award 1990), Phi Kappa Phi (Scholar of Yr. 2002). Achievements include the discovery and description of 10 species of fish new to science from North American fresh waters. Home: 203 S Wedgewood Ln Carbondale IL 62901-2147 Office: So Ill Univ Dept Zoology Carbondale IL 62901-6501 E-mail: burr@zoology.siu.edu.

BURR, DAVID BENTLEY, anatomy educator; b. Findlay, Ohio, June 28, 1951; s. Willard Bentley and Dorothy Eleanor (Beiler) B.; m. Lisa Marie Pedigo; children: Kathryn Lise, Michael David, Erik Johan. BA, Beloit Coll., 1973; MA, U. Colo., 1974, PhD, 1977. Instr. anatomy U. Kans. Med. Ctr., Kansas City, 1977-78, asst. prof. anatomy, 1978-80; asst. prof. anatomy and orthop. surgery W.Va. U., Morgantown, 1980-83, assoc. prof., 1983-86, prof., 1986-90; chmn. dept. anatomy and cell biology, prof. anatomy, bioengring. and orthopedic surgery Ind. U., Indpls., 1990—, chmn. dept. cell biology. Mem. adv. bd. dirs. Primate Found. Am., Tempe, Ariz., 1978—; cons. County Med. Examiner, Morgantown, 1983-89; mem. Adv. Group for the Treatment Human Remains, USDA, Monongahela Nat. Forest Svc., 1989; cons. NASA, 1990-91, Am. Inst. Biol. Sci., NAS, 1990—, U.S. Congress Office Tech. Assessment, 1990; mem. biochemistry study sect. Arthritis found., 1992-95; spl. grants rev. com. NIH, 1996-2000. Author: Structure, Function & Adaptation of Compact Bone, 1989, Skeletal Tissue Mechanics, 1998, Musculoskeletal Fatigue and Stress Fracture, 2001, Bridging the Gap Between Dental and Orthopaedic Implants, 2002; mem. editl. bd. Bone, 1993—, Jour. Bone and Mineral Metabolism, 1994—, Jour. Biomech., 1999—, Calcif. Tiss. Int., 2000—; contbr. articles to profl. jours. Pres. First Ward Sch. PTA, Morgantown, 1987—88; sec. Cub Scout Pack Com., 1989; chmn. troop com. Boy Scouts Am., 1993—95; linesman Morgantown Soccer League, 1988; sec. Classic Ragtime Soc., 1997—98; clk. witness and svc. First Friends Meeting, 1999—2001; mem. adminstrv. bd. Epworth United Meth. Ch., Indpls., 1992—93. Rsch. grantee NIH, 1988—, Orthopedic Rsch. and Edn. Found., 1985-86. Mem.: Internat. Soc. for Musculoskeletal and Neuronal Interactions (bd. dirs. 1999—2000, 2002—), Assn. Anatomy, Cell Biology and Neurobiology Chairpersons (pres. 2001—02), Am. Anatomy Assn. (exec. com. 1998—2001, chmn. jour. trust fund com. 2002—), Orthop. Rsch. Assn. (chmn. membership com. 2002—03), Internat. Soc. Bone Mineral Rsch., Am. Soc. Bone Mineral Rsch. Avocations: piano, softball, racquetball, stamps, reading. Office: Ind U Sch Medicine Dept Anat & Cell Biology 635 Barnhill Dr Indianapolis IN 46202-5126 E-mail: dburr@iupui.edu.

BURR, EDWARD BENJAMIN, life insurance company executive, financial executive; b. Worcester, Mass., Dec. 19, 1923; s. Guy Weatherbee and Bertha Mary (Clark) B., m. Mary Elizabeth Hayes, Sept. 2, 1944 (div. Sept. 1970); children: Susan Jean Burr Williams, Nancy Carol Burr Montanaro; m. Kay Frances Flanagan, Nov. 1, 1970 (div. 1992); children: Kristine Kay (dec.), Kelly Anne Carter. BA, Bowdoin Coll., 1945; MBA, U. Pa., 1948; grad., Am. Coll. Life Underwriters, 1951. CLU. Dir. Inst. Life Ins., N.Y.C., 1948-54; exec. dir. Investment Co. Inst., N.Y.C., 1954-58; exec. v.p., dir. One William Street Fund, N.Y.C., 1958-62; pres., dir. William Street Sales, Inc., N.Y.C., 1958-62; pres., vice chmn. Anchor Corp., Elizabeth, N.J., 1964-78; chmn. bd. Anchor Nat. Life, Phoenix, 1965-85, hon. chmn., 1985—; chmn. bd. Anchor Nat. Fin. Services, Phoenix, 1971-85, hon. chmn., 1986—; pres. United Planners Fin. Services Am., 1987-95. Trustee Scottsdale Meml. Hosp., Ariz., 1985-95, chmn., 1990-91; dir. Ariz. Cmty. Found., 1985-93. With U.S. Army, 1943-46, ETO. Decorated Bronze Star, Silver Star Mem. Am. Soc. CLUs, Nat. Assn. Life Underwriters, Phoenix Met. C. of C. (bd. dirs. 1982-88), Scottsdale Club at Gainey Ranch, Camelback Golf Club. Home: 7331 E Griswold Rd Scottsdale AZ 85258-2731 Office: United Planners Group 7333 E Doubletree Ranch Rd Scottsdale AZ 85258-2042 E-mail: benburr@aol.com.

BURR, FRANCIS HARDON, lawyer; b. Nahant, Mass., July 21, 1914; AB cum laude, Harvard U., 1935, LL.B, 1938, LL.D., 1982. Bar: Mass. 1938. Assoc. Ropes & Gray, Boston, 1938-47, ptnr., 1947-87, of counsel, 1988—. Dir. emeritus AMR Corp., Corning, Inc., Raytheon Co. Hon. trustee Mass. Gen. Hosp., McLean Hosp.mem. dir. Humane Soc., Commonweath of Mass.; dir. emeritus Cotting Sch. Fellow Harvard Coll., 1954-82; sr. fellow Harvard Coll., 1971-82 Fellow AAAS, Am. Bar Found; mem. ABA, Boston Bar Assn., Am. Law Inst. Office: Ropes & Gray One International Pl Boston MA 02110 E-mail: fhburr@ropesgray.com.

BURR, RICHARD M. congressman; b. Charlottesville, Va., Nov. 30, 1955; m. Brooke Fauth; children: Tyler, William. BA in Comm., Wake Forest U., 1978. Nat. sales mgr. Carswell Distributing, 1978-94; state co-chmn. N.C. Taxpayers United, 1993-98; mem. U.S. Ho. of Reps. from 5th N.C. dist., 1995—; vice chair energy and commerce com., mem. internat. rels. com., intelligence com. Co-chmn. Partnership for Drug Free NC; bd. dirs. Brenner Children's Hosp. Republican. Office: US House Reps 1526 Longworth Ho Office Bldg Washington DC 20515-3305*

BURR, RONALD EDWIN, publisher; b. Chgo., Oct. 5, 1949; m. My Hanh Duong-Tran. AB in Polit. Sci., Ind. U., 1972, MBA in Fin., 1976. Circulation mgr. The Am. Spectator, Bloomington, Ind., 1970—75, bus. mgr., 1975—79, sr. pub., 1979—80, gen. mgr., 1980—81, pub. Arlington, Va., 1981—97; COO CHQ.com, 1997—2001; pres. Red Line Mktg. LLC, Vienna, Va., 1979—. Mng. ptnr. Lemley Yarling & Co., Chgo., 1976—; bd. dirs., Launchspace Publs. Mem. Ind. Hist. Soc., Cath. Press Assn. Roman Catholic. Office: Red Line Mktg LLC PO Box 156 Vienna VA 22183-0156 E-mail: Ronaldeburr@hotmail.com.

BURR, TIMOTHY FULLER, lawyer; b. New Bedford, Mass., Oct. 18, 1952; s. John Thayer and Joan (Ames) B.; m. Marguerite Conti, Feb. 28, 1981; children: Emily Ames, Lisa Conti, David Thayer. AB, Harvard U., 1975; JD, U. Miami, 1979. Bar: La. 1979, Tex. 1993, Fla. 1996, U.S. Supreme Ct., U.S. Cir. Ct., U.S. Dist. Ct. Admiralty and litigation atty. Galloway, Johnson, Tompkins, Burr & Smith, New Orleans, Houston, Lafayette, Gulf Breeze, 1979—, mng. dir. firm New Orleans, Gulf Breeze, 1987—. Past chmn. St. Tammary Parish Zoning Bd.; mem. Gulf Breeze Devel. Rev. Bd.; pres. Optimist Club Gulf Breeze, Fla., 2001-02. Mem. La. Bar Assn., Tex. Bar Assn., Fla. Bar Assn., Maritime Law Assn. U.S., Tammany Yacht Club, Pensacola Yacht Club. Republican. Home: 281 Plantation Hill Rd Gulf Breeze FL 32561-4050 Office: 1101 Gulf Breeze Pky Ste 2 Gulf Breeze FL 32561-4468

BURRAGE, BILLY MICHAEL, lawyer, retired judge; b. Durant, Okla., June 9, 1950; BSBA, Southeastern State U., 1971. Bar: Okla. 1980, U.S. Dist. Ct. (ea. dist.) Okla. 1980, U.S. Ct. Appeals (10th cir.) 1980, U.S. Supreme Ct. 1982, U.S. Dist. Ct. (no. dist.) Okla. 1993. Legal intern, 1974—75; assoc. Stamper & Otis, 1975—93; ptnr. Stamper, Otis & Burrage, 1982—94; dist. judge US Dist. Ct. No. and Ea. Dists., 1994—2001; chief judge US Dist. Ct. Ea. Dist., 1996—2001; of counsel Taylor, Burrage, Foster, Mallett, Downs & Ramsey, Claremore, Okla., 2002—. Contbr. articles to profl. jours. Fellow: Am. Coll. Trial Lawyers, Okla. Bar Found. (trustee); mem.: ABA, Southeastern Okla. Bar Assn., Pushmataha County Bar Assn., Okla. Bar Assn. (pres. 1990, v.p., bd. govs. 1983—87). Office: Taylor Burrage Foster Mallett Downs & Ramsey PO Box 309 Claremore OK 74018 Office Fax: 918-343-4900.*

BURRELL, ORVILLE RICHARD (SHAGGY), popular musician; Albums Boombastic, 1995 (Best Reggae Album Grammy award, 1996), Midnite Lover, 1997, Hot Shot, 2000, Mr. Lover Lover: The Best of Shaggy Part 1, 2002, Hot Shot Ultramix, 2002, Lucky Day, 2002. Office: c/o Geffen Records 2220 Colorado Ave. Santa Monica CA 90404*

BURRES, CARLA ANNE, medical technologist; b. Lawrence, Kans., Feb. 18, 1938; d. Emil Bowen Robison and Emma Annabelle (Boots) R.; m. Kenneth Lee Burres, Aug. 24, 1956; children: Cara Burres Jones, Katrina Burres Heinzen, Heather Burres Petry. BA, Ctrl. Meth. Coll., 1972; BS, U. Mo., 1982. Tchr. biology and chemistry Glasgow (Mo.) H.S., 1977-80; rsch. specialist Cytogenetics Lab., U. Mo. Hosp., Columbia, 1980; med. technologist Cooper County Hosp., Boonville, Mo., 1982-89, ARC, Columbia, 1989—. Editor: Preachers, Pioneers, Professors, Printers, 1997. Mem. Soc. for Better Fayette (Mo.) Cmty., 1995—, Cmty. Task Force, Fayette, 1997; sec. bd. dirs. Wesley Found., Fayette, 1995—. Mem. Am. Soc. Clin. Pathologists (assoc., cert. med. technologist). Democrat. Methodist. Avocations: gardening, photography, hiking, travel, reading. Home: 320 S Main St Fayette MO 65248-1269

BURRI, BETTY JANE, research chemist; b. San Francisco, Jan. 23, 1955; d. Paul Gene and Carleen Georgette (Meyers) B.; m. Kurt Randall Annweiler, Dec. 1, 1984. BA, San Francisco State U., 1976; MS, Calif. State U., Long Beach, 1978; PhD, U. Calif. San Diego, La Jolla, 1982. Research asst. Scripps Clinic, La Jolla, 1982-83, research assoc., 1983-85; research chemist Western Human Nutrition Rsch. Ctr., USDA, San Francisco, 1985-99, Davis, Calif., 1999—; adj. prof. nutrition dept. U. Nev., 1993-98, U. Calif., 2000—. Mem. steering com. Carotenoid Rsch. Interaction Group, 1994-97. Co-editor Carotenoid News, 1995-99; contbr. articles to profl. jours. Grantee NIH, 1982, 85, USDA, 1986, Spinal Cord Rsch. Found., 1998, Am. Chem. Soc., 1998-2002; affiliate fellow Am. Heart Assn., 1983, 84. Mem. Assn. Women in Sci. (founding dir. San Diego chpt.), N.Y. Acad. Sci., Carotenoid Rsch. Interaction Group, Internat. Carotenoid Soc. Office: Western Human Nutrition Rsch Ctr 229 Cruess Hall 1 Shields Ave Davis CA 95616 E-mail: bburri@whnrc.usda.gov.

BURRIDGE, MICHAEL JOHN, veterinarian, educator, research director; b. St. Albans, Eng., Apr. 27, 1942; came to U.S., 1973; s. Arthur Wilfred Bailey and Georgina Augusta (Davis) Burridge; m. Desree Margaret Wiggins, Aug. 13, 1973 (div. Sept. 1981); m. Karen Maureen Bengtsson, Jan. 1, 1983; 1 child, Christina Michelle. BVM&S, U. Edinburgh, Scotland, 1966; MPVM, U. Calif., Davis, 1974, PhD, 1976. Rsch. asst. East African Trypanosomiasis Rsch. Orgn., Tororo, Uganda, 1966; vet. practitioner Grant and Arnold, Woking, Eng., 1967-68; animal health officer Food & Agr. Orgn., Kabete, Kenya, 1968-73; grad. rsch. asst. U. Calif., Davis, 1973-76; assoc. prof. U. Fla., Gainesville, 1976-82, prof., 1982—, chmn. dept., 1984-93. Mem. com. on animal health NAS, Washington, 1980-83; cons. World Bank, Zaire, 1982, USAID, India, 1987, 91; cons. vet. medicine Williams & Wilkins, Balt., 1982-99; bd. dirs. Internat. Laveran Found., Annecy, France, 1991-94. Editor: Impact of Diseases on Livestock Production in the Tropics, 1984. Grantee U.S. AID, 1985—. Achievements include co-invention of attractant decoy for tick control, self-medicating applicators for parasite control, and diagnostic tests and vaccines for rickettsial diseases. Home: 10021 SW 67th Dr Gainesville FL 32608-6304 Office: U Fla Dept Pathobiology PO Box 110880 Gainesville FL 32611-0880 E-mail: burridgem@mail.vetmed.ufl.edu.

BURRILL, KATHLEEN R. F. (KATHLEEN R. F. GRIFFIN-BURRILL), Turkologist, educator; b. Canterbury, U.K., Mar. 8, 1924; d. William Henry and Ruby Amy (Webber) Griffin; children: Anne Ruth, Jane Ruth. AM, Columbia U., 1957, PhD, 1964; cert., Mid. East Inst., Columbia U, 1959. Officer of Brit. Coun., Ankara, Turkey, U.K., 1947-55; lectr. to prof. Middle East and Asian langs. and cultures Columbia U., N.Y.C., 1957-2000, prof. emerita, 2000—. Author: The Quatrains of Nesimi, Fourteenth-Century Turkic Hurufi Poet; co-editor Archivum Ottomanicum, 1984-95; contbr. articles to profl. jours. and encys. Recipient rsch. and travel award, Coun. Rsch. Humanities, 1966—67; fellow, Columbia U., 1957—59, Ford Found., 1959—60, Am. Rsch. Inst. in Turkey, summers, 1967, 1975. Fellow: Mid. East Studies Assn. (dir. 1974—76, founding fellow); mem.: Am. Assn. Tchrs. Turkic Langs. (pres. 1986—2002, hon. pres. 2003—), Mid. East Inst. (Washington), Brit. Soc. Mid. East Studies, Inst. Turkish Studies (governing bd. 1995—2001, founding assoc.), Turkish Studies Assn. (dir. 1974—76).

BURRIS, BILL BUCHANAN, JR., automotive marketing executive; b. San Diego, Jan. 7, 1957; s. Bill Buchanan Sr. and Marjorie Ellen (Halliburton) B. BA in Biology, Westmont Coll., 1981; postgrad., Heriot-Watt U. Svc. technician Mesa Porsche Audi Ferrari, La Mesa, Calif., 1981, Alan Johnson Porsche Audi, Inc., San Diego, 1981-82; svc. trainer Volkswagen Am., Inc., Culver City, Calif., 1982-84; sr. svc. trainer, dist. svc. mgr. Porsche Cars N.Am., Inc., Reno, 1984-88; mgr. nat. svc. tng. Jaguar Cars, Inc., Mahwah, N.J., 1988-90; tech. and body tng. devel. mgr., exec. coord. tech. svcs., tech. svcs. mgr., field ops. mgr., mgr. Ctr. for Customer Knowledge, Toyota Motor Sales, U.S.A., Inc., Torrance, Calif., 1991—2002; interactive mktg. magr. Lexus divsn. Toyota, Torrance, Calif., 2002—. Author: Training Value and Statistical Analysis, 1991. Exec. advisor Jr. Achievement Inc., 1993. Mem. Soc. Automotive Engrs. (subcom. 1988—), Am. Mgmt. Assn. Avocations: auto racing, home improvement. Office: Lexus a Divsn of Toyota 19001 S Western Ave Torrance CA 90501-1106

BURRIS, BOYD LEE, psychiatrist, psychoanalyst, physician, educator; b. Knoxville, Tenn., Jan. 28, 1930; s. Fred Roosevelt and Mildred Blanche Burris. BS, U. Tenn., Knoxville, 1951; MD, U. Tenn., Memphis, 1952. Diplomate in psychiatry Am. Bd. Psychiatry and Neurology; cert. in psychoanalysis. Tng. and supervising analyst Balt.-Washington Inst. for Psychoanalysis, Washington, 1974—, co-dir., 1980-86; clin. prof. psychiatry and behavioral scis. George Washington U. Sch. Medicine, Washington, 1983—; clin. prof. psychiatry Georgetown U. Sch. Medicine, Washington, 1990—; mem. bd. trustees Ctr. for Advanced Psychoanalytic Studies, Princeton, N.J., Aspen, Colo., 1982—, pres. bd. trustees and dir., 1994—2003; pvt. practice psychiatry and psychoanalysis Washington, 1960—. Active staff George Washington U. Hosp., 1963-96; cons. Potomac Found. for Mental Health, Bethesda, Md., 1969-78, St. Elizabeth's Hosp., Washington, 1969-88. Contbr. chpt. to book, articles to profl. jours. Lt. comdr. M.C., USN, 1954-56. Mem. Am. Psychiat. Assn. (chair tellers com. 1987-88), Am. Psychoanalytic Assn. (bd. on profl. standards 1982-86, 2000-2002), Balt./Washington Soc. for Psychoanalysis (pres. 1978-79). Home: 3100 Rolling Rd Chevy Chase MD 20815-4038 Office: 4545 42nd St NW Ste 310 Washington DC 20016-4623

BURRIS, CRAVEN ALLEN, retired college administrator, educator; b. Wingate, N.C., Sept. 11, 1929; s. Craven Cullom and Virginia Neulin (Currie) B.; m. Jane Russell Burris, June 19, 1955; children: Christa Cullom, David Allen. AA, Wingate Coll., 1949; BS, Wake Forest U., 1951; BDiv, Southeastern Bapt. Sem., Wake Forest, N.C., 1958; MA, Duke U., 1959, PhD, 1964. Prof. history and govt. Gardner-Webb U., Boiling Springs, N.C., 1958-66; prof. history, govt. and interdisciplinary studies St. Andrews Presbyn. Coll., Laurinburg, N.C., 1966-69; v.p., dean of coll., prof. history and politics Meredith Coll., Raleigh, N.C., 1969-98, ret., 1998, acting pres., 1971. Contbr. articles to profl. jours. Precinct ofcr. State Conv. del., N.C. Dem. Party, 1969, 71; pres., dir. Tammy Lynn Found./Retarded Children, Raleigh, 1980—; chmn. Raleigh Hist. Dists. Commn., 2000-2001. Lt. USNR, 1951-55, Italy and Atlantic Fleet. Recipient Disting. Alumni award Wingate U., 1983, Fulbright Study Trip, U.S. Govt., Pakistan, 1973, Study Trip USSR, 1988, Rsch. Brit. Mus. and Libr., 1963, 97. Mem. Civitan Internat. (v.p. bd. dirs. 1970—), Lions Club (editor 1965), Masons. Baptist. Avocations: choral singing, tennis, racquetball, golf, sailing, gardening. Home: 1322 Duplin Rd Raleigh NC 27607-3721 Office: Meredith Coll 3800 Hillsborough St Raleigh NC 27607-5237

BURRIS, DARREL GENE, retired company executive; b. Springfield, Ill., Aug. 6, 1932; s. Roy L. and Hilma Emilia (Helgeson) B.; m. Bonnie Jean, June 25, 1960. AA, Springfield Jr. Coll., 1953; BS, Okla. State U., 1964. Commd. 2d lt. USAF, 1954, advanced through grades to col., 1974, comdr. 67th Field Maintenance Squadron, 1973-75; air attache Def. Intelligence Agy. Am. Embassy, Oslo, 1976-79; asst. dep. comdr. ops. 363rd Tactical Reconnaissance Wing USAF, Shaw AFB, S.C., 1979-80, asst. vice wing comdr. 363rd Tactical Reconnaissance Wing, 1980-81, program mgr. F-100 engring. Tactical Air Command/Logistics Langley AFB, Va., 1981-83, 1983; sr. tech. specialist Northrop/Grumman Corp., Hawthorne, Calif., 1983-86, tech. mgr., 1986-93; ret., 1993—. Lutheran. Avocation: golf. Home: 501 Bizzy Ln Burnet TX 78611-5810 E-mail: dburris@tstar.net.

BURRIS, HARRIET LOUISE, emergency physician; b. Alexandria Bay, N.Y., Apr. 7, 1949; d. Robert Barker and Harriet Louise (Dorman) Burtch; m. John Samuel Burris Jr., Nov. 30, 1974; children: Elizabeth Jane, Katherine Ann. SB, MIT, 1972; MD, SUNY, Syracuse, 1976. Diplomate Am. Bd. Family Practice, Am. Bd. Emergency Medicine, Nat. Bd. Med. Examiners; cert. added qualification in geriatrics. Resident in family practice St. Joseph's Hosp. Health Ctr., Syracuse, 1976-79; pvt. practice Cazenovia, N.Y., 1979-81; staff MD emergency dept. Middlesex Hosp., Middletown, Conn., 1982-83; staff MD family practice Cmty. Health Care Plan, Wallingford, Conn., 1983-84; staff MD emergency dept. Middlesex Med. Ctr.-Shoreline divsn. Middlesex Hosp., Essex, Conn., 1984—, acting med. dir., 1994. Fellow Am. Acad. Family Physicians; mem. Handweavers Guild Conn. (libr.). Avocations: knitting, handweaving, needle arts. Home: 422 Westland Ave Cheshire CT 06410-3142 Office: Middlesex Med Ctr-Shoreline 260 Westbrook Rd Essex CT 06426-1513

BURRIS, JAMES FREDERICK, federal research administrator, educator; b. Mauston, Wis., Apr. 15, 1947; s. James Duane and Margaret Katherine (Jones) B.; m. Christine Tuve, July 3, 1971; 1 child, Cameron William Tuve. AB, ScB, Brown U., 1970; MD, Columbia U., 1974. Diplomate Am. Bd. Internal Medicine, Subspecialty Bd. Geriatrics, Am. Bd. Clin. Pharmacology. Intern Roosevelt Hosp., N.Y.C., 1974-75; resident in internal medicine Georgetown U. Med. Ctr., Washington, 1977-79; fellow in hypertension VA Med. Ctr., Washington, 1979-81; asst. prof. Sch. Medicine, Georgetown U., Washington, 1981-86, assoc. prof., 1986-91, coord. MD/PhD program, 1988-94, prof., 1991-97; clin. prof., 1997—; asst. dean Sch. Medicine, Georgetown U., Washington, 1987-90; assoc. dean Sch. Medicine Georgetown U., 1990-97, dir. continuing profl. edn., 1994-97; dep. chief R&D officer Vets. Health Adminstrn., U.S. Dept. Vets Affairs, Washington, 1997—. Bd. dirs. Inst. for Clin. Rsch., Washington, 1989-92; bd. regents Am. Bd. Clin. Pharmacology, 1992-98, 2002—; rsch. adminstr. cert. coun.; rsch. assoc. hypertension unit VA Med. Ctr., Washington, 1981-92; vis. investigator Centre Hospitalier, U. Vaudois, Lausanne, Switzerland, 1982-83; dir. clin. rsch. Cardiovasc. Ctr. No. Va., Falls Church, 1988-92; under-sec. health's exec. performance award U.S. Dept. of Vet. Affairs, 1999, 2000. Mem. editl. bd. Jour. Clin. Pharmacology, Jour. Am. Geriat. Soc., Clin. Pharmacology and Therapeutics; contbr. over 200 articles to profl. jours. Cubmaster Boy Scouts Am., 1995-98, asst. scoutmaster, 1998—. Lt. comdr. USPHS, 1975-77. Recipient svc. award ARC, 1970, outstanding svc. citation DAV, 1987, meritorious svc. award Am. Heart Assn., 1994, Cubmasters award Boy Scouts Am., 1998, James E. West award, 1997, Scouter's Tng. Key award, 2000, Vicennial medal Georgetown U., 2000; commd. officer student tng. and extern program scholar USPHS, 1973-74; rsch. fellow Found. for Rsch. of Cardiovascular Diseases, Lausanne, 1983. Fellow: ACP, Am. Coll. Cardiology, Am. Coll. Clin. Pharmacology (bd. regents 1990—95, 1998—, Disting. Svc. award 1992), Am. Coll. Preventive Medicine, Am. Geriatrics Soc.; mem.: AMA (physician's recognition award 1982, 1985, 1988, 1991, 1994, 1997, 2001), Am. Heart Assn. (v.p. 1995—96, rsch. com. 1994—96, chmn. rsch. peer rev. com. 1992—94, bd. dirs. Nation's Capital affiliate 1994—97, fellow couns. on high blood pressure rsch., circulation, epidemiology, fellow coun. clin. cardiology), Sigma Xi. Achievements include education and research in hypertension, hyperlipidemia, preventive cardiology and clinical pharmacology; grants and contracts management and regulatory affairs and technology transfer administration; direction of continuing professional education programs; federal research policy development and program implementation. Office: Vets Health Adminstrn (12A) Dept VA 810 Vermont Ave NW Rm 775 Washington DC 20420-0001 E-mail: james.burris@hq.med.va.gov.

BURRIS, JANICE ELAINE, educational administrator; b. Omaha, July 3, 1964; d. Isreal and Pearlie Mae Beaugard; m. Lonnie Burris, June 29, 1991. BS, Creighton U., 1986, MS, 1999; MEd, Lesley Coll., Omaha, 1999. Cert. tchr., Nebr. Educator Omaha Pub. Schs., 1986-99, instructional facilitator, 1999-2000, counselor, 2000—. Mem. Met. Reading Coun. (rep.), Urban League, Alpha Kappa Alpha. Democrat. Home: 13020 Patrick Cir Omaha NE 68164-3938 E-mail: jebburris@aol.com.

BURRIS, JOHN EDWARD, academic administrator, biologist, educator; b. Feb. 1, 1949; s. Robert Harza and Katherine (Brusse) Burris; m. Sally Ann Sandermann, Dec. 21, 1974; children: Jennifer, Margaret, Mary. AB, Harvard U., 1971; postgrad., U. Wis., 1971—72; PhD, U. Calif., San Diego, 1976. Asst. prof. biology Pa. State U., University Park, 1976—83, assoc. prof. biology, 1983—85, adj. assoc. prof., 1985—89, adj. prof., 1989—2001; pres. Beloit College, Beloit, Wis., 2000—. Dir. bd. biology NRC, Washington, 1984—89; exec. dir. Commn. Life Scis., 1988—92, mem., 1993—97; dir., CEO Marine Biol. Lab., Woods Hole, Mass., 1992—2000; pres.-elect Am. Inst. Biol. Scis., 1995, pres., 96; chmn. adv. com. student sci. enrichment program Burroughs Wellcome Fund, 1995—2002; life and microgravity scis. and applications adv. com. NASA, 1997—2001; trustee Krasnow Inst., 1999—2002; bd. dirs. Radiation Effects Rsch. Found., Wis. Found. Ind. Colls. Trustee Grass Found., 2001—. Mem.: AAAS (bd. dirs. 2002—), Naples Stazione Zoologica, Consiglio Sci., Phi Beta Kappa. Office: 700 College St Beloit WI 53511 E-mail: burrisj@beloit.edu.*

BURRIS, LAUREN BAYLERAN, business owner; b. Detroit, Mar. 30, 1952; d. Haig Aram and Dirouhi (Halajian) Bayleran; m. William James Burris, Feb. 14, 1981; children: Taron, Ian. BBA, U. Mich., 1973; MBA, Wayne State U., 1978. Sales rep. IBM Corp., Detroit, 1973-76; assoc. dir. U. Mich., Dearborn, 1976-78; owner Bayleran & Burris, Inc., Orchard Lake, Mich., 1978—, L.B. Burris & Co., Inc., Orchard Lake, 1982—, Servicelease, Inc., Orchard Lake, 1989—; pres. Burtech, Inc., Orchard Lake, 1997—. Cons. Rapidata, Southfield, Mich., 1980-82. Editor: A Practical Armenian & English Book, 1971. Head pub. rels. com. Oakland County C. of C., Pontiac, Mich., 1983; core leader Cmty. Bible Study, 1994—. Mem. Wayne State U. Alumnae Assn. (pres. Detroit chpt. 1981-83), Alpha Phi. Republican. Avocations: piano, gardening.

BURRIS, REBECCA FRANCES, nursing educator; b. Dallas, May 31, 1951; d. William James Butts and Jessie Mae Porter; m. Raymond Morris Kassouf (div. Aug. 1990); children: Elizabeth Joanne Gunsolus, Katherine Marie Parnell, Jeremy Michael Kassouf; m. Dale Edward Burris, Nov. 21, 1990. BSN, Northwestern State U., Shreveport, La., 1978; MSN, Northwestern State U., 1991; PhD, U. Ark., Little Rock, 2000. RN Ark. Staff nurse Shreveport Med. Ctr., 1979, 1986—91; instr. Northwestern State U., Shreveport, 1991; asst. prof. nursing Ark. Tech. U., Russellville, 1991—96, assoc. prof. nursing, 1996—2003, prof. nursing, 2003—, head dept. nursing, 2001—. Project evaluator, cons. Yell County Rural Health Consortium, Danville, Ark., 2000—; rsch. assoc. Program Against Teen Chewing/U. Ark. Med. Ctr., Little Rock, 1998—99; lectr. in field. Contbr. Mem. Campaign for Tobacco Free Kids, 1999—, Ark. for Nursing, 2000—, Nurse Adminstrs. of Nursing Edn. Programs, 2000—. Fellow Leadership for Acad. Nursing fellow, Am. Assn. Colls. Nursing, 2002; scholar Am. Nurses Found. scholar, 1999—2000. Mem.: ANA, Sigma Theta Tau (chpt. pres. 2002—), Ark. Nurses Assn., So. Nursing Rsch. Soc. Presbyterian. Avocations: canoeing, sailing, hiking, kayaking. Office: Ark Tech Univ 402 West O St [ ]Russellville AR 72801

BURRIS, ROBERT HARZA, biochemist, educator; b. Brookings, S.D., Apr. 13, 1914; s. Edward T. and Mabel T. (Harza) Burris; m. Katherine Irene Brusse, Sept. 12, 1945; children: Jean Carol, John Edward, Ellen Louise. BS, S.D. State Coll., 1936, D.Sc., 1966; MS, U. Wis., 1938, PhD, 1940. NRC fellow Columbia U., 1940—41; faculty U. Wis., Madison, 1941—, prof., 1951—84; chmn. biochemistry Coll. Agr., 1958—70, W.H. Peterson prof. biochemistry, 1976—84, prof. emeritus, 1984—. Recipient Charles Thom award, Soc. Indsl. Microbiology, 1977, Nat. Medal of Sci., 1980, Carty award, NAS, 1984, Wolf award in Agr., 1985; fellow Guggenheim Found., Cambridge U., 1954. Mem.: NAS, AAAS, Am. Soc. Plant Physiologists (pres. 1960, Stephen Hales award 1968, Charles Reid Barnes award 1977), Indian Nat. Sci. Acad. (fgn. assoc.), Am. Soc. Microbiology, Biochem. Soc., Am. Philos. Soc., Am. Soc. Biochemistry and Molecular Biology, Am. Chem. Soc. (Spencer award 1990). Home: 6225 Mineral Point Rd Madison WI 53705 E-mail: burris@biochem.wisc.edu.*

BURRIS, TERRY EUGENE, ophthalmologist, corneal specialist; b. Enid, Okla., Jan. 26, 1952; s. Wiley Eugene and Elizabeth B.; m. Tima Burris; 4 children. BS, MD, Pitts. State U., 1974. Diplomate Am. Bd. Ophthalmology. Dir. corneal and external disease svcs., dept. ophthalmology Naval Hosp., Oakland, Calif., 1982-86; cons. corneal and external diseases, dept. ophthalmology Pacific Med. Ctr., San Francisco, 1984-86; chief and founder Cornea and External Disease Svc. Devers Eye Inst., Portland, Oreg., 1986-90; med./surg. dir. Lions Eyebank of Oreg., Devers Eye Inst., Portland, 1986-90; dir., founder Lions Eyebank of Oreg., Eyebank Rsch. Lab., 1986-90; pres. we. region Eyebank Assn. of Am., 1989-91, mem. eyebank accreditation bd., 1990—; assoc. clin. prof. ophthalmology Casey Eye Inst./Oreg. Health Sci. U., Portland, 1998—; founding ophthalmologist Northwest Corneal Svcs., Portland, 1990—. Cons. sci. medicine adv. bd. Keravision, Inc., 1987—2001; tech. cons. Chiron Ophthalmics, 1988—98; prin. investigator Intrastromal Corneal Ring for Phase II and III Protocol Keravision, Inc., 1995—2002. Comdr. M.C., USNR. Avocations: collecting minerals, writing music. Office: Northwest Corneal Svcs 6950 SW Hampton St Ste 150 Portland OR 97223-8380 E-mail: nwcornea.com.

BURRIS, VALLON LEON, JR., sociologist, educator; b. Beeville, Tex., May 8, 1947; s. Vallon Leon, Sr. and Phyllis Bertha (Tatro) B.; m. Beverly Lynn Hudeck, Mar. 8, 1969 (div. 1978). BA, Rice Univ., 1969; MA, Princeton Univ., 1972, PhD, 1976. Asst. prof. CUNY, N.Y.C., 1976-77; from asst. prof. to prof. Univ. Oreg., Eugene, 1977-92, prof., 1992—, assoc. dept. head, 2001—. Editor Critical Sociology, 1991-97; assoc. editor Social Sci. Quar., 1983-93, Am. Sociol. Rev. 1992-95; contbr. over 40 articles to profl. jours. Mem. Am. Sociol. Assn., Phi Beta Kappa. Office: U Oreg Dept Sociology Eugene OR 97403 E-mail: vburris@oregon.uoregon.edu.

BURRITT, BARBARA, artist; b. Meadville, Pa., Apr. 22, 1947; d. Robert Henry and Gertrude Leone (Kennedy) B.; children: Shane P. Jernigan, Erin A. Jernigan. AA, Ctr. Creative Studies, 1968; BFA, Mpls. Coll. Art & Design, 1980; postgrad., Royal Coll. Art, England, 1992. With K.T.C.A. TV, St. Paul, 1981; courtroom illustrator W.C.C.O. TV, Mpls., 1981-82; arts cons. Cir. Fine Arts Gallery, San Francisco, 1983-84; asst. dir. art Vorpal Art Gallery, San Francisco, 1984; coord. vis. svcs. Mpls. Inst. Arts, 1988-92; tutor art St. Paul, 1998—; artists, leather crafts White Raven Visual Arts, St. Paul, 1993—. Author: Arising from the Ashes, 1992, Blue Electric Monkey, 2003. Art facilitator Wisdom Cirs., Minn., 1994—. Mem. Visionary Artists No. Calif. Avocation: renaissance festival artisan. Home: 7203 N Mohawk Ave Portland OR 97203

BURROUGHS, CHARLES EDWARD, lawyer; b. Milw., June 9, 1939; s. Edward Albert and Ann Monica (Bussman) B.; m. Kathleen Walton, Jan. 30, 1965; children— James, Michael, Lauri, Stephanie. B.S., U. Wis.-Madison, 1962, LL.B., 1965; LL.M., George Washington U., 1968. Bar: Wis. 1965, U.S. Dist. Ct. (ea. and we. dists.) Wis. 1965, U.S. Ct. Clms. 1967, U.S. Ct. Mil. Apls. 1967, U.S. Ct. Apls. (7th cir.) 1969, U.S. Supreme Ct. 1968. Assoc., Porter & Porter, Milw., 1969-71, Purtell, Purcell, Wilmot & Burroughs, 1971-86; ptnr. VonBriesen & Purtell, 1986-91, Hinshaw & Culbertson, Milw. Served to capt. U.S. Army, 1965-69. Mem. ABA, AHLA, HFMA, State Bar Wis. (pres. health law sect.). Roman Catholic. Club: Milw. Athletic. Home: 10937 N Hedgewood Ln Mequon WI 53092-4907

BURROUGHS, PAMELA GAYLE, information systems specialist; b. Dayton, Ohio, July 31, 1957; d. Dale Davis and Anita Madge (Allen) Hallsted; m. Donald W. Burroughs, Oct. 7, 1978; children: Kristin Rene, Kevin Wayne. Diploma, Jewish Hosp. Sch. Nursing, 1977. RN, Ohio. Staff nurse Epp Meml. Hosp., Cin., 1977-78; relief charge nurse ICU, Clermont Mercy Hosp., Batavia, Ohio, 1978-90, supr. patient care, 1990-95, coord. nursing edn., 1991-92, staff nurse ICU, 1993-94, edn. instr., 1992-94, info. svcs. nursing coord., 1994-96, clin. info. sys. specialist, 1996—. E-mail: gburroughs@fuse.net., pgburroughs@health-partners.org.

BURROUGHS, SUSAN MARIE, industrial and organizational psychologist, educator; b. Des Plaines, Ill., Dec. 16, 1969; d. James Edward and Dorothy Ann (Luszcz) B. BA with honors, Eastern Ill. U., 1992; MA with honors, Roosevelt U., 1995; PhD with honors, U. Tenn., 2001. Intern Human Rsch. and Data, Palatine, Ill., 1991; intern HR dept. Eastern Ill. U., Charleston, Ill., 1992, London House, Rosemont, Ill., 1994—95; cons. psychologist to industry, tchr., 1994—; Asst. Prof. mgmt. Roosevelt U., Chgo./Schaumburg, Ill., 2000—. Author: Nat. Safety Coun., 2001; author: (with M. Bing) Jour. Org. Beh., 2001; author: (with J. Bishop and K.D. Scott) Jour. of Mgmt., 2000; author: (with L. Eby) Jour. Cmty. Psychology, 1998; author: (with T. Allen and M. Poteet) Jour. Vocat. Behavior, 1997; author: (with J. Jones) Plant Svcs., 1995, Occupational Health/Safety, 1995; contbr. chapters to books, numerous presentations in field, papers under jour. rev.; contbr. chpts. to textbooks. Recipient APA Dissertation Rsch. award, 2000, Walter Melville Bonham Meml. Endowment award, 1999, Bus. Admin./Finance Fellowship award, 1998, Student Travel awards, 1997—2000, Doctoral Consortium Rep., 1999, Internat. Personnel Mgmt. Assn. Assessment Coun. Paper Finalist, 1997; grantee Scholarly Rsch. grantee, 1999; scholar Roosevelt U. Grad. scholar, 1994, Community/Econ. Devl. Assn. scholar, 1990—91, James J. McGrath Humanities Endowment scholar, 1990, Faculty Senate scholar, 1990, Ctr. for Advancement of Rsch. Methods/Analysis Junior scholar, 1998; recipient various rsch. awards and grants. Mem. APA, Acad. Mgmt., Chgo. Indsl./Orgnl. Psychologists, Soc. Human Resource Mgmt., Soc. Indsl./Orgnl. Psychology, So. Mgmt. Assn., others. Roman Catholic. Avocations: theater, museums, drawing, music. Home: 707 N Prospect Manor Ave Mount Prospect IL 60056-2051 Office: Roosevelt Univ Coll Business Adminstrn 1400 N Roosevelt Blvd Schaumburg IL 60173-4348 Fax: 847-619-4852. E-mail: susanmburr@aol.com.

BURROUGHS, TOM L. state representative; b. Kansas City, Kansas, Nov. 21, 1954; m. Cathie Burroughs; 3 children. Student, Kans. City C.C., 1988, Friends U. Kans. With Colgate Palmolive, 1978—; mem. Kans. Ho. of Reps., 1997—. Chair Colgate-Palmolive Employees Credit Union. Candidate Kans. State Ho. of Reps., 1990, Kans. Senate, 1992. Mem.: Wy-Jo Chpt. Credit Unions, Oil-Chem. Atomic Workers Internat. Union. Democrat. Office: 284-W State Capitol 300 SW 10th Ave Topeka KS 66612 Address: 3131 S 73d Terr Kansas City KS 66106-5162*

BURROW, GERARD NOEL, physician, educator; b. Boston, Jan. 9, 1933; s. William and Noelle Elvira (Money) B.; m. Ann Huntington Rademacher, June 22, 1956; children: Peter Noel, Elisabeth Huntington, Sarah Rogers. BA, Brown U., 1954; MD, Yale U., 1958. Diplomate Am. Bd. Internal Medicine. From asst. prof. to prof. Yale U. Sch. Medicine, New Haven, 1966-76; prof. dept. medicine U. Toronto, Ont., Can., 1976-81, Sir John and Lady Eaton prof. medicine, 1981-88, chmn. dept., 1981-88; physician-in-chief Toronto Gen. Hosp., 1981-88; vice-chancellor for health scis., dean U. Calif. Sch. Medicine, San Diego, 1988-92; prof. dept. medicine U. Calif., San Diego, 1988-92; dean Yale U. Sch. Medicine, New Haven, 1992-97; prof. dept. medicine Yale U., New Haven, 1992-97, David Paige Smith prof. medicine, 1997—2002; dean emeritus Yale U. Sch. Medicine, 2002—; pres., CEO Sea Rsch. Found., Mystic, Conn., 2002—. Author: The Thyroid Gland in Pregnancy, 1972; editor: (with Ferris) Medical Complications During Pregnancy, 1975, 82, 88, 94, 99 (with Duffy). Bd. dirs. Nat. Med. Fellowships. Fellow ACP, Royal Coll. Physicians (Can.); mem. Assn. Am. Physicians, Am. Thyroid Assn., Inst. Medicine of NAS. Office: Sea Rsch Found 55 Coogan Blvd Mystic CT 06355-3289

BURROW, PAUL IRVING, secondary education educator; b. Iowa City, Iowa, Aug. 16, 1955; s. George Irving and Elizabeth Zane (Miller) B.; m. Nancy Kay Rader, Sept. 8, 1979; children: Rachel, Timothy. BA, Drake U., 1976, MA, 1981. Tchr. Spanish, social studies Adair (Iowa) -Casey Schs., 1977-78, Oskaloosa (Iowa) Sr. H.S., 1978—. Bd. dirs. Iowa State Employee's Benefits Assn., chmn. 2002—; exec. bd. Crisis Intervention Svcs., Oskaloosa, 1996-2000; mem. coun. Boy Scouts Am., Oskaloosa, 1988-95; pastor Kirkville United Meth. Ch., 1999—, Hispanic Ministries, Central United Meth. Ch., Oskaloosa, 2001—. Mem. Am. Coun. Tchrs. Fgn. Langs., Iowa Fgn. Lang. Assn. (pres. 1985-87), Iowa Edn. Assn. (exec. bd. 1997—), Oksaloosa Edn. Assn. (spokesperson 1985-2000, grievance chair 1998—, Tchr of Yr. 1992). Democrat. Methodist. Avocations: computers, genealogy, camping, travel. Home: 2212 Lynndale Rd Oskaloosa IA 52577-9129 Office: 1816 N 3rd St Oskaloosa IA 52577

BURROW, WILLIAM HOLLIS, II, dermatologist; b. Walla Walla, Wash., Nov. 19, 1945; s. William Hollis and Patricia (Hoke) B.; m. Lafon Walcott, Jan. 29, 1967; children: William H. III, Kristina, Jamey. BA in Chemistry, Vanderbilt U., 1967; MD, U. Miss., 1973. Bd. cert. in dermatology. Dermatology resident U. Ala., Birmingham, 1974-77; pvt. practice Jackson, Miss., 1977—. V.p. Young Life, Jackson, 1990, Downtown YMCA Bd., Jackson, 1991. Fellow AMA, Am. Acad. Dermatology, So. Med. Assn.; mem. Alpha Omega Alpha. Avocations: golf, gardening, being a grandfather. Office: 1006 Treetops Blvd Ste 101 Jackson MS 39232-7645

BURROWES, ROBERT ARTHUR, transportation consultant, travel-tour operator; b. Bozeman, Mont., Dec. 26, 1919; s. Douglas Henry and Florence May Burrowes; m. Dorthalee Vervil, Aug. 14, 1945 (div. 1956); children: James Douglas, Harold Leslie; m. Annie May Mortimore, Aug. 28, 1958. Clk. exec. dept. East Bay Transit Co., Oakland, Calif., 1938-42; with traffic dept. Bamberger Electric R.R., Salt Lake City, 1942-43; traffic mgr. Pacific Greyhound Lines, San Francisco, 1943-51, Yosemite Gray Line, San Francisco, 1951-61; owner, mgr. Lincoln Bus Line, Stockton, Calif., 1961-72; dir. transp. Culver City (Calif.) Mcpl. Bus. Line, 1972-77; exec. dir. Humboldt Transit Authority, Eureka, Calif., 1977-85; transit cons., Calif., 1985—. Contbr. articles to motor bus mags. Mem. Lyon County Mus. Soc., chmn., 1974-80; mem. State Transp. Com., Carson City, Nev., 1986—. Mem. Am. Sunbathing Assn. (life), Nev. Hist. Soc., Motor Bus Soc., Pacific Bus Mus., Profl. Car Soc., Bay area Electric Railway Assn. (life). Republican. Avocation: yerington senior citizens. Home: 500 Fairview St Yerington NV 89447-3231

BURROWS, BERTHA JEAN, retired academic administrator; b. Brush, Colo., June 15, 1930; d. John and Marie Pabst; m. Leslie R. Burrows, Sept. 2, 1951; children: Paul Eric, Amy Susan, Julie Diane, David Arthur. BA in Bus., U. Colo., 1952. Sec. Dental Found. Colo., Denver, 1969—70, John Boswick, MD, Denver, 1970—72; adminstrv. cons. dept. contg. edn. U. Colo. Sch. Dentistry, Denver, 1975—76; asst. dir. vol. svcs. U. Colo. Health Sci. Ctr., 1977—80; sec. Denver Neurosurg. Assn., Denver, 1981—83, ret., 1983. Part-time bookkeeper Clark & Co., Denver, 1981—83; mem. various coms. U. Colo. Hosp., Denver, 1999—. Vol. U. Colo. Hosp., Denver, 1970—; treas. U.

Colo. Hosp. Gift Shop, 1997—, bd. mgrs., 1987—. Mem.: Colo. Assn. Healthcare Auxilians and Vols. (treas. 2000—01, chmn. gift shop 2002—03), U. Colo. Srs. Assn. (pres. 2002—). Home: 6911 E Iliff Place Denver CO 80224

BURROWS, BRIAN WILLIAM, research and development manufacturing executive; b. Burnie, Tasmania, Australia, Nov. 15, 1939; came to U.S., 1966; s. William Henry and Jean Elizabeth (Ling) B.; 1 child, Karin; m. Penny Nathan Kahan, 1998. BSc, U. Tasmania, 1960, BSc with honors, 1962; PhD, Southampton U., 1966. Staff scientist Tyco Labs., Inc., Waltham, Mass., 1966-68; lectr. Macquarie U., Sydney, Australia, 1969-71; chef de sect. Battelle-Geneva, Switzerland, 1971-75; group leader Inco, Ltd., Mississauga, Ont., Can., 1976-77; program mgr., lab. dir. Gould, Inc., Rolling Meadows, Ill., 1977-86; v.p. rsch. and tech. USG Corp., Chgo., 1986—. Co. rep., Indsl. Rsch. Inst., Washington. Contbr. articles to tech. jours.; patentee in field. Fellow: AAAS; mem.: IEEE, Am. Chem. Soc., Union League Club. Home: 927 Longmeadow Ct Barrington IL 60010-9391 Office: USG Rsch Ctr 700 N Us Highway 45 Libertyville IL 60048-1268 E-mail: bburrows@usg.com.

BURROWS, DONALD ALBERT, artist, painter, photographer, dean; b. Chgo., June 26, 1937; s. Charles Fredrick and Bertha Lillian (Olesen) B.; m. Philomena Durkin, Mar. 3, 1962 (div. 1983); children: Jennifer Maria, Charles Fredrick, Quentin Connor; m. Charlyn Butterfield, Apr. 2, 1995. BFA, Sch. of the Art Inst. of Chgo., 1961, MFA, 1963. Dir. Mobile (Ala.) Art Mus., 1964-66, Ft. Worth Art Mus., 1966-67, Ctr. for Creative Studies, Detroit, 1967-68; prof. humanities City Colls. of Chgo., 1968-83; assoc. dean Harrington Inst., Chgo., 1974-84; acad. dean Ray Coll. of Design, Chgo., 1986-93; prin. artist, designer Misaine/Chaleur, Inc., Gardena, Calif., 1990—, Modern Classic Artworks, Lexington; pres., CEO ChyCogo and Co., Ltd., Willowbrook, Ill., 1987—. One-man shows include Hansen Gallery, Chgo., 1986, Elmhurst (Ill.) Coll., 1986, Galleria Renata, Chgo., 1988. Mem. Am. Soc. Interior Designers, Alumni Assn. Sch. of Art Inst. Chgo., Alumni Assn. U. Chgo., Art Inst. Chgo. (Ryerson Fgn. Traveling fellow, 1961-63). Democrat. Home: 717 Maplewood Ct Unit D Willowbrook IL 60527-7539

BURROWS, EDWIN G. education educator; b. Detroit, Mich., May 15, 1943; s. Edwin G. Burrows and Gwenyth Lemon; m. Mary Patricia Adamski, Aug. 5, 1978; children: Matthew, Katherine. PhD, Columbia U., 1964—72. Prof. history Bklyn Coll., 1972—2000, Broeklundian prof. history, 2001—; disting. prof. history Bklyn. Coll., Bklyn., 2003—; vis. disting. prof. history Hofstra U., 2002—03. Bd. of dirs. Dyckman Farmhouse Mus., NYC, 2000—; cons. Fraunces Tavern Mus., NYC, New-York Hist. Soc., NYC. Co-author: (book) Gotham: A History of New York City (Pulitzer Prize in History, 1999). Recipient Wash. Irving medal, St. Nicholas Soc. NY, 2000, The Brendan Gill prize, The Mcpl. Art Soc. of NY, 1999, Presbyn. Writer of the Yr., Presbyn. Writers Guild, 2001, Presdl. medal, Hofstra U., 2001. Fellow: Soc. of Am. Historians; mem.: Inst. of Early Am. History and Culture, Orgn. of Am. Historians. Home: 14 Clipper Dr Northport NY 11768 Office: Depart of History / Bklyn Coll Bedford Ave & Ave H Brooklyn NY 11210 E-mail: eburrows@brooklyn.cuny.edu.

BURROWS, EDWIN GLADDING, retired broadcaster, writer, poet; b. Dallas, July 23, 1917; s. Millar Burrows, Irene B. (Gladding); m. Gwenyth Lemon, 1940 (div. 1971); children: Edwin Gwynne, Daniel William, David John; m. Beth Elpern, Dec. 7, 1973. BA, Yale U., 1938; MA, U. Mich., 1940. Program dir. Sta. WWJ-FM, Detroit, 1940-43, Sta. WPAG, Ann Arbor, Mich., 1946-48; program dir., mgr. Stas. WUOM-WVGR, U. Mich., Ann Arbor, 1948-70, exec. prodr., 1973-82; dir. Nat. Ctr. for Audio Experimentation, U. Wis., Madison, 1970-73; ret., 1982. Condr. poetry readings through Mich., 1965—82; poetry readings State of Wash., 1986—; helped charter radio divsn. Nat. Ednl. Radio of Nat. Assn. Ednl. Broadcasters, former region III dir., chmn. bd., 1965; chmn./mem. bd. network adv. com. Nat. Assn. Ednl. Broadcasters; lobbyist for inclusion of radio in Pub. Broadcasting Act of 1967. Author: (poetry) The Arctic Tern and Other Poems, 1957, Man Fishing, 1970, Kiva, 1976, Properties: A Play for Voices, 1979, The House of August, 1985, (chapbooks) The Crossings, 1976, On the Road to Bailey's, 1979, Handsigns for Rain, 1989, The Birds Under the Earth, 1997, Sailing As Before, 2001; contbr. poetry to anthologies, poems to over 150 jours. Lt. USN, 1943—46. Recipient Ohio State awards, 1953, 1954, 1955, 1956, 1971, 1974, Borestone Mountain poetry award, 1964, 1st ann. poetry award Ascent, 1987, donated his papers to U. Md. at College Park Librs., 1991; fellow Yaddo Found., 1963, 1966.

BURROWS, ELIZABETH MACDONALD, religious organization executive, educator; b. Portland, Oreg., Jan. 30, 1930; d. Leland R. and Ruth M. (Frew) MacDonald. Certificate, Chinmaya Trust Sandeepany, Bombay; PhD (hon.), Internat. U. Philosophy and Sci., 1975; ThD, Christian Coll. Universal Peace, 1992. Ordained to ministry First Christian Ch., 1976. Mgr. credit Home Utilities, Seattle, 1958, Montgomery Ward, Crescent City, Calif., 1963; supr. Oreg. dist. tng. West Coast Tele., Beaverton, 1965; pres. Christ Ch. of Universal Peace, Seattle, 1971—, prof. religion, also bd. dirs.; pres. Archives Internat., Seattle, 1971—; v.p. James Tyler Kent Inst. Homeopathy, 1984-95; sec. Louis Braille Inst. for the Blind, 1995—. Author: Crystal Planet, 1979, Pathway of the Immortal, 1980, Odyssey of the Apocalypse, 1981, Harp of Destiny, 1984, Commentary for Gospel of Peace of Jesus Christ According to John, 1986, Seasons of the Soul, 1995, Voyagers of the Sand, 1996, The Song of God, 1998, Hold the Anchovies, 1996, Pilgrim of the Shadow, 1998, Maya Sangh and the Valley of the White Ones, 2001, The Secret Jesus Scroll, 2002, Poetry Chapbook, 2002, Visions, 2002, Maya Sangh and the Valley of the White One. Recipient Pres. award for literary excellence CADER, 1994, 95, 97, Diamond Homer award Famous Poets Soc., 1998, Pub.'s Choice award Poets of the New Era, 2002. Mem. Internat. Speakers Platform, Internat. New Thought Alliance, Cousteau Soc., Internat. Order of Chivalry, The Planetary Soc. Home: 10529 Ashworth Ave N Seattle WA 98133-8937 E-mail: Starbase2001@earthlink.net. *Oneness with God is mankind's ultimate vision. This results in a profound journey which covers strange and wonderful worlds beyond mortal boundaries. To reach oneness is to achieve more than anyone can imagine, or more than anyone has ever dreamed.*

BURROWS, HENRY PETER, III, secondary education educator; b. Selma, Ala., Jan. 26, 1944; s. Henry Peter Jr. and Josepine (Porter) B.; m. Dinah Shore, Aug. 26, 1983. BA in English, U. Del., 1967; BS in Edn., Auburn U., Montgomery, Ala., 1996; MA in History, U. Ala., 1986. Cert. tchr., Ala.; cert. airline trasnport pilot, command pilot. Commd. 2d lt. USAF, 1967, advanced through grades to lt. col., 1986, fighter pilot/staff officer, 1967-88, ret., 1988; airline pilot Pan Am. World Airways, Miami, Fla., 1989-91; tchr. math. Autauga County Bd. Edn., Prattville, Ala., 1996—. Contbr. articles and short stories to mags.; mem. editl. bd. Ala. Jour. Math., Montgomery, 1996—. Decorated DFC, Air medal; Chancellor's scholar Auburn U., 1996. Mem. NEA, Ala. Edn. Assn., Math. Assn. Am., Phi Kappa Phi, Kappa Delta Pi, Phi Alpha Theta. Avocations: coin collecting, photography, jogging, reading. Office: Prattville Jr HS 1135 N Chestnut St Prattville AL 36067 Home: 102 Jordon Crossing Prattville AL 36067

BURROWS, JAMES, television and motion picture director, producer; b. L.A., Dec. 30, 1940; s. Abe Burrows. BA, Oberlin Coll.; MFA, Yale U. Off-Broadway prodns.: dir. (motion picture) Partners, 1982, (TV film) More Than Friends, 1978, (TV pilots) Lou Grant, Dear John, Night Court, Wings, Roc, Frasier, Friends, Newsradio, Third Rock from the Sun, Caroline in the City, Stark Raving Mad, Madigan Men, The Weber Show/ Cursed, Dexter Prep; co-creator, (TV series) The Mary Tyler Moore Show, 1976-76, The Bob Newhart Show, 1975-77, Taxi, 1978-82; co-creator, co-exec. producer, dir. Cheers, 1982-93, exec. producer, dir. Will & Grace, 1998-. Recipient Dirs. Guild Am. award for comedy direction, 1984, 91, 94, 99, Emmy awards NATAS for dir. in comedy series Taxi, 1979-80, 81-82 seasons, Cheers, 1982-83, 90-91 seasons; Emmy award as co-producer Cheers, 1982-83, 83-84, 89-90, 90-91 seasons; Emmy award as director of a Comedy Series for Fraiser, 1994, American Comedy award for Lifetime Achievement, 1996. Office: care Paramount TV Prodns 5555 Melrose Ave # Bung1 Los Angeles CA 90038-3112

BURROWS, JOHN (JACK) NEWTON, music educator; b. Winchester, Mass., Mar. 10, 1947; s. William Mead and Dorothy Newton Burrows; m. Janeen Renee Hayes, July 22, 1972; children: Michael Christian, Robert William. MusB with distinction, Ind. U., 1974; 30 hours over Masters (in music), Butler U., 1979—84; MSc in music edn., Ind. U., 1974—79. Cert. tchg. Life Lic. State of Ind., 1974. Mid. sch. band dir./gen. music Frankfort Mid. Sch., Ind., 1974—. Staff mem. of summer music camps Future Musicians of Ind./Gt. Lakes Music Camp, 1987—. Coach (soccer, basketball and baseball) Boys and Girls Club, 1987—94; H.S. soccer coach Frankfort Sr. H.S., 1994—2002; lead trumpet player Fun Time Band, 1985—2002; trumpet player Lafayette Citizens Band, 2000—02; asst. scout master Boy Scouts of Am. Troop 320, 1992—2002; youth dir. St. Matthew United Meth. Ch., 1976—91, pres. of men's orgn., 1975—79; pres. Ch. Men's Orgn., 1975—79; fin. com. mem. St. Matthew United Meth. Ch., 1985—88, choir mem., 1974—2002, adminstrv. bd. mem. at large, 1989—91, orch. and hand bell mem., 1982—2002. E-5 U.S. Army, 1968—71, Ft. Benjamin Harrison, Ind., IN. Recipient Bands and students receiving first divsn. ratings at contest, Ind. State Sch. Music Assn., 1974—2002. Mem.: Music Educators Nat. Conf., Ind. U. Alumni Assn. (life), Pi Kappa Lambda (hon.). Methodist. Avocations: golf, soccer, swimming, sports, travel. Home: 600 South Maish Road Frankfort IN 46041 Office: Frankfort Middle School 329 North Maish Road Frankfort IN 46041 Office Fax: 765-659-6260. Personal E-mail: burrows@geetel.net. E-mail: burrowsj@fhs.frankfort.k12.in.us.

BURROWS, JOHN EDWARD, communications company executive; b. Englewood, N.J., Aug. 6, 1950; s. Laurence McCallum and Pauline Hannah (McClave) B. BA in Journalism, Rutgers U., 1972. From staff asst. to account exec. Ogilvy & Mather Inc., N.Y.C., 1977-80; mgr. sales devel. CBS Radio Spot Sales, N.Y.C., 1980-81; dist. dir. affiliate relations CBS Radio Network, N.Y.C., 1981-84, dir. affiliate relations, 1984-86, v.p. affiliate relations, 1986-87; v.p. news and sports affiliate relations CBS Radio Networks, N.Y.C., 1987-89; broadcast cons. Hackensack, N.J., 1989-91; broadcast cons., classical piano instr. Norfolk, Conn., 1991—. Author: A Country Heart, 1983. Episcopalian. Avocations: golf, writing, cross-country skiing, genealogy. Home: PO Box 623 10 Laurel Ln Norfolk CT 06058-1135 E-mail: JEBurrows@aol.com.

BURROWS, JON HANES, lawyer; b. Frederick, Okla., July 12, 1946; s. John Henry and Eula Elizabeth (Trull) B.; m. Katie Lea Royal, July 13, 1969; children: Justin Hanes, Kelly Elizabeth. BME, U. Okla., 1968, MME, 1969; JD, U. Tex., 1976. Bar: Tex. 1976, U.S. Dist. Ct. (we. dist.) Tex. 1978, U.S. Dist. Ct. (no. dist.) Tex. 1989; cert. residential and comml. real estate law Tex. Bd. Legal Specialization. Ptnr. Burrows & Cure, Temple, Tex., 1976-78; pvt. practice Temple, 1978-81; ptnr. Burrows & Baird, Temple, 1982-85; pres. Burrows, Baird, Miller & Crews, PC, 1985-98; judge Bell County, Belton, Tex., 1999—. Mem. faculty in real estate law Temple Jr. Coll., 1980 89. Treas., bd. govs. Temple Civic Theatre, 1980; pres. Western Hills Elem. PTO, 1982; mem. human studies subcom. VA Hosp., 1983-86; bd. dirs. Temple United Way, 1983-86, 93-98, campaign chmn., 1992; trustee Temple Coll., 1989-98. Capt. USAF, 1969-73, col. USAFR, ret. 2000. Mem. ABA, State Bar Tex., Bell-Lampasas-Mills Counties Bar Assn., Temple C. of C. (bd. dirs. 1993-98, chmn. 1996-97), Lions (bd. dirs. 1980-86, pres. 1986-87), Phi Alpha Delta. Baptist. Home: 709 Clover Ln Temple TX 76502-4817 Office: Bell County Courthouse PO Box 768 Belton TX 76513-0768

BURROWS, KATHY S. health facility administrator; b. Springfield, Ill., Dec. 30, 1957; d. Leslie Taylor Cullers and Nancy Ann Neuber Cullers; m. Charles Anthony Cady, Oct. 28, 1982 (div. Jan. 1986); 1 child, Leslie Ann Cady; m. James Anthony Burrows, May 21, 1988. BBA, U Iowa, 1988, MS in Health Admin., 1999. Program asst. U Iowa, Iowa City, 1988—99; fiscal admin. mgr. Baumet Eisner Neuromedical Inst., Ft. Lauderdale, Fla., 2000—01; exec. dir. The Mind Inst. Mental Illness and Neuroscience Discovery, Albuquerque, 2001—. Mem.: Soc. of Rsch. Admin., Assn. of Fund Raising Profl. (assoc.). Republican. Avocations: swimming, reading, crafts. Office: The Mind Institute 801 University Blvd SE Suite 200 Albuquerque NM 87106

BURROWS, KENNETH DAVID, lawyer; b. Bklyn., Mar. 26, 1941; s. Selig S. and Gladys (Spatt) B.; m. Erica Johng, Aug. 5, 1989. BA, Brown U., 1967; JD, Fordham U., 1970. Bar: N.Y. 1971, Conn. 1973, U.S. Dist. Ct. (so. dist.) N.Y. 1972, U.S. Dist. Ct. Conn. 1994, U.S. Sureme Ct. 1973. Assoc. Phillips, Nizer, Benjamin, Krim & Ballon, N.Y.C., 1970-77; ptnr. Kleinberg, Kaplan, Wolff, Cohen & Burrows, N.Y.C., 1977-79, Burrows & Poster, N.Y.C., 1980-89, Burrows & Franzblau, N.Y.C., 1990-91; arbitrator small claims ct. City of N.Y., 1975-95; lectr. Practising Law Inst., 1996—; spl. master Supreme Ct. State of N.Y., N.Y. County, 1980-89; arbitrator U.S. Dist. Ct. (ea. dist.) N.Y., 1994—; mediator U.S. Dist. Ct. (so. dist.) N.Y., 1994—; ptnr. Bender Burrows & Rosenthal LLC, NYC, 2003—. Mem. Appellate Divsn. 1st Dept. Com. on Law Guardians. Served with USCGR, 1960-68. Mem. ABA, N.Y. State Bar Assn., Assn. Bar City N.Y., Am. Acad. Matrimonial Lawyers, N.Y. County Lawyers Assn., Am. Arbitration Assn. (mem. nat. arbitrators panel 1973-97). Office: Bender Burrows & Rosenthal 451 Park Ave S New York NY 10016 E-mail: burrows@pipeline.com.

BURROWS, MAILE LEILANI, court clerk; b. Leesburg, Fla., Oct. 2, 1979; d. Roberto Luis Burrows and Cathy Diane Kirby, James Dexter Kirby (Stepfather). Excellence in Customer Service Nat. Cable Tng. Inst. (Arapahoe C.C.), 2002. Customer account exec. Comcast Comm., Leesburg, Fla., 1999—2002; ct. clk. Clk. of Circuit and County Courts, Lake County Fla., 2002—. Team coord. Comcast Comm. Relay for Life Team, Leesburg, Fla., 2002. Personal E-mail: mlbsn99@aol.com.

BURROWS, MICHAEL DONALD, lawyer; b. Oak Park, Ill., May 23, 1944; s. Milford Denton and Helen Jean (Spitali) B.; m. Sandi Miller, Feb. 6, 1982; 1 child, Matthew Denton. BA, Williams Coll., 1967; JD, N.Y. Law Sch., 1973. Bar: N.Y. 1974, U.S. Dist. Ct. (ea. and so. dists.) N.Y. 1974, U.S. Ct. Appeals (2d cir.) 1978, U.S. Supreme Ct. 1981. Assoc. Baker & McKenzie, N.Y.C., 1973-80, ptnr., 1980-95, of counsel, 1995-99, mem. internat. exec. com., 1986-88; ptnr. Winston & Strawn, N.Y.C., 1999—, exec. com., chmn. N.Y. Litigation dept., 2000—. Co-author: The Practice of International Litigation, 1992. With USMC, 1968-70. Mem. ABA, Assn.of Bar of City of N.Y. Office: Winston & Strawn 200 Park Ave New York NY 10166-0005

BURROWS, ROBERT PAUL, optometrist; b. Chehalis, Wash. s. Fremont O. and Pauline A. (Kostick) B.; m. Marilyn Burrows. BS in Visual Sci., Pacific U., 1979, OD, 1981. Assoc. optometric physician L.E. Hedgen, O.D. & Assocs., Chehalis, 1981-86; ptnr. Lewis County Eye & Vision Assocs., Chehalis, 1986—. Active United Way, 1981—. Rsch. grant PTU, 1980. Mem.: Wash. Assn. Optometric Physicians, Am. Optometric Assn. (charter contact lens sect., recognition award 1984—2003), Twin City C. of C., Kiwanis (dir. 1984—85, 1989—90, 2000—03), Omega Epsilon Phi. Methodist. Office: 1179 S Market Blvd Chehalis WA 98532-3427 E-mail: l.c.eye@localaccess.com.

BURROWS, SUZETTA CECILE, medical librarian; d. Werner and Clara Martha Geiger; m. John Joseph Burrows, Jan. 22, 1967; 1 child, Joseph John. MS in Libr. Sci., Columbia U., 1968. Libr. cons. Eliot Health Scis. Books, Inc., Long Island City, NY, 1974—76; libr. dir. Meml. Sloan-Kettering Cancer Ctr., New York, NY, 1967—74; head of cataloging/assoc. reference libr. U. Miss. Med. Ctr., Jackson, Miss., 1977—80; vice chmn., dept. of the libr. and biomed. comm. U. Miami Sch. Medicine, Miami, Fla., 1980—. Dir.: (website) Point-of-Care Team-based Information System (Nat. Libr. of Medicine Info. Systems Grant, 1998), (medical school curriculum component) Evidence-based Medicine/Use of the Biomedical Literature (Jour. of the Med. Libr. Assn., 2003), (website) Southeast Florida AIDS Network (Jour. of the Med. Libr. Assn., 1993); contbr. articles to profl. jours. and conf. procs. Vestry mem. St. Johns Episc. Ch., Hollywood, Fla., 2000—01. Mem.: Med. Libr. Assn. (chair Med. Sch. Libr. 1996—97, chair so. chpt. 1990—91). Avocation: sailing. Office: U Miami Med Libr PO Box 016950 Miami FL 33101

BURROWS, WILLIAM E. journalist, educator, writer; b. Phila., Mar. 27, 1937; s. Eli William and Helen B.; m. Joelle Bentley Hodgson, Nov. 19, 1966; 1 child, Lara Julie. BA, Columbia U., 1960, MA, 1962. Reporter The Times-Dispatch, Richmond, Va., 1965-66, The Washington Post, 1966-68, The N.Y. Times, 1968-69, The Wall St. Jour., N.Y.C., 1969-71; travel writer Fielding Publs., Mallorca, Spain, 1971-73; prof. journalism NYU, 1974—, founder, dir. grad. Sci. and Environ. Reporting Program. Author: Deep Black, 1986, Exploring Space, 1990, This New Ocean, 1998; contbg. editor Air & Space/Smithsonian Inst., Washington, 1993—. Recipient excellence award Air & Space Writers Assn., 1991. Mem. AAAS, Nat. Assn. Sci. Writers, Am. Astron. Soc. (bd. govs. 1999, Eugene M. Emme award 2000), Century Assn. Avocations: astronomy, cooking, classical music. Office: NYU Sci Writing Program 10 Washington Pl New York NY 10003-6604

BURR-STIENON, ELAINE, writer, minister, private school educator; d. Henry Leonard and Verna Ruth (Buyer) Burr; m. Francis Michael Stienon, Jan. 23, 1958; children: Christopher Stienon, Burr Stienon, Ruth Lane Stienon. Attended, Interlochen Center for the Arts, Interlochen, MI., 1952—54; BA, U. Mich., 1954—57; courses in creative writing, extension sch., Cambridge, MA, 1958—58. Tchr. of mus. self employed, Salt Lake City, 1973—78, Glendale, Calif., 1978—2003. Mng. editor Ensign Pub. House, Glendale, Calif., 1988—2003. Author: Lightning in the Fog, 1977, Ut. Spring, 1979, The Light of the Morning, 1988, short stories, 1952—90. Recipient Hopwood Award, U. Mich, 1957, writing award, Nat. Scholastic, 1952, Nat. Honor Soc., 1952—53. Mem.: Nat. Writers Assn., John Whitmer Hist. Assn., Mormon History Assn. Democrat. Community Of Christ. Avocations: music, history, art, photography, reading. Home and Office: 1241 Irving Ave Glendale CA 91201-1305 Home Fax: 818-956-5395. E-mail: Epburr@hotmail.com.

BURRUS, DANIEL ALLEN, research company executive, consultant; b. Portland, Oreg., Aug. 22, 1947; s. Joe Howard and Mary Kathleen B. BS, U. Wis., Oshkosh. Founder, pres. Burrus Media Prodns., Brookfield, Wis., 1978-80, Burrus Powered Gliders, Waukesha, Wis., 1980-82, Midwest Skynasaurs, Waukesha, 1982-84, Ultrasports Inc., Waukesha, 1982-84, Burrus Research Assocs., Inc., Milw., 1983—. Cons. various corps., assns. and univs.; speaker in field. Author, editor: Tech. Futures Newsletter, 1985—93, Technotrends Newsletter, 1993—; author: (audio tape learning sys.) The Future of Education, 1985, Beyond Megatrends, 1985, Teaching Creativity, 1986, Futureview: A Look Ahead, 1986, 1988, Maximimizing your Creativity, 1989, Reengineering Yourself, 1995, The New Tools of Technology, 1990, Technotrends, 1993, Desining Thriving Schools, 2001; co-author: Medical Advances, 1990, Environmental Solutions, 1990, Advances in Agriculture, 1990, Insights into Excellence, 1992; editor: Applied Sci. Rev., 1985, 1988; writer, dir., prodr.: films Deja Vu, 1972, Phantasmagoria, 1972, The New Adventures of Superman, 1972; author: Designing Thriving Schools, 2000, The Advantage Business Strategy Game, 2000; contbr. Mem. AAAS, Internat. Personal Robot Assn. (founding), Internat. Ctr. Profl. Speaking (founding, bd. dirs.), Nat. Speakers Assn. (bd. dirs. 1991-96, cert. speaking profl., Profl. Speakers Hall of Fame 1992). Avocations: film making, photography, mountain climbing, flying, scuba diving. Office: Burrus Rsch Assocs 557 Cottonwood Ave Ste 106 Hartland WI 53029-2347 E-mail: office@burrus.com.

BURRUS, JOHN N(EWELL), sociology educator; b. Gilmer, Tex., Jan. 23, 1920; s. Herman Clifford and Beulah (Blalack) B.; m. Sarah Gray. AB, U. Miss., 1942; MA, La. State U., 1944, PhD, 1950; postgrad., U. Minn., 1945-47, Vanderbilt U., 1947-48. Asst. prof. sociology U. Miss., Oxford, 1943-45; instr. Vanderbilt U., Nashville, 1947-48; rsch. assoc. rural sociology La. State U., Baton Rouge, 1948-50; asst. prof. U. Fla., Gainesville, 1950-51, U. So. Miss., Hattiesburg, 1951-52, assoc. prof., 1952-57, prof., 1957-70, Disting. Univ. prof. sociology, 1970-83, Disting. Univ. prof. sociology emeritus, 1982—, chmn. dept. sociology, 1951-70, chmn. dept. sociology and anthropology, 1978-80; disting. univ. prof. emeritus Sociology and Anthropology, U. So. Miss., 1982—. Author: monographs Differential Mortality in Mississippi, 1951, (with M. King, H. Pedersen) Mississippi's People, 1955, Mississippi Life Tables, 1950-51, 54, Composition of Population of the Coastal Counties; books (with T.L. Smith) Social Problems, 1955, (with others) A Legacy of Knowledge: Sociological Contributions of T. Lynn Smith, 1980; contbr. chpts., articles to profl. jours, books including History of Mississippi (2 vols.), 1973, Ency. Brit., 15th edit., Ency. Brit. sect. on Miss., 1974. Bd. dirs. Hattiesburg Area Hist. Soc., 1971-73, S. Central Miss. chpt. A.R.C., 1961-71. Miss.-Ala. Sea Grant Consortium grantee, 1973-74 Mem. So. Sociol. Soc. (mem. exec. com. 1955-58), Rural Sociol. Soc., Population Reference Bur., Sigma Chi, Phi Kappa Phi, Alpha Kappa Delta, Pi Gamma Mu, Omicron Delta Kappa. Clubs: Kiwanian (dir. Hattiesburg 1975-76). Home: 1305 Windsor Dr Hattiesburg MS 39402-2852

BURRUS, ROBERT LEWIS, JR., lawyer; b. Richmond, Va., Sept. 16, 1934; s. Robert Lewis and Bessie (Hart) B.; m. Ann Williams, Aug. 1, 1964; children: David Curran, Peter Tandy, Lewis Graves BA, U. Richmond, 1955; LLB, Duke U., 1958. Bar: Va. 1958. Assoc. McGuire Woods LLP, Richmond, Va., 1959-63, ptnr., 1963—, chmn., 1990—. Bd. dirs. CSX Corp., Richmond, Smithfield Foods, Smithfield, Va., S&K Famous Brands, Richmond. Trustee U. Richmond, past rector; trustee Va. Mus. Fine Arts, Va. Hist. Soc.; bd. visitors Duke U. Law Sch., Durham, N.C.; past chmn. State Coun. Higher Edn. for Va.; past dir., chmn. exec. com. Richmond Renaissance; past bd. dirs. Richmond Children's Mus., Circuit City Found.; past mem. Govs. Commn. Intercollegiate Athletics, 1991-92; past pres. St. Christopher's Sch. Found., Richmond; adv. com. Mt. Vernon's Ladies' Assn. Recipient Charles S. Rhyne award Duke U., 1998, Alumni of Yr. award U. Richmond, 1998, Silver Hope award Nat. Multiple Sclerosis Soc., 2000, Humanitarian award Nat. Conf. for Cmty. and Justice, 2001, Trustees Disting. Svc. award U. Richmond, 2002. Fellow Am. Bar Found., Va. Bar Found.; mem. ABA, Va. Bar Assn. (chmn. corp. law com. 1975-77, chmn. bus. sect. 1976-77), Richmond Bar Assn., Va. Hist. Soc. (trustee), Commonwealth Club, Chgo. Club, Country Club Va., Bull and Bear Club, Kinloch Golf Club, Forum Club, Omicron Delta Kappa. Episcopalian. Home: 220 Ampthill Rd Richmond VA 23226-2235 Office: McGuireWoods LLP One James Ctr Richmond VA 23219 E-mail: rburrus@mcguirewoods.com.

BURRUSS, TERRY GENE, architect; b. Dec. 30, 1950; s. Alvin Eugene and Fern (Pelton) B.; m. Merilyn Kloss, Dec. 20, 1981; children: Mamie Christine, Gracie Aline. BArch, BA, U. Ark., 1973. Registered architect, Ark. Intern architect firm Robinson and Wassell, Inc., Little Rock, Ark., 1973-75; practice architecture Evo-Tech Prodn., Little Rock, Ark., 1976-78, I.D.E.A., Eureka Springs, Ark., 1976-78; architect Store Planning Assocs., San Francisco, 1978; assoc. Design 3, Architects, Little Rock, 1979; v.p., divsn. mgr. Mehlburger, Tanner, Renshaw and Assocs., Little Rock, 1980-84; v.p. Mehlburger, Tanner, Robinson & Assocs., Little Rock, 1984-87; pres. Terry Burruss Architects, Little Rock, 1987—. Instr. Hatha Yoga Community Edn. Program, 1976-77, St. Francis House, Little Rock, 1978, Parapsychology Ctr., 1978-79; vis. prof. constrn. mgmt. program U. Ark., Little Rock, 1999-00; mem. Ark. Environ. Barriers Coun. Author: Flow Gently Sweet Alpha, 1972, Inflatables, an Alternative to the Deflated Classroom, 1973, Accessibility Guidelines for Meeting and Lodging Facilities, 1981, Housing for the Developmentally Disabled, 1986. Chmn. ministerial rels. Unity Ch. of Little Rock, 1986-87, pres. bd. dirs., 1987; pres. Montessori Children's Ctr. Parent Tchrs. Orgn., 1986-87; pres. Unity Ch., 1987, Ctrl. High Neighborhood Assn., 1989-90; chmn. Gov.'s Mansion Area, 1998-2000; mem. bd. adjustment City of Little Rock, 2003—. Mem. AIA (state chmn. 1981), U. Ark. Alumni Assn., Little Rock Jaycees (dir. 1981-83, sec. 1982-83, chmn. TV auction 1982), Alpha Phi Omega, Pi Kappa Alpha. Home: 12 Tallyho Ln Little Rock AR 72227-2416 Office: 1202 Main St Ste 230 Little Rock AR 72202-5076

BURSCH, DANIEL W. astronaut; b. Bristol, Pa., July 25, 1957; s. Dudley and Betsy Bursch; m. Roni J. Patterson; 4 children. BS in Physics, U.S. Naval Acad., 1979; grad. with distinction, U.S. Naval Test Pilot Sch., 1984; MS in Engring. Sci., Naval Postgrad. Sch., 1991. Commd. ensign USN, 1979, advanced through grades to capt.; flight officer Pensacola, Fla.; pilot Attack Squadron 34, USS John F. Kennedy, 1981; project test flight officer; flight instr. U.S. Naval Test Pilot Sch.; strike ops. officer Cruiser-Destroyer Group 1, 1984; aeronautical engring. duty officer; astronaut NASA, Houston, 1990, with Astronaut Office Ops. Devel. Br., chief of astronaut appearances, spacecraft communicator, astronaut aboard Internat. Space Sta., 2001. Decorated Navy Commendation medal, Navy Achievement medal. Mem.: U.S. Naval Acad. Alumni Assn. Achievements include logged over 2,900 flight hours in over 35 different aircraft; logged over 746 hours in space; mission specialist STS-51 (1993), STS-68 (1994) and STS-77 (1996). Avocations: tennis, softball, skiing, woodworking, windsurfing. Office: Astronaut Office/CB NASA Johnson Space Ctr Houston TX 77058

BURSEY, MAURICE M. chemistry educator; b. Balt., July 27, 1939; s. Reginald Price and Edna Frances (Moyer) B.; m. Joan Marie Tesarek, Dec. 28, 1970; children— John Thomas Kieran, Sara Helen Moyer. BA, Johns Hopkins U., 1959, MA, 1960, PhD, 1963. Lectr. Johns Hopkins U., Balt., 1963-64; asst.

prof. Purdue U., Lafayette, Ind., 1964-66; asst. prof. chemistry U. N.C., Chapel Hill, 1966-69, assoc. prof., 1969-74, prof., 1974-96, prof. emeritus, 1996—. Editor Mass Spectrometry Revs., 1990-93; contbr. articles to profl. jours. Recipient various research grants. Fellow Am. Inst. Chemists, Royal Soc. Chemistry (assoc.); mem. Am. Chem. Soc. (bd. dirs. 1993-2001), Am. Soc. Mass Spectrometry, Alpha Chi Sigma (Grand Master Alchemist nat. pres. 1986-88). Democrat. Roman Catholic. Home: 101 Longwood Pl Chapel Hill NC 27514-9584 E-mail: mauricebursey@aol.com.

BURSHTAN, JOHN WILLIS, television producer; b. Cedar Rapids, Iowa, July 4, 1958; s. Alvin and Ann Carol (Lichtenstein) B.; children: Eduard (Erik), Marina. BS in Mass. Comm., Miami U., Oxford, Ohio, 1980. Prodr./dir. WKEF TV, Dayton, Ohio, 1978-81, QUBE Interactive TV/Warner Cable Comm., Cin., 1981-85, promotions mgr., 1985-87; prodr., dir., writer Paradise Prodrs. Group, Inc., L.A., 1987-91; prodr./dir. mktg. and devel. Rocky Mountain PBS, Denver, 1991-95, exec. prodr. sta. and cultural affairs, 1995—. Recipient Nat. Cable TV Assn. Ace award for Swordquest, 1983, Emmy award Gov.'s Trophy for Vietnam: We Remember, 1984, Heartland Emmy awards, 1992, 93, 94, 95, 96, 97, 98, 99, 2000, 01, 02, NEA award for Really Short Shows, 1994, Gold plaque, Chgo. Internat. Film Festival, 1994,CINE Golden Eagle award for Klondike and Snow: A Tale of Twin Polar Bears, 1997, others, Wrangler Award for Spirit of Colo. Cowboys, 2002. Mem. Writers Guild of Am. West,. Office: Rocky Mountain PBS 1089 Bannock St Denver CO 80204-4067

BURSKY, HERMAN AARON, lawyer; b. Bklyn., Jan. 16, 1938; s. Abraham S. and Anna R. (Polstein) B.; m. Dolores Kelner, Sept. 3, 1961; children: Daniel Jay, Jennifer Dina. BA, B in Hebrew Lit., Yeshiva U., 1959; LLB, Cornell U., 1962. Bar: N.Y. 1963. Assoc. Levin & Weintraub, N.Y.C., 1963-69; atty. CIT Fin. Corp., N.Y.C., 1969-70; assoc. Otterbourg, Steindler, Houston & Rosen, P.C., N.Y.C., 1970-71; ptnr. Shea & Gould, N.Y.C., 1971-91, Rosenman & Colin, N.Y.C., 1991-98; counsel Fischbein, Badillo, Wagner and Harding, 2000—. Contbg. author: Practical Guide to Bankruptcy and Debtor Relief, 1964. Served as pvt. U.S. Army, 1962-63. Mem. ABA, N.Y. State Bar Assn., Fed. Bar Council, Assn. Comml. Fin. Attys., N.Y. County Lawyers Assn. (bankruptcy com. 1973-80). Clubs: Inwood Country (N.Y.). Jewish. Home: 25 Muriel Ave Lawrence NY 11559-1810 Office: Fischbein Badillo Wagner Harding 909 3rd Ave Fl 18 New York NY 10022-4731

BURSLEY-HAMILTON, SUSAN, secondary school educator; b. Redbank, N.J., May 6, 1955; d. Robert Kelly and Irene Magdolin (Connell) Bursley; m. Raymond Hamilton, June 20, 1981; 1 child, Rob. BA in Edn., No. Ariz. U., 1978, MA, 1988. Asst. prin. Kingman Jr. High Sch., Ariz. Order Eastern Star scholar. Mem. Am. Fedn. Tchrs.

BURSON, CHARLES W. federal official, former state attorney general; b. Memphis; m. Marion 1971; children: Clare, Kate. BA, U. Mich., 1966; MA, Cambridge U., England, 1968; JD, Harvard U., 1970. Assoc. Burson & Burson and Burson & Walkup, Memphis; ptnr. Wildman, Harrold, Allen, Dixon, & McDonnell, Memphis, 1981-88; atty. gen. State of Tenn., Nashville; counsel to v.p. Office of V.P., Washington, 1993-99, chief of staff to v.p., 1999—. Del. Tenn. Constl. Conv., 1977, (chmn. State Spending Limitation Com.). Mem. Nat. Assn. Attys. Gen. (pres. 1994-95, chair FTC working group, mem. exec. com. securities group, chair consumer protection com. 1990-91, vice chair securities working group, Wyman award 1994), Tenn. Bd. Law Examiners (past pres.). Office: Exec Office of VP 278 Old Exec Office Bldg NW Washington DC 20501-0001

BURSON, HAROLD, public relations executive, director; b. Memphis, Feb. 15, 1921; s. Maurice and Esther (Bach) Burson; m. Betty Ann Foster, Oct. 30, 1947; children: Scott, Mark. BA, U. Miss., 1940; DHL (hon.), Boston U., 1988. Corr., reporter Memphis Comml. Appeal, 1938—40; dir. Ole Miss News Bur., Oxford, Miss., 1939—40; dir. pub. rels. H.K. Ferguson Co., N.Y.C., 1941—43; chmn. Burson-Marsteller, N.Y.C., 1953—; bd. dirs., mem. exec. com. Young & Rubicam, N.Y.C.; pub. affairs adviser to Pres. Ronald Reagan, 1989—94; mem. adv. coun. Emory U. Bus. Sch., Medill Sch. Journalism Northwestern U., U. So. Calif. Sch. Journalism; trustee Ab. Fortas Meml. Fund, Kennedy Ctr.; hon. prof. Fudan U., Shanghai, 1999; vis. prof. Leeds Met. U., Yorkshire, 2001; exec.-in-residence U. Ky. Coll. Commn., 2000. Chmn. bd., mem. exec. com. Nat. Coun. on Econ. Edn.; bd. dirs., exec. com., v.p. pub. info. Nat. Safety Coun., 1968—76; bd. dirs. Kennedy Ctr. Prodns., Washington, Catalyst Inc., 1978—89; former trustee World Wildlife Fund, 1979—81, Found. for Pub. Rels. Rsch. and Edn.; trustee Hackley Sch., Tarrytown, NY, 1968—76; chmn. pvt. sector pub. rels. com. USIA; mem. Fine Arts Commn., 1981—85; exec. com. Young Astronauts Coun., 1984—88; adv. bd. Bus. Coun. for Internat. Understanding; pres. coun. N.Y. Acad. Sci.; trustee World Environ. Ctr. Named Pub. Rels. Profl. of Yr., Pub. Rels. News, 1977, 1989, Most Influential Person in Pub. Rels. in 20th Century, PR Week, 1999, to U. Miss. Hall of Fame, 1980; recipient Gold Anvil award, Pub. Rels. Soc. Am., 1980, Horatio Alger award, 1986, Arthur Page award, 1990, Lifetime Achievement award, Inside PR, 1993, Alexander Hamilton award for lifetime achievement in pub. rels., Inst. Pub. Rels. Mem.: Horatio Alger Assn., N.Y. Acad. Med. (trustee 2003), Am. Philatelic Soc., N.Y. Soc. Security Analysts, Internat. Pub. Rels. Assn., Am. Pub. Rels. Assn., Blue Key Club, Econ. Club N.Y. (exec. com.), Scarsdale Golf Club, Overseas Press Club, Mid-Am. Club, Omicron Delta Kappa. Office: Burson-Marsteller 230 Park Ave S New York NY 10003-1513 E-mail: harold_burson@nyc.bm.com.

BURSTEIN, ALAN STUART, lawyer; b. Detroit, Sept. 21, 1940; s. Harry S. and Florence (Rosen) B.; m. Margery E. Gordon, June 23, 1963; children: Mark Albert, Florence Beth, Robert Gordon. BA, U. Mich., 1962, JD, 1965. Assoc. counsel to majority leader N.Y. State Senate, Albany, 1971-73; ptnr. Hiscock & Barclay, Syracuse, N.Y., 1965-85, Scolaro, Shulman, Cohen, Fetter & Burstein, Syracuse, 1985—. Bd. dirs. Penfield Mfg. Co., Syracuse; former mem. 5th Dist. Grievance Com. Bd. dirs. Pub. Broadcasting Coun., Syracuse, 1977-84; v.p. Temple Adath Yeshurun; past pres. Syracuse Jewish Fedn. Named Outstanding Young Man Syracuse Jaycees, 1976; recipient Community Leadership award Syracuse Jewish Fedn., 1980, Community Svc. award B'nai Brith. Mem. ABA, N.Y. State Bar Assn., Onondaga County Bar Assn. (past bd. dirs.), Century Club. Republican. Jewish. Avocations: tennis, boating, fishing, reading. Home: 100 Old Farm Rd Fayetteville NY 13066-2526 Office: 90 Presidential Plz Syracuse NY 13202-2240 E-mail: aburstein@scolaro.com.

BURSTEIN, ELIAS, physicist, educator; b. N.Y.C., Sept. 30, 1917; s. Samuel and Sarah (Plotkin) B.; m. Rena Ruth Benson, Sept. 19, 1943; children—Joanna Bliss, Sandra Joy, Miriam Stephanie. AB, Bklyn. Coll., 1938; A.M., U. Kans., 1941; postgrad., MIT, 1941-43, Cath. U., 1946-48; DTech (hon.), Chalmers U. Tech., Göteborg, Sweden, 1982; DSc (hon.), Bklyn. Coll., 1985, Emory U., 1994, Ohio State U., 1999. Physicist Crystal br. U.S. Naval Research Lab., 1945-58, head semiconductor br., 1958; prof. physics U. Pa., Phila., 1958-82, Mary Amanda Wood prof. physics, 1982-88, emeritus, 1988—. Jubilee vis. prof. physics Chalmers U. Tech., Goteborg, 1981; mem. solid state scis. adv. panel NRC-NAS, 1971-80, chmn., 1977-79, condensed matter physics adv. com. Internat. Ctr. for Theoretical Physics, 1990-96, Trieste; com. on sci. and the arts, Franklin Inst., 1994—; Miller Inst. vis. rsch. prof. physics U. Calif., Berkeley, 1996. Founding editor Solid State Comms., 1963, sec. bd. editors, 1963-69, editor-in-chief, 1969-1992; co-editor Comments on Solid State Physics, 1971—; patentee in field. Recipient Navy Civilian Meritorious Service award, 1957; John Price Wetherill medal Franklin Inst., 1979; Guggenheim fellow, 1980; Alexander Von Humboldt Sr. U.S. Scientist award, 1988-90, 92-93. Fellow AAAS, Am. Phys. Soc. (sec.-treas. div. solid state physics 1956-61, Isakson prize 1986), Optical Soc. Am.; mem. Nat. Acad. Scis., Phi Beta Kappa, Sigma Xi. Clubs: Internat. House Japan (Tokyo). Office: U Pa Dept Physics Philadelphia PA 19104 E-mail: burstein@physics.upenn.edu.

BURSTEIN, MERWYN JEROME, lawyer; b. Springfield, Mass., Apr. 6, 1938; s. Rubin Meyer and Sylvia (Burke) B.; m. Ruth B. Burstein, July 31, 1966; children: David, Judith, Jeffrey. BA in Psychology, Am. Internat. Coll., 1959; LLB, Boston Coll., 1960; JD, New Eng. Sch. Law, 1962. Bar: Mass. 1963, U.S. Dist. Ct. Mass. 1963, U.S. Dist. Ct. Conn. 1979, U.S. Tax Ct. 1981. Ptnr. Michelman & Burstein, Springfield, 1963-70; pvt. practice law Springfield, 1970-73; sr. ptnr. Burstein & Dupont, Springfield, 1973-88, Burstein Law Offices, 1988—. Pres., treas. Burstein Springfield Investment Assocs., 1963—. Author: (pamphlet) You and the Law, 1963. Class chmn. alumni fund raising drive Am. Internat. Coll., 1969-76m life mem. Alumni Varsity Club; vice chmn. Longmeadow (Mass.) Dem. Com.; active Beth El Temple and Jewish Cmty. Ctr., Springfield. Mem. ATLA, Mass. Bar Assn., Hampden County Bar Assn., Masons, Shriners. Home: 29 Willett Dr Longmeadow MA 01106-2037 Office: 1331 E Columbus Ave Springfield MA 01105-2539

BURSTEIN, MICHAEL CLIFFORD, management consultant; b. Washington, June 10, 1942; s. Edward Marion and Ethel Kaplan Burstein; m. Laurel Douglass Crooks, Dec. 20, 1973; 1 child, Adam. BA in Math., Johns Hopkins U., 1967; MS in Ops. Rsch., George Wash. U., ., 1969; PhD in Managerial Econ. & Decision Scis., Northwestern U., 1977. Prin. scientist Indsl. Tech. Inst., Ann Arbor, Mich., 1985—88; vis. assoc. prof. ops. mgmt. U. of Mich., Sch. of Mgmt., Ann Arbor, 1989—90; adj. assoc. prof. ops. mgmt. Yale U, Sch. of Mgmt., New Haven, 1991—92; assoc. prof. ops. mgmt., dir. Ctr. Bus. Competitiveness U. Wis., Milw., 1992—95; cons. Milw., 1996—97; CEO, pres. T.I.P.E., Inc., Westhampton, Mass., 1998—. Fellow Yale U., Jonathan Edwards Coll., New Haven, 1991—92. Co-editor and contbr. (book) Manufacturing Strategy: The Research Agenda for the Next Decade, 1990; assoc. editor: Mgmt. Sci., 1985—90, Internat. Jour. Flexible Mfg. Sys., 1986—2000, IIE Transactions, 1986—90; editl. bd. Engring. Economist, 1986—89. Chair Cub Scout Pack Com., Dexter, Mich., 1986—87; mem. Zoning Bd. of Appeals, Westhampton, Mass., 2001—03, Planning Bd., Pelham, Mass., 1982—85. With U.S. Army, 1965—70. Mem.: Soc. Mfg. Engrs. (chair prodn. systems & mgmt. tools tech. com. 2001—02), Soc. Concurrent Product Devel. (program com. mem. 2000—02, co-chmn. ann. conf. 2002—03, Outstanding Contbr. 2002), CAMI Consortium (academic rev. panelist, cost mgmt. sys. program 1986—88), Omicron Delta Epsilon, Alpha Pi Mu, Tau Beta Pi. Judaism. Avocations: bicycling, hiking, cross country skiing, music, snowshoeing. Home: 632 Warrenwright Rd Belchertown MA 01007-9747 Office: TIPE Inc 632 Warrenwright Rd Belchertown MA 01007 Home Fax: 413-237-3459; Office Fax: 413-253-3459. E-mail: mcb.tipe@worldnet.att.net.

BURSTEIN, NEIL ALAN, lawyer; b. N.Y.C., June 24, 1951; s. Edward Stuart and Pauline (Linksman) B. B.S., Union Coll., Schenectady, 1973; J.D., Albany Law Sch., 1976; LL.M., NYU, 1983. Bar: N.Y. 1977, U.S. Dist. Ct. (so. dist.) N.Y. 1981. Assoc. Clayman, Mead & Gallo, Schenectady, 1976-78; gen. atty. Waldes Kohinour, Inc., Long Island City, N.Y., 1978-81; assoc. counsel Saks Fifth Ave., N.Y.C., 1981-86, mng. atty. Trans World Airlines Inc., 1986 , legis. counsel to N.Y. state senator A. Frederick Meyerson, Albany, 1973-76. Contbr. chpt. to Entertainment Law (Selz & Simensky), 1983, articles to profl. jours. William C. Saxton scholar Albany Law Sch., 1973. Mem. Assn. Bar City N.Y., ABA, N.Y. State Bar Assn. Home: 305 E 86th St New York NY 10028-4702 Office: Trans World Airlines 605 3rd Ave New York NY 10158-0180

BURSTEIN, RICHARD JOEL, lawyer; b. Detroit, Feb. 9, 1945; s. Harry Seymour and Florence (Rosen) B.; m. Gayle Lee Handmaker, Dec. 21, 1969; children: Stephanie Faith, Melissa Amy. Grad., U. Mich., 1966; JD, Wayne State U., 1969. Bar: Mich. 1969, U.S. Ct. Appeals (ea. dist.) Mich. 1969. Ptnr. Smith Miro Hirsch & Brody, Detroit, 1969-81, Honigman Miller Schwartz & Cohn, Detroit, 1981-96. Bd. dirs. Sandy Corp., Troy, Mich.; bd. dirs. Met. Affairs Corp., Detroit; co-chmn. Artrain. Mem. Am. Coll. Real Estate Lawyers. Office: Honigman Miller Schwartz & Cohn 32270 Telegraph Rd Ste 225 Bingham Farms MI 48025

BURSTEIN, SHARON ANN, corporate communications specialist, designer; b. Schenectady, N.Y., July 18, 1952; d. Harold Edward and Lois Ida (Hesner) Rieck; m. Richard Lyle Burstein, Sept. 8, 1985; 1 child, Alexandra Blaire. BA, Nat. Lewis U., 1974; postgrad., Russell Sage Coll., 1974-78, Union Coll., 1980. Cert. tchr., N.Y. Elem. tchr. Saratoga Springs (N.Y.) Schs., 1974-80; ednl. cons. Whitcomb Assocs., Boston, 1980-81; ednl. mktg. specialist Monroe Sys. for Bus., Newington, Conn., 1981-83; nat. mktg. mgr. Victor Techs., Hartford, Conn., 1983, Exclusives, Boston, 1984-85; dir. pub. rels. Lawrence Group, Albany, N.Y., 1985-87, dir. corp. comm., 1987-88, v.p., 1988-89, v.p investors rels. N.Y.C., 1987-89; pres. S.A. Burstein & Assocs., Albany, 1989—, Neswick Ct., 1994-99. Adj. prof. Russell Sage Coll., Troy, N.Y., 1994-99; exec. prodr. Carmine's Television Show-NBC; cons. N.Y. Assn. Bus. Ofcls., 1982-83. Editor: Helpline newspaper, 1985, 87; co-prodr. Playing It Safe, 1986 (Nori award 1987), To Be As Independent As You Can be (Nori award 1989), Cookbook Capital Connoisseur (Nori award 1989), Camp Ever Young (Nori award 1993); acted in TV comml., 1981 (Addy award 1982); prodr. Carmine's Table TV Show (NBC). Bd. dirs. Multiple Sclerosis Soc., Albany, 1986, Mohawk Pathways Girl Scouts U.S.; active N.Y. Spl. Olympics, 1987; v.p. bd. dirs. Capital Repertory Theater Guild, 1999—. Mem. Nat. Investor Rels. Inst., Am. Mgmt. Assn., Assn. Profl. Communicators, Nat. Assn. Investment Clubs, Tennis Industry Assn., Albany C. of C. (women's bus. coun.), Steuben Club, Women's Press Club, Kappa Delta Pi. Democrat. Avocations: writing, tennis, golf, skiing, reading. Home: 4 Birch Hill Rd Loudonville NY 12211-2004

BURSTEIN, STEPHEN DAVID, neurosurgeon; b. Bklyn., Apr. 10, 1934; s. Moe and Anna (Bloch) B.; m. Ronnie Sue Deutsch, Oct. 8, 1972; 1 dau., Alissa Aimee. BA with distinction, U. Mich., 1954; MD, SUNY, Bklyn., 1958; MS in Neurosurgery, U. Minn., Rochester, 1965. Diplomate Am. Bd. Neurol. Surgery. Surg. intern Johns Hopkins Hosp., Balt., 1958-59; neurosurgery fellow Mayo Clinic, Rochester, 1961-65; chief dept. neurosurgery South Nassau Cmty. Hosp., Oceanside, N.Y., 1980—, pres. med. staff, 1980-82. Chief dept. neurosurgery Franklin Gen. Hosp., Valley Stream, N.Y., 1980—; prin. Neurol. Surgery & Neurology, P.C., Freeport, N.Y., 1965—. Contbr. articles to med. jours. Bd. dirs. South Nassau Cmty. Hosp., 1978—. Lt. USNR, 1959-61. Recipient Neurosurg. Travel award Mayo Found., 1966. Fellow ACS; mem. L.I. Hearing and Speech Soc. (bd. dirs.), N.Y. State Neurosurgeons Soc. (bd. dirs.), N.Y. State Neurosurg. Soc. (pres. 1981-82, exec. dir.), Sigma Xi, Alpha Omega Alpha. Jewish. Avocations: theatre, travel. Home: 57 Princeton St Williston Park NY 11596 Office: Neurol Surgery PC 88 S Bergen Pl Freeport NY 11520-3510 E-mail: neurofree@aol.com.

BURSTEN, STUART LOWELL, physician, biochemist; b. L.A., Jan. 19, 1953; s. Leo and Goldie (Zeff) B.; m. Colleen Sue Thompson, May 4, 1980; children: Elisa Michelle, Shawna Mariel, Tiana Marie; m. Lesley Domino, Mar. 26, 2000. BS in Biology, AB Psychology, Stanford U., 1975; MD, Yale U., 1980. Diplomate Am. Bd. Internal Medicine, Am. Bd. Nephrology. Intern Boston City Hosp., 1980-81; resident internal medicine U. Wash., Seattle, 1981-83, fellow nephrology, 1983-85, postdoctoral rsch. fellow, nephrology, 1985-86; acting instr. U. Wash. Sch. Medicine, 1986-88, asst. prof. medicine, 1988-92, clin. asst. prof. medicine, 1992-94, clin. assoc. prof. medicine, 1994-2001; co-dir., second messenger protein chemistry divsn. Cell Therapeutic, Inc., Seattle, 1992-95, prin. scientist, lipid biology and biochemistry, 1995-2000; prin. cons., rsch. dir. Inst. Lipid Studies, 2000—. Contbr. articles to profl. jours.; patentee. Rsch. dir. Friends of Snoqualmie Valley, Wash., 1986-89. Nat. Merit Found. scholar 1971, Nat. Grocers Assn. scholar, 1971, S&H Green Stamps Assn. scholar 1971; grantee NIH, 1975-78; recipient Northwest Kidney Found. Rsch. award, 1988-89, Nat. Inst. Arthritis, Diabetes, Digestive, and Kidney Diseases fellowship, 1985-86, others. Fellow: ACP; mem.: AAAS, Am. Stats. Assn., Am. Chem. Soc., Am. Soc. Nephrology, N.Y. Acad. Scis., Am. Fedn. Med. Rsch., Am. Heart Assn. Achievements include discovering that theobromine-based alkyl chains with patentable substitutions result in modulation of fatty acid and lipid peroxidative metabolism in mammalian cells, which in turn results in profound protection against acute inflammation and oxidant injury - this has introduced or is introducing an entire new class of compounds for treatment of a broad range of human diseases, including renal and liver disease, and protection against acute immune damage and the side effects of radiation; in addition, related compounds have been found to have potent anti-tumor activity based on interaction with lipid-directed enzymes. Office: Inst Lipid Studies 22287 Mulholland Hwy #325 Calabasas CA 91302

BURSTON, RICHARD MERVIN, business executive; b. Brookline, Mass., Oct. 31, 1924; s. Mark and Anita (Andrews) B.; m. Phoebe Harvey Hopkins, Aug. 29, 1958; children: Abby Lyn, Seth Hopkins, Joshua Craig, Mark Andrews, Amanda Lee. BA, Bowdoin Coll., 1949; MBA, Harvard U., 1952. Mgr. beauty dept. Kendall Co., Boston, 1953-58; regional sales mgr. M. Pier Co., Ft. Lauderdale, Fla., 1958-59; nat. sales mgr. Ozon Products, Inc., Bklyn., 1959-63; v.p., co-founder Burston/Larkin Assocs., Stamford, Conn., 1964-88; pres., CEO Excalibur, Inc., Stamford, 1981-88; founder, pres. Burston Inc., Stamford, 1987-98, cons., 1999—. Dir. Nat. Beauty and Barber Reps. Assn., N.Y.C., 1973-74, Louv Yacht Yard, Norwalk, Conn., 1969-73; cons. Ruckel Mfg., Inc., N.Y.C., 1969-87. Dir. Roxbury-Riverbank Little League, Stamford, 1971-82; fundraiser Bowdoin Coll., Brunswick, Maine, 1983-90, mem. alumni coun., 1994-98, pres., 1997-98. Lt. USNR, 1943-46, PTO. Recipient Man of Yr. award United Beauty Supply Corp., Bridgeport, Conn., 1983, Polar Bear award, 2003. Mem. Beauty and Barber Supply Inst., Am. Beauty Assn., Kents Hill Sch. Alumni Assn. (bd. dirs. 1994-2000, trustee 1994—), Miramichi Rod and Gun Club Inc. (pres. 2002), High Head Yacht Club (dir. 1997-2000). Republican. Jewish. Avocation: fly fishing. Home: 408 High Head Rd Harpswell ME 04079-2917 Office: Burston Inc 45 Church St Stamford CT 06906-1711 E-mail: dpburst@clinic.net.

BURSTYN, HAROLD LEWIS, lawyer; b. Boston, Feb. 26, 1930; s. Julius and Zena (Pezrow) B.; m. Joan Netta Jacobs, Aug. 19, 1958; children: Judith, Gail, Daniel. AB, Harvard Coll., 1951; MS, U. Calif., 1957; PhD in History of Sci., Harvard U., 1964; JD, Rutgers U., 1987. Registered patent atty. Instr. Brandeis Univ., Waltham, Mass., 1962-65; asst., assoc. prof. Carnegie-Mellon U., Pitts., 1966-73; dean, prof. Wm. Paterson U., Wayne, NJ, 1973-77; historian U.S. Geol. Survey, Reston, Va., 1976-84; cons. J & H Assocs., Syracuse, N.Y., 1984—; assoc. Melvin & Melvin, Syracuse, 1987-91; ptnr. Morrison Law Firm, Mt. Vernon, N.Y., 1991-95; of counsel McGuire Law Offices, Syracuse, N.Y., 1995-96; patent atty. USAF Rsch. Lab., Rome, N.Y., 1996-2001; affiliated with Hancock & Estabrook LLP, Syracuse, NY, 2001—. Vis. investigator Woods Hole Oceanog. Inst., 1961-76; cons. Coll. Marine Studs, U. Del., 1970; vis. lectr. Rutgers U., Piscataway, N.J., 1977-87; mem. Marine Biol. Lab., Woods Hole, Mass., 1983—; adj. prof. elec. engring. and computer sci., Syracuse U., 1995—. Author: At the Sign of the Quadrant, 1957, 1957; assoc. articles editdor Law Practice Mgmt., 1994—2001; contbr. articles to profl. jours. With USN, USNR, 1952-55. Mem. ABA, Fed. Bar Assn., Am. Assn. Advt. Sci., The Fla. Bar, N.Y. State Bar Assn., Am. Arbitration Assn. (cert.), Computer Law Assn., Am. Intellectual Property Law Assn. Home: 216 Bradford Pkwy Syracuse NY 13224-1767 Office: Link Hall 115 Syracuse Univ Syracuse NY 13244 E-mail: burstynh@iname.com.

BURSTYN, JOAN NETTA, education educator; b. Leicester, Eng., Mar. 6, 1929; d. David Edward and Nellie (Wachman) Jacobs; m. Harold L. Burstyn, Aug. 19, 1958; children: Judith, Gail, Daniel. BA with honors, U. London, 1950, cert. of edn., 1952, acad. diploma in edn., 1958, PhD, 1968. Tchg. fellow edn. Harvard U., Cambridge, Mass., 1959-64; lectr. U. Pitts., 1967; lectr. psychology and edn. Carnegie Mellon U., Pitts., 1967-68, instr., 1968, asst. prof., 1969-74, dir. tchr. edn., 1970-74; assoc. prof., chairperson dept. edn. Douglass Coll., Rutgers U., New Brunswick, N.J., 1974-81, prof. edn., 1981-85, dir. women's studies program, 1981-85; dean sch. edn. Syracuse (N.Y.) U., 1986-89, prof. cultural founds. of edn. and of history, 1986—2003, sr. rsch. assoc., 2002—03, dir. violence prevention project, 1997-98, prof. emeritus, 2003—. Co-dir. Fund for Improvement of Post-Secondary Edn. Grant, 1983-85; vis. prof. Monash U., Australia, summer 1989; Emens disting. prof. Ball State U., 1996; dir. Nat. Endowment for Humanities Pilot grant, 1980-82; seminar rsch. assoc., Syracuse (N.Y.) U., 2002-03 Author: Song Cycle, 1976, Victorian Education and the Ideal of Womanhood, 1980, Waiting for the Lame Horse, 1987; co-author: Preventing Violence in Schools: A Challenge to American Democracy, 2001; editor: Preparation for Life?, 1986, Desktop Publishing in the University, 1991, Educating Tomorrow's Valuable Citizen, 1996; editor-in-chief Past and Promise: Lives of New Jersey Women, 1990; contbr. articles to profl. jours.; assoc. editor Signs: Jour. of Women in Culture and Soc., 1974—89; mem. editl. bd.: Jour. Women in Culture and Soc., 1980—89, History of Edn. Quar, 1982—86, History of Higher Edn. Ann., 1989—, Issues in Edn., 1983—87, Syracuse U. Press, 1991—94, Ednl. Founds., 2000—, Jour. Sch. Violence, 2001—. Mem. adv. bd. nurse-midwifery ednl. program U. Medicine and Dentistry N.J., 1978-83; bd. dirs. Children's Sch. Sci., Woods Hole, Mass., 1977-80; assoc. dir. N.E. Council Women in Devel., 1981-82; mem. joint com. Am. Hist. Assn. and Can. Hist. Assn., 1978-81. Recipient grant-in-aid John F. Kennedy Sch. Govt. and Bunting Inst., 1964-65; Marion Talbot fellow AAUW, 1965-66; recipient Faculty Merit award Rutgers U., 1977, 81. Fellow AAAS; mem. AAUW, Am. Hist. Assn., Am. Ednl. Rsch. Assn. (com. on freedom of inquiry and human rights 1984-86, pubs. com. 1986-89), History of Edn. Soc. U.S. (pres. 1985-86), Am. Ednl. Studies Assn. (chmn. publs. com. 1984-85, v.p. 1993-94, pres.-elect 1994-95, pres. 1995-96). Office: Syracuse U Sch Edn 350 Huntington Hl Syracuse NY 13244-0001 E-mail: jburstyn@syr.edu.

BURT, ALVIN MILLER, III, anatomist, cell biologist, educator, writer; b. Bridgeport, Conn., Aug. 14, 1935; s. Alvin Miller and Esther Louise (Carey) B.; m. Dorothy Hanlin, July 15, 1961 (div.); children: Constance Walker, Carolyn Marie; m. Judith Nath, July 13, 1991; 1 stepchild, Stephen Jacob Nath. BA, Amherst Coll., 1957; PhD (USPHS fellow 1960-61), U. Kans., 1962. Asst. prof. anatomy Med. Coll. Va., Richmond, 1962-63; instr. Yale U. Med. Sch., 1963-66; mem. faculty Vanderbilt U. Med. Sch., 1966—, prof. anatomy, 1974-85, prof. cell biology, 1985-2000, prof. cell biology emeritus, 2000—; prof. cell biology Nursing Sch. Vanderbilt U., Nashville, 1994-2000, prof. cell biology in nursing emeritus, 2000—; sole proprietor Creative Manuscripts and CM Web Graphics, Hendersonville. Vis. scientist Agrl. Research Council, Inst. Animal Physiology, Babraham, Cambridge, Eng., 1972-73 Author: Textbook of Neuroanatomy, 1993; contbr. articles to profl. jours. Vestryman Episcopal Ch. of Advent, Brentwood, Tenn., 1977-81, sr. warden, 1979-81, lay reader, chalice bearer, 1975-87, tchr. adult classes, mem. diocesan lay ministry com., 1981-85; lay reader, chalice bearer St. Philips Episcopal Ch., Donelson, Tenn., 1989-92, vestryman, 1991-92, mem. diocesan total ministry com., 1990-93; mem. Stephen Ministry Diocese of Tenn., 1991—; dir. pastoral care St. Ann's Episcopal Ch., Nashville, 1993-96, lay reader, 1994—, chalice bearer, 1996—, vestryman, 2002—; mem. steering com. Interfaith AIDS Ministry, 1994-96; vol. ombudsman rep. Mid Cumberland Human Resources Ctr., 2001—. Recipient Research Career Devel. award USPHS, 1968-73 Mem. Am. Assn. Anatomists, Am. Soc. Neurochemistry, Human Anatomy & Physiology Soc., Internat. Soc. Neurochemistry, Internat. Brain Rsch. Orgn., Soc. Neurosci., Tenn. Outdoor Writers Assn. (v.p. 1985-86, pres.-elect 1986-87, pres. 1987-88, chmn. bd. dirs. 1988-89), Southeastern Outdoor Press Assn. (Webmaster 2002-), Bass Anglers Sportsmens Soc., Tenn. Spoonplugging Club (bd. dirs. 1980-88, editor newsletter 1980-85), Sigma Xi. Home and Office: 149 Bay Dr Hendersonville TN 37075-4040

BURT, BILLY GEORGE, oil company professional; b. New Orleans, Feb. 19, 1954; s. James Henry and Irene Mary Burt; m. Katherine Wilson, July 23, 1972 (div. Oct. 1980); children: Keith Burt, Raymond Burt; m. Deborah Gaye Gibson, Apr. 15, 1983 (div. Nov. 1985); children: Billy Burt Jr., Brandon; m. Samantha Hile, Oct. 12, 1989; children: Stephanie, Justin. Student, Lamar U., 1988-92, Tex. A&M U., 1992-99; BS in Chemistry, Trinity Coll., 2001. Operator Crown Cen. Petroleum, Pasadena, Tex., 1978-86, Basell USA Inc., Pasadena, 1988—. Mem., capt. fire brigade Basell USA Inc., Pasadena, 1988—. Sgt. USAF, 1975—77. Republican. Roman Catholic. Avocation: Avocations: art, music, sports. Office: Basell USA Inc 12001 Bay Area Blvd Pasadena TX 77507-1309 Home: 2109 Moss Creek Ln Pearland TX 77581 E-mail: bbillburt@netzero.net.

BURT, JEFFREY AMSTERDAM, lawyer; b. Phila., Apr. 27, 1944; s. Samuel Matthew and Esther (Amsterdam) B.; m. Sandra Cas, Dec. 17, 1967; children: Stephen, Daniel, Jonathan, Andrew. BA, Princeton, 1966; LLB, Yale U., 1970; MA in Econs., 1970. Bar: Md. 1971, DC 1971. Law clk. to judge U.S. Ct. Appeals (4th cir.), Balt., 1970-71; assoc. Arnold & Porter, Washington, 1971-77; ptnr., 1978—. Adj. prof. law Georgetown U., 1987-95; frequent lectr. Pres., Green Acres, Inc. Ind. Sch., Rockville, Md., 1984-86. Author: (with others) International Joint Ventures, 1986, 2nd edit., 1992; co-editor: Joint Ventures with Internat. Ptnrs., 1997. Mem. ABA (co-chairperson NIS Law Com. Sect. Internat. Law and Practice 1992-98), Russian Am. C. of C. (dir., sec.). Office: Arnold & Porter 555 12th St NW Washington DC 20004-1206

BURT, JOHN HARRIS, bishop; b. Marquette, Mich., Apr. 11, 1918; s. Bates G. and Emily May (Bailey) B.; m. Martha M. Miller, Feb. 16, 1946; children: Susan, Emily, Sarah, Mary. BA, Amherst Coll., 1940, D.D. (hon.), 1960; BA, Va. Theol. Sem., 1943, B.D., 1967; D.D., Youngstown U., 1958, Kenyon Coll., 1967. Boys worker Christodora House, N.Y.C., 1940-41; ordained to ministry Episcopal Ch., 1943; canon Christ Ch. Cathedral; rector St. Paul's Ch., St. Louis, 1943-44; chaplain to Episc. students U. Mich., 1946-50; rector St. John's Ch., Youngstown, Ohio, 1950-57, All Saints Ch., Pasadena, Calif., 1957-67;

bishop coadjutor Ohio, 1967-68; Episc. bishop of Ohio, 1968-84. Pres. So. Calif. Council Chs., 1962-65; mem. bd. Ch. Soc. Coll. Work, 1964-71; chmn. clergy deployment bd. Episc. Ch., 1971-73 Co-author: World Religions and World Peace, 1969, Joy in the Struggle - Memoirs of Ecumenical Dialogue, 1993; author: Economic Justice and the Christian Conscience, 1987. Pres. Youngstown Coordinating Coun., 1953-56, Pasadena Cmty. Coun., 1964-66; trustee Pomona Coll., 1963-66, Va. Theol. Sem., 1967-72, Colgate-Rochester Div. Sch., 1968-84, Kenyon Coll., 1967-84; bd. dirs. United Way L.A., 1964-67, Cleve. Urban Coalition, 1968-70, Ams. for Energy Independence, 1975-85; bd. dirs. Nat. Com. Against Censorship, 1974—; chmn. bd. dirs. St. John's Home for Girls, Painesville, Ohio, 1968-84; governing bd. Nat. Coun. Chs., 1970-81; mem. Com. on Ch. Order, Consultation of Ch. Union, 1980-88; chmn. com. on theology Episc. Ch. House Bishops, 1973-80; chmn. Urban Bishops Coalition, 1977-93, Faith and Order Commn. Ohio Coun. Chs., 1970-74; bd. dirs. Episcopal Ch. Pub. Co., 1985-92, pres., 1990-92; chmn. commn. ecumenical rels. Episc. Ch., 1973-79, also chmn. commn. mid. judicatories, cons. on ch. union, 1975-79; chmn. com. human affairs and health Episc. Ch., 1982-85; chmn. Bishops Com. Nat. and Internat. Affairs, 1982-85; chmn. Ecumenical Gt. Lakes Project on Econ. Crisis, 1983-89; chmn. Presiding Bishop's Com. Christian-Jewish Rels., 1986-91; pres. Nat. Christian Leadership Conf. on Israel, 1988 99; mem. ch. rels. com. U.S. Holocaust Meml. Coun., 1989-96; mem. Ecumenical Consultation on New Religions Movements, 1985-87; bd. dirs. Ams. for Med. Progress, Inc., 1992-95. Chaplain USNR, 1943-46. Recipient Arvona Lynch Human Relations award Youngstown, 1956; Rissica Human Relations award Jewish War Vets., 1966; Pasadena Community Relations award, 1967; Cleve.'s Simon Bolivar award, 1972; Pitts.'s Thomas Merton award, 1978; Human Rights award Ohio br. ACLU, 1980; Ecumenical Leadership award Christian Ch. (Disciples of Christ), 1986, Am. Jewish Com. award, 1991. Mem. Phi Gamma Delta. Episcopalian. Home: Middle Island Point Rd # 25 Marquette MI 49855-9726

BURT, MARVIN ROGER, financial advisor, investment manager; b. L.A., Mar. 5, 1937; s. Henry Howard Burt and Iris Faith (Green) Welton; m. Joy Lee Rougk, July 20, 1958; children: Sandra Marie, Scott Marvin. BA, UCLA, 1958; MPA, George Washington U., 1965, D in Pub. Adminstrn., 1969. Cert. fin. planner. Mgmt. trainee Bank Am., L.A., 1961-62; program analyst Dept. Def., Washington, 1962-65, Exec. Office Pres., Washington, 1965-66; mem. sr. rsch. staff Resource Mgmt. Corp., Bethesda, Md., 1966-67; sr. cons. Peat Marwick Mitchell, Washington, 1967-68; cons. Potomac, Md., 1968-69; mem. sr. staff Urban Inst., Washington, 1969-72; pres. Burt Assocs., Inc., Bethesda, 1972—2002, Inst. Human Resources Rsch., Bethesda, 1973-82; asst. v.p. Sci. Applications Internat., McLean, Va., 1982-85; chmn. bd. Burt Assocs., Inc., Bethesda, 1972—. Cons. Govt. Agys., Washington, 1965—82. Author: Options for Improving the Care of Neglected and Dependent Children, 1971, Policy Analysis, 1974, A Comprehensive Emergency Services System for Neglected and Abused Children, 1977, Drug Abuse, 1979, Children of Heroin Addicts, 1980; contbr. Mem. Cmty. Coordinated Child Care, Bethesda, 1976—77, Montgomery County Drug. Abuse Adv. Com., 1990—92; chmn. coun. on ministries North Bethesda (Md.) United Meth. Ch., 1975—76, 1981—82, chmn. bd. dirs., 1977—78, bd. dirs., 1986—92, lay del. to ann. conf., 1989, chmn. staff-parish rels. com., 1990—92, chmn. fin. conf., 2001—; bd. dirs. Mental Health Assn. Montgomery County, 2002—03. Grantee, USPHS, 1977—82. Fellow: AAAS; mem.: Registry Fin. Planning Practitioners, Inst. Cert. Fin. Planners (dean mid-atlantic conf. 1995), Internat. Assn. Fin. Planning (v.p. nat. capital chpt. 1987—89), Ops. Rsch. Soc. Am. (chmn. tech. sect. 1979—80), Avenel Commn. Assn. (pres. 1998—2000, bd. dirs. 1996—2001), Bethesda/Chevy Chase C. of C. (chmn. small bus. com. 1990—91, v.p. small bus., bd. dirs. 1991—93), Potomac Rotary (pres. 1991—92, bd. dirs. 1987—93, pres. Potomac Rotary Charities, Inc. 1992). Avocations: hiking, backpacking, golf, skiing. Home: 5 Willow Gate Ct Bethesda MD 20817-4110 Office: Burt Assocs Inc 6010 Executive Blvd Ste 900 Rockville MD 20852

BURT, ROBERT AMSTERDAM, lawyer, educator; b. Phila., Feb. 3, 1939; s. Samuel Matthew and Esther (Amsterdam) B.; m. Linda Gordon Rose, June 14, 1964; children: Anne Elizabeth, Jessica Ellen. AB, Princeton U., 1960; BA in Jurisprudence, Oxford (Eng.) U., 1962, MA, 1968; JD, Yale U., 1964, MA (hon.), 1976. Bar: D.C. 1966, Mich. 1973, U.S. Supreme Ct. 1971. Law clk. to chief judge U.S. Ct. Appeals D.C., 1964-65; asst. gen. counsel Office President's Spl. Rep. Trade Negotiations, 1965-66; senatorial legis. asst., 1966-68; assoc. prof. law U. Chgo. Law Sch., 1968-70; assoc. prof., then prof. law U. Mich. Law Sch., 1970-76; prof. law in psychiatry U. Mich. Med. Sch., 1973-76; Southmayd prof. Yale U. Law Sch., 1976-93, Alexander M. Bickel prof., 1993—. Spl. master U.S. Dist. Ct. Conn., 1987-92, 95. Bd. dirs. Benhaven Sch. Autistic Persons, New Haven, 1977—, chmn., 1983-96; bd. dirs. Judge David L. Bazelon Ctr. for Mental Health Law, 1985—, chmn., 1990-2000; mem. adv. bd. Project on Death in Am., Open Soc. Inst., 1994—; bd. dirs. Slifka Ctr. for Jewish Life at Yale, 1996—. Rockefeller fellow, 1976, John Simon Guggenheim fellow, 1997-98. Mem. Inst. Medicine (coun. 1992-94). Democrat. Jewish. Home: 66 Dogwood Cir Woodbridge CT 06525-1254 Office: Yale U Sch Law PO Box 208215 127 Wall St New Haven CT 06511-6636 E-mail: robert.burt@yale.edu.

BURT, ROBERT GENE, lawyer, educator; b. Tucson, Sept. 7, 1944; s. Jack A. and Eva Grace (Colton) B.; m. Stasia Payne, June 7, 1968; children: Jason R., Ashley A. AA, N.Mex. Mil. Inst., Roswell, 1964; BA, U. Ariz, 1965, JD, 1972; LLM in Taxation, Georgetown U., 1973. Bar: Ariz. 1972, D.C. 1973, Oreg. 1977. Appeals atty., spl. asst. to asst. atty. gen. tax div. U.S. Dept. Justice, 1973-75, trial atty., 1975-77; sole practice, Portland, Oreg., 1978; ptnr. Robert G. Burt, P.C., Portland, 1978-80, Burt & Hagen, P.C., Portland, 1980-85, Burt & Day, P.C., Portland, 1985-86; shareholder Burt & Assocs. P.C., Portland, 1986—; adj. prof. Lewis and Clark Coll.; editor: Professional Insight column, 1990-94. Capt. U.S. Army, 1967-71. Decorated Silver Star, Bronze Star with two oak leaf clusters, Purple Heart with one oak leaf cluster, Army Commendation medal with 4 oak leaf clusters, Air Medal with oak leaf cluster. Recipient Spl. Meritous award U.S. Dept. Justice, Washington, 1975. Mem. ABA, Oreg. Bar Assn. (chmn. taxation sect 1988-89, chmn. CPA's joint com. 1989-90), Multnomah County Bar Assn., Oreg. Trial Lawyers Assn., Nat. Health Lawyers Assn., Oreg. Soc. Hosp. Attys., Ariz. State Bar, D.C. Bar. Episcopalian. Clubs: Multnomah Athletic (Portland). Office: 1515 SW 5th Ave Ste 600 Portland OR 97201-5449

BURT, ROBERT NORCROSS, retired diversified manufacturing company executive; b. Lakewood, Ohio, May 24, 1937; s. Vernon Robert and Mary (Norcross) B.; m. Lynn Chilton, Apr. 19, 1969; children: Tracy, Randy, Charlie. BSChemE, Princeton U., 1959; MBA, Harvard U., 1964. With Mobil Oil Corp., N.Y.C. and Tokyo, 1964—68; dir. corp. planning and acquisitions Chemetron Corp., Chgo., 1968—70, mgr. internat. div., 1970—73; dir. corp. planning FMC Corp., Chgo., 1973—76, v.p. agrl. chems. group Phila., 1976—83, v.p. def. group San Jose, Calif., 1983—88, exec. v.p. Chgo., 1988—90, pres., 1990—91, chmn., CEO, 1991—2001. Bd. dirs. Phelps Dodge, Pfizer. Bd. dirs. Rehab. Inst. Chgo., 1991—; trustee Orchestral Assn. of Chgo. Symphony Orch., 1992—, vice chmn., 1995-99. Lt. USMC, 1959-62. Mem. Bus. Roundtable (policy com., chmn. environ. task force 1993-99, chmn. 1999-2001), Ill. Bus. Roundtable (vice chmn. 1999-2001). Avocations: reading, golfing, spectator sports. Home: 5 Kent Rd Winnetka IL 60093-1815

BURT, WALLACE JOSEPH, JR., insurance company executive; b. Burlington, Iowa, Apr. 1, 1924; s. Wallace Joseph and Lela (Catlow) B.; m. Alice Olmsted, June 22, 1946; children: Lockwood, David, Virginia. student Iowa State Coll., 1942, U. Wis., 1945. V.p., dir. 1st Ins. Fin. Co., Des Moines, 1946-50, Northeastern Ins. Co., Hartford, Conn., 1950-59; pres., owner Hail Reinsurance Mgmt., Inc., Ormond Beach, Fla., 1960-89; chmn. Burt & Scheld, Inc., Ormond Beach, 1961-89; chmn. U.S. br. Hamburg Internat. Reins. Co., 1976-81; chmn. First N.Y. Syndicate Corp., 1979-89, W.J. Burt Mgmt., Inc., N.Y.C., 1979-89; pres. Ormond Reins. Co., 1976-92, Oceanside RE Group, Inc., 1989; dir., v.p. Barnett Bank, Ormond Beach; underwriting mem. Lloyd's of London; dir. N.Y. Ins. Exchange, 1983-84. Trustee, pres. Ormond Beach Meml. Hosp. Served to 1st lt. USAAF, World War II. Decorated D.F.C., Purple Heart, Air medal with 5 oak leaf clusters. Home: 222 Riverside Dr Ormond Beach FL 32176-6504 Office: 140 S Atlantic Ave Ormond Beach FL 32176-6689

BURTCH, JACK WILLARD, JR., lawyer; b. Youngstown, Ohio, Dec. 11, 1946; s. Jack Willard and Elizabeth Bentley (Robinson) B.; m. Susan Lee Thielemann, June 21, 1969; children: Anson James, Douglas Robinson. BA, Wesleyan U., 1969; JD, Vanderbilt U., 1972. Bar: Va. 1973. Assoc. Hunton and Williams, Richmond, Va., 1973-80; ptnr. McSweeney, Burtch & Crump PC, Richmond, Va., 1980—2000, Va. Law & Govt. Affairs PC, Richmond, Va., 2001—. Active Episc. Diocese Va.; bd. dirs. Church Schools Diocese of VA, 1999—. Capt. USAR, 1972-80. Republican. Home: 3205 Hawthorne Ave Richmond VA 23222-2518 Office: Va Law & Govt Affairs PC PO Box 8088 1015 E Main St 4th Fl Richmond VA 23223-0088 E-mail: jb@vlga.com.

BURTLESS, GARY THOMAS, economist, consultant; b. Cayuga County, N.Y., Apr. 11, 1950; s. Charles Bernie and Patricia Ann (MacCone) B.; m. Elise Kathe Bruml, Nov. 27, 1976; children: Andrew B., Matthew B. BA, Yale U., 1972; PhD, MIT, 1977. Economist Office Sc., HEW, Washington, 1977-79, U.S. Dept. Labor, Washington, 1979-81; John D. and Nancy C. Whitehead chair in econ. studies Brookings Instn., Washington, 1981—. Vis. prof. pub. affairs U. Md., College Park, 1993; cons. various orgns., 1981—, U.S. Dept. Lab., 1985—, World Bank, Washington, 1990-97. Author: Can America Afford To Grow Old, 1989, Growth With Equity: Economic Policymaking for the Next Century, 1993, Globaphobia: Confronting Fears about Open Trade, 1998; co-editor Jour. Human Resources, 1988-96, A Future of Lousy Jobs?, 1990, Five Years After: Long Term Effects of Welfare-to-Work Programs, 1995, Does Money Matter? Effect of School Resources, 1996, Work, Health and Income Among the Elderly, 1997, Aging Societies: The Global Dimension, 1998; mem. editl. bd. Jour. Policy Analysis and Mgmt., 1999—; contbr. articles to profl. jours. Commn. mem. panel on fin. adequacy Trustees Social Security, 1989; mem .tech. panel Adv. Coun. on Social Security, 1994—95; mem. com. on health and safety needs of older workers NAS, 2001—. Recipient Leontief prize Ea. Econ. Assn., 1978. Mem.: Assn. Pub. Policy Analysis & Mgmt., Nat. Acad. Social Ins. (commn. mem. panel on Social Security notch 1988, panel on privatizing Social Security 1997—98), Am. Econ. Assn. Avocations: history, hiking. Office: Brookings Instn 1775 Massachusetts Ave NW Washington DC 20036-2103 E-mail: brookinfo@brook.edu.

BURTNICK, RONALD, software consultant, educator; b. Stuttgart, Germany, Nov. 9, 1946; came to U.S., 1947. s. Robert Brennan and Ellen (Wondratchek) B.; m. Alice Galofaro, June 21, 1975; children: Katherine, Megan, Michael. AAS, Middlesex County Coll., Edison, N.J., 1970; BA, Montclair State U., 1972, MA, 1973; EdS, Rutgers U., 1982. Asst. dir. student ctr. Montclair State U., 1972-73; from coord. reg. vet. tng. ctr. to dir. N.J. vet. edn. Kean U., Union, NJ, 1973—76; assoc. dir. ctr. adult devel. Rutgers U. Grad. Sch. Edn., 1976-79; coord. mgmt. inst. Adelphi U., Garden City, N.Y., 1979-80; mgmt. trainer Thomas J. Lipton, Inc., Englewood Cliffs, N.J., 1980-83; mgr. computer auditing tng. Deloitte, Touche, N.Y.C., 1983-88; adjunct prof. Raritan Valley Community Coll., Somerville, N.J., 1989-94, Northampton Community Coll., Bethlehem, Pa., 1989-94; dir. training tech. KBI Systems, Mountainside, N.J., 1990-93; cons. Clinton, N.J., 1993-94; trng. dir. Hertz Corp., Park Ridge, N.J., 1994-96; sales engr. TALX Corp., Clark, N.J., 1996-98; cons. SAP Am., Parsippany, 1998—2002; instr. Rutgers U. Gov.'s Sch. for Engring. and Tech., Piscataway, NJ, 2002—; bus. tech. tchr. North Brunswick (N.J.) Twp. H.S., 2002—. Cons. U.S. Office of Edn., Washington, 1975-76. Active mem. Clinton (N.J.) Pub. Sch. PTA, 1990-91; exec. com. Middlesex County Coll. Alumni Assn., Edison, N.J., 1989—, Rutgers U. Grad. Sch. Edn. Alumni Assn., New Brunswick, N.J., 1988—. With U.S. Army, 1966-68. Mem. ASTD (chair career counseling com. 1979 94), Inst. Cert. Profl. Mgrs. Avocations: weight lifting, fitness, computers, fooseball, volleyball. Home: 23 Marudy Dr Clinton NJ 08809-1220 Office: Raider Rd North Brunswick NJ 08902

BURTON, AL, producer, director, writer; b. Chgo. s. D. Chester and Isabelle (Olenick) G.; m. Sally Lou Lewis, Jan. 8, 1956; 1 dau., Jennifer. BS cum laude, Northwestern U. Exec. v.p. creative affairs Norman Lear-Embassy Communications, Inc., 1973-83; exec. producer-cons. Universal TV, 1983-92; exec. prodr., v.p. syndication Castle Rock Entertainment, 1992-95; pres. Al Burton Prodns., Beverly Hills, Calif., 1995—. Bd. dirs. Pilgrim Group Funds; adv. bd. Samantha Smith Found. Producer Johnny Mercer's Mus. Chairs, 1952-55, Oscar Levant Show, 1955-61; creative producer Teen-Age Fair, 1962-72; exec. producer Charles in Charge, CBS-TV, 1984-85, Tribune Entertainment, 1986-91, Together We Stand, CBS-TV, 1986-87, Nothing Is Easy, 1987-88, The New Lassie, The Family Channel, 1989-92 (Outstanding Family Classic award Youth in Film 1994), Out of the Blue, Tribune Entertainment, 1995-96, Win Ben Stein's Money, Disney, Comedy Ctrl., 1997— (Cable Ace nomination, Emmy nomination 1998, 99, 2001, shared 2 Emmys, 1998, Emmy award for Outstanding Game Show 1999); creative supr. Mary Hartman, Mary Hartman, Fernwood 2Night, America 2Night; prodn. supr. One Day At a Time, Facts of Life, Silver Spoons, The Jeffersons, Square Pegs, Different Strokes; composer-lyricist theme songs for Facts of Life, Different Strokes, Charles in Charge, The New Lassie (Genesis award, 1992), Together We Stand, Nothing Is Easy; cons. Domestic Life CBS-TV, 1983-84, Alan King Show, 1986. Shared Emmy honors for outstanding comedy series All in the Family, 1978-89, Producers award Nat. Coun. for Families and TV, 1984, Jackie Coogan award for Oustanding Contbn. to Youth through Entertainment, 1991; honored for Different Strokes, NCCH, 1979-80; honored by Calif. Gov.'s Com. for employment of the handicapped for Facts of Life, 1981-82, for Charles in Charge, 1988; recipient Youth in Film award Charles in Charge, 1990, The New Lassie, 1994, Genesis award for portrayal animal issues The New Lassie, 1992; spl. commendation Entertainment Industries Coun. for The New Lassie and Charles in Charge, 1990. Mem. AFTRA, Chmn.'s Coun. of Caucus for Producers, Writers and Dirs., Dirs. Guild Am., Writers Guild Am., Acad. TV Arts and Scis., Acad. Magical Arts. *I believe that, in order to achieve success, one should make an occupation of his or her hobby.*

BURTON, ALAN HARVEY, city official; b. Chgo., Mar. 26, 1952; s. Harvey C. and Lois (Fitzpatrick) B.; (div. Oct. 1987); children: Douglas Alan, Marla Joy. Bs, Western Ill. U., 1974, MS, 1986. Recreation supr. Park Ridge (Ill.) Park Dist., 1974-75; dir. parks and recreation York Ctr. Park Dist., Lombard, Ill., 1975-78, City of Berwyn, Ill., 1978-82, adminstr., 1982-86; dir. parks and recreation Norridge (Ill.) Park Dist., 1986-93, recreation bur. chief City of Orlando, Fla., 1993-96; dir. leisure svcs. City of Ormond Beach, Fla., 1996—. Chmn. Berwyn Bus. Commn., 1984-86; cons. Berwyn Devel. Corp., 1986-88, chair FRPA fin. taskforce. Mem. Suburban Cook County Spl. Olympics, Franklin Park, Ill., 1983; hon. EMT Ill. Dept. Pub. Health, 1984; mem. at large Boy Scouts Am., La Grange, Ill., 1986, chmn. dist. nominating com.; rep. West Cen. Mcpl. Conf., Western Springs, Ill., 1987; pres. United Way of Harwood Heights (Ill.)/Norridge, 1990; active Fla. Conservation Corps., 1994, Birthplace of Speed Centennial Com., 2000; bd. dirs. Ormond Art Mus.; bd. mem. Ormond Meml. Art Mus. Recipient Arbor Day award Ill. Assn. Park Dists., 1977, Individual Merit award, 1986, Gold Medal finalist Nat. Sporting Goods Found., 1991, 92, 93, 2002, Faculty award FRPA, 1999, Al Monaco Cmty. Svc. award. Mem. Nat. Park and Recreation Assn. (U.S. del. to Japan, youth at risk sect., so. regional rep.), Nat. Soc. Fundraising Execs., Fla. Recreation and Park Assn., Ill. Park and Recreation Assn. (issues com., long-range planning com., Meritorious Svc. award 1990, Facility Showcase award for skatebd. design), Northeastern Ill. Planning Commn. (open space com. 1991-92), Fla. Park and Recreation Assn., West Suburban Spl. Recreation Assn. (bd. dirs. 1991), Jackson Hole Conservation Alliance, Berwyn Hist. Soc., Kiwanis Club of Ormond Beach (bd. dirs., Internat. George F. Hixson fellow, v.p.). Lutheran. Avocations: bowling, theater, genealogy, biking, science fiction. Home: 915 Ocean Shore Blvd Apt 707 Ormond Beach FL 32176-8307 E-mail: burton@ormondbeach.org.

BURTON, ARTHUR HENRY, JR., insurance company executive; b. Phila., Jan. 24, 1934; s. Arthur H. and Gertrude May B.; m. Gail M. Burton, Sept. 6, 1955; children: Bradford, Steven, Robert, John. AB, Princeton U., 1955; grad. Exec. Program, Columbia U., 1967. C.L.U. With Prudential Ins. Co. Am., 1968—; assoc. dir. group ins. Newark, 1968-70; dir. group ins. Chgo., 1970-75; v.p. group ins. Mpls., 1975-78; v.p. Newark, 1978-80, Parsippany, N.J., 1980-81; pres. Cen. Atlantic ops. Ft Washington, Pa., 1981-83; pres. North Cen. ops. Mpls., 1983-88; asst. to chmn. Prudential-Bach Securities, N.Y.C., 1988; sr. v.p. human resources Prudential, Newark, 1988-89; ret., 1992. Vice chmn. Prudential Securities, 1990-92; sr. advisor Seabridge Investment Advisors, LLC, 1997. Trustee United Way SE Pa., Phila., 1982-83; bd. dirs. World Affairs Council, 1982-83, Chgo. Area Council, 1983-86, United Way Mpls., 1987—; counties chmn. United Way S.E. Pa., 1982-83. Served to 1st lt. U.S. Army, 1956-57. Mem. Ins. Fedn. Pa. (bd. dirs., chmn. 1981-83), Ins. Fedn. Minn. (exec. com. 1983—), Mpls. C. of C. (bd. dirs. 1983-87), Pa. Economy League (bd. govs. 1981-83), First Inf. Corp. (bd. dirs. 1990—). Clubs: Princeton of N.Y., Merion Cricket (Phila.), Windsor (Vero Beach, Fla.). Republican. Episcopalian. Home: 3425 Windsor Blvd Vero Beach FL 32963-4714

BURTON, BARBARA ABLE, psychotherapist; b. Columbia, S.C. d. Eugene Walter Able and Mary Louise (Chadwick) Cantelou; 1 child, Stacia Louise. BA in Psychology, Ga. State U.; MSW, U. Ala., 1970. Diplomate Am. Bd. Examiners in Clin. Social Work, Internat. Acad. Behavioral Medicine, Counseling and Psychotherapy. Assoc. exec. dir. Positive Maturity, Inc., Birmingham, Ala., 1970—72; comm. orgn. planner Cmty. Svc. Coun., Inc., Birmingham, 1972—75; mem. adj. faculty U. Ala., Tuscaloosa, 1975—77; dir. Ensley Outpatient Drug Abuse Clinic, Birmingham, 1975—77; dir. Sch. Social Work, Miles Coll., Birmingham, 1977—78; program mgr. and clin. cons. Goodwill Industries Ala., Birmingham, 1977—81; pvt. practice New Orleans, 1983—. Cons. Omega Internat. Inst., New Orleans, 1988-94. Author: Love Me, Love Me Not, and Other Matters That Matter, 1990. Past chmn. policy and program com. Birmingham Urban League, mem. Ala. Adv. Com. on Social Svcs., Ala. Com. for Devel. Higher Ed., Ala. Conf. Social Work. NIMH fellow Inst. on Human Sexuality, U. Hawaii, 1976. Mem. NASW (diplomate in clin. social work), Am. Assn. Sex Educators, Counselors and Therapists, Pvt. Practitioners Unit of New Orleans, Acad. Cert. Social Workers, Internat. Platform Com., Psi Chi. Avocations: creative writing, reading, interior design. Office: 110 Country Club Dr Covington LA 70433

BURTON, BARRY LAWSON, librarian, educator; b. Ulverston, Cumbria, Eng., Dec. 30, 1942; s. William Lawson and Runah (Sandwell) B.; m. Wendy Fay Monks, Dec. 4, 1970 (dec. Oct. 1997); children: Jodi, Nigel Robin, Simon Lawson. BA, U. Keele, 1965. Reference office Flinders U., Australia, 1966-67; chief libr. Salisbury Coll. Advanced Edn., 1968-71; dep. univ. libr. Makerere U., Uganda, 1972; libr. Hong Kong Polytechnic U., 1973—. Pres. Internat. Fedn. for Info. and Documentation, Commn. for Asia and Oceania, 1981-88. Editor Directory of Professional Associations and Learned Societies in Hong Kong, 1988—; contbr. articles to profl. jours. Mem. Hong Kong Libr. Assn. (chmn. 1975), Libr. Assn. Australia (assoc.), Chartered Mgmt. Inst., Chartered Inst. Libr. and Info. Profls., Hong Kong Wine Soc. (chmn. 1983—). Avocation: wine judging. Home: 1811 Convention Plaza Apts 1 Harbour Rd Wanchai Hong Kong Office: Hong Kong Polytech U Univ Librarian Kowloon Hong Kong E-mail: lbbarry@polyu.edu.hk.

BURTON, BERNARD OTTWAY, lawyer; b. Axton, Va., Mar. 12, 1916; BS in Commerce, U. N.C., 1941; Indsl. Adminstr. Degree, Harvard U., 1943; JD, U. N.C., 1945. Bar: N.C. 1945, U.S. Dist. Ct., 1948. Counsel Randolph County Airport Commn., Asheboro, N.C., 1948-50; spl. right-of-way N.C. Hwy. Commn., Asheboro, N.C., 1965-68; sole-practice Ottway Burton PA, Asheboro, N.C., 1945—. Dir. N.C. R.R. Co., 1964-68. With Med. Svc. Corps., 1934-37. Mem.: ABA, N.C. Bar Assn., Shriners, Masons. Democrat. Methodist. Avocations: gardening, photography, golf, history. Office: Ottway Burton PA 115 Worth St Asheboro NC 27203-5517

BURTON, CHARLES HENNING, lawyer; b. Washington, Nov. 25, 1915; s. Charles Henry and Bessie R. (Harrell) B.; m. Mary Sheppard, Sept. 6, 1941; children: Nancy Leigh Burton Wysling, Susan C. Burton Roberts, Mary Ellen Burton Graves, Charles S. Attended, George Washington U., 1937-41; LLB, Am. U., 1936, LLM, 1937. Bar: DC 1936, Md. 1957. Gen. counsel D.C. Unemployment Compensation Bd., 1938-42; mem. firm MacCracken & O'Rourke, Washington, 1946-50; mem. Law Offices Robert Ash, Washington, 1950-56; gen. partner Bauersfeld, Burton, Hendricks and Vanderhoff, Bethesda, Md., 1956—. Ltd. ptnr. A.W.S. Assocs., S & H Assocs.; pres., dir. North Shore Corp., Links, Inc., Charles H. Burton, P.A.; dir. Mattos, Inc., Sisk Mailing Svc. Inc., Sisk Fulfillment, Inc.; gen. counsel Bapt. World Alliance, McLean, Va., 1958, Calvary Bapt. Ch., 1950. Bd. dirs. Jovius Found., Mustard Seed Found., F.W. Harris Found. for Personal Evangelism; trustee Kendall Mission Fund; v.p. Cen. Union Mission; nat. chmn. World Peace Through Law of World Jurist Assn. Comdr. USNR, 1942-46. Fellow Am. Bar Found.; mem. Am. Bar Assn. (editor Young Lawyer 1946-48, nat. sec. Jr. Bar 1949, nat. vice-chmn. 1950, nat. chmn. 1951, ho. of dels. 1952-59), Sigma Chi, Sigma Nu Phi. Clubs: Montgomery County Country. Home: 21600 Davis Mill Rd Germantown MD 20876-4418 Office: Bauersfeld Burton Hendricks & Vanderhoff 7101 Wisconsin Ave Ste 1011 Bethesda MD 20814-4805

BURTON, CHARLES VICTOR, physician, surgeon, inventor; b. N.Y.C., Jan. 2, 1935; s. Norman Howard and Ruth Esther (Putziger) B.; m. Joy Burton; children— Matthew, Timothy, Andrew, Dawn, Stacy, Chad. Student, Johns Hopkins U., Balt., 1952-56; MD, N.Y. Med. Coll., 1960. Diplomate Am. Bd. Neurol. Surgery, Nat. Bd. Med. Examiners, Am. Bd. Forensic Medicine, Am Bd. Spinal Surgery. Intern surgery Yale U. Med. Ctr., 1961-62; asst. resident neurol. surgery Johns Hopkins Hosp., Balt., 1962-66, chief resident, 1966-67; assoc. chief surgery, chief neurosurgery USPHS Hosp., Seattle, 1967-69; vis. research affiliate Primate Ctr., U. Wash., 1967-69; asst. prof. neurosurgery Temple U. Health Scis. Ctr., Phila., 1970-73, assoc. prof., 1973-74, neurol. research coordinator, 1970-74; dir. dept. neuroaugmentive surgery Sister Kenny Inst., Mpls., 1974-81, med. dir. Low Back Clinic, 1978-81; med. dir. Inst. for Low Back Care, Mpls., 1981-96; sr. med. dir. Inst. Low Back and Neck Care, Mpls., 1996—. Biomed. Instrumentations Internat., Ltd., 1988-92; co-chmn. Joint Neurosurg. Com. on Devices and Drugs, 1973-77; chmn. adv. panel on neurologic devices FDA, 1974-77, Internat. Standards Orgn., 1974-76; mem. U.S. Biomed. Instrumentation Del. to Soviet Union, 1974; co-chmn. Am. Bd. Spine Surgery. Editor Neuroorthopedics jour., 1987-1998, editor The Burton Report; editor-in-chief www.burtonreport.com, 2000—. Research fellow Nat. Polio Found., 1956, HEW, 1958; neurosurg. fellow Johns Hopkins Hosp., 1960-61, 62-67, 69-70 Fellow ACS (exec. com. Minn. chpt. 1989-92); mem. Congress Neurol. Surgeons (chmn. com. materials and devices 1972-79), Am. Assn. Neurol. Surgeons, Minn. Neurosurg. Soc., AAAS, ASTM (chmn. com. materials 1973-78), Internat. Soc. Study of Lumbar Spine (exec. com. 1986-89), N.Am. Spine Soc. (exec. com. 1987-91, chmn. com. on profl. conduct 1991-92, dir. coun. mem. affairs 1992-94, bd. dirs. 1990 94), Am. Nat. Standards Inst. (med. device tech. adv. bd 1973-78), Am. Bd. Spine Surgery (bd. dirs. 1997—, vice chair 2002—, chair ethics com. 1998—), Philadelphia County Med. Soc. (med.-legal com. 1970-74), Minn. Med. Assn. (Gold medal award for best sci. presentation at 1975 meeting, subcom. on med. testimony 1978—), Hennepin County Med. Soc. (med.-legal com. 1975—), Mpls. Acad. Medicine, Cor et Manus Soc., Profl. Assn. Diving Instrs. (underwater photography splty. diver), Am. Back Soc., Twin Cities Spine Soc. (pres. 1994-95), Back Pain Assn. Am. (hon. chmn. 1995—), Am. Bd. Sinal Surgery (bd. dirs. 1997, chmn. ethics com., v.p. 2002—, chmn. med.-legal com., co-chmn. 2002—), Johns Hopkins U. Alumni Assn. (pres. Minn. chpt. 1988-92), Yale Surg. Soc., Alpha Epsilon Delta. Achievements include patents for surgical devices, operating room fiberoptic headlights, clinical therapy systems and techniques. Home: 148 W Lake St Excelsior MN 55331-1744 Office: Inst Low Back and Neck Care 2800 Chicago Ave Minneapolis MN 55407-1318

BURTON, DAN L. congressman; b. Indpls., June 21, 1938; m. Barbara Jean Logan, 1959; children: Kelly, Danielle Lee, Danny Lee II. Mem. Ind. Ho. Reps., Indpls., 1967-68, 77-80, Ind. State Senate, 1969-70, 81-82; owner ins. and real estate firm, 1968—; mem. U.S. Congress from 5th Ind. dist. (formerly 6th), 1983—. Mem. internat. rels. com.; chmn. govt. reform and oversight com. Pres. Vols. of Am.; pres. Ind. Christian Benevolent Assn., Com. for Constl. Govt., Family Support Ctr. Served with U.S. Army, 1957-58. Republican. Office: US Ho of Reps 2185 Rayburn Ofc Bldg Washington DC 20515-1406*

BURTON, DARRELL IRVIN, engineering executive; b. Ashtabula, Ohio, Sept. 21, 1926; s. George Irvin and Barbara Elizabeth (Streyle) B.; m. Lois Carol Warkentien, Apr. 14, 1951; children: Linda Jean Burton Clinton, Lisa Ann Burton Watts, Lori Elizabeth Burton Admokom. BS in Radio Engring., Chgo. Tech. Coll., 1954. R&D engr. Motorola, Inc., Chgo., 1951-60; devel. engr. Hallicrafters, Chgo., 1960-62; chief engr. TRW, Inc., Des Plaines, Ill., 1962-65; devel. engr. Warwick, Niles, Ill., 1965-68; systems mgr. Admiral Corp., Chgo., 1968-76; elec.-electronics lab. mgr. Montgomery Ward & Co., Chgo., 1976-82; staff engr. Wells-Gardner Electronics Corp., Chgo., 1982-85; sr. engr. Zenith Electronics Corp., Chgo., 1985-91, ret., 1991; pres. Burton Electronics Co., Elmhurst, Ill., 1992—. Tchr. electronics and math. Pres. Addison Homeowners

Assn., 1958-60, v.p., 1960-62; mem. Addison Plan Commn., 1960-63; mem. bd. edn. Immanuel Luth. Sch., 1985-87, dir. audio/video ministry, 1973-98, ret., 1998, v.p., 1997, pres., 1998; elder Immanuel Luth. Ch., 1999-2002. Lutheran. Home: 112 Lawndale Ave Elmhurst IL 60126-3522

BURTON, DONALD JOSEPH, chemistry educator; b. Balt., July 16, 1934; s. Lawrence Andrew and Dorothy Wilhelmina (Koehler) B.; m. Margaret Anna Billing, June 21, 1958; children— Andrew, Jennifer, David, Julie, Elizabeth. BS, Loyola Coll., Balt., 1956; PhD, Cornell U., 1961; postgrad., Purdue U., 1961-62. Asst. prof. chemistry dept. U. Iowa, Iowa City, 1962-67, assoc. prof., 1967-70, prof., 1970—, Roy Carver/Ralph Shriner prof. chemistry, 1989—. Recipient Gov.'s Sci. Medal for Sci. Achievement, 1988; Japanese Soc. for Promotion Sci. fellow, 1979 Mem. Am. Chem. Soc. (chmn. fluorine divsn. 1978, award for creative work in fluorine chemistry 1984, Midwest Chemistry award 1990, ACS divsn. Fluorine Chemistry Disting. Svc. award 2003), Chem. Soc. London, Sigma Xi, Alpha Chi Sigma. Home: 4304 Oakridge Trl NE Iowa City IA 52240-7735 Office: U Iowa Dept Chemistry Iowa City IA 52242 E-mail: donald-burton@uiowa.edu.

BURTON, EARL GILLESPIE, III, lawyer; b. St. Louis, Sept. 20, 1952; s. Earl Gillespie Jr. and Patricia Joan B.; 1 child, Sara Frances; m. Suzanne Mohr. BBA in Fin., U. Mo., 1976, JD, 1980. Bar: Mo. 1980. Legal intern Mo. Atty. Gen., Jefferson City, 1978-80; assoc. gen. counsel Clayton (Mo.) Brokerage Co., 1980-86; pvt. practice, Clayton, 1987-97; with tax dept. Grace Advisors, Inc., St. Louis, 1997—2002; pvt. practice, 2002—. Trustee Gateway chpt. Leukemia Soc. Am., St. Louis, 1988-89. Mem. Mo. Bar Assn., Order of Barristers. Avocations: fishing, weightlifting, piano. Home: 7212 Dale Ave Apt A Saint Louis MO 63117-2321 Office: 7212A Dale Saint Louis MO 63117-2321 E-mail: egb3_98@yahoo.com.

BURTON, FRED CLIFFORD, visual artist, educator; b. Diablo Heights, Panama, Apr. 19, 1945; came to U.S., 1950; s. Royal Clifford Burton and Marjorie Junita Wheeler; m. Stella Giordanengo, Feb. 18, 1987 (div. 1992). BFA, Wichita State U., 1968; MA, Kent State U., 1969; MFA, Wichita State U., 1975. Instr. Midwe. State U., Wichita Falls, Tex., 1979-81; asst. prof. art U. No. Iowa, Cedar Falls, 1983-86; prof. art Memphis Coll. Art, 1987—. Vis. prof. art, Radford (Va.) U., summer 1987, vis. faculty AICA N.Y. Studio Program, N.Y.C., 1990, Penland (N.C.) Coll. Art, summer 1994; artist in residence, Michael Karolyi Found., Vence, France, 1977, 78, 81, Altos de Chavon, Dominican Republic, 1983, Tyrone Guthrie Ctr., Annaghmakkerig, Ireland, Millay Colony for Arts, Inc., Steepletop, Austerlitz, N.Y., 1984, Ragdale Found., Lake Forest, Ill., 1985, Workspace Fellowship, Woodstock (N.Y.) Sch. Art, 1986, Tougaloo Art Colony, Jackson, Miss., 2001. Illustrator: For Reasons of Music, 1994; mem. editl. adv. bd., Collegiate Press, San Diego, 1995—. Office: Memphis Coll Art Overton Park 1930 Poplar Ave Memphis TN 38104

BURTON, FREDDA JEAN, writer, artist; b. Deadwood, S.D., Dec. 3, 1941; d. Albert Hjalmer and Mardie Dagmar (Hanson) Anderson; m. Theodore Allen Burton, Aug. 5, 1961. BA, Wash. State U., 1967; MFA in Fine Arts, So. Ill. U., 1972, MFA in Creative Writing, 1998. Contbr. short stories to various publs. Mem.: Women into Scandinavian Heritage (v.p. 1999—2000, treas. 2000—01, pres. 2002—), N.W. Writers Assn., Western Rosemalers. Democrat. Avocations: travel, clay sculpting, swedish painting, photography. Home: 732 Caroline St Port Angeles WA 98362 E-mail: fjburton@olypen.com.

BURTON, GARY, musician; b. Anderson, Ind., Jan. 23, 1943; s. Wayne and Bernice Burton; m. Catherine Goldwyn, July 12, 1975; children: Stephanie Clare, Samuel John. Ed., Berklee Coll. Music, Boston Conservatory Music. Vibraphone player, leader jazz group, 1967—; instr. Berklee Coll. Music, 1972-84, dean, 1985—. Rec. artist, including Alone At Last, 1972 (Grammy award, 1972), Artist's Choice, 1988. Named Jazzman of Yr., Downbeat Mag., 1968; recipient Downbeat Mag. Poll, 1968—86, Grammy award, 1972, 1978, 1979, 1999. Office: care Ted Kurland Assos 173 Brighton Ave Allston MA 02134-2003

BURTON, GLENN WILLARD, geneticist; b. Clatonia, Nebr., May 5, 1910; s. Joseph Fearn and Nellie (Rittenburg) Burton; m. Helen Maurine Jeffryes, Dec. 16, 1934; children: Elizabeth Ann Fowler, Robert Glenn, Thomas Jeffryes, Joseph William, Richard Bennett. BS, U. Nebr., 1932, DSc (hon.), 1962; MS, Rutgers U., 1933, PhD, 1936, DSc (hon.), 1955. With USDA and U. Ga. at Tifton Exptl. Sta., 1936—, prin. geneticist, 1952—, chmn. div. agronomy, 1950—64; Univ. Found. prof. U. Ga., 1957. Mem. Tift County Bd. Edn., 1953—58. Recipient 1st Ann. Agrl. award, So. Seedsman Assn., 1950, Sears-Roebuck Rsch. award, 1953, 1960, Superior Svc. award, USDA, 1955, 1st Ford Almanac Crops and Soils Rsch. award, 1962, Disting. Svc. award, 1980, Pres.'s award for Disting. Fed. Civilian Svc., 1981, Nat. Medal of Sci., 1983, named Man of Yr., So. Agriculture Progressive Farmer, 1954, named to Hall of Fame, USDA ARS, 1987, numerous other awards and citations. Fellow: Am. Soc. Agronomy (v.p. 1961, pres. 1962, Stevenson award 1949, John Scott award 1957); mem.: Nat. Acad. Sci., Am. Soc. Range Mgmt., Am. Genetic Assn., Gamma Sigma, Alpha Zeta, Sigma Xi. Home: 421 10th St W Tifton GA 31794-3917 Office: USDA Coastal Plain Experimental Station Tifton GA 31794

BURTON, JEFF, race car driver; b. June 29, 1967; m. Kim Burton; 1 child, Kimberle Paige. Named Orange County Speedway champion, 1987, South Boston Most Popular Driver, Va., 1988, 4-time winner, NASCAR Busch Grand Nat. Divsn. series, 1989—92, quilified, 6th NASCAR Winston Cup, London, N.H., 1993, NASCAR Rookie of Yr., 1994, 3 top-10 finishes, 6th NASCAR Winston Cup, London, N.H., 1994, 2 top-10 finishes, 1995, 6 top-10 finishes, 1996, winner, Winston Cup, Tex., 1997, Winston Cup, London, Va., 1997, Winston Cup, Martinsville, Va., 1997, 13 top-10 finishes, Winston Cup, 1998, 18 top-5 finishes, 1998, winner, InterState Batteries 500, 1997, Hanes 500, 1997, Jiffy Lube 300, 1997, 1998, 1999, DuraLube/KMart 500, 1999, Exide NASCAR 400, 1998, Las Vegas 400, 1999, Transsouth Fin. 400, 1999, Coca-Cola 600, 1999, Pepsi So. 500, 1999, Pop Secret 400, 1999, CarsDirect-.com 400, 2000, 21-time winner, NASCAR Winston Racing Series. Avocations: basketball, boating.

BURTON, JOHN, state official; b. Ohio, Dec. 15, 1932; 1 child, Kimiko. Student, San Francisco State Coll., San Francisco Law Sch. Mem. Calif. Ho. of Reps., 1964-74, 88-96, U.S. Congress, 1974-82, Calif. Senate from 3rd dist., 1997—; Pres. pro tem Calif. Senate, 1998—. Founder Point Reyes Wilderness Area, Farallon Marine Sanctuary. Named Legislator of Yr. Calif. Abortion Rights Action League, Animal Rights Legislator of Yr.; recipient Community United Against Violence award, Sean Mcbride award, award Ancient Order of Hibernians. Office: State Capitol Rm 205 Sacramento CA 95814 also: 601 Van Ness Ave Ste 2030 San Francisco CA 94102-6310*

BURTON, JOHN BRYAN, music educator; b. Lubbock, Tex., Nov. 10, 1948; s. John Clark and Geraldine (Wolf) B. B in Music Edn., West Tex. State U., 1970; MA, Western State Coll. Colo., 1973; D in Music Edn., U. So. Miss., 1986. Dir. bands, humanities Jal (N.Mex.) Schs., 1978-79; dir. bands, gen. music Bronte (Tex.) Schs., 1979-80; dir. bands Comfort (Tex.) Schs., 1980-82; dir. high sch. band, music coord. Kirbyville (Tex.) Ind. Schs., 1982-84; grad. asst. U. So. Miss., Hattiesburg, 1984-86; asst. prof. music, dir. bands, music theatre dir. Frostburg (Md.) State U., 1986-91; prof. music edn. West Chester (Pa.) Univ., 1991—, coord. grad. studies, 1997—, dir. post baccalaureate tchr. cert. program, 2001—. Panelist Symposium on Native Am. Musics, Coll. Music Soc. 33d Nat. Meeting, Washington, 1990; curriculum cons. Prince Georges County Schs., Upper Marlboro, Md., 1991, other Mid-Atlantic schs.; guest condr. Allegany County Honor Band, Tri-State Honor Band, 1986-87, Allegany County Band, Bedford County Band, Mineral County Band, 1987-88, Allegany Solo and Ensemble Festival Harford County Intermediate Bands Festival, 1990-91; presenter conf. Ea. divsn. Music Educators Nat. Conf., 1993, 95, 97, 99, 2001, 03, So. divsn., 1994, Internat. Kodaly Soc. Conf., Am. Orff-Schulwerk Assn., Orff 100 Internat. Conf. on Music and Dance, Melbourne, Australia, 1995, Internat. Soc. for Music Edn., Amsterdam, 1996, Internat. Soc. for Music Edn. Commn. on Cmty. Music Making, Liverpool, 1996, many others; lectr. nat. meeting Music Educators Nat. Conf., 1992, 94, 96; cons. Native Am. music, 1993, 94, nat. chair, editor Social Scis. Rsch. Group Soc. for Rsch. in Music Edn., 1994-96; edit. adv. bd. mem. Tchg. Music, 1996-98; keynote lectr. World Conf. Internat. Soc. Music Edn., 1994, 96, 98, 2000, 01, 02; mem. ISME Commn. on cmty. music activity, Durban, South Africa, 1998; mem. exec. bd. Soc. for Music Tchr. Edn. (ea. rep.), 1998—; presenter and lectr. in field; vis. prof. U. Washington, 1995, Ga. State U., 1995, Trenton State Coll., 1996, U. Okla., 1996, U. Nebr., 1997, U. Sioux Falls, 1997, Rider U., 1998. Assoc. editor: Scholars, 1994-2001; author: moving Within the Circle: Contemporary Native American Music and Dance, 1993, Music of the Minority Nationalities of the People's Republic of China, 1989, When the Earth Was Like New: Songs and Stories of the Western Apache, 1994, Songs of A Living Apache Tradition: The Musical Life of Chesley Goseyun Wilson, 1994, (with Maria P. Kreiter) Native American Flute Music, 1997; co-author: Welcome to Mussomeli: Italian Children's Songs, 1999; contbg. author: Multicultural Perspectives in Music Education, 2d edit., 1996, Getting Started with Teaching Multicultural Music, 1996, Making Connections: Multicultural Traditions and the National Standards in Music Education, 1996, Strategies for Teaching: General Music K-4, 1996, Strategies for Teaching: General Music 5-8, 1996, Strategies for Teaching: General Music 9-12, 1996, Strategies for Teaching: Beginning and Middle Level Band Grades 5-8, 1996, Strategies for Teaching: High School Band, 1996, Strategies for Teaching: College Methods Class, 1996, Strategies for Teaching: High School Chorus, 1996, Many Seeds, Different Flowers--The Music Education Legacy of Carl Orff, 1997, On the Sociology of Music Education, 1997; mem. editl. bd. Music Edn. Internat., 2001--; contbr. songs to World of Children's Song, 1993, lessons and photographs to The Music Connection, 1995, songs and lessons to Share the Music, 1995, World Music and Music Education: Facing the Issue, 2002, Making Music (classroom music texttbook series), song transcriptions to OAKE Multicultural Songs, Dances and Games, 1995, articles to profl. jours. Mem. Nat. Band Assn., Music Educators Nat. Conf. (presenter nat. meeting 1992, 94, 96, 98, 2000, 2002), Australia Soc. Music Educators, Pa. Music Educators Assn., Coll. Band Dirs. Nat. Assn., Coll. Music Soc., Soc. for Ethnomusicology (chair edn. com. 1999—), Associated Photographers Internat., Audubon Soc., Amnesty Internat., Phi Mu Alpha, Alpha Chi, Kappa Delta Pi, Kappa Kappa Psi. Avocations: photography, travel, gardening. Home: 441 Webb Rd Chadds Ford PA 19317-9125 Office: West Chester U Sch Music West Chester PA 19383-0001 E-mail: jburton3@wcupa.edu.

BURTON, JOHN CAMPBELL, university dean, educator, consultant; b. N.Y.C., Sept. 17, 1932; s. James Campbell and Barbara (French) B.; m. Jane Garnjost, Apr. 6, 1957; children: Eve Bradley, Bruce Campbell. BA, Haverford Coll., 1954; MBA, Columbia U., 1956, PhD, 1962. C.P.A., N.Y. Staff acct. Arthur Young & Co., N.Y.C., 1956-60; prof. acctg. and fin. Grad. Sch. Bus. Columbia U., N.Y.C., 1962-72, Ernst & Young prof. acctg. and fin., 1978—, dean Grad. Sch. Bus., 1982-88. Chief acct. SEC, Washington, 1972-76; dep. mayor fin. City of N.Y., 1976-77; bd. dirs. Scholastic Inc.; dir., chmn. audit com. Commerce Clearing House Inc., 1979-95, First Pa. Corp.-First Pa. Bank, 1982-85; mem. adv. and valuation com. Warburg-Pincus Venture Capital Funds; mem. U.S. Comptroller Gen. Cons. Panel, 1978-95; bd. dirs. Accts. for Pub. Interest, 1978-85. Editor: Corporate Financial Reporting: Conflicts and Challenges, 1969, Corporate Financial Reporting: Ethical and Other Problems, 1972, (with Russell Palmer and Robert Kay) Handbook of Accounting and Auditing, 1981, The International World of Accounting: Challenges and Opportunities, 1981; co-mng. editor Acctg. Horizons, 1989-91; author: Accounting for Business Combinations, 1970, (with W.T. Porter) Auditing: A Conceptual Approach, 1971, and others; contbr. articles to profl. jours. Pres., trustee Millbrook Sch. (N.Y.), 1958-88; trustee ex officio Am. Assembly, 1982-88. Recipient Disting. Scholar award Hofstra U., 1975; Ford Found. fellow, 1961-62 Mem. AICPA (coun. 1980-83), Am. Acctg. Assn. (acad. v.p. 1980-82), Am. Fin. Assn., Am. Econ. Assn., Fin. Execs. Inst., Assn. Govtl. Accts., Nat. Assn. Securities Dealers (pub. gov. 1990-94), Met. Club (N.Y.C.), Lake Sunapee Yacht Club (N.H.). Clubs: Metropolitan (N.Y.C.); Lake Sunapee Yacht (N.H.). Home: 130 East End Ave Apt 12A New York NY 10028-7553 E-mail: jburton996@aol.com.

BURTON, JOHN JACOB, retired real estate company executive appraiser; b. NYC, Dec. 31, 1912; s. Fannie (Rosenfeld) Burton; m. Sylvia R. Carlin, Oct. 12, 1940 (dec. 1981); children: Frances Lee, Barbara, Spencer, Gerald K. BS in Physics with honors, LI U., l935, DSc (hon.), l987; MAI, Columbia U., l937. Lic. real estate broker, Fla. With Manpower Commn. Sci. and Specialized Pers., NJ, l942-46, Manpower Commn. Sci. and specialized Pers., NY, 1942—46; owner, mgr. John J. Burton Real Estate, Mortgages & Appraisals, Boston, l946-50, John J. Burton Gen. Real Estate & Appraisals, Hollywood, Fla., 1950-92; ptrn. Am. Title Corp., 1992—95, ret., 1995. Personal aide col. to gov. State of Mass., 1966-68; trustee Broward County Investment Trust, Dania, Fla.; co-founder Technion, Israel. A founder Jewish Chapel at US Mil. Acad. West Point, NY; mem. exec. com. Broward County Rep. Com., 1958-74; mem. Presdl. Commns., 1986, 92. Recipient Presdl. Medals of Merit, 1985, 90, 93, Rep. Presdl. Legion of Merit, 1985, 94, US Presdl. Commn., Pres. Ronald Reagan, 1986, US Presdl. Commn., Pres. George Bush, 1992; commd. col. by Pres., 1986. Mem. AAAS, Internat. Orgn. Real Estate Appraisers (sr.), Nat. Assn. Real Estate Appraisers (cert.), Fla. Assn. Cert. Real Estate Appraisers, US Navy League Commodore, Security and Intelligence Fund. (founder), Naval Intelligence Profls., Mil. Order of the World Wars (life mem.), Masons (32 degree), Shriners, B'nai B'rith. Jewish. Avocations: science, philanthropy. Home: 2470 N Park Rd Apt 328S Hollywood FL 33021-3753

BURTON, JOHN PAUL (JACK BURTON), lawyer; b. New Orleans, Feb. 26, 1943; s. John Paul and Nancy (Key) Burton; m. Anne Ward; children: Jennifer, Michele Kfouri, Marcos Maiken, Susanna, Derek, Catherine. BBA magna cum laude, La. Tech. U., 1965; LLB, Harvard U., 1968. Bar: N.Mex. 1968, U.S. Dist. Ct. N.Mex. 1968, U.S. Ct. Appeals (10th cir.) 1973, U.S. Supreme Ct. 1979. Assoc. Rodey, Dickason, Sloan, Akin & Robb, Albuquerque, 1968-74, dir., 1974—, chmn. comml. dept., 1980-81, mng. dir. Santa Fe, 1986-90. Settlement facilitator N.Mex. Second Jud. Dist., 1997—. Co-author: Boundary Disputes in New Mexico, 1992, Unofficial Update on the Uniform Ltd. Liability Co. Act, 1994. Pres. Brunn Sch., 1987—89; active Nat. Coun. Commrs. on Uniform State Laws, 1989—, drafting com. UCC Article 5, 1990—95, UCC Article 9, 1993—95, UCC Articles 2 and 2A, 1999—2001; active Power-of Sale Forcclosure Act, 1999—2002, Uniform Ltd. Liability Co. Act, 1993—95, Legis. Coun., 1991—99, divsn. chmn., 1993—95, 1999—2001, 1995—99; chmn. drafting com. on uniform durable powers of atty. Nat. Coun. Commrs. on Uniform State Laws, 2003—; joint editl. bds. Uninc. Bus. Orgns., 1994—95, Trust and Estates Acts, 1999—2001. Fellow Am. Coll. Real Estate Lawyers; mem. ABA, Am. Law Inst. (rep. to UCC Article 5 drafting com. 1992-95), Am. Coll. Mortgage Attys., Am. Arbitration Assn. (mem. comml. panel arbitrators), N.Mex. State Bar Assn. (chmn. comml. litig. and antitrust sect. 1985-86). Office: Rodey Dickason Sloan Akin & Robb PA PO Box 1357 Santa Fe NM 87504-1357 E-mail: jpburton@rodey.com.

BURTON, JOSEPH RANDOLPH, lawyer; b. Houston, Sept. 10, 1951; s. Joseph Milburn and Lee (Hillegeist) B.; m. Regina Helen O'Brien, Mar. 13, 1982; children: Cara Eileen, Ross Andrew. BS, Yale U., 1974; JD, South Tex. Coll., Houston, 1982. Bar: Tex. 1983, U.S. Dist. Ct. (so. and ea. dists.)Tex. 1983, U.S. Supreme Ct. 1996. Asst. dist. atty. Harris County Dist. Atty's Office, Houston, 1984-87; litigation assoc. Kennedy, Sanford, Kuhl & Hackney, Houston, 1987-90; ptnr. Moerer & Burton, Houston, 1990—. Contbr. articles to profl. jours.; featured on TV shows, including ABC News Prime Time Live, 20/20, HBO, Discovery Channel, Donahue, Good Morning Am. Founder, spokesperson Justice for Children, Houston, 1987—, Citizens Response Group; bd. dirs. Houston Area Women's Ctr., 1987-89, Aid to Victims of Domestic Abuse, 1987, Children's Trust Fund of Tex. Coun., 1994-98; child advocate mem. Tex. Child Fatality Rev. Com. Recipient AIA Pres.'s award, 1998, Victims' Resource Inst. with U. Houston Kim Houston award, 1999; named Outstanding Young Lawyer of Houston, Houston Young Lawyers' Assn., 1987-88, Mayor's award Outstanding Vol. Svc., 1998, e-town Achievement award, 2002; finalist 5 Outstnding Young Houstonians, Houston Jr. C. of C., 1988. Fellow Tex. Bar Found.; mem. ABA, Houston Bar Assn., South Tex. Coll. of Law Alumni Assn., Garland Walker Inns of Ct. Democrat. Avocation: golf. Home: 18418 Snowwood Dr Spring TX 77388-5100 Office: Moerer and Burton 440 Louisiana St Ste 1150 Houston TX 77002-1634

BURTON, KATHLEEN T. mental health services professional; b. Lynn, Mass., Jan. 29, 1962; d. Charles W. and Mary L. (Mayer) Burton. BA in Psychology/Comm., Notre Dame Coll., South Euclid, Ohio, 1985; MEd in Counseling, Cleve. State U., 1990, EdS in Counseling, 1991; postgrad., Saybrook Inst., 1998—. Cert. rational marriage and family therapist, diplomate cognitive-behavioral therapy. Human rels. & devel. coord. Kaiser Permanente, Cleveland Heights, Ohio, 1984—87; counselor Cleve. Treatment Ctr., 1989—90; tchg. asst., counselor intern Cleve. State U., 1989—91; cmty. trainer Woodland (Calif.) Cmty. Options, 1991—95; mental health profl., psychologist intern Davis, Calif., 1992—95; pvt. practice mental health profl. Woodland, Calif., 1995—2001; undergrad. psychology instr. Computer Quest Ltd., 2003. Group facilitator human sexuality course dept. psychiatry Davis Med. Sch., 1994—2001; group leader, facilitator anxiety, phobias and panic Woodland Sr. Ctr., 1993—99; mental health cons., creator Mental Health Matters, Pub. TV, 1995; founder Sr./Youth Fair, Woodland, 1995; mental health writer Davis Enterprise; lectr. anxiety, phobias, panic, drug addictions, Moscow, Kiev, 1994. Author: (poetry) Hold on Tight; contbr. articles to profl. jours. Recipient 1st pl., Nat. Future Design Competition, 1984. Mem.: ACA, Internat. Assn. Marriage Family Counselors, Nat. Assn. Cognitive Behaviorial Therapists. Roman Catholic. Avocations: gardening, dancing, camping, hiking. Home: 2180 Wascana Ave Lakewood OH 44107

BURTON, LAVON D. education educator; b. Abilene, Tex., Sept. 5, 1957; d. Floyd Lewis and Jane Evelyn Duncan; m. Brian Keith Burton; children: Tyler, Briana. BS inEdn., Abilene Christian U., 1981, MEd, 1997. Cert. profl. tchg. Tex., edn. agy. adminstrn. Tex. Tchr. Abilene (Tex.) Ind. Sch. Dist., 1981—86, instr. acad. advance, 1987—94, acad. advance program dir., 1994—. Troop leader Girl Scouts of Am., Abilene, 1996—2002; vol. in pub. schs., orgn. mem. Abilene Ind. Sch. Dist., 1992—2002; youth adv. team mem. Hillcrest Ch. of Christ, Abilene, 1999—2002, Bible class tchr., 1979—2002, drama writer, dir., 1997—2002; Chair bd. dirs. Paramount Theater Children's Performing Arts Series, Abilene, 1997—2002; mem., soloist Hillcrest Singers, Abilene, 1986—2002; PTA exec. bd. dirs. Taylor Elem. Sch., Abilene, 1994—2002, Franklin Mid. Sch., Abilene, 1998—2001. Named Vol. of the Yr., Abilene Cultural Affairs Coun., 1999. Mem.: Big Country Coun. of Tchrs. Math. and Sci., Nat. Coun. Tchrs. of Math. Church Of Christ. Avocations: piano, singing, sewing, reading. Business E-Mail: burtonl@acu.edu.

BURTON, LAWRENCE DEVERE, agriculturist, educator; b. Afton, Wyo., May 27, 1943; s. Lawrence VanOrden and Maybell (Hoopes) B.; m. Arva Merrill, Nov. 20, 1967; children: LauraLee, Paul, Shawn, Renee, Kaylyn, Kelly, Pratt. BS, Utah State U., 1968; MS, Brigham Young U., 1972; PhD, Iowa State U., 1987. Agr. tchr. Box Elder County Sch. Dist., Brigham City, Utah, 1967-68, Morgan County Sch. Dist., Morgan, Utah, 1968-70, Minidoka County Sch. Dist., Rupert, Idaho, 1972-79, Cassia County Sch. Dist., Declo, Idaho, 1979-84; instr. Iowa State U., Ames, 1984-87; area vocat. edn. coord. Idaho State Div. Vocat. Edn., Pocatello, 1987-88, state supr. agrl. sci. and tech. Boise, 1988-97; dir. rsch. Idaho State Divsn. Vocat. Edn., Boise, 1997-99; mem. telecomm. coun. Idaho State Bd. Edn., 1997-98, mem. coun. acad. affairs and programs, 1997—; instrnl. dean Coll. So. Idaho, Twin Falls, 2000—. Biochem. cons. rep. Ctr. for Occupational Rsch. and Devel., Waco, Tex., 1989-94; chmn. Nat. Task Force, Agrl. Edn. Ind. Study Honors program, 1993; mem. Nat. Task Force, Environ. Edn., 1996. Author: Agriscience and Technology, 1991, 97, Ecology of Fish and Wildlife, 1995, Introduction to Forestry Science, 1998, Agriscience, Fundamentals and Applications, 2000; contbr. articles to profl. jours. Vice-chmn. Minidoka County Fair Bd., Rupert, Idaho, 1977-80. Mem. Am. Vocat. Assn., Am. Vocat. Info. Assn., Nat. Vocat. Agrl. Tchrs. Assn., Idaho Vocat. Agrl. Tchrs. Assn. (pres. 1981-82, Adminstr. of Yr. 1989), Am. Vocat. Info. Assn., Nat. Assn. Suprs. Agrl. Edn. (western v.p. 1990-91, nat. pres. 1993-94), Gamma Sigma Delta, Alpha Zeta. Mem. Lds Ch. Home: 802 Sunrise Blvd N Twin Falls ID 83301-4247 Office: Coll So Idaho PO Box 1238 Twin Falls ID 83303-1238

BURTON, LESLIE ANNE, psychologist; b. N.Y.C. BA, Queens Coll., 1977; MS, U. Chgo., 1983, PhD, 1985. Lic. psychologist, N.Y., Calif. Intern Columbia U. Coll. Physicians and Surgeons, N.Y.C., 1983-84; fellow in psychology Cornell U. Med. Coll., 1984-86; asst. prof. psychology in neurosci. Cornell U. Med. Coll./Burke Rehab. Hosp./N.Y. Hosp., White Plains, 1986-90; asst. prof. psychology Fordham U., Bronx, N.Y., 1994-99, assoc. prof. psychology, 1999—. Adj. assoc. prof. psychology in neurosci. Cornell U. Coll. N.Y. Hosp., N.Y.C., 1995—. Contbr. articles to profl. jours. Mem. APA, Internat. Neuropsychol. Soc., Nat. Acad. Neuropsychology, Cognitive Neurosci. Soc., N.Y. Acad. Scis. Office: Fordham U Psychology Dept 441 E Fordham Rd Bronx NY 10458-9993

BURTON, MALINDA DAUGHERTY, school librarian; b. Lexington, Ky., July 19, 1954; d. Charles Walter and Barbara Ann (Hunter) Daugherty; m. Robert Allen Williams Jr., Sept. 1, 1972 (div. Feb. 1990); children: Christopher Allen, Casey Ann; m. Daniel Wayne Burton, July 21, 1990; stepchildren: Karen Nicole, Daniel Todd. BA in Elem. Edn., U. Ky., 1974, MA in Elem. Edn., 1981, MS in Libr. Sci., 1998. Sch, media libr. Eastern Elem. & Sadeville, Georgetown, Ky., 1975-76, Nicholasville (Ky.) Elem. Sch., 1977—. Acad. team coach Nicholasville Elem., 1987-90; contest mgr., gov., cup, acad. competition Nicholasville Elem. Sch. and Jessamine County Elem. Sch., 1989, tech. com. mem., 1990—. Active Ronald McDonald House, Lexington, 1980-83, parent support group Spl. Care Nursery-Ctrl. Bapt. Hosp., Lexington, 1980-82; libr. vol. Southland Christian Ch., Lexington, 1992—; v.p. Jessamine County Edn. Assn., 2001-03. Excellence grantee Jessamine County Edn. Found., 1987, Edn. Found. Awards grantee, 1992, 93. Mem. Ky. Libr. Assn., Ky. Edn. Assn., Ctrl. Ky. Sch. Media Assn., Ctrl. Ky. Edn. Assn. Democrat. Avocations: reading, swimming, shelling, snorkeling, travel. Office: Nicholasville Elem Sch 414 W Maple St Nicholasville KY 40356-1295

BURTON, MARY LOUISE HIMES, computer specialist; b. Altoona, Pa., Oct. 4, 1948; d. Paul Silas and Clara Marie (Bettwy) Himes; m. Carl Hansel Burton, Aug. 28, 1983; children: Michael, Edward, Carla. AA, Mt. Aloysius Jr. Coll., 1968; BS in Edn., Slippery Rock U., 1970; MLS magna cum laude, U. Pitts., 1982. Cataloguer Slipper Rock (Pa.) U., 1968-70; cataloguer, children's librn. Altoona Area Pub. Libr., 1970-71; dir. libr. svcs. Altoona Hosp., 1971-83; project coord. Coll. of Physician of Phila., 1983-84; med. libr. VAMC, Coatesville, Pa., 1984-85, acting chief libr. svc., 1985-86, chief libr. svc., 1986-94; asst. chief IRM, 1994-96, computer specialist, 1996—. Mem. Nat. Adv. Group for Info. Security, 1991-2001, vice chmn., 1996-98; security officer Automated Info. Sys., 1988—; local resource libr. Mideastern Regional Med. Libr. Program, Phila., 1976-82, Greater Northeastern Regional Med. Libr. Program, N.Y.C., 1983-93; master instr. MS office, 2000. Mem. United Ch. of Christ. Mem. Spl. Librs. Assn., Pa. Libr. Assn. (chmn. spl. librs. divsn. and bd. dirs. 1980-82, 85-86, 89-90), Med. Libr. Assn., Acad. Health Info. Profls. (sec. DV-MUG 1996), VFW Aux., Assn. Health Info. Profls., Consortium Health Info. (pres. 1990-93). Avocations: vocalist, organist, pianist. Home: 5495 Highview Dr Gap PA 17527-9553 Office: VAMC 1400 Blackhorse Hill Rd Coatesville PA 19320-2096 E-mail: marylou.burton@med.va.gov/home., chmlburton@aol.com.

BURTON, MICHAEL LADD, anthropology educator; b. Long Beach, Calif., June 6, 1942; s. Warren Nathan Burton and Dorothy Brent (Braden) Asquith; children: Melissa, Christopher; m. Ellen Greenberger, Aug. 26, 1979. BS in Econs., MIT, 1964; PhD in Anthropology, Stanford U., 1968. Rsch. fellow Harvard U., 1968-69; asst. prof. U. Calif., Irvine, 1969-76; rsch. fellow U. Nairobi, Kenya, 1973-74; assoc. prof. U. Calif., Irvine, 1976-83, prof., 1983—, chmn., dept. anthropology, 1986-91, 2003—; dir. Program Internat. Studio, 2001—. Contbr. articles to profl. jours. NSF grantee, 1981-89, 91-93. Mem. Am. Anthropol. Assn., Soc. for Cross-Cultural Rsch., Soc. Econ. Anthropology, Soc. Applied Anthropology, Assn. Social Anthropology of Oceania. Home: 10 Morning Sun Irvine CA 92612-3715 Office: U Calif Dept Anthropology Irvine CA 92697-5100 E-mail: mlburton@uci.edu.

BURTON, PAUL FLOYD, social worker; b. Seattle, May 24, 1939; s. Floyd James and Mary Teresa (Chovanak) B.; m. Roxanne Maude Johnson, July 21, 1961; children: Russell Floyd, Joan Teresa. BA, U. Wash., 1961, MSW, 1967. Juvenile parole counselor Divsn. Juvenile Rehab. State of Wash., 1961-66; social worker VA, Seattle, 1967-72; social worker, cons. Work Release Program, King County, Wash., 1967-72; supr., chief psychiatry sect. Social Work Svc. VA, Topeka, 1972-73; pvt. practice Topeka and L.A., 1972—; chief social work svc. VA, Sepulveda, Calif., 1973-98; assoc. dir. Cmty. Care Svcs., VA Greater L.A. Healthcare System, 1998—2001, dir. cmty. residential care, 2001—. EEO coord. Med. ctr., 1974-77. Mem. NASW (newsletter edito Puget Sound chpt. 1970-71), Acad. Cert. Social Workers, Ctr. for Studies in Social

Functioning, Soc. Social Svc. Leaders Healthcare, Assn. VA Social Workers (founder 1979, charter mem. and pres. 1980-81, newsletter editor 1982-83, 89-91, pres. elect 1993-95, pres. 1995-97, newsletter editor 2000-2002, treas. 2003). Home: 14063 Remington St Arleta CA 91331-5359 Office: 16111 Plummer St Sepulveda CA 91343-2036

BURTON, PEGGY, advertising and marketing executive; b. N.Y.C. BSBA, NYU, 1960. Freelance TV producer, N.Y.C., 1964-67; TV producer Young & Rubicam, N.Y.C., 1967-69; sr. acct. exec. Daniel & Charles, N.Y.C., 1969-74; ptnr., v.p. Bruderer Hartnett Advt. Agy., N.Y.C., 1974-76; dir. Comm. Am. Express Co., N.Y.C., 1976-83; pres. advt. Dreyfus Corp., N.Y.C., 1983-95; pres. Burton Commns. Multi Media, N.Y.C., 1995—. Vol. Met. Mus. Art; bd. dirs. Nat. Sch. Com. Econ. Edn., Mallon Fund. Mem. Internat. Advt. Assn., N.Y. New Media Assn., Fin. Women's Assn., Fgn. Policy Assn., Bus. Execs. for Nat. Security, NYU Gallatin Arts Com., N.Y. Athletic Club, Nat. Arts Club. Address: 220 Central Park S New York NY 10019-1417

BURTON, RANDALL JAMES, lawyer; b. Sacramento, Feb. 4, 1950; s. Edward J. and Bernice Mae (Overton) B.; m. Kimberly D. Rogers, Apr. 29, 1989; children: Kelly Jacqueline, Andrew Jameson. BA, Rutgers U., 1972; JD, Southwestern U., 1975. Bar: Calif. 1976, U.S. Dist. Ct. (ea. dist.) Calif. 1976, U.S. Dist. Ct. (no. dist.) Calif. 1990, Supreme Ct. 1991. Assoc. Brekke & Mathews, Citrus Heights, Calif., 1976; pvt. practice Sacramento, 1976—93; ptnr. Burton & White, Sacramento, 1993—; judge pro tem Sacramento Samll Claims Ct., 1982—. Bd. dirs. North Highlands Recreation and Park Dist., 1978—86, Family Svc. Agy. Sacramento, 1991—96; active local bd. 22 Selective Svc., 1982—2001; active 20-30 Club Sacramento, 1979—90, pres., 1987. Recipient Disting. Citizen award Golden Empire Coun., Boy Scouts Am. Mem.: Sacramento Young Lawyers Assn., Sacramento Bar Assn., Rotary (pres. Foothill-Highlands club 1980—81). Presbyterian. Office: 1540 River Park Dr Ste 224 Sacramento CA 95815-4609

BURTON, RAYMOND CHARLES, JR., retired transportation company executive; b. Phila., Aug. 29, 1938; s. Raymond Charles and Phyllis (Clifford) B.; m. Madeline Ann Starmann, Feb. 13, 1999; children: Carolyn Starmann, Raymond Starmann. BA, Cornell U., 1960; MBA, U. Pa., 1963. Various operating positions Santa Fe Ry. Co., 1963-68, asst. controller, 1968-69; asst. treas. Santa Fe Industries, Chgo., 1969-74; asst. v.p. planning, treas. Burlington No., Inc., 1974-79, v.p. and treas., 1979-82; v.p. planning Internat. Harvester Co., Chgo., 1982; chmn., pres., CEO, TTX Co., Chgo., 1982-2000; pres., CEO, Railbox Co., Railgon Co., Chgo., 1982-2000; ret., 2000. 1st lt. U.S. Army, 1960-61. Mem.: Met. Club. Republican. Presbyterian.

BURTON, RICHARD IRVING, orthopedist, educator; b. Providence, Sept. 18, 1936; s. Kenneth Gould and Edith Irving (Vayro) B.; m. Margaret Ann Leaman, Apr. 5, 1961; children: Thomas Kenneth, Douglas Leaman. BA, Amherst Coll., 1958; MD, Harvard U., 1962. Diplomate Am. Bd. Orthopaedic Surgery (examiner 1980—, bd. dirs. 1989-98). Intern U. Rochester, N.Y., 1962-63, resident in surgery, 1963-64; resident in orthopedic surgery Harvard U., 1966-70; fellow in hand surgery Roosevelt Hosp., N.Y.C., 1970-71; asst. prof. Cleve. Clinic Found., 1971-72, head sect. surgery of hand, 1971-74, assoc. prof., 1973-74; mem. faculty U. Rochester Med. Sch., 1974—, head sect. surgery of hand, 1974—2003, prof. orthopedics, 1979—, Marjorie Strong Wehle prof. orthopedics, 1995-2000, dean's prof., 2000—02, assoc. chmn. dept. orthopedics, 1981-88, chmn., 1988—2000, acting chmn. dept. neurol. surgery, 2000—02, sr. assoc. dean for acad. affairs, 2002—; sr. assoc. orthopedist Strong Meml. Hosp., Rochester, 1974-79, orthopedist, 1979—; sr. assoc. dean for acad. affairs U. Rochester Med. Sch., 2002—. Chmn. cert. of added qualifications com. Am. Bd. Orthopaedic Surgery, 1994-98. Assoc. editor Jour. Hand Surgery, 1980-84; contbr. articles to profl. jours., chpts. to books. Mem. exec. com. Monroe County chpt. Am. Arthritis Found., 1983-86; elder Presbyn. Ch. Buswell Disting. Svc. fellow, U. rochester, 1980-81. Recipient Exec. of Yr. award Profl. Secs. Internat., Flower City chpt., 1981. Mem. ACS, AAAS, Am. Acad. Orthopedic Surgeons (chmn. hand and wrist com. 1986-89, orthopedic resources com. 1989-91), Am. Bd. Orthop. Surgery (dir. 1988-98), Am. Bd. Med. Specialties (voting rep. 1995-98), Am. Soc. Surgery of the Hand (coord. divsn. edn. 1982-85, coun. 1985-89, chmn. membership com. 1991, v.p. 1990, pres.-elect 1991, pres. 1992), Am. Orthopedic Assn. (exec. com. 1986, resident rsch. conf. com. 1987-89, chair 1989, membership com. 1989-92, chmn. 1992, exec. com. 1992, forward planning com. 1996-99), Interurban Orthopedic Soc., Am. Rheumatism Assn., Eastern Orthopedic Assn., Monroe County Med. Soc., N.Y. State Med. Soc., Rochester Acad. Medicine, Rochester Orthopedic Soc., Soc. N.Y. State Orthopedic Surgeons, J. William Littler Soc., Amherst Alumni Assn., Harvard U. Med. Sch. Alumni Assn. Home: 7869 Hidden Oak Pittsford NY 14534-9607 Office: U Rochester Med Ctr Deans Office Box 706 601 Elmwood Ave Rochester NY 14642-0001

BURTON, RICHARD JAY, lawyer; b. N.Y.C., May 4, 1949; s. Melvin F. Burton and Shirley (Burton) Silber; m. Truly Demetra Dourdis, June 11, 1972; 1 child, Marc Aaron. BA, George Washington U., 1971; JD, U. Miami, 1974. Bar: Fla. 1974, D.C. 1976, U.S. Supreme Ct. 1979. Founder Med. Commn. on Human Rights, Washington, 1969-71; adminstrv. aide Fla. Legis., 1973-74; gov. affairs liaison Dade County Fla. Legis., 1974; assoc. Richard H.W. Maloy and Assocs., Coral Gables, Fla., 1974-76; atty., advisor FAA, Washington, 1976-77; assoc. Pompan, Rumizen & Reynolds, Washington, 1978-79, Donald M. Murtha and Assocs., Washington, 1978-79; ptnr. Schoninger, Siegfried, Kipnis, Burton & Sussman PA, Miami, Fla., 1979-82; sole practice Miami, 1982—; gen. counsel Rexall Sundown Inc., 1982-90. Guest lectr. U. Miami Sch. of Law, Coral Gables, 1982. Mem. Am. Arbitration Assn. Constr. law panel, 1974—, Builders Assn. S. Fla., legis. com. 1980—, Builder Industry Polit. action com.; fire commr. Met. Dade County, 1988, 92, vice chmn., fire commr., 1989-90. Mem. ABA, D.C. Bar Assn., Fed. Bar Assn., Fla. Bar Assn. (constr. law com.). Democrat. Jewish. Avocations: skiing, scuba diving, tennis. Home: 1000 W Island Blvd Apt 1109 Miami FL 33160

BURTON, ROBERT CLYDE, science educator; b. Borger, Tex., Feb. 27, 1929; s. Earl and Edith Belle Burton; m. Betty Jean Hill, Oct. 6, 1951; children: Randall L., Roger E., Jana S. Cornett, Jill E. Brown. BA, Tex. Tech U., 1957, MA, 1959; PhD, U. N.Mex., 1965. From asst. prof. to assoc. prof. W. Tex. State U., Canyon, 1959—63, prof., dept. head, 1966—76, prof. geology, 1976—89; prof. Temple U., Tokyo, 1989—91; prof. emeritus W. Tex. A&M U., Canyon, 1991—. Owner Geomag Surveys, Canyon, 1970—. Contbr. articles to profl. jours. Sgt. USAF, 1948—52. Recipient Favorite Prof. award, W. Tex. State Coll., Canyon, 1960. D-Conservative. Presbyterian. Avocation: golf. Home: 711 Taylor Lane Canyon TX 79015 Personal E-mail: rcbbjb1@cox.net.

BURTON, ROBERT GENE, printing and publishing executive; b. Pontiac, Mich., Apr. 4, 1939; s. Earl R. and Verna L. Burton; m. Paula M. Suwanski, May 26, 1972; children: Robert Gene Jr., Michael, Joseph. BS, Murray (Ky.) State U., 1962; MA, U. Tenn., 1964; postgrad., U. Chgo., 1964, U. Ala., 1965—67; D (hon.), Murray State U., 1968, U. Conn., 2000. From salesman to nat. sales dir. SRA/IBM Corp., Dallas and Chgo., 1967—76; from midwest dir. to mktg. dir. CBS, Chgo. and N.Y.C., 1976—78, v.p. mktg., 1978—79, v.p. ops. N.Y.C., 1978—79; v.p. pub. ABC, N.Y.C., 1980, pres. leisure mags., 1980—81, group v.p. spl. interest pub., 1981, pres., 1981—91; v.p. Capital Cities/ABC, Inc., 1991; chmn. bd., pres., CEO World Color Press Inc., 1991—99; pres., CEO Moore Corp., 2000—01, chmn., pres., CEO, 2001—02, Burton Mgmt. Group., LLC, 2003—. Mem. adv. bd. NYU Bus. Press. Trustee Eagle Hill Sch., Greenwich, Conn.; mem. bd. overseers U. Conn. Sch. Bus. Adminstrn.; past trustee Murray State U., Boy Scouts Am. Nat. Mus., Murray; former chmn. Nat. Bible Week/Laymen's Nat. Bible Assn.; former pub. industry chmn. Juvenile Diabetes Found.; bd. dirs. Cancer Care of Conn.; bd. advisors Breast Cancer Alliance; bd. dirs. Kentuckians of N.Y., Burton Charitable Found., NYU, past pres. adv. bd.; bd. dirs. Murray State U. Coll. Bus. and Pub. Affairs, past dean's adv. coun. Named to Murray State Football Hall of Fame; recipient award, Spl. Achievement Soc. and Athletic Hall of Fame, West Frankfort, Ill., Oak award, Ky. Advocates for Higher Edn. Mem.: Assn. Bus. Pubs. (past chmn.), Greenwich (Conn.) Country Club, Washington Nat. Press Club. Republican. Baptist.

BURTON, RUSSELL ROHAN, aerospace scientist, researcher; b. Chico, Calif., Jan. 15, 1932; s. Russell Huntt and Merle (Rohan) B.; m. M. Ruth Ferguson, Nov. 8, 1958 (div. Dec. 1979); children: Robert Paul, Russell Patrick Douglas; m. Sharon Lea Milton, Aug. 8, 1983; children: Jennifer Paige, Heather Lea. BS, U. Calif., Davis, 1954, DVM, 1956, MS, 1965, PhD, 1970. Pvt. practice, Grover City, Calif., 1956-62; rsch. physiologist U. Calif., Davis, 1962-71, Brooks AFB, Tex., 1971-80; chief aerospace rsch. br. USAF Sch. of Aerospace Medicine, Brooks AFB, Tex., 1980-88, chief scientist, 1988-91, chief scientist crew systems directorate, 1991-96; chief scientist Armstrong Lab., Brooks AFB, 1995-97; sr. scientist human effectiveness directorate Air Force Rsch. Lab., Brooks AFB, 1997-99, ret., 1999; prof. emeritus, 1999—. Cons. NASA, Johnson Space Ctr., Ames Rsch. Ctr., 1980—, cons. adv. group Aerospace R&D, Paris, 1987-92, mem. panel, 1992-97; com. chair, project officer, custodian Air Standardization Coord. Com., Washington, 1984-91. Co-author: High G Physiological Protection Tng. (AGARD-AG-322), 1990, Adaptation to Acceleration Environments, 1996; co-author, editor: Cervical Spinal Injury from Repeated Exposures to Sustained Acceleration (RTO-TR-4), 1999; contbr. chpts. to books, articles to profl. jours. Recipient Sci. Achievment award RTO/NATO, 1998, Outstanding Civilian Svc. medal USAF, 1999, Examplary Civilian Svc., 1998. Fellow Aerospace Med. Assn. (Tuttle award 1976, Environ. Sci. award 1980, Liliencrantz award 1988, USAF Basic Rsch. award 1988); mem. AAAS, Am. Physiol. Soc. (editorial bd. 1976-78), Aerospace Physiol. Soc. (pres. 1982), Safety and Flight Equipment (editor jour. 1993-98), Sigma Xi (pres. local chpt. 1988). Avocations: jogging, cooking, watercolor painting. Home: 16203 Avenida Del Luna San Antonio TX 78232-2526 Fax: 210-490-1327. E-mail: russebrt@aol.com.

BURTON, SIGRID, artist; b. Pasadena, Calif., June 20, 1951; d. Eugene John and Elizabeth Sigrid (Monell) B.; m. Michael Fellowes Brennan, May 20, 1983. Student, U. Calif., Berkeley, 1969-71, UCLA, 1970; BA, Bennington Coll., 1973. One-person shows include Ivory Kimpton Gallery, San Francisco, 1984, 87, Martha White Gallery, Louisville, 1984, Patricia Hamilton, N.Y., 1986, 88, Hokin Kaufman Gallery, 1987, 90, Eve Mannes Gallery, 1987, Hamilton Gallery, Santa Monica, 1990, Jean Albano Gallery, Chgo., 1993, State St. Gallery, Sarasota, 1998, Rockefeller Arts Ctr., SUNY, Fredonia, 2001, Baum Gallery, U. Ctrl. Ark., 2003, Flatfile Contemporary, Chgo., 2003, Waterworks Visual Arts Ctr., Salisbury, NC, 2004; exhibited in group shows at Leubsdorf Gallery, Hunter Coll., N.Y.C., 2001, Hofstra Mus., Hofstra Univ., 2000, Art Ctr. Coll. Design, 1986, Hokin Kaufman Gallery, 1987, 90, Adelphi U., 1988; represented in permanent collections Bucknell U., Met. Museum of Art, N.Y.C., Auberge Du Soleil, Calif., Bank of the South, Atlanta, Citicorp, N.Y.C., Coca Cola Corp., Atlanta, Prudential Life Ins., Newark, John and Mable Ringling Mus., Sarasota, Fla., Lewis & Clark Coll., Portland. Recipient Richard and Hinda Rosenthal Found. award, Am. Acad., Inst. Arts and Letters, N.Y.C., 1977; Bellagio Study Ctr. fellow Rockefeller Foun d., Lake Como,Italy, 1985, Indo-Am. Sr. Rsch. fellow, 1994-95. Democrat. E-mail: sigridburton@aol.com.

BURTON, TIM, film director; b. Burbank, Aug. 25, 1958; Student Calif. Inst. Arts (Disney Fellowship), 1979—80. Cartoon artist Disney Prodn., apprentice animator. Film dir. Vincent, 1982, Frankenweenie, 1984, Pee-Wee's Big Adventure, 1984, Beetlejuice, 1988, Batman, 1989, Edward Scissorhands, 1990, Batman Returns, 1992, Ed Wood, 1994, Mars Attacks, 1996, Sleepy Hollow, 1999, Planet of the Apes, 2001; prodr. The Nightmare Before Christmas, 1993, Cabin Boy, 1994, Batman Forever, 1995, James and the Giant Peach, 1996, others; dir. TV film Aladdin, Faerie Tale Theatre series; appeared in film Singles, 1992; author: My Art & Films, 1993, The Melancholy Death of Oyster Boy and Other Stories, 1997. Office: Chapman Bird & Grey 1990 S Bundy Dr Ste 200 Los Angeles CA 90025-5240*

BURTON, WARD, professional race car driver; b. South Boston, Va., Oct. 25, 1961; married; m. Tabitha Burton; children: Sarah, Jeb. Student, Elon Coll. Race car driver NASCAR Busch Series Grand Nat. Divsn., 1990, Bill Davis Racing, High Point, NC. Achievements include winner Winston Cup, 1995; 23 top 5 career starts; 37 top 10 stars in 148 races; career finishes include 5 top 5 finishes and 24 top 10 finishes in 146 races; winner N.C. Motor Speedway, 1995; AC Delco 400, 1995; Mall.com 400, 2000. Avocations: wildlife conservation, hunting. Office: c/o Bill Davis Racing 301 Old Thomasville Rd High Point NC 27260-8190

BURTON, WILLIAM JOSEPH, engineering executive; b. Gaffney, S.C., Mar. 22, 1931; s. Emory Goss and Olivia (Copeland) B.; m. Joan Holland Burton, Sept. 26, 1987. BSME, U. S.C., 1957, MSME, 1964; PhDME, Tex. A&M U., 1970. Registered profl. engr., Tenn., Fla. Sr. dynamics engr. Lockheed-Ga. Co., Marietta, 1957-62; sr. project engr. Allison div. GM Corp., Indpls., 1964-67; asst. prof., researcher Tex. A&M U., College Station, 1968-70; asst. prof. U. Tenn., Knoxville, 1970-74; projects mgr. Tenn. Valley Authority, Chattanooga, 1974-79; program mgr. Dept. Navy, Washington, 1979-94; chair equal employment opportunity com. Chesapeake divsn. Naval Facilities Engring. Command, Washington, 1982—83; cons. engr. Ocean and Power Applications, Lakeland, Fla., 1993—. Lectr. in field nat. and internat. audiences; adj. prof. mech. and aerospace engring., energy conversion tech. U. Tenn., Knoxville, 1974—75; speaker and presenter, various venues and topics. Author: On the Heating Surface Effects of Nucleate Boiling Data Correlation, 1964, The Effects of Surface Roughness on the Wave Forces on a Circular Cylindrical Pile, 1970; author more than 50 articles on ocean engring., power and propulsion, aircraft structures, planning and economics, ethics. Secretary, mem. hospitality com. Exch. Club, Knoxville, 1975, bd. dirs., 1976; coord. charitable campaign Naval Facilities Engring. Com., Washington, 1982. With U.S. Army, 1951-53. Recipient Occupation medal, 1952, Nat. Def. Svc. medal U.S. Army, 1953, Antarctic Svc. medal U.S. Dept. of Navy, 1962, Wisdom award of honor, 2000; Eminent Wisdom fellow Scroll of Wisdom Hall of Fame, 2000. Fellow ASME (organizer, chmn. tech. sessions for internat. confs. 1982-87, chmn. exec. com. ocean engring. divsn. 1985, mem.-at-large energy resources bd. 1986-92, chmn. com. honors & awards energy resources bd. 1992-98, com. on tech. planning coun. on engring. 1992-94, fellow peer rev. bd. 1992-97, rep. energy resources bd. to nat. nominating com. 1998—, Golden Cert. ocean engring. divsn. 1989), Va. Soc. Profl. Engrs. (no. Va. regional coun. 1988); mem. AAAS, NSPE (pres.-elect Fairfax chpt. 1988), Soc. Mfg. Engrs., Soc. Naval Architects and Marine Engrs., S.C. Hist. Soc., Nat. Trust for Historic Preservation, Polk County (Fla.) Hist. Assn., VFW, Marine Tech. Soc., The Univ. South Caroliniana Soc., Sigma Xi. Baptist. Avocations: travel, bicycling, classic guitar, golf, tennis. Home: 307 Miramar Dr Lakeland FL 33803-2633 Office: Naval Facilities Engring Svc Ctr East Coast Detachment 901 E M St SE 218 Wash Navy Yard Washington DC 20374-0001 E-mail: wmburton@hotmail.com.

BURWEN, BARBARA R. painter; b. Mass., Aug. 30, 1934; d. Barnet and Martha Y. (Gordon) Wallace; m. Richard S. Burwen, May 27, 1956; children: Diane S., Dale R., Russell W. BS, Boston U., 1956, EdM, 1958. mem. Depot Square Gallery, Lexington, Mass., 1993-96. One-woman shows include West Tisbury (Mass.) Field Gallery, 1988, 89, Martha's Vineyard Nat. Bank, Chilmark, Mass., 1990, Nineteen Marsh Street Gallery, Stamford, Conn., 1992, Piper Gallery, Lexington, Mass., 1995, Depot Square Gallery, Lexington, 1995, 96; group shows include N.Am. Open Show, 1990, 92, 94, Doshi Ctr. for Contemporary Art, Harrisburg, 1995, Copley Soc. of Boston Juried Show, 1995, 25th Internat. Exhbn. of the La. Watercolor Soc., 1995, Rocky Mountain Nat. Show 1994, 1996, Ky. Watercolor Soc. Nat. Show 1993, 95, others.; published in "Best of Watercolor, 1995, Best of Watercolor 2, 1997, Abstracts in Watercolor, 1995, Creative Expressions, 1997, Watercolor Expressions, 1999; radio guest Sonja Tonkajoy Show, 1995. Recipient First award N.Am. Open Show, 1992, award of honor Niagara Frontier Watercolor Soc., 1992, Windsor Newton award and Silver Brush Ltd. award Ky. Watercolor Soc., 1995, Forstall award 25th Internat. Exhbn. of the La. Watercolor Soc., 1995, Vance Kirkland award Rocky Mountain Nat., 1996. Mem. New Eng. Watercolor Soc. (Guild of Boston Artists award 1993, 2d prize 1994, North Shore Art Assn. award 1995, Gold medal 1996), Concord Art Assn., Cambridge Art Assn. Avocations: skiing, bicycling, tennis. Home: 12 Holmes Rd Lexington MA 02420-1917

BURZYNSKI, JAMES BRADLEY, state legislator; b. Christopher, Ill., July 13, 1955; m. Judy Burzynski; 2 children. BA, Ill. Wesleyan Coll. Ill. state sen. Dist. 35, 1990. Chair licenced activities com.; mem. state govt.ops. com., exec. appts. com. Address: 505 Dekalb Ave Sycamore IL 60178-1719*

BURZYNSKI, NORMAN STEPHEN, editor; b. Pitts., Nov. 21, 1928; s. Ladislaus and Eleanor Marie B.; m. Ann Louise Adams, June 11, 1951; children: Michael Derek, Stephanie Ann, Eric Adams, Karen Ruth, John Kerstan, Joan Lorraine. BA in Journalism, U. Pitts., 1953; MS in Bus. Adminstrn., George Washington U., 1971; A. Applied Sci. summa cum laude in Aviation Tech.— Airport Mgmt., No. Va. Community Coll., Manassas, 1977, A. Applied Sci. summa cum laude in Aviation Tech.— Air Traffic Control, A. Applied Sci. magna cum laude in Comml. Art, 1982. Editor corporate publs. PPG Industries, Pitts., 1958-72, pub. relations rep., 1972-73; air res. forces liaison officer Office of Info., U.S. Air Force, Washington, 1968-72; chief Office of Info., U.S. Air Force Res., 1973-76; editor The Officer, Res. Officers Assn. U.S., Washington, 1976-95. Editor Civil War Camera, Luray, Va., 1998—. Served to lt. U.S. Army, 1951-52; to col. USAF, 1968-76. Mem. Res. Officers Assn., Air Force Assn., Aircraft Owners and Pilots Assn., Exptl. Aircraft Assn., Aviation and Space Writers Assn. Home: 4 Jackson Dr Luray VA 22835-9606 E-mail: f64fotography@yahoo.com.

BURZYNSKI, STANISLAW RAJMUND, internist; b. Lublin, Poland, Jan. 23, 1943; came to U.S., 1970; s. Grzegorz and Zofia Miroslawa (Radzikowski) B. MD with distinction, Med. Acad., Lublin, 1967, PhD, 1968. Tchg. asst. Med. Acad., 1962-67, intern, resident, 1967-70; rsch. assoc. Baylor U., 1970-72, asst. prof., 1972-77; pvt. practice specializing in internal medicine Houston, 1977—; pres. Burzynski Clinic, 1979—. Dir. Burzynski Rsch. Lab., 1977-83; pres. Burzynski Rsch. Inst., Inc., 1983-2002. Contbr. articles to profl. jours. Nat. Cancer Inst. grantee, 1974, West Found. grantee, 1975. Mem. AMA, AAAS, Am. Assn. Cancer Rsch., Harris County Med. Soc., Polish Nat. Alliance (pres. Houston chpt. 1974-75), Soc. Neurosci., Tex. Med. Assn., Sigma Xi. Roman Catholic. Achievements include discovery of antineoplastons components of biochem. def. system against cancer; described structure of Ameletin, 1st substance known to be responsible for remembering sound in animal's brain; invented new treatment for cancer, AIDS, viral infections, autoimmune diseases, neurofibromatosis, and Parkinson's disease; gene silencing theory of aging. Home: 20 W Rivercrest Dr Houston TX 77042-2127 Office: 9432 Old Katy Rd Ste 200 Houston TX 77055-6330 E-mail: info@burzynskiclinic.com.

BUS, JAMES STANLEY, toxicologist; b. Kalamazoo, Mich., June 27, 1949; s. Charles J. and Sena (Wolthuis) B.; m. Gerda W. Hekman, Apr. 20, 1974; children: Sara E., Timothy J., Brian M. BS in Medicinal Chemistry, U. Mich., 1971; PhD in Pharmacology, Mich. State U., 1975. Diplomate Am. Bd. Toxicology (v.p., pres. 1985-87). NIH predoctoral trainee Dept. Pharmacology, Mich. State U., East Lansing, 1971-75; asst. prof. environ. health U. Cin., 1975-76; scientist I (biochem. toxicologist) Chem. Industry Inst. Toxicology, Research Triangle Park, N.C., 1977-84, scientist II (biochem. toxicologist), 1984-86; assoc. dir. pathology/toxicology, dir. drug metabolism rsch. The Upjohn Co., Kalamazoo, 1986-89; toxicology rsch. lab. Dow Chem. Co., Midland, Mich., 1989-91, project mgr., 1992-93, rsch. mgr., tech. dir., 1994—2001, dir. external tech., 2001—. Adj. assoc. prof. curriculum in toxicology U. N.C., Chapel Hill, 1984-88; adj. prof. pharmacology/toxicology Mich. State U. East Lansing, 1987—; toxicology expert Am. Conf. for Govtl. Indsl. Hygienists, Cin., 1993-2002; safety assessment bd. advisors Merck, Sharp & Dohme Lab., West Point, Pa., 1985-86; bd. sci. counselors EPA, 1996-2003, NTP, 1997-2001; bd. dirs. CIIT. Co-editor: Patty's Industrial Hygiene and Toxicology, Vol. 3B, 1995; assoc. editor Toxicology and Applied Pharmacology, 1989-92, speciality editor, 2003—; editl. bd. Reproductive Toxicology, 1986-96; contbr. articles to profl. jours. Bd. trustees Covenant Coll., Lookout Mountain,. Ga., 1984-87. Recipient Robert A. Scala award, Environ. Occupl. Health Sci. Inst., Rutgers U., 1999, Disting. Alumni award, Mich. State U. Dept. Pharmacol. Toxicology, 2001. Mem. Soc. Toxicology (pres. 1996-97, Achievement award 1987), Am. Soc. for Pharmacology and Exptl. Therapeutics, Teratology Soc., Am. Conf. Govt. Indsl. Hygiene (mem. chem. substances threshold limit value com. 1993-2002), Nat. Acad. Scis. (emerging issues and data on environ. contaminants com. 2002—). Republican. Achievements include research dealing with mechanisms of chemical toxicity, including oxidant and glutathione mediated toxicities. Office: Dow Chemical Co Toxicology Rsch Lab 1803 Bldg Midland MI 48674-0001 E-mail: jbus@dow.com.

BUS, ROGER JAY, lawyer; b. Kalamazoo, Mich., Oct. 15, 1953; s. Charles J. and Sena (Wolthuis) B.; m. Lida Margaret Sell, Aug. 27, 1977; children: Emily Lynn, Stephen Charles. Student, Calvin Coll., 1971-73; BA, U. Mich., 1975; JD, U. Toledo, 1979. Bar: Mich. 1979, U.S. Dist. Ct. (we. dist.) Mich. 1979. Law clk. to presiding justice Kalamazoo Cir. Ct., 1978; intern Toledo Legal Aid, 1979; staff atty. Legal Aid Bur. SW Mich., Kalamazoo, 1979-81; assoc. Stanley, Davidoff & Gray, Kalamazoo, 1981-83; owner, atty. Debt Relief Law Ctr., Kalamazoo, 1983—. Deacon Ref. Bapt. Ch., Kalamazoo, 1983-85; precinct del. Kalamazoo County Reps., 1986-88; bd. dirs., atty. Kalamazoo Gospel Mission, 1983-86, v.p., 1997—, bd. dirs., 1996—, chmn. bd., 2000-02; adult Sunday sch. tchr. Calvary Bible Ch., elder, 1988-91, 92-98, elder clk., 1989-91, 97, 98, missions coun., 1999—; mem. missions team Richland Bible Ch., 2000—, adult Sunday Sch. tchr., 2001--, elder, 2002--; team mem. Operation Mobilization, Grenada, 2002. Mem. Fed. Bar Assn. (lectr. western dist. Mich. bankruptcy div. 1990-92, 97, 2001, spkr. we. dist. Mich. 2001), Am. Bankruptcy Inst., Mich. Bar Assn., Kalamazoo County Bar Assn., Nat. Assn. Chpt. 13 Trustees. Avocations: global missions, reading, religious book collecting, gospel music, evangelism. Home: 5330 Stoney Brook Rd Kalamazoo MI 49009-3850 Office: Debt Relief Law Ctr 903 E Cork St Kalamazoo MI 49001-4875

BUSBEE, KLINE DANIEL, JR., law educator, lawyer; b. Macon, Ga., Mar. 14, 1933; s. Kline Daniel and Bernice (Anderson) B.; children: Rodgers Christopher, Jon Edward. BBA, So. Meth. U., 1961, JD, 1962. 70ptnr. Worsham, Forsythe, Sampels & Busbee, Dallas, 1962; ptnr. Locke, Purnell, Rain & Harrell, P.C., Dallas, 1970-98, Gibson, Dunn & Crutcher, Dallas, 1998-99. Adj. prof. law So. Meth. U. Sch. Law, 1974—83, 1992, 2003, sr. fellow Inst. Internat. Banking and Fin., 2001—; adj. prof. pub. internat. law U. Tex. Grad. Sch. Mgmt., Dallas; bd. dirs. Atmos Energy Corp.; vis. sr. fellow Ctr. for Comml. Law Studies, Queen Mary U. London, 2001—, Brit. Inst. Internat. and Comparative Law, Russell Sq., 2001—. Mem.: ABA, Dallas Com. on Fgn. Rels., Tex. Bar Assn., Dallas Petroleum Club, Snowmass Club, Dallas Country Club. Home: 4360 San Carlos St Dallas TX 75205-2052 E-mail: danbusbeelaw@msn.com.

BUSBY, DAVID, lawyer; b. Ada, Okla., Jan. 29, 1926; s. Orel and Hope B.; m. Mary Beth Baker, June 9, 1962; children: Helen Hope Busby Burleigh, Alison Sears Busby Vareika, Robert David, John Orel. BA, 1948; LL.B., Okla. U., 1951. Bar: Okla. 1950, D.C. 1959, N.Y. 1959, U.S. Supreme Ct. 1959. Assoc. Busby, Harrell & Trice, Ada, 1951-55; counsel Subcom. on Automobile Mktg. Practices, Com. on Interstate and Fgn. Commerce, U.S. Senate, Washington, 1955-58, Subcom. Fgn. Commerce, 1958; ptnr. Hays, Busby & Rivkin, N.Y.C., 1958-77, Busby, Rehm & Leonard, 1977-87; of counsel Dorsey & Whitney, Washington, 1988—. Trade advisor Ministry of Fin., Republic of Latvia, 1996; lectr., Moscow, Kiev, Chisinev, Kampala, 1995-98; mem. accountability rev. bd. terrorist attack on U.S. Embassy, Dar Es Salaam, 1998-99. Mem. Nat. Motor Vehicle Safety Adv. Coun., 1966-68; pres. League Young Dems. of Okla., 1951; city judge, Ada, 1952-53; bd. dirs. Legal Aid Soc. D.C.; mem. Washington Nat. Cathedral chpt., 1984-91. Served with USNR, 1944-46. Mem. ABA (chmn. standing com. on customs law 1973-76), Fed. Cir. Bar Assn. (bd. dirs.), Customs and Internat. Trade Bar Assn. (bd. dirs.), Nat. Cathedral Assn. (bd. trustees 1992-96), Met. Club. Episcopalian. Office: Dorsey & Whitney 1001 Pennsylvania Ave NW Washington DC 20004-2505 E-mail: busby.david@dorseylaw.com.

BUSBY, EDWARD OLIVER, retired dean; b. Macomb, Ill., June 22, 1926; s. Lynn John and Pauline (Hoebel) B.; m. Lois E. Tehan, June 17, 1950; children: Thomas L., John E., Paula L. BS, U. Wis., 1950, MS, 1962, PhD, 1971. Resident engr. Wis. Hwy. Commn., 1950-51; asst. city engr. City of LaCrosse, Wis., 1951-53; sales engr. Wis. Culvert Co., 1953-59; lectr. civil engring. U. Wis., Madison, 1959-66; dean Coll. Engring. U. Wis.-Platteville, 1966-84, dean emeritus, 1985—. Mem. Wis. Examining Bd. for Profl. Engrs., 1981-84; v.p. Platteville Area Indsl. Devel. Corp., 1977-80; vis. prof. U. Tenn., 1984-85; treas. U. Wis.-Platteville Found., 1989-95. Contbr. articles in field to profl. jours. Served with U.S. Navy, 1944-46. NSF fellow, 1970-71 Fellow ASCE (chmn. profl. registration com. 1985-86); mem. Wis. Soc. Profl. Engrs. (pres. 1972-73), Nat. Soc. Profl. Engrs. (nat. dir. 1976-81, vice chmn. engrs. edn. 1971-73) Republican. Home: 7628 Widgeon Way Madison WI 53717-1805

BUSBY, JUSTIN BRETT, lawyer; b. Austin, Tex., Apr. 12, 1973; s. Russell Clyde and Jan (Weaver) Busby; m. Erin Glenn Busby, Nov. 16, 2002. AB summa cum laude, Duke U., 1995; JD, Columbia U., 1998. Bar: NY 1999, Tex. 2001. Law clk. to Judge Gerald B. Tjoflat U.S. Ct. Appeals, 11th Cir., Jacksonville, Fla., 1998-99; law clk. to Justices Byron R. White and John Paul Stevens Supreme Ct. of U.S., Washington, 1999-2000; assoc. appellate litigation Hogan Dubose & Townsend, Houston, 2000—. Senator and exec. com. mem. Columbia U. Senate, 1997-98; mem. acad. affairs com. of bd. trustees Duke U., Durham, N.C., 1993-95, chief justice student gove., 1993-95; mem. Round Table Cmty. Svc. House, Durham, 1992-95. Recipient Young B. Smith Torts prize Columbia Law Sch., 1996, Griffith Univ. Svc. award Duke U., 1995; James Kent scholar, 1998. Mem. Phi Beta Kappa. Avocations: violin playing, reading, travel, art and architectural history, community service. Home: 3511 Yupon St Houston TX 77006 Office: Mayer Brown Rowe & Maw 700 Louisiana #3600 Houston TX 77002 E-mail: jbbusby@alumni.duke.edu.

BUSBY, MARJEAN (MARJEAN BUSBY), retired journalist; b. Kansas City, Mo., Jan. 31, 1931; d. Vivian Eric and Stella Mae (Lindley) Phillips; m. Robert Jackson Busby, Apr. 11, 1969 (dec. Feb. 1989). B.J., U. Mo., 1952. With Kansas City Star Co. (Knight Ridder purchased 1997), 1952-2000, editor women's news, 1969-73, assoc. Sunday editor, People Sect. editor, 1973-77, fashion editor, 1978-81, feature and home writer, 1981-2000; ret., 2000. Mem. Fashion Group (1st recipient Kansas City appreciation award 1978), LSV, Mortar Board, Soc. Profl. Journalists, Friends of Art, Belle of Am. Royal Orgn., Kappa Alpha Theta (pres. Alpha Mu chpt. 1951-52) Presbyterian. Home: 9804 Mercier St Kansas City MO 64114-3860

BUSBY, MORRIS D. former ambassador; b. Memphis; married; 2 children. BA, Marshall U.; MS, George Washington U.; postgrad., U.S. Naval Destroyer Sch., Def. Intelligence Sch., Naval War Coll. With USN, various locations including Vietnam, 1971-73; mem. staff Office of Coord. of Ocean Affairs, dir. Office Oceans and Polar Affairs, dep. asst. sec. ocean affairs, amb. oceans and fisheries affairs Dept. of State, 1973-81, alt. rep. to conf. on disarmament, 1981-83, dep. chief of mission Mexico City, 1984-87, founder, office head assistance program for Nicaraguan resistance, 1987-88, prin. dep. asst. sec. inter-Am. affairs, 1987-88, spl. envoy to C.Am., sr. dep., 1988-89; head counter-terrorism Dept. State, 1989-91; amb. to Colombia Dept. of State, Bogota, 1991-94; pres. BGI, Internet Cons. Svcs., 1994—. Bd. dirs InVision Techs., Newark, Calif., 1998—. Decorated Bronze Star; recipient 3 Presdl. Meritorious Svc. awards Govt. Colombia Gran Cruz de Boyaca. Office: BGI Inc PO Box 1189 Mathews VA 23109-1918

BUSCEMI, PETER, lawyer; b. Bklyn., Sept. 25, 1950; s. Vincent and Ilse (Griesser) Buscemi; m. Judith Ann Miller, June 27, 1981. BA, Columbia U., 1969, JD, 1976; MA, Princeton U., 1971. Bar: N.Y. 1977, D.C. 1979, U.S. Supreme Ct. 1980, U.S. Dist. Ct. (D.C. dist.) 1981, U.S. Ct. Appeals (D.C. cir.) 1981, U.S. Dist. Ct. (so. dist.) N.Y. 1982, U.S. Ct. Appeals (5th and 11th cirs.) 1982, U.S. Ct. Appeals (2d cir.) 1985, U.S. Ct. Appeals (fed. cir.) 1986, U.S. Ct. Appeals (3d and 4th cirs.) 1990, U.S. Ct. Appeals (6th cir.) 1993, U.S. Ct. Appeals (1st cir.) 1994, U.S. Ct. Appeals (7th cir.) 1995, U.S. Ct. Appeals (10th cir.) 1998. Law clk. to Hon. Carl McGowan U.S. Ct. Appeals (D.C. cir.), Washington, 1976-77; asst. to solicitor gen. U.S. Dept. Justice, Washington, 1977-81; spl. asst. U.S. atty. U.S. Atty.'s Office, Alexandria, Va., 1980; assoc. Paul, Weiss, Rifkind, Wharton & Garrison, Washington, 1981-86, Morgan, Lewis & Bockius, LLP, Washington, 1986-87, ptnr., 1987—. Home: 5215 Chamberlin Ave Chevy Chase MD 20815-6646 Office: Morgan Lewis & Bockius LLP 1111 Pennsylvania Ave NW Washington DC 20004 E-mail: pbuscemi@morganlewis.com.

BUSCH, ANN MARIE HERBAGE, medical/surgical nurse; b. Roseburg, Oreg., Jan. 24, 1958; d. Robert Canfield and Magdaline Mary (Tuchscherer) Herbage; m. John Patrick Busch, June 27, 1981; children: Rebecca Ann, Michael Robert. BSN summa cum laude, U. Portland, 1980; MSN, U. Calif., San Francisco, 1985. RN Oreg., Calif., cert. clin. specialist in med.-surg. nursing, wound, ostomy, continence nurse, CPR instr. Staff nurse IV Stanford (Calif.) U. Hosp., 1981-88, acting nursing ednl. coord., 1986-87; coord./educator RN refresher program DeAnza Coll., Cupertino, Calif., 1986-88; med-surg. clin. nurse specialist Cmty. Hosp. Los Gatos (Calif.), 1988-92; surg. clin. nurse specialist Palo Alto (Calif.) VA Med. Ctr., 1992-95; liver transplant clin. nurse specialist VA Med. Ctr., Portland, Oreg., 1995—. Cons. patient pathways U. So. Calif. Hosp., 1990—91; asst. clin. prof. dept. physiol. nursing U. Calif., San Francisco, 1993—; primary faculty Oreg. Health Scis. U. Sch. Nursing, 1995—; spkr. in field. Contbr. articles to profl. jours. Recipient disting. nursing rsch. utilization award, VA, 1993, Clin. Nurse Specialist of Yr. award, Nat. Assn. Clin. Nurse Specialists, 2002. Mem.: ANA, Oreg. Coun. Clin. Nurses Specialists Group (chair 1999—2002), Oreg. Nurses Assn. (bd. dirs. 2002—), Nat. League Nursing, Internat. Transplant Nurses Assn., Am. Soc. Parenteral and Enteral Nutrition, Wound, Ostomy and Continence Nurses Soc., Blue Key, Delta Epsilon Sigma, Sigma Theta Tau. Home: 1310 Stonehaven Dr West Linn OR 97068-1867 Office: Portland Vet Affs Med CtrLiver Transplant (P-3-Liver) PO Box 1034 3710 SW US Veterans Hosp Rd Portland OR 97207 E-mail: ann.busch@med.va.gov.

BUSCH, ANNIE, library director; b. Joplin, Mo., Jan. 6, 1947; d. George Lee and Margaret Eleanor (Williams) Chancellor; 1 child, William Andrew Keller. BA, Mo. U., 1969, MA, 1976. Br. mgr. St. Charles (Mo.) City Coun. Libr., 1977-84, Springfield/Greene County (Mo.) Libr., 1985-89, exec. dir., 1989—. Exec. bd. Mo. Libr. Network Corp., St. Louis, 1991-96. Mem. adv. bd. Springfield Pub. Sch. Found., 1992-94; pres. Ozarks Regional Info. On-Line Network, Springfield, 1993-98; mem. Gov.'s Commn. on Informational Tech.; exec. bd. Mo. Rsch. and Edn. Network, pres., 1996-97; bd. dirs. Ozarks Pub. TV, 1994-2000, Every Kid Counts; mem. task force Mo. Goals 2000, 1995, Mo. Census 2000 Complete Count commn., 1999-00; coord. com. Springfield Vision 20/20; mem. Cmty. Task Force, Springfield, 1993-98, Cmty. Partnership of the Ozarks, 1998; adv. bd. St. John's Health Sys., Boys and Girls Town, Good Cmty. Task Force, 1999-2002; chair Sec. of State Adv. Coun., 2001—; mem. adv. com. So. Mo. State U. Coll. Humanitites and Pub. Affairs. Mem.: ALA, Springfield Rotary (pres. 1998—99), Springfield Area C. of C. (bd. dirs.), Pub. Libr. Assn., Mo. Libr. Assn. (pres. 1993—94, exec. bd. 1990—94). Office: Springfield-Greene Cty Libr PO Box 760 Springfield MO 65801-0760 E-mail: annie@mail.sgcl.org.

BUSCH, ARTHUR ALLEN, lawyer, educator; b. Flint, Mich., July 25, 1954; s. William Allen and Anna Elizabeth (York) B.; m. Bernadette Marie-Therese Regnier, Aug. 28, 1982. BA, Mich. State U., 1976, MLIR, 1977; JD, T.M. Cooley Law Sch., 1982. Bar: Mich. 1982, U.S. Dist. Ct. (ea. dist.) Mich. 1984. Supr. pers. Nat. Gypsum Co., Gibsonburg, Ohio, 1977-78; instr. Mich. State U., East Lansing, 1980-82; pvt. practice Flint, 1982-92; instr. C.S. Mott C.C., Flint, 1978—. Counsel Flint Cty Coun., 1982-84; cons. labor atty. City of Flint, 1984; prosecutor Genesee County, 1993—. Commr. Genesee County, 1986-92, mem. planning com., pks. and recreation; active Valley Area Agy. on Aging. Mem. Mich. Bar Assn., Genesee County Bar Assn. Democrat. Baptist. Office: 200 Courthouse Flint MI 48502

BUSCH, AUGUST ADOLPHUS, III, brewery executive; b. St. Louis, June 16, 1937; s. August Anheuser and Elizabeth (Overton) Busch; m. Susan Marie Hornibrook, Aug. 17, 1963 (div. 1969); children: August Adolphus IV, Susan Marie II; m. Virginia L. Wiley, Dec. 28, 1974; children: Steven August, Virginia Marie. Student, U. Ariz., 1957—58, Siebel Inst. Tech., 1960—61. With Anheuser-Busch, Inc., St. Louis, 1957—, pres., 1974—75; chmn. bd., pres., CEO Anheuser Busch Cos., Inc., St. Louis. Bd. dirs. SBC Comms., Emerson Electric Co. Exec. bd. St. Louis Boy Scouts Am.; bd. dirs. United Way Greater St. Louis. Mem.: Log Cabin Club, St. Louis Country Club. Office: Anheuser-Busch Cos Inc 1 Busch Pl Saint Louis MO 63118-1852

BUSCH, BEVERLY GAIL, English language educator, literature educator, instructional resource center administrator; b. Boston, Oct. 27, 1948; d. Andrew Earl Thompson and Martha Bartlett; m. Peter Raymond Busch, Apr. 15, 1972; children: Cheyenne J., Carin S., Luke W. BA, U. Mass., 1970; MA, Middlebury Coll., 1978; MPhil, Drew U., 1981, PhD, 1986. Cert. English tchr. Mass., NJ. Adj. faculty mem. Coll. St. Elizabeth, Madison, N.J., 1981-83, Centenary Coll., Hackettstown, N.J., 1981-83; coord. ministries program Phillipsburg (N.J.) Alliance Ch., 1995-99; adj. prof. English Warren County Cmty. Coll., Washington, N.J., 1995-99; prof. English Somerset Christian Coll., Zarephath, NJ, 1999—, dir. Instructional Resource Ctr. Author poetry and inspirational articles; mem. editl. adv. bd.: Collegiate Press, 2002—03. Mem. Greenwich Twp. Bd. Edn., Stewartsville, N.J., 1995-99; pres. Greenwich Twp. Parent Tchr. Orgn., 1989-92, Parents On Site, 1994-96. Mem.: MLA, NJ Coun. Tchrs. English, Nat. Coun. Tchrs. English, Drew U. Alumni Assn., Middlebury Coll. Alumni Assn., U. Mass. Alumni Assn. Republican. Avocations: walking, biking, crafts. Home: 113 Kennedy Mill Rd Stewartsville NJ 08886

BUSCH, BRITON COOPER, historian, educator; b. LA, Sept. 5, 1936; s. Niven and Phyllis (Cooper) B.; m. Deborah B. Stone, Aug. 16, 1958 (div. 1984); children: Philip Briton, Leslie Cooper; m. S. Jill Harsin, June 4, 1985. AB, Stanford U., 1958; MA, U. Calif. at Berkeley, 1960, PhD, 1965. Instr. Colgate U., 1963-65, asst. prof. history, 1965-68, assoc. prof. history, 1968-73, prof., 1973-78, William R. Kenan, Jr. prof., 1978—2003, dept. chmn., 1980-85, dir. div. social scis., 1985-91, William R. Kenen Jr. prof. emeritus, 2003—. Mem. coun. Internat. Commn. of Maritime History, 1996-2000. Author: Britain and the Persian Gulf, 1894-1914, 1967, Britain, India and the Arabs 1914-1921, 1971, Mudros to Lausanne: Britains Frontier in West Asia 1918-1923, 1976, Master of Desolation: The Reminiscences of Capt. Joseph J. Fuller, 1980, Hardinge of Penshurst: A Study in The Old Diplomacy, 1980, Alta California 1840-1842: The Journal and Observations of William Dane Phelps, Master of the Ship Alert, 1983; The War Against the Seals: A History of the North American Seal Fishery, 1985; Fremont's Private Navy: the 1846 Journal of Capt. W.D. Phelps, 1987, Whaling Will Never Do For Me: The American Whaleman in the 19th Century, 1994, (with B.M. Gough) Fur Traders From New England: The Boston Men, 1787-1800, 1996; editor: Canada and the Great War: Western Front Association Papers, 2003; book rev. editor Am. Neptune, 1991-2003. Woodrow Wilson fellow, 1963; Nat. Endowment for the Humanities fellow, 1967-68; Social Sci. Research Council fellow, 1968-69 Mem. Am. Hist. Assn., Royal Soc. Asian Affairs, Mid. East Inst., Mid. East Studies Assn., Western Front Assn., Soc. Mil. History (book prize com. 1996-98, chair 1998-2000), N.Am. Soc. Oceanic History (exec. coun. 1983-88, v.p. 1988-91, pres. 1991-92, 95-98, chmn. book award com. 1987-92, book prize 1984, 86, 94, 97). Home: PO Box 154 Hamilton NY 13346-0154 Office: Colgate U Dept History 13 Oak Dr Hamilton NY 13346-1383

BUSCH, DANIEL ADOLPH, geologist, educator; b. St. Paul, May 31, 1912; s. Karl George Adolph and Lulu Elizabeth Busch; m. Emilie Louise Finch; children: Daniel Andrew(dec.), David Arthur. BSc, Capital U., 1934; MA, Ohio State U., 1936, PhD, 1939; DSc (hon.), Capital U., 1960. Instr. U. Pitts., 1938—42; with Pa. Geol. Survey, Pitts., 1943—44, Huntley & Huntley Petroleum Cons., Pitts., 1944—46; sr. rsch. geologist Carter Rsch. Lab., Tulsa, Okla., 1946—51; chief geologist Zephyr Petroleum Co., Tulsa, Okla., 1951—54; petroleum geology cons. Tulsa, Okla., 1955—89; ret., 1989. Vis. prof. geology U. Okla., Norman, 1964—74; lectr. Oil & Gas Cons., Internat., Tulsa, 1967—89; lectr. in field; cons. in field. Author: (book) Stratigraphic Traps in Sandstones - Exploration Techniques, 1974 (Robert Dott Best Publ. award, 1975), Exploration Methods for Sandstone Reservoirs, 1985. Fellow: Geol. Soc. Am. (sr.); mem.; Am. Assn. Petroleum Geologists (hon.; v.p. 1966—67, pres. 1973—74, Matson award 1959, Leverson award 1971, Sidney Powers medal 1982, Monroe Cheney award 2003, Am. Registry of Outstanding Profls. 2003—), Sigma Xi. Avocations: travel, gardening, investments. Home: 3757 S Wheeling Ave Tulsa OK 74105

BUSCH, DAVID FREDERICK, internist; b. Chgo., Apr. 12, 1943; s. Albert E. and Vera Ellman Busch; m. Cathy Lynne Anderson, Sept. 16, 1984; 1 child, Bailey Anderson. AB, Stanford U., 1964; MD, U. Chgo., 1968. Diplomate Am. Bd. Internal Medicine with subspecialty in infectious diseases, lic. physician Calif. Med. resident U. Cin. Hosp., 1968—70, 1972—73; infectious diseases fellow VA Hosp. Wadsworth, L.A., 1973—75; staff physician, asst. prof. VA Hosp. Wadsworth/UCLA, 1975—77; infectious diseases cons. San Francisco, 1977—; internal medicine resident program dir., assoc. dir. Children's Hosp./Calif. Pacific Med. Ctr., San Francisco, 1982—2002; chief infectious diseases divsn. Calif. Pacific Med. Ctr., 1999—, chmn. instl. rev. bd., 2002—. Mem. editl. bd. Clin. Infectious Diseases, 1997—2000. Lt. comdr. Med. Corps USN, 1970—72. Fellow: Infectious Diseases Soc. Am. (chmn. bd. state/regional chpt. 1994—96, prin. investigator, bd. dirs. Emerging Infections Network 1996—), ACP; mem.: Am. Soc. Microbiology. Office: Infectious Diseases Assoc Med Group 2100 Webster St #404 San Francisco CA 94115

BUSCH, FREDERICK MATTHEW, writer, literature educator; b. N.Y.C., Aug. 1, 1941; s. Benjamin and Phyllis (Schnell) B.; m. Judith Burroughs, Nov. 29, 1963; children: Benjamin, Nicholas. BA, Muhlenberg Coll., Allentown, Pa., 1962, LittD (hon.), 1980; MA, Columbia U., 1967. Writer for mags., N.Y.C., and Greenwich, Conn., 1966—; from instr. to prof. Colgate U., Hamilton, N.Y., 1966-87, Fairchild prof. lit., 1987—2003, writer in residence, 2003—. Acting dir. Program in Creative Writing U. Iowa, Iowa City, 1978-79. Author: 25 books including Sometimes I Live in the Country, 1986, Absent Friends, 1989, Harry and Catherine, 1990, Closing Arguments, 1991, Long Way From Home, 1993, The Children in the Woods: New and Selected Stories, 1994 (PEN/Faulkner award nomination, 1995), Girls, 1997, (essays) A Dangerous Profession, 1998, (novel) The Night Inspector, 1999 (PEN/Faulkner award nomination, NBCC award nomination, 2000); editor: (anthology) Letters to a Fiction Writer, 1997, (stories) Don't Tell Anyone, 2000, A Memory of War, 2003; numerous other essays and short stories. Recipient Nat. Jewish Book award for fiction, Jewish Book Coun., 1986, Fiction award, AAAL, 1986, PEN/Malamud, 1991, Award of Merit, AAAL, 2001; fellow, Guggenheim Found., 1981—82, Ingram Merrill Found., 1981—82. Mem.: AAAS, PEN, Am. Acad. Arts & Scis., Authors Guild Am., Writers Guild Am.

BUSCH, JOHN ARTHUR, lawyer; b. Indpls., Mar. 23, 1951; s. John L. and Betty (Thomas) B.; m. Barbara Ann Holt, June 23, 1973; children: Abigail, Elizabeth, Amanda, Rachel. BA, Wabash Coll., 1973; JD, Duke U., 1976. Bar: Wis. 1976, U.S. Dist. Ct. (ea. we. dists.) Wis., U.S. Ct. Appeals (5th and 7th cirs.) 1976. Assoc. Michael, Best & Friedrich, Milw., 1976-83, ptnr., 1983—; chmn. litigation dept. Michael Best & Friedrich, Milw., 1990-95, mgmt. com., 1995-2001, mng. ptnr. Milw. office, 2003—. Mem. ad hoc com. on alternative dispute resolution Milw. Cir. Ct., ad hoc com. on multidisciplinary practices State Bar, mem. bd. govs., 2001—. Treas. North Shore Rep. Club, Milw., 1984-85, vice chmn., 1985-86, chmn., 1987-89; del. Rep. State Conv., Milw., 1986; mem. local rules adv. com. Ea. dist., Wis.; mem. com. Fed. Bench Bar. Master Am. Inns of Ct.; mem. ABA, Wis. Bar Assn. (v.p. edn1. devel. 2002—), Milw. Bar Assn. Home: 1025 E Lyon St Milwaukee WI 53202 Office: Michael Best & Friedrich 100 E Wisconsin Ave Ste 3300 Milwaukee WI 53202-4108 E-mail: jabusch@mbf-law.com.

BUSCH, JOYCE IDA, small business owner; b. Madera, Calif., Jan. 24, 1934; d. Bruno Harry and Ella Fae (Absher) Toschi; m. Fred O. Busch, Dec. 14, 1956; children: Karen, Kathryn, Kurt. BA in Indsl. Arts & Interior Design, Calif. State U., Fresno, 1991. Cert. interior designer, Calif. Stewardess United Air Lines, San Francisco, 1955-57; prin. Art Coordinates, Fresno, 1982—, Busch Interior Design, Fresno, 1982—. Art cons. Fresno Community Hosp., 1981-83; docent Fresno Met. Mus., 1981-84. Treas. Valley Children's Hosp. Guidance Clinic, 1975-79, Lone Star PTA, 1965-84,; mem. Mothers Guild San Joaquin Mem. H.S., 1984-88. Mem. Am. Soc. Interior Designers. Clubs: Sunnyside Garden (pres. 1987-88). Republican. Roman Catholic. Avocations: gardening, art history.

BUSCH, KURT, race car driver; b. Las Vegas, Nev., Aug. 4, 1978; s. Tom and Gaye Busch. Race car driver Roush Racing, Concord, NC. Named NASCAR Hobby Stock Rookie of Yr., Champion, 1996, Featherlite S.W. Series Rookie of the Yr., 1998, Featherlite S.W. Series Champion, 1999, Craftsman Truck Series Rookie of the Yr., 2d in points, 2000. Office: Roush Racing 7050 Aviation Blvd Concord NC 28027-8196

BUSCH, KYLE, counseling administrator; b. Erie, Pa., Apr. 4, 1960; AS in Bus. Adminstrn., Behrend Coll., 1982; BS in Econs. (hon.), Edinboro U., 1987; MS in Counseling Psychology, Gannon U., 1992. Cert. secondary sch. counselor, rehab. counselor. Author: (Book) Drive the Best for the Price ..., 2000.

BUSCH, LAWRENCE MICHAEL, sociologist, researcher; b. N.Y.C., Mar. 27, 1945; s. Raymond and Carol Cecilia (Lewis) B.; Karen V. Hagberg, Dec. 30, 1966; children: Lisa Marion, Rachel Valaria. BA, Hofstra U., 1965; MS, Cornell U., 1972, PhD, 1974. Asst. prof. sociology U. Ky., Lexington, 1974-79, assoc. prof., 1979-85, prof., 1985-90, Mich. State U., 1990-96, univ. disting. prof., 1997—. Cons. U.S. AID, Washington, 1978—; mem. sci. adv. bd. CIRAD (French Fgn. Aid Agy.), 1990-96. Co-author: Science, Agriculture Politics of Research, 1983, Food Security in the U.S., 1984, The Agricultural Scientific Enterprise, 1986, Plants, Power, and Profit, 1991, Making Nature, Shaping Culture: Plant, Biodiversity in Global Context, 1995, The Eclipse of Morality, 2000; editor: Science and Agricultural Development, 1981. Grantee NEH, 1981, NSF, 1982, 86, 92, 96, 98, 2001, USDA, 1985, 87, 94, USAID, 2001, 02; recipient Chevalier de l'Ordre du Merite Agricole, French Govt., 2001—. Fellow AAAS; mem. Rural Sociol. Soc. (pres. 1997-98), Am. Sociol. Assn., Soc. for Food, Agr. and Human Values (pres. 1989-90). Office: Mich State U Dept Sociology East Lansing MI 48824

BUSCH, MICHAEL, state legislator; b. Balt., Jan. 4, 1947; BS, Temple U., 1970. Tchr., coach St. Mary's H.S., 1973-79; adminstr. youth athletics Anne Arundel County, Md., 1979—; del. dist. 30 Md. State Delegation, 1987—, ho. spkr., 2003—, mem. judiciary com., 1987-91, dep. majority whip, 1993, chmn. econ. matters com., 1994—, mem. legis. policy com., 1994—, mem. rules and exec. nominations com., 1994—. Joint oversight com. on state employees health ins., 1994; mem. environtl. assessment subcom., 1995, gov.'s task force on cmty. health networks, 1994; joint oversight com. on state econ. devel. inititatives, co-chmn. 1995; join com. on health care delivery and financing, 1995, house chmn.; spl. joint house com. on competitive taxation and econ. devel., 1996. Chmn. Anne Arundel County Delegation, 1992-93; mem. St. Mary's Sch. Bd., 1992—; bd. trustees The Md. Hist. Trust, 1995. Named Coach of the Yr., 1978, Man of Yr., Anne arundel County Lacrosse Assn., 1982, Legislator of Yr., Anne Arundel County Nurses assn., 1989; recipient Presdl. Citation, Md. Recreation and Parks Assn., 1989. Office: State House H 101 Annapolis MD 21401*

BUSCH, MILDRED MOORMAN, music educator; b. Dallas, Jan. 8, 1920; d. Cull Cade Moorman and Lila Love; m. Theodore Norman Busch, June 3, 1946 (div. 1954); 1 child, Kathryn Anne Busch Garcia. MusB, BA, Baylor U., 1940; MA, West Tex. A&M U., 1954. Cert. piano and music theory. Head piano dept. San Marcos (Tex.) Acad., 1940—41; tchg. fellow in piano Baylor U., 1942—43; piano instr. Conservatory of Musical Arts, Amarillo, Tex., 1943—52; freelance piano instr. Amarillo, 1952—54; pub. rels. Betty Smith Assoc., NYC, 1954—55; freelance piano instr. Amarillo, 1955—. Composer piano teaching pieces. Vol. N.W. Tex. Hosp., Amarillo, USO, Amarillo; pianist Amarillo Little Theatre; vol. Meals on Wheels, Amarillo. Mem.: Amarillo Music Tchrs. Assn., Friends of Planned Parenthood (life), Magna Charta Dames and Barons. Presbyterian. Avocations: doll collecting, cats, charity work, church activities. Home and Office: 6717 Adirondack Trail Amarillo TX 79106

BUSCH, NANCY ELIZABETH, artist, educator; b. Manitowoc, Wis., Sept. 7, 1944; d. Edgar Wilhelm and Dorothy Janette (Blust) Putz; m. Charles Nels Busch, Aug. 21, 1965; 1 son, Alexander. BA in Journalism, U. Mich., 1966; student, Birmingham Bloomfield Art Assn, 1978-88, Ctr. for Creative Studies, 1985; postgrad., U. Mich., 1987-88; MFA, Wayne State U., 1990. Sales rep. Grosse Pointe News, Mich., 1966-68; pres. Nels Advt. Co., Birmingham, Mich., 1968-75, Busch & Morris, Birmingham, 1975-80, Busch & Assocs., Birmingham, 1980-88; prof. Instituto Federico Brandt, Caracas, Venezuela, 1991-93; artist, tchr. MFA program U. Vt., 2003. Cons. U. Mich. Devel. Bd., Ann Arbor, 1973-80. One-woman shows include Wayne State U., Mich., 1990, Sala Mendoza, Caracas, 1991, 93, Galeria Diners, Bogota, 1993-94, Galeria Ruth Benzacar, Buenos Aires, 1996, Centro Cultural Borges, Buenos Aires, 1996, Joseph Borges Museo, Caracas, Venezuela, 1998; group shows include Creative Arts Ctr., Pontiac, Mich., 1990, Wayne State U., Mich., 1990, Willis Gallery, Detroit, 1990; pvt. collections include Aco Corp. Collection, Caracas, Univ. de los Andes, Bogota, Columbia, Museo de Arte Contemporaneo, Bogota. Recipient award of Excellence Nat. Pub. Rels. Soc. am., 1975-80, Design award Internat. Graphics, 1980. Mem. Econs. Club of Detroit, Adcraft Club of Detroit, Am. Mktg. Assn., Southeastern Mich. Hosp. Assn. (awards for concept and creative devel. in reports, brochures and other collateral materials 1975-80), Am. Hosp. Assn., Mich. Hosp. Assn. (awards for reports, brochures and othe materials 1975-80).

BUSCHANG, PETER HEINZ, dental educator; b. Cologne, Germany, June 23, 1951; s. Heinz G. Buschang and Ellen Pfendt; m. Joyce A. Hayne, July 17, 1972; children: Nicholas, Rebecca, Emily. BA, U. Tex., 1976, MA, 1978, PhD, 1980. Rsch. assoc. U. Montreal, Que., Canada, 1983-88; prof. Baylor Coll. Dentistry Tex. A&M U. Sys., 1988—. Postdoctoral fellow U. Conn. Health Scis. Ctr., Farmington, 1980-83. Contbr. over 100 articles to profl. jours., chpts. to books. With U.S. Army, 1969-72. Decorated Army Commendation medal. Mem. Am. Assn. Physical Anthropology, Internat. Assn. Dental Rsch., Human Biology Coun. (assoc. editor 1988—), Phi Beta Kappa, Phi Kappa Phi. Home: 615 Willowbrook Cir Duncanville TX 75116 Office: Dept Orthodontics 3302 Gaston Ave Dallas TX 75246 E-mail: jabuschang@msn.com., phbuschang@tambcd.edu.

BUSCHBACH, THOMAS CHARLES, geologist, consultant; b. Cicero, Ill., May 12, 1923; s. Thomas Dominick and Vivian (Smiley) B.; m. Mildred Merle Fletcher, Nov. 26, 1947; children— Thomas Richard, Susan Kay, Deborah Lynn BS, U. Ill., 1950, MS, 1951, PhD, 1959. Geologist, structural geology, stratigraphy, underground storage of natural gas Ill. Geol. Survey, 1951-78; coordinator New Madrid Seismotectonic Study, U.S. Nuclear Regulatory Commn., 1976-85; research prof. geology St. Louis U., 1978 85; geologic cons. Champaign, Ill., 1985—. Served to lt. comdr. USNR, 1942-47 Fellow Geol. Soc. Am. Home: 604 Park Lane Dr Champaign IL 61820-7631 Office: PO Box 1608 Champaign IL 61824-1608 E-mail: tcbusch@aol.com.

BUSCHE, ROBERT MARION, chemical engineer, consultant; b. St. Louis, June 14, 1926; s. Ferdinand and Irma (Seim) B.; m. Norma Jean Nickles, Sept. 17, 1950 (div. Mar. 1978); children: Robert Eric, David Clay, Kristin Anne, Amy Ellen; m. Emma Elizabeth Ruch, June 21, 1980. BSChE, Washington U., St. Louis, 1948, MSChE, 1949, DSc in Chem. Engring., 1952. Project engr. coal-to-oil demonstration br. U.S. Bur. Mines, Louisiana, Mo., 1950-53; rsch. supr. plastics dept. rsch. divsn. E.I. DuPont de Nemours & Co. Inc., 1953-62, tech. svcs. supr. plastics dept. mktg. divsn., 1962-64, tech. mgr. devel. dept. heat transfer products divsn., 1964-68, staff cons. devel. dept. mgmt. svcs. divsn., 1968-74, planning cons. cen. rsch. dept. life scis. divsn., 1974-85; pres. Bio En-Gene-Er Assocs. Inc., Wilmington, 1985—. Adj. prof. chem. engring. U. Pa., Phila., 1983—; adv. bd. Nat. Solar Energy Plan, Mitre Corp., Washington, 1980-85; adv. bd. liaison com. Forest Products Lab., Madison, Wis.; adv. bd. NSF cellulose hydrolysis program N.C. State U., Raleigh, 1980-82. Contbr. articles to profl. jours. Deacon, elder Presbyn. ch., Wilmington and Orange, Tex., 1957—; dist. and coun. mem. Delmarva coun. Boy Scouts Am., Wilmington, 1959—; bd. dirs. New Castle Cotillion, Wilmington, 1989-91. With U.S. Army, 1944-46. Heerman's fellow Washington U., 1948, Honor scholar, 1943; recipient Order of Merit award Del-Mar-Va coun. Boy Scouts Am., 1970, Silver Beaver award, 1974, Wood Badge award, 1974, God and Svc. award, 1998. Mem. AIChE, Am. Chem. Soc., Am. Mensa, Intertel, Tau Beta Pi, Tau Kappa Epsilon, Alpha Chi Sigma, Alpha Phi Omega, Phi Eta Sigma. Republican. Home and Office: 533 Rothbury Rd Wilmington DE 19803-2439 E-mail: rmbusche@aol.com.

BUSCHKE, HERMAN, neurologist; b. Berlin, Oct. 15, 1932; came to U.S., 1934, naturalized, 1945; s. Franz Julius and Ruth Helen (Minkowski) B.; children: Thomas, Katherine; m. Bertelle Selig, 1993. BA, Reed Coll., 1954; MD, Western Res. U., 1958. Diplomate: Am. Bd. Psychiatry and Neurology. Intern Bronx (N.Y.) Mcpl. Hosp. Center, 1958-59, resident in neurology, 1959-62; asst. instr. neurology Albert Einstein Coll. Medicine, Bronx, N.Y., 1961-62, asso. prof., 1969-74, prof., 1974—, prof. neurosci., 1974—; practice medicine specializing in neurology Bronx, N.Y., 1969—. Staff mem., attending neurologist Hosp. of Albert Einstein Coll. of Medicine; instr. medicine Stanford U., 1962-63, asst. prof., 1963-69 Named Lena and Joseph Gluck Disting. Scholar in Neurology, 1973. Office: Albert Einstein Coll Medicine Saul R Korey Dept Neurology 1300 Morris Park Ave Bronx NY 10461-1926 E-mail: buschke@aecom.yu.edu.

BUSCHMANN, SIEGFRIED, manufacturing executive; b. Essen, Germany, July 12, 1937; s. Walter and Frieda Maria (von. Stamm) B.; m. Rita Renate Moch, May 7, 1965; children: Verena, Mark. Diploma, Wilhelms U. Various exec. positions Thyssen AG, Duesseldorf, Germany, 1964-82; pres. Thyssen Holding Corp., Troy, Mich., 1982-99; chmn. ThyssenKrupp USA, Inc., 1999—; sr. v.p. The Budd Co., Troy, 1982-83, sr. v.p., CFO, 1983-86, vice chmn., CFO, 1986 89, chmn., CEO, 1989—2001, chmn. bd., 2001—02. Chmn. exec. bd. Thyssen Budd Automotive GmbH, Essen, Germany, 1997—99; v.chmn., exec. bd. Thyssen Krupp Automotive AG, Bochum, Germany, 1999—2001, mem. supervisory bd., 2001—. Avocation: golf. Office: Thyssenkrupp USA Inc PO Box 5084 3155 W Big Beaver Rd Troy MI 48007-5084

BUSCH-VISHNIAC, ILENE JOY, mechanical engineering educator, researcher; b. Phila., Jan. 28, 1955; d. Leonard and Ruth (Rudnick) Busch; m. Ethan Tecumseh Vishniac, June 13, 1976; children: Cady Anne, Miriam Rachel. BA in Math. magna cum laude, BS in Physics magna cum laude, U. Rochester, 1976; MSME, MIT, 1978, PhD in Mech. Engrng., 1981. Mem. tech. staff acoustics rsch. dept. Bell Labs., 1980-82; asst. prof. mech. engrng. U. Tex., Austin, 1982 86, assoc. prof., 1986-91, prof., assoc. chmn. mech. engrng. for acad. affairs, 1991-95, Harry H. Power prof., 1994-98; dean Whiting Sch. of Engrng. Johns Hopkins U., 1998—. Cons. AT&T Bell Labs., 1982-84, Nat. Inst. Justice, 1988, Body, Vickers, Daniels, 1989-93, to Tex. atty. gen., 1989-95; also others; mem. vis. com. dept. mech. engrng. MIT, 1993-99; presdl. young investigator NSF, 1985; numerous presentations to profl. soc. mtgs., workships, confs.; numerous invited lectures; chmn. session on micro-automation, sensing and hardware issues Internat. Symposium on Robotics and Mfg., 1992, mem. mfg. program com., 1994; numerous others. Author: Electromechanical Sensors and Actuators, 1999; contbg. author: Handbook of Acoustics, 1992; contbr. numerous articles to sci. jours. Program mentor YWCA, 1989; speaker Tex. Energy Sci. Symposium for H.S.'s, 1989, Austin Sci. Acad., 1989, 90; speaker, session chmn. Expanding Your Horizons Workshop, 1991. Recipient Curtis McGraw rsch. award Am. Soc. for Engrng. Edn., 1994, best paper award in mfg. Internat. Symposium on Robotics and Mfg., 1994; fellow Fannie and John Hertz Found., MIT, 1976-80, GM Found. Centennial tchg. fellow in mech. engrng., 1985; grantee NSF, 1983—, Univ. Rsch. Inst., 1983-85, U. Tex. Bur. Engrng. Rsch., 1983-85, Office Naval Rsch., 1985-87, Bosque Found., 1986-88, Semicondr. Rsch. Corp., 1987-90, GM, 1988-89, Tex. Instruments, 1989, Tex. Dept. Transp., 1994—; others. Fellow Acoustical Soc. Am. (v.p. 1997-98, tech. com. on engrng. acoustics 1982—, tech. com. on noise 1982—, exec. com. 1988-91, com. on status of women in the Soc. 1992—, chmn. Austin chpt. 1986, nominating com. 1989, Lindsay award 1987); mem. ASME (micro-mech. sys. panel dynamic sys. and control div. 1992—, Outstanding Mech. Engrng. Faculty Advisor award 1983), Inst. Noise Control Engrng. (assoc.), Soc. Women Engrs. (achievement award 1997), AAUW, Golden Key, Phi Beta Kappa. Achievements include patent on electret transducer with a selectively metallized backplate, with a variably charged electret foil, with a variable electret foil thickness, with a variable effective air gap, with a variable actual air gap; integrated capacitive microphone, electret transducer for blood pressure monitoring, six degree-of-freedom optical sensor. Office: Johns Hopkins U NEB 120 3400 N Charles St Baltimore MD 21218-2680 E-mail: ilenebv@jhu.edu.

BUSDICKER, GORDON G. retired lawyer; b. Winona, Minn., Oct. 12, 1933; s. Harry John and Edna Mae (Rogers) B.; m. Noreen Decker; children— Karla E., Pamela J., Alison G., Neal A. BA, Hamline U., St. Paul, 1955; JD, Harvard U., 1958. Bar: Minn. Atty. Aluminum Co. of Am., Pitts., 1958-61; assoc. Faegre & Benson, Mpls., 1961-67, ptnr., 1967-99, ret., 1999. Trustee Hamline U., St. Paul, 1973— Mem. ABA, Minn. Bar Assn., Interlachen Golf Club. Republican. Congregationalist. Avocations: boating, geanealogy. Home: 3833 Abbott Ave S Minneapolis MN 55410-1036 E-mail: busdick1@mn.rr.com.

BUSECK, PETER R. geochemistry educator; s. Paul M. and Edith G. (Stern) Buseck; m. Alice E. Bien, June 20, 1960; children: Lori, David, Susan, Paul. AB, Antioch Coll., 1957; MA, Columbia U., 1959, PhD, 1962. Fellow Geophys. Lab. Carnegie Inst., Washington, 1961-63; mem. faculty depts. chemistry and geology Ariz. State U., Tempe, 1963—, Regents' prof., 1989—. Vis. prof. geology Oxford (Eng.) U., 1970-71, Stanford (Calif.) U., 1979-80, U. Paris, 1986-87; spl. asst. to dir. NSF, 1994-95; mem. sci. staff Office of Sci. and Tech. Policy, White House, 1994-95, vis. scholar, Dept. Earth & Planetary Scis., Harvard U., 2001-2. Contbr. articles to profl. jours. Fellow, NSF, 1970—71. Fellow AAAS, Geol. Soc. Am., Meteorite Soc., Mineral Soc. Am.; mem. Am. Geophys. Union, Geochem. Soc., Microbeam Soc., Can. Mineral Soc., Microscope Soc. Am., Am. Crystallographic Assn. Office: Ariz State U Dept Geol Scis Tempe AZ 85287-1404 E-mail: pbuseck@asu.edu.

BUSELMEIER, BERNARD JOSEPH, insurance company executive; b. Detroit, Feb. 10, 1956; s. Bernard August and Rita Mathilda (Cook) Buselmier; m. Carolyn Diane Karamon, Mar. 22, 2003; 1 child, Andrew Joseph. BBA in Acctg., U. Detroit, 1980, MBA, 1990. Various fin. positions ins. group Auto Club Mich., Dearborn, Mich., 1974-81; various fin. positions Motors Ins. Corp., Detroit, 1981-89, treas., 1989-98, v.p., treas., 1993-98; exec. v.p., CFO, Integon Corp., Winston-Salem, N.C., 1998-99; CFO GMAC Ins. Personal Lines, St. Louis, 1999—. Office: GMAC Ins Personal Lines One GMAC Insurance Plaza Earth City MO 63045

BUSELT, CLARA IRENE, religious organization administrator; b. Detroit, Jan. 30, 1921; d. Andrew and Bernice (Marcian) Kochanowski; m. Michael Leo Buselt, Apr. 18, 1940; children: Edwin, Nancy, Robert, John, Jane. Student, MacGregor Beauty Coll., Kansas City, 1939. Cosmetician various beauty shops, Leavenworth, 1940-45; surp. dir. Sch. Lunch Program Sacred Heart Cafeteria, Immaculata High, Leavenworth, 1957-68; dietetic worker VA Med. Ctr., Leavenworth, 1968-81; office clk. Storage Box Inc., Leavenworth, 1987—. Sr. Times corr., photographer Leavenworth Times, 1990—. Photographer (contest) Congress Americas, 1986. Mem. Sr. Coun. Park and Recreation, Leavenworth, 1988, Sr. Citizen Inc. Kitchen Band, 1993—. Recipient Gov. and First Lady Vol. award Gov. of Kans., 1990, Sr. Citizen of Yr. award Leavenworth County Coun. on Aging, 1994, Sr. Citizen award Am. Assn. Ret. Persons, 1995; named Silver Haired Legislator Leavenworth County, 1993. Mem. Am. Assn. Ret. Persons (recording sec. 1995-96, v.p. 2000-02, chair 2002-03, pres. 2002—), Women's Div. C. of C., Parish Council Sacred Heart Ch., Sacred Heart Alter Soc. (pres. 1977-87), Am. War Mothers (state pres. 1983-85, nat. color bearer 1985-87, nat. chaplain 1987-89), Cath. Literary Club (pres. 1983-85), Sch. Food Svc. Assn. (charter pres. 1958), St. John Hosp. Guild (pres. 1975-76), Loyal Christian Benefit Assn. (br. pres. 1977-88, nat. trustee 1981—), Daughters Isabella, Arch Diocese Coun. (pres. 1981-83), Nat. Assn. Ret. Fed. Employees, Loyal Christian Benefit Assn. (br. pres. 1977—), Leavenworth County Coun. Aging (chair adv. coun. aging), Wyandotte/Leavenworth Area Agy. in Aging (chair adv. coun. 2002), Ret. Eagles Activity Club (v.p. 1991-93, pres. 1993—). Avocations: volunteer work, sewing, photography, tap dancing, ballroom dancing. Home: 1413 S 16th St Leavenworth KS 66048-2914 *In my lifetime I have found that you must place your trust in God, and have a positive attitude; there is good in every person, but sometimes someone has to bring it out.*

BUSER, CAROLYN ELIZABETH, correctional education administrator; b. St. Paul, June 14, 1946; d. Jerome Alfred and Ella Caroline (Anderson) B.; m. Richard John Ward, Sept. 17, 1977; children: John Jerome Buser Ward, Carl Alfred Buser Ward. BA in English, Carleton Coll., 1968; MS in Spl. Edn., U. Md., 1985, PhD in Ednl. Policy and Adminstrn., 1996. Correctional tchr. Md. Div. Correction, Hughesville, 1970-74, Balt., 1974-76; correctional edn. supr. Md. Dept. Edn. Md. Penitentiary, Balt., 1976-80, Md. Correctional Instn., Jessup, 1980-88; correctional edn. supr. Md. Dept. Edn., Md. correctional pre-release program Md. Correctional Instn. for Women, Jessup, 1988-94; field coord. correctional edn. Md. Dept. Edn., 1994-2001, dir. correctional edn., 2001—. Cons. Am. Correctional Assn., Laurel, Md., 1980; Md. state dir. Correctional Edn. Assn., Laurel, 1988-90; program supr. Prison Literacy, Nat. Inst. Corrections, Washington (designated exemplary program, 1986), mem. editl. rev. bd. Jour. Correctional Edn., 2002—. Mem. editl. rev. bd. Jour. Correctional Edn., 2002—. Fellow Edn. Behaviorally Disorded Students, U. Md., 1985. Mem.: Md. Assn. Adult Cmty. and Continuing Edn., Correctional Edn. Assn. (sec. 1986, edit. bd. Jour. Correctional Edn. 2002—), Phi Kappa Phi. Office: Md State Dept Edn 200 W Baltimore St Ste 1 Baltimore MD 21201-2595 E-mail: cbuser@msde.state.md.us.

BUSEY, ROXANE C. lawyer; b. Chgo., June 15, 1949; BA cum laude, Miami U., 1970; MAT, Northwestern U., 1971, JD, 1975. Bar: Ill. 1975. Ptnr. Gardner, Carton & Douglas, Chgo. Mem. ABA (chair health com., antitrust sect. 1989-92, antitrust sect. coun. 1992-95, officer 1995-2003, chmn. antitrust sect. 2001-2002), Ill. State Bar Assn. (chair antitrust coun. 1984-85), Chgo. Bar Assn. (chair antitrust sect. 1990-91). Office: Gardner Carton & Douglas LLP 191 N Wacker Ste 3000 Chicago IL 60606 E-mail: rbusey@gcd.com.

BUSFIELD, ROGER MELVIL, JR., retired trade association executive, educator; b. Ft. Worth, Feb. 4, 1926; s. Roger Melvil and Julia Mabel (Clark) B.; m. Jean Wilson, Mar. 26, 1948 (div. Oct. 1960); children: Terry Jean, Roger Melvil III, Timothy Clark; m. Virginia Bailey, Dec. 1, 1962 (dec. July 1991); 1 child, Julia Lucille; m. Addie Howard Davis, June 17, 1995. Student, U. Tex., 1943, 46; BA, Southwestern U., 1947, MA, 1948; PhD, Fla. State U., 1954. Asst. prof. Southwestern U., 1947-49; instr. U. Ala., 1949-50, Fla. State U., 1950-54; asst. prof. speech Mich. State U., 1954-60; editl. svcs. specialist Oldsmobile divsn. Gen. Motors Corp., Lansing, Mich., 1960; gen. publs. supr. Consumers Power Co., Jackson, Mich., 1960-61; assoc. dir. Mich. Hosp. Assn., Lansing, 1961-73; exec. dir. Ark. Hosp. Assn., Little Rock, 1973-81, pres., 1981-94, pres. emeritus, 1994—. Adj. prof. health svcs. mgmt. Webster U., 1979-97. Author: The Playwright's Art, 1958, Arabic transl., 1964, (with others) The Children's Theatre, 1960; editor Theatre Arts Bibliography, 1964; contbr. articles to profl. jours.; author profl. motion picture scenarios. Trustee Ctrl. Mich. U., 1967-73, chmn., 1970; mem. Mich. Gov.'s Commn. on Higher Edn., 1972-74; mem. Ark. Gov.'s Emergency Med. Svcs. Adv. Coun., 1975-94, chmn., 1978-84; mem. Ark. Gov.'s Task Force on Rural Hosps., 1988-89, Ark. Dept. of Health Long Range Planning Com., 1988-89; chmn. AIDS adv. com. Ark. Dept. Health, 1990-97; mem. Ark. Gov.'s Task Force Health Care Reform, 1993-96; chmn. Health Data Task Force, Ark. Resources Comm., 1994-95; mem. adv. bd. Ark. Pediat. Facility, 1995-96. Served with USMC, 1943-46. Named Tex. Outstanding Author, Theta Sigma Phi, 1958; recipient Disting. Alumnus award Southwestern U., 1971, Senate-House Concurrent Resolution of Tribute, Mich. Legis., 1973, Bd. Trustees award Am. Hosp. Assn., 1994, Merit award Ark. Hosp. Assn., 1994. Mem. Am. Soc. Assn. Execs., Ark. Soc. Assn. Execs. (pres. 1981-82), Pub. Rels. Assn. Mich. (pres. 1966), Speech Comm. Assn., Am. Coll. Health Care Execs., State Hosp. Assn. Exec. Forum (sec., treas. 1989, pres. 1991), Am. Hosp. Assn. (coun. legis. 1975-77, coun. allied and govtl. rels. 1983-86), San Gabriel Writers League (pres. 2000-01), Rotary (Little Rock). Methodist. Home: PO Box 2267 Georgetown TX 78627-2267 E-mail: areembee@aol.com.

BUSH, BARBARA PIERCE, former First Lady of the United States, volunteer; b. Rye, N.Y., June 8, 1925; d. Marvin and Pauline (Robinson) Pierce; m. George Herbert Walker Bush, Jan. 6, 1945; children: George Walker, John Ellis, Neil Mallon, Marvin Pierce, Dorothy Walker. Student, Smith Coll., 1943-44; hon. degrees, Stritch Coll., Milw., 1981, Mt. Vernon Coll., Washington, 1981, Hood Coll., Frederick, Md., 1983, Howard U., Washington, 1987, Judson Coll., Marion, Ala., 1988, Bennett Coll., Greensboro, N.C., 1989, Smith Coll., 1989, Morehouse Sch. Medicine, 1989. Oper. & facilities div. Dept. Administration, Washington, 1992; with Office of George Bush, Washington, 1992—. Author: C. Fred Story; Millie's Book; Barbara Bush: A Memoir, 1994. Hon. chair adv. bd. Reading is Fundamental; hon. mem. Bus. Coun. for Effective Literacy; mem. adv. coun. Soc. of Meml. Sloan-Kettering Cancer Ctr.; hon. mem. bd. dirs. Children's Oncology Svcs. of Met. Washington, The Washington Home, The Kingsbury Ctr.; hon. chmn. nat. adv. coun. Literacy Vols. of Am., Nat. Sch. Vols. Program; sponsor Laubach Literacy Internat.; nat. hon. chmn. Leukemia Soc. of Am.; hon. mem. bd. trustees Morehouse Sch. of Medicine; hon. nat. chmn. Nat. Organ Donor Awareness Week, 1982-86; pres. Ladies of the Senate, 1981-88; mem. women's com. Smithsonian Assocs., Tex. Fedn. of Rep. Women, life mem., hon. mem.; hon. chairperson for the Nat. Com. on Literacy and Edn. United Way, Barbara Bush Found. for Family Literacy, 1989-, Washington Parent Group Fund, Girls Clubs of Am., 10th anniversay Harvest Nat. Food Bank Network; hon. chmn. Nat. Com. for the Prevention of Child Abuse and Childhelp U.S.A.; hon. pres. Girl Scouts U.S; hon. chair Nat. Com. for Adoption; mem. bd. trustees Mayo Clinic Found.; hon. chair Read Am., Boarder Baby Project; mem. bd. visitors M. D. Anderson Cancer Ctr.; hon. chair Leukemia Soc. Am., Children's Literacy Initiative; hon. mem. Reading is Fundamental; ambassador at large Americares; honorary mem. Barbara Bush Found. for Family Literacy. Recipient Nat. Outstanding Mother of Yr. award, 1984, Woman of Yr. award USO, 1986, Disting. Leadership award United Negro Coll. Fund 1986, Disting. Am. Woman award Coll. Mt. St. Joseph, 1987, Free Spirit award Freedom Forum, 1995. Mem. Tex. Fedn. Rep. Women (life), Internat. II Club (Washington), Magic Circle Rep. Women's Club (Houston), YWCA. Episcopalian.*

BUSH, CHRISTINE GAY, dental hygienist; b. Toledo, Dec. 31, 1951; d. Jack G. and Virginia Aileen (Doyle) Tornga; m. John Howard Mosher, May 11, 1974 (div. July 1990); children: Heather Kristen, Andrew Jacob; m. Robert Milton Counts, July 5, 1991 (dec. Mar. 1993); m. Charles T. Bush II, June 16, 1998. BS in Dental Hygiene, U. Mich., 1974. Registered dental hygienist, Nat. Bd. Dental Examiners, Ind. State Bd. Dentistry, Fla. State Bd. Dentistry, Mich. State Bd. Dentistry. Asst. supr. dental hygiene Ind. U., South Bend, Ind., 1974-75; expanded functions hygienist South Bend Dental Ctr., 1975; periodontal hygienist Dr. John B. Lehman, South Bend, 1976-82, Dr. Cristene Maas, Longwood, Fla., 1983-84, Dr. Richard Altman, Orlando, Fla., 1984-85; dental hygienist Dr. H. Raymund Barcus, Winter Park, Fla., 1984—2000; periodontal hygienist Dr. Michael Abufaris, 2000—. Adj. instr. So. Coll., Orlando, 1984. Med./dental mission Wekiva Presbyn. Ch., Honduras, 1987, 89, Diocese of Orlando, Dominican Republic, 1994, 95, Fla. Hosp. Found., Jamaica, 1997; deacon Presbyn. Ch., 1992; mem. Festival of Orchs. League. Mem.: Greater Orlando Dental Hygiene Assn. (sec. 1986—87), Messiah Soc., Festival of Orches Fras League, U. Mich. Club Orlando (treas. 1998—2001), Alpha Chi Omega (chpt. pres. 1995—97, Lyre editor 1997—98, 2000—01, pres. Gamma Upsilon Gamma chpt. 1998—99). Republican. Roman Catholic. Avocations: cross-stitch, playing piano, reading. Office: Dr Michael Abufaris Periodontics 201 N Lakemont Ave Ste 600 Winter Park FL 32792

BUSH, DONNA, forensic toxicologist; b. Balt., Apr. 18, 1954; d. Francis Joseph and Dorothy Theresa (Koris) B. BS in Chemistry, Loyola Coll., Balt., 1976; MS in Medicinal Chemistry, U. Md., Balt., 1980; MS in Environ. Toxicology, Johns Hopkins U., 1984; PhD in Forensic Toxicology, U. Md., Balt., 1988. Diplomate Am. Bd. Forensic Toxicology. Sr. technologist, clin. and forensic toxicology Md. Med. Lab., Inc., Balt., 1978-85; tech. dir. U.S. Army Forensic Toxicology Drug Testing Lab., Ft. Meade, Md., 1987-89; chief of drug testing, Divsn. Workplace Programs Ctr. for Substance Abuse Prevention, Rockville, Md., 1989—. Exec. sec. Drug Testing Adv. Bd., Substance Abuse and Mental Health Svcs. Adminstrn., Rockville, 1989—; faculty Am. Soc. Addiction Medicine, Bethesda, Md., 1992—, Fla. Sch. Addiction Studies, Tallahassee, 1991—, Southeastern Sch. Alcohol and Other Drug Studies, 1993—; invited lectr. internat. venues and confs.; dir. Nat. Lab. Certification Program. Contbr. chpts. to books, numerous articles to refereed profl. jours. and conf. procs., including Jour. Analytical Toxicology, Pharmacologist, Jour. Nat. Cancer Inst., Radiation Rsch., Sci., others. Recipient Nat. Rsch. Svc. awards, NIH, 1980-82. Fellow Am. Acad. Forensic Scis.; mem. Soc. Forensic Toxicologists (Ednl. Rsch. award 1986), Internat. Assn. Forensic Toxicologists, Am. Chem. Soc., Rho Chi. Office: Workplace Programs SAMHSA 5600 Fishers Ln Rockwall II Ste 815 Rockville MD 20857

BUSH, EUGENE NYLE, pharmacologist, research scientist; b. McKeesport, Pa., Apr. 14, 1952; s. Nyle E. and Rosalia M. (Merlino) B.; m. Janet Rosemary Ruscitto, May 7, 1977; children: Stephen Michael, Rebecca Renee, Timothy George. BS in Pharmacy, U. Pitts., 1977, PhD in Pharmacology, 1981. Registered pharmacist, Pa., Ill. Tchg. asst. U. Pitts., 1978-81; staff pharmacist Western Pa. Hosp., Pitts., 1977-81; pharmacologist II Abbott Labs., 1981-84, pharmacologist I, 1984-87, sr. rsch. sci., 1986-88, rsch. investigator, 1988-89, group leader, endocrine pharmacol., 1989-91, sr. group leader endocrine pharmacol., 1991-97, assoc. Volwiler rsch. fellow, 1996—. Co-author numerous publs.; contbr. articles to profl. jours. Mem.: Am. Coll. Clin. Pharmacology, Am. Diabetes Assn., Am. Pharm. Assn., Endocrine Soc., Nat. Eagle Scout Assn., Sigma Xi. Republican. Roman Catholic. Avocations: gardening, photography, computers, bicycling. Home: 816 Bedford Ct Libertyville IL 60048-3002 Office: Abbott Labs R47M Bldg AP13A/2 100 Abbott Park Rd North Chicago IL 60064-6126 E-mail: gene.bush@abbott.com.

BUSH, FRED MARSHALL, JR., lawyer; b. Newhebron, Miss., Jan. 25, 1917; s. Frederick Marshall Sr. and Elizabeth Stewart (Buck) B.; m. Katie Ruth Field, May 8, 1942; children: Frederick Marshall III, Carl J., Richard S. AA, Hinds Jr. Coll., 1935; BS, U.S. Naval Acad., 1939; LLB, U. Miss., 1950. Bar: Miss. 1948, U.S. Dist. Ct. Miss. 1948, U.S. Ct. Appeals (5th and 11th cirs.) 1948, U.S. Supreme Ct. 1965. Commd. ensign USN, 1939, advanced through grades to capt., resigned, 1948, with Res., 1948-60; ptnr. Fant & Bush, Holly Springs, Miss., 1950-60, Mitchell, McNutt, Bush, Lagrone & Sams, Tupelo, Miss., 1962-89, Phelps Dunbar, Tupelo, Miss., 1989—. Bd. dirs. Miss. Bd. Econ. Devel., Jackson, Miss., 1960-68, exec. dir., 1960-62; bd. dirs. Tenn.-Tombigbee Waterway Devel. Authority, Columbus, Miss., 1980-84. Fellow Miss. Bar Found. (chmn. 1978); mem. ABA (ho. of dels. 1986-87, 89-90), Miss. Bar Assn. (pres. 1986-87, various coms. and offices), Miss. Def. Lawyers Assn. (pres. 1973-74). Lodges: Rotary (pres. local club 1954-55). Episcopalian. Office: Phelps Dunbar PO Box 1220 Tupelo MS 38802-1220 E-mail: bushf@phelps.com.

BUSH, FREDERICK MORRIS, federal official; b. Newport News, Va., Feb. 6, 1949; s. Morris and Dorothy Montony B.; m. Catherine Marie Murphy, Sept. 10, 1977, children— Alexander Murphy Morris, Taylor McGrath, Channing Barbara and Margaret Montony (twins). BA, U. Colo., 1971; MA in Internat. Studies, Am. U., 1974. Clk. Republican policy com. U.S. Senate, 1971-73; legis. asst. Ho. of Reps., 1973; asst. to fin. chmn. Rep. Nat. Com., 1973-74; dep. fin. dir. Pres. Ford Com., 1975-77; nat. fin. dir. George Bush for Pres., 1979-80; asst. sec. commerce for tourism; dep. Chief of Staff to v.p.; pres. Bush & Co.; commr. gen. U.S.A. Universal Expn., Seville, Spain, 1991-92; U.S. amb., commr. gen. Expo 92, Seville, 1992—; dir. devel. Woodrow Wilson Internat. Ctr. for Scholars, Washington. Founder Rep. Assocs. Chgo.; trustee Am. Ctr. Internat. Leadership; dep. fin. chmn. for George Bush for Pres.; fin. chmn. San Diego host com. Rep. Nat. Conv.; fin. chmn. Reps. Abroad; fin. chmn. Washington bdi. com. 2012 Olympic Games, 1998—; devel. dir. Woodrow Wilson Internat. Ctr. for Scholars, 1998—. Address: Home: 8208 Kerry Rd Chevy Chase MD 20815-4808 E-mail: bushfred@wwic.si.edu.

BUSH, GAIL, library educator, school librarian; b. Chgo., May 2, 1952; d. George William and Norma T. Fish; m. Robert K. Bush, Sept. 7, 1978; children: Matthew Thomas, Claire Anne. BA in Anthropology magna cum laude, U. Ill., 1973, MS in Libr. Sci., 1977; PhD in Ednl. Psychology, Loyola U., Chgo., 2001. Cert. libr. media, Ill. Head libr. Nat. Coll. Edn. (now Nat.-Louis U.), Chgo., 1977-79; corp. libr. mgr. Heidrick & Struggles, Chgo., 1979-82; grad. rsch. instr., ref. libr. Nat. Coll. Edn., Wilmette, Ill., 1982-92; curriculum libr. Maine Twp. H.S. West, Des Plaines, Ill., 1992—2002; dir. sch. libr. media program Dominican U., River Forest, Ill., 2002—, assoc. prof., 2002—. Editions advisory Bd., ALA, 2002-; Teacher Libr. Advisory Bd., 2002-; goals 2000 cons. Loyola U. Chgo., 1997-2000, lectr., 1998—; pub. cons. Greenwood Press, Westport, Conn., 2000-2002; info. lit. cons. Great Plains Network, Lincoln, Nebr., 1999-2000; mem. adv. bd. Knowledge Quest, 2003—. Author: The School Buddy System: the Practice of Collaboration; mem. editl. bd. Am. Assn. Sch. Librs., 1997-2000; contbr. articles to profl. jours. including Ednl. Leadership, Knowledge Quest, Sch. Libr. Jour., NASSP Bull., tchr.-libr. Voice Youth Advocates, Ill. Reading Coun. Jour. Named Sch. Libr. of Yr. North Suburban Libr. Sys., 1999; Shoah Visual History Found. fellow, 2001—. Mem. ALA, ASCD, Am. Assn. Sch. Librs. (Nat. Sch. Libr. Media Program of Yr. 1996), Internat. Reading Assn., Am. Ednl. Rsch. Assn., Freedom to Read Found., Beta Phi Mu, Phi Delta Kappa. Office: Dominican Univ 7900 W Division St River Forest IL 60305 E-mail: gbush@dom.edu.

BUSH, GEORGE ARTHUR, illustrator; b. Reading, Pa., Jan. 10, 1953; s. Legrand Easton Bush and Joan Marie Fix; m. Lorraine Daniella Brinit, Sept. 22, 1973. A in Comml. Art, Art Inst. Pitts., 1972; BS in Comml. Art, LaRoche Coll., 1975. Cover illustrator various pubs. including Bantam, N.Y.C., 1975—2000, Ballantine, N.Y.C., Dell, Doubleday, Harper Harlequin, Warner, Putnam, Simon & Schuster, Tor, Leisure, Franklin Mint, Bradford Exch., Danbury Mint, TV Guide, Marvel Comics. Book covers, Bradford Exchange Collectors Plate Series, pre-prodn. art for Bram Stoker's Dracula movie; contbr. art and stories; (art used in Deep Impact film), 1998. Republican. Lutheran. Avocations: electronics, movies, carpentry. Home and Studio: 5701 Church Lane Rd Reading PA 19606 E-mail: gabush@verizon.net.

BUSH, GEORGE HERBERT WALKER, 41st President of the United States; b. Milton, Mass., June 12, 1924; s. Prescott Sheldon and Dorothy (Walker) B.; m. Barbara Pierce, Jan. 6, 1945; children: George W., John E., Neil M., Marvin P., Dorothy W. Koch. BA in Econs., Yale U., 1948; numerous other hon. degrees. Co-founder Bush-Overbey Oil Devel. Co., 1951; Co-founder, dir. Zapata Petroleum Corp., Midland, 1953-59; pres. Zapata Off Shore Co., Houston, 1956-64, chmn. bd., 1964-66; mem. 90th-91st Congresses from 7th Dist. Tex., 1967-71, Ways and Means com.; U.S. amb. to UN, 1971-73; chmn. Rep. Nat. Com., 1973-74; chief U.S. Liaison Office Peking, People's Republic China, 1974-75; dir. CIA, 1976-77; adj. prof. adminstrv. sci. Rice U., Houston, 1978; v.p. served under Pres. Ronald Reagan U.S., 1981-89, President of the U.S., 1989-93. Bd. visitors M.D. Anderson Cancer Ctr., Houston. Del. Rep. Nat. Conv., 1964, 69; Rep. candidate U.S. senator from Tex., 1964, 70. Lt. (j.g.), pilot USN, WWII. Decorated D.F.C., Air medals (3). Republican. Office: 10000 Memorial Dr, Ste 900 Houston TX 77024-3422

BUSH, GEORGE WALKER, 43d President of the United States; b. July 6, 1946; s. George Herbert Walker and Barbara (Pierce) B.; m. Laura; children: Barbara and Jenna (twins). BA in History, Yale U., 1968; MBA, Harvard U., 1975. Chmn., CEO Spectrum 7 Energy Corp., Midland, Tex., 1980—86; dir. Harken Energy Corp. (formerly Spectrum 7 Energy Corp.), Midland, Tex., 1985—86; mng. gen. ptnr. Tex. Rangers (baseball franchise), 1989—94; gov. State of Tex., Austin, 1994—2000; President of the United States, 2001—. Pilot Texas Air Nat. Guard, 1968—70. Recipient Big D award Dallas All Sports Assn., 1989. Republican.*

BUSH, JANICE, principal; b. Detroit, Oct. 23, 1947; d. James and Annie Bush. BA, Western Mich. U., 1968; MA, Wayne State U., 1972, PhD, EdD, Wayne State U., 1997. Cert. tchr. Mich. Tchr. Detroit Pub. Schs., 1969—78, tchr., coord., 1979—84, instr. specialist, 1985, asst. prin., 1985—95, prin., 1975—. Editl. bd. Profl. Women's Network, Detroit, 1988—89; bd. govs. Wayne State U., Coll. of Edn., Detroit, 1988—89; bd. dirs. IN Site, Detroit, 1992. Recipient Golen Apple award, State of Mich., 2000. Mem.: Delta Sigma Theta Sorority (exec. bd. 1966—). Avocations: travel, reading, investment club.

BUSH, JOHN B. circuit judge; b. Montgomery, Ala., June 15, 1956; s. John W. and Gail H. Bush; children: Julie, Ben, David. BS, Auburn U., 1978; JD, Cumberland Sch. Law/Samford U., 1981, 1981. Atty. Cleveland, Booth & Bush, Attys., Prattville, Ala., 1982-83, Moore, Kendrick et al, Attys., Montgomery, 1983-86; cir. judge State of Ala. 19th Jud. Cir., Wetumpka, 1986—. Bd. dirs. Grandview YMCA, Millbrook, Ala., 1995—01. Mem. Ala. Cir. Judges Assn. (bd. dirs., sec./treas. 2003-04), Millbrook Men's Club. Republican. Baptist. Avocation: hunting. Office: 8935 Us Highway 231 Rm 232 Wetumpka AL 36092-8256 E-mail: john.b.bush@att.net.

BUSH, JOHN ELLIS (JEB BUSH), governor; b. Midland, Tex., Feb. 11, 1953; m. Columba Bush; children: George, Noelle, Jeb. B.Latin Am. Affairs, U. Tex. Co-founder Codina Group, Miami, Fla., 1981—, pres., COO; Sec. of commerce State of Fla., 1987—88; gov. State of Fla., Tallahassee, 1998—. Vol. Miami Children's Hosp., United Way of Dade County, Dade County Homeless Trust; founder Found. for Fla.'s Future, 1995, chmn.; co-founder Liberty City Charter Sch. Republican. Roman Catholic. Office: Office of the Governor The Capitol Tallahassee FL 32399-0001 E-mail: fl_governor@eog.state.fl.us.*

BUSH, LARRY DON, communications company administrator; b. Sulphur Springs, Tex., June 8, 1945; s. Robert Lawson and Margret Laverne (Davis) B.; m. Opal June Chamberlain, Jan. 15, 1965 (div. Nov. 1969); 1 child, Laura Michelle; m. Kathleen Ann Merkel, May 4, 1974; children: Angela Dawn, Andrea Danielle. BBA summa cum laude, Dallas Bapt. U., 1993. Engrng. technician Tex. Instruments, Richardson, 1962-65; sys. engr. Sci. control Corp., Carrollton, Tex., 1965-69; from course developer to competitive analyst Southwestern Bell, Dallas, 1972—99, competitive analyst, 1999—2000; dir. sales engrng. nat. carrier sales Carrier Access Corp., Rockwall, Tex.,

2001—02; bus. cons. ML Murphy and Assocs., Rockwall, Tex., 2002—. Tchr. New Covenant World Outreach, 1997—99; assoc. pastor Internat. Spirit of Truth, Nevada, Tex., 2000—02; dir. Ministries Spirit of Truth, Plano, Tex., 1999—2000. Mem. Soc. Competitive Intelligence Profls., Tex. Soc. Telephone Engrs., Tex. Telephone Pioneers, Alpha Chi, Alpha Sigma Lambda, Delta Mu Delta. Republican. Avocations: woodworking, electronics. Home and Office: 1096 Midnight Pass Rockwall TX 75087-7200 E-mail: larrybush@sbcglobal.net.

BUSH, MARILYN WOLIN, management consultant, software engineer; b. Phila., Dec. 2, 1948; d. Louis and Minnie (Goldsmith) Wolin; m. Ronald Bush, Dec. 14, 1969; 1 child, Charles Max. BSEE, U. Pa., 1969. Rsch. asst. Cavendish Labs. Cambridge (Eng.) U., 1970; electronic engr. Dept. Def., 1970-75; project mgr. Trans. Sys. Ctr., Cambridge, Mass., 1975-82; software product assurance mgr. NASA Jet Propulsion Lab. Calif. Inst. Tech., Pasadena, 1982-92. Vis. scientist Software Engring. Inst., Carnegie Mellon U., Pitts., 1992-94, 95-96; tutor Winthrop House, Harvard U., Cambridge, Mass. Co-author: The Capability Maturity Model: Guidelines for Improving the Software Process, 1995; contbr. articles to profl. jours. Mem. Mass. High Tech. Coun., Boston. Recipient awards NASA, 1991. Mem. IEEE (nat. adv. com. on edn., program com. internat. conf.), IEEE Computer Soc. (nat. exec. com. tech. com.), Boston Profl. Coun. (founding pres. 1981-82). Avocations: jogging, travel. E-mail: m.w.bush@ieee.org.

BUSH, MARJORIE EVELYNN TOWER-TOOKER, educator, media specialist, librarian; b. Atkinson, Nebr., Mar. 12, 1925; d. Albert Ralph and Vera Marie (Rickover) Tower-Tooker; m. Louis T. Genung, Feb. 2, 1944 (dec. Jan. 1982); 1 child, Louis Thompson; m. Laurence Scott Bush, Sept. 22, 1984; 1 stepchild, Roger A. Student, U. Nebr., 1951, Wayne State Coll., 1942-47; BA, Colo. State Coll., 1966, U. No. Colo., 1970; postgrad., Doane Coll., 1967-68, U. Utah, 1973-74, PhD (hon.), 1973; MA in Tchg., Hastings (Nebr.) Coll., 2000. Elem. tchr. Atkinson Pub. Schs., 1958-69; adminstr. librs. and audiovisual comm. Clay County Dist. I-C, Fairfield, Nebr., 1972-81; media specialist Albion (Nebr.) City Schs., 1981—. Mem. Neb. Gov.'s White House Conf. on Libraries. Chmn. edn. adminstrv. bd. Park Hill United Meth. Ch., Denver, also pres.; sec. Denver Symphony Guild, Colo. Symphony Guild, 1990-96. Mem. NEA (life), ALA, AAUW, ASCD, Nat. Coun. Tchrs. English, Nebr. Edn. Assn., Colo. Edn. Assn., Nebr. Libr. Assn., Nebr. Ednl. Media Assn., Mountain Plain Libr. Assn., Assn. Childhood Edn. Internat., Assn. Ednl. Comm. & Tech., Internat. Visual Literacy Assn., Nat. Coun. Exceptional Children, Alumni Assn. U. No. Colo. (life charter), Women Educators Nebr., United Meth. Women (pres.), Am. Legion Aux., Nebr. Lay Citizens Assn. (exec.), Am. NAt. Cowbelles, Nebr. Cowbelles, Internat. Platform Assn., LWV, Women's Soc. Christian Svc., Ak-Sar-Ben, Windsor Gardens Club (Denver), Opti-Mrs. Club (pres.), Optimists Internat., Columbine Optimists (pres. 1987-88), Ea. Star. Address: 1003 E 9th St Hastings NE 68901-4140

BUSH, SISTER MARY KATHLEEN, social worker; b. Newport, Ky., July 7, 1935; d. Rollin James and Margaret Mary (Flynn) Bush. AB in Elementary Edn., Villa Madonna Coll., Covington, Ky., 1965; MEd, Xavier U., Cin., 1969; MSW, U. Ky., 1981. Lic. clin. social worker, Ky.; entered Sisters of Divine Providence Ky., 1951. Tchr. Christ the King Sch., Lexington, Ky., 1953-61, St. Philip Sch., Melbourne, Ky., 1961-62, St. Vincent de Paul Sch., Newport, 1962-64, Holy Family Sch., Ashland, Ky., 1964-66, St. Camillus Acad., Corbin, Ky., 1966-71, Christ the King Sch., Lexington, 1971-74; prin. Corpus Christi Sch., Newport, 1974-78; tchr. Our Lady of Providence High Sch., Newport, 1979-80; clin. social worker Cath. Social Svc., Covington, 1981—. Cons. in field; mem. No. Ky. Task Force on Child Sexual Abuse, 1992-94. Mem. adv. team Multidisciplinary Case Cons. Team Child Abuse, No. Ky., 1982-83, team mem., 1983-96; mem. adv. team social work dept. Thomas More Coll., Ft. Mitchell, 1985-86; mem. Outreach to African-Am. Diocese of Covington, 1987-96; mem. pub. def. com. No. Ky. Bar Assn., 1990-92; bd. dirs. for setting up children's advocacy ctr. No. Ky. Advs. for Children, 1993-94; mem. Diocesan pastoral ministry formation bd. Diocese of Covington, 1996—. Recipient various awards. Mem. NASW (Social Worker of Yr. No. Ky. chpt. 1983), Assn. for Psychol. Type. Democrat. Roman Catholic. Office: Cath Social Svc Bur 3629 Church St Covington KY 41015-1430 E-mail: kaybush@hotmail.com.

BUSH, MICHAEL KEVIN, lawyer; b. Davenport, Iowa, May 23, 1952; s. Roy Alvin and A. Carmelita (Gilroy) B.; m. Kathleen M. Grace, Nov. 26, 1977; children: Kelly Anne, Daniel Stephen, Brendan Michael. BA, U. Notre Dame, South Bend, Ind., 1974; JD, Valparaiso (Ind.) U., 1977. Bar: Iowa 1977, U.S. Dist. Ct. (no. dist.) Iowa 1980, U.S. Ct. Appeals (7th cir.) 1980, U.S. Dist. Ct. (ctrl. dist.) Ill. 1983, U.S. Ct. Appeals (8th cir.) 1996, U.S. Supreme Ct. 1990, Ill. 1999. Mem. Wells, McNally & Bowman, Davenport, 1977-80; prosecutor Scott County Atty.'s Office, Davenport, 1980-82; mem. Henninger & Henninger, Davenport, 1979-82; founding ptnr. Walton, Creen & Bush, Davenport, 1982-86; ptnr. Carlin, Hellstrom & Bittner, Davenport, 1987—; sr. ptnr. Bush, Motto, Creen, Hoffman and Koury, Davenport, 2000—. Recipient Iowa Trial Lawyer's Public Justice award, 2001. Mem. ATLA (sustaining mem.), Am. Bd. Trial Advocates (assoc.), Iowa Assn. Trial Lawyers (Pub. Justice award 2000), Million Dollar Advocates Forum, Iowa Bar Assn., Scott County Bar Assn., Am. Coll. Barristers (sr. counsel). Roman Catholic. Avocation: tennis. Home: 2806 E 42nd Ct Davenport IA 52807-1576 Office: Carlin Hellstrom & Bittner 5505 Victoria Ave Ste 100 Davenport IA 52807

BUSH, NORMAN, research and development executive; b. N.Y.C., Dec. 10, 1929; s. Louis and Ida (Trembola) B.; m. Audrey Faith Blumberg, Dec. 28, 1952; children: Stewart Alan, I. Jeffrey, Ellen Gail Dash. BBA, CUNY, 1951, MBA, 1952; PhD, N.C. State U., 1962. Statistician Army Chem. Ctr., Edgewood, Md., 1952-56, RCA Svc. Co., Patrick AFB, Fla., 1956-58, DBA and ICF, Melbourne, Fla., 1962-64, Pan Am Airlines, Patrick AFB, Fla., 1964-72; div. mgr. ENSCO Inc., Melbourne, Fla., 1972-83, pres., chief oper. officer Springfield, Va., 1983-94, chmn. bd., 1989-95. Contbr. articles to statis. jours. With U.S. Army, 1952-54. Mem. Am. Statis. Assn. Republican. Avocation: travel. Office: PO Box 410279 Melbourne FL 32941-0279

BUSH, RAYMOND T. accountant, corporate professional; b. Providence, R.I., Sept. 7, 1939; s. Raymond F. and Regina C. (Pearl) B.; m. Barbara Ann Cormier, May 31, 1962; children: Laura Jean, Raymond F., Matthew T., James J., Michael. BS in Acctg. and Fin., Bryant Coll., 1960. CPA, R.I. Auditor USDA, Providence, 1960-66; audit supr. KPMG Peat Marwick LLP, Providence, 1966-69; mgr. system and audit Ludlow Corp., Needham Heights, Mass., 1969-71, asst. treas., 1971-73, v.p., gen. mgr., 1973-80; pres. Recticel Foam Corp., Needham Heights, 1980-83; sr. v.p. fin. and adminstrn. Maguire Group Inc., Providence, 1983—. Dir. Ocean State Bus. Devel.; pres. East Atlantic Casualty Co. Ltd.; cons. Bryant Coll. Small Bus. Devel. Ctr. Mem. R.I. Indsl. Recreational Bldg. Authority; trustee Providence Pub. Libr. Fellow R.I. Soc. CPA's; mem. Am. Inst. CPA's. Roman Catholic. Home: 3 Hayfield Ln Cumberland RI 02864-4114 Office: Maguire Group Inc 225 Foxborough Blvd Foxboro MA 02035-2885

BUSH, RICHARD CLARENCE, III, think-tank associate; b. Chgo., Nov. 21, 1947; s. Richard Clarence Jr. and Mary Ethlyn (Ball) B.; m. Martha Virginia Hodge, June 21, 1969; children: Sharmon Melissa Kellet, Andrew Milton. BA, Lawrence U., Appleton, Wis., 1969; MA, Columbia U., 1973, M Philosophy, 1975, PhD, 1978. Program assoc. China Coun., Asia Soc., N.Y.C., 1977-79, Washington, 1979-81; staff cons. fgn. affairs com. U.S. Ho. of Reps., Washington, 1983-95; nat. intelligence officer East Asia, Washington, 1995-97; chmn., mng. dir. Am. Inst. in Taiwan, Rosslyn, Va., 1997—2002; sr. fellow, dir. Ctr. for N.E. Asian Policy Studies, Brookings Instn., 2002—. Author: The Politics of Cotton Textiles in Kuomintang China, 1927-37, 1982; co-compiler The People's Republic of China: A Basic Handbook, 1979, 81, 82; editor Brookings Northeast Asia Survey, 2002-03, 2003. Sgt. U.S. Army, 1970—72. Democrat. E-mail: rbush@brookings.edu.

BUSH, ROBERT BRADFORD, corporate lawyer; b. Indpls., June 13, 1953; s. Robert Leland and Mary Corrine (Burton) B.; m. Denise Marquette, June 14, 1975; children: Christopher, Keith, Matthew. BS, U.S. Naval Acad., 1975; JD, Ind. U., Bloomington, 1983. Bar: Ind. 1983, U.S. Dist. Ct. (no. and so. dists.) Ind. 1983, U.S. Ct. Appeals (7th cir.) 1984, U.S. Dist. Ct. (so. dist.) Ill. 1988. Ptnr. Ice, Miller, Donadio & Ryan, Indpls., 1983-99; assoc. gen. counsel Cmty. Hosps. of Ind., Inc., Indpls., 2000—. Contbr. articles to profl. jours. Lt. comdr. USN, 1975-80. Mem. ABA, Ind. Bar Assn., Indpls. Bar Assn., Order of Coif. Republican. Office: Cmty Hosps of Indiana Inc Admin/Legal 1500 N Ritter Ave Indianapolis IN 46219-3027 E-mail: RBush@ecommunity.com.

BUSH, ROBERT G. food service executive; b. 1926; s. Merlin G. B.; married. Grad., U. Wis., 1950. Exec. Schreiber Foods, Inc. and predecessor co., Green Bay, Wis., 1948-62, officer, 1962-77, v.p., 1977-78, pres., COO, 1978-85, chmn., CEO, 1985-89, chmn., 1989—. Office: Schreiber Foods Inc 425 Pine St Green Bay WI 54301-5179

BUSH, ROBERT THOMAS, shipping company executive; b. Newbury, Berkshire, Eng., May 18, 1928; came to U.S., 1968; s. Randolph George and Catherine Ellen (Benger) B.; m. Haydee Ojeda, Jan. 23, 1966; children: Allan David, Linda Martha, Grace Katherine. Master Mariner, Southampton (Eng.) U., 1953. Shipmaster Burmah Oil Co., Rangoon, Burma, 1955-60; marine surveyor Sydney, Australia, 1960-68; terminal supt. Exportadora De Sal, Cedros Island, Mex., 1968-70; marine mgr. Balfour Williamson, London, 1970-73; sr. marine advisor Aramco, Saudi Arabia, 1974-76; ops. mgr. Mercantile & Marine (Tex.) Inc., Houston, 1976-80; sr. marine advisor Phillips Petroleum Co., Bartlesville, Okla., 1980-86; gen. mgr. Universe Tankships (Del.) Inc., N.Y.C., 1986-94; pres. Neptune Marine Consultants (Ams.) Inc., Dickinson, Tex., 1994—. Contbr. numerous articles to profl. jours. Charter mem. Better World Soc., Washington, 1988; tutor Literacy Vols. Am., Edison, N.J., 1988—; founder Friends of the Sea, N.Y., 1991. Felow Nautical Inst. London; mem. N.Y. Acad. Sci. Avocations: reading, history, walking. Home: 3065 Overland Trl Dickinson TX 77539-5970 E-mail: neptune18@earthlink.net.

BUSH, ROBERTA B. psychotherapist, accountant; b. Watertown, NY, Dec. 23, 1937; d. Robert King and Barbara P. (Wiggins) Banks; m. Marvin D. Bush, Feb. 28, 1959 (div. 1977). BA, Glenville State Coll., 1977; MS, W.Va. U., Morgantown, 1985. Lic. profl. therapist W.Va. Acct. GE Plastics, Parkensburg, W.Va., 1959—77; lit. vol. Parkensburg, 1977—89; outpatient site head Abraxas, Parkensburg, 1989—95; psychotherapist Westbrook Health Svc., Parkensburg, 1996—97; ret., 1997. Pres., bd. dirs. Lit. Vol. Program of Wood City, Parkersburg. Mem.: Profl. Women's Assn. (pres., bd. dirs., Hall of Fame 1995). Episcopalian. Home: 111 Canterbury Dr Parkersburg WV 26104-8057

BUSH, SANDI TOKOA, elementary school educator; b. Albany, Ga., Aug. 1, 1953; d. Charlie and Beauty (Miller) Bush; 1 child, Allen. BS, Barry U., Miami, 1983; MS, Nova U., 1987; PhD, Union Inst., 2001, U. Cin., 2001. Cert. tchr. Fla. Counselor Health and Rehab. Svcs., Miami, Fla., 1979-86; tchr. Dade County Pub. Schs., Miami, 1986—. Tchr., tutor Ind. Children's Group, Miami, 1987—; co-chmn. Hall of Fame Dade County Sch. Bd., 1986—, world difference, 1987—. Author: (book) World of Poetry Anthology The Sun, 1991; co-author: Experiences with Discrimination: From Deep Within, 1998; contbr. articles to profl. jours. Mem.: Nova U. Assocs., Nova U. Alumni Assn. (mem. recruitment com. 1987—88, Recognition award 1988), Smithsonian Assocs. (Recognition award 1988), Am. Mus. Natural History (assoc.). Avocations: reading, classical music, walking, jogging, tennis.

BUSH, SARAH LILLIAN, historian; b. Kansas City, Mo., Sept. 17, 1920; d. William Adam and Lettie Evelyn (Burrill) Lewis; m. Walter Nelson Bush, June 7, 1946 (dec.); children: William Read, Robert Nelson. *Ms. Bush's son, Bill, is a researcher at Sun Microsystems Laboratories, where he has worked on various implementations of the Java programming language. He started the KVM project, which has put Java on millions of mobile devices around the world. Before joining Sun, Bill was a founder and principal scientist of Intrinsa Corporation, where he invented software analysis technology that is used by Microsoft to improve the quality and security of all its products. Her son, Bob, is a summa cum laude graduate of Harvard College with a masters degree from Stanford. He is currently a geologist who works in Houston, Texas applying and developing computer applications to geological problems.* AB, U. Kans., 1941; BS, U. Ill., 1943. Clk. circulation dept. Kansas City Pub. Library, 1941-42, asst. librarian Paseo br., 1943-44; librarian Kansas City Jr. Coll., 1944-46; substitute librarian San Mateo County Library, Woodside and Portola Valley, Calif., 1975-77; various temporary positions, 1979-87; owner Metriguide, Palo Alto, Calif., 1975-78. Author: Atherton Lands, 1979, rev. edition 1987. Editor: Atherton Recollections, 1973. Pres., v.p. Jr. Librarians, Kansas City, 1944-46; courtesy, yearbook & historian AAUW, Menlo- Atherton branch (Calif.) Br.; asst. Sunday sch. tchr., vol. Holy Trinity Ch., Menlo Park, 1955-78; v.p., membership com., libr. chairperson, English reading program, parent edn. chairperson Menlo Atherton High Sch. PTA, 1964-73; founder, bd. dirs. Friends of Atherton Community Library, 1967-2002, oral historian, 1968-2002, chair Bicentennial event, 1976; bd. dirs. Menlo Park Hist. Assn., 1979-82, oral historian, 1973-2002; bd. dirs. Civic Interest League, Atherton, 1978-81; mem. hist. county commn. Town of Atherton, 1980-87; vol. Allied Arts Palo Alto Aux. to Children's Hosp. at Stanford, 1967—, oral historian, 1978—, historian, 1980—; vol. United Crusade, Garfield Sch., Redwood City, 1957-61, 74-88, Encinal Sch., Menlo Park, Calif., 1961-73, program dir., chmn. summer recreation, historian, sec.; vol. Stanford Mothers Club, 1977-81, others; historian, awards chairperson Cub Scouts Boy Scouts Am.; founder Atherton Heritage Assn. 1989, bd. dirs., 1989—, dir., 1989-94; mem. Guild Gourmet, 1971—, Mid Peninsula History Consortium, 1993-95; oral historian St. Andrew's Ch., Saratoga, Calif., 2003—. Recipient Good Neighbor award Civic Interest League, 1992. Mem. PTA (life). Episcopalian. Avocations: gourmet cooking, entertaining, reading.

BUSH, SARGENT, JR., English language educator; b. Flemington, N.J., Sept. 22, 1937; s. Sargent and Marion Louise (Roberts) B.; m. Cynthia Bird Greig, June 18, 1960; children: Charles Sargent, James Jonathan. AB, Princeton U., 1959; MA, U. Iowa, 1964, PhD, 1967. Asst. prof. English Washington and Lee U., Lexington, Va., 1967-71; asst. prof. English U. Wis., Madison, 1971-73, assoc. prof., 1973-79, prof., 1979—, John Bascom prof. English, 1997—, chmn. dept. English, 1980-83, assoc. dean for humanities, Coll. Letters and Sci., 1989—94, 1999. Vis. prof. U. Warwick, Coventry, Eng., 1983-84. Author: (wth George H. Williams, Norman Pettit and Winfried Herget) Thomas Hooker: Writings in England and Holland, 1626-1633, 1975, The Writings of Thomas Hooker: Spiritual Adventure in Two Worlds, 1980, (with Carl J. Rasmussen) The Library of Emmanuel College, Cambridge, 1584-1637, 1986; editor Jour. of Sarah Kemble Knight in Journeys in New Worlds: Early American Women's Narratives, 1990, The Correspondence of John Cotton, 2001; contbr. articles to profl. jours. With U.S. Army, 1959-60, 61-62. Fellow Coop. Program in Humanities, 1969-70, Am. Coun. Learned Socs., 1974, Inst. for Rsch. in Humanities, 1978, Mass. Hist. Soc. rsch. fellow, 1990, Peterson fellow Am. Antiquarian Soc., 2002; grantee NEH, 1969, 86, Am. Philos. Soc., 1979, 97. Mem. MLA, Am. Lit. Assn., Soc. Early Americanists, Nathaniel Hawthorne Soc., Cambridge Bibliog. Soc., Assn. Documentary Editing, Melville Soc., Thoreau Soc., New Eng. Hist. Geneaol. Soc., SHARP. Presbyterian. Home: 4146 Manitou Way Madison WI 53711-3014 Office: U Wis Helen C White Hall Madison WI 53706

BUSH, SPENCER HARRISON, metallurgist, consultant; b. Flint, Mich., Apr. 4, 1920; s. Edward Charles and Rachel Beatrice (Roser) B.; m. Roberta Lee Warren, Aug. 28, 1948; children: David Spencer, Carl Edward. Student, Flint Jr. Coll., 1938-40, Ohio State U., 1943-44, U. Mich., 1946-53. Registered profl. engr., Calif. Asst. chemist Dow Chem. Co., 1940-42, 46; assoc. Engring. Rsch. Inst., U. Mich., 1947-53; research asst. Office Naval Rsch., 1950-53, instr. dental materials, 1951-53; metallurgist Hanford Atomic Products Operation, Gen. Electric Co., 1953-54, supr. phys. metallurgy, 1954-57, supr. fuels fabrication devel., 1957-60, metall. specialist, 1960-63, cons. metallurgist, 1963-65; cons. to dir. Battelle Pacific N.W. Labs., Richland, Wash., 1965-70, sr. staff cons., 1970-83, sr. staff scientist, 1985-2000; pres. Rev. & Synthesis Assocs., cons., 1983—. Lectr. metall. engring. Ctr. for Grad. Study U. Wash., 1953-67, affiliate prof., 1967-78; chmn., mem. com. study group on pressure vessel materials Electric Power Rsch. Inst., 1974-78; cons. U. Calif. Lawrence Livermore Labs., 1975-79, Integral Fast Reactor U. Chgo., 1984-94; chmn. com. on reactor safeguards U.S. AEC, 1971; mem. Wash. Bd. Boiler Rules, 1972-85; mem. spec. adv. com. for Argonne Nuc. Tech. Pgm., U Chgo. 1994-2002; chmn. piping design com. Joint NRC/Pressure Vessel Rsch. Coun., 1982-90, PVRC Peer Rev. on ASME Code Simplification, exec. com., 1982—, mem. steering com. on fatigue, 1992—, hon. emeritus mem., 1999; mem. nuclear safety rsch. rev. com. NRC, 1988-94; mem. high level waste structural integrity panel Dept. Energy Brookhaven Nat. Lab., 1992-97. Contbr. tech. articles to profl. jours. Served with U.S. Army, 1942-46. Recipient Silver Beaver award Boy Scouts Am.; Am. Foundrymens Soc. fellow, 1948-50; Regents prof. U. Calif., Berkeley, 1973-74 Fellow ASME (hon., bd. nuc. codes and stds. 1983-2000, chmn. sec. XI 1985-90, hon. mem. subcom. XI 1995, exec. bd. NDE divsn. 1984-90, chmn. 1987-88, nat. nominating com. 1988-90, Langer award 1983, Melvin R. Green Codes & Stds. medal 1997), ASM (life, chmn. program coun. 1966-67, trustee 1967-69, chmn. fellow com. 1968), Am. Nuc. Soc. (adv. editl. bd. nuc. applications 1965-77, bd. dirs. 1984-87, Thompson award 1987); mem. AIME (chmn. ann. seminar com. 1967-68), ASTM (Gillette lectr. 1975), Am. Soc. Nondestructive Testing (Mehl lectr.), Nat. Acad. Engring., Sigma Xi, Tau Beta Pi, Phi Kappa Phi. Home and Office: 630 Cedar Ave Richland WA 99352-3632 E-mail: shb2544@bossig.com.

BUSH, STANLEY GILTNER, secondary school educator; b. Kansas City, Mo., Nov. 4, 1928; s. Dean Thomas and Sallie Giltner (Hoagland) B.; m. Barbara Snow Adams, May 23, 1975 (dec. Mar. 1994); stepchildren: Deborah Gayle Duclon, Douglas Bruce Adams. BA, U. Colo., 1949, MA, 1959, postgrad., 1971, U. Denver, 1980, 85, 90. Tchr. Gering (Nebr.) Pub. Schs., 1949-51, 54-57, Littleton (Colo.) Pub. Schs., 1957-91. Emergency plan dir. City of Littleton, 1961—; safety officer Littleton Pub. Schs., 1968—; founder, chief Arapahoe Rescue Patrol, Inc., Littleton, 1957-92, search mission coord., 1975—; pres. Arapahoe Rescue Patrol, Inc., 1957—, Expedition, Inc., Littleton, 1973—; owner Emergency Rsch. Cons., 1990—. Contbr. chpts. to Boy Scout Field Book, 1984; co-author: Managing Search Function, 1987; contbr. articles to profl. jours. Safety advisor South Suburban Parks Dist., Littleton, 1985—; advisor ARC, Littleton, 1987—, Emergency Planning Com., Arapahoe County, Colo., 1987—; coord. search and rescue Office of Gov., Colo., 1978-82; state judge Odyssey of the Mind, 1996-97; steering com. on homeland security Metro Denver Mayors Office, 2002—. Sgt. U.S. Army, 1951-54. Shell Oil Co. fellow, 1964; recipient Silver Beaver award Boy Scouts Am., 1966, Vigil Order of Arrow, 1966, Award of excellence Masons, 1990, Service to Mankind award Arapahoe Sertoma, 1999. Mem. Nat. Assn. for Search and Rescue (life, Hall Foss award 1978), Colo. Search and Rescue Bd., NEA (life). Methodist. Avocations: mountaineering, wilderness emergency care, emergency services. Home: 2415 E Maplewood Ave Littleton CO 80121-2817 Office: Littleton Ctr 2255 W Berry Ave Littleton CO 80165-0001 E-mail: sbsbush@aol.com.

BUSH, WILLIAM ARDEN, federal agency administrator; b. Ogallala, Nebr., Feb. 1, 1948; s. James L. and Phyllis M. (Sullivan) Bush; m. Carol L. Jensen, June 14, 1970; 1 child, Daniel Arden. A in Bus. Adminstr., Northeastern Jr. Coll., 1969; BSBA, Kearney State Coll., 1972, MBA, 1981; MS in Acct., Okla. City U., 1987. CPA Okla. Gen. mgr., contr. Sullivan-Bush Dept. Store, Ogallala, 1972-73, ptnr., 1973-79; grad. tchg. asst. in acctg. Kearney (Nebr.) State Coll., 1980-81; job office mgr. South Prairie Constrn. Co., Oklahoma City, 1981; agt. IRS, Enid, Oklahoma City, 1981-87, supr. Oklahoma City, 1987—99, agent, 1999—. Pres. W.A. Bush Investment Advisor, Ogallala, 1974—75; instr. supplemental acctg. Rose State Coll., 1990—99; adj. prof. Rose State Jr. Coll., 1990—99. Wrestling coach Ogallala Jaycees, 1975; leader Cub Scouts Am., Ogallala, 1976; chmn. bd. trustees Congl. Ch., Ogallala, 1974. Mem.: Big Mac Sports (Ogallala) (chmn. com. 1978—79), Masons, Rotary (1st v.p. 1979). Republican. Avocations: studying, reading, travel. Home: 11321 N Shannon Ave Oklahoma City OK 73162-2149 Office: IRS 55 N Robinson Ave Ste A Oklahoma City OK 73102-9237

BUSH, WILLIAM GLENN, manufacturing company executive, engineer; b. Lakeland, Fla., Nov. 28, 1937; s. William Baker and Lois (Collins) B.; m. Ruby Joyce King, June 10, 1960; children: Wesley Glenn, William Stuart, Brian Lewis. B in Indsl. Engring., Ga. Inst. Tech., 1960. Registered profl. engr., Calif. Indsl. engr. Procter & Gamble, Perry, Fla., 1960-61, FMC Corp., Lakeland, 1961-62, shop foreman, 1962-63, supr. mfg. engring., 1963-65, mgr. prodn. control, 1966-70, mgr. mfg., 1970-72, gen. mgr. ops. Riverside, Calif., 1972-75, div. gen. mgr. Fairmont, W.Va., 1975-79, corp. dir. bus. planning Chgo., 1979-80, group exec., 1980-81, corp. v.p., 1981-89; chief engr. Durand Machinery, Woodbury, Ga., 1965-66; dir. engring. Mark Industries, Brea, Calif., 1990-92; dir. product engring. Indsl. Dynamics Inc., Torrance, Calif., 1992-1999; cons. engr., 1999—. Bd. govs. mfrs. div. Am. Mining Congress, 1976-78; chmn. bd. dirs. BS&B Engring., 1985-86. Mem. agrl. adv. com. U. Calif., Riverside, 1974-75; mem. adv. bd. Ga. Inst. Tech., 1988-91; bd. dirs. Riverside C. of C., 1973-75, United Way, Riverside, 1973-75, Fairmont C. of C., 1977-79. Mem.: SAR, NSPE, Soc. Descendants Wash.'s Army Valley Forge, Sons of the Revolution, Nat. Soc. Sons Am. Colonists. Republican. Presbyterian. Home and Office: 201 Ocean Ave # 1502B Santa Monica CA 90402

BUSH, WILLIAM MERRITT, lawyer; b. Long Beach, Calif., June 23, 1941; s. Lloyd Merritt and Barbara Ann (Bufkin) B.; m. Dorothy Irene Vasvary, June 25, 1966; children: Steven Merritt, Amy Elizabeth. BA, Stanford U., 1963; JD, U. Calif., Hastings, 1966. Bar: Calif. 1967, U.S. Dist. Ct. (ctrl. dist.) Calif. 1967, U.S. Dist. Ct. (so. dist.) Calif. 1976. Assoc. Dannemeyer & Tuohey, Fullerton, Calif., 1967, Miller, Bush & Minnott, Fullerton, Calif., 1967-69, ptnr., 1970-88; pvt. practice Fullerton, Calif., 1989—. Human rels. commr., City of Fullerton, 1971-77; mem. site coun., Fullerton H.S., 1986-88. Fellow Am. Acad. Matrimonial Lawyers; mem. Orange County Bar Assn. (dir. 1982-85), Calif. State Bar (mem. family law cons. group, family law sect. 1979, mem. family law adv. commn. 1979-85, chmn. commn. 1982-85, bd. legal specialization 1982-89, chmn. 1987-88). Republican. Methodist. Avocations: computers, walking, body surfing. Office: 110 E Wilshire Ave Ste 210 Fullerton CA 92832-1945 E-mail: wmbushesq@lawbush.com.

BUSH, YVONNE, writer, counselor; b. Madelia, Minn., Jan. 29, 1935; d. Guy Pearl and Frances Louise (Traver) Burk; m. William Clarence Bush; children: Donald, Steven, Billie Jean Vogel, Thomas Bush Lovelace, Tami li Robbins, Christopher Clark. AA Edn., Yavapai Coll., 1985; BA, Prescott Coll., 1989, MA, 1999. Cert. EMT 1987, St. Joseph's Med. Center/Newborn,Child Normal Devel. 1983, Feeding and Swallowing Disorders of Infancy; Assessment and Mgmt. 1991, Fetal Alcohol Syndrome/Instructor 1993, Parenting the Teen Years 1987, Understanding Aids 1987, Failure to Thrive, Infant Mental Health 1988, Breast Cancer Self examination/Instructor 1983. Office mgr. Allen's New Way Retail Grocery Store, Prescott, Ariz., 1980—82; head cashier K Mart, Prescott, 1982—83; case mgr. Cath. Social Services of Yavapai, Prescott, Ariz., 1987—90, Ariz. Dept. of Econ. Security, Prescott, 1990—98. Trust com. The Acker Trust Bd., Prescott, 1983—85; organizer, co-leader Scholls Cmty. Orgn., Scholls, 1978—80; bd. dirs. Sierra Comm., Inc., Prescott; charter mem. Ariz. Pub. Svc. Project Voice, Phoenix; bd. dirs. Child Haven, Prescott Crisis Nursery; den mother Boy Scouts of Am., Rowland Heights, 1965—66; bd. dirs. Affordable Constrn., Inc. Prescott; leader women's ministries Alliance Bible Ch., Prescott, Ariz. Author: Bonding and Attachment, 2001, Beyond Tears, A Book To Encourage Women, 2002. Small claims hearing officer Prescott Justice Ct., 1998—2003. Mem.: Prescott Pub. Library/Friends of the Libr. Conservative.

BUSHARA, KHALAFALLA O, neurologist; b. Khartoum, Khartoum, Sudan, Mar. 28, 1963; s. Omer Bushara and Aziza Kaballo; m. Magda Amin, Nov. 21, 1989; children: Omar, Sarrah. MB, BS, MRCP (UK), U. Khartoum, Khartoum, Sudan, 1988. Diplomate American Board of Neurology 1999. Contbr. articles (Wis. neurol. Soc., 1995). Grantee for clin. studies, NIH, Dept. of Veterans Affairs, Minn. Med. Found., 2000—03. Achievements include research in First to describe the effect of botulinum toxin injections on sweating in humans. First to describe octanol use in humans with tremor; First To Describe The Association Between Wheat Allergy And Hereditary (Polyglutamine) Diseases. Office: Minneapolis VA Medl Ctr One Veterans Drive Minneapolis MN MN 55 Office Fax: 612-727-5693. E-mail: busha001@umn.edu.

BUSHEE, WARD, newspaper editor; b. Redding, Calif., 1949; m. Claudia Bushee; children: Ward Gardiner, Mary Standish. BS in History, San Diego State U., 1971. Sports editor Gilroy (Calif.) Dispatch, 1973—75; asst. city editor/sports editor/reporter/copy editor The Californian, Salinas, Calif., 1975—79; sports editor Marin County (Calif.) Ind. Jour., 1979—82; asst. content editor sports USA Today, Arlington, Va., 1982—85; asst. mng. editor sports Westchester (N.Y.) Suburban Newspapers, 1985—86; exec. editor Argus Leader, Sioux Falls, SD, 1986—90; editor Reno (Nev.) Gazette-Jour., 1990—99, Cin. (Ohio) Enquirer, 1999—2002, Ariz. Republic, Phoenix,

2002—, v.p. news, 2002—. Named Editor of Yr., 1992, 97, Gannett Co., Inc., Pres.'s Ring winner 1992-97, 99-2001. Mem. Nev. Press Assn. (pres. 1993, 94, API discussion leader 1996). Office: Arizona Republic 200 E Van Buren St Phoenix AZ 85001*

BUSHEY, ALAN SCOTT, retired insurance holding company executive; b. Peoria, Ill., Apr. 16, 1930; s. Leo James and Luella Frederica (Brunnenmeyer) B. BA, Augustana Coll., Rock Island, Ill., 1952; MBA, Stanford U., 1954. Asst. prof. mktg. and stats. San Jose State Coll., Calif., 1958-59; dir. econ. and mktg. rsch. Continental Casualty Co., Chgo., 1959-68; asst. v.p. CNA/Ins., Chgo., 1968-72; v.p. CNA Fin. Corp., Chgo., 1972-74, USLIFE Corp., N.Y.C., 1974-84, sr. v.p., 1984-88, exec. v.p., 1988-97. Bd. dirs. Ecumenical Inst., Chgo., 1963-74. Served to lt. (j.g.) USNR, 1954-57 Mem. Nat. Assn. Bus. Economists (coun. 1973-76), Life Ins. Mktg. Rsch. Assn. (chmn. mkt. rsch. com. 1985-87, vice chmn. rsch. coun. 1994, chmn. adv. svcs. coun. 1995), Am. Statis. Assn. (bd. dirs. Chgo. chpt. 1965-67), LOMA (strategic mgmt. com. 1987-93), Brit. Schs. and Univs. Found. (bd. dirs. 1993—, hon. sec. 1995-97, pres. 1997-2001, chmn. 2001—), Caledonian Found. USA (trustee 2000—), Sarasota Yacht Club. Republican. Lutheran. Home: 340 S Palm Ave # 122 Sarasota FL 34236-6741

BUSHINSKY, JAY (JOSEPH MASON), journalist, radio/TV correspondent, columnist; b. Buffalo, N.Y., Dec. 8, 1932; s. Joshua M. and Malka (Coralnik) B.; m. Dvora Apte, Dec. 30, 1952; children: Jesse, Aviv, Dahlia. BA, Queens Coll., 1955; MS in Edn., Yeshiva U., N.Y.C., 1959; MS in Journalism, Columbia U., 1963. Mcpl. reporter Times Herald/Record, Middletown, N.Y., 1963-64; copy editor Miami (Fla.) Herald, 1964-66; spl. corr. Chgo. Daily News Fgn. Svc.; corr. Westinghouse Broadcasting Co., 1967—69; Tel Aviv bur. chief Westinghouse Broadcasting Co. (now Infinity), 1969—; corr. Chgo. Sun-Times, Tel Aviv, 1978-85, Middle East bur. chief, columnist, 1986-96; Jerusalem bur. chief Cable News Network, 1980-85; corr. Independent News Network, 1985-87, WWOR-TV, N.Y.C., 1987, Sta. WPIX-TV, N.Y.C., 1991-94, Global TV Network (Can.), 1993—95, Toronto Sun, 1994—, Fox TV Network, 1995—, Boston Herald, 1998-99; diplomatic corr. The Jerusalem Post, 1997-98. Tchr. social studies L.I. City (N.Y.) H.S., 1958-59, William C. Bryant H.S., N.Y.C., 1959-62; lectr. journalism Tel Aviv U., 1966-70, Bar Ilan U., 1993—; asst. prof. journalism U. Mo., 1978—1986. Corr., columnist The Daily Herald, 1996-2001. Served with AUS, 1955-57. Chgo. Newspaper Guild award for investigative reporting for expose of Nazi war criminals in U.S., 1978; co-recipient Media award for econ. understanding Amos Tuck Sch. Bus. Adminstrn., Dartmouth Coll., 1979; named to Chgo. Journalism Hall of Fame, 2002. Mem. Fgn. Press Assn. in Israel (chmn. 1968-71), Overseas Press Club Am. (award for Best Radio Spot News Reporting from Abroad to Group W Foreign News Service for coverage of Yom Kippur War in Mideast, Joint citation 1974). Home and Office: Rehov Hatsafon 5 Savyon 56530 Israel

BUSHKIN, MERLE JEROME, investment banker; b. Dayton, Ohio, Mar. 21, 1935; s. Charles D. and Eva (Flegel) B.; m. Leone Edricks, Aug. 6, 1961; children: Elizabeth Bushkin Schnitzer, Nancy Louise. AB, Harvard U., 1956, MBA, 1960. Mgmt. cons. Cresap, McCormick & Paget, N.Y.C., 1960-64; planning and mktg. positions Mobil Oil Corp., N.Y.C., 1964-70; fin. v.p., treas., corp. sec. Wollensak, Inc., Rochester, N.Y., 1970-71; v.p., mgr. mergers and acquisitions, CBWL-Hayden Stone Inc. (predecessor of Shearson Lehman Brothers Inc.), N.Y.C., 1971-72; pres. Bushkin Assocs., Inc., N.Y.C., 1972—. Lectr. in field. Mem. Harvard Club N.Y., Woodstock Country Club. Home: 86 Caterson Ter Hartsdale NY 10530-2605 Office: Bushkin Assocs Inc PO Box 111 White Plains NY 10602-0111 Address: PO Box 639 Brownsville VT 05037 E-mail: mbushkin@bushkin.com.

BUSHNELL, DANIEL S. lawyer. Ptnr. Kirton, McKonkie & Bushnell, Salt Lake City. Office: Kirton McKonkie & Bushnell 330 S 3rd E # D Salt Lake City UT 84111-2525

BUSHNELL, GEORGE EDWARD, III, lawyer; b. Detroit, Feb. 18, 1952; s. George Edward Jr. and Elizabeth (Whelden) B.; m. Eileen Mary Maguire, Sept. 16, 1989; children: Ann-Elizabeth, Emily Spears, George Edward. BA, Bucknell U., 1974; JD, Emory U., 1981. Bar: Ga. 1981, D.C. 1983, N.Y. 1986. Vol. U.S. Peace Corps, Burkina Faso, 1974-76, tng. dir., 1976-77; staff asst. to hon. Lucien Nedzi U.S. Ho. of Reps., Washington, 1977-78; assoc. Duncan, Allen and Mitchell, Washington, Ivory Coast, Congo, 1981-85, Shearman & Sterling, N.Y.C., 1985-91; corp. counsel Joseph E. Seagram & Sons, Inc., N.Y.C., 1991-2001; v.p., corp. counsel Vivendi Universal S.A., N.Y.C., 2001—. Mem. ABA, N.Y. State Bar Assn. Home: 1075 Park Ave Apt 2A New York NY 10128-1003 Office: Vivendi Universal 800 3rd Ave New York NY 10022-7604

BUSHNELL, PRUDENCE, diplomat, management consultant; b. Washington, Nov. 26, 1946; d. Gerald Sherman and Bernice Edna (Duflo) B.; m. Richard Alan Buckley, Oct. 26, 1979. BA, U. Md., 1969; MS, Russell Sage Coll., 1980. Bi-lingual sec. Embassy of Morocco, Washington, 1969-70; chief sec. U. Md., College Park, 1970-72; tng. mgr. Legal Svcs. Tng. Program, Washington, 1972-76; dir. Cultural Learning Concepts, Dallas, 1976-81; mgr. adminstrv. ops. U.S. Consulate Bombay, U.S. Embassy, Dakar, 1982-86; dir. exec. devel. Fgn. Svc. Inst., Washington, 1986-89; dep. chief mission U.S. Embassy Dakar, Dept. State, Washington, 1989-92; dep. asst. sec. for African affairs Dept. State, Washington, 1993-96; U.S. amb. to Kenya Dept. of State, Nairobi, 1996-99, U.S. amb. to Guatemala, 1999—. Avocations: gardening, walking, writing.

BUSHOR, MARK ELDON, pastor, writer, consultant; b. St. Louis, Aug. 22, 1954; PhD, Southwestern Bapt. Theol. Sem., Ft. Worth, 1998. Assoc. pastor St. Mark United Meth. Ch., Cleburne, Tex. Office: 1109 W Henderson St Cleburne TX 76033-8723

BUSHWICK, NATHANIEL LEWIS, translator, researcher; b. N.Y.C., Jan. 24, 1949; s. Samuel and Doris Ruth Bushwick; m. Marguerite Brom; children: Zvi Eliezer, Yizhak, Hodaya, Shmuel. BA, Yeshiva Coll., 1970; MA, MS, Yeshiva U., 1973; PhD, Binghamton U., 1995. Pres., founder Nathan Bushwick Inc., Scranton, Pa., 1984—. Mem. adj. faculty Pa. State U., Dunmore, 1987—2001; translator, anthologist Moznaim Pub., N.Y.C., 1989—97. Author: Understanding the Jewish Calendar, 1989; translator: Torah Anthology - Book of Joshua, 1990, Torah Anthology - Book of Judges, 1991, Torah Anthology - Book of Kings I, 1994, Torah Anthology - Book of Kings II, 1997, The Commentary of Rabbenu Nissim ben Reuven Gerondi on Mesechet Nedarim, 2000; contbr. articles to profl. jours. Avocations: painting, sculpture.

BUSIG, RICK HAROLD, mining executive; b. Vancouver, Wash., June 21, 1952; s. Harold Wayne and Ramona (Riley) B. AA, Clark Coll., Vancouver, 1972; BA in Econs., U. Wash., 1974. Acct. Universal Svcs., Seattle, 1975-78; acct., acctg. mgr., controller Landura Corp., Woodburn, Oreg., 1978-80; asst. controller Pulte Home Corp., Laramie, Wyo., 1980-81; treas., controller Orcal Cable, Inc., Sparks, Nev., 1981-82; controller Saga Exploration Co., Reno, Nev., 1982—. Acct. Sterling Mine Joint Venture, Beatty, Nev., 1982-95. Del. Nev. State Dem. Conv., Reno, 1984, 94, Las Vegas, 1988. Recipient Spaatz award CAP. Mem. AICPA, Wash. Soc. CPA's, Oreg. Soc. CPA's, Del. Nev. State Dem. Conv., Reno, 1984, 94, Las Vegas, 1988. Recipient Spaatz award CAP. Mem. AICPA, Wash. Soc. CPA's, Oreg. Soc. CPA's. Home: 2735 Lakeside Dr Apt A Reno NV 89509-4254 Office: Saga Exploration Co 2660 Tyner Way Reno NV 89503-4926 E-mail: rickb@sierra.net.

BUSKIRK, DANIEL D. animal scientist, educator; b. Fort Wayne, Ind., June 14, 1965; s. Marvin D and Ann M Buskirk; m. Jennifer Runyan, June 13, 1987; children: Lauren, Janna, Wesley. BS, Purdue U., West Lafayette, IN, 1987, MS, 1987—89; PhD, U. of Ill., Urbana-Champaign, IL, 1996. Cert. Profl. Animal Scientist 1996. Assoc. prof. Mich. State U., East Lansing, Mich., 1996—. Office: Mich State Univ 2265C Anthony Hall East Lansing MI 48824

BUSKIRK, ELSWORTH ROBERT, physiologist, educator; b. Beloit, Wis., Aug. 11, 1925; s. Ellsworth Fred and Laura Ellen (Parman) B.; m. Mable Heen, Aug. 28, 1948; children: Laurel Ann Buskirk Wiegand, Kristine Janet Buskirk Hallett. Student, U. Wis., 1943; BA, St. Olaf Coll., Northfield, Minn., 1950; MA, U. Minn., 1951, PhD, 1954. Lab. and tchg. asst. Lab. Physiol. Hygiene, U. Minn., 1951-53; rsch. fellow Life Inst. Med. Rsch. Fund, 1953-54; physiologist Environ. Rsch. Ctr., Natick, Mass., 1954-57, Nat. Inst. for Arthritis, Metabolic and Digestive Diseases, NIH, Bethesda, Md., 1957-63; prof. applied physiology Pa. State U., University Park, 1963-92, dir. Lab. Human Performance Rsch., 1963-92, Marie Underhill Noll prof. Human Performance, 1988-92, emeritus, 1992—. Mem. sci. adv. com. Pres.' Coun. on Phys. Fitness, 1959-61; mem. applied physiology study sect. divsn. rsch. grants NIH, 1964-68, 76-80; mem. com. on interplay of engrng. with biology and medicine NAS-NAE, 1968-74, 82-88; mem. rsch. com. Pa. Heart Assn., 1970-73, 82 86, 87-89, 90-95; mem. Pa. Gov.'s Coun. on Phys. Fitness and Sports, 1978-82; mem. com. on mil. nutrition rsch. NAS/NRC, 1982-90; mem. clin. scis. study sect. divsn. rsch. grants NIH, 1989-92, spl. reviewer, 1992-99; mem. Def. Women's Rsch. Com. IOM, NAS-NRC, 1995. Sect. editor Jour. Applied Physiology, 1974-78, assoc. editor, 1978-84; co-editor Sci. and Medicine in Sports and Exercise, 1974, editor, 1973-75; editor-in-chief, 1984-88, cons., editor, 1989-94; mem. editl. bd. Physician and Sports Medicine, 1974-85, Jour. Cardiopulmonary Rehab., 1980-2000, Underseas and Hyperbaric Medicine, 1988-95, Am. Jour. Clin. Nutrition, 1982-92, Jour. Gerontology, 1982-92, Exptl. Gerontology, 1989-98; also over 250 articles on physiology, revs. to sci. jours. Bd. visitors Sargent Coll., Boston U., 1976-92; bd. dirs. Ctr. Cmty. Hosp., Pa., 1966-70, sec., 1971-72, v.p., 1973, pres., 1974-75. Served with U.S. Army, ETO. Recipient Disting. Alumni award St. Olaf Coll., 1969, Daggs Svc. award Am. Physiol. Soc., 2000; rsch. grantee NIH, 1963 92, U.S. Olympic Com., 1965-68, USAF, 1965-69, Pa. Dept. Health, 1966-67, Pa. Heart Assn., 1966, 76-80, NSF, 1968-70, Nat. Inst. Occupl. Safety and Health, 1969-74; NATO sr. fellow in sci., 1977; named to Athletic Hall of Fame, St. Olaf Coll., 2000. Mem. AAAS, AAPHERD, ASHRAE, Aerospace Med. Assn., Am. Acad. Phys. Edn., Am. Coll. Sports Medicine (citations 1973, 75, Honor award 1984, editl. award 1989, 93, Mid-Atlantic regional chpt. Svc. award 1991), Am. Inst. Nutrition, Am. Physiol. Soc. (pres. environ. and exercise sect. 1987-91, com. on coms. 1988-92, Honor award environ. exercise physiology sect. 1993, Daggs award 2002), Am. Heart Assn. (coun. on epidemiology), N.Y. Acad. Scis., NIH Alumni Assn., Pa. Heart Assn. (rsch. com. 1988-94), Am. Diabetes Assn., Coun. Biology Editors (Healthy Am. Fitness Leaders award 1992), Centre Hills Country Club. Lutheran. Home: 216 Hunter Ave State College PA 16801-6947 Office: Pa State U 119 Noll Lab University Park PA 16802-6900

BUSKY, DONALD FRANK, political science educator; b. Phila., Oct. 3, 1951; s. Robert and Lena Ida Busky. BA, Temple U., 1978, MA, 1980, PhD, 1988. Lectr. Temple U., Phila., 1980-90; adj. prof. Drexel U., Phila., 1987-95, Camden County Coll., Blackwood, N.J., 1998—. Author: Democratic Socialism: A Global Survey, 2000, Communism in History and Theory, 3 vols., 2002. Local chairperson Socialist Party of Greater Phila., 1978-2002; state chairperson Socialist Party of Pa., 1988-2000, editor of The Red City News (later renamed The Keystone Socialist and then The Red Penn., 1979-2002, editor of The Weird News, 1989-2003. Mem. Am. Polit. Sci. Assn. Home: 7393 Rugby St Philadelphia PA 19138 Office: Camden County Coll Rm 208 Madison Hall PO Box 200 College Dr Blackwood NJ 08012 E-mail: caimans@yahoo.com.

BUSNER, PHILIP H. retired lawyer; b. Bklyn., Mar. 26, 1927; s. Joseph and Ray (Grajewer) B.; m. Naomi Marcia Greenfield, June 24, 1951; children: Joan Alexandra, Carey Elizabeth. BA cum laude, NYU, 1949; LLB, Harvard U., 1952. Bar: N.Y. 1953, U.S. Dist. Ct. (so. dist.) N.Y. 1956, U.S. Dist. Ct. (ea. dist.) N.Y. 1958, U.S. Ct. Appeals (2d cir.) 1956, U.S. Supreme Ct. 1974. Assoc. Rein, Mound & Cotton, N.Y.C., 1953, Hess, Mela, Segall, Popkin & Guterman, N.Y.C., 1954-55, Carroad & Carroad, N.Y.C., 1955-72; ptnr. Young, Sonnenfeld & Busner, N.Y.C., 1972-75, Sonnenfeld & Busner, N.Y.C., 1976-78, Sonnenfeld, Busner & Weinstein, N.Y.C., 1978-85, Sonnenfeld, Busner & Richman, N.Y.C., 1986-88; pvt. practice Great Neck, N.Y., 1989-97; ret., 1998. Trustee Asthmatic Children's Found. N.Y., 1978-87; adminstrv. judge N.Y.C. Dept. Transp., 1989-93; arbitrator N.Y.C. Civil Ct., 1990-92, Nassau County Dist. Ct., 1990-95, Suffolk County Dist. Ct., 1990-93. With USAAF, 1945-47. Mem. Am. Arbitration Assn. (arbitrator 1990-92), Phi Beta Kappa. Home: One Todd Dr Sands Point NY 11050

BUSQUETS, MIGUEL ANTONIO, ophthalmologist; b. Hyannis, Mass., July 14, 1971; s. Miguel Salvador and Anne Healy Busquets; m. Gretchen Elizabeth Gruener; children: Talia children: Marisa. BA magna cum laude, Harvard U., 1992; MD, Duke U., 1996. Med./surg. intern Carilion Roanoke (Va.) Meml. Hosps., 1996—97; ophthalmology resident Washington U., St. Louis, 1997—2000; vitreoretinal fellow Barnes Retina Inst., St. Louis, 2000—02; vitreoretinal specialist/cons. Assocs. in Ophthalmology, Pitts., 2002—. Lectr. in field. Contbr. articles to profl. jours. Recipient Rosenbaum Rsch. award, Washington U., 1999; grantee Lawrence grant, Retina Rsch. Found., 1999. Mem.: AMA, Allegheny Councy Med. Soc., Pa. Med. Soc., Mo. Soc. Eye Physicians and Surgeons, Assn. for Rsch. in Vision and Ophthalmology, Am. Acadamy Ophthalmology. Achievements include research and publication in photodynamic therapy for choroidal neovascularization. Avocations: marathon running, swimming. Office: 500 Lewis Run Rd Ste 218 Pittsburgh PA 15122 Personal E-mail: MGMBusquets@aol.com.

BUSS, DANIEL FRANK, environmental scientist; b. Milw., Jan. 13, 1943; s. Lynn Charles and Pearl Elizabeth (Ward) B.; m. Ann Makal, Jan. 22, 1977; children: Jessica, Jonathan. BS, Carroll Coll., 1965; MS in Biology, U. Wis., 1972, MS in Environ. Engrng., 1977, P.D.D. in Environ. Engrng., 1985. Registered profl. engr., Wis. Dir. limnological studies Aqua-Tech, Inc., Waukesha, Wis., 1969-72; project mgr. environ. studies Point Beach Nuclear Plant, Two Creeks, Wis., 1972-76; assoc., dir. aquatic studies environ. sci. div. Camp Dresser & McKee, Inc., Milw., 1977—, dir. indsl. service, 1978-90, office mgr., coord. for environ. assesments, 1990—. Lectr. on nuclear power and environ., environ. auditing; mgr. hazardous waste superfund projects, dredge disposal planning projects; asbestos insp., mgmt. planner EPA, 1988, also nat. accounts mgr. for performance of environ. site assessments for property trans.; instr. environ. site assments according to domestic and internat. stds. with consideration of bus. environ. risk for real property. Author: An Environmental Study of the Ecological Effects on Lake Michigan of the Thermal Discharge from the Point Beach Nuclear Plant, 1976, Environmental Auditing-- A Systematic Approach, 1984; contbr. articles to profl. jours, chpts. to books and environmental site investigation protocols for ASTM, ASCE and other soc. guidance documents. Mem. ASCE (chmn. site constrn. and remediation implementation manual task com.),Am. Nuclear Soc. (sec.-treas. Wis. sect., program mgr. waste disposal studies, program mgr. for remedial programs involving jet fuel and deicer contamination at Gen. Mitchell Internat. Airport), Midwest Soc. Electron Microscopists, Internat. Soc. Theoretical and Applied Limnology and Oceanography, Internat. Assn. Gt. Lakes Rsch., Am. Indsl. Hygiene Soc., Nat. Assn. Environ. Profls., Fed. Water Pollution Control Adminstrn., Cons. Engrs. Coun. (chmn. liaison com. Ill. and Chgo. Bar Assn., mem. com. for devel. site investigation manual ASCE, assn. ASCE com. to develop remedial design, feasibility study manual), Am. Assn. Environ. Engrs. (diplomate 1990, cert. hazardous materials mgr. 1988, hazard control mgr. 1988), Program mgr. design, construction mgmt., oper. UV/Oxidation system (used for treating herbicide contaminated ground water in Wisconsin), Am. Acad. Environ. Engrs. (Wis. state rep.), Glendale Wis. Econ. Devel. Com. and Bus. Coun., Sigma Xi. Home: 5543 N Shasta Dr Milwaukee WI 53209-4924 also: 330 E Kilborn Ste 1219 Milwaukee WI 53202

BUSS, EDWARD GEORGE, geneticist; b. Concordia, Kans., Aug. 28, 1921; s. George E. and Kathryn (Luginsland) B.; m. Dorothy Ruth Arvidson, May 7, 1949; children: Ellen, Norman. BS, Kans. State Coll., 1943; MS, Purdue U., 1949, PhD, 1956. Grad. rsch. teaching asst. Purdue U., West Lafayette, Ind., 1946-49; asst. prof. Colo. A&M Coll., Ft. Collins, 1949-55; instr. Purdue U., 1955-56; assoc. prof., prof. Pa. State U., University Park, 1956-86, prof. emeritus, 1987—. Cons. P.T. Anputraco Ltd., Surabaya Indonesia, 1987-94; sr. scientist Biopore Inc., State College, Pa., 1987-94; Fulbright lectr., Sierra Leone, West Africa, 1988. Co-author: Meat Production in Turkeys, 1990; contbr. articles to profl. jours. Vol. Internat. Exec. Svc. Corps., Egypt, 1995. Mem. Am. Genetic Assn. (coun. mem.), Am. Inst. Biological Scis. (gov. bd., exec. com.), AAAS (fellow 1962); Poultry Sci. Assn. (fellow 1988), World's Poultry Sci. Assn. Democrat. Home: 1420 S Garner St State College PA 16801-6330 Office: Pa State U Dept Poultry Sci 213 Henning Bldg University Park PA 16802-3501

BUSS, KATHLEEN E. music educator; b. Boulder, Colo., May 31, 1957; d. Frank F. Priest and Charlee M. Amis; m. Harry Dean Buss, June 19, 1980; 1 child, Charles Harlan. MusB in Piano Pedagogy, U. Colo., 1979. Tchr. aid Mountain Shadows Montessori, Boulder, Colo., 1979—80, 1991—92; adminstrv. asst. Haddock Ins. Agy., Boulder, 1980—84; pvt. lic. day care provider Boulder and Niwot, 1984—90; child care referral svc. staff City of Boulder, 1990—91; part-time pvt. piano tchr. Kathy's Piano Studio, Boulder and Niwot, 1976—, full time pvt. piano tchr. Niwot, 1992—. Recipient award, Nat. Guild Piano Tchrs., 1975, Paderewski Gold medal, 1975. Mem.: Boulder Area Music Tchr. Assn. (2nd v.p. 1993—95), Nat. Federated Music Tchrs. (festival chair 1997, pres. 2001—02), Music Tchrs. Nat. Assn. Lutheran. Avocations: running, hiking, skiing, snowshoeing, antiques. Home and Office: PO Box 342 Niwot CO 80544

BUSS, SAMUEL RUDOLPH RUDOLPH, mathematics educator, researcher; b. New Haven, Conn., Aug. 6, 1957; s. Martin John and Nancy Jane (Macpherson) B.; m. Teresa Paula Thacker, June 7, 1980; children: Stephanie, Ian. BS in Math. and Physics, Emory U., 1979; MA in Math., Princeton U., 1982, PhD in Math., 1985. VLSI engr. Proximity Designs Corp. (now Franklin Electronic Pub.), 1980-82; researcher Math. Scis. Rsch. Inst., Berkeley, Calif., 1985-86; instr. U. Calif., Berkeley, 1986-88, asst. prof. math. San Diego, 1988-90, assoc. prof., 1990-93, prof. math., 1993—. Co-organizer workshop on feasible math., Ithaca, 1989; organizer workshops on proof theory, complexity and logic, San Diego, 1990, Prague, 1991. Author: Bounded Arithmetic, 1986, 3D Computer Graphics: A Mathematical Introduction with Open GL, 2003; editor: Archive for Mathematical Logic, Lecture Notes in Logic; co-editor: Feasible Mathematics, 1990; author, editor: Handbook of Proof Theory, 1998; patentee in field; contbr. articles to profl. jours. NSF fellow, 1979-80, 82-84, 85-88, Sloan Found. fellow, 1984-85; NSF grantee, 1988—. Mem.: American Mathematical Society, Association for Computing Machinery, IEEE Computer Society, Association for Symbolic Logic. Achievements include patents on associative memory circuit system and method, on methods for minimum-cost matchings. Office: U Calif San Diego Math Dept La Jolla CA 92093

BUSSARD, CARMEN ADELAIDE, speech professional; b. Portland, Oreg., May 31, 1931; MusB, Coll. of the Pacific, 1952. Cert. speech and hearing specialist Calif., elem. edn. tchr. Calif. Speech and lang. therapist Hudson Sch. Dist., Calif., 1963—66, Saddleback Valley Sch. dist., Mission Viejo, Calif., 1968—91; organist St. Stephen's Episc. Ch., La Habra, Calif., Peace Luth. Ch., Tustin, Calif. Author: (book) Martin Shellabarger, 1994, Asa Canterbury, 1998, Joseph Vance, 1998, The Littler Family, 2001. Mem.: Colonial Dames of the 17th Century, DAR, Mu Phi Epsilon, Pi Kappa Lambda, Phi Kappa Phi.

BUSSARD, JANICE WINGEIER, retired educator, inventor; b. Lowell, Mich., Mar. 2, 1925; d. Carl L. and E. May (Velzy) Wingeier; m. James W. Bussard, June 15, 1947; children: Jane, Jody, Jiselle, Jill. BS, Western Mich. U. 1946. Cert. secondary edn. tchr., Mich. Bus. edn. tchr. Spring Lake (Mich.) H.S., 1965-86; inventor Spring Lake, Mich., 1987-97. Achievements include 10 issued patents in U.S. and 1 in Canada in the field of holography. Mfr. holographic labels for security, authentication and decoration for applications to any substrate. Home: 201 N Fruitport Rd Spring Lake MI 49456-0193

BUSSARD, ROBERT WILLIAM, physicist; b. Washington, Aug. 11, 1928; s. Marcel Julian and Elsa Mathilda (Griesser) B.; m. Dolly H. Gray, 1981; children: Elise Marie, William Julian, Robert Lee, Virginia Lesley Bussard Barausky. BS in Engring., UCLA, 1950, MS in Engring., 1952; MS in Physics, Princeton U., 1959, PhD in Physics, 1961. Design engr. Falcon program Hughes Aircraft Co., 1949-51; mech. engr. aircraft nuclear propulsion project Oak Ridge Nat. Lab., 1952-55; alt. group leader nuclear rocket program Los Alamos Sci. Lab., 1955-62, alt. leader laser div., 1971-73; dir. nuclear systems staff, asst. dir. mechanics div. Space Tech. Labs., TRW Inc., Redondo Beach, Calif., 1962-64; assoc. mgr. research and engring., corp. chief scientist Electro-Optical Systems div. Xerox Corp., Pasadena, Calif., 1964-69; with CSI Corp., Los Angeles, 1969-70; mgr. Cherokee Assocs., Pasadena, Calif., 1970-72; asst. dir. div. controlled thermonuclear research U.S. AEC, Washington, 1973-74; founder, pres., chmn. Energy Resources Group (ERG), Inc., Arlington, Va., 1974-86, Internat. Nuclear Energy Systems Co. (INESCO), Inc., La Jolla, Calif. and McLean, Va., 1976-84; sr. scientist PSR Corp., Arlington, Va., 1985-89; founder, tech. dir. Energy/Matter Conversion Corp. (EMC2), San Diego, 1984—. Cons. NATO, 1960-64, U.S. Dept. Energy, 1974-78, Los Alamos Sci. Lab., 1973-88, dir. ctrl. intelligence, 1971-78; lectr. UCLA, 1960-69, U. Fla., 1962-64 Author: (with R.D. DeLauer) Nuclear Rocket Propulsion, 1958, Fundamentals of Nuclear Flight, 1965; editor: Nuclear Thermal and Electric Rocket Propulsion, 1967; contbr. articles to profl. jours. Fellow AIAA; mem. Am. Phys. Soc., Internat. Acad. Astronautics. Clubs: Princeton (N.Y.C.); Cosmos (Washington), Capitol Hill (Washington). Achievements include patentee space nuclear propulsion, power generation, fusion and fission power, solar power systems. Office: Ste 103 9705 Carroll Center Rd San Diego CA 92126-6505 E-mail: emc2qed@compuserve.com. *The future is constructed in a fashion and to a scale envisioned by those who perceive what it might be, and who work to make these visions happen. At any one time, only a few thousand people are working to shape the world of tomorrow from the tools, techniques, and ideas of today. I hope with God's grace to help this work, to improve the lot of man and ensure the survival and growth of humankind in such a way that the freedom of all people might be preserved and extended for future generations.*

BUSSE, EILEEN ELAINE, special education educator; b. Green Bay, Wis., Oct. 16, 1957; d. Ervin F. Dohl and Elaine I. (Behnke) Richmond; m. John F. Busse, July 5, 1980; children: Jessica Lynn, Jeremy John. BS in Elem. and Spl. Edn., U. Wis., Eau Claire, 1979; MS in Spl. Edn., U. Wis., Whitewater, 1985. Cert. tchr. elem. and spl. edn. Tchr. spl. edn.-mentally retarded Ithaca (Wis.) Pub. Schs., 1979-80; spl. edn. tchr. Walworth County CDEB, Whitewater, Wis., 1980—, Lakeview Elem. Sch., 1991-2000, Whitewater H.S., 2000—; summer sch. instr. St. Thomas U., 2003. Coop. tchr. U. Wis., Whitewater, 1988—; summer sch. tchr. U. St. Thomas, St. Paul, Minn., 2003. Author: Student Owned Spelling, 1991, II, 1992, III, 1994. Mem. First English Luth. Ch. edn. com., Whitewater, 1990-95, 98—, chmn. edn. com., 1993-95, mem. ch. coun., 1993-94, 97—; active Girl Scouts U.S.A., 1992-2000; advisor sr. high youth 1st English Luth. Ch., 1998—. Recipient Excellence in Edn. award U.S. Dept. Edn., 1984-85, Recognized spl. educator, 1998. Mem. Coun. for Exceptional Children, Wis. Assn. Children with Behavioral Disorders, Milw. (Wis.) County Zool. Soc., Delta Kappa Gamma. Avocations: reading, travel, gardening. Home: 455 Ventura Ln Whitewater WI 53190-1548 Office: Whitewater HS 534 S Elizabeth St Whitewater WI 53190

BUSSE, EWALD WILLIAM, psychiatrist, educator; b. St. Louis, Aug. 18, 1917; s. Frederick Ewald and Emily Louise (Stroh) B.; m. Ortrude Helen Schnaedelbach, July 18, 1941; children: Ortrude Susan Busse White, Barbara Ann, Ewald Richard, Deborah Emily Busse Bragg. AB, Westminster Coll., 1938, ScD (hon.), 1960; MD, Washington U., St. Louis, 1942. Diplomate Am. Bd. Psychiatry and Neurology, Am. Bd. Qualification in Clin. Neurophysiology. Intern St. Louis City Hosp., 1942; resident in neuropsychiatry and psychiatry McCloskey Gen. Hosp., Temple, Tex., 1943-46, Colo. Psychiat. Hosp., Denver, 1946-48; faculty, head dept. psychosomatic medicine U. Colo., Denver, 1950-53; prof. Duke U. Med. Ctr., Durham, N.C., 1953-65, J.P. Gibbons prof. psychiatry, 1965-87, chmn. dept., 1953-74, dir. Ctr. for Study Aging, 1957-70, assoc. provost, dean Sch. Medicine, 1974-82, dean emeritus, 1982—; pres., CEO N.C. Inst. Medicine, 1987-94, pres. emeritus, 1994—. Mem. council Nat. Inst. on Aging, Bethesda, Md., 1979-83; chmn. geriatrics and gerontology adv. com. VA, 1981-86 Author, editor: Behavior and Adaptation in Late Life, 1969, 2d edit., 1977, Handbook of Geriatric Psychiatry, 1980, 2d edit., 1994, Part II, Vol. II-Psychiatry Update, 1983, The Duke Longitudinal Studies, 1985, Aging: The Universal Human Experience, 1987, Geriatric Psychiatry, 1989, (textbook) Geriatric Psychiatry, 1996; author: Cerebral Manifestations of Cardiac Dysrhythmias, 1979. Mem. N.C. State Commn. on Care of Elderly, Raleigh, 1968-73; mem. Durham County Commn. in Mental Health, 1971-74; pres. biomed. rsch. panel White Ho. Conf. on Aging, 1975-76, sect. chmn. del., 1978-81; mem. sci. adv. bd. Alliance for Aging Rsch., 1986—; bd. dirs. Greater Durham United Way, 1987-92. Maj. U.S. Army, 1943-46. Recipient Brookdale Found. award, 1982, Alumni Achievement award Westminster Coll., 1984, Disting. Alumni award Washington U., 1992, Pioneer award Govs. Commn. on Reduction of Infant Mortality, 1993; Busse Bldg. named in his honor Duke U., 1985; Busse Internat. Rsch. award endowed, 1990; Ewald Busse award created in his honor N.C. Dept. Human Resources, 1990; Busse Lecture endowment, 1995. Wash. U. Alumni Aohmist,2002. Fellow Am. Psychiat. Assn. (pres.

1971-72, chmn. ethics com. 1981-85, Jack Weinberg Meml. award, Warren Williams award 1987, Disting. Service award 1988), Am. Geriatrics Soc. (pres. 1975-76 Allen Thewlis award), Gerontol. Soc. Am. (pres. 1967-68 Freeman award), ACP (Menninger award 1971), Southeastern Med. Dental Soc. (pres. 1978-80); mem. Internat. Assn. Gerontology (pres. 1983-89, Sandoz prize1983), World Psychiat. Assn. (ethics com.), N.Y. Acad. Medicine (Salmon award 1980). Clubs: Hope Valley; Beech Mountain (N.C.). Lodges: Rotary/Durham; Masons. pres., 1972-73. hon. mem., 2002. Gov. N.Y. Ordin at 7th Long Land Pine, 2002. Home: 2701 Pickett Rd Apt 4049 Durham NC 27705 Office: Duke U Med Ctr PO Box 2948 Durham NC 27715-2948*

BUSSE, LEONARD WAYNE, banker, financial consultant; b. Chgo., June 29, 1938; s. Edwald William and Elsie Helen (Weidner) B.; m. Gretchen Guam Beal, Sept. 7, 1963; children: Whitney Lee, Carter Douglas. BS, Purdue U., 1960; postgrad., Northwestern U., 1964-67. CPA, Ill. With Continental Ill. Corp., Chgo., 1963-88, v.p., 1973-81, sr. v.p., 1981-85, head internat. banking dept., 1985; exec. v.p. Continental Bank, Chgo., 1985-88; cons. The Busse Group, Vail, Colo., 1989-93; pres., CEO The Pacific Bank, San Francisco, 1993-94, also bd. dirs., 1994; CEO, bd. dirs. First Citizen Bank Ltd., Port of Spain, Trinidad, 1994-96; CFO, bd. dirs. Worldbridge Broadband Svcs., Denver, 1998-2000; v.p. fin. Open Access Broadland Network, Denver, 1999-2001; sr. advisor Headwaters MB, Denver, 2001—; dir. Exabyte Corp., Boulder, Colo., 2002—. Bd. dirs. McGraw Wildlife Found., Elgin, Ill., 1982-92, Vectra Banking Corp., Denver, 1993-94. Mem. AICPA. Republican. Lutheran. Avocations: skiing, hunting, biking, fishing.

BUSSEWITZ, ROY JON, lawyer, pharmacist; b. Hartford, Wis., Mar. 19, 1944; s. Reginald Max and Bernice (Kadolph) B.; m. Joyce Ann O'Donnell, Aug. 24, 1980; children: Kathleen Ann, Christine Marie. BS in Pharmacy, U. Wis., 1967; JD, Valparaiso U., 1973. Bar: Wis. 1973. Prof. health law U. Wis., Milw., 1973-78; legal cons. State of Wis., Madison, 1978; legis. asst., health U.S. Senator Gaylord Nelson, Washington, 1979—80; legis. counsel Am. Health Care Assn., Washington, 1981; exec. dir. Nat. Assn. Med. Equipment Suppliers, Alexandria, Va., 1982—83; dir. govt. rels. Nat. Assn. Pvt. Psychiat. Hosps., Washington, 1984; dir. fed. govt. affairs Glaxo Inc., Alexandria, 1984-88; cons. 1988-91; v.p. managed care/telecomms. Nat. Assn. Chain Drug Stores, Alexandria, 1991—. Bd. dirs., mem. working group Electronic Data Interchange, Nat. Coun. Prescription Programs. Mem. Wis. Bar Assn. Avocations: tennis, golf, gardening, photography. Home: 1103 Potomac Ln Alexandria VA 22308-2534 Office: 413 N Lee St Alexandria VA 22314-2301 E-mail: rbussewitz@nacds.org.

BUSSEY, GEORGE DAVIS, psychiatrist; b. Salta, Argentina, Apr. 14, 1949; s. William Harold and Helen (Wygant) B.; m. Moira Savage, July 26, 1975; children: Andrew Davis, Megan Elizabeth. BS, U. Denver, 1969; MD, Ea. Va. Med. Sch., 1977; JD, U. Hawaii, 1993. Diplomate in psychiatry, forensic psychiatry and addiction psychiatry Am. Bd. Psychiatry and Neurology. Intern Eastern Va. Grad. Sch. Medicine, 1977-78; resident Ea. Va. Grad. Sch. Medicine, 1978-79, Vanderbilt U. Hosp., Nashville, 1979-81; staff psychiatrist Hawaii State Hosp., Kaneohe, 1981-82; asst. prof. dept. psychiatry U. Hawaii, Honolulu, 1982-84; dir. adult svcs. Kahi Mohala Hosp., Ewa Beach, Hawaii, 1983-89; assoc. med. dir. Queens Healthcare Plan, Honolulu, 1988-94, v.p., 1997—2001; med. dir. Queen's Health Mgmt., Honolulu, 1994—2001; med. dir. behavioral scis. First Health of the Carolinas, Pinehurst, NC, 2001—, sr. med. dir., 2002. Clin. assoc. prof. Dept. Psychiatry U. Hawaii, Honolulu, 1990. Mem. U. Hawaii Law Rev., 1991-93; contbr. articles to profl. jours. Fellow Am. Psychiat. Assn., Hawaii Psychiat. Soc. (treas. 1982-83, pres. 1985-87), N.C. Psychiat. Assn.; mem. Am. Coll. Physician Execs. (cert.). Office: First Health of the Carolinas 155 Memorial Pinehurst NC 28374

BUSSGANG, JULIAN JAKUB, electronics engineer; b. Lwow, Poland, Mar. 26, 1925; came to U.S., 1949, naturalized, 1954; s. Joseph and Stephanie (Philipp) B.; m. Fay Rita Vogel, Aug. 14, 1960; children: Jessica Edith, Julia Claire, Jeffrey Joseph. B.Sc. in Engring., U. London, 1949; S.M. in Elec. Engring., MIT, 1951; PhD in Applied Physics, Harvard U., 1955. Mem. tech. staff Lincoln Lab., MIT, Lexington, 1951-55; mgr. applied rsch. RCA, Burlington, Mass., 1955-62; pres. Signatron, Inc., Lexington, 1962-87; pvt. practice cons. Lexington, 1988—. Vis. lectr. Harvard U., 1964; lectr. Northeastern U., Boston, 1962-65; mem. Mass. del. White House Conf. on Small Bus., 1980. Assoc. editor: Radio Sci., 1976-78; translator: The Last Eyewitnesses: Children of the Holocaust Speak, 1998; contbr. chpts. to books, also articles; patentee in field. Mem. Town Mtg., Lexington, 1975-93; mem. alumni coun. MIT, 1965-72; bd. overseers Mus. of Sci., Boston, 1989-95; vol. exec. Internat. Exec. Svc. Corps., 1993, 94, 95. With Free Polish Forces, 1942-46. Fellow IEEE (life fellow, chmn. Boston sect. 1994-95). Home and Office: 2 Forest St Lexington MA 02421-4911 *I was a child-refugee, an adolescent-soldier, a student-immigrant, a young engineer and an adult entrepreneur. In every phase of my life I was blessed with the friendship and support of many wonderful people from various walks of life. Even in the darkest moments I had faith that each of us could improve the world a little.*

BUSSIERE, BRUCE EMILE, protective services official; b. Holyoke, Mass. s. Emile Oscar Jr. and Beverly Ann B.; m. Lyn Madlyn, Nov. 29, 1981; children: Heather Ann, Zachary Joseph, Courtney Lyn, Brittney Marie. AS, Springfield Tech. C.C., 1990. Correctional officer Conn. Dept. Corrections, Somers, 1981-87, lt., shift supr., 1982-90, lt. ops. Enfield, 1990-93, capt., staff comdr. Windsor Locks, 1993-95, capt. ops. Somers, 1995-96, chief tactical ops. Wethersfield, 1996—. Head coach Agawam (Mass.) Youth Football, 1996—; coach Agawam Little League, 1994-2002; asst. coach Agawam High Sch. Football, 1996—. Mem. U.S. Correctional Tactical Officers Assn. (pres. 1999-2001), Am. Football Coaches Assn., Nat. Youth Sports Coun. Republican. Roman Catholic. Avocations: reading, football, baseball, hockey. Home: 30 Elbert Rd Agawam MA 01001 Office: Conn Dept Corrections 24 Walcott Hill Rd Wethersfield CT 06109 E-mail: bruce.bussiere@po.state.ct.us.

BUSSIERE, EMILE R. lawyer; b. Manchester, N.H., May 16, 1932; s. Joseph and Emere (Gagnon) B.; m. Joan H. Blais, Aug. 16, 1969; children— Jaqueline, Denise, Emile R., Michelle, Christine. J.D., Boston Coll., 1954. Bar: N.H. 1954. U.S. commr. U.S. Dist. Ct. N.H., 1959-63; county atty. County of Hillsborough (N.H.), 1963-68; practice law, Manchester. Democratic nominee for Gov. N.H., 1968. Served to pfc. U.S. Army, 1956-58. Mem. N.H. Bar Assn. Roman Catholic. Office: 15 North St Manchester NH 03104-3016

BUSSIERE, LINDA ROSE, writer, historian; b. Bklyn., Dec. 9, 1953; d. Joseph Gary and Mary (Barbera) Salvato; m. Mark Evans Bussiere, Aug. 18, 1973; children: Anthony Salvato, Angela Francesca. Grad., Chelsea (Mass.) H.S., 1971. Town historian Town of Rindge, N.H., 1985—. Cmty. svc. coord. for troubled youths, 1997—. Author: Promise to the South, 1994, Wilder Creek, 1995, Nightmare in New Hampshire, 1997, How to Eat Cheap Cookbook, 1998, Chronicles of My Miserable Life, 1999. Vol. Jaffrey/Rindge Sch. Dist., 1985—; exec. officer, bd. dirs. Rindge Hist. Soc., 1992—, curator Rindge Mus., 1993—. Recipient various awards Jaffrey Rindge Sch. Dist., 1992, 93, 94. Mem. 101st Airborne Divsn., VFW Aux. Roman Catholic. Avocations: herbology, medieval and renaissance music, gardening. Home: 2 Fieldstone Ln Rindge NH 03461-3903

BUSSINO, MELINDA HOLDEN, human services administrator; b. Boston, Apr. 20, 1946; d. Sharon Virtulan and Grace (Fitzgerald) Holden; m. Louis Logue Doyle, Feb. 14, 1974 (dec. Oct. 1980); children: Sarah, Joseph; m. Fred John Bussino, Sept. 22, 1998 (dec. Jan. 2000). BA in Psychology, U. N.H., 1968. Dir. outreach and tng. Stratford County Cmty. Action, Somersworth, N.H., 1968-73; trainer, cons. New Eng. Regional Comm., Boston, 1971-73; office mgr. Beacon Banjo Co., Westminster, Vt., 1980-88; asst. to pastor United Meth. Ch., Brattleboro, Vt., 1985-89; exec. dir. Brattleboro Area Drop In Ctr., 1989—; cons. Putney, Vt., 1994—. Chmn. Brattleboro Human Resource Coun., 1990—; bd. dirs., past pres. Vt. Affordable Housing Coalition, 1990—, Vt. Campaign to End Child Hunger, 1991-99; housing commr. Windham Regional Commn., Brattleboro, 1995—; organizer, bd. dirs. N.H. Low Income Advocacy Coun., 1972-73, Operation Low Income People, N.H., 1969-73; adv. coun., bd. dirs. Vt. Protection Advocacy, Montpelier, Vt., 1995-2001; vice chair Westminster (Vt.) Planning Commn., 2003—. Recipient Vt. Woman of Distinction award, 1996, Humanitarian award Brattleboro Pastoral Counseling Ctr., 2001. Democrat. Methodist. Avocations: gardening, cooking, grandchildren, skiing. Home: PO Box 387 Putney VT 05346-0387 Office: Brattleboro Area Drop In Ctr PO Box 175 Brattleboro VT 05302-0175 E-mail: badic@together.net.

BUSSMAN, DONALD HERBERT, lawyer; b. Lakewood, Ohio, July 15, 1925; s. Herbert L. and Hilda L. (Henrichs) B. PhB, U. of Chgo., 1947, JD, 1951. Bar: Ill. 1951. Atty. Swift & Co., Chgo., 1950-84; pvt. practice Chgo., 1985—. With U.S. Army, 1944-46. Mem. ABA, Chgo. Bar Assn., Am. Assn. of Individual Investors, Club Internat. (Chgo.). Office: Ste 2102 860 N Dewitt Pl Chicago IL 60611-5780

BUSSONE, FRANK JOSEPH, bank executive, television broadcaster; b. Pontiac, Ill. s. Joseph Dominick and Olma Francis (DesCarpentrie) B.; m. Karen Marie Watson, May 27, 1972; 1 child, R.J. BS, Bradley U., 1964, MA, 1966; PhD, U. So. Calif., 1968. Adminstr. Bradley U., Peoria, Ill., 1969-77; v.p., COO Dirksen Congl. Ctr., Pekin and Washington, 1977-80; pres., CEO Sta. WEEK-TV, Peoria, 1980-86; exec. v.p. Eagle Broadcasting Co., N.Y.C., 1985-86; pres., CEO The Proctor Found., Peoria, 1986—2000. TV broadcaster ESPN SportsChannel, Chgo., 1972—; anchor TV broadcaster Ill. State Basketball Tournament, 1980—91; dir., officer BankPlus, Ill., 2001—; bd. dirs. St. Jude, Memphis; motivational spkr., 1970—. Author: The Tag Line, 1975; editor: Surprising Peoria, 1990; columnist for various newspapers, 1982—. Bd. dirs. Am. Heart Assn., Springfield, Ill., 1991—; TV host St. Jude Telethons, Ill., 1980-86; mem. Presdl. Task Force, Washington, 1988; speaker Bush for Pred. Campaign, Ill., 1988, Edgar for Gov. Campaign, Ill., 1990; mem. Bradley U. Community Bd., 1982—. Recipient Love a Child award Neighborhood House, Peoria, 1987, Citation of Hon. City of L.A., 1968; named to Bradley U. Hall of Fame, 1989, Ill. Basketball Hall of Fame Ill. Coaches Assn., 1983, One of Outstanding Young Men in Am. Mem. Ill. Hosp. Assn., The Dirksen Soc., Creve Coeur Club, Mt. Hawley Country Club, Downtown Rotary Club. Roman Catholic. Avocations: tennis, jogging, reading, cooking, writing. Home: 53 Hyde Park Dr Morton IL 61550-9534 Office: 4100 W Willow Knolls Dr Peoria IL 61615 E-mail: fjbussone@hotmail.com.

BUSSY, CARVEL DE, retired military officer, educator; b. Champaign, Ill., Oct. 29, 1919; s. Martin Kaucher Busey and Raye Hanley; m. Elisabeth de Bussy, Oct. 9, 1960 (dec. Oct. 1998); m. Shirley de Bussy Aug. 31, 1999; children: Bruce, Yvonne. BA, Ohio State U., 1940, MA, 1942; PhD, Cath. U., 1969. Commd. 2d lt. U.S. Army, 1942, advanced through grades to lt. col., ret.; mil. attaché Am. Embassy, Saigon, Indochina, 1954-56; prof. D.C. Tchrs. Coll., Washington, 1967-79, Cath. U., Washington, 1980—, Georgetown U., Washington, 1997—. Translator, editor East European Monographs, Columbia U. Press, Bradenton, Fla., 1987—, Return to the Center, 1993, Crime at Mayerling, 1995; adv. bd. Am. Biog. Inst., Raleigh, N.C., 1995—; comms. commn. Interallied Confederation of Res. Officers, Brussels, 1978—. Author: Prague Sunset, 1998. Chmn., divsn. fgn. langs. D.C. Tchrs. Coll., Washington, 1974-79. Named Officier Acad. Palsm Rep. of France, 1991, Chevalier, 1983. Mem. MLA (life), Res. Officers Assn. (commn. mem. 1978—), Union Interalliée (diplomatic), Diplomatic and Consular Officers (ret.), Officers Club, German Studies Assn. (sect. chmn.), Rocky Mountain Modern Lang. Assn. (sect. chair 1980—), Phi Beta Kappa, Phi Alpha Theta, Eta Simga Phi, Phi Eta Sigma. Avocations: music, piano, equitation. Home: 3901 Connecticut Ave NW Washington DC 20008 Office: Met Coll Cath U of Am Michigan Ave NE Washington DC 20064

BUST, JEFFRY D. manufacturing executive; BSME, U.S. Naval Acad.; MBA, Harvard U. Pres. Manitowoc Cranes, Inc., Lattice Crane Group; sr. exec. Harnischfeger Corp., FMC Engring.; pres., COO Grove Crane, Shady Grove, Pa., chmn., CEO, 1999—. Office: Grove Worldwide PO Box 21 Shady Grove PA 17256-0021

BUSTAMANTE, CRUZ M. lieutenant governor; b. Dinuba, Calif., Jan. 4, 1953; s. Cruz and Dominga Bustamante Jr.; m. Arcelia De La Pena; children: Leticia, Sonia, Marisa. BA, Fresno State U. Past intern for Congressman B.F. Sisk, Washington; formerly with Fresno employment and tng. commn. City of Fresno, past program dir. summer youth employment tng. program, 1977—83; past dist. rep. Congressman Rick Lehman and Assemblyman Bruce Bronzan State of Calif.; mem. Calif. State Assembly, 1993, spkr. of assembly, 1996-98; lt. gov. State of Calif., 1998—. Mem. U.S. Census Monitoring Bd. Trustee Calif. State U.; regent U. Calif.; mem. State Lands Commn.; vice chair Aerospace States Assn. Named Legislator of Yr. Assn. Mexican Am. Educators, U. Calif. Alumni Assn.; recipient True Am. Role Model award Mexican Am. Polit. Assn., Calif. Coastal Hero award, Pres.'s award NAACP, Friend of Labor award Mexican Am. Polit. Assn. Democrat. Office: State Capitol Rm 1114 Sacramento CA 95814 also: 300 S Spring St Ste 12702 Los Angeles CA 90013 Address: 2550 Mariposa Mall Rm 5006 Fresno CA 93721 also: 701 B St San Diego CA 92101 Office Fax: 916-323-4998., 213-897-7156., 559-445-5415., 619-525-4071. E-mail: Cruz.Bustamante@ltg.ca.gov.

BUSTAMANTE, DONALD D. information systems administrator, consultant; b. Las Vegas, Aug. 11, 1953; s. Pete J. and Mary M. Bustamante. BS in Chemistry summa cum laude, N.Mex. State U., Las Cruces, 1975, MBA, 1981. Dir. Computer Ctr., Luna Vo-Tech Inst., Las Vegas, N.Mex., 1981-87; project mgr. N.Mex. State U., 1987—. Mgmt. cons., 1981—; info. sys. cons., 1981—; session chair 1st Internat. Conf. on Multi-Sensor Multi-Source Data Fusion; sci. program com. Internat. Conf. on Data Fusion. Contbr. numerous articles to profl. jours. Mem. IEEE, IEEE Computer Soc., Am. Meteorol. Soc. (sci. and tech. adv. bd. on artificial intelligence 1998—), Mensa. Office: NMex State U PO Box 30002 Las Cruces NM 88003-8002

BUSTAMANTE, NESTOR, lawyer; b. Havana, Cuba, Apr. 20, 1960; came to the U.S., 1961; s. Nestor and Clara Rosa (Sanchez) B.; m. Marilyn Gonzalez, Sept. 20, 1986; children: Tiffany Alexandra, Nestor C. AA, U. Fla., 1980, BS in Journalism, 1982, JD, 1985. Bar: Fla. 1986, U.S. Dist. Ct. (so. dist.) Fla. 1989, U.S. Supreme Ct. 1991. Asst. state atty. State Atty.'s Office 11th Cir., Miami, 1986-88; juvenile serious offender prosecutor State Atty.'s Office, Miami, 1987-88, spl. prosecutor, gang prosecutor, 1987-88; asst. divsn. chief State Atty.'s Office-11th Jud. Cir., Miami, 1987-88; of counsel Fernandez-Caubi, Fernandez & Aguilar et al., Miami, 1988-89; atty. Ferencik, Libanoff, Brandt and Bustamante PA, Ft. Lauderdale, Fla., 1989—, ptnr., 1996—. Mem. code and rules of evidence com. The Fla. Bar, 1989—90, jud. evaluation com., 2000; vice chmn. Dade County Constrn. Trades Qualifying Bd.; adj. faculty dept. constrn. mgmt. Fla. Internat. U. Contbr. articles to newsletters. Mem. Miami-Dade Constrn. Trades Qualifying Bd. Named Hon. mem. Quien es Quien Publs., Inc., N.Y.C., 1990. Mem. ATLA (scoring judge nat. finals student trial advocacy competition 1994, 95), Fed. Bar Assn., Dade County Bar Assn. (mem. juvenile divsn. com. 1988-92, mem. media and pub. rels. com. 1989-91, mem. constrn. law com. 1990-91), Phi Delta Phi, U. Fla. Alumni Assn. Office: Ferencik Libanoff Brandt & Bustamante PA 150 S Pine Island Rd Ste 400 Fort Lauderdale FL 33324-2667 E-mail: flbbnb@mindspring.com.

BUSTER, JOHN EDMOND, gynecologist, medical researcher; b. Oxnard, Calif., July 18, 1941; s. Edmound B. and Beatrice (Keller) B. Student, Stanford U., 1959-62; MD, UCLA, 1966. Diplomate Am. Bd. Obstetrics and Gynecology. Intern Harbor UCLA Med. Ctr., Torrance, Calif., 1966-67, resident, 1967-71, rsch. fellow, 1971-73, faculty, 1975—; prof. ob-gyn. UCLA Sch. Medicine, 1983, U. Tenn., Memphis, 1987-94; prof. ob-gyn., dir. divsn. reproductive endocrinology Baylor Coll. Medicine, Houston, 1994—; div. divsn. reproductive endocrinology UCLA Sch. Medicine. Examiner Am. Bd. Ob-Gyn. Contbr. articles to profl. jours. Served to lt. col. U.S. Army, 1973-75. Mem. Am. Gynecologic and Obstet. Soc., Soc. for Gynecologic Investigation. Presbyterian. Office: Baylor Coll Medicine 6550 Fannin St Ste 801 Houston TX 77030-2739 E-mail: jbuster@bcm.tmc.edu.

BUSTIN, EDOUARD JEAN, political scientist, educator; b. Hollogne aux Pierres, Belgium, Apr. 9, 1933; came to U.S., 1961; s. Maurice and Mariette (De Graeve) B.; m. Francine Lekeu, Apr. 13, 1957 (dec. 1984); children: Denis, Olivier; m. Marisol Maura, Nov. 16, 1991. Cand.Phil., U. Liege, 1953, D. en Droit, 1956, Lic.Sc. Diplomat., 1957. Asst. in pub. law and adminstrn. U. Liege, 1956-59; atty. in Liege, 1956-59; sr. lectr., then vis. prof. U. Officielle du Congo, 1959-71; vis. lectr. polit. sci. UCLA, 1961-63; mem. faculty Boston U., 1963—, prof. polit. sci., 1970—, chmn. dept., 1977-82, 86-87, asso. African Studies Ctr., 1963—. Dir. Francophone Africa Rsch. Group, 1993—; vis. prof. U. de Bordeaux, 1996-97. Author: Lunda Under Belgian Rule: The Politics of Ethnicity, 1975; co-author: Five African States: Responses to Diversity, 1963. Decorated officer Palmes Académiques (France). Mem. African Studies Assn., Centre d'Etudes d'Afrique Noire, Inst. Africain. Home: 57 Columbine Rd Milton MA 02186-1724 Office: 270 Bay State Rd Boston MA 02215-1403 E-mail: ebustin@bu.edu.

BUSTIN, GEORGE LEO, lawyer; b. Perth Amboy, N.J., Feb. 10, 1948; s. George and Agnes W. (Bulvanoski) B.; m. Halina Orestovna Kaniuka, July 9, 1979; children: Michael G., Alexander G. AB summa cum laude, Princeton U., 1970; JD magna cum laude, Harvard U., 1973. Bar: N.Y. 1973, U.S. Dist. Ct. (so. dist.), U.S. Ct. Appeals ((2nd cir.), 1974. Assoc. Cleary, Gottlieb, Steen & Hamilton, N.Y.C., 1973-81, ptnr., 1982-84; vis. prof. Princeton (N.J.) U., 1991; ptnr. Cleary, Gottlieb, Steen & Hamilton, Brussels, 1984-90, 1992—; chair Brussels chpt. Internat. divsn. N.Y. State Bar Assn., 1996—. Chair Princeton Alumni Schs. Com., Belgium, 1998—; dir. Sabre Found. (Europe) S.p.r.l.; co-chair Fall 2003 meeting ABA section Internat. Law and Practice. Author: Business Transactions with the USSR, 1975, International Business Transactions, 1980, International Financial Law Review, 1990, Insights, 1990. Mem. Cercle Gaulois Artistique et Litteraire, Harvard Law Sch. Assn. (sec. Brussels 1989-92), Am. European Union Assn. (pres.'s group), N.Y. State Bar Assn., Assn. Bar City N.Y. (co-chair coms. on rels. with European bars 2001—), Ordre Francais du barreau de Bruxelles, Brussels Sports Assn. (bd. dirs. 1996-98), Commn. des membres associés du barreau de Bruxelles (ABA liaison rep. 2001—). Home: 39 Rue de La Gendarmerie 1380 Lasne Belgium Office: Cleary Gottlieb Steen & Hamilton 57 Rue de La Loi 1040 Brussels Belgium

BUSTOS, RUDOLPH R. health facility administrator; s. Maria T. and Jose R. Bustos; 1 child, Alan Otto-Raymond. BA, Westfield State Coll., 1968; MEd, Springfield Coll., 1971; PhD, Capella U., 2001—. LCSW Mass., 2002; cert. sch. psychologist Mass., 1974, S.C., 2001. Supr. Mass. Dept. Social Svcs., South Yarmouth, 1980—98; coord. psychoeducational svcs. High Plains Mental Health Ctr., Hays, Kans., 2001—. Lectr. Petach Tikvah Day Care Ctr. for Elderly, Israel, 2000—00; adj. prof. Limestone Coll., Gaffney, SC, 2000—01, Ft. Hays State U., Hays, 2001—; presenter in field. Actor: (plays) Jesus Christ Superstar. Grant writer Cherokee County ARC, Gaffney, 2000—01, Cherokee Suicide Intervention Ctr., 2000—01, Cape Cod Therapeutic Riding Ctr., Brewster, Mass., 1998—2000; sixth degree black belt U.S. Karate Assn., Sagamore, Mass., 1996. With U.S. Army, 1968—70. Mem.: AAUP (assoc.), Coun. Exceptional Children (assoc.), Am. Ednl. Rsch. Assn. (assoc.), U.S. Karate Assn. (life). Achievements include development of Virtual Course: Teaching Young Hispanic CHildren with Special Needs; research in Survey research about MIT's OpenCourseWare; Distance Education in the Military; Presidential Sports Award in Karate, 1994; Black Belt in Karate 1987. Office: Fort Hays State U 600 Park St Hays KS 67601 Personal E-mail: rbustos@fhsu.edu. E-mail: rbustos@fhsu.edu.

BUSWELL, ARTHUR WILCOX, physician, surgeon; b. Oklahoma City, Jan. 6, 1926; s. Albert Currier and Enid May (Scott) B.; B.Sc., U. Okla., 1950, M.D., 1952; m. Loleta JoAnn Sherrill, June 11, 1950; children— Arthur Lee, Robert Joseph, Barbara JoAnn, Brian A., Gayla, Richard; m. 2d, Jane Marie Fuksa, Mar. 1, 1969. Intern. Fitzsimons Army Hosp. Aurora, Colo., 1952-53; surg. resident Wesley Hosp., Oklahoma City, 1954-55; practice medicine and surgery, Hennessey, Okla., 1955-63; dep. surgeon, Fort Wainwright and Yukon Command, 1963-65; chief staff Kingfisher (Okla.) Community Hosp., 1956-57; supt. health Kingfisher County, 1960-61; chief profl. service Bassett Army Hosp., 1963-65; div. surgeon 1st Armored Div., Ft. Hood, Tex., 1965-67, 1st Inf. Div., Republic of Vietnam, 1967-68; med. project officer U.S. Army Combat Devels. Command, Experimentation Command, Ft. Ord, Calif., 1968-72, also chief human factors div. and chief experimentation div. of experimentation command; chief profl. services Reynolds Army Hosp., Ft. Sill, Okla., 1972-73; comdr. med. dept. activities Ft. Stewart, Ga., 1973-77; chief profl. services Kenner Army Hosp., Ft. Lee, Va., 1977-78; comdr. med. dept. activities, Alaska, 1979-83; adj. asst. prof. med. scis. Baylor U., 1973— . Pres., Ft. Stewart Sch. Bd., 1977; bd. dirs. Ft. Stewart Fed. Credit Union, 1977, Chisholm Trail Mus., 1986—, Friends of Librs. in Okla., 1987—; mem. Kingfisher Meml. Libr. Bd.; pres. Friends of Libr. for Kingfisher County, 1984-88. Served with AUS, 1944-46, 1st lt. U.S. Army, 1952-54, maj. to col., 1961-83. Decorated Legion of Merit with 2 oak leaf cluster, Soldier's medal, Bronze Star for Valor with oak leaf cluster, Meritorious Service medal, Air medal with 3 oak leaf clusters, Army Commendation medal; Gallantry cross with palm, Honor medal 1st class (both Vietnam); named to Kingfisher High Sch. Hall of Fame, 1987, Citizen of the Yr. Kingfisher C. of C., 1988. Fellow Royal Soc. Health; mem. Am., Okla. State (mem. no. dels.), Aerospace, Army Aviation (charter) med. assns., Assn. Mil. Surgeons U.S., Garfield-Kingfisher County Med. Soc. Home: PO Box 703 Kingfisher OK 73750-0703

BUSWELL, DEBRA SUE, small business owner, programmer, analyst; b. Salt Lake City, Apr. 8, 1957; d. John Edward Ross and Marilyn Sue (Patterson) Potter; m. Randy James Buswell, Aug. 17, 1985; 1 child, Trevor Ryan. BA, U. Colo., Denver, 1978. Programmer, analyst Trail Blazer Systems, Palo Alto, Calif., 1980-83; data processing mgr. Innovative Concepts, Inc., San Jose, Calif., 1983-86; owner Egret Software, Milpitas, Calif., 1986—. Mem.: IEEE. Home and Office: 45701 Vineyard Ave Fremont CA 94539-4817 E-mail: dbuswell@attbi.com.

BUSWELL, JAMES OLIVER, III, retired education educator, retired academic administrator; b. Milw., Jan. 12, 1922; s. James Oliver, Jr. and Helen (Spaulding) Buswell; m. Kathleen Marie Witmer, Feb. 14, 1945; 1 child, James O. IV. BA, Wheaton Coll., 1948; MA, U. of Pa., 1952; PhD, St. Louis U., 1972. Instr. Nat. Bible Inst., N.Y.C., 1948; asst. prof. Shelton Coll., 1948—54; from assoc. to full prof. Wheaton Coll., 1954—59; prof Nyack Coll., 1960—62, Wheaton Coll., 1962—65, St. John's U., 1967—73, Trinity Coll., 1973—75, Wheaton Coll., 1974—80; prof., v.p. academic affairs William Carey Internat. U., 1981—2001. Bd. mem. Trans World Radio, Carey, NC, 1960—, Ameritribes (formerly Navajo Gospel Misssion), Tucson, 1981—, Emmanuel Bible Coll., 1981—2001, William Carey Internat. U., 1995—. Author: (book) Slavery, Segregation and Scripture, 1964; contbr. numerous articles and book reviews in var. publications. Lt. (1st.) USMC, 1942—46, PTO. Grantee Danforth Found., Columbia U., 1959. Fellow: Am. Anthrop. Assn., Am. Sci. Affiliation (pres. 1984); mem.: Evang. Missiological Soc. Republican. Presbyterian. Avocations: music, books, am. indians, christian missions. Home: 1017 Eddy Ct Wheaton IL 60187-4455

BUTCHER, AMANDA KAY, retired university administrator; b. Lansing, Mich., Oct. 25, 1936; d. Foster Eli and Mayme Lenore (Taft) Stuart; m. Claude J. Butcher, Aug. 24, 1957; 1 child, Mary Beth. BS in Bus., Cen. Mich. U., 1981. Office asst. Dept. Dairy Sci., East Lansing, Mich., 1966-76; bus. mgr. dept. pathology Coll. Vet. Medicine Mich. State U., East Lansing, 1976-96. Mem. Adminstrv. Profl. Suprs. Assn. (v.p. 1982), Adminstrv. Profl. Assn. East Lansing (pres. 1976-80). Avocations: photography, antiques, bowling. Home: 610 Emily Ave Lansing MI 48910-5404

BUTCHER, ANN PATRICE, elementary school educator; b. Aurora, Ill., May 14, 1965; d. Harry Neal and Patsy JoAnn (Smith) Patterson; m. Steven James Butcher, July 14, 1990; children: Todd Merrill, Seth Richard-James, Zacharry Neal. BA, Aurora U., 1989; MA, No. Ill. U., 1994; EdD in Leadership in Curriculum and Instrn., Aurora U., 2003. Cert. in elem. edn., curriculum and supervision. Elem. sch. tchr. Sch. Dist. #129, Aurora, 1989—; gifted tchr. Aurora U., 1993—. Tchr. Adv. Bd. for Sci. Edn., Sci.-Tech./Physics of Aquatic Animals, Aurora; Impact II adv. bd. Ill. Math. and Sci. Acad., Aurora, 1991, Leadership Inst. Integrating Internet, Instrn. and Curriculum participant, instr. Fermi Acceleration Lab., Batavia, Ill.; mem. consortium Aurora Cmty. Edn., 1996—; dir. programs Scholars program Aurora U., 1996—. Recipient Impact II grant, Ill. Math. and Sci. Acad./State of Ill., 1991, 1992, Best in West award, 2001, Honor Roll of Tchrs. award, Assn. Sci. and Tech. Ctrs., Washington, 1996; grantee, Aurora Found., 1993. Mem. NEA, Ill. Edn. Assn., Ill. Sci. Tchrs. Assn., Ill. Reading Coun., Aurora Cmty. Edn. Consortium, Kappa Delta Pi. Lutheran. Avocations: physical fitness, aerobics, running, weight training. Home: 805 Acorn Dr North Aurora IL 60542-3030 Office: Fearn Elem Sch 1600 Hawksley Ln North Aurora IL 60542 E-mail: butch4@interaccess.com.

BUTCHER, BOBBY GENE, retired military officer; b. Mineral Wells, W.Va., Apr. 30, 1936; s. John Franklin and Anna Pearl (Hersman) B.; m. Patricia Maureen O'Keefe, Dec. 15, 1961 (dec. Dec. 1996); 1 child, Lisa Lee Butcher Clardy. BS, W.Va. U., 1958; grad., USN Flight Sch., 1960; postgrad., USMC Amphibious Warfare Sch., 1966-67, USMC Command and Staff Coll., 1973-74. Commd. 2d lt. USMC, 1959, advanced through grades to maj. gen., 1989; officer in charge USMC Officer Selection Office, Phila., 1971-73; ops. officer Marine Attack Tng. Squadron 102, Yuma, Ariz., 1974, exec. officer, 1974-76, comdg. officer, 1976-77; ops. officer Marine Corps Air Sta., Yuma, 1977-79; ops. plans officer 3d Marine Div., Camp Courtney, Okinawa, 1979-80; comdg. officer Marine Aviation Weapons and Tactics Squadron One, Yuma, 1980-82; participant Dept. State Sr. Seminar, Arlington, Va., 1982-83; asst. chief staff, plans and policy, comdr. Naval Striking and Support Forces, So. Europe, Naples, Italy, 1983-86; asst. wing comdr. 3d Marine Aircraft Wing, El Toro, Calif., 1986-87; comdg. gen. 6th Marine Expeditionary Brigade, Camp Lejeune, N.C., 1987-89; dir. ops. U.S. Pacific Command, Honolulu, 1989-91; comdg. gen. Landing Force Command, Coronado, Calif., 1991-92. Cons. specializing in Marine Corps and joint mil. matters. Decorated Def. D.S.M., D.S.M., Def. Superior Svc. medal, Legion of Merit, DFC, Bronze Star with combat V, Air medals (15); recipient various other unit and personal medals and ribbons. Mem. The Ret. Officers Assn. (nat. bd. dirs.), Flying Leatherneck Hist. Found. (chmn. bd. dirs.), USS Midway Mus. (bd. dirs.), The Early and Pioneer Naval Aviators' Assn. (Golden Eagles). Republican. Methodist. Home: 110 Carob Way Coronado CA 92118-2433 E-mail: thunderBGB@san.rr.com.

BUTCHER, BRUCE CAMERON, lawyer; b. N.Y.C., Feb. 17, 1947; s. John Richard and Dorothy Helen (Wehner) B.; m. Kathryn Ann Fiddler, Oct. 12, 1979; 1 child, Kristen Ann. BS, Belknap Coll., 1969; JD, St. John's U., N.Y.C., 1972. Bar: N.Y. 1973, U.S. Dist. Ct. (so. dist.) N.Y. 1974, La. 1980, U.S. Dist. Ct. (ea. dist.) La. 1980, U.S. Ct. Appeals (5th and 11th cirs.) 1981, Tex. 1993. Assoc. Laporte and Meyers, N.Y.C., 1972-73; asst. chief contract and comml. litigation divsn. Corp. Counsel's Office City of N.Y., 1973-79; ptnr. Chaffe, McCall, Phillips, Toler & Sarpy, New Orleans, 1980-84; prin. Bruce C. Butcher, P.C., Metairie, La., 1985-93; of counsel Smith Martin & Schneider, New Orleans, 1993-94; gen. coun. The Vulcan Group, Birmingham, Ala., 1994-95, Favalora Constructors, Inc., 1995—2002; gen. counsel Tailgators Restaurant, LLC, New Orleans, 1994-99; pvt. practice Law Offices of Bruce Cameron Butcher & Assocs., New Orleans, 1999—. Mem. ABA (regional chmn. pub. report 1975, state chmn. pub. contracts sect. 1984-95, cert. of performance 1975), La. Bar Assn., Am. Arbitration Assn. (mem. arbitration panel U.S. Coun. on Internat. Bus. Arbitration 2001—), New Orleans Country Club, New Orleans Athletic Club, Crescent Club. Home: 402 Julia St Ste 307 New Orleans LA 70130-3689 Office: 402 Julia St Ste 307 New Orleans LA 70130-3689 E-mail: bbutch@bellsouth.net.

BUTCHER, HARRY WILLIAM, educational administrator, educator, historian; b. Frederick, Okla., May 15, 1948; s. Harry William Hobbs and Alice Marie (Brownrigg) Butcher Able; m. Susan Mary Howell, Nov. 11, 2000; children: Jonathan Hobbs, Megan Rachel. BS, Okla. State U., 1970, postgrad., 1971. Cert. tchr. Tex., 2002. Agt. Pinkerton, Inc., Oklahoma City, 1971-73, mgr. investigation Dallas, 1973-75, mgr. Baton Rouge, 1975-77, Memphis, 1977-78, mgr., dist. Houston, 1978-79, v.p. Mark Lipman Divsn. Memphis, 1979-84, regional dir. Dallas, 1984-88, dir., group investigation Ft. Worth, 1988-89, dir. nat. accounts, 1990-91; v.p. domestic and internat. sales, 1991-96; sr. v.p. domestic and internat. sales Pinkerton, Inc., Ft. Worth, 1996-99, sr. v.p. strategic accounts, 1999-2000; founder, exec. dir. Ctr. for Edn., 2000—; educator Ft. Worth Ind. Sch. Dist., 2000—. Mem. Am. Mgmt. Assn. (pres.'s assn.), Pres.'s Club (Minot Dodson award for outstanding leadership 1997), Tex. Hist. Soc., Golden Key Soc., Nat. Trust Historic Preservation, Phi Alpha Theta. Republican. Episcopalian. Avocations: teaching young people, gardening, historical studies.

BUTCHER, JACK ROBERT (JACK RISIN), manufacturing executive, film producer, actor; b. Akron, Ohio, Dec. 10, 1941; s. William Hobart and Marguerite Bell (Dalton) Butcher; m. Gloria Jean Hartman, June 1, 1963 (dec. July 1995); children: Jack R. II, William H.(dec.), Charlotte Jean. BA in Math., Jacksonville U., 1964; cert. in mgmt. consulting, Akron U., 1979; cert. in paralegal, CCT Inst., 1990; cert. in radio broadcasting, Chaffey Coll., 1994. Pres. Portableacher Corp., Hesperia, Calif., 1977—; v.p. Nice Day Products, Hesperia, 1980-85; pres. Mark Profl. Mgmt. and Design Co., Hesperia, 1983—, Nice Day Products, Hesperia, 1985—; owner Movie Funding Without Risk Co., 1996—; pres. Vallivue Prodns., Phelan, Calif., 2000—; co-owner Rizinn Consolidated Holdings Corp., 2001—. Co-owner JB Scale Co., Hesperia, 1991—. Actor, voice-overs and commls. : Film Industry Workshop Sch. Acting, 1995—99; author: (poems) Something Good, 1978, Forever My Valentine, 1996. Mem.: SAG, Internat. Platform Assn. (bd. govs. 1996—, Silver Bowl award 1995), Royal Order of Jesters, Shriners, Masons. Achievements include patents in field. Avocations: hunting, travel, designing, acting, commercial voice-overs. Home and Office: PO Box 3524 Hesperia CA 92340-3524

BUTCHER, PAUL, communications executive; COO Mitel Networks, Kanata, Canada. Spkr. in field. Office: Mitel Networks Corp 350 Legget Dr Kanata ON K2K 2W7 Canada

BUTCHER, RUSSELL DEVEREUX, author, photographer; b. Bryn Mawr, Pa., Feb. 8, 1938; s. Devereux and Mary Frances (Taft) B.; m. Pamela Richards, Apr. 12, 1967 (div. 1993); children: Pamela Marie (dec.), Neill Devereux, Wendy Nan; m. Karen T. Black, Nov. 29, 1997. BA, U. Colo., 1960; postgrad., U. Mich., 1960-61. Rsch. editor Sierra Club, San Francisco, 1961-65; editl. writer N.Y. Times, 1963-79; publicity writer Save-the-Redwoods League, San Francisco, 1963-65; conservation specialist Nat. Audubon Soc., N.Y.C., 1965-66; chief pub. rels. and publs. Mus. of N.Mex., Santa Fe, 1967-69; freelance writer, photographer, author, 1969-80. Conservation zoning cons. Town of Mount Desert (Maine), 1978-79, S.W. and Calif. rep. Nat. Parks and Conservation Assn., 1980-90, Pacific S.W. regional dir., 1990-93. Author: Maine Paradise, 1973, New Mexico: Gift of the Earth, 1975, The Desert, 1976, Field Guide to Acadia National Park, Maine, 1977, Exploring Our National Parks and Monuments, 9th edit., 1995, Exploring Our National Historic Parks and Sites, 1997, America's National Wildlife Refuges, A Complete Guide, 2003; author, compiler: Guide to National Parks (8 regional guides), 1999; mem. editl. bd. Audubon mag.; manuscript editor KC Publs., 1985-88; contbr. articles to environ. jours. Mem. Ariz. Strip Dist. adv. coun. U.S. Bur. Land Mgmt., 1983—90; bd. dirs. Friends Saguaro Nat. Park, 1997—2002, Rincon Inst., 2002—. Nat. Parks and Conservation Assn. fellow, 1993-99. Mem. Save-the-Redwoods League (life), Nat. Parks and Conservation Assn., Maine Audubon Soc. (pres. Down East chpt. 1978-80, trustee 1979-80), Friends of Lake Dist. Eng. (life), Sierra Club (life). Episcopalian (Vestryman 1978-81). Address: 5948 N Misty Ridge Dr Tucson AZ 85718-3438

BUTCHKES, SYDNEY, artist; b. Covington, Ky., Oct. 13, 1922; s. Isadore and Bertha (Gussis) B. Student, Cin. Art Acad., 1936-40, Art Students League, N.Y.C., 1940-42, New Sch., 1957-59. Exhibited one-man shows, Amel Gallery, N.Y.C., 1966, Bertha Schaefer Gallery, N.Y.C., 1969, 71, 73, Benson Gallery, Bridgehampton, N.Y., 1971, 76, 80, 86, 89, 91, 96, 2000, Alonzo Gallery, N.Y.C., 1978, Touchstone Gallery, N.Y.C., 1982, Bace Gallery, Southampton, 1993; Bujese Gallery, E. Hampton, 1998, 2000; group shows Mus. Modern Art, N.Y.C., 1964, San Francisco Mus., 1967, Inst. Contemporary Art, Boston, 1969, Robert Elkon Gallery, N.Y.C., 1974, 76, Brenda Taylor Gallery, N.Y.C., 2000, Celadon Gallery, Watermill, N.Y., 2002; pub. collections: Bklyn. Mus., Cin. Mus. Art, Wadsworth Atheneum, Hartford, Conn., Met. Mus. Art, N.Y.C., Nat. Collection of Smithsonian Inst., Washington, Newark Mus. Served with U.S. Army, 1942-45. Hon. fellow Am. Craft Council; mem. Abstract Am. Artists Home: Sagg Main St Sagaponack NY 11962-9999

BUTCHKO, HARRIETT HAYS, food products executive, physician; b. Athens, Ga., Mar. 31, 1950; d. William Jackson and Carolyn Ross Hays; m. Gregory Michael Butchko, July 8, 1972; children: Karin Hayston, Jeffrey Maston. Student, Canal Zone Coll., Balboa, 1968—69; BS, U. Ga., 1972; MD, Northwestern U., 1982. Diplomate Nat. Bd. Med. Examiners, 1984. Intern, resident Northwestern U., 1982—85; assoc. dir. clin. rsch. G.D. Searle & Co., Skokie, Ill., 1985—86, The NutraSweet Co., Skokie, 1986—91, dir. clin. rsch. and regulatory affairs Deerfield, Ill., 1991—97, v.p. med. and sci. affairs and chief med. officer Evanston, Ill., 2000—; sr. dir. global regulatory coordination Monsanto Co., Skokie, 1997—2000. Bd. dirs. Internat. Food Info. Coun., Washington, Calorie Control Coun., Atlanta. Editor: (book) The Clinical Evaluation of a Food Additive: Assessment of Aspartame; contbr. chapters to books, articles to profl. jours. Fellow: Am. Coll. Nutrition; mem.: AMA, Am. Acad. Neurology (assoc.), Phi Beta Kappa. Republican. Avocations: creating stained glass windows, collecting american brilliant cut glass, collecting antiques. Office: The NutraSweet Company 1801 Maple Ave Evanston IL 60201 Office Fax: 847-491-6109. E-mail: harriett.h.butchko@nutrasweet.com.

BUTCHVAROV, PANAYOT KRUSTEV, philosophy educator; b. Sofia, Bulgaria, Apr. 2, 1933; s. Krustyu Panayotov and Vanya (Tsaneva) B.; m. Sue Graham, Sept. 28, 1954; children: Vanya, Christopher. BA, Robert Coll., Istanbul, 1952; MA, U. Va., 1954, PhD, 1955. Instr. philosophy U. Balt., 1955-56; asst. prof. U. S.C., 1956-59; asso. prof. Syracuse U., 1959-66, prof., 1966-68; vis. prof. U. Iowa, 1967-68, prof., 1968—, chmn. dept. philosophy, 1970-77; univ. found. disting. prof., 1995—. Vis. prof. U. Miami, Coral Gables, Fla., 1979-80; Simon lectr. U. Toronto, 1984; guest prof. Akad. für Philosophie, Liechtenstein, 1997. Author: Resemblance and Identity, 1966, The Concept of Knowledge, 1970, Being Qua Being, 1979, Skepticism in Ethics, 1989, Skepticism About the External World, 1998; editor: Jour. Philosophical Rsch., 1993—; mem. editl. bd.: Midwest Studies in Philosophy, Philos. Monographs; contbr. numerous articles and revs. to profl. jours. Mem. Am. Philos. Assn. (program com. 1971, chmn. 1975, nominating com. 1978, chmn. 1993-94, pres. ctrl. div. 1992-93), Ctrl. States Philos. Assn. (v.p. 1987-88, pres. 1988-89), Phi Beta Kappa. Home: 2507 Princeton Rd Iowa City IA 52245-3721 E-mail: panayot-butchvarov@uiowa.edu.

BUTEL, JANET SUSAN, research scientist, virology educator; b. Overbrook, Kans., May 24, 1941; d. Floyd Charles and Berniece (Humbert) B.; m. David Yates Graham, Mar. 31, 1967; children: Susan Kathleen, David Peter. BS summa cum laude, Kans. State U., 1963; PhD with honors, Baylor U., 1966. Postdoctoral fellow Baylor Coll. Medicine, Houston, 1966-68; asst. prof. Houston, 1968-72; assoc. prof. Baylor U. Coll. Medicine, Houston, 1972-76, prof., 1976-95, head divsn. molecular virology, 1989-2000, disting. svc. prof., 1995—, Joseph L. Melnick prof. virology, 1986, chmn. dept. molecular virology and microbiology, 2000—. Mem. study sect. NIH, Bethesda, Md., 1980—84; mem. bd. sci. counselors Nat. Cancer Inst., Bethesda, 1980—84; mem. coun. Nat. Inst. Arthritis and Infectious Diseases, 1994—98; mem. external adv. coun. Am. Cancer Soc., 1998—2001. Contbg. editor: Lange Med. Microbiology, 1987—; contbr. sci. articles to profl. jours. Grad. fellow NSF, 1963-66; rsch. grantee NIH, 1973—. Mem. AAAS, Am. Assn. for Cancer Rsch., Am. Soc. for Cell Biology, Am. Soc. for Microbiology (div. chair 1990-91, group IV rep. 1993-95), Am. Soc. for Virology, Internat. Assn. Breast Cancer Rsch. (bd. govs. Lakewood, Colo. 1987-91), Sigma Xi. Office: Baylor Coll Medicine 1 Baylor Plz Houston TX 77030-3411

BUTENHOFF, SUSAN, public relations executive; b. N.Y.C., Jan. 13, 1960; BA in Internat. Rels. with hons., Sussex U., Eng.; MPhil, Wolfson Coll., Cambridge U., Eng. Account exec. Ellen Farmer Prodns., 1984-85, Ketchum Pub. Rels., N.Y.C., 1988-90, v.p., account supr., 1990-91; prin., CEO Access Pub. Rels., San Francisco, 1991—, pres., CEO. Mem. Pub. Rels. Soc. Am. Office: Access Comm 101 Howard St Fl 2D San Francisco CA 94105-1629

BUTERA, ANN MICHELE, consulting company executive; b. Bayside, N.Y., Apr. 27, 1958; d. Gaetano Thomas and Josephine (Inserro) B. BA, L.I. U., 1979; MBA, Adelphi U., 1982. Dept. mgr. Abraham & Straus Stores, Huntington, N.Y., 1978-80; mgmt. cons. Chase Manhattan Bank N.A., Lake Success, N.Y., 1980-83, Nat. Bankcard Corp., Melville, N.Y., 1983-84; pres. Whole Person Project, Inc., Elmont, N.Y., 1984—. Bd. dirs. Nassau County coun. Girl Scouts U.S., 1985-95. Recipient Bus. Achievement award Women on the Job, 1990. Mem. NAFE, ASTD, Fin. Women Internat., L.I. Networking Entrepreneurs (pres. 1984-91), Inst. Internal Auditors, Assn. Govt. Auditors, L.I. Ctr. for Bus. and Profl. Women, World Futurists Soc. Republican. Roman Catholic. Avocations: tennis, dancing, gardening. Home and Office: Whole Person Project Inc 82 Cerenzia Blvd Elmont NY 11003-3631 E-mail: annbutera@cs.com.

BUTHMAN, NANCY SMITH, nurse practitioner, critical care nurse; b. Chgo. d. Robertson and Ruth (Metcalf) Smith; m. G.B. Bostock, Aug. 1955 (dec. 1964); m. A.J. Buthman, Sept. 18, 1965 (div. 1977); children; David, Daniel, Mark, John, Jay, Lisa, Jim. BA in Psychology, Drew U., 1956; BSN, Rush U., 1977; MS in Mgmt. and Orgnl. Behavior, Ill. Benedictine Coll., 1988; MSN, Fla. Internat. U., 1996; postgrad., George Washington U., 1999. RN, Ill., Fla; cert. adult and family nurse practitioner; cert. instr. BLS and ACLS, Am. Heart Assn. Staff nurse surg. floor Rush Presbyn. St. Luke's Hosp., Chgo., 1977-78, staff nurse surg. ICU, 1978-80, asst. head nurse surg. ICU, 1980-81; critical care instr. Edgewater Hosp., Chgo., 1981-82; unit mgr. ICU/critical care unit Luth. Gen. Hosp., Chgo., 1982-89; staff nurse cath. lab. Sarasota (Fla.) Meml. Hosp., 1989-90; dir. ICU and cardiac care unit Cape Coral (Fla.) Hosp., 1990-95; clin. coord. subacute care unit Integrated Health Svcs., Ft. Myers, Fla., 1995-96; nurse practitioner Family Health Ctrs., Ft. Myers, Fla., 1997—. Instr. St. Francis U., Joliet, Ill., 2000. Author, dir. video and teaching booklet: Mock Code, 1984 (Hon. Mention Critical Care award), Mock Code II, 1986. Mem. mem. disaster med. assistance team U.S. Dept. Emergency Preparedness. Mem. AACN (cert. RN), Sigma Theta Tau. Avocations: family, reading, guitar, water sports. Home: 1705 W Savona Parkway Cape Coral FL 33914 E-mail: nbuthman@aol.com.

BUTKEVIČIENÉ, BIRUTE, librarian; b. Joniškis, Lithuania, Aug. 20, 1938; d. Juozas and Sofija (Boreikaitė) Lipeika; m. Antanas Kuzminskas, Dec. 14, 1963 (dec. Jan. 19, 1969); 1 child, Arvydas; m. Boleslovas Butkevičius, May 25, 1975 (dec. Nov. 7, 1993). Librarian, Vilnius U., 1962. Head regional libr. Varniai (Lithuania) Regional Libr., 1962-63; libr. Vilnius U. Libr., 1963-66, head dept., 1966-67, bibliographer, 1968-70, head dept., 1971-77, dep. dir., 1978-85, acting dir., 1985-91, dir., 1991—. Mem. Assn. Lithuanian Librs., Women Assn. of Lithuanian Univs., Club of M. Mažvydas, Lithuanian Acad. Librs. Assn., Assn. XXVII Bibliophiles. Avocation: gardening. Office: Vilniaus Univ Biblioteka Universiteto 3 2633 Vilnius Lithuania E-mail: birute.butkeviciene@mb.vu.lt.

BUTKI, BRIAN DAVID, psychologist, educator; b. Dearborn, Mich., May 18, 1970; s. Alice Mary Gibson and Julius Jerome Butki; m. Erin Rae Chandler, Aug. 9, 1997; 1 child, Alisha Rae. BS, U. Wyo., Laramie, 1988—92, MSEd, 1992—93; PhD, U. N.C., Greensboro, 1994—98. Asst. prof. So. Ill. U., Edwardsville, 1998—; therapeutic recreation dir. Youth Focus, Inc., Greensboro, NC, 1998—99. Owner and dir. P.E.A.K. Performance Cons., Glen Carbon, Ill., 1998—. Tng. dir. Spl. Olympics of Ill., Highland, 1999—; dir. Metro East Humane Soc., Edwardsville, Ill., 2000—. Recipient Greensboro Grad. Award, State of N.C., 1994—98. Mem.: ASPCA, Am. Alliance of Health, Phys. Edn., Recreation, and Dance, Soc. of Behavioral Medicine, Assn. for the Advancement of Applied Sport Psychology, Phi Beta Kappa. Avocations: cycling, travel, music, reading, hiking. Home: 44 Jason Dr Glen Carbon IL 62034 Office: PO Box 1126 Siue Edwardsville IL 62026-1126 Home Fax: 618-650-3699. Personal E-mail: bbutki13@yahoo.com. E-mail: bbutki@siue.edu.

BUTKO, VLADIMIR YURYEVICH, physicist, researcher; b. Leningrad, Russia, Jan. 30, 1966; came to the U.S., 1998; s. Yurii Alexseievich and Elena Petrovna Butko; m. Irina Stanislavovna, Apr. 7, 1989 (div. Mar. 1998), remarried, July 17, 1999; 1 child, Aleksey. MS with honors, Leningrad Poly. INst., 1989; PhD, Ioffe Physics Tech. Inst., Russian Acad. Sci., St. Petersburg, 1997. Cert. engr.-physicist. Probational rschr. Ioffe Physics Tech. Inst., Russian Acad. Sci., St. Petersburg, 1989-91, jr. sci. rschr., 1991-97, postdoctoral rschr., 1997—; postdoctoral rschr. dept. physics and astronomy La. State U., Baton Rouge, 1998-2001; long term vis. staff mem. Los Alamos Nat. Lab., 2001—. Contbr. articles to profl. jours. Mem. Am. Phys. Soc. Avocations: reading, chess. Office: Los Alamos Nta Lab MST-9 MS-K774 PO Box 1633 Los Alamos NM 87545-4001

BUTLER, ALICE CLAIRE, rehabilitation nurse; b. Lander, Wyo., Sept. 9, 1925; d. Donald A. and Violet C. (Carney) Sherlock; m. Harry Wallace Butler, July 25, 1948 (dec. Feb. 1994); children: Gladys Norene, Linda Marie, Christine Janet, Mary Alice(dec.), David Paul, Anna Louise, Rebecca Ruth, Philip Clyde, John Glenn, James Sheldon. ADN, Penn Valley C.C., 1976; AA, Kansas City (Mo.) Jr. Coll., 1949; BA in Elem. Edn., U. Mo., Kansas City, 1986. RN, Mo. Charge nurse Rehab. Inst., Kansas City, 1981—2001; asst. dir. nursing Children's Mercy Hosp., Kansas City, 1977-81; staff relief nurse Clara Manor Nursing Home, Kansas City; part-time nursing coord. Park Lane Med. Ctr., Kansas City; rehab. nurse Bapt. Luth. Med. Ctr., 2001—. Mem. Assn. Rehab. Nurses (cert.), Mo. League for Nursing, Nat. League for Nursing. Home: 4311 Campbell St Kansas City MO 64110-1621

BUTLER, ALISON, agricultural studies educator, researcher; b. N.Y.C., May 5, 1960; d. Sandra Ada and Wallace Butler, Rita Butler (Stepmother); m. Eric Ryan Lindsay, May 30, 1999. BA, Sonoma State U.; MS, U. Oreg., 1988, PhD, 1989. Economist Fed. Res. Bank of St. Louis, 1989—93; vis. asst. prof. George Washington U., 1993—95; asst. prof. Fla. Internat. U., Miami, 1995—99; assoc. prof. Kent State U., Ohio, 1999—2003, Willamette U., 2003—. Vis. scholar Swiss Nat. Bank, Zurich, 1990—91, Fed. Res. Bank of St. Louis, 1997—2000, Fed. Res. Bank of Cleve., 2000—03. Author: (article) Jour. of Internat. Econs., Can. Jour. of Econs. (Nominated for best article of yr., 1997), Econ. Jour. Tchg. Fellowship, U. of Oreg., 1984—89. Mem.: So. Poverty Law Ctr., Am. Econ. Assn. Avocation: independent movies. Office: Asst Prof Dept of Econ Willamette Univ Salem OR 97301 Office Fax: 503-370-6720. E-mail: abutler@willamette.edu.

BUTLER, ARTHUR D. retired economics educator; b. Detroit, Oct. 13, 1923; s. Dwight and Gertrude Mae (Byers) B.; m. Kathleen Lehman, Sept. 3, 1945; children: Terese Kay, Pamela Ann, Sandra Sue. BA, Manchester Coll. (North Manchester, Ind.), 1944; MA, U. Minn., 1946; PhD, U. Wis., 1951. Lectr. U. Buffalo, 1949-52, asst. prof. econs., 1952-57, assoc. prof., 1957-61, prof., 1961—89, acting dean, 1960-63; provost social scis. SUNY-Buffalo, 1973-78; cons. U.S. Senate, Washington, 1976-78; ret., 1989. Author: Labor Economics and Institutions, 1961, Impact of the Fiscal System, 1968, State and Local Government Payrolls, 1968; editor: Selections in Economics, 1958. Bd. dirs. Housing Opportunities Made Equal, Buffalo, 1983— . Fulbright prof. U. Zambia, 1978-79; recipient Outstanding Alumnus award Manchester Coll., 1982 Fellow Japan Soc. for Promotion Sci. Home: 735 Renaissance Dr Apt 124 Buffalo NY 14221-8041

BUTLER, BRIAN, podiatric physician; b. N.Y.C., Mar. 30, 1949; s. William Leland and Mary Theresa (O'Leary) B.; m. Catherine Mary Collins; children: Irene, Matthew, Beth. BA, St. Francis Coll., Bklyn., 1970; MA, Manhattan Coll., Riverdale, N.Y., 1973; D in Podiatric Medicine, N.Y. Coll. Podiatric Medicine, 1981; postgrad., Columbia U., 1994—. Lic. podiatrist, N.Y.; diplomate Am. Bd. Podiatric Orthopedics. Resident in surgery Joint Diseases North Gen. Hosp., N.Y.C., 1982; Fellow advanced mgmt. program for clinicians NYU, 1987; asst. to pres. govt. affairs N.Y. Coll. Podiatric Medicine, N.Y.C., 1979-82, assoc. prof. cmty. medicine, 1988—; chm. dept. podiatry/foot surgery Bklyn. Hosp. Ctr., 1994—2003; chief podiatry Victory Meml. Hosp., Bklyn., 1992-95. Adj. asst. prof. medicine N.Y. Med. Coll., Valhalla, 1984-92; asst. clin. prof. surgery NYU Sch. Medicine, 1996—; asst. clin. prof. podiatric medicine and surgery Weill Med. Coll., Cornell U., 1999—; chmn., pres. adv. bd. N.Y. Coll. Podiatric Medicine, 1991, chmn. curriculum reform commn., 1992; chmn. coun. SUNY Health Sci. Ctr. at Bklyn., 1997-2000. Author: Woodrow Wilson's Entry Upon the American Political Scene, 1973; contbg. author: Surgical Management of the Diabetic Patient, 1995; contbr. articles to profl. jours. Pres., chmn. bd. U.S. Cath. Hist. Soc., N.Y.C., 1984—, EN EL Inc., Med. Mission to Guatemala, Roman Cath. Diocese of Bklyn., 1992-96; bd. dirs. Rachmiel Levine Diabetes Found., Westchester County Med. Ctr., N.Y., 1984-90, Angel Guardian Home for Children, Bklyn., 1988-2000; sec., bd. trustees Catholic Charities, Roman Cath. Diocese of Bklyn., 1991—; past chmn. Bishop's Lay Com. for Charity. Named Outstanding Young Man in Am., U.S. Jaycees, Washington, 1981, Knight of Malta Sovereign, Mil. Order Malta, Rome, 1982; recipient The Franciscan Spirit award St. Francis Coll., Bklyn., 1990, Pub. Svc. award N.Y.C. Transit Police Dept./Police Benevolent Assn., 1994, Alumni Achievement award St. Francis Coll., N.Y.C., 2002. Fellow Am. Coll. Foot Orthopedists, N.Y. Acad. Medicine; mem. Am. Podiatric Med. Assn., N.Y. State Podiatric Med. Assn. (peer rev. and pub. affairs and legis. coms., Disting. Svc. award student chpt. 1981), N.Y. Athletic Club. Democrat. Home: 77 Sagamore Rd Bronxville NY 10708-1506 Office: 1 Hanson Pl Brooklyn NY 11243 E-mail: tbhcbutler@aol.com.

BUTLER, CAROL KING, advertising executive; b. Charlotte, N.C., May 29, 1952; d. Charles Snowden Watts and Marion (Thomas) King; m. James Rodney Butler, Aug. 12, 1972 (div. 1975). Student, U. N.C., Greensboro, 1970-72; BA in Theatre, U. N.C., Charlotte, 2000. Sales rep. Sta. WKIX, Raleigh, NC, 1978-82, N.C. Box, Inc., Raleigh, 1982-84; radio sales account exec. Sta. WRAL-FM, Raleigh, 1984-88, team sales mgr., 1989; prin. Butler-Smith Assocs., Raleigh, 1988-89; ind. programming and video prodr. Raleigh, 1989-90; prin., freelance presentation/video script writer, 1991—. Sales mgr. BW Territory Lifetouch, 1996; creative cons. Creative Comms., 1997—98; writer, artist, photographic enhancer, 2000; writer, cons., playwright, 2003—. Democrat. Mem. Unity Ch. Avocations: water-skiing, feral cat rescue, boating, photography, rollerblading. Home: 1948 Maryland Ave Charlotte NC 28209 E-mail: cbcats@comporium.net.

BUTLER, CHARLES FRANCIS, cardiac surgeon; b. N.Y.C., July 24, 1943; s. Francis DeSales and Juanita Elizabeth (Staggers) B.; m. Penelope Johnson; children: Charles, Erin, Brendan. BA, St. Joseph U., 1965; MD, U. Ala., 1971, PhD, 1974. Diplomate Am. Bd. Gen. Surgery, Am. Bd. Thoracic Surgery. Fellow surgery Peter Bent Brigham Hosp., Boston, 1971-73; fellow in surgery Mayo Clinic, Rochester, Minn., 1974-77; fellow in cardiac surgery U. Utah, Salt Lake City, 1977-79; dir. cardiac surgery St. Francis Hosp., Monroe, La., 1979-81; cardiac surgeon Borgess Hosp., Kalamazoo, Mich., 1981-86; dir. cardiac surgery Bronson Meth. Hosp., Kalamazoo, 1986—. Dir. rsch. Next Wave, Inc., Kalamazoo, 1991—; med. dir. Heritage Products Co., Inc., Mich., 1995—; med. cons. UpJohn/Pharmacia, Kalamazoo, 1996—; bd. dirs. Am. Heart Assn., Kalamazoo, 1983—, pres., 1987—88; bd. dirs. Inst. Music and Neurologic Function, Beth Abraham Health Svcs., NY, 1999—; mem. music therapy and heart transplant rsch. bd. Temple U. Author: Dignity or Despair, 1989, Can You Afford to Grow Old?, 1993; contbr. chpts. to books, articles to profl. jours. Pres. Am. Heart Assn., Kalamazoo, 1992-93. Maj. USAF, 1972-79. Superior scholarship award Med. Coll. Ala., 1971. Fellow ACS, Am. Coll. Cardiology, Internat Coll. of Surgeons (vice regen 1990-93), Am. Coll. of Chest Physicians (critical care com. 1992-93); mem. Soc. Thoracic Surgeons. Home: 2130 S Park St Kalamazoo MI 49001-3657

BUTLER, CHARLES RANDOLPH, JR., federal judge; b. N.Y.C., Mar. 28, 1940; BA, Washington and Lee U., 1962; LLB, U. Ala., 1966. Assoc. Hamilton Butler Riddick and LaTour, Mobile, Ala., 1966-69; asst. pub. defender Mobile County, 1969-70, dist. atty., 1971-75; ptnr. Butler and Sullivan, Mobile, 1975-84, Hamilton Butler Riddick Tarlton and Sullivan P.C., Mobile, 1984-88; dist. judge U.S. Dist. Ct. (so. dist.) Ala., Mobile, 1988-94, 2003—, chief dist. judge, 1994—2003. Adj. prof. criminal justice program U. So. Ala., 1972-76; mem. jud. coun. 11th cir., 1994-2003, jud. conf. com. on criminal law, 1993-99, jud. conf. com., 1999-2002; past liaison mem. to long-range planning com. of the AO; past mem. program and adminstrn. subcom., planning for the future and automation subcom., probaton and pretrial umbrella group; mem. exec. com. Jud. Conf. of U.S., 1999-2002. Lst lt. USAR, 1962-64. Named One of Outstanding Young Men of Am., Mobile County Jaycees, 1971. Office: US Dist Ct 113 Saint Joseph St Mobile AL 36602-3683

BUTLER, COLETTE M. minister; b. Chgo., Mar. 26, 1959; d. Eugene Rivers and Constance Bateman; m. Daryl Lee Butler, July 15, 1993; children: Natasha, Cynthinia, Lanina, Angeline, Darrell, Kimberly. Cert. of completion, Midwest Bible Coll., 1999; cert. of ordination, Holy Trinity, 2001. Cashier/payroll Burt's Shoe Store, Chgo., 1975—80; data entry First Nat. Bank/Bank One, Chgo., 1980—85; customer svc., receptionist Preferred Care Network, Chgo., 1986—90; customer svc. Culinary, Chgo., 1991—94; owner Mr. B's Auto Repair, Chgo., 1995; sec. Bank of Am., Chgo., 1999—2000; founder, pres., shepherd All Nations Kingdom of God, Chgo., 1997. Pharmacy advisor Healthstar, Chgo., 1989—90; fundraiser cons. Corner Stone, Chgo.; ministerial bd. Lighthouse, Chgo., 1999—2000. Author: Bone of His Bone, 2001; contbr. articles. Organizer Mind, Body & Spirit Ministries, Chgo., 2001, recovery

shepherd, 2001, feeding & clothing adminstr., 2002, pres., 1999—2003, founder. Avocations: sewing, crocheting, reading. Office: All Nations Kingdom of God PO Box 368603 Chicago IL 60609 Fax: 773-498-6209. E-mail: allnationskingdomofgod@netzero.net.

BUTLER, DAVID, lawyer; b. St. Paul, June 11, 1930; s. Francis David and Alida (Bigelow) B.; m. Diana Dodge Duffy, Aug. 29, 1952 (div. 1957); children: Anne, Lawrence David; m. Barbara Williams Clark, July 12, 1958; children: Molly Elizabeth, Peter, Katherine BA, Princeton U., 1952; LLB, Harvard U., 1957. Bar. Colo. 1958, U.S. Dist. Ct. Colo. 1958. Assoc. Holland & Hart, Denver, 1957-63, ptnr., 1963-95, chmn. mgmt. com., 1990-95; of counsel, 1996—. Gen. counsel 1st Interstate Bank Denver, 1984-86; bd. dirs. UMB Bank Colo., Denver. Mem. bd. editors Harvard Law Rev., 1955-57. Chmn. lawyers adv. com. United Way, Denver, 1989—94; trustee Graland Country Day Sch., Denver, 1971—79, Legal Aid Found., Colo., 1991—97, chmn., 1993—97, Colo. Planning Group for Legal Svcs. to the Poor, 1995—2002; bd. dirs. Met. Denver Legal Aid Soc., 1971—74; founder Colo. Lawyers Trust Account Fund, 2000—; chmn. Colo. Access to Justice Commn., 2003—. 1st lt. U.S. Army, 1952—54. Mem. ABA, Colo. Bar Assn. (chmn. tax sect. 1970, Jacob V. Schaetzel pro bono award 2002), Denver Bar Assn. Office: Holland & Hart 555 17th St Ste 2900 Denver CO 80202-3979

BUTLER, DAVID ALFRED, music educator; b. Chattanooga, Tenn., Aug. 16, 1968; s. Wayne Alfred Butler, Elberta Ruth (Carroll) Butler; m. Jamie Lee Crews, Aug. 17, 1991; 1 child, Jessica Anne. BS in Music Edn., Tenn. Technol. U., 1991. Asst. dir. band Hixson H.S., Hixson, Tenn., 1991—94; dir. bands Chattanooga Sch. for Arts and Scis., Chattanooga, 1994—. Tubist Chattanooga Symphony, Chattanooga Concert Band. Composer (arranger music for tuba) ; contbr. Mem.: East Tenn. Sch. Band and Orch. Assn. (band chmn. 1999—), Internat. Tuba-Euphonium Assn., Nat. Band Assn., Phi Beta Mu. Office: Chattanooga Sch for Arts & Scis 865 E Third St Chattanooga TN 37403

BUTLER, DAVID GEORGE, obstetrician, gynecologist; b. Bklyn., Dec. 27, 1939; s. Joseph I. and Margaret Frances (Kiley) B.; m. Mary Ann Casey, June 13, 1964; children: Mary, Jean, David, Kevin, Susan. BS in Biology, Coll. of the Holy Cross, 1961; MD, SUNY, Bklyn., 1965. Diplomate Am. Bd. Ob-Gyn. Intern St. Vincents-N.Y. Med. Ctr., N.Y.C., 1965-66, resident in ob-gyn., 1966-70; attending physician Englewood Hosp., 1972—, Holy Name Hosp., 1972—; pvt. practice. Dir. ob-gyn. Holy Name Hosp., Teaneck, NJ, 1990—96, Teaneck, 1990—96. Mem. ACOG, Am. Assn. Gynecol. Laporoscopists. Home: 6 Ridge Rd Norwood NJ 07648-2416 Office: 420 Grand Ave Englewood NJ 07631-4141

BUTLER, DONALD K. lawyer; b. Newport News, Va., Feb. 4, 1944; s. Grover Cleveland Butler and Nettie Louise (Peele) Vince; married Jan. 29, 1965 (div.); 1 child, Robin Player Michelsen; m. Chena Allison, Sept. 15, 1979; children: Allison Peele, Charlotte Louise. BA, U. Richmond, 1966, JD, 1970. Bar: Va. 1970. Assoc., ptnr. Cole, Wells & Bradshaw, Richmond, Va., 1970-78; pvt. practice Richmond, 1978-81; ptnr. ButlerCook L.L.P., Richmond, 1981—. Lectr. on family law at seminars and law schs. Contbr. articles to law revs. Named one of Best Lawyers in Am. for 20 Yrs. Mem. Va. State Bar (bd. govs. 1978-82, chmn. family law sect. 1980-81), Va. Trial Lawyers Assn. (chmn. family law sect. 1993), Richmond Bar Assn., Am. Acad. Matrimonial Lawyers (pres. Va. chpt. 1997-99). Avocations: golf, cooking. Office: Morano Colan Cook and Butler 526 N Boulevard Richmond VA 23220-3309 E-mail: vafamlaw@aol.com.

BUTLER, DOUGLAS JOHN, physician; b. Greensboro, N.C., Nov. 23, 1954; s. John C. and Jeannette D. B. BA magna cum laude, Miami Univ., 1975; MD, Ohio State, 1978. Diplomate Am. Bd. Family Practice. Family medicine resident Moses Cone Hosp., Greensboro, 1978-81; attending physician, pvt. practice Ashe Meml. Hosp., Jefferson, N.C., 1981-93; emergency dept. physician Lake Norman Reg. Medical Ctr., Mooresville, N.C., 1993; emergency dept. medical dir. Alexander Cmty. Hosp., Taylorsville, N.C., 1993-2000, chief of staff, 1999; locum tenens physician Indian Health Svc., 2000—; attending physician Old Fort Med. Clinic/The McDowell Hosp., Marion, NC, 2001—02. Chief of staff Ashe Meml. Hosp., Jefferson, N.C., 1982-83. Author: Ashe County Discovering the Lost Province, 1993; contbr. articles to profl. jours. Chmn. Ashe County EMS Coun., Jefferson, 1986-91. Mem. Am. Heart Assn. (pres. Ashe County chpt. 1986-91), Jefferson Rotary Club. Avocations: photography, mountaineering, travel. Office: RR 1 Box 140A Crumpler NC 28617-9801

BUTLER, FREDERICK GEORGE, retired drug company executive; b. Greenwich, Conn., Mar. 25, 1919; s. Harold Nassau and Rosa (Rhinhart) B.; m. Sarah Lou Allred, Sept. 23, 1945; children: Pamela Sue, Frederick Houston (dec.). AB, Middlebury (Vt.) Coll., 1941; MBA, Columbia U., 1947. CPA, N.Y. With Price Waterhouse & Co. (C.P.A.'s), 1941-42, 47-49; with McKesson & Robbins, Inc., N.Y.C., 1949-63, asst. comptroller, 1952-61, comptroller, 1961-63; controller Bristol-Myers Co., N.Y.C., 1963-66, v.p., controller, 1966-69, v.p. ops., 1970-76. Pioneered developement of bar code (compatible universal product code and nat. drug code) for supermarket automated checkout scanning and inventory control. Village mayor, Briarcliff Manor, N.Y., 1969-71. Served to comdr. USNR, 1942-46, 51-52. Mem. Fin. Execs. Inst., Fairfield Mountains Club (Bald Mountain and Apple Valley, N.C.), Pres.'s Club, Hillsdale (Mich.) Coll., Chi Psi. Methodist. Home: 6825 Davis Blvd Apt 219 Naples FL 34104-5325 E-mail: frdbutler@aol.com.

BUTLER, GEORGE BERGEN, chemistry educator; b. Liberty, Miss., Apr. 15, 1916; s. Benjamin Franklin and Estelle (McGehee) B.; m. Josephine Eldridge, June 4. 1944; children: George Bergen, Barbara Butler Ward. Cert., S.W. Miss. Jr. Coll., 1936; BA, Miss. Coll., 1938, DSc (hon.), 1986; PhD, U. N.C., Chapel Hill, 1942. Instr. organic lab. Miss. Coll., Clinton, 1937-38; instr. analytica lab. U. N.C., Chapel Hill, 1938-40, rsch. fellow, 1940-42; rsch. chemist Rohm & Haas Co., Inc., Phila., 1942-46; prof. chemistry, rsch. prof. U. Fla., Gainesville, 1946-90, dir. Ctr. Macromolecular Sci. and Engring., 1970-90, prof. emeritus, 1990—. Mem. panel on nation's potential for basic rsch. in chemistry Nat. Rsch. Coun., Washington; cons. Chemstrand Corp., PCR Inc., Atlantic Refining Inc., Calgon divsn. Merck, Inc., Allied Chem. Co., Internat. Minerals and Chem. Co., Proctor and Gamble, indsl. and govtl. labs. Editl. bd. Macromolecular Syntheses, 1961-95, Jour. Macromolecular Sci.-Chemistry, 1966-90; adv. bd. Jour. Polymer Sci., 1966-86; organizer, co-editor Jour. Macromolecular Sci. - Reviews, 1966-98, Reviews in Macromolecular Chemistry, 1967-68; editl. adv. bd. Macromolecules, 1968-69. contbr. articles to profl. jours. Recipient Fla. Blue Key award, 1965, Disting. alumnus award Miss. Coll., 1993. Fellow Am. Inst. Chemists (pres. Fla. chpt.); mem. AAAS, Am. Chem. Soc. (councilor Fla. sect. 1949-51, chmn. 1954-55, gen. chmn. 1958, award for Outstanding Rsch. and Tchg. 1963, Herty medal 1978, Polymer award 1980, Stone award 1983, So. chemist 1985, Flory Polymer Edn. award 1990), Fla. Acad. Scis. (bd. dirs., medal 1982), Sigma Xi (pres. 1962-63, award 1961), N.Y. Acad. Scis. Republican. Presbyterian. Avocations: weekend farming, fishing, traveling. Office: U Fla Dept Chemistry PO Box 117200 Gainesville FL 32611-7200

BUTLER, IAN JOHN, neurologist; b. Adelaide, Australia, Sept. 19, 1941; came to U.S., 1972; s. John Alfred and Susan Pearl (Matters) B.; m. Patricia Mary Gordon, Feb. 28, 1969; children: Sarah, Katherine, Philip. MBBS, U. Adelaide, 1964. Diplomate Am. Bd. Psychiatry and Neurology. Resident Adelaide (Australia) Childrens Hosp., 1966-67; med. registrar Royal Childrens Hosp., Victoria, Australia, 1968; fellow neurology U. Melbourne, Victoria, 1969; sr. house officer Hosp. for Sick Children, London, 1970; registrar U. Wales Hosp., Cardiff, 1971; resident neurology, asst. prof. Johns Hopkins Univ. Hosp., Balt., 1972-76; assoc. prof. neurology U. Tex., Houston, 1976-79, prof. neurology and pediatrics, 1979—. Prof. pediatrics dept. M.D. Anderson Cancer Ctr., Houston, 1980—; assoc. prof. Grad. Sch. Biomed. Scis., U. Tex. Health Sci. Ctr., Houston, 1978—; cons., dir. neuromuscular clinic Shrine Hosp., Houston; lectr. in field. Mem. editl. bd. Jour. Child Neurology, 1987—, assoc. editor, 1990—; contbr. articles to profl. jours. Chmn. prof. adv. com. Ctr. for Retarded, Inc., 1981—, bd. govs. mem., 1981—. Grantee Huntington Chorea Found., 1977-79, NSF, 1978, March of Dimes, 1978-80, Am. Parkinson Disease Assn., 1980-83, Epilepsy Ctr. Baylor Coll. Medicine, 1984-86, 88-93, Brandt Family Found., 1986, Meadows Found., 1986-91, Muscular Dystrophy Assn., 1988-90, 90-91, 91-93, NIH, 1989-94, 91-94, Shriner Hosp. for Crippled Children, 1990-93, 93-94, 95-97, 96-99, NASA, 1991-93. Fellow Royal Soc. Medicine, Royal Australasian Coll. Physicians; mem. AAAS, Am. Neurol. Assn., Assn. Rsch. in Nervous and Mental Disease, Am. Acad. Neurology, Soc. Neurosci., Internat. Child Neurology Assn., Child Neurology Soc., N.Y. Acad. Scis., Tex. Med. Assn., Harris County Med. Soc., Houston Pediatric Soc., Houston Neurol. Soc., Alpha Omega Alpha. Episcopalian. Avocations: music, reading, tennis. Home: 2200 Glen Haven Blvd Houston TX 77030-3606 Office: Univ Tex Dept Neurology 6431 Fannin St Ste 7044 Houston TX 77030-1501

BUTLER, JACK FAIRCHILD, semiconductors company executive; b. El Centro, Calif., July 18, 1933; s. Jack Orval and Dorothy (Marsh) B.; m. Colette Alice Guerard, Sept. 6, 1959; children—Alice, Jack, Michael, Patricia. Student, San Jose State Coll., 1951-54; BS, U. Calif., Berkeley, 1959, MS, 1960, PhD, 1962. Research staff mem. Mass. Inst. Tech., Lincoln Lab., Lexington, Mass., 1962-68; staff scientist Gen. Dynamics Corp., Pomona, Calif., 1968-71; sr. staff mem. Arthur D. Little, Inc., Cambridge, Mass., 1971-74; co-founder, co-owner, dir., pres. Laser Analytics, Inc., Lexington, 1974-81; founder, owner, dir., pres. Butler Research and Engring., Inc., 1981-85; co-founder, co-owner, dir., pres. San Diego Semicondrs., Inc., 1985-91, Aurora Techs. Corp., 1991-95; co-founder, co-owner, pres. Digirad (formerly Aurora Techs. Corp.), 1995-98; ret., 1998. Contbr. articles to sci. jours. Served with USMC, 1954-57. Mem. IEEE (life), AAAS, Am. Inst. Physics (life), Gen. Soc. Mayflower Descs. (life).

BUTLER, JAMES ROBERTSON, JR., lawyer; b. Cleve., May 29, 1946; s. James Robertson and Iris Davis (Welborn) B. AB magna cum laude, U. Calif., Berkeley, 1966, JD, 1969. Bar: Calif. 1970, U.S. Tax Ct. 1977, U.S. Supreme Ct. 1980, Nev. 1997. Chmn. real estate dept. and Global Hospitality Group Jeffer, Mangels, Butler & Marmaro, LLP, L.A. and San Francisco, 1982—. Founder, chmn. JMBM Global Hospitality Group Briefing Series, 1991—, ULI Los Angeles Hospitality Product Coun., 2000—; expert panelist on hospitality industry topics NYU Hospitality Industry Investment Conf., UCLA Hospitality Investment Conf., Calif. Soc. CPAs ann. hospitality confs., 1992, 93, 94, 95; spkr., panelist Robert Morris Assocs. Nat. Conf., Chgo., 1989, nat. ann. conf. Ind. Bankers Assn. Am., 1992; frequent guest expert securities, real estate and banking various TV programs, 1985—; participant comml. real estate workouts workshop FDIC & RTC Nat. Tng. Conf., San Antonio, 1989, San Diego, 1990; adv. bd. Bur. Nat. Affairs, Washington. Author: Arbitration in Banking, A Robert Morris Associates State of the Art Book, 1988, Lender Liability: A Practical Guide, A BNA Special Report, 1987; editor Global Hospitality Advisor 1991—, Banking Law Report Capital Adequacy series, 1985, Global Hospitality Advisor, 1991—, Calif. Law Rev.; co-chmn. adv. council Money and Real Estate: The Jour. of Lending, Syndication, Joint Ventures, and the Third Market; contbr. chpt., Mapping the Minefield--Lender's Liability, The Workout Game, Solutions to Problem Real Estate Loans, 1987; contbr. more than 100 articles to profl. jours, chaps. to books. Mem. Am. Arbitration Assn., Comml. Arbitration Panel; founding dir. Liberty Nat. Bank; Charter Adv. bd. dirs., Adv. Council of the Banking Law Inst. Recipient Kraft Prize U. Calif., 1966; Bartley Cavenaugh Crum scholar U. Calif. Sch. Law, 1969. Mem. ABA (corp., banking and bus. law sect., taxation sect.), Urban Land Inst. (chmn. hospitality product coun., exec. com. L.A. Dist. coun. 2000—), Internat. Soc. Hospitality Cons., L.A. County Bar Assn., Century City Bar Assn. (chmn. fin. instn. sect. 1990-91), Beverly Hills Bar Assn., Calif. League of Savs. Instns. (chmn. arbitration com. 1987, 88), Young Pres.' Orgn. (internat. hospitality conference, Milan, 2001). Avocations: personal computers (beta reviewer for various software developers including, microsoft). E-mail: jbutler@jmbm.com.

BUTLER, JANNETTE SUE, human resources professional; b. Eugene, Oreg., Mar. 15, 1960; d. Robert Eugene and Dorothy Marilyn (Irvin) Butler. BS in Hotel Adminstrn., U. Nev., Las Vegas, 1982. Cert. health promotion dir., sr. profl. in human resources. Pers. mgmt. trainee The Sheraton Corp., San Diego, 1982-83, dir. pers. Palm Coast, Fla., 1983-85, dir. human resources Dallas, 1985-89; corp. dir. human resources Hilton Reservations Worldwide, Carrollton, Tex., 1989-95; human resource cons. Symantec Corp., Eugene, Oreg., 1995-97; mgr. human resource Microsoft Corp., Redmond, Wash., 1997-99, sr. mgr. human resource, 1999—2000, group human resources mgr., 2000—01, human resource dir., 2001—. Mem., vol. Nat. Multiple Sclerosis Soc., Redmond Police Dept., 2001—; mem. steering com. Lane County Career Ctrs. Recipient Volunteerism award Lodging Industry Tng. Ctr., 1988. Mem. Soc. for Human Resource Mgmt., Northwest Human Resource Mgmt. Assn. (pres. elect 1997), Inst. for Internat. Human Resource Mgmt., Eugene C. of C. (edn. com.). Episcopalian. Avocations: boating, gardening, skiing. Office: Microsoft One Microsoft Way Redmond WA 98052

BUTLER, JILL LAUREN KRAFT, internist, educator; b. Bronx, N.Y., Jan. 10, 1965; d. David Werner and Anita Toni (Rankow) Kraft; m. Robert George Butler III, Oct. 2, 1994; children: Yehuda, Yocheved, Esther. BA in Biology, Princeton U., 1986; MD, SUNY, Stony Brook, 1992. Lic. physician, N.Y. Intern, then resident in internal medicine Montefiore Med. Ctr., Bronx, 1992-95, chief resident in primary care, 1994-95, asst. attending physician, 1995—, asst. attending physician primary care adult medicine, 1997—; asst.attending physician dept. medicine and asthma ctr. North Ctrl. Bronx Hosp., 1995-97; asst. prof. medicine Albert Einstein Coll. Medicine, Bronx, 1995—. Mem. Am. Coll. Physicians. Jewish. Avocations: child rearing, jewish studies. Office: Montefiore Med Ctr 111 E 210th St Bronx NY 10467-2401

BUTLER, JODY TALLEY, gifted education educator; b. Columbus, Ga., Mar. 14, 1958; d. Bill Ray and Jacqueline (Hay) T.; m. Danny Butler. BS in Edn., West Ga. Coll., 1979, MEd, 1982; EdD, Auburn U., 1988. Cert. tchr., Ga. Tchr. Cen. Primary Sch., Carrollton, 1979-88; tchr. gifted student program QUEST Cen. Middle School, Carrollton, 1988-98; co-owner Hay's Mill Antiques, Ga., 1994—; QUEST tchr. Roopville Elem., Mt. Zion Elem., 1998-2000; tchr. of gifted Carrollton Elem. Sch., 2000—. Mem. handbell choir Carrollton Presbyn. Ch. Mem. Internat. Reading Assn., Profl. Assn. Ga. Educators, Carroll County Cmty. Chorus, Phi Delta Kappa (Dissertation of Yr. award 1989), Phi Kappa Phi, Alpha Gamma Delta. Presbyterian. Avocations: antiques, travel, music, writing, guitar. Office: Carrollton Elem Sch 401 Ben Scott Blvd Carrollton GA 30117

BUTLER, JOHN EDWARD, biomedical sciences educator, consultant; b. Rice Lake, Wis., Jan. 10, 1938; s. Edward W. and Ida (Fredrick) B.; children: Kirsten Diane Butler Bennett, Brian Miller. BS in Chemistry and Biology, U. Wis., River Falls, 1961; PhD in Zoology and Biochemistry, U. Kans., 1965. Ranger, naturalist U.S. Nat. Park Svc., Crater Lake, Oreg., 1961-63; tchg. asst. U. Kans., Lawrence, 1961-66; rsch. biologist USDA, Washington, 1968-71; asst. prof. microbiology U. Iowa, Iowa City, 1971-74, assoc. prof., 1974-80, prof., 1980—, dir. Iowa biotech. tng. program, 1984-89, dir. grad. studies dept. microbiology, 1996—. Cons. devel. immunology. Editor: The Ruminant Immune System, 1981, Immunochemistry of Solid-phase Immunoassay, 1991; mem. editl. bd.: Analytical Biochem., Develop. & Comparative Immunology; contbr. more than 180 articles and revs. to sci. jours. Recipient citation Inst. for Sci. Info., 1983; Max Planck fellow, Mariensee, Germany, 1972-74, Fogarty internat. fellow NIH-Fogarty Ctr., 1981-82. Mem.: Soc. Mucosal Immunity, Am. Assn. Immologists, Stearman Restorers Assn. Avocations: flying, bicycle touring. Office: U Iowa Dept Microbiology Bowen Sci Bldg 51 Newton Rd Iowa City IA 52242-1109 E-mail: john-butler@uiowa.edu.

BUTLER, JOHN MUSGRAVE, financial consultant, consultant; b. Bklyn., Dec. 6, 1928; s. John Joseph and Sabina Catherine (Musgrave) Butler; m. Ann Elizabeth Kelly, July 9, 1955; children: Maureen, John, Ellen, Suzanne. BA cum laude, St. John's U., 1950; MBA, NYU, 1951. CPA N.Y., Ill. Sr. acct. Lybrand, Ross Bros. & Montgomery (CPAs), N.Y.C., 1953-59; sr. auditor ITT Corp., N.Y.C., 1959-62; asst. to contr. Dictaphone Corp., Bridgeport, Conn., 1962-63, contr. Bridgeport, Rye, NY, 1964-68; v.p. acctg. Chgo. & North Western Ry. Co., 1968-69, v.p. fin. and acctg., 1969-72, Chgo. and North Western Transp. Co., 1972-79, sr. v.p. fin. and acctg., 1979-89, dir., 1976-89, trustee, 1978-82, acting sr. v.p. fin. and acctg., 1994; sr. v.p. fin. and acctg., dir. CNW Corp., 1985-89; cons. in fin. and acctg. for bus., 1989—; instr. fin. DePaul U., Chgo., 1989—2001. Dir. Cath. Med. Mission Bd., N.Y.C., 1998—2000. With USCGR, 1951—53. Mem.: Fin. Execs. Inst. Roman Catholic. Office: 119 E Palatine Rd Ste 206 Palatine IL 60067-5132

BUTLER, JON TERRY, computer engineering educator, researcher; b. Balt., Dec. 26, 1943; s. Herbert Harriss and Vera Esse (Buck) B.; m. Susan Beth Wood, Feb. 24, 1968 (div. Aug. 1996); 1 child, Anne Elizabeth; m. Fujiko Sakaguchi, Jan. 31, 1998. BEE, Rensselaer Poly. Inst., 1966, M in Engring., 1967; PhD, Ohio State U., 1973. Registered profl. engr., Ohio. NRC postdoctoral assoc. Air Force Avionics Lab., Wright-Patterson AFB, Ohio, 1973-74; sr. postdoctoral assoc. Naval Postgrad. Sch., Wright-Patterson AFB, Ohio, 1980-81; assoc. prof. Northwestern U., Evanston, Ill., 1974-87; prof. Naval Postgrad. Sch., Monterey, Calif., 1987—, Navalex Chair prof., 1985-87. Editor: Multi-Valued Logic in VLSI, 1991; contbr. articles to profl. jours. Capt. USAF, 1967-70. Recipient Faculty Performance award Naval Postgrad. Sch., 1990-93. Fellow IEEE; mem. IEEE Computer Soc. (chmn. multiple-valued logic com. 1980-81, Disting. vis. 1982-86, press editor 1986-90, editor-in-chief Computer mag. 1991-92, editor-in-chief Computer Soc. Press 1993-97, chmn. Computer Soc. fellows evaluation com. 1999, chmn. Computer Soc. transactions ops. com. 1998-99, chmn. Computer Soc. Press ops. com. 2000—, Meritorious Svc. award 1988, 92, TAB Pioneer award 1989, cert. appreciation 1982, 89, 91, 95, 96, 99, 2000, Disting. Svc. award 1995, Third Centennial medal 2000, bd. govs. 1991-97). Presbyterian. Avocation: jogging. Office: Naval Postgrad Sch Dept Elec Computer Engring Code EC-BU Monterey CA 93943-5121

BUTLER, JONATHAN PUTNAM, architect; b. Portchester, N.Y., June 6, 1940; s. Jonathan Fairchild and Mary Elizabeth (Putnam) Butler; m. Deborah Day Rogers, Mar. 18, 1967; children: Jonathan Rogers, Pauline Washburn, Benjamin Putnam, Cynthia Day. BA, Princeton U., 1962, MFA, 1965; MArch, Columbia U., 1966. Designer, programmer, planner Skidmore, Owings & Merrill, Architects, N.Y.C., 1968-71; ptnr. Rogers, Butler, Burgun & Shahine, N.Y.C., 1971-79; pres. Butler, Rogers & Baskett, N.Y.C., 1979—. Bd. dirs. Woodlawn Cemetary, Bronx, N.Y., Search & Care, N.Y. Landmarks Preservation Found. Mem AIA, N.Y. Soc. Architects, N.Y. State Assn. Architects, Columbia Archtl. Alumni Assn., Nat. Coun. Archtl. Registration Bds. (cert.), Union Club, Princeton Club. Home: 14 West Ln Niantic CT 06357-3716 Office: Butler Rogers & Baskett 475 10th Ave Fl 5 New York NY 10018-1139 E-mail: jbutler@brb.com.

BUTLER, KEITH ARNOLD, psychologist, software researcher; b. L.A., Dec. 22, 1945; s. John Harold and Phyllis Alder (Falke) B.; m. Janis Lynn Mowry, Dec. 23, 1972 (div. Jan. 1981); 1 child: John Keith; m. Ann Marie Kimball, Jan. 30, 2000. BA, Calif. State U., Long Beach, 1972; PhD in Exptl. Psychology, Tufts U., Medford, Mass., 1980. Lectr. Emmanual Coll., Boston, 1975-77; mem. tech. staff Bell Telephone Labs., 1978-81; tech. fellow The Boeing Co., Bellevue, Wash., 1981—. Tutorial lectr. SIGCHI Conf., 1989—, gen. co-chair, New Orleans, 1991; tech. fellow Boeing Tech., Seattle, 1999. Contbr. articles to profl. jours. Founding bd. mem. Citizens for Better Schs., Snoqualmie, Wash., 1989-91. With U.S. Army, 1967-69. Mem. Assn. Computing Machinery. Congregationalist. Achievements include development of an engineering method for the design of usable human-computer interfaces; leadership in developing industrywide standard for software product usability; design of the experiment which revealed the role of beta-estradiol in male reproductive behavior. Office: Boeing Phantom Works M&CT PO Box 3707 MS 7L-40 Seattle WA 98124-2207

BUTLER, MANLEY CALDWELL, retired lawyer; b. Roanoke, Va., June 2, 1925; s. W.W.S. Butler Jr.; m. June Nolde, June 26, 1950; children: Manley, Henry, James, Marshall. AB, U. Richmond, 1948; JD, U. Va., 1950; LLD (hon.), Washington & Lee U., 1978. Bar: Va. 1950. Mem. Va. Ho. Dels., 1962-72, minority leader; mem. 92d-97th Congresses from 6th Va. dist., Judiciary Com., Com. on Govt. Ops., Woods, Rogers & Hazlegrove, P.L.C., 1983—99; ret., 1999. Mem. Nat. Bankruptcy Rev. Commn., 1995-97. Lt. USNR, 1943-46. Fellow Am. Bar Found., Am. Coll. Bankruptcy, Va. Law Found.; mem. ABA, Va. Bar Assn., Va. State Bar Assn., Roanoke Bar Assn., Am. Bankruptcy Inst., Raven Soc. Order of Coif, Phi Beta Kappa, Tau Kappa Alpha, Omicron Delta Kappa, Phi Gamma Delta. Episcopalian. Home: Unit 202 4434 Pheasant Ridge Rd Roanoke VA 24014-5279 E-mail: nuniepapa@cox.net.

BUTLER, MARGARET KAMPSCHAEFER, retired computer scientist; b. Evansville, Ind., Mar. 7, 1924; d. Otto Louis and Lou Etta (Rehsteiner) Kampschaefer; m. James W. Butler, Sept. 30, 1951; 1 child, Jay. AB, Ind. U., 1944; postgrad., U.S. Dept. Agr. Grad. Sch., 1945, U. Chgo., 1949, U. Minn., 1950. Statistician U.S. Bur. Labor Statistics, Washington, 1945-46, U.S. Air Forces in Europe, Erlangen and Wiesbaden, Germany, 1946-48, U.S. Bur. Labor Statistics, St. Paul, 1949-51; mathematician Argonne (Ill.) Nat. Lab., 1948-49, 51-80, sr. computer scientist, 1980-92; dir. Argonne Code Ctr. and Nat. Energy Software Ctr. Dept. Energy Computer Program Exch., 1960-91; spl. term appointee Argonne Nat. Lab., 1993—. Cons. AMF Corp., 1956-57, OECD, 1964, Poole Bros., 1967. Author: Careers for Women in Nuclear Science and Technology, 1992; editor Computer Physics Communications, 1969-80; contbr. (chpt.) The Application of Digital Computers to Problems in Reactor Physics, 1968, Advances in Nuclear Sci. and Technology, 1976; contbr. articles to profl. publs. Treas. Timberlake Civic Assn., 1958; rep. mem. nomination com. Hinsdale (Ill.) Caucus, 1961-62; coord. 6th dist. ERA, 1973-80; del. Rep. Nat. Conv., 1980; bd. mgr. DuPage dist. YWCA Met. Chgo., 1987-90; mem. computer and info. sys. adv. bd. Coll. DuPage, 1987-95; mem. industry adv. bd. computer sci. dept. Bradley U., 1988-91; vice chair Ill. Women's Polit. Caucus, 1987-90; chair voter's svc. LWV, Burr-Ridge-Willowbrook, 1991-93; vol. Morton Arboretum, 1997—, Friends of Indian Prairie Pub. Libr., 2000-2002; mem. LaGrange Park Friends Libr., 2002-. Recipient cert. of leadership Met. YWCA, Chgo., 1985, Merit award Chgo. Assn. Technol. Socs., 1988; named to Fed. 100, 1991; named Outstanding Woman Leader of DuPage County Sci., Tech. and Health Care, 1992. Fellow Am. Nuclear Soc. (mem. publs. com. 1965-71, bd. dirs. 1976-79, exec. com. 1977-78, chmn. bylaws and rules com., 1979-82, profl. women in ANS com. 1991-93, reviewer for publs., spl. award math. and computer divsn. 1992); mem. Assn. Computing Machinery (exec. com., sec. Chgo. chpt. 1963-65, publs. chmn. nat. conf. 1968, reviewer for publs.), Assn. Women in Sci. (pres. Chgo. area chpt. 1982, nat. exec. bd. 1985-87), Nat. Computer Conf. (chmn. Pioneer Day com. 1985, tech. program chmn. 1987). Independent. Home: 107 Brewster Lane La Grange Park IL 60526-6003 *My goal is the removal of barriers restricting individuals from achieving their full potential and the furtherance of individual rights.*

BUTLER, MERLIN GENE, physician, medical geneticist, educator; b. Atkinson, Nebr., Aug. 2, 1952; s. Garold Melvin and Berdena June (Sandall) B.; m. Ranae Ilene Kisker, Oct. 2, 1976; children: Michelle Ranae, Brian Gene. BA with very high distinction, Chadron State Coll., 1974, BS with very high distinction, 1975; MD, U. Nebr., Omaha, 1978; MS, U. Nebr., Lincoln, 1980; PhD, Ind. U., Indpls., 1984. Supervising physician Med. Info. Svcs., Omaha, 1978-80; rsch. assoc. dept. biology U. Notre Dame, South Bend, Ind., 1983-84; med. dir. North Ctrl. Ind. Regional Genetics Ctr., South Bend, 1983-84; dir. cytogenetics Meml. Hosp., South Bend, 1983-84; NIH postdoctoral fellow dept. med. genetics Sch. Medicine Ind. U., Indpls., 1980-83, adj. asst. prof. dept. med. genetics Sch. Medicine, 1984; asst. prof. dept. pediatrics Sch. Medicine Vanderbilt U., Nashville, 1984-90, dir. regional genetics program Sch. Medicine, 1984-98, dir. Cytogenetics Lab. dept. pediatrics Sch. Medicine, 1989-98, assoc. prof. dept. pediatrics, 1990-98, assoc. prof. dept. pathology, 1991-98, investigator John F. Kennedy Ctr. Rsch. on Edn. and Human Devel., Peabody Coll., 1987-98; assoc. dir. Inst. Behavior and Genetics; assoc. prof. dept. orthopedics Vanderbilt U., 1994-98. Adj. assoc. prof. dept. pediatrics Meharry Med. Coll., Nashville, 1988-98; genetics cons. Baptist Hosp., Nashville, 1985-98, Westside Hosp., Nashville, 1985-98, Nashville Gen. Hosp., 1985-98, chief, section of Med. Genetics and Molecular Medicine, Children's Mercy Hosp., Kansas City, Mo., 1998—, William R. Brown prof., chmn., 1998—, prof. dept. pediats., U. Mo.-Kansas City Sch. Medicine; mem. epidemiology genetic diseases subcom. Ind. State Bd. Health, 1983-84; faculty interviewer Vanderbilt U., 1987; peer reviewer Am. Jour. Human Genetics, Am. Jour. Med. Genetics, Clin. Genetics, Am. Jour. Diseases of Children, Dysmorphology and Clin. Genetics, Am. Jour. Mental Retardation, Jour. Pediatrics, So. Med. Jour., Human Mutations, Cancer Genetics and Cytogenetics, Pediatrics, Genomics, Prader-Willi Perspectives; mem. ad-hoc grant review com. NIH, 1990—, craniofacial assessment team Vanderbilt U., 1992-98; lectr., presenter in field. Author: Fragile X Syndrome: A Major Cause of X-Linked Mental Retardation, 1988, 1989; author: (with others) Genetics for the Medically Oriented, 1983, Novak's Textbook of Gynecology, 11th edit., 1988, Birth Defects Encyclopedia, 1990, Prader-Willi Syndrome and Other Chromosome 15q Deletion Disorders,

1992, Human Genetics: New Perspectives, 1994, 1992 International Fragile X Conference Proceedings, 1992, Prader-Willi and Angelman Syndromes Examples of Genetic Imprinting in Man, 1994, Prader-Willi Syndrome: A Guide for Parents and Physicians, 1995, Prader-Willi Syndrome: Clinical and Genetic Findings, 2000' editor: Genetics of Developmental Disabilities, 2003, Management of Prader-Willi Syndrome, 2003; mem. editorial bd. Prader-Willi Perspectives, 1992—; contbr. numerous articles to profl. jours. including Nature and New England Jour. Medicine. Grant reviewer March of Dimes Birth Defects Found., 1985—. Recipient Disting. Svc. award Chadron State Coll., 1986, Teaching award Osler Inst., 1989; grantee Univ. Rsch. Coun., 1985, 92-93, Tenn. Dept. Mental Health and Mental Retardation, 1986-91, Clin. Nutrition Rsch. Unit, 1986-88, Joseph P. Kennedy, Jr. Found., 1988, Clin. Rsch. Ctr. Meharry Med. Coll., 1989-98, Dept. Pathology, 1992-93, Orthopedic Rsch. Edn. Found., 1993-95, NIH, 1995—; Cancer Rsch. grantee Ind. U. Med. Ctr., 1980, Biomed. Rsch. Support grantee, 1985, 88, 89—, Clin. Rsch. grantee March of Dimes Birth Defects Found., 1987, 88, 90-92, Lyle V. Andrews Meml. scholar, 1974. Fellow Am. Coll. Med. Genetics (founder, diplomate, lab. practice subcom. 1993); mem. AMA (Physician Recognition award 1984, 87, 00), AAAS, Am. Bd. Med. Genetics (cert. clin. genetics and clin. cytogenetics), Am. Genetics Assn., Am. Soc. Human Genetics (cytogenetics resource com. 1992-97), Am. Fedn. Clin. Rsch., Coll. Am. Pathologists (cytogenetics resource com. 1992-97, molecular pathology resource com. 1993-97), So. Med. Assn., Davidson County Pediatric Soc., Metro. Med. Soc., Prader-Willi Syndrome Assn. (med. rsch. task force 1985—, diagnostic task force 1991—, sci. adv. bd. 1991—, chair 2000—), N.Y. Acad. Scis., Sigma Xi, Phi Chi. Avocations: gardening, camping, fishing, collecting sports memorabilia. Home: 6410 Hillside St Shawnee KS 66218-9070 Office: Children's Mercy Hosp 2401 Gillham Rd Kansas City MO 64108-4698 E-mail: mgbutler@cmh.edu.

BUTLER, MICHAEL FRANCIS, lawyer; b. Pitts., Aug. 17, 1935; s. Frank J. and Mary M. (Montgomery) B. BA magna cum laude, Harvard U., 1957; LLB, Yale U., 1960. Bar: Pa., D.C. Mem. Kirkpatrick & Lockhart, Pitts., 1960-69; asst. gen. counsel for domestic and internat. bus., then dep. gen. counsel U.S. Dept. Commerce, Washington, 1969-73; v.p., gen. counsel Overseas Pvt. Investment Corp., Washington, 1973-75; gen. counsel Fed. Energy Adminstrn., Washington, 1975-77; ptnr. Andrews & Kurth, Washington, 1977-92. Bd. dirs., chmn. audit com. Three Rivers Bancorp, Inc., Three Rivers Bank & Trust Co.; mem. adv. com. Fagan & Co.; mem. panel of arbitrators Dispute Settlement Ctr., Internat. Energy Agy., Paris; past mem. or chmn. U.S. dels. to OECD coms., Berne Union, Adminstrv. Conf. of U.S. Contbr. articles to profl. publs. Past vice chmn. class spl. gifts com. Harvard Coll. and Yale Law Sch., past bd. dirs., sec. Three Rivers Arts Festival, Pitts.; past bd. dirs. Bryce Harlow Found. Fellow Am. Bar Found. (life); mem. ABA (past chmn. com. on fgn. investment in U.S. internat. law sect.), Am. Arbitration Assn. (mem. comml. panel of arbitrators), Pa. Bar Assn., D.C. Bar Assn., Allegheny County Bar Assn., Am. Law Inst., Am. Judicature Soc., Am. Soc. Internat. Law, Internat. Bar Assn., Washington Fgn. Law Soc., Inter-Am. Bar Assn., Harvard Club West Pa. (past sec.), Harvard Club of D.C. (past bd. dirs.), Met. Club, Rolling Rock Club (Ligonier, Pa.), Harvard-Yale-Princeton Club (Pitts.). Republican. Presbyterian. Home and Office: 2214 Massachusetts Ave NW Washington DC 20008-2812

BUTLER, MICHAEL WARD, economics educator; b. Great Bend, Kans., June 11, 1939; s. George Ward and Mary Jane (Lambert) B.; m. Regina Ann Hammond, Sept. 8, 1995; 1 child, Alexander Ward. BSBA, Fort Hays State U., 1963, MS in Econs., 1964; PhD in Econs., U. Ark., 1974. Diplomate Am. Bd. Forensic Examiners. Data processing sales rep. IBM, Wichita, Kans., 1964-66; instr. econs. Butler County C.C., El Dorado, Kans., 1964-70; asst. prof. econs. U. North Ala., Florence, 1973-75, assoc. prof. econs., 1975-78, prof. econs., 1978-97, dean coll. bus., 1997-2001; dean Coll. Bus. and Profl. Studies, Angelo State U., San Angelo, Tex., 2001—. Referee Jour. Forensic Econs., Kansas City, Mo., 1988—; editl. adv. Ark. Bus. Econs. Rev., Fayetteville, Ark., 1976-99; editl. bd. Am. Bd. of Forensic Examiners, Springfield, Mo., 1995-98; mem. mgmt. adv. com. Wise Alloys, L.L.C., 1999-2001; pres. Region 3, Assn. of Collegiate Bus. Schs. and Programs, 1999-2000; bd. dirs. Wells Fargo Cmty. Bank; chmn. Concho Valley Ctr. for Entrepreneurship. Editor: Jour. Legal Econs., 1991—. Bd. govs. Soc. Litig. Economists, 2000-02. Recipient Outstanding Achievement award Am. Higher Ed., 1985, Disting. Svc. award Ala. C. of C., Montgomery, 1976. Mem. Assn. Collegiate Bus. Schs. and Programs (pres. region 3 1999-2000), Nat. Assn. Forensic Economists, Am. Coll. Forensic Examiners, Am. Rehab. Econs. Assoc. (adv. bd. 1992-94), MidSouth Acad. Econs. and Fin. (pres. 85-86), Am. Acad. Econ. Fin. Experts (pres. 1994-96, svc. award 1995), Am. Econs. Assn., Am. Statis. Assn., San Angelo C. of C. Avocations: wine collecting, boating. Home: 3101 Clearview Dr San Angelo TX 76904 Office: Angelo State U PO Box 11030 University Station San Angelo TX 76909

BUTLER, NANCY TAYLOR, gender equity specialist, program director; b. Newport, RI, Oct. 31, 1942; d. Robert Lee and Roberta Claire (Brown) Taylor; m. Edward M. Butler, Aug. 22, 1964; children: Jeffrey, Gregory, Katherine. AB, Cornell U., 1964. Asst. dir. Career Equity Assistance Ctr. for Tng. Coll. of N.J., 1990-98; owner Equity Resources, Tinton Falls, N.J., 1993—. Mem. N.J. Gender Equity Adv. Comm., 1995—, sec., 1996-2000, chair, 2000—. Editor Equity Exch., 1991—. Monmouth County dist. ethics com. Supreme Ct. N.J., 1987-91; pres. Vol. Ctr. Monmouth County, Red Bank, 1985-89; mem. Cornell U. Coun., Ithaca, N.Y., 1987-91, 94—, adminstrv. bd., 1996—, vice-chair, 2001—; dir. Cornell Assn. Class Officers, 1991-97; chair Cornell Alumni Trustee Nominating Com., 1994. Recipient Woman of Achievement award Commn. on Status of Women, 1988, Women's History Tribute NOW-N.J., 1995, Woman Leader award N.J. Assn. Women Bus. Owners, 1996. Mem. AAUW (life; pres. N.J. chpt. 1988-90, Edn. Found. Named Gift 1982, 83, 84, 86, 87, 89, 91), Nat. Coalition for Sex Equity in Edn. Home: 20 Cedar Pl Tinton Falls NJ 07724-2807

BUTLER, NAOMI WITMER, librarian, educator; b. Boonsboro, Md., Aug. 25, 1934; d. Howard David and Lavina Lucy (Faulders) Witmer; m. Philip Anthony Butler, Sept. 7, 1962. AB, Shepherd Coll., 1957; MS in Libr. Sci., U. N.C., 1966; AGS, U. Md., 1988. Libr. media specialist Frederick (Md.) County Schs., 1957-67, 68-69; asst. prof. Shippensburg (Pa.) U., 1967-68, Shepherd Coll., Shepherdstown, W.Va., 1969-70; sch. outreach liaison Md. State Dept. Edn., Baltimore, 1970-95; coord. Educators Lit. Corps, Boonsboro, Md., 1995—; tng./advocacy coord. We. Md. Pub. Librs., 1996—. Mem. Delta Kappa Gamma. Avocations: reading, traveling, water sports. Home and Office: 109 David Dr Boonsboro MD 21713-1055

BUTLER, OCTAVIA ESTELLE, free-lance writer; b. Pasadena, Calif., June 22, 1947; d. Laurice and Octavia Margaret (Guy) B. AA, Pasadena City Coll., 1968; student, Calif. State U., Los Angeles, 1969—. Free-lance writer, Los Angeles, 1975—. MacArthur fellow, 1995. Author: Patternmaster, 1976, Mind of My Mind, 1977, Survivor, 1978, Kindred, 1979, Wild Seed, 1980, Clay's Ark, 1984, Dawn, 1987, Adulthood Rites, 1988, Imago, 1989, Parable of the Sower, 1993, Bloodchild, 1995, Parable of the Talents, 1998; also sci. fiction short stories. Recipient fifth prize Writer's Digest Short Story Contest, 1967, Creative Arts Achievement award L.A. YWCA, 1980, Sci. Fiction (Hugo) Best Novelette award World Sci. Fiction Conf., 1985, Best Short Story award World Sci. Fiction Conv., 1984, Nebula Best Novelette award Sci. Fiction Writers Am., 1985, Locus Best Novelette award, 1985, Best Novelette award Sci. Fiction Chronicle Reader, 1985, Nebula award for Best Novel, Sci. Fiction and Fantasy Writers Am., 2000; fellow John D. and Catherine T. MacArthur Found., 1995. Mem. Sci. Fiction Writers Am., Nat. Writers Union. Address: PO Box 25400 Seattle WA 98165-2300

BUTLER, ORTON CARMICHAEL, earth science educator, climatologist; b. Millersburg, Ohio, June 9, 1923; s. Maxon Henry Butler and Atossa Ruth Carmichael; m. Betty Ellen Johnson, Sept. 15, 1951; children: Marilyn Jean, Kathryn Ellen. BA, Oberlin Coll., 1948; MA, Clark U., 1951; PhD, Ohio State U., 1969. Rsch. analyst, China specialist U.S. Army Engr. Strategic Intelligence, Washington, 1951-60; prof. Memphis State U. (now U. Memphis), 1960-81; prof. emeritus U. Memphis, 1981. Author: (book) An Introductory Soils Laboratory Handbook, 1979, other publs. Cpl. U.S. Army, 1942-46, PTO. Mem. Masons. Republican. United Ch. of Christ. Avocations: tree farming, gardening, golf.

BUTLER, PATRICK HAROLD, communications executive; b. Hartselle, Ala., Oct. 25, 1949; s. Arthur L. and Christine (Stewart) B.; m. Donna Therese Norton, Sept. 10, 1977; children: Katharine, Anna, Sydney. Student, U. Tenn., 1967-69, 74, Am. U., 1993, MA in Comm., 1996; postgrad. Cert. in Fin. and Acctg., U. Pa., 1997. Reporter Chattanooga Times, 1968-69; asst. dir. pub. info. Appalachian Regional Commn., Washington, 1969-70; press sec. U.S. Rep. Wilmer D. Mizell, Washington, 1970 75; speechwriter to Pres. The White House, Washington, 1975-77; dir. corp. pub. relations Bristol-Myers Co., N.Y.C., 1978; spl. asst. U.S. Sen. Rep. leader, Washington, 1978-80; staff v.p. RCA Corp., N.Y.C. and Washington, 1980-82; pres. Patrick Butler and Co., Washington, 1982-85; v.p. Times Mirror, Washington, 1985-91, Washington Post Co., 1991—; founder and pres. Newsweek Prodns., Inc., 1997—. Cons. to chief of staff The White House, 1987; lectr. Mt. Vernon Coll., Washington, 1979; guest lectr. Brookings Inst., 1985, 87, U. Va., 1988; mem. adj. faculty Am. U., 1996—. Author, editor numerous articles newspapers, mags. Bd. govs. Ford's Theatre, Washington, 1987-91; mem. Nat. Coun. on Humanities, 1988-94, chmn. pub. programs com.; bd. trustees Found. Nat. Archives, Alfred U. Children's Charities Found.; bd. visitors Coll. Comm. and Info. U. Tenn.; chmn. dean's coun. Sch. Comm. Am. U. Mem. Kenwood Club. Avocation: golf. Office: Washington Post Co 1150 15th St NW Washington DC 20071-0002

BUTLER, PAUL BASCOMB, JR., lawyer; b. Charleston, S.C., Nov. 27, 1947; s. Paul B. and Mary Anna (Tisdale) B.; m. Virginia Eldridge, June 14, 1969; children: Jeffrey Bryan, Robert Paul. BA, Emory U., 1969, MDiv cum laude, 1972, JD with distinction, 1976. Bar: Ga. 1976, Fla. 1977; ordained to ministry United Meth. Ch., 1970. United Meth. Ch., 1970—; assoc. min. First United Meth. Ch., Phoenix, 1972-73; assoc. Swift, Currie, McGhee and Hiers, Atlanta, 1976-79; ptnr. Butler Pappas, Tampa, Fla., 1979-97, of counsel, 1998—. Chancellor Fla. Ann. Conf. United Meth. Ch., 1997—. Contbr. articles to profl. jours. Chair com. on new church devel. Fla. annual conf. United Meth. Ch., 1996-2000, chair bd. missions and ch. ext. Tampa dist. United Meth. Ch., Inc., 1992-96; pastor Temple Terrace United Meth., Tampa, 1998-2000, sr. pastor, 2000-02; vision pastor Tampa Dist. United Meth. Ch., 2002-; bd. dirs. United Meth. Ch. Found., 1999-2000. Mem. ABA (chmn. Nat. Inst. sect. of trial tort and ins. practice 1987-89, ho. of dels. 1993-95, coun. mem. sect. of trial tort and ins. practice 1990-93, chmn. task force on civil justice reform, chmn. property ins. law com. 1985-86, editor So. Region Annotated Homeowner's Policy), Fedn. of Def. and Corp. Counsel (dean Litigation Mgmt. Coll. 1996-98, chair litigation mgmt. coll. adv. coun. 1998-2000, bd. deans 2000—), Def. Rsch. Inst. (chmn. ins. law com. 1989-92, chmn. Amcus com. 1994-97, bd. dirs. 1995-98, vice chair law inst. 1998-99, chair law inst. 1999-2001, immediate past chair 2001-), Fla. Def. Lawyers Assn., Hillsborough County Bar Assn., Internat. Assn. Def. Counsel (vice chair property ins. com. 1993-96), Assn. Def. Trial Attys. Clubs: Temple Terr. (Fla.) Golf and Country. Democrat. Avocations: golf, tennis. Office: Butler Pappas Ste 1100 6200 W Courtney Campbell Cswy 1100 Tampa FL 33607-5946 E-mail: pbutler@butlerpappas.com.

BUTLER, PAUL THURMAN, retired religious studies educator; b. Springfield, Mo., Nov. 17, 1928; s. Willard Drew and Verna Lois (Thurman) B.; m. Gale Jynne Kinnard, Nov. 20, 1948; children: Sherry Lynne, Mark Stephen. ThB, Ozark Bible Coll., 1961, M Bibl. Lit., 1973; ThD, Theol. U. Am., 1990. Ordained to ministry Christian Ch., 1958. Noncommd. officer USN, 1946-56; mem. staff Amphibious Forces Pacific, 1947-50; mem. CTF 90 Korean War, 1950-51; mem. guided missile unit 41 Guided Missile Unit 41, Point Mugu, Calif., 1951-56; ret., 1956; min. Washington Christian Ch., Lebanon, Mo., 1958-60; registrar Ozark Christian Coll., Joplin, Mo., 1960-92, prof. Bible and philosophy, 1960-98; ret., 1998. Min. Westside Christian Ch., 1960-63, North Joplin Christian Ch., 1969-71. Author: The Gospel of John, 1961, The Minor Prophets, 1968, Daniel, 1976, Isaiah, 3 vols., 1978, Esther, 1979, The Gospel of Luke, 1981 (transl. into Korean, French, Portuguese, East Indian-Tamil), Revelation, 1982, I Corinthians, 1984, II Corinthians, 1986, What the Bible Says about Civil Government, 1990, Approaching the New Millennium—An Amillennial Look at A.D. 2000, 1997; also author 8 geneal. family histories: Butlers, Thurmans, Ganns, Alleys, Painters, Kinnard, Driefuses, Vincents. Recipient Outstanding Alumnus award Ozark Christian Coll., 1992. Mem. SAR (nat. chaplain gen. 1991-92, pres., sec. Mo. Soc. chpt., pres. Sgt. Ariel Nims chpt.), Nat. Soc. Sons. Colonial New Eng., Nat. Soc. Sons and Daus. Pilgrims, Ret. Officers Assn. (hon.), Am. Legion, Mo. Territorial Pioneers, Mo. Geneal. Soc., Tenn. Geneal Soc., Tenn. Pioneer Ancestors, Joplin Hist. Soc., Gann Family Hist. Soc. (pres. 1993-95). Republican. Home: 2502 Utica St Joplin MO 64801-1246

BUTLER, PETER JOSEPH, lawyer; b. New Orleans, Oct. 19, 1935; s. Peter Butler and Catherine (Browne) B.; m. Billie Butler, Jan. 30, 1960; children: Peter, Tommy, Julie. BBA, Loyola U., New Orleans, 1957; LLB, Loyola U., 1959. Bar: La., U.S. Supreme Ct., U.S. Ct. Appeals (5th cir.), U.S. Ct. Appeals (11th cir.), U.S. Tax Ct., U.S. Ct. Claims, U.S. Dist. Ct. La.; CPA, La. Law clk. Orleans Parish Civil Dist. Ct., New Orleans, 1959-60, U.S. Dist. Ct. (ea. dist.) La., New Orleans, 1960-62; assoc./ptnr. Sehrt, Boyle & Wheeler, New Orleans, 1962-70; mng. ptnr. Butler, Heebe & Hirsch, New Orleans, 1970-88; mem. exec. com. Sessions, Fishman, Boisfontaine, Nathan, et al, New Orleans, 1988-90; shareholder Locke Purnell Rain Harrell, Dallas/New Orleans, 1990-95, Deutsch, Kerrigan & Stiles, 1995-96; spl. counsel Breazeale, Sachse & Wilson, LLP, 1997—. Mem. faculty, mem. adv. bd. Loyola Law Sch., New Orleans; mem. disciplinary com., mem. civil justice adv. group U.S. Dist. Ct. (ea. dist.) La. Mem. ABA, Fed. Bar Assn., La. State Bar Assn., La. Soc. CPAs. Office: 909 Poydras St Ste 1500 New Orleans LA 70112-4016

BUTLER, QUINCY GASQUE, musician; b. Winchester, Va., May 31, 1935; d. Quincy Damon and Ruth Lavinia (Beaty) Gasque; m. Raymond Kenneth Butler, June 23, 1956; children: Ruth Wendell Butler Forstall, Raymond Kenneth III, Damon Gasque, Courtney Canair Ashmore. BA cum laude, Randolph-Macon Women's Coll., 1956; AA summa cum laude, No. Va. C.C., 1982; MM, Cath. U. Am., 1985; student, Westminster Choir Coll. Social studies tchr., 1956-57; music dir., founder handbell program, bell camp and concerts St. Alban's Episcopal Ch., Annandale, Va., 1976—91, 1996—2000, mem. vestry, 1996-97; chorus tchr. No. Va. C.C., 1986; dir. Musica Viva Oratorio Soc. Washington, 1989-90; founder, music dir. Alban Chorale, 1989—; piano tchr. Falls Church, Va., 1961—. Judge Nat. Piano Guild Auditions; clinician local and nat. level teaching various classes in handbell techniques. Vol. Jr. League No. Va., chmn. thrift shop, pres., 1976-77; mem. Dominion Guild, Inc., projects chmn., 1995-96. Mem.: Oratorio Soc. Washington (singer 1985—98), Choral Arts Soc. (singer 1965—76), Am. Guild English Handbell Ringers Inc. (chmn. area III festival conf. 1989—91, chmn. area III 1991—93, nat. bd. dirs. 1990—93, chmn. adult festival conf. area III 1994—95, membership chmn. area III 2000—), No. Va. Music Tchrs. Assn., Nat. Assn. Music Tchrs., Am. Coll. Musicians (cert. piano tchr.), Phi Beta Kappa. Episcopalian. Avocations: needlework, travel. Home and Office: 3613 Bent Branch Ct Falls Church VA 22041-1005 E-mail: kgbutler@erols.com.

BUTLER, RAYMOND ARCHIBALD, cartographer; b. Windsor, Va. s. J. Butler and Odie Underwood; m. Phyllis Jane Holden, June 1942; children: David Holden, Pamela Rae Butler Chryst, Keith Underwood, Melanie Butler Post. Student, Syracuse U., 1932—36. Asst. to Admiral Byrd, 1939—41; chief of Arctic Unit Aero Med. Lab., Wright Field; cartographer of Antarctic Projects Rsch. Ctr., Washington. Recipient Spl. Medal of Honor, Rear Admiral Richard E. Byrd, 1947. Mountain named in his honor at South Pole. Democrat. Baptist. Avocations: birdwatching, hiking, camping, painting oil landscapes. Home: 5433 Pigeon Hill Rd Spring Grove PA 17362

BUTLER, REX LAMONT, lawyer; b. New Brunswick, N.J., Mar. 24, 1951; s. Ekker and Beatrice (Curry) B.; m. Stephanie Butler; children: Nijel Jaibrun, Vikteria Lamontra, Octavia Reneè Lamontra, Synclaire Lamontra. AA with honors, Fla. Jr. Coll., 1975; BA, U. North Fla., 1977; JD, Howard U., 1983. Bar: Alaska 1983, U.S. Dist. Ct. Alaska 1983, U.S. Ct. Appeals (9th cir.) 1984, U.S. Ct. Appeals (D.C. cir.) 1984, U.S. Supreme Ct. 1996. Assoc. M. Ashley Dickerson, Inc., Anchorage, 1983-84; profl. legis. asst. State of Alaska, Juneau, 1984, asst. atty. gen. Anchorage, 1984-85; pvt. practice Anchorage, 1985—. Adj. prof. law Anchorage C.C., 1985; adj. prof. U. Alaska, Anchorage, 1990—; mem. State Ct. Criminal Pattern Jury Instructions Com., 1997; chmn. lawyer rep. com. Alaska 9th Cir. Judicial Conf., 1997-98. Pres. Alaska Black Caucus, Anchorage, 1986, bd. dirs., 1987-88; gen. counsel NAACP, Anchorage, 1985-87, life mem.; commr. Anchorage Telephone Utility, 1985-87; trustee Anchorage Sr. Ctr., Inc., 1985-87, Shiloh Missionary Bapt. Ch., Anchorage, 1985-87; bd. dirs. Ctr. Drug Problems, Anchorage, 1985-86, Alaska Civil Liberties Union, 1987-88; active fin. com. Dem. Cen. Com. Alaska. With USN, 1969-73. Named one of Outstanding Young Men Am., 1984; recipient Cert. Appreciation, African Relief Campaign, 1985. Mem. ABA, Nat. Bar Assn., Nat. Assn. Criminal Defense Lawyers, Alaska Bar Assn., Assn. Trial Lawyers Am., Anchorage Bar Assn., Alaska Trial Lawyers Assn., Lions Internat., Omega Psi Phi (dist. counselor 1995-96, 98—). Democrat. Home: PO Box 200025 Anchorage AK 99520-0025 Office: 745 W 4th Ave Ste 300 Anchorage AK 99501-2157 Fax: 907-276-3306. E-mail: rexattys@alaska.net.

BUTLER, ROBERT MOORE, JR., podiatrist; b. Camp Lejeune, N.C., Mar. 21, 1949; s. Robert Moore and Virginia Lee (Keen) B. BA in Anthropology, U. Calif., Santa Barbara, 1971; BS in Med. Scis., Calif. Coll. Podiatric Medicin, San Francisco, 1975; DPM, Calif. Coll. Podiatric Medicin, 1976. Diplomate Am. Bd. Podiatric Surgery, Am. Bd. Podiatric Orthop. and Primary Podiatric Medicine (examinations com. 1993-95). Pvt. practice, San Diego, 1977-78, U.S. Army Reynolds Army Med. Ctr., Ft. Sill, Okla., 1978-80, U.S. Army 97th Gen. Hosp., Frankfurt, Germany, 1980-83; cons. in podiatry to commdg. gen. 7th Med. Command, 1980-83; with U.S. Army Walter Reed Army Med. Ctr., Washington, 1984-85, VA Med. Ctr., Alexandria, La., 1985—. Clin. instr. Calif. Coll. Podiatric Medicine, San Francisco, 1978-80. Maj. USAR, ret. Decorated Army Commendation medal, 1981; recipient Expert Field Med. badge 3d Bat., U.S. Army, 1984. Fellow Am. Coll. Foot and Ankle Surgeons, Am. Coll. Foot and Ankle Orthop. and Medicine, Am. Acad. Pain Mgmt.; mem. Am. Podiatric Med. Assn. (del. ho. of dels. 1985-96, budget com. 1994-96). Avocation: snow skiing. Office: VA Med Ctr Alexandria LA 71306

BUTLER, ROBERT NEIL, gerontologist, psychiatrist, writer, educator; b. N.Y.C., Jan. 21, 1927; s. Fred and Easter (Dikeman) B.; m. Diane McLaughlin, Sept. 2, 1950; children: Ann Christine, Carole Melissa, Cynthia Lee; m. Myrna I. Lewis, May 17, 1975; 1 dau., Alexandra Nicole. BA, Columbia U., 1949, MD, 1953; hon. degree, U. So. Calif., U. Gothenburg, Sweden. Intern St. Lukes Hosp., N.Y.C., 1953-54; resident U. Calif. Langley Porter Clinic, 1954-55, NIMH, 1955-56, research psychiatrist, 1955-62; founder geriatric unit Chestnut Lodge, 1958, adminstr., 1958-59; research psychiatrist Washington Sch. Psychiatry, 1962-76; dir. Nat. Inst. on Aging, NIH, 1976-82; prof. geriatics and adult devel. Mt. Sinai Sch. Medicine, N.Y.C., 1982—. Dir. Internat. Longevity Ctr., 1990—, pres., CEO, 1998—; mem. faculty George Washington U. Med. Sch., Washington, 1962-82, Howard U. Sch. Medicine; cons. NIMH, 1967-76, U.S. Senate Spl. Com. on Aging. Author (with others): Human Aging, 1963; author: (with Myrna I. Lewis) Aging and Mental Health, 1973, 5th edit., 1998; author: Why Survive? Being Old in America, 1975, reissue, 2002, Sex After Sixty, 1976; author: (with A. Bearn) The Aging Process, 1985; author: (with Herbert Gleason) Productive Aging, 1985; author: (with Myrna I. Lewis) Love and Sex After Forty, 1986; author: Modern Biological Theories of Aging, 1987, Human Aging Research, 1988, The Promise of Productive Aging, 1990, Who is Responsible for My Old Age?, 1993; author: (with Myrna I. Lewis) Love and Sex After Sixty, 3d edit., 1993; author: (with Jacob Brody) Delaying the Onset of Late Life Dysfunction, 1995; author: (with Howard Fillit) Cognitive Decline, Strategies for Prevention, 1997; author: (with Laude Jasmin) Longevity and Quality of Life, 1999; author: (with Lawrence Grossman and Mia Oberlink) Life in an Older America, 1999; author: (with Myrna I. Lewis) The New Love and Sex After Sixty, 4th edit., 2002; editor: Geriatrics, 1986—2000; mem. editl. bd.: Jour. Geriatric Psychiatry. Sec. Nat. Ballet of Washington, 1962-75; chmn. D.C. Advisory Commn. on Aging, 1969-72; bd. dirs. Nat. Council on Aging, Mildred and Claude Pepper Found. Served with U.S. Maritime Service, 1945-47. Recipient Pulitzer prize for gen. nonfiction, 1976, Leo Laks award, 1976; McIntyre award, 1977, Allied-Signal award, Gustav O. Lienhard award Inst. Medicine NAS, 1996; others. Fellow Am. Psychiat. Assn., Am. Geriatrics Soc. (founding mem.); mem. Group for Advancement Psychiatry (trustee 1974-76), Gerontol. Soc., Forum for Profls. and Execs. (founding) Clubs: Cosmos (Washington); Century (N.Y.C.). Office: Internat Longevity Ctr 60 E 86th St New York NY 10028-1009 E-mail: morrissenb@ilcusa.org. *To always stretch the limits of the possible through personal relationships, scholarship, science, writing, action and political activism. To work toward making life a work of art. To do no harm.*

BUTLER, ROBERT OLEN, writer, educator; b. Granite City, Ill., Jan. 20, 1945; s. Robert Olen Sr. and Lucille Frances (Hall) B.; m. Carol Supplee, Aug. 10, 1968 (div. Jan. 1972); m. Marylin Geller, July 1, 1972 (div. July 1987); 1 child, Joshua Robert; m. Maureen Donlan, July 21, 1987 (div. Mar. 1995); m. Elizabeth Dewberry, Apr. 23, 1995. BS summa cum laude in Oral Interpretation, Northwestern U., 1967; MA in Playwriting, U. Iowa, 1969; postgrad., New Sch. Social Rsch., 1979-81; LHD, McNeese State U., 1994. Editor-in-chief Energy User News, N.Y.C., 1975-85; assoc. prof. fiction writing McNeese State U., Lake Charles, La., 1985—93, prof., 1993—2001; Francis Epps prof. Fla. State U., 2001—. Summer faculty Iowa Summer Writing Festival U. Iowa, Port Townsend (Wash.) Writers Conf., New Orleans Writers' Conf., Southampton Writers' Conf., Long Island U., N.Y., Hofstra U. Summer Writing Conf., Hempstead, N.Y., others, 1988—. Author: The Alleys of Eden, 1981 (also wrote screenplay 1991-92), Sun Dogs, 1982, Countrymen of Bones, 1983, Fragments, 1984, On Distant Ground, 1985, Wabash, 1987, The Deuce, 1989, (short story collection) A Good Scent from a Strange Mountain, 1992 (Pulitzer Prize for fiction 1993, Richard and Hinda Rosenthal Found. award Am. Acad. Arts & Letters 1993, nominee PEN/Faulkner award 1993, Notable Book 1993 Notable Books Coun. Am. Libr. Assn.), They Whisper, 1994, Tabloid Dreams, 1996, The Deep Green Sea, 1998, Silver Rose Anthology: Award-Winning Short Stories, 2001, 02, Fair Warning, 2002; author numerous short stories; works translated to 12 langs.; contbr. articles, book reviews to jours., newspapers, screenplays. Sgt. U.S. Army, 1969-72, Vietnam. Recipient Emily Clark Balch award best work fiction, 1990 Va. Quar. Rev., 1991, TuDo Chinh Kien award outstanding contbns. Am. culture by Vietnam vet. Vietnam Vets. Am., 1987, Medal of Merit, Lotos Club, 1996; grantee NEA, 1994; fellow John Simon Guggenheim Found., 1993. Mem. PEN, WGAWest. Office: English Dept Fla State U 411 Williams Bldg Tallahassee FL 32306-1580 Office Fax: 850-644-0811. E-mail: rbutler@english.fsu.edu.*

BUTLER, ROBERT THOMAS, retired advertising executive; b. Westmont, N.J., Feb. 22, 1925; s. John T. and Kathryn M. (Donehower) B.; m. Eleanore MacIndoe, May 4, 1950; children— R. Mark, Kathryn J., Elizabeth Anne. BS, Temple U., Phila., 1951. Market research mgr. James Lees Carpet Co., 1951-53; v.p. N.W. Ayer, Phila., 1953-74; pres. Gray & Rogers, Phila., 1975-90. Served with USCG, 1943-46. Mem.: St. David's (Pa.) Golf, Merion Cricket (Haverford, Pa.). Republican. Episcopalian.

BUTLER, RONALD B. pathologist; b. Jackson, Wyo., Oct. 27, 1929; s. Albert Nathan Butler and Mary Edna Bay; m. Carole Henderson, Sept. 30, 1954; children: Elaine Velina, Bryan Ronald, Kendall Ray, Daniel Lee, Tamara Sue, Jeffrey David. BS, U. Utah, 1953, MD, 1958. Diplomate Am. Bd. Pathology, Am. Bd. Anatomic and Clin. Pathology. Intern Thomas D. Dee Meml Hosp., Ogden, Utah, 1958; resident Salt Lake City (Utah) Hosp., 1958—62; pathologist U.S. Army Hosp., Fort Leonard Wood, Mo., 1962—64, Utah Valley Regl. Med. Ctr., Provo, 1964—90; physician Alpha Therapeutic, Provo, 1991—2001. Capt. U.S. Army, 1962—64. Home: 436 W 1680 S Orem UT 84058-7546

BUTLER, SAMUEL COLES, lawyer, director; b. Logansport, Ind., Mar. 10, 1930; s. Melvin Linwood and Jane Lavina (Flynn) B.; m. Sally Eugenia Thackston, June 28, 1952; children: Samuel Coles, Leigh F., Elizabeth J. AB magna cum laude, Harvard U., 1951, LLB magna cum laude, 1954. Bar: D.C. 1954, Ind. 1954, N.Y. 1957. Law clk. to Justice Minton U.S. Supreme Ct., 1954; assoc. Cravath, Swaine & Moore, N.Y.C., 1956-60, ptnr., 1961—. Trustee Vassar Coll., 1969-77, N.Y. Pub. Libr., 1979—, chmn. bd., 1999—; trustee Am. Mus. Natural History, 1989-93, The September 11 Fund, 2001—; chmn. Harvard Coll. Fund, 1977-85; bd. overseers Harvard U., 1982-88, pres. bd., 1986-88; bd. dirs. Culver Ednl. Found., 1981-2001. With U.S. Army, 1954-56. Mem. Coun. Fgn. Rels. Home: 1220 Park Ave New York NY 10128-1733 Office: Cravath Swaine & Moore 825 8th Ave New York NY 10019-7475

BUTLER, SHEILA MORRIS, occupational health nurse; b. Paducah, Ky., Sept. 12, 1944; d. Edwin Morris and Beatrice Aileen (Hobbs) Word; m. Benjamin Edward Butler, Dec. 4, 1976; 1 child, Michelle Renee. ADN, Paducah Jr. Coll., 1966. Cert. occupational health nurse, Am. Bd. Occupational Health,

occupational hearing conservationist. Staff nurse Marshall County Hosp., Benton, Ky., 1966-67; shift nursing supr. Parkview Hosp., Dyersburg, Tenn., 1967-69, obstet. nursing supr., 1969-72; clin. nursing instr. State of Tenn. Dept. of Edn., Nashville, 1968-69; charge nurse Dravo-Groves-Newberg, Hamlettsburg, Ill., 1972-74; surg. nurse Western Bapt. Hosp., Paducah, Ky., 1974-76; ophthalmic asst. Dr. Harry Abell, Jr., Paducah, Ky., 1976-83; occupational health cons. self-employed, Paducah, Ky., 1983-86; plant nurse Air Products & Chemicals, Inc., Calvert City, Ky., 1986—. Bd. dirs. Nat. Nurses Soc. on Addiction, 1983-84; bd. dirs. Am. Bd. Occupational Health Nurses, 1994-2001, treas., 1997-99, chair Cohn adv. bd., 1999-2000; sec. Jackson Purchase Oper. Nurses, Paducah, 1975-76; cmty. asst. panel Agy. for Toxic Substance and Disease Registry of CDC, Atlanta, 1991-94; pres. Jackson Purchase Occupational Health Nurse, 1993-96. Mem. Nat. Arbor Day Found. Named Student Nurse of Yr., Circle K-Paducah Jr. Coll., 1966, Ky. Col., Gov. Louie B. Nunn, 1971—; recipient Chem. Group Recognition award Air Products & Chems., 1990, 91. Mem. NAFE, Am. Assn. Occupational Health Nurses (pres. Jackson Purchase sect. 1993-95), Civil Def. of McCracken County, Order of Ea. Star, Esther # 5 Ruth, Daus. of the Nile Neith Temple, Chinese Shar-Pei Club of Am. Democrat. Baptist. Avocations: bicycling, swimming, gardening, needle work. Home: 248 Hayes St Benton KY 42025-6649 Office: Air Products & Chemicals PO Box 97 Calvert City KY 42029-0097 E-mail: swb912@mchsi.com.

BUTLER, SHERYL L. systems engineer, consultant; d. Edwin and Marteena Newcomb; children: Janet Tanner, Heather Glenn, Melissa Smith. AS in Electronic Tech., Met. C.C., Omaha, Nebr., 1980; BS in Computer Info. Systems, Bellevue U., Bellevue, Nebr., 1997. MCSE Microsoft, 2000, cert. MCP and internet Microsoft, 2000. Systems engr. Kellogg Co., Omaha, 1992—98; pres. OOPS Tech, Inc., Bellevue, Nebr., 1996—. Engring. technician Kellogg Co., Omaha, 1980—85, assoc. engr., 1985—91. Mem.: NAFE, Project Mgmt. Inst. E-mail: sbutler@oopstech.net.

BUTLER, SUSAN RUTH, clinical psychologist; b. Montreal, Quebec, Canada, Dec. 20, 1937; d. William Eric and Daisy Mabel Maria (Weeks) B. BEd, McGill U., 1959, MA, 1963; PhD, U. London, 1971. Head therapist McGill Montreal Children's Hosp. Learning Ctr., 1962—; sr. lectr. spl. edn. U. Sydney, Australia, 1972—; prof. McGill U., Montreal, Canada. Cons. psychologist Great Ormond St. Hosp. for Children, London, 1967—, Royal Alexandra Hosp. for Children, Sydney, 1972—; adviser Sydney Inst. Edn., 1979—, U. Western Sydney, 1989-91, Dept. Edn. Australia, 1989-91. Author: Spotlight China, 1981, Reading Assistance Tutorial Pack for children, 1990, R.A.T. Bags for Teenagers, 1991, R.A.T. Race Executive Pack for Adults, 1991; editor: Exceptional Child, 1990. Recipient Italian award for Rsch. Govt. of Italy, 1985; Fulbright Sr. Scholar award 1985-86; Spl. Fellow Pediatric Psychiatry Meml. Sloan Kettering Cancer Ctr., NYC, 1986—; grantee U. Sydney, 1987—. Mem. Australian Psychol. Soc. (bd. dirs.), Australian Inst. Pvt. Clin. Psychology, British Psychol. Soc., Harvard U. Assn., McGill U. Alumnae Assn. Avocations: swimming, skiing, camping, interior decorating, photography, watercolor, motorcycling. Home: Unit 82 108 Elizabeth Bay New South Wales Australia 2011 Office: U Sydney Faculty of Edn McGill U 805A 1212 Pine Ave Montreal QC Canada H3G 1A9 E-mail: susan.butler@mcgill.ca.

BUTLER, TARYN DARNELLA, systems analyst; b. Washington, Feb. 10, 1971; d. Paul Ignatious and Linda Gray Butler. BS in Math., Morgan State U., 1993; MA in Applied Math., U. Md., 1998. Tchg. asst. U. Md., College Park, 1995—96; intern Analytical Svcs., Inc. (ANSER), Arlington, Va., 1995—96; tech. staff mem. SETA Corp., McLean, Va., 1996—97; analyst Systems Planning and Analysis, Inc. (SPA), Alexandria, 1997—2000; systems analyst Integrated Systems Analysts, Inc. (ISA), Arlington, Va., 2000—01; analyst Metron Aviation, Inc., Herndon, Va., 2001—. Vol. AJ Howell County Coun. Campaign, Upper Marlboro, Md., 2002—02. Named Modern-Day Tech. Leader, U.S. Black Engr. and Info. Tech. mag., 2003. Mem.: Inst. for Ops. Rsch. and the Mgmt. Scis. (assoc.). Achievements include research in fairness model for air traffic management. Avocations: attending live music shows, attending plays and musicals, attending sporting events, listening to music, home improvement projects. Office: Metron Aviation Inc Ste 200 131 Elden St Herndon VA 20170 Home Fax: 301-868-6238; Office Fax: 703-456-0133. E-mail: butler@metronaviation.com.

BUTLER, THOMAS WILLIAM, retired health and social services administrator; b. Aiken, S.C., Aug. 29, 1933; s. Eddie and Lillie Mae B.; BA, Adelphi U., 1958; MS in Social Work, Columbia U., 1964; MPA, NYU, 1970; children: Kathi Susan, Thomas William, Michael David. Case supr. Nassau County (N.Y.) Dept. Social Svcs., 1959-67; exec. asst. Joint Legis. Com. on Problems of Public Health Svcs., Medicare, Medicaid and Compulsory Health Ins., N.Y. State, 1967-69; dir. cmty. affairs N.Y.C. Health and Hosps. Corp., 1969-72; with div. alcohol, drug abuse and mental health Public Health Service, Dept. Health and Human Svc., N.Y.C., 1972-95, regional cons. for mental health, 1972-79, regional supr. substance abuse and mental health, 1979-81, co-acting dir. Region II, N.Y.C., 1981, chief health services, 1981-85, chief primary care health services, 1985-86, chief planning, evaluation and data mgmt. services, 1986-95, acting dir. grants mgmt., 1987-88, dep. dir., Divsn. of Health Svcs. Delivery, 1992-95, ret., 1995; guest lectr. NYU, 1977, Grad. Sch. Mgmt. and Urban Professions, New Sch. for Social Rsch., 1977-95. Mem. alumni bd. Columbia U., 1964-67, 76-78, 81-84, Columbia U. Sch. of Social Work rep. Alumni Fedn., 1975-78; bd. dirs. NCCJ, N.Y.C., 1978-80, 80— . Served with U.S. Army, 1954-56; ETO. Recipient Internat. Service award Salvation Army, 1978; univ. athletic scholar, 1952-54, 56-58, univ. acad. scholar, 1952-54. Mem. N.Y. U. Alumni, Adelphi Alumni, Acad. Cert. Social Workers, Nat. Assn. Social Workers, Child Welfare League Am., Am. Legion. Author: Community Organization: A Case Study, 1970; contbr. articles to profl. publs.; inventor in field. Home and Office: 14 N Ferndale Pl Montauk NY 11954 also: 52 Udall Dr Great Neck NY 11020-1530

BUTLER, VINCENT PAUL, JR., physician, educator; b. Jersey City, Feb. 16, 1929; s. Vincent Paul and Ruth Eilene (Lynch) B. AB, St. Peter's Coll., 1949; MD, Columbia U., 1954. Intern Presbyn. Hosp., N.Y.C., 1954-55, resident, 1955-56, 58-59, asst. physician, 1963-68, asst. attending physician, 1968-71, asso. attending physician, 1971-74, attending physician, 1974—; trainee clin. immunology U. Rochester Med. Center, 1959-61; research fellow immunochemistry dept. microbiology Columbia U., 1961-63, asst. prof. medicine, 1963-70, assoc. prof., 1970-74, prof., 1974-98, prof. emeritus, 1999—, spl. lectr., 1999—. Asst. vis. physician 1st med. div. Bellevue Hosp., N.Y.C., 1963-68, Harlem Hosp., N.Y.C., 1968-88; mem. VA Merit Rev. Bd. in Immunology, 1974-77, chmn., 1976-77; mem. immunol. sci. study sect. NIH, 1979-83, chmn., 1980-83 Mem. rsch. com. Arthritis Found., 1986-91, chmn., 1989-91; bd. trustees St. Peter's Prep. Sch., Jersey City, 1985-93, chmn., 1991-93. Lt. M.C. USN, 1956-58. Helen Hay Whitney Found. fellow, 1960-63; Arthritis Found. investigator, 1963-68; Josiah Macy, Jr. Found. scholar dept. zoology Univ. Coll., London, 1979-80; recipient Research Career Devel. award NIH, 1968-73; Joseph Mather Smith prize Columbia U. Coll. Physicians and Surgeons, 1973; Irma T. Hirschl Charitable Trust Career Scientist, 1973-78 Fellow AAAS; mem. Assn. Am. Physicians, Am. Soc. Clin. Investigation, Am. Assn. Immunologists, Am. Soc. Pharmacology and Exptl. Therapeutics, Am. Heart Assn., N.Y. Heart Assn., Am. Fedn. Med. Research, Harvey Soc. Roman Catholic. Home: 66 Tulip St Summit NJ 07901 Office: 630 W 168th St New York NY 10032-3702

BUTLER, WILLIAM JOSEPH, lawyer, educator; b. Brighton, Mass., Mar. 22, 1924; s. Patrick Lawrence and Delia (Conley) B.; m. Jane Hays, Dec. 22, 1945; children: Arthur Hays, Patricia. Student, Harvard U., 1946, NYU, 1949; DHL (hon.), U. Cin., 1988. Bar: N.Y. 1950. Assoc. Hays, St. John, Abramson & Schulman, N.Y.C., 1949-53; ptnr. Butler, Jablow & Geller, N.Y.C., 1953—. Spl. counsel in landmark case on school prayer tried in Supreme Ct. ACLU, DC, 1962; lectr. Practicing Law Inst., 1966; sec., dir., gen. counsel Walco Nat. Corp., FAO Schwartz, N.Y.C., 1961—85; internat. legal observer to South African Elections, 1994; mem. faculty Salzburg Seminar, Austria, 1989, UN Devel. Program, Poland, 1992, Woodrow Wilson Sch. of Pub. and Internat. Affairs, Princeton U., 2000—01; spl. regional adv. for N.Am. on human rights UN High Commr. Mary Robinson, 1998. Author: Human Rights and the Legal System in Iran, 1976, The Decline of Democracy in the Phillipines, 1977, Human Rights in United States and United Kingdom Foreign Policy, Guatemala, a New Beginning, 1987, Palau; A Challenge to the Rule of Law in Micronesia, 1988, The New South Africa - The Dawn of Democracy, 1994; contbr. papers to U. Cin. Law Libr., articles to profl. jours. Mem. commn. urban affairs Am. Jewish Congress, 1965-70; dir. emeritus N.Y. Civil Liberties Union, Internat. League for Human Rights; exec. com. League to Abolish Capital Punishment; standing com. human rights World Peace Through Law Ctr., Geneva; chmn. adv. com. Morgan Inst. Human Rights, U. Cin. Sch. Law; internat. legal observer Internat. Human Rights Orgn., Internat. Criminal Tribunal for Former Yugoslavia in the Hague, The Netherlands, 1996—, others; faculty Salzburg (Austria) Seminar, 1989; UN Devel. Prog. to Poland, 1992. With U.S. Merchant Marine Svc., 1942—45. Recipient Spl. Citation for contbn. to cause of religious freedom, 1962, William J. Butler Medal of Human Rights award, Urban Morgan Inst. Human Rights U. Cin., 1999. Mem. Internat. Commn. Jurists (Geneva) (chmn. exec. com., dir., pres. Am. Assn., UN rep.), Coun. on Fgn. Rels., ABA, Assn. Bar City N.Y. (bd. dirs. ctr. internat. policy, chmn. com. internat. human rights), Inter-Am. Assn. Democracy and Freedom, Internat. Law Assn. (Am. br.), Am. Soc. Internat. Law, Harvard Club (N.Y.C.), U. Club Dublin. Home: 24 E 10th St New York NY 10003-5965 Office: 280 Madison Ave New York NY 10016-0801

BUTLER, WILLIAM LANGDON, manufacturers representative; b. Indpls., Jan. 26, 1939; s. Edward Morris Jr. and Louise Hughes (Dyer) B.; m. Grace Caroline Gage, Dec. 28, 1961; children: Mary Dyer, William Langdon Jr. BA, Middlebury Coll., 1962. With J.J. Newberry Co., N.Y.C., 1961-63; owner Butler Sales Assocs., Summit, N.J., 1965-66; regional mgr. Hi-Fashion Inc., Atlanta, 1966-67; chief exec. officer, owner Butler Sales & Mktg. Inc., Summit, 1967-80; regional sales mgr. Trina Inc., Fall River, Mass., 1980-82, v.p. sales, 1982-87, v.p. gen. mdse. divsn., 1987-97; pres., owner Butler Sales Assocs., 1998—. Coach Jr. Raider Football League, Fanwood, N.J., 1968; trustee Summit Jaycee Found., 1970. Served to 1st lt. U.S. Army, 1963-65. Named One of Outstanding Young Man of Am. Jaycees, 1971. Mem. N.J. NG Assn., Summit Jaycees (Outstanding Dir. award 1970, Key Man award 1970), Soc. for Preservation Barbershop Quartet Singing in Am. (bd. dirs. Westfield 1972-74), Sigma Phi Epsilon. Republican. Presbyterian. Avocations: barbershop quartet singing, philately, spectator sports. Home: 125 Russell Rd Fanwood NJ 07023-1063

BUTLER, WILLIAM THOMAS, college chancellor, physician, educator; b. Boston, Aug. 10, 1932; s. Albert Quigg and Elizabeth West (Viskniskki) B.; m. Marilou Beutel, Apr. 26, 1957; children: Marilyn West, Thomas Charles, Robin Eileen; m. Carol Ann Pike, Nov. 23, 1977. AB, Oberlin Coll., 1954; MD, Western Res. U., 1958; grad. program for health systems mgmt., Harvard U., 1974, A.M.P., 1979. Intern and asst. resident in internal medicine Mass. Gen. Hosp., Boston, 1958-61, clin. fellow in medicine, 1960-61, resident in internal medicine, 1964-65; research fellow in bacteriology and immunology Harvard Med. Sch., 1960-61; clin. assoc. Lab. Clin. Investigations, Nat. Inst. Allergy and Infectious Diseases, NIH, Bethesda, Md., 1961-62, chief clin. assoc., 1962-63, clin. investigator, 1963-64, acting head clin. immunology sect., 1965-66; asst. prof. Baylor Coll. Medicine, Houston, 1966-68, assoc. prof., 1968-71, prof. microbiology and immunology, prof. internal medicine, 1971—, asso. dean, 1973-74, dean admissions, 1974-77, acting exec. v.p., 1976-77, exec. v.p., dean, 1977-79, pres., 1979-96, chancellor, 1996—. Mem. spl. med. adv. group VA, 1981-91, chmn., 1984-91; bd. dirs. C.R. Bard Inc., 1988-2003, Lyondell Chem. Co., chmn. bd., 1997—; mem. Am. Quality and Productivity Ctr., 1991—, chmn. S.W. CEO Coun., 1997-98, mem., 1994—. Mem. forward planning com. Tex. Med. Ctr., 1981-96; bd. dirs. South Main Ctr. Assn., exec. com., 1980-94, chmn., 1989-91, coun. advisors, 1994—; past assoc. chmn. key group United Way Campaign, Flagship Divsn., group chmn., 1990; mem. Houston Econ. Summit Host Com., 1990; bd. dirs. Blvd. Oaks Civic Assn., 1982-85, Sci. Engring. Fair of Houston, 1985—. United Way Tex. Gulf Coast, trustee, 1993-99, exec. com. 1998-99; nat. bd. dirs. Points of Light Found., 1995—; mem. coordinating bd. Tex. Coll. and Univ. System, Health Professions Edn. Adv. Com., 1984-95, chmn., 1988-95, rsch. adv. com., 1987-90; mem. The Houston Forum, 1981—, bd. govs., 1983-92, 96—; mem. Tex. Sesquicentennial Celebration Com., 1984-86; mem. bd. edn. blue ribbon com. Houston Ind. Sch. Dist., 1986; adv. bd. Covenant House Tex., 1987-90; HISD City-Wide Com., 1987; vice-chmn. health svcs., 1990 U.S. Savs. Bond Program. Mem. AMA, Am. Assn. Immunologists, Am. Soc. Clin. Investigation, N.Y. Acad. Scis., Infectious Diseases Soc. Am., Inst. Medicine, Nat. Acad. Scis. (membership com. 1992-96, sect. 12 1992—, vice chmn., 1992-94, chmn. 1994-96, com. on prevention and control of sexually transmitted diseases 1995-96, chmn. 1995-96), Assn. Acad. Health Ctrs., Assn. Am. Med. Colls. (chmn. coun. deans 1987-89, adminstrv. bd. 1983-90, exec. coun. 1984-92, mgmt. edn. programs planning com. 1986-96, chmn.-elect 1989-90, chmn. 1990-91, project 3000x2000 implementation com. chmn. 1991—, nominating com. chmn. 1982), Harris County Med. Soc., Houston Acad. Medicine, Tex. Med. Assn. (adv. coun. med. edn.), Houston C. of C. (bd. dirs. 1981-82, 83-89), Greater Houston Partnership, Inc. (bd. dirs. 1989, 92-99, co-chair healthcare task force 1994-97, bus. issues adv. com. 1994-99, govtl. rels. adv. com. 1995-97), Points of Light Found. (nat. bd. dirs. 1995—), Houston Ptnrs. Com. (co-chmn. 1991- 92), Houston Mus. Nat. Sci. (ex officio 1989-94), River Oaks Country Club, Doctors' Club (bd. govs. 1980-84, pres. 1982), Harvard Bus. Sch. of Houston Club, Sigma Xi, Alpha Omega Alpha. Methodist. Achievements include research numerous publs. on infectious disease and immunology. Office: Baylor College of Medicine 1 Baylor Plz Ste 177A Houston TX 77030-3498

BUTMAN, HARRY RAYMOND, clergyman, writer; b. Beverly, Mass., Mar. 20, 1904; s. John Choate and Elsie Louise (Raymond) B.; m. Jennette Alice Stott, Jan. 5, 1929; children: Beverly, Raymond, Jack, Jennette. BD, Bangor Sem., 1928; postgrad., U. Vt., 1933; DD (hon.), Piedmont Coll., 1955. Ordained to ministry Congregational Ch., 1932. Minister Federated Ch., Edgartown, Mass., 1932-37, Congl. Ch., Randolph, Mass., 1937-45, Allin Congl. Ch., Dedham, Mass., 1945-53, Ch. of the Messiah, L.A., 1953-78; interim minister First Congl. Ch., L.A., 1978-81, cons., 1982—. Moderator Nat. Assn. Congl. Christian Chs., 1963, chmn. exec. com., 1958, 59, 74; editor, The Congregationalist, 1967-68; chmn. Internat. Congl. Fellowship, London, 1977-81. Author: History of Randolph, 1942, Far Islands, 1954, Preamble to Articles of Assn. for Nat. Assn. Congl. Christian Chs., 1956, The Measure of the Immeasurable, 1967, The Lord's Free People, 1968, Serve with Gladness, 1971, The Theology of Congregationalism, 1975, The Chislehurst Thanksgiving, 1976, The Argent Year, 1980, World Book Ency., Manuscript of Nat. Assn. Congl. Christian Chs., 1981, The Desert Face of God, 1985, Brown Boy, 1987, The Good Beasts, 1991, The Soul's Country, 1994, Symbols of Our Way, 1994, A Quiet and Durable Joy, 1996, A Long Green Flash, 2000, A Thinking Man's Faith, 2000; contbr. articles to profl. jours. Named for Best Patriotic Sermon Freedoms Found., 1972; honoree of the Harry R. Butman Endowed Chair of Religion and Philosphy Piedmont Coll., Demorest, Ga., 1994; prelate The Soc. of Descendants of Knights of the Most Noble Order of the Garter, 1972—. Republican. Avocations: boating, desert driving. Home: 2451 Soledad Canyon Rd Acton CA 93510-2416

BUTORAC, FRANK GEORGE, librarian, educator; b. Crosby, Minn., Feb. 12, 1927; s. Frank and Mary (Paun) B.; m. Mary Regis McGowan Ratigan, Apr. 8, 1972; stepchildren: Helen Elizabeth, Nicholas. AB, U. Mich., 1950, AM, 1956, AMLS, 1958; postgrad., Cornell Law Sch., 1950-51, Harvard U., 1953; postgrad. in philosophy, U. Notre Dame, 1959, 60-62; postgrad. in theology, Holy Cross Coll., 1962-66; postgrad., Cath. U., 1963, Georgetown U., 1965, NYU, 1968-70, 79-81, Cambridge U., 1975, Oxford U., 1989, postgrad., 1995, postgrad., 2003, Trinity Coll., Dublin, 1990. With exec. tng. program U.S. Rubber, Mishawaka, Ind., 1952-53; tchr. 6th grade Jefferson Sch., Wayne, Mich., 1953-54; tchr. social studies Slauson Jr. H.S., Ann Arbor, Mich., 1954-55; supervising tchr. social studies Lincoln Consol. H.S., Ea. Mich. U., Ypsilanti, 1955-57; circulation libr., engring. libr. U. Mich., Ann Arbor, 1958-59; joined Congregation of Holy Cross, 1959; postulant U. Notre Dame, 1959; seminarian and temporary profession, 1959-66; novice Sacred Heart Novitiate, Jordan, Minn., 1959-60; registrar Mercer C.C., Trenton, N.J., 1966-68, asst. dir. cmty. and ext. svcs., 1968-70, dir. evening and ext. ops., 1970-71, dir. spl. programs, 1971-74, dir. libr. svcs., 1974-84, chmn. libr. tech. program, 1974-84, dir. libr. devel., 1984-87, libr., 1987—. Cons. libr. edn., libr. mgmt. Pres. U. Mich. Clubs Coun. 2d Dist., 1991-93; chmn. U. Mich. Newman Ctr. Fund Drive, 1958; professed Secular Franciscan Order Monastery of St. Clare, Bordentown, N.J., 1984, Third Order Dominican, 2003—; ann. participant Yale U.-Hopkins summer seminar program, 2000—. Bd. dirs. U. Mich. Alumni Assn., 1995-98; chmn. Anna B. Stokes Found., Trenton, 1972; dean's adv. com. Cornell Law Sch., 1972-73; mem. N.J. State Adv. Com. on Aging, 1971; mem. Mich. State Ctrl. Com. Young Democrats, 1949-50. Served with USN, 1944-47. Recipient Tall Cedars of Lebanon award for Cmty. Svc., Trenton, 1974. Mem. ALA, N.J. Libr. Assn. (exec. bd. 1977-78), Purnell Sch. Parents Assn., Cornell Law Assn., Bennington Coll. Parents Assn., Pine Manor Coll. Parents Assn., U. Mich. Ctrl. N.J. (pres. 1987-91), Mensa, English Speaking Union, Nassau Club (Princeton, N.J.), Princeton Club (N.Y.C.), Trenton Lions Club (pres. 1972), Trenton Torch Club (pres. 1972), Cornell Club Ctrl. N.J. (pres. 1977-78), Marines' Meml. Club (San Francisco), Cath. Alumni Club Trenton (pres. 1968), Theta Delta Chi, Phi Delta Phi, Phi Delta Kappa, Kappa Delta Pi, Alpha Phi Omega. Republican. Roman Catholic. Home: 6 Mercer St Princeton NJ 08540-6808 Office: 1200 Old Trenton Rd Princeton Junction NJ 08550-3407

BUTRIMOVITZ, GERALD PAUL, financial planner, securities analyst, investment advisor; b. Detroit; BA, Wayne State U., 1969; MSc, Ohio State U., 1973; PhD, U. Md., 1977; postgrad., U. Wash., 1978; postgrad. Inst. for Legis. Assts., Nat. Def. U., 1978; postgrad., Golden State U., 1985. CFP, registered prin., NASD; registered investment advisor. Sr. aide U.S. Congress, Washington, 1978—80; writer bills on fiscal budgets and health, 1979; asst. prof., affiliate in health policy U. Calif.-San Francisco, 1980-82, biotechnology analyst, cons., 1982-84, Mt. Zion Hosp., San Francisco, 1984; pres. Gerald Butrimovitz and Assocs. Adv. Svcs. Developed NIH Clin. Nutrition Insts. Program, 1977-80; dir. polit. mobilization Am.-Israel Pub. Affairs Com. Leadership Coun., San Francisco; fin., investment and endowment coms. Jewish Children and Family Svcs.; past bd. dirs. Jewish Community Ctr., Jewish Community Relations Coun.; bd. dirs. Hebrew Free Loan of San Francisco; active San Francisco Estate Planning Coun., Santa Clara Estate Planning Coun. Recipient seal, Dalbar Inc., 1998—2002; fellow Congl. Sci. fellow, AAAS, 1978—80. Fellow Nat. Acad. Clin. Biochemists; mem. Fin. Planning Assn. (bd. dirs.), Internat. Fedn. Tech. Analysts, Am. Assn. Individual Investors (bd. dirs., founder fin. planning, 1983-88), Tech. Securities Analysts Assn. (pres. emeritus 1990, co-dir. mentor program 1991-92, dir. long range planning com. 1992-93, chmn. 1994-97), Internat. Fedn. of Tech. Analysts (bd. dirs. 1999—), Coll. for Fin. Planning, Inst. CFPs, Internat. Bd. Standards Practices for CFPs, Internat. Fedn. Tech. Analysts, Sigma Xi.

BUTSCH, JOHN LORD, surgeon, educator; b. Rochester, Minn., Mar. 5, 1934; AB, Princeton U., 1956; MDCM, McGill U., 1960; MS in Surgery, U. Minn., 1967. Diplomate Am. Bd. Surgery. Intern U. Hosp., Ann Arbor, Mich., 1960-61; resident surgery Mayo Clinic, Rochester, 1961-65; clin. asst. dept. surgery Buffalo Gen. Hosp., 1968-70, clin. assoc. dept. surgery, 1970-72, asst. surgeon, 1972-78, assoc. surgeon, 1978-85, surgeon, 1985—; asst. attending surgeon Buffalo Children's Hosp., 1970-78, assoc. attending surgeon, 1978—; asst. attending surgeon Erie County Med. Ctr., 1983-96; from instr. in surgery to clin. prof. surgery SUNY, Buffalo, 1968—2002, clin. prof. surgery, 2003—; pub. health physician II N.Y. State Dept. of Health, Buffalo, 1980—. Chmn. com. ER Buffalo Gen. Hosp., 1970-72; mem. first year com. med. students SUNY Buffalo, 1982-89, ad hoc com. guidelines acad. promotions, 1985-86, med. faculty coun., 1987-93; team physician Buffalo Sabres Hockey Team, 1973-99; med. dir. Republic Steel Corp., 1973-82; med. cons. Niagara Mohawk Power Corp., 1974—; med. dir. Buffalo Forge, 1986-95, Clearing Niagara, 1994-98; rschr., lectr. in field. Contbr. articles to profl. jours. Bd. govs. Buffalo Tennis & Squash Club, 1987-89; mem. parents coun. St. Lawrence U., 1989-93; mem. Thursday Club Literary Soc., 1995—. Capt. U.S. Army, 1966-68. Fellow ACS (pres. western N.Y. chpt. 1982, exec. coun. 1983-85); mem. Soc. Internat. de Chirugie, Collequim Intertnat. Chirurgiae Digestivae, Ctrl. Surg. Assn. (membership com. 1994-97, chmn. audit com. 2002), Soc. for Surgery of the Alimentary Tract, Am. Trauma Soc., Univ. Assn. Emergency Med. Svcs., James Priestley Surg. Soc. (v.p. 1983-85), Surgeon's Travel Club (sec./treas. 1991-98). Home: 174 Soldiers Pl Buffalo NY 14222-1259 Office: 869 Delaware Ave Buffalo NY 14209-2099

BUTT, CHARLES CLARENCE, food service executive; b. Houston, Tex., 1938; BS in Econs., U. Pa., 1959; grad. advanced mgmt. program, Harvard U. Pres. H.E.B. Grocery Co., San Antonio, 1971-84; chmn., CEO H.E. Butt Grocery Co., San Antonio, 1984—. Dir. Tex. Commerce Bancshares, 1974-89. Mem. bd. overseers The Wharton Sch.; mem. bd. dirs. of the assocs, Harvard Bus. Sch.; chmn. adv. coun. U. Tex. Marine Sci. Inst., 1976-86; chmn. M.D. Anderson Cancer Hosp. ann. campaign, 1981; mem. coord. bd. Tex. Coll. and Univ. Sys., 1978-83, chmn. faculty salaries com.; mem. Harvard Bus. Sch.'s Bd. Dirs. of Assocs.; dir. Tex. Commerce Bancshares, 1974-89. Recipient Conservation award Winedale Hist. Ctr., U. Tex., Amanda Cartwright Taylor award San Antonio Conservation Soc., Mr. South Tex. award Washington's Birthday Celebration Assn., 1996. Mem. Order of the Alamo, San Antonio German Club, Argyle Club, Corpus Christi Yacht Club, Nantucket Yacht Club, N.Y. Yacht Club. Avocations: sailing, historical preservation, photography. Office: H E Butt Grocery Co 646 S Main Ave San Antonio TX 78204-1210 Office Fax: 210-938-8169.*

BUTT, EDWARD THOMAS, JR., lawyer; b. Chgo., Oct. 27, 1947; s. Edward T. and Helen Kathryn (Guy) B.; m. Leslie Laidlaw Hilton, Oct. 20, 1972; children: Julie Guy, Andrew McNaughton. BA, Lawrence U., 1968; JD, U. Mich., 1971. Bar: Ill. 1971, U.S. Dist. Ct. (no. dist.) Ill. 1971, Wis. 1975, U.S. Dist. Ct. (ea. dist.) Wis. 1978, U.S. Ct. Appeals (7th cir.) 1978, U.S. Ct. Claims 1982, U.S. Ct. Appeals (6th cir.) 1986, U.S. Ct. Appeals (6th cir.) 1987, Mich. 1997. Assoc. Wildman, Harrold, Allen & Dixon, Chgo., 1971-75, 76-78, ptnr., 1979-94, Lund & Butt, S.C., Minocqua, Wis., 1975-76; of counsel Swanson, Martin & Bell, Chgo. and Wheaton, Ill., 1994—. Bd. dirs. Constl. Rights Found., Chgo. Mem. ABA, State Bar Wis., State Bar Mich., 7th Cir. Bar Assn., Def. Rsch. Inst., Crystal Lake Yacht Club, Crystal Downs Country Club. Avocations: distance running, sailing, golf. Home: Michabou Shores 1006 Tiba Rd Frankfort MI 49635-9216 also: 3903 Forest Ave Western Springs IL 60558-1049 Office: Swanson Martin & Bell 2525 Cabot Dr Ste 2041420 Lisle IL 60532

BUTT, SAMEER, filmmaker, writer; s. Khalida and Yusuf Butt. Mem./market maker Am. Stock Exch., N.Y.C., 1996—99; dir. of prodn. IndiePlanet/Urban Box Office, N.Y.C., 1999—2000. Pres. NY Spice Film Co., N.Y.C., 2000—. Actor: (films) Atomic Tabasco (Acad. Award[00a9], 1998); prodr.(writer): (documentary news spl.) Islamabad: Rock City; dir.(co-producer): (documentary) Becoming Muslim: Submitting to Allah in Am.; contbr. comedy The Daily Show; dir.: (documentary) Dollars and $ex; creator, writer : (situation comedy) New York Spice. Home: 334 East 55th St #4 New York NY 10022 Office: NY Spice Film Co 334 East 55th St #4 New York NY 10022 E-mail: sameerybutt@hotmail.com.

BUTT, WILLIAM, corporate financial executive; Exec. mng. dir., co-head Can. investment and corp. banking BMO Nesbitt Burns Inc., Toronto. Office: BMO Nesbitt Burns 1 First Canadian Pl Toronto ON Canada M5X 1H3

BUTTA, DEENA CELESTE, librarian; b. Chgo., June 1, 1950; d. Joseph James and Michaline Ann (Pabisinski) Weglarz; m. William C. Hartray, Apr. 21, 1974 (div. 1983); m. Raymond Peter Butta, June 2, 1984; children: Alexander Michael, Maris Michael, Philip Adrian. BA, Northwestern U., 1972; MLS, Rosary Coll., River Forest, Ill., 1978. Mem. staff Evanston (Ill.) Pub. Libr., 1969-79; libr. Triton C.C., River Grove, Ill., 1981, Libr. of Health Scis., U. Ill., Chgo., 1982-85; family day care provider Starchild Daycare, Chgo., 1985—, also bd. dirs.; staff mem. Des Plaines (Ill.) Pub. Libr., 1995-97, Glenview (Ill.) Pub. Libr., 1997—. Counselor Bach Flower Soc., Lynbrook, N.Y., 1987—; mem. Day Care Action Coun., Chgo., 1985-97; treas. Echo 33, Chgo., 1988—; Reiki III practitioner; co-founder CARETAKERS, 1996. Panelist TV series Man's Ultimate Destiny, 1992; interviewed for A&E The Unexplained. Presenter Day of Prayer, Monastic Interreligious Dialogue, others; dancer Old Town Renaissance Consort, 1983—. Mem. Fellowship of Isis (priestess, del. representing fellowship to Parliament of the World's Religions), Eleusis of Chgo. (planning and facilitating com. FOI ann. convs.), Bach Flower Remedy Soc., Sacred Dance Guild, Chgo. Calligraphy Collective. Avocations: art, dance, flower remedies, needlecraft, calligraphy. Mailing: PO Box 257996 Chicago IL 60625-7996

BUTTARO, LUCIA, language educator, consultant; b. Bklyn., May 21, 1963; d. Giuseppe Buttaro and Maria Christina Vuotto-Buttaro. BS Inst. de Enseranza Superior Daguerre, Buenos Aires, 1986; MS in edn., Fordham U., NYC, 1996, PhD, 1999. Instr. English High Lyceum of English Culture, Buenos Aires,

1982—85, Cambridge Inst., Buenos Aires, Aeon Eng. Conversation Sch., Toyahoshi, Japan, 1990—91, Alpha English Sch., Toyahoshi, Japan, 1991—92; GED lectr. Spanish Bronx Coll. CUNY, 1992—98; adj. prof. Baruch Coll. CUNY, 1995—; literacy cons. NYC Dept. of Edn., Bklyn., 2001—; asst. prof. Fordham U., NYC, 1999—, Kingsborough Coll. CUNY, Bklyn., 1999—. Del. Acad. Scholars Program, Shanghai, 2002—03; ESL med. instr. Action for Russian Immigrants, Bklyn., 1994—; mem. writing across the curriculum com. CUNY; mem. com. on admissions Kingsborough Coll. CUNY, mem. academic standing com. Contbr. articles to profl. jours., presentations to profl. conferences. Recipient PSC CUNY Rsch award program, 2002—03; grantee Fulbright Tchr. and Adminstr. Exch. Program, 2002—03. Mem.: ENLACE (bd. dir. 1999—), Phi Delta Kappa. Democrat. Roman Catholic. Avocations: travel, photography. Home: 1395 E Second St Brooklyn NY 11230 Office: Kingsborough College 2001 Oriental Blvd Brooklyn NY 11235 Fax: 713-368-4879. E-mail: lbuttaro@kbcc.cuny.edu.

BUTTARS, GERALD ANDERSON, librarian; b. Logan, Utah, Oct. 12, 1939; s. Thomas James and Mary (Anderson) B.; m. Jeannie Webb, June 3, 1966; children: Brian Gerald, Angela. BS, Utah State U., 1967; MLS, Brigham Young U., 1970. Dir. libr. for blind and phys. handicapped Utah State Libr., Salt Lake City, 1965—. Recipient Disting. Svc. awards Utah Coun. for Blind, 1979, Brigham Young U., 1986, Francis Joseph Campbell award and citation ALA, 1998. Mem. ALA, Utah Libr. Assn. (exec. sec. 1972-87), Nat. Fedn. Blind, Am. Coun. for Blind. Republican. Mem. Lds Ch. Home: 4749 W 3280 S Salt Lake City UT 84120-1566 Office: Utah State Libr Blind & Physically Handicapped Program 250 N 1950 W Ste A Salt Lake City UT 84116-7901 E-mail: gbuttars@utah.org.

BUTTE, ATUL JANARDHAN, pediatric endocrinologist; s. Janardhan and Mangala Butte; m. Tarangini Deshpande. MD, Brown U., 1995. Diplomate Am. Bd. Pediat. Software engr. Microsoft Corp., Redmond, Wash., 1989; sys. software engr. Apple Computer, Inc., Cupertino, Calif., 1990; rsch. scholar Howard Hughes Rsch. Med. Inst./NIH, Md., 1993—94; asst. in endocrinology, attending physician Children's Hosp., Boston, 2001—02; instr. pediat. Harvard Med. Sch., Boston, 2001—. Founder, sci. advisor Xpogen, Inc., Cambridge, Mass., 2000—, Genstruct, Inc., Cambridge, 2001—. Recipient Outstanding Spkr. award, Am. Assn. Clin. Chemistry, 2002; fellow, Merck / MIT, 2000; grantee Scholar-In-Tng. award, Am. Assn. Cancer Rsch., 2001; Farley fellow, Children's Hosp., 1999, clin. scholar, Lawson Wilkins Pediatric Endocrine Soc., 2001. Mem.: Endocrine Soc., Am. Med. Informatics Assn. Achievements include patents pending for system and method for mining data from database using relevance networks. Office: Children's Hosp 300 Longwood Ave Boston MA 02115

BUTTENHEIM, EDGAR MARION, publishing executive; b. Yonkers, N.Y., Dec. 23, 1922; s. Edgar J. and Marian R. (Voorhees) B.; m. Mary Elizabeth Robertson, Aug. 22, 1947; children: Margaret Collier, Anne Robertson, Elizabeth Gay, Martha Bradford. AB magna cum laude, Princeton U., 1943; MBA, NYU, 1955. Instr. Hotchkiss Sch., Lakeville, Conn., 1946-47; with Buttenheim Pub. Corp., Pittsfield, Mass., 1947-74, exec. v.p., 1963-68, pres., 1969-75, Morgan-Grampian Pub. Co. subs. Morgan-Grampian Ltd., 1975-76, Buttenheim Assocs., Pittsfield, 1976-79; exec. v.p. Springhouse (Pa.) Corp., 1979-87; mgmt. cons. Nat. Exec. Svc. Corps, N.Y.C., 1987-95; advisor to pres. William Patterson Coll., Wayne, N.J., 1990-91. Adj. prof. mgmt. Union Coll., Schenectady, Rider Coll., Lawrenceville, N.J., autumn, 1987; adj. lectr. MS in pub. degree program Pace U., N.Y.C., 1986-94. Mem., Westchester County Rep. Com., 1957-61; candidate for Mass. Legislature, 1978. 1st lt., F.A. AUS, 1943-46, 51-52. Decorated Bronze Star; McAllister fellow Medill Sch. Journalism Northwestern U., Evanston, Ill., 1984. Mem. Phi Beta Kappa. Home and Office: 8 Hedge Row Rd Princeton NJ 08540-5055 E-mail: libgeg@aol.com.

BUTTENWIESER, LAWRENCE BENJAMIN, lawyer; b. NYC, Jan. 11, 1932; s. Benjamin Joseph and Helen (Lehman) B.; m. Ann Harriet Lubin, July 13, 1956; children— William Lawrence, Carol Helen Sharp, Jill Ann Schloss, Peter Lubin BA, U. Chgo., 1951, MA, 1955; JD, Yale U., 1956; DHL (hon.), Yeshiva U., 1974. Bar: NY 1956. Assoc. Rosenman & Colin, NYC, 1956-66, ptnr., 1966—2002; counsel KMZ Rosenman, 2002—. Chmn., bd. dir. Gen. Am. Investors Co., Inc., NYC Past pres., trustee Associated YM-YWHAs of Greater NY; past v.p., dir. Citizens Housing and Planning Coun. of NY; past treas., dir. City Ctr. of Music and Drama, Inc.; past dir. Coun. on Social Work. Edn.; past trustee Dalton Sch. ; past. hon. chmn. bd., trustee, past pres. Fedn. Jewish Philanthropies NY; past chmn. bd., trustee Montefiore Med. Ctr.; past gen. campaign chmn. United Neighborhood Houses NY; past trustee, NY Acad. Sci.UJA/Fed. Joint Campaign; past chmn., past trustee Am. Jewish World Svc.; past chmn., trustee Citizens Budget Commn.; dir. Playwrights Horizons Inc.,trustee U. Chgo. Mem. Assn. Bar City of NY Office: KMZ Rosenman Fl 21 575 Madison Ave Fl 21 New York NY 10022-2511 E-mail: lawrence.buttenwieser@kmzr.com.

BUTTERBRODT, JOHN ERVIN, real estate executive; b. Beaver Dam, Wis., Feb. 14, 1929; s. Ervin E. and Josephine M. (O'Mare) B.; m. June Rose Bohalter, Sept. 27, 1952; children— Claire, Daniel, Larry. U. Agriculture short course, 1946-47. Cert. tchr. real estate, rental weatherization inspector, real estate appraiser, sr. profl. appraiser; internat. cert. farm appraiser; cert. gen., lic. appraiser, Wis. Vice-pres. Pure Milk Assn., 1967-69; pres. Asso. Milk Producers, Inc. Chgo., 1969-75, State Brand Creameries, Madison, Wis., 1970—, Wis. Real Estate Co., Wis. Real Estate of Burnett Inc., 1978—, Sunset Hills Golf & Supper Club Inc., 1979—; chmn. bd. Realty World-Wis. Real Estate, Inc., 1985—; treas. Real Estate Cons., 1983—. Dir. Town Mut. Ins. Co., Central Milk Sales, Central Milk Producers Coop. Pres. Sch. Bd., 1968; Bd. dirs. Nat. Milk Producers Fedn., Central Am. Coop. Fedn., World Dairy Expo. Recipient Am. Farmer degree Future Farmers of Am., 1949, hon. degree, 1973; Outstanding Wis. Farmer award, 1965; Outstanding Wis. 4-H Alumni award, 1973; named Realtor of Yr., 1979 Mem. United Dairy Industry Assn. Republican. Office: 1708 N Spring St Beaver Dam WI 53916-1106

BUTTERFIELD, ALEXANDER PORTER, former business executive, government official; b. Pensacola, Fla., Apr. 6, 1926; s. Horace Bushnell and Susan A. (Alexander) B.; m. Charlotte Mary Maguire, Sept. 9, 1949 (div. Jan. 1985); children: Leslie Carter (dec.), Alexander Porter Jr., Susan Carter Holcomb, Elisabeth Gordon Buchholz. BS, U. Md., 1956; MS, George Washington U., 1967; PhD (hon.), Embry-Riddle U., 1973. Commd. 2d lt. USAF, 1949, advanced through grades to col., 1966, fighter pilot, fighter-gunnery instr., weapons officer, mem. Skyblazers (U.S. jet aerobatic team Europe), 1949-53; aide to comdr. 4th Allied Tactical Air Force NATO, 1954-55; ops. officer interceptor squadron, 1955-56; asst. prof. USAF Acad., 1957-59; sr. aide to comdr.-in-chief U.S. Pacific Air Forces, 1959-62; comdr. fighter squadron Okinawa, 1962-63; comdr. tactical reconnaissance task forces, 1963-64; tactical air warfare policy planner USAF hdqrs., 1964-65; mil. asst. to spl. asst. sec. def., 1965-66; student Nat. War Coll., 1966-67; sr. U.S. mil. rep., comdr. in chief Pacific rep. Australia, 1967-69; retired, 1969; dep. asst. Pres. Richard M. Nixon, 1969-73; sec. to Cabinet, 1969-73; adminstr. FAA, 1973-75; lectr. Ethics in Govt. Am. Program Bur., 1975-76; exec. v.p., chief oper. officer, dir. Internat. Air Svc. Co. Ltd., 1977-79; pres., chief oper. officer, dir. Calif. Life Corp., 1979-80. Chmn. GMA Corp., Global Network Inc., 1981-82; chmn., chief exec. officer Armistead & Alexander, Inc., 1983-94; bd. dirs. Aloha Airlines Inc. Contbr. articles to profl. jours. and nat. mags.; mem. editorial bd. L.A. County Mus. Natural History mag. Terra, 1983-86. Presidentially apptd. mem. Nat. Armed Forces Mus. adv. bd. Smithsonian Instn., 1970-76; bd. dirs. Internat. Flight Safety Found., L.A. County Mus. Natural History, 1981-85; mem. mil. sci. expedition to South Pole, 1968; leader of U.S. govt. industry del. to Moscow for ministerial level talks on tech. and trade, 1973; key witness U.S. senate select com.'s hearings on Watergate, 1973, and before U.S. Ho. of Reps. Judiciary Com. during its deliberations of impeachment of Pres. Richard Nixon, 1974. Decorated Legion of Merit, DFC, Air medal with 3 bronze oak leaf clusters, Bronze Star. Mem. Am. Film Inst., Screen Actors Guild, Coun. for Excellence in Govt., Tailhook Assn., Air Force Assn., Bel-Air Country Club (L.A.), Univ. Club (San Diego).

BUTTERFIELD, BRUCE SCOTT, publishing, communications and education executive, consultant; b. N.Y.C., Feb. 4, 1949; s. Richard Julian and Mary (Hart) B.; m. Karin Lynn Wittlinger, June 20, 1986; children: Elizabeth Holly, Timothy Hart. BA cum laude, Amherst Coll., 1971; MA, Harvard U., 1972; MBA, U. Conn., 1977; advanced cert. in journalism and creative fiction, Newspaper Inst. Am, 1981. Mng. editor, adminstr. Golden Press/Western Pub. Co., N.Y.C., 1972-77; v.p., pub. Scholastic Inc., N.Y.C., 1978-83; pres. Longman-Addison Wesley Pub. Group/Pearson PLC, White Plains, N.Y., 1984-93, Prentice Hall Regents/Simon & Schuster/Viacom Inc., Upper Saddle River, NJ, 1993-97; CEO, pres. VirtualEd, Inc., 2002—. Author: Fantasy and the Free School Thought: E.B. White and His Literature for Children, A Plea for Fantasy; Our Real Work Can't Be Drudgery; editor various books including: ABC's Wide World of Sports, Buccaneers; Book of the Mysterious, Chroma-Schema, Calculator Games; Children's Bible Stories, Oh Heavenly Dog, The Watcher in the Woods. Named Most Valuable Semi-Pro Pitcher, Bergen Highlanders, 1969, All New Eng. Baseball Pitcher, 1971, All Am. Baseball Pitcher, 1971, named to U. Conn. Bus. Sch. Hall of Fame, 1998; recipient Wall St. Jour. Achievement award; Nat. Fedn. Music award; J.F. Kennedy Brotherhood Essay award; Gardener Fletcher fellow; St. Clair Meml. fellow; Amherst Coll. fellow. Mem. Beta Gamma Sigma, Phi Delta Kappa, Phi Delta Sigma.

BUTTERFIELD, CHARLES EDWARD, JR., educational consultant; b. Urbana, Ill., Mar. 31, 1928; s. Charles E. and Bessie J. (Winters) B.; m. Gayle Coberley, Jan. 27, 1952; children: Jeffrey M., Carey J. BS in Biology, Chemistry, Physics, Psychology, Edn., U. Ill., 1951, MS, 1953; postgrad., Duke U., 1958, No. Ill. U., 1958-59, Mich. State U., 1959, 64-65, 72, Knox Coll., 1962, Fla. State U., 1969, U. Colo., 1970. Field exec. Nottawa Trails coun. Boy Scouts Am., Battle Creek, Mich., 1953-54; instr. sci. Gardner (Ill.)-South Wilmington Twp. H.S., 1954-59; pub. rels. cons., edn.l. cons. Dresden Nuclear Power Plant, Consol. Edison, Braidwood, Ill., 1958—60; biology coord. Lake Park H.S., Medinah, Ill., 1959 65; sr. sci. project editor Singer/Random House Pub. Co., N.Y.C., 1965-68; sci. supr. K-12 Ramsey (N.J.) Pub. Schs., 1968-82; sci. edn. cons., 1981—; pres., CFO, Shield Cons., 1977—. Instr. radiation physics N.W. Cmty. Hosp., Arlington Heights, Ill., 1963-65; cons. Rand McNally Pubs., 1972-80; peer reviewer NSF proposals, 1979-84; mem. sci. adv. bd. Raintree Publs., Milw., 1981-86; assoc. Thomas A. Edison Found., 1981-88; condr. various workshops for sci. tchrs., 1965—. Contbg. author: NSSA Sourcebook for Science Supervisors, 2nd edit., 1976, 3rd edit., 1988. Pres. Bd. Edn., Gardner, Ill., 1956-57; pres. Foxwood Village Fedn. Mfrd. Home Owners of Fla., 1988-90; co-project dir., fin. officer suprs. programs NSF/NSSA/PEEC, 1979-83; treas., bd. dirs. Highland Fairways Property Owners Assn., 1993-96, 99-2002, fin. cons., 1996—; judge Seiko Youth Challenge, 1994, 95. With USN and USMC, 1946-48. Recipient Allendale (N.J.) Cmty. Lifesaving award, 1976; NSF/AAAS fellow Mich. State U., 1964-66, fellow 1st Southeastern NASA Aerospace Conf., 1961. Fellow AAAS; mem. NEA, ACLU, Nat. Sci. Ednl. Leadership Assn. (mem. exec. com. 1974-80, pres. 1977-78, sr. staff mem. various other confs. U. Calif. at San Diego, 1979, U. Iowa 1979-80, supr. nat. elections 1982-2000, mem. editl. adv. bd. 1986-91, Outstanding Svc. award 1990, 98, 1st hon. lifetime exec. bd. mem. award for outstanding svc. 2000—), Nat. Sci. Tchrs. Assn. (exec. bd. 1977-78, Disting. Svc. Sci. Edn. citation 1981), Am. Humanist Assn., N.J. Sci. Tchrs. Assn., N.J. Sci. Suprs. Assn. (Disting. Svc. award 1982), Ramsey Suprs. Assn. (founding pres. 1980-81), Bergen County Sci. Suprs. Assn. (pres. 1971-73, Outstanding Svc. award 1974, 78), Sch. Sci. and Math. Assn., Am. Inst. Biol. Scis. (cons. biological sci. curriculum study 1965—), Nat. Assn. Biol. Tchrs., Coun. Elem. Sci. Internat., Assn. Edn. Tchrs. Sci., N.J. Prins. and Suprs. Assn., Am. Assn. Notaries, Nat. Notary Assn., U. Ill. Alumni Assn., Fla. So. Coll. Sixth Man Club, Cmty. Assns. Inst., 1st Marine Divsn. Assn., Fleet Marine Force Combat Med. Pers. Assn., Am. Legion, USN Meml. Found., Lakeland (Fla.) C. of C., Mensa, Masons, DeMolay Internat. (chevalier), Order of Ea. Star, Humanist Assn. West Ctrl. Fla. (charter), Norwalk H.S. Alumni Assn., U. Ill. Alumni Assn., Psi Chi. Office: 22 Spring Ave Oakland NJ 07436-1930 E-mail: chargayb2@earthlink.net.

BUTTERFIELD, DEBORAH KAY, sculptor; b. San Diego, May 7, 1949; m. John Buck; 2 children. BA, U. Calif., Davis, 1971, MFA, 1973; D.Fine Arts (hon.), Mont. State U., 1998, Rocky Mountain Coll., Billings, Mont., 1997. Asst. prof. sculpture U. Wis., Madison, 1975-76, Mont. State U., Bozeman, 1979-81, adj. prof., 1981-84. One-man shows include Lowe Mus. Art U. Miami, Coral Gables, Fla., 1992, San Diego Mus. Art, 1996; exhibited in groups shows U. Mus. Berkeley, Calif., 1974, Whitney Mus. Am. Art, N.Y., 1979, Albright-Knox Gallery, Buffalo, 1979, Israel Mus., Jerusalem, 1980, Arco Ctr. Visual Art, 1981, Walker Art Ctr., Mpls., 1982, Dallas Mus. Fine Arts, 1982, Oakland, 1983, Chgo., 1985, Contemporary Art Ctr., Honolulu, 1986, Whitney Mus., 1988, Contemporary Art Mus., Honolulu, 1993, Seattle Mus. Art, 1994, The White House, Washington, Yale U., New Haven, Conn., 1997; represented in permanent collections Whitney Mus. Am. Art, N.Y., San Francisco Mus. Contemporary Art, Israel Mus., Jerusalem, Walker Art Ctr., Mpls., Met. Mus. Art, N.Y., Hirshhorn Mus., Washington, Seattle Art Mus., UCLA Sculpture Garden; commd. Copley Square, Boston, Portland (Oreg.) Airport, Denver Art Mus., Kansas City (Mo.) Zoo, White House, Washington, 2000, Monte Carlo, Monaco, 2000, Smithsonian Instn., Washington, San Francisco Internat. Airport. Nat. Endowment Arts grantee, 1977, 80, Guggenheim grantee, 1980; Commission Portland Internat. Airport.

BUTTERFIELD, G. K., JR., former state supreme court justice; b. Wilson, N.C., Apr. 27, 1947; s. G. K. and Addie (Davis) Butterfield; children: Valeisha Monique, Jenetta Lenai. BS, NC Central U., 1971, JD, 1974. Sr. ptnr. law firm, 1974—88; resident judge NC Superior Ct Dist 7B, 1988—2001; assoc. justice Supreme Ct. N.C., 2001.*

BUTTERFIELD, JAMES T. small business owner; b. Galion, Ohio, July 9, 1951; s. Carlos and Ethel Louise (Miller) B.; m. Mary Anne Shaffo, May 17, 1986; children: Jacob Alan, Emily Lauren. Cert. plumbing insp., backflow insp., cert. pipe welder, EPA cert. refrigerant handling technician, lic. low pressure steam operator, cert. automatic sprinkler installer, lic. plumbing contractor, Ohio; lic. hydronics contractor, Ohio, N.C., elec. contractor, Ohio, heating, ventilating, air conditioning contractor, Ohio. Apprentice Don Barnett Plumbing, Galion, Ohio, 1968-69, Rinehart Plumbing and Heating, Galion, 1969-71; owner Butterfield Plumbing and Heating, Galion, 1972—, Galion Sheet Metal, 1982—. Mem. Am. Soc. Sanitary Engrs., Ohio Assn. Plumbing Insps. Home: 375 W Atwood St Galion OH 44833-2553 Office: Butterfield Plumbing and Heating PO Box 33 Galion OH 44833-0033 E-mail: bfield@richnet.net., Mengdu@netscape.net.

BUTTERFIELD, MARGARET ANNE DAVIS, music educator, vocalist; d. James Emerson and Mary Anne Jackson Davis; m. Stuart James Butterfield, June 6, 1982; children: Steven James, James Emerson. MusB in Music Edn., Cath. U. Am., 1978; MusM in Voice Performance, Manhattan Sch. of Music, 1982. Singer N.Y.C. Opera Nat. Co., 1980—87; asst. to exec. dir. Am. Sch. Classical Studies at Athens, Princeton, NJ, 1983—96; soloist N.Y.C. Opera Edn. Dept., NY, 1990—93; dir. vocal program Lawrenceville Sch., NJ, 1994—2003; upper sch. choir dir. Wilmington Friends Sch., Del., 2003—. Singer (soprano soloist): (premiere recording) Six Paripari by Walter Winslow; singer: The Princeton Singers, 1995—, Fuma Sacra, 1998—. Recipient State Winner, Nat. Fedn. of Music Clubs, 1979, Regional Semi-finalist, Met. Opera Nat. Coun., 1986, Finalist, Luciano Pavarotti 2nd Internat. Vocal Competition, 1995; Merit Scholarship, Manhattan Sch. of Music, 1980—82. Mem.: Am. Choral Directors Assn., SAG, Am. Guild Musical Artists, Sigma Alpha Iota (life). Presbyterian. Home: 3301 Cross Country Dr Wilmington DE 19810 E-mail: mbutterfield@wilmingtonfriends.org.

BUTTERFIELD, MARIAN ISBEY, psychiatrist, researcher; b. Detroit, Dec. 17, 1958; d. William Field and JoAnne (O'Dowd) Isbey; m. Kevin William Butterfield; children: Corrie Caitlin, William Jackson. BA in Biology, Kalamazoo Coll., 1980; MPH, U. N.C., 1986, MD, 1990. Diplomate Am. Bd. Psychiatry and Neurology. Resident in psychiatry, 1990—94; dir. of women's mental health program Durham VAMC-Duke U Sch Medicine, NC, 1994—2001; clin. assoc. dept psychiatry and behavioral scis. Duke U. Sch. Medicine, 1994—98, clin. asst. prof., 1998—; asst. prof. Duke U. Sch. of Medicine, 2002—. Contbr. articles to profl. publs. Recipient Women's Health Excellence award for Clin. Excellence, Nat. Assn. Women's Health, 2000; grantee, Dept. Veterans Affairs, 1998—2002, 2001—. Mem.: Assn. Women Psychiatrists, Am. Psychiat. Assn. (vice chair of sci. program com. 1998—2001, Marian I. Butterfield award named in her honor 2002). Avocations: painting, reading, writing. Office: Durham VAMC/Duke U 508 Fulton St Ste 116A Durham NC 27705

BUTTERKLEE, NEIL HOWARD, lawyer; b. Bklyn., Mar. 17, 1958; s. Samuel and Edith (Uday) B.; m. Arlene Marie Eberle, July 5, 1982. BA, SUNY, Stony Brook, 1980, MS, 1982; MBA, Adelphi U., Garden City, N.Y., 1987; JD, N.Y. Law Sch., 1992. Bar: Conn. 1992, N.Y. 1993, D.C. 1994, U.S. Dist. Ct. (ea. and so. dists.) N.Y. 1993, U.S. Ct. Appeals (D.C. cir.) 1997, U.S. Supreme Ct., 1997. Tech. writer Consolidated Edison Co. N.Y. Inc., N.Y.C., 1982-83, analyst, 1983-89, sr. analyst, 1989-93, atty., 1993-95, staff atty., 1995-99, sr. staff atty., 1999—2002, sr. atty., 2002—. Editor: Law Review. Recipient Scholarship N.Y. Law Sch., N.Y.C., 1988-92; nationally ranked fencer U.S. Fencing Assn., 1984-88. Mem. ABA, N.Y. State Bar Assn., Conn. Bar Assn., Assn. Bar City N.Y., Energy Bar Assn. Avocations: golf, writing. Office: Consolidated Edison Co NY 4 Irving Pl Rm 1815 New York NY 10003-3598 E-mail: butterklee@coned.com.

BUTTERMAN, JAY RONALD, lawyer; b. N.Y.C., June 15, 1958; s. Louis and Ellen (Schmeltzer) B. BA, Vassar Coll., 1983; JD, Yeshiva U., 1988. Bar: N.J. 1988, N.Y. 1989, U.S. Dist. Ct. (so. dist.) N.Y. 1991, U.S. Dist. Ct. (ea. dist.) N.Y. 1996, U.S. Dist. Ct. N.J. 1988, U.S. Supreme Ct. 2002. Assoc. Hoffinger Friedland Dobrish Bernfeld & Hasen, N.Y.C., 1988-91; sole practitioner N.Y.C., 1991-95; mng. ptnr. Law firm of Jay R. Butterman, N.Y.C., 1995-99; sr. ptnr. Butterman, Kahn & Gardner, LLP, 1999—. Recipient Outstanding Acad. Achievement award Acad. Am. Matrimonial Lawyers, 1988. Mem. ABA, ATLA, N.Y. State Bar Assn., Assn. Bar City N.Y. Democrat. Avocations: oriental art, antiquarian books. Office: 425 Park Ave Fl 26 New York NY 10022-3506

BUTTERMAN, STEVEN FRED, language educator, researcher; b. Montreal, Quebec, Canada, Feb. 11, 1970; s. Norman Butterman and Marilyn Silver. BA, U Colo., 1993; MA, U Wis., 1996, PhD, 2000. Tchg. asst. U Wis., Madison, 1994—98; seminar instr. Jung Soc. of Austin, Austin, Tex., 1994; head tchg. asst. U Wis., 1996—98; sr. instr., coord. Beloit (Wis.) Coll., Beloit, Wis., 1996—2000; lectr. U Wis., 1998—2000; asst. prof. portuguese U Miami, Coral Gables, Fla., 2000—. Co-chair Awards Com., Coral Gables, Fla., 2002—; mem. editl. adv. bd. Odisseia: Ciencias Humanas, Letras E Artes, Natal, Brazil, 2002—; v.p. Centro Cultural Brasil-USA, Miami, Fla., 2003—. Contbr. ; author: Perversions on Parade: Brazilian Lit. of Transgression and Post Modern Anti-Aesthetics in Glauco Mattoso. Recipient Brazilian Internatl. Press Award, 2003, Nat. Endowment for the Humanities, Ariz. State U, 2002. Mem.: Control Cultural Brasil-USA (v.p. 2003), Latin Am. Studies Assn. (assoc.), Modern Lang. Assn. (assoc.). Avocations: music, hiking, creative writing, poetry, foreign languages. Office: University of Miami Dept of Foreign Langs & Lit Coral Gables FL 33124-4650

BUTTERS, JOHN PATRICK, educator, tour director; b. Janesville, Wis., Jan. 11, 1933; s. John William and Mary Helen (Tracey) B.; m. Collette Helen Jung, Apr. 20, 1963; children: Blair John, Laura Lisbeth. BA, U. Wis., 1955. cert. travel counselor. Traffic supr., field training Pan Am. Airways, Chgo., 1958-64; ops. mgr. incentives Lerios/E.F. MacDonald, San Francisco, 1964-67; retail agy. mgr. Bungey Travel, Palo Alto, Calif., 1967-68; dist. sales mgr. Lissonne Lindeman, San Francisco, 1968-71; group travel mgr., Wis. div. Am. Automobile Assn., Madison, 1971-75; owner, v.p., sec. Travel/ease Inc., Madison, 1975-88; owner, pres. Travel Learn, Ltd., Madison, 1981-90; sr. curriculum specialist Inst. Cert. Travel Agts., Wellesley, Mass., 1989-93; free lance tour coord., tour escort Gretchen Petersen Tours, Inc., Madison, Wis., 1993-2000, Van Galder Tour and Travel, Janesville, Wis., 1996—. Cons. Madison Area Tech. Coll., 1982-88, Rockford (Ill.) Bus. Coll., 1988-90; treas. Capital Area Travel Soc., Madison, 1973-77. Editor: Travel Industry Mktg., 1990, Travel Industry Bus. Mgmt., 1992, U.S.A.-Can., 1992, Pacific Rim, 1993, Latin Am., 1994; contbr. articles to profl. jours. Program chmn. The Travel Club, Madison, 1973-77; bd. trustees St. Andrew's Soc., Madison, 1976-88 (treas. 1975-79); chmn. mus. svc. coun. Rock County Hist. Soc., Janesville, Wis., 1985-89; trustee Schumacher Farm Conservancy, Waunakee, Wis., 1984—. Mem. Inst. Cert. Travel Agts. (life), U. Wis. Alumni, Madison Club. Avocations: travel, reading, geneology, history, geography. Home: 1328 Oakland Ave Janesville WI 53545-4243 Office: Van Galder Tour and Travel 20 S Main St Janesville WI 53545-3959

BUTTERWORTH, DAVID GARDNER, lawyer; b. Bryn Mawr, Pa., Nov. 13, 1957; m. Susan Vinson Cauffman, May 16, 1987; children: D. Gardner, Henry M. BA in Chemistry, Conn. Coll., 1980; MS in Chemistry, Drexel U., 1986; JD, Villanova U., 1989. Bar: Pa., 1989; U.S. Dist. Ct. (ea. dist.) Pa. 1994. Chemist Rohm & Haas, Springhouse, Pa., 1980-86; atty. Morgan Lewis & Bockius, Phila., 1989-97, Miller Dunham & Doering, Phila., 1997-98, Butterworth & Campbell PC, Phila., 1998-2000; sole practitioner, 2000—; pres., CEO Biosolids Ventures, Inc., 2000—. Editor-in-chief Villanova Environ. Law Jour., 1989. Mem. Environmental Profl. Assn. of Phila. Region (sec., treas. 1996-2001). Office: 103 Sibley Ave PO Box 146 Ardmore PA 19003-0146 E-mail: dgb@dgbutterworth.com., dgb@biosolids-ventures.com.

BUTTERWORTH, MICHAEL, computer programmer; b. Hartford, Conn., July 4, 1942; s. Oliver and Miriam (Brooks) B.; m. Carol Ann Hastings, Aug. 6, 1966; 1 child, Beth. BS, Dartmouth Coll., 1963; MS, Stanford U., 1968, Rensselaer Poly. Inst., 1994. Statistician Univ. Calif. Med. Ctr., San Francisco, 1968-70; statistician, demographer Greater Hartford Process, 1970-75; mktg. specialist ADVO-System, Inc., Hartford, 1975-77, programmer, 1978-79; sr. software engr. Gerber Systems Tech., South Windsor, Conn., 1979-91; dir. info. sys., election and survey unit CBS News, 1994—. Contbr. articles to profl. jours. Sec. Arts of Tolland (Conn.), Inc., 1979-84, pres. 1985-93. Mem. Assn. Computing Machinery. Home: 106 Cedar Swamp Rd Tolland CT 06084-3610

BUTTERWORTH, RITAJEAN HARTUNG, broadcast executive; b. 1931; m. Fred R. Butterworth; 5 children. Bd. dirs. Corp. Pub. Broadcasting, Washington, 1992—. Chmn. bd. Corp. Pub. Broadcasting, 1995—96, vice chmn., 2001; treas., bd. dirs. Discovery Inst., 1990—2002. Mem. coun. Annenberg/CPB Project; active Children's Orthop. Hosp., Child Ryther Ctr., Seattle, 1989—91; mem. merit selection panel U.S. Dist. Ct. ea. dist., Wash.; Wash. state dir. Senator Slade Gorton, 1981—86, 1988—90; bd. trustees Wash. U., Bellingham, 1969—77, sec., vice chmn., chmn. bd.; mem. NPR Bd., 1977—85; sec., vice chmn.; mem. adv. bd. Sta. KUOW-FM, Seattle, 1985—88, KCTS, Seattle, 1989—. Office: Corp Pub Broadcasting 401 9th St NW Washington DC 20004-2128

BUTTERWORTH, ROBERT A. dean, former state attorney general; b. Passaic, N.J., Aug. 20, 1942; m. Marta Prado. BA, BS, U. Fla., 1965; JD, U. Miami, 1969. Prosecutor, Fla., 1970—74; circuit and county judge, 1974—78; adj. prof. Nova Univ. Grad. Sch. Criminal Law, 1976—78; sheriff Broward County Sheriff's Office, 1978—82; head Fla. Dept. Hwy. Safety and Motor Vehicles, Tallahassee, 1982—84; mayor City of Sunrise, 1984—87; atty. gen. State of Fla., Tallahassee, 1987—2002; sr. judge Broward County, Fla., 2002—; dean St. Thomas Univ. Law Sch., Fla., 2003—. Democrat. Office: St Thomas U Law Sch 16400 NW 32nd Ave Miami FL 33054

BUTTIGIEG, JOSEPH J. banking executive; BBA, U. Notre Dame; JD, Detroit Coll. Various to sr. v.p. Manufacturer's Bank, Detroit, 1972-89, exec. v.p., 1989-91; exec. v.p. global corp. banking Comerica, Inc., Detroit, 1995-99, vice-chmn. bus. bank, 1999—. Office: Comerica Inc Comerica Twr/500 Woodward A Detroit MI 48226

BUTTLAR, RUDOLPH OTTO, retired college dean; b. Chgo., Dec. 31, 1934; s. Otto Robert and Lucille Ann (Blasnig) B.; m. Lois Jacqueline Mercier, June 5, 1955; children— Michael Robert, Andrew Scott, John David. BS in Chemistry, Wheaton (Ill.) Coll., 1956; PhD in Inorganic Chemistry, Ind. U., 1962. Mem. faculty Kent (Ohio) State U., 1962-96, asso. prof. chemistry, 1971-96; dean Kent (Ohio) State U. (Coll. Arts and Scis.), 1975-96. Adminstrv. cons., 1996—. Mem. Am. Chem. Soc., Am. Sci. Affiliation. Baptist. Home: 5936 Horning Rd Kent OH 44240-4140 E-mail: rbuttlar@neo.rr.com.

BUTTLER, JOHN HOWLAND, retired judge, retired arbitrator; b. Bridgeport, Conn., Aug. 4, 1923; s. Frank Delano and Ruth Curtis Buttler; m. Ann Elizabeth Stover, 1947; children: Suzanne, John, Dana, Elizabeth, Barbara. BA, Dartmouth Coll., Hanover, N.H., 1947; LLB, Columbia U., N.Y.C., 1950. Bar: D.C., Oreg. 1951. Atty. Hardy, Buttler & McEwen, Portland, Oreg., 1951—77;

appellate judge Ct. of Appeals, State of Oreg., 1977—92, pro-tem, 1992—97; arbitrator, 1993—98. Mem. Oreg. Bd. of Bar Examiners, 1966—69, Oreg. Bar Trial Com. Apptd. citizen Bd. of Parole, Oreg., 1959—65; bd. dirs. Portland Jr. Symphony, Portland City Club. Lt. (j.g.) Air Corps USN. Mem.: Oreg. Bar Assn., Multnomah Athletic Club. Democrat. Avocations: photography, tennis, gardening, fly fishing, woodworking. Home: 3131 NW Skyline Blvd Portland OR 97229-3865

BUTTNER, JEAN BERNHARD, diversified financial services company executive; b. New Rochelle, N.Y., Nov. 3, 1934; d. Arnold and Janet (Kinghorn) Bernhard; m. Edgar Buttner, Sept. 13, 1958 (div.); children: Janet, Edgar Arnold, Marianne. BA, Vassar Coll., 1957; cert. bus. adminstrn., Harvard-Radcliffe program, 1958; Montessori diploma, Coll. Notre Dame, Belmont, Calif., 1967; D Bus. Adminstrn. (hon.), U. Bridgeport, 1994. Past v.p. Buttner Cos., Oakland, Calif.; pres. Value Line Inc. (subs. Arnold Bernhard & Co., Inc.), N.Y.C., 1985, chmn., pres., CEO, 1988—; chmn., CEO, pres. Arnold Bernhard & Co., Inc., 1988—; chmn., pres. Compupower, 1988—, Value Line Securities, Inc., 1988—, Value Line Distbn. Ctr., Inc., 1994—, Value Line Pub., Inc., 1988—, Vanderbilt Advt., Inc., 1988—. Chmn., pres. Value Line Mut. Funds. Editor-in-chief Value Line Rsch. Ctr., The Value Line 600, The Value Line Investment Survey-Small and Mid-Cap Edition, The Value Line Mut. Fund Survey, The Value Line No-Load Fund Advisor, The Value Line Options Survey, The Value Line Convertibles Survey, The Value Line Spl. Situations Svc., Value Line Select, Value Line Investment Survey for Windows, Value Line Mut. Fund Survey for Windows, Value Line Daily Options, Convertibles Data File, DataFile and DataFile II, Estimates and Projections, Value Line on Microfiche, Value Line Insight, Value Line Industry Watch; web editor: www.ValueLine.com. Past trustee Skidmore Coll.; past pres. Piedmont Sch. Bd.; past dir. Berkeley Montessori Sch.; mem. N.Y.C. Partnership, Com. of 200; past mem. adv. coun. Stanford Bus. Sch.; past mem. The Presdl. Roundtable; past vis. com. for bd. overseers Harvard Bus. Sch.; past bd. dirs. Harvard Bus. Sch. Club Greater N.Y.; past west coast admissions rep. Vassar Coll.; past trustee Radcliffe Coll., Harvard U., Williams Coll., Emma Willard Sch., Coll. Prep. Sch. Com. for Econ. Devel. Named one of N.Y.'s 75 Most Influential Women in Business, Crain's, 1996, One of N.Y.'s 100 Most Influential Women in Business, Crain's, 1999; recipient Alumni Achievement award, Harvard U. Grad. Sch. Bus. Adminstrn., 1995, Alumnae award Choate Rosemary Hall, Wallingford, Conn., 1995, Emma Lazarus award Associated Builders and Owners of N.Y., Inc., 1996; Life Achievement award Emma Willard Sch., 1998. Mem. Harvard Bus. Sch. Club Greater N.Y., Harvard Bus. Sch. Assn. (bd. dirs.). Republican. Congregationalist. Avocations: reading, swimming, biking, tennis, skiing. Office: Value Line Inc 220 E 42nd St Fl 6 New York NY 10017-5891 E-mail: jbb@valueline.com.

BUTTON, GLENN MARSHALL, aeronautical engineer; b. L.A., June 26, 1958; s. Albert Ronald Button and Laurel Lang (Bluske) Ratkay; m. Mary Josephine Puetzer, May 16, 1981; children: Nichole Elisabeth, Jessica Sarah, Laura Marie. BS in Physics, Ariz. State U., 1980. Counselor Adventure Unlimited Ranches, Buena Vista, Colo., 1977; aerodynamics engr. aircraft divsn. Northrop Grumman Corp., Hawthorne, Calif., 1980-82, structures rsch. engr. aircraft divsn., 1982-85, engring. specialist aircraft divsn., 1986-91, database application software developer B-2 divsn. Pico Rivera, Calif., 1991-92, lead configuration specialist, design application software aircraft divsn.; prin. GMB Assocs. Mktg., Cypress, Calif., 1988—; electronic process devel. prin. engr., scientist Long Beach (Calif.) divsn. The Boeing Co., 1996-98, supplier integration mgr., 1998—99, electronic contractual supplier data program mgr., 2000—; with eBusiness, 2000—. Aerodynamics cons. Kachina Racing, Tempe, Ariz., 1977-93; software cons. Aeromax, Cypress, 1989—; internat. tech. data mgmt. cons., 1998—. Contbr. articles to sci. jours. Pres. Villas Figueroa Homeowners Assn., Carson, Calif., 1983; tchr. Sea Coast Grace Ch., Cypress, Calif., 1990—. Mem. Soc. Automotive Engrs., Boeing Long Beach Mgmt. Assn. Republican. Mem. Christian Ch. Avocations: cycling, teaching, skiing, reading, mountain climbing. Home: 10441 Santa Elise St Cypress CA 90630-4234 Office: The Boeing Co D801-0042 3855 N Lakewood Blvd Long Beach CA 90846-0003 E-mail: gmbassoc@bww.com., glenn.m.button@boeing.com.

BUTTON, JOE WADE, civil engineer, researcher, consultant; b. Nacagdoches, Tex., Oct. 19, 1944; s. Joseph Berry and Nora B. (Wade) B.; m. Shirley Lou Williams, July 3, 1964; children: Tammy Annette, Wendy Jo. BS in Chem. Engring., Tex. A&M U., 1972, MS in Civil Engring., 1984. Registered profl. engr., Tex. Sr. rsch. engr., head materials & pavement divsn. Tex. Transp. Inst., Tex. A&M U., College Station. Internat. engring. cons.; chmn. Expert Task Group Strategic Hwy. Rsch. Program, Washington, 1990-93; cons. Nat. Coop. Hwy. Rsch. Bd., 1991—. Author: pubs. on proceedings and papers at profl. confs. and meetings, 1982—. Pres. Brazos chpt. Tex. Soc. Profl. Engrs., Bryan, 1982. Recipient Army Commendation medal, U.S. Army, Bryan, Tex., 1980, 91, Meritorious Svc. medal, U.S. Army, Houston, 1991. Mem. Transp. Rsch. Bd., Am. Soc. for Testing and Materials, Nat. Soc. Profl. Engrs., Assn. Asphalt Paving Technologists. Republican. Baptist. Home: 4616 Midsummer Ln College Station TX 77845-9358 Office: Tex A&M Univ Tex Transp Inst College Station TX 77843-0001

BUTTON, RENA PRITSKER, public affairs executive; b. Providence, Feb. 15, 1925; d. Isadore and Esther (Kay) Pritsker; m. Daniel E. Button, Aug. 16, 1969; children by previous marriage: Joshua, Bruce, David Posner. Student, Pembroke Coll., 1942-45; BS, Simmons Coll., 1948; postgrad., Union U., 1968-69. Spl. asst. to U.S. Rep., 1967-69; spl. projects coord. United Jewish Appeal, 1971-74; exec. dir. Nat. Coun. Jewish Women, Inc., N.Y.C., 1974-76; pres. Button Assos., N.Y.C., 1976—; exec. v.p. Catalyst, N.Y.C., 1980-82; pres. Button & Button, Albany, N.Y., 1982—. Adv. coun. N.Y. State Senate Minority, 1980—; exec. dir. N.Y. State Coun. on Alcoholism and Other Drug Addictions, 1990-93; pres., founder Two Together, A Pilot Reading Program for Young People, 1997-2003. Co-producer, moderator: TV pub. affairs program Speak For Yourself, Albany, N.Y., 1963-66. Chair pub. affairs com. Marymount Manhattan Coll.; past bd. dirs. Albany YWCA, Albany Coun. Chs. Devel. Corp., World Affairs Coun., Planned Parenthood Assn. Albany; trustee Jerusalem Women's Seminar, Citizens for Family Planning, N.Y. Com. Integrated Housing, Hist. Albany Found. Ctr. for Counseling, Town of Bethlehem Pub. Libr., 1999; pres. Sr. Svc. Ctr. Albany Area, Two Together, 1997; bd. dirs. Com. Modern Cts.; exec. dir. N.Y. Head Injury Assn., 1993-96; candidate N.Y. State Assembly 102d Dist., 1996; trustee Albany Symphony Orch., 2002—. Mem. Siasconset Casino Club, Univ. Club. Clubs: Siasconset Casino (Siasconset, Mass.), Univ. (Albany). Home and Office: 16 Spruce Ct Delmar NY 12054-2614 E-mail: rbutton96@aol.com.

BUTTON, RICHARD TOTTEN, television and stage producer, former figure skating champion; b. Englewood, N.J., July 18, 1929; s. George and Evelyn Bunn Totten B.; children: Edward Totten, Emily Rada. BA, Harvard U., 1952, LLB, 1956; LHD (hon.), Buena Vista Coll., 1988. Dir. Decorative Arts Trust, 1979-80. Commentator ABC Sports; creator The Superstars sports competitions, The World Profl. Figure Skating Championships; prodr. Broadway shows: Sweet Sue, 1987, Artist Descending a Staircase, 1989; nat. spokesperson Brain Injury ASsn. Am., 2003. Author: Dick Button on Skates, 1955, Instant Skating, 1964; contbr. articles to various mags. Pres. Richmondtown Restoration, Inc., 1968-77. U.S. figure skating champion, 1946-52; world figure skating champion, 1948-52; European figure skating champion, 1948; Olympic gold medalist, 1948, 52; recipient James E. Sullivan award, 1949, Emmy award for outstanding sports personality-analyst, 1980-81; named to U.S. Olympic Hall of Fame. Mem. Bar Assn. D.C., Skating Club N.Y., Skating Club Boston, Phila. Skating Club. Office: 765 Park Ave New York NY 10021

BUTTON, TOM, information technology executive; married; 6 children. BSEE, Princeton U. With IBM; assoc. cons. Boston Cons. Group; from program mgr. to corp. v.p. Microsoft, Redmond, Wash., 1988, corp. v.p. developer tools. Avocations: coaching little league baseball, coaching little league soccer, coaching little league softball. Office: One Microsoft Way Redmond WA 98052-6399

BUTTREY, DONALD WAYNE, lawyer; b. Terre Haute, Ind., Feb. 6, 1935; s. William Edgar and Nellie (Vaughn) B.; children: Greg, Alan, Jason; m. Karen Lake, Mar. 23, 1985. BS, Ind. State U., 1956; JD, Ind. U., 1961. Bar: Ind. 1961, U.S. Dist. Ct. 1961, U.S. Ct. Appeals (7th cir.) 1972, U.S. Tax Ct. 1972, U.S. Supreme Ct. 1972. Law clk. to chief judge Steckler, U.S. Dist. Ct. So. Dist. Ind., 1961-63; mem. McHale, Cook & Welch, P.C., Indpls., 1963—2001, pres., 1986-93, chmn., 1993—2001; of counsel Wooden & McLaughlin, LLP, 2001—. Chmn. Ctrl. Region IRS-Bar Liaison Com., 1984; mem. jud. nominating com. Marion County Mcpl. Ct., 1993-96; mem. Estate Planning Coun. Indpls., 1990—. Note editor Ind. Law Jour., 1960-61. Trustee Ind. State U., 1992-2000, v.p. bd., 1997-2000; bd. dirs. Ind. State U. Found., 1991—. With AUS, 1956-58, Korea. Fellow Am. Coll. Tax Counsel, Am. Bar Found., Ind. State Bar Found., Indpls. Bar Found. (pres. 1993-96, Buchanan award 1999); mem. ABA (taxation, real property, probate and trust sect., liaison IRS-Bar Liaison com., taxation sect. 1995-96), Ind. State Bar Assn. (bd. govs. 1994-96, taxation, real property, probate and trust sect., chmn. taxation sect. 1982-83), Indpls. Bar Assn. (pres. 1990, mem. probate, taxation sects.), Highland Golf and Country Club, Indpls. Athletic Club (bd. dirs. 1982-88), Skyline Club, Univ. Club (bd. dirs. 1997-2000). Presbyterian. E-mail: dbuttrey@woodmaclaw.com.

BUTTRICK, HAROLD, architect; b. Bryn Mawr, Pa., Jan. 2, 1931; s. Charles Edgar and Constance (La Boiteaux) B.; m. Ann Octavia White, Sept. 3, 1955; children: John Ward, Jerome Chanler, Mary Constance, Sarah Elizabeth, Catherine. Student, The Sorbonne, Paris, 1950-51; AB, Harvard U., 1953, MArch, 1959. Cert. NCRB. Prin. Harold Buttrick & Assocs., N.Y.C., 1963-75, Smotrich Platt & Buttrick, N.Y.C., 1975-76, Buttrick White & Burtis, N.Y.C., 1976-97, Murphy Burnham & Buttrick, N.Y.C., 1998—. Prin archtl. works include Corpus Christi Monastery, Nairobi, Kenya, 1967, Green Vale Sch., Iselin Ctr., Glen Head, N.Y., 1971, Trans World Airlines 747 Hangar, John F. Kennedy Airport, 1971, Carter Giraffe House, Bronx Zoo, 1981, 42 Tower Records Stores, 1982—, St. Thomas Choir Sch., N.Y.C., 1987, Central Park projects, Loeb Boathouse, 1986, Ballplayers Refreshment Stand, 1990, Outdoor Performance State in Bushnell Park, Hartford, Conn., restoration of the Pulitzer Fountain and Grand Army Plz., 1990, The Charles A. Dana Discovery Ctr., 1993, Battery Park City Authority Offices, 1996, Trinity Mid. Sch., N.Y.C., 1998. Bd. dirs. N.Y. Soc. Libr., 1989-93. Recipient Preservation League of N.Y. State awards, 1990-91, 96, City Club of N.Y. Bard awards Loeb Boathouse, 1986, St. Thomas Choir Sch., 1990, Ballplayers Refreshment Stand, 1992. Fellow AIA (Honor award 1972, Brick in Architecture award 1991, 95), N.Y. State Assn. Architects; mem. Century Assn; mem., bd. dirs. Pks. Council, N.Y., 2000—. Office: Murphy Burnham & Buttrick 48 W 37th St New York NY 10018

BUTTS, CAROL HENDERSON, human resources specialist, consultant; b. Anniston, Ala., Feb. 11, 1946; d. William Edward and Mary (Hill) Henderson; m. Robert Russell Butts, Feb. 12, 1976 (div. Mar. 1989); children: Jabe Bowden, Deborah Ann Miller. BA, Jacksonville State U., 1970. From pers. counselor to tng. dir. Norrell, Inc., Atlanta, 1971-77; creative dir. TV Tempo Stevens County, Toccoa, Ga., 1978-82; gen. mgr. Niermann Pers. Svcs., Atlanta, 1983-87; dir. tng. and continuing edn. KOT Pers., Atlanta, 1987-90; gen. mgr., v.p. med. divsn. Prestige Pers. Svcs., Norcross, Ga., 1990-94; dir. med. divsn. MedPro Pers., Atlanta, 1994-95; pres. MedStat, Inc., Alpharetta, Ga., 1995—. Pres. Habitat for Humanity, 1996—97. Recipient Editor's Choice award, Internat. Libr. Poetry, 2001—02, Poet of Merit award, 2002. Fellow: Nat. Assn. Pers. Cons., Am. Biog. Inst.; mem.: NOW, NAFE (pres. 1996—97), NAUW (pres. 1996—97), Ga. Assn. Pers. Cons. (chair, Disting. Cons. of Yr. 1978), Jacksonville State U. Alumni Assn. (Alumni fo the Yr. nominee 1997), Sigma Tau Alpha, Alpha Xi Delta. Avocations: reading, writing, poetry, fishing, water sports.

BUTTS, EDWARD PERRY, civil engineer, environmental consultant; b. Ukiah, Calif., July 29, 1958; s. Edward Oren Butts and Orvilla June (Daily) Hutcheson; m. JoAnne Catherine Zellner, Aug. 14, 1978; children: Brooke C., Adam E. Cert. continuing studies in Irrigation Theory and Practices, U. Nebr., 1980. Registered profl. civil and environ. engr., Oreg., Wash., cert. water rights examiner, Oreg., sprinkler irrigation designer, pump installer, Oreg., registered gen. contractor, Oreg., Wash., control sys. engr., Oreg., lic. pump installation contractor, Oreg., diplomate, Am. Bd. Engring. and Tech., Am. Coll. Forensic Examiners, Am. Acad. Environ. Engrs., cert. plant engr., Assoc. Facilities Engring., bd. cert. environ. engr. Technician Ace Pump Sales, Salem, Oreg., 1976, Stettler Supply Co., Salem, 1976-78, assoc. engr., 1978-86, chief engr., 1986—90, v.p. engring., 1990-97, pres., 1997—2003, chief engr., 2003—. Profl. engr. exam. question reviewer Nat. Coun. Engring. Examiners, Clemson, SC, 1989—; profl. engr. exam. supr. Oreg. State Bd. Engring. Examiners, Salem, 1986—96; mem. Marion County Water Mgmt. Coun., 1993, Oreg. Drinking Water Adv. Com., 1999; mem. blue ribbon com. Oreg. Dept. Environ. Quality, 2003—; mem. Oreg. State Bd. Examiners Engring. and Land Surveying; editl. adv. bd. Pumps & Systems mag., 2001. Contbr. articles to profl. jours. including Jour. Pub. Works Mag., AWWA Opflow, Pumps and Sys.; columnist Water Well Jour. Coach Little League Coach Basketball Leage, Turner, Oreg., 1990-94; vol. Jr. Achievement; presdl. bus. commn. Nat. Rep. Congrl. Com., 2002—. Recipient Merit award Am. City and County Mag., 1990, Cmty. Vol. citation City of Keizer, Oreg., 1993, Cert. of appreciation Oreg. State Bd. Engring. Examiners, 1996, Commendation letter City of Salem, 1996, Application Design award Spraying Systems Co., 1996, Apex award Most Improved Jour.,Oreg. Republican of the Yr., 2001, Meritorius Svc. medal Nat. Rep. Congressional Com., 2001-02, Presdl. Bus. Commn., 2002. Mem. ASCE, ASME, NSPE, IEEE, Am. Pub. Works Assn., Assn. Groundwater Scientists and Engrs., Nat. Ground Water Assn., Oreg. Groundwater Assn., Profl. Engrs. Oreg. (mid-Willamette chpt. v.p. 1990-91, pres. 1992-93, state v.p. 1993-95, state pres.-elect 1995-96, state pres. 1996-97, nat. dir. 1999-2000, Young Engr. of Yr. award 1993-94), Am. Water Works Assn., Oreg. Assn. Water Utilities (bd. dlrs. 1998—, Friend of Rural Water award 2002). Republican. Achievements include devel. of system used to install multiple pumps in water wells. Office: 1810 Lana Ave NE Salem OR 97303-3116 E-mail: stettlers@juno.com.

BUTTS, HERBERT CLELL, retired dentist, educator; b. Dover, Tenn., Aug. 24, 1924; s. Sidney Lewis and Georgia (Sawyer) B.; m. Quay Coker; children: Marla Lyce, April Chyrese, Dawn Denise, Sidney Coker. Student, U. Tenn. Jr. Coll., 1942-43, Memphis State U., 1946-47; DDS, U. Tenn., 1950; MS, U. Iowa, 1966. Pvt. practice dentistry, Memphis, 1950-58; mem. faculty Coll. Dentistry, U. Tenn., Memphis, part-time 1950-58, 58-60, assoc. dean acad. affairs, 1978-81, spl. advisor to dean, 1986-2000; ret., 2000; fgn. svc. officer, dental edn. advisor State Dept. Fgn. Aid program, San Salvador, El Salvador, 1960-64; assoc. prof. St. Louis U. Sch. Dentistry, 1966-67; prof., chmn. dept. operative dentistry Coll. Dental Medicine, Med. U. S.C., Charleston, 1967-70, asst. dean for admissions and student affairs, 1970, 72-74, acting dean, 1971; editor-in-chief ADA, Chgo., 1974-77; dean Sch. Dental Medicine So. Ill. U., Alton, 1981-86. Editor U. Tenn. Coll. Dentistry Bull., 1990-2000. With USNR, 1943-46. Recipient Outstanding Alumnus award U. Tenn. Coll. Dentistry, 1975. Mem. ADA, Tenn. Dental Assn. (fellowship award 1993), Memphis Dental Soc., Am. Coll. Dentists (pres. Tenn. sect. 1994, sec.-treas. Tenn. sect. 1995-98), Internat. Coll. Dentists, Am. Assn. Dental Schs., Ala. Dental Assn. (hon.), Am. Assn. Women Dentists (hon.), Omicron Kappa Upsilon. Home: 1360 Peabody Ave Memphis TN 38104-3636

BUTTS, HUGH FLORENZ, physician, psychiatrist, psychoanalyst; b. N.Y.C., Dec. 2, 1926; s. Lucius Cornelius and Edith Eliza Butts; m. June Dobbs, June 9, 1953 (div. Dec. 1971); children: Lucia Irene, Florence, Eric Hugh; m. Clementine Riggsbee, Dec. 11, 1971; children: Sydney Clementine, Samantha Florenz, Heather Marguerita. BS, CCNY, 1949; MD, Meharry Med. Coll., 1953. Diplomate Am. Bd. Psychiatry and Neurology. Intern Morrisania Hosp., 1956; resident Bronx VA Hosp., 1958; psychiatry instr. Columbia U., N.Y.C., 1962-65, assoc. prof. psychiatry, 1965-67, asst. clin. prof. psychiatry, 1967-74; mem. faculty Columbia Psychoanalytic Clinic, N.Y.C., 1962-87, supervising and tng. analyst, 1968-87; lectr. Columbia Coll., N.Y.C., 1969-71; instr. Seek program CCNY, N.Y.C., 1972-74. Prof. psychiatry Albert Einstein Coll. Medicine, Bronx, 1974-81; cons. Altanta U. Sch. Social Work, 1970-74; vis. prof. psychiatry Meharry Med. Coll., Nashville, 1980-82; dir. Bronx Psychiat. Ctr., 1974-79; 1st dept. commr. N.Y. State Office Mental Health, Albany, N.Y., 1975-76; chmn. adv. bd. The Med. Herald, 1991-2002. Pres., founder Clementine Pub. Co., 1989, Lit. Mind Assocs., 1989; author 3 books; contbr. more than 200 articles to profl. jours. With USAAF, 1944-45. Recipient Spl. Merit award Assn. for Psychoanalytic Medicine, 1967; travel fellow Ford Found., 1972. Fellow: NY Acad. Scis., Am. Psychiat. Assn. (life); mem.: Am. Psychoanalytic Assn. Avocations: gardening, fishing, antique collecting, playing the violin, writing. Office: 350 Central Park W New York NY 10025-6547 E-mail: hfbuttsmd@aol.com.

BUTTZ, CHARLES WILLIAM, outdoor advertising executive; b. Aberdeen, S.D., Aug. 8, 1932; s. Ward Leland and Mary Baker (Eddy) B.; m. Teresa Margarita Castro, July 28, 1956; children: Jean, Teresa, Charles, William, James. BCE, Rensselaer Polytech Inst., 1956; MBA, U. Conn., 1974. Registered profl. engr. N.Y., N.J. Chief engr. Kuala Lumpur (Malaysia) Transp. Study, 1963-64; project mgr. Tippetts Abbett McCarthy Stratton Engrs., N.Y.C., 1956-65; mgmt. cons. Booz, Allen and Hamilton, N.Y.C., 1965-67; dir. Knight, Gladieux and Smith Cons., N.Y.C., 1967-74; group mgr. Boeing Computer Svcs. Cons., N.Y.C., 1974-76; v.p. Middlesex Rsch. Ctr., Washington, 1976-77; pres. Eastern Shelter-All Inc., Mountainhome, Pa., 1977—, N.J. Shelter-All Inc., Columbia, N.J., 1980—, Regional Shelter-All Inc., Buck Hill Falls, Pa., 1985—. Instr. mktg. U. Conn., Stamford, 1975-76. Pres. St. Paul's Housing Corp., Norwalk, Conn., 1974-77; com. mem. Alfred Dater Coun. Boy Scouts Am., Stamford, 1970-77; v.p., camp chmn. Darien (Conn.) United Way, 1974; v.p., sec. Darien Young Mens Christian Assn., 1974-77; dir. United Way Monroe County, Tannersville, Pa., 1984-97. Maj. USAR, 1956-70. Recipient MBA Scholar award, Wall St. Jour., 1974. Mem. ASCE, Pa. Soc., Inst. Transp. Engrs., Am. Legion, Army and Navy Club. Episcopalian. Home: Cottage 266 Buck Hill Falls PA 18323 Office: Ea Shelter-All Inc PO Box 152 Mountainhome PA 18342

BUTTZ, GABRIELA I, chemical engineer, artist; b. London, Eng., Dec. 17, 1972; arrived in U.S., 1973; d. Donald L and Angelina I. Buttz. BS in Chem. Engring., Rensselaer Polytech.Inst., Troy, N.Y., 1995. Tech. cons. Oracle Corp., Bethesda, Md., 1996—2000, tech. cons. Boston, 1997—2000, patent agt. San Francisco, 2000—. Spkr. and cons. Coalition on New Office Tech., Boston, 1998—2000; hon. spkr. U.S. Congl. Panel, Washington, 1998—2000; hon. spkr. and guest Soc. Hispanic Profl. Engrs., San Francisco, 2000—01; mem. Presdl. Task Force on Minorities in Engring. and Scis.; guest spkr. congl. testimony on Ams. with Disabilities Act and ergonomic stds., 2000. Muralist, jeweler, La Flor de la Vida, 1995 (Commissioned by the El Paso Silver Company, 1999); musician: (prin. violinist) Rensselaer Symphony, 1990, Carnegie Hall Symphony Performance, 1988. Recipient Rensselaer Scholarship, Rensselaer Polytech. Inst., 1990—94; grantee Study Grant, Nat. Action Coun. on Minorities in Engring. and Sci., 1993—95, Mobil Grant, Mobil Corp., 1993—95. Mem. DAR, Am. Intellectual Property Assn., Soc. Women Engrs., Soc.Hispanic Profl. Engrs., Rensselaer Alumni Assn. (life; Secretary 1992—93).

BUTZ, BRADLEY MITCHELL, music educator; b. Oak Park, Ill., Mar. 7, 1952; s. Frank Lee and Josephine Mitchell Butz; m. Carol Eve Thrun, June 28, 1975; children: Holly Ann, Kelly Sue. BFA, U. of Wis., Milw., 1975; M of Music Edn., VanderCook Coll. of Music, Chgo., 1998. Instrumental music educator Wilmette (Ill.) Pub. Sch. Dist. 39, 1990—; pres. Sales Essentials Mfg. Co., Elk Grove Village, Ill., 1980—91. Bass player Civic Orch. Chgo., 1975—80. Home: 293 Columbia Ave Des Plaines IL 60016 Office: Highcrest Mid Sch 569 Hunter Rd Wilmette IL 60091 Office Fax: 847-256-0083. Personal E-mail: butzb@nttc.org. E-mail: butzb@nttc.org.

BUTZ, GENEVA MAE, pastor; b. Emmaus, Pa., May 11, 1944; d. Edwin F. and Arlene E. (Engler) B. BA, Hood Coll., 1966; MRE, Union Theol. Sem., 1968; D Divinity (hon.), Ursinus Coll., 1994. Ordained clergywoman United Ch. of Christ, 1972. Dir. Christian edn. United Ch. of Christ, Palos Verdes, Calif., 1968-72; mng. editor Youth mag., United Ch. Bd. for Homeland Ministries, Phila., 1972-75; affiliate rep. Ecumenical Community of Taizé, France, New Zealand, Australia, Indonesia, India and others, 1975-77; parish worker Temple Presbyn. Ch., Phila., 1978-83; pastor Old First Reformed Ch., United Ch. Christ, Phila., 1984—2003; assoc. conf. minister Pa. SE Conf. United Ch. Christ, 2003—. Bd. dirs. Met. Christian Coun. of Phila., 1985-96, 98—; chair Ch. and Ministry Com., Phila. Assn. United Ch. Christ, 1983-86; cons. Auburn Theol. Sem., N.Y.,, 1988-89; coord. 5-Day urban seminar for incoming students Lancaster Theol. Sem., 1986-93, The Small Ch. and Cultural Change, Bangor Theol. Sem., 1988; mem. adv. com. on evangelism and membership growth priority United Ch. Christ, 1989=90; team chair Toward the 21st Century, A Church-wide Planning Process for the United Ch. Christ, 1990-93; spkr. Faith Journey, consultation XVI in Parish Ministry for United Ch. Christ Clergy, Orlando, Fla., 1991; guest preacher Nat. Cathedral, Washington, 1993; commencement spkr. Lancaster Theol. Sem., 1996; sabbatical visitor to ch. in Indonesia through Common Global Mission Bd. (Disciples of Christ/United Ch. Christ), 2001. Author: Color Me Well, 1986, Christmas Comes Alive, 1988, Christmas in All Seasons, 1995; contbr. Women Pray, Karen Roller, Ed, 1986. Bd. dirs. Bethesda Project, Inc., Phila., 1986-98, Phila. Religious Leadership Devel. Fund, 1988-98, Maternity Care Coalition, Phila., 1999—; del. Gen. Synod-United Ch. Christ, Cleve., Ft. Worth, Providence, Kansas City, 1987-89, 99-2001; ecumenical del. Gen. Assembly Presbyn. Ch. (USA), 1989; adv. bd. Seamen's Ch. Inst., Phila., 1992-2003; trustee Lancaster Theol. Sem., 1992—; 2d v.p. Met. Christian Coun. Phila., 1998—. Named One of 85 People to Watch, Phila. Mag., 1985, One of 7 Clergy Leading U.S. Constl. Bicentennial Parade, 1987, Valiant Woman of Yr., Ch. Women United, 1991; recipient Human Rels. award, NCCJ, Phila., 1985; fellow Merrill fellow, Harvard Div. Sch., 1993. Mem. Nat. Orgn. of Women, Ch. Women United of Greater Phila., Old Phila. Clergy, Assn. United Arts and Religion, Phila. Assn. (ministrial standing). Democrat. Office: Old 1st Reformed Ch 151 N 4th St Philadelphia PA 19106 E-mail: gbutz@psec.org. *Being religious is so simple that as adults we find it hard to achieve. Children do it easily. We need to work with children so we don't destroy their natural religious inclination. The future of the faith lies in our ability to evoke the innate religious sensitivity in all people.*

BUTZ, OTTO WILLIAM, political science educator; b. Floesti, Romania, May 2, 1923; came to U.S., 1949, naturalized, 1959; s. Otto E. and Charlotte (Engelmann) B.; m. Velia DeAngelis, Sept. 13, 1961. BA, U. Toronto, 1947; PhD, Princeton U., 1953. Asst. prof. polit. sci. Swarthmore Coll., 1954-55; asst. prof. politics Princeton U., 1955-60; asso. editor Random House, N.Y.C., 1960-61; prof. social sci. San Francisco State Coll., 1961-67; academic v.p. Sacramento State Coll., 1967-69, acting pres., 1969-70; pres. Golden Gate U., 1970-92; pres. emeritus, 1992—. Author: German Political Theory, 1955, The Unsilent Generation, 1958, Of Man and Politics, 1960, To Make a Difference—A Student Look at America, 1967. Recipient Calif. State Colls. Outstanding Tchr. award, 1966 Mem. Am. Polit. Sci. Assn. Office: 536 Mission St San Francisco CA 94105-2921

BUX, WILLIAM JOHN, lawyer; b. Wadsworth, Ohio, Nov. 10, 1946; s. William J. and Helen M. (Sybelnik) B.; m. Linda Alice Zenar, Feb. 13, 1971. BSME, Ohio State U., 1969, MS, 1970; JD, So. Meth. U., 1977. Bar: Tex. 1977, U.S. Dist. Ct. (so. dist.) Tex. 1978, U.S. Ct. Appeals (5th cir.) 1978, U.S. Dist. Ct. (no. dist.) Tex. 1980, U.S. Dist. Ct. (ea. and we. dists.) Tex. 1981, U.S. Ct. Appeals (11th cir.) 1981, U.S. Supreme Ct. 1982; cert. Labor & Employment Law Tex. Bd. Legal Specialization. Assoc. Vinson & Elkins, Houston, 1977-85; ptnr. Hughes & Luce, Dallas, 1985-93; shareholder Locke Purnell Rain Harrell, Dallas, 1994-97; ptnr. Liddell, Sapp, Zivley, Hill & La Boon, Houston, 1997-98, Locke, Liddell & Sapp, Houston, 1999—. Author: Developing and Enforcing Drug and Alcohol Abuse Work Rules: A Primer for Texas Employers, 1984. Sec. So. Meth. U. Law Sch. Alumni Council, Dallas, 1986-88. Capt. USAF, 1971-74. Mem. ABA, Tex. Bar Assn. (chmn. labor and employment law sect. 1992-93), Houston Bar Assn., 5th Cir. Bar Assn. Republican. Roman Catholic. Home: 2511 Westgate St Houston TX 77019-6609 Office: Locke Liddell & Sapp 600 Travis St 3400 JP Morgan Chase Twr Houston TX 77002-3095

BUXBAUM, ALEXANDRA, photographer; b. Evanston, Ill., Mar. 1, 1962; d. Brigitte (Zenger) Kaeske; m. Michael Victor Buxbaum, Nov. 7, 1982. Student, Truman Coll., 1982-83, Columbia Coll., 1983-86. Photographer Pioneer Press, Wilmette, Ill., 1986-88, ADA, Chgo., 1988—, Black Star Pub. Co., N.Y.C., 1988—, Christian Sci. Monitor, Boston, 1988—, Kraft Gen. Foods, Glenview, Ill., 1989—, Agence France Presse, Washington, 1988—, L.A. Times, 1989—; freelance photographer Chgo., 1986—. Career day guest panel Forest Hosp., Des Plaines, Ill., 1988—, Women Employed, Chgo., 1989; manage support team of photographers for freelance work, 1993—; owner/operator Fine Art Gallery, 1995—; lectr. Skokie Photographic Soc., 1996; guest grant panelist Chgo. Dept. Cultural Affairs, 1999-2000; invited juror Art Fair, 1999-2000.

Exhibited in group show at Chgo. Pub. Libr., 1986; internat. pub. photographer in over 12 countries, 1993-2000. Recipient award of Excellence, Photographers Forum, 1986, award of Excellence, Northshore Art League, 1994, 95, 3rd place Brownsville Art League/Fine Art Mus.-Internat. Art Show, 1995. Mem. Women in Communications, Inc. Avocations: etching, drawing, writing, reading, swimming. Address: 1303 W Chicago Ave Chicago IL 60622-5706 E-mail: stolenbuick@hotmail.com.

BUXBAUM, RICHARD M. law educator, lawyer; b. 1930; AB, Cornell U., 1950, LLB, 1952; LLM, U. Calif., Berkeley, 1953; Dr. (hon.), U. Osnabrück, 1992, Eötvös Lorand U., Budapest, Hungary, 1993. Bar: Calif. 1953, N.Y. 1953. Practice law pvt. firm, Rochester, N.Y., 1957-61; prof. U. Calif., Berkeley, 1961—, dean internat. and area studies, 1993-99. Hon. prof. U. Peking, 1998. Editor-in-chief Am. Jour. Comparative Law. Property commn. mem. Found. for Responsibility, Remembrance, and the Future, Germany, 2001—. Recipient Humboldt prize, 1991, German Order of Merit, 1992, Officier Arts et Lettres, France, 1997, Order of Rio Branco, Brazil, 1998. Mem. AAAS, German Soc. Comparative Law (corr.), Coun. on Fgn. Rels. Office: U Calif Sch Law 888 Simon Hall Berkeley CA 94720-0001 E-mail: bux@uclink.berkeley.edu.

BUXBAUM, ROBERT C(OURTNEY), internist; b. Milw., Dec. 16, 1930; s. Edwin C. and Lillian (Tousman) B.; m. Ann S. Shocket, Dec. 26, 1955; children: Laura, Carl, Paula, Margaret. AB, Harvard U., 1952; MD, U. Pa., 1956. Diplomate Am. Bd. Internal Medicine, Am. Bd. Hospice and Palliative Medicine. Intern Henry Ford Hosp., Detroit, 1956-57; officer USPHS, San Carlos Apache Res., Ariz., 1957-59; resident, rsch. fellow U. Wis. Hosp., Madison, 1959-63; from rsch. assoc. to instr. Harvard Med. Sch., Boston, 1963-69, asst. prof. medicine, 1969—. Internist Harvard Cmty. Health Plan (now Harvard Vanguard Med. Assocs.), Boston, 1969—; cons. health policy; founding mem. Mass. Compassionate Care Coalition, 1999—, pres., 2003—. Author: Sports for Life, 1979; contbr. articles to profl. jours. V.p. Mass. Compassionate Care Coalition, 2000—03, pres.; chmn. Gov.'s Com. on Fitness, Mass., 1975—80. Fellow ACP. Mem. Am. Acad. Hospice and Palliative Medicine. Avocations: playing oboe, swimming, skiing. Office: Harvard Vanguard Med Assocs Faultner Hosp 1153 Centre St 6th Fl Boston MA 02130 E-mail: robert_buxbaum@hms.harvard.edu.

BUXTON, BARRY MILLER, museum director, historical author, educator; b. Blowing Rock, N.C., Aug. 5, 1949; s. Augustin Kinnard and Carrie (Miller) B.; m. Deborah Keyes, June 15, 1984; children: Loren Augustin, Peter I. BS, Appalachian State U., 1971, MA, 1973; PhD, U. Nebr., 1976. Cert. tchr., N.C. Dean Southeast C.C., Lincoln, Nebr., 1977-81; exec. dir., dir. press Appalachian Consortium, Boone, N.C., 1982-90; exec. dir. Health Adventure Mus., Asheville, N.C., 1991-95; dir. Mus. Health and Med. Sch., Houston, 1995-98; pres., CEO Eighth Air Force Heritage Mus., Savannah, Ga., 1998-2000; v.p. for instnl. advancement Savannah Coll. Art and Design, 2000—. Cons. Howard Hughes Med. Inst., Chevy Chase, Md., 1993-95, Girl Scouts U.S., N.Y.C., 1984; prin. rschr. Nat. Park Svc., Asheville, 1987-90; project dir. Nat. Humanities Coun., Washington, 1986-87. Author: (history) A Village Tapestry, 1989, Moses H. Cone, 1987, Mabry Mill Historic Study, 1989, The Brenegar Cabin, 1988. Trustee Tex. A&M U., Inst. Bioscis., Houston, 1996-98, YMCA, Savannah, Ga., 1998-99, Bethesda Home for Boys, 2000—, Lucas Theater, 2003—; mem. policy coun. Tex. Med. Ctr., Houston, 1995-98, chmn., 2003, chmn. bd. dirs.; bd. dirs. Conv. and Visitors Bur., Savannah, 1998-99, C. of C. Sanavannah, 2002—; bd. dirs. N.C. Health Alliance, 1993-95, Savannah Econ. Devel. Authority, 1998-99; v.p. Project ASSIST, 1994-95. Recipient Cmty. Historian of Yr. award N.C. Soc. Historians, 1989, Disting. Svc. award N.C. Soc. Historians, 1987; named Outstanding Fund Raiser, Nat. Soc. Fundrising Execs., 1996; Lovill fellow Appalachian State U., 1971. Mem. Houston Museums Assn. (v.p., 1996-98), N.C. Sci. Museums (v.p. 1993-95). Republican. Episcopalian. Avocations: tennis, bicycling, hiking, landscape architecture, history. Home: 114 W Gaston St Savannah GA 31401-4903 Office: PO Box 3146 a622 Dreyton St Savannah GA 31402-3146 E-mail: bbuxton@scad.edu.

BUXTON, DOUGLAS FRANCISCO, ophthalmologist, educator; b. N.Y.C., Nov. 5, 1952; s. Jorge Norman and Amalia (Gonzalez) B. BA, Yale U., 1975; postgrad., Columbia U., 1977; MD, Cornell U., 1982. Diplomate Am. Bd. Ophthalmology, Nat. Bd. Med. Examiners; diplomate in cataract/implant surgery, penetrating keratoplasty, and laser in situ keratomileusis Am. Bd. Eye Surgery. Intern St. Vincent's Hosp. and Med. Ctr., N.Y.C., 1982—83; resident N.Y. Eye and Ear Infirmary, N.Y.C., 1983—86, fellow in cornea and external disease, 1986—88, assoc. attending, 1986—; asst. attending surgeon dept. ophthalmology Manhattan Eye, Ear and Throat Hosp., N.Y.C., 1988—; clin. assoc. prof. ophthalmology N.Y. Med. Coll., 1991—. Contbr. articles to profl. jours. Fellow Am. Acad. Ophthalmology; mem. Am. Coll. Eye Surgeons, Am. Soc. Cataract and Refractive Surgeons, Castroviejo Cornea Soc., N.Y. Intra-Ocular Lens Implant Soc., Pan Am. Assn. Ophthalmology, N.Y. Keratorefractive Soc. Office: NY Eye and Ear Infirmary 310 E 14th St Ste 403 New York NY 10003-4201 Fax: (212) 353-5772.

BUYER, STEVEN EARLE, congressman, lawyer; b. Rensselaer, Ind., Nov. 26, 1958; m. Joni Geyer; children: Colleen, Ryan. BS in Bus. Adminstrn., The Citadel, 1980; JD, Valparaiso U., 1984. Officer Med. Svc. Corps U.S. Army, 1980, spl. att to U.S. Atty., 1984-87; atty., 1988—92; dep. atty. gen., 1987-88; legal counsel 22nd Theater Army, Saudi Arabia, 1990-91; legal advisor U.S Armed Forces/Western Enemy Prisoner of War Camps/War Crimes Interrogations, Saudi Arabia, 1991; mem. 103d Congress from 4th Ind. Dist., 1993—. Mem. com. on energy & commerce, U.S. Ho. of Reps.; mem. health, Energy and Air quality, environment & hazardous materials subcoms.; mem. com. on vet.'s affairs, chmn. subcom. oversights & investigations. Natl. Gaurd and Reserve Components Caucus Decorated Bronze Star. Republican. Office: US Ho Reps 2230 Rayburn HOB Washington DC 20515-1405*

BUYERS, JOHN WILLIAM AMERMAN, agribusiness and specialty foods company executive; b. Coatesville, Pa., July 17, 1928; s. William Buchanan and Rebecca (Watson) B.; m. Elizabeth Lindsey; children: Elsie Buyers Viehman, Rebecca Watson Buyers-Basso, Jane Palmer Buyers-Russo. BA cum laude in History, Princeton U., 1952; MS in Indsl. Mgmt., MIT, 1963. Div. ops. mgr. Bell Telephone Co. Pa., 1953-66; dir. ops. and personnel Gen. Waterworks Corp., Phila., 1966-68, pres., chief exec. officer Phila, 1971-75; v.p. adminstrn. Internat. Utilities Corp., Phila., 1968-71; pres., chief exec. officer, dir. C. Brewer and Co., Ltd., Honolulu, 1975—, chmn. bd., 1982—; chmn., CEO D. Buyers Enterprises, LLC, 2001—. Chmn. Calif. and Hawaiian Sugar Co., 1982-84, 86-90; pres., chmn. bd. Buyco, Inc., 1986—; mem. Hawaii Joint Coun. Econ. Edn., Japan-Hawaii Econ. Coun.; bd. dirs. BancWest, First Hawaiian Bank, John B. Sanfilippo & Sons, Inc., Outrigger Hotels and Resorts, ML Macadamia Orchards, L.P. Trustee U. Hawaii Found., Hawaii Prep. Acad., 1986—; chmn. bd. dirs. Hawaii Visitors Bur., 1990-91; mem. Gov.'s Blue Ribbon Panel on the Future of Healthcare in Hawaii; bd. dirs. Hawaii Sports Found., 1990-95; mem. adv. group to U.S. Dist. Ctr. With USMC, 1946-48. Sloan fellow MIT, 1962-63. Mem. Hawaiian Sugar Planters Assn. (chmn. bd. dirs. 1980-82, dir.), c. of C. Hawaii (chmn. bd. dirs. 1981-00), Nat. Alliance Bus. (chmn. Hawaii Pacific Metro chpt. 1978), Cap and Gown Club (Princeton), Hilo Yacht Club, Oahu County Club, Pacific Club, Waialae County Club, Prouts Neck (Maine) County Club, U.S. C. of C. (mem. food and gr. com. 1991—), Beretania Tennis Club. Presbyterian. Office: D Buyers Enterprises LLC PO Box 1826 Papaikou HI 96781-1826 E-mail: JWABuyers@dbuyers.com.

BUYNY, MARIANNE JO, eating disorders therapist, addictions counselor; b. Connellsville, Pa., Mar. 19, 1949; d. Marion Alyowich and Stella Louise (Sowinski) Marchewka; m. Jerome Michael Buyny, Oct. 21, 1972; children: Janean Estell, Jared Michael, Allison Victoria. BA in Psychology and Sociology, Alliance Coll., Cambridge Springs, Pa., 1971; MA in Psychology, Marywood Coll., Scranton, Pa., 1976; postgrad., C.C. Allegheny County, Pitts., 1985. Cert. allied addictions practitioner; cert. clin. criminal justice specialist, masters addictions counselors; cert. rsch. integrity. Med. social worker Schneider Home Health Care Agy., Inc., Pitts., 1985-87; mental health specialist Intercare, Hillside Psychiat. Ctr., McKeesport, Pa., 1987-91, Intercare, Lakewood Psychiat. Hosp., Canonsburg, Pa., 1991-95; psychol. specialist counselor III, Med. Ctr. U. Pitts. Med. Ctr., 1995—; clin. cmty. instr. U. Pitts., 1998—. Sr. rsch. assoc. Western Psychiat. Inst. and Clinic, Pitts., 1990—; therapist Willough at Naples, Naples, Fla., 1994-97; asst. dir. in tng. of Group Psychotherapy and Psychodrama, Pitts., 1991-96; reconstrn. therapist, Pitts., 1991-93; ednl. conf. cons. dialectical behavior therapy/coaching skills, 1998—; instr. C.C. Allegheny County, Pitts., 1985—. Mem. Dance Therapy Assn., Pi Gamma Mu, Lambda Alpha. Home: 978 Highfield Rd Bethel Park PA 15102-1071 E-mail: buynym@msx.upmc.edu.

BUYSE, LEONE KARENA, orchestral musician, educator; b. Oneida, N.Y, Feb. 7, 1947; d. Leonard Cornelius and Ione Esther (Hinman) B.; m. Michael Fanning Webster, Sept. 7, 1987. MusB, Eastman Sch. Music, Rochester, N.Y., 1968; MusM, Emporia (Kans.) State U., 1980; cert., Paris Conservatory, 1971. 2d flute and piccolo Rochester Philharm. Orch., 1971-78; asst. prin. flute San Francisco Symphony, 1978-83, Boston Symphony Orch., 1983-90, acting prin., 1990-93; prin. flute Boston Pops Orch., 1983-90; prof. flute U. Mich., Ann Arbor, 1993-97; prof. flute and chamber music Shepherd Sch. Music, Rice U., Houston, 1997—. Mem. faculty Boston U., 1983-93, Tanglewood Inst. of Boston U., Lenox, Mass., 1984-94, New Eng. Conservatory, 1988-93. Fulbright grantee, Paris, 1968-69. Mem. Nat. Flute Assn. (bd. dirs. 1985-86, conv. program chmn. 1987), Greater Boston Flute Assn. (founder, pres. 1992-93), Mu Phi Epsilon (winner internat. competition 1970), Pi Kappa Lambda. Avocations: physical fitness, gardening, vegetarian cuisine. Office: Rice University Shepherd Sch of Music PO Box 1892 Houston TX 77251-1892 E-mail: lbuyse@rice.edu.

BUYSSE, PAUL HENRI MARIA, trading company executive; b. Mar. 17, 1945; s. Eugene and Germain (Van Hecke) Buysse; children: Frank, Pia, Ann, Sophia, Thomas. Asst. to mng. dir., gen. mgr. Brit. Leyland, Antwerp, 1976-79; gen. mgr. Poclain Belgium, Aartselaar, 1979-81; mng. dir. Tenneco Belgium N.V., Aartselaar, 1981-88; regional dir. J I Case Benelux, Aartselaar, 1984-86, J I Case Europe North, 1986-88; group mng. dir. Hansen Transmissions Internat., 1988—. Group chief exec. BTR Industries Ltd., 1989, regional chief exec., 1994—98; dir. BTR Internat. Ltd., 1991; CEO Vickers plc, 1998—2000; chmn. Bekaert N.V., 2000. Named a Knight, Order of Leopold, Belgium, 1988, Cmdr., 2001, Cmdr. of the Brit. Empire, 1997, Baron, King Albert II of Belgium, 1998; named an Officer in the Order of Orange-Nassau, The Netherlands, 1994, Hon. Dean of Labour, Belgium, 1994, Officer in the French Nat. Order of Merit, 1996. Home: Sparrendreef 104 8300 Knokke Belgium Office: Bekaert N V Diamant Bldg A Reyerslaan 80 1030 Brussels Belgium

BUYST, ERIK CESAR, economic history educator; b. Schoten, Belgium, July 2, 1960; s. Adhemar D. and Eveline A. (Kerremans) B.; m. Helga A. De Doncker, Aug. 29, 1997. PhD in History, U. Leuven, Belgium, 1988; MA in Econs., Northwestern U., 1989. Sr. economist Kredietbank-Brussels, 1989-93; assoc. prof. U. Leuven, 1993-95, prof. econ. history, 1995—. Cons. in field. Author: An Economic History of Residential Building in Belgium, 1992; contbr. articles to profl. jours. Laureate, Belgium Royal Acad. Arts and Scis., Brussels, 1989. Mem. Fondation Univ. Brussels. Office: U Leuven Ctr Econ Studies Naamsestraat 69 B-3000 Leuven Belgium E-mail: erik.buyst@econ.kuleuven.ac.be.

BUZACOTT, JOHN ALAN, engineering educator; b. Sydney, N.S.W., Australia, May 21, 1937; emigrated to Can., 1967; s. Alan Ernest and Jean Elizabeth (Bingle) B.; m. Ursula Schulmerich, Sept. 7, 1963; children: Alan J., Kimberly A. BSc, U. Sydney, 1957, BE, 1959; MSc, U. Birmingham, Eng., 1962, PhD, 1967; Dr. honoris causa (hon.), Tech. U. Eindhoven, 2001. Engr. Associated Elec. Industries, Rugby, Eng., 1959-61; ops. research systems officer A.E.I. Hotpoint Ltd., London, 1963-64; asst. prof. U. Toronto, 1967-71, assoc. prof., 1971-77, prof., 1977-83, U. Waterloo, Ont., Can., 1984-91, York U., North York, 1991—2002, prof. emeritus, 2002—. Author: Scale in Production Systems, 1982, Stochastic Models of Manufacturing Systems, 1993; corr. editor: Canadian Jour. Info. Processing and Ops. Research, 1974-78. Mem. Can. Operational Rsch. Soc. (pres. 1983-84), Inst. for Ops. Rsch. and Mgmt. Sci., Prodn. and Ops. Mgmt. Soc. (pres. 1999). Home: 68 Divadale Dr Toronto ON Canada M4G 2P2 Office: York U Schulich Sch Bus North York ON Canada M3J 1P3 E-mail: jbuzacot@schulich.yorku.ca.

BUZAK, EDWARD JOSEPH, lawyer; b. Jersey City, Apr. 20, 1948; s. Edward and Nellie (Scalone) B.; m. Gail Marie Capizzi, July 24, 1971; children: Craig E., Lindsay T. BA, Union Coll., 1970; JD, Georgetown U., 1973. Bar: N.J. 1973, D.C. 1974. Assoc. Villoresi & Flanagan, Boonton, N.J., 1973-75; ptnr. Villoresi & Buzak, Boonton, 1976-82; pvt. practice, Montville, N.J., 1983—. Trustee Housing Partnership of Morris County, Morristown, N.J., 1992—. Contbr. articles to profl. jours. Chmn. affordable housing com., asst. counsel N.J. State League of Municipalities, Trenton, N.J., 1986—; asst. counsel N.J. Planning Ofcls., 1998-2000. Mem. Assn. Environ. Authorities (chmn. legis. com. 1986-2000), N.J. Inst. Local Govt. Attys.(pres.), N.J. Bar Assn. (chmn. local gov. com. 1985-87). Roman Catholic. Avocations: running, skiing, music, reading. Office: 150 River Rd Ste N4 Montville NJ 07045-8920

BUZALJKO, GRACE WILSON, retired editor; b. Cambridge, Mass., Nov. 4, 1922; d. Charles and Elizabeth (Douglas) Wilson; m. Ahmed Buzaljko, Mar. 9, 1963 (div. Mar. 1980). BA cum laude, St. Mary Coll., Leavenworth, Kans., 1944; postgrad., U. Pitts., 1945-46, New Sch. for Social Rsch., 1949-50. Promotions asst. Pitts. Press, 1945-48; manuscript editor John Wiley & Sons, N.Y.C., 1948-52, Harcourt Brace Jovanovich, N.Y.C., 1952-60, U. Calif. Press, Berkeley, 1960-67; adminstrv. editor Harcourt Brace Jovanovich, San Francisco, 1967-72; editor dept. anthropology U. Calif., Berkeley, 1973-88; ret., 1988. Editor: (books) Yurok Myths (A. L. Kroeber), 1976, Karok Myths (A. L. Kroeber and E. W. Gifford), 1980; contbr. articles to profl. jours. Co-clk. Berkeley Soc. of Friends Meeting, 1988—90. Mem.: AAUW (v.p., program chmn. Berkeley br. 1981—83, legis. chmn. 1988—94), Am. Anthrop. Assn., Miwok Archeol. Preserve of Marin. Avocations: gardening, walking. Home: Grand Lake Gardens 401 Santa Clara Ave Apt 219 Oakland CA 94610

BUZARD, DAVID ANDREW, lawyer; b. Evanston, Ill., Dec. 8, 1961; s. Clifford Howard and Mary Louise (Dole) B.; children: Clémentine, Victor. Student, Carleton Coll., 1980-82; BA in Linguistics, Northwestern U., 1984; JD, Tulane U., 1990. Bar: Ill. 1991, Va. 1997, U.S. Ct. Mil. Appeals 1991, U.S. Ct. Appeals (4th cir.) 1991, U.S. Dist. Ct. (ea. dist.) Va. 1997, U.S. Dist. Ct. (no. dist.) Ill. 1998, U.S. Supreme Ct. 1998; cert. qualified guardian ad litem for incapacitated adults, Va. Supreme Ct. Law clk. U.S. Atty.'s Office, New Orleans, 1988-90; judge advocate U.S. Navy, 1990-97; assoc. Glasser & Glasser, PLC, Norfolk, Va., 1997-98, Bennett & Zydron, P.C., Virginia Beach, Va., 1998—. Adj. asst. prof. Old Dominion U., 2002; lectr. law and ethics U.S. Joint Forces Staff Coll., 2002-03; counsel Alliance Française Chapitre de Grasse, Norfolk, Va., 1996—; judge Jessup Internat. Law Moot Ct. Competition, 1998. Contbr. articles to profl. jours. Lt. USN, 1990-97; lt. comdr. USNR, 1998—. Nat. Merit scholar. Mem. ATLA (fed. tort liability and mil advocacy sect., nursing homes litigation group), Va. State Bar (bd. govs. mil. law sect.), Virginia Beach Bar Assn., Va. Trial Lawyers Assn. (del. 2003—), Norfolk and Portsmouth Bar Assn. (founder, chair mil. law and lawyers com. 1997-2002, Walter E. Hoffman award 2001), Judge Advocates Assn., DAV, Naval Res. Assn., Pan European Orgn. Personal Injury Lawyers Avocations: civic activities, travel. Office: Bennett & Zydron PC 120 S Lynnhaven Rd Virginia Beach VA 23452 E-mail: dbuzard@bandzlaw.com.

BUZARD, JAMES ALBERT, healthcare management consultant; b. Warren, Ohio, Nov. 2, 1927; s. Milton Vogan and Mary Cora (Matthews) B.; m. Caroline L. Jansen, July 28, 1951; children: Catherine A. Sazdanoff, James M. BS, Kent (Ohio) State U., 1949; MA, U. Buffalo, 1951, PhD, 1954. Rsch. biochemist, then dir. R & D Norwich (N.Y.) Pharmacal Co., 1954—68; dir. devel., then exec. v.p. G.D. Searle & Co., Skokie, Ill., 1968—79, also bd. dirs.; exec. v.p. Merrell Internat./Richardson Merrell Inc., Wilton, Conn., 1979—81, Merrell Dow Pharm., Inc., Cin., 1981—89; v.p. corp. affairs, mergers & acquisitions Marion Merrell Dow Inc., 1989-90; ret., 1990; mgmt.-health care cons., 1990—. Bd. dirs. Meridian Diagnostics Inc., Cin.; chmn. emeritus Biostart, Cin., Ohio. Contbr. 40 articles to profl. jours. With USNR, 1945-46, 51-55. Named Ohio Entreprenuer Yr., 1998. Republican. Roman Catholic. Avocations: woodworking, golf, gardening, painting.

BUZARD, KURT ANDRE, ophthalmologist; b. Lakewood, Colo., Apr. 9, 1953; s. Donald Keith and Sonja Marie (Vik) B.; m. Carol Ann Moss, Aug. 4, 1989. BA in Math. and Physics, Northwestern U., 1975; MA in Applied Physics, Stanford, U., 1976; MD, Northwestern U., 1980. Diplomate Am. Bd. Ophthalmology, Nat. Bd. Med. Examiners. Intern medicine L.A. County-U. So. Calif. Med. Ctr., 1980-81; resident Jules Stein Eye Inst. UCLA, 1982-85; fellow cornea/refractive surgery Richard C. Troutman, MD, 1985-86; ophthalmologist, corneal specialist Las Vegas, Nev., 1986—. Staff physician Rancho Los Amigos Hosp., 1981-82; clin. asst. prof. div. ophthalmology dept. surgery U. Nev. Sch. Medicine, 1988—; clin. asst. prof. dept. ophthalmol. medicine Tulane U. Med. Ctr., New Orleans, 1991; med. dir. S.W. Eye Procurement Ctr., Las Vegas, 1989—; affiliate Humana Hosp.-Sunrise, 1989—, Las Vegas Surg. Ctr., 1989—, Las Vegas Surg. Ctr., Med. Ctr. So. Nev., 1989—; assoc. staff Valley Hosp., Las Vegas, 1986—; mem. med. adv. bd. Donor Orgn. Referral Svc.; internat. hon. advisor Tung Wah Ea. Hosp., Hong Kong, 1999-2003. Author: (with Richard Troutman) Corneal Astigmatism: Etiology, Prevention and Management, 1992, (with Miles Friedlander and Jean Luc Febbraro) The Blue Line Incision and Refractive Phacoemulsification, 2000; mem. editorial bd. Refractive and Corneal Surgery, 1992—; contbr. articles to profl. jours. Mem. Las Vegas C. of C., 1989. Recipient Rsch. award Jules Stein Inst., L.A., 1985. Fellow Am. Acad. Ophthalmology (Honor award 1999), Am. Coll. Surgeons; mem. Am. Soc. Cataract and Refractive Surgery, AMA, Assn. for Rsch. in Vision and Ophthalmology, Castroviejo Soc., Colombian Soc. Ophthalmology (corr.), Eye Bank Assn. of Am.-Paton Soc., Internat. Soc. for Eye Rsch., Internat. Soc. Refractive Keratoplasty (long-range planning com., alternative rep. to Am. Acad. Ophthalmology, bd. dirs. 1992-94), Pan Am. Assn. Ophthalmology, Pan Am. Implant Assn., Phi Eta Sigma, Phi Beta Kappa. Avocations: computers, photography. Office: 7135 W Sahara Ave Las Vegas NV 89117-2828

BUZASH, MICHAEL D. Romance languages educator; s. Mike and Flora (Urden) B. Student, U. Mex., Mexico City, 1952; BA in French and Spanish, Ind. State U., 1953; MA in Romance Langs., U. Western Res., 1960; postgrad., U. Wis., 1963-69; Cert. de Stage, Purdue U., 1984, 86, U. Wis., 1993, Mich. State U., 1994, U. Ill., 1995. Cert. superior rating Am. Coun. on Tchg. of Fgn. Langs., 1986. Tchr. French, Spanish, English Lawrence H.S., 1954-59; dir. pilot program in French and Spanish honors Lawrence Jr. H.S., 1956-57; dir. French honors program Ind. State U., summers 1980-97, assoc. prof. Romance langs., 1959-98. Del., presenter, chair internat. symposia; presenter in field; leader symposia and workshops. Author: Exercices Pratiques de Français Oral, 1983-90, Repetition et Acquisition Pratique, 1983-95, Revision Pratique de Français, 1980-96, honors edit., 1981, 89-90, 94-96; contbr. chpt. to book: From Third World to One World, 1988, Proceedings of Black Studies Conferences, 1989-91; contbr. papers and book revs. to varied rsch. procs. and profl. jours.; contbr. poetry to anthologies. Mem. Friends of Cunningham Libr.; v.p. Terre Haute Symphony Assn., 1970-72, 1965-67, Swope Art Mus., Indpls. Art Mus.; hon. mem. Hoosiers for Econ. Devel., 1982. Mem. AAUP, MMLA, Internat. Book Distbr. Ltd., Am. Translators Assn., Am. Assn. for Advancement of Core Curriculum, Am. Assn. Romanian Studies, Am. Assn. Tchrs. of French (Ind. chpt.), Am. Coun. on Tchg. of Fgn. Langs. (25-Yr. pin 1995), Ind. Fgn. Lang. Tchrs. Assn., European Studies Conf., Vigo County Ret. Tchrs. Assn. (treas. 2000--), Vigo Co. Hist. Soc. (life), Cen. States Conf. of Tchg. of Fgn. Langs., Univ. Club, Ind. State U. Alumni Assn. (charter life), Nat. Soc. of Sycamores, Masons, Blue Key (faculty advisor 1979-95), Phi Sigma Iota (life, sec. 1959-62, faculty advisor 1963-77, nat. v.p. 1971-75), Kappa Delta Pi, Theta Alpha Phi (awards for svc. and honor in tchg. 1969, 75, 89, 94, 96, 97, 98). Avocations: reading, traveling, gardening, translating, writing. E-mail: flbuza@isugw.indstate.edu.

BUZBEE, RICHARD EDGAR, retired newspaper editor; b. Fordyce, Ark., Aug. 16, 1931; s. Edgar Andrew and Helen Koester (Darling) B.; m. Marie Palmer, Apr. 16, 1955; children: Robert Edgar, William Bruce, James Palmer, John Richard. B.J., BA, U. Mo., 1954. Mgmt. intern Harris Newspaper Group, Chanute (Kans.) Tribune, Burlington (Iowa) Hawk-Eye, also Olathe (Kans.) News, 1957-63; editor, pub. Olathe News, 1963-79, Hutchinson (Kans.) News, 1979-93; ret. Hutchinson Pub. Co., 1993. Hon. chmn. bd. dirs. Hutchinson Pub. Co., 1993—; ptnr. Radine Enterprises, Olathe. Pres. Olathe C. of C., 1969, Olathe United Way, 1968, Johnson County chpt. ARC, 1978-79; chmn. Johnson County Scholarship Found., 1968; mem. Olathe Public Bldg. Commn. 1, 1964-65, 2, 1978-79; co-chmn. Olathe Home-for-Christmas from Vietnam Project, 1969-72; mem. bd. Hutchinson Public Library, 1980-87, chmn., 1982-83; bd. dirs. Hutchinson Symphony Assn., 1980-88, pres. 1987. Served to lt. (j.g.) USNR, 1954-57. Mem. Am. Soc. Newspaper Editors, William Allen White Found., Greater Hutchinson C. of C. (chmn. 1988), Rotary (bd. dirs. 1981-83), Phi Beta Kappa. Clubs: Rotary. (dir. 1981-83). Republican. Methodist. Home: 4 Crescent Blvd Hutchinson KS 67502-5541 E-mail: dick@buzbee.net.

BUZUNIS, CONSTANTINE DINO, lawyer; b. Winnipeg, Man., Can., Feb. 3, 1958; came to U.S., 1982; s. Peter and Anastasia (Ginakes) B. BA, U. Man., 1980; JD, Thomas M. Cooley Law Sch., 1985. Bar: Mich. 1986, U.S. Dist. Ct. (ea. and we. dists.) Mich. 1986, Calif. 1986, U.S. Dist. Ct. (so. dist.) Calif. 1987, U.S. Supreme Ct. 1993. Assoc. Church, Kritselis, Wyble & Robinson, Lansing, Mich., 1986, Neil, Dymott, Perkins, Brown & Frank, San Diego, 1987-94, ptnr., 1994—. Arbitrator San Diego County Mcpl. and Superior Cts.; judge pro tem San Diego Mcpl. Ct. Sec., treas. Sixty Plus Law Ctr., Lansing, 1985; active Vols. in Parole, San Diego, 1988—; bd. dirs. Hellenic Cultural Soc., 1993-98. Mem. Mich. Bar Assn., Calif. Bar Assn., San Diego County Bar Assn., Desert Bar Assn., So. Calif. Def. Coun., State Bar Calif. (gov. 9th dist. young lawyers divsn. 1991-94, 1st v.p. 1993-94, pres. 1994-95, bd. govs. 1995-96) San Diego Barristers Soc. (bd. dirs. 1991-92), San Diego Def. Lawyers Assn. (bd. dirs. 2003-), Risk Ins. Mgmt. Soc. (assoc.), San Diego Ins. Adjusters Assn. (assoc.), Pan Arcadian Fedn., Order of Ahepa (chpt. bd. dirs., v.p. 1995-98, chpt. pres. 2001—), Hellenic Cultural Soc., Phi Alpha Delta. Home: 3419 Overpark Rd San Diego CA 92130-1865 Office: Neil Dymott Perkins Brown & Frank 1010 2nd Ave Ste 2500 San Diego CA 92101-4959 Fax: 619-238-1562. E-mail: cbuzunis@neil-dymott.com.

BUZZARD, STEVEN RAY, lawyer; b. Centralia, Wash., May 22, 1946; s. Richard James and Phylis Margaret (Bevington) B.; m. Joan Elizabeth Merrow, Nov. 11, 1967; children: Elizabeth Jane, Richard Wolcott, James Merrow. BA, Cen. Wash. State Coll., 1972; postgrad., U. Wash., 1973; JD, U. Puget Sound, 1975. Bar: Wash. 1975, U.S. Dist. Ct. (we. dist.) Wash. 1976, U.S. Supreme Ct. 1979, U.S. Tax Ct. 1983. Assoc. Shires, Kruse, Wallace, Roper & Kamps, Port Orchard, Wash., 1975-77; ptnr. Buzzard & O'Connell, Centralia, 1978-80, Buzzard & Tripp, Centralia, 1980-94, Buzzard & Assoc., Centralia, 1994—. City atty. Mossyrock, Wash., 1979-94, Vader, Wash., 1989-96, Bucoda, Wash., 1989-99; judge Centralia, 1980-84, Winlock, Wash., 1983—; sec. Consol. Enterprizes Inc., Centralia, 1986-88; judge Chehalis (Wash.) Mcpl. Ct., 1998—, Winlock Mcpl. Ct., 1983—, Napavine Mcpl. Ct., 2001—, Vader Mcpl. Ct., 2001—; past pres. Reliable Enterprises, Inc. Chmn. bd. dirs. Lewis County Cmty. Svcs., Chehalis, Wash., 1981-84; bd. dirs. Lewis County United Way, 1993-95; mem. adv. bd. Centralia Sch. Dist., 1995—; founding mem., trustee, treas. Dollars for Scholars, Scholarship Found., 1997-2002. Mem. ABA (rural judges com. 1986), Wash. State Bar Assn. (ct. rules com. 1992-), Lewis County Bar Assn. (past pres.), Assn. Trial Lawyers Am., Wash. State Trial Lawyers Assn., Wash. State Govt. Lawyers Bar Assn. (former trustee), Wash. State Dist. and Mcpl. Ct. Judges Assn. (dist. and mcpl. rural judges com.), Wash. Bd. Jud. Adminstrn. (best practices com. 2001—, ct. improvement com., 2001-), Dist. and Mcpl. Judges Assn. (dist. and mcpl. rural judges com., ct. improvement com., long range planning com.), Kiwanis (pres.-elect 1991, pres. 1992-93, Disting. Past Pres. award 1994), Elks (trustee Centralia 1981—). Avocations: running, boating, hiking, biking, fishing. Office: Buzzard & Assoc 314 Harrison Ave Centralia WA 98531-1326 Fax: (360) 330-2078.

BUZZELLI, CHARLOTTE GRACE, educator; b. Mar. 21, 1947; d. Edmund Albert and Sarah Agnes (Russo) Buzzelli. BS, U. Akron, 1969, MS in Edn., 1976. Tchr. St. Anthony Sch., Akron, 1969-76; program coord., tchr. Akron Montessori Sch. Continuing Edn. Program, Eastwood Ctr., Akron, 1976-77; dir. edn. Fallsview Psychiat. Hosp., Ohio Dept. Mental Health, Cuyahoga Falls, 1977-92, developer job tng. partnership grant program and spl. needs handicapped grant program, 1992-97; tng. coord. N.E. regional & program educator children svcs. Ohio Dept. Mental Health State Operated Svcs., 1992—97. Spl. edn. svcs. developer and educator cmty svcs. div. North Coast Behavioral Healthcare Sys., Ohio Dept. Mental Health, 1997-2002; tchr. adult basic lit. edn. program Akron City Sch. Dist., 1992—; developer Akron City Schs. Project Rise Homeless Youth Family Literacy Program, 2001—; cons. in field; pioneered first spl. edn. program in Ohio for adult state psychiat. hosp.;

developed 1st community-based adult basic edn. program in state instn. in Ohio; program cons. state operated svcs. State of Ohio; participant U. Hawaii Study Tours Rsch. Projects, Internat. Edn. and East Asia Pi Lambda Theta Orient Study Tour, Manoa campus, 1990, spl. edn. rsch. U. Ark., 1976. Developer literacy evaluation program Project Rise Homeless Youth, Akron, Ohio, 1991—; mem. gospel meets Symphony chorus Akron Symphony Orch. Gospel Choir, 1996—; mem. choir Diocese of Cleve., St. John's Cathedral, Mass of Jubilee Gospel Choir, 1998, 2000. Named Ohio Tchr. of Yr., 1979; recipient A Key award, U. Akron, Urban Light award for outstanding svc., 2001, Cmty. Svc. Achievement award, Italian Am. Soc., Cmty. Collaboration award, Summit County Housing Network, 2003. Mem. CEC (coun. pres.), ASCD, Assn. Children with Learning Disabilities, Internat. Reading Assn., U. Akron Alumni Assn., Univ. Club, Akron Women's City Club, Coll. Club of Akron, Pi Lambda Theta (pres.), Phi Delta Kappa, Delta Kappa Gamma, Gamma Beta (pres.), Kappa Kappa Iota. Avocations: pet therapy to children and adults with disabilities, reading, travel, writing, singing, creating community resources for spl. edn. students and mental health clients. Home: 662 Dayton St Akron OH 44310-2301 Office: Adult Basic Literacy Edn Profl Devel Acad 785 Carnegie Ave Akron OH 44314

BUZZELLI, DENNIS KEVIN, mechanical engineer; b. Jersey City, Apr. 8, 1946; s. Albert F. and Mildred G. (Corrado) B. B of Engring., Stevens Inst. Tech., 1969; MSME, Poly. Inst. N.Y., 1973. Propulsion engr. Grumman Aero. Corp., Bethpage, N.Y., 1969-70; project engr. Ducon Co. divsn. U.S. Filter Corp., Mineola, N.Y., 1970-77, Metco Inc. divsn. Perkin-Elmer, Westbury, N.Y., 1977-83, East/West Ind., Farmingdale, N.Y., 1983-84, Airborn Instruments Lab. divsn. Eaton Corp., Farmingdale, N.Y., 1984-89, Radiation Dynamics, Inc., Farmingdale, NY, 1989—91; mgmt. info. sys. data input, programming and supr. Nassau Case Mgmt., Hicksville, NY, 1993—98; with Centura Group Inc., Farmingdale, NY, 1998—. Patentee plasma spray nozzle, electronic module locking mechanism. Mem. ASME (Stevens chpt. v.p. 1968-69), AIAA. Roman Catholic. Home: 38 Fairway Dr Old Bethpage NY 11804-1740 E-mail: dennisbu@juno.com.

BUZZELLI, JAMES RAYMOND, pharmaceutical company executive; BSBA, U. S.C. 1992; postgrad. Oxford (Eng.) U., 1999; MBA, Wake Forest U., Winston-Salem, N.C., 2000. Sales mgr. Pioneer Electronics, Charlotte, N.C., 1993-97; product mgr. Pharmacia Corp., Peapack, N.J., 1997-2001; sr. product mgr. Orgonon Inc., West Orange, NJ, 2001—.

BUZZI, RUTH, comedienne; b. Westerly, R.I., July 24, 1936; d. Angelo Peter and Rena Pauline (Macchi) B.; m. Kent Perkins, Dec. 10, 1979. Student, Pasadena Playhouse Coll. of Theatre Arts, 1954-57; pvt. study dance, drama and voice. Appeared on Broadway in Sweet Charity; appeared in N.Y. theater prodns. including Misguided Tour; network TV appearances include Garry Moore Show, Rowan and Martin's Laugh-In, Dean Martin Roasts, Trapper John, M.D., Medical Center, Alice, The Entertainers, Carol Burnett and Friends, Flip, Donnie and Marie, The Dean Martin Comedy Hour, Tony Orlando and Dawn, Day of Our Lives, Passions, 2003, The Jamii Foxx Show, Diagnosis Murder, The Muppet Show, Sesame Street, That Girl, The Monkees, Saved By the Bell, Love Boat, The Munsters Today, Masquerade, Adam 12, Major Dad, Here's Lucy; films include Freaky Friday, 1972, Skatetown, U.S.A., 1977, The Apple Dumpling Gang Rides Again, 1979, The Villain, 1979, The North Avenue Irregulars, 1979, Surf II, 1984, Bad Guys, 1986, Dixie Lanes, 1988, Diggin Up Business, 1990; TV movies In Name Only, 1969; featured commedienne in mus. revues; filmed TV commls. for various sponsors. Recipient Golden Globe award, Image award NAACP; named to R.I. Hall of Fame; inducted into Broadcasting Hall of Fame; nominee 5 Emmy awards. Mem. DAR (hon.). Address: c/o AMR Ste 438 5042 Wilshire Blvd Los Angeles CA 90036

BYAM, M(ARIE) ELIZABETH, data processing management consultant; b. Cooperstown, N.Y., Oct. 31, 1949; d. Harmon Leigh and Elizabeth Virginia (Baldo) B. BA, Ga. State U., 1972; postgrad., Columbia So. Sch. Law, 1976-78; MBA, U. N.Mex., 1997. Cert. Systems Profl. Programmer Coastal States Life Ins. Co., Atlanta, 1973-75; programmer, analyst So. Airways, Atlanta, 1975-76; cons. computer programming Atlanta, 1978-82; sr. cons., field mgr. Computer Dynamics, Woodland Hills, Calif., 1983-84; owner, prin. cons. MEB Assocs., Winnetka, Calif., 1984-92; enterprise applications program mgr. Intel Corp., Rio Rancho, N.Mex., 1992-97; dir. bus. solutions Explore Reasoning Systems, 1998—2001. Frequent speaker on career planning and info. processing techs. for schs., profl. confs. and meetings. Guest co-host Ms. Biz radio show, 1987. Bd. dirs. Opera Guild So. Calif., Los Angeles, 1984-88. Mem. Data Processing Mgmt. Assn. (publs. dir. L.A. chpt. 1988, treas. 1989, pres. 1990, nat. chair legis. affairs com. 1990-91), Assn. Women in Computing (pres. L.A. chpt. 1985-87, nat. conf. chmn. 1986), Project Mgmt. Inst., Sierra Club. Republican. Avocations: reading sci. fiction and mysteries, film. Office: 3771 Mazewood Ln Fairfax VA 22033-1342 E-mail: ebyam@msn.com.

BYARS, MERLENE HUTTO, accountant, visual artist, writer, publisher; b. West Columbia, SC, Nov. 8, 1931; d. Gideon Thomas and Nettie (Fail) Hutto; m. Alvin Willard Byars, June 10, 1950 (dec.); children: Alvin Gregg, Robin Mark, Jay C., Blaine Derrick; m. Fred W. Klutzow, Dec. 10, 1999. Student, Palmer Coll., Midlands Tech., U. S.C., 1988—; diploma in Journalism, Internat. Corr. Sch., 1995, Longridge Writers Group, 1995. Acct. State of SC, 1964-93; ret., 1993; pres. Merlene Hutto Byars Enterprises, Cayce, 1993—. Designer Collegiate Licensing Co., US Trademark, 1989—; mem. Thinktank for Ret. Employees, U. SC Edn. Found., 1998-2003. Pub. Lintheads, 1986, Olympia-Pacific: The Way It was 1895-1970, 1981; Did Jesus Drive a Pickup Truck, 1993, Fate, Faith and Fortitude, 2003; The Plantation Era in South Carolina; pub., produr. (play) Lintheads and Hard Times, 1986; creator quilt which hung in SC State Capital for bicentennial celebration, 1988, designer Saxe Gotha Twp. Flag, 1993; author: The State of South Carolina Scrap Book, Orangeburg District, 1990, A Scrap Book of SC, Dutch Fork, Saxe Gotha, Lexington County, 1994, The Plantation Era of SC, 1996; exhibited art at Oxford (Eng.) U., 1997, Internat. Congress on Arts and Comm., 1997, Sonesta Hotel, New Orleans, 1998—; exhibited art and book From My Scrap Book of the State of SC, Xlibris publ. new book by Merlene Hutts Byars (Klutzow), 2003, Fate, Faith and Fortitude, Life of F.W. Klutzaw, MD., Four Seasons, The Ritz, 1999—; exhibited genealogy and art work St. John's Coll., Cambridge U., July 15-22, 2001. Life mem. Women's Missionary Soc., United Luth. Ch., 1954—; mem. edn. found. U. SC, 1969-93; treas. Airport HS Booster Club, 1969-76; sec. Saxe Gotha Hist. Soc., Lexington County, 1994-96; mem. USC Edn. Found., Think-Tank for 2001 fundraising campaign/ret. faculty and staff, 1998-2001; rep. Cayce Hist. Com. at Am. Biographical Inst./Internat. Biographical Ctr. Congress, New Orleans, 1998. Recipient numerous awards for quilting SC State Fair, 1976—, Cert. for rose rsch. test panel Jackson and Perkins, 1982, Foremost Women in Comm. award, 1969-70, Cayce Amb. award, City of Cayce, 1994. Fellow Internat. Biog. Assn. (dep. dir. gen. 1999—), U. SC Soc., U. SC Thomas Cooper Libr. Soc.; mem. Cayce Mus. History (contbr. books, award for contribution 1987), SC State Mus., Town and Country Assn., Univ. SC Soc., Nat. Mus. Women in the Arts, Kiwanis Internat. Avocations: history, geneologist, reading, sewing, traveling. Home: PO Box 3387 West Columbia SC 29171-3387 E-mail: needle1@msn.com.

BYARS, WALTER RYLAND, JR., lawyer; b. Birmingham, Ala., Oct. 5, 1928; s. Walter Ryland and Essie (Hopper) B.; m. Mildred Lucile Rhodes, Dec. 22, 1950; children: Debra Leigh Byars Patterson, Walter Ryland III, Rebecca Lynn Byars Pradat, John Baxter. BS, U. Ala., 1948, LLB, 1952, JD, 1969. Bar: Ala. 1952, U.S. Ct. Appeals (5th and 11th cirs.), U.S. Dist. Ct. (no., mid. and so. dists.) Ala., U.S. Supreme Ct. Pvt. practice, Troy, Ala., 1953-57; atty. legal dept. So. Bell. Tel. & Tel. Co., Atlanta, 1957-59, gen. atty. Birmingham, 1959-68; ptnr. Steiner, Crum & Baker, 1968—; city atty. Montgomery, Ala., 2002—; ptnr. Steiner, Crum & Byars, PC, Montgomery, 2003—. Bd. editors Ala. Law Rev., 1951-52. Lt. (j.g.) USNR, 1952-53. Fellow Am. Bar Found., Internat. Soc. Barristers (gov. 1977-83, sec.-treas. 1979-80, 2d v.p. 1980-81, 1st v.p. 1981-82, pres. 1982-83), Am. Coll. Trial Lawyers; mem. ABA (Young Lawyers past mem. exec. council, com. chmn.), Ala. Bar Assn. (pres.-elect 1983-84, pres. 1984-85, past pres. Young Lawyers, past sect. chmn., past com. chmn.), Pike County Bar Assn. (past pres.), Birmingham Bar Assn. (past com. chmn.), Montgomery County Bar Assn. (past com. chmn., bd. dirs. 1976-79, v.p. 1978, pres. 1979), Ala. Law Inst. (council), Montgomery Area Com. of 100, Masons, Sigma Chi, Phi Alpha Delta. Methodist. Home: 1744 Fairforest Dr Montgomery AL 36106-2602 Office: Regions Bank Bldg PO Box 668 Montgomery AL 36101-0668 E-mail: wbyars@steinercrum.com.

BYAS, TERESA ANN URANGA, customer service representative, interior designer; b. Plainview, Tex., Mar. 20, 1955; d. Adam T. and Lucy (Sandoval) Uranga; m. Wesley W. Byas, Sept. 11, 1972 (div. 1992); children: Chad W., Christina Ann. Student, Tex. Wesleyan U., 1983—, Tarrant County Coll., Ft. Worth, various yrs., student, 95, 97, 99. Teller Allied Nat. Bank (now named 1st Interstate), Ft. Worth, 1985-87, Nowlin Savs. and Loans (now named Comerica), Ft. Worth, 1987-88; missionary United Meth. Ch. Global Bd. World Missions, Brazil, 1988-91; asst. mgr. Bag 'n Baggage, Ft. Worth, 1991-92, store mgr., 1992-93; med. record clerical coord. Total Home Health Svcs., Inc., Ft. Worth, 1993-94; nurses aide Total Home Svcs. In Med. Home Health, 1994-96, Nurture Care, Ft. Worth, 1995-96; customer svc. staff Home Depot, Ft. Worth, 1996-98, 1998-2000, interior decorator Pembroke Pines, Fla., 2000, design cons. Arlington, Tex., 2000—. Mem. Women's Polit. Caucus, Ft. Worth, United Meth. Women's Group; hon. mem. Westcliff United Meth. Women's Group (chpt. named in her honor 1991); mem. Brother Sister Orgn., Ft. Worth. Mem. Am. Bus. Women's Assn. Democrat. Avocations: photography, reading, writing, fluent in spanish and portuguese. Home: 2509 Spanish Trail Apt 313 Arlington TX 76016 Office: Design Cons 4611 S Cooper St Arlington TX 76017

BYBEE, CHARLES FORREST, writer, poet; b. Davis County, Iowa, May 28, 1920; Grad., Capitol Radio Engring. Inst., Washington, 1948. Engr. CIA, Washington; freelance writer, poet Winter Haven, Fla. Author: One Man's Family, 1995, Life is a Poem, 2002; contbr. poetry to nat. anthologies and newspapers. Address: Apt 411 1225 Havendale Blvd NW Winter Haven FL 33881-1388

BYBEE, JAY SCOTT, judge, federal agency administrator; b. Oakland, Calif., Oct. 27, 1953; s. Rowan Scott and Joan (Hickman) B.; m. Dianna Jean Greer, Feb. 15, 1986; children: Scott, David, Alyssa, Ryan. BA, Brigham Young U., 1977, JD, 1980. Bar: D.C. 1981, U.S. Ct. Appeals (4th cir.) 1983, U.S. Supreme Ct. 1985, U.S. Ct. Appeals (5th cir.) 1986, U.S. Ct. Appeals (2d, 9th, 10th and D.C. cirs.) 1987. Law clk. to judge U.S. Ct. Appeals (4th cir.), 1980-81; assoc. Sidley & Austin, Washington, 1981-84; atty. advisor U.S. Dept. Justice, Washington, 1984-89; assoc. counsel to Pres. of U.S. The White House, 1989-91; prof. law La. State U., Baton Rouge, 1991-98, U. Nev., Las Vegas, 1999—2000; asst. atty. gen. off. legal counsel U.S. Dept. Justice, Washington, 2001—02; judge U.S. Ct. Appeals (9th cir.), San Francisco, 2003—. Contbr. articles to profl. jours. Missionary Mormon Ch., Santiago, Chile, 1973-75. Edwin S. Hinckley scholar, Brigham Young U., 1976-77. Mem. Phi Kappa Phi. Avocations: piano, all sports, reading. Office: US Ct of Appeals PO Box 193939 San Francisco CA 94119-3939*

BYBEE, PAUL JOSEPH, zoologist, educator; b. Ogden, Utah, June 2, 1952; m. Shirley I.M. Bybee. AS, Weber State U., 1981, BSc in Zoology, 1984; MSc in Ecology, Brigham Young U., 1991, PhD in Zoology, Vertebrate Paleontology and Evolution, 1997. Assoc. prof. sci. Utah Valley State Coll., Orem, Utah, 2000—03, prof., 2003—. Home: 320 E 1075 N Springville UT 84663-3133

BYBEE, RODGER WAYNE, science education administrator; b. San Francisco, Feb. 21, 1942; s. Wayne and Mary Genevieve (Mungon) B.; m. Patricia Ann Brovsky, May 28, 1966. BA, Colo. State Coll., 1966; MA, U. No. Colo., 1969; PhD, NYU, 1975. Tchr. sci. Greeley (Colo.) Pub. Schs., 1965-66; instr. sci. U. No. Colo., Greeley, 1966-70; teaching fellow NYU, N.Y.C., 1970-72; instr. edn. Carleton Coll., Northfield, Minn., 1972-75, asst. prof., 1975-81, assoc. prof., chmn. dept., 1981-85; assoc. dir. Biol. Scis. Curriculum Study, Colorado Springs, 1986-95, acting dir., 1992-93; exec. dir. Ctr. Sci., Math. and Engring. Edn. NRC, Washington, 1995-99; exec. dir. BSCS, Colorado Springs, Colo., 1999—. Mem. adv. bd. for sci. assessment Nat. Assessment Ednl. Progress, Princeton, N.J., 1987-89, 92-93, 95-96; mem. adv. bd. Social Sci. Edn. Consortium, Boulder, Colo., 1987-90; chairperson working group on curriculum NRC project on Nat. Sci. Ednl. Stds., 1993-95; chmn. Sci. Framework 2006, Orgn. Econ. Coop. and Devel., Paris, France. Author: numerous books; contbr. numerous articles to profl. jours. NSF grantee, 1986—. Fellow AAAS (mem.-at-large 1987-90, chair sect. Q 1993-94, coun. del.), Nat. Assn. Rsch. Sci. Teaching (rsch. coord. 1986-89). Home: PO Box 563 Frisco CO 80443-0563 Office: BSCS 5415 Mark Dabling Blvd Colorado Springs CO 80918-3842 E-mail: rbybee@bscs.org.

BYCZKOWSKI, JANUSZ ZBIGNIEW, toxicologist; b. Gdansk, Poland, May 29, 1947; came to U.S., 1979; s. Stanislaw and Halina (Osterczy) B.; m. Janina K. Slosarska, Aug. 6, 1977; children: Ian S., L. Peter. MSc in Toxicology, Acad. Medicine, Gdansk, 1970, PhD in Pharmacology, 1975, DSc in Biochem. Pharmacology, 1979. Diplomate Am. Bd. Toxicology. Cancer rsch. scientist dept. exptl. therapeutics Roswell Park Meml. Inst., Buffalo, 1979-80, 1985-87; adj. asst. prof. pharmacology Acad. Medicine Gdansk, 1980-83; pharmacologist and dir. of pharmacy Internat. Red Cross and Red Crescent, Tobruk, Libya, 1983-84; asst. prof. and rsch. scientist Coll. Pub. Health U. South Fla., Tampa, 1987-91; project scientist and study dir. ManTech. Environ. Tech., Inc., Dayton, Ohio, 1991-98; sr. toxicologist TN&A Inc., Cin., 1998-99, ind. cons., 1999—; health risk assessment specialist Ohio EPA, Columbus, 2000—. Editorial reviewer Bull. Environ. Contamination and Toxicology, Reno, Nev., 1989—, Free Radical Biology and Medicine, Baton Rouge, 1989—, Placenta, Manchester, Eng., 1991—; dean Polish Sect. N.Y. Coll. Advanced Studies, 2002—; hon. prof. Albert Schweitzer Internat. U., 2000—. Contbr. articles to profl. publs., chpts. to books. Active mem. Solidarity, Poland, 1980-83. Recipient Rsch. award 1st degree Sci. Soc. Gdansk, 1975, Polish Pharmacol. Soc., 1977, Ministry Health and Social Welfare of Poland, 1977. Mem. AAAS, Soc. for Rsch. on Polyunsaturated Fatty Acids (pres. 6th sci. meeting 1992—, travel grantee 1992), N.Y. Acad. Scis., Oxygen Soc., Soc. Toxicology, Soc. for Risk Analysis (councilor Ohio chpt. 1994—). Achievements include finding mechanism of action of DDT on mitochondrial respiration; discovery of NAD-Dependent mode of action of vanadium, co-oxygenation of benzopyrene by lipoxygenase; developing physiologically-based pharmacokinetic model for lactational transfer of chemicals; consulting for U.S. Govt. Home: 212 N Central Ave Fairborn OH 45324-5006 E-mail: jbyczkowski@netscape.net.

BYCZYNSKI, EDWARD FRANK, lawyer, financial executive; b. Chgo., Mar. 17, 1946; s. Edward James and Ann (Ruskey) B.; children: Stefan, Suzanne. BA, U. Wis., 1968; JD, U. Ill., 1972; Cert. de Droit, U. Caen (France), 1971. Bar: Ill. 1972, U.S.Dist. Ct. (no. dist.) Ill. 1972, U.S. Supreme Ct. 1976. Title officer Chgo. Title Inst. Co., 1972-73; ptnr. Haley, Pirok, Byczynski, Chgo., 1973-76; pres. Alderstreet Investments, Portland, Oreg., 1976-82, Nat. Tenant Network, Portland, 1981—. Asst. regional counsel SBA, Chgo., 1973-76; pres. Bay Venture Corp., Portland, 1984—. Contbr. articles to profl. jours. Mem. ABA, Ill. Bar Assn. Independent. Home: PO Box 2377 Lake Oswego OR 97035-0614 Office: 525 1st St Ste 105 Lake Oswego OR 97034-3100 E-mail: efb@ntnnet.com.

BYE, KERMIT EDWARD, federal judge, lawyer; b. Hatton, N.D., Jan. 13, 1937; s. Kermit Berthrand and Margaret B. (Brekke) Bye; m. Carol Beth Soliah, Aug. 23, 1958; children: Laura Lee, William Edward, Bethany Ann. BS, U. N.D., 1959, JD, 1962. Bar: N.D. 1962, U.S. Dist. Ct. N.D. 1962, U.S. Ct. Appeals (8th cir.) 1969, U.S. Supreme Ct. 1974, Minn. 1981. Dep. securities commr. State of N.D., 1962—64, spl. asst. atty. gen., 1964—66; asst. U.S. atty. U.S. Atty.'s Office, Dist. N.D., 1966—68; ptnr. Vogel Brantner Kelly Knutson Weir & Bye, Fargo, ND, 1968—2000; judge U.S. Ct. Appeals (8th cir.), Fargo, 2000—. Contbr. articles. Chmn. Red River Human Svcs. Found., 1980—83; S.E. Mental Health and Retardation Ctr., Inc. Fellow: Am. Bar Found.; mem.: ABA (state del. 1986—95, bd. govs. 1999—2001, state del. 2002—), Minn. Bar Assn., Cass County Bar Assn., N.D. State Bar Assn. (pres. 1983—84). Lutheran. Office: 655 1st Ave N Ste 330 Fargo ND 58102

BYE, MICHAEL ROBERT, pulmonologist, educator; b. Bklyn., N.Y., July 30, 1948; children: Sarah Elizabeth, Rachel Peninah, Naomi Chana, Ezra Samuel. BA, SUNY, Buffalo, 1970, MD, 1976. Diplomate Nat. Bd. Med. Examiners. Intern, resident in pediat. Children's Hosp. Buffalo, NY, 1976—79, fellow, pediatric pulmonology, 1979—82; asst. prof. pediat. Temple U., Phila., 1982—85; assoc. prof. pediat. Albert Einstein Coll. Medicine, Bronx, NY, 1985—94; prof. clin. pediat. Columbia U., New York, NY, 1994—. Acting dir., pediatric pulmonary medicine Morgan Stanley Children's Hosp. of N.Y. Presbyn., N.Y.C., NY, 1997—; dir., pediatric pulmonary medicine Albert Einstein Coll. Medicine, Bronx, NY, 1985—94; guest editor Pediatric Annals; editl. bd. Pediatric Pulmonology. Contbr. chapters to books, articles and revs. to profl. jours. Treas. Teaneck Baseball Orgn., NJ, 1998. Fellow: ACP, Am. Coll. Cardiol. Physicians; mem.: Assn. Am. Physicians. Achievements include research in early descriptions of diagnosis and pattern of lung disease in children with AIDS. Avocation: softball coaching. Office: Columbia U/ Childrens Hosp 3959 Broadway CH7S New York NY 10032 E-mail: mb255@columbia.edu.

BYE, RANULPH DEBAYEUX, artist, author; b. Princeton, NJ, June 17, 1916; s. Arthur Edwin and Mary C. (Heldring) B.; m. Mary DuBois McCarty, May 24, 1941 (div. 1981); children: Dennis L., Barbara D., Stephen G., Catherine M.; m. Glenna C. Lange, Oct. 16, 1983. Diploma, Phila. Mus. Sch. Indsl. Art, 1938; student, Art Students League, N.Y.C., 1940-41; D Pub. Svc. (hon.), Bucks County C.C., Newtown, Pa., 1994. Assoc. prof. painting Moore Coll. Art, Phila., 1949-79. Condr. watercolor workshop in Eng. and Ireland, 1987, Maine Coast Art Workshop, 1990. One-man shows include Newman Galleries, Phila, Hahn Gallery, Phila., Woodmere Art Mus., Chestnut Hill, Phila., 2002; retrospective at Woodmere Art Mus., 2002; group shows Am. Watercolor Soc., Allied Artists, NYC, NAD, Phila. Waercolor Club; represented in permanent collections Smithsonian Instn., Davenport, Iowa, Mcpl. Art Gallery, Reading, Pa., James A. Michener Art Mus., Doylestown, Pa., Pub. Mus., Temple U. Sch. Pharmacy, Phila., Munson, Williams Proctor Inst., Utica, NY, Mus. Fine Arts, Boston, William Penn Mus., Harrisburg, Pa.; author, illustrator: The Vanishing Depot, 1973, rev. edit., 1983, 3d edit., 1994, Ranulph Bye's Bucks County, 1989, Ranulph Bye's Collection of Old Firehouses, 2000; author: (with Margaret Bye Richie) Victorian Sketchbook, Painting Buildings in Watercolor, 1994. Served with U.S. Army, 1942-45. Recipient numerous awards including Gold medal Nat. Arts Club, 1963, Nat. Arts Club Award, 1988, Newman Galleries award, Mems.' Show award NJ Water Color Soc., 1991, 3d award with merit Pa. Watercolor Soc., Keystone medal and award, 1996, Patrons Purchase award Watercolor U.A.S., Springfield, Mo., 1997, Salmagundi members' medal, 1999. Mem. NAD (nat. academician 1994, cert. of merit, Adolph and Clara Obrig prize 1993), Am. Watercolor Soc. (6 awards 1964-92, Dolphin Allow 1985), Phila. Watercolor Club (Franklin Mint award 1988, 90, Savoir Faire prize 1993), Allied Artists Am. (Strathmore award 1986, Henry Gasser Meml. award 1989), Nat. Acad. N.Y., Salmagundi Club (34 awards 1958—), Phila. Water Color Soc. (disting.). Mem. Soc. Of Friends. Home: PO Box 362 Mechanicsville PA 18934-0362 *I felt fortunate in being able to pursue a career of my own choice; painting and interpreting my enviornment in landscape and genre subjects. I am a watercolorist in the tradition of American realism— the impressionist school of Sargent and Homer. My concern for architectural preservation caused me to publish two books on this theme. One with illustrations of bygone railroad stations and another on Victorian structures, hoping to enlighten the public's awareness of our architectural heritage.*

BYEARS, LATASHA, professional basketball player; b. Aug. 12, 1973; Student, N.E. Okla. A&M Jr. Coll., 1992—94; grad., DePaul U., 1996. Basketball player Faenza, Italy, 1996—97, Beskijas, Turkey, 1996—97; basketball player Sacramento Monarchs Women's NBA, 1997—. Vol. Meals on Wheels. Office: Sacramento Monarchs One Sports Pky Sacramento CA 95834

BYEFF, PETER DAVID, hematologist, oncologist; b. Nov. 27, 1948; s. Herbert Isaac and Ruth Helen (Wolfe) B.; m. Gail Schneider, Apr. 2, 1982. BA, U. Pa., 1970; MD, Johns Hopkins U., 1974. Diplomate Am. Bd. Internal Medicine (subcert. in med. oncology and hematology), Nat. Bd. Med. Examiners. Intern Georgetown U. Hosp., Washington, 1974-75, resident in internal medicine, 1975-77; vis. fellow in hematology and oncology Columbia-Presbyn. Med. Ctr., N.Y.C., 1977-81, Damon Runyon-Walter Winchell oncology fellow, 1977-81. Instr. Coll. Physicians and Surgeons, Columbia U., N.Y.C.; assoc. prof., attending physician U. Conn.; attending physician Bradley Meml. Hosp., Southington, Conn., New Britain (Conn.) Gen. Hosp., med. dir. George Bray Cancer Ctr.; sr. investigator Gynecologic Oncology Group; prin. investigator Eastern Cooperative Oncology Group, Nat. Surg. Bowel and Breast project. Office: Bradley Med Bldg 55 Meriden Ave Ste 1-a Southington CT 06489-3237 also: 40 Hart St New Britain CT 06052-1743

BYEKWASO, SERAPIO, statistician, researcher; s. John Muwanga and Anastansia Namuli. BS in Stats., Makerere U., Kampala, Uganda, 1985; MS in Statis. Computing, Am. U., Washington, 1989; PhD in Stats., Am. U., 1994. Instr. Am. U., 1991—94; statis. cons. World Bank, Washington, 1994—95; instr. U. New Orleans, 1995—97; sr. statistician Conway/Milliken and Assocs., Chgo., 1997—98; rsch. specialist Nat. Data Corp., Newtown, Pa., 1998—99; dir. mktg. scis. Rsch. Internat., Chgo., 1999—. Contbr. Fellow, UN, 1987—89. Mem.: Am. Mktg. Assn., Am. Statis. Assn. Roman Catholic. Home: 5650 N Sheridan Rd Chicago IL 60660 Office: Rsch Internat Ste 2511 875 N Michigan Ave Chicago IL 60660 Office Fax: 312-787-4156. Personal E-mail: sgkwby1@aol.com. E-mail: s.byekwaso@research-int.com.

BYER, DIANA, performing arts company executive; b. Trenton, NJ, Aug. 31, 1946; d. Fred and Norma (Handis) B. Student, Juilliard Sch., 1964—66. Soloist Manhattan Festival Ballet, N.Y.C., 1972, Les Grands Ballet Canadiens, Montreal, Can., 1975; dir. Ballet Sch. of N.Y., N.Y.C., 1978—, N.Y. Theatre Ballet, 1978—. Dir., founder Project LIFT scholarship program for children living N.Y.C. homeless shelters, 1989—. Helen Weiselberg scholar Nat. Arts Club, 1988, 90, 93 Achievements include being subject of Lincoln Ctr. presentation Dreams on a Shoestring, 1992. Office: NY Theatre Ballet 30 E 31st St New York NY 10016-6825 E-mail: balletfore@aol.com.

BYER, HAROLD GEORGE, civil/environmental engineer; b. Phila., May 23, 1943; s. Harold G. and Estelle (Mirtz) B.; m. Susan C. Buchter, Apr. 24, 1976. AS in Engring., Cmty. Coll. Phila., 1972; BS in Civil Engring., Drexel U., 1975; MS, U. Pa., 1997. Sect. chief, engr. U.S EPA, Phila., 1975-87; project dir., mgr. R.F. Weston, Inc., West Chester, Pa., 1987-95; project dir. DuPont Environ. Remediation, Wilmington, Del., 1995-96; ind. environ. cons. Phila., 1997—. Policy adviser U.S. EPA, 1984-86. Adv. coun. Frankford Hosp., Phila., 1987-97; dir. Northwood Civic Assn., Phila., 1986-89; pres. Pa. State Ch. Youth Orgn., 1980-81. Served in U.S. Army, 1965-69, PTO, Korea, Japan. Mem. ASCE (bd. dirs. 1977-81), NRA, Nat. Soc. Tax Profls., Am. Water Works Assn., Masons., Rep. Nat. Com. Presbyterian. Avocations: skiing, photography, fishing, backpacking, geology. Home: 1129 Allengrove St Philadelphia PA 19124-2901

BYER, ROBERT LOUIS, applied physics educator, university dean; b. Pasadena, Calif., May 9, 1942; s. Herbert Louis and Wilfrie (Schulz) B.; m. Eva Maria Guzsella, Aug. 15, 1964; children: Scott, Douglas, Mark, Evi-Lynn. BA in Physics, U. Calif., Berkeley, 1964; MS in Applied Physics, Stanford U., 1967, PhD in Applied Physics, 1969. Scientist Spectra Physics, Mountain View, Calif., 1964-65; asst. prof. Stanford (Calif.) U., 1969-74, assoc. prof., 1974-79, prof., 1979—, chair dept. applied physics, 1980-83, assoc. dean humanities and sci., 1984-86, dean rsch., 1987-92, chair dept. applies physics, 2000—. Bd. dirs. Lightwave Electronics Corp., Mountain View, Polystor, Gen. Lasertronics Corp. Contbr. 350 articles to profl. jours.; holder over 30 patents. Recipient Arthur L. Schawlow Awd. 1998, NAS award 2000. Fellow IEEE (millennium medal 2000), AAAS, Am. Phys. Soc., Optical Soc. Am. (Adolph Lomb medal 1972, bd. dirs. 1986-89, v.p. 1992, pres.-elect 1993, pres. 1994); mem. NAE, Lasers and Electro-Optic Soc. (pres. 1984), Calif. Coun. on Sci. and Tech. (vice chmn.). Office: Stanford University Dept of Applies Physics Stanford CA 94305 E-mail: Byer@Stanford.edu.

BYER, THEODORE SCOTT, accountant; b. Trenton, N.J., Oct. 2, 1957; s. Fred and Norma (Handis) B.; m. Marcy Pam Steier, Aug. 8, 1981; children: Sarah, Tara, Hallie. BA, Muhlenberg Coll., 1979; MBA, Rider Coll., 1986. CPA; cert. fin. planner. Auditor State of N.J., Trenton, 1979-80; staff acct. Louis H. Linowitz and Co., Trenton, 1980-82; supr. Amper, Politzner & Mattia, Flemington, N.J., 1982-88; tax mgr. Price Waterhouse, N.Y.C., 1988-90; sr. mgr. Salomon & Co., P.C., N.Y.C., 1990-94; ptnr. Mintz, Rosenfeld & Co., Fairfield, N.J., 1994—. Co-author: Taxation of Foreign Nationals in the United States, 1990; editor: Selecting and Installing Medical Practice Computer Software, 1996. Fellow N.J. State Soc. CPAs (co-founder Hunterdon-Warren chpt.); mem.

AICPA, N.Y. State Soc. CPAs. Avocations: avid reader, music, computers. Home: 87 Cedar Ln Berkeley Heights NJ 07922-2400 Office: Mintz Rosenfeld & Co 60 Route 46 E Fairfield NJ 07004-3007 E-mail: tbyer@mintzrosenfeld.com.

BYERLY, CARL WESLEY, music educator, academic administrator; b. Columbus, Ohio, Apr. 6, 1960; s. Donald Byerly and Patricia Ann Shank; m. Thayer Jeannine Simar, Oct. 22; children: Carl Weston, Neiman Christian. BA in Ch. Music, Jackson Coll. Ministries, Jackson, Miss., 1981; B in Music Edn., Miss. Coll., Clinton, 1983; MA in Music, U. Tex., Tyler, 1985; PhD in Choral Conducting, Clayton U., Mo., 1987. Cert. music tchr. Mich. Music dir. South Flint Tabernacle, Mich., 1991—97, Tabernacle Christian Acad., Mich., 1991—97; prof. music Mott C.C., Flint, Mich., 1991—93; founder, coord. Midwest Music Ministry Encounter, Pontiac, Mich., 1991—2001, Mich. Charter Sch. Fine Arts Camp, Grand Blanc, Mich., 2000—; adminstr. fine arts Woodland Park Acad., Grand Blanc, 1997—; prof. music U. Mich., Flint, 1993—. Chmn. music divsn. Spring Fest Arts Festival, Grand Blanc, 2000—03; head choral dir. Music In the Parks/Flint Symphony Orch., 1992—; bd. dirs., music dept. Grand Blanc Arts Coun., 1999—; pianist for Pres. Gerald Ford, 1976; dir. U. Mich. Gospel Choir, Flint; numerous nat. TV performances. Dir.(exec. prodr.): (recording CD) Colorblind/U, Mich. Flint Gospel Choir, 2001 (nomination outstanding choir Nat. Gospel Truth Mag. Music awards, Las Vegas, 2002), Come On Home, 1996; musician: (recording) Make a Joyful Noise, 1978 (Grammy award nomination, 1979); performer: Nat. Stellar Awards, 2002. Hon. bd. dirs. Gospel Music Workshop of Am., Flint, 1998—2002. Recipient Drum Major award, Mayor of Flint, 1996. Mem.: Mich. Elem. and Mid. Sch. Prins. Assn. Republican. Apostolic. Avocations: fishing, hunting, antiques. Home: 1459 Wiggins Rd Fenton MI 48430 Office: Woodland Park Acad 9127 S Saginaw Rd Grand Blanc MI 48430

BYERLY, RADFORD, JR., science policy official; b. Houston, May 22, 1936; s. Radford and Garvis N. (Cook) B.; m. Kathryn Jester, May 13, 1960 (div. 1980), children: Laura, Hamilton, Charles; m. Carol Ann Ries, Apr. 10, 1987. BA, Williams Coll., 1958, MA, 1960; PhD, Rice U., 1967. Sr. engr. No. Rsch. & Engring. Co., Cambridge, Mass., 1961-63; postdoctoral fellow U. Colo., Boulder, 1967-69, dir. Ctr. for Space and Geoscis. Policy, 1987-91; physicist, mgr. Nat. Bur. Standards, Washington, 1969-75; mem. profl. staff com. on sci. and tech. U.S. Ho. of Reps., Washington, 1975-87, chief of staff, com. on sci. and tech., 1991-93; v.p. pub.policy U. Corp. for Atmosphere Rsch., Boulder, 1993-94; dir. Roberts Inst., Boulder, 1993-94; vis. scholar Ctr. for Sci. and Tech. Policy Rsch., 2001—. Mem. space sta. adv. com. NASA, 1988-91, space sci. adv. com., 1987-91, 93-98; mem. adv. com. on space launch industry OTA, 1993-95; mem. bd. assessment NIST NAS, 1993-2000, mem. NAS com. on Dept. Energy peer rev. 1997-98, mem. com. environ. R & D, 2000-01, mem. com. on staged respository strategies, 2001-03; hon. lectr. Mid-Am. State Univs. Assn., 1988-89. Editor Space Policy Reconsidered, 1989, Space Policy Alternatives, 1991, Prediction: Science, Decision Making, and the Future of Nature, 2000; contbr. articles to profl. jours. NSF fellow, 1963-67. Fellow AAAS (com. on sci. engring. and pub. policy 1998—); mem. AIAA (chmn. civil space subcom. 1988-89), Assn. Univs. Rsch. in Astronomy (bd. dirs. 1998—, pers. policy com. 2002—), Am. Phys. Soc., Phi Beta Kappa, Sigma Xi (pres. U. Colo. chpt. 1995-97). Avocations: skiing, hiking, gardening. Home: 3870 Birchwood Dr Boulder CO 80304-1419 E-mail: hrbyerly@comcast.net.

BYERRUM, RICHARD UGLOW, college dean; b. Aurora, Ill., Sept. 22, 1920; s. Earl Edward and Florence (Uglow) B.; m. Claire Somers, Apr. 3, 1945; children: Elizabeth, Mary, Carey. AB, Wabash Coll., 1942, D.Sc. (hon.), 1967; PhD, U. Ill., 1947. Teaching asst. U. Ill., 1942-44; research asso. U.S. Chem. Corps, toxicity dept. U. Chgo., 1944-47; faculty Mich. State U., East Lansing, 1947—, prof. biochemistry, 1957-91, prof. emeritus, 1991—; acting dir. Mich. State U. (Inst. Biology and Medicine), 1961-62; dean Mich. State U. (Coll. Natural Sci.), 1962-86. Author: (with others) Experimental Biochemistry, 1956; Editorial bd.: (with others) Phytochemistry, 1961-81; Contbr. (with others) numerous articles to profl. jours. Mem. Project Hope, 1961— ; Trustee Mich. Health Council, 1961—, pres., 1966. Travel grantee Internat. Congress Biochemistry, Vienna, 1958; Travel grantee Internat. Congress Biochemistry, Montreal, 1959 Mem. Am. Chem. Soc. (lectr. vis. scientist program, awards com., visitor for com. profl. tng.), N. Central Assn. Colls. and Secondary Schs., A.A.A.S., Am. Soc. Plant Physiologists (trustee, exec. com.), Am. Soc. Biol. Chemists, Soc. Exptl. Biology and Medicine, Mich. Acad. Arts, Sci. and Letters, Phi Beta Kappa (pres. local chpt. 1962), Sigma Xi (awards com., Jr. Research award Mich. State U. chpt. 1958), Phi Kappa Phi (pres. 1968-69), Phi Lambda Upsilon, Alpha Chi Sigma, Beta Theta Pi. Achievements include patent in cancer tumor inhibiting material. Home: 2407 Sapphire Ln East Lansing MI 48823-7264

BYERS, CHARLES FREDERICK, public relations executive, marketing executive; b. Johnstown, Pa., Jan. 30, 1946; s. Walter Hayden and Mary Ann Elizabeth (Succop) B.; m. Vicki Louise Beard, June 3, 1967 (div. Apr. 1992); children: Natalie L., Tamara N., Valerie A.; m. Janette Lanora Buck, Apr. 23, 1993. BS in Journalism, Ohio U., 1968; MA in Mass Comm., U. Tex., 1969. Gen. reporter Springfield (Ohio) Daily News, 1967-68; promotion specialist GE, Chgo., 1969-71; account supr. Burson-Marsteller, Chgo., 1971-78; group v.p. Carl Byoir & Assocs., Chgo., 1978-82, gen. mgr. Atlanta, 1982-85; pres. Camp-Byers Pub. Rels., Atlanta, 1985-91; client svc. dir. Kalman Comm., L.A., 1991-92; v.p., COO Hayes Pub. Rels., San Jose, Calif., 1992-95; mktg. comms. mgr. Actel Corp., Sunnyvale, Calif., 1995-98; dir. comm. TSMC, San Jose, 1998—2002, dir. worldwide brand mgmt., 2002—. Pres. Hoffman Estates (Ill.) Jaycees, 1976; dir., treas. Brookcliffe Home Owners Assn., 1988-89; comm. chair Ga. Heart Assn., Atlanta, 1990; bd. dirs. NorCal Lacrosse Found., 1999, 2000. Recipient Golden Trumpet, Chgo. Publicity Club, 1980, Golden Quill (award for excellence in bus. comm. programming), Internat. Assn. Bus. Comm., 2000. Mem. Pub. Rels. Soc. Am. (accredited pub. rels. practitioner, bd. dirs. Silicon Valley chpt. 1993, v.p. chpt. 1994, pres.-elect 1995, pres. 1996, del. nat. assembly 1997, 99, bd. dirs. L.A. chpt. 1992, Silver Anvil award 1978, 2000, Compass award Bay Area chpts. 1997, 2000, North Pacific Dist. del. 2001), Fabless Semiconductor Assn. (chair program com. 2002-03). Avocations: lacrosse official, golf, photography, tennis, tropical fish. Office: TSMC USA 2585 Junction Ave San Jose CA 95134

BYERS, ELIZABETH, education educator; b. Cedar Rapids, Iowa, Mar. 22, 1964; d. Charles A. Byers and Mary Ann Hetherington-Byers. BA in Music, BA in English and Speech, Coe Coll., 1986; MA in Rhetorical Studies, U. Iowa, 1988, MA in English Edn., 2002. Tchg. asst. in pub. speaking U. Iowa, Iowa City, 1987—88, rsch. asst., 1987, tchg. asst. bus. and profl. speaking, 1987—88, art history teaching asst., 2000; English/speech instr. Kirkwood C.C., Iowa City, 1988—89; English and speech instr. Mt. Mercy Coll., Cedar Rapids, 1989—93; elem. edn. instr. Iowa Wesleyan Coll., Mt. Pleasant, 2001—. ESL tutor Kirkwood C.C., Iowa City, 1988—93, Mt. Mercy Coll., 1988—93; pub. speaking cons., Iowa City, 1988—93. Grad. student editor: Basil Blackwell Companion, 1989; editor: Communicating, 1992, author web page for postsecondary tchrs. Vol. Habitat for Humanity, Iowa City, 1999—2001, Cath. Worker House, Cedar Rapids, 1990—93. Mem.: DAR (Good Citizenship award 1982), Mu Phi Epsilon, Pi Lambda Theta (Teaching Excellence award 2001), Phi Beta Kappa. Home: PO Box 156 Morning Sun IA 52640-0156

BYERS, FRANK MATTHEW, surgeon; b. Bridgeport, Conn., Mar. 30, 1933; s. Matthew Francis and Esther H. (Rosson) B.; m. Patricia Hauft; 1 child, Robert R. Grad., Duke U., 1955, MD, 1958. Surg. intern and resident Duke U. Hosp.; resident U. Fla.; pvt. practice surgery St. Petersburg, Fla., 1965-98; ret., 1998. Fellow ACS, Am. Coll. Chest Physicians; mem. Internat. Soc. Cardiovasc. Surgeons, Soc. Thoracic Surgeons, So. Thoracic Surg. Assn., Alpha Omega Alpha. Avocations: boating, golfing, motorcycling. E-mail: ByersF@aol.com.

BYERS, GEORGE WILLIAM, retired entomology educator; b. Washington, May 16, 1923; s. George and Helen (Kessler) B.; m. Martha Esther Sparks, Feb. 25, 1945 (div. 1953); children: George William, Carolyn Sylvia; m. Gloria B. Wong, Dec. 16, 1955; children: Bruce Alan, Brian William, Douglas Eric. BS, Purdue U., 1947; MS, U. Mich., 1948, PhD, 1952. Asst. prof. dept. entomology U. Kans., Lawrence, 1956-60, curator Snow Entomol. Mus., 1956-83, dir., sr. curator, 1983-88, assoc. prof., 1960-65, prof. entomology, 1965-88, prof. dept. systematics and ecology, 1969-88, chmn. dept. entomology, 1969-72, 84-87, ret., 1988. Vis. prof. Mountain Lake Biol. Sta. U. Va., alt. summers, 1961-92, U. Minn. biol. sta., 1970. Author: several book chpts.; contbr. articles to profl. jours. With U.S. Army, 1942-46, 53-56, WWII and Korea; lt. col. M.S.C., USAR, ret. Rackham fellow U. Mich., 1952-53; NSF grantee, 1958-87, 97-99. Mem. Entomol. Soc. Am. (editl. bd. Annals 1967-72, chmn. 1971-72), Entomol. Soc. Can., Ctrl. States Entomol. Soc. (pres. 1958-59), Entomol. Soc. Washington, Soc. Systematic Biology (editor Syst. Zool. jour. 1963-66), Phi Beta Kappa, Phi Kappa Phi, Sigma Xi. Avocations: invertebrate paleontology, photography, ornithology. Home: 909 Holiday Dr Lawrence KS 66049-3006 Office: U Kans Entomology Divsn Natural History Mus Lawrence KS 66045-7523 E-mail: ksem@ku.edu.

BYERS, KEITH THOMAS, librarian, educator; b. Laurel, Miss., Nov. 13, 1952; s. Theodore Kenneth and Alma Gladys B. ABA, Orangeburg-Calhoun Tech. Coll., 1973; BS in Mech. Engring., S.C. State U., Orangeburg, 1980, MEd in Maths., 1988; M in Libr. and Info. Scis., U. S.C., 1999; MDiv in Ministry, Erskine Theol. Seminary, 1997. Cert. tchr., S.C., cert. librarian S.C. Libr. Bd. Security guard Pinkerton's Inc., Orangeburg, 1973-80; devel. mech. engr. Bell Telephone Labs., Norcross, Ga., 1980-84; libr. asst. Erskine Coll. and Sem., Due West, S.C., 1997, Luth. Theol. So. Sem., Columbia, S.C., 1998-99; libr. intern S.C. State U., Orangeburg, 1999; reference dept. Orangeburg Co. Pub. Libr., 2000—. Contbr. articles to Christian Observer; inventor test probe, hand tool. Mem.: ALA, Travelers Protective Assn., SC Libr. Assn., Am. Theol. Libr. Assn., Am. Forestry Assn. (life), Clowns of Am. (life), Alpha Kappa Mu. Presbyterian. Avocations: electronics, fishing, gardening, mechanics, woodworking. Home: 1635 Central St Orangeburg SC 29115-3321

BYERS, MATTHEW T(ODD), lawyer, educator; b. Ridley Park, Pa., May 30, 1963; s. Richard Lynn and Joyce Ann (Ralston) B.; m. Lori Byers; children: Amanda Michelle, Amber, Helen, David, Saren, Loren. BA, U. N. Mex., 1985, JD, 1990. Bar: N.Mex. 1990, U.S. Dist. Ct. N.Mex. 1991, U.S. Ct. Appeals (10th cir.) 1991, U.S. Tax Ct. 1991, Pa. 1997. Staff Los Alamos (N.Mex.) Nat. Lab., 1989—90; assoc. Marek, Francis & Byers, P.A., Carlsbad, N.Mex., 1990—2001, ptnr., 1998—2001; assoc. Forry, Ullman, Ullman & Forry, Reading, Pa., 1997; pvt. practice Matthew T. Byers, Carlsbad, N.Mex., 2001—. Assoc. editor N. Mex. U. Law Review, 1990. Bd. dirs. United Way of Carlsbad, 1990-93. Recipient Cert. of Achievement Renaissance Program, Carlsbad, 1991. Mem. ABA, State Bar Assn. N.Mex., Eddy Cty. Bar Assn. (pres. 1993), George L. Reese Jr. Inn of Court, Pa. Bar Assn. Democrat. Baptist. Avocations: softball, music, reading. Office: 211 W Mermod Carlsbad NM 88220

BYERS, NINA, physics educator; b. Los Angeles, Jan. 19, 1930; d. Irving M. and Eva (Gertzoff) B.; m. Arthur A. Milhaupt, Jr., Sept. 8, 1974 (dec.). BA in Physics with highest honors, U. Calif., Berkeley, 1950; MS in Physics, U. Chgo., 1953, PhD, 1956; MA, U. Oxford, Eng., 1967. Research fellow dept. math. physics U. Birmingham, Eng., 1956-58; research assoc., asst. prof. Inst. Theoretical Physics and dept. physics Stanford, 1958-61; asst. then assoc. prof. physics UCLA, 1961-67, prof. physics, 1967—. Mem. Sch. Math., Inst. Advanced Studies, Princeton, N.J., 1964-65; ofcl. fellow Somerville Coll., Oxford, 1967-68, Janet Watson vis. fellow, 1968-74; faculty lectr., mem. dept. theoretical physics Oxford U., 1967-74, sr. vis. scientist, 1973-74; official fellow and tutor in physics, Somerville Coll. John Simon Guggenheim Meml. fellow, 1964-65, Sci. Rsch. Coun. fellow Oxford U., 1978, 85. Fellow AAAS (mem-at-large physics sect., com. on freedom and responsibility 1983-86), Am. Phys. Soc. (councillor-at-large 1977-81, panel pub. affairs 1980-83, vice-chmn. forum on physics and soc. 1981-82, 2002--, chmn. 1982-83, vice-chmn. forum on history of physics 2002-03, chair-elect, 2003--); mem. Fedn. Am. Scientists (nat. coun. 1972-76, 78-80, exec. com. 1974-76, 78-80). Achievements include research in theory of particle physics and superconductivity; history of physics; contributions of 20th century women to physics. Office: U Calif Dept Physics Los Angeles CA 90095-0001

BYERS, PAUL HEED, television news producer, consultant; b. Balt., Mar. 6, 1943; s. Paul Horatio and Corinne May (Gardner) B.; m. Frances Regina Barbour, June 10, 1967. BA, Am. U., 1966; MS with honors, Columbia U., 1967. Reporter, cameraman Sta. WTOP-TV, Washington, 1961-65; assignment editor, prodr. Post-Newsweek Stas., Washington, 1969-74; asst. assignment editor CBS News, Washington, 1974-75, dep. fgn. editor N.Y.C., 1975-78, bur. mgr., 1978-83, prodr., 1983-85; coordinating prodr. NBC News, Washington, 1985-87; pres. Gateway Video Svcs. Inc., Washington, 1987—; assoc. prof. comms. Marymount U., Arlington, Va., 1988—. Dir. Health Vols. Overseas, Washington, 1986-89. With U.S. Army, 1967-69. Columbia U. internat. fellow, 1966-67. Mem. Nat. Press Club, Sigma Delta Chi, Kappa Tau Alpha. Episcopalian. Avocations: camping, photography, sailing. Office: Gateway Video Svcs Inc 5418 Hawthorne Pl NW Washington DC 20016-2667

BYERS, STEVEN JOHN, health facility administrator; b. Branson, Mo., Aug. 27, 1959; s. John Benjamin and Saundra June Byers; m. Anita Eileen Reed, Nov. 19, 1983; children: Matthew Reed, Alyssa Noelle. BS in Bus. Comm., S.W. Mo. State U., 1981; MPA, U. Mo., Kansas City, 1984. Cert. fund raising exec. Profl. Cert. Bd., Alexandria, Va., 1998. Rsch. dir. Kansas City (Mo.) Consensus, 1984—87; dir. pub. and regional affairs Children's Mercy Hosp., Kansas City, 1987—95, sr. dir. devel. adminstrn., 1995—. Author: The Life of Your Time, 2001 (Booklist Top 10 Christian Novels, 2001). Mem.: Assn. Fund Raising Profls.

BYERS, WALTER, athletic association executive; b. Kansas City, Mo., Mar. 13, 1922; s. Ward and Lucille (Hebard) B.; children: Ward, Ellen, Frederick. Student, Rice U., 1939-40, U. Iowa, 1940-43. News reporter United Press Assn. (later U.P.I.), St. Louis, 1944, U.P.I., Madison, Wis., 1945, sports editor Chgo., 1945, asst. sports editor N.Y.C., 1946-47; also fgn. sports editor; dir. Big Ten Conf. Service Bur., Chgo., 1947-51; exec. asst. NCAA, Chgo., 1947-51, exec. dir., 1951-52, Kansas City, Mo., 1952-73, Shawnee Mission, Kans., 1973-87, exec. dir. emeritus, 1988-90. Pres. Byers Seven Cross Ranch, Inc., Emmett, Kans., 1974—, Ironwood Seven Cross Ranch, Inc., Hatfield, Mo., 1992-2002, Volland, Kans., 2002—, Byers Land and Cattle Co., Mission, Kans., 1996—; mgr. Byers Ranches, Limited Liability Co., 1997. With M.C. AUS, 1944. Home and Office: PO Box 96 Saint Marys KS 66536

BYFIELD, BERT A. conservative humanitarian novelist; b. Lansing, Mich., Mar. 9, 1943; s. Virgil Albert and Frances Mary Pitts; m. Theresa Anne Baldassare, Dec. 2, 1972 (div. Dec. 1996); children: Cyndee, Maria, Catherine, Charity; m. Barbara Lloyd Scott, May 16, 1998. Author Caravela Books, Henrietta, N.Y., 1995—. Author: Rage of the Bear, 1995, Scream of the Eagle, 1999, Last Stand at Perekop, 2001, Father Gregory, 2003, Koba, 2003. Organizer Computer People for Peace, 1968-70. With USN, 1960-64. Russian Orthodox. Avocations: computer programming, computer games. Office: Caravela Books 134 Goodburlet Rd Henrietta NY 14467-9503 E-mail: bbww@caravelabooks.com.

BYFIELD, RITA RAE, nursing educator, family nurse practitioner; b. Bartlesville, Okla., Mar. 30, 1950; d. Bill R. and Beverly A. (Loper) Nichols; m. Michael U. Byfield, May 31, 1969; children: Sean, Kristi, Katee. ADN, Tulsa Jr. Coll., 1977; BSN, Pittsburg (Kans.) State U., 1989; MEd in Health Occupations, U. Cen. Okla., 1993; MS in Nursing/Family Nurse Practitioner, Pittsburg (Kans.) State U., 1997. RN, Okla., Kans.; cert. ACLS; cert. nurse oper. rm., CPR instr.; advanced RN practitioner. Operating room nurse Jane Phillips Med. Ctr., Bartlesville, 1976; nursing asst. III St. Francis Hosp., Tulsa, 1974; allied health instr. Tri-County Vocat. Sch., Bartlesville, Okla., 1990, practical nursing instr., 1991-94; nursing prof., nurse practitioner Okla. Wesleyan U., 1994-2000; family nurse practitioner Coffeyville (Kans.) Regional Med. Ctr., 2000—; adj. nursing prof. BSN completion program So. Nazarene U., Tulsa, 2000—. Named New Health Profl. of Yr. Okla. Vo-Tech. System, 1994. Mem.: ANA, Pittsburg State U. Nursing Alumni (bd. dirs. 1992—2000, sec.), Okla. Vocat. Edn. Assn., Okla. Nurse Practitioners Assn., Okla. Nursing Assn., Am. Acad. Nurse Practitioners, Am. Acad. Nurse Practitioners, Am. Coll. Nurse Practitioners, Kappa Delta, Gamma Upsilon Nursing Honor Soc., Sigma Theta Tau. Home: 912 S Cherokee Ave Bartlesville OK 74003-5024 E-mail: ritaraern@aol.com.

BYFORD, EMMA, rancher; b. Marlin, Tex., Jan. 30, 1918; d. Joseph and Emma (Conner) Watkins; m. Ray Homan Byford, Sept. 2, 1937 (dec. 1980). Stenographer, sec. Waco (Tex.)-McLennan County Health Unit, 1944-50; sec. to plant mgr. Owens-Illinois Glass Co., Waco, 1950-54; co-owner, office mgr. Byford Machine & Tool, Waco, 1956-76; owner Byford Ranch, Clifton, Tex., 1963—. Methodist.

BYINGTON, DIANE B. social work educator; b. Atlanta, Sept. 5, 1951; d. Claude H. and Ruth (Singleton) B.; 1 child, Joel Blum. BA, Calif. State U., 1974; MSW, Fla. State U., 1977, PhD, 1982. Clin. counselor Med. U. of S.C., Charleston, 1974-75; program evaluator Apalachee Mental Health, Tallahassee, 1977-80; program adminstr. Dept. Adminstrn., Tallahassee, 1982-83; rsch. assoc. Fla. State U., Tallahassee, 1983-84; program mgr. Health & Rehabilitative Svcs., Tallahassee, 1984-86; asst. prof. East Carolina U., Greenville, N.C., 1986-89; assoc. prof. U. Denver, 1989—. Democrat. Mem. Boulder Friends

BYKANOV, ALEXANDER N. research scientist; b. Moscow, Apr. 20, 1957; arrived in U.S., 1998; s. Nickolay Bykanov and Valentina Bykanova; m. Svetlana A. Laricheva, Oct. 15, 1977 (div. Aug. 1987); 1 child, Denis; m. Lioudmila G. Barkova, Oct. 8, 1987. BS, MS, Moscow Inst. Physics and Tech., 1980, PhD of Physics, 1988. Engr. Sci. Prodn. Assn. Istok, Fryazino, Russia, 1980—87; lead engr. Design Office for Automatic Sys., Samara, Russia, 1987—89; sr. rsch. scientist Moscow Inst. Physics and Tech., Moscow, 1989—98, Artann Labs, Inc., North Brunswick, NJ, 1998—2000, Sci. Rsch. Lab, Inc., Somerville, Mass., 2000—. Cons. Ctr. Ecology and Plasma Rsch., Moscow, 1990—98. Author: Encyclopedia of PC, 1997. Mem.: Soc. Advancement of Material and Process Engring. Achievements include patents in field. Avocations: skiing, kayaking, guitar. Office: Science Rsch Lab 15 Ward St Somerville MA 02143

BYLES, ROBERT VALMORE, manufacturing company executive; b. Robeline, La., Dec. 7, 1937; s. Robert S. and Ann (Murray) B.; m. Mary E. Hornsby, Sept. 14, 1954; children: Robert V. Jr., Rebecca Kay, Raymond Gale, Aaron Blake. Student, Northwestern State U., Natchitoches, La., 1955-57, La. Tech. U., 1957-58. Ptnr. Byles Bros. Welding and Tractor Co., Many, La., 1960-72; owner, pres. R.V. Byles Industries, Many, 1972-80, R.V. Byles Enterprises, Inc., Many, 1980—; ptnr. Byles Internat., Shreveport, La., 1984-92; pres. West La. Hot Mix Asphalt, Inc., Many, 1986-96. Bd. dirs. Sabine Med. Ctr. Hosp. Bd., 1994—, chair, 1997, 98, 99, 2000. Chmn. Sabine Parish Dem. Exec. Com., 1968-79; mem. Rep. State Cen. Com., 1979-94, 2002—; chief Many Fire Dept., 1965-69. Served with USN, 1959-60. Named one of Outstanding Young Men Am., 1970. Mem. La. Assn. Bus. and Industry, Am. Soc. Concrete Constrn., Nat. Fedn. Bus. and Industry, Sabine Parish C. of C. (bd. dirs. 1966-2000, pres. 1969-70), Many Jaycees (pres. 1970-71, Outstanding Young Men of Am. 1970). Lodges: Shriners (pres. 1988). Republican. Baptist. Avocations: flying, swimming, scuba diving, tennis. Office: RV Byles Enterprises Inc 1751 Robby St Many LA 71449-3361

BYLINSKY, GENE MICHAEL, magazine editor; b. Belgrade, Yugoslavia, Dec. 30, 1930; s. Michael Ivan and Dora (Shadan) B.; m. Gwen Gallegos, Aug. 14, 1955; children: Tanya, Gregory. BA in Journalism, La. State U., 1955. Staff reporter Wall St. Jour., Dallas, 1957-59, San Francisco, 1959-61, N.Y.C., 1961; sci. writer Nat. Observer, Washington, 1961-62, Newhouse Newspapers, Washington, 1962-66; bd. editors Fortune Mag., N.Y.C., 1966—2001, contbg. writer, 2002—. Author: The Innovation Millionaires, 1976, Mood Control, 1978, Life in Darwin's Universe, 1981, Silicon Valley, High Tech Window on the Future, 1985. Served with AUS, 1956. Recipient 21st Ann. Albert Lasker Med. Journalism award, 1970, Deadline award Sigma Delta Chi, 1970, 72, 79, spl. commendation AMA, 1967, 68, 72, Journalism award, 1974, Claude Bernard Sci. Journalism award Nat. Soc. Med. Rsch., 1973, 74, James T. Grady award for interpreting chemistry to pub. Am. Chem. Soc., 1976, Am. Space Writers Assn. award, 1976-79, Bus. Journalism award U. Mo.-Columbia, 1984, Journalism award Am. Assn. Engring. Socs./Engring. Found., 1995, hon. mention award, 1970, 71, hon. mention award AAAS-Westinghouse Corp., 1975, 76, 77, hon. mention award Overseas Press Club, 1988. Mem. Nat. Assn. Sci. Writers, N.Y. Acad. Scis. Mem. Russian Orthodox Ch. Office: Fortune Magazine Time and Life Bldg Rockefeller Plz New York NY 10020-2002 E-mail: gmbylinsky@aol.com.

BYNES, FRANK HOWARD, JR., physician; b. Savannah, Ga., Dec. 3, 1950; s. Frank Howard and Frenchye (Mason) B.; m. Janice Ratta, July 24, 1987; children: Patricia, Frenchye. BS, Savannah State Coll., 1972; MD, Meharry Med. Coll. Resident gen. surgery Staten Island (N.Y.) Hosp., 1978-82; resident internal medicine N.Y. infirmary Beekam Downtown Hosp., N.Y.C., 1983-86; dir. medicine USAF Sheppard Regional Hosp., Sheppard AFB, Tex., 1986-87; pvt. practice internal medicine N.Y.C., 1987-90; attending physician Bronx (N.Y.) Lebanon Hosp., 1990-93; pvt. practice internal medicine Savannah, Ga., 1994—. Maj. USAF, 1986-87. Mem. AMA, AAAS, ACP, N.Y. Acad. Scis., Assn. Mil. Surgeons of U.S., Alpha Phi Alpha.

BYNOE, PETER CHARLES BERNARD, real estate developer, lawyer; b. Boston, Mar. 20, 1951; s. Victor Cameron Sr. and Ethel May (Stewart) B.; m. Linda Jean Walker, Nov. 20, 1987. BA, Harvard U., 1972, JD, MBA, Harvard U., 1976. Bar: Ill. 1982; cert. real estate broker, Ill. Exec. v.p. James H. Lowry & Assocs., Chgo., 1977-82; chmn., chief exec. officer Telemat Ltd., Chgo., 1982—; mng. dir. Howard Ecker & Co. Real Estate, Chgo., 1986-87; of counsel Davis, Barnhill & Galland, Chgo., 1987-88; exec. dir. Ill. Sports Facilities Authority, Chgo., 1988-92; mng. gen. ptnr. Denver Nuggets, 1989-92; ptnr. Piper Rudnick, Chgo., 1995—. Bd. dirs. Uniroyal Tech. Corp., Jacor Comms., Ind., TransAfrica Forum. Chmn. Chgo. Landmarks Commn., 1995; vice chmn. Goodman Theater; dir. Chgo. Econ. Club, Ill. Sports Facilities Authority; trustee Rush-Presbyn. St. Luke's Med. Ctr.; bd. overseers Harvard U. Mem. East Bank Club. Democrat. Avocations: squash, tennis, racquetball, skiing, travel, golf. Office: Piper Rudnick 203 N La Salle St Ste 1800 Chicago IL 60601-1210

BYNUM, GAYELA A. public affairs specialist; b. Sulphur, Okla., Oct. 28, 1945; d. Martin Cleveland and Birdie Burnett Sparks Word; m. Ronald Orr Bynum, June 6, 1965 (div. Apr. 1983); children: William Blaine, Bradley Word; m. Robert F. Hannon, Oct. 28, 1995. Student, U. Okla., 1963-66; BA, U. Ark., 1969; postgrad., George Washington U., 1991-93. Lic. real estate agt., legal asst. Supr. NAS, Jacksonville, Fla., 1972-79; mgmt. analyst Chief Naval Ops., Washington, 1979-85; pres. Gayela Bynum & Assocs., Washington, 1985-88, The Carpet Bagger, Ltd., Oklahoma City, 1997—; pub. affairs advisor HUD, Washington, 1988—. Treas. Globint, LLC, Carefree, Ariz., 199-2002, Globe Car, Ltd., Wilmington, Del., 1998-2002; exec. v.p. Sea Spur, Ltd., Wilmington, 1997—; internat. cons. Mideast Presdl. Candidate, Washington, 1988. Vice chmn. The Opera Camerata, Washington, 2001—02; fundraiser various polit. campaigns, 1985—88; mem. Congl. Steering Com., Washington, 1985—88; bd. govs. Summer Opera Theater, Washington, 2003—. Mem.: DAR, Nat. Press Club (mem. spkrs. com. 1996—2000, newsmakers com. 2001—02, bd. govs. 2002—). Avocations: running, sailing, aerobics, music, painting, crafts. Home and Office: 5902 Mount Eagle Dr Apt 408 Alexandria VA 22303-2516

BYNUM, MAGNOLIA VIRGINIA WRIGHT, retired secondary school educator; b. Waynesboro, Ga., Jan. 10, 1934; d. George and Edith Arilee (Williams) Wright; m. Marvin Bynum, Sept. 17, 1955 (dec. Oct. 1977). BS in Bus. Edn., N.C. A&T State U., Greensboro, N.C., 1956; postgrad., NYU, 1964—65; MS in Edn., CUNY, Bklyn., 1985, Adv. Cert. Guidance & Counseling, 1986. Engring. adminstr. Radio Receptor Co., Bklyn., 1957—59; data processing staff NYU, N.Y.C., 1959—64; tchr., dean, counselor Lincoln H.S., Jersey City, 1964—92; ret., 1992. Adj. prof. CUNY, Bklyn., 1986—90; asst. to Congressman Edolphus Towns, 10th Congl. Dist., Bklyn., 1982—90; counselor incentive program dept. human resources Bklyn. Coll., 1992—93; cons. Parent Advocacy, Medgars Evers Coll., Bklyn., 1984—85. Editor-in-chief (newsletter) Cornerstone Torch, 1993—97. Mem. Cmty. Coalition for Edn., Greensboro, NC, NAACP; spearheaded Hard of Hearing campaign, Bklyn.; women's day chairperson New Zion Missionary Bapt. Ch., Greensboro, NC; chairperson bd. dirs. Chama Child Devel., Bklyn., 1983—91, Cornerstone Day Care Ctr., Bklyn., 1991—97. Named to Faculty Achievement Hall of Fame, Lincoln H.S., 1981; recipient Outstanding Cmty. Svc. award, Bklyn. Coll. Grad. Students,

1984, citations, Congl. Record, 1990, 1997; scholar Myers Jacob Guidance & Counseling scholar, 1984. Mem.: Alpha Kappa Alpha, Phi Delta Kappa, Kappa Delta Pi. Baptist. Avocations: reading, travel, singing. Home: 563 Summerwalk Rd Greensboro NC 27455

BYNUM, RICHARD CARY, author, former publisher; b. Atlanta, Mar. 15, 1937; s. Paul Cary and Ethel Avious (Rutherford) B.; m. Brenda Sue Storey, Apr. 12, 1964; children: Brennon Franklin, Quinlan Ashby. BFA, U. Ga., 1962; MA, CUNY, 1973. Prodn. editor Holt, Rinehart and Winston, N.Y.C., 1965-67; publ. mgr. Assn. Am. U. Presses, N.Y.C., 1967-69; mng. editor R.R. Bowker Co., N.Y.C., 1969-73; founding dir. Ga. State U. Bus. Press, Atlanta, 1973-95; ret. Ga. State U., 1997. Co-dir. So. Poets Theatre, 1974-87. Author: Cabbagetown: 3 Women, 1984, Six Short Plays, 1993, The Chinaberry Tree and Other Poems, 2002; editor: Scholarly Books in America, 1968-69. With USAR. Recipient John Golden award CUNY, 1972, Sparks award Ga. State U., 1985, medal AAUP, 1995. Mem. Dramatists Guild. Avocations: reading, sports, city lore.

BYNUMN, JEANETTE LYNN, holistic health nurse; b. Providence, June 14, 1947; d. Herman David and Carmela Rosemary (Coletta) Harris; m. R.J. Walsh, Dec. 16, 1967 (div. 1983); children: Robert A., Shawn M.; m. Robert Raymond Hansel, Mar. 21, 1991 (div. 1996); m. William D. Bynumn, June 1996 (dec. 1998). AA, R.I. Jr. Coll., 1968; BSN, U. Tex., Arlington, 1981; student, Clayton Coll. Natural Health, Birmingham, Ala., 2002—. RN, Tex., RNC; cert. chemotherapy nurse. Staff nurse Osteo. Med. Ctr., Ft. Worth, 1981-82; charge nurse Duncan Meml. Hosp., Ft. Worth, 1983; supr. Northwest Hosp., Ft. Worth, 1983-85; staff nurse St. Joseph Hosp., Ft. Worth, 1985-86; relief charge nurse All Saint's Hosp., Ft. Worth, 1986-87; staff nurse, asst. supr., staff devel. John Peter Smith Hosp., Ft. Worth, 1987-93; home infusion therapy nurse AACU Care Infusion, Burleson, Tex., 1993-96; peripherally inserted ctrl. catheter line specialist John Peter Smith Hosp., Ft. Worth, 1992; adminstr., corp. dir. nursing PrimeCare, Inc., Ft. Worth, 1997-98, labor and delivery nurse/relief charge, 1998—2002; pres., CEO Wolf Spirit-A Holistic Co., Willow Park, Tex., 2002—. Mem. test devel. com. for gen. practice ANCC, 1995-98. Mem. Nat. Alaska Native Am. Indian Nurses Assn. Roman Catholic. Avocations: crafts, breeding paint horses, sewing. Home and Office: 101 Crown Rd Willow Park TX 76087-9061

BYRAMJEE, ASPI MINOO, surgeon; b. Nairobi, Kenya, May 4, 1944; MD, Royal Coll. Phys. and Surg., Ireland, 1969. Diplomate Am. Bd. Surgery. Intern Meml. Hosp., Albany, N.Y., 1969-70; resident in surgery Mt. Sinai Hosp., Cleve., 1970-74; fellow in cardiovascular surgery St. Josephs Hosp., Phoenix, 1974-76; mem. staff Kaiser Hosp., Cleve., Cleve. Clinic. Fellow ACS. Office: Ohio Permanente Med Group 10 Severance Cir Cleveland Heights OH 44118

BYRD, ANDREW WAYNE, investment company executive; b. Nashville, Apr. 16, 1954; s. Benjamin F. and Allison (Caldwell) B.; m. Marianne Menefee; children: Marianne, Valere, Andrew Jr. BA, Vanderbilt U., 1976, JD, 1979; LLM, Georgetown U., 1981. Bar: Tenn., 1979, U.S. Dist. Ct. (mid. dist.) Tenn. 1979, U.S. Supreme Ct. 2001. Atty. Stokes & Bartholomew, Nashville, 1981-84; exec. v.p. Gen. Cap Am. Inc., 1987-94, Gen. Capital Corp., Nashville, 1984-89, pres., 1989-94, Andrew W. Byrd & Co., LLC, 1994—. Chmn., bd. dirs. Multi-Link, Inc., Lexington, Ky., Albertville (Ala.) Quality Foods, Inc., Precision Boilers, Inc., Morristown, Tenn., So. Quality Meats, Inc., Pontotoc, Miss. Mem. Leadership Nashville, 1984-85; deacon 1st Presbyn. Ch., 1982-92; bd. dirs. Tenn. divsn. Am. Cancer Soc., 1982-88, 92-97, Cheekwood, 1987-93; bd. dirs. Boy Scouts of Am., Mid. Tenn. Coun., 1995—, v.p. manpower, 2002—; bd. dirs. Exch. Club Charities, 2003—; bd. dirs. Vanderbilt Children's Hosp., 1987-93, chmn., 1991-93. Mem. ABA, Tenn. Bar Assn., Nashville Bar Assn., Nashville Area C. of C. (bd. dirs. 2003—), Cumberland Club Nashville, Exch. Club (pres. 1993-94). Democrat. Avocations: tennis, gardening, travel. Home: 4419 Harding Pl Nashville TN 37205-4530 Office: Andrew W Byrd & Co LLC 201 4th Ave N Ste 1250 Nashville TN 37219-2092

BYRD, BETTY RANTZE, writer; b. Oklahoma City, July 8, 1949; d. Rolande Brown and Mary Louise Haner; m. Gordon Peter Rantze (div.); 1 child, Elizabeth Chase Rantze; m. William James Byrd, Sept. 16, 1995; 1 child, Kortnee. BA, U. Ariz., 1974; legal asst. cert., Capital U., 1975. Society editor The Spectator Newspaper, Columbus, Ohio, 1974—75; paralegal Paul Bran-Pub. Defender, Lewisburg, Pa., 1976—77. Author: Trinity's Daughter, 2002; actor: appeared in numerous commls., films, TV. Vol. Salvation Army, Meals-on-Wheels, San Diego, Spl. Olympics, San Diego, Family Recovery Ctr., San Diego. Mem.: AFTRA, SAG, Rancho Santa Fe Literary Soc., Nat. Charity League. Avocations: photography, golf, travel, walking, scrapbooks. Home and Office: PO Box 2593 Rancho Santa Fe CA 92067

BYRD, CHARLES EVERETT, clergyman; b. Brinkerhoff, N.Y., Mar. 19, 1909; s. James Edward and Mamie (Lovelle) B.; m. Violetta Eleanor Price. AB, Howard U., 1932; MDiv, Union Theol. Sem., 1935; MA, Columbia U., 1947; D of Ministry, Drew U., 1978. Pastor Cen. Bapt. Ch., Salt Point, N.Y., 1939-47, Mt. Zion Bapt. Ch., Green Haven, N.Y., 1936-52, Ebenezer Bapt. Ch., Poughkeepsie, N.Y., 1947-52; program rep. Am. Bapt. Svc. Corp., Valley Forge, Pa., 1969-74; chaplain Dutchess County Jail, Poughkeepsie, 1974-89. Author: Review of the Policies of the Baptist Home in Light of the Theology of Service, 1978. Bd. dirs. Bapt. Home, Rhinebeck, N.Y., 1976-94, Dutchess County Office Aging, Poughkeepsie, 1976-94, The Rural and Migrant Ministry, New Paltz, N.Y., 1980-94, Dutchess County Mental Health Assn., Poughkeepsie, 1981—. With USAAF, 1943-46; lt. col. USAF, 1952-68. Decorated Commendation medal with oak leaf cluster; recipient Marist Coll. Pres. award, 1997. Mem. Dutchess Interfaith Coun. (Disting svc. medal 1987), Rotary (sr. active mem.). Home: 3030 Park Ave Apt 5e15 Bridgeport CT 06604-1163 *During the time of my prayers prior to very high risk cancer surgery, the third with 2 in 1987, my courage and faith grew as I reached the point that nothing could change or diminish the goodness of God to me over the past 78 years.*

BYRD, CHRISTINE WATERMAN SWENT, lawyer; b. Oakland, Calif., Apr. 11, 1951; d. Langan Waterman and Eleanor (Herz) Swent; m. Gary Lee Byrd, June 20, 1981; children: Amy, George. BA, Stanford U., 1972; JD, U. Va., 1975. Bar: Calif. 1976, U.S. Dist. Ct. (ctrl., so. no., ea. dists.) Calif., U.S. Ct. Appeals (9th cir.). Law clk. to Hon. William P. Gray, U.S. Dist. Ct., L.A., 1975-76; assoc. Jones, Day, Reavis & Pogue, L.A., 1976-82, ptnr., 1987-96; asst. U.S. atty. criminal divsn. U.S. Atty.'s Office-Cen. Dist. Calif., L.A., 1982-87; ptnr. Irell & Manella, L.A., 1996—. Mem. Calif. Law Revision Commn., 1992-97. Author: The Future of the U.S. Multinational Corporation, 1975; contbr. articles to profl. jours. Mem.: ABA (Vice Chmn. ADR Advocacy in Litigation 2003—), Assn. Bus. Trial Lawyers (bd. govs. 1996—99), 9th Jud. Cir. Hist. Soc. (bd. dirs. 1986—, pres. 1997—2002), Century City Bar Assn. (bd. govs. 2001—), Stanford Profl. Women Los Angeles County, Am. Arbitration Assn. (large and complex case panel 1992—, nat. energy panel 1998—, bd. dirs. 1999—), Women Lawyers Assn. Los Angeles County, Los Angeles County Bar Assn., Calif. State Bar (com. fed. cts. 1985—88), Stanford U. Alumni Assn. Republican. Office: Irell & Manella LLP 1800 Ave Of Stars Ste 900 Los Angeles CA 90067-4276

BYRD, ELLEN STOESSER, school nurse administrator; b. Dayton, Tex., Dec. 10, 1941; d. Edward Joseph and Nina Mae (Cannon) Stoesser; m. C. Robert Byrd, June 6, 1964; children: Byron, Preston, Aaron, Robyn. BSN, Baylor U., 1964. RN, Tex. Nurse Parkland Hosp., Dallas, 1964-65; nurse gyn. svcs. Baylor U. Med. Ctr., Dallas, 1965-66; charge nurse med./surg. Collin Meml. Hosp., McKinney, Tex., 1967-68; nurse newborn nursery St. Paul Hosp., Dallas, 1972; pvt. duty nurse Dist. 4 Tex. Nurse Assn., Dallas, 1976; sch. nurse Dallas Ind. Sch. Dist., 1989-90; home health nurse Rehab Home Care, DeSoto, Tex., 1994-98; dermatology nurse Dallas Bapt. U., 1999—2001, dir. health svcs., campus nurse, 2001—; sch. nurse Richardson (Tex.) Ind. Sch. Dist. Mem. adv. bd. Baylor U. Sch. Nursing, Dallas, 1994—, chmn. adv. bd. 1999—; advisor Baylor U. Woman's Coun., Dallas, 1995—, pres., 1994-95. Author: History of Dallas CPA Wives, 1983, Biography of Mae Stoesser, 1988, Byrd Family 25 Years, 1990. Program chmn. Freedom Found. Valley Forge, Dallas, 1986-89; centennial circle chmn. Dallas County Heritage Soc., Dallas; deacon Cliff Temple Bapt. Ch., 1988; v.p. DeSoto Svc. League, 1990; pres. Dallas CPAs Wives Club, 1984-85; mem. Richardson Jr. League. Recipient W.T. White Meritorious Svcs. award Baylor U. Alumni Assn., 1996. Mem. Richardson Jr. League, Presbyn. Presby Ptnrs. Repubican. Baptist. Avocations: european travel, grandchildren. Home: 304 Prince Albert Ct Richardson TX 75081-5059 Office: Dallas Bapt Univ 3000 Mountain Creek Pkwy Dallas TX 75211-9299 Fax: 972-234-8448.

BYRD, EVA WILSON, communications executive; Dir. media Bates Health World, New York, NY, 1994—, v.p., dir. media. Office: Girgenti Hughes Butler & McDowell Fl 8 100 Ave of the Americas New York NY 10013-1687

BYRD, GARY ELLIS, lawyer; b. Dothan, Ala., Mar. 8, 1957; m. Emily Marie Reid; children: Elizabeth, Virginia and Victoria (twins). BS in Pre-Law and Am. History summa cum laude, Troy State U., 1979; JD, U. Ala., 1982. Bar: Ga. (no. and middle dists.) 1983, U.S. Dist. Ct. (no. and so. dists), Ga., U.S. Ct. Appeals. Pntr. Bishoff & Byrd, Talbotton, Ga., 1982-86; assoc. Bunn & Kirby, Hamilton, Ga., 1993—, 1993-96; ptnr. Bunn & Byrd, Hamilton, Ga., 1996—2000; city atty. Woodland, Ga., 1986—, Geneva, Ga., 1988—, Shiloh, Ga., 1994—; ptnr. Bunn, Byrd, Newsom & Hix, 2001—. Chmn. bd. dirs. Talbot County Law Libr., Talbotton, 1992-2003; bd. dirs. Harris County Law Libr., Hamilton, 1998-2003. Contbr. numerous articles to newspapers and profl. jours., chpt. to book; author City of Woodland city code, 1986, City of Geneva charter, 2000, City of Shiloh charter, 2001. Bd. dirs. Chattahoochie-Flint RESA, Americus, Ga., 1986-87, Pine Mountain Regional Arts Coun., Manchester, Ga., 1986-88; pres., chmn. exec. com. Talbot County 2000 Group, Talbotton, 1987-88; coach debate team dept. social studies Manchester (Ga.) H.S., 1982; chmn. appropriations com. Harris County YMCA, Hamilton, 1994-2000, 2002-03, bd. dirs. 1994-2000, 2002-03; mem. budget com. City of Talbotton, 1989-92, councilman, 1985-92, mem. policy adv. com., 1986-92, vol. fireman, 1982-93; ct. apptd. adminstr. City of Geneva, Ga., 1992; mem. adv. com. Am. Security Coun., Washington, 1976-82; dir. Harris County Indigent Def. Program, 1999-2003. Recipient Outstanding Svc. award Talbot County Jaycees, 1983, Mem. Ga. Bar Assn., Ga. Mcpl. Assn. (atty.'s sect.), Talbot County C. of C. (chmn. membership com. 1992-93, bd. dirs. 1993), Harris County C. of C. (bd. dirs. 2000-02), Troy State U. Alumni Assn. (membership com. East Ala./West Ctrl. Ga. chpt. 1993-99, Rotary (chmn. internat. svc. com. 2002-03), Phi Kappa Phi, Phi Alpha Theta (State Hist. Rsch. award 1979). Author, City of Geneva, GA Charter, 2000; Author, City of Shiloh, GA Charter, 2001. Avocations: model trains, stock car racing. Home: PO Box 119 Hamilton GA 31811-0119 Office: 103 N College St PO Box 489 Hamilton GA 31811-0489

BYRD, HARRY FLOOD, JR., newspaper executive, former senator; b. Winchester, Va., Dec. 20, 1914; s. Harry Flood and Anne Douglas (Beverley) B.; m. Gretchen B. Thomson, Aug. 9, 1941 (dec. Oct. 1989); children: Harry, Thomas Thomson, Beverley. Student, Va. Mil. Inst., 1931-33, U. Va., 1933-35; hon. LL.D., L.H.D., D. Internat. Service. Editor Winchester Evening Star, 1935—81; pub. Harrisonburg (Va.) Daily News-Record, 1937—2000; Pres., dir. Rockingham Pub. Co., from 1946; dir. A.P., 1950-66; v.p., mem. exec. com.; mem. Va. Senate, 1947-65; mem. U.S. Senate from Va., 1965-83, chmn. subcom. on taxation. Author Va. automatic tax reduction law. Mem. Va. Dem. Ctrl. Com., 1940-66. Served to lt. comdr. USNR, 1942-46. Recipient Honor medal Freedoms Found.; named to Va. Comms. Hall of Fame. Mem. VFW, Va. Press Assn. (Man of Yr.), Am. Legion, Masons (33 degree, insp. gen. hon.). Clubs: Rotarian, National Press, Army-Navy. Office: Rockingham Pub Co Inc 2 N Kent St Winchester VA 22601-5038

BYRD, ISAAC BURLIN, fishery biologist, fisheries administrator; b. Canoe, Ala., Mar. 14, 1925; s. Isaac Britt and Mary Adline (Wright) B.; m. Marjorie Fé Elmore, Sept. 24, 1949; children— Cathy Ann, Teresa Carol, Gary Curtis. BS, Auburn U., 1948, MS, 1950. Chief fisheries sect. Ala. Dept. Conservation, 1951-65; fed. aid coordinator fisheries research and devel. Bur. Comml. Fisheries, Dept. Interior, 1965-70; chief div. state-fed. relationships, fisheries research, devel. and mgmt. Nat. Marine Fisheries Service, St. Petersburg, Fla., 1970-85, asst. regional dir. S.E. Region, 1985-91, ret., 1991. Adminstr. Internat. Fisheries Agreement (for U.S. shrimp fishermen to fish Brazilian coastal waters), 1975-76; mem. adv. com. to organize 1st fishery mgmt. councils and to develop initial fed. policies under Fisheries Conservation and Mgmt. Act 1976 (for marine fisheries in fisheries conservation zone of U.S.); chmn. Gulf of Mexico State/Fed. Fisheries Mgmt. Bd., 1985-86, 88-89; chmn. South Atlantic State/Fed. Fisheries Mgmt. Bd., 1990-91 Contbg. author: McCanes Standard Fishing Ency., Internat. Angling Guide, 1965; contbr. articles to sci. jours. Served with USAAF, 1943-46. Recipient Gov. Ala. award outstanding tech. accomplishments conservation, 1964 Fellow Am. Inst. Fishery Research Biologists; mem. Am. Fisheries Soc. (pres. So. div. 1958, pres. 1965-66, asso. editor trans. 1955-58), World Mariculture Soc. (dir. 1972-73), Internat. Assn. Fish and Wildlife Agys., Gulf and Caribbean Fisheries Inst., Inland Comml. Fisheries Assn., Phi Kappa Phi, Omicron Delta Kappa, Gamma Sigma Delta, Alpha Zeta, Alpha Gamma Rho. Methodist. Achievements include initiating the 1st fisheries mgmt. and fisheries research program in state for Ala. Dept. Conservation. Home: 11105 7th St E Treasure Island Saint Petersburg FL 33706

BYRD, JAMES EVERETT, lawyer; b. Cin., Aug. 1, 1958; BS, U. Dayton, Ohio, 1980, JD cum laude, 1984. Law clk. U.S. Dist Ct. (so. dist.), Ohio, 1983; assoc. Smith & Schnacke, Dayton, 1984-89; v.p., gen. counsel Internat. Cargo Svcs., Virginia Beach, Va., 1989-91; assoc. Beale, Balfour et al., Richmond, Va., 1991-92; corp. counsel Huffy Corp., Dayton, 1992-94; ind. corp. legal cons., 1994-95; assoc. gen. counsel Lexis Nexis divsn. Reed Elsevier, Inc., Dayton, 1995—. Pres. Condominium Owners Assn., Dayton, 1995-99. Mem. ABA, Ohio Bar Assn., Va. Bar Assn. Office: Lexis Nexis 9443 Springboro Pike Miamisburg OH 45342-4425 E-mail: james.e.byrd@lexisnexis.com.

BYRD, JEFFERY, performance artist; b. Russellville, Ala., Nov. 11, 1964; s. J. R. Byrd and Carrie Jean Logan. BFA, U. Ala., Tuscaloosa, 1987; MFA, U. Fla., Gainesville, 1989. Prof. art U. No. Iowa, Cedar Falls, 1989—; assoc. prof. art Oberlin (Ohio) Coll., 1995—96; vis. prof. art U. Ala., Tuscaloosa, 1999—2001. Vis. artist U. Montevallo, Ala., 1997, U. South Fla., Tampa, 1997, Oreg. Coll. Art and Craft, Portland, Oreg., 2002, Herron Sch. Art, Indpls., 2002; instr. Penland (N.C.) Sch. Craft, 2001. Performance art piece, How Wang Fo (Indpls. Installation Festival Merit Award, 1997); singer: (opera) Lunar Opera by Pauline Oliveros (performed at Lincoln Ctr., NYC, 2000), (performance/chamber work) Selections from the Songbooks by John Cage; performance art piece, How Wang Fo (Cleve. Int'l Performance Art Fest Featured Artist, 1998), performance art piece/solo chamber opera, Raft of the Medusa (selection New West Electro Acoustic Musicians Organiztion Festival San Diego State Univ, 2002), performance art piece, Holding the Universe, Stone Above the Sky, Countless Days, Endless Nights, Holding the Universe. Profl. Devel. grantee, Iowa Arts Coun., 1994, 1998, 1999. Mem.: Coll. Art Assn.

BYRD, JOAN EDA, film librarian; b. May 12, 1942; BFA, Howard U., 1965; MLS, Cath. U. Am., 1976; MA, New Sch. for Social Rsch. Reference librarian Bklyn. Pub. Libr., 1985-87, sr. librarian, 1987-89; sr. film librarian N.Y. Pub. Libr., N.Y.C., 1989-93, supervising librarian, 1993—. E-mail: jbyrd@nypl.org.

BYRD, JOHNNIE, JR., state legislator; b. Brewton, Ala., Feb. 8, 1951; BS in Bus. Adminstrn., Auburn U., 1973; JD, U. Ala., 1976. Mem. Fla. Ho. of Reps., Tallahassee, 1996—, mem. econ. impact, govt. svc., fiscal responsibility couns., also govtl. responsibility, justice couns., ho. spkr., 2003—. Mem. Kiwanis (past pres.), Greater Plant City C. of C. (past pres.), Friends of Brewton Meml. Libr. (past pres.). Republican. Office: Fla Capitol 402 S Monroe St Tallahassee FL 32399-6526 also: 121 N Collins St Ste 202 Plant City FL 33566-3311 E-mail: byrd.johnnie@leg.state.fl.us.*

BYRD, JOSEPH, composer; b. Louisville, Dec. 19, 1937; s. J. H. and Dian Nall Byrd; m. Beni Bennett, 1984; 1 child, Clarissa Elizabeth. MusB, U. Ariz., 1959; MA in Music and Composition, Stanford U., 1960; student, Morton Feldman and John Cage, 1960—63; postgrad., UCLA, 1963—66. Sec. Virgil Thomson, 1961—63; staff arranger Capital Recs., 1963; founder The New Music Wrokshop, 1963—66; assoc. music Coll. Redwoods, Humboldt County, Calif. Composer (arranger): (films) Lions Love, Health, The Long Riders, (commls.) the first nat. Dr. Pepper campaign, (TV series) CBS Evening News with Dan Rather; arranger, producer: Jazz, 1978. Mailing: 1681 Henry Ln Mckinleyville CA 95519

BYRD, LARRY DONALD, behavioral pharmacologist; b. Salisbury, N.C., July 14, 1936; s. Donald Thomas and Mildred (Gardner) B.; m. Corrinne Williams, Dec. 23, 1961; children: Kay, Lynn, Renee, Andrew. AB, E. Carolina U., Greenville, N.C., 1962; MA, E. Carolina U., 1964; PhD, U. N.C., 1968; postgrad., Harvard U., 1967-70. Faculty E. Carolina U., 1962-64; tchg. and rsch. asst. exptl. psychology U. N.C., Chapel Hill, 1964-67; rsch. fellow pharmacology, instr. psychobiology Harvard Med. Sch., 1967-70; assoc. scientist Lab. Psychobiology New Eng. Reg. Primate Rsch. Ctr., 1969-74; psychobiologist, chmn. divsn. primate behavior Yerkes Primate Rsch. Ctr., Emory U., Atlanta, 1974-79, assoc. rsch. prof., chmn. divsn. primate behavior, 1979-80, lectr. dept. psychology, 1974-81, assoc. rsch. prof., chief divsn. behavioral biology, 1980-82, prof., chief divsn. behavioral biology, 1982-97, prof. dept. pharmacology, 1995-97; prof. emeritus, 1998. Adj. prof. dept. psychology Emory U., 1981-97; cons. Dept. Pharmacological and Physiol. Scis. U. Chgo., 1973, MIT Press, Cambridge, 1975, Nat. Ctr. for Toxicological Rsch. FDA, Jefferson, Ark., 1976-77, S.W. Found. for Rsch. and Edn., San Antonio, 1977, Naval Aerospace Med. Rsch. Lab. U.S. Naval Air Sta., Pensacola, Fla., 1977, G.D. Searle and Co., Skokie, Ill., 1986, Battelle Meml. Inst., Columbus, Ohio, 1989-94; mem. spl. rev. com. Contract Rev. Unit Nat. Inst. on Drug Abuse, Lexington, Ky., 1979-81, mem. spl. rev. com. biomed. rsch. rev. com., 1981-82, spl. rev. cons. clin., behavioral and psychosocial rsch. rev. com., 1981-82, mem., 1982-85, chmn., 1984-85, others; spl. rev. cons. dept. medicine and surgery VA, Washington, 1983, NSF, Washington, 1984, div. of rsch. resources NIH, Washington, 1983, mem. spl. study sect. div. rsch. grants, 1984, panel mem. Workshop on Implemenation of Pub. Health Svc. Policy on Humane Care and Use of Lab. Animals, 1989, others; panel mem. USPHS Animal Welfare Forum Alcohol, Drug Abuse and Mental Health Adminstrn., 1985; active numerous other career related orgns. Editorial bd. Jour. Exptl. Analysis of Behavior, 1969-79, 87-91; assoc. editor Jour. Exptl. Analysis of Behavior, 1970-76; cons. editor Am. Jour. Primatology, 1980-83; editor Psychopharmacology Newsletter, 1976-82; editorial advisor Jour. Pharmacology and Exptl. Therapeutics, Jour. Exptl. Analysis of Behavior, others; contbr. numerous articles to profl. jours. Mem. sci. adv. com. Nat. Families in Action, 1991-95. Recipient Outstanding Alumnus award, E. Carolina U., 1977, Disting. Alumnus award, U. N.C., 1987. Fellow AAAS, Am. Psychol. Assn. (exec. com. psychopharmacology divsn. 1976-95, neurobehavioral toxicity test standards com. 1980-97, coord. Young Psychopharmacologist award 1985-95, bd. sci. affairs com. on animals in rsch. and ethics 1990-93); mem. Assn. for Assessment and Accreditation Lab. Animal Care (trustee 1990-98, exec. com. 1991-98, sec. 1993, vice chmn. 1994-96, chmn. 1996-98), Am. Soc. Pharmacology and Exptl. Therapeutics, Nat. Families in Action (sci. adv. com. 1991-95), Am. Soc. Primatologist, Behavioral Pharmacology Soc. (pres. 1984-86), Soc. Exptl. Analysis of Behavior (v.p. 1975-76, bd. dirs. 1970-78), European Behavioral Pharmacology Soc., Southeastern Pharmacology Soc., Am Pub. Health Assn., Behavioral Toxicology Soc., Southeastern Assn. for Behavior Analysis, Internat. Study Group Investigating Drugs as Reinforcers, Emory Neurosci. Group, Phi Sigma Pi. Home: 2730 Camp Branch Rd Buford GA 30519-4455 E-mail: lbyrd@emory.edu.

BYRD, LLOYD GARLAND, civil engineer; b. Atlanta, May 6, 1923; s. Lloyd Porter and Gladys Ardee (Daniell) B.; m. Jeanne Mae Parkhurst, Jan. 23, 1943; children: Gary Daniell, Donna Jeanne, Jeffrey Alan, Julie Anne. BCE, Ohio State U., 1950. Staff engr. Ohio Dept. Hwys., Columbus, 1949-52; maintenence engr. Ohio Turnpike Commn., Berea, 1952-60; assoc. editor Pub. Works Publs., Ridgewood, N.J., 1960-63; ptnr. Byrd, Tallamy, MacDonald & Lewis, Falls Church, Va., 1963-72; sr. v.p., mgr. Byrd, Tallamy, MacDonald & Lewis div. Wilbur Smith & Assocs., Falls Church, 1972-84; interim dir. Strategic Hwy. Rsch. Program, Washington, 1984-86; pvt. practice Washington, 1986-99. Chmn. group 3 coun. Transp. Rsch. Bd., Washington, 1972-76, chmn. overview com.; ex-officio governing bd. NRC, Washington, 1989-95; mem. bd. cons. Eno Found., Westport, Conn., 1986-89; mem. report rev. com. NRC, 1997—. Co-author: Street and Highway Maintenance Manual: American Public Works Association, 1985; assoc. editor: Handbook of Highway Engring., 1975; chmn. pub. affairs coun. Am. Assn. Engring. Socs., 1992. Chmn. Fairfax County (Va.) Human Rights Commn., 1978-79; pres. Fairfax County C. of C., 1975-76; bd. dirs. Hospice of Carolina Foothills, Inc. Recipient Disting. Alumnus award Ohio State U. Coll. Engring., 1978, Roy W. Crum award Transp. Rsch. Bd., Washington, 1986, P.D. McLean Meml. award Road Gang, Washington, 1989, Disting. Lectr. award, 1998, Transp. Rsch Bd. Fellow ASCE (pres. nat. capital sect. Washington 1976-77, nat. bd. dirs. N.Y.C. 1979-82, Wilbur S. Smith award 1985, Francis C. Turner Lecture award 1995)); mem. NAE, Am. Pub. Works Assn., Univ. Club (Washington), Tryon (N.C.) Country Club, Rotary Club. Republican. Congregationalist. Avocations: golf, bridge. E-mail: lgbyrd@aol.com.

BYRD, LORENDA SUE, nursing administrator; b. Eureka, Ill., Jan. 31, 1941; d. Denver C. and Sadie M. (Van Sickle) Aucutt; m. Larry L. Byrd, Jan. 2, 1984; children: Scott, Ellen, Leslie, Brian. Diploma, Meth. Hosp. Cen. Ill. Sch., Peoria, 1962; BSN, McKendree Coll., 1981; MSN, So. Ill. U., Edwardsville, 1990. RN, Ill., Mo.; cert. nursing adminstr. ANCC. Staff nurse Charleston Community Hosp., 1962-65; mem. faculty Mennonite Hosp. Sch. Nursing, Bloomington, Ill., 1965-76; head nurse emergency rm. Belleville (Ill.) Meml. Hosp., 1976-80; nurse mgr. med.-surg. oncology dept. St. Elizabeth Med. Ctr., Granite City, Ill., 1980-87; assoc. dir. patient svcs. Alexian Bros. Hosp., St. Louis, 1988-91; dir. nursing St. Joseph Hosp.-West, Lake St. Louis, Mo., 1991-96, v.p. patient svcs., 1996-97; chief nursing officer Lucy Lee Healthcare Sys, Poplar Bluffs, Mo., 1998-2000, Three Rivers Healthcare, 2000-01, Jefferson Meml. Hosp., Festus, Mo., 2001—. Adv. bd. Jefferson Coll., 2001—02. Mem. "We Can 2000" Cmty. Orgn., Wentzville, Mo., 1992-95, Bus. and Profl. Women, Wentzville, 1993-94. Mem.: St. Louis Coun. Nurse Execs. (pres.-elect 1993, pres. 1994), Mo. Orgn. Nurse Execs., Am. Orgn. Nurse Execs., C. of C. Lake St. Louis (sec. 1994—, bd. dirs. 1994, 1996), Twin City Optimus, O'Fallen (Mo.) Rotary (sec. 1995, pres.-elect 1996), Sigma Theta Tau.

BYRD, MARC ROBERT, designer, florist; b. Flint, Mich., May 14, 1954; s. Robert Lee and Cynthia Ann (Poland) B.; m. Bonnie Jill Berlin, Nov. 25, 1975 (div. June 1977). Student, Ea. Mich. U., 1972-75; grad., Am. Floral Sch., Chgo., 1978; BS, postgrad., U. Redlands, 2002—. Gen. mgr., dir. floral shops; designer Olive Tree Florist, Palm Desert, Calif., 1978-79, Kayo's Flower Fashions, Palm Springs, 1979-80; owner, designer Village Florist, Inc., Palm Springs, 1980-85; pres. Mon Ami Florist, Inc., Beverly Hills, 1986-87; gen. mgr. Silverio's, Santa Monica, 1987; gen. mgr., hotel florist, creative dir. Four Seasons Hotel, Beverly Hills, 1988-90; pres. Marc Fredericks, Inc., Beverly Hills, 1990-97; event florist Marc Byrd of Floral Works, L.A., 1997—2002, Marc Byrd Holiday Decor, 2002—. Author: Celebrity Flowers, 1989. Del., Dem. County Conv., 1972, Dem. County Conv., 1972, Dem. State Conv., 1972, Dem. Nat. Conv., 1972. Mem. Soc. Am. Florists, So. Calif. Floral Assn., Desert Mus., Robinson's Gardens. Democrat. Episcopalian. Avocations: skiing, tennis, community service. Fax: (323) 962-9275. E-mail: marcbyrd@earthlink.net.

BYRD, MARY JANE, education educator; b. Topeka, Apr. 21, 1946; d. Vernon Thomas and Mary Elizabeth (Caldwell) Wharton; m. Gerald David Byrd, June 24, 1965; children: Kari, Juli, Cori. BS, U. So. Ala., 1980, MBA, 1984; D of Bus. Adminstrn., Nova Southeastern U., 1991. Dental asst. Gerald E. Berger, DMD, Mobile, Ala., 1963-65; dental hygienist Robert P. Hall, DMD, Mobile, Ala., 1965-66; teller Am. Nat. Bank, Mobile, Ala., 1972-75; office mgr. Byrd Surveying, Inc., Mobile, Ala., 1975-80; div. acct. cafeteria Morrison, Inc., Mobile, Ala., 1980-82; mgmt. cons. pvt. practice Mobile, Ala., 1982-84; lectr. acctg. U. South Ala., Mobile, Ala., 1984; asst. prof. acctg. & mgmt. Univ. Mobile, Mobile, Ala., 1984-89; assoc. prof. acctg. and mgmt. Mobile Coll., 1989-95; prof. mgmt., 1995—. Reviewer Internat. Jour. Pub. Adminstrn., 1991—; dir. Nat. Assn. Accts., Mobile, 1986-89. Author: Supervisory Management Study Guide/Southwestern, 1993, 97, Small Business Management; An Entrepreneur's Guide to Success/Irwin, 1994, 4th edit. 2003, Human Resource Management, Dame, 1995; contbr. articles to profl. jours. Named Assoc. of the Month, Home Builders Assn., 1986, Charles S. Dismukes Outstanding Mem., Nat. Assn. Accts. Mem. AAUW, Acad. Mgmt., Am. Bus. Women Assn., Mortgage Lenders Assn., So. Acad. Mgmt. Office: Univ Mobile PO Box 13220 Mobile AL 36663-0220 E-mail: janebyrd@free.umobile.edu.

BYRD, MILTON BRUCE, college president, former business executive; b. Boston, Jan. 29, 1922; s. Max Joseph and Rebecca (Malkiel) B.; m. Susanne J. Schwerin, Aug. 30, 1953; children: Deborah, Leslie, David. AB cum laude,

Boston U., 1948, MA, 1949; PhD, U. Wis., 1953; postgrad. (fellow), U. Mich., 1961-62. Teaching asst. English U. Wis., 1949-53; instr., asst. prof. English Ind. U., 1953-58; asst. prof., asso. prof. humanities So. Ill. U., 1958-62, head div. humanities, 1958-60, supr. acad. advisement, 1959-60, asso. dean, 1960- 62; v.p. acad. affairs No. Mich. U., 1962-66; pres. Chgo. State U., 1966-74; provost Fla. Internat. U., 1974-78; pres. Adams State Coll., Alamosa, Colo., 1978-81; v.p. corp. devel. Frontier Cos., Anchorage, 1981-85; pres. Charter Coll., 1985—. Bd. dirs Chgo. Council for Urban Edn., Union for Experimenting Colls. and Univs., Am. Assn. State Colls. and Univs., Resource Devel. Council Alaska, Alaska Commn. Econ. Edn.; v.p. Common Sense for Alaska, Inc.; former pres. Alaska Support Industry Alliance. Author: (with Arnold L. Goldsmith) Publication Guide for Literary and Linguistic Scholars, 1958; contbr. to profl. jours. Vice chmn. Alaska Commn. on Postsecondary Edn. Served with USAAF, 1943-46. Mem. MLA, Nat. Council Tchrs. English, Coll. English Assn., Am. Studies Assn., AAUP, Fla. Assn. Univ. Adminstrs. (former pres.), Rocky Mountain Athletic Conf. (former pres.), Assn. for Higher Edn., Pub. Relations Soc. Am., NEA, Alaska Press Club, Mich. Edn. Assn., Phi Beta Kappa, Phi Delta Kappa. Clubs: Rotary. Office: # 120 2221 E Northern Lights Blvd Anchorage AK 99508-4143 E-mail: mbyrd@chartercollege.edu.

BYRD, ROBERT CARLYLE, senator; b. North Wilkesboro, N.C., Nov. 20, 1917; s. Cornelius Sale and Ada (Kirby) B.; m. Erma Ora James, May 29, 1937; children: Mona Carole (Mrs. Mohammad Fatemi), Marjorie Ellen (Mrs. John Moore). Student, Beckley Coll., Concord Coll., Morris Harvey Coll., 1950-51, Marshall U., 1951-52, BA in Polit. Sci. summa cum laude, 1994; JD cum laude, Am. U., 1963. Mem. W.Va. Ho. of Reps., 1947-50, 83d-85th Congresses from 6th W.Va. dist., W.Va. Senate, 1951-52; U.S. senator from W.Va., 1959 ; senate majority leader, 1977-80, 87-88; senate minority leader, 1981-86. Mem. appropriations com., armed svcs. com., rules and adminstrn. budget com., senate Dem. steering and coord. com. Author: The Senate, 1789-1989, 4 vols., 1989-94, The Senate of the Roman Republic: Addresses on the History of Roman Constitutionalism, 1995; contbr. articles to profl. jours. Recipient Disting. Svc award Radio and TV News Dirs. Assn. 1986; named Most Influential Mem. U.S. Senate, U.S. News and World Report Poll, 1979, Legislator of Yr. Nat. Coal Assn., 1986, West Virginian of the 20th Century, 2001. Mem. Country Music Assn. (hon.) Lodges: Masons (33 degree). Democrat. Baptist. Office: US Senate 311 Hart Bldg Washington DC 20510-0001 also: 300 Virginia St Ste 2630 Charleston WV 25301

BYRD, RONALD DALLAS, civil engineer; b. Reno, Nov. 30, 1934; s. Eugene Richard and Helen Madelyn (Hursh) B.; m. Irene Josephine Phenix, Sept. 19, 1953; children: Kevin Gregory, Helen Christine, Stephanie Irene. BSCE, U. Nev., 1960. Registered profl. engr., Nev., Calif., Oreg., Wash., Idaho., Wyo. Staff engr. Sprout Engrs., Sparks, Nev., 1960-64, design engr., 1964-67, office mgr. Seattle, 1967-70; exec. v.p. Sea, Inc., Seattle, 1970-72, Sparks, 1972-97; v.p. Stantech Cons. Inc. SW, 1997-98, Stantec Cons. Inc., 1998-99, sr. cons., 1999—. Bd. dirs. Am. Cons. Engrs. Coun. Nev., 1987-95, pres., 1993-94, nat. dir. 1994-95. Fellow ASCE (sec. 1966-67); mem. NSPE (bd. dirs. 1983-86), Am. Pub. Works Assn., U. Nev. Reno Enginrg. Alumni Assn. (sec. 1985-86), U. Nev. Reno Alumni Assn. (pres. 1989-90), Kiwanis (pres. Sparks club 1965-66), Rotary (pres. Federal Way, Wash. club 1971-72, bd. dirs. Reno Sunrise 1992-98, pres. 1996-97), Elks, Masons. Republican. Methodist. Home: 30 Ocelet Way Reno NV 89511-4751 Office: Stantec Cons Inc 6980 Sierra Ctr Pkwy Ste 100 Reno NV 89511 E-mail: rbyrd@stantec.com.

BYRD, STEPHEN FRED, human resource consultant; b. Charleston, S.C., June 12, 1928; s. Paul Fred and Dorothy B.; m. Margaret A. McAulay, Apr. 15, 1955; children: Owen, Susan. Student, CCNY, 1945-48; LLB, N.Y. Law Sch., 1951. Bar: N.Y. 1951. Corp. indsl. rels. rep. Pan Am. Airways, 1957-62, Sinclair Oil Corp., 1962-64; v.p. employee rels. indsl. chems. div. Allied Chem. Corp., 1964-68; v.p. indsl. rels. and pers. Internat. Nickel Co., Ltd., 1968-72; sr. v.p. human resources Schering-Plough Corp., Madison, N.J., 1973-88; cons. Right Assocs., Parsippany, N.J., 1988-90. Author: Front Line Supervisors Labor Relations Handbook, 1962, Management Strategy in Collective Bargaining, 1964. Bd. dirs. United Fund Morris County, N.J., Big Bros. Morris County, Morristown YMCA, 1962-63; chmn. Madison council Boy Scouts Am., 1975-76; trustee Drew U., Madison, N.J., 1976-80. With AUS, 1952-53, Korea. Mem. Indsl. Relations Research Assn., N.Y. Law Sch. Alumni Assn. Home and Office: 23 Academy Rd Madison NJ 07940-2001 E-mail: pmbstudio@worldnet.att.net.

BYRD, STEPHEN TIMOTHY, lawyer; b. Roanoke Rapids, N.C., July 4, 1957; s. William Timothy and Betty Faye (Davis) B.; m. Sandra Jean Sain, May 6, 1989; children: Rachel Leigh, Samuel Davis, Kelly Elizabeth. BSBA, U. N.C., 1979, JD, 1984. CPA N.C.; bar: N.C. 1984; cert. specialist in estate planning and probate law. AV rating Martindale-Hubbell,Inc.; staff acct. Peat Marwick & Mitchell, Raleigh, N.C., 1980-81; assoc. Petree, Stockton & Robinson, Winston-Salem, N.C., 1984-88, Raleigh, 1988-89; ptnr. Manning, Fulton & Skinner, P.A., Raleigh, 1989—. Contbg. author: Jour. of Partnership Taxation, 1989; author, lectr. partnership & LLC topics for N.C. Bar Found., Nat. Bus. Inst., 1994. Unit chmn. United Way Wake County, Raleigh, 1988, 93, mem. allocation rev. com. 1994-97; mem. adminstrv. coun. Crossroads Fellowship Ch., Raleigh, 1995—. Named to Wake County Vol. Lawyers Program Honor Roll. Mem. N.C. Bar Assn. (exec. coun. young laywers divsn. 1987-92, dirs. 1990-92, tax sect. newsletter editor 1989-91, coun. 1990-93, 94-97, sec. 1991-92, 97-98, chmn. tax sect. CLE com. 1995-96, legis. com. 1996-98, treas. 1996-97, tax sect. vice chair 1998-99, chair 1999-2000), N.C. Forestry Assn. (taxation com.), Wake County Estate Planning Coun., Raleigh C. of C. (amb. 1990-93, bd. advisors 1996-99). Republican. Avocations: basketball, golf. Office: Manning Fulton & Skinner Ste 500 3605 Glenwood Ave Raleigh NC 27612-4954 E-mail: byrd@manningfulton.com.

BYRD, THOMAS RUSSELL, medical educator; b. Palo Alto, Calif., Mar. 9, 1942; s. Oliver Erasmus and Jennie Christine (Sonnichsen) B.; children: Patrick, Kristina, Jaime Lynn, Jenna. AA, Menlo Coll., 1961; BS in Health Sci., Calif. State U., San Jose, 1963; MA in Health Edn., Stanford U., 1965. Cert. state c.c. tchg. credential Calif. Tchr. Palo Alto (Calif.) Unified Sch. Dist., 1966-68; prof. De Anza Coll., Cupertino, Calif., 1968—2002. Mem. free med. treatment teams Interplast (Stanford U.), 1976—80, fundraiser, 1976—86; mobile tng. instr. Transp. Security Adminstrn., 2002—. Author: Medical Readings on First Aid, 1971, Medical Readings on Counseling and Psychological Services, 1971, Medical Readings on Family Life, 1971, Medical Readings on Vision, Speech and Hearing, 1971, Medical Readings on Nutrition, 1971, Medical Readings on Heroin, 1972, Medical Readings on the Heart, 1973, Medical Readings in Health Sciences, 1974, In Case of Emergency, 1976, Preventive Health Concepts, 1976, Health Sciences: Selected Medical Readings, 1979, Addictive Awareness, 1990, Lives Written in Sand, 1997. Vol. instr., trainer in lic. oxygen adminstrn., AED, bio/hazard protection, CPRFPR and emergency response ARC, 1966—; vol. health caregiver live-in, 1995—. Mem.: Calif. Assn. Alcohol and Drug Abuse Educators (lic. educator), U.S. Masters Swimming (nat. champ long distance open water swim Capitola to Santa Cruz 6 mile 1998, All Am. honours for long distance open water swimming competition 1998). Democrat. Avocations: landscaping, gardening, open water swimming, writing. Home: 1533 Madrono Ave Palo Alto CA 94306-1016 E-mail: t.byrd@sbcglobal.net.

BYRD, WARREN EDGAR, II, lawyer; b. Bogalusa, La., Dec. 28, 1950; s. H. Warren and Martha Helen (Conner) B.; m. Arlene Dianne Calcote, June 16, 1974; children: Lauren Elizabeth, Matthew Warren. BS, La. State U., 1973, JD, 1978. Bar: La. 1978, U.S. Dist. Ct. (mid., ea. and we. dists.) La. 1978, U.S. Ct. Appeals (5th cir.) 1978. Law clk. Judge E. Gordon West U.S. Dist. Judge, Baton Rouge, La., 1978-80; assoc. Due, Dodson & de Gravelles, Baton Rouge, 1980-81, Wray, Robinson & Kracht, Baton Rouge, 1981-83; asst. atty. gen. La. Dept. Justice, Baton Rouge, 1983-88; assoc. Adams and Reese, Baton Rouge, 1988—, ptnr., 1992—. Speaker Nat. Bus. Inst., Baton Rouge, 1991-92, Fed. Publs. Seminar, New Orleans, 1993, Exec. Enterpriser Seminar, New Orleans, 1994, environ. law seminar La. State U., Baton Rouge, 1997. Bd. dirs. Audubon Coun. Girl Scouts, Baton Rouge, 1986-94, 3d v.p. 1990-91 (Thanks Badge 1990, honor award 1990, Vol. award 1997); soccer referee USSF, NISOA, LHSAA. Named to, La. State U. Track and Field Ofcls. Hall of Fame. Mem. Fed. Bar Assn. (Baton Rouge chpt. treas. 1980-86), La. State Bar Assn. (environ. law sect. coun. 1997, v.p. 2003—), Baton Rouge Bar Assn. (ADR com. 1990—, chmn. com. 1993-95), La. State U. Track and Field Ofcls. Assn., Greater Baton Rouge C. of C. (govtl. fiscal affairs com.). Avocations: running, soccer referee, weightlifting, track. Office: Adams and Reese Bank One Ctr N Twr 19th Fl 451 Florida St Baton Rouge LA 70801-1700

BYRKETT, GARY LEE, hospital engineer; b. Indianapolis, Aug. 21, 1950; s. Robert Harry and Betty Lou Byrkett; m. Sharon Kay Arvin, Oct. 20, 1984. BS in Interdisciplinary Engring., Purdue U., 1972. Plant mgr. St. Francis Hosp. and Health Ctrs., Beech Grove, Ind., 1975—. Chmn. Ind. Coun. on Ind. Living, Indpls., 1996—99; co-chmn. Accessing Tech. Through Awareness Ind., Indpls., 1991—92; pres. Ctrl. Ind. chpt. Muscular Dystrophy Assn., Indpls., 1981—85; bd. mem. Indpls. Resource Ctr. For Independant Living, 1990—97. Recipient Outstanding Achievment ward, Muscular Dystrophy Assn., 1997. Mem.: ASME, Assn. of Energy Enginneers, Assn. of Facility Engineers, Nat. Fire Protection Assn. Methodist. Avocations: motor sports, jazz. Office: St Francis Hospl and Health Ctrs 1600 Albany Beech Grove IN 46107 Office Fax: 317-783-8415. E-mail: gary.byrkett@ssfhs.org.

BYRNE, C. WILLIAM, JR., athletics program director; b. Boston; m. Marilyn Kent; children: Bill, Greg. BBA, Idaho State U., 1967, MBA, 1971. Dir. alumni rels. Idaho State, 1971—76; exec. dir. Lobo Club, U. N.Mex., Albuquerque, 1976-79; asst. athletic dir. San Diego State U., 1980-82; assoc. dir., adminstr. Duck Athletic Fund, U. Oreg., Eugene, 1983-84, dir. athletic dept., 1984-92; dir. athletics U. Nebr., Lincoln, 1992—. Named Ctrl. Region NACDA/Continental Athletic Dir. Yr., Hall of Champions dedicated in his honor, Autzen Stadium, 1993, Nat. Fundraiser Yr., Nat. Athletic Fundraisers Assn. Mem. Nat. Assn. Collegiate Dirs. of Athletics (exec. com., pres.), U.S. Collegiate Sports Coun. (v.p., bd. dirs.), All-Am. Football Found. (v.p.), Football Assn. (bd. dirs.), NCAA (spl. events com., mktg. com., cert. com.). Office: Tex A&M Univ Athletics Dept PO Box 30017 College Station TX 77842-3017

BYRNE, CAROL CUNKLE, medical/surgical nurse; b. York, Pa., Feb. 5, 1948; d. Paul Vincent and Gracella Cunkle; ; m. Thomas Joseph Byrne, Sept. 2, 2000; children: Noel Michele Lane Mumford, Paul Christian Lane. Student in pre-nursing and edn., U. Dubuque, 1966—68; student in practical nursing, Harry B. Ward Vocat. Ctr., Riverhead, N.Y., 1977—79. LPN, N.Y. State U. Camp counselor, waterfront instr. Fireplace Lodge, East Hampton, NY, 1966—69; lifeguard Town of East Hampton, NY, 1974—76; park EMT Cedar Point County Park, East Hampton, NY, 1977—79; nursing staff Southampton (N.Y.) Hosp., 1981—92; office nurse East Hampton Family Medicine, Amagansett, NY, 1994—2001, Dr. Cannon's Office, Wainscott, NY, 2002—. Author: Remember the Red Book, 2002. EMT fire depts., East H ampton and Springs, NY, 1976—81; CPR instr. ARC and Am. Heart Assn., 1977—80; emergency rm. vol. Southampton Hosp., 1977—80. Mem.: DAR, Am. Legion Post 419 (aux.). Roman Catholic. Avocations: writing, Sketching, music, sports.

BYRNE, DANIEL WILLIAM, biostatistician, educator; b. Bklyn., Jan. 21, 1958; s. Thomas Edward and L.M. (Collins) B.; m. Loretta Marie May, June 22, 1985; children: Michael, Virginia. BA in Biology, SUNY, Albany, 1983; MS in Biostatistics, N.Y. Med. Coll., 1991. Programmer, med. software dept. surgery N.Y. Med. Coll., Valhalla, 1983-84; computer/data analyst N.Y. Med. Coll., Westchester County Med. Ctr. and affiliate hosps., 1984-87; rsch. asst. prof. dept. surgery N.Y. Med. Coll., Valhalla, 1988-98, rsch. asst. prof. dept. cmty. and preventive medicine, 1996-99; founder, med. rsch. cons. Byrne Research, Ridgefield, Conn., 1989-99; dir. biostats. GCRC Vanderbilt U., 1999—. Author: Publishing Your Medical Research Paper: What They Don't Teach in Medical School, 1997; author, programmer various software including Trauma Management System, 1990, Occupational Stress Database, 1990, contbr. numerous articles to med. jours. Mem.: Biometric Soc., Am. Statis. Assn. Roman Catholic. Home: 407 Landrake Close Franklin TN 37069-4347 Office: AA-3228 Med Ctr N 1161 21st Ave S Nashville TN 37232-2195

BYRNE, DONN ERWIN, psychologist, educator; b. Austin, Tex., Dec. 19, 1931; s. Bernard Divine and Rebecca (Singleton) B.; m. Lois Ann Pugsley, Sept. 12, 1953 (div. 1978); children: Keven Singleton, Robin Lynn; m. Kathryn Kelley, Aug. 17, 1979 (div. 1996); children: Lindsey Kelley, Rebecka Byrne Kelley. BA, Calif. State U., Fresno, 1953, MA, 1956; PhD, Stanford U., 1958. Instr. psychology Calif. State U., San Francisco, 1957-59; asst. to assoc. prof. psychology U. Tex., Austin, 1959-66, prof. psychology, 1966-69, dir. exptl. personality program, 1963-69, asst. dept. chmn., 1964-66; prof. psychology Purdue U., West Lafayette, Ind., 1969-79, chmn. social personality program, 1972-78; prof. psychology SUNY, Albany, 1979-91, disting. prof., 1991-01, chmn. social-personality program, 1980-84, 90-99, chmn. dept., 1984-89, disting. prof. emeritus, 2001—. Vis. prof. psychology Stanford U., Palo Alto, Calif., 1966-67, U. Hawaii, Honolulu, 1968; panel mem. NSF grad. fellowship program NRC, 1972; NIH participant Inst. Sex Research Summer Program, 1974; G. Stanley Hall lectr. Am. Psychol. Assn., 1981 Author: (with H.C. Lindgren) Psychology: An Introduction to the Study of Human Behavior, 1961, 4th edit., 1975, (with P. Worchel) Personality Change, 1964, An Introduction to Personality: A Research Approach, 1966, 3d edit., 1981, (with M.L. Hamilton) Personality Research: A Book of Readings, 1966, The Attraction Paradigm, 1971, (with R.A. Baron and W. Griffitt) Social Psychology, 1974, (with R.A. Baron) 10th edit., 2003, (with R.A. Baron, B.H. Kantowitz) Psychology: Understanding Behavior, 1977, 2d edit., 1980, (with L.A. Byrne) Exploring Human Sexuality, 1977, (with W.A. Fisher) Adolescents, Sex, and Contraception, 1983, (with K. Kelley) Alternative Approaches to the Study of Sexual Behavior, 1986, (with K. Kelley) Exploring Human Sexuality, 1992; contbr. numerous articles to psychol. jours. and chpts. to anthologies. Grantee NSF, NIMH, U. Tex. Rsch. Inst., USAF, others; recipient Disting Sci. Achievement award Soc. for Scientific Study of Sexuality, 1989. Mem. Midwestern Psychol. Assn. (pres. 1979-80), Soc. for Sci. Study Sexuality (pres. 1990-93), Festschrift at U. Conn. Home: 15 Indian Hill Rd Feura Bush NY 12067-2602 E-mail: vyaduckdb@aol.com. *All of us are seeking the ultimately impossible aims of happiness and self-satisfaction. The former is achieved, however fleetingly, by sensual pleasures and by reaching a series of challenging but attainable goals. Satisfaction depends not only on attaining such goals, but also on the unoriginal but golden ideal of treating other individuals with the same measure of fairness and kindness that we desire from them.*

BYRNE, GEORGE MELVIN, physician; b. Aug. 1, 1933; s. Carlton and Esther (Smith) B.; m. Joan Stecher, July 14, 1956; children: Kathryne, Michael, David; m. Margaret C. Smith, Dec. 18, 1982; m. Barbara Barrett, May 19, 2001. BA, Occidental Coll., 1958; MD, U. So. Calif., 1962. Diplomate Am. Bd. Family Practice. Intern Huntington Meml. Hosp., Pasadena, Calif., 1962-63, resident, 1963-64; family practice So. Calif. Permanente Med. Group, 1964-81; physician-in-charge Pasadena Med. Office, 1966-81; asst. dir. family practice residency Kaiser Found. Hosp., L.A., 1971-73; clin. instr. emergency medicine Sch. Medicine U. So. Calif., 1973-80; v.p. East Ridge Co., 1983-84, sec., 1984; dir. Alan Johnson Porsche Audi, Inc., 1974-82, sec., 1974-77, v.p., 1978-82. Bd. dirs. Kaiser-Permanente Mgmt. Assn., 1976-77, mem. regional mgmt. com. So. Calif. Lung Assn., 1976-77; mem. pres.'s cir. Occidental Coll., L.A. Drs. Symphony Orch., 1975-80; mem. profl. sect. Am. Diabetes Assn. Fellow Am. Acad. Family Physicians (charter); mem. AMA, Calif. Med. Assn., L.A. County Med. Assn., Calif. Acad. Family Physicians, Internat. Horn Soc., Quarter Century Wireless Assn., Am. Radio Relay League (Pub. Svc. award), Sierra (life), So. Calif. Dx Club. Home: 528 Meadowview Dr La Canada Flintridge CA 91011-2816

BYRNE, GRANVILLE BLAND, III, lawyer; b. San Antonio, Jan. 26, 1952; s. Granville Bland and Mary (Dowling) B.; divorced; children: Peyton Smith, Fulton Buckner; m. Monique Renée Wise, 1999. AB, U. N.C., Chapel Hill, 1974; JD, Harvard U., 1978. Bar: Ga. 1978, U.S. Dist. Ct. (no. dist.) Ga. 1978, U.S. Ct. Appeals (5th cir.) 1978, U.S. Ct. Appeals (11th cir.) 1981. Assoc. Swift, Currie, McGhee & Hiers, Atlanta, 1978-84, ptnr., 1984-94; prin. Byrne Eldridge, Moore & Davis, P.C., Atlanta, 1994—99, Byrne, Moore & Davis, PC, Atlanta, 1999—2002, Byrne & Davis, PC, Atlanta, 2003—. Bd. dirs. Compeer Atlanta, Inc., chmn., 1993-, 1996-2002; bd. dirs. Cagle's, Inc. Elder, mem. session 1st Presbyn. Ch. Atlanta, 1993-96, 99-2002. Mem. ABA, Ga. Bar Assn., Atlanta Bar Assn. Democrat. Presbyterian. Home: 3555 Castlegate Dr NW Atlanta GA 30327-2601 Office: Byrne & Davis PC 3340 Peachtree Rd NE Atlanta GA 30326-1000 E-mail: gbb@bmdlaw.net.

BYRNE, GREGORY WILLIAM, lawyer; b. Chgo., Aug. 18, 1939; s. William Daniel and Theresa (Gregory) B.; m. Debra Demert, Oct. 12, 1984; children: Kathleen Minde, Gregory W. Jr., Julianna Rowe, Elizabeth Hering. AB, U. S.C., 1968; JD, Harvard U., 1971. Bar: Oreg. 1971, U.S. Dist. Ct. Oreg. 1971, U.S. Ct. Appeals (9th cir.) 1973, U.S. Supreme Ct. 1990, U.S. Ct. Fed. Claims 1993. Enlisted USMC, 1959, advanced through grades to capt., 1965, resigned, 1967; sole practice Portland, Oreg., 1971—. Judge pro tem Multnomah County Cts., Portland, 1983-90; dir. Harvard Legis. Rsch. Bur., 1970-71; adj. scholar Cascade Policy Inst., 2002. Mem. Multnomah Bar Assn. Republican. Office: 5550 SW Macadam Ave Portland OR 97201 E-mail: gbyrne@att.net.

BYRNE, JAMES FREDERICK, banker; b. Fairmont, N.C., July 30, 1931; m. Daphne Martin, July 22, 1955; children— Paula Jean, Daphne Ann, Laura BS, Wake Forest U., 1953; MBA, U. N.C., 1959. Ptnr. Byrne-Floyd Realty, Fairmont, N.C., 1961-80; v.p., city exec. So. Nat. Bank, Fairmont, 1963-69, mgr. master charge Lumberton, N.C., 1969-71, v.p., dir. mktg., 1971-77, sr. v.p., dir. customer services, 1977-83, exec. v.p., 1983, exec. v.p., dir. retail banking, 1985-89, sr. exec. v.p., chief adminstrv. officer, 1989-94. Mem. endowment bd. Pembroke State U., N.C., 1985-87, chmn. libr. bd., 1995-96. Pres. Am. Lung Assn. of N.C., Wilmington, 1971, Raleigh, 1972, N.C. rep. dir., N.Y., 1977 89; nat. v.p. Am. Lung Assn., 1989. Recipient Vol. of Yr. award Am. Lung Assn. of N.C., 1972-90, Nat. Humanitarian award, 1993. Mem. Bank Mktg. Assn., N.C. Bankers Assn., Shrine Club (pres. 1996-97), Rotary (pres. 1968), Masons. Home: 905 Dogwood Dr Fairmont NC 28340-2115

BYRNE, JEFFREY EDWARD, pharmacology researcher, educator, consultant; b. Mpls., July 15, 1939; s. Maurice Charles and Edna F. (Kinney) B.; m. Janice Grove, Feb. 1, 1960 (dec. Apr., 1976); children: Christopher, Maura; m. Margaret Ann Kaiser, June 17, 1978, 1 child, Jason. BA, U. N.D., 1962; MA, U. S.D., 1964, PhD, 1966. Sr. rsch. assoc. Bristol-Myers Co., Evansville, Ind., 1969-81, prin. rsch. scientist, 1981-87; sr. rsch. scientist II Bristol-Myers Squibb Co., Wallingford, Conn., 1987-91, Princeton, N.J., 1991-94; cons. in field, 1994—; computer software programmer/database applications developer, 1995-2000. Adj. faculty Ind. U. Sch. Medicine, Evansville, 1972-81, Evansville U. Sch. Nursing, 1972-81. Contbr. articles to profl. jours.; author (with others) books. Mem. Am. Heart Assn., Internat. Soc. for Heart Rsch. Lutheran. Achievements include discovery of Encainide, an antiarrythmic drug. Home: 5411 Ironwood Dr Newburgh IN 47630-3126 E-mail: jbyrne1@adelphia.net.

BYRNE, JOHN EDWARD (JEB BYRNE), writer, retired government official; b. N.Y.C., Jan. 15, 1925; s. Harry Theodore and Mary Elizabeth (Whelen) B.; m. Beverly Ann McKinley, Mar. 31, 1951; children— Peter J., David F., John P., Michael T. BA, Marquette U., 1949; MA, George Washington U., 1973, PhD, 1987. News service corr. UPI, Milw., 1949-50, Albany, N.Y., 1951, Portland, Maine, 1951-56, Augusta, Maine, 1956-58; gov.'s press sec., state promotion ofcl. State of Maine, Augusta, 1959-60; exec. GSA, Washington, 1961-80; dir. fed. register Nat. Archives and Records Adminstrn., Washington, 1980-88. Fulbright scholar Alexander Turnbull Libr., Wellington, New Zealand, 1989. Served to 2d lt. USAAF, 1943-45 Roman Catholic. Home: 2104 Marthas Rd Alexandria VA 22307-1823

BYRNE, JOHN JOSEPH, surgeon; b. Morristown, N.J., Sept. 30, 1916; MD, Harvard Univ., 1941. Intern Boston City Hosp., 1941-42, resident surgery, 1942-44, dir. rsch. lab., 1948-93, chief surgeon 3rd surg., 1948-93; prof. surgery Boston U., 1960-93. Fellow ACS; mem. Am. Surg. Assn., Am. Soc. Surgery of the Hand. E-mail: jbyrne9648@aol.com.

BYRNE, JOHN MICHAEL, energy and environmental policy educator, researcher; b. Chgo., Nov. 2, 1949; s. Michael Thomas and Mabel Victoria (Cranford) B.; m. Elizabeth Maria Garey, Aug. 9, 1975; children: Brian, Tara. BA in Econs., U. Del., 1971, MA, 1973, PhD in Urban Affairs and Pub. Policy, 1980. Asst. prof. Urban Affairs and Pub. Policy, U. Del., Newark, 1982-86, assoc. prof., 1986-92, prof., 1992—, dir. Energy Policy Rsch. Group, 1981-84, dir. Ctr. for Energy and Environ. Policy, 1984—, chair Urban Affairs and Pub. Policy grad. program, 1992-96. Apptd. environ. policy advisor Korea Nat. Assembly, 1998—; co-exec. dir. Joint Inst. for a Sustainable Energy and Environ. Future, 1999—. Co-editor: Energy and Cities, 1985, The Politics of Energy R&D, 1986, Energy and Environment: The Policy Challenge, 1992, Governing the Atom: The Politics of Risk, 1996, Environmental Justice, 2002; mem. editl. bd. Bull. of Sci., Tech. and Soc., 1995—; contbg. author: 2nd and 3rd Assessment Reports of the Intergovtl. Panel on Climate Change, 1995—. Bd. dirs. Urban Environ. Ctr., 1997—, Environ. Market Solutions, Inc., 2002—. Grantee ESMAP/World Bank, 1990-91, U.S. Dept. Energy/Nat. Renewable Energy Lab., 1991-2001, UNIDEL Found., 1992, U.S. EPA, 1994, 97-2001, Asia Found., 1995, Inst. Internat. Edn., 1996-97, W. Alton Jones Found., 1997-2002, U.S. Dept. Energy, 2002—, Blue Moon Fund, 2003—; recipient Fulbright Sr. Lectr./Rschr. award, 1995. Mem. IEEE Social Implications of Tech. Affiliate, Nat. Assn. Sci., Tech. and Society (adv. bd. 1991—). Avocations: music, woodworking, hiking. Office: U Del Ctr Energy & Environ Policy Newark DE 19716-7301

BYRNE, JOHN VINCENT, higher education consultant; b. Hempstead, N.Y., May 9, 1928; s. Frank E. and Kathleen (Barry) B.; m. Shirley O'Connor, Nov. 26, 1954; children: Donna, Lisa, Karen, Steven. AB, Hamilton Coll., 1951, JD (hon.), 1994; MA, Columbia U., 1953; PhD, U. So. Calif., 1957. Research geologist Humble Oil & Refinery Co., Houston, 1957-60; assoc. prof. Oreg. State U., Corvallis, 1960-66, prof. oceanography, 1966—, chmn. dept., 1968-72, dean Sch. Oceanography, 1972-76, acting dean research, 1976-77, dean research, 1977-80, v.p. for research and grad. studies, 1980-81, pres., 1984-95; adminstr. NOAA, Washington, 1981-84; pres. Oreg. State U., 1984-95; higher edn. cons. Corvallis, 1996—. Program dir. oceanography NSF, 1966-67; exec. dir. Kellogg Commn. on Future of State and Land Grant Univs., 1996-2000; dir. Harbor Br. Ocean Inst., Oregon Coast Aquarium. Recipient Carter teaching award Oreg. State U., 1964. Fellow AAAS, Geol. Soc. Am.; mem. Geol. Soc. Am., Am. Geophys. Union, Sigma Xi, Chi Psi. Home: 3190 NW Deer Run St Corvallis OR 97330-3107 Office: Autzen House 811 SW Jefferson Ave Corvallis OR 97333-4506 E-mail: john.byrne@orst.edu.

BYRNE, JUDY SUSANNE, writer, educator; b. Great Falls, Mont., Mar. 18, 1950; d. Patrick John and Lila Mae Byrne. Student, Coll. Litteraire U., Avignon, France, 1970; BA, Mont. State U., 1972, MEd, 1982. Mid. sch. tchr. Lewistown (Mont.) Sch. Dist. 1, 1972—97; substitute tchr. Fergus County pub. sch., Lewistown, 1997—. Adj. instr. Coll. Gt. Falls, 1978—79, No. Mont. Coll., Havre, 1990—93, Carroll Coll., Helena, 2003, Mont. State U., 2001, mem. adv. coun., 1991—95, student tchr. supr., Billings, 2003; cons. in field; co-creator state stds. writing instrn. Mont. pub. schs. State Office Pub. Instrn., Helena, 1998; supr. student tchr. U. Mont., Missoula, 2002, Bozeman, 02. Contbr. articles to profl. jours., columns in newspapers; author: (newspaper column) A Class Act (Outstanding Media award, 1999); contbg. author (book) What America's Teachers Wish Parents Knew, 1993; editor: LEA Link Newsletter, 1985—95 (Outstanding Local Media award, 1992); dir., performer, co-author (plays) As the Whistle Blows, Lewistown, Mont., 1998; dir.: (plays) Centennial Story, 1999; actor: Annie, 2000, The Sound of Music, 2001; dir., actor (variety show) Luck o' the Irish, Lewistown, Mont., 1999, 2000; dir.: The Wizard of Oz, 2002. Student selection coord. Am. Field Svc., Lewistown, 1979—93; campaign chmn. Myers for Exec. Com. of the NEA, Great Falls, 1990—91; election judge Fergus County, Lewistown, 1997—2003. Grantee Title III Innovative Edn. Incentive grant, U.S. Dept. of Edn., 1976. Mem.: AARP, NEA (life), Mont. Theater Edn. Assn., Mont. Assn. Lang. Teachers, Mont. Assn. Tchr. English Lang. Arts, Mont. State U. Alumni Assn. (life), Phi Delta Kappa, Delta Kappa Gamma. Avocations: skiing, golf, photography, reading, travel. Personal E-mail: judyb@lewistown.net.

BYRNE, MICHAEL JOSEPH, manufacturing executive; b. Apr. 3, 1928; s. Michael Joseph and Edith (Lueken) Byrne; m. Eileen Kelly, June 27, 1953; children: Michael Joseph, Nancy, James, Thomas, Patrick, Terrence. BSC in mktg., Loyola U., Chgo., 1952. Sales engr. Emery Industries, Inc., Cin., 1952—59; with Pennsalt Chem. Corp., Phila., 1959—60; pres. Oakton Cleaners, Inc., Skokie, Ill., 1960—70, Datatax Inc., Skokie, Ill., 1970—74, Midwest Synthetic Lubrication Products, 1978—, Pure Water Sys., 1984—, Superior Tax Svc., 1984—. With U.S. Army, 1946—48. Mem.: AIM, Toastmasters Internat., VFW, Alpha Kappa Psi. Home: PO Box 916 Prospect Heights IL 60070-0916

BYRNE, NOEL THOMAS, sociologist, educator; b. San Francisco, May 11, 1943; s. Joseph Joshua and Naomi Pearl (Denison) B.; m. Dale W. Elrod, Aug. 6, 1989. BA in Sociology, Sonoma State Coll., 1971; MA in Sociology, Rutgers U., 1975, PhD in Sociology, 1987. Instr. sociology Douglass Coll., Rutgers U., New Brunswick, N.J., 1974-76, Hartnell Coll., Salinas, Calif., 1977-78; from lectr. to assoc. prof. dept. mgmt. Sonoma State U., Rohnert Park, Calif., 1978-94, chmn. dept. of mgmt., 1990-91, from. assoc. prof. to prof. sociology dept., 1994—, chmn. dept. sociology, 1997—2002; cons. prof. Emile Durkheim Inst. for Advanced Study, Grand Cayman, B.W.I., 1990-93. Chair of faculty Sonoma State U., 2002—03, chair acad. senate, 2002—03. Contbr. articles and revs. to profl. lit. Recipient Dell Pub. award Rutgers U. Grad. Sociology Program, 1976, Louis Bevier fellow, 1977-78. Mem. AAAS, Am. Sociol. Assn., Pacific Sociol. Assn., N.Y. Acad. Sci., Soc. for Study Symbolic Interaction (rev. editor Jour. 1980-83), Soc. for Study Social Problems, Commonwealth Club. Democrat. Home: 4773 Ross Rd Sebastopol CA 95472-2114 Office: Sonoma State U Dept Sociology Rohnert Park CA 94928 E-mail: noel.byrne@sonoma.edu.

BYRNE, PATRICIA CURRAN, small business owner; b. Tannersville, N.Y., Mar. 17, 1915; d. Michael Edward and Catherine Mary (Keogh) Curran; m. Owen Perry Byrne, July 6, 1939 (dec. Sept. 3, 1970); children: Sharon Byrne Van Dyke, Maureen E., Kevin O., Brian H., Sean M. BA, Hunter Coll., 1936; MS in Edn., SUNY, New Paltz, 1975. Tchr. elem. sch. H.T. Ctrl. Sch., N.Y., 1937-41, 52-53; mgr., co-owner restaurant Curran's Tavern, Tannersville, N.Y., 1953-70, owner-operator, 1970—. Democrat. Roman Catholic. Avocations: skiing, walking, swimming, poetry. Address: PO Box 201 Tannersville NY 12485-0201

BYRNE, PAUL ADAMS, pediatrician, educator; b. Norwood, Ohio, Feb. 14, 1933; s. Randolph E. and Anna A. (Rape) Byrne; m. Shirley A. Dominetto, Oct. 11, 1957; children: James, Lisa, Paul G., Michael, Dan, Tom, Mary, Kathleen, Anne, Mark, Amy, Jennifer. BS, Xavier U., Cin., 1953; MD, St. Louis U., 1957. Diplomate Am. Bd. Pedriat. From instr. to clin. prof. pediat. St. Louis U., 1961—81; clin. prof. pediat. Creighton U., Omaha, 1981—86; prof., chmn. pediat. dept. Oral Roberts U., Tulsa, 1986—89; prof. pediat. Med. Coll. Ohio, Toledo, 1990—. Pres. Catholic Med. Assn., 1997—98; dir. neonatology St. Charles Mercy Hosp., Oregon, Ohio. Home: 577 Bridewater Dr Oregon OH 43616 Office: St Charles Mercy Hosp 2600 Navarre Ave Oregon OH 43616

BYRNE, RAYMOND HARRY, electrical engineer; b. Baton Rouge, La., Dec. 12, 1965; s. Harry C. Jr. and Judite K. (Kamarauskas) B. BSEE, U. Va., 1987; MSEE, U. Colo., 1989; PhD, U. N.Mex., 1995. Mem. tech. staff Sandia Nat. Labs., Albuquerque, 1989—. Adj. prof. U. N.Mex., Albuquerque, 1996—. Named N.M. qualifier mid-amateur USGA, 1996, 98, 99, Sun Country Amateur Golf Assn. Match Play Champion, 2002. Mem. IEEE (chmn., vice chmn., sec., treas. Albuqueque sect. 1992—, Third Millennium medal 2000), Sun Country Amateur Golf Assn. (bd. dirs. 2000—, sec. 2000-2002, treas. 2002—), Four Hills Country Club (golf com. chmn. 1997), Sandia Golf League (A-League Dir. 1992-95), North Eubank Ski Club (pres., v.p., winter trips treas. 1989-2000), U.S. Golf Assn. (sr. amateur com. 2001-), Tau Beta Pi, Eta Kappa Nu, Sigma Xi. Avocations: golf, skiing, mountain biking, roller-blading. Office: Sandia Nat Labs MS 0501 PO Box 5800 Albuquerque NM 87185-0501

BYRNE, RICHARD HILL, counselor, educator; b. Lancaster, Pa., Aug. 3, 1915; s. Jacob Hill and Mary Deborah (Allwein) B.; m. Magdalene Antoinette Wardell, June 12, 1954; children— Christopher, Mary, Matthew, Peter AB, Franklin and Marshall Coll., 1938; MA, Columbia U., 1947, Ed.D., 1952. Tchr. several sch. systems, Lancaster County, Pa., 1939-42; counselor Allegany County Schs., Cumberland, Md., 1949-50; state guidance supr. State of N.H., Concord, 1950-51; assoc., then prof., chmn. counseling dept. U. Md., College Park, 1951-82, prof. emeritus, 1983—, resident grad. prof. Upper Heyford, Eng., 1982-84, Boston U., Germany, 1984-86. Cons. U.S. Dept. Labor, Washington, 1964-68; cons. in guidance numerous sch. systems, Md., Pa., Va., 1951-82; dir. interprofl. research ctr. on pupil services, College Park, Md., 1963-68 Author: The School Counselor, 1963, Guidance: A Behavioral Approach, 1977, Becoming a Master Counselor, 1994. Served to capt. U.S. Army, 1942-46, ETO Mem. Am. Psychol. Assn., Md. Personnel and Guidance Assn. (1st pres. 1957-58) Home: 1390 Ventnor Ave Tarpon Springs FL 34689-2731

BYRNE, ROBERT EUGENE, chess columnist; b. N.Y.C., Apr. 20, 1928; s. Frank and Elizabeth Eleanor (Cattelier) B.; m. Florence Mary Dolley, Sept. 8, 1954 (div. Feb. 1971); children: Benjamin (dec.), Thomas Edward; m. Ursula Maria von Krebs, Sept. 11, 1971. BA, Yale U., 1952; postgrad., Ind. U., 1952-60. Chess reporter N.Y. Daily News, N.Y.C., 1971-72; chess columnist N.Y. Times, 1972—. Mem. U.S. Olympiad teams U.S. Chess Fedn., New Windsor, N.Y., 1952-84, capt., 1984, U.S. chess champion, 1972, quarter finalist world chess championship; world chess champion Internat. Chess Fedn., Geneva, 1974; U.S. Open champion U.S. Chess Fedn., New Windsor, 1960, 63, 66, comm. for IBM on Deep Blue chess computer project. Author: Beginning Chess, 1972, Both Sides of the Chessboard, 1972, The Road to the World Championship, 1976, (calendar) The Chess Calendar, 1998, 99, 2000, N.Y. Times Book of Great Chess Victories and Defeats, 1990. Mem. U.S. Chess Fedn. (Fred Cramer award for excellence in journalism best newspaper column 2000), Manhattan Chess Club (hon. bd. dirs. 1980—). Avocations: opera, ballet, archaeology, tennis. Home and Office: 16 Rockledge Ave Scarborough NY 10510

BYRNE, ROBERT WILLIAM, lawyer; b. Frankfurt, Germany, Dec. 12, 1958; s. Robert Patrick and Anne Lise (Brondelsbo) B. BA, Rutgers U., 1981; JD, Seton Hall U., 1984; LLM, Golden Gate U., 2002. Bar: N.J. 1984, U.S. Dist. Ct. N.J. 1984, D.C. 1986, U.S. Ct. Appeals (3d cir.) 1987, U.S. Ct. Appeals (D.C. and fed. cirs.) 1988, (11th cir.), 1993, U.S. Dist. Ct. D.C. 1989, U.S. Supreme Ct. 1989, N.Y. 1991, U.S. Dist. Ct. (so. and ea. dists.) N.Y. 1991, Fla. 1992, U.S. Dist. Ct. (no. and mid. dists.) Fla. 1992, Calif. 2001., U.S. Dist. Ct. (no. dist.) Calif. 2001, U.S. Ct. Appeals (9th cir.) 2001. Law clk. to Judge Sylvan G. Rothenberg, Superior Ct. Passaic County N.J., 1984-85; asst. prosecutor Bergen County, N.J., 1985-88; assoc. Harwood Lloyd, Hackensack, NJ, 1988-90, Mudge Rose Guthrie Alexander & Ferdon, N.Y.C., 1990-91; sr. assoc. O'Connor, Reddy & Jensen, N.Y.C., 1991-92; pvt. practice Panama City, Fla., 1992-94; v.p., gen. counsel Bay Bank & Trust Co., Panama City, Fla., 1994-2000; dep. atty. gen. Calif. Dept. Justice, San Francisco, 2002—. Contbr. Seton Hall Legislative Jour., 1983-84. Mem. Phi Alpha Delta, Pi Sigma Alpha. Democrat. Lutheran. Home: 267 Roosevelt Way San Francisco CA 94114-1431 Office: 455 Golden Gate Ave Ste 11000 San Francisco CA 94102-7004 Fax: 415-703-5480. E-mail: robert.byrne@doj.ca.gov.

BYRNE, SHAUN PATRICK, law enforcement mediator; b. Atlantic City, Aug. 22, 1963; s. Warren Patrick and Donna Mae (Curlott) B. Student, Nat. Acad. Paralegals, Egg Harbor, N.J., 1991; AS, Cumberland County Coll., Vineland, N.J., 1994; BA in Criminal Justice, Stockton State Coll., Pomona, N.J., 1995; grad., Widener U. Sch. Law, 2000. Bar: (N.J., Pa.) 2000. Police officer Atlantic City Police Dept., 1984-85; with trade union, 1986-91; sr. detective Jamesway Corp., Secaucus, N.J., 1991-95; law clk. Atlantic County Pub. Def. Office, 1999-2000. Security advisor P.S.I., Inc.; paralegal, 1991-92; mediation counselor Criminal Justice Inst., 1995—; deputy gen. dir. Internat. Biog. Ctr., 1999; mediator U.S. Post Office, 1998—. Martial arts trainer/demonstrator Fighting Dragons Dojo, Atlantic City, 1980-97; high sch. presentations on violence/drugs, Vineland, 1995; Oceanview vol. firefighter, 2003—. Named Outstanding Person 20th Century Internat. Biog. Ctr., 1997; Am. Biog. Inst. fellow, 1998. Republican. Roman Catholic. Avocations: martial arts, kick boxing, scuba diving, weight training. Home: PO Box 1081 Absecon NJ 08201-5081 E-mail: p8s2i2@earthlink.net.

BYRNE, THOMAS J. lawyer; b. Rochester, N.Y., June 17, 1944; m. Brenda C. Byrne, June 4, 1994; children: Thomas, David, Heather. AB, U. Rochester, 1967; JD, U. Denver, 1976. Bar: Colo. 1977, Calif. 1977, U.S. Ct. Appeals (10th cir.) 1977, U.S. Dist. Ct. Colo. 1977, U.S. Dist. Ct. (so. dist.) Tex. 1990, N.Y. 1990, U.S. Ct. Appeals (3d cir.) 1992, U.S. Dist. Ct. (ea. dist.) Pa. 1992, U.S. Dist. Ct. (ea. dist.) Va. 1992, U.S. Ct. Appeals (4th cir.) 1993, U.S. Dist. Ct. (no. dist.) Ill. 1993, U.S. Dist. Ct. Ariz. 1993, U.S. Dist. Ct. Utah 1996, U.S. Dist. Ct. (so. dist.) N.Y. 1997. Law clk. Dist. Ct. Colo., Denver, 1976-77; assoc. Ullstrom Law Offices, Denver, 1978-83; ptnr., Denver mgr. Conklin & Adler, Ltd., Denver and Chgo., 1983-86; mng. ptnr. Byrne, Kiely & White LLP, Denver, 1986—. Mem. fin. com. Citizens for Romer, Denver, 1990—. Capt. USAF, 1967-73. Mem. ABA (tort and ins. practice sect., vice chair aviation and space law com., litigation sect., forum on air and space law), Internat. Bar Assn., Colo. Bar Assn., Denver Bar Assn., State Bar Calif., N.Y. State Bar Assn., Def. Rsch. Inst., Colo. Def. Lawyers Assn., Nat. Bus. Aircraft Assn., Lawyer-Pilot Bar Assn., Aviation Ins. Assn. Avocations: flying, travel, sports. Office: Byrne Kiely & White LLP 1120 Lincoln St Ste 1300 Denver CO 80203-2140

BYRNE-DEMPSEY, CECELIA (CECELIA DEMPSEY), journalist; b. L.A., Aug. 7, 1925; d. John Joseph and Margaret Agnes (Frakell) B.; m. John Dempsey, Mar. 25, 1951 (dec. June 1981); children: Margaret, Elizabeth, John, Cecelia, Cathrine, Patricia, Bridget, Charles, Mary Teresa. Student, Immaculate Heart Coll., 1944; BA in Psychology, Calif. State U., Northridge, 1975, BA in Journalism, 1978, MA in Mass Communication, 1992. Staff Lockheed Aircraft Corp., Burbank, Calif., 1943—, Office Naval Rsch., San Francisco, 1947—; with Sisters of Mercy, Burlingame, Calif., 1945—, Sisters of Presentation, San Francisco, 1949—; mem. staff Calif. State U., Calif., 1976—. Rschr., journalism historian early Am. newspapers, 1978—. Author: The Meaning Index: A Model for Early American Newspaper Indexing: a research guide, 1992. Mentor 4-H Club; past mem. Urban Corp., L.A. Mem. Mensa, Kappa Gamma Delta. Republican. Jewish. Avocations: poetry, gardening, philosophical meditation.

BYRNES, CHRISTOPHER IAN, academic dean, researcher; b. N.Y.C., June 28, 1949; s. Richard Francis and Jeanne (Orchard) B.; m. Catherine Morris, June 24, 1984; children: Kathleen, Alison, Christopher. BS, Manhattan Coll., 1971; MS, U. Mass., 1973, PhD, 1975; D (hon.) of Tech., Royal Inst. Tech., Stockholm, 1998. Instr. U. Utah, Salt Lake City, 1975-78; asst. prof. Harvard U., Cambridge, Mass., 1978-81, assoc. prof., 1981-85; rsch. prof. Ariz. State U., Tempe, 1985-89; prof., chmn. dept. systems sci. and math. Washington U., St. Louis, 1989-91, dean engring. and applied sci., 1991—. Adj. prof. Royal Inst. Tech., Stockholm, 1985-90; cons. Sci. Sys., Inc., Cambridge, 1980-84, Sys. Engring., Inc., Greenbelt, Md., 1986; sci. advisor Sherwood Davis & Geck, 1996-98, Aucsyn Venture Capital Cernium Inc., 2002-; mem. NRC; bd. dirs., chmn. compensation com. Belden Inc.; chmn. bd. dirs. Ctr. for Emerging Techs.; pres., bd. dirs. WUTA, Inc. Editor: (book series) Progress in Systems Control, 1988—01, Foundations of Systems and Control, 1998—2001; Nonlinear Synthesis, 1991, 13 other books; contbr. numerous articles to profl. jours., book revs. Recipient Best Paper award, IFAC, 1993. Fellow: IEEE (Geroge Axelby award 1991), Acad. Sci. St. Louis, Japan Soc. for Promotion Sci.; mem.: AAAS, Regional Chamber for Growth Assn. (vice chmn. tech., chmn. Tech. Gateway Alliance 2000—03), Royal Swedish Acad. Engring. Sci. (fgn.), Am. Math. Soc., Soc. Indsl. Applied Math. (program com. 1986—89), Tau Beta Pi, Sigma Xi. Avocations: cooking, fishing, travel. Office: Washington U Sch Engring and Applied Sci 1 Brookings Dr Saint Louis MO 63130-4899 E-mail: Chrisbyrnes@seas.wustl.edu.

BYRNES, JAMES BERNARD, museum director, consultant; b. N.Y.C., Feb. 19, 1917; s. Patrick J.A. and Janet E. (Geiger) B.; m. Barbara A. Cecil, June 10, 1946; 1 son, Ronald L. Student, N.A.D., 1936-38, Am. Artist Sch., 1938-40, Art Students League, 1940-42, U. Perugia, Italy, 1951, Inst. Meschini, Rome, 1952. Art tchr. mus. activity program N.Y.C. Bd. Edn., 1936-40; indsl. designer Michael Saphier Assos., N.Y.C., 1940-42; audio visual specialist USNR, 1944—45; with L.A. County Mus., 1946-47, assoc. curator modern contemporary art, 1947-48, curator, asst. to dir., 1948-53; dir. Colorado Springs Fine Arts Center, 1954-55; from assoc. dir. to dir. N.C. Mus. Art, 1956-60; dir. New Orleans Mus. Art, 1961-71, dir. emeritus, 1989—; dir. Newport Harbor Art Mus., Newport Beach, Calif., 1972-75. Vis. lectr. U. Fla., 1961, Newcomb Coll., Tulane U., 1963; art cons. Author: Masterpieces of Art, W.R. Valentiner Memorial, 1959, Tobacco and Smoking in Art, 1960, Fetes de la Palette, 1963, Edgar Degas, His Family and Friends in New Orleans, 1965, Odyssey of an Art Collector, 1966, Art of Ancient and Modern Latin America, 1968, The Artist as Collector of Primitive Art, 1975, also numerous mus. catalogs. Decorated knight Order Leopold II (Belgium); recipient Isaac Delgado Meml. award New Orleans Mus. of Art, 1998. Mem. Am. Soc. Interior Design (hon. life), Am. Soc. Appraisers (sr.), Appraisers Assn. Am. Office: James B Byrnes and Assocs 7820 Mulholland Dr Los Angeles CA 90046-1223

BYRNES, JO ANN, professional relations administrator; b. Paterson, N.J., Dec. 12, 1949; d. George J. and Josephine (Balady) Hajjar. BA, Douglas Coll., 1974; MSW, NYU, 1976. Cert. ACSW; lic. clin. social worker. Dir. social svcs. Vis. Homemakers, Jersey City, Summit Ridge, West Orange, N.J.; pvt. practice family counselor; dir. social svcs. Raritan Bay Med. Ctr.; pub. rels. coord. Compassionate Care Hospice, Clifton, N.J. Home: 176 Harvest Ln Lincoln Park NJ 07035-2047

BYRNES, MICHAEL FRANCIS, podiatrist; b. Chgo., Aug. 11, 1957; s. Edward and Dorothy Franchi; m. Debra Michelle Moody, July, 31, 1982. BA, Loyola U., Chgo., 1979; D in Podiatry Medicine, Ill. Coll. Podiatry Med., 1984. Diplomate Am. Bd. Podiatric Surgery. Practice medicine specializing in podiatrics Ridgeland Foot Clinic., Chgo., 1984—. Surgeon Mercy Surg. Ctr., Justice, Ill., 1984—, Holy Cross Hosp., 1987—, Palos Cmty. Hosp., 1997—; assoc. prof. Dr. Scholl Coll. Podiatric Medicine; mem. sci. and med. staff Mercy Hosp. and Med. Ctr. Contbr. case reports to Jour. Foot Surgery, 1985. Bd. dirs. Animal Welfare League, Chgo., 1993—, chief fin. officer, 1998-99, 2000-01. Precinct capt. 49th Dem. Ward., Chgo., 1976-80. Winner state skating championship, 1980; recipient commendation Oaklawn Police Dept., 1995, VFW award Oaklawn Post, 1995, Courage award The Wizard of Oz on Ice, TNT Prodns., 1995, Clark Oil award, 1995. Fellow Am. Coll. Foot Surgeons; mem. Am. Podiatric Med. Assn., Ill. Podiatric Med. Assn. (co-chmn. legis. com. 1985-86, del.), Am. Acad. Podiatric Sports Medicine. Roman Catholic. Avocation: skating. Home: 203 Kenmare Dr Burr Ridge IL 60527-5299 Office: 9941 Southwest Hwy Oak Lawn IL 60453-3767 E-mail: mbyrnes@pol.net.

BYRNES, RICHARD JAMES, lawyer; b. Newark, Jan. 14, 1947; s. L. George and A. Marie (Ellis) B. A.B., Rutgers U., 1968; J.D., NYU, 1976. Bar: N.Y. 1976. Assoc. Weil, Gotshal & Manges, N.Y.C., 1976-77, Shearman & Sterling, N.Y.C., 1977-81; assoc. Hawkins, Delafield & Wood, N.Y.C., 1981-83, ptnr. 1984-85; sr. v.p. and co-mgr. William E. Pollack & Co., Inc., N.Y.C., 1985— ; ptnr. Kutak, Rock & Campbell, Washington, 1985—; dir. Pub. Space Collaborative, N.Y.C. Counsel N.Y. Sch. for Circus Arts, N.Y.C., 1978— . Served to capt. U.S. Army, 1968-71. Mem. ABA (internat. law com. 1983—, internat. fin. transactions com. 1984—, internat. trade com. 1984—), N.Y. Bar Assn., Am. Mgmt. Assn., Internat. Law Inst. (assoc.), Internat. Bar Assn., Inter-Am. Bar Assn. Office: William E Pollock & Co Inc 160 Water St New York NY 10038-4922

BYRNES, ROBERT WILLIAM, secondary school educator; b. Morristown, N.J., July 30, 1948; s. Robert Sinon and Mary Loraine (Benz) B.; m. Sherri Lynn Ackerman. BA in Secondary English, Newark State Coll., 1970; MA in English, Fairleigh Dickinson U., 1995. Cert. tchr. English 7-12, N.J. Tchr. Deptford Twp. (N.J.) Bd. Edn., 1971-72; tchr. English Dover (N.J.) Bd. Edn., 1972—. Cadet supr. N.J. Track and Field Ofcls. Assn., 2001—. Mem. sewer Ban Relief Com., Denville, N.J., 1980, Zeek Rd. Recreation Planning Commn., Denville, 1980; girl's sch. rep. N.J. Cath. track Conf., Kearny, 1983-89, treas., 1990—. Recipient Svc. award N.J. Cath. Track Conf., 1988, Morris County Track Coaches Assn., 1997. Mem. Dover Edn. Assn. (v.p. 1999-2003). Avocations: track and field, golf, reading, art. Home: 5 Snyder Ave Denville NJ 07834-2135 Office: Dover High Sch 100 Grace St Dover NJ 07801-2697

BYRNES, THOMAS RAYMOND, JR., osteopath; b. Ft. Meade, Md., Aug. 18, 1956; s. Thomas Raymond and Jeanne Marie (Lavis) Byrnes; m. Kathleen Ann Jory, Jan. 7, 1983; children: Erin Marie, Christopher Mason. Student, Tanana Valley C.C., Fairbanks, Alaska, 1977-85, U. Alaska, 1978-85; BSc in Sports Medicine, Pepperdine U., 1983; DO, Kirksville Coll. Osteo. Medicine, 1992. Cert. athletic trainer, 1995; Diplomate Am. Bd. Family Practice, 1972. Human performance lab. technician, athletic trainer Pepperdine U., Malibu, Calif., 1980—83; asst. athletic trainer U. Alaska, Fairbanks, 1983-85; spl. edn. tchrs. aide North Star Borough Sch. Dist., Fairbanks, 1985-87; OMM teaching fellow Kirksville (Mo.) Coll. Osteo. Medicine, 1989-92; resident Warren Hosp., Phillipsburg, N.J., 1992-95; family practice physician, med. supr. Soldier Family Health Clinic, Fort Stewart, Ga., 1995-98; chief family practice svc. Winn Army Cmty. Hosp., Ft. Stewart, 1998; CEO Coastal Ga. Osteo. Health Care Assn. Inc., Richmond Hill, Ga., 1999—; med. dir. REDICARE, Richmond Hill, 1999—; CEO, pres. So. Light Osteo. Wellness and Healthcare Assocs., Inc., 2002—. Maj. U.S. Army. Mem. Am. Acad. Osteopathy, Am. Osteo. Assn., Am. Acad. Family Practitioners, Cranial Acad. Avocations: family, philosophy, mechanical tinkering, walking, skiing. Office: REDICARE PO Box 1979 4164 Us Highway 17 Richmond Hill GA 31324-3306

BYRNES, WILLIAM JOSEPH, lawyer; b. Bklyn., Apr. 11, 1940; s. William James and Margaret Mary (English) B.; m. Catherine Belle Rollings, Aug. 15, 1970 (dec. 2002); children: Jennifer, Suzanne. BS, Fordham U., 1961; JD, Yale U., 1964. Bar: N.Y. 1965, D.C. 1970, Va. 1992. Atty. AEC, Washington, 1964-68; internat. mgr. Comm. Satellite Corp., Washington, 1968-70; ptnr. Haley, Bader & Potts, Arlington, Va., 1970-95; of counsel Irwin Campbell & Tannenwald, Washington, 1995-96; pvt. practice, McLean, Va., 1997—; v.p. Shared Spectrum Co. Author: Telecommunications Regulation: Something Old and Something New in the Communications Act: A Legislative History of the Major Amendments, 1934-1996, 1999; co-author: The Common Carrier Provisions--A Product of Evolutionary Development in A Legislative History of the Communications Act, 1989, Decency Redux: The Curious History of the New FCC Broadcast Indecency Policy, 1989, A New Telecommunications Paradigm, 1993; bd. dirs. Great Falls Players; mem. Elden Street Players, Rockville Little Theatre, Am. Music Stage, Sterling Playmakers, Vienna Theater Co. Candidate Fairfax County Bd. Suprs., 1995; bd. dirs. McLean Citizens Assn (ex. pres.) Recipient cert. U.S. Atomic Energy Commn., 1967. Mem. Fed. Comms. Bar Assn., Va. State Bar, D.C. Bar Assn. Avocations: acting, videography. Office: 7921 Old Falls Rd Mc Lean VA 22102-2414

BYROM, FLETCHER LAUMAN, chemical manufacturing company executive; b. Cleve., July 13, 1918; s. Fletcher L. and Elizabeth (Collins) B.; m. Marie L. McIntyre, Feb. 17, 1945; children: Fletcher Lauman, Carol A. Byrom Conrad, Susan J. Byrom Evans. BS in Metallurgy, Pa. State U., 1940. Sales engr. Am. Steel & Wire Co., Cleve., 1940-42; procurement and adminstrv. coord. Naval Ordnance Lab., also Bur. Ordnance and Research Planning Bd., Navy Dept., 1942-47; from asst. to gen. mgr. Tar Products divsn. Koppers Co., Inc., Pitts., 1947-82, pres., 1960—70, chmn., 1970—82; mgr. Micasu Tungsten LLC, 2000—. Mem. Pitts. br. Fed. Res. Bd. Cleve., 1962-68, chmn., 1966-68, N.Y. Stock Exch., 1980-86; mem. bd. govs. Com. Devel. Am. Capital; bd. dirs. Purecycle Corp., pres., bd. dirs. Micasu Corp. Bd. dirs. Allegheny Conf. on Cmty. Devel., v.p., 1970-83; chmn. Hershey Med. Ctr., 1970-73; chmn. Pres.'s Export Coun., 1974-79, Pub. Edn. Fund, 1980-85; chmn. bd. trustees Presbyn.-Univ. Hosp., 1972-83, Kiskiminetas Springs Sch., 1971-82; trustee Carnegie Mellon U., 1975-81, Allegheny Coll., 1969-79, Pa. State U., 1970-73; former trustee, Inst. Advanced Study, Inst. for Future Mem., Hudson Inst., Keystone Ctr.; trustee Conf. Bd., 1962-82, lifetime chancellor, 1968—; mem. pres.'s circle NAS, chmn., 1999-2000; trustee Com. for Econ. Devel., chmn. bd. dirs., 1978-84. Recipient Disting. Civilian Service award U.S. Navy Dept., Disting. Alumnus Pa. State U., David Ford McFarland award Pa. State U., 1979, Alumni Achievement award Harvard U. Bus. Sch., 1981, William Metcalf award West Pa. Engring. Soc., 1985; Woodrow Wilson Edn. Found. vis. fellow, Pa. State U. fellow. Mem. Pa. State U. Alumni Assn. (pres. 1965-66), Coun. Retired CEO's, Duquesne Club (Pitts.), Links Club (N.Y.C.), Phi Kappa Psi. Presbyterian. Home and Office: 305 Village Heights Dr Apt 328 State College PA 16801 E-mail: fmicasu3@aol.com.

BYROM, JOE ALAN, lawyer; b. Duncan, Okla., Nov. 6, 1949; s. Joe Lane and Dorothy Adelle (Norton) B.; m. Carla Peters, June 25, 1977; children: Celeste Elizabeth, Russell Patrick. BA, U. Tex., 1972; JD, So. Meth. U., 1975. Bar: Tex. 1975, U.S. Dist. Ct. (no. and ea. dists.) Tex. 1976, U.S. Ct. Appeals (5th and 11th cirs.) 1981, U.S. Supreme Ct. 1985. Assoc. Blassingame & Osburn, Dallas, 1975-81, ptnr., 1981-88; ptnr. Brill, Siney and Hohmann, Dallas, 1989—. Mem. Assn. Trial Lawyers Assn. Am., Tex. Bar Assn., Dallas Bar Assn., Phi Delta Phi. Methodist. Home: 3505 Mockingbird Ln Dallas TX 75205-2225 Office: Brill Siney & Hohmann 2980 Lincoln Pla 500 N Akard St Dallas TX 75201-3320

BYRON, BEVERLY BUTCHER, former congresswoman; b. Balt., July 27, 1932; d. Harry C. and Ruth Butcher; m. Goodloe E. Byron, 1952 (dec.); children: Goodloe E. Jr., Barton Kimball, Mary McComas; m. B. Kirk Walsh, 1986. Student, Hood Coll., 1962-64. Mem. 96th-102nd Congresses from 6th Md. dist., 1979-93; Presdl. appt. to base closing and realignment commn., 1993. Bd. dirs. McDonnell Douglas, Constellation Energy Group, Blue Cross/Blue Shield, UNC Corp., Farm and Mech. Nat. Bank, LMI, Def. Adv. Commn. on Women in the Mil.; exec. panel Chief of Naval Ops.; adv. bd. NASA, A.F. Meml. Found. State treas. Md. Young Dems., 1962, 65; bd. assocs. Hood Coll.; bd. visitors USAF Acad., 1980-87; trustee Mt. St. Mary's Coll.; bd. dirs. Frederick County chpt. ARC; sec. Frederick Heart Assn., 1974-79; mem. Frederick Phys. Fitness Commn.; chmn. Md. Phys. Fitness Commn., 1979-89; mem. Frederick County Landmarks Found.; bd. dirs. Am. Hiking Soc.; bd. dirs. Adventure Sports Inst., 1992—; bd. advisors Internat. Studies Frostburg State U., 1990—, Am. Volkssport Assn., 1991—; mem. bd. vis. U.S. Naval Acad., 1995—, chair, 1997-2002; chair TedCo. Recipient Pres.'s medal John Hopkins U. Democrat. Episcopalian. Home: 306 Grove Blvd Frederick MD 21701-4813

BYRON, E. LEE, real estate broker; b. Gt. Falls, Mont., Oct. 1, 1945; d. Chase and Mary Lee (Evans) Kimball; m. H. Thomas Byron Jr., May 18, 1966 (dec. 2000); children: H. Thomas Byron III, Chase K. (dec. June 2002), Lee-Hayes. AB, Smith Coll., 1967; MA, Monterey Inst. Fgn. Studies, 1971; Montessori cert., St. Nicholas. Ctr., London, 1971. Lic. real estate broker, Fla. Lectr. Monterey (Calif.) Inst. Fgn. Studies, 1971-72; founder, dir., owner Children's Sch. and Summer Dynamics, Auburn, Ala., 1975-79; instr. Child Study Ctr. Auburn U., 1973-79; hosp. dir. Fruitville Vet. Clinic, Sarasota, Fla., 1980-93; broker assoc. Michael Saunders & Co., Sarasota, 1993—. Founder, adv. bd. mem. Guaranty Bank, North Port, Fla., 1987-99; owner, ptnr. Lee Ventures Real Estate Partnership, Sarasota, 1984-99; presenter in field, organizer discussion panels. Co-author: Preschool Theme Lesson Plans, 1975. Bd. dirs. Jr. League, Sarasota, 1981-90; bd. dirs. Pine View Assn. PTA, 1981-90, chmn., 1984-85; bd. dirs. Teen Ct., Sarasota, 1990—, Fla. Sch. Bd. Assn., cert., 1993; bd. dirs. Taxpayers Assn. Sarasota County, 1995-99, pres., 1996-97; bd. dirs. Civic League Sarasota, 1995-2001, 2nd v.p., 1997-98, 1st v.p., 1998 99, pres., 1999-2000; chmn. Sarasota County Exceptional Student Edn. Sch. Adv. Bd., 1984-90; mem. Pine View Sch. Adv. Com., 1994-98, chmn., 1994-97; bd. dirs. Consortium for Children and Youth, Sarasota, 1986—, pres., 1993-97; vice chair Action Task Force Venice (Fla.) 20/20, 1995-97, Children and Youth Svcs. Adv. Com., 1993-2001, chair, 1996-98, vice chair, 1999-2000; bd. dirs. Sarasota County Human Svcs. Adv. Commn., 2002-; co-chmn. Pres.'s Spl. Com. Exceptional Edn. Fla. Sch. Bd. Assn., 1992-93; mem. Bishop's Com. Sexual Misconduct Cath. Diocese, Venice, 1994-95, Multi-Stakeholder's Group (Future Land Planning East Sarasota County), 1995-99; mem. adv. com. Fla. House Inst., 1998—; mem. Sarasota County Sch. Bd., 1990-94; bd. govs. Big Bros./Big Sisters of the Suncoast, 1998—, Fla. Women's Alliance, 1994-2000, Sarasota Women's Alliance, 2001—; eucharistic minister St. Patrick's Ch., 1995—. Recipient Sustainer of Yr. award Sarasota Jr. League, 1993, Cmty. Svc. award, 1995; Women of Power award Nat. Coun. Jewish Women, 1997; named one of 100 Vols. for 100th birthday, Internat. Assn. Jr. Leagues, 1996. Mem. Sarasota Assn. of Realtors (program com. 1995-99, govt. affairs com. 2001—), Nat. Assn. Realtors (Grad. Realtor Inst. 1996). Republican. Roman Catholic. Avocations: reading, swimming, skiing. Home: 653 Sinclair Dr Sarasota FL 34240-9367 Office: Michael Saunders & Co 5100 Ocean Blvd Sarasota FL 34242-1693 E-mail: lee@sarasota.com.

BYRON, ERIC HOWARD, sculptor, museum researcher and administrator; b. N.Y.C., Jan. 14, 1948; s. Melville and Ruth (Levine) Byron. BA, Beloit Coll., 1970; postgrad., Hunter Coll., 1972-75, YIVO Inst./Columbia U., 1972-76; MA, Goddard Coll., 1979; postgrad, NYU, 1985. Founder, dir. The Synagogue Rescue Project, Inc., N.Y.C., 1974-85; mus. technician South St. Seaport Mus., N.Y.C., 1992-93, Statue of Liberty Nat. Monument/Ellis Island Immigration Mus, N.Y.C., 1993—. Lectr. sr. citizens N.Y. Tech. Inst., 1982; coord. oral history project Brookdale Ctr. on Aging, Hunter Coll., N.Y.C., 1982, discography project Ellis Island Mus. Immigration, 1997—. Exhibited in group shows at Ward-Nasse Gallery, 1975-76, Detail, N.Y.C., 1989, Nathaniel's Music Box, N.Y.C., 1989, Civilization, 1989, Am. Craftsman, 1989-90, Dinosaur Hill, N.Y.C., 1990, Mus. Am. Folk Art, N.Y.C., 1990, Mark Milliken Gallery, N.Y.C., 1990, Faith Nightengale Gallery, San Diego, 1991-92, Whitney Mus., N.Y.C., 1992; sculpture, performer Washington Sq. Pk., 1989-2001; coord. The Ellis ISland Immigration Discography Project, 1997—.featured on PBS Channel 13

City Arts, 1998, also on Nat. Pub. Radio, 1999. Fellow Brookdale Ctr. on Aging, N.Y.C., 1985; recipient archeology award Profl. Archeologists N.Y.C., 1997. Mem.: N.Y. State Archaeol. Assn. (Met. chpt.), Nat. Steroscopic Assn., Nat. Trust Historic Preservation. Home: 411 E 10th St Apt 15F New York NY 10009-4212 Office: Statue of Liberty Nat Mus Liberty Island New York NY 10004-1467

BYRON, FREDERICK WILLIAM, JR., physicist, educator, university vice chancellor; b. Manchester, N.H., July 8, 1938; s. Frederick William and Anna (Muir) B.; m. Edith Iselin, June 23, 1961; children: Kenniston, Alexander deNeufville. AB, Harvard U., 1959; PhD, Columbia U., 1963. Acting asst. prof. U. Calif., Berkeley, 1963-65, asst. prof., 1965-66, U. Mass., Amherst, 1966-69, assoc. prof., 1969-74, prof., 1974—, head dept. physics and astronomy, 1975-79; dean U. Mass. (Faculty Natural Scis. and Math.), Amherst, 1979-93; coordinating dean U. Mass. (Coll. of Arts and Scis.), Amherst, 1989-91; vice chancellor rsch. and econ. devel. U. Mass., Amherst, 1994—. Bd. dirs. Reg. Tech. Corp., 2003—. Author: (with Robert W. Fuller) The Mathematics of Classical and Quantum Physics, 1970; contbr. articles to profl. jours. Alfred P. Sloan Found. fellow, 1965-67; Fulbright research scholar, 1973-74 Fellow Am. Phys. Soc. Office: U Mass 512 Goodell Bldg Amherst MA 01003 E-mail: byron@resgs.umass.edu., fredbyron@yahoo.com.

BYRON, RITA ELLEN COONEY, travel executive, publisher, real estate agent, civic leader, photojournalist, writer; b. Cleve. d. Harry James and Marie (Hakey) Cooney; m. Carl James Byron Jr., Nov. 27, 1954 (dec.); children: Carey Lewis, Carl James, Bradford William. Student, Cleve. Coll., 1954, Western Res. U., 1955, John Carroll U., 1956; PhD (hon.), Colo. State Christian Coll., 1972. Mgr. European Immigration Dept. U.S. Steamship Lines, Cleve., 1956; real estate agt. W.I. White Realtor Inc., Shaker Heights, Ohio, 1965—67, J.P. Malone Realtors Inc., Shaker Heights, Ohio, 1967—70, Thomas Murray & Assocs., Shaker Heights, Ohio, 1971—76, Mary Anderson Realty, Shaker Heights, Ohio, 1978—79, Barth Brad & Andrews Realtors Inc., Shaker Heights, Ohio, 1979—, Heights Realty, Shaker Heights, Ohio, 1986—. V.p., co-owner Your Connection to Travel, Kent, Ohio, 1980—; v.p., gen. mgr. World Class Travel Agy., 1985; dir. Travel One divsn. Quaker Sq., Akron, Travel Trends for Singles, 1985, Playhouse Sq. Travel, 1986, World Class Internat., 1986. Co-pub., exec. editor: The Single Register (pub. documentary book The Fall of the Wall, 1989), other publs.; featured in numerous publs. Mem. women's com. Cleve. Mus. Art, 1969—; mem. Friendship Force Ohio, 1969—; co-chmn. Cleve. Invitational Figure Skating Competition, 1972—; chmn. Gold Rush Rush, U.S. Ski Team, 1982, Cleve. benefit U.S. Olympic Teams, Midas; originator Exceptional Single Person's Connectiosn Unltd.; founder, coord. Singled Out Club; co-ptnr., adv. bd. The Service Service; benefit chmn., patroness varioous balls and fundraising events; vol. Foster Parents, Inc., Coun. on World Affairs, Bellefaire Home for Spl. Children, Big Sisters Greater Cleve., Camp Cheerful, Chisholm Ctr., Children's Diabetic Camp Ho Mita Koda, Young Audiences; adv. trustee Friends of Fairmount Theatre of the Deaf; mem. Greater Cleve. Growth Assn. Mem.: Cleve. Real Estate Bd., Coun. on Small Enterprises, Growth Assn., North Coast Exec. Women's Network, Globetrotters Internat. Fedn. Women's Travel Orgns., Travel Age Exch., English Speaking Union (jr. bd.), Garden Ctr. Greater Cleve., Wightman's Cup Women's Com., U.S. Figure Skating Assn. (chmn. benefits), Western Res. Hist. Soc., Friends Cleve. Pub. Libr., U.S. Ski Ednl. Found., Cleve. Coun. World Affairs, UN Assn. of U.S., Holden Arboretum Soc., Photographic Soc. Am., Cleve. Photographic Soc. (bd. dirs. 1989), Camera Guild (exec. bd. trustees 1989), Assoc. Photographers, Nat. Hist. Mus. Photo Soc., Archeol. Soc., Cleve. Astron. Soc., Nature Artists Soc., Kodochrome Adventure Soc., Cuyahoga Valley Nat. Pk. Photo Club (assoc. photographer, various photography awards), Sanctuary Marsh Photo Club;, Photocrafters, Photography Club, Met. Parks Club, Shaker Lakes Nature Club, Chagrin Valley Photo Club, East Berlin Photo Club, Internat. Chagrin Valley Camera Club, Himalaya Yeti (1987 Nepal Expdn.), Tibet, Mongolia and China Explorers' Club, Intrepid Traveler Club, Arctic Circle, Cleve. Wellesley Club, Mid-Day Club, Gilmour Acad. Women's Club, Women's City Club, Towne Hall Club, Communicator's Club, Cleve. Advt. Club, Suburban Ski Club, Colony Beach and Racquet Club, Broadmoor World Arena Figure Skating Club, Cleve. Skating Club. Home: 752 White Pine Tree Rd # 208 Venice FL 34292 Office: World Class Travel 3520 Ingleside Rd Cleveland OH 44122-5002 also: Es Turo Edificio Kontiki Majorica Balearic Islands Spain

BYRON, WILLIAM JAMES, author, management educator, researcher, former university president; b. Pitts., May 25, 1927; s. Harold J. and Mary I. (Langton) B. AB in Philosophy, St. Louis U., 1955, Ph.L., 1956, MA in Econs, 1959; S.T.B., Woodstock Coll., 1960, S.T.L., 1962; PhD in Econs, U. Md., 1969; cert., Harvard U. Inst. Ednl. Mgmt., 1974. Joined S.J., 1950, ordained priest Roman Cath. Ch., 1961. Tchr. math. Scranton (Pa.) Prep. Sch., 1956-58; manpower rsch. fellow Dept. Labor, 1965-66; asst. prof. econs. Loyola Coll., Balt., 1967-69; assoc. prof. social ethics, rector Woodstock Coll., Woodstock Jesuit Community, 1967-73; dean Coll. Arts and Scis. Loyola U., New Orleans, 1973-75; pres. U. Scranton, 1975-82, Cath. U. Am., Washington, 1982-92; rsch. assoc. Georgetown U., 1992-93, Disting. prof. mgmt. Sch. of Bus., 1993—2000; rsch. prof. Sellinger Sch. Bus., Loyola Coll. in Md. Author: Toward Stewardship: An Interim Ethic of Poverty, Pollution and Power, 1975, Quadrangle Considerations, 1989, Take Your Diploma and Run, 1992, Finding Work Without Losing Heart, 1995, The 365 Days of Christmas, 1996, Answers from Within, 1998, Jesuit Saturdays, 2000; editor: Causes of World Hunger, 1982; contbr. numerous articles to profl. jurs. Bd. dirs. Fed. City Coun., Joint Commn. on Accreditation Healthcare Orgns., U. San Francisco, Loyola Coll. in Md., Balt. With U.S. Army, 1945-56. Mem. Am. Econs. Assn., Am. Soc. Christian Ethics, Assn. Cath. Colls. and Univs., Phi Beta Kappa, Alpha Sigma Nu Mailing: 4603 Millbrook Rd Baltimore MD 21212

BYRUM, LINDA KLUBER, artist; b. Aurora, Ill., Nov. 20, 1954; d. Ronald Edward Kluber and Barbara Jean (Shephard) Nussbaum; m. Steven Stuart Rabin (div.); m. Jeffrey Z. Byrum, July 15, 1988. Student, So. Ill. U., Carbondale, 1975, Waubonsee CC, Sugar Grove, Ill., 1984. Artist, DeKalb, Ill., 1996—. Mem. artist Fox Valley Art Coun., Geneva, 1992—. One-woman shows include Nat. Mus. Women Arts, Egyptian Theatre, DeKalb, Ill., 1999, exhibited in group shows, 1999. Philanthropy officer, programs dir. Kishwaukee Valley Art League, Sycamore, Ill., 1996—. Mem.: Nat. Mus. Women in Art, Oil Pastelists Assn. Internat. (artist). Avocations: art, hiking, camping, jewelry making, photography. Home and Office: 920 N 7th St Dekalb IL 60115-2569 Personal E-mail: lindabyrum@comcast.net.

BYRUM-SUTTON, JUDITH MIRIAM, accountant; b. Bismarck, N.D., Sept. 24, 1943; d. Adolph Mathew and Gertrude Cecelia (Lechner) H.; m. Richard W. Byrum, July 30, 1965 (div. Oct. 1984); children: Thomasin Jane, Toby Oliver; m. Danny D. Jansen, Oct. 21, 1989 (dec. Nov. 1989); m. Jack N. Sutton, June 26, 1993. BS in Acctg., Ariz. State U., 1967. CPA, Ariz., Kans. Underwriter Gt. SW Fire Ins. Co., Mesa, Ariz., 1963-65; staff auditor Touche Ross & Co., London, 1967-69, Arthur Andersen & Co., Kansas City, Mo., 1970-71; treas. John J. Peterson Real Estate, Overland Park, Kans., 1971-75; internal auditor Bus. Men's Assurance Co., Kansas City, 1975-78; owner Judith H. Byrum, CPA, Chartered, 1978—; ptnr. G.R. Starbuck & Co. P.A., Leawood, Kans., 1996—. Contbr. articles to newsletter. Mem. adv. bd. Rockhurst Coll. Women's Ctr., Kansas City, 1977; mem. Congressman Larry Winn II Small Bus. Com., Washington, 1977-80; treas. Trinity Luth. Ch., Mission, Kans., 1990-94. Mem. AICPA (legis. liaison), Am. Woman's Soc. CPAs (treas., v.p. Chgo. 1977-83), Am. Soc. Women Accts. (pres. Kansas City 1980-81), Kans. Soc. CPAs (com. mem. 1977—, pres., v.p., treas. Metro chpt. 1989—, bd. dirs. 1994-97), Kansas City Women's C. of C. (v.p. 1980), Beta Alpha Psi. Avocations: skiing, golf, reading, gardening, hunting. Office: 4601 College Blvd Ste 160 Leawood KS 66211-1678

BYSIEWICZ, SUSAN, secretary of state; b. New Haven, Conn. BA magna cum laude, Yale Coll., 1983; JD, Duke U., 1986. Corp. atty. White & Case, N.Y., 1986-88, Robinson & Cole, Hartford, Conn., 1988-92; with law dept. Aetna Life and Casualty, 1992-94; state rep. 100th dist. judiciary com. State of Conn., 1992-98, chair govt. adminstrn. and elections com., 1995-98, Sec. of State, 1998—. Author: Ella: A Biography of Governor Ella T. Grasso, 1984. Conn. Bar Assn., N.Y. Bar Assn. Democrat. Address: Rm 104 State Capitol Hartford CT 06106 E-mail: susan.bysiewicz@po.state.ct.us.*

BYSTRYN, JEAN-CLAUDE, dermatologist, educator; b. Paris, May 8, 1938; arrived in U.S., 1949, naturalized, 1958; s. Iser and Sara Bystryn; m. Marcia Hammill, May 14, 1972; children: Anne, Alexander. BS, U. Chgo., 1958; MD, NYU, 1962. Diplomate Am. Bd. Deratology, Am. Bd. Immunodermatopathology. Intern Montefiore Hosp., N.Y.C., 1962-63, resident in medicine, 1963-64; resident in dermatology NYU Sch. Medicine, N.Y.C., 1966-69, USPHS postgrad. tng. fellow in immunology, 1968-72, asst. prof. clin. dermatology, 1971—72, assoc. prof., 1976-84, prof., 1984—. Asst. dispensary physician Albany Med. Coll., 1964—66; asst. attending physician Univ. Hosp., N.Y.C., 1969—; asst. vis. dermatologist Bellevue Hosp. Ctr., N.Y.C., 1969—; dir. melanoma program NYU Kaplan Cancer Ctr., N.Y.C.; dir. Immunofluorescence Lab. NYU Med. Sch., N.Y.C. Contbr. articles to profl. jours. Mem. adv. bd. Skin Cancer Found., Vitiligo Found., Nat. Alepecia Areata Found., Am. Skin Assn., Nat. Pemphigus Found. Lt. comdr. USPHS, 1964—66. Recipient Irma T. Hirschl Rsch. Career award, AOA; Ford Found. fellow, 1954—58, NIH grantee, 1970—. Mem.: N.Y. Dermatol. Soc. (dir.), Soc. Investigative Dermatology, Am. Assn. Cancer Rsch., Am. Assn. Immunologists, Am. Acad. Dermatology, Am. Dermatology Assn. Office: NYU Med Ctr U Hosp 530 1st Ave New York NY 10016-6402

BYUN, MICHAEL, plastic surgeon; b. Tokyo, May 2, 1965; s. Justine and Terresa Byun; m. Michelle Seo Byun, 1 child, Hannah. BS, U. Calif., Irvine, 1988; MD, Northwestern U., 1992. Clin. instr. Northwestern U., Chgo., 1997—98, chief resident, 1997—98; dir. Chgo. Cosmetic Surgery, Chgo., 1998—; founder Michael Byun MD, SC, Chgo., 1998—; plastic surgeon TKI Wellness Ctr., Chgo., 1999—; asst. prof. Rush U., Chgo., 2000—02. Attending physician Luth. Gen. Hosp., Park Ridge, Ill., 1998—, Swedish Covenant Hosp., Chgo., 1998—. Contbr. articles to profl. jours. Attending plastic surgeon charitable orgn., Chgo., 2001. Recipient Young Scientist award, Iksong Found., 1988, award, Mayor of Chgo., 2001. Mem.: AMA, Chgo. Med. Soc. Avocations: skiing, golf. Office: Chicago Office 1 E Erie Ste 510 Chicago IL 60611 also: Northbrook Office 1775 Walters Ste 100 Northbrook IL 60062

BYUN, THAK-SANG, research scientist, educator; b. Taegue, Keong-Sang-Book-Do, Republic of Korea, July 7, 1963; s. Young-Sang Byun and Soon-Yim Kim; m. Jin-Sook Hong, Nov. 11, 1990; children: Hyo-Yul, Woo-Yul. PhD, Korea Advanced Inst. of Sci. and Tech., Taejon, 1992. Sr. rschr. Korea Atomic Energy Rsch. Inst., Taejon, Republic of Korea, 1992—98; rsch. prof. Oak Ridge (Tenn.) Nat. Lab., U. of Tenn., 1999—. Contbr. scientific papers to profl. jours. Achievements include patents for improved method for material processing. Home: 109 Golfcrest Ln Oak Ridge TN 37830 Office: Oak Ridge Nat Lab PO Box 2008 Bethel Valley Rd Oak Ridge TN 37831-6151

BYYNY, RICHARD LEE, academic administrator, physician; b. South Gate, Calif., Jan. 6, 1939; s. Oswald and Essa Burnetta (McGinnis) B.; m. Jo Ellen Garverick, Aug. 25, 1962; children: Kristen, Jan, Richard. BA in History, U. So. Calif., 1960, MD, 1964. Intern and resident in internal medicine Columbia Presbyn. Med. Ctr., N.Y.C., 1964-66, chief resident, 1968-69; fellow in endocrinology Vanderbilt U., Nashville, 1969-71; asst. prof. medicine U. Chgo., 1971-74, head div. internal medicine, 1972-77, assoc. prof., 1975-77; prof. internal medicine U. Colo., Denver, 1977—, head divsn. internal medicine, 1977-94, vice-chmn. dept. medicine Health Scis. Ctr., 1977-85, exec. vice chancellor, 1994-95, v.p. acad. .affairs, 1995-97, chancellor Boulder, 1997—. Med. dir. ambulatory care, 1990-92; mem. Coun. on Econ. Devel., Boulder, Colo. Author: A Clinical Guide in the Care of Older Women, 1990, 95; contbr. numerous articles to profl. jours., chpts. to textbooks, monographs. Pres. Ill. Council Continuing Med. Edn., Ill., 1976-77; bd. dirs. Denver affiliate Am. Heart Assn., 1987-98 (pres. 1994-95), Boulder Com. Hosp., 1997—, Bank of Boulder, Boulder Econ. Coun., arm of Boulder C. of C., U.S. Coun. on Competitiveness Big 12 Conf. Served to capt. USAF, 1966-68. Recipient Merck award U. So. Calif., 1964; Am. Coun. Edn. fellow, 1992-93. Fellow ACP; mem. AAAS, Soc. for Gen. Internal Medicine (pres. 1979-80), Am. Soc. Hypertension, Western Soc. Clin. Investigation, Endocrine Soc., Am. Fedn. for Clin. Rsch., Am. Coun. Edn. (commn. leadership instl. effectiveness), Alpha Omega Alpha (bd. dirs. 1996—). Clubs: U. Club Denver; Arapahoe Tennis (Englewood, Colo.), Boulder Country Club. Avocations: tennis, skiing, running, surfing, sailing. Home: 2900 Park Lake Dr Boulder CO 80301-5139 Office: Office of Chancellor Regent Adminstrv Ctr Room 301 Campus Box 17 Boulder CO 80309-0017 Fax: 303-492-8866. E-mail: richard.byyny@colorado.edu.

BZYMEK, ZBIGNIEW MARIAN, educator; b. Warsaw, Aug. 5, 1935; came to U.S., 1981; s. Stefan and Stefania (Turek) Bzymek; m. Danuta Jaworska, Oct. 22, 1966; children: Malgorzata, Dorota, Zbigniew Wojciech. *Immediate family — wife: Danuta Jaworska — Bzymek, MD, Medical Academy, Warsaw Poland, UConn-Hartford Hospital Surgery Program, Yale Dept. of Plastics Surgery, Instructor of Plastic Surgery 1991-92, currently a plastic surgeon practicing in Connecticut; daughter: Malgorzata Bzymek, PhD, research fellow at Harvard University; daughter: Dorota Bzymek, MD, Medical Academy, Warsaw Poland, presently living in the US; son: Zbigniew W. Bzymek, BA, Bowdoin College, Radclif Publishing School at Harvard University, UConn Daily Campus-editorial page editor 1993, writer-plays, essays, poems, articles, presently a film directing student, Film School, Lodz, Poland.* MS in Engring., Politechnika Warszawska, Warsaw, Poland, 1959, PhD in Engring. Sci., 1967; MS in Engring., U. Mich., 1961. Asst. Politechnika Warszawska, 1961, sr. asst., 1961-67, adj. prof., 1967-73, docent, 1973-81; assoc. prof., dir. CAD & CAM, Expert Sys. Lab. U. Conn., Storrs, 1981—. Cons. Head Mgmt. Ctr. for Hwy. Data Processing, 1978-81; designer bridge sect. Transproject, Warsaw, 1961-63. Author: (Hungarian and Polish) Application of Computers in Structural Analysis, 1966, others; translator (from Russian): Structural Analysis by Means of Digital Computers, 1970; editor (monthly) Drogownictwo, 1977-81; head editor Rsch. Reports on Automatization of Structural Design, 1974-81; contbr. numerous articles to profl. jours. Recipient 1st Prize for Design Competition Soc. of Transp. Engrs., 1974, Hon. mention, 1974. Mem. ASME (2nd Nat. Design award), Internat. Orgn. for Sci. and Tech. (chmn. CAD/CAM com. 1987-92), N.Y. Acad. Scis., Assn. for Computers Machinery (spl. interest group graphics 1982), Polish Acad. of Sci. (mem. civil engring. com., computer graphics pioneer, award 1976), Soc. of Bldg. Engrs. (Stefan Bryla award 1977). Achievements include research in computer graphics, structural analysis, and bridge and machine design. Avocations: tennis, skiing, sailing, coin collecting. Home: 260 Codfish Falls Rd Storrs Mansfield CT 06268-1407 Office: U Conn 191 Auditorium Rd Storrs Mansfield CT 06269-9012 E-mail: bzymek@uconnvm.uconn.edu.

CAAMANO, KATHLEEN ANN FOLZ, gifted and talented educator; b. Rozellville, Wis., Dec. 20, 1944; d. Joseph and Isabel Ann (Brost) Folz; m. Gerald J. Caamano, Aug. 10, 1968; children: Michelle, David. BS, U. Wis., Stevens Point; MA, Ctrl. Mich. U. Cert. tchr., Ill. Tchr. Midland (Mich.) Pub. Schs., 1968-74, Newark (Ohio) City Schs., 1974-77, Minooka (Ill.) Sch. Dist., 1986—, coord. gifted edn. Pres. Camelot Homeowners Assn., Joliet, Ill.; tutor Big Bros./Big Sisters Assn. Will County; voter registrar Will County, Joliet. Recipient Those Who Excel award Ill State Bd. Edn. Mem. Internat. Reading Assn., Ill. Edn. Assn. (tchr. rep), Gifted Edn. Coun., Ill. Assn. Ednl. Rsch. and Evaluation, Will County Reading Coun., Delta Kappa Gamma (v.p.), Beta Sigma Phi (pres.). Roman Catholic. Avocations: travel, reading, golf, bridge. Home. 22257 S Galahad Dr Joliet IL 60431-7611

CABALLERO, RAYMOND CESAR, former mayor; b. El Paso, Tex., Feb. 6, 1942; s. Elmira (Hernandez) C.; m. Dorothy Jean McGill, Sept. 4, 1965 (div. Nov. 1988); children: Theresa, Jennifer, Deborah, Raymond, Elizabeth; m. Mary Hull BBA, U. Tex., El Paso, 1963; JD, U. Tex., Austin, 1967; LLM, George Washington U., 1972; MPA, Harvard U., 1990. Bar: Tex. 1966, Calif. 1972. Asst. U.S. atty U.S. Dept. Justice, El Paso, 1967-69, trial atty. tax div. Washington, 1969-73; ptnr. Pearson & Caballero, El Paso, 1974-81, Caballero & Ortega, El Paso, 1981—97, of counsel, 1997—2001; mayor City of El Paso, 2001—03. Chmn. El Paso County Dem. Party, 1974-76. Fellow Am. Coll. Trial Lawyers; mem. El Paso County Bar Assn. (past pres.). Democrat. Office: City of El Paso 2 Civic Center Plaza El Paso TX 79901*

CABALLERO, SHARON, academic administrator; m. Roger Caballero. BS Journalism/English, San Diego State U., 1968; MA Secondary Edn., U.S. Internat. U., 1976, EdD Ednl. Leadership, 1980. Dir. pub. rels. & mktg. Southwestern Cmty. Coll., Chula Vista, Calif., 1984—85; assoc. exec. dir. Calif. Assn. Cmty. Colls. (now Cmty. Coll. League Calif.), 1985—87; dean, communs. & fine arts Grossmont Coll., El Cajon, Calif., 1988—91; asst. supt. & v.p. acad. svcs. Rio Hondo Cmty. Coll. Dist., 1991—97; pres. San Bernardino Valley Coll., 1997—2002, N.Mex. Highlands U., Las Vegas, N.Mex., 2002—. Mem. Arrowhead United Way, Bernardino Valley Coll. Found., Victor Valley Women's Club, KVCR-FM/TV Found.; San Bernardino C. of C.; chmn. journalism dept., instr. mass media, telecommunications coll. newspaper. Named Calif. Woman of Yr. 58th Dist., 1994. Mem.: Cailf. Cmty. Colls. Exec. Bd. (CEO mem. bd. 1995—), Mgmt. Devel. Commn. Assn. of Calif. Cmty. Coll. Adminstrs. (chair 1989—), Am. Assn. Women in Cmty. & Junior Colls. (nat. v.p. for profl. devel. 1987—89, nat. pres. 1989—91), Rotary. Office: NMex Highlands U 701 S Mt Vernon Ave San Bernardino CA 92410

CABALQUINTO, LUIS CARRAZCAL, freelance writer; b. Magarao, Camarines Sur, Philippines, Jan. 31, 1935; came to U.S., 1968; s. Geminiano and Irene (Carrazcal) C. BA in Journalism, U. Philippines, 1967; postgrad., Cornell U., 1968-71, NYU, 1982-84. Editor Office Philippine Pres., Manila, 1960-66; editor, instr. U. Phillipines, Los Baños, 1966-75; customer svc. rep. Pfizer Inc., N.Y.C., 1980-90; pvt. practice N.Y.C., 1990—. Author: The Dog-eater and Other Poems, 1989, The Ibalon Collection, 1991, Dreamwanderer, 1992, Bridgeable Shores, 2001, Moon Over Nagarao, New and Selected Poems, 2003. Recipient Dylan Thomas Poetry award New Sch. Social Rsch., 1979, Poetry prize Acad. Am. Poets, 1985, fiction prize Philippine Graphic Mag., 1992; fellow N.Y. Found. Arts, 1989. Mem. Poetry Soc. Am., Poets Writers, Writers Cmty., Am. PEN. Avocations: fishing, movies, gardening, sports, travel. Home and Office: 1 Stuyvesant Oval MF New York NY 10009-2101 E-mail: DonLuisC@aol.com.

CABANA, ROBERT D. astronaut; b. Mpls., Jan. 23, 1949; m. Nancy Joan Shimer; children: Jeffrey, Christopher, Sarah. BS in Math., U.S. Naval Acad., 1971; grad., Naval Flight Officer Tng., Pensacola, Fla., 1972, U.S. Naval Test Pilot Sch., 1981. Commd. ensign USN, advanced through grades to col.; bombardier/navigator Marine Air Wings, Cherry Point, NC and Iwakuni, Japan; naval aviator 2d Marine Aircraft Wing, Cherry Point; project mgr., X-29 advanced then. demonstrator project officer, test pilot Naval Air Test Ctr., Patuxent River, Md.; asst. ops. officer Marine Aircraft Group Twelve, Iwakuni; flight software coord Astronaut Office Space Shuttle, NASA, dept. chief aircraft ops. Johnson Space Ctr., lead astronaut Shuttle Avionics Integration Lab., spacecraft communicator, chief astronaut appearances, chief Astronaut Office, dep. dir. flight crew ops., mgr. internat. ops. Internat. Space Sta. Program, dir. Human Space Flight Programs, Russia. NASA lead rep. Russian Aviation and Spacy Agy. Decorated DFC, Def. Superior Svc. medal, Def. Meritorious Svc. medal, Meritorious Svc. medal; recipient award, DAR, 1976, De La Vaulx medal, Fedn. Aeronautique Internat., 1994, Nat. Intelligence Medal of Achievement. Mem.: Assn. Space Explorers, Soc. Exptl. Test Pilots (assoc.). Achievements include four space flights; logged over 1,010 hours in space; pilot on STS-41 Discovery (Oct. 6-10, 1990), STS-53 Disco (Dec. 2-9, 1992); mission comdr. STS-65 Columbia (July 8-23, 1994) and STS-88 Endeavour (Dec. 4-15, 1998). Avocations: jogging, softball, sailing, woodworking, cycling. Office: Astronaut Office/CB NASA Johnson Space Ctr Houston TX 77058

CABANAS, ELIZABETH ANN, nutritionist, educator; b. Port Arthur, Tex., Oct. 27, 1948; d. William Rosser and Frances Merle (Block) Thornton. BS, U. Tex., 1971; MPH, U. Hawaii, 1973; PhD, Tex. Woman's U., 2001. Registered dietitian; cert. diabetes educator. Clin. nutritionist Family Planning Inst. Kapiolani Hosp., Honolulu, 1972-74; dietitian Kauikeolani Children's Hosp.-Pacific Inst. Rehab. Medicine, Honolulu, 1974-75; asst. food service adminstr. San Antonio Ind. Schs., 1975-89; coord. equipment and facilities Dallas Ind. Sch., 1990-91; nutritionist SureQuest Solutions in Software, Richardson, Tex., 1990-91; nutritionist div. endocrinology, metabolism and hypertension, clin. studies unit rsch. nutritionist, asst. prof. dept. health promotion & gerontology U. Tex. Med. Br., Galveston, 1991—2002. Lectr. nutrition U. Hawaii, Honolulu, 1974-75, St. Mary's U., San Antonio Coll., 1984-90; adj. faculty Tex. Woman's U., 1994; cons. nutritionist, 1980—; presenter in field. Contbr. papers to profl. jours. Vol. ARC, Brooke Army Med. Ctr., Saddle Light Ctr. for Therapeutic Riding, Habitat for Humanity. Recipient diabetes educator recognition Eli Lilly & Co., 1994. Mem. Am. Dietetic Assn., Am. Assn. Diabetes Educators (chair holistic care specialty practice group 1997-98), Assn. Sch. Bus. Ofcls. Internat., Nutrition and Food Svc. Mgmt. Com., Am. Diabetes Assn. (adv. com. U. Tex. Med. Br. children's diabetes mgmt. program 1993-98, mem. Galveston County diabetes support group 1991-99, Disting. Svc. award 1995, mem. Galveston County Outreach adv. com., UTMB rep. 1996-98), Coun. Nutritional Scis. and Metabolism (profl. sect., non-peer rev. com. 1993-94), Tex. Sch. Food Svc. Assn. (dist. bd. dirs. 1977-78), Tex. Nutrition Coun. (nominating com. 1996-97, 2d v.p. 1997-99, sports and cardiovasc. nutritionists practice group, Tex. gerontol. nutritionists practice group), Houston Area Dietetic Assn. (legis. network com. 1995-99), San Antonio Dietetic Assn., San Antonio Sch. Food Svc. Assn. (com. chmn. 1975-89), Tex. Assn. Sch. Bus. Ofcls., Tex. Restaurant Assn., San Antonio Area Food Svc. Adminstrs. Assn. (pres. 1989-90), Assn. Profls. in Positions of Leadership in Edn., Dallas Dietetic Assn. (cons. nutritionists practice group, chmn. 1990-91), Harris County Biofeedback Soc., San Antonio Mus. Assn., Randolph C. of C., Grand Opera House, Galveston (patron), Galveston Hist. Found., Phi Kappa Phi. Avocations: perpetuation of hawaiian culture, nordic skiing, equestrian sports, art, dixieland jazz.

CABBABE, EDMOND BECHIR, plastic and hand surgeon; b. Aleppo, Syria, Feb. 21, 1947; Came to U.S., 1973; s. Bechir Wahid and Samia (Hamoui) C.; m. Rima Gorab, Apr. 22, 1973; children: Nabil, Samer, Monica. BS in Physics, Chemistry Biology, Damascus U. Sch. Scis., 1967, MD, 1972. Diplomate Am. Bd. Surgery, Am Bd. Plastic Surgery, cert hand surgery. Surg. intern St. Mary of Nazareth Hosp., Chgo., 1973-74; surg. resident U. Tenn., Chattanooga, 1974-78; resident in plastic surgery St. Louis U., 1978-80, asst. prof., 1980-86, asst. clin. prof., 1986-98, assoc. clin. prof., 1998—, clin. prof., 2003—; practice medicine specializing in plastic surgery Plastic Surgery Cons., St. Louis, 1986—, pres., 1994-95, 97—; chief plastic surgery St. Anthony Med. Ctr., St. Louis, 1990-95, 2000—, De Paul Health Ctr., St. Louis, 1991—. Chief plastic surgery John Cochran VA Hosp., St. Louis, 1981-86; dir. cleft palate clinic Cardinal Glennon Children's Hosp., St. Louis, 1984-86; mem. adv. com. Healthlink CompMgmt., vice chmn., 1997-2001; mem. adv. bd. to Senator Christopher Bond, chmn. small bus. com. U.S. Senate, 1995-98 Editor: St. Louis Met. Medicine, 1991-93; mem. editl. bd.: Missouri Medicine, 1999—; contbr. articles to profl. jours. Mem. Arab Am. Anti Discrimination Com., Washington, 1982—. Fellow: ACS; mem.: AMA, Am. Soc. Aesthetic Plastic Surgery, St. Louis Area Soc. Plastic Surgeons (pres. 1993—95), St. Louis Soc. for Med. and Sci. Edn. (trustee 1991—93, pres. 1995), St. Louis Met. Med. Soc. (pres. 1995), Mo. Assn. Plastic Surgeons (pres. 2000—02), Mo. State Med. Assn. (treas. 1996—99, councilor 1999—2000, vice chmn. coun. 2000—01, chmn. council 2001—02, pres. elect 2003—), Nat. Arab Am. Med. Assn. Found. (chmn. 1999), Nat. Arab Am. Med. Assn. (pres. 1995), St. Louis Arab Am. Med. Assn. (pres. 1985—86), Am. Assn. Hand Surgery (sci. program com.), Am. Soc. Plastic and Reconstructive Surgeons (sci. program com). Roman Catholic. Avocations: writing, fitness exercises, antiques, photography. Home: 1249 Takara Ct Saint Louis MO 63131-1013 Office: Plastic Surgery Cons Ltd 10004 Kennerly Rd Ste 200 Saint Louis MO 63128-2174

CABELL, BEN B. retired pediatrician, naval officer; b. Honolulu, July 22, 1935; s. Gerald Frank Cabell and Merle Gore Bryan; m. Ann Alda Ellefson, June 20, 1959 (div. Jan. 1972); children: Laura Ashley, Bryan Chastain; m. Evalyn Ann Woods, Oct. 6, 1975; 1 child, Scott David. BS optime merens, U. of South, 1955; MD, Tulane U., 1959. Diplomate Am. Bd. Pediat. Commd. ensign USN Med. Corps., 1958, advanced through grades to capt., 1979, active duty flight surgeon, 1960-65; resident in pediat. U. Ark. Med. Ctr., Little Rock, 1965-67; pvt. practice pediatrician Ft. Smith, Ark., 1967-90; active duty flight surgeon USNR Med. Corps., Pensacola, Fla., 1990-2000, ret., 2000. Clin. asst. prof. pediat., U. Ark. Health Scis., 1968-90; cons. in pediat. Area Health Edn. Ctr., Ft. Smith, 1980-90, Sebastian County Health Dept., 1968-90, Ark. State Crippled Children's divsn., 1967-90; sr. med. examiner and aircraft accident investigator, FAA, 1969—; med. dir., Brownwood Life Care Ctr., Ft. Smith, 1986-90. Bd. dirs., Spl. Learning Ctr. for Children with Learning Disabilities, Ft. Smith, 1970-76, chmn., 1971-72; bd. dirs. Ft. Smith Symphony Assn., 1968-72, 80-82, chmn., 1970-72; dist. rep. Ark. Arts Coun., 1970-82, 86-90, chmn., 1971-72, 80-82; bd. dirs. Sebastian County United Way, 1985-88. Decorated Navy Commendation medal, Meritorious Svc. medal with gold star. Fellow Am. Acad. Pediat.; mem. So. Med. Assn. E-mail: bcabell@earthlink.net.

CABELL, ELIZABETH ARLISSE, psychologist; b. Bryan, Tex., Apr. 14, 1947; d. John David Kernodle and Jeanne Forrest (McCluer) Riley; m. Kent E. Johnson, Dec. 23, 1967 (div. May 1972); m. Donald Allen Cabell, May 19, 1978; children: Ryan, Andrew. BA with honors, U. Tex., 1968; MA, U. Colo., 1973, PhD, 1977. Lic. sch. psychologist. Vocat. trainer Mary Lee Sch. Spl. Edn., Austin, Tex., 1968-69; employment counselor Colo. Div. Employment, Denver, 1971-73; sch. psychologist Aurora (Colo.) Mental Health Ctr./Aurora Pub. Schs., 1974-76, Douglas County Schs., Castle Rock, Colo., 1976-77, Jefferson County Schs., Lakewood, Colo., 1977-80, Denver Pub. Schs., 1980-82; coord. spl. learning support program/learning disabled adult Community Coll. of Denver, 1983-89; sch. psychologist Denver Pub. Schs., 1989—. Mem. faculty part-time Met. State Coll., Denver, 1984-86; mem. grad. faculty part-time U. Colo., Denver, 1977-81, 86-89; presenter in field. U.S. Dept. Edn. grantee, 1987-89. Mem. APA, Colo. Soc. Sch. Psychologists (treas. 2002-04), Colo. Assn. for Gifted and Talented, Autism Soc. Am. (bd. dirs. Colo. chpt. 1996-2001), Littleton Assn. for Gifted and Talented (bd. dirs. 1996-98), Nat. Kidney Found. (living donor 2001). Democrat. Home: 4271 E Links Pwky Littleton CO 80122

CABIOGLU, NESLIHAN, surgeon; d. Saniye and Kemal Mustafa Cabioglu. MD, U. of Istanbul, Faculty of Medicine, Turkey, 1994. Lic. Gen. Surgeon Turkey, 2000. Attending physician Haseki Rsch. Hosp., Istanbul, Turkey, 2001; postdoctoral fellow MD Anderson Cancer Ctr., Houston, 2001—02, MD Anderson Cancer Ctr., Dept. of Cancer Biology, Houston, 2002—. Surg. residency U. of Istanbul, Faculty of Medicine, Dept. of Gen. Surgery, Turkey, 1995—2000. Author pubs. in med. lit. Clin. scholar in Breast Cancer, Astra Zeneca Drug Co., 2000. Mem.: Am. Assn. of Cancer Rsch. (assoc.). Office: MD Anderson Cancer Ctr Knight Rd 7777 Houston TX 77054 Personal E-mail: neslicab@yahoo.com. E-mail: ncabiogl@mdanderson.org.

CABLE, CHARLES ALLEN, mathematician; b. Akeley, Pa., Jan. 15, 1932; s. Elton Thomas and Margaret (Fox) C.; m. Mabel Elizabeth Yeck, Dec. 19, 1955; children: Christopher A., Carolyn E. BS, Edinboro State Coll., 1954; M.Ed., U. N.C., 1959; PhD in Math., Pa. State U., 1969. Instr. math. Interlaken High Sch., N.Y., 1954-55, Tidioute High Sch., Pa., 1957-58; asst. prof. math Juniata Coll., Huntingdon, Pa., 1959-67; assoc. prof. dept. math. Allegheny Coll., Meadville, Pa., 1969-75, prof. dept. math., 1975-96, chmn. dept., 1970-90. Editorial reviewer: Math. Mag., 1975-80; assoc. editor: Focus, 1981-85. Served with AUS, 1955-57. Gen. Elec. fellow, 1958; NSF fellow, 1959, 61, 68, 73; NDEA fellow, 1969 Mem. Am. Math. Soc., Math. Assn. Am. (chmn. Allegheny Mountain chpt. 1973-75, bd. govs. 1981-84, mem. newsletter editorial com. 1981-85, com. on student chpts. 1987-93, publs. com. 1983-86), AAUP. Republican. Presbyterian. Home: 199 Jefferson St Meadville PA 16335-1108 Office: Allegheny Coll N Main St Meadville PA 16335

CABLE, DANA GERARD, psychologist; b. Sewickley, Pa., Aug. 27, 1943; s. Boyd and Jean (Clover) C.; m. Sylvia Kaufman, Mar. 19, 1977; children: David, Jennifer. AB, W.Va. Wesleyan Coll., 1965; MA, W.Va. U., 1971, PhD, 1972. Lic. psychologist; cert. grief therapist, death educator. Rsch. asst. W.Va. Wesleyan Coll., Buckhannon, 1965-68; instr. W.Va. U., Morgantown, 1968-71, vis. asst. prof., 1971-72; prof. psychology, thanatology Hood Coll., Frederick, Md., 1972—; pvt. practice, 1974—. Author: Death and Dying, 1983; mem. editl. bd. Am. Jour. of Hospice and Palliative Care, 1988—. Mem. Md. Commn. on Aging, 1979-83; bd. dirs. Citizens Nursing Home, Frederick, 1977-82, 87-93, 94—, Daybreak Adult Day Care Ctr., Frederick, 1988-94, Hospice of Frederick County, 1991—, bd. pres., 1998—, cons., 1981—. NDEA fellow, 1968-72; recipient Svc. award Assn. for Death Edn. and Counseling, 1982, Clin. Practice award Assn. for Death Edn. and Counseling, 1995, Alumni Achievement award W.Va. Wesleyan Coll., 2002. Mem. APA, Assn. Death Edn. (bd. dirs. 1981-87, 90-93), Gerontol. Soc., Internat. Platform Assn., Md. Gerontol. Assn. (bd. dirs. 1981-83), Capital Dist. Kiwanis (gov. 1990-91, Kiwanian of Yr.), Kiwanis Internat. (internat. chmn. tng. and leadership devel. 1993—, trustee 2002—), Elks. Republican. Avocations: travel, writing. Home: 8605 Pinecliff Dr Frederick MD 21704-6619 E-mail: danagcable@adelphia.net.

CABLE, DAVID GEORGE, cardiologist, surgeon; b. Cedar Falls, Iowa, Dec. 31, 1965; s. George Melvin and Claudette Cable; m. Anne Eleanor Frevert, Aug. 9, 1966; children: Calvin James, Spencer George. BS, Iowa State U., 1988; MD, U. of Iowa, 1993. Physician Mayo Clinic, Rochester, Minn., 1993—. Recipient Nygaard Travel award, 1998, Donald C. Balfour Alumni award for Meritorious Rsch., Mayo Clinic Alumni Assn., 1999, Nygaard Travel award, 1999. Achievements include research in Nitric oxide synthase gene therapy human coronary artery bypass grafts; Therapy for radial coronary artery bypass graft vasospasm; Minimally invasive saphenous vein harvesting for coronary artery bypass grafting. Office: Mayo Clinic and Mayo Foundation 200 First Street Rochester MN 55905 Home Fax: 507-255-7378; Office Fax: 507-255-7378. Personal E-mail: cable.david@mayo.edu. E-mail: cable.david@mayo.edu.

CABLE, JOHN FRANKLIN, lawyer; b. Hannibal, Mo., Dec. 22, 1941; s. John William and Dorothy (Stanley) C.; m. Leslie Gibbs, Apr. 5, 1965; children: Coventry, Tory, John. AB, Stanford U., 1964; LLB, Harvard U., 1967. Bar: Oreg. 1967. Assoc. Miller, Nash, Wiener, Hager & Carlsen, Portland, Oreg., 1967-73, ptnr., 1973—. Office: Miller Nash LLP 111 SW 5th Ave Fl 35 Portland OR 97204-3604 E-mail: cable@millernash.com.

CABLE, MABEL ELIZABETH, urban planner, artist; b. Sewickley, Pa., May 23, 1935; d. Andrew Lee and Josephine (James) Yeck; m. Charles Allen Cable, Dec. 19, 1955; children: Christopher A., Carolyn E. BS, Edinboro U., 1958; M in Urban-Regional Planning, U. Pitts., 1982. Tchr. Mount Union (Pa.) Jr.-Sr. High Sch., 1964-69; graphics illustrator Crawford County Planning Commn., Meadville, Pa., 1974-79, planner, 1979-86, asst. dir. planning, 1987-94; ret., 1994. Exhibitor Foothills Art Gallery, Golden, Colo., 1986-87, Pastimes Gallery, Meadville, Pa., 1987-99. Bd. dirs. Penn Lakes coun. Girl Scouts U.S.A., Meadville, 1974-79; pres. John Brown Heritage Assn., Meadville, 1985-88; mem. adv. coun. Pa. Community Devel. Block Grant Com., Harrisburg, 1987-94, chmn., 1990-94, Mem. Am. Inst. of Cert. Planners, Am. Planning Assn., Pa. Planning Assn. Home: 199 Jefferson St Meadville PA 16335-1108

CABLE, PAUL ANDREW, lawyer; b. N.Y.C., Apr. 13, 1939; s. Sydney W. and Karen A. (Petersen) C.; m. Diana Kathleen Sybil Lee, June 17, 1972. B.A., Wesleyan U., 1961; M.A. in Econ., U. Manchester, 1963; LL.B., Harvard U., 1966. Bar: D.C. 1967, N.Y. 1970, Calif. 1976. Assoc., Anderson, Mori & Rabinowitz, Tokyo, Japan, 1966-69, Anderson & Martin, N.Y.C., 1969-70; ptnr. Anderson, Martin & Cable, 1970-72, Whitman & Ransom, N.Y.C. and Los Angeles, 1972-93; ptnr. Whitman, Breed, Abbott & Morgan, N.Y.C., 1993—. Contbg. author: International Business Operations, 1974, East-West Trade Transactions, 1976, International Trade, 1983, 3rd. edit., 1991. Marshall scholar, Brit. Govt., 1961-63. Mem. N.Y. City Bar Assn. (coms.), D.C. Bar Assn., Calif. Bar Assn., Phi Beta Kappa (hon.). Clubs: Stanwich; Harvard. Home: 38 Birch Ln Greenwich CT 06830-3913 Office: Whitman Breed Abbott & Morgan 200 Park Ave New York NY 10166-0005

CABOT, HUGH, III, painter, sculptor; b. Boston, Mar. 22, 1930; s. Hugh and Louise (Melanson) C.; m. Olivia P. Taylor, Sept. 8, 1967. Student, Boston Mus., 1948, Ashmolean Mus., Oxford, England, 1960, Coll. Ams., Mexico City, 1956, San Carlos Acad. Portrait, landscape painter. Author (illustrator): Korea I (Globe); one-man shows include U.S. Navy Hist. and Records Dept., U.S. Navy Art Gallery, The Pentagon, Nat. War Mus., Washington, La Muse de la Marine, Paris, exhibited in group shows at Tex. Tri-State, 1969, Represented in permanent collections Starmont Vail Med. Ctr., Topeka, Kans., Tucson Med. Ctr., Harwood Found., Taos, N.Mex., Washburn U., Topeka, U. Ariz., Tucson, Chandler (Ariz.) Ctr. Arts, Booth Western Mus. Art, Cartersville, Ga.; Ofcl. artist for Korean War. With USN, Korean War. Named Artist of Yr., Scottsdale, Ariz., 1978, 30th ann. Mem. Salmagundi Club (N.Y.C.).

CABOT, LEWIS PICKERING, manufacturing company executive, art consultant; b. Sept. 6, 1937; s. John Moors and Elizabeth (Lewis) C.; m. Judith Ogden, July 1, 1960 (div. 1974); children: Elizabeth Lewis, Edward Ogden, Timothy Pickering; m. Susan Knight, July 15, 1978; children: James Eliot, Alexander Lee. AB, Harvard U., 1961, MBA, 1964. Trainee F.S. Moseley & Co., Boston, 1961-62; analyst John P. Chase, Inc., Boston, 1964-68; prin. Gardner & Preston Moss, Boston, 1968-73; chmn., pres. Artcounsel, Inc., Portland, Maine, 1973—; chmn., CEO Southworth Internat. Group, Inc., Portland, Maine, 1977—; pres. ZY-AX Realty, Portland, Maine, 1977—. Chmn. Shellback Corp., 1984-93; pres., chmn. Maine Art Leasing, 1988—; bd. dirs. Material Handling Roundtable; trustee NE Pooled Common Fund, Princeton, N.J., 1972-94. Trustee, pres. Soc. Arts and Crafts, Boston, 1962-66; trustee Phila. Maritime Mus., 1963-68, Mus. Fine Arts, Boston, 1966-90, Mus. Am. Folk Art, N.Y.C., 1973-77, Maine Coll. Art, 1982-91, Portland (Maine) Mus. Art, 1994—, Storm King Art Ctr., Mountainville, N.Y., 1961-72, Maine Maritime Mus., 1997—. Mem. com. Harvard U. Art Mus., Cambridge, Mass., 1982-88; bd. dirs. Maine State Music Theater, 1996-2001. Mem. Met. Club (Washington), Somerset Club (Boston), N.Y. Yacht Club (N.Y.C.). Office: Southworth Internat Group 11 Gray Rd Falmouth ME 04105-2027 E-mail: lpc@southworthproducts.com.

CABOT, LOUIS WELLINGTON, foundation trustee; b. Boston, Aug. 3, 1921; s. Thomas Dudley and Virginia (Wellington) C.; m. Mabel Hobart Brandon, 1997. AB, Harvard U., 1943, MBA, 1948; LLD (hon.), Norwich U., 1961. With Cabot Corp., 1948-96, pres., 1960-69, chmn. bd., 1969-86; chmn. Brookings Instn., Washington, 1986-92, hon. trustee; chmn. Cabot Wellington, LLC; trustee Cabot Family Trust, VWC Found. Bd. dirs. Owens-Corning Fiberglas Corp., 1961-91, Wang Labs Inc., 1982-91, New Eng. Tel. & Tel., 1965-82, R.R. Donnelley & Sons Co., 1965-91; bd. dirs. Fed. Res. Bank Boston, 1970-78, chmn., 1975-78; U.S. rep. 15th Plenary Session UN Econ. Commn. for Europe, 1960; mem. bus. ethics adv. coun. Dept. Commerce, 1961-63; dir., New Eng. chmn. Nat. Alliance Businessmen, 1970-72, Boston chmn., 1968-69; chmn. Sloan Commn. on Govt. and Higher Edn., 1977-80; mem. Pres.'s Blue Ribbon Commn. on Def. Mgmt., 1985-86; mem. Def. Sec.'s Commn. on Base Realignment and Closure, 1988; dir. Nat. Coun. for U.S.-China Trade, 1978-82. Mem. bd. overseers Harvard U., 1970-76; chmn. Harvard Coll. Fund Coun., 1963-65; pres. Beverly (Mass.) Hosp., 1958-61; chmn. Com. Corp. Support Pvt. Univs., 1977-83; trustee Norwich U., 1952-77, Mus. of Sci., Boston; corp. mem. MIT; trustee Woods Hole Oceanographic Inst., Northeastern U Conservation Internat. & Island Inst. Fellow: Am. Acad. Arts and Scis. (v.p.); mem.: NAS (pres. cir., co-chmn. 1992—95), Coun. Fgn. Rels., NY Yacht Club, Met. Club, Comml. Club (Boston) (pres. 1970—72), Somerset Club, Harvard Club, Sigma Xi, Phi Beta Kappa. Office: Cabot-Wellington LLC 70 Federal St Boston MA 02110-1906

CABOT, STEPHEN JAY, lawyer; b. Phila., Nov. 21, 1942; s. Charles and Roslyn (Levin) C.; m. Patti D. Gilberg, June 26, 1966 (div. Dec. 1996); children: Michele, Jennifer; m. Anna M. Farmer, Dec. 21, 1996. BS in Econ., Villanova U., 1964; JD, U. Pa., 1967. Bar: Pa. 1967. Field atty. Nat. Labor Rels. Bd., Pitts., 1967-69; labor atty. Obermayer, Rebmann, et al, Phila., 1970-72; ptnr., chmn. labor rels. and employment law Pechner, Dorfman et al, Phila., 1973-87; sr. ptnr., chmn. labor rels. and employment law Myerson & Kuhn, N.Y.C., Phila., 1987-89; labor atty. Summit Rovens, N.Y.C. and Phila., 1990; sr. ptnr., chmn. labor rels. and employment law Harvey, Pennington, Cabot, Griffith & Renneisen, Phila., 1991—, chmn. labor rels. and employment law dept. Cons. Bottom Line Bus., N.Y.C., 1980—; mem. labor rels. com. U.S. C. of C., Washington, 1982-86; lectr. in field. Author: Labor Management Relations Act Manual: A Guide to Effective Labor Relations, 1978, Labor Relations Guidebook: Practical Techniques for Managing Workplace Issues, 1988, Everybody Wins, 1998; contbg. editor: The Developing Labor Law for the ABA, 1980—, Phila. Bus. Jour, 1995; mem. editl. adv. bd.: McKnight's Long Term Care News, 2001—. Mem. ABA, Fed. Bar Assn., Soc. Human Resource Mgmt., Am. Coll. Health Care Admintrs. (Educator of Yr. 1985), Pa. Bar. Assn., Phila. Bar Assn. Avocations: golf, jogging, hiking, biking, weight lifting. Office: Harvey Pennington Cabot Griffith & Renneisen 1835 Market St Fl 29 Philadelphia PA 19103-2968 E-mail: scabot@harvpenn.com.

CABRANES, JOSÉ ALBERTO, judge; b. Mayaguez, P.R., Dec. 22, 1940; s. Manuel and Carmen López Cabranes; m. Kate Stith, Sept. 15, 1984; children: Alejo, Benjamin José;children from previous marriage: Jennifer Ann, Amy Alexandra. AB, Columbia U., 1961; JD, Yale U., 1965; MLitt in Internat. Law, Cambridge (Eng.) U., 1967; LLD (hon.), Colgate U., 1988. Bar: N.Y. 1968, D.C. 1975, U.S. Dist. Ct. Conn. 1976. Assoc. Casey, Lane & Mittendorf, N.Y.C., 1967—71; assoc. prof. law sch. Rutgers U., Newark, 1971—73; spl. counsel to gov. P.R., head Office Commonwealth P.R., Washington, 1973—75; gen. counsel Yale U., New Haven, 1975—79; judge U.S. Dist. Ct. Conn., New Haven, 1979—94, chief judge, 1992—94; judge U.S. Ct. Appeals (2nd cir.), 1994—. Mem. Pres.'s Commn. White House Fellowships, 1993—96, Pres.'s Commn. Mental Health, 1977—78; U.S. del. Conf. Security and Coop. in Europe, Belgrade, 1977—78; bd. dirs. James Madison Meml. Fellowship Found., 1995—2003; founding mem. P.R. Legal Def. and Edn. Fund, 1972, chmn. bd., 1977—80; cons. to sec. Dept. State, 1978; mem. Fed. Cts. Study Com., 1988—90; instr. history P.R. Colegio San Ignacio de Loyola, Rio Piedras, PR, 1962; supr. in internat. law Queens' Coll., Cambridge U., 1966—67. Author: Citizenship and the American Empire, 1979; co-author (with Kate Stith): Fear of Judging: Sentencing Guidelines in the Federal Courts, 1998 (Cert. of Merit, ABA); author: articles on law and internat. affairs. Trustee Yale U., 1987—99, Yale-New Haven Hosp., 1978—80, 1984—87, Colgate U., 1981—90, Century Found., N.Y.C., 1983—2000, Columbia U., 2000—, Fed. Jud. Ctr., 1986—90; mem. Coun. on Fgn. Rels.; bd. dirs. Aspira of N.Y. (Puerto Rican edn. agy.), chmn., 1971—73. Recipient Life Achievement award, Nat. P.R. Coalition, 1987, John Jay award, Columbia Coll., 1991, Life Achievement award student divsn., Nat. Hispanic Bar Assn., 1991, Learned Hand medal for excellence in fed. jurisprudence, Fed. Bar Coun., 2000; Kellett rsch. fellow, Columbia Coll. at Cambridge U., 1965—67. Fellow: ABA, Mex.-Am. Lawyers Assn. (Spl. Recognition award 1994); mem.: Nat. Hispanic Bar Assn., Am. Law Inst., Conn. Bar Assn. (Naruk Jud. award 1993). Roman Catholic. Office: US Ct of Appeals US Courthouse 141 Church St New Haven CT 06510-2030

CABRERA, JOAO B.D. information scientist; b. Rio de Janeiro, Aug. 29, 1964; s. Arthur S. and Carmen D. Cabrera. BSEE, Aero. Inst. Tech., Sao Jose dos Campos, Brazil, 1985; M Engring. in Control Engring., Tokyo Inst. Tech., 1990; PhD in Elec. Engring., Yale U., 1997. Elec. engr. Promon, Inc., Sao Paulo, Brazil, 1986, sr. elec. engr. Campinas, Brazil, 1990—91; rsch. engr. Scientific Systems Co., Inc., Woburn, Mass., 1996—2001, sr. rsch. engr., 2001—02, group leader, info. systems, 2002—. Contbr. chapters to books, articles to profl. jours. and conf. procs. Mem.: IEEE.

CABRERA, LUIS FELIPE, software architect; b. Santiago, Chile, Dec. 22, 1951; came to U.S., 1975; s. Luis H. and Marlinda Codoceo; m. Marcelle O. Stagno, Dec. 28, 1972; children: Valentina, Luis. PhD, U. Calif., Berkeley, 1981. Rsch. staff mem. IBM, San Jose, 1985-95; software architect Microsoft Corp., Redmond, Wash., 1996—. Contbr. articles to tech. pubs.; inventor in field. Fulbright scholar, 1975. Fellow IEEE. Office: Microsoft Corp 1 Microsoft Way Redmond WA 98052-8300

CABRERA, QUINCY RODOLFO, minister, educator; b. Lingle, Wyo., Feb. 14, 1943; s. Pedro Cabrera and Sarah Garcia; m. Ruth Estrada, Nov. 4, 1966 (dec. 1980); children: Pablo, Juan, Sarai; m. Maria Esther, July 26, 1985; children: Rodolfo, Esther, Caleb, Joshua. MEd, L.A. State U., 1965; PhD, U. Autonoma de Mex., Mex. City, 1968; DD, Fuller Theol. Seminary, 1994. Tchr., missionary Assemblies of God Bible Seminary, Tijuana, Baja, Mex.,Calif, tchr. theology L.A., 1980-92; pastor New Life Christian Ctr., L.A., 1992—. Author: The Holy Trinity, 1980, Essentials of Preaching, 1986. Pres. Mex. Am. Political Assn., L.A., 1982-87; mem. Police commn., L.A., 1997, L.A. City Council, 1998; bd. edn. L.A. Unified Sch. Dist., 1998-2000; bd. mem. YMCA, L.A., 2001. Recipient Latino of Yr. award Hispanic Mag., 1995. Democrat. Avocations: mountain climbing, boating. Home: 1410 Perez Lane Los Angeles CA 90033 Office: El Adalid Ministries PO Box 432399 San Diego CA 92143-2399

CABRERA-JIMENEZ, JORGE ALBERTO, scientific researcher; b. Mexico, Apr. 15, 1940; s. Enrique Bernardo Cabrera-Vega and Maria de Los Angeles Jimenez-Gonzalez-Arratia; div.; children: Cristina-Elena, Alberto-Manuel, Socorro, Ana-Laura, Cecilia. Diploma in Biology, Nat. Autonomous U. Mexico, 1966, MS in Biology, 1976, DS in Biology, 2001. Rsch. asst. Inst. Biology, Nat. Autonomous U. of Mexico, 1959-65, rschr., 1965—. Prof. Nat. Autonomous U. of Mexico, 1962-87; coord. Trust for the Devel. of the Aquatic Fauna, Mexico, 1973-74; project evaluator Nat. Coun. Sci. and Technology, Mexico, 1988-95. Project leader Pioneer Mexican Scientific Rsch./Shrimp and Fish Biology for Aquaculture in Mexico, 1968 (Econ. prize 1971); designer: first Mexican exptl. farm for shrimp and fish aquaculture, 1971 (econ. prize 1972), others. Originator Latin Am. Assn. for Aquaculture, fin. sec. 1977; promoter Mex. Assn. of Aquaculturist, others. Fellow UNESCO, U. Miami, 1964; recipient scholarships and grants in field, numerous medals in field. Mem. World Mariculture Soc., Latin Am. Assn. Aquaculture, N.Y. Acad. Sci., AAAS, others. Avocations: salon dancing, playing piano, poetry, sculpting, table tennis. Office: Inst De Biologia UNAM Apartado Postal 20-239 01000 Mexico City Mexico

CABRERA-TRUJILLO, REMIGIO, research scientist; s. Remigio Cabrera-Aguirre and Juana Trujillo-Barriga; m. Luz Maria Diaz-Rivera, June 8, 1996. PhD in Physics magna cum laude, U. Autonoma Metropolitana, Mexico City, 1998. Tchg. asst. physics dept. U. Autonoma Metropolitana, Mexico City, 1992—94; rsch. assoc. physics dept. U. Fla., Gainesville, 1999—. Vis. PhD student Syddansk U., Odense, Denmark, 1995—97. Contbr. sci. articles to profl. jours. Mem.: AAAS, Am. Phys. Soc., Alachua Astronomy Club (program coord., sec. 2001—02). Office: U Fla Dept Physics Gainesville FL 32611-8435

CACAYORIN, EDWIN D. diagnostic and interventional neuroradiologist; b. Philippines, Apr. 21, 1947; m. Donna Lee Miller; children: Edward Ross Corrin, Laura Jean Corrin. MD, Far Ea. U. Inst. of Medicine, Philippines, 1971. Cert. Added Qualification (CAQ) in Neuroradiology Am. Bd. of Radiology, 1996, diplomate Radiology Am. Bd. of Radiology, 1978. Radiologist, spl. procedures Western Pa. Hosp., Pitts., 1977—79; asst. prof. of radiology SUNY Health Sci. Ctr., Syracuse, NY, 1980—82, chief of neuroradiology, 1982—92, prof. of neurosurgery, 1989—92; med. dir. and neuroradiologist Ctrl. Tex. Imaging Ctr., St. David's Med. Ctr., Austin, Tex., 1992—98; diagnostic, interventional neuroradiology Allegheny Gen. Hosp., Pitts., 1993—94; prof., chief of neuroradiology St. Louis U. Hosp., St. Louis, 1998—2001, U. Tex. Health Sci. Ctr., Hermann Hosp., Houston, 2001—. Reviewer Am. Jour. of Neuroradiology, 1987—97; exec. com. appointment, dept. of radiology SUNY Health Sci. Ctr. at Syracuse, 1988—92; reviewer Radiographics, 1990—95; pres. Capital Imaging Assn., Austin, Tex., 1994—95; reviewer Radiology, 2003—; fellowship neuroradiology U. Pittsburgh under Charles Kerber and Arthur Rosenbaum, 1980. Lecturer (various scientific presentations); contbr. chapters to books, articles various profl. jours. Recipient Physician's Recognition award, AMA, 1980, Cert. of Merit, Am. Roentgen Ray Soc., 1981, Legislative Resolution, Senatorial Commendation, SUNY, NY State Senate, 1987, Outstanding Tchr. award, St. Louis U. Radiology Residents, 1999-2000, Summa Cum Laude award on stroke, ASNR, Vancouver, CA, 2002. Mem.: Am. Soc. of Neuroradiology, Radiol. Soc. of N.Am. Achievements include research in embolization of vascular lesions of the central nervous system with n-butyl cyanoacrylate. Clinical trial sponsored by Tri-Point Medical LP (completed); balloon dilitation of cerebral vessels in spasm. Clinical trial sponsored by Interventional Therapeutics Corp. (completed); currently involved in innovative endovascular treatment of strokes and intracranial aneurysms. Avocations: travel, music. Office: UT Health Sci Ctr Houston TX

CACCAMISE, ALFRED EDWARD, real estate executive; b. LeRoy, N.Y., June 9, 1919; s. Joseph Peter and Rose Marie (Petrella) C.; m. Louise Ball, July 7, 1974. Student, Officers' Candidate Sch., Camp Davis, N.C., 1943, Cen. Calif. Comml. Coll., 1946-47. Lumber co. and hardware store owner, Chili, N.Y., 1956-65; motel owner DeLand, Fla., 1965-71; real estate salesman, 1974-75; real estate investments co. owner, 1972—; real estate broker Alliance Realty, DeLand, 1976—. Served with U.S. Army, 1940-46. Recipient John McCready award Community Outreach Services, DeLand, 1979, 81. Mem. Nat. Assn. Realtors, Fla. Assn. Realtors, DeLand and West Volusia Bd. Realtors (bd. dirs. 1978-79, grievance com. chmn. 1983, bldg. com. chmn. 1985-87), Alhambra Villas Home Owners' Assn. (pres. 1979-80), DeLand C. of C., DeLand Com. of 100. Lodges: Kiwanis (Sav-a-Life chmn. 1977, membership chmn. 1979), Lions (charter). Democrat. Roman Catholic. Avocations: golf, traveling, reading. Home: PO Box 241 Deland FL 32721-0241 Office: Alliance Realty 1122 N Woodland Blvd Deland FL 32720-2250

CACCAMISE, GENEVRA LOUISE BALL (MRS. ALFRED E. CACCAMISE), retired librarian; b. July 22, 1934; d. Herbert Oscar and Genevra (Green) Ball; m. Alfred E. Caccamise, July 7, 1974. BA, Stetson U., 1956; MLS, Syracuse U., 1967. Tchr. grammar sch., Sanford, Fla., 1956-57; tchr. elem. sch. Longwood, Fla., 1957-58; tchr., libr. Enterprise (Fla.) Sch., 1958-63; libr. media specialist Boston Ave. Sch., DeLand, Fla., 1963-83; head media specialist Blue Lake Sch., DeLand, 1983-87; ret., 1987. Author: Volusia County manual Instructing the Library Assistant, 1965, Echoes of Yesterday: A History of the DeLand Area Public Library, 1912-1995, 1995, A Quest for Beauty: A History of the Garden Club of DeLand, Florida, 1927-97, 1997, Index to Reflections: West Volusia County, 100 Years of Progress, 2002, (compilation) The Minutes and Memorials of the Old Settlers of DeLand, Fla., 1882-1916, 2003. Charter mem. West Volusia Meml. Hosp. Aux., DeLand, 1962-81; leader Girl Scouts U.S., 1955-56; area dir. Fla. Edn. Assn., Volusia County, 1963-65; bd. dirs. Alhambra Villas Home Owners Assn., 1972-75; trustee DeLand Pub. Libr., 1977-86, sec., 1978-80, v.p., 1980-82, pres., 1982-84; v.p. Friends of DeLand Pub. Libr., 1987-88, 98—, bd. dirs., 1987—, pres., 1989-90, 95-97, newsletter editor 1992-95, 99—; charter mem. Guild of the DeLand Mus. Art, 1988—, v.p., 1990, pres., 1991-92, co-rec. sec., 1997-98, mus. bd. dirs., 1991-95; co-orgn. chmn. Friends DeLand Mus. Art, 1993. Mem. AAUW (2d v.p. chpt. 1965-67, rec. sec. 1961-65, 78-80, pres. 1980-82, parliamentarian 1982-84), Assn. Childhood Edn. (1st v.p, 1965-66, corr. sec. 1963-65), DAR (chpt. registrar 1969-80, asst. chief page Continental Congress, Washington 1962-65), Fla. Libr. Assn., Bus. and Profl. Women's Club (corr. sec. DeLand 1968-71, 2d v.p. 1969-70), Stetson U. Alumni Assn. (class chmn. for ann. fund dr. 1968), Volusia County Assn. Media in Edn. (treas. 1977), Volusia County Ret. Educators Assn. (pres. Unit II 1988-90, scholarship chmn. 1992-95), Soc. of Mayflower Descendants (lt. gov. Francis Cook Colony 1988-90), Pilgrim John Howland Soc., Colonial Dames XVII Century, Magna Carta Dames, Nat. Soc. New Eng. Women (v.p. Daytona Beach Colony 1990-91), Nat. League Am. Pen Women (corr. sec. 1996-98, 2000—, pres. 1998-2000), Hibiscus Garden Cir. (treas. 1988-89, v.p. 1990-93, 96-97, pres. 1997-99, treas. 2001-2003), Nat. Soc. U.S. Daus. of 1812 (rec. sec. Peacock chpt. 1989-90), West Volusia Hist. Soc. (sec. 1996, libr. 1993—, v.p. 2000-02, pres. 2002-03, bd. dirs., Historian of Yr. 2002), Fla. Hist. Soc., DeLand Garden Club (corr. sec. 1993-95, editor newsletter 1993-95, v.p. 1997-99), Delta Kappa Gamma (pres. Beta Psi chpt. 1982-84). Address: PO Box 241 Deland FL 32721-0241

CACCESE, MICHAEL STEPHEN, lawyer; b. Penn Valley, Pa., Nov. 21, 1954; s. Frederick D. and Mary J. Caccese; m. Barbara Mitchel, Jan. 7, 1978; children: Stephen M., Michelle L. BA, Pa. State U., 1977; JD, Temple U., 1980. Bar: Pa. 1980, Va. 1993, U.S. Dist. Ct. (we. dist.) Va. 1997, Mass. 2001. Corp. counsel Federated Ivestors, Inc., 1980-83; sr. v.p., assoc. counsel Frank Russell Co., Tacoma, 1983-93; sr. v.p., gen. counsel, sec. Assn. for Investment Mgmt. and Rsch., Charlottesville, Va., 1993-2000; ptnr. Kirkpatrick & Lockhart, Boston, 2001—. Mem. editl. bd. Villanova Jour. Law and Investment Mgmt., 1997—, Jour. for Performance Measurement, 1997—. Mem. ABA, Boston Soc. Security Analysts, Assn. for Investment Mgmt. and Rsch. Home: 34 Choate Ln Ipswich MA 01938 Office: Kirkpatrick & Lockhart 75 State St Boston MA 02109 E-mail: mcaccese@kl.com.

CACCIATORE, RONALD KEITH, lawyer; b. Donaldsville, Ga., Feb. 5, 1937; s. Angelo D. and Myrtice E. (Williams) C.; children: Rhonda, Donna, Rex. Student, Spring Hill Coll., 1955-56; BA, U. Fla., 1960; JD, 1963. Bar: Fla. 1963, U.S. Supreme Ct. 1969. Asst. state atty. 13th Jud. Cir., 1963-65; pvt. practice Tampa, Fla., 1967. Lectr. criminal law; mem. 13th Jud. Cir. Jud. Nominating Commn., 1976-80, chmn., 1980; mem. Fed. Judiciary Adv. Commn. Fla., 1987—. Trustee Hillsborough C.C., 1979-83, chmn., 1982-83. Fellow Am. Coll. Trial Lawyers; mem. Hillsborough County Bar Assn. (pres. 1975-76, chmn. trial lawyers sect. 1983-85, Herbert G. Goldburg Meml. award 1991), Fla. Bar Assn. (chmn. criminal law sect. 1977-78), Fla. Coun. Bar Pres.'s (chmn. 1979-80), Fed. Bar Assn. (pres. Tampa Bay chpt. 1985-86, fed. jud. nominationcom. Fla. 1999—, George C. Carr Meml. award Tampa Bay chpt. 1996), Master of the Bar, White-Ferguson Inn, Herbert G. Goldburg Criminal Law Am. Inn of Ct. (pres. 2000—), Am. Inns of Ct., Palma Ceia Golf and Country Club, University Club.

CACCIATORE, S. SAMMY, lawyer; b. Tampa, Fla., Aug. 2, 1942; s. Sam and Margarita C.; m. Carolyn Michels, Aug. 10, 1963; children: Elaine Michel, Sammy Michel. BA, JD, Stetson U., DeLand, Fla., 1966. Bar: Fla. 1966, U.S. Ct. Appeals (5th cir.) 1967, U.S. Supreme Ct. 1971, U.S. Ct. Appeals (11th cir.) 1981, U.S. Dist. Ct. (mid. dist. 1966) Fla. Asst. public defender 9th jud. cir. State of Fla., State of Fla., 1966; assoc. firm Orlando, Fla., 1966-67; pvt. practice Melbourne, Fla., 1967—; ptnr. Nance, Cacciatore, Hamilton, Barger, Nance & Cacciotore, Melbourne, Fla., 1970—. Mem. 5th Dist. Appellate Nomination Commn., 1979-83; mem. Fla. Med. Malpractice Adv. Com., 1982; mem. jud. nominating commn. Fla. Supreme Ct. 1986-90, mem. Superior Ct. jury instrn. com., 2001—; bd. overseers Stetson U. Coll. Law, 1995—, Stetson Univ., trustee, 2000—; lectr. in field. Contbr. articles to profl. jour., chpt. to books. Trustee A. Max Brewer Meml. Law Libr., Brevard County, Fla., 1972-76, chmn., 1972-75. Mem. ABA, ATLA, Am. Law Inst., Internat. Acad. Trial Lawyers, Am. Bd. Profl. Liability Lawyers, Am. Bd. Trial Advocates, Nat. Bd. Trial Advocacy, Acad. Fla. Trial Lawyers (bd. dir. 1970—, pres. 1984-85, Pres.'s award 1983), Internat. Acad. Trial Lawyers Assn. (adminstrn. of justice com. 1989), Fla. Bar (bd. govs. 1994-99, exec. com. 1995-99, vice chmn. advt. task force 1995-97, budget com. 1994-97, chmn. 1996, mem. exec. com. trial lawyer sect. 1975, chmn. constl. revision com. 1997—, mem. legis. com. 1995-99, chmn. 1998-99, mem jury instrn com. Fla. Supreme Ct., 2001—), So. Trial Lawyers Assn., Stetson Lawyers Assn. (1st v.p. 1992-93, pres.-elect 1994-95, pres. 1995-96), Brevard County Bar Assn. (bd. dir., Pres.'s award 1975), Vassar Carlton Inn of Ct. (emeritus), Eau Gallie Yacht Club (gov., vice commodore 1981-82, commodore 1983-84). Democrat. Roman Catholic. Office: 525 N Harbor City Blvd Melbourne FL 32935-6837 *The law is a living, growing institution of our lives. Lawyers need to remember this and nurture its development as one would a child. It should grow straight and strong for the benefit of the people.*

CACCIATORE, SAMMY MICHEL, lawyer; b. Melbourne, Fla., June 18, 1968; s. Carolyn and Sammy C.; m. Joey Lynn Hoffmeier, June 6, 1992; children: Maddison Paige, Claire Ashlynn, Charles Edwin. BA in Psychology, Stetson U., 1990; MHS in Rehab. Counseling, U. Fla., 1992; JD, Stetson U. Coll. Law, 1995. Bar: Fla. Asst. state's atty. Office of State's Atty. 18th Jud. Cir., Melbourne, 1995—97; assoc. Nance, Cacciatore et al, Melbourne, 1998—2002, ptnr., 2002—. Mem. Fla. Bar Assn., Brevard County Bar Assn. (sec. 1997—). Avocations: water skiing, fishing. Home: 799 Malibu Ln Indialantic FL 32903-4763 Office: Nance Cacciatore et al 525 N Harbor City Blvd Melbourne FL 32935-6890

CACCIATORE, SHAREN WENDY, educational administrator; b. Boston, Mass., Feb. 18, 1960; d. Frederick Everett Robertson and Doris Marie McLean; m. Carmelo Cacciatore, Mar. 19, 1978; children: John, Carmelo, Alfonso, Catherine. BA Humanities, Stonehill Coll., Easton, MA, 1999; MA Edn., Harvard U., Cambridge, MA, 2000. Founder / dir. / pres. The Story Train, Inc., Middleboro, Mass., 1994—; treas. / adminstrv. officer Cacciatore Bros., Inc., Middleboro, Mass., 1985. Dir. The Story Train Literacy Ctr., Middleboro, Mass., 2000—. Contbr. articles to profl. publs. Recipient Hon. Award Recognition, The Nat. Dean's List, 1999. Fellow: Internat. Reading Assn., Religious Studies and Philos. Assn., The Am. Philos. Assn., Nat. Coun. Teachers English, Phi Delta Kappa Internat. Achievements include patents for 501C-3 non-profit status awarded, US IRS, The Story Train, Inc., 1995; Service Mark awarded from US Patent and Trademark Office: The Story Train website, 1997. Avocations: creative writing, volunteering. Office: The Story Train Literacy Center 353 West Grove Street Middleboro MA 02346 Office Fax: 508-946-4054. E-mail: stytrain@ici.net.

CACCIAVILLAN, AGOSTINO, cardinal; b. Vicenza, Italy, Aug. 14, 1926; JCD, Pontifical Lateran U.; JD, State U., Rome. Ordained priest Roman Cath. Ch., 1949, archbishop, 1976. Joined diplomatic svc. Holy See, Rome, 1959; served The Philippines, Spain, Portugal in Vatican Secretariat of State, until 1976; Titular Archbishop of Amiterno Italy, 1976; apostolic pro-nuncio, 1976-81, 1981-90; joint appointment to Nepal, 1985-90. Apptd. Apostolic pro nuncio to U.S. and Permanent Observer of the Holy See to O.A.S., 1990-98; pres. adminstrn. of Patrimony of the Apostolic See, 1998-2002; cardinal, 2001. Roman Catholic.

CACCIOLA, PATRICK BARRY, art association administrator; b. White Plains, NY, Oct. 6, 1960; s. Theresa Barry and Anthony Roland Cacciola. MusB, Manhattanville Coll., 1979—83. Fund Raising and Devel. for Non-Profit Orgn. Marymount Coll. / Tarrytown, NY, 2001, Excellence in Non-Profit Leadership and Mgmt. Learning Inst. for Non-Profit Orgn.,Madison, Wis., 1999. Music tchr. Osborn Elem. Sch., Rye, NY, 1983—85; art dir. The Ink Spot, Chappaqua, NY, 1985—94; program dir. Arts Coun. of Rockland, Spring Valley, NY, 1994—. Judge for student visual arts competition Holocaust Mus. & Study Ctr., Spring Valley, NY, 1996—2002; competition judge for nat. libr. pub. rels. coun. Valley Cottage Libr., NY, 1998—99; workshop presenter NY State Coun. on the Arts, N.Y.C., 1999—, grant panelist, 1999—2002. Musician: (vocal soloist) Presented solo Lieder/Song Recitals at various locations, (baritone soloist in Am. premiere) Vivaldi Te Deum; musician: (vocal soloist) various choral/instrumental groups; musician: (musical theater) Various Musical Revues and Cabaret Performances, (vocal soloist) Performed works by Virgil Thompson for composer at Manhattanville College graduation where Thompson received honorary degree in 1983. Adv. bd. chairperson to county exec. on lesbian, gay, bi-sexual, transgendered constituents Westchester County Govt., White Plains, 2002—03; bd. mem. WestFair Chamber Singers, White Plains, NY, 1997—98; graphic designer/vol. N.Y. State Art Educators Assn., White Plains, 2001—03. Avocations: 20th century vocal music, graphic design, interest in children's book illustration and cartooning. Home: 75 Peiro Dr Yonkers NY 10710 Office: Arts Council of Rockland 7 Perlman Dr Spring Valley NY 10977 Office Fax: 845-426-3203. Personal E-mail: pbcny@aol.com. E-mail: acor@ucs.net.

CACERES, AILEEN, physician; b. N.Y.C., Apr. 23, 1972; d. Victor and Adanisa (Santana) C. BA, Boston U., 1994, MPH, 1996; MD, Robert Wood Johnson Med. Sch., Piscataway, N.J., 2002. Nutrition cons. Gen. Nutrition Ctr., Orlando, Fla., 1991-92; patient advocate Franciscan Children's Hosp., Boston, 1992; rsch. asst. Boston U., 1992-94; program asst. N.Am. Indian Ctr., Boston, 1994-95; rsch. asst. Boston U., 1995-96; rsch. staff assoc. Columbia U., N.Y.C., 1996—; resident Albert Einstein Med. Sch., Montefiore Med. Ctr., 2002—. Cons. Boston U., 1995-97, Mt. Sinai Med. Ctr., N.Y.C., 1996-97; lectr. in field. Contbr. articles to profl. jours., chpts. to books. Internat. health coord. Family Health Group-RWJMS, Piscataway, 1997; pub. health advocacy coord. ob-gyn. interest group RWJMS, 1999—. Rutledge Cook fellow N.J. State Dept. Health and Sr. Svcs., 1998. Mem. AMA, APHA, Nat. Coun. Internat. Health, Mass. Pub. Health Assn., Med. Soc., N.J., Hispanic Fedn. N.Y.C. Avocations: travel, advocacy for women's health and issues related to medically and socially underprivileged. Home: 700 Riverside Dr Apt 6D New York NY 10031-3129 E-mail: cacereai@hotmail.com.

CACERES, FRANKLIN THOMAS, writer; b. N.Y.C., July 8, 1946; s. Frank Caceres and Louise Caamano; m. Magali Zayas; children: Anthony Caceres, German Gomez, Zaira Gomez. BBA, Manhattan Coll., 1969; MA, U. South Fla., 1998; postgrad., Clayton Coll. Natural Health. Regional credit mgr. Carrier Air Conditioners, Inc., Clearwater, Fla., 1988—94; asst. acad. dean Hillsborough C.C., Mac Dill AFB, Fla., 1994—96; mgmt. sys. analyst Hillsborough County Bd. Commrs., Tampa, Fla., 1996—. Cons. Hispanic Bus. Initiative Fund, Tampa, 1996—. Author: (novels) Because They Were, 2002, Chronic Nights, 2003; contbr. articles. Mem. So. Poverty Law Ctr., Montgomery, 2000—, Hillsborough Alliance for Citizens with Disabilities, Tampa, 1996—, Nat. Coun. La Raza, Washington, 2000—. With U.S. Army, 1969—71. Mem.: Paralyzed Vets. Am., Mystery Writers Am., Nat. Multiple Sclerosis Soc., Tampa Writers' Alliance, Fla. Writers' Assn., League United Latin Am. Citizens, Phi Kappa Phi. Roman Catholic. Avocation: woodworking. Personal E-mail: caceresf@novel-guy.com. Business E-Mail: caceresf@hillsboroughcounty.org.

CACHIA, PIERRE JACQUES, Middle East languages and culture educator, researcher; b. Fayoum, Egypt, Apr. 30, 1921; came to U.S., 1975; s. François and Anna Rachel (Axler) C.; m. Phyllis Barbara Oyston, Mar. 20, 1953; children: Susan Margaret, Philip Greville, Helen Frances; m. Merle McNeill Dalziel, Sept. 26, 1992. BA, Am. U., Cairo, 1942; PhD, U. Edinburgh, 1951. Mem. faculty Am. U., Cairo, 1946-48, U. Edinburgh, Scotland, 1949-75; prof. Middle East langs. and cultures Columbia U., N.Y.C., 1975-91, chmn. dept. Middle East langs. and cultures, 1980-83, prof. emeritus, 1991—. Author: Taha Husayn, 1956, Popular Egyptian Narrative Ballads, 1989, An Overview of Modern Arabic Literature, 1990, The Arch Rhetorician: A Handbook of Late Arabic Badi', 1998, Arabic Literature - An Overview, 2002; co-author: History of Islamic Spain, 1965, 1977, 1992, 1996, Landlocked Islands: two alien lives in Egypt, 1999; translator (by Tawfiq al-Hakim). The Prison of Life, 1992; translator: (by Yahya Haqqi) Blood and Mud, 1999; compiler The Monitor-Arabic Grammatical Terms, 1973; editor: The Book of the Demonstration by Eutychius, Vol. 1, 1960, Vol. 2, 1961; co-editor: Islam: Past Influence and Present Challenge, 1979, Jour. Arabic Lit., 1970—96; contbr. encys., Orientalist jours., Great Lit. of Ea. World, African Writers, Life Writing. Grantee NEH, 1977; grantee Smithsonian Instn., 1979; fellow Am. Research Ctr. in Egypt, Cairo, 1982; fellow Woodrow Wilson Ctr., Washington, 1991-92. Mem.: Union Européenne d'Arabisants et d'Islamisants, Brit. Soc. Middle Eastern Studies, Am. Assn. Tchrs. Arabic, Middle East Studies Assn., Am. Oriental Soc. E-mail: pjc1@columbia.edu.

CACIOPPO, JOHN TERRANCE, psychology educator, researcher; b. Marshall, Tex., June 12, 1951; s. Cyrus Joseph and Mary Katherine (Kazimour) Cacioppo; m. Barbara Lee Andersen, May 17, 1981 (div. 1998); children: Christina Elizabeth, Anthony Cyrus; m. Wendi L. Gardner, Sept. 8, 2001. BS in Econs., U. Mo., Columbia, 1973; MA in Psychology, Ohio State U., 1975, PhD in Psychology, 1977. Asst. prof. psychology U. Notre Dame, Ind., 1977-79, U. Iowa, Iowa City, 1979 81, assoc. prof., 1981-85, prof. psychology, 1985-89, Ohio State U., 1989-98, Univ. chaired prof. psychology, 1998-99; Tiffany-Margaret Blake disting. svc. prof. U. Chgo., 1999—. Vis. faculty Yale U., 1986, U. Hawaii, 1990, U. Chgo., 1998—99; tng. grant dir. NIMH Social Psychology, 1993—98; co-dir. Inst. for Mind and Biology, 1999—; dir. Social Psychology Program, 1999—. Author, editor: 10 books; editor: Psychophysiology, 1994—97; mem. editl. bd.: various prof. jours.; contbr. articles over 270 to profl. jours. Active John D. and Catherine T. MacArthur Found. Network on Mid-Body Integrations, 1995-98; bd. dirs. Ohio State U. Rsch. Found., 1993-98 Recipient Early Career Contbn. award Psychophysiology, 1981, Troland Rsch. award NAS, 1989, Disting. Sci. Contbr. Psychophysiol., Soc. Psychophysiol. Rsch., 2000; NSF grantee, 1979—, Campbell award Soc. Personality and Social Psychology, 2000. Fellow: APA (past pres. 2 divsns., Disting. Sci. Contbn. award 2002), Acad. Behavioral Medicine Rsch., Am. Psychol. Soc. (keynote spkr. ann. meeting 2002, bd. dirs. 2002—); mem.: AAAS, Am. Acad. Arts and Scis., Soc. Exptl. Psychologists, Soc. Exptl. Social Psychology, Soc. Personality and Social Psychology (pres. 1995), Soc. Psychophysiol. Rsch. (bd. dirs. 1985—88, officer 1991—94, pres. 1992—93, bd. dirs. 1998—2000), Sigma Xi (nat. lectr. 1996—98). Office: U Chgo Dept Psychology Chicago IL 60637

CACOSSA, ANTHONY ALEXANDER, Romance languages educator; b. Newburgh, NY, Jan. 29, 1935; s. Salvatore and Franceschina (Scicchitano) C.; m. Anna Iaccino, Apr. 10, 1969. BA, Johns Hopkins U., 1955; MA, Syracuse U., 1956; D Modern Langs., U. Catania, Italy, 1969. Teaching asst. Syracuse (N.Y.) U., 1956-57; asst. prof., chmn. fgn. langs. Coppin State Coll., Balt., 1959-65; asst. prof. to prof. modern langs., coord. Italian studies Towson State U., Balt., 1965-83; adj. prof. Romance langs. and ESL Greenwich U., Hilo, Hawaii, 1989—2000; core faculty advisor in edn. Walden U., Mpls., 1990—96. Vis. tchr. Newburgh (NY) Free Acad., 1956; vis. lectr. Loyola Coll., Balt., 1967; accredited and chartered profl. cons. fgn. lang. edn. and curriculum design, Balt., 1983—; Fulbright lectr. Colombia, 1965, Italy, 1968-69, Costa Rica, 1972-73. Author: A Bergamask Parody of Guarini's Il Pastor Fido, 1972, Italian trans., 1973; contbr. articles to profl. jours. Fellow in Italian NEH, Stanford (Calif.) U., 1979; East European studies fellow Am. Coun. Learned Socs., UCLA, 1986. Mem. AAUP, Sigma Delta Pi (hon.). Home and Office: 316 E Melrose Ave Apt B Baltimore MD 21212-2913 E-mail: antalfra@aol.com.

CADDELL, FOSTER, artist; b. Aug. 2, 1921; s. Foster and Clara (Bamford) C.; m. June A. Kaufmann, Apr. 10, 1943 (dec. Feb. 1989); m. Gail L. Marchant, Feb. 14, 1993. Student, R.I. Sch. Design, 1940-43; pvt. study with, Peter Helck, Robert Brackman, Guy Wiggins. Artist Providence Lithograph Co., R.I., 1939-52; freelance illustrator, 1951-65; owner, instr. Foster Caddell's Art Sch., Voluntown, Conn., 1958—. One-man shows Providence Art Club, 1948, 63, South County (R.I.) Art Assn., 1967, Slater Mus., Norwich Acad., 1976, Heritage Plantations of Sandwich, 1985; group shows include Springfield Mus. Fine Arts, 1962-77, Am. Watercolor Soc., 1973, NAD, 1973, Am. Artists Profl. League (awards 1953, 71, 72, 89, 90, 91), Acad. Artists Am. (awards 1968, 73, 75), Slater Mus., Norwich Acad., 1975-80, Providence Art Club (award 1978, 79, 92), Nat. Arts Club, 1978, Internat. Soc. Artists (award 1978), Soc. des Pastellists de France, 1987, The Monmouth (N.J.) Mus., 1994, Brown U. Libr., Providence, 1995, Pastel Soc. No. Fla. (award 1996), Pastel Soc. Am. (elected Hall of Fame 1998), Beijing Acad. Fine Arts, 1997, others; specialist in portraiture, 1965—; author: Keys to Successful Landscape Painting, 1976, Keys to Successful Color, 1979, Keys to Painting Better Portraits, 1982, Oil Painting Techniques, 1983, Landscape Painting Techniques, 1984, Foster Caddell's Keys to Successful Landscape Painting, 1993, Pastel Interpretations, 1993, The Art of Pastel Portraiture, 1996, Best Pastels II, 1998, Best of Sketching and Drawing, 1998, Pastel Jour. 2000, Pastel Artists Internat. 2001; work on display at pastelsocietyofamerica.org, Conn. Soc. Portrait Artists, ctpastelsociety.com. Served as artist USAAC, WWII. Recipient award, Norwich Acad., 1947, Ogunquit Art Ctr., 1949, Conservative Painters R.I., 1962, Salmagundi Club, 1973, 1980, No. Fla. Pastel Soc., 1996, Award of Excellence, Mystic Seaport Maritime Gallery, 1996, Best of Show award, Mystic Art Assn., 1997, award, Conn. Pastel Soc., 1990—94, 1998, 1999, Honor award, 2001, 2002, 2003. Mem. Oil Painters of Am., Washington Soc. of Portrait Artists (award 1998), Lyme Art Assn., Providence Art Club, Am. Artists Profl. League, Acad. Artists Am., Am. Soc. Portrait Artists, Salmagundi Club, Pastel Soc. Am. (award 1990, 91, 92, 93, 94, 98, 99), Internat. Soc. of Portrait Artists, Conn. Soc. Portrait Artists (award 2003). Address: 47 Pendleton Hill Rd Voluntown CT 06384-1920 Fax: 860-376-9583.

CADDELL, JOHN A. lawyer; b. Tuscumbia, Ala., Apr. 23, 1910; s. Thomas Arthur and Florence Lee (Huff) C.; m. Lucy Bowen Harris, Sept. 1, 1935; children— Thomas A., Lucinda Lee, Henry Harris and John A. (twins). AB, U. Ala., 1931, LLB, 1933, LLD (hon.), 1982. Bar: Ala. bar 1933. Since practiced in, Decatur. Sec., dir. Southeastern Metals Co., Inc., Birmingham, 1946-68; chmn. bd. First Nat. Bank Decatur, 1976-81; City atty., Decatur, 1936-59; counsel com. investigating campaign expenditures U.S. Ho. of Reps., 1944; bd. commrs. Ala. State Bar, 1939-54, Jud. Council Ala., 1946-58; mem. bd. Bar Examiners Ala., 1949, 50 Mem. Ala. Democratic Exec. Com., 1938-50; Trustee U. Ala., 1954-79, also pres. pro tem, 1974-78. Fellow Am. Coll. Trust and Estate Counsel, Am. Coll. Trial Lawyers, Am. Bar Found.; mem. ABA, Ala. Bar Assn. (pres. 1951-52), Morgan County Bar Assn., U. Ala. Alumni Assn. (pres. 1953), Decatur C. of C. (pres. 1943-44), Ala. Acad. Honor, Pi Kappa Alpha, Omicron Delta Kappa, Phi Delta Phi. Democrat (mem. Ala. exec. com. 1938-50). Presbyn. (elder). Clubs: Athletic, U. Alabama, Decatur Kiwanis (pres. 1939). Home: PO Box 2688 Decatur AL 35602-2688 Office: 214 Johnston St SE Decatur AL 35601 2516 E-mail: jcaddell2200@aol.com.

CADDY, DEBORAH CAROL RUNYAN, social worker; b. Arkadelphia, Ark., Jan. 24, 1958; d. Dean and Marilyn (Yancey) Runyan; m. Rod Caddy, May 26, 1979; 1 child, Hallie Kaitlin. BA, Ouachita Bapt. U., 1980; MS Social Work, U. Tex., Arlington, 1986. Dir. rape crisis program Women's Ctr. Tarrant County, Ft. Worth, 1986—. Mem. NASW, Alpha Delta Mu. Office: Womens Ctr Tarrant County 1723 Hemphill Fort Worth TX 76110-0860

CADDY, EDMUND H.H., JR., architect; b. N.Y.C., Apr. 17, 1928; s. Edmund Harrington Homer and Glenna Corinne (Garratt) C.; m. Mary Audrey Ortiz, Dec. 22, 1951; children— Edmund Harrington Homer III, Mary Elizabeth. BA, Princeton, 1952, M.F.A. (grad. sch. fellow), 1955. With Louis E. Jallade, N.Y.C., 1949-53, Eggers & Higgins, N.Y.C., 1953-55; dir. design Dalton-Dalton Assocs., Cleve., 1955-60; assoc. Raymond & Rado, N.Y.C., 1960-68; gen. ptnr. Raymond & Rado and Ptnrs., N.Y.C., 1968-72, Raymond, Rado, Caddy & Bonington, P.C., N.Y.C., 1972-80, pres., 1980-83; project mgr. Robinson, Mills & Williams, San Francisco, 1983-87, McCue, Boone, Tomsick, San Francisco, 1987-88, O'Brien-Kreitzberg, San Francisco, 1988-90; Sverdrup Corp., 1990-94; archtl. design cons., 1994—. Apptd. by Pres. John F. Kennedy to adv. com. arts John F. Kennedy Ctr. Performing Arts, 1963-70; mem. archtl. adv. commn. N.Y.C. C.C., CUNY, 1979-83. Works include Suburban Hosp, Cleve., 1957, J.M. Smucker Co, Salinas, Cal., 1957, Brookpark (Ohio) City Hall, 1959; Cleve. Transit System addition, 1959, administrn. bldg., Met. Water Treatment System, Saigon, 1960, Franklin D. Roosevelt High Sch, N.Y.C., 1963, Crown Heights Intermediate Sch, N.Y.C., 1966, engring. complex design, Stony Brook Campus, State U. N.Y., 1970, Sibley's dept. stores, Syracuse, N.Y., 1973, Rochester Downtown Devel. Study, 1975, R.H. Macy & Co. dept. store, Stamford, Conn., 1979; project mgr. Main Postal Facility, San Francisco, 1985, Univ. Ctr., U. Calif., Irvine, 1987, Santa Clara (Calif.) County CourtHouse, Ft. Mojave Resort Devel., 1991-94. Pres. bd. trustees Montclair (N.J.) Cmty. Hosp., 1973-80. Served with USMC, 1946-48, USMCR, 1948-53. Mem. AIA, Tower Club (Princeton), Racquet and Tennis Club (N.Y.C.) Home: 1999 Baldwin Way Bolingbrook IL 60490-6551

CADDY, MICHAEL DOUGLAS, lawyer; b. Long Beach, Calif., Mar. 23, 1938; s. Frank Edward and Tabitha (Miles) C. BS in Fgn. Svc., Georgetown U., 1960; JD, NYU, 1966. Bar: DC 1970, Tex. 1979. Practiced in, Washington and, Tex.; exec. dir. com. on pub. affairs McGraw-Edison Co., N.Y.C., 1960-61; asst. to lt. gov. State of N.Y., 1962-65; asst. to exec. v.p. NAM, N.Y.C., 1966-67; Washington liaison Gen. Foods Corp., 1968-70; assoc. Gall, Lane, Powell & Kilcullen, 1970 74; legis. counsel Nat. Assn. Realtors, Washington, 1975 76; atty. Office Tex. Sec. of State, Austin, 1980-81. Author: The Hundred Million Dollar Payoff, 1974, How They Rig Our Elections, 1975, Understanding Insurance, 1984, Legislative Trends in Insurance Regulation, 1985, Exploring America's Future, 1987. Mem. Rep. County Com., N.Y.C., 1965-66; nat. dir. Young Ams. for Freedom, 1960-62. Scholar Intercollegiate Studies Inst., 1957-59. Mem.: FBA, ACLU, ABA, ATLA, Nat. Lesbian and Gay Law Assn., Nat. Trust Hist. Preservation, People for Am. Way, Supreme Ct. Hist. Soc., Nat. Coun. Crime and Delinquency, Internat. Platform Assn., Am. Acad. Polit. and Social Sci., Am. Econ. Assn., Assn. Former Intelligence Officers, Am. Judicature Soc., Stonewall Lawyers Assn. Houston, Houston Bar Assn. Office: 7941 Katy Fwy Ste 296 Houston TX 77024-1924 E-mail: douglascaddy@justice.com.

CADE, NANCY JEAN, history and political science educator; b. Indpls., June 21, 1955; d. Fred William Jr. and Evelyn Jean Meyer; m. John Joseph Cade, Dec. 30, 1989. BS, Ball State U., 1977, MA, 1979, PhD, 1987. Adj. instr. Ball State U., Muncie, Ind., 1983, Anderson (Ind.) Coll., 1985; asst. prof. history and polit. sci. Pikeville (Ky.) Coll., 1986-90, assoc. prof. history and polit. sci., 1990-98, prof. history and polit. sci., 1998—. Mem.: Am. Polit. Sci. Assn., Orgn. Am. Historians, Pike County Humane Soc., U.S. Humane Soc., Am. Soc. for Prevention of Cruelty to Animals, Phi Alpha Theta, Pi Gamma Mu. Democrat. Lutheran. Home: 1938 Raccoon Rd Raccoon KY 41557 Office: Pikeville Coll Dept Polit Sci Pikeville KY 41501 E-mail: ncade@pc.edu.

CADE, WALTER, III, artist, musician, singer, actor; b. N.Y.C. s. Walter Cade and Helen (Henderson) Brehon. Student, Arts Students League, Inst. Modern Art. Appeared in (plays) Amen Corner, Hatful of Rain, Jim Pavone & the Buzz Bomb, Mary Mary, Don't Bother I Can't Cope, Harlequinade, The Story of Ulysses, Mateus, Which Way America, Poetry Now Subway Cinema, (films) Cotton Comes to Harlem, Education of Sonny Carson, Claudine, Now, Angel Heart, The Wiz, FX, (T.V.) Joe Franklin Show, Positively Black, Soul, Sammy Davis Telethon, June Rolands, Musical Chairs, Big Blue Marble; one man shows include: Ocean County Coll., 1977, Jackson State U., 1980, Phoenix Gallery, Atlanta, 1982, Olin Mus. Art, Bates Coll., Maine, 1993, U.S. Nat. Tennis Ctr., Arthur Ashe Stadium, U.S. Open, NY, 1997, 98, 99, Sande Webster Gallery, Pa., 2000, others; 2-man shows include: Lewiston-Auburn Coll., Maine, 1993, others; 3 man shows include: Suffolk Community Coll., 1987; group shows include Whitney Mus., 1971, Corcoran Gallery, 1972, Black Expo, N.Y.C., 1973, Miss. Mus. Fine Art, 1991, Roanoke (Va.) Mus. Fine Art, 1982, Tampa Mus., 1982, Hunter Mus. Art, 1983, Tucson Mus. Art, 1983, New Eng. Fine Arts Inst., Maine, 1993, Lewiston-Auburn Coll., 1994; represented in permanent collections Fine Arts Mus. South, Bruce Mus., Virginia Beach Art Mus., Rockefeller Found., Peter A. Juley and son Collection, Smithsonian Inst. Nat. Mus. Am. Art, others. Recipient numerous awards for paintings, 1978—, including best in show award Las Olas Art Festival, 1980, Arts Festival Atlanta, 1981, Bruce Mus., 1983, 84, 94, 1st prize, Fine Arts Mus. South, 1982. Mem. SAG, Artists Equity. Avocations: motorcycling, martial arts. Home: 17203 119th Ave Jamaica NY 11434-2261

CADENHEAD, ALFRED PAUL, lawyer; b. LaGrange, Ga., Oct. 14, 1926; s. Roy E. and Omie (Bishop) C.; m. Sara Davenport, Oct. 14, 1945; children: Steven Paul, David James. Jr. coll. certificate, W. Ga. Coll., 1944; LL.B., Emory U., 1949. Bar: Ga. 1949. Sr. counsel, ptnr. Hurt, Richardson, Garner, Todd & Cadenhead, Atlanta; with Hurt, Richardson, 1977-92; now of counsel Fellows, Johnson & La Briola, Atlanta, 1993—. Pres. Atlanta Legal Aid Soc., 1958 Pres. Met. Atlanta Mental Health Assn., 1964-65, Ga. Assn. Mental Health, 1968; past trustee Queens Coll., Charlotte, N.C.; lifetime trustee West Ga. Found. Served with paratroops U.S. Army, 1944-46. Recipient West Ga. Coll. Disting. Svc.award, 1993, Emory U. Law Sch. Disting. Alumnus award, 1996, Ben F. Johnson Pub. Svc. award Ga. State U., 1999, Founders award State U. West Ga., 2001. Fellow ABA, Am. Acad. Matrimonial Lawyers, Am. Coll. Trial Lawyers, Internat Soc. Barristers; mem. State Bar Ga. (past bd. govs.), Atlanta Bar Assn. (pres. 1970-71, Charles E. Watkins award for disting. and sustained svc. 1992, Leadership award 2000), Atlanta Estate Planning Coun. (pres. 1976). Presbyterian. Home: 6305 Riverside Dr NW Atlanta GA 30328-3646 Office: South Tower Peachtre Ctr Ste 2300 225 Peachtree St NE Atlanta GA 30303-1731

CADES, STEWART RUSSELL, lawyer, communications company executive; b. Phila., Jan. 16, 1942; s. Ralph E. and Lillian G. (Mann) C. BS in Econs., U. Pa., 1964, LLB, 1967; MEd, Temple U., 1971. Bar: Pa. 1971. Sole practice, Phila. and Bala-Cynwyd, Pa., 1971—; chmn. bd. Porcupine Communications Co., Phila., 1971—. Pres. Nairn U.S. Holdings divsn. Stewart Nairn Group P.L.C., 1980-86; bd. dirs. Cloche Assocs., Inc., Andrews & Leith, Ltd., ACM Worldwide, Ltd.; mng. dir. Overseas Strategic Consulting; chmn. bd. dirs. Towne Met., Inc., 1985-92, pres. Election judge Montgomery County, Pa., 1975—77; ct. vol. probation dept. Ct. Common Pleas Phila. County, 1972—74; vice-chmn. Montgomery County Planning Commn., 1980—95; bd. dirs. Southeastern Pa. Transit Authority, 1991—97, trustee, 1991—97, pension com., 1991—97, chmn. real estate com., 1991—97; mem. adv. bd. City of Phila. Airport, 1996—, mem. exec. com., 2000—01; bd. dirs. Friends of Phila. Mus. Art, 1985—91, Juvenile Law Ctr., SEPTA Transit Mus.; mem. assocs. adv. bd. Phila. Mus. Art, 2001—; trustee Pa. Acad. Fine Arts, 1992—2002; bd. dirs. Found. Arch., 1999—2002, Conservation Ctr. Art and Hist. Artifacts, 2000—; sec., sch. chmn. alumni undergrad admissions U. Pa., 1978—2001, alumni pres. Class of '64, 1975—90; v.p. Fabric Workshop. Mem.: ABA, Montgomery County Bar Assn., Phila. Bar Assn. (ct. house & detention facilities com. 1983—86), Pa. Bar Assn., Print Club (bd. govs. 1978—98, hon. bd. 1999—). Office: 191 Presidential Blvd Bala Cynwyd PA 19004-1207

CADGE, WILLIAM FLEMING, gallery owner, photographer; b. Phila., May 5, 1924; s. Arthur and Janet (Fleming) C.; m. Anne Marie English, Feb. 5, 1949; children: Stephen Anthony, Jeffrey John, Catherine Anne. Student, Phila. Coll. Art, 1945-49. Free-lance designer, Phila., 1949-50; asst. art dir. Eve. Bull., Phila., 1950-52, Woman's Home Companion, 1952-56; art dir. Doyle, Dane & Bernbach (advt.), N.Y.C., 1956-57; asso. art dir. McCall's mag., 1959-61; art dir. Redbook mag., 1961-75; owner, mgr. Jeff and Bill Cadge Photography; owner Pinwheel Studio and Gallery, Cape May, N.J., 1989—. Cons. art dir. Think Mag. Photog. covers nat. and European mags., also editorial and adwt. illustration. Served with RAF, 1941-43; with USAAF, 1943-45. Recipient 2 gold medals, 8 award distinctive merit Art Director's Club N.Y.; 1 gold medal; 1 award distinctive merit Art Director's Club Phila.; 1 award excellence Art Director's Club N.J.; also N.J. 2 awards of excellence.; 1 award outstanding achievement for 1966 Soc. Illustrators; 1 gold medal, 1971, 72; 5 awards excellence Type Director's Club N.Y.; 1 award excellence for 3 consecutive issues of Redbook in 1966, 1969; 1 award excellence for 3 consecutive issues of Redbook in 1966 Soc. Publ. Designers; also 1 award excellence best typography in 1966, and award distinctive merit for 3 consecutive issues Redbook, 1970; awards excellence CA Mag. Show, 1967, 68; awards excellence Soc. Publ. Designers, 1968; awards excellence Soc. Illustrators, 1968, 1977; gold medal Art Dirs. Club Show, 1977 Mem. Soc. Illustrators, Art Dirs. Club N.Y. (exec. bd. 1966-68) Home and Office: 174 Charter Cir Ossining NY 10562-6012

CADIEUX, CHESTER, gas industry executive; b. 1932; BBA, U. Okla., 1954. Salesman Maneke-Kinzie Printing Co., Tulsa, Okla., 1954—58; CEO QuikTrip, Tulsa, Okla., 1958—. Office: QuikTrip Corp PO Box 3475 Tulsa OK 74101-3475*

CADIEUX, ROGER JOSEPH, physician, mental health care executive; b. Bay Shore, N.Y., Feb. 7, 1945; m. Kathryn Cadieux; children: Kevin, Kristin. BS, Northwestern State U., 1973; MD, La. State U., 1977. Cert. geriatric psychiatrist, RN anesthetist. Intern, then resident in psychiatry Coll. Medicine Pa. State U., Hershey, 1977-81, psychogeriatric fellow, instr. Coll. Medicine Milton S. Hershey Med. ctr., 1980-81, asst. prof. dept. psychiatry, 1981-93, assoc. prof. psychiatry, 1993-99; clin. prof. psychiatry, 1999—; dir. geriatric assessment program Pa. State U. Coll. Medicine, 1992-98; psychiat. cons. Jewish Home of Harrisburg, 1985—, Homeland Ctr. of Harrisburg, 1993—; program dir. Pa. Dept. Aging, 1986—, physician cons., 1987—; pres. Commonwealth Affiliates, P.C., 1992—. Contbr. articles to profl. jours. Fellow Am. Bd. Psychiatry and Neurology (disting., diplomate); mem. Am. Psychiat. Assn., Am. Geriatric Soc., Am. Assn. for Geriatric Psychiatry, Acad. Sleep Disorders Medicine, Alpha Omega Alpha. Office: 2215 Forest Hills Dr Harrisburg PA 17112-1099

CADIGAN, ELISE, social worker; b. Topeka, Mar. 8, 1947; d. Grattan C. Huckabee and Virginia (Ross) Huckabee Specht; m. Glenn Koski, 1989; children: Kent, Matthew, Drew. BS, Washburn U., 1972; MSW, Kans. U., 1977. Bd. cert. diplomate clin. social work; lic. clin. social worker, Ill. Adj. prof. social work Ottawa (Kans.) U., 1977-78; social worker Lawrence (Kans.) Sch. Dist., 1978-79, Harlem Sch. Dist., Loves Park, Ill., 1979-82; pvt. practice Glenwood Evaluation and Treatment Ctr., Rockford, Ill., 1980—. Mgr. adolescent svcs. Swedish Am. Hosp., Rockford, 1984-88; adj. faculty U. Ill., Rockford. Bd. dirs. Big Bros./Big Sisters, Rockford, 1980-85, Rock River Valley United Way, 1997-2003, Cmty. Fedn. No. Ill.. 2003; bd. dirs. Children's Devel. Ctr., 1986-94, pres., 1992-93; mem. bd. counselors Rockford Coll.; mem. adv. bd. U. Kans. Sch. Social Welfare; sr. warden St. Anskars Episcopalian Ch., 1996-98. Mem. NASW (Ill. chpt. ethics com. 1995—, dist. chair 1983-85, Dist. Social Worker of Yr. award 1985), Rockford Area Substance Abuse Coun. (Cmty. Vol. of Yr. award 1988), Rockford Jr. League, Rockford Womans Club (dept. pres. 1997 98), Rotary Internat. (asst. dist. gov. 1999 2001, pres. Downtown Rockford club 1999-2000, dist. 6420 Leadership Trainer 2001—, bd. dirs. 1994-96, 97-2001), Phi Delta Kappa Avocations: downhill skiing, travel, music. Office: Glenwood Ctr 2823 Glenwood Ave Rockford IL 61101-3599 Fax: 815-968-4656. E-mail: jhawks77@charter.net.

CADLE, JERRY NEAL, lawyer; b. Swainsboro, Ga., June 3, 1951; s. F.H. and Eugenia (Baker) Cadle; m. Paula Kay Ferre, Dec. 27, 1971; children: Ivy Neal, Donald Jacob, Jean Marie. Student, Mid. Ga. Coll., 1969—70, Ga. So. Coll., 1970—71; BBA, U. Ga., 1972, JD, 1975. Bar: Ga. 1975, U.S. Dist. Ct. (so. dist.) Ga. 1975, U.S. Tax Ct. 1976, U.S. Ct. Appeals (11th cir.) 1981. Assoc. Rountree & Rountree, Swainsboro, 1975—76; ptnr. Rountree & Cadle, Swainsboro, 1977—87, Rountree Cadle & McNeely, Swainsboro, 1987—. Commr. Emanuel County, 1997—2000; chmn. Emanuel County Commn., 2000. Chmn. East Georgia Coll. Found., 1990—2000; pres. Swainsboro Devel. Corp., 1977—; deacon First Bapt. Ch., Swainsboro, 1983—85, 1987—, chmn. deacons, 1988—89, chmn. bd. trustees, 1984—85; bd. dirs. Emanuel County 4-H Found., 1975—2003, v.p., 1979—2003. Mem.: Mid. Jud. Cir. Bar Assn. (sec.-treas. 1978, 1983, pres. 1988), Ga. Sch. Bd. Attys. Assn., Swainsboro Country Club (dir. 1981—85, pres. 1984). Home: 957 W Main St Swainsboro GA 30401 Office: Rountree Cadle & McNeely 130 S Main St Swainsboro GA 30401-3618

CADMAN, EDWIN CLARENCE, dean, health facility administrator, medical educator; b. Bandon, Oreg., May 14, 1945; s. Edwin Herbert Cadman and Gloria (Ranellie) Wilson; children: Tim, Kevin, Brian. AB, Stanford U., 1967; MD, U. Oreg., 1971. Intern in internal medicine Stanford (Calif.) U. Hosp., 1971-74; fellow in oncology Yale U., New Haven, 1974-76, asst. prof. medicine, 1976-79, assoc. prof. medicine, 1979-83, prof., chmn. medicine, 1987-94, prof., 1994—; prof. medicine, dir. Cancer Rsch. Inst. U. Calif., San Francisco, 1983-87, vice chmn. dept. medicine, 1985-87; chief of staff, sr. v.p. med. affairs Yale New Haven Hosp., 1994—99; dean John A. Burns Sch. of Med. Univ. of Hawaii, 1999—. Pror. Am. Cancer Soc., 1985-87. Contbr. over 300 articles to profl. jours. Basketball coach Novato (Calif.) Park and Recreation, 1985. Capt. USNG, 1972-78. Recipient Gold Headed Cane award U. Oreg. Med. Sch., 1971. Fellow AAAS, ACP; mem. AFCR (pres. 1984-86), ASCI, AAP, ASCO/AACR, AOA. Avocations: running, fishing, reading. Home: 2954 Makalei Pl Honolulu HI 96815-4743 Office: John A Burns Sch Med 1960 E West Rd Honolulu HI 96822

CADMAN, WILSON KENNEDY, retired utility company executive; b. Wichita, Kans., Sept. 7, 1927; s. Wilson K. and Ethel Louise (Wheeler) C.; m. Mary Roslyn Rowley, Nov. 22, 1950; children: Elizabeth Louise, Cadman Haywood, Robert Wilson. AB, Wichita State U., 1951, postgrad., 1953, Okla. State U., 1965. With Kans. Gas & Electric Co., Wichita, 1951-92, mgr. Wichita divsn., 1967-70, v.p., 1970-79, pres., 1979-92, chief exec. officer, 1981-92, also chmn. bd. dirs.; ret., 1992. Sr. advisor Barr Devlin & Assocs. Investment Bankers, N.Y.C.; bd. dirs. Bank IV of Wichita, El Paso (Tex.) Electric Co., Columbia Energy Group, Herndon, Va., Clark/Bardes Inc., Dallas, Broadbande2e.com, Newport Beach, Calif., Ponca Products Mfg., Wichita, Kans. Bd. govs. Wichita State U. Endowment Assn.; bd. dirs. Wichita State U. Athletic Scholarship Orgn.; mem. Gov.'s Task Force on High Tech. Devel., Mayor's Econ. Adv. Council, Kans. Water Resources Council. Served with USN, 1945-46. Mem. Edison Electric Inst., Wichita Area Devel. (exec. com.), Wichita State U. Endowment Assn., Wichita Club, Wichita Country Club, Univ. Club, Crestview Country Club, Kiwanis, Phi Lambda Psi. Home: The Cloisters 8905 E Douglas Wichita KS 67207 also: PO Box 160-583 33 Hidden Village Big Sky MT 59716

CADOGAN, DAVID PHILLIP, aerospace engineer, researcher; b. Ann Arbor, Mich., Nov. 25, 1963; s. Lydia Ann Olson and Ronald Lee Cadogan, Gene Gilbert Olson (Stepfather) and Janice Cadogan(Stepmother); m. Heather Ann Lotrich; 1 child, Connor Thomas. BS, Western Mich. U., 1981—86. Mgr. rsch. & devel. ILC Dover Inc., Frederica, Del., 2001—, sr. design engr., 1986—2001. Chmn. AIAA Gossamer Spacecraft Program Com., Washington D.C., 2000—. Achievements include patents for braking mechanism for spacecraft component deployment. Office: ILC Dover Inc One Moonwalker Rd Frederica DE 19946-2080 Office Fax: 302-335-0762. E-mail: cadogan@ilcdover.com.

CADY, BLAKE, surgical oncologist; b. Washington, Dec. 27, 1930; s. John Parmalee and Elizabeth (Blake) C.; children: Brian, Suzanne, Pamela. AB, Amherst Coll., 1953; MD, Cornell U., 1957. Diplomate Am. Bd. Surgery; lic. physician, Mass., NY, RI. Intern Tufts Surg. Svc. Boston City Hosp., 1957-58, resident Tufts Surg. Soc., 1958-59, resident Harvard Surg. Svc., 1961-65; USPHS clinic cancer trainee Meml. Hosp. for Cancer and Allied Diseases, N.Y.C., 1965-67; fellow in surgery Cornell U. Med. Coll., 1965-67; fellow Sloan-Kettering Inst., 1965-67; staff surgeon Lahey Med. Clinic, Burlington, Mass., 1967-81; mem. surg. staff New Eng. Deaconess Hosp., Boston, 1967-97; chief surg. oncology New Eng. Deaconess, Boston, 1982-97; prof. surgery Brown U. Med. Sch., Providence, 1997—. Surg. liaison Dana Farber Cancer Ctr., Boston, 1982—; cons. surgery Uganda Cancer Inst., Kampala, Uganda, East Africa, 1971; assoc. clin. prof. surgery Harvard Med. Sch., 1975-82, assoc. prof., 1982-91, prof. 1991-97, emeritus prof., 1997—; dir. Breast Health Ctr., Women and Infants Hosp., Providence, 1997-2003. Editor emeritus: Surgical Oncology Clinic of North America; mem. editl. bd. several jours.; contbr. over 300 articles to profl. jours. Bd. dirs. Mass. div. Am. Cancer Soc., 1974, pres., 1991-93, nat. bd. dirs., 1993-99, chmn. tobacco policy com., 1991-93; chmn. bd. dirs. Tobacco Control Resource Ctr., 1994—, Planned Parenthood League Mass., 1984-85; chmn. Mass. Coalition for Healthy Future, 1991-93, Tobacco Control Oversight Coun. Mass.; pres. James Ewing Found., 1988. Lt. M.C., USN, 1959-61. Recipient Lemuel Shattuck medal Mass. Pub. Health Assn., 1983, 96; ann. nat. divsn. award Mass. divsn. Am. Cancer Soc., 1984, Disting. Svc. award, 2000. Mem. AMA, ACS (Mass. chpt., spl. rep. to regional cancer control com. subcom., regional cancer control com.), Am. Surg. Assn., Soc. Surg. Oncology (program chmn. nat. meetings 1980, 81, chmn. rsch. com. 1980-82, sec. 1984-86, v.p. 1986-87, pres.-elect 1987-88, pres. 1988, chmn. exec. com. 1989-90), Soc. Head and Neck Surgeons (program com. 1980, Hayes Martin lectr. 1998), Am. Assn. Endocrine Surgeons (v.p. 1982, local arrangements chmn. 1988, exec. coun. 1986-90, sec.-treas. 1991-94, pres. 1998), New Eng. Cancer Soc. (treas. 1976-83, sec. 1983-87, pres. 1991), New Eng. Surg. Soc. (recorder 1989, pres. 1995-96), Soc. for Surgery Alimentary Tract, Boston Surg. Soc. (pres. 1993), Halstead Soc. Avocations: sailing, traveling. Home: 24 Walnut Pl Brookline MA 02445-6710 Office: Univ Surg Assocs APC-110 593 Eddy St Providence RI 02903 Office Fax: 401-868-2313. Business E-Mail: bcady@usasurg.org.

CADY, EDWIN HARRISON, English language educator, author; b. Old Tappan, N.J., Nov. 9, 1917; s. Edwin Laird and Ethel Sprague (Harrison) C.; m. Norma Woodard, Aug. 31, 1939; children: Frances (Mrs. Edward Hitchcock, dec.), Elizabeth (Mrs. Larry Saler). AB, Ohio Wesleyan U., 1939, LittD (hon.), 1964; MA, U. Cin., 1940; PhD, U. Wis., 1943; LittD (hon.), Oklahoma City U., 1967; LHD (hon.), Georgetown U., 1989. Instr. English U. Wis., 1945, Ohio State U., 1946; from asst. prof. to prof. Syracuse U., 1946-59; Rudy prof. English Ind. U., 1959-73; prof. English Duke U., 1973-87, Andrew W. Mellon prof. humanities, 1975-87, prof. emeritus, 1987—. Vis. prof. Am. lit., Uppsala and Stockholm, Sweden, 1951-52 Author: The Gentleman in America, 1949, The Road to Realism: The Early Years, 1837-1885, of William Dean Howells, 1956, The Realist at War: The Mature Years, 1885-1920, of William Dean Howells, 1958, Stephen Crane, 1962, rev. edit., 1980, John Woolman: The Mind of the Quaker Saint, 1965, The Light of Common Day, 1971, The Big Game: College Sports and American Life, 1979, Young Howells and John Brown, 1985. Editor: (with H.H. Clark) Whittier on Writers and Writing, 1950, Literature of the Early Republic, 1950, rev. edit, 1969, (with L. Ahnebrink) An Anthology of American Literature, 1953, (with L.G. Wells) Stephen Crane's Love Letters to Nellie Crouse, 1954, (with F.J. Hoffman and R.H. Pearce) The Growth of American Literature, 1956, W.D. Howells, The Rise of Silas Lapham, 1957, Corwin K. Linson, My Stephen Crane, 1958, (with D.L. Frazier) The War of the Critics Over William Dean Howells, 1962, W.D. Howells, The Shadow of a Dream and An Imperative Duty, 1962, William Cooper Howells, Recollections of Life in Ohio, 1963, The American Poets, 1800-1900, 1966, (with D.F. Hiatt) W.D. Howells, Literary Friends and Acquaintance, 1968, Nathaniel Hawthorne, The Scarlet Letter, 1969, W.D. Howells as Critic, 1973, (with C. Anderson and L. Budd) Toward a New American Literary History; Essays in Honor of Arlin Turner, 1980, (with N.W. Cady) Critical Essays on W.D. Howells, 1866-1920, 1983, A Modern Instance, 1984; (with Louis J. Budd) On Whitman: The Best from American Literature, On Mark Twain: The Best from American Literature, 1987, On Emerson: The Best from American Literature, On Melville: The Best from American Literature, 1988, On Faulkner: The Best from American Literature, 1989, On Dickinson: The Best from American Literature, 1989, On Hawthorne: The Best from American Literature, 1990, On Henry James: The Best from American Literature, 1990, On Robert Frost: The Best from American Literature, 1991, On Humor: The Best from American Literature, 1991, On Howells: The Best From American Literature, 1993, On Poe: The Best From American Literature, 1993, W.D. Howells, Pebbles, Monochromes, and Other Modern Poems, 1891-1916, 2000; gen. editor: A Selected Edition of W.D. Howells, 1966-68; assoc. editor: Am. Lit. mag, 1973—; chmn. bd. editors, 1979-86, mng. editor, 1986-87. Mem. exec. com. Center Am. Editions, 1964-68; mem. U.S. Nat. Commn. for UNESCO, 1969-71. Served with Am. Field Service, 1943-44, Italy; with USNR, 1945. Recipient citation Ohio Wesleyan U., 1991; Guggenheim fellow, 1953-54, 75-76 Mem. MLA (chmn. Am. lit. sect. 1979, Jay B. Hubbell medal Am. lit. sect. 1990), Guild Scholars, Am. Antiquarian Soc., Phi Beta Kappa, Omicron Delta Kappa, Phi Gamma Delta. Episcopalian. Home: 2701 Pickett Rd Apt 1232 Durham NC 27705-5649

CADY, ELWYN LOOMIS, JR., medico legal consultant, educator; b. Ames, Iowa, Feb. 21, 1926; s. Elwyn Loomis Sr. and Annabel (Lacey) C.; m. Jane Carolyn Elliott, Jan. 27, 1964 (dec. Dec. 1989); children: James Anson, Kathryn Anne; stepchildren: Martin Norman Jensen III, Paul Elliott Jensen. BS in Medicine, U. Mo., 1955; JD, Tulane U., 1951. Bar: Mo. 1951, U.S. Supreme Ct. 1965. Sci. comml. tchr., athletic dir. and coach Vermillion (Kans.) Rural High Sch., 1948-49; pvt. practice Kansas City, St. Louis, Independence, Mo., 1951—; dir. law-medicine program U. Kansas City, 1951-56; asst. dir. Law-Sci. Inst. U. Tex., Austin, 1956-57, sec. Law-Sci. Acad. Am., 1956-57; of counsel Koenig & Dietz, St. Louis, 1959-74; gen. counsel Elliott Oil, Inc., Independence, 1966—, Overland Park Dry Cleaners, Inc. Mem. com. on mgmt. Ea. Jackson County Planned Parenthood Clinics, Independence, 1970-75. Author: (book) Law and Contemporary Nursing, 1961, 1st. rev. edit., 1963; Author: (with others) Immediate Care of the Acutely Ill and Injured, 1974, Cardiac Arrest and Resuscitation, 1958, 4th rev. edit., 1974, West's Federal Practice Manual, 1960, rev. 2nd edit., 1989, Gradwohl's Legal Medicine, 1954; book reviewer: sci. books and films. Legal Counsel Friends of the Truman Campus, U. Mo.-Kansas City, Independence, 19 87-97, Cmty. Assn. for the Arts, Independence, 1991—; charter mem. Friends of Nat. Frontier Trails Ctr., Independence, 1990—, Independence Hist. Trails City Com., 1991—. With U.S. Army, 1944-45, ETO. Fellow Harry S. Truman Libr. Inst. for Nat. and Internat. Affairs (hon.), Am. Acad. Forensic Sci. (ret.); mem. AAAS (life), Nat. Geog. Soc. (life), Am. Legion (past comdr., judge adv., chaplain, chmn. state blood donor program, chmn. dist. oratorical contest), Mo. Writers' Guild (past pres., historian), Soc. Mayflower Descs. (gov. Heart of Am. colony), Phi Alpha Delta (life), Phi Beta Pi, Tau Kappa Epsilon. Home and Office: 1919 Drumm Ave Independence MO 64055-1836

CADY, JACK ANDREW, writer, educator; b. Columbus, Ohio, Mar. 20, 1932; s. Donald Victor and Pauline Lucille Cady. BSc, U. Louisville, 1961. Writer-in-residence Pacific Luth. U., Tacoma, 1983—96; ret., 1996. Author: (novels) The Night We Buried Road Dog, 1998, (nonfiction) The American Writer, 2000, The Hauntings of Hood Canal, 2001; contbr. articles to profl. jours. With U.S. Coast Guard, 1952—56. Recipient Nebula award, Nebula Awards Com., 1993, Bram Stoker award, Horror Writers Assn., 1993, Atlantic prize for short fiction, Iowa prize for short fiction, World Fantasy award, award, Nat. Lit. Anthology; fellow fellowship, Nat. Endowment for the Arts. Home: PO Box 872 Port Townsend WA 98368-0872 Personal E-mail: erewhon@olympus.net.

CADZOW, JAMES ARCHIE, engineering educator, researcher; b. Niagara Falls, N.Y., Jan. 3, 1936; s. John Francis and Mildred Lois (Lankis) C.; m. Alice Ruby Bissell, June 21, 1958; children: Gregory C., Patricia A., Robert J., Debra L., James C. BSEE, U. Buffalo, 1958; MSEE, SUNY, Buffalo, 1963; PhDEE, Cornell U., 1964. Engr. U.S. Army R&D Labs., Ft. Monmouth, N.J., 1958-59; design engr. Bell Aerosystems, Wheatfield, N.Y., 1959-61; rsch. asst. Cornell Aeronautical Labs., Cheektowaga, N.Y., 1961-62; prof. SUNY, Buffalo, 1964-77, Va. Poly. Inst., Blacksburg, 1977-81; rsch. prof. Ariz. State U., Tempe, 1981-88; Centennial prof. Vanderbilt U., Nashville, 1988—. Author: Discrete-Time and Computer Control, 1970, Discrete-Time Systems, 1973, Signals, Systems and Transforms, 1985, Foundation of Digital Signal Processing, 1987; contbr. articles to profl. jours. Recipient Spectral Estimation Disting. award Rome (N.Y.) Air Devel. Ctr., 1978, 79; Joshua Gibbs fellow Cornell U., 1962-64; NIH fellow, 1972-73. Fellow IEEE; mem. IEEE Signal Processing Soc. (Sr. award 1990), Sigma Xi, Phi Kappa Phi. Roman Catholic. Avocations: basketball, reading, crossword puzzles, tennis. Office: Vanderbilt U Dept Elec Engrng Nashville TN 37235

CAEMMERER, RICHARD RUDOLPH, art educator; b. St. Louis, Mo., Mar. 17, 1933; s. Richard Rudolph and Dorothy Elizabeth Caemmerer; m. Elizabeth Carolyn Schmidt, Aug. 23, 1958; children: David, Katherine, Michael, Matthew. BFA, Washington U., St. Louis, 1954; diploma, Heidelberg U., 1961; MFA, Ind. U., 1966. Prof. Art Valparaiso U., Valparaido, Ind., 1958—80; founder, dir. Grunewald Guild, Leavenworth, Wash., 1980—. Vis. prof. Akademie der Bildenden Kunste, Karlsruhe, Germany, 1961—62, Makerere U., Kampala, Uganda, 1970—71, Grad. Theol. Union, Berkeley, Calif., 1990—91, Luth. Sch. Theology, Chgo., 1983—; cons. Liturgical art and design Cath. Archdiocese Chgo., 1965—80. Author: Visual Art in the Life of the Church, 1983. Bd. dirs. Wheat Ridge Found., Chgo., 1968—73. Pfc U.S. Army, 1956—58. Named Danforth Assoc., Danforth Found., 1968—72; recipient Cert. of award, AIA; Disting. scholar, Staley Found., 1986—87. Lutheran. Avocation: conducting annual overseas art/theology study pilgrimages. Home: 19003 River Rd Leavenworth WA 98826 Office: Grunewald Guild 19003 River Rd Leavenworth WA 98826

CAESAR, GODFREY WRENSFORD, biologist, educator; b. Georgetown, Guyana; Student, Queen's Coll., Georgetown; DSc, DePaul U., 1977. Ind. rschr. Contbr. articles to profl. jours. Avocations: dancing, jogging, cooking. Address: 209 W 137th St New York NY 10030-2406

CAESAR, VANCE ROY, newspaper executive; b. New Kensington, Pa., Dec. 22, 1944; s. Jack Raymond and Norma Norine (Wiles) C.; m. Carol Ann Richards, Apr. 22, 1967; 1 son, Eric Roy BSBA, The Citadel, 1966; MBA, Fla. Atlantic U., 1969; grad., Stanford U. Exec. Program, 1982; PhD in Organizational Psychology Mgmt., Walden U., 1994. From asst. to gen. mgr. to consumer mktg. dir. Miami Herald, Fla., 1970-77; assoc. editor Detroit Free Press, 1977-78; sr. v.p., gen. mgr. Long Beach Press-Telegram, Calif., 1978-88; pres. P.C.H. Publs., 1989-93, Treasure Coast Newspapers Inc., 1992-93; chmn. The Vance Caesar Group, 1994—. Bd. dirs. Meml. Med. Ctr., Silverado Sr. Living Inc., Am. Women Econ. Devel., Rancho Los Alamitos; chmn. Sch. Bus. Adminstrn. Calif. State U., Long Beach; vice-chmn. adv. bd. Bus. Roundtable; exec. com. mem. Boy Scouts Am., Long Beach, Internat. Forum for Corp. Dirs.; chmn. Long Beach Bus. Devel. Group, So. Calif. Profl. Assocs.; pres., bd. dirs. Profl. Coaches & Mentors Assn.; bd. dirs. Orange County Venture Network, Accelerate Bus. Devel. Corp. Mem.: World Trade Ctr. Assn., Am. Newspaper Pubs. Assn., Long Beach Area C. of C., Rotary, Old Ranch Country Club, Long Beach Yacht Club, Assn. at Long Beach, Citadel Alumni Assn., Stanford Bus. Sch. Alumni Assn. (pres.). Home: 110 Ocean Ave Seal Beach CA 90740-6027

CAETANO, RAUL, psychiatrist, educator; b. São Paulo, Brazil, May 5, 1945; came to U.S., 1978; s. Silvestre Vieira and Vera Vieira (Barbosa) C.; m. Patrice Vaeth, Sept. 30, 1995; children: Izabel, Lauren, Helena. MD, U. Rio de Janeiro, 1969, diploma in psychiatry, 1971; MPH, U. Calif., Berkeley, 1979, PhD, 1983. Psychiatrist Pinel Hosp., Rio de Janeiro, 1969-73; asst. prof. State U., Rio de Janeiro, 1969-73; rsch. psychiatrist Inst. Psychiatry U. London, 1973-76; asst. prof. Inst. Psychiatry, Rio de Janeiro, 1976-78; vis. scholar Alcohol Rsch. Group, Berkeley, 1978-83, assoc. scientist to sr. scientist, 1983-94, dir., 1992—. Adj. prof. Sch. Pub. Health, U. Calif., Berkeley, 1991-98; assoc. dir. Calif. Pacific Med. Ctr. Rsch. Inst., San Francisco, 1992-93; prof., asst. dean Sch. Pub. Health, U. Tex., 1998—. Contbr. articles to profl. jours. WHO fellow, 1973-76; rsch. grantee Nat. Inst. Alcohol Abuse and Alcoholism, 1985—. Mem. APHA, Am. Coll. Epidemiology, Rsch. Soc. Alcoholism. Roman Catholic. Office: V8112 5323 Harry Hines Blvd Dallas TX 75390-9128 E-mail: raul.caetano@utsouthwestern.edu.

CAFARO, PATRICIA L. nurse practitioner, nurse, clinical administrator; b. Berwyn, Pa, June 16, 1957; d. Orlie Crawford and Yoneka Tamura Cookingham; m. Victor Paul Cafaro Jr., Nov. 27, 1979. Diploma, RN, St. Margaret Meml. Hosp., 1984; BSN, Pa. State U., 1993; MSN, U. Pitts., 1997; postgrad. in Psychology/Mental Health, Va. Commonwealth U., 2001. Cert. family nurse practitioner, asthma educator, asthma care provider. Clin. nurse U. Pitts. Med. Ctr., 1994, patient care mgr., asst. head nurse, 1994-97, nurse practitioner cardiac st, 1997-98; family nurse practitioner Med. Coll. of Va. Hosp., Richmond, 1998-99, asthma nurse practitioner, 1999—. Team leader Cerner orders/results task force Med. Coll. of Va. Hosp., 1999—. Vol. Family Advocacy Clinic, Richmond, 2000. Mem. Va. Coun. of Nurse Practitioners, Am. Acad. of Nurse Practitioners Assoc. Asthma Educators, Am. Lung Assn. Va. Asthma Coalition, Ctrl. Va. Asthma Coalition (founder), Coun. Advanced Practice Nurses (founder). Avocations: stamp collecting, gardening, reading, collecting matchbooks. Office: Med Coll Va Hosp PO Box 985861 401 N 12th St Richmond VA 23298-5861 E-mail: pcafaro@mcvh-vcu.edu.

CAFFEE, H. HOLLIS, plastic surgery educator; b. Oneida, Ky., May 8, 1943; BS, U. Fla., 1964, MD, 1968. Asst. prof. U. Fla., Gainesville, 1977-81, assoc. prof., 1981-88, prof. surgery, 1988—, chief plastic and reconstructive surgery, 1995—. Chief plastic surgery VA Hosp., Gainesville, 1977-95. Contbr. articles to profl. jours. Capt. U.S. Army Med Corps, 1970-72. Mem. Am. Soc. Plastic Surgeons, Am. Soc. for Surgery of the Hand, Southeastern Soc. Plastic and Reconstructive Surgeons (bd. mem. 1989-94), Plastic Surgery Ednl. Found. (bd. mem. 1988-93). Avocation: sailing. Office: U Fla Coll Medicine 1600 SW Archer Rd Gainesville FL 32610-3001

CAFFEE, LORREN DALE, lawyer; b. Decatur, Ind., Oct. 22, 1947; s. Howard Dale and Maxine Faye (Smith) C.; m. Mary Katherine Hostetler, May 25, 1968 (div. Apr. 1982); children: Liesl Katherine, Evan Dale, Colin Dale (dec.); m. Mary Jannice Dyer, June 14, 1986. BA, Bluffton Coll., 1969; JD, Georgetown U., 1972. Bar: Ind. 1972, U.S. V.I. 1994, U.S. Dist. Ct. (no. dist.) Ind. 1974. Pvt. practice, Decatur, 1972-73, 74-76; assoc. DeVoss & DeVoss Law Offices, Decatur, 1973-74; judge Adams County Ct., Decatur, 1976-84, Adams Superior Ct., Decatur, 1985-90, Adams Cir. Ct., Decatur, 1991-99; assoc. A.J. Weiss & Assoc. Law Office, 1999—2002; of counsel Law Offices of Norman P. Jones, 2003—. Mem. county ct. com. Ind. Jud. Ctr., 1978-88, chmn., 1983-86; mem. juvenile benchbook com. Jud. Conf. of Ind., 1991-99, bd. dirs., 1995-99. Bd. dirs. Ind. Right to Life, 1974-76; mem. constn. and by-laws com. Ind. Young Reps. Fedn., 1974, of counsel, 1975-76; chmn. Adams County Young Reps., 1973-76. Mem. Ind. State Bar Assn., Adams County Bar Assn. (pres. 1975-76), Ind. Judges' Assn., Am. Judges Assn., Nat. Coun. Juvenile and Family Ct. Judges, Federalist Soc. Lutheran. Avocations: jazz music, aviation, sports cars, art, reading. Home: PO Box 11479 St Thomas VI 00801-4479 Office: Law Offices of Norman Jones 4002 Raphune Hill Ste 407 St Thomas VI 00802

CAFFEE, VIRGINIA MAUREEN, executive assistant; b. Kansas City, Mo., Feb. 25, 1948; d. Frederick Arthur Gladden and Ethel Elizabeth (Keithly) Courier; m. Marcus Pat Caffee, May 31, 1975; 1 child, Katheryn Elizabeth. Student, Ctrl. Mo. State U., 1966-73, Okla. State U., 1977-78; BBA in Bus. Edn., Sam Houston State U., 1985. Cert. profl. sec., 1975. Land abstractor Johnson County Title Co., Warrensburg, Mo., 1967-68; dept. sec., bus. placement office Ctrl. Mo. State U., Warrensburg, 1968-69; exec. sec. European Exchange System, Giessen, Germany, 1969-70; confidential sec. Consolidated Freightways, Kansas City, 1972-73; exec. sec. Behring Internat., Houston, 1974-75; sr. sec. Tenneco Oil Co.-E&P, Houston, 1979-84; exec. sec. St. Petersburg (Fla.) Hilton & Towers, 1989-90; adminstrv. mgr. Tampa Bay Engring., Clearwater, Fla., 1990-92; office mgr., WP trainer Marcus Caffee, Consulting, Largo, Fla., 1992-95; sr. adminstrv. asst. BMH Inc., Dallas, 1995-97; exec. sec. GTE Comms. Corp., Irving, Tex., 1997-2000, mem. Internet coun., 1999—2000; exec. asst. Verizon-ESG, 2000—02, human resources bus. ptnr., 2001—. Ad hoc instr. St. Petersburg (Fla.) Jr. Coll., 1993, Profl. Secs. Internat. chpt. liaison for CPS rev. course, 1993-94; presenter in field. Editor (performance programs) Suncoast Singers, 1991-94 (Cmty. Svc. award Arts Coun. Co-op 1993), Clearwater Cmty. Chorus, 1993-95, Ft. Worth Civic Chorus, Fall 1995, (newsletters) Clearwater Sparkler, 1992-93 (1st pl. award 1993), Fla. Divsn. The Secretariat, 1993-94; editor: Livin, Lovin, Laughin, 1995, Texana Newsletter, 1997-98; webmaster T-L Divsn., 1997—. Sec. Montgomery County Choral Soc., Conroe, Tex., 1986-88, publicity co-chmn., 1987-89; pres. Anona Meth. Ch. Choir, Largo, 1990-91; mem. adv. bd. Mountain View C.C., Dallas, 1999. Named Sec. of Yr. Profl. Secs. Internat. Inc. Clearwater chpt., 1994; recipient Mo. State Tchrs. scholarship Mo. Congress Parents and Tchrs., 1966. Mem. CPS Acad., Internat. Assn. Adminstrv. Profls. (chmn. secs. week, sec. Clearwater chpt. 1992-93, pres. 1994, chmn. seminar and v.p. Clearwater chpt. 1992-93, workshop spkr. Fla. divsn. 1993, program spkr. St. Petersburg chpt. 1993, alt. del. to internat. conv. 1993, 96, 98, del. to internat. conv. 1999, alt. del. to divsn. meeting 1993, 94, del. dist. conv. 1994, 98, Sec. of Yr. 1994-95, del. Fla. divsn. meeting 1995, program spkr. Trinity chpt. 1996, del. Tex.-La. meeting 1996, 97, 98, 99, divsn. treas. Tex.-La. divsn. 1996, v.p. 1997-98, pres.-elect 1998-99, pres. 1999-00, workshop spkr. internat. conv. Chgo. 2000), CPS Soc. Tex. (roster chmn. 1983-85); Soc. Human Resource Mgmt., Women's Assn. Verizon Employees. Republican. Methodist. Avocations: choral singing, sewing, movies, ensemble singing performances. Home: 218 Oakmont Dr Trophy Club TX 76262-5472 E-mail: gcaffee@mccinternet.com.

CAFFERTY, PASTORA SAN JUAN, public policy educator; b. Cienfuegos, Las Villas, Cuba, July 29, 1940; arrived in US, 1947; d. Jose Antonio and Hortensia (Horruitiner) San Juan; m. Michael Cafferty, Apr. 13, 1971 (dec. 1973); m. Henry P. Russe, Aug. 18, 1988 (dec. 1991). BA, St. Bernard Coll., 1967; MA, George Washington U., 1969, PhD, 1971; DHC, Columbia Coll., 1987. Instr. George Washington U., Washington, 1967-69; asst. to sec. U.S.

Dept. Transp., Washington, 1969-70, U.S. HUD, Washington, 1970-71; asst. prof. U. Chgo., 1971-76, assoc. prof., 1976-83, prof., 1983—. Bd. dirs. Kimberly-Clark Corp., Dallas, Peoples' Energy Corp., Chgo., Waste Mgmt. Inc., Houston, Harris Bankmont and subs., Chgo. Author: The Politics of Language: The Dilemma of Bilingual Education for Puerto Ricans, 1981, Backs Against The Wall, 1983, The Dilemma of American Immigration, 1983, Hispanics in the U.S.A., 1985, 2d edit., 1992, Hispanics: An Agenda for 21st Century, 1999, 2d edit., 2002. Bd. dirs. Lyric Opera Assn., Chgo., 1990—, Rush Presbyn. St. Luke's Med. Ctr., 1993— White House fellow U.S. Govt., 1969-70. Mem. Chgo. Yacht Club. Democrat. Roman Catholic. Office: U Chgo 969 E 60th St Chicago IL 60637-2677

CAFFEY, H(ORACE) ROUSE, university official, agricultural consultant; b. Grenada, Miss., Mar. 24, 1929; s. C. Horace and Anna Belle (James) C.; m. Lois (Granger) Stevens, Mar. 13, 1999; children: Brenda, Jerry, Belle, Rex. BS, Miss. State U., 1951, MS, 1955; PhD, La State U., 1959. Agronomist in charge rice project Miss. Agrl. Exptl. Sta., Stoneville, 1958-62; supt. La. State U. Rice Sta., La. Agrl. Exptl. Sta., Crowley, 1962-70; assoc. dir., prof. La. State U., La. Agrl. Exptl. Sta., Baton Rouge, 1970-79; vice-chancellor adminstrn. La. State U. Agrl. Ctr., 1979-80, vice-chancellor internat. programs, 1980-81; chancellor La. State U., Alexandria, 1981-84, La. State U. Agr. Ctr., 1984-97; pres., CEO Caffey Internat. Inc., 1997—. Internat. rice cons. AID, World Bank, other orgns., 1965—; mem. pub. health study team Nat. Acad. Sci., Washington, 1973-74; mem. adv. bd. Bd. Regents Masters Plan Higher Edn., Baton Rouge, 1977; Nat. co-chair joint coun. for Food and Agr., 1989-94, Internat. Sci. and Edn. Coun., 1986-90; chmn. Nat. Assn. State Univs. and Land Grant Colls. divsn. Agr. Budget Com., 1989. Contbr. chpts. to books, articles to profl. jours. Pres. Internat. Rice Festival, Crowley, 1968; bd. dirs. Boy Scouts U.S.A., United Way, others. Served to 1st lt. U.S. Army, 1951-54. Recipient Internat. award of Merit Gamma Sigma Delta, 1970, 81; honoree Internat. Rice Festival, 1974; named Man of Yr. Crowley C. of C., 1969-70, Progressive Farmer Man of Yr. in Svc. to La. Agr., 1986, Outstanding Alumnus Coll. Agr. of La. State U., 1992, Alumnus of Yr., La. State U., 1993, Outstanding Alumnus of Yr., Coll. Agr., Miss. State U., 1993. Mem. Sigma Xi, Gamma Sigma Delta, Phi Delta Kappa, Omicron Delta Kappa, Phi Delta Phi, Phi Zeta. Lodges: Masons; Rotary. Democrat. Baptist. Home: 10471 Barry Dr Baton Rouge LA 70809-3265 Office: Chancellor Emeritus La State U 4560 Essen Ln Baton Rouge LA 70809-3424 E-mail: hrcaffey@agctr.lsu.edu.

CAFFEY, JAMES ENOCH, civil engineer; b. Rockdale, Tex., May 5, 1934; s. Enoch Arden and Leevicy Viola (Stephens) C.; m. Patricia Louise Latham, June 4, 1960; children: Jeffrey E., Jeanne Erin, Jerald E. BSCE, Tex. A&M U., 1955, MSCE, 1956; PhD, Colo. State U., 1965. Registered profl. engr., Tex. Prof. U. Tex., Arlington, 1959-74; dept. head Turner, Collier & Braden, Inc., Houston, 1974-76; assoc. Rady and Assocs., Inc., Ft. Worth, 1976-85; pres. Caffey Engring., Inc., Arlington, 1985—; asst. city engr. City of Arlington, 1991-97, environ. mgr., 1997—2001. Adv. bd. Cancer Rsch. Found. North Tex., Arlington, 1990-91. Capt. USAF, 1956-59; mem. USAFR, 1959-68. Fellow ASCE (life mem.), Am. Water Resources Assn. (charter, bd. dirs. 1973-75), Assn. State Floodplain Mgrs. (nat. cert.); mem. NSPE, Am. Geophys. Union, Water Environment Fedn., Am. Inst. Hydrology (profl.), Kiwanis, Phi Eta Sigma, Tau Beta Pi, Phi Kappa Phi, Chi Epsilon, Sigma Xi. Baptist.

CAFIERO, JAMES S. state legislator, lawyer; b. North Wildwood, N.J., Sept. 21, 1928; m. Patricia E. Campbell; children: Jamey, Drew, Stephen. BA, Princeton U., 1950; JD, U. Pa., 1953. Ptnr. Cafiero, Balliette & Balliette, Wildwood, N.J., 1954—; asst. prosecutor Cape May County, N.J., 1958-60; solicitor City of North Wildwood, Boroughs West Wildwood and Woodbine, N.J.; mem. N.J. Gen. Assembly, Trenton, 1968-72, N.J. Senate, Dist. 1, Trenton, 1972-82, 90—. Rep. majority whip, 1973-82, minority leader, 1976-77; bd. dirs. Marine Nat. Bank. Past pres. Cape May County Young Reps. Club. Mem. ABA, Wildwood Jr. C. of C., Cape May County Cmty. Concerts Assn., Kiwanis, Navy League. Home: PO Box 789 Wildwood NJ 08260-0789 Office: 3319 New Jersey Ave Wildwood NJ 08260-2323*

CAGE, ALLIE M. communications executive; b. Memphis, Feb. 2, 1953; d. Ernest Hampton Sr. and Robie Lee (Bynum) Cage. BS, Cornell U., 1975; MBA, Tenn. State U., 1986. Pres., owner Profl. Svc., Inc., Memphis, 1981-83; dir. tutorial ctr. Tenn. State U., Nashville, 1984-85; rsch. assoc. Inst. African Affairs, Nashville, 1986-88; ptnr. Cage, Smith & Assocs., Nashville, 1988-91; mktg. dir. So. Colour, Inc., Brentwood, Tenn., 1994—; owner, pres. Cage Comm. Co., Madison, Tenn., 1988—. Bd. dirs. So. Colour, Inc. Author: (weekly publ.) Rap Sheet, 1983—86; co-author: (pub., cassette rec.) Arbitration, 1975; freelance reporter various newspapers, 1986—. Bd. dirs. Rainbow Coalition Davidson County, Tenn., 1984—, Nat. Coalition to Save Black Colls., Nashville, 1986—; pres. Lit. Soc., 1991—; publicity coord., vol. coord. Unity Build Habitat for Humanity, project dir. Ecumenical Build 2002; publicity coord., vol. coord. Unity Build Bldg. Together for Christ, 1999—; min. in tng. St. Luke CME Ch., Nashville, min. Named to So. Women in Pub. Svc., Stennis Ctr. Pub. Svc. and Miss. U. for Women, 1992. Mem.: NAACP (life), Am. Mgmt. Assn., Nat. Hook-Up Black Women. Democrat. Avocations: travel, reading, tennis, volleyball, music. Office: 510 Heritage Dr Unit 25 Madison TN 37115-6001 E-mail: amcage@msn.com.

CAGE, JACK HAYS, executive search consultant; b. San Francisco, Mar. 15, 1953; s. James Gilliam and Audrey (Shade) C.; children: Catherine, Anna. BS, U.S. Mil. Acad., 1975; MA, Columbia U., 1981, PhD, 1982. Commd. 2d lt. U.S. Army, 1975, advanced through grades to Col., 1995, ret., 1997; mng. dir. Sullivan & Co., N.Y.C., 1997-99; ptnr. Heidrick & Struggles, N.Y.C., 1999—, co-head global ins. tech. practice. Ptnr. Fin. Svcs. Info. Tech., N.Y.C., 1997—; CIO, chief tech. officer Ins. Tech. Practice. Recipient Bronze Star U.S. Army, 1989, 3 Legion of Merit awards U.S. Army. Mem. Assn. Exec. Search Cons. Avocations: personal investment, information systems, travel. Office: Heidrick & Struggles 40 Wall St Fl 48 New York NY 10005-2301

CAGE, NICOLAS (NICOLAS COPPOLA), actor; b. Long Beach, Calif., Jan. 7, 1964; m. Patricia Arquette, 1995 (div. 2001); m. Lisa Marie Presley, 2002 (div. 2002). Actor: (feature films) Fast Times At Ridgemont High, 1982, Valley Girl, 1983, Rumble Fish, 1983, Racing with the Moon, 1984, Birdy, 1984, The Boy in Blue, 1986, The Cotton Club, 1984, Peggy Sue Got Married, 1986, Raising Arizona, 1986, Moonstruck, 1988, Vampire's Kiss, 1989, Never on a Tuesday, 1989, Tempo di Uccidere, 1989, Fire Birds, 1990, Wild at Heart, 1990, Zandalee, 1991, Honeymoon in Vegas, 1992, Time to Kill, 1992, Amos & Andrew, 1993, Red Rock West, 1993, Deadfall, 1993, Guarding Tess, 1994, It Could Happen to You, 1994, Trapped in Paradise, 1994, Kiss of Death, 1995, Leaving Las Vegas, 1995 (Best Actor award L.A. Film Critics 1995, Best Actor award N.Y. Film Critics 1995, Golden Globe award for best actor 1996, Acad. award for best actor 1996), The Rock, 1996, The Funeral, 1996, Con Air, 1997, Face Off, 1997, Welcome to Hollywood, 1998, Snake Eyes, 1998, City of Angels, 1998, 8MM, 1999, Bringing Out the Dead, 1999, Gone in 60 Seconds, 2000, Family Man, 2000, Captain Corelli's Mandolin, 2001, Windtalkers, 2002, Adaptation, 2002, Matchstick Men, 2003; Prod.: (films) Shadow of the Vampire, 2000, Sonny (also dir.), 2002, The Life of David Gale, 2003. Office: Saturn Films 9000 W Sunset Blvd Ste 911 West Hollywood CA 90069-5809 also: Creative Artists Agy 9830 Wilshire Blvd Beverly Hills CA 90212-1804*

CAGGIANO, ERNEST CHRISTOPHER, funeral director; b. Boston, Oct. 12, 1934; s. Ernest Patrick and Grace (Ferrara) C.; m. Annette Marie Piscitelli, Feb. 9, 1963; children: Lisa Grace Graham, E. Christopher, Peter Anthony, Mark J.T. BS in Biology, Boston Coll., 1955; A. in Embalming, New Eng. Inst., Boston, 1956. Lic. funeral dir., Mass. Funeral dir. and embalmer Ernest P. Caggiano & Son, Inc., Winthrop, Mass., 1956—, pres., 1971—, Caggiano Ambulance Svc., Inc., Winthrop, Mass., 1971-86; instr. in embalming New Eng. Inst., Boston, 1960-72. Trustee and mem. audit com. Advantage Bank, Winthrop, 1973-93. Trustee Winthrop Hosp., 1978-93; treas. Winthrop Housing Authority, 1993—; former mil. a.d.c. to gov. State of Mass.; col. Mass. Def. Force; capt. comdg. 285th Ancient and Hon. Arty. Co., Boston, 1993-94. Decorated Knight of Malta Mil. Order of Malta, 1983. Mem. Nat. Funeral Dirs. Assn., Mass. Funeral Dirs. Assn., Boston Latin Sch. Alumni Assn. (trustee 1993), K.C. (chancellor 1952—), Rotary (past pres., dist. trustee, Paul Harris medal 1992), Order Sons of Italy (sec.). Republican. Roman Catholic. Avocations: military history, coin collecting, travel, small arms instructing. Home and Office: 147 Winthrop St Winthrop MA 02152-2665 Home: 555 SE 6th Ave Apt 10B Delray Beach FL 33483-5246 E-mail: caggiano@pipeline.com.

CAGGIANO, JOSEPH, advertising executive; b. N.Y.C., Oct. 22, 1925; s. Daniel Joseph and Lucia (Gaudiosi) C.; m. Catherine Marie Gilmore, Aug. 28, 1948; children— Cathleen, Mary Yvonne. BBA, Pace Coll., 1953. Chief accountant Criterion Advt. Co., N.Y.C., 1947-57; treas. Emerson Foote, Inc., N.Y.C., 1957-67; became sr. v.p. Bozell & Jacobs, Inc. (now Bozell, Jacobs, Kenyon & Eckhardt Inc.), N.Y.C., 1967, exec. v.p. finance and adminstrn. Omaha, 1971-91, vice chmn. bd., chief financial officer, 1991-97; vice chmn. bd. dirs. emeritus Bozell, Jacobs, Kenyon & Eckhart Inc., 1991—, ret., 1998. Bd. dirs. St. Mary's Coll., Omaha Zool. Soc. Served with USNR, 1943-46, ETO, PTO. Mem. N.Y. Credit and Financial Mgmt. Assn., Omaha Zool. Soc. (dir.) Home: 9731 Fieldcrest Dr Omaha NE 68114-4932 *Luck in business is best defined as preparation meeting opportunity while always keeping a positive attitude. Dedication and fairness to a cause is mandatory. There are few short cuts to success in business or meaningful relationships with family and friends; and still fewer gray areas. It would have been impossible to achieve any degree of success without the help and understanding of my wife and family.*

CAGINALP, AYDIN S. lawyer; b. Ankara, Turkey, Aug. 2, 1950; AB, Ind. U., 1972; JD, Tulane U., 1974; LLM in Taxation, NYU, 1975. Bar: N.Y. 1976, U.S. Dist. Ct. (so. and ea. dists.) N.Y. 1976, U.S. Tax Ct. 1976. Atty., mem. ptnrs. com. Alston & Bird LLP, N.Y.C. Bd. editors Tulane U. Law Rev., 1973-74. Mem. ABA (taxation sect.). Address: Alston & Bird LLP 90 Park Ave New York NY 10016-1301

CAGLE, WILLIAM REA, librarian; b. Hollywood, Calif., Nov. 15, 1933; s. Howard Clinton and Eunice (Colcord Althouse) C.; m. Terry Lucinda Conrad, Jan. 17, 1975; children by previous marriage: Michael Stewart, Chantal Gabrielle, Mark Christopher, Monique Antoinette. AB in English, UCLA, 1956, MLS, 1962; postgrad., Oxford U., 1959-60. Asst. to librarian Henry E. Huntington Library and Art Gallery, San Marino, Calif., 1960-62; librarian for English Ind. U. Libraries, Bloomington, 1962-67, asst. Lilly librarian, 1967-75, acting Lilly librarian, Lilly librarian, 1977-97. Dir.'s acad. adv. com. Harry Ransom Humanities Rsch. Ctr. U. Tex.; mem. adv. bd. U. S.C. Ctr. for Literary Biography; adv. bd. Maine Women Writers Collection U. New England. Author: A Matter of Taste, 1990, revised and enlarged, 1999, Two Hundred and Fifty Years of the British Novel: 1740-1989, 1990, American Books on Food and Drink, 1998, 150 Years of the American Short Story, 1998, Lit Check: The Center for Literary Biography Online Checklist, University of South Carolina, www.cla.sc.edu/engl/litcheck/litcheck.html; contbr. to Printing and the Mind of Man, 1967; editor Ind. U. Bookman, 1966-89; mem. adv. bd. Dictionary Lit. Biography, Cambridge edit. Joseph Conrad, Bibliography of United States Literature, Chadwyck-Healey American Poetry Full-Text Database; mem. editl. bd. Pitts. Series in Bibliography; contbr. articles to profl. jours. Trustee Carver Meml. Libr., Searsport, Maine, Camden Pub. Libr.; mem. collection adv. bd. Kinsey Inst. Sex, Gender and Reprodn. With U.S. Army, 1956—59. Mem.: Assn. Internat. de Biliophilie, Benjamin Franklin Guild (bd. govs.), Baxter Soc., Lincoln Soc., Caxton Club (Chgo.), Grolier Club (N.Y.C.), Century Club. Home: 56 Mountain St Camden ME 04843 E-mail: caglet@acadia.net.

CAGUIAT, CARLOS JOSE, health care administrator, Episcopal priest; b. N.Y.C., Jan. 23, 1937; s. Carlos C. and Carmen (Rovira) C.; m. Julianna Skomsky, Aug. 29, 1958; children: Stephen D., Jonathan J., Sarah E. Caguiat Borthwick. BA, CCNY, 1958; MDiv, Gen. Theol. Sem., 1965; MPA, NYU, 1976. Ordained priest Episcopal Ch., 1965. Curate St. Christopher Chapel, N.Y.C., 1965—68; vicar St. Christopher's Chapel, N.Y.C., 1968—71; exec. dir. project for human comm. Episcopal Diocese of N.Y., N.Y.C., 1971-73; project mgr. ambulatory care/cmty. rels. N.Y.C. Health and Hosps. Corp., 1973-76, regional coord. for adminstrn./ops., 1975-76; assoc. dir. adminstrn./ops. Morrisania Neighborhood Family Care Ctr., Bronx, N.Y., 1976-78, adminstr., 1978-81; adminstrv. dir. Clin. Ctr., Mich. State U., East Lansing, 1981-90; regional v.p. St. Francis Acad., Lake Placid, NY, 1990—2002, strategic planning and ventures v.p. Saranac Lake, NY, 1999—2002. Chair decentralized unit of several parishes, N.Y.C.; mem. Diocese of N.Y. Pension Bd., Ecumenical Commn., Budget Com., 1967-81; vice chair North Country Behavioral Health Devel. Corp., 1997-98, chair, 1999-2002. Chair Two Bridges Settlement Housing Corp.; bd. dirs. Settlement Housing Fund., 1969-73; pres. Mid-Mich. South Health Sys. Agy., 1985-88. Infantry and Intelligence Officer, U.S. Army. Fellow Am. Coll. Health Care Execs., Am. Hosp. Assn., Lake Placid Rotary (bd. dirs., v.p., 2002, pres. 2003—), Lakeside House (bd. dirs.). Home: 20 Oakwood Pl Saranac Lake NY 12983 E-mail: CarlosC@st-francis.org.

CAHILL, CHARLES ADAMS, III, psychiatrist; b. Milw., Mar. 2, 1930; s. Charles Adams and Beatrice Cahill. BA, Harvard U., 1951, MD, 1955. Diplomate Am. Bd. Psychiatry and Neurology. Intern U. N.C. Med. Ctr., Chapel Hill, 1955-56; resident in psychiatry Menninger Found., Topeka, 1956-58, Bellevue Hosp., N.Y.C., 1960-61; cons. psychiatrist fed., state and local govtl. agys., Wis., 1961—. Mem. legis. coun. mental health subcom. Wis. State Legislature, Madison, 1966-69; examiner Am. Bd. Psychiatry and Neurology, midwestern U.S., 1982-88. Contbr. to book TM, 1972 (Gambrinus award 1974); contbr. articles to profl. jours. Lt. USNR, 1958-60, lt. col. USAR, 1983-87, ret. Recipient outstanding Pub. Svc. award Wis. County Human Svcs. Assn., 1996. Fellow Am. Psychiat. Assn. (disting. life); mem. Wis. Psychiat. Assn. (councilor 1978-79), Harvard Club (Milw.). Avocations: performing arts, local hist. socs. Home and Office: W235S4478 Amber Ct Waukesha WI 53189-7977

CAHILL, CHARLES L. retired university administrator, chemistry educator; b. El Reno, Okla., Feb. 23, 1933; m. Dorotha Ann Cleek, Feb. 14, 1954; children: Steven Charles, Terri Ann, Susan Beth. AB in Chemistry, Okla. Bapt. U., 1955; MS in Biochemistry, U. Okla., 1957, PhD in Biochemistry, 1961. Rsch. asst., biochemist Vets. Hosp., Sch. Medicine, U. Okla., Oklahoma City, 1955-57; NIH predoctoral fellow Sch. Medicine, U. Okla., Oklahoma City, 1957-60; clin. chemist med. arts labs. Oklahoma City U., 1960-61, asst. prof. chemistry, 1961-63, asst. prof., chmn. dept., 1963-67, assoc. prof., chmn. dept., assoc. dean Coll. Arts and Sci., 1967-69, prof. chemistry, assoc. dean, dir. rsch., 1970-71; vice chancellor for acad. affairs U. N.C., Wilmington, 1971-85, provost, vice chancellor for acad. affairs, 1985-92, prof. chemistry, 1992-2000, prof. emeritus, 2000—; ret. Mem. Rotary. Avocations: bass fishing, hunting, golf.

CAHILL, GERARD ALBIN, university educator; b. N.Y.C., Dec. 21, 1936; s. Albin G. and Susan E. (Maschenic) C.; m. Lea D. Chandler, Jan. 29, 1993. BS in Elec. Engring., Manhattan Coll., 1958; MBA, CCNY, 1962; PhD, NYU, 1973. Registered profl. engr., N.Y. With Lucent Tech., N.Y.C., 1959-67; divsn. contr. Gen. Dynamics Corp., Orlando, Fla., 1967-68; corp. contr. Smithfield Corp., Washington, 1968-69; v.p. HETRA Co., Melbourne, Fla., 1969-71, CODI Corp., Fairlawn, N.J., 1971-73; v.p. fin., treas. Cablecom-Gen. Inc., Denver, 1973-81; sr.v.p. Capital Cities Cable Inc., Bloomfield Hills, Mich., 1981-82; sr. v.p. Simmons Comm., Inc., Stamford, Conn., 1982-85; prof. Westfield (Mass.) State Coll., 1986-87, Fla. Inst. Tech., 1987—. Cons. in field. Ford Found. fellow, 1965. Mem. NSPE, Nat. Assn. Forensic Economists, Ea. Econ. Assn., Suntree Country Club. Office: 208 Versailles Dr Melbourne FL 32951 E-mail: gcahill@fit.edu.

CAHILL, HARRY AMORY, diplomat, educator; b. N.Y.C., Jan. 10, 1930; s. Harry Amory and Elaine Olga (Loumena) C.; m. Angelica Margarita Ravazzoli, Dec. 12, 1956; children— Alan, Daniel, Sylvia, Irene, Madeleine, Steven BA, Manhattan Coll., N.Y.C., 1951; postgrad., Johns Hopkins U., 1964-65; MS, George Washington U., Washington, 1972. Sales exec. Johns Manville Corp., N.Y., 1954-56; fgn. service officer U.S. Dept. of State, Washington, 1956-59, Oslo, 1959-61, Warsaw, 1961-64, Belgrade, Yugoslavia, 1965-68, Montevideo, Uruguay, 1968-71, Lagos, Nigeria, 1975-78, Colombo, Sri Lanka, 1979-81; dir. comml. service U.S. Dept. Commerce, 1982-83; U.S. consul gen. Dept. of State, Bombay, 1983-87; U.S. Mission to UN, dep. U.S. rep. UN Econ. and Social Coun., N.Y.C., 1987-89; pres. Amory Assoc., Inc., McLean, Va., 1990—, World of Film Found., N.Y.C., 1990-2000. Prof. George Mason U., 1982, Pepperdine U., 1992—, Georgetown U., 1995; cons. U.S. Dept. State, 1991—, U.S. Dept. Def., 1999—. Author: The China Trade and U.S. Tariffs, 1973. Pres. Hinduja Found., NYC, 1993—2002. Woodrow Wilson Nat. Fellowship found. fellow, 1990-93. Mem. Am. Fgn. Svc. Assn. Roman Catholic. Avocation: photography. Office: 1240 Daleview Dr Mc Lean VA 22102-1539

CAHILL, JOHN T. consumer products company executive; AB in Econs., MBA in Bus. Adminstrn., Harvard U. CFO RKO Pictures; v.p. corp. fin., asst. treas. PepsiCo, 1989—93, sr. v.p., treas., 1997—98; sr. v.p. fin., CFO KFC, 1993—96; sr. v.p., CFO PepsiCo N.Am., 1996—97; exec. v.p., CFO Pepsi Bottling Group, 1998—2000, pres., COO, 2000—. Bd. dirs. U.S.-Russia Bus. Coun., Woodward/White Pub. Co. Mem.: Grocery Mfrs. Am. (industry affairs coun.), Nat. Soft Drink Assn. (chmn.). Office: Pepsi Bottling Group Inc 1 Pepsi Way Somers NY 10589-2201*

CAHILL, KEVIN MICHAEL, physician, educator; b. NYC, May 1936; s. John and Genevieve (Campion) C.; m. Kathryn M. McGinity; children: Kevin, Sean, Christopher, Brendan, Denis. AB cum laude, Fordham U., 1957; MD, Cornell U., 1961; DTM&H, London Sch. Tropical Medicine, 1963; LLD (hon.), Iona Coll., NY, LeMoyne Coll.; DSc (hon.), NY Med. Coll., St. John's U., NY; LHD (hon.), Villanova U., Pa.; LittD (hon.), Fordham U.; LLD (hon.), Niagara U., NY, U. Liverpool, Eng.; LHD (hon.), U. Cul. Am., Nicaragua, Marymount Coll., Coll. Boca Raton, Am. Coll. Switzerland, Geneva, Georgetown U.; MD (hon.), Nat. Autonomous U. Nicaragua, Managua; DSc (hon.), Seton Hall U.; LLD, LHD, Manhattanville Coll. Diplomate Am. Bd. Microbiology, Am. Bd. Preventive Medicine. Dir. clin. tropical medicine, head dept. epidemiol. US Naval Med. Rsch. Unit, Cairo, 1963-65; assoc. prof. microbiology, clin. medicine NY Med. Coll., NYC, 1965-67; clin. prof. pub. health, preventive medicine U. NJ, Newark, 1971-95; pres. Ctr. Internat. Health Coop., NYC; dir. tropical disease ctr. Lenox Hill Hosp., NYC; pvt. practice NYC; Univ. prof., dir. Inst. Internat. Humanitarian Affairs, Fordham U., NYC; chief med. advisor for counterterrorism NY Police Dept. Mem. scientific adv. coun. Am. Found. Tropical Medicine, 1966-74; med. adv. African-Am. Inst., N.Y.C., 1967-77, Will Rogers Meml. Fund, N.Y., 1970-87; mem. com. pub. health N.Y. Acad. Medicine, 1974-80; advisor on health Govt. N.Y. State, 1975-81, chmn. health planning commn., 1975-81, chmn. health rsch. coun., 1975-81; sr. mem. N.Y. Bd. Health, 1981-93; sr. cons. UN Med. Svc., 1970-97; Alfred Gellhorn prof. CUNY, 1980-81; clin. prof. tropical medicine, parasitic diseases, medicine NYU; prof. chmn. dept. internat. health, tropical medicine Royal Coll. Surgeons, Dublin, Ireland; clin. prof. medicine Seton Hall U., N.J.; cons. tropical diseases St. Vincent's Hosp. and Health Ctr., N.Y.C.; med. adv. Cath. Relief Svc., Balt., Cath. Med. Mission Bd., N.Y.; spl. advisor to spkr. and health com. chmn. N.Y. City Coun.; impartial specialist tropical medicine N.Y. State, Workmen's compensation Bd. Author: Tropical Diseases in Temperate Climates, 1964, Health on the Horn of Africa, 1970, Medical Advice for the Traveler, 1970, 3d edit., 1977, Clinical Tropical Medicine Vol. 1, 1970, 2d edit., 1972, The Untapped Resource: Medicine & Diplomacy, 1973, Clinical Tropical Medicine Vol. 11, 1973, Teaching Tropical Medicine, 1973, Tropical Diseases: A Handbook for Practitioners, 1975, 2d edit., 1976, Health and Development, 1975, Health in New York State, 1977, Irish Essays, 1980, Somalia: A Perspective, 1980, Threads for a Tapestry, 1981, Famine, 1982, The AIDS Epidemic, 1983, The American-Irish Revival, 1984, A Bridge to Peace, 1988, Un Pont Vers La Paix, 1989, Un Puente Tendido Hacia La Paz, 1989, Imminent Peril: Public Health in Declining Economy, 1991, A Framework for Survival, 1993, 2d edit., 1999, Clearing the Fields: Solutions to the Global Land Mines Crisis, 1994, Silent Witnesses, 1995, Preventive Diplomacy, 1996, 2d edit., 2000; co-author: (with W. O'Brien) Pets and Your Health, 1987, Tropical Medicine: A Clinical Text, 1989, 3d edit., 1990, The Open Door: Health and Foreign Policy, 1999; Medicine Tropicale: Precis Clinique, 1990, (with H. Gilles) Tropical Medicine, 2001, Basics of International Humanitarian Missions, 2002, Emergency Relief Operations, 2003; Traditions, Values and Humanitarian Action, 2003;contbr. over 250 articles to profl. jour. Trustee Fordham U., NYC, 1968-74, Mt. St. Vincent Coll., NYC, 1968-74. Lt. US Navy, 1962-65. Lehman fellow, 1959, Royal Free Hosp. fellow, 1960-61, Hosp. Tropical Diseases fellow, 1962-63; recipient Highest Order, Govt. Sudan, Govt. Somalia, 1968, with sash, 1972, Colles medal Royal Coll. Surgeons, Xavier award Jesuit Order, Pres.'s medal Niagara U., Miguel Larenega Order, Order of Miguel Ramirez Goyena, Govt. Nicaragua, Internat. award Pan Am. Med. Assn., Health Scis. award SUNY, Assn. Retarded Children medal, Order of Merit, Knights of Malta, Disting. Svc. award Am.-Jewish Congress, Grand Cross Pro Merito Melitensi, The Vatican, Bicentenial medal Georgetown U., Order of Carlos Finlay, Havana. Fellow Am. Coll. Chest Physicians, Am. Coll. Preventive Medicine; Am.-Irish Hist. Soc. (pres.-gen. 1974—), Royal Coll. Physicians Ireland; mem. NY Soc. Tropical Medicine (pres. 1990-92), Hist. Soc. of Kerry/Cork (pres.). Office: 850 5th Ave New York NY 10021-5802 E-mail: CIHCNYC@aol.com.

CAHILL, LAURENCE ROY, JR., customer service administrator; b. Wichita Falls, Tex., Sept. 7, 1944; s. Laurence Roy and Mildred Louise Cahill; m. JoEllen Cahill, May 8, 1982. AS, Amarillo Coll., Tex., 1971—74; BBA, W. Tex. A&M U., Canyon, 1985. Mgr., prin. customer svc. Xcel Energy, Roswell, N.Mex., 1964—. Mem. adv. bd. Ea. N.Mex. Med. Ctr., Roswell, 1998—, N.Mex. CC; mem. N.Mex. Work Force Devel. Bd., 1998. Treas. Roswell C. of C., 2003; commr. City of Roswell Planning Commn., 2003; treas. Chaves County Devel. Found., Roswell, 2003. Named Workhorse of Yr., Roosevelt County Commn., 1988, Caring Citizen of the Month, Chaves County Commn., 2002; recipient Chamber Support award, Roswell C. of C., 2002. Mem.: Pecos Valley Rotary Club (bd. mem. 1999—2002). Republican. Avocations: woodworking, gardening, golf, travel. Home: 2607 Serenata Dr Roswell NM 88201 Office: Xcel Energy 111 E 5th St Roswell NM 88201 Office Fax: 505-625-5461. Business E-Mail: roy.cahill@xcelenergy.com.

CAHILL, MICHAEL CLARK, linguist; b. Albuquerque, Feb. 7, 1954; s. James Buchanan and Ruth (Clark) C.; m. Virginia Kuczun, July 28, 1984; children: Deborah, Laura, Stephen. BS in Biochemistry, Iowa State U., 1977; MA in Linguistics, U. Tex., Arlington, 1985; PhD in Linguistics, Ohio State U., 1999. Tchr. Newell (Iowa) H.S., 1977-82; linguist, Bible translator Summer Inst. Linguistics, Ghana, W. Africa, 1983 93, internat. linguistics coord. Dallas, 1999—. Mem. Com. Endangered Langs. and Their Preservation, Washington, 2000—, chmn., 2003. Mem. Linguistic Soc. Am., W. African Linguistic Soc. Office: Summer Inst Linguistics 7500 W Camp Wisdom Rd Dallas TX 75236 E-mail: mike_cahill@sil.org.

CAHILL, THOMAS ANDREW, physicist, educator; b. Paterson, N.J., Mar. 4, 1937; s. Thomas Vincent and Margery (Groesbeck) C.; m. Virginia Ann Arnoldy, June 26, 1965; children: Catherine Frances, Thomas Michael. BA, Holy Cross Coll., Worcester, Mass., 1959; PhD in Physics, U. Calif., Los Angeles, 1965. Asst. prof. in residence U. Calif., Los Angeles, 1965-66; NATO fellow, research physicist Centre d'Etudes Nucleaires de Saclay, France, 1966-67; prof. physics U. Calif., Davis, 1967-94; acting dir. Crocker Nuclear Lab., 1972, dir., 1980-89. Dir. Inst. Ecology, 1972-75; cons. NRC of Can., Louvre Mus. UN Global Atmospheric Watch, 1990—; mem. Internat. Com. on PIXE and Its Application, Calif. Atty. Gen., Nat. Audubon Soc., Mono Lake Com. Author: (with J. McCray) Electronic Circuit Analysis for Scientists, 1973; editor Internat. Jour. Pixe, 1989—; contbr. articles to profl. jours. on physics, applied physics, hist. analyses and air pollution. Prin. investigator IMPROVE Nat. Air Pollution Network., 1987-97; co-dir. Crocker Hist. and Archeol. Projects; head U. Calif. Delta Group, Davis, 1997-. OAS fellow, 1968, Japanese Nat. Rsch. fellow, Kyoto, 1992. Mem. Am. Phys. Soc., Air Pollution Control Assn., Am. Assn. Aerosol Rsch., Sigma Xi Democrat. Roman Catholic. Home: 1813 Amador Ave Davis CA 95616-3104 Office: U Calif Dept Applied Sci One Shields Ave Davis CA 95616

CAHILL, VIRGINIA ARNOLDY, lawyer; b. Summit, NJ, Dec. 18, 1942; d. Francis R. and Roberta (Dearing) A.; m. Thomas A. Cahill, June 26, 1965; children: Catherine Frances, Thomas Michael. BS, St. Louis U., 1964; MA, U. Calif., Davis, 1968, JD, 1981. Bar: Calif. 1981, U.S. Dist. Ct. (ea. dist.) Calif. 1981, U.S. Dist. Ct. (no. dist.) Calif. 1984, U.S. Ct. Appeals (9th cir.) 1984, U.S. Supreme Ct. 1995. Law clk. to judge U.S. Dist. Ct. (ea. dist.) Calif., Sacramento, 1981-83; assoc. McDonough, Holland & Allen, Sacramento, 1983-88, ptnr., 1988-2001, co-chair environ. law sect., 1991-2001; dep. atty. gen. Calif. Dept. Justice, Sacramento, 2001—. Lectr. water law U. Calif., Davis, 1985, 93-96, 2000-03, vis. prof. Law Sch., 2001. Pres. Davis Cmty. Meals,

1997. Mem. Calif. Bar Assn. (co-chair natural resource subsect. real property sect. 1995-97), Order of Coif. Office: Office Atty Gen 1300 I St Sacramento CA 95814-2919 E-mail: virginia.cahill@doj.ca.gov.

CAHIR, JOHN JOSEPH, meteorologist, educational administrator; b. Scituate, Mass., Oct. 8, 1933; s. Jeremiah Francis and Mary Eleanor (Duggan) C.; m. Mary Anne Louise Schrott, Dec. 1, 1962; children: Ellen, William, Kathryn, Barton. BS in Meteorology, Pa. State U., 1961, PhD, 1971. Meteorologist trainee, meteorologist U.S. Weather Bur., 1956-64; instr. meteorology Pa. State U., University Park, 1965-70, asst. prof., 1971-74, assoc. prof., 1975-79, prof., 1980—2002; assoc. dean Coll. Earth and Mineral Scis., Pa. State U., University Park, 1980-93; vice provost, dean for undergrad. edn. Pa. State U., University Park, 1993—2002; emeritus, 2002—. Vis. prof. St. Augustine's Coll., Va. State Coll.; cons. in field; mem. Commn. for Atmospheric Scis., World Meteorol. Orgn. (UN), 1986-97, alt. prin. U.S. del. to 9th session, Sofia, Bulgaria, 1986, del. to 10th session, Offenbach, Fed. Republic Germany, 1990, 11th session, Geneva, 1994; mem. com. on info. sys. for ports and harbors Marine Bd., NRC, 1985; Earth Sci. Adv. com. U. Space Rsch. Assn., 1987-93, convenor, 1992-93; mem. policy adv. com. Coop. Program for Meteorol. Edn. and Tng. (COMET), U. Corp. for Atmospheric Rsch., 1988-92, chair, 1996-99, mem. adv. panel, 1996-2000, vis. scientist, 2003—; instnl. mem. The Coll. Bd., 1993-2002. Co-author: Principles of Climatology, 1969, The Atmosphere, 1975, 78 81; editor: Monthly Weather Rev., 1977-80; contbr. papers, research reports to profl. publs. Bd. dirs. Pa. Coll. Tech., Williamsport, 1994—, Standards for Success, Washington, 2001-02. Served with USN, 1958-60. Fellow Nat. Ctr. Atmospheric Research, 1974 Fellow Am. Meteorol. Soc. (chmn. com. on weather forecasting and analysis 1979-80, seal of approval for TV weathercasting, nat. councillor 1986-89, chmn. com. on undergrad. awards 1986, nominating com. 1990-91, chmn. 1991, investment com. 1997—, chair 1999—); mem. Royal Meteorol. Soc., Am. Geophys. Union, Nat. Weather Assn. (pres. 1981-82, Svc. award 1979), Am. Assn. Univs. (task force on Undergrad. Edn. 1999-2002). Home: 952 Robin Rd State College PA 16801-4138 Office: 617 Walker Bldg University Park PA 16802-1505

CAHN, JEFFREY BARTON, lawyer; b. N.Y.C., Jan. 1, 1943; s. Harold Leon and Vivian (Loewy) C.; m. Miriam Epstein, Jan. 22, 1965; children: Lauren Samantha, Vanessa Shari. BA, Ind. U., 1964; JD, Rutgers U., 1967. Bar: N.J. 1967, U.S. Dist. Ct. N.J. 1967, U.S. Ct. Appeals (3d cir.) 1971, U.S. Supreme Ct. 1971, U.S. Tax Ct. 1973, U.S. Ct. Appeals (D.C. cir.), 1979, N.Y. 1980, U.S. Ct. Appeals (9th cir.) 1981, U.S. Claims Ct. 1981, U.S. Dist. Ct. (so. dist.) N.Y. 1992, U.S. Dist. Ct. (ea. dist.) N.Y. 1994, U.S. Ct. Appeals (2nd cir.) 1998. Law clk. to sr. presiding judge Appellate Div. N.J. Superior Ct., Trenton, N.J., 1967-68; assoc. Schapira, Steiner & Walder, Newark, 1968-72; ptnr. Sills, Cummis, Radin, Tischman, Epstein & Gross, Newark, 1972—. Author: (with others) New Jersey Transaction Guide, Vol. 12, 1993, The Use of Another's Trademark: A Review of the Law in The United States, Canada, and Western Europe, 1997; co-author, editor: Trademark Law Basics Coursebook, 2001; rsch. editor: Rutgers Law Rev., 1966-67; cons. editor Trademark Administration, 1999; contbr. articles to profl. jours. Mem. ATLA, ABA, N.J. State Bar Assn., Essex County Bar Assn., Internat. Trademark Assn. (publs. bd., 2002, projects editl. bd. 2001-), N.Y. State Bar Assn. (sect. intellectual property, chair copyright law com.), Am. Intellectual Property Law Assn., N.J. Intellectual Property Law Assn., Phi Delta Phi (Outstanding Grad. 1967). Jewish. Home: 72 Winged Foot Dr Livingston NJ 07039-8229 Office: Sills Cummis Radin Tischman Epstein & Gross Legal Ctr 1 Riverfront Plz Fl 13 Newark NJ 07102-5401

CAHN, JOHN WERNER, metallurgist, educator; b. Germany, Jan. 9, 1928; arrived in U.S., 1939, naturalized, 1945; s. Felix H. and Lucie (Schwarz) C.; m. Anne Hessing, Aug. 20, 1950; children: Martin Charles, Andrew Blender, Lorie Selma. BS, U. Mich., 1949; PhD, U. Calif. at Berkeley, 1953; DSc (hon.), Northwestern U., 1990, U. d'Evry, France, 1996. Instr. U. Chgo., 1952-54; with research lab. Gen. Electric Co., 1954-64; prof. metallurgy MIT, 1964-78; ctr. scientist Nat. Inst. Standards and Tech. (formerly Nat. Bur. Standards), 1978—, sr. fellow, 1984—. Vis. prof. Isreli Inst. Tech., Haifa, 1971—72, 1980; cons. in field, 1986—; chmn. Gordon Conf. Phys. Metallurgy, 1964; affil. prof. physics U. Wash., Seattle, 1984—; rsch. fellow Japan Soc. Promotion of Sci., 1981—82. Research and articles on surfaces and interfaces, thermodynamics, phase changes, quasicrystals. Recipient Dickson prize, Carnegie Mellon U., 1981, Gold medal, U.S. Dept. Commerce, 1982, Von Hippel award, Materials Rsch. Soc., 1985, Stratton award, Nat. Bur. Stds., 1986, Michelson-Morley prize, Case Western Res. U., 1991, William Hume-Rothery award, Minerals, Metals and Materials Soc., 1993, Harvey prize, Israel Inst. Tech., 1995, Nat. Medal of Sci., 1998, Bakhuis-Roozeboom medal, Netherlands Acad. Sci., 1999, Heyn medal, German Materials Soc., 2001, Bower award, Franklin Inst., 2002; fellow Guggenheim Found., 1960. Fellow: Am. Soc. Metals Internat. (Saveur award 1989), Am. Inst. Metallurg. Engrs., Am. Acad. Arts and Scis.; mem.: Japan Inst. Metals (gold medal 1994), Indian Meterials Rsch. Soc. (hon.), Am. Ceramics Soc. (hon.), NAE, NAS. Home: 6610 Pyle Rd Bethesda MD 20817-5454 Office: Nat Inst Standards And Tech Gaithersburg MD 20899-8555

CAHN, RICHARD CALEB, lawyer; b. Bklyn., June 11, 1932; s. Irving and Pearl (Abel) C.; m. Vivian Isabel Meksin, Dec. 24, 1961; children: Michael, Lisa, Daniel, Sara. AB, Dartmouth Coll., 1953; LLB, Yale U., 1956; U. London, 1959. Bar: NY 1956, Fla. 1966, US Supreme Ct. 1960. Student asst. US atty. So. Dist. NY, NYC, 1955; atty. U.S. Dept. Justice, Washington 1956-57; ptnr. Cahn & Cahn, LLP, Melville, NY; prin. asst. dist. atty. Suffolk County (NY), 1965-66; dep. atty. Town of Huntington (NY), 1966-68; spl. counsel towns of Smithtown, Islip, Brookhaven, Babylon, Southhampton (NY), 1967-68, Islip, NY, 1976-83, Huntington, NY, 1981-92; counsel Brentwood Sch. Dist., 1977-82, 86-90; spl. counsel Amityville Sch. Dist., 1978-79, Village of North Hills, 1978-79, Merrick Pub. Library; adj. prof. Touro Coll., 1987-90, 93—; hearing officer NY State Edn. Dept., Nassau and Suffolk Counties, 1971-77; spl. dist. atty. Suffolk County, 1972; participant World Peace Through Law Conf., 1967, Malpractice Mediation Panel, 2d dept., 1974-84, Gov.'s Jud. Nominating Com. 2d dept., 1975-81; screening com. bankruptcy judges U.S. Dist. Ct. Dist. NY, 1976-81, screening com. US magistrates, 1977-81; regional counsel SUNY, Stony Brook, 1972-90. Bd. dirs. Stony Brook Found., 1974-86, Ea. Dist. Civil Litigation Fund, 1982-86; del. Moscow Conf. on Law & Jurisprudence, 1990; trustee Adelphi U., 1997—. Fellow Soc. Values in Higher Edn., 1984-96; mem. ABA, NY Bar Assn. (ho. of dels. 1981-83, chmn. condemnation, zoning and property use com. 1989—), Suffolk County Bar Assn. (pres. 1981-82), Fed. Bar Assn., Am. Judicature Soc., Fed. Bar Council (v.p. 1982-84, trustee 1984-89), Huntington Lawyers Club. Contbr. articles to profl. jours.; mem. editl. bd. Yale Law Jour., 1954. Office: 445 Broadhollow Rd Ste 332 Melville NY 11747 Personal E-mail: rcahn@aol.com. Business E-Mail: rcahn@cahnlaw.com.

CAHN, STEVEN MARK, philosopher, educator; b. Springfield, Mass., Aug. 6, 1942; s. Judah and Evelyn (Baum) C.; m. Marilyn (Ross), May 4, 1974. AB, Columbia U., 1963; PhD, U. Mo., 1966. Vis. instr. Dartmouth Coll., 1966; vis. prof. U. Rochester, Rochester, NY, 1967; asst. prof. philosophy Vassar Coll., Poughkeepsie, NY, 1966-68, NYU, N.Y.C., 1968-71, assoc. prof., 1971-73, dir. grad. studies, 1972, dir. under grad. studies, 1971-73; prof., chmn. dept. philosophy U. Vt., Burlington, Vt., 1973-80, adj. prof. philosophy, 1980-83; dean grad. studies, prof. philosophy Grad. Sch. and Univ. Ctr., CUNY, 1983—, provost, v.p. for acad. affairs, 1984-92, acting pres., 1991; program officer Exxon Edn. Found., N.Y.C., 1978-79; assoc. dir. Rockefeller Found., N.Y.C., 1979-81, acting dir. humanities, 1981-82; dir. div. gen. programs NEH, Washington, 1982-83. Pres. John Dewey Found., 1983— ; cons., panelist NEH, 1975-82 Author: Fate, Logic, and Time, 1967, 82, A New Introduction to Philosophy, 1971, 86, The Eclipse of Excellence: A Critique of American Higher Education, 1973, Education and the Democratic Ideal, 1979, Saints and Scamps: Ethics in Academia, 1986, rev. 1994, Philosophical Explorations: Freedom, God and Goodness, 1989, Puzzles & Perplexities: Collected Essays, 2002; editor: (with Frank A. Tillman) Philosophy of Art and Aesthetics: From Plato to Wittgenstein, 1969, The Philosophical Foundations of Education, 1970, Philosophy of Religion, 1970, Classics of Western Philosophy, 1977, 6th edit., 2002, New Studies in the Philosophy of John Dewey, 1977, Scholars Who Teach: The Art of College Teaching, 1978, (with David Shatz) Contemporary Philosophy of Religion, 1982, (with Patricia Kitcher and George Sher) Reason at Work: Introductory Readings in Philosophy, 1984, 3d edit., 1995, Morality, Responsibility and the University: Studies in Academic Ethics, 1990, Affirmative Action and the University: A Philosophical Inquiry, 1993, (with Joram G. Haber) Twenty first Century Ethical Theory, 1995, The Affirmative Action Debate, 1995, 2nd edit., 2002, Classic and Contemporary Readings in the Philosophy of Education, 1997, Classics of Modern Political Theory: Machiavelli to Mill, 1997, (with Peter Markie) Ethics: History, Theory, and Contemporary Issues, 1998, 2nd edit., 2001, Exploring Philosophy: An Introductory Anthology, 2000, Classics of Political and Moral Philosophy, 2002, (with David Shatz) Questions About God, 2002, (with Tziporah Kasachkoff) Morality and Public Policy, 2003, (with Maureen Eckert and Robert Buckley) Knowledge and Reality, 2003, Philosophy for the 21st Century: A Comprehensive Reader, 2003; gen. editor Issues in Acad. Ethics, 1994—, Critical Essays on the Classics, 1997—, Blackwell Philosophy Guides, 20001, Blackwell Readings in Philosophy 2001—. Chmn. standing com. on tchg. philosophy Am. Philos. Assn., 1985-90, del. Am. Coun. Learned Socs., 1998-2002. Home: 100 W 57th St New York NY 10019-3302 Office: CUNY Grad Sch U Ctr 365 5th Ave New York NY 10016-4334

CAHOON, BETH ANN, special education educator; b. Fillmore, Utah, Aug. 5, 1960; d. Fred Claudell Cahoon and Margaret Elizabeth Robison-Cahoon. MEd, U. Utah, 2000. Cert. elem. edn. Utah State Office Edn., 1997. Store mgr. JB's Restaurant, Cedar City, Utah, 1987—89, night mgr. St. George, Utah, 1989—92; severe spl. edn. tchr. La Verkin (Utah) Elem., 1997—. Office: Washington County Sch Dist 121 W Tabernacle Saint George UT 84770

CAI, LU, biomedical scientist; b. Changchun, China, May 4, 1958; came to U.S., 1999; s. Peisheng Cai and Chunlian Zhang; m. Luping Guo, July 7, 1959; children: Luwa, Amy. MD, Norman Bethune U. Med. Scis., Changchun, China, 1983; PhD, Jilin U., Changchun, 1990. Rsch. assoc. U. louisville, 1999-2000, rsch. asst. prof., 2001—. Cons. dir. dept. toxicology Sch. Preventive Medicine, Jilin U., 1998. Contbr. over 50 articles to profl. jours. Office: U Louisville MDR Bldg Rm 535 511 S Floyd St Louisville KY 40202 Fax: (502) 852-6904. E-mail: lcai1@hotmail.com.

CAI, TIANXI, science educator; b. Ruian, Zhejiang, China, July 2, 1977; d. Xiaowan Cai and Xiaoxiang Xie. DSc, Harvard U., 1999. Asst. prof. U. Wash., Seattle, 2000—02, Harvard U., Boston, 2002—. Recipient Robert B. Reed award, Harvard U., 1997. Mem.: Am. Statis. Assn. Office: Harvard U Dept of Biostatistics 655 Huntington Ave Boston MA 02115

CAI, TING, biomedical scientist; b. Anda, Heilongjiang, China, Nov. 2, 1973; d. Shanmi Cai and Guiru Wang; m. Haojie Wang. MD, Shanghai Med. U., 1997, MS, 2000. Grad. clin. intern Shanghai Med. U., 1996—97, tchg. asst., 1997—98, rsch. asst., 1997—2000; asst. rschr. Chinese Nat. Human Genome Ctr., Shanghai, 2000—01; rsch. assoc. Med. Coll. Ohio, Toledo, 2001—. Contbr. articles to sci. jours. Mem.: Am. Soc. Biochemistry and Molecular Biology, Biophysical Soc., Sigma Xi. Avocations: cooking, travel. Business E-Mail: tcai@mco.edu.

CAI, WEIZHONG (WILL CAI), electronics engineer, researcher, physicist; b. Shanghai, June 28, 1969; arrived in U.S., 1994; s. Xin-fang Cai and Ding-zhen Chen; m. Jenny Zheng. BS in Physics, Fudan U., 1991; PhDEE, Pa. State U., 2000. Rschr., asst. to dir., editor-in-chief NSPL Ann. Report Nat. Surface Physics Lab. of China, Shanghai, 1991—94; grad. rschr. Pa. State U., University Park, 1994—2000; sr. semiconductor rschr. ON Semiconductor Corp. (former divsn. Motorola), Phoenix, 2000—. Mem. 21st Internat. Conf. on the Physics of Semiconductors Local Orgn. Com., Shanghai, 1992, mem. 4th Internat. Conf. on the Surface of Semicondrs., 93; tech. reviewer Am. Vacuum Soc., Research Triangle Park, NC, 1999—; book editor Transworld Rsch. Publ., Kerala, India, 2002—; invited lectr. Fudan U., China, 2001. Editor: III-V Semiconductor Heterostructures: Physics and Devices, 2003; contbr. chapters to books, over 35 articles to profl. jours. Recipient Judge award, Pa. Jr. Acad. Sci, 1997, Grad. Travel award, 39th Electronic Material Conf., Ft. Collins, Colo., 1997; grantee with Prof. D. L. Miller, Tyco Internat. Co., 1998—2000. Mem.: IEEE, The Electrochemical Soc., Surface Analysis Soc. Japan, Inst. Physics U.K. (assoc.), Sigma Xi. Achievements include invention of a new passivation technique for GaAs surfaces; patents in field of of semiconductors in U.S. and China; patents pending in field. Office: ON Semiconductor Co 5005 E McDowell Rd MD AE100 Phoenix AZ 85008 Business E-Mail: will.cai@onsemi.com.

CAILLÉ, ANDRÉ, public service company executive; b. Saint-Luc, Que., Can., Sept. 11, 1943; s. Jean-Paul C.; m. Lyse Senécal; children: Daniel, Guillaume, Marc-Vincent. BSc, U. Montreal, Que., Can., 1965, MSc, 1966, PhD in Phys. Chemistry, 1968. Dir. Fed./Provincial Com. on St. Lawrence River, Quebec, 1975-77, Environ. Protection Services, Quebec, 1978-79, dep. minister, 1980-82; sr. v.p. adminstrn. and pub. affairs Gaz Metro., Montreal, 1983-85, exec. v.p., 1985-87; pres., CEO Hydro-Quebec, Montreal, Que., 1987-96, 96—. Chmn. bd. Noverco Inc.; bd. dirs. Hydro-Que. Internat., Conseil Des Gouverneurs De La Federation Quebecoise Du Saumon Atlantique, World Energy Coun., Enbridge Energy, Conf. Bd. Can. Office: Hycro-Que 75 René-Levesque Blvd W Montreal QC Canada H2Z 1A4 Fax: 514-289-3659. E-mail: caille.andre@hydro.9c.ca.

CAIN, B(URTON) EDWARD, chemistry educator; b. Batavia, N.Y., Sept. 11, 1942; s. Burton Leo and Bettie S. (Williams) C. BA, SUNY, Binghamton, 1964; PhD, Syracuse U., 1971. Biochemist Onondaga County (N.Y.) Pub. Health Labs., Syracuse, N.Y., 1971-72; chemist O'Brien & Gere Cons. Engrs., Inc., Syracuse, N.Y., 1972-74; asst. prof. chemistry Nat. Tech. Inst. Deaf, Rochester (N.Y.) Inst. Tech., N.Y., 1974-80, assoc. prof. dept. chemistry, 1980-84, prof., 1984—; asst. chemistry dept. head Rochester Inst. Tech., 1981-87, 88—. Reader Advanced Placement chemistry exams. Ednl. Testing Svc., June 1987, 88, 89, 90, 91, 92. Author: The Basics of Technical Communicating, 1988; contbr. articles to profl. jours. Reviewer grant proposals coll. sci. instrument program NSF, 1987, instrumentation and lab. improvement program NSF, 1992. Recipi ent Eisenhart Outstanding Tchr. award, 1980. Mem. Am. Chem. Soc., AAAS, AAUP, Nat. Sci. Tchrs. Assn., Nat. Assn. Deaf, Conf. Am. Instrs. for Deaf, Registry of Interpreters for Deaf, Sigma Xi, Phi Lambda Upsilon, Gamma Epsilon Tau (Tchr. of Yr. award 1983). Home: 200 East Ave Apt 1105 Rochester NY 14604-2633 Office: 85 Lomb Memorial Dr Rochester NY 14623-5603 E-mail: becsch@rit.edu.

CAIN, COLEEN W. writer, educator; b. Birmingham, Iowa, Sept. 2, 1916; d. Marida Irwin Cain and Effie Levina Walters; m. James Cazort McClurkin, Feb. 5, 1937 (dec. Jan. 1938); m. James Robert Cazort, Dec. 24, 1942 (div. Oct. 1970); 1 child, Sidney Cain; m. Eugene Everett Bauer, Nov. 3, 1974 (div. Feb. 1984). BA in Journalism, U. Ark., 1938. Cert. real estate agt. Wash., 1946, Ark., 1948. Tech. writer Manpower, Inc., Huntsville, Ala., 1966—69; editor, arts reviews Huntsville Times, 1969—70; fgn. news corr. Jour. Am., Bellevue, Wash., 1980—83; instr. Beijing Fgn. Langs. Inst., 1981—83; lectr. Continuing Edn. Bellevue & South Seattle C.C., 1983—88; pres., owner Cain-Lockhart Press, Issaquah, Wash., 1985; instr. Issaquah Cmty. Ctr., 1996, North Bellevue Cmty. Sr. Ctr., 1997—. Author: Beth Bauer's Enjoy China More, 1985, 1986, 115 Jet Stories for Your Briefcase, 2001, (novels) Wild Blue, 1st of WWII Series, 2002. Singer Seattle Symphony Chorale, New Orleans Opera Soc., Cascadian Chorale, Huntsville Cmty. Chorus; mem. 47th dist. Democrats, Bellevue, 1972; alt. del. King County Democrats, Seattle, 1992; election judge Westlake Precinct, Issaquah, 1991—98; mezzo soloist in choirs, chorales. Recipient cert. of excellence, City of Bellevue Parks and Cmty. Svcs. Dept., 2001. Mem.: Northwest Bookfest (author spkr. 2001), Seattle Free Lances (treas. 1997—98, adviser 2001), Pacific Northwest Writers Assn. (critique editor 1995—99, 3rd place nonfiction award 1976). Democrat. Presbyn. Avocation: music. Home: 19510 S E 51st St Issaquah WA 98027-9327 Personal E-mail: colcain@foxinternet.com.

CAIN, DAVID LEE, corporate executive; b. Morgantown, W.Va., Oct. 14, 1941; s. David Melvin and Dorothy Eleanor (Burchinal) C.; children: Diana Jo, Michael Allen, Mark Aaron. BSME, W.Va. U., 1965. Adminstrn. mgr. Value Engring. Co., Alexandria, Va., 1968-72; gen. mgr. Walker Iron Works, Woodbridge, Va., 1972-75; owner, mgr. Dyna Products, Richmond, Va., 1975-78; adminstrn. mgr. VSE Corp., Alexandria, 1978-83; sr. v.p. The Orkand Corp., Falls Church, Va., 1983—. Vol. youth progs., various orgns., 1965—; head coach freshman wrestling team, W.Va., U., Morgantown, 1965, asst. coach varsity wrestling team, 1965; judge various pageants in Va., N.C., S.C., Md., Del., Pa., 1984—; mem. Rep. Nat. Com., 1990—. Capt. U.S. Army, 1965-68. Recipient scholarship W.Va. U., 1961-64, Disting. Student grant, ROTC, 1963-64, Disting. Mil. Grad., 1964-65. Mem. Nat. Contracts Mgmt. Assn. Methodist. Avocations: gardening, sports, collections. Office: The Orkand Corp 7799 Leesburg Pike Ste 700 Falls Church VA 22043-2413 E-mail: dcain@orkand.com., caindavid@aol.com.

CAIN, DONALD EZELL, judge; b. San Marcos, Tex., Oct. 8, 1921; s. Erie Montclair and Betty Belle (Howell) C.; m. Betty Anne Culberson, June 14, 1952; children: David, Dale Cain Husen, Donald Ezell, Randolph. A.S., North Tex. Agrl. Coll., 1941; BBA, U. Tex., 1943, LL.B., 1948; postgrad., Nat. Jud. Coll., Reno, 1974, 78, 82. Bar: Tex. 1948. With contracts dept. Convair, Ft. Worth, 1948-50; pvt. practice law Pampa, Tex., 1951-76; county atty. Gray County, Tex., 1955-68; county judge, 1971-77; dist. judge 223rd Dist. Ct. Tex., 1977-91; sr. dist. judge State of Tex., 1991—. Pres. Adobe Walls coun. Boy Scouts Am., 1957-59; bd. dirs. Pampa United Fund, 1956-60. Served from ensign to lt. USNR, 1943-46; as lt., 1950-51. Recipient Silver Beaver award Boy Scouts Am., 1958 Fellow Tex. Bar Found.; mem. ABA, Tex. Bar Assn., Gray County Bar Assn. (pres. 1968), Am. Judicature Soc., Tex. Judges and Commrs. Assn., Panhandle County Judges and Commrs. Assn. (pres. 1975), Pampa C. of C. (dir. 1959-60), Phi Alpha Delta. Clubs: Masons, Rotary (pres. 1958-59), Pampa Country. Democrat. Baptist. Home: 2321 Chestnut Dr Pampa TX 79065-2910

CAIN, DOUGLAS MYLCHREEST, lawyer; b. Chgo., Sept. 8, 1938; s. Douglas M. Jr. and Louise C. (Coleman) C.; m. Constance Alexis Adams Moffit, Apr. 18, 1970; children: Victoria Elizabeth Moffit, Alexandra Catherine Moffit. AB, Harvard U., 1960; JD with distinction, U. Mich., 1966; LL.M., N.Y. U., 1970. Bar: Colo. 1966, U.S. Ct. Appeals (10th cir.) 1972, U.S. Supreme Ct. 1972. Assoc. Sherman & Howard, L.L.C., Denver, 1966-72, ptnr., 1972-93; equity mem., 1993—; chmn. policy council Sherman & Howard, Denver, 1984-87; adj. prof. law U. Denver, 1972-78. Mem. Rocky Mountain Estate Planning Council, pres., 1976-77 Assoc. editor: Mich. Law Rev, 1964-66; contbr. articles to profl. jours. Bd. dirs. Craig Hosp. Found., 1980-86, v.p., 1984-85, pres., 1986-87, 88-89; bd. dirs. Colo. Jud. Inst., 1990-96, chmn., 1992-93; bd. dirs. Colo. chpt. Am. Diabetes Assn., 1993, Breathe Better Found., 1993—, Colo. Coun. Econ. Edn., 1996-98, Fortune Found., 1998—; mem. Estate Planning Seminar Group. With USN, 1960-63. Fellow Am. Coll. Tax Coun., Am. Coll. Trust and Estate Counsel; mem. ABA, Colo. Bar Assn. (gov. 1980-82), Greater Denver Tax Coun. Assn. (v.p. 1987, pres. 1988), Assn. Harvard Alumni (regional dir. 1978-81), Rocky Mountain Harvard Club (pres. 1977-78, 92-93), Denver Country Club, Mile High Club, Rotary. Home: 1960 Hudson St Denver CO 80220-1459 Office: Sherman & Howard LLC 633 17th St Ste 3000 Denver CO 80202-3665

CAIN, EDDIE, army officer; b. Apr. 1, 1948; BS in Chemistry, Jackson State U. Commd. 2d lt. U.S. Army, 1971, advanced through grades to brig. gen., 1998; chem. officer 1st Cavalry Divsn., Ft. Hood, Tex., 1987-88; polit.-mil. affairs officer Office of Sec. of State, Washington, 1988-90; comdr. 23d Chem. Bn., 9th U.S. Army, Korea, 1990-92; detailed to U.S. Army War Coll., Carlisle Barracks, Pa., 1992-93; dep. comdr. U.S. Army Chem. Materiel Destruction Agy., Aberdeen Proving Ground, Md., 1993-94; comdr. U.S. Army Chem. Activity Pacific, Johnston Island, 1994-95; chem. officer III Corps, Ft. Hood, 1995-98; joing program mgr. Biol. Def., Falls Church, Va., 1998—. Decorated Legion of Merit, Army Commendation medal, others. Office: Biol Def 5201 Leesburg Pike Ste 1200 Falls Church VA 22041-3269

CAIN, GEORGE HARVEY, lawyer, business executive; b. Washington, Aug. 3, 1920; s. J. Harvey and Madeleine (McGettigan) C.; m. Patricia J. Campbell, Apr. 23, 1946 (div.); children: George Harvey, James C., John P., Paul J.; m. Constance S. Collins, Aug. 10, 1985 BS, Georgetown U., 1942; JD, Harvard U., 1948. Bar: N.Y. 1949, Ohio 1972, Conn. 1977, U.S. Supreme Ct. 1995. Practiced law, N.Y. State, 1949-71, 73-76; pvt. practice, 1972-73; sec., gen. counsel Nat. Carloading Corp., 1949-54; mem. firm Spence & Hotchkiss, 1954-55; gen. atty., asst. sec. Cerro Corp., 1955-68, sec., gen. atty., 1968-72; v.p., gen. counsel Pickands Mather Co., Cleve., 1971-73; v.p., sec., gen. counsel Flintkote Co., White Plains, N.Y., 1973-76, Stamford, Conn., 1976-80; spl. counsel Day, Berry & Howard, Hartford and Stamford, Conn., 1980-82, ptnr. Stamford, 1983-90, of counsel, 1991—. Sec. Cerro Sales Corp., 1955-71; bd. dirs., sec. Leadership Housing Sys., Inc., 1970-71; bd. dirs., gen. counsel Atlantic Cement Co., Inc., 1962-71; bd. dirs. Hajoca Corp., 1975-79, Polymer Bldg. Sys., Inc.; adj. prof. U. Bridgeport Law Sch., 1983-86. Author: Turning Points: New Paths and Second Careers for Lawyers, 1994, Law Firm Partnership: Its Rights and Responsibilities, 1995, 2nd edit., 1999, Law Partnership Revisited, 2002. Served to 1st lt. USAAF, 1942-46; to capt. USAF, 1951-52. Fellow Am. Bar Found.; mem. ABA (chair sr. lawyers divsn. 2002—), N.Y. State Bar Assn., N.Y.C. Bar Assn., Ohio Bar Assn., Conn. Bar Assn., Am. Law Inst., Am. Soc. Corp. Secs., Georgetown U. Alumni Assn. (mem. Alumni senate), Harvard Club N.Y., Dutch Treat Club. Home: 14 Burnt Hill Rd Farmington CT 06032-2039 Office: Day Berry & Howard City Place I Hartford CT 06103-3499 E-mail: cainghsr@worldnet.att.net.

CAIN, JAMES NELSON, arts school and concert administrator; b. Arcadia, Ohio, Jan. 6, 1930; s. Alfred Ray and Gladys Eliza (Cruikshank) C.; m. Marthellen Jones, June 12, 1950; children— Nelson, Jennifer, Richard, Elizabeth. AB, Ohio State U., Columbus, 1955. Dir. Prestige Concerts, Inc., Columbus, 1948-62; exec. dir. Music Assos. Aspen, Inc., Colo., 1962-68; from asst. mgr. to mgr. St. Louis Symphony Orch., 1968-80; v.p. St. Louis Conservatory and Schs. Arts, 1980-94. Home: 2 Nantucket Ln Saint Louis MO 63132-4111 E-mail: JNCain@prodigy.com.

CAIN, JUDITH SHARP, mathematics consultant; d. Sturdy O. and Erna E. Sharp; children: Jason Charles, Crystal Heather, Jeffrey Ronald. MEd, U. of LA at Lafayette, 1986—2002. Cert. tchr. State of La., 1984, Supervision of Instruction State of La., 2002, adminstrv. cert. State of La., 2003. Lead tchr., connected math. project Lafayette Parish Sch. Bd., Lafayette, La., 1999—, presenter - workshops and inservices, 1997—; estimator Sellers, Dubroc & Assoc., Inc., Civil Engineers, Lafayette, La., 1972—81; tchr., mid. sch. math. Lafayette Parish Sch. Bd., Cathedral Carmel Sch., Lafayette, La., 1984—99. Math. workshop cons./tchr. trainer Various sch. districts, La., 1999—; com. mem. Grade Level Expectations La. Dept. of Edn., 2003. Author: (pub. ednl. program evaluation) An evaluation of the Connected Math. Project. Mem. St. Anne's Cath. Ch., Youngsville, La. Named Tchr. of Yr., Lafayette Parish, 2000; named an Outstanding Tchr., Diocese of Lafayette, 1993—94. Mem.: Assn. for Supervision of Curriculum Devel., NEA, La. Teachers of Math., Nat. Coun. Teachers of Math. Office: Lafayette Parish Sch Bd 805 Teurlings Dr Lafayette LA 70501 Office Fax: 337-289-1997. Personal E-mail: judycain@excite.com.

CAIN, KAREN MIRINDA, musician, educator; b. Anna, Ill., Feb. 25, 1944; d. James Paul and Margaret Camilla (Sinks) C. MusB, So. Ill. U., 1966, MusM in Voice and Choral Conducting, 1967; postgrad., Trinity Coll., Washington, 1985. Cert. music tchr., Md. Choral music tchr., Prince George's County, Md., 1969-71; music tchr. class piano Montgomery County, Md., 1972-89; music tchr., founder of studio Rockville, Md., 1972—; co-founder, dir., arranger, profl. madrigal ensemble The Renaissance Revelers, 1985—. Choral music dir. and soloist various chs. and synagogues, Rockville, Md., 1972-92; soprano soloist, sect. leader Grace Luth. Ch., Washington, 2000—; singer Paul Hill Chorale, Washington, 1982-90, mem. chorale staff, music theory instr., 1984-90; contbr. minstrel and history guilds, performer, mem., Md. Renaissance Festival, 1987—. Dir., editor: (CD) Renaissance Romance, 1994 (CD) Journey into Light, 2002; arranger choral works featured on Renaissance Romance, Journey Into Light; dir.: performances at The Lutheran Reformation Svc. held at The Washington Nat. Cathedral, 1995, The White House, Kennedy Ctr.; co-author (with John Sinks): Sinks: A Family History, 1980. Mem. AAUW, Md. Music Tchrs. Assn., Montgomery County Class Piano Tchrs. Assn., Mu Phi Epsilon. Home and Office: 862 College Pkwy # T-1 Rockville MD 20850-1938

CAIN, LOUIS PERKINS, III, economist, educator; b. Chgo., May 30, 1941; s. Louis Perkins Jr. and Mary (Dale) C.; m. Rochelle Ann Osborn, June 17, 1967; 1 child, Lauren Elizabeth. AB, Princeton U., 1963; MA, Northwestern U., 1966, PhD, 1969. Instr. Ill. Inst. Tech., Chgo., 1967-68; asst. prof. econs. Loyola U., Chgo., 1968-73, assoc. prof., 1973-79, prof., 1979—. Adj. prof. Northwestern U., Evanston, Ill., 1990—; cons. in field, 1978—. Editor, author: Business

Enterprise and Economic Change, 1973; author: Sanitation Strategy for a Lakefront Metropolis, 1978, American Economic History, 6th edit., 2003. Bd. dirs. Ill. Sch. Dist. 37, Wilmette, 1987-91. Mem. Am. Econ. Assn., Bus. History Conf. (trustee 1972-75, 88-91), Cliometric Soc. (assoc. editor 1990-2000, chmn. bd. trustees 2000—), Econ. History Assn. (editl. bd. 1989-94, trustee 1994-98), Ill. Econs. Assn. (trustee 2000-01, pres. 2002-03), Princeton Club Chgo., Beta Gamma Sigma, Omicron Delta Epsilon. Office: Loyola U 820 N Michigan Ave Chicago IL 60611-2147

CAIN, MARCENA JEAN BEESLEY, retail executive; b. Kingman, Kans., May 1, 1935; d. Albert Eugene and Stella Wanda (Ruthowski) Beesley; m. Kenneth B. Cain, Aug. 4, 1951; children: Kenneth Thomas, David Raymond. With AMVETS Thrift Stores, Washington, 1971—, asst. dir., 1971—87, exec. adminstr., 1987—; pres., asst. dir. AMVETS Value Village Thrift Stores, Balt. Ptnr. Bank St. Joint Venture Realty, Del-Mar Realty, Oakland Ctr. Partnership Ltd., 1987; pres. Famlity Thrift Ctr., Inc.; v.p. 4 corps; chmn. bd. dirs. Alamo II Thrift Stores, 1993. DC area rep. PTA Valley Forge Mil. Acad. Named Woman of the Yr., Balt.'s Best BPW, 1981; recipient Disting. Citizen's citation, Howard Co., 1987, Gov.'s citation, State of Md., 1987, Dedicated Svc. award, Seat Pleasant, Md., 1987, Congl. cert. Merit, 1991, 1992, AMVETS Dept. Md. Freestate award, 1994, Silver Helmet Spl. award for cmty. svc., 2003. Mem.: DAV Aux. (past nat. historian), Affiliated Mchts. Assn. Balt. (past pres.), Govanstown Mchts. Assn. (rec. sec.), Highlandtown Mchts. Assn. (bd. dirs. 1980, pres. 1981, 1983—84, chmn. bd. dirs. 1982, 1984—85), Highlandtown Businessmen Assn., Bus. and Profl. Women's Club, Kiwanis. Republican. Christian Scientist. Office: 3424 Eastern Ave Baltimore MD 21224-4121

CAIN, MICHAEL HANEY, lawyer; b. Chicoutimi, Que., Can., Mar. 26, 1929; s. Murray Vincent and Anna Marie (Feeney) C.; children: Murray, Evelyn. BA, McGill U., 1950, B.C.L., 1953. Bar: Que. 1954. Sr. ptnr. firm Cain Lamarre Casgrain Wells and predecessors, Chicoutimi, 1954-71, 72—; judge Mcpl. Ct., Chicoutimi North, 1965-70; justice Superior Ct. Que., Chicoutimi, Quebec City, 1971-72; Queen's Counsel, 1972. Mem. Canadian Inst. for Adminstrn. of Justice; mem. Adv. Com. Nomination Fed. Jud. Appointments Que., 1994-99; mem. inquiry com. Can. Jud. Coun.; founding pres. Found. U. Quebec at Chicoutimi Inc., 1969; bd. dirs. Found. Roland Saucier Inst.; dir., Bar of Que. Ins. Fund, 1986, v.p., 1991-96; dir. Sta. CJPM-TV, Inc. Founding mem. Que. Human Rights Commn., 1976-83; pres. com. on discipline Order of Nurses of P.Q.; pres. arbitration bd. Ministry of Edn. P.Q. Decorated Order of Can.; recipient Golden Jubilee medal, 2003. Mem.: Aboriginal Ednl. Found., Found. Jerzy & Phillida Brochocki, Found. Pierre & Gisele Laberge Charitable Found. (pres.), Bar of Saguenay (batonnier 1969—70, 1970—71), Am. Coll. Trial Lawyers, Can. Bar Assn. (v.p. Que. 1973—74, pres. 1974—75), Que. Bar Assn. (Merit medal 1996), Order of Can. Home: 1786 Des Maristes Chicoutimi QC Canada G7H 7M2 Office: 255 Racine St E Chicoutimi QC Canada G7H 6J6 E-mail: michaelh.cain@clcw.qc.ca.

CAIN, R. WAYNE, sales, finance and leasing company executive; b. 1937; BA, Wayne State U., 1959; LLB, N.Y.U., 1962. Lawyer Cleary, Gottlieb, Steen & Hamilton, 1962-63; with Chrysler Corp., Chrysler Fin. Corp., 1965-81; asst. treas. Navistar Internat. Corp., 1981-85; v.p., treas. Navistar Fin. Corp., 1985—2001, sr. v.p. fin., 2001—; v.p., treas. Harco Leasing Co., Inc. Del. With USAF, 1963-65. Office: Navistar Fin Corp 2850 W Golf Rd Rolling Meadows IL 60008-4050

CAIN, THOMAS ROBERT, interventional radiologist; b. Sullivan, Mo., Sept. 4, 1951; s. Noble William and Evelyn (Scott) C.; m. Emily Hamlin, Mar. 7, 1984; children: Geoffrey, Amy, Natalie. BA, U. Calif., Berkeley, 1973; MPH, UCLA, 1974; MD, U. So. Calif., 1978. Diplomate in radiology and in cardiovasc. and interventional radiology Am. Bd. Radiology. Intern Cedars-Sinai Med. Ctr., L.A., 1978-79; resident UCLA Med. Ctr., L.A., 1980-83, Northridge Hosp. Med. Ctr., 1983-85; ptnr., mem. staff Western Roentgenologic Assocs., Northridge, Calif., 1985-94; dir. nonvascular interventional rdiology sect. Christ Hosp. and Med. Ctr., Oak Lawn, Ill., 1997—; ptnr. Oak Lawn Radiologists, S.C., 1994—; fellow Am. Coll. Nuclear Medicine, 2000—. Asst. prof. U. So. Calif.; dir. Advanced Med. Imaging Svcs., 1987-88, Panorama Cmty. Hosp., 1989-92, Northridge Diagnostic Ctr., 1992-94, Pacifica Hosp. of the Valley, Sun Valley, Calif., 1991-94; com. mem. Christ Hosp. Med. Ctr. Fellow Am. Coll. Nuc. Medicine; mem. AMA, Radiol. Soc. N.Am., Soc. Cardiovasc. and Interventional Radiology, Salerni Collegium, Chgo. Med. Soc. Office: Christ Hospital Med Ctr 4440 W 95th St Oak Lawn IL 60453-2699 E-mail: trc@spininternet.com.

CAIN, TIM J. lawyer; b. Angola, Ind., July 12, 1958; s. Nancy J. (Nichols) C.; m. Debra J. VanWagner, Feb. 28, 1976; children: Christine M., Stephanie L., Katherine S., Jennifer A. BA in Polit. Sci. with honors, Ind. U., 1980; JD, Valparaiso U., 1984; MBA, Ind. Wesleyan U., 1991; LLM in Internat. Bus. and Trade with honors, John Marshall Law Sch., 2001. Bar: Ind. 1984, U.S. Dist. Ct. (no. and so. dists.) Ind. 1984, U.S. Supreme Ct., 2002. Assoc. Hartz & Eberhard, LaGrange, Ind., 1984-85; pub. defender LaGrange Cir. Ct., 1985-86; sr. assoc. Eberhard & Assocs., LaGrange, 1985-86; chief dep. to Pros. Atty.'s Office, LaGrange, 1986-87; ptnr. Eberhard & Cain, LaGrange, 1986-89; pvt. practice LaGrange, 1989-95; pros. atty. La Grange (Ind.) County, 1991—2002; ptnr. Williams and Cain, Ft. Wayne, Ind., 2002—. Asst. atty. La Grange County, La Grange; atty. Town of Shipshewana, Ind., 1984-93. Coach Orland (Ind.) Little League, 1977-79, Prairie Hts. Baseball, LaGrange, 1986-90; pres. Prairie Hts. H.S. Dollars for Scholars, LaGrange, 1989; active LaGrange County Coun. on Aging, 1989-91, Prairie Hts. At-Risk Students Com., 1989—, LaGrange County 4-H Fair Assn., 1993-97. Mem.Ind. Bar Assn., LaGrange County Bar Assn. (sec.-treas. 1986-87, v.p. 1987-89, pres. 1990-93). Clubs: Exchange (pres. 1988-89). Republican. Home: 360 S 900 E Lagrange IN 46761-9529 Office: 110 W Berry Ste 1910 Fort Wayne IN 46802 E-mail: tim@williams-cain.com.

CAIN, VERNON, retired information services executive; b. Bisbee, Ariz., Jan. 5, 1947; BS, No. Ariz. U., 1969; MBA with honors, Roosevelt U., 1984. Pres. U.S. holdings Dawson Holdings PLC, Oregon, Ill., 1985-96, CEO, mng. dir. info. svcs. group, 1996-2000. Mem. Am. Libr. Assn. Home: 4505 W Sunset Dunes Pl Tucson AZ 85743-8345 E-mail: verncain@aol.com.

CAIN, WILLIAM STANLEY, experimental psychologist, educator, researcher; b. N.Y.C., Sept. 7, 1941; s. William Henry and June Rose (Stanley) Cain; m. Claire Murphy, Oct. 30, 1993; children: Justin, Alisonstepchildren: Michael, Jennifer, Courtney. BS, Fordham U., 1963; MSc, Brown U., 1966, PhD, 1968. From asst. fellow to fellow John B. Pierce Lab., New Haven, 1967-94; from instr. to assoc. prof. dept. epidemiology, pub. health, and psychology Yale U., New Haven, 1967-84, prof., 1984-94; prof. otolaryngology U. Calif., San Diego, 1994—. Mem. sensory disorders study sect. NIH, Bethesda, Md., 1991—95; mem. sci. adv. bd. Ctr. Indoor Air Rsch., Linthicum, Md., 1991—99. Mem. editl. bd. Chem. Senses, 1985—94, mem. editl. adv. bd. Indoor Air, 1990—2000, Physiology and Behavior, 1995—96; editor: 5 books, 1971—; contbr. articles to profl. jours. Recipient Jacob Javits/Claude Pepper award, NIH, 1984, Sense of Smell Rsch. award, Fragrance Rsch. Fund, 1986. Fellow: ASHRAE (Crosby Field award 1984), APA, Acad. Indoor Air Rsch.; mem.: N.Y. Acad. Scis. (pres. 1986), Assn. Chemoreception Scis. (exec. chmn. 1983—84). Home: 4459 Nabal Dr La Mesa CA 91941-7168 Office: U Calif Dept Surgery 9500 Gilman Dr Rm Mc957 La Jolla CA 92093-0957

CAINE, MICHAEL, actor; b. London, Mar. 14, 1933; s. Maurice and Ellen Frances Marie Micklewhite; m. Patricia Haines, 1954; children: Dominique, Natasha; m. Shakira Baksh, 1973. Asst. stage mgr. Westminster Repertory, Horsham, England, 1953; actor Lowestoft Repertory, 1953-55, Theatre Workshop, London, 1955. Actor: What's It All About?: An Autobiography, 1993, (numerous TV appearances):, 1957—63, : (plays) Next Time I'll Sing for You, 1963; (films) A Hill in Korea, 1956, How to Murder a Rich Uncle, 1958, Zulu, 1964, The Ipcress File, 1965, Alfie, The Wrong Box, Gambit, 1966, Hurry Sundown, 1967, Woman Times Seven, 1967, Deadfall, 1967, The Magus, 1968, Battle of Britain, 1968, Play Dirty, 1968, The Italian Job, 1969, Too Late the Hero, 1970, The Last Valley, 1971, Get Carter, 1971, Zee & Co., 1972, Kidnapped, 1972, Pulp, 1972, Sleuth, 1973, The Black Windmill, 1974, Marseilles Contract, 1974, The Wilby Conspiracy, 1974, Fat Chance, 1975, The Romantic Englishwoman, 1975, The Man Who Would Be King, 1975, Harry and Walter Go to New York, 1975, The Eagle Has Landed, 1976, A Bridge Too Far, 1976, Silver Bears, 1976, The Swarm, 1977, California Suite, 1978, Beyond the Poseidon Adventure, 1979, Dressed to Kill, 1980, The Island, 1980, The Hand, 1981, Victory, 1981, Deathtrap, 1982, Educating Rita, 1983, Beyond the Limit, 1983, The Jigsaw Man, 1984, The Holcroft Covenant, 1984, Blame It On Rio, 1984, The Whistle Blower, 1985, Hannah and Her Sisters, 1986 (Acad. award for best supporting actor, 1987), Water, Sweet Liberty, 1986, Mona Lisa, 1986, Half Moon Street, 1986, Jaws The Revenge, Surrender, 1987, Without a Clue, 1988, Dirty Rotten Scoundrels, 1988, Shock to the System, 1989, Bullseye!, 1990, Jekyll and Hyde, 1990, Mr. Destiny, 1990, Noises Off, 1991, The Muppets Christmas Carol, 1992, On Deadly Ground, 1994, Bullet to Beijing, 1995, Blood and Wine, 1996, Curtain Call, 1997, Blue Ice, 1993, Little Voice, 1998 (Golden Globe), Debtors, 1999, Cider House Rules, 1999 (Acad. award for best supporting actor), Quills, 1999, Shiner, 2000, Get Carter, 2000, Miss Congeniality, 2000, Last Orders, 2001, Quicksand, 2001, The Quiet American, 2002 (Acad. award nomination, 2002), Austin Powers 3, 2002, The Actor, 2003, Secondhand Lions, 2003, The Statement, 2003; actor, exec. prodr.: (films) The Fourth Protocol, 1987; actor: (TV miniseries) Jack the Ripper, 1988, World War II: When Lions Roared, 1994 (Emmy nominee for Lead Actor in a Miniseries, 1994). Named Companion of Order of the Brit. Empire, 1992, Sir Michael Caine, 2000, Knight, Queen of Eng., 2000. Office: care Pam PR Inc 4401 Wilshire Blvd Los Angeles CA 90010-3728 also: Chelsea Harbour London England

CAINE, PHILIP DAVID, retired military officer, author; b. Chadron, Nebr., July 3, 1933; s. Clifford M. Caine and Eulah Ann Robertson; m. Doris E. Caine, Aug. 1, 1954; children: Barbara, Virginia, Jennifer. BA, U. Denver, 1955; MA, Stanford U., 1963, PhD, 1966; grad., Air War Coll., 1972, Nat. War Coll., 1978. Tchr. Denver Pub. Schs., 1955; commd. 2nd lt. USAF, 1955, advanced through grades to brig. gen., 1992, pilot, 1956-72, prof. history USAF Acad., 1963-69, 1970-78, head project CHECO 7th Air Force, 1969-70, prof. Nat. Def. U. Washington, 1978-80, dep. comdt. cadets USAF Acad., 1980-92, ret., 1992. Sr. fellow Nat. Def. U., Washington, 1987; sr. Mil. Sch. Rev. Bd., Washington, 1987. Author: Eagles of the RAF, 1991 (Blue Line award 1992), American Pilots in the RAF, 1993 (Mil. Book Club selection 1993), Spitfires, Thunderbolts and Warm Beer, 1995 (Mil. Book Club selection 1995), Aircraft Down!, 1997 (Mil. Book Club selection 1997). Dir. Woodmoor Improvement Assn., Monument, Colo., 1972-74; trustee/sec. Falcon Found., USAF Academy, Colo., 1996—; sec. Friends of the Acad. Libr., USAF Academy, 1998—. Decorated Commendation medals USAF, 1968, 87, Bronze star USAF, 1970, Meritorious Svc. medals USAF, 1980, 87, Legion of Merit USAF, 1992. Mem. Air Force Assn., Order of Daedalians. Avocations: travel, woodworking, writing, art. Home: 19060 Pebble Beach Way Monument CO 80132-8931 E-mail: PhilDC1@aol.com.

CAINE, RAYMOND WILLIAM, JR., retired public relations executive; b. Fall River, Mass., June 30, 1932; s. Raymond W. and Emma (Gardella) C.; m. Sharon G. Henry, Nov. 10, 1956; children: Karen, Kimberly, Patrick, Peter. BS, Providence Coll., 1956. Sr. v.p. advt., pub. relations Creamer, Dickson, Basford, N.Y.C. and Providence, 1966-74; v.p. pub. rels. Blue Cross (Blue Shield), Providence, 1974-80; v.p. corp. communications Textron, Inc., Providence, 1980-94. Contbr. articles to profl. jours. Bd. dirs. R.I. Commodores, 1987—, Newport Preservation Soc., Newport Hist. Soc.; trustee The Miriam Hosp. Recipient Bell Ringer award Publicity Club Boston, 1971, 72. Mem. Pub. Rels. Soc. Am. (bd. dir. 1971-73), Machinery and Allied Products Inst. (pub. rels. coun.), Newport Reading Rm. Avocations: golf, home remodeling.

CAINE, STANLEY PAUL, college administrator; b. Huron, SD, Feb. 11, 1940; s. Louis Vernon and Elizabeth (Holland) C.; m. Karen Anne Mickelson, July 11, 1964; children: Rebecca, Kathryn, David. BA, Macalester Coll., 1962; MS, U. Wis., 1964, PhD, 1967; LLD, Hanover Coll., 2000; LittD, MacMurray Coll., 2003. Asst. prof. history Lindenwood Coll., St. Charles, Mo., 1967-71; from asst. to assoc. prof. history DePauw U., Greencastle, Ind., 1971-77; prof. history, v.p. for acad. affairs Hanover (Ind.) Coll., 1977-89; pres. Adrian (Mich.) Coll., 1989—. Bd. dirs. NCAA Coun., 1995-96, vice chair mgmt. coun. divsn. III, 1997-99, pres.'s coun., 1999-2002; cons., evaluator North Ctrl. Assn., 1984—. Author: The Myth of a Political Reform, 1970; contbr. to book The Progressive Era, 1974; co-editor: Political Reform in Wisconsin, 1973. Bd. dirs. Nat. Assn. Schs., Colls. and Univs. of United Meth. Ch., 1994-97, 2000—, pres., 2002-03; mem. Lenawee Tomorrow, Adrian, 1989—. Recipient D.C. Everest prize Wis. State Hist. Soc., 1968; Woodrow Wilson fellow, 1962-63, Nat. Presbyn. fellow Presbyn. Ch. U.S., 1963-65 Mem. Orgn. Am. Historians, Nat. Assn. Ind. Colls. Univs. (bd. dirs. 1997-2000), Rotary. Methodist. Avocations: sports, reading. Office: Adrian Coll Office of Pres 110 S Madison St Adrian MI 49221-2518

CAINE, STEPHEN HOWARD, data processing executive; b. Washington, Feb. 11, 1941; s. Walter E. and Jeanette (Wenborne) C. Student, Calif. Inst. Tech., 1958-62. Sr. programmer Calif. Inst. Tech., Pasadena, 1962-65, mgr. sys. programming, 1965-69, mgr. programming, 1969-70; pres. Caine, Farber & Gordon, Inc., Pasadena, 1970—; gen. mgr. Gatekeeper Systems, Pasadena, 1995—. Lectr. applied sci. Calif. Inst. Tech., Pasadena, 1965-71, vis. assoc. elec. engring., 1976, vis. assoc. computer sci., 1976-84; dir. San Gabriel Valley Learning Ctrs., 1992-95. Mem. Pasadena Tournament of Roses Assn., 1976—, vice chmn. com., 1996-2000, chmn. com., 2000—. Mem. AAAS, IEEE, Nat. Assn. Corrosion Engrs., Am. Ordnance Assn., Assn. Computing Machinery, Athanaeum Club (Pasadena), Houston Club. Home: 77 Patrician Way Pasadena CA 91105-1039

CAIRE, WILLIAM, biologist, educator; b. Savannah, Ga., Nov. 3, 1946; s. James Andrew and Anna Elizabeth (Rahn) C.; children: William James, Jacob Wooldridge, Samuel Rahn. AA, Howard Coll., Big Spring, Tex., 1966; BS, Tex. Tech. U., 1969; MS, U. North Tex., 1972; PhD, U. N.Mex., 1978. Tchr. math. and sci. J.L. Long Jr. High Sch., Dallas, 1969-70; biologist U.S. Fish and Wildlife Svc., Ft. Collins, Colo., 1974; rsch. assoc. U. Mo., Sullivan, 1975-76; prof. biology U. Ctrl. Okla., Edmond, 1976—, asst. dean Coll. Math. and Sci., 1992-96, dean Coll. Math. and Sci., 2000—. Cons., spkr. in field. Author: Mammals of Oklahoma, 1989; reviewer jour. articles; contbr. articles to profl. jours. Grantee NSF grant, U. Ctrl. Okla. Mem. Southwestern Assn. Naturalists, Am. Soc. Mammalogists, Okla. Acad. Sci. Avocations: golf, woodworking, gardening. Home: 10774 Coyote Cir Arcadia OK 73007-9206 Office: U Ctrl Okla Dept Biology Edmond OK 73034 E-mail: wcaire@wcok.edu.

CAIRNS, DIANE PATRICIA, motion picture executive; b. Fairbanks, Alaska, Mar. 2, 1957; d. Dion Melvin and Marsha Lala (Andrews) C. BBA, U. So. Calif., 1980. Literary agt. Sy Fischer Agy., L.A., 1980-85; sr. v.p. Internat. Creative Mgmt., L.A., 1985-96; sr. v.p. prodn. Universal Pictures, L.A., 1996-97. Mem. NOW, NARAL, Acad. Motion Picture Arts and Scis., Women's Action Coun., Amnesty Internat., L.A. County Mus. of Art, Mus. of Contemporary Art (L.A.), Mus. TV and Radio (L.A.).

CAIRNS, DONALD FREDRICK, engineering educator, management consultant; b. Coulterville, Ill., Sept. 9, 1924; s. Fred Barton and Elsie Loretta (Barbary) C.; m. Marion Grace Huey, Sept. 2, 1950; 1 son, Douglas Scott. BS, U. Ill., 1950; MBA, St. Louis U., 1966, PhD, 1972. Registered profl. engr. Mo., Ill., Md. Asst. engr. Mo. Pacific R.R. Co., St. Louis, 1950-56; project engr., plant engr., asst to pres., v.p. Granite City (Ill.) Steel Co., 1956-79; pres. Nat. Inter-Tech Inc. (subs. Nat. Intergoup, Inc.), St. Louis, 1979-84; chmn. bd. Nat. Engrs. and Assocs., Inc., 1984-90; prof. engring. ret. Washington U., St. Louis, 1990-95, dean Sch. Tech. and Info. Mgmt., 1992-93. Pres., chmn. bd. Indsl. Waste Control Coun.; mem. Mo. Bd. Architects, Profl. Engrs. and Land Surveyors, 1983; former guest lectr. Washington U. Grad. Sch. Bus.; adj. prof. mgmt., U. Mo., St. Louis, 1989-91; chmn. Webster Groves (Mo.) City Planning Commn., 1958; mem. St. Louis Country Traffic Commn., 1960-61, Webster Groves Bus. Devel. Commn., 1962, St. Louis County Charter Commn., 1979; mem., chmn. St. Louis County Planning Commn., 1968-76. Pres., dir. Edgewood Children's Ctr., 1963—72; dir. Webster Oaks Place, 2000; dir., pres. condominium assn. Served with U.S. Army, 1943—46. Decorated Bronze star; recipient recognition for control of air pollution Pres.'s Johnson and Nixon, 1970. Mem.: ASCE (life), Southwestern Ill. Indsl. Assn. (chmn. bd.), Air Pollution Control Assn., Am. Iron and Steel Inst., Assn. Iron and Steel Engrs. (life), Whitemore Ho. Club, Valley View Golf Club (Bozeman, Mont.), Algonquin Golf Club. Home: 1115 Webster Oaks Ln Saint Louis MO 63119-4661

CAIRNS, ELTON JAMES, chemical engineering educator; b. Chgo., Nov. 7, 1932; s. James Edward and Claire Angele (Larzelere) C.; m. Miriam Esther Citron, Dec. 26, 1974; 1 dau., Valerie Helen; stepchildren: Benjamin David, Joshua Aaron. BS in Chemistry, Mich. Tech. U., Houghton, 1955; BS in Chem. Engring, 1955; PhD in Chem. Engring. (Dow Chem. Co. fellow, univ. fellow, Standard Oil Co. Calif. grantee, NSF fellow), U. Calif., Berkeley, 1959. Phys. chemist GE Rsch. Lab., Schenectady, 1959-66; group leader, then sect. head chem. engring. div. Argonne (Ill.) Nat. Lab., 1966-73; asst. head electrochemistry dept. GM Rsch. Labs., 1973-78; assoc. lab. dir., dir. energy and environment divsn. Lawrence Berkeley Nat. Lab., Calif., 1978-96, C.D. Hollowell meml. lectr., 1996, head, Energy Conversion and Storage Program, 1982—; prof. chem. engring. U. Calif., Berkeley, 1978—. Cons. in field; mem. numerous govt. panels; Croft lectr. U. Mo., 1979. Author: (with H.A. Liebhafsky) Fuel Cells and Fuel Batteries, 1968; mem. editor bd. Advances in Electrochemistry and Electrochm. Engring., 1974—; divsn. editor Jour. Electrochem. Soc., 1968-91; regional editor Electrochimica Acta, 1984-99, editor, 2000—; contbr. articles to profl. jours.; patentee in field. Recipient IR-100 award, 1968, Centennial medal Case Western Res. U., 1980, R&D 100 award, 1992, Melvin Calvin medal of distinction Mich. Technol. U., 1998; named McCabe lectr. U. N.C., 1993; grantee DuPont Co., 1956. Fellow Am. Insts. Chemists, Electrochem. Soc. (chmn. phys. electrochem. divsn. 1981-84, v.p. 1986-89, pres. 1989-90, Francis Mills Turner award 1963); mem. AIChE (chmn. energy conversion com. 1970-94), AAAS, Am. Chem. Soc., Internat. Soc. Electrochemistry (chmn. electrochem. energy conversion divsn. 1977-85, U.S. nat. sec. 1983 89, v.p. 1984-88, pres. 1999-2000), Intersoc. Energy Conversion Engring. Conf. (steering com. 1970—, gen. chmn. 1976, 90, 97, program chmn. 1983, co-chair internat. meeting on lithium batteries 2002), Sigma Xi (pres. Berkeley chpt. 2002-03). Home: 239 Langlie Ct Walnut Creek CA 94598-3615 Office: Lawrence Berkeley Nat Lab 1 Cyclotron Rd Berkeley CA 94720-0001 E-mail: ejcairns@lbl.gov., cairns@cchem.berkeley.edu.

CAIRNS, JAMES DONALD, lawyer; b. Chelsea, Mass., Aug. 7, 1931; s. Stewart Scott and Kathleen (Hand) C.; m. Alice Crout Cairns, June 18, 1988; children from previous marriage: Douglas S., Timothy H., Pamela S., Heather M. AB, Harvard U., 1952; JD, Ohio State U., 1958. Bar: Fla. 1974, Ohio 1958, U.S. Dist. Ct. (no. dist.) Ohio 1975, U.S. Tax Ct. 1963. Ptnr. Squire, Sanders & Dempsey, Cleve., 1958-95, Spieth, Bell, McCurdy & Newell, Cleve., 1995—. Served to lt. (j.g.) USNR, 1952-55. Mem. ABA, Am. Coll. Trust and Estate Counsel, Fla. Bar Assn., Ohio State Bar Assn., Bar Assn. Greater Cleve., Union Club, Edgewater Yacht Club, Shoreby Club. Democrat. Episcopalian. Office: Spieth Bell McCurdy Newell 2000 Huntington Bldg 925 Euclid Ave Cleveland OH 44115-1408 E-mail: dcairns@spiethbell.com.

CAIRNS, JAMES ROBERT, mechanical engineering educator; b. Indpls., Feb. 4, 1930; s. John Joseph and Agatha Bertha (Krebs) C.; m. Catherine I. DiCicco, Feb. 6, 1954; children: James Robert, Steven J., Michael P., Daniel F., Timothy E., Robert B. BS in Mech. Engring, U. Detroit, 1954; MS in Engring, U. Mich., 1959, PhD, 1963. Registered profl. engr., Mich. cert. energy mgr. Instr. U. Detroit, 1954-57, U. Mich., Ann Arbor, 1957-63, asst. prof. Dearborn, 1963-65, asso. prof., 1965-68, prof. mech. engring., 1968—, chmn. engring. div., 1964-73, acting dean, 1973-75, dean, 1975-81. Cons. and expert witness in product liability litigation. Contbr. articles to profl. jours. Ford Faculty fellow, 1960-63 Mem. ASME, ASHRAE, Assn. Energy Engrs., Am. Soc. Engring. Edn., Common Cause, Tau Beta Pi, Pi Tau Sigma. Roman Catholic. Home: 836 Dover Dr Dearborn Heights MI 48127-4144 Office: 4901 Evergreen Rd Dearborn MI 48128 2406 E-mail: bcairns@dhol.org.

CAIRNS, SARA ALBERTSON, physical education educator; b. Bloomsburg, Pa., July 18, 1939; d. Robert Wilson and Sara (Porter) Albertson; m. Thomas Cairns, Apr. 13, 1968. BS in Edn., Pa. State U., 1961; MS in Edn., West Chester U., 1965. Cert. tchr., Pa., Del., prin., Del.; adaptive p.e. specialist. Phys. edn. tchr., coach Cen. Columbia County High Sch., Bloomsburg, Pa., 1961-64; phys. edn. tchr. Christina Sch. Dist., Newark, Del., 1964—, coord. adult edn., 1998—. Cons. U. Del., Newark, 1984—, coop. tchr., 1965—; area coord. New Castle (Del.) County Parks and Recreation, 1973—; presenter in field. Contbr. articles to profl. publs. Chair Leasure Elem. Sch. campaign United Fund, 1987-91. Recipient Outstanding Svc. award New CAstle County Parks and Recreation, 1985. Mem. NEA, AAUW, AAHPERD, Del. Assn. Health, Phys. Edn., Recreation and Dance (v.p. dance 1991-94, exec. bd.), Del. State Edn. Assn. Democrat. Presbyterian. Avocations: toy poodles, beach, walking. Home: 40 Vansant Rd Newark DE 19711-4839 Office: Leasure Elem Sch 1015 Church Rd Newark DE 19702-5102

CAJACOB, DANIEL EMERSON, otolaryngologist; b. Toledo, Ohio, Jan. 13, 1955; s. Edward John and Ruth CaJacob; m. Suzanne Ellen CaJacob, Nov. 1, 1980; children: Daniel II, Nicholas, Molly, Libby, Trey. BS in Chemistry, John Carroll U., 1977; MD, U. Cin., 1981. Diplomate Am. Bd. Otolaryngology. Resident in gen. surgery Albany (N.Y.) Med. Ctr. Hosps., 1981-83, resident in otolaryngology, 1983-86, chief resident, 1985-86; otolaryngologist ENT Assocs. in Cin., Inc., 1986-94, Group Health Assocs., Cin., 1994—. Presenter in field. Contbr. articles to profl. jours. John Carroll U. scholar. Fellow ACS, Am. Acad. Otolaryngology/Head and Neck Surgery; mem. AMA, Cin. Soc. Otolaryngology (pres. 1998-99), Cin. Acad. Medicine (trustee coun. 1991-94, chmn. young physicians com. 1988-93, mem. sch. partnership com. 1990-94, membership com. 1994-98, constitution and bylaws com. 1996-99), Ohio State Med. Assn. (del. 1988-91, mem young physicians com. 1988-93, jud. and profl. rels. com. 1990-93, state legis. com. 1991-93). Avocations: sailing, family. Home: 1133 Hearthstone Dr Cincinnati OH 45231-5717 Office: Group Health Assocs 2915 Clifton Ave Cincinnati OH 45220-2402 E-mail: daniel_cajacob@cgha.com.

CAJORI, CHARLES FLORIAN, artist, educator; b. Palo Alto, Calif., Mar. 9, 1921; s. Florian Anton and Marion (Haines) C.; m. Barbara Grossman, June 23, 1967; children: Marion, Nicole. Student, Colo. Coll., 1939-40, Cleve. Art Sch., 1940-42, Columbia, 1946-48, Skowhegan Sch., 1947, 48. Instr. Notre Dame of Md., Balt., 1950-56, Cooper Union, N.Y.C., 1956-59, 60-65; vis. artist U. Calif., Berkeley, 1959; instr. N.Y. Studio Sch., N.Y.C., 1964-69, 85—, Yale U., New Haven, 1989, prof. Queens Coll., N.Y.C., 1965 86. Co-founder Tanager Gallery, N.Y.C., 1952, N.Y. Studio Sch., N.Y.C., 1964; one-man shows include Howard Wise Gallery, N.Y.C., 1963, Bennington (Vt.) Coll., 1969, Landmark Gallery, N.Y.C., 1974, 81, Ingber Gallery Ltd., N.Y.C., 1976, Am. U., Washington, 1977, 88, Gross McCleaf Gallery, Phila., 1983, 85, N.Y. Studio Sch., N.Y.C., 1988, Cen. Conn. State U., New Britain, Conn., 1992, Dartmouth Coll., N.H., 1996, N.Y. Studio Sch., 2000, Paessagio Gallery, West Hartford, Conn., 2002; exhibited in numerous group shows including Chgo. Art Inst., 1964, Whitney Mus., N.Y.C., 1965, Artists Choice, 1977, 3-man show, Loeb Ctr., NYU, N.Y.C., 1970, Wadsworth Atheneum, Hartford, Conn., 1983, Bruce Mus., Greenwich, Conn., 1989, New Britain Mus., 1990; represented in permanent collections including Am. U., Washington, Del. Art Ctr., Wilmington, Met. Mus. Art, N.Y.C., Mitchner Collection, Austin, Tex., NYU, N.Y.C., U. N.Mex., Albuquerque, Walker Art Ctr., Mpls., Whitney Mus., Geigy Chem. Corp. Ardsley, N.Y., Snite Mus., U. Notre Dame, Ind., Honolulu Art Acad., Hirshhorn Mus., Washington, Met. Mus. Art, N.Y.C., Ark. Art Ctr., Little Rock. Served with USAAF, 1942-46. Recipient Distinction in Arts award Yale U., 1959, purchase awards Longview Found., 1962, purchase awards Ford Found., 1963, purchase awards Childe-Hassam, 1975, 76, 80, award for painting Inst. Arts and Letters, N.Y.C., 1970, Louis Comfort Tiffany award, 1979, Altman Figure prize Nat. Acad., 1983, 87, 94, 2000; Guggenheim fellow, 2001; Fulbright grantee, 1952-53, Nat. Endowment Arts grantee, 1981. Mem. NAD, Coll. Art Assn. Home: 2338 Litchfield Rd Watertown CT 06795-1005 Office: NY Studio Sch 8 W 8th St New York NY 10011-9002

CALABRESE, ANTHONY, marine biologist; b. Providence, Feb. 25, 1937; BS, U. R.I., 1959; MS, Auburn U., 1962; PhD in Zoology, Ecology, U. Conn., 1969. Fishery biologist Nat. Oceanic & Atmospheric Adminstrn., Nat. Marine Fisheries Svc., 1962—. Mem. Am. Fisheries Soc., Nat. Shellfisheries Assn. (sec.-tres. 1974-76, v.p. 1976-77, pres. elect 1977-78, pres. 1978-79), World Aquaculture Soc. Achievements include research on aquaculture and the development of biological information concerning the effect of pollutants on marine organisms, including shellfish, finfish and crustaceans, to provide a basis for environmental management. Office: Nat Marine Fisheries Svc NE Fisheries Sci Ctr Milford Lab 212 Rogers Ave Milford CT 06460-6435 E-mail: anthony.calabrese@noaa.gov.

CALABRESE, KAREN ANN, artist, educator; b. N.Y.C., May 27, 1952; d. Daniel Alexander and Janet Russell (Anderson) McKnight; m. Joseph Salvatore Calabrese, Apr. 27, 1974; children: Joseph S. Jr., Brian Patrick. Art cert., Ridgewood Sch. Art, 1973. Paste-up artist, designer Ridge Type Svc., Ridgewood, NJ, 1973—77; artist, prodn. mgr. Ea. Art, Garfield, NJ, 1977—81; various jobs, freelance artist, 1981—; art tchr., 1995—, Phoenix Sch. Art, Vernon, NJ, 1998—. Exhibited in group shows at Highland Lakes Country Club, 1999—2001 (1st Pl. award, 1995, Hon. mention, 1999, 2000), Pub. Gallery, 1995 (Juried Show award, 2000), 1998—2001, (Juried Show award, 1999, 2001), Lake Mohawk Country Club, Sparta, N.J., 1995 (Juried Show award), Skylands Assn., Ringwood, N.J., 1997 (Juried Show award), Drue Chryst Gallery, Sparta, 1999, Perona Farms, Andover, N.J., 1999, Sussex County C.C., 2001— (Juried Show award), Sussex-Warren Winter Show, 2002—, Flying Pig Gallery, Sussex, NJ, 1999—. Recipient 1st Pl. award, Decorative Artist's Workbook Mag., 1998, 3d Pl. award, 22d Ann. Warwick Valley Telephone Directory Cover Competition. Avocations: photography, hiking, hunting, fishing, physical fitness.

CALABRESE, LEONARD M. social services administrator, director; b. Cleve., Nov. 22, 1946; s. Anthony O. and Mary M. (Buzzelli) C. BA magna cum laude, John Carroll U., 1968; MA summa cum laude, Northwestern U., Evanston, Ill., 1974; postgrad., Northwestern U., 1974-78. Cons. in neighborhood devel. Cuyahoga C.C., 1977; assoc. prof. U. Akron (Ohio), 1977-88; cons. in human resources City of Cleve., 1978; exec. dir. Commn. on Cath. Community Action, Cleve., 1987—. Ofcl. election observer Nicaragua Elections, 1990; Segundo Montes lectr. John Carroll U., 1993; presenter Internat. Thomas Merton Soc. Conf., 1995; mem. interfaith civic and religious leaders del. to Israel, 1996. Co-author: Multicultural Diversity Training Manual, 1989; prodr. TV videos, 1985, 88. Active Witness for Peace, 1984, 86; chmn. Consumer Adv. Panel, Cleve., 1989-92; commr. Cleve. Poverty Commn., 1990-93; mem. Nat. Urban Ministry Bd., 1993—; bd. dirs. Greater Cleve. Interreligious Task Force on Ctrl. Am., 1991-95, Wings of Hope, Cleve., 1991-95; trustee Collinwood Art Coun., 1990-95, trustee Greater Cleve. Substance Abuse Initiative, 1995—; trustee, chair program com., exec. com. Cleve. City Club, 1996—, v.p. 2000, pres., 2001-2002, convernor, coun. of pres., 2003—; mem. Ohio adv. coun. Trust Pub. Land, 2000—, Clean Ohio Rev. com, City of Cleve. Cuyahoga County Welfare Reform Coun., 1997-98; chmn. Clergy and Laity Concerned, Cleve., 1984-85; nat. bd. Roundtable Action Dirs., 1995—; mem. Cleve. Workers Rights Bd., 1994—, Cleve. Mus. Art; trustee Bridge Found., 1998-2000, RTA Dowtown Adv. Com.; mem. St. Cecilia Parish, Intercultural Cmty. Coun.; trustee, mem. exec. com. Greater Cleve. Roundtable; co-founder Small Bus. Support Ctr., 1989; bd. advisors Northeastern Neighborhood Devel. Corp., 1999-2002; mem. adv. coun. Trust for Pub. Land Ohio; dir. outreach team Earnnned Income Tax Credit Co.; leadership adv. coun. Cleve. Pub. Libr., 2003—, bd. trustees. Named Consumer of Year, Ohio Consumers Coun., Columbus, 1990; recipient William Evans New Frontier award, 1991, Civic Svc. award Citizens League Greater Cleve., 1996, Urban Issues award, Northern Ohio Live Mag., 2001; Leadership Study grantee Louisville Inst., 1998. Mem. United Nations Assn. of USA (Greater Cleve. chpt.), Greater Cleve. Coun. on World Affairs. Avocations: music, movies, reading, poetry. Office: Commn Cath Community Action 1027 Superior Ave E Cleveland OH 44114-2503

CALABRESE, ROSALIE SUE, arts management consultant, writer; b. N.Y.C., Feb. 17, 1938; d. Julius and Florence (Tuck) Hochman; m. Anthony J. Calabrese, June 15, 1960 (div.); 1 child, Christopher. BA in Journalism, CCNY, 1959. Asst. news editor Electronic News, N.Y.C., 1960; asst. to publicist Abner Klipstein, N.Y.C., 1963; asst. to producer Leonard Field, N.Y.C., 1964; mgr. Am. Composers Alliance, N.Y.C., 1969-85, exec. dir., gen. mgr., 1985-94; dir. Rosalie Calabrese Mgmt., N.Y.C., 1983—. Music advisor Phyllis Rose Dance Co., N.Y.C., 1987—, also bd. dirs.; sec. bd. dirs. Am. Composers Orch., N.Y.C., 1987-93; pres., bd. dirs. 1st Ave. Ensemble, 1993—, Golden Fleece Ltd., 1994—; bd. dirs. Friends Am. Composers, treas., 1991-94; adv. bd. Downtown Music Prodns., 1991—, Joan Miller's Dance Players, N.Y.C., 1991-94, Copland House, 1996-97; mem. editl. adv. bd. New Music Connoisseur Mag., 2002-; mem. music com., Estate Project for Artists with AIDS, 2001-. Author, lyricist: (musicals) A Hell of An Angel, Simone, Not in Earnest, Murdering Macbeth, Pop Life, Does Anyone Here Speak Arabic?, Friends and Relations, Double-Play, C-R; assoc. prodr., treas. box office: (play) Courtyard, 1959, The Mime and Me; co-prodr.: various plays at White Lake (N.Y.) Playhouse, also packaged tours for Prodn. Assocs.; dir. The Bagel Baker's Daughter, 1999, night club acts for Florence Hayle; mem. editl. adv. bd. New Music Connoisseur Mag., 2002--; contbr. short stories and poetry to lit., nat. mags. and anthologies. Mem.: Poetry Soc. Am., Poets and Writers, Broadcast Music Inc., Dramatists Guild. Office: Rosalie Calabrese Mgmt PO Box 20580 New York NY 10025-1521 E-mail: rcmgt@yahoo.com.

CALABRESI, GUIDO, judge, law educator; b. Milan, Oct. 18, 1932; s. Massimo and Bianca Maria (Finzi Contini) C.; m. Anne Gordon Audubon Tyler, May 20, 1961; children: Bianca Finzi Contini, Anne Gordon Audubon, Massimo Franklin Tyler BS in Analytical Econs., Yale U., 1953, LLB, 1958, MA (hon.), 1962; BA in Politics, Philosophy and Econs., Oxford U., 1955, MA in Politics, Philosophy and Econs., 1959; LLD (hon.), Notre Dame U., 1979, Villanova U., 1984, U. Toronto, 1985, Boston Coll., 1986, Cath. U. Am., 1986, U. Chgo., 1988, Conn. Coll., 1988, Chgo.-Kent-I.T.T., 1989, William Mitchell Coll. Law, 1992, Princeton U., 1992, Detroit Mercy Sch. Law, 1994, Seton Hall U., 1995, Albertus Magnus Coll., 1995, Lewis and Clark Coll., 1996, St. John's U., 1997, Pace U., 1998, Iona Coll., 1998, Roger Williams U., 1999, Hofstra U., 1999, N.Y. Law Sch., 1999, Skidmore Coll., 2000, Colby Coll., 2001, U. San Diego, 2001, Dott. Ius SD (hon.), U. Turin, Italy, 1982; JD (hon.), U. Pavia, Italy, 1987, U. Stockholm, 1993; PhD (hon.), U. Haifa, Israel, 1988; DPhil, U. Tel Aviv, 1998; LHD (hon.), U. New Haven, 1989, Williams Coll., 1991, Quinnipiac Coll., 1993; DSc in Politics (hon.), U. Padua, Italy, 1990; Dott. Jur. (hon.), U. Bologna, Italy, 1991, U. Milan, 1998. Bar: Conn. 1958. Asst. instr. dept. econs. Yale U., New Haven, Conn., 1955-56; law clk. to Hon. Hugo Black U.S. Supreme Ct., Washington, 1958-59; asst. prof. Yale U. Law Sch., 1959-61, assoc. prof., 1961-62, prof., 1962-70, John Thomas Smith prof. law, 1970-78, Sterling prof. law, 1978-95; prof. emeritus, lectr. Yale U., 1995—; dean Yale U. Law Sch., 1985-94, Sterling prof. law emeritus, lectr., 1995—; judge U.S. Ct. Appeals 2d cir., New Haven, 1994—. Fellow Timothy Dwight Coll., 1960—; vis. prof. Harvard U. Law Sch., 1969-70, Japan Am. Studies Seminar, Kyoto-Doshisha Univs., summer 1972, European U. Inst., Florence, Italy, 1979; Arthur L. Goodhart prof. legal sci. Cambridge U., also fellow St. John's Coll., 1980-81. Author: The Costs of Accidents: A Legal and Economic Analysis, 1970; (with P. Bobbitt) Tragic Choices, 1978; A Common Law for the Age of Statutes, 1983 (ABA citation of merit, Order of Coif Triennial Book award); Ideals, Beliefs, Attitudes and the Law: Private Law Perspectives on a Public Law Problem (Silver Gavel award ABA), 1985; contbr. articles to profl. jours. Hon. trustee Hopkins Grammar Sch., pres. 1976-80; trustee St. Thomas More Chapel, Yale U.; vice-chmn. bd. trustees Carolyn Found., Minn. Rhodes scholar, 1953; named one of Ten Outstanding Young Men Am., U.S. Jaycees, 1962; recipient Laetare Medal, U. Notre Dame, 1985, Marshall-Wythe medal Coll. William and Mary, 1985, award for outstanding rsch. in law and govt. Fellows of Am. Bar Found., 1998, Thomas Jefferson medal in law Jefferson Found./U. Va. Law Sch., 2000. Fellow Am. Acad. Arts & Scis., Associazione Italiana di Diritto Comparato, Brit. Acad. (corr.), Royal Swedish Acad. Scis. (fgn.), Nat. Acad. dei Lincei (fgn.), Acad. delle Sci. di Torino (fgn.); mem. Conn. Bar Assn., Assn. Am. Law Schs. (exec. com. 1986-89), Am. Philos. Soc. Home: 639 Amity Rd Woodbridge CT 06525-1206 Office: US Ct Appeals 2d Cir 157 Church St New Haven CT 06510-2100*

CALABRESI, PAUL, oncologist, educator, pharmacologist; b. Milan, Apr. 5, 1930; U.S. citizen; married; three children. BA, Yale U., 1951, MD, 1955; MD (hon.), U. Genova (Italy), 1996. Diplomate Am. Bd. Internal Medicine (sec.-treas. 1982-84). Intern Harvard Med. Svc., Boston City Hosp., 1955—56, asst. resident, 1958—59; project assoc. U. Wis., 1956—58; from instr. to assoc. prof. medicine and pharmacology Yale U., 1960—68; prof. med. sci. Brown U., 1968—83, chmn. dept. medicine, 1974—93, prof., chmn. emeritus, 1993—; clin. prof. pharmacology Coll. Pharmacy, U. R.I., Kingston, 1977—; prof. pharmacology R.I. Hosp., 1981—. Field investigator Nat. Cancer Inst., NIH, 1956—60, mem. cancer chemotherapy collaborative program rev. com., 1965—66, bd. sci. counselors, 1983—88; mem. Pharmacol.-Toxicol. Rev. Com., Nat. Inst. Genetic Med. Sci., 1967—70, exptl. therapeutic study sect., 1972—76, chmn., 1975—76; rsch. fellow dept. medicine Yale U., 1959—60, head divsn. clin. pharmacology and chemotherapy, dir. clin. pharmacol. rsch. ctr., 1965—67; vis. scientist U. Lausanne, Switzerland, 1966—67; physician-in-chief, chmn. dept. medicine Roger Williams Gen. Hosp., Providence, 1968—91, v.p. acad. affairs, 1977—91; mem. rsch. coun. and drug rsch. bd. NAS, 1968—75; mem. sci. group on evaluation and testign of drugs for mutagenicity, principles and problems WHO, 1971; cons. Study Group Hycanthone, 1971; counselor Environ. Mutagen Soc., 1971—74; chief medicine Women and Infants Hosp. R.I., 1974—80; cons. Miriam Hosp., Meml. Hosp., Providence VA Med. Ctr., R.I. Hosp., St. Joseph's Hosp., 1974—; mem. Sci. and Pub. Affairs Com., Am. Assn. Cancer Rsch., 1983—; mem. Nat. Cancer Adv. Bd., Nat. Cancer Inst., 1991—, chmn., 1991—94, mem. pres.'s cancer panel, 1995—; dir. divsn. clin. pharmacology R.I. Hosp., 1994—; dir. Brown-Tufts Cancer Ctr., 1997—; vis. prof. numerous univs. Fellow Eleanor Roosevelt Internat. Cancer fellow, Am. Cancer Soc., 1966—67; scholar Burroughs Wellcome scholar clin. pharmacology, 1964—68. Master: ACP (sci. program com. 1975—78, clin. pharmacol. com. 1977—82, chmn. 1978—82); mem.: Am. Soc. Clin. Pharmacology and Therapeutics (38th Oscar B. Hunter Meml. award 1995), Am. Cancer Soc. (St. George medal 1996), Am. Assn. Clin. Rsch., Am. Fedn. Clin. Rsch., Am. Soc. Clin. Oncology (pres. 1969—70), Am. Soc. Pharmacology and Exptl. Therapeutics, Am. Soc. Hematology, Inst. Medicine-NAS. Office: Rhode Island Hosp Aldrich Bldg Rm 124 593 Eddy St Providence RI 02903-4923

CALABRO, JOSEPH JOHN, III, physician; b. Carbondale, Pa., Sept. 4, 1955; s. Joseph J. and Judith A. (Fidati) C.; children: Lia Jude, J. John. IV. Secondary cert., Scranton Prep. Sch., 1973; BS in Biology cum laude, U. Scranton, 1977; DO, Phila. Coll. Osteo. Medicine, 1981. Intern Tripler Army Med. Ctr., Honolulu, 1981-82; resident in emergency medicine Madigan Army Med. Ctr., Tacoma, Wash., 1984-86; chief dept. ambulatory care and emergency med. svcs. Letterman Army Med. Ctr., San Francisco, 1986-90; asst. clin. prof. Sch. Nursing U. Calif., San Francisco, 1987-89; attending physician San Francisco Gen. Hosp., 1987-91; asst. clin. prof. U. Calif. Sch. Medicine, San Francisco, 1987—; chmn. dept. emergency medicine Jersey Shore Med. Ctr., Neptune, N.J., 1990-92, Beth Israel Med. Ctr., Newark, 1992-98, residency program dir. emergency medicine, 1993-98; asst. clin. prof. U. Medicine and Dentistry of N.J., 1991—, dir. emergency svcs.; chmn. dept. emergency medicine West Hudson Hosp., Kearny, N.J., 1994—, St. Michael's Med. Ctr., Newark, 1995-98; assoc. prof., chmn. dept. emergency medicine Seton Hall U. Sch. Grad. Med. Edn., 1998—. Chmn. San Francisco City and County Emergency Med. Care Com., 1988-90; chmn. emergency med. care com. San Francisco chpt. Am. Heart Assn., 1989-90; pres., founder N.J. Inst. Med. Rsch., 1995—; pres., founder, CEO Physicians' Practice Enhancement, LLC, 1994—; assoc. clin. prof. N.Y. Coll. Osteo. Medicine, 1997—. Reviewer Jour. AMA, Jour. EMS, Annals of Emergency Medicine, Rescue, Acad. Emergency Medicine. Lt. col. U.S. Army, 1990-96. Mem. AMA, Am. Coll. Emergency Physicians (N.J. chpt. bd. dirs., sec. 1995-96, treas. 1994-95, pres.-elect 1996-97, pres. 1997-98, chmn. EMS/trauma com., chmn. emergency medicine residency com., chmn. practice mgmt. com., nat. ACEP-EMS com. 1988-96, nat. emergency medicine practice com. 1996—), Am. Coll. Osteo. Emergency Physicians (bd. dirs. 1993-99, sec. 1995-97), Am. Osteo. Assn., Assn. Mil. Surgeons U.S., Soc. Acad. Emergency Medicine, Nat. Assn. EMS Physicians, Phi Lambda Upsilon. Roman Catholic. Home: 15 Hance Rd Fair Haven NJ 07704-3206 Office: 66 W Gilbert St Ste 100 Red Bank NJ 07701-4918

CALALANG, SESINANDO SEBASTIAN, retired obstetrician-gynecologist; b. The Philippines, 1934; s. Esteban Eugenio and Consuelo (Sebastian) C.; m. Rita Ann Hollar, June 17, 1963; children: Carolyn, Steven, Deborah. AA, Letran Coll., Manila, The Philippines, 1953; MD, Far Eastern U., Manila, The Philippines, 1959. Intern Womens Hosp., Balt., 1960-61; resident Balt. City Hosps., 1961-64; fellow gynecol. endocrinology SUNY-Syracuse, 1964-65; attending ob-gyn. Cmty. Gen. Hosp., Syracuse, 1969-99; asst. prof. SUNY-Syracuse, 1970-99. Chmn. dept. ob-gyn. Cmty. Gen. Hosp., Syracuse, N.Y., 1984-89. Fellow Am. Coll. Obstetricians & Gynecologists; mem. AMA, Am. Soc. Reproductive Medicine, Am. Colposcopy Soc., Am. Fertility Soc. Republican. Roman Catholic.

CALAMAR, GLORIA, artist; b. N.Y.C., Sept. 7, 1921; d. Louis B. and Dina (Cotter) Calamar; m. R.L. Redgate, Aug. 22, 1950 (div. 1972); children: Chris James, Steven Clay, Michael Cotter. Cert., Otis Art Inst., L.A., 1943; student, Art Students League, N.Y.C., 1944-45; BA in Art History, State Univ. Coll. N.Y. at New Paltz, 1970. Instr. art history and painting Orange County (N.Y.) Community Coll., 1964-69; instr. art history Mt. St. Mary Coll., Newburgh, N.Y., 1968-69; instr. painting Santa Barbara City Coll., 1975-80. Judge Hallmark Art Contest, N.Y., 1968; lectr. Woodstock (N.Y.) Sch. Art, 1994; color slide lectr. throughout world. Artist in water color, oil, pen and ink, 1946—; one woman shows include Georgetown U., 1974, Portland (Oreg.) C.C., 1973, Willamette U., 1972, U. Oreg., 1971-72, U. Calif. at Berkeley, 1969, Santa Barbara (Calif.) Mus. Art, 1950, Musèe d'Art Moderne de la Ville de Paris, 1967, Galèrie de la Madeleine, Brussels, Belgium, 1964, Landau Gallery, Beverly Hills, Calif., 1953, Parnassus Sq., Woodstock, N.Y., 1978, Ibiza, Balearic Islands, Spain, 1978, Santorini, Greece, 1980, Beaux Arts Ctr., Tunis, Tunisia, 1981, Alkamal Gallery, Jerusalem, Israel, 1981, Jaisalmer, India, 1984, Women's Cmty. Bldg., Santa Barbara, 1986, Jewish Cmty. Ctr., San Francisco, 1986; group shows include Delgado Mus., New Orleans, 1950, San Francisco Art Assn., 1953, L.A. County Mus. Art, 1954, Bertrand Russell Centenary Invitational, London, 1972-73, Woodstock Art Assn., 1978, Faulkner Gallery Santa Barbara, 1992, 93; curated Santa Barbara Visual Artists League Exhbn., 1993, 94; book, video Tar Pits Park Landmark Proposal, Portola Sycamore Tree Landmark Proposal, Carpinteria Airport Landmark Proposal, Juarez-Hosmer Adobe Landmark Proposal, Leaping Greyhound Bridge Landmark Proposal, Los Clavelitos Landmark Proposal, Los Cruces Adobe Landmark Proposal, De la Cuesta Adobe Landmark Proposal; painted the facade of Wells Cathedral, 1999-00, producer video TV program; author: Traveling Artist, 1995; prodr. TV video series Traveling Artist; contbr. articles to publs; prodr. (video) The Traveling Artist, 1996—. Curator Visual Artists League Exhbn., Santa Barbara, 1992, 93, 94, 95; mem. Santa Barbara County Hist. Landmark Adv. Commn. Nat. Endowment for Arts grantee, 1980-81; recipient Calif. Gov.'s Historic Preservation award Santa Barbara County Hist. Landmark Adv. Commn., 1999. Mem. Woodstock (N.Y.) Art Assn. (life), Alumni Assn. Otis Art Inst. (L.A.), Art Students League N.Y. (life), Santa Barbara Visual Artists League. *Many people have told me that I am a strong painter and add in the same breath— like a man. Others have asked me which comes first— my work or my children. I wonder how many male artists have been evaluated or interrogated in the same way. To the former I say thank you for the evaluation of strength but to be a woman artist does not preclude this ingredient. To the latter (I say) one interest supports the other and each is given priority at different times. Much in the same way that food and drink are necessary to the whole person and each is given priority at different times.*

CALAMARO, RAYMOND STUART, lawyer; b. Cairo, May 28, 1944; came to U.S., 1947, naturalized, 1960; s. Albert and Charlotte (Golub) C.; m. Jaana Pirinen; 1 child, Alexander M. AB, Cornell U., 1966; JD, NYU, 1969. Bar: N.Y. State 1970, U.S. Supreme Ct. 1975, D.C. 1976. Legis. dir. Sen.Gaylord Nelson, Washington, 1973-75; exec. dir. Com. for Pub. Justice, N.Y.C., 1975-76; adj. faculty New Sch. Social Rsch., N.Y.C., 1976; staff profl. Carter/Mondale Transition Team, Washington, 1976-77; dep. asst. atty. gen. Office Legis. Affairs, Dept. Justice, Washington, 1977-79; pvt. practice Washington and Brussels, 1979-95; team leader Clinton-Gore Transition Team, 1992-93; ptnr. Hogan & Hartson, Washington, 1995—. U.S. vice-chmn. U.S.-Korea Com. on Bus. Coop., 1997-99. Recipient Royal Order of Polar Star King Carl XVI Gustav, Sweden, 1989. Mem. Met. Club (Washington), St. Albans Tennis Club (Washington). Home: 5073 Lowell St NW Washington DC 20016-2616 Office: Hogan & Hartson 555 13th St NW Ste 800E Washington DC 20004-1161 also: rue de l'Industrie 26 1040 Brussels Belgium E-mail: RSCalamaro@HHLaw.com.

CALAME, BYRON EDWARD, journalist; b. Appleton City, Mo., Apr. 14, 1939; s. Harry Franklin and Gladys Verl (Neal) C.; m. Kathryn Lee Boehm, June 9, 1962; children: Christine Lee, Jonathan David. B.J., U. Mo., 1961; MA in Polit. Sci, U. Md., 1966. Staff reporter Wall St. Jour., 1965-74, bur. mgr., 1974-87, asst. mng. editor, 1985-87, sr. editor, 1987-92, dep. mng. editor, 1992—. Thomas Jefferson disting. vis. lectr. U. Mo., Columbia, 1997. Served to lt. USN, 1961-65. Recipient Faculty-Alumni award U. Mo., Columbia, 1996. Mem. Am. Soc. Newspaper Editors, Soc. Am. Bus. Editors and Writers (bd. govs., Disting. Achievement award 2002). Office: Wall Street Journal 200 Liberty St New York NY 10281-1003 E-mail: barney.calame@wsj.com.

CALARCO, N. JOSEPH, theater educator; b. N.Y.C., Mar. 19, 1938; s. Charles and Vincenza (Marrara) C.; m. Margot Demarais, Mar. 1964 (div. 1981); children: Deidre L., Joseph V. AB, Columbia U., 1959, MA, 1962; PhD, U. Minn., 1966. Instr. U. Minn., Mpls., 1964-66; asst. prof. U. Calif., Berkeley, 1966-68; from asst. prof. to prof. theatre Wayne State U., Detroit, 1968—; artistic dir. Wayne State Playwrights' Workshop, 1992-94. Pres. TransArt Prodns., N.Y.C., 1982-86; cons. in field. Author: Tragic Being: Apollo and Dionysus in Western Drama, 1968; (play) Telephone: A Play in Three Calls, 1990, The Tragedy of Ajax, 1992, beethoven is..., 2001 (Nat. New Play award 2002); prin. theorist of tragedy: Tragedy and Tragic Theory: An Analytical Guide, 1992; contbr. articles to profl. jours.; dir. 50 theatrical prodns. (Best Play of Decade award 1970-80). Bd. dirs. City of Troy (Mich.) Bicentennial Ethnic Festival, 1976. Recipient Theatre Achievement award Detroit Free Press, 1996. Mem. Dramatists Guild, AAUP, Soc. Stage Dirs. and Choreographers, Assn. Theatre in Higher Edn. Avocations: weight training, photography, music. Home: 1826 Eastport Dr Troy MI 48083-1719 Office: Wayne State U Dept Theatre Detroit MI 48202 E-mail: njc31@columbia.edu.

CALARCO, VINCENT ANTHONY, specialty chemicals company executive; b. NYC, May 29, 1942; s. George Michael and Madeline J. Calarco; m. Linda Joyce Maniscalco, Apr. 10, 1971; children: David V., Christopher G. BS, Polytech. U. N.Y., 1963; MBA, Harvard U., 1970. With Crompton & Knowles Corp, pres., CEO, 1985—, chmn. bd., 1986—. Bd. dirs. Newmont Mining, Con Edison, The Hosp. of St. Raphael. Trustee Poly. U. With U.S. Army, 1966—68. Mem.: Chem. Heritage Found. (vice chmn., trustee, exec. com.), Nat. Found. for History of Chemistry (trustee, exec. com.,), Am. Chemistry Coun. (chmn. bd. internat. com., chmn. Office of Chem. Industry Trade Advisor), Am. Soc. Chem. Industry (chmn. Am. sect. 1998—99, pres. 1998—2000), Am. Chem. Soc., Harvard Bus. Sch. Club. Office: Crompton Corp 199 Benson Rd Middlebury CT 06749

CALATCHI, RALPH FRANKLIN, investment banker, writer; b. Alpes-de-Haute Provence, France, Apr. 18, 1944; came to U.S. 1969; s. Mony and Odette (Calef) C.; children: Sophie C., Rafaela C., Ralph C. M of Econ., U. Law and Econs., Paris, 1970; MBA, Columbia U., N.Y.C., 1970; PhD in Econs., U. Paris, 1973; degree in Chinese Lang., Cambridge U., 1980, Bejing U., 1982. Head new bus. sect. Kuhn Loeb & Co., N.Y.C., 1970-72; mgr. The Nikko Securities Co., Ltd., Tokyo, Paris, 1973-75; dir., chmn.'s alt. Sociedad Financiera Union C.A., Caracas, Venezuela, 1975-83; chmn. and chief exec. officer Wood Gundy Calatchi China Investments, Ltd., Shanghai, Toronto, Hong Kong, 1984-87, Calatchi Investments Ltd., London, 1987-89; pres. Calatchi Capital Corp., Ft. Lauderdale, 1990—; spl. advisor to bd. dirs. Banco Union S.A., Caracas, Venezuela, 1994—95. Author, editor: Property Finance: An International Perspective, 1992; co-founder, editor: The Action Letter Inc., 1993—94; chief editor: World Property Finance Atlas: Comparing and contrasting commercial real estate in 25 countries, 1997. Founding mem., chmn. adv. com. Cmty. Redevel. Agy., City of Pompano Beach, Fla., 2002—, mem. budget rev. com., 1995—; mem. adv. bd. Sand and Spurs Equestrian Park, 1995—, chmn. Avocations: golf, flying, skiing. Home: 4116 W Palm Aire Dr Apt 161B Pompano Beach FL 33069-4145

CALAWAY, DENNIS LOUIS, insurance company executive, real estate broker, financial executive; b. Helena, Ark., Dec. 10, 1960; s. Carl Jr. and Mary Jean Calaway; m. Elizabeth Anne Suiter, July 16, 1988. BS in Bus. Adminstrn., Ark. State U., 1983, MBA, 1988, grad. leaders program, 1999. Registered health underwriter; life underwriter tng. coun. fellow; lic. real estate broker, Ark.; registered employee benefit cons.; cert. profl. in human resources. Ops. mgr. Churchill Truck Lines, Jonesboro and Litte Rock, Ark., 1983-85; rep. Mut. of Omaha Cos., Jonesboro, 1985-88; pres. Profl. Ins. Svcs., Inc., 1988—; gen. agt. State Life Ins. Co. of Ind., Time Ins. Co. and United Am. Ins. Co., 1988—, Security Gen. Life Ins. Co., 1989—, GPM Life Ins. Co., 1991—; prin. broker Calaway Realty Co., 1992—; pres. Profl. Fin. Svcs., Inc., 1993—; CFO, Davis Electric Motors, Inc., 1993-94; co-founder TDI Bearing & Supply, Inc., 1994; account exec., indsl. benefit cons. Health Choice of Jonesboro, Inc./Meth. Hosp. of Jonesboro, 1995-98; with First American Group, 1998; benefits specialist Allstate Fin., 2001—. Benefit cons. Health Choice of Jonesboro, 1995, bus. instr. Ark. State U., 1995, 98-, Sterling Coll., 1997, S.W. Baptist U., 1997-99. Chief counsellor Columbian Squire Cir., 1988-93, 2000-; mem. pastoral coun. Blessed Sacrament Cath. Ch., 1990-92, founder, pres. Soc. St. Therese, 1975—; mem. fin. com. Blessed Sacrament Cath. Sch., 1994-95; asst. cubmaster Boy Scouts Am., 1998-99, chmn. pack com., 1999—, treas. troop com., 2000-2001, chmn. troop com., 2002-. Fellow Life Underwriters Tng. Coun. (instr. 1990-91, moderator 1991, 1998, chmn. 1991-92, Amb. Club, Silver Club); mem. Nat. Assn. Health Underwriters, Nat. Soc. Human Resource Mgmt., N.E. Ark. Soc. Human Resource Mgmt. (v.p. legis. affairs 1997-98, v.p. programs 1999, pres. 2000), Gen. Agts. and Mgrs. Conf., Nat. Assn. Life Underwriters, Ark. State Assn. Life Underwriters (state health chmn. 1997-98), Jonesboro Assn. Life Underwriters (sec.-treas. 1986-88, pres.-elect 1988-89, pres. 1989-91, health chmn. 1992—), Govs. Partnership for Chldn's and Families (bd. dirs. 1997-2001), Assn. Health Ins. Agts., World Safety Orgn. (v.p. membership 1996-97), KC (treas. 1982-83, 84-87, faithful scribe 1983-84, faithful navigator 1986-88, grand knight 1981-83, faithful adm. 1989-90, faithful trustee 1991—, Ark. youth dir. 1989-92, chmn. Ark. squires 1989-92, 2001-, Knight of Yr. award 1982, 88), Lions, Jerry Suiter Found. (bd. dirs. 1998—), Beta Gamma Sigma, Omicron Delta Epsilon, Gamma Iota Sigma. Home: PO Box 1 State University AR 72467-0001 Office: Profl Ins Svcs Inc PO Box 419 Jonesboro AR 72403-0419 also: CSA Mktg Inc PO Box 130 State University AR 72467-0130

CALCAGNIE, KEVIN FRANK, lawyer; b. Glendale, Calif., Feb. 27, 1955; s. Frank Calcagnie Jr. and Margaret Mildred (Bierman) Jones; m. Peggy Melinda Malmberg, Jan. 2, 1982; children: Kelly Shea, Sean Frank. BSBA, Calif. State U., Fullerton, 1977; JD, Western State U., 1983. Bar: Calif. 1983, U.S. dist. Ct. (ea., so. and cen. dists.) Calif. 1983, U.S. Ct. Appeals (9th cir.) 1983, U.S. Supreme Ct. 1987. Ptnr. Robinson, Calcagnie & Robinson, Newport Beach, Calif., 1982—. Instr. paralegal studies Fullerton Coll., 1990. Author: (with others) Products Liability Litigation: Product Studies, 1996, A Guide to Toxic Torts, 1987; contbr. articles to profl. jours. Recipient Am. Jurisprudence awards Bancroft Whitney Pub., San Francisco, 1981. Mem. ABA, ATLA, Consumers Attys. of Calif. (bd. govs. 1993-98), Orange County Trial Lawyers Assn. Roman Catholic. Office: Robinson Calcagnie & Robinson 620 Newport Center Dr Fl 7 Newport Beach CA 92660-6420 E-mail: kcalcagnie@rcrlaw.net.

CALCAMUGGIO, LARRY GLENN, lawyer; b. Toledo, Feb. 9, 1951; s. Glenn L. and Darlene M. (Brown) C.; m. Diane L. Seagert, June 30, 1973; children: Jeffrey, Todd, Scott. BBA, U. Toledo, 1973, JD, 1977. Bar: Ohio 1977, U.S. Dist. Ct. Ohio 1979, U.S. Tax Ct. 1984. Auditor Blue Cross N.W. Ohio, Toledo, 1973-75; trust officer Ohio Citizens Bank, Toledo, 1975-78; assoc. Brown, Baker, Schlageter & Craig, Toledo, 1979-80; ptnr. Rohrs, Rimelspach & Calcamuggio, Toledo, 1980-82; trust officer new bus. BancOhio Nat. Bank, Toledo, 1982-84; pvt. practice Toledo, 1984-94; ptnr. Sprenger, Douglas and Calcamuggio Attys., Toledo, 1994-95; pvt. practice Toledo, 1996—. Mem. adv. com. legal assisting tech. U. Toledo, 1980-92, instr., 1987-89. Coach Little League Baseball, 1986-92; trustee Luth. Social Svcs., Toledo, 1989-92, sec. 1992; trustee Luth. Homes Soc. Found., 1997—, Interfaith Hospitality Network of Metro Toledo, 2000-2001. Mem. NRA, Ohio Bar Assn., Toledo Bar Assn., Toledo Estate Planning Coun., Nat. Fedn. Ind. Bus., Toledo Planned Giving Coun. Lutheran. Avocations: shooting, hunting, gun collecting, choir singing. Office: Ste 4 4149 Holland-Sylvania Rd Toledo OH 43623-2590

CALCATERRA, EDWARD LEE, construction company executive; b. St. Louis, Mar. 26, 1930; s. Frank John and Rose Theresa (Ruggeri) C.; m. Patricia Jean Marlow, July 4, 1953; children— Christine, Curtis, David, Richard, Tracy BSC.E., U. Mo., Rollo, 1952. Registered profl. engr., Mo. Estimator J.S. Alberici Constrn. Co., St. Louis, 1955-57, mgr. project, 1957-63, v.p. ops., 1963-71, sr. v.p., 1971-76, exec. v.p., 1976-91, pres., 1991-96; exec. dir. J.S. Albenci Constrn. Co., St. Louis, 1996—. Bd. dirs. Cardinal Ritter Inst., St. Louis, 1980-83; bd. regents Rockhurst Coll., Kansas City, Mo., 1983—. Served with U.S. Army, 1953-55 Mem. Assoc. Gen. Contractors St. Louis (pres. 1980) Roman Catholic.

CALDER, CLIVE, music company executive; Chmn., CEO The Zomba Group of Cos., N.Y.C. Office: Zomba Group 137-139 W 25th St New York NY 10001-7200

CALDER, IAIN WILSON, publishing company executive; b. Scotland, Feb. 27, 1939; arrived in U.S., 1967, naturalized; s. William and Charlotte G. (West) C.; m. Jane Brownlea Bell, Apr. 17, 1965; children: Douglas William, Glen Robert Bell. Student pub. schs., Falkirk, Scotland. Reporter Falkirk Sentinel, 1955-56, Stirling Jour., 1956, Falkirk Mail, 1956-60, Glasgow Daily Record, 1960-64; London bur. chief Nat. Enquirer, 1964-67, articles editor, 1967-73, exec. editor, 1973-75, editor, 1975-91, pres., 1976-95, editor-in-chief, 1991-95, editor emeritus, 1995-97; exec. v.p. pub. Am. Media Inc., 1994-97. Dir. Am. Media, Inc./Nat. Enquirer; Disting. lectr Fla. Atlantic U. Bd. dirs. Bethesda Hosp. Found., 1997—.

CALDER, KENT EYRING, political science educator, diplomat; b. Salt Lake City, Apr. 18, 1948; s. Grant H. and Rose (Eyring) C.; m. Toshiko Matsuura; children: Mari, Ryan. BA with honors, U. Utah, 1970; AM, Harvard U., 1972, PhD, 1979. Staff mem. U.S. Ho. of Reps., Washington, 1968-69; tchg. fellow Harvard U. Dept. of Govt., Cambridge, Mass., 1972-74; rsch. economist U.S. Fed. Trade Commn., Washington, 1974-78; vis. fellow U. Tokyo, 1977—78; exec. dir. U.S.-Japan Program Harvard U., Cambridge, 1979-80, lectr., 1979-83; asst. prof. Woodrow Wilson Sch., Princeton (N.J.) U., 1983—89, tenured faculty, 1989—2003, dir. U.S.-Japan program, 1990—2003; Edwin O. Reischauer prof. East Asian Studies Johns Hopkins U., Washington, 2003—, dir. Reischauer Ctr. East Asian Studies Washington, D.C., 2003—. Internat. adv. bd. Japanese Ministry of Fin., Inst. of Fiscal and Monetary Policy, Tokyo, 1987-96, Japan chair Ctr. for Strategic and Internat. Studies, Washington, 1989-91, 96; spl. advisor to U.S. Amb. to Japan, 1996-2001; mem. Bretton Woods Com., 2001—; mem. nat. U.S. adv. bd. Japan Found., 2003--. Author: Crisis and Compensation, 1988 (Ohira and Arisawa Meml. prizes 1990), Japan's Changing Role in Asia, 1992, Strategic Capitalism, 1993, Pacific Defense, 1996 (Mainichi Asia-Pacific Grand prize 1997); co-author: The Eastasia Edge, 1982. Instr. Japan Soc. U.S.-Japan Leadership Program, N.Y.C., 1988-91, U. Pa. Wharton Sch. Internat. Forum, 1990—; trustee Princeton in Asia, 1987-95; mem. Coun. on Fgn. Rels., 1990—, internat. adv. bd. Waseda U. Sch. Asia-Pacific Studies, 1998—, World Econ. Forum East Asia Summits, 1998—, Bretton Woods Com., 2001—. 1st lt. U.S. Army, 1975-76. Named Fulbright Faculty Fellow and Doctoral Fellow, 1985-86, 75-76, Faculty Research Fellow The Japan Found., 1984, Graduate Prize Fellow Harvard U., 1970-74. Mem. Am. Polit. Sci. Assn., Assn. for Asian Studies, Phi Beta Kappa, Phi Kappa Phi (Sparks Fellow 1970-71, Gibbs Fellow 1970), OECD Tide 2000 Club. Avocations: stamp collecting, collecting classic African musical instruments, tennis. Home: 197 Shadybrook Ln Princeton NJ 08540-4135 Office: Sch Adv Internat Studies 1619 Mass Ave NW Washington DC 20036-1984 E-mail: kcalder@jhu.edu.

CALDER, ROBERT AUSTIN, preventive medicine physician, administrator; b. Beloit, Wis., May 21, 1954; s. John T. and Rosemary A. (Austin) C.; m. Daphne R. Calder, Aug. 17, 1979; children: Heather, Joseph. BS, U. Wis., 1979; MD, Med. Coll. Wis., 1982; MS, U. Wis., Milw., 1984. Diplomate Am. Bd. Preventive Medicine. Chief, preventive medicine U.S. Army, Ft. Sill, Okla., 1985-87; epidemiologist Fla. Dept. Health, Tallahassee, 1987-90; assoc. dir. Merck & Co., Inc., West Point, Pa., 1990-91, dir., 1992-93, sr. dir., 1993-98, exec. dir., 1999—. Capt., U.S. Army, 1985-87. Eagle Scout, 1970. Fellow Am. Coll. Preventive Medicine. Roman Catholic. Avocation: sailing. Home: 905 Farwell Dr Madison WI 53704 Office: Merck & Co Inc 4 Westbrook Corp Ctr Westchester IL 60154 E-mail: robert_calder@merck.com.

CALDER, ROBERT MAC, aerospace engineer; b. Vernal, Utah, Oct. 16, 1932; s. Edwin Harold and Sydney (Goodrich) C.; m. Yoshiko Iemura, Feb. 14, 1959; children: Suzanne, Alex, Irene, John. BSChemE, U. Utah, 1956, MS in Math. and Geology (NSF grantee), 1967; postgrad., U. Wash., 1964, Utah State U., 1965, U. Iowa, 1966. Cert. secondary tchr., Utah. Tchr. Utah Pub. Schs., 1958-79. V.p. Sydney Corp., Bountiful, Utah, 1958-82; sr. engr. aero. div. Hercules Inc., Magna, Utah, 1979—. Designed and built 200 ft. long bridge across Green River, Brown's Park, Utah, 1967; owner RMC Enterprises, Nations Imports; cons. in field, 1960—; cultural exchange participant to Israel, Egypt, 1983, 87. Author: Power Requirements for Laboratory Mixers, 1956, Academic Preparation of Utah's Secondary Mathematics Teachers, 1967. Active Boy Scouts Am., 1945-75, attended World Scout Jamboree in France, 1947, instr., Philmont Scout Ranch, 1972, asst. scoutmaster Nat. Jamboree Troop, 1973; instr. hunter safety and survival, Utah Dept. Fish and Game, 1964-74; state advisor U.S. Congl. Adv. Bd., 1982—; mem. Rep. Nat. Com. Capt. USAF, 1956-70. Mem. AIAA, NRA (life), Am. Quarter Horse Assn., Internat. Platform Assn., Oratorio Soc. Utah, The Planetary Soc., Hercules Toastmasters Club (treas. 1980, v.p. edn. 1981, pres. 1982), N.Am. Fishing Club (life), mem. LDS Ch. Mem. Lds Ch. Achievements include building of 220-foot long bridge across Green River in Brown's Park, Utah, 1967. E-mail: mcalder32@hotmail.com.

CALDERA, LOUIS EDWARD, academic administrator, former federal official; b. El Paso, Tex., Apr. 1, 1956; s. Benjamin Luis and Soledad (Siqueiros) C.; m. Eva Orlebeke Caldera. BS, U.S. Mil. Acad., 1978; JD, MBA, Harvard U., 1987. Bar: Calif. 1987. Commd. 2nd lt. U.S. Army, 1978, advanced through ranks to capt., 1982, resigned commn., 1983; assoc. O'Melveny & Myers, L.A., 1987-89, Buchalter, Nemer, Fields & Younger, L.A., 1990-91; deputy county counsel County of L.A., 1991-92; mem. Calif. State Assembly, 46th Dist., L.A., 1992-97, chmn. banking and fin. com.; mng. dir., COO Corp. for Nat. Svc., Washington, 1997-98; Sec. of the Army Washington, 1998—2001; vice chancellor, univ. advancement Calif. State U., 2001—03; pres. Univ. New Mexico, Albuquerque, 2003—. Democrat. Roman Catholic. Office: Univ New Mexico Albuquerque NM 87131*

CALDERO-FIQUEROA, ANA JHANILCA, language educator; b. San Juan, P.R., Jan. 14, 1963; d. Jose Luis Caldero and Maria Mercedes Fiqueroa. BA in Spanish Lang., U. Ctrl. Fla., 1984; MA in Spanish Lit., U. Wis., 1988. Fgn. lang. prof. Valencia C.C./West, Orlando, Fla., 1989—. Faculty advisor Valencia Internat. Students, Orlando, 2001—. Prodr.: (Hispanic heritage theater celebration) Garcia Lorca: Homage to the Spanish Poet, (Hispanic heritage celebration) Homage to Jose Marti, Homage to Spanish Poets/Generation of 98, (homage to the music of Cuba & P.R.) Two Islands in a Sea of Music, (Hispanic heritage celebration) Women in Arts; author: (short story) From the Distance (3d pl. short story competition, 1990), The Dream Searcher (hon. mention short story category, 1992). Avocations: travel, reading, writing. Office: Valencia CC-West Campus 1800 S Kirkman Rd PO Box 3028 Orlando FL 32811 E-mail: acaldero@valenciacc.edu.

CALDERON, MARK A. artist, sculptor; b. Bakersfield, Calif., Oct. 31, 1955; s. Julian Paul and Patricia Ruth Calderon. BA with distinction, San Jose (Calif.) State U., 1978. Artist and sculptor. Solo exhbns. include Seattle Art Mus., 1987, Jamison/Thomas Gallery, N.Y.C., 1990, Greg Kucera Gallery, Seattle, 1985, 88, 91, 94, 96, 99, Nancy Hoffman Gallery, N.Y.C., 1999. Recipient Betty Bowen Meml. award Seattle Art Mus., 1986, Seattle Artists award Seattle Arts Commn., 1997; WESTAF/NEA regional fellow for visual arts, Santa Fe, 1993; Art Matters Inc. fellow, 1989, 95; Painters and Sculptors grantee Joan Mitchell Found., Inc., N.Y.C., 2001. Democrat. Avocations: yoga, hiking, camping. Home: 924 26th Ave Seattle WA 98122-4916

CALDERON, RONALD, state official; b. Montebello, Calif., Aug. 12, 1957; m. Ana Calderon; children: Jessica, Zachary. Student, Western State U. Law; BA, UCLA, 1980. Owner fin. svcs. sales and mktg. firm; mgr. mfg. industry; mortgage banker; real estate agt.; chief of staff Assemblyman Ed Chavez; state assembly mem. Dist. 58 Calif. State Assembly, 2002—. Mem. appropriations com.; mem. banking and fin. com.; mem. govtl. orgn. com.; mem. ins. com.; mem. utilities and commerce com. Mem. La Merced Elem. Sch. PTA, 1998—; bd. dirs. L.A. Econ. Devel. Corp., 1998—, N.E. Cmty. Clinic, 1999—; mem. Gangs Out of Downey, 2001—. Democrat. Mailing: Rm 2179 PO Box 942849 Sacramento CA 94249 Office: Ste 100 400 N Montebello Blvd Montebello CA 90640

CALDERON, SILA M. governor; b. San Juan, Sept. 23, 1942; 3 children. B in polit. sci. with honors, Manhattanville Coll.; MPA, U. P.R. Worked for Sec. of Labor; spl. asst. econ. devel. and labor for Gov. Hernández Colón, 1974; chief of staff Gov. Hernández Colón, 1985, sec. interior, sec. state, 1988; mayor City of San Juan, 1996—2000; gov. PR, 2000—. Bd. dirs. Banco Popular P.R. Named Outstanding Woman of Yr., PR C. of C., 1975, 1985, 1987, Puerto Rican Products Assn., 1986, PR chpt. Am. Assn. Pub. Works, 1988. Mem.: Sister Isolina Ferré Found. Democrat. Office: Off de Gobierno Calle Fortaleza #52 PO Box 9020082 San Juan PR 00902-0082*

CALDERWOOD, JAMES ALBERT, lawyer; b. Washington, Dec. 4, 1941; s. Charles Howard and Hilda Pauline (Dull) C.; m. Joyce M. Johnson, 1987 BS, U. Md., 1964; JD cum laude, George Washington U., 1970; postgrad., Oxford Ctr. Mgmt. Studies, Oxford, Eng., 1977. Bar: Md. 1970, D.C. 1973, U.S. Supreme Ct. 1974. Trial atty. antitrust div. U.S. Dept. Justice, Washington, 1970-73; spl. asst. U.S. Atty., 1973, trial atty. antitrust div., 1973-79; ptnr. Grove, Jaskiewicz, Gilliam & Cobert, Washington, 1979-90, Zuckert, Scoutt, Rasenberger, Washington, 1990—. Mem. faculty Transp. Law Inst. U. Denver; adj. prof. Washington Coll. Law, Am. U., 1983, 86; faculty Internat. Law Inst., 1995—; gen. counsel Soc. Govt. Economists. Contbr. articles to profl. jours. Served to capt. USAF, 1964-68, George Washington U. Law Ctr. scholar, 1969. Mem. ABA (Achievement award 1973), Fed. Bar Assn. (nat. co chmn. council young lawyers 1972-73, chmn. regulated industries com. 1976-79), Fed. Energy Bar Assn. (chmn. antitrust com. 1985-86, 93-95), Transp. Lawyers Assn. (chmn. antitrust com. 1998-03, chmn. transp. security com. 2003—); Assn. for Transp. Law, Logistics & Policy (pres. D.C. chpt. 1998-99), Md. Bar Assn., D.C. Bar Assn., U. Md. Alumni Assn. (pres. elect 1984-85, pres. 1985-86) Coll. Bus Alumni Club (pres. 1980-81), Nat. Press Club, Pi Sigma Alpha, Delta Sigma Pi, Delta Theta Phi. Episcopalian. Home: 5518 Western Ave Chevy Chase MD 20815-7122 Office: Zuckert Scoutt & Rasenberger 888 17th St NW Ste 600 Washington DC 20006-3309 E-mail: jacalderwood@zsrlaw.com.

CALDWELL, ANN B. music educator; b. Anniston, Ala., July 12, 1947; d. Byron Brenford and Bernice New Boyd; m. John Harold Harmon, Mar. 22, 1969 (div. Sept. 28, 1983); children: Heather, John Harold II; m. Bobby Ted Caldwell, Aug. 14, 1987. MusB in Edn., Birmingham (Ala.) So. Coll., 1969; MusM in Edn., Jacksonville (Ala.) U., 1975. Music tchr. elem. sch. Auburn (Ala.) City Schs., 1969; choral dir. Oxford (Ala.) HS, 1969—74; instr. music So. Union State C.C., Wadley, Ala., 1974—89, dir. music, 1989—. Choir dir. First United Meth. Ch., Wedowee, Ala., 1999—; exec. dir. Miss. So. Union Scholarship Pageant, Wadley, 1984—; mem. nat. forum advisors Mid-Am. Prodns., Inc., N.Y.C., 1996—97 Dir.: (choral group) The So. Union Sound, Carnegie Hall, NYC, 1993—2003. Mem.: Wedowee Music Club (past pres.), Delta Kappa Gamma, Kappa Delta Epsilon, Delta Zeta. Methodist. Avocations: music, reading, crossword puzzles. Home: 524 Conty Road 29 Wedowee AL 36278 Office: Southern Union State Cmty Coll PO Box 1000 Wadley AL 36276-1000

CALDWELL, ANN WICKINS, academic administrator; b. Rochester, N.Y., Dec. 3, 1943; d. Ralph Everett and Constance Ann (McCoy) Wickins; m. Herbert Cline Caldwell, Sept. 17, 1966; children: Constance Haley Blacklow, Robert James. BA in English Lit., U. Mich., 1965. Reporter Democrat & Chronicle, Rochester, 1961-64; asst. to dean Harvard Grad. Sch. of Edn., Cambridge, Mass., 1965-70, editor alumni quarterly, 1968-71; freelance editor, writer Harvard U. and Radcliffe, Cambridge, 1971-73; assoc. sec. Philips Acad., Andover, Mass., 1973—80; v.p. for planning and resources Wheaton Coll., Norton, Mass., 1980-90; assoc. dir. Mus. Fine Arts, Boston, 1990-91; v.p. for devel. Brown U., Providence, 1991-97; pres. MGH Inst. Health Professions, Boston, 1997—. Chair bicentennial com. Newburyport, Mass., 1974—76; citizens adv. com. Pub. Sch., Newburyport, 1979—80; bd. dirs. Am. Laryngological Voice Rsch. & Edn. Found.; trustee Women's Edn. and Indsl. Union, Boston, 1988—91, John Hope Settlement Ho., Providence, 1997—. Mem.: Women in Devel. Boston (founder, pres. 1984—86), Coun. for Advancement and Support of Edn. (trustee, sec. dist. 1 1985—87, trustee, sec. nat. 1987—89), Boston Club, Chilton Club, Phi Delta Kappa. Avocations: sailing, skiing, travel, reading. Office: Charlestown Navy Yard 36 First Ave Boston MA 02129-4724 E-mail: acaldwell@mghihp.edu.

CALDWELL, BARRETT SCOTT, industrial engineering educator; b. Phila., Sept. 25, 1962; s. Shirl C. and Jacqueline H. (Horsey) C.; m. Shanta Wilson Hartsough, Sept. 1, 1986 (div.); children: Piers Hartsough C., Kyrie Eleison Hartsough C. BS in Aero. & Astronautics, BS in Humanities, MIT, 1985; MA in Psychology, U. Calif., Davis, 1987, PhD in Social Psychology, 1990. Grad. student lectr. U. Calif., Davis, 1985-90; asst. prof. U. Wis., Madison, 1990-97, assoc. prof., 1997—2000, Purdue U., West Lafayette, Ind., 2000—. Author: (book) Social Processes in Isolated Groups of U.S. Park Service Rangers, 1990; contbr. articles to Behavior and Info. Tech. and Human Factors. Mem. ministry and counsel Madison Quakers Monthly Meeting, 1992-94; dir., Ind Space Grant Consortium, 2001—. Recipient Minority Rsch. Initiation award NSF, Madison, 1994, grad. fellowship NSF, Davis, 1985, Ameritech Faculty fellowship, Madison, 1991. Mem. Human Factors and Ergonomics Soc. (co-chair tech. program com.). Avocation: rowing. Office: Purdue U-Sch of Indsl Engring 315 N Grant StRm 228D Lafayette IN 47907-2023

CALDWELL, BETTYE MCDONALD, education educator, director; b. Smithville, Tex., Dec. 24, 1924; d. Thomas Milton and Juanita (Mayes) McDonald; m. Fred T. Caldwell, Jr., June 8, 1947; children: Paul Frederick, Elizabeth Lanier. BA, Baylor U., 1945; MA, U. Iowa, 1946; PhD, Washington U., St. Louis, 1951. Research assoc. Upstate Med. Ctr., Syracuse, N.Y., 1959-65; prof. edn. Syracuse U., 1965-69; prof. U. Ark., Little Rock, 1969-78, Disting. prof., 1978-93; prof. pediatrics U. Ark. Med. Sci., 1993—. Belding prof. Found. for Child Devel., 1987-88; bd. dirs. First Comml. Bank, Little Rock. Editor: Child Devel. Jour., 1968-72, Rev. Child Devel. Research, III, 1973, Infant Education, 1977; contbg. editor: Working Mother, 1984—. Bd. dirs. Ark. Advs., Little Rock, 1977-85; bd. dirs. Child Care Action Campaign, Ark. Early Childhood Commn. Recipient Woman of Yr. award Ladies Home Jour., 1976, Alumna of Yr. award Baylor U., 1980, Excellence award U. Ark., 1990, Disting. Svc. award Nat. Gov.'s Assn., 1990, Distinction award Ark. Profl. Women, 1991, Dolly Madison award for lifelong contbn. to devel. and well being of infants, 2001. Mem. Fellow Soc. Rsch. in Child Devel. (governing bd. 1977-81, Disting. Contbns. award 1993); mem. Nat. Assn. for Edn. Young Children (pres. 1982-84), Kappa Delta Pi (laureate chpt. 1977—). Democrat. Home: 21 Saint Andrews Dr Little Rock AR 72212-2908 Office: College of Education UALR 2801 S University Little Rock AR 72204

CALDWELL, BILLY RAY, geologist; b. Newellton, La., Apr. 20, 1932; s. Leslie Richardson and Helen Merle (Clark) C.; m. Carolyn Marie Heath; children: Caryn, Jeana, Craig. BA, Tex. Christian U., 1954, MA, 1970. Cert. petroleum geologist, cert. profl. geologist. Geologist Geol. Engring. Svc. Co., Ft. Worth, Tex., 1954-60; sci. tchr. Ft. Worth and Lake Worth Sch. Dists., 1960-63; mgr. Outdoor Living, 1963-71; instr. geology Tarrant County Coll., Ft. Worth, 1971—. Petroleum and environ. geologist cons., Ft. Worth, 1971—. Bd. dirs. Ft. Worth and Tarrant County Homebuilders Assn., 1973; mem. Ft. Worth Environ. Coun. Named Dir. of Yr. Ft. Worth Jaycees, 1966-67. Mem. Am. Inst. Profl. Geologists, Am. Assn. Petroleum Geologists, Geol. Soc. Am., Ft. Worth Geol. Soc. Republican. Baptist. Avocations: travel, church work, enrichment lecturing on cruise ships. Home: 305 Bodart Ln Fort Worth TX 76108-3804 Office: PO Box 150989 Fort Worth TX 76108-0989 E-mail: bcgeology@aol.com.

CALDWELL, CHARLES M. federal judge; b. 1954; BS, Evansville U., 1976; JD, Northwestern U., 1979. Asst. U.S. trustee U.S. Dist. Ct. (so. dist.) Ohio, 1988-93; staff atty. bankruptcy divsn. Adminstrv. Office U.S. Cts., Washington, 1986-88; bankruptcy judge U.S. Bankruptcy Ct., Columbus, 1993—. Office: US Bankruptcy Ct 170 N High St Columbus OH 43215-2403 Fax: 614-469-5506.

CALDWELL, CICELY, human resources specialist, consultant; b. East Orange, N.J., Apr. 25, 1970; d. Frank Thompson and Helena V. Caldwell-Smith. AA, Centenary Coll., 1990; BA in Comm. with emphasis in Speech, Rider U., 1992; MA in Corp. & Org. Comm., Fairleigh Dickinson U., 2000. Cert. PHR (Profl. H.R.). Office mgr. NeuMed, Lawrenceville, NJ, 1993—96; employee rels. rep. Am. Preferred Provider Plan, Inc., Newark, 1996—97; benefits adminstr. Watson Pharma, Morristown, NJ, 1997—2000; human resources mgr. Wire One Tech., Inc., Hillside, NJ, 2000—02; sr. human resources rep. Martindale-Hubbell, New Providence, NJ, 2002—. Tutor Literacy Vol. Am., Westfield, NJ, 2002—; mem. Sr. Usher Bd., Rahway, NJ, 1998—. Mem.: Soc. H.R. Management. Avocations: travel, reading, personal and professional devel.. Personal E-mail: ccaldwellphr@hotmail.com.

CALDWELL, COURTNEY LYNN, lawyer, real estate consultant; b. Washington, Mar. 5, 1948; d. Joseph Morton and Moselle (Smith) Caldwell. Attended, Duke Univ., 1966-68, U. Calif., Berkeley, 1967, 1968-69; BA, U. Calif., Santa Barbara, 1970, MA, 1975; JD (hon.), George Washington Univ., 1982. Bar: D.C., 1984; Wash., 1986; Calif., 1989. Jud. clk. U.S. Ct. Appeals for 9th Cir., Seattle, 1982-83; assoc. Arnold and Porter, Washington, 1983-85, Perkins Coie, Seattle, 1985-88; dir. western ops. Edn. Real Estate Svc., Inc., Irvine, Calif., 1988-91, sr. v.p., 1991-98; ind. cons., Orange County, Calif., 1998—. Bd. dir. Univ. Town Ctr. Assn., 1994; bd. dir. Habitat for Humanity, Orange County, 1993-94, chair legal com., 1994. Named Nat. Law Ctr. Law Rev. scholar, 1981-82. Mem. Calif. Bar Assn. Avocation: fgn. languages. Home and Office: 140 Cabrillo St 15 Costa Mesa CA 92627 E-mail: clcaldwell@earthlink.net.

CALDWELL, ELWOOD FLEMING, food scientist, educator; b. Gladstone, Man., Can., Apr. 3, 1923; s. Charles Fleming and Frances Marion (Ridd) C.; m. Irene Margaret Sebille, June 13, 1949; children: John Fleming, Keith Allan; m. Florence Annette Zar, June 23, 1979. BS, U. Man., 1943; MA in Food Chemistry, U. Toronto, 1949, PhD in Nutrition, 1953; MBA, U. Chgo., 1956. Chemist Lake of the Woods Milling Co., Can., 1943-47; research chemist Can. Breweries Ltd., Toronto, Ont., 1948-49; chief chemist Christie, Brown & Co. div. Nabisco, Toronto, 1949-51; research assoc. in nutrition U. Toronto, 1951-53; with Quaker Oats Co., Barrington, Ill., 1953-72, dir. research and devel., 1969-72; prof., head dept. food sci. and nutrition U. Minn., St. Paul, 1972-86, exec. assoc. to dean Coll. Agr., 1986-88; dir. sci. svcs. Am. Assn. Cereal Chemists, 1988-94, analysis svcs. coord., 1994-98; exec. editor Cereal Foods World, 1986-91; chmn. bd. Dairy Quality Control Inst., Inc., St. Paul, 1972-88, R. & D. Assocs. for Mil. Food & Packaging, Inc., San Antonio, 1970-71; chmn. evening program in food sci. Ill. Inst. Tech., Chgo., 1965-69. Contbr. articles to sci. jours. Chmn. North Barrington (Ill.) Bd. Appeals, 1966-69, mayor, 1969-72; vice-chmn. Barrington Area Council Govts., 1972; bd. dirs. Family Guidance Barrington, 1971-72. Recipient cert. of appreciation for civilian service U.S. Army Materiel Command, 1970. Fellow Am. Assn. Cereal Chemists (Geddes Meml. award 1996), Inst. Food Technologists (Chmn.'s Svc. award Chgo. sect. 1975, Chmn.'s award Minn. sect. 1977, Calvert L. Willey Disting. Svc. award 1991); mem. Am. Assn. Family and Consumer Scis., AOAC Internat. (Reference Material Achievement award 2002), Kiwanis, Phi Tau Sigma (nat. pres. 1980-81), Gamma Sigma Delta (award of merit 1988), Phi Upsilon Omicron. Republican. Lutheran.

CALDWELL, GAIL, book critic; b. Amarillo, Tex., Jan. 20, 1951; d. Bill M. and Ruby C. BA, U. Tex., 1978, MA in Am. Studies, 1980. Instr. U. Tex., Austin, to 1981; book critic, book editor Boston Globe, 1985—. Judge Radcliffe Bunting Fiction Fellowship; nominator Irish-Times/Aer Lingus Internat. Fiction Prize; mem. Pulitzer jury fiction, 1991 (chmn. of jury 1995 & 1997). Recipient Pulitzer Prize for criticism, 2001. Mem. PEN New Eng. (bd. dirs.), Nat. Book Critics Circle. Office: The Boston Globe PO Box 2378 135 Morrissey Blvd Boston MA 02125-3338

CALDWELL, GARNETT ERNEST, lawyer; b. Houston, July 2, 1934; s. William Ernest and Ethel Leona (Jones) C. BA, U. Tex., Houston, 1957, JD, 1959. Bar: Tex. 1958. Pvt. practice law, Houston, 1959-64; ptnr. Ginther, Erwin, Dillard & Caldwell, Houston, 1964-65, Prappas, Caldwell & Moncure, Houston, 1965-77, Caldwell & Baggott, Houston, 1977-82, Caldwell, Wallis, Pruitt & Baggott, Houston, 1982; pvt. practice Houston, 1982-85, 87-90, Houston and Galveston, 1990—; ptnr. Caldwell & Lareau, 1985-87. Lectr. govt. U. Houston, 1961-62 2d lt. U.S. Army, 1957, lt. col. Res., 1977—. Decorated knight and knight comdr. Royal Yugoslavian Order St. John of Jerusalem. Mem. Galveston County Bar Assn., Houston Bar Assn., Houston Bankruptcy Conf., Res. Officers Assn., Houston Early Music Soc., Delta Theta Phi. Roman Catholic. Home and Office: 1619 Post Office St Galveston TX 77550-4813

CALDWELL, GILBERT RAYMOND, III, lawyer; b. Newton, Iowa, June 14, 1952; s. Gilbert Raymond and Frances Elizabeth (Ellingsworth) C.; m. Jeanne Sharon Myerscough, Dec. 23, 1974; 1 son: Kyle Myerscough. BA, U. Tulsa, 1974, JD, 1977. Bar: Iowa 1978, U.S. Dist. Ct. (no. and so. dists.) Iowa, U.S. Supreme Ct. 1988. Asst. city prosecutor, legal intern City of Tulsa, 1976-77; asst. county atty. Jasper County, Iowa, 1978; ptnr. Caldwell, Caldwell & Caldwell, Newton, 1979; bd. dirs. Prevent Child Abuse Iowa, 2000—03, v.p., 2003. Presenter in field, magistrate appointing commn. 2003-. Contbr. Iowa Juvenile Law Manual, 1990. Rep. precinct chmn. Fairview Twp., Iowa, 1982-83; legis. study com. on family cts. in Iowa, Iowa Supreme Ct., 1990, select com. to review ct. practices in child welfare matters, 1997; mem. Coun. on Chemically Exposed Children, 1990, 98; mediator, bd. dirs. Prairie City-Monroe Sch. Edn. Found. 1998-99; facilitator Improving Representation in Child in Need of Assistance Cases conf., 1998; faculty panel Practical Solutions to Family Law Ethical Problems seminar, 1993; faculty substance abuse conf., 1993; bd. dirss. Prevent Child Abuse Iowa, 2000-2003, v.p., 2003; adoption seminar presenter, NBI, 1999, 2003. Mem. ABA (young lawyers divsn., exec. coun. family law, child advocacy and protection com., juvenile justice exec. com., family law sect., juvenile law and needs of children com., mental health com., gen. practice sect., vice-chmn. family law com. 1990-92, regional coord. juvenile law update 1988-90, pres. 5A judicial dist. 1991-92), Am. Judicature Soc., Iowa State Bar Assn. (young lawyers divsn. 1982-89, exec. coun. 1987-89, chmn., v.p. juvenile law com., co-chmn. membership and minority affairs, chmn. family law sect. 1991-92, 98-99, exec. coun. family law sect, 1990-92, litigation sect. practice aides com., vice-chair mental health com., gen. practice sect., family law com. 1990-92, chair family and juvenile law sect., 1991-92, 98-99, exec. coun. family and juvenile law sect., 1997-98, family law resource panel vol. lawyers project 1997—), Jasper County Bar Assn. (pres. 1989-90), Iowa Mcpl. Atty.'s Assn., Iowa Trial Lawyers Assn., Assn. Trial Lawyers Am., Nat. Assn. Counsel for Children, Prevent Child Abuse (bd. dirs. 2000-03, v.p. 2003), Newton Jaycees (sec. 1978-79, pres. 1979-80), Newton C. of C., Iowa Jaycees (state legal coun. 1979-80), Monroe Community Club, Jasper County Farm Bur., Kiwanis Noon Club (faculty panel family law seminar 1993, chair com. family and juvenile law sect. 1993-94, bd. dirs. 2003—), Iowa Mcpl. Atty.'s Assn. Home: RR 2 Monroe IA 50170-9802 Office: Caldwell Caldwell & Caldwell 102 1st St N Newton IA 50208-3226

CALDWELL, JOHN ALVIS, JR., experimental psychologist; b. New Orleans, June 16, 1955; s. John Alvis and Patsy Ruth (Richardson) C.; m. Jo Lynn Woodard, July 18, 1981. BA cum laude, Troy State U., 1976; MS in Psychology, U. South Ala., 1979; PhD in Psychology, U. So. Miss., 1984. Psychologist II Eufaula (Ala.) Adolescent Adjustment Ctr., 1979-80, coord. drug-free clinic, 1980-81; asst. dir. behavioral med. lab. Children's Hosp. Nat. Med. Ctr., Washington, 1984-86; rsch. psychologist U.S. Army Aeromed. Rsch. Lab., Ft. Rucker, Ala., 1986—2002; vis. scientist NASA Ames Rsch. Ctr., Moffett Field, Calif., 2001—02; prin. rsch. psychologist Air Force Rsch. Lab., Brooks AFB, Tex., 2002—. Sec., chief edn. working group 19 NATO Adv. Group R&D, 1991-94; math. and sci. adv. com. mem. Troy State U., 1992-2002; adj. faculty U.S. Army Sch. Aerospace Medicine, 1996—; mem. spkrs. bur. Nat. Sleep Found., 1996—, mem. sci. coun., 1999—; instr. Army Aviation Psychology course, Ft. Rucker, 1998-2002; instr. U.S. Army Aviation Pre-Command Course, 1997-2002; chmn. sci. rev. com. U.S. Army Aero. Rsch. Lab., 1996-2000; sci. cons. sustained ops. rsch. and policy groups, 1999-2001; prepared and distributed unique edni. brochures on aviator fatigue; sleep expert USA Today/Nat. Sleep Found. 1999 Hotline; lead sci. cons. on pharmacol. fatigue mgmt. USAF Sustained Ops. Working Group, 1999-2002; mem. com. metabolic monitoring techs. for mil. field application Inst. Medicine, Nat. Acads., 2003. Spl. guest editor Biol. Psychology, Amsterdam, 1994; jour. referee Aviation Space and Environ. Medicine, 1992—, mem. editl. rev. bd., 2001-03; referee Jour. Exptl. Psychology, 1998-99; contbr. articles to profl. jours. Dir. ch. choir St. John Cath. Ch., Enterprise, Ala., 1991-97; vol. counselor Wiregrass Emergency Pregnancy Svc., Daleville, Ala., 1992; mem. Enterprise cmty. choir, 1991, St. Luke's Meth. Ch. Christmas choir, Enterprise, 1995-97; mem. U.S. Army Aeromed. Rsch. Lab. Choir, Ft. Rucker, 1992-93; mem. spl. choir Enterprise Ch. LDS, 1993-94; mem. ch. choir St. Columba Cath. Ch.,

Dothan, Ala., 1998; mem. Dothan (Ala.) Cmty. Choir, 1999-2000, Enterprise Cmty. Choir, 1999; music leader Our Lady of Loretto Cath. Ch., Ft. Rucker, Ala., 1999. Recipient writing award U.S. Army Aviation Med. Assn., 1996. Mem. AAAS, Aerospace Med. Assn., Sigma Xi, Psi Chi. Republican. Roman Catholic. Achievements include conducting the first aviator performance study of the new stimulant modafinil, the first controlled study of performance sustaining effects of dextroamphetamine in helicopter pilots, first in-flight helicopter pilot evaluation of the chem. def. antidote atropine sulfate, first studies on the feasibility of monitoring helicopter pilot brain activity during actual flight conditions, first controlled study on the effects of fatigue in F-117 pilots. Home: 7430 Legend Point San Antonio TX 78244 Office: Air Force Rsch Lab APRL/HEPM 2485 Gillingham Dr Ste 25 Brooks AFB TX 78235 E-mail: lynn_john81@hotmail.com.

CALDWELL, JOHN L. international company executive; b. Algiers, Algeria, Mar. 5, 1940; m. Nina C. McClain; 1 child, Ian. BA, U. Md., 1965; MA, George Washington U., 1966. Liaison to comdr.-in-chief NATO Fontainebleau, France, 1960-64; exec. sec., staff dir. Task Force World Shortages, Mex.-U.S. Com., East-West Trade Task Force, 1966-73; exec. sec. European Community-U.S. Bus. Council, 1972-75, Adv. Council Japan-U.S. Econ. Relations, 1970-73; dir. Center for Internat. Bus. Relations, 1973-77; mgr. internat. div. U.S. C. of C., 1977—81, v.p. internat., 1981—82; sr. v.p. Carl Byoir & Assocs., Washington, 1982—87; mng. dir. U.S. Trading Co., 1987—; pres. U.S. Trading & Investment Co., Washington, 1987—2002, Cameron Internat., LLC, 2003—. Mem. bd. advisors Landegger Internat. Bus. Diplomacy program Georgetown U.;mem. internat. coun. Elliott Sch. Internat. Affairs, George Washington U.; bd. dirs. ConSyGen; past chmn. bd. dirs. Taipei-Washington Coord. Coun.; past chmn. internat. com. Greater Washington Bd. Trade; bd. dirs., chmn. Nat. Ctr. Therapeutic Riding, Citizens Network for Fgn. Affairs; councillor Atlantic Coun. U.S. Bus. Basics; adj. prof. George Mason U.; lectr. Elliott Sch. Internt. Affairs, George Washington U. Mem. U.S. C. of C. (internat. policy com., chmn. Africa task force). Office: Cameron Internat LLC 3256 Prospect St NW Washington DC 20007 E-mail: jcaldwell@caminter.com.

CALDWELL, JOHN THOMAS, JR., communications executive; b. Sewickley, Pa., July 30, 1932; s. John Thomas and Helen Oliva (Chanto) C.; m. Margery Eleanor Hill, Dec. 31, 1971. AB, U. Pitts., 1955; postgrad., Mich. State U., U. Mich., Harvard U. Sch. Bus. Mem. prodn. staff Sta. WKAR-TV, East Lansing, Mich., 1955-56, dir., 1957, prodr., 1958, prodn. mgr., 1959-62; distbn. mgr. Nat. Ednl. TV, Inc., Ann Arbor, Mich., 1962-64; v.p. distbn. and ops., 1964-66; ops. mgr. Sta. WGBH, Boston, 1966-70; gen. mgr. Sta. WGBY-TV, Springfield, Mass., 1971-79; pres., gen. mgr. Sta. WTVS-TV, Detroit, 1979-83; dir. electronic communication, corp. pub. affairs Ford Motor Co., Dearborn, Mich., 1983-86, dir. internal comm., pub. affairs, 1986-94; v.p. bus. comm. planning Convergent Media Systems, 1995-98; pres. The Caldwell Co., Grosse Pointe, Mich., 1998—. Bd. dirs. Public Broadcasting Service, 1977-81, Sta. WTVS-TV, 1979-92. Bd. dirs. Detroit Symphony Orch., 1979—87, Mich. Cancer Found., 1980—96, Boys and Girls Clubs Mich., 1981—84, Springfield (Mass.) Symphony Orch., 1975—79; mem. U. Mich. Cmty. Adv. Bd., 1979—88, Mich. State Film, TV and Rec. Arts Adv. Coun., 1984—86; bd. dirs. Karmanos Cancer Inst., 1986, Mich. Info. Tech. Network, 1995—2001, Karmanos Cancer Found., 2002—. Woodrow Wilson fellow, 1981 Mem. Nat. Acad. TV Arts and Sci., Mich. Corp. Public Broadcasting (dir. 1979-83), Internat. TV Assn., Economic (Detroit) Club, Grosse Pointe Yacht Club, Skyline Club, Marina Club at Jonathon's Landing, Jupiter, Fla. Home: 874 Lake Shore Rd Grosse Pointe Shores MI 48236-1273

CALDWELL, JOHN WARWICK, lawyer; b. Dayton, Ohio, May 19, 1949; s. Curtis Philip and Elizabeth L. (Warwick) C.; m. Janet Hudson, June 14, 1975; children: Philip E., Katherine E., Sarah A. BA, Rice U., 1971; MA, Johns Hopkins U., 1975; JD, Villanova U., 1978. Bar: Pa. 1978, U.S. Dist. Ct. (ea. dist.) Pa. 1978, (mid. dist.) 1990, U.S. Ct. Appeals (3rd cir.) 1980, (fed. cir.) 1983, U.S. Supreme Ct., 1986, U.S. Patent and Trademark. From assoc. to ptnr. Woodcock Washburn LLP, Phila., 1978—, chmn. patent prosecution and client counseling practice group. Nat. spkr. in field. Author: The Effects of Gatt Upon Patent Property, 1994, Biotechnology Patents, 1994, Five Ways to Improve the Examination of Biotechnology Patents, 1994, Voo Doo Diligence, 1994, ALI-ABA Videotape: Development in the Law of Copyrights, 1992, Artists' Guide to Copyrights, Patents and Trade Secrets, 1985, 2d edit., 1995; author monograph; contbr. to series Science and the Law, Am. Chem. Soc. Bd. dirs. Phila. Vol. Lawyers for Arts, 1978-80. Robert Welch Found. scholar, 1968-71. Mem. ABA, Internat. Trademark Assn., Licensing Execs.' Soc., Pa. Bar Assn., Phila. Bar Assn. (fed. cts. com.), Phila. Intellectual Property Law Assn. (chmn. antitrust com. 1983-85, treas. 1978-80, 95-97, pres.-elect 1998-99, pres. 1999-2000), Copyright Soc. U.S. (nat. trustee 1999—, co-chair Phila. chpt.). Republican. Presbyterian. Avocations: sailing, golf. Office: Woodcock Washburn Kurtz Mackiewicz & Norris 1 Liberty Place 46th Flr Philadelphia PA 19103 E-mail: Caldwell@Woodcock.com.

CALDWELL, JOHN WINSTON, III, petroleum engineer; b. Gainesville, Fla., Nov. 21, 1955; s. John Winston Jr. and Barbara T. (Thostenson) C.; m. Melissa Ann Myers, June 26, 1981; children: Graham Colin, Alexandra Alyssa, Evan Benjamin. BSCE, U. Idaho, 1977. Registered profl. engr., Okla. Prodn. engr. Texaco, Inc., Hobbs, N.Mex., 1978-80; drilling/prodn. engr. Southland Royalty Co., Farmington, N.Mex., 1980-82, reservoir engr. Oklahoma City, 1982-84, Houston, 1985; sr. reservoir engr. Meridian Oil Inc., Billings, Mont., 1986, regional joint interest engr., 1987, regional reservoir engr. Farmington, N.Mex., 1988-89, regional drilling engr., 1990-95, regional planning engr., 1996-97, divsn. team leader, 1997-2000, divsn. prodn. mgr., 2000—01, sr. engring. advisor, 2002—. Expert witness on reservoir issues in Okla., Tex., Colo., N.D., Mont., N.Mex., Ark. State Oil Commns. Mem. Soc. of Petroleum Engrs. Achievements include leading drilling team in engineering horizontal wells in San Juan Basin, use of geoservice measurement while drilling, N2 membrane drilling, slimhole horizontal R/C, and leading team in exploiting shale gas in San Juan Basin, currently division lead in benchmarking and instituting best practices in all phases of oil and gas operations. Home: 4109 Saint Michaels Dr Farmington NM 87401-0806 Office: Burlington Resources Oil and Gas Inc 3401 E 30th St Farmington NM 87402-8807 E-mail: jcaldwell@br-inc.com.

CALDWELL, JONI, psychology and women's studies educator, small business owner; b. Chgo., Aug. 8, 1948; d. Bruce Wilver and Eloise Ethel (Ijams) C. BS in Home Econs. Edn., Mich. State U., 1970; MA in Psychology, U. San Francisco, 1978. Cert. high sch. and coll. tchr., Mich. Instr. Northwestern Mich. Coll., Traverse City, 1972-78, Mott Community Coll., Flint, Mich., 1974-78; tchr. Grand Blanc (Mich.) High Sch., 1970-73, Clio (Mich.) High Sch., 1974-78; parent educator, vol. coord. Family Resource Ctr., Monterey, Calif., 1981-82; owner, gen. mgr. Futons & Such, Monterey, 1982—; instr. psychology Hartnell Coll., Salinas, Calif., 1993-96; spl. project dir. YWCA, 1996-97. Instr. women's studies and psychology Monterey Peninsula Coll., 1997—, Cabrillo Coll., 2000—. Bd. dirs., v.p., pres. Ch. Religious Sci., Monterey, 1984-87; mem. bd. stewards Pacific Coast Ch., Monterey, 1988-92, v.p.; bd. dirs. YWCA, Monterey, 1986-88, mem. nominating com., 1995-98, pers. comm., 1996-2001; vol., fund raiser Buddy Program, 1992-97; membership com. Profl. Womens Network, 1989—; founder Women's Spiritual Journeys, 1999—. Named Woman of the Yr. for Empowering Other Women, 2001. Mem. AAUW (state del., 1997, co-chair equity comm., 1998—, bd. dirs. 1998—), NOW (life), Nat. Womens Studies Assn., New Monterey Bus. Assn. (past pres., bd. dirs. 1984-95, v.p. 1993-97), Monterey C. of C. (cons. workshop com. 1985-87, Small Bus. Excellence award 1990), Nat. Coalition Bldg. Inst. (del. First Women's Conv. 1998). Avocations: skiing, sailing, skin diving, remodeling houses, travel, hiking. Home: 29 Portola Ave Monterey CA 93940-3731 Office: Futons & Such 475 Alvarado St Monterey CA 93940-2722 E-mail: jonic@redshift.com.

CALDWELL, JUDY CAROL, advertising executive, public relations executive, consultant, writer, designer; b. Nashville, Dec. 28, 1946; d. Thomas and Sarah Elizabeth Carter; 1 child, Jessica. BS, Wayne State U., 1969. Tchr. Bailey Mid. Sch., West Haven, Conn., 1969-72; editorial asst. Vanderbilt U., Nashville, 1973-74; editor, graphics designer, field researcher Urban Observatory of Met. Nashville, 1974-77; account exec. Holden and Co., Nashville, 1977-79; bus. tchr. Federated States of Micronesia, 1979-80; dir. advt. Am. Assn. for State and Local History, Nashville, 1980-81; dir. prodn. Mktg. Communications Co., Nashville, 1981-83; ptnr. Victory Images of Tenn., Inc., Nashville, 1990-92; sr. tech. advisor UN, 2002; owner, pres., writer, designer Ridge Hill Corp., Nashville, 1983—. E-mail: ridgehillcorp@comcast.net.

CALDWELL, KIRK, state representative; b. Waipahu, Hawaii, 1952; m. Donna Tanoue; 1 child, Maya. BA in Econs., Tufts U., Mass.; MA in Law and Diplomacy, Fletcher Sch. of Law and Diplomacy, Mass.; JD, U. of Hawaii, 1978. Economist Inst. of Sugar and Alcohol, Sao Paulo, Brazil, 1975—76; legis. asst. U.S. Senator Daniel K. Inouye, Washington, 1978—81; law clk. Hawaii Supreme Ct. Justice William S. Richardson, Honolulu, 1982—83; staff Majority Leader Russell Blair, State House of Reps., Honolulu, 1984; atty. Ashford & Wriston, Honolulu, 1984—, ptnr., 1991—, mng. ptnr., 1997—99. Dir., officer Hawaii Justice Found., Legal Aid Soc. of Hawaii, Friends of the Judiciary History Ctr., Young Lawyers Divsn. of the Hawaii State Bar Assn.; mem. Aloha Unite Way Fund Drives, Kaimuki Neighborhood Bd., Honolulu, Manoa Neighborhood Bd., Honolulu. Democrat. Office: State Capitol Rm 406 415 S Beretania St Honolulu HI 96813 Fax: 808-586-8479. E-mail: repcaldwell@Capitol.hawaii.gov.*

CALDWELL, LINDA E. critical care nurse; b. Spencer, Iowa, June 23, 1954; d. George W. and Elaine Wava (Parks) D.; m. Bill Caldwell, June 25, 1988. ADN, Cumberland County Coll., 1984; EMT, Cumberland Adult Edn., 1986. RN; cert. EMT. Staff nurse Newcomb Med. Ctr., Vineland, NJ; head nurse Leesburg State Prison, Delmont, NJ; charge nurse, ICU South Jersey Hosp. Divsn., Millville, NJ, 1991—; co-owner P.S. & L. Emergency med. tech. Bridgeton Ambulance Svc. Mem. EOF (past pres.), AACN. Home: PO Box 976 Millville NJ 08332-0976 E-mail: linda4847@aol.com.

CALDWELL, LOUISE PHINNEY, historical researcher, community volunteer; b. Dallas, Sept. 19, 1938; d. Carl Lawrence and Louise (Snow) Phinney; m. Josef Caldwell, Sept. 8, 1962; children: Mattie Caldwell Roberts, Jane Barron Caldwell Jackson, Josef Caldwell Jr., Charles Phinney Caldwell. Grad., The Hockaday Sch., 1956; student, Sweet Briar Coll., 1956-57. Owner retail bus., Dallas, 1965-75; project chmn. Mus. of Dallas History-Fair Park, 1985—; interim dir. Dallas Hist. Soc., 1990, chmn., 1991-93, pres., 1987-91, life trustee, 1991; friends of the bd. Dallas Publ. Libr., 2003. Membership chair trustee com. Tex. Assn. Mus., Austin, 1986-88; mem.-at-large Women's Coun. Dallas County, 1991—; adv. 36th Inf. Divsn. Mus. Com., Camp Mabry, Austin, Tex.; v.p., treas. Hist. Inquiry, Inc., 1992—. Author rsch. project 150 Years of Lone Star Cuisine, 1986. Mem. Dallas County Hist. Commn., 1989-90; chmn. Awards for Excellence in Cmty. Svc., Dallas, 1983-89; founding co-chmn. Jubilee Dallas! Celebrating 150 Years, 1990-91; mem. charter bd. dir. Friends of Fair Park, Dallas, 1985-91; mem. Crystal Charity Ball Com.; chmn. Festival Shakespeare, 1994. Recipient Heritage award Dallas County Heritage Soc., 1982. Fellow Dallas Hist. Soc. (chmn. Fellows 1982-84), Mayflower Soc., Nat. Soc. of Colonial Dames, Daus. of Republic of Tex. (chpt. v.p. 1991-92), Dallas Woman's Club, Dallas Garden club, Independant Hist. documents, book, Charter 100. Democrat. Episcopalian. Avocations: collects & catalogues, antique glass trade beads, folk art of hispanic southwest.

CALDWELL, LYNTON KEITH, social scientist, educator; b. Montezuma, Iowa, Nov. 21, 1913; s. Lee Lynton and Alberta (Mace) C.; m. Helen A. Walcher, Dec. 21, 1940; children: Edwin Lee, Elaine Lynette. PhB, U. Chgo., 1935, PhD, 1943; MA, Harvard U., 1938; LLD (hon.), Western Mich. U., 1977. Asst. prof. govt. Ind. U., South Bend, 1939-44, dir. advanced studies in sci., tech. and public policy Bloomington, 1965—, Arthur F. Bentley prof. polit. sci., 1971-84, prof. pub. and environ. affairs, 1970—; dir. research and publs. Council of State Govts., 1944-47; faculty U. Chgo., 1945-47; prof. polit. sci. Syracuse U., 1947-54; dir. Pub. Adminstrn. Inst. for Turkey and Middle East, UN, Ankara, 1954-55; prof. polit. sci. U. Calif., Berkeley, 1955-56. Mem. environmental adv. bd. C.E., 1970—; mem. Sea Grant adv. panel NOAA, 1971—; panel mem. Office Tech. Assessment, 1977—; cons. U.S. Senate Com. on Interior and Insular Affairs, 1969—, UN, 1973-74, UNESCO, 1975—, Army Environ. Policy Inst., 1991—, Nat. Com. on New Directions for Nat. Wildlife Refuge System, 1990—; mem. Nat. Commn. on Materials Policy, 1971—, Nat. Acad. Scis. Com. on Internat. Environ. Programs, 1970—; chmn. com. internat. law, policy and adminstrn. IUCN, 1969-77; mem. Internat. Coun. Environ. Law, 1985—; mem. sci. adv. bd. Internat. Joint Commn., 1984-91; Franklin lectr. Auburn U., 1972; Disting. Profl. lectr. U. Ala., 1981, William and Mary, 1991, U. Houston, 1992. Author: Administrative Theories of Hamilton and Jefferson, 1944, 2d edit., 1988, Environment: A Challenge to Modern Society, 1970, In Defense of Earth, 1972, Environmental Policy and Administration, 1975, Citizens and the Environment, 1976, Science and the National Environmental Policy Act, 1982, International Environmental Policy: From the 20th to the 21st Century, 1984, 3d edit., 1996, Biocracy: Public Policy and the Life Sciences, 1987, Perspectives on Ecosystem Managment for the Great Lakes, 1988, Between Two Worlds: Science, The Environmental Movement and Policy Choice, 1990, (with K. Schrader-Frechette) Policy for Land: Law and Ethics, 1993, Ecologia: Ciencia y politica medioambiental, 1993, Environment as a Focus for Public Policy, 1995, The National Environmental Policy Act: An Agenda for the Future, 1998; co-editor: Environmental Policy: Transnational Issues and National Trends, 1997, The National Environmental Policy Act: Agenda for the Future, 1999; mem. bd. editors Environ. Conservation Jour., 1973-93, Natural Resources Jour., 1973—, Sci., Tech. and Soc., 1979-91, Environ. Profl. Jour., 1981-89, Politics and the Life Scis., 1982-96, Colo. Jour. Internat. Environ. Law and Policy, 1990—, Ambiente y Recursos Naturales (Argentina), 1985—, Environmental Awareness (India), 1989—, Duke U. Law and Policy Forum, 1991—, Environ., 1993-95, Global Environ. Politics, 1999—. Bd. govs. The Nature Conservancy, 1959-65, Shirley Heinze Environ. Fund., Global Environ. and Energy in the 21st Century, 1988—. Recipient Sagamore of Wabash award State of Ind., 1980, H. and M. Sprout award Internat. Studies Assn., 1985, Global 500 award UN Environ. Programme, 1991, Disting. Svc. award Ind. U., 2001, Spirit of Philanthropy award Ind. U. Press, 2001; grantee Conservation Found., 1968-69, NSF, 1963—, Conservation and Research Found., 1969-70, U.S. Office Edn., 1973; guest fellow Woodrow Wilson Internat. Ctr. for Scholars Smithsonian Instn., 1971-72, East-West Ctr. fellow, 1981; named to Royal Order of Crown Thailand. Fellow AAAS; mem. Am. Soc. Pub. Adminstrn. (William Mosher award 1966, Laverne Burchfield award 1972, Marshall E. Dimock award 1981), Nat. Acad. Pub. Adminstrn., Royal Soc. Arts, Nat. Acad. Law and Social Scis. (hon. Cordoba, Argentina chpt.), Internat. Assn. for Impact Assessment (Rose Hulman Inst. Tech. award for outstanding achievement 1989), Am. Polit. Sci. Assn. (John M. Gaus award 1996), Natural Resource Coun. of Am. (Nat. Environ. Quality award 1997), Policy Studies Orgn. (Aaron Wildavsky book award 1996). Home: 4898 E Heritage Woods Rd Bloomington IN 47401-9175 Office: Indiana Univ Sch Pub & Environ Affairs Bloomington IN 47405 E-mail: lkcaldwe@indiana.edu.

CALDWELL, MARY ELLEN, English language educator; b. El Paso, Ark., Aug. 6, 1908; d. Clay and Mabel Grace (Coe) Fulks; m. Robert Atchison Caldwell, Feb. 22, 1936; 1 child, Elizabeth. PhB, U. Chgo., 1931, MA, 1933. Instr. English U. Ark., Fayetteville, 1940-42, U. Toledo, 1946-48; from instr. to asst. prof. to assoc. prof. U. N.D., Grand Forks, 1952-79, assoc. prof. emeritus, 1979—, prof. ext. divsn., 1979-2000. Author: North Dakota Division of the American Association of University Women, 1930-63, A History, 1964; co-author: The North Dakota Division of the American Association of University Women, 1964-84, 2d vol., 1984; contbr. revs. and articles to scholarly jours. Sec. citizen's com. Grand Forks Symphony Assn., 1960-66. Mem. AAUW (life, N.D. state pres. 1968-70), P.E.O., MLA (life), Soc. for Study of Midwestern Lit. (bibliography staff 1973-2002, MidAm. award for disting. contbns. to study of midwstern lit. 2000), Linguistic Cir. of Man. and N.D. (pres. 1981), Melville Soc. Democrat. Episcopalian. Home: 514 Oxford St Grand Forks ND 58203-2847

CALDWELL, MICHAEL FRANCIS, psychologist; b. Kansas City, Kans., Oct. 12, 1952; D in psychology, U. of Denver, 1988. Diplomate Am. Coll. of Forensic Medicine, 1996. Lectr. U. of Wis. - Madison, 1998—; sr. psychologist Mendota Juvenile Treatment Ctr., Madison, Wis., 1987—. Forensic cons. Michael F. Caldwell, PsyD, Middleton, Wis., 1987—. Grant, Office of Juvenile Justice and Delinquency Prevention, 1997—99, Office of Justice Assistance, OJJDP, 2001, 2002, 2002—03, 2003—. Mem.: APA. Catholic. Achievements include research in effective treatment of serious and violent juvenile offenders. Office: Michael F Caldwell PsyD PO Box 628043 Middleton WI 53562 E-mail: mfcaldwell@wisc.edu.

CALDWELL, NAOMI RACHEL, library media specialist, educator; b. Providence, Mar. 31, 1958; d. Atwood Alexander II and Juanita (Johnson) Caldwell; 1 child, William Earl Wood. BS, Clarion State Coll., 1980; MSLS, Clarion U. Pa., 1982; postgrad., Tex. A&M U., 1986-87, Providence Coll., 1990-92; PhD in Libr. and Info. Studies, U. Pitts., 2002. Cert. tchg. libr.; cert. libr. media specialist. Asst. dir., adult svcs. libr. Oil City (Pa.) Pub. Libr., 1984-85; microtext reference libr. Sterling C. Evans Libr., Tex. A&M U., College Station, 1985-87; libr. media specialist Nathan Bishop Mid. Sch., Providence, 1987-92; libr. sci. doctoral fellow dept. libr. sci. Sch. Libr. and Info. Sci. U. Pitts., 1992-94; sch. library media specialist Feinstein H.S. for Pub. Svc., Providence, 1994-99; asst. prof. U. R.I. Grad. Sch. Libr. Info. Studies, 2002—. Mem. discovery award com. U.S. Bd. on Books for Young People, 1994; mem. com. R.I. Children's Book Award, 1990—92, R.I. Read-Aloud, 1990—92; participant Native Am. and Alaskan Native Pre-Conf. to White House Conf. on Librs. and Info. Scis., Washington, 1991, George Washington U. Nat. Indian Policy Ctr. Forum on Native Am. Librs. and Info. Svcs., Washington, 1991; participant, spkr. Internat. Indigenous Librs. Forum, Auckland, New Zealand, 1999; hon. del. White House Conf. on Libr. and Info. Svcs., Washington, 1991; bd. dirs. Ocean State Freenet; mem. exec. bd. R.I. Ednl. Media Assn., 1996—97; cons. Am. Coll. Testing, 1995—; mem. exec. bd. Native Am. child literacy program If I Can Read, I Can Do Anything, 2001—; mem. Coalition Libr. Advocates, 2002—; presenter in field. Mem. editl. adv. bd., reviewer : Multicultural Rev., 1991—; mem. adv. bd. Native Ams. Info. Dir., 1992, OYATE, 1992—, Gale Ency. Multicultural Am., Native N.Am. Ref. Libr.; mem. exec. bd.: OYATE, 2001—; reviewer Clarion Books, Greenwood Press, Random House, Harcourt Brace Trade Divsn., Browndeer Press, Oryx Press; contbr. articles to profl. jours. Mem. State of R.I. Libr. Bd., 1996-97, Spl. Presdl. Adv. Com. on Libr. of Congress, 1996-97; mem. nominating com. R.I. chpt. Girl Scouts of Am., 1998-99. Mem.: ALA (councilor-at-large 1992—96, chmn. com. on status of women in librarianship 1995—97, nominating com. 1996—97, legis. assembly 1996—98, councilor-at-large 1996—2000, assembly on planning and budget 1998—99, presdl. task force spectrum program, com. on coms. 1999—2000, spectrum jury com. 2001—02, com. on diversity 2001—03, presdl. ad hoc com. 2002—), R.I. Coalition of Libr. Advs. (sec. 2003), Native Am. N.E. Librs., Worcraft Cir. Native Writers and Storytellers, Windwalker Coalition, Libr. Adminstrn. Mgmt. Assn., Spl. Librs. Assn., Am. Assn. Sch. Librs., Am. Indian Libr. Assn. (new mems. round table publicity com. 1986, new mems. round table minority recruitment com. 1986—88, OLOS libr. svcs. for Am. Indian people subcom. 1986—88, ALCTS micropub. com. 1988—90, OLOS libr. svcs. for Am. Indian people subcom. 1990—91, pres. 1990—94, mem. coun. com. on minority concerns 1991—92, chmn. 1992—94, sec. 1994—96, mem. coun. com. on minority concerns 1994—96, book award task force 2002—03). Home: 475 Sowams Rd Barrington RI 02806-2745 Office: U RI Grad Sch Libr and Info Studies 11 Rodman Hall Kingston RI 02881 E-mail: inpeacencw@aol.com.

CALDWELL, PHILIP, retired automobile manufacturing company executive, retired financial services company executive; b. Bourneville, Ohio, Jan. 27, 1920; s. Robert Clyde and Wilhelmina (Hemphill) C.; m. Betsey Chinn Clark, Oct. 27, 1945; children: Lawrence Clark, Lucy Hemphill Caldwell-Stair (Mrs. Thomas O. Stair), Désirée Caldwell Armitage (Mrs. William F. Armitage, Jr.). BA in Econs., Muskingum Coll., 1940, HHD (hon.), 1974; MBA, Harvard U., 1942; DBA (hon.), Upper Iowa U., 1978; LLD (hon.), Boston U., 1979, Ea. Mich. U., 1979, Miami U., 1980, Davidson Coll., 1982, Ohio U., 1984, U. Mich., 1984, Lawrence Inst. Tech., 1984. Served to lt. USNR, 1942-46; civilian Navy Dept., 1946-53, dep. dir. procurement policy div., 1948-53; with Ford Motor Co., 1953-90, v.p., gen. mgr. truck ops., 1968-70; pres., dir. Philco-Ford Corp. subs., 1970-71, v.p. mfg. group N.Am. automotive ops., 1971-72; chmn., CEO Ford of Europe, Inc., 1972-73, exec. v.p. internat. automotive ops., 1973-77; dir. Ford of Europe Inc., Ford Latin Am., Ford Mideast and Africa, Ford Asia Pacific, 1973-85; vice chmn. bd. Ford Motor Co., 1977-79, dep. CEO, 1978-79, pres., 1978-80, CEO, 1979-85, chmn. bd. dirs., 1980-85, dir., 1973-90, Ford Motor Credit Co., Ford of Can., 1977-85; mem. Ford European Adv. Coun., 1976-88, chmn., 1987-88; sr. mng. dir. Lehman Bros. Inc., N.Y.C., 1985-98. Chmn. bd. dirs. Mettler-Toledo, Inc., 1996-98; bd. dirs. Russell Reynolds Assoc., Inc., The Mex. Fund, Mettler-Toledo, Inc., Waters Corp., Castech Aluminum Group, Inc., 1994-96, Chase Manhattan Corp., Chase Manhattan Bank NA, 1982-85; Digital Equipment Corp., 1980-95; Federated Dept. Stores Inc., 1984-88; The Kellogg Company, 1985-92; Shearson Lehman Bros. Holdings, 1985-93; Specialty Coatings Grp. Inc., 1991-93, Zurich Am. Ins. Group, 1987-99; Zurich Reinsurance Ctr. Holdings, 1993-97; mem. policy com. The Bus. Roundtable, 1980-85, Bus. Coun., 1980-2001, Com. for Econ. Devel., 1979—, Conf. Bd., 1979—, Trilateral Commn., 1979-86; mem. U.S. Trade Rep. Adv. Com. for Trade Negotiations, 1983-85; mem. Pres.'s Export Coun., 1985-89; mem. Mex.-U.S. Bus. Com., 1985—; adv. coun. Japan-U.S. Econ. Rels., 1981-85; dir. Japan Soc., 1983-89, vice chmn., chmn. exec. com. 1987-89; mem. motor truck com. Automobile Mfg. Assn., 1964-70; mem. transp. com. U.S. C. of C., 1968-77; mem. U.S. coun. Internat. C. of C., 1973-77, U.S. Coun. for Internat. Bus., 1977-85; mem. internat. adv. com. Chase Manhattan Bank, 1979-85; mem. Coun. Fgn. Rels., 1985—; mem. Zurich Fin. Svcs. Group U.S. Adv. Bd., 1999-2001. Trustee Muskingum Coll., 1967—, Winterthur Mus. and Gardens, 1986-2000; dir. Harvard Bus. Sch. Assocs., 1977-93; dir. Inst. Europeen de Adminstrn. des Affaires (INSEAD), 1978-81, chmn. U.S. adv. bd., 1979-84, mem. internat. coun., 1983-2002; bd. advisors The Jerome Levy Econs. Inst., 1988-2001; bus. adv. coun. Kent State U., 1968-70; mem. Merrill-Palmer Inst., 1971-81, New Detroit, Inc., vice-chair, 1977-85, Detroit Renaissance, 1979-85, dir. Detroit Symphony Orch., 1974-85; charter mem. Bus. Higher Edn. Forum, 1979-84; dir. Citizens Rsch. Coun. of Mich., 1980-85; hon. bd. mem. Plan Internat. USA, 1989—; dir. Econ. Club of Detroit, 1977-86. Recipient 1st William A. Jump Meml. award, 1950, Meritorious Civilian Svc. awardUS Navy Dept., 1953, Disting. Svc. Alumni award Muskingum Coll., 1978, Internat.Exec. of Yr. award Sch. Mgmt. Brigham Young U., 1983, Bus. Statesman of Yr. award Harvard Bus. Sch. Club Greater N.Y., 1984, Businessman of Yr. award Harvard Bus. Sch. Club Columbus, Ohio, 1984, Alumni Achievement award Harvard Bus. Sch.,1985; named Automotive Industry Leader of Yr. Automotive Hall of Fame, 1984; Harvard Bus. Sch. Philip Caldwell Professorship of Bus. Adminstrn. named in his honor, 1990; named Statesman of Yr. Harvard Bus. Sch. Club Detroit, 1991; elected laureate Nat. Bus. Hall of Fame, 1995. Mem. The Links, River Club (N.Y.C.). Office: Ford Motor Co W Bldg 225 High Ridge Rd Stamford CT 06905-3000 Fax: 203-357-8241.

CALDWELL, RODNEY KENT, lawyer; b. Washington, Feb. 19, 1937; s. Rodney Huntington and Marion Elizabeth Caldwell; m. Marjorie Lee Zink, Apr. 15, 1965 (div. 1975); children: Dana Kent, Susan Ashley; m. Yolanda Silva, June 22, 1979; 1 child, David Huntington. BChemE, U. Va., 1959; JD, U. Houston, 1969. Bar: Tex. 1969, U.S. Supreme Ct. 1975. With Howrey Simon Arnold & White, LLP (formerly Arnold, White & Durkee), Houston, 1970—. Author: Patent Litigation: Procedure & Tactics, 1978-84. Lt. USAF, 1959-62. Fellow Tex. Bar Found., Houston Bar Found.; mem. ABA, Am. Intellectual Property Law Assn., Internat. Bar Assn., Internat. Intellectual Property Assn., Univ. Club., Army and Navy Club. Methodist. Home: 4021 Ella Lee Ln Houston TX 77027-3910 Office: Howrey Simon Arnold & White LLP 750 Bering Dr Houston TX 77057-2198 E-mail: caldwellr@howrey.com.

CALDWELL, ROSSIE JUANITA BROWER, retired library service educator; b. Columbia, S.C., Nov. 4, 1917; d. Rossie Lee and Henrietta Olivia (Irby) Brower; m. Harlowe Evans Caldwell, Aug. 6, 1943 (dec. 1983); 1 adopted dau., Rossie Laverne Caldwell Jenkins. BA magna cum laude, Claflin U., 1937; MS, S.C. State Coll., 1952; MSLS, U. Ill., 1959. Tchr. libr. Reed St. H.S., Anderson, S.C., 1937-39, Emmett Scott H.S., Rock Hill, S.C., 1939-42, Wilkinson H.S., Orangeburg, S.C., 1942-43, libr., 1945-57; civilian pers. War Dept., Tuskegee Army Air Field, 1943-45; asst. prof., then assoc. prof. libr. svc. dept. S.C. State U., Orangeburg, 1957-83. Co-editor (mag.) Trinity United Meth. Women; contbg. author book in field; author articles. Assoc. mem. Orangeburg Regional Hosp. Aux.; mem. Historical Soc. S.C.; trustee, Christian adv. United Meth. Ch. in S.C., 1978—86; co-chair history and archives com. Trinity United Meth. Ch. Recipient Presdl. citation Claflin Coll., 1989, Links award for cmty. achievement, 1998, numerous ann. vol. work citations; Founders Day honoree, 1994,

Heritage Club award Claflin U., 2000; named to Claflin Coll. Hall of Fame, 1997; Woman of Yr., United Meth. Women, 2003. Mem. NAACP (life), ALA (continuing life mem.), ALA Black Caucus (emeritus), AAUP (emeritus), VFW Aux. (life), Nat. Women's History Mus. (charter, Washington), S.C. Libr. Assn. (hon.), AAUW (editor Orangeburg br. bull.), Friends of the Libr. (Orangeburg County), Palmetto Med. Dental Pharm. Assn. Aux. (historian, state pres., Woman of Yr. 1972, Spl. Longevity award 2003), Links Club (archivist, historian), As You Like It Bridge Club, Daus. of Isis, Claflin Univ. Forerunners Club (coord., founder 1987), Golden Scholarship Club (co-founder 1987), Sigma Pi Phi (archousa, Claflin queen 1935-37, emeritus queen 1999), Phi Delta Kappa (emeritus mem.), Alpha Kappa Alpha (life mem.; Golden Soror 2001), Omega Psi Phi (Omega Lambda Sigma chpt. Scroll of Honor 1988), Beta Phi Mu (mem. internat. Libr. hon. soc., mem. libr. sci. soc.). Home: 1320 Ward Ln NE Orangeburg SC 29118-1342 E-mail: bojal@hotmail.com.

CALDWELL, SARAH, opera producer, conductor, stage director and administrator; b. Maryville, Mo., Mar. 6, 1924; Student, U. Ark., Hendrix Coll., New Eng. Conservatory, Berkshire Music Ctr., Tanglewood, Mass.; D. Mus. (hon.), Harvard U., Simmons Coll., Bates Coll., Bowdoin Coll. Mem. faculty Berkshire Music Ctr.; dir. Boston U. Opera Workshop, 1953-57; created dept. music theater Boston U.; founded Boston Opera Group (later became Opera Co. of Boston), 1957, sinced served as artistic dir. and condr., 1968—; disting. prof. dept. music U. Ark., Fayetteville, 1999—. Asst. to Boris Goldovsky in direction of New Eng. Opera Co.; operatic directorial debut with Rake's Progress, Opera Workshop, 1953; operatic debut as condr. with Opera Group of Boston, 1957, Carnegie Hall debut with Am. Symphony Orch., 1974; condr. and/or dir. maj. opera cos. in U.S., including N.Y. Met. Opera, Dallas Civic Opera, Houston Grand Opera, N.Y.C. Opera; condr. with maj. orchs. including: Indpls. Symphony, Milw. Symphony, Am. Symphony, N.Y. Philharmonic; condr. at Ravinia Festival, 1976. Recipient Rogers and Hammerstein award. Achievements include 1st woman to appear as conductor with the Met. Opera, N.Y.C., 1976. Address: 651 W Wilson St Fayetteville AR 72701-9070 also: 651 N Wilson Ave Fayetteville AR 72701-3346 Office: Univ Ark MB 201 Dept Music Fayetteville AR 72701

CALDWELL, STRATTON FRANKLIN, kinesiology educator; b. Mpls., Aug. 25, 1926; s. Kenneth Simms and Margaret Mathilda (Peterson) C.; m. Mary Lynn Shaffer, Aug. 28, 1955 (div. May 1977); children: Scott Raymond, Karole Elizabeth; m. Sharee' Deanna Ockerman, Aug. 6, 1981; 1 stepchild, Shannon Sharee' Calder. Student, San Diego State Coll., 1946-48; BS in Edn. cum laude, U. So. Calif., 1951, PhD in Phys. Edn., 1966; MS in Phys. Edn., U. Oreg., 1953. Teaching asst. dept. phys. edn. UCLA, 1953-54, assoc. in phys. edn., 1957-65, vis. asst. prof. phys. edn., 1967; dir. phys. edn. Regina (Sask., Can.) Young Men's Christian Assn., 1954-56; tchr. sec. grades, dir. athletic Queen Elizabeth Jr.-Sr. High Sch., Calgary, Alta., Can., 1956-57; asst. prof. phys. edn. San Fernando Valley State Coll., Northridge, Calif., 1965-68, assoc. prof., 1968-71; prof. phys. edn. dept. kinesiology Calif. State U., Northridge, 1971-90, prof. kinesiology, 1990-92, prof. kinesiology emeritus, 1992. Vis. asst. prof. phys. edn. UCLA, 1967; vis. assoc. prof. phys. edn. U. Wash., Seattle, 1968, U. Calif., Santa Barbara, 1969. Author (with Cecil and Joan Martin Hollingsworth) Golf, 1959, (with Rosalind Cassidy) Humanizing Physical Education: Methods for the Secondary School Movement Program, 5th edit., 1975; also poetry, book chpts., articles in profl. jours., book revs. With USN, 1944-46. Recipient Meritorious Performance and Profl. Promise award Calif. state U., 1986, 87, 89, Disting. Teaching award, 1992; AAPHERD fellow, 1962, Am. Coll. Sports Medicine fellow, 1965, Can. Assn. for Health, Phys. Edn., and Recreation fellow, 1971. Fellow Am. Alliance for Health, Phys. Edn., Recreation and Dance (Centennial Commn. 1978-85, cert. appreciation 1985), Am. Coll. Sports Medicine; mem. Calif. Assn. for Health, Phys. Edn., Recreation and Dance (pres. L.A. coll. and univ. unit 1969-70, v.p. phys. edn. com. 1970-71, mem. editorial bd. CAHPER Jour. 1970-71, mem. forum 1970-71, Disting. Svc. award 1974, Honor award 1988, Verne Landreth award 1992), Nat. Assn. for Phys. Edn. in Higher Edn. (charter), Sport Art Acad., Nat. Assn. for Sport and Phys. Edn., N.Y. Acad. Scis., N.Am. Soc. for Sports History, Sport Lit. Assn., Acad. Am. Poets, Phi Epsilon Kappa (Svc. award 1980), Alpha Tau Omega (charter, Silver Circle award 1976, Golden Circle award 2001), Phi Delta Kappa, Phi Kappa Phi, others. Republican. Mem. Christian Ch. Avocations: reading, writing. Home: 80 N Kanan Rd Oak Park CA 91377-1105 *The consummate teacher is the artist who consistently attempts to deepen and enrich human experience, to weave the fabric of feeling, mood, attitude and idea into a tailor-made garment of personal meaning.*

CALDWELL, THOMAS HOWELL, JR., accountant, financial management consultant; b. Wichita Falls, Tex., Feb. 5, 1934; s. Thomas Howell and LaVerne Louise C.; m. Bernell Irons, Apr. 12, 1968 (div. Jan. 1979); 1 child, Thomas Howell III (dec.). BA in Religion, Baylor U., 1956; postgrad., Tex. Christian U., 1958-63, North Tex. State U., 1973-75; LLD (hon.), London Inst. Applied Rsch., 1994. Cert. internal auditor. Tech. writer Gen. Dynamics, Ft. Worth, 1956-60; asst. dir. pers. Harris Hosp., Ft. Worth, 1960-62; with fiduciary tax sect. lst Nat. Bank, Ft. Worth, 1962-64; jr. acct. various CPA's, Dallas, 1964-65; auditor Def. Contract Audit Agy., Dallas, 1965-74; tax appraiser, mcpl. acct. City of McKinney, Tex., 1974-75; systems acct. USDA, Dallas, 1975-83; auditor U.S. Army C.E., Dallas, 1983-86; acct. rep. IRS, Dallas, 1986-87; systems acct. Def. Fin. & Acctg. Svc., Dallas, 1987-93; fin. mgmt. cons. Caldwell Fin. Mgmt. Cons., Dallas, 1993—. Mem. Airport Amb. Vol. Program, Dallas Ft. Worth Internat. Airport, 1999—. Mem. jr. bd. lst Bapt. Ch., Dallas. With USAFR, 1957-63. Mem. Descs. Vets. Mexican War, (bd. dirs., treas.), Baylor U. Ex-Students Assn., Masons, Shriners, Scottish Rite. Republican. Avocations: flying, dogs, watching football, church. Home and Office: 10822 Pagewood Dr Dallas TX 75230-4468

CALDWELL, TONI LUCILLE, b. Chambersburg, Pa., June 25, 1953; d. Herbert Leroy Waters and Ruth Virginia (Webb) Richardson; children: D. Marquis Henry, Sharif Q. Student, Am. U., 1973—74, Rutgers U., Newark, 1981—83; BS in Mgmt., Caldwell Coll., 2001, MS cum laude in Contemporary Mgmt., 2003. Legal sec. Kleinfield, Kaplan & Becker, Washington, 1974-76, Budd Larner Gross Rosenbaum Greerberg & Sade, Short Hills, NJ, 1988-93; office mgr. Smith & Howard Assocs., Washington, 1976-78; adminstrv. mgr., corp. treas. Common Bros. USA, N.Y.C., 1978-79; adminstrv. asst. to exec. dir.-supr. automobile equipment N.J. Transit Corp., Newark, 1980-85; ind. contractor, 1985-88; campaign mgr. Com. To Elect Corinna Kay Williams, East Orange, NJ, 1993; mgr. chambers ops. U.S. Dist. Ct. for N.J., Newark, 1996—2002, mediation adminstr., 1993-96; pres., CEO, InHim Charities, Inc., East Orange, 1997—2002; exec. dir., CEO Tri-City People's Corp., East Orange, 2002—. Exec. v.p. N.J. chpt. Conf. Minority Transp. Ofcls., 1982—85; adj. prof. Gibbs Coll., 2003—. Pres. East Orange H.S. PTA, 1991—95, sec.-treas., 1995—2002; chmn. East Orange Unified Coun. PTAs and PTOs, 1992—2002; sec. bd. dirs. East Orange Police Athletic League, 1993—96; chmn. bd. mgmt. East Orange YMCA, 1993—97, chmn. minority achievers bd. govs., 1993—97; bd. dirs. Met. YMCA of Oranges, 1996—97; pres. Essex County Coun. PTAs, 1996—2002; chair, bd. dirs. Tri-City Peoples Corp., 1996—2002; treas. Newark Cmty. Devel. Network, 2003—. Named Ward Woman of Yr., East Orange City Coun., 1993, 2d Ward Unsung Hero, 1997; recipient Mayor's Adult Vol. Cmty. Svc. award, City of East Orange, 1987, Cmty. Svc. award, Essex County Bd. Chosen Freeholders, 1998, numerous awards, PTA and East Orange Sch. Dist. Mem.: LWV (dir. voters svcs. East Orange chpt. 1997—). Democrat. Avocations: reading, music. Office: Tri City Peoples Corp 55 Washington St East Orange NJ 07017 E-mail: Tonicald@aol.com., tcaldwell@tri-citypeoples.org.

CALDWELL, WALLACE CAUGHEY, physicist, engineer; b. Britt, Iowa, Sept. 9, 1918; s. Harry Vincent and Julia Leona Caldwell; m. Beth Caldwell, Feb. 8, 1948 (dec. Dec. 6, 1995); children: Linda R. Caldwell Gahring, Gregory G.; m. LaVaune Wood, Aug. 1, 1998. BS in Physics, Iowa State U., 1939, MS in Physics, 1940; PhD in Physics, Cornell U., 1948. Student aide Iowa State U., Ames, 1935-39, tchg. asst., 1939-41, Cornell U., Ithaca, N.Y., 1941-43; computation cli. Met. Life Ins. Co., N.Y.C., summer 1941; student engr. Western Electric Co., summer 1942; staff mem. radiation lab. MIT, 1943-46; tchg. asst. Cornell U., 1946, NRC predoctoral fellow, 1946-48; asst. prof. Iowa State U., Ames, 1948-51; cons. The Bendix Corp., Teterboro, N.J., 1951-52, chief engr. Eatontown, N.J., 1952-55, mgr. Holmdel, N.J., 1955-62; dir. Collins Radio Co., Cedar Rapids, Iowa, 1962-70; budget officer Bd. Regents, Des Moines, Iowa, 1970-83; adj. prof. Iowa State U., 1983-93, adj. prof. emeritus, 1993—. Co-author: Microwave Duplexers, 1946, Physics-The Root Science, 1995. Del. Rep. Party, 1980. Mem. Kiwanis (treas. 1980-97), Pi Mu Epsilon, Phi Kappa Phi, Sigma Xi. Methodist. Avocations: music, skiing, ice skating, boating, traveling. Home: 3524 Grand Ave Des Moines IA 50312-4300 Office: Iowa State Univ 2229 Lincoln Way Ames IA 50011-0001

CALDWELL, WALTER EDWARD, editor, small business owner; b. L.A., Dec. 29, 1941; s. Harold Elmer and Esther Ann (Fuller) Caldwell; m. Donna Edith Davis, June 27, 1964; 1 child, Arnie-Jo. AA, Riverside (Calif.) City Coll., 1968. Sales and stock profl. Sears Roebuck & Co., Riverside, 1963-65; dispatcher Rohr Corp., Riverside, 1965-67; trainee Aetna Fin., Riverside, 1967-68, mgr. San Bruno, Cal., 1968-70, Amfac Thrift & Loan, Oakland, Calif., 1970-74; free lance writer San Jose, Calif., 1974-76; news dir. Sta. KAVA Radio, Burney, Calif., 1977-79; editor-pub. Mountain Echo, Fall River Mills, Calif., 1979-81. Co-author: (book) Yearbook of Modern Poetry, 1976. Participant Am. Leadership Conf., San Diego, 1989; pres. United Way, Burney, 1979, co-chmn., 1977, chmn., 1979; disaster relief worker ARC, Redding, Calif., 1988—91, disaster action team leader, 1991—95; bd. dirs. Shasta County Women's Refuge, Redding, 1988—91, Shasta County Econ. Devel. Task Force, 1985—86, exec. bd. dirs., 1988; leader Girl Scouts U.S., San Jose, 1973—76; announcer various local parades; trustee Mosquito Abatement Dist., Burney, 1978—87, 1989—, chmn., 1990—; commr. Burney Fire Protection Dist., 1987—91, v.p., 1990, pres., 1991; chmn. Burney Basin Days Com., Calif., 1983—95, Hay Days Com., 1995—96; alt. commr. Local Agy. Formation Commn. Shasta County, 1995—; mem. Intermountain Hospice, 1998 ; del. Farmers and Ranchers Congress, St. Louis, 1985; candidate Shasta County Bd. Suprs., 1992; bd. dirs. Shasta County Econ. Devel. Corp., 1986—90, Crossroads, 1985; pres. Intermountain Devel. Corp., 1989. With USMC, 1959—63. Mem.: Calif. Newspaper Pubs. Assn., Fall River Valley C. of C. (bd. dirs. 1991, pres. 1995), Burney Basin C. of C. (advt. com. 1982, Cmty. Action award 1990—93), Shriners (sec.-treas. 1992—94), Masons (master 1995), Moose, Lions (student spkr. chmn. Fall River 1983—97, co-chmn. disaster com., newsletter chmn. dist. 4-C1 1989—91, 1st v.p. 1991, pres. 1992), Rotary (pres. 1977—78, chmn. bike race 1981—85), Am. Legion (2d vice comdr. 2000—02, post boys state chmn. 2001—02, citation of recognition 1987, Cmty. Action award 1989, 1993). Republican. Avocations: photography, painting, archaeology. Office: Mountain Echo Main St Fall River Mills CA 96028 also: PO Box 224 Fall River Mills CA 96028-0224 E-mail: mtecho@shasta.com.

CALDWELL, WESLEY STUART, III, lawyer, lobbyist; b. Teaneck, N.J., June 3, 1946; s. Wesley S. Jr. and Helen Skrek C.; m. Theresa Hale, Apr. 20, 1970 (div. Jan. 1988); children: Ashley Hale, Ferris Elena; m. J.R. Dillenback, May 27, 1988. BA in Liberal Arts, Fairleigh Dickinson U., 1968; JD, Rutgers U., 1975. Bar: N.J. 1975, U.S. Dist. Ct. N.J. 1975, U.S. Supreme Ct. 1992. Dep. atty. gen. N.J. Atty. Gen.'s Office, Trenton, 1975-78; assoc. gen. counsel Prudential Reins. Co., Newark, 1978-79; v.p. Am. Ins. Assn., N.Y.C., 1979-86; ptnr. LeBoeuf, Lamb, Greene & MacRae, Newark, 1986-95, Caldwell Megna & Brewster, Trenton, 1995-97, Caldwell Megna, Trenton, 1997—2001; atty. Wesley S. Caldwell III Law Offices, Trenton, 2002—. Regulatory counsel AFLAC, Columbus, Ga., 1991—, Clarendon Ins., N.Y.C.; others. With U.S. Army, 1969-72. Mem. N.J. Bar Assn. (past chmn. ins. law sect.). Avocations: golf, pocket billiards. Home: 1266 River Rd Titusville NJ 08560-1603 Office: 224 W State St Trenton NJ 08608-1002 E-mail: wscaldwell@inslawcaldwell.com.

CALDWELL, WILLARD E. psychologist, educator; b. Flushing L.I., N.Y., July 10, 1920; s. Howard Eugene and Lillian (Warner) C. AB in Psychology, U. Fla., 1940, MA in Psychology, 1941; PhD in Psychology, Cornell U., 1946; postgrad., Washington Sch. Psychiatry, 1948-53. Lic. psychologist, D.C. Grad. asst. psychology U. Fla., Gainesville, 1940-41; teaching asst. Psychology Dept. Cornell (N.Y.) U., 1943-46; prof. psychology, dept. chmn. Mary Baldwin Coll., Staunton, Va., 1947-48; asst. prof., assoc. prof., prof. psychology The George Washington U., Washington, 1948-85, prof. emeritus psychology, 1985—. Psychotherapist. Editor, contbg. author: Principles of Comparative Psychology, 1960; contbr. over 50 articles to profl. jours. Pvt. U.S. Army, 1941-42. Mem. APA, Am. Psychol. Soc., D.C. Psychology Assn., Internat. Soc. Biometeorology. Republican. Episcopalian. Avocations: swimming, gardening, traveling. Home: Apt 316 1101 New Hampshire Ave NW Washington DC 20037-1509

CALDWELL, WILLIAM EDWARD, educational administration educator, arbitrator; b. Providence, Aug. 18, 1928; s. James E. and Eva E. (Barker) C.; m. Doris E. Parlee, June 17, 1950; children: William E., Donna E., Allen E. BA in Math., Ea. Nazarene Coll., 1950; MEd in Secondary Edn., U. N.H., 1957; PhD in Ednl. Adminstrn., NYU, 1968. Cert. prin., supt.; arbitrator. Tchr. math., dir. music, coach pub. schs., Berwick, Maine, 1950-54; tchr. math., supr. pub. schs. Valley Stream, N.Y., 1954-61; guidance counselor, prin. pub. schs. Manchester, Conn., 1961-67; dir. secondary tchr. tng. U. Hartford, Conn., 1967-69; exec. dir. Pa. Sch. Study Coun., University Park, 1970-78; prof. ednl. adminstrn. Pa. State U., University Park, 1969—, pres. faculty coun., 1985-86, ombudsman Coll. Edn., 1986-90, chmn. edn. adminstrn. program, 1987-90, chmn. adminstrn., policy, founds. and internat. edn., 1990-93, prof. emeritus, 1993—. State dir. mediation Commonwealth of Pa., Harrisburg, 1979-80; conciliator, fact finder Pa. Labor Rels. Bd., Harrisburg, 1971—; arbitrator AAA, FMCS, Pa. Labor Rels. Bd., 1971—. Author: Collective Negotiation in Public Education, 1970, Agreement, Policy for Principal/Supervisor, 1983; mem. editl. bd. Jour. Individual Employment Rights, 1993—; contbr. articles to profl. jours., chpts. to books, author reports. Nat. del. Am. Assn. Sch. Adminstrs., Washington, 1976, 77, 79; bd. dirs. Fed. Credit Union, Manchester, Conn., 1963-67, Appalachian Ednl. Lab., Charleston, W.Va., 1970-78; examiner Pa. Civil Svc. Commn., Harrisburg, 1972-79. Lt. col. USMCR, ret. 1988. Recipient Commendation award Pa. Sch. Bds. Assn., 1980, Acad. Achievement award NYU, 1969, Outstanding Svc. award Commonwealth Pa., 1973, Outstanding Svc. award Pa. Dept. Labor, 1987, Excellence in Instrn. award Pa. Sch. Study Coun., 1994, William E. Caldwell Excellence in Adminstrn. award Pa. Sch. Study Coun., 1997—. Mem. Am. Ednl. Rsch. Assn. (presenter), Pa. Assn. Secondary Sch. Prins. (rsch. chmn., Commendation award 1983, Excellence in Edn. award 1986).

CALDWELL, WILLIAM FRANK, aerospace project manager, mechanical engineer; s. Frank Leroy and Carol Ida Caldwell; m. Lee Ann Ainsworth, June 24, 1989; children: Melanie Rae, Lauren Amanda, Jared William. Degree in mech. engring.(hon.), U. of Calif., Davis, 1988, Stanford U., Palo Alto, Calif., 1995. Registered profl. engr., Calif. State Bd. of Registration for Profl. Engrs. Aerospace project mgr. NASA Ames Rsch. Ctr., Moffett Field, Calif., 1989—. Contbr. articles to profl. jours. (IEEE Transactions Prize Paper award, 1992). Mem.: ASME (assoc.), Pi Mu Epsilon, Tau Beta Pi, Outstanding Coll. Students of Am. Soc. Office: NASA Ames Rsch Ctr Mail Stop 213-4 Moffett Field CA 94035

CALDWELL, ZOE, actress, director; b. Hawthorn, Victoria, Australia, Sept. 14, 1933; m. Robert Whitehead, 1968; 2 sons: Sam, Charlie. Attended, Meth. Ladies Coll., Melbourne, Australia. Dorothy F. Schmidt Vis. Eminent Scholar in Theatre, Fla. Atlantic U., 1989-93. Theater debut as mem. of Union Theatre Repertory Co., Melbourne, 1953; other appearances in The Madwoman of Chaillot, Goodman Theatre, Chgo., 1964, The Way of the World, The Caucasian Chalk Circle, Mpls., Slapstick Tragedy, N.Y.C., 1966 (Best Supporting Actress Tony award 1966), Antony and Cleopatra, Richard III, The Merry Wives of Windsor, Stratford, Ont., Can., Shakespeare Festival, 1967, The Prime of Miss Jean Brodie, 1967 (Best Actress Tony award 1968), Colette, N.Y.C., 1970, A Bequest to the Nation, London, 1970, The Creation of the World and Other Business, N.Y.C., 1972, Love and Master Will, Washington, 1973, The Dance of Death, N.Y.C., 1974, Long Day's Journey Into Night, N.Y.C., Washington, 1976, Medea, N.Y.C., 1982 (Best Actress Tony award), Lillian, 1986, Come A-Waltzing With Me, A Perfect Ganesh, 1993, Master Class, 1995 (Best Actress Tony award 1996); dir. (plays): An Almost Perfect Person, N.Y.C., 1977, Richard II, Stratford, Ont., 1979, These Men, off-Broadway, 1980, The Taming of the Shrew, Hamlet, Am. Shakespeare Theatre, 1985, Vita and Virginia, N.Y.C., 1995. Decorated Order Brit. Empire; recipient Theatre World award, 1966, John Gielgud award Shakespeare Guild/Folger Shakespeare Libr., 1998, Linda Wilson Lifetime Achievement award for Excellence in the Theatre U. Fla., 1998, Bernard B. Jacobs Excellence in the Theatre award/U.J.A. Fedn. N.Y., 1999, medal of distinction Barnard Coll., 1999. Address: Whitehead Stevens 1501 BroadwaySte 1614 New York NY 10036

CALDWELL-SMITH, GAETANA LEE, writer; d. Ennis Combs Caldwell and Maria Esperanza Ilya-Salituri Sanchez Hill; children: Roark Smith, Terrence Smith, Douglas Smith. BA cum laude, San Francisco State U., 1994. Comml. ins. underwriter Fireman's Fund Ins. Co., San Francisco, 1978—84; account rep. Marsh & McLennan Ins. Co., San Francisco, 1984—97; theatre writer Socialist Action Newspaper, San Francisco, 1998—2002. Author: (solo performance plays) The Cynthia Trilogy: Part I, The Sign, 1996 (1st prize Dominican Players, San Rafael, Calif., 1998); actor: (solo perfornace) The Cynthia Trilogy: Part I, The Sign, 1996 (2nd prize Dominican Players, San Rafael, Calif., 1998). Mem.: Wild Plum (writer 2001—02), San Francisco Bay Area Theatre Critics Cir. (theatre writer 2001—02). Avocations: swimming, bicycling, hiking.

CALE, CHARLES GRIFFIN, lawyer, private investor; b. St. Louis, Aug. 19, 1940; s. Julian Dutro and Judith Hadley (Griffin) C.; m. Jessie Leete Rawn, Dec. 30, 1978; children: Whitney Rawn, Walter Griffin, Elizabeth Judith. BA, Principia Coll., Elsah, Ill., 1961; LLB, Stanford U., 1964; LLM, U. So. Calif., 1966. Bar: Calif. 1965. Pvt. practice, L.A., 1965—90; ptnr. Adams, Duque & Hazeltine, L.A., 1970—81, Morgan, Lewis & Bockius, L.A., 1981—91. Bd. dirs., co-chmn., CEO World Cup USA 1994, Inc., L.A., 1991. Group v.p. sports L.A. Olympic Organizing Com., 1982-84; assoc. counselor U.S. Olympic Com., 1985, spl. asst. to pres., 1985-89, asst. to pres, dir. olympic del., 1989-92; bd. dirs. Century 21 Real Estate-Can. Ltd., 1995-97, Rapattoni Corp., 2001—, Foresters Equity Services Corp., 2001—. Trustee St. John's Hosp. and Med. Ctr., Santa Monica, Marymount H.S.; asst. chief de mission U.S. Olylmpic Team, 1988; bd. dirs. Hallum Prevention of Child Abuse Fund, 1976-96. Recipient Gold medal of Youth and Sports, France, 1984. Mem. State Bar Calif., Calif. Club, L.A. Country Club, The Beach Club, Ind. Order Foresters (bd. dirs. 1993-2001), Eagle Springs Golf Club, Country Club of the Rockies. Office: PO Box 688 Pacific Palisades CA 90272-0688

CALEGARI, MARIA, ballerina; b. N.Y.C., Mar. 30, 1957; d. Richard A. and Marion (Gentile) C. Student, DuPons Dance Studio, Queens, 1960-66, Ballet Acad., 1966-71, Sch. Am. Ballet, 1971-74. Mem. corps de ballet N.Y.C. Ballet, 1974-81, soloist, 1981-83, prin., 1983-94; guest artist Richmond Ballet, 1996—; artistic dir. dance Conn. Conservatory of the Performing Arts, New Milford, 2002—; artistic dir. The Maria Calegari Schl of Ballet, New Milford, Conn., 2003—. Artist-in-residence Richmond Ballet, Richmond Ctr. for Dance, State Ballet of Va., 1997—98, Conn. Cons. of Performing Arts, New Milford, 1999—. Dancer in N.Y.C. Ballet's Balanchine Celebration, 1993, Celebrating Balanchine, Kennedy Ctr., 1995. Repétiteur George Balanchine Trust. Recipient Alumni award Profl. Children's Sch., 1986. Address: 404 Richardsville Rd Carmel NY 10512-3771 E-mail: mcale50064@aol.com.

CALENOFF, LEONID, radiologist; b. Vienna, Aug. 24, 1923; arrived in U.S., 1957, naturalized, 1962; s. Albert and Anna (Prover) C.; m. Miriam Arnon, Oct. 30, 1955; children— Jean Zucker, Deborah Lipoff. MD, U. Paris, 1955. Diplomate Am. Bd. Radiology. Intern Jewish Hosp., Cin., 1958; resident in radiology U. Ill. Med. Center, Chgo., 1959-61; asst. radiologist Ill. Research and Ednl. Hosp., Chgo., 1961-64; chief radiology Chgo. State Hosp., 1963-68; dir. radiology Sheridan Gen. Hosp., Chgo., 1964-68; attending radiologist West Side VA Hosp., Chgo., 1963-68, Rehab. Inst. Chgo., 1974-89, chief diagnostic radiology, 1974-86; attending radiologist Northwestern Meml. Hosp., Chgo., 1968—2003, chief outpatient diagnostic radiology, 1979—2003, vice chmn. dept. radiology, 1991-96; chief diagnostic radiology Passavant Pavillion of Northwestern Meml. Hosp., 1972-79; asst. prof. radiology Northwestern U. Med. Sch., 1970-73, assoc. prof., 1973-78, prof., 1978—2003, prof. emeritus, 2003—. Author articles in field, chpts. in books.; Editor: Radiology of Spinal Cord Injury, 1981. Fellow Am. Coll. Radiology; mem. Radiol. Soc. N.Am., Am. Roentgen Ray Soc. Home: 1515 N Astor St #18A Chicago IL 60610-1627 E-mail: l-calenoff@northwestern.edu.

CALETTI, DEB L. writer; b. San Rafael, Calif., June 16, 1963; d. Paul Albert Caletti and Evelyn Ann Siler; children: Samantha Bannon, Nicholas Bannon. BA in Journalism, U. Wash., 1985. Mem. adv. bd. Bellevue (Wash.) C.C. Ctr. for Liberal Arts; spkr. and lyricist. Author: The Queen of Everything, 2002, Honey, Baby, Sweetheart, 2003. Literary fellow, Artist Trust-Wash. State Arts Commn., 2001. Mem.: PEN USA, Amnesty Internat. Avocations: painting, writing.

CALEVAS, HARRY POWELL, management consultant; b. Williamsburg, Va., Nov. 18, 1918; s. Gus and Elizabeth (Powell) C.; m. Betty Nicoolette Chronaker, July 4, 1939 (wid. Nov. 1989); children: Phillip H., Stanley P.; m. Jenny Steele. Diploma in mech. engring., Case Sch. Applied Scis., Cleve., 1939; MBA, Pacific Western U., 1980, DBA, 1985. Lic. real estate broker, real estate property mgr., Fla. Real Estate Commn. V.p., gen. mgr. Radisson Hotel, Mpls., 1949-53; v.p. Banker Life & Casualty, Chgo., 1953-63; pres. Fla. Bd. Trade, Ft. Lauderdale, 1963-95. Author: Condominium Management Handbook, 1985, The Wandering Moon, 1994, Positive Way to Profit, 1965; author twelve cookbooks/internat. food recipes. Capt. Merchant Marines, ATO. Mem. Am. Legion, SAR, Decendants George Washington, Optimist Club (bd. dirs. 1990-96). Republican. Baptist. Avocations: writing, golf, travel, tennis. Home: 1010 S Ocean Blvd Apt 803 Pompano Beach FL 33062-6630 Fax: 954-782-2023.

CALFEE, JOHN BEVERLY, retired lawyer; b. Cleve., May 2, 1913; s. Robert M. and Alwine (Haas) C.; m. Nancy Leighton, Feb. 8, 1944; children: John Beverly Jr., David L., Peter H., Mark E. Grad., Hotchkiss Sch., 1931; BA, Yale U., 1935; LLB, Western Res. U., 1938. Bar: Ohio 1939. Sr. ptnr. Calfee, Halter & Griswold, Cleve., 1939-86, ret., 1987. Dir. civil def., Cleveland Heights, 1951; active Cuyohoga County Rep. Fin. Com., 1978—81; mem. Ohio N.W. Ordinance Bicentennial Commn., 1986. Maj. AUS, 1942—46. Mem. ABA, Ohio Bar Assn., Cleve. Bar Assn., Ohio Hist. Soc. (trustee 1988-97 Presbyterian. Home: 4892 Clubside Rd Cleveland OH 44124-2539 *A person has many guiding principles, but if I am limited to the main one, it would be the motto of Hawken School, my first preparatory institution in Cleveland—"Fair Play." This is a term which for me has become translated into a game goal to be ambitiously sought and achieved by hard work. The effort applied must be honest in thought as well as deed and in achieving it a firm purpose is the motivating concept, tempered by respect for the other person's viewpoint.*

CALFEE, WILLIAM LEWIS, lawyer; b. Cleveland Heights, Ohio, July 12, 1917; s. Robert Martin and Alwine (Haas) C.; m. Eleanor Elizabeth Bliss, Dec. 6, 1941; children: William R., Bruce K., Cynthia B. BA, Harvard Coll., 1939; LL.D., Yale U., 1946. Bar: Ohio 1946. Assoc. Baker & Hostetler, Cleve., 1946-56, ptnr., 1957-90, of counsel, 1990-92. Bd. dirs. Growth Assn. Greater Cleve., 1979-92; trustee Greater Cleve. United Appeal; pres. Health Fund Greater Cleve. Served to lt. col. M.I., U.S. Army, 1941-45. Decorated Legion of Merit; decorated Order of Brit. Empire Mem. ABA (ho. of dels. 1980-93), Ohio Bar Assn., Bar Assn. Greater Cleve. (trustee 1980-93, pres. 1979-80), Nat. Conf. Bar Pres. (exec. coun. 1982-85), Ohio C. of C. (bd. dirs. 1993), Mayfield Country Club (pres.), Union Club, Pepper Pike Club. Republican. Episcopalian. Home: 2845 SOM Center Rd Chagrin Falls OH 44022-6653

CALHAMER, ALLAN BRIAN, retired postal worker; b. Hinsdale, Ill., Dec. 7, 1931; s. Timothy Michael and Helen Augusta (Morton) C.; m. Hilda Camelia Morales, Sept. 1, 1967; children: Tatiana, Selenne. AB, Harvard U., 1953. Lectr. on game of diplomacy and diplomatic history Keio U., 1997. Author: Calhamer on Diplomacy, 2000; contbr. articles to profl. jours.; inventor Game of Diplomacy (named to Prod. Hall of Fame, Acad. of Adventure Game Design 1993; named to Hall of Fame by Games Mag.; Diplomacy named Game of Yr. by Games & Puzzles 1977). Avocations: strategic games, reading, writing. Home: 501 N Stone Ave La Grange Park IL 60526-5523 E-mail: abcalhamer@yahoo.com.

CALHOUN, CRAIG JACKSON, social scientist, educator; b. Watseka, Ill., June 16, 1952; s. Jay Robert and Audrey Thelma (Jackson) C.; m. Pamela Frances DeLargy, Aug. 2, 1980. BA, U. So. Calif., 1972; MA, Columbia U., 1974, U. Manchester (Eng.), 1975; D Phil, Oxford U. (Eng.), 1980. Rsch. assoc. Columbia U., N.Y.C., 1972-74; instr. U. N.C., Chapel Hill, 1977-80, asst. prof. sociology, 1980-85, assoc. prof., 1985-89, prof. sociology and history, 1989-96; prof. NYU, 1996—, chair dept. sociology, 1996-99; pres. Social Sci. Rsch.

Coun., N.Y.C., 1999—. Tech. advisor U.S. AID, Govt. of Sudan, 1984-86; dir. program in social theory and cross-cultural studies U. N.C., 1989-95, office of internat. programs 1990-93, chmn. curriculum in internat. studies, 1990-93, dir. Univ. Ctr. for Internat. Studies, 1993-96; vis. prof. dept. sociology, U. Oslo, 1991-97; vis. fellow Swedish Collegium for Advanced Study in Social Scis., 1994; rsch. fellow Ctr. for Transcultural Studies-Ctr. for Psychosocial Studies, Chgo., 1983; Irene Flecknoe Ross lectr., UCLA, 1994-5; Harry Bridges lectr. U. Wash., 1995, Howard W. Beers lectr. U. Ky., 1997, Benjamin J. Meaker Disting. vis. prof. U. Bristol, 2000. Author: The Question of Class Struggle, 1982; co-author: Sociology, 1988, Neither Gods Nor Emperors: Students and the Struggle for Democracy in China, 1995, Critical Social Theory: Culture, History, and the Challenge of Difference, 1995, Nationalism, 1997; editor: The Anthropological Study of Education, 1976: Habermas and the Public Sphere, 1992, Sociological Theory, 1994-99, Hannah Arendt and the Meaning of Politics, 1997, Dictionary of the Social Science, 2002, Understanding September 11, 2002; contbr. numerous articles to profl. jours. Recipient Kellogg Found. fellow, 1982-85; R.J. Reynolds Fund award U. N.C. 1985, Disting. Contrbn. to Scholarship award Am. Sociol. Assn. Fellow Royal Anthrop. Inst.; mem. Am. Sociol. Assn. (chair sect. comparative hist. sociology 1984-85, chair com. on internat. sociology 1988-92, chair sect. on theoretics of sociology, 1991-92; coun. mem. 2000—), Sociol. Rsch. Assn., Soc. for Comparative Rsch. Address: SSRC 810 7th Ave New York NY 10019-5818 Office: NYU Dept Sociology 269 Mercer St New York NY 10003-6633

CALHOUN, DONALD EUGENE, JR., federal judge; b. Columbus, Ohio, May 15, 1926; s. Donald Eugene and Esther C.; m. Shirley Claggett, Aug. 28, 1948; children: Catherine C., Donald Eugene III, Elizabeth C. BA in Polit. Sci., Ohio State U., 1949, JD, 1951. Bar: Ohio 1951. Pvt. practice, 1951-68; ptnr. Folkerth, Calhoun, Webster, Maurer & O'Brien, 1968-82, Guren, Merritt, Feibel, Sogg & Cohen, 1982-84; of counsel Lane, Alton, Horst, 1984-85; judge U. S. Bankruptcy Ct., Columbus, 1985-99, ret., 1999, recalled, 2000—. Gen. counsel Ohio Conf. United Ch. of Christ, 1964-85 Chmn. City-wide Citizens Com. for Neighborhood Seminars on Sch. Program and Fin., 1963; mem. Columbus Bd. Edn., 1963-71, pres., 1966, 70. With USNR, 1944-46. Mem. Columbus Bar Assn. (pres. 1967-68, Community Svc. award 1972), Nat. Conf. Bar Pres., Am. Arbitration Assn., Columbus Jaycees (life), Athletic Club, Masons. Congregationalist. Office: US Bankruptcy Ct 170 N High St Columbus OH 43215-2403

CALHOUN, JOHN ALFRED, social services administrator; b. Phila., Dec. 1, 1939; s. John Alfred and Helen Fordham (Webster) C.; m. Ottilia Klenota, May 29, 1971; children: Byron, Hollis. BA, Brown U., 1962; M in Div., Episcopal Div. Sch., Cambridge, Mass., 1965; MPA, Harvard U., 1986; DHL (hon.), Heidelberg Coll., 2001. Tchr. Phila. pub. schs., 1965-66; program adminstr. Action for Boston Community Devel., 1966-70; v.p. Tech. Devel. Corp., Boston, 1970-73; exec. dir., founder Justice Resource Inst., Boston, 1973-76; commr. Mass. Dept. of Youth Svcs., Boston, 1976-79, U.S. Adminstrn. for Children, Youth and Families, Washington, 1979-81; v.p., dir. Ctr. for Govtl. Affairs Child Welfare League, Washington, 1981-83; pres., CEO Nat. Crime Prevention Coun., Washington, 1983—. V.p. Internat. Ctr. for the Prevention of Crime; bd. dirs. Ctr. for Internat. Leadership, D.C., Pacific Ctr. for Violence Prevention, The Nat. Assembly of Voluntary Health and Social Welfare Ags., Childrens Trust Neighborhood Initiative; assoc. in edn. Harvard U., 1978; moderator Aspen Inst., 1980—; founder Pre-trial Diversion Programs, Mass., Urban Ct. Mediation Cmty. Sentencing, Mass., Cmty. Responses to Drug Abuse, 10 Sites Across the U.S.; mem. U.S. Atty. Gen.'s Coordinating Coun. on Juvenile Justice; founder Youth as Resources., Mass. and Ind., Ctr. for Faith and Svc., Teens, Crime and the Cmty.(nationwide); adv. bd. Nat. League of Cities Children and Youth subcom. Author: What, Me Evaluate?, 1986; editor: Crime in Urban Communities, 1986, Making a Difference, 1985, Reaching Out: School-based Community Service Programs, Teen Crime and the Community, National Service and Public Safety: Partnerships for Safer Communities, Taking the Offensive: How Seven Cities Did It, Changing Communities Through Faith in Action:Crime Prevenation in the New Millenium, Philantrophy and Faith; contbr. articles to profl. jours. Coach McLean (Va.) Youth; tchr. confirmation class Louisville Presbyn. Ch., McLean; state chmn. Mass. Adolescent Task Force, 1978; chmn. Mass. State of the Family Task Force, 1979; pres. Franklin Flaschner Found., 1978; treas. Met. Beaverbrook Area Mental Health Bd.; bd. advisors U. Mass. Coll. Cmty. Pub. Svc., 1979; bd. dirs. Edna Stein Acad., Boston, Pekinese Island Sch., Woods Hole, Mass.; mem. adv. bd. Va. Dept. for Children, 1990-94. Littauer fellow Harvard U. Kennedy Sch. of Govt., 1986; recipient award of Recognition Am. Arbitration Assn., 1978, award of Recognition, U.S. Office Juvenile Justice and Delinquency Prevention, 1998, Spirit of Crazy Horse award Reclaiming Youth Internat., 2002. Mem. Am. Probation/Parole Assn. (prevention com.). Democrat. Episcopalian. Avocations: photography, tennis, gardening, coaching, skiing. Home: 921 Mackall Ave Mc Lean VA 22101-1617 Office: Nat Crime Prevention Coun Office Pres & CEO 13th Fl 1000 Connecticut Ave NW Washington DC 20036-5302

CALHOUN, JOHN C., JR., academic administrator; b. Betula, Pa., Mar. 21, 1917; s. John C. and Martha (Rowe) C.; m. Ruth Elizabeth Huston, June 10, 1941; children: John, Emily, Mary Beth, Ruth Ellen. BS in Petroleum and Natural Gas Engring., Pa. State U., 1937, MS, 1941, PhD, 1946; DSc (hon.), Ripon Coll., 1975. Research asst., instr. petroleum and natural gas engring. Pa. State U., 1937-46, prof., head dept. petroleum and natural gas engring., 1950-55; assoc. prof., then prof. Sch. Petroleum Engring., U. Okla., 1946-50, chmn., 1948-50; dean Sch. Engring. Tex. Agrl. and Mech. Coll., College Station, 1955-57; dir. Engring. Expt. Sta., Engring. Ext. Service Tex. Agrl. and Mech. U., College Station, 1955-57, v.p. engring., 1957-59, vice chancellor for engring., 1959-60, vice chancellor for devel., 1960-63, v.p. programs, 1965-71, Disting. prof. petroleum engring., 1965-83, dir. Office Sea Grant Programs, 1968-72, dean geoscis., 1969-71, v.p. acad. affairs, 1971-77, exec. vice chancellor for programs Tex. A&M U. System, 1977-80, dep. chancellor for engring., 1980-83; dir. Crisman Inst. Petroleum Reservoir Mgmt., 1984-87; dep. chancellor for engring. emeritus Tex. A&M U. Sys., College Station, 1983—; asst., sci. advisor to sec. Dept. Interior, Washington, 1963-65. Vice chmn. Engring. Coll. Rsch. Coun., 1959-62; mem. Fed. Coun. for Sci. and Tech., 1963-65, Presdl. Task Force on Oceanography, 1969, Nat. Adv. Coun. on Oceans and Atmosphere, 1971-72, Tex. Coastal and Marine Coun., 1972-83; acting dir. Office Water Resources Rsch., 1964; mem. environ. pollution panel Pres.'s Sci. Adv. Com., 1964-66; chmn. com. on oceanography NAS, 1967-70, chmn. ocean sci. affairs bd., 1970-72; chmn. Pres.'s Santa Barbara Oil Spill Panel and Panel on Union Oil Lease, 1969; mem. adv. panel Internat. Decade Ocean Exploration, NSF, 1970-72; mem. nat. adv. coun. on minorities in engring. Nat. Acad. Engring., 1973-74; mem. naval studies bd. Nat. Acad. Scis., 1974-79; bd. dirs. Inst. Nautical Archeology, 1976-86; dir. Tex. Petroleum Rsch. Com., 1978-82; cons. So. Regional Edn. Bd., 1953-54, Pa. Dept. Forests & Waters, 1955, World Bank, 1978-85, Coun. Internat. Edn. Exch., 1988-92; mem. rsch. coordination panel Gas Rsch. Inst., 1977-82; mem. adv. com. on mining and mineral resources rsch. Dept. Interior, 1987-94. Author: Fundamentals of Reservoir Engineering, 1953; contbr. articles to profl. jours. Chmn. Coll. Sta. United Fund, 1961; trustee U. Corp. for Atmospheric Rsch., 1969-71, chmn. bd., 1968-71; trustee Tex. Agrl. and Mech. Rsch. Found., 1961-82, Tex. Inst. for Rehab. and Rsch., 1981-82; bd. dirs. EDUCOM, 1966-69, Houston Area Rsch. Ctr., 1982-83; exec. dir., pres. Gulf Univs. Rsch. Corp., 1966-69. Recipient 15th Sea Grant award Sea Grant Assn., 1984, Lifetime Achievement award Dwight Look Coll. Engring., Tex. A&M U., 2001; alumni fellow Pa. State U., 1976. Fellow AAAS, Marine Tech. Soc. (pres. 1975-76), Am. Soc. Engring. Edn. (v.p., dir. 1968-72, pres. 1974, Centennial medallion 1993, Collins award 1996); mem. Nat. Acad. Engring., Engrs. Coun. Profl. Devel. (bd. dirs. 1964-67), Engrs. Joint Coun. (bd. dirs. 1972-77), AIME (hon.), Soc. Petroleum Engrs. (pres. 1964, DeGolyer medal 1982, Anthony F. Lucas Gold medal 1997), Am. Assn. Engring. Socs. (mem. exec. com. internat. affairs coun. 1980-81), Sigma Xi, Tau Beta Pi, Sigma Gamma Epsilon, Phi Kappa Phi, Tau Kappa Epsilon. Presbyterian. Home: 1106 Ashburn Ave College Station TX 77840-2502

CALHOUN, JOHN R. lawyer; b. Fairfield, Iowa, Nov. 22, 1933; m. Elizabeth Calhoun; four children. BA in Polit. Sci., U. Iowa, 1956, JD, 1958. Bar: Iowa, 1958, Calif. 1960, U.S. Ct. Appeals (9th cir.) 1987, U.S. Ct. Appeals (fed. cir.) 1997, U.S. Dist. Ct. (cen. dist.) Calif. 1960, U.S. Supreme Ct. 1963, U.S. Ct. Mil. Appeals 1963. Commd. 2d lt. U.S. Army Res., 1958, advanced through grades to col., JAG Corp., ret., 1988; atty. U.S. Securities and Exch. Commn., 1960, Automobile Club of So. Calif., 1960-61; dep. dist. atty. L.A. Dist. Atty.'s Office, 1961-62; dep. city prosecutor Long Beach (Calif.) City Prosecutor's Office, 1962-67; dep. city atty. Long Beach City Atty.'s Office, 1967-78, asst. city atty., 1978-85, city atty., 1985-98; commr., v.p. Long Beach Harbor Commn., 1999—. Decorated Legion of Merit, Meritorious Svc. medal. Mem. Calif. Bar Assn., Long Beach Bar Assn. (bd. govs. 1974-75, 87-88), Rotary, Res. Officers Assn., Long Beach Area C. of C., Phi Delta Phi, Phi Delta Theta. Home: 4011 Chestnut Ave Long Beach CA 90807-3207

CALHOUN (GAYLE), LINDA MARGARET, music educator; b. Moline, Ill., Dec. 13, 1947; d. Garnett Noel and Betty Lou Gayle; m. Wayne Earlson Calhoun, Jr., Mar. 24, 1938. BS in Music Edn., East Tex. State U., 1965—70; MA, Ctrl. Mich. U., 1974—75. Cert. tchr. of music in piano Music Teachers Nat. Assn., 2002. Elem. music tchr. Kaufman Ind. Sch. Dist., Tex., 1970—73, Dept. of Def. Dependent Schools, Lajes, Portugal, 1973—79, Irving Ind. Sch. Dist., Tex., 1979—80; sec. IBM Mktg. Edn., Dallas, 1980—81; systems engr. IBM, Dallas, 1981—84, account mktg. rep. Tampa, Fla., 1984—92; ind. piano instr. Bella Vista, Ark., 1992—. Pres. Welcome Wagon, Bella Vista, Ark., 1992—94, N.W. Ark. Symphony, Fayetteville, 1993—96. Mem.: Music Teachers Nat. Assn., Ark. State Music Teachers Assn. (chmn. of state auditions 2001—03), NW Ark. Music Teachers Assn. (treas. 1992—2003). Independent. Avocations: reading, travel, piano, needlecrafts.

CALHOUN, LYLA LEA, clinical social worker, consultant; b. Holdrege, Nebr., July 3, 1934; d. Lyle Curtis and Bula Beatrice (Kent) Spongberg; m. Donald Ray Calhoun, Mar. 6, 1954; children: Dennis Blake, Sheryl Ann Calhoun Montford, Shaun Patrick, Scott Alan Student, Friends U., Wichita, Kans., 1952-53; BA, Wichita State U., 1974; MS in Social Adminstrn., Case Western Res. U., 1986. Diplomate in Clin. Social Work, lic. ind. social worker, Ohio. Social worker ARC, Wichita, 1973-75, Mo. Dept. Human Svcs., Union, 1977-78; clin. social worker Cath. Social Svc. Bur., Medina, Ohio, 1981—2001, Cornerstone Psychol. Svcs., Medina, 1993—2001, Wholeness Ministry, Medina United Meth. Ch., 2000—. Cons. Hospice Medina County, Medina, 1986-91, Tri County Home Health, 1993-95, Medina County Health Dept., 1989-96. Mem. adv. bd. Medina County Ext. Agy., 1985-93, Adult Edn. Joint Vocat. Sch., Medina, 1989-96, Dept. Human Svcs., Medina, 1989-91; bd. dirs. ARC, Medina, 1980-90. Mem. NASW, Ohio Assn. Social Workers, Mental Health Profls. of Medina County (program chmn. 1990-93, pres. 1994-95). Republican. Mem. Christian Ch. (Disciples Of Christ). Avocations: grandchildren, reading music, travel. Home: 5700 Jason Oval Medina OH 44256-6878 Office: Medina United Meth Ch 260 S Court St Medina OH 44256

CALHOUN, NOAH ROBERT, oral maxillofacial surgeon, educator; b. Clarendon, Ark., Mar. 23, 1921; s. Noah and Della (Sherman) Calhoun; m. Cecelia Christopher, Oct. 19, 1950; children: Stephen Marc, Cecelia Noel. DDS, Dental Sch., Howard U., 1948; M.Dental Sci., Tufts Med. and Dental Sch., 1955. Oral surgeon VA Hosp., Tuskegee, Ala., 1950—52, Kessler AFB, Biloxi, Miss., 1952—53; chief dental service VA Hosp., Tuskegee, Ala., 1955—57, oral surgeon, asst. chief dental surgeon Washington, 1964—74; chief dental service, oral surgeon VA Med. Center, Washington, 1974—; prof. oral surgery Dental Sch., Howard U., Washington, 1966—92, Georgetown U., Washington, 1975—93; prof. emeritus Dental Coll. Howard U., 1992—. Dir. Tuskegee Red Cross, Ala., 1962—64; chmn. Nat. Concerned VA Dentists, 1975, Inst. Medicine-NAS, 1975. Sect. editor Current Lit. in Internat. Oral/Maxillofacial Surgery, 1986, mem. editl. bd. Jour. Oral and Maxillo-facial Surveys, 1993; contbr. articles. Mem. fin. com. St. Michael Ch., Silver Spring, Md. Mem.: NAACP (trustee D.C. chpt.), ADA, Inst. Medicine-NAS, Am. Coll. Dentistry, Internat. Coll. Dentistry, Am. Soc. Oral and Maxillofacial Surgeons (Audio Visual award 1978), Bridge Masters of Washington (pres.), Omicron Kappa Upsilon. Roman Catholic. Office: Dental Coll Howard U Washington DC 20001

CALHOUN, PEGGY JOAN, fundraising executive; b. La Salle, Ill., Sept. 14, 1957; d. Floyd Anthony and Sophia (Regula) Sarwinski; m. James R. Calhoun, Apr. 19, 1989; children: (twins) Robert Blair and Christina Sophia. Student, Ill. Valley C.C., Oglesby, 1975, So. Ill. U., 1976, 77; MA, St. Mary's Coll., Minn., 1994. Assoc. dir. United Way, Sarasota, Fla., 1979-85; devel. dir. Boy Scouts Am., Sarasota, 1985-86; assoc. campaign dir. United Way, Ft. Lauderdale, Fla., 1986-87; dir. devel. YMCA, Sarasota, 1987-88, Salvation Army, Ft. Lauderdale, 1988-91, Diabetes Rsch. Inst. Found., U. Miami Sch. Medicine, 1992-93; pres. Calhoun & Co., Inc., Ft. Lauderdale, 1993—; prin. Miller, Calhoun & Co., Inc. Instr. Nova U., Ft. Lauderdale, Barry U., 1996—. Com. mem. United Way, 1988-91. Mem.: Pub. Rels. Soc. Am. (bd. dirs. 1991—93, pres. 1993), Broward Planned Giving Coun. (bd. dirs. 1991), Women's Exec. Com., Assn. Fund Raising Profls. (advanced cert. fund raising exec., pres. bd. dirs. 1985, bd. dirs. 1990—97, pres. 1996), Am. Mothers of Twins, Jr. League. Republican. Avocations: water sports, reading, travel. Home and Office: 2741 NE 57th Ct Fort Lauderdale FL 33308-2723

CALHOUN, SCOTT DOUGLAS, lawyer; b. Aurora, Ill., May 1, 1959; s. Ellsworth L. Calhoun and Mary Louise (Mummert) Wire; m. Gloria Jean Fulvi, Aug. 1, 1987; 1 child, John Daniel. BA cum laude, Knox Coll., 1981; JD, Coll. of William and Mary, 1984. Bar: Ga. 1984, U.S. Dist. Ct. (no. dist.) Ga. 1984, U.S. Ct. Appeals (11th cir.) 1984. Assoc. Swift, Currie, McGhee & Hiers, Atlanta, 1984-90, ptnr., 1990-92; pvt. practice Atlanta, 1992-94; prin. Byrne, Eldridge, Moore & Davis, PC, Atlanta, 1994-95; ptnr. Mozley, Finlayson & Loggins, Atlanta, 1996—. Spkr. in field. Bd. dirs. Atlanta Symphony Assocs., 1991-97, Wildwood Civic Assn., Atlanta, 1991-98; elder Trinity Presbyn. Ch., Atlanta, 1994-97, 2001—. Mem. Mortar Bd. Avocations: golf, music. Office: Mozley Finlayson & Loggins 5605 Glenridge Dr NE Ste 900 Atlanta GA 30342-1380 E-mail: scalhoun@mfllaw.com.

CALICO, PAUL B. lawyer; b. Berea, Ky., Aug. 24, 1954; s. Thruman E. and Norma Jean (Brandenberg) C.; m. Ann Carol Rutherford, June 2, 1979; children: Austin Clay, Molly Elizabeth. Magna cum laude, Western Ky. U., 1976; JD with distinction, U. Ky., 1980. Bar: Ohio 1980, Ky. 1981, U.S. Dist. Ct. (so. dist.) Ohio 1980, U.S. Dist. Ct. ea. dist.) Ky. 1981. Ptnr. Strauss & Troy, LPA, Cin., 1980—. Mediator The Ctr. for Resolution Disputes, Inc.; spkr. in field. Contbr. articles to profl. jours. Trustee Collaborative Law Ctr., Women Helping Women, Inc., Vol. Lawyers Found., past pres.; adminstrv. bd. dirs., fin. com. sec. Anderson Hills United Meth. Ch. Decorated Order of Coif U. Ky. Mem. ABA, Ohio Bar Assn., Ohio Acad. Civil Trial Attys., Ky. Bar Assn., Ky. Acad. Trial Attys., Cin. Bar Assn. (arbitrator 1982—, participant vol. lawyers for the poor project 1983—, common peas ct. com. 1985—, Alt. Dispute resolution com., employment law com. 1990—, ct. appeals com. 1987—), No. Ky. Bar Assn., Ohio Valley Scottish Soc. (trustee). Home: 900 Birney Ln Cincinnati OH 45230-3718 Office: Strauss & Troy Fed Res Bldg 150 E 4th St Cincinnati OH 45202-4018 E-mail: pbcalico@strauss-troy.com.

CALICO, ROBERT A. dean; BS in Aerospace Engring., U.Cin., Ohio, 1966; MS in Aerospace Engring., U.Cin., 1968, PhD in Aerospace Engring., 1971. Aerospace design engr. Advanced Systemes Br. LTV Aerpspace, Dallas, 1966—68; instr. dept. aerospace engring. U. Cin., Ohio, 1969—72; from asst. prof. to prof. Air Force Inst. Tech., Wright AFB, Dayton, Ohio, 1972—, dean Grad. Sch. Engring., 1990—. Named Disting. Alumni, U. Cin. Coll. Engring., Disting. Engr., Engring. and Sci. Found. Dayton. Fellow: AIAA (assoc.); mem.: Engring and Sci. Found. (bd. trustees), Am. Soc. Engring. Edn., Sigma Xi, Sigma Gamma Tau, Tau Beta Pi. Office: USAF Inst Tech Office of Pub Affairs Wright Patterson AFB Dayton OH 45433-7765

CALIFANO, JOSEPH ANTHONY, JR., lawyer, public health policy educator, writer; b. Bklyn., May 15, 1931; s. Joseph Anthony and Katherine (Gill) C.; m. Hilary Paley Byers, 1983; children by previous marriage: Mark Gerard, Joseph Anthony III, Claudia Frances; stepchildren: Brooke A. Byers, John Fredric Byers IV. BA, Holy Cross Coll., 1952; LLB, Harvard U., 1955. Bar: N.Y. 1955, U.S. Supreme Ct. 1966, D.C. 1969. With firm Dewey Ballantine, N.Y.C., 1958-61; spl. asst. to gen. counsel Dept. Def., 1961-62; spl. asst. to sec. Army, 1962-63; gen. counsel Dept. Army, 1963-64; spl. asst. to sec. and dep. sec. Def., 1964-65; spl. asst. to Pres. of U.S., 1965-69; ptnr. Arnold & Porter, Washington, 1969-71, Williams, Connolly & Califano, Washington, 1971-77; sec. HEW, 1977-79; ptnr. Califano, Ross & Heineman, Washington, 1980-82; sr. ptnr. Dewey Ballantine, Washington, 1983-92; prof. pub. health policy Columbia U. Schs. Medicine and Pub. Health, N.Y.C., 1992—; chmn., pres. Nat. Ctr. on Addiction and Substance Abuse at Columbia U., N.Y.C., 1992—. Bd. dirs. ADP, Inc., Viacom Inc.; gen. counsel Dem. Nat. Com., 1971—72. Author: The Student Revolution: A Global Confrontation, 1969, A Presidential Nation, 1975, Governing America: An Insiders Report from the White House and the Cabinet, 1981, The 1982 Report on Drug Abuse and Alcoholism, America's Health Care Revolution, 1986, The Triumph and Tragedy of Lyndon Johnson, 1991, Radical Surgery: What's Next for America's Health Care, 1995, (with Howard Simons) The Media and the Law, 1976, The Media and Business, 1978. Trustee Urban Inst., Am. Ditchley Found., Century Fund, Nat. Health Mus.; bd. govs. N.Y. and Presbyn. Hosp. Inc.; chmn. Inst. Social and Econ. Policy in Mid. East, Harvard U., 1983-98. Recipient Distinguished Civilian Svc. award Dept. Army, 1964; Man of Year award Justinian Soc. Lawyers, 1966; Disting. Pub. Svc. medal Dept. Def., 1965; named One of Ten Outstanding Young Men of America, 1966. Mem. N.Y. State Bar Assn., D.C. Bar Assn., Met. Club (Washington), Century Assn., Univ. Club.

CALIFANO, III, JOSEPH, physician; b. Washington; s. Joseph Califano, Jr. and Trudy Kendrew; m. Elizabeth Califano, May 0, 1990; children: Joseph Califano, IV, Peter Califano. BA, Amherst Coll., Mass., 1985; MD, Harvard Med. Sch., Boston, 1993. Cert. Am. Acad. of Otolarynogology-Head and Neck Surgery, 2000. Asst. prof. Johns Hopkins Hosp., Balt., 2000—. Recipient Clinician Scientist award, Damon Runyan Cancer Rsch. Found., 2001. Mem.: Am. Head and Neck Soc. Achievements include research in Molecular Biology Of Head And Neck Cancer. Office: Johns Hopkins Med Instn 01 N Caroline St 6th Fl Baltimore MD 21287-0910

CALIGIURI, JOSEPH FRANK, retired engineering executive; b. Columbus, Ohio, Feb. 13, 1928; s. Frank and Angeline Josephine (Gentile) C.; m. Barbara Jane Delaney, June 15, 1948 (dec. 1996); children: Mark, Timothy, Jeffrey, Anderw; m. Tanya Alberta Condon, June 24, 1998. BSEE, Ohio State U., 1949, MSEE, 1951. Chief engr. Sperry Gyroscope Co., Gt. Neck, N.Y., 1966-69; v.p. engring. Guidance and Control Sys. divsn. Litton Industries, Inc., Woodland Hills, Calif., 1969-71, pres., 1971-77, v.p. parent co., 1974-77, sr. v.p., group head Beverly Hills, Calif., 1977-81, exec. v.p., head advanced electronics group, 1981-93; ret., 1993. Bd. dirs. Titan Corp., Intracel Corp., Phillip Mark Cos. Home: 1353 Oak Grove Pl Westlake Village CA 91362-4248

CALIN, WILLIAM, literature educator; b. Newington, Conn., Apr. 4, 1936; BA, Yale Coll., New Haven, Conn., 1957; PhD, Yale U., New Haven, 1957—60. Instr. Dartmouth Coll., Hanover, NH, 1960—62, asst. prof., 1962—63, Stanford U., Stanford, Calif., 1964—65, assoc. prof., 1965—70, prof., 1970—73, U. Oreg., Eugene, 1973—88; grad. rsch. prof. U. Fla., Gainesville, 1988—. Vis. prof. U. Poitiers (France), 1982, 84; Edwin Arnold vis. prof. Whitman Coll., Walla Walla, Wash., 1987. Author: The Old French Epic of Revolt:, Minority Literatures and Modernism: Scots, Breton, and Occitan, 1920-1990, Aux Portes du Poème, The Epic Quest: Studies in Four Old French Chansons de Geste, La Chanson de Roland, A Poet at the Fountain: Essays on the Narrative Verse of Guillaume de Machaut, Crown, Cross and Fleur-de lis: An Essay on Pierre Le Moyne's Baroque Epic Saint Louis, A Muse for Heroes: Nine Centuries of the Epic in France (Gilbert Chinard First Lit. Prize; and ALA, Outstanding Academic Book for 1984, 1981), In Defense of French Poetry: An Essay in Revaluation, The French Tradition and the Literature of Medieval England (ALA, Outstanding Academic Book, 1995). Named rsch. prof., U. of Fla. Rsch. Found., 1998—2001; recipient Soci dou Felibrige, Lou Felibrige, 1991; Guggenheim fellow, 1962—63, sr. rsch. fellow, Am. Coun. Learned Socs., 1996—97, Grant-in-Aid, 1963—64, 1968, grantee, Am. Philos. Soc., 1970, Can. Fedn. Humanities, 1981, Fulbright Found., 1982, ind. study and rsch. fellow, NEH, 1984—85, vis. rsch. fellow, Clare Hall, Cambridge, 1984—85, Summer Inst. for Tchg. of Lit. and History fellow, NEH, 1985, sr. rsch. grant, Fulbright Found., 1987—88, vis. rsch. fellow, Inst. for Advanced Studies in the Humanities, U. of Edinburgh, 1997, U. Toronto, 2000. Mem.: MLA (pres. medieval French divsn. 1981, pres. Provençal and Catalan divsn. 1989, 2001), South Atlantic Modern Lang. Associaion (pres. internat. courtly lit. soc. divsn. 1990—91), Assn. Internat. d'Etudes Occitanes (internat. v.p. 1983—2002), Internat. Guillaume de Machaut Soc. (pres. 1987—99), Soc. Internat. Rencesvals (pres. Am. br. 1973—76). Episcopalian. Avocations: collecting antiquarian books, collecting antique porcelain china, european travel. Home: 5352 NW 9th Ln Gainesville FL 32605-4475 Office: U Fla PO Box 117405 Gainesville FL 32611-7405 Office Fax: 352-392-5679. Personal E-mail: wcalin@rll.ufl.edu. E-mail: wcalin@rll.ufl.edu.

CALINESCU, ADRIANA GABRIELA, museum curator, art historian; b. Bucharest, Romania, Dec. 30, 1941; came to U.S., 1973; d. Nicolae and Tamara Gane; m. Matei Alexe Calinescu, Apr. 29, 1963; children: Irena, Matthew. BA, Cen. Lyceé, Bucharest, 1959; MA in English, U. Bucharest, 1964; MLS, Ind. U., 1976, MA in Art History, 1983. Asst. prof. Inst. Theater and Cinema, Bucharest, 1967-73; rsch. assoc. Ind. U. Art Mus., Bloomington, 1979-83, Thomas T. Solley curator ancient art, assoc. scholar, 1992—. Vis. assoc. mem. Am. Sch. Classical Studies, Athens, Greece, 1984. Author: The Art of Ancient Jewelry, 1994; author, co-editor: Ancient Art from the V. G. Simkhovitch Collection, 1988; editor: Ancient Jewelry and Archaeology, 1996. NEA fellow, 1984; grantee Salzburg Seminar, 1970, NEA, 1987, 93, Kress Found., 1991, Internat. Rsch. and Exchanges Bd., 1991. Mem. Am. Inst. Archaeology, Classical Art Soc., Beta Phi Mu. Office: Ind U Art Mus E 7th St Bloomington IN 47405

CALINGAERT, MICHAEL, nonprofit organization executive; b. Detroit, Sept. 17, 1933; s. George and Dorothy C.; m. Efrem Funghi, June 20, 1962; children: Alexander, Daniel, Nicholas. BA, Swarthmore Coll., 1955; postgrad., U. Cologne, Fed. Republic Germany, 1955-56, U. Calif., Berkeley, 1963-64. Commd. fgn. svc. officer Dept. State, 1956, intelligence rsch. specialist, 1957-58; vice consul Am. consulate gen. Mogadiscio, Somalia, 1959—61; econ. officer Am. consulate gen. Bremen, Germany, 1961-63; econ. officer Am. Embassy, Colombo, Sri Lanka, 1964-68; chief food policy div. Dept. State, Washington, 1968-72; econ. counselor Am. Embassy, Tokyo, 1972-75, econ./comml. min. Rome, 1975-79; dep. asst. sec. for internat. resources and food policy Dept. State, 1979-83; econ. min. Am. Embassy, London, 1983-87; vis. sr. fellow Nat. Planning Assn., Washington, 1987-89, sr. fellow, 1993-97; non-resident sr. fellow Atlantic Coun. U.S., 1989; dir. of European ops. Pharm. Mfrs. Assn. (U.S.), Belgium, 1989-93; dir. The Monnet-Madison Inst., Brussels, 1994-97; exec. dir. Coun. for U.S. and Italy, 1997—2003, exec. v.p., 2003—. Rsch. fellow Inst. for European Studies, Free U. Brussels, 1994-98, mem. polit. sect., 1998—; guest scholar The Brookings Inst., 1996—. Author: The 1992 Challenge from Europe: Development of the European Community's Internal Market, 1988, European Integration Revisited: Progress, Prospects, and U.S. Interests, 1996; contbr. numerous articles to profl. jours. Recipient Meritorious Honor award Dept. State, 1971, Superior Honor award, 1981 Mem. Am. Fgn. Svc. Assn., Royal Inst. Internat. Affairs, Inst. Affari Internat. Office: The Brookings Inst 1775 Massachusetts Ave NW Washington DC 20036-2103

CALINGER, RONALD STEVE, historian; b. Aliquippa, Pa., Apr. 6, 1942; s. Thomas H. and Mary (Blicha) Calinger; m. Betty Jeanne Mikulecky, Dec. 21, 1974; children: John Michael, Anne Sun Nyeo. AB summa cum laude, Ohio U., 1963; MA, U. Pitts., 1964; PhD, U. Chgo., 1971. Assoc. editor scis. A.N. Marquis Publ. Co., Chgo., 1966-68; mem. faculty Rensselaer Poly. Inst., Troy, N.Y., 1969-85, assoc. prof. history, 1975-85, chmn. dept. history and polit. sci., 1977-82, dean Undergrad. Coll., 1982-85; dean sch. arts scis. Cath. U. Am., Washington, 1985-87, assoc. to ordinary prof. history, 1987—. Author: (book) Gottfried Wilhelm Leibniz, 1976, A Contextual History of Mathematics: Up to Euler, 1999, (electronic book) A Study Guide for a Contextual History of Mathematics, 2001; co-author: Dictionary of Twentieth Century World Politics, 1993; editor: (book) Classics of Mathematics, 1982, Classics of Mathematics, rev. edit., 1995, Vita Mathematica, 1996; contbr. ; sect. editor: History and Pedagogy of Math. newsletter, 1989—98; contbr. articles and revs. to scholarly jours. Recipient Henry Schuman Prize, 1968, Austrian Cross Scis. & Arts 1st Class, 1996, Foley Outstanding Educator of the Yr. award, Nat. Bd. Dir. Aplha Delta Gamma, 2001; grantee German Marshall Fund, 1987, 1989, NSF, 1995, 1996, 1998, Hitachi, Internat. Virtual Inst. Hist. Studies Math., 1998—2001. Mem.: Math. Assn. Am. (hist. maths. com.), Atlantic Coun. (acad. assoc.), History Sci. Soc. (Washington rep. 1991—), Am. Hist. Assn., The Euler Soc. (chancellor 2001—), Phi Beta Kappa. Roman Catholic. Achievements include research in the history of mathematics; biographies of Leonhard Euler and Gottfried Leibniz; development of Newtonian science and competing Leibniz-

Wolffian thought in 18th century Brandenburg-Prussia and Russia; the University Berlin Mathematics Seminar under Kummer-Weierstrass, and Imperial Austria. Home: 12806 Lacy Dr Silver Spring MD 20904-2916 E-mail: calinger@cua.edu.

CALIO, ANTHONY JOHN, scientist, business executive; b. Phila., Oct. 27, 1929; s. Antonio and Mary Emma (Cappuccio) C.; m. Jenanne L. Murphy. BA, postgrad., U. Pa., 1953, Carnegie Inst. Tech., 1959; ScD (hon.), Washington U., St. Louis, 1974; postgrad. (Sloan fellow), Stanford U., 1974-75. With Westinghouse Electric Corp., Pitts., 1956-59; chief nuclear physics sect. Am. Machine & Foundry Co., Alexandria, Va., 1959-61; v.p. Mt. Vernon Rsch. Co., 1961-63; electronic rsch. task group NASA Hdqrs., Washington, 1963-64; chief rsch. engring. NASA (Electronics Rsch. Ctr.), Boston, 1964-65; chief instrumentation and systems integration br. NASA Hdqrs., Washington, 1965-67, asst. dir. planetary exploration, 1967-68; dir. sci. and applications NASA Johnson Space Ctr., Houston, 1969-75; dep. assoc. adminstr. office space scis. NASA Hdqrs., Washington, 1975-77, assoc. adminstr. Office of Space and Terrestrial Applications, 1977-81; dep. adminstrn. NOAA Dept. Commerce, 1981-84, under sec. for oceans and atmosphere, 1984-87; sr. v.p. Planning Rsch. Corp., McLean, Va., 1987-90; from exec. v.p. to sr. v.p. Hughes Info. Tech. Corp., Reston, Va., 1991-97; sr. v.p. Hughes Info. Tech. Sys., 1996-97; pres. Space Sys., 1996-97, Hughes Info. Tech. Sys., 1997-99; ret., 1999. With U.S. Army, 1954-56. Recipient Group Achievement award (2) NASA, 1969, Exceptional Service medal, 1969, Apollo Achievement award, 1970, Exceptional Sci. Achievement medal, 1971, Lunar Sci. Team award, 1973, Disting. Service medal, 1973, 81, presdl. rank of Disting. Exec., 1980 Fellow AIAA, Am. Astron. Soc.; mem. Am. Geophys. Union. Home: 4920 Scurlock Rd Freeland WA 98249-9632

CALIP, ROGER, writer, educator; b. Manila, Sept. 19, 1941; came to U.S. 1968; s. Generoso and Paula (Echalar) C. LittB in Journalism, U. Santo Tomas, Manila, 1961; Lic. Es Lettres, U. Paris, 1968; MA in Sociology, U. Conn., 1972, MA in French, 1977. Proofreader Robinson & Cole, Hartford, Conn., 1986-90; contbg. editor The Business Times, East Hartford, Conn., 1986-88; contbg. writer The Hartford News, Hartford, 1988-90; tchr. of writing Manchester (Conn.) C.C., 1988-98, West Hartford Continuing Edn., 1999—; freelance bus. writer Hartford Courant, Conn., 2001—03; contbg. writer Hartford Mag., 2003. Adj. instr. sociology Tunxis C.C., Farmington, Conn., 1992-94; adj. instr. French Mitchell Coll., New London, Conn., 1998-99. Contbr. articles and essays to mags. and newspapers. Recipient Rank 14 Top 100 Articles Writer's Digest, 1980, 2d Pl. short story Hartford Advocate, 1996. Mem.: Assn. Writers and Writing Programs. Roman Catholic. Avocation: reading. Home and Office: 19 Fennbrook Rd West Hartford CT 06119-2205 E-mail: rcalip2265@aol.com.

CALIRI, DAVID JOSEPH, retired lawyer, insurance agent; b. Lawrence, Mass., Dec. 12, 1929; s. Joseph and June Hazel (Rothera) C.; m. Saralou Debnam, Aug. 29, 1958; children: Linda, Donna, Paul, James, John. AB, Harvard Coll., 1951; LLB, Harvard U., 1954. Bar: N.J. Assoc. Gardner & Williams, Passaic, N.J., 1957-59, ptnr., 1959-64, Williams, Gardner, Caliri, Miller & Otley, Wayne, N.J., 1964-71, Williams, Caliri, Miller & Otley, Wayne, 1971-86; N.C. life, health, long-term care and Medicare ins. agt.; in-house counsel Capital Transactions Group, 2001—. Author: The Pine and the Thistle, 1989. Pres. bd. edn., Wayne, 1964-70; chmn., mem. Scholarship and Honors Bd., Wayne, 1972-86; dir. Lenni-lenape coun. Girl Scouts Am., 1970-82; coord. Presbytery of the Palisades, Teaneck, N.J., 1974-76; chmn. Moore County Dem. Party, 1992-97; elder Bethesda Presbyn. Ch., 1988-91, 93-95, mem. gov.'s com. Recognition of State Employees, N.C., 1993—; moderator Outdoor Ministries divsn., 2000-03, Presbytery of Coastal Carolina, 2002. With U.S. Army, 1955-56. Avocations: computing, writing, camping, vol. work. Home: 700 E Indiana Ave Southern Pines NC 28387-6643

CALISE, WILLIAM JOSEPH, JR., lawyer; b. N.Y.C., May 22, 1938; s. William Joseph and Adeline (Rota) C.; m. Elizabeth Mae Gagne, Apr. 16, 1966; children: Kimberly Elizabeth, Andrea Elizabeth. BA, Bucknell U., 1960; MBA, JD, Columbia U., 1963. Bar: N.Y. 1963, D.C. 1981. Assoc., then ptnr. Chadbourne & Parke, NYC, 1967—94; sr. v.p., gen. counsel, sec. Rockwell Automation, Inc., Milw., 1994—. Dir. Henry St. Settlement, N.Y.C., 1977-94; mem. Allendale (N.J.) Sch. Bd., 1977-80. Capt. U.S. Army, 1964-66. Mem. Assn. Bar N.Y.C., Milw. Club. Roman Catholic. Office: Rockwell Automation Inc 777 E Wisconsin Ave Milwaukee WI 53202-5300 E-mail: wjcalise@corp.rockwell.com.

CALISHER, HORTENSE (MRS. CURTIS HARNACK), writer; b. N.Y.C., Dec. 20, 1911; d. Joseph Henry and Hedvig (Lichtstern) C.; m. Curtis Harnack, Mar. 23, 1959; children by previous marriage: Bennet Hughes, Peter Heffelfinger. AB, Barnard Coll., 1932; LittD (hon.), Skidmore Coll., 1980, Grinnell Coll., 1986; LittD, Adelphi U., 1988. Adj. prof. English Barnard Coll., N.Y.C., 1956-57. Vis. lectr. State U. Iowa, 1957, 59-60, Stanford U., 1958, Sarah Lawrence Coll., Bronxville, N.Y., 1962, 67; adj. prof. Columbia U., N.Y.C., 1968-70, CCNY, 1969; vis. prof. lit. SUNY, Purchase, 1971-72, Brandeis U., 1963-64, U. Pa., 1965; Regent's prof. U. Calif., 1976; vis. prof. Bennington Coll., 1978, Washington U., St. Louis, 1979, Brown U., spring 1986; lectr., Fed. Republic of Germany, Yugoslavia, Rumania, Hungary, 1978; guest lectr. U.S./China Arts Exch., Republic of China, 1986. Author: (novels) False Entry, 1961, Textures of Life, 1962, The New Yorkers, 1969, Journal from Ellipsia, 1965, Queenie, 1971, Standard Dreaming, 1972, Eagle Eye, 1973, On Keeping Women, 1977, Mysteries of Motion, 1984, The Bobby-Soxer, 1986 (Kafka prize U. Rochester 1987), Age, 1987, (under pseudonym Jack Fenno) The Small Bang, 1992, In the Palace of the Movie-King, 1994, In the Slammer with Carol Smith, 1997; (novellas) The Railway Police, 1966, The Last Trolley Ride, 1966; short stories include In The Absence of Angels, 1951, Tale for the Mirror, 1962, Extreme Magic, 1963, Collected Stories, 1975, Saratoga Hot, 1985; autobiography: Herself, 1972; memoir: Kissing Cousins, 1988; contbr. short stories, articles, revs. to Am. Scholar, N.Y. Times, Harpers, Yale Rev., New Criterion, others. Guggenheim fellow, 1952, 55; Dept. of State Am. Specialists's grantee to S.E. Asia, 1958; recipient Acad. of Arts and Letters award, 1967, Nat. Council Arts award, 1967, Lifetime Achievement award Nat. Endowment for the Arts, 1989. Mem. Am. Acad. Arts and Letters (pres. 1987-90), PEN (pres. 1986-87). Office: care Marion Boyars Publishers 237 E 39th St New York NY 10016-2110 *Going back over one's work, one can see from earliest times certain para-forms emerging. If one is crazy, these are idées fixes: if one is sane these are systemic views. A mind is not given but makes itself, out of whatever is at hand and sticking-tape—and is not a private possession but an offering . . . I had always had to write everything, no matter the subject, as if my life depended upon it. Of course—it does. (from— Herself: An Autobiographical Work.)**

CALKINS, DAVID ROSS, physician, medical educator; b. Kansas City, Kans., May 27, 1948; s. Leroy Adelbert and Emily Virginia (Kyger) C.; m. Susan Spalding Rice, Sept. 22, 1989; 1 child, Christopher Ross. AB, Princeton (N.J.) U., 1970; MD, MPP, Harvard U., 1975. Diplomate Am. Bd. Internal Medicine. Intern U. Wash., Seattle, 1975-76; resident in medicine Beth Israel Hosp., Boston, 1976-78, from asst. to assoc. in medicine, 1981-96; fellow White House, Washington, 1978-79; spl. asst., dep. exec. sec. HHS, Washington, 1979-81; from instr. to asst. prof. medicine Harvard Med. Sch., Boston, 1981-96; from instr. to asst. prof. Harvard Sch. Pub. Health, Boston, 1985-96, dir. profl. programs dept. health policy and mgmt., 1985-96; chief div. gen. internal medicine, med. dir. ambulatory svc. New Eng. Deaconess Hosp., Boston, 1991-96; assoc. dean for primary care U. Kans. Sch. Medicine, Kansas City, 1996-98, from assoc. prof. to prof. internal and preventive medicine, 1996-99, sr. assoc. dean for edn., 1998-99; assoc. prof. medicine Harvard Med. Sch., Boston, 1999—, assoc. dean for clin. programs, 1999—2003. W.K. Kellogg Found. fellow, 1987. Office: 25 Shattuck St Boston MA 02115-6027 Business E-Mail: david_calkins@hms.harvard.edu.

CALKINS, EVAN, physician, educator; b. Newton, Mass., July 15, 1920; s. Grosvenor and Patty (Phillips) C.; m. Virginia McC. Brady, Sept. 9, 1946; children: Sarah Calkins Oxnard, Stephen, Lucy McCormick, Joan, Benjamin, Hugh, Ellen Rountree, Geoffrey, Timothy. Grad., Milton Acad., 1939; AB, Harvard U., 1942, MD, 1945. Intern, asst. resident medicine Johns Hopkins, 1946-47, 48-50; chief resident physician Mass. Gen. Hosp., 1951-52, mem. arthritis unit, 1952-61; NRC fellow med. scis. Harvard, 1950-51, instr., asst. prof. medicine, 1952-61; practice medicine, specializing in rheumatology Boston, 1951-61, Buffalo, 1961—; prof. medicine SUNY, Buffalo, 1961-94, prof. emeritus, 1994—, chmn. dept. medicine, 1965-77; head dept. medicine Buffalo Gen. Hosp., 1961-68; dir. medicine E.J. Meyer Meml. Hosp., 1968-78; head gerontology sect. Buffalo VA Med. Ctr., 1978-90; head div. geriatrics/gerontology SUNY-Buffalo, 1978-90. Founder, pres. Network in Aging of Western N.Y., Inc., 1980-83; cons. Nat. Inst. Arthritis and Metabolic Diseases Tng. Grants Com., 1958-62, Program Project Com., 1964-68, Nat. Instn. Spl. Study Sect. for Health Manpower, 1969-77, for Behavioral Medicine, 1978-79; mem. acad. awards com. Nat. Inst. on Aging, 1979-80, mem. nat. adv. coun., 1985-88; dir. Western N.Y. Geriatric Edn. Ctr., 1983-88, co-dir., 1988-90; dir. Multidisciplinary Ctr. on Aging SUNY-Buffalo, 1989-90, prof. family medicine, 1987-94; sr. physician and coord. geriatric programs Health Care Plan, 1990-97; ptnr. Promedicus Health Group, 1998-2001; co-dir. WNY/Rochester Osteoporosis Ednl. Resource Ctr., 1999; pvt. practice rheumatology and geriatrics, 2001—. Editor: Handbook of Medical Emergencies, 1945, Geriatric Medicine, 1983, Practice of Geriatrics, 1986, 2d edit., 1991, New Ways to Care for Older People: Building Systems Based on Evidence, 1998; contbr. articles to profl. jours. Pres. Nat. Assn. Geriatric Edn. Ctrs., 1992-93. Capt. M.C. AUS, 1943-45, 46-48. Recipient Presdl. citation for Community Service, 1983 Fellow ACP (master 1989, Laureate award N.Y. Upstate chpt. 1998), Am. Coll. Rheumatology (founder, pres. 1967-68, master 1986), Gerontol. Soc. Am. (chair clin. med. sect. 1989, Freeman award 1991), Am. Geriatrics Soc. (Milo D. Leavitt award 1986); mem. Am. Clin. and Climatological Assn. (v.p. 1987), Am. Soc. Clin. Investigation, Assn. Am. Physicians, Soc. Medicine Argentina (hon.), Argentine Soc. Gerontology and Geriatrics (hon.), Soc. Fellows John Hopkins U., Alpha Omega Alpha. Home: 3799 Windover Dr Hamburg NY 14075-6338 Office: Village Rheumatology 17 Long Ave Ste 110 Hamburg NY 14075-6388

CALKINS, HUGH, foundation executive; b. Newton, Mass., Feb. 20, 1924; s. Grosvenor and Patty (Phillips) C.; m. Ann Clark, June 14, 1955; children: Peter, Andrew, Margaret, Elizabeth. AB, LLB, Harvard U., 1949, D in Law (hon.), 1985. Bar: Ohio 1950. Law clk. to presiding judge U.S. Ct. Appeals (2d cir.), N.Y.C., 1949-50; law clk. to justice Felix Frankfurter U.S. Supreme Ct., Washington, 1950-51; from assoc. to ptnr. Jones, Day, Reavis & Pogue, Cleve., 1951-90; tchr. elem. schs. Cleve. City Sch. Dist., 1991-94. Contbr. articles on fed. income tax to profl. jours. Mem. Cleve. Bd. Edn., 1965-69; assoc. dir. Pres.'s Commn. on Nat. Goals, Washington, 1960; mem., pres., fellow Harvard U., 1968-85; mem. task forces Cleve. Summit on Edn., 1990-94; pres., trustee Initiatives in Urban Edn., 1991—. Capt. USAF, 1943-46. Mem. ABA (chmn. tax sect. 1985-86), Am. Law Inst. (coun.), City Club, Cleve. Skating Club, Rowfant Club, Phi Beta Kappa. Democrat. Unitarian Universalist. Home and Office: 3345 N Park Blvd Cleveland OH 44118-4258

CALKINS, JERRY MILAN, anesthesiologist, educator, administrator, biomedical engineer; b. Benkelman, Nebr., Sept. 10, 1942; s. Robert Thomas and Mildred Rachel (Stamm) C.; m. Connie Mae Satterfield, Oct. 17, 1964; children: Julie Lynn, Jenifer Ellan. BSChemE, U. Wyo., 1964, MSChemE, 1966; PhD in Chem. Engring., U. Md., 1971; MD, U. Ariz., 1976. Diplomate Am. Bd. Anesthesiology. Lectr. engring. U. Md., College Park, 1970-71; asst. prof. engring. Ariz. State U., Tempe, 1971-73; asst. prof. anesthesiology U. Ariz., Tucson, 1979-84, assoc. prof., 1984; assoc. prof., vice chmn. dept. U. N.C., Chapel Hill, 1984-86; clin. assoc. U. N.Mex., Albuquerque, 1986-88, chmn. dept. anesthesiology Lovelace Med. Ctr., 1986-88; chmn. dept. anesthesiology Maricopa Med. Ctr., Phoenix, 1988-98; clin. prof. anesthesiology U. Ariz., 1988—; v.p. med. affairs Metasensors, Inc., 1998—; med. staff Mayo Clinic, Scottsdale, Ariz. Adj. assoc. prof. indsl. engring. N.C. State U., 1984-86; adj. faculty Ariz. State U. Coll. Engr., 1988—; dir. med. engring. lab. Harry Diamond Labs., Washington, 1968-71; cons. Bur. Med. Devel., FDA, Washington, 1977-86; asst. prof. engring., bd. dir. advanced biotech. Lab. Ariz. Health Sci. Ctr., Tucson, 1979-84 Co-author: Future Anesthesia Delivery Systems, 1984, High Frequency Ventilation, 1986; editor Annals Biomed. Engring., 1979, Clin. Monitoring, 1984— ; contbr. numerous articles to profl. jours., chpts. to books Chmn., bd. dirs. Gladys Taylor McGary Med. Found., 1999—. Recipient Outstanding Tchr. award Upjohn Co., 1979; spl. fellow NIH, 1970 Mem. AMA, AICE, Am. Soc. Anesthesiologists, Am. Soc. Artificial Internal Organs, Closed and Lowflow Anesthesia Systems Soc. (pres. 1986-88), Soc. Tech. Anesthesia (pres. 1993—), Ariz. Med. Assn., Ariz. Soc. Anesthesiology (v.p. 1998), Am. Found. Med. Acupuncture (pres. 1992), Maricopa County Med. Assn., Masons, Sigma Xi. Republican. Avocations: swimming; skiing; tennis; golf; model railroading. Office: Conjer Inc 5915 E Caron Cir Paradise Valley AZ

CALKINS, MARK R. tenor, educator; b. Mounds Park, Minn., Aug. 16, 1961; s. Richard B. and Eileen M. Calkins; m. Cynthia Lawrence, Mar. 17, 1985; children: Rowan, Shannon. MusB, Concordia Coll., 1983; MusM, U. Colo., 1987. Tenor London Classical Players, 1996, Raoul Co./Kennedy Ctr., Washington, 1997, Sacramento Opera, 2001, Opera Columbus, Ohio, 2001, Piedmont Opera, Winston-Salem, NC, 2002, Tacoma Opera, 2003; instr. voice Northwestern Coll., St. Paul, 2001—. Instr. voice U. N.D., Grand Forks, 2001, U. Colo., Boulder, 1998, No. Utah State U., 1996. Singer: Lyric Opera Ctr. for Am. Artists, 1987—90, Ctrl. City Opera Co., 1985—86; singer: (TV prodn.) (Operas) Under the Arbor by Robert Greenleaf. Mem.: Coll. Music Soc., Am. Guild Musical Artists, Nat. Assn. Tchrs. of Singing. Republican. Lutheran. Avocations: boating, bicycling, yoga. Office: Northwestern Coll 3003 N Snelling Ave Saint Paul MN 55113-1598*

CALKINS, RALPH NELSON, economics educator; b. Albuquerque, Apr. 28, 1926; s. Fred Myron and Luella (McDonald) C.; m. Ruth J. (Thatcher) Calkins, Jan. 8, 1949; children: Alison, Paul, Patricia. BBA, U. N.Mex., 1947, MA, 1949; PhD, Columbia U., 1963. Instr. econs. Bloomfield (N.J.) Coll., 1949-53, dean, 1953-67; assoc. prof. U. Alaska, Fairbanks, 1967-68; prof. dept. econs. and bus. adminstrn. Hanover (Ind.) Coll., 1968-91, prof. emeritus, 1991. Author: (CD) The Gradual Encroachment-Capitalism As We Know It, 2003. With USN, 1944-46. Mem. AAAS, Am. Econ. Assn., Am. Solar Energy Soc., Union of Concerned Scientists (sponsor), Ind. Acad. Social Scis. (bd. dirs. 1985-88). Democrat. Home: 7424 Edith Blvd NE Albuquerque NM 87113-1202 Office: Hanover Coll Faculty Office Bldg Hanover IN 47243

CALKINS, RICHARD M. lawyer; b. 1931; BA, Dartmouth Coll., 1953; JD, Northwestern U, 1959. Bar: Ill. 1959. Law clk. US Ct. Appeals, 7th Cir., Chgo., 1959—61; assoc. Chadwell, Keck, Kayser, Ruggles, McLaren, Chgo., 1961—68, ptnr., 1968—69, Burditt & Calkins, Chgo., 1969—78; prof. John Marshall Law Sch., 1978—80; prof. law, dean Drake U, 1980—. Served USAR. Mem.: Order Coif. Office: Drake U Law Sch 25th University Ave Des Moines IA 50314-3118

CALKINS, SUSAN W. state supreme court justice; Grad., U. Colo.; JD, U. Maine. Staff atty., exec. dir. Pine Tree Legal Assistance; judge Maine Dist. Ct., 1980-90, chief judge, 1990—94; judge Maine Superior Ct., 1995—98; justice Maine Supreme Jud. Ct., 1998—. Office: Maine Judicial Center 65 Stone St Augusta ME 04330*

CALKINS, SUSANNAH EBY, retired economist; b. Bucyrus, Ohio, Jan. 16, 1924; d. Samuel L. and Mae (McClure) Eby; m. G. Nathan Calkins, Nov. 19, 1949 (dec.); children: Helen E. (dec.), Margaret S. Van Auken, Sarah A. (dec.), Abigail Calkins Aguirre. AB, Goucher Coll., 1945; MS in Econs. (Univ. scholar 1946-47), U. Wis., 1947. Fiscal analyst U.S. Bur. Budget, 1945-50; economist U.S. Council Econ. Advisors, 1950-51, U.S. Office Price Stabilization, 1951-53, U.S. Bur. Budget, 1953-55; cons. U.S. Adv. Commn. on Intergovtl. Rels., Washington, 1972-73, 74-75, cons. on counter-cyclical aid programs, 1977-78, sr. analyst, 1979-87, exec. asst. to dir., 1987-89. Cons. revenue sharing Brookings Instn., Washington, 1973-74. Author: (with R. Nathan and A. Manvel) Monitoring Revenue Sharing, 1975. Sponsor S.S. Goucher Victory, Balt., 1945; bd. dirs. Bread for the City, 1994-2002. Mem. Am. Econs. Assn., George Towne Club (Washington), Phi Beta Kappa. Presbyterian. Home: 6504 Dearborn Dr Falls Church VA 22044-1115

CALL, MERLIN WENDELL, lawyer; b. Long Beach, Calif., Nov. 25, 1931; s. True and Bernice (Johnson) C.; m. Kathryn J. Gage, Dec. 22, 1956 (div.); children: Christopher, Lori. AB, Stanford U., 1951, JD, 1953. Bar: Calif. 1953. Assoc. Tuttle & Taylor, L.A., 1955-60, ptnr., 1960-2000; sr. counsel Shapiro, Borenstein & Dupont, Santa Monica, Calif., 2000—02. Bd. visitors Stanford Sch. Law, 1987-90. Chmn. bd. trustees Westmont Coll., Santa Barbara, Calif., 1988—94, The Fuller Found., Pasadena, Calif., 1987—94, Mission Aviation Fellowship, Redlands, Calif., 1974—78, Gospel Broadcasting Assn., 1967—78, De Pree Leadership Ctr., 2001—; mem. Town Hall Calif., L.A., 1958—; trustee Fuller Theol. Sem., Pasadena, 1963—78, 1983—, chmn., 2001—; trustee China Connection, 2001—, Westmont Coll., Santa Barbara, Calif., 1984—, The Fuller Found., 1987—, Mission Aviation Fellowship, Redlands, Calif., 1963—78. Mem. Phi Beta Kappa, Order of Coif. Home: 1660 La Loma Rd Pasadena CA 91105-2158 Office: 225 S Lake Ave Ste 300 Pasadena CA 91101- E-mail: mwcall@earthlink.net., mwcalllaw@polarisnet.net.

CALL, NEIL JUDSON, corporate executive; b. Detroit, June 15, 1933; s. Judson Francis and Glennys Jean (Amluxen) C.; m. Jane E. Rathslag, Feb. 4, 1956; children: Laura, Keith; m. Eleanor Ann King, Nov. 23, 1978. BBA, U. Mich., 1955, MBA, 1956. C.P.A., Mich. With Hogan Juengel & Harding (C.P.A.'s), Detroit, 1956-61, Ford Motor Co., Dearborn, Mich., 1961-65; with Ford Motor Credit Co., Dearborn, 1965-67, Gulf & Western Industries Inc., N.Y.C., 1968-86, v.p., 1970-79, sr. v.p., 1979-83, exec. v.p., 1983-84, D.F. King & Co., Inc., N.Y.C., 1986-89, Dewe Rogerson Inc., N.Y.C., 1990-92, Mackenzie Ptnrs., Inc., N.Y.C., 1992—. Bd. dirs. So. Fin. Bancorp. Bd. dirs. Lower Fla. Keys Hosp. Dist., 2000—. Served with U.S. Army, 1956-58. Home: 1500 Atlantic Blvd Apt 307 Key West FL 33040-5071 Office: Mackenzie Ptnrs Inc 105 Madison Ave New York NY 10016-7002 E-mail: nandecall@aol.com.

CALLAGHAN, BARNEY, secondary school educator; b. Richwood, W.Va., June 15, 1950; s. T. Paul and Gloria A. Callaghan. BA in English, Bradley U., 1974; MS in Recreation Adminstrn., Aurora U., 2001. Cert. H.S. tchr. Ill. Resource tchr. Indian Trail Jr. H.S., Addison, Ill., 1974—75; English tchr., coach St. Anthony H.S., Effingham, Ill., 1977—78, Cumberland H.S., Toledo, Ill., 1978, St. Teresa Acad., Decatur, Ill., 1979—81, Griffin H.S., Springfield, Ill., 1981—82, Kaneland H.S., Maple Park, Ill., 1985—. Mem.: NEA, Ill. Edn. Assn., Hi-Pointers. Democrat. Avocations: writing, hiking. Office: Kaneland HS 47W326 Keslinger Rd Maple Park IL 60151

CALLAGHAN, DAN O. lawyer; b. Charleston, W. Va., June 24, 1935; s. Brooks B. and Rebekah M. (Myers) Callaghan; m. Margaret L. Errington, Aug. 31, 1958; children: Michael O., Stephen O. BS commerce, U. Va., 1957; LLB, 1962. Bar: W. Va. 1962, US Dist. Ct. (so. dist.)/W. Va. 1963, US Supreme Ct. 1969, US Dist. Ct. (no. dist.)/W. Va. 1971, US Ct. Appeals (4th cir.) 1981. Ptnr. Callaghan & Callaghan, W.Va., 1962—81, Callaghan & Callaghan, Ruckman & Vaughan, Charleston, 1981—; dir. Cherry River Nat. Bank, 1973—. Served USN, 1958—59, served USNR, 1959—67. Mem.: Richwood C. of C. (W. Va. pres. 1972—73), Nicholas County Bar Assn., Trial Lawyers Assn., W. Va. State Bar Assn. (grievance com. 1980—), Assn. Trial Lawyers Am., ABA (numerous com.), Cherry Hill Country (Richwood). Democrat. Meth. Office: W Va State Bar E-400 State Capitol Charleston WV 25305

CALLAGHAN, GEORGANN MARY, lawyer; b. Bklyn., June 25, 1944; d. George Louis and Jean (Russo) Carpenito; m. Matthew John Callaghan, June 7, 1969; children: Matthew, Michael, Christian. BS in Hist. Studies, SUNY Empire State Coll., 1994; JD, Pace U., 1999. Bar: Conn. 1999, N.Y. 2000, D.C. 2000. Adminstr. Wood & Scher, Scarsdale, 1986—99, atty., 1999—2001; assoc. Colucci & Umans, 2001—. Exec. com. Boy Scouts Am. Mem. ABA, N.Y. State Bar Assn., Westchester County Bar Assn., Conn. Bar Assn., D.C. Bar Assn., Westchester Women's Bar Assn., Scarsdale Town and Village Club. Home: 49 Carman Rd Scarsdale NY 10583-6328 Office: Colucci & Umans 670 White Plains Rd Scarsdale NY 10583

CALLAGHAN, JOHN WILLIAM, JR., information technology manager, retired military officer; b. Frankfurt, Germany, Nov. 20, 1953; s. John William and Virginia Timberman Callaghan; m. Vivian Anne Simmons, Apr. 20, 1957; children: John William III, Virginia Keyes, Samuel Brooks. BS in Math and Physics, Campbell U., N.C., 1979; MA in Security Mgmt., Webster U., St. Louis, 1996; EdD, George Wash. U., Washington, D.C., 2001—. Comptrollership, U.S. Dept. of Def., 1988; Counter Terrorism U.S. Dept. of Def., 1989. Army officer inf. and counter terrorism Various Units to include Army Rangers, SF Detachment Delta (planning HQ), 82d Airborne Div, 2d Inf. Div Korea, Dep. J-3 Haiti Op Uphold Democracy, U.S. and Korea, 1979—97; sr. program analyst Ballistic Missile Def. Orgn., Sr. Budget Analyst, Pentagon, Futron Corp., Arlington, Va., 1997—99; sr. sys. integrator Discoverer II, Joint Space Based Radar Intelligence Program, Pentagon, SRS Technologies Corp., Arlington, Va., 1999—2000; site mgr., sr. program analyst Joint Urban Warfare & Counter Terrorism, Joint Chiefs of Staff, Pentagon- SRS Technologies Corp., Arlington, Va., 2000—01; sr. program mgr. Anti- Terrorism, Homeland Security, U.S. Dept. of Interior, Veridian, Fairfax, Va., 2001—03; sr. bus. area mgr. Counter Terrorism & Intelligence Ops. Support Svcs. Harris Corp, Alexandria, Va., 2003—. Vice nat. comdr. Korean Veteran's of Am., Washington, 1999—2003. Maj. U.S. Army, 1972—97. Scholar George Wash. U. Excellence in Edn., Dept. of Higher Edn., 2001—03. Mem.: The Ret. Officer Assn. (assoc.). Conservative. Roman Catholic. Achievements include Vice Nat. Comdr. Korean Def. Veteran's of Am. (U.S. Congressionally approved Vet. organization). Avocations: running, reading history, outdoor work. Home: 8211 Greeley Blvd Springfield VA 22152 Office: Harris Corp 1201 E Abingdon Ste 500 Alexandria VA 22314 Office Fax: 703-739-1779. E-mail: john.callaghan@harris.com.

CALLAGHAN, MARY ANNE, secondary school educator; b. Seattle, Mar. 14, 1947; d. John Joseph and Catherine Clara (Emard) C.; m. David Michael Buerge, Mar. 8, 1975; children: David John, Catherine Emily. BA in English Lit., U. Wash., 1970, Teaching Cert., 1973. Standard Wash. state teaching certification. Tchr. tng. intern Hazen H.S., Renton, Wash., 1968-70, tchr. English, 1970-71; tchr. English, theology Forest Ridge Sch. of the Sacred Heart, Bellevue, Wash., 1971-93, dean of students, 1988-92; tchr. English, theology Holy Cross H.S., Everett, Wash., 1993—, student life v.p., 1995-98, Archbishop Murphy H.S. (formerly Holy Cross H.S.), 1999. Chair English dept. Forest Ridge H.S. and Holy Cross H.S., 1980—; mem. accreditation team Holy Name Acad., Seattle, 1991, O'Dea H.S., Seattle, 1995; insvc. presenter for Archdiocese of Seattle, 1992, 93, 98. Vol. Christian Movement for Peace, Montreal, Quebec, 1972; sch. bd. mem. St. Catherine Parish, Seattle, 1984-90. Recipient grants to initiate ethnic awareness programs Religious of the Sacred Heart, 1982, grant to study Asian lit. NEH, 1988. Mem. Nat. Cath. Edn. Assn., Nat. Coun. Tchrs. English. Roman Catholic. Avocations: film, hiking, teaching classes on grief. Office: Archbishop Murphy HS PMB # 6132 12911 39th Ave SE Everett WA 98208-6159 E-mail: mcallaghan@archbishopmurphyhs.org.

CALLAHAN, ALSTON, physician, author; b. Vicksburg, Miss., Mar. 16, 1911; s. Neil and Effie (Alston) C.; m. Eivor Holst, Feb. 23, 1941; children: Kristina Alice, Patrick Alston, Michael Alston, Timothy Alston, Karin Eivor, Kevin (dec. 1961). AB, Miss. Coll., 1929; MD, Tulane U., 1933, MS in Ophthalmology, 1936; RSM, Tulane U., London, 1990. Diplomate Am. Bd. Ophthalmology. Intern Charity Hosp., New Orleans, 1933-35, resident in ophthalmology, 1936-37; hon. mem. emeritus Eye Found. Univ. Hosps, Birmingham, Ala., 1959—; also founder Callahan Eye Found. Hosp., Birmingham, Ala., 1964; co-developer Rsch. and Profl. Office Bldg. E.F. Hosp., 1985-87; founder Internat. Retinal Rsch Found., Inc., Birmingham, 1997. Author: Surgery of the Eye, Injuries, 1950, Surgery of the Eye, Diseases, 1956, Reconstructive Surgery of the Eyelids and Ocular Adnexa, 1966, (with M. Callahan) Ophthalmic Plastic Surgery, 1979; contbr. articles to profl. jours. Served to capt. M.C., AUS, 1944-46 Recipient award Ala. Acad. Honor, 1996; named Tulane Alumnus of Yr., 1997, to Ala. Healthcare Hall of Fame, 1998. Fellow ACS, Royal Australian Coll. Ophthalmology (hon.); mem. Am. Acad. Ophthalmology, So. Med. Assn. (emeritus), Am. Soc. Ophthal. Plastic Surgery, Alpha Omega Alpha, Sigma Alpha Epsilon. Clubs: Mountain Brook, The Club, Metropolitan, Explorers. also: Internat Retinal Rsch Found Inc 700 18th St S Ste 511 Birmingham AL 35233-3802 Office: 1720 University Blvd Birmingham AL 35233-1816

CALLAHAN, BILL, professional football coach; b. Chicago, July 31, 1956; m. Valerie Callahan; 4 children. Coach Oakland Raiders, 2002—, offensive line coach, 1999, Phila. Eagles, 1995—97, Univ. Wis., 1990—94; offensive coord. So. Ill. Univ., 1989. Office: Oakland Raiders 1220 Harbor Bay Pky Alameda CA 94502

CALLAHAN, BILLY T. writer, secondary school educator; b. Queens, NY, Sept. 20, 1970; s. Thomas Leo and Alice Brady Callahan; m. Gretel Sarah Salzmann, June 29, 2002. BA in Comm., Seton Hall U., 1995. Tchr. English Ranney Sch., Tinton Falls, NJ, 2003—. Author: Muckraker, 1999. Mem. Celebrations Com., Garwood, NJ, 2003. Home: 211 2nd Ave Apt 1-L Garwood NJ 07027

CALLAHAN, CONSUELO MARIA, federal judge; b. Palo Alto, Calif., June 9, 1950; married; 2 children. BA, Leland Stanford Jr. Univ., 1968—72; JD, McGeorge Sch. of Law, Univ. of the Pacific, 1972—75; grad LLM, Univ. of Va. Sch. of Law, 2002—. Bar: Calif. 1975. Dep. city atty. City of Stockton, Stockton, Calif., 1975—76; dep. dist. atty. Dist. Atty. Office, San Joaquin County, Calif., 1976—82, sup. dist. atty., 1982—86; ct. comm. Mcpl. Ct. of Stockton, Stockton, Calif., 1986—92; judge San Joaquin County Superior Ct., San Joaquin, Calif., 1992—96; Assoc. judge Ct. of Appeal, State of Calif., Calif., 1996—2003; judge, U.S. Court of Appeals (9th. cir.), 2003—. Recipient Award for Criminal Justice Programs, Gov., Susan B. Anthony Award for Women of Achievement, Stockton Peacemaker of the Yr., 1997, Mexican-Am. Hall of Fame, San Joaquin County, 1999. Office: US Ct Appeals 95 Seventh St San Francisco CA 94103*

CALLAHAN, DANIEL JOHN, biomedical researcher; b. Washington, July 19, 1930; s. Vincent Francis and Anita (Hawkins) Callahan; m. Sidney Cornelia de Shazo, June 5, 1954; children: Mark Sidney, Stephen Daniel, John Vincent, Peter Thorn, Sarah Elisabeth, David Lee. BA, Yale U., 1952; MA, Georgetown U., 1957; PhD, Harvard U., 1965; DSc (hon.), U. Medicine and Dentistry of N.J., 1981; DHL (hon.), U. Colo., 1990, Williams Coll., 1992, Oreg. State U., 1997. Exec. editor The Commonweal, N.Y.C., 1961—68; staff assoc. Population Council, 1969—70; co-founder, pres. The Hastings Ctr., 1969—96, dir. internat. programs, 1997—; resident scholar Aspen Inst. Humanistic Studies, 1975. Vis. asst. prof. religion Temple U., 1964; vis. asst. prof. religious studies Brown U., 1965; vis. prof. theology Marymount Coll., 1966; vis. prof. U. Pa., 1970; sr. fellow Harvard Ctr. for Population and Devel. Studies, 1996; cons. med. ethics, jud. coun. AMA, 1972—82, ACP, 1979—; spl. cons. Commn. on Population Growth and Am. Future, 1970—71, NEH, 1979; hon. prof. Charles U. Med. Sch., Prague, 1997—; sr. fellow Harvard Med. Sch., 1998—. Author: The Mind of the Catholic Layman, 1963, Honesty in the Church, 1965, The New Church, 1966, Abortion: Law, Choice and Morality, 1970, Ethics and Population Limitation, 1971, The Tyranny of Survival, 1973, The Teaching of Ethics in the Military, 1982, Setting Limits: Medical Goals in an Aging Society, 1987, What Kind of Life: The Limits of Medical Progress, 1990, The Troubled Dream of Life: Living with Morality, 1993, False Hopes: Why America's Quest for Perfect Health is a Recipe for Failure, 1998, What Price Better Health: Hazards of the Research Imperative, 2003; also essays, articles: ; co-editor: Christianity Divided: Protestant and Roman Catholic Theological Issues, 1961, Ethical Issues in Human Genetics, 1973; editor: Federal Aid and Catholic Schools, 1964, Secular City Debate, 1966, The Catholic Case for Contraception, 1969, The American Population Debate, 1971, Science, Ethics and Medicine, 1976, Knowledge, Value and Belief, 1977, Morals, Science and Sociality, 1978, Knowing and Valuing, 1979, Ethics Teaching in Higher Education, 1980, Ethical Issues in Population Aid, 1980, The Roots of Ethics, 1981, Ethics in Hard Times, 1981, Ethics, the Social Sciences and Policy Analysis, 1983, Abortion: Understanding Differences, 1984, Applying the Humanities, 1985, Representation and Responsibility, 1985, A World Growing Old, 1995, What Price Mental Health?, 1995, Promoting Healthy Behavior, 2000, The Role of Complementary and Alternative Medicine, 2002, What Price Better Health, 2003; mem. editl. adv. bd.: Tech. in Soc., 1981—, mem. adv. bd.: Ency. of Life Scis., 1982, Sci., Tech. and Human Values, 1979—, Bus. and Profl. Ethics, 1981, Criminal Justice Ethics, 1982, Environ. Ethics, 1982, Jour. Bioethics, 1985—96. Mem. nat. adv. bd. Health Promotion Program, Henry J. Kaiser Family Found., 1987—91, N.Y. Panel and HIV Screening, 1987; adv. com. to dir. Ctr. for Disease Control, DHHS; mem. N.Y. Coun. for Humanities, 1975—79, Nat. Book Award Com., 1975, N.Y. State Health Adv. Coun., 1975—76; selection com. Ford-Rockefeller Program in Population Policy, 1975—78, Rockefeller Found. Program in Humanities, 1980; elector Nat. Medal for Lit., 1979—83; pub. mem. Am. Bd. Med. Specialties, 1982—87, N.Y. Sci. Policy Assn., 1985—91; mem. N.Y. Task Force on Life and Law, 1985—87; trustee U. Pa. Med. Ctr., 1987—91; mem. adv. com. on sci. integrity HHS, 1991—93. Named one of 200 Outstanding Young Men Leaders, Time mag., 1974; named one of 200 Outstanding Young Men Leaders, 1974; recipient Thomas More medal, 1970, Career Achievement award, Soc. Bioethics and Med. Humanities, 2001, Daryl J. Mase Disting. Leadership award, 1987, Book of Yr. award, Am. Jour. Nursing, 1987, Henry Knowles Beecher award, The Hastings Ctr., 1989, James H. Hamilton Book award, Am. Coll. Health Care Execs., 1990, Pres. Cabinet award, U. Tex., 1995, Scientific Freedom and Responsibility award, AAAS, 1995, Joseph Leiter award, Nat. Libr. of Medicine, 1999, ARCHON award, Sigma Theta Tau Internat. Honor Soc. of Nursing, 1999, Washington Irving Book award for Fals Hopes, 1999, Thomas More medal, 1970, Career Achievement award, Soc. Bioethics and Med. Humanities, 2001, Daryl J. Mase Disting. Leadership award, 1987, Book of Yr. award, Am. Jour. Nursing, 1987, Henry Knowles Beecher award, The Hastings Ctr., 1989, James H. Hamilton Book award, Am. Coll. Health Care Execs., 1990, Pres. Cabinet award, U. Tex., 1995, Scientific Freedom and Responsibility award, AAAS, 1995, Joseph Leiter award, Nat. Libr. of Medicine, 1999, ARCHON award, Sigma Theta Tau Internat. Honor Soc. of Nursing, 1999, Washington Irving Book award for False Hopes, 1999, Movison prize for sci. and society, MIT; fellow nat. fellow, Bus. Enterprise Trust, 1989—95, nat., 1989—95; scholar Tekolste scholar, Ind. Hosp. Assn., 1986, Tekolste, 1986. Fellow: AAAS (Sci. Freedom and Responsibility award 1996); mem.: Soc. for Study Social Biology (bd. dirs. 1987—95), Inst. Medicine of NAS, Am. Assn. for Advancement Humanities, Harvard Grad. Soc. (coun. 1989—92). Home: PO Box 260 Ardsley On Hudson NY 10503-0260 Office: The Hastings Ctr 21 Malcolm Gordon Rd Garrison NY 10524-5555

CALLAHAN, DANIEL JOSEPH, surgeon, consultant; b. Balt., Sept. 28, 1945; s. Thomas Daniel and Mary Catherine C.; m. Barbara Joan Danahy, Nov. 24, 1979; 1 child, Daniel Joseph, Jr. BA, LaSalle Coll., 1967; MD, Thomas Jefferson U., 1971. Asst. prof. plastic and reconstructive surgery St. Louis U., 1977-80, founder, divsn. hand clinic; chief surgery, vice chief of med. staff St. Petersburg (Fla.) Gen. Hosp., 1992; chief plastic surgery Sunrise Med. Ctr., Freeport, Bahamas, 1995-97; clin. cons., 1997—. Contbr. articles to profl. jours. Mem. AMA, AAAS, N.Y. Acad. Scis. Achievements include first successful multi-digit microvascular reimplantation in Missouri, 1977.

CALLAHAN, DEBRA JEAN, professional society administrator; b. Burbank, Calif., June 4, 1958; d. Robert Bascom and Betty Jean Callahan. Student, Calif. State Poly. U., San Luis Obispo, 1976-79; BA magna cum laude, U. Calif., Santa Barbara, 1981. Legal asst. Loo, Merideth & McMillan, L.A., 1982-83; field staff Mondale for Pres., Washington, 1984; dep. state campaign mgr. Mondale-Ferraro Com., Kansas City, Mo., 1984; regional polit. dir. League of Conservation Voters, Portsmouth, N.H., 1985-86; dep. campaign mgr. Kent Conrad for U.S. Senate, Bismarck, N.D., 1986; exec. asst. to Senator Kent Conrad, Washington, 1986-87; dep. nat. polit. dir. Gore for Pres., Washington, 1987-88; exec. dir. Ams. for the Environment, Washington, 1988-90; campaign mgr. Re-election Rep. Howard Wolpe (D-Md.), 1990; policy cons. Nat. Toxics Campaign, 1991—; program dir. W. Alton Jones Found., 1992-95; exec. dir. Brainerd Found., Seattle, 1995-96; pres. League of Conservation Voters, Washington, 1996—. Polit. cons. League of Conservation Voters, 1988. Field dir. Hands Across Am., St. Louis, 1986; bd. dirs. World Resources Inst., 1998—, Earth Day Network, 1999—. U. Calif. Dept. Environ. Studies scholar, Santa Barbara, 1981, Alumni award, 1998. Avocations: travel, reading, scuba diving, cycling, music. Office: League of Conservation Voters 1920 L St NW Ste 800 Washington DC 20036-5045

CALLAHAN, EDWARD WILLIAM, chemical engineer, retired manufacturing executive; b. N.Y.C., July 17, 1930; s. William Patrick and Clara (Schultz) C.; m. Barbara Jane Willmarth, Nov. 23, 1985; children: Susan Lynne, Kevin Foster. B.Ch.E., Cornell U., 1953. Engr. Solvay div. Allied Chem. Corp., Syracuse, N.Y., 1953-65, dir. comml. devel., 1965-66; asst. to pres. Allied Signal Corp., N.Y.C., 1966-70, gen. mgr. environ. services Morristown, N.J., 1970-78, v.p. health, safety and environ. scis., 1978-95; ret. Bd. dirs. Am. Cancer Soc., Morristown, 1982-84; trustee Ind. Coll. Fund. of N.J., 1988-94. Mem.: Chem. Mfrs. Assn. (chmn. environ. mgmt. com. 1978—82), Am. Indsl. Health Coun. (dir. 1978—91), Chem. Industry Inst. Toxicology (dir. 1974—91, Conf. Bd. environ. com. chmn. 1994—95), World Environ. Ctr. (bd. dirs. 1992—98), Internat. Environ. Forum (chmn. 1986—94), Laurel Links Country Club, Quantuck Beach Club, Quogue Field Club, Jonathan's Landing Golf Club, Shinnecock Yacht Club, Union Club, F & AM (Holland Loge No. 8). Home: 16940 Bay St Apt 207 N Jupiter FL 33477-1207

CALLAHAN, GERALD WILLIAM, lawyer, oil company executive; b. 1936; BA, Gannon Coll., 1960; JD, Washington U, St. Louis, 1965. Assoc. McAlevy & Welch, 1966—71, Breene, Frame & Magee, 1967; trust officer 1st Seneca Bank & Trust Co., 1968—71; asst. sec., corp. legal counsel Quaker State Oil Refining Corp., Oil City, Pa., 1971—79, v.p., corp. legal counsel, 1979—85, v.p. counsel and corp. sec., 1985—93, v.p. gen. counsel, sec., 1993—. USMC, 1954—56. Office: Quaker State Corp 700 Milam St Houston TX 77002-2806 Address: Quaker Sate Corp 700 Milam St Houston TX 77002-2806

CALLAHAN, JOHN JOSEPH, lawyer; b. Toledo, Feb. 5, 1922; s. Hugh and Anna (Mackin) C.; m. Joyce Teague, Apr. 18, 1953. BA, John Carroll U., 1949; LLB, U. Mich., 1952. Bar: Ohio 1952, U.S. Supreme Ct. 1966, U.S. Mil. Ct. Appeals 1966, U.S. Ct. Appeals (6th cir.) 1973. Assoc. Burgess & Callahan, Toledo, 1952-72, Openlander, Callahan & Connelly, Toledo, 1972-77; ptnr. Secor, Ide & Callahan, Toledo, 1977-92; prin. John J. Callahan Law Office, Toledo, 1992—99; of counsel McHugh, Denune and McCarthy, Sylvania, Ohio, 1999—. Served to Maj. USAF, 1942-46. Fellow ABA, Ohio State Bar Assn., Toledo Bar Assn. (pres. 1969-70). Democrat. Roman Catholic. Home: 4203 Eaglehurst Rd Sylvania OH 43560-3410 Office: 5580 Monroe St Sylvania OH 43560-2561

CALLAHAN, J(OHN) WILLIAM (BILL CALLAHAN), judge; b. Rockville Centre, N.Y., Feb. 8, 1947; s. Peter Felix and Catherine L. (Walbroehl) C. BA, Mich. State U., 1971, JD cum laude, 1974. Atty. Bank of Commonwealth, Detroit, 1974-76; assoc. Hoops & Hudson, P.C., Detroit, 1976-79, Tyler & Canham, P.C., Detroit, 1979-80, Stark & Reagan, P.C., Troy, Mich., 1980-81; pvt. practice Farmington Hills, Mich., 1981-86; mem. Plunkett & Cooney, P.C., Detroit, 1986-96; judge Wayne County Cir. Ct., Detroit, 1996—. Bd. dirs. Vietnam Vets. Am. Chpt. 9, Detroit, 1981-85. With USMC, 1967-69, Vietnam. Mem. Detroit Bar Assn. Office: 1813 City-County Bldg Detroit MI 48226

CALLAHAN, LEEANN LUCILLE, psychologist; b. San Diego, Calif., Dec. 7, 1950; d. Charlie A. Olsen and Dolores A. (Libke) Turner; m. Chuck Callahan, Oct. 31, 1970; children: Clint, Devin, Chet. BS/MS in Psychology, San Diego State U., 1983; PhD in Psychology, USIU, San Diego, 1990. Lic. clin. psychologist. Clin. dir. Sharp Cabrillo Hosp., San Diego, 1989-91, Charter Hosp., San Diego, 1991-93; psychologist San Diego, 1989—. Preferred provider Charter Hosp., San Diego, 1990—, speakers bur., 1990—; staff psychologist Sharp Cabrillo Hosp., San Diego, 1989-92. Editor Parentteen Mag.; contbr. articles to profl. jours. Pres. PTA, San Diego, 1985; citizen adv./city coun. City of San Diego, 1987; vol. Poway Unified Sch. Dist., San Diego, 1975—; speaker Rotary, San Diego, 1994. Recipient Citizen of Yr. award, Sigma Chi, 1997. Mem. APA, Calif. State Psychol. Assn. Office: 9320 Carmel Mountain Rd Ste D San Diego CA 92129-2159

CALLAHAN, MARILYN JOY, social worker; b. Portland, Oreg., Oct. 11, 1934; d. Douglas Q. and Anona Helen Maynard; m. Lynn J. Callahan, Feb. 27, 1960 (dec.); children: Barbara Callahan Baer, Susan Callahan Sewell, Jeffrey Callahan. BA, Mills Coll., 1955; MSW, Portland State U., 1971, secondary teaching cert., 1963. Bd. cert. diplomate in clin. social work. Developer, adminstr. ednl. program Oreg. Women's Correctional Ctr., Oreg. State Prison, Salem, 1966-67; mental health counselor Benton County Mental Health, Corvallis, Oreg., 1970-71; inst. tchr. Hillcrest Sch., Salem, Oreg., 1975-81; social worker protective svcs. Mid- Willamette Valley Sr. Svcs. Agy., Salem, 1981-88; psychiat. social worker dept. forensics Oreg. State Hosp., 1988-93; pvt. practice treatment of adult male and female sexual offenders Salem, 1987—; pvt. practice in care/mgmt. of elderly, 1987—2000. Panel mem. Surgeon Gen.'s N.W. Regional Conf. on Interpersonal Violence, 1987; speaker in field; planner, organizer Seminar on Age Discrimination, 1985. Mem. NASW (past mem. bd. dirs. Oreg. chpt.), Am. Acad. Forensic Scis., Acad. Cert. Social Workers (lic. clin. social worker), Assn. for Treatment Sex Abusers, Oreg. Gerontol. Assn., Catalina 27 Nat. Sailing Assn., Mid-Valley Alzheimers Assn. (bd. dirs. 1998—). Office: 780 Commercial St SE Ste 304 Salem OR 97301-3455 E-mail: mcallahan55@aol.com.

CALLAHAN, MICHAEL THOMAS, lawyer, writer, arbitrator, construction executive, consultant; b. Kansas City, Mo., Oct. 7, 1948; s. Harry Leslie and Venita June (Yohn) C.; m. Stella Sue Paffenbach, Mar. 21, 1970; children: Molly Leigh, Michael Kroh. BA, U. Kans., 1970; JD, U. Mo., 1973, LLM, 1979; postgrad., Temple U., 1976-77. Bar: Kans. 1973, N.J. 1975, Mo. 1977. V.p. T.J. Constrn., Inc., Lenexa, Kans., 1973-74; sr. cons. Wagner-Hohns-Inglis, Inc., Mt. Holly, N.J., 1974-77, v.p. Kansas City, Mo., 1977-86; exec. v.p. CCL Constrn. Cons., Overland Park, Kans., 1986-88, pres., 1988—. Adj. prof. U. Kans., Iowa State U.; arbitrator, lectr. in field, author; chmn. CCL Pacific Corp.; pres. Handcrafted Wines Kans., Inc. Home: 9011 Delmar St Shawnee Mission KS 66207-2343 Office: CCL Constrn Cons 4600 College Blvd Ste 104 Overland Park KS 66211-1606

CALLAHAN, NORTH, author, educator; b. near Sweetwater, Tenn., Aug. 7, 1908; s. Robert B. and Naomi (North) C.; m. Jennie Waugh, Sept. 27, 1939 (div. 1970); m. Helen Pemberton Jones, July 5, 1974; children: Mary Alice, North. AB cum laude, U. Chattanooga, 1930, LHD, 1964; postgrad., U. Tenn., 1930-32; MA, Columbia U., 1950; PhD, NYU, 1955. Educator, 1930-34; ednl. pub. relations counselor TVA-Civilian Conservation Corps., 1934-37; reporter, columnist, spl. writer, editor Chattanooga Times, Chattanooga News, Knoxville Jour., Tyler (Tex.) Courier-Times, Morning Telegraph; N.Y.C. corr. Dallas News, 1939-44; writer syndicated column So This is New York, 1943-68; pub. relations cons. various firms and orgns., N.Y.C., 1954-55; prof. Am. hist., head soc. sci. dept. Finch Coll., N.Y.C., 1956-57; assoc. prof. NYU, 1957-62, prof. history, 1962-73, prof. emeritus, 1973—. Vis. lectr. Brit. univs., 1965; vis. prof. U. Tenn., 1973. Author: The Army, 1941, The Armed Forces as a Career, 1947, Smoky Mountain Country, 1952, Henry Knox: General Washington's General, 1958, Daniel Morgan, Ranger of the Revolution, 1961, Royal Raiders: the Tories of the American Revolution, 1963, Flight from the Republic (Vol. II), 1967, Carl Sandburg, a Biography, 1970, 2d edit., 1987, George Washington: Soldier and Man, 1972, TVA: Bridge Over Troubled Waters, 1980; (novels) Peggy, 1983, Daybreak, 1985, Thanks Mr. President: The Trail-Blazing Second Term of George Washington, 1991, (play) George Washington Visits Chattanooga, 1994; editor Army Life mag., 1943-46, Europe's View of America, 1954; contbg. editor So. Observer mag.; composer (with Norman Cloutier) Voice of the Army, adopted by War Dept. as ofcl. song Army Recruiting Service; editor-in-chg. History of Mountain City Club, Chattanooga, 1998. Mem. N.Y.C. Bicentennial Hist. Commn.; supr. army radio show Voice of Army; chmn. U. Tenn. Lupton Libr. Friends, 1992-94, Chattanooga chmn., U. Tenn. Commemoration Ceremonies George Washington, 1998; Served from 1st Lieut. to Lieut. Col. AUS, 1940-46. Penfield fellow NYU, 1954-55; recipient NYU Founders Day Honors award, 1956, Am. Revolution Round Table placque Henry Knox, 1958; vis. scholar Huntington Library, 1960; named Disting. Alumnus U. Tenn., 1983; requested to submit personal videotape of WWII experiences by Library of Congress, 2002. Fellow Am. Studies Assn.; mem. Am. Hist. Assn., Soc. Hist. Assn., Am. Acad. Polit. and Social Sci., So. Soc. (historian), Civil War Round Table N.Y. (pres. 1954-55), Tenn. Soc. N.Y. (historian), Conf. Brit. Studies, Tenn. Hist. Soc., Am. Revolution Round Table (chmn.), Writer's Group, Princeton Club (founder, chmn.), Chattanooga Golf and Country Club, Mountain City Club, Delta Sigma Phi, Kappa Tau Alpha, Theta Alpha Phi, Delta Theta Phi, Kappa Tau Alpha, Sigma Delta Chi. Home: 600 Pine St Chattanooga TN 37402-1712

CALLAHAN, RALPH WILSON, JR., advertising agency executive; b. Anniston, Ala., Apr. 14, 1942; s. Ralph Wilson and Ida Bell (Price) C.; m. Cathryn Vann Holman, Feb. 16, 1981; 1 dau., Meeghan Crabtree. BA, U. Va., 1964; M. Fgn. Trade, Am. Grad. Sch. Internat. Mgmt., 1966. Acct. exec. Young and Rubicam, Inc., N.Y.C., 1967-70, v.p., acct. supr., 1971-78; sr. v.p. Henderson Advt., Greenville, S.C., 1978-80, exec. v.p., 1980-81, pres. & CEO, 1981—. Gov. so. region Am. Assn. Advt. Agys., N.Y.C., 1981— ; chmn. Carolinas council Am. Assn. Advt. Agys., Greenville, 1982 Vice pres. Met. Arts Council, Greenville, 1982; bd. visitors The McCallie Sch., Chattanooga, 1983. Served to 2d lt. USAR, 1963-65. Mem. Am. C. of C. of Netherlands (pres. 1970), Greenville C. of C. (dir. 1983), Omicron Delta Kappa, Phi Beta Kappa Clubs: Union League (N.Y.C.); Apawamis (Rye, N.Y.); Greenville Country. Episcopalian. Home: 2 Woodland Way Cir Greenville SC 29601-3824 Office: Henderson Advt Inc 60 Pointe Cir Greenville SC 29615-3568

CALLAHAN, RICKEY DON, business owner; b. Dallas, Mar. 17, 1956; s. Dayton Easton and Alice Jane (Holloway) C. AA, Eastfield Coll., 1976; BA in Polit. Sci., U. Tex.-Dallas, 1978; MBA in Gen. Mgmt., Amber U., 1986. Cert. secondary tchr., Tex. Real estate assoc. ERA Sage Realty, Inc., Dallas, 1979-80, First Mark Real Estate, Dallas, 1980-81; adminstrv. asst. Dallas Precious Metal Plating, Inc., Garland, Tex., 1981-84; legis. asst. to state rep. Alvin R. Granoff, Dallas, 1984-87; owner, broker Callahan Properties, Dallas, 1987—. Pres. Dallas County East Dem. Orgn., 1986-88, Clean Dallas-S.E., Inc., 1987-88, Tex. Jr. C. of C. Found.; bd. dirs. Dallas Conv. and Visitors Bur., 1995-98; mem. Dallas Bond Campaign Com., 1995; bd. dirs. S.E. Emergency Food Ctr., 1996-99, v.p. 1998-99; treas. Pleasant Grove Hist. Soc., 2000-02. Mem. Nat. Assn.Realtors, Tex. Assn. Realtors, North Tex. Comml. Assn. of Realtors (arbitration panel), S.E. Dallas C. of C. (bd. dirs. 1987—, vice chmn. econ. devel. 1991-92, chmn. 1994-95, vice chmn. 2002-03), U. Tex. Dallas Alumni Assn., Amber U. Alumni Assn., Tex. Jaycees (dist. dir. 1981-82, Prestigious J.C.I. Senator award #38931, pres. Mesquite chpt. 1980-81, 82-83, bd. dirs. Dallas 1990-91), Phi Theta Kappa. Democrat. Baptist. Avocations: scuba diving, guitar, genealogy, reading, attending football games. Office: Callahan Properties 8344 E R L Thornton Fwy Ste 308 Dallas TX 75228-7134

CALLAHAN, ROBERT JEREMIAH, retired judge, mediator; b. Norwalk, Conn., June 3, 1930; s. Jeremiah J. and Elizabeth A. (Connolly) C.; m. Dorothy B. Trudel, Jan. 24, 1959; children: Sheila, Kerry, Denise, Janine, Patrick, Megan, Jane, Robert Jr. BS in History and Govt., Boston Coll., 1952; JD, Fordham U., 1955. Judge Cir. Ct. Conn., 1970-75, Ct. Common Pleas, Conn., 1975-76, Conn. Superior Ct., 1976-85; assoc. justice Conn. Supreme Ct., 1985-96, chief justice, 1996-99; ret., 1999. Judge trial referee Superior Ct., Stamford, Conn.; mem. Bd. Pardons, Conn., 1985-87. Served with U.S. Army, 1956-58. Recipient Fordham U. Sch. Law Dean's medal of recognition, 1986, Fordham Law Alumni Assn. medal of excellence, 1997, Fordham Disting. Alumnus award, 1998, U. Conn. Alumni Assn. Disting. Svc. award, 1998. Roman Catholic. Office: Superior Ct 123 Hoyt St Stamford CT 06905

CALLAHAN, ROBERT JOHN, JR., lawyer, arbitrator; b. St. Louis, July 3, 1923; s. Robert John and Elizabeth Mae Deck (Gentner) C.; m. Dorothy Foley, Apr. 18, 1958 (dec. Nov. 1980); m. Barbara Kelsall Couture, May 22, 1982. Grad., Chaminade Coll., 1941; BS in Bus. Adminstrn., Washington U., 1944; JD cum laude, Notre Dame U., 1948. Bar: Mo. 1948, U.S. Ct. Appeals (fed. cir.) 1951, U.S. Supreme Ct. 1955, U.S. Ct. Mil. Appeals. Ptnr. Callahan and Callahan, St. Louis, 1948-56; sole practice St. Louis, 1956—. Contbr. articles to legal jours. Candidate for judge St. Louis County Cir. Ct., 1960. Served with FBI and USCGR, 1944-45; former liaison officer USAF Acad. Served to capt. JAGC, USAFR. Coro fellow. Mem. ABA, Lawyers Assn. of St. Louis, St. Louis Bar Assn., Am. Assn. Trial Lawyers, Notre Dame U. Law Assn., U. Notre Dame Alumni Assn., Nat. Panel Consumer Arbitrators, Ret. Air Force Officers Assn., Phi Delta Theta. Republican. Roman Catholic. Office: 32 Normandy Dr Lake Saint Louis MO 63367-1502

CALLAHAN, SONNY (H.L. CALLAHAN), former congressman; b. Mobile, Ala., Sept. 11, 1932; m. Karen Reed; children: Scott, Patrick, Shawn Cushing, Chris, Cameron (dec.), Kelly Thomas. Grad., McGill Inst. Pres., chmn. bd., chief exec. officer Finch Cos., Mobile and Montgomery, Ala., 1964-84; mem. Ala. Ho. of Reps., 1970-78, chmn. Mobile County delegation; mem. Ala. Senate, 1978-82, U.S. Congress from 1st Ala. dist., 1985—2002; mem. appropriations com.; chmn. subcom. on energy and water devel. Served with USN, 1952-54 Mem. Mobile Area C. of C., Ala. Movers Assn., Ala. Trucking Assn., Kiwanis, Optimists. Republican.

CALLAHAN, THOMAS JAMES, lawyer; b. Cleve., Jan. 21, 1957; s. Thomas Joseph and Lucille Dorothy (DeVries) C.; m. Laura Jean Schwartz, Oct. 13, 1979; children: Thomas, Michael. BS cum laude in Acctg., Duke U., 1979; JD cum laude, Case Western Reserve U., 1985. Bar: Ohio 1985, U.S. Ct. Appeals (6th cir.) 1987, U.S. Tax Ct. 1987, U.S. Dist. Ct. (no. dist.) Ohio 1987, U.S. Ct. Fed. Claims 1987, U.S. Ct. Appeals (fed. cir.) 2000, U.S. Supreme Ct. 2000; CPA, Ohio 1981. Staff sr. acct. Price Waterhouse, Cleve., 1979-82, mgr., 1985-86; assoc. Thompson Hine LLP, Cleve., 1986-96, ptnr., 1997—, leader tax practice. Bd. dirs. The Ultrasonic Solution, Inc., Solon, Ohio. Vice chair allocations com. United Way Svcs., Cleve., 1992-96; mem. arbitration com. Cuyahoga Ct. Common Pleas, Cleve., 1989—. Fellow: Am. Coll. Tax Counsel; mem.: AICPA, ABA (tax sect., vice chair adminstrv. practice com.), Cleve. Tax Inst. (program chair 1999, chair 2001, exec. com. 1999—2002), Cleve. Bar Assn. (spkr. 1994—, chmn. gen. tax com. 1999), Tax Club Cleve. (bd. dirs. 2000, treas. 2001, v.p. 2002—03), Rotary Club of Cleve. Office: Thompson Hine LLP 3900 Key Ctr 127 Pub Sq Cleveland OH 44114-1216 E-mail: tom.callahan@thompsonhine.com.

CALLAHAN, THOMAS JAY, petroleum engineer, geologist, consultant; b. Denver, Feb. 14, 1949; s. Mark Allen and Marjorie Jean (christian) C.; divorced; 1 child, Christian Thomas. Student, Tex. A&M U., 1967-71; BS in Physics and Math., U. La., 1974, BS in Petroleum Engring., 1981, MS in Geology, 1994. Cert. field engr., field engr.-petrology, computer field engr., registered fundamentals engr., 1981; cert. tchr. physics and math. Reservoir engr. Aminoil Co., Lafayette, La., 1976-78, 81-83, Tenneco Oil Co., Lafayette, La., 1978-81; cons. engr. I.H. Delatte & Assocs., Dave Casey & Assocs., Lafayette, 1983-87; rsch. and tchg. asst. U. La., Lafayette, 1987-94; asst. geoscientist Conoco, Unocal, Lafayette, 1989-93; field geologist Petrolog Corp., Lafayette, 1994-98, 2002—03, Stokes & Spiehler, Lafayette, 1996-98; cons. geoscientist Landmark Graphics Corp., New Orleans, 1998-99; field engr. Schlumberger/Anadrill, Youngsville, 1999—2001; field geologist Stratagraph, Inc., 2003—. Tchr. Lafayette Parish H.S. Sys., 1974-76, 85-86; mem. Tex. A&M corps cadets, 1967-1969. Active Salvation Army, 1971-98, First Bapt. Ch., Lafayette, 1983-, Ascension Episcopal Ch., 2003—; leader Civil Air Patrol, 1974-77, others. Recipient Aerospace Engr. Seminar award, 1967; Estwing Geology scholar, 1990, L.G.S. Geology scholar, 1991, S.I.P.E.S. Geology scholar, 1991, G.C.A.G.S. Geology scholar, 1992. Mem. AIAA, Soc. Petroleum Engrs., Am. Assn. Petroleum Geologists, Nat. Petroleum Engrs. Honor Soc., Nat. Earth Sci. Honor Soc., Nat. Physics Honor Soc., Phi Kappa Phi. Avocations: biblical studies, sculpting, visual arts, athletics, nutrition.

CALLAHAN, TIMOTHY J. lawyer, investment advisor; b. Yokohama, Japan, Jan. 6, 1948; parents Am. citizens; s. Frank T. and Jane A. Callahan; m. Margan Raphael, Aug. 15, 1970; children: Katie E., Zachary P., Carmen C., Elizabeth G. BS in Commerce, U. Va., 1970; JD, Cath. U., 1974. Bar: Va. 1974. Atty./assoc. Simmonds, Coleburn, Towner and Carman, Arlington, Va., 1974-76, Farley, Harrington & Sickels, Fairfax, Va., 1977-79; atty., ptnr. Merrell & Callahan, McLean, Va., 1980-87, Clary, Lawrence, Lickstein and Moore, Falls Church, Va., 1987-91, Tener & Callahan, Vienna, Va., 1992-2000, McCandlish & Lillard PC, Vienna, Va., 2000—. Bd. dirs. Joe Gibbs' Youth for Tomorrow, Manassas, Va., 1997, Fresta Valley Christian Sch., Marshall, Va., 1987—; adminstr. I Found It campaign, Washington, 1976. Mem. Christian Legal Soc., Fin. Planning Assn., No. Va. Estate Planning Coun. Republican. Evangelical Christian. Office: McCandlish & Lillard PC 11350 Random Hills Rd Ste 500 Fairfax VA 22030

CALLAHAN, VINCENT FRANCIS, JR., state legislator, publisher; b. Washington, Oct. 30, 1931; s. Vincent Francis and Anita (Hawkins) C.; m. Dorothy Helen Budge, Aug. 27, 1960; children: Vincent Francis III, Elizabeth Lauren, Anita Marie, Cynthia Helen, Robert Bruce. BS in Fgn. Svc., Georgetown U., 1957; LHD (hon.), No. Va. C.C., 1997. Pres. Callahan Publs., 1957-2000; mem. Va. Hos. of Dels., 1968—, minority leader, 1982-85, chmn. appropriations com. Author eight books including: Missle Contracts Guide, 1958, Space Guide, 1959, Underwater Defense Handbook, 1963, Military Research Handbook, 1963. Candidate for lt. gov. Va., 1965; state fin. chmn. Rep. Party of Va., 1966-68; candidate for U.S. Congress, 1976; chmn. No. Va.

Cmty. Found. With USMC, 195-53; as lt. USCGR, 1959-63. Mem. U.S. Naval Inst., Nat. Press Club, Kiwanis (past pres. McLean, Va.). Republican. Roman Catholic. Office: PO Box 1173 Mc Lean VA 22101-1173 E-mail: dcalla5475@aol.com.

CALLAN, JAMIE, writer, educator; b. Long Island, N.Y., Jan. 26, 1954; d. John Joseph and June Vaughn Callan; m. Eugene Charles Silver, June 20, 1981 (div. Jan. 26, 1994). BA, Bard Coll., 1975; MA, Goddard Coll., 1980; MFA, U. Calif., L.A., Calif., 1992. Script devel. Paramount Pictures, L.A., 1992—94; instr. U. Calif., L.A., 1994; fiction tchr. Ednl. Ctr. for the Arts, Fairfield, Conn., 1995—. Adj. prof. Fairfield (Conn.) U., 1994—; writing instr. NYU, N.Y.C., 1995—; adj. prof. Wesleyan U., Middletown, Conn., 2001—. Author: Over the Hill At Fourteen, 1982, The Young and The Soapy, 1984, Just Too Cool, 1987, short stories. Mem.: Pen Am. Ctr., Author's Guild. Democrat. Unitarian. Avocations: dancing, yoga, theater, reading, travel.

CALLAN, JOSEPH PATRICK, social service administrator; b. Washington, July 29, 1944; s. G. Christopher and Mary Jane (Gorsuch) C.; m. Judith Marie Bell, June 14, 1980; children: Kimberly Jane, Kathleen Marie. AA, St. Petersburg (Fla.) Jr. Coll., 1964; BA, U. So. Fla., 1972, MSW, 1985; MS, Nova U., 1985. Group work supr. Eckerd Found., Clearwater, Fla., 1968-72, dir. tng., 1977-83; coord. Collier County Mental Health, Naples, Fla., 1972-76; pvt. practice psychotherapy Tampa, Fla., 1985—; dir., owner Univ. Psychotherapy Group, P.A., Tampa, 1987—. Psychotherapist Employee Assistance Programs and Sex Therapy, Tampa, 1987—; vis. faculty U. So. Fla., Tampa, 1987—; clin. dir. Traverse Equestrian Therapy Program for traumatized youth, Tampa, 1995—; pres. Tng. and Edn. Ctr., Naples, 1972-77, Immokalee (Fla.) Adult Refuge, 1972-77; cons. social svcs. agys. Tampa area, 1987—. Sgt. U.S. Army, 1966-71. Mem. NASW, Am. Acad. Clin. Sexologists, Fla. Soc. Clin. Social Work, Collier County Assn. Retarded Citizens (charter), U. So. Fla. Social Work Alumni Assn. (pres. 1986-88), N.Am. Handicapped Riding Assn., Equine Assisted Growth and Learning Assn., Phi Kappa Phi, Pi Gamma Mu. Avocation: horseback riding. Home: 3450 Lake Padgett Dr Land O'Lakes FL 34639-6514 Office: Univ Psychotherapy Group PA 10730 N 56th St Ste 210 Temple Terrace FL 33617-3615 E-mail: jandjcallan@juno.com.

CALLAN, RICHARD JOHN, elementary school educator; b. Indpls., Dec. 8, 1953; s. John B. and Bernice (Burns) C. BS, Ind. U., Indpls., 1977, MS, 1985. Cert. elem. tchr. Tutor Indpls. Pub. Schs., 1974-76, tchr., 1977-81; tchr. 3d grade Franklin Twp. Schs., Indpls., 1981—. Edn. cons. Ind. Dept. Edn., summer, 1990, 98, mem. proficiency guide writing team, 1991, 97; lectr. various workshops, seminars; co-chmn. "Make and Take It" com. Nat. Coun. Tchrs. of Math. conv., 1994; trainer Math. Assessment: The Hoosier Alternative, 1994; mem. edn. expert panel in sci. and math. U.S. Dept. Edn., 1998—; lectr. in math. edn. Franklin (Ind.) Coll. Author: (with others) Improving Students' Learning and Attitudes, Multi-Cultural Education, 1992, Indiana Department of Education Mathematics and Assessment Guide, 1992, Mathematics Assessment, The Hoosier Alternative (M.A.T.H.A.), 1994, Mission Mathematics: Workshops on Linking Aerospace and the NCTM Standards, 1997, Math, Literature and Unifix, 2001, Math, Literature and Manipulation, 2001. Faculty rep. Bunkerhill PTO 1989-92. Grantee Ind. Dept. Edn., 1990—; recipient William J. Garrett award, 1976, Outstanding Young Men of Am. award Ind. U., Presdl. award for Excellence NSF and Ind. Dept. Edn., 1993, Presdl. award for Excellence in Sci. and Math. Teaching, 1995, NASA Ednl. Workshop for Elem. Sch. Tchrs. award, 1995. Mem. NEA, ASCD, Ind. State Tchrs. Assn., Ind. Coun. Tchrs. Math. (exec. bd. 1992-96, reviewer jour. 1993, co-chair fall conf. 1997—, profl. devel. chair 2000—), Nat. Coun. Tchrs. Math. (arithmetic tchr. referee 1990-96, chair ctrl. regional program 2003), Franklin Twp. Edn. Assn. (pres. 1989-90, 91-92, 98-2000, cen. discussion team 1989-92), Ind. U. Alumni Assn., Cen. Ind. Coun. Tchrs. Math. (exec. bd. 1992—, pres. 1991), South Ctrl. Ind. Coun. Tchrs. Math., Ind. State Tchrs. Assn., Ind. U. Edn. Alumni Assn. (steering com., chair 1978-79), Soc. Elem. Presdl. Awardees (math. rep. 1997-2003). Fax: (317) 882-0067. E-mail: rcallan@iquest.net.

CALLAN, TERRENCE A. lawyer; b. San Francisco, Sept. 20, 1939; s. Harold A. and Viola A. (Briese) C.; m. Gail R. Raine, Apr. 20, 1968; 1 child, Ryan T. BA, U. San Francisco, 1961; JD, U. Calif. Hastings Coll. Law, San Francisco, 1964. Bar: Calif. 1965, U.S. Dist. Ct. (no. dist.) Calif. 1965, U.S. Ct. Appeals (9th cir.) 1965, U.S. Dist. Ct. (cen. dist.) Calif. 1970, U.S. Supreme Ct. 1975, U.S. Dist. Ct. (so. dist.) Calif. 1981, U.S. Dist. Ct. (ea. dist.) Calif. 1996. Rsch. asst. Pillsbury, Madison & Sutro, San Francisco, 1964-65, assoc., 1965-72, ptnr., 1973—. Dir. sec., gen. counsel Presidio Soc., 1981-94; dir., sec., legal counsel Ft. Point and Presidio Hist. Assn., 1984—; trustee Hastings Coll.Law 1066 Found., Mildred E. Stearns Found. Mem. ABA, Calif. State Bar Assn. (past chmn., exec. com. antitrust and trade regulation sect.), San Francisco Bar Assn. (past mem. judiciary com., antitrust, 9th cir. no. dist. merit screening com. for bankruptcy judgeships), Lawyers Club San Francisco (bd. govs.), U. Calif. Alumni Assn., Hastings Coll. of the Law Annual Campaign (nat. chair), U. San Francisco Alumni Assn. (bd. govs., pres.-elect), Order of Coif, Green and Gold Club (former chmn. bd. dirs.), U. San Francisco Club, Phi Alpha Delta. Roman Catholic. Office: Pillsbury Winthrop LLP PO Box 7880 San Francisco CA 94120-7880

CALLANAN, KATHLEEN JOAN, retired electrical engineer; b. Detroit, Feb. 10, 1940; d. John Michael and Grace Marie (Kleehammer) C. BSE in Physics, U. Mich., 1963; postgrad., Northeastern U., 1963-65; MSEE, U. Hawaii, 1971; diploma in Japanese lang., St. Joseph Inst. Japanese, Tokyo, 1973; cert. in mgmt., Boeing Mil. Airplane Co., 1985. Religious missionary Maryknoll Sisters St. Dominic, 1966-79; vis. scholar Sophia U., Tokyo, 1976-79; elec.-eletronic components engr. Boeing Mil. Airplane Co. (later Boeing Def. and Space Group), Wichita, Kans., 1979-83, instrumentation design engr., 1983-85, strategic planner for tech., 1985-86, rsch. and engring. tech. supr., 1986-87, electromagnetic effects avionics mgr., 1987 89, elec. and electronics mgr., 1989, design tech. support mgr., 1990-92, engring. leader, 1992-95, ret., 1995. Contbr. articles to profl. jours. Mem. Rose Hill Planning Commn., Kans., 1982-85; coord. Boeing Employees Amateur Radio Soc., Wichita, 1982-83, sec., 1991. Fellow Soc. Women Engrs. (sr. mem.; sect. rep. 1981-83, sect.-treas. 1985-86, regional bd. dirs. 1983-85, sect. pres. 1987-88); mem. Quarter Century Wireless Assn. (comms. com. 1985 86), Assn. Old Crows (bd. dirs. 1988-91, chpt. pres. 1991), Toastmasters (local pres. 1985-86, competent toastmaster 1985), Nat. Soc. DAR (registrar Estero Island chpt. 2000—). E-mail: kjcallanan@callanan.org.

CALLANAN, LAURA PATRICE, foundation executive; b. St. Louis, June 25, 1965; d. James Carson and Mary Ann (Plati) C.; m. Romulus Zachariah Linney, Mar. 8, 1996. BA, Barnard Coll., 1987; MPA, Columbia U., 1991. Devel. assoc. Lincoln Ctr. Theater, N.Y.C., 1987-88; devel. mgr. Am. Ballet Theatre, N.Y.C., 1988-89; assoc. Lehman Bros., N.Y.C., 1990-94, JP Morgan Securities Inc., N.Y.C., 1994-95; asst. v.p. Moody's Investors Svc., N.Y.C., 1995-96; assoc. treas. Lila Wallace-Reader's Digest Fund, N.Y.C., 1996-98, DeWitt Wallace-Reader's Digest Fund, N.Y.C., 1996-98; assoc. dir. investments Rockefeller Found., N.Y.C., 1998—. Treas. bd. dirs. Signature Theatre Co., N.Y.C., 1993-98; cons. Alliance for the Arts, N.Y.C., 1996; mem. investment com. Am. Acad. Arts and Letters, 2002—. Treas. N.Y. Found. for Arts, N.Y.C., 2002—; bd. dirs. Rhizome.org, N.Y.C., 2002—. Home: 289 Dales Bridge Rd Germantown NY 12526-5222

CALLANDER, BRUCE DOUGLAS, journalist, freelance writer; b. Malone, N.Y., Dec. 23, 1923; s. Douglas Newton and Blanche Keller (Redfield) C.; m. Imogene A. O'Malley, Nov. 23, 1979; children by previous marriage— Richard Scott, John Byron AB with cert. in Journalism, U. Mich., Ann Arbor, 1948. Indsl. editor Kaiser Frazer Co., Willow Run, Mich., 1948-50; pub. relations officer U.S. Air Force, Ohio, Md., 1951-52; assoc. editor Air Force Times, Washington, 1952-67, mng. editor, 1967-72, editor Springfield, Va., 1972-85; freelance writer, mil. historian Mullett Lake, Mich., 1986—. Served to capt. USAF, 1942-45, 51-52; Italy. Recipient Hopwood awards U. Mich., 1945, 48; Freedom Found. award, 1982. Mem.: St. Andrews Soc. (Washington). Avocations: painting; sculpting; woodworking; playing the flute.

CALLANDER, KAY EILEEN PAISLEY, business owner, retired education educator, writer; b. Coshocton, Ohio, Oct. 15, 1938; d. Dalton Olas and Dorothy Pauline (Davis) Paisley; m. Don Larry Callander, Nov. 18, 1977. BSE, Muskingum Coll., 1960; MA in Speech Edn., Ohio State U., 1964, postgrad., 1964-84. Cert. elem., gifted, drama, theater tchr., Ohio. Tchr. Columbus (Ohio) Pub. Schs., 1960-70, 80-88, drama specialist, 1970-80, classroom, gifted/talented tchr., 1986-90, ret., 1990; sole prop. The Ali Group, Kay Kards, 1992—. Coord. Artists-in-the Schs., 1977-88; cons., presenter numerous ednl. confs. and sems., 1971—; mem., ednl. cons. Innovation Alliance Youth Adv. Coun., 1992—. Producer-dir., Shady Lane Music Festival, 1980-88; dir. tchr. (nat. distbr. video) The Trial of Gold E. Locks, 1983-84; rep., media pub. relations liason Sch. News., 1983-88; author, creator Trivia Game About Black Americans (TGABA), exhibitor of TGABA game at L.A. County Office Edn. Conf., 1990; presenter for workshop by Human Svc. Group and Creative Edn. Coop., Columbus, Ohio, 1989. Benefactor, Columbus Jazz Arts Group; v.p., bd. dirs. Neoteric Dance and Theater Co., Columbus, 1985-87; tchr., participant Future Stars sculpture exhibit, Ft. Hayes Ctr., Columbus Pub. Schs., 1988; tchr. advisor Columbus Coun. PTAs, 1983-86, co-chmn. reflections com., 1984-87; mem. Columbus Mus. Art, Citizens for Humane Action, Inc.; mem. supt.'s adv. coun. Columbus Pub. Schs., 1967-68; presenter Young Author Seminar, Ohio Dept. Edn., 1988, Illustrating Methods for Young Authors' Books, 1986-87; cons. and workshop leader seminar/workshop Tchg. About the Constitution in Elem. Schs., Franklin County Ednl. Coun., 1988; sponsor Minority Youth Recognition Awards, 1994. Named Educator of Yr., Shady Lane PTA, 1982, Columbus Coun. PTAs, 1989, winner Colour Columbus Landscape Design Competition, 1990; Sch. Excellence grantee Columbus Pub. Schs.; Commendation Columbus Bd. Edn. and Ohio Ho. of Reps. for Child Assault Prevention project, 1986-87; first place winner statewide photo contest Ohio Vet. Assn., 1991; recipient Muskingum Coll. Alumni Disting. Svc. award, 1995. Mem. ASCD, AAUW, Assn. for Childhood Edn. Internat., Ohio Coun. for Social Studies, Franklin County Ret. Tchrs. Assn., Nat. Mus. Women in the Arts, Ohio State U. Alumni Assn., U.S. Army Officers Club, Navy League, Liturgical Art Guild Ohio, Columbus Jazz Arts Group, Columbus Mus. Art, Nat. Coun. for Social Studies, Columbus Art League, Columbus Maennerchor (Damen sect.). Republican. Avocations: painting, photography, swimming, golfing, playing piano and organ. Home: 9131 Indian Mound Rd Pickerington OH 43147 E-mail: pais1609@aol.com.

CALLARD, CAROLE CRAWFORD, librarian, educator; b. Charleston, W.Va., Aug. 8, 1941; d. William O. and Helen (Shay) Crawford; children: Susan Lynne, Annie Laurie. BA in Am. History, U. Charleston, 1963; MLS, U. Pitts., 1966; MA in Social Founds., Ea. Mich. U., 1978; grad., Nat. Inst. for Geneal. Rsch., 1997. Tchr. Blessed Sacrament Sch., South Charleston, W.Va., 1962-64; grad. trainee W.Va. Libr. Commn., Charleston, 1964-65; reference libr. Tompkins County Pub. Libr., Ithaca, N.Y., 1966-69; head libr. U.S. Embassy, Addis Ababa, Ethiopia, 1969-70; head govt. documents Haile Sellassie U., Addis Ababa, 1970-71; br. libr. Ann Arbor (Mich.) Pub. Libr., 1973-83; documents libr. U. Mich., Ann Arbor, 1983-84; pub. svcs. supr. Libr. of Mich., Lansing, 1984-95; depository libr. inspector Govt. Printing Office, 1995-96; librarian Allen Co. Pub. Libr., Ft. Wayne, Ind., 1996-97; specialist Libr. of Mich., Lansing, 1997—; adj. prof. libr. info. sci. Wayne State U., Mich., 2003—; instr. Nat. Inst. for Geneal. Rsch., 1999, adj. prof., 2003—. Chair around the world, around the campus U. Mich. Faculty Women's Club, Ann Arbor, 1974-76; tchr. genealogy Holt Pub. Schs., Okemos Pub. Schs., 1990-92, Lansing Cmty. Schs., 2000, Washtenaw C.C., 1992-94; lectr., Libr. Info. Sci., Wayne State U., 2003; judge Mich. history Day, 1991, 93, 94; genealogy chair Abrams Found., 1997—. Author: Index to 150th Anniversary Issue Ithaca Jour., 1967, Guide to Local History, Sources in the Huron Valley, 1980; editor: Sourcebook of Michigan, 1986, Michigan Cemetery Atlas, 1991, Michigan 1870 Census Index, 1991-95, Michigan Cemetery Sourcebook, 1994, Government Documents for Genealogists Historians and Archivists, 1998; column editor Mich. History Mag. and Chronicle; contbr. articles to profl. jours. Membership chair LWV, Ann Arbor; v.p. Geneal. Soc. Washtenaw County, Mich., 1993, pres., 1993-94; v.p. Palatines to Am., 1987-90, Washtenaw Libr. Club, 1982-83; pres. Mich. Staff Assn., Lansing, 1985-86; pres. Govt. Documents Roundtable of Mich., pres., 1992-93; pres. Mich. Data Base Users Group, 1992-93; chmn. book sale Friends of Ann Arbor Pub. Libr. Recipient Notable Document award Govt. Documents Roundtable of Mich., 1991, Paul Thurston Documents award Govt. Documents Roundtable of Mich., 1993, Cert. of Merit Assn. State and Local History, 1995, Mich. Geneal. Coun., Libr. of Mich. Found. and Abrams Found. award, 1996; grantee U. Pitts., 1966, prof. staff grantee Ann Arbor Pub. Schs., 1980, edn. found. grantee Mich. Libr. Assn., 1982. Mem. ALA (state and local documents com., mem. genealogy com. 2000—, instr. genealogy pre-conf. 2001—02, mem. local history com. 2002-, chmn. genealogy pre-conf. 2003—), AAUW (corr. sec., historian 1973-74, 82-83), DAR (corr. sec. Lansing chpt., Sarah Angell Caswell chpt. chair, registrar CAR Seimes Microfilm), Children of Am. Revolution, Internat. Soc. Brit. Genealogy (trustee 1994-96), Mich. Libr. Assn. (chmn. govt. documents sect. 1982-84, leadership acad. 1991-93), Spl. Librs. Assn., D.C. Libr. Assn., Va. Libr. Assn., Fedn. Genealogy Socs. (del., corr. sec. 1986-87, v.p. regional affairs 1989-92), Nat. Genealogy Soc. (instr. devel. com. 1988-90, chmn. instns. com. 1992—, archives and libr. com. 1993-94), Mich. Geneal. Coun. (ofcl. good will ambassador 1995—, P. William Filby award 2003), Mich. Libr. Assn. Avocations: storytelling, reading, travel, genealogy. E-mail: ccallard@michigan.gov.

CALLARD, DAVID JACOBUS, investment company executive; b. Boston, July 14, 1938; s. Henry Hadden and Clarissa Cooley (Jacobus) C.; m. Deborah Winston, 1960 (div. 1982); children: Owen Winston, Francis Jacobus, Anne Lloyd, Elizabeth Hadden, Samuel Porter; m. Mary R. Morgan, July 14, 1990. AB, Princeton U., 1959; postgrad., Union Theol. Sem., 1964-65; JD, NYU, 1969. With Morgan Guaranty Trust Co., N.Y.C., 1959-61, asst. v.p., 1965-69, v.p., 1970-72; gen. ptnr. Alex Brown & Sons, Balt., 1972-84; mng. dir., 1984-89; bd. dirs. Alex Brown Inc., Balt., 1984-89; pres. Wand Ptnrs. Inc., N.Y.C., 1991—; chmn. Pelican Investment Mgmt., Inc., Boston, 2002—, N.Y.C., 2002—. Chmn. Paragon Holdings, Inc., ACSIS, Inc., 1992—; bd. dirs. Fulcrum Analytics, Inc. Bd. dirs. Union Theol. Sem., N.Y.C., Episcopal Charities of Diocese of N.Y.; trustee Rockefeller Bros. Fund, Pictet Funds; dep. exec. dir. Pres.'s Commn. on All Vol. Armed Forces, 1969-70. Lt. USMC, 1961-64. Boothe Ferris fellow, 1964-65 Mem. Union Club, Knickerbocker Club, Elkridge (Balt.). Democrat. Episcopalian.

CALLARI, EMILY DOLORES, artist; b. N.Y.C., Aug. 30, 1920; d. Joseph and Italia Lena (Ciraolo) C. Grad. high sch., Elmhurst, N.Y.; student, Art Students League, N.Y.C., 1950-60; studied under master artists, N.Y.C., 1955-65. Artist showroom Hollywood Jewelry Co., N.Y.C., 1947-60; adminstrv. cashier States Marine Co., N.Y.C., 1960-70; sec. Salmagundi Art Club, N.Y.C., 1970-73, Artists Fellowship, N.Y.C., 1970-73; tchr. Venice Recreation, Sarasota County, Fla., 1974-80, Venice (Fla.) Art Ctr., 1974—. Tchr. Venice Art Ctr., 1974-97. One-woman shows include Fin. Inst., Fla., 1973-77, Caldwell Trust Co., Venice, 1996; group shows include Wall St. Art Assn., 1964-68, Nat. Acad. N.Y.C., 1959, Art Travel Award Exhibits, London, Amsterdam and Paris, 1968-69, Venice Art Ctr., 1974-97; represented in permanent collections at Venice Art Ctr., Big Brothers and Big Sisters, Venice, Fla., Women's Support and Enrichment Ctr., Venice. Active VFW Aux., Italian-Am. Club, Sarasota Arts Coun., Friends of Venice Art Ctr; donated paintings Big Bros., Big Sisters, Women's Support & Enrichment Ctr. Recipient 1st Place award nat. show, Flushing, N.Y., 1968. Mem. Nat. Mus. Women in Arts (charter), Art Students League (life), Catherine Lorillard Wolfe Art Club, Venice (Fla.) Art Ctr. Home and Office: 606 Home Park Rd Venice FL 34292-2827

CALLAWAY, BEN ANDERSON, journalist; b. Oakland, Calif., Mar. 16, 1927; s. Owen M. and Aulis (Anderson) C.; m. Patricia Hurd, Apr. 7, 1951; children: Randall Owen, Karen Anne Franks. Student, Stanford, 1946-47; BA, Denison U., 1950. Sports writer, wildlife editor Denver Post, 1950-57; with Phila. Daily News, 1957-80, sports editor, 1961-70, outdoor columnist, 1961-80; outdoor editor Phila. Inquirer, 1980-91, editor fishing reports, 1992—2000; outdoor columnist Courier-Post, 1992—2001. Exec. editor Metro East Outdoor News, 1973-77; co-editor Penn-Jersey Outdoor Sportsman, 1976-77; free-lance mag. writer-photographer; commentator Sta. KYW, 1972-95. Sports chmn. Phila. United Fund, 1966-70; active local Boy Scouts Am., Eagle, 1942. Served with USNR, 1945-46. Recipient Henshall award Am. Fishing Tackle Mfrs. Assn., 1964, Old Salt award N.J. Resort Assn., 1967, Johnson Deep Woods award, 1977; gold medal Pa. Fish and Game Protective Assn., 1978; McCulloch Outdoor Writing award, 1978 Mem. Phila. Sports Writers Assn. (pres. 1968-70), Denver Sports Writers and Broadcasters Assn. (pres. 1957), Outdoor Writers Am. (dir. 1976-79, 89—92, Pa. Outdoor Writers, Boating Writers Internat. (dir. 1976-85), Met. N.Y. Rod and Gun Editors, N.J. Outdoor Writers Assn. (v.p. 1982-86, pres. 1988-91), Blue Key, Beta Theta Pi, Pi Delta Epsilon, Omicron Delta Kappa. Presbyn. (elder) and Meth. Address: 146 Buckingham Dr Southampton NJ 08088

CALLAWAY, CLIFFORD WAYNE, physician; b. Easton, Md., May 28, 1941; s. Charles Herschel and Anna Agnes (Stradley) C.; 1 child, David Wayne; m. Jackie Chalkley. BA, U. Del., 1963; MD, Northwestern U., 1967. Diplomate Am. Bd. Internal Medicine, Am. Bd. Endocrinology, Diabetes and Metabolism, Am. Bd. Nutrition. Resident internal medicine Northwestern U. Med. Ctr., Chgo., 1967—69, Mayo Grad. Sch. Medicine, Rochester, Minn., 1971—73, advanced clin. resident endocrinology, 1973—75; assoc. cons. Mayo Clin., 1975—78, cons. endocrinology, 1978—85, dir. nutrition and lipid clins., 1980—85; rsch. assoc. Harvard Med. Sch., Boston, 1976—78; dir. ctr. clin. nutrition George Washington U., Washington, 1986—88; sr. sci. cons. Food & Nutrition Bd., NRC/NAS, Washington, 1987—88; pvt. practice Washington, 1988—. Author 4 books; contbr. articles to profl. jours. Acting exec. sec. nutrition coordinating office HHS, Washington, 1980. Mayo Found. scholar, 1976-78. Mem. Am. Soc. Clin. Nutrition (treas. 1988), Am. Bd. Nutrition (mem. bd. dirs. 1983-89, 93-98, sec.-treas. 1984-86, v.p. 1986-88), Am. Inst. Nutrition (chair and various coms.), Am. Dietetics Assn. (hon.), Am. Osler Soc. (bd. dirs.), Am. Assn. Clin. Endocrinologists (bd. dirs. 1992-95), Cen. European Ctr. for Health and Environment (bd. dirs. 1993—). Achievements include development and writing of dietary guidelines for Americans(USDA/DHHS). Office: 2311 M St NW Ste 301 Washington DC 20037-1468 Business E-Mail: cwcallaway@aol.com.

CALLAWAY, DAVID JAMES EDWARD, physicist, protein chemist, bioinformaticist, expedition mountaineer; b. Milw., Sept. 11, 1956; s. James E. and Sharon Callaway. BS, Calif. Inst. Tech., 1977; MS, U. Wash., 1979, PhD, 1981. Rsch. assoc. Argonne (Ill.) Nat. Lab., 1981-83; sci. assoc. CERN, Geneva, 1983-84; rsch. assoc. Los Alamos (N.Mex.) Nat. Lab., 1984-85; asst. prof. Rockefeller U., N.Y.C., 1985-90, assoc. prof., 1990-96; prof. Picower Inst., Manhasset, NY, 1996—2001, dir. of lab. of computational medicine and bioinformatics, 1996—2001; investigator North Shore LIJ Rsch. Inst., 2002—; prof. neurology NYU Sch. Medicine, 2003—. Adj. prof. Rockefeller U., N.Y.C., 1996—. Energy commr., Woodridge, Ill., 1981-83. Mem. AAAS, Am. Soc. for Biochemistry and Molecular Biology, Am. Alpine Club, Am. Phys. Soc., European Phys. Soc., Am. Soc. Biochemistry, Molecular Biology, Am. Chem. Soc. Achievements include research on high energy physics, superconductivity, nuclear physics, neutron scattering, surface physics, protein folding, macromolecular simulation, rational drug design, Alzheimer's disease, computational physics and bioinformatics. Office: North Shore/LIJ Rsch Inst 350 Community Dr Manhasset NY 11030-3849

CALLAWAY, HOWARD HOLLIS, business executive; b. La Grange, Ga., Apr. 2, 1927; s. Cason Jewell and Virginia (Hand) C.; m. Elizabeth Walton, June 11, 1949; children: Elizabeth Callaway Considine, Howard Hollis Jr., Edward Cason, Virginia Callaway Martin, Ralph Walton. Student, Ga. Inst. Tech., 1944-45; BS, U.S. Mil. Acad., 1949. Commd. 2d lt. AUS, 1949, advanced through grades to 1st. lt., 1952; resigned, 1952; mem. 89th Congress from 3d Ga. dist.; U.S. sec. Army Washington, 1973-75; campaign mgr. Pres. Ford Com., 1975-76; dir. Crested Butte (Colo.) Mountain Resort, 1975—. Pres. Nat. 4-H, mem. svc. com.; former chmn. bd. trustees Ida Cason Callaway Found., Pine Mountain, Ga., Freedoms Found. at Valley Forge; former mem. bd. regents Univ. Sys. Ga.; Rep. candidate for gov. of Ga., 1966; candidate Rep. primary for U.S. Senate from Colo., 1980; chmn. Colo. Rep. Com., 1981-87, chmn. GOPAC, 1987-93; mem. Def. Base Realignment and Closure Commn., 1992; chmn. tourism com. Ga. Dept. Industry, Trade and Tourism, 2001--. 1st lt. inf. U.S. Army, 1949-52. Mem. World Pres.' Orgn. (past pres.), Young Pres.' Orgn. (past pres.), Chief Execs. Orgn., Capital City Club (Atlanta), Piedmont Driving Club (Atlanta), Bohemian Club (San Francisco), Phi Delta Theta, Phi Kappa Phi. Episcopalian. Home: Callaway Gardens Pine Mountain GA 31822

CALLAWAY, JULIENNE MORRISS, financial consultant; b. N.Y.C., May 31, 1965; d. John Michael and Judy (Mauser) Morriss; m. John Patrick Callaway, Nov. 4, 1995; children: James Michael, Emeline Hanna, Madeleine Judy. BA, Georgetown U., 1987; MBA, Columbia U., 1993. Cert. CFA. Paralegal Davis Polk & Wardwell, N.Y.C., 1987—90; assoc. Taylor Rafferty Assoc., N.Y.C., 1990—91, Brown Bros. Harriman & Co., N.Y.C., 1993—94; equity rschr. Morgan Stanley & Co., Inc., N.Y.C., 1994—96; risk mgr. G.E. Capital Corp., Stamford, Conn., 1996—99; ret., 1999. Mem.: Georgetown U. Alumni Assn. (comm. chmn. 1997).

CALLAWAY, KAREN A(LICE), journalist; b. Daytona Beach, Fla., Sept. 5, 1946; d. Robert Clayton III and Alice Johnston (Webb) Callaway. BS in Journalism, Northwestern U., 1968. Copy editor Detroit Free Press, 1968-69; asst. woman's editor, features copy editor, news copy editor, asst. makeup editor Chgo. Am. and Chgo. Today, 1969-74; asst. makeup editor Chgo. Tribune, 1974-76, asst. news editor, 1976-81, assoc. news editor spl. sect., 1981-2000, assoc. news editor vertical publs., 1993-2000, asst. news editor spl. sect., 2000—. Adviser Jr. Achievement Tribune sponsored co., Chgo., 1976—77; editor Infant Mortality sect., 1989; vis. prof. student chpt. Soc. Profl. Journalists, Northwestern U., 1989. Chmn. Class of 1968 20th reunion Northwestern U., Evanston, Ill., 1989, seminar day com., 1989—90, chmn., 1991; alumni bd. Medill Sch. Journalism, Evanston, Ill., 1991—99; vol. Northwestern U. Settlement Assn., Evanston, Ill. Mem.: Soc. Profl. Journalists, Chgo. Headline Club, Kappa Delta. Methodist. Avocations: swimming, cooking, travel. Office: Chicago Tribune 435 N Michigan Ave Ste 500 Chicago IL 60611-4041 Business E-Mail: kcallaway@tribune.com.

CALLAWAY, LINDA MARIE, special education educator; b. Upland, Calif., June 21, 1940; d. Elwyn T. and Fladger Idell (Flake) Bice; m. David Barry Callaway, May, 1957 (div. sept. 1962); children: Tess Callaway Tyler, Darren Francis. B in English, Calif. State U., Fullerton, 1975; MEd Adminstrn., Calif. State U., L.A., 1991. Cert. tchr. L.A. County Office Edn., 1984—88; resource specialist spl. edn. Pomona (Calif.) Unified Sch. Dist., 1990—. Presenter U. St. Petersburg, Russia, 2002. Mem. Soc. Of Friends. Avocations: traveling, jewelry making. Home: 2225 Brescia Ave Claremont CA 91711-1807 Office: Pomona HS Pomona Unified Sch Dist 475 Bangor St Pomona CA 91767-2449

CALLEGARI, WILLIAM A., JR., lawyer, mediator; b. Baton Rouge, La., Sept. 3, 1961; s. William A. and Ann T. (Roy) C.; m. Denise Bordelon, Dec. 17, 1993; children: Will, Michael, John, Elizabeth. BA, La. State U., 1982; MBA, Emory U., 1985; JD, South Tex. Coll. Law, Houston, 1993. Bar: Tex. 1994. Comml. loan rep. Tex. Commerce Bank, Houston, 1985-86; project mgr. AM-TEX Corp., Houston, 1986-90, project devel. mgr., 1990-94; seconded atty. Vinson & Elkins, LLP, Houston, 1995-96; v.p., sec., gen. counsel S T Environ. Svcs., Houston, 1994-97; sole practitioner Houston, 1997—; fee atty. Stewart Title Co., 2001—. Mem. Alpha Tau Omega. Office: 15040 Fairfield Village Dr Ste 200 Cypress TX 77433 E-mail: wcj1304@msn.com.

CALLEN, JAMES DONALD, plasma physicist, nuclear engineer; b. Wichita, Kans., Jan. 31, 1941; s. Donald Dewitt and Bonnie Jean (Walton) C.; m. Judith Carolyn Chinn, Aug. 26, 1961; children: Jeffrey Scott, Sandra Jean. BS in Nuclear Engring., Kans. State U., 1962, MS in Nuclear Engring., 1964; PhD in Nuclear Engring., MIT, 1968. Postdoctoral fellow Inst. for Advanced Study, Princeton, N.J., 1968-69; asst. prof. aeros. and astronautics MIT, Cambridge, 1969-72; mem. rsch. staff fusion energy divsn. Oak Ridge (Tenn.) Nat. Lab., 1972-74, group leader, 1974-75, head plasma theory sect., 1975-79; prof. nuc. engring. and physics U. Wis., Madison, 1979-86, D.W. Kerst prof. engring. physics and physics, 1986—. Mem. editor. bd. Nuc. Fusion Jour., 1978-97; assoc. editor divsn. plasma physics Phys. Rev. Letters Jour., 1980-85; contbr. over 165 articles to profl. jours. Recipient Dept. of Energy Disting. Assoc. award, 1988, Disting. Career award Fusion Power Assocs., 2002; named to Coll. Engring. Hall of Fame, Kans. State U., 1991; Fulbright fellow Tech. Hogesch., Eindhoven, Netherlands, 1962-63; Guggenheim fellow, 1986. Fellow Am. Phys. Soc. (chmn. divsn. plasma physics 1986), Am. Nuc. Soc.; mem. NAE, AAAS. Office: Univ of Wisconsin 1500 Engineer Dr 521 ERB Madison WI 53706-1609 Business E-Mail: callen@engr.wisc.edu.

CALLEN, JEFFREY PHILLIP, dermatologist, educator; b. May 30, 1947; s. Irwin R. and Rose P. (Cohen) C.; m. Susan B. Manis, Dec. 21, 1968; children: Amy, David. BS, U. Wis., 1969; MD, U. Mich., 1972. Diplomate Am. Bd. Internal Medicine, Am. Bd. Dermatology. Intern, resident in internal medicine U. Mich., Ann Arbor, 1972-75, intern, resident in dermatology, 1975-77; from asst. clin. prof. to dir. residency tng. program U. Louisville Sch. Medicine, 1977-84, dir. residency tng. program, 1984-88; chief dermatology svc. Louisville VA Hosp., 1984-93, prof., chief dermatology divsn., 1988—. Author: Manual of Dermatology, 1980, Cutaneous Aspects of Internal Disease, 1981, Neurology Clinics North America, 1987, Dermatologic Signs of Systemic Disease, 1988, 3d edit., 2003, Color Atlas of Dermatology, 1993, 2d edit., 2000, Current Practice of Dermatology, 1995; editor: Clinics in Rheumatic Disease, 1982, Dermatologic Clinics, 1985, 89, 2002, Medical Clinics of North America, 1982, 84, 86, 89; editor-in-chief Dermavision video program; mem. editl. bd. Internat. Jour. Dermatology, 1990-95; asst. editor Internat. Jour. Dermatology, 1993-95, Jour. Am. Acad. Dermatology, 1995-; editor spl. issues of jours. in field. Bd. dirs. Actor's Theater of Louisville, 1982-91, 92-98, 2000—, sec., 1986-87, Ky. Arts and Crafts Found., 1991-97; bd. govs. JB Speed Art Mus., 1995-2003. Fellow ACP, Am. Acad. Dermatology (chmn. audio/visual edn. com., task force therapeutic agts., internal med. symposium 1978-83, chmn. sci. and tech. exhibits 1986-89, dir. various symposiums, mem. coun. sci. assembly 1993-98, chair 1997-98, chair com. to evaluate ann. meeting, 1999-2003, vice chair coun. on edn. 2002-2003, chair coun. on edn. 2003—, v.p.-elect 2003—, bd. dirs. 1995-99, mem. exec. com. 1997-99, co-chair program for 21st century 1999-2000, chair psoriasis edn. conf. 2002), Am. Coll. Rheumatology (founder, chair skin disease study group 1996-98, 2000-02); mem. AMA, Am. Fedn. Clin. Rsch., Am. Dermatol. Assn., Dermatology Found. (trustee 1984-90), Louisville Theatrical Assn. (bd. dirs. 1999-2002). Achievements include research on condition in which systemic disease has cutaneous manifestations, lupus erythematosus, psoriasis, dermatomyositis. Office: U Louisville Dept Dermatology 310 E Broadway Ste 200 Louisville KY 40202-1745

CALLENBACH, ERNEST, writer, editor; b. Williamsport, Pa., Apr. 3, 1929; m. Christine Leefeldt, May 19, 1978; children: Joanna, Hans. Ph.B., U. Chgo., 1949, MA, 1953. Editor Film Quar., U. Calif. Press, Berkeley, 1958-91, editor books, 1958-91. Author: Living Poor With Style, 1971, rev. as Living Cheaply With Style, 2000, Ecotopia, 1975, Ecotopian Ency. for the Eighties, 1981, Ecotopia Emerging, 1981, Publisher's Lunch, 1989, Earth's Ten Commandments, 1990, Bring Back the Buffalo!, 1995, Ecology: A Pocket Guide, 1998; co-author: The Art of Friendship, 1979, Citizen Legislature, 1985, Humphrey the Wayward Whale, 1986, EcoManagement, 1993. Mem. Nat. Writers Union. Address: care Banyan Tree Books 1963 El Dorado Ave Berkeley CA 94707-2441

CALLENDER, CLIVE ORVILLE, surgeon; b. N.Y.C., Nov. 16, 1936; s. Joseph and Ida (Burke) C.; m. Fern Irene Marshall, May 25, 1968; children: Joseph, Ealena, Arianne. AB, Hunter Coll., 1959, DSc (hon.), 1998; MD, Meharry Med. Coll., 1963. Diplomate Am. Bd. Surgery. 1970. Intern U. Cin., 1963-64; asst. resident Harlem Hosp., N.Y.C., 1964-65, Howard U. and Freedmans Hosp., Washington, 1965-66, 67-68, chief resident, 1968-69, instr. dept. surgery, 1969-71; asst. resident Meml. Hosp. for Cancer and Allied Diseases, N.Y.C., 1966-67; cons. surgery Port Harcourt Gen. Hosp., Nigeria, 1970, 71; med. officer D.C. Gen. Hosp., 1970-71; NIH postdoctoral rsch. and clin. transplant fellow U. Minn., 1971-73; asst. prof. surgery Howard U. Med. Coll., Washington, 1973-76, assoc. prof., 1976-81, prof. surgery, 1981—, vice-chmn. dept. surgery, 1980-95, chmn. dept. surgery, 1996—, LaSalle D. Leffall, Jr. prof. surgery, 1996—, dir. transplant ctr., 1973—. Transplantation cons., Bermuda, 1977, V.I., 1978, 82-86; cons. Ethiopian Surg., Amenity Med. Sch., 1984; G.P.A. Ford Meml. lectr., 1978; mem. task force on organ procurement and transplantation HEW, 1984; testifier com. on labor and human resources U.S. Senate, 1983; mem. end stage renal disease study com. Inst. Medicine, 1989-90, com. on xenograft transplantation: ethical issues and pub. policy Inst. of Medicine, 1995-96, to the Sec. Health, 1990-94; mem. Inst. of Medicine Com. on Non-Heart-Beating ORgan Transplantation II, 1999; fellowship in liver transplantation Pitts. U., 1986-87; founder, prin. investigator Nat. Minority Organ and Tissue Transplant Edn. Program, 1991—. Mem. editl. adv. bd. New Directions, 1974-91, Contemporary Dialysis and Nephrology Jour., 1993-95, Clin. Transplant Proceedings, 1998—, Am. Jour. Kidney Disease, 2001—); contbr. articles to med. jours. Testifier for Ho. of Reps. Com. on Appropriation, U.S. Congress, 1992, others; councillor Soc. Organ Sharing, 1993, sec., 1995; chmn. tissue com. D.C. chpt. ARC, 1993-95; bd. trustees, Hunter Coll. Found., 2000. Recipient Hoffman LaRoche award, 1961, Charles Nelson Gold medal, 1963, Hudson Meadows award, 1963, Charles R. Drew Rsch. award, 1969, Daniel Hale Williams award, 1969, William Alonzo Warfield award, 1977, Howard U. Faculty Outstanding Unit award, 1982, 1st Humanitarian award Cmty. of Caring Ctr., 1990, Disting. Svc. award Surg. Sect. Nat. Med. Assn., 1990, Howard U. Health Affairs Disting. Svc. award, 1984, Outstanding Svc. award Dialysis and Transplant Support, Inc., 1993, Howard U. Legacy of Leadership in Health award, 1995, 11th ann. Minds in Motion award Sci. Skills Ctr., 1993, Edler Garnet Hawkins Humanitarian award Bronx Urban League, 1993; appreciation plaque for 1st renal transplant in V.I., Gov. St. Thomas, 1983, plaque for outstanding contbns. V.I. Legislature, 1984; named to Hunter Coll. Hall of Fame, 1989, Practitioner of Yr., Nat. Med. Assn., 1989, Scroll of Merit, Nat. Med. Assn., 1998, 1 of 10 Outstanding African Am. Male, WHMM-TV, Washington, 1994, 1 of 133 Gifts to the World Alumni Achievers, CUNY, 1995, Pearl Watson Meml. award for excellence in health care delivery Carribbean Am. Intercultural Orgn., Inc., 1995, Pioneer in Edn. award Inst. for Ind. Edn., 1995, Kidney Patients medal of Excellence 2nd Am. Assn., 1997, Fellow ACS (LaSalle D. Leffall, Jr. award 1998, Mary McLeod Bethune Legacy award, 2000), Am. Coll. Surgeons (bd. govs. 1994-00); mem. D.C. Med. Soc. (past vice chmn., chmn. surg. sect. 1994—, bd. trustees 1995), Internat. Soc. Organ Sharing (sec. 1993—), Transplantation Soc., Am. Soc. Transplantation Surgeons (chmn. membership com. 1986, organ placement com. 1991, mem. ethics com. 1995-97), N.Y. Acad. Medicine, Am. Assn. Kidney Patients (bd. dirs. 1998), Nat. Assn. Former Foster Care Children Am. (bd. dirs. 1998-99), Nat. Kidney Found. (nat. bd. dirs. 1991-94, nat. capital area 1977-90), Am. Surg. Assn., Am. Coun. on Transplantation (bd. dirs.), Nat. Med. Assn., Soc. Surg. Assn., Inst. Cellular Therapeutics (adv. bd.), United Network of Organ Sharing (vice-chair 1996-98, chair 1998-00), Soc. Black Acad. Surgeons (pres. elect 1998-01, pres. 2001—), Alpha Omega Alpha, Alpha Phi Omega, Alpha Phi Alpha. Home: 509 Kimblewick Dr Silver Spring MD 20904-6341 Office: 2041 Georgia Ave NW Washington DC 20060-0001 E-mail: ccallender@fac.howard.edu.

CALLENDER, JOHN FRANCIS, lawyer; b. Jacksonville, Fla., May 3, 1944; s. Francis Louis and Ethel (McLean) C.; m. Susan Carithers, June 13, 1969; children: John Francis Jr., Susanna McLean. AB cum laude, Davidson Coll., 1966; MA, U. N.C., 1969; JD with distinction, Duke U., 1976. Bar: Fla. 1976, U.S. Supreme Ct. 1982, cert.: Fla. Bar Assn. (civil trial lawyer). Asst. states atty. State of Fla., Jacksonville, 1980-81; ptnr. Turner, Ford & Callender, P.A., Jacksonville, 1981-84; pvt. practice Jacksonville, 1984—. Pres. Mental Health Clinic Jacksonville, Inc., 1985; bd. dirs. Vol. Jacksonville, Inc., 1981-84, AANR Edn. Found., Inc., 2003—. Served with U.S. Army, 1970-73. Fellow Am. Soc. Papyrologists, 1969. Mem.: ATLA, ABA, Jacksonville Bar Assn., Fla. Bar, Acad. Fla. Trial Lawyers, Phi Beta Kappa Alumni Assn. N.E. Fla. (treas. 1996—99, pres. 1999—2000), Am. Mensa Ltd., River Club, Fla. Yacht Club, Rotary Club (pres. 1997, asst. dist. gov. 1999—2002, dist. sec. 2002—03). Democrat. Episcopalian. Avocations: sailing, windsurfing, fishing, tennis, swimming. Home: 1745 Woodmere Dr Jacksonville FL 32210-2233 Office: 1301 Riverplace Blvd Ste 2105 Jacksonville FL 32207-9027 E-mail: jcallend@fdn.com.

CALLENDER, NORMA ANNE, psychology educator, counselor; b. Huntsville, Tex., May 10, 1933; d. C.W. Carswell and Nell Ruth (Collard) Hughes Bost; m. B.G. Callender, 1951 (div. 1964); remarried 1967 (div. 1973); children: Teresa Elizabeth, Leslie Gemey, Shannah Hughes, Kelly Mari; m. E Purfurst, June 1965 (div. Aug. 1965). BS, U. Houston, 1969; MA, U. Houston at Clear Lake, 1977; postgrad., U. Houston, 1970, Tex. So. U., 1971, Lamar U., 1972-73, U. Houston-Clear Lake, 1979, 87, 89-93, St. Thomas U., 1985, 86, Aerospace Inst., NASA, Johnson Space Ctr., 1986, U. Houston-Clear Lake, summer 98, San Jacinto Coll., 1988, postgrad., 1989, postgrad., 1994, postgrad., 2001, postgrad., 2002; PhD, Cornerstone U., 1998; postgrad, San Jacinto (Tex.) Coll., 2003. Cert. profl. reading specialist, Tex.; lic. profl. counselor. Tchr. Houston Ind. Schs., 1969-70; co-counselor, instr. Ellington AFB, Houston, 1971; tchr. Clear Creek Schs., League City, Tex., 1970-86; owner, dir. Bay Area Tutoring and Reading Clinic, Clear Lake City, Tex., 1970—, Bay Area Tng. Assocs., 1982-98, Bay Area Family Counseling, 1995—; cons., LPC intern Guidance Ctr. Pasadena (Tex.) Ind. Sch. Dist., 1993-95. Part-time instr. San Jacinto Coll., Pasadena, 1980-81, 91-93; univ. adj. U. Houston, Clear Lake, 1986-91; founder, editor BATA Books Pub., 1997—; cons. in field. Contbr. poetry to profl. jours. State advisor U.S. Congl. Adv. Bd., 1985-87; vol., bd. dirs. Family Outreach Ctr., 1989-92; vol. Bay Area Coun. on Drugs and Alcohol, Nassau Bay, Tex., 1993-94; bd. dirs. Ballet San Jacinto, 1985-87; adv. bd. Cmty. Ednl. TV, 1990-92. Recipient Franklin award U. Houston, 1965-67; Delta Kappa Gamma/Beta Omicron scholar, 1967-68, PTA scholar, 1973, Berwin scholar, 1976, Mary Gibbs Jones scholar, 1976-77, Found. Econ. Edn. scholar, 1976, Insts. Achievement Human Potential scholar, Phila., 1987. Mem.: ACA, Internat. Reading Assn., Clear Creek Educators Assn. (past, honorarium 1976, 1977, 1985), Leadership Clear Lake Alumni Assn. (charter, program and projects com. mem. 1986—87, edn. com. 1985), U. Houston Alumni Assn. (life), Phi Theta Kappa, Phi Delta Kappa, Kappa Delta Pi, Psi Chi (life), Phi Kappa Phi (life). Mem. Life Tabernacle Ch. Office: 1234 Bay Area Blvd Ste R Houston TX 77058-2538

CALLETON, THEODORE EDWARD, lawyer, educator; b. Newark, Dec. 13, 1934; s. Edward James and Dorothy (Dewey) C.; m. Elizabeth Bennett Brown, Feb. 4, 1961; children: Susan Bennett, Pamela Barritt, Christopher Dewey.; m. Kathy E'Beth Conkle, Feb. 22, 1983; 1 child, James Frederick. BA, Yale U., 1956; LLB, Columbia U., 1962. Bar: Calif. 1963, U.S. Dist. Ct. (so. dist.) Calif. 1963, U.S. Tax Ct. 1977. Assoc. O'Melveny & Myers, L.A., 1962-69, Agnew, Miller & Carlson, L.A., 1969, ptnr., 1970-79; pvt. practice L.A., 1979-83; ptnr. Kindel & Anderson, L.A., 1983-92, Calleton & Merritt, Pasadena, Calif., 1992-99, Calleton & Trytten, Pasadena, 1999—2002; pvt. practice Pasadena, 2002—. Academician Internat. Acad. Estate and Trust Law, 1974—; lectr. Calif. Continuing Edn. Bar, 1970—96, U. So. Calif. Tax Inst., 1972, 76, 91, Calif. State U., L.A., 1974—93, Practicing Law Inst., 1976—86, Am. Law Inst., 1985; bd. dirs. UCLA/Continuing Edn. of Bar Estate Planning Inst., 1979—; adj. prof. Golden Gate U. Law Sch., 1997—2000, Loyola U. Sch. Law, 2002—. Author: The Short Term Trust, 1977, A Life Insurance Primer, 1978, Calleton's Wills and Trusts, 1992—2003; co-author: California Will Drafting Practice, 1982, Tax Planning for Professionals, 1985, California Estate Planning, 2002; contbr. articles to profl. jours. Chmn. Arroyo Seco Master Planning Commn., Pasadena, Calif., 1970-71; bd. dirs. Montessori Sch., Inc., 1964-68, chmn., 1966-68, Am. Montessori Soc., N.Y.C., 1967-72, chmn., 1969-72; trustee Walden Sch. of Calif., 1970-86, 90-94, chmn., 1980-86; trustee Episc. Children's Home of L.A., 1971-75; bd. dirs. L.A. Master Chorale Assn., 1989-94, San Gabriel Valley Coun., Boy Scouts of Am., 2002—. Lt. USMC, 1956-59. Fellow Am. Coll. Trust and Estate Counsel; mem. L.A. County Bar Assn. (chmn. taxation sect. 1980-81, chmn. probate and trust law sect. 1981-82, Dana Latham Meml. award 1996), Aurelian Honor Soc., Elihu, Beta Theta Pi, Phi Delta Phi. Home: 301 Churchill Rd Sierra Madre CA 91024-1354 Office: 200 S Los Robles Ave Ste 678 Pasadena CA 91101-4600 E-mail: ted@calletonlaw.com.

CALLEY, JOHN, motion picture company executive, film producer; b. N.J., 1930; m. Olinka Schoberova, 1972 (div.) m. Meg Tilly, 1995; 4 stepchildren, Emily, David, Will, Sabrina. Dir. nighttime programming, dir. programming sales NBC, 1951-57; prodn. exec. and TV producer Henry Jaffe Enterprises, 1957; v.p. radio and TV Ted Bates Advt. Agy., 1958; exec. v.p., film producer Filmways, Inc., 1960-69; with Warner Bros., Inc., Burbank, Calif., 1969-87, exec. v.p. world-wide prodn., 1969-75, pres., 1975-80, vice chmn. bd., 1977-80, cons., 1980-87; film prodr., 1987—; pres., COO, United Artists Pictures, 1993-96; pres., CEO, Sony Pictures Entertainment, Inc., Culver City, Calif., 1996—98, chmn., CEO, 1998—2003. Office: care Sony Pictures Entertainment Inc 10202 Washington Blvd Culver City CA 90232-3119

CALLICOATTE, TROY D. loss control consultant; s. Norman V. and Charlotte J. Callicoatte; m. Sarah C. Pell, Oct. 21, 1970; children: Sarah M., Cody D., Brianna D. A of Computer Info. Systems, Bossier Parish C.C., La., 1989—93; MBA, La. Tech U., 1996—2001; PhD in Mgmt., NOVA Southeastern U., 2001—. Police Officer La. POST Cert., 1991. Dep. sheriff Caddo Parish Sheriff's Office, Shreveport, La., 1991—94; detective/police officer Shreveport Police Dept., 1994—2001; loss control cons. Summit Consulting Inc., Shreveport, La., 2001—. Den helper Cub Scouts, Blanchard, La., 2000—02. Mem.: Acad. of Mgmt. (corr.). Mem. Methodist Ch. Avocations: walking, travel, reading, family time, church. Office: Summit Consulting Inc 9434 Interline Ave Baton Rouge LA 70809-1911 Office Fax: 225-926-4102. Personal E-mail: tdcallicoatte@aol.com. E-mail: tcallicoatte@summitholdings.com.

CALLICOTT, JOHN BAIRD, philosopher, educator; b. Memphis, May 9, 1941; s. Burton H. and Evelyne Baird Callicott; m. Nancy Archer, 1963 (div. 1985); m. Frances Moore Lappé, 1985 (div. 1990); 1 child, Burton. BA, Rhodes Coll., 1963; MA, Syracuse U., 1966, PhD, 1972. Instr. U. Memphis, 1966-69; from asst. prof. to prof. U. Wis., Stevens Point, 1969-95; prof. philosophy U. North Tex., Denton, 1995—. V.p. Ctr. for Environ. Philosophy, 1980—. Author: In Defense of the Land Ethic, 1989, Earth's Insights, 1994, Beyond the Land Ethic, 1999. Mem.: Internat. Soc. Environ. Ethics (pres. 1994—2000). Avocation: outdoor aesthetics. Home: 1402 Kenwood Dr Denton TX 76205 Office: Dept Philosophy and Religion Studies U North Tex Denton TX 76203-0920 E-mail: callicott@unt.edu.

CALLIER, MARIA CECILE, writer, actress; BA in English Edn., U. No. Colo., 1979. Cert. secondary tchr. English. Broadcast journalist and prodr. various TV and pub. radio sta. programs, Colo., 1983—; freelance writer Colo., 1993—; pub. rels. dir. and grantwriter Grand River Hosp. Dist., Rifle, Colo., 1997-98; pub. rels. writer Colo. Mountain Coll., Glenwood Spring, Colo., 1997—; prepaid legal svcs. assoc. and group benefits cons. Westminster, Colo., 1995—98, 2001—. Tchr. various schs. in Denver area and Roaring Fork Valley, 1979-96; sales and mktg. rep. various radio stas. Colo., 1986—; local coord. and cmty. counselor, Acad. Yr. Am., Am. Inst. Foreign Study, 1991—, Au Pair in Am., 1992-97; local coord. Multiple Sclerosis Walk, Glenwood Springs, Colo., 1998. Appeared in (films) Christmas Vacation '95, Murder in High Places, He's Still There, Endangered Species; (TV shows) Unsolved Mysteries, Sky Merchant Home Shopping Program; provides voiceover and narration for various TV and radio commls.; publicist, ghostwriter Glenwood Springs Ctr. for the Arts, 2000—. Mem. SAG, NAFE, Nat. Writer's Union. Home and Office: Apt 432 7402 Church Ranch Blvd Westminster CO 80021-5413 Office Fax: 303-438-6250. E-mail: mariacecile@aol.com., ccallier@prepaidlegal.com.

CALLIES, DAVID LEE, lawyer, educator; b. Chgo., Apr. 21, 1943; s. Gustav E. and Ann D. Callies; m. Laurie Breeden, Dec. 28, 1996; 1 child, Sarah Wayne. AB, DePauw U., 1965; JD, U. Mich., 1968; LLM, U. Nottingham, England, 1969. Bar: Ill. 1969, Hawaii 1978, U.S. Supreme Ct. 1974. Spl. asst. states atty., McHenry County, Ill., 1969; assoc. firm Ross, Hardies, O'Keefe, Babcock & Parsons, Chgo., 1969-75, ptnr., 1975-78; prof. law Richardson Sch. Law, U. Hawaii, Honolulu, 1978—; Benjamin A. Kudo prof. law U. Hawaii, Honolulu, 1995—. Mem. adv. com. on planning and growth mgmt. City and County of Honolulu Coun., 1978-88, mem. citizens adv. com. on State Functional Plan for Conservation Lands, 1979-93. Author: (with Fred P. Bosselman) the Quiet Revolution in Land Use Control, 1971 (with Fred P. Bosselman and John S. Banta) The Taking Issue, 1973, Regulating Paradise: Land Use Controls in Hawaii, 1984, (with Robert Freilich and Tom Roberts) Cases and Materials on Land Use, 1986, 3d edit., 1999, Preserving Paradise: Why Regulation Won't Work, 1994 (in Japanese 1994, in Chinese 1999), Land Use Law in the United States, 1994; editor: After Lucas: Land Use Regulation and the Taking of Property Without Compensation, 1993, Takings! Land Development Conditions and Regulatory Takings: After Dolan and Lucas, 1995, (with Hylton, Mandelker and Franzese) Property Law and the Public Interest, 1998, 2nd edit., 2003 (with Kotaka) Taking Land, 2002, (with Curtin and Tappendorf) Bargaining For Development: A Handbook, 2003; co-editor Environ. and Land Use Law Rev., 2000—. Named Best Prof., U. Hawaii Law Sch., 1990-91, 91-92; Mich. Ford Found. fellow U. Nottingham (Eng.), 1969, life mem. Clare Hall, Cambridge U., 1999. Fellow Am. Inst. Cert. Planners, Am. Planning Assn.; mem. ABA (chmn. com. on land use, planning and zoning 1980-82, coun. sect. on state and local govt. 1981-85, 95—, exec. com. 1986-90, sec. 1986-87, chmn. 1989-90), Am. Law Inst., Am. Planning Assn., Hawaii State Bar Assn. (chair, real property and fin. svc. sect., 1997), Am. Bar Found., Ill. Bar Assn., Internat. Bar Assn. (coun. Asia Pacific Forum 1993-96, co-chair Acads. Forum 1994-96, chair 1996-98), Nat. Trust for Hist. Preservation, Royal Oak Soc., Lambda Alpha Internat. (pres. Aloha chpt. 1989-90, internat. v.p. Asia-Pacific region 2001—, Internat. Mem. of Yr. 1994). Home: 1532 Kamole St Honolulu HI 96821-1424 Office: U Hawaii Richardson Sch Law 2515 Dole St Honolulu HI 96822-2328 E-mail: dcallies@hawaii.edu.

CALLIGAN, WILLIAM DENNIS, retired life insurance company executive; b. Hibbing, Minn., Mar. 21, 1925; s. Raymond George and Ann Matilda (Olson) C.; m. Aletha E. Cornelius, Dec. 21, 1949; children— Ann M., Timothy M. BA, Yankton (S.D.) Coll., 1949. With N.Y. Life Ins. Co., 1953—, dir. mass market products, 1963-77, v.p. pensions, 1977-87. Mem. Internat. Found. Employee Benefit Plans, Inc. Served with USMC, World War II. Home: 66 Noe Ave Madison NJ 07940-2835

CALLINAN, TOM, editor; Corr. St. Cloud (Minn.) Daily Times, 1975; various positions Little Falls (Minn.) Daily Transcript, 1977—83; from asst. city editor to mng. editor Argus Leader, Sioux Falls, Minn., 1983—86; editor Lansing (Mich.) State Jour., 1986—91; exec. editor Fort Myers News-Press, 1991—94; editor Dem. and Chronicle and Times-Union, Rochester, NY, 1994—2000, v.p. news, 1994—2000; editor The Ariz. Republic, Phoenix, 2000—02, Cin. (Ohio) Enquirer, 2002—, v.p. news, 2002—. Named Gannett's Editor of Yr., 1997; recipient six Gannett Pres.'s Rings in News. Office: Cincinnati Enquirer 312 Elm St Fl 18 Cincinnati OH 45202-2724*

CALLIS, JERRY JACKSON, veterinarian; b. Parrot, Ga., July 28, 1926; s. Samuel Clayton and Sue (Glover) C.; m. Loisanne Roon, July 23, 1964 (dec. Aug. 1996); 1 child, Fredrick Alan. Student, North Ga. Coll., 1943-44; D.V.M., Auburn U., 1947; MS, Purdue U., 1949, D.Sc. (hon.), 1979, Southampton Coll., 1980. With U.S. Dept. Agr., 1948-88; veterinarian-in-charge of research Plum Island Animal Ctr., 1953-56; asst. dir. Plum Island Rsch. Ctr., 1956-63, dir., 1963-87; sr. rsch. advisor Agrl. Rsch. Svc., 1987-88; cons. on animal health, 1988—. Cons. Pan Am. Health Orgn., 1968—. Mem. AAAS, AVMA. Home: PO Box 537 Southold NY 11971-0537 E-mail: jcallis@hamptons.com.

CALLISON, CHARLES STUART, retired foreign service officer, development economist; b. Boonville, Mo., July 11, 1939; s. Charles Hugh Callison and Ruth Marie (Ecord) Woolsey; m.m Michelle My-Dung Pham, Sept. 29, 1965; children: Cynthia Thuy-Tien, Patricia Mong-Tuyen, Clarissa Thien-Huong. BS in Fgn. Svc., U. Md., 1961; cert. Vietnamese lang. course, Defense Lang. Inst., 1964; MA in S.E. Asian Studies, Yale U., 1969; PhD in Devel. Econs., Cornell U., 1976. Asst. prof. econs. Ohio U., Athens, 1973-74; econ. advisor Office of Vietnam Affairs Agy. for Internat. Devel. (AID), Washington, 1974-76; econ. advisor Bicol River Basin Devel. program AID, Naga City, Philippines, 1976-79, program economist Manila, 1979-82, program economist regional office Nairobi, Kenya, 1982-84, chief analysis div., 1984-87, dep. assoc. asst. adminstr. Office Policy Devel. Washington, 1987-90, counselor Sr. Fgn. Svc., 1987, dep. exec. dir. bd. for internat. food and agrl. devel. (BIFAD), 1990-91, dep. exec. dir. Agy. Ctr. for Univ. Coop. in Devel., 1991-93, dir. Office of Econs. and Enterprise Dhaka, Bangladesh, 1993-95, ret., 1995; chief of party, devel. econs policy reform analysis team Nathan Assocs. Inc., Cairo, 1996-99, exec. officer, 1999-2000, chief of party, 2000, chief of party, Partnership for Econ. Growth Project Jakarta, Indonesia, 2001—. Bd. govs. Mgrs. Network, AID, Washington, 1990-92. Author: Land-to-the-Tiller in the Mekong Delta, 1983; editor-in-chief 1960 Terrapin Yearbook, 1959-60; editl. bd. Fgn. Svc. Jour., 1990-93. Bd. dirs. Internat. Sch., Makati, Manila, 1980-82, Am. Internat. Sch., Dhaka, 1993-95. Capt. USAF, 1961-67, Vietnam. Decorated Bronze Star, Air Force Commendation medal; Vietnamese Air Force Honor medal; recipient fellowships Yale U., 1967-69, Cornell U., 1969-71 73, Ford Found., South Vietnam, 1971-73, Meritorious Honor award AID, 1993. Mem. Am. Econ. Assn., Am. Fgn. Svc. Assn. (v.p. for AID 1993), Phi Kappa Phi, Omicron Delta Kappa, Scabbard & Blade, Phi Eta Sigma, Sigma Alpha Epsilon (chpt. corres. sec. 1958-61). Democrat. Mem. Christian Ch. (Disciples Of Christ). Avocations: photography, genealogy, jogging. Home: 53 Trumbull St West Haven CT 06516-7029 Office: Setiabudi Atrium Plaza Setiabudi Jalan HR Rasuna Said Kuningan Jakarta 12920 Indonesia E-mail: stu@pegasus.or.id.

CALLISON, JAMES W. former lawyer, consultant, airline executive; b. Jamestown, N.Y., Sept. 8, 1928; s. J. Waldo and Gladys A. C.; m. Gladys I. Robinson, Oct. 3, 1959; children: Sharon Elizabeth, Maria Judith, Christopher James. AB with honors, U. Mich., 1950, JD with honors (Overbeck award 1952, Jerome S. Freud Meml. award 1953), 1953. Bar: D.C. 1954, Ga. 1960, U.S. Supreme Ct., 1961. Atty. Pogue & Neal, Washington, 1953-57; with Delta Air Lines, Inc., Atlanta, 1957-93, v.p. law and regulatory affairs, 1974-78, sr. v.p., gen. counsel, 1978-81, sr. v.p., gen. counsel, corp. sec., 1981-88; sr. v.p. legal and corp. affairs, sec. Delta Air Lines Inc., 1988-90; sr. v.p. corp. and external affairs Delta Air Lines, Inc., 1990-91, sr. v.p. corp. affairs, 1991-93; ret., 1993; cons. Inman Deming Internat., Washington. Contbr. articles to legal jours.; asst. editor: Mich. Law Rev, 1952-53. Bd. dirs. St. Joseph's Mercy Found. (chmn. planned giving com.); mem. adv. bd. Atlanta Union Mission. Recipient Papal Pro Ecclesia Et Pontifice award, 1966. Mem. State Bar Ga. (chmn. corp. counsel sect. 1989-90, mem. emeritus), Atlanta Bar Assn. (life), Atlanta Athletic Club, Order of Coif. Home: 2034 Dunwoody Club Way Dunwoody GA 30338-3024

CALLISON, JAMES WILLIAM, lawyer; b. Albemarle County, Va., Dec. 24, 1955; s. James Crofts and Jan (Richelsen) C. AB, Oberlin Coll., 1977; JD, U. Colo., 1982; LLM, Yale U., 2000. Law clk. to judge Dist. Ct. Colo., Boulder, 1982; ptnr. Moye, Giles, O'Keefe, Vermeire & Gorrell, Denver, 1982-96, Faegre & Benson L.L.P., 1997—. Lectr. law U. Denver, 1988-90; adj. prof. U. Colo. Law Sch., 1997—. Author: Partnership Law and Practice, 1992, Limited Liability Companies, 1994; contbr. articles to profl. jours. Mem. Leadership Denver, 1989-90, Denver Community Leadership Forum, 1991. Mem. ABA (bus. law sect., tax sect.), Colo. Bar Assn. (tax sect., exec. council 1986—, chmn. 1988-89), Denver Bar Assn., Order of Coif. Democrat. Home: 4622 S Vine Way Cherry Hills Village CO 80110-6045 Office: Faegre & Benson LLP 1700 Lincoln St Ste 3200 Denver CO 80203 E-mail: wcallison@faegre.com.

CALLISTER, LOUIS HENRY, JR., lawyer; b. Aug. 11, 1935; s. Louis Henry and Isabel (Barton) C.; m. Ellen Gunnell, Nov. 27, 1957; children: Mark, Isabel, Jane, Edward, David, John Andrew, Ann. BS, U. Utah, 1958, JD, 1961. Bar: Utah 1961. Asst. atty. gen., Utah, 1961; sr. ptnr. Callister Nebeker & McCullough, Salt Lake City, 1961—2002, of counsel, 2002—. Bd. dirs. Am. Stores Co., 1985-97, Quailbluff Devel. Co., 1971-2000; Vice-chmn. Salt Lake City Zoning Bd. Adjustment, 1979-84; bd. govs. Salt Lake Valley Hosps., 1983-91; treas. exec. com. Utah Rep. Com., 1965-69; chmn. Utah chpt. Rockefeller for Pres. Com., 1964-68; sec., trustee Salt Lake Police/Sheriff Hon. Cols., 1982-97; trustee, mem. exec. com. Utah Econ. Devel. Corp., 1992—, chmn., 1998-2000; trustee U. Utah, 1987-99, vice-chmn., 1989-99, bd. dirs. U. Utah Hosp., 1993-99; trustee Grand Canyon Trust, 2001—. Mem. Lds Ch. Home: 3860 Highland Ct Bountiful UT 84010-3365 Office: Callister Nebeker & McCullough Gateway Tower E Ste 900 Salt Lake City UT 84133-1102 E-mail: Lhcallister@cnmlaw.com.

CALLISTER, RONDA, management and human resources educator; b. Washington, Sept. 20, 1955; d. Jack Earl and Marilyn (Humphreys) Roberts; m. Michael Scott Callister, May 8, 1976; children: Christine, Corinne, Amber, Sarah. BS, Brigham Young U., 1977; MBA, U. Utah, 1980; PhD, U. Mo., 1996. V.p. Roberts' Wall Furniture, Salt Lake City, 1977-84; instr. Salt Lake C.C., Salt Lake City, 1984-87; v.p. Cmty. Water Co., Salt Lake City, 1988-91; rsch. and tchr. asst. U. Mo., Columbia, 1991-96; asst. prof. mgmt. and human resources Utah State U., Logan, 1996—2002, assoc. prof. mgmt. and human resources, 2002—. Adv. bd. Sunshine Terr., Logan, 1999; mem. Citizens Adv. Bd. for Parks and Recreation, Logan City, 1999; mem. Women and Gender Rsch. Inst., Logan, 1999-2002. Contbr. articles to profl. jours. Bd. dirs. Alta Canyon Recreation, Sandy, Utah, 1981-91, chair, 1987-90; mem. Water Adv. Bd., Sandy City, 1982-84. Irwin fellow, State Farm Found. fellow, 1996; New Faculty Rsch. grantee Utah State U., 1999, Women and Gender Rsch. grantee, 1999-2000, 02. Mem. Lds Ch. Avocations: skiing, walking. Home: 1633 Mountain Rd Logan UT 84321-6744 Office: Utah State U 3555 Old Main Hl Logan UT 84322-3555

CALLO, JOSEPH FRANCIS, writer; b. N.Y.C., Dec. 16, 1929; s. Joseph Francis and Mary Ellen (Brennan) C. (Mary Walsh C. stepmother); m. Susan Catherine Jones, June 10, 1952 (div. Nov. 1978); children: Joseph Francis III, James D., Mary Ellen, Kathleen E., Patricia A.; m. Sally Chin McElwreath, Mar. 17, 1979; 1 stepson, Robert Joseph McElwreath. BA, Yale U., 1952. Account exec. firm Joseph F. Callo Inc., N.Y.C., 1952-58; v.p. Potts-Woodbury Inc., N.Y.C., 1958-60, also dir., 1958-60; pres. Callo & Carroll Inc., N.Y.C., 1960-74; chmn. bd. dirs., creative dir. Callo Berger Albanese Inc., N.Y.C., 1974-75; TV prodr. NBC-TV, also PBS, 1976-78; exec. v.p. Albert Frank/FCB, Inc., N.Y.C., 1978-81; sr. v.p. Grey Advt., 1981-83, Muir Cornelius Moore, Inc., 1983-84. Ptnr. Leeward Islands Yacht Charters, 1980-83; adj. assoc. prof. comm. arts St. John's U., N.Y.C., 1965-78; mem. mktg. rev. group USN, 1973-74. Author: Legacy of Leadership: Lessons from Admiral Lord Nelson, 1999, Nelson Speaks, 2001, Nelson in the Caribbean, 2002. Bd. advisors Nat. Maritime Hist. Soc. Served with USNR, 1952—54, rear adm. Res. Mem.: Soc. Nautical Rsch. (Gt. Britain), Surface Navy Assn. (founding pres. greater NY chpt.), The Naval Club (London), Yale Club of N.Y. Home: 330 E 38th St Apt 25A New York NY 10016-2727

CALLON, MARGARET JOANN, writer, minister; b. Brown County, Ind., Aug. 30, 1946; d. Sanford Sherman Marshall and Essie Rosemary Jacob; m. Ralph Stephen Callon, Sept. 14, 1964; children: Steven, Carolyn, Roy. Lic. minister Ind., 1982. Activity coord. Welcome Nursing Facility, Franklin, Ind., 1977—88; prin., owner Variety Gift Shop, Nashville, 1988—92; nursing asst. Brown County Cmty. Care, Nashville, 9202; song writer Hilltop Records, Hollywood, Calif., 2002—; minister Gospel Revelation, Inc., Connersville, Ind., 1982—. Author: Guardian Angel In The Midst Of Life's Tempest, 2000, (songs) Little Angels God Has Lent, 2000, I See Love Written Everywhere, 2001. Avocations: hiking, bowling, visiting elderly. Home and Office: 7815 SR 135 N Morgantown IN 46160

CALLOW, ALLAN DANA, surgeon; b. W. Somerville, Mass., Apr. 9, 1916; s. Edward Rol and Carrie (Fowles) C.; M. Eleanor Magee (dec. 1986); children: Beverly Ann Callow Nelson, Susan Diane Callow Moseley, Allan Dana Jr.; m. Una Scully Ryan, May 26, 1989; stepchildren: Tamsin Smith, Amy Ryan. BS, Tufts U., 1938, MS, 1948, PhD in Physiology, 1952; MD, Harvard, 1942, DSc (hon.), 1987. Intern Boston City Hosp., 1942-43; rsch. fellow, resident in gen. and vascular surgery Tufts New Eng. Med. Ctr., Boston, 1947-51, vice chmn. dept. surgery, 1966-82; cons. vascular surgery, dir. Vascular Surgery Rsch. Group, TNEMC, 1982-90; prof. surgery vascular div. Washington Univ Sch Medicine, St. Louis, 1990-94; rsch. prof. medicine, surgery Boston U. Med. Ctr., 1995—. Mem. Whitaker Inst. Advanced Cardiovascular Rsch.; spl. fellow vascular diseases Mayo Clinic, Rochester, Minn., 1948-49; instr. to prof. surgery Tufts U. Sch. Medicine, Boston, 1948-64; cons. to surgeon gen. Med. Corps, U.S. Navy, also civilian community hosps.; mem. study com. div. med. scis. NRC, 1969-72 Author: Carotid Surgery, 1996; editor: Vascular Surgery, 1995; assoc. editor Jour. Vasc. Surgery, 1969—; contbr. articles on vascular surgery, gen. surgery, med. edn. to profl. jours. Trustee Tufts U., 1971—, chmn. bd., 1977-87; trustee Civic Edn. Found., Lincoln Filene Center; chmn. bd. deacons Wellesley Congl. Ch., 1962-66. With M.C. USNR, 1943-46, PTO; rear adm. Res. (ret.). Decorated Legion of Merit; recipient award Hellenic Internat. Red Cross, Predl. medal Tufts U. Mem. Internat. Cardiovascular Soc. (sec.-gen. 1967-77, pres. 1977-79, pres. N.Am. chpt. 1974-75), A.C.S. (gov. 1974—, pres. Mass. chpt. 1973), New Eng. Surg. Soc., AMA (ho. dels. 1966-70), New Eng. Soc. Vascular Surgery (pres. 1977-78), Soc. Vascular Surgery (pres. 1986), Soc. Biomaterials (Clemson award 1988), Boston Surg. Soc. (pres. 1978), Mass. Med. Soc., Mass. Soc. Med. Rsch. (pres. 1988—), Am. Surg. Assn., European Soc. Vascular Surgery, So. Vascular Assn., Assn. Med. Consultants to Armed Forces, Navy Inst., Navy League, Navy Res. Officers Assn., Phi Beta Kappa, Sigma Xi, Delta Upsilon, Alpha Omega Alpha; hon. mem. Hellenic, Mexican, Argentine socs. angiology, Italian, Belgian surg. socs., European Soc. Cardiovascular Surgery. Clubs: Union (Boston), Wardroom (Boston). Home: 329 Hammond St Chestnut Hill MA 02467-1207 Office: Boston U Med Ctr 80 E Concord St Boston MA 02118-2307

CALLOW, KEITH MCLEAN, judge; b. Seattle, Jan. 11, 1925; s. Russell Stanley and Dollie (McLean) C.; m. Evelyn Case, July 9, 1949; children: Andrea, Douglas, Kerry. Student, Alfred U., 1943, CCNY, 1944, Biarritz Am. U., 1945; BA, U. Wash., 1949, JD, 1952. Bar: Wash. 1952, D.C. 1974. Asst. atty. gen., Wash., 1952; law clk. to justice Supreme Ct. Wash., 1953; dep. pros. atty. King County, 1954-56; ptnr. Little, LeSourd, Palmer, Scott & Slemmons, Seattle, 1957-62, Barker, Day, Callow & Taylor, 1964-68; judge King County Superior Ct., 1969-71, Ct. of Appeals Wash., Seattle, 1972-84, presiding chief judge, 1985-90; justice State Supreme Ct. Wash., Olympia, 1985-90, chief justice, 1989-90; cons. Prior-Martech, 1998—. 2d v.p. Conf. of Chief Justices; Booneville Power Admin. Rate Hearings Officer, 1995-96; lectr. bus. law U. Wash., 1956-62, Shefelman Disting. lectr., 1991; faculty Nat. Jud. Coll., 1980, Seattle U. Environ. Law, 1992, 94-95; co-organizer, sec. Coun. of Chief Judges of Cts. of Appeals; Rep. of Estonia, 1993-96, advisor Nat. Ct. and Ministry of Justice; advisor Kyrgyzstan, Kazakhstan, Georgia, Armenia, 1997; presenter in field. Editor-in-chief Commercial Law Desk Book, 1992-95; editor works in field. Chief Seattle coun. Boy Scouts Am.; adviser Gov. Health Care Commn. State of Washington, 1991-92; pres. Young Men's Rep. Club, 1957. With AUS, 1943-46. Decorated Purple Heart; recipient Brandeis award Wash. State Trial Lawyers Assn., 1981, Douglas award, 1990. Fellow Am. Bar Found.; mem. ABA (chmn. com. on judiciary 1984-90), Wash. State Bar Assn. (mem. exec. com., appellate Judges Conf.), D.C. Bar Assn., Seattle-King County Bar Assn., Estate Planning Coun., Navy League, Rainier Club (sec. 1978, trustee 1989-92), Forty Nine Club (pres. 1972), Masons, Rotary, Psi Upsilon, Phi Delta Phi.

CALLOW, WILLIAM GRANT, retired judge; b. Waukesha, Wis., Apr. 9, 1921; s. Curtis Grant and Mildred G. C.; m. Jean A. Zilavy, Apr. 15, 1950; children: William G., Christine S., Katherine H. PhB in Econs, U. Wis., 1943, JD, 1948. Bar: Wis.; cert. for Fla. mediation. Asst. city atty., Waukesha, 1948-52; city atty., 1952-60; county judge, 1961-77; justice Supreme Ct. Wis., Madison, 1978-92. Asst. prof. U. Minn., 1951-52; mem. faculty Wis. Jud. Coll., 1968-75; Wis. commr. Nat. Conf. Commrs. on Uniform State Laws, 1967—; arbitrator Wis. Employment Rel. Commn.; arbitrator-mediator bus. disputes; arbitration and mediation nat. and internat. res. judge, 1992—. With USMC, 1943-45, with USAF, 1951-52, Korea. Recipient Outstanding Alumnus award U. Wis., 1973 Fellow Am. Bar Found.; mem. ABA, Dane County Bar Assn., Waukesha County Bar Assn. Episcopalian. Fax: 608-241-9923, 715-588-3452, 941-642-8889. E-mail: wgc@mymailstation.com., justice4@newnorth.net.

CALLOWAY, MARK T. lawyer, former prosecutor; married. Grad. in Polit. Sci., N.C. State U., 1980, JD, 1983. Bar: N.C. 1983, U.S. Dist. Ct. (we., mid., ea. dists.) N.C., U.S. Ct. Appeals (4th cir.), U.S. Supreme Ct. Rsch. asst. to Hon. Jack L. Cozort N.C. Ct. Appeals; law clk. to Hon. Robert D. Potter U.S. Dist. Ct. (we. dist.) N.C.; assoc., then ptnr./shareholder James, McElroy & Diehl, P.A., Charlotte, N.C., 1987-94; U.S. atty. for we. dist. N.C. U.S. Dept. Justice, Charlotte, 1994—2001; partner Alston & Bird, LLP, Charlotte, NC, 2001—. Office: Alston & Bird LLP Bank Amer Plz Ste 4000 101 S Tryon St Charlotte NC 28280 Office Fax: 704-444-1111.

CALLSEN, CHRISTIAN EDWARD, medical device company executive; b. 1938; married. AB, Miami U., 1959; MBA, Harvard U., 1966. With Cole Nat. Corp., Cleve., 1966-87, various mgmt. and v.p. positions, 1966-87, exec. v.p., 1983-87; pres. Hyatt Legal Svcs., Cleve., 1987-90, Profl. Vet. Hosps., Detroit, 1991, Profl. Med. Mgmt., Cleve., 1992—, Applied Med. Tech., Cleve., 1993-96; chmn., CEO Allen Med. Sys., Cleve., 1995-99; pres. Polymer Concepts, Inc., 1999; dir. Sight Resources Corp. Lt. USN, 1959-64. Home: 235 College St Hudson OH 44236-2908 Office: 7561 Tyler Blvd Ste 8 Mentor OH 44060-4867 E-mail: cec235@aol.com.

CALLUM, MYLES, magazine editor, writer; b. Lynn, Mass., Apr. 4, 1934; s. Abraham Edward and Ann Edith (Caswell) C.; m. Suzanne Connellis, Apr. 22, 1967 (div. 1974); children— Deborah, Jennifer. Student, U. Conn., 1951-53, N.Y. U., 1958-61. Pvt. investigator, Stamford, Conn., 1958-59; assoc. editor Leisure mag., N.Y.C., 1959-60; asst. editor Good Housekeeping mag., N.Y.C., 1961-63, assoc. editor, 1963-69, dir. spl. publs. divsn., 1969-70; mng. editor Better Homes and Gardens, Des Moines, 1971-75; assoc. editor TV Guide, Radnor, Pa., 1977-86, sr. editor., 1986-91, sr. writer N.Y.C., 1991-96, contbg. editor, 1996-97. White Ho. cons., writer Fed. health programs, 1968; constructor crossword puzzles, 1998—. Author: Body-Building and Self-Defense, 1961, Body Talk, 1972, also articles. Served with CIC AUS, 1955-57. Mem. Mensa, U.S. Chess Fedn., Greater Phila. Search and Rescue. Home: 2367 Julio Ln Santa Rosa CA 95401-5725

CALMAN, CRAIG DAVID, writer, actor, director; b. Riverside, Calif., June 11, 1953; Student, Pacific U., Forest Grove, Oreg., 1971-72, U. de Querétaro, Mex., 1972-73; BA in Motion Picture/TV, UCLA, 1975. Sr. admitting worker UCLA Med. Ctr., 1974-76; actor/playwright Old Globe Theatre, San Diego, 1977-78, Off Broadway and regional, N.Y.C. and East Coast, 1979-86; exec. asst. various film/TV studios and law firms, L.A., 1986-89, Orion Pictures Corp., L.A., 1989-90; dir. staged readings L.A., 1991—, The Transcription Co., 1998—. Actor with starring roles (TV and film) ADP Industrial, Teamwork, Macbeth, Flesteron in Amazonia, co-starring roles in Commercial Break, Sullivan's Travels; actor with co-starring/lead roles (theatre) in Book of the Dead, Dark Lady of the Sonnets, Hamlet, Rosencrantz and Guildenstern are Dead, Much Ado About Nothing, Too True to be Good, Henry V, Richard III, The Rivals, Merchant of Venice, A Day for Surprises, The Tavern, The Earrings of Madame De..., The Firebugs, and others; columnist World Wide Web mag. FilmZone, 1995-97. Author play/screenplays: The Turn of the Century, Strangled Nocturne, Skidoo Ruins, Life Without Father, Patterns Woven In A Park; author novel: The Turn of the Century; author one-act plays, screenplays, full-length plays, poetry; writer asst. Hal Roach, Bel Air, Calif., 1987-88. Vol. book reader Recording for the Blind, L.A., 1991—. Recipient Old Globe Theatre Atlas award for best actor in a comedy role for Too True to be Good, 1977-78; Helene Wurlitzer Found. of N.Mex. Writers Residency grantee, 1988; finalist Walt Disney fellowship program, 1992, Chesterfield Film Writers Project, 1997. Mem. SAG, Actors Equity Assn., Actors Studio West (playwright/dir. unit 2000—). Office: 6632 Lexington Ave PMB # 77 Los Angeles CA 90038-1306 E-mail: craigcalman@earthlink.net.

CALMAN, ROBERT FREDERICK, mining executive; b. Mineola, N.Y., May 14, 1932; s. William Arthur and Ida (Albersworth) C.; m. Susan Jean Raphael, June 20, 1959 (div. 1978); children: Andrew Frederick, Camille, Matthew Alexander; m. Doris Sumerson, June 9, 1979. BA, Yale U., 1954; MS, MIT, 1967. With Chase Manhattan Bank, N.Y.C., 1954-61, asst. treas., 1961; with Mobil Oil Corp., N.Y.C., 1961-70, treas. N.Am. div., 1964-68, treas. Internat. div., 1968-69; v.p. finance, treas. IU Internat. Corp., Phila., 1970-72, group v.p. devel., 1972-74, exec. v.p., 1974-78, vice chmn., 1978-85, chmn. fin. com., dir., 1986-88; chmn., dir. Echo Bay Mines Ltd., Edmonton, Alta., Can., 1981-96. Bd. dirs. Corp. Cons. Group, Ltd., Bank of N.Y. Trust Co. of Fla., The Gold Inst., Am. Mining Congress; lectr. NYU, 1968-69. Author: Linear Programming and Cash Management/Cash Alpha, 1968. Pres., Phila. chpt. Nat. Found. for Ileitis and Colitis, Inc., 1974-75; pres., mem. bd. govs. Soc. Alfred P. Sloan Fellows; dir. alumni fund, mem. corp. devel. com. Mass. Inst. Tech. Served to 1st lt., arty. AUS, 1955-57. Recipient E.P. Brooks prize Mass. Inst. Tech., 1967. Mem. Phi Beta Kappa, Phi Gamma Delta. Republican. Christian Scientist. Office: 241 S 6th St Apt 2302 Philadelphia PA 19106-3736 E-mail: BobCalman@compuserve.com.

CALMENSON, MARVIN, retired surgeon; b. Aberdeen, S.D., 1914; MD, Rush Med. Coll., 1938. Diplomate Am. Bd. Surgery. Intern Emanuel Hosp., Portland, Oreg., 1938-39; surg. fellow Mayo Fedn., Rochester, Minn., 1943-46; ret. Fellow ACS; mem. AMA.

CALNAN, ARTHUR FRANCIS, ophthalmologist; b. Boston, Mar. 11, 1926; s. Augustine Francis and Mary Ellen (Callahan) C.; m. Jeanne Elizabeth Faber, Nov. 27, 1954; children: Kathleen, Diane, Barbara, Jeffrey, Douglas, David. BS, Tufts U., 1946, MD, 1950; MS, U. Pa., 1954. Diplomate Am. Bd. Ophthalmology, Am. Bd. Med. Examiners. Rotating intern St. Louis City Hosp., 1950-51; resident ophthalmology, rsch. fellow Wills Eye Hosp., Phila., 1954-55, resident, 1955-57; preceptorship Trygye Gundersen MD, Boston, 1957-65; chair ophthamology dept. Lahey Clinic, Boston, 1965-70; sr. mem. South Suburban Ophthalmology, Hingham, Mass., 1970—. Clin. instr. ophthalmology Tufts U. Sch. Medicine, 1958; mem. active staff ophthalmology South Shore Hosp., Weymouth, Mass., 1960—; jr. assisting surgeon ophthalmology Carney Hosp., Dorchester, Mass., 1963—; asst. ophthalmology Milton (Mass.) Hosp., 1973—. Mem. Plymouth County Rep. Club. Served to capt. USAF, 1950-53. Recipient Humanitarian of Yr. award Vis. Nurse Assn., 1992. Mem. AMA, Internat. Assn. Ocular Surgeons, Am. Acad. Ophthalmology, Am. Intra-Ocular Implant Soc., New Eng. Ophthalmol. Soc., Mass. Soc. Ophthalmic Physicians and Surgeons, Mass. Med. Soc., Norfolk-South Med. Soc., Am. Soc. Cataract and Refractive Surgeons, Am. Soc. Contemporary Ophthalmology, Contact Lens Assn. Ophthalmologists, Mass. Eye and Ear Infirmary Alumni Assn., Wills Eye Hosp. Alumni Assn., Erie Soc., Clan Gillean Assn., South Shore C. of C., Air Force Assn., Guild St. Luke. Roman Catholic. Avocations: travel, gardening, music. Home: 170 Old Oaken Bucket Rd Scituate MA 02066-4435 Office: S Suburban Ophthalmology 31 Derby St Hingham MA 02043-3706 E-mail: afcalnan@yahoo.com.

CALODNY, ALAN LEE, retired pharmacist; b. Bklyn., Feb. 27, 1934; s. Benjamin Lewis and Rose C.; m. Akie Luckhoo (dec. May 1990). BS in Pharmacy, Bklyn. Coll. Pharmacy, 1955; MS in Hosp. Pharmacy Adminstrn., L.I. Univ., 1973. Pharmacist Whelan Drug Stores, N.Y.C., 1956-57, C&M Pharmacy, Bklyn., 1957-58; asst. chief pharmacist L.I. Jewish Hosp., Glen Oaks, N.Y., 1958-59; chief pharmacist Parsons Hosp., Flushing, N.Y., 1959-84; pharmacist N.Y. State Dept. Corrections, 1984-90, Bronx-Lebanon Hosp., N.Y., 1989-93. Life mem. Cancer Care, Inc., Flushing, 1977; alumni assn. bd. dirs. Arnold and Marie Schwartz Coll. Pharmacy. Mem. Am. Pharm. Assn., N.Y. State Coun. Health Sys. Pharmacists, L.I. Soc. Health Sys. Pharmacists, Rho Chi. Democrat. Jewish. Avocations: philately, study of outer space/ufos, study of animals and natural history, geography. Home: 82-59 268th St Floral Park NY 11004

CALOGERO, PASCAL FRANK, JR., judge; b. New Orleans, Nov. 9, 1931; s. Pascal Frank and Louise (Moore) C.; children— Deborah Ann Calogero Applebaum, David, Pascal III, Elizabeth, Thomas, Michael, Stephen, Gerald, Katie, Chrissy. Student, Loyola U., New Orleans, 1949-51, JD, 1954; ML in the Jud. Process, U. Va., 1992; LLD (hon.), Loyola U., New Orleans, 1991. Bar: La. Ptnr. Landrieu, Calogero & Kronlage, 1958-69, Calogero & Kronlage, 1969-73; gen. counsel La. Stadium and Expn. Dist., 1970-73; assoc. justice Supreme Ct. La., New Orleans, 1973-90, chief justice, 1990—. Mem. La. Democratic State Central Com., 1963-71; mem. subcom. on del. selection La. Dem. Party, 1971; del. Dem. Nat. Conv., 1968. Served to capt. JAGC U.S. Army, 1954-57. Recipient Disting. Jurist award La. Bar Founds., 1991; Judge Bob Jones Meml. award, Am. Judges Assn., 1995. Mem. ABA, La. Bar Assn., New Orleans Bar Assn., Greater New Orleans Trial Lawyers Assn. (v.p. 1967-69), Order of the Coif. Office: Supreme Ct La 301 Loyola Ave New Orleans LA 70112-1814 E-mail: icaloger@lasc.org.

CALORE, PAUL, retired writer; b. Providence, Apr. 5, 1938; s. Enrico Calore, Ida Marie Ann Calore; m. Cecelia Ferreira, Apr. 18, 1964; children: Vickie Noel, Stephen, Cheryl Calore-Abatacola. BA magna cum laude, Johnston & Wales U., 1976. Ops. br. chief Def. Logistics Agy., Needham, Mass., 1981—93. Author: Land Campaigns of the Civil War, 2000, Naval Campaigns of the Civil War, 2002. Mem.: Civil War Ctr., Civil War Preservation Trust. Avocations: collector Civil War memorabilia, travel. Personal E-mail: paulcalore1@wmconnect.com.

CALSBEEK, FRANKLIN, health promotion educator; b. Rock Valley, Iowa, Dec. 20, 1931; s. August and Rena (Bakker) C.; m. Ula Kay Oosterbaan, June 8, 1963; children: Leslie Joan, Leah Rae, Laurel Beth. AA, Northwestern Coll., Orange City, Iowa, 1952; BS, Augustana Coll., 1956; MS, U. Ill., 1961; EdD, U. Oreg., 1969. Cert. health edn. specialist. Tchr., coach Illiana Christian High Sch., Lansing, Ill., 1956-62; prof. health sci. Dordt Coll., Sioux Center, Iowa, 1962-74; asst. dean Sch. Edn., S.W. Tex. State U., San Marcos, 1981-85, prof. health edn., 1978—. Assoc. dir. AIDS consortium Tex. Coll. and Univ.; cons. Tex. Edn. Agy. and Nat. Evaluation System, Inc., Amherst, Mass., 1985, 86, 89; researcher in field. Contbr. articles to profl. jours. Coun. mem. 1st Christian Reformed Ch., Sioux Ctr. With U.S. Army, 1953-55. Fellow Am. Sch. Health Assn., Tex. Pub. Health Assn., Tex. Sch. Health Assn. (bd. dirs. 1985-89); mem. Assn. for Advancement Health Edn., Tex. Assn. for Health, Phys. Edn., Recreation and Dance (v.p. 1974-78, pres. 1991-92). Avocations: music, travel, stained glass, fishing, reading.

CALTER, PAUL ARTHUR, mathematician, educator, writer; b. N.Y.C., June 18, 1934; s. Arthur and Frances (Bankowitz) Calcaterra; m. Margaret Jolind Carey, May 13, 1959; children: Amy, Michael. BS in Engring., The Cooper Union, N.Y., 1962; MS in Mech. Engring., Columbia U., 1966; MFA in Sculpture, Norwich U., 1993. Lab. technician Columbia U., 1952-60; devel. engr. Kollsman Instrument Corp., 1960-65; sr. project engr. Intertype Co., Bklyn., 1965-68; prof. math. Vt. Tech. Coll., 1968-89, prof. emeritus, 1990—, dir. Summer Math. Insts., 1989—. Vis. prof. math. Dartmouth Coll., 1997. Author: Problem Solving with Computers, 1973, Magic Squares, 1977, Schaum's Outline of Technical Mathematics, 1979, Technical Mathematics, 1983, 4th edit., 2000, Practical Math Handbook for the Building Trades, 1983, Mathematics for Electricity and Electronics, 1984, Mathematics for Computer Technology, 1986, Technical Calculus, 1988, 2d edit., 1999, Technical Mathematics with Calculus, 1984, 4th edit., 2000, Introductory Algebra and Trigonometry, 1997. With U.S. Army, 1957-59. Recipient Ralph Horton Meml. award in Sci., 1952; vis. scholar Dartmouth Coll., 1995. Mem. Am. Math. Assn. 2-Year Colls., Math. Assn. Am., Nat. Coun. Tchrs. Math., Assistance, Coll. Art Assn., New Eng. Math. Assn. 2-Year Colls., Internat. Sculpture Soc. Avocations: sculpture, painting, mountaineering. Home: 108 Bluebird Ln Randolph Center VT 05061-9733 E-mail: pcalter@sover.net.

CALTRIDER, PAUL GENE, pharmaceutical company executive, microbiologist; b. Mineral Wells, W.Va., Jan. 14, 1935; s. Caroll Lesta and Ora V. (Cooper) C.; m. Virginia D. Deem, Oct. 20, 1956; children: Jeffrey D., Steven P., Beth A. BS in Biology, Glenville State Coll., 1956; MS in Plant Pathology, W.Va. U., 1958; PhD in Plant Pathology, U. Ill., 1962. Sr. microbiologist Eli Lilly & Co., Indpls., 1962-66, mgr. tech. svcs., 1966-70, Clinton, Ind., 1970-76, mgr. fermentation devel. Indpls., 1976-80, dir. biochem. devel. and tech. svc., 1980-94; cons. in fermentation tech. Zionsville, Ind., 1995—. Author: (with others) Antibiotics Vol. I, 1967; contbr. articles to scholarly and profl. jours. Mem. Zool. Soc., Indpls. Mem. Am. Soc. Microbiology, Am. Chem. Soc., Soc. Indsl. Microbiology, Optimists (pres. Zionsville, Ind. chpt. 1991), Sigma Xi. Republican. Achievements include patent for Tylosin Production.

CALVA, ROBERT BARAQUIEL, music educator; b. Witchita, Sept. 15, 1959; s. Erma Mae and Robert Calva. Cert. Musicians Inst., Hollywood, 1992, Svc. Calif., 2002. Git instr. Musicians Inst., Hollywood, Calif., —; music instr. Delian Music, Culver City, Calif. Musician The Missing Links, LA. Author: (book) Texas Blues Guitar. Mem. Berachah Ch., Houston, 1980—2003. Conservative. Avocations: reading, fitness, natural healing, history, movies. Home: 12300 Sherman Way #182 North Hollywood CA 91605 Office: Musicians Inst 1655 McCadden Pl Hollywood CA 90028 Home Fax: 323-462-6978; Office Fax: 323-462-6978. Personal E-mail: rbcalva@hotmail.com. E-mail: robertc@mi.edu.

CALVANI, TERRY, lawyer; b. Carlsbad, N.Mex., Jan. 29, 1947; s. Torello Howard and Mary Virginia (Hawkins) C.; m. Mary Virginia Anderson, May 3, 1969; m. 2d, Judith Thompson, Aug. 28, 1980; children: Dominic Mario, Torello Howard. BA, U. N.Mex., 1969; JD with distinction, Cornell U., 1972. Bar: N.Mex. 1972, Calif. 1972, Tenn. 1978, D.C. 1992, U.S. Dist. Ct. N.Mex. 1972, U.S. Dist. Ct. (no. dist.) Calif. 1972, U.S. Dist. Ct. (mid. dist.) Tenn. 1978, U.S. Dist. Ct. D.C. 1994, U.S. Ct. Appeals (9th cir.) 1972, U.S. Ct. Appeals (6th cir.) 1977, U.S. Ct. Appeals (5th cir.) 1981, U.S. Ct. Appeals (11th cir.) 1981, U.S. Ct. Appeals (D.C. cir.) 1994, U.S. Supreme Ct. 1985. Tchg. fellow Stanford U. Law Sch., 1972-73; asst. prof. law Vanderbilt U. Sch. Law, Nashville, 1974—77, assoc. prof., 1977—80, prof., 1980—83; assoc. Pillsbury, Madison & Sutro (now Pillsbury Winthrop LLP), San Francisco, 1973-74, ptnr., 1990—2002; mem. The Competition Authority Republic of Ireland, 2002. Vis. prof. law U. Va., Charlottesville, 1981—82; of counsel Haksell Slaughter & Young, Birmingham, 1980—83; commr. U.S. F.T.C., 1983—90; acting chmn., 1985—86; lectr. Harvard U. Sch. Law, 1998—2002; sr. lectrg. fellow Duke U. Sch. Law, 2000. Author: (with John Siegfried) Economic Analysis and Antitrust Law, 1979, 2d edit., 1988; bd. editors Antitrust Bull., 1982—, Bur. Nat. Affairs RICO Report, 1986-96. Mem.: ABA (chmn. spl. com. to study antitrust penalties and damages antitrust sec 1979—82, chmn. Robinson-Patman com. antitrust sect. 1981—83, coun. mem. 1985—86), Adminstrv. Conf. U.S. 1985-90, Am. Law Inst. (coun. mem. 1990—93), 6th Jud. Conf. (life), Malahide Tennis and Croquet Club (Dublin Coll.), Richland County Club (Nashville), Riverside Country Club (Carlsbad), The G.C. Club Tenn. (Nashville), The Club (Birmingham), Pacific Union Club (San Francisco), Colonnade Club (Charlottesville), Olympic Club (San Francisco), The Stephen's Green Club (Dublin), Order of the Coif. Roman Catholic. Office: Competition Authority Parnell Ho 14 Parnell Sq Dublin Ireland Fax: +353 1 804 5401. E-mail: tc@tca.ie.

CALVANO-SMITH, RITA, journalist, small business owner; b. Pasadena, Calif., Jan. 11, 1948; d. Alfred Augustus and Rose Lucille (DeFazio) Calvano; m. Clifford R. Smith, Nov. 6, 1992. BA in Journalism, San Diego State U., 1972, MA in Am. Studies, 1976. Reporter The Daily Californian, El Cajon, Calif., 1972—76, San Diego Tribune, 1977-92; instr. Fashion Careers of Calif., San Diego, 1993-97, Fashion Inst. Design & Merchandising, San Diego, 1993, Mira Costa C.C., Oceanside, Calif., 1992-93; pres., owner Make Mine Petite, San Diego, 1992—. Vol. instr. San Diego Journalism Project, 1996; mem. fashion prodn. com. Crawford H.S., 1994-2003. Editor/writer PS Features, San Diego, 1996—, Fancy Publs., 1997-2003, caregiverzone.com. Recipient Cmty. Svc. award AAUW, LaMesa, Calif., 1970's, Feature Writing award AP, 1970's, Ring of Truth award Copley Press, 1980's. Democrat. Avocation: travel nationally and internationally.

CALVER, RICHARD ALLEN, retired college dean; b. Chillicothe, Ohio, Feb. 16, 1939; s. Robert K. Calver and Catherine Mae (Roush) Bryan; m. Susan Jane Yost, Oct. 9, 1988. Student, U. Hawaii, 1959-61; BSBA, W.Va. U., 1963; MS in Bus., Va. Commonwealth U., 1970; C.A.G.S.E., Va. Tech. U., 1983, EdD in C.C. Edn., 1984. Mgmt. trainee Sears Roebuck & Co., 1963, Reuben H. Donnelley Corp., 1963-64, state publs. and customer rels. mgr., 1964-68; state job analyst Va. Divsn. pers., Richmond, 1968-70; dean adminstrv. svcs. S.W. Va. C.C., Richlands, 1970-88, Thomas Nelson C.C., Hampton, Va., 1988—2002, interim pres., 1994-95, spl. asst. to pres., 2002—. Mem. accreditation teams So. Assn. Colls. and Schs., 1976-95, Mid. States Assn., 1983-94. Mem. Lebanon (Va.) Town Coun., 1978-82; mem. spl. edn. adv. com. Russell County Sch. Bd., 1984-88, Va. Peninsula Inst. Leadership Inst. Program, 1989; mem. Greater Williamsburg Area Crossroads planning com., 1999—. With USAF, 1957-61. Mem. Nat. Assn. Coll. and Univ. Bus. Officers, Nat. Coun. C.C. Bus. Officers (Regional Outstanding Bus. officer 1990, nat. bd. dirs. 1985-94), So. Assn. Coll. and Univ. Bus. officers, Ea. Assn. Coll. and U. Bus. Officers, Coll. and Univ. Pers. Assn., Lions (pres. Lebanon club 1976-77), Shriners (pres. club 1974-75), Scottish Rite (32d degree), Masons, Delta Tau Delta, Phi Kappa Phi, Phi Theta Kappa (hon.). Methodist. Home: 5509 N Mallard Run Williamsburg VA 23188-9415 Office: 161C John Jefferson Sq Williamsburg VA 23185

CALVERLEY, JOHN ROBERT, physician, educator; b. Hot Springs, Ark., Jan. 14, 1932; s. John A. and Della (O'Neill) C.; m. Alice Mae Feller, Dec. 27, 1953; children: Mark (dec.), David. BS, U. Oreg., 1953, MD, 1955. Diplomate: neurology Am. Bd. Psychiatry and Neurology (dir. 1977-84, sec. 1981-83, v.p. 1983-84). Intern U. Iowa, Iowa City, 1955-56, resident in neurology, 1956; resident in internal medicine Mayo Found., Rochester, Minn., 1957, neurology resident, 1957-59; mem. faculty dept. neurology med. br. U. Tex., Galveston, 1964—, assoc. prof. med. br., 1966-70, prof. med. br., 1970—, chief div. neurology med. br., 1967-73, chmn. dept. neurology med. br., 1973—2002, interim chmn. dept. psychiatry, 1989-90, prof. neurology med. br., 2002—. Cons. neurology USAF, 1965-94, nat. cons. to surgeon gen., 1976-94. Capt. M.C. USAF, 1957-64. Served to capt. M.C. USAF, 1957-64. Mem. Tex. Med. Assn., Am. Acad. Neurology (exec. bd. 1983-86), Am. Neurol. Assn., Assn. Univ. Profs. of Neurology (pres. 1993-94). Home: 711 Harborside Way Kemah TX 77565-2387 Office: U Tex Med Br Dept Neurology 301 University Blvd Galveston TX 77555-5302 Fax: 409-772-6940. E-mail: jcalverl@aol.com., jcalverl@utmb.edu.

CALVERT, C(LYDE) EMMETT, former state agency administrator; b. Lexington, Ky., Feb. 24, 1937; s. Emmett I. and Minnie (Hall) C.; m. Violet Stafford, Sept. 22, 1962; children: Emmett Bradford, Eric Brandon. BS in Commerce and Acctg., U. Ky., 1959. Rsch. asst. U. Ky., Lexington, 1959; from auditor to audit mgr. Ky. Revenue Cabinet, Lexington, 1959-87, sec. Frankfort, 1987-91. Bd. dirs. Ky. Housing Corp., Frankfort, Ky. Workers Compensation Funding Commn., Frankfort, State Property and Bldg. Commn., Frankfort, Commonwealth Venture Fund, Ky. Employees Deferred Compensation System, Frankfort, 1991-94. Mem. tax com. Ky. Farm Bur., Louisville, 1991; vol. non-profit schs., Lexington; coach, league ofcl. various sport orgns., Lexington, 1975-86. Recipient Cert. of merit Office Vocat. Rehab., 1990. Mem. Southeastern Assn. Tax Adminstrs., Fedn. Tax Adminstrs., Lexington Yacht Club. Democrat. Presbyterian. Avocations: boating, woodworking, brick laying. Home: 3536 Castlegate Wynd Lexington KY 40502-7701

CALVERT, DAVID VICTOR, soil science educator; b. Chaplin, Ky., Feb. 26, 1934; s. Stanford Byron and Willia Neal Calvert; m. Joyce Faye LeMay, July 27, 1957; children: Victor Neal Calvert, Yvonne Carole Calvert. BS, U. Ky., 1956, MS, 1958; PhD, Iowa State U., 1962. Cert. profl. soil scientist, Am. Registry of Cert Profls. in Agronomy, Crops and Soils, Ltd. Grad. rsch. asst. U. Ky., Lexington, 1956-58, Iowa State U., Ames, 1958-62; asst. prof. soil and water sci. U. Fla., Ft. Pierce, 1962-68, assoc. prof., 1968-76, prof., 1976—, dir. Indian River Rsch. & Edn. Ctr., 1979-94. Ofcl. collaborator S.E. region USDA, Athens, Ga., 1965-79; cons. World Bank, Jamaican Sch. Agr., Kingston, 1970-71; cons. soil sci. Coun. for Agrl. Sci. and Tech., St. Louis. Contbr. over 175 articles to profl. jours. including Soil Sci. Soc. Am. Proceedings, Jour. Agrl., Food Chem., Jour. Environ. Quality, Soil Sci., Proceedings Internat. Soc. Citriculture. Recipient Soil-Water-Air-Plant grant USDA Agrl. Rsch. Svc., Fla., 1968-80; grantee EPA, 1970-73, Water Quality Rsch. City of Okeechobee, Fla., 1990-93, St. Johns and South Fla. Water Mgmt. Dists., Palatka and West Palm Beach, 1993-96; award Fla. Dept. Agr. and Consumer Svcs., Tallahassee, 1996—; recipient Rsch. Achievement award Fla. Fruit and Vegetable Assn., 1979, Agrl. Hall of Fame award Saint Lucie County Farm Bur., 1997; U. Ky. fellow; named Outstanding Conservationist of Yr., Soil Conservation Svc. USDA, Fla., 1983, Disting. Out-of-State Alumnus for the U. Kys. Coll. of Agrl., 1997. Fellow Am. Soc. Agronomy; mem. Soil Sci. Soc Am., Internat. Soc. Soil Sci., Am. Soc. for Hort. Sci., Coun. of Agrl. Sci. and Tech., Soil and Crop Sci. Soc. Fla. (pres. 2000), Fla. State Hort. Soc. (hon. membership award 1997), Internat. Soc. Citriculture, Rsch. Ctr. Adminstrs. Soc., Am. Soc. Agronomy, Farmhouse Fraternity, Scovell Soc. U. Ky. (charter mem.), Sigma Xi, Gamma Sigma Delta, Alpha Zeta. Achievements include contbns. to development and deployment of working water quality standards to guide growers using low-volume sprinkler and micro irrigation systems; development of a soil and water management strategy for control of nitrates and phosphates leaching from citrus groves into surface and ground water. Home: 1007 Grandview Blvd Fort Pierce FL 34982-4323 Office: U Fla IFAS Indian River Rsch & Edn Ctr 2199 South Rock Rd Fort Pierce FL 34945-3138 E-mail: dvcalvert@mail.ifas.ufl.edu.

CALVERT, DELBERT WILLIAM, energy executive; b. Bosworth, Mo., Jan. 29, 1927; s. William McKinley and Ruby Leona (Berrier) Calvert; m. Mary Lee Brown, Feb. 10, 1947 (div. Mar. 1971); children: Gary D., Danial L.; m. Melva Allen Hurst, Sept. 4, 1971; stepchildren: Holly Hurst, Allen Hurst. BSCE, U. Mo., 1952. Asst. mgr. supply and transp. divsn. Phillips Petroleum Co., Bartlesville, Okla., 1952-63; asst. to v.p. Tex. Ea. Transmission Corp., Houston, 1963-65; mgr. diversification dept. No. Natural Gas Co., Omaha, 1965-68; pres. Williams Bros. Pipe Line Co., Tulsa, 1968-71; exec. v.p. The Williams Cos., Tulsa, 1971-85, also bd. dirs.; chmn. bd. Williams Energy Co., 1975-79, also bd. dirs.; chmn., CEO, Agrico Chem. Co., Tulsa, 1977-85, also bd. dirs. Pres. Wiliams Techs., Inc., 1992—97; chmn. bd. dirs. Black Mesa Pipeline Co., 1996—97, adv. dir., 1997—98. Apptd. to gov.'s agroindustry policy commn., 1987—; mem. exec. bd. Indian Nations coun. Boy Scouts Am., 1969—, pres., 1974—76; mem. U. Mo. Devel. Fund, 1969—, chmn., 1972—73; bd. dirs. Goodwill Industries Tulsa. With AUS, 1945—47. Mem.: Potash and Phosphate Inst. (dir. 1982—85), Fertilizer Industry Assn. (chmn. bd.), Am. Petroleum Inst. (gen. com. div. transp. 1971), Okla. Petroleum Coun. (dir. 1968—, pres. 1977—78), Mo. U. Civil Engring. Acad. Disting. Alumni (Pipe Liner of Yr. 1998), Garden of Gods Club (Colorado Springs, Colo.), Univ. Club (Columbia, Mo.), Waikoloa (Hawaii) Village Golf Club, Pi Mu Epsilon, Chi Epsilon, Tau Beta Pi. Home: PO Box 384690 Waikoloa HI 96738

CALVERT, GORDON LEE, retired legal association executive; b. Wardensville, W.Va., Sept. 2, 1921; s. Aaron Lee and Ada (Brill) C.; m. Margaret James, June 9, 1945; children— Gordon R., Roger L., Walter R. BA with distinction, George Washington U., 1943, JD with distinction, 1945. Bar: D.C. 1946. Assoc. firm Covington & Burling, Washington, 1944-46; with Investment Bankers Assn. Am., Washington, 1946-71, exec. dir., gen. counsel, 1966-71; exec. v.p., gen. counsel Securities Industry Assn., 1972; v.p., gen. counsel N.Y. Stock Exchange, Washington, 1973-76; exec. dir. comml. collection agy. sect. Comml. Law League Am., Washington, 1976-92. Author: Fundamentals of Municipal Bonds, 1959, Digest of Investments of State Pension Funds, 1960, Digest of State Laws Regulating Debt Collection Agencies, 1977, 81. Mem. ABA, Order of Coif, Pi Kappa Alpha, Phi Delta Phi, Omicron Delta Kappa, Met. Club (Washington), Columbia Country Club (Chevy Chase, Md.). Presbyterian. Home: 6712 Michaels Dr Bethesda MD 20817-2220

CALVERT, JACK GEORGE, atmospheric chemist, educator; b. Inglewood, Calif., May 9, 1923; s. John George and Emma (Eschstruth) C.; m. Doris Arlene Breimon, Nov. 8, 1946; children: Richard John, Mark Steven. BS in Chemistry, UCLA, 1944, PhD, 1949. Mem. faculty Ohio State U., 1950-81, prof. chemistry, 1960-81, Kimberly prof. chemistry, 1974-81, prof. emeritus, 1981—, chmn. dept., 1964-68; sr. scientist Nat. Ctr. Atmospheric Rsch., Boulder, Colo., 1982-94, sr. rsch. assoc., 1994—2002, sr. scientist emeritus, 2002—. Vis. scientist Oak Ridge (Tenn.) Nat. Lab., Environ. Scis. Divsn., 2002—; cons. air pollution tng. com. USPHS, 1964-66, World Innovation Found.; mem. Nat. Air Pollution Control Manpower Devel. Com., 1966-69, chmn., 1968-69; bd. dirs. Gordon Rsch. Confs., 1969-71; mem. air pollution control rsch. grants com. EPA, 1970-72, chmn., 1971-72, mem. chemistry and physics adv. com., 1973-75; chmn. air pollution com. Conservation Found., 1968-70; mem. air conservation commn. Am. Lung Assn., 1973-75; chmn. EPA environ. chemistry/physics grants rev. panel, 1979-83; mem. State of Colo. Air Quality Control Commn., 1987-90, Disting. Acad. Adv. Group of Auto/Oil Air Quality Improvement Rsch. Program, 1989-96; mem. panel on atmospheric effects of aviation NRC/NAS, 1995-98, mem. com. on ozone potential of reformulated gasoline, 1997-99; atmospheric chemistry tech. implementation panel Am. Chem. Coun., 1998—. Author: (with J. N. Pitts, Jr.) Photochemistry, 1966, Graduate School in the Sciences, 1972; also articles. Ensign USNR, 1944-46. Named Honor Prof. of Year Coll. Arts and Scis., Ohio State U., 1957; recipient Alumni award for disting. tchg., 1961, Disting. Rsch. award, 1981; fellow NRC Can., 1949; Guggenheim fellow, 1977-78 Fellow Ohio Acad. Sci., Am. Inst. Chemists, Am. Geophys. Union; mem. AAUP, Am. Chem. Soc. (award for creative rsch. in environ. sci. and tech. 1981, Columbus sect. award 1981), Air Pollution Control Assn. (Chambers award 1986), Phi Beta Kappa, Sigma Xi, Pi Mu Epsilon, Phi Lambda Upsilon, Alpha Chi Sigma. Achievements include research on photochemistry, reaction kinetics, atmospheric chemistry, mechanisms free radical reactions. E-mail: jgcalvert@aol.com., calvert@ucar.edu., calvertj@ornl.gov.

CALVERT, JAMES FRANCIS, manufacturing company executive, retired admiral; b. Cleve., Sept. 8, 1920; s. Charles Spence and Grace (Gholson) C.; m. Nancy Ridgeway King, Aug. 9, 1942 (dec. Dec. 1965); children: James, Margaret (dec.), Charles; m. Margaretta Sergeant Harrison, Apr. 8, 1968. Student, Oberlin Coll., 1937-39, D.Sc. (hon.), 1960; BS in Elec. Engring., U.S. Naval Acad., 1942. Commnd. ensign U.S. Navy, 1942, advanced through grades to vice-adm., 1970; served on 9 war patrols in submarines PTO, World War II; comdr. diesel submarine U.S.S. Trigger, 1952-55; comdr. nuclear power submarine U.S.S. Skate, 1957—60, engaged in polar ops., 1958, 59; (1st submarine to break through ice and surface in Arctic Ocean), 1958; (1st ship to surface at North Pole), 1959; dir. politico-mil. policy Navy Dept., 1965-67; comdr. Cruiser-Destroyer Flotilla Eight, 1967-68; supt. U.S. Naval Acad., Annapolis, Md., 1968-72; comdr. U.S. First Fleet, 1972-73; ret., 1973; asst. to chmn. bd. Texaco Inc., N.Y.C., 1973-74; v.p. Combustion Engring., Inc., Stamford, Conn., 1974-75, v.p. ops., 1975-84, dir., 1975-84; chmn. bd. Aqua-Chem. Inc., Milw., 1989-93. Corp. mem. Woods Hole Oceanographic Inst. Author: Surface at the Pole, 1960 (paperback edit. 1996), A Promise to Your Country, 1961, The Naval Profession, 1965, Silent Running, 1995. Decorated D.S.M. (2), Silver Star (2), Bronze Star (2), Legion of Merit (4), Navy Commendation ribbon, Dept. Def. Commendation medal; French Govt. Merite Maritime; recipient Presdl. Unit citation. Mem. U.S. Naval Acad. Alumni Assn., U.S. Naval Inst., Univ. Club (N.Y.C.), N.Y. Yacht Club, Chesapeake Bay Yacht Club (Easton, Md.).

CALVERT, JAY H., JR., lawyer; b. Charleston, S.C., Mar. 19, 1945; m. Ann E., June 14, 1969; children: Amanda, Emily, Sarah. BA, Amherst (Mass.) Coll., 1967; JD, U. Va., 1970. Bar: Pa. 1970, U.S. Dist. Ct. (ea. dist.) Pa. 1970, U.S. Ct. Appeals (3d cir.) 1971, U.S. Dist. Ct. (mid. dist.) Pa. 1973, U.S. Ct. Appeals (2d cir.) 1980, U.S. Ct. Appeals (8th cir.) 1987, U.S. Supreme Ct. 1989, U.S. Dist. Ct. Ariz. 1994, U.S. Dist. Ct. (we. dist.) Pa. 2000. Assoc. Morgan, Lewis & Bockius LLP, Phila., 1970—78, ptnr., 1987—89, exec. ptnr., 1987—90; mem. firm governing bd. Morgan Lewis & Bockius LLP, Phila., 1989—94; mng. ptnr. Morgan, Lewis & Bockius LLP, Phila., 1990—94, mem. exec. com., 1997—98, sr. ptnr. litigation sect., 1990—, mgr. litigation sect., 1996—99. Trustee Agnes Irwin Sch., Rosemont, Pa., 1988-94, Leukemia and Lymphoma Soc. Am., Phila., 1982—; bd. dirs. St. David's Nursery Sch., Wayne, Pa., 1980-94; chmn. devel. com. Phila. Zool. Soc., 1993-96, chmn. facilities, exhibits and safety com., 1997-2001, bd. dirs., 1992—, vice-chmn. bd. dirs., 1994-96.; mem. ann. fund campaign com. Inglis House, 1998—. Mem. ABA, Pa. Bar Assn., Phila. Bar Assn., Lawyers Club of Phila. Avocations: biking, gardening, hiking, horseback riding, animal husbandry. Office: Morgan Lewis & Bockius LLP 1701 Market St Philadelphia PA 19103-2903 Office Fax: 215-963-5299. E-mail: jcalvert@morganlewis.com.

CALVERT, JAY WYNN, plastic surgeon; b. Newark, N.J., Aug. 19, 1968; s. Peter Jeffrey and Marie E. Szem; m. Kris Lee Calvert, Mar. 21, 1998. BA, Vanderbilt U., 1990; MD, Cornell U., 1994. Diplomate Am. Bd. Plastic Surgery. Gen. surgery resident U. Pitts., 1994-97, rsch. fellow, 1997-99; founder, cons. Gen. Tissue Therapeutics, Inc., Pitts., 1999—; plastic surgery fellow U. Pitts., 1999—2002; asst. prof. clin. surgery U. Calif., Irvine, 2002—. Adj. prof. robotics Carnegie Mellon U., Pitts., 1997-2001. Author: (book chpt.) Plastic Surgery Secrets, 1997; contbr. articles to med. jours. Recipient 1st prize Robert H. Ivy Soc., 1998, Best Sci. Paper, Ohio Valley Plastic Surgery, 1997; rsch. grantee Pitts. Tissue Engring., 1998, Office of Naval Rsch., 1997. Mem. AMA, Pitts. Athletic Assn., The Cornell Club, Jacksonville Golf and Country Club. Avocations: marathon running, playing guitar, traveling. Office: Divsn Plastic Surgery Bldg 55 Rm 110 101 The City Dr Orange CA 92868 E-mail: jcalvert@uci.edu.

CALVERT, JON CHANNING, family practice physician; b. Sonora, Calif., May 17, 1941; s. Floyd Raymond and Aloha Jean (Fernandes) C.; m. Lynnette Laurene Jacobson, June 6, 1970; children: Joshua and Stephen (twins). AB, Stanford U., 1963; MS, MD, Baylor U., 1968, PhD in Anatomy and Cell Biology, postdoctoral fellow in anatomy, Baylor U., 1970. Diplomate Am. Bd. Family Practice, Am. Bd. Ob-gyn. Intern Meth. Hosp., Houston, 1970-71; pvt. practice medicine Houston, 1971-73; asst. prof. anatomy and cell biology Baylor U., 1970-73; asst. prof. family practice Med. Coll. Ga., Augusta, 1973-75, assoc. prof., 1975-77, prof., 1977-82, chmn. dept., 1976-81; prof. family medicine Oral Roberts U. Sch. Medicine, Tulsa, 1982-88, chmn. dept., 1982-87, prof. dept. anatomy, 1982-88, assoc. dean clin. scis., 1984-87; chief dept. cmty. and family medicine City of Faith Med. and Rsch. Ctr., Tulsa, 1982-87; prof., chmn. dept. family medicine U. Okla. Coll. Medicine, Tulsa, 1988-92; resident in ob-gyn. U. Okla. Coll. Med., Tulsa, 1992-95; prof. family medicine, ob-gyn. U. Okla. Coll. Medicine, Tulsa, 1995—. Mem. Gov.'s Joint Bd. Family Practice, 1976-81; chmn. Ga. Fedn. Family Practice Residency Programs, 1976-77; mem. Ga. Dept. Human Resources Adv. Coun. on Phys. Health Needs of Children and Youth, 1977-78; med. dir. Tri-County Health System, Inc., 1981-82, HMO of Okla., 1985-86; mem. family medicine del. to China, 1983 Mem. bd. deacons Covenant Presbyn. Ch., 1979-81; chmn. bd. govs., COO, City of Faith Med. and Rsch. Ctr., Inc., 1987-88. Fellow ACOG, Am. Acad. Family Physicians; mem. AMA, AAAS, Am. Assn. Med. Colls., So. Soc. Anatomists, So. Med. Assn. (chmn. family practice sect. 1977-78), Ga. Acad. Family Physicians (Disting. Svc. award 1975), Soc. Tchrs. Family Medicine, Sci. Rsch. Soc. N.Am., Christian Med. Soc., Tulsa County Med. Soc. Office: U Oklahoma Coll of Medicine Tulsa OK 74129

CALVERT, KEN, congressman; b. Corona, Calif., June 8, 1953; AA, Chaffey Coll., 1973; BA Econs., San Diego State U., 1975. Corona/ Norco youth chmn. for Nixon, 1968, 82; county youth chmn. rep. Vesey's Dist., 1970, 43d dist., 1972; congl. aide to Rep. Vesey, Calif., 1975-79; gen. mgr. Jolly Fox Restaurant, Corona, Calif., 1975-79, Marcus W. Meairs Co., Corona, Calif., 1979-81; pres., gen. mgr. Ken Calvert Real Properties, Corona, Calif., 1981—; Reagan-Bush campaign worker, 1980; co chmn. Wilson for Senate Campaign, 1982, George Deukmejian election, 1978, 82, 86, George Bush election, 1988, Pete Wilson senate elections, 1982, 88, Pete Wilson for Gov. election, 1990; mem. U.S. Congress from 43rd Calif. dist., 1993—, U.S. Congress from 44th dist., 2003—; mem. armed svcs., resources, sci. com. Former v.p. Corona/ Norco Rep. Assembly; chmn. Riverside Rep. Party, 1984-88, County Riverside Asset Leasing; bd. realtors Corono/ Norco Exec. bd. Corona Community Hosp. Corp. 200 Club; mem. Corona Airport adv. commn.; adv. com. Temescal/ El Cerrito Community Plan. Mem. Riverside County Rep. Winners Circle (charter), Lincoln Club (co-chmn., charter, 1986-90), Corona Rotary Club (pres. 1991), Elks, Navy League Corona Norco, Corona C. of C. (pres. 1990), Norco C. of C., Monday Morning Group, Corona Group (past chmn.), Econ. Devel. Ptnrship., Silver Eagles (March AFB support group, charter). Republican. Office: US Ho of Reps 2201 Rayburn Ho Office Bldg Washington DC 20515-0001 also: Office of Ken Calvert 3400 Central Avenue Suite 200 Riverside CA 92506*

CALVERT, LAURA CRISTINA, private school educator; b. Miami, Fla., May 6, 1963; d. Alfredo and Marta Garcia; m. Jeffrey Calvert; children: Maria-Cristina, Jeffrey. BA, U. Md., College Park, 1985; postgrad., U. Cen. Fla., 1997—. Tchr. Spanish and French Chopticon H.S., Morganza, Md., 1985—88; tchr. Spanish Souderton (Pa.) Area Schs., 1990—91, St. Lukes Luth. Sch., Slavia, Fla., 1996—97, Lake Highland Pre., Orlando, Fla., 1998—, chair fgn. lang. grade 8-12, 2000—, coord. Spanish program pre-K-12, 2001—. Leader Girl Scouts Am., Orlando, 1996—2001; mem. WMFE T.V. Comm. Adv. Bd., Orlando, 1996—97. Mem.: Fla. Fgn. Lang. Assn., MLA, Am. Assn. of Tchrs. of Spanish and Portugese. Avocations: gardening, art, hiking, cooking, reading.

CALVERT, LOIS PRINCE, health facility administrator, geriatrics nurse; b. Lawrenceburg, Tenn., June 27, 1948; d. Virgil Miller and Beulah Mae (Fox) Prince; m. Albert Sidney Johnson, Sept. 26, 1970 (div. 1985); children: Kelly Nicole Johnson, Kristopher Scott Johnson; m. Malon Sherman Calvert, Oct. 19, 1990. Student, Bapt. Hosp. Sch. Nursing, 1966-67, Belmont Coll., 1966-67; ADN cum laude, Columbia State C.C., 1970; cert. in nursing home adminstrn., George Washington U., 1985. RN Ala., Tenn. Psychiat. nurse, staff RN Bapt. Meml. Hosp., Memphis, 1970-71; staff RN, psychiat. staff nurse VA Hosp., Memphis, 1971-73; DON svc. Lawrenceburg (Tenn.) Health Care Ctr., 1975-80, nursing home adminstr., 1980-85; case mgr., aide supr., staff RN Lawrenceburg Home Health Agy., 1985-86; staff RN, case mgr. home health patients, coord. home health Mid-South Home Health Agy., Florence, Ala., 1986-87; DON svcs. Lawrenceburg Manor, Inc., 1987-96, adminstr., 1996-98; gero-psychiatric nurse Lifesprings Unit, Hillside Hosp., Pulaski, Tenn., 1998-2000; nurse mgr. gero-psych lifespring unit Hillside Hosp., Pulaski, Tenn., 2000—. Paramed. examiner ASB-Meditest, Nashville, 1989—; mem. NCLEX panel, item reviewer LPN State Bds., 1993. Sustaining membership chmn. Lawrence County coun. Girls Scouts U.S., 1977—78; vol., bd. dirs. Lawrence County chpt. ARC, 1995, disaster health chmn.; mem. Lawrence County Health Coun., 1998—; pianist, dir. youth choir E. Edn. Meth. Ch., 1985—94; mem. choir Mt. Moriah Cumberland Presbyn. Ch.; v.p., founding mem. NG Family Support Group 1/115 FA Bn., 1996—97, publicity chmn., 1998. With Tenn. NG, 1997—98. Recipient Molly Pitcher award, NG Arty. Assn., 1998. Fellow: Am. Coll. Health Care Adminstrs. (profl. cert.); mem.: Nat. Assn. Dirs. Nursings Adminstrs. (founding mem. Tenn. chpt., corr. sec. 1995), Tenn. Employee Rels. Com., Beta Sigma Phi (Girl of the Yr. 1973, 1976). Avocations: piano, painting, cross stitch, basket weaving. Home: 800 Old Agnew Rd Pulaski TN 38478 Office: Hillside Hosp Lifesprings Geropsych Unit 1265 W College St Pulaski TN 38478-3640

CALVERT, LOIS WILSON, civic worker; b. Hartford, Conn., Sept. 12, 1924; d. Royal Wouldhave and Evelyn Charlotte (Danielson) Wilson; m. Wallace Erdix Calvert, Mar. 29, 1947; children: Pamela, Gary, Craig and David (twins). Grad., Bryant Coll., 1943. Registrar of voters Town of Simsbury, Conn., 1982—. Mem. Simsbury Com. on Aging, 1980—89, Friends of Simsbury Libr.; trustee Simsbury Cemetery Assn., 1987—, Simsbury Land Trust, 1984—88; justice of the peace Town of Simsbury, 1985—, mem. design rev. bd., 1989—93; mem. constl. conv. bicentennial commn. Hometown Hero, 1986, awards selection com., 1996, 1999; mem. tourism com. Town of Simsbuy, 1994—96, 1996—98, 1999—2002, ann. report com., 1994, 1995, 325th ann. com., 1995; judge Regional History Day, 1993—96, 1997—98, 1999; vol. Hartford Symphony Talcott Mountain Music Festival, 1996—97, 1999; mem. Bridge of Flowers Com., 1997—; coord. Simsbury Visitors Ctr., 1998; del. 6th dist. Dem. Conv., Bristol, Conn., 1984—86; alt. Conn. Dem. Conv. for Gov., Hartford, 1986; del. State Dem. Conv., 1990, 1992; bd. dirs. Simsbury Hist. Soc., 1978—86, mng. dir., 1978—98, mem. hist. sites com., 1998—. Named a Simsbury Woman Hartford Woman mag., 1987. Mem. Registrar of Voters Assn. Conn., Soc. of Mary and John. Congregationalist. Avocations: knitting, needle-point, travel. Home: 28 Riverside Rd Simsbury CT 06070-2517

CALVERT, MATTHEW JAMES, lawyer; b. Lynchburg, Va., Apr. 24, 1953; s. George Edward and Helen Owen Calvert; m. Helen Baldwin Saer, Oct. 3, 1981; children: McQueen Saer, Anne Russell, Helen Hardie. BA, Washington & Lee U., 1975, JD, 1979. Bar: Va. 1980, Ga. 1995. Law clk. to hon. John Minor Wisdom 5th Cir. Ct. Appeals, La., 1979-80; assoc. Hunton & Williams, Richmond, Va., 1980-87, ptnr. Richmond and Atlanta, 1987—, chmn. pro bono com. Atlanta, 1995—. Chmn. young lawyers sect. Richmond Bar Assn., 1987-88; 6th dist. disciplinary com. Va. State Bar, Richmond, 1993-94. Editor-in-chief Washington & Lee Law Rev., 1978-79. Chmn. workplace com. Metro Coalition on Drugs, Richmond, 1990-93; major gifts com. Woodruff Arts Ctr., Atlanta, 1995—. Recipient Dir.'s award FBI, Richmond, 1993, Charles R. Yates award for fundraising leadership Woodruff Arts Ctr., Atlanta, 1998. Avocations: camping, hunting, golfing. Office: Hunton & Williams 600 Peachtree St NE Ste 4100 Atlanta GA 30308-2217

CALVERT, PETER DEANE, neuroscientist, medical educator; b. Milw., Aug. 11, 1964; PhD, U. Wis., 1995. Fellow Med. Sch. Harvard U., Boston, 1996—2001, instr. Med. Sch., 2001—. Mem.: Biophysical Soc. (assoc.). Office Fax: 617-573-4290. Personal E-mail: pdcalvert@meei.harvard.edu. E-mail: pdcalvert@meei.harvard.edu.

CALVERT, WILLIAM PRESTON, radiologist; b. Warrensburg, Mo., July 2, 1934; s. William Geery and Elizabeth (Spaulding) C.; m. Mary Kay Kersh, Apr. 4, 1976. BS, MIT, 1956; MD, U. Pa., 1960. Diplomate Am. Bd. Nuclear Medicine, Am. Bd. Radiology. Intern Pa. Hosp., Phila., 1960-61, resident in medicine, 1961-62, 64-66, chief med. resident, chief resident physician, 1965-66; resident in gastroenterology U. Miami, 1966-67, NIH fellow in gastroenterology, 1967-68, resident in radiology, 1968-71; radiologist Meml. Hosp., Hollywood, Fla., 1971-72; chief dept. radiology Larkin Gen. Hosp., South Miami, Fla., 1972-80, radiologist, 1980-89, Jackson Meml. Hosp., U. Miami, 1989-93, Univ. Hosp., Tammarac, Fla., 1993-95; part-time radiologist Northern Navajo Med. Ctr., Shiprock, N.Mex., 1995-2000; ret., 2000. Clin. instr. radiology U. Miami Sch. Medicine, 1971-76, clin. asst. prof. radiology, 1984-88, clin. assoc. prof. radiology, 1988-94. Bd. dirs. Wediko Farms Children's Svcs., Carbondale, Ill. Served with M.C., USAF, 1962-64. Mem. AMA, Fla. Med. Assn., Fla., Greater Miami radiol. socs., Soc. Nuclear Medicine, Radiol. Soc. N.Am., Explorers Club.

CALVIN, ALLEN DAVID, psychologist, educator; b. St. Paul, Feb. 17, 1928; s. Carl and Zelda (Engelson) C.; m. Dorothy VerStrate, Oct. 5, 1953; children: Jamie, Kris, David, Scott. BA in Psychology cum laude, U. Minn., 1950; MA in Psychology, U. Tex., 1951, PhD in Exptl. Psychology, 1953. Instr. Mich. State U., East Lansing, 1953-55; asst. prof. Hollins Coll., 1955-59, assoc. prof., 1959-61. Dir. Britannica Ctr. for Studies in Learning and Motivation, Menlo Park, Calif., 1961; prin. investigator grant for automated tchg. fgn. langs. Carnegie Found., 1960; USPHS grantee, 1960; pres. Behavioral Rsch. Labs., 1962-74; prof., dean Sch. Edn., U. San Francisco, 1974-78; Henry Clay Hall prof. orgn. and leadership, 1978—; prof. Pacific Grad. Sch. Psychology, 1984-2001. Author textbooks. Served with USNR, 1946-47. Mem. Am. Psychol. Assn., AAAS, Sigma Xi, Psi Chi. Home: 1645 15th Ave San Francisco CA 94122-3523 Office: Pacific Grad Sch Psychology 935 E Meadow Dr Palo Alto CA 94303-4233 E-mail: a.calvin@pgsp.edu.

CALVIN, DONALD LEE, business executive, stock exchange consultant; b. Mount Olive, Ill., Nov. 10, 1931; m. Louise Elinor Peterson, Mar. 28, 1952; children: Jane Calvin Palasek, Sally Anne Calvin Salvaterra. Student, Ea. Ill. U., 1950-54, LLD, 1990; LLB, U. Ill., 1956. Bar: Ill. 1956. Atty. Office Sec. of State of Ill., Springfield, 1957-58, securities commr., 1959-62; syndicate mgr. A.C. Allyn & Co., Chgo., 1962-63; atty. F.I. DuPont & Co., Chgo., 1963-64; exec. asst. civic and govt. affairs N.Y. Stock Exch., N.Y.C., 1964-65, v.p., 1966-77, sr. v.p., 1977-79, exec. v.p. pub. affairs, 1979-85, exec. v.p. internat., 1986-87; chmn. Internat. Bus. Enterprises, Inc., N.Y.C., 1987—. Advisor to chmn. Chgo. Bd. Options Exch., Geneva Stock Exch., 1987—96; advisor to pres. Fedn. Internat. des Bourses de Valeurs, Paris, 1989—98, Kuala Lampur Stock Exch., 1991—, São Paulo (Brazil) Stock Exch., 1993—, Stock Exch. of Hong Kong, 1995—98, Cairo and Alexandria, Egypt Stock Exchs., 1997—; others in N. Am., Europe, S. Am., Asia; chmn. bd. dirs. Cin. Stock Exch., 1993; bd. dirs. Internat. Fin. Ctr. and Exch. of Curacao, sec. hist. soc.; bd. dirs. Nat. Coun. on Econ. Edn. With USMCR, 1951-56, Mem. ABA, Internat. Bar Assn., Ill. State Bar Assn., Chgo. Bar Assn., Am. Law Inst., Met. Club N.Y.C., Stock Exch. Luncheon Club, Manhasset Bay Yacht Club (Port Washington, N.Y.). Home: 4 Knolls Ln Manhasset NY 11030-1630 E-mail: calvindonaldl@aol.com.

CALVIN, DOROTHY VER STRATE, computer company executive; b. Dec. 22, 1929; d. Herman and Christina (Plakmyer) Ver Strate; m. Allen D. Calvin, Oct. 5, 1953; children: Jamie, Kris, Bufo, Scott. BS magna cum laude, Mich. State U., 1951; MA, U. San Francisco, 1988, EdD, 1991. Mgr. data processing Behavioral Rsch. Labs., Menlo Park, Calif., 1972-75; dir. Mgmt. Info. Sys. Inst. for Profl. Devel., San Jose, Calif., 1975-76; sys. analyst, programmer Pacific Bell Info. Sys., San Francisco, Calif., 1976-81, staff mgr., 1981-84; mgr. applications devel. Data Architects Inc., San Francisco, Calif., 1984-86; pres. Ver Strate Press, San Francisco, Calif., 1986—. Instr., Downtown C.C., San Francisco, 1980-84, Cañada C.C., 1986-92, Skyline Coll., 1988-92, City Coll. of San Francisco, 1992—; mem. computer curriculum adv. coun. San Francisco City Coll., 1982-84. V.p. LWV, Roanoke, Va., 1956-58. Pres. Bulliss Purissima Parents Group, Los Altos, Calif., 1962-64; bd. dirs. Vols. for Israel, 1986-87. Mem. IEEE Computer Soc., Assn. Sys. Mgmt., Assn. Women in Computing, Phi Delta Kappa. Democrat. Avocations: computing, gardening, jogging, reading. Office: Ver Strate Press 1645 15th Ave San Francisco CA 94122-3523 E-mail: dcalvin2@aol.com.

CALVIN, JAMES ELDON, JR., cardiologist, educator, researcher; b. Winchester, Mass., Aug. 9, 1951; s. James Eldon Calvin and Carol Morgan Whittaker; m. Sadie Anne Ryan, Aug. 18, 1973; children: James Eldon III, Kaelen Anne. MD, Dalhousie U., Halifax, N.S., Can., 1975. Diplomate Am. Bd. Internal Medicine, Am. Bd. Cardiology, Am. Bd. Critical Care Medicine. Resident in internal medicine U. Western Ont., London, Can., 1975-80; fellow in cardiology U. Ottawa, Ont., 1980-81, asst. prof. medicine, 1983-88, assoc. prof., 1988-91; fellow in cardiology U. Calif., San Francisco, 1981-83; assoc. prof. medicine Rush Med. Coll., Chgo., 1991—; chmn. divsn. adult cardiology Cook County Hosp., Chgo., 1999—. Dir. CCU U. Ottawa Heart Inst., 1989-91, Rush-Presbyn.-St. Lukes Med. Ctr., Chgo., 1991-98; mem. adv. bd. Registry Acute Coronary Syndrome, 1999. Editor: Yearbook of Critical Care Medicine, 1995—, Resource Utilization in Cardiovascular Disease, 1999; contbr. over 100 articles, edits. and revs. to med. jours. Recipient young investigator award Soc. Critical Care Medicine, 1986, internal medicine rsch. award, 1990; rsch. fellow Med. Rsch. Coun. Can., 1981-83; rsch. scholar Ont. Heart and Stroke Found., 1983-90. Fellow Am. Coll. Cardiology, Am. Heart Assn., Royal Coll. Physi-

cians and Surgeons Can.; mem. ACP. Avocations: guitar, skiing. Office: Cook County Hosp Divsn Adult Cardiology 1835 W Harrison St Chicago IL 60612-3785 E-mail: jcalvin@rpslmc.edu.

CALVIN, JAMES WILLARD, thoracic and vascular surgeon; b. Oakland, Calif., Dec. 7, 1929; s. George Fairchild and Mary Norris Calvin; m. Claudine Deprez (div. 1971); m. Carrie Carman, 1973; children: Carolyne, Frances, Sophie. BA, Stanford U., 1951; MD, MChir, McGill U., 1955. Diplomate Nat. Bd. Med. Examiners, Am. Bd. Surgery, Am. Bd. Thoracic Surgery spl. qualifications gen. vascular surgery. Intern Stanford (Calif.) U., 1955-56, resident dept. surgery, 1959-63, chief resident dept. surgery, 1963-64; group practice Sansum Med. Clinic, Santa Barbara, Calif., 1964-66; pvt. practice Thoracic and Cardiovascular Med. Group, Inc., Ventura, Calif., 1966-95. Bd. dirs. Rehab. Inst. Santa Barbara, bd. trustees; scientific adv. coun. Ramus Med. Technologies, Carpinteria, Calif., 1996-2001; hosp. staff Cmty. Meml. Hosp., Ventura. Contbr. articles to profl. jours. With USAF, 1956-58. NIH rsch. fellow, 1960-61. Fellow ACS (rep. hosps. of Ventura County 1980-87), Am. Coll. of Chest Physicians; mem. AAAS, AMA, Am. Cancer Soc. (Ventura county chpt., bd. dirs. 1969-72), Am. Heart Assn. (coun. on cardiovascular diseases), Am. Lung Assn., Am. Thoracic Soc., Calif. Med. Assn., Internat. Cardiovascular Soc. (N.Am. chpt.), N.Am. Soc. for Pacing and Electrophysiology, Samson Thoracic Surg., Soc. for Clin. Vascular Surgery, Soc. for Thoracic Surgeons, So. Calif. Vascular Surg. Soc., Ventura County Heart Assn. (pres. 1965), Ventura County Med. Soc. (pres. 1979, bd. govs. 1975-81). Home: 47-515 Via Florence La Quinta CA 92253 Fax: 760-564-4840.

CALVIN, STAFFORD RICHARD, academic administrator; b. St. Paul, Apr. 6, 1931; s. Carl and Zelda Ida (Engelson) C.; m. Nancy Goldbert (div. 1984); m. Rochelle Ann Schaffer, Nov. 26, 1988; children: Lawrence, Carlton, Loran. BA, U. Minn., 1952; MFA, U. Mexico City, 1954. Pres. Sibley Co., St. Paul, 1953-58, Dealers Distbrs., St. Paul, 1958-65; v.p. Internat. Sys. Assn., N.Y.C., 1965-70, Carlson Cos., Mpls., 1970-74; CEO Calstar, Mpls., 1974-85; v.p. Acad. Learning Ctrs., Inc., St. Paul, 1988-90; pres. Calvin Acad., St. Paul, 1991—. Founder Inst. Essential Edn. Author: Save Your Child, 1989. Democrat. Jewish. Avocations: performing arts, biking, rafting. Office: Calvin Acad 2574 Highway 10 NE Mounds View MN 55112-4032

CALVIN, WILLIAM HOWARD, neurophysiologist; b. Kansas City, Mo., Apr. 30, 1939; s. Fred Howard and Agnes (Leebrick) C.; m. Katherine Graubard, Sept. 1, 1966. BA, Northwestern U., 1961; PhD, U. Wash., 1966. Affiliate prof. psychiatry U. Wash., Seattle, 1966—. Author: Inside the Brain, 1980, The Throwing Madonna, 1983, The River That Flows Uphill, 1986, The Cerebral Symphony, 1989, The Ascent of Mind, 1990, How the Shaman Stole the Moon, 1991, Conversations with Neil's Brain, 1994, How Brains Think, 1996, The Cerebral Code, 1996, Lingua ex Machina, 2000, A Brain for All Seasons, 2002. Pres. ACLU of Wash., 1973-74. NIH rsch. grantee, 1967-84; recipient Gov.'s Writing prize State of Wash., 1984, 88, Book prize for Sci. Phi Beta Kappa, 2002. Fellow Am. Psychol. Soc.; mem. Soc. for Neurosci., Internat. Brain Rsch. Orgn., N.Y. Acad. Sci., Internat. Soc. for Human Ethology, Lang. Origins Soc., Am. Assn. Phys. Anthropologists, Internat. Astronom. Union. Achievements include research in neurobiology and anthropology. Office: Univ Wash PO Box 351800 Seattle WA 98195-1800

CALVO, ROQUE JOHN, professional society administrator; b. Allentown, Pa., Sept. 26, 1958; s. Rocco John and Ruth Hattie (Zimpfer) C.; m. Marianne Willever, Feb. 27, 1982; children: Amy Elizabeth, Roque John. BS, Lebanon Valley Coll., 1980; MBA, Rider U., 1986. Actg. supv. Electrochem. Soc., Inc., Pennington, N.J., 1980-82, asst. exec. dir., 1982-91, exec. dir., 1991—. Adv. bd. Fedn. Materials Socs., Washington, 1991—; meeting adv. bd. Starwood Hotels and Resorts Worldwide. Mem. Am. Soc. Assn. Execs., Coun. Engring. and Sci. Society Execs. (task force in mem. satisfaction 1992-94, bd. dirs. 1995-2002, pres. 2000-01), N.J. Soc. Assn. Execs. Avocations: golf, basketball, tennis, reading. Office: Electrochemical Soc Inc 65 S Main St Pennington NJ 08534-2827 E-mail: rcalvo12@aol.com.

CAMACCI, MICHAEL A. commercial real estate broker, development consultant; b. Youngstown, Ohio, Feb. 6, 1951; s. Martin B. and Viola F. (Conti) C.; m. Susan Hawkins, Oct. 18, 1985; 1 child, Michael Philip. BBA, Youngstown Coll., 1974. Cert. bus. analyst. Acct. U.S. Steel Corp., Youngstown, 1969-80; mgr. sales Soc. Realty, Boardman, Ohio, 1980-81; dir. sales Pop-ins Maid Services, Columbiana, Ohio, 1981-82; bus. broker Eranco Assocs., Girard, Ohio, 1982-86; pres. JMC Realty, Inc., Youngstown, 1986-99; pres., broker Camacci Real Estate, 1986—; pres. Hillview Nursing Home, 1988-99, Valley View Nursing Home, 1990-99, Pyramid Printing, Inc., 1991-99; dir. Crestview Nursing & Rehab. Facility, 1999—2002; CEO Van Fossan & Assoc., 2000—. Pres. Wedgewood Property Mgmt., Inc., 4682 North, LLC, 55 West, LLC, 1997-2002, 19th Hole Investments, 1997-2002; pres. CRE Holding Corp., 1996; pres. 20 West, LLC, 1998—, pres. Goldco Internat., 1997—. Downtown Partners, Landmark Real Estate Svcs, Inc., 1998—, pres. CPR, LLC, 2003-. Mem. Youngstown-Warren Regional Growth Alliance; v.p. Austintown Growth Found., 1994-96. Served with U.S. Army, 1971-77. Mem. BBB, Am. Health Care Assn., Ohio Health Care Assn., Nat. Assn. Printers and Lithographers, Internat. Coun. Shopping Ctrs., Youngstown-Warren Area C. of C., Columbiana Area C. of C., Mahoning County Home Builders Assn., Downtown Ptnrs. Democrat. Roman Catholic. Office: Camacci Real Estate Inc 5533 Mahoning Ave Youngstown OH 44515-2316

CAMACHO, FELIX PEREZ, governor; b. Guam, Oct. 30, 1957; s. Carlos G. and Lourdes Perez Camacho; m. Joann Gumataotao Garcia Camacho; children: Jessica Lourdes, Felix James, Maria Amparo. Degree in Bus. Adminstrn. and Fin., 1980. Ins. mgr. property casualty divsn. Pacific Fin. Corp.; account adminstr. IBM; gov., Guam, 2002—. Mem.: Nat. Coun. State Legislators, Asian Pacific Parliamentarian Union. Republican. Roman Catholic. Office: Office of the Governor PO Box 2950 Hagatna GU 96932

CAMACHO, GEORGE, internist; b. Savannah, Ga., Nov. 20, 1952; s. D. F. and Carmen Camacho; m. Dolores Knight, Dec. 27, 1974; children: Christopher George, Heather Ashley. BS, U. Houston, 1977; MD, Tex. Tech. Health Scis. Ctr., 1980. Cert. Am. Bd. Internal Medicine. Internal medicine intern Shands Hosp., Jacksonville, Fla., 1984-85, resident, 1985-87. Mem. internal medicine adv. bd. Specialty Hosp., Jacksonville, Fla., 1994—, mem. hosp. bd., 1997-98, ethics com., 1994—; pharmacy and therapeutics Meml. Hosp., Jacksonville, 1994-96. Fellow ACP; mem. AMA (Physicians Recognition award 1998, 99), Fla. Med. Soc. Republican. Roman Catholic. Avocations: baseball, basketball, water sports, kids. Office: Internal Medicine Assocs 3627 University Blvd S Ste 415 Jacksonville FL 32216-4299 E-mail: gcamach@bellsouth.net.

CAMACHO, HECTOR, boxer; b. Bayamon, P.R., May 24, 1942; Lightweight champion, 1983; WBO Jr. Welterweight title, 1991; middleweight champion, 1996.

CAMACHO, HENRY FRANCIS, accountant; b. Somerville, Mass., May 1, 1930; s. Martin F. and Marie D. (Castanha) C.; m. Audrey A. Camacho, Dec. 12, 1954; children: Creda, Robert, Liza, Peter, Cindra, Melissa. BSBA, Boston U., 1954; MS, Bentley U., Boston, 1957. CPA, Mass. Acct. J.T. Ferland & Co., Danielson, Conn., 1954-55; sr. acct. Starr, Finer, Starr, Boston, 1955-57; revenue agt. IRS, Boston, 1957-64, systems analyst Andover, Mass., 1964-71; with spkrs. bur., 1965-85; chief tech. br. IRS, Andover, Mass., 1971-75, chief disclosure, 1976-81, chief data security, 1981-85; pvt. practice Lawrence, Mass., 1986—. Adj. prof. Merrimack Coll., North Andover, Mass., 1965—. No. Essex Community Coll., Haverhill, Mass., 1975-82. Contbr. articles to profl. jours. Sgt. USMC, 1950-52. Mem. AICPA (small practitioners adv. com., seminar instr. 1986-92), Mass. CPA Soc. (fed. taxation com. 1985-93, mem. spkrs. bur. 1992—). Roman Catholic. Avocations: reading, golf, fishing, gardening, traveling. Home: 15A River St Seabrook NH 03874-4848 Office: 33 Main St Unit 212 Salisbury MA 01952-1216

CAMARA, JOAN ELLEN, dean; b. Fall River, Mass. d. Dimas Miguel and Alice Reis Camara; m. Charles John Jordan III, May 24, 1980; children: Alexander Bradley Jordan, Daniel Ross Jordan. JD (cum laude), Suffolk U., 1978; BA, Polit. Sci. in Polit. Sci. (magna cum laude), U. of Mass., 1973. Atty./ptnr. Peppard, Littman & Camara, Fall River, Mass., 1980—89; EEO investigator, decision writer Delany, Siegel & Zorn Assocs., Boston, 1995—; dir. paralegal studies program Dean Coll., Franklin, Mass., 1996—99; interim dean sch. bus. Roger Williams U., Bristol, RI, 2001—02. Adj. faculty Dean Coll., Franklin, Mass., 1995—99, Roger Williams U., Bristol, RI, 1998—99; presenter in field. Co-author: (professional publication) Strategic Marketing Planning Made Easier: An Imbricative Analysis Case Study; author: 'A Student's Guide to Law & Government On The Internet, (pedagogical publication) Law On The Internet. Mem. RI State Advs. Gifted Talented Edn., 1992—95. Recipient Excellence in Tchg. award, Alpha Chi, 2000. Mem.: AAUW, Am. Mktg. Assn., Sigma Beta Delta. Avocations: reading, travel, cooking. Office: Roger Williams University One Old Ferry Road Bristol RI 02809 Office Fax: 401-254-3545. E-mail: jcamara@rwu.edu.

CAMARA, VINCENT ANTONIN REGINALD, mathematician, educator, statistician, researcher; arrived in U.S., 1992; s. Athanase and Lucie Camara; m. Gislhaine Claire P. Soivilus. BSc in Math., U. Dakar, 1984, MS in Pure Math., 1986; MS in Applied Math., U. North Fla., 1994; PhD in Math. and Option Statis., U. South Fla., 1997. Stats. educator U. of NC, Charlotte, NC, 1997—98; math. and stats. educator U. of South Fla., Tampa, Fla., 1998—2001, St. Leo U., Largo, Fla., 2001—. Presenter Joint Statis. Meetings, N.Y.C., 2002—. Contbr. articles to profl. jours.; mem. editl. bd.: Jour. Modern Applies Statis. Methods. Mem.: The Risk Analysis Soc., The Bayesian Statis. Soc., Am. Statis. Assn., Phi Kappa Phi, Pi Mu Epsilon. Home: 8799 Bardmoor Boulevard Unit 201 Largo FL 33777 Personal E-mail: gvcamara@ij.net. Business E-Mail: vincent.camara@saintleo.edu.

CAMBEL, JOSEPH ANDREW, design engineer; b. Bklyn., N.Y., Apr. 1, 1946; s. John Leo and Mary Lavinia Campbell; m. Chong Ae Lee, Jan. 1, 1973; 1 child, Nunilo Marie. BE in Marine Engring., SUNY, 1967. Marine engr. Marine Engrs., Bklyn., 1967—74; design engr. Gibbs & Cox Inc., N.Y.C., 1974, Stone & Webster, N.Y.C., 1974—78, Gibbs & Cox Inc., N.Y.C., 1978, Wegman Engrs., N.Y.C., 1978—80; cons. engr. Camco Consultants, Bklyn., 1980—. Home: 3602 Mermaid Ave Brooklyn NY 11224

CAMBON, ELISE MURRAY, music educator, musician; b. New Orleans, Feb. 27, 1917; d. Maurice Cornelius Cambon and Marie Camilia Murray. BA, Tulane U., 1939, PhD, 1975; postgrad., Benedictine Abbey of Solesmes, France, 1955; MusM, U. Mich., 1947. Organist, music dir. St. Louis Cathedral, New Orleans, 1941—; instr. music Ursuline Coll., New Orleans, 1949—51, Ursuline Acad., New Orleans, 1942—49, McGhee Sch., New Orleans, 1951—61; prof. music Loyola U., New Orleans, 1959—82, founding chmn. dept. liturgical music Coll. Music. Condr. St. Louis Cathedral Choir in Europe, England and Ireland. Coord. choirs and brass choir One Shell Sq. La. Philharm. Orch., New Orleans, 1989—. Recipient 1st prize musicol. rsch., Mu Phi Epsilon, 1975—76, Order of Chevalier des Arts et Lettres, French Govt., 1983; grantee, Schlieder Found., 1959, for concert tours, Archdiocese of New Orleans and St. Louis Cathedral, 1987—98; Fulbright scholar, Hochschule Musik in Frankfurt-am-Main, Germany, 1951—53. Mem.: Bach Oratorio Soc. (founding mem.), Am. Guild Organists (founding mem., dean). Roman Catholic.

CAMBONE, STEPHEN A. federal agency administrator; BA in Polit. Sci., Cath. U., 1973; MA in Polit. Sci., Claremont Grad. Sch., 1977, PhD in Polit. Sci., 1982. Staff mem. office of dir. Los Alamos Nat. Lab., 1982—86; dep. dir. strategic analysis SRS Techs. (Washington Ops.), 1986—90; dir. for strategic def. policy Office of Sec. Def., 1990—93; sr. fellow in polit.-mil. studies Ctr. for Strategic and Internat. Studies, 1993—98; staff dir. Commn. to Assess the Ballistic Missile Threat to U.S., 1998; dir. rsch. Inst. for Nat. Strategic Studies, Nat. Def. U., 1998—2000; staff dir. Commn. to Assess U.S. Nat. Security Space Mgmt. and Orgn., 2000—01; spl. asst. Sec. and Dep. Sec. Def., 2001; prin. dep. under Sec. Def. for Policy Dept. of Def., Washington, 2001—02, dir of program analysis and evaluation, 2002—. Office: Dir Program Analysis and Eval Dept of Defence Washington DC 20301-2000*

CAMBRE, RONALD C. mining executive; m. Gail Cambre. BSCE, La. State U.; postgrad., Harvard U. Chmn. bd. Rio Tinto Minera SA; various positions, including pres., CEO Freeport-McMoRan Resource Ptnrs. subs. Freeport-McMoRan Inc., 1964-93; v.p., sr. technical adviser to chmn. Freeport-McMoRan Inc., 1988-93; vice chmn., CEO, bd. dirs. Newmont Mining Corp., Denver, 1993—, pres., 1994—, chmn. bd. dirs., 1995—. Vice chmn., CEO, chmn. bd. dirs. Newmont Gold Co. subs. Newmont Mining Corp. Office: Newmont Mining 1700 Lincoln St Denver CO 80203

CAMBRICE, ROBERT LOUIS, lawyer; b. Nov. 23, 1947; s. Eugene and Edna Bertha (Jackson) C.; m. Christine Jackson, Jan. 7, 1972; children: Bryan, Graham. BA cum laude, Tex. So. U., 1969; JD, U. Tex., 1972. Bar: Tex. 1973, U.S. Dist. Ct. (so. dist.) Tex. 1975, U.S. Ct. Appeals (5th cir.) 1975, U.S. Ct. Appeals (11th cir.) 1981, U.S. Supreme Ct. 1981. Asst. atty. City of Houston, 1974-76; pvt. practice, Houston, 1976-81; asst. atty. Harris County, Tex., 1981-85, City of Houston, 1986—, sr. trial atty. legal dept., 1990-92, chief def. litigation dept., 1992—. Earl Warren fellow, 1969-72. Mem. ABA, NAACP, Nat. Bar Assn., Alpha Kappa Mu. Roman Catholic. E-mail: Robert.Cambrice@cityofhouston.net.

CAMEL, MARK HOWARD, neurological surgeon; b. St. Louis, May 30, 1955; s. H. Marvin and Greta (Hahn) C.; m. Linda J. Chiswick, May 3, 1987; children: Andrew, Matthew, Edward. BA, U. Rochester, 1977; MD, Washington U., St. Louis, 1981. Diplomate Am. Bd. Neurol. Surgery. Intern in gen. surgery Barnes Hosp., 1981-82, resident in neurol. surgery, 1982-86; fellow in neurol. surgery Washington U., 1986-87; pvt. practice, Greenwich, Conn., 1987—. Mem. Congress Neurol. Surgeons (exec. com. 1992—, v.p. 1995), New Eng. Neurol. Soc. (bd. dirs.), Belle Haven Club. Office: Orthopaedic and Neurol Surgery Specialists 6 Greenwich Office Park Greenwich CT 06831-5151

CAMERIUS, JAMES WALTER, marketing educator, corporate researcher; b. Chgo., June 14, 1939; s. Wilbert Albert and Violet Elna (Johnson) C. BS, No. Mich. U., 1961; MS, U. N.D., 1963, postgrad., U. Okla., 1974-77. From instr. to assoc. prof. No. Mich. U., Marquette, 1963-90, prof. mktg., 1990—. Lectr. in field; mem. adv. bd. S.E. Advanced Tech. Edn. Consortium. Newsletter editor N.Am. Case Rsch. Assn.; bd. rev., editl. rev. bd. Bus. Case Jour.; mem. internat. editl. adv. bd. Jour. SMET Edn. Cir. lay rep. Luth. Ch.-Mo. Synod, 1987-89; pres. Redeemer Luth. Ch., Marquette, 1989-90, sec. to ch. coun., 1990-92, bd. elders, 1993-98, v.p., 2000-2001, pres. 2001-02; mktg. track chair N.Am. Case Rsch. and Mktg. Assn., 1997-2003. Recipient MAGB Disting. Prof. award, 1995; Rsch. grantee Direct Selling Edn. Found., 1987-2002, Walker L. Cisler Sch. No. Mich. U., 1990, Filene Rsch. Inst., 1994; named Outstanding Case Reviewer, Case Rsch. Jour., 1998. Fellow Acad. Mktg. Sci.; mem. Am. Mktg. Assn., Soc. Case Rsch. (v.p. 1990-91, case workshop dir. 1999, pres.-elect 2000, pres. 2001-2002, archivist 2002—), N.Am. Case Rsch. Assn. bd. dirs. (midwest rep.), World Assn. for Case Method Rsch. and Application (case colloquium dir. 1997—), WACRA Adv. bd., Econ. Club, Alpha Kappa Psi (Alumni award). Democrat. Home: 171 Lakewood Ln Marquette MI 49855-9543 Office: No Mich U Mktg Dept Marquette MI 49855

CAMERON, ALASTAIR GRAHAM WALTER, astrophysicist, educator; b. Winnipeg, Man., Can., June 21, 1925; came to U.S., 1959, naturalized, 1963; s. Alexander Thomas and Airdrie Edna (Bell) C.; m. Elizabeth Aston MacMillan, June 11, 1955. B.Sc., U. Man., 1947; PhD, U. Sask., 1952, D.Sc. (hon.), 1977; A.M. (hon.), Harvard U., 1973. Asst. prof. physics Iowa State Coll., Ames, 1952-54; asst., asso. and sr. research officer Atomic Energy Can., Ltd., Chalk River, Ont., 1954-61; sr. research fellow Calif. Inst. Tech., Pasadena, 1959-60; sr. scientist Goddard Inst. Space Studies, N.Y., 1961-66; prof. space physics Yeshiva U., 1966-73; prof. astronomy Harvard U., Cambridge, Mass., 1973-97, Donald H. Menzel prof. astrophysics, 1997-99, Donald H. Menzel rsch. prof. astrophysics, 1999—; sr. rsch. scientist Lunar and Planetary Lab., U. Ariz., 2000—. Chmn. Space Sci. Bd., 1976-82, Nat. Acad. Scis. Contbr. articles to profl. jours. Recipient J. Lawrence Smith medal NAS, 1988, Disting. Pub. Service medal NASA, 1983. Mem. NAS, AAAS, Am. Phys. Soc., Am. Geophys. Union (Harry H. Hess medal 1989), Am. Astron. Soc. (Russell lectr. 1997), Internat. Astron. Union, Meteoritical Soc. (Leonard medal 1994). Office: Lunar and Planetary Lab 1629 E University Blvd 527A Tucson AZ 85721 E-mail: acameron@lpl.arizona.edu.

CAMERON, ALEX BRIAN, accounting educator; b. Fresno, Calif., Nov. 20, 1943; s. Alexander Archer and Francette (Maize) C.; m. Judy Lea Helphrey, June 7, 1969; children: Michelle, Michael. BA, Eastern Wash. U., 1969, MBA, 1970; PhD, U. Utah, 1982. CPA, Wash.; cert. in mgmt. acctg. Mgr. prodn. planning Bunker Hill Mining Co., Kellog, Idaho, 1970-77; asst. prof. Wash. State U., Pullman, 1978-79; assoc. prof. Eastern Wash. U., Cheney, 1981-87, prof., 1987—, chmn. dept. acctg., 1988-89, assoc. dean, 1990-97, interimm v.p. bus. and fin., 1998-99, interim dean Coll. Bus. and Pub. Adminstrn., 1999-2001. Contbr. articles to profl. jours. Avocations: sailing, golf, volleyball. Home: 15212 Pinnacle Ln Veradale WA 99037-9163 Office: 668 N Riverpoint Blvd Spokane WA 99202-1677

CAMERON, ANN M. language educator; b. Fargo, N.D., Dec. 18, 1950; d. Edwin Frank and Helen Charlotte Baumler; m. G. Bruce Cameron, July 26, 1972; children: Caitlin E., Lily J. BA in Humanities, Mich. State U., 1971, MA in English, 1972; PhD in English, Purdue U., 2000. Instr. English, Ind. U., Kokomo, 1977—82, asst. prof., 1983—2000, assoc. prof., 2001—. Author: Sidekicks in American Literature, 2002. Mem.: MLA, Am. Lit. Soc. of MLA, Soc. Early Americanists, Phi Beta Kappa. Office: Ind U Kokomo 2300 S Washington PO Box 9003 Kokomo IN 46904-9003

CAMERON, CATHERINE ISABELLA, community volunteer; b. Mar. 25, 1928; PhD, U. Wis., 1975; MBA, De Paul U., 1985. Dir., faculty adult edn. grad. program R.I. Coll., Providence, 1973-76; mem. grad. faculty Fed. U. Brazil, Santa Maria, 1977-79; coord., faculty HRD grad. program Nat. Louis U., Evanston, Ill., 1980-87; mgr. rsch. dept. Rotary Internat., Evanston, 1987-89; ret. Founding pres. Friendship Force Chgo., 1996; vol. Field Mus., The Saints, Srs. Abroad. Mem.: AARP, Servas. Home: No 916 5555 N Sheridan Rd Apt 916 Chicago IL 60640-1654

CAMERON, CHARLES HENRY, supervisory petroleum engineer; b. Greeley, Colo., Oct. 21, 1947; s. Leo Leslie and Naomi Tryphena (Phillips) C.; m. Cheryl Christine Debelock, Aug. 30, 1969; 1 child, Ericka Dawn. AS, Mesa State Coll., 1968; BS in Geology, Mesa Coll., 1978; AS in Hazardous Materials Tech., Front Range C.C., Wesminister, Colo., 1990. Cert. info. resource mgmt. approving ofcl. (CIAO), 1998. Retardation technician Colo. State Home and Tng. Sch., Grand Junction, 1967-69; journeyman carpenter Brotherhood of Carpenters and Joiners, Grand Junction, 1969-76; hydrocompaction mgr. Colo. Dept. Hwys., Grand Junction, 1975-77; rsch. geologist Occidental Oil Shale, Inc., Grand Junction, 1977-78; geol. engr. Cleveland Cliffs Iron Co., Morgantown, W.Va., 1978-81; tech. advisor Ute Indian Tribe, Ft. Duchesne, Utah, 1981-86; ops. mgr. Charging Ute Corp., Golden, Colo., 1986-87; cons. Golden, 1987-90; petroleum engr. U.S. Dept. Interior/Bur. of Indian Affairs, Ft. Duchesne, 1990—2003, hazardous material mgr., freedom of info./privacy act coord., 1990-2000, minerals/realty officer, 1994, natural resources officer, 1996—, ADP com. chmn., LAN adminstr., PL 93-638 com. chmn. grants/loan mgr., 1999-2000, GIS committeeman, 1994, supervisory petroleum engr., realty officer, br. of realty, 2000—. Minerals specialist Phoenix area Bur. Indian Affairs, Y2K coord. U&O Agency computer systems upgrade project, 1998, acting realty officer, 1999. Contbr. articles to profl. jours. Mem. Colo. Oil Field Investigators Assn., Vernal (Utah) C. of C., Internat. Platform Assn. Avocations: photography, fishing, hunting, antiques, motorcycling. Home: 255 East 200 North Vernal UT 84078-1713 Office: BIA Uintah Ouray Agy 988 S 7500 E PO Box 130 MS 410 Fort Duchesne UT 84026-0130 E-mail: charlescameron@bia.gov., cameron@hotmail.com.

CAMERON, DANIEL FORREST, communications executive; b. Santa Monica, Calif., Mar. 8, 1944; s. Dan W. and Bonnie (Forrest) C.; m. Sharon Tompos, June 1, 1968; children: Daniel Christian, Stephen Forrest. BSBA, U. Tulsa, 1974; MBA, Morehead (Ky.) State U., 1978, MA, 1981; PhD, U. Ky., 1989. Editor Appalachian News-Express, Pikeville, Ky., 1976-77; coord. mining tech. program Pikeville (Ky.) Coll., 1977-78, Morehead State U., 1978-85; dir. devel. and pub. rels. Monte Cassino Sch., Tulsa, 1986-89; exec. dir. coll. advancement Coll. Osteo. Medicine Okla. State U., Tulsa, 1989-92; pres. D. Forrest Cameron and Assocs., Tulsa, 1992—. Editor: Kentucky Underground Coal Mine Guidebook, 1985; editor, pub. Greater Tulsa Reporter Newspapers (Union Boundary, Jenks Gazette, Owasso Rambler, Broken Arrow Express, Tulsa Free Press and Bixby Breeze), 1993—. Pres. Comet Jr. Athletic Assn., Tulsa, 1989; co-founder Collegiate Assn. for Mining Edn., Lexington, Ky., 1983; bd. dirs. U. Tulsa Golden Hurricane Club, 1993-99, Camp Fire Boys and Girls of Green Country Coun., Inc., 1999-2002. Mem. Tulsa Press Club (bd. dirs. 2000—), Metro. Tulsa C. of C. (mem. small bus. coun.), U. Tulsa Alumni Assn., U. Ky. Alumni Assn., Tulsa Green Country Rotary Club (pres. 1994-95). E-mail: fcameron@gtrnews.com.

CAMERON, DORT, electronics executive; b. 1945; m. Elizabeth Cameron. Grad., Middlebury Coll. With Drexel Burnham Comml. Paper, Inc., Dallas, 1966—84, pres.; with Investment Ltd. Partnership, Greenwich, Conn., 1984—99, mng. gen. ptnr.; chmn. Entex Info. Svcs., Rye Brook, NY, 1993—99; trustee emeritus Middlebury Coll. Bd. mem. Rippowan Cisqua Sch. Westchester Land Trust. Office: Airlie Group 115 E Putnam Ave Greenwich CT 06830-5643*

CAMERON, DUNCAN HUME, lawyer; b. Brandon, Man., Can., May 26, 1934; s. Donald Ewen and Jean Carruthers (Rankine) Cameron; m. Caroline I. Gilbert, 1975; children: Sarah, Anne. BA cum laude, Harvard U., 1956; LLB, Columbia U., 1959, PhD, 1965. Bar: N.Y. 1959, D.C. 1967, U.S. Supreme Ct. 1970. Assoc. Paul, Weiss, Rifkind, Wharton & Garrison, 1959-62; atty. office gen. counsel AID U.S. Dept. State, Washington, 1963-67, legal advisor mission to Dominican Republic, 1966; ptnr. Appleton, Rice & Perrin, 1967-71; mng. ptnr. Cameron & Hornbostel, Washington, 1972—2001, ptnr., 1972—. Adj. prof. Law Ctr., Georgetown U., Washington, 1970—80, Washington, 1989—2002, adj. prof. Sch. Fgn. Svc., 1973—88; vis. prof. Victoria U., New Zealand, 1986; vis. lectr. INCAE, Costa Rica, 2001—. Contbr. articles to profl. jours. Bd. dirs. Pan Am. Sch. Agr., 1986—2002, chmn. bd. dirs., 1991—97, trustee emeritus, 2002—; bd. dirs. Washington Tennis Found., 1995—99. Mem.: ABA, Washington Fgn. Law Soc. (bd. govs. 1988—90), Hist. Soc. Washington (bd. dirs. 1999—), Chilean Am. C. of C. Washington (pres. 1992—96, bd. dirs. 1992—), Cosmos Club. Home: 3532 Chesapeake St NW Washington DC 20008-2957 Office: Cameron & Hornbostel 818 Connecticut Ave NW Washington DC 20006-2702 E-mail: dcameron@cameron-hornbostel.com.

CAMERON, FRED E. band director, composer; b. Laurinburg, N.C., Apr. 7, 1949; s. Ernest and Loraine Cameron; m. Sherry L. Gibbs, Dec. 29, 1978; children: Heather, Samantha. BS, Pembroke State U., 1976. Dir. bands Franklin County H.S., Rocky Mount, Va., 1976—79, Lake City (S.C.) H.S., 1979—81, Lumberton (N.C.) H.S., 1981—85, St. Pauls (N.C.) H.S., 1985—90; min. music Cornerstone Assembly of God, Lumberton, 1986—92; dir. bands Fairmont (N.C.) H.S., 1990—2000; min. music 1st Assembly of God, Bladenboro, NC, 1992—94, Good Shepherd Cmty. Ch., Lumberton, 1994—; dir. bands West Bladen H.S., Bladenboro, NC, 2000—. Adjudicator All-Am. Judges Assn., Lumberton, SC, 1975—, Concert Band Adjudication Panel, Lumberton, NC, 1984—2002; band clinician New Creation Music, Lumberton, NC, 1972—. Composer: (marching band music) Fanfare for Rockets, 1970, (concert band) In the Beginning God Created...., 1996, Suite for Concert Band, 1994, (church music) We Bless You Lord, 1990, (concert march) The Final Chapter, 2001. Named Outstanding Young Educator, Lumberton Jaycees, 1981, Nat. Flag Tchr. of Yr., Psi Omega Psi, 1973. Mem.: Southeastern Dist. Band Assn., Nat. Band Assn., N.C. Music Educators Assn., Music Educators Nat. Conf., Phi Mu Alpha. Assembly Of God. Avocations: golf, stamp collecting, coin collecting, travel, writing. Home: 1213 Patton St Lumberton NC 28358 Office: West Bladen H S 1600 Hwy 410 Bladenboro NC 28320 Office Fax: 910-863-2000. Personal E-mail: FCbandman@nc.rr.com. Business E-Mail: FCbandman@nc.rr.com.

CAMERON, GLENN NILSSON, mortgage company executive; b. Orange, N.J., Apr. 20, 1956; s. John Richardson and Alma (Nilsson) Cameron. BA in History, Wheaton (Ill.) Coll., 1978; ThM in Bibl. Studies, Dallas Theol. Sem., 1983. Lic. real estate broker Tex., mortgage broker. Real estate developer shopping ctrs. and apts. Hunsicker & Assocs., Dallas, 1983-85; dir. comml. investment brokerage Donald Kinney & Assocs., Dallas, 1985-86; dir. sales So. Classical Homes/Northtown Sq., Dallas, 1986-87, Glenn Cameron & Co., Residential Real Estate Brokerage, Dallas, 1987-90; broker assoc. Realty

Execs., Residential Real Estate Brokerage, Plano & Dallas, Tex., 1990-95; dir. sales Martin Raymond Homes, Inc., 1995—98; sr. mortgage fin. officer Consumer Direct Mortgage, Dallas, 1998-2000; CEO Mortgage Lending Assocs., Dallas, 2000—. Mem. So. Meth. U. Internat. Friendship Program, 1985—87, Lone Star Masters Swim Team, 1983—89, North Dallas Aquatics, 1989—93, Tex. Human Rights Found., Human Rights Campaign Fund; vol. Lifewalk, Contact Counseling Line, Black Tie Dinner, AIDS Svcs., Denton County; HIV counselor. Named Outstanding Young Man of Am., 1983—87. Mem.: Realty Execs. Internat., Dallas Songwriters Assn., Collin County Assn. Realtors, Greater Dallas Assn. Realtors, Tex. Assn. Realtors, Nat. Assn. Realtors, DFW Fed. Club (bd. dirs.), Exec. Club. Avocations: sports, volunteer work, writing, composing music, piano. Home: 4433 Cole Dallas TX 75205 Office: Mortgage Lending Assocs 3878 Oak Lawn Ave Ste 520 Dallas TX 75219

CAMERON, GORDON MURRAY, chemical engineer; b. New Liskeard, Ont., Can., Apr. 9, 1932; s. Murray and Vera Alice (Strader) C.; m. Marie Therese Skutezky, Feb. 2, 1963; children: Barbara, Ian, Vera, Ewen. BSc, Royal Mil. Coll. Can., Kingston, Ont., 1953; BS with honors, Queen's U., Kingston, 1954; PhD in Chem. Engring., U. Del., 1962. Registered prof. engr. With CIL Inc., 1960-73, Chemetics Internat. Ltd., 1960-73, tech. mgr., 1974-75, Toronto, 1975-87, dir. tech., 1987, v.p. tech., 1987-88; pres. Cecebe Technologies Inc., Burk's Falls, Ont., Can., 1988—. Mem. heat transfer com. Nat. Research Coun. of Can., Ottawa, Ont., 1966-70. Contbr. 20 tech. articles to profl. jours.; inventor, patentee in field. Mem. Can. Soc. Chem. Engring., Am. Inst. Chem. Engrs., Metall. Soc. Presbyterian. Avocations: golfing, travel. Home: 460 Chapman Dr RR 3 Burks Falls ON Canada POA 1C0

CAMERON, HEATHER ANNE, publishing executive; b. Montreal, Quebec, Can., Mar. 12, 1951; came to U.S., 1981; d. Douglas George and Jeanne Sutherland (Thompson) C.; m. Ward Eric Shaw, Dec. 20, 1980; 1 child, Geoffrey Cameron. BA, Queen's U., Kingston, Ont., Can., 1973; MLS, McGill U., Montreal, 1977. Head reference and bibliography sect. Nat. Libr. Can., Ottawa, 1977-80; head editl. dept. Librs. Unltd., Inc., Denver, 1981-86; v.p. acquisitions and editl. devel. ABC-CLIO, Inc., Santa Barbara, Calif., 1986-92, pres., pub. Santa Barbara, Denver and, Eng., 1992-97; v.p., gen. mgr. West-group, San Francisco, 1997—. Bd. dirs. Friends of Librs. U.S.A., v.p., 1996, pres., 1997—. Mem. ALA (com. chair 1993—), Friends of Librs., USA (dir. 1994—, pres. 1997-2000), Amnesty Internat., Phi Beta Mu. Office: West Group 50 California St Fl 19 San Francisco CA 94111-4624 E-mail: heather.cameron@thomson.com.

CAMERON, HUGH C. career officer; BA in Bus. Adminstrn. and Mgmt., E. Carolina U., 1972; student pilot tng., Reese AFB, Tex., 1972-73; student, 474th Tactical Fighter Wing, Nellis AFB, Nev., 1976-77; MA in Mgmt., U. No. Colo., 1977; student, Squadron Officer Sch., 1978, Armed Forces Staff Coll., 1984, 56th Tactical Tng. Wing, MacDill AFB, Fla., 1984, Nat. War Coll., 1989. Commd. 2d lt. USAF, 1972, advanced through grades to brig. gen., 1996; T-38 instr. pilot Reese AFB, 1973-76; F-111E aircraft comdr. and instr. pilot 20th Tactical Fighter Wing, Royal Air Force, Upper Heyford, Eng., 1977-80; F-111E instr. pilot and wing exec. officer 27th Tactical Fighter Wing, Cannon AFB, N.Mex., 1980-82; aide to comdr. 12th Air Force, Bergstrom AFB, Tex., 1982-83; ops. officer 35th Tactical Fighter Squadron, Kunsan Air Base, S. Korea, 1984-85; stationed at Nellis AFB, 1985-88; plans officer Hdqs. U.S. Ctrl. Command, MacDill AFB, 1989-91; comdr. 51st Ops. Group, Osan Air Base, S. Korea, 1991-93; insp. gen Hdqs. Pacific Air Forces, Hickam AFB, Hawaii, 1993-94; comdr. 8th Fighter Wing, Kunsan Air Base, 1994-95, 3rd Wing, Elmendorf AFB, Alaska, 1995-96, Air Force Ctr. Quality and Mgmt. Innovation, Randolph AFB, Tex., 1996-98; vice comdr. 9th Air Force, dep comdr. U.S. Ctrl. Command Air Forces, Shaw AFB, S.C., 1998—. Decorated Legion of Merit with oak leaf cluster, Bronze Star. Office: 9 AF/CV 524 Shaw Dr Ste 200 Shaw A F B SC 29152-5031

CAMERON, J. ELLIOT, retired parochial educational system administrator; b. Panguitch, Utah, Feb. 9, 1923; s. B.A. and Leonia (Sargent) C.; m. Maxine Petty, Dec. 23, 1942; children— Bruce, Kim, Kerry Lynn, Preston. BS, MA, Brigham Young U., 1946-49, EdD, 1966. High sch. prin., supt. schs., Duchesne, Sevier, Utah, 1949-56; later pres. Snow Coll., Ephraim, Utah, 1956-58; dean students Utah State U., 1958-62; dean of student life, prof. edn., v.p. student svcs. Brigham Young U., Provo, Utah, 1962-80, pres. Hawaii campus, 1980-86; commr. ch. ednl. system LDS Ch., 1986-89, ret., 1989. With AUS, WWII. Mem. NEA, Nat. Assn. Student Personnel Adminstrs., Phi Delta. Kappa. Mem. Ch. of Jesus Christ of Latter-day Saints.

CAMERON, JAMES, film director, screenwriter, producer; b. Kapuskasing, Ont., Can., Aug. 16, 1954; s. Philip and Shirley Cameron; m. Sharon Williams, 1974 (div. 1985); m. Gale Ann Hurd, 1985 (div. 1989); m. Katheryn Bigelow, 1989 (div. 1991); m. Linda Hamilton, 1997 (div. 1999); 1 child: Suzy Amis. Grad. in Physics, Calif. State U., Fullerton. Head Lightstorm Entertainment, Burbank, Calif., 1992—; CEO Digital Domain, 1993—. Art dir. Battle Beyond the Stars, 1980, prodn. designer Galaxy of Terror, 1981, creator spl. effects Escape from New York, 1981; dir.: (films) Piranha II: The Spawning, 1981, Terminator 2 3-D, 1996; (TV films) Earthship, 2001; screenwriter Rambo: First Blood Part II, 1985, Strange Days, 1995, exec. prodr. Point Break, 1991, dir., screenwriter Xenogenesis, 1978, The Terminator, 1984, Aliens, 1986, The Abyss, 1989, dir., prodr., editor (films) Titanic, 1997 (Academy award for Best Picture and Best Dir., 9 others, 1997), dir., prodr. Ghosts of the Abyss, 2002, (TV) Expedition Bismarck, 2002, dir., prodr., screenwriter Terminator II: Judgement Day, 1991 (6 Academy award nominations, Ray Bradbury award for dramatic screenwriting, 5 Saturn awards Acad. Sci. Fiction, 5 MTV Movie awards, People's Choice award), True Lies, 1994, writer, exec. prodr. (TV series) Dark Angel, 2000—; author (films): Terminator 3: Rise of the Machines, 2003; prodr.(films): Volcanos of the Deep Sea, 2003. Office: Lightstorm Entertainment 919 Santa Monica Blvd Santa Monica CA 90401-2704*

CAMERON, JOHN CLIFFORD, lawyer, health science facility administrator; b. Phila., Sept. 17, 1946; m. Eileen Duffy, July 12, 1975; children: Christopher, Meghan. BA, U. Pitts., 1969; MBA, Temple U., 1972; JD, Widener U., 1976; LLM, NYU, 1980. Bar: Pa. 1977, N.J. 1977, Md. 1995. Asst. adminstr. Phila. Psychiatric Ctr., 1972-76; jud. clk. to presiding justice N.J. Superior Ct., Newark, 1976-77; asst. adminstr. St. Elizabeth Hosp., Elizabeth, N.J., 1977; v.p. corp. legal affairs Methodist Hosp., Phila., 1978-94; solicitor, 1988-94; legal cons. North Penn Hosp, Lansdale, Pa., 1994-95; counsel, legal adminstr. Hodes, Ulman, Pessin & Katz, P.A., Towson, Md., 1995-96; asst. to pres. Temple U. Health Sys., Phila., 1996—; asst. sec. Neumann Med. Ctr., Phila., 1997—2002, Jeanes Hosp., Phila., 1997—, Northwood Nursing Home, Phila., 1997—2002, Temple Physicians, Inc., Phila., 1997—, Temple Univ. Hosp., Phila., 1997—, Lower Bucks Hosp., Bristol, Pa., 1997—2002, Episcopal Hosp., Phila., 1997—, Temple U. Children's Med. Ctr., Phila., 1997—2002, Northeastern Hosp., Phila., 1997—, Temple Continuing Care Ctr., Phila., 1997—2002. Sec. Suthbrelt Properties, Ltd., Phila., 1981-94, Asbury Corp., Wilmington, Del., 1982-94, Healthmark, Inc., Moorestown, N.J., 1982-94, Meth. Hosp. Nursing Ctr., Phila., 1983-94; asst. sec. various hosps. and nursing homes, 1997—, instr. Grad. Sch. Mgmt., Pa. State U., 1991—; instr. mgmt. dept. Neumann Coll., 1991-96; instr. bus. divsn. Rosemont Coll., 1995-96. Contbr. articles to profl. jours. Mem. campaign United Way, Phila., 1979-94; mem. health and welfare com. United Meth. Eastern Pa. Conf., 1978-94; advisor Explorer Post, Boy Scouts Am., 1988-94; mem. steering com. Golden Cross, Phila., 1984-94; sec. Tredyffrin Twp. Park and Recreation Bd., 1987-95; alumni rep. Widener U.; mem. environ. adv. com. and open space task force Tredyffrin Twp., 1991-95. Fellow Am. Coll. Healthcare Execs. (chmn. bylaws com. 1995-96); mem. ABA, N.J. Bar Assn., Pa. Bar Assn., Phila. Bar Assn., Am. Hosp. Assn., Hosp. Assn. Pa., Swedish Colonial Soc. (bd dirs. 1992—, gov. 1993-95), Sons of Union Vets. of Civil War, SAR. Avocations: swimming, music. Home: 1410 Church Rd Malvern PA 19355-9714

CAMERON, JOHN GRAY, JR., lawyer; b. Detroit, July 28, 1949; s. John Gray and Helen Jane (Schueler) C.; m. Ann Elizabeth Dargus, June 19, 1976; children— Clara Katherine. A.B., Albion Coll., 1971; J.D. cum laude, Wayne State U., 1974. Bar: Ill. 1974, Mich. 1978, Colo. 1998, N.C. 1999, U.S. Ct. Appeals (8th cir.) 1975, U.S. Dist. Ct. (ea. dist.) Mo. 1975, U.S. Dist. Ct. (no. dist.) Ill. 1975, U.S. Dist. Ct. (we. dist.) Mich. 1978, U.S. Ct. Appeals (6th cir.) 1980. Law clk. U.S. Ct. Appeals, St. Louis, 1974-75; assoc. Isham, Lincoln & Beale, Chgo., 1975-78; ptnr. Warner, Norcross & Judd, Grand Rapids, Mich., 1978— ; instr. Seidman Sch. Bus., Grand Valley State Coll., Allendale, Mich., 1979-85, Mich. Inst. Continuing Legal Edn., 1980-82; lectr. Mich. Bar, 1983. Author: Michigan Real Property Law: Principles and Commentary, 1984, 2nd edit. 1993, Michigan Real Estate Forms and Practice, 1988, A Practioner's Guide to Construction Law, 2000; contbg. author: Michigan Real Estate Form Book, 1982-83. Bd. dirs. Urban Inst. Contemporary Art, Grand Rapids, 1980-82; trustee East Congl. Ch., Grand Rapids, 1985-88, Mary Free Bed Hosp. and Rehab. Ctr., 1997—. Mem. ABA, Mich. Bar Assn., Grand Rapids Bar Assn., Grand Rapids Bar Found., Am. Land Title Assn., Omicron Delta Epsilon. Republican. Club: U. Home: 56 Campau Cir NW Grand Rapids MI 49503-2658 Office: Warner Norcross & Judd 900 Old Kent Bldg Grand Rapids MI 49503-2487

CAMERON, JUDITH LYNNE, secondary education educator, hypnotherapist; b. Oakland, Calif., Apr. 29, 1945; d. Alfred Joseph and June Estelle (Faul) Moe; m. Richard Irwin Cameron, Dec. 17, 1967; 1 child, Kevin Dale. AA in Psychol., Sacramento City Coll., 1965; BA in Psychol., German, Calif. State U., 1967; MA in Reading Specialization, San Francisco State U., 1972; postgrad., Chapman Coll.; PhD, Am. Inst. Hypnotherapy, 1987. Cert. tchr., Calif. Tchr. St. Vincent's Cath. Sch., San Jose, Calif., 1969-70, Fremont (Calif.) Elem. Sch., 1970-72, LeRoy Boys Home, LaVerne, Calif., 1972-73, Grace Miller Elem. Sch., LaVerne, Calif., 1973-80, resource specialist, 1980-84; owner, mgr. Pioneer Take-out Franchises, Alhambra and San Gabriel, Calif., 1979-85; resource specialist, dept. chmn. Bonita H.S., LaVerne, Calif., 1984; mentor tchr. in space sci. Bonita Unified Sch. Dist., 1988-99, rep. LVTV; owner, therapist So. Calif. Clin. Hypnotherapy, Claremont, Calif., 1988—. Bd. dirs., recommending tchr., asst. dir. Project Turnabout, Claremont, Calif.; Teacher-in-Space cons. Bonita Unified Sch. Dist., LaVerne, 1987-99; advisor Peer Counseling Program, Bonita High Sch., 1987—; advisor Air Explorers/Edwards Test Pilot Sch., LaVerne, 1987—; mem. Civil Air Patrol, Squadron 68, Aerospace Office, 1988-92; selected amb. U.S. Space Acad.-U.S. Space Camp Acad., Huntsville, Ala., 1990; named to national (now internat.) teaching faculty challenger Ctr. for Space Edn., Alexandria, Va., 1990; regional coord. East San Gabiel Valley Future Scientists and Engrs. of Am.; amb. to U.S. Space Camp, 1990; mem. adj. faculty challenger learning ctr. Calif. State U., Dominguez Hills, 1994, state edn. accreditation team, 2000; rep. ceremony to honor astronauts Apollo 11, White House, 1994; exec. bd. Bonita Unfied tchrs. assoc., 1995— (negotiating team, 1998—); flight dir. mission control, Challenger learning ctr., Long Beach, Ca., 2002—. Vol. advisor Children's Home Soc., Santa Ana, 1980-81; dist. rep. LVTV Channel 29, 1991; regional coord. East San Gabriel Valley chpt. Future Scientists and Engrs. of Am., 1992; mem. internat. invesigation Commn. UFOs, 1991; field mem. Ctr. for Search for Extraterrestrial Intelligence, 1996; tchr., leader Ctr. for the Study Extraterrestrial Intelligence, 1997—. Recipient Tchr. of Yr., Bonita H.S., 1989, continuing svc. award, 1992; named Toyolaa Tchr. of Yr., 1994. Mem. NEA, AAUW, Internat. Investigations Com. on UFOs, Coun. Exceptional Children, Am. Psychol. Assn., Calif. Assn. Resource Specialists, Calif. Elem. Edn. Assn., Calif. Tchrs. Assn., Calif. Assn. Marriage and Family Therapists, Planetary Soc., Mutual UFO Network, Com. Sci. Investigation L5 Soc., Challenger Ctr. Space Edn., Calif. Challenger Ctr. Crew for Space Edn., Orange County Astronomers, Chinese Shar-Pei Am., Concord Club, Rare Breed Dog Club (L.A.), gardening club of Am., ctr. for the extraterrestrial intelligence, diplomat, 1997. Republican. Avocations: skiing, banjo, guitar, flying, astrophotography. Home: 3257 La Travesia Dr Fullerton CA 92835-1455 Office: Bonita High Sch 115 W Allen Ave San Dimas CA 91773-1437

CAMERON, KAY, conductor, music director, arranger; b. Robbins, N.C. d. Joe and Gladys (Hussey) C. MusB, U. N.C., 1972, MusM, 1973. Music dir. Kennedy Ctr. For the Performing Arts, Washington, 1994—; condr. Words and Music, Musicals in Concert; music supr. Sondheim Celebration. Tchr. Richmond Pub. Schs., Va., 1973-77; music dir., condr. broadway and nat. tours, N.Y., 1978-1996; arranger, orchestrator musicals and TV, 1979-1996; vis. lectr. U. N.C., Wilmington, 1997-98; condr. concert featuring Cy Coleman, Kennedy Ctr. Opera House Orch. Music dir., condr. State Fair, The Will Rogers Follies, Phantom, The King and I, On The 20th Century, Sugar Babies, Showboat, The Sound of Music, Salute To The Broadway Composer, The Sound Of Rodgers And Hammerstein, New Moon, La Cage Aux Folles (opera) Amelia Goes To The Ball, Candide, Die Fledermaus, Hansel and Gretel, The Medium, Madama Butterfly, The Telephone, others; arranger, orchestrator Show Boat on PBS, United Nations 40th Anniversary, Herman & Soundheim Together, (compositions) A Christmas Carol, Heroes, others. Mem. Am. Fedn. Musicians. Home: 121 Loder Ave Wilmington NC 28409 E-mail: kcameron@kennedy-center.org.

CAMERON, KIRK MACGREGOR DRUMMOND, statistician; b. Glendale, Calif., Oct. 27, 1962; s. Paul Drummond and Virginia May (Rusthoi) C.; m. Kelly Mitchell, May 21, 1994; chilre: Kaitlyn Gray, Kit MacGregor, Kyle Henry, Kristyn Virginia. BS in Math., U. Nebr., 1984; MS in Statis., Stanford U., 1989, PhD in Statis., 1990. Statis. cons. Family Rsch. Inst., Colorado Springs, Colo., 1983—; sr. statis. Sci. Applications Internat. Corp., McLean, Va., 1990-95; pres., statis. cons. Macstat Cons., Colorado Springs, 1995—. Bd. dirs. Family Rsch. Inst., editor, 1995—. Contbr. articles to profl. jours.; contbr. scientific papers. Youth counselor McLean Bible Ch., 1991-94; Sunday sch. leader Village Seven Presbyn., Colorado Springs, 1995—2002; county del. El Paso County Rep. Conv., Colorado Springs, 1998. NSF Grad. fellow, 1984, Pew Found. Teaching fellow, 1990. Mem. Am. Statis. Assn., Inst. Math. Stats., Phi Beta Kappa. Avocations: rock collecting, guitar, hiking, camping, tennis. E-mail: kcmacstat@qwest.net.

CAMERON, LUCILLE WILSON, retired dean of libraries; b. Nashua, N.H., Dec. 21, 1932; d. Hugh Alexander and Louise Perham (Baldwin) C.; m. James Robert Doris, Aug. 19, 1976; children: Glenn A. Browning, Gail W. Browning, Valerie B. Cruickshank. BA, U. R.I., 1964, MLS, 1972. Social case worker R.I. Dept. Pub. Assistance, Providence, 1964-70; asst. circulation libr. U. R.I. Libr., Kingston, 1970-72, reserve libr., 1972-73, reference/bibliographer, 1973-88, head reference unit, 1983-86, chair pub. svcs., 1988-89, interim dean, 1989-90, dean, 1990—, dean emerita. Bd. trustees North Scituate (R.I.) Pub. Libr., 1995, pres., 1996. Co-author: Labor and Industrial Relations Journals and Serials, 1989; contbr. articles to profl. jours. Bd. trustees North Scituate (R.I.) Pub. Libr., 1995—, pres., 1996—. Recipient Computerized Intergrated Libr. System award Champlin Founds., Providence, 1989, 90, 91, Coll. Tech. Libr. Program award U.S. Dept. Edn., Washington, 1990, Disting. Alumna award Grad. Sch. Libr. and Info. Studies, U. R.I., Kingston, 1991. Mem. ALA, Assn. Coll. and Rsch. Librs., Consortium R.I. Acad. and Rsch. Librs., Higher Edn. Libr. Info. Network (chair), Univ. Press New England (gov.), North Scituate (R.I.) Pub. Libr. Assn. (bd. trustees 1995—, pres. 1996—), Alpha Kappa Delta.

CAMERON, MARY EMILY, pediatrics nurse, nursing researcher; b. Newark, Mar. 22, 1948; d. Donald Eugene and Clara Preston (Zink) C. BSN, Duke U., 1970; pediatric nurse practioner cert., Ind. U., Indpls., 1973; MS, Boston U., 1985; PhD, U. Pa., 1996. RN Pa. Nurse practioner United Health Svcs., Clairfield, Tenn., 1973-74; insvc. dir. Jellico (Tenn.) Community Hosp., 1974-75; instr., nurse practioner East Tenn. State U. Coll. Medicine, Kingsport, 1975-76, 79-82; staff nurse Holston Valley Med. Ctr., Kingsport, Tenn., 1976-79; pediat. nurse practitioner East Tenn. Coll. Medicine, Johnson City, 1979—82; charge nurse Boston City Hosp., 1982-86; sect. chair Boston City Hosp. Sch. Practical Nursing, 1984-85; instr. U. Mass Sch. Nursing, Boston, 1985-86; teaching and rsch. asst. U. Pa. Sch. Nursing, Phila., 1986-91, clin. rsch. coord., 1991-94; asst. prof. pediatric nursing Temple U., Phila., 1994-96; lectr. Burlington County Coll., N.J., 1996-99; asst. prof. nursing Rutgers U., Camden, NJ, 1999—2001; program mgr. NINR grant U. Pa., 2001—03. Lectr. Mass. Emergency Med. Svcs., Boston, 1983-85; nurse mgr. Children's Rehab. Hosp., Phila., 1986-87; staff nurse Children's Seashore House, Phila., 1988-90; cons. U. Pa. Sch. Nursing, 1991-94. Contbr. articles to profl. jours. Ch. instr., choir mem. Springfield, Pa., 1987-94, Moorestown, N.J., 1994—. Fellow Nat. Assn. Pediatric Nurse Assocs. and Practitioners (hon., CPNA); mem. ANA (cert. maternal-child health nurse, pediatric nurse), Soc. Pediatric Nurses. Methodist. Avocations: original needlework, camping. E-mail: maryemily.cameron@att.net.

CAMERON, NICHOLAS ALLEN, diversified corporation executive; b. Phila., Jan. 6, 1939; s. Nicholas Guyot and Katherine (Rogers) C.; m. Leslie Wood, Dec. 14, 1974; children: Christopher Wilson, Pamela Wilson. BS, Yale U., 1960. Treas. Allied Corp., Morristown, N.J., 1979-81, v.p. and treas., 1981-82, v.p. fin., 1982-83, v.p. planning and devel., 1983-85; sr. v.p. planning, devel. and adminstrn. Allied-Signal Inc., Morristown, N.J., 1985-86; sr. v.p. tech. and bus. devel. Bendix Aerospace-Allied-Signal, Inc., Arlington, Va., 1986-87; group pres. Allied-Signal Aerospace, 1988; sr. v.p. ops. svcs. Allied-Signal, Inc., Morristown, N.J., 1988-90, sr. v.p., gen. mgr. chem. intermediates, 1990-95. Bd. dirs. Morristown Meml. Health Found., 1996—2001, United Way of Morris County, Morristown, N.J., 1980-86, 90-98, campaign chmn., 1991, chief vol. officer, 1993-95, bd. chmn., 1996-98; bd. dirs. Morris 2000, 1990-97, 99—, chmn., 1993-96; mem. adv. bd. Morristown Hosp., 1998—; commr. Morris County Park Commn., 1999-2004. Mem. Morris County C. of C. (bd. dirs. 1975-86, 1990-98), Tau Beta Pi. Clubs: St. Elmo Soc. (New Haven); Morris County Golf. Republican. Episcopalian. Home and Office: 27 Kitchell Rd Morristown NJ 07960 E-mail: ncame1639@aol.com.

CAMERON, NINA RAO, lawyer, government official; b. N.Y.C., Apr. 28, 1925; d. Paul and Grace (Malatino) Rao; m. John D. Cameron, Jan. 9, 1950 (div.); 1 child, Scott; m. Robert M. Gewald. BA, Manhattanville, 1945; LLB, Bklyn. Law Sch., 1950; JD, U. Mex., 1968. Bar: N.Y. 1951, U.S. Ct. Appeals (2nd cir.) 1962, U.S. Supreme Ct. 1966. Pvt. practice, N.Y.C., 1951, 55, 90—; atty. adviser U.S. Immigration and Naturalization Svc., N.Y.C., 1952-54, dist. counsel, 1968-84, spl. counsel, 1985-90; asst. dir. commerce City of N.Y., 1956-58; asst. commr. dept. pub. events, dir. UN Consular Corps Coms. N.Y.C., 1958-65; law sec. Supreme Ct. State of N.Y., 1967; dep. asst. sec. Dept. of Interior, 2002—. Chmn. govt. officials com. Internat. Debutante Ball, 1980—. Decorated Orden de Ruben Dario (Nicaragua), Order Nacional al Merito (Ecuador), Order of Merit (Italy), Officers Cross of Merit (Germany), Order of the Brilliant Star (China), Officer of the Natural Order of the Cedar (Lebanon); recipient Amita award to Women of Outstanding Achievement of Italian Ancestry, 1956, Vespu CCI award to Outstanding Ams. of Italian Ancestry, 1957, award Soc. Fgn. Consuls in N.Y., 1961, 63, award for community svc. JFK Libr. for Minorities of Am. Heritage, 1972. Mem. Am. Soc. Italian Legions of Merit (bd. dirs., officer), Am. Immigration Lawyers' Assn. Republican. Roman Catholic. Avocations: gardening, theatre. Office: 58 W 58th St New York NY 10019-2502

CAMERON, PAUL DRUMMOND, research facility administrator; b. Pitts., Nov. 9, 1939; s. Nelson Drummond and Veronica (Witco) C.; m. Virginia May Rusthoi BA, L.A. Pacific Coll., 1961; MA, Calif. State U., L.A., 1962; PhD, U. Colo., 1966. Asst. prof. psychology Stout State U., Menomonie, Wis., 1966-67, Wayne State U., Detroit, 1967-69; assoc. prof. psychology U. Louisville, 1970-73, Fuller Grad. Sch. Psychology, Pasadena, Calif., 1976-79; assoc. prof. marriage and family U. Nebr., Lincoln, 1979-80; pvt. practice psychologist Lincoln, 1980-83; chmn. Family Rsch. Inst., Washington, 1982-95, Colo. Springs, 1995—. Reviewer Am. Psychologist, Jour. Gerontology, Psychol. Reports; presenter, witness, cons. in field. Author: Exposing the AIDS Scandal, 1988, The Gay 90's, 1993; contbr. articles to profl. jours. Mem. Ea. Psychol. Assn., Nat. Assn. for Rsch. and Treatment of Homosexuality. Republican. Lutheran. Achievements include investigation of health effects of second-hand tobacco smoke; investigation of first comprehensive national random sample of sexuality; documented abbreviated lifespan of homosexuals; documented poorer parenting by homosexuals. Office: Family Rsch Inst PO Box 62640 Colorado Springs CO 80962-2640

CAMERON, RITA GIOVANNETTI, writer, publisher; b. Washington; d. Joseph Angelo and Adeline Katherine (Fochett) C. BS with honors, U. Md., 1957; MEd, Am. U., Washington, 1962; DEd, Nova U., 1978. Tchr. D.C. pub. schs., Washington, 1959-64; prin. Prince George's County (Md.) Pub. Schs., 1964-73, 76-84; supr. instrn. K-12 Prince George's County pub. schs., 1973-76; free-lance writer ednl. materials Media, Materials Inc., Balt., 1965-75, Learning Well, Balt., 1995, World Class Learning Materials, Inc., Balt., 2000; free-lance writer travel articles AAA, Washington, 1978-83; owner, pub. Sch. House Global Enterprises, Fort Washington, Md., 1980—. Presenter, cons. to sch. systems and ednl. orgns., 1985—. Author: Let's Learn About Maryland and Prince George's County, 1970, Let's Learn About Maryland, 1972, 95, Super Sub! Or How to Substitute Teach in Elementary School, 1974, AAA Travel articles and Traffic Safety Teacher Guide Grades 4-6, 1982, 83; author, pub.: The Master Teacher's Plan and Record Book, 1985, The School House Encyclopedia of Educational Programs and Activities, 1991; author, publisher and nat. marketer of 88 social studies and sci. ednl. materials for students grades 4-10; developer/owner School House Global Enterprises Pub. Co. Food preparer So Others Might Eat, Washington, 1985—, food preparer for Missions of Charity Home for AIDS Victims, Washington, 1992—, sponsor Christian Found. for Children and Aging. Recipient Outstanding Citizenship award DAR, 1954, Nat. Tchr. award Expedition Nat. Tchr. Awards Program, 1960-61, Outstanding Tchr. Sci. award D.C. Coun. Engring. and Archtl. Soc. and Washington Acad. Scis., 1964, Outstanding Educator of Yr. award Prince George's County Bd. Edn., 1982-83, Am. Hist. award DAR, 1987, Outstanding Contbn. to Bicentennial Leadership Project award Couns. for Advancement of Citizenship, 1989. Mem. U. Md. Alumni Assn., Am. U. Alumni Assn., Nova U. Alumni Assn., Nat. Press Club, Phi Kappa Phi. Roman Catholic. Avocations: art, music, theater, antiques, travel. Office: Sch House Global Enterprises PO Box 441028 Fort Washington MD 20749-1028 Fax: 301-292-9744. *In one form or another, I have been a teacher all my life. It's been an enormous responsibility, matched only by enormous satisfaction. The knowledge, skills, love for learning, and feelings of self-worth given to students are among the finest gifts they will ever receive.*

CAMERON, ROY EUGENE, scientist; b. Denver, July 16, 1929; s. Guy Francis and Ilda Annora (Horn) C.; m. Margot Elizabeth Hoagland, May 5, 1956 (div. July 1977); children: Susan Lynn, Catherine Ann; m 2d Carolyn Mary Light, Sept. 22, 1978. BS, Wash. State U., 1953, 54; MS, U. Ariz., 1958, PhD, 1961. Research scientist Hughes Aircraft Corp., Tucson, 1955-56; sr. scientist Jet Propulsion Lab., Pasadena, Calif., 1961-68, mem. tech. staff, 1969-74; dir. research Darwin Research Inst., Dana Point, Calif., 1974-75; dep. dir. Land Reclamation Lab. Argonne Ill. Nat. Lab., 1975-77, dir. energy resources tng. and devel., 1977-85; sr. staff scientist Lockheed Environ. Systems and Techs. Co., Las Vegas, Nev., 1986-95; quality assurance officer Lockheed Engring. and Scis. Co., Las Vegas, Nev., 1990-95; bioremediation lab. mgr. TAD Lockheed, 1991-95; environ. advisor Mashantucket (Conn.) Pequot Tribal Nation, 1995-96. Cons. Lunar Receiving Lab. Baylor U., 1966-68, Ecology Ctr. Utah State U., Desert Biome, 1970-72, U. Alaska Tundra Biome, 1973-74, U. Maine, 1973-76, numerous others; mem. Nat. Agr. Rsch. and Extension Users Adv. Bd., 1986-92; tribal rep. stormwater phase 2 subcom. U.S. EPA, 1995-98, cons. sci. adv. bd., 1996—; mem Vols. on Overseas Coop. Assistance, Bolivia, 1997, 99, 2000. Contrb. articles to sci. books; participated in 7 Antarctic expdns. Served with U.S. Army, 1950-52, Korea, Japan. Recipient 3 NASA awards for tech. briefs, EPA award of Excellence for global climate program, 1988; Paul Steere Burgess fellow U. Ariz., 1959; grantee NSF, 1970-74; Dept. Interior, 1978-80. Mem. AAAS, Soil Sci. Soc. Am., Am. Chem. Soc., Am. Soc. Microbiology, Am. Soc. Agronomy, Antarctican Soc., Soil and Water Conservation Soc. Am., World Future Soc., Internat. Soc. Soil Sci., Coun. Agrl. Sci. and Tech., Am. Inst. Biol. Sci., Am. Geophys. Union, Sigma Xi. Lutheran. E-mail: royecameron@yahoo.com.

CAMERON, THOMAS WILLIAM LANE, investment company executive; b. Newton, Mass., Feb. 19, 1927; s. Percy G. and Mary W.D. (Mitchell) C.; m. Carol Louise Soliday, June 17, 1950; children: Helen Delone, Thomas Mitchell (dec.). AB cum laude, Harvard, 1948, MBA, 1951. With sales dept. Procter & Gamble, Boston, 1951-53; with Hopper, Soliday, & Co., Inc., Phila., 1953-66, ptnr., 1961—, pres., 1966-72, chmn., 1972-83; dir. Hopper, Soliday & Co., Inc., 1983-86; sr. v.p. Interstate/Johnson Lane, Johns Island, SC, 1986—99; chmn. Sovereign Investors Inc., 1979-91; vice chmn. John Hancock Sovereign Investors, 1991-96; chmn. Cameron & Assocs., Inc., 1999—. Chmn. Phila.-Balt.-Washington Stock Exch., 1970-74, bd. govs., 1963-75. Bd. mgrs. Franklin Inst., 1970-90, chmn., 1978-81; bd. dirs. Holling Cancer Ctr., Med. U. S.C., 1992—. Served with USNR, 1944-46. Mem.: Waynesborough Country (Paoli, Pa.) (pres. 1965-67); Harvard (Phila.) (pres. 1965-66), Harvard Bus. Sch. (Phila.) (pres. 1962-64). Home: 332 Catbrier Ct Johns Island SC 29455-5618 Office: Cameron & Assocs Inc 1894 Andell Bluff Blvd Johns Island SC 29455-8222

CAMERON, WILLIAM DUNCAN, plastics company executive; b. Harrell, N.C., June 14, 1925; s. Paul Archiebald and Atwood (Herring) C.; m. Betty Gibson, Oct. 3, 1953; children: Phillip MacDonald, Colleen Kay. Student, Duke U., 1945-49. Chmn. emeritus Reef Industries, Inc., Houston. Pres. bd. trustees Trinity Epsicopal Sch., Galveston, Tex., 1981-82; trustee William Temple Found., 1987-90. Served with U.S. Army, 1943-45. Mem. Houston C. of C. (chmn. mfg. com. 1967), Rotary, Galveston Artillery, Bob Smith Yacht Club. Home: 3614 Acorn Wood Way Houston TX 77059-3741 Office: Reef Industries Inc 9209 Almeda Genoa Rd Houston TX 77075-2339

CAMERON, WILLIAM WESLEY, investment executive; b. Gypsym, Kans., Jan. 2, 1953; m. Judy D. Blair, Apr. 26, 1984. BSEE, Tulane U., 1974; MBA in Fin., U. Pa., 1978. CFP. Engr. IBM, Manassas, Va., 1974-76; prin. Am. Mgmt. Sys., Arlington, Va., 1978-87; account mgr. The Acacia Group, Fairfax, Va., 1993-97; pres. Blair Cameron Assocs., Arlington, 1987-98; ptnr. Blair Cameron Assocs., LLC, Barboursville, 1998—; pres. Third Millennium Advisors, Inc., Barboursville, 1997—. Office: Third Millennium Advisors Inc 4493 Stony Point Rd Barboursville VA 22923-2119

CAMERON-GODSEY, MELINDA A. BRANTLEY, artist; b. El Dorado, Ark., Jan. 3, 1954; d. Austin Van and Jamie Lou (Middleton) Brantley; m. James Stephen Cameron, Jan. 5, 1973 (div. Nov. 1985); children: Kelly Van Cameron, Courtney Y. Cameron; m. William Paul Godsey, Jan. 1, 1995. BFA, La. Tech. U., 1979. Registered interior designer Ark. One-woman shows include San Diego Internat. Exhbn., 1985 (Best of Show award), Southwestern Water Soc., Dallas, 1985 (2 awards), Watercolor Art Soc., Houston, 1985, 1987, Ariel Gallery, N.Y.C., 1986, Dishman Art Gallery, Beaumont, Tex., 1987, Hot Springs (Ark.) Art Ctr., 1988, South Ark. Art Ctr., El Dorado, 1988, 1991, 1995, Ark. River Valley Art Ctr., Russellville, 1989, Adirondacks Nat. Exhbn., N.Y., 1989, Riverside Art Gallery, Shreveport, 1990, Salmagundi Club, N.Y.C., 1999, others, U.S. Senator Blanche Lincoln, Washington D.C., 2003—; art work published in: Am. Artist's Ann. Publ., Watercolor 90, Crazyhorse, 1990, 1997, Poet's Market, others. Named Ark. Woman Artist, Russell State Bldg., Washington. Mem.: Southwestern Watercolor Soc., Mid-So. Watercolor Soc. (signature mem.), Knickerbockers Artists. Episcopalian. Home and Office: 1217 Cypress Dr El Dorado AR 71730-3668 E-mail: z@melindacamerondesigns.com.

CAMERON JR, EDWARD JOHN, engineer; b. Tracey, Calif., Aug. 7, 1976; s. Edward John and Emiko Cameron. BSc in mech. engring., Worcester Poly. Inst., 1995—99. Nuc. plant engr. Knolls Atomic Power Lab., Ballston Spa, NY, 1999—, fleet support engr., 2002—03. Firefighter Round Lake Fire Dept., NY, 2001—03. Mem.: ASME (assoc.), AIAA (assoc.). Home: 10 D Maclyn Meadows Ballston Lake NY 12019 Office: Knolls Atomic Power Laboratory 350 Atomic Project Rd Ballston Spa NY 12020

CAMERY, JOHN WILLIAM, computer engineer; b. Cin., Feb. 5, 1951; s. Donald Otis and Mary Lynne (Edgington) C. BA, U. Cin., 1972; MS, Carnegie-Mellon U., 1974. Mathematician U.S. Army Material Systems Analysis Agy., Aberdeen Proving Grounds, Md., 1973; student asst. engring. spectrum analysis task force Fed. Comms. Commn., Park Ridge, Ill., 1974; mathematician U.S. Army Comms. Electronics-Engring. Agy., Washington, 1975-83; computer specialist U.S. Army Mgmt. Systems Analysis Agy., Washington, 1983; mathematician Def. Comms. Agy., Washington, 1983-86; programmer, analyst Gen. Scis. Corp., Laurel, Md., 1986-87; software engr. Sygnetron Protection Systems, Timonium, Md., 1987-88, Automation Cons., Inc., Balt., 1988-89, RDA Logicon, Leavenworth, Kans., 1989-2001; sr. systems analyst Battle Simulation Ctr. Anteon Corp., Wheeler Army Air Field, Hawaii, 2001—. Cons. Martin Marietta Ocean Systems Ops., Glen Burnie, Md., 1988—. Carnegie-Mellon U. fellow, 1972-73. Mem. Am. Math. Soc., Societe Mathematique de France, Soc. for Indsl. and Applied Math., European Math. Soc., Internat. Platform Assn., Imperial Hawaii Vacation Club, Greater Cin. Amateur Radio Club. Republican. Mem. Christian Ch. Avocations: music, dancing, swimming, electronics, travel. Home: 94-647 Kauakapuu Loop Mililani HI 96789-1832 Office: Anteon Corp PO Box 861563 Wahiawa HI 96786-1563 E-mail: jcamery@west.anteon.com.

CAMFIELD, WILLIAM ARNETT, art educator, educator; b. San Angelo, Tex., Oct. 29, 1934; s. William Augustus and Frances Maurine (Arnett) C.; m. Virginia Anne Kindig, June 1, 1958; children: Lynn Alexia, Paul Justin, Mark Arnett. BA, Princeton U., 1957; MA, Yale U., 1961, PhD, 1964. Asst. to assoc. prof. U. St. Thomas, Houston, 1964-69; assoc. prof. to prof. Rice U., Houston, 1969—2002, Joseph and Joanna Nazro Mullen prof., 1980, prof. emeritus, 2002—. Mem. art adv. coun. Princeton (N.J.) U., 1975-91; advisor Archives Am. Art, Tex. area, Houston, 1980-85. Author: Francis Picabia, 1979; author/curator exhbns. Francis Picabia at Guggenheim Mus., 1970, Tabu Dada, Kunsthalle Berne, 1983, Marcel Duchamp: Fountain, Menil Coll., Houston, 1989, Max Ernst: Dada and the Dawn of Surrealism, MOMA, 1993, The Paintings of Frank Freed, Museum of Fine Arts, Houston, 1996. Bd. dirs. Citizens for Good Schs., Houston, 1966-68; deacon, elder St. Phillip Presbyn. Ch., Houston, 1974-80; juror/advisor various civic art projects, Houston; trustee Mus. Fine Arts, Houston, 1979-88, The Eleanor and Frank Freed Found. Capt. arty. U.S. Army, 1957-59. Fellow Am. Coun. Learned Socs., 1973-74, NEH, 1981, John Simon Guggenheim Found., 1988-89; Am. Philos. Soc. grantee, 1965. Mem. Coll. Art Assn., Tex. Conf. Art Historians (co-founder 1978-79). Democrat. Avocations: jogging, reading, travel. Office: Rice U 6100 Main St Houston TX 77005-1892

CAMIC, DAVID EDWARD, lawyer; b. Indpls., June 11, 1954; s. Edward Franklin Camic and Carolyn (Hooker) Camic-Longland. BA, Aurora U., 1982; postgrad., DePaul U., 1982-83; JD cum laude, John Marshall Law Sch., 1987. Bar: Ill. 1987, U.S. Dist. Ct. (no. dist.) Ill. 1990, N.Y. 1996. Ptnr. Camic, Johnson, Wilson & McCulloch P.C., Aurora, Ill., 1987—. Mem. faculty, lectr. Aurora U.; lectr. in criminal law Regional Police Tng., Aurora, 1987—. Contbr. articles to profl. jours. Chmn. Rape Def. Seminar, Aurora, 1986. Named Man of Yr. Todays Orgn. Youth, 1987. Mem. ATLA, ABA, Ill. Bar Assn. (past-chair criminal justice sect.), Kane County Bar Assn. (past chair criminal law com., bd. dirs. 2000-01), Nat. Assn. Criminal Lawyers, Phi Delta Phi. Office: Camic Johnson Wilson & McCulloch PC 546 W Galena Blvd Aurora IL 60506-3855

CAMILLERI, LOUIS C. consumer goods company executive; With Philip Morris, 1978—, various postiions in Europe, 1978—95, sr. v.p. corp. planning, 1995, pres., CEO Kraft Foods Internat., 1995—96; sr. v.p., CFO Philip Morris Companies Inc., 1996—2002; pres., CEO Altria Group (formerly Philip Morris Companies Inc.), 2002—. Office: Altria Group 120 Park Ave New York NY 10017-5592*

CAMILLERI, MICHAEL, lawyer, educator; b. N.Y.C., July 16, 1953; s. Joseph and Lena (Calatozzo) C.; m. Debralyn Fisher, Aug. 5, 1989; children: Bryan, Brandon, Brooke. BA, L.I. U., 1974; JD, Fordham U., 1977. Bar: N.Y. 1978. Sr. v.p., gen. counsel Nat. Coun. Compensation Ins., N.Y.C., 1978-91; ptnr. Adorno & Zeder, Miami, 1991-99; pres. Ameritrust Ins. Group, Boca Raton, Fla.; principal Preferred Ins. Capital Cons., Boca Raton, Fla., 2001—; pres. Newport Star Reins. Co. Pres. Ins. Data Resources, 1997-2000; cons. Family Counseling Ctr., Bklyn., 1980-85; adj. prof. law Coll. Ins., N.Y.C., 1981-91; arbitrator civil ct., N.Y.C., 1983-91. Author: Matthew Bender's Accident and Health Law, 1989; editor: Werbel's N.Y. Worker's Compensation Law, 1986-94. Mem. ABA, N.Y. State Bar Assn., D.C. Bar Assn., Profl. Bowlers Assn. Office: PICC Ste 415 2101 NW Corporate Blvd Boca Raton FL 33431

CAMING, H. W. WILLIAM, lawyer, consultant; b. N.Y.C., Sept. 22, 1919; s. Arthur and Anne Winifred (Hayman) C.; m. Kathleen Marie White, Feb. 16, 1951; 1 child, Patricia Reynolds. BS summa cum laude, NYU, 1938; JD, Harvard U., 1941; LLM, NYU, 1956. Bar: N.Y. 1943, U.S. Dist. Ct. (so. dist.) N.Y. 1950, ICC 1954, FCC 1957. With office corp. counsel Brit. Ministry of Supply Mission, N.Y.C., Washington and Ottawa, Ont., Can., 1941-43; chief prosecutor and dep. dir. polit. ministries div. Office of U.S. Chief of Counsel for War Crimes, Nuremburg, Ger., 1946-49; spl. asst. atty. gen. State of N.Y., 1950-52; atty. Bell Telephone Labs., N.Y.C., 1953-57; labor counsel long lines dept. AT&T, N.Y.C., 1957-65, chief co. spokesman, sr. counsel in charge privacy and corp. security, 1965-76, Basking Ridge, NJ, 1977-84; cons. war crimes trials, privacy matters, info. tech. and corp. security, 1984—. Mem. nat. adv. bd. Ctr. Info. Tech. and Privacy Law of John Marshall Law Sch., Chgo., 1983-88; lectr., panelist symposia internat. war crimes trials, and privacy matters, 1975—. Columnist Dubois (Pa.) Courier-Express, 1949-50; contbr. articles to profl. publs. Mem. Summit (N.J.) Bd. Edn., 1969-73, 85-88, pres., 1972; mem. adv. panels Congl. Office Tech. Assessment, 1987-88; mem. U.S. Privacy Coun. Served to capt. USAAF, 1943-46; capt. JAGC, USAR, 1946-53; PTO, CBI. Mem. ABA (chair com. privacy of criminal justice sect. 1981-83, vice chmn. 1980, 84-85, advisor on privacy matters to chair criminal justice sect. 1985-97), U.S. C. of C. (panel on privacy 1978-82, com. working group transborder data flow C. of C.'s U.S. and Can. 1984-85), U.S. Council Internat. Bus. (com. mem.), Nat. Dist. Attys. Assn., Computer Profls. for Social Responsibility, JAG Assn., Harvard Law Sch. Assn., Brotherhood of St. Andrew, Mil. Order World Wars, Organized Res. Corps Assn., Belmont Golf Club (Bermuda), Phi Beta Kappa. Republican. Episcopalian. Office: 17 Knob Hill Dr Summit NJ 07901-3024

CAMINITI, DONALD ANGELO, lawyer; BA magna cum laude, Rutgers U., 1973, JD, 1976. Bar: N.J. 1976, D.C. 1977, N.Y. 1980; cert. civil trial atty. N.J. Supreme Ct., cert. trial lawyer Nat. Bd. Trial Advocacy. Ptnr. Breslin & Breslin, P.A., Hackensack, N.J., 1977—; counsel Housing Authority of Bergen County, 1977—; asst. counsel Twp. of River Vale, 1977-80; counsel Housing Devel. Corp. Bergen County, 1978—, North Bergen Rent Leveling Bd., 1980—, North Bergen Housing Authority, 1980-84, Englewood Housing Authority, 1991—, Fort Lee Housing Authority, 1993—; spl. counsel Dept. Housing and Urban Devel., N.J., 1990—; counsel Guttenberg Housing Authority, 1995—. Master Morris Pashman Inns Ct., 1998—; speaker in field. Author: (with others) Products Liability Practice Guide, 1988. With USAF, 1966-70. Mem.: ATLA (parliamentarian N.J. chpt. 1984—85, seminar com. chmn. 1984—87, chmn. edn. com. 1990—91, v.p. 1990—91, 2d v.p. 1991—92, 1st v.p. 1992—93, pres.-elect 1993—94, pres. 1994—95, bd. govs. 2001—), ABA, Am. Bd. Trial Adv., Nat. Bd. Trial Adv., Bergen County Bar Assn., N.Y. Bar Assn., D.C. Bar Assn., N.J. Bar Assn., Phi Beta Kappa. Office: Breslin and Breslin PA 41 Main St Hackensack NJ 07601-7087 Home: 7 Parkwood Ln Mendham NJ 07945-2201

CAMINITI, KENNETH GENE, professional baseball player; b. Harford, Calif., Apr. 21, 1963; Grad., H.S., San Jose, Calif. With Houston Astros, 1987—94; 3d baseman San Diego Padres, 1995—98; with Houston Astros, 1998—. Named to Coll. All-Am. Team, The Sporting News, 1984, All-Star Team, Nat. League, 1994; recipient Nat. League's Most Valuable Player award, Baseball Writers' Assn. Am., 1996

CAMISHION, RUDOLPH CARMEN, physician; b. Riverside, N.J., July 16, 1927; m. Nancy Muzzarelli, June 28, 1952; children: Germain, Sandra, Lisa, Nancy, Janice. BS, St. Joseph's Coll., 1950; MD, Jefferson Med. Coll. of Phila., 1954. Cert. Am. Bd. Surgery, 1960, Bd. of Thoracic Surgery, 1961, Bd. Gen. Vascular Surgery, 1983. USNR Petty Officer, 1944-46; intern Cooper Hosp., Camden, N.J., 1954-55; resident in surgery Jefferson Med. Coll. Hosp., Phila., 1955-59; trainee Nat. Cancer Inst., 1958-59, 1959-62; asst. in surgery Jefferson Med. Coll., 1959-60, instr. in surgery, 1960-62, asst. prof. surgery, 1963-64; cons. thoracic surgery VA Hosp., Phila., 1963-66; assoc. prof. surgery Jefferson Med. Coll., 1964-67, prof. surgery, 1967-73; prof., head dept. surgery Robert Wood Johnson Med. Sch., Camden, 1973-91, prof. surgery, 1991—. Numerous medical presentations. Recipient Surgical Excellence award, 1991, rev. Clarence E. Shaffrey, S.J., award, 1991. Mem. Acad. Surgical Rsch., Am. Assn. Advancement of Sci., Am. Assn. for Thoracic Surgery, AAUP, Am. Coll. Chest Physicians, ACS, AHA, AMA, Am. Thoracic Soc., Am. Surgical Assn., Pa. Assn. for Thoracic Surgery, Phila. Acad. of Surgery, Camden County Med. Soc., Soc. of Univ. Surgeons, Soc. for Vascular Surgery, Vascular Soc. N.J., Eastern Vascular Soc., Soc. Clin. Vascular Surgery, Southeastern Surgical Cong., N.J. Chpt. Am. Coll. Surgeons, Alpha Omega Alpha. Office: R Wood Johnson Med Sch 3 Cooper Plz Rm 411 Camden NJ 08103-1438

CAMMA, ALBERT JOHN, neurosurgeon; b. Cleve., Dec. 27, 1940; s. August and Amelia (Catalioti) C.; m. Sheryl Virginia Doptis, Aug. 27, 1966 (div. Jan. 1986); children: August Leon, Albert David; m. Rebecca Ann Wenzel July 27, 1996; stepchildren: Joshua Wenzel, Nicholas Wenzel, Jaime Wenzel. BS cum laude, John Carroll U., 1963; MD, Western Res. U., 1967; MBA, Capital U., 1997. Diplomate Am. Acad. of Pain and Mgmt., Am. Bd. Neurol. Surgeons, Nat. Bd. Med. Examiners. Intern, surg. resident U. Pitts., 1967-69, resident in neurosurgery, 1971-75; pvt. practice in neurosurgery Zanesville, Ohio, 1975—. Trustee Zanesville YMCA, 1976-82; bd. dirs. Ohio Rails-to-Trails; pres. bd. dirs. Muskingum Recreational Trail, 1994-2001. With M.C., USN, 1969-71. Mem. AMA, AAAS, Ohio State Med. Assn., Am. Pain Soc., Am. Acad. Pain Medicine, Am. Back Soc., Am. Assn. Advance Sci., Am. Coll. Angiology, N.Y. Acad. Scis., Muskingum County Acad. Medicine (pres. 1996-97), Congress Neurol. Surgeons, Am. Acad. Thermology, Midwest Pain Soc., Soc. Behavioral Medicine, ACS, Am. Assn. Neurol. Surgeons, Ohio State Neurosurg. Soc. (bd. dirs. 1985-87, treas. 1987-89, v.p. 1989-91, pres. 1991-92), Mid-Atlantic Neurosurg. Soc., Am. Pain Soc., Am. Acad. Scis., Am. Soc. Neuroimaging. Office: Neurosurg Assn SE Ohio 855 Bethesda Dr Zanesville OH 43701-1894 E-mail: acamma@ee.net.

CAMMACK, ANN, librarian, secondary school educator; b. Akron, Ohio, Sept. 24, 1947; d. Matthew John and Anna (Maxim) Klinovsky; m. Robert Floyd Cammack, Sept. 27, 1969; children: Lisa Ann, Holly Ann, Noël Ann, Monica Ann. BA, Youngstown State U., 1969; MLS, Tex. Woman's U., 1995, PhD, 2001. Cert. tchr. secondary sch. Ohio, elem. and secondary sch., Tex. English tchr. Struthers (Ohio) City Schs., 1969-83; asst. cataloger Amon Carter Mus., Ft. Worth, 1997, 2000—01. Life mem. Tex. Parent Tchrs. Assn., historian Arlington, 1991-92. Doctoral fellow Tex. Woman's U., 1996. Mem. AAUW, ALA, Ladies Aux. VFW, Tex. Libr. Assn., Youngstown State U. Alumni Assn., Beta Phi Mu. Avocation: golf.

CAMMACK, TRANK EMERSON, retired university dean; b. Columbus, Kans., July 11, 1919; s. Levi Jackson and Ida Maud (Hull) C. Student, N.E. Okla. Jr. Coll., 1936-37; BS, U. Okla., 1940, MA, 1941; Huebner fellow in ins. edn., U. Pa., 1941-43. Fin. statistician SEC, Phila., 1943-48, Washington, 1948-49; prof. fin. U. Ill., Urbana, 1949-90, assoc. dean charge undergrad. program Coll. Commerce and Bus. Adminstrn., 1968-90. Author: (with Robert I. Mehr) The Insurance Contract and Its Analysis, 1950, Principles of Insurance, 1952. Mem. Champaign County Democratic Central Com., 1962-78; chmn. Champaign Dem. Orgn., 1966-68. Mem. AAUP, Am. Risk and Ins. Assn., Royal Econ. Soc. Methodist. Home: 1704 W Green St Champaign IL 61821-3721

CAMMAKER, SHELDON IRA, lawyer; b. N.Y.C., Apr. 26, 1939; s. Jack Robert and Anne (Benjamin) C.; children: Joshua, Meredith. BA magna cum laude, Brandeis U., Waltham, Mass., 1961; JD cum laude, Harvard U., 1964. Bar: N.Y. 1965, U.S. Dist. Ct. (so. dist.) N.Y. 1961. Assoc. Botein Hays & Sklar, N.Y.C., 1964-70, ptnr., 1971-87; exec. v.p., gen. counsel Emcor Group, Inc., Norwalk, Conn., 1987—. Office: Emcor Group Inc 301 Merritt Seven Norwalk CT 06851-6214

CAMMARATA, ANGELO, surgical oncologist; b. Italy, 1936; s. Giuseppe and Giuseppina (Ruggiero) C.; m. Diane M. Donner, Apr. 25, 1965; children: Joseph, Marisa, Michael, Christina. BA, Upsala Coll., 1958; MD, N.Y. Med. Coll., 1962. Diplomate Am. Bd. Surgery. Intern N.Y. Polyclin. Hosp., N.Y.C., 1962; resident, chief resident Met. Hosp. N.Y.C., 1963-67, asst. surgeon, 1968—; resident in surgery Meml. Hosp. Cancer and Allied Diseases, N.Y.C., 1967-68; assoc. surgeon, attending surgeon, chief breast surgery Cabrini Med. Ctr., N.Y.C.; attending surgeon Beth Israel North Hosp., N.Y.C.; instr. surgery N.Y. Med. Coll., N.Y.C., 1968-74, clin. asst. prof. surgery, 1974—. Vis. attending surgeon Met. Hosp. Ctr., N.Y.C. Contbr. articles to profl. jours. Fellow ACS, Internat. Coll. Surgeons; mem. AMA, N.Y. Cancer Soc., N.Y. Met. Breast Cancer Group, N.Y. Acad. Scis., Meml. Alumni Soc., Alpha Club. Office: 55 E 87th St New York NY 10128-1043

CAMMARATA, JOAN FRANCES, Spanish language and literature educator; b. Bklyn., Dec. 22, 1950; d. John and Angelina Mary (Guarnera) Cammarata; m. Richard Montemarano, Aug. 9, 1975. BA summa cum laude, Fordham U., 1972; MA, Columbia U., 1974, MPhil, 1977, PhD, 1982. Preceptor Columbia Coll., NYC, 1974-82; adj. instr. Fordham U., NYC, 1980-81; adj. asst. prof. Iona Coll., New Rochelle, NY, 1982-84; asst. prof. Manhattan Coll., Riverdale, NY, 1982-90, assoc. prof., 1990-96, prof., 1996—. Author: Mythological Themes in the Works of Garcilaso de la Vega, 1983; editor: Women in the Discourse of Early Modern Spain, 2003; mem. editl. bd. Modern Lang. Studies; editl. reviewer D.C. Heath; contbr. articles and revs. to profl. jours. Fellow arts and sci. Columbia U., 1972-75; grantee Manhattan Coll., 1985, 91, NEH, 1987, 88, Spain's Min Edn. Culture, 1997—; Rsch. Fellowship grantee NYU Faculty Seminars, 1992, 94; named univ. assoc. Faculty Resources Network Program NYU, 1985—; Andrew Mellon Found. vis. scholar, 1990; scholar-in-residence NYU, 1991-92, 97-98. Mem.: MLA (mem. del. assembly), N.Y. State Assn. Fgn. Lang. Tchrs., Am. Assn. Tchrs. Spanish and Portugese, Assn. Internat. de Hispanistas, Renaissance Soc. Am., Inst. Internat. de Lit. Iberoamericana, South Atlantic, South Ctrl. and Midwest MLA, N.E. MLA (rsch. fellow 1991, v.p. 1997—98, pres. 1998—), Am. Coun. Tchg. of Fgn. Langs, Cervantes Soc. Am., Hispanic Inst. Roman Catholic. Avocations: piano, gardening, writing, needlework. Office: Manhattan Coll Bronx NY 10471

CAMMARATA, RICHARD JOHN, financial advisor; b. Boston, June 29, 1950; s. Dominic Joseph and Anna Mary (Masone) C. BA, Stonehill Coll., 1972. Mgr. Ace Fence Co., South Boston, 1972-83; fin. advisor, investor self-employed Randolph, Mass., 1983—. Mem. Am. Security Coun., Nat. Adv. Bd., Boston, Va., 1988—. Mem. Rep. Presdl. Task Force, Washington, 1987—, Rep. Nat. Com., Washington, 1984—, GOPAC, Washington, 1984—. Mem. N.Y. Acad. Scis., AAAS. Republican. Roman Catholic. Home and Office: 47 Eugenia St Randolph MA 02368-1950

CAMMAROSANO, JOSEPH RAPHAEL, economist, educator; b. Mt. Vernon, NY, Mar. 12, 1923; s. Louis Raphael and Mary Nancy (Sansone) C.; m. Rosalie Nancy Esposito, Nov. 22, 1952; children: Louis, Nancy, Joseph. Student, Stanford U., 1943-44; BS cum laude, Fordham U., 1947, PhD, 1956; MA, N.Y.U., 1949. Insp. U.S. Bur. Customs, 1948-50; asst. prof. Iona Coll., 1950-55, Fordham U., Bronx, N.Y., 1956-60, assoc. prof., 1962-67; dir. Inst. Urban Studies, 1964—84, prof. econs., 1967—93, prof. emeritus, chmn. dept. econs., 1969, exec. v.p., 1969-75, 85-88, acting fin. v.p., treas., 1984-85; fiscal economist U.S. Bur. of Budget, Washington, 1961-62. Fiscal cons. N.Y. State Temp. Commn. on Constl. Conv., 1957—58, N.Y. State Spl. Legis. Com. on Revision and Simplification of the Constn., 1958—60, N.Y. State Tax Structure Study Com., 1962—70, N.Y. State Temp. Commn. on the Constn., 1966—67, N.Y. Bell Tel. Co., 1960; cons. N.Y.C. Econ. Devel. Adminstrn., 1969, Cmty. Coun. Greater N.Y., 1971—74; vice chmn. Regional Manpower Adv. Com. to U.S. Secs. Labor and HEW, 1970—73, chmn., 1973—74, cons. ACTION, Fed. Agy. for Vol. Svc., 1976, N.Y.C. Pub. Devel. Corp., 1979—81, Office of Edn. Roman Cath. Diocese of N.Y., 1981—87; mem. adv. com. Ind. Budget Office City of N.Y., 1990—92; higher edn. cons. U. Md., 1980, Malcolm-King Coll., 1982—89, Manhattan-Marymount Coll., 1987—89. Author: Highway Finance in New York State, 1958, A Profile of the Bronx Economy, 1967, A Plan for the Redevelopment of the Brooklyn Navy Yard, 1968, The Long Range Forecasting of Telephone Demand, 1960, Industrial Activity in the Inner City: A Case Study of the South Bronx, 1981, The Contributions of John Maynard Keynes to Foreign Trade Theory and Policy, 1987. Trustee Fordham Rd. Devel. Corp., 1969—85, St. Joseph's Coll., Bklyn., 1974—80, Cathedral Coll., Douglaston, NY, 1969—85, Bronx Inter-Neighborhood Housing Corp., 1975—88, AAPC; mem. ednl. policies com. bd. trustees L.I. U., Greenvale, NY, 1977—85. With U.S. Army, 1943—46, ETO. Mem. Am. Econ. Assn., Phi Delta Kappa. Home: 120 Archer Ave Apt 2C Mount Vernon NY 10550-1423

CAMMERMEYER, MARGARETHE, retired medical/surgical nurse; b. Oslo, Mar. 24, 1942; arrived in U.S., 1951; d. Jan and Margrethe (Grimsgaard) Cammermeyer; m. Harvey H. Hawken, Aug. 1965 (div. 1980); children: Matthew Hawken, David Hawken, Andrew Hawken, Thomas Hawken; life ptnr. Diane Divelbess. BS, U. Md., 1963; MA, U. Wash., 1976, PhD, 1991. RN Wash. Enlisted U.S. Army, 1961, advanced through grades to capt., 1965, resigned, 1968; staff nurse VA Hosp., Seattle, 1970-73, clin. nurse specialist in neurology, epilepsy, 1976-81; clin. nurse specialist in neuro-oncology VA Med. Ctr., San Francisco, 1981-86, clin. nurse specialist in neuroscis., nurse rschr. Tacoma, 1986-96; ret., 1996. Asst. chief nurse, supr. Army Res. Hosp., Oakland, Calif., 1985—88. Co-author: Neurological Assessment for Nursing Practice, 1984 (named Book of Yr. ANA), Serving in Silence, 1994; co-editor, contbg. author: Core Curriculum for Neuroscience Nursing, 1990, 1993; contbr. articles to profl. jours.; host radio-Internet talk show, 1999—2001. Hon. bd. Ctr. Study of Sexual Minorities in Mil., Svc. Mem.'s Legal Def. Network. Capt. to col. USAR, 1972—88, col. Wash. N.G. U.S. Army, 1988—97. Decorated Bronze Star; named Woman of the Yr., Woman's Army Corps Vets. Assn., 1984, Nurse of the Yr., VA, 1985; recipient Presdl. cert. for Outstanding Cmty. Achievement Vietnam Era Vets., 1979, Woman of Power award, NOW, 1993, 1998, Human Rights award, ANA, 1994, Disting. Alumna award, U. Wash. Nursing Assn., 1995. Mem.: Am. Vets. for Equal Rights. Home and Office: 4632 S Tompkins Rd Langley WA 98260-9695 E-mail: grethe@cammermeyer.com.

CAMMISA, REBECCA, filmmaker, photographer; b. Sleepy Hollow, N.Y. d. Sebastine and Elvira Cammisa. BFA in Photography, Pratt Inst., 1988; postgrad., Neighborhood Playhouse Sch. Theatre, 1989—90. Freelance documentary photographer, 1991—98; dir., prodr., camerawoman documentary films, 1998—. Dir., prodr., camerawoman : (documentaries) Sister Helen, 2003; Exhibited in group shows at UN Gallery, N.Y., 1994, exhibitions include Barrett House Gallery, Poughkeepsie, N.Y., 1995, Ceres Gallery, N.Y., 1996, one-woman shows include Barrett House Gallery, Poughkeepsie, 1996, The Photography Gallery, U. Notre Dame, Ind., 1996, exhibitions include Longwood Arts Gallery, 1997. Named Future Star, Emerging Leica Photographers, LeicaView Mag.; recipient Charles A. Dana Photography award, 1986, Documentary Directing award, Sundance Film Festival, 2002, Golden Hugo award for best documentary film, Chgo. Internat. Film Festival, 2002, Jury prize for best documentary film, Newport Film Festival, 2002, Best Documentary Film award, Westchester Film Festival, 2002, Nashville Film Festival, 2002; Artists' grant, Rauschenberg/Change Inc., 1996, Media grant, N.Y. State Coun. on the Arts, 2001, Photography fellow, N.Y. Found. for the Arts, 1998, Women Dirs. Workshop fellow, Am. Film Inst., 2003. Mem.: Acad. TV Arts and Scis. Home: Apt 2C 294 Riverside Dr New York NY 10025-5216

CAMNER, HOWARD, author, poet; b. Miami, Fla., Jan. 14, 1957; s. Edward I. and Ida (Puldy) C.; m. Susan Clara Camner, July 29, 2000; 2 children. BA in English, Fla. Internat. U., 1982; LittD (hon.), London Sch. Applied Rsch., 1995. Cert. English tchr., Fla. Editor Southwind Mag., Miami, Fla., 1976-78; performance poet Writers' Exch., N.Y.C., 1979-81; freelance writer various publications, Miami, 1982-84; screenwriter Harris Prodns., L.A., 1985-89; TV prodr., host Century Cable, L.A., 1986-88; writing instr. Dade County Schs., Miami, 1990—. Author: (poems) Notes from the Eye of a Hurricane, 1979, Transitions, 1980, Scattered Shadows, 1980, Road Note Elegy, 1980, A Work in Progress, 1981, Poetry from Hell to Breakfast, 1981, Midnight at the Laundromat, 1983, Hard Times on Easy Street, 1987, Madman in the Alley, 1989, Stray Dog Wail, 1991, Banned in Babylon, 1993, Jammed Zipper, 1994, Bed of Nails, 1995, Brutal Delicacies, 1996, Hiss, 2000; contbg. author Bristol Banner Books Anthology Series; contbr. to anthology: Florida in Poetry, 1995, also over 100 lit. collections. Mem. Nat. Writers Assn., Acad. of Am. Poets, Poets and Writers, Inc., Poetry Soc. of Am., So. Fla. Poetry Inst., Authors Guild. Home: 10440 SW 76th St Miami FL 33173-2903 E-mail: hcamner@aol.com.

CAMOUGIS, GEORGE, health, safety and environmental consultant; b. Concord, Mass., May 10, 1930; s. Charles George and Angeliki (Georgekopoulou) C.; m. Irene Andreson, Nov. 18, 1961; children: Caroline A., Elizabeth M., Sarah A. BS magna cum laude, Tufts U., 1952; MA, Harvard U., 1957, PhD, 1958. Asst. prof. physiology Clark U., 1958-62, assoc. prof., 1962-64, affiliate prof., 1964-79; sr. neurophysiologist Astra Pharm. Products, Inc., Worcester, Mass., 1964-66, head sect. neuropharmacology, 1966-68; pres., rsch. dir., dir. New Eng. Rsch., Inc., Worcester, 1968-88; sr. cons. New Eng. Indsl. Waste, Inc., 1988-89; v.p., compliance officer Am. Reclamation Corp., 1989-96. Cons. Bd. Radioactive Wast Mgmt. NAS, 1987-92, numerous state and fed. agys. including Army C.E., Fed. Hwy. Adminstrn., U.S. Dept. Interior, EPA; cons. Mass. Dept. Mental Health, 1997—; affiliate prof. Worcester Poly. Inst., 1970-82; adj. prof. toxicology Tufts U. Sch. Vet. Medicine, 1981-84; panelist NSF; mem. corp. Bermuda Biol. Sta. for Rsch., 1968-85; lectr. in field, U.S., Can.; mem. Worcester Sci. Ctr. Planning Com., 1963. Author: Nerves, Muscles and Electricity, 1970, Environmental Biology for Engineers, 1981; contbr.

numerous articles to profl. jours., 1959—; patentee drug; cons. editor Acad. Press, Inc., 1978; mem. editl. adv. bd. Hazardous Waste Mgmt., 1983-90. Bd. dirs. Worcester Children's Friend Soc., 1968-92, v.p. 1978-84, pres. 1984-87. With USNR, 1952-54, Korea. Virginia B. Gibbs scholar, 1954-55; E.L. Mark fellow, 1956, USPHS fellow, 1957-58; NIH grantee, 1962-64, Office Naval Rsch. grantee, 1963-64; recipient Sci. Achievement award Worcester Engring. Soc., 1985. Mem. AAAS, Biophys. Soc., Am. Physiol. Soc., N.Y. Acad. Scis., ASTM, Soc. Environ. Toxicology and Chemistry, Harvard Club (Boston), Phi Beta Kappa, Sigma Xi. Republican. Greek Orthodox. Home and Office: 7 Wheeler Ave Worcester MA 01609-1707

CAMP, ALETHEA TAYLOR, executive and organizational design consultant; b. Wingo, Ky., Nov. 12, 1938; d. Wayne Thomas and Ethel Virginia (Austin) Taylor; children: Donna Paul, Sean Richard. BA, Murray State U., 1961; MA, So. Ill. U., 1975. Tchr. McLean and Hopkins (Ky.) County Schs., 1961-64; instr. homebound Harrisburg (Ill.) Community Sch. Dist., 1971-73; counselor evaluation Coleman Rehab. Ctr., Shawneetown, Ill., 1974-75; counselor corrections and parole Dept. Corrections, State Ill., Springfield, 1975-77, supr. casework, 1977, supr. parole, 1977-80, asst. warden programs Hillsboro, 1980-84, warden, 1984-91; correctional program specialist Nat. Inst. Corrections, Washington, 1991-95; exec. and orgnl. cons. Camp-Blair Consulting, Inc., 1995—2002, CAUCAsoft, Inc., 2003—. Mem.: NAFE, Assn. Women Execs. in Corrections (exec. dir. 1998—2001), Am. Correctional Assn. Avocations: gardening, sailing, traveling, extensive walking. E-mail: ataylorcamp@compuserve.com.

CAMP, CLIFTON DURRETT, JR., rancher, retired publishing executive; b. Trenton, Ky., Aug. 2, 1927; s. Clifton Durrett and Virginia (McElwain) C.; m. Mary Jane Peters, June 9, 1950; children: Daniel Durrett, Thomas Clifton, Pamela Jane, Emily Ann. BS, U. Ky., 1950. Sr. acct. Sheldon, Curry and Masterson, St. Petersburg, Fla., 1950-54; asst. contr. Times Pub. Co., St. Petersburg, 1954-57, contr., 1957-71, treas., 1960-73, v.p. adminstrn., 1967-73, sec., 1969-85, bus. mgr., 1974-82, sr. v.p., 1982-88, also bd. dirs.; owner, pub. Sumter County Times, Bushnell, Fla., 1973-76, Wildwood Herald Express, Bushnell, 1973-76; owner Oakwood Ranch, Bushnell, 1981-88. Bd. dir. Poynter Inst. for Media Studies, St. Petersburg; sec. Mod. Graphic Arts, St. Petersburg, 1976-87, also bd. dirs.; pres. Fla. Trend, Inc., St. Petersburg, 1984-87, bd. dirs. Fla. Press Ctr., Tallahassee, 1980-87, pres., 1984; bd. dirs. Congl. Quar., Inc., Washington, 1986-88; bd. dir. Poynter Libr. U. South Fla. Treas. United Way, St. Petersburg, 1965-68; bd. dirs. Salvation Army Adv. Bd., 1970-78, Bayfront Med. Ctr., 1981-87, St. James United Meth. Ch., Tampa, 1995—. With USN, 1945-46. Mem. Fla. Press Assn. (bd. dirs. 1982-87), Internat. Newspaper Fin. Execs. (bd. dirs. 1964-70), Hunters Green Country Club (Tampa).

CAMP, DAVE, congressman; b. Midland, Mich., July 9, 1953; m. Nancy Keil, Sept. 10, 1994; children: Andrew David, Lauren. BA, Albion (Mich.) Coll., 1975; JD, U. San Diego, 1978. Bar: Mich., Calif., D.C., U.S. Supreme Ct., U.S. Dist. Ct. (ea. dist.) Mich., U.S. Dist. Ct. (so. dist.) Calif. With Riecker, Van Dam, Looby & Barker, 1978-90; spl. asst. atty. gen., 1980-84; adminstrv. asst. to Congressman Bill Schuette, 1985-87; state rep. 102nd Dist. Mich., 1989-91; mem. U.S. Congress from 10th (now 4th) Mich. dist., 1991—; mem. ways and means com., asst. minority whip; mem. Ho. Select Com. on Homeland Security. Chmn. Spkrs. Correction Day Com. Mem. ABA, Midland County Bar Assn. Republican. Office: US Ho of Reps 137 Cannon Bldg Washington DC 20515-2204*

CAMP, DELPHA JEANNE, counselor; b. Yakima, Wash., Apr. 20, 1937; d. George Emerson and Emilie Loraine (Rivard) Stevens; m. George Ernest Mills, Aug. 13, 1960 (dec. 1975); children: Adriene Phillips, Stacey Harcus, Ryan, Tiffany; m. James Clell Camp, June 24, 1978; children: Catherine Thompson (dec.), Wayne (dec.), Darla Coolman, John, Janna Barnes. BEd, Gonzaga Univ., 1959; MS, Univ. Oreg., 1977. Lic. profl. counselor; cert. in death, dying and bereavement. Tchr. Riverside Sch. Dist., Milan, Wash., 1959-61, Cheney (Wash.) Sch. Dist., 1968-70; asst. prof. Univ. Oreg., Eugene, 1979-92; pvt. practice Eugene, 1992—. Mem. faculty Marylhurst (Oreg.) U., 1992—2002. Mem. Assn. for Death Edn. and Counseling (bd. dirs. 1990-93, co-chair conf. 1994, 2002, 1st v.p. 1998-99, pres. 1999-00, Svc. award 1990), Am. Mental Health Counselors Assn., Oreg. Mental Health Counselors Assn. Avocations: reading, classical music. Home: 440 E 39th Ave Eugene OR 97405-4722 Office: 317 W Broadway Ste 217 Eugene OR 97401-2890 E-mail: deljcamp@aol.com.

CAMP, DONALD EUGENE, experimental photographer, educator; b. Meadville, Pa., July 28, 1940; s. Ira Guy and Martha Gladys (Irving) C.; m. Marie Josephé Dumont, Nov. 26, 1966; children: Stephanie Martha Helené, Dorothea Rae. BFA, Tyler Sch. Art, Phila., 1987; MFA, Tyler Sch. Art, 1989. Staff photographer Phila. Bulletin, 1972-81; asst. prof. Tyler Sch. of Art, Phila., 1989-91, Slippery Rock (Pa.) U., 1992—. Dir. Future Faculty Fellowship program Temple U., Phila., 1990—91; vis. asst. prof. Ursinus Coll., Collegeville, Pa., 2000—, artist in-residence, vis. asst. prof. art, 2002—; mem. bd. overseers Inst. Contemporary Art, U. Pa., 2002—. One person exhbns. include Nat. Mus. The Gambia, 2000, Smithsonian, 2000, Anacostia Mus. and Ctr. for African Am. History and Culture, 2000, Reflections In Black. 1840-Present, 2000; photographs have appeared in many popular magazines including Ebony, News Week, People; represented in numerous pub. collections including ARCO collection, Phila. Mus. Art, and Schaumberg Ctr. for Black Culture, N.Y.C., Pa. Conv. Ctr., U. Mich. Mus. of Art; appeared in Face to Face Exhbn. Nat. Jewish Am. Mus. in Phila., U. Mich. Mus. Art, 1998, Inst. Contemporary Art, U. Pa., 1999. Mem. Spiritual Assembly of Bahais of Phila., 1981—, Interfaith Support Group, Phila., 1989-92. Recipient Future Faculty fellowship Temple U., Phila., 1988, Eugene Feldman award The Print Club, 1983; named Pa. Visual Artist fellow, 1990, Smithsonian Am. Artist Oral History, 1991, PEW Charitable Trust resident artist to the Am. Acad. in Rome, 1994; John Simon Guggenheim Found. fellow, 1995-96, fellow NEA, Pew Charitable Trust fellow, Pa. Coun. for the Arts fellow. Mem. Soc. Photographic Educators (bd. dirs. 1990-94, chmn., founder multicultural caucus, 1990-93), Recherche. Avocations: baha'i promotion, magic. Home: 4511 Spruce St Philadelphia PA 19139-4526 E-mail: doncamp@cartel.net.

CAMP, HAZEL LEE BURT, artist; b. Gainesville, Ga., Nov. 28, 1922; d. William Ernest and Annie Mae (Ramsey) Burt; m. William Oliver Camp, Jan. 24, 1942; children: William Oliver, David Byron. Student, Md. Inst. Art, 1957-58, 62-63. Exhibitions include Muscarelle Mus. of Art Coll. of William and Mary, Williamsburg, Va., 1998—99, Susquehanna U. Lore A. Degenstein Gallery, Pa., 1994, Nat. League of Am. Pen Women Cork Gallery, Lincoln Ctr., N.Y.C., 1994, Suffolk Art League, 1994, 1996—2001, Town Hall Gallery, Epe, The Netherlands, 1999, Piedmont Art Assn, Martinsville, Va., 2000, one-woman shows include Ga. Mus. Art, Rockville Art Mus., Coll. Notre Dame (Balt.), U. Md., Balt. Vertical Gallery, Cleveland Meml. Gallery (Balt.), Unicorn Gallery, 1982, Hampton Ctr. for Arts and Humanities (Va.), 1985, Bendann Art Gallery, Balt., 1980, Cultural Art Ctr. On the Hill Gallery, Yorktown, Va., 1995, Cultural Art Ctr. on the Hill Gallery, Yorktown, Va., 2000—03, others; juried shows include Peale Mus., Balt., Wilmington (Del.) Fine Arts Ctr., Smithsonian Inst., City Hall Gallery, Balt., 1982, Balt. Watercolor Soc., 1983, 1994—95, Arts Club, Washington, 1987—96, Strathmore Hall Arts Ctr., Maryland, 1997—2002, Fells Point Gallery, Balt., 2000, 2002, Hampton Bay Days Raddison Hotel Gallery, 1988, Twentieth Century Gallery, Williamsburg, Va., 1989—2003, D'Art Ctr., Norfolk, Va., 1989, Virginia Beach Ctr. for Arts, 1990, Verona, 1991, William King Regional Arts Ctr. ., Abingdon, Va., 1992, 2002, Lore A. Degenstein Gallery, Pa. Watercolor Soc., 1994, Longwood Ctr. Visual Arts, Farmville, Va., 1995, Fine Arts Ctr., Lynchburg, Va., 1996, Va. Watercolor Soc., Martinsville, Va., 2000, Yorktown Cultural Arts Ctr., 1991—2003, Furman U., 1992, Goucher Coll., Hermitage Found. Mus., Norfolk, 1994, 1998, 2000, Francis Land House Tidewater Artists Assn., Va. Beach, 1994, Salmagundi Club, N.Y.C., 1995, The Nat. League of Am. Pen Women; Miniature Art Soc. Fla., 1999, 2001, St. Petersburg Mus. Fine Arts, 2000, Dunedin Fine Arts Ctr., 2002, Gulf Coast Mus. Art, Fla., 2003, exhibitions include Seaside Art Gallery, Nags Head, NC, 2001, 2002, Miniature Painters, Sculptors and Gravers Soc. Washington, 1987—2002. Recipient 3d prize Nat. Biennial Exhibit, Tulsa, 1966, 1st prize Md. Chpt. Artists' Equity, 1967, St. Mary's County Art Assn., 1964, 67, 1st prize still life Cape May, N.J., 1969, Catonsville (Md.) C.C., 1969, Nat. League Am. Pen Women Exhibit at St. John's Coll., 1969, Best in Show York (Pa.) Art Assn. Gallery, 1972, 2nd award Md. Inst. Alumni Founding Chpt., Balt., 1976, Best in Show Three Arts Club, Balt., 1978, hon. mention Rehoboth Art League, Del., 1983, 93, Adelia E. Chiswell 2nd award, 1996, purchase award Old Point Nat. Bank, Hampton, Va., 1985, merit award Hampton (Va.) City Hall, 1986, Juror's Choice award Twentieth Century Gallery, Williamsburg, Va., 1987, Award of Excellence Md. State Biennial Eliminations of Nat. League Am. Pen Women at Essex C.C., 1989, Montgomery Coll., Rockville, Md., 1987, hon. mention Nat. Miniature Show, Jackson, Tenn., 1991, Suffolk Art League, 1992, award Eagleton's Inc., 1996, 1st prize Virginia Heritage Exhibit, Yorktown Arts Found., 1998, hon. mention award Tidewater Art Assn., Norfolk, 1999, The Willows award Suffolk Art League Juried Exhibit, 1999. Mem. Nat. League Am. Pen Women (pres. Carroll bd. 1968-70, editor The Quill 1975-76, Carroll br. 1982-83, rec. sec. nat. exec. bd. 1979-80, nat. nominating com. 1982, Md. art chmn. 1982, illustrator Nat. Roster 1990 and The Pen Woman mag. 1995), Rehoboth Art League (Adelia E. Chiswell 2d award 1996), Del. Hampton Arts League, Va. Watercolor Soc. (signature artist mem.), Balt. Watercolor Soc. (signature artist life mem., hon. mention 1982, sec. 1978-80), Peninsula Fine Arts Ctr., 20th Century Gallery (Williamsburg), Yorktown Cultural Arts Ctr., Tidewater Art Assn., Miniature Painters, Sculptors and Gravers Soc. of Washington, Suffolk Art League, Hampton (Va.) Arts League, Miniature Art Soc. Fla., Pa. Watercolor Soc. Methodist. Home: 2 Bayberry Dr Newport News VA 23601-1006 *I might say that persistance, coupled with any talent that I have, has been the greatest factor in achieving some of the goals that I set for myself in the fine arts field.*

CAMP, J. HOLDEN, history educator; b. Holyoke, Mass., Jan. 26, 1942; s. J. Holden and Mary Catherine Camp; m. Henriette E.A.H. Camp, Oct. 20, 1972; children: Marisha, J.H. III. BA in History, Am. Internat. Coll., 1964, MA in History, 1966; MBA, U. Hartford, 1976. Assoc. prof. history U. Hartford, Conn., 1967—, asst. dean, 1982-90, chmn. humanities dept. Hillyer Coll., 1992—. Organist Grace Ch., Holyoke, Mass., 1962-72; pres. Salmon Brook Hist. Soc., 1995—; sec. ZBA, Granby, Conn., 1990-2002, chmn., 2002—. Mem. New Eng. Hist. Assn. Republican. Congregationalist. Avocations: hiking, music, reading, gardening, research. Office: U Hartford 200 Bloomfield Ave West Hartford CT 06117-1545

CAMP, JEFFERY MARK, Web specialist, military officer; b. Glens Falls, N.Y., Dec. 14, 1964; s. Leroy Phillip and Karen Gray Camp; m. Andrea Marie Gallo, Sept. 11, 1990. AS, City Colls. Chgo., 1989; BS, Siena Coll., 1993; postgrad., DePaul U., 1999—. IBM cert. AS/400 solutions sales; IBM cert. RS/6000 solutions sales; IBM cert. AS/400 solutions design; IBM cert. RS/6000 SP sales. Sr. AS/400 sales specialist IBM Corp., Atlanta, 1995-2000, sr. Web server specialist Chgo., 2000—. Capt. U.S. Army, 1983-2001. Republican. Roman Catholic. Avocations: marathons, travel. Home: 1415 W Cuyler Ave Chicago IL 60613 Office: IBM Corp Ste 300 2000 Spring Rd Oak Brook IL 60523-1848 Home Fax: 773-529-3987. E-mail: jeffcamp@us.ibm.com., jcamp@flashcom.net.

CAMP, JOHN CLAYTON, lawyer; b. Arab, Ala., Sept. 23, 1923; s. Roy Hubert and Alice Mellie (Cox) C.; m. Frances Elizabeth Spencer, Nov. 3, 1944; children: John, Elizabeth Camp Bower, Martha Camp Cox, Charles. Student, Birmingham-So. Coll., 1940-42, U. Ala., 1943, Auburn U., 1944; JD, La. State U., 1948. Bar: La. 1948, U.S. Supreme Ct. 1958, D.C. 1974. Assoc. Thompson, Lawes and Cavanaugh, Lake Charles, La., 1948-55; ptnr. Camp, Carmouche, Barsh, Gray, Hoffman & Gill, Lake Charles, 1955-84, Camp, Barsh & Tate, Washington, 1984-94, Patton Boggs LLP, Washington, 1994—. Active Internat. Top Mgmt. Roundtable Confs., London, Milan, Amsterdam, Brussels, Frankfurt, Rome, Dusseldorf, Ditchley Park, Stockholm and Toronto, 1982-87. Mem. Presdl. Trade Commn. to People's Republic of China, 1979; trustee Athens (Greece) Coll., 1985-91; mem. exec. com., vice chmn. Meridian House Internat., 1986-96; past mem. med. ctr. adv. coun. George Washington U. With USAF, 1943-46; bd. advs. Internat. Mgmt. and Devel. Inst., Fowler McCracker Commn. (chmn. policy planning group, 1982-87); pres., mem. exec. com. Metro USO, 1989-92; bd. exec. com. Wolf Trap Found., 1984-91. Mem.: ABA, Southwestern La. Bar Assn., La. State Bar Assn., D.C. Bar Assn., Congl. Country Club. Democrat. Presbyterian. Avocations: golf, photography, reading. Office: Patton Boggs LLP 2550 M St NW Ste 800 Washington DC 20037-1301 Home: Apt CT 411 3122 Gracefield Rd Silver Spring MD 20904-5804

CAMP, JOSEPH SHELTON, JR., film producer, director, writer; b. St. Louis, Apr. 20, 1939; s. Joseph Shelton and Ruth Wilhelmena (McLaulin) C.; m. Andrea Carolyn Hopkins, Aug. 7, 1960; children: Joseph Shelton III, Brandon Andrew. BBA, U. Miss., 1961. Jr. account exec. McCann-Erickson Advt., Houston, 1961-62; owner Joe Camp Real Estate, Houston, 1962-64; account exec. Norsworthy-Mercer, Dallas, 1964-69; dir. TV commls. Jamieson Film Co., Dallas, 1969-71; founder, pres., writer, producer, dir. feature films Mulberry Square Prodns., Inc., Dallas, 1971-90, Gulfport, Miss., 1991-94, Chapel Hill, N.C., 1994—. Producer, dir., writer films including Benji, 1974, Hawmps, 1976, For the Love of Benji, 1977, The Double McGuffin, 1979, Oh Heavenly Dog, 1980, Benji The Hunted, 1987; TV spls. The Phenomenon of Benji, 1978, Benji's Very Own Christmas Story, 1978, Benji at Work, 1980, Benji (Takes a Dive) at Marineland, 1981; TV series Benji, Zax and the Alien Prince, 1983; author: Underdog, 1993. Bd. trustees Piney Woods Country Life Sch., Warren Wilson Coll.; adv. bd. N.C. Sch. of Arts, Sch. of Film Making. Mem. Dir.'s Guild Am., Writer's Guild Am. Home: 31336 Cove Lantern Dana Point CA 92629 *I hope that I have been able to help people in a troubled time to lose themselves for a moment in a piece of entertainment and, when it's over, to feel better for having done so, to have a new respect for persistence in achieving objectives and a new feeling of hope and happiness in their lives. I hope to inspire others to follow their dreams with passion and persistence, to reach further than they might have otherwise.*

CAMP, KIMBERLY N. museum administrator, artist; b. Camden, N.J., Sept. 11, 1956; d. Hubert E. and Marie (Dimery) C.; m. Seydou Coulibaly, Apr. 1997 (div.). BA, U. Pitts., 1978; MS, Drexel U., 1986. Dir. artistic design project City Camden, 1984-86; program dir. Pa. Coun. on Arts, Harrisburg, 1986-89; dir. exptl. gallery Smithsonian Instn., Washington, 1989-94; pres. Mus. African Am. History, Detroit, 1994-98; exec. dir., CEO Barnes Found., Merion, Pa., 1998—. Evaluator Am. Assn. Mus., Washington, 1994—; panel chair Nat. Endowment for Arts, Washington, 1991-92; vice chair, bd. dirs. Assn. Am. Cultures, Washington, 1987-89. One-woman shows include Clifton Art Ctr., N.J., Glouchester County Coll., Deptford Township, N.J., Passaic Count C.C., Paterson, N.J., Diggs Gallery, Winston-Salem, N.C., Galerie Francois, Washington, Banneker Douglass Mus., Annapolis, Md., 3d Bienniel Nat. Black Arts Festival, Atlanta, Manchester Craftsmen's Guilde, Pitts., Caribbean Cultural Ctr., N.Y.C., Jr. Black Acad. Arts and Letters, Dallas, Walt Whitman Ctr. Arts and Humanities, Camden, Longwood Gardens, Kennett Square, Pa., Art Mus. Western Va., Raonoke, Harrison Mus. African Am. Culture, Roanoke, 1994; represented in permanent collections J.B Speed Art Mus., Manchester Craftsmen's Guild, Reader's Digest, Camden Hist. Soc.; mng. editor Nat. Conf. Artists Phila. Chpt. newsletter, 1980-84. Bd. dirs. Bus. Vols. for Arts, 1994-97. Recipient Nat. Svc. award Nat. Conf. Artists, 1984, Arts Achievement award City of Camden, 1984, Cmty. Svc. award Assn/ Negro Bus. and Profl. Women, 1985, Builders of Cmty. award Camden County Cultural and Heritage Commn., 1986, Purchase award J.B. Speed Art Mus., 1988, Spirit of Detroit award Detroit City Coun., 1994; Arts Internat. grantee Ctr. Internat. Exch. Scholars, 1994, Roger L. Stevens Nat. Arts award Carnegie Mellon U. H. John Heinz Sch. Mgmt., 1999; fellow Kellogg Nat. Leadership Program, 1994-97. Mem. Assn. Am. Cultures (bd. dirs. 1989—), Am. Assn. Museums (bd. dirs. 1995-97), Links, Inc., N.J. Coun. on Arts. Office: The Barnes Found 300 N Latch's Ln Merion Station PA 19066-1729

CAMP, RICHARD J. ecologist, statistician, researcher; b. Anchorage, Dec. 6, 1965; s. Chester V. and Yvonne E. Camp; m. J. Kiko Camp, 2002. BS, U. Minn., 1991; MS, Colo. State U., 1995. Cert. in conservation biology Program in Ecol. Studies, Colo. State U. Rsch. assoc. Colo. State U., Ft. Collins, 1991-97; quality assurance specialist New Belgium Brewing Co., Inc., Ft. Collins, 1997-98; devel. coord. Obsessive-Compulsive Found., Inc., New Haven, 1998-99; computer/biol. technician Colo. Natural Heritage Program, Ft. Collins, 1999; rsch. project coord. Rsch. Corp., U. Hawaii, Hawaii National Park, 1999—. Mem. ornithol. adv. com. Hawaii Heritage Program, 2000-2002; adv. mem. Hawaii Forest Bird Recovery Team, U.S. Fish and Wildlife Svc., 1999-2002; grad. student rep. faculty coun. internat. program Colo. State U., Ft. Collins, 1992-93. Contbr. articles to sci. jours. Named Regional Rep. Hugh O'Brian Youth Leadership, 1982, Outstanding Sophomore, 1982, Mem. of Yr., Future Farmers of Am., 1984; student fellow Concordia Coll., 1984. Mem. Am. Ornithologists' Union, Am. Soc. Naturalists, Soc. for Conservation Biology (sci. presentation selector ann. meeting 1995, 2001), Pacific Conservation Biology, Western N.Am. Naturalist, Hawaii Audubon Soc., Xeries Soc., Xi Sigma Pi. Avocations: long-distance running, cooking, longboard surfing, travel. Home: PO Box 281 Volcano HI 96785 Office: Pacific Island Ecosystem Rsch Ctr Bldg 344 PO Box 44 Hawaii National Park HI 96718 E-mail: rick_camp@usgs.gov.

CAMP, THOMAS EDWARD, retired librarian; b. July 12, 1929; s. Charles Walter and Annie Laura (Brazzel) C.; m. Elizabeth Anne Sowar, Sept. 4, 1952; children: Anne Winifred, Thomas David. BA, Centenary Coll., Shreveport, 1950; MLS, La. State U., 1953. Binding asst. La. State U. Library, Baton Rouge, 1951-53; circulation librarian Perkins Sch. Theology Bridwell Libr., So. Meth. U., Dallas, 1955-57; librarian Sch. Theology, U. of South, Sewanee, Tenn., 1957-93. Assoc. univ. librarian, 1976-93, acting univ. librarian, 1981-82. C-author: Using Theological Libraries and Books, 1963; contbr. articles to profl. jours. Pres. Franklin County Assn. for Retarded, 1971-72. Served with AUS, 1953-55. Mem. ALA, Am. Theol. Library Assn. (exec. sec. 1965-67), Tenn. Library Assn. Democrat. Episcopalian. Home: 209 Carruthers Rd PO Box 820 Sewanee TN 37375-0820 E-mail: ecamp@sewanee.edu.

CAMPAGNA, DIANNA GWIN, real estate broker; b. Pueblo, Colo., Mar. 9, 1948; d. Everett Paul Gwin and Ava Mariea (Calvert) Johnson; m. Michael E. Campagna. Staff asst. The White House, Washington, 1971-77, exec. asst. to counsel, 1981-89; sales agt. Rand Real Estate, Alexandria, Va., 1977-79, Pagett Real Estate, Alexandria, 1979-81; assoc. broker WJD & Assocs., Alexandria, 1985-93; assoc. broker, asst. mgr. adminstrn. Long & Foster Realtors, 1993-96; prin. broker, v.p. Century 21 Campaigne, 1996-98; mng. broker Century 21 New Millennium, 1998-99; planner Mgmt. Bus. Planning Sys., Alexandria, 1999—2001; prin. dir., exec. secretariat Dept. HUD, Washington, 2001—03; mgr. ops. Nat. Commn. on Terrorist Attacks Upon the U.S., 2003—. Exec. aide to chmn. Edward Lowe Industries, Inc., 1990—91. Del. Va. Rep. Conv., 1981, 1982, 1984. Roman Catholic. Home: 311 Park Rd Alexandria VA 22301-2737

CAMPAGNA, RICHARD SAMUEL, investment management executive; b. Oct. 22, 1967; BS, Duke U., 1989; MBA, Harvard Bus. Sch., 1994. Analyst Morgan Stanley, N.Y.C., London, Tokyo, 1989-92; prin. McKinley Capital, N.Y.C., 1994-96; sr. analyst Manning & Napier, Rochester, NY, 1996—2001; mng. dir. Shaker Investments, Cleve., 2001—.

CAMPAGNA, TIMOTHY NICHOLAS, institute executive; b. Chgo., June 8, 1957; s. Nicholas and Dorothy (Hoffmeister) C.; m. Diana Lynn Czarny, Aug. 1, 1981; children: Maria, Joseph. BA, Lewis U., Romeoville, Ill., 1980, MA, 1985. Basketball referee NCAA and Ill. High Sch. Assn., 1976-95; asst. dir. housing Lewis U., 1978-80; tchr. Fairmont Jr. High Sch., Lockport, Ill., 1979-80; tchr., therapist Guardian Angel Home, Joliet, Ill., 1980-82; assoc. dean students DeVry Inst. Tech., Lombard, Ill., 1982-84, dean students, 1984-87, dean adminstrv. svcs. Irving, Tex., 1987-93, dean evening coll., dir. Ctr. Bus. and Industry Ednl. Svcs., 1993-95, dean enrollment mgmt. and mktg., 1994-95; v.p. Am. Inst. Commerce, Davenport, Iowa, 1995-97; pres. Westwood Coll. Tech., 1997-2000, Denver Tech. Coll., 2000-01, DeVry U., 2001—. Mem. sch. bd. Holy Family Nazareth; mem. nominating bd. Outstanding Men and women of Am. Coach Nativity of Our Lord Basketball Team, Hyland Hills Youth Hockey Team, St. Louis 2001 Planning Com.; vol. YMCA. Named Tchr. of Yr., Fairmont Jr. High Sch., 1980, Adminstr. of Yr., DeVry Inst. Tech., 1984. Mem. Nat. Assn. Student Pers. Adminstrs., Am. Assn. Coll. Registrars and Admissions Officers, Nat. Assn. Fgn. Student Advisors, Nat. Assn. Coll. and Univ. Bus. Officers, Denver C. of C., CEO Network. Roman Catholic. Avocations: golf, travel. Office: DeVry Univ 1870 W 122d Ave Westminster CO 80234 E-mail: tcamp@rmi.net., tcampagna@den.devry.edu.

CAMPAGNOLO, ANN-CASEY, retail executive; b. Newport, R.I., July 17, 1972; d. Eugene Louis and Kathleen Ellen (Laughlin) C. BS in Agr. and Resource Econs., U. Md., 1995. Asst. buyer petites Bloomingdale's, N.Y.C., 1995-96; asst. buyer Salon Z Saks Fifth Ave., N.Y.C., 1996-97, assoc. buyer sportswear, 1997-98, store planner casual, 1998-99, corp. planner ready-to-wear divsn., 1999-2001, dir. corp. merchandise planning, 2001—02, sr. dir. planning and allocation mens and cosmetics, 2002—03, sr. dir. planning and allocation designer, childrens and home, 2003—. Bd. dirs., treas. Saks Fifth Ave. Employee Fed. Credit Union, 2002—. Mem. Jr. League N.Y. Mem.: Order of Omega (Outstanding Chpt. Pres. award 1994), Gamma Phi Beta (Province collegiate dir. 1996—2001, sec. alumnae N.Y.C. chpt. 1995—96, pres. Beta Beta chpt. 1993—94). Republican. Roman Catholic. Avocations: cooking, reading, traveling. Office: Saks Fifth Ave 12 E 49th St 9th Fl New York NY 10017-1088

CAMPAIGNE, LINDA MARY, special education educator; b. Niagara Falls, N.Y., Dec. 17, 1948; d. Howard Albert and Mary Ellen (Eckel) C. BA, Tarkio Coll., 1973. Tchr. spl. edn. Brownsville (Tex.) Ind. Sch. Dist., 1980-81, 1985-89; program asst. Retama Manor, Brownsville; case mgr. Lancaster (Tex.) Residential Ctr., 1989-90; tchr. spl. edn. Wilmer-Hutchins Ind. Sch. Dist., Dallas, 1990-95. Author of poems. Recipient Assn. Retarded Citizens Vol. award, 1979, Inst. Achievement Human Potential citation, 1974. Mem. Coun. Exceptional Children, Order Ea. Star. Avocations: reading, swimming, bowling, crafts, needlework. Home: 10317 Andover Dr Dallas TX 75228-2701 E-mail: lcampaigne@hotmail.com.

CAMPANA, PHILLIP JOSEPH, German language educator; b. Jersey City, Apr. 10, 1941; s. Ralph Joseph and Alberta Alphonsine (Lepis) C.; m. Paulette Monique Beauregard, Apr. 20, 1968 (div. Apr. 19, 1978); children: Lisa Marie, Michael Phillip. BA in German magna cum laude, St. Peters Coll., Jersey City, 1962; postgrad. (Fulbright scholar), U. Saarbrücken, Germany, 1962-63; PhD, Brown U., 1970. Instr. German St. Peter's Coll., Jersey City, summer 1964; grad. asst. in German Brown U., Providence, 1965-67; assoc. prof. German Tenn. Tech. U., Cookeville, 1970-74, prof. German, 1974—, chmn. dept. fgn. langs., 1970—2003, founder and 1st dir. English Lang. Inst., 1977, dir. Interactive Videodisc Project, 1984-94. State chmn. So. Conf. on Lang. Tchg., 1981-85; reviewer grant proposals (EESA, Title II) Tex. Coord. Bd. for Higher Edn., 1986, U.S. Dept. Edn., 1987; evaluator Nat. Tchrs. Exam in German for Ednl. testing Svc., 1990; lectr., presenter in field. Assoc. editor Schatzkammer, 1980-89, cons. editor, 1990-93, editl. bd., 1993—; evaluator: the materials Ctr. of Am. Assn. Tchrs. German, 1980-81, Modern Lang. Jour., Fgn. Lang. Annals, Seminar; mem. editl. bd. Unterrichtspraxis, 2000—; book rev. editor Unterrichtspraxis, 2002—; contbr. numerous articles and revs. to profl. jours. Mem. faculty adv. group on master plan for higher edn. Tenn. Higher Edn. Comm., 1973, steering com. on tchr. edn., 1983-84; chmn. Tenn. Bd. Regents Task Force on Improvement of Quality in Tchr. Edn., 1982; mem. Com. on Bus. and Fiscal Affairs, Tenn. Bd. Regents, 1975-76. Recipient Outstanding Faculty award in Tchg., Tenn. Tech. U., 1976, Goethe-Inst. award, 1977, 84, 99, Nat. Endowment for the Humanities, 1981, Meritorious Svc. award Nat. Coun. State Suprs. of Fgn. Langs., 1981, Svc. award Rural Educators Alliance for Lang., 1993, Outstanding Faculty award for Profl. Svcs., Tenn. Tech. U., 1995; Fulbright scholar, 1962-63, 80, 88; Woodrow Wilson fellow, 1962-64, NDEA fellow, 1963-66; grantee Tenn. Tech., 1984, 86-87, 87-88, 88-89, Govt. of Germany, 1983, Tenn. Higher Edn. Commn., 1986-87, 88, 89, 97, 98, 99, Tenn. Bd. Regents, 1989, Tenn. Humanities Coun., 1990. Mem. AAUP, MLA, Am. Assn. Tchrs. German (Tenn. chpt. pres. 1975-77, treas. 1980-92, cert. of Merit award 1982), Tenn. Fgn. Lang. Tchg. Assn. (bd. dirs. 1974-77, 80-81, 82-85, 98-2001, pres. 1977-80, mem. com. 1990-96, rep. Ctrl. States Conf. bd. 1990-93, Jacqueline C. Elliott award 1984), Ctrl. States Conf. on Tchg. Fgn. Langs. (chmn. 1984-87, bd. dirs. 1979-80, 81-84, 91-94, adv. coun. 1978—, co-editor annual volume 1995, co-chair Leadership CSC, 1995-96), Am. Coun. on Tchg. Fgn. Langs. (exec. coun. 1985-86, 91-94, chmn. pub. com. 1993-94, Florence Steiner award 1987), Tenn. Fgn. Lang. Inst. (bd. govs. 1986-2001, v.p., sec.-treas.), Tenn. Coun. Internat. Edn. (bd. dirs. 1976-78), Ill. Fgn. Lang. Tchrs. Assn. (mem. adv. bd. 1986-88, nominating com. 1987-88, Land of Lincoln Svc. award 1986, 87), Consortium for German in S.E. (founding mem., treas. 1991-96), Omicron Delta Kappa. Roman Catholic. Home: 1135 Meadow Rd Cookeville TN 38501-2035 Office: Tenn Tech U Dept Fgn Langs PO Box 5061 Cookeville TN 38505-0001 E-mail: pcampana@tntech.edu.

CAMPANELLI, RICHARD M. federal agency administrator; m. Shannon Campanelli; 3 children. BS in Economics, U. Va.; JD, U. Va. Law Sch. Trial atty., Spl. Litigation Section of the Civil Rights Divsn. U.S. Dept. Justice; mem., S. Africa Working Group U.S. Dept. State, sr. spl. asst. to atty. gen., 1987—89; atty. Gammon & Grange, PC, McLean, Va., 1989—; adj. prof. George Mason U.; dir., Office of Civil Rights U.S. Dept. Health and Human Svcs., 2002—. Office: Office for Civil Rights US Dept Health and Human Svcs 200 Independence Ave SW Rm 509F HHH Bldg Washington DC 20201

CAMPANIE, SAMUEL JOHN, lawyer; b. Oneida, N.Y., May 30, 1952; s. Samuel G. Campanie and Kathryn A. McCarthy Warner, stepson George A. Warner; m. Susan Noyes Garner, June 14, 1975; children: Joseph Warner, Abigail Noyes. AB cum laude, Colgate U., 1974; JD, Albany Law Sch., 1978; postgrad., Syracuse U., 1982—. Bar: N.Y. 1979, U.S. Dist. Ct. (no. and we. dists.) N.Y. 1994. Assoc. Kiley, Feldman, Whalen, Devine & Patane, Oneida, 1977-81; mgr. Mid-east and African divs. Oneida (N.Y.) Ltd. Silversmiths, 1981-83, mgr. export div., 1982-85, mgr. export and mil. divs., 1985; ptnr. Kohn, Moseman, Campanie, Oneida and Remsen, 1986-88; county atty. Madison County, N.Y., 1987—; dir. Kiley, Feldmann, Whalen, Devine & Patane P.C., Oneida, 1988-2000; mem., pres. Campanie & Wayland-Smith PLLC, Sherrill, N.Y., 2000—. Dir., counsel, Madison Oneida County Indian Land Claim Litigation Task Force, 1999—; accredited rep. Svc. Core of Retired Execs./Active Core Execs., Utica, N.Y., 1979-90; cons. to various firms, 1985-89; pvt. cons. practice Kenwood Assocs. Internat., Oneida, 1986-89. Mem. City of Oneida Planning Commn., 1979-91, chmn. 1990-91; legislator Madison County Bd. Suprs., Wampsville, N.Y., 1986-87; bd. dirs. Madison County Indsl. Devel. Agy., 1986-90, Oneida-Madison Red Cross, 1979-87, Mansion House Svc. Corp., 1988-98, pres. 1997-98; mem. platform com. N.Y. State Rep. Com., Albany, 1986; mem. exec. com. Madison County Rep. Com., 1979-87; chmn. City of Oneida Rep. Com., 1979-87; mem. N.Y. State Oneida Lake Adv. Com., 1986—, chmn., 1988—. Named one of Outstanding Young Men in Am., 1985. Mem. ABA, N.Y. State Bar Assn., Madison County Bar Assn., N.Y. State County Attys. Assn. (dir. 1988—, pres. 1989-90, treas. 1997—), Oneida Jaycees. Republican. Roman Catholic. Avocations: sailing, biking, skiing, reading, computers. Home: 209 Kenwood Ave Oneida NY 13421-2809 Office: Campanie & Wayland-Smith PLLC PO Box 70 60 E State St Sherrill NY 13461 Fax: (315) 363-1952. E-mail: nybizlawyer@yahoo.com., sjclaw@twcny.rr.com., sjc@mad.co.ny.us.

CAMPANIZZI, JANE, consulting company executive; b. Wheeling, W.Va., Nov. 27, 1947; d. Peter and Jean (Ciesielka) Campanizzi; m. William Harry Mook, Dec. 31, 1978. MA, Ohio State U., 1971, PhD, 1978. Cert. quality analyst. Instr. Barnesville (Ohio) Schs., 1968-70, Columbus (Ohio) Schs., 1971-76; cons. State of Ohio, Columbus, 1978-81; analyst OCLC Inc., Dublin, Ohio, 1981-85; pres. JCM Enterprises, Columbus, 1985—. Bd. dirs. Application Innovations Corp., Columbus, Rapi-Serv Cash Systems, Columbus; trustee Artreach Gallery, Columbus, Small Bus. Council, 1987—. Editor Quali-News newsletter, 1986; contbr. articles to profl. jours. Mem. com. Columbus Area Leadership Program, 1985—, sci./math adv. com. Columbus Schs., 1986; convenor Nat. Issues Forum, Dayton, Ohio, 1986—. Mem. Am. Soc. Quality Control, Quality Assurance Inst., AAAS, Columbus C. of C. (exec. club). Clubs: Faculty Ohio State U., Capital. Roman Catholic. Avocations: astronomy, electronics. Home: 4453 Masters Dr Columbus OH 43220-4284

CAMPAS, ANNA PENELOPE, civil engineer, architect; b. Balt., Nov. 21, 1949; d. William and Katy (Hondros) Campas; children: Thomas William, Scott Stratton. BArch, Rensselaer Polytech. Inst., 1972; BSCE, Union Coll., 1977. Registered profl. engr., architect, N.Y.; accredited profl. leadership in energy and environ. design profl. Staff architect-engr. GE Co., Schenectady, N.Y., 1972-73; architectural designer Fay Evans, P.C., Troy, N.Y., 1974-75, Golub Corp., Schenectady, 1975-77, Einhorn, Yaffee, Prescott, P.C., Albany, N.Y., 1979-80; jr. engr. N.Y. State Office Gen. Svc., Design and Constrn. Group, Albany, 1980-82, asst. bldg. structural engr., 1982-87, sr. bldg. structural engr., 1987—, mem. green bldg. working group for NY State exec. order 111, team leader design & constrn. green bldg. coun. Bd. dirs. Montessori Sch. of Albany, 1990-92. Vol. Susan G. Komen Breast Cancer Race for the Cure. Mem. Bethlehem Music Assn. (membership chmn., treas., co-pres.). Home: 41 Darroch Rd Delmar NY 12054-3916 E-mail: anna.campas@ogs.state.ny.us.

CAMPASINO, ELLEN MARIE, elementary school educator; b. Titusville, Pa., Aug. 30, 1950; d. Frank and Helen (Lowicki) Campasino. BS in Elem. and Early Childhood Edn., Edinboro U., 1972, cert. in elem. and early childhood edn., 1978. 1st grade tchr. St. Titus Sch., Titusville, 1975-76, 4th grade tchr., 1976-77, 3rd grade tchr., 1977—. Coaching tchr. St. Titus Tchr. Induction Program, Titusville, 1989—90, asst. to prin., 1993—; mentor tchr., 2000—01. Mem. ministry tng. program Diocese of Erie; min. hospitality St. Walburga Parish, Roman Cath. Ch., Titusville. Recipient Svc. award, Diocese of Erie, 1988, 1990, 1996, 25 Yrs. of Svc. award, 2000—01. Avocations: reading, doll collecting, embroidery. Office: St Titus Sch 528 W Main St Titusville PA 16354-1598

CAMPBELL, ADDISON JAMES, JR., writer; b. Dilliner, Pa., Dec. 16, 1933; s. Addison James Campbell and Nora Lee (Marshall) Reynolds; m. Fumie Murashige, Oct. 13, 1962; 1 child, Gary Clark Campbell. Pres. Action Bolt Corp., Houston, 1965-72. Author: Nanci's World, Ukelele Lil of Lihue, The Object; co-author: Fumie Murashige Campbell, 1994; contbr. numerous articles and research papers to profl. jours. Sgt. USMC, 1952-55. Recipient recognition award for Adult Correction Officer for Island of Kauai, State of Hawaii, 1987, 88.

CAMPBELL, ALLAN MCCULLOCH, bacteriology educator; b. Berkeley, Calif., Apr. 27, 1929; s. Lindsay and Virginia Margaret (Henning) C.; m. Alice Del Campillo, Sept. 5, 1958; children— Wendy, Joseph. BS in Chemistry, U. Calif. at Berkeley, 1950; MS in Bacteriology, U. Ill., 1951; PhD, 1953; PhD hon. degree, U. Chgo., 1978, U. Rochester, 1981. Instr. bacteriology U. Mich., 1953-57; research asso. Carnegie Inst., Cold Spring Harbor, N.Y., 1957-58; asst. prof. biology U. Rochester, N.Y., 1958-61, assoc. prof., 1961-63, prof., 1963-68; prof. biol. sci. Stanford (Calif.) U., 1968—. Barbara Kimball Browning prof. humanities and scis., 1992—. Author: Episomes, 1969; co-author: General Virology, 1978; editor Gene, 1980-90, mem. editl. bd., 1990—; assoc. editor Virology, 1963-69; assoc. editor Ann. Rev. Genetics, 1969-84, editor, 1984—; spl. editor Evolution, 1985-88; editl. bd. Jour. Bacteriology, 1966-72, Jour. Virology, 1967-75, New Biologist, 1989-92. Served with AUS, 1953-55. Recipient Research Career award USPHS, 1962-68 Mem. Nat. Acad. Scis., Am. Acad. Arts and Scis., Am. Soc. Microbiology, Soc. Am. Naturalists, Genetics Soc. Am., AAAS, Am. Acad. Microbiology. Democrat. Home: 947 Mears Ct Stanford CA 94305-1041 Office: Stanford U Dept Biol Scis Stanford CA 94305 E-mail: AMC@stanford.edu. *I've always thought that each individual has some contribution to human knowledge that he is uniquely suited to make. So I try to be organized and to avoid doing things that I expect will get done, anyway, by others. And, of course, everything worthwhile requires hard work.*

CAMPBELL, ANDRÉ RENAY, surgical educator, internist; b. N.Y.C., May 5, 1958; s. Ronald Ivan and Ether Sylvia Campbell Walker; m. Gillian Pearl Otway, May 11, 1991; 1 child, André Renay Jr. AB, Harvard U., 1980; MD, U. Calif., San Francisco, 1985. Diplomate Am. Bd. Internal Medicine, Am. Bd. Surgery, Am. Bd. Surg. Critical Care. Intern in internal medicine Columbia-Presbyn. Med. Ctr., N.Y.C., 1985-86, resident in internal medicine, 1986-88, resident in gen. surgery, 1988-91, chief resident in gen. surgery, 1991-92, fellow in surg. critical care, 1992-93; clin. instr. surgery U. Calif.-San Francisco Gen. Hosp., 1993-94, asst. prof., 1994-2000, assoc. prof. surgery, 2000—. Contbr. articles to med. jours., including Jour. Trauma, Jour. AMA; also chpt. Grantee NIH, 1974-97. Fellow ACS, ACP, Southwestern Surg. Congress, Am. Assn. for Surgery of Trauma, Pacific Coast Surg. Assn., Soc. Critical Care Medicine, Nat. Med. Assn., Assn. for Acad. Surgery. Avocations: playing the trumpet, jazz, reading, computers. Office: San Francisco Gen Hosp Dept Surgery Ward 3A 1001 Potrero Ave San Francisco CA 94110-3594 E-mail: acampbell@stghsurg.ucst.edu.

CAMPBELL, ANDREA S. writer; b. Lakewood, Ohio, Jan. 3, 1949; AAS in Criminal Justice, Garland County C.C., Hot Springs, Ark., 1997. Diplomate Am. Coll. Forensic Examiners. Forensic sci. artist, 1999—; author, 1989—. Forensic artist Ark. State Crime Lab. Author: (book) Legal Ease: A Guide to Criminal Law, Evidence and Procedure, 2002, Making Crime Pay: A Writer's Guide to Criminal Law, Evidence, and Procedure, 2002, Perfect Party Games, 2001, Rights of the Accused, 2000; contbg. editor: The Simian Newsletter, First Draft Newsletter. Fellow: Am. Coll. Forensic Examiners; mem.: Sisters in Crime, Internat. Assn. for Identification (Ark. bd. dirs.), Mystery Writers of Am., Am. Soc. Journalists and Authors.

CAMPBELL, ANDREW WILLIAM, immunotoxicology physician; b. Beirut, Apr. 3, 1948; s. William Alexander and Gisela (Landes) C.; children: Denia Giselle, Michelle Elise, Colin Alexander, Ian William. BA in Pre-med., Psychology, Franklin Piere Coll., Rindge, N.H., 1970; MD, U. Autonoma de Guadalajara, Mex., 1974. Diplomate Am. Bd. Family Practice, Am. Bd. Forensic Examiners, Am. Bd. Forensic Medicine. Intern Pediat. Hosp. Infantil, Ob-gyn., Clin. Santa Monica, Guadalajara, Mex., 1974-75, Pub. Health Dept., Guadalajara, Mex., 1975-76; resident gen. surgery Orlando (Fla.) Regional Med. Ctr., 1977-78; resident family practice Med. Coll. Ga., Augusta, 1978-81; pvt. practice family physician Two Physician Practice, Sarasota, Fla., 1981, with former chief surgeon Eisenhower Med. Ctr., Augusta, Ga.; pvt. practice Augusta, Wrens and Louisvlle, Ga., 1983-84, Houston, 1985—; med. dir. Med. Ctr. for Immune and Toxic Disorders, Houston, 1993—. Staff mem. Meml. City Med. Ctr., West Houston Med. Ctr., Spring Branch Med. Ctr.; chmn. dept. family practice Sam Houston Meml. Hosp., Houston, 1987, chmn. credentials com., 88, mem. exec. com., 1987—89; internat. cons. and med. expert on artificial implants, toxic exposure and occupl. medicine; lectr. and spkr. at Artificial Implants and Toxic Exposure Symposia; mem. faculty U. Tex. Sch. Medicine, 1993—98. Contbr. numerous articles to profl. jours.; made numerous presentations to sci. meetings; author: (with others) Health Effects of Toxic Chemicals, 1994, Textbook of Nephrology (2 vols.), 1995; co-editor Internat. Jour. Occupl. Medicine and Toxicology, 1992-95; mem. editl. bd. Toxicology and Indsl. Health, 1994-95. Founder Clinic for the Indigent, St. John Vianney Ch., Houston, 1987; bd. trustees Sam Houston Meml. Hosp., 1987-93. Recipient Consumer's Choice award Am. Nurses in Bus. Assn., Houston, 1994. Fellow: Am. Acad. Family Physicians; mem.: AAAS, Am. Assn. Immunologists, Indoor Air Quality Assn. of Tex., Tex. Med. Assn., Am. Bd. Forensic Examiners, Harris County Med. Soc., So. Med. Assn., Soc. Mucosal Immunology, Internat. Soc. Neuroimmunology, Am. Acad. Clin. Toxicology, Am. Coll. Occupl. and Environ. Medicine, Tex. Acad. Family Physicians. Republican. Avocations: golf, collecting pipes, collecting pens. E-mail: md@immunotoxicology.com.

CAMPBELL, ANITA JOYCE, computer company executive; b. Jefferson City, Mo., Sept. 24, 1953; d. George Rigsby and Betty Jean (Heade) Sanders; m. Michael Joseph Campbell (div. 1986); children: Kim Erik Seaver, Daniel Joseph Campbell. AAS in Computer Sci., Lincoln U., Mo., 1985; BA in Psychology, Maryville U., 1998. Student lab. mgr. Lincoln U., 1985; integrated systems analyst Xerox Corp., St. Louis, 1988-89, ins. industry project mgr., western region ops. mgmt. staff, 1990-91, advanced product specialist, western regions ops. mgmt., 1991, advanced solutions tech. mgr., western region ops. mgmt., 1992-93, tech. market project mgr., rsch. & engring, integrated systems orgn., 1993-94, tech. mktg. mgr. integrated solutions, systems sales and support, 1994-95; tech. con., integrated document solutions Integrated Document Solutions, 1995-96; project mgr. state and local govt. Xerox Profl. Document Svcs., Bridgeton, Mo., 1996-97; project mgr. govt. practice Xerox Profl. Svcs., 1997-99, opportunity mgr. cons. and sys. integration, 1999—; program mgr. GraphicArts Solutions Xerox Document Svcs.; program mgr. graphic arts solutions Document Solutions Group; prin. document solutions practice Xerox Connect, St. Louis, 2000-01, solutions architect, 2001; IT rschr. Wyeth BioPharma, Berkeley, Mo., 2001—03; bus. analyst KV Pharms., 2003—. Co-developer Delta Plan, 1988. Office staff campaign mgr. for Carter-Mondale Reelection Com., Washington, 1989-90; waterfront dir. Spl. Olympics, Lake of the Ozarks, Mo., 1987; bd. dirs. ARC, Jefferson City, 1986. Avocations: reading, swimming. Home: 912 Leawood Dr Saint Louis MO 63126-1114 Office: Wyeth BioPharma 4777 LeBourget Berkeley MO 63134

CAMPBELL, ANN MARIE, artist; b. Burbank, Calif., June 14, 1956; d. Stephen and Ann Marie (Luis) C.; children: Richard Arthur, Robert Campbell, Victoria Ann. BA in Painting, Sculpture, Graphic Arts, UCLA, 1980. Spkr. Mural Art Seminar, ASID Student Career Forum, 1995. Artist: (murals) The Pickle Barrel, 1992, Old World Sky with Angels, 1996, Cottage Garden, 1995, Two Street Window, 1996, Heather's Jazz Band, 1996, California Groaning Board, 1997, History of Virgin Records, 1997, Christ Crucufied, 2000, numerous others throughout U.S. and Can., San Francisco, N.Y., L.A., Las Vegas, Orlando, Fla., Dallas, Phoenix, New Orleans, Denver, Chgo., Columbus, Ohio, Miami, Fla., and Vancouver, B.C., Can., St. Anthony Ch., El Segundo, Calif. Mem. Nat. Soc. Mural Painters, Am. Soc. Portrait Artists, Alpha Lambda Delta. Roman Catholic. Office: PO Box 581 Folsom CA 95763-0581 E-mail: AmcArtist@aol.com.

CAMPBELL, ARTHUR ANDREWS, retired government official; b. Bklyn., Feb. 8, 1924; s. Arthur Monroe and Jo Ethel (Andrews) C.; m. Nancy Elizabeth Pyle, Jan. 28, 1961; children— Julia, Tay. AB, Antioch Coll., 1948; postgrad., Columbia U., 1947-50. Editorial clk. Met. Life Ins. Co., N.Y.C., 1950-52; statistician U.S. Bur. of Census, Washington, 1952-56; asso. research prof. Scripps Found. for Research in Population Problems, Miami U., Oxford, Ohio, 1956-64; chief natality stats. br. Nat. Center for Health Stats., Washington, 1964-68; dep. dir. Center for Population Research, NIH, Bethesda, Md., 1968-94; ret., 1994. Co-author: Family Planning, Sterility, and Population Growth, 1959, Fertility and Family Planning in the U.S, 1966, Trends and Variations in Fertility in the U.S, 1968, Manual of Fertility Analysis, 1983. Served with USN, 1943-46. Recipient Meritorious Service award U.S. Dept. Commerce, 1957; Dir.'s award NIH, 1976 Fellow Am. Statis. Assn.; mem. Population Assn. Am. (pres. 1973-74), Internat. Union for Sci. Study Population.

CAMPBELL, AUDREY LEIGH, communications professional; b. Cleve., Oct. 30, 1959; d. Odis E. and Winnie R. Campbell. BS in Journalism, Ohio U., Athens, 1982; MBA in Internat. Mgmt., Baldwin-Wallace Coll., Berea, Ohio, 1999. TV announcer and news reporter WOUB-TV, Athens, Ohio, 1980—81; radio sta. sec. WQAL-FM, Cleve., 1981—82, radio sta. adminstrv. asst., sec., 1981—82; radio advt. traffic WJW-AM, Cleve., 1982—85, adv. traffic dir., 1983—86; media rels. rep., news editor Bus. Wire, Cleve., 1985—2001; billing supr. WWWE-AM-WDOK-FM, 1985—86; news editor Bus. Wire, Cleve., 1986—88, newsroom supr., sr. editor, 1988—90, media rels. rep., 1990—2001; sr. assoc. corp. comm. Convergys Corp., Cin., 2001—02, 2001—02, nat. media rels. specialist, 2002—. Instr. Warrensville Heights (Ohio) Adult Edn. Dept., 1985-94. Author: Campbell Family Photos, 1994. Mem. Internat. Assn. Bus. Comm., Nat. Assn. Black Journalists (bd. mem., rec. sec. 1998), Press Club Cleve. (bd. dirs.). Baptist. Avocations: piano, bowling, travel, reading. Office: Convergys Corp PO Box 1638 Cincinnati OH 45201-1638 E-mail: ALcambell@aol.com.

CAMPBELL, BALLARD CROOKER, JR., historian, educator; b. East Orange, N.J., Nov. 30, 1940; s. Ballard Crooker and Ruth A. (Boman) Campbell; m. Wendy E. Kent, Dec. 26, 1965 (div. May 1980); children: Cynthia Ann, Erica Lynn; m. Eugenie F. Benoit, Oct. 15, 1988. BA in Polit. Sci., Northwestern U., 1962; MA in History, Northeastern U., 1964; PhD of History, U. Wis., 1970. From instr. to assoc. prof. Northeastern U., Boston, 1969—82, prof. History, 1982—. Pres. Soc. for Historians of Gilded Age and Progressive Era, 2002—. Author: Representative Democracy, 1980, Growth of American Government, 1995; editor: The Human Tradition in the Gilded Age and Progressive Era, 2000, American Presidential Campaigns and Elections, 2003; contbr. Fellow, Am. Coun. Learned Socs., 1982, Charles Warren Ctr. Harvard U., 1976—77; grantee, Am. Philos. Soc., 1971, 1982. Mem.: Social Sci. Hist. Assn. (exec. com. 1996—99), Orgn. Am. Historians, Am. Hist. Assn. Office: Northeastern Univ History Dept 360 Huntington Ave Boston MA 02115

CAMPBELL, BEN NIGHTHORSE, senator; b. Auburn, Calif., Apr. 13, 1933; m. Linda Price; children: Colin, Shanan. BA, Calif. U., San Jose, 1957. Educator Sacramento Law Enforcement Agy.; mem. Colo. Gen. Assembly, 1983-86, U.S. Ho. Reps., 1987-93; senator from Colorado U.S. Senate, 1993—. Rancher, jewelry designer, Ignacio, Colo. Chief No. Cheyenne Tribe. Named Outstanding Legislator Colo. Bankers Assn., 1984, Man of Yr. LaPlata Farm Bur., Durango, Colo., 1984; named one of Ten Best Legislators Denver Post/Channel 4, 1986. Mem. Am. Quarter Horse Assn., Am. Brangus Assn., Am. Indian Edn. Assn. Republican. Office: US Senate 380 Russell Senate Office Bldg Washington DC 20510-0001*

CAMPBELL, BERT LOUIS, lawyer, mediator, arbitrator; b. Tyler, Tex., Aug. 11, 1939; s. Bert M. and Jocelyn M. (Day) C.; m. Mary Ann Suatoni, July 17, 1965; children: Stephen, Brian, Rebecca. BA, U. Tex., 1961, B in Journalism, JD, U. Tex., 1970. Ptnr. Vinson & Elkins, Houston, 1970—2001. Writer, lectr. in field. Trustee Cullen Found. Lt. (j.g.) USN, 1963-66. Mem. ABA, Tex. Bar Assn., Houston Bar Assn., Am. Health Lawyers Assn. (ADR panel), Am. Arbitration Assn., Atty.-Mediators Assn. Office: 3017 Nottingham Blvd Houston TX 77005

CAMPBELL, B(OBBY) JACK, university official; b. Ft. Worth, Oct. 12, 1929; s. Jack Bryan and Ruby Opal (Lamberth) C.; m. Frances Carol Alexander, Aug. 24, 1957; children: Carol Stuart Davis, John William Campbell. BA, Tex. Christian U., 1951, MA, 1953; PhD, U. N.C., 1960. Asst. dir. U. N.C. Inst. of Govt., Chapel Hill, 1957-59; chief accident rsch. br. Cornell U. Aero. Lab., Buffalo, 1959-66; dir. U. N.C. Hwy. Safety Rsch. Ctr., Chapel Hill, 1966-91, sr. investigator, dir. emeritus, 1992—. Chmn. com. accident stats. Nat. Safety Coun., 1964-68; chmn. nat. motor vehicle safety adv. coun. U.S. Dept. Transp., 1975-76, mem., 1987-89, chmn. nat. driver register adv. com., 1983-86; chmn. panel on automotive assessment into 21st century U.S. Congress Office Tech. Assessment, 1976-77; chmn. com. to study CB radios on buses NRC, 1983-84, mem. com. to identify measures to improve safety of sch. bus transp., 1987-88; chmn. Global Traffic Safety Trust, Melbourne, Australia, 1988-92; lectr. or cons. in Australia, Azerbaijan, Brazil, Can., China, Denmark, Dominica, France, India, Hong Kong, Japan, Republic of Korea, Malawi, Malaysia, New Zealand, Russia, Saudi Arabia, Spain, Switzerland, Uruguay. Author: Driver Improvement: The Point System, 1958, Reducing Traffic Injury: A Global Challenge, 1988; (with others) Reflections on the Transfer of Highway Safety to Developing Nations, 1998, Collier's Encyclopedia, 1962, Human Factors in Technology, 1963, Trauma and the Automobile, 1966, Traffic Safety: A National Problem, 1967, Key Issues in Highway Loss Reducation, 1970, Restraint Technologies: Rear Seat Occupant Protection, 1987; contbr. numerous articles to profl. jours. SFC. U.S. Army, 1948-49. Recipient Leadership award Nat. Gov. Safety Rep. Orgn., 1997, Gerin Medal for Rsch. Internat. Assn. for Accident and Traffic Medicine, 1992, Gustafson Leadership award Hwy. Users Fedn., 1989, Volvo Internat. Traffic Safety award, 1988, Volvo Pub. Safety award 1984, Disting. Svc. award Am. Assn. for Automotive Medicine, 1978, N.C. Pub. Health Assn., 1972, Alvah Lauer award Human Factors Soc., 1976, Met. Rsch. award Commendation Nat. Safety Coun., 1971, 60. Avocations: astronomy, classical music, opera, sports. Home: 502 Belmont St Chapel Hill NC 27517-3000

CAMPBELL, BRIAN SCOTT, army officer; b. Union City, Pa., Mar. 14, 1959; s. Paul Ralph and Beverly Jean (Allen) C.; m. Susan Carol Palone, Nov. 26, 1988. BS, Edinboro U. Pa., 1980; postgrad., U. Scranton, 1980-81; DO, Phila. Coll. Osteo. Medicine, 1985; MPH, U. Tenn., 1992, U.S. Army Command & Gen. Staff Coll., 1996. Diplomate Am. Bd. Preventative Medicine, Am. Osteo. Bd. Preventive Medicine, Nat. Bd. Examiners for Osteo. Physicians and Surgeons, Pa. State Bd. Examiners. Enlisted USMC, 1976; commd. 2d lt. U.S. Army, 1981, advanced through grades to col., 2001; comdr. U.S. Army Aeromed. Rsch. Lab., 2001—. Asst. adj. prof. preventive medicine and biometrics Uniformed Svcs. U. Health Scis., Bethesda, Md. Author: Special Operations Forces Medical Handbook, University of Tennessee Wellness Handbook; contbr. articles to profl. jours. Instr. Baize Sch. Karate, Clarksville, Tenn., 1988-96; res. dep. sheriff Hillsborough County, Fla., 1997-2001. Health Professions scholar, 1981; decorated Bronze Star, Def. Meritorious Svc. medal. Mem.: NRA (patron), United Bujutsu Fedn. (black belt), U.S. Judo Assn. (patron life, black belt), Assn. Mil. Osteo. Physicians and Surgeons, Am. Osteo. Assn., Am. Osteo. Coll. Occupl. and Preventive Medicine, Aerospace Med. Assn., Soc. U.S. Army Flight Surgeons (life), N. Am. Hunting Club (life), Beta Beta Beta. Republican. Avocations: martial arts, science fiction, hunting, shooting.

CAMPBELL, BRUCE, geologist; BS in Geophysics, Tex. A&M U., 1986; PhD in Geology and Geophysics, U. Hawaii, 1991. Rsch. asst. dept. geology and geophysics U. Hawaii, Honolulu, 1986—91, postdoctoral fellow, 1991—92; geophysicist Ctr. for Earth and Planetary Studies, Nat. Air and Space Mus., Washington, 1992—, chmn., 1998—2002. Vis. scientist Astrogeology Br. U.S. Geol. Survey, Flagstaff, Ariz., 1987; vis. scientist Arecibo Obs., 1989, Nat. Astronomy and Ionosphere Ctr., Cornell U., 1992; discipline scientist Planetary Instrument Definition and Devel. Program NASA, Washington, 1996—98. Grantee Planetary Geology and Geophysics Program grantee, NASA, 1993—, Planetary Astronomy Program grantee, 1998—99, Lunar and Asteroid Data Analysis Program grantee, 1996—97, Venus Data Analysis Program grantee, 1993—94, ESA ERS-1 Program grantee, 1994—97. Mem.: Am. Astron. Soc. (divsn. of planetary scis.), Am. Geophys. Union (planetology divsn. sec. 1996—98). Achievements include research in radar remote sensing of volcanic and impact crater deposits on Venus and the moon, Venus geologic mapping and development of improved radar scattering models for planetary surfaces. Office: Nat Air and Space Mus Ctr for Earth and Planetary Studies MRC 315 Smithsonian Instn Washington DC 20560-0315

CAMPBELL, BRUCE ALAN, corporate and executive coach; b. Washington, Jan. 19, 1944; s. Albert Angus and Jean Lorraine (Winter) C.; m. Jennifer Lee Drew, May 3, 1968 (div. Dec. 1986); children: Kirsten, Robert; m. Lorna Marion Wise Ekholm, Aug. 21, 1993. BA, Oberlin Coll., 1966; MA, U. Mich., 1968, PhD, 1971. Asst. prof. to assoc. prof. U. Ga., Athens, 1971-83, dir. survey rsch. ctr., 1981-83; v.p. Marktrend Mkt. Rsch., Vancouver, Canada, 1983-84; pres., CEO Campbell Goodell Traynor Consul, Vancouver, Canada, 1984—2000; sr. cons. CGT Rsch. Internat. (formerly named Campbell Goodell Traynor Consul), Vancouver, Canada, 2000—02; v.p. Corp. Insights, Inc., Vancouver, 1992-96; pres. Argus Strategies, Ltd., Vancouver, 1988—. Dir. Downtown Vancouver Assn., 1989-96, pres., 1994-96, mem. adv. bd., 1996—; dir. Parking Corp. of Vancouver, 1992-2000, v.p., 1994-96, chmn. bd., 1996-98; bd. dir s. Downtown Vancouver Bus. Improvement Assn., 1994-96; mem. Vancouver Econ. Devel. Commn., 1996. Author: The American Electorate, 1979, profl. jours. Avocations: musical theatre, minor hockey officiating. Office: Argus Strategies Ltd 2224 W 15th Ave Vancouver BC Canada V6K 2Y7 E-mail: bcampbell@argusstrategies.com.

CAMPBELL, BRUCE CRICHTON, hospital administrator; b. Balt., July 21, 1947; s. James Allen and Elda Shaffer (Crichton) C.; m. Linda Page Cottrell, June 28, 1969; children: Molly Shaffer, Andrew Crichton. BA, Lake Forest Coll., 1969; M.H.A., Washington U., St. Louis, 1973; D.P.H., U. Ill., 1979. Adminstrv. asst. Passavant Meml. Hosp., Chgo., 1970-71; adminstrv. resident Albany (N.Y.) Med. Center Hosp., 1972-73; adminstrv. asst. Rush-Presbyn.-St. Luke's Med. Center, Chgo., 1973-75, asst. administr., 1975-77, asst. v.p., 1977-79, v.p. adminstrv. affairs, 1979-83; chmn. dept. health systems mgmt. Rush U., Chgo., 1977-81, dean Coll. Health Scis., 1981-83; exec. dir. U. Chgo. Hosps. and Clinics, 1983-85; lectr. Grad. Sch. Bus., U. Chgo., 1983-85; pres. Campbell Assocs., Chgo., 1985-92; exec. v.p. Ill. Masonic Med. Ctr., Chgo., 1993, pres., 1993-2000; chief exec. Advocate Luth. Gen. Hosp., Park Ridge, Ill., 2000—. W.K. Kellogg Found. fellow, 1977; Leadership Greater Chgo. fellow, 1984-85 Fellow Am. Coll. Healthcare Execs.; mem. Young Adminstrs. Chgo. (pres. 1977), Assn. Univ. Programs in Health Adminstrn., Am. Hosp. Assn., Ill. Hosp. Assn., Chgo. Hosp. Council. Office: Advocate Luth Gen Hosp 1775 Dempster St Park Ridge IL 60668

CAMPBELL, BRUCE HEGSTAD, otolaryngologist, educator; b. Chgo., Mar. 10, 1955; s. Ray W. and Thora H. C.; m. Kathryn Campbell, Sept. 8, 1979; children: Daniel, Sarah, David, Rebekah. BS in Biology, Purdue U., 1976; MD, Rush Med. Coll., Chgo., 1980. Intern St. Luke's Hosp., Milw., 1980-81; resident in otolaryngology Med. Coll. Wis., Milw., 1981-85, prof. otolaryngology, 1987—; fellow in head and neck surgery M.D. Anderson Cancer Ctr., Houston, 1985-87. Office: MCW Otolaryngology 9200 W Wisconsin Ave Milwaukee WI 53226

CAMPBELL, BRUCE HENRY, chemist; b. Madison, S.D., Oct. 27, 1940; s. Frank Leonard and Orville Estelle (Fulwider) C.; m. Karen Kay Tosch, May 12, 1963; children: Byron, Brandon, Bryson, Karissa. BS, U. Kans., 1962; MA, U. S.D., 1964; PhD, U. Tex., 1967. Asst. prof., then assoc. prof. U. So. Miss., Hattiesburg, 1967-72; postdoctoral fellow Clarkson Coll. Tech., Potsdam, N.Y., 1972-74; rsch. chemist J. T. Baker Chem. Co., Phillipsburg, N.J., 1974-81, Am. Cyanamid, Stamford, Conn., 1981-93; with CyTec Ind., Inc., 1993-2000; gen. co-mgr. R&T Pure Trust, Douglasville, Ga., 2001—. Adj. prof. Sacred Heart U., Fairfield, Conn., 1993—; mem. food chems. codex com. NAS/NAt. Acad. Medicine, Washington, 1977-82; cons. in field, 2000—. Editor, contbr.: Organic Electrochemistry, 1974; contbr. articles to profl. jours.; editor jour. Critical Revs. in Analytical Chemistry, 1972-83. Mem. adv. bd. chem. dept. U. So. Miss., 1994—. Mem. Am. Chem. Soc. (chmn. Lehigh Valley sect. 1980, chmn. Western Conn. sect. 1991, chair for near infrared nat. discussion group, pres. coun. for near infrared spectroscopy 2003—), Mensa (officer), Masons (officer 1970-72). Avocations: golf, bridge. Home: 9036 Green Valley Ct Douglasville GA 30134 E-mail: airconsulting@prodigy.net.

CAMPBELL, BRUCE IRVING, lawyer; b. Mason City, Iowa, July 7, 1947; s. E. Riley Jr. and Donna May (Andresen) C.; children: Anne, John; m. Beverly J. Evans. BA, Upper Iowa U., 1969; JD, Harvard U., 1973. Bar: Iowa 1973, U.S. Dist. Ct. (so. dist.) Iowa 1973, U.S. Dist. Ct. (no. dist.) Iowa 1974, U.S. Tax Ct. 1976, U.S. Ct. Appeals (8th cir.) 1977, U.S. Ct. Claims 1982. Shareholder Davis, Brown, Koehn, Shors & Roberts, P.C., Des Moines, 1973—. Adj. prof. law Drake U., Des Moines, 1974-90. Trustee Upper Iowa U., Fayette, 1978—, chair bd. trustees, 1992—2002; sec., dir. Iowa Natural Heritage Found., 2001—. Mem. ABA, Iowa State Bar Assn., Polk County Bar Assn. Republican. Home: 62 Meadowbrook Cir Cumming IA 50061-1014 Office: Davis Brown Koehn Shors & Roberts PC 666 Walnut St Ste 2500 Des Moines IA 50309-3904 E-mail: bruce.campbell@lawiowa.com.

CAMPBELL, BYRON CHESSER, publishing company executive; b. Evanston, Ill., Feb. 6, 1934; s. Chesser Milburn and Hallie (Calhoun) C.; m. Barbara Mace, Aug. 16, 1958 (div. Apr. 1982); children: Evan, Aimee Campbell Grey; m. Meta Pierce, Aug. 13, 1983; stepchildren: Marc Wise, Meier Wise, Matthew Wise, Miles Wise. BA, Yale U., 1955; MBA, Harvard U., 1959. Various positions Burlington (Vt.) Free Press, 1959-61, prodn. mgr., asst. labor rels. mgr. Chicago Tribune, 1961-68, prodn. mgr., 1970-73; bus. mgr. Chicago Today, 1968-70; asst. to pres. Tribune Co., 1973-75; pres., gen. mgr. Area Publs. Corp., Merrill Printing Co., Chgo., 1975-77; pres., chief exec. officer News and Sun-Sentinel Co., Ft. Lauderdale, Fla., 1977-83; pres., pub. L.A. Daily News; pres., chief exec. officer Tribune Newspapers West, Inc., L.A., 1983-87; pres., pub. The Record, Hackensack, N.J.; v.p. Macromedia Inc., Hackensack, 1988-91. Bd. dirs. Home News Pub. Co., New Brunswick, N.J., Newspapers of New Eng., Concord, N.H., George W. Prescott Pub. Co., Quincy, Mass., Journal-Star Printing Co., Lincoln, Nebr., Freedom Comm., Inc., Irvine, Calif. Bd. dirs. Lyric Opera Chgo., Newberry Libr. Chgo., Sta. WPBT, Miami, Fla., Rush-Presbyn.-St. Luke's Med. Ctr., Chgo.; bd. dirs., campaign chmn. United Way of Bergen County, 1989-91; adv. bd. Bergen 2000; bd. dirs., pres., campaign chmn. United Way of Broward County, Fla.; bd. dirs., chmn. San Fernando Valley Cultural Found., L.A.; bd. dirs., pres. Chgo. Youth Ctrs., Broward Community Blood Ctr.; bd. dirs., exec. com. Broward Workshop; bd. dirs. United Way, L.A., campaign chmn. San Fernando Valley; bd. dirs., 1st v.p. Ft. Lauderdale Symphony. Lt. USN, 1955-57. Mem. AP (nominating com.), Am. Newspaper Pubs. Assn. (govt. affairs com., newsprint com. 1989-92), Am. Press Inst. (bd. dirs. 1984-93), Inland Press Assn. (pres., bd. dirs.), Greater L.A. C. of C. (bd. dirs.), Econ. Club (Chgo.), Yale Club (Chgo., bd. dirs., pres.), Lotos Club (N.Y.C.), Univ. Club (Chgo., bd. dirs., admissions com.), Saddle and Cycle Club (Chgo., bd. dirs., admissions com.), Lauderdale Yacht Club (Ft. Lauderdale, Fla.), Ristigouche Salmon Club (Matapedia, Que.). Avocations: tennis, wine, fly fishing, travel, golf. E-mail: bccampbell@webtv.net.

CAMPBELL, CARL DAVID, oil industry executive; b. Oklahoma City, July 4, 1959; s. David Gwynne and Janet Gay (Newland) C. BBA, U. Okla., 1982. Cert. profl. landman. Land cons. Leede Exploration, Oklahoma City, 1978, 79; lease broker W.M. Bryan, Inc., Oklahoma City, 1980, 81; corp. sec., land mgr. Earth Hawk Exploration, Inc., Oklahoma City, 1980-96, v.p., 1996—; landman PetroCorp, Oklahoma City, 1983-87, mid-continent divsn. landman, 1987-91, Gulf Coast divsn. landman Houston, 1991-92, Gulf, Rockies, Can. divsn. landman, 1993-2000; pres. Concorde Resources, L.L.C., Houston, 2000—. Mem. Cherokee Nation Okla., Tahlequah, 1979—; contbg. charter mem. Houston Mus. Fine Arts. Mem. Am. Assn. Petroleum Landmen, Houston Assn. Petroleum Landmen, Canadian Assn. Petroleum Landmen, Okla. Ind. Petroleum Assn., Okla. City Assn. Petroleum Landmen, Houston Soc., U. Okla. Found. Assocs., First Families East Tenn. (charter), Clan Campbell of N.Am., Cherokee Nation of Okla., First Families of the Cherokee Nation (charter), First Families of the Twin Territories, Cherokee Hist. Soc. (charter mem. heritage coun. 1982—), Houston Mus. Fine Arts (contbg. charter patron mem.), Aircraft Owners and Pilots Assn., Phi Gamma Delta. Republican. Presbyterian. Avocations: biking, flying, travel, scuba diving, golf. Home: 1701 Hermann Dr Ste 2702 Houston TX 77004-7368 Office: Concorde Resources LLC 808 Travis Ste 1444 Houston TX 77002 Fax: 713-224-6096. E-mail: carl@concorderesources.com.

CAMPBELL, CARL LESTER, banker; b. Sunbury, Pa., Apr. 10, 1943; s. Claude L. and Viola W. Campbell; m. Mary E. Bingaman, June 5, 1965; children: Carla L., Craig L. BS, Susquehanna U., 1965; postgrad., Stonier Grad. Sch. Banking, 1978. Br. mgr. asst. v.p. Tri-County Nat. Bank, Middleburg, Pa., 1965-72; asst. v.p. adminstrn. Pa. Nat. Bank, Pottsville, 1972-74, adminstrv. v.p., 1974-80, sr. v.p., 1980-81, exec. v.p., 1981-82, pres. chief exec. officer, 1982-86; pres., chief exec. officer Keystone Fin., Inc., Harrisburg, Pa., 1986-98, chmn., CEO, 1998-2000; vice chmn. M&T Bank, Harrisburg, 2000—. Office: M & T Bank 23 N Front St Harrisburg PA 17101

CAMPBELL, CAROL SUE, sociology, social work, psychology, and criminal justice educator; b. Jacksonville, Fla., July 3, 1956; d. William Arthur and Juantia May (Vickery) C. BA, Valdosta State Coll., 1977, MS, 1979; PhD, La. State U., Baton Rouge, 1985, MSW, M. Criminal Justice, 1987. Cert. Acad. Cert. Social Workers, bd. cert. social worker, profl. counselor, La. Instr. La. State U., Eunice, 1982-88; asst. prof. Valdosta (Ga.) State Coll., 1988-89; asst.prof., coord. La. Coll., Pineville, 1989-92; asst. prof. McNeese State U., Lake Charles, La., 1992—. Therapist Anglewood Clinic, Baton Rouge, 1985-88, Profl. Counseling Specialties, Inc., Lake Charles, 1996—; instr. La. State U., Eunice, 1990—; mem. Project Independence Adv. Com., Rapides Parish, La., 1991-92. Contbr. articles and revs. to profl. publs. Mem. NASW (pub. rels. 1991-92, chair 1994—). Alpha Kappa Delta (sponsor). Avocations: gardening, antique collection. Office: McNeese State Univ Dept Social Scis Lake Charles LA 70609-0001

CAMPBELL, CATHERINE ELLEN, French language educator; b. Cleve., Jan. 7, 1948; d. Malcolm Freeman and Ruth Campbell. AB, Mt. Holyoke Coll., 1969; MA, Colgate U., 1970; PhD, U. Mo., Columbia, 1982. Tchr. Whitesboro (N.Y.) H.S., 1970, Poland (N.Y.) Ctrl. Sch., 1970-73; tchg. asst. U. Mo., Columbia, 1974-82; prof. French Cottey Coll., Nevada, Mo., 1982—. Author: The French Procuress, 1984; editor/translator: The Widow (La Veuve), 1993; reviewer scholarly jours. Mem. Am. Assn. Tchrs. of French, Renaissance Soc. Am., Assn. of Literary Scholars and Critics, 16th Century Studies Conf., Alpha Mu Gamma (reg. v.p. 1997—). Home: 412 Main St Nevada MO 64772 Office: Cottey Coll 1000 W Austin Blvd Nevada MO 64772-2763

CAMPBELL, CATHERINE LYNN, elementary school educator; b. Lynchburg, Va., Mar. 16, 1961; d. Tomie Eawell Campbell and Barbara (Arthur) McCraw. BA, Sweet Briar Coll., 1983; MEd in Adminstrv. and Supervision, U. Va., 2003. Cert. elem. tchr., NK-8 tchr. VA. Tchr. Amherst (Va.) County Pub. Schs., 1984—. Mem. Va. Real Estate Bd. Common Interest Properties. Mem.: ASCD, Va. Edn. Assn., NEA, Nat. Honor Soc. Avocations: horseback riding, raising quarter horses. Home: 139 Cedar Crest Dr Ste 107 Madison Heights VA 24572-2366 Office: Amherst County Pub Schs Amherst VA 24521

CAMPBELL, CHARLES ALTON, business executive; b. Brunswick, Ga., Mar. 10, 1944; s. Rayford Monroe and Cecelia Elizabeth (Camilla) C.; m. Mary Alla Traber, Aug. 15, 1970; children: Christine Beensen, Elizabeth Traber, Charles Traber. B Indsl. Engring., Ga. Inst. Tech., 1966; MBA, Harvard U., 1973. Mgr. ops. projects Camak Lumber Ops., ITT Rayonier, Thomson, Ga., 1974-75, mgr. ops. projects Wood Products Group N.Y.C., 1975-77, dir. chems. devel. parent co., 1977-79, dir. operational planning and control Seattle, 1979-80; pres. Fox Mfg. Co., Rome, Ga., 1980-81, Camtec, Inc., Rome, 1981-88; chmn. bd. Universal Ceramics, nc., Adairsville, Ga., 1984-87; exec. v.p. Saunders, Inc., Birmingham, Ala., 1987-88, pres. CEO, 1988-90; pres. N.Am. Tech. Corp., Birmingham, 1990—. Lt. CE, USNR, 1967-69. Mem. Downtown Rotary (Birmingham, Ala.) Swim and Tennis Club, The Club. Episcopalian. Home: 3725 Briar Oak Cir Birmingham AL 35223-2826 Office: NAm Tech Corp PO Box 43462 Birmingham AL 35243-0462

CAMPBELL, CHARLES EDWARD, lawyer; b. Atlanta, Jan. 12, 1942; s. Borden Burr and Bonnie (McPherson) C.; m. Ann Grovenstein, Apr. 12, 1976; 1 child, Garrett McPherson. Student, Emory U., 1960-61; BA, MA, U. Ga., 1964; JD, Georgetown U., 1971. Bar: Ga. 1972. Legis. asst. to U.S. Sen. Richard B. Russell, Washington, 1965-67; exec. sec., 1967-69; adminstrv. asst., 1969-71; assoc. Heyman & Sizemore, Atlanta, 1971-73, ptnr., 1974-77, Hicks, Maloof & Campbell, Atlanta, 1977-98, McKenna Long & Aldridge LLP (formerly Long, Alridge & Norman, LLP), 1998—. Trustee Richard B. Russell Found., 1978—, mem. exec. com., 1980—, chmn., 1990—. Fellow Am. Coll. Trial Lawyers, Am. Coll. Bankruptcy; mem. Ga. Bar Assn. (mem. legis. com. 1978-79), Southeastern Bankruptcy Law Inst., Inc. (bd. dirs., pres. 1993-94). Home: 2485 Dellwood Dr NW Atlanta GA 30305-4075 Office: McKenna Long & Alridge LLP 303 Peachtree St NE Ste 5300 Atlanta GA 30308-3264

CAMPBELL, CHERYL ANN, social worker; b. St. Louis, Sept. 14, 1956; d. Henry Francis and Carol Jean (Buckner) Bazile; children: Carol Louise, Robert Lamont II. BSW, Mo. Valley Coll., 1977; MSW, Washington U., St. Louis, 1980. Cert. social worker, Mo.; lic. clin. social worker, Mo. Juvenile officer Jackson County Juvenile Ct., Kansas City, Mo., 1976; counselor Joint Community Program, St. Louis, 1979, St. Louis Comprehensive Health Ctr., 1979; social svc. counselor Human Devel. Corp., 1977; caseworker St. Louis County Div. Family Svcs., 1979; tchr. St. Louis Community Coll., 1980-84; dep. juvenile officer Family Ct. of St. Louis County, Clayton, Mo., 1977-80, detention supr., 1980-92, delinquency svc. mgr., 1992-95, detention supt., 1995-99, dir. of detention, 1999—; pvt. practice therapist St. Louis, 1987-92. Speaker in field; researcher in crisis intervention techniques. Author manual: Crisis Intervention, 1987. Mem. NASW (nat. com. on women's issues 1985-88), St. Louis County Juv. Justice Assn. Democrat. Roman Catholic. Avocations: walking, bowling. Home: 1677 Ryall Ct Florissant MO 63031-1145 Office: St Louis County Family Ct 501 S Brentwood Blvd Saint Louis MO 63105-2522

CAMPBELL, CLAIRE PATRICIA, nurse practitioner, educator; b. Jan. 10, 1933; d. Hugh Paul Campbell and Clara Louise Campbell. Student, So. Meth. U., 1956-57; BS in Nursing, U. Tex. Sch. Nursing, Galveston, 1959, Family Nurse Pracitioner, 1979, cert., 1984, 89, 99; MS in Nursing, Tex. Woman's U. Sch. Nursing, 1971. Staff nurse Parkland Meml. Hosp., Dallas County Hosp Dist., 1955-70; head nurse gen. surgery, chest surgery, neurosurgery orthopedics and internal medicine, until 1970; instr. nursing Tex. Woman's U. Sch. Nursing, Dallas, 1971-72; rschr. nursing diagnosis Dallas, 1972-77; FNP Otis Engring. Health Svc., Dallas, 1979-86; nurse pracitioner pain mgmt. program Dallas Rehab. Inst., 1986-95, HealthSouth SubAcute Unit, Dallas, 1995-97, Heath-South Med. Ctr.-Rehab., Dallas, 1997—. Adj. asst. prof. U. Tex. Sch. Nursing, Arlington, 1976-98; cons. nursing diagnosis. Author: Nursing Diagnosis and Intervention in Nursing Practice, 1st edit., 1978, 2d edit., 1984. Mem.: ANA, Tex. Nurses Assn. Roman Catholic.

CAMPBELL, CLYDE DEL, academic administrator; b. Wheeling, W.Va., Apr. 1, 1930; s. Clyde William and Vera (Speidel) C.; m. Joan Luhan, Aug. 25, 1956; 1 child, Leslie Ann Campbell. BS, BA, West Liberty Coll., 1953; MS, N.C. State U., 1955; PhD, W.Va. U., 1958. Instr. chemistry West Liberty (W.Va.) State Coll., 1958-61; sr. research chemist Mobay Chem. Co., New Martinsville, W.Va., 1961-67; prof. chemistry, chmn. sch. natural sci. West Liberty State Coll., 1967-70, assoc. acad. dean. 1970-73, dean adminstrn., 1973-82, acad. dean, 1982-84, pres., 1984-95; interim pres. Jefferson C.C., Steubenville, Ohio, 1998—. Patentee in field; contbr. articles to profl. jours. Mem., pres. Ohio County Bd. Edn., W.Va., 1966-72, W.Va. Intercollegiate Athletic Conf., 1986-95; bd. dirs. Oglebay Inst., Wheeling, 1985—. Mem. Am. Chem. Soc., W.Va. Acad. Sci., Phi Lambda Upsilon, Alpha Chi Sigma, Sigma Xi. Clubs: Blue Pencil (Wheeling). Lodges: Rotary. Avocations: jogging, golf, numismatics, music. Home: 199 Clearview Ave Wheeling WV 26003-6755

CAMPBELL, COLIN DEARBORN, economist, educator; b. Cooperstown, N.Y., Feb. 10, 1917; s. James Samuel and Marion (Jennings) C.; m. Rosemary Garst, June 18, 1949; children— William Garst, Janet Adele. BA, Harvard, 1938; MA, U. Iowa, 1941; PhD, U. Chgo., 1950; MA, Dartmouth, 1965. Instr. Rensselaer Poly. Inst., Troy, N.Y., 1946-47; asst. prof. Drake U., Des Moines, 1949-51; economist CIA, 1952-54, FRS, 1954-56; prof. econs. Dartmouth Coll., Hanover, N.H., 1956-87, prof. econs. emeritus, 1987—. Dir. Dartmouth Nat. Bank, 1961-88, Student Loan Mktg. Assn., 1973-75; adj. scholar Am. Enterprise Inst., 1974-87; mem. U.S. Tax Adv. Group to Republic Korea, 1959-60. Author: (with R.G. Campbell and E.G. Dolan) Money, Banking and Monetary Policy, 1987; contbr. to profl. jours. Served to capt., Ordnance Corps AUS, 1941-46, 51-53. Mem. Am. Econ. Assn., Mont Pelerin Soc. Home: 9 N Park St Hanover NH 03755

CAMPBELL, COLIN GOETZE, foundation president; b. N.Y.C., Nov. 3, 1935; s. Joseph and Marjorie (Goetze) C.; m. Nancy Nash, June 20, 1959; children: Elizabeth, Jennifer, Colin, Blair. AB, Cornell U., 1957; JD, Columbia U., 1960; LLD (hon.), Amherst Coll., 1972, Williams Coll., 1973, Dickinson Coll., 1982, U. Hartford, 1983, Wesleyan U., 1989, Conn. Coll., 1990, Fairfield U., 1999; DHL (hon.), Trinity Coll., 1981, Georgetown U., 1984; PhD in Pub. Sci. (hon.), Cedar Crest Coll., 1997. Bar: Conn. 1961. Atty. Cummings & Lockwood, Stamford, Conn., 1960-62; asst. to pres. Am. Stock Exch., N.Y.C., 1962-63, sec., 1963-64, v.p., 1964-67; adminstrv. v.p. Wesleyan U., Middletown, Conn., 1967-69, exec. v.p., 1969-70, pres., 1970-88, pres. emeritus, 1988—; pres. Rockefeller Bros. Fund, 1988-2000; chmn., pres. Colonial Williamsburg (Va.) Found., 2000—. Bd. dirs. Pitney Bowes, Sysco Corp. Trustee NY Hist. Soc. Mem. Am. Acad. Arts and Scis., Coun. on Fgn. Rels., Century Assn., Knickerbocker Club, Psi Upsilon, Phi Delta Phi. Episcopalian. Home: Coke-Garrett House 465 E Nicholson St Williamsburg VA 23185 Office: Colonial Williamsburg Found PO Box 1776 Williamsburg VA 23187-1776 E-mail: ccampbell@cwf.org.

CAMPBELL, COLIN HERALD, former mayor; b. Winnipeg, Man., Can., Jan. 18, 1911; s. Colin Charles and Aimee Florence (Herald) C.; m. Virginia Paris, July 20, 1935; children: Susanna Herald, Corinna Buford, Virginia Wallace. BA, Reed Coll., 1933. Exec. sec. City Club of Portland, 1934-39; alumni sec., dir. endowment adminstrn. Reed Coll., 1939-42; exec. sec. N.W. Inst. Internat. Rels., 1940-42; supr. contract, engr. Kaiser Co., Inc., 1942-45; asst. pers. dir. Portland Gas & Coke Co., 1945-48; dir. indsl. rels. Pacific Power & Light Co., Portland, 1948-76. Mem. Oreg. Adv. Com. on Fair Employment Practices Act, 1949-55; trustee, chmn., pres. Portland Symphonic Choir, 1950-54; trustee Portland Civic Theater, 1941-54; bd. dirs. Portland Symphony Soc., 1957-60, Cmty. Child Guidance Clinic, 1966-68; active United Way, 1945-75; bd. dirs. Contemporary Crafts Assn., 1972-76, treas., 1975-76; bd. dirs. Lake Oswego Corp., 1961-65, 71-73, 74-76, corp. sec., 1964, pres., 1973-74, treas., 1975-76; mem. Com. on Citizen Involvement, City of Lake Oswego, 1975-77; chmn. Bicentennial Com., Lake Oswego, 1975-76; sec.-treas. Met. Area Comms. Commn., 1980-85; treas. Clackamas County Cmty. Action Agy., 1980-82, chmn., 1982-85; mem. fin. adv. com. West Clackamas County LWV, 1974-76, 78-80; councilman City of Lake Oswego, 1977-78, mayor, 1979-85, chmn. libr. growth task force, 1987-89, chmn. hist. rev. bd., 1990-92; chmn. energy adv. com. League Oreg. Cities, 1982-84; mem. adv. bd., chmn. fin. com. Lake Oswego Adult Cmty. Ctr., 1985-88; pres. Oswego Heritage coun., 1992-95, sec., 1995-96, treas., 1997-99, dir., 2000, dir. emeritus, 2001—; mem. County Blue Ribbon Com. on Law Enforcement, 1987-89; mem. fee arbitration panel Oreg. State Bar Assn., 1995-2000. Mem. Edison Electric Inst. (exec. com.), N.W. Electric Light and Power Assn., Lake Oswego C. of C. (v.p. 1986-87, chmn. land use com. 1990-91), Nat. Trust for Hist. Preservation, Hist. Preservation League Oreg., Oreg. Hist. Soc., McLoughlin Meml. Assn., Oswego Heritage Coun. (pres. 1992-94, 95-96, treas. 1997-99, editor 1992-2003), Clackamas County Hist. Assn., Rotary (treas. Lake Oswego chpt. 1990-93). Republican. Presbyterian. Home: Apt 306 17440 Holy Names Dr Lake Oswego OR 97034-5143

CAMPBELL, COLIN KYDD, electrical and computer engineering educator, researcher; b. St. Andrews, Fife, Scotland, May 3, 1927; s. David Walker and Jean (Hutchison) C.; m. Vivian Gwyn Norval, Apr. 17, 1954; children— Barry, Gwyn, Ian B.Sc. in Engring. with honors, St. Andrews U., 1952; S.M., MIT, 1953; PhD, St. Andrews U., 1960; D.Sc., U. Dundee, 1984. Registered profl. engr., Ont. Communications engr. Fgn. Office and Diplomatic Wireless Service, London, Eng., 1946-47; communications engr. Brit. Embassy, Washington, 1947-48; electronics engr. Atomic Instrument Co., Cambridge, Mass., 1954-57; asst. prof. elec. and computer engring. McMaster U., Hamilton, Ont., Can., 1960-63, assoc. prof. elec. and computer engring., 1963-67, prof. elec. engring., 1967-89, prof. elec. and computer engring., 1989—, prof. emeritus. Vis. scholar Ctr. for Power Electronic Sys., Va. Poly. Inst. and State U., Blacksburg, 2000, 02. Author: Surface Acoustic Wave Devices and Their Signal Processing Applications, 1989, Surface Acoustic Wave Devices for Mobile and Wireless Communication, 1998; contbr. numerous articles to profl. jours. Served with Brit. Army, 1944-46 Recipient The Inventor insignia Can. Patents and Devel. Ltd., 1973, invitation fellow Japan Soc. for Promotion of Sci., 1995, rsch. fellow Rand Afrikaans U., South Africa, 1995. Fellow Royal Soc. Can. (Thomas Eadie medal 1983), Engring. Inst. Can., Royal Soc. Arts London, IEEE (life); mem. Sigma Xi Mem. Ch. of England. Club: Royal Canadian Mil. Inst. (Toronto) Avocation: fishing. Home: 160 Parkview Dr Ancaster ON Canada L9G 1Z5 Office: McMaster U Elec Computer Engring 1280 Main St W Hamilton ON Canada L8S 4K1 E-mail: colin.kydd.campbell@sympatico.ca.

CAMPBELL, COLIN MCLEOD, journalist; b. Boston, Nov. 25, 1945; s. Peter Archibald and Elizabeth Blalock (Black) C.; m. Caroline P. Bethea, Aug. 25, 1973 (div. 1991); 1 child, Colin Gray; m. Deborah L. Scroggins, Feb. 20, 1993; 2 children; Anna Barrington, Elizabeth Baker. BA, U. Calif, Berkeley. Assoc. editor Psychology Today mag., 1973-77; mng. editor Sports Afield mag., 1977; sr. editor Human Nature mag., 1978, mng. editor, 1979; editl. writer The N.Y. Times, 1979-81, reporter, 1981, 84-86, Bangkok bur. chief, 1982-84; fgn. corr. The Atlanta Jour. - Constn., 1987-90, columnist, 1990—. Recipient Human Rights Reporting award Overseas Press Club, 1988, Robert F. Kennedy Journalism award, 1988; Assoc. fellow Yale U., 1986—. Mem. The Johnsonians Club. Office: The Atlanta Jour - Constn 72 Marietta St NW Atlanta GA 30303-2804 E-mail: ccampbell@ajc.com.

CAMPBELL, COURTNEY SCOTT, humanities educator; b. El Paso, Tex., Dec. 12, 1956; s. Robert Sanders and Karen Hinckley Campbell; m. Marie Elaine Chudleigh, May 21, 1982; children: Juliette, Jason, Scott, Cassandra. BA, Yale U., 1981; MA, U. Va., 1984, PhD, 1988. Assoc. for religion Hastings Ctr., Briarcliff Manor, NY, 1987—90; prof. Oreg. State U., Corvallis, 1990—, chair dept. philosophy, 2002—. Editor: What Price Parenthood, 1991, Duties to Others, 1996. Recipient Media award, Hudson Valley Mag., 1989. Mem. Lds Ch. Avocations: mountain climbing, hiking, golf, photography, cycling. Home: 3660 SW Country Club Dr Corvallis OR 97333 Office: Oreg State U 208 Hovland Hall Corvallis OR 97331 Office Fax: 541-737-2571. Business E-Mail: ccampbell@orst.edu.

CAMPBELL, DAVID GEORGE, ecologist, researcher, author; b. Decatur, Ill., Jan. 28, 1949; s. George Robert and Jean Blossom C.; m. Karen S. Lowell; 1 child, Tatiana Claire. BA, Kalamazoo Coll., 1971; MS, U. Mich., 1973; PhD, Johns Hopkins U., 1984. Exec. dir. Bahamas Nat. Trust, Nassau, 1974-77; ecologist N.Y. Bot. Garden, Bronx, 1984-88, leader Amazon Expdns., 1974-92, research fellow, 1989—; prof. biology, Henry R. Luce prof. nations-global environ. Grinnell (Iowa) Coll., 1991—. Adj. prof. U. Nanjing, China, 1993—; prof. Semester at Sea, 1997; prof. Grinnell-in-London, 1999; cons. Internat. Union for Conservation of Nature, 1978-79, leader Maya forest project, Belize, 1993-96; biologist and lectr. M.V. World Discoverer in Amazon and Antarctic, 1981-87, I.B. Yamal to North Pole, 1995; biologist Brazilian Antarctic Expdn., 1987-88. Author: The Ephemeral Islands, 1978, The Crystal Desert, 1992, Islands in Space and Time, 1996; editor: Floristic Inventory of Tropical Countries, 1989; contbr. articles to profl. jours. Recipient Fulling award Soc. Econ. Botany, 1987, Houghton Mifflin Lit. fellow, 1992, Pen/Martha Albrand award for nonfiction, 1993, John Burroughs medal, 1994; Guggenheim fellow, 1989. Fellow Linnean Soc. London, Royal Geog. Soc. London, Explorers Club Office: Grinnell Coll Dept Biology Grinnell IA 50112

CAMPBELL, DAVID GWYNNE, petroleum executive, geologist; b. May 2, 1930; s. Lois Raymond Henager and La Vada (Ray) Henager Campbell; m. Janet Gay Newland, March 1, 1958; 1 child, Carl David. BS, Tulsa U., 1953; MS, U. Okla., 1957. Geologist Lone Star Producing Co., Oklahoma City, 1957-65; dist. geologist, geol. cons. Tenneco Oil Co., Oklahoma City, 1965-77; exploration mgr. Leede Exploration, Oklahoma City, 1977-80; pres. Earth Hawk Exploration, Inc., Oklahoma City, 1980—. Divsn. exploration mgr. PetroCorp., Inc., Oklahoma City, 1983-92, divsn. gen. mgr. 1992-96; cons. Jr. Achievement, Oklahoma City, 1996—; active U. Okla. Sch. Geology and Geophysics Alumni 1985—, bd. dirs. adv. coun. 1988-90, sec. 1990-91, vice chmn., 1991-92, chmn., 1992-93. Contbr. articles to Jour. Cherokee Studies. Active Last Frontier Coun. Boy Scouts Am., 1960-73, edn. chmn. Eagle Dist. 1963-67; gubernatorial appointee Native Am. Cultural and Edn. Authority, 2002—. Recipient Cert. of Appreciation award Nat. Exch. Club, Oklahoma City, 1999. Mem. AAAS, Internat. Assn. Energy Economists, Soc. Ind. Profl. Earth Scientists (pres. Okla. chpt. 1988, chmn. 1989, chmn. pollt. affairs com. 1991), Soc. Profl. Well Log Analysts, Am. Assn. Petroleum Geologists (hon. mem. 1995, chmn. house of dels. 1981-82, house of dels. mem.-at-large 1982—, exec. com. 1981-82, 90-91, found. trustee assoc. 1983—, corp. mem. Am. Assn. Petroleum Geologists Found. 1996—, mem. adv. coun. 1984-87, councillor mid-continent sect. 1984-87, nominating com. 1984-85, 86-87, astrogeology com. 1984—, mem. liaison subcom. astrogeology com. 1984, honors and awards com. 1984-85, 85-86, adv. bd. Treatise of Petroleum Geology 1986-91, nat. membership adv. coun. 1987-90, membership com. chmn. mid-continent sect. 1987-90, Disting. Svc. award 1989, nat. v.p. 1990-91, cand. nat. pres.-elect. 2000-2001, mid-continent councillor energy minerals divsn. 1992-94, chmn. com. of coms. 1992-98, mem. com. of coms. 1992—, charter mem. divsn. Environ. Geoscis. 1992), Okla. City Geol. Soc. (hon. life mem. 1992, pub. rels. chmn. Spkrs. Bur. 1963-64, chmn. stratigraphic code com. 1967-68, presdl. appointee 1969-70, advt. mgr. Shale Shaker 1969-71, rep. to AAPG Ho. of Dels. 1980-86, bylaws and incorp. rev. com. 1986), Okla. City Geol. Found. (founding pres. 1993-98, bd. dirs. 1993-2001), Ind. Petroleum Assn. Am. (Okla. chpt. regulatory affairs com. 1991-93), Okla. City Assn. Petroleum Landmen, Houston Geol. Soc., Tulsa Geol. Soc., Petroleum Exploration Soc. Great Britain, Okla. City Petroleum Club (bd. dirs. 1987-90, 1995-98, sec. 1989, 2d v.p. 1990, chmn. membership com. 1988-90), Geol. Soc. Moscow, N.Y. Acad. Scis., Okla. City C. of C., Okla. Hist. Soc., Cherokee Nat. Hist. Soc. (devel. com. 1987-95, bd. trustees nat. soc. 1983-96), Ctr. Am. Indian (bd. dirs. 1988-92), Red Earth Indian Ctr. (bd. dirs. 1992—, co-founder Red Earth Amb. of Yr. award, chmn. auction 1993, v.p. 1994-97, pres. 1997-98, Spirit award, 1999), Gubernatorial appointee to Native Am. Cultural and Edn. Authority, 2002; Nat. Mus. Am. Indian, Am. Indian Cultural Soc., Houston Mus. Fine Arts, Okla. Pilots Assn., Exptl. Aircraft Assn., Aircraft Owners and Pilots Assn., First Families of Twin Ters., Clan Campbell of N. Am., Sigma Xi, Pi Kappa Alpha. Home: 6109 Woodbridge Rd Oklahoma City OK 73162-3220 Office: Earth Hawk Exploration Inc PO Box 2396 Oklahoma City OK 73101-2396 E-mail: earthhawk1@sbcglobal.net.

CAMPBELL, DAVID JAMES, hospital administrator; b. Syracuse, N.Y., Oct. 29, 1946; married. BA, Mich. StateU., 1969; MA, U. Mich., 1971. Adminstr. St. Joseph Mercey Hosp., Ann Arbor, Mich., 1970; adminstrv. fellow U. Mich. Hosps., Ann Arbor, Mich., 1971-73, asst. to dir., 1973-74, asst. dir., 1974-76, assoc. dir., 1976-78; adminstr. svcs. Henry Ford Hosp., Detroit, 1978-82; adminstrv. dir. Metro Hosp. & Health Ctrs., Detroit, 1978-82; exec. v.p., COO Allegheny Gen. Hosp., Pitts., 1982-84, pres., 1984-86; exec. v.p., COO Allegheny Health Systems, Pitts., 1986-87, Detroit Med. Ctr., Mich., 1988-90, pres., CEO, 1990—99; pres. and CEO Saint Vincent's Med. Ctrs. of N.Y., 2000—. Home: 27 Oxford Rd Grosse Pointe MI 48236-1835 Office: 130 W 12th St New York NY 10011

CAMPBELL, DEBRA LYNN, marketing and new venture consultant; b. Phoenix, Apr. 8, 1954; d. Joseph David and Elaine Lucinda (Krueger) C.; m. J. Frederick Stillman III, Oct. 26, 1985; 1 child, J. Frederick Stillman IV. BS, U. Ariz., 1975; MBA, Harvard U., 1980. Brand mgr. Procter & Gamble Co., Cin., 1975-78; project mgr. Dunham & Marcus, N.Y.C., 1980-81; v.p. Cox, Lloyd Assocs., N.Y.C., 1981-83; cons. Am. Cons. Corp., N.Y.C., 1983-85, dir., 1985-87, dir., CFO, 1987-88, pres., COO, 1988-90; pres. DCA, 1990—2002; COO Hudson River Group, Valhalla, NY, 2002—. Pres. 173-175 Tenants' Corp.; Treas. Cathedral Guild St. John the Divine Ch. Recipient Reggie award Promotion Mktg. Assn. Am. (Reggie award 1986, 87, 90). Mem.: Nat. Sculpture Soc. (treas.). Avocations: travel, collecting American Indian art, golf, tennis. Office: Hudson River Group 465 Columbus Ave Valhalla NY 10595-1336

CAMPBELL, DEMAREST LINDSAY, artist, interior designer, writer; b. N.Y.C., June 4, 1951; d. Peter Stephen III and Mary Elizabeth (Edwards) C.; m. Dale Gordon Haugo, Apr. 7, 1978. BFA in Art History, MFA in Asian Art History, MFA in Theatre Design. Designer murals and residential interiors Campbell and Haugo Design Cons., San Francisco, 1975—; chargeman scenic artist Am. Conservatory Theatre, 1976—. Designed, painted and sculpted over 250 prodns. for Broadway, internat. opera, motion pictures. Mem. NOW, Asian Art Mus. Soc., San Francisco, Mem. NOW, United Scenic Artists, Scenic & Title Artists and Theatrical Stage Designers, Internat. Alliance of Theatrical Stage Employees, Scenic, Title and Graphic Artists (Local 816), Sherlock Holmes Soc. London, Amnesty Internat., Nat. Trust for Hist. Preservation (Gt. Britian and U.S.A. chpt.), Fine Arts Mus. Soc. San Francisco, Shavian Malthus Soc. (charter Gt. Britian chpt.), Humane Soc. of U.S. (millennium mem.). Avocations: medical history, pre-twentieth century military history.

CAMPBELL, DENNIS MARION, educator, university administrator, theologian; b. Dalhart, Tex., Aug. 23, 1945; s. Francis Marion and Margaret (Osterberg) C.; m. Leesa Heydenreich, June 13, 1970; children: Margaret Heyden, Robert Trevor. AB, Duke U., 1967, PhD, 1973; BD, Yale U., 1970; DD (hon.), Fla. So. U., 1986. Ordained to ministry United Meth. Ch., 1974. Min. Trinity United Meth. Ch., Durham, N.C., 1973-74; chmn. dept. religion Converse Coll., Spartanburg, S.C., 1974-79; dir. continuing edn. Div. Sch. Duke U., Durham, 1979-82, prof. theology, 1982—, dean. Div. Sch., 1982-97; headmaster Woodberry Forest (Va.) Sch., 1997—. Mem. Oxford (Eng.) Inst. Theol. Studies, 1982, 87, 92, Denver, 1996; gen. conf. United Meth. Ch., Balt., 1984, St. Louis, 1988, Louisville, 1992; del. World Meth. Coun., Nairobi, Kenya, 1987, World Coun. Chs. 7th Assembly, Canberra, Australia, 1991. Author: Authority and the Renewal of American Theology, 1976, Doctors, Lawyers, Ministers: Christian Ethics in Professional Practice, 1982, The Yoke of Obedience: The Meaning of Ordination in Methodism, 1988, Who Will Go For Us?, 1994. Chmn. Protection of Human Subjects Com.; bd. dirs. Family Health Internat., Research Triangle Park, 1986—, Internat. Coalition Boys Schs; bd. visitors Perkins Sch. Theology So. Meth. U., Dallas, 1987—; overseers com. Harvard U., 1992—. Mem. Am. Theol. Soc., Am. Acad. Religion, Soc. Christian Ethics, Assn. Theol. Schs. (accrediting com. 1986—), Phi Beta Kappa, Omicron Delta Kappa. Methodist. Home: PO Box 48 Woodberry Forest VA 22989-0048 Office: The Residence Woodberry Forest VA 22989-0048

CAMPBELL, DIANA BUTT, lawyer; b. Ayer, Mass., Nov. 14, 1943; d. Lester A. and Genevieve P. (Ash) Butt; m. James W. Campbell, Feb. 3, 1961; children: James R., Lisa J., Alan D. BS magna cum laude, Suffolk U., 1980; JD, New Eng. Sch. Law, 1984. Bar: Mass. 1984, U.S. Dist. Ct. Mass. 1986, U.S. Supreme Ct. 1988. Editor Danvers (Mass.) State Hosp. Newsletter, 1977, Mass. Press Assn. Bull., 1978-79; mediator, case coord. Salem (Mass.) Mediation Program, 1979-83; legal adv. Help for Abused Women and Their Children, Salem, 1980-82; pvt. practice, Hamilton, Mass., 1984—. Mem., chair Hamilton Housing Authority, 1975-80; vol. Danvers State Hosp., 1978-92; mem. Cape Ann Area bd. Dept. Social Svc., Beverly, Mass., 1982-84; merit badge counselor Boy Scouts Am., Hamilton, 1984-93; assoc. mem. Hamilton Cable Adv. Bd., 1987-91; bd. dirs. United Way of North Shore, Beverly, 1988-94; adv. bd. of money mgmt. program North Shore Elder Svcs., 1993—; mem. adv. coun. SeniorCare, Inc. 2001—. Mem. Nat. Acad. Elder Law Attys., Assn. Trial Lawyers Am., Mass. Acad. Trial Lawyers, Mass. Bar Assn., Soc. Profl. Journalists, Essex County Bar Assn., Salem Bar Assn., North Shore Women Lawyers' Assn., Kiwanis (pres. 1990-91). Avocations: volkssporting, photography, travel. Home: 30 East St Topsfield MA 01983 Office: 65 Railroad Ave South Hamilton MA 01982-2218

CAMPBELL, DOUGLAS, physician; b. Rockville Centre, N.Y., Dec. 12, 1954; s. Nelson M. and Martha C. BS, U. Ga., 1976; MD, Med. Coll. of Ga., 1981. Emergency med. physician Wellstar Phys. Group, Marietta, Ga., 1992—, internal medicine practice, 1999—. Mem. ACP. Avocation: travel.

CAMPBELL, EARL DUNCAN, computer consultant; b. Berkeley, Calif., Sept. 5, 1946; s. Thomas S. and Mary (Hanlon) Campbell; m. Kathleen L. Gavin, Aug. 17, 1968 (div. May 1985); children: Kelly Lora, Heather Marie; m. Janice M. Holl, Oct. 31, 1992. AA in Philosophy, Monmouth U., W. Long Branch, N.J., 1970, BS in Acctg., 1972; MBA, Baruch U., N.Y.C., 1974. Cert. sys. analyst IBM, 1969. With Johnson & Johnson, New Brunswick, NJ, 1974—79; pres. SMS Consulting, Woodbridge, NJ, 1979—95, Campbell & Rathsam, Matawan, NJ, 1995—2003. Bus. and computer cons., Chgo., San Francisco, N.Y.C., 1979—2003. Sgt. USAF, 1964—68. Named N.J. Businessman of Yr., Bus. Adv. Coun., 2002. Mem.: Benevolent and Protective Order of Elks (exalted ruler 1982—83). Office: Campbell and Rathsam Inc 11 Morganville Rd Matawan NJ 07747 Office Fax: 732-583-8974. E-mail: earlcampbell@msn.com.

CAMPBELL, EDWARD ADOLPH, judge, electrical engineer; b. Boonville, Ind., Jan. 16, 1936; s.Revis Allen and Sarah Gertrude (Hunsaker) C.; m. Nancy Colleen Keys, July 26, 1957; children: Susan Elizabeth Campbell Frisse, Stephen Edward, Sara Lynne. BEE, U. Evansville, 1959; JD, Ind. U., 1965; grad. Nat. Coll. Dist. Attys., U. Houston, 1972; grad. Nat. Jud. Coll., U. Nev., 1978; grad. Am. Acad. Jud. Edn., U. Va., 1979; grad., Ind. Jud. Coll., 1981; grad. Ind. Grad. Program for Judges, Ind. Jud. Ctr., 1999. Bar: Ind. 1965, U.S. Dist. Ct. (so. dist.) Ind. 1965, U.S. Ct. of Customs and Patent Appeals 1967, U.S. Supreme Ct. 1973, U.S. Ct. Appeals (fed. cir.) 1982. Patent examiner U.S. Patent Office Digital Computer Divsn., Washington, 1959-60; patent adv. U.S. Naval Avionics, Indpls., 1960-65; patent atty. Gen. Elec. Co., Ft. Wayne, Ind., 1965-66; ptnr. Weyerbacher & Campbell, attys., Boonville, Ind., 1966-71; pros. atty. 2nd Jud. Cir., Warrick County, Ind., 1971-77; judge Warrick Superior Ct. No. 1, 1977-2001; sr. judge Ind. State Trial Cts., 2001—. Fellow Ind. Bar Found.; mem. IEEE, Ind.State Bar Assn., Evansville Bar Assn., Warrick County Bar Assn., Ind. Judges Assn., Nat. Coun. Juvenile and Family Ct. Judges, Ind. Coun. Juvenile and Family Ct. Judges, Warrick County C. of C. (bd. dirs. 1978-84, 97—), Lions Club, Sigma Pi Sigma, Phi Delta Phi. Democrat. Methodist. Home: 911 Julian Dr Boonville IN 47601-9556

CAMPBELL, EDWARD CLINTON, small business owner, violin maker; b. Scranton, Pa., May 24, 1929; s. Raymond Pyne and Mercedes Ruth (Simmons) C.; m. Mary Ringwald Dunfee, Sept. 1, 1954. BS in Engring., Pa. State U., 1955. Supr. order sect. Square D Electric Co., Inc., Detroit, 1955-59; propr., master violin maker Chimneys Violin Shop, Boiling Springs, Pa., 1960; operator Chimneys Sch. Violin Making. Lectr. various colls.; luthier in residence Internat. String Conf., Pa. State U. String Conf., N.J. chpt. Am. String Tchrs. Assn., Nat. Sch. Orch. Assn.; dir. Chimneys Violin Makers Ann. Workshop, Tucson; chmn., host. Violin Soc. Am. Conv., 1995; coord. activities Leonard Rose Cello Competition and the 6th Cello Congress, May 2001; host, chmn. 29th Ann. Conf. of Violin Soc. Am., 2001. Co-author: The Chimneys Violin Maker's Workshop-Book I, 1989, Book II, 1990, Book III, 1992; contbr. articles to Viol mag., Instrumentalist Mag. Pres. bd. dirs., fundraiser Amelia S. Givin Libr., Mt. Holly Springs, Pa., 1980-89. With USN, 1946-50. Recipient Grand Prize (14), Gold medal (3), Cert. of Merit (11), Internat. Violin Makers Competition, Gold Medal award Ministry of Culture, Peoples Republic of China, 1992; violins made by Edward Campbell exhibited at Renwick Gallery, Smithsonian Instn., 1978-79 and Oberlin Mus., Oberlin U., Ohio, 1987-88. Mem. Violin Soc. Am. (bd. dirs., sec., chmn., host 15th ann. conv., 20th ann. conf., 10th internat. competition, 1992, 23d ann. conf. 1995, coord. activities with 1st World String Quartet Congress 1987, 89, with Leonard Rose Cello Competition 1993, with 1st World Cello Congress 1988, coord. activities Leonard Rose Cello Competition and 6th Am. Cello Congress 2001, contbr. articles to jour.), So. Calif. Violin Makers Assn. (charter), Am. String Tchrs. Assn., Catgut Acoustical Soc. (spkr. joint conv. with Guild Am. Luthiers), Pa. String Tchrs. Assn., Boiling Spring Allenberry Club (pres. 1969), Lions (pres. Mt. Holly Springs club 1963-64, 85-86, 88-89), Clan Campbell (dep. commr. ctrl. Pa.) Republican. Methodist.

CAMPBELL, EDWARD JOSEPH, retired machinery company executive; b. Boston, Feb. 21, 1928; s. Edward and Mary (Doherty) C.; divorced; children: Gary, Kevin, Diane. BSME, Northwestern U., 1952, MBA, 1959. With Am. Brakeshoe Co., 1952-58, Whirlpool Corp., 1958-65; gen. mgr. Joy Mfg. Co., 1965-67; exec. v.p. J.I. Case Co. subs. Tenneco, Inc., 1968-78; pres., chief exec. officer Newport News Shipbuilding & Dry Dock Co. subs. Tenneco, Inc., Va., 1979-91; pres. J.I. Case Co. subs. Tenneco Inc., Racine, Wis., 1992-94. Bd. dir. Global Marine, Zurn Industries, Titan Internat., ABS Group; chmn. Campbell Enterprises. Mem. bd. and adv. coun. Webb Inst., Northwestern U., William & Mary Coll., U. Wis. Vet. Medicine Sch., Hampden & Sydney Coll.; chmn. Navy League US Found., elected ato NAE 1986 (Nat. Acad. of Engrng., With USNR, 1946-48. Home: 1 Deepwood Dr Unit A1 Racine WI 53402-2868 Office: PO Box 8 Racine WI 53401-0008

CAMPBELL, EDWARD WALLACE, nutritionist; b. Elizabeth, N.J., June 29, 1939; s. Edward Wallace Sr. and Dorothy Mae (Fairchild) C.; m. Phyllis A. Vecere, Sept. 27, 1959 (div. 1985); children: Diane Theresa, Christina Marie. PhD, Am. Coll., 1988, DLitt, Wellington U., 1990; MD, Open Internat. U., 1991, DSc, 1992; diploma, Lyons Med. Lab. Sch. Diplomate Internat. Coll. Acupuncture, Am. Coll. Manipulation and Nutrition, Inst. for Human Biomechanics, Am. Bd. Nutrition and Clin. Nutrition; cert. wellness counselor; Australian postgrad. cert. in acupuncture. Pvt. practice, 1974-94; dean of students Nat. Nutrition Inst., Oak Park, Ill., 1988-92; exec. dir. Am. Bd. Nutritional and Naturopathic Cert., Toms River, N.J., 1989-92; dir. R & D Vitagenics Rsch., Brick, N.J., 1990-95; dir. rsch. World AIDS Rsch. Inc., 1995—. Spkr. Nat. Health Fedn., 1987-93; prof. Open Internat. U. Author: Orthomolecular Protocol for Morbid Obesity with Adjunctive Congestive Heart Failure, 1987, Orthomolecular Protocols for the Physician, 1988, The Etiology of Hyperlipoproteinemia, 1990, Nutritional Management of Peripheral Vascular Diseases, 1991; contbg. editor: Am. Nutrition Cons. Assn. Jour., 1988-93. Assoc. mem. Am. Mus. Nat. History; mem. Lighthouse at Community Med. Ctr., Nat. Arbor Day Found., Rep. Nat. Com., Washington, 1980—; del. Rep. Party Platform Planning Com., Washington 1991-92, Presdl. Trust, Washington, 1992; campaign trustee Rep. Presdl. Task Force, Washington, 1987, 93. Fellow Found. for Complementary Medicine, Commonwealth (U.K.) Inst. Natural Medicine, Medicina Alternativa Sci. Soc., The Homeopathic Found.; mem. AARP (ret. tchrs. divsn.), Internat. Assn. Holistic Health and Medicine, Am. Nutrition Cons. Assn., Nat. Health Fedn., Am. Assn. of Nutritional Cons., Wilson Ctr. Assocs., Homeopathy and Homotoxicology Symposium, Va. Sheriffs Inst., Law Enforcement Alliance Am., Am. Legion, Senators Club, Clan Campbell Soc. Methodist. Avocations: hunting, fishing, motorcycle riding, chess, numismatism. *One's achievements are of no importance when accomplished without regard for morality and ethics.*

CAMPBELL, EDWARD WILSON (NED CAMPBELL), theater director, actor; b. Martinsburg, W.Va., Nov. 13, 1948; s. V. Wilson and Ruth Sargent Campbell; m. Kamal E. Burjorjee; 1 child, Malloree. BA in English, U. Md., 1970; MS in Human Resource Mgmt., Troy State U., 1980. Counselor Ga. Dept. of Human Resources, Columbus, 1981—85; playwright Columbus, Ga., 1985—. Adv. bd. mem. theater dept. Columbus State U., 1997—. Author: (plays) Ollie Utz is Free, 1999, Hauncho's Xellent Xmas (Jackie White Meml. award Columbia Entertainment Co., 1996), The Bluefeather Beastie (finalist for three nat. playwriting awards, 1995); actor: (plays) Shadowlands, (U.S. Army recruiting comml.), 1995; author: (plays) Haunco the Hamster, 1992 (Shubert Fendrich Meml. award for Playwriting Excellence, 1992, DeepSouth New Play award); actor: (TV films) Selma, Lord Selma, 1998; (films) The Fighting Temptations, 2002, Something to Talk About, 1995; (plays) Macbeth, The Crucible, The Passion of Dracula, The Diary of Anne Frank, St. Elmo; dir.: Ollie Utz is Free, 1999, Foxfire, 2000, Shadowlands, 2002. Mem.: Mensa, Dramatists Guild. Home and Office: 2007 Iris Dr Columbus GA 31906-1630

CAMPBELL, EDWIN DENTON, consultant; b. Boston, June 25, 1927; s. William Edwin and Mildred (Altmiller) C.; m. Crystal Cousins, 1973; children: Geraldine, Linda, David, Sean, Jennifer. Grad., Bentley Coll., Boston, 1948; CAS, Harvard U., 1971; EdD, 1975. CPA, Mass. Mgr. Arthur Andersen & Co. (C.P.A.s), Boston, 1948-53; v.p. Lab. for Electronics, Inc., Boston, 1953-62, also dir.; exec. v.p. Itek Corp., Lexington, Mass., 1962-70, dir., 1962-83; pres. Edn. Devel. Ctr., Newton, Mass., 1971-76, trustee, 1971—; pres. Gulf Mgmt. Inst. div. Gulf Oil Corp., Boston, 1976-83; on loan as exec. v.p. Nat. Alliance of Bus., Washington, 1983-86; dean sch. bus. Adelphi U., Garden City, N.Y., 1986-87; trustee Ednl. Testing Svc., Princeton, N.J., 1983-87, v.p., 1987-89; exec. dir. Coalition of Essential Schs., Annenberg Inst. for Sch. Reform, Brown U., Providence, 1990-96; prin. Padanaram Assocs., Inc., 1996—2001. Interim exec. dir. Plimoth Plantation, 1997; bd. dirs. ARtworks!; mem. faculty Bentley Coll., Boston, 1956-58. Cons. editor: Change, 1980-98. Trustee Bentley Coll., 1963—, New Bedford Whaling Mus., 1996—, Friends Acad., 1996—2002, Ptnrs. in Edn., Inc., 1997-99; v.p. Mass. Assn. Mental Health, 1965-68, bd. dirs., 1962-73; mem. Mass Commn. Vocat. Rehab., 1966-68, Coll. Bd. Commn. on Pre-coll. Counseling, 1984-86; mem. vis. com. Harvard Sch. Edn., 1977-83; mem. fin. com. Town of Carlisle, Mass., 1965-68; trustee Boston Urban Found., 1969-75, Mass. Taxpayers Found., 1962-68, Fenn Sch., 1970-75, OSTI, Inc., 1971-76, Lesley Coll., 1972-76, Mass. Advocacy Ctr., 1975-76. Served with USMC, 1943-45, PTO. Mem. Assn. Industries Mass. (pres. 1967-69, now dir.), Harvard Club Boston, Cosmos Club Washington (D.C.), New Bedford Yacht Club.

CAMPBELL, EUGENE PAUL, retired public health administrator; b. St. Paul, July 22, 1907; s. Eugene Paul and Fan (Berry) C.; m. Reba Lowe, Oct. 3, 1936; 1 child, Marilyn Joyce. BA in Zoology, UCLA, 1929; MD, Johns Hopkins U., 1933; MPH, U. Pa., 1942. Intern Balt. City Hosp., 1933-34, asst. resident in medicine, 1935; practice medicine specializing in preventive medicine, 1939—; ward officer Communicable Disease sect. Walter Reed Hosp., Washington, 1935-39; asst. prof. epidemiology U. Pa. Sch. Pub. Health, Phila., 1939-42; chief of Coop. Health Program Guatemala, 1942; field dir. South Am. Coop. Health Programs, 1943-45; chief Coop. Health Program Brazil, 1945-55; dep. chief pub. health divsn. ICA, Washington, 1955-57; dir. Office of Pub. Health, Washington, 1959-62; chief pub. health divsn. AID, New Delhi, 1962-65; health attache Am. Embassy, India, 1962-65; chief pub. health divsn. AID, Brazil, 1966-70; ret., 1970; now cons. V.p. Internat. Environ. Services, Inc., 1985— ; mem. U.S. del. WHO Gen. Assembly, 1957, 58, 60; cons. and promoter improved quality of pub. drinking water and child health. Bd. dirs. Am. Sch., Rio de Janeiro, Brazil, Strangers Hosp., Rio de Janeiro. Decorated grand ofcl. Order Med. Merit, Brazil, 1955; recipient Meritorious Service citation U.S. Govt., 1956, Merit citation Nat. Civil Service League, 1958. Fellow APHA, ACP; mem. Royal Acad. Tropical Medicine and Hygiene, Am. Soc. Tropical Health and Hygiene, Indian Assn. Advancement Med. Edn., Royal Soc. Health, Brazilian Soc. Hygiene, Washington Soc. for History of Medicine (pres. 1979-80), Antarctican Soc. U.S.A. Home: 1001 Middleford Rd Seaford DE 19973-3638

CAMPBELL, F(ENTON) GREGORY, college administrator, historian; b. Columbia, Tenn., Dec. 16, 1939; s. Fenton G. and Ruth (Hayes) C.; m. Barbara D. Kuhn, Aug. 29, 1970; children: Fenton H., Matthew W., Charles H. AB, Baylor U., 1960; postgrad., Philipps U., Marburg/Lahn, Germany, 1960-61; MA, Emory U., 1962; postgrad., Charles U., Prague, Czechoslovakia, 1965-66; PhD, Yale U., 1967; postgrad., Harvard U., 1981. Rsch. staff historian Yale U., New Haven, 1966-68, spl. asst. to acting pres., 1977-78; asst. prof. history U. Wis., Milw., 1968-69; asst. prof. European history U. Chgo., 1969-76, spl. asst. to pres., 1978-87, sec. bd. trustees, 1979-87, sr. lectr., 1985-87; pres., prof. history Carthage Coll., Kenosha, Wis., 1987—. Fellow Woodrow Wilson Internat. Ctr. for Scholars, Smithsonian Instn., Washington, 1976-77; participant Japan Study Program for Internat. Execs., 1987; bd. dirs. Thrivent Mut. Funds, Johnson Family Mut. Funds, Prairie Sch., United Health Systems, Wis. Author: Confrontation in Central Europe, 1975; joint editor Akten zur deutschen auswartigen Politik, 1918-1945, 1966-96; contbr. articles and revs. to profl. jours. Fulbright grantee, 1960-61, 73-74; Woodrow Wilson fellow, 1961-62; U.S.A.-Czechoslovakia Exch. fellow, 1965-66, 73-74, 85. Mem. Mid-Day Club (Chgo.), Coun. on Fgn. Rels. (NYC), Phi Beta Kappa, Omicron Delta Kappa. Home: 623 17th Pl Kenosha WI 53140-1360 Office: Carthage Coll Kenosha WI 53140-1360 E-mail: poc@carthage.edu.

CAMPBELL, FINLEY ALEXANDER, geologist, consultant; b. Kenora, Ont., Can., Jan. 5, 1927; s. Finley McLeod and Vivian (Delve) C.; m. Barbara Elizabeth Cromarty, Oct. 17, 1953; children— Robert Finley, Glen David, Cheryl Ann. B.Sc., Brandon Coll., U. Man., Can., 1950; MA, Queen's U., Kingston, Ont., 1956; PhD, Princeton U., 1958. Exploration and mining geologist Prospectors Airways, Toronto, 1950-58; asst. and asso. prof. geology U. Alta., Can., 1958-65; prof., head dept. geology U. Calgary, Alta., 1965-69, v.p. capital resources, 1969-71, v.p. acad., 1971-76, prof. geology, 1976-84, v.p. priorities and planning, 1984-88, prof. emeritus, 1988—; geol. cons., 1988—. Bd. dirs., vice chmn. Can Energy Research Inst. Contbr. articles on geol. topics to profl. jours. Bd. dirs. Calgary Olympic Devel. Assn.; mem. minister's adv. bd. Tyrrell Mus. Palaeontology. Decorated Queen's Jubilee medal Can.; recipient Commemorative medal for 125th Anniversary of Can., Geology medal Brandon U. Honor Soc.; Sir James Dunne fellow, 1955-56; Princeton Alumni fellow, 1957-58. Fellow Royal Soc. Can.; mem. Assn. The Univ. of Calgary (pres. emeritus), Geol. Assn. Can., Mineral Assn. Can., Soc. Econ. Geologists, Assn. Profl. Geologists Alta., Am. Mineral Soc. Royal Soc. Can., Can. Inst. Mining and Metallurgy, Brandon Univ. Alumni Assn. (reg. dir., Disting. Svc. award Hockey Hall of Fame 1994), Glenmore Yacht Club, Silver Springs Golf and Country Club, Clearwater Bay Yacht Club. Home: 3408 Benton Dr NW Calgary AB Canada T2L 1W8 Office: U Calgary Dept Geology and Geophysics Calgary AB Canada T2N 1N4 E-mail: campbelf@ucalgary.ca.

CAMPBELL, FRANCES HARVELL, foundation administrator; b. Goldston, N.C. d. George Henry and Evelyn (Meggs) Harvell. BS magna cum laude, U. Md., 1982; postgrad., Fla. State U., 1997—99. Asst. to Congressman Claude Pepper U.S. Ho. of Reps., 1966-80, staff dir., 1980-89; dir. Claude Pepper Ctr., 1996—; dir., prs. Mildred and Claude Pepper Found., 1989—. Exec. dir. Franklin D. Roosevelt Meml. Commn., 1988-92. Del. White House Conf. on Aging; v.p. Dem. Women of Capitol Hill, 1982—83; bd. dirs. Fla. State U. Found., 1995—2001, Nat. Com. to Preserve Social Security and Medicare, Econ. Club Fla., 1993—99, Fla. Assn. Non-profit Orgns., Zonta, Killearn Homeowners Assn.; v.p. LWV. Mem. ACLU, AAUW, Tiger Bay Club, Zonta, Economic Club of Fl., Phi Kappa Phi, Alpha Sigma Lambda. Avocations: orchid culture, reading, travel, the Arts. Home: 3943 Leane Dr Tallahassee FL 32309-2210 Office: 636 W Call St Tallahassee FL 32304-1122 E-mail: francescampbell6@aol.com.

CAMPBELL, FRANCIS JAMES, retired chemist; b. Toledo, Ohio, July 29, 1924; s. Herbert J. and Florence E. (Kelch) C.; m. Elizabeth P. Savage, Aug. 21, 1948; children: Nancy, MaryLou, Joan, Kathryn, Janice, James, Daniel. BS in Chem. Engring., U. Toledo, 1948. Cert. profl. chemist. Chemist Dow Chem. Co., Midland, Mich., 1948-53; chemist Dow Corning Corp., Midland, 1953-58, Naval Rsch. Lab., Washington, 1958-93; retired, 1993. Chmn. radiation effects on elec. insulation com. Internat. Electrotech. Commn., Geneva, 1974-85 House com. mem. Ind. Living for Handicapped, Inc., Washington, 1983-92; No. Va. chmn. Joint Bd. on Sci. and Engring. Edn., Washington, 1965-92. With U.S. Army, 1943-45. Recipient Research Publs. award Naval Research Lab., 1982, USN Meritorious Civilian Svc. award, 1997; decorated D.F.C., Air medal with 2 oak leaf clusters, Asiatic-Pacific Theater ribbon, WWII victory medal; inducted into Edward Drummond Libbey High Sch. Hall of Fame, Toledo, 1996; inducted as hon. fellow Washington Acad. Scis., 1999. Fellow IEEE (life); mem. IEEE Dielectrics and Elec. Insulation Soc. (Eric O. Forster award for Disting. Svc. 1992), Am. Chem. Soc., Am. Legion, Sigma Xi. Achievements include patents on thermal control coatings and battery packaging to prolong satellite life; research in thermal aging and multi-factor effects on reliability of electrical insulation of wire and cable, radiation curing of polymer matrix composites and adhesives, and in radiation damage in organic materials; in identifying the failure mechanisms in Kapton insulated wires that were responsible for a high number of electrical fires in Naval aircraft. Home: 2412 Crest St Alexandria VA 22302-2715

CAMPBELL, FREDERICK HOLLISTER, retired lawyer, historian; b. Somerville, Mass., June 14, 1923; s. George Murray and Irene Ivers (Smith) C.; m. Amy Holding Strohm, Apr. 14, 1951; 1 child, Susan Hollister. AB, Dartmouth Coll., 1944; JD, Northwestern U., 1949; postgrad., Indsl. Coll. Armed Forces, 1961-62; MA in History, U. Colo., 1984, PhD in History, 1993. Bar: Ill. 1950, U.S. Supreme Ct. 1967, Colo. 1968. Joined USMC, 1953, advanced through grades to lt. col., 1962; assoc. editor Callaghan and Co., Chgo., 1949-50; pvt. practice Colorado Springs, Colo., 1968-88; ptnr. Gibson, Gerdes and Campbell, 1969-79; pvt. practice, 1980-88; gen. counsel 1st Fin. Mortgage Corp., 1988-96; vice-chmn., corp. sec. 1st Fin. Mortgage Corp., 1993-96; hon. instr. history U. Colo., Colorado Springs, 1986—. Judge adv. USMC, Camp Lejeune, N.C., Korea, Parris Island, S.C., 1950-67, El Toro, Calif., Vietnam, Washington, 1950-67; vis. instr. Colo. Coll., 1993-95, asst. prof., 1996—. Author: John's American Notary and Commissioner of Deeds Manual, 1950; contbr. articles to profl. jours. Mem. Estate Planning Coun., Colorado Springs, 1971—81, v.p., 1977—78; trustee Frontier Village Found., 1971—77; precinct committeeman Rep. Party, 1971—86; del. Colo. State Conv., 1972, 1974, 1976, 1980; bd. dirs. Rocky Mountain Nature Assn., 1975—2001, pres., 1979—92; bd. dirs.. Rocky Mountain Nat. Park Assocs., 1986—2001, v.p., 1986—92, sec., 1992—95; bd. dirs. Colorado Springs Symphony Assn., 2002—. Mem. Colo. Bar Assn., El Paso County Bar Assn. Am. Arbitration Assn., Marines Meml. Club, Phi Alpha Theta. Congregationalist.

CAMPBELL, G. DOUGLAS, medical educator; b. Jackson, Miss., May 20, 1951; s. Guy D. and Margaret F. Campbell. Student, U. Miss., 1969-72, MD, 1976. Resident U. Miss. Sch. Medicine, Jackson, 1976-79, instr. dept. internal medicine, 1979-80, asst. dir. student health, 1979-81, asst. prof. dept. internal medicine, 1980-81; fellow U. Tex. Health Sci. Ctr., San Antonio, 1981-83; asst. prof. dept. internal medicine U. Ark. for Med. Scis., Little Rock, 1985-90, asst. prof. dept. microbiology and immunology, 1987-90; assoc. prof. dept. medicine La. State U. Med. Ctr., Shreveport, 1990—2002, program dir. pulmonary diseases dept. medicine, 1990-95, acting chief divsn. pulmonary and critical care medicine, 1992-94, chief divsn. pulmonary and critical care medicine, 1994-99; dir., divsn. pulmonary critical care U. of Miss., Sch. of Medicine, Jackson, Miss., 2002—. Staff physician med. svc. VA Med. Ctr., Jackson, 1979-81, dir. diabetes sect., 1980-81, med. student coord. med. svc., 1980-81, asst. environ. health officer, 1980-81; staff physician med. svc. John L. McClellan VA Hosp., Little Rock, 1985-90; staff physician med. svc. Overton Brooks VA Hosp., Shreveport, 1990—2002. Named Outstanding Young Men in Am., 1981; recipient Disting. Svc. award Disabled Am. Vets., 1990; postdoctoral fellowship in microbiology and infectious diseases U. Calgary Health Sci. Ctr., 1983-85. Fellow ACP, Am. Coll. Chest Physicians; mem. Am. Thoracic Soc., Sigma Xi. Office: UMC Pulmonary Division 2500 N State St Jackson MS 39216-4505

CAMPBELL, GEORGE, JR., physicist, administrator; s. George Washington and Lillian (Britt) C.; m. Mary Schmidt, Aug. 24, 1968; children: Garikai, Sekou, Britt. BS, Drexel U., 1968; PhD, Syracuse U., 1977; postgrad., Yale U., 1988; D (hon.), Drexel U., 2000, Coe Coll., 2002. Sr. faculty Nkumbi Internat. Coll., Kabwe, Zambia, 1969-71; staff scientist AT&T Bell Labs., Holmdel, N.J., 1977-83, third level mgr., 1983-89; pres., CEO Nat. Action Coun. for Minorities in Engring., Inc., N.Y.C., 1989-2000; Porth disting. lectr. U. Mo.-Rolla, 1993, 99; pres. Cooper Union for the Advancement of Sci. and Art, N.Y.C., 2000—. Adv. bd. U.S. Sec. of Energy, Washington, 1990-93, NRC Com. on Women in Sci. and Engring., 1991-95, Coll. Engring. Cooper Union, Sta. WGBH-TV Discovering Women series, 1993-94, Merck Inst. Sci. Edn., 1993-99; mem. nat. commn. Ill. Inst. Tech., 1994; pres. Coalition for Equity and Access to Sci., Tech., Engring. and Math., 1996-97. Co-editor: Access Denied: Race, Ethnicity and the Scientific Enterprise, 2000, Access Denied: Race, Ethnicity and the Scientific Enterprise, 2000; contbr. chpts. to books, articles to profl. jours. including Phys. Rev. D, Jour. Math. Physics, Issues in Sci. and Tech., Procs. IEEE Globecom, Black Issues in Higher Edn., Black Collegian, Chronicle of Higher Edn., NACME Rsch. Letter, AAAS Sci. and Tech. Policy Yearbook, 1995; commentator Nightly Bus. Report, 1993—. Bd. dirs. N.Y. Hall of Sci., 1994—, Oak Ridge Assoc. Univs., 1993-99, Crossroads Theater Co., 1990-95,

Consolidated Edison, Inc., 2000—, Montefiore Med. Ctr., 2001-; mem. NSF adv. bd. Comprehensive Regional Ctr. for Minorities, N.Y. chmn., 1990-93; trustee, mem. exec. com. Rensselaer Poly. Inst., Troy, N.Y., 1991—; chmn. N.Y.C. Chancellor's Task Force on Sci. Edn., 1992-93; task force on minorities in sci. Nat. Inst. Environ. Health Scis./AAAS, 1994; bd. govs. All Nations Alliance for Minority Participation in Sci. and Engring., 1995-2000; trustee Poly. U., Bklyn., 1997-2000; mem. Pres.' Info. Tech. Adv. Com. Socio-Econ. and Workforce Panel, 1998—; mem. Congl. Commn. on Advancement of Women and Minorities in Sci. and Tech., 1999-2000. Recipient George Arents Pioneer medal in physics Syracuse U., 1993, Drexel U. Centennial medal, 1992, Presdl. award for excellence in math., sci. and engring. mentoring, 1996, EPIC award U.S. Dept. Labor, 1998, Disting. Svc. award for sci. and tech. Poly. U., 1999; named Black Achiever in Industry, YMCA, N.Y.C., 1987; Simon Guggenheim scholar Guggenheim Found., Phila., 1963-67. Fellow AAAS (com. on sci., engring. and pub. policy 1990-96), N.Y. Acad. Scis. (pres. coun. 1991—), ; mem. Am. Phys. Soc. (pres. cir. 1997—), Nat. Acad. Scis., Nat. Acad. Engring. and Inst. Medicine, Nat. Acad. Engring. (steering com. on engr. of 2020), Sigma Pi Sigma. Achievements include extending bootstrap model to SU(4)-symmetric strong interaction physics; responsible for third generation satellite 3 power system development. Office: The Cooper Union 30 Cooper Sq New York NY 10003-7125 E-mail: campbell@cooper.edu.

CAMPBELL, GEORGE EMERSON, lawyer; b. Piggott, Ark., Sept. 23, 1932; s. Sid and Mae (Harris) C.; m. Anna Claire Janes, June 22, 1960 (dec. Mar. 1971); children: Dianne, Carole; m. Joan Stafford Rule, Apr. 7, 1973. JD, U. Ark., Fayetteville, 1955. Bar: Ark. 1955, U.S. Supreme Ct. 1971. Law clk. to judge Ark. Supreme Ct., 1959-60; mem. Rose Law Firm, P.A., Little Rock, 1960—; Del. 7th Ark. Constl. Conv., 1969-70; regional v.p. Nat. Mcpl. League, 1974-86. Mem. Ark. Ednl. TV Commn., 1976-92, chmn., 1980-82, 88-91; bd. dirs. Ark. Ednl. TV Found., 1984-92, chmn., 1988-91. Chmn. bd. Pulaski County Law Libr., 1980—; bd. dirs. Ark. Arts Ctr., 1991-95, sec. 1992-93), Ark. Symphony Orch. Soc., 1982-87, Ark. Capital Corp., pres. 2001-; bd. dirs. Ark. Cert. Devel. Corp., Downtown Partnership, 1978-2002; bd. dirs. Youth Home Inc., 1986-92, pres., 1991-92. With USNR, 1955-77, comdr. ret. Fellow Am. Bar Found.; mem. ABA, Ark. Bar Assn., Pulaski County Bar Assn., Am. Law Inst. (life mem.), Am. Judicature Soc., Nat. Assn. Bond Lawyers. Office: Rose Law Firm PA 120 E 4th St Little Rock AR 72201-2893 Office Fax: 501-375-1309. E-mail: gcampbell@roselawfirm.com.

CAMPBELL, GEORGE VAN PELT, sociology and religion educator; b. Jackson, Tenn., Apr. 15, 1953; s. George Edward and Constance Van Pelt Campbell; m. Karen P. Underwood, Oct. 9, 1952; children: Derek V., Joanna G. BS, Bryan Coll., Dayton, Tenn.; PhD, U. Pitts., 1990—99; ThM, Dallas Theol. Seminary. Temp. asst. prof. religious studies Ind. U. Pa., Indiana, Pa., 1999—2000; asst. prof. sociology and religion Grove City Coll., Grove City, Pa., 2000—. Chair, religion and culture study group Evang. Theol. Soc., 1999—2002. Contbr. articles to jour. Bd. mem. Grace Cmty. Food Pantry, Grove City, Pa., 2001—03. Recipient Participant in Scholars' Seminar, Morality, Culture, and the Power of Religion in Social Life, Pew Charitable Trusts, 2001. Mem.: Evang. Theol. Soc. Presbyterian Christian. Avocations: American Civil War study, travel, musical theater. Home: 128 Garden Ave Grove City PA 16127 Office: Grove City Coll 100 Campus Dr Box 2567 Grove City PA 16127 Office Fax: 724-458-3852. E-mail: gvcampbell@gcc.edu.

CAMPBELL, GILBERT SADLER, surgery educator, surgeon; b. Toronto, Ont., Can., Jan. 4, 1924; s. Gilbert S. and Ellen (Thorson) C.; m. Dorothy Jean Nugent, Sept. 18, 1947 (div. 1960); children: Kathryn Ellen, Rebecca Sadler, Thomas Kim, William Riley; m. Joan Louise Hancock, Sept. 28, 1961; children: Susan Muffin, John Gilbert. Student, Hampden Sydney Coll., 1939-40; BA, U. Va., 1943, MD, 1946; MS, U. Minn., 1949, PhD, 1954. Intern U. Minn. Hosps., Mpls., 1946-47, tchg. asst., 1947-49, researcher Am. Cancer Soc., 1951-53, sr. surgery resident, 1953-54; instr. physiology U. Minn., Mpls., 1948-49, instr. surgery, 1954-55, asst. prof., 1955-58; prof. surgery U. Okla., Oklahoma City, 1958-65; prof. surgery and thoracic surgery U. Okla. Med. Ctr., Oklahoma City, 1958-65; prof. surgery, chief thoracic surgery U. Ark. for Med. Scis., Little Rock, 1965-90; cons. surgery Little Rock VA Hosp, 1965-90, Ark. Children's Hosp., Little Rock, 1973-90; mem. courtesy staff Ark. Bapt. Med. Ctr., Little Rock, 1972-90; prof. emeritus, 1990—. Contbr. articles in field to med. jours. Served to capt. U.S. Army, 1949-51. Decorated Purple Heart, Bronze Star with oak leaf cluster, Silver Star with oak leaf cluster U.S. Army; Mary R. Markle scholar, 1954-59; recipient Horsley prize U. Va., 1954; named Surgery Alumnus of Yr. U. Minn., 1983. Mem. Am. Assn. Thoracic Surgery, AMA (ho. of dels. 1976-82), Am. Physiol. Soc., Am. Surg. Assn., Halsted Soc. (pres. 1978), Internat. Cardiovascular Soc. (v.p. N. Am. Chpt. 1973), Societe Internationale de Chirurgie, Soc. Thoracic Surgeons, Soc. Univ. Surgeons, Soc. Vascular Surgery, So. Surg. Assn. (1st v.p. 1981), Western Surg. Assn., S.W. Surg. Congress (pres. 1980), Raven Soc., Alpha Omega Alpha Home: 66 River Ridge Rd Little Rock AR 72227-1526

CAMPBELL, GREGORY AUGUST, engineering educator, consultant; b. Providence, Sept. 18, 1941; s. Gordon Raymond and Vita (Carstensen) C.; m. Susann Wardwell, Sept. 8, 1962; children: Sara, Gordon. BS, U. Maine, 1964, PhD, 1969. Assoc. sr. rsch. engr. GM Rsch. Lab., Warren, Mich., 1968-71, sr. rsch. engr., 1971-74, staff rsch. engr., 1974-78, sr. staff rsch. engr., 1978-81; supr. polymer fabrication R&D Mobil Chem., Edison, N.J., 1981-84; assoc. prof. Clarkson U., Potsdam, N.Y., 1984-96, prof., chair chem. engring., 1996-98, dean of engring., 1998—2000; prof. chem. engring., 2000—. Cons. Mobil Chem., 1986—; dir. polymer fabrication Ctr. for Advanced Material Processing, Potsdam. NASA fellow U. Maine, 1965-68. Mem. AAAS, Am. Inst. Chem. Engrs., Soc. Plastics Engrs. Achievements include patents for Novel Foam Process Electropainting; Temperature Measurement and Process Stability Analysis and Control; developed new concept for foam nucleations, and for new screw-pump extender. Office: Clarkson U Dept Chem Engring Potsdam NY 13699-0001

CAMPBELL, HELEN WOERNER (MRS. THOMAS B. CAMPBELL), librarian; b. Indpls., Oct. 17, 1918; d. Clarence Julius and Gertrude Elizabeth (Colley) Woerner; student Ind. U., 1935-38; B.S., Butler U., 1967; m. Thomas B. Campbell, Jan. 17, 1942; 1 dau., Martha (Mrs. L. Kurt Adamson). Asst. order librarian Ind. U., Bloomington, 1937-42; librarian Ind. U. Sch. Dentistry, Indpls., 1942-46, cataloger, part-time, 1960-65, asst. librarian, 1965-66, librarian, 1966-80. Mem. Med. Library Assn., Spl. Libraries Assn. (chpt. pres. 1972-73). Home: Apt 206 5354 W 62nd St Indianapolis IN 46268-4483

CAMPBELL, HENRY CUMMINGS, librarian; b. Vancouver, C., Can., Apr. 22, 1919; s. Henry and Margaret (Cummings) C.; m. Sylvia Woodsworth, Sept. 13, 1943; children— Shiela (Mrs. David Macrae), Bonnie, Robin. BA, U. B.C., 1940; BLS, U. Toronto, 1941; MA, Columbia U., 1949. Librarian, film producer Nat. Film Bd., Can., 1941-46; with Secretariat UN, N.Y., 1946-48, UNESCO, Paris, 1949-56; chief librarian Toronto (Can.) Pub. Library, 1956-78; gen. mgr. Cinfolink Svcs., Toronto, 1994—. Lectr. U. Toronto Sch. Libr. Sci., 1970-71; cons. on info. systems and libr. svcs. Canadian Govt. Social Sci. Rsch. Coun. Can., UNESCO; active State Sci. and Tech. Commn., Beijing, China, 1991—, China Internet Info. Svcs., 1997—. Author: How To Find Out About Canada, 1967, Canadian Libraries, 1972, rev. edit., Early Days on the Great Lakes, 1971, The Public Library in the Urban Metropolitan Setting, 1973, Development of Public Library Systems and Services, 1982, Computer Information Systems in the People's Republic of China, Cinfolink Directory of Information Services in China and Hong Kong, 1993-94, 1993, Cinfolink Annual Review of Information Services in China, 1995-96, 1996, Looking for Harrison, 1993, Cinfolink China Internet Directory, 2002, (with Joachim Wieder) IFLA: A History 1927-2002, 2002. Recipient Prof. Kawla award for Library and Info. Sci., 1984 Fellow IFLA (hon.); mem. Internat. Assn. Met. City Librs. (pres. 1971-74), Canadian Libr. Assn. (pres. 1973-74), Ont. Continuing Edn. Assn. (pres. 1966), Fedn. Can.-China Friendship Socs. (pres. 1985-88), Ex Libris Assn. (pres. 2002—). E-mail: cinfo@ican.net.

CAMPBELL, HUGH BROWN, JR., judge; b. Charlotte, N.C., Feb. 19, 1937; s. Hugh Brown and Thelma Louise (Welles) C.; m. Mary Irving Carlyle, Nov. 3, 1962; children: Hugh B. III, Irving Carlyle, Thomas Lenoir. AB, Davidson Coll., 1959; JD, Harvard U., 1962. Atty. Craighill, Rendleman, Charlotte, 1964-77, Weinstein & Sturges, Charlotte, NC, 1977-94, Cansler Lockhart Charlotte, 1995-2000; judge N.C. Ct. Appeals, Raleigh, 2001—02, 26th Jud. Dist. Ct., Charlotte, 2003—. Chmn. Jury Commn., Mecklenburg County, N.C., 1985-97; exec. com. County Bar Assn., Mecklenburg County, 1989-92, civil cts. com. chair, 1990-92. Rep. N.C. House Reps., Raleigh, 1969-71; legis. liaison Charlotte/Mecklenburg County, Raleigh, 1971-72; state chmn. N.C. Zoo Bond Campaign, 1972; chmn. Carolinas Med. Ctr. Bond Campaign, 1976. Col. JAG U.S. Army, 1962-64, Res., 1964-92. Decorated Legion of Merit, Meritorious Svc. medal (2); Honored Order of Hornet, Mecklenburg County, 1976. Mem. N.C. Bar Coun. (exec. com., chair ethics 1981-90), Planned Parenthood Charlotte (bd. dirs., chmn. 1980-81), YMCA Charlotte (adv. bd. 1992—), Rotary Club E. Charlotte (pres. 1976-77). Democrat. Episcopalian. Avocations: tennis, swimming, hiking, reading, politics. Home: 1428 Scotland Ave Charlotte NC 28207-2561 Office: 26th Jud Dist 700 E 4th St Charlotte NC 28202

CAMPBELL, IAN DAVID, opera company director; b. Brisbane, Australia, Dec. 21, 1945; came to U.S., 1982; m. Ann Spira; children: Benjamin, David. BA, U. Sydney, Australia, 1967. Prin. tenor singer The Australian Opera, Sydney, 1967-74; sr. music officer The Australia Council, Sydney, 1974-76; gen. mgr., stage dir. The State Opera of South Australia, Adelaide, 1976-82; asst. artistic adminstr. Met. Opera, N.Y.C., 1982-83; gen. dir. San Diego Opera, 1983—. Guest lectr. U. Adelaide, 1978; guest prof. San Diego State U., 1986—; cons. Lyric Opera Queensland, Australia, 1980-81; bd. dirs. Opera Am., Washington, 1986-95, 1997-2001, chmn., 2001—; chmn. judges Met. Opera Auditions, Sydney, 1989, Masterclasses, Music Acad. of the West, 1993-96. Producer, host San Diego Opera Radio Program, 1984-2001, At the Opera with Ian Campbell, 2001--; stage director La Boheme, 1981, The Tales of Hoffmann, 1982 (both in South Australia), Falstaff (San Diego Opera), 1999, Cavalleria Rusticana/Pagliacci (Santa Barbara Grand Opera), 1999, Il Trovatore (San Diego Opera), 2000, Tosca (San Diego Opera), 2002. Mem., bd. dirs. San Diego Conv. and Visitors Bur., 1997-2002. Recipient Peri award Opera Guild So. Calif., 1984; named Headliner of Yr., San Diego Press Club, 1991, Father of Yr., San Diego, 1997. Fellow: Australian Inst. Mgmt.; mem.: Rotary, San Diego Press Club. Avocation: golf. Office: San Diego Opera 1200 3rd Ave Fl 18 San Diego CA 92101-4112

CAMPBELL, JACK JAMES RAMSAY, microbiology educator; b. Vancouver, C., Can., Mar. 29, 1918; s. Murdoch and Margaret (Campbell) C.; m. Emily Ann Fraser, Sept. 4, 1942; children: Sheila Merle, Ann Ross. BSA, U. B.C., Vancouver, 1939; PhD, Cornell U., 1944. Research assoc. chem. warfare Dept. Def., Kingston, Ont., Can., 1944-46; mem. dairying dept. U. B.C., 1946-65, prof., head microbiology dept., 1965-82. Fellow Royal Soc. Can., AAAS; mem. Am., Can. socs. microbiology, Sigma Xi, Phi Kappa Phi, Alpha Delta, Sigma Tau Upsilon. Home: 3949 W 37th St Vancouver BC Canada V6N 2W4

CAMPBELL, JACQUELYN C. community health nurse; b. Camden, N.J., Aug. 2, 1946; d. Joseph and Dorothy (Cutler) Bowman; 1 child, Christina, Bradley. BSN, Duke U., 1968; MSN, Wright State U., 1980; PhD in Nursing, U. Rochester, 1986. RN, Mich. Instr. Sinclair Community Coll., Dayton, Ohio, 1976-79, Wayne State U. Coll. Nursing, Detroit, 1980-82, mem. faculty, 1984—, assoc. prof., 1988—; teaching asst. U. Rochester (N.Y.) Sch. Nursing, 1982-84; Anna D. Wolf Endowed Prof., Sch. Nursing Johns Hopkins U., associate dean for the Ph.D. program and res., Sch. Nursing. Mem. violence rev. panel NIMH, Washington, 199—. Co-author: Nursing Care of Victims of Family Violence, 1984 (AJN Book of Yr.); editor and co-author: Sanctions and Sanctuary:Cultural Perspectives on the Beating of Wives, 1992; mem. editorial bd. to sci. jours.; contbr. articles to profl. jours. V.p., bd. dirs. Women's Justice Ctr., Ann Arbor, Mich., 1987—; pres. Coun. on the Status of Women, Detroit, 1988-92; support group facilitator My Sister's Place, Detroit, 1989-92; mem. adv. bd. Wayne County Adv. Bd. Interpersonal Violence, Detroit, 1991-92, adv. panel Robert Wood Johnson Found., Princeton, N.J., 1990-92; prin. investigator NIH, NCNR, 1990—. Recipient First ward NIH, 1987-92; W.K. Kellogg Found., 1990-93. Mem. ANA (chair task force on violence 1991-92), APHA, Am. acad. Nursing, a.A.N. award 1988), Inst. Medicine, Midwest Nursing Rsch. Soc. (Helen Werley new investigator 1992), Nursing Rsch. Consortium on Violence and Abuse, Nursing Network on Violence Against Women. Democrat. Avocation: tennis. Office: Johns Hopkins Univ Sch of Nursing 525 N Wolfe St Baltimore MD 21205-2110

CAMPBELL, JAMES ALBERT BARTON, association executive, retired marketing executive; b. Chattanooga, Tenn., Nov. 2, 1940; s. James Harry and Elizabeth Tipton (Johnson) C.; m. Julia Madge Clark, Sept. 12, 1964; children: Richard Barton, Julia Clark. BS, Princeton U., 1962; grad., U.S. Army Command Gen. Staff Coll., 1975, U.S. Army War Coll., 1985. Devel. engr. DuPont Co., Wilmington, Del., 1964-66; mktg. specialist Formex Co., Greeneville, Tenn., 1966-67; field sales engr. Reynolds Metals Co., Richmond, Va., 1967-70, regional sales rep. Charlotte, N.C., 1970-74, mktg. mgr. Richmond, 1975-81, mgr. market planning, 1982-84, market group mgr., 1984-86, mktg. svcs. mgr., 1986-93, mgr. sales and mktg. svcs., 1994-96, mem. pres.'s task force on corp. definition, 1996, mem. process definition team, 1996; ret., 1996; dir. membership and ROTC affairs Res. Officer Assn., Washington, 1997-2000, Eastern region mktg. dir., 2000—01. Founder, owner Priceless Pages Christian Bookstore, Richmond, Va., 1983—90; mem. light postal vehicle task force Aluminum Assn., N.Y.C., 1978—79; advisor Marine Pleasure Boat Assn., Chgo., 1984. Pres. Res. Officers Assn., Richmond, 1987, area 3 dir., 1988, state v.p. Army, 1992-93; exec. com. Assn. U.S. Army, Richmond, 1988-90; mil. advisor State of Va. Com. Employer Support Guard and Res.; mem. exec. com. Young Life, 1988-92; bd. dirs. Encounter Ministries; elder local Presbyn. Ch. Col. USAR ret. Decorated Legion of Merit, Meritorious Svc. medal with three oak leaf clusters, Army Commendation medal, Army Achievement medal with oak leaf cluster. Mem. SCV (Ga. comdr. 1969-70, Va. lt. comdr. 1992-96, chmn. nat. strategy planning com. 1994-96, chmn. centennial nat. conv. 1996), Gideons Internat. (local pres., v.p., sec. 1969-90), Jeb Stuart Camp (comdr. 1991-92), Ball Cmty. Mus. of the Confederacy (trustee 2001), Res. Officers Assn. (pres. MG Jeb Stuart chpt. 2000 02), ROA Nat. Exec. Com., 2002-2004, The Mus. of the Confederacy (com. mem. 1996-2001, exec. dir. 2002—), Scottish Clan Campbell Soc. N.Am. (trustee). Avocations: history lectr., strategy gaming. Home: 2211 Heathland Dr Midlothian VA 23113-4183 E-mail: colbert@earthlink.net.

CAMPBELL, JAMES L. military career officer; b. Ft. Benning, Ga., Aug. 16, 1949; m. Carol Anderson; children: Scott, Casey. Grad., U. Mo.; BS in Phys. Edn., 1971; MS in Phys. Edn., U. Ill.; MA in Nat. Security & Strategic Studies, Naval War Coll.; grad., U.S. Army Command & Gen. Staff, Naval War Coll. Commd. 2nd lt. U.S. Army, advanced through grades to brig. gen.; dir. instrn. dept. phys. edn. U.S. Mil. Acad.; with 15th Battalion, 4th combat support tng. brigade U.S. Army, Ft. Jackson, S.C., co. comdr. 1st Battalion, 32d Infantry, 2nd Infantry Divsn. Camp Casey, Korea, rifle platoon leader, reconnaissance platoon leader, comdr. 4th Bn., 27th Inf., 25th Inf. Divsn. (Light), ACofS, G3, 9th Inf. Divsn. (Motorized) Ft. Lewis, Wash., dep. chief staff I Corps, chief of staff, comdr. 1st Brigade, 10th Mountain Divsn., exec. officer to the chief of staff, comdr. Joint Task Force-Full Acctg., asst. divsn. comdr., 25th Inf. Divsn. (Light), asst. divsn. comdr. (ops.), 25th Inf. Divsn. (Light), 1998—. Decorated Def. Superior Svc. medal with oak leaf cluster, Legion of Merit with 2 oak leaf clusters, Bronze star, Meritorious Svc. medal with 3 oak leaf clusters, Army Commendation medal, Army Achievement medal.

CAMPBELL, JAMES R. transportation executive; b. July 16, 1941; s. Ray E. and Anne Louise (Wooten) Campbell. BS, U. Houston, 1965; postgrad., Case Western Res. U., 1967-68, Yale U., 1990. Personnel asst. The Standard Oil Co., Cleve., 1966-68; dir. equal opportunity programs Turner Constrn. Co., Cleve., 1968-73; employment project dir. Nat. Assn. Drug Abuse Problems, N.Y.C., 1973-74; exec. dir. The Cuyahoga Plan Ohio, Cleve., 1974-77; dir. EEO compliance and cmty. activities the continental Group, Inc., Stamford, Conn., 1978-85; cons. human resources James Campbell & Assocs., Inc., 1985-88; asst. v.p. strategic human resource planning MTA N.Y.C. Transit, Bklyn., 1990—93, acting dep. v.p. employee resources, 1993—96, asst. v.p. employee resources, 1988—90; v.p. adminstrn. MTA Long Island Bus, Garden City, NY, 1996—. Expert witness HUD, 1970, U.S. Ho. of Reps. subcom., 1972. Contbr. Chmn. task force, mem. steering com. Cleve. Fedn. Cmty. Devel. Manpower Planning & Devel. Commn., 1971—73; mem. cmty. adv. bd. Cleve. Press, 1972; mem. Pres.'s com. Employment of People With Disabilities, 1985—91. With USAF, 1958—62, Japan. Recipient Key to City, Cleve., 1970, Outstanding Cmty. Svc. award, Urban League Cleve., 1972. Mem.: ASTD, N.Y. Human Resources Planning Soc., Pers. Accreditation Inst., Soc. Human Resources Mgmt. (life-time profl. cert. advanced level), Human Resource Assn. N.Y., St. Andrew's Soc. N.Y. State, Clan Campbell Edn. Found. (trustee 2000—), Clan Campbell Soc. (dep. commr. N.Y.C. 1998—2000, trustee 2000—, N.Am. chpt.), N.Y. Caledonian Club (chieftain 1999, trustee 2000—02, chief 2001—02), Omicron Delta Kappa (circle v.p. 1965, Gold Key 1965). Home: 504 W 110th St Apt 8-d New York NY 10025-2008 Office: MTA LI Bus 700 Commercial Ave Garden City NY 11530-6410 E-mail: jamesrcampbell1@rcn.com.

CAMPBELL, JAMES ROBERT, retired bank executive; b. Rochester, Minn., May 24, 1942; s. Donald William and Alice Marie (Gray) C.; m. Carmen Dawn Starkson, July 11, 1964; children: Peter Ian, Kathryn Ann. BS in Bus, U. Minn., 1964. Comml. banking officer Norwest. Nat. Bank Mpls., 1964-67, asst. v.p., 1967-71, sr. v.p. nat. dept., 1976-79, pres., COO, 1984-86; pres., dir. Lease N.W., Inc., Mpls., 1971-75, Norwest Bank Omaha N.A., 1979-82; regional pres. Norwest Corp.-Norwest Banks, 1982-84; pres., CEO Wells Fargo Bank, Mpls., 1986-95, chmn. bd. dirs., 1995—2002; chmn. bd. Norwest Bank Minn. N.A., Mpls., 1995-98; ret., 2002. Group exec. v.p. Wells Fargo & Co., 1998—2002; exec. v.p. Norwest Corp.; bd. dirs. Allianz U.S.A., Marvin Lumber & Cedar Co., Allina Health Sys., Cretex Cos. Inc., Lifetouch, Inc. Bd. dirs. Mpls. Inst. Arts, U. Minn. Found., United Way Mpls. Mem.: World Pres. Orgn., Minn. Exec. Orgn., Bay Colony Golf Club, Spring Hill Golf Club, Mpls. Club (bd. dirs.), Minikahda Club. Presbyterian. Home: 5521 Woodcrest Dr Minneapolis MN 55424-1651 E-mail: James.r.campbell@wellsFargo.com.

CAMPBELL, JAMES SARGENT, lawyer; b. Chgo., Sept. 19, 1938; m. Mary Tydings Eager, Sept. 3, 1960; children: Catherine, Julia, John. BA summa cum laude, Yale U., 1960; LLB, Stanford U., 1964. Bar: DC 1966. Carnegie teaching fellow Yale U., 1960-61; law clk. to Hon. William O. Douglas U.S. Supreme Ct., 1964-65; spl. asst. antitrust div. Dept. of Justice, 1967-68; gen. counsel Nat. Commn. Causes and Prevention Violence, 1968-69; assoc. Wilmer, Cutler & Pickering, Washington, 1965-67, 70-71, ptnr., 1972-2000, of counsel, 2001—. Cons. Office of Sec. HUD, 1977—78, HHS, 1979. Author, editor: book Law and Order Reconsidered, 1970, Doctor Faustus: Archetypal Subtext at the Millenium, 1999. Trustee Eastern Shore Chamber Music Festival, 2000—, pres., 2002—; co-chair Eastern Shoreway Alliance, 2003—; mem. vestry Wye Parish, 2003—. Mem.: MLA, ABA, Save Our County (Queen Anne's), Cosmos Club, Elizabethan Club, Phi Beta Kappa, Order of Coif. Office: Wilmer Cutler & Pickering 2445 M St NW Washington DC 20037-1420

CAMPBELL, JANE LOUISE, mayor; b. May 19, 1953; d. Paul and Joan (Brown) C.; m. Hunter Morrison, Dec. 8, 1984; children: Jessica Elizabeth, Catherine Joanna. BA in History, U. Mich., 1974; MS in Urban Studies, Cleve. State U., 1980. Mem. State of Ohio Ho. of Reps. 11th dist., Columbus, 1984—92, majority whip, 1992—2000; mayor City of Cleve., 2001—. Apptd. mem. Nat. Com. on Welfare Reform; mem. Cuyahoga County Plan Commn., Fin. and Appropriations Com., Ways and Means Com., Aging and Housing Com.; active Nat. Coun. State Legislators, vice-chair Human Svcs. Com., Children, Families and Youth Com., past pres. Women's Network, mem. Federal Budget and Taxation Com.; chair Abused, Neglected Children Oversight Com.; vice-chair Select Com. on Child Abuse and Juvenile Justice, 1989; mem. gov. task force on Adolescent Sexuality and Pregnanacy, 1986, com. to Study Ohio's Sch. Found. Program Distribution of State Funds to Sch. Dists., 1991; exec. dir. Friends of Shaker Square, 1982-84; nat. field dir. ERAmerica, 1979-82; founding dir. Womenspace, 1975-79. Elder Heights Christian Ch. Recipient Legislative Leadership award Ohio Psychological Assn., 1986, Legislative award Ohio Hunger Task Force, 1987, Recognition award Ohio Primary Care Assn., 1987, Dean's Disting. Alumni award Cleve. State Univ., 1987, Hall of Fame award Nat. Senior Citizens, 1988, State Public Official of the Year award Ohio Chpt. Nat. Assn. of Social Workers, 1988, Found. award Ohio Chpt. ACLU, 1988, Legislative award Ohio Assn. of Counseling and Devel., 1989, Ohio Assn. of County Bds. of Mental Retardation/Developmental Disabilities award, 1989, Cancer Fighter award Ireland Cancer Ctr., 1990, Legislative award Ohio Human Svcs. Dirs. Assn., 1990, Hosephine Irwin award Womenspace, 1991, Spcl. Recognition award Providence House, 1991, Citizen award Ohio Assn. for the Edn. of Young Children, 1991, Legislator of the Year award Greater Cleve. Nurses Assn., 1991, Legilsative award Nat. Assn. of Sch. Psychologists, 1992, Outstanding Svc. award Public Children's Svcs. Assn., 1992., numerous others. Democrat. Office: Cleveland City Hall 601 Lakeside Ave Rm 202 Cleveland OH 44114

CAMPBELL, JANE TURNER, retired realtor, retired secondary school educator; b. Macon, Mo., July 8, 1931; d. Thomas Freeman and Rena Ellen (Vandiver) Turner; m. Duard Ray McDonald, Aug. 25, 1952 (div. 1955); m. Ian MacCallum Campbell, Mar. 28, 1958; children: Colin Turner, Clay Ian. BS in Edn., U. Mo., 1953; postgrad., San Diego State Coll., 1955-57, UCLA, 1958. Cert. secondary sch. tchr. Calif., Ill., N.J., lic. real estate salesperson, broker N.J., Pa., N.J., Mo. Tchr. Hallsville (Mo.) HS, 1953-54; co-owner McDonalds' Clothiers, Wewoka, Okla., 1954-55; tchr., class advisor Imperial (Calif.) HS, 1955-58, Temple City (Calif.) HS, 1958-59; prof. Coll. San Mateo, Calif., 1965-70, McHenry County Coll., Crystal Lake, Ill., 1972-76, Waubonsee Coll., Aurora, Ill., 1976-79; tchr., adminstr. Purnell Sch., Pottersville, NJ, 1980-86; realtor Sig Kuhne Realtors, Milford, NJ, 1986-89, Burgdorff Realtors, Inc., Pittstown, NJ, 1989-94; ret., 1994. Co-founder Audio, Verbal and Tutorial Ctr. McHenry County Coll., 1975—77. Author: (book) Shorthand I, Shorthand II, Shorthand III, Office Procedures I, Bookkeeping I, Bookkeeping II, Bookkeeping III, Medical Secretary, Legal Secretary, Office Procedures II, Business Materials, Business Law, Office Machines I, Office Machines II. Chair Holland Twp. Hist. Preservation Commn., 1989—95; chairperson Delaware Valley Autumn Antique Show, Holland, NJ, 1988—93; chair Christmas Project, Hunterdon County, NJ, 1988—. Mem.: N.J. Assn. Realtors, Hunterdon County Bd. Realtors (Cmty. Svc. award 1988), Golden Talents (pres., v.p., trustee 1988—91), Holland Twp. Women's Club (chairperson Clarence Carter Night 1988), Pi Beta Phi (province pres.). Republican. Episcopalian. Avocations: swimming, boating, antiques. Home: PO Box 443 1929 S Sweetwater Garden City UT 84028 Fax: 435-946-3508.

CAMPBELL, JESSIE KATHERINE, mathematician, educator; b. Whittier, Calif., May 5, 1977; d. Kenneth E. and Dorothy Elizabeth Campbell. BS in math, biology, Buena Vista U., 1999. Academic asst. Buena Vista U., Storm Lake, Iowa, 1996—99; grad. tchg. asst. Iowa State U., Ames, 1999—. Liberal. Presbyterian. Avocation: acting. Office: Iowa State U 400 Carver Hall Ames IA 50011 Personal E-mail: campbelljk@hotmail.com.

CAMPBELL, JILL FROST, university official; b. Buffalo, July 29, 1948; d. Jack and Elaine Mary (Hamilton) Frost; m. Gregory H. Campbell, May 31, 1969; children: Geoffrey, Kimberly, Kristina. BS, SUNY, Brockport, 1970, MSED, 1981; PhD, U. Buffalo, 1997. From acct. clk. bursar's office to asst. v.p. SUNY, Brockport, 1974—2003, asst. v.p. student affairs, 2003—. Chmn. web redesign com. SUNY, Brockport; mem. enrollment ops. group SUNY, Brockport, 1997-99, mem. metroctr. com. for student svcs., 1997-98, chair campus com. on profls.' roles and rewards, 1997-98, campus jud. officer, 1997-99, mem. coll. rev. panel, 1995—, coll. com. profl. evaluation, 1995—, strategic planning com., 1995-97, mem. retention com., 1998—, mem. presdl. scholars com., 1998-99, mem. strategic planning implementation com. on retention, 1999-2000, mem. strategic planning implementation com. on systemic change, 1999-2000, mem. alumni follow-up survey adv. com., 1999-2000, coord. alumni placement survey, 2000-, mem. transfer articulation group, 1999—, mem. acad. advisement task force, 2000-01, mem. enrollment mgmt. divsn. budget rev. com., 2000, chmn. alumni survey consulting group, 2000-02, mem. coll. tech. coun., 2003-. Mem. exec. com. Nativity Home Sch. Assn., Nativity Blessed Virgin Sch., Brockport, 1985-87, mem. sch. pub. rels. and mktg. com., 1985-88, mem. ch. festival com., 2001—; mem. Friends of Brockport Athletics, 1985-2000; coach Brockport Youth Summer Soccer, 1988-91; host family Assn. for Teen-Age Diplomats, 1995-96; mem. com. Chancellor's Award for Excellence in Profl. Svc., Brockport, 1989-90; liaison Brockport Child Care Ctr., 1995-96. Grantee United Univ. Professions, 1985, 90, 93, 94, 2000, 01. Mem. NAFE, Nat. Assn. Instl. Rsch. (mem. exec. com., co-originator and discussion leader books and current issues 1985-87, co-author profl. file, presenter papers, presenter panels 1979-87), SUNY Assn. Instl. Rsch. and Planning Officers (mem. exec. com., presenter papers, presenter panels 1984-87), North East Assn. Instl. Rsch. (mem. exec. com., sec. 1985-87, presenter papers, presenter panels 1978-87), Nat. Coun. Univ. Rsch. Adminstrs., Internat. Conf. for Women in Higher Edn. (presenter 1992), SUNY Brockport Alumni Assn., Brockport

Profl. Women's Group, Rsch. Found. Cen. Office (users group 1987-90, sponsored program comm. com. 1990-97, 4-yr. rsch. coun. 1988-93, vice chmn. 1991, chmn. 1992, univ. colls. rsch. coun. 1993-97), N.Y. State Transfer Articulation Assn. (presenter 1998, 2003, mem. conf. com. 2001-03, nominations com., 2001-02, registration 2001-03), N.Y. State/United Univ. Professions (Excellence award 1990, 2003). Home: 5129 Redman Rd Brockport NY 14420-9601 Office: SUNY Brockport Seymour 224 350 New Campus Dr Brockport NY 14420

CAMPBELL, JOANN CAVO, social worker; b. Cetara, Salerno, Italy, Dec. 2, 1950; BA, SUNY, Oneonta, 1972; MSW, Ariz. State U., 1977. Cert. social worker, N.Y. Family therapist Family Svcs. of Greater Utica, N.Y., 1977-84; case mgmt. supr. Cath. Charities of Utica-Rome, Utica, 1980-85, coord. clin. svcs., 1985-88, dir. social svcs., 1988-92; pvt. practitioner of social work Utica, 1992—; clin. program coord. Oneida County Alcohol and Substance Abuse Svcs., Utica, 1993-97; N.Y. State trainer for mandated child abuse reporters Madison-Oneida BOCES, Verona, NY, 1990—; social worker New Hartford (N.Y.) Ctrl Sch. Dist., 1997-99, Whitesboro (N.Y.) Ctrl. Sch. Dist., 1999—. Vice chair social work adv. bd. Utica Coll., 1978-83; treas., co-chair, chair Mohawk Valley Com. for Prevention of Child Abuse and Neglect, Utica, 1977—; bd. dirs., treas., sect. N.Y. State chpt. Nat. Com. for Prevention of Child Abuse, Albany, 1982-90. Chair program com. Hugh R. Jones Sch. PTA, Utica, 1991-94. Recipient Teddy Bear award N.Y. state chpt. Nat. Com. for Prevention of Child Abuse, 1990, Outstanding and Dedicated Svc. award Cath. Charities, 1990. Republican. Roman Catholic. Office: 75 Oriskany Blvd Whitesboro NY 13492-1323

CAMPBELL, JOHN B. T., III, state official; b. L.A., Calif., July 19, 1955; m. Catherine Campbell; 2 children. Tax acct. Ernst & Young; pres., CEO Campbell Automotive Group, 1985—95, Saturn of Orange County, 1990—99; chair, CEO Saab of Orange County, 1999—; state assembly mem. Dist. 70 Calif. State Assembly, 2000—. Chair Orange County Overall Econ. Devel. Program Com.; mem. Calif. Rep. State Cen. Com.; vice-chair budget com. Mem. Turtlerock Sch. Site Coun.; pres. Young Pres. Orgn. Mem.: Nat. Automobile Dealers Assn., Calif. Soc. CPAs. Republican. Presbyterian. Mailing: Rm 6027 PO Box 942849 Sacramento CA 94249 Office: Ste 220 18952 MacArthur Blvd Irvine CA 92612

CAMPBELL, JOHN CARL, retired engineering educator; b. Wilsey, Kans., Apr. 20, 1920; s. Alfred Wray and Zoa May (Henderson) C.; m. Eula Marie Hagan, Aug. 31, 1941 (div. 1978); children: Frederick J., Chris J., Victor C.; m. Roberta Louise DeVoe, Feb. 14, 1980. BS in Agrl. Engring. with honors, Kans. State U., 1947; MS in Agrl. Engring., Oreg. State U., 1949. Registered profl. engr., Oreg., cert. safety profl. of the Ams. Ext. specialist agrl. engring. U. Ill., Champaign, 1954—55, Oreg. State U., Corvallis, 1948—54, assoc. prof. gen. engring., 1955—66, head dept. gen. engring., 1966—77, dir. safety, 1978—85, prof. emeritus, 1985—. Safety engring. cons. Rust Engring. Co., Albany, Oreg., 1978—79, Daniels Atty. at Law, Albany, 1980—81; civil engr. Bur. Reclamation, Salem, Oreg., 1960—61. Author: (novels) The New Blend, 1972; contbr. articles to sci. jours. Capt. arty. U.S. Army, 1942—46, Philippines. Democrat. Avocations: travel, birdwatching. Home: #481 702 S Meridian Apache Junction AZ 85220 E-mail: campbellj106@cs.com.

CAMPBELL, J(OHN) JETTE, corporate finance executive; b. Raleigh, N.C., Sept. 22, 1947; s. Richard Jette and Janet (Bullard) C.; m. Sally Worthington, Aug. 31, 1968 (div. Dec. 1991); children: Ashley Maree Rosilier, Heather Janette, John Jette; m. Linda Edwards, Oct. 5, 1993; 1 child, Coleman David. BS in Bus. Adminstrn., Auburn U., 1969, postgrad., 1969-70, Harvard U., 1985, 87, 90, cert. mgmt program Grad. Sch. Bus., 1990; DHL (hon.), Paul Quinn Coll., 1992. CPA, Tex. From assoc. to ptnr. Arthur Andersen Co., Houston and Austin, 1970-83; co. founder, dir. The Rubicon Group, 1983-86; ptnr. Watson Group, Austin, 1983-86; pres. Internat. Conservation Sys. Inc., Austin, 1986-87; cons. Campbell & Assocs., Austin, 1987-88; ptnr. KMPG Peat Marwick, Dallas, 1988-91; CFO Europe Pepsi Foods Internat., London, 1992; contr. Frito Lay, 1993-94; CFO Griffin Corp., Valdosta, Ga., 1994-98, Griffin LLC, Valdosta, 1998-99, v.p. corp. devel., treas., 1999—. Vice chmn. Tex. State Gov.'s Small Bus. Task Force, 1979-82 Bd. dirs. Jaycees, Houston, 1974-78, exec. v.p., 1975-76; arts commr. City of Austin, 1984-85; bd. trustees St. Edwards U., 1984-90; bd. dirs. Ballet Austin, 1980-88, treas., 1981-83, v.p., 1984-86; bd. dirs. Laguna Gloria Art Mus., 1982-88, v.p fin., 1984-86; bd. dirs. Capitol Area coun. Boy Scouts Am., 1983-88, v.p., 1985-88, pres.-elect, 1988, asst. scoutmaster 1988-92, scoutmaster troop 35, Dallas, 1992-94, exec. bd. Alapaha Area coun., Valdosta, Ga., 1994—, v.p., 1995-98, pres., 1999; mem. 1980-81 class Leadership Austin, chmn. alumni, 1982-84, chmn. program, 1984-85, rep. mem. on C. of C. bd., 1984-85; trustee Paul Quinn Coll., Dallas, 1989-94, chmn. exec. com., 1990-92; trustee Stetson U. Music Sch., Deland, Fla., 1996-2001, vice-chmn., 1997-2001; trustee Valdosta Tech. Coll. Found., 2001-. Recipient Key Man award Jaycees, 1976, Silver Beaver Boy Scouts Am., 1997; named Outstanding Young Man in Am., 1975-80 Republican. Methodist. Avocations: camping, travel, music, theater. Home: 217 E Brookwood Pl Valdosta GA 31602-3854 E-mail: jette.campbell@Griffinllc.com.

CAMPBELL, JOHN M. judge; b. Wooster, Ohio, Aug. 5, 1953; m. Nicola Welsh Wilson; 1 child. BA, Yale Coll., 1975; student, Columbia U., 1978-79; JD, Yale U., 1981. Bar: D.C. 1983, U.S. Ct. Appeals (4th cir.) 1985, U.S. Ct. Appeals (1st cir.) 1987, U.S. Ct. Appeals (D.C. cir. 1995). Law clk. Judge Jon O. Newman, Hartford, Conn., 1981-82; assoc. Arnold and Porter, Washington, 1982-84; trial atty. pub. integrity sect. Dept. of Justice, Washington, 1985-91; chief pub. corruption-govt. fraud sect. Office of U.S. Atty. for D.C., Washington, 1991-97; assoc. judge Superior Ct., Dist. of Columbia, Washington, 1997—. Editor-in-chief Yale Law Jour. Mem. ABA, D.C. Bar Assn.

CAMPBELL, JOHN MORGAN, retired chemical engineer; b. Virden, Ill., Mar. 24, 1922; S. John M. and Ione Marie (Whittler) C.; m. Gwendolyn Thompson, Aug. 27, 1945; children: John Morgan, Robert, Charles. BS in Chem. Engring, Iowa State U., 1943; MS, U. Okla., 1948, PhD, 1951. Devel. engr. and supr. E.I. duPont de Nemours & Co., Inc., 1943-46; spl. instr. chem. engring U. Okla., 1946-50; tech. adviser to v.p. Black Sivalls and Bryson, Oklahoma City, 1951-54; mem. faculty U. Okla. Sch. Petroleum Engring., 1954-69, chmn. dept., 1956-63, Erle P. Halliburton prof., 1963-69, dir., 1969, Petroleum Research Center, 1964-69. Pres. John M. Campbell & Co. (engring. counselors, mgmt. consultants), 1968-82; chmn. bd. Petrotech Ltd., Petroleum Learning Programs Ltd. Author: Oil Property Evaluation, 1959, Effective Technical Communications, 1969, Decision Methods For Petroleum Investments, 1969, Gas Conditioning and Processing, 2 vols., 1970, 6th edit., 2000, The Professional - From Puberty to Senility, 1970, Effective Communication for the Technical Man, 1972, Petroleum Reservoir Property Evaluation, 1973, Mineral Property Economics (3 vols.), 1978, Petroleum Evaluation for Financial Disclosures, 1983, Analysis and Management of Petroleum Investments, 1987, Successful Communication Strategies and Practices, 2000, Analysis and Management of Risky Investments, 2001; also numerous articles, chpts. in books. Recipient Hanlon award Gas Processors Assn., 1987, Disting. Achievement award Iowa State U., 1988, Disting. Grad. award Okla. U. Mem. NAE, AIME (hon. mem. 1994, exec. com. coun. edn., mineral industries econs. award 1989), Soc. Petroleum Engrs. (hon. mem. 1994, J.F. Caril award 1978, Arps award 1989), Am. Arbitration Assn. (arbitration panel), Internat. Petroleum Inst. (pres. 1968-82), Sigma Alpha Epsilon, Phi Lambda Upsilon, Pi Epsilon Tau. Clubs: Lion. Home: 6 Rustic Hills St Norman OK 73072-7411

CAMPBELL, JOHN RICHARD, pediatric surgeon; b. Pratt, Kans., Jan. 16, 1932; s. John Ross and Laura (Harkrader) C.; m. Susan Charlotte Baker, June 9, 1962; children: Kathryn, John Richard, George Ridgway. BA, U. Kans., 1954, MD, 1958. Diplomate Am. Bd. Surgery with cert. of spl. qualifications in pediatric surgery. Rotating intern Hosp. U. Pa., 1958-59; resident in gen. surgery U. Kans. Hosp., 1959-63; resident in pediatric surgery Children's Hosp. of Phila., 1965-67; asst. instr. U. Pa. Med. Sch., 1965-67; mem. faculty U. Oreg. Health Scis. Ctr., Portland, 1967—, prof. surgery emeritus, 2000, prof. surgery and pediatrics emeritus, 2000—, chief pediatric surgery, prof. emeritus surgery and pediats., 2000—; surgeon-in-chief Doernbecher Children's Hosp., Portland, 1967-99. Cons. VA, Shriners Crippled Children's hosps., Alaska Native Med. Ctr., Anchorage. Served to lt. comdr. M.C. USNR, 1963-65. Mem. A.C.S., Soc. Acad. Surgeons, Am. Acad. Pediatrics, Am. Pediatric Surg. Assn., Pacific Assn. Pediatric Surgeons, North Pacific Pediatric Soc., North Pacific Surg. Assn., Pacific Coast Surg. Assn., Portland Acad. Pediatrics, Portland Surg. Soc. Presbyterian. Office: Oreg Health Scis Univ 745 SW Gaines St # Cdw7 Portland OR 97239-2901 E-mail: campbell@ohsu.edu.

CAMPBELL, JOHN ROY, animal science educator, academic administrator; b. Goodman, Mo., June 14, 1933; s. Carl J. and Helen (Nicoletti) C.; m. Eunice Vieten, Aug. 7, 1954; children: Karen L., Kathy L., Keith L. BS, U. Mo., 1955; MS, U. Mo., Columbia, 1956, PhD, 1960. Instr. dairy sci. U. Mo., Columbia, 1960-61, asst. prof., 1961-65, assoc. prof., 1965-68, prof., from 1968; assoc. dean, dir. resident instrn. Coll. Agr. U. Ill., Urbana-Champaign, 1977-83, dean Coll. Agr. Urbana, 1983-88; pres. Okla. State U., Stillwater, 1988-93. Author (with J.F. Lasley): The Science of Animals That Serve Humanity, 1969, The Science of Animals That Serve Humanity, 3d edit., 1985; author: In Touch with Students, 1972; author: (with R.T. Marshall) The Science of Providing Milk for Man, 1975; author: Reclaiming A Lost Heritage...Land-Grant and Other Higher Education Initiatives for the Twenty-First Century, 1985, Dry Rot in the Ivory Tower, 2000; author: (with M.D. Kenealy and K.L. Campbell) Animal Sciences...The Biology, Care and Production of Domestic Animals, 2002. Recipient Superior Tchg. award Gamma Sigma Delta, 1967, Internat. award for disting. svc. to agr., 1985, Disting. Svc. award Coll. Osteo. Medicine Okla. State U., 1992. Fellow Am. Dairy Sci. Assn. (dir. 1975-78, 80-86, pres. 1980-81, Ralston Purina Disting. Tchg. award 1973, Award of Honor 1987); mem. Nat. Assn. Coll. Tchrs. Agr. (Ensminger Interstate Disting. Tchr. award 1973, Teaching fellow 1973, Disting. Educator award 1990, Nat. Assn. State and Univ. and Land-Grant Colls. (commns. on home econs. and vet. medicine, com. on water resources, coun. of presidents), Okla. Futures, Gamma Sigma Delta. Office: Okla State U 201AS Stillwater OK 74078-0001 Personal E-mail: jcampbell.author.educator@mchsi.com. Business E-Mail: bale@okstate.edu.

CAMPBELL, JOHN WILLIAM, prosecutor; b. Honolulu, Jan. 6, 1955; s. George Willis and Leona Ruth Campbell; m. Lisa Jo Hale, Dec. 31, 1984. BA in Polit. Sci. and History, Washburn U., 1977; JD, U. Kans., 1979, MPA, 1980. Bar: Kans. 1979, U.S. Dist. Ct. Kans. 1979, U.S. Ct. Appeals (10th cir.) 1986, U.S. Supreme Ct. 1986, U.S. Ct. Appeals (D.C. cir.) 1992. Asst. county atty. Ford County Atty.'s Office, Dodge City, Kans., 1979-80; asst. atty. gen. Kans. Atty. Gen.'s Office, Topeka, 1981-86, dep. atty. gen., 1986-95, sr. dep. atty. gen., 1995—2003, gen. counsel Kans. Dept. Ins., 2003—. Chmn. Gov.'s Indian Gaming Group, Topeka, 1995; trustee Western Hills Bapt. Ch., Topeka, 1997-2000. Recipient Gen. Pres.'s award Nat. Assn. Attys., 2000, Marvin award Nat. Assn. Attys., 2001. Mem. Kans. Bar Assn., Topeka Bar Assn. Republican. Avocations: motorcycles, reading.

CAMPBELL, JOHN YOUNG, economics educator; b. London, May 17, 1958; came to U.S., 1979; s. Alexander Elmslie and Sophia Anne (Sonne) C.; m. Susanna Peyton, Apr. 28, 1984; children: Graham, Malcolm, Naomi, Sophia. BA, Oxford (Eng.) U., 1979; PhD, Yale U., 1984. Asst. prof. econs. Woodrow Wilson Sch. Princeton (N.J.) U., 1984-89, prof. econs. and pub. affairs Woodrow Wilson Sch., 1989-94; Otto Eckstein prof. applied econs. Harvard U., Cambridge, Mass., 1994—; mng. ptnr. Arrowstreet Capital, LP. Contbr. articles to profl. jours. NSF grantee, 1988; Alfred P. Sloan rsch. fellow, 1989. Fellow Am. Acad. Arts and Scis.; mem. Am. Econ. Assn., Am. Fin. Assn., Econometric Soc. Avocation: choral singing. Office: Harvard U Dept Econs Littauer Ctr 213 Cambridge MA 02138

CAMPBELL, JONATHAN WESLEY, astrophysicist, aerospace engineer; b. Alexander City, Ala., Sept. 1, 1950; s. Harry Underwood and Sarah Ruth Campbell; m. Charlotte Clift, June 5, 1999; children from previous marriage: Jason Jonathan, Christopher Sanders, Benjamin Robert. BS disting. mil. grad., Auburn U., 1972, MS, 1974, U. Ala., 1988, PhD, 1992. Cert. flight instr. Coop. engr. Pratt & Whitney Aircraft, West Palm Beach, Fla., 1968-70; instr. physics Auburn U., 1972-74; astrophysicist, aerospace engr. Missile and Space Intelligence Ctr., Huntsville, Ala., 1978-80; space scientist, supervisory aerospace engr. propulsion, exec. asst. to dir., lead engr. space telescope fine guidance sensor NASA/Marshall Space Flight Ctr., Huntsville, Ala., 1980—; pres. Redstone Aerospace Inc. Cons. Starflight Assocs. Part-time pastor United Meth. Ch.; sheriff's dep. Sheriff's Res. Ret. col. USAF Res. Decorated Legion of Merit; recipient Eagle Scout award, Presdl. Cert. Appreciation. Mem. AIAA, Air Force Assn., Res. Officer Assn., Aircraft Owners and Pilots Assn., Scabbard and Blade, Tau Beta Pi, Sigma Gamma Tau, Sigma Pi Sigma. Home: PO Box 295 Harvest AL 35749-0295 Office: NASA E51 Marshall Space Flight Ctr Huntsville AL 35812

CAMPBELL, JOSEPH JOHN, financial services executive; b. Harrisburg, Pa., May 24, 1947; s. John Patrick and May (Murray) C.; m. Susan Jane Ott, Jan. 28, 1966; children: John William, Allison Susan. BA in Econs., Allentown Coll. of St. Francis de Sales (now DeSales U.), 1970; Advanced Mgmt. Cert., U. Pitts., 1980. Computer and systems profl. Gen. Acceptance Corp., Allentown, Pa., 1968-70; v.p. sys. planning and devel. Fin.Am. Corp. (Bank Am. Corp.), 1970-83; v.p. sys. devel. and strategic planning Chrysler First, 1983-87; sr. v.p., chief info. officer Dollar Dry Dock Bank, N.Y.C., 1987-90; sr. v.p., retail bank opers. and tech. Citicorp/Citibank, N.Y.C., 1990-91, sr. v.p. mortgage opers. and tech. St. Louis, 1991-93; exec. v.p. Home Ins. Co., N.Y.C., 1993-95; exec. v.p., chief info. officer Zurich Risk Mgmt. Svcs./Zurich Fin. Group, N.Y.C., 1995—. Mem. Pres.'s Coun. Allentown Coll. of St. Francis de Sales, 1988—; owner Breakthrough Fitness Ctrs., Hilton Head Island and Bluffton, S.C., Pilates of Hilton Head. Inventor computer system in fin. field. Mem. Allentown Coll. of St. Francis de Sales Alumni Assn. (pres. 1981-85, Alumnus of Yr. award 1986). Avocations: golf, tennis, raquetball. Home: 54 Deer Hill Rd Redding CT 06896-2331 Office: Zurich Risk Mgmt Svcs 2540 Rte 130 Ste 109 Cranbury NJ 08512

CAMPBELL, JOSEPH LEONARD, trade association executive; b. Independence, Mo., 1938; BS in Acctg., U. Kans., 1960, MS in Acctg., 1963. CPA, Mo. Audit mgr. Arthur Young & Co., Kansas City, Mo., 1962-75; v.p., sec., treas. Assoc. Wholesale Grocers, Kansas City, Kans., 1975—. Active Boy Scouts Am., Overland Park, Kans., 1983-93. Mem. AICPA. Office: Associated Wholesale Grocers Inc PO Box 2932 Kansas City KS 66110-2932

CAMPBELL, JOSEPHINE ANNE CONRAD, news service executive; b. Evansville, Ind., Jan. 31, 1927; d. Owen McIntyre and Josephine Anne (Greene) C.; m. Donald Herman Campbell, Mar. 15, 1946 (dec. Mar. 3, 1988); children: Kathleen Mary, Carolyn Margret, Deborah Jean. Student, George Washington U., 1980-81. Cub reporter Daytona Beach (Fla.) News-Jour., 1944-45; copy boy Washington Post, 1945-46; copy editor World Report Mag., Washington, 1946-47; mem. pub. rels. staff AMVETS, Washington, 1952-53; pub. rels. person Govt. Pakistan, Washington, 1953-55; Washington and UN corr. Daily NAWA-I-WAQT, Lahore, Pakistan, 1955-56; writer, editor USIA, 1956-86; founder, CEO Ecotopics Internat. News Svc., Ocean City, Md., 1986-98, Willits, Calif., 1998—. Columnist Prince George's Jour., 1994-2000. Chair White House/Justice Dept. Task Force on Sex Discrimination USIA Press Svc.; mem. Gov.'s Task Force to Examine State Pension Investment in South Africa, 1987; v.p. Am. Fedn. Govt. Employees, AFL-CIO, Local #1812, 1969—78, del. nat. conv., 1974—76; del. founding conf. Coalition Labor Union Women, 1974; mem. Prince George's County Exec. Com., NCCJ, 1980—84; rep. Ocean City State Coastal and Watershed Resources adv. Com., 1991—98; mem. steering com., commr. Worcester County Commn. for Women, 1995—98; mem. Friends of Ocean City Libr., Friends of Willits Libr., 1999—; mem. citizen's adv. bd. The Willits News, 1999—2000, op-ed writer, 1999—. Jefferson fellow George Washington U., Washington, 1980-81. Mem. NAACP (3d v.p. Worcester County 1992-98; Sonoma County, Calif. br. 1999—), ACLU (mem.Prince George county, Md., exec. bd. 1975-81, chmn., 1977-80, chair Mendocino County, Calif. 1985-88, exec. bd. 2003—), Nat. Press Club, Press Club San Francisco, Washington Ind. Writers, Dog Writers Assn. Am., Women's Inst. Freedom of Press, Conservation Voters, Worldwatch, Nat. Resources Def. Coun., Women's Club Ocean City (2d v.p. 1996), Marine's Meml. Club. Democrat. Roman Catholic. Avocations: photography, poetry writing, political activism. Fax: 707-456-0713.

CAMPBELL, KARLYN KOHRS, speech and communication educator; b. Blomkest, Minn., Apr. 16, 1937; d. Meinhard and Dorothy (Siegers) Kohrs; m. Paul Newell Campbell, Sept. 16, 1967 (dec. Mar. 1999). BA, Macalester Coll., 1958; MA, U. Minn., 1959, PhD, 1968. Asst. prof. SUNY, Brockport, 1959-63; with The Brit. Coll., Palermo, Italy, 1964; asst. prof. Calif. State U., L.A., 1966-71; assoc. prof. SUNY, Binghamton, 1971-72, CUNY, 1973-74; prof. comms. studies U. Kans., Lawrence, 1974-86, dir. women's studies, 1983-86; prof. comms. studies U. Minn., Mpls., 1986—, dept. chair, 1993-96, 99—. Inaugural Gladys Borchers lectr. U. Wis., Madison, 1974. Author: Critiques of Contemporary Rhetoric, 1972, rev. edit., 1997, Form and Genre, 1978, The Rhetorical Act, 1982, rev. edits. 1996, 2002, The Interplay of Influence, 1983, rev. edits., 1987, 92, 96, 2000, Man Cannot Speak for Her, 2 Vols., 1989, Deeds Done in Words, 1990, Women Public Speakers in the United States, 1800-1925: A Bio-Critical Sourcebook, 1993, Women Public Speakers in the United States, 1925—: A Bio-Critical Sourcebook, 1994; editor Quar. Jour. Speech, 2001--; co-editor: Guilford Revisioning Rhetoric series, 1995-2000; mem. editl. bd. Comm. Monographs, 1977-80, Quar. Jour. Speech, 1981-86, 92-94, editor, 2001—, Critical Studies in Mass Commn., 1993-99, Rhetoric and Pub. Affairs, 1997-2000, Philosophy and Rhetoric, 1988-93; contbr. articles to profl. jours. Recipient Woolbert Rsch. award, 1987, Winans-Wichelns Book award, 1990, Ehninger Rsch. award, 1991; Tozer scholar Macalester Coll., 1958, Tozer fellow, 1959; fellow Shorenstein Barone Ctr., JFK Sch. of Govt., Harvard, 1992; Disting. Woman scholar U. Minn., 2002. Mem. Nat. Comm. Assn. (disting. scholar award 1992, Francine Merritt award for significant contbns. to the lives of women in comm. 1996 Women's Caucus), Ctrl. States Speech Comm. Assn., Rhetoric Soc. Am., Phi Beta Kappa, Pi Phi Epsilon. Office: U Minn Dept Comm Studies 225 Ford Hall 224 Church SE Minneapolis MN 55455 E-mail: campb003@umn.edu.

CAMPBELL, KATHLEEN CHARLOTTE MURPHEY, audiology educator, administrator, researcher; b. Sioux Falls, S.D., Mar. 20, 1952; d. Chester Humphrey and Ruth Maxine (Thompson) Murphey; m. Craig Anthony Campbell, Nov. 15, 1975. BA, S.D. State U., 1973; MA, U. S.D., 1977; PhD, U. Iowa, 1989. Cert. audiologist. Clin. grad. asst. dept. communication U. S.D., Vermillion, 1976-77; regional audiologist II British Columbia Ministry Health, Cranbrook, 1977-82; audiologist II dept. otolaryngology head and neck U. Iowa, Iowa City, 1983-88, rsch. asst. dept. speech, pathology and audiology, 1985; doctoral fellow Health Svcs. R&D, VA, Iowa City, 1987-88; prof. div. otolaryngology dept. surgery So. Ill. U. Sch. Medicine, 1989—, prof., 1996—. Cons. Packer Engring., Naperville, Ill., 1992—. Editorial cons. Am. Jour. Audiology, 1992; reviewer Annals of Otolaryngology, 1992; contbr. articles to profl. jours. Mem. Midamerica Playwrights Theatre, Springfield, Ill., 1989—, Sierra Club, Springfield, 1989—. Recipient Clin. Investigator Devel. Award grant NIH, 1990, Small Bus. Innovative Rsch. grant NIH, 1990, Ctrl. Rsch. Coun. grant So. Ill. U., 1991, Children's Miracle Network award So. Ill. U., 1991, 92, Alzheimer Disease Ctr. grant So. Ill. U. Sch. Medicine, 1992, James A. Shannon Dir.'s award NIH, 1997-99. Mem. Am. Speech-Lang.-Hearing Assn., Am. Acad. Audiology, Assn. Rsch. in Otolaryngology, Am. Acad. Otolaryngology-Head/Neck Surgery (assoc.), Mensa. Achievements include development of of a device for treatment of Meniere's disease; research in in electrocochleography and perilymphatic fistual; patents for for otoprotective agents for ototoxicity. Office: SIU Sch Medicine PO Box 19629 Springfield IL 62794-9629

CAMPBELL, KENNETH EUGENE, JR., vertebrate paleontologist, ornithologist; b. Jackson, Mich., Nov. 4, 1943; s. Kenneth Eugene and Betty Louise (Duffey) C. BS, U. Mich., 1966, MS, 1967; PhD, U. Fla., 1973. Research asso. Fla. State Mus., Gainesville, 1972-74; asst. prof. zoology U. Fla., Gainesville, 1974-77, asst. prof. geology, 1975-77; curator vertebrate paleontology/ornithology Natural History Mus. Los Angeles County, L.A., 1977—. Acting dir. George C. Page Mus., 1995-96. Contbr. articles to sci. publs. Mem. AAAS, Am. Ornithologists' Union, Assn. Tropical Biology, Cooper Ornithol. Soc., Soc. Vertebrate Paleontology, Wilson Ornithol. Soc., Asian Paleontology and Evolution Soc. (pres. 2000-), Sigma Xi. Office: Natural History Mus 900 Exposition Blvd Los Angeles CA 90007-4057 E-mail: kecampbe@bcf.usc.edu.

CAMPBELL, KEVIN PETER, physiology and biophysics educator, researcher; b. Bklyn., Jan. 19, 1952; s. Miller Jerome and Anna L. (Telesco) C.; m. Anna A. Derragon, Jan. 5, 1974; children: Colleen, Kerry, David. BS in Physics, Manhattan Coll., 1973; MS, U. Rochester, 1976, PhD, 1979. Grad. fellow U. Rochester (N.Y.), 1973-77, teaching asst., 1976-78; Elon Huntington Hooker fellow dept. radiation biology and biophysics, U. Rochester (N.Y.), 1977-78; Med. Rsch. Coun. postdoctoral fellow U. Toronto, Ont., Can., 1978-81; asst. prof. dept. physiology and biophysics U. Iowa, Iowa City, 1981-85, assoc. prof., 1985-88, prof., 1988—, Found. Disting. prof., 1989—, Howard Hughes Med. Inst. investigator, 1989—. Mem. editorial bd. Jour. Biol. Chemistry, Circulation Rsch., Cell Calcium; reviewer for Nature, Jour. Clin. Investigation, Jour. Cell Biology, Proc. NAS, Archives Biochem. and Biophysics, Molecular Pharmacology, Biophys. Jour.; contbr. numerous articles and abstracts to profl. jours. Patentee immunogen conjugates and use; co-patentee in field. Grantee NIH, NSF, NATO, Muscular Dystrophy Assn., 1981—; recipient Amgen award Am. Society of Biochemistry and Molecular Biology, 1994 Mem. AAAS, Biophys. Soc. (officer 1988—), N.Y. Acad. Scis., Soc. Gen. Physiologists, Am. Physiology Soc., Am. Soc. Cell Biology, Am. Soc. Biochem. Chemists, Am. Heart Assn. (established investigator, coun. high blood pressure rsch., cell transport and metabolism rsch. study com. 1989—), Inst. of Medicine, Sigma Xi (Bendix award), Phi Beta Kappa. Roman Catholic. Office: U Iowa HHMI 400 Eckstein Med Rsch Ctr Iowa City IA 52242

CAMPBELL, LARRY L. state representative; b. Flint, Mich., May 17, 1955; m. Gwendolyn G. Campbell; 2 children. Degree in Bus., So. Nazarene U.; MBA in Bus., MidAm. Nazarene Coll. Banker; owner, pres. Evening Star Inc., Brighter Day Ministries; mem. Kans. Ho. of Reps., 1997—. Mem. Olathe City Coun., 1991—95; mayor Olathe, 1995—97. Republican. Office: 514-S State Capitol 300 SW 10th Ave Topeka KS 66612 Address: 15803 S Avalon Olathe KS 66062*

CAMPBELL, LEONARD M. lawyer; b. Denver, Apr. 12, 1918; s. Bernard Francis and May (Moran) C.; m. Dot J. Baker, Sept. 23, 1944; children: Brian T., Teri Pat, Thomas P. AB, U. Colo., 1941, LLB, 1943. Bar: Colo. 1943. Of counsel Gorsuch, Kirgis, Campbell, Walker and Grover, 1948-88, sr. ptnr., 1951 88; city atty. Denver, 1951-53; of counsel Gorsuch, Kirgis LLC, 1989—, Cons. pub. utility matters Colo. Mcpl. League. Mem. Denver Charter Com., 1947; mgr. Safety and Excise for Denver, 1947-48; chmn. Denver Com. Human Relations, 1954; mem. Denver Planning Bd., 1950-51; mem. Bd. Water Commrs., Denver, 1965-70, pres., 1968-69; mem. Gov.'s Com. on Jud. Compensation, 1972; chmn. U. Colo. Law Alumni Devel. Fund, 1962. Served with USAAF, 1943-46. Mem. ABA, Colo. Bar Assn. (pres. 1978-79, Award of Merit 1967), Denver Bar Assn. (pres. 1969), Am. Coll. Trial Lawyers, Cath. Lawyers Guild Denver (pres. 1962, St. Thomas More award 1978), Nat. Inst. Mcpl. Law Officers (v.p. 1952), Colo. Judicial Inst. (Chancellor Chester Alter award 1987). Clubs: Denver Athletic (Denver) (sec. 1960-61, pres. 1962), Cherry Hills Country (Denver). Democrat. Roman Catholic. Home: 3447 S Birch St Denver CO 80222-7212 Office: Gorsuch Kirgis LLP Tower One 1515 Arapahoe St Ste 1000 Denver CO 80202-2120

CAMPBELL, LESLIE CAINE (CAINE CAMPBELL), writer, historian; b. New Orleans, June 5, 1932; s. George Alexander and Nell Ruble C.; m. Bettye Bryan, June 10, 1961; children: Cathryn Campbell Jordan, Roxane Campbell Rose. BS in Bus., Miss. State U., 1954; MA in History, U. Miss., 1964, PhD in History, 1967. Chmn. div. humanities Ark. Coll., Batesville, 1967-68; assoc. dean Sch. Arts and Scis. Auburn (Ala.) U., 1968-86, dean Coll. Liberal Arts, 1986-88, prof. history and journalism, 1988-92. Hartman lectr. U. Miss., 1983. Author: Two Hundred Years of Pharmacy, 1976 (Am. Inst. History of Pharmacy award 1977), A Reminder of Stones, 2001; contbg. author: Research Institutions and Learned Societies, 1982, Foundations, 1984; contbg. editor Nat. Forum, 1987-92; newsman NBC News-TV and Radio, 1962-66. With USN, 1955—58. NSF fellow, 1966; Challenge grantee NEH, 1980. Mem. Am. Assn. Univ. Adminstrs. (bd. dirs. 1987-90), Assn. Ala. Coll. Adminstrs. (pres. 1988). Office: 126 Summerhill Hoschton GA 30548

CAMPBELL, LEVIN HICKS, judge; b. Summit, N.J., Jan. 2, 1927; s. Worthington and Louise (Hooper) Campbell; m. Eleanor Saltonstall Lewis, June 1, 1957; children: Eleanor S., Levin H., Sarah H. AB cum laude, Harvard U., 1948, LLB, 1951; postgrad., Nat. Coll. State Judiciary, 1970; LLD (hon.), Suffolk U., 1975; LLD (hon.), Colby Coll., 1982. Bar: D.C. 1951, Mass. 1954. Assoc. firm Ropes & Gray, Boston, 1954—64; mem. Mass. Ho. of Reps.,

1963—64; asst. atty. gen. State of Mass., 1965—66, spl. asst. atty. gen., 1966—67, 1st asst. atty. gen., 1967—68; assoc. justice Superior Ct. of Mass., 1969—72; judge U.S. Dist. Ct. Mass., Boston, 1972, U.S. Ct. Appeals (1st cir.), Boston, 1972—, chief judge, 1983—90, sr. judge, 1992—. Fellow Inst. of Politics J.F. Kennedy Sch. Govt. Harvard U., 1968—69, study group leader, 1980; faculty chmn. law sessions Salzburg Seminar in Am. Studies, 1981. Pres. Cambridge 9 Neighborhood Assn., 1960—62; treas. Cambridge Ctr. for Adult Edn., 1961—64; campaign chmn. Cambridge United Fund, 1965; mem. bd. overseers Boston Symphony Orch., 1969—75, 1977—80; pres. bd. overseers Shady Hill Sch., 1969—70; mem. vis. com. Harvard U. Press, 1958—64; v.p. Cambridge Cmty. Svcs.; corp. mem. SEA Ednl. Assn., 1982—; trustee Colby Coll., Waterville, Maine, 1981—90, 1991—99, Asheville (N.C.) Sch., 1987—98; overseer U.S. Constn. Mus. 1st lt. (j.g.) U.S. Army, 1951—54, Korea. Mem.: ABA, Mass. Hist. Soc. (coun. 1993—96, v.p. 1996—99, pres. 2000—02, coun. 2003—), U.S. Jud. Conf. (ct. adminstrn. com. 1975—83, chmn. subcom. on supporting pers. 1980—83, exec. com. 1985—90, ad hoc com. study jud. conf. 1987, fed. ct. study com. 1988—90, chmn. com. to rev. cir. coun. conduct and disability orders 1989—94, nat. commn. on jud. discipline and removal 1991—93), Boston Bar Assn., Mass. Bar Found. (long range planning com. 1999—2000), Am. Bar Found., Am. Law Inst. Office: US Ct of Appeals US Courthouse 1 Courthouse Way Ste 6720 Boston MA 02210-3008

CAMPBELL, LEWIS B. aerospace technology executive; b. 1946; BS in Mech. Engring., Duke U. Various mgmt. positions Gen. Motors, 1968-88, v.p., gen. mgr. Flint automotive divsn. Buick-Oldsmobile-Cadillac group, 1988-91, v.p., gen. mgr. GMC truck divsn., 1991-92; exec. v.p., COO Textron Inc., 1992-94, pres., COO, 1994-98, chmn., CEO, 1998—2001, chmn., pres., CEO, 2001—. Office: Textron Inc 40 Westminster St Providence RI 02903

CAMPBELL, LILLIE SPURGIN, social worker; b. Frederick, Okla., Mar. 22, 1942; m. John C. Campbell, June 25, 1966; children: Russell, Matthew. BA, Okla. Bapt. U., 1964; MSW, Washington U., St. Louis, 1966. Lic. master social wroker, advanced clin. practitioner, Tex. Psychiat. social worker Convalescent Hosp. for Children, Rochester, N.Y., 1967-69; adminstrv. dir. GLO Day Care Ctr., Abilene, Tex., 1971-72; exec. dir. Abilene Girls Home, 1974; prof. McMurry Coll., Abilene, 1976-83; staff social worker Hendrick Med. Ctr., Abilene, 1985-86; coord. social svcs. Hospice of Abilene Inc., 1987-91. Pvt. practice, Abilene Profl. Ctr., 1983—; cons. Woods Psychiat. Inst., Abilene, 1979-82; social work cons. Hendrick Home for Children, 1983-84; ct. cons. 326th Dist. Family Ct., Abilene, 1983—; dir. social svcs. Hospice of the Big Country, Abilene, 1992-98. Mem. planning com. United Way of Abilene, 1978-83, coordinating coun., 1980-83, sec. 1987-88; active work com. Juvenile Justice Assn., Abilene, 1980-87 Mem. NASW (state nominating com. 1983-85, 89-91, diplomate in clin. social work), Acad. Cert. Social Workers, Am. bd. examiners Clin. Social Work (cert. diplomate). Baptist. Office: Abilene Profl Ctr 1215 ES 11th Ste C Abilene TX 79602 E-mail: jlcampbe@nts_online.net.

CAMPBELL, LINZY LEON, molecular biology researcher, educator; b. Panhandle, Tex., Feb. 10, 1927; s. Linzy Leon and Eula Irene (McSpadden) C.; m. Alice P. Dauksa, Feb. 7, 1953. BA in Bacteriology and Chemistry, U. Tex., 1949, MA, 1950, PhD, 1952. Rsch. scientist U. Tex., 1947-51; predoctoral rsch. fellow NIH, 1951-52; postdoctoral rsch. fellow Nat. Microbiol. Inst., U. Calif. at Berkeley, 1952-54; asst. prof., then assoc. prof. Wash. State U., 1954-59; assoc. prof. Western Res. U. Sch. Medicine, 1959-62; sr. rsch. fellow USPHS, 1959-62; prof. microbiology U. Ill. at Urbana, 1962-72, head dept., 1963-71, dir. Sch. Life Scis., 1971-72; prof. microbiology, provost and v.p. acad. affairs U. Del., Newark, 1972-88, univ. rsch. prof. molecular bioscis., 1988-89, Hugh M. Morris rsch. prof. molecular bioscis., 1989—. Editorial bd.: Jour. Bacteriology, 1961-65; editor, 1964-65, editor-in-chief, 1965-77; Contbr. articles to profl. jours. Served with USNR, 1944-46. Fellow AAAS; mem. Am. Soc. Microbiology (chmn. publ. bd. 1965-80, councilor at large 1962-64, v.p. 1972-73, pres. 1973-74), Am. Soc. Biochemistry and Molecular Biology. Office: U Delaware Dept Biology 400 Morris Library Newark DE 19717 E-mail: campbell@udel.edu.

CAMPBELL, L(OUIS) LORNE, mathematics educator; b. Winnipeg, Man., Can., Oct. 20, 1928; s. Elgin Smith and Jonina Solveig (Johnson) C.; m. Eha Johanson, June 12, 1954; children: Ian, Barry, Barbara. BSc, U. Man., 1950; MS, Iowa State U., 1951; PhD, U. Toronto., 1955. Def. sci. officer Def. Rsch. Bd., Ottawa, Ont., Can., 1954-58; asst. prof., then assoc. prof. U. Windsor, Ont., Can., 1958-63; assoc. prof., then prof. Queen's U., Kingston, Ont., Can., 1963-96, prof. emeritus, 1996—, head dept. math and stats., 1980-90. Contbr. articles to profl. publs. Fellow IEEE; mem. Can. Math. Soc. (treas. 1982-85), Can. Statis. Soc., Am. Math. Soc. Home: 153 Byron Crescent Kingston ON Canada K7M 1J2 Office: Queens U Dept Math and Stats Kingston ON Canada K7L 3N6 E-mail: campblll@mast.queensu.ca.

CAMPBELL, MAGDA, child psychiatrist, researcher, educator; b. Subotica, Yugoslavia, Jan. 22, 1928; arrived in U.S., 1957; d. Bela and Marija (Lipoženčic) Pijuković; m. Francis P. Campbell, July 2, 1961; children: Maria D., John F. MD, U. Belgrade, Yugoslavia, 1953. Diplomate in psychiatry and child psychiatry Am. Bd. Psychiatry and Neurology. From tchg. asst. to prof. psychiatry NYU, N.Y.C., 1963-95, prof. emeritus, 1995—; dir. divsn. child adolescent psychiatry, 1987-91; dir. tng. edn., 1990-91. Co-author: Child and Adolescent Psychopharmacology, 1985, Clinical Evaluation of Psychotropic Drugs for Psychiatric Disorders, 1993; contbr. over 225 articles to profl. jours., chpts. to books. Grantee NIMH, 1973-95. Fellow: Am. Psychiatric Assn., Am. Coll. Neuropsychopharmacology (life; emeritus), Am. Acad. Child Adolescent Psychiatry (life). Office: NYU Med Ctr Dept Psychiatry 550 1st Ave New York NY 10016

CAMPBELL, MARGARET SUSAN, defender; b. Painesville, Ohio, July 15, 1969; d. Alan Maxted and Marlene Sue Campbell. BS, Miami U., 1991; JD, Ohio Northern U., 1994. Bar: Ohio, U.S. Dist. Ct. (no. dist.), U.S. Supreme Ct. Asst. pub. defender Lake County Pub. Defenders, Painesville, Ohio, 1995—. Instr. Lake Erie Coll., Painesville, 1997-1999. Mem. Ohio Bar Assn., Ohio Assn. Criminal Def. Lawyers, Ohio Women's Bar Assn. Avocations: international travel, cooking. Office: Lake County Pub Defenders Office 125 E Erie St Painesville OH 44077-3948

CAMPBELL, MARIA BOUCHELLE, state official; b. Mullins, S.C., Jan. 23, 1944; d. Colin Reid and Margaret Minor (Perry) C. Student, Agnes Scott Coll., 1961-63; AB, U. Ga., 1965, JD, 1967. Bar: Ga. 1967, Fla. 1968, Ala. 1969. Pvt. practice law, Birmingham, Ala., 1968-94; law clk. U.S. Cir. Ct. Appeals, Miami, Fla., 1967-68; assoc. Cabaniss, Johnston and Gardner, 1968-73; sec., counsel Ala. Bancorp., Birmingham, 1973-79; sr. v.p., sec., gen. counsel AmSouth Bancorp., 1979-84, exec. v.p., gen. counsel, 1984-94, AmSouth Bank, 1984-94; exec. asst. to rector Parish of Trinity Ch., N.Y.C., 1994-99; lawyer, mediator Sirote & Permutt, 1999-2001; cabinet ofcl., supt. of banks State of Ala., Montgomery, 2001—. Bd. trustees Ptnrship for Women's Health Columbia U., 1996-2000; bd. dirs. Leake and Watts Childrens Svcs., Inc., 1997-99; lectr. continuing legal edn. programs; cons. to charitable orgns. Exec. editor Ga. Law Rev, 1966-67. Bd. dirs. St. Anne's Home, Birmingham, 1969-74, chancellor, 1969-74; bd. dirs. Children's Aid Soc., Birmingham, 1970-94, 1st v.p., 1988-90, pres., 1990-92; trustee Canterbury Cathedral Trust in Am., 1992—. Discovery 2000 Children's Mus., 1991-94, Soc. for Propagation of Christian Knowledge, 1991-93; bd. dirs. NCCJ, 1985-94, 99-2002, state chair, 1990-93; bd. dirs. Positive Maturity, 1976-78, Mental Health Assn., 1978-81, YWCA, 1979-80, Op. New Birmingham, 1985-87, pers. com., 1987-90, v.p., 1990-94; bd. dirs. Soc. for the Fine Arts U. Ala., 1986-89, Baptist Hospital Found. of Birmingham Inc., 1994-95, Alliance for Downtown N.Y., 1995-99, chair affordable housing initiative region 2020, 2000-01, Habitat for Humanity of Birmingham, 2000-02; commr. Housing Authority, Birmingham Dist., 1980-85, Birmingham Partnership, 1985-86, Leadership Birmingham, 1986—, program com., 1989-90, co-chair program com., 1990-91, mem.'s coun., 1999-2002; mem. pres. adv. coun. Birmingham So. Coll, 1988-92, chair bd. overseers Masters Program, 1990-94; mem. pres.'s cabinet U. Ala., 1990-95; trustee Ala. Diocese Episcopal Ch., 1971-72, 74-75, mem. canonical revision com., 1973-75, 89-91, liturg. commn., 1976-78, treas., chmn. dept. fin., 1979-83, 2000—; mem. coun., 1983-87, chancellor, 1987-91, cons. on stewardship edn., 1981-94, dep. to gen. conv., 1985, 88, 91; mem. Standing Commn. on Constn. and Canons, 1988-94; vestryman St. Luke's Episcopal Ch., 1991-94; bd. advisors So. region of Am. Soc. Corp. Secs., pres., 1992-94; cmty. advisor Jr. League Birmingham, 1992-93; mem. adv. bd. Cahaba River Soc., 1991-94; trustee St. Andrew's Sewanee Sch., 1998—; commr. Ala. Securities Commn., 2001—; bd. dirs. Ala. Agrl. Commn., 2001—; bd. dirs. Ala. Housing Fin. Authority, 2001--; bd. regents Univ. of the South, 2002-. Named One of Top 10 Women in Birmingham, 1989, One of Top 5 Women in Bus., 1993. Mem. ABA, State Bar Ga., Fla. Bar, Ala. Bar Assn., Birmingham Bar Assn., Am. Corp. Counsel Assn. (bd. dirs. Ala. 1984-89), Assn. Bank Holding Cos. (chmn. lawyers com. 1986-87), Greater Birmingham C. of C. (bd. dirs. 1988-94, exec. com. 1992-94, vice chmn., gen. counsel 1993-94), Kiwanis, The Church Club N.Y., Order of St. John of Jerusalem, Summit Club. Office: State of Ala State Banking Dept 401 Adams Ave Ste 680 Montgomery AL 36130 E-mail: mcampbell@bank.state.al.us.

CAMPBELL, MARY KATHRYN, chemistry educator; b. Phila., Jan. 20, 1939; d. Henry Charles and Mary Kathryn (Horan) C. AB in Chemistry, Rosemont Coll., 1960; PhD, Ind. U., 1965. Instr. Johns Hopkins U., 1965-68; asst. prof. chemistry Mt. Holyoke Coll., South Hadley, Mass., 1968-74, assoc. prof., 1974-81, prof., 1981—; vis. scholar U. Paris VII, 1974-75; vis. prof. U. Ariz., 1981-82, 88-89. Mem. panel on grad. fellowships NSF, 1979-81 Author: Biochemistry, 1991, 4th edit., 2002; co-author: Understand! Biochemistry, 1999; contbr. articles to profl. jours. Fellow Woodrow Wilson Found., 1960, NSF, 1960-64, NIH, 1964-65; grantee in field Mem. Am. Chem. Soc., AAAS, AAUP, Sigma Xi Office: Mt Holyoke Coll 50 Coll St Dept Chemistry South Hadley MA 01075

CAMPBELL, SISTER MAURA, religious studies and philosophy educator; b. Bayonne, N.J. d. Patrick John and Helena Marie (Collins) C. BS, Seton Hall U., 1940, MA, 1945, Providence Coll., 1953, D in Religious Edn. (hon.), 1985; PhD, St. Mary's Sch. Theology, Notre Dame, Ind., 1955; postgrad., Marquette U., Ottawa U., 1969, Cath. U. Am., 1970-71. Joined Dominican Order, Roman Cath. Ch., 1927. Tchr. elem. and secondary schs., 1930-42; dir. postulants Mt. St. Dominic, Caldwell, NJ, 1955-59, dir. scholastics, 1959-69; mem. faculty Caldwell Coll., 1955—, prof. religious studies, 1957-86, prof. emerita, 1986—, chmn. dept., 1969—89, pres. faculty counsel, 1986-89. Permanent rep. internat. Cath. edn. office UN Non-Govtl. Orgns., 1969—; cons. Thomas Edison State Coll., 1962-2002; v.p. internat. Cath. orgns. N.Y. Info. Ctr., 1978, pres., 1987-90; permanent rep. World Assembly Internat. Cath. Edn. Office, Bangkok, 1982; participant Women's Forum, Nairobi, Kenya, 1985, Mexico City, 1986, Madrid, 1993, Rome, 1994; participant World Congress of Office of Cath. Internat. Edn., Rome, 1994; del. Fourth Internat. UN Conf. Women, Beijing, 1995; Roman Catholic rep. World Coun. Religions, 1986-88. Mem. editl. bd. The Cath. Adv. Mem. Ecumenical/Interfaith Commn. Archdiocese of Newark, 1986-90; elected mem. exec. bd. Non-Govtl. Orgn./Dept. Pub. Info. at UN, 1988-90. Recipient Recognition award for outstanding achievement in higher edn. State of N.J., 1989, Jubilee medal Archdiocese of Newark, 1994, Disting. Svc. award Sacred Heart Inst., 1994, Peace Initiative award First Dominican Sisters, 1995, Jubilee Medal Pro Meritis, Archdiocese of Newark, 1995, Office of Cath. Internat. Edn. award for representation at UN, 1998, Redemptors Mater award 1999, Woman of Distinction award Soroptimist Internat., 2000, Fidelity to Mission award Cath. Internat. Edn. Conf., Brazil, 2002; named Ambassador for Peace, World Fedn. Women for Peace, 2002. Mem. Dominican Edn. Assn. (past pres.), Coll. Theology Soc. (past v.p., sec.), Am. Acad. Religion, Religious Edn. Assn., Cath. Theology Soc., Coun. Religion and World Affairs, Theta Alpha Kappa (hon. mem. alumnus 1989, Veritas award 1989, Outstanding Prof. award 1989). Home: St Catherine Convent 7 Ryerson Ave Caldwell NJ 07006-6199 Office: Caldwell Coll 9 Ryerson Ave Caldwell NJ 07006-6109 E-mail: smaura@caldwell.com.

CAMPBELL, MICHAEL HARRY, psychologist, academic administrator; b. Orlando, Fla., Oct. 30, 1969; s. Donald Fisher and Sylvia Knight Campbell. BA in Psychology and L.Am. Studies, New Coll. of Fla., 1991; MS in Geography, Fla. State U., 1993; PhD in Counseling Psychology, U. Fla., 1998. Lic. psychologist Fla. Grad. asst. inpatient psychiatry U. Fla. Coll. Medicine, Gainesville, 1995—96; psychol. intern U. of Wyo., Laramie, 1996—97; adj. instr. psychology U. of Tampa, Fla., 1997—98; lic. psychologist/post-doctoral resident Counseling and Wellness Ctr. New Coll. of Fla., Sarasota, 1998—2000, dir. residential life, 2000—, adj. asst. prof. psychology, 2000—; consulting psychologist Coastal Behavioral Healthcare, Sarasota, 2001—. Team leader, resident program evaluation project North Fla. Evaluation and Treatment Ctr., Gainesville, 1996; cons. LeBon & Associates, P.A., Miami, Fla., 1998—2000. Author: (book chapter) Clinical Psychology. In I'm a People Person: A Guide to Human Services Professions, 2002, (test reviews (2) The Buros Mental Measurements Yearbook, 2001. Mem. Fla. Local Adv. Coun., Sarasota, 2002; trustee New Coll. Found., Sarasota, 1991—94. Recipient Fubright grant, Inst. for Internat. Edn., 1991, U. Grad. fellowship, Fla. State U., 1992, Grinter fellowship, U. of Fla., 1993—94, Threadgill Dissertation fellowship, 1997. Mem.: APA (Grad. Student Travel Award 1994), Fla. State U. Geography Students' Assn. (v.p. 1991—92), Southeastern Assn. of Housing Officers, Nat. Assn. Student Pers. Administrators, Assn. Coll. and U. Housing Officers-International, Internat. Critical Incident Stress Found., Sara-Mana Critical Incident Stress Mgmt. Team, New Coll. Alumni Assn. (sec. 1994—99, pres. 1999—2002), St. Andrew Soc. of Sarasota, Phi Kappa Phi, Phi Beta Kappa. Office: New Coll of Florida 5700 North Tamiami Tr Sarasota FL 34243-2197 Office Fax: 941-359-4308. Personal E-mail: mcampbell@ncf.edu. E-mail: mcampbell@ncf.edu.

CAMPBELL, NAOMI SYLVIA, lawyer; b. Newark, Nov. 17, 1925; d. Isidore and Esther Charner; m. Charles Melton Campbell, Dec. 25, 1947; 1 child, Lori Margaret. BS in Bus. Adminstrn., Upsala Coll., East Orange, N.J., 1947; JD, U. Chgo., 1957. Bar: Ill., N.Y., Hawaii, D.C. Prof. bus. law Fairleigh Dickinson U., 1959-62; ptnr. Sterry, Mah & Campbell, Honolulu, 1966; judge Family Ct., Honolulu, 1966-70; head family support divsn. Dept. of Corp. Counsel, Honolulu, 1971-95. Bd. dirs. Legal Aid Soc., Honolulu. Lt. col., legal officer U.S. CAP, Honolulu; chmn. Teen Intervention Program, Honolulu; docent Iolani Palace, Honolulu; chmn. Teen-Age Assembly; mem. adv. com. McKinley High Young Parents Program. Mem. Hawaii State Bar Assn. Avocations: tai chi, line dancing, yoga, hula dancing. Home: 441 Mananai Pl Apt E Honolulu HI 96818-5345

CAMPBELL, NEAL FRANKLIN, music educator; b. Pittsboro, N.C., Jan. 27, 1953; s. Owen Riley and Aline Grey (Mangum) C.; m. Gwynn McLaurine Callis, May 13, 1996. MusB, Manhattan Sch. Music, 1983, MusM, 1985, D of Mus. Arts, 1996. Asst. organist All Saints' Ch., Chevy Chase, Md., 1973-76; organist, choirmaster St. Peter's Ch., Phila., 1976-77, St. George's By the River, Rumson, N.J., 1977-80, Christ Ch., Bloomfield, N.J., 1980-85, St. Stephen's Ch., Richmond, Va., 1985—; adj. asst. prof. music U. Richmond, 1997—. Author: Music and Life of Harold Friedell, 1996; performer recordings, radio and TV. Recipient Bronson Ragan award Manhattan Sch. Music, 1983. Mem. Am. Guild Organists (dean 1989-90, chair recital com. 1995-96, nat. coun. 2000—), Assn. Anglican Musicians, Organ Hist. Soc., Royal Coll. Organists (London), Ch. Club N.Y. Episcopalian. Office: 6000 Grove Ave Richmond VA 23226-2601 E-mail: ncampbell@ststephensch.org., ncampbel@richmond.edu.

CAMPBELL, PATRICIA ANN, artist; b. Camp Atterbury, Ind., July 12, 1953; d. Walter Samuel Campbell and Juanita Young-Campbell-Blackwell-Curtright; m. Wesley Derek Fissinger; m. Richard Abraham Sinclair (dec. July 31, 1999); m. John Rawlings III, Dec. 24, 1981 (div. Mar. 6, 1986); m. Ronald Ray Sale, Nov. 24, 1971 (div. July 6, 1981); children: Chastity Sale-Campbell, Freedom Sale-Hankins, Hope Sale-Sinclair-DuFour. AA, NW Ark. C.C., 1993. Manager-advertising dir. Sinclair Guttering, Rogers, Ark., 1986—95; buyers asst. Wal-Mart Inc., Bentonville, Ark., 1994—95; owner/operator Bargains "A" Plenty-Retail Store, Bentonville, Ark., 1992—95., Garfield, Ark., 1998—. Independent. Avocations: astrology, taking care of terminally ill. Home: 19318 Ford Rd Garfield AR 72732 Personal E-mail: oknarkie@email.com.

CAMPBELL, PATTON, stage designer, educator; b. Omaha, Sept. 10, 1926; s. Ralph Harold and Frances Lorraine (Patton) C. BA, Yale U., 1950, MFA, 1952. Instr. costume design and history Barnard Coll., 1955-57; instr. scenery, costume design and history NYU, 1962-67; assoc. prof. Columbia U., 1967-91, SUNY, Purchase, 1975—2002; vis. lectr. Bklyn. Coll., 1973-74, 80, 86-89, Brandeis U., 1975-76, 82-83. Faculty New Sch., 1985; vis. prof. So. Methodist U., 1986, SUNY, Stony Brook, 1987; lectr. O'Neill Ctr., Suffolk Community Colls., 1987, Ohio U., 1996, So. Meth. U., Dallas, 1996, 97, Easton, Conn. Libr., 1997. Designer: costumes for plays and operas including 27 Wagons Full of Cotton, Playhouse Theatre, 1955, Trouble in Tahiti, 1955, Fallen Angels, 1956, A Hole in the Head, Plymouth Theatre, 1957, All American, Winter Garden Theatre, 1962, Wuthering Heights, N.Y.C. Opera, 1959, The Mikado, 1959, The Inspector General, 1960, Natalia Petrovna, 1964, Katya Kabonova, 1964, Capriccio, 1965, Lizzie Borden, 1965, La Traviata, 1966, The Pirates of Penzance, 1968, Carry Nation, 1969, Susannah, 1971, The Ballad of Baby Doe, 1988 (PBS), La Belle Helene, 1976, The Student Prince, 1980, La Traviata, 1981, Il Tabarro, Gianni Schicchi, Juilliard Opera Theatre, N.Y.C., The Lady from Colorado, 1964, Madame Butterfly, Central City (Colo.) Opera, 1964, After The Fall, Nat. Co., Wilmington, Del., 1964, Oliver!, 1964, Man of La Mancha, ANTA Washington Square, 1965 (Tony award nominee), On A Clear Day You Can See Forever, Nat. Co. Cleve., 1966, Loot, Biltmore Theatre, 1968, Der Rosenkavalier, Santa Fe Opera, 1968, Tosca, Santa Fe Opera, 1969, Cosi Fan Tutte, 1969, The Fisherman and His Wife, Opera Co. of Boston, 1970, Scarlett, Imperial Theatre, Tokyo, 1970, Between Time and Timbuktu (on PBS), 1972, Gone With The Wind, Drury Lane Theatre, London, 1972, Regina, Houston Grand Opera, 1980, Merry Wives of Windsor, So. Meth. U., The Mighty Casey and Gianni Schicchi, Glimmer Glass Opera Theatre, Cooperstown, N.Y., 1986, Teddy and Alice, Omaha Playhouse, 1990; costumes and scenery The Rake's Progress, Santa Fe Opera, 1957, Ariadne auf Naxos, 1957, La Boheme, 1958, Capriccio, 1958, Falstaff, 1958, Fledermaus, 1959, The Abduction From The Seraglio, 1959, The Makropoulos Affair, N.Y.C. Opera, 1970, H.M.S. Pinafore, 1975; exhibited in shows at Wright Hepburn Gallery, 1969, Praha Quedrennial, 1985, 89, Omaha Playhouse, 1986, Gone with the Wind Mus., 1993. Served with USN, 1944-46. Mem. United Scenic Artists. Episcopalian.

CAMPBELL, PAUL, III, lawyer; b. Chattanooga, Feb. 1, 1946; children: Paul IV, Kolter M. BA, Vanderbilt U., 1968; MA, Middlebury Coll., 1972; postgrad., So. Meth. U., 1971-72, Emory U., 1972-73; JD, U. Tenn., 1975. Bar: Tenn. 1976, Ga. 1977. Tchr. English St. Mark's Sch., Dallas, 1968-72; ptnr. Campbell & Campbell, Chattanooga, 1976-98; mem. Witt, Gaither & Whitaker, Chattanooga, 1998—2002, Shumacker Witt Gaither & Whitaker, Chattanooga, 2002—. Adj. prof. English, U. Tenn., Chattanooga, 1976, adj. prof. law, 1979-81, adj. prof. pre-trial litigation, Knoxville, 1996, adj. prof. pol. schi., 2002-; mem. Tenn. Ct. of Judiciary, 1995-2003; mem. Tenn. Jud. Evaluation Guidelines Commn., 1994-95. Author: Tennessee Admissibility of Evidence in Civil Cases, 1987; co-author: Tennessee Automobile Liability Insurance, 1986, 95, 96, 99, 2002; editor-in-chief Tenn. Law Rev., 1975; contbr. articles to profl. jours. Bd. mgrs. YMCA Youth Residential Ctr., 1977-80; mem. McCallie Sch. Alumni Coun., 1987-93, U. Tenn. Dean's Alumni adv. coun. law coll., 1979—; trustee, Harbison Found., 1994-96; bd. Cmty. Found. Greater Chattanooga, 2002-. Recipient Am. Jurisprudence award U. Tenn., 1974, U. Ten. Coll. Law Pub. Svc. award, 1995; Alumni Achievement award McCallie Sch., 1994. Mem. ABA, Am. Bar Found., Tenn. Bar Assn. (bd. govs. 1985-94, pres. 1992-93, ho. del., 2002-), Tenn. Bar Found., Chattanooga Bar Found., Chattanooga Bar Assn. (bd. govs. 1983-85), State Bar Ga., Fed. Bar Assn. (dir. chpt. 1983-88), Fed. Defense and Corp. Counsel, Def. Rsch. Inst., Internat. Assn. Def. Counsel, Order of Coif, Phi Kappa Phi. Office: Shumacker Witt Gaither & Whitaker 736 Market St Ste 1100 Chattanooga TN 37402-4856

CAMPBELL, RICHARD ALDEN, electronics company executive; b. Bend, Oreg., July 31, 1926; s. Corlis Eugene and Lydia Amney (Peck) C.; m. Edna Mary Seaman, June 12, 1948; children: Stephen Alden, Douglas Niall (dec.), Carolyn Joyce. BS in Elec. Engring., U. Ill., 1949, MS in Elec. Engring., 1950. With TRW Inc., Redondo Beach, Calif., 1954-87, exec. v.p., 1979-87; bus. cons., profl. co. dir. Rolling Hills Estates, Calif., 1987—. Patentee in radio communications. Bd. dirs. U. Ill. Found., Hugh O'Brian Youth Leadership. With USN, 1944-46. Recipient Alumni Honor award U. Ill. Coll. Engring. Mem. IEEE (life), Am. Electronics Assn. (pres. 1969, dir. 1970), Phi Kappa Phi, Tau Beta Pi, Eta Kappa Nu, Sigma Tau, Pi Mu Epsilon, Phi Eta Sigma, Rolling Hills Country Club, Rancheros Visitadores Club, Los Caballeros Club. Republican.

CAMPBELL, RICHARD BRUCE, lawyer; b. Phila., Jan. 5, 1947; s. George B. and Edith (Neithammer) C.; m. Patricia Ann James, Mar. 7, 1981; children: Ron Martin, Rebecca Joi. BA, U. S.C., 1968, JD, 1974. Bar: U.S. Dist. Ct. S.C. 1975, U.S. Ct. Appeals (4th cir.) 1976, U.S. Ct. Appeals (5th cir.) 1983, Colo. 1985, U.S. Dist. Ct. Colo. 1986, U.S. Ct. Appeals (fed. cir.) 1989, Fla. 1989, U.S. Dist. Ct. (mid. dist.) Fla., U.S. Ct. Appeals (11th cir.) 1992. Law clk. to presiding justice U.S. Dist. Ct., Columbia, S.C., 1975; ptnr. Henderson & Salley, Aiken, S.C., 1975-80; atty. TVA, Knoxville, 1980-85; ptnr. Wells, Love & Scoby, Boulder, Colo., 1986-89; shareholder Carlton, Fields, Ward, Emmanuel, Smith & Cutler, P.A., Tampa, Fla., 1989—. Lectr. in field. Contbr. articles to profl. jours. Served to capt. USAF, 1968-72. Mem. ABA, Am. Arbitration Assn. (panelist), Fla. Bar Assn., Colo. Bar Assn., Hillsborough County Bar Assn. Avocations: travel, skiing, photography. Office: Carlton Fields Ward Emmanuel Smith & Cutler PC PO Box 3239 Tampa FL 33601-3239 E-mail: rcamp@carltonfields.com.

CAMPBELL, RICHARD P. lawyer; b. Boston, June 17, 1947; s. William Thomas and Mary Patricia (O'Brien) C.; m. Barbara Lydon; children: Rochard, Sean, Lauren. BA, U. Mass, 1970; JD cum laude, Boston Coll., 1974. Bar: N.J. 1974, U.S. Dist. Ct. N.J., 1974, Mass. 1977, U.S. Dist. Ct. R.I. 1979, U.S. Dist. Ct. Maine, U.S. Ct. Appeals (1st cir.) 1980, Fla., 1984, Maine, 1986, U.S. Supreme Ct. 1991, U.S. Dist. Ct. Conn. 1997, R.I. 1997. Assoc. Shanley & Fisher, Newark, 1974-77, Nutter McClennen & Fish, Boston, 1979-81, Craig & Macauley, Boston, 1979-81; shareholder, 1981-83; founder Campbell, Campbell, Edwards & Conroy, Boston, 1983—. Chmn. bd. overseers Boston Coll. Law Sch. Contbr. articles to profl. jours. Recipient Founders medal Boston Coll. Law Sch., 1995. Mem. ABA (chmn. products liability com., tort and ins. practice sect. 1990-91, task force on tort liability systems 1991—, chmn., acamedician practitioner task force, 1993-94, chmn. TIPS ann. meeting 1994, long range planning com. 1995-96, TIPS coun. 1996-2002, task force autochoice legis. 1997-99, vice-chmn. 1999-2001, chmn. 2001-02), Fed. Bar Assn. (pres. Mass. chpt. 1993-94), Am. Coll. Trial Lawyers, Mass. Bar Assn. (chmn. white collar crime com. criminal just. sect., co-chmn. lawyer advt. com. 1993-96, bd. dels. 1993-98), Mass. Def. Lawyers Assn. Lwyers for Civil Justice, Def. Rsch. Inst. (prod. liability com. 1984—, amicus curaie com. 1995-97), Assn. for Advancement of Automotive Med. (life), Product Liabilty Adv. Counc. (exec. counc. 1993-97, sustaining), Nat. Assn. Criminal Def. Lawyers, Nat. Bd. Trail Advocacy (cert. civil trial adv.), Internat. Assn. of Def. Couns. (chmn. toxic and hazardous substances litigation com. 1992-94, chair open forum com. 1994-95, exec. com. 1996-99, chair CLE bd. 1996-98), Civil Justice Adv. Grp., Notre Dame Acad., Hingham, Mass. (bd. dirs. 1998—), Ireland C of C in US (bd. dirs. 1996), Cath. Charities (bd. dirs.). Algonquin Club, Hawk's Nest Golf Club (Vero Beach, Fla.), Univ. Club, Bay Club Hatherly Country Club. Office: 1 Constitution Plz Boston MA 02129-2025

CAMPBELL, ROBERT, architect, writer; b. Buffalo, Mar. 31, 1937; s. R. Douglas and Amy (Armitage) C.; m. Janice Jaye Gold, Feb. 2, 1969 (div. 1990); 1 child, Nicholas. AB magna cum laude with highest honors, Harvard U., 1958, MArch, 1967; MS in Journalism, Columbia U., 1960. Registered architect, Mass. Writer, editor Parade mag., 1960-63; designer Benjamin Thompson Assocs., 1968-69; assoc. Sert Jackson & Assocs., 1967-75; architecture critic Boston Globe, 1973—; pvt. practice architecture Cambridge, Mass., 1975—. Cons. Am. Acad. Arts and Scis., Whitehead Inst., Boston Symphony Orch., Isabella Stewart Gardner Mus., Mayors Inst. for City Design, City of San Francisco; lectr. in field; mem. vis. faculty U. N.C. Sch. Architecture, Charlotte, 1979-94; Sam Gibbons Eminent scholar U. South Fla., 1993-2002; vis. scholar MIT, 1991-94; Max Fisher vis. prof. U. Mich., 2002; artist-in-residence Am. Acad. Rome, 1997. Author: Cityscapes of Boston: An American City Through Time; contbg. editor Architectural Record mag., Preservation mag.; contbr. articles to profl. jours.; published poet, photographer. Mem. Mid-Cambridge Neighborhood Assn.; propr. Boston Athenaeum. Recipient Francis Kelley prize, 1967, Pulitzer Prize for Criticism, 1996; named Julia Amory Appleton traveling fellow, 1967, Nat. Endowment for Arts design fellow, 1975; Nat. Arts Journalism Program sr. fellow Columbia U., 2003; grantee Graham Found., 1991, 2003. Fellow AIA (nat. design com., medal for criticism 1980), Am. Acad. Arts and Scis.; mem. Boston Archtl. Ctr. (hon. life), Boston Soc. Architects, Am. Archtl. Found. (bd. regents), Cambridge Club, St. Botolph

Club, Tavern Club, Examiner Club, Century Assn. (N.Y.C.), Saturday Club, Phi Beta Kappa. Democrat. Address: 52 Antrim St Cambridge MA 02139-1102 Fax: 617-576-4784. E-mail: Robert@RCampbell.net.

CAMPBELL, ROBERT CHARLES, minister, theology educator; b. Chandler, Ariz., Mar. 9, 1924; s. Alexander Joshua and Florence (Betzner) C.; m. Lotus Idamae Graham, July 12, 1945; children: Robin Carl, Cherry Colleen. AB, Westmont Coll., 1944; BD, Eastern Baptist Theol. Sem., 1947, ThM, 1949, ThD, 1951, DD (hon.), 1974; MA, U. So. Calif., 1959; postgrad., Dropsie U., 1949-51, U. Pa., 1951-52, NYU, 1960-62, U. Cambridge, Eng., 1969; DLitt (hon.), Am. Bapt. Sem. of West, 1972; HHD (hon.), Alderson-Broaddus Coll., 1979; LHD (hon.), Linfield Coll., 1982; LLD (hon.), Franklin Coll., 1986. Ordained to ministry Am. Bapt. Ch., 1947; pastor 34th St. Bapt. Ch., Phila., 1945-49; instr. Eastern Bapt. Theol. Sem., Phila., 1949-51; asst. prof. Eastern Coll., St. Davids, Pa., 1951-53; assoc. prof. N.T. Am. Bapt. Sem. of West, Covina, Cal., 1953-54, dean, prof., 1954-72; gen. sec. Am. Bapt. Chs. in U.S.A., Valley Forge, Pa., 1972-87; pres. Eastern Bapt. Theol. Sem., Phila., 1987-89, ret. Vis. lectr. Sch. Theology at Claremont, Calif., 1961-63, U. Redlands, Calif., 1959-60, 66-67, Fuller Theology Seminary, Calif., 1992-97; Bd. mgrs. Am. Bapt. Bd. of Edn. and Publ., 1956-59, 65-69; v.p. So. Calif. Bapt. Conv., 1967-68; pres. Am. Bapt. Chs. of Pacific S.W., 1970-71; Pres. N.Am. Bapt. Fellowship, 1974-76; mem. exec. com. Bapt. World Alliance, 1972-90, v.p., 1975-80; mem. exec. com., gov. bd. Nat. Council Chs. of Christ in U.S.A., 1972-87; del. to World Council of Chs., 1975, 83, mem. central com., 1975-90. Author: Great Words of the Faith, 1965, The Gospel of Paul, 1973, Evangelistic Emphases in Ephesians, Jesus Still Has Something To Say, 1987. Baptist. Home: 125 Via Alicia Santa Barbara CA 93108-1769

CAMPBELL, ROBERT DAVID, minerals and metals executive; b. Teaneck, N.J., May 5, 1947; s. Robert Wesley and Phyllis May Julich; m. Elizabeth I. Young, June 15, 1978; 1 child, Ariel. BS, Syracuse U., 1969. Trader C. Tennant Sons & Co., N.Y.C., 1969-73, Cargill, N.Y.C., 1974-75; mng. dir. Amalgamated Metal Corp., Zug, Switzerland, 1975-80; pres. Amalgamet Inc., N.Y.C., 1978-80; v.p. Samincorp Inc., N.Y.C., 1980-84; pres. RST Resources, Inc., N.Y.C., 1984-93; pres., CEO Global Minerals & Metals Corp., N.Y.C., 1993—. Mem. N.Y. Copper Club, Metropolitan Club, Cannon Point South (dir. 1983-95). Avocations: tennis, scuba, sailing, skiing. Home: 45 Sutton Pl S New York NY 10022-2444

CAMPBELL, ROBERT EMMETT, retired health care products company executive, medical association administrator; b. Passaic, N.J., 1933; Grad., Fordham U., 1955, Rutgers U., 1962. Vice chmn., dir. Johnson & Johnson, New Brunswick, N.J., ret., 1995. Chmn. bd. trustees Fordham U., 1992-98, Robert Wood Johnson Found., 1999—; chmn. bd. dirs. Cancer Inst. N.J., 1995—. Home: 40 Lake Dr North Brunswick NJ 08902-4830 Address: Robert Wood Johnson Found Rte 1 & College Rd E PO Box 2316 Princeton NJ 08543-2316

CAMPBELL, ROBERT GORDON, music educator; b. Camden, Ark., May 24, 1922; s. Charles Milton and Edith Harriet (Newman) C.; m. Nancy Brough Patterson, May 27, 1947; children: Shirley, Catherine, Gordon, Betty. BA, Hendrix Coll., 1943; BMus, U. Tex., 1948, MMus, 1950; PhD, Ind. U., 1966. Mus. instr. U. Tex., Austin, 1950-52, So. Ark. U., Magnolia, 1952-55, asst. prof., 1955-57, assoc. prof., 1957-64, prof. music, 1964-87, prof. emeritus, 1987—, chmn. divsn. fine arts, 1964-80, hon. prof., 1987. Pres. bd. dirs. So. Ark. Symphony, El Dorado, 1967-68. With USAAF, 1943-46, ETO. Named in honor Campbell Music Listening Libr., 2001. Mem. Mus. Tchrs. Nat. Assn. (exec. bd. dirs. 1968-72), Ark. State Mus. Tchrs. Assn. (pres. 1967-68, Outstanding Coll. Tchr. award 1980), Am. Musicol. Soc., Coll. Mus. Soc., Mus. Libr. Assn., Pi Kappa Lambda, Phi Mu Alpha Sinfonia. Democrat. Presbyterian. Avocations: swimming, bird watching. Home: 508 Margaret St Magnolia AR 71753-2530 Office: So Ark U PO Box 9398 Magnolia AR 71754-9398

CAMPBELL, ROBERT HEDGCOCK, investment banker, lawyer; b. Ann Arbor, Mich., Jan. 16, 1948; s. Robert Miller and Ruth Adele (Hedgcock) C.; m. Katherine Kettering, June 17, 1972; children: Mollie DuPlan, Katherine Elizabeth, Anne Kettering. BA, U. Wash., 1970, JD, 1973. Bar. Wash. 1973, Wash. State Supreme Ct. 1973, Fed. 1973, U.S. Dist. Ct. (we. dist.) Wash. 1973, Ct. Appeals (9th cir.) 1981. Assoc. Roberts & Shefelman, Seattle, 1973-78, ptnr., 1978-85; sr. v.p. Lehman Bros., Inc., Seattle, 1985-87, mng. dir., 1987—. Bd. dirs. Pogo Producing Co., 1999—; dir., treas. Nat. Assn. Bd. Lawyers, Hinsdale, Ill., 1982-85; pres., trustee Wash. State Soc. Hosp. Attys., Seattle, 1982-85; mem. econs. dept. vis. com. U. Wash., 1995-97; mem. Law Sch. dean's adv. bd. U. Wash., 1999—. Contbr. articles to profl. jours. Trustee Bellevue (Wash.) Schs. Found., 1988-91, pres., 1989-90; nation chief Bellevue Eastside YMCA Indian Princess Program, 1983-88; trustee Wash. Phikeia Found., 1983-91, Sandy Hook Yacht Club Estates, Inc., 1993-98; mem. Wash. Gov.'s Food Processing Coun., 1990-91. Mem. U. Wash. Varsity Swimming Alumni Bd. Republican. Avocations: skiing, wind surfing, bike riding, physical fitness, golf. Home: 8604 NE 10th St Medina WA 98039-3915 Office: Lehman Bros Bank of America Tower 701 5th Ave Ste 7101 Seattle WA 98104-7016 E-mail: ibe2ski@msn.com., rhcampbe@lehman.com.

CAMPBELL, RONALD NEIL, retired magazine designer; b. Morristown, N.J., Mar. 7, 1926; s. Carroll Francis and Emily Ruth (Peters) C.; m. Jule Gallina, Sept. 22, 1956; 1 son, Bruce G. B.F.A., R.I. Sch. Design, 1951. With Fortune mag., N.Y.C., 1952-82, art dir., 1974-82; ret. Freelance writer Sports Illustrated, CASE Currents, Graphis mag.; freelance graphic designer, lectr., 1951—; mem. adv. bd. Internat. Editorial Design Forum; design cons. Harvard Mag., 1985-95, Harvard Bus. Rev., 1987-90. Served with USNR, 1944-46. Recipient merit awards Art Dirs. Club N.Y., merit awards Comm. Arts Mag., merit awards Art Direction Mag., Page One award Am. Newspaper Guild, 2 Silver awards Editl. Design Forum, N.J. State Disting. Svc. medal, 2003. Mem. Soc. Illustrators (Gold and Silver medals), Am. Inst. Graphic Arts (merit awards), Soc. Publ. Designers (hon. bd. dirs., merit awards), Univ. and Coll. Designers Assn., U.S.S. Bon Homme Richard Assn. Home: 37 Barton Hollow Rd Flemington NJ 08822-5929 Office: 136 Waverly Pl Apt 8A New York NY 10014-6822

CAMPBELL, ROY TIMOTHY, JR., lawyer; b. Newport, Tenn., Aug. 8, 1927; s. Roy Timothy and Polly Vance (Brittain) C. LLB, U. Tenn., 1950. Bar: Tenn. 1951, U.S. Dist. Ct. Tenn. 1953, U.S. Ct. Appeals (6th cir.) 1962. Pvt. practice, Newport, 1951-64; atty. Town of Newport, 1963—92; with Campbell & Hooper, Newport, 1964—. Bd. dirs. Mchts. and Planters Bank, Fed. Defender Svcs. for Ea. Dist. Tenn.; mem. Tenn. Senate, 1983. Bd. dirs. Indsl. Devel. Bd., Newport, 1964—; pres. Union Cemetery, Newport; now chmn. Newport Utilities Bd.; chmn. adminstrn. bd. First United Meth. Ch., Newport, 1980-82; sec.-treas. Cocke County Rep. Exec. Com., Tenn., 1964—. With U.S. Army, 1946-47. Mem. Cocke County Bar Assn. (pres. 1973-74), Civic Club, Lions (Lion of Yr. 1980-81). Office: 335 E Main St Newport TN 37821-3131

CAMPBELL, RUSSELL BRUCE, mathematics educator; b. Hartford, Conn., Sept. 18, 1952; s Andrew Burr and Marian Priscilla (Champlin) C. ScB/ScM, Brown U., Providence, 1974; MS, Stanford U., 1976, PhD, 1979. Asst. prof. math. Purdue U., W. Lafayette, Ind., 1979-83, U. No. Iowa, Cedar Falls, 1983-88, assoc. prof., 1988—. Assoc. editor Theoretical Population Biology, 1991—; contbr. numerous articles to profl. jours. Mem. Am. Math. Soc., Math. Assn. Am., Am. Soc. Naturalists, Genetics Soc. Am., Soc. for Study Evolution, Sigma Xi.

CAMPBELL, RUTH ANN, budget analyst; b. La Plata, Md., Aug. 25, 1948; d. Lawrence Gilbert Pilkerton and Eleanor Garrettei (Swann) Pilkerton-Grimm; m. Joseph Harvey Campbell, May 22, 1970 (dec. Oct. 1989); children: Joseph Lawrence, Timothy Craig. Clk.-stenographer Gen. Svcs. Adminstrn., Washington, 1966-68, sec., stenographer, 1968-70, program asst., 1970-71, adminstrv. asst. Mpls., 1971-72, Washington, 1974-75, program analyst, 1975-78, corr. specialist, 1978-79, program analyst, 1979, budget analyst, 1979—. Sec. Fed. Women's Program/Gen. Svcs. Adminstrn., Washington, 1981—82, PTA, Waldorf, Md., 1981—83; treas. Cub Scout pack Boy Scouts Am., La Plata, Md., 1982—87, Athletic Boosters Club, 1993—94; sec. Warrior Stadium Steering Com.; team capt. Thursday Nite Mixed Bowling League, 1976—; mem. vestry Christ Ch., Wayside, 1990—94, 2000—, treas. Woman's Guild, 1990—. Mem. Am. Assn. Budget and Program Analysis. Episcopalian. Avocations: bowling, camping, horseshoes, travel, reading. Home: 7305 Saint Marys Ave La Plata MD 20646-3968 Office: Gen Svcs Adminstrn Bldg 4 Rm 1105 Washington DC 20406-0001 E-mail: ruthann.campbell@gsa.gov.

CAMPBELL, SARAH, elementary education educator, special education specialist; b. Altavista, Va., Jan. 4, 1940; d. Charlie and Emma Francis (Morgan) Dalton; m. James Campbell, June 12, 1961; children: Saunta, Sidra. AA, Altantic Community Coll., 1976; BA magna cum laude, Glassboro State Coll., 1978; nursery sch. cert., Rutgers U.; spl. edn. cert., Glassboro State Coll., 1986; grad., Garden State Bible Sch., Pleasantville, N.J., 1994. Cert. tchr., NJ; asst. chaplain, Bapt. Ch.; ordained to ministry Bapt. Ch., 1995. Tchr. Head Start program Atlantic Human Resources, Inc., Atlantic City; ednl. area supr. Head Start program Adriatic Day Care Ctr., Atlantic, N.J.; head tchr., mgr. Atlantic Human Resources, Ind./Adriatic Day Care Ctr., Atlantic. Edn. con. Pleasantville (N.J.) Day Care Ctr. Past pres. dist. 8 Second Bapt. Ch.; choir libr. Gt. Choir; co-dir. children's ministry; tchr. Bible studies Greater Exodus Missionary Bapt. Ch. Mem. ASCD, Nat. Assn. Edn. Young Children.

CAMPBELL, SCOTT KENNETH, management educator; b. Athens, Ga., Sept. 7, 1969; s. Kenneth Claude and Barbara Lula Campbell; m. Katalin Kovacs Campbell, Dec. 4, 1975; 1 child, Alexandra Michelle. PhD, Auburn U., 2002. Asst. prof. Ga. Coll. and State U., Milledgeville, Ga., 2001—. Vol. U.S. Peace Corps, Szeged, Hungary, 1995—97. Home: 1652 Pine Valley Rd Milledgeville GA 31061 Office: Ga Coll and State U 420 Akinson Hall Milledgeville GA 31061

CAMPBELL, SCOTT ROBERT, lawyer, former food company executive; b. Burbank, Calif., June 7, 1946; s. Robert Clyde and Jenevieve Anne (Olsen) C.; m. Teresa Melanie Mack, Oct. 23, 1965; 1 son, Donald Steven. BA, Claremont Men's Coll., 1970; JD, Cornell U., 1973. Bar: Ohio 1973, U.S. Dist. Ct. (so. dist.) Ohio 1974, Minn. 1976, Calif. 1989, U.S. Dist. Ct. (no. dist.) Calif. 1989, U.S. Ct. Appeals (9th cir.) 1989, U.S. Dist. Ct. (cen. and so. dists.) Calif. 1990, U.S. Ct. Appeals (5th cir.) 1991, U.S. Tax Ct. 1991, U.S. Ct. Appeals (fed. cir.) 2001. Assoc. Taft, Stettinius & Hollister, Cin., 1973-76; atty. Mpls. Star & Tribune, 1976-77; sr. v.p., gen. counsel, sec. Kellogg Co., Battle Creek, Mich., 1977-89; ptnr. Furth Fahrner Mason, San Francisco, 1989-2000, Zelle, Hofmann, Voelbel, Mason & Gette, LLP, San Francisco, 2000—. U.S. del. ILO Food and Beverage Conf., Geneva, 1984; participant, presenter first U.S.-USSR Legal Seminar, Moscow, 1988; speaker other legal seminars. Mem. ABA, Ohio Bar Assn., Minn. Bar Assn., Calif. Bar. Assn. Office: Zelle Hofmann Voelbel Mason& Gette LLP 44 Montgomery St Ste 3400 San Francisco CA 94104-E-mail: srclaw@ix.netcom.com., scampbel@zelle.com.

CAMPBELL, SELAURA JOY, lawyer; b. Oklahoma City, Mar. 25, 1944; d. John Moore III and Gyda (Hallum) C. AA, Stephens Coll., 1963; BA, U. Okla., 1965; MEd, Chapel Hill U., 1974; JD, N.C. Cen. U., 1978; postgrad. atty. mediation courses, South Tex. Sch. of Law, Houston, 1991, Atty. Mediators Inst./Dallas, Dallas, 1992. Bar: Ariz 1983; lic. real estate broker, N.C.; cert. tchr. N.C. With flight svc. dept. Pan Am. World Airways, N.Y.C., 1966-91; lawyer Am. Women's Legal Clinic, Phoenix, 1987. Charter mem. Sony Corp. Indsl. Mgmt. Seminar, 1981; guest del. Rep. Nat. Conv., Houston, 1992; judge all-law sch. mediation competition for Tex., South Tex. Sch. Law, Houston, 1994. Mem. N.C. Cen. U. Law Rev., 1977-78. People-to-People del. People's Republic of China, 1987; guest del. Rep. Nat. Conv., Houston, 1992. Mem. Ariz. Bar Assn., Humane Soc. U.S., Nat. Wildlife Fedn., People for the Ethical Treatment of Animals, Amnesty Internat., Phi Alpha Delta. Republican. Episcopalian. Avocations: climbed Mt. Kilimanjaro, 1983, also Machu Pichu, Peru, Mt Kenya, Africa, horseback riding, photography. Home: 206 Taft Ave Cleveland TX 77327-4539

CAMPBELL, SHARON MILLIGAN, mathematician, educator; b. Tyler, Tex., Jan. 22, 1948; 1 child, Kimberly Ann. AA, Tyler Jr. Coll., 1968; BA, Stephen F. Austin State U., 1970, MS, 1972. Tchr. math. U. Tex., 1975—94, Robert E. Lee H.S., 1972—2002, Tyler Jr. Coll., 2002—. Mem.: Tex. C.C. Tchrs. Assn., Tex. Ret. Tchrs. Assn., Nat. Coun. Tchrs. Math., Tex. Coun. Tchrs. Math., East Tex. Coun. Tchrs. Math., Am. Math. Assn., Math. Assn. Am., Tex. Classroom Tchrs. Assn., Tex. State Tchrs. Assn., Alpha Delta Kappa.

CAMPBELL, SOPHIE ANN ORISZKO, manager and senior health care consultant; b. Sewickley, Pa., Dec. 20, 1957; d. John and Sophie (Zapola) Oriszko; m. William Henry Campbell Jr., May 10, 1980; children: Christopher William, Nicholas John. BSN, U. Pitts., 1979, MSN, 1986. RN; cert. rehab. nurse; cert. nurse assessment coord. Staff nurse trauma Allegheny Gen. Hosp., Pitts., 1979-80; staff nurse, clin. supr. D. T. Watson Rehab. Hosp. for Children and Adults, Sewickley, 1980-87; clin. dir. neuro/vent and head injury Greater Pitts. Rehab. Hosp., 1987-90; dir. adult rehab. nursing The Rehab. Inst., Pitts., 1990-93; rehab. program dir. Olsten Kimberly Quality Care, 1993-94; post acute care cons. The Polaris Group, Hingham, Mass., 1994-99; sr. healthcare cons./mgr. Parente Randolph, LLC, Wilkes-Barre, Pa., 1999—. Instr. Pa. State U. br. campuses, Monroeville, Beaver, and St. Francis Hosp., 1991-94. Mem.: Am. Assn. Nurse Assessment Coords., Assn. Rehab. Nurses (pres. 1993), Sigma Theta Tau. Republican. Byzantine Catholic. Home: 145 Lawnview Dr Freedom PA 15042-2215 Office: Parente Randolph LLC 46 Public Sq Wilkes Barre PA 18701-2609 E-mail: scampbell@parentenet.com.

CAMPBELL, STANLEY CLINTON, retired school system administrator, retired military officer; b. Mpls., Aug. 26, 1922; s. Harry Clayton and Minnie Louise (Adamson) Campbell; m. Violette Margaret Saylor, June 12, 1944 (dec. Mar. 28, 2002); children: Gail, Tamara, Dean, Amy. BS in polit. sci., U. Minn., 1947, MA in Am. history, 1949; PhD in ednl. adminstrn., U. Wis., 1961. Cert. chief sch. admnstr. Pa., 1969, Ind., 1969. Elem. tchr. Eatonville Elem. Sch., Minn., 1948—49; prin. Spring Grove HS, Minn., 1950; prin. jr. HS Wilmar Pub. Sch., Minn., 1952—55; prin. HS Stoughton Pub. Sch., Wis., 1955—56, supt. 1956—59; rsch. assoc. U. Wis., Madison, 1959—61; supt. Rose Tree Media Sch., Media, Pa., 1961—69, Indpls. Pub. Sch., 1969—72; ret., 1972. Chmn. Jr. Achievement, Media, Pa., 1960, edn. cons. com., 1960; county chmn. White House Conf. Children and Youth, Media, Pa., 1965. Lt. col. U.S. Army, 1943—47, ETO, lt. col. U.S. Army, 1950—52, Korea. Recipient First Ann. Svc. award, Kiwanis Club of Media, Pa., 1964; fellow Wis. Sch. Adminstr. Assn., 1959; grantee Shankland scholarship, Am. Assn. Sch. Adminstr., 1960. Democrat. Methodist. Achievements include research in planning and design of school buildings. Avocations: running, hunting, fishing, cooking, carpentry.

CAMPBELL, STEWART FRED, foundation executive; b. St. Louis, June 29, 1931; s. Archibald Stewart and Charlotte (Ehrmann) C.; m. Ann Abbey Hudson, Dec. 18, 1954; children: Karen Ann, Deborah Ann. BS, Lehigh U., Bethlehem, Pa., 1954; MBA, NYU, 1961. With Mfrs. Hanover Trust Co., N.Y.C., 1958-64, asst. sec., 1962-64; with Duke Endowment, N.Y.C., 1964-79, asst. treas., 1967-73, treas., 1973-79; sec.-treas. Alfred P. Sloan Found., N.Y.C., 1979-86, fin. v.p., sec., 1986—. Treas. Doris Duke Trust, 1973-79, Angler B. Duke Meml., Inc., 1973-79, Nanaline H. Duke Fund, 1973-79; asst. treas. Duke Power Co., 1968-75; bd. dirs. Skytop Lodge, Inc., 1992—, v.p., 1993-95, chmn. bd., 1995-2000. Treas. Essex unit N.J. Assn. Retarded Children, 1967-72, trustee, 1966-74; trustee Meml. Home of Upper Montclair, 1987-96, pres., 1990-95. Mem. Delta Phi. Clubs: Rockefeller Center (N.Y.C.); Montclair Golf; Skytop (Pa.). Home: 3 Wendover Rd Montclair NJ 07042-3031

CAMPBELL, TERENCE WARREN, forensic psychologist; b. Chgo., Sept. 9, 1943; s. Jess Frank and Dorothy Agnus C.; m. Constance Lee, Aug. 20, 1966 (div. July 1, 1977); m. Sharon Kay, Aug. 20, 1982; children: Elisabeth, Derek. BS, Western Mich. U., 1965; PhD, U. Md., 1970. Staff to chief psychologist Md. Penitentiary, Balt., 1970-72; pvt. practice Sterling Heights, Mich., 1972—. Adj. asst. prof. Loyola Coll., Balt., 1969-72; asst. prof. Mercy Coll., Detroit, 1972-80; cons. Macomb County Cir. Ct., Mount Clemens, Mich., 1972-81, 90-94, Lifeline-Doc.'s Hosp., Detroit, 1989-91; adv. bd. mem. FMS Found., Phila., 1993—, Nat. Assn. Consumer Protection in Mental Health, Salt Lake City, 1994—, Nat. Parental Alienation Found., Washington, 2000-01. Author: Beware The Talking Cure, 1994, Smoke & Mirros: The Devastating Effects of False Sexual Abuse Claims, 1998, Cross-Examining Experts in the Behavioral Sciences, 2001. Fellow Am. Psychol. Soc.; mem. Am. Psychology-Law Soc., Am. Assn. Applied & Preventive Psychology, Am. Assn. Marriage and Family Therapy. Office: Terence W Campbell PhD PD 4105 Metro Pkwy Ste 103 Sterling Heights MI 48310

CAMPBELL, THOMAS J. chiropractor, legislator; b. Bklyn., Oct. 27, 1954; s. Charles Marvin and Edna Mary (Sacer) C.; m. C. Lynn Hearn, July 2, 1983. AA in Social Scis., Fla. Tech. U., 1974; BA in Police Sci. and Adminstrn., Seattle U., 1977; DC, Life Chiropractic Coll., 1983; postgrad. in orthopedics, L.A. Chiropractic Coll., 1984-90. Diplomate Am. Acad. Pain Mgmt.; cert. chiropractic rehab. dr. Nat. Bd. Chiropractic Examiners-Physiotherapy; lic. chiropractor, Wash., Fla. Pvt. practice Chiropractic Spinal Care, Inc., 1984—. Mem. Wash. State Ho. of Reps., 1993-96, 99-. With inf. U.S. Army, 1977-79, capt. USAR/ARNG, 1979-85. Recipient Appreciation for Svc. award Chiropractic Disciplinary Bd., 1989-93, Gov. Appreciation Certificate Wash. State Disciplinary Bd., Legislator of Yr. award Wash. State Labor Coun., 1999, Wash. State Trial Attys., 1999, Wash. State Vet. Assn., 1994, Wash. State Nurses Assn., 2000, others. Fellow Internat. Coll. Chiropractors; mem. Am. Chiropractic Assn. (alt. del. House of Dels. 1988-92), Wash. State Chiropractic Assn. (chmn. mem. com. 1984-85, dist. 4A 1985-86, dir. exec. bd. 1985-88, vice-chmn. disciplinary bd. 1990-93, legislative affairs com. 1986, Pres. award 1985, Dist. of the Yr. award 1985-86, Chiropractor of Yr. 1987, 89-91, 2001, Appreciation award 1994, Exceptional Svc. award 1994), Wash. State Chiropractic Assn., Pierce County Chiropractic Assn., Chiropractic Rehab. Assn. (bd. dirs.). Republican. Avocations: scuba diving, boating, fishing. Home: PO Box 443 Spanaway WA 98387-0443 E-mail: thomasjcampbell@qwest.net.

CAMPBELL, THOMAS CORWITH, JR., economics educator; b. Enfield, Va., Mar. 19, 1920; s. Thomas Corwith and Pearl (Gravatt) C.; m. Burdine Gordon, Apr. 17, 1943; children— Thomas Corwith III, Maxwell Gordon. AB, Lynchburg Coll., 1942; MA, U. Pitts., 1947, PhD, 1948; student, U. Wis., summer 1947. Mem. faculty W.Va. U., 1948—, asst. to asso. prof., 1948-58; asst. dean Coll. Commerce, 1955-64, prof., 1958-80, dean, 1964-68; vis. prof. Va. Commonwealth U., 1980-91. Contbr. articles to profl. jours. Adviser to Ministry of Econ. Planning and Devel. Govt. of Kenya, 1968-70; economist U.S. Bur. Mines, 1974-77, Dept. of Energy, 1977— ; Chmn. Gov.'s Council Econ. Advisers, 1963-65; mem. Charleston Regional Export Expansion Council, 1964— . Served to lt. USNR, 1942-46; capt. Res. Mem. Am. Econ. Assn., AAUP, Soc. Cincinnati, Beta Gamma Sigma. Mem. Christian Ch. Home: 4014 Fauquier Ave Richmond VA 23227-4040

CAMPBELL, TIMOTHY REID, financial services company executive; b. Sparta, Ill. s. Floyd and Dorothy Campbell; m. Sara Campbell; children: Timothy Scott, Catherine Elizabeth. AB, MacMurray Coll, 1968; postgrad., U. Ill., 1968-69, U. Hartford, 1972; MA in Adminstrn., U. Ill. at Springfield, 1975; grad., Pub. Affairs Inst., 1995. V.p. govt. affairs Travelers Ins. Cos., Hartford; v.p. govt. rels. Travelers Group, N.Y., v.p. state govt. rels.; sr. v.p., dir. state govt. rels. divsn. Citigroup, 1998-2000, sr. v.p. state govt. rels. divsn., 2000—02; sr. v.p. govt. rels. Travelers Property Casualty Corp., Hartford, Conn., 2002—. Bd. dirs. Ins. Fedn. Pa.; mem. exec. com. Nat. Conf. State Legislatures, Denver, 1976-78; chair governing bd. Manifesto Ins. Group, Tallahassee, Fla., 1992-98. Trustee MacMurray Coll., Jacksonville, Ill., 1976-83, 94-99; dir. Sci. Mus. Conn., West Hartford, 1994, 97-2000; apptd. by gov. to Conn. Adv.Commn. on Intergovtl. Rels., 1996—. Inducted into Samuel K. Gove Ill. Legis. Internship Hall of Fame, 1995. Mem. Am. Soc. Pub. Adminstrn. Avocations: reading, travel. Office: Travelers Property Casualty Corp 1 Tower Sq Hartford CT 06183-0001

CAMPBELL, TODD J. judge; b. Rockford, Ill., 1956; BA cum laude, Vanderbilt U., 1978; JD with high honors, U. Tenn., 1982. Bar: Tenn. 1982. With Gullett, Sanford, Robinson & Martin, Nashville, 1982-92; counsel to Vice Pres. of U.S., Washington, 1993-95; with Doramus & Trauger, Nashville, 1995; judge U.S. Dist. Ct., Nashville, 1996-. Democrat.

CAMPBELL, TOM, former congressman, dean; b. Chgo., Aug. 14, 1952; s. William J. and Marie Campbell; m. Susanne Martin. BA, MA in Econs. with highest honors, U. Chgo., 1973, PhD in Econs. with highest dept. fellowship, 1980; JD magna cum laude, Harvard U., 1976. Law clk. to Judge George E. MacKinnon U.S. Ct. Appeals (D.C. cir.), 1976-77; law clk. to Justice Byron R. White U.S. Supreme Ct., Washington, 1977-78; assoc. Winston & Strawn, Chgo., 1978-80; White Ho. fellow Office Chief of Staff, Washington, 1980-81; exec. asst. to dep. atty. gen. Dept. Justice, Washington, 1981; dir. Bur. Competition FTC, Washington, 1981-83; mem. 101st, 102nd, 104th, 105th, 106th Congresses from Calif. 12th Dist., 1989—93; mem. com. on sci., space and tech., com. on judiciary, banking, fin. and urban affairs; mem. com. internat. rels., com. on banking, joint eco. com. 104th-106th Congress from Calif. 15th Dist., 1995-2001; mem. Calif. State Senate, 1993-95; dean U. Calif., Berkeley, 2002—. Prof. Stanford Law Sch., 1983-2002. Referee Jour. Polit. Economy, Internat. Rev. Law and Econs. Mem. ABA (antitrust sect., coun. 1985-88, program chmn. 1983-84), Coun. on Fgn. Rels., World Affairs Coun. No. Calif. (chair 2003—). Republican.

CAMPBELL, TROY DAVID, officer; b. Kendallville, Ind., July 26, 1964; s. Jerry L. and Marsha Ann (Henney) C.; stepmother: Kristy Ann Rhead; m. Dawn Suzanne Krumwiede, Aug. 2, 1986; children: Meaghann Michelle, Trevor Scot. BS in aerospace tech., Ind. State Univ., 1986; MS in aerospace tech., Embry-Riddle Aeronautical Univ, 1997. Lic. comml./instrument pilot. FB-111 radar navigator 393 BMS, Pease AFB, N.H., 1989-90; F111F weapon systems officer, radar stike officer 492 Tactical Fighter Squadron, RAF Lakenheath, England, 1990—92; F 15E Weapon Systems Officer/training officer 492 Fighter Squadron, RAF Lakenheath, 1992-94; 48 FW Strike Plans officer/F 15E weapons systems officer 48 Operational Support Squadron, RAF Lakenheath, 1994-96; F 15 Tactical electronic warfare Suite Program mgr. 36 Engineering & Test Squadron, Eglin AFB, Fl., 1996-98; major US Air Force, Seymour Johnson AFB, NC, 1998—2001; chief 4 FW operational plans.F 15E weapons systems officer 4 Fighter Wing Plans and Evaluations, Seymour Johnson AFB, NC, 1998—2002; air liaison officer, asst. dir. ops. 9 Air Support Ops. Squadron, Ft. Hood, Tex., 2002—. Pastor Parrish Rels Com., Salem United Methodist Ch., Goldsboro, N.C., 2000-2001. Named U.S. Air Force in Europe Bowling champion Ramstein Air Base, Germany, 1995. Mem. Air Force Assn., Aircraft Owners and Pilot Assn., Moose Lodge, Gideons Internat., Am. Legion, Vets. Fgn. Wars, Meth. Men. Methodist. Avocations: bowling, sports, flying, scuba diving. Office: 9 ASOS/ADO 90042 Clarke Rd Killeen TX 76544-5056 E-mail: troy.campbell@hood.army.mil., tcampbell@hot.rr.com.

CAMPBELL, VINCENT BERNARD, judge, lawyer; b. Rochester, N.Y., Nov. 1, 1943; s. Paul and Lucy C.; m. Geraldine Miceli, July 4, 1970; children: Dina, Tracy. BS, Syracuse U., 1965, LLD, 1968. Bar: N.Y. 1969. Lawyer Goldman and Shinder, Rochester, N.Y., 1970-74, Vincent B. Campbell Law Firm, Rochester, N.Y., 1974—; businessman Flower City Builders Supply Corp., Rochester, N.Y., 1974—; real estate developer V.R.J.D. Devel. Inc., 40 West Ave. Properties, Rochester, N.Y., 1970—; judge Town of Greece, N.Y., 1994—. V.p. Monroe County Legislature, Rochester, 1976-88; N.Y. state committeeman Rep. Party, Rochester, 1988-93; town councilman Town of Greece, 1990-94; bd. trustees N.Y. Chiropractic Coll., Seneca Falls, N.Y., 1992; econ. devel. com. Nazareth Coll., Rochester, 1991-93. Recipient Robert Roantree award Syracuse Credit Mfrs. Assn., 1965, Am. Jurisprudence award Lawyers Coop., 1969; named Legislator of the Yr., Monroe County Conservative Party, 1983-84. Mem. ABA, N.Y. State BarAssn., Monroe County Bar Assn., N.Y. State Magistrate's Assn., Rochester Yacht Club. Avocations: sailing, golfing, hunting, winemaking.

CAMPBELL, WILLIAM, research analyst, educator, artist; Student, Bryn Mawr Conservatory Music, 1984-86. Print shop asst. Independence Hall Nat. Park, Phila., 1986; vis. instr. Gifted Opportunity Ctr., Lynchburg, Va., 1997; rsch. analyst The Beckley Found., 1998—. Instr. Fellowship Christian Acad., Madison Heights, Va., 1997-99, Gifted and Talented Devel. Ctr., Charlotte, N.C., summer 1998. Pubished artwork: Angel, 1984, After Leonardo DaVinci Abound With Blessings, 2000. Alt. del. Rep. Nat. Conv., San Diego, 1996; credentialed guest Rep. Nat. Conv., Phila., 2000; vice-chmn. Campbell County

(Va.) Rep. Com., 1996, 98—, chmn., 1996-98; legis. dist. chmn. 22nd Dist. Rep. Com., 1997-98. Recipient Cert. of Recognition, Gov. Va., Richmond, 1997. Mem. Nat. Assn. for Gifted Children. Reformed Episcopalian. Avocations: Scrabble, military history, polo.

CAMPBELL, WILLIAM AUBREY, law educator; b. Springfield, Mo., Mar. 30, 1940; s. Aubrey and Clastel (Richardson) C.; m. Lynnette Humphreys, June 29 1963; children: Alistair, Anne, Katherine. BA, Rhodes Coll., 1962; LLB, Vanderbilt U., 1965. Bar: N.C. 1976. Asst. prof. U. N.C., Chapel Hill, 1965-66, assoc. prof., 1969-74, prof. pub. law and govt., 1974-91, Gladys Hall Coates prof. pub. law govt., 1991-2001, emeritus prof., 2001—. Mem. com. on contraceptive rsch. NAS, Washington, 1988-90. Author: Property Tax Collection, 1988, Guidebook for North Carolina Registers, 1994, (with others) Healthcare Facilities Law, 1991. Bd. dirs., pres. Conservation Trust for N.C., Raleigh, 1992-2002. Lt. USN, 1966-69. Mem. N.C. Bar Assn. (coun. real property sect. 1994-97). Democrat. Presbyterian. Office: U NC Chapel Hill Inst Govt Cb 3330 Knapp Bldg Chapel Hill NC 27599-0001

CAMPBELL, WILLIAM BUFORD, JR., materials engineer, chemist, forensic consultant; b. Clarksdale, Miss., Nov. 23, 1935; s. William Buford and Bertha Lucille (Atkins) C.; m. Joan E. Stakem, June 29, 1963 (div. 1983); children: Lisa Anne, William Buford III, Heather Katherine, Matthew Rush-(dec.); m. Marcia L. Dickert, Mar. 1, 2003. B in Ceramic Engring., Ga. Inst. Tech., 1958, MS in Engring., 1960; AM in Mineralogy, Inorganic Chemistry, Harvard U., 1962; PhD in Materials Engring., Ohio State U., 1967; postgrad., MIT, 1963-65, Ohio State U., 1969-72, NYU, 1980. Registered profl. engr., Ga., Ala., Tenn. Asst. prof. dept. ceramic engring. Ohio State U., Columbus, 1967-69, assoc. prof., 1969-74; chief biomed. engring. dept. Doctor's Hosp., Morristown, Tenn., 1974-76; assoc. prof. engring. sci. and mechanics U. Tenn., Knoxville, 1974-77; assoc. prof. orthopaedic surgery U. Tenn. Coll. Medicine, Memphis, 1974-77; sr. ptnr. Campbell, Churchill, Zimmerman & Assocs., Cons., Knoxville, 1977-84; cons., pvt. practice Biomed. Engring. and Forensic Sci., Knoxville, 1984—; adj. prof. Coll. Applied Sci., East Tenn. State U., 1998—. Ptnr. Brae Arden Farms Ltd., Phila., Tenn., 1979-83, tech. dir., chief exec. officer Southeastern Mobility Co., Inc., Phila., Tenn., 1977-84; founder Biomed. Systems Inc., Knoxville, 1986; project engr. TVA, 1987-89; dir. EPRI Ctr. for Materials Fabrication, Battelle Meml. Inst., Columbus, Ohio, 1989-90, dir., program mgr. Innovation and Tech. Transfer, Battelle Meml. Inst., Columbus, 1990; mng. ptnr. Performance Cons., Knoxville, Tenn., 1991-2002; v.p. Accurate Automation Corp., Chattanooga, 2002. Patentee: Holds 3 U.S. Patents; contbr. articles to profl. jours. Mem. adminstrv. bd. Bearden United Meth. Ch., 1982-85; chmn. exec. com. The Ch. of the Redeemer, Concord, Tenn., 1985-87; mem. fin. com. Americans for Responsible Govt, 1984-85, fin. com. 50th Am. Presdl. Inaugural, 1984-85, Nat. Adv. Bd. on Tech. and the Disabled; trustee Lakeshore Mental Health Insts., Dept. Mental Health, State of Tenn., 1986—; bd. dirs. Direct Braille Slate Fund, 1998—, Vols. of Am., Knoxville, 1987-90; mem. bldg. com. and exec. com. Hist. Tenn. Theater Found., 1997—; mem. adv. bd. Knoxville Mus. Art, 1987-88; bd. dirs., mem. exec. com. Tenn. Tech. Devel. Corp.; mem. Tenn. Sci. and Tech. Adv. Coun., State Tenn., 1993-98. Lt. col. Tenn. State Guard, 1995—. Recipient Cert. Recognition, NASA, 1973, Freeman award Am. Coun. for the Blind, 1976, Recognition award ASTM, 1997. Fellow Am. Inst. Chemists (cert. chemist), Am. Acad. Forensic Sci., Am. Ceramic Soc. (abstracter and reviewer 1962—, nat. programs and meetings com. 1968-72, div. chmn. 1969-70, other offices, life mem.); mem. ASTM (liaison mem. for ceramics and med., surg. materials and devices 1975—, Recognition award 1997—), Nat. Soc. Profl. Engrs., Am. Soc. for Engring. Edn., Am. Soc. for Nondestructive Testing, Nat. Inst. Ceramic Engrs. (life), Phi Lambda Upsilon, Tau Beta Pi (Eminent Engr. 1974), Sigma Xi (rsch. awards 1958, 60, 71), KERAMOS, others. Republican. Office: Accurate Automation Corp 7001 Shallowford Rd Chattanooga TN 37421 E-mail: wcampbell@accurate-automation.com.

CAMPBELL, WILLIAM EDWARD, mental hospital administrator; b. Kansas City, Kans., June 30, 1927; s. William Warren and Mary (Bickerman) C.; m. Joan Josselyn Larimer, July 26, 1952; children: William Gregory, Stephen James, Douglas Edward. Student, U. Nebr., 1944-45, MS, 1975; student, U. Mich., 1945, Drake U., 1948; BA, U. Iowa, 1949, MA, 1950; PhD in Psychology, U. Nebr., Lincoln, 1980. Psychologist Dept. Pub. Instrn., State of Iowa, 1951-52; hosp. adminstr. Mental Health Inst., Cherokee, Iowa, 1952-68; dir. planning and rsch. Dept. Social Svcs., State of Iowa, 1968-69; supt. Glenwood Resource Ctr. (formerly Glenwood State Hosp. Sch.), Iowa, 1969—, Clarinda Mental Health Inst., Iowa, 1979—; assoc. prof. mental health adminstrn. Northwestern U., Chgo., 1982—; pres., bd. dirs. River Bluffs Cmty. Mental Health Ctr. Dir. Shared Mental Health Svcs., Clarinda/Glenwood; founder, chmn. Regional Drug Abuse Adv. Coun.; adj. prof. Sch. Pub. Health U. Minn., also preceptor grad. students in mental health adminstrn.; vis. faculty Avepane U., Caracas, Venezuela; adj. prof. Coll. Medicine and Health Adminstrn. Tulane U.; mem. vis. staff dept. psychiatry U. Nebr. Med. Ctr.-Creighton U. St. Joseph Med. Ctr. Author works in field. UN spl. cons. to Venzuela for UNESCO; bd. dirs. Polk County Mental Health; v.p., bd. dirs. Mercy Hosp., Coun. Bluffs, Iowa; state pres. United Cerebral Palsy; charter mem., bd. dirs. Pub. Broadcasting Sta. KIWR, Council Bluffs, Iowa, Glenwood-Mills County Econ. Devel. Found., Inc., 1985—; chartered mem., bd. dirs. Mills County Econ. Devel., 1987, Glenwood Resource Ctr., 1993—; apptd. State of Iowa Dept. Human Svcs. Exec. Mgmt. Team, 1997; charter mem., organizer Loess Hills Alliance, 1998—, mem. land protection, econ. devel. and long range planning coms., 1999—. Served with AUS, 1944-46; col. Res. Decorated Army Commendation medal; recipient Meritorious Service medal U.S. Army, 1982. Fellow Assn. Mental Health Adminstrs. (nat. com. chmn. 1970); mem. Assn. Med. Adminstrs., Am. Hosp. Assn. (nat. governing bd. psychiat. services sect., charter panelist nat. adv. panel on mental health services, mem. governing body psychiat. services sect.), Iowa Hosp. Assn., Health Planning Council of Midlands, Assn. Univ. Programs in Health Adminstrn. (mem. nat. task force on edn. of mental health adminstrs.), Am. Assn. on Mental Deficiency (chmn. adminstrn. sect. Region 8), Nat. Rehab. Assn., Assn. for Retarded Children, Mental Health Assn., Phi Beta Kappa. Office: Office of Supt Glenwood Resource Ctr Glenwood IA 51534

CAMPBELL, WILLIAM H. career officer; b. Kaukauna, Wis., Jan. 5, 1940; Commd. U.S. Army, advanced through grades to lt. gen., 1997, dir. info. info. sys. command, control, comm. and computers, 1997—. Office: Office Dir Info Sys for Command Control Comm and Computers 107 Army Pentagon Washington DC 20310-0107

CAMPBELL, WILLIAM HENRY, JR., federal agency administrator; b. Quincy, Mass., Mar. 12, 1947; s. William Henry and Alice Elizabeth (Cleary) C.; m. Pamela Jeanne Beall, Mar. 29, 1974; children: Jennifer Anne, John Matthew. BS in Engring., Mass. Maritime Acad., 1967; Dipl. Mgmt., Indsl. Coll. Armed Forces, Washington, 1984; MS in Tech. Mgmt., Johns Hopkins U., Balt., 1987. Chief engr. U.S. Merchant Marine, 1967-73; chief main propulsion br. George G. Sharp, Inc., Hyattsville, Md., 1973-75; sr. mech. engr. USCG, Washington, 1975-77, chief sys. tech. div., 1980-85; investigator-in-chg. Nat. Transp.. Safety Bd., Washington, 1977-80; dep. comdr. engring. quality Naval Supply Sys. Command, Washington, 1985-91; chief procurement mgmt. and sr. competition advocate USCG, 1991—2000; dep. asst. sec. for finance, dep. CFO Dept. Veterans Affairs, Washington, 2000—02, asst. sec. mgmt., CFO, 2002—, acting asst. sec of Veterans Affairs for human resources & adminstr., 2003—. Contbr. articles to profl. jours. Recipient Engring. award Brotherhood of Marine Officers, 1967, Disting. Svc. award Nat. Transp. Safety Bd., 1980, Equal Opportunity award U.S. DOT, 1983, Superior Civilian Svc. medal USN, 1991. Mem. Mass. Maritime Acad. Alumni Assn., Indsl. Coll. Armed Forces Alumni Assn., Johns Hopkins U. Alumni Assn. Democrat. Avocations: history, philosophy, economics. Office: Dept Veterans Affairs 810 Vermont Ave NW Rm 200 Washington DC 20420*

CAMPBELL, WILLIAM J. lawyer; b. Grand Junction, Colo., Feb. 10, 1945; s. Timothy Samuel and Narcissa Cooke C.; m. Marsha Logan Campbell, June 16, 1979; children: John Bradford Geiger, Elizabeth Weir Geiger, Anne Wentworth Campbell, Amy Logan Campbell. BA cum laude, Colo. Coll., 1967; JD, U. Colo., 1971. Bar: Colo. 1971, U.S. Dist. Ct. Colo. 1971. Shareholder Bradley, Campbell, Carney & Madsen, P.C., Golden, Colo., 1971-95; ptnr. Faegre & Benson LLP, Denver, 1995—. Mem. U. Colo. Law Rev., 1970-71. Bd. trustees Colo. Colo.; mem. St. Andrews Vestry; bd. dirs. World Trade Ctr., Denver. Named Outstanding Young Lawyer, First Jud. Dist. Bar Assn., 1982; Boettcher scholar Boettcher Found., 1963-67; Grad. fellow Rotary Found., 1969. Mem. ABA, Colo. Bar Assn., Colo. Assn. Corp. Counsel, Phi Beta Kappa. Republican. Episcopalian. Avocation: golf. Home: 6781 Lupine Cir Arvada CO 80007 Office: Faegre & Benson LLP 3200 Wells Fargo Ctr 1700 Lincoln St Denver CO 80203

CAMPBELL, WILLIAM O'NEAL, retired physician; b. McCaysville, Ga., May 22, 1928; s. Martin Hoyt Campbell and Pauline Kimsey; m. Reba Kathern Hughes, June 14, 1961; 1 child, Martin Lee. AA, Tenn. Wesylan Coll., 1948; MD, U. Tenn. Memphis, 1962. Diplomate Am. Acad. Family Physicians. Resident Carraway Meth. Hosp., Birmingham, Ala., 1965; family physician Copperhill, Tenn., 1965—77; staff physician Tenn. Valley Authority, Chattanooga, 1977—94; ret., 1994. Cons. U. So. Ala. Med. Mus., Mobile, Med. Mus., Foley, Ala. Mem.: AMA, Med. Collectors Assn., Chattanooga and Hamilton County Med. Soc., Alpha Omega Alpha, Alpha Epsilon Delta. Home: 4900 Bal Harbor Dr Chattanooga TN 37416

CAMPBELL, WILLIAM STEEN, publishing executive, writer, speaker; b. New Cumberland, W.Va., June 27, 1919; s. Robert N. and Ethel (Steen) C.; m. Rosemary J. Bingham, Apr. 21, 1945 (dec. Dec. 1992); children: Diana J., Sarah A., Paul C., John W. Grad., Steubenville (Ohio) Bus. Coll., 1938. Cost acct. Hancock Mfg. Co., New Cumberland, 1938-39; cashier, statistician Weirton Steel Co., W.Va., 1939-42; travel exec. Am. Express Co., N.Y.C., 1946-47; adminstr., account exec. Good Housekeeping mag., 1947-55; pub. Cosmopolitan mag., 1955-57; asst. dir. circulation Hearst Mags., N.Y.C., 1957-61; gen. mgr. Motor Boating mag., 1961-62; v.p., dir. circulation Hearst Mags., 1962-85; pres. Internat. Circulation Distbrs., 1978-81, Mags., Meetings, Messages, Ltd., 1986—. With Periodical Pubs. Svc. Bur. subs. Hearst Corp., Sandusky, Ohio, 1964-85, v.p., chief exec., 1964-69, pres., chief exec., 1970-85; dir. Audit Bur. Circulations, 1974-86, Periodical Pubs. Svc. Bur., 1964-85, Nat. Mag. Co., Ltd., London, Randolph Jamaica Ltd., Omega Pub. Corp. Fla., Hearst Can. Ltd., 1964-85; former chmn. Ctrl. Registry, Mag. Pubs. Assn.; chmn. bd trustees Hearst Employees Retirement Plan, 1971-85; mem. pres.'s coun. Brandeis U., 1974-94; chmn. nat. corp. and found. com. U. Miami, 1979-85; dir. Broadway Assn., 1985-90, v.p., 1988-90; keynote spkr. Fifth Ann. Hospitality Industry Luncheon, Santa Barbara, Calif., 1996. Bd. dirs. Santa Barbara Rep. Club, 1993-94, Lobero Theatre Found., 1994-96, v.p., 1995-96. Lt. col. USAF, 1942-46, ETO. Recipient Lee C. Williams award Mag. Fulfillment Mgrs. Assn., 1974, Torch of Liberty award Anti-Defamation League, 1979. Mem. Campbell Clan Soc., Mil. Order of World Wars (chaplain), Masons, Cosmopolitan Club (chaplain). Home and Office: 1150 Coast Village Rd Santa Barbara CA 93108-2722

CAMPE, RÜDIGER, humanities educator; b. Hagen, Germany, Sept. 4, 1953; arrived in U.S., 2000; s. Andreas and Lore Campe; m. Petra Scharre Campe, July 7, 1988. PhD, U. Freiburg, Germany, 1986. Asst. prof. U. Essen, Germany, 1986—88, 1990—96, Johns Hopkins U., Balt., 1988—90, prof., 2001—. Recipient award in the humanities, ABY Warburg-Found., Hamburg, Germany. Office: Johns Hopkins U 3400 N Charles St Baltimore MD 21218 Business E-Mail: rcampe@jhu.edu.

CAMPEAU, RICHARD JOHN, JR., internal medicine and radiology educator; b. New Orleans, Mar. 30, 1944; s. Richard John Campeau Sr. and Shirley Claire Lequay; m. Erin E. Boh, Aug. 1, 1980 (div. Oct. 1986); m. Nathalie Jacqueline DuBois, Oct. 16, 1996; 1 child, Anastasia. BS, La. State U., 1966, MD, 1969. Diplomate Am. Bd. Internal Medicine, Am. Bd. Nuclear Medicine. Intern Tulane U., 1969-70, resident in internal medicine, 1970-72; fellow in nuclear medicine Johns Hopkins Hosp., 1972-73; asst. chief nuclear medicine svcs. VA Med. Ctr., Miami, Fla., 1973-74; asst. prof. radiology U. Miami, 1974-76, asst. prof. radiology, chief imaging divsn., 1975-76; dir. sect. nuclear medicine Tulane U., 1976—, assoc. prof. clin. radiology, 1976-92, assoc. prof. clin. internal medicine, 1982-92, prof. clin. radiology and internal medicine, 1992—. Cons. in nuclear medicine VA Med. Ctr., New Orleans, 1976-86, staff physician, 1986—; med. dir. nuclear medicine tech. program Delgado C.C., New Orleans, 1991—; cons. staff physician Our Lady of the Lake Regional Med. Ctr., Baton Rouge, La., 1998—. Mem. edit bd. Clin. Nuclear Medicine, 1987—; contbr. numerous articles to profl. jours. Mem. Am. Heart Assn., Am. Soc. Nuclear Cardiology, European Assn. Nuclear Medicine, Inter Am. Coll. Radiology, Am. Telemedicine Assn., Am. Coll. Nuclear Medicine, Soc. of Chefs of Acad. Nuclear Medicine Sects., Assn. Univ. Radiologists, Am. Inst. Ultrasound in Medicine, Soc. Nuclear Medicine, Am. Coll. Nuclear Physicians, Musser-Burch Soc., Alpha Omega Alpha, Phi Delta Epsilon. Democrat. Avocations: music, wine collecting, physical fitness, backgammon, cooking. Office: Dept Radiology SL-54 1430 Tulane Ave New Orleans LA 70112 E-mail: richard.campeau@tulane.edu.

CAMPELLO, FLORENCIO LENNOX, artist; b. Guantanamo, Us Naval Base, Cuba, Sept. 6, 1956; s. Florencio and Ana Olivia Campello; m. Catriona Trafford Fraser; 1 child, Callum Fraser-Sharp; m. Mary Bridgett Strasser (div. Sept. 8, 1993); children: Vanessa, Elise. BS Math., BS Art, U. Wash., 1981; MS, Naval Postgrad. Sch., Monterey, Calif., 1987. Art critic Dimensions Mag., Norfolk, Va., 1994—99, Visions Mag. for the Visual Arts, Virginia Beach, Va., 1995—2000; info. warfare advisor KSI, Arlington, Va., 1997—; art critic Crier Media, Alexandria, Va., 1999—, Washingtonpost.com, 2001—, Cultureflux Mag., 2001—, DC One Mag., 2002—, Art Krush, 2003—. Advisor D.C. Arts & Humanities Commn., Washington, 1999—2001; guest curator Athenaeum, Alexandria, Va., 2001, Greater Reston Arts Ctr., Reston, Va., 1997, Gallery West, Alexandria, Va., 1997, League of Fairfax Artists, Fairfax, Va., 2000; assoc. dealer Sothebys.com. Artwork, Body of Works, 1970 (Our Lady of Loretto Art Medal, 1970), original artwork, America Desnuda, 1981 ("Prix de Peinture de Raymond Duncan" Musee des Duncan. Paris, France, 1981), drawing, 1981 (Silver Medal, "Salon of the 50 States." Musee des Duncan. Paris, France, 1981), watercolor, Road Near Memmuir, Scotland, 1990 ("Most Popular Award." 42nd North Wynd River Art Show. Wyoming, 1990), etching, Mujertrees, 1980 (First Prize (Printmaking). Whipple Gallery National. Marshall, MN., 1980), watercolors, Edzell Castle, 1991 (First Prize (Watercolors). Montana Art Society. Billings, Montana, 1991), charcoal drawing, Feral Mermaid, 1995 (Best of Show. 20th Princess Anne Art Show. Virginia Beach, VA, 1995), Female Nude, 1996 (Best of Show. Festival in the Park. Roanoke, Virginia., 1996), one-man shows include The Hub Gallery, 1979, Arts Northwest Gallery, Wash., 1981, Galeria Sevillana, Spain, 1984, Warehouse Gallery, Scotland, 1992, Chevrier's Presidio Gallery, Calif., 1993—94, Fraser Gallery, Washington, D.C., 1996—99, 2001, 49 West, Md., 1997, Eklektikos Gallery, Washington, D.C., 2000. Decorated Meritorious Svc. medal USN, Navy Commendation Medal (4), Navy Achievement Medal (2); recipient second prize, Bellgrade Art Festival, 1997, 1998. Mem.: Art Dealers Assn. of Greater Washington.

CAMPER, JOHN JACOB, speech writer; b. Toledo, Sept. 8, 1943; m. Cleraine Uguccioni, Mar. 27, 1971 (div. May 1981); 1 child, Sarah; m. Mary C. Galligan, Jan. 9, 1988; 1 child, Joseph. BA, Kenyon Coll., 1964. Reporter Detroit News, 1965-68; reporter, critic Chgo. Daily News, 1968-78; editorial writer Chgo. Sun-Times, 1979-84; dept. head external relations Regional Transp. Authority, Chgo., 1984-85; media coord. Chgo. World's Fair Authority, 1985; reporter Chgo. Tribune, 1985-90; assoc. chancellor for pub. affairs U. Ill., Chgo., 1990-97; dep. press sec., speech writer Mayor of Chgo., 1997—; v.p. Chgo. Pub. Rels. Forum, 1995-97, pres., 1997-98. Bd. dirs. Family Svc. Mental Health Ctr. of Oak Park and River Forest, 1990-97. Recipient Peter Lisagor award Chgo. Headline Club, 1983, UPI award, Chgo., 1983, Stick-O-Type, Chgo. Newspaper Guild, 1983, Nat. Assn. Black Journalists award, 1987. Home: 1846 W Newport Ave Chicago IL 60657-1024 Office: 502 City Hall 121 N Lasalle St Chicago IL 60602-1202 E-mail: jcamper@cityofchicago.org.

CAMPER, JOHN SAXTON, public relations and marketing executive; b. Trenton, N.J., Apr. 24, 1929; s. Thomas Emory and Mildred Ruth (Burke) C.; m. Ferne Arlene Clanton; children: Susan Jennifer, John Saxton III. BS in History and Econs., U. Nebr., 1968. Enlisted U.S. Army, 1948, commd. to 1st lt., advanced through ranks to maj., 1972, ret., 1972; regional mktg. officer First Bank System, Mont., 1978-83. Lectr., instr. mktg. and advt. pub. rels.; pres. Camper Comm., Helena, 1983—; dir. Profl. Devel. Ctr., Mont., 1984-91. Decorated Legion of Merit. Mem. Helena Advt. Fedn. (1st pres., founder), Rotary Internat. (dist. gov. 1998-99). Methodist. Fax: (406) 443-0310. E-mail: jarl@mcn.net.

CAMPHOR, JAMES WINKY, JR., educational administrator; b. Balt., Mar. 16, 1927; s. Emma Rosetta (Lewis) Butler; m. Lillie Mae Gilliard (div. Sept. 1976); children: Yvonne, Michael, Yolande; m. Florine Alston Camphor, Aug. 10, 1980. BS, Coppin Coll., 1951; MA, Coppin State Coll., 1971. Tchr. Dept. Edn., Balt., 1951-53, Dept. Juvenile Svcs., Chettenham, Md., 1953-75, demonstration tchr., 1972-75; behavior specialist Dept. Health and Mental Hygiene, Montgomery County, Md., 1975-87, ednl. supr., 1987—. Cons. Fantastic Buddies Travel, Balt., 1980-94. Co-author: (study) Social Studies in the Training School, 1963. Mem. adv. bd. Foster Grandparents Assn., Prince George County, Md., 1991—94, Nat. Assn. Sickle Cell Disease, Balt., 1984—94, chmn. Walk-A-Thon, 1991; pres. Am. Fedn. State County Mcpl. Employees Assn., Assn. State County Employees Montgomery County, 1991; mem. adv. com. capital campaign Coppin State Coll., 1998—2002, mem. cmty. fundraising coalition, 2002—, pres. nat. alumni assn., 2002—; supt. Sunday sch. Emmanuel Cmty. Ch., Balt., 1945. Recipient Cmty. Svc. award Nat. Assn. Sickle Cell Disease, 1988, Presdl. citation Nat. Assn. in Higher Edn., 1992, Gov.'s Citation award William Donald Shafer, Annapolis, Md., 1994, Commitment to Edn. award City Coun. of Balt., 1994. Mem. Black Profl. Men Inc., Bus. and Profl. Coun. (pres. 1989-94), Cmty. Men (cmty. mem., bus. mgr. 1985-92), Lucky Ten Inc. (charter, pres. 1990-94), Elks, Phi Beta Sigma (pres. 1990-94). Democrat. Avocations: reading, tutoring, traveling, collecting pipes, singing. Home: 3308 Lauri Rd Baltimore MD 21244-1324 Office: Dept Health and Mental Hygiene 3100 Gracefield Rd Silver Spring MD 20904-1870

CAMPHOUSE, MARK DAVID, music educator, composer, conductor; b. Oak Park, Ill., May 3, 1954; s. William Henry and Esther C.; m. Elizabeth Ann Curtis, June 20, 1982; children: Elizabeth Curtis Camphouse, Briton Curtis Camphouse. B in Music, Northwestern U., 1975, M in Music, 1976. Vis. instr. music U. Okla., Norman, 1976-77, St. Cloud (Minn.) State U., 1977-78; asst. prof. music Blackburn Coll., Carlinville, Ill., 1980-84; music dir. and conductor N.Mex. Music Festival, Taos, 1978-82; assoc. prof. music Radford (Va.) U., 1984-99; prof. music, 2000—; assoc. dir. Va. Govs. Sch. Arts, Radford, 1986-89; acting dean music New World Sch. Arts, Miami, Fla., 1998-99. Author: Composers on Composing for Band, composer: 15 published works for symphonic bands. Recipient Outstanding Faculty award, State Coun. Higher Edn. Va., 2002. Mem. Nat. Band Assn. (1st Prize music composition 1991, bd. dirs. 1998—), Am. Bandmasters Assn., Music Edn. Nat. Conf., Am. Symphony Orch. League, Coll. Band Dir. Nat. Assn. Republican. Methodist. Avocations: racquetball, flag collecting. Home: 106 Hidden Valley Dr Radford VA 24141-3912 Office: Radford U Dept Music PO Box 6968 Radford VA 24142-6968 E-mail: mcamphou@radford.edu.

CAMPION, DANIEL RAY, editor; b. Oak Park, Ill., Aug. 23, 1949; s. Raymond Edward and Wilma Frances (Dougherty) C. AB, U. Chgo., 1970; MA, U. Ill., Chgo., 1975; PhD, U.Iowa, 1989. Indexer Libr. Resources, Inc., Chgo., 1971-72; prodn. editor Encyc. Britannica, Chgo., 1972-74; tchg. asst. U. Ill., Chgo., 1974-76; editl. asst. Follett Pub. Co., Chgo., 1977-78; tchg. and rsch. asst. U. Iowa, Iowa City, 1978-84; sr. test devel. assoc. ACT, Inc., Iowa City, 1984—. Vis. asst. prof. English U. Iowa, 1991-95. Author: (poems) Calypso, 1981, Peter De Vries and Surrealism, 1995; co-editor: Walt Whitman: The Measure of His Song, 1981, 2d edit. 1998. Mem. U. Ill. Pres. Coun., Urbana, 1992—, Mus. Contemporary Art, Chgo., 1996—; life mem. Art Inst. Chgo., 1973—. Recipient Festival of Arts Poetry award U. Chgo., 1967, All Nations Poetry award Triton Coll., River Grove, Ill., 1975, Ill Arts Coun. Literary award, Chgo., 1979, Sustainer Achievement award U. Ill., 1994-95. Mem. Nat. Coun. Tchrs. English, Midwest Modern Lang. Assn., MLA, Soc. Study Midwestern Lit., Authors Guild, Sierra Club, Cousteau Soc., Modern Poetry Assn., Acad. of Am. Poets. Office: ACT 2201 N Dodge St Iowa City IA 52243-0001 E-mail: dan.campion@act.org.

CAMPION, JANE, director, screenwriter; b. Wellington, New Zealand; d. Richard and Edith Campion. BA in Anthropology, Victoria U., Wellington, 1975; Diploma of Fine Arts, Chelsea Sch. Arts, London, 1979; degree, Sydney Coll. Arts, 1979; Diploma in Direction, Australian Film and T.V. Sch., Sydney, 1984; DLitt (hon.), Victoria U., 1999. Adj. prof. Sydney Coll. Arts, 2000. Dir., screenwriter Peel: An Exercise in Discipline, 1982 (also editor, Palme d'Or short film category Cannes Internat. Film Festival 1986, Diploma of Merit Melbourne Film Festival, 1983, finalist Greater Union awards, Australian Film Inst. awards 1983-84), A Girl's Own Story, 1983 (with Gerard Lee, Rouben Mamoulian award 1984, Best overall short film Sydney Film Festival 1984, Unique Artist Merit Melbourne Film Festival 1984, Best Direction, Best Screenplay, Best Cinematography Australian Film Inst. 1984, First Prize Cinestud Amsterdam Film Festival, 1985, Best Film Cinestud 1985, First Prize Festival and Press prize), writer/dir. Mishaps of Seduction and Conquest, 1984-85, Passionless Moments (also prodr., dir., writer, with Gerard Lee and dir. photography, Unique Artist Merit Melbourne Film Festival 1984, Best Exptl. Film Australian Film Inst. 1984, Most Popular Short Film Sydney Film Festival 1985), screened at Cannes Un Certain Regard, 1986, After Hours, 1984 (XL Elders award Best Short Fiction, Best Short Fiction Melbourne Internat. Film Festival 1985), Dancing Daze (TV series), 1985, (TV movie) Two Friends, 1986 (Golden Plaque TV category Chgo. Internat. Film Festival 1987, Best Dir., Best Telemovie, Best Screenplay Australian Film Inst. awards 1987, screened at Cannes in Un Certain Regard, 1986, Edinburgh Film Festival, Sydney and Melbourne Film Festival, 1986), Sweetie, co-writer, dir. 1988, (Georges Sadoul prize Best Fgn. Film, Best Dir., Best Actress, Best Film Australian Critics awards 1990, New Generation award L.A. Film Critics, 1990, Best Fgn. Film Spirit of Independence awards 1990), An Angel at my Table, 1990 (Byron Kennedy award Australian Cinema 1990, Spl. Jury prize, Elvira Notari award Best Woman Dir., Agia Scuola Italian Min. Culture, Best Film Si presci award Panel Internat. Critics, Best Film O.C.I.C. award Christian journalists, Best Film for Young Audiences Cinema e Ragazzi Italian film critics prize, Critics award Toronto Film Festival, Most popular film in the Forum, Otto Debelius prize Berlin Film Festival, Best Fgn. Film, Spirit of Independence Awards, Venice Film Festival, World Premiere, 1990); writer, dir. The Piano, 1993 (Palme d'Or Cannes Internat. Film Festival 1993, Academy Award Best Original Screenplay 1994, Best Picture, Best Dir., Best Cinematography nominations, Acad. Awards, Australian Film Inst. awards, Australia Film Critics, Southeastern Film Critics Assn., others, Best Fgn. Film Chgo. Film Critics, Caesar awards (2000 WIN award, Wimfemme Film Festival Women's Image Network); composer: Feel the Cold, 1983, (play) The Portrait of A Lady, 1996, Holy Smoke, 1998-99 (Best Film Francesco Pasinetti award, pres. Internat. jury Mostra Internat. Art Cinematography Festival Venice Film Festival, 1997, Nat. Union Film Journalists, nominated Best Costume Acad. awards 1997, nominated Best Supporting Actress Acad. awards 1997; dir. In the Cut, 2002-03. Office: HLA Mgmt Pty Ltd 87 Pitt St Redfern NSW 2016 Australia also: PO Box 1536 Strawberry Hills NSW 2012 Australia

CAMPION, RENÉE, lawyer; b. Balt. BS, U. Md., 1980; JD, U. Balt., 1987. Bar: Md. 1987; cert. mediator. Atty. Legal Aid Bur., Inc., Balt., 1988-96; pvt. practice Balt., 1996—. Mem.: ABA, Bar Assn. Balt. City, Women's Law Ctr., Balt. County Bar Assn., Md. State Bar Assn., Women's Bar Assn. Office: 401 Washington Ave Ste 803 Towson MD 21204-4905 E-mail: rlcesq8080@aol.com.

CAMPION, ROBERT THOMAS, manufacturing company executive; b. Mpls., June 23, 1921; s. Leo P. and Naomi (Revord) C.; m. Wilhelmina Knapp, June 8, 1946; 1 son, Michael. Student, Loyola U., Chgo., 1939-41, 46-48. C.P.A., Ill. With Alexander Grant & Co., Chgo., 1946-57, ptnr., 1954-57; with Lear Siegler, Inc., Santa Monica, Calif., 1957—, pres., 1971-85, chief exec. officer, dir., 1971-86, chmn., 1974-86; pvt. investor, 1987—. Served with AUS, 1942-46. Mem. AICPA, Ill. Soc. CPAs, Bel Air Country Club, Jonathan Club, La Quinta Country Club. Republican. Office: Blair House # 406 10490 Wilshire Blvd Los Angeles CA 90024-4646

CAMPION, THOMAS FRANCIS, lawyer; b. Bklyn., Aug. 15, 1935; s. Thomas Francis and Genevieve Agnes (Schantz) C.; m. Virginia Grosscup, Aug. 21, 1965; children: Caroline, Michael. AB, Fordham U., 1957; LLB, Cornell U., 1961. Bar: N.J. 1961, U.S. Dist. Ct. N.J. 1961, U.S. Ct. Appeals (3d cir.) 1965,

U.S. Supreme Ct. 1966, U.S. Dist. Ct. D.C. 1970, N.Y. 1988. Law clk. to judge Appellate Div.-Superior Ct. N.J., 1961-62; assoc. Shanley & Fisher, Newark and Morristown, NJ, 1962-67, ptnr. Morristown, 1968-99, Drinker, Biddle & Shanley, LLP, Florham Park, NJ, 1999—2002, Drinker, Biddle & Reath, LLP, Florham Park, NJ, 2003—. Bd. on trial atty. cert. N.J. Supreme Ct., 1982—89, chmn., 1987—89, chmn. disciplinary oversight com., 1994—2001, vice chmn. commn. on rules of profl. conduct, 2001—. Contbr. articles to profl. jours. Mem. N.J. Gov.'s Mgmt. Commn., 1970. 1st lt. USAR, 1957-61. Fellow Am. Bar Found., Am. Coll. Trial Lawyers; mem. ABA, N.J. Bar Assn. (past chmn. jud. and county prosecutor appointments com., civil cts. task force), Essex County Bar Assn., Morris County Bar Assn., Assn. Fed. Bar N.J. (pres. 1980-82), Univ. Club (N.Y.C.). E-mail: thomas.campion@dbr.com.

CAMPO, DAVE, professional football coach; Football coach various Colls., 1971-89; asst. coach to head coach Dallas Cowboys, 1989—2002; defensive coord. Cleveland Browns, 2003—. Office: Cleveland Browns 76 Lou Groza Blvd Berea OH 44017*

CAMPOLETTANO, THOMAS ALFRED, international contract manager; b. Long Island City, N.Y., Feb. 13, 1946; s. Barney and Mary (Felner) C.; m. Kathy Lee Clemons, Mar. 19, 1989; 1 stepchild, Christopher; children by previous marriage: Lisa, Jennifer, Tricia. AAS, Nassau Coll., 1971; BA, U. South Fla., 1977; postgrad., Am. Grad. U., 1980-85, Touro Coll., 1980-85; internat. contracting cert., George Washington U., 1998. Cert. profl. contract mgr. Cost/price analyst Grumman Aero. Corp., Bethpage, N.Y., 1963 70; sr. cost/price analyst Potter Instrument Co., Plainview, N.Y., 1970-73; prin. fin. analyst, govt. liaison Space Systems div. Honeywell, Inc., Clearwater, Fla., 1973—, sr. contracts mgr. Honeywell Aerospace and Electronics, 2002—. Prof. Honeywell Fed. Contracting Tng. program (recipient 1992 Honeywell Fin. Achievement award). Author: Profit Proposal Initiatives, 1990; co-author: Weighted Guidelines Profit, 1984. With USN, 1963-66, Vietnam, 7th Fleet Flag Commendation, Combat Air Ops., 1965. Recipient Apollo Space Program commendation, NASA, 1969. Mem. Nat. Contract Mgmt. Assn., Fin. Exec. Inst. (mem. com. on govt. bus. 1985), Def. Industry Offset Assn. Republican. Roman Catholic. Avocation: golf. Office: Honeywell Inc 13350 Us Highway 19 N Clearwater FL 33764-7290 E-mail: tom.a.campolettano@honeywell.com.

CAMPOS, ELIZABETH BALLI, lawyer; b. McAllen, Tex., Oct. 9, 1970; d. S. Balli; m. Julio A. Campos; 1 child, Jacob Alex. BBA in Mgmt., Tex. A&M U., 1995; JD, Tex. So. U., Houston, 1998. Bar: Tex. 1998. Law clk. Howard Singleton & Assocs., Houston, 1996-97, Harris County Atty.'s Office, Houston, 1997-98, 61st Dist. Ct., Houston, 1998; atty. Law Office of Manuel Solis, Houston, 1999—. Mem. State Bar Tex., Tex. Young Lawyers Assn., Mex.-Am. Bar Assn. Roman Catholic. Avocation: water sports. Office: Law Office of Manuel E Solis 6657 Navigation Blvd Houston TX 77011-1341

CAMPOS, JORGE, professional soccer player; b. Acapulco, Guerrero, Mexico, Oct. 15, 1966; s. Alvaro Campos Gonzalez and Lucina Navarrete de Campos. Goalkeeper Dolphins of Acapulco, Mexico, 1984—85, Cruz Azul, Mexico, Pumas, Mexico, L.A. Galaxy, Atlante FC, Mexico, Mexican Nat. Team, 1991; champion Concacaf, 1989; second pl. Am. Cup, 1993; champion Gold Cup, 1993, USA Cup, 1996. Named Best Goalkeeper, Mex. League, 1991, 1992, 1993, 1994, 1995; recipient Mexican championship medal, UNAM, 1991, league runners-up medal, Am. MLS, L.A. Galaxy, 1996. Avocations: surfing, basketball, volleyball, tennis, music. Office: Club Deportino Socialy Cultural Cruz Azw AC Antiguo Camino Xochimilco No 100 La Noria CP 16030 Mexico

CAMPOS, NORA, government official; b. Dallas, July 9, 1959; d. Secundino and Rosa Elia Campos; (div. Aug. 1990); 1 child, Valerie Lee Martinez. BA in Social Sci., U. North Tex., 1991; MPA in Pub. Mgmt., U. Tex., Dallas, 2000; postgrad., U. Tex., 2000—. Taxpayer svc. rep. IRS, Dallas, 1986-87, tax technician, 1987-88, pub. affairs specialist, 1988-91, quality rev. analyst, 1991-94, taxpayer edn. specialist, 1994—. Coord. territory vol. income tax assistance, tax counseling for the elderly coord. IRS, Dallas.; mem. minority youth bus. retreat com. Minority Bus. Devel. Agy., Dallas, 1995—, mem. Minority Enterprise Devel. Week com., 1995—. Author: Volunteer Coordinator's Handbook, 1999. Asst. troop leader Girl Scouts U.S.A., Dallas, 1991—; mem. bd. Jesuit-Ursuline Ranger Band Boosters, Dallas, 2000—; vol. El Club Capri, Dallas. Mem. ASPA, Acad. polit. Sci., Assn. Vol. Adminstrs. Roman Catholic. Avocations: music, reading, needlecrafts. Home: 4342 Bonham St Dallas TX 75229 Office: IRS 1100 Commerce 6610DAL Dallas TX 75242 E-mail: nora.campos@irs.gov.

CAMPOS, ROEL C. commissioner; b. Harlingen, Texas, 1949; m. Mini Villarreal; children: David, Daniel. BS, US Air Force Acad., 1971; MBA, UCLA, 1972; JD, Harvard Law Sch., 1979. Commr. US SEC, Washington, 2002—; owner El Dorado Comm., Houston, 1995; fed. prosecutor US Attorney's Office, Los Angeles, 1985—89; attorney pvt. practice, 1990—95. Officer USAF. Office: 450 Fifth St NW Washington DC 20549*

CAMPOS-PONS, MARIA MAGDALENA, artist; b. Matanzas, Cuba, 1959; Student, Nat. Sch. Art, Havana, Cuba, 1980, Higher Inst. Art, 1985, Mass. Coll. Art, 1988. Prof. aesthetic and painting Higher Inst. Art, Havana, Cuba, 1986-89; asst. curator The Space Gallery, 1992. Co-coord. aesthetic and fine art seminar Revolution and Culture Mag., Cuba, 1989—90; vis. prof. RISD, 1994, Mass. Coll. Art, Boston, 1995, Boston, 96, Sch. Mus. Fine Arts, Boston, 1997; juror numerous competitions; curatorial project Articule Gallery, Montreal, 1991, Inst. Contemporary Art, Boston, 1992. One-woman shows include Gallery L, Havana, 1985, Kennedy Bldg. Gallery Mass. Coll. Art, Boston, 1988, CAstle of Royal Force, Havana, 1989, Embassy Cultural House, London, Ont., 1990, Banff Ctr. Arts, Can., 1990, SOHO 20 Gallery, N.Y.C., 1991, Gallery Burning, Montreal, Can., 1991, Burnaby Art Gallery, B.C., Can., 1991, Gallery La Ctrl./Powerhouse, Montreal, 1992, Akin Gallery, Boston, 1993, Latin Am. Gallery, N.Y.C., 1993, Gallery North Miami Dade C.C., 1994, Bunting Inst. Radcliffe Coll., Mass., 1994, Martha Schneider Gallery, Chgo., 1996, The Caribbean Cultural Ctr., N.Y.C., 1997, The Photographers Gallery, Saskatoon, Can., 1997, U. Antioquia and Centro Colombo Am., Colombia, 1997, Ambrosino Gallery, Coral Gables, Fla., 1997, Martha Schneider Gallery, Chgo., 1997, Mario Diacono Gallery, Boston, 1997, Hallwalls, Buffalo, 1998, Mus. Modern Art, N.Y.C., 1998, exhibited in group shows at Ctr. Fine Arts, Miami, 1996, DNA allery, Provincetown, Mass., 1996, Craiger/Dane Gallery, Boston, 1997, Addison Gallery Am. Art Philips Acad., Andover, Mass., 1997, Smithsonian, Washington, 1997, 1998, Nat. Gallery Can., Ottawa, 1998, numerous others, Represented in permanent collections; performer: The Seven Powers Come by the Sea, 1992, La Voz del Silencio/The Voice of Silence, 1993, Letter to my Mother, 1994, 1995, 1996, others; reviewer in field, contbr. carticles to profl. jours. Office: care Schneider Gallery 230 W Superior St Chicago IL 60610-3595

CAMPOVERDE, REBECCA O. federal agency administrator; b. Ecuador;, naturalized, U.S. married; 1 child. Grad., Northwestern U. Reporter, Tex.; with Dallas Ind. Sch. Dist.; legis. asst. to Rep. Steve Bartlett Washington; chief of staff to two successive dep. secs. U.S. Dept. Edn., dep. chief of staff to sec. Lamar Alexander; dir. comm. U.S. Ho. of Reps., dep. staff dir. com. on edn. and the workforce; asst. sec. legis. and congl. affairs Dept. Edn., Washington, 2001—. Cons. trade matters; mem. Bush-Cheney transition team U.S. Dept. Edn. Office: Dept Edn Legislation and Congl Affairs 400 Maryland Ave SW Washington DC 20202-3100

CAMPRIELLO, CHRISTINA MATTHEWS, lawyer, librarian; b. Niskayuna, NY, Aug. 25, 1948; d. Philip R. and Ann Williamson Matthews; m. Austin V. Campriello, June 2, 1968; children: Austin M., Lucia W., Susan C. BA, Barnard Coll., 1972; JD, Fordham U., 1978. Bar: NY 79. Editl. asst. United Presbyn. Ch. USA, N.Y.C., 1969—72; assoc. dir. Dem. Coalition, N.Y.C., 1972—75; census coord. Pleasantville (NY) Sch. Dist., 1990—; pvt. practice law Pleasantville, 1990—; libr. asst. Scarsdale (NY) Sch. Dist., 2002—. Editor Recollections, Inc., Hawthorne, NY, 1999—2001. Chmn. Pleasantville Fund for Learning, 1994—2001; pres. Bedford Rd. Sch. PTA, Pleasantville, 1988—2000. Recipient Outstanding Vol. award, Pleasantville Sch. Dist., 1998. Presbyterian. Home: 40 Nannahagan Rd Pleasantville NY 10570

CAMSTER, BARON OF See WIEMANN, MARION JR.

CANADA, MARK ALAN, English educator, researcher; b. Indpls., Aug. 21, 1967; s. Alan Richard and Mary Frances C.; m. Lisa Michelle Henry, Sept. 23, 1989; children: Esprit, Will. BA, Ind. U., 1989; MA, U. N.C., 1994, PhD, 1997. Copy editor Johnson County Daily Jour., Franklin, IN, 1989-91, News-Sentinel, Fort Wayne, Ind., 1991-92; assoc. prof. English U. N.C., Pembroke, 1997—. Contbr. articles to profl. jours. Mem. Poe Studies Assn., Phi Beta Kappa. Avocations: outdoors, exercise, travel. Office: U NC at Pembroke One University Dr Pembroke NC 28372-1510 Fax: 910-521-6688. E-mail: mark.canada@uncp.edu.

CANADA, MARY WHITFIELD, retired librarian; b. Richmond, Va., June 13, 1919; d. Waverly Thomas and Ruth Bradshaw (Smith) C. BA magna cum laude, Emory and Henry Coll., 1940; MA in English, Duke U., 1942; BS in L.S., U. N.C., 1956. Asst. circulation dept. Duke U. Library, 1942-45, undergrad. librarian, 1945-55, reference librarian, 1956-85, asst. head reference dept., 1967-79, head dept., 1979-85; ret., 1985. Contbr. articles to profl. jours. Mem. exec. com. Friends of Duke U. Library. Duke U. grantee Can., 1979, 81 Mem. ALA (life; initiated performance evaluation discussion group), Southeastern Library Assn. (sec. coll. and univ. sect., chmn. nominating com. reference services div., also chmn. div.), N.C. Library Assn. (chmn. nominating com., chmn. newspaper com., chmn. coll. and univ. sect.), Alumni Assn. Sch. Library Sci. U. N.C. (pres.), Va. Hist. Soc. (life), Va. Geneal. Soc., DAR (chpt. regent), Friends of Va. State Archives, Campus club (Duke U.), Planning Adv. Com. N. Cen. Durham, Va. Mus. Beta Phi Mu. Methodist. Home: 1312 Lancaster St Durham NC 27701-1132

CANADAY, DORIS CHARLENE, retired traffic representative; b. Island Branch, W.Va., Aug. 4, 1932; d. Doy A. and Virgie (Haynes) Nichols; m. Frederick M. Canaday, Mar. 27, 1958 (div. 1963); 1 child, Tammy J. Canaday-Slike. Grad. high sch., Charleston, W.Va. With selecting dept. Owens-Illinois, Inc., Charleston, 1950-56, packer selecting dept./clk. typist various adminstrv. depts., 1956-58, steno clk. adminstrv. svc., 1958-62, clk. typist corrugated dept. Forest Products div., 1962, steno clk. svc. dept. Clarion, Pa., 1963-74; traffic mgr. Owens-Brockway GC, a Unit of Owens Illinois, Clarion, 1974-93; retired, 1993. Former mem. supervisory com. OnIzed Fed. Credit Union, Clarion, 1976. Mem. North-Cen. Pa. Traffic Club (bd. dirs. 1989-92), OnIzed Club, Clarion OnIzed Quarter Century Club, Gold Emblem Club. Republican. Presbyterian. Avocations: international travel, network marketing. Home: 32 Woodlawn Ave Clarion PA 16214-1250

CANADAY, RICHARD A. lawyer; b. Alton, Ill., Aug. 26, 1947; AB, Stanford U., 1969; JD, U. Calif., 1973. Bar: Oreg. 1973, Wash. 1987. Ptnr. Miller Nash LLP, Portland, Oreg. Mem. ABA, Oreg. State Bar, Wash. State Bar Assn. Office: Miller Nash LLP 111 SW 5th Ave Ste 3500 Portland OR 97204-3638 E-mail: rich.canaday@millernash.com.

CANADY, ALEXA IRENE, pediatric neurosurgeon; b. Lansing, Mich., Nov. 7, 1950; d. Clinton Jr. and Hortense (Golden) C.; m. George Davis, June 18, 1988. BS, U. Mich., 1971, MD cum laude, 1975; DHL (hon.), Marygrove Coll., 1994, U. Detroit, 1997; DSc (hon.), Ctrl. Mich. U., 1999, U. So. Conn., 1999. Diplomate Am. Bd. Neurol. Surgery. Intern in surgery Yale U., New Haven, 1975-76; resident in neurosurgery U. Minn., Mpls., 1976-81; fellow in pediatric neurosurgery Children's Hosp. Pa., Phila., 1981-82; instr. neurosurgery U. Pa., Phila., 1981-82; staff neurosurgeon, instr. neurosurgery Henry Ford Hosp., Detroit, 1982-83; asst. dir. neurosurgery Children's Hosp. Mich., Detroit, 1986-87, chief of neurosurgery, 1987-97; assoc. prof. neurosurgery Wayne State U., Detroit, 1988-91, vice chmn. neurosurgery, 1991—2001; prof. neurosurgery, 1997—2001. Clin. instr. neurosurgery Wayne State U. Sch. Medicine, 1985, mem. internal rev. com. dept. anatomy, 1988, chmn. search com. dept. neurosurgery, 1989, internal rev. com. dept. neurology, 1991-92, 125th anniversary celebration com., 1992, internal rev. com. dept. pediat., 1993, chmn. search com. dept. ophthalmology, 1992-93, internal rev. com. dept. neurosurgery, 1994; chmn. neurobil. devices panel, FDA; vis. prof. Med. Coll. S.C., 1990; cons. neurol. devices panel Med. Devices Adv. Com., FDA, 1994; mem. surg. com. Children's Hosp. Mich., chmn. operating room subcom. surg. com., intensive care unit com., med. record com., med. exec. com.; mem. med. staff Children's Hosp. Mich., William Beaumont Hosp, Royal Oak and Troy, Mich., Harper-Grace Hosps., Detroit, Hutzel Hosp., Detroit, Sinai Hosp., Detroit, Huron Valley Hosp., Milford, Mich., Crittenton Hosp., Rochester Hills, Mich., St. John Hosp. and Med. Ctr., Detroit; presenter various profl confs. in U.S. and internat. Contbr. chpts. to books. Mem. Mich. Head Injury Alliance, Mich. Myelodysplasia Assn.; bd. dirs. Inst. Am. Bus., 1986-88. Recipient Citation Women's Med. Assn., 1975, Candace award Nat. Coalition 100 Black Women, N.Y., 1986, Golden Heritage award, 1989, Leonard F. Sain Esteemed Alumni award U. Mich., 1990, Disting. Alumni award Everett H.S., Pres.'s award Am. Med. Women's Assn., 1993, Variety Heart award for Med., Sci. and Tech. Variety Club, 1994, Shining Star award Colgate-Palmolive Co./Starlight Found., 1994, Golden Apple award Roeper Sch., 1995, Athena award Alumni Assn. U. Mich., 1995; named Outstanding Young Woman in Am., 1977, Top 100 Bus. & Profl. Women of Am., 1985, Woman of Yr. Detroit Club Nat. Assn. Negro Bus. & Profl. Women's Club, Inc., 1986; named to Mich. Woman's Hall of Fame, 1989; grantee Am. Cancer Soc., 1979, Minn. Med. Found., 1979, Am. Cancer Soc., 1981-82, Widman Found. Early Intervention Treatment and Follow-Up of Infants with Post-hemorrhagic Hydrocephalus, 1984-85, Neuropsychol. Recovery and Family Adaptation to CHI Children's Hosp. Mich., 1987-88, Hydrocephalus Induced Endocrinopathies: Morphologic Correlates Children's Hosp. Mich., 1989, 91. Mem. AMA, ACS, Am. Assn. Neurol. Surgeons, Congress Neurol. Surgeons, Am. Soc. Pediatric Neurosurgery, Nat. Med. Assn. Detroit Med. Soc., Mich. Assn. Neurol. Surgeons (sec. 1992-93, v.p. 1994-95, pres. 1995-96), Transplantation Soc. Mich. (adv. bd. 1993-94), Mich. State Med. Soc. (child abuse and neglect divsn. 1986), Southeastern Mich. Surg. Soc. (sec. 1986-87), Soc. Crit. Care Medicine, Wayne County Med. Soc. (ethics com., pub. affairs com., law com.), U. Mich. Med. Ctr. Alumni Soc., Delta Sigma Theta. Office: 6064 Forest Green Rd Pensacola FL 32505 E-mail: alexacanady@aol.com.

CANADY, CHARLES TERRENCE, lawyer, former congressman; b. Lakeland, Fla., June 22, 1954; m. Jennifer Houghton, Oct. 1996. BA, Haverford Coll., 1976; JD, Yale U., 1979. Mem. 44th dis. Fla. Ho. of Reps., 1984-90, mem. Marketable Record Title Act Study Commn., 1985-86, majority whip, 1986-88, mem. crime prevention and law enforcement study com., 1987-88; mem. U.S. Congress from 12th Fla. dist., 1993-2001; gen. counsel Gov. Jeb Bush, Fla., 2001—. Mem. counsel Ctrl. Fla. Regional Coun., 1983-84. V.p. United Cerebral Palsy, Polk County, 1982-83; bd. dirs. Big Brothers & Big Sisters, 1984-85. Recipient Allen Morris award Fla. Ho. of Reps., 1986, Legislator of the Yr. Fla. Assn. Realtors, 1986, Spec Leadership award Save Our Home and Lands, 1986; named Most Valuable Legislator in Growth Mgmt. Fla. Regional Coun. Assn. Mem. ABA, Lakeland Bar Assn., Lakeland C. of C., Winter Haven C. of C. Republican. Presbyterian.

CANAGARAJAH, R. SUDHARSHAN, economist; b. Jaffna, Northern, Sri Lanka, Sept. 23, 1960; m. Angeline Canagarajah, May 15, 1967; 1 child, Joanna. PhD, Cambridge U., England, 1991. Sr. economist The World Bank, Wash., 1993—. Home: 4715 Brightwood Rd Olney MD 20832 Office: The World Bank 1818 H St N W Washington DC 20433 Home Fax: 202-473-8262. Personal E-mail: scanagarajah@worldbank.org.

CANALES, JAMES EARL, JR., foundation administrator; b. San Francisco, Nov. 6, 1966; s. James Earl Canales Sr. and Maritsa M. (Solorzano) Espinoza. BA, Stanford U., 1988, MA, 1989. English tchr., class dean San Francisco Univ. H.S., 1989-91, dir. admissions, 1991-93; program assoc. The James Irvine Found., San Francisco, 1993-95, program officer, spl. asst. to pres., 1995-97, chief adminstrv. officer, corp. sec., 1997-99, v.p., corp. sec., 1999—2003, pres, CEO, 2003—. Vice chair, bd. dirs. Nat. Ctr. for Nonprofit Bds., Washington; chmn. bd. dirs. KQED, Inc.; bd. regents, St. Ignatius Coll. Preparatory, 2001-03. Chair, bd. dirs. Larkin St. Youth Ctr., San Francisco, 1992-99; bd. dirs., Nat. Assn. for Cmty. Leadership, Indpls., 1994-97; trustee San Francisco Day Sch., 1996-99. Andrew W. Mellon Edn. Found. fellow, 1988-89. Mem. Stanford Alumni Assn. (bd. dirs. 1997—, vice chmn. 2001-03, chmn. 2003--). Democrat. Roman Catholic. Home: 21 Carmel St San Francisco CA 94117-4332 Office: One Market Steuart Tower St Ste 2500 San Francisco CA 94105 E-mail: jcanales@irvine.org.

CANAN, ELIZABETH LEVY, health facility administrator; b. Coffeyville, Kans., Feb. 26, 1963; d. Joe Lynn and Patsy Sue (Pote) Levy. BA in Pers. Adminstrn., U. Kans., 1985; M of Hosp. and Health Care Adminstrn., U. Minn., 1987. Adminstrv. resident Rochester (Minn.) Meth. Hosp., 1986; adminstrv. trainee Mayo Found., Rochester, 1987-90; systems analyst Mayo Clinic, 1990—93, planning analyst, 1992—98; admin. health sys. Mayo Health Sys. Adminstrn., Rochester, 1998—. Mem.: Kappa Alpha Theta Alumni. Methodist. Avocations: tennis, golf, water skiing. Home: 3117 Tremont Lane SW Rochester MN 55902 Office: Mayo Clinic 200 1st St SW Rochester MN 55905-0002

CANAN, THOMAS MICHAEL, lawyer; b. Appleton, Wis., Mar. 22, 1964; s. Michael Edward and Jean Ellen (McLaughlin) C.; m. Elizabeth Jane Levy, Aug. 5, 1989; children: Katherine, William. BA, U. Wis., Eau Claire, 1986; JD, U. Minn., 1989. Bar: Minn. 1989, U.S. Dist. Ct. Minn. 1990. M.J. Murdock fellow Washington Legal Found., 1987; student atty. Civil Practice Clinic, Mpls., 1987-88; summer assoc. Davis & Kuelthau, Milw., 1988; rsch. asst. Minn. Ho. of Rep. Rsch. Dept., Mpls., 1988-89; jud. clk. Olmsted County Dist. Ct., Rochester, Minn., 1989-90; assoc. Streater, Murphy, Gernander, Winona, Minn., 1990-91; asst. city atty. City of Rochester, Minn., 1991-99; pvt. practice Rochester, 1999—. Presenter in field. Presenter of various programs including Domestic Abuse Prosecution, Abating Gang Graffiti, Criminal Law Update. Tour guide Olmsted County Hist. Soc., Rochester, 1991-96; vol. Rochester Pk. and Recreation, 1989-93, Woodside Nursing Home, Rochester, 1993-97. Mem. Minn. State Bar Assn., Olmsted County Bar Assn. (v.p.), Kiwanis, Lions (1st v.p.). Avocations: bicycling, swimming, sea kayaking. Home: 3117 Tremont Ln SW Rochester MN 55902-6316 Office: Merchants Exchange Bldg 18 3rd St SW Ste 200 Rochester MN 55902-3022 E-mail: tomcanan@worldnet.att.net.

CANAPARY, HERBERT CARTON, insurance company executive; b. Bklyn., Dec. 1, 1932; s. Edward Paul and Alice G. (Brennan) C.; m. Mary E. Dolan, May 6, 1961; children: Patrick, Ellen, Ann, Jennifer Henriksen. BBA, Manhattan Coll., 1954; MS in Fin., Columbia U., 1957. With Manhattan Life Ins. Co., N.Y.C., 1957-80, asst. sec., 1961-70, 2d v.p., 1970-79, v.p., treas., 1974-80; v.p. investments Union Labor Life Ins. Co., Washington, 1981—, MRCo., 2000—, GBL Holdings, Inc., 2000. Roman Catholic. Home: One Goshen Ct Gaithersburg MD 20882 Office: 111 Massachusetts Ave NW Washington DC 20001-1461 also: 1300 Market St Wilmington DE 19801

CANARINA, OPAL JEAN, nurse, administrator, educator, consultant, lecturer; b. Geneva County, Ala., Mar. 21, 1936; d. O. Lee and L. Ellen (Box) Peacock; m. Miles Steven Bajcar, June 27, 1953 (div.); children: Debra Lynn-Wilson; Wayne Steven; m. Arnold R. Canarina, June 19, 1965 (dec. 1998); children: Catherine Mary, Christopher John, Charles Benjamin. B.S.N. summa cum laude, George Mason U., Fairfax, Va., 1976, M.S.N., Vanderbilt U., 1981. R.N., Va., Tenn., Ky., Okla., Utah, Miss., Fla. Staff and charge nurse Georgetown U. Hosp., Washington, 1976; charge nurse ob-gyn Vanderbilt U. Hosp., Nashville, 1976-77; charge nurse labor and delivery svc. Baptist Hosp., Nashville, 1977-80; asst. prof. dept. baccalaureate nursing Austin Peay State U., Clarksville, Tenn., 1981-83; dir. nursing svcs. Meml. Hosp., Guymon, Okla., 1983-85; dir. Women's Ctr./Maternal-Child Nursing, McKay-Dee Hosp. Ctr., Ogden, Utah, 1985-87; dir. nursing Jeff Anderson Regional Med. ctr., Meridian, Miss., 1987-89, program mgr., dir. Women's Ctr. Univ. Community Hosp., Tampa, Fla., 1990-91; adminstrv. dir. women's health svcs. Scripps Meml. Hosp., La Jolla, Calif., 1991-92; asst. adminstr., prof. Hart County Hosp., Hartwell, Ga., 1992-94; cons. to middle Tenn. and No. Utah areas health and nursing issues; cons. quality assurance Al Hada Hosp, TAIF, Saudi Arabia, 1992, assoc. adminstr. nursing, 1992-99, ret., 1999. Recipient cert. of excellence R.N.s on campus George Mason U., 1976. Mem. ANA (cert. in nursing adminstrn. 1989), NAFE, Am. Orgn. Nurse Execs., Am. Coll. Health Care Execs. (internat. assoc.), Tenn. Nurses Assn. (legis. chmn. dist. 13, 1982-83, pres. 1982), Va. Nurses Assn. (Student Nurse of Yr. award 1975), Sigma Theta Tau, Alpha Chi.

CANARY, NANCY HALLIDAY, lawyer; b. Cleve., Apr. 21, 1941; d. Robert Fraser and Nanna (Hall) Halliday; m. Sumner Canary, Dec. 1975 (dec. Jan. 1979). BA, Case Western Res. U., 1963; JD, Cleve. State U., 1968. Bar: Ohio 1968, Fla. 1972, U.S. Dist. Ct. (no. dist.) Ohio 1975, U.S. Supreme Ct. 1974, U.S. Dist. Ct. (so. dist.) Fla. 1994. Law clk. to presiding judge Ohio Ct. Appeals, Cleve., 1968—69; ptnr. McDonald, Hopkins & Hardy, Cleve., 1969—83, Thompson, Hine, LLP, Cleve., 1984—2002. Trustee Beck Ctr. for Cultural Arts, Lakewood, Ohio, 1980—90, Ohio Motorists Assn., 1989—95, Ohio Chamber Orch.; trustee, mem. devel. adv. com. Fairview Gen. Hosp., Cleve., 1980—96; chairperson Sumner Canary Lectureship com. Case Western Res. U. Law Sch.; sec. bd. govs. Churchill Ctr., Washington, 2000—02; bd. dirs. Comerica Bank & Trust Co., F.S.B., 1993—2000. Mem. Ohio State Bar Assn., Cleve. Bar Assn., Palm Beach County Bar Assn., Estate Planning Coun. Cleve., Estate Planning Coun. Palm Beach County, Gulf Stream (Fla.) Golf Club, Westwood Country Club (Cleve.). Republican. Avocations: music, horseback riding, collecting Churchill books. Home: Unit 1806 12500 Edgewater Dr Cleveland OH 44107-1677 also: 200 N Ocean Blvd Delray Beach FL 33483-7126 Office: 125 Worth Ave # 117 Palm Beach FL 33480

CANAVAN, CHRISTINE ESTELLE, state legislator; b. Dorchester, Mass., Jan. 25, 1950; m. Paul Canavan; 2 children. Grad., Massasoit C.C., 1983; BS summa cum laude, U. Mass., 1988. RN, Mass., 1988. Mem. Mass. Ho. of Reps., Boston, 1993—, mem. human svcs. and elderly affairs com., vice chair joint healthcare, mem. steering policy and scheduling com., mem. spl. legis. com. on foster care. Mem. Brockton (Mass.) Sch. Com., 1990-94, vice chmn., 1992-2000. Mem. South Shore Nurses Assn., Polish White Eagles. Democrat. Roman Catholic. Home: 29 Mystic St Brockton MA 02302-2825 Office: Mass Ho of Reps Mass State House Rm 34 Boston MA 02133

CANAVAN, FRANCIS, priest, educator; b. N.Y.C., Oct. 27, 1917; BS, Forham Univ., 1939; PhL, St. Louis Univ., 1944; MA in Polit. Sci., Fordham Univ., 1947; STL, Woodstock Coll., 1951; PhD in Polit. Sci., Duke Univ., 1957. Tchr. Regis H.S., NY, 1944—45, Canisus Coll., Buffalo, 1945—46, St. Peter's Coll., Jersey City, 1956—60; assoc. editor America, 1960—66; tchr. Fordham Univ., 1966—88, emeritus, 1988—. Author: The Political Reason of Edmund Burke, 1960, Freedom of Expression: Purpose as Limit, 1984, Edmund Burke: Prescription and Providence, 1986, The Political Economu of Edmund Burke, 1995, The Pluralist Game: Pluralism, Liberalism, and the Moral Conscience, 1995; contbr. articles to profl. jour.; editor: The Ethical Dimension of Political Life, 1983. Rockefeller Found. Fellowships in Polit. and Legal Theory, 1954—55, 1961—62, Earhart Found. rsch. Fellowships, 1979—80, 1984—85, 1992—93, Nat. Endowment for the Humanities Fellowship, 1991—92. Roman Cath. Office: Loyola-Faber Hall Fordham Univ Bronx NY 10458

CANAVAN, GREGORY H. science educator; BS in Math., USAF Acad., 1965; MA in Applied Sci., U. Calif.-Davis, 1967, PhD in Applied Sci., 1969; MBA in Energy Econs., Auburn U., 1975. Rschr.Air Force Weapons Lab., 1969—74, program mgr. for advanced laser and sensor rsch. Def. Advanced Rsch. Projects Agy., 1975—77; White House fellow Dept. Energy, 1977—78; dep. chief, staff group to the chief of staff USAF, 1978—79; dir. Office of Inertial Fusion, Dept. Energy, 1979—81; assoc. physics divsn. leader for fusion programs Los Alamos Nat. Lab., N.Mex., 1981—83, asst. physics divsn. leader, 1983—86, sr. sci. advisor, 1986—. Mem. def. policy bd. Dept. of Def., 1990—92; mem. def. tech. panel White House Sci. Coun., 1982—88; mem. Commn. on Discriminate Deterrence, 1985—87; mem. directed energy panel Strategic Def. Adv. Com., 1983—90. Chmn. bd. Hertz Found. Recipient Award for Outstanding Tech. Contbn. to Applied Sci., Hertz Found., 1977; fellow, White House fellow, 1987—88. Fellow: APS; mem.: AAAS. Office: Los Alamos Nat Lab Physics Divsn Office Los Alamos NM 87545

CANAVOR, FREDERICK CHARLES, JR., lawyer; b. N.Y.C., Mar. 29, 1944; s. Frederick Charles Sr. and Leila (Armstrong) C.; m. Allison Arthur, Nov. 23, 1987; children: Victoria, Rachel Lee, Elaine Elizabeth. BS, Syracuse U., 1965; JD, St. John's U., 1971; LLM, NYU, 1972; MBA, Golden Gate U., 1981. Bar: N.Y. 1972, Calif. 1976, D.C. 1977, Wash. 1978. With Arthur Andersen & Co., N.Y.C., 1971-72; asst. dist. atty. Kings County Dist. Atty., Bklyn., 1972-75; spl. asst. atty. Atty. Gen. State N.Y., N.Y.C., 1975-76; atty. Wettrick, Toulouse, Lirhus & Hove, Seattle, Wash., 1978-86; prosecuting atty. San Juan County, Friday Harbor, Wash., 1986-95; atty. Appel & Glueck, P.C., Seattle, 1995-99;

legal cons., 2000—. Author: Rape One, 1982. With U.S. Army, 1967-69. N.Y. War Svc. scholar N.Y. State, 1969, Regents scholar, 1961. Avocations: travel, writing. Office: PO Box 2231 Vashon WA 98070-2231 E-mail: fare@wolfenet.com.

CANBY, WILLIAM CAMERON, JR., judge; b. St. Paul, May 22, 1931; s. William Cameron and Margaret Leah (Lewis) Canby; m. Jane Adams, June 18, 1954; children: William Nathan, John Adams, Margaret Lewis. AB, Yale U., 1953; LLB, U. Minn., 1956. Bar: Minn. 1956, Ariz. 1972. Law clk. U.S. Supreme Ct. Justice Charles E. Whittaker, 1958—59; asso. firm Oppenheimer, Hodgson, Brown, Baer & Wolff, St. Paul, 1959—62; asso., then dep. dir. Peace Corps, Ethiopia, 1962—64, dir., 1964—66; asst. to U.S. Senator Walter Mondale, 1966; asst. to pres. SUNY, 1967; prof. law Ariz. State U., 1967—80; judge U.S. Ct. Appeals (9th cir.), Phoenix, 1980—96, sr. judge, 1996—; chief justice High Ct. of the Trust Ter. of the Pacific Islands, 1993—94. Bd. dirs. Ariz. Ctr. Law in Pub. Interest, 1974—80, Maricopa County Legal Aid Soc., 1972—78, D.N.A.-People's Legal Svcs., 1978—80; Fulbright prof. Makerere U. Faculty Law, Kampala, Uganda, 1970—71. Author: American Indian Law, 1998; note editor: Minn. Law Rev., 1955—56; contbr. articles to profl. jours. Precinct and state committeeman Dem. Party Ariz., 1972—80; bd. dirs. Ctrl. Ariz. Coalition for Right to Choose, 1976—80. With USAF, 1956—58. Mem.: Maricopa County Bar Assn., State Bar Ariz., Order of Coif, Phi Beta Kappa. Office: Sandra Day O'Connor US Courthouse 401 W Washington St SPC 55 Phoenix AZ 85003-2156

CANCE, WILLIAM GEORGE, surgery educator; b. Waterbury, Conn., June 14, 1957; MD, Duke U., 1982. Diplomate Am. Bd. Surgeons. Intern Barnes Hosp., Washington U., St. Louis, 1982-83, resident in gen. surgery, 1983-84, 86-88; fellow in surg. oncology Meml. Sloan Kettering Cancer Ctr., 1988-90; asst. prof. surgery U. N.C., Chapel Hill, 1990-95, chief sect. surg. oncology, 1993—, assoc. prof. surgery, 1995-99, prof. surgery, 1999—, James F. Newsome M.D. Endowed term prof. in surg. oncology, 1998—2002, Hector MacLean disting. prof. cancer rsch., 2002. Mem. staff U. N.C. Hosps., 1990—. Fellow ACS (George H.A. Clowes Jr. Meml. Rsch. Career Devel. award 1994); mem. Assn. Acad. Surgery, Soc. Surg. Oncology, Soc. Univ. Surgeons, Am. Surg. Assn., Soc. Clin. Surgery. Office: Univ of Fla Dept of Surgery PO Box 100286 1600 SW Archer Rd Rm 6172 Gainesville FL 32610-3001 E-mail: cance@surgery.ufl.edu.

CANCIAMILLA, JOSEPH, state legislator; b. Pittsburg, Calif., Apr. 19, 1955; m. Laura Canciamilla. BA, St. Mary's Coll., 1978; JD, John F. Kennedy Sch. Law, 1986. Mem. sch. bd. Pittsburg Sch. Dist., 1973—87; lawyer, 1986—; mayor, councilman City of Pittsburg, 1987—96; county supr. Contra Costa County, 1996—2000; mem., dist. 11 Calif. State Assembly, 2000—. Co-owner Pittsburg Funeral Chapel, 1992—; chair Water, Parks and Wildlife Com.; mem. Arts, Entertainment, Sports, Tourism, and Internet Media Com., Budget Com., Govtl. Orgn. Com. Mem.: State Bar Calif., NAACP (life), Young Mens Inst., Italian Am. Club. Democrat. Mailing: PO Box 942849 Rm 2141 Sacramento CA 94249-0011 Office: 815 Estudillo St Martinez CA 94553*

CANCRO, ROBERT, psychiatrist, educator; b. NYC, Feb. 23, 1932; s. Joseph and Marie E. (Cicchetti) C.; m. Gloria Costanzo, Dec. 8, 1956; children: Robert, Carol. Student, Fordham U., 1948-51; MD, SUNY, 1955. Intern Kings County Hosp., Bklyn., 1955-56, resident in psychiatry, 1956-59; attending staff Gracie Sq. Hosp., N.Y.C., 1959-66; clin. instr. SUNY Downstate Med. Ctr., Bklyn., 1959-66; staff psychiatrist Menninger Found., Topeka, Kans., 1966-69; cons. Topeka State and VA Hosps., 1967-69; prof. dept. psychiatry U. Conn. Health Ctr., Farmington, 1970-76; prof., chmn. dept. psychiatry NYU Med. Ctr., 1976—; dir. N.S. Kline Inst. Psychiat. Research, 1982—. Cons. psychiat. edn. br. NIMH; biol. scis. sect. NIMH. Editor 10 books; Contbr. articles on schizophrenia to profl. jours. Recipient Freida Fromm-Reichmann award, 1975, Strecker award, 1978, Dean award, 1981, Lehmann award, 1992. Fellow A.C.P., Am. Coll. Psychiatrists, Am. Psychiat. Assn.; mem. Am. Psychol. Assn., Assn. Am. Med. Colls., Am. Assn. Social Psychiatry (pres. 1984-86), N.Y. Acad. Scis., AAAS, AMA. Home: 118 Mclain Rd Mount Kisco NY 10549-4932 Office: NYU Med Ctr 550 1st Ave New York NY 10016-6402 E-mail: robert.cancro@med.nyu.edu.

CANDA, EDWARD R. social work educator; b. Dec. 8, 1954; s. Frank W. and Anne R. C.; m. Hwi-Ja Canda, Aug. 5, 1977. BA in Anthropology summa cum laude, Kent State U., 1976; MA in Religious Studies, U. Denver, 1979; PhD in Social Welfare, Ohio State U., 1986. Edn. coord. and counselor unaccompanied minor refugee pgm. Luth. Social Svcs. of Cen. Ohio, Columbus, 1982-83, supr. unaccompanied minor refugee program, 1983; cons. Transcultural Family Inst., Columbus, 1982-86; grad. tchg. fellow Sung Kyun Kwan U., Seoul, 1976-77; asst. prof. social welfare U. Iowa, Iowa City, 1986-89, U. Kans., Lawrence, 1989-92, assoc. prof. social welfare, 1992-99, prof. social welfare, 1999—, chair PhD program in social welfare, 2000—. Cons. editor Jour. Social Work Edn., 2001—02. Author: Contemporary Human Behavior Theory: A Critical Perspective for Social Work, 1998, Spiritual Diversity in Social Work Practice, 1999; editor: Spirituality in Social Work: New Directions, 1998, Transpersonal Perspectives on Spirituality in Social Work, 2001; editor spl. issue Reflections: Narratives of Profl. Helping, 1995. Bd. dirs. Kans. Friends of Religious Studies, Lawrence, 1998—, exec. bd. 1999—; dir. for Internat. Course on Spirituality and Social Work, Inter-Univ. Ctr., Dubrovnik, Croatia, 1998—. Mem. Soc. for Spirituality and Social Work (founder, bd. dirs. 1990—), NASW, Coun. on Social Work Edn. Avocation: world percussion. Office: Univ Kans Sch Social Welfar Twente Hall Lawrence KS 66045-7587 E-mail: edc@ku.edu.

CANDAGE, HOWARD EVERETT, insurance management consultant, agent, broker; b. Blue Hill, Maine, Sept. 23, 1952; s. Aubrey Llewellyn and Evelyn Edsley (Carter) C.; m. Jeri-Lynn Moore, Nov. 3, 1979; children, Chelsea Alyssa, Curran Aubrey. CPCU, cert. assoc. in marine ins. mgmt., cert. ethics trainer, Inst. for Global Ethics. Ind. comml. fisherman, Blue Hill, Maine, 1970-79; ins. agt. J.T. Rosborough, Inc., Ellsworth, Maine, 1979-80, W.C. Ladd & Sons, Inc., Rockland, Maine, 1980-86, br. mgr. Damariscotta, Maine, 1986-89, resident v.p., 1988-90; ptnr. Cole-Harrison Agy. of Maine, Inc./Atlantic Yacht Insurers, Ltd., Kennebunk, 1990-93; mktg. mgr. Hanover Ins. Co. Maine, Scarborough, 1993-96; owner Ins. Resources, Gorham, Maine, 1996-98; pres. H.E. Candage, Inc., Portland, Maine, 1998—. Pres., Maine Marine Industry Assocs., Freeport, 1982-83; appointed adj. faculty Ctrl. Maine Tech. Coll., 1998—; dean sch. bus. Ind. Ins. Agts. Am. Virtual U.; underwriting mem. comml. fishing vessel safety adv. coun. USCG, 2003—. Recipient Chmn's. award Am. Assn. Mng. Gen. Agts., 1992. Mem. Am. Soc. Appraisers, Am. Mgmt. Assn. (cert.), Soc. Chartered Property and Casualty Underwriters (treas. Maine chpt. 1990-92, v.p. 1992-93, pres.-elect 1993-94, pres. 1994-95), Nat. Soc. of Chartered Property and Casualty Underwriters (nat. chpt. affairs com.), Ind. Ins. Agts. Assn. Maine (chmn. com. 1983-84, 91-92, bd. dirs. 1990-93, Young Agt. of Yr. 1987), Soc. Ins. Rsch., Soc. Ins. Counselors (cert.), Am. Soc. Appraisers. Avocations: woodworking, travel, photography. Home: 6 Meadow Crossing Dr Gorham ME 04038-2058 Office: Marine Trade Ctr 2 Portland Fish Pier Ste 214 Portland ME 04101-4698 E-mail: howard@candage.com., hcandage@insurancemergers.com.

CANDELARIA, NASH, writer; b. L.A., May 7, 1928; s. Ignacio Nuanez and Flora Rivera Candelaria; m. Doranne Godwin, Nov. 27, 1955; children: David, Alex. BS, UCLA, 1948. Rsch. chemist Don Baxter, Inc., Glendale, Calif., 1948-52; tech. editor N.Am. Aviation, Inc., Downey, Calif., 1953-54; promotion supr. Beckman Instruments, Inc., Fullerton, Calif., 1954-59; promotion specialist Northrop Nortronics, Anaheim, Calif., 1959-65; account exec. Hixon Jorgensen Advt. Agy., L.A., 1965-67; advt. and sales promotion mgr. Varian Assocs., Palo Alto, Calif., 1967-82; pvt. practice fiction writer Palo Alto, 1982-85; mktg. writer Daisy Sys., Mountain View, Calif., 1985-87; mktg. comm. mgr. Hewlett-Packard Co., Palo Alto, 1987-92; ret., 1992; pvt. practice fiction writer, 1992—. Lectr. Rutgers U., Newark, 1987. Author: Memories of the Alhambra, 1977, Not by the Sword, 1982 (Am. Book award 1983), Inheritance of Strangers, 1985, The Day the Cisco Kid Shot John Wayne, 1988, Leonor Park, 1991, Uncivil Rights and Other Stories, 1998; author of short stories, novels and articles. 1st lt. USAF, 1952-53. Mem. Nat. Assn. for Chicana and Chicano Studies (Cert. of award 1983), Western Writers Am., PEN Internat. Writers Assn., Sin Fronteras/Writers Without Borders. Avocations: writing, reading, investments. Home: 206 Spruce St Santa Fe NM 87501 E-mail: nashcan@aol.com.

CANDELAS, GRACIELA C. biologist, educator; b. Mayaguez, P.R., Oct. 3, 1922; d. Teobaldo Casanova and Carmen Vivó; children: Gustavo, Carmen, Teresa. BS, U. P.R., Rio Piedras, 1944; MA, Duke U., 1959; PhD, U. Miami, 1966. Instr. biol. scis. and gen. studies U. P.R., Rio Piedras, 1951—57, instr. biology dept. biology, 1959—61, asst. prof. dept. biology, 1961—65, assoc. prof. dept. biology, 1966—71, prof. biology, 1971—, radiation security officer, 1966—92. Rsch. asst. Duke Marine Lab., Beaufort, NC, 1957; instr. isotopic techniques P.R. Nuc. Ctr., Rio Piedras, 1959—61, dir. Radiology Summer Inst., 1962, assoc. scientist I radioisotope divsn., 1966—71; lectr. NSF Traveling Lectr. Program, 1961—63; rsch. assoc. marine biology program U. P.R., Mayaguez, 1962—65; vis. prof. devel. biology Syracuse (N.Y.) U., 1969—70; prof. cell and molecular biology Med. Coll. Ga., Augusta, 1971—74; vis. prof. cell and molecular biology CCNY, N.Y.C., 1974—75; guest investigator cell biology Rockefeller U., N.Y.C., 1976—78, vis. prof. cell biology, 1979—80; mem. policy adv. com. Nat. Inst. Dental Rsch., NIH, 1985—88; reviewer competitive proposals NSF and Office Naval Rsch., 1986—; cons. in field; reviewer various jours. Contbr. chapters to books, articles to profl. jours. Mem. steering com. Arts Mgmt. Initiative, 1987—89; bd. dirs. San Juan Art Students League, 1980—86, 1987—92; pres. bd. dirs. Art Students League, 1984—86, 1988—90; bd. dirs. Centro Documentacion Arte Latinoamericano, 1985—86, Museo de Arte Contemporaneo, 1987—89; devel. dir. San Juan Art Students League, 1986—92; bd. mem. Voluntarios por las Artes, 1989—; dir. Nat. Endowment for the Arts Advancement Program San Juan Students League, 1989—92. Recipient Spl. Sci. award, Inst. P.R., 1985; grantee in field; faculty fellow, NSF, 1964—66. Mem.: AAAS, Assn. Biomolecular Resources, Caribbean Biotechnology Soc., Whitman Soc., Royal Entomol. Soc. London, N.Y. Acad. Scis., Soc. Iberoamericana de Biologia Celular (del.), Internat. Soc. Devel. Biology, Fedn. Am. Socs. for Exptl. Biology, Internat. Fedn. Cell Biologists, Am. Soc. for Cell Biology, Internat. Cell Rsch. Orgn., Sigma Xi. Avocations: music, art collecting. Office: Univ PR PO Box 23360 San Juan PR 00931-3360

CANDER, LEON, retired physician; b. Phila., Oct. 7, 1926; s. Joseph Harry and Anna (Glick) C.; m. Geraldine Piontkowski, Dec. 11, 1954; children, Alan Drew, Harris Scott. MD, Temple U., 1951. Rsch. fellow in physiology Grad. Sch. Medicine, U. Pa., 1952-56; resident in medicine Beth Israel Hosp., Boston, 1956-58; asst. in medicine Harvard U. Med. Sch., Boston, 1957-58, sr. instr. medicine Tufts U. Med. Sch., Boston, 1958-60; asst. prof. medicine Hahnemann Med. Coll., Phila., 1960-63, assoc. prof., 1963-66; prof., chmn. dept. physiology and medicine U. Tex. Med. Sch., San Antonio, 1966-72; chmn. dept. medicine, dir. med. edn. Daroff div. Albert Einstein Med. Ctr., Phila., 1972-80; prof. medicine Jefferson Med. Coll., Phila., 1972-89; head sect. of chest diseases, dir. med. edn. Daroff div. Albert Einstein Med. Ctr., Phila., 1980-88; clin. prof. medicine Hahnemann Med. Coll., Phila., 1985—2002; head sect. of chest diseases Mt. Sinai Hosp., Phila., 1988-96, ret., 2002. Mem. Nat. Adv. Coun. on Black Lung; nat. cons. U.S. Dept. Labor Black Lung Program, 1978—. Soc. Editor: (with J. H. Moyer) Aging of the Lung, 1963. Research fellow Nat. Acad. Scis., 1954-55 Fellow ACP; mem. Am. Thoracic Soc., Am. Physiol. Soc. Home: 317 Cherry Ln Wynnewood PA 19096-1710

CANDIB, MURRAY A. business executive, retail management consultant; b. Chelsea, Mass., Sept. 16, 1915; s. Jacob and Fannie (Einbinder) C.; m. Claudette Aggie, Oct. 8, 1972 (dec. Dec. 1991); children: Nancy, Rachel, David, Caroline; m. Maureen Davis, July 30, 1995. BA, Boston U., 1950. Founder King's Dept. Store Inc., 1949; Pres. Canco Enterprises, Worcester, Mass. Credited with being the pioneer of self-service dept. stores; subject of articles in Fortune Mag., Harvard Bus. Rev. and profl. jours. Founder, life trustee, soc. mem. Mt. Sinai Hosp., Miami Beach, Fla.; benefactor Miami Heart Inst.; bd. dirs. Temple Emanu-El, Miami Beach; charter mem. Rep. Presdl. Task Force, 1981—, U.S. Senatorial Club, 1981—, Nat. Rep. Senatorial Com.; mem. Fla. Victory Com. Brandeis U. fellow, 1966; recipient Human Relations award Am. Jewish Com., Nat. Community Service award Jewish Theol. Sem. of Am., 1965, Man of Yr. award Mental Health Clinic, Mt. Sinai Hosp., N.Y.C., Man of Yr. award Boys Wear Industry of N.Y., Hall of Fame award U. Mass. Mem. Am. Heart Assn., Shriners, Masons, Westview Country Club Miami. Avocations: tennis, golf, painting, boating. Office: 306 Main St Worcester MA 01608-1550

CANDIDO, A. MICHAEL, contracting company executive, real estate manager; b. Falls Church, Va., June 23, 1953; s. Albert Babbitts and Rose Marie (Naturale) C.; m. Joyce Mary Baratta, Sept. 27, 1975; children: Rosalie, Elizabeth, Jacqueline, Allison. BA in Acctg., William Paterson U., 1975. Office mgr. J. Moore & Co., Livingston, N.J., 1973-79, v.p., 1979-95, pres., 1995—, Essex Realty Co., Cedar Grove, N.J., 1991—. Adj. prof. Kean U. N.J., Union, 1988-93. Mem. Essex Fells (N.J.) Zoning Bd., 1995—, vice-chmn., 2001—; trustee Steamfitters Local 475, Warren, N.J., 1995—; chmn. bldg. and grounds com. Notre Dame Ch., No. Caldwell, N.J., 1997—; active MCAA Industry Fund, Washington, 1999—; mem. MCA Legis. Com., 2000—. Mem.: ASHRAE, Mech. Contractors Assn. NJ (treas. 1998—2000, v.p. 2000—02, pres. 2002—), Mech. Contractors Assn. (treas. polit. action com. 1998, mem. legis. com. 2000—, Mentoring Program Man of Yr. award 2003), Internat. Soc. Pharm. Engrs., Bay Head Hist. Soc., Essex Fells Country Club. Roman Catholic. Avocations: golf, photography, books, music, fishing. Office: J Moore & Co 118 Naylon Ave Livingston NJ 07039-1006 E-mail: mikecandido@jmoore.com.

CANDIDO, ARTHUR ALDO, publishing and distribution company executive; b. Corona, Queens, N.Y., June 6, 1960; BA, CUNY, 1982. Ops. mgr. Scholium Internat. Inc., Port Washington, N.Y., 1982-91, pres., 1991—. Mem. Spl. Librs. Assn., Am. Booksellers Assn. Office: Scholium Internat Inc PO Box 1519 Port Washington NY 11050-7519

CANDLAND, D. STUART, lawyer; b. Madison, Wis., Sept. 6, 1942; s. Don Charles and Dorothy Jane (Nelson) C.; m. Evelyn McComber, Dec. 3, 1982; children: Ashley, Tara Lynn, Brett. BA with honors, Brigham Young U., 1967; JD, U. Calif., Berkeley, 1970. Bar: Calif. 1971, U.S. Dist. Ct. (no. dist.) Calif. 1971, U.S. Ct. Appeals (9th cir.) 1971. Dep. atty. gen. State of Calif., San Francisco, 1970-73; dep. dist. atty. Solano County Dist. Atty.'s Office, Fairfield, Calif., 1973-75; assoc. Law Offices of M. Craddick, Walnut Creek, Calif., 1976-78; ptnr. Craddick, Candland & Conti, Danville, Calif., 1979—. Asst. prof. law Armstrong Sch. Law, Berkeley, 1971-77. Mem. ABA, Assn. Def. Counsel, Contra Costa County Bar Assn. Office: Craddick Candland & Conti Ste 260 915 San Ramon Valley Blvd Danville CA 94526-4021

CANDLAND, DOUGLAS KEITH, educator; b. Long Beach, Calif., July 9, 1934; s. Horace George and Erma Louise (Downing) C.; m. Mary Homrighausen, June 18, 1959; children: Kevin, Christopher, Ian. AB, Pomona Coll., 1956; PhD, Princeton U., 1959. Rsch. fellow U. Va., 1959-60, Delta Primate Ctr., 1967-68, Pa. State U., 1968-69, U. Stirling, Scotland, 1972-73, Cambridge (Eng.) U., 1977-78: Fulbright fellow U. Mysore (India), 1983; asst. prof. psychology Bucknell U., 1960-64, assoc. prof., 1964-67, prof., 1967—85, prof. animal behavior, 1985—2002, prof. emeritus, 2002—. Presdl. prof., 1973-80, head program in animal behavior, 1968—2002, pres. div. teaching of psychology, 1976-77, head dept. psychology, 1970-75, Class of 1956 lectr., 1971. Vis. scholar U. Calif., Berkeley, 1996-97. Author: Exploring Behavior, 1961, Psychology: The Experimental Approach, 1968, 2d edit., 1978, Emotion, Bodily Change, 1961, Emotion, 1979, Feral Children and Clever Animals, Reflections on Human Nature, 1993, Fossils of the Mind, 2000, Handbook of Comparative Psychology, 1998; editor: Rev. Gen. Psychology, 2002—; contbr. chpts. to profl. books; editor The Primates, 1968-78, Animal Behavior, 1979-89; assoc. editor Animal Learning and Behavior, 1976-84, Teaching of Psychology, 1976-84, Am. Jour. Primatology, 1980-84; cons. editor Jour. Comparative Psychology, 1988-94; documentary film featured scientist: The Boy Who Was Raised With Monkeys, 1999, The Rise of Animal Rights, 2001. Bd. dirs. Wildlife Preservation Trust Internat. (chmn. conservation 1989-94), Pa. Cinema Register, 1976-79, 86-89. Recipient award Lindback Found., 1971; Harriman award Bucknell U., 1979 Fellow Am. Psychol. Assn. (award for disting. contbn. to edn. 1978); mem. Brit. Psychol. Assn., Psychonomic Soc., Internat. Soc. Primatologists, Animal Behavior Soc. (chmn. policy and planning, Disting. Contbn. to Edn. award 1999). Home: 125 Stein Ln Lewisburg PA 17837-1742 Office: Bucknell U Lewisburg PA 17837 E-mail: dcandlan@bucknell.edu.

CANDLER, JAMES NALL, JR., lawyer; b. Detroit, Jan. 25, 1943; s. James Nall and Lorna Augusta (Blood) C.; m. Jean Ward McKinnon, Mar. 8, 1974; children: Christine, Elizabeth, Anne. AB, Princeton U., 1965; JD, U. Mich., 1970. Bar: Mich. 1970. Assoc. Dickinson Wright PLLC, Detroit, 1970-77, ptnr., 1977—. Adj. prof. real estate planning U. Detroit Sch. of Law, 1975-80. Bd. dirs. Detroit Inst. Ophthalmology Grosse Pointe Park, Mich., 1983—, chmn., 1994—. Lt. USNR, 1965-67. Mem. Internat. Assn. Attys. and Execs. in Corp. Real Estate, State Bar Mich. (chmn. real property law sect. 1998-99), Am. Coll. of Real Estate Lawyers, Grosse Pointe Club (chmn. 1987-89), Country Club of Detroit. Republican. Avocations: sailing, golf, platform tennis. Home: 211 Country Club Dr Grosse Pointe Farms MI 48236-2901 Office: 500 Woodward Ave Ste 4000 Detroit MI 48226-3416 E-mail: jcandler@dickinson-wright.com.

CANDLISH, MALCOLM, manufacturing company executive; b. Liverpool, Eng., Aug. 23, 1935; came to U.S., 1963; s. Norman Dennis and Jane Jefferson (Grieves) C.; m. Jasmine Rosemary Cresswell, Apr. 15, 1963; children: Fiona, Vanessa, Sarah, John. BSc, London Sch. Econs., 1956. Mgr. mktg., asst. mgr. prodn. Beecham Products, Brazil, Eng., 1958-63; product mgr. Colgate Palmolive, N.Y.C., 1963-65; prin. McKinsey and Co., N.Y.C., Cleve., Toronto, Melbourne and Sydney, Australia, 1965-77; pres., sr. v.p. mktg. Wilson Sporting Goods, Chgo., 1977-83; pres. Samsonite Corp., Denver, 1983-89; chmn., CEO Sealy, Inc. (formerly Ohio Mattress Co.), Cleve., 1989-92, First Alert, Inc., Aurora, IL, 1992-98. Bd. dirs. Mile High United Way, Denver, 1985-89. Lt. British Army, 1956-58. Mem. Luggage and Leather Goods Mfrs. Am. (bd. dirs. 1984-89), Econ. Club (founding mem.). Avocations: lit., philosophy, sports.

CANDOTTI, FABIO, geneticist; MD summa cum laude, U. Brescia, Italy, 1987. Diplomate in pediats. and pediat. allergy and immunology Am. Bd. Pediats.; lic. physician, Italy. Med. staff fellow dept. pediatrics U. Brescia, Italy, 1988-89; enlisted Italian Army Sch. of Medicine, Florence, 1989; resident in pediatrics U. Brescia, 1989-92, staff mem. Bone Marrow Transplantation Unit, 1990-91, postdoctoral fellow Lab. of Biotechnology, 1991-92; postdoctoral fellow Metabolism Br. NCI, NIH, Bethesda, Md., 1992-94; postdoctoral fellow Clin. Gene Therapy Br. NHGRI/NIH, Bethesda, 1994-96. Lectr. Italian Nat. Health Svc. Nursing Sch., Brescia, 1991-92; asst. prof. dept. pediatrics U. Brescia, 1996-97; tenure-track investigator NHGRI/NIH, Bethesda, 1998—; mem. animal care and use com. NHGRI, 1998-2002, vice chair animal care and use com., 2003-, NIH gene therapy interest group steering com., 1998—, NHGRI liaison to NIH Office of Biotechnology Activities, 1999—; attending physician dept. pediatrics, Brescia City Hosp., Italy, 1996-97, Clin. Ctr., NIH, Bethesda, 1998—; investigator in field. Co-author: (book) The Child: Health and Disease, 1993; mem. editl. bd. Exptl. Hematology; contbr. articles to profl. jours., books, and publs. Physician, lt. Italian Army, 1988—. Recipient fellowship Italian Nat. Health Svc., 1988, Assn. for Child with Cancer, Brescia, 1990-91, Fondazione Golgi, Brescia, 1992-94; recipient awards nat. Ctr. for Human Genome Rsch. Scientific Retreat, Airlie, Va., 1995, 96, NIH Merit award, 1999, others; grantee in field. Mem. Internat. Soc. for Exptl. Hematology, Italian Soc. Pediatrics, Working Group on Human Genetics, Italian Soc. Pediatric Immunology and Allergy, European Soc. Gene Therapy, Am. Assn. Immunologists, Am. Soc. Gene Therapy, European Soc. Immunodeficiencies, Pan Am. Group for Immunodeficiency, Clin. Immunology Soc. Office: 49 Convent Dr 49/3A20 Bethesda MD 20892 E-mail: fabio@nhgri.nih.gov.

CANDREIA, PEGGY JO, financial analyst; b. Pawhuska, Okla., Aug. 23, 1944; d. Joseph Leonard and Wilma Jane (Brook) C. Student, U. Ozarks, 1965. Supr. credit and collections Credit Bur. Bartlesville, Okla., 1965-69; credit rep. Shell Oil Co., Tulsa, 1969-88; owner, mgr. Gorgeous Car Care, Tulsa, 1988-90; date coord. H.A. Chapman Children's Ctr., Tulsa, 1990—; fin. analyst H.A. Chapman Inst., Children's Med. Ctr., Tulsa, 1990—, fin. coord. Children's Med. Network Telethon, 1994—2002; data coord. Hillcrest Healthcare System, 2002—. Founder local chpt. Parents and Friends of Lesbians and Gays, Tulsa, 1988-90; v.p. Tulsa Oklahomans for Human Rights, 1988-89; bd. dirs. Follies Rev., Tulsa, 1993-97, Broken Arrow Cmty. Playhouse, 1998-99; mem. steering com., sec., treas., Names Project, Tulsa, 1990—, co-chmn. ctrl. region logistics, Washington, 1996. Republican. Roman Catholic. Avocations: designing homes, travel, skiing, fundraising, drawing. Home: 1525 N College Ave Tulsa OK 74110-2719

CANDRIS, LAURA A. lawyer; b. Frankfort, Ky., Apr. 5, 1955; d. Charles M. and Dorothy (King) Sutton; m. Aris S. Candris, Dec. 22, 1974. AB with distinction in polit. sci., Transylvania Coll., 1975; postgrad., U. Pitts., 1975-77, U. Fla., 1977-78; JD, U. Pitts., 1978. Bar: Fla. 1978, U.S. Dist. Ct. (mid. dist.) Fla. 1978, U.S. Ct. Appeals (4th cir.) 1980, Pa. 1981, U.S. Dist. Ct. (we. dist.) Pa. 1982, U.S. Ct. Appeals (3d cir.) 1983. Assoc. Coffman, Coleman, Andrews & Grogan, Jacksonville, Fla., 1978-80, Manion, Alder & Cohen, Pitts., 1981-85, Eckert, Seamans, Cherin & Mellott, Pitts., 1985-86, ptnr., 1987-96, vice chmn. labor and employment law dept, mem. practice mgmt. com., mem. strategic planning com.; ptnr. Meyer Unkovic & Scott, LLP, Pitts., 1996—, chair labor, employment law and employee benefits sect., mem. litigation and transactions depts. Contbr. over 30 articles to profl. jours. including Compensation and Benefits Rev., Forum Reporter, Employment Law Inst. manuals, Ref. Manual for the 34th Ann. Mid-West Labor Law Conf. Dynamic Bus. Mem. O'Hara Twp., 1986—90, O'Hara Twp. Planning Commn., 1990; bd. dirs. Tri-State Employers Assn., 1991—93, Parent and Child Guidance Ctr., 1991—2001, v.p., 1998—99, mem. exec. com., 1998—2001, pres., 1999—2000, sec., 2000—01; treas., mem. exec. com. SMC Bus. Couns., 1993—94, bd. dirs., 1993—96, Big Bros. & Big Sisters Greater Pitts., 1998—, v.p. planning, 2001—02, mem. exec. com., 2001—, v.p. adminstrn., 2003—; bd. dirs. The Whale's Tale, 2000—01; bd. dirs., mem. exec. com. The FamilyLinks, 2000—01. Nat. Merit Found. scholar 1972-75; named Ky. Col., 1974. Mem.: ABA (EEO com. labor sect., labor and employment law com. litigation sect.), Pitts. Human Resources Assn., Allegheny County Bar Assn. (coun. on professionalism 1990—2000, employment and fed. cts. sect., women in the law div., hqrs. com. and pers. subcom.), Pa. Bar Assn. (elected mem. employment sect.), Fla. Bar Assn. Republican. Avocations: skiing, traveling, bicycling, reading. Office: Meyer Unkovic & Scott LLP 1300 Oliver Bldg Pittsburgh PA 15222 E-mail: lac@muslaw.com.

CANE, BARBARA HAAK, lawyer; b. Mineola, N.Y., Mar. 5, 1945; d. Robert A. and Julia C. Haak; m. Mark A. Cane; children: Laura J., Jacob H.D. AB magna cum laude, Harvard U., 1966; MA, Columbia U., 1969; JD cum laude, Suffolk U., Boston, 1980. Bar: N.Y. 1985, Mass. 1980, U.S. Ct. Appeals (1st cir.), U. S. Dist. Ct. Mass. 1981, U.S. Supreme Ct. 1986. Law clk. Mass. Appeals Ct., 1980-81; assoc. Brown, Rudnick, Freed & Gesmer, Boston, 1981-84; corp. counsel Grand Met, USA, Montvale, N.J., 1984-86; v.p. legal and environ. affairs Polychrome Corp., Yonkers, N.Y., 1986-90; pvt. practice Nyack, N.Y., 1991—. Lectr. Coll. City N.Y.; pro-bono lectr. WNET-13, Leave a Legacy Rockland. Hospice, others. Writer monthly column The Rockland Jewish Reporter, 1994-99. Treas., bd. dirs. RSVP Internat., 1998-2000; trustee Harvard Hillle; co-chair N.Y. Friends of Harvard-Radcliffe Hillel; past chair endowment com. UJA-Fedn. Rockland County; profl. adv. com. WNET 13. Mem. N.Y. State Bar Assn., Rockland County Bar Assn., Women's Bar Assn., N.Y.C. Bar Assn., Rockland County Women's Network, Planned Giving Group Greater N.Y., Nat. Coun. Planned Giving. Office: 8 Hart Pl Nyack NY 10960-2010 E-mail: bhcane@aol.com.

CANE, DAVID E. chemistry educator; b. N.Y.C., Sept. 22, 1944; BA, Harvard U., 1966, AM, 1967, PhD, 1971. NIH Postdoctoral fellow Eidgenossische Technische Hochschule NIH, Zurich, Switzerland, 1971-73; asst. prof. Brown U., Providence, 1973-78, assoc. prof., 1978-80, prof., 1980—, chmn. dept. chemistry, 1983-89, Vernon K. Krieble prof. chemistry, 1992—. Vis. prof. U. Chgo., 1980, Technion, Haifa, Israel, 1994-95, U. Calif. San Francisco, 1998-99, U. Louis Pasteur, Strasbourg, France, 1999; cons. Smith Kline and French Labs., Phila., 1984-85, Lederle Labs., Pearl River, N.Y., 1986-88; sci. adv. bd. KOSAN Biosci., San Francisco, 1996—; chmn. Gordon Conf. Natural Products, New Hampton, N.H., 1982; co-chmn. Gordon Conf. Enzymes, Coenzymes & Metabolic Pathways, Meriden, N.H., 1996. Mem. editl. bd. Bioorganic Chemistry, 1983—, Jour. Antibiotics, 1983—, Chem. Revs., 1987-89, Topics in Sterochemistry; assoc. editor Jour. Organic Chemistry, 1995—; contbr. articles to profl. jours. Recipient Rsch. Career Devel. award NIH, 1978-83, Prelog medal ETH, Zurich, 2002; fellow Japan Soc. Promotion Sci., 1983, Alfred P. Sloan Found., 1978, Prelog medal of Eidgenossische Technische Hochschule, Zürich, 2002; NIH Fogarty Sr. Internat. fellow, 1989, 99; John Simon Guggenheim Meml. Found. fellow, 1990; Disting. Vis. fellow Christ's

Coll., U. Cambridge, 1989-90; recipient Fulbright Grant-in-Aid, 1990. Mem. Am. Chem. Soc. (Ernest Guenther award 1985, Arthur C. Cope Scholar Award, 2000), Royal Soc. Chemistry (Simonsen lectr. 1990-91), Kitasato Inst. (Microbial Chemistry medal, 1995).

CANE, MARILYN BLUMBERG, lawyer, educator; b. Rockville Center, N.Y., Feb. 26, 1949; d. Howard Godfrey and Lilly Ruth (Goldberg); m. Edward M. Cane, Dec. 24, 1970 (div.); children: Daniel Eric, Jonathan Marc Howard; life ptnr. Karen E. Michaels, June 18, 2001. BA magna cum laude, Cornell U., 1971; JD cum laude, Boston Coll., 1974. Bar: N.Y. 1975, U.S. Dist. Ct. (so. dist.) N.Y. 1975, U.S. Ct. Appeals (2d cir.) 1976, Conn. 1977, Fla. 1981. With Reavis & McGrath, N.Y.C., 1974-76, Badger, Fisher & Assocs., Greenwich, Conn., 1977-80; counsel Corp Components divsn. GE, Fairfield, Conn., 1980-81; with Gunster, Yoakley & Assocs., Palm Beach, Fla., 1981-83; asst. prof. law Nova Southeastern U., Fort Lauderdale, Fla., 1983-85, assoc. prof. law, 1985-88, prof. law, 1988—. Author: Securities Arbitration: Law and Procedure, 1991; contbr. articles to profl. jours. Dir. Jewish Cmty. Day Sch. Palm Beach County, West Palm Beach, Fla., 1983-88; mem. adv. com. Conn. Banking Commn., Hartford, 1979-81; trustee Temple Beth Torah, Wellington, Fla., 1985-87, 92-98, Sta. WXEL, 1992—. Fellow Am. Bar Found.; mem. ABA (bus. law sect., bank holding cos. subcom.), Fla. Bar Assn., (advisor exec. coun. bus. law sect. 1988—, chair corp./securities com. bus. law sect. 1992-93, vice chair 1999-2000), Am. Law Inst., Order of Coif, Human Rights Campaign. Home: 1580 NW 100th Terr Plantation FL 33322 Office: Nova Southeastern U Law Ctr 3305 College Ave Fort Lauderdale FL 33314-7721 E-mail: canem@nsu.law.nova.edu.

CANE, MARK ALAN, oceanography and climate researcher; b. Bklyn., Oct. 20, 1944; s. Philip and Ida Deborah C.; m. Barbara Jane Haak, Oct. 28, 1968; children: Laura, Jacob. BA, Harvard U., 1965, MS, 1968; PhD, MIT, 1975. Earth scientist NASA, 1975-79; assoc. prof. oceanography MIT, Cambridge, 1979-84; Doherty sr. scientist Lamont Doherty Earth Obs. of Columbia, Palisades, N.Y., 1984-97; G. Unger Vetlesen prof. earth and climate scis. Columbia U., N.Y.C., 1998—. Contbr. articles to profl. jours. Organizer Student Non-Violent Coord. Conv., Ala., 1965. Recipient Cody award, Scripps Inst. Oceanography. Fellow Am. Acad. Arts & Scis., Am. Meteorol. Soc. (Sverdup gold medal 1993), Am. Geophys. Union; mem. Oceanography Soc., N.Y. Acad. Scis. Democrat. Jewish. Achievements include prediction of climate variations known as El Nino and the Southern Oscillation. Office: Lamont Doherty Earth Obs Rte 9W Palisades NY 10964 E-mail: mcane@ldeo.columbia.edu.

CANE, WILLIAM EARL, nonprofit organization executive; b. San Francisco, Aug. 15, 1935; s. Joseph Earl and Mae M. (McDermott) C.; m. Patricia Ann Mathes (div. 1997). MDiv, St. Patrick's Sem., 1973; ThD, San Francisco Theol., 1976. Assoc. pastor St. Joseph Ch., Cupertino, Calif., 1960-65; dir. St. Benedict Ctr., San Francisco, 1966-72; prof. Grad. Theol., Berkeley, Calif., 1973-79; dir. IF, Santa Cruz, Calif., 1975—; editor Integrities, Santa Cruz, 1985—. Pres. Assn. Priests Union, San Francisco, 1970-72; bd. dirs. Gaia Ctr., Santa Cruz; lectr. in field. Author: Thru Crisis to Freedom, 1980, Circles of Hope, 1992, Passing on the Spirit, 2002; contbr. articles to profl. jours. Founder Friends of the Deaf, San Francisco, 1970; co-founder Santa Cruz (Calif.) Sanctuary, 1987. Grantee Rascob Found., San Francisco, 1970, Santa Cruz (Calif.) Cmty. Found., 1988, Mervyn's Found., 1988, Eschaton Found., Santa Cruz, 1994. Avocations: gardener, water diviner, tennis, chef. Home and Office: 3015 Freedom Blvd Watsonville CA 95076-0436

CANEDAY, ARDEL BRUCE, religious studies educator, writer; b. Mpls., Jan. 16, 1950; s. Herbert Victor and Della Mildred Caneday; m. Lois Mae Neal, Aug. 5, 1950; children: John Murray, David Ryan. BA, Bryan Coll., 1973; MDiv, Grace Theol. Sem., Winona Lake, Ind., 1973, ThM, 1978; PhD, Trinity Evang. Div. Sch., Deerfield, Ill., 1991. Sr. pastor Grace Cmty. Ch., King City, Mo., 1985—87; vis. prof. N.T. lit. Trinity Internat. U., Deerfield, 1989—91, Grace Theol. Sem., Winona Lake, 1991—92; prof. N.T. lit. Northwestern Coll., St. Paul, 1992—. Instr. mosaic adult class Bethlehem Bapt. Ch., Mpls., 1997—; ajd. prof. N.T. lit. Bethel Theol. Sem., St. Paul, 1997—. Author: (non-fiction) The Race Set Before Us: A Biblical Theology of Perseverance and Assurance. Precinct caucus mem. Rep. Party, Grand Rapids, Mich., 1979—82. Tchg. fellow, Trinity Evang. Div. Sch., 1989—91. Mem.: Inst. for Bibl. Rsch., Soc. Bibl. Lit., Evang. Theol. Soc. (assoc.; pres. for midwest region 2002—03), The Ctr. of the Am. Expt. (assoc.). Republican. Avocations: history, hiking, travel, furniture making. Office: Northwestern College 3003 Snelling Ave N Saint Paul MN 55113

CANELLI, JEANNE, early childhood educator; b. Framingham, Mass., June 9, 1948; d. Francis J. and Jeanne T. (Landry) Keefe; m. Gerard P. Canelli, Aug. 5, 1972; children: Gerry Jr., Jill, Jennifer. BS in Elem. Edn., Framingham State Coll., 1970; MS, Wheelock Coll., 1987; PhD, Lesley Coll., 1999. Cert. tchr. in elem. edn., moderate spl. needs, young children with spl. needs, Mass. Tchr. Holliston Pub. Schs., 1970-73, Bellingham (Mass.) Pub. Schs., 1980-81; dir., head tchr. ECDC Sherborn (Mass.) Presch., 1981-87; assoc. prof. dept. edn., dir. child devel. lab. Framingham State Coll., 1987—. Validator Nat. Acad. Early Childhood Programs, 1993—; tchg. fellow Lesley Coll. Grantee Mass. Dept. Edn. Mem. Nat. Assn. Edn. Young Children (founder, pres. Framingham chpt.), Mass. Assn. Early Childhood Eucators, MetroWest Assn. for Edn. of Young Children (pres.). E-mail: jccdl@aol.com.

CANEPA, JOHN CHARLES, banking consultant; b. Newburyport, Mass., Aug. 26, 1930; s. John Jere and Agnes R. (Barbour) C.; m. Marie Olney, Sept. 13, 1953; children: Claudia, John J., Peter C., Milissa L. AB, Harvard U., 1953; MBA, NYU, 1960. With Chase Manhattan Bank, N.Y.C., 1957-63; sr. v.p. Provident Bank, Cin., 1963-70; past pres., chmn. bd., CEO Old Kent Fin. Corp., Grand Rapids, Mich., 1970-95; past pres., past chief exec. officer Old Kent Bank & Trust Co., Grand Rapids, 1970-95; consulting prin. Crowe Chizek, Grand Rapids, Mich., 1995—. Served with USN, 1953-57. Office: Crowe Chizek 400 Riverfront Plaza Grand Rapids MI 49503 E-mail: jcanepa@crowechizek.com.

CANES, BRIAN DENNIS, retirement benefits systems specialist; b. London, July 14, 1945; arrived in U.S., 1982; s. Jules Joel C. and Freda Rica (Gavronsky) C; m. Melanie Maxine Segal, June 29, 1969; 1 child, David. B.Sc, U. Witwatersrand, Johannesburg, Republic of South Africa, 1967; student, Inst. Actuaries, London. Systems mgr. Shepley & Fitchett Consulting Actuaries, Johannesburg, 1968-75; asst. v.p. William M. Mercer Ltd., Toronto, Ont., Can., 1975-80, controller, 1980-82; prin. Mercer Consulting, N.Y.C., 1982—87; sr. systems cons. Watson Wyatt Worldwide, N.Y.C., 1987—93; asst. dir. systems Ernst & Young ABC, N.Y.C., 1993-96; sr. mgr. Ernst & Young Mgmt. Cons., 1996-99; v.p. actuarial and econs. Golden Retirement Resources, N.Y.C., 1999—. Office: Golden Retirement Resources Inc 500 5th Ave Fl 32 New York NY 10110 E-mail: brian@canes.net.

CANES, MICHAEL EDWIN, research economist; b. Jerusalem, Dec. 24, 1941; came to U.S., 1943; m. Mary Patricia Ferron, July 11, 1970; children: Brandice, David, Aran. BS, U. Chgo., 1963, MBA, 1965; MSc, London Sch. Econs., 1966; PhD, UCLA, 1970. Economist The Ctr. for Naval Analyses, Arlington, Va., 1969-72; asst. prof. U. Rochester (N.Y.), 1972-74; sr. economist and dep. dir. Am. Petroleum Inst., Washington, 1974-78, dir., 1978-82, v.p. and chief economist, 1982-2000; sr. rsch. fellow The Logistics Mgmt. Inst., McLean, Va., 2000—. Contbr. articles to profl. jours. Mem. Am. Economic Assn., Internat. Assn. of Energy Economists, Western Economic Assn. Office: Logistics Mgmt Inst 2000 Corporate Rdg Mc Lean VA 22102-7805 E-mail: mcanes@lmi.org.

CANESTRARI, RONALD, state legislator; Assemblyman dist. 106 N.Y. State Assembly, 1989—. Address: 717 Legislative Office Bldg Albany NY 12248-0001 E-mail: Canestr@Assembly.State.NY.US.

CANES-WRONE, BRANDICE, political scientist, educator; b. Washington, Jan. 25, 1971; d. Michael and Mary Pat Canes; m. David A. Wrone. PhD, Stanford U., 1998; AB, Princeton Univ., 1993. Asst. prof. of polit. sci. MIT, Cambridge, Mass., 1998—2002; vis. asst. prof. of polit. sci. Calif. Inst. of Tech., Calif., 2001—02; assoc. prof. of polit. sci. Northwestern U., Ill., 2002—. Editl. bd. mem. Presdl. Studies Quar. Author: (scholarly articles) American Political Science Review, American Journal of Political Science, Journal of Politics, among other journals (Patrick J. Fett Award, 1997). Fellow EPA Sci. to Achieve Results Fellowship, EPA, 1997—98. Mem.: Midwest Polit. Sci. Assn., Am. Polit. Sci. Assn. Office: Northwestern Univ 601 University Pl Scott Hall Evanston IL 60208

CANFIELD, ANDREW TROTTER, lawyer, writer; b. NYC, Apr. 30, 1953; s. Edward Francis and Janet Powell (Trotter) C.; m. Marguerite Southworth Dove, May 30, 1987; children: Augusta Phillips, Lilian Sinclair. BA in History, U. Va., 1976; JD, Am. U., 1991. Bar: Pa. 1991, D.C. 1993. Rsch. assoc. Planning Rsch. Corp., McLean, Va., 1977-79; legal asst. Casey, Scott and Canfield P.C., Washington, 1979-88, law clk., 1988-91, assoc., 1991-93, Canfield and Smith, Washington, 1993-94, of counsel, 1994—. Technical and legal writer on solar energy, environ. law, manufactured housing, computer products liability and govt. timber contracts, 1976—. Republican. Episcopalian. Avocations: history, audio, photography, poetry, skiing. Home: PO Box 819 261 Falls Rd Shelburne VT 05482-6357

CANFIELD, CHERYL LUCAS, epidemiologist; d. Paul Keith and Joanne Bissonette Lucas; m. Raymond Gordon Canfield; 1 child, Raymond Gordon Jr. BA, SUNY, Buffalo, 1983, MS in Epidemiology, 1988. Epidemiologist Ecology and Environment, Lancaster, NY, 1991—95; corp. compliance officer Ind. Health Assn., Williamsville, NY, 1995—. Strategic planner Univ. Heights Cmty. Devel. Assn., Buffalo, 2000—03; pres. West Main Block Club, Buffalo, 1996—2003. Mem.: Health Care Compliance Assn. Avocations: international travel and cultures, pen and ink rendering, rollerblading, community activism. Office: Ind Health Assn 511 Farber Lakes Dr Williamsville NY 14221 Address: 9660 High St Clarence Center NY 14032

CANFIELD, CONSTANCE DALE, retired accountant, retired medical/surgical nurse; b. Fairmont, W.Va., May 2, 1940; d. Robert Alman and Dorothy Jane (Motter) C. Flight nurse diploma, Sch. Aerospace Med., 1967; BS in Acctg., Rollins Coll., 1979; student, Stetson U., 1975-76, Fla. Inst. Tech., 1976-77; grad., Army Comd. Gen. Staff Coll., Ft. Levenworth Kans., 1991. RN Fla.; registered Nurse Fla. Prin. C. D. Canfield, Acct., Melbourne, Fla., 1979-90; acct. C.D. Canfield, Acct., Melbourne, Fla., 1991—2002; ret., 2002. Gov.'s appointee Women in Mil. for Am. Meml. Found., Washington, 1991; gov.'s escort Fla. Freedom Festival, Inc., Tallahassee, 1991; state coord. VietNam Women's Meml. Project, Inc., Washington, 1986—; adminstrv. bd. United Meth. Ch., Melbourne, 1987—; musician Melbourne Mcpl. Band, 1980-90, Space Coast Philharmonic Orch., 1986-87; vol. Habitat for Humanity. With USAF, 1963-70, U.S. Army, 1970-75, lt. col., 1989-2000, ret. With USAF, 1963—70, with U.S. Army, 1970—75, lt. col. U.S. Army, 1989—2000. Decorated Air Force Commendation medal, Army Commendation medal, Fla. Meritorious Svc. medal. Mem. AACN, Nat. Soc. Tax Profls., Nat. Soc. Pub. Accts., Fla. Assn. Ind. Accts. (sec. space coast chpt. 1992-93), Internat. Biog. Assn. (life), VFW (life), Vietnam Vets. of Brevard, Inc. (life), N.G. Officers Assn., Fla. Hist. Soc., U.S. C. of C., Internat. Lions Club (pres. local club). Republican. Avocations: fishing, camping, music, show cars.

CANFIELD, EDWARD FRANCIS, lawyer, business executive; b. Phila., Apr. 7, 1922; s. Frank James and Eunice C. (Sullivan) C.; m. Janet Powell Trotter, 1952 (div. 1991); children: Andrew Trotter, Janet Powell; m. Margaret Harvey O'Brien, 1993. BA, St. Joseph's U., 1943; JD, U. Pa., 1949. Bar: Pa. 1949, D.C. 1972. Practice in, Phila., 1949-51; with RCA, 1953-60, Philco-Ford Corp., 1960-69, corp. dir. govt. planning and mktg., 1961-69; pres. Leisure Time Industries, Inc., 1969; mng. ptnr. Casey, Scott & Canfield, 1971-93; ptnr. Canfield & Smith, Washington, 1993—. Lt. comdr. USNR, ret. Mem. Fed. Bar Assn., D.C. Bar Assn., Phila. Bar Assn., Congl. Country Club (Bethesda, Md.), Overbrook Golf Club (Bryn Mawr, Pa., Atlantic City (N.J.) Country Club. Home: 1 Andover Rd Haverford PA 19041-1002 Office: Canfield & Smith 910 17th St NW Ste 800 Washington DC 20006-3604 also: 117 S 17th St Philadelphia PA 19103-5025

CANFIELD, JAMES, artistic director; Art dir. Oreg. Ballet, Portland, 1988—. Office: Oregon Ballet 818 SE 6th Ave Portland OR 97214-2329

CANFIELD, JOHN DOUGLAS, English educator, writer, consultant; b. Washington, Feb. 4, 1941; s. Austin Francis and Gertrude Canfield; m. Pamela Eden Crotty, Sept. 7, 1963; children: Robert Alan, Bret Douglas, Colin Geoffrey. AB, U. Notre Dame, 1963; MA in Tchg., Yale U., 1964; MA, Johns Hopkins U., 1966; PhD, U. Fla., 1969. Tchr. Radnor (Pa.) Sr. H.S., 1964-65; grad. asst. tchg. Johns Hopkins U., Balt., 1965-66; asst. prof. UCLA, 1969-74; assoc. prof. U. Ariz., Tucson, 1974-79, prof., 1979-94, Regents' prof., 1994—. Author: Nicholas Rowe and Christian Tragedy, 1977, Word as Bond in English Literature from the Middle Ages to the Restoration, 1989, Tricksters and Estates: On the Ideology of Restoration Comedy, 1997 (Outstanding Acad. Book award Choice Mag., 1997), Heroes and States: On the Ideology of Restoration Tragedy, 1999, Mavericks on the Border: The Early Southwest in Historical Fiction and Film, 2000, The Broadview Anthology of Restoration and Early Eighteenth Century Drama, 2001, The Graying of the Sixties, 2002, The Baroque in English Neoclassical Literature, 2003, Violence and the Secular, 2003; mem. editl. bd. Jour. Early Modern Cultural Studies, Eighteenth-Century Studies, 1996—99, Restoration, 1982—2001, editor-in-chief, 2001—. Coach, referee Am. Youth Soccer Orgn., 1983—. Recipient Tchg. Excellence award Burlington Resources Found., 1991, Sherill Creative Tchg. award U. Ariz. Found., 1993, Ariz. Prof. of Yr., Coun. for Advancement and Support of Edn., 1993; Nat. Endowment for Humanities fellow, 2001-02. Mem. MLA (chair exec. com. divsn. on restoration and early 18th century Brit. lit.), Am. Soc. 18th Century Studies (chair Clifford Prize com. 1990-91), Western Soc. 18th Century Studies (exec. sec. 1972-74), Group for Early Modern Cultural Studies (co-founder). Democrat. Avocations: poetry, hunting, soccer. Home: 1802 W Ahmed Ave Tucson AZ 85704-1202 Office: Univ Ariz Dept English 445 Modern Lang Bldg 67 Tucson AZ 85721-0001 Fax: 520-621-7397. E-mail: dcanfield@dakotacom.net., jdcanfie@u.arizona.edu.

CANFIELD, JUDY S. psychologist; b. N.Y.C., May 15, 1947; d. Arthur and Ada (Werner) Ohlbaum; m. John T. Canfield (div.); children: Oran David, Kyle Danya. BA, Grinnell Coll., 1963; MA, New Sch. Social Rsch., 1967; PhD, U.S. Internat. U., 1970. Psychologist Mendocino State Hosp., Talmage, Calif., 1968-69, Douglas Coll., New Westminster, BC, Can., 1971-72, Family & Childrens Clinic, Burnaby, BC, Can., 1971-72; psychologist, trainer, cons. VA Hosp., Northampton, Mass., 1972-75; dir. New England Ctr., Amherst, Mass., 1972-76; dir., psychologist Gateways, Lansdale, Pa., 1977-78; asst. prof., psychologist Hahnemann Med. Ctr., Phila., 1978-84; pres., dir. Inst. Holistic Health, Phila., 1978-85; psychologist, cons. Berkeley, Calif., 1986—. Mem. task force, tng. com. Berkeley Dispute Resolution Svc., 1986-89; mem. measure H com. Berkeley United Sch. Dist., 1987-88. Mem. APA, Nat. Register Health Svc. Providers in Psychology, Nat. Assn. Advancement Gestalt Therapy (steering com. 1990), Calif. Psychol. Assn., Alameda County Psychol. Assn. (info.-referral svc. 1989—), Assn. Humanistic Psychology. Avocations: piano, horseback riding, ice skating. Office: 2031 Delaware St Berkeley CA 94709-2121

CANFIELD, ROBERT CLEO, lawyer; b. St. Joseph, Mo., Sept. 10, 1938; s. Robert Charles Canfield and Nadine (Ressler) Thomas; m. Patricia Joan Harms, June 8, 1958; children: Tamara, Robert, Michael. AB, DePauw U., 1960; LLB, U. Mich., 1963. Bar: Mo. 1963, U.S. Dist. Ct. (we. dist.) Mo. 1964. Assoc. Watson, Ess, Marshall & Enggas, Kansas City, Mo., 1963-72, ptnr., 1972-92; sr. v.p., gen. counsel, sec. DST Sys., inc., Kansas City, 1992—. Mem. exec. bd. Boy Scouts Am., Kansas City, 1982—. Mem. ABA, Mo. Bar Assn., Kansas City Club. Republican. Methodist. Home: 9722 Sagamore Rd Shawnee Mission KS 66206-2314 Office: DST Systems Inc 333 W 11th St Kansas City MO 64105-1634

CANGEMI, JOHN RICHARD, physician; b. Jersey City, Feb. 21, 1954; s. Vito Francis Cangemi and Agnes Grimes McMahon; m. Lila Mae Headington, Oct. 17, 1981; children: David John, Lindsay Headington, Christina Headington. BA, Brown U., 1975, MD, 1978. Diplomate Am. Bd. Internal Medicine, Am. Bd. Gastroenterology. Intern, resident Mayo Clinic, Rochester, Minn., 1978-81, staff cons., 1984-88; fellow in gastroenterology John Hopkins Hosp., Balt., 1981-84; staff cons. Mayo Clinic, Jacksonville, Fla., 1988—, chair dept. edn., 1999—. Contbr. articles to profl. jours. Vol. sch. bd. Jax County Day Sch., Jacksonville, 1990-99. Mem.: ACP, Brown Med. Assn., Fla. Gastroenterol. Soc., Fla. Med. Assn., Crohn's and Colitis Found. Am., Am. Gastroent. Assn., Am. Coll. Gastroenterology. Office: Mayo Clinic 4500 San Pablo Rd S Jacksonville FL 32224-3899

CANGEMI, JOSEPH PETER, psychologist, consultant, educator; b. Syracuse, N.Y., June 26, 1936; m. Amelia Elena Santaló, Oct. 6, 1962; children: Michelle, Lisa Ann. BS, SUNY, Oswego, 1959; MS, Syracuse U., 1964; EdD, Ind. U., 1974; LittD (hon.), William Woods U., 1996; LittD honoris causa, Moscow State U., 2001. Diplomate Am. Bd. Vocat. Experts, Am. Bd. Forensic Examiners, Am. Coll. Counselors; diplomate in profl. counseling Am. Acad. Forensic Examiners, Internat. Acad. Behavioral Medicine, Counseling and Psychotherapy; cert. sch. psychologist, counselor, N.Y. Instr. Syracuse Pub. Schs., 1959-60, vocat. rehab. coord., rsch. assoc., 1961-65; instr., asst. dir. Carol Morgan Sch., Santo Domingo, Dominican Republic, 1960-61; asst. head basketball coach SUNY C.C., Syracuse, 1962-63, lectr., chmn. dept. psychology evening-extension divsn., 1962-65, vis. lectr., 1966; supr. edn. Orinoco Mining divsn. U.S. Steel Corp., Ciudad Piar, Venezuela, 1965-66, supr. tng. and devel. Puerto Ordaz and Ciudad Piar, Venezuela, 1966-68; asst. prof. psychology Western Ky. U., Bowling Green, 1968-75, assoc. prof., 1975-79, prof., 1979—. Project dir. U. Los Andes, Merida, Venezuela, Inter-Am. Devel. Bank, Washington, Western Ky. U., 1975-77; cons. R.R. Donnelley & Sons, Coca Cola, Gould Corp., Eaton Corp., Firestone Tire and Rubber Co., Uniroyal/Goodrich Tire and Rubber Co., Gen. Tire and Rubber Co., Jefferson Smurfit, Std. Products, Tyson Foods, others; host Conversation program Western Ky. U. Divsn. Radio, TV Film, 1968-71. Author: Higher Education and the Development of Self-Actualizing Personalities, 1977, La Administracion Participativa, 1983, (with Casimir Kowalski) Perspectives in Higher Education, 1983, Higher Education in the United States and Latin America, 1983, (with George Guttschalk) Effective Management, 1980, (with Casimir Kowalski and Jeffrey Claypool) Participative Management: Employee Management Cooperation, 1985, Chinese edit., 1990, (with Mario Noronha) Marketing Y Venda, Portuguese edit., 1992, (with Casimir Kowalski) Andersonville Prison, Lessons in Organizational Failure, 1993, (with Carl Kreisler) Raymond C. Gibson-Distinguished Kentuckian, Renowned Educator and Statesman: An Anthology, 1996, (with Mario Noronha, Casimir Kowalski, George Guttschalk) Falhas Organizaciones, Portuguese edit., 1996, (with Tatyana Ushakova and Casimir Kowalski) Leadership for the 21st Century, Russian edit., Russian Academy of Sciences, Leadership Behavior, 1998; editor: Educator's Svc. Bull., 1971-72, Psychology and Edn.: An Interdisciplinary Jour., 1977—, Jour. Human Behavior and Learning, 1983-90, Orgn. Devel. Jour., 1983-89; mem. editl. bd. Archivos Panamenos de Psicologia, 1968-88, Coll. Student Jour., 1973—, Faculty Rsch. Bull. of Western Ky. U., 1977-88, Jour. Instructional Psychology, 1977—, Counseling and Values, 1979-84, Technol. Horizons in Edn. Jour., 1979-92 Edn., 1976—, Jour. Fgn. Psychology, Russia, 1996—, Chinese Jour. Applied Psychology, 1999—, Forensic Examiner, 1998—; contbr. over 400 articles, chpts. to profl. publs. Trustee William Woods U., 1988—; past bd. dirs. COCITE (Cooperativa de Ensino Superior de Technicas Avancadas de Gestao e Informatica) Technol. U., Lisbon; mem. Ho. of Goa, Lisbon, Portugal, 1996-97. Recipient certs. and awards U.S. Army Armor Sch., 1974; Eaton Corp., 1974, 76, Brazilian Acad. Humanities, 1976, Nat. Autonomous U. Nicaragua, 1976, ICETEX, Colombia, 1977, Colombian Nat. Assn. Indsl. Engrs., 1977, Decreto award City of Bucaramanga, Colombia, 1976, 77, Quality Control Assn., 1979, Decreto award State of Santander, Colombia, 1977, Excellence in Productive Tchg. award Western Ky. U. Coll. Edn., 1979, 91, 99, Firestone Tire and Rubber Co. award, 1978, 81, Profl.-Tech. Socs. award, 1983, Coll. Student Jour. and Models of Excellence award, 1983, Disting. Pub. Svc. award Western Ky. U., 1983, Excellence in Pub. Svc. award Coll. Edn., 1983, Disting. Alumnus award SUNY, Oswego, 1983; award from Uniroyal-Goodrich Tire and Rubber Co., 1986, Excellence in Rsch. and Creativity award Coll. Edn., Western Ky. U., 1987, United Rubber Workers/Internat. Brotherhood Elec. Workers and Firestone Tire & Rubber Co. award, 1991; featured personality Orgn. Devel. Jour., 1989, Jour. Edn. award, Project Innovation, 1992 (featured on cover in summer issue); Bridgestone-Firestone award Valencia, Venezuela, 1994, Outstanding Contbn. award Southea. divsn. Redman Industries, 1996. Mem. ACA (regional chmn. com. internat. edn. 1976 life), Nat. Vocat. Guidance Assn. Profl., Internat. Coun. Psychologists (past area chmn. Ky.), Assn. Specialists in Group Work (charter), Panamanian Psychol. Assn. (hon.), Ky. Acad. Arts and Scis. (life), Internat. Assn. Edn. and Vocat. Guidance, Nat. Assn. Gifted (bd. dirs. 1973), Colombian Nat. Soc. Indsl. Engrs. (hon.), Romanian Acad. Scis. (hon.), Internat. Registry Orgn. Devel. Profls., RODP, InterAm. Soc. Psychology, Acad. Mgmt., Soc. Psychology in Mgmt., Capitol Arts Assn., Alumni Assn. SUNY-Oswego, Ind. U. Alumni Assn. (life), Gold Key, Pi Kappa Delta, Psi Chi, Sigma Delta Psi, Sigma Tau Delta, Phi Delta Kappa. Clubs: Bowling Green Country. Home: 1409 Mt Ayr Cir Bowling Green KY 42103-4708 Office: Western Ky U Dept Psychology Bowling Green KY 42101 Fax: 270-842-0432. E-mail: joseph.cangemi@wku.edu.

CANGEMI, MICHAEL PAUL, accountant, financial executive, writer; b. Bklyn., May 5, 1948; s. Ignatius and Mary (Chimento) C.; m. Maria D. Ruscitti, Nov. 23, 1974; children: Michael Jason, Marc Ignatius. BBA, Pace U., 1970. CPA, N.Y.; cert. info. systems auditor. Asst. to v.p. ops. Blair & Co., N.Y.C., 1966-70; prin. Arthur Young & Co., N.Y.C., 1970-80; v.p. Phelps Dodge Corp., N.Y.C., 1980-88; ptnr., nat. dir. EDP auditing BDO Seidman, 1988-92; from sr. v.p., CFO to CEO Etienne Aigner Inc., Edison, NJ, 1992—2002; pres., CEO, bd. dirs. Etienne Aigner Group, Edison, 2002—. Lectr. in field. Author: Managing the Audit Function-A Corporate Audit Department Procedures Guide, 1993, 2d edit., 1995, 3rd edit., 2003; contbg. author: The Handbook for EDP Auditing, 1986; co-author: Auditing in an EDP Environment; contbr. articles to profl. jours. Mem. AICPA, N.Y. State Soc. CPAs (data processing com. 1979-80, computer usage and data processing com. 1980-82), EDP Auditors Assn. (internat. bd. dirs. 1982-89, trustee 1982-89, v.p. edn. 1982-84, exec. v.p. 1984-85, assn. and found. pres. 1985-86, pres. N.Y. chpt. bd. dirs. 1978-86, 2d v.p., 1979-80, 1st v.p. 1983, nominating com. 1982-86, conf. site selection com. 1981-82, editor Info. Sys. Control Jour., 1987—, editor-in-chief, 1992—, assoc. editor EDPACS, (newsletter) The EDP Audit, Control and Security, 1988-94, J.J. Wasserman award 1987, Eugene M. Frank award 1989, Michael P. Cangemi best article-best book award, 1996), Fin. Execs. Inst., Inst. Internal Auditors (program devel. com. for 1986 conf. 1984-86, bd. govs. N.Y. chpt. 1986-92, mem. bd. rsch. advisors 1987-93, pres. N.Y. chpt. 1989-90, trustee rsch. found. 1994-2000), Soc. for Info. Systems Quality (bd. dirs. 1987-88), Arthur Young Businessmen's Assn. (bd. dirs. 1982-89, v.p. 1985-89), Metuchen (N.J.) Golf and Country Club. Roman Catholic. Home: 18 Fishel Rd Edison NJ 08820-3217 Office: Etienne Aigner 47 Brunswick Ave Edison NJ 08817-2081 also: Info Systems Audit & Control Assn 3701 Algonquin Rd Ste 1010 Rolling Meadows IL 60008-3124

CANHAM, PRUELLA CROMARTIE NIVER, retired educator; b. Statesboro, Ga., Dec. 4, 1924; d. Esten Graham and Mary Lee (Jones) Cromartie; m. Robert E. Niver June 4, 1946 (div. 1965) m. David L. Canham July 26, 1985; 1 child, Peddy Niver Hayhurst Moran. BS in Bus. and Music, Ga. So. U., 1944, postgrad., various univs. tchr. voice, piano, chorus and bus. career maths. North Ft. Myers H.S., Fla.; former sec. Statesboro Air Base, Ga., Warner Robbins Air Base, Macon, Ga.; former tchr. Westside Sch., Bulloch County, Ga., Southside Sch., Opelika, Ala. Mem. Singers Club of L.I.; guest spkr., panelist various cultural orgns. in Fla. and so. states; soloist various chs. and schs.; music cons. local theater groups; mem. Fla. State Secondary Music Instructional Materials Coun. Nominee Gannett Found. Heart of Gold Humanatarian award, 1981; named Vocal Solo. Lit. Music Specialist State of Florida, Lee County Florida Tchr. of the Year, 1987, nominee Nat. Tchr. Hall of Fame, 1998; recipient Nat. Libr. Poet's Editor's Choice award, 1994; cert. Appreciation Nat. Park Trust, 1995, Lee County Sch. Dist. Fla., 1991, numerous awards in 2002, including: ABI Hall of Fame, Great Minds of 21st Century, Poet of Year, Internat. Poet Merit and Honored Mem., 500 Founders of 21st Century, Internat. Biographical Ctr. Living Legions, 1000 Great Scholars, Worlds Lifetime Achievement award, Companion of Honor, Internat. Peace Prize, Am. Medal of Honor; Nobel Prize for Oustanding Achievement and Contbr. to Humanity, 2002. Mem. AAAS, Am. Ch. Dirs. Assn., Fla. Music Educator Assn., Music Educator's Nat. Conf., Lee County Alliance of the Arts (charter), Fla. Vocal Assn. (past coord., state bd.), Nat. Assn. of Tchrs. of Singing in Am. and Cand., So. Fla. Symphony and Chorus Assn., Am. Guild of Organists, Fla. League of the Arts (past pres. and

bd. dirs., hon. life, 1998—), Lee County Retired Tchrs. Assn., Fla. Vocal Assn., Am. Choral Assn., Internat. Soc. Poets (disting. mem. 1994, merit award, 1995), Profl. Women's Adv. Bd., others. Home: 1271 Burtwood Dr Fort Myers FL 33901-8711

CANIATO, MICHELE, music educator, composer, conductor; MusB, Boston U, 1991, MusM, 1994, Mus D, 1998. Faculty Creative Arts, Reading, Mass., 1990—93; instr. Cmty. and Adult Edn., Brookline, Mass., 1993—94; music tchr. Watertown Pub. Sch., Watertown, Mass., 1995—97; dir. jazz ensemble Boston U, 1995—2001; music dir. Boston U Acad., 1996; artist in residence Adria Conservatory, Italy, 1998; asst. prof. of music Fitchburg State Coll., Fitchburg, Mass., 2000—. Adv. bd. Ctr. for Italian Culture, Fitchburg, Mass., 2000—; advisor internat. edn. Fitchburg State Coll., Fitchburg, Mass., 2000—; guest condr. Indian Hill Music Ctr., Littleton, Mass., 2001. Contbr. ; composer (music oratorio): Three Meditations, 1998. Mentor to youth Boston Ctr. for the Arts, 1998; vol. preconcert lectures Centerstage, Boston, 2002. Grantee Marion and Jasper Whiting award, Found. Grant, 2002. Master: Am. Soc. Composers, Authors and Pub.; mem.: Soc. for Music Theory, Internat. Assoc. Jazz Edn. (assoc.), Pi Kappa Lambda (hon.). Avocations: hiking, swimming, bicycling, reading. Office: Fitchburg State College 160 Pearl Street Fitchburg MA 01420

CANIPAROLI, VAL WILLIAM, choreographer, dancer; b. Renton, Wash., Sept. 12, 1951; s. Francisco and Leonora (Marconi) C. Student, Wash. State U., 1969-71, San Francisco Ballet Sch., 1971-72. Dancer San Francisco Opera, 1973, San Francisco Ballet, 1973—; co-dir. OMO, San Francisco, 1985; resident choreographer San Francisco Ballet, 1983—, Ballet West, 1993—97, Tulsa Ballet, 2001—. Choreographer (ballets) Street Song, 1980, Pacific Northwest Ballet, Seattle, 1980, 91, The Bridge, 1998, Love-lies-Bleeding, 1982, Aria, 1998, Slow, 1998, Ciao Marcello, 1997, Hamlet and Ophelia, 1985, In Perpetuum, 1990, Aubade, 1985 (Isadora Duncan award 1986), Narcisse, 1987, Ririe Woodbury Dance Co., 1988, Ritual, 1990, A Door is Ajar, 1990, Jacob's Pillow Dance festival, 1990, Pulcinella, 1991, Concerto Grosso, 1992, Seeing Stars, 1993, Lady of the Camellias, 1993, Ballet West, 1994, Lambarena, 1995, Capriccio, Chgo. Lyric Opera, 1994, Bow Out, 1995, San Francisco Symphony Pops, 1995-96, Prawn Watching, 996, Djangology, 1997, Open Veins, 1998, Book of Alleged Dances, 1998, Going for Baroque, 1999, Attention Please, 1999, The Nutcracker, 2001, Torque, 2001, Jaybird Lounge, 2001, Death of a Moth, 2001, Unspoken, 2002, No Other, 2002, boink!, 2002, Gustave's Rooster, 2003, others. Recipient Isadora Duncan award, 1987, 97, 2001, Choo-San Goh and H. Robert Magee Found. award for choreography, 1994, 97; Nat. Endowment Arts fellowship grantee, 1981-88. Fellow Calif. Arts Coun. Coreographers. Avocations: music, theatre, dance. Home: 81 Lansing St Apt 405 San Francisco CA 94105-2647 Office: San Francisco Ballet 455 Franklin St San Francisco CA 94102-4471

CANIVEZ, GARY LYNN, psychologist, educator; b. Chgo., Nov. 17, 1960; s. Lynn and Carol (Busser) C. BS, Bemidji State U., 1982; MS in Edn., So. Ill. U., 1985, PHD, 1987. Lic. psychologist, Ariz.; cert. sch. psychologist, nat., Ariz., Ill. Sch. psychologist Deer Valley Unified Sch. Dist. #97, Phoenix, 1987-90, Tempe (Ariz.) Sch. Dist. #3, 1990-95; asst. prof. Ea. Ill. U., Charleston, 1995-98, assoc. prof., 1998—2003, prof., 2003—. Adj. prof. No. Ariz. U., Flagstaff, 1988-95; sport psychologist Ea. Ill. U., Charleston, 1995—; sport psychologist, cons. Apex Sport Psychology Svcs., Charleston. Mem. editl. bd. Psychology in the Schs., 1997—; reviewer Sch. Psychology Rev., 1997—; contbr. articles to profl. jours. Recipient Past Pres. award Ariz. Assn. Sch. Psychologists, Phoenix, 1993, Max Jones Meml. Rsch. award Ariz. Assn. Sch. Psychologists, 1993; grantee NIH/NIMH Grant IR15MH066829-01, 2002—. Mem. APA, Nat. Assn. Sch. Psychologists, Ill. Sch. Psychologists Assn. (trainer rep. 1997-99, 2000-03, rsch. chair 2000-03). Home: 2409 8th St #24 Charleston IL 61920-4124 Office: Ea Ill Univ 600 Lincoln Ave Charleston IL 61920-3011 E-mail: glcanivez@eiu.edu.

CANIZARES, CLAUDE ROGER, astrophysicist, educator; b. Tucson, June 14, 1945; s. Orlando and Stephanie (Bolan) C.; children: Kristen, Alexander. BA, Harvard U., 1967, MA, 1968, PhD, 1972. From rsch. staff to assoc. provost MIT, Cambridge, 1971—2001, assoc. provost, 2001—. Assoc. dir. NASA-Chandra X-ray Obs. Ctr.; chair NRC Space Studies Bd., 1994-2000; chair space sci. adv. com. NASA, 1993-94, mem. Space Earth Sci. Adv. Com., Washington, 1986-88; mem. adv. coun. NASA, 1992-2000; mem. astron. and astrophysics survey com. NRC, Washington, 1989-91; trustee Assoc. Univs., Inc., 1997—; mem. Air Force Sci. Adv. Bd., 1999—; mem. bd. on physics and astronomy NRC, 2001—. Contbr. articles over 170 to profl. jours. Royal Soc. vis. fellow, Cambridge, Eng., 1981-82, Alfred P. Sloan Found. fellow, 1980-84; NASA grantee, 1975—. Fellow Am. Phys. Soc.; mem. NAS, AAAS, Am. Astron. Soc., Internat. Astron. Union, Internat. Acad. Astronautics, Phi Beta Kappa, Sigma Xi. Achievements include first implementation of studies in x-ray spectroscopy and plasma diagnostics of supernova remnants, clusters of galaxies. Office: MIT 77 Massachusetts Ave 3-234 Cambridge MA 02139-4309 E-mail: crc@mit.edu.

CANN, JOHN PEARCE, III, educator; b. Richmond, Va., Feb. 13, 1941; s. John Pearce Jr. and Virginia Waddy C.; m. Courtenay Williams, June 20, 1970 (div. Aug. 1999); children: John, James. BA, U. Va., 1963, MBA, 1970; MA, Georgetown U., 1993; PhD, King's Coll. London, 1996. Chmn. Rand Bus. Systems, Richmond, Va., 1985-87; pres. CMO Metal Supply, Richmond, Va., 1987-88, Coastal Builders, Richmond, Va., 1988-93; asst. prof. USMC Command and Staff Coll., Quantico, Va., 1997-99, assoc. prof., 1999—. Author: Counterinsurgency in Africa: The Portuguese Way of War, 1961-1974, 1997; N.Am. editor War Studies Jour., 1997-2000. Bd. dirs. Poe Found., Richmond, 1970, Historic Richmond Found., 1970. Capt. USN Res., 1963-93. Decorated Def. Superior Svc. medal, Medal Dom Afonso Henriques; recipient Overseas Rsch. Student award, London, 1994. Mem. Internat. Inst. Strategic Studies, Internat. Conf. Group Portugal, Royal African Soc., London Rowing Club, Country Club Va. Episcopalian. Avocation: rowing. Home: 904 Oronoco St Alexandria VA 22314-2235 Office: USMC Command and Staff Coll 2076 South St Quantico VA 22134-5068 E-mail: jackcann@earthlink.net.

CANN, NANCY TIMANUS, retail yacht sales executive; b. Balt. d. E. Frank Timanus and Ruth F. (Herman) Schell; m. Craig Shimer; children: Justin Ronald, Heather Sharp, Heath Shimer. Grad., Balt. Bus. Coll., 1967. Pres. Crusader Yacht Sales, Inc., Annapolis, Md., 1982—. Bd. dirs. Bayfarers. Bd. dirs. Chesapeake Region Accessible Boating, 2003—. Mem. Yacht Architects and Brokers Assn. (v.p. 1989-91, 92-94, chmn. membership com. 1989-92, bd. dirs. 1992-99, pres. 1994-96, boat dealer adv. com. 1999—), bd. dir. Chesapeake Region Accessible Boating, 2003-. Avocation: boating. Home and Office: 7078 Bembe Beach Rd Annapolis MD 21403-3616 E-mail: nancy@crusaderyachts.com.

CANN, SHARON LEE, retired health science librarian; b. Ft. Riley, Kans., Aug. 14, 1935; d. Roman S. and Cora Elon (George) Foote; m. Donald Clair Cann, May 16, 1964. Student, Sophia U., Tokyo, 1955-57; BA, Calif. State U., Sacramento, 1959; MSLS, Atlanta U., 1977; EdD, U. Ga., 1995. Cert. health scis. libr. Recreation worker ARC, Korea, Morocco, France, 1960-64; shelflister Libr. Congress, Washington, 1967-69; tchr. Lang Ctr., Taipei, Taiwan, 1971-73; libr. tech. asst. Emory U., Atlanta, 1974-76; health sci. libr. Northside Hosp., Atlanta, 1977-85, libr. cons., 1985-86; libr. area health edn. ctr., learning resource ctr. Morehouse Sch. Medicine, 1985-86; edn. libr. Ga. State U., 1986-93; dir. libr. svcs. Ga. Bapt. Coll. Nursing, 1993-99, ret., 1999. Author: Life in a Fishbowl: A Call To serve, 2003; editor Update, publ. Ga. Health Scis. Libr. Assn., 1981; contbr. articles to publs. Chmn. Calif. Christian Youth in Govt. Seminar, 1958. Named Alumni Top Twenty Calif. State U., Sacramento, 1959. Mem. ALA, Med. Libr. Assn. (bookkeeper So. chpt. 1996-98, credentialing com. 1996-2000, nursing and allied health sect. continuing edn. chair 1998-2000, hon. life), Spl. Libr. Assn. (dir. South Atlantic chpt. 1985-87), Ga. Libr. Assn. (spl. libr. divsn. chmn. 1983-85), Ga. Health Scis. Libr. Assn. (chmn. 1981-82, hon. life), Atlanta Health Sci. Libr. (chmn. 1979, 95), Am. Numis. Assn., ARC Overseas Assn., Audubon Soc., Women in Mil. Svc. for Am., Suncity Hilton Health Computer Club (v.p. 2003). Home: 69 Plymouth Ln Bluffton SC 29909-5062 E-mail: sharoncann@aol.com.

CANN, STEVEN J. political science educator; b. Oct. 30, 1944; BS, N.D. State U., 1970, MA, 1972; PhD, Purdue U., 1977. Assoc. prof. Idaho State U., Pocatello, 1977-85; prof. polit. sci. Washburn U., Topeka, 1985—. Author: Administrative Law (3d edit.); Contbr. to profl. jours. Vol. Topeka Victim/offender mediation project. With USN, (E-4) 1966-68. Mem. Am. Soc. Pub. Adminstrn. (bd. dirs., past pres. Kans. chpt.), Am. Polit. Sci. Assn., The Am. Acad. Polit. Sci. Office: 1700 SW College Ave Topeka KS 66621-0001 E-mail: zzcann@washburn.edu.

CANNADY, TERESA LYNN, lawyer; b. Albertville, Ala., Aug. 16, 1963; d. Verlon Gene and Martha Ellen Cannady. AS, Snead State C.C., Boaz, Ala., 1982, 84; BS in Acctg., Jacksonville State U., 1988; JD, U. Ala., Tuscaloosa, 1991. Bar: Ala. 1991. Law clk. to Judge Inge Johnson, Tuscumbia, Ala., 1991-92; sole practitioner Albertville, 1992-97; atty. Engel, Walsh & Assocs., Mobile, Ala., 1997-98; gender issues legal specialist ABA.CEELI, Almaty, Kazakhstan, 1998—. Contbr. poetry to mags. Mem. Alice Meadows Coun., Mobile, 1998; bd. dirs. Salvation Army Women's Shelter, Mobile, 1998; chmn. bd. Big Bros./Big Sisters Marshall County, 1995. Mem. ABA, Ala. Bar Assn., Marshall County Bar Assn. Avocations: playing piano, writing poems and short stories. Home: 534 Seifullin Apt 172 Almaty Kazakhstan Office: ABA/CEELI 740 15th St NW Washington DC 20005-1019

CANNELL, ELIZABETH ANN MAY, interior designer; b. Easton, Pa., May 11, 1936; d. Jack Bertle and Margaret (Peifer) May; m. John Redferne Cannell, May 28, 1960; children: John Jr. (dec.), James, William AB, Vassar Coll., 1958; student, N.Y. Sch. Interior Design, 1973-75. Owner, mgr. Betty Ann Cannell Interior Design, Montclair, N.J., 1976-81, 85—, Singapore, 1981-85. Docent Nat. Mus., Singapore, 1983-85; trustee Montclair Art Mus., 1997—. Mem. Jr. League Montclair-Newark, Garden Club of Montclair. Clubs: Vassar of Essex County. Republican. Episcopalian. E-mail: cannells@worldnet.att.net.

CANNELL, JOHN REDFERNE, lawyer; b. Cambridge, Mass., Apr. 3, 1937; s. John and Thyra (Larson) C.; m. Elizabeth Ann May, May 28, 1960; children: John R. Jr. (dec.), James C., William H. AB, Princeton U., 1958; LLB, Columbia U., 1961. Bar: NY 1961. Assoc. Simpson Thacher & Bartlett, NYC, 1961-70, ptnr., 1970-95, of counsel, 1996—. Gov. Am. Bus. Coun., Singapore, 1982-85, vice chmn., 1984-85; dir. Mattapoisett Casino, 2002--. Trustee Kessler Inst. for Rehab., West Orange, NJ, 1986-97, vice chmn., 1989-92, chmn., 1992-95; trustee Henry H. Kessler Found., 1992—, chmn., 1996-99; trustee Marcus Ward Home, Maplewood, NJ, 1996—; dir. Kessler Rehab. Corp., 1992—, Kessler Med. Rehab. Rsch. and Edn. Corp., 1997—; bd. dir. New Alternatives for Children, Inc., 1996—. Mem. Montclair Golf Club (trustee 2001—), Univ. Club, Bay Club (Mattapoisett). Episcopalian. Avocations: squash, golf. Office: Simpson Thacher & Bartlett 425 Lexington Ave Fl 17 New York NY 10017-3903

CANNELL, ROBERT QUIRK, former agricultural sciences educator; b. Isle of Man, Mar. 20, 1937; married; 2 children. BSc in Agrl. with 1st class honors, King's Coll., U. Durham, Newcastle-upon-Tyne, U.K., 1959; PhD, U. Newcastle-upon-Tyne, 1968. Agronomist fertilizer devel. sect. Shell Chem. Co. Ltd., London, 1959-61; lectr. crop physiology dept. agr. U. Newcastle-upon-Tyne, 1961-70; rsch. fellow, Fulbright scholar dept. agronomy/plant genetic U. Minn., St. Paul, 1968-69; prin. sci. officer, head field studies dept. Agrl. and Food Rsch. Coun., Letcombe Lab., Oxfordshire, 1970-84; dir. Welsh Plant Breeding Sta., prof. agrl. botany U. Coll. Wales, Aberystwyth, 1984-87; prof., head crop and soil environ. scis. Va. Poly. Inst. and State U., Blacksburg, 1987-94, dir. Va. Agrl. Expt. Sta., assoc. dean rsch., 1994-99; ret. Internat. cons., lectr. in field; mem. FAO panel of experts on agrl. mechanization, Rome, 1981; assessor for U.K. Overseas Devel. adminstrn. on conservation tillage project, 1980, 82 Contbr. numerous articles and abstracts to profl. jours., chpts. to books; editl. bd. Agrl. Water Mgmt., Soil and Tillage Rsch. Recipient Pres.'s award Va. Turfgrass Coun., 1992. Fellow Inst. Biology; mem. Brit. Soc. Soil Sci., Inst. Biology London, Internat. Soc. Soil Sci., Internat. Soil Tillage Rsch. Orgn. E-mail: robertcannell@manx.net.

CANNEY, DONALD LADD, museum administrator, historian, writer; b. Manchester, Conn., Sept. 25, 1947; s. Ladd Lee and Helen Burnsed Canney; m. Janice Suzanne Pound, Jan. 25, 1972; 1 child, Brendan Ladd Hatfield. BA, Ga. So. Coll., 1969. Tchr. Marantha Christian Sch., Columbus, Ohio, 1974; editl. asst. Blue and Gray mag., Columbus, Ohio, 1984—86; hist. rsch. cons. and writer Columbus and Washington, 1986—91; mus. collections registrar US Coast Guard Hdqs., Washington, 1991—. Rsch. cons. US Navy Meml. Found., Washington, 1988—89, Coastal Heritage Soc., Savannah, Ga., 1990—92, Nat. Civil War Mus., Columbus, Ga., 1999—2002. Author: (books) The Old Steam Navy Vol. I: Frigates, Sloops and Gunboats, 1815-1885, 1990, The Old Steam Navy Vol. 2: The Ironclads, 1842-1885, 1993, US Coast Guard and Revenue Cutters, 1790-1935, 1995, Lincoln's Navy: The Ships, Men and Organization, 1861-1865, 1998 (Bookman News' A List of Exceptional Books of 1998), Sailing Warships of the US Navy, 2001; contbr. articles to mil. jours. Staff sgt. USAF, 1969—73. Avocations: photography, model building. Home: 12618 Kornett Ln Bowie MD 20715 Office: US Coast Guard Curatorial Svcs USCG Headquarters Washington DC 20593

CANNING, JOHN RAFTON, urologist; b. Evanston, Ill., Dec. 5, 1927; s. Claude E. and Martha C. Canning; m. Elizabeth Learned, Sept. 11, 1948; 1 dau., Sarah Blee; m. Jacqueline Maartense, Apr. 3, 1970; children— John R., Richard, Roberta. BA, Lake Forest (Ill.) Coll., 1951; MD, Northwestern U., 1955, MS, 1956. Diplomate: Am. Bd. Surgery, Am. Bd. Urology. Intern St. Luke's Hosp., Chgo., 1955; resident in gen. surgery VA Hosp., Hines, Ill., 1956-60, resident in urology, 1966-68; chest fellow Presbyn.-St. Luke's Hosp., Chgo., 1963; asst. chief vascular surg. sect. VA Hosp., Hines, 1960-66, asst. chief urology surg. sect., 1968, chief urology, 1969—86; asst. prof. urology Loyola U. Stritch Sch. Medicine, Maywood, Ill., 1969 82, prof. urology, 1982—, chmn. dept., 1979-86; attending urologist Cook County Bur. Health, 1995—. Fellow A.C.S.; mem. AMA, Ill. Urol. Soc. (exec. com.), Chgo. Urol. Soc. (pres. exec. com.), Chgo. Med. Soc., Soc. Univ. Urologists. Clubs: Chgo. Yacht. Office: Loyola U Stritch Sch Medicine Dept Urology Maywood IL 60153

CANNING, MICHAEL PAUL, movie reviewer, film essayist; b. Fargo, N.D., May 15, 1941; s. William Myles and Gladys Marie (O'Brien) C.; m. Judith May Jones, Dec. 26, 1964; children: Elizabeth Sarah, Rachel Deborah. BA in Maths., N.D. State U., 1963, Tübingen U., Germany, 1963-64, Free U., Berlin, Germany, 1964. Fgn. svc. officer USIA, Washington, 1965-93, insp., 1994—98; movie reviewer Hill Rag, Washington, 1993—. Chmn. young officers policy panel, 1970-71; mem. sr. seminar Dept. State, Washington, 1986-87. Contbr. articles to profl. jours.; mem. editl. bd. Fgn. Svc. Jour., Washington, 1970-72. Mem., supporter Capitol Hill Arts Workshop, Washington, 1978—; vol. Food & Friends, Washington, 1994—. Scholar German Acad. Exch. Svc., Bad Godesberg, 1963-64. Mem.: Capitol Hill Restoration Soc. (bd. dirs. 2002—), Sr. Seminar Alumni Assn. (bd. dirs. 2002—), Pub. Diplomacy Found. (bd. dirs. 2003—), USIA Alumni Assn. (pres. 2001—), Am. Polit. Sci. Assn., Am. Fgn. Svc. Assn. Avocations: theater, classical music, painting, drawing. Home: 21 5th St SE Washington DC 20003-1119

CANNISTRARO, NICHOLAS, JR., newspaper executive; b. Waltham, Mass., Oct. 7, 1939; s. Nicholas and Audrey Phyllis (Hager) C.; m. Margaret Clement Clark, Sept. 30, 1961; children: Melissa Greer Salvesen, Margaret Clement Miller. BA, Harvard U., 1961. Account exec. Young & Rubicam, N.Y.C., 1965-68; account supr. Erwin Wasey Co., N.Y.C., 1968-69; product mgr. Gillette Co., Boston, 1969-71; v.p. mktg. Bristol-Myers Corp., N.Y.C., 1971-82; v.p. advt. and mktg. Washington Post, 1982-92, sr. v.p., 1992-92; sr. v.p., chief mktg. officer Newspaper Assn. Am., Vienna, Va., 1993-96; pres., gen. mgr. The Newspaper Nat. Network, N.Y.C., 1997—; chmn. bd. Annapolis Techs., Inc., Balt., 1999—. Bd. dirs. Md. Hall for Creative Arts Found., Advt. Coun. Lt. USN, 1961-65. Mem. Annapolis Yacht Club, Naval Acad. Sailing Squadron, N.Y. Yacht Club. Republican. Avocations: sailing, offshore racing. Home: 1865 Milvale Rd Annapolis MD 21401-5922 Office: Newspaper Nat Network 20 W 33rd St New York NY 10001-3305 E-mail: cannn@nnn-haa.com., nickbuzzi@aol.com.

CANNON, ALICE GRACE, counselor; b. Greenville, N.C., Nov. 3, 1949; d. Carl William Hannah and Lula Estelle Briley; children: Mary Alice Cannon Blankenship, Laren Jay. PhD, DD, Progressive Universal Life Ch., 2000. Commd. 2d lt. USAF, 1973, advanced through ranks to staff sgt., 1980, ret., 1993; clk. U.S. Postal Svc., Norfolk, Va., 1994—97, ret.; min. Progressive Universal Life Ch., Sacramento, 2000—, counseling practitioner, 2001—, min., 2000; counselor practioner, 2001. Staff sgt. USAF, 1983, Greneda Invasion, staff sgt. USAF, 1991—92, Desert Storm. Mem.: AARP, Air Force Meml. Assn., Disabled Vets. Assn. Avocations: Black Belt in Tae Kwan Do, reading, museums, travel, music. Home: 50 Brook Meadow Ln La Grange NC 28551 E-mail: snowy777@msn.com.

CANNON, BENJAMIN WINTON, lawyer, business executive; b. Muncie, Ind., Sept. 17, 1944; s. Zane William and Gloria Gene (Phillips) C.; m. Diane Joan Koenig, June 24, 1967; children: Matthew Zane, Christine Elizabeth, Leslie Joan, Todd Graham. BA, Western Mich. U., 1965; postgrad., Notre Dame Law Sch., 1966-67; JD, Wayne State U., 1969; MBA, Mich. State U., 1979. Bar: Mich. 1970, Ill. 1981, Ohio 1994. Law clk. labor rels. staff Gen. Motors Corp., Detroit, 1966-69; tax atty. Plante & Moran CPAs, Southfield, Mich., 1969-71; atty. Burroughs Corp. (Unisys), Detroit, 1971-72; assoc. Nine and Maister, Attys., Bloomfield Hills, Mich., 1972-73; atty. Chrysler Fin. Corp., Troy, Mich., 1973-78, sr. atty., 1978-80; dep. gen. coun. DF Industries Inc., Long Grove, Ill., 1980-81; asst. gen. counsel, asst. sec. COMDISCO, Inc., Rosemont, Ill., 1981-82, pres. internat. group, 1982-86, v.p. capital equipment, 1986-90, v.p. gen. mgr. venture capital group, 1990-92; v.p. gen. counsel, sec., v.p. human resources LDI Corp., Cleve., 1992-94; v.p. Realtors Info. Network, 1995-96; pvt. practice Barrington, Ill., 1996—98, Bus. Lawyers Internat., Palatine, Ill., 1998—. Instr. law Oakland U., Rochester, Mich., 1980; legal counsel and cons. in field. Mem. Ill. Bar Assn., Assn. Corp. Counsel Am., Am. Soc. Corp. Secs., Gray's Inn Legal Soc., Omicron Delta Kappa, Kappa Delta Pi. Republican. Presbyterian. Home: Apt 5 751 Pennsylvania Dr Palatine IL 60074-1978 E-mail: cannon007@att.net.

CANNON, CHARLES CURTIS, JR., military career officer; b. Jasper, Ala., Feb. 19, 1943; m. Karen McFadden Cannon; children: Dianne, Curtis. Grad., U. Tex., Arlington; BA in History, Fla. Inst. Tech., 1967, MS in Logistics Mgmt., 1976; advanced operational fellowship, Army Command/Gen. Staff Coll., 1985. Commissioned. 2nd lt. U.S. Army, 1967, advanced through grades to maj. gen., 1995, various positions including exec. officer petroleum distbn.; logistics programmer Dept. of the Army, asst. exec. officer to dep. chief of staff for logistics, divsn. support command exec. officer 1st Cavalry Divsn., 1982, advance operational fellow, 1985-87, dir. bulk fuels 200th Theater Army Material Mgmt. Ctr., comdr. 8th Inf. Divsn. (Mechanized) Support Command, chief logistics planning divsn. on the joint staff, 1991-92, comdr. 3d Corps Support Command, 1992-94, vice dir. for logistics Joint Staff, 1994-96, comdr. for support, Implementation Force, 1996, asst. dep. chief of staff for logistics Washington, 1996-99. Decorated Def. Disting. Svc. medal, Army Disting. Svc. medal, Def. Superior Svc. medal, Legion of Merit with two oak leaf clusters, Bronze Star medal with V device and three oak leaf clusters, Purple Heart, Def. Meritorious Svc. medal, Army Meritorious Svc. medal with four oak leaf clusters, Air medal, Army Commendati on medal with V device and five oak leaf clusters, Army Achievement medal. Office: US Army Material Command Washington DC 20310-0500

CANNON, CHRISTINE ANNE, veterinarian; b. Chgo., Nov. 13, 1952; d. Joseph Phillip and Mildred Eileen (Toll) C.; divorced. BS in Animal Sci., Purdue U., 1974; BS in Vet. Medicine, U. Ill., 1975, DVM, 1977. Vet. Bellemore Animal Hosp., Granite City, Ill., 1977-79, Humane Soc. of Mo., St. Louis, 1979-81, Wheaton Way Vet. Hosp., Bremerton, Wash., 1981-82, Rose Hill Animal and Bird Hosp., Kirkland, Wash., 1982-83; relief vet. Wash., 1983-87; vet., owner Bird and Exotic Pet Care Clinic, Lynnwood, Wash., 1987-92; vet. owner A Pet Care Clinic, Mountlake Terrace, Wash., 1992—. Lectr. Pet Industry Joint Adv. Coun., 1996—. Asst. editor Avian Emergency Care A Manual for Emergency Clinics, 1990. Group leader Canine Coll., Kirkland, 1986-87; mentor Project Discovery, Edmonds, Wash., 1989, 95-96; leader Explorer scout troop Boy Scouts Am., St. Louis, 1981; chair King County Animal Control Citizens Adv. Com., 1991-97; bus. cons. Jr. Achievement, 1994-95, 95-96. Mem. AVMA, Assn. Avian Veterinarians (pub. rels. com. 1989-95, chmn. client edn. com. 1995-96), Wash. State Vet. Med. Assn. (editors and pub. com. newsletter), Seattle-King County Vet. Med. Assn. (rep. South Snohomish chpt. 1990—, chmn. ethics com. 1991-94, pres. 1995-97), Finch Lovers Puget Sound (co-founder, sec.-treas. 1987-91), Avicultural Soc. Puget Sound, N.W. Exotic Bird Soc., Pacific N.W. Herpetological Soc., Rotary (charter Mountlake Terrace, sgt.-at-arms 1994-96, cmty. svc. dir. 1997-2000, Lake Forest Pk. chpt. 2000—, sgt.-at-arms, 2003—), Assn. N.W. Avian Vet. (co-founder 1989—, pres. 1994-96). Avocations: reading, camping, aquarium keeping, gardening, dog training. Office: A Pet Care Clinic 23502 56th Ave W Mountlake Terrace WA 98043-5204

CANNON, CHRISTOPHER BLACK, congressman; b. Salt Lake City, Utah, Oct. 20, 1950; m. Claudia Fox, 1978; 8 children. BS and law degree, Brigham Young U. Bar: Utah 1980. Asptd. asst. assoc. solicitor Dept. Interior, 1983—84, assoc. solicitor, 1984—86; cons. to Asst. Sec. Productivity, Tech. and Innovation Dept. Commerce, 1986—87; co-owner Geneva Steel, Orem, Utah, 1987—90; owner Cannon Industries, Inc., 1990—95; Utah fin. chmn., 1995—96; mem. nat. fin. com. Lamar Alexander for Pres., 1995—96; mem. US Congress, 3rd Utah dist., 1996—; chmn. Subcom. on Commercial and Adminstrv. Law; mem. Com. on Govt Reform. Mem. Resources, Judiciary, and Sci. coms. Mem. nat. fin. com., Utah fin. chmn. Pres. George Bush Re-election Campaign, 1991—92; del. Rep. Nat. Conv., 1992, 1996; fin. chmn. Utah Rep. Party, 1991—92. Republican. Office: 51 S University Ave Ste 317 Provo UT 84606 also: 118Cannon House Office Bldg Washington DC 20515 Business E-Mail: cannon.ut03@mail.house.gov.*

CANNON, CHRISTOPHER PAUL, cardiologist; b. N.Y.C., Sept. 28, 1960; MD, Columbia U., 1986. Diplomate Am. Bd. Internal Medicine, Am. Bd. Cardiovasc. Disease. Intern Presbyn. Hosp., N.Y.C., 1986-87, resident in internal medicine, 1987-89; fellow in cardiology Brigham & Womens Hosp., Boston, 1989-92; asst. prof. medicine Harvard U., Boston, 1993—2002, assoc. prof., 2002—. Hosp. appt.: Brigham & Women's Hosp., Boston. Mem. Am. Coll. Cardiology, Am. Coll. Chest Physicians, Am. Heart Assn., Mass. Med. Soc. Office: Brigham & Womens Hosp Cardiovascular Divsn 75 Francis St Boston MA 02115-6106

CANNON, CRIS A. protective services official; b. Birmingham, Ala., Feb. 27, 1960; s. Thurmond Gray and Elaine Patricia (Deal) C.; m. Barbara Jean Bent. Cert. police firearms instr. NRA; peace officer cert., Ohio, Ala.; lic. class C pvt. investigator Ohio. Police officer Dayton (Ohio) Police Dept., 1984-88, Springville (Ala.) Police Dept., 1988-89; chief police Ashville (Ala.) Police Dept., 1989-97; sgt. Sinclair C.C. Campus Police, Dayton, 1997—. Owner Cannon Confidential Investigations, Dayton, 1998-99. Author: A Picture History of the Great Dayton Flood, 1999. Sgt. USAF, 1978-82. Recipient Legion of Honor for Line of Duty Injury, Am. Police Hall Fame, Miami, Fla., 1989, Disting. Svc. medal Am. Police Hall Fame, Miami, 1989, Silver Star for Bravery, Am. Police Hall Fame, Miami, 1989. Mem. NRA, Am. Legion, USAF Wright-Patterson AFB Officers Club, Cherokee Tribe N.E. Ala., Cherokee Warriors' Soc. Avocations: motorcycling, sailing, golfing, archery, muzzleloading. Home: 3824 Cleveland Ave Dayton OH 45410 Office: Sinclair CC 444 W 3d St Dayton OH 45402 E-mail: cig45@earthlink.net.

CANNON, DAVID C. mechanical engineer, consultant; b. Raleigh, N.C., Sept. 27, 1937; s. Doyle L. and Katherine C. (Coker) Cannon; m. Patsy Sturgeon, Feb. 12, 1977; children: Patricia, Mary, Ann, Katherine, John, Ben. BSME, Clemson U., 1959; MSME, Case Inst., 1965. Registered profl. engr., S.C. Sr. project engr. Sonoco Products Co., Hartsville, SC, 1965-87; pres. Edisto Shrimp Co., Edisto Island, SC, 1987-92, Edisto Seafarms, Inc., Edisto Island, 1993—2001. Pres. Edisto Beach Property Owners Assn., 2002—03. 1st lt. Ordnance Corps U.S. Army, 1960—68. Mem.: ASME, Global Aquaculture Alliance, S.C. Shrimp Growers Assn., S.C. Aquaculture Assn., World Aquaculture Soc. Methodist. Achievements include patents for square column form; die cutter feeder; disposable beer keg. Home and Office: PO Box 370 Edisto Island SC 29438 E-mail: dccannon@earthlink.net.

CANNON, DAVID JOSEPH, lawyer; b. Milw., Aug. 6, 1933; s. George W. and Florence (Dean) c.; m. Carol Nevins, Mar. 10, 1962; children: Charles, Courtney. BS, Marquette U., 1955, JD, 1960. Bar: Wis. 1960, U.S. Dist. Ct. (ea. dist.) Wis. 1960, U.S. Ct. Appeals (7th cir.) 1969, U.S. Ct. Appeals (8th cir.) 1976, U.S. Dist. Ct. (we. dist.) Wis. 1976, U.S. Ct. Appeals (5th cir.) 1978, U.S.

Ct. Appeals (4th cir.) 1997. Atty. Cannon & Cannon, Milw., 1960-66; asst. dist. atty. Milw. County Dist. Atty., 1966-68, dist. atty., 1968; U.S. atty. Dept. Justice Ea. Dist. Wis., Milw., 1969-73; ptnr. Michael, Best & Friedrich, Milw., 1973—. Home: 1520 Sunset Dr Elm Grove WI 53122-1629 Office: Michael Best & Friedrich 100 E Wisconsin Ave Ste 3300 Milwaukee WI 53202-4108

CANNON, DAVID PRICE, video executive, advertising consultant; b. Pitts., Mar. 1, 1946; s. Daniel Willard and Ann Marshall (Price) C.; m. Jaymee Denise Ives, May 20, 1967 (div. Jan. 1971); m. Joanne Marie Hauck, Jan. 5, 1973; children: Jesse Rhys, Ashley Dunbar. BA in Am. Civilization, U. Miami, 1969. Media dir. Lasky Advt., Bloomfield, N.J., 1969-70, v.p., creative dir., 1972-75; freelance writer Montclair, N.J., 1975-77; v.p., copywriter Edwin Bird Wilson, N.Y.C., 1977-78, assoc. creative dir., 1978-80; owner, pres. Collective Unconscious, Inc., Upper Montclair, N.J., 1979—; producer Video Encore, Upper Montclair, 1979—; cameraman Videotape Highlights of Your Life, Upper Montclair, 1979—; creative dir. Tollin Advt./Graphics 55/Block Advt./Morello Design, NJ, 1984—. Cons. Fuji, Samsung, Apple and Scena Videotapes, N.Y.C., 1981-99, Burett Swiss Sports Watches, 1996—; promotion cons. Goodtimes Home Video, N.Y.C., 1986-90; audio/video prodr. Cath. Girls band, Newark, 1983; mgr. Distractions rock band, 1991-92, Caution rock band, 1992; instr. advt. Credit Suisse/N.Y., N.Y.C., 1987. Author: (novelty catalog) Cat's Pajamas Swell Stuff, 1983—; creator (comic persona) The Corporate Jester, 1980; contbg. to William Safire's lang. compendium Coming to Terms, 1991; asst. editor Supplicant Fanzine, 1996—; contbr. articles to profl. jours.; pioneered the use of video tape recs. in courtroom, delivery room, other events. Contbg. researcher U.S. Ho. of Reps. Select Com. on Assassinations, Washington, 1978. Recipient numerous Town Crier awards Fin. Advt. and Mktg. Assn. N.Y., 1974-78, N.J. Ad Club awards, 1990, 91, 92, 93, 97, Percy award N.J. Healthcare Pub. Rels. Soc., 1996, Penny award Bank Mktg. Assn., 2000, award Art Dirs. Club of NJ, 1996, 2002. Home and Office: 9 Carriage Way Montclair NJ 07042-2118

CANNON, FREDERICK SCOTT, water engineer, educator, consultant; b. Mar. 30, 1954; s. Robert Hamilton and Dorothea (Alta) Cannon; m. Lizabeth Ann Lehman, Oct. 27, 1979; children: Scott Joseph, Amy Marie, Christy Rose. BS, U. Calif., Davis, 1977; MS, Stanford U., 1978, Engr., 1980; PhD, U. Ill., 1993. Registered chem. engr., civil engr., mech. engr., Calif., Colo. Engring. aide Bur. of Reclamation, Yuma, Ariz., 1974—75; lab. tech. Stanford U., Calif., 1978—80; engr. Montgomery Engrs., Phoenix, 1980—81; project engr. Brown & Caldwell, Pasadena, Calif., 1981—84; project mgr. McLaughlin Water Engrs., Denver, 1984—90; rsch. asst. U. Ill., 1990—93; asst. prof. Pa. State U., State College, 1993—99, prof., 1999—. Mem. editl. adv. bd.: Jour. Am. Water Works Assn.; contbr. articles to profl. jours. Mem.: Am. Assn. Environ. Engring. Profs., Toastmasters, Tau Beta Pi. Office: Pa State Univ Civil & Environ Dept 212 Sackett Engring Bldg State College PA 16802 E-mail: fcannon@psu.edu.

CANNON, G. ALAN, mathematician, educator; b. Houston, Tex., July 16, 1966; s. Henry Timothy and Lynette Lisbony Cannon. BS Math. Sci., BS Curriculum and Instrn., Tex. A&M U., Coll. Sta., Tex., 1988, MS Math., 1990, PhD Math., 1995. Cert. Sec. Tchg. Tex., 1988. Grad. tchg. asst. Tex. A&M U., Coll. Sta., Tex., 1988—95; asst. prof. of math. Southeastern La. U., Hammond, La., 1995—2001; vis. prof. of math. U. Klagenfurt, Klagenfurt, Austria, 2001—01; assoc. prof. of math. Southeastern La. U., Hammond, La., 2001—. Contbr. articles to prol. jour. Recipient McDonald's Grad. Asst. Tchg. Award, Tex. A&M U., 1992, Guseman Award (Tchg. and Svc.), Tex. A&M U. Dept. of Math., 1995, Hon. Mem., Southeastern La. U. Student Govt. Assn., 2000. Mem.: Nat. Coun. of Tchrs. of Math., Math. Assn. of Am., Am. Math. Soc., Project Kaleidoscope, Pi Mu Epsilon Math. Avocations: movies, travel. Office: Dept Math Southeastern La Univ SLU 10687 Hammond LA 70402 E-mail: acannon@selu.edu.

CANNON, GARLAND, linguist, educator; b. Fort Worth, Dec. 5, 1924; m. Patricia Richardson, 1947; children— Margaret, India, Jennifer, William. BA in English, U. Tex., 1947, PhD in English Linguistics, 1954; MA in English, Stanford U., 1952. Instr. U. Hawaii, Honolulu, 1949-52; instr. U. Tex., Austin, 1952-54, U. Mich., Ann Arbor, 1954-55; asst. prof. speech U. Calif.-Berkeley, 1955-56; acad. dir. Am. U. Lang. Ctr., Bangkok, 1956-57; asst. prof. English U. Fla., Gainesville, 1957-58; vis. prof. linguistics U. P.R., 1958-59; asst. prof. linguistics Columbia U., N.Y.C., 1959-62; dir. English lang. program for Afghanistan, Kabul, 1960—62; assoc. prof. Northeastern Ill. U., Chgo., 1962-63, Queens Coll., CUNY, 1963-66; assoc. prof. English Tex. A&M U., College Station, 1966-68, prof. English, 1968—; vis. prof. humanities U. Mich., 1970-71; vis. prof. linguistics Kuwait U., 1979-81. Vis. prof. linguistics Inst. Teknologi Mara, Kuala Lumpur, 1987; vis. summer prof. Cambridge U., 1980, Oxford U., 1974, MIT, 1969, U. Wash., 1967; lectr. throughout world Author: Sir William Jones, Orientalist: A Bibliography, 1952, Biography, 1964, A History of the English Language, 1972, An Integrated Transformational Grammar of the English Language, 1978, Sir William Jones: A Bibliography of Primary and Secondary Sources, 1979, Historical Change and English Word-Formation, 1987, Oriental Jones: The Life and Mind of Sir William Jones, 1990, Arabic Loanwords in English, 1994, (with A. Pfeffer) German Loanwords in English, 1994, Japanese Loanwords in English, 1996, (with A. Kaye) Persian Loanwords in English, 2001; editor: The Letters of Sir William Jones, 1970 (Book of Yr. Sunday London Telegraph 1970); editor: The Collected Works of Sir William Jones, 1993, Objects of Enquiry: The Life and Influences of Sir William Jones, 1995; contbr. numerous articles to profl. jours. Recipient Disting. Achievement award Tex. A&M U., 1972; Indian Govt. grantee, 1984; Linguistic Soc. Am./Am. Council Learned Socs. grantee, 1984; Am. Philos. Soc. grantee, Eng., 1964, 66, 74 Mem. MLA (exec. com. gen. linguistics discussion group 1982-85, chmn. 1984, 85, exec. com. present-day-English 1986-89, 94-97, exec. com. lexicography 1986-89, chmn. 1989, rep. to del. assembly 1985-88), Am. Dialect Soc. (exec. coun. 1989-93), Dictionary Soc. N.Am., South Asian Lit. Assn. (pres. 1979-85). Office: Tex A&M U Dept English College Station TX 77843-0001

CANNON, GRACE BERT, immunologist; b. Chambersburg, Pa., Jan. 29, 1937; d. Charles Wesley and Gladys (Raff) Bert; m. W. Dilworth Cannon, June 3, 1961 (div. 1972); children: Michael Quayle Cannon, Susan Radcliffe Cannon Antolin, Peter Bert Cannon. AB, Goucher Coll., 1958; PhD, Washington U., St. Louis, 1962. Fellow Columbia U., N.Y.C., 1962-64, Columbia U. Coll. Physicians and Surgeons, N.Y.C., 1964-65; staff fellow NIH Nat. Cancer Inst., Bethesda, Md., 1966-67; cell biologist Litton Bionetics, Inc., Kensington, Md., 1972-80, head immunology sect., 1980-85; dir. sci. ImmuQuest Labs., Inc., Rockville, Md., 1985-88; pres. Biomedical Analytics, Inc., Rockville, Md., 1988-2001; mgr. ATLIS Fed. Svcs., Inc., Rockville, Md., 1991-95, dir. Silver Spring, Md., 1995-97; sr. assoc. United Info. Sys., Inc., Bethesda, Md., 1998—2000. Mem. contract rev. coms. Nat. Cancer Inst., 1983-87. Contbr. articles to profl. jours. Mem. Pub. Svc. Health Club, Bethesda, Md., 1984—, sec., 1990-2000. Grantee USPHS, 1959-65, NSF, 1959. Mem. AAAS, Am. Assn. for Cancer Rsch., N.Y. Acad. Sci., Sigma Xi. Home and Office: 2708 Oak Rd # 36 Walnut Creek CA 94597

CANNON, HERBERT SETH, investment banker; b. Bklyn., Dec. 3, 1931; s. Joseph and Gertrude (Kimmel) C.; m. Edith Marks, June 20, 1954; children: Naomi Sue, Nina Louise. BA, Washington and Jefferson Coll., 1953; student, Cornell U. Law Sch., 1953-54; LL.B., Fordham U., 1960. Salesman Manhattan Scalloping & Embroidery Co., N.Y.C., 1956-57; stock broker Hirsch & Co., N.Y.C., 1956-61, Wineman, Weiss & Co., N.Y.C., 1961-62; pres. Weis, Voisin, Cannon, Inc., N.Y.C., 1963-70; chmn. bd. Elgin Nat. Industries, Inc., N.Y.C., 1967-70; chmn. bd., pres. Cannon, Jerold & Co., Inc., 1970-73; chmn. bd. PUD Industries, Inc., 1971-83, CitiWide Capital Corp., 1984-88, CitiWide Securities Corp., 1984-88, pres. Cannon Enterprises Inc., real estate devel., investment bankers and fin. cons., Boca Raton, Fla., 1975-93; chmn. bd. Holistic Services Corp., 1979-83; pres. HSC Consulting, Inc., 1997—. Past trustee Washington and Jefferson Coll. Served with AUS, 1954-56. Mem. Young Pres. Orgn., World Bus. Council, Metro Pres. Orgn. Home and Office: 23402 Savona Ct Boca Raton FL 33433-6935 Office Fax: 561-361-0515. E-mail: HSC0039@aol.com. *Make it happen.*

CANNON, HUGH, lawyer; b. Albemarle, N.C., Oct. 11, 1931; s. Hubert Napoleon and Nettie (Harris) C.; m. Jo Anne Weisner, Mar. 21, 1988. AB, Davidson Coll., 1953; BA, Oxford U., 1955, MA, 1960; LLB, Harvard U., 1958. Bar: N.C. 1958, D.C. 1978, S.C. 1979. Mem. staff U. N.C. Inst. Govt., Chapel Hill, 1959; mem. firm Sanford, Phillips, McCoy & Weaver, Fayetteville, N.C., 1960; asst to Gov. of N.C., Raleigh, 1961; dir. adminstrn. State of N.C., 1962-65, state budget officer, 1963; mem., mng. ptnr. Sanford, Cannon, Adams & McCullough, Raleigh, 1965-79; pvt. practice Charleston, S.C., 1979—; mem. Everett, Gaskins, Hancock and Stevens attys., Raleigh, 1990—; v.p. gen. counsel Palmetto Ford, Inc., Charleston, 1979—. Author: Cannon's Concise Guide to Rules of Order, 1992. Parliamentarian NEA, 1965 ; mem. nat. adv. coun. Am. Inst. Parliamentarians; pres. Friends of Coll., Raleigh, 1963; alt. de. Dem. Nat. Conv., 1964, chief parliamentarian, 1976, 80, 84, 88, 92, 96; bd. govs. U. N.C., 1972-81; trustee Davidson Coll., 1966-74, N.C. Sch. Arts, 1963-72; mem. sch. bd. Charleston County, 2000—. Rhodes scholar, 1955. Mem. Phi Beta Kappa, Omicron Delta Kappa, Phi Gamma Delta. Episcopalian. Home: PO Box 31820 Charleston SC 29417-1820 Office: 1625 Savannah Hwy Charleston SC 29407-2236

CANNON, J. TIMOTHY, psychology educator, neuroscientist; b. Scranton, Pa., Aug. 26, 1949; s. Thomas F. and Nancy (Culkin) C.; m. Brooke J. Szuhay, Nov. 17, 1984; children, Jaye A., Linnea F.; children from previous marriage: Christina M., Sean T., Michael R. BS, U. Scranton, 1971; PhD, U. Maine, 1977. Postdoctoral fellow UCLA, 1977-81; prof. psychology U. Scranton, 1981—, dir. neurosci., 1987—, assoc. chair, 1987-2000. Chair IACUC, Scranton, 1985—. Contbr. articles to profl. jours. Named State of Pa. Prof. of Yr., Coun. for Advancement and Support of Edn., 1995; NSF ILI grantee, 1992. Mem. Internat. Assn. for Study of Pain, Soc. for Neurosci., Am. Psychol. Soc. Office: U Scranton Dept Psychology Alumni Meml Hall Scranton PA 18510-4596

CANNON, JOE LOUIS, retired orthodontist; b. Jan. 27, 1929; MS, DDS, U. Tenn., Memphis, 1957. Pvt. practice orthodontist, Memphis, 1957-98; ret. Col. USAF, 1949—53, Korea. Decorated Purple Heart, Legion of Merit, Disting. Flying Cross, Air Medal with three oak leaves. Home: 4834 Fleetview Ave Memphis TN 38117-3225

CANNON, JOHN, investment consultant; b. Phila., Jan. 17, 1930; s. John F. and Anne (Carlin) C.; m. Edythe Marple Grebe, Aug. 16, 1952; children: John III, Lynne, Anne. BS, U. Pa., 1954; MBA, Drexel Inst. Tech., 1956. Fin. analyst Bishop & Hedberg, Inc., Phila., 1956-58; rep. Stone & Webster Securities Corp., Phila., 1958-62; nat. sales mgr. mcpl. bond dept. Hallowell & Sulzberger, Phila., 1962-64; pres., dir. AMA Investment Advisers, Inc., Blue Bell, Pa., 1964-91, AMA Family Funds, Inc., Blue Bell, 1967-71, AMA Money Fund, 1982-91, Med. Tech. Fund., Inc., 1979-88, Emerging Med. Tech. Fund, 1984-88; dir. AMA Svcs. Inc., 1986-91; fin. svcs. bus. cons. Ambler, Pa., 1999—. Bd. dirs. Neuberger & Berman Funds, Oppenheimer Convertible Securities Fund, Oppenheimer/Rochester Fund Mcpls.; v.p. Janney, Montgomery, Scott, Inc., 1972-73; chmn., bd. dirs. CDC Capital Mgmt., Inc., Blue Bell, 1998-99. With USMCR, 1950-51. Mem. Fin. Analysts Am., Phila. Securities Assn., No-Load Mut. Fund Assn. (gov. 1979-89), Mfrs. Golf and Country Club (Oreland, Pa., pres. 1988-90), Royal Palm Yacht and Country Club (Boca Raton, Fla., treas.), Masons. Home: 531 Willow Ave Ambler PA 19002-6013

CANNON, JOHN, III, lawyer; b. Phila., Mar. 19, 1954; s. John and Edythe (Grebe) C. BA, Denison U., 1976; JD, Dickinson Sch. Law, 1983. Bar: Pa. 1983, Hawaii 1986, U.S. Dist. Ct. (ea. dist.) Pa. 1983, U.S. Ct. Appeals (3d cir.) 1985. Account exec. PRO Services, Inc., Flourtown, Pa., 1976-79, br. officer mgr. Pitts., 1979-80; law clk. Montgomery County Ct. of Common Pleas, Norristown, Pa., 1983-84; assoc. Rawle & Henderson, Phila., 1984-88; comml. litigation counsel CIGNA Corp., Phila., 1988-90; counsel fin. svcs. divsn. CIGNA Internat., Phila., 1990-93, sr. counsel, 1993-95, v.p., sr. counsel, 1995-97, sr. v.p., chief counsel, 1997-2000, CIGNA Healthcare, Bloomfield, Conn., 1999—2003, Conn. Gen. Life Ins. Co., Bloomfield, Conn., 1999—2003; sr. v.p. pub. affairs, assoc. gen. counsel CIGNA Corp., Phila., 2003—. V.p. Life Ins. Co. N.Am.; trustee U.S.-China Legal Coop. Fund, Washington, 1998—. Comments editor Dickinson Internat. Law Ann., 1983. Mem. ABA, Pa. Bar Assn., Hawaii State Bar Assn., Kappa Sigma (pres. 1975-76), Gamma Xi (v.p., trustee 1982-86). Republican. Episcopalian. Office: Cigna Corp 1650 Market St Philadelphia PA 19192

CANNON, JONATHAN Z. lawyer, educator; m. Alice P. Cannon; children: Ariel, Maia A., Benjamin Z. BA summa cum laude, Williams Coll., 1967; postgrad., Oxford U., 1967-68; JD cum laude, U. Pa., 1974. Law clk. U.S. Ct. Appeals (D.C. cir.), 1974-75; assoc. Beveridge & Diamond, P.C., 1975-80, ptnr., 1980-86; dep. gen. counsel, litigation and regional ops. Office Gen. Counsel, U.S. EPA, Washington, 1987; dep. asst. adminstr. Office Enforcement and Compliance Monitoring, U.S. EPA, Washington, 1987-88, Office Solid Waste and Emergency Response, U.S. EPA, Washington, 1988-89, acting asst. adminstr., 1989; ptnr. Beveridge & Diamond, P.C., 1990-92; dir. Gulf of Mexico Program U.S. EPA, Washington, 1992-93, acting asst. adminstr. Office Policy, Planning & Evaluation, 1993, acting dep. adminstr., spl. advisor to adminstr., 1993, asst. adminstr., CFO, Office Adminstrn. and Resource Mgmt., 1993-95, gen. counsel, 1995-98; prof. U. Va. Sch. Law, Charlottesville, 1998—. Lectr. environ. law U. Va. Sch. Law, 1983-87, 97—; adj. prof. environ. law Washington and Lee Law Sch., 1982-83. Office: U Va Sch Law 580 Massie Rd Charlottesville VA 22903-1738 E-mail: jzc8j@virginia.edu.

CANNON, JOSEPH A. steel products company executive, political party official; b. Salt Lake City, July 31, 1941; BA in Polit. Sci., Brigham Young U., 1974, JD cum laude, 1977. Asst. adminstr. EPA, 1981-85; assoc. Pillsbury, Madison & Sutro, Washington, 1985-87; dir. Geneva Steel Holdings Corp., Vineyard, Utah, 1987—, chmn. bd. dirs., 1987—, pres., 1987-91, CEO, 1991—. Chmn. Utah Rep. Party, 2001—. Mem. Am. Iron and Steel Inst. (dir., mem. policy and planning com.), N.Am. Steel Coun. Republican. Mem. LDS Ch. Office: Geneva Steel Holdings Corp 10 S Geneva Rd Vineyard UT 84058 also: Utah Rep Party 117 E South Temple Salt Lake City UT 84111*

CANNON, LOUIS SIMEON, journalist, author; b. N.Y.C., June 3, 1933; s. Jack and Irene (Kohn) C.; m. Virginia Oprian, Feb. 2, 1953 (div. 1983); children: Carl, David, Judy, Jack; m. Mary L. Shinkwin, Sept. 7, 1985. Student, U. Nev., 1950-51, San Francisco State U., 1951-52. Reporter Lafayette Sun, Calif., 1957; editor Newark (Calif.) Sun, 1957-58, Merced Sun Star, Calif., 1958-60, Contra Costa Times, Calif., 1960-61, San Jose (Calif.) Mercury News, Calif., 1961-69; Sacramento corr. San Jose Mercury News, Calif., 1965-69; Washington corr. Ridder Pubs., Washington, 1969-72; reporter The Washington Post, 1972-96, spl. corr., 1997-99. Author: Ronnie and Jesse, 1969, The McCloskey Challenge, 1972, Reporting: An Inside View, 1977, Reagan, 1982, President Reagan: The Role of a Lifetime, 1991, rev. and updated 2000, Official Negligence: How Rodney King and the Riots Changed Los Angeles and the LAPD, 1998, The Presidential Portfolio: Ronald Reagan, 2001, Governor Reagon: His Rise to Power, 2003. Recipient Gerald R. Ford prize Gerald Ford Libr., 1988, Merriman Smith award White House Corrs. Assn., 1986, Aldo Beckman award, 1984, Washington Journalism Rev. award, 1985, Disting. Reporting of Pub. Affairs award Am. Polit. Sci. Assn., 1968, Lifetime Achievement award Ctr. for Calif. Studies at Calif. State U., Sacramento, 2001. Mem. Soc. of Profl. Journalists, Authors Guild. Home: PO Box 436 Summerland CA 93067-0436 E-mail: cannonlou@hotmail.com.

CANNON, LYNNE MARPLE, investment management company executive; b. Phila., Oct. 14, 1955; d. John and Edythe (Grebe) C.; m. Richard W. Baksa, 1999. BA, Ohio Wesleyan U., 1977. Employee PRO Svcs. Inc., Flourtown, Pa., 1979-82, asst. sec., 1982-86; v.p. AMA Investment Advisers Inc. (formerly PRO Svcs. Inc.), Blue Bell, Pa., 1986-92; v.p., sec. AMA Family of Funds, Inc., 1986-92; v.p. Independence Capital Mgmt., Inc., Horsham, Pa., 1992-95, Independence Capital Group of Funds, Inc., 1992-95; sr. v.p. relationship mgmt. FPS Svcs., Inc., King of Prussia, Pa., 1995-98; v.p. client svcs. PFPC Inc., King of Prussia, 1998—. Dir. devel. Stratton Mgmt., Inc., 1995—; chmn. sml. funds com. Investment Co . Inst., 1994-99; dir. The Stratton Funds, Inc., Plymouth Meeting, Pa., 1995—, FPS Broker Svcs., Inc., 1996-98. Vol. Plant Ambler Inc., Pa., 1983-2002. Mem. Mut. Fund Edn. Alliance (bd. govs. 1990-91), Phila. Saddle Club (bd. dirs., v.p.), Wodehouse Soc. Republican. Episcopalian. Home: Twin Hills Farm 115 Hess Rd Collegeville PA 19426 Office: PFPC Inc 760 Moore Rd King Of Prussia PA 19406

CANNON, MAJOR TOM, special education educator; b. Anniston, Ala., Nov. 11, 1932; s. Thomas Albert and Sallie Mae (James) C. BA in Liberal Arts, Samford U., 1961; postgrad., So. Bapt. Theol. Sem., 1961-62, Tulane U., 1962-63, Auburn U., 1963-64; MEd in Counseling, U. Ga., 1968; postgrad., U. S.C., 1971, 81, 84, Francis Marion Coll., 1979—80, Western Md. Coll., 1980, S.C. State Coll., 1981-85, U. Charleston, 1993, The Citadel, Charleston, S.C., 1996-97, Charleston So. U., Francis Marion Coll., 2000, postgrad., 2003. Cert. prin., guidance counselor, spl. edn. tchr., psychology, S.C. English tchr. North Whitfield H.S., Dalton, Ga., 1964-65, Savannah (Ga.) H.S., 1965-66; guidance counselor Savannah Pub. Schs., 1966-79; dir. spl. svcs. Marlboro County Sch. Dist., Bennettsville, S.C., 1979-80, coord. programs for handicapped, 1980-81; tchr. trainable mentally retarded Edisto Mid. Sch., Orangeburg, S.C., 1981-86; tchr. learning disabled Norman C. Toole Mid. Sch., Charleston, S.C., 1986-88, Berkeley Mid. Sch., Moncks Corner, S.C., 1988-97, chmn. dept. spl. edn., 1991-94; specialist learning disabilities Berkeley County Sch. Dist., Moncks Corner, 1995-97; resource C.E. Murray H.S., Greeleyville, S.C., 1997—. Labor resources technician City of Savannah, 1979; presenter in field; mem. Strategic Planning Com. for Berkeley County Sch. Dist., 1993-97, Sch. Improvement Coun., 1996-97. Contbr. poetry to Great Poems of the Western World, 1990, Our World's Favorite Gold and Silver Poems, 1991, Perceptions, 1994, Am. Poetry Annual, 1994; author resource manuals and videotaped lessons. Charter Rep. Nat. Com., 1992—, Rep. Presdl. Task Force, 1989—, Rep. Nat. Commn. on Am. Agenda, 1996, Nat. Rep. Senatorial Com., 1990—; at-large del. Rep. Party Platform Planning Com.; mem. Ga. Com. on Children and Youth, 1968. With USN, 1953-57. Recipient Nat. Def. Edn. award U.S. Office of Edn., 1966-67, GE Found. award, 1971, Rep. Presdl. Legion of Merit, 1992-2001, Rep. Presdl. award, 1994, Rep. Presdl. Order of Merit, 1997. Mem. ASCD, ASPCA, AARP, Acad. Am. Poets, Nat. Authors Registry, Coun. for Exceptional Children, Am. Pers. and Guidance Assn., Am. Sch. Counselors Assn. (Ga. coord.), Nat. Assn. Sch. Counselors., Am. Legion, VFW (life), Ga. Assn. Educators, Ga. Pers. and Guidance Assn., Palmetto Tchrs. Assn., Sierra Club, Nature Conservancy, Nat. Resources Def. Coun., World Wildlife Soc., Defenders of Wildlife, Rainforest Alliance, Ocean Conservancy, Nat. Trust for Hist. Preservation, Civil War Preservation Trust, Environ. Def., Heritage Found., Nat. Pks. Conservancy Assn., Humane Soc. U.S., Phi Delta Kappa, Kappa Delta Pi. Republican. Baptist. Avocations: coin collecting, pets, scientific experiments, historical studies. Home: 324 Tulane Dr Ladson SC 29456-6235

CANNON, MARK WILCOX, government official, business executive; b. Salt Lake City, Aug. 29, 1928; s. Joseph Jenne and Ramona (Wilcox) C.; m. Ruth Marian Dixon, Dec. 28, 1956 (div. Jun. 1992); children: Lucile, Mark, Kristen Cannon Brown. m. Betty Ann Schomann, June 25, 1993. Student, Deep Springs Coll., 1944-46; BA, U. Utah, 1949; MA, Harvard U., 1954, MPA, 1955, PhD, 1961. Missionary Ch. Jesus Christ of Latter-Day Saints, Argentina, 1949-52; rsch. analyst Utah Found., 1953; sec. Utah Sch. Merit Study Com., 1954; instr. Brigham Young U., 1955, chmn. dept. polit. sci., 1961-64; mem. staff U.S. Senator W.F. Bennett, 1961, 62-63; adminstrv. asst. to U.S. congressman Henry A. Dixon, 1956-61; mem. staff Inst. Pub. Adminstrn., N.Y.C., 1964-72, dir. urban devel. program, 1964-65, dir. internat. programs, 1965-68, dir., 1968-72; adminstrv. asst. to chief justice of U.S., 1972-85; staff dir. Commn. on Bicentennial of U.S. Constn., 1985-88; vice chmn., bd. dirs. Geneva Steel; exec. v.p. Geneva Devel., 1988-89; vice chair Cannon Industries, 1989-96. Venture capitalist, 1989—; guest scholar Woodrow Wilson Internat. Ctr. for Scholars, 1989. Author: (with R. Joseph Monsen) The Makers of Public Policy: American Power Groups and Their Ideologies, 1965; (with others) Partnership for Progress: Atlanta-Fulton County Consolidation, 1969, Urban Government for Valencia, 1973, Views From The Bench: The Judiciary and Constitutional Politics, 1985; contbg. author: Development Administration in Latin America, 1973; contbr. articles to profl. jour.; mem. editorial bd. Judicature, 1975-76. Trustee Inst. Pub. Adminstrn. Recipient ann. award Western Polit. Sci. Assn., 1963 Mem. Nat. Acad. Pub. Adminstrn., Internat. Studies Assn. (sec. 1962-63). Home: 8360 Greensboro Dr Apt 917 Mc Lean VA 22102-3543 E-mail: mwcannon@erols.com. *Much of my motivation, orientation, and values stem from a conviction of the masterful leadership of a perfect personal God who is exemplary in His knowledge and utilization of eternal laws to promote the eternal progress and happiness of each human being, partially by providing a complicated earthly learning environment and by permitting people to deal freely with individual and social problems, thereby providing laboratory opportunities for the flourishing of character, knowledge, and wisdom.*

CANNON, MICHAEL R. manufacturing executive; b. 1953; V.p. S.E. Asia ops. Imprimis Tech.; sr. v.p. Syquest Tech. Inc.; various positions including v.p. mobile & desktop bus. unit IBM, v.p. product design, v.p. worldwide ops.; pres., CEO Maxtor, 1996—. Office: Maxtor 510 Cottonwood Dr Milpitas CA 95035

CANNON, OCTAVIA MANETTA, obstetrician-gynecologist; b. Shelbyville, Tenn., Feb. 8, 1967; d. Harvey and Roberta C. BS, Johnson C. Smith U., 1988; D in Osteopathic Medicine, Nova Southeastern U., 1995. Fellow Am. Bd. Osteopathe Ob-Gyn. Intern (chief) Mich. Hosp. Med. Ctr., Detroit, 1995-96; resident St. John Health Systems, Detroit, 1996-99; dir. women's health physician Gaston Co. Health Dept., Gastonia, N.C., 1999—. Clin. faculty Mich. State U. Coll. Osteopathic Medicine, East Lansing, 1996-2001, nat. rep. ACOOG Residency Eval. Com., Pontiac, Mich., 1996-98, postgrad. physician Sec. co-chair Nat. Med. Assn., Washington, D.C., 2002—. AMA Women's Political Action Com., 1997—, Minority Awareness Com., 1997—; vol. Charolette-Meck Pub. Sch., 2000—. Recipient Best Case (OB/Gyn) Presentation award St. John Health Systems, 1997; named one of Outstanding Young Women of Am., 1988, 91, 95. Mem. Am. Coll. Osteopathic OB/Gyn. (cert.), Am. Osteopathic Assn., Am. Med. Assn., Nat. nominating com. Outstanding Young Men of Am. Democrat. Methodist. Avocations: reading, listening to music, creative writing, watching football and basketball. Office: Gaston Co Health Dept 991 W Hudson Blvd Gastonia NC 28052-6430 E-mail: ocgyn@aol.com.

CANNON, PATRICK D. federal offical, broadcaster; married; five children. Comm. specialist Mich. Dept. Labor, Bur. Workers' Disability; staff rsch. specialist; dir. Senate Cul. Office, Audio Comm. Divsn.; exec. dir. Mich. Commn. Disability Concern, Lansing, 1988-97, Mich. Commn. Blind, Lansing, 1997—. Bd. dirs. Capital Area Transp. Authority; mem. Pres.'s Com. Employment People with Disabilites; apptd. U.S. access Bd., 1995; presentor in field. Mem. Pres.'s com. Employment of People with Disabilities, Gov.'s com. People with Disabilities, Access Bd., 1995—, Advanced Am. with Disabilities Act Tng. Network, Capital Area Ctr. Indep. Living, All Peoples' Theater, Riverwalk Theater; bd. trustees BoarsHead Theater, Capitol Area Transp. Authority; co-chair Gov.'s State Am. with Disabilites Act Implementation Task Force; chair Mich. Am. with Disabilities Act Steering Com.; trainer Windmills; active People's Theatre, Easter Seal Soc., St. Vincent Home. Mem. Nat. Rehab. Assn.. Avocations: baseball, movies, theater, hotdogs, sunshine. Office: Mich Commn Blind PO Box 30652 Lansing MI 48909-8152

CANNON, PATRICK FRANCIS, public relations executive; b. Braddock, Pa., Mar. 2, 1938; s. Peter J. and Kathleen (Donnelly) C.; children by previous marriage: Patrick F. Jr., Elizabeth Kathleen; m. Jeanette Krema, Nov. 22, 1986. BA, Northwestern U., 1969. Ops. mgr. Compact Industries, Albert Lea, Minn., 1968-72; pub. info. dir. Dept. Pub. Works, Chgo., 1970-72; acct. exec. Humes & Assocs., Chgo., 1972-77; freelance journalist, cons. Oak Park, Ill., 1977-79; mgr. pub. rels. and prodn. Lions Clubs Internat., Oak Brook, Ill., 1979-2001; pvt. comms. cons., writer, 2001—. Editor: Water in Rural America, 1973, Wastewater in Rural America, 1974, We Serve: A History of the Lions Clubs, 1991; contbr. articles to profl. jours. and mags.; exec. producer, writer (pub. TV documentaries) With Very Little...Blindness Prevention in Developing Countries, 1991, The Search for Light, 1993, A Dangerous Time for Kids, 1997. Exec. dir. Civic Arts Coun. Oak Park, 1977-79; bd. dirs. interpreter coun. Oak Park Tour Ctr., 1978-82, mem. vol. svc. com. Frank Lloyd Wright Home and Studio Found., 1988-94, mem. pub. programs com., 1995-96, chmn. Wright Plus Housewalk, 1996; mem. bd. advisors U.S. Internat. Film and Video Festival; mem. internat. bd. advisors World Media Festival. Named PR All Star 1996, Inside PR Mag.; recipient awards Publicity Club of Chgo., PRSA, Internat. Assn. of Bus. Comms., U.S. Film and Video Festival, others. Mem. Lions (pres. 1983-84). Roman Catholic. Avocations: history, horse racing. Home and Office: 243 Iowa St Oak Park IL 60302-2347 E-mail: patnette@aol.com.

CANNON, ROBERT EUGENE, library director; b. Dec. 20, 1945; s. Wendell Eugene and Louise Marie (Bredehoeft) C.; m. Miriam Ruth Hillson, May 25, 1974; 1 child, Alexander BA in Music, Calif. State U., L.A., 1967; postgrad., Ariz. State U., 1967-68; MS in Lib. Sci., U. So. Calif., 1970; M in Pub. Adminstrn., San Diego State U., 1978. Adult svcs. libr. Tucson Pub. Libr., 1969-70, Altadena Libr. Dist., 1970-71; head tech. processing, regional coord. San Diego County Libr., 1971-76; asst. dir. Tulare County Libr., Visalia, Calif., 1976-78; dir. Kern County Libr., Bakersfield, Calif., 1978-86; exec. dir. Pub. Libr. of Charlotte and Mecklenburg County, 1986—2003; dir. librs. divsn. Broward County, Ft. Lauderdale, Fla., 2003—. Mem. bd. dirs. Mecklenburg County Law & Govt. Libr., Inc., 1992—; sec., treas. Pub. Libr. Charlotte & Mecklenburg County, 1986—; sec. Mus. New South, 1991-93, bd. dirs., 1991-97. Former mem. Leadership Charlotte; founder Novello Festival of Reading, 1991—, ProSearch Info. Svc., 1991—96, Internat. Bus. Libr., 1994—2003, Virtual Libr., 1995—2000, Virtual Village Comm. Ctr., 2000—, BizLink, 1998—, (wwebsites) Readers Club, 1999—, StoryPlace, 2000—, Brarydog.net, 1999—, BookHive, 1999—; co-founder Charlotte's Web, 1995—2000; bd. vis. Sch. Info. and Libr. Sci. U. N.C., Chapel Hill; bd. vis. Johnson C. Smith U.; mem. steering com. Charlotte Alliance Info. Referral Svcs., 1995—97; mem. Internat. Network Pub. Librs. Bertelsman Found., Germany, 1996—; mem. leadership group Charlotte Reads, 2001—03; mem. steering com. Leave a Legacy, 1998—2003; mem. Leadership Cir. United Way of Ctrl. Carolinas, 1997—; co-founder Novello Festival Press, 2000—; founder ImaginOn: The Joe and Joan Martin Ctr., 2003—, ImginOn.org, 2003—; bd. dirs. Smart Start of Charlotte Mecklenburg, 2000—03. Named N.C. Libr. Dir. of Yr., N.C. Pub. Libr. Dirs. Assn, 1995, Local Hero, Creative Loafing newspaper; recipient Pegasus award, Pub. Rels. Soc. Am., 1998. Mem. ALA, N.C. Libr. Assn., Charlotte/Mecklenburg Coalition for Literacy, 1988-89, Kern County Hist. Records Commn. (vice chmn. 1978-86), Southeastern Libr. Assn. (treas., chmn. conf. com. 1993-95), Mecklenburg Hist. Assn., Cultural Edn. Collaboration (bd. dirs. 1998-2000). Office: Pub Libr Charlotte & Mecklenburg County 310 N Tryon St Charlotte NC 28202-2176

CANNON, ROBERT HAMILTON, JR., aerospace engineering educator; b. Cleve., Oct. 6, 1923; s. Robert Hamilton and Catharine (Putnam) C.; m. Dorothea Alta Collins, Jan. 4, 1945 (dec. Apr. 1988); children: Philip Gregory, Douglas Charles, Beverly Jo, Frederick Scott, David John, Joseph Collins, James Robert; m. Vera Berlin Crie, May 27, 1989. BS, U. Rochester, 1944; Sc.D. (du Pont fellow), MIT, 1950. Rsch. engr. Baker Mfg. Co., Evansville, Wis., 1946-50; instr. MIT, 1949-50; research engr. Bendix Aviation Research Labs., Detroit, 1950-51; with Autonetics div. N.Am. Aviation Inc., Downey, Calif., 1951-57, supr. automatic flight control systems, 1951-54, systems engr. inertial nav. instruments and systems, 1954-57; assoc. prof. mech. engring. MIT, 1957-59; mem. faculty Stanford U., 1959-74, prof. aeros. and astronautics, 1962-74, dir. Guidance and Control Lab., 1960-69; chief scientist USAF, 1966-68; asst. sec. U.S. Dept. Transp. Washington, 1970-74; chmn. div. engring. and applied sci. Calif. Inst. Tech., Pasadena, 1974-79; Charles Lee Powell prof. aeronautics and astronautics Stanford U., 1979—, chmn. dept., 1979-90, dir. aerospace robotics lab., 1980—97, dir. emeritus, 1997—; chmn. sci. adv. com. to CEO GM, 1979-84. Mem. Draper Corp., 1975—; vice chmn. sci. adv. bd. USAF, 1968-70; chmn. assembly engring. NRC, 1974-75, chmn. energy engring. bd., 1975-81, com. on nuclear and alt. energy sources, 1975-78, aeros. and space engring. bd., 1975-79, 85-92, governing bd., 1976-78, ocean studies bd., 1991-94; chmn. Gen. Electric Space Sta. Adv. Bd., 1985-87; chmn. Pres.'s Com. on Nat. Medal of Sci., 1984-88; chmn. NASA Flight Telerobotic Servicer Commn., 1987-91; tech. adv. coun. Boeing Corp., 1984-94, R.R. Donnelley, 1984-89, Comsat, 1985-87, United Techs. Corp., 1989-92; commn. underwater vehicles Marine Bd. Author: Dynamics of Physical Systems, 1967; also articles. Served to lt. (j.g.) USNR, 1944-46. Fellow AIAA (dir. 1968-70), Am. Acad. Arts and Scis., Internat. Acad. Astronautics; mem. Nat. Acad. Engring. (councillor 1975-81), Sigma Xi, Theta Chi (chpt. pres. 1943-44), Tau Beta Pi. Presbyterian. Achievements include devel. hydrofoil boats, automatic flight control, inertial guidance instruments and systems, space vehicle control, drag free satellite, gyro test of gen. relativity, tech. assessment of climatic impact of stratospheric flight, wave-actuated upwelling pump, flexible robot and space robot control systems, underwater free-flying robots, autonomous task-commanded helicopter, nat. energy alternatives. Office: Stanford U Dept Aeronautics & Astronautics Durand Bldg Rm 357 Stanford CA 94305-8468

CANNON, THOMAS ROBERTS, lawyer; b. Durham, N.C., May 22, 1940; s. Edward Lee and Elizabeth Hendren (Roberts) C.; m. Martha Craig White, Feb. 19, 1966; children: Caroline Craig, Thomas Roberts Jr. AB, U. N.C., 1962, JD, 1965; postgrad., U. Va., 1962-63. Bar: N.C. 1965, U.S. Dist. Ct. (we. dist.) N.C. 1969, U.S. Ct. Appeals (4th cir.) 2000; cert. specialist in family law. Ptnr. Helms, Cannon, Henderson & Porter, P.A., Charlotte, NC, 1985—2000, Horack, Talley, Pharr & Lowndes, Charlotte, 2000—. Served with USNR, 1968-89. Recipient John Motley Morehead scholarship, 1958-62. Fellow Am. Acad. Matrimonal Lawyers; mem. ABA, N.C. Bar Assn. (chmn. family law sect. 1982-83), N.C. State Bar (bd. legal specialization, family law certification com. 1988-94), Charlotte Country Club, Charlotte City Club, Soc. of the Lees of Va.. Presbyterian. Home: 2611 Beretania Cir Charlotte NC 28211-3635 Office: 301 S College St Ste 2600 Charlotte NC 28202-6044 E-mail: tcannon@horacktalley.com.

CANNON, WILLIAM BERNARD, retired university educator; b. Cascade, Iowa, Nov. 10, 1920; s. Charles Bernard and Irma (White) C.; m. Jeanne Adair Ketchum, Aug. 16, 1944; children: Julia, Dominic, William, Robert. Ph.B., U. Chgo., 1947; MA, 1949. Budget examiner Bur. Budget, 1951-54, 59-62; asst. v.p. U. Chgo., 1954-59, v.p. programs and projects, 1968-74; dean Lyndon B. Johnson Sch. Pub. Affairs, U. Tex. at Austin, 1974-75; v.p. bus. and fin. U. Chgo., 1976-83, prof., 1976-89, prof. emeritus, 1989—. Asst. chief, office legis. reference for health, edn. and welfare programs Bur. Budget, 1962-65, chief edn., manpower and sci. div., 1965-67; dep. chmn. Nat. Endowment for the Arts, 1968 Mem. selection com. Rockefeller Pub. Service Awards, 1976-81; mem. Midwest selection com. H.S. Truman Scholarship Program, 1977-87. Served with AUS, 1943-46. Mem. Phi Beta Kappa. Home: 2102 Bowman Ave Austin TX 78703-2306

CANO, KRISTIN MARIA, lawyer; b. McKeesport, Pa., Oct. 27, 1951; d. John S. and Sally (Kavic) C. BS in Biochemistry, Pa. State U., 1973; MS in Forensic Sci., George Washington U., 1975; JD, Southwestern U., 1978; LLM in Securities Regulation, Georgetown U., 1984. Bar: Calif. 1978, U.S. Dist. Ct. (cen., no. and so. dists.) Calif. 1984, U.S. Dist. Ct. Ariz., 1988, U.S. Supreme Ct. 1988, U.S. Ct. Appeals (9th cir.) 1992. Assoc. Yusim, Cassidy, Stein & Hanger, Beverly Hills, Calif., 1979-81, Walker and Hartley, Newport Beach, Calif., 1981-82, Milberg, Weiss, Bershad, Spethrie & Lerach, San Diego, 1984; pvt. practice Newport Beach, 1984—. Bd. dirs., v.p. Sandcastle Community Assn., Corona del Mar, Calif., 1987-97; active Leadership Tomorrow Class of 1994. Mem. Orange County Bar Assn., Balboa Bay Club. Democrat. Roman Catholic. Avocations: ballet, ice skating, bicycling, photography, golf. Office: 1 Corporate Plaza Dr Ste 110 Newport Beach CA 92660-7924 E-mail: cano@securities-law.com.

CANO, MARIO STEPHEN, lawyer; b. Miami, Fla., Sept. 2, 1953; s. Mario Arturo Cano and Irene H. Moreno; m. Johanna Marie Van Rossum, Oct. 13, 1979. AA, Miami Dade Jr. Coll., 1973; BA, Fla. Internat. U., 1975; JD, U. Santa Clara, 1978. Bar: Fla. 1979, U.S. Dist. Ct. (so. dist.) Fla. 1979, U.S. Ct. Claims 1979, U.S. Tax Ct. 1979, U.S. Ct. Mil. Appeals 1979, U.S. Ct. Appeals (9th cir.) 1979, U.S. Dist. Ct. (no. and mid. dists.) Fla. 1980, U.S. Dist. Ct. (no. dist.) Calif. 1980, U.S. Ct. Appeals (3d cir.) 1980, U.S. Ct. Internat. Trade 1981, U.S. Ct. Appeals (11th cir.) 1981, U.S. Ct. Appeals (6th and 10th cirs.) 1983, U.S. Supreme Ct. 1983, Nebr. 1984, U.S. Dist. Ct. Nebr. 1984, U.S. Dist. Ct. (no. dist.) Okla. 1984, U.S. Dist. Ct. Hawaii 1984, U.S. Ct. Appeals (2d, 4th, 5th, 7th 8th and D.C. cirs.) 1984, N.Y. 1985, U.S. Dist. Ct. (no., we., ea. and so. dists.) N.Y. 1985, U.S. Ct. Appeals (1st cir.) 1987, U.S. Dist. Ct. (no. and so. dist.) Tex. 1988, U.S. Dist. Ct. (ea. dist.) Wis. 1988, U.S. Dist. Ct. (we. dist.) Pa. 1988, U.S. Dist. Ct. (no. dist.) Ill. 1991, Mass., 1998, U.S. Dist. Ct. Mass. 1999. Assoc. Orta and Assocs., Miami, 1979-80, Law Office of J. Ramirez, Coral Gables, Fla., 1980, Law Office of I.G. Lichter, Miami, 1980-82, Gelb & Spatz, Miami, 1982; pvt. practice Coral Gables, 1982—. Mem. Am. Immigration Lawyers Assn., Cuban Am. Bar Assn., Nat. Assn. Criminal Def. Lawyers. Democrat. Office: Ste 600 2121 Ponce De Leon Blvd Coral Gables FL 33134-5222 Fax: 305-567-0423.. E-mail: canolawmiami@msn.com.

CANO-BALLESTA, JUAN, Spanish language educator; b. Murcia, Spain, Mar. 12, 1932; s. José Cano and Marcelina Ballesta; m. Mercedes Cano, Sept. 12, 1969. PhD, Ludwig Maximilian U., Munich, 1961. Lektor U. Göttingen, Germany, 1962-65; asst. prof. Spanish Yale U., New Haven, 1966-71; assoc. prof. Boston U., 1971-75; prof. U. Pitts., 1976-83; Commonwealth prof. U. Va., Charlottesville, 1983—2001, acting chmn. dept. Spanish and Italian, 1984-85, prof. emeritus, 2001—. Author: La Poesia de Miguel Hernández, 1962, La poesia española entre pureza y revolución, 1972, 2d edit. 1996, Literatura y tecnologia; las letras españolas ante la revolución industrial, 1981, 2d edit., 1999, Las estrategias de la imaginacion, 1994; editor: Poesia y prosa de guerra de Miguel Hernández, 1977, En torno a Miguel Hernández, 1978, Articulos sociales, politicos y de critica literaria de Mariano J. de Larra, 1982, El rayo que no cesa de Miguel Hernández, 1988, Viento del pueblo de Miguel Hernández, 1989, Nuevas amistades de J. Garcia Hortelano, Poesía española reciente (1980-2000), 2001, La mentria de las sombras critica cinematografica de Juan Gil-Albert, 2003. Fellow Morse Research Soc. Yale U., 1968-69, Am. Council Learned Socs., Madrid, 1975-76, Ctr. for Advanced Studies U. Va., 1983-84. Mem. MLA, Internat. Assn. Hispanists, Southeastern Medieval Assn., Am. Assn. Tchrs. Spanish and Portugese. Office: 115 Wilson Ct Charlottesville VA 22901-2941

CANONI, JOHN DAVID, lawyer; b. Newton, Mass., May 11, 1939; s. John Joseph and Olga Elizabeth (Mangini) C.; m. Katherine Ariadna Bryant, Aug. 18, 1962; children: Lisa Ann, Peter Christopher, John Charles, Scott Francis. BA, Amherst Coll., 1960; LLB, Yale U., 1963. Bar: N.Y. 1964, U.S. Ct. Appeals (2d cir.) 1966, U.S. Ct. Appeals (3d cir.) 1967, U.S. Ct. Appeals (4th cir.) 1968, U.S. Ct. Appeals (1st cir.) 1969, U.S. Supreme Ct. 1971, U.S. Ct. Appeals (7th cir.) 1972. Assoc. Townley & Updike, N.Y.C., 1963-71, ptnr., 1971-95, Nixon Peabody LLP, N.Y.C., 1995—. Mem. Lt. Gov.'s Task Force on Plant Closings, N.Y., 1984-85. Mem. N.Y. State Bar Assn. (chmn. labor & employment law sect. 1983-84), Yale Club. Republican. Roman Catholic. Home: 20 High Meadows Mount Kisco NY 10549-3847 Office: Nixon Peabody LLP 437 Madison Ave New York NY 10022-7001 E-mail: jcanoni@aol.com., jcanoni@nixonpeabody.com.

CANSLER, LESLIE ERVIN, retired newspaper editor; b. Hickory, N.C., Sept. 10, 1920; s. Leslie Ervin and Mabel Pearl (Braswell) C.; m. Maria Muriel Olwell, Aug. 19, 1944 (div.); children: David, Robert, James.; m. Elizabeth Marie Walters; 1 dau., Leslie Anne. BA, Wake Forest U., 1941. News editor Daily Advance, Elizabeth City, N.C., 1941; reporter Raleigh (N.C.) Times, 1941-42, 46, city editor, 1946-47; with News-Jour. Co., Wilmington, Del., 1947-88, day mng. editor, 1966-68, mng. editor, 1968-76, assoc. Sunday editor, 1976-79, Sunday editor, 1979-80, assoc. editor, 1980-89. Served with USNR, 1942-45. Mem. Sigma Phi Epsilon. Republican. Episcopalian. Home: 11 Bristol Way New Castle DE 19720-3906

CANTALUPO, CLAUDIO, neuroscientist, researcher; b. Bologna, Emilia-Romagna, Italy, June 19, 1964; s. Giorgio Cantalupo and Paola Grandi. BS, U. Padua, Italy, 1993; MS, PhD, U. Memphis, 2000. Contbr. articles to profl. jours. (APA Brenda Milner award, 2002). Recipient Exceptional Academic Achievement Award, Phi Kappa Phi, 2000; grantee GIAR grant, Sci. Rsch. Soc. (Sigma Xi), 2000. Mem.: So. Soc. Philosophy and Psychology (assoc.), Am. Psychol. Soc. (assoc. Brenda Milner Award for exceptional pub. work in the field of behavioral neurocience 2002). Achievements include research in simlarities between the human and great ape brain. Office: Yerkes Rsch Ctr Emory U 954 Gatewood Rd Atlanta GA 30329 Office Fax: 404-727-3270. E-mail: ccantal@rmy.emory.edu.

CANTALUPO, JIM, food products executive; married; 2 children. With Arthur Young & Co., 1966—74; controller McDonald's Corp., 1974—75, v.p., 1975—81, sr. v.p., 1981—85, zone mgr., 1985; pres. McDonald's Internat., 1987—97, CEO, 1991—, chmn., 2003—. Bd. dirs. Sears, roebuck and Co., Rohm and Haas Co., Ill. Tool Works, INc., World Bus. Chgo., Chgo. Coun. Fgn. Rels. Trustee Ronald McDonald House Charities. Mem.: Nat. Multiple Sclerosis Soc. (past chmn., hon. trustee), Internat. Fedn. Multiple Sclerosis Socs. (past pres.). Office: McDonalds Corp McDonalds Plaza Oak Brook IL 60523*

CANTARELLA, JASON H. mathematician, educator; b. Buffalo, N.Y., May 1972; BA, Vassar Coll., 1993; PhD, U. Pa., Phila., 1999. Asst. prof. U. Ga., Athens, 1999—. Contbr. articles to profl. jours. Nat. Def. Sci. and Engring. Grad. fellow, Army Rsch. Office, 1993—99, Math. Scis. Postdoctoral Rsch. fellow, NSF, 1999—2002, Individual Investigator grantee, 2002—, Faculty Rsch. grantee, U. Ga. Rsch. Found., 2002. Mem.: Phi Beta Kappa (Mu chpt.). Office: Univ Ga Math Dept DW Brooks Dr Athens GA 30602 Office Fax: 706-542-5907. E-mail: cantarella@math.uga.edu.

CANTELLA, VINCENT MICHELE, stockbroker; b. Boston, Oct. 27, 1917; s. Michele and Josephine (Sapienza) C.; m. Josephine R. Castanien, Nov. 19, 1944; children: Betsy Ann, David V., Steven M. BS, Boston U., 1939. Mng. ptnr. Cantella & Co., Boston, 1952-74; ptnr. Josephthal & Co., Boston, 1974-78, 1974-78; pres. Cantella & Co. Inc., 1979, 1979-97, chmn., 1997—. Mem. Boston Stock Exchange, 1953—, bd. govs., mem. exec. com., 1963-74, 79-91, chmn. exec. com., 1971-73, chmn. bd. govs., 1973-74; pres. Boston Stock Exchange Clearing Corp., 1964-68; mem. Midwest Stock Exchange, 1965-72, Pacific Coast Stock Exchange, 1965-78, N.Y. Stock Exchange, 1969-78, Detroit Stock Exchange, 1963-76, P.B.W. Stock Exchange, 1970-73, Am. Stock Exchange, 1972-75. Ret. Maj. USMC, World War II. Mem.: The Bay Club Boston, The N.Y. Stock Exc. Luncheon Club, Boston Athletic Club. Home: 635 Lewis Wharf Boston MA 02110-3924 Office: 2 Oliver St Boston MA 02109-4901

CANTELON, JOHN EDWARD, retired university chancellor; b. Warroad, Minn., June 20, 1924; s. Arthur Edward and Georgia (Turnbull) C.; m. Joy Elizabeth Norton, Aug. 16, 1953; children: Barbara Jean, Charles Norton. Student, U. Man., 1941-42; BA, Reed Coll., 1948; PhD, Oxford U., 1951; D.H.L., Hebrew Union Coll.-Jewish Inst. Religion, 1972. Ordained to diocese of Oreg., 1952; pastor Fairmont Presbyn. Ch., Eugene, Oreg., 1952-53; mem. staff Christian Assn., U. Pa., 1953-57; asso. sec. div. higher edn. United Presbyn. Ch., Phila., 1957-60; univ. chaplain, asso. prof. U. So. Calif., 1960-67; prof. U. So. Calif. Sch. Relgion, 1967-70; vice provost, dean U. So. Calif. Coll. Letters, Arts and Scis., 1972-76; v.p. undergrad. studies U. So. Calif. (Coll. Letters, Arts and Scis.), 1972-76, Bicentennial prof., 1976; provost, v.p. for acad. affairs Central Mich. U., Mt. Pleasant, 1976-86, prof., 1976-89, provost emeritus, 1986; v.p. for acad. affairs Walden U., 1991-94, chancellor, 1995-99, chancellor emeritus, 1999—. Pres. Middle Mich. Devel. Corp. Author: Higher Education and the Campus Revolution, 1969, Terrorism and the Moral Majority, 1984. Served with AUS, 1943-46. Recipient Gov. Gen.'s medal acad. excellence Neepawa Collegiate Inst., 1941 Mem. Newcomen Soc., Univ. Club, Phi Beta Kappa, Phi Kappa Phi, Blue Key, Skull and Dagger, Sigma Iota Epsilon. Home: Portland Plz # 1201 1500 SW 5th Ave Portland OR 97201-5458 E-mail: jcantelo@teleport.com.

CANTELON, PHILIP LOUIS, historian; b. Ft. Wayne, Ind., Nov. 7, 1940; s. Philip Eccles and Marie (Gehrke) C.; m. Eileen S. McGuckian, Feb. 14, 1989. AB, Dartmouth Coll., 1962; MA, U. Mich., 1963; PhD, Ind. U., 1971. Asst. prof. Williams Coll., Williamstown, Mass., 1968-77; Fulbright prof. Kyushu Nat. U./Seinan Gakuin U., Fukuoka, Japan, 1978-79; pres., CEO, History Assocs. Inc., Rockville, Md., 1980—. Adj. prof. Cath. U., 2002; exec. sec. Nat. Coun. Pub. History, Washington, 1979-81, Soc. History in Fed. Govt., Washington, 1979-80, pres., 1995-96; chmn. Montgomery County Hist. Preservation Commn., 1985-91; pres. Montgomery County Hist. Soc., Rockville, 1991-95, Peerless Rockville Historic Preservation, Ltd., 1996-2002. Author: Crisis Contained, 1980, The History of MCI, 1993, The Roadway Story, 1996, Never Stand Still: The History of Consolidated Freightways and CNF Transportation Inc., 1999, The History of Mere Point: 1878-2003, 2003; editor: The American Atom, 1989, Corporate Archives and History, 1993. Mem.: Oral History Assn., Orgn Am. Historians (chmn. com. on rsch. and access to his. documentations 1999), Cosmos Club (admissions com. 1993—94, bd. mgmt. 1995—99, v.p. 1999—2000, pres. 2000—01, bd. mgmt. 2001—02, chair). Home: 11807 Dinwiddie Dr Rockville MD 20852-4459 Office: History Assocs Inc 300 N Stonestreet Ave Rockville MD 20850 E-mail: pcantelon@historyassociates.com.

CANTERBERY, E. RAY, economics educator; b. Corning, Ark., May 26, 1935; s. Otis R. and Virginia Elizabeth (House) C.; m. Carolyn; children: Kathryn Lynn, Jennifer Ann. AB, So. Ill. U., 1957, MA, 1959; PhD, Washington U., St. Louis, 1966. Mkt. analyst Gardner Advt., St. Louis, 1959-60; statistician Fed. Reserve Bank, St. Louis, 1961-62; asst. prof. econs. Ariz. State U., Tempe, 1964-65; asst. prof. econs U. Md., College Park, 1965-69; assoc. prof. econs. Simon Fraser U., Vancouver, B.C., Can., 1969, Fla. State U., Tallahassee, 1970-72, prof. econs., 1972—. Cons. economist U.S. Dept. State, Washington, 1966, 69, UN, Vienna, Austria, 1982-84, Ben Johnson Assocs., Tallahassee, 1986—; bd. dirs. Genamax, Inc., R & D Co., Fla. Inst. for Econ. Justice, 2000—. Author: Foreign Exchange Capital Flows and Monetary Policy, 1965, Economics on a New Frontier, 1968, The Making of Economics, 1976, 4th edit., 2003, The Literate Economist, 1995, Wall Street Capitalism, 2000, Chinese edit., 2003, A Brief History of Economics, 2001, Portuguese edit., 2003, Korean edit., 2003, Black Box Inc., 2000. With U.S. Army, 1953-55. Recipient Harry S. Truman Scholar, 2000-01. Mem. Am. Econs. Assn., Ea. Econs. Assn. (pres. 1987-88, bd. dirs. emeritus 1989, life), Internat. Trade and Fin. Assn. (bd. dirs. 1994-96, pres. 1998-99), So. Econ. Assn., The Acad. Polit. Sci., N.Y. Acad. Scis., Nat. Tax Assn. Office: Fla State U 258 Bellamy Bldg Tallahassee FL 32306

CANTERBURY-COUNTS, W. DOUGLAS, psychologist; b. Lancaster, Pa. s. William L. Jr. and Marion E. (Winters) Counts; m. Belinda Jaya Canterbury, Mar. 12, 1977; 1 child, William Andrew Hanuman. BA, So. Calif. Coll., 1979; MDiv, Ea. Bapt. Theol. Sem., 1983; PhD, Temple U., 1989. Pvt. practice roofing contractor, Calif. & Pa., 1976-88; counselor Pathways Counseling Svc., Swarthmore, Pa., 1985-86; psychotherapist, clin. coord. dept. medicine Temple U., Phila., 1985-88; pvt. practice clin. psychologist Lake Worth and Sebastian, Fla., 1989—. Lectr. Temple U., Coll. Edn., Phila., 1983-86; adj. prof. Fla. Atlantic U., Boca Raton, 1990—; cons. Goodwill Industries, Inc., West Palm Beach, Fla., 1995—, River Sch., Sebastian, 1995—; founder, dir. Ctr. for Sacred Psychology, 1992. Contbr. articles to profl. jours. County del. Delaware County Crisis Intervention and Suicide Prevention, Media, Pa., 1981-83; chairperson bereavement com. Fla. chpt. NAMES Project AIDS Meml. Quilt, Sebastian, 1997—; bd. dirs. River Fund, Sebastian, 1997—; mem. Coun. Interfaith Call, World Tibet Day Found. Sgt. USMC, 1969-75. Mem. APA, Nat. Acad. Neuropsychology, Fla. Psychol. Assn., Ctr. for Jungian Studies SE Fla, Inc. (v.p. 1990-96). Democrat. Avocations: t'ai chi ch'uan, [illegible], camping, white water rafting. Office: PO Box 1365 Roseland FL 32957-1365 Fax: 253-390-3985. E-mail: sacredpsyc@aol.com.

CANTILLI, EDMUND JOSEPH, safety engineering educator, translator, writer, consultant; b. Yonkers, N.Y., Feb. 12, 1927; s. Ettore and Maria (deRubeis) C.; m. Nella Franco, May 15, 1948; children: Robert, John, Teresa. AB, Columbia U., 1954, BS, 1955; cert., Yale Bur. Hwy. Traffic, 1957; PhD in Transp. Planning and Engring., Poly. Inst. Bklyn., 1972; postgrad. in urban planning and pub. safety, NYU, 1968-71. Registered profl. engr., N.Y., N.J., Calif.; profl. planner, N.J.; bd. cert. safe ty profl. (BCSP); bd. cert. planner (AICP); bd. cert. forensic engr. (BCFE). Supervising engr. safety rsch. and studies Port Authority of N.Y. & N.J., 1955-69; prof. transp. and safety engring. Poly. U., N.Y.C., 1969-90; pres. Urbitran Assocs., 1973-81; exec. dir., chmn. bd. Internat. Inst. for Safety Trans., Inc., 1977—; pres. EJC Safety Assocs., Inc., 1989—. Tchr. Italian, algebra, traffic engring., urban planning, transp. planning, urban and transp. geography, land use planning, aesthetics, environment, indsl., traffic and transp. safety engring., human factors engring., ethics for engrs.; cons. transp. and traffic safety engring., community planning, traffic engring., transp. planning, accident reconstrn., environ. impacts, 1969—; vis. prof. transp. safety engring. Inst. Superior Técnico, Lisbon, 1987-97; advisor to doctorate students Poly. U., CUNY, 1969-94, Politecnico di Milano, U. Trieste, Italy, 1980—; consulting forensic engr., accident reconstructionist, expert witness transp. accident litigation including hwy. traffic, railroad, rail rapid transit, pedestrian accidents, 1969—. Translator (Italian-English autobiog. Joseph Tusiani): The Difficult Word; The New Word; The Ancient Word, 1988; author: Programming Environmental Improvements in Public Transportation, 1974, Transportation and the Disadvantaged, 1974, Transportation System Safety, 1979; editor: Transportation and Aging, 1971, Pedestrian Planning and Design, 1971; editor, contbr.: Traffic Engineering Theory and Control, 1973; editor and calligrapher There Is No Death That Is Not Ennobled by So Great A Cause, 1976; contbr. over 200 articles to profl. jours. and trade jours.; developer daylight running lights, methods of severity evaluation of accidents, identification, priority-setting and treatment of roadside hazards, transp. system safety methodology; expert systems for improving traffic safety; introduced diagrammatic traffic signs, collision energy-absorption devices. With U.S. Army, 1945-49, 50-51. Fellow ASCE, Inst. Transp. Engrs., Nat. Acad. Forensic Engrs.; mem. NSPE, Am. Planning Assn. (charter), Am. Inst. Cert. Planners (cert.), Am. Soc. Safety Engrs., N.Y. Acad. Scis., Nat. Assn. Profl. Accident Reconstrn. Specialists, Internat. Assn. for Accidents and Traffic Medicine, Human Factors Soc., N.Y. Acad. Scis., System Safety Soc., Sigma Xi. Home: 134 Euston Rd West Hempstead NY 11552-1024 Office: PO Box 63 Franklin Square NY 11010-0063 E-mail: ejcsafety@aol.com., insafetran@aol.com., cantoxxv@aol.com.

CANTLIFFE, DANIEL JAMES, horticulture educator; b. N.Y.C., Oct. 31, 1943; s. Sarah Lucretia Keesler C.; m. Elizabeth F. Lapetina, June 5, 1965; children: Christine, Deanna, Danielle, Cheri. BS, Delaware Valley Coll., Doylestown Pa., 1965; MS, Purdue U., 1967, PhD, 1971. Asst. prof. horticulture U. Fla., Gainesville, 1974-76, assoc. prof., 1976-81, prof., 1981—, asst. chair dept., 1983-84, acting chair dept., 1984-85, chmn. dept., 1985-92, acting chair dept. fruit crops, 1991-92, chair dept. hort. scis., 1992—. Vis. prof. U. Hawaii, Honolulu, 1979-80; sci. cons. Sun Seeds Genetics, Hollister, Calif., 1987, Pillsbury Co., 1987—, Teltech Inc., Bloomington, Minn., 1988—, DNAP, Monsanto, Seed Dynamics, Ball Seed Co., Sybron Chem., Dow Agro Scis. Contbr. articles to profl. jours. and conf. procs., chpts. to books. Recipient rsch. award Fla. Fruit and Vegetable Assn., Orlando, 1986, Alumni Achievement award Delaware Valley Coll., Doylestown, 1990, Distinguished Agrl. Alumni award Purdue Univ., 1999. Fellow Am. Soc. Hort. Sci. (v.p. rsch. 1991-92, pres.-elect 1993-94, pres. 1994-95, chmn. 1995-96, Outstanding Grad. Educator award 1991, Best Paper Vegetable Sect. 1992, Membership Recruitment award 1996, Outstanding Rsch. award 1997, vegetable publ. award 1997, So. Region Leadership and Adminstrn. award 2000), Crop Sci. Soc. Am. (Seed Sci. award 1997); mem. Fla. State Hort. Soc. (v.p. vegetable sect. 1984-85, pres. 1991-92, chmn. exec. com. 1992-93, best paper vegetable sec. 1990, 92, 93, 2001, 2003, profl. excellence program award 1996, USDA Group Hon. award for Excellence 1997, Internat. Soc. Hort. Sci. (chair sect. of vegetables), Crop Sci. Soc. Am., Fla. Seed Assn. (hon.), Internat. Soc. Horiculture, Am. Soc. Plant Physiologists, Am. Soc. Agronomy, Internat. Soc. Tropical Horticulture, Bot. Soc. Am., N.Am. Strawberry Growers Assn., Plasticulture Soc. Am., Sigma Xi, Delta Tau Alpha, Phi Kappa Phi, Gamma Sigma Delta, Phi Beta Delta. Office: U of Fla Hort Scis Dept PO Box 110690 1251 Fifield Hall Gainesville FL 32611-0690

CANTON, MAMIE RUTH, humanities educator; b. San Augustine, Tex. d. Otto Fox and Mary (Jenkins) Canton; m. Arnett Bertrand Caviel (div.); 1 child, Sheila Ann Hubbard. BA, MA, San Francisco State U. Instr. San Francisco State U., 1970—72; lectr. San Jose State U., Calif., 1974—83, Skyline Coll., San Bruno, Calif., Canada Coll., Redwood City, Calif., 1981, Menlo Coll., Atherton, Calif., 1980—81; instr. No. Essex Cmty. Coll., Haverill, Mass., 1998. Program tutor Lesley U., Cambridge, Mass., 1994—; tutor, curriculum supr. Boston Learning Ctr., Dorchester, Mass., curriculum supr., 1997—. Chair, deaconness bd. Third Bapt. Ch., San Francisco, 1979—82, libr., 1972—79, social chmn., 1979—86, mem., Bapt. Tng. Union, 1964—89. Mem.: MLA, Nat. Coun. Tchrs. of English. Avocation: writing. Home: 49 Driscoll Dr Boston MA 02124-5501 Office: PO Box 870185 Milton Village MA 02187-0185 E-mail: cantoneast@aol.com.

CANTONE, VIC, political cartoonist; b. N.Y.C., Aug. 7, 1933; Grad., Sch. Art and Design, N.Y.C., 1952, Art Instrn. Schs., Inc., Mpls., 1978; AA cum laude, Nassau Coll., Garden City, N.Y., 1978; BA, Hofstra U., 1979, postgrad., 1985—. Cartoonist, courtroom artist Newsday, Garden City, NY, 1954—59; polit. cartoonist/caricaturist N.Y. Daily News, 1959—91, Editor & Pub. mag., 1973—78; syndicated polit. cartoonist/caricaturist Rothco Cartoon Syndicate, 1980—91, King Features/N.Am. Syndicate, 1991—2002, ArtistMarket.com Syndicate, 2002—; corp. cartoonist/caricaturist Wall St. Jour. Nat Broadcast Syndicate report Sta. WPIX-TV, 1982—83. Bd. dirs., curator Hofstra U.

Internat. Environ. Polit. Cartoon Exhibit, 1990; lectr. on media, terrorism; courtroom artist WPIX-TV, CableVision News 12, 1991-2000, polit. cartoonist/caricaturist O'Dwyer's PR Mag., 1987-2003, Bklyn. Papers Pub, 1996-2001. Permanent collections include 3 U.S. Presdl. librs.; author books and articles; curator, exhibitor Smithsonian Instn., U.S.A. Tour, Internat. Polit. Cartoons on the Environment, 1992-96. Recipient Bicentennial Trophy award, Aux. Am. Legion, 1976, Golden Press award, 1979, Fourth Estate award, Am. Legion, 1976, Valley Forge Honor cert., Freedoms Found., 1976, George Washington Honor medal, 1978, cert. of recognition, NCCJ, 1977, Patriotic Svc. award, U.S. Dept. Treasury, 1978, Honor Legion award, N.Y.C. Police Dept., 1994, 1996, The Deadline Club award, 1999; Fulbright scholar, 1987. Mem.: Nat. Cartoonists Soc., N.Y.C. Deadline Club (exec. coun. 1999—), Soc. Profl. Journalists (spkrs. bur. 1999—), N.Y. Press Club (bd. govs. 1995—99), Assn. Am. Editl. Cartoonists. *The political cartoonist is a powerful political weapon in that a public image can be shaped. Therefore, the burden of responsibility rests heaviest upon the political cartoonist to triumph in common sense, over myths and hysteria, over nostalgia or paranoia.*

CANTONI, LOUIS JOSEPH, psychologist, poet, sculptor; b. Detroit, May 22, 1919; s. Pietro and Stella (Puricelli) C.; m. Lucile Eudora Moses, Aug. 7, 1948; children: Christopher Louis, Sylvia Therese. AB, U. Calif., Berkeley, 1946; MSW, U. Mich., 1949, PhD, 1953. Personnel mgr. Johns-Manville Corp., Pittsburg, Calif., 1944-46; social caseworker Detroit Dept. Pub. Welfare, 1946-49; counselor Mich. Div. Vocat. Rehab., Detroit, 1949-50; conf. leader, tchr. psychology, coordinator family and community relations program Gen. Motors Inst., Flint, Mich., 1951-56; from assoc. prof. to prof., dir. rehab. counseling Wayne State U., Detroit, 1956-89. Author books and monographs including: The 1939-1943 Flint Michigan Guidance Demonstration, 1953, Marriage and Community Relations, 1954; (with Mrs. Cantoni) Counseling Your Friends, 1961, Supervised Practice in Rehabilitation Counseling, 1978, Writings of Louis J. Cantoni, 1981, Essays, Theses and Projects in Rehabilitation Counseling, 1989; (with Mrs. Cantoni) Theoretical Underpinnings of Practice in Family Service Agencies, 1990; (poetry) With Joy I Called to You, 1969, Gradually The Dreams Change, 1979, A Festival of Lanternes, 1994; editor: Placement of the Handicapped in Competitive Employment, 1957; poetry editor Cathedral Digest, 1973-75; co-editor: Preparation of Vocational Rehabilitation Counselors Through Field Instruction, 1958; prin. editor: (poetry) Golden Song Anthology, 1985; editor jours. Mich. Rehab. Assn. Digest, 1961-63, Grad. Comment, 1963-64; bibliography, books and reprints placed in Reuther Libr. Archives Wayne State U., Detroit; contbr. articles, revs., poems, comments, abstracts, and illustrations to jours. Judge Mich. regional and nat. essay and poetry contests, 1965-77; bd. dirs. Mich. Rehab. Assn., 1962-64, 78-79, Mich. Rehab. Conseling Assn., 1985-87. 2d lt. AUS, 1942-44. Recipient award for leadership and service Mich. Rehab. Assn., 1964, Mich. Rehab. Counseling Assn., 1985, 87, 88, Outstanding Service award Mich. State Bd. Edn., 1989, South and West ann. poetry award, 1970, Meritorious Service award Wayne State U., 1971, 81, 86, 87, 89, Excellence in Poetry award Pig's Wing Press, 1997, Edizioni Universum Author of the Yr. award, 2000. Fellow AAAS; mem. AAUP, APA, Coun. of Rehab. Counselor Educators (sec. 1957-58, chmn. 1965-66), Nat. Rehab. Assn., Nat. Congress of Orgns. of the Physically Handicapped, Nat. Assn. of the Physically Handicapped, Nat. Alliance for the Mentally Ill, Am. Inst. Econ. Rsch., Poetry Soc. Am., Mich. Rehab. Assn. (pres. 1963-64), Detroit Rehab. Assn. (pres. 1958), Mich. Counseling Assn., Mich. Career Devel. Assn., Mich. Assn. for Humanistic Edn. and Devel. (Outstanding Svc. award 1997), Mich. Employment Counselors Assn., Mich. Assn. for Marriage and Family Counseling, Internat. Inst. Met. Detroit, World Poetry Soc. (Edwin A. Falkowski Meml. award 1990), Acad. Am. Poets, Detroit Inst. Arts, Friends of Detroit Pub. Libr., Friends of Marshall M. Fredericks Sculpture Gallery, Soc. for Study of Midwestern Lit., U.S. Hist. Soc., Italic Studies Inst., USN Meml., Internat. Sculpture Ctr., Nat. Sculpture Soc., Sculptors Guild Mich., Lladro Collectors Soc., Birmingham-Bloomfield Art Ctr., Psychology and the Arts, Poetry Soc. Mich. (Outstanding Svc. award 1984), Detroit Film Soc., Detroit Zool. Soc., Poetry Resource Ctr. Mich., Univ. Club, Scarab Club (Detroit), Phi Kappa Phi, Phi Delta Kappa. Democrat. Episcopalian. Achievements include research in theory and practice of counseling and psychotherapy, psychosocial aspects of disabling conditions, therapeutic and vocational counseling with disabled persons; workplace accommodation for the disabled, vocational rehabilitation of the severely disabled. Home: 2591 Woodstock Dr Detroit MI 48203-1062 *His destination, when he set out, was pure poetry, although he did not recognize it. He came to cherish the gifts of sun, rain, a walk in the woods, a brightening smile. His wife radiates the clear beauty of mature women. His children, albeit circuitously, took on his values. He feels near to man and God and views death as another beginning. He has reached his destination many times and welcomes sunset as well as sunrise, conflict as well as calm. He knows now that much of his life has been pure poetry.*

CANTOR, ALAN BRUCE, management consultant, computer software engineer; b. Mt. Vernon, N.Y., Apr. 30, 1948; s. Howard and Muriel Anita C.; m. Judith Jolanda Szrka, Mar. 1, 1987; 1 child, Alec Brandon. BS in Social Scis., Cornell U., 1970; MBA, U. Pa., 1973. Mgmt. cons. M & M Risks Mgmt. Svcs., N.Y.C., 1974-78; nat. svcs. officer spl. projects divsn. Marsh & McLennan Risk Mgmt. Svcs., L.A., 1980-81; sr. v.p. sr. cons. prin. Warren, Mc Veigh & Griffin, Inc., 1981-82; founder, pres. Cantor & Co., 1982—; founder, ptnr., mng. dir. Beacon Health Informatics, LLC, 2002—. Co-mgr. Air Travel Rsch. Group, N.Y.C., 1977-79; instr. risk mgmt. program Am. Mgmt. Assn.,; lectr. Risk and Inst. Mgmt. Soc. Conf., 1975-87, Med. Edn. Spkrs. Bur. of So. Calif., 19990--; seminars How to Use Spreadsheets in Risk Mgmt., 1986-89, How to Use Computers in Risk Mgmt., 1989-93. Copyright airline industry model; contbr. articles to profl. jours.; creator, developer, copyright RISKMAP risk mgmt. software products, 1982-2002, Riskmap Windows version, copyright 2000-2002, Exposure Base Mgmt. System (EBMS), 1985, 86, patient care monitoring system, 1985-92, Med. Quality Mgmt. Systems Plus, 1991-2002, MQMS Plus Windows version, 1997-2003, COLTS corp. overal legal tracking system, 1984, 86, 87, 89, 90, 91, 93, 94, RISKMAP ins. schedules system, 1989. Cons., vol. Urban Cons. Group, N.Y.C.; elder Beverly Hills Presbyn. Ch., 1991—; co-project dir. East European Orphans Toy Ministry, 1999—. Mem. Cornell Alumni Assn. N.Y.C. (bd. govs., program chmn.), Cornell Alumni Assn. So. Calif., Wharton Bus. Sch. Club (N.Y.C., chmn., mem. adv. com. L.A.), L.A. Athletic. Office: Cantor & Co 9100 Wilshire Blvd Beverly Hills CA 90212-3415

CANTOR, ARNOLD, labor relations official; b. Rochester, N.Y., Jan. 4, 1927; s. Samuel Abraham and Bessie (Brightman) Cantor; m. Meriam Renee Teichner; children: Nadine, Duane, Paul, Glenn, Erica. BMusic, U. Rochester, N.Y., 1949; M in Music, U. Rochester, 1953; MA in Sociology, CCNY, 1995; PhD in Sociology CUNY, 1997. Cert. clarinet performer Eastman Sch. of Music. Tchr. instrumental music Rochester Pub, Schs., NY, 1949—57, dean of students, 1957—62, v. prin. h.s., 1962—68, prin., 1968—70; exec. dir. Profl. Staff Congress CUNY, 1970—95. Adj. asst. prof. Baruch Coll. CUNY, 1996—. Mem.: AAUP (mem. exec. com. 1969—), N.Y. State United Tchrs. (bd. dirs. 1961—70, pres. Rochester tchrs. assn 1963—65), Am. Fedn. Tchrs. (Disting. Svc. award 1994). Democrat. Jewish. Achievements include Led Rochester Tchrs. Assn. to 1st collective bargaining contract agreement in N.Y. state outside of N.Y.C. Avocations: music, photography. Home: 122 Philip Pl Hawthorne NY 10532-2108

CANTOR, BERNARD JACK, lawyer; b. N.Y.C., Aug. 18, 1927; s. Alexander J. and Tillie (Henzeloff) Cantor; m. Judith L. Levin, Mar. 25, 1951; children: Glenn H., Cliff A., James E., Ellen B., Mark E. BME, Cornell U., 1949; JD, George Washington U., 1952. Bar: DC 1952, U.S. Patent Office 1952, Mich. 1952, registered: U.S. (patent atty.), Can. Examiner U.S. Patent Office, Washington, 1949-52; pvt. practice Detroit, 1952-88; ptnr. firm Harness, Dickey & Pierce, Troy, Mich., 1988—. Lectr. in field. Contbr. articles to profl. jours. Mem. exec. coun. Detroit area Boy Scouts Am., 1972—. With U.S. Army, 1944—46. Recipient Ellsworth award patent law, George Washington U., 1952, Shofar award, Boy Scouts Am., 1975, Silver Beaver award, 1975, Disting. Eagle award, 1985. Fellow: Mich. State Bar Found.; mem.: ABA, Am. Technion Soc. (bd. dirs. Detroit 1970—), Cornell Engring. Soc., Am. Arbitration Assn. (arbitrator), Am. Intellectual Property Law Assn., Mich. Patent Law Assn., Oakland Bar Assn., Detroit Bar Assn., Mich. Bar Assn. (dir. econs. sect., arbitrator State of Mich. grievance com.), Beta Sigma Rho, Phi Delta Phi, Pi Tau Sigma. Home: 5685 Forman Dr Bloomfield Hills MI 48301-1154 Office: Harness Dickey & Pierce 5445 Corporate Dr Troy MI 48098-2683 Office Fax: 248-641-0270.

CANTOR, CHARLES ROBERT, biochemistry educator; b. Bklyn., Aug. 26, 1942; s. Louis and Ida Dianne (Banks) C. AB summa cum laude, Columbia U., 1963; PhD, U. Calif., Berkeley, 1966. Asst. prof. chemistry Columbia U., N.Y.C., 1966-69, assoc. prof. chemistry and biol. scis., 1969-72, prof., 1972-81, prof., chmn. genetics and devel., dep. dir. Comprehensive Cancer Ctr. Coll. Phys. and Surgs., 1981-89; dir. Human Genome Ctr. Lawrence Berkeley Lab, 1988-90; prof. molecular biology U. Calif., Berkeley, 1989-92; prof. biomed. engring. Boston U., 1992—, chmn., 1994-98, dir. Ctr. for Advanced Biotech, 1992—; prof. pharmacology, 1995—; prin. scientist human genome project Dept. Energy, 1990-92; chief sci. officer Sequenom, Inc., 1998—; also bd. dirs., 2000—. Sherman Fairchild vis. scholar Calif. Inst. Tech., 1975-76; mem. biophysics and biophys. chemistry study sect. NIH, 1971-75; mem. cell and molecular basis of disease rev. com. Nat. Inst. Gen. Med. Scis., 1977-81, coun. mem., 1986-89; mem. ozone update com. NRC, 1983, mem. rsch. opportunities in biology com., 1985-89, com. on the human genome, 1986-89, com. on bits of power, 1995-96; trustee Cold Spring Harbor Lab., 1977-83; mem. proposal rev. panel Stanford Sychrotron Radiation Lab., 1976-88; mem. U.S. Nat. Commn., Internat. Union Pure & Applied Biophysics, 1986-94, vice chmn., 1988-91, chmn., 1991-94; sci. adv. bd. Hereditary Disease Found., 1987-89; mem. coun. Human Genome Orgn., 1989-92, v.p. 1990-92, pres. America's, 1991-98; chmn. DOE Department of energy Human Genome Coordinating com., 1989-92; adv. com. Searle Scholars program, 1987-93, chair, 1993-94, mem. adv. com. program in parasite biology MacArthur Found., 1990-93; mem. sci. adv. coun. Roswell Park Cancer Inst. 1992-98; sci. adv. com. European Molecular Biology Lab., 1989-94; bd. sci. counselors Nat. Ctr. for Biotechnology Info., Nat. Libr. Medicine, 1990-95; cons. Incyte Pharm. Inc., 1992-98, Genelabs, Inc., 1988 , Samsung Advanced Inst. Tech., 2000—, mem. coun. Internat. Union Pure and Applied Biophysics, 1993-99; vis. com. biology Brookhaven Nat. Lab., 1986-89; bd. dirs. and chair sci. adv. com. Avitech Diagnostics, Inc. (formerly ATGC Inc.), 1992-1997; mem. nomenclature com. IUBMB, 1989—; chair adv. com. European Bioinformatics Inst., 1993-94; mem. USDA Genome Adv. Com., 1992-98; co-chair biotech. adv. coun. Fisher Sci., 1994—; mem. biology adv. com. Lawrence Livermore Nat. Lab., 1995—, chair 2000—; chair sci. adv. com. Sequenom, Inc., Sequenom Instruments GmbH, 1995—, mem. sci. adv. com., Aclara, Inc., Caliper, Inc., 1996—, ExSar, Inc. (formerly Carta, Inc., formerly Thermaphore, Inc.), 1999—, bd. dirs.; bd. dirs. SelectX, Inc., Plexus, Inc., The Molecular Scis. Inst.; mem. sci. adv. com., Odyssey Inc., 2002-; pres. Biochemist, Inc., 2001-2002; mem. FASEB consensus conf. on fed. funding, 1995-2000; quest scholar Quest Diagnostics, Inc., 1997-99; mem. biotech. coun. DOE, 1996-99; mem. unconventional pathogen countermeasures adv. com. DARPA (Defense Advanced Projects Research Agency, 1996-2000; adj. prof. biomed. engring., U. Calif., San Diego, 2002—. Author: (with Paul R. Schimmel) Biophysical Chemistry, I, II, III, (with Cassandra L. Smith) Genomics; assoc. editor Ann. Rev. Biophysics, 1983-93. Trustee Assoc. Univs. Inc., 1999-2000; bd. dirs. Keystone Confs., 1999-2001. Recipient Fresenius award Phi Lambda Upsilon, 1972; Eli Lilly award in biol. chemistry Am. Chem. Soc., 1978; Alfred P. Sloan fellow, 1969-71; Guggenheim fellow, 1973-74; Nat. Cancer Inst. outstanding investigator grantee, 1985, Analytica prize, 1988; ISCO prize, 1989, Sober prize ASBMB, 1990. Fellow AAAS, Biophys. Soc. (mem. coun. 1977-81, Emily Gray prize 2000, fellow 2000); mem. Am. Acad. Arts and Scis., Nat. Acad. Sci., Am. Soc. Biol. Chemists, Am. Chem. Soc., Soc. Analytical Cytology, Harvey Soc., Am. Soc. Human Genetics, Biomed. Engring. Soc., Japanese Biochem. Soc. (hon.). Home: 526 Stratford Ct Apt E Del Mar CA 92014-2767 Office: Sequenom Inc 3595 John Hopkins Ct San Diego CA 92121 E-mail: ccantor@sequenom.com.

CANTOR, DAVID JULES, economist; b. N.Y.C., Nov. 17, 1935; s. Nathan and Sadye Ruth (Schwartz) C.; m. Cynthia A. Crook, May 29, 1992. AB, Boston U., 1957, AM, 1958; MA, Harvard U., 1961, PhD, 1967. Asst. prof. Boston U., 1961-71; economist Unido, Vienna, 1968-70; assoc. prof. Nasson Coll., Sanford, Maine, 1971-75; assoc. dean Golden Gate U., Sacramento, 1976-77; energy analyst Calif. Energy Commn., Sacramento, 1977-78; economist Planning Rsch. Corp., McLean, Va., 1978-80, Congl. Rsch. Svc., Washington, 1980—99. Jewish. Avocations: music, reading. Home: 531 W Cherrywood Dr Sun Lakes AZ 85248-6327

CANTOR, DONALD JEROME, lawyer; b. Stamford, Conn., May 11, 1931; s. Albert Adelbert and Lillian (Schoenfield) C.; m. Lois Levin (div.); children: Rachel, Elizabeth, Michael, Aeron; m. Patricia Kirby, June 19, 1977; children: Jonathan, Stephanie. AB, Harvard Coll., 1953, LLB, 1959. Bar: Conn. 1959. Lawyer Gilman & Marks, Hartford, Conn., 1959-60, Levin & Hultgren, Hartford, 1960-64; ptnr. Levin, Hultgren & Cantor, Hartford, 1964-71, Hyman & Cantor, Hartford, 1971-76, Hyman, Cantor & Seichter, Hartford, 1976-85, Hyman, Cantor, Seichter & Klau, Hartford, 1985-92, Hyman, Cantor & Klau, Hartford, 1992-98, Hyman & Cantor, P.C., Hartford, 1998—. Corporator Mt. Sinai Hosp., Hartford; lectr. U. Conn. Law Sch., Hartford; founder, first pres. Conn. League Abortion Law Reform; co-founder, counsel Gender Identity Clin. Author: Escape From Marriage, 1971; co-author: Child Custody, 1989; contbr. articles to Am. Jurisprudence Trials, Atlantic Monthly, The Humanist. Founder, 1st pres. Conn. League for Abortion Law Reform; co-founder., counsel Gender Identity Clinic. Mem. Conn. Bar Assn., Hartford County Bar Assn. (chmn. family rels. sect. 1972-73), Tolland County Bar Assn. Jewish. Avocations: crossword puzzles, travel, reading, softball, children. Home: 49 High Farms Rd West Hartford CT 06107-1544 Office: Hyman & Cantor PC 21 Oak St Ste 310 Hartford CT 06106-8021

CANTOR, ERIC I. congressman; b. Richmond, Va., June 6, 1963; m. Diana Marcy Fine; children: Evan, Jenna, Michael. BA, George Washington U., 1985; JD, Coll. William & Mary, 1988; MS, Columbia U., 1989. Mem. Va. State Legis., 1992-2001, co-chair claims. com., 1992-2001, mem. cts. of justice, 1992-2001, mem. gen. laws com., 1992-2001, mem. corp. ins. & banking com., 1992-2001, mem. sci. & tech. com., 2000-2001; mem. U.S. Congress from 7th Va. dist., 2001—; mem. fin. svcs. com., internat. rels. com.; house asst. majority whip, 2001—; chmn. congress. task force on terrorism and warfare, 2001—. Republican. Jewish. Office: 329 Cannon House Office Bldg Washington DC 20515-4607*

CANTOR, IRVIN VICTOR, lawyer; b. Richmond, Va., June 9, 1953; s. Leo Joseph and Mary Frances (Cohen) C. BS, U. Va., 1975, JD, 1978. Bar: Va. 1978. Law clk. Va. Supreme Ct., Richmond, Va., 1978-79; ptnr. Rilee Cantor Arkema Edmonds (now Cantor, Arkema, P.C.), Richmond, Va., 1979—, World Class, Inc., Richmond, 1983—. Bd. dirs. Richmond Tennis Patrons, Tennis Found. Richmond, Hist. Richmond Found. Zeta Beta Tau Nat. Found. scholar, 1973. Mem. Am. Bd. Trial Advocates, Nat. Head Injury Found., Brain Injury Assn. Va. (bd. dirs. 2002—), Va. Bar Assn., Richmond Bar Assn., Va. Trial Lawyers Assn. (bd. govs. 1992—, legis. chmn. 1993—, v.p. 1997-99, pres.-elect 2001, pres. 2002—), Richmond Trial Lawyers, U. S. Tennis Assn., U. Va. Alumni Assn., Westwood Racquet Club. Office: Cantor Arkema & Edmonds PO Box 561 Richmond VA 23218-0561 E-mail: icantor@cantorarkema.com.

CANTOR, JAMES ELLIOT, lawyer; b. Detroit, Mar. 14, 1958; s. Bernard J. and Judith (Levin) C.; m. Susan Elaine Finger, Dec. 26, 1983; children: Tilly Samantha, Brian Alexander. BS in Natural Resources, U. Mich., 1980; JD, Cornell U., 1986. Bar: Alaska 1986. Assoc. Perkins Coie, Anchorage, 1986-91; asst. atty. gen. environ. sect. Alaska, Atty. Gen.'s Office, Anchorage, 1991-98, supervising atty. transp. sect., 1998—, chief asst. atty. gen., 2003—. Mem. Eagle River (Alaska) Pk. and Recreation Bd. of Suprs., 1989-95, chmn., 1991-92; dir. Anchorage (Alaska) Trails and Greenways Coalition, 1994-97; commr. Municipality of Anchorage, The Municipality of Anchorage Heritage Land Bank Adv. Commn., 1999—, chmn., 2002-2003. Mem. Anchorage Inn of Ct. Avocation: dog sled racing. Office: Atty Gen Office 1031 W 4th Ave Ste 200 Anchorage AK 99501-5903

CANTOR, LOUIS, lawyer; b. Atlantic City, N.J., Sept. 17, 1921; s. Joseph B. and Miryl (Ginsberg) C.; m. Olga Yovu, Sept. 12, 1947; children— Diana Louise Dorman, David Joseph. B.S. in Social Scis., CCNY, 1942; J.D., Columbia U., 1949. Bar: N.Y. 1949, D.C. 1967, U.S. Dist. Ct. (so. and ea. dists.) N.Y. 1951. Assoc. Sol A. Herzog, N.Y.C., 1949-53, Max E. Greenberg, N.Y.C., 1953-67; sr. ptnr. Greenberg, Cantor, Trager & Toplitz, N.Y.C., 1968—; bd. dirs., sec. CCNY Alumni Fund, N.Y.C., 1980—; nat. chmn. Am. Red Mogen David for Israel, N.Y.C., 1980— . Served to cpl. U.S. Army, 1943-46, CBI. Mem. N.Y. County Lawyers Assn., N.Y. State Bar Assn., ABA. Jewish. Club: Robert F. Wagner, Sr. Democratic (pres. 1959-62). Office: Greenberg Cantor & Reiss 100 Church St New York NY 10007-2601

CANTOR, MELVYN LEON, retired lawyer; b. Boston, Aug. 13, 1942; s. Manuel and Adeline (Raffel) C.; m. Susan Gershen, June 7, 1964 (div. Jan. 1981); children: Matthew, Douglas; m. Kathryn Gabler, Jan. 3, 1982; 1 child, Joanna. BA, U. Vt., 1964; LLB magna cum laude, U. Pa., 1967. Bar: N.Y. 1969, U.S. Dist. Ct. (so. and ea. dists.) N.Y. 1971, U.S. Ct. Appeals (2nd cir.) 1971, U.S. Ct. Appeals (3d cir.) 1974, U.S. Ct. Appeals (5th cir.) 1986, U.S. Supreme Ct. 1987. Law clk. to Hon. Stanley A. Weigel U.S. Dist. Ct., San Francisco, 1967-68; assoc. Simpson, Thacher & Bartlett, N.Y.C., 1968-74, ptnr., 1974-97; of counsel, 1998—. Adj. prof. Yeshiva U. Benjamin Cardozo Sch. Law, N.Y.C., 1977-81, lectr. in law, Columbia U. Contbr. numerous articles to profl. jours. Fellow Am. Coll. Trial Lawyers; mem. ABA, Am. Law Inst., Bar Assn. of City of N.Y., Fed. Bar Coun. Office: Simpson Thacher & Bartlett 425 Lexington Ave Fl 14 New York NY 10017-3903

CANTOR, NANCY, academic administrator; b. NYC; m. Steven Brechin; children: Maddy, Archie. AB, Sarah Lawrence Coll., 1974; PhD in Psychology, Stanford U., 1978. Faculty, chair dept. psychology Princeton (NJ) U., 1991—96; dean Horace H. Rackham Sch. Grad. Studies, vice provost for acad. affairs U. Mich., Ann Arbor, 1996—97, provost, exec. v.p. acad. affairs, 1997—2001; chancellor U. Ill.-Urbana-Champaign, 2001—. Mem. adv. bd. NSF; mem. com. on nat. needs in biomed. and behavioral sci. rsch. NRC, mem. com. on women in sci. and engring. Co-author (or co-editor): 3 books; contbr. Recipient Woman of Achievement award, Anti Defamation League. Fellow: Soc. for Personality and Social Psychology, APA (Disting. Sci. award for early career contbn. in psychology), Am. Psychol. Soc.; mem.: Am. Assn. for Higher Edn. (vice chair bd. dirs.), Am. Acad. Arts and Sci., Inst. of Medicine of NAS. Office: Univ Ill-Urbana-Champaign 320 Swanlund Adminstrn Bldg 601 E John St Champaign IL 61820

CANTOR, NORMAN FRANK, history educator, writer; b. Winnipeg, Man., Can., Nov. 19, 1929; came to U.S., 1951, naturalized, 1968; s. Max W. and Elizabeth (Niznick) C.; m. Mindy Mozart, Aug. 25, 1957; children: Howard, Judith. BA with honors, U. Man., 1951; MA, Princeton U., 1953, PhD (Porter Ogden Jacobus fellow), 1957; postgrad. (Rhodes scholar), Oxford (Eng.) U., 1954-55; LL.D. (hon.), U. Winnipeg, 1973. Instr. Princeton U., 1955-59, asst. prof. history, 1959-60; asso. prof. Columbia U., 1960-65, prof., 1965-66; Leff prof. Brandeis U., 1966-70; disting. prof. SUNY, Binghamton, 1970-76, provost for grad. studies, 1974-75, v.p. acad. affairs, 1975-76; vice chancellor for acad. affairs U. Ill., Chgo., 1976-78; dean faculty Arts and Sci. NYU, 1978-81, prof. history, sociology and comparative lit., 1981-87; prof. emeritus, 1999—; dir. Inst. Cultural Analysis NYU, 1981-87; Fulbright prof. Tel Aviv U., 1987-88. Affiliated prof. NYU Sch. Law, 1982-88; vis. disting. prof. Adelphi U., 1988-89; lectr. Inst. for Secular Jewish Humanism, Farmington Hills, Mich., 1996—. Author: Church, Kingship and Lay Investiture, 1958, Medieval History, 1963, How to Study History, 1967, The English, 1968, Western Civilization, 1972, Twentieth Century Culture, 1988, Inventing the Middle Ages, 1991, The Civilization of Middle Ages, 1993, The Medieval Reader, 1994, Medieval Lives, 1994, The Sacred Chain, 1994, The Jewish Experience, 1997, The American Century, 1997. Imagining the Law, 1997, Encyclopedia of the Middle Ages, 1999, In the Wake of the Plague (N.Y. Times Bestseller), 2001. Am. Council Learned Socs.-Can. Council fellow, 1960. Fellow Royal Hist. Soc.

CANTOR, PAMELA CORLISS, psychologist; b. N.Y.C., Apr. 23, 1944; d. Alfred Joseph and Eleanor (Weschler) C.; m. Howard Feldman, Sept. 11, 1969; children: Lauren Jaye, Jeffrey Lee. BS cum laude, Syracuse U., 1965; MA, Columbia U., 1967, PhD, 1972; postgrad., Johns Hopkins U., 1969-70, Harvard U., Boston, 1973-74. Assoc. prof. psycholoyg Boston U., 1970-80; instr. Radcliffe Inst., Harvard U., 1977-78; pvt. practice clin. psychology, South Natick, Mass., 1980—. Mem. faculty Med. Sch., Harvard U.; lectr. in field, also TV and radio appearances Author: Understanding a Child's World—Readings in Infancy through Adolescence, 1977; cons. editor Suicide and Life-Threatening Behavior; columnist For Parents Only; contbr. articles to profl. jours., chpts. to hanbooks. Mem. statewide adv. bd. Mass. Gov.'s Office for Children, 1980—; mem. adv. bd. Samaritans of Boston; pres. Nat. Com. Youth Suicide Prevention; mem. Presdl. Task Force on Youth Suicide, HHS. Mem. APA, Am. Assn. Suicidology (pres. 1985-86, bd. dirs.), Am. Orthopsychiat. Assn., Mass. Psychol. Assn. Home: 6 Phillips Pond South Natick MA 01760

CANTOR, RICHARD ALAN, lawyer; b. Terre Haute, Ind., Dec. 25, 1949; s. Oscar Edwin and Irene (Miller) C. B.A., Tulane U., 1972; J.D., Northeastern U., 1979. Bar: Fla. 1981, D.C. Press aide to Congressman Philip Ruppe, Washington, 1973-74; spl. asst. to Congressman James Mann, Washington, 1974-75; legis. cons., Washington, 1975-76; assoc. gen. counsel Oil Investment Inst., Washington, 1979-82, exec. dir., gen. counsel, 1982-86, Triad Artists, Los Angeles, 1987; atty., advisor office chief counsel Urban Mass Transp. Adminstrn., 1988—. Editorial bd. Petroleum Investment News, 1983-85. Fin. coordinator Buchanan for Senate Campaign, Washington, 1980; treas. Energy Edn. Com., Washington, 1982-85. Served with Air NG., 1972. Mem. ABA, State Bar Fla., U.S. Supreme Ct. Bar. Jewish. Office: 400 7th St SW Washington DC 20590-0001

CANTOR, RICHARD IRA, physician, corporate health executive; b. N.Y.C., Jan. 25, 1944; s. Jacob Alvin and Sarah Cantor; m. Patricia Ann Honeycutt, June 7, 1970. AB, NYU, 1965; MD, Med. Coll. Va., 1970; postgrad., Bellevue Hosp. Ctr., N.Y.C., 1970-73. Diplomate Am. Bd. Internal Medicine. Intern Bellevue Hosp. Ctr., N.Y.C., 1970-71, resident, 1971-73; internist N.Y. Med. Group, N.Y.C., 1973-76; asst. med. dir. substance abuse programs Bellevue Hosp., 1973-76, med. dir. substance abuse programs, 1976-79; med. dir. Med Plan, N.Y.C., 1979-84; employee health unit Equitable Life Assurance Soc. U.S., N.Y.C., 1984-87; v.p., dir. health and med. svcs. Citibank, N.Y.C., 1988-89, v.p., dir. health, med. and staff svcs., 1989-91, v.p., corp. med. dir., 1991-98, Citigroup, N.Y.C., 1998—. Teaching asst. in medicine N.Y.U. Med. Ctr., N.Y.C., 1970-73, asst. prof. clin. medicine, 1983—; attending physician Cabrini Med. Ctr., N.Y.C., 1973-76, Bellevue Hosp. Ctr., 1973—; chmn. policy adv. bd. N.Y.C. Methadone Maintenance Treatment Programs, 1976-77; med. cons. Am. Fedn. State, County, and Mcpl. Employees, N.Y.C., 1979-84. Columnist Ask Your Med Plan Doctor, Pub. Employee Press, 1980-84. NIH trainee in endocrinology Med. Coll. Va., 1968. Mem. ACP, AMA, Am. Coll. Occupl. and Environ. Medicine, Royal Soc. Medicine (London), Am. Coll. Physician Execs., N.Y. Occupl. Med. Assn. (exec. com. 1997), Med. Execs., Med. Soc. County N.Y., Med. Soc. State N.Y., Nat. Corp. Med. Assocs., Internat. Soc. Travel Medicine, Med. Dirs. Forum, Phi Beta Kappa, Alpha Omega Alpha, Sigma Zeta. Office: Citibank 399 Park Ave New York NY 10022-4699

CANTOR, RUSTY SUMNER, artist; b. N.Y.C., Aug. 6, 1927; s. Charles and Mollie (Kaufman) Sumner; m. Paul Arthur Cantor, Aug. 30, 1953 (dec. Sept. 1980); children: Lesley Cantor-Fallihee, Matt Geoffrey. Presenter in field. Solo exhibits include Inst. of Am. Indian Art Mus., Santa Fe, 1984, Mill Valley (Calif.) City Hall, 1991, AIA, Oakland, Calif., 1994, Bade Mus., Berkeley, Calif., 1996, SoMar, San Francisco, 1997, The Atrium @ 600 Townsend, 1999, C.G. Jung Inst., San Francisco, 2002, New Assiemo, Prato, Italy, 2003, NAWA, NYC, 2003, PRSG, San Francisco, 2003, others; two-person show Gallery on the Rim, San Francisco, 1995, Christensen Heller Gallery, Oakland, 2001, ; group exhibits include Lynnhouse Gallery, East Bay Bronze, Antioch, Calif., 1995, Fourth World Congress on Women, Beijing, 1995, Berkeley (Calif.) Art Ctr., 1995, Ritz Carlton Sculpture Gallery, San Francisco, 1995, NAWA Lever House, N.Y.C., 1995, ISE Art Found., N.Y.C., 1996, Bechtel Gallery Stanford U., 1996, NAWA Traveling exhibit, 1996—; Prieto Gallery, Mills Coll., Oakland, 1996, N.A.W.A., Soho, N.Y., 1996, 99, Somar, San Francisco, 1999, Group-ISE Found., Soho, N.Y., 2000, Discovery Mus., Bridgeport, Conn, 2001, CIIS, S.F.C.A., Halbert Biannual Appalachian State U., Mill Valley, Calif., New Assioma Art Ctr., Prato, Italy, 2003, numerous others; represented in collections Nat. Mus. Women in the Arts, Washington, Inst. Am. Indian Art Mus., Santa Fe, Am. Embassy, New Delhi, Art in Embassies Program, Washington, Many Horses Gallery, L.A., numerous pvt. collections. Group leader Inst. of Noetic Scis.; pres. N.C. Womens Caucus for the Arts (nat. bd. dirs., v.p. Pacific region). Recipient Lifetime Achievement award Women's Caucus for Art. Mem. Nat.

Assn. Women Artists, Women's Caucus for Art (bd. dirs.), Pacific Rim Sculptor Group. Avocations: reading, traveling, theatre, cinema, writing. Home: # 14 940 Dwight Way Berkeley CA 94710-2537 E-mail: rustycan@lmi.net.

CANTOR, SAMUEL C. lawyer, company executive; b. Phila., Mar. 11, 1919; s. Joseph and Miryl (Ginzberg) C.; m. Dorothy Van Brink, Apr. 9, 1943; children: Judith Ann Stone, Barbara Ann Palm. BSS, CCNY, 1940; JD, Columbia, 1943. Bar: N.Y. 1943, U.S. Dist. Ct. (so. and ea. dists.) N.Y. 1951, U.S. Supreme Ct 1969, D.C. 1971. Asst. dist. atty., N.Y.C., 1943-48; legislative counsel N.Y. State Senate; counsel N.Y.C. Affairs Com. N.Y. State Senate, 1949-59; mem. firm Newcomb, Woolsey & Cantor, Newcomb & Cantor, N.Y.C., 1951-59; 1st dep. supt. ins. State of N.Y., 1959-64, acting supt. ins., 1963-64; 2d v.p., gen. solicitor Mut. Life Ins. Co. N.Y., 1964-66, v.p., gen. counsel, 1967-72, sr. v.p., gen. counsel, 1973-74, sr. v.p. law and external affairs, 1974-75, sr. v.p. law and corp. affairs, 1975-78, exec. v.p. law and corp. affairs, 1978-84; counsel Rogers & Wells, 1984-89. Bd. dir. Mut. Life Ins. Co N.Y., Mony Reins. Corp., Monyco, Inc., Key Resources, Inc., Mony Advisors, Inc.; chmn. exec. com. N.Y. Life Ins. Guaranty Corp., 1974-84; mem. spl. com. on ins. holding holding cos. N.Y. Supt. Ins., 1967, N.Y. State select com. pub. employee pensions, 1973 Contbr. articles to Golf and other mags., legal and ins. jours. Fellow Am. Bar Found.; mem. Ins. Fedn. N.Y. (pres. 1967-68), Am. Bar Assn., N.Y. State Bar Assn., Am. Life Conv. (v.p. N.Y. State 1965-70), Am. Coun. Life Ins. (chmn. legal sect. 1977, chmn. legis. com. 1977-78, N.Y. State v.p. 1977-84), Health Ins. Assn. Am. (chmn. govt. rels. com. 1975, chmn. health care com. N.Y. State 1974-80), Assn. Life Ins. Counsel (dir.), Am. Judicature Soc., Bar Assn. City N.Y., N.Y. Law Inst., Nat. Attys. Assn., N.Y. State Dist. Attys. Assn., Union Internationale des Avocats, Columbia U. Law Sch. Alumni Assn. (dir.) Clubs: Mason. (N.Y.C.), University (N.Y.C.); Met., Univ. (Washington); Fort Orange (Albany, N.Y.); Sawgrass Country, Marsh Landing, Ponte Vedra (Fla.); La Costa Country (Carlsbad, Calif.); Confrérie des Chevaliers du Tastevin; Fairview Country (Greenwich, Conn.); Royal Dornoch Golf (Scotland), Am. Seniors Golf Assn., U.S. Golf Assn. (committeeman). Home: 10 Audubon Ln Greenwich CT 06831-2501 also: 34 Little Bay Harbor Dr Ponte Vedra Beach FL 32082-3707

CANTRELL, DOUGLAS EUGENE, history educator, author; b. Whitewood, Va., May 24, 1959; s. Charles Anderson Cantrell and Norma Lovus Davis; m. Lisa Ann Sanders, July 29, 1988. BA, Berea Coll., 1982, MA, U. Ky., 1985. Student tchr. Harlan (Ky.) High Sch., 1983; grad. asst. U. Ky., Lexington, 1983-87, instr. history, 1988, Elizabethtown (Ky.) C.C., U. Ky., 1987-91, asst. prof. history, 1991—96, assoc. prof., 1996—2003, prof., 2003—. Presenter in field. Author: American Dreams and Realities: A Retelling of the American Story, The Western Dream of Civilization, HIstorical Perspectives: A Reader and Study Guide; co-editor: Ky. History Jour., 1987; contbr. articles to profl. jours. Mem. Ky. Hist. Soc., Ky. Assn. Tchrs. History (mem. exec. bd. 1991—, pres. 1994—), Orgn. Am. Historians, So. Hist. Assn., Appalachian Studies Assn., Filson Club. Avocations: breeding tropical fish, bass fishing. Home: 220 Ruby Dr Elizabethtown KY 42701-4632 Office: Elizabethtown CC 600 College Street Rd Elizabethtown KY 42701-3053

CANTRELL, GEORGIA ANN, realtor; b. Hall, Ky., May 26, 1950; d. Melvin Johnson and Liza Ann (Collins) Johnson; children: David Cantrell, Jr., Mary Elizabeth Cantrell Riley. Grad. h.s., Fedcreek, Ky. Cert. realtor Ky. Owner Cantrell Supply, Winchester, Ky., 1979—2000; realtor Coldwell Banker Mc Mahan, Winchester, Ky., 1995—. Recipient Leadership award, Winchester-Clark Co. C. of C., 1996. Mem.: Boonesboro Lions Club, Million Dollar Club (life). Baptist. Avocations: travel, reading, walking. Home: 330 Runnymeade Dr Winchester KY 40391 Office: Coldwell Banker Mc Mahan 920 Bypass Rd Winchester KY 40391 Office Fax: 859-744-1601. Personal E-mail: gcantrell@coldwellbanker.com .

CANTRELL, JOSEPH SIRES, chemistry educator; b. Parker, Kans., July 31, 1932; s. Joseph Sires and Alta Fern (Collins) C.; m. Margaret Joyce Herr, Aug. 17, 1958; children: Mark Alan, Kenneth Aaron, Keith Floyd. AB, Emporia (Kans.) State U., 1954; MS, Kans. State U., 1958, PhD, 1961. Scientist, chemist Procter and Gamble Co., Cin., 1961—65; asst. prof. chemistry Miami U., Oxford, Ohio, 1965—68, assoc. prof., 1968—80, prof., 1980—2002, emeritus prof., 2002—. Cons. Mound Lab., EG and G, Miamisburg, Ohio, 1982—, Lawrence Livermore (Calif.) Nat. Lab., 1984— Contbr. numerous articles to profl. jours. Cubmaster pack 937, Boy Scouts Am., Hamilton, Ohio, 1978-80, com. chmn. troop 956, 1980-86, scoutmaster troop 930, Oxford, 1986-89, dist. commr. Dan Beard coun., 1970—. Sgt. U.S. Army, 1954-56. Fellow Ohio Acad. Sci., 1981, Inst. Environ. Sci., 1988. Mem. AAAS, Am. Chem. Soc. (chmn. Cin. sect. 1983-84), Electrochem. Soc. (Masons (master Oxford 1969, 76), Sigma Xi (pres. Miami U. chpt. 1980-81). Methodist. Avocations: camping, hiking, stamp collecting, oil painting. Home: 1364 Morman Rd Hamilton OH 45013-4366

CANTRELL, LANA, actress, singer, lawyer; b. Sydney, Australia, Aug. 7, 1943; d. Hubert Clarence and Dorothy Jean (Thistlethwaite) C. JD, Fordham Law Sch., 1993. Bar: N.Y. 1994. Former of counsel Ballon Stoll Bader & Adler, N.Y.C.; assoc. Sendroff & Assocs. PC, N.Y.C., 1996—. Singer supper clubs, TV programs, Australia, 1958-62; U.S. debut: TV show The Tonight Show, NBC, 1962; rec. artist RCA and Polydor Records, 1967— (Grammy award as Most Promising New Female Artist, Nat. Assn. Rec. Arts and Scis. 1967); recs. include Lana!, Act III, And Then There Was Lana, The Now of Then! Pres. Thrush, Inc.; U.S. rep. Internat. Song Festival, Poland, 1966, UN Internat. Women's Year Concert, Paris, France, 1975. Decorated Order of Australia, 2003; recipient 1st prize Internat. Song Festival Poland, 1966; 1st Internat. Woman of Yr. award Feminist Party, 1973 Office: 300 E 71st St New York NY 10021-5234

CANTRELL, ROBERT WENDELL, otolaryngologist, head and neck surgeon, educator; b. Neosho, Mo., Apr. 25, 1933; s. Lloyd L. and Ruby R. (Moffett) Cantrell; m. Young Hi Lee, Feb. 6, 1964; children: Mark L., Elizabeth L., Victoria L., Robert Wendell, Jr. Student, U.S. Naval Acad., 1952—55; AB, George Washington U., 1956, MD, 1960. Diplomate Am. Bd. Otolaryngology 1969. Intern N.Y. Hosp-Cornell U., 1960—61; resident in otolaryngology Nat. Naval Med. Center, Bethesda, Md., 1965—69; chmn. dept. otolaryngology Naval Regional Med. Center, San Diego, 1969—76; Fitz-Hugh prof. dept. otolaryngology-head and neck surgery U. Va., Charlottesville, Va., 1976—; acting v.p., provost U. Va. Health Scis. Ctr., Charlottesville, Va., 1995—96, v.p., provost, 1996—2001; dir. Va. Health Policy Ctr., Charlottesville, Va., 2001—. Bd. dirs. Am. Bd. Otolaryngology, 1980—98, exec. v.p., 1990—98. Mem. editl. bd. Laryngoscope, 1976—88, Annals of Otology, Rhinology and Laryngology, 1977—88, Am. Jour. of Otolaryngology, 1978—82, Archives of Otolaryngology, 1979—88; contbr. articles. Mayor City of Oakmont, Md., 1968—69. Capt. USN, 1961—76, capt. USNR, 1976—91. Recipient Huron W. Lawson prize, 1960; fellow, Am. Heart Assn., 1959. Mem.: Am. Otol. Soc., Am. Laryngol. Assn. (coun. 1988—90, treas. 1990—95, pres.-elect 1995, pres. 1996—97), Am. Broncho-Esophagological Assn. (pres. 1988—89), Soc. Univ. Otolaryngologists (pres. 1982), Am. Soc. Head and Neck Surgery (pres. 1985—86), Triological Soc. (v.p. So. sect. 1989—90, Mosher award 1974), Am. Acad. Facial Plastic and Reconstructive Surgery (v.p. So. sect. 1980—83), Am. Acad. Otolaryngology-Head and Neck Surgery (pres. 1987), AMA, Alpha Omega Alpha. Home: 1925 Owensville Rd Charlottesville VA 22901-8824 Office: Va Health Policy Ctr PO Box 800789 Charlottesville VA 22908-0789

CANTRELL, SCOTT, newspaper music critic; b. Ft. Smith, Ark., Nov. 14, 1949; s. Bert Thomas and Elizabeth Winstel (Scott) C. BFA, So. Meth. U., 1971; MS, Rensselaer Poly. Inst., 1974. Prodr., announcer Sta. WMHT, Schenectady, N.Y., 1973-86; music critic Times Union, Albany, N.Y., 1981-87, Rochester, N.Y., 1987-90; classical music editor Kansas City (Mo.) Star, 1990-99; music critic Dallas Morning News, 1999—. Freelance contbr. N.Y. Times, High Fidelity, Musical Am., Ovation, Classical and various other publs., 1973—; organist, choirmaster various chs., Albany, 1971-87. Recipient Deems Taylor award ASCAP, 1987, 89. Mem. Am. Guild of Organists, Music Critics Assn. N.Am. (exec. bd. 1989-2001, pres. 1993-97). Episcopalian. Avocations: travel, art, architecture, reading, cuisines. Office: The Dallas Morning News PO Box 655237 Dallas TX 75265-5237 E-mail: scantrell@dallasnews.com.

CANTRELL, SHARRON CAULK, principal; b. Columbia, Tenn., Oct. 2, 1947; d. Tom English and Beulah (Goodin) Caulk; m. William Terry Cantrell, Mar. 18, 1989; 1 child, Jordan; children from previous marriage: Christopher, George English, Steffenee Copley. BA, George Peabody Coll. Tchrs., 1970; MS, Vanderbilt U., 1980; EdS, Mid. Tenn. State U., 1986. Tchr. Ft. Campbell Jr. High Sch., Columbia, Tenn., 1970-71, Whitthorne Jr. High Sch., Columbia, Tenn., 1977-86, Spring Hill (Tenn.) High Sch., 1966—. Mem. NEA, AAUW (pres. Tenn. divsn. 1983-85), Maury County Edn. Assn. (pres. 1983-84), Tenn. Edn. Assn., Assn. Preservation Tenn. Antiquities, Maury Alliance, Friends of Children's Hosp., Rotary (bd. dirs.), Phi Delta Kappa. Mem. Ch. of Christ. Home: 5299 Main St Spring Hill TN 37174-2495 Office: Spring Hill High Sch 1 Raider Ln Columbia TN 38401-7346

CANTRICK, ROBERT BIRDSALL, music educator, academic administrator; b. Adrian, Mich., Dec. 8, 1917; s. George Townsend and Laura Elizabeth (Birdsall) C.; m. Margaret Amelia Gesell, July 16, 1943; children: Robert Allen, Joel Walter, Anthony Gesell, Timothy Townsend, Susan Birdsall, Catherine Volker. BA, U. Rochester, 1938, MA, 1946; PhD, U. Iowa, 1959. Condr. Juilliard Sch. Music, N.Y.C., 1946; asst. prof. Furman U., Greenville, S.C., 1946-51; apprentice condr. under George Szell Cleve. Orch., 1951-52; asst. prof. Carnegie-Mellon U., Pitts., 1952-55, Cornell Coll., Mt. Vernon, Iowa, 1955-59; head divsn. fine arts Jacksonville (Ala.) State U., 1959-64; dean sch. fine arts Wis. State U., Stevens Point, 1964-67; dir. arts and humanities SUNY Coll. at Buffalo, 1967-69, prof. music, 1969—85. Composer of symphonic, vocal and chamber music; restored Holst's Hammersmith to concert band repertoire; contbr. articles to profl. jours. Founder, condr. Greenville (S.C.) Symphony Orch., 1948-51. With U.S. Army, 1942-45. Grantee Carnegie Found., 1948, 49; fellow Berkshire Mus. Ctr., 1950, Ford Found., 1951-52, U.S. Office Edn., 1967, SUNY Rsch. Found., 1970, 71. Mem. Am. Music Ctr., Am. Soc. Aesthetics, Soc. Composers, Music Educators Nat. Conf., Soc. Music Theory, Nat. Flute Assn., Phi Beta Kappa. Home: 159 Bidwell Pkwy Buffalo NY 14222-1203

CANTRIL, ALBERT H(ADLEY), public opinion analyst; b. N.Y.C. s. Hadley and Mavis Katherine Cantril; m. Susan Bradford Davis. AB, Dartmouth Coll., 1962; PhD, MIT, 1966. Asst. to Bill Moyers The White House, Washington, 1965-67; cons. to dir. Bur. of the Budget, Washington, 1967; spl. asst. to asst. sec. East Asian and Pacific affairs Dept. of State, Washington, 1967-69; exec. sec., com. on def. social sci. rsch. Nat. Acad. Scis., Washington, 1969-70; cons. Dem. Nat. Com. and candidates Washington, 1971-74; dir. rsch. Commn. Op. of U.S. Senate, Washington, 1975-76; pres. Nat. Coun. on Pub. Polls, Washington, 1976-81, Bur. Social Sci. Rsch., Inc., Washington, 1981-86; fellow and rsch. fellow Inst. of Politics Harvard U., Cambridge, Mass., 1986-88; cons. ABA Comprehensive Legal Needs Survey, 1989-96; cons. pub. opinion rsch. with Susan Davis Cantril ACLU Found., 1991-93, Woodrow Wilson Internat. Ctr. for Scholars, 1996-2000. Mem. editl. adv. bd. Pub. Opinion Quar., 1985-89; trustee Nat. Coun. on Pub. Polls, 1982-94; adj. prof. internat. politics Fletcher Sch. Law and Diplomacy, Tufts U., Medford, Mass., 1991-94. Author: The Opinion Connection: Polling, Politics and the Press, 1991, Agenda for Access: The American People and Civil Justice, 1996; co-author: Hopes and Fears of the American People, 1971, Polls: Their Use and Misuse in Politics, 1972, 2d edit., 1980, Live and Let Live: American Public Opinion about Privacy at Home and at Work, 1994, Reading Mixed Signals: Ambivalence in American Public Opinion About Government, 1999; editor: Polling on the Issues, 1980, Psychology, Humanism and Scientific Inquiry: The Selected Essays of Hadley Cantril, 1988. Recipient Mecklin award Dartmouth Coll., 1962. Mem. Am. Assn. Pub. Opinion Rsch. Avocations: jazz, tennis.

CANTÚ, NORMA V. law educator, former federal official; b. Brownsville, Tex., Nov. 2, 1954; BS summa cum laude, Pan Am. U., 1973; JD, Harvard U., 1977. Bar: Tex. 1978, U.S. Dist. Ct. (so. dist.) Tex. 1979, U.S. Dist. Ct. (we. dist.) Tex. 1981, U.S. Ct. Appeals (5th and 11th cirs.) 1982, Calif. 1985, U.S. Ct. Appeals (10th cir.) 1986, U.S. Dist. Ct. (no. dist.) Tex. 1992. Tchr. English, Brownsville, 1974, San Antonio, 1979; intern Office of Atty. Gen. Tex., 1977-78; atty. Mex. Am. Legal Def. and Ednl. Fund, 1979—93, regional counsel, 1985-93; asst. sec. for civil rights Office for Civil Rights U.S. Dept. of Edn., Washington, 1993—2001; prof. law and edn. U. Tex., Austin, Tex., 2001—. U.S. rep. OAS Commn. on Children, 1999—2001. Officer Avance Parent Child Tng. Program, 1990; bd. dirs. Hispanic Health Policy Devel. Program, 1992, MALDEF, 2001—02, Mex. Am. Leadership Coun., 2002—, Leadership San Antonio, 1992—. Named to San Antonio Women Hall of Fame, Women in Sports Edn. Hall of Fame. Office: U Tex at Austin Sch Law Townes Hall Rm 3118M 727 E Dean Keeton St Austin TX 78705 Home: 140 Twinleaf Ln San Antonio TX 78213

CANTWELL, CHRISTOPHER WILLIAM, artist; b. Atwater, Calif., Dec. 24, 1960; s. Donald Byron and Ann Louise Cantwell; m. Susan Rebecca Moore, Sept. 19, 1982 (div. 1997); children: Claire Elyse Moore, Katie Lynn Moore. Owner, artist Christopher W. Cantwell Woodworks, Modesto, Calif., 1979-82, Oakhurst, Calif., 1982—. Cons. Internat. Union for conservation of Natural Resources, Cambridge, Eng., 1991—. Contbr. art book Jewelry Boxes, 1996; exhibited at Del Mano Gallery, 1990, 98, 99, Furniture Soc. Conf., San Francisco, 1998, Del Mano, 1999, Laguna Art Mus., 1999, Orange County Mus. Art, 2000, OXO Tower, London, England, 2001, Collins Gallery, Glasgow, Scotland, 2002; represented in permanent collections Irving Lipton Collection, Robert Bohlen Collection, White House Ornament Collection. Youth advisor Oakhurst Luth. Ch., 1992-96. Mem. Am. Craft Coun., World Wildlife Fund, Program for Belize, Good Wood Alliance (CITES Liaison 1994—), Box Art Soc. (pres. 1999—). Democrat. Avocations: rock climbing, skiing, surfing. Home and Office: PO Box 1736 Oakhurst CA 93644-1736

CANTWELL, DON, artistic director; b. Charleston, S.C., July 10, 1935; s. James Richard Jr. and Helen (Thompson) C.; m. Patricia Downs; children: Kimberly S., Dewey C. Jr., Joshua Paul. Grad. high sch., Charleston. Dir. Charleston Ballet Sch., 1969—; artistic dir. Charleston Ballet Theatre, 1969—. Mem. Southeastern Ballet Assn. (v.p. 1981-82, 85-86, pres. 1983-84, 86-87, chmn. bd. 1984-85, 87-88). Office: Charleston Ballet Theatre 477 King St Charleston SC 29403-6231

CANTWELL, JOHN WALSH, advertising executive; b. Fall River, Mass., July 16, 1922; s. William J. and Esther (Walsh) C.; m. Evelyna Dyson; children from previous marriage: Sharon, Peter, Paul. BS in Econs., Holy Cross Coll., 1944; MA, Georgetown U., 1945; postgrad., Columbia U., 1949-50. Asst. sales mgr. Internat. Milling Co., 1947-48; v.p. mgmt. supr. Compton Advt., N.Y.C., 1948-60; sr. v.p. mgmt. supr. Sullivan, Stauffer Colwell & Bayles, N.Y.C., 1960-65; pres., CEO Pritchard, Wood (advt.), N.Y.C., 1965-68, Parkson Advt. Agy., Inc., 1968-69; sr. v.p. J.B. Williams Co., Inc., 1968-69; pres. Jack Cantwell, Inc., 1970—; chmn., CEO Dolphin Med. Acoustics, Ltd., 1997-99; CEO Essex Labs., Ltd., Ft. Lauderdale, 1999—. Office: Essex Towers 340 Sunset Dr Ste 1405 Fort Lauderdale FL 33301-2653

CANTWELL, MARIA E. senator; b. Oct. 13, 1958; d. Rose and Paul Cantwell. BA Public Policy, Miami U. of Ohio. State repr. Dist. 44, Wash., 1987—92; mem. 103rd Congress from 1st Wash. dist., Washington, 1993—2000; owner pub. rels. firm.; U.S. senator from Wash., 2001—. Democrat. Office: 717 Hart Senate Bldg Washington DC 20510*

CANTWELL, ROBERT, lawyer; b. Buffalo, Sept. 12, 1931; s. Thomas and Helen (Robinson) C.; m. Barbara Hurlbert, Oct. 19, 1963; children: Robert, Helen Virginia, Sara Elizabeth. AB, Cornell U., 1953, JD, 1956; LLM, NYU, 1959. Bar: N.Y. State bar 1956. Assoc. firm Jaeckle, Fleischmann & Mugel (and predecessor firm), Buffalo, 1956-62; mem. legal dept. Colgate-Palmolive Co., N.Y.C., 1962-68, London dep. gen. counsel, 1972-73, v.p., gen. counsel, 1973-86, sec., 1974-86; v.p., sec., gen. counsel Roblin Industries, Inc., Buffalo, 1968-72; ptnr. Serchuk, Wolfe and Zelermyer, White Plains, N.Y., 1986-87, Cantwell and Chen, N.Y.C., 1988-89; pvt. practice Greenwich, Conn., 1989—. Mem. ABA, N.Y. State Bar Assn., Assn. of Bar of City of N.Y., Am. Soc. Corp. Secs., Saturn Club (Buffalo), Belle Haven, Greenwich Horseneck Club. Home and Office: 5 Meadow Dr Greenwich CT 06831-4504

CANTWELL, WILLIAM PATTERSON, lawyer; b. Saranac Lake, N.Y., Dec. 2, 1921; s. Francis Barry and Genevieve (Godfrey) C.; m. Hendrika Antonia Bestebreurtje, June 19, 1947; children: Peter F., Rebecca D., Christopher A. BA with highest honors, Williams Coll., 1942; JD, Yale U., 1948. Bar: N.Y. 1948, Colo. 1953. Assoc. Moot, Sprague, Marcy & Gulick, Buffalo, 1948-52, Holland & Hart, 1953-64; ptnr. Sherman & Howard, 1964-87, of counsel, 1988-95. Vis. lectr. law U. Denver, 1956-60, 64-65, U. Colo., 1962, 87, U. Miami, 1976; lectr. various continuing legal edn. insts. and legal meetings; reporter on Uniform Marital Property Act Nat. Conf. Commrs. on Uniform State Laws, 1980-83. Contbr. articles to profl. jours. Recipient Treat award Nat. Coll. Probate Judges for Probate Excellence, 1983 Mem. ABA (ho. of dels. 1964-66, 73-78, chmn. real property probate and trust law sect. 1971-72), Am. Coll. Trust and Estate Counsel (pres. 1975-76, Trachtman lectr. 1980), Colo. Bar Assn. (pres. 1970-71, gov. 1959-65, chmn. taxation law sect. 1959-60, probate and trust law sect. 1960-61), Denver Bar Assn. (pres. 1962-63, award of merit 1969), Order of Coif (hon.). Home: 700 West 140 North Driggs ID 83422

CANUP, JAMES W.C. lawyer; b. Washington; s. William C. and Mireille R. Canup; m. Winnie Perilla, May 30, 1987; children: Elise, William, Ann Charlotte. BA, U. Va., 1980; JD, Washington & Lee U., 1984; LLM, Georgetown U., 1992. Bar: Va. 1984, Md. 1987, D.C. 1987. Sr. atty.-advisor Chief Counsel, IRS, Washington, 1987-93; assoc. Brown & Wood, LLP, Washington, 1993-95; ptnr. McGuire Woods, LLP, Richmond, Va., 1996—. Mem. Nat. Assn. of Real Estate Investment Trusts (govt. rels. com. 1994—), Mortgage-Backed Securities Industry Group, Jr. Achievement of Ctrl. Va. Inc. (bd. dirs. 1999—). Office: McGuire Woods LLP One James Ctr 901 E Cary St Richmond VA 23219-4057

CANYON, STEVEN, financial officer; b. Nov. 3, 1961; BS, Calif. State U., Northridge, 1985. C.F.O. Paracelsus Healthcare, 1991-93; v.p. fin. Friendly Hills Health Care Network, La Habra, Calif., 1993-96; regional C.F.O. Tenet Integrated Physician Svcs., Calif., 1996-97; principal Greater Pacific Med. Mgmt., Huntington Beach, Calif., 1997—. Office: Principal Greater Pacific Med Mgmt 15061 Springdale St Ste 204 Huntington Beach CA 92649-1104

CANZONIER, WALTER JUDE, shellfish aquaculturist; b. New Brunswick, N.J., Feb. 6, 1936; s. Joseph V. and Mary M. (Patterson) C. BS, St. Peter's Coll., Jersey City, 1957; postgrad., Rutgers U., 1957-64. Teaching asst. dept. zoology Rutgers U., New Brunswick, N.J., 1958-59, rsch. asst. dept. oyster culture, 1960-67, rsch. assoc., 1968-71, 81-87; rsch. fellow Inst. Marine Biology, CNR, Venice, Italy, 1971-77, dir. Coastal Resources Applied Rsch. Lab., Venice, 1977-80; dir. R & D, Aquarius Assocs., Port Noris, N.J., 1987—. Mem. tech. coms. Italian Ministry Sanità and Ministry Merchant Marine, 1974-80, Interstate Shellfish Sanitation Conf., 1980—; cons. on marine sci. UNESCO, France, 1978—. Contbr. over 45 articles to sci. jours. in N.Am., Europe and Asia. Organizer, treas. Point Pleasant Beach (N.J.) Taxpayers Assn., 1963-70; bd. dirs. N.E. Regional Aquaculture Ctr., 1992-2003, N.J. Taskforce for Revitalization of Shellfish Industry, 1997, N.J. Aquaculture Adv. Coun., 2000—. Recipient numerous grants from pub. agys. in N.Am. and Europe, 1971—. Mem. Nat. Shellfisheries Assn., Soc. Invertebrate Pathology, World Aquaculture Soc. N.J. Aquaculture Assn. (trustee 1989—, pres. 1991—). Achievements include development of shellfish sanitation guidelines and regulations for state and national health agencies in North America and Europe; design of marine research and aquaculture facilities in Asia, Europe and North America; advocacy for legis. to promote comml. aquaculture devel. Home: 44 Cowart Ave Manasquan NJ 08736-3102 Office: Aquarius Assocs PO Box 662 Port Norris NJ 08349-0662

CAO, DAC-BUU, software engineer; b. Ninh Hoa, Khanh Hoa, Vietnam, Feb. 21, 1949; came to U.S., 1980; s. Thuan and Tiep Thi (Le) C.; m. Amy My-Hao Luong, Nov. 11, 1967; children: Valerie Phuong-Bao, Jesse Chau, Mike Minh-Chau. B of Law, U. Saigon, Vietnam, 1972; BS in Computer Sci., U. Calif., Irvine, 1985; MS in Computer Sci., West Coast U., L.A., 1991. Spl. corr. Progress Daily News, Saigon, 1965-69, mng. editor, 1969-72; asst. editor Dem. Daily News, Saigon, 1973-74; programmer, analyst Eaton Corp., Costa Mesa, Calif., 1981-85; system design engr. EPC Internat., Newport Beach, Calif., 1985-89; sr. application specialist McDonnell Douglas System Integration, Cypress, Calif., 1989-91; sr. systems engr. Unigraphics div. EDS Corp., 1991-98; mgr. TAC Systems Devel., Unigraphics Solutions, Cypress, 1998—. Author: (Vietnamese) Tien Don Yeu Dau, 1969, Ngon Doi Tuyet Vong, 1970. Recipient Vietnamese Journalism award Nat. Press Coun., U.S. Govt., 1966, Systems Integration MVP award McDonnell Douglas Corp., 1990. Mem. Assn. for Computing Machinery, N.Y. Acad. Scis. Republican. Buddhist. Achievements include invention of protector for motor vehicles; design of cellular air time tracking system. pager tracking system. Office: Unigraphics Solutions 10824 Hope St Cypress CA 90630-5214

CAO, GUOHONG, computer science educator; b. Hebei, China, Oct. 14, 1968; came to U.S., 1994; s. Zhongjie Cao and Xiaocai Liu; m. Lihong Huang, Oct. 9, 1996; children: Jeffrey, Jasmine. BS, Xian Jiaotong U., 1990; MS, Ohio State U., 1997, PhD, 1999. Computer engr. Inst. of Data Processing Tech., Beijing, 1990-93, group leader, 1993-94; rsch. assoc. Fla. Internat. U., Miami, 1994-96; rsch. asst. Ohio State U., Columbus, 1996-99; asst. prof. Pa. State U., State College, 1999—. Software engr. Comtech Corp., Wesserville, Ohio, 1997. Contbr. articles to profl. jour. Presdl. fellow Ohio State U., 1999; NSF career awardee, 2001. Mem. IEEE, Assn. for Computing Machinery. Avocations: chess, bridge, basketball, football. Office: Dept Computer Sci/Engring Pa State U State College PA 16802 E-mail: gcao@cse.psu.edu.

CAO, (FRANCIS) KHANG VAN, small business owner, poet; b. Vung Tau, Vietnam, Apr. 15, 1967; s. Thiet Van Cao and Huong Thi Nguyen; m. Tam Thanh Cao, Feb. 10, 1996; children: Jasmine Diem-Lien, Luke The-Luc, Nicholas The-Quyen. BS in Gen. Sci. cum laude, BA in Theology cum laude, Divine Word Coll., Epworth, Iowa, 1990; AA in Libr. Tech., Rancho Santiago Coll., Santa Ana, Calif., 1993. Bilingual tchr. Vermilion Parish Sch. Bd., Abbeville, La., 1994—97; owner TJ Food Mart, Abbeville, La., 1997—. Songwriter (songs) Love Songs for Everyone Forever Vols. 1, 2, & 3, poet (poetry) Love Beyond Looks: My Little Book of Poems, The Sun Is Up/Down (2nd Pl., 1984). Mem.: La. Songwriters Assn. Office: TJ Food Mart 900 S State St Abbeville LA 70510 Personal E-mail: sirfrancis111@yahoo.com. E-mail: franciscao@cox-internet.com.

CAO, L. CHARLIE, structural engineer, consultant; b. Jiangsu, Peoples Republic of China, 1959; BS, S.E. U., Nanjing, China, 1982, MS, 1985; PhD, U. Colo., 1996. Registered profl. engr., Calif., Colo., Wash. Cons. on projects including seismic upgrading of I. Magnin Bldg., Oakland, Calif.; prin. Unistress Engring. Group, Calif. Contbr. articles to profl. jours. including Jour. Structural Engring. Recipient Sci. and Tech. Hon. award China State Shipbuilding Co., 1990, medal of excellence, China State Commn. Engring. Software Appraisal, 1988. Recipient Outstanding Project award, Nat. Coun. Structural Engrs. Assns., 2001, Structural Engring. Excellence award, Structural Engrs. Assn. Calif., 2001. Mem. ASCE (Arthur M. Wellington prize 1997), S.E. of Structural Engrs. Assn. of Calif.

CAO, LI, social studies educator, educator; s. Changming Cao and Huazhi Peng; m. Grace Xiang Li, Dec. 26, 1984; 1 child, Jennifer Jianqin. PhD, McGill U., Montreal, QC Canada, 2001. Asst. prof. St. Mary's U. Minn., Mpls., 2000—01; asst. prof. ednl. psychology State U. West Ga., Carrollton, Ga., 2001—. Sr. rsch. assoc. AXDEV Corp., Brossard, Quebec, Canada, 1997—99. Recipient Dean's awards, Queen's U., Kingston, Ont. Can., 1994, Grad. awards, Queen's U. Kingston, Ont. Can., 1995; fellow Royal Bank fellowship, Royal Bank, 1997; grantee Rsch. grant, Found. for Info. and Rsch. Que., 1997; scholar Guang Hua scholarship, Guang Hua Found., 1991. Mem.: AAUP, Can. Soc. Study of Edn., Ea. Region of Ednl. Rsch. Assn., Am. Ednl. Rsch. Assn. Avocations: running, travel, reading. Office: State U West Ga 1600 Maple St CEPD Carrollton GA 30118 Office Fax: 770-836-4645. Personal E-mail: lcao@westga.edu. E-mail: lcao@westga.edu.

CAO, WEIMING, mathematician, educator; b. Jingjiang, Jiangsu Province, China, 1963; PhD, Shanghai U. Sci. and Tech., Shanghai, China, 1989. Asst. prof. U. Tex. at San Antonio, 1996—99; rsch. assoc. Simon Fraser U., Van Couver, Canada, 1995—96; post-doc rsch. fellow U. Manitoba, Winnipeg, Canada, 1990—94; lectr. Shanghai U. Sci. and Tech., Shanghai. Recipient First Class prize Sci. and Tech. Progress award, Min. Edn. China, 1991. Office: Dept Math U Tex San Antonio San Antonio TX 78249

CAOUETTE, DAVID PAUL, public relations executive; b. Sanford, Maine, Aug. 6, 1960; s. Paul Henry and Barbara (Stackpole) C. BA with distinction, U. Maine, Orono, 1983. Editor employee communications Union Mutual Life Ins. Co., Portland, Maine, 1981-84, pub. rels. acct. exec., 1984-85; mgr. employee communications UNUM Life Ins. Co., Portland, 1985-87; v.p., mgr. communications Integrated Resources, Inc., N.Y.C., 1987-89; asst. dir. corp. communications Fin. Guaranty Ins. Co., N.Y.C., 1989—; a.v.p. corp. comms. GE Capital/FGIC, N.Y.C., 1989-94; corp. comms. dir. AT&T Capital, Morristown, N.J., 1994-98; fin. comm. dir. AT&T Corp., Basking Ridge, NJ, 1998—2001; v.p. corp. media rels. and fin. comms. AT&T Wireless Svcs. Corp., Redmond, Wash., 2001—. Ptnr., co-founder Interactive Communications, Inc., Merrick, N.Y., 1989—. Recipient 1st place bronze award Fin. World Ann. Report Competition, 1994, Grand award ARC awards, 2002, Best of Show NIRI, Seattle, 2002. Mem. Internat. Assn. Bus. Communicators, Pub. Rels. Soc. Am., Nat. Investor Rels. Inst. Democrat. Roman Catholic. Office: AT&T Wireless Svcs 16331 NE 72d Way Redmond WA 98052 Home: 803 197th Ave SE Sammamish WA 98075-7499 E-mail: david.caouette@attws.com.

CAPACCIO, MATTEO, social worker, health facility administrator; b. Bklyn., Feb. 24, 1961; s. Matteo Capaccio, Maria Annunciata D'Accordo; life ptnr. Carmela Carrubba, Apr. 1, 1999. B in Profl. Studies, Audrey Cohen Coll., 1995; MSW, Hunter Coll., 1998. Cert. social worker N.Y. Case mgr. The Bridge, Inc., N.Y.C., 1992—97; program dir. Argus Cmty., Bronx, NY, 1997—98; mental health coord. Promesa, Inc., Bronx, 1998—99; dir. social svcs. Casa Promesa, Bronx, 1999—2000; sr. assoc. dir. Guidance Ctr. Bklyn., Inc., 2000—02, dir., 2002—03; crisis counselor Project Liberty program Inst. for Cmty. Living, Inc., Bklyn., 2003—. Recipient Above and Beyond Award, Promesa Found., 1999. Mem.: Acad. Cert. Social Workers, Hunter Coll. Sch. Social Work Alumni Assn. (bd. dirs. 2001—). Avocations: skydiving, long-distance running. Office: Inst for Cmty Living 2581 Atlantic Ave Brooklyn NY 11207 Office Fax: 718-280-8113.

CAPALBO, CARMEN, theater director and producer; b. Harrisburg, Pa., Nov. 1, 1925; s. Joseph and Concetta (Riggio) C.; m. Patricia McBride, July 9, 1950 (div. June 1961); children: Carla, Marco. Student, Yale Sch. Drama. Prodns. include: dir., co-prodr. (plays) Juno and the Paycock, Shadow and Substance, Dear Brutus, Awake and Sing!, The Threepenny Opera, The Potting Shed, A Moon for the Misbegotten, The Cave Dwellers, The Rise and Fall of the City of Mahagonny; dir. (opera) The Good Soldier Schweik, (plays) A Connecticut Yankee, Seidman and Son, The Strangers, Enter Solly Gold, Slowly, By Thy Hand Unfurled; original dir.: The Sign in Sidney Brustein's Window, The Chosen; also TV prodn. The Power and the Glory; story cons.: Studio One, 1951-52; cons. The Bronx: After the Fires, Conversation with Eddie, 1983; prodn. mgr. Emlyn Williams as Charles Dickens, 1952-53, Jean-Louis Barrault-Madeleine Renaud Co., 1952; dir., prodr., writer 200 radio plays. Served with U.S. Army, 1944—45. Decorated Bronze Star, Purple Heart; recipient spl. Tony award 1956, Obie award 1956. Mem. League N.Y. Theatres, Dirs. Guild Am., Soc. Stage Dirs. and Choreographers, Dramatists Guild, League OffBroadway Theatres (co-founder 1958, exec. bd. 1958-60). Address: 500 2nd Ave New York NY 10016-8606

CAPALDI, ELIZABETH ANN DEUTSCH, psychological sciences educator; b. N.Y.C., May 13, 1945; d. Frederick and Nettie (Tarasuck) Deutsch; m. Egidio J. Capaldi, Jan. 20, 1968 (div. May 1985) AB, U. Rochester, 1965; PhD, U. Tex., 1969. Asst. prof. dept. psychol. scis. Purdue U., West Lafayette, Ind., 1969-74, assoc. prof., 1974-78, prof., 1979-86, asst. dean Grad. Sch., 1982-86, head dept. psychol. scis., 1983-88, sec.-treas. council of grad. dept. psychology, 1986-88; prof. U. Fla., Gainesville, 1988-2000, provost, v.p. acad. affairs, 1996-99; provost SUNY, Buffalo, 2000—. Spl. asst. to pres., U. Fla., 1991-96. Author: Psychology, 1989, 4th edit., 1996; cons. editor Jour. Exptl. Psychology, 1991-96; assoc. editor Psychonomic Bull. Rev., 1993-98; contbr. articles to profl. jours. NIMH grantee, 1984-94, NSF grantee, 1995-98. Fellow AAAS, APA, Am. Psychol. Soc. (mem. governing bd. 1991-96, pres. 1999); mem. Psychonomic Soc. (mem. governing bd. 1992-97), Midwestern Psychol. Assn. (sec.-treas. 1988-90, pres. 1991), Sigma Xi. Office: SUNY Univ at Buffalo Office of Provost 562 Capen Hall Buffalo NY 14260-1600

CAPALDI, LARRY SYLVESTRO, business educator; b. N.Y.C., Sept. 22, 1942; s. Leonard and Alesia C.; 1 child, Lance. BBA, CCNY, 1965; MA, Ctrl. Mich. U., 1974; D in Bus. Adminstrn., Nova U., 1981. Cert. procurement educator. Commd. 2d lt. USAF, 1965; advanced through grades to maj.; dep. chief def. contract adminstrv. svc. area, 1978-80; contracting officer AVCO sys. divsn. Wilmington, Mass., 1980-82; ret. USAF, 1985; acquisition support mgr. hqrs. Air Force Contract Mgmt. Div. Albuquerque, 1982-85; prof. Webster U., Albuquerque, 1985—; assoc. staff mem. BDM Corp., Albuquerque, 1986-88; negotiation cons. Capaldi Cons., Albuquerque, 1988—; prof. Navajo Indian Nation, Window Rock, Ariz., 2000-2001; with Albuquerque (N.Mex.) Police Dept., 2003—. Contbr. articles to jours. Vol. Albuquerque Little Theatre, 1984—; docent Rio Grande Zoo, Albuquerque, 1983—; mus. dir. Toy Train Operating Soc., Albuquerque, 1997-2000; election vol. Heather Wilson Election Coun., Abuquerque, 1998-2000. Avocations: hot air ballooning, scuba diving. Home: 7115 Montano Rd NW Albuquerque NM 87120 Fax: 897-7279. E-mail: profspqr@comcast.net.

CAPALDO, GUY, obstetrician, gynecologist; b. Bisaccia, Italy, Jan. 1, 1950; came to U.S., 1958; s. Arturo Nunziante and Maria Carmela (Ciani) C.; m. Kathy Nicita, Apr. 20, 1985. BSEE magna cum laude, U. Dayton, 1972; MS, Ohio State U., Columbus, 1973; MD, Med. Coll. Ohio, 1978. Diplomate Am. Bd. Ob-Gyn; cert. clin. densitometrist Internat. Soc. Clin. Densitometry. Research asst. Ohio State U., 1973-75; resident in ob-gyn Med. Coll. Ohio, Toledo, 1978-82; practice medicine specializing in ob-gyn Mansfield, Ohio, 1982—. Chief ob-gyn. dept. Mansfield Gen. Hosp., 1985—; lab. dir. Mansfield (Ohio) Ob-Gyn Assocs. Contbr. articles to profl. jours. Clinic physician Plan Parenthood, Mansfield, 1982—. Pres. scholar U. Dayton, 1968-72, Univ. fellow Ohio State U., 1972-75. Fellow Am. Coll. Ob-Gyn; mem. AMA, Ohio State Med. Assn., Richland County Med. Soc. Avocations: reading, fishing, traveling, golfing. Office: Mansfield Ob-Gyn Assocs 500 S Trimble Rd Mansfield OH 44906-3483

CAPANNA, ALBERT HOWARD, neurosurgeon, neuroscientist, lawyer; b. Utica, N.Y., May 12, 1947; m. Dawn McLouth; children: Christine, Alicia, Albert II, Danielle, Gabriella, Guy, Brianna, Gianna, Beau, Bianca. BA, U. Tex., 1970; MD, Wayne State U., 1974; JD, U. Nev., 2001. Med. intern St. John Hosp., Detroit, 1974, resident in gen. surgery, 1974-75; resident in neurosurgery Wayne State U., Detroit, 1975-79; fellow in microneurosurgery U. Zurich, 1979; stereotactic fellow U. Paris, 1980; fellow in pediatric neurosurgery Hosp. for Sick Children, Toronto, 1980; pvt. practice Las Vegas, Nev., 1980—; clin. asst. prof. neurosurgery sch. medicine U. Nev., 1983—. Chief staff Sunrise Hosp., Las Vegas, 1993-94; chief neurosurgery Univ. Med. Ctr., Las Vegas; clin. prof. U. Nev. Sch. Medicine, 1991—. Mem.: Rocky Mountain Neurosurg. Soc. (sec. 1998—2001, pres. 2002—03). Office: Internat Neurosci Cons Ste 302 2320 Paseo Del Prado Las Vegas NV 89102-4358

CAPANOLI, BRIAN MARIO, sales executive; b. Grand Rapids, Minn., Sept. 5, 1960; s. Mario Stevenson and Patricia Ann Capanoli. Student, U. Minn., 1980—84; A in Applied Sci., Hibbing C.C., 1996. Peer counselor Ctr. for Independent Living, Hibbing, Minn., 1989—92; diction coach, transl. Hibbing C.C., 1993—2003, theater asst., 1994—96; dist. mgr. Hibbing Daily Tribune, 1997—2001; salesperson Wal-Mart, 2001—. Author: (book) The Cycle, 2002 (Five Minutes of Fame award). Chairperson Hibbing Human Rights Commn., Hibbing, 1986—92; sec. Across Hibbing Adv. Bd., Hibbing, 1992—95; adv. bd. Access Hibbing; office asst. Dem. Farmer UBR Party, Hibbing, 1996—. Avocations: learning foreign languages, reading, bicycling. E-mail: briancap@cpinternet.com.

CAPASSO, FEDERICO, physicist; b. Rome, June 24, 1949; came to U.S., 1976; D in Physics summa cum laude, U. of Rome, 1973; D in Electronic Engrng. (hon.), U. Bologna, Italy, 2003. Researcher Fondazione Bordoni, Rome, 1974-76; vis. scientist Bell Labs., Holmdel, N.J., 1976-77, mem. tech. staff, 1977-78, Lucent Technologies (formerly AT&T), Murray Hill, N.J., 1978-87, head quantum phenomena and device rsch. dept., 1987-97, head semicondr. physics rsch. dept., 1997-2000, v.p. phys. rsch., 2000—; Gordon McKay prof. applied physics, Vinton Hayes sr. rsch. fellow elec. engring. Harvard U., 2003—. Co-chmn. Internat. Semiconductor Device Rsch. Symposium, Charlottesville, Va., 1995; chmn. Internat. Conf. on Advances in Semiconductors and Superconductors, Newport Beach, 1988, 90; program co-chmn. Picosecond Electronics and Optoelectronics Conf., Lake Tahoe, 1987; program com., mem. of 20 internat. confs.; invited lectr. at over 140 internat. confs. Editor 4 books; mem. editl. bd. Il Nuovo Cimento, Applied Physics Letters, Semiconductor Sci. and Tech.; holder 38 U.S. patents, more than 50 fgn. patents; contbr. over 300 articles to profl. jours. Recipient award N.Y. Acad. Scis., 1993, Gold medal Heinrich Welker Meml., 1994, Vinci Excellence award LMVH, 1995, medal Materials Rsch. Soc., 1995, Electronics Letters Premium award Inst. of Elec. Engrs. (London), 1995, Bell Labs. fellow award, 1997, John Price Wetherill medal Franklin Inst., 1997, Rank prize, 1998, Capitolium prize, 1998, Alessandro Volta Meml. medal, 1999, Willis Lamb medal in laser physics, 2000; named hon. mem. Franklin Inst., 1997, Goff Smith Prize, U. of Mich., 2003. Fellow AAAS (Newcomb Cleveland prize 1995), IEEE (David Sarnoff award 1991, W. Streifer Sci. Achievement award), IEEE Lasers Electrooptics Soc., Am. Phys. Soc., Optical Soc. Am. (Robert Wood prize 2001), Internat. Soc. for Optical Engring., Am. Acad. Arts and Scis., Inst. of Physics (Duddell medal 2001); mem. NAE, NAS, European Acad. Sci.

CAPASSO, NICHOLAS JOHN, curator, art historian, public art expert; b. Alexandria, Va., Nov. 16, 1959; s. Nicholas Salvatore and Clio Maria (Di-Napoli) C.; m. Andrea Maxim Southwick, July 25, 1992. BA magna cum laude in Art History, Clark U., Worcester, Mass., 1982; MA in Art History, Rutgers U., 1984, PhD in Art History, 1998. Teaching asst. Rutgers U., 1986-88, lectr., summer 1988, Rochester Inst. Tech., fall 1988; assoc. curator, curator DeCordova Mus. and Sculpture Park, Lincoln, Mass., 1990—. Guest curator Fire and Ice, Attleboro (Mass.) Mus., 1993, Sculpture Walk '93, Larz Anderson Park, Brookline, Mass., 1993, Seventh Annual Sculpture Exhibition, Bradley Palmer State Park, Topsfield, Mass., 1993, Relief Printmaking in the 1980s: Prints and Blocks from Rutgers Archives for Printmaking Studios, Jane Voorhees Zimmerli Art Mus., New Brunswick, N.J., 1988, Arts Afloat, Boston Children's Mus., 1998, Just the Thing, Woodson Mus., Wausau, Wis., 1998, Contemporary Outdoor Sculpture, City of Boston, 1997; pub. art juror. Editor: Sculpture Park Guide, 1991, 92; editor-in-chief: Rutgers Art Review, The Journal of Graduate Research in Art History, 1986; contbr. articles to profl. jours.; lectr. in field. Bd. chair Urban Arts Inst., Mass. Coll. Art. Recipient Samuel H. Kress travel fellowship in history of art, 1990-91, Smithsonian predoctoral fellowship Nat. Mus. Am. Art, 1989-90, Univ. Grad. fellowship Rutgers U., 1987-88, Spl. Grad. fellowship Rutgers U., 1982-86. Mem. Am. Assn. Museums, Assn. Historians Am. Art, Coll. Art Assn., New Eng. Mus. Assn., Internat. Sculpture Ctr., Phi Beta Kappa. Office: DeCordova Mus & Sculpture Park 51 Sandy Pond Rd Lincoln MA 01773 E-mail: ncapasso@decordova.org.

CAPASSO, ROBERT, financial executive; b. Bridgeport, Conn., Dec. 8, 1954; s. Patrick and Helen Capasso; m. Beverly Capasso, May 12, 1978; children: Robert, Thomas. BS in Acctg., Sacred Heart U., 1976; MS in Taxation, Fla. Internat. U., 1994. CPA, CFP, cert. mgmt. acct., Fla. V.p., CFO Stresscon, Hialeah, Fla., 1985-92; CFO Rinker Materials Corp., West Palm Beach, Fla., 1992-99; v.p. fin. CSR Am.-Pipe Concrete Products, West Palm Beach, 1999—2001, Rinker Materials of Fla., West Palm Beach, 2001—. Office: Rinker Materials-Fla 1501 Belvedere Rd West Palm Beach FL 33406-1501 E-mail: bcapasso@yahoo.com.

CAPE, FRANCIS, artist; b. Lisbon, Portugal, Dec. 19, 1952; arrived in US, 1993; s. Donald Paul and Cathune Agnes Cape; m. Liza Phillips, July 2, 1960. BA, Cambridge (Eng.) U., 1974; BFA, City and Guilds of London Art Sch., 1982; MFA, U. London, 1991. Apprentice wood and stone carver Dick Reid, Master Carver, York, England, 1974—79. Artist in residence Amherst (Mass.) Coll., 2002—02. Exhibitions include The Showroom, London, 1993, Andrea Rosen Gallery, NY, 1996, Sculpture Ctr., 1997, reviewed in:, New York Times, Art in America, New Yorker, etc, exhibitions include P.S.1 Contemporary Art Ctr., NY, 2000, Statements, Art Basel, Switzerland, 2000, P.S.1 Contemporary Art Ctr., NY, 2002, Mary Boone Gallery, 2002, Aldrich Mus., 2002. EMT Tusten (N.Y.) Vol. Ambulance Svc., 2002—03. Recipient Award in Sculpture, The Louis Comfort Tiffany Found., 2001. Avocation: hiking.

CAPE, JAMES ODIES E. fashion designer; b. Detroit, Nov. 18, 1947; s. Odies E. and Juanita K. (Brandon) C. Student, Henry Ford C.C., 1973-75, Am. Acad. Dramatic Arts, N.Y.C., 1975-76, Pace U., 1977-78. Trapeze artist Mills Bros. Circus, 1962; skater Ice Capades, 1971-72; creator, dir., instr. skating program City of Southfield, Mich., 1972, 73; haute couture designer James E. Cape & Assocs., Dearborn, Mich., 1986—. Mem. Marji Kunz scholarship award com. Wayne State U., Detroit. Film reviewer Times-Herald Newspapers, 1989-90; clothing designs pub. in various mags. and newspapers; creations for TV and stage including the Emmys, The Am. Music Awards, Dick Clark-ABC Prodns., Showtime Spl. "Aretha", Trump Castle, Atlantic City, The Chgo. Theater, Kennedy Ctr., Washington, Radio City Music Hall; co-prodr. Eartha Kitt, A Night in Paris; spl. commd. designs various celebrities; spl. publicity creations for Detroit Inst. Arts, Am. Lung Assn.; producer, host TV show "Town Talk." Recipient Pre-silver, bronze medals U.S. Figure Skating Assn., 1969, Citation award City of Dearborn, 1994, Wayne County (Mich.) Resolution award, 1993, Spl. Tribute award State of Mich. Ho. of Reps., 1994, Page award Herald Newspapers, 1999-2000. Mem. AFTRA, Actors Equity, Soc. for Cinephiles. Home: James E Cape & Assocs 500 N Rosevere Dearborn MI 48128 E-mail: JamesECape@aol.com.

CAPECCHI, MARIO RENATO, geneticist, educator; b. Verona, Italy, Oct. 6, 1937; BS, Antioch Coll., 1961; PhD in Biophysics, Harvard U., 1967. Soc. fellows, jr. fellow biophysics Harvard U., 1966-69, from asst. prof. to assoc. prof. biochemistry med. sch., 1969-73; prof. Biology U. Utah, 1973-88; prof. human genetics U. Utah Sch. Medicine, Salt Lake City, 1989—; investigator Howard Hughes Inst./U. Utah, Salt Lake City, 1988—; disting. prof. human genetics Howard Hughes Inst./U.Utah, 1993—. Mem. bd. sci. counselors Nat. Cancer Inst. Recipient Biochemistry award, Am. Chem. Soc., 1969, Intrnat award, Gairdner Found., Can., 1990, Alfred P. Sloan Jr. prize, Gen. Motors Corp., 1994, Molecular Bioanalytics prize, 1996, Kyoto Prize in Basic Schs., 1996, Franklin medal, Franklin Inst., 1997, Baxter award, AAMC, 1988, Horace Mann Disting. Alumni award, Antioch Coll., 2000, Premio Phoenix-Anni Verdi award, Associazione Anni Verdi, 2000, 33d Jimenez-Diaz prize, Fundacion Concita Rabago de Jiminez-Diaz, 2001, Albert Lasker award Basic Med. Rsch., 2001, Laureate of the Nat. Medal of Sci. award, 2001, Utah Gov.'s Medal of Sci. and Tech. award, 2002, Wolf prize in Medicine, 2002—03, Pezcollar Found. Internat. Cancer Rsch. award, Am. Assn. Cancer Rsch., 2003. Mem. NAS, Am. Biochem. Soc., Am. Soc. Biol. Chemistry, Am. Soc. Microbiology, Molecular Med. Soc., N.Y. Acad. Sci., Soc. Devel. Biology, Internat. Genome Soc., Genetics Soc. Am., Am. Acad. Microbiology, European Acad. Scis. Achievements include research in gaining an understanding of how the information encoded in the gene is translated by the cell, elucidating the mechanism of genetic recombination in mouse embryo-derived stem (ES) cells, developing gene targeting in the mouse, gaining an understanding of embryonic and neuronal mammalian development through the use of gene targeting. Office: Howard Hughes Med Inst Univ Utah 15 N 2030 E Rm 5100 Salt Lake City UT 84112-5331 E-mail: mario.capecchi@genetics.utah.edu.

CAPECELATRO, MARK JOHN, lawyer; b. New Haven, June 2, 1948; s. Ralph Ettore and Elaine (Scialla) C.; m. Jane Beals, June 19, 1971; children: Christopher Beals, Kate Rowley, Jonathan Mark. BA, Colgate U., 1970; JD, U. Conn., 1973. Bar: Conn. 1973. Assoc. Ells, Quinlan, Eddy & Robinson, Canaan, Conn., 1973-77; ptnr. Ells, Quinlan & Robinson, Canaan, 1977-90, Capecelatro & Nelligan LLP, Canaan, 1991—2001; pvt. practice, 2002—, Bd. advisors Canaan Nat. Bank, 1982—; mortgage counsel People's Bank, Canaan and Hartford, Conn., 1983—; trustee Sharon (Conn.) Hosp., 1984-91, vice chmn., 1990-91, chmn. exec. com., 1990-91; trustee Salisbury Congl. Ch., 1990-98, 2000—, vice chmn., 1990-93, chmn., 1993-2000, 2002—, fin. com., 1998—. Bd. dirs. Housatonic Homemaker Health Aide, West Cornwall, Conn., 1977-80, Housatonic Day Care Ctr., Inc., Lakeville, Conn., 1981-90, Salisbury Pub. Health Nursing, Lakeville, 1983-85, Salisbury Vol. Ambulance Svcs., Inc., 1997-2003, Salisbury Winter Sports Assn., 1983-87, Salisbury (Conn.) Congl. Ch.; mem. adv. com. Parkside Med. Svcs. Corp., 1988-93. Mem. ABA, Conn. Bar Assn., Litchfield County Bar Assn., Model A Ford Club Am. Republican. Avocations: guitar, fishing, canoeing. Home: 196 Belgo Rd Lakeville CT 06039-1003 Office: 117 Main St Canaan CT 06018-1045 Address: PO Box 1045 Canaan CT 06018 Office Fax: 860-824-9869. E-mail: mjc@mohawk.net.

CAPEHART, BARNEY LEE, industrial and systems engineer; b. Galena, Kans., Aug. 20, 1940; s. Samuel Alfred and Mary Jane (Bliss) C.; m. Lynne Carol Fowler, Sept. 2, 1961; children: Thomas David, Jeffrey Donald, Cynthia Diane. BSEE, U. Okla., Norman, 1961, MEE, 1962, PhD, 1967. Instr. elec. engring. U. Okla., 1965-67; mem. tech. staff Aerospace Corp., San Bernardino, Calif., 1967-68; asst. prof. indsl. and systems engring. U. Fla., Gainesville, 1968-72; assoc. prof. indsl. engring. U. Tenn., 1972-73; assoc. prof. indsl. and systems engring. U. Fla., 1973-79, prof., 1979—, asst. chmn., 1987-88. Cons. Martin Marietta Corp., U.S. Naval Tng. Device Ctr., State of Fla., Hicks and Assocs., Casazza, Schultz & Assocs.; nat. lectr., Assn. Energy Engrs.; expert witness in energy and safety cases; chmn. Regional Energy Action Com., 1977-79; Region IV adv. group on appropriate tech. Dept. of Energy, 1978-80; mem. Local Energy Action Program, 1980-81; cons. U.S. Dept. Energy, Dep. Asst. Sec. for Bldg. Techs., Washington, 1989-90. Author books in field; editor Internat. Jour. Energy Systems, 1985-88; contbr. articles to profl. jours. Pres. Fla. League Conservation Voters, 1984-86; grad. Leadership Gainesville, 1984; dir. Energy Analysis and Diagnostic Ctr. U. Fla., 1990-95; dir. U. Fla. Indsl. Assessment Ctr., 1995-99. Decorated Air Force Commendation medal; Barney Capehart Day proclaimed by Alachua County, Fla., May 26, 1987, City of Gainesville, Dec. 21, 1987; recipient Palladium medal Am. Assn. Engring. Socs., 1988; inducted into Assn. Energy Engrs. Hall of Fame. Fellow AAAS, IEEE (energy com. 1988-90), Inst. Indsl. Engrs. (dir. energy mgmt. divsn. 1986-87); mem. Audubon Soc. (Fla. chpt. Conservationist of Yr. 1987), Fla. Conservation Found., Assn. Energy Engrs., Fla. Blue Key, Sigma Xi, Sigma Tau, Alpha Pi Mu, Tau Beta Pi, Eta Kappa Nu. Home: 1601 NW 35th Way Gainesville FL 32605-4846 Office: U Fla Dept Indsl & Systems Engring 303 Weil Hall Gainesville FL 32611-2083 E-mail: energydoc1@aol.com.

CAPELL, CYDNEY LYNN, editor; b. Jacksonville, Fla., Dec. 20, 1956; d. Ernest Clary and Alice Rae (McGinnis) C.; m. Garrick Philip Martin, July 16, 1983 (div. Jan. 1988). BA, Furman U., 1977. Mktg. rep. E.C. Capell & Assocs., Greenville, S.C., 1977-80; sales rep. Prentice-Hall Publs., Cin., 1980-81; sales, mktg. rep. Benjamin/Cummings, Houston, 1981-83; sales rep. McGraw-Hill Book Co., Houston, 1983-85, engring. editor N.Y.C., 1985-87; acctg. and infosys. editor Bus. Pubs., Inc., Plano, Tex., 1988-89; sr. editor Gorsuch Scarisbrick Pubs., Scottsdale, Ariz., 1989-90; editor-in-chief rsch. dept. Rauscher, Pierce, Refsnes Stock Brokers, 1990-94; editor-in-chief, dir. mktg. Marshall & Swift, L.A., 1994-98; sr. mng. editor Pearson Custom Pub., Tulsa, 2000—. Editor Talon mag., 1972; news editor Paladin newspaper, 1977. Named Rookie of Yr. McGraw-Hill Book Co., 1985. Mem. NOW, NAFE, Women in Pub., Women in Comm., Mensa. Republican. Avocations: tennis, ballet.

CAPELLAN, ANGEL, small business executive; b. Zorraquin, Spain, Apr. 10, 1942; s. Sotero Capellan and Damasa Gnozalo; m. Sonia C. Guadalupe, Aug. 27, 1971; children: Carlos Manuel, Amaya Isabel. Licentiate degree, U. Madrid, 1968; MA, NYU, 1969, MA, 1970, PhD, 1977. Tchr. Colegio Santa Maria, Spain, 1962-66; instr. Spanish Hunter Coll., N.Y.C., 1969-78; dir. lang. arts South Bronx campus Sch. New Resources, Coll. New Rochelle, N.Y.C., 1978-83; assoc. dean Eugenio Maria de Hostos Community Coll., N.Y.C., 1983-84; pres. LEA, Book Distbrs., N.Y.C., 1984—. Judge CEPI Literary Prizes, N.Y.C., 1972-89; founder, pub. Españoles en USA, Inc. Contbr. articles to profl. jours.; author of book revs., poems, and stories; author: Hemingway and the Hispanic World, 1985, Paisajes renacidos, 1982; contbg. author: Gran enciclopedia Rialp, Tomo 20, 1974, Tomo 23, 1974; founder, publisher Espanoles en USA; pres. Españoles en USA, Inc., 1998—. Pres. Coun. Spanish Residents N.Y. Consular Area, 1997—; U.S. rep. Gen. Coun. for Emigration, Madrid, 1998—. Juan March fellow Juan March Found., Madrid, 1969-70, Fulbright scholar Fulbright Found., 1968-69; Elias Ahuja fellow Fulbright Found., Madrid, 1968-69. Mem. MLA, Am. Assn. Tchrs. Spanish and Portuguese, Am. Booksellers Assn., Assn. Empresarios Y Profesionales (U.S., Spain). Roman Catholic. Avocations: reading, stamp collecting, writing. Home and Office: 17023 83rd Ave Jamaica NY 11432-2101

CAPELLAS, MICHAEL D. telecommunications industry executive; Chief info. officer Compaq Computer Corp., Houston, 1998-99, pres., CEO, chmn., 1999—2002; pres. Hewlett-Packard Co., 2002; CEO, chmn WorldCom Inc., 2002—.

CAPELLI, JOHN PLACIDO, nephrologist, educator; b. Hammonton, N.J., May 23, 1936; s. John L. and Marie C.; m. Patricia Ann Verna, Nov. 4, 1961; children: John L., Elizabeth Ann, David S. BS in Biology, Villanova U., 1958; MD, Jefferson Med. Coll., 1962. Diplomate: Am. Bd. Internal Medicine (Nephrology). Intern Michael Reese Hosp., Chgo., 1962-63; resident Thomas Jefferson U. Hosp., 1963-65, NIH fellow in nephrology, 1965-67, Martin E. Rehfuss chief resident internal medicine, 1967-68; practice medicine specializing in nephrology Haddonfield, N.J., 1968—; clin. prof. medicine U. Medicine and Dentistry N.J., 1995—; pres. Lourdes Med. Assn., P.A. and Health Mgmt. Svcs. Orgn., Inc., 1995—, Nephrology Network for N.J., P.C., 1995—. Dir. div. clin. pharmacology Jefferson Med. Coll., Phila., 1968-69; dir. hemodialysis unit Our Lady of Lourdes Med. Ctr., Camden, N.J., 1969—, dir. div. nephrology and transplantation, 1974—, chief of staff, 1980-86, v.p. med. affairs, 1987-2001, sr. v.p. med. affairs, 2002—; clin. prof. medicine Thomas Jefferson U., Phila., 1974— ; mem. chronic renal disease adv. com. N.J. Dept. Health, 1969-79, chmn., 1971-73, 74-75; pres. Health Mgmt. Svcs. Orgns., Inc., 1995—, N.J. Renal Mgmt., 1996—. Discovered extra-renal source of renin in uterus, 1968; contbr. articles to med. jours. Named to Order of Knights St. Gregory, 1995. Mem. Am. Soc. Nephrology, Internat. Soc. Nephrology, Renal Physicians Assn. (pres. 1977-79), AMA, Med. Soc. N.J., Am. Soc. Artificial Internal Organs, Southeastern Organ Procurement Found., Nat. Kidney Found. Roman Catholic. Office: Haddon Renal Med Specialists 35 Kings Hwy E Haddonfield NJ 08033-2009

CAPELLOS, CHRIS SPIRIDON, chemist; b. Athens, Greece, Oct. 22, 1934; came to U.S., 1966, naturalized, 1976; s. Spiridon Em. and Melpo Christou (Christidou) C.; m. Helen Nicholaou Sakkoulas, Dec. 3, 1959; children: Melina, Maria. BS in Chemistry, Athens, 1959; DIC in Nuc. Tech., Imperial Coll., London U., 1962; PhD, London U., 1965. Rsch. assoc. Brookhaven (N.Y.) Nat. Lab., 1966-68, assoc. chemist, 1968, vis. assoc. chemist, 1968-72; sr. rsch. chemist energetic materials divsn. Armament R&D Command, Dover, N.J., 1968—, sr. scientist, 1972—. Vis. scientist Davy Faraday Lab., Royal Inst., 1970-71; NRC rsch. advisor; bd. dirs. NATO Advanced Study Inst., 1980, 85; mem. tech. adv. panel to Army Rsch. Office for Univ. Rsch. Initiative, 1987—; vice-chmn. Gordon Rsch. Conf. on Energetic Materials for 1990, chmn., 1992. Author: Kinetic Systems, 1972, Japanese transl., 1978; editor NATO Conf. Procs., 1980, 86; contbr. writings to sci. jours.; contbr. numerous sci. papers to nat. and internat. meetings. Served with Greek Army, 1965-66. USAF Office Sci. Rsch. fellow, 1962-65; NATO awardee, 1979-80, 83; recipient various awards and commendations. Mem. Am. Chem. Soc., Radiation Rsch., N.Y. Acad. Scis., Sigma Xi (pres. Picatinny chpt.). Home: 11 Cambridge Rd Morris Plains NJ 07950-1529 E-mail: cristeleni@aol.com.

CAPEN, CHARLES CHABERT, veterinary pathology educator; b. Tacoma, Sept. 3, 1936; s. Charles (Kenneth) and Ruth (Chabert) C.; m. Sharron Lee Martin, June 27, 1968. DVM, Wash. State U., 1960; MS, Ohio State U., 1961, PhD, 1965. Instr. dept. vet. pathology Ohio State U., Columbus, 1962—65, asst. prof. dept. vet. pathology, 1965—67, assoc. prof., 1967—70, prof., 1970—, prof. endocrinology Coll. Medicine, 1972—, chmn. dept. vet. pathobiology, 1981—94, chmn., 1982—94, interim chmn. dept. bioscis., 1994—97; chmn., 1997—2002. Israel Doniach Meml. lectr. Brit. Endocrine Soc. meeting, Manchester, 1989; plenary lectr. Italian Soc. Endocrinology Congress, Pisa, 1995. Editor: (series) Animal Models of Human Disease, 1979—96; mem. editl. bd. : Lab. Investigation, 1988—; Vet. Pathology, 1986—87; Am. Jour. Pathology, 1984—88; Exptl. and Toxicologic Pathology, 1990—; Food and Chem. Toxicology, 1993—; Drug and Chem. Toxicology, 1994—; Toxicology and Ecotoxicology News, 1993—; Handbook on Rat Tumor Pathology WHO/IARC, 1991—96. Mem. Opera Columbus, 1982—, Columbus Symphony Assn., 1972—. Named Disting. U. prof., Ohio State U., 2001; recipient Disting. scholar award, 1993, Dean's Tchg. Excellence award for grad. edn., Coll. Vet. Medicine, 1993, Disting. Vet. Alumnus award, Wash. State U., 1997,

Career Achievement award in canine rsch., Am. Vet. Med. Found., 1997. Mem.: AVMA (Nat. Borden rsch. award 1975, small animal rsch. award 1984, Gaines rsch. award 1987, excellence in canine rsch. award 1995, George Scott Meml. award of Toxicology Forum 1997), Soc. Toxicol. Pathologists (pres. 1997—98), U.S. Can. Acad. Pathology (coun. 1989—92), Inst. Medicine/NAS, Am. Coll. Vet. Pathologists (disting. mem., diplomate) (coun. 1975—81, pres. 1978—79). Avocations: traveling, wildlife and nature photography. Office: The Ohio State U Dept Vet Bioscis 1925 Coffey Rd Columbus OH 43210-1005

CAPERS, GREGG, secondary school educator, musician; b. Bronx, N.Y., Jan. 21, 1961; s. Joe Simon and Evelyn Delores Capers; m. Alberta Amber Lloyd, Jan. 21, 1966; children: George Steven Bush, Christina Lillian Bush, Anthony Tony Burno. Bachelors Degree(hon.), Bowie State U., 1983; Assoc. Degree, Comml. Programming Unlimited, N.Y.C., 1985; cert., Trident Tech. Coll., Charleston, S.C., 1988. Min. praise and worship God's Positive Minds, Phila., 1998—2003; tchr. Del. Valley Charter H.S., Phila., 1999—. Musical and choir dir. Inspirational Words Of Life, Phila., 1999—. Min. music Ministers of Praise, Phila. Recipient John Phillip Sousa Award For Music Excellence, USMC, 1980. Democrat. Home: 6740 Old York Rd Philadelphia PA 19126 Office: Inspirational Words Of Life 6740 Old York Rd Philadelphia PA 19126 Personal E-mail: greg.alberta@verizon.net. E-mail: greg.alberta@verizon.net.

CAPERTON, ALBERT FRANKLIN, retired newspaper editor; b. Hemphill, W.Va., Dec. 31, 1936; s. Albert Harrison and Viola (Hicks) C.; m. Elizabeth Moreland, Jan. 29, 1960; children— Catherine Elizabeth, Robert Harrell B., Northwestern State U., 1962; M.Jour., Columbia U., 1965; cert. Advanced Mgmt. Program, Harvard U., 1982. Reporter Richmond News Leader, Va., 1962-64; reporter St Petersburg Times, Fla., 1965-67, Tampa Tribune, Fla., 1967-69; asst. city editor Miami Herald, Fla., 1969-72, Broward County editor, 1972-75; exec. editor Macon Telegraph & News, Ga., 1975-78, Virginian-Pilot & Ledger Star, Norfolk, 1978-84; mng. editor Indpls. News, 1984-90, Indpls. Star, 1990-95; exec. editor Indpls. Star and News, 1995-99, Indpls. Star, 1999-2000. Pres. Crossroads of Am. coun. Boy Scouts Am., Indpls., 1991-92; chmn., bd. trustees Christian Theol. Sem., 1999-2003. With USAF, 1954-57. Mem.: Rotary. Mem. Diciples of Christ. Avocations: reading, tennis. Home: 6432 Landborough North Dr Indianapolis IN 46220-4351 E-mail: acape1066@aol.com.

CAPERTON, BOB W. risk manager; b. Marlin, Tex., Feb. 1, 1942; s. Clyde Milton and Cecil Inez Caperton; m. Sandra Jo Longacre, Dec. 21, 2002; children: Christian, Joey. BBA, U. Tex., 1964. Corp. dir. ins. ETMF Freight Sys., Dallas, 1974—80; corp. risk mgr. Comml. Metals Co., Dallas, 1980—. With U.S. Army, 1964—72. Mem.: Dallas Claims Assn., Tex. Claims Assn., Dallas-Ft. Worth Risk and Ins. Mgmt. Methodist. Avocation: big game hunting. Office: Comml Metals Co PO Box 1046 Dallas TX 75221

CAPERTON, RICHARD WALTON, photographer, automobile repair company executive, educator, consultant; b. Waynesburg, Pa., Jan. 11, 1948; s. Walton Greene Caperton and Sareta (Campbell) Garetson; children: Richard Walton Jr., Christa Elizabeth, Joseph Allen, Stephanie Gabrielle; m. Linda L. Burgess, July 4, 1999; 1 stepchild: Melinda Carlson. Grad. high sch., Naples, Fla. Asst. mgr. W.T. Grant Co., Naples, 1967-75; pres., chief exec. officer, gen. mgr. R&R Automotive Inc., Naples, 1975-95, CEO, 1996; pres., chief exec. officer AAMGO Auto Parts Inc., Naples, 1987-91; pres. Caperton Properties, 1977—2000, Nu U Mktg., 1991-95, Caperton Consulting, 1994-96. Instr. Walker Tech. Inst., 1996-97; advt. cons. Edwards Publs., 1998; owner Rick Caperton Photography, Anderson, S.C., 2000—. Bd. dirs. East Naples Civic Assn., 1979-80; v.p. Fla. Sports Park, Naples, 1997, pres., 1997-98, bd. dirs., 1987—, dir. emeritus; mem. adv. bd. Walker Tech. Inst., 1991-95; apptd. to Fla. New Motor Vehicle Arbitration Bd., 1994-97. Fellow Automobile Svc. Assn., Rotary (bd. dirs. Naples East 1987-96, v.p. Naples East 1990-91, pres. 1996-97), mem. Greater Anderson Rotary. Republican. Methodist. Avocations: golf, scuba diving, boating, shooting. Office: 1701 Broadway Lake Rd Anderson SC 29621 E-mail: rikcapertonphoto@cs.com.

CAPESTRO, SUSAN, musician, educator, composer; b. N.J., Nov. 24, 1956; d. John Augustine and Esther Mabel Burdge Capestro. MusB in Music Edn. and Performance, Ithaca Coll., 1980; MusM in Piano Performance & Pedagogy, Northwestern U., 1984. French Horn performer The Shore Brass Quintette, Pt. Pleasant Beach, N.J., 1972-75, Garden State Philharm. Orch., Toms River, N.J., 1973-74, N.J. All State Band, 1975, Ithaca (N.Y.) Coll. Orch., 1976-79; piano performer various solo recitals, 1978-92; piano performer Orrington Hotel, Evanston, Ill., 1984, Sacred Heart Parish, Newton, Mass., 1994—, Sounds of Swing Big Band, Belmont, Mass., 1995—; synthesizers performer Ibrahima Camara African Pop Ensemble, Boston, 1998—2001. Piano tchr. Northwestern U. Sch. Music, Evanston, 1983-84; piano and composition tchr. Capestro Music Studio, Watertown, Mass., 1985—; guest lectr. piano pedagogy Boston U. Grad. Sch. Music, 1988; adjudicator piano performance competition N.H. Music Tchrs. Assn., 1987, New Eng. Pianoforte Tchrs. Assn., Boston, 1996-97. Recipient Annual award ASCAP Popular Awards Panel, N.Y.C., 1999, 2000, 2001, 2002, 1999 Hall of Fame award Pub. Edn. Found., Point Pleasant Beach, N.J., 1999. Mem. Music Tchrs. Nat. Assn. (nat. cert. tchr. music), Mass. Music Tchrs. Assn. (treas. 1985-86, pres. 1987-88, adjudicator composition contest 1993-99, adjudicator piano performance competition 1995-97, Commd. Composer 2001). Avocations: sports, gardening. Office: Capestro Music PO Box 164 New Town MA 02456-0164

CAPEZZA, MICHELLE, lawyer; b. Edison, NJ, Dec. 21, 1971; d. Michael J. Capezza and Lenora Capezza-Byrne. BA with high honors, Rutgers Coll., 1993; JD, Seton Hall U., 1996. Bar: N.J. 1996, N.Y. 1997. Jud. clerk N.J. Superior Ct., New Brunswick, 1996-97; staff atty. The Ayco Co. LLP, Albany, N.Y., 1997-98; assoc. Salomon Smith Barney, N.Y.C., 1998-99, Proskauer Rose, LLP, N.Y.C., 1999-2000, Pitney Hardin Kipp & Szuch, LLP, Morristown, N.J., 2000—. Mem. editl. bd. Seton Hall Law Rev., 1994—95, asst. editor, 1995—96. Mem. ABA, N.Y. State Bar Assn., N.J. Bar Assn., Phi Beta Kappa. Avocations: music, art, foreign languages, gourmet cooking. Office: Pitney Hardin Kipp & Szuch LLP PO Box 1945 Morristown NJ 07962-1945 Business E-Mail: mcapezza@pitneyhardin.com.

CAPICE, PHILIP CHARLES, television production executive; b. Bernardsville, N.J., June 24, 1931; s. Philip Joseph and Angelina Mary (Togno) C. BA, Dickinson Coll., 1952; M.F.A., Columbia U., 1954. Production supr., assoc. program dir. Benton & Bowles Inc., N.Y.C., 1954-64, Vice pres. in charge program devel., 1965-69; dir. spl. programs CBS-TV Network, N.Y.C., 1969-74; sr. v.p. creative affairs Lorimar Prodns., Burbank, Calif., 1974-78; pres. Lorimar TV, Burbank, Calif., 1978-79; ind. producer Lorimar Productions, Culver City, Calif., from 1979; pres., chief exec. officer Raven's Claw Productions, Los Angeles, Calif. Since 1974, exec. producer Dallas, Eight Is Enough, The Blue Knight, Two Marriages, Helter Skelter, Sybil (Emmy Award, 1977, Peabody Award, 1977), Green Eyes (Peabody Award, 1978, Humanitas Prize, 1978), Eric, Widow, Studs Lonigan, A Man Called Intrepid, The Runaways, The Prince of Central Park, A Question of Guilt, Some Kind of Miracle (Christopher Award, 1978), Returning Home, Conspiracy of Terror, Hunter, Married: The First Year, The Rivermen, Mary and Joseph: A Love Story, The Stranger Within, A Matter of Life and Death, Bunco, Some People Like Us, Private Sessions, others. Trustee Dickinson Coll. Recipient Emmy award, 1977, Peabody award, 1977, 78. Mem. Acad. TV Arts and Scis., The Caucus for Producers, Writers and Dirs.

CAPITAN, WILLIAM HARRY, university president emeritus; b. Owosso, Mich., Feb. 7, 1933; s. Harry and Anthe (Sarris) C.; m. Dolores Marie Randolph, Sept. 19, 1959; children: Rita, Edwin. BA, U. Mich., 1954; postgrad., Queens U.; postgrad. (Ulster Am. fellow), 1954-55; MA, U. Minn., 1958, PhD, 1960. Registered mediator 2001, lic. Capt. USCG, auxiliary USCG, 2001. Instr. philosophy U. Minn., 1959-60, U. Md., 1960-62; asst. prof., assoc. prof., chmn. dept. Oberlin (Ohio) Coll., 1962-70; dean fine arts, v.p. acad. affairs, acting pres. Saginaw Valley State U., U. Ctr., Mich., 1970-74; v.p. acad. affairs, dean faculty, acting pres. W.Va. Wesleyan Coll., Buckhannon, 1974-79; pres. Ga. Southwestern U/, Americus, 1979-95; pres. emeritus Ga. Southwestern Coll., Americus, 1996—. Adj. prof. U. Ga., 1996. Author: Introduction to the Philosophy of Religion, 1972, Speak For Yourself, 1987; editor: (with D.D. Merrill) Metaphysics and Explanation, Art, Religion, and Mind, 1967, The Ethical Navigator, 2000. Trustee Charles L. Mix Meml. Fund, Inc., 1979—96; pres. Americus Sumter County C. of C., 1985; v.p. Hellenic-Am. C. of C., Atlanta; lay reader Episcopal Ch., Americus, Ga.; bd. dir. Saginaw Symphony Orch., 1970—74; Project Save; Buckhannon C. of C.; Sumter County United Way. Am. Council Lerned Socs. fellow Paris, 1967-68 Mem. Am. Soc. Aesthetics, Am. Philos. Assn., Rotary (pres. 1990-91), Beta Theta Phi, Omicron Delta Kappa, Phi Kappa Phi, Phi Delta Kappa. Episcopalian. Office: GA Southwestern State U Americus GA 31709 *Clarity of objectives, persistence, and Christian respect for persons have guided me in whatever of value I have accomplished. My failures came when I wasn't very clear about what I was doing. America rewards, supports, and buoys up those with initiative. This is why my parents were able to go from "rags to riches" and I from illiterate to lettered. We Americans help one another, and we shape our institutions to help, too. May we ever remain so.*

CAPITANO, NICHOLAS, television producer; s. Malinda and Nelson Capitano; m. Melissa Poole, Dec. 28, 1973; 1 child, Gia. BA, Aurora U., 2003. Prodr. WAND-TV, Decatur, Ill., 1994—97; exec. prodr. WXII-TV, Winston-Salem, NC, 1997—. Instr. Salem Coll., Winston-Salem, NC, 2002. Author: (poetry) New Millennium Poets, The Sound of Poetry, Theatre of the Mind. Office: WXII-TV 700 Coliseum Dr Winston Salem NC 27106 Office Fax: 336-721-0865.

CAPITO, SHELLEY MOORE, congresswoman; b. Glen Dale, WV, Nov. 26, 1953; m. Charles L. Capito, Jr.; children: Charles, Moore, Shelley. BS in zoology, Duke U., 1975; MEd, U. Va., 1976. Career counselor West Va. State Coll.; dir. Ednl. Info. Ctr. West Va. Bd. Regents; mem. West Va. House of Delegates, 30th dist., 1996—2000, U.S. Ho. of Reps. from 2nd WV dist., 2001—; minority chair health and human resources committee; mem. judiciary committee., banking commitee, insurance committee. Mem. 107th Congress House Banking and Fin. Svcs. com., House Transportation and Infrastructure com., House Small Bus. com. Mem. YWCA (past pres.), Cmty. coun., Kanawha Valley, West Va. Interagency Coun. Early Intervention. Republican. Mem. First Presbyn. Ch. Office: 1431 Longworth House Office bldg Washington DC 20515-4802*

CAPIZZI, MICHAEL ROBERT, prosecutor; b. Detroit, Oct. 19, 1939; s. I.A. and Adelaide E. (Jennelle) C.; m. Sandra Jo Jones, June 22, 1963; children: Cori Anne, Pamela Jo. BS in Bus. Adminstrn., Ea. Mich. U., 1961; JD, U. Mich., 1964. Bar: Calif. 1965, U.S. Dist. Ct. (so. dist.) Calif. 1965, U.S. Ct. Appeals (9th cir.) 1970, U.S. Supreme Ct. 1971. Dep. dist. atty., Orange County, Calif., 1965-68; head writs, appeals and spl. assignments sect., 1968-71; asst. dist. atty., dir. spl. ops., 1971-86; legal counsel, mem. exec. bd. Interstate Organized Crime Index, 1971-79, Law Enforcement Intelligence Unit, 1971-95, chief asst. dist. atty., 1986-90, dist. atty., 1990-99. Instr. criminal justice Santa Ana Coll., 1967-76, Calif. State U., 1976-87. Commr. City Planning Commn., Fountain Valley, Calif., 1971-80, vice chmn. 1972-73, chmn. 1973-75, 79-80; candidate for Rep. nomination Calif. Atty. Gen., 1998. Fellow Am. Coll. Trial Lawyers; mem. Nat. Dist. Attys. Assn. (bd. dirs. 1995-96, v.p. 1996-99), Calif. Dist. Attys. Assn. (outstanding prosecutor award 1980, v.p. 1995, pres. 1996), Calif. Bar Assn., Orange County Bar Assn. (chmn. cts. com. 1977, chmn. coll. of trial advocacy com. 1978-81, bd. dirs. 1977-81, sec.-treas. 1982, pres. 1984). Office: PO Box 1938 Santa Ana CA 92702-1938 E-mail: mrclaw@socal.rr.com.

CAPIZZI, ROBERT LAWRENCE, physician; b. Phila., Nov. 20, 1938; s. Nunzio B. and Nancy (Gatto) C.; m. Barbara Ann Kain, July 10, 1965; children: Robert, Marc, Tara Ann, Mary Catherine BS, Temple U., Phila, 1960; MD, Hahnemann Med. Coll., Phila., 1964. Asst. prof. medicine and pharmacology Yale U., New Haven, 1972-75, assoc. prof. medicine and pharmacology, 1975-77, acting chief sect. med. oncology, 1976-77; chief div. med. oncology U. N.C., Chapel Hill, 1977-79, co-dir. div. hematology and oncology, 1980-82; dir. Comprehensive Cancer Ctr., sect. head hematology and oncology Bowman Gray Sch. Medicine, Wake Forest U., Winston-Salem, N.C., 1982-91; exec. v.p. worldwide R&D U.S. Bioscience, West Conshohocken, Pa., 1991-96; Magee prof., chmn. dept. medicine Jefferson Med. Coll., Phila., 1996—. Mem. study sect. Cancer Clin. Investigation Rev. Com., NIH, 1982-85 Served to maj. U.S. Army, 1969-72 Investigator, Howard Hughes Med. Inst., Yale U., 1976-77; recipient Faculty Devel. award Pharm. Mfrs. Assn., Yale U., 1974-76 Mem. Am. Soc. Clin. Oncology (program com. 1983, membership com. 1983), Am. Fedn. Clin. Research (program com. 1983), Piedmont Oncology Assn. (bd. dirs. 1982-91, chmn. 1985-91), Am. Soc. Clin. Investigation Roman Catholic. Mailing: 2027 Spruce St Philadelphia PA 19103

CAPLAN, EDWIN HARVEY, university dean, accounting educator; b. Boston, Aug. 24, 1926; s. Henry and Dorothy (Nathanson) C.; m. Ramona Hootner, June 20, 1948; children— Gary, Dennis, Jeffrey, Nancy BBA, U. Mich., 1950, MBA, 1952; PhD, U. Calif., 1965. CPA, Calif., Mich. Ptnr. J.J. Gotlieb & Co., CPAs, Detroit, 1953-56; prof. acctg. Humboldt State U., 1956-61, U. Oreg., 1964-67; prof. U. N.Mex., Albuquerque, 1967-91, assoc. dean Sch. Mgmt., 1982-83, dean Sch. Mgmt., 1989-90, prof. emeritus, 1991—. Cons. in field. Contbr. articles to profl. jours. 1st lt. U.S. Army, 1944-46. Mem. AICPA, Am. Acctg. Assn., Inst. Mgmt. Accts. Home: 8201 Harwood Ave NE Albuquerque NM 87110-1517

CAPLAN, ELINOR, Canadian provincial legislator, former cabinet minister; b. Toronto, Ont., Can., 1944; m. Wilf Caplan; children: David, Mark, Zane, Meredith. Pres. Elinor Caplan and Assocs., 1973-78; alderman Ward 13 City of North York, 1978-85; mem. Ont. Legislature, 1985-97, chief opposition whip; minister Ministry of Health, Toronto, 1987-90; critic for health and women's issues; mem. Ho. of Commons Dist. Thornhill, Ont., 1997—; Min. of Citizenship and Immigration Canada, 1999—2002; Min. of National Revenue, 2002—. Chmn. Mgmt. Bd. of Cabinet, chmn. of cabinet Peterson Govt.; minister Govt. Svcs., mem. Standing Com. on Health, Standing Com. on Pub. Accounts Past chmn. North York Coun. Com., Human Resources Adv. Coun., Rapid Transit Subcom.; past mem. North York Bd. of Health; past vice chmn. North York Interagy. Coun. Mem. North York Bus. Assn. (founder, past chmn. devel. and econ. growth com.). Office: House of Commons 658 Confederation Bldg Ottawa ON Canada K1A OA6

CAPLAN, HUBERT IRWIN, medical educator; b. Boston, Sept. 15, 1931; s. Abraham Nathan and Goldie Marion (Pantell) C.; m. Raynor Doris Bornstein, June 21, 1952; children: Susan Paula, Jeanne Marcia, Donna Beth. Ed., Harvard U., 1952; MD magna cum laude, Tufts U., 1955. Intern Boston City Hosp., 1955-56; resident N.E. Med. Ctr., 1958-59, fellow rheumatology, 1959-60; resident Boston VA Hosp., 1960-61; dir. Tufts tchg. program & chief medicine Jewish Meml. Hosp., Boston, 1966-70; assoc. clin. prof. medicine Sch. Medicine Tufts U., 1970—; chief rheumatology Newton-Wellesley (Mass.) Hosp., 1977-87; pvt. practice Newton. Pres. Lakes Environ. Assn., Bridgton, Maine, 1982-90, v.p., 1978-82. Capt. U.S. Army, 1956-58. Fellow ACP, Am. Coll. Rheumatology; mem. Mass. Med. Soc., Charles River Dist. Med. Soc. (v.p. 1998-2000, pres. 2000-03, alt. trustee 2003—), Alpha Omega Alpha. Jewish. Avocations: photography, classical music, collector of samovars. Office: 2000 Washington St Newton MA 02462-1650

CAPLAN, JESSICA MARIE, small business owner, artist; b. Cleve., Aug. 11, 1969; d. Harry Walter Caplan and Susan Elaine Klein. BFA, Carnegie Mellon U., 1991. Asst. mgr. Crystal Dragon Gallery, Madrid, N.Mex., 1992—94; owner, dir. Humana Gallery, Madrid, 1994—96; owner, tchr. Sun Studios, Santa Fe, 1996—97; owner, pres. Jezebel, Inc., Santa Fe, 1997—. Spkr. Arts Coun. U. Pa., 1990. Inventor glass slumping process. Office: Jezebel Gallery 236 Delgado St Santa Fe NM 87501

CAPLAN, JUDITH SHULAMITH LANGER-SURNAMER, genealogist, poet, researcher, editor, educator; b. Brooklyn, NY, Feb. 3, 1945; d. Rabbi Samuel Langer, Gladys Surnamer Langer; m. Neil Howard Caplan, M.D.; children: Hillel N., Baruch I. BA English, Brooklyn College, Brooklyn, NY, 1962—66; Masters in Communications/Television, Syracuse University, Syracuse, New York, 1967—68. Genealogist Up, Roots! Genealogy Research Services, Long Beach, NY, 1995—Now; LitvakSIG Online Journal Editor LitvakSIG, 27 West Penn Street, NY, 1997—Now; English Teacher Springfield Gardens High School, Springfield Gardens, NY, 1985—2001, Far Rockaway High School, Far Rockaway, NY, 1983—83, George W. Wingate High School, Brooklyn, NY, 1969—72, Andries Hudde Junior High School, Brooklyn, NY, 1966—67; Hebrew School Teacher Temple Israel, Long Beach, NY, 1983—85; Hebrew Teacher Merrick Jewish Center, Merrick, NY, 1982—85, Congregation Sherith Israel, Atlanta, 1978—79, Congregation Beth Jacob, Atlanta, 1975—77. Contbr. Book of Poetry, Poetry and Memoirs, Genealogy Article in AVOTAYNU, Genealogy Article, Genealogy Article on LitvakSIG (Online), Genealogy Article, Introduction to Database, and Database, Talk. Mem.: Jewish Genealogy Society of Long Island, Jewish Genealogy Society of New York, Association of Professional Genealogists. Home: 27 West Penn Street Long Beach NY 11561-4003 Office: Up, Roots! Genealogy Research Services 27 West Penn Street Long Beach NY 11561-4003 Personal E-mail: Judith27@aol.com. Business E-Mail: Judith27@aol.com.

CAPLAN, LINCOLN, journalist; b. New Haven, Apr. 19, 1950; m. Susan L. Carney; 1 child, Molly. BA, Harvard U., 1972, JD, 1976; postgrad., Cambridge (Eng.) U., 1972-73. Staff writer New Republic, Washington, 1975-76; law clk. Conn. Supreme Ct., Hartford, 1976-77; mgmt. cons. Boston Cons. Group, 1977-79; White House fellow U.S. Dept. energy, Washington, 1979-80; staff writer New Yorker, N.Y.C., 1980-92; conbrg. writer Newsweek, N.Y.C., 1993-95; editor spl. projects U.S. News and World Report, Washington, 1996-98; Knight sr. journalist Yale Law Sch., New Haven, 1998—; editor., pres. Legal Affairs, New Haven, 2000—. Author: The Insanity Defense, 1984, The Tenth Justice, 1987, An Open Adoption, 1990, Skadden, 1993, Up Against the Law, 1997. Recipient Silver Gavel award ABA, 1985, Pope Journalism award Pope Found., 1992; Guggenheim fellow, 1989; Harvard-Cambridge scholar, 1972. Home: 115 Blake Rd Hamden CT 06517 Office: Legal Affairs 254 Elm St New Haven CT 06511

CAPLAN, LOUIS ROBERT, neurology educator; b. Balt., Dec. 31, 1936; s. Carl Clarence and Bess Pauline (Cohen) C.; m. F. Brenda Fields, Nov. 28, 1963; children: Laura, Daniel, Jonathan, David, Jeremy, Benjamin. BA cum laude, Williams Coll., 1958; MD summa cum laude, U. Md., 1962. Diplomate Am. Bd. Internal Medicine, Am. Bd. Psychiatry and Neurology. Intern to jr. asst. resident Boston City Hosp., 1962-64; resident Harvard Neurol. Unit, Boston, 1966-69; cerebrovascular fellow Mass. Gen. Hosp., Boston, 1969-70; neurologist Beth Israel Hosp., Boston, 1970-78; asst. prof. Harvard Med. Sch., Boston, 1970-78, prof. neurology, 1999; chief neurologist Michael Reese Hosp., Chgo., 1978-84; prof. neurology U. Chgo., 1980-84; chief neurologist New England Med. Ctr., Boston, 1984-97; prof., chmn. dept. neurology Tufts U., Boston, 1984-97, prof. medicine, 1989-97; neurologist Beth Israel Deaconess Med. Ctr., Boston, 1998—; prof. neurology Harvard Med. Sch., 1999—. Author: stroke: A Clinical Approach, 1986, 3rd edit., 2000, Consultations in Neurology, 1987, The Effective Clinical Neurologist, 2nd edit., 2001, Vertebrobasilar Arterial Disease, 1993; author: (with others) Cerebral Small Artery Disease, 1993; author: Management of Persons with Stroke, 1993, Brainstem Localization and Function, 1993, Intercerebral Hemmorhage, 1994, Family Guide to Stroke, 1994, Brain Ischemia-Basic Concepts and Clinical Relevance, 1995, Stroke Syndromes, 2nd edit., 2001, Posterior Circulation Disease, 1996, Neurologic Disorders: Course and Treatment, 1996, 2d edit., 2003, Primer on Cerebrovascular Diseases, 1997; author: (with others) Clinical Neurocardiology, 1999; author: Uncommon Causes of Stroke, 2001, Striking Back at Stroke--A Doctor-Patient Journal, 2003; contbr. over 500 articles to profl. jours.; contbr. more than 500 articles to profl. jours. Bd. dirs. Solomon Schecter Day Sch., Boston, 1977-78, Chgo., 1983-85. Capt. U.S. Army, 1962-64. Recipient House Officer Teaching prize Michael Reese Hosp., 1980. Fellow Am. Acad. Neurology, Am. Neurol. Assn., Stroke Coun. Am. Heart Assn. (chmn. 1987-89, sci. adv. com. 1990—), Royal Soc. of Medicine; mem. Coun. Med. Specialties Socs. (rep. 1982-90), Chgo. Neurol. Soc. (chmn. 1984-85), Boston Soc. Neurology and Psychiatry (pres. 1988-89), Chgo. Heart Assn. (chmn. stroke com. 1979-84), Australian Neurol. Soc. (hon.), German Neurol. Assn. (hon.), Phi Beta Kappa, Alpha Omega Alpha. Democrat. Jewish. Office: Beth Israel Deaconess MC Dept Neurology 330 Brookline Ave Palmer 127 Boston MA 02215-5400

CAPLAN, RONALD MERVYN, gynecologist, obstetrician; b. Montreal, Dec. 12, 1937; came to U.S., 1971; s. Philip and Betty (Gamer) C.; m. Marilyn Gail Amdur, Dec. 23, 1962; children: Randy Sue, Gordon. BSc, McGill U., Montreal, 1958, MD CM, 1962. Resident Royal Victorial Hosp., Montreal, 1963-67; instr. ob-gyn McGill U., 1968-71; practice medicine specializing in ob-gyn Montreal, 1968-71, N.Y.C., 1971—; mem. attending staff Royal Victoria Hosp., Montreal, 1968-71; asst. attending physician in ob-gyn N.Y. Hosp., N.Y.C., 1971, now assoc. attending physician. Clin. assoc. prof. ob-gyn NY Weill Cornell Med. Coll. Editor: (with William J. Sweeney, III) Advances in Obstetrics and Gynecology (Williams, Wilkins), 1978, Principles of Obstetrics, 1982. Fellow ACS, Am. Coll. Obstetricians and Gynecologists, Royal Coll. Surgeons (Can.); mem. AMA, N.Y. Med. Soc., Soc. Reproductive Surgeons, Griffis Faculty Club of Cornell U. Office: 12 E 69th St New York NY 10021-4923

CAPLAN, SUSAN ROBIN, artist, writer, educator; b. Boston, July 23, 1965; d. Edwin Stanley and Sandra Betty (Primack) C. AS, Massasoit C.C., Brockton, Mass., 1988; BA in English, Curry Coll., Milton, Mass., 1990; MA in Profl. Writing, U. Mass., North Dartmouth, 1995. Artist Horizon House, Norwood, Mass., 1986-91; instr. English, U. Mass. Dartmouth, North Dartmouth, 1992-94; artist Learning Express, Canton, Mass., 1989-92, Norwood, 1993-97; instr. English, Dean Coll., Franklin, Mass., 1994-97; tchr., naturalist Mass. Audubon Soc. Wildlife Sanctuary, Sharon, 1997—. Instr. creative writing Canton Evening Sch., 1998—. Wiccan. Avocations: creativity, mythology, tarot reading, belly dancing.

CAPLES, RICHARD JAMES, dance company executive, lawyer; b. Balt., June 7, 1949; s. Delphin Delmas and Louise Skinner (Leigh) C. BA, Yale U., 1971; MA, Johns Hopkins U., 1974; JD, Cornell U., 1977. Bar: N.Y. 1978, U.S. Dist. Ct. (so. and ea. dists.) N.Y. 1978. Assoc. Donovan Leisure Newton & Irvine, N.Y.C., 1977-81, Shearman & Sterling, N.Y.C., 1981-83; exec. dir. Santa Fe Festival Theater, 1983-84, Lar Lubovitch Dance Co., N.Y.C., 1984—; dir. Doug Varone and Dancers, N.Y.C., 1995—, Dance/USA, Washington, 1995—2002, also sec. bd., 1998-2000, treas., 2000—02, Project Ballet Theater, 2000—, Artists Cmty. Fed. Credit Union, 2002—. Treas. Park 58 Corp., N.Y.C., 1989—, pres. 1994—; dir. Dean Dance and Music Found., N.Y.C., 1981-84. Mem. Am. Soc. Internat. Law, N.Y. State Bar Assn., Assn. Bar City of N.Y. (com. on copyright 2002—, com. on art law, 2003—), Am. Coun. on Germany, Johns Hopkins Alumni Assn. (bd. dirs. N.Y.C. chpt. 1988-92), Univ. Club, Yale Club, Johns Hopkins Club (Balt.) Episcopalian. Home: 470 Park Ave New York NY 10022-1903 Office: Lar Lubovitch Dance Co 229 W 42d St 8th Fl New York NY 10036-7299 E-mail: DickCaples@aol.com., lubovitch@aol.com.

CAPLICE, NOEL M. cardiologist, researcher; s. James M. and Margaret B. Caplice; m. Katie M. Kearney, May 25, 1990; children: Ross J., Samuel K. MB, BCh, Nat. U. of Ireland, 1986. Lic. Minn. Licensure Bd., 1999. Author: (med. rsch.) Growth factors released after angioplasty (Young Investigator award, Australian Cardiac Soc., 1996). Fellow Coll. of Physicians, Royal Australian Coll. of Physicians, 1996, Royal Coll. of Physicians, Ireland, 2001. Achievements include discovery of Stent for cell-based gene delivery.

CAPLIN, JERROLD LEON, health physicist; b. Phila., Jan. 25, 1930; s. Samuel Harry and Katherine (Socloff) C.; children: Sally C. Daniels, Patricia Graham Reed. AB, Temple U., 1951, postgrad., 1952-53, Vanderbilt U., 1951-52. Supervisory health physicist U.S. Army C.E., Ft. Belvoir, Va., 1959—61; health physicist radiation protection stds. AEC, U.S. Nuc. Regulatory Commn., Washington, 1961—81, environ. projects mgr., 1971—72; ret., 1981; cons., 1981—. Guest lectr. radiation sci. Georgetown U. Grad. Sch., 1987-97; sr. scientist Advanced Sys. Tech., Inc., 1993-97; photographer, newspaper editor, sci. writer, 1983—; sr. tech. editor Advanced Technologies and Labs. Internat., Inc., 2000-03. Co-author, editor Manual Respiratory Protection Against Airborne Radioactive Materials, 1976. Active Nat. Mus. of Women in Arts, Friends of the Nat. Zoo, Friends of the Kennedy Ctr. Lt. USNR, 1953-58. AEC Radiol. Physics fellow, Vanderbilt U., Oak Ridge Nat. Lab., 1951—52. Mem. AAAS, ASTM, Am. Nat. Stds. Inst., Am. Conf. Gov. Indsl. Hygienists (chmn. com. 1977-83), Am. Assn. Physics Tchrs., Am. Film Inst., Nat. Ctr. Sci. Edn. (assoc.), Internat. Radiation Protection Assn., U.S. Naval Inst., Nat. Wildlife Fedn., Nat. Geog. Soc., Nat. Trust for Hist. Preservation, Health Physics Soc., Smithsonian Instn. (resident assoc. 1970—), Wilderness

Soc., Libr. Congress Assocs., Com. Sci. Investigation of Claims of the Paranormal Assoc. Home and Office: 9 Goodport Ln Gaithersburg MD 20878-1001 E-mail: jcaplin001@aol.com.

CAPLIN, MORTIMER MAXWELL, lawyer, educator; b. N.Y.C., July 11, 1916; s. Daniel and Lillian (Epstein) C.; m. Ruth Sacks, Oct. 18, 1942; children: Lee Evan, Michael Andrew, Jeremy Owen, Catherine Jean. BS, U. Va., 1937, LLB, 1940; JSD, NYU, 1953; LLD (hon.), St. Michael's Coll., 1964. Bar: Va. 1941, N.Y. 1942, D.C. 1964. Law clk. to Hon. Armistead M. Dobie U.S. Ct. Appeals (4th cir.), Richmond, 1940-41; assoc. Paul, Weiss, Rifkind, Wharton & Garrison, N.Y.C., 1941-42, 45-50; prof. law U. Va., Charlottesville, 1950-61, vis. prof. law, 1965-87, prof. emeritus, 1988—; ptnr. Perkins, Battle & Minor, Charlottesville, 1952-61; U.S. commr. IRS, Washington, 1961-64; sr. ptnr. Caplin & Drysdale, Washington, 1964—. Mem. Pres.'s Task Force on Taxation, 1960; bd. dirs. Danaher Corp., Washington, Fairchild Corp., Dulles, Va., Presdl. Realty Corp., White Plains, N.Y., Environ. and Energy Study Inst.; mem. pub. rev. bd. Arthur Andersen & Co., Chgo., 1980-88; reorgn. trustee Webb & Knapp, Inc., 1965-72. Author: Proxies, Annual Meetings and Corporate Democracy, 1953, Doing Business in Other States, 1959; editor-in-chief Va. Law Rev., 1939-40; contbr. numerous articles on tax and corp. matters to profl. jours. Past chmn. bd. dirs. Nat. Civic Svc. League, Am. Coun. on Internat. Sports; past chmn. nat citizens adv. com. Assn. Am. Med. Colls.; trustee Arena Stage, U. Va. Law Sch. Found., Wolf Trap Found. Performing Arts, Shakespeare Theatre, Washington, Arena Stage, Washington, Peace Through Law Found., Washington, bd. overseers U. V.I.; chmn. adv. bd. Hospitality and Info. Svc., Washington; chmn. Coun. for Arts, U. Va.; past pres. Atlantic Coast Conf.; emeritus trustee George Washington U.; mem. bd. visitors U. Va., 1992-97; pres., bd. dirs. Indigent Civil Litigation Fund. Decorated mem. initial landing force Normandy Invasion USN; recipient, Va. State Bar and Va. Soc. CPAs award, 1960, Achievement award, Tax Soc. of NYU, 1962, Judge Learned Hand Human Rels. award, Am. Jewish Com., 1963, 1993, Alexander Hamilton award, U.S. Treasury Dept., 1964, Disting. Svc. award, Tax Execs. Inst., 1964, medal in law, U. Va. Thomas Jefferson Found., 2001. Fellow Am. Bar Found., Am. Tax Policy Inst., Am. Coll. Tax Counsel; mem. ABA (ho. of dels. 1980-92, mem. fed. jud. com. 1993-96, ALI-ABA com. continuing profl. edn., chair DC Fellows), Nat. Conf. of Lawyers and CPAs, Am. Law Inst. (life), N.Y. State Bar Assn., Va. Bar Assn., D.C. Bar Assn., D.C. Bar Found. (adv. com.), Univ. Club (Washington), Fed. City Club (bd. govs.), Colonnade Club (Charlottesville), Order of Coif, Phi Beta Kappa, Phi Beta Kappa Assocs., Omicron Delta Kappa. Democrat. Jewish. Avocations: swimming, tennis, hiking. Home: 5610 Wisconsin Ave Apt 18E Chevy Chase MD 20815-4415 Office: One Thomas Circle NW Washington DC 20005-5802 E-mail: mmc@capdale.com.

CAPLINGER, PATRICIA ELLEN, family nurse practitioner; b. St. Louis, Oct. 6, 1956; d. Julius G. and Wanda L. (Guthrie) Kissel; child from previous marriage, Jeremy Michael Frederiksen; m. Ray E. Caplinger, Dec. 26, 1995. ADN, St. Louis C.C., 1977; BSN, U. State N.Y., 1982; FNP, U. Colo., Denver, 1985. RN, Colo.; CNOR, CNRN; cert. family nurse practitioner. Med. case mgmt. supr. Intracorp., Denver; clin. mgr. Rehab. Svcs. Corp., Eureka, Calif.; family nurse practitioner Burre Clinic, Eureka; pvt. practice Eureka; dir. PM&R Marian Health Ctr., Sioux City, Iowa; family nurse practitioner St. John's Physicians and Clinics, Lebanon, Mo. Mem. ANA (nursing scholar), ARN, AANP. Home: 23241 Red Oak Dr Lebanon MO 65536-5895

CAPLOW, THEODORE, sociologist, educator; b. N.Y.C., May 1, 1920; s. Samuel Nathaniel and Florence (Israel) C.; m. Margaret Mary Pettit, 1981. AB, U. Chgo., 1939; PhD, U. Minn., 1946; LLD, Ball State U., 2003. Mem. faculty U. Minn., 1945-60; prof. sociology Columbia U., 1961-70; chmn. dept. sociology U. Va., Charlottesville, 1970-78, 84-86, Commonwealth prof., 1973—. Vis. prof. U. Bordeaux, France, 1950, U. Aix-Marseille, France, 1951, U. Utrecht, Netherlands, 1954-55, Stanford, 1957, P.R., 1959, U. Bogota, Colombia, 1962, Sorbonne, Paris, France, 1968-69, Institut d'Etudes Politiques, Paris, 1983, U. Rome, 1984, U. Oslo, 1986; pres. Mendota Research Group Inc., 1957-65 Author: Sociology of Work, 1954, Principles of Organization, 1964, Two Against One, 1968, L'Enquête Sociologique, 1970, Toward Social Hope, 1975, Peace Games, 1989, American Social Trends, 1991, Perverse Incentives, 1994; sr. author: The Academic Marketplace, 1957, The Urban Ambience, 1964, Middletown Families, 1982, All Faithful People, 1983, Recent Social Trends in the United States, 1960-90, 1991, Systems of War and Peace, 1995, Sociologie Militaire, 2000, The First Measured Century, 2001, Leviathen Transformed, 2002. With AUS, 1943-45, PTO. Decorated Purple Heart. Mem. Tocqueville Soc. (pres. 1979-83), Am. Sociol. Assn. (sec. 1983-86), Farmington Hunt Club Albemerle Yacht Club,(Charlottesville), Century Club (N.Y.C.), Tarratine Club (Dark Harbor, Maine). Home: Twin Springs 793 Reas Ford Rd Earlysville VA 22936-2306 E-mail: tc@virginia.edu.

CAPO, RAFAEL V. lawyer; b. San Juan, PR, Jan. 22, 1951; s. Rafael and Edith (Zayas) Capo; m. Ines Garcia, Dec. 31, 1977; 1 child, Ines A. BA cum laude, U PR, 1970; JD magna cum laude, 1973; LLM, Yale U., 1974; postgrad., Columbia U., 1974. Bar: PR 1974. Assoc. Jose H. Pico Law Offices, Hat Rey, PR, 1974, Francis, Doval, Colorado & Carlo, Hato Rey, 1975; sole practice Hato Rey, 1976—77; dir. Office Indsl. Tax Exemption, Hato Rey, PR, 1977—81; dep. counsel to v.p. Bush v.p. Bush, Washington, 1981—83; dep. gen. counsel US Export-Import Bank, Washington, 1983; chmn. fin. com. PR Rep. Com., 1980; del. Rep. Nat. Conv., Detoit, 1980. Contbr. articles. Fellow ITT fellow, 1974, Fomento fellow, 1974. Mem.: Tax Inst. Am., Nat. Tax Assn., PR Bar Assn., ABA, Am. Cancer Soc. Roman Catholic. Home: 6424 Wishbone Ter Cabin John MD 20818-1700

CAPOBIANCO, ANTHONY G. physician; b. Somerville, Mass., Feb. 19, 1928; MD, Georgetown U., 1952. Diplomate Am. Bd. Surgery. Intern Boston City Hosp., 1952-53, resident in surgery, 1953-54, 56-59; mem. staff Met. West Med. Ctr., Natick, Mass. Fellow ACS; mem. Boston Soc. Surgery, Mass. Med. Soc. Office: 205 Newbury St Framingham MA 01701-4581

CAPODILUPO, JEANNE HATTON, public relations executive; b. McRae, Ga., May 3, 1940; d. Lewis Irby and Essee Elizabeth (Parker) Hatton; m. Raphael S. Capodilupo, Jan. 21, 1967. Grad., Dale Carnegie Inst., 1976. Sec. A.R. Clark Acct., Fernandina Beach, Fla., 1958-59; receptionist, girl Friday Sta. WNDT-TV, N.Y.C., 1960-62, Coy Hunt and Co., N.Y.C., 1962-69; clk. Woodlawn Cemetery, Bronx, N.Y., 1969-71, historian, cmty. affairs coord., 1971-84, editor newsletter, 1979—, asst. to pres., 1984-99, dir. pub. rels., 1984; grad. asst. Dale Carnegie Inst., 1977-78. Rschr. Woodlawn Cemetery's Hall of Fame; contbr. articles to Collier Encyclopedia, 1985; contbr. articles to profl. jours. Chmn. ann. Adm. Farragut Honor Ceremony, Bronx, 1976—; founder, chmn. Toys for Needy Children, 1983-97; bd. dirs. Bronx Mus. Arts, v.p., 1983-84; pres. Bronx Coun. Arts, 1987-90, Network Orgn. Bronx Women, 1997-98; adv. bd. Salvation Army, 1985, Bronx Arts Ensemble, 1985; bd. mgrs. Bronx YMCA, 1985, vice-chmn., 1989—; bd. dirs. Bronx Urban League, 1985, Bronx Coun. on Arts, 1985, pres. 1987-90; active Bronx Landmarks Task Force, 1994—. Recipient award citation VFW, 1976, Voice of Democracy Program judge's citation, 1980, Disting. Community Svc. award N.Y.C. Council, II Leone di Sanmarco award Italian Heritage & Culture Com. Bronx, 1989, Lifetime Achievement Humanitarian award Bronx Coun. on Arts, 1999-2000; named Woman of Yr., YMCA, Bronx, 1986, Network Orgn. Bronx Women, 1986, Jeanne and Ray Capodilupo named as Mr. & Mrs. Bronx 1989-90 proclaimed by Borough Pres., named Pioneer of the Bronx, 1992, Citizen of Yr. Bronx Club, 1995; recipient cert. appreciation Dale Carnegie Inst., 1977, Outstanding Citizenship award Bronx N.E. Kiwanis Club, 1981, Service to Youth award YMCA of Bronx, 1983; recipient proclamation City Council of N.Y., Italian Heritage and Culture Com. of the Bronx, 1989; Outstanding Cemeterian award Am. Cemetery Assn., 1987-88; Citation of Merit Bronx Borough Pres.'s Office, 1988; Spl. Hons. for Outstanding Vol. Work Ladies Aux. Our Lady of Mercy Med. Ctr.; named Hon. Grand Marshall Bronx Columbus Day Parade, 1987-89, Bronx Meml. Day Parade, 1989; apptd. to comm. celebrating 350 yrs. of the Bronx by Borough Pres., recipient Pioneer award for Women's History Month for Outstanding Humanitarian Svcs., 1991, Lifetime Achievement award Bronx YMCA, 1999-2000, Role Model award Columbus Alliance, 2000; Jeanne Hatton Capodilupo Day proclaimed by Bronx Borough Presdl. Proclamation, 1999. Mem. Bronx County Hist. Soc., Network Orgn. Bronx Women (pres. 1997-99), Women in Communication, Bronx C. of C. (sec. 1988), YMCA (life mem.), N.Y. Press Club, Italian Big Sisters Club, Women's City Club, Order Eastern Star. Methodist. Office: Woodlawn Cemetery Webster Ave at 233 St Bronx NY 10470-0075

CAPOLARELLO, JOE R. photojournalist; b. Bklyn., Sept. 6, 1961; s. Carmelo and Grace (Auditore) C. Cert. news prodn. and tech., Inst. New Cinema Artists, N.Y.C., 1981; cert. TV News Video Workshop, U. Okla., Norman, 1986; cert. TV News Feature Workshop, Internat. Film & TV Workshops, Rockport, Maine, 1987; cert. Leadership in Broadcast Photojournalism, The Poynter Inst. for Media Studies, St. Petersburg, Fla., 1992. Photojournalist, videotape editor, field producer W.Va. Jour. Sta. WSWP-TV, Beckley, W.Va., 1982-83; photojournalist Eyewitness News Sta. WABC-TV, N.Y.C., 1983; photojournalist Bus. Times, ESPN, N.Y.C., 1984, Broadcast News Svc., N.Y.C., 1984, Cable News Network, Inc., N.Y.C., 1984—, Entertainment Tonight, Paramount Pictures Corp., N.Y.C., 1988-91, Fox News at Seven, The Ten O'Clock News, Sta. WNYW-TV, N.Y.C., 1988-91, USA Today: The Television Show, Grant Tinker/Gannett East Prodns. Inc., N.Y.C., 1988-89, Preview: the best of the new, TV Program Enterprises, N.Y.C., 1990; photojournalist Personalities Twentieth Century Fox Film Corp., N.Y.C., 1991. Mem. Acad. TV Arts and Scis., Nat. Hon. Broadcasting Soc., TV and Radio Working Press Assn., Nat. Press Photographers Assn. Democrat. Avocation: traveling. Home: 1 Liberty St Little Ferry NJ 07643-2303 Office: Cable News Network 5 Penn Plz Fl 21 New York NY 10001-1810 E-mail: joecapolarello@hotmail.com.

CAPON, EDWIN GOULD, church organization administrator, clergyman; b. Boston, Apr. 1, 1924; s. Gould and Helen (Wood) C.; m. Norma Jean Wilcoxson (div. Jan. 1971); children: Peter Lawrence, Jonathan Edwin; m. Esther Constance Nicastro, Sept. 5, 1975. AB, Harvard U., 1947; STM, Andover-Newton Theol. Sem., 1949. Ordained to ministry Swedenborgian Ch., 1949. Min. Bridgewater (Mass.) New Ch., 1948-51, Elmwood (Mass.) New Ch., 1949-55, Detroit New Ch., Royal Oak, Mich., 1977-79; v.p. Swedenborg Sch. Religion, Cambridge, Mass., 1953-55, pres. Cambridge and Newton, Mass., 1955-77; pastor San Francisco Swedenborgian Ch., 1979-90; interim min. St. Paul Swedenborgian Ch., 1991-92, min., 1992-94; pres. The Swedenborgian Ch., Newton, 1992-98, chmn. coun. mins., 1956-67. Trustee Urbana (Ohio) U., 1966-80, 92-99; v.p. Mass. Coun. Chs. Mem. Swedenborgian Ch. Avocations: hiking, mountain climbing in new england.

CAPONE, ALPHONSE WILLIAM, retired industrial executive; b. Pitts., Oct. 22, 1919; s. Aniello and Mary (Manzione) C.; m. Eleanor M. Polis, Aug. 16, 1947 (dec. Nov. 1972); 1 child, Margaret Ellen; m. Alvira L. Petty, July 5, 1975. BBA, Duquesne U., 1942; postgrad., Harvard U., 1959, Am. U. Sch. Internat. Service, Washington, 1965, Brookings Instn., 1966. With Koppers Co., Inc., Pitts., 1946-84, mgr. fin. dept. internat. ops., 1964-67, asst. treas., 1958-67, v.p., chief fin. officer, treas., 1967-77, sr. v.p., chief fin. officer, 1978-84. Chmn. bd. Gordon Terminal Svc. Co., Aeolian Enterprises, Inc., Latrobe, Pa., 1993—. Bd. dirs. Duquesne U., chmn., 1979-87. Served to lt. USNR, 1943-46. Mem. AICPA, Pa. Inst. CPAs, Fin. Execs. Inst. (dir., pres. Pitts. chpt. 1974-75), Pitts. C. of C., World Affairs Council Pitts., Duquesne U. Alumni Assn. (past pres., gov.), Am. Mgmt. Assn. (v.p. charge fin. council 1977-79), Machinery and Allied Products Inst. (fin. council), Conf. Bd. (council fin. execs.), Harvard Advanced Mgmt. Assn., Harvard Bus. Sch. Assn. Pitts., Duquesne Club. Home and Office: PO Box 4540 Eighty Four PA 15330-0540

CAPONE, HELEN DIANA, retired internist; b. Romanow, Poland, June 1, 1927; came to U.S., 1951; d. Zygmunt Louis and Monica Jachimowski Preisler, m. Maurice Anthony Capone (dec.). Jan. 16, 1954; children: Maurice Charles, Marcus James, Matthew Peter, Martha Helen, Michael Paul, Martin Thomas. MD, U. Ottawa, Ont., 1951. Diplomate Am. Bd. Internal Medicine. Rotating intern Ottawa Gen. Hosp., 1950-51; resident in pathology D.C. Gen. Hosp., Washington, 1952; resident in internal medicine Sisters of Charity Hosp., Buffalo, N.Y., 1951-52, D.C. Gen. Hosp., Washington, 1953-54; sr. resident in internal medicine Boston City Hosp, 1954-55; med. officer Walter Reed Army Med. Ctr., Washington, 1955-60, 72-77, asst. chief med. clin., 1977-78, chief med. clin., 1978-82; pvt. practice in internal medicine Bethesda, Md., 1961-72, Clinton, Md., 1982-95, Colonial Beach, Va., 1989-99; retired, 1999. Fellow ACP. Republican. Roman Catholic. Avocations: stamp collecting, antiques, coins, gardening.

CAPONE, LUCIEN, JR., management consultant, former naval officer; b. Bristol, R.I. s. Lucien and Louise Dolores (Malafronte) C.; m. Charlotte Loretta Lammers, July 22, 1950; children: Lucien, Judith Ann. BS, U.S. Naval Acad., 1949; grad., Naval Postgrad. Sch., 1955, Indsl. Coll. Armed Forces, 1967; MS in Bus. Adminstrn, George Washington U., 1967, postgrad., 1970-71. Commd. ensign USN, 1949, advanced through grades to rear adm., served on destroyers Atlantic Fleet, 1949-54, mem. staff Office Chief Naval Ops. Dept. of Navy, 1955-57, exec. officer U.S.S. Huse, 1957-59, staff, comdr. Middle East Force, 1959-61, head plans, programs, and requirements br. Naval Communications System Hdqrs., 1961-63; comdg. officer U.S.S. Hammerberg, 1963-64; dep. chief of staff Def. Comm. Agy., Washington, 1964-66; comdg. officer U.S.S. Dahlgren, 1967-69; asst. comdr. plans, programs, requirements Naval Telecommunications Command USN, Washington, 1969-72; comdg. officer U.S.S. Richmond K. Turner, 1972-74; dep. dir. nat. mil. command system tech. support Def. Comm. Agy., Washington, 1974-76, dir. command and control tech. ctr., 1976-78; dep. dir. command and control Def. Communications Agy. USN, 1976-78; dir. Inter-Am. Def. Coll., Washington, 1978-79; exec. Booz, Allen & Hamilton, Inc., McLean, Va., 1979-97, v.p., 1983-88, sr. v.p., 1988-97, bd. dirs., operating coun., 1988-97. Decorated Legion of Merit, Def. Superior Service medal with oak leaf cluster. Mem. IEEE, AIAA, Armed Forces Communications and Electronics Assn. (past pres. D.C. chpt.). Office: Booz Allen & Hamilton Inc 8283 Greensboro Dr Ste 700 Mc Lean VA 22102-3838 E-mail: capone_luke@bah.com.

CAPONE, LUCIEN, III, lawyer; b. Balt., June 10, 1951; s. Lucien Jr. and Charlotte (Lammers) C.; m. Julia Smith, Oct. 17, 1950; children: William Justice, Margaret Grey. BA, N.C. State U., 1973; JD, Wake Forest U., 1977. Bar: NC, DC, US Ct. Appeals (4th cir.), US Ct. Mil. Appeals, US Supreme Ct.; cert. flight instr. Asst. atty. gen. NC Dept. Justice, Raleigh, 1977-86, spl. dep. atty. gen., 1986-91; Univ. counsel U. NC Greensboro, 1991—. Bd. dir. CACREP, Alexandria, Va., 1995-2000. Comdr. JAGC, USN, 1982—. Mem. Nat. Assn. Coll. and Univ. Attys. (bd. dirs.), N.C. Bar Assn. Avocation: teaching flying. Office: U NC 1000 Spring Garden St Greensboro NC 27402-6170 E-mail: caponel@uncg.edu.

CAPONIGRO, JEFFREY RALPH, public relations counselor; b. Kankakee, Ill., Aug. 13, 1957; s. Ralph A. and Barbara Jean (Paul) C.; m. Ellen Colleen Kennedy, Oct. 15, 1982; children: Nicholas J., Michael J. BA, Ctrl. Mich. U., 1979. Sports reporter Observer and Eccentric newspaper, Rochester, Mich., 1974-75, Mt. Pleasant (Mich.) Times, 1975-77, Midland (Mich.) Daily News, 1977-79; acct. exec. Desmond & Assocs., Oak Park, Mich., 1979-80; v.p. Anthony M. Franco, Inc., Detroit, 1980-84; chmn., pres., CEO Shandwick USA (formerly Casey Comm. Mgmt., Inc.), Southfield, 1984—95; founder & CEO Caponigro Public Relations Inc., Detroit, 1995—. Contbr. author: Best Sports Stories, 1978. Mem. Pub. Rels. Soc. Am. (accredited, Detroit chpt., nat. accrediation bd.). Home: 5790 Springbrook Dr Troy MI 48098-5352 Office: Caponigro Public Relations Ste 900 4000 Town Ctr Southfield MI 48075-1410

CAPORALE, D. NICK, lawyer; b. Omaha, Sept. 13, 1928; s. Michele and Lucia Caporale; m. Margaret Nilson, Aug. 5, 1950; children: Laura Diane Stevenson, Leland Alan. BA, U. Nebr.-Omaha, 1949, M.Sc., 1954; JD with distinction, U. Nebr.-Lincoln, 1957. Bar: Nebr. 1957, U.S. Dist. Ct. Nebr. 1957, U.S. Ct. Appeals 8th cir. 1958, U.S. Supreme Ct. 1970. Judge Nebr. Dist. Ct., Omaha, 1979—82, Nebr. Supreme Ct., Lincoln, 1982—98; of counsel Baird Holm Law Firm, 1998—. Lectr. U. Nebr., Lincoln, 1982-84, 2000—. Pres. Omaha Community Playhouse, 1976. Served to 1st lt. U.S. Army, 1952-54, Korea. Decorated Bronze Star; recipient Alumni Achievement U. Nebr.-Omaha, 1972 Fellow Am. Coll. Trial Lawyers, Internat. Soc. Barristers; mem. Order of Coif. Office: Baird Holm Law Firm 1500 Woodmen Tower Omaha NE 68102 E-mail: ncaporale@bairdholm.com.

CAPOUANO, ALBERT D. lawyer; b. Montgomery, Ala., 1945; BS, U. Ala., 1967, JD, 1970; LLM in Taxation, NYU, 1971. Bar: Ala. 1970, Fla. 1973. Mem. Dean, Mead, Egerton, Bloodworth, Capouano & Bozarth P.A., Orlando, Fla. Mem. Fla. Bar, Ala. State Bar. Office: Dean Mead Egerton Bloodworth Capouano & Bozarth 800 N Magnolia Ave # 1500 PO Box 2346 Orlando FL 32802-2346 E-mail: acapouano@deanmead.com.

CAPOZZI, LOU, public relations executive; CEO Manning, Selvage & Lee, N.Y.C. Office: Manning Selvage & Lee 79 Madison Ave Fl 4 New York NY 10016-0018

CAPOZZIELLO, MARTHA M. medical/surgical nurse; b. NYC, Mar. 6, 1966; d. Teodoro and Marta Capozziello. BSN, Hunter Coll., 1987; M in Nursing Adminstrn. Summa cum laude, U. New England, 1999. Cert. Registered Nurse Anesthetist. RN Bellevue Hosp., NYC, 1987—95, Sloane-Kettering Hosp., NYC, 1994—95, NYU Med. Ctr., NYC, 1997—99; CRNA Presbyn. Med. Ctr, U. Pa., Phila., 2000—02, Bapt. Hosp. South Miami, South Miami, Fla., 2002—. Mem.: New Eng. Assn. of Nurse Anesthetists, N.Y. Acad. Sci., Am. Assn. Nurse Anesthetists (Goldie Brangman scholar 1998, NEANA scholar 1999), Sigma Theta Tau.

CAPP, MICHAEL PAUL, physician, educator; b. Yonkers, N.Y., July 1, 1930; s. Michael and Mary (Bybel) Capp; m. Constance Whitehead, Jan. 4, 1989; children: Marianne, Michael, Steven, John. BS, Roanoke Coll., Salem, Va., 1952; MD, U. N.C., 1958. Diplomate Am. Bd. Radiology. Lab. instr. physics Roanoke Coll., 1952; tchg. asst. Grad. Sch. Physics, Duke U., 1952—54; intern in pediat. Duke U. Med. Ctr., 1958—59, resident in radiology, 1959—62, assoc. in radiology, 1962, asst. prof., 1963—66, assoc. prof., 1966—70, dir. diagnostic divsn., dept. radiology, 1967—70, asst. prof. pediat., 1968—70, radiologist in charge pediatric cardiology, 1962—70; dir. Duke U. Med. Ctr. (Pediatric Radiology Program), 1965—70, Duke Med. Center (Med. Students Teaching Program Diagnostic Radiology), 1965-66; prof., chmn. dept. radiology U. Ariz. Coll. Medicine, Tucson, 1970—93, prof. emeritus, 1993—; chief of staff Ariz. Med. Ctr., Univ. Hosp., 1971—73; exec. dir. Am. Bd. of Radiology, Tucson, 1993—2001. Mem. NRC com. on Radiology James Picker Found., 1972. Contbr. articles to profl. jours. Mem.: NAS, AMA, Inst. Medicine, Soc. for Chmn. Acad. Radiology Depts. (pres. 1977), Soc. for Pediatric Radiology, Eastern Radiol. Soc. (sci. program chmn. 1967, v.p. 1973—), Pima County Med. Soc., N.Y. Acad. Scis., N.Am. Soc. Cardiac Radiologists (pres. 1975), Radiol. Soc. N.Am. (chmn. sci. exhibits com. 1976—79), Am. Bd. Radiology (treas. 1982—85, v.p. 1985, pres. 1987—89, exec. dir. 1993—), Am. Heart Assn. (pres. coun. on cardiovasc. radiology 1976—78), Am. Assn. Univ. Radiologists (exec. com. 1970, Gold medal 1988), Am. Roentgen Ray Soc. (pres. 1990), Am. Coll. Radiology, Sigma Pi Sigma. Office: U of Arizona Coll of Med 1501 N Campbell Ave PO Box 245017 Tucson AZ 85724

CAPPARELLI, RALPH C. state legislator; b. Chgo., Apr. 12, 1924; s. Ralph and Mary (Drammis) C.; m. Cordelia Capparelli; children: Ralph, Valerie. BS, No. Ill. U. 1st v.p. 41st Ward Dem. Orgn., Chgo., 1965—; Ill. state rep. Dist. 13, 1971—. Asst. majority whip, ex officio mem. Com. Intergovt. Coop. Com., exec. mem. Fin. Inst. Com. and Transp. and Motor Vehicles Com., Ill. Ho. of Reps.; supr. recreation Chgo. Pk. Dist., 1953-67; advisor Columbia Bank, Chgo., 1967—; sec.-treas. Jefferson Travel, 1968—; former tchr. Decorated Battle Star. Mem. Nat. Recreation Soc., Ill. Recreation Soc., Lions, K.C. (4th degree), Eagles, Am. Legion, Sigma Nu. Office: 7452 N Harlem Ave Chicago IL 60631-4404*

CAPPE, MELVIN SAMUEL, economist; b. Toronto, Ont., Canada, Dec. 3, 1948; s. David and Patricia (Wise) C.; m. Marline Linda Pliskin, Nov. 5, 1971; children: Daniel, Emily. BA, U. Toronto, 1971; MA, U. Western Ont., 1972. Sr. analyst, chief Treasury Bd. Secretariat, Ottawa, Ont., 1975-78; chief Dept. Fin., Ottawa, 1978-82; asst. dept. minister Consumer & Corp. Affairs, Ottawa, 1982-90; dep. sec. Treasury Bd. Secretariat, Ottawa, 1990-94; dep. minister Environment Canada, Ottawa, 1994-96; dep. min. Human Resources Devel. Canada, 1996-99; clerk of the Privy Coun., sec. of Cabinet Ottawa. Office: Langevin Block Rue Wellington St Ottawa ON Canada K1A 0A3

CAPPEL, CONSTANCE, educational consultant, writer; b. Dayton, Ohio, June 22, 1936; d. Adam Denison and Mary Louise (Henry) C.; m. R.A. Montgomery Jr., June 16, 1962 (div. Apr. 1980); children: Raymond A. Montgomery III, Anson Cappel Montgomery. BA, Sarah Lawrence Coll., 1959; MA, Columbia U., N.Y.C., 1961; PhD, Union Inst. and Univ., Cin., 1991. Editor Newsweek, N.Y.C., 1961-63, Vogue, N.Y.C., 1964-66; grad. prof. Goddard Coll., Plainfield, Vt., 1975-79; founder, chief exec. officer, pub. Vt. Crossroad Press, Waitsfield, 1972-82; comml. realtor Investmark, Dayton, 1983—85; prin., founder, CEO Cappel Cons., San Francisco, 1986-94; bus. advisor U.S. Peace Corps, Lodz, Poland, 1994-96; mgr. Price Waterhouse Nieruchomości, Warsaw, 1996-97; dir. devel. Conflict Resolution Catalysts, Montpelier, Vt., 1997; tchr. trainer U.S. Peace Corps., Kazakhstan, 1998; pres. Newport (N.H.) Earth Inst., 1999; faculty Norman Rockwell Mus., 2000—02; PhD adj. prof. UI & U, 2003—. Adj. faculty PhD program Union Inst. and Univ., 2002—03. Author: Hemingway in Michigan, 1966 (paperback 1977, 99), Vermont School Bus Ride, 1977, Utopian Colleges, 1999, Sweetgrass and Smoke, 2002. Founder Women's Rights Project/ACLU, Vt., 1973-74; mem. grad. alumni/ae bd. The Union Inst. and Univ., 1992-94, 99—, sec., 1993; v.p. bd. Chief Andrew Blackbird Mus., 2002—, bd. mem. 2002—, Harbor Springs Hist. Soc., 2002—. McDowell Colony fellow, Peterborough, N.H., 1972, 74. Mem.: NEARA, Archl. Conservancy. Petoskey Audabon Soc., Archaeol. Conservancy, Audubon Soc., Mich. Hemingway Soc., Hemingway Soc., Great Lakes Lighthouse Keepers Assn., PEN Am. Ctr. Democrat. Episcopalian. Office: 524 Pine St Harbor Springs MI 49740

CAPPELLI, PETER H. human resources educator; b. Utica, N.Y., Sept. 7, 1956; s. Henry Achilles and Elvie MaeDell C.; m. Virginia Hale McKinnie, June 1, 1985; children: Michael, Robert. BS, Cornell U., 1978; DPhil, Oxford U., 1983; MA, U. Pa., 1990. Postdoctoral fellow MIT, Cambridge, mass., 1981-82; asst. prof. U. Ill., Champaign, 1982-83; assoc. prof. U. Calif., Berkeley, 1990; co-dir Nat. Ctr. Ednl. Quality of Workforce Ctr. Human Resources Wharton Sch., Phila., 1991—. Vis. prof. London Sch. Econs., 1993, Boconni U., Milan, 1993. Author: Change at Work, 1997, The New Deal at Work, 1999. Staff mem. Sec. Labor's Commn. on Workforce Quality, Washington, 1988-90. Office: The Wharton Sch U Pa Philadelphia PA 19104-6358

CAPPELLO, EVE, speaker, trainer, author; b. Sydney, Australia; d. Nem and Ethel Shapira; children: Frances Soskins, Alan Kazdin. BA, Calif. State U., Dominguez Hills, 1974; MA, Pacific Western U., 1977, PhD, 1978. Singer, pianist, L.A., 1956-76; profl. devel. and mgmt. staff tng. Calif. Inst. Tech., 1977—; instr. Calif. State U., St. Mary's Coll., U. So. Calif., Loyola Marymount U.; founder, pres. A-C-T Internat.; founder WIN Internat. Invited speaker World Congress Behavior Therapy, Israel, Melbourne U., Australia; newspaper columnist, 1976—. Author: Let's Get Growing, 1979, The Professional Touch, 1988, 3d edit., 2000, Dr Eve's Garden, 1984, Act, Don't React, 4th edit. 2000, The Game of the Name, 1985, The Perfectionist Syndrome, 1990, Why Aren't More Women Running the Show?, 1994, Great Sex After 50, 2d edit., More Great Sex After 50, 2003; contbr. articles to profl. jours. Named to Bus. and Profl. Women Internat. Hall of Fame, 1994. Mem. Internat. Platform Assn. (bd. dirs., affirmative action com., bd. govs.), Toastmasters (area gov.), Alpha Gamma. E-mail: dreve@earthlink.net.

CAPPETTA, PAMELA GUYLER, counselor; b. Huntington, Pa., May 16, 1949; d. Thomas Winslow and Lois Olene (Lukens) G.; m. Christopher John Boll, Aug. 16, 1969 (div. Aug. 1985); 1 child, Kirstin Boll Kochanek; m. Robert Christopher Cappetta, May 4, 1991. BS, Shippensburg U., 1971; MEd, Coll. William & Mary, 1980, EdD, 1990. Lic. profl. counselor, Va.; lic. marriage and family therapist, Va. Social worker York-Poquoson Social Svcs., Grafton, Va., 1981-84; coord. PACES family counseling ctr. Coll. William & Mary, Williamsburg, Va., 1984-87; family therapist TMJ rsch. ctr. Med. Coll. Va., Sch. Dentistry, 1984-88; clin. assoc., counselor Family Living Inst., Williamsburg, Va., 1985-88; clin. asst. prof. Med. Coll. Va., Sch. Dentistry, Richmond, Va., 1990-94; med. family therapist Norge Family Practice, Williamsburg, 1992-94; co-owner, counselor Family Living Inst., 1988-94; allied health prof. Williamsburg Place, 1993—; counselor pvt. practice, Williamsburg, 1995—. Dir. coord.

Transitions, Williamsburg, 1992-94; holotropic breathwork practitioner, Williamsburg, 1996—; faculty Asheville (N.C.) Body-Mind Clinic, 1999—. Contbr. articles to profl. jours. Vol. Va. Breast Cancer Found., Williamsburg, 1995—; bd. dirs. Va. Cancer Pain Initiative, Richmond, 1996. Mem. ACA, Am. Acad. Pain Mgmt., Nat. Bd. of Cert. Counselors, Va. Counseling Assn., Assn. Transpersonal Psychology, Assn. for Holotropic Breathwork Internat. (cert.), Internat. Soc. for Study of Dissociation, Acad. for Eating Disorders. Democrat. Avocations: travel, reading, walking dogs. Office: 161-B John Jefferson Rd Williamsburg VA 23185-5640 E-mail: drpamm@mindspring.com.

CAPPIELLO, ANGELA, meeting and marketing manager; b. New Hyde Park, N.Y., July 6, 1954; d. Augustine and Angela (Tamburello) C. Cert. meeting and conv. mgmt., NYU, 1988, cert. assn. mgmt., cert. food and beverage mgmt., NYU, 1989, cert. travel mgmt., 1990, cert. hotel and motel mgmt., 1991, cert. in fin. controls, 1992, cert. mgmt. practices, 1998. Cert. meeting profl., assn. exec. Mgr. meetings and convs. N.Y. Libr. Assn., N.Y.C., 1987-89; conf. coord. ASCE, N.Y.C., 1989; mgr. meetings and confs. Coun. Cons. Orgns., N.Y.C., 1990-91; asst. to pres. Goodstein Devel. Corp., N.Y.C., 1991-93; asst. meetings mgr. Nat. Episcopal Ch., N.Y.C., 1993-96, dir. grants program, 1996-99; mgr. meetings and confs. SCP Communications, N.Y.C., 1999—. Mem. Meeting Profls. Internat. (bd. dirs. N.Y. chpt. 1991-93), Nat. Assn. for Advancement Fat Acceptance (bd. dirs. 1983-86). Home: 36 New Hyde Park Rd New Hyde Park NY 11040-4935 Office: SCP Communications 134 W 29th St New York NY 10001-5304 E-mail: apcmeetings@worldnet.att.net.

CAPPITELLA, MAURO JOHN, architect; b. N.Y.C., July 11, 1934; s. Gaetano and Maria (D'Errico) Cappitella; m. Christine Wilhelmine Otte, Oct. 11, 1964; children: Mark, Christina, Nicole. BS in Architecture, CCNY, 1956; postgrad., Columbia U., 1960-62; M in Urban Planning, NYU, 1967. Registered arch., N.Y., N.J., lic. Nat. Coun. Archtl. Registration Bds., profl. planner, N.J. Designer Garfinkel & Marenberg, N.Y.C., 1956-57; arch. Western Electric Co., Inc., N.Y.C., 1957-68. Cons. arch., Norwood, NJ, 1968—76, Upper Saddle River, NJ, 1976—. Served to 1st lt. U.S. Army, 1957—59. Mem.: AIA (N.J. liaison rep. to N.J. State Bd. Archs. 1997), Archs. League No. N.J. (bd. dirs. 1980—83, sec. 1984—85, v.p. 1985, 1st v.p. 1986, pres.-elect 1987, pres. 1988, bd. dirs. 1989—91, pres. 1993, bd. dirs. 1994—96, Dir. of the Yr. award 1980, 1981, Anton Vegliante award 1993), N.J. Soc. Archs. (bd. dirs. 1983—84, 1987—89, 1993—96), Saddle River Valley Investment Club (pres. 2003—), Soc. 3d U.S. Inf. Divsn. U.S. Army, Saddle River Tennis Club, Rotary. Republican. Roman Catholic. Office: 332 E Saddle River Rd Upper Saddle River NJ 07458-2108 E-mail: baron332@optonline.net.

CAPPO, JOSEPH C. journalist, writer; b. Chgo., Feb. 24, 1936; s. Joseph V. and Frances (Maggio) Caciopppo; m. Mary Anne Cappo, May 7, 1967; children: Elizabeth, John. BA, DePaul U., 1957. Reporter Hollister Publs., Wilmette, Ill., 1961-62, Chgo. Daily News, 1962-68, bus. columnist, 1968-78; columnist Crain's Chgo. Bus., 1978—, pub., 1979-89, editor at large, 2003—; v.p. Crain Comm., Inc., 1981-89, sr. v.p. group pub., 1989-95, sr. v.p. internat., 1996—2003; pres. Crain Comms. of Mex., 2001—02; editor at large Crain Comms., Inc., 2003—. Pub. Advt. Age, 1989—92, publishing dir., 1992—99; dir. Assn. Area Bus. Publs., 1982—88, pres., 1985—86. Author: Future Scope: Success Strategies for the 1990's and Beyond, 1990, The Future of Advertising: New Clients, New Media, New Consumers in the Post Television Age, 2003. Bd. dirs. Off the Street Club, Chgo., 1981—, Chgo. Advt. Fedn., 1987-93, Mus. Broadcast Comm., 1984-90, Ill. Coun. on Econ. Edn., 1990-95. With U.S. Army, 1959-61. Recipient award Ill. Press Assn., 1962, (with other Daily News staffers) Nat. Headliner award, 1966, Disting. Alumni award DePaul U., 1975, Page One award Chgo. Newspaper Guild, 1978, Peter Lisagor award Sigma Delta Chi, 1978, Outstanding Achievement award in comm., Justinian Soc. Lawyers, 1979, Champion award YWCA of Met. Chgo., 1984, Media Svc. award Chgo. Lung Assn., 1990, Dante award Joint Civic Com. Italian-Ams., 2003. Mem.: Bus. and Econ. Writers (bd. govs. 1984—89), Econ. Club (Chgo.), Internat. Advt. Assn. (world bd. 1994—, sr. v.p. 1996—98, world pres. 1998—2000), Delta Mu Delta (hon.). Roman Catholic. Office: Crain Communications Inc 360 N Michigan Ave Chicago IL 60601-3806

CAPPS, ETHAN LEROY, oil company executive; b. Sherman, Tex., Dec. 2, 1924; s. Ethen Daniel and Annie Mae (Anderson) C.; m. Emily Ann Tyson, Sept. 8, 1951; children— Richard LeRoy, Nancy Elizabeth. BS, Tex. A&M U., 1948; grad., Advanced Mgmt. Program, Harvard U., 1965. C.P.A., Tex. With Tenn. Gas Transmission Co., Houston, 1948-59, asst. treas., budget dir., 1960-61; chief acct. Midwestern Gas Transmission Co., Houston, 1959; v.p. Tenneco Corp., Houston, 1961-63; adminstrv. v.p., controller Tenneco Oil Co., Houston, 1963-73; v.p., treas. Tenneco Inc., 1974-84, v.p. fin. mgmt. devel. and ins. and loss control, 1984-86, ret., 1986. Elder First Presbyn. Ch., Houston. Mem.: Petroleum (Houston), Racquet (Houston). Home: 6206 Cedar Creek Dr Houston TX 77057-1804

CAPPS, JAMES LEIGH, II, lawyer, reserve military career officer; b. Brunswick, Ga., 1956; s. Thomas Edwin Sr. and Betty Marie C.; m. Nancy Ann Fisher, 1978; children: Bonnie Lynn, James Leigh III. AA, Seminole C.C., Sanford, Fla., 1976; BA in History, U. Cen. Fla., 1981; JD, U. Fla., 1987. Bar: Fla. 1987, U.S. Ct. Mil. Appeals 1988, Colo. 1990, U.S. Ct. Appeals (4th cir.) 1997. Enlisted USAF, 1976, advanced through grades to maj., 1995, med. svc. specialist, 1977-79, air weapons dir., 1982-84, claims officer, 1987-88, area def. counsel, 1988-90, dep. staff judge adv. Onizuka AFB, Calif., 1990-93; atty. office of state atty. 18th Jud. Ct., Sanford, Fla., 1994; assoc. Dominick Salfi Law Offices, Maitland, Fla., 1993-94; res. judge adv. Moody AFB, Ga., 1993-99; of counsel Dominick Salfi Law Offices, Maitland, Fla., 1994—; pvt. practice, 1996—; res. judge adv. Patrick AFB, Fla., 2000—; civilian contract specialist for Naval Air Warfare Ctr. USN, Orlando, Fla., 1999—. Assigned to 16th Air Force Hdqs., Aviano AFB, Italy, Operation Joint Endeavor, 1996; atty. Vietnam Vets. Ctrl. Fla., 1998-99; implementation force Dayton Peace Accords UN. Maj. USAFR, 1993—. Recipient McCarthy award for legal svc. Air Combat Command, 1995. Mem. DAV, VFW. Democrat.

CAPPS, JASON SCOTT, education educator, researcher; b. Kans. City, Mo., June 10, 1975; s. Raymond Lee and Rhonda Jean Capps; m. Tonya Jo Ryan, July 20, 1996. BS in Sociology, S.W. Mo. State U., 1993—97; MA in Sociology, U. of Kans., 1998—2001. Writing cons., eng. dept. U. of Kansas, Kans., 1998—; asst. instr., sociology dept. U. of Kans., 1999—. Editor Social Thought and Rsch. (dept. sociology academic jour.), U. of Kans. Recipient Alpha Kapp Delta-Sociology honor soc., S.W. Mo. State U., 1997. Mem.: Internat. Soc. of Polit. Psychology, Am. Soc. of Criminology, Pacific Sociol. Assn., Am. Sociol. Assn., Midwest Sociol. Soc., Phi Lambda Theta. Green Party. Office: U of Kans 716 Fraser Hall Lawrence KS 66045-2172

CAPPS, LARRY LYNN, school librarian; b. Liberal, Kans., Aug. 27, 1950; s. Charles Andrew and Mary Edna Capps; m. Janet Sue Smith, Jan. 9, 1971; children: Heather Lynn, Larry Lynn Capps II. BA in Edn., Northeastern State U., 1972; MLS, U. Okla., 1980. Tchr. H.S. French and English Weleetka (Okla.) Pub. Schs., 1972—73; tchr. H.S. English, libr. Bowlegs (Okla.) Pub. Schs., 1973—83; libr., yearbook, acad. bowl teams Dale (Okla.) Pub. Schs., 1983—. Mem.: NEA, Okla. Jr. Acad. Bowl Assn. (treas., membership chmn. 1997—), Okla. Acad. Coaches Assn., Okla. Edn. Assn. Republican. Baptist. Avocations: stamp collecting, coin collecting, television, movies, music. Office: Dale Pub Schs 300 Smith Ave Dale OK 74851

CAPPS, LOIS RAGNHILD GRIMSRUD, congresswoman, former school nurse; b. Ladysmith, Wis., Jan. 10, 1938; d. Jurgen Milton and Solveig Magdalene (Gullixson) Grimsrud; m. Walter Holden Capps, Aug. 21, 1960 (dec.); children: Lisa Margaret, Todd Holden, Laura Karolina. BSN with honors, Pacific Luth. U., 1959; MA in Religion, Yale U., 1964; MA in Edn., U. Calif., Santa Barbara, 1990. RN, Calif.; cert. sch. nurse, Calif.; jr. coll. instr., Calif. Asst. instr. Emanuel Hosp. Sch. Nursing, Portland, Oreg., 1959-60; surgery flr. nurse Yale/New Haven Hosp., 1960-62, head nurse, out patient, 1962-63; staff nurse Vis. Nurse Assn., Hamden, Ct., 1963-64; sch. nurse Santa Barbara (Calif.) Sch. Dists., 1968-70, 77-98; dir. teenage pregnancy and parenting project Santa Barbara, 1985-86; mem. U.S. Congress from 23rd Calif. dist., Washington, 1998—. Mem. commerce com., former mem. sci. com., internat. rels. com; mem U.S. Congress, campaign finance reform task force, budget task force, Calif. ISTEA task force, congrl. caucus women's issues, congrl. task force tobacco and health, diabetes caucus, congrl. caucus on the arts, House com. on the budget; instr. Santa Barbara City Coll., 1990—. Bd. dirs. Am. Heart Assn., Santa Barbara, 1989—, The Adoption Ctr., Santa Barbara, 1986-90, Family Svc. Agy., Santa Barbara, 1994—, Stop AIDS Now, Santa Barbara, 1994—, Santa Barbara Women's Polit. Com., 1991—; instr. CPR, first aid, ARC, Santa Barbara, 1985—; bd. dirs. Pacific Luth. Theol. Sem. Democrat. Lutheran. Office: US House of Reps 1707 Longworth Ho Office Bldg Washington DC 20515-0001 Home: 1216 State Street Suite 403 Santa Barbara CA 93101 Fax: 202-225-5632. E-mail: lois.capps@mail.house.gov.*

CAPPS, PHILLIP LEWIS, music educator; b. Greenville, SC, Nov. 13, 1951; s. Furman Lewis and Edna Capps; m. Kathryn Coad, Nov. 22, 1978; 1 child, Grace Kathryn. BA, Lander Coll., 1977; MA in Edn., The Citadel, 1990. Cert. tchr. Edn. Dept. SC, 1978. Music educator Pickens (S.C.) Schs., 1978—79, Berkeley S.C. County Sch. Dept., Moncks Corner, 1980—90, math educator, 1990—91, band educator, 1992—. Mem.: SC Music Educators (assoc.), Low Country Winds (assoc.). Office: Sangaree Intermediate School 201 School House Ln Summerville SC 29483

CAPPS, RICHARD HENRY, retired minister; b. Columbia, S.C., June 22, 1944; s. Henry Eddie and Maude Cecile (Simpson) Crapps; m. Joyce Dianne Wood, Aug. 2, 1968; children: Richard Henry (Hank) Jr., Elizabeth Cecille. AA, North Greenville Coll., 1965; BA, Furman U., 1967; ThM with honors, New Orleans Bapt. Theol. Sem., 1970, DMin, 1978. Ordained minister So. Bapt., 1965. Pastor Fairfield Bapt. Ch., Winnsboro, S.C., 1964-68, Society Hill Bapt. Ch., Oakvale, Miss., 1969-71, First Bapt. Ch., Gaston, S.C., 1971-79, interim pastor Cheraw, S.C., 1968; sr. pastor Laurel Bapt. Ch., Greenville, S.C., 1979-82; dir. missions South Roanoke Bapt. Assn., Greenville, 1982-93, Liberty Bapt. Assn., Thomasville, N.C., 1993-98; area dir. Piedmont/Western NC Prison Fellowship, Winston-Salem, N.C., 1999; min. missions and outreach Forsyth Park Bapt. Ch., Winston-Salem, N.C., 2000, sr. pastor, 2000—03; sr. pastor, missions min. Marketplace Ministries Fellowship, SBC, Winston-Salem, 2003—. S.S. enlargement campaign cons. S.C. Bapt. State Conv., 1981-82; PACT cons. N.Am. Mission Bd., Atlanta, 1988-95; state disaster relief coord. N.C. Bapt. Men., Cary, 1989-93; ch. growth cons. Bapt. State Conv. of N.C., Cary, 1996-98. Contbr. articles to profl. publs. Bd. dirs. Greenville Boys Choir, 1986-90, Transplant Recipient Suport Sys., Pitt County Meml. Hosp., Greenville, 1991-93; mem. Greenville Choral Soc., 1990-93; mem. religion in schs. task force Pitt County Schs., Greenville, 1993; vice chmn. chaplains bd. Davidson Correction Ctr., Lexington, N.C., 1996-98; vol. greeter ARC, 2000—. Recipient Am. Legion award, 1965, Vol. of the Year, Davidson Correctional Ctr., 1997, Northwestern N.C. chpt. ARC, 2000. Mem. Dir. of Missions Conf. (pres. 1986-87, treas. 1987-98), Thomasville C. of C., Lexington Ministerial Assn., Gaston Ruritan Club (chaplain 1973-77), Am. Numis. Assn., Nat. Probation and Parole Assn., Sierra Club. Democrat. Avocations: African violets, roses, antiques/collectibles, walking, collecting stamps and coins. Home: 198 Creekside Dr High Point NC 27265-9209 Office: Days Inn PO Box 5808 Winston Salem NC 27113-5808

CAPPS, THOMAS EDWARD, utilities company executive, lawyer; b. Wilmington, N.C., Oct. 31, 1935; s. Edward S. Jr. and Agnes (Rhodes) C.; m. Jane Paden, Sept. 13, 1963; children: Ashley R., Leigh C. AB, U. N.C., 1958, JD, 1965. Bar: Fla. 1975, N.C. 1966. Sr. counsel Carolina Power & Light Co., Raleigh, N.C., 1970-74; v.p., gen. counsel Boston Edison Co., 1974-75; sr. ptnr. Steel Hector & Davis, Miami, Fla., 1975-84; exec. v.p. Va. Power, Richmond, 1984-86; pres. Dominion Resources, Inc., Richmond, 1986—, chief exec. officer, 1990—, chmn. bd. dirs., 1992—, now vice chmn. Bd. dirs. Bassett (Va.) Furniture Industries, Inc., NationsBank Corp., Petersburg Long Distance, Inc. Bd. dirs. Va. Blood Svcs., 1986. Lt. USCG, 1959-62. Mem. ABA, Bd. of Bar Overseers, N.C. Bar Assn., Fla. Bar Assn., Mass. Bar Assn. Episcopalian. Office: Dominion Resources Inc PO Box 26532 Richmond VA 23261-6532

CAPPUCCIO, RICHARD, language educator; b. N.Y.C., Apr. 29, 1952; s. Louis and Rose Cappuccio; m. Ann H. Marshall. BA, CUNY, 1970, MS, 1976. Tchr. English Grover Cleveland H.S., Erasmus Hall H.S.; faculty of English Temple U., Phila.; tchr. English The Hill Summer Program. Tchg. fellow Acad. of Am. Poets. Author: The Gaze, 1995, Wig, 1996, Chapbook Blues, 1997. Recipient vis. scholar Princeton U., Nat. Endowment for the Arts, 1993; scholar vis. scholar Northwestern U., 1990. Mem.: Unterberg Poetry Ctr., Katherine Mansfield Birthplace Soc. Avocation: bibliophile.

CAPRARO, FRANZ, accountant; b. Uder-Eichsfeld, Thuringia, Germany, Nov. 19, 1941; came to U.S., 1959; s. Ernst Capraro and Lia (Loeschmann) Baeuscher; m. Daniela DiPauli, Dec. 26, 1964; 1 child, Monica L. BBA cum laude, U. Miami, 1964. CPA Fla. Ptnr. Deloitte Haskins & Sells (name now Deloitte & Touche), Miami, 1966-84; exec. v.p. The Wolfson Initiative Corp., Miami, 1984-95; v.p. The Novecento Corp., Miami, 1984-95, Washington Storage Co., Miami, 1984-95, The Foundlings, Inc., Miami Beach, 1984-95, The Hampton Roads, Inc., Miami Beach, 1984-95; pvt. practice acctg. Davie, Fla., 1995-96; ptnr. Grau & Co., P.A., Miami, 1996—. Treas. The Jour. of Decorative and Propaganda Arts, Miami, 1986-98; attended Nat. Security Forum, U.S. Air War Coll., Montgomery, Ala., 1993. Mem. exec. com. U. Miami Citizens Bd., Coral Gables, 1987—; treas. Mitchell Wolfson Family Found., Miami, 1985—; bd. dirs. Louis Wolfson II Media History Ctr., Miami, 1987-95; trustee Greater Miami Opera Fin. Com., 1991-96. 1st lt. U.S. Army Fin. Corps, France, 1965-66. Recipient Certificate of Appreciation City of Miami Beach, 1987; named Honorary Conch City of Key West, 1987. Mem. AICPA, Fla. Inst. CPAs, Schlaraffia Costa Aurea (treas. 1986-87), U.S. Air War Coll. Alumni Assn. (life). Roman Catholic. Avocations: reading, travel. Home: 2821 SW 116th Ave Fort Lauderdale FL 33330-1418 Office: Grau & Company PA PH 2 1110 Brickell Ave Miami FL 33131

CAPRIATI, JENNIFER MARIA, professional tennis player; b. N.Y.C., Mar. 29, 1976; d. Stefano and Denise (Deamicis) Capriati. Profl. tennis player, 1990—. Winner: (jr. singles) French Open, 1989, U.S. Open, 1989, (jr. doubles, with McGrath) Italian Open, 1989, Wimbledon, 1989, (singles) P.R. tournament, 1990, San Diego, 1991, Can. Open, 1991, (doubles, with M. Seles) Italian Open, 1991, Strasbourg, 1999; finalist (singles) Phila., 1990; semifinalist (jr. singles) French Open, 1988, (singles) Wimbledon, 1991, U.S. Open, 1991, Boca Raton, 1991, German Open, 1991; recipient Gold medal 1992 Olympics, named Sportswoman of the Year by US Olympic Comm., 2001, winner Grand Slam Singles, 2002. Avocations: dancing, swimming, reading, music, golf. Office: Internat Mgmt Group care Barbara Perry 22 E 71st St New York NY 10021-4975

CAPRIGLIONE, RALPH RAYMOND, geologist, educator; b. Chgo., Dec. 7, 1968; s. Peter C. and Helen T. (Benthey) C. BS in Earth Sci., Northeastern Ill. U., 1994. Geologist Indsl. Comml. Environ., Lansing, Ill., 1994-95; field technician Environ. Monitoring and Technologies, Morton Grove, Ill., 1995-96; geologist Integrated Environ. Solutions, Schererville, Ind., 1996-98, Bradburne Briller & Johnson, LLC, Chgo., 1998-2000; acct. mgr. Staff Mgmt., Skokie, Ill., 2000—01, Sioux Falls, 2001—02, sr. acct. mgr. Waseca, Minn., 2002—. Adj. prof. Moraine Alley C.C., Palos Hills, Ill., 1998-2001; geographic clk. Bur. of the Census, Chgo., 1999-2000. Sec. Spl. Forces Assn., Chgo., 1995—; mem. Chgo. Coun. on Fgn. Rels. Mem. Chgo. Acad. Scis. Republican. Roman Catholic. Avocations: astronomy, scuba diving, off-road driving, exercise, rifle shooting. Home: 409 8th St NE Waseca MN 56093

CAPRIO, ANTHONY S. academic administrator; b. Providence, Apr. 12, 1945; s. Salvatore and Esther (Iafrati) C. BA, Wesleyan U., 1967; MA, Columbia U., 1969, PhD, 1973; BA (hon.), Western New Eng. Coll., 2000. Asst. prof. langs. and fgn. studies Lehman Coll., CUNY, Bronx, 1971-76; assoc. prof. Cedar Crest Coll., Allentown, Pa., 1976-80; prof., administr. Am. U., Washington, 1980-89; provost Oglethorpe U., Atlanta, 1989-96; pres. Western New Eng. Coll., Springfield, Mass., 1996—. Mem. Nat. Humanities Faculty, 1977—. Author: Reflets de la femme, 1973, En Français, 1976, 3d edit., 1985; contbr. over 100 articles to profl. jours., chpts. to books. Trustee Willie Ross Sch. for the Deaf, 1999—, Springfield Symphony Orch., 1998—; bd. dirs. Springfield Adult Edn. Coun., 1999-2002, Greater Springfield Convention and Visitors Bureau, 1999—, Pioneer Valley Econ. Devel. Coun., 2000—, Springfield Sch. Vols., 2000—, Tuition Exch. Inc., 1994—, Mass. Mentoring Partnership, 2001—; exec. com. Assn. Ind. Colls. and Univs. in Mass., 1999-2002; mem. cabinet Cmty. United Way of Pioneer Valley, 1998—; co-chair Leadership Coun. of Springfield Mentoring Partnership, 1998—; corporator Springfield Libr. and Mus. Assn., 1998—; task force on workforce devel. Pioneer Valley Planning Commn., 1998—; pres. Cooperating Colls. of Greater Springfield, 2000—; accreditation com. ABA, 2002—. Recipient Adminstr.-Faculty award for outstanding performance Am. U., 1984, Disting. Adminstr. and Educator award Greater Washington Assn. Fgn. Lang. Educators, 1986. Mem. Am. Translators Assn., Am. Assn. Higher Edn., Am. Assn. Univ. Adminstrs., Soc. Coll. and Univ. Planning, Phi Beta Kappa, Omicron Delta Kappa, Phi Beta Delta, Phi Beta Kappa (fellow), others. Office: Western New Eng Coll Office of President 1215 Wilbraham Rd Springfield MA 01119-2612

CAPRIOLE, SISTER CARMEN MARIA, geriatric nurse; b. Methuen, Mass. d. Morris and Constance (Magri) C. Diploma, Burbank Hosp., 1978; AAS, Maria Coll., 1972; BSN, Worcester (Mass.) State Coll., 1982; MS, Springfield Coll., 1990. RN, Mass.; cert. gerontology nurse, wound care nurse. Asst. head nurse Meml. Hosp., Worcester, 1978-81; staff devel. coord. Bancroft House Health Care, Worcester, 1982-86; community health nurse Easter Seals Soc., Worcester, 1986-87; missionary nurse leper colony Peoples Republic of Benin, 1987-88; staff devel. coord. Lincoln Nursing & Rehab. Ctr., Worcester, 1990-91; dir. nursing Lincoln Nursing and Rehab. Ctr., Worcester, Mass., 1991-92; dir. nursing edn. Keystone Nursing and Rehab. Ctr., Leominster, Mass., 1991-93; dir. health and edn. Jewish Healthcare Ctr., Worcester, Mass., 1994—. Capt. Army Nurse Corps USAR, 1991—2001. Mem. APiC (cert. gerontology nurse, nursing adminstrn.), Sigma Theta Tau (Epsilon Beta chpt.). Home: 31 Indian Hill Rd Worcester MA 01606-2609 Office: Jewish Healthcare Ctr 629 Salisbury St Worcester MA 01609-1120

CAPRON, ALEXANDER MORGAN, lawyer, educator, philosopher; b. Hartford, Conn., Aug. 16, 1944; s. Willaim Mosher and Margaret (Morgan) Capron; m. Barbara A. Brown, Nov. 9, 1969 (div. Dec. 1985); 1 child, Jared Capron-Brown; m. Kathleen West, Mar. 4, 1989; children: Charles Spencer West Capron, Christopher Gordon West Capron, Andrew Morgan West Capron. BA, Swarthmore Coll., 1966; LLB, Yale U., 1969; MA (hon.), U. Pa., 1975. Bar: D.C. 1970, Pa. 1978. Law clk. to presiding judge U.S. Ct. Appeals, Washington, 1969—70; lectr., rsch. assoc. Yale U., 1970—72; asst. prof. law U. Pa., 1972—75, vice dean, 1976, assoc. prof., 1975—78, prof. law and human genetics, 1978—82; exec. dir. Pres.'s Commn. for Study of Ethical Problems in Med. and Biomedical and Behavioral Rsch., Washington, 1980—83; prof. law, ethics and pub. policy Law Ctr. Georgetown U., Washington, 1983—84, inst. fellow Kennedy Inst. Ethics, 1983—84; Topping prof. law, medicine and pub. policy U. So. Calif., LA, 1985—89, Univ. prof., 1989—, prof. medicine and law, 1991—, Henry W. Bruce prof. equity, 1991—; co-dir. Pacific Ctr. for Health Policy and Ethics, LA, 1990—; dir. ethics and health WHO, 2002—03, dir. ethics, trade, human rights and law, 2003—. Mem. bd. advisors Am. Bd. Internal Medicine, 1985—95, chmn., 1991—95; cons. NIH, mem. subcom. on human gene therapy, 1984—92, mem. recominent DNA com., 1990—95; chmn. Congrl. Biomedical Ethics Adv. Commn., 1987—91; mem. Joint Commn. on Accreditation of Healthcare Orgns., 1994—, mem. ethics adv. com., 1984—85; mem. Nat. Bioethics Adv. Commn., 1996—2001. Author (with Katz): Catastrophic Diseases: Who Decides What?, 1976; author: (with others) Genetic Counseling: Facts, Values and Norms, 1979, Law, Science and Medicine, 1984, supplements, 1987, 1989, 2d edit., Treatise on Health Care Law, 1991; contbr. articles to profl. jours. Bd. mgrs. Swarthmore Coll., 1982—85; bd. trustees The Century Found. Fellow: AAAS, Hastings Ctr. (Inst. Soc., Ethics and Life Scis., bd. dirs. 1975—98), Am. Coll. Legal Medicine (hon.); mem.: AAUP (exec. com. Pa. chpt.), Am. Soc. Law, Medicine and Ethics (pres. 1988—89), Inst. Medicine of NAS (bd. dirs. 1985—90), Swarthmore Coll. Alumni Soc. (v.p. 1974—77). Office: SDE/ETH WHO Avenue Appia 20 1211 Geneva 27 Switzerland E-mail: capron@who.int.

CAPRON, JOHN M. lawyer; b. Mt. Vernon, Ohio, Apr. 14, 1942; AB, Kenyon Coll., 1964; LLB, U. Pa., 1967. Bar: Pa. 1968, Ga. 1971. Mem. Fisher & Phillips, Atlanta. Mem. Federalist Soc. (labor and employment sect.), Employers' Resource Group, Inc. (v.p.), State Bar Ga. Office: Fisher & Phillips 945 E Paces Ferry Rd NE Atlanta GA 30326-1372

CAPSHAW, TOMMIE DEAN, judge; b. Oklahoma City, Sept. 20, 1936; m. Dian Shipp; 1 child, Charles W. BS in Bus., Oklahoma City U., 1958; postrad., U. Ark., 1958-59; JD, U. Okla., 1961. Bar: Okla. 1961, Wyo. 1971, Ind. 1975. Assoc. Looney, Watts, Looney, Nichols and Johnson, Oklahoma City, 1961-63, Pierce, Duncan, Couch and Hendrickson, Oklahoma City, 1963-70; trial atty., v.p. Capshaw Well Service Co., Liberty Pipe and Supply Co., Casper, Wyo.; adminstrv. law judge Evansville, Ind., 1973-75, 96-99; hearing office chief adminstrv. law judge Chgo., 1975-96; acting regional chief adminstrv. law judge, 1977-78; sr. adminstrv. law judge, 1999—. Acting appeals coun. mem., Arlington, Va., 1980, acting chief adminstrv. law judge, 1984; mem. faculty U. Evansville, 1977, So. Ill. U. Sch. Law, 1988—, So. Ind. U., 1990; lectr. in field. Author: A Manual for Continuing Judicial Education, 1981, Practical Aspects of Handling Social Security Disability Claims, 1982, Judicial Practice Handbook, 1990, A Quest for Quality, Speedy Justice, 1991; contbr. numerous articles to profl. jours., chpt. to textbook. Mem. adv. coun. Boy Scouts Am., scoutmaster, den leader, 1969—, Nat. Jud. Coll. U. Nev.; bd. dirs. Casper Symphony, 1972-73, Casper United Fund, 1972-73, Midget Football Assn., Casper, 1972-73, German Twp. Water Dist., 1984-85; pres. Evansville Unitarian Universalist Ch., 1984-86; performer Evansville Philharmonic Orch., 1986-98; bd. dirs. German Twp. Vol. Fire Dept., 1998—. Recipient Kappa Alpha Order Ct. of Honor award, 1962, Silver Beaver award Boy Scouts Am., 1980, presentation for vol. svc. contbg. betterment of cmty. Office Hearings and Appeals, 1992, presentation outstanding jud. mentor tng. Supreme Ct. Iowa, 1992, presentation disting. mentor tng. Fla. Jud. Coll., 1992, Robert V. Payant award Nat. Jud. Coll., 2002. Mem. Okla. Bar Assn., Okla. County Bar Assn. (v.p. 1967), Wyo. Bar Assn., Evansville Bar Assn. (jud. rep. 1986-87, James Bethel Gresham Freedom award 1988), Young Lawyers Assn., Assn. Adminstrv. Law Judges HHS (bd. dirs. 1979-82, Tic Vickery award 1998), Oklahoma City U. Alumni Assn. (bd. dirs. 1965). Home: 6105 School Rd # 6 Evansville IN 47720

CAPSTAFF, GENEVIEVE MACKEEBY, humanities educator; b. Paterson, N.J., Nov. 5, 1916; d. John Wesley and Josephine Claire (Pinckney) MacKeeby; m. Albert Lant Capstaff, Nov. 3, 1934 (div. Apr. 1945); 1 child, Judith Capstaff Heinrich. PhB, DePaul U., 1963, MA, 1968; CAS, No. Ill. U., 1973; PhD, Columbia Pacific U., 1975. Tchr. English, Reavis H.S., Burbank, Ill., 1966-68; prof. humanities Moraine Valley C.C., Palos Hills, Ill., 1968-86, prof. emeritus, 1986—, adj. prof., 1986-99. Lectr., spkr. in field; owner, mgr. Haar Baron Kennels. Contbr. articles to German Shorthair Pointer News, Am. Kennel Club Gazette, 1964—. Mem. AAUW, German Wirehaired Pointer Club Am. (dir. 1960—), German Wirehaired Pointer Club Ill. (dir. 1963-90, 98—, treas. 1995-96, pres. 1997). Republican. Anglican. Avocations: breeding, showing and hunting german wirehaired pointers. Home: 13909 Will Cook Rd Orland Park IL 60467-1237 E-mail: haarbaron@aol.com.

CAPUANO, MICHAEL EVERETT, congressman; b. Somerville, Mass., 1952; s. Andrew and Rita (Garvey) C.; m. Barbara Teebagy, 1974; children: Michael, Joseph. BA in Psychology, Dartmouth Coll., 1973; JD, Boston Coll., 1977; postgrad., Boston U. Bar: Mass. 1977. Alderman Ward 5, Somerville, 1977-79; alderman-at-large, 1985-89; mayor, 1990-99; congressman 8th Dist. Mass., 1999—. Mem. Ho. Dem. Leadership team (regional whip), com. fin. svcs., subcoms. on Captial Mkts., Securities and Govt. Sponsored Enterprises, banking subcom. housing and cmty. mem. Ho. Dem. steering and policy com., com. transp. and infrastructure, subcom. allocation, hwys. and transit and aviation. Elected congressman Nov. 1998 with 82% of the vote. Democrat. Office: 1232 Longworth Hob Washington DC 20515-0001*

CAPUTO, DANIEL VINCENT, psychologist; b. N.Y.C. s. Pasquale and Hortense C. AB, Bklyn. Coll., 1954; PhD, U. Ill., 1961. Registered psychologist, Nat. Register of Health Providers in Psychology; lic. psychologist, N.Y. Prof. med. psychology Wash. U., St. Louis, 1959-64; prof. psychology Queens Coll., CUNY, Flushing, 1964—, prof. emeritus, 1998—, chair dept. psychology, 1974-77; rsch. assoc. St. Vincent's Med. Ctr., S.I., N.Y. Pvt. practice clin. psychology, 1973—. Contbr. to Infants Born at Risk, 1979, Pre-term Birth: Relevance to Optimal Psychological Development, 1981, Multivariate Analysis of the Type A Personality, 1981. Rsch. grantee NIMH, 1963. Fellow N.Y. Acad. Scis.; mem. APA, Eastern Psychol. Assn., N.Y. State Psychol. Assn. (rep. exec.

com. 1981-83), Biofeedback Soc. Am. (cert.). Roman Catholic. Office: 16-07 150th St Whitestone NY 11357-2545 also: Queens Coll Dept of Psychology Kissena Blvd Flushing NY 11367 E-mail: drdvcaputo@aol.com.

CAPUTO, DAVID ARMAND, university president, political scientist educator; b. Brownsville, Pa., Aug. 30, 1943; s. Armand and Marie E. (Smalstig) C.; m. Alice M. Glotfelty, June 27, 1964; children: Christopher, Elizabeth, Jeffrey. BA, Miami U., Oxford, Ohio, 1965; MA, Yale U., 1967, MPhil, 1968, PhD, 1970. Mem. faculty Purdue U., 1969—, prof. polit. sci., 1977—, head dept., 1978-87, dean Sch. Liberal Arts, 1987-95; pres. Hunter Coll., CUNY, N.Y.C., 1995-2000, Pace U., N.Y.C., 2000—. Author: Urban America: The Policy Alternatives, 1976; co-author: Urban Politics and Decentralization, 1974; editor: Politics of Policy-Making in America, 1977. Ruling elder Ctrl. Presbyn. Ch., Lafayette, Ind., 1981—; trustee Madison Ave. Presbyn. Ch., N.Y.C., 2000—. Woodrow Wilson nat. fellow, 1965-66; NSF faculty fellow, 1977; Fulbright fellow, Italy, 1985; Lilly fellow, 1985; Bologna chair Fulbright sr. fellow, Italy, 1993. Mem. Am. Polit. Sci. Assn., Am. Soc. Public Adminstrn., Midwest Polit. Sci. Assn., So. Polit. Sci. Assn., Phi Beta Kappa, Omicron Delta Kappa. Office: Pace Univ One Pace Plz New York NY 10038 E-mail: dcaputo@pace.edu.

CAPUTO, GREGORY MICHAEL, physician, educator; b. May 18, 1954; s. Joseph Vincent and Mary (Pisapia) C.; m. Leesa, June 10, 1978; children: Jennifer, Michael. BA in Biol. Sci., U. Del., 1976; MD, U. Md., 1980. Diplomate Am. Bd. Internal Medicine, Am. Bd. Infectious Disease. Intern Thomas Jefferson U. Hosp., Phila., 1980-81, clin. asst. prof. dept. medicine, 1987-90; resident Milton S. Hershey Med. Ctr., Pa. State U. Coll. Medicine, Hershey, Pa., 1981-83, fellow divsn. infectious diseases, 1983-84; from asst. prof. to prof. medicine Pa. State U., Hershey, 1990-98, prof., 1998—; chief divsn. gen. internal medicine Milton S. Hershey Med. Ctr., Hershey, Pa., vice-chief dept. medicine, 2002—. Staff Med. Ctr. Del., Wilmington, 1985-90, Alfred I. duPont Inst., Wilmington, 1990-95, U. Hosp., Milton S. Hershey Med. Ctr., 1990—, med. dir. diabetes amputation prevention program, 1993-99, dir. Cecil County Lyme Disease Clinic, Elkton, 1988-90; cons. Assn. Acad. Health Ctrs., Am. Lyme Disease Found., 1992—; vis. scholar Johns Hopkins Ctr. for Preventive Cardiology, 2001-02; lectr. in field. Author: (chpt.) Comprehensive Textbook of Pulmonary Medicine, 1991, The Foot in Diabetes, 2d edit., 1994; co-author: (chpt.) Comprehensive Textbook Pulmonary Medicine Update, 1995, (computer program) The Prevention Guides for Clinicians and Patients, 1996; co-editor: Medical Consultation, 1997; reviewer New Eng. Jour. Medicine, Internal Medicine Jour., Clin. Infectious Diseases, Diabetes Care; contbr. articles to profl. jours. Recipient Fletcher Brown award, 1975, Disting. Physician award, 1995; Harvard Med. Sch. fellow, 1984-85, C. Everett Koop Inst. fellow Dartmouth Coll., 1996, 97; Ellis scholar, 1976, vis. scholar Johns Hopkins Med. Instns., 2001-02. Fellow ACP; mem. Am. Soc. Microbiology, Soc. Gen. Internal Medicine, Am. Diabetes Assn., Phi Beta Kappa, Phi Kappa Phi, Beta Beta Beta, Alpha Omega Alpha. Avocations: music, tennis, hiking. Office: Milton S Hershey MC Divsn Gen Int Med MC HU15 500 University Dr Hershey PA 17033

CAPUTO, JOSEPH ANTHONY, retired university president; b. Jersey City, May 10, 1940; s. Anthony and Virginia (Bennett) C.; m. Linda Mary Ryan, Sept. 4, 1965; children: Christine D., David R. BS, Seton Hall U., 1962, MS, 1964; PhD, U. Houston, 1967; hon. degree, Univ. North London, 2002. Research assoc. Duke U., Durham, N.C., 1967-68; prof. dept. chemistry SUNY Coll.-Buffalo, 1968-77, chmn. dept. chemistry, 1974-77; dean sch. sci. and math. S.W. Tex. State U., San Marcos, 1977-79, v.p. acad. affairs, 1979-81; pres. Millersville (Pa.) U., 1981—2003. Mem. task force on transfer articulation Mid. States Commn. on Higher Edn., 1993-94, visitation team chair, 1987-92; mem. State Sys. Higher Edn. Commn. of Pres., 1981—, vice chair, 1982-84, chmn., 1984-86, mem.-at-large, 1995-96; bd. dirs. Acad. for Profession of Tchg., 1987-89; mem. Task Force on Acad. Quality and Enrollment Mgmt., chair, 1988-90; mem. tchr. edn. accreditation coun. Coun. of Ind. Colls., 1997. Contbr. numerous articles to profl. jours. Chmn. bd. Pa. State Athletic Conf., 1983, mem., 1981—; mem. Gov. Transition Team, 1982; mem. adv. bd. Commonwealth of Pa. Ben Franklin Partnership Program, 1983, N.E. Tier Ben Franklin Tech. Ctr., 1988; bd. dirs. Lancaster Area Arts Coun., 1987-89, Lancaster Gen. Hosp. Found., 1989—, Harrisburg U. Ctr. Consortium, 1987-92, Lancaster Chamber Commerce and Industry, 1985-88, Urban League Lancaster County, 1988-93, St. Joseph Hosp. Neumann Svcs., Inc., 1983-85, Econ. Devel. Coun. Lancaster, 1997—, SICO Found., 1997—; mem. capital allocations com. Lancaster Gen. Health Alliance Fin., 1995, strategic planning and mktg. com., 1995-96; mem. Pa. Adv. Coun. for Migrant Edn., 1988-92; mem. 30th anniversary com. of 100, Lancaster County Human Rels. Commn., 1994; hon. chair Lancaster br. NAACP, 1990, Spanish Am. Civic Assn., mem. capital campaign com., 1988, 96-97. Recipient Elaine J. Washington award Urban League of Lancaster County, 1994; SUNY Rsch. Found. fellow and grantee, 1969-70, 73-74; NSF grantee, 1972-73, 75-77; Am. Chem. Soc. grantee, 1969-72; Sigma Xi grantee, 1976. Mem. AAAS, Am. Chem. Soc., Am. Assn. State Colls. and Univs. (com. on profl. devel. 1988-92, vice chair 1991, chair 1992, found. bd. dirs. 1984-87, policies and purposes com. 1982-85, 94-97, 98—), Am. Coun. on Edn. (Commn. on Leadership Devel. 1992-95, exec. com. 1996—), Pa. Assn. Colls. and Univs. (treas. 1991, v.p. 1992, chmn. 1993-94, bd. dirs. 1991-95, Commn. for Univs. 1981—, vice chair 1982-84, chmn. 1984-86), Renaissance Group (exec. com. 1994-96, chair 1994-95), Sigma Xi, Phi Sigma Pi, Phi Eta Sigma, Phi Kappa Phi.

CAPUTO, KATHRYN MARY, paralegal; b. Bklyn., June 29, 1948; d. Fortunato and Agnes (Iovino) Villacci; m. Joseph John Caputo, Apr. 4, 1976. AS in Bus. Adminstrn., Nassau C.C., Garden City, N.Y., 1989. Legal asst. Jacob Jacobson, Oceanside, N.Y., 1973-77; legal asst., office mgr. Joseph Kaldor, P.C., Franklin Square, N.Y., 1978-82, William H. George, Valley Stream, N.Y., 1983-89; exec. legal asst., office adminstr. Katz & Bernstein, Westbury, N.Y., 1990-93; sr. paralegal and office adminstr. Blaustein & Weinick, Garden City, N.Y., 1993—. Instr. adult continuing edn. legal sec. procedures Lawrence (N.Y.) H.S., 1992—. Spl. events coord. Bklyn.-Queens Marriage Encounter, 1981, 82, 83, 85, 86; mem. Lynbrook Civic Assn., St. Raymond's R.C. Ch. Pastoral Coun., 1999-2002, sec. 2000-02, Renew 2000, mem. rev. bd.; mem. St. Vincent DePaul Soc., sec., 2001—. Mem. L.I. Paralegal Assn. Avocations: traveling, reading, theatre, gardening. Office: Blaustein & Weinick 1205 Franklin Ave Garden City NY 11530-1629 E-mail: kacapbwparalgl@hotmail.com.

CAPUTO, LUCIO, trade company executive; b. Monreale, Italy, May 22, 1935; came to U.S., 1967. s. Giuseppe and Gioacchina (Spinnato) C.; m. Maria Luisa Mayr, Oct. 5, 1967; 1 child, Giorgio. Law degree, Palermo U., 1957, journalism degree, 1958, degree in polit. sci., 1960, postgrad. econs., 1961. Bar: Italy, 1961. Journalist, Italy, 1950-65; assoc. Studio Legale Caputo-Orlando, Palermo, Sicily, 1960-62; ofcl. Italian Fgn. Trade Inst., 1962-82; market rschr. Libya, Cyprus, 1963; dep. trade commr. London, 1964-67; dir. study mission S.E. Asia, 1967; Italian trade commr. Phila., 1967-71, N.Y.C., 1972-82; founder Italian Wine Promotion Ctr., N.Y.C., 1975—, Italian Tile Ctr., N.Y.C., 1979—, Italian Fashion Ctr., N.Y.C., 1980—, Italian Shoe Ctr., N.Y.C., 1981—, ITAL Trade Ctr., N.Y.C., 1981—. Pres. Ital Trade USA Corp., 1982-86; pres. Italian Wine and Food Inst., 1984—; organizer ann. Italian Week on 5th Ave., N.Y.C.; pres., bd. dirs. Gruppo Esponenti Italiani, 1974—. Signer agreement between Italy and People's Republic of China, 1967; editor trade mags.: Italy Presents, Quality (English, French, Spanish, German), 1962-64; contbr. articles to Italian mags. and newspapers. Mem. adv. bd. Italy-Am. C. of C., 1972-82; U.S. rep. Verona Fair Orgn., 1980—; chmn. Internat. Trade Ctr., Inc., 1987—; exec. dir. Gruppo Ristoratori Italiani, 1988-90; vice chmn., bd. dirs. Nat. Wine Coalition, 1990-95; chmn. bd. dirs. European Wine Coun., 1993—, chmn. bus. adv. coun. for gov., 1996—; mem. adv. coun. Princeton U. Lt. Italian Air Force, 1959-61. Named Cavaliere Ufficiale nell'Ordine al Merito della Repubblica Italiana, 1972, Commendatore, 1981, Grande Ufficiale, 1996, Cavaliere di Gran Croce, 2003. Mem. Sommelier Soc. Am., Italian Sommelier Soc., Italian Bar Assn., Italian Journalist Assn., Fgn. Consular Assn. Phila., Soc. Fgn. Consuls N.Y., Am. Soc. Italian Legions of Merit (chmn. bd. dirs.), Assn. Pres. of Maj. Italian-Am. Orgns. (bd. dirs.). Office: Lincoln Bldg 60 E 42d St Ste 1341 New York NY 10165 Mailing: PO Box 789 New York NY 10150 Fax: 212-867-4114. E-mail: iwfi@aol.com.

CAPUTO, PHILIP JOSEPH, author, journalist; b. Chgo., June 10, 1941; s. Joseph and Marie Ylonda (Napolitan) C.; m. Jill Esther Ongemach, June 21, 1969 (div. 1982); children: Geoffrey Jacob, Marc Antony.; m. Marcelle Lynn Besse, Oct. 30, 1982 (div. 1985); m. Leslie Blanchard Ware, June 4, 1988. BA in English, Loyola U., Chgo., 1964. Mem. staff Chgo. Tribune, 1968-72; fgn. corr. Europe, Middle East, USSR, 1972-77; freelance writer, 1977—. Author: A Rumor of War, 1977, Horn of Africa, 1980, Del Corso's Gallery, 1983, Indian Country, 1987, Means of Escape, 1991, Equation for Evil, 1996, Exiles, 1997, The Voyage, 1999; contbr. to N.Y. Times, L.A. Times, Boston Globe, Nat. Geog. Adventure, others. Served with USMCR, 1964-67, Vietnam. Recipient award Ill. AP, Ill. United Press award, Green Gavel award ABA, Overseas Press Club award, Pulitzer prize, Sidney Hillman award, others. Mem. Authors Guild. Democrat. Roman Catholic. Address: care Aaron Priest Lit Agy 708 3rd Ave New York NY 10017-4201

CAPUTO, THOMAS ANTHONY, obstetrician, gynecologist; b. Newark, N.J. s. Anthony Ralph and Pauline Cascella C.; m. Particia Eileen Kempton, Oct. 6, 1965; children: Caroline, Christine, Anthony. BS, Holy Cross Coll., 1961; MD, U. N.J., Newark, 1965. Diplomate Am. Bd. Gynecol. Oncology, Am. Bd. Ob-Gyn. and Gynecol. Oncology. Intern Newark City Hosp., 1965 66; resident The Martland Hosp. U. Medicine and Dentistry N.J., 1966-69; fellow gynecologic oncology dept. ob-gyn. Emory U., Atlanta, 1972-74; dir. gynecologic oncology Albany Med. Ctr. Hosp./Albany Med. Coll., 1974-82; dir. gynecologic oncology, attending physisian N.Y. Hosp.-Cornell Med. Ctr., 1982—. Major U.S. Army, 1969-72. Office: Cornell Med Ctr NY Hosp 525 E 68th St New York NY 10021-4870 Fax: 212-746-3179

CAPUTO, WAYNE JAMES, surgeon, podiatrist; b. Newark, Feb. 18, 1956; s. James Vincent and Jennie (DeMaio) C.; m. Phyllis A. Grillo, Nov. 20, 1984; children: Karla, Stefanie. BS in Biology, Syracuse U., 1978; DPM, N.Y. Coll. Podiatric Medicine, 1982. Diplomate Am. Bd. Podiatric Surgery. Clin. asst. prof. N.Y. Coll. Podiatic Medicine, N.Y.C., 1984-89; chief dept. podiatric surgery Clara Maass Med. Ctr., Belleville, N.J., 1987—, Columbus Hosp., Newark, 1995—. Dir. residency in podiatric surgery Union (N.J.) Hosp., 1990—. Contbr. articles to profl. jours. Fellow ACFS, Am. Coll. Dermatologists. Office: Clara Maass Profl Med Ctr 5 Franklin Ave Belleville NJ 07109-3532

CARABALLO, DIMAS J. music educator; b. Habana, Cuba, Oct. 3, 1962; arrived in U.S., 1967; s. Jose Caraballo and Marta Suarez. AA in piano performance, Broward Cmty. Coll.; BA in piano performance, U Miami; MusM, U Mich. Vis. assoc. prof. of Dance in the Dance Dept. U Mich., Ann Arbor, 1996—99; Master Instr. Piano Pvt. Practice. Adjudicator, The Northe Am. Internat. Invitational Piano Competition, The Mich. Music Tchr. Assoc. Piano Examinations, The Vivace Piano Competition, The Nat. Fedn. of Music Clubs Piano Solo Div., The Margaret Denise Scholarship Competition; guest artist to raise money for Nat. Philippino Nurses Assn. Annual Scholarship Fund; guest artist Plymouth Symphony, Plymouth, Mich. Co-dir.: (ballets) The Netherlands Dance Co. - Jiri Kylian, Master, The Gyori Ballet Gyori Nenzeti Szinhaz Theatre Annual Concert, The Dance Theater of Harlem, The Am. Ballet Theater of N.Y. Recipient First Place, Southeast Fla. Chopin Competition, Annual Fort Lauderdale Piano Concerto Competition, Mich. Music Tchr. Assn. Collegiate Level State Competition, Germania Piano Concerto Competition, Finalist, Young Keyboard Artist Competition. Master: Am. Music Guild; mem.: Music Nat. Tchr. Assn. (assoc.), Mich. Music Tchr. Assn. (assoc.). Home: 44105 Lee Ann Lane S Canton MI 48187

CARABALLO, WILFREDO, assemblyman; b. Yabucia, P.R., Jan. 1, 1947; BA in Philosophy, St. Joseph's Seminary and Coll.; JD, NYU Sch. of Law. Assemblyman N.J. Gen. Assembly, 1996—, assoc. minority leader, 1998—2001; parliamentarian, 2002—. Mem. South Orange Maplewood Bd. of Edn., 1987—90; pub. adv., pub. defender, NJ, 1990—92; arbitrator BBB; atty., law prof. Seton Hall U. Sch. of Law. Mem. Am. Assn. of Law Schs., Dehere Found., Martin Luther King Commemoration Com. of N.J.; bd. dirs. Puerto Rican Legal Def. Edn. Fund; former v.p. South Orange-Maplewood Bd. of Edn.; mem. South Orange City Budget Adv. com. Democrat. Office: 371 Bloomfield Ave 2d Fl Newark NJ 07107*

CARABELLO, BLASE ANTHONY, cardiology educator; b. Reading, Pa., Aug. 5, 1947; s. Charles Anthony and Fern June (Houck) C.; m. Susan Jane Beidman, Aug. 15, 1970 (div. June 1977); 1 child, Charles; m. Catherine Wheatley, Apr. 9, 1989; children: Nicholas, Blaise. BA, Gettsburg Coll., 1969; MD, Temple U., 1973. Diplomate Am. Bd. Internal Medicine, Am. Bd. Cardiology. Intern in Medicine Mass. Gen. Hosp., Boston, 1973-74, resident in Medicine Harvard Med. Sch., 1974-75, sr. resident in Medicine Harvard Med. Sch., 1975-76; fellow in Cardiology Peter Bent Brigham Hosp., Boston, 1976-78, cardiologist, 1978-79; asst. prof. Medicine U. Va. Hosp., Charlottesville, 1979-81; dir. Diagnostic Cardiology Temple U., Phila., 1981-85; prof. Medicine Med. U. S.C., Charleston, 1985-95, dir. clin. rsch., 1990-99; Charles Ezra Daniel prof. medicine U. S.C., Charleston, 1995-99; chief of med. svcs. Houston VA Med. Ctr., 1999—; vice chmn. medicine Baylor Sch. of Medicine, Houston, 1999—. Author: Cardiology Pearls, 1993; contbr. articles to profl. jours. Beta-Blockade grantee Pub. Health Svc., 1988-89, Dept. Va. Pub. Health grantee, 1989-94. Fellow Am. Coll. Cardiology, Am. Heart Assn. (coun. on circulation, chmn. com. on cardiac catheterization); mem. Am. Soc. Clin. Investigation, Best Doctors in Am., Alpha Omega Alpha. Avocation: fine dining. Home: 5303 Huisache St Bellaire TX 77401-4933 Office: VA Hosp Dept Medicine Houston TX 77030

CARABIAS LILLO, JULIA, government official; b. Mexico City, Mex., 1954; BA, MA, Nat. Autonomous, 1981. Sec. Environ., Natural Resources & Fisheries, Mexico, 1998—. Prof. sci. Nat. Autonomous U., 1981, U. Coun. UNAM, 1989-93; pres. Nat. Ecol. Inst.; mem. Coun. Nat. Solidarity Program; mem. adv. coun. Nat. Conservation Fund. Office: Sec Environ Natural Resourc Arillo Periferico Sur 4209 14210 Col Jardines Montana Mexico

CARAHER, MICHAEL EDWARD, systems analyst; b. Indpls., Dec. 22, 1953; s. Gregory Thomas and Mary Margaret (Shevlin) C.; m. Jan. 6, 1979 (div. 1986); children: Joseph Michael, Erin Michelle; m. Vicky L. Caraher, July 14, 2000. BA, Butler U., Indpls., 1976. Systems mgr. Alexander Typesetting, Indpls., 1984-88; systems specialist for Weimer Graphics divsn. Shepard Poorman Comm. Corp., Indpls., 1988-94, sys. mgr., 1994-96; sys. mgr., network adminstr. Ind. State Budget Agy., Indpls., 1996—. Vice precinct committeeman Ind. Dem. Party, Indpls., 1972-78, precinct committeeman, 1994. Mem. Ancient Order of Hibernians. Democrat. Roman Catholic. Home: 9772 Innisbrook Blvd Carmel IN 46032

CARALEY, DEMETRIOS JAMES, political scientist, educator, writer; b. N.Y.C., June 22, 1932; s. Christopher and Stella (Psaras) C.; children (from previous marriage): James Christopher (dec.), David Andrew, Anne Leslie; m. Vilma Mairo Bornemann; 1 child, Lisa Anne. BA summa cum laude, Columbia U., 1954, PhD, 1962. Mem. faculty Barnard Coll. and Columbia U., N.Y.C., 1959—, prof. polit. sci., 1968—, Janet H. Robb prof. social scis., 1980—; editor Polit. Sci. Quar., 1973—; dir. Grad. Program in Pub. Policy and Adminstrn. Columbia U., 1978-85, chmn. Barnard dept. polit. sci., 1965-95; pres. Acad. Polit. Sci., 1992—. Vis. scholar Russell Sage Found., 1995-96. Author: Politics of Military Unification, 1966, New York City's Deputy Mayor— City Administrator, 1966, Party Politics and National Elections, 1966, (with R. H. Connery) Governing the City, 1969, City Governments and Urban Problems, 1977, American Political Institutions in the 1970's, 1976, (with M.A. Epstein) The Making of American Foreign and Domestic Policy, 1978, Doing More With Less, 1982, (with R.H. Connery) National Security and Nuclear Strategy, 1983, The President's War Powers, 1984, Volatilities in the New World Politics, 1993, Critical Issues for Clinton's Domestic Agenda, 1994, (with B.B. Hartman) American Leadership, Ethnic Conflict, and the New World Politics, 1997, The New American Interventionism, 1999, September 11, Terrorist Attacks and US Foreign Policy, 2002; contbr. American Politics and Public Policy, 1978, Urban Policymaking, 1979. Mem. North Tarrytown Zoning Bd. Appeals, 1970-71; mem. North Tarrytown Bd. Trustees, 1971-73, dep. mayor and acting mayor, 1972-73; chmn. North Tarrytown Planning Bd., 1977-79. Served with USNR, 1954-56. Mem. Am. Polit. Sci. Assn., Acad. Polit. Sci. (bd. dirs., pres. 1992—), Phi Beta Kappa. Club: University (N.Y.C.). Democrat. Office: Columbia Univ Barnard Coll Dept Polit Sci New York NY 10027 also: Acad Polit Sci/Polit Sci Quar 475 Riverside Dr Ste 1274 New York NY 10115-1299 E-mail: DC121@columbia.edu.

CARAM, DOROTHY FARRINGTON, educational consultant; b. McAllen, Tex., Jan. 14, 1933; d. Curtis Leon and Elena (Santander) Farrington; m. Pedro C. Caram, June 7, 1958 (dec. Aug. 2000); children: Pedro M., Juan D., Hector L., Jose M. BA, Rice U., 1955, MA, 1974; EdD, U. Houston, 1982; postgrad., U. Madrid, 1957. Tchr. Houston Ind. Sch. Dist., 1955-56, 56-60, St. Mark's Episcopal Ch., Houston, 1964-65; substitute tchr. St. Vincent De Paul Cath. Sch., Houston, 1965-68; mgr. med. office Houston, 1983; dir. Fed. Home Loan Bank, Little Rock, 1976-82; pres. Inst. Hispanic Culture, Houston, 1983, 93, chmn. bd., pres., 1984; with Houston Ednl. Excellence Program, 1980. Mem. task force Tex. Edn. Agy., 1981-83; mem. adv. coun. Nat. Inst. Neurol. and Communicative Disorders and Stroke, 1972-76; pres. IDM Satellite Comm. of Tex. Divsn., Inc., 1990, chmn. bd., 1998—99 asst. to pres. U. Houston, 1991-94, ret., 1994. Mem. coun. Miller Theater, Houston, 1976—, adv. bd. emeritus, 2000-; bd. dirs. Houston Pops, 1983-87, United Way Tex., 1991-94; mem. task force Quality Integrated Edn., Houston, 1972; bd. dirs. United Way Tex., Gulf Coast, 1989-95, mem. exec. bd., sec.; mem. Civil Commn. Houston, 1983-85; bd. mgrs. Harris County Hosp. Dist., 1988-90; founder, bd. dirs. Houston Hispanic Forum, 1985, pres., 1989-90; chmn. bd. Teatro Bilingue de Houston, 1989-90; pres. Mexican Cultural Inst. Houston, Inc., 1997; bd. dirs. Southmain Ctr. Assn., 1998—, Harris County Hosp. Dist. Found., 1997—, Houston Ind. Sch. Dist. Found., 1996-2002, chmn. peer com. magnet and vanguard schs., 1996—; mem. adv. bd. Theater Under Stars, Career and Recovery, Jobs for Progress of Tex. Gulf Coast, Inc., AAMA; bd. dirs. Majestic Seas Aquarium, 1998-99; bd. dirs., treas. Colonial Homes Found. for Youth, 1999; mem. Mil. and Hospitler Order of St. Lazarus of Jerusalem, 1982-; pres. Braes Rep. Women, 2002—, precinct judge, 1998—; v.p. edn. bd. Houston Grand Opera, 2001—. Recipient Willie Velasquez Outstanding Hispanic Citizenship award, 1994, Dorothy F. Caram Leadership award Blueprint-United Way Tex. Gulf Coast, 2000, 2001-02, Woman of Vision award Delta Gamma Found., 2003; named Vol. of Yr., United Way Tex. Gulf Coast, 1992, Outstanding Alumnus, Coll. Edn, U. Houston, 2000, Woman of Vision, Delta Gamma Found., 2003; decorated Lady in Court of Isabel La Catolica by King Carlos (Spain), 1984. Mem. Cedars Club (pres. 1978). Roman Catholic. Home: 2603 Glen Haven Blvd Houston TX 77025-2132 E-mail: dcaram@worldnet.att.net.

CARAM, EVE LA SALLE, English educator, writer; b. Hot Springs, Ark., May 11, 1934; d. Raymond Briggs and Lois Elizabeth (Merritt) La Salle; m. Richard George Caram, Apr. 19, 1965 (div. Apr. 1978); 1 child, Bethel Eve. BA, Bard Coll., 1956; MA, U. Mo., 1977. English instr. Stephens Coll., Columbia, Mo., 1974,79-82; fiction writing grad. instr. Sch. Profl. Writing U. So. Calif., L.A., 1982-87; English lit. and writing instr. Calif. State U., Northridge, 1983—; sr. fiction writing instr. The Writers' Program UCLA, 1983—. Fiction contest judge Calif. State U., Long Beach, 1992, 94, writer's conf. spkr., 1985-87, 94; spkr., mem. panel Tex. Am. Studies Assn., Wichita Falls, 1998. Author: (novel) Dear Corpus Christi, 1991, 2d edit., 2001, Wintershine, 1994, Rena, A Late Journey, 1999; editor: Palm Readings, Stories from Southern California, 1998; fiction editor West/Word, 1991. Mem. AAUP, Assn. Calif. State Profs., Nat. Assn. Tchrs. English, Poets and Writers, PEN Ctr. U.S.A. West. Democrat. Avocations: swimming, beach walks, outdoors. Home: 3400 Ben Lomond Pl Apt 121 Los Angeles CA 90027-2952 Office: UCLA Ext The Writers' Program 10995 Le Conte Ave Los Angeles CA 90095-3001 also: Calif State U English Dept 1811 Nordoff Northridge CA 91330-0001 E-mail: ecaram1@earthlink.net.

CARAMANA, EDWARD J. physicist; b. Reading, Pa., Nov. 24, 1949; s. James E. and E. Louise Caramana; m. Christina M. Rizzo; 1 child, Cynthia L. SB in Physics, MIT, 1971; MS in Physics, U. Colo., 1975, PhD in Physics, 1979; postgrad., Princeton U., 1979. Mem. staff various divsns. Los Alamos (N.Mex.) Nat. Lab., 1979—, now with computer and computational sci. divsn. Author: Physics of Fluids; contbr. articles to sci. jours. including Jour. of Computational Physics. Mem. Am. Phys. Soc. Avocations: weight lifting, pool/billiards, motorcycles, early 20th century psychology. Office: Los Alamos Nat Lab MS D413 Los Alamos NM 87545 E-mail: ejc@lanl.gov.

CARAMEROS, GEORGE DEMITRIUS, JR., natural gas company executive; b. El Paso, Tex., Mar. 1, 1924; s. George Demitrius and Esperanza (Purdy) C.; m. Verna Narcissus Easterling, May 26, 1944; children: Cecille (Mrs. George Shannon), Cynthia (Mrs. John Blevins), Cathy (Mrs. David Patton), George Demitrius III, Carl. BA, U. Tex., El Paso, 1947. With El Paso Natural Gas Co., 1948-80; mgr. new projects devel. subs. El Paso Products Co., 1957-60; mng. dir. El Paso Europe-Afrique, Paris, France, 1960-65; adminstrv. asst. to chmn. bd. El Paso Natural Gas, N.Y.C., 1965-66; asst. v.p. El Paso Natural Gas Co., N.Y.C., 1966-70, v.p., 1970-73; exec. v.p. El Paso Europe-Afrique, N.Y.C., 1973-75, The El Paso Co., 1975-78, vice chmn., 1978-80; pres. El Paso LNG Co., Houston, 1975-78, chmn., 1978-80, also bd. dirs.; chmn. Internat. Gas Devel. Corp., 1980-85. V.p. Groupe Internat. des Importateurs de Gaz Nauel Liquifie, 1988-92. Served with AUS, World War II. Decorated Bronze Star, Combat Inf. badge. Mem. Interstate Natural Gas Assn. Am. (dir.), Lakeside Country Club. Presbyterian. Home: 660 Shartle Cir Houston TX 77024-5503 Office: 1200 Smith St Ste 1760 Houston TX 77002-4310

CARAS, JOSEPH SHELDON, life insurance company executive; b. Lawrence, Mass., Aug. 3, 1924; s. Joseph and Bessie Esther (Kasanoff) C.; m. Adele Salett, June 8, 1947 (dec. 2002); children: Richard, David, Susan. BA, Bowdoin Coll., 1948. CLU. With Met. Life Ins. Co., 1949-55; asst. mgr. Waltham, Mass., 1951-55; with New Eng. Mut. Life Ins. Co., 1955-88; 2d. v.p. mktg. Boston, 1967-71; sr. v.p. mktg. services, 1971-81; sr. v.p. mktg., 1982-88, ret., 1989; pres. New Eng. Nat. Life, 1981-86; dir. New Eng. Nat. of N.Y., Covenant Life Ins. Co., InterNEL Corp. Exec. dir. Nat. Fin. Mktg. Group, 1988-93. Mem. Swampscott (Mass.) Town Meeting, 1972-78; past pres. Temple Emanu-El, Marblehead, Mass. Served with USAAF, 1943-45. Decorated Air medal. Mem. Life Ins. Mktg. Research Assn. (past chmn. sales com. and mktg. services com.), Agy. Mgmt. Tng. Council, Assn. Advanced Life Underwriters, Nat. Assn. Life Underwriters, Am. Soc. C.L.U.'s. Home: 11602 Losano Dr Boynton Beach FL 33437-1927

CARASIK, MICHAEL, writer, researcher; b. Chgo., Dec. 2, 1952; m. Janice Sara Yaffa. BA, New Coll., Sarasota, Fla., 1973; BJS, MAJS, Spertus Coll., 1986; MA, PhD, Brandeis U., 1996. Rschr. Marquis Who's Who, Chgo., 1973—74; sr. programmer Inst. for Computers in Jewish Life, Chgo., 1981—85; editor/pub. Jour. Jocular Studies, Brookline, 1987—92; dir. Inst. for Implied Rsch., Phila., 1990—; darshan Gershman Y Congregation, Phila. V.p. Ctr. City Eruv Corp., Phila., 2001—02. Grantee, Bruckner Found., 2001—03.

CARASSO, ALFRED SAM, mathematician; b. Alexandria, Egypt, Apr. 9, 1939; arrived in US, 1962; s. Samuel and Renee (Ades) Carasso; m. Beatrice Kozak, June 12, 1964; children: Adam Leonard, Rachel Lisa. BSc in Physics, U. Adelaide, Australia, 1960; PhD in Math., U. Wis., 1968. Meteorologist Bur. Meteorology, Adelaide, 1960-62; rsch. asst. grad. sch. U. Wis., Madison, 1962-68; asst. prof. math. Mich. State U., East Lansing, 1968-69, U. N.Mex., Albuquerque, 1969-72, assoc. prof., 1972-76, prof., 1976-81; mathematician Nat. Inst. Standards and Tech., Gaithersburg, Md., 1982—. Vis staff mem Los Alamos Nat Lab, N.Mex., 1972—81, consult Inst Def Analyses's Ctr Computing Scis, 1996—. Contbr. articles to profl jours. Mem.: Soc Indust and Applied Math, Am Math Soc, Cosmos Club. Jewish. Achievements include development of basic results in analysis and computation of ill-posed evolution equations, integral equations and deconvolution, holomorphic semigroups; invention of "slowly divergent" schemes in inverse heat conduction, and "APEX" and "BEAK" methods in blind image deblurring; development of "slow evolution" constraint in ill-posed continuation problems; applications in system identification, nondestructive evaluation, inverse heat transfer, image reconstruction; patents for "SECB method" in image deblurring; discovery of useful property of heavy-tailed Lévy stable laws in blind sharpening of wide classes of images, including astronomical, Landsat and scanning electron microscope images, MRI and PET brain scans. Office: Nat Inst Stds and Tech Math & Computational Scis Gaithersburg MD 20899-0001 E-mail: alfred.carasso@nist.gov.

CARAVASOS, NIALENA, lawyer; b. Ridley Park, Pa., Oct. 20, 1966; BS in Econs. with honors, U. Pa., 1988; JD, Boston U., 1993. Bar: Mass. 1993, Pa. 1994, U.S. Dist. Ct. (ea. dist.) Pa. 1997, U.S. Ct. Appeals (3rd cir.) 1997, U.S. Supreme Ct. 1997. Law clk. to presiding judge Lisa Aversa Richette Ct. Common Pleas, Phila., 1995-97; assoc. F. Emmett Fitzpatrick, P.C., Phila., 1997—. CLE speaker at 2000 Criminal Law Symposium, Pa. Bar Inst. Edward F. Hennessey scholar; recipient Commencement award, Am. Jurisprudence award in Criminal Trial Practice. Mem. Pa. Bar Assn., Hellenic Lawyers Assn. Phila., Phila. Bar Assn. (criminal justice sect.), Fed. Bar Assn. (criminal law com.). Office: 926 Public Ledger Bldg 610 Chestnut St Philadelphia PA 19106 E-mail: nialena@toplaw.com.

CARAVATT, PAUL JOSEPH, JR., communications company executive; b. New Britain, Conn., Dec. 13, 1922; s. Paul Joseph and Bessie (Avery) C.; m. B. Laura Bennett, June 22, 1946; children— Cynthia Diane, Suzanne Laura. AB, Dartmouth, 1945, MBA, 1947. With Nat. Dairy Assn., 1947-49, Young & Rubicam, 1949-50; advt. mgr. Hunting and Fishing mag., 1950-52, Biow Co., 1952-56; v.p. Ogilvy, Benson & Mather, 1956-59; sr. v.p. Foote, Cone & Belding, 1960-64, LaRoche, McCaffrey & McCall (advt. agy.), N.Y.C., 1964-66; pres. Carl Ally, Ind. (advt. agy.), N.Y.C., 1966-67; chmn. bd., chief exec. officer Marschalk Co., Inc. (mem. Interpublic Group of Cos.), N.Y.C., 1967-69; sr. v.p., dir. Interpub. Group Cos., N.Y.C., 1970-72; pres., chief exec. officer, dir. Caravatt Communications, 1971-86, Newtel World Communications, N.Y.C., 1971-86; pres., chief exec. officer Caravatt Mktg., Wilton, Conn., 1986—; pres. Caravatt Mktg. Group, 1998—. Exec. dir. Vision Fund, The Lighthouse, 1994—97. Mem. SAR, Spl. Interest Video Assn. (pres., exec. dir. 1988-97), Newcomen Soc., Univ. Club (N.Y.C.), Ednl. Found. of Spl. Interest Marketers and Prodrs. (pres. 1997—), Zeta Psi. Congregationalist. Home: 274 Westport Rd Wilton CT 06897-4723 E-mail: caramktg@optonline.net.

CARBALLO, FERNANDO ANTHONY, gastroenterologist, hepatologist; b. Chgo., Nov. 29, 1961; s. Fernando T. and Carmen L. (Lamas) C.; m. Noreen Patricia Henehan, June 4, 1988; children: Sarah, Andrew, Carmen. BS in Biology, Loyola U., Chgo., 1983; MD, Autonomous U., Guadalajara, Jalisco, Mexico. Diplomate Am. Bd. Internal Medicine and Gastrenterology. Fifth Pathway N.Y. Med. Coll., Valhalla, 1989-90; internal medicine intern West Suburban Hosp. Med. Ctr., Oak Park, Ill., 1990-91; internal medicine resident MacNeal-Rush Presbyn. St. Luke's Med. Ctr., Chgo., 1993-95; fellow in digestive disease Rush Presbyn. St. Luke's Med. Ctr., Chgo., 1993-95; gastroenterologist, hepatologist Sterling Rock Falls Clin., Sterling, Ill., 1995-97, Summit Digestive Disease and Liver Specialists, Oakbrook Terrace, 1998—. Cons. Credentials Com., KSB Hosp., Dixon, Ill., 1996-97, Quality Assurance and Improvment Com., CGH Hosp., Sterling, 1996-97. Mem. AMA, Am. Gastroenterol. Assn., Am. Coll. Gastroenterology, Am. Soc. for Gastrointestinal Endoscopy. Republican. Roman Catholic. Avocations: computers, golf. Office: Milw Digestive Disease Cons 2901 W River Pky Ste 414 Milwaukee WI 53215

CARBALLO, JUAN-ANTONIO, research scientist; b. Madrid, Nov. 29, 1970; s. Juan-Antonio Carballo-Gallego and Maria-Cruz Herrero. BS, MS in Telecomms. Engring., Poly. U. Madrid, 1994; MBA, Coll. des Ingenieurs, Paris, 1995; PhD, U. Mich., 2000. Info. sys. cons. Andersen Cons., Madrid, 1992—93; bus. cons. Electricite de France, Paris, 1994—95; staff mem. rsch. divsn. IBM Corp., Austin, Tex., 2000—. Mem. voting com. Virtual Socket Interface Alliance, Los Gatos, 2001; mem. Design Automation Tech. Com., Poughkeepsie, NY, 2001—; mem. program com. Electronic Design Processes Workshop, Monterey, 2001—. Contbr. paper to conf. proceedings. Fellow, Coll. des Ingenieurs, 1994—95. Mem.: IEEE. Home: 2601 Scofield Ridge Pky #827 Austin TX 78727 Office: IBM Rsch 11501 Burnet Rd Austin TX 78758 Home Fax: 6037545754; Office Fax: 6037545754. Personal E-mail: jantonio@us.ibm.com. Business E-Mail: jantonio@us.ibm.com.

CARBARY, JONATHAN LEIGH, lawyer; b. Elgin, Ill., Nov. 6, 1949; s. Warren Edward and Barbara Jean (Leigh) C.; m. Janice Kay Weingartner, Dec. 29, 1973; children: Nicole, Dana, Jonathan. BA, Knox Coll., 1972; JD, Hamline U., 1978. Bar: Ill. 1978, U.S. Dist. Ct. (no. dist.) Ill. 1979. Assoc. Robert A. Chapski, Ltd., Elgin, 1978-83; ptnr. Roeser, Vucha & Carbary, Elgin, 1984-96; pvt. practice Elgin, 1996—. 1st lt. U.S. Army, 1972-73. Recipient Am. Jurisprudence award Lawyer Co-op Pub. Co., 1978. Mem. Ill. State Bar Assn., Kane County Bar Assn. Republican. Home: 11 N 205 Johnstown Rd Elgin IL 60123 Office: 1814 Grandstand Pl Elgin IL 60123-4981 E-mail: jcarbary@msn.com.

CARBAUGH, JOHN EDWARD, JR., lawyer; b. Greenville, S.C., Sept. 4, 1945; s. John Edward and Mary Lou (McCarley) C.; m. Mary Middleton Calhoun: children: John, Martha, Leacy, Miller. BA, U. of South, 1967; JD, U. S.C., 1973, postgrad., 1967-69, Georgetown U., 1977-79. Bar: S.C. 1973, U.S. Ct. Appeals (4th cir.) 1982, U.S. Supreme Ct. 1982. With White House Staff, Washington, 1969-70; campaign dir. re-elect Thurmond campaign Washington, 1970-73; legis. asst. U.S. Senate, Washington, 1974-82; pvt. practice Washington, 1982—. Bd. dirs. Westech. Internat., Inc., Washington Watch, Inc., Splty. Materials and Mfg., Inc., Tech. Holdings, Inc., The Stealth Corp., Inc.; mem. Pres. Commn. on Econ. Justice, Washington, 1985-87 Author: The Revisionists, 1991, We Need Each Other: U.S.-Japan Relations Approach the 21st Century, 1992; co-author: A Program for Military Independence, 1980; contbr. articles to profl. jours. Rep. Nat. Platform Staff, 1976, 80, 84, 88, 92, 96; Presdl. Transition Team, 1980-81. Sgt. USAR, 1969-77. Mem. Met. Club. Republican. Presbyterian. Avocations: tennis, travel, horticulture. Address: 1300 N 17th St Ste 1100 Arlington VA 22209

CARBINE, JAMES EDMOND, lawyer; b. Scotts Bluff, Nebr., June 3, 1945; s. Edmond Horace Carbine and Mabel (Porterfield) Hukle; m. Marianne Lemly, Aug. 5, 1972; 1 child, Matthew. BA, Mich. State U., 1967; JD, U. Md., 1972. Bar: Md. 1972. Assoc. Weinberg and Green, Balt., 1972-79, ptnr., 1980-96, chmn. litigation dept., 1985-95; pvt. practice Balt., 1996—. Panel mem. Nat. Press Club Symposium, 1974. Reporter Govs. Landlord Tenant Commn., Md., 1973-76; mem. Mayor's Bus. Roundtable, Balt., 1983-85; bd. dirs. Greater Homewood Community Corp., Balt., 1980-82; trustee Roland Park Found., 1986-87; bd. dirs. Md. Vol. Lawyers Svc., 1991-2002. With U.S. Army, 1968-70. Named one of Outstanding Young Men Am., Jaycees, 1977. Mem. ABA (computer litigation com., corp. coun. com., co-chair trial practice com. 1994-97), Md. Bar Assn., Balt. City Bar Assn., Nat. Press Club (panelist 1974). Avocation: outdoor sports. Office: 111 S Calvert St Ste 2700 Baltimore MD 21202-6143

CARBO, TONI (TONI CARBO BEARMAN), information scientist, educator; b. Middletown, Conn., Nov. 14, 1942; d. Anthony Joseph and Theresa (Bauer) Carbo; m. David A. Bearman, Nov. 14, 1970 (div. Nov. 1995); 1 child, Amanda Carole Bearman Rochon; m. Clark Coolidge, July 7, 1962 (div. Apr. 1966). AB, Brown U., 1969; MS, Drexel U., 1973, PhD, 1977. Bibliog. asst. Am. Math. Soc., Math. Revs., 1962-63; supr. Brown U. Phys. Scis. Library, Providence, 1963-66, 67-71; subject specialist U. Wash. Engring. Library, Seattle, 1966-67; teaching and research asst. Drexel U., Phila., 1971-74; exec. dir. Nat. Fedn. Abstracting and Info. Svcs., Phila., 1974-79; cons. for strategic planning and new product devel. Instn. Elec. Engrs., London, 1979-80; exec. dir. U.S. Nat. Commn. on Libraries and Info. Sci., Washington, 1980-86; prof. U. Pitts. Sch. Info. Sci., 1986—, dean, 1986—2002. Adv. com. U.S. Dept. Commerce, Patent and Trademark Office, 1987—90; trustee Engring. Info., Inc., 1985—87; Lazerow lectr. U. Ind., 1984, U. Toronto, 1999; Schwing lectr. La. State U., 1988; lectr. No. Ohio Am. Soc. Info. Sci./Spl. Librs. Assn., 1990, Beta Phi Mu, Phila., 1992; Sigma chpt. lectr. Drexel U., Phila.; U.S. adv. coun. Nat. Info. Infrastructure, 1994—96; U.S. del. G-7 Info. Soc. Conf.; bd. dirs. Pa. Info. Hwy. Consortium; Miles Conrad lectr. Nat. Fedn. Abstracting & Info. Svcs., 1997; Biennial Srygley lectr. Fla. State U., 1997; Nasser Sharify lectr. Pratt U., 1997; mem. Nat. Conf. Lawyers and Scientists, 2000—06; Cunningham lectr. Vanderbilt U., 2002; lectr. in field. Co-editor: Internat. Info. and Libr. Rev., 1989—92; editor, 1993—; mem. editl. bds. profl. jours.; contbr. articles to profl. jours. Mem. presdl. adv. com. Carnegie Libr. Pitts.; bd. dirs. Greater Pitts. Literacy Coun. Recipient Disting. Alumni award, Drexel U. Coll. Info. Studies, 1984, 100 Most Disting. Alumni award, 1992, 100th Anniversary medal, Drexel U., 1992, Silver Anniversary award, U.S. Nat. Commn. Librs. & Info. Sci., 1996, Leadership award in Sci. and Tech., YWCA Greater Pitts., 2000; fellow Madison Coun., Libr. Congress, 2002—03. Fellow: AAAS (chmn. sect. T 1992—93, coun. 1997—99), Spl. Librs. Assn. (rsch. com. 1987—92, internat. rels. com. 1991), Inst. Info. Scientists, Nat. Fedn. Abstracting and Info. Svcs. (hon.); mem.: ALA (coun. 1988—92, 50th Anniversary Honor Roll 1996), Internat. Women's Forum Western Pa., Assn. Libr. and Info. Sci. Edn. (bd. dirs. 1996—2000, pres. 1997—98, Profl. Contbn. to Libr. and Info. Sci. Edn. award 2002), Internat. Fedn. Info. and Documentation (co-chair U.S. nat. com. 1990—2000, chair global info. infrastructure and superhighways taskforce 1993—96, mem. coun., chair info. structures and policies com. 1997—2000), Nat. Info. Stds. Orgns. (bd. dirs. 1987—90), Pa. Libr. Assn. (adv. bd. Pa. Gov.'s Conf. libr. and info. svcs. 1996, Disting. Svc. award 1996), Am. Soc. Info. Sci. (chmn. networking com., chmn. 50th ann. conf., pres. 1989—90, chmn. planning and nominations com. 1990—91, Watson Davis award 1983), 3 Rivers Connect (bd. dirs., exec. com. 1998—, vice chair 1999—2002, interim chair 2003—), Ctr. Democracy and Tech. (bd. dirs. 1996—, chair 1999—2002), Laurel Initiative (bd. dirs. 1990—93). Home: 263 Maple Ave Pittsburgh PA 15218-1523 Office: 135 N Bellefield Ave Pittsburgh PA 15213-2609 Fax: 412-648-7001. E-mail: tcarbo@mail.sis.pitt.edu.

CARBON, MAX WILLIAM, nuclear engineering educator; b. Monon, Ind., Jan. 19, 1922; s. Joseph William and Mary Olive (Goble) C.; m. Phyllis Camille Myers, Apr. 13, 1944; children: Ronald Allen, Jean Ann, Susan Jane, David William, Janet Elaine. BSME, Purdue U., 1943, MS, 1947, PhD, 1949. With Hanford Works divsn. GE, 1949-55, head heat transfer unit, 1951-55; with rsch. and advanced devel. divsn. Avco Mfg. Corp., 1955-58, chief thermodynamics sect., 1956-58; prof., chmn. nuclear engring. and engring. physics dept. U. Wis. Coll. Engring., Madison, 1958-92, emeritus prof., collateral faculty, 1992—, acting assoc. dean for rsch., 1995-96. Group leader Ford Found. program Singapore, 1967-68; mem. adv. com. on reactor safeguards, 1975-87; chmn. spl. com. for integral fast reactor U. Chgo., 1984-94, chmn. spl. adv. com. for nuclear tech. program Argonne (Ill.) Nat. Lab., 1995-2002; mem. INPO Nat. Nuclear Accrediting Bd., 1990-94; mem. nuclear safety rev. and audit com. Kewaunee Nuclear Power Plant, 1993-96. Author: Nuclear Power: Villain or Victim, 1997. Capt. ordnance dept. AUS, 1943-46. Named Disting. Engring. Alumnus, Purdue U. Fellow Am. Nuclear Soc.; mem. AAAS, Sigma Xi, Tau Beta Pi. Office: U Wis Engring Rsch Bldg Madison WI 53706 E-mail: carbon@engr.wisc.edu.

CARBONE, ROSE ELAINE, mathematics educator; b. Wilkinsburg, Pa., Sept. 17, 1948; d. Bruno Bernard and Rose Marie (Nagoda) Balest; m. John James Carbone, Oct. 21, 1972; children: Caren, Catherine, Maria. BS in Math. Edn., Indiana U. of Pa., 1970, MEd in Math., 1974; EdD, U. Pitts., 1998. Cert. tchr., Pa. Tchr. Greater Latrobe (Pa.) Sch. Dist., 1970-75; instr. Westmoreland County C.C., Youngwood, Pa., 1977-79, Pa. State U., 1978, 91-92; instr. math. dept. Indiana U. of Pa., 1982, 96; instr. in math. Seton Hill Coll., 1986; math. specialist Indiana U. of Pa., 1989-90, program coord., 1993-98; asst. prof. dept. math. Clarion U. of Pa., 1998—2001, assoc. prof., 2001—. Mem. Clarion Cmty. Choir, 1999—; Clarion Walk chair Juvenile Diabetes Rsch. Found., 2002 Named Civic Leader of the Yr., Indiana Community Civic Clubs, 1986. Mem. ASCD, AAUP, Nat. Coun. Tchrs. Math., Pa. Coun. Tchrs. Math., Math. Coun. Western Pa., Am. Math. Soc., Assn. Math. Tchr. Educations, Assn. Math. Tchrs. Northwestern Pa., State Sys. Higher Edn. Math. Assn., Math. Assn. Am., Am. Diabetes Assn. (bd. dirs. parent support group Indiana County chpt. 1985-95, treas. 1983, v.p., 1984, pres. 1985, chmn. bd. dirs. 1986, sec. 1990-93, state bd. dirs. 1990-93), Clarion Civic Club (rec. sec. 2000-01, edn. chair 2001, scholarship chair 2001--), Phi Delta Kappa (v.p. program 2000, 01, pres. 2002--), Pi Mu Epsilon. Roman Catholic. Avocations: singing, nautilus, travel, photography, gardening. Home: 1309 Robinwood Dr Clarion PA 16214-8803 E-mail: ecarbone@clarion.edu.

CARBONELL, JOSEFINA, federal agency administrator; b. Cuba; 1 child, Alfredo. Student, Fla. Internat. U. With Little Havana Activities and Nutrition Ctrs., Dade County, Fla., 1972—, pres., CEO; asst. sec. for adminstrn. on aging Dept. HHS, Washington, 2001—. Recipient Citizen of Yr. award, Miami, 1992, Charles Whited Spirit of Excellence award, Miami Herald, 1993, Cmty. Svc. award, Nat. Alliance for Hispanic Health, 1995, Monsignor Bryan Walsh Outstanding Human Svc. award, United Way, 1997, Commrs. Team award, Social Security Adminstrn., 1997, Claude Pepper Cmty. Svc. award, 2001; fellow in health mgmt., John F. Kennedy Sch. Govt., Harvard U. Office: Dept HHS Adminstrn on Aging 330 Independence Ave SW Washington DC 20201

CARBUTO, NICHOLAS, music educator; b. Glen Cove, N.Y., Oct. 23, 1956; s. Anne Carbuto; m. Judy Venezio, June 17, 1979; children: Lauren, Nicholas Richard. MS in Music Edn., L.I. U., 1982. Band dir. Freeport Pub. Schs., NY, 1992—99, Glen Cove Schs., 1999—. Interfaith min. Office: Robert M Finley Mid Sch Forest Ave Glen Cove NY 11542

CARCATERRA, LORENZO GABRIEL, writer; b. N.Y.C., Oct. 16, 1954; s. Mario and Raffaela Carcaterra; m. Susan J. Toepfer, May 16, 1981; children: Katherine Marie, Nicholas Gabriel. BS, St. John's U., 1976. News editor, copyboy, clk., reporter N.Y. Daily News, N.Y.C., 1976—83; sr. writer Time, Inc., N.Y.C., 1983—84; freelance writer, 1984—88; mng. editor CBS-Grosso/Jacobson Prodns., Top Cops, N.Y.C., 1990—94; freelance writer N.Y.C., NY, 1990—, L.A., 1990—. CEO One Punch Prodns., N.Y.C., 1997—. Author: A Safe Place, 1993, Sleepers, 1995, Apaches, 1997, Gangster, 2000, (screenplays) Street Boys, 2002, Dreamer, 1996, Doubt, 1997, Ringers, 1998, The Force, 1999, Law & Order, 2003—. Recipient Leone Di San Marco award, Lehman Coll., Bronx, N.Y., 1994. Mem.: Mystery Writers Am., Authors Guild, Writers Guild Am. East, Internat. Nat. Assn. Crime Writers. Republican. Roman Catholic. Avocations: running, weight-lifting, travel, book collecting, sports.

CARCIERI, DONALD L. governor; b. Conn., Dec. 16, 1942; m. Sue Carcieri; 4 children. Degree in Internat. Rels., Brown U. Tchr.; various positions including exec. v.p. Old Stone Bank; head West Indies ops. Cath. Relief Svcs., Kingston, Jamaica, 1981—83; various positions including CEO Cookson Am., RI, 1983, joint mng. dir. Cookson Group Worldwide; gov. RI, 2002—. Mem. Cath. Relief Svcs. Leadership Coun.; former chair R.I. Math./Sci. Edn. Coalition; co-founder Acad. Children's Sci. Ctr., East Greenwich; dir. Providence Ctr., RI. Republican. Roman Catholic. Office: Office of the Gov State House Rm 115 Providence RI 02903*

CARD, ANDREW H., JR., federal official; b. Brockton, Mass., May 10, 1947; s. Andrew Hill and Joyce (Whitaker) C.; m. Kathleene Marie Bryan; 3 children. BS in Engring., U. S. C., 1971; MA, LLD (hon.), Mount Ida Coll. and Assumption Coll.; MA, DPA (hon.), Curry Coll.; postgrad., Mass. Maritime Acad. Structural design engr. Maurice Reidy Engrs., Inc., 1971-72, David M. Berg, Inc., 1972-75; held several elected and appointed offices Holbrook, Mass., 1971-82; rep. Gen. Ct. of Commonwealth of Mass., 1975-82; v.p. CMIS Corp., Vienna, Va., 1983; spl. asst. to Pres. Ronald Reagan for Intergovtl. Affairs The White House, 1983-87; N.H. campaign mgr. for George Bush, 1987-88; dep. asst. to Pres. Ronald Reagan, dir. Office of Intergovtl. Affairs, 1988; asst. to Pres. and dep. chief of staff The White House, 1989-92; sec. U.S. Dept. Transp., Washington, 1992—93; pres., CEO Am. Automobile Mfrs. Assn., Washington, 1992—98; v.p. of Govt. Relations General Motors, 1999—2000; chief of staff The White House, Washington, 2000—. Mem. adv. commn. on intergovtl. relations, 1988; head of task force Federal relief effort Hurricane Andrew So. Fla., 1992. Candidate for gov., Mass., 1983. With USN, 1965-67. Named one of Nation's Outstanding Legislators, Nat. Rep. Legislators' Assn., 1982. Office: Chief of Staff 1600 Pennsylvania Ave NW Washington DC 20502*

CARD, CLAUDIA FALCONER, philosophy educator; b. Madison, Wis., Sept. 30, 1940; d. Walter Munro and Achsah Susan (Falconer) C. BA, U. Wis., 1962; AM, Harvard U., 1964, PhD, 1969. From instr. to prof. philosophy U. Wis., Madison, 1966—. Author: Lesbian Choices, 1995, The Unnatural Lottery: Character and Moral Luck, 1996, The Atrocity Paradigm: A Theory of Evil, 2002; editor: Feminist Ethics, 1991, Adventures in Lesbian Philosophy, 1994, The Cambridge Companion to Simone de Beauvoir, 2003; guest editor: Hypatia, 1992; co-editor: Religious Commitment and Salvation, 1974; editl. bd. book series Columbia U. Press, 1989—; editor book series U. Press Kans., 1997—; editor jours. Ethics, 1989-92, Hypatia, 1989—; adv. bd. jour. Social Theory and Practice, 1989—; contbr. articles to profl. jours. Fellow Woodrow Wilson, 1962-63, 65-66, NEH, 1974-75, Vilas, 1989-91. Fellow Am. Coun. Learned Socs.; mem. Am. Philos. Assn. (mem. various coms. 1975—), Soc. Women in Philosophy, Soc. for Lesbian and Gay Philosophy (co-chair 1988-90), Nat. Women's Studies Assn., Inst. for Rsch. in Humanities (sr. fellow), Internat. Assn. Women Philosophers, Internat. Genocide Soc.Sierra Club. Avocations: classical piano, swimming, t'ai chi, bicycling. Office: U Wis Dept Philosophy 600 N Park St Madison WI 53706-1403

CARD, ORSON SCOTT (BYRON WALLEY), writer; b. Richland, Wash., Aug. 24, 1951; s. Willard Richards and Peggy Jane (Park) C.; m. Kristine Allen, May 17, 1977; children: Geoffrey, Emily, Charles, Zina. BA in Theater, Brigham Young U., 1975; MA in English, U. Utah, 1981. Editor Brigham Young U. Press, Provo, Utah, 1974-76; assoc. editor Ensign mag., Salt Lake City, 1976-78; sr. editor Compute! Publs., Greensboro, N.C., 1983; game design cons. Lucasfilm Games, 1989-92. Instr. Brigham Young U., U. Utah, U. Notre Dame, Appalachian State U., Clarion West Writer's Workshop, Cape Code Writers Conf., Antioch Writers Workshop; columnist "You Got No Friends in This World", Science Fiction Review, 1979-86, "Book to Look For", Fantasy and Science Fiction, 1987—, "Gameplay", Compute!, 1988—. Author: (fiction) Capitol, 1978, Hot Sleep, 1978, A Planet Called Treason, 1979, Songmaster, 1980 (Hamilton/Brackett award 1981), Unaccompanied Sonata and Other Stories, 1981, Hart's Hope, 1982, The Worthing Chronicle, 1983, A Woman of Destiny, 1983, Ender's Game, 1985 (Nebula award 1985, Hugo award 1986, Hamilton/Brackett award 1986), Speaker For The Dead, 1986 (Nebula award 1986, Hugo award 1987, Locus award 1987), Hatrack River, 1986 (Hugo award nomination 1986, World Fantasy award 1987), Wyrms, 1987, Seventh Son, 1987 (Locus award best fantasy 1988, Hugo award nomination 1988, World Fantasy award nomination 1988), Cardography, 1987, Eye for Eye, 1987 (Hugo award 1988, Locus award nomination 1988), Treason, 1988, Red Prophet, 1988 (Locus award 1989), Prentice Alvin, 1989, Folk of the Fringe, 1989, The Abyss, 1989, Maps in a Mirror, 1990, The Worthing Saga, 1990, Xenocide, 1991, The Memory of Earth, 1992, Lost Boys, 1992, The Call of Earth, 1992, The Changed Man, 1992, Flux, 1992, Cruel Miracles, 1992, Monkey Sonatas, 1993, The Ships of Earth, 1993, A Storyteller in Zion, 1993, Earthfall, 1994, (with David Dollahite) Turning Hearts, 1994, (with Kathryn H. Kidd) Lovelock, 1994, Earthborn, 1995, Alvin Journeyman, 1995 (Locus award 1996), Pastwatch: The Redemption of Christopher Columbus, 1996, Children of the Mind, 1996, Treasure Box, 1996, Stone Tables, 1997, Homebody, 1998, Heartfire, 1998, Enchantment, 1999, Ender's Shadow, 1999, First Meetings: in the Enderverse, 2003; (nonfiction) Listen, Mom and Dad, 1978, Saintspeak, 1981, Ainge, 1982, Characters and Viewpoint, 1988, How to Write Science Fiction and Fantasy, 1990 (Hugo award for non-fiction 1991); (plays) The Apostate, 1970, In Flight, 1970, Across Five Summers, 1971, Of Gideon, 1971, Stone Tables, 1973, A Christmas Carol, 1974, Father, Mother, Mother, and Mom, 1974, Liberty Jail, 1975, Rag Mission, 1977, Fresh Courage Take, 1978, Elders and Sisters, 1979, Wings, 1982; editor: Dragons of Darkness, 1981, Dragons of Light, 1983; author numerous audio and videoplays; contbr. short stories and essays to Fantasy & Sci. Fiction, Windows Sources and other mags. Recipient John W. Campbell award World Sci. Fiction Conv., 1978, Hugo award nominations World Sci. Fiction Conv., 1978, 79, 80, Nebula award nominations Sci. Fiction Writers of America, 1979, 80, Utah State Inst. of Fine Arts prize, 1980. Mem. Sci. Fiction Writers Am., Authors Guild. Democrat. Mem. Lds Ch. Office: c/o Tor Books 175 5th Ave Fl 14 New York NY 10010-7703*

CARD, ROBERT GORDON, federal agency administrator; b. Yakima, Wash. Bachelor's, U. Wash.; M in Environ. and Civil Engring., Stanford U. Exec. v.p. CH2M Hill, Inc.; pres., CEO Kaiser-Hill Co., Colo.; under sec. energy, sci., and environment Dept. Energy, Washington, 2001—. Office: Dept Energy Energy Sci and Environment 1000 Independence Ave SW Washington DC 20585-0001

CARDAMONE, RICHARD J. judge; b. Utica, N.Y., Oct. 10, 1925; s. Joseph J. and Josephine (Scala) Cardamone; m. Catherine Baker Clarke, Aug. 28, 1946. BA, Harvard U., 1948; LLB, Syracuse U., 1952. Bar: N.Y. 1952. Pvt. practice, Utica, 1952—62; judge N.Y. State Supreme Ct., 1963—71, judge appelate divsn. 4th dept., 1971—81; judge U.S. Ct. Appeals (2d cir.), Utica, 1981—. Lt. (j.g.) USNR, 1943—46. Mem.: Oneida County Bar Assn., N.Y. State Bar Assn., Am. Law Inst. Roman Catholic. Office: US Ct Appeals 10 Broad St Utica NY 13501-1233

CARDELLA, JOHN F. radiologist; b. Feb. 21, 1954; s. John and Eva Cardella; m. Kay Cardella, June 10, 1978; children: John Thomas, Michael John. BS in Med. Scis., U. Mich., 1975, MD, 1978. Chief interventional radiology Met. Med. Ctr., Mpls., 1985—89, Pa. State U., Hershey, 1989—99; chmn. radiology SUNY Upstate Med. Ctr., Syracuse, 1999—. Contbr. articles to profl. publs. and electronic media, chpts. to books. Named Reviewer of Distinction, Jour. Vascular Interventional Radiology. Fellow: Am. Heart Assn. (cardiovascular coun.), Soc. Cardiovasc./Inerventional Radiology (chmn. stds. of practice com. 1999—); mem.: Am. Roentgen Ray Soc., Radiol. Soc. N.Am.

CARDEN, CONSTANCE, law educator, lawyer; b. D.C., July 15, 1944; d. George Alexander and Constance (Sullivan) C.; m. John Dinsmore Adams, Jun. 7, 1975 (div. Jun. 1988); 1 child, Elizabeth; m. Bernard Lawrence Goldstein, Aug. 7, 1998. BA, Radcliffe Coll., 1966; MA in Teaching, Harvard Grad. Sch. Edn., 1967; JD, N.Y. Univ., 1972. Bar: N.Y. 1973. Assoc. Webster & Sheffield, N.Y.C., 1972-73; law clerk U.S. Dist. Judge Kevin Thomas Duffy, N.Y.C., 1973-74; staff atty. Legal Aid Soc., N.Y.C., 1974-81; sr. staff atty. Legal Svcs. for the Elderly, N.Y.C., 1981-90; dir. litig. Bklyn. Neighborhood Office Legal Aid Soc., N.Y.C., 1990-96; supervising atty. gen. legal svcs. N.Y. Legal Assistance Group, N.Y.C., 1997-98, dir. spl. litig., 1998—. Revson fellow, City Coll. N.Y. Law Sch., N.Y.C., 1981-82; adj. asst. prof., Bkln. Law Sch., N.Y.C., 1985-86; adj. prof., Pace Law Sch., White Plains, NY, 1993—. Author, editor: Medical Assistance in New York State, 1988, revised annually. Pres., Project Greenhope Svcs. for Women, N.Y.C., 1986-97; bd. dirs. Medicare Rights Ctr., 1988-95, Correctional Assn., Osborne Assn., N.Y.C., Project Greenhope Svcs., 1986—. Recipient Legal Svcs. award, Bar Assn. City of N.Y., 1990. Mem. Century Assn., Canterbury Choral Soc., Essex Hunt Club. Avocations: running, singing, foxhunting, playing piano, reading. Home: 115 E 90th St New York NY 10128-1509 Office: New York Legal Asst Group 130 E 59th St New York NY 10022-1302 E-mail: ccarden@nylag.org.

CARDEN, ZACHARY FRANK, JR., dentist; b. Chattanooga, June 19, 1941; s. Zachary Frank and Mable (Torbett) C.; m. Anne Fowler, Jan. 28, 1967; children: Heather Anne, Zachary Frank III. BS, Carson-Newman Coll., 1963; med. technologist, Erlanger Hosp., Chattanooga, 1964; DDS, U. Tenn., 1974. Med. technologist Erlanger Hosp., Chattanooga, 1964-65, 68-70; pvt. practice Chattanooga, 1974—. Pres. Civic Art League, Chattanooga, 1980. Capt. U.S. Army, 1965-68. Mem. ADA, Am. Acad. Oral Medicine (Oral Medicine award 1974), Tenn. Dental Assn. (del. 1983-85, chmn. coun. on ethics, by-laws and jud. affairs 1999—, v.p. 2000—, sci. editor Tenn. Dental Assn. Jour., Fellowship award 2002), Lookout Dental Study Group (pres. 1975), 3d Dist. Dental Soc. (chmn. peer rev. 1983-85, trustee for Hamilton County 1996, treas. 1997-98), Chattanooga Area Dental Soc. (treas. 1997-98, sec. 1998-99, pres.-elect 1999, pres. 2000-01), Chattanooga Craniomandibular Study Group (pres. 1985-86). Republican. Methodist. Avocations: watercolor and oil painting, golf. Office: Lake Hills Profl Bldg 4216 Cross St Chattanooga TN 37416-3334

CARDENAS, ALBERTO R. lawyer; b. Havana, Cuba, 1948; BS, Fla. Atlantic U., 1969; JD, Seton Hall U., 1974. Bar: Fla. 1974, U.S. Supreme Ct. 1980, U.S. Dist. Ct. (so. dist.) Fla. 1992. Atty. Tew Cardenas Rebak Kellogg Lehman Damaria & Tague, LLP, West Palm Beach. Bd. dirs. Dade County Commrs., City of Miami; chmn. Fla. Rep. Party, 1999-2003; policy coord. Office of the Pres.-Elect, Dept. of Commerce, 1980-81; chmn. Presdl. Adv. Com. on Small and Minority Bus. Affairs, 1981-84; mem. adv. com. on internat. trade U.S. Senate, 1985-86, mem. Pres. Bush's Commn. on Trade Policy, 1991-93; dir. Performing Arts Ctr. Trust; trustee The Wolfsonian Found. Office: Miami Ctr 201 S Biscayne Blvd 26th Flr Miami FL 33131 Fax: 561-820-8295. E-mail: AC@Tewlaw.com.*

CARDENES, ANDRES JORGE, violinist, music educator; b. Havana, Cuba, May 2, 1957; came to U.S., 1958; s. Andres Manuel and Arlene (Cuevas) C. Student, Ind. U., 1975-80; diploma, Meisterkurse Zurich, Switzerland, 1977. Asst. prof. music Ind. U., Bloomington, 1980-82; prof. music Espoo Festival, Helsinki, Finland, 1982; prof. U. Utah, Salt Lake City, 1982-85; prof. music U. Mich., 1987-89. Mem. artistic com. Utah Symphony, Salt Lake City, 1983-85; cons. in field; bd. dirs. Intermountain-West Music Festival, Salt Lake City, 1984-88; artistic dir. Strings in the Mountains Chamber Music Festival,

Steamboat Springs, Colo.; prof. violin studies Carnegie Mellon U., 1989—. Concertmaster Utah Symphony, Salt Lake City, 1982-85, San Diego Symphony, 1985-86, Pitts. Symphony, 1987—; concert violin soloist, 1981—; 1985-86; editor: Concerto by Ramiro Cortes, 1983; performer worldwide Nuclear Arms Freeze, 1980—. Cultural amb. UNICEF, 1980—; chmn., co-founder Underprivileged Arts Student San Diego Soc.; cultural chmn. Make-a-Wish Found. of Pitts. Recipient Bronze medal Queen Elizabeth Internat. Violin Competition, Brussels, 1980, Bronze medal Sibelius Internat. Violin Competition, Helsinki, 1980, Bronze medal Tchaikovsky Internat. Violin Competition, Moscow, 1982, Bronze medal Internat. Violin Competition, Indpls., 1986, Pitts. Classical Artist of Yr., 1998, Starling Found. endowed chair Carnegie-Mellon U., 1998, Shalom awrd Kollell Found. Mem. Young San Diegans Soc. (bd. dirs.). Clubs: Machista (Bloomington) (pres. 1978—). Roman Catholic. Home: 4729 Bayard St Pittsburgh PA 15213-1707 Office: Pittsburgh Symphony Orch Heinz Hall 600 Penn Ave Ste 1 Pittsburgh PA 15222-3259

CARDER, PAUL CHARLES, retired advertising executive; b. Oak Park, Ill., Jan. 27, 1941; arrived in Can., 1967; s. Lawrence E. and Irene (Zahler) C.; children from previous marriages: Greg Lawrence, Tracy Allison, Leigh Rebecca Kamping-Carder, Amanda Rachel Kamping-Carder. BA, U. Mich., 1962; MBA, Harvard U., 1964. Account exec. Ogilvy & Mather, N.Y.C., 1964-65; v.p. Ogilvy & Mather Can., Ltd., Toronto, Ont., Can., 1966-73; v.p., dir. client svcs. Doyle Dane Bernbach, Toronto, 1974-77; sr. v.p., mng. dir. Vicker & Benson, Ltd., Toronto, 1978-83; pres., CEO Carder Gray Advt., Inc., Toronto, 1983-90, DDB Needham Worldwide, Toronto, 1990-94; ret., 1994; dean, faculty Bus. and Creative Arts George Brown Coll., Toronto, 1999—2002. Adj. prof., Queen's U. Sch. Bus., 1995—96; prin. Paladin Co.; dir. mktg. and bus. devel. Davies, Ward, Phillips & Vineberg, 2003—. Bd. dirs. Nat. Ballet Can., Toronto, 1984-90, Thousand Islands Playhouse, 1995—, Heart and Stroke Found. of Ont., 1997—, Toronto Cmty. Found., 2000—. Mem. Inst. Can. Advt. (dir., treas. 1988-90), dir. Harvard Bus. Sch. Club of Toronto. Liberal party of Ontario. Avocations: tennis, skiing. Office: Davies WArd Pillips & Vineberg 44th Fl 1 First Canadian Pl Toronto ON Canada M5X 1B1 Personal E-mail: pcarder@sympatico.ca.

CARDIERI, ALEXANDER M. music specialist, music educator; b. Brooklyn, NY, May 9, 1953; s. Alexander Sr. and Mary Cardieri; m. Filis A. DeRodio, Jan. 14, 1978; children: George, Alexis. MusB, Manhattan Sch. of Music, New York, NY, 1976, MusM, 1980. Cert. Eng. as a second lang. Tchr. (min. of music) Bklyn. Diocese, Bklyn., 1979—84, Queens, NY, 1979—84; tchr. (music) St. Joseph HS, Bklyn., 1981—84, Patagonia Sch., Patagonia, Ariz., 1985—95, tchr. (band dir.), 1985—95; music specialist Nogales Ltd. Sch. Dist., Nogales, Ariz., 1995—96, Sunnyside Ltd. Sch. Dist., Tucson, 1996—; adj. music instr. Pima Comm. Coll., Tucson, 1996—. Pianist Anthony's In the Catalinas Restaurant, Tucson, 1989—. Author: (Thesis) An Anthology and Approach to Ear Training Through the Use of Familiar Tunes, 1979. Recipient Who's Who Among Am. Tchr., 1990, O.M. Hartsell Excellence in Tchg. Music award, 2003; grantee tech. grant, Sunnyside Found./ AZ, 2002. Mem.: MENC: The Nat. Assoc. for Music Ed. Republican. Roman Catholic. Achievements include General Music Curriculum co-writer; Sunnyside Ltd. Sch. Dist. Career Ladder Level III tchr. Avocations: computers, hiking, aerobics. Home: 12770 E Wentworth Ct Vail AZ 85641 E-mail: alexc@sunnysideud.k12.az.us.

CARDIFF, ROBERT DARRELL, pathology educator; b. San Francisco, Dec. 5, 1935; s. George Darrell and Helen (Kohfield) C.; m. Sally Joan Bounds, June 23, 1962; children: Darrell, Todd, Shelley. BS, U. Calif., Berkeley, 1958, PhD, 1968; MD, U. Calif., San Francisco, 1962. Intern King's County Hosp., Bklyn., 1962-63; resident in pathology U. Oreg., Portland, 1963-66; NIH fellow U. Calif., Berkeley, 1966-68, mem. faculty med. sch. Davis, 1971—, prof. pathology med. sch., 1977—, chair dept. pathology, 1990-96; dir. Ctr. for Med. Informatics U. Calif. Davis Healthcare System, Davis, 1996-98; chair Med. Informatics Grad. Group, 2002—; faculty Ctr. for Comparative Medicine U. Calif. Davis Healthcare System, Davis. Mem. sci. adv. bd. Contra Costa Cancer Fund, Walnut Creek, Calif., 1985-99; mem. Univ.-Wide AIDS Task Force, Berkeley, 1984-87; vis. prof. Sun-Yat Sen U. Med. Sci., Peoples Republic of China, 1985, 93, Harvard Med. Sch., 1990, U. Calif. San Diego, 1998-99. Mem. editorial bd. Human Pathology, 1992—, Tumor Markers, 1992—, Internat. Jour. Oncology, 1992—, Jour. Mamglnd Biol. and Neoplasia, 1998—; contbr. articles to profl. jours. Lt. col. U.S. Army, 1968—71. Recipient Triton Rsch. award Triton Bioscis., Inc., 1985, Kaiser Found. Teaching award U. Calif. Med. Sch., Davis, 1985, Disting. Teaching award U. Calif., Davis, Saduk award Peralta Cancer Inst., 1986, Faculty Rsch. award U. Calif. Med. Sch., 1988, Affirmative Action award U. Calif. Davis Med. Ctr., 1991, others. Master: AAUP (exec. com. 1983—85); mem.: No. Calif. Pathology Soc. (pres. 1990—96), Sacramento Pathology Soc. (bd. dirs. 1985—96), Internat. Assn. Breast Cancer (bd. dirs. 1984—96), Internat. Acad. Pathology, Pluto Soc., Sigma Xi. Avocations: basketball, skiing, jogging. Office: U Calif-Davis Ctr for Comparative Medicine 98 County Rd & Hutchison Dr Davis CA 95616

CARDILE, PAUL JULIUS, fine arts dealer; b. N.Y.C., July 30, 1948; s. Julius Joseph and Mary Lola (Contrucci) C. BA, Queens Coll., N.Y.C., 1969, MA, 1971; MPhil, Yale U., 1974, PhD, 1976. Asst. prof. SUNY, Albany, 1975-76, Newcomb Coll., New Orleans, 1976-77, Cleve. State U., 1977-78; asst. prof., mus. dir. Denison U., Granville, Ohio, 1978-84; owner Cardile Galleries, N.Y.C., 1984—. Appraiser Assn. of Am., N.Y.C., 1985—, bd. dirs., 1995—. Author: Paintings in Churches and Sacred Places in Cortona, 1982; contbr. articles to profl. jours. Historian Orthodox Knights Hospitaller of St. John of Jerusalem. Humanities fellow NEH, 1982-83. Mem. Portuguese Heritage Found. (adv. coun. 1991—). Republican. Roman Catholic. Home: 880 5th Ave # 6H New York NY 10021-4951 Office: RF Stuart 444 Park Ave S New York NY 10016

CARDIN, BENJAMIN LOUIS, congressman; b. Balt, Md, Oct. 5, 1943; s. Meyer M. and Dora (Green) C.; m. Myrna Edelman, Nov. 24, 1964; children: Michael, Deborah. BA cum laude, U. Pitts., 1964; JD (hon.), U. Md., 1967; LLD (hon.), U. Balt., 1990, U. Md., 1993, Balt. Hebrew U., 1994, Goucher Coll., 1996. Bar: Md. 1967. Mem. Md. Ho. of Del., 1967-86; pvt. practice law Balt., 1967-87; chmn. ways and means com. Md. Ho. of Del., 1974-79, spkr. of house, 1979-86; mem. 100-108th Congresses from 3d Md. Dist., Washington, 1987—; asst. Dem. whip 100-107th Congresses from 3d Md. Dist., Washington, ways and means com., human resources and social security subcoms., 1991—, steering com. Dem. caucus, 1991—, com. on stds. and ofcl. conduct, 1991-97; chair orgn., study and review com. of Dem. caucus, 1997—; Homeland Security Comm., 2003. Chmn. MD Legal Svc. Corp., 1988-95; commr. Commn. on Security and Cooperation in Europe, 1993—. Contbr. articles to profl. jour. Bd. visitors U. Md. Sch. Law, 1993—; trustee St. Mary's Coll., 1988-99, Goucher Coll., 1999—. Recipient Small Bus. Coun. of Am. Congrl. award, 1993, 99, Jacob K. Javits award Am Psychiat. Assn., 1999, Md. Psychiatric Soc. Friend of Psychiatry Award, 1988; Common Cause of Md. Ann Hogan Meml. Award, 1087; Rep. of Yr. award Nat. Assn. Police Orgn., 1998, Md. Bar Found. Vernon Eney award, 1996, Md. Save Our Streams' Living Stream award, 1996, Digestive Disease Nat. Coalition Publ. Policy Leadership award, 1996, The Coalition for a Lead Safe Environment, Alliance to End Childhood Lead Poisoning, the H. John Heinz III Nat. Leadership Award, 1994; ABA Pro Bono Publico Award, 1989; Hunting S. Williams award, 1995, H. John Heinz III Nat. Leadership award, 1994, Nat. Multiple Sclerosis Soc. Rep. of the Yr. award, 1993, Israel Freedom award, 1992, U. Md. Law Sch. Alumni Assn. Cardin Pro Bono award, 1990, Congl. Advocate of Yr. award Child Welfare League of Am., 2000; named to Concord Coalition's Deficit Hawk Honor Roll, 1998, 99, The Am. Med. Assoc. Dr. Nathan Davis Award for Publ. Svc., 1999; Congressional Advocate of the Yr. Award, Child Welfare League of Am, 2000; Nat. Leadership Award for Svc. to Children and Families, Casey Family Svc., 2000; Congressional Leadership Award, the Am. Coll. of Emerg. Physicians, 2001; Congressional Champion Award, The Nat. coalition for Cancer Rsch., 2002; Legislator of the Yr., Am. Assoc. of Health Plans, 2003. Mem. ABA (Pro Bono Public award 1989), Md. Bar Assn., Baltimore City Bar Assn. Democrat. Jewish. Office: US Ho Reps 2207 Rayburn Bldg Washington DC 20515-2003 Fax: 202-225-9219.*

CARDIN, FREDERICK, investment banker; b. Charlotte, N.C., July 28, 1946; s. Frederick Armand Cardin and Kate Elizabeth Rose. BA summa cum laude, Tufts U., 1968; MBA with distinction, Harvard U., 1970, Doctorate, 1974. Faculty mem. internat. fin. Harvard Bus. Sch., Cambridge, 1970; dir. Cambridge Rsch. Inst., 1974-81; founder, CEO O'Deli Corp., San Francisco, 1985-90; mng. dir. Harvard Growth Strategies, Newport Beach, Calif., 1995—. Mem. adv. bd. Absorbent Industries, Inc., Portland, Oreg., 2000-02, RPost, Ltd., Bermuda, 2001—, Arkeia, 2002—; bd. dirs. Whitney Info. Network, 2003-. Recipient 1st prize Greater Boston Regional Sci. Fair, 1968. Avocations: reading, travel. Office: Harvard Growth Strategies PO Box 9035 Newport Beach CA 92658

CARDIN, SUZETTE, nursing educator; b. Attleboro, Mass., Feb. 4, 1950; d. Wilfred W. and Vera E. (Broadbent) C.; m. Edward R. Barden, May 10, 1986; children: Luke Edward, Helen Elizabeth. Diploma, Children's Hosp. Sch. Nursing, Boston, 1970; BSN, Southeastern Mass. U., 1974; MS, U. Md., 1978; DNSc, UCLA, 1995. RN, Calif. Nursing instr. Fall River (Mass.) Diploma Sch. Nursing, 1974-76; staff nurse SICU Johns Hopkins Hosp., Balt., 1977-78; dir. critical care nursing Med. Ctr. Hosp. Vt., Burlington, 1978-83; nurse mgr. UCLA Med. Ctr., 1984-98, performance improvement coord., 1998-99; asst. adj. prof. UCLA Sch. Nursing, 1998—. Co-editor: Personnel Management in Critical Care Nursing, 1989, Critical Care Nursing, 1992, 96; mem. editl. bd. Dimensions of Critical Care Nursing, 1989—, Clin. Issues in Critical Care Nursing, 1989-92, AONE Leadership Perspectives, 1993-96. Recipient award Profl. Businesswomen, 1973, award Maxicare Ednl. & Rsch. Found., 1993, Nurse Mgr. Leadership Excellence award AONE, 1994. Fellow Am. Acad. Nursing, Am. Heart Assn. (coun. cardiovasc. nurses comms. com. 2001-03, advocacy com. 2003—); mem. AACN (chair various coms., co-editor CCRN newsletter 1985-86, cert. com. 1984-85, liaison AANN cert. bd. 1986-88, pres. Vt. chpt. 1979-81, program com. 1987-88, NTI com. 1987-88, leadership devel. workgroup 1999-2002), Children's Hosp. Alumnae Assn., Sigma Theta Tau (co-editor newsletter Gamma Tau chpt. 1987-89). Home: 2102 Farrell Ave Redondo Beach CA 90278-1819 E-mail: scardin@sonnet.ucla.edu.

CARDINAL, ROGER JOSEPH, tax specialist; b. Thompson, Conn., Apr. 25, 1950; s. Gerard O. and Adrienne (Lafleur) Cardinal; m. Diane McCormick; children: Jason, Daniel. BS in Acctg., U. Mass., Dartmouth, 1978; MS in Taxation, Bentley Coll., 1985. CPA, Mass. Sr. tax acct. Arthur Andersen & Co., Boston, 1978-81; mgr. corp. tax State St. Bank & Trust Co., Boston, 1981-90, v.p. product tax, 1990—2003; prin. Ernst & Young LLP, 2003—. Mem. IRS Info. Reporting Program Adv. Com., 1992-94, chmn. 1993; mem. Northea. U. MS in Taxation Program Adv. Coun., 1993—; speaker, lectr. Bank Tax Inst., N.Y.C., 1987—, Bank Adminstrn. Inst., Chgo., 1985—, Mass. Bankers Assn., Boston, 1983—; adj. assoc. prof. Bentley Coll., Waltham, Mass., 1986; mem. U. Mass. Dartmouth Acctg. and Fin. Adv. Coun., 1997—. Mem. AICPA, Mass. Soc. CPAs. Home: # 2334 500B Falls Blvd Quincy MA 02169 Office: Ernst & Young LLP 200 Clarendon St Boston MA 02116

CARDINALE, GERALD, state legislator; b. Bklyn., Feb. 27, 1934; s. Gaspar and Mary (Modica) C.; m. Carole Nina Petrullo, 1959; children: Marisa, Christine, Kara, Gary, Nicole. BS, St. John's U., 1955; DDS, NYU, 1959. Dentist, Ft. Lee, N.J., 1959—; asst. prof. dentistry Columbia U., N.Y.C., 1971-80; mayor Town of Demarest, N.J., 1974-79; mem. N.J. Gen. Assembly, Trenton, 1980-81, N.J. Senate, Trenton, 1982—. Minority whip N.J. Senate, 1985, asst. minority leader, 1987, dep. majority leader, 1994—. Trustee Dumont Cmty. Ctr. for Mental Health, 1976; vol. Bergen-Passaic unit for Retarded Citizens; mem. Demarest Planning Bd. Mem. ADA, Ft. Lee Athletic Club, Elks. Republican. Office: 350 Madison Ave Cresskill NJ 07626-1342*

CARDINALE, PHILIP JOHN, lawyer, educator; b. Bklyn., Dec. 14, 1948; s. Alerio A. and Louise D. Cardinale; m. Susan Marie Porreco, Aug. 19, 1972; children: Philip Jr., Cristina, Joseph. AB, Georgetown U., 1970, MA, 1971, JD, 1973. Bar: N.Y., U.S. Dist. Ct. (ea. dist.) N.Y. 1974. Asst. dist. atty. Suffolk County (N.Y.) Dist. Atty.'s Office, Riverhead, 1973-80; ptnr. Cardinale & Cardinale, Jamesport, NY, 1980—; assoc. adj. prof. Suffolk County C.C., Selden, NY, 1978—. Councilman Town of Riverhead, 1997-2001; trustee Riverhead Lib., 1996-2002. Mem. Rotary. Roman Catholic. Home: 785 Peconic Bay Blvd Riverhead NY 11901-5906 Office: Cardinale & Cardinale 1451 Main Rd Jamesport NY 11947

CARDINALI, ALBERT JOHN, lawyer; b. N.Y.C., Apr. 24, 1934; s. John and Ines (Clara) C.; m. June DuRose Seaman; children: Kathleen, John, Raymond, Kenneth, Scott, Jeffrey. BA, CCNY, 1955; LL.B., Columbia U., 1958; LL.M., NYU, 1965. Bar: N.Y. 1961. Asso. Thacher, Proffitt & Wood, N.Y.C., 1960-68, partner, 1969—. Served with AUS, 1958-60. Mem. ABA, N.Y. State Bar Assn., Assn. Bar City N.Y. Clubs: Shenorock Shore (Rye, N.Y.); University (N.Y.C.). E-mail: acardinali@tpwlaw.com.

CARDMAN, LAWRENCE SANTO, physics educator, research administrator; b. Mt. Vernon, N.Y., Oct. 7, 1944; s. Michael L. and Alice (Willis) C.; m. Helen-Andrea Fox; children: Andrew Lawrence, Michael Allan, Zena Maria. BA, Yale U., 1966, PhD in Physics, 1972. Instr. physics Yale U., New Haven, 1971—72, rsch. assoc., 1972; NAS/NRC postdoctoral fellow Nat. Bur. Stds., 1972—73; asst. prof. U. Ill., Urbana, 1973—78, assoc. prof., 1978—82, prof., 1982—95, adj. prof., 1995—, co-prin. investigator nuc. physics lab. Champaign, 1982—89, 1992; dep. assoc. dir. physics Continuous Electron Beam Accelerator Facility, Newport News, Va., 1993—96; assoc. dir. for physics Thomas Jefferson Nat. Accelerator Facility, Newport News, Va., 1996—; prof. U. Va., Charlottesville, 2002—. Vis. scientist Centre D'Etudes Nucleaire Saclay, France, 1980-81, Continuous Electron Beam Accelerator Facility, Newport News, Va., 1989-90; adj. prof. Coll. William and Mary, Williamsburg, Va., 1995—. Nat. Acad. Scis.-NRC Postdoctoral Rsch. fellow, 1972-73. Fellow Am. Phys. Soc.; mem. Sigma Xi. Avocations: woodworking, electronics, computers, cooking. E-mail: cardman@jlab.org.

CARDNO, DONALD BARRY, retired personnel director; b. Winnipeg, Manitoba, Can., Jan. 5, 1936; s. Frederick Noble and Pearl Lillian C.; m. Sallie Ann Waterman, Feb. 12, 1955; children: Scott G., Ross A. BA, Calif. State U., San Francisco, 1959, Calif. State U., Sacramento, 1964. Personnel analyst State of Calif., Sacramento, 1959-64; employee relations mgr. Calif. State Employees Assn., Sacramento, 1964-74; capt. sailing vessel "Peregrine", 1974-77; dir. personnel Oakland (Calif.) Housing Authority, 1977-80; dir. personnel and labor relations City of Vallejo (Calif.), 1980-88. Served with USMC, 1959. Mem. Internat. Personnel Mgmt. Assn., N. Calif. Mcpl. Personnel Mgrs. Group. Lodges: Rotary. Democrat. Avocations: sailing, flying. Home: San Miguel de Allende Guanajuato Mexico

CARDONA, MANUEL, physics educator; b. Barcelona, Catalonia, Spain, July 9, 1934; s. Juan and Angela (Castro) C.; m. Inge Hecht; children: Michael, Angela, Steven. Licenciado en Ciencias, U. Barcelona, 1955; DSc, U. Madrid, 1958; MSc, Harvard U., 1958, PhD, 1959; degree (hon.), Brown U.; Dr. (hon.), U. Autónoma de, Madrid, 1985, U. Autónom de Barcelona, 1985, U. Regensburg, Germany, 1994, Sherbrooke U., Can., 1994, U. La Sapienza, Roma, 1995, U. Toulouse, 1998, U. Thessaloniki, 2001, Masaryk U., Brno, 2002. Mem. tech. staff RCA Labs, Zurich, Switzerland, 1959-61, Princeton, N.J., 1961-64; assoc. prof. physics Brown U., Providence, 1964-66, prof. physics, 1966-71; dir. Max Planck Inst. for Solid State Rsch., Stuttgart, Germany, 1971-2000, emeritus, 2000—. Adj. prof. U. Stuttgart, 1973—, U. Konstanz, 1990—; lectr. Air New Zealand, 2001; mem. French Nat. Com. for Evaluation Sci. Rsch., 1999—2001. Editor-in-chief Solid State Comm., Oxford, Eng., 1992—; mem. bd. editors Physica Status Solidi, Berlin, 1971—; assoc. editor Phys. Rev. Letters, Upton, N.Y., 1989-92; editor Solid State Sci. Series Springer, 1975—; author: Modulation Spectroscopy, 1969, Fundamentals of Semiconductors, 1995, 3d edit., 2001; others; contbr. numerous articles to profl. jours. Recipient N. Monturiol medal, Govt. of Catalonia, 1984, Great Cross of Order of Alfonso X el Sabio, Spain, 1987, Principe de Asturias Found. award, 1988, J.M. Marci von Kronland medal, Czechoslovak Spectroscopic Soc., Prague, 1989, Sci. prize, Catalonian Sci. Found., 1990, Medaglia Teresiana, U. Pavia, Italy, 1992, Italgas prize, 1993, Max Planck Rsch. prize, 1994, Ernst Mach medal, Czech Phys. Soc., 1999, Sir Nevill Mott medal and prize, Inst. Physics, London, 2001; fellow, World Innovation Found., 2001. Fellow: Inst. of Physics (London), Am. Phys. Soc. (Frank Isakson prize 1984, John Wheatley award 1997); mem.: NAS of U.S. (ordinary mem.), Internat. Union Pure and Applied Physics (chmn. semicondrs. commn. 1996—2002), Royal Acad. Scis. of Spain (corr. mem.), Academia Europaea, Mex. Acad. Scis. (corr.), German Phys. Soc., European Phys. Soc., Acad. Scis. of Barcelona (corr. mem.). Lutheran. Office: Max Planck Inst Heisenbergstr 1 70569 Stuttgart Germany

CARDONA, RODOLFO, Spanish language and literature educator; b. San Jose, Costa Rica, Jan. 17, 1924; came to U.S., 1943, naturalized, 1950; s. Jose Ismael and Julia (Cooper) C.; m. Electra Ducas, Aug. 1, 1954; children: Eleni Maria, Alexander Xavier, Michael Anthony, Christopher Pericles. BA, La. State U., 1946; PhD, U. Wash., Seattle, 1953. Consul of Costa Rica, San Diego, 1943-44; asst. instr. fine arts and Spanish La. State U., 1946-47; asst. prof. Am. Inst. Fgn. Trade, Phoenix, 1947-48; instr. U. Wash., 1948-53; hon. consul Costa Rica, Seattle, 1948-53, asst. prof. Western Res. U., also hon. consul Cleve., 1953-56; asst. prof., then assoc. prof. Chatham Coll., Pitts., 1956-60; prof., then chmn. dept. Hispanic langs. U. Pitts., 1961-69; hon. consul Costa Rica, Pitts., 1956-69; prof. Spanish, chmn. dept. Spanish and Portuguese U. Tex., Austin, 1969-78; Univ. prof., dir. Univ. Profs. Program Boston U., 1978-88, prof. emeritus, 1991—. Resident dir. Internat. Inst., Madrid, 2000—. Author: Ramón: A Study of Gómez de la Serna and His Works, 1957; co-author: Visión del esperpento; editor: Novelistas españoles de hoy, 1959, La sombra de Benito Pérez Galdós, 1964, Doña Perfecta, 9th edit., 1984, Greguerias, 9th edit., 1997, La viuda blanca y negra by R. Gomez de la Serna, 1988, Galdós ante la literatura y la historia, 1998; Novelistas españoles de postguerra, 1977; co-editor: Teatro selecto de Galdós, 1973; founder, editor: Anales galdosianos; contbr. articles to profl. jours. Andrew Mellon postdoctoral fellow, 1960-61; grantee Am. Council Learned Socs., 1967-68; grantee Univ. Research Inst., 1973-74; fellow Nat. Endowment Humanities, 1973-74 Mem. Phi Beta Kappa, Phi Kappa Phi, Pi Mu Epsilon, Phi Sigma Iota. Mem. Eastern Orthodox Ch. Home: 17 Beethoven St Boston MA 02119-3108 also: Miguel Angel 8 28010 Madrid Spain E-mail: rcardona@iie.es.

CARDONE, BONNIE JEAN, freelance photojournalist; b. Chgo., Feb. 21, 1942; d. Frederick Paul and Beverly Jean Rittschof; m. David Frederick Cardone, June 9, 1963 (div. 1978); children: Pamela Susan, Michael David. BA, Mich. State U., 1963. Editorial asst. Mich. State Dental Assn. Jour., Lansing, 1963-64; asst. editor Nursing Home Adminstr. mag., Chgo., 1964-65, Skin Diver Mag., L.A., 1976-77, sr. editor, 1977-81, photographer, 1981—, exec. editor, 1981-97, editor, 1997-99; mystery novelist, 1999—. Author: Fireside Diver, 1993; co-author: Shipwrecks of Southern California, 1989. Named Woman Diver of Yr. Women's Scuba Assn., 1999; recipient Calif. Scuba Svc. award St. Brendan Corp., 1999; named to Women Diver's Hall of Fame, 2000, Women's Scuba Assn. Mem. Calif. Wreck Divers Club (Wreck Divers Hall of Fame, 2003), Hist. Diving Soc. (bd. dirs. 1997-2001). E-mail: bjcardone@hotmail.com.

CARDOSO, ANTHONY ANTONIO, artist, educator; b. Tampa, Fla., Sept. 13, 1930; s. Frank T. and Nancy (Mesina) C.; m. Martha Rodriguez, 1954; children: Michele Denise, Toni Lynn. BS in Art Edn., U. Tampa, 1954; BFA, Minn. Art Inst., 1965; MA, U. South Fla., 1975; PhD in Art, Elysion Coll. Calif., 1981. Art instr., head fine arts dept. Jefferson H.S., Tampa, 1952-67, Leto H.S., Tampa, 1967—; art and humanities supr. Hillsborough County Sch., Tampa, 1985—91. Bd. dirs., supr. art Hillsboro County Schs.; rep. Tampa Art Council; artist, 1952-87. One-man shows include Warren's Gallery, Tampa, 1974, 75, 76, Tampa Realist Gallery, Tampa, 1975; group shows include Rotunda Gallery, London, Eng., 1973, Raymon Duncan Galleries, Paris, France, 1973, Brussells (Belgium) Internat., 1973; represented in permanent collections Minn. Mus., St. Paul, Tampa Sports Authority Art Collection, Tampa Arts' Coun.; executed murals Tampa Sports Authority Stadium, 1972, Suncoast Credit Union Bldg., Tampa, 1975. Recipient Prix de Paris Art award Raymon Duncan Galleries, 1970, Salon of 50 States award Ligoa Duncan Gallery, NYC, 1970, Latham Found. Internat. Art award, 1964, XXII Bienniel Traveling award Smithsonian Instn., 1968-69, Purchaase award Minn. Mus., 1971, 1st award Fla. State Fair, 1967, Gold medal Accademia Italia, 1981-82, Medallion Merit, Internat. Parliament, Italy, 1984, Statue of Vittoria award for centro studi and richerche, Italy, 1988, Accademia D'Europa, Premio Palma D'Oro D' Europa, Italy, 1989—, El Prado Gallery, 1990—, Merit award Festival Arts Hillsborough County Tampa, 1994-2002, El Prado Gallery, Tampa, 1999-2003. Democrat. Roman Catholic. Office: El Prado Art Gallery 3208 W Nassau St Tampa FL 33607-5145

CARDOSO, DINORA CARIDAD, education educator; b. Havana, Cuba, June 12, 1959; arrived in U.S., 1968; d. Gaudencio and América Cardoso; m. Keith Lungwitz, May 25, 1996. BA, Calvin Coll., Mich., 1981; MA, U. of South Fla., 1985; PhD, U. of Tex., 1997. Spanish and english tchr. Bradenton Christian Sch., Fla., 1981—86; Spanish tchr. Sarasota HS, Fla., 1986—88; prof. Calvin Coll., Grand Rapids, Mich., 1988—92; asst. instr. U. of Tex., Austin, 1992—95; vis. prof. Spanish Tex. A&M, Corpus Christi, 1995—96; asst. instr. LA City Coll., 1997—98; asst. prof. spanish Tex. Luth. U., Seguin, 1998—2001, Pepperdine U., Malibu, Calif., 2001—. Translator: (poetry book) Austin International Poetry Festival, Voices of Land and Sea.; author: (edited volume) The Ties That Bind: Questioning Family Dynamics and Family Discourse in Hispanic Literature and Film., (journal) Cuaderno internacional de estudios hispánicos y lingüística I.I., 2001, (conf. procs.) Literatura, historia e identidad: Los discursos de la cultura hoy. Big sister Big Bros./Big Sisters, San Antonio, 1999—2001; choir mem. Woodland Hills Cmty. Ch., Calif., 2001, adult ministries bd., 2002. Recipient Edn. award, Clairol Mentor's Program, 1991; fellow, Pepperdine U., 2002—03; grantee Academic Devel. Grant, Tex. Luth. U., 1998, 1999, 2000, Dean's Rsch. Grant, Pepperdine U., 2002. Mem.: Am. Coun. for Tchg. of Fgn. Langs., MLA, Phi Kappa Phi. Office: Pepperdine U 24255 Pacific Coast Hwy Malibu CA 90263 Office Fax: 310-506-7518. E-mail: dinora.cardoso@pepperdine.edu.

CARDOZA, DENNIS, congressman; b. Atwater, Calif., Mar. 31, 1959; m. Kathleen McLoughlin; children: Joey, Brittany, Elaina. BA, U. Md., 1983. Intern Rep. Martin Frost, Washington; mem. Calif. Assembly, 1996—2002; congressman 18th Dist. Calif. U.S. Ho. Reps., 2003—, mem. agr. com., mem. com. on resources, mem. com. on sci. Mem. Atwater City Coun., 1984, Merced City Coun., 1994. Named Legis. of Yr., Calif. Sheriff's Assn., 2001, Calif. Sherrif's Assn., 2002, U. Calif., 2001, Small Bus. Roundtable, 2001, Small Bus. Assn., 2001. Democrat. Office: 503 Cannon House Office Bldg Washington DC 20515-0518

CARDOZIER, VIRGUS RAY, higher education educator; b. Montgomery, La., Apr. 2, 1923; s. James C. and Lelia M. C.; m. Nancy Pattison Fyfe, Dec. 29, 1955. BS, La. State U., 1947, MS, 1950; PhD, Ohio State U., 1952; postgrad., U. Mich., 1967. Adult edn. tchr. and supr. La. schs., 1947-50; edn. specialist in industry, 1952-57; assoc. prof. U. Tenn. Coll. Edn., Knoxville, 1957-60; prof., chmn. rural edn. U. Md., College Park, 1960-70, prof. higher edn., 1968-70; v.p. for acad. affairs U. Tex. of Permian Basin, Odessa, 1970-74, prof. higher edn. and behavioral sci., 1970-82, pres., 1974-82; sr. acad. policy adviser U. Tex. System, 1982-83; prof. higher edn. U. Tex., Austin, 1983-97, prof. emeritus, 1997—. Vis. prof. Pa. State U., 1968; vis. scholar UCLA, 1983; cons. in field. Author: American Higher Education: An International Perspective, 1987, Colleges and Universities in World War II, 1993, The Mobilization of the United States in World War II, 1995; co-author, editor: Important Lessons from Innovative Colleges and Universities, 1993, University of Texas-Permian Basin: A History, 1998; contbr. articles to profl. jours. Bd. dirs. Am. Assn. State Colls. and Univs., 1981-82. With U.S. Army, 1943-45, PTO. Named Outstanding Grad. Ohio State U. Centennial Celebration, 1969. Mem. Am. Sociol. Assn., Am. Assn. for Higher Edn., Acad. Polit. and Social Scis., Assn. for Study of Higher Edn., Nat. Assn. of Scholars, Phi Delta Kappa, Omicron Delta Kappa. Office: U Tex Coll Edn Austin TX 78712

CARDOZO, BENJAMIN MORDECAI, lawyer; b. N.Y.C., May 15, 1915; s. Sidney Benjamin and Eva Cecile (Mordecai) C.; m. Barbara Ruth Schaffer, Sept. 21, 1941; children: Enid Cardozo Lamen, Ellen Cardozo Sonsino. BA, Dartmouth Coll., 1937; postgrad., Columbia U., 1938; JD, NYU, 1941. Bar: N.Y. State bar 1942, U.S. Supreme Ct. bar 1947, Conn. bar 1954. Mem. staff Moreland Commn. Workmen's Compensation Investigation, N.Y. State, 1941, Office Alien Property, U.S. Dept. Justice, Washington, 1946-49; assoc. Cardozo & Nathan, N.Y.C., 1949-51, Cardozo & Cardozo, P.C., N.Y.C., 1952—; pvt. practice, N.Y.C. Mem. ABA, New York County Lawyers Assn., Assn. Bar City N.Y., Yale Club, Met. Club. Home: 325 E 79th St New York NY 10021-0954 Office: 488 Madison Ave Rm 1100 New York NY 10022-5702

CARDOZO, RICHARD NUNEZ, marketing, entrepreneurship and business educator; b. Mpls., Feb. 13, 1936; s. William Nunez and Miriam (Honig) C.; m. Arlene Rossen, June 29, 1959; children: Miriam, Rachel (dec.), Rebecca. AB,

Carleton Coll., 1956; MBA, Harvard U., 1959; PhD (Ford Found. fellow, Kaiser fellow), U. Minn., 1964. Asst. prof. bus. adminstrn. Harvard U., 1964-67; assoc. prof. mktg. U. Minn., 1967-71, prof., 1971—2000, Curtis L. Carlson chair in entrepreneurial studies, 1987-2000, prof. entrepreneurial studies, strategic mgmt., 2000—02, prof. emeritus, 2002—; dir. Ctr. for Exptl. Studies in Bus., 1969-73, chmn. dept. mktg., 1975-78; dir. Case Devel. Ctr., 1980-2000, Entrepreneurial Studies Ctr., 1987-2000. Dir. Nat. Presto Industries, Brownstone Distbg.; Fulbright lectr. Hebrew U., Jerusalem, 1980; vis. prof. bus. adminstrn. Harvard U., Grad. Sch. Bus., 1982-83; adj. prof. U. Miami, 2003—; cons. in field. Author: (with others) Problems in Marketing, 4th edit, 1968; Product Policy: Cases and Concepts, 1979; contbr. articles to profl. jours. Served with USAR, 1961. Fulbright fellow London Sch. Econ., 1956-57 Mem. Am. Mktg. Assn., AAAS, Product Devel. and Mgmt. Assn., Acad. Mgmt. Home: 1007 Pine Tree Trail Stillwater MN 55082-5918 also: 202A Sunrise Dr Key Biscayne FL 33149 E-mail: dickcardozo@aol.com.

CARDUCCI, JUDITH WEEKS BARKER, artist, former social worker; b. Norwood, Mass., Feb. 25, 1935; d. Harold O. and Catherine E. (Stone) Barker; m. Dewey J. Carducci, June 22, 1961; 1 child, David E.B. BA, U. Maine, 1956; MS, Columbia U., 1958. Coor. psychiatry and social work programs Cleve. VA Med. Ctr., Brecksville, Ohio, 1964-94; now artist, 1994—. Instr. art workshops, Cuyahoga Valley Art Ctr., Cuyahoga Falls, Ohio. Mag., Am. Artists Mag., 1997, 2001, Artist's Mag., 1998, 2000, book, The Best of Portrait Painting, 1998, Internat. Artist, 1999, 2000, Pastel Artist Internat., 1999, 2001, Pastel Jour., 1999, book, Beautiful Things, 2000, Paint! Figure & Portrait, 2000, juried art shows include, State Tchrs. Retirement Sys., 1997, 1998 (Purchase award, 1997), Pastel Soc. Am., Nat. Arts Club, Am. Artists Profl. League, Salmagundi Club, Hilton Head Art League, Grand Exhbn., Akron, Portrait Soc. Am., Reston, Va., Degas Pastel Soc., New Orleans, Pastel Soc. of the West Coast, Calif., Butler Inst. Am. Art, Youngstown, Ohio, KLH Fine Art Competition, Bennington (Vt.) Ctr. Fine Art, Cahoon Mus. Am. Art, Mass., Lexington (Ky.) Art League (Best of Show), Cin. Art Club, one-woman shows include Gallery 732, Akron Women's City Club, 1997, Hudson (Ohio) Galleries, 1997, Akron Jewish Cmty. Ctr., 1997, Moos Gallery, Western Res. Acad., Ohio, exhibited in group shows at Churski Gallery, Bath, Ohio, 1996, 1997, 1998, 1999, 2000, 2001, 2002, Weerhoff Gallery, Georgetown, Va. Represented in permanent collections Ohio Edn. Assn., State Tchrs. Retirement Sys., Rep. Sav. Bank, Hudson Libr. and Hist. Soc., Cuyahoga Valley Youth Ballet, Hudson C. of C., City of Hudson, Case-Barlow Hist. Farm, Cleve. State U., Hosp. for Spl. Surgery., N.Y.C., U. Maine Mus. Art. Recipient Best of Show nat. pastel competition award LaFond Galleries, Best of Show Portrait Soc. Am. Internat. Competition, 1999, Lexington Art League Nat. Show. Mem.: Hudson Soc. Artists (pres. 1996—97), Am. Artists Profl. League, Portrait Soc. Am. (charter), Akron Soc. Artists (Best of Show award), Degas Pastel Soc. (award of Excellence 1998, Patrons Purchase award 2001, Daler-Rowney award 2001), Pastel Soc. Am. (Art Times award, David B. Korostoff Purchase award, Merit award 2002), Cin. Art Club (Internat. Artist award), Salmagundi Club, Phi Kappa Phi, Phi Beta Kappa. Home: 197 Sunset Dr Hudson OH 44236-3347 E-mail: djcarducci@aol.com.

CARDUCCI, MICHAEL ANTHONY, oncologist, educator; b. Orlando, Fla., Aug. 4, 1961; s. Alexander Thomas and Millicent Jeanne (Worth) Carducci; m. Mary Katherine Bowling. AB, Georgetown U., 1983; MD, Wayne State U., 1988. Diplomate Nat. Bd. Med. Examiners, Am. Bd. Internal Medicine, Am. Bd. Med. Oncology. Resident in internal medicine U. Colo. Health Scis. Ctr., Denver, 1989-91, chief resident, 1991-92; sr. clin. fellow med. oncology Johns Hopkins U. Hosp., Balt., 1992-95, postdoctoral rsch. fellow, 1993-95, instr. oncology and urology, 1995-96, asst. prof. oncology and urology, 1996-2001, assoc. prof. oncology and urology, 2001—, dir. drug devel., 2001—. Mem. ACP, AACR, Am. Soc. Clin. Oncology (Young Investigators award 1995), Am. Urol. Assn. Fellow ACP; mem. Am. Assn. Cancer Rsch. Office: Johns Hopkins U IM89 Bunting-Blaustein 1650 Orleans St Baltimore MD 21231-1000

CARDUS, DAVID, physician; b. Barcelona, Aug. 6, 1922; arrived in U.S., 1957, naturalized, 1969; s. Jaume and Ferranda (Pascual) C.; m. Francesca Ribas, July 19, 1951; children: Hellena, Silvia, Bettina, David. BA, BS, U. Montpellier (France), 1942; MD magna cum laude, U. Barcelona, 1949, diploma in cardiology, 1956; D honoris causa, Autonomous U. Barcelona, 1993. French Govt. fellow dept. cardiology Hosp. Boucicaut and Hosp. de la Pitié, Paris, 1953-54; fellow U. Manchester, 1957; rsch. assoc. Lovelace Found., Albuquerque, 1957-60; NIH trainee Summer Inst. Math. for Life Scientists U. Mich., 1966; mem. active med. staff Inst. for Rehab. and Rsch. Baylor Coll. Medicine, Houston, from 1960, prof. dept. rehab., from 1969, prof. dept. physiology, from 1973, dir. Biomath. Program, 1966-69, dir. biomath. com. Sch. Grad. Studies, 1968-69, head exercise lab., from 1960, head cardiopulmonary lab., from 1969. Adj. prof. math. scis. Rice U., 1970—, adj. prof. stats., 1989—. Chmn. bd. dirs. Inst. Hispanic Culture, Houston; vice chmn. Gordon Conf. on Biomaths., 1970; pres. Am. Inst. Catalan Studies, 1980—. Recipient 1st prize for exhibit Am. Urol. Assn., 1967, 1st prize for sci. exhibit 5th Internat. Am. Cong. of Rehab. Medicine, 1968, Gold medal for demonstration use of computers and telecomm. in rehab. 6th Internat. Congress Phys. Medicine and Rehab., 1972, August Pi Sunyer prize Inst d' Estudis Catalans, 1968, Elisabeth and Sidney Licht award for sci. writing Am. Congress Phys. Med. and Rehab., 1980, Narcis Monturiol medal Generalitat de Catalunya, Spain, 1985, Catalunya Enfora prize Inst. Catalan de Cooperación Iberoamericana Fundación Bertran, 1987, Commendation of Isabel la Católica (Spain), 1980, Creu de Sant Jordi Generalitat de Catalunya, 1992, Joan d'Alos award Centre Cardiovascular Sant Jordi, Barcelona, Spain, 1996. Mem. Am. Coll. Cardiology, Am. Coll. Chest Physicians, Am. Coll. Sports Medicine, Am. Congress Rehab. Medicine, Am. Physiol. Soc., Am. Statis. Assn., Internat. Soc. for Gravitational Physiology (pres. 1993), Fedn. Am. Socs. Exptl. Biology, Royal Acad. Medicine Catalonia (hon.), Spanish Profls. in Am. (pres. 1984-85), N.Y. Acad. Scis., Societat Catalana Biologia, Royal Acad. Medicine Catalonia (hon.), Sigma Xi. Home: Spring, Tex. Died June 1, 2003; Barcelona, Catalonia.

CARDWELL, GUY ADAMS, retired language educator; b. Savannah, Ga., Nov. 14, 1905; s. Guy Adams and Ethel Mae (Parmalee) Cardwell; m. Margaret Randolph Bullitt, Dec. 21, 1935 (dec. Oct. 1991); children: Evelyn Bullit(dec.), Margaret Randolph, Ethel Parmele(dec.), Lucy; m. Blanche Butler Marshall, May 7, 1992 (dec. Apr. 1995). AB, U. N.C., 1926, PhD, 1936; AM, Harvard U., 1932. Instr., asst. prof. Wake Forest U., 1936-38; asst. prof., prof. Tulane U., 1938-45; prof., head English Dept. U. Md., 1945-49, Washington U., St. Louis, 1949-68; prof. SUNY, Albany, 1968-71. Vis. prof. Duke U., U. N.C., U. Vienna, U. Buenos Aires, Nat. U. Mex., Am. U., Paris, King's Coll., Cambridge U. Author: Twins of Genius, 1953, Der Amerikanische Roman, 1954, Charleston, S.C., Periodicals, 1960, The Man Who Was Mark Twain, 1991; editor: The Uncollected Poems of Henry Timrod, 1942, Readings From the Americas, 1947, Life on the Mississippi, 1968, Mississippi Writings, 1982, The Innocents Abroad; Roughing It, 1984; contbr. articles, poems, essays, stories to profl. jours., quars. Home: 1010 Waltham St Apt 546B Lexington MA 02421-8066

CARDWELL, HAROLD DOUGLAS, SR., retired rehabilitation specialist; b. Varnell, Ga., July 17, 1926; s. Arlie Amber and Hettie Ellen (Eledge) C.; m. Priscilla Dean Rumley, July 3, 1954; children: Harold Douglas, Jr., Ruth Ellen Cardwell-Landau. AA, Daytona Beach C.C., 1972; student, U. Fla., 1970; BA, Fla. Tech. U., 1974; postgrad., Clemson U., 1975. Registered landscape architect, Fla. Chem. operator Fercleve Chem. Corp., Oak Ridge, Tenn., 1945-46; draftsman C.M. Price Constrn. Co., Daytona Beach, Fla., 1947-48; bookkeeper, expediter W.A. Cardwell Constrn. Co., Gatlinburg, Tenn., 1948-49; office mgr., sales rep. J.H. Gordon Lumber Co., St. Augustine, Fla., 1949-51; asst. mgr. King Bros. Lumber Co., St. Augustine, 1951-56; pvt. practice landscape architect Port Orange, Fla., 1956-67; sr. rehab. specialist State of Fla. Divsn. of Blind Svcs., Daytona Beach, 1967-99, ret., 1999. Vice chmn. Daytona Beach Preservation Bd., 1987-98; adv. mem. task force Daytona Beach City Govt., 1987; vice chmn. Volusia County Hist. Commn., Deland, Fla., 1989-92; mem. adv. bd. Volusia County Hist. Preservation Bd., Deland, 1992-94; adv. mem. Flagler Centennial Com., Tallahassee, Fla., 1986; pres. Fla. Anthropol. Soc., Gainesville, 1988-89; chmn. Daytona Beach Preservation Bd., 1998—. Recipient Historian of Yr. award Volusia County Hist. Commn., 1988, Lazarus award for Preservation, Fla. Anthropol. Soc., 1988. Mem. Am. Hort. Therapy Assn. (registered hort. therapist, nat. treas. 1978-80), Fla. Nurserymen and Growers Assn. (bd. dirs. 1963-64, 68-69), Halifax Hist. Soc. (bd. dirs. 1974—), Fla. Hist. Soc., Lions (Pres.' award in leadership Port Orange/South Halifax club 1988). Democrat. Methodist. Avocations: history, anthropology, historical tools, pre-historic tools, writing, research. Home: 1343 Woodbine St Daytona Beach FL 32114-5740

CARDWELL, KATHLEEN R. music educator, pianist; b. Charleston, S.C., Dec. 30, 1950; d. Luther Kenneth and Annie Mae (Courtney) Rayner; m. J. Harry Cardwell, Dec. 22, 1978; 1 child, Adrian Lloyd. BA in piano performance, Bapt. Coll., Charleston, S.C., 1972; MusM in piano pedagogy, U. S.C., Columbia, 1980. Cert. profl. tchr. Music Tchrs. Nat. Assn. Concert artist/factory rep. Kawai Am. Corp., 1985—89; ind. piano instr. Charleston, SC, 1967—80, Atlanta, 1980—2000, Murphy, NC, 2000—; freelance ch. pianist/organist, 1965—2000; pianist Friendship Bapt. Ch., Murphy, NC, 2000—. Pres. Gwinnett Music Tchrs. Assn., Atlanta, 1993—95, Cherokee Music Tchrs. Assn., Atlanta, 1996—98; competition judge Ga. Music Tchrs. Assn., Nat. Fedn. of Music Tchrs., Am. Coll. of Musicians. Instr. women's self-def. Martial Hearts, Inc., Atlanta, 1997—2000, Friendship Bapt. Ch. Sch. of Tae Kwan Do, Murphy, NC, 2000—. Mem.: N.C. Music Tchrs. Assn., North Fulton Music Tchrs. Assn. (founder and pres. 1998—2000, piano scholarship established in name 2000). Avocations: horseback riding, martial arts.

CARDWELL, KENNETH HARVEY, architect, educator; b. Los Angeles, Feb. 15, 1920; s. Stephen William and Beatrice Viola (Duperrault) C.; m. Mary Elinor Sullivan, Dec. 30, 1946; children: Kenneth William, Mary Elizabeth, Ann Margaret, Catherine Buckley, Robert Stephen. AA, Occidental Coll.; AB, U. Calif.-Berkeley; postgrad., Stanford U. Lic. architect, Calif. Draftsman Thompsen & Wilson Architects, San Francisco, 1946-48, Michael Goodman, Architect, Berkeley, Calif., 1949; architect W.S. Wellington, Architect, Berkeley, 1950-59; prin. Kolbeck, Cardwell, Christopherson, Berkeley, 1960-66; prof. dept. arch. U. Calif.-Berkeley, 1950-82; prin. Kenneth H. Cardwell Architect, Berkeley, 1982—. Author: Bernard Maybeck, 1977. Pres. Civic Art Commn., Berkeley, 1963-65; mem. Bd. Adjustments, 1967-69, Alameda County Art Commn., 1969-72. Served to 1st lt. USAAF, 1941-45. Decorated D.F.C.; decorated Air medal with 3 oak leaf clusters; Rehman fellow, 1957; Graham fellow, 1961; recipient Berkeley citation U. Calif., 1982. Fellow: AIA; mem.: Berkeley Hist. Soc. (pres. 1997—2000), Alpha Rho Chi. Home and Office: 1210 Shattuck Ave Berkeley CA 94709-1413

CARDWELL, MICHAEL STEVEN, physician, lawyer; b. Salem, Ind., Apr. 3, 1954; s. Carlie and Gladys Cardwell; m. Dannette Marie Littell, Oct. 8, 1983; children: R. Roxanne, Michael S. II. BS, Purdue U., 1974; MD, Ind. U., 1978; MPH, St. Louis U., 1991; JD, U. Toledo, 1992; MBA, Bowling Green State U., 1997. Diplomate Am. Bd. Ob-Gyn, Am. Bd. Maternal-Fetal Medicine, Am. Bd. Diagnostic Sonography. Intern, resident U. Ill. St. Francis Hosp. Med. Ctr., Peoria, Ill., 1979—82; fellow Baylor Coll Medicine, Houston, 1982—84; dir. maternal-fetal medicine Rockford (Ill.) Meml. Hosp., 1984—86, Bapt. Hosp., Nashville, 1986—88, U. Mo., Columbia, 1988—90; with The Toledo Hosp., 1990—92; dir. Maternal Fetal Medicine St. Vincent Med. Ctr., Toledo, 1991—96; dir. maternal fetal medicine Riverside Hosp., 1996—2001. Advisor Mo. Low Birth Weight Program, Jefferson City, Mo., 1988—; physician advisor Planned Parenthood Ctrl. Mo., Columbia, 1988—90, Planned Parenthood, N.W. Ohio, 1990—; peer reviewer New Eng. Jour. Medicine, 1988—; mem. Perinatal Adv. Com., Jefferson City, 1989—90; asst. clin. prof. Meharry Med. Coll., Nashville, 1986—88; asst. prof. U. Mo., Columbia, 1988—90; mem. clin. faculty Med. Coll. Ohio, Toledo, 1990—; clin. instr. Ohio U. Sch. Osteopathy, 1993—. Contbr. articles to med. jours. Leader 4-H Club, Hardinsburg, Ind., 1968-72; asst. scoutmaster Boy Scouts Am., Livonia, Ind., 1970-72. Recipient teaching award Am. Acad. Family Practice, 1984. Fellow Am. Coll. Obstetricians and Gynecologists, Am. Coll. Preventive Medicine; mem. AMA, APHA, Soc. Perinatal Obstetricians, So. Med. Assn., Ohio Perinatal Assn., Alpha Omega Alpha. Republican. Mem. Christian Ch. (Disciples Of Christ). Avocations: travel, americana. Home: 7863 Brint Rd Sylvania OH 43560 Office: 3335 Meijer Dr Toledo OH 43617 Office Fax: 419-842-0792.

CARDWELL, NANCY LEE, editor, writer; b. Norfolk, Va., Apr. 2, 1947; d. Joseph Thomas Cardwell and Martha (Bailey) Underwood BA in Econs., Duke U., 1969; MS in Journalism, Columbia U., 1971. Copy editor Wall Street Jour., N.Y.C., 1971-73, reporter, 1973-76, editor fgn. dept. and Washington bur., 1977-80, night news editor, 1981-83, nat. news editor, 1983-87, asst. mng. editor, 1987-89; sr. editor Bus. Week mag., N.Y.C., 1989-91; editor Habitat World, Habitat for Humanity Internat., Americus, Ga., 1991-94; freelance editor/writer, 1994—. Episcopalian.

CARDWELL, SANDRA GAYLE BAVIDO, university admissions professional; b. Vinita, Okla., July 14, 1943; d. Amos Calvin Wilkins and Gretta Odell (Pool) Wilkins Kudlemyer; m. Phillip Patrick Bavido, Nov. 26, 1964 (div. Dec. 1973); 1 child, Phillip Patrick Bavido Jr.; m. Max Loyd Cardwell, Jan. 18, 1979 (div. Apr. 1992). AA, Tulsa Jr. Coll., 1973; BS cum laude, U. Tulsa, 1975. Sec. with various cos., 1966-69; sec. U.S. Dept. Fgn. Langs., West Point, N.Y., 1969-70; dep. ct. clk. civil div. Tulsa County Dist. Ct., Tulsa, 1975-76, dep. ct. clk. U.S. Passport Office, 1976-77; broker-assoc. Gordona Duca, Inc., Realtors, Tulsa, 1977-91; mem. admissions staff St. Francis Hosp., Tulsa, 1997—2000; univ. admissions profl. Oral Roberts U., Tulsa. Mem. Polit. Action Com., Tulsa, 1980—; vol. children's rights and child abuse legis. and statutes.; bd. of trustees Asbury United Meth. Ch., 2003—. Mem. AAUW, Tulsa Met. Bd. Realtors, Okla. Bd. Realtors, Tulsa Christian Women's Club (contact advisor 1988-89), Stonecroft Ministries (life publs. 1987-88), United Meth. Women (bd. dirs. 1986-87), Phi Theta Kappa (pres.), Pi Sigma Alpha (treas. 1974). Republican. Methodist. Avocations: piano, boating, gardening, reading, walking. Home: 3908 S St Louis Tulsa OK 74105-3317 Office: Oral Roberts U 7777 S Lewis Ave Tulsa OK 74171

CARDWELL, THOMAS AUGUSTA, III, research scientist, retired career officer, executive; b. Oklahoma City, July 25, 1943; s. Thomas Augusta Jr. and Hilda Ogreta (Box) C.; m. T.J. Hopkins, 1992; children: Jill Suzanne, Mark Christopher, Robert M. Hopkins, Kevin D. Hopkins. BBA, Tex. A&M U., 1965; MS, U. So. Calif., 1976; PhD, Pacific Western U., L.A., 1988; DLitt (hon.), London Inst. for Applied Rsch., 1993. Commd. 2d lt. USAF, 1965, advanced through grades to col., 1982; ret., 1993; F-4 fighter pilot 390th Tactical Fighter Squadron USAF, Da Nang Air Base, Republic of Vietnam, 1967; F-106 pilot 11th Fighter Interceptor Squadron USAF, Duluth, Minn., 1968-72, ASTRA dep. chief staff for sys. and logistics Washington, 1973-74, dir. acad. tng. and pubs. Interceptor Weapons Sch. Tyndall AFB, Fla., 1974-77, program and planning officer Washington, 1977-81, dep. comdr. ops. 323d Flying Tng. Wing Mather AFB, Calif., 1982-84; chief strategy div. Orgn. of Joint Chiefs of Staff, Washington, 1984-85; comdr. 601st Tactical Control Wing USAF, Semach Air Base, Germany, 1985-87; asst. dep. chief staff for plans and prog. U.S. Air Forces in Europe, Ramstein Air Base, Germany, 1987-88; dep. asst. chief staff and vice comdr. Air Force Ctr. for Studies and Analyses, Washington, 1988-90; comdr. Air Force Studies and Analyses Agy., Washington, 1990-93; sr. program mgr. joint and comml. programs Sci. Applications Internat. Corp., McLean, Va., 1993-95, divsn. mgr. command and control ops.; v.p., ops. mgr. C2 Ops., McLean, Va., 1995-96; v.p. internat. and comml. bus. devel. ADSI Ops., 1996-97; v.p. info. tech., internat. sys. ops. McLean, 1997—2002; v.p., dep. ops. mgr., divsn. mgr. internat. sys. ops, 2002—. Lectr. in field. Author: Command Structure for Theater Warfare, 1984, 2d edit., 1991, Air Land Combat -- An Organization for Joint Warfare, 1992, Global Reach -- Global Power, 1995; contbr. articles to profl. jours. Donor Washington Performing Arts Soc.; mem. Washington Opera Guild, Wolf Trap Assocs., Kennedy Ctr. Stars, Libr. Congress Assocs., Corcoran Gallery of Art, Air Mus. Britain (founder). Decorated Legion of Merit, DFC, Air Medal. Mem. Nat. Air and Space Soc. (founder), Studies and Analyses Assn., Air Force Assn., Red River Valley Fighter Pilot Assn., Air Force Mus., Mil. Ops. Rsch. Soc., Assn. Former Students Tex. A&M U., Air War Coll. Alumni Assn., Armed Forces Communication and Electronics Assn., Tex. State Soc. Washington, Tex. Breakfast Club of Washington, Assn. Old Crows, Am. Legion, VFW, Order of Daedalians (flight adj. 1978-80, vice flight capt. 1987-88), Mil. Order of World Wars. Republican. Episcopalian. Home: 3025 John Vaughan Rd Williamsburg VA 23185 Office: Sci Applications Internat Corp 1710 SAIC Dr Mc Lean VA 22102-3701 E-mail: cardwellt@saic.com.

CARE, TERRY, state legislator, lawyer; b. Oklahoma City, Jan. 12, 1947; m. Jenny Lockhart; 1 child, Diana. Student, Clark Coll., Vancouver, Wash., Foothill Coll., Los Altos, Calif.; BA in History, JD, U. N.Mex. Mem. Nev. Senate, Dist. 7, 1998—; mem. govt. affairs com., judiciary com., transp. com. Nev. Senate. Mem. Nev. State Coun. Sr. Citizens; chmn. Nev. State Dem. Party, 2001-03. Served with inf. U.S. Army, 1966-69. Mem. Nev. Bar Assn., Clark County Bar Assn., DAV, Am. Legion. Democrat. Address: 4371 Woodcrest Rd Las Vegas NV 89121-4946 Office: Ste 496 1785 E Sahara Ave Las Vegas NV 89104 E-mail: tcare@sen.state.nv.us.*

CAREK, DONALD J(OHN), child psychiatry educator; b. Sheboygan, Wis., Aug. 10, 1931; s. Peter and Rose (Gergisch) C.; m. Frances M. Schaefer, Jan. 28, 1956; children: Carla, Thomas, Therese, Peter, Mary Beth, Christopher MD, Marquette U., 1956. Diplomate Am. Bd. Psychiatry and Neurology (examiner in child psychiatry, psychiatry). Intern Walter Reed Army Hosp., 1956-57; resident U. Mich. Hosps., 1959-63; pediatrician Fort Meyer Dispensary, Arlington, Va., 1958-59; instr. psychiatry U. Mich., Ann Arbor, 1962-65, asst. prof., 1965-66; dir. day care Children's Psychiat. Hosp., Ann Arbor, 1965-66; assoc. prof. psychiatry and pediatrics Med. Coll. Wis., Milw., 1966-74, acting chmn. div. human behavior, 1970-73, prof. psychiatry, 1974-76; pres. med. staff Milw. Psychiat. Hosp., 1971-73; prof. psychiatry and pediatrics, chief youth divsn. Med. U. S.C., Charleston, 1976-96, emeritus prof. psychiatry, 1996—. Co-author: Guide to Psychotherapy, 1966; author: Principles of Child Psychotherapy, 1972; mem. editorial bd. Am. Jour. Child & Adolscent Psychiatry, 1988-93; contbr. articles to profl. jours. Bd. dirs. Cedarcrest Girls Residential Treatment Ctr., 1969-71. Capt. USAR, 1956-59. Fellow Am. Acad. Child Psychiatry (com. on adolescent psychiatry 1979-85, com. on psythotherapy 1986-90), Am. Psychiat. Assn., Am. Coll. Psychiatrists (membership com. 1991-94, 95-98); mem. AMA, Am. Orthopsychiatry Assn., AAAS, Am. Psychosomatic Soc., Soc. Profs. Child Psychiatry, S.C. Med. Assn. (mental health com. 1992-93), S.C. Dist. Cr. Am. Psychiat. Assn., Charleston County Med. Soc., S.C. State Bd. Med. Examiners (med. disciplinary commn. 1992-95), Alpha Omega Alpha, Alpha Sigma Nu, Best Doctors in America Southeast Region, 1995. Fellow Am. Acad. Child Psychiatry (life, com. on adolscent psychiatry 1979-85, com. on psychotherapy 1986-90), Am. Psychiat. Assn., Am. Coll. Psychiatrists (membership com. 1991-98); mem. AMA, AAAS, Am. Orthopsychiatry Assn., Am. Psychosomatic Soc., Soc. Profs. Child Psychiatry, S.C. Med. Assn. (mental health com. 1992-93), S.C. Dist. Cr. Am. Psychiat. Assn., Charleston County Med. Soc., S.C. State Bd. Med. Examiners (med. disciplinary commn. 1992-95), Alpha Omega Alpha, Alpha Sigma Nu. Roman Catholic. Home: 47 Sowell St Mount Pleasant SC 29464-2681 Office: Med Univ SC 171 Ashley Ave Charleston SC 29425-0001 E-mail: djfmcarek@aol.com.

CAREKLAS, JOHN ORESTES, secondary school educator; b. St. Louis, Mo., May 19, 1952; s. Orestes George and Bessie Careklas. BS in Edn., U. Mo., 1974; MEd, U. Mo., St. Louis, 1980; cert. in physics and math. tchg., U. Mo. Tchr. Ritenour H.S., Overland, Mo., 1974—. Greek Orthodox. Office: Ritenour HS 9100 St Charles Rock Rd Saint Louis MO 63114

CARELLA, J(OSEPH) DINO, printing company executive; b. Belleville, Ill., Oct. 26, 1955; m. Yan Zeng; 1 child, Bryan Anthony. AS in Bus., Waubonsee Community Coll., 1975; BS in Bus. Mktg., No. Ill. U., 1977. Pres., founder JDC Mktg. Internat., Geneva, Ill., 1977-84; mktg. dir. Acctg. Mgmt. Services, Aurora, Ill., 1984-85; founder, co-owner Orion Specialty Printing, Geneva, Ill., 1986—; founder, owner WacBac Bds., 2001—; pres., co-owner Nanning Grove Trading Co., Ltd., 2002—. Author: 30 Small Business Mistakes, 1981. Organizing and founding mem. Sugar Grove Chamber Commerce and Industry, 1991, bd. dirs., 1991-94, pres., 1992-94; coach Tri-Cities Soccer Assn. Mem. Printing Industries Am., Am. Entrepreneurs Assn., Internat. Traders Assn., Waubonsee Community Coll. Alumni Assn. (v.p. 1985-87, pres. 1987-89, founding bd. dirs. 1983), Phi Theta Kappa. Roman Catholic. Avocations: camping, fishing, sailing, soccer. Office: Orion Specialty Printing PO Box 361 Geneva IL 60134-0361 E-mail: OSP77@aol.com.

CAREN, ROBERT POSTON, aerospace company executive; b. Columbus, Ohio, Dec. 25, 1932; s. Robert James and Charlene (Poston) C.; m. Linda Ann Davis, Mar. 27, 1963; children: Christopher Davis, Michael Poston. BS, Ohio State U., 1953, MS, 1954, PhD, 1961. Sr. physicist N.Am. Aviation, Columbus, 1959-60; assoc. research scientist research and devel. div. Lockheed Missiles and Space Co., Inc., Palo Alto, Calif., 1962-63, research scientist, 1963-66, sr. mem. research lab., 1966-69, mgr. def. systems space systems div., 1969-70, mgr. infared tech. R & D div., 1970-71, research dir., 1972-76, chief engr., 1976-86, v.p. gen. mgr. R & D div., 1986—, corp. v.p. sci. and engring., 1987-98; chmn. LITEX Inc., 1998—2000. Bd. dirs. LITEX Corp., Superconducting Tech. Inc.; mem. U.S./Israel Sci. and Tech. Commn., 1997—. Contbr. articles to profl. jours.; patentee in field. Fellow AIAA, AAAS, AAS, Soc. Automotive Engrs.; mem. NAE, IEEE (sr.), Am. Def. Preparedness Assn. (past chmn. rsch. divsn.), Am. Phys. Soc., Aerospace Industries Assn. (past chmn. tech. and ops. coun.), Calif. Coun. on Sci. and Tech., Sigma Pi Sigma, Pi Mu Epsilon. Home: 6039 Gleneagles Cir San Jose CA 95138-2372 Office: 15260 Ventura Blvd Ste 2250 Sherman Oaks CA 91403-5338 E-mail: rcaren@sprynet.com.

CARESS, ROBERT SEYMOUR, personnel consultant; b. N.Y.C., Mar. 6, 1917; s. David C. and Dinah (Feldman) C.; m. Ruth Klein, Feb. 23, 1941; children: Barbara, Jane, Jeffrey. BS, CCNY, 1936; MA, NYU, 1938. V.p. Klein Inst., N.Y.C., 1946-61; pres. Caress, Gilhooly & Kestin, N.Y.C., 1961—. Contbr. articles to profl. jours. With USN, 1944-46. Avocation: clarinettist. Home: 115 E 9th St New York NY 10003-5414 Office: Caress Gilhooly Kestin Inc 276 5th Ave New York NY 10001-4509

CARESS, TIMOTHY CHARLES, lawyer; b. Indpls., June 30, 1969; s. John Hugh and Marianna (Milani) C.; m. Megan Theresa Ryan, Dec. 31, 1994. BA in Journalism, Ind. U., 1991, JD summa cum laude, 1994. Bar: Ind. 1994, U.S. Dist. Ct. (no. and so. dists.) Ind. 1994. Legal writing instr. Sch. of Law Ind. U., Indpls., 1995—96; assoc. Yosha Ladendorf Krahulik & Weddle, Indpls., 1994—96; ptnr. Cline Farrell Christie Lee & Caress, Indpls., 1996—. Mem. sect. Inadequate Security Litig. Group, Mpls., 1995—, Attys. Info. Exch. Group, 1998—, Elec. Accident Group, 1998—. Editor Ind. Law Rev., 1993-94; contbr. (civil summaries) The Ind. Lawyer, 1995—. Chmn. annual fund drive Chatard H.S., Indpls., 1995—; moot ct. judge Sch. of Law Ind. U., Indpls., 1994—. Named Forrest E. Jump scholar Howard County Bar Assn., 1992-94. Mem. ABA, ATLA, Ind. Trial Lawyers Assn., Ind. State Bar Assn. Office: Cline Farrell Christie Lee & Caress 951 N Delaware St Indianapolis IN 46202 E-mail: tim@cfcl-law.com.

CARET, ROBERT LAURENT, academic administrator; b. Biddeford, Maine, Oct. 7, 1947; s. Laurent J. and Anne (Santorsola) C.; m. Elizabeth Zoltan; children: Colin Ready, Katherine Ready, Katalyn Ford, Kellen Ford. BA, Suffolk U., 1969; PhD, U. N.H., 1974; DSc (hon.), Suffolk U., 1996; DHL (hon.), Nat. Hispanic U., 1997. Dean Towson (Md.) State U., Coll. Natural and Math. Scis., 1981-87; prof. chemistry Towson (Md.) State U., 1994—, assoc. v.p., 1985-86, exec. asst. to pres., 1986-87, provost, exec. v.p., 1987-95; pres. San Jose (Calif.) State U., 1995—2003, Towson (Md.) State U., 2003—. Author: (with A.S. Wingrove) Quimca Organica, 1984, Organic Chemistry, 1981, (with P. Plante) Myths and Realities in Higher Education Administration, 1990, (with K. Denniston and J.J. Topping) Principles and Applications of Organic and Biological Chemistry, 1995, 2d edit., 1997, Principles and Applications of Inorganic, Organic and Biological Chemistry, 1992, 3d edit., 2000, Foundations of Inorganic, Organic and Biological Chemistry, 1995; contbr. articles to profl. jours. Chmn. Baltimore County Higher Edn. Adv. Bd., Towson, 1989-1994; co-chmn. Balt. Sci. Fair/Kiwanis, Towson, 1983-88; bd. dirs. San Jose Repertory Theater, 1995-2001, bd. dirs. San Jose Opera, Calif. State U. Inst., 1995-2003. Recipient Employee Incentive award, State of Md., 1987, Outstanding Chemistry Tchr. award, Md. Inst. Chemists, 1971, Award for Excellence, Suffolk U. Gen. Alumni Assn., 1986, Tomas Rivera Leadership award, Nat. Hispanic U., 1999, Univ. Partnership award, 2002, Outstanding Pres. award, All Am. Football League, 2001; Albert W. Diniak fellow, U. N.H., 1972, Lester A. Pratt fellow, 1972. Mem. AAUP (Towson State U. chpt., exec. com. 1978-81, v.p. 1975-80, divsn. and dept. rep. 1975-80), Am. Assn. Higher Edn., Am. Assn. Univ. Adminstrs. (Md. membership rep. 1986-1989), EDUCOM (instl. rep. 1986-87), Am. Chem. Soc. (Chesapeake sect. alt. counselor

1979-87, exec. com. 1978-87, mem.-at-large 1978-79, com. mem. 1978-87), Am. Coun. Edn. (Leadership Commn., 2000, Internat. Commn., 1997), Am. Assn. State Colls. and Univs. (adv. bd. 1986—, Kellogg Leadership bd., state rep. 1989-1989, joint venture Silicon Valley bd. dirs. 1997-2003, co-chair econ. devel. team 1996-98, co-chair econ. prosperity coun. 1998-2000), Silicon Valley Mfg. Group (bd. dirs. 1988-2003), San Jose C. of C. (bd. dirs. 1995-2001, Leadershipin Excellence award 1999), Sigma Xi (Towson State U. chpt. pres. 1975-76), Sigma Zeta, Phi Beta Chi, Omicron Delta Kappa. Avocations: jogging, tae kwan do, cross country skiing, golf. Office: Towson Univ 8000 York Rd Towson MD 21252-0001 Office Fax: 410-704-3488.

CARETTI, RICHARD LOUIS, lawyer; b. Grosse Pointe, Mich., Dec. 17, 1953; s. Richard John and Doris Eleanor (Evans) C.; m. Lori Beth Resnick, Oct. 14, 1983; children: Katherine Lynn, Kristin Doris, Carly Makenna, Kendall Ricki. BA, Wayne State U., 1975; JD magna cum laude, Detroit Coll. Law, 1980. Bar: Mich. 1980, U.S. Dist. Ct. (ea dist.) Mich. 1980, U.S. Ct. Appeals (6th cir.) 1982, U.S. Supreme Ct. 1989. Assoc. and ptnr. Dickinson, Wright, Moon, Van Dusen & Freeman, Detroit, 1979-95; ptnr. Strobl, Cunningham, Caretty & Sharp, Bloomfield Hills, Mich., 1996—2002; judge Macomb County Cir. Ct., Mich., 2002—. Mem. ABA, Detroit Bar Assn., Def. Rsch. Inst., Mich. Def. Trial Counsel, Assn. Def. Trial Counsel, Macomb County Bar Assn., Delta Theta Phi. Clubs: Detroit Athletic (club open raquetball champion). Roman Catholic. Avocations: raquetball, softball, golf. E-mail: richard.caretti@co.macomb.mi.us.

CAREY, ALIDA LIVINGSTON, political scientist, writer, reporter; b. Phila., June 29, 1928; d. Henry Reginald and Margaret Howell (Bacon) C.; m. Isaac Kleinerman, Febr. 29, 1964 (div. Aug. 1967). Attended, Chatham (Va.) Hall Sch., 1947, Grad. Inst. of Internat. Studies, Geneva, Switzerland, 1949-50, U. Geneva; BA, Smith Coll., Northampton, Mass., 1951. Promotion mgr. The Reporter Mag., N.Y.C., 1951-52; rschr., writer Newsweek Mag., N.Y.C., 1952-54; rschr. Edward R. Murrow series "See It Now" CBS-TV, Paris, 1954; reporter, writer Agence France-Presse, Paris, 1955; nat. U.S. correspondent The Reporter Mag., N.Y.C., 1968; reporter, writer Forbes Mag., N.Y.C., 1969-70. Freelance writer various publs. including N.Y. Times Sunday Mag., Christian Sci. Monitor, The Guardian of London, The N.Am. Rev., 1955—. Contbr. numerous articles to profl. jours. and papers. Mem. Com. to Oppose Sale of Saint Bartholomew's Ch., Inc., N.Y., 1986-91, European Union Studies Ctr., CUNY; vol. Saint James Ch. Soup Kitchen, N.Y., 1986—. Mem. ACLU, French Inst./Alliance Francaise, Mcpl. Art Soc., Editl. Freelancers Assn., N.Y. Pub. Libr. Friends, N.Y. Coalition Profl. Women in Arts and Media, Inc., French-Am. Found. Avocations: music, theater, film, photography. Office: 200 E 74th St Apt 4H New York NY 10021-3606

CAREY, ANTHONY MORRIS, lawyer; b. Balt., May 31, 1935; s. Anthony Morris and Louise (Waterman) C.; m. Eleanor MacKey, Oct. 7, 1967. AB, Princeton U., 1957; LLB, Harvard U., 1963; MLA, Johns Hopkins U., 1970. Bar: Md. 1963, U.S. Dist. Ct. (fed. dist.) Md. 1965, U.S. Supreme Ct. 1968. Assoc. Venable, Baetjer & Howard, Balt., 1963-67, ptnr., 1972-79, 87—; former chmn. environ. dept., asst. atty. gen. State of Md., Balt., 1967-69; spl. asst. for energy affairs HUD, Washington, 1979-81; pres. Carey-Tidewater, Inc., Balt., 1981-86; regional dir., gen. counsel HEC Energy Corp., Balt., 1986-87. Former bd. dirs. Carey Machinery Supply Co., Inc., Balt.; former bd. dirs. Eberhard Faber, Inc; former exec. sec. Md. Bd. Ethics. Former trustee Citizen's Planning and Housing Assn.; former dir. Nat. Civic League, Denver, 1979-90; chmn. bd. trustees Balt. Sch. for the Arts Found., current chmn. emeritus bd. overseers; vice chmn. Lillie Carroll Jackson Mus.; trustee, sec. Robert Garrett Fund for Surg. Treatment of Children; mem. Balt. City Commn. on Resource Conservation and Recycling. With USAF, 1957-60. Mem. ABA, Md. State Bar Assn., Balt.City Bar Assn., Ivy Club, Hamilton St. Club. Democrat. Episcopalian. Avocations: skiing, hiking, reading. Office: Venable Baetjer & Howard 1800 Merc Bank & Trust Bldg 2 Hopkins Plz Ste 2100 Baltimore MD 21201-2982

CAREY, ARTHUR BERNARD, JR., editor, writer, columnist; b. Phila., May 16, 1950; s. Arthur Bernard and Mary Louise (Lynch) C.; m. Katherine Ann White, Apr. 14, 1973 (div. Feb. 1980); m. Tanya Marie Walters, July 17, 1982; 1 child, Edward Lynch AB, Princeton U, 1972; MS, Columbia U., 1975. Editor Fedn. Telephone Workers of Pa., Phila., 1972-74; reporter Bucks County Courier Times, Levittown, Pa., 1975-77, Phila. Inquirer, 1977—. Author: In Defense of Marriage, 1984, The United States of Incompetence, 1991; editor: That's Livin', 1984 Term trustee The Episcopal Acad., Merion, Pa., 1982-88, alumni trustee, 1990-93; mem. com. to nominate alumni trustees Princeton U., 1989-92. Recipient Edward J. Meeman Conservation award Scripps-Howard Found., 1977, Best Story of the Yr. award Nat. Conf. Sunday Mags., 1983, George Washington Honor medal Freedoms Found., 1984, Disting. Journalism award Epilepsy Found. Am., 1997, Robert Joplin Sci. Writers award Am. Orthopedic Foot and Ankle Soc., 1998; Robert E. Sherwood Traveling fellow Columbia U., 1975; best feature story Pa. Soc. Newspaper Editors, 1986, 91. Mem. Soc. Profl. Journalists (best newsfeature N.J. chpt. 1979) Democrat. Episcopalian. Avocations: running, weight lifting, carpentry, antique jeeps. Home: 928 Clover Hill Rd Wynnewood PA 19096-1631 Office: Phila Inquirer 400 N Broad St Philadelphia PA 19130-4099 E-mail: acarey@phillynews.com.

CAREY, AUDREY LANE, interior designer, motivational speaker, educator; b. Spokane, Wash., Sept. 26, 1936; d. Glen Howard and Beatrice M. (Olsen) L.; m. Willard Keith Carey, July 4, 1959; children: Natalie Kay, Robert Lane, Willard Arthur. BS with honors in Home Econs., Wash. State U., 1958; postgrad., U. Wash., 1958, Ea. Oreg. State Coll., 1960—. Tchr. high sch. home econs., Coulee City, Wash., 1958, Reardan, Wash., 1958-59; substitute tchr. LaGrande (Oreg.) Pub. Schs., 1960-65; nutrition instr. Ea. Oreg. State Coll., 1968-71; owner, mgr. Audrey Lane Carey Studio Interior Design, LaGrande, 1973-85. Spkr. in field. Vol. mgmt. tng. U. Colo., 1988, Nat. Vol. Conf., 1987, 88; family task force rep. 13 western states and Guam N.G. Assn. U.S., 1986-89; active St. Peter's Episcopal Ch., 1960—, sr. warden, 2002; youth activities dir. City LaGrande, 1959-60; v.p., bd. dirs. Grande Ronde Symphony, 1960-64; den mother Blue Mountain coun. Boy Scouts Am., 1970; leader 4-H Club, 1983; advisor EOSC Canterbury Club, 1961-65; campaign chmn. Union County, Sec. State, 1976, 80; pres. Union County Rep. Women, 1968; advisor Rainbow Girls, 1974-78; sponsor S.E. Asian Family, 1980-84; mem. Gov.'s Higher edn. Mission, 1985; Ea. Oreg. chmn. Employer Support of Guard and Res. Family Readiness Program, 1985; mem. bd. trustees Oreg. State Libr., 1986-94, chair, 1993-94; trustee Ea. Oreg. U., 2002—; creator family support program Nat. Guard families in U.S.; exec. com. Ea. Oreg. U. Bd. Trustees. Recipient Patrick Henry citation Nat. Guard Assn. U.S., 1994; Viola Coulter scholar, 1957. Mem. Am. Soc. Interior Designers, PEO (past pres., charter mem. 1962—), Kappa Alpha Theta (rush bd. chmn. 1960-84), Phi Kappa Phi, Pi Lambda Theta, Omicron Nu. Republican. Episcopalian.

CAREY, CATHERINE ANITA, artist, art educator; b. Washington, Sept. 27, 1960; d. Charles William Carey and Geraldine Elizabeth Sheil; m. Brian Elliot Slnofsky. Student, Corcoran Sch. Art, 1976—78; BFA, Va. Commonwealth U., 1982. Fine art painter, Escondido, 1982—; graphic artist Circuit City Stores, Inc., Richmond, Va., 1985—87, Circuit City stores, Inc., Walnut, Calif., 1987—89; art dir. W. Coast Cmty. Newspapers, Encinitas, Calif., 1989—91; freelance art dir. Elements Graphic Design, Escondido, 1991—; tchr. Art Methods and Materials Show, Pasadena, Calif., 1998—; workshop leader Golden Door, Escondido, 2001—; tchr., owner The Glass House Art Studio, Escondido, 2001—. Workshop leader Daler-Rowney Art Mfr., 1998—; workshop demonstration artist Savoir Faire, San Diego, 2000—. Exhibitions include Paintings from Giverny France, La Jolla, Calif., 2000, Paintings by Cathy Carey, Escondido, Calif., 2001, Impressions of Mission Trails, San Diego, 2002, Color Harmony and Contrast, Escondido, Calif., 2003, one-woman shows include Expressive Colors, Escondido Artists Gallery, 2003; author: The Philosophy of Color, 2003. Organizer art shows for children, Encinitas, 1990—91, San Diego, 1999—2000, 2000—01. Recipient Blue Ribbon, San Dieguito Art Club, 1990, Honorable Mention, San Diego Watercolor Soc., 2000, Escondido Art Assn., 2001. Master: Scripps Ranch Art Club (pres. 2000—01, founder 2000). Avocations: hiking, photography, swing dancing, gardening, cooking. Office: Glass House Studio 2048 Ridgecrest Pl Escondido CA 92029 Fax: 760-489-9149. E-mail: element@abac.com.

CAREY, CHARLES WILLIAM, JR., historian, educator; b. Norfolk, Va., June 16, 1951; s. Charles William and Jean (Sheil) Carey; m. Deborah Ann Lane, June 15, 1974; children: Billy, Beth, Jeff, Diana. BA in English, U. Va., 1973; MA in History, Va. Tech., 1995. Adj. instr. History Ctrl. Va. C.C., Lynchburg, 1995—. Adj. instr. History Lynchburg Coll., 1997—2001, Va. Tech., Blacksburg, 2003. Author: American Inventors, Entrepreneurs, and Business Visionaries, 2002, The Mexican War: "Mr. Polk's War", 2002, Emancipation Proclamation, 2000, George Washington Carver, 1999, Life Under Soviet Communism, 2003, Eugene V. Debs: Outspoken Labor Leader and Socialist, 2003; contbg. author: Ency. Am. Polit. History, 2001, Ency. Am. Scandal, 2001, Ency. of U.S. in Nineteenth Century, 2000, Ency. Nationalism, 2000, Am. Nat. Biography, 1999, Chronology of World Slavery, 1999, Macmillan Ency. World Slavery, 1998. Democrat. Roman Catholic. Avocation: canoeing. Home and Office: 1102 Biltmore Ave Lynchburg VA 24502

CAREY, CHASE, broadcast executive; BA, Colgate U., 1976; MBA, Harvard U., 1981. Sr. v.p. Columbia Pictures, 1981—88; exec. v.p. & CFO Fox Inc., 1988—92, COO, 1992—94; chmn. & CEO Fox TV Group, 1994—96; co-COO News Corp., 1997—2002. Office: Hughes Electronics Corp Communications PO Box 956 El Segundo CA 90245-0956*

CAREY, DEAN LAVERE, fruit canning company executive; b. Biglerville, Pa., Nov. 29, 1925; s. Earl E. and Ann Olivia (Newman) C.; m. Doris M. Dugan, July 21, 1949; children: Philip D., Juanita Ann. BS, U. Pitts., 1949. With Knouse Foods Corp., Inc., Peach Glen, Pa., 1949—, contr., 1955-59, asst. gen. mgr., 1960-62, gen. mgr., 1963-65, pres., 1966—, also dir. Dir. Blue Cross, Harrisburg, Pa.; chmn. Capital Blue Cross, Harrisburg. Served with USNR, 1944-46. Mem. Pa. Chamber Bus. and Industry (bd. dirs.). Clubs: Am. Legion, Masons, Shriners. Lutheran. Office: Knouse Foods Coop Inc 800 Peach Glen Idarille Rd Peach Glen PA 17375-0001

CAREY, DREW, actor; b. Cleve., May 23, 1958; Acting debut on The Tonight Show, 1991; actor: (film) Coneheads, 1993, (TV movies) Freaky Friday, 1995, Sex, Drugs and Freedom of Choice, 1998; (TV series) The Drew Carey Show, 1995—; host Whose Line Is It Anyway?, 1998—; actor, prodr.: Whose Line is it Anyway?, 1998, (film) The Big Tease, 1999; exec. prodr. (TV movie) Geppetto, 2000, TV guest appearances include The Torkelsons, 1991, Late Night with Rita Sever, 1998, Star Search, 1988, George Carlin Show, 1995, Lois & Clark: The New Adventures of Superman, 1993, Home Improvement, 1991, Ellen, 1994, Sabrina, the Teenage Witch, 1996, Weird Al Show, 1997, Dharma & Greg, 1997, Larry Sanders Show, 1992, star comedy spls. for Showtime: Full Frontal Comedy, Drew Carey, Human Cartoon; author: Dirty Jokes and Beer, 1997; host 25th Ann. Am. Music Awards, 1999. Recipient Editor's Choice award, TV Guide, 1999, People's Choice award for best actor in a new series, CableACE award.

CAREY, DUANE GENE (DIGGER), astronaut; b. St. Paul, Minn., Apr. 30, 1957; m. Cheryl Ann Tobritzhofer. BSc in Aerospace Engring. & Mechanics, U. Minn., 1981, MSc in Aerospace Engring., 1982. Commn. lt. USAF, 1981, advanced through grades to lt. col., 1998; stationed at Torrejon Air Base, Spain, 1988—91; student USAF Test Pilot Sch., Edwards AFB, Calif., 1991—92; experimental test pilot Edwards AFB, 1992—96; astronaut candidate NASA, Houston, 1996—98, with spacecraft sys./ops. branch, 1998—. Pilot STS-109 Hubble Space Telescope Svc. Mission, 2002. Mem.: Air Force Assn., Nat. Space Soc., Am. Motorcyclist Assn. Avocations: motorcycling, travel, racing motocross, camping, reading science fiction. Office: Astronaut Office NASA Johnson Space Center Houston TX 77058

CAREY, EDWARD JOHN, utility executive; b. N.Y.C., Jan. 16, 1944; s. Edward John and Mary Elizabeth (Hopkins) C.; m. Maureen A. McCullough, June 4, 1977; children: Christine, Caroline. BA, Fordham U., 1971. With N.Y. Central R.R., 1962-68; with Consol. Edison Co., N.Y.C., 1968-99; ret., 1999. Past bd. dirs. Salvation Army, Greater N.Y. Adv. Bd. Home: 17 Richmond Hls Irvington NY 10533-2301

CAREY, EDWARD JOHN, insurance company executive; b. Kansas City, Aug. 12, 1947; s. Joseph George and Nelda (Roy) C.; m. Dana Marie LeMay, Mar. 30, 1985; children: Bridget C., Edward J. Jr., William T. BS in Polit. Sci., Rockhurst Coll., 1973. Multi line claims adjuster Safeco Ins. Co., Kansas City, 1973-79; risk mgr. Dolphin Titan Internat., Houston, 1980-85, Pennzoil Co., Houston, 1985-89; ins. broker Arthur J. Gallagher Co., Houston, 1989-99; ptnr. John L. Wortham & Son LLP Ins., Houston, 1999—. Instr., assoc. risk mgmt. designation Risk and Ins. Mgmt. Soc., Houston, 1985-95. Charter mem., bd. dirs. Offshore Energy Ctr. Soc., Galveston, Tex., 1996; scout leader Boy Scouts Am., Houston, 1999. With USMC, 1966-70. Mem. Houston Club, Univ. Club, Lakeside Country Club. Roman Catholic. Avocations: golf, private pilot, collecting books on albrecht durer.

CAREY, EDWARD MARSHEL, JR., accounting company executive; b. Washington, Pa., June 12, 1942; s. Edward Marshel and Mildred Elizabeth (Bradley) Carey; m. Naomi Ruth Davis, June 1, 1964; children: Martha Ann, Mary Louise. BS in Bus. Adminstrn., Greenville (Ill.) Coll., 1964. Acct. GM Corp., Anderson, Ind., 1964—68, supr. acctg., 1968—70; staff acct. Carter, Kirlin & Merrill LLP, Indpls., 1970—74, ptnr., 1974—87, mng. ptnr., 1988—2000, tax ptnr., 2001—. Pres. CKM Mgmt., Inc., Indpls., 1985—. Mem.: AICPA (dir. Indpls. chpt. 1977—83, treas. 1978—79, pres. 1979—80), Inst. Internal Auditors (dir.), Am. Mgmt. Assn., Nat. Assn. Accts., Greenville Coll. Alumni Assn. (dir., treas. Ind. chpt. 1980—82), Indpls. Athletic Club. Republican. Methodist. Home: 215 Royal Oak Ct Zionsville IN 46077-1039 Office: Carter Kirlin & Merrill LLP CPAs 9102 N Meridian St Ste 555 Indianapolis IN 46260-1809

CAREY, ELEANOR MACKEY, lawyer, financial consultant; b. Providence, Jan. 31, 1942; d. Joseph A. and Margaret D. Mackey; m. Anthony M. Carey, Oct. 7, 1967. BA in Polit. Sci., Wellesley Coll., 1963; JD, U. Md., 1973. Bar: Md. 1973, U.S. Supreme Ct. 1980. Dep. atty. gen. Atty. Gen. Office of Md., Balt., 1979-87; on air legal reporter WJZ-TV Channel 13, Balt., 1987-88; pres. Multi Media Ednl. Tech., 1988-91; pvt. practice Balt., 1988-95; spl. counsel Gov. State of R.I., Providence, 1991-93; ptnr. Brand Lowell & Ryan, Washington, 1995-96; sr. counselor Gov. of Md., Annapolis, 1996-98; pres. Gov.'s Workforce Investment Bd., Balt., 1998—2003, Eleanor Carey & Assocs., 2003—. Candidate for Atty. Gen. of Md., 1986, 94. Recipient Kathleen Kennedy Townsend Women in Govt. Svc. award, 1999; named one of Warfield's Md.'s Top 100 Women, 1998, 2000, 02; inducted into Cir. of Excellence. E-mail: ellie.carey@verizon.com.

CAREY, ELLEN, artist; b. N.Y.C., June 18, 1952; BFA, Kansas City Art Inst., 1976; MFA, SUNY, Buffalo, 1978. Assoc. prof. of photography Hartford Art School, U. of Hartford, Hartford, CT. One woman shows include Concord Gallery, N.Y.C., 1985, Zone, Springfield, Mass., 1986, Real Art Ways, Hartford, Conn., 1986, Art City, N.Y.C., 1986, Simon Cerigo, N.Y.C., 1987, Internat. Ctr. of Photography, N.Y., 1987, John Good Gallery, N.Y.C., 1989, Schnider-Bluhm-Loeb Gallery, Chgo., 1990, Nat. Acad. of Scis., Washington, 1992, Jayne H. Baum Gallery, N.Y.C., 1992, 94, Gallery 954, Chgo., 1994, Nina Freudenheim Gallery, Buffalo, N.Y., 1995, Mus. Contemporary Photography, Chgo., 2002; exhibited in numerous group shows including Dayton (Ohio) Art Inst., 1993, The Dallas Mus. of Natural History, 1993, Rochester Mus. of Sci. Ctr., Rochester, 1993, L.A. Mus. of Natural History, Charles and Emma Frye Art Mus., Omniplex Sci. Ctr., Seattle, 1993, Fernback Mus. of Natural History, Atlanta, 1993, Calif. Acad. of Scis., 1993, Cleve. Mus. of Natural History, 1993, Tatischeff Gallery, N.Y.C., 1993, Mus. of Modern Art, 1994, U. N.C., Greensboro, 1993-94, Herter Gallery, U. Mass., Amherst, Mass., 1993-94, Palazoo de Exhbns., Rome, 1993-94, Art Inst. of Chgo., 1994, Caldwell (N.J.) Coll., Artspace, New Haven, Conn., 1994, Akron Art Mus., 1994, Ansel Adams Ctr. for Photography, San Francisco, 1994, Park Avenue Atrium, N.Y.C., 1994, Charter Oak Cultural Ctr., Hartford, 1995, Kingsborough Cmty. Coll. Art Gallery, Bklyn., 1995; represented in permanent collections Albright-Knox Art Gallery, Art Inst. of Chgo., Bell Atlantic, Bklyn. Mus. of Art, Chase Manhattan Bank, Coca Cola Corp., First Bank of Mpls., Fogg Mus., Harvard U., Internat. Ctr. of Photography, Mus. of Fine Arts, many others; contbr. articles to profl. jours. Office: Hartford Art School U of Hartford 200 Bloomfield Ave Hartford CT 06117-1545 Home: 155 Kenyon St Hartford CT 06105

CAREY, ERNESTINE GILBRETH (MRS. CHARLES E. CAREY), writer, lecturer; b. N.Y.C., Apr. 5, 1908; d. Frank Bunker and Lillian (Moller) Gilbreth; m. Charles Everett Carey, Sept. 13, 1930; children: Lillian Carey Barley, Charles Everett. BA, Smith Coll., 1929. Buyer R. H. Macy & Co., N.Y.C., 1930-44, James McCreery, N.Y.C., 1947-49. Carey writer and lectr. Book reviewer, 1949—, syndicated newspaper articles, 1951, (with Lillian Moller Gilbreth) (McElligott medallion Assn. Marquette U. Women 1966); author: Jumping Jupiter, 1952, Rings Around Us, 1956, Giddy Moment, 1958, Off and Away, 1998, Blubby, 1999, (with Frank B. Gilbreth, Jr.) Cheaper by the Dozen, 1949 (Prix Scarron French Internat. Humor award 1951, over 52 translations), Belles on Their Toes, 1951; contbg. author: Smith Voices—Selected Works by Smith College Women, 1990, 99; lifetime papers represented in collections at Smith Coll.; also mag. articles and book revs. Bd. dirs. Right to Read, Inc., 1968—, co-chmn., 1967; lay adv. com. Manhasset (N.Y.) Bd. Edn.; trustee Manhasset Pub. Libr., 1953-59, v.p., 1956-59; trustee Smith Coll., 1967-72; active in care-preservation and current student use of Frank B. and Lillian M. Gilbreth lifetime papers at Purdue U., Smith Coll. and internationally. Montgomery award Friends of Phoenix Pub. Libr., 1981, honored guest Ariz. Lib. Friends, 1994; recipient Internat. Mgmt. award: the Gilbreth Medal, Soc. for Advancement of Mgmt., 1996. Mem. Authors Guild Am. (life mem., mem. guild council 1955-60), PEN, North Shore Club, Smith Coll. Club (asst. chmn. scholarship com. L.I. chpt. 1950-59), Smith Coll. Club (vice chmn. scholarship com. Phoenix chpt.). Home: 701 W Herbert Ave # 115 Reedley CA 93654-3941

CAREY, FRANCIS JAMES, investment banker; b. Balt., Mar. 24, 1926; s. Francis James and Marjorie (Armstrong) C.; m. Emily Norris Large, June 8, 1956 (dec. Apr. 1997); children: Francis James III, Elizabeth P. Carey Boden, Henry Augustus, Emily Norris, Frances Carey MacMaster. Student, Princeton, 1943-44; AB, U. Pa., 1945, JD, 1949. Bar: Pa. 1950. Law sec. to justice Supreme Ct. Pa., 1950-51; with firm Reed Smith Shaw & McClay, Phila., 1951-87, counsel, 1987-92; chmn., CEO, bd. dirs. Carey Diversified LLC, N.Y.C., 1998-2000; vice chmn., chmn. exec. com., bd. dirs. W.P. Carey & Co. LLC, 2000—; pres., bd. dirs. W.P. Carey Internat. LLC, 2000—. Mem. faculty U. Pa., 1946-47; bd. mgrs., mem. exec. com. Western Savs. Bank, 1970-82; pres., bd. dirs. W.P. Carey & Co.Inc., Carey Fiduciary Advisors Inc., Corporate Property Assocs. 12 Inc. and affiliates, Carey Institutional Properties, Inc., 1987-98; pres., trustee W.P. Carey Found., 1990—; mem. bus. adv. com. Bus. Coun. for UN, 1994—; trustee Investment Program Assn., 1990-2000, chmn., 1998-2000; mem. Senatorial Trust, 1992—. Mem. Com. of Seventy, Phila., 1957-58; mem. Lower Gwynedd Twp. (Pa.) Planning Commn., 1962-75, sec., 1962-65; trustee Germantown Acad., Fort Washington, Pa., 1961—, pres., 1966-72; overseer Sch. Arts and Scis., U. Pa., 1983-90; mgr. Law Alumni Soc., U. Pa., 1962-66. Served to lt. USNR, 1943-45, PTO. Mem. ABA, Pa. Bar Assn. (chmn. real property, probate and trust law sect. 1966-67, chmn. conf. group to cooperate with Pa. Land Title Assn. 1970-77), Phila. Bar Assn. (chmn. com. on civil legislation 1962), Soc. Mayflower Descendants in State of N.Y., Fourth Street Club, St. Anthony Club (Phila.), Sunnybrook Golf Club (Plymouth Meeting, Pa.), Racquet & Tennis Club, The Brook Club, St. Anthony Club (N.Y.), Abenakee Club (Biddeford Pool, Maine), Biddeford Pool Yacht Club. Republican. Episcopalian. Home: 485 Lewis Ln Ambler PA 19002-5116 Office: WP Carey & Co LLC 50 Rockefeller Plz Fl 2 New York NY 10020-1607 E-mail: fcarey@wpcarey.com.

CAREY, GERALD JOHN, JR., retired research institute director emeritus, former air force officer; b. Bklyn., Oct. 1, 1930; s. Gerald John and Madeline (McNamara) C.; m. Joan Bennett, Apr. 24, 1954; children: Gerald John, III, Cathleen, John Kevin, Daniel. BS, U.S. Mil. Acad., 1952; MS in Aero. Engring, Tex. A&M U., 1961. Commd. 2d lt. USAF, 1952, advanced through grades to maj. gen., 1978; pilot trainee Victoria, Tex., 1953; flight instr. Laredo, Tex., 1954-56; asst. air attache Tokyo, 1958-61; aero. engr. Air Force Systems Command, Andrews AFB, Md., 1963-66; flight comdr. Seymour Johnson AFB, 1967; ops. officer Udorn, Thailand, 1969-70; wing comdr. 1st and 56th Tactical Fighter Wings, Tampa, Fla., 1973-75; asst. dep. chief of staff ops. Tactical Air Command Hdqrs., Langley AFB, Va., 1975-78; comdr. USAF Tactical Air Warfare Center, Eglin AFB, Fla., 1978-81; ret., 1981; emeritus assoc. dir. Rsch. Inst. Ga. Inst. Tech., Atlanta, 1981—. Mem. USAF Sci. Adv. Bd., 1995. Decorated Legion of Merit, D.S.M., D.F.C. with 2 oak leaf clusters. Mem. Air Forces Assn., Daedalians, Tau Beta Pi, Sigma Gamma Tau. Office: Ga Inst Tech Rsch Inst Atlanta GA 30332-0001

CAREY, HUGH L. lawyer, former governor; b. Bklyn. s. Dennis and Margaret C. Carey; m. Helen Owen Carey, Feb. 27, 1947 (dec. Mar. 1974); children: Alexandria, Christopher, Susan, Peter(dec.), Hugh(dec.), Michael, Marianne, Nancy, Helen, Paul, Kevin, Thomas;children: Donald, Bryan. JD, St. John's U. Mem. NY Ho. of Rep., 1960—74; dep. whip; gov. NY, 1974—82; exec. v.p. W.R. Grace & Co., 1987; of counsel Whitman & Ransom. Col. infantry N.Y.N.G., WWII. Decorated Bronze Star Medal, Croix de Guerre, Inf. Combat badge. Office: WR Grace & Co 919 18th St NW Ste 400 Washington DC 20006-5503 also: Whitman & Ransom 200 Park Ave Rm 2700 New York NY 10166-0005

CAREY, JAMES HENRY, banker; b. Elizabeth, N.J., May 22, 1932; s. Charles C. and Adelyne (Bilyeu) C.; m. Nancy Mershon Ferrenz, Aug. 14, 1954; children: Jane Meredith, Christopher James, George Mershon, David James. BA cum laude, Brown U., 1953; postgrad., Sch. Bus. Adminstrn., N.Y. U., 1956-59. With Chase Manhattan Bank, N.Y.C., 1955-86, asst. v.p., 1961-63, v.p., 1963-68, exec. v.p., 1976-86, Hambro Am. Bank & Trust Co., N.Y.C., 1968-69, pres., 1969-72, also bd. dirs.; pres., chmn. bd. First Empire Bank N.Y. (formerly Hambro Am. Bank & Trust Co.), N.Y.C., 1972-75; exec. v.p. Chase Manhattan Corp., N.Y.C., 1976-86; pres., CEO The Berkshire Bank N.Y., N.Y.C., 1989-92; mng. dir. Briarcliff Fin. Assocs., N.Y.C., 1992—. Bd. dirs. Midland Co., Airborne Freight Corp., S.G. Asset Mgmt. Variable Series Funds, Inc. Bd. dirs. The Rayburn Found., Am. Mus. Flyfishing, U.S. Com. for UNICEF. Lt. (j.g.) USNR, 1953-55. Mem. The Dorset (Vt.) Field Club, Mid Ocean Club (Bermuda), The Sky Club, Phi Beta Kappa, Delta Tau Delta. Episcopalian. Home: PO Box 859 Manchester VT 05254-0859 Office: Briarcliff Fin Assocs PO Box 859 Manchester VT 05254-0859 E-mail: jhcarey@together.net.

CAREY, JAMES ROBERT, educator; b. Jefferson, Iowa, Oct. 26, 1947; s. Robert Donald and Laverna Elizabeth Carey; children: Bryce, Ian, Meradith. BS, Iowa State U., 1973; MS, Iowa State University, 1975; PhD, U. Calif., Berkelely, 1980. Asst. prof. U. Calif., Davis, 1980, assoc. prof., 1987—92, prof., 1992—. Mem. Ctr. for the Econs. and Demography of Aging, U. Calif., Berkeley. Author: Applied Demography for Biologists, 1993, Longevity Records: Life Spans of Mammals, Birds, Amphibians, Reptiles and Birds, 2001, Longevity: The Biology and Demography of Life Span, 2002; contbr. articles to profl. jours. Staff sgt. U.S. Army Mountain Ranger Camp, 1967—69. Fellow: AAAS; mem.: Gerontol. Soc. Am., Population Assn. Am. Office: Univ Calif Dept Entomology Davis CA 95616 Office Fax: 530-752-1537. Personal E-mail: jrcarey@ucdavis.edu. Business E-Mail: jrcarey@ucdavis.edu.

CAREY, JOHN, lawyer, judge; b. Phila., June 11, 1924; s. Henry Reginald and Margaret Howell (Bacon) C.; m. Patricia F. Frank, Feb. 24, 1951; children: Henry Frank, John, Douglas, Jennifer Patricia. Grad., Milton Acad., 1942; BA, Yale U., 1947; LL.B., Harvard U., 1949; LL.M. in Internat. Law, N.Y.U., 1965; LL.D., U. W.I., 1985. Bar: Pa. 1950, N.Y. 1957. Practiced in, Phila., 1949-55; asst. dist. atty., 1952-54; cons. spl. com. fed. loyalty-security program Assn. Bar City N.Y., 1955-56; ptnr. Coudert Bros., 1961-87; justice N.Y. Supreme Ct., 1987; judge Westchester County Ct., White Plains, N.Y., 1988-94; mem. faculty NYU Law Sch., 1966-73; jud. hearing officer N.Y. State, 1995—. Author: UN Protection of Civil and Political Rights, 1970; editor: United Nations Law Reports, 1966—. Mem. Rye (N.Y.) City Coun., 1964-68, 72-74, mayor, 1974-82; alt. mem. UN Subcommn. on Prevention Discrimination and Protection of Minorities, 1966-82, 84-91, mem. 1983; alt. U.S. rep. UN Human Rights Commn., 1968; trustee Little Harbor Chapel, Portsmouth, N.H. Mem. ABA, N.Y. State Bar Assn., Assn. Bar City N.Y., Am. Soc. Internat. Law (v.p. 1987-88), Coun. on Fgn. Rels., Phi Beta Kappa. Home and Office: 860 Forest Ave Rye NY 10580-3145 Office: County Ct House White Plains NY 10601 E-mail: jncarey@westnet.com.

CAREY, JOHN, English language educator, literary critic; b. London, Apr. 5, 1934; s. Charles William and Winifred Ethel (Cook) C.; m. Gillian Mary Booth, Aug. 13, 1960; children: Leo, Thomas. BA, St. John's Coll., Oxford, Eng., 1957; PhD, Oxford U., 1960. Lectr. Christ Church Coll., Oxford, 1958-59; rsch. fellow Balliol Coll., Oxford, 1959-60; tutorial fellow Keble Coll., Oxford, 1960-64, St. John's Coll., 1964-75; Merton prof. English lit. Oxford U., 1976-2001. Prin. book reviewer Sunday Times, London, 1977—; hon. fellow St. John's Coll., Balliol Coll., Oxford, fellow British Acad., 1996. Author: Milton, 1969, The Violent Effigy, 1973, Thackeray: Prodigal Genius, 1977, John Donne: Life, Mind and Art, 1981, Original Copy: Selected Reviews and Journalism, 1987, The Faber Book of Reportage, 1987, The Intellectuals and the Masses, 1992, The Faber Book of Science, 1995, The Faber Book of Utopias, 1999, Pure Pleasure, 2000. Served to lt. Brit. Army, 1953-54. Fellow Royal Soc. Lit. Avocations: bee-keeping, gardening, swimming. Home: 57 Stapleton Rd Headington Oxford England Office: Merton Coll Oxford England

CAREY, JOHN ANDREW, investment company executive; b. Glendale, Calif., May 27, 1949; s. John Nelson and Dorothea Ruth (Bordwell) C.; m. Harriet Ruth Stolmeier, June 19, 1982; children: Julia Scott, Elizabeth Bordwell. BA, Columbia U., 1971; AM, Harvard U., 1972, PhD, 1979. Chartered fin. analyst. Teaching fellow Harvard U., Cambridge, Mass., 1973-78; sr. council rep. Yankelovich, Skelly & White, Stamford, Conn., 1977-79; analyst Pioneer Investment Mgmt., Inc., Boston, 1979-81, sr. analyst, 1981-83, v.p., 1983-98, sr. v.p., 1998—2002, exec. v.p., 2002—. V.p. Pioneer Scout, Inc., Boston, 1984-89, v.p. Pioneer Fund, 1987—, Pioneer Equity-Income Fund, 1992—, Pioneer Income Fund, 1994-96, Pioneer Variable Contract Trust, 1995—. Author: Judicial Reform in France before the Revolution of 1789, 1981. Treas. Newton Hist. Soc., Mass., 1983—87, Musicians of the Old Post Rd, 1998—; trustee Longy Sch. Music, 2001—. Mem.: Boston Security Analysts Soc., Assn. for Investment Mgmt. and Rsch., Boston Athenaeum, Harvard Club of Boston. Republican. Episcopalian. Home: 14 Yarmouth Rd Wellesley Hills MA 02481-1249 Office: Pioneer Investment Mgmt Inc 60 State St Fl 18 Boston MA 02109-1800

CAREY, JOHN CLAYTON, pediatrician, medical geneticist; b. Balt., 1946; MD, Georgetown U., 1972. Diplomate Am. Bd. Med. Genetics, Am. Bd. Pediatrics. Prof. pediatrics U. Utah Med. Ctr., Salt Lake City. Co-author: Medical Genetics, 1988, 3d edit., 2003, Care of the Child with Trisomy 18/13, 1996, rev. edit. 2000. Softly Written, Softly Spoken, 2002; editor-in-chief Am. Jour. Med. Genetics; contbr. over 190 articles to profl. jours. Med. advisor Support Orgn. Trisomy 18, 13 and Related Disorders, Utah Birth Defects Network, Pregnancy Risk Line. Office: U Utah Med Ctr Pediatrics 2C412 SOM 50 N Medical Dr Salt Lake City UT 84132-0001 E-mail: john.carey@hsc.utah.edu.

CAREY, JOHN EDWARD, information services executive; b. Albany, N.Y., Sept. 21, 1949; s. John Edward and Lillian Rose (Murdock) C.; m. Nicolette Anne Yianilos, Oct. 26, 1974; children: Theodore, Anna. BA, Tulane U., 1971. Pres. FOI Svcs., Inc., Rockville, Md., 1976-95, Gaithersburg, Md., 1995—. Office: FOI Svcs Inc 11 Firstfield Rd Gaithersburg MD 20878-1704 E-mail: jcarey@foiservices.com.

CAREY, JOHN JESSE, academic administrator, religion educator; b. Ft. Wayne, Ind., Oct. 13, 1931; s. Edmund Othmar and Frieda Louise (Jesse) C.; m. Sally Ann Stanback, Mar. 30, 1954 (div. Dec. 1967); children: Sarah, Mary Lynn, Beth; m. Mary Charlotte McCall, May 22, 1969; children: Joanna, Jessica. AB, Duke U., 1953, PhD, 1965; BD, Yale U., 1956, MST, 1957. Ordained to ministry Presby. Ch. Chaplain Catawba Coll., Salisbury, N.C., 1957-60; univ. chaplain Fla. State U., Tallahassee, 1960-62, assoc. dean students, 1962-63, asst. dean Grad. Sch., 1965-66, dean of students, 1966-67, v.p. student affairs, 1967-68, prof. religion, 1968-86; pres. Warren Wilson Coll., Swannanoa, N.C., 1986-88; Pendergrass prof. religion Fla. So. Coll., Lakeland, 1988-89; Wallace M. Alston prof. Bible and religion Agnes Scott Coll., Decatur, Ga., 1989-91, emeritus prof. religious studies, 1999—. Author: Carlyle Marney: A Pilgrim's Progress, 1980; editor: The Death of God Debate, 1967, Tillich Studies, 1975, Kairos and Logos, 1978, Theonomy and Autonomy, 1984, Doing and Being, 1988, The Sexuality Debate in North Am. Chs. 1988-95, 1995. Recipient Standard Oil Co. Excellence in Teaching award, Fla. State U., 1973, R.R. Oglesby Disting. Service award, Fla. State U., 1980. Mem. Soc. for Values in Higher Edn. Clubs: Yale (N.Y.C.). E-mail: Jessecarey@aol.com.

CAREY, JOHN LEO, lawyer; b. Morris, Ill., Oct. 1, 1920; s. John Leo and Loretta (Conley) C.; m. Rhea M. White, July 15, 1950; children: John Leo III, Daniel Hobart, Deborah M. BS, St. Ambrose Coll., Davenport, Ia., 1941; JD, Georgetown U., 1947, LLM, 1949. Bar: Ind. 1954, DC 1947, Ill. 1947. Legislative asst. Sen. Scott W. Lucas, 1945-47; spl. atty. IRS, Washington, 1947-54; since practiced in South Bend; ptnr. Barnes & Thornburg, 1954—, now of counsel; law prof. taxation Notre Dame Law Sch., 1968-90. Trustee LaLumiere Prep. Sch., Laporte, Ind. Served with USAAF, World War II; to lt. col. USAF, Korean War. Decorated D.F.C., Air medal. Mem. ABA (bd. govs. 1986-89, treas. 1990-93), Ind. Bar Assn. (pres. 1976-77), St. Joseph County Bar Assn., Signal Point Country Club, Quail Valley City Club. Home: # 114 1250 W Southwinds Blvd Vero Beach FL 32963 Office: 600 1st Source Bank Ctr 100 N Michigan St South Bend IN 46601-1630

CAREY, JOHN PATRICK, III, lawyer; b. N.Y.C., Oct. 31, 1955; s. John Patrick Jr. and Emily Carey; m. Jane Alden Hopkins, 1980; children: William Nelson, Timothy Jarvis, John Patrick IV. AB, Georgetown U., 1978, JD, 1983. Bar: N.Y. 1984, D.C. 1985. Asst. to pres. Georgetown U., Washington, 1978-80; law clk. to Hon. June L. Green U.S. Dist Ct. for D.C., Washington, 1983-85; assoc., of coun. Paul, Hastings, Janofsky & Walker, Washington, 1985-93; chief counsel Office of Presdl. Pers., The White House, Washington, 1993; gen. counsel Fed. Emergency Mgmt. Agy., Washington, 1993-97; sr. exec. v.p., regulatory counsel MBNA Am. Bank, N.A., Wilmington, Del., 1997—; mem. adv. coun. IRS, Washington, 1998-2000. V.p., pres., trustee South Kent (Conn.) Sch. Corp., 1991-98, 99—. Assoc. counsel pers. office Office of Presdl. Transition, Washington, 1992-93; bd. govs. Georgetown U., 1988-92; trustee Wilmington Music Sch., 1997-98; dir. Russian Ballet Theatre of Del., 1997-98; bd. dirs. Georgetown U. Child Devel. Ctr., 2000—; Del. Symphony Orch., 2000—. Georgetown U. Law Ctr. law fellow, 1982-83. Mem. ABA, D.C. Bar, Georgetown U. Alumni Assn. (senator 1992—). Democrat. Roman Catholic. Office: MBNA Am Bank NA 1100 N King St Wilmington DE 19884-0001

CAREY, KATHLEEN, economist; b. Syracuse, NY, Aug. 26, 1949; d. James Francis and Mary Collar Carey; m. Steven Edgar Ferrey, June 25, 1988; children: Cameron Alec Ferrey, Curran Andrew Ferrey. BA, LeMoyne Coll., Syracuse, NY, 1971; MAT, Harvard U, Cambridge, MA, 1972; PhD, Boston U, Boston, MA, 1987. Math. tchr. Cambridge Pub. Sch., Cambridge, Mass., 1972—80; asst. prof. Wellesley Coll., Wellesley, Mass., 1986—89; econ. VA Mgmt. Sci. Group, Bedford, Mass., 1989—; asst. prof. Boston U Sch. of Pub. Health, Boston, 1999—. Author: (jour. articles) indsl.,agrl., health svc. and social econ. Avocation: piano. Office: VA Mgmt Sci Group 200 Springs Rd Bedford MA 01730

CAREY, KATHRYN ANN, foundation administrator, editor, consultant; b. LA, Oct. 18, 1949; d. Frank Randall and Evelyn Mae (Walmsley) Carey; m. Richard Kenneth Sundt, Dec. 28, 1980. BA in Am. Studies with honors, Calif. State U., L.A., 1971; postgrad., Georgetown U., Boston Coll. Cert. comml. pilot instrument rated, advanced cert. corp. cmty. rels. Tutor Calif. Dept. Vocat. Rehab., L.A., 1970; tchg. asst. U. So. Calif., L.A., 1974-75, UCLA, 1974-75; claims adjuster Auto Club So. Calif., San Gabriel, 1971-73; corp. pub. rels. cons. Carnation Co., L.A., 1973-78; cons., adminstr. Carnation Cmty. Svc. Award Program, 1973-78; pub. rels. cons. Vivitar Corp., 1978; sr. advt. asst. Am. Honda Motor Co., Torrance, Calif., 1978-84; exec. dir. Am. Honda Found., 1984—, Honda Philanthropy, Office of the Ams., 1996—. Adminstr. Honda Involvement Program; mgr. Honda Dealer Advt. Assns., 1978—84; cons. in field. Asst. editor: Friskies Rsch. Digest, 1973—78; editor: Vivitar Voice, 1978, Honda Views, 1978—84, Found. Focus, 1984—, Instrument Pilots' Survival Manual (Rod Machado), 1991; contbg. editor: Newsbriefs and Momentum, 1978—. Recipient Silver award, Wilmer Shields Rich award, Coun. Founds. Excellence in Comm., 1995, 2003, Gold award, 1997, 2001, award of Excellence, Soc. Tech. Comm., 1995, Merit award, 1996, 1997, 1999, 2001, Apex award, Excellence in Comm., 1997—2001, 2003; scholar, Calif. Life Scholarship Found., 1967. Mem.: Affinity Group on Japanese Philanthropy (pres.), Coun. on Founds., So. Calif. Assn. Philanthropy, Pub. Rels. Soc. Am., Advt. Club L.A., Calif. Advs. Nursing Home Reform (officer, sec./treas., treas. bd. dirs. 1997—), Elsa Wild Animal Appeal, Humane Soc. U.S., Am. Humane Assn., Ocicats Internat., Greenpeace, L.A. Soc. Cruetly to Animals, Aircraft Owners and Pilots Assn., Am. Quarter Horse Assn., Ninety-Nines. Office: Am Honda Found 1919 Torrance Blvd Torrance CA 90501-2722 E-mail: kathryn_carey@ahm.honda.com.

CAREY, KEITH GRANT, editor, publishing executive; b. Oakland, Calif., Jan. 13, 1958; s. Richard William and Juanita May (Yost) C.; m. Lois Lynn Schuricht, Oct. 15, 1994. BA in History with honors, San Jose State U., 1980. Tchr. Chaparral H.S., Las Vegas, 1981-82; pers. mgr. Grecian Health Spa, Palo Alto, Calif., 1982-83, Palos Verdes Health Spa, San Pedro, Calif., 1983-86; prodn. mgr., mng. editor U.S. Ctr. World Mission, Pasadena, Calif., 1986—. Mng. editor Global Prayer Digest, 1992—. Avocations: cooking, jogging. Office: USCWM Global Prayer Digest 1605 E Elizabeth St Pasadena CA 91104-2721 E-mail: KeithCarey@uscwm.org.

CAREY, LOIS J. psychotherapist; b. Pitts., Aug. 7, 1927; d. Robert Gray Doeblin and Thelma (Pettit) Harris; m. David Carey, June 22, 1947; children: David, Norman, Arlene Keiser. BS, Columbia U., 1973, MS, 1974. Diplomate Am. Bd. Examiners, Am. Bd. Clin. Social Work. Pvt. practice, specializing in sand play therapy, Upper Grandview, N.Y., 1980—; dir. Ctr. for Sandplay Studies, East Coast Sandplay Assn. Workshop leader in U.S., Can., South Africa, Greece, Holland, Ireland; adj. prof. play therapy Hofstra Univ., 2003—. Author: Sandplay Therapy with Children and Families, 1999; co-editor: School-Based Play Therapy, Family Play Therapy; contbr. articles to profl. jours. Recipient Lifetime Achievement award N.Y. Assn. Marriage and Family Therapy, 1999. Mem. NASW, Am. Assn. Marriage and Family Therapy (past pres. West/Mid-Hudson), Assn. for Play Therapy (pres. N.Y. br.). Avocations: clay, writing. Home: 254 S Boulevard Nyack NY 10960-4125 E-mail: ljcarey@spyral.net.

CAREY, MARGOT BECKMANN, fundraiser; b. Cin., Feb. 22, 1960; d. Emil Hans and Beatrice Christina (Sciarra) Beckmann; m. David Mitchell Carey, Nov. 28, 1981 (dec. Oct. 2001); children: Caydan, Spencer. BS, Skidmore Coll., 1983; postgrad., Ctr. on Philanthropy, Indpls. Program and devel. dir. Bethesda Episcopal Ch., Saratoga Springs, N.Y., 1989—. Trustee Bethesda Vestry, Saratoga Springs, Home of the Good Shepherd, Saratoga Springs; mem. Flower and Fruit Mission, Saratoga Springs, 1987, Caroline St. Home Sch. Assn., Saratoga Springs, 1995, Bethesda Altar Guild, Saratoga Springs, 1985; den mother cub scouts Boy Scouts Am., Caroline St. Sch., 1998-99; mem. Skidmore Coll., Saratoga Springs, 1986-99. Mem. Assn. Fundraising Prodls., Women in Devel. in the N.E. N.Y. Republican. Episcopalian. Avocations: tennis, aerobic exercise, swimming, sailing, reading. Office: Bethesda Episcopal Ch 41 Washington St Saratoga Springs NY 12866-4116

CAREY, MARTIN CONRAD, gastroenterologist, molecular biophysicist, educator, medical geneticist; b. Clonmel, Ireland, June 18, 1939; came to U.S., 1967; s. John Joseph and Alice (Broderick) C.; m. Garcia Antonieta Fernandez, July 1, 1972 (div. 1987); children: Julian Albert, Dermot Martin. MB, BCh BAO with 1st class honors, Nat. U. Ireland, 1962, MD, 1981, DSc, 1984; AM (hon.), Harvard U., 1989; LLD (hon.), Nat. U. Ireland, 1992. Intern St. Vincent's Hosp., Dublin, Ireland, 1962-63, resident, 1965-67, Nat. Maternity Hosp., Dublin, Ireland, 1963, St. Luke's Hosp., Dublin, Ireland, 1964, Queen Charlotte's Hosp., London, 1964; asst. prof. medicine Boston U. Sch. Medicine, 1973-75, Harvard U. Med. Sch., Boston, 1975-79, assoc. prof., 1979-88, Lawrence J. Henderson assoc. prof. health sci. & Tech., 1979-88, 88-91, faculty mem. grad. sch. arts & scis., 1983—, assoc. mem. dept. cellular & molecular physiology, 1983—, prof. medicine, 1988—, prof. health sci. & tech., 1991—. Mem. staff Brigham and Women's Hosp., Boston, 1975—; McIlrath guest prof. Royal Prince Alfres Hosp., U. Sydney, Australia, 1987; cons. Gipharmex S.A., Milan, 1984—87, Dow Chem. Co., Midland, Mich., 1984—87, Merix, Inc., Needham, 1986—96, Oculon, Cambridge, 1987—95, Ciba-Giegy, Summit, NJ, 1988—93, Labs. Fournier, Dijon-Diax, 1992—93, Hoechst AG (now Aventis), Frankfurt, 1993—2002, GelTex, Inc., 1993—, Merck & Co., 2001—, Dublin (Ireland) Molecular Medicine Centre, 2001—, Mpex Biosci., Inc., San Diego, 2002—, Chrysalis Biotech., Inc., Galveston, Tex., 2003—. Author: Bile Salts and Gallstones, 1974, Hepatic Excretory Function, 1975; assoc. editor Jour. Lipid Rsch., 1978-81; mem. editl. bd. Am. Jour. Physiology, 1976-81, Gastroenterology, 1983-88, Hepatology, 1981-84; contbr. articles to profl. jours.; patentee in field. Recipient Acad. Career Devel. award NIH, 1976, Merit award, 1986, Adolf Windaus prize Falk Found., 1984, Huddinge Sikhuis medal Karolinska Inst., Stockholm, 1992, Fitzgerald medal U. Coll., 1993, Ismar Boas medal German Soc. for Digestive and Metabolic Diseases, 2002; postdoctoral fellow Boston U. Sch. Medicine, 1968-73, Guggenheim Found. fellow, 1974, Fogarty Internat. fellow NIH, 1968, Fulbright fellow, 1967-68. Fellow AAAS, Royal Coll. Physicians Ireland; mem. Gastroenterology Rsch. Group (vice chmn., steering coms.), Am. Soc. Clin. Investigation, Am. Gastroent. Assn. (disting. achievement award 1990, William Beaumont prize 2000), Am. Oil Chemists Soc., Biophys. Soc., Interurban Clin. Club, Am. Assn. Physicians, Royal Irish Acad. (hon.), St. Botolph Club (Boston). Roman Catholic. Office: Brigham and Womens Hosp Div Gastroenterology 75 Francis St Boston MA 02115-6106 E-mail: mccarey@rics.bwh.harvard.edu.

CAREY, MICHAEL EMMETT, neurosurgeon, educator; b. Hartford, Conn., Mar. 30, 1934; s. Thomas C. and Elizabeth (Kelly) C.; m. Betty Oseid, Apr. 28, 1962; children: Thomas, Elizabeth, Sarah. BA, Yale U., 1956; MD, Cornell U., 1960; MS, U. Minn., 1970. Diplomate Am. Bd. Neurol. Surgery. Intern in gen. surgery U. Minn. Hosps., Mpls., 1960-61, resident in gen. surgery, 1961-62, resident in neurosurgery, 1962-67, Mayo Clinic, Rochester, Minn., 1965; pvt. practice Hartford, Conn., 1967-68; chief neurosurgery 312th-91st Evacuation Hosp., Chu Lai, Vietnam, 1968-69, William Beaumont Gen. Hosp., El Paso, Tex., 1969-70; asst. prof. neurosurgery La. State U. Med. Ctr., New Orleans, 1970-74, assoc. prof., 1974-78, prof., 1978—; chief of neurosurgery 148th Evacuation Hosp., El Quasumah, Saudi Arabia, 1991. Mem. promotions com., La. State U., 1985-88, clin. faculty assembly organizer, 1986-87, pres. faculty assembly, 1989-90, del. to faculty assembly, 1990-93; cons. in neurosurgery U. Conn., 1967-68, Vietnam Head Study Group Walter Reed Army Hosp., Washington, 1985, Desert Storm Neurosurg. Conf., Chandler, Ariz., 1991; mem. staff Charity Hosp., New Orleans, Meml. Hosp., New Orleans, Univ. Hosp., New Orleans, Children's Hosp., New Orleans; vis. prof. U. Ky., Lexington, 1976, Med. Coll. Va., Richmond, 1985, U. B.C., Vancouver, 1986, Tufts U., Boston, 1988, Wayne State U., Detroit, 1996, La. State U., Shreveport, 1997; presenter in field; cons. Natick Soldier Ctr., 1999. Editorial reviewer Jour. Surg. Neurology; contbr. numerous articles to profl. jours. Mem. D-Day Museum Bd. Dirs., New Orleans, 1993-94. With USAR, 1970-96, Col., 1978-96. Decorated Legion of Merit, Bronze Star, Purple Heart. Fellow ACS; mem. AMA (medal of valor 1994), Congress of Neurol. Surgeons, Am. Assn. Neurol. Surgeons, Soc. Neurol. Surgeons, Soc. Univ. Neurosurgeons, Neurosurg. Soc. Am., Internat. Soc. CBF and Metabolism (founder), So. Neurosurg. Soc. (chmn. membership com. 1985-87), La. Neurosurg. Soc. (pres. 1982-83), La. State Med. Soc., Orleans Parish Med. Soc., Am. Epilepsy Soc. Avocation: sailing. Office: La State U Med Ctr Dept Neurosurgery 1542 Tulane Ave Dept New Orleans LA 70112-2825 E-mail: ehulbe@lsuhsc.edu.

CAREY, MILBURN ERNEST, musician, educator; b. Marion, Ind., Feb. 25, 1912; m. Elizabeth Bilsborrow, Aug. 7, 1935 (dec. Oct. 18, 1985); children: Jane, Don, Phil; m. Mary Jane Gragg, June 12, 1988. BS, MusB, U. Ill., 1935, M in Music, 1943; MA, EdD, Columbia U., 1955. Mng. dir. Tri-State Music Festivals, 1935-82; prof. music Phillips U., 1935-81, also dir. Fine Arts Sch., Disting. prof. emeritus music, dir. emeritus Fine Arts Sch., 1981—, Disting. mem. faculty; musician Enid-Phillips (Okla.) Symphony Orch. Vis. prof. music various univs. incl. Columbia, Purdue, Ill., Wis., Ohio, Kans., Colo., Tex., Mich., Interlochen Nat. Mus. Camp; organizer, conductor local choir and instrument ensemble on 4 European tours, Caribbean Cruise and Mexico; dir. Enid Legionettes Drum and Bugle Corps; bandleader 189th Field Arty. and 45th Inf. Div. bands, Enid; adjudicator, guest conductor 25 states, Europe and Japan; vocal soloist in several local chs.; served as TV color commentator parades, Interlochen, Mich., sustained local radio program. Author: Basic Oboe Method, 1938, Flute Duet Album, 1962, History, Activities and Personnel of the 189th Field Artillery Band, 1926-42, 1992, 7 Minute Looks at 100 World Cities Visited, 1993, Book of ABA Prayers, 1998; arranged numerous compositions for band and orch., various instrumental ensembles. Apptd. pres. Enid Armory Bd., 1944; pres. Enid Bd. Edn., 2 terms; mem. John Philip Sousa Found. com. for Selecting Outstanding H.S. Bands, Okla. Bicentennial Com.; del. World Music Coun. Conv., Czechoslovakia, 1978; condr. Enid Cmty. Band; mng. dir. Ann. Tri-State Music Festivals, 1935-85; dir. music First United Meth. Ch., Enid, 1943-83. Named Mr. Tri-State, State of Okla., 1972, Enid Citizen of Yr., Salvation Army, 1973, Disting. Alumnus Alumni of Phillips U.; recipient plaque DuQuesne U., Pitts., 1965, plaque U. Tex. Interscholastic League, 1982, Orpheus award Nat. Sinfonia Frat., 1973, Okla. Arts award Gov. Boren, 1976, St. Cecilia award U. Notre Dame, 1985, Hon. Alumnus award Phillips U., Pres.'s plaque Nat. Cath. Band Assn., 1996; honored with Dr. Milburn Carey Day, May 8, 1982, Mayor and City Council of Enid and Okla. Gov. Nigh and Senate; name engraved on Plaque of John Philip Sousa Stage, Kennedy Ctr., Washington, 1965; elected to Okla. Bandmasters Hall of Fame, 1972, Okla. Music Edn. Hall of Fame, 1988; bandstand named in his honor Humphrey Heritage Village adjoining Cherokee Strip Mus., 1993; proclaimed Cherokee Chief Longbranch, 1984; decorated Medal of Honor Mid-West Internat. Instrumental Music Clinic Chgo., 1995; named Disting. Friend, Phillips U. Alumni and Friends Assn., 1999. Mem. Am. Choral Dirs. Assn., Enid Concert Assn. (past pres.), Enid Music Tchrs. Assn. (past pres.), N.Am. Band Dirs. (chmn. coordinating coun. 1964), Am. Bandmasters Assn. (hon. life 1998), N.Am. Band Dir. Coord. Coun. (chmn. 1963), Music Educators Nat. Conf., Okla. Music Educators Assn., Phi Mu Alpha-Sinfonia, Pi Kappa Lambda, Beta Theta Pi, Phi Beta Mu (internat. hon. life pres., nominated Hall of Fame Alpha chpt., Internat. Hall of Fame from Internat. Sch. Bandmasters Fraternity, 2001), Mu Kappa Alpha, Kappa Kappa Psi (hon.), Bandmasters Fraternity. Avocation: travel in 50 states and on 6 continents. Home: 2405 Eden Terrace 2500 Woodside Dr Arlington TX 76016-1306

CAREY, PAUL RICHARD, biophysicist; b. Dartford, Kent, Eng., June 17, 1945; arrived in Can., 1969; s. Charles Richard and Winifred Margaret (Knight) C.; m. Julia Smith, Sept. 4, 1966 (div. May 1991); children: Emma, Sarah, Matthew; m. Marianne Pusztai, Mar. 7, 1992. BS in Chemistry with honors, U. Sussex, Eng., 1966, PhD, 1969. Postdoctoral fellow Nat. Rsch. Coun., Ottawa, Ont., Can., 1969-71, rsch. officer, 1971-94; mgr. Ctr. for Protein Structure Design, head protein lab. Inst. for Bio. Scis., Ottawa, Ont., Can., 1987-93; prof. dept. biochemistry Case Western Res. U., 1995—, dir. Cleve. Ctr. Structural Biology, 2000—. Mem. internat. adminstrv. com. Internat. Conf. on Lasers and Biol. Molecules, 1987—, adj. prof. Dept. Biochemistry, U. Ottawa, 1987-94, prof., 1994; prof. dept. biochemistry Case Western Reserve U. Author: Biochemical Applications of Raman and Resonance Raman Spectroscopies, 1982; contbr. over 190 articles to profl. jours.; patentee in field. Fellow Chem. Inst. Can.; mem. Am. Chem. Soc., Can. Protein Engring. Network (Adminstrv. body 1990-93), Internat. Network Protein Engring. Ctrs. Achievements include first demonstration of resonance Raman spectroscopy providing vibrational spectrum of a substrate or drug in active site of an enzyme; generation of first quantitative relationship between active site bond lengths and reactivity by combining resonance Raman spectroscopy, enzyme kinetics and x-ray crystallography; elucidation of mechanism of sunlight degradation of biological insecticide from B. thuringiensis; research on use of lasers in fingerprint detection. Office: Case Western Res U Dept Biochemistry Cleveland OH 44106-4935 E-mail: carey@biochemistry.cwru.edu.

CAREY, PETER KEVIN, reporter; b. San Francisco, Apr. 2, 1940; s. Paul Twohig and Stanleigh M. (White) C.; m. Joanne Dayl Barker, Jan. 7, 1978; children: Brendan Patrick, Nadia Marguerite. BS in Econs., U. Calif., Berkeley, 1964. Reporter San Francisco Examiner, 1964, Livermore (Calif.) Ind., 1965-67, editor, 1967; aerospace writer, spl. projects and investigative reporter San Jose (Calif.) Mercury, 1967—. Recipient Pulitzer prize for internat. reporting Columbia U., 1986, George Polk award L.I. U., 1986, Investigative Reporters and Editors award, 1986, staff Pulitzer prize for gen. reporting, Columbia U., 1990, Thomas L. Stokes award Washington Journalism Ctr., 1991, Malcolm Forbes award Overseas Press Club of Am., 1993, Gerald Loeb award UCLA Grad. Sch. Mgmt., 1993, Best of the West, First Amendment Funding Inc., 1993, 95, Pub. Svc. award Calif. Newspapers Pub. Assn., 1996, Fairbanks award for pub. svc. AP, 1996; NEH profl. journalism fellow, Stanford U., 1983-84. Mem. Internat. Consortium of Investigative Journalists, Soc. Profl. Journalists, Investigative Reporters and Editors. Avocation: classical piano. Office: San Jose Mercury-News 750 Ridder Park Dr San Jose CA 95131-2432 E-mail: pcarey@sjmercury.com.

CAREY, ROBERT GEORGE, lawyer; b. Oil City, Pa., Sept. 22, 1934; s. James Herbert and Mary Catherine (Lonergan) C.; children— Leslie Erin, Jason Andrew. B.A., Gannon U., 1961; J.D., Temple U., 1967. Bar: Del. 1967, U.S. Dist. Ct. Del. 1968, U.S. Ct. Appeals (3d cir.) 1970, Pa. 1980, U.S. Supreme Ct. 1982. Assoc., Prickett Jones Elliott Kristol & Schnee and predecessors, Wilmington, Del., 1967-70, ptnr., 1970-85; pvt. practice, Wilmington, 1985—; counsel to Gov. Del., Dover, 1973-74; vice chmn. Del. Agy. to Reduce Crime, Office Gov. Del., Dover, 1974-77; chmn. Del. Gov.'s Crime Reduction Task Force, Dover, 1974-77; chmn. Del. Gov.'s Juvenile Justice Task Force, Dover, 1974-77; chmn. Council on Police Standards and Goals, 1979-82. Served with USAF, 1954-57. Mem. Del. Bar Assn. (ins. com. 1970-84, jud. selections com. 1975—, nominating com. 1980-84, vice chmn. fee dispute counciliation and mediation com. 1984—, gen. legislation com. 1985—), Pa. Bar Assn., ABA, Assn. Trial Lawyers Am., Del. Trial Lawyers Assn., Nat. Assn. R.R. Trial Counsel, Def. Research Inst., Am. Judicature Soc., VFW. Democrat. Roman Catholic. Clubs: University and Whist, Rodney Sq., Concord Country (Wilmington). Lodge; K.C. Office: 1401 Pennsylvania Ave Ste 101 Wilmington DE 19806-4125 Home: Apt 206 2304 Riddle Ave Wilmington DE 19806-2163

CAREY, ROBERT MUNSON, medical educator, physician; b. Lexington, Ky., Aug. 13, 1940; s. Henry Ames and Eleanor Day (Munson) C.; m. Theodora Vann Hereford, Aug. 24, 1963; children: Adonice Ames, Alicia Vann, Robert Josiah Hereford. BS, U. Ky., 1962; MD, Vanderbilt U., 1965; Doctor Honoris Causa, Fed. U. Ceara, Brazil, 1998. Diplomate Am. Bd. Internal Medicine, Am. Bd. Endocrinology and Metabolism, Nat. Bd. Med. Examiners. Intern in medicine U. Va. Hosp., Charlottesville, 1966; jr. asst. resident in medicine N.Y. Hosp.-Cornell Med. Ctr., N.Y.C., 1968-69, sr. asst. resident, 1969-70; instr. endocrinology, dept. medicine Vanderbilt U. Sch. Medicine, Nashville, 1970-72; postdoctoral fellow in medicine St. Mary's Hosp. Med. Sch., London, 1972-73; asst. prof. internal medicine, endocrinology and metabolism U. Va. Sch. Medicine, Charlottesville, 1973-76, assoc. prof., 1976-80, prof., 1980—, James Carroll Flippin prof. medical sci. and dean, 1986—2002, prof. u., 2002—, David A. Harrison III disting. prof. medicine, 2002—, assoc. dir. Clin. Rsch. Ctr., 1975-86, prof., dean emeritus, 2002—, head. div. endocrinology and metabolism, dept. internal medicine, 1978-86, chmn. gen. faculty, chmn. med. adv. com., chmn. exec. com., 1986—. Attending staff U. Va. Hosp., Charlottesville, 1973—, pres. clin. staff, 1977-79, vice chmn. med. policy com., 1986—, adv. bd. 1986—; mem. study sect. on exptl. cardiovascular scis. NIH, 1982-85; mem. cardiovascular and renal adv. com. USDA, 1988—; vis. prof. div. nephrology, U. Miami Med. Sch., Fla., 1979, 83, 84, Hosp. das Clinicas da Univ., Fed. do Ceara, Forteleza, Brazil, 1981, hypertension div. Mt. Sinai Sch. Medicine, N.Y.C., 1981, div. pediatric endocrinology N.Y. Hosp.-Cornell Med. Ctr., 1981, dept. endocrinology St. Vincent's Hosp., Univ. Coll., Dublin, Ireland, 1982, depts. physiology and endocrinology Mayo Grad. Sch. Medicine, Rochester, Minn., 1984, div. rsch. Cleve. Clinic Found., 1984, Genentech, Inc., San Francisco, 1984, divs. endocrinology and metabolism U. Mass., U. Pa. Sch. Medicine, Boston U. Med. Sch., 1984, U. N.C. Sch. Medicine, 1985, Harvard Med. Sch., Boston, 1987, Jefferson Med. Coll., 1988; Bley Stein vis. prof. endocrinology U. So. Calif., 1987; Pfizer vis. prof. in pharmacology U. Chgo., 1988; co-organizer 3d Internat. Meeting on Peripheral Actions of Dopamine, Charlottesville, 1989; v.p. Va. Ambulatory Surgery, Inc., 1986—; speaker, presenter numerous nat. and internat. profl. meetings and congresses. Author: (with E.D. Vaughn) Adrenal Disorders, 1988; co-editor: Hypertension: An Endocrine Disease, 1985; mem. editorial bd. Jour. Clin. Endocrinology and Metabolism, 1981-84, Hypertension jour., 1983-84, Am. Jour. Physiology: Heart and Circulatory Physiology, 1987-89, Am. Jour. Hypertension, 1987—; author over 150 articles, revs., papers for profl. jours., contbr. 19 chpts. to books. Mem. exec. com. and fin. com. U. Va. Health Services Found., 1986—; bd. dirs. Va. Kidney Stone Found., Inc., 1986—, The Harrison Found., Inc. U. Va., 1986—, Dyslexia Ctr., Charlottesville, 1986—. Surgeon (lt. comdr.) USPHS, 1966-68, res., 1968—. Recipient Attending Physician of Yr. awrd dept. internal medicine U. Va. Med. Ctr., 1983-84, Disting. Alumnus award and

Founder's medal Vanderbilt U.; USPHS fellow Vanderbilt U., 1970-72; recipient numerous NIH grants as co-prin. and prin. investigator, 1972—; named to Hall Disting. Alumni, U. Ky., 2000. Master ACP (program com. regional meeting 1987); fellow Coun. for High Blood Pressure Rsch. AHA (program com. 1984-86, exec. and long rang planning coms. 1992—; chair-elect 2002-); mem. Inst. Medicine of NAS, Am. Heart Assn. (established investigator 1975-80), Va. affiliate Am. Heart Assn. (bd. dirs. 1977-83, pres. 1979-80, Disting. Service award), The Endocrine Soc. (fin. com. 1988—, chair devel. com. 1991-92), Am. Fedn. Clin. Rsch. (so. sect. councilor 1978-81, nominating com. 1982), So. Soc. Clin. Investigation (nominating com. 1982, sec.-treas. 1985-86), Inter-Am. Soc. for Hypertension, Am. Soc. Clin. Investigation, Am. Clin. and Climatol. Assn., Am. Soc. Hypertension (intersocietal affairs com. 1986—), Internat. Soc. Hypertension, Assn. Am. Physicians, AMA, Albemarle County Med. Soc., Med. Soc. Va., Assn. Am. Med. Coll.s Coun. of Deans, Inst. of Medicine, Nat. Acad. of Scis., The Raven Soc., Alpha Omega Alpha (Disting. Med. Alumnus award Vanderbilt U. 1994). Home: Pavilion Vi East Lawn Charlottesville VA 22903 Office: U Va Sch Medicine PO Box 801414 Charlottesville VA 22908-1414

CAREY, RONALD, former labor union leader; b. N.Y.C., Mar. 22, 1936; m. Barbara Murphy; 5 children. Pres. local union Internat. Brotherhood of Teamsters, Long Island City, NY, 1967—, pres. Washington, 1992-99. Avocations: swimming, diving, fishing.

CAREY, SARAH COLLINS, lawyer; b. N.Y.C., Aug. 12, 1938; d. Jerome Joseph and Susan (Atlee) Collins; m. James J. Carey, Aug. 28, 1962 (div. 1977); 1 child, Sasha; m. John D. Reilly, Jan. 27, 1979; children: Sarah Reilly, Katherine Reilly. BA, Radcliffe Coll., 1960; LLB, Georgetown U., 1965. Bar: D.C. 1966, U.S. Supreme Ct. 1977. Soviet specialist USIA/U.S. Dept. State, 1961-65; assoc. Arnold & Porter, Washington, 1965-68; asst. dir. Lawyers Com. for Civil Rights, Washington, 1968-73; ptnr. Heron, Burchette, Ruckert & Rothwell/predecessor firms, Washington, 1973-90; chair CIS Practice Steptoe and Johnson, Washington, 1990-99; chair CIS Practice, sr. ptnr. internat. Squire, Sanders & Dempsey, Washington, 1999—. Cons. Ford Found., 1975—83; bd. dirs. Yukos Oil Co., 2001—. Chair bd. dirs. Eurasia Found., 1994—; bd. dirs. Russia-Am. Enterprise Fund, 1993—95, Def. Enterprise Fund, 1994—2001, Georgetown U. Sch. Law Inst. Pub. Representation, 1971—85, Am. Arbitration Assn., 1975—82, Women's Fgn. Policy Group. Mem.: Atlantic Coun., Coun. Fgn. Rels. Democrat. Office: 1201 Pennsylvania Ave NW Washington DC 20004-2401 E-mail: scarey@ssd.com.

CAREY, SCOTT M, music educator; b. Rahway, Nj, Mar. 12, 1968; s. Robert Earl and Susan Marie Carey; m. Kimberly Mae Groves, Aug. 1, 1998; children: Kaitlyn Alexa, Kristopher Michael. BM, Susquehanna U, Selinsgrove, PA, 1990. Band and chorus dir. Our Lady of Lourdes Reg HS, Shamokin, Pa., 1990—97; band dir. Shikellamy Sch. Dist., Sunbury, Pa., 1997—. Asst. marching band dir. Selinsgrove HS, Selinsgrove, Pa., 1990—90; marching instr. Mifflinburg HS, Mifflinburg, Pa., 1991—97, Shikellamy HS, Sunbury, Pa., 1992—97. Mem.: Pa. State Educators Assoc, Pa. Music Educators Assoc. Home: 111 Madison Ave Northumberland PA 17857 Office: Shikellamy High School 6th and Walnut Sts Sunbury PA Office Fax: 570-286-3775.

CAREY, SHIRLEY ANNE, nursing consultant; b. Syracuse, N.Y., Sept. 27, 1939; d. John Crotty and Eva Mae (Pratt) Walsh; m. John Paul Carey, July 23, 1966; children: Jason Leo, Jonathan Paul, Jennifer Anne. BSN, Nazareth Coll., 1961. RN Calif. Charge nurse surg. svcs. L.A. County Hosp., 1962-64; instr. nursing L.A. County-U. So. Calif. Med. Ctr. Sch. Nursing, 1964-70; rschr., developer nursing edn. films Concept Media, Irvine, Calif., 1971—2003, prodn. and sales coord., 1999—; cmty. health educator Huntington Beach Hosp. and Med. Ctr., Calif., 1983—; nursing cons., health educator, writer Huntington Beach, 1988—; dir. staff devel. Columbia Huntington Beach, 1995-99, Columbia San Clemente Hosp. and Med. Ctr., San Clemente, Calif., 1995-99. Bd. trustees Huntington Beach City Sch. Dist., 1990—2003, clk., 1993, 97, 2001, pres., 1993, 98, 2002, 03. Author (ednl. video): Impaired Mobility, 1993, Basic Patient Care, 1994, Infection Control, 1995, Elderly Issues: Nutrition, Falls and Abuse, 2002; coord. : (films) Human Development: Conception to Neonate, 1992; Human Development: First 21/2 Years, 1992; The Vulnerable Child, 2000; Birth to 2 1/2, 2001; Young Children With Developmental Challenges (Autism, ADHD), 2001; Nutrition in Young Child, 2002; Nutrition in Infant, 2002; coord.: films Infection in Elderly, 2003. Mem., past officer Orange County Adoptive Parents, Calif., 1975—80; active Girl Scouts Am., Costa Mesa, Calif., 1984—98, PTA, Huntington Beach, 1976—; bd. dirs. West Orange County Consortium Spl. Edn., Huntington Beach, 1991—92, clk., 1992; active Huntington Coalition Against Substance Abuse, 1999—2000, Orange County Com. on Sch. Dist. Orgn., 1994—, v.p., 1997, pres., 1998—; pres., bd. dirs. Harry W. Montague Basketball Meml. Scholarship Com., Huntington Beach, 1989—; sec., bd. dirs. Huntington Beach Sister City Assn., 1993—95; commr. Huntington Beach Cmty. Svcs. Commn., 1994—2000, v.p., 1996—97; active Huntington Beach Children's Needs Task Force, 1995—, chair, 2000—02; active Huntington Beach Collaboration, 1997—2001; exec. bd. dirs. Huntington Beach PRIDE/DARE Found., 1995—, v.p., 1998, 2002, chair, 2000—01; founder, coord. Substance Abuse and Violence Edn. Task Force, 2001—03. Recipient Hon. Svc. award PTA, 1989, 2d Pl. award Am. Jour. Nursing Film Festival, 1994, 96, Gold Svc. award Orange Svc. Ctr. Coun., 1994; named Finalist AMA Internat. Film Festival, 1996. Mem.: AAUW (exec. bd. dirs. Huntington Beach chpt. 1996—2001, co-pres. 1997—98, Calif. pub. policy com. 1998—2000, honoree Huntington Beach br. 1998), Calif. Sch. Bd. Assn. (legis. network 1990—, del. assembly 1993—, nomination com. 1999), Nat. Sch. Bd. Assn. (fed. rels. network 1993—97), Orange County Sch. Bds. Assn. (v.p. 2001, pres. 2002), AHA (bd. dirs. Huntington Valley divsn. 1996—98). Avocations: travel, music, working with children and teenagers. Home and Office: 21142 Brookhurst St Huntington Beach CA 92646-7407

CAREY, STEPHANIE L. systems engineer, educator; b. Miami, Fla., July 31, 1973; d. Stephen C. and Joan D. Lutton; m. Craig E. Carey, Oct. 7, 2000. B. U. Fla., 1996; M. U. Miami, 2000. Rsch. assoc. U. Miami, Fla., 1996—2000; sys. engr. Peak Performance, Denver, 2001—. Adj. instr. Front Range C.C., Boulder, Colo., 2002—. Vol. Denver Children's Hosp., 2002—. Mem.: AAUP. Home: 2076 Concord Ln Superior CO 80027*

CAREY, THOMAS HILTON, advertising agency executive; b. Oak Park, Ill., Aug. 31, 1944; s. James Patrick and Caroline Hale (Hilton) C.; m. Barbara Lynn Hardy, Sept. 13, 1969; children: Christopher, Colleen, Jill. BA, Holy Cross, 1966; MS in Journalism, Northwestern U., 1967. Account mgr. Benton & Bowles Inc., N.Y.C., after 1967; sr. v.p., mng. dir. D'Arcy Masius Benton & Bowles, N.Y.C., exec. v.p. internat. div., until 1990; now pres., COO BBDO N.Y., N.Y.C., BBDO N.Am., N.Y.C., until 2000; exec. v.p. Monicom Group, N.Y.C., 2000—. Office: 437 Madison Ave New York NY 10022-7001

CAREY, WILLIAM BACON, pediatrician, educator; b. Phila., Dec. 6, 1926; s. Henry Reginald and Margaret (Bacon) Carey; m. Ann Lord McDougal, July 21, 1956; children: Katharine Blayney, Laura Bacon, Elizabeth McDougal. BA, Yale U., 1950; MD, Harvard U., 1954. Diplomate Am. Bd. Pediatrics. Intern Phila. Gen. Hosp., 1954-55; resident in pediatrics Children's Hosp. of Phila., 1955-57, 59-60; dir. sect. on behavioral pediatrics Children's Hosp. Phila., 1989—; practice medicine specializing in pediatrics Media, Pa., 1960-89. Instr. pediat. U. Pa. Sch. Medicine, Children's Hosp. Phila., 1961—73, assoc. in pediat., 1973—79, clin. asst. prof., 1979—82, clin. assoc. prof., 1982—90, clin. prof., 1990—. Co-editor: (book) Developmental-Behavioral Pediatrics, 1983, 1992, 1999, Clinical and Educational Applications of Temperament Research, 1989, Prevention and Early Intervention: Individual Differences as Risk Factors for the Mental Health of Children, 1994; author (with S. C. McDevitt): Coping with Children's Temperament: A Guide for Professionals, 1995; author: (with M. Jablow) Understanding Your Child's Temperament, 1997; contbr. articles to profl. jours.; developer Infant Temperament Questionnaire, 1970, co-developer Toddler Temperament Scale, 1978, Behavioral Style Questionnaire, 1976, Middle Childhood Temperament Questionnaire, 1980, Early Infancy Temperament Questionnaire, 1990, BASICS Behavioral Adjustment Scale, 2002. Pres. Friends of Wyck (House), Germantown, Phila., 1980—; bd. dirs. Benchmark Sch., Media, Pa., 1989—. Capt. M.C. U.S. Army, 1957—59. Recipient Wistar-Haines award, 2001. Fellow: Am. Acad. Pediat. (Rsch. grantee 1975, 1980, 1985, Aldrich award 1991, Practitioner Rsch. award 1992); mem.: Coll. Physicians Phila., Phila. Pediatric Soc. (bd. dirs. 1969—71), Soc. Devel. and Behavioral Pediat. (exec. coun. 1983—85, pres-elect 1989—90, pres. 1990—91), Ambulatory Pediatric Assn., Soc. Rsch. Child Devel., Am. Pediat. Soc., Inst. Medicine NAS, Franklin Inn Club, Phi Beta Kappa. Home: 511 Walnut Ln Swarthmore PA 19081-1140 E-mail: carey@email.chop.edu., wbcarey@worldnet.att.net.

CAREY, WILLIAM POLK, investment banker; b. Balt., May 11, 1930; s. Francis J. and Marjorie A. (Armstrong) C. Grad., Pomfret Sch., 1948; student, Princeton, 1948—50; BS in Econs., Wharton Sch., U. Pa., 1953; DSc (hon.), Ariz. State U., 1998, CUNY, 2003. V.p., gen. mgr. A. J. Orbach Co., Plainfield, NJ, 1955—58; prin. W. P. Carey & Co., Bloomfield, NJ, 1958—63; pres., dir. Internat. Leasing Corp., N.Y.C., 1959—89; chmn. exec. com., dir. Hubbard, Westervelt & Mottelay, Inc. (now Merrill Lynch Hubbard, Inc.), N.Y.C., 1964—67; dept. head Loeb, Rhoades & Co. (now Lehman Bros.), N.Y.C., 1967—71; vice chmn. investment banking bd., dir. corporate finance duPont Glore Forgan Inc., 1971—73; pres., dir. W.P. Carey & Co., Inc. and affiliates, N.Y.C., 1973—83, chmn., 1983—; gen. ptnr. Corp. Property Assocs. (CPA), N.Y.C., 1978—97, chmn. CPA series of pub. ltd. partnerships and real estate investment trusts, 1979—. Chmn. Carey Instnl. Properties, N.Y.C., 1991—, W.P. Carey & Co. LLC, W.P. Carey Internat. LLC, 2000—; chmn. exec. com. Carey Diversified LLC, 1997-2000; adv. com. U.S. Treasury Dept., 1986-92; exec. in residence Harvard Bus. Sch., 1999; advisor W.P. Carey Sch. Bus., Ariz. State U. Trustee Johns Hopkins U., Newcomer Soc.; adv. bd. Johns Hopkins Sch. Advanced Internat. Studies; life trustee Gilman Sch. Balt., Pomfret Sch., Conn.; trustee, mem. exec. com. Rensselaerville (N.Y.) Inst., 1979—; chmn. bd. trustees Oxford Mgmt. Ctr. Assocs. Coun., 1984-94, hon. trustee 1994—; mem. coun. mgmt. Templeton Coll., Oxford U., 1970-95; chm. St. Elmo Found., W.P. Carey Found., Pa. Inst. for Econ. Rsch., 2001—; dir. (hon.) Edmund Niles Huyck Preserve; mem. leadership com. James A. Baker III Inst. for Pub. Policy Rice U.; gov. Nat. Assn. Real Estate Investment Trusts, 1993-97; chmn. bd. overseers Rensselaerville Inst. Conf. Ctr., 2000—. 1st lt. USAF, 1953-55. Estab. William Polk Carey prize in econs., Carey term chairs in econs. and fin. U. Pa., Carey chair in math. Pomfret Sch., Carey prize in math. Calif. Inst. Tech., Armstrong law prize Ariz. State U. Mem. Soc. Mayflower Descs. (gov. emeritus), White's (London), The Pilgrims, The Brook, Newcomen Soc., Racquet and Tennis Club, Univ. Club, Penn Club (N.Y.), St. Elmo Club (Phila. and N.Y.C.), Maryland Club (Balt.), Harvard Faculty Club (Cambridge), N.E. Harbor Fleet (N.E. Harbor, Maine), Johns Hopkins Club, Delta Phi. Episcopalian. Home: 525 Park Ave New York NY 10021-8141 also: Fullerlea Rensselaerville NY 12147 Office: 50 Rockefeller Plz New York NY 10020-1605

CARFAGNA, VINCENT O. physician; b. Syracuse, NY, Feb. 15, 1931; s. Cosmo and Livia Irma (Franceschetti) Carfagna; m. Bernice Irene Czerwinski, July 2, 1960; children: Michael Dominick, Catherine Ann, Christopher Cosmo Casimir. BS, LeMoyne Coll., 1953; MD, Creighton U., 1959. Diplomate Am. Bd. Family Practice. Intern, gen. practice resident Mercy Hosp., Buffalo, 1959—61, attending physician, 1961—, chmn. pharmacy and therapeutics, 1981—91, chmn. dept. family practice, 1997—. Sch. physician East Aurora (NY) Pub. Schs., 1963—96, on-field football med. officer, 1963—95. With U.S. Army, 1953—58. Named Man of Hr., East Aurora Jaycees; recipient Outstanding Svc. Plaque, East Aurora Football Boosters, Golden Stethoscope award, Erie County chpg. NY State Acad. Family Physicians. Fellow: Am. Acad. Family Physicians. Roman Catholic. Avocations: tennis, gardening, Nordic skiing. Office: 323 Main St East Aurora NY 14052 Fax: 716-655-4476.

CARFORA, JOHN MICHAEL, economics educator, academic administrator; b. New Haven, Conn., July 24, 1950; s. John Michael and Rose Mary (Mitro) C.; m. Linda Louise Palmer, July 22, 1972; 1 child, Rachel Ellen. BS, U. New Haven, 1973, MPA, 1975; MS in Econs. and Polit. Sci., London Sch. Econs., 1978; AM, Dartmouth Coll., 1985; EdM, Harvard U., 1993. Rsch. asst. London Sch. Econs. and Polit. Sci., 1980-81; lectr. polit. sci. Albertus Magnus Coll., New Haven, 1982-83; lectr. econs. and quantitative analysis U. New Haven, 1982-83; program cons. Dartmouth Coll., 1984-85, asst. prof. internat. econ. Sch. Internat. Tng., 1985-90; v.p. rsch. and acad. affairs, dir. Soviet-Am. projects Global-Genesis, Internat. Cons., 1989-91, dir. east and west projects, 1992-94; asst. dean for rsch. and sponsored programs Ind. State U., Terre Haute, 1994-95; dir. grants and sponsored programs Simmons Coll., Boston, 1995-97; assoc. dir. grants and contracts Dartmouth Coll., Hanover, NH, 1997—2002; dir. office rsch. & sponsored programs Boston Coll., 2002—. Ednl. cons. USSR Acad. Mgmt., Moscow, 1991-92; vis. asst. prof. U.S. Dept. Def., Europe, 1979-80; vis. sr. lectr. Poly. of Ctrl. London, 1980; vis. asst. prof. internat. rels. So. Conn. State U., New Haven, 1982; cons. Commonwealth Acad. Mgmt., Moscow, 1992-94; lectr. in field. Editl. bd. Rsch. Mgmt. Rev.; contbr. articles to profl. jours. With USAR, 1970-76. Recipient Roy E. Jenkins award, 1972; fellow Radio Free Europe-Radio Liberty, 1979, Internat. Rsch. and Exchs. Bd., 1981-84. Mem. ASTD, AAUP, Am. Assn. Advancement Slavic Studies, Nat. Assn. Fgn. Student Advisors (internat. educators), Am. Acad. Polit. Sci., Am. Econ. Assn., Am. Polit. Sci. Assn., Am. Assn. for Higher Edn., Am. Assn. for Adult and Continuing Edn., Nat. Coun. Univ. Rsch. Adminstrs., Acad. Polit. Sci., N.E. Slavic Assn., Soc. Rsch. Adminstrs., Royal Acad. Pub. Adminstrn. (Eng.), Atlantic Econ. Soc., Am. Friends of the London Sch. Econs. (Conn. program chmn. 1981-85, N.H.-Vt. program chmn. 1985-87, alumni bd. dirs. 1983-92). Office: Office Sponsored Programs Boston Coll Chestnut Hill Chestnut Hill MA 02467 E-mail: carfora@bc.edu.

CARGILL, PAULA MARIE, social worker, gerontologist; b. Henrietta, N.C., Sept. 18, 1943; d. John Edwin and Mabel Anne (Bridges) C. BA in Sociology/French, Winthrop Coll., 1965; MSW, So. Bapt. Theo. Sem., 1973; MS in Social Work, U. Louisville, 1975; grad. in gerontology, U. Mich., 1983. Lic. clin. practice social worker, lic. nursing home adminstr. Social worker Connie Maxwell Children's Home, Greenwood, S.C., 1965, 70-71; tchr. French secondary pub. schs., N.C., S.C., 1965-70; instr. sociology and French North Greenville Coll., Tigerville, S.C., 1973-74, adj. assoc. instr., 1973-85; clin. social worker S.C. Dept. Mental Health, Simpsonville, 1975-77; social work supr. J Health Care Ctr., Inc., Simpsonville, 1977-84, S.C. Dept. Corrections, Greenville, 1984-89, 90-91; exec. dir. Grady H. Hipp Nursing Ctr., Greenville, S.C., 1989-90; access and in-home program dir. Sr. Action, Greenville, 1991-92; social worker S.C. Dept. Health and Environ. Control, 1992; social work cons. Interim Healthcare, 1992-96; dir. social work Richard Michael Campbell Vets. Nursing Home, Anderson, S.C., 1993; social worker, nursing home and rehab. agy. cons. Aging Cons. Svcs., Greenville, 1982—; ctr. dir. Choice Cmty. Mental Health, Greenville, 1996-97; social worker Bon Secours St. Francis Homecare, Greenville, 1997-2000; bereavement coord. Bon Secours St. Francis Hospice, 2001—. Contbr. articles to religious mag. Bd. dirs. Greenville County Alcohol/Drug Abuse Commn., 1981-84, Ch. Cmty. Ministries, Greenville Bapt. Assn., 1982-2000, Grady H. Hipp Nursing Ctr., 1985-89, Rolling Green Village Retirement Ctr., 1990-91, 97-2000, Upstate Alzheimer's Assn., 1990-92, 94-2000, mem. edn. com., 2000—; bd. dirs. Greenville County Mental Health Assn., 1999-2000; mission action cons. So. Bapt. Conv., 1982-83; coun. mem. Bapt. Women, Greenville, 1979-81, 88-91. Mem. NASW (bd. dirs. S.C. chpt. 1976-77, 79-81, 83-85, 90-91, 2002—), S.C. Health Care Assn., Alumni Leadership Greenville. Avocations: building dollhouses and antique doll furniture, foreign languages, travel, walking. Home and Office: 1 Kenilworth Dr Greenville SC 29615-2320

CARGILL, ROBERT MASON, lawyer; b. Atlanta, Nov. 15, 1948; s. George Slade Jr., and Emma Elizabeth (Matthews) C.; m. Sharon McEver, June 12, 1971; children: Ansley Lauren, Kristin Lucille. BS summa cum laude, Ga. Inst. Tech., 1970; JD magna cum laude, Harvard U., 1973. Bar: Ga. 1973, D.C. 1975. Assoc. atty. Hansell & Post, Atlanta, 1976-81, ptnr., 1981-89, Jones Day, Atlanta, 1989—. Lt. USNR 1973-76. Mem. Swedish Am. C. of C. Atlanta (bd. dirs.), Swiss Am. C. of C. (bd. dirs. Atlanta chpt.), World Trade Ctr. Atlanta (bd. dirs.), Cherokee Town Country Club. Methodist. Avocations: tennis, travel. Home: 230 Colewood Way NW Atlanta GA 30328-2923 Office: Jones Day 303 Peachtree St NE Ste 3500 Atlanta GA 30308-3263 E-mail: rcargill@jonesday.com.

CARGILL, THOMAS FRANK, economist, educator; b. Oakland, Calif., May 24, 1942; s. Otto Oscar and Jennie (Marchi) C.; m. Mary Jean Medeiros, Aug. 9, 1964; 1 child, Michele Anne. AA, City Coll. San Francisco, 1962; BS in Econs., U. San Francisco, 1964; MA in Econs., U. Calif., Davis, 1965, PhD, 1968. Asst. prof. Purdue U., West Lafayette, Ind., 1969-73; assoc. prof. U. Nev., Reno, 1973-78, prof., 1978—. Vis. scholar Comptr. of Currency, Washington, 1980, Hoover Instn., Stanford, Calif., 1983, Bank Japan, Tokyo, 1984, Fed. Res. Bank San Francisco, 1985—86, 2001, 02, FDIC, Washington, 1988, Bank Korea, 1997—98. Author: Money, the Financial System, and Monetary Policy, 1991; (with Gillian G. Garcia) Financial Reform in the 1980's, 1985; (with Shoichi Royama) The Transition of Finance in Japan and the United States, 1988, Central Bank Independence and Regulatory Responsibilities: The Bank of Japan and the Federal Reserve, 1989; (with Michael Hutchison and Takatoshi Ito) The Political Economy of Japanese Monetary Policy, 1997, Financial Policy and Central Banking in Japan, 2000, (with Naoyuki Yoshino) Postal Savings and Fiscal Investment in Japan: The PSS and the FILP, 2003. Ford Found. Dissertation fellow, 1967. Mem. Am. Econ. Assn. Office: U Nev Dept Of Econs Reno NV 89557-0207

CARGILL, URSULA BARDOT, university official; b. Buffalo, Aug. 2, 1963; d. Alton Elmore and Madge Evelyn (Bullard) C. BS, Morgan State U., Balt., 1981, MBA, 1983; PhD, SUNY, Buffalo, 1994. Zone mgr. Ford Motor Co., Dearborn, Mich., 1986-90; assoc. dean admission Colgate U., Hamilton, N.Y., 1994-98, coord. multicultural recruitment, coord. transfer admissions, 1994-98; dir. undergrad. acad. svcs. Stern Sch. Bus. NYU, 1998-99; edn. planner N.J. State Dept. Edn., Piscataway, 1999—. Contbg. author: High School to Employment Transition, 1994. Bd. trustees Liberation in Truth Unity Fellowship Ch., Newark, 1994—; bd. dirs. Foothills Coun. Girl Scouts U.S.A., 1997-98; planning assoc. N.J. Dept. Edn.; founder United Fellowship Ch. of Greater Newark, 2003. Office: 45 Lakeside Dr N Piscataway NJ 08854-4205 Address: PO Box 1445 Trenton NJ 08607-1445 E-mail: ucargill@hotmail.com.

CARGO, DAVID FRANCIS, lawyer; b. Dowagiac, Mich., Jan. 13, 1929; s. Francis Clair and Mary E. (Harton) C.; children: Veronica Ann, David Joseph, Patrick Michael, Maria Elena Christina, Eamon Francis. AB, U. Mich., 1951, M of Pub. Adminstrn., 1953, JD, 1957. Bar: Mich. 1957, N.Mex. 1957, Oreg. 1974. Practice in, Albuquerque, 1957; asst. dist. atty., 1958-59; mem. N.Mex. Ho. of Reps., 1962; gov. N.Mex., 1967-71; practice law, 1970-73, Portland, Oreg., 1973-83. Dir. N.Mex. Lottery Authority; mem. Interstate Compact. Chmn. Four Corners Regional Commn., 1967-71, Oil and Gas Conservation Commn.; chmn. N.Mex. Young Reps., 1959-61, Clackamas County Rep. Ctrl. Com.; mem. Israel Bond Com.; former mem. bd. govs. St. John Coll.; bd. dirs. Albuquerque Tech. Vocat. Sch.; chmn. governing bd. Albuquerque Tv.I. C.C.; mem. Albuquerque City Pers. Bd.; adv. bd. mem. N.Mex. State Fair; exec. bd. Found. for Open Govt. With AUS, 1953-55; bd. dirs. N.M. State Libr. Found.; elected state chair libr. bond chmn., 2002; pres. Calvin Coolidge Found. and Libr. Named Man of Yr. Albuquerque Jr. C. of C., 1964, Congregation Albert Brotherhood Man of Yr., 2001, 2002; recipient Outstanding Conservationist award N.Mex. Wildlife Assn., 1969, 70; David F. Cargo Libr., Mora, N.Mex., named in his honor. Mem. Mich. Bar Assn., Oreg. Bar Assn., N.Mex. Bar Assn., Albuquerque Bar Assn., Isaac Walton League (past v.p. N.Mex.), World Affairs Coun. Oreg. (pres.), Interstate Oil and Gas Compact, Isaak Walton League Oreg., Hispano C. of C., Am. Leadership Conf. (bd. dirs.), Nat. Fedn. Blind, Calvin Coolidge Presidential Found. (nat. bd. mem.), Oegon State Film Commn. Home: 6422 Concordia Rd NE Albuquerque NM 87111-1228

CARGO, WILLIAM IRA, retired ambassador; b. Detroit, Feb. 27, 1917; s. Ira Wiles and Nina (Lathrop) C.; m. Margaret Grace Ludwig, June 21, 1938; children: David Paul, Ruth. AB, Albion Coll., 1937, LLD, 1963; AM, U. Mich., 1938, PhD, 1941; student Russian lang., Naval Tng. Sch., Boulder, Colo., 1944-45; LLD, Waynesburg Coll., 1970. Instr. polit. sci. U. Mich., 1941-42, Colo. Coll., 1942-43; staff Dept. State, 1943-78, Bur. UN Affairs, 1946-53, dep. dir. office dependent area affairs, 1952; assigned Nat. War Coll., 1953-54; adviser U.S. delegations Gen. Assembly, Trusteeship Council Sessions, 1946-53; alternate U.S. rep. UN Com. on Non-self-governing Terrs., 1952; U.S. rep. UN vis. mission Trust Terrs. Tanganyika, Italian Somaliland, Ruanda-Urundi, 1951; assigned to U.S. Mission to NATO and European regional orgns. in connection with spl. internat. trade problems, Paris, 1954-57; dep. dir. Office of UN Polit. and Security Affairs, Dept. State, 1957-58, dir., 1958-61; dep. U.S. rep. Internat. Atomic Energy Agy., Vienna, 1961-63; dep. chief of mission, minister-counselor Am. embassy, Karachi and Rawalpindi, Pakistan, 1963-67; dep. U.S. rep. to NATO minister, Brussels, 1967-69; career minister U.S. Fgn. Service, 1969; dir. policy planning staff Dept. State, Washington, 1969-73; US amb. to Nepal, 1973—76; sr. insp. Fgn. Service Inspection Corps., Washington, 1976-78, cons., 1979-83; adviser U.S. delegation UN Gen. Assembly, 1957, Gen. Conf. of IAEA, Vienna, 1958, alt. U.S. rep., 1961, 62; adviser U.S. del. Conf. Discontinuance Nuclear Weapons Tests, Geneva, 1959; vice-chmn. U.S. del. Conf. to Amend Single Conv. Narcotic Drugs, Geneva, 1972. Co-author: (autobiography) Wherever the Road Leads, 1997. Served with USNR, 1944-46. Recipient Meritorious Service award Dept. State, 1958 Mem. AAAS, Phi Beta Kappa, Delta Sigma Rho, Phi Mu Alpha, Am. Fgn. Svc. Assn., DACOR. Methodist. Home: Vantage House # 313 5400 Vantage Point Rd Columbia MD 21044-2696

CARHART, HOMER W(ALTER), retired research scientist; b. Orange, Calif., May 21, 1914; s. Walter D. and Ethel (Shepherd) C.; m. Julia M. Holzapfel, June 15, 1940; children: Martha Jean, David Henry. BS, Dakota Wesleyan U., 1934; MA, U. S.D., 1935; PhD in Organic Chemistry, U. Md., 1939. Asst. prof. Gallaudet Coll., Washington, 1939-42; rsch. chemist Naval Rsch. Lab., Washington, 1942-52, head fuels br., 1952-70, head chem. dynamics br., 1970-86, dir. Navy Tech. Ctr. for Safety and Survivability, 1986-94, sr. scientist emeritus, 1994—. Mem. sec. of treas. Blue Ribbon Com. on Tanker Hazards, 1962-63; USN mem., del. Am., Brit., Can., and Australian Quadripartite Coms. on Fuels, 1964-94; mem. USN Working Group in Submarine Atmosphere Control, 1966-71; mem. Nat. Acad. Scis./NRC Com. on Hazardous Materials, 1966-75, chmn. Elec. Hazards Panel, 1966-75, chmn. Electrostatics Panel, 1969-75, chmn. indsl. hazards com., 1982-89; fire panel mem., spl. cons. NASA Apollo 204 (Fatal) Fire Rev. Bd., 1967; mem. exec. group, dir. Navy Labs. Planning Panel for Enhanced Aircraft Carrier Survivability, 1967-68; chmn. USN Panel on Hydrogen as a Potential Fuel, 1973, USN Inter-Labs. Com. on Pers. Adminstrn., 1973-75; chmn. dir. Navy Labs. Advanced Tech. Objectives Working Group for Fire Rsch., 1973-76; mem. Coordinating Rsch. Coun. Diesel Com., 1950-66; chmn. Ignition Quality Investigation Group, 1956-66, Compression Ignition Adv. Group, 1960-65; chmn. Aviation Fuel Safety Task Force (Adv. to FAA), 1974-76; chmn. NAS/NRC Com. on Indsl. Hazards, 1982-89; mem. Dept. of Labor Joint Soviet/Am. Task Force on Safety in the Chem. Industry, 1991. Contbr. articles to profl. publs.; patentee in field. Recipient USN Meritorious Civilian Svc. award, 1945, Dept. of Navy Recognition of Achievement award, 1975, USN Superior Civilian Svc. award, 1965, USN Disting. Civilian Svc. award, 1979, Winning Team, Federally Employed Women, Inc. award, 1989, Robert Dexter Conrad award for outstanding achievemnet in naval sci. and engring., 1991, Naval Rsch. Lab. Lifetime Achievement award, 1994, Harry C. Bigglestone award for excellence in written comm. of fire protection concepts, 1990, Jack Bono Engring. Comms. award, 1995, Ann. Homer W. Carhart award for excellence in damage control/fire protection established by Chief of Naval Ops; elevated to rank of Meritorious Sr. Exec. by Pres. Bush, 1989, Naval Rsch. Lab. Award for Innovation, 1998. Mem. Am. Chem. Soc. (alt. councilor 1954-56), Chem. Soc. Washington (mgr. 1953, mem. com. on rels. and status com. 1954, chmn. budget com. 1957, chmn. edn. com. 1965-66, chmn. long range planning com. 1967-70), Combustion Inst. (charter), U.S. Naval Inst., Naval Submarine League, Surface Navy Assn., Navy League U.S., Phi Kappa Phi, Sigma Xi. Avocations: musical composition, plant hybridization, photography. Office: Naval Rsch Lab Code 6108 Washington DC 20375-0001

CARHUAPOMA, JUAN RICARDO, critical care neurologist, researcher; b. Lima, Peru, Sept. 1, 1965; s. Cirilo Carhuapoma and Enedina Fernandez, m. Elizabeth Ann Sutherland, May 15, 1997; 1 child, Ethan. MD, Cayetano Heredia Peruvian U., 1991. Intern Henry Ford Hosp., Detroit, 1993-94, neurology resident, 1994-97; neuro ICU fellow Johns Hopkins U. Sch. Medicine, Balt., 1997-99, mem. neurology faculty, 1999-2000, Columbia U. Coll. Physician and Surgeons, N.Y.C., 2000—01; mem. faculty neurology and neurol. surgery Wayne State U., Detroit, 2001—. Cons. IC USA, Balt., 2000—. Contbr. articles to profl. jours., chpts. to books. Recipient Daland Fellowship Am. Philosophical Soc., 1999-2001. Mem. AAN, Am. Heart Assn., Soc. Critical Care Medicine. Office: Columbia U Box 209 710 W 168th St New York NY 10032 Home: 42695 Savoy Ct Northville MI 48167 Fax: 212-305-2792. E-mail: jcarhuap@med.wayne.edu.

CARIGNAN, CLAUDE, astronomer, educator; b. Montreal, Dec. 20, 1950; s. Philippe and Gilberte (Frenette) C.; m. Lucie Houde, Aug. 1972 (div. Oct. 1985); children: Stephane, Veronik, Marilis. MSc, U. Montreal, 1978; PhD, Australian Nat. U., Canberra, 1983. Fellow Kapteyn Lab., Groningen, Holland, 1983-85; rsch. fellow U. Montreal, 1985-90, asst. prof., 1990-91, assoc. prof., 1991-97, prof., 1997—. Dir. de L'Observatoire Du Mont Megantic; bd. dirs. CFHT. Contbr. articles to profl. jours. Mem. Can. Astron. Soc. (bd. dirs. 1992-96, future radio astronomy nat. facility com. 1995-97), Am. Astron. Soc. Achievements include research in neutral hydrogen in galaxies from radio synthesis observations, detailed kinematics, mass distribution and properties of dark matter in spiral and dwarf galaxies. Home: 290 ch Des Mille-Feuilles St St Sauveur PQ Canada J0R 1R7 Office: U Montreal Dept Physics CP 6128 Succ Centre Ville Montreal QC Canada H3C 3J7

CARINO, AURORA LAO, psychiatrist, hospital administrator; b. Angeles, The Philippines, Jan. 11, 1940; came to U.S., 1967; d. Pedro Samson and Hilaria Sanchez (Paras) Lao; m. Rosalito Aldecoa Carino, Dec. 2, 1967; children: Robert, Edwin, Antoinette. AA, U. of the East, Manila, 1961; degree in medicine, U. of the East, Quezon City, The Philippines, 1966. Lic. psychiatrist N.Y., Va., Conn., Fla.; cert. Am. Bd. Psychiatry and Neurology. Resident in pediatrics U. of the East-R.M. Meml. Hosp., Quezon City, 1966-67; rotating intern Stamford (Conn.) Hosp., 1967-68; resident in psychiatry Norwich (Conn.) Hosp., 1968-71, staff psychiatrist, 1971-75; staff psychiatrist, unit chief, acting clin. dir. Harlem Valley Psychiat. Ctr., Wingdale, N.Y., 1975-80; svc. chief Fla. State Hosp., Chattahoochee, 1982-83; unit chief Hudson River Psychiat. Ctr., Poughkeepsie, N.Y., 1983-89, dep. med. dir., acting clin. dir., 1989-90, asst. to clin. dir., 1990-93, dep. med. dir.-admissions, 1993-97. Cons. Dept. Mental Hygiene, Dutchess County, Poughkeepsie, 1976—. Mem. Am. Psychiat. Assn. Republican. Roman Catholic. Avocations: gardening, country music, recording/listening to spiritual enhancement. Home: 10 Millbank Rd Poughkeepsie NY 12603-5112

CARINO, LINDA SUSAN, business consultant; b. San Diego, Nov. 4, 1954; d. DeVona (Clarke) Dungan. Student, San Diego Mesa Coll., 1972-74, 89-90. With Calif. Can. Bank, San Diego, 1974-77, from ops. supr. to ops. mgr., 1977-82; asst. v.p. ops. mgr. First Comml. Bank (formerly Calif. Can. Bank), 1982-84; v.p. data processing mgr. First Nat. Bank, 1984-91; v.p. conversion adminstr. Item Processing Ctr. Svc. Corp., Denver, 1991-92; mgr. computer ops. FIserv, Inc., Van Nuys, Calif., 1992-93; v.p., data processing mgr. So. Calif. Bank, La Mirada, 1993-94, v.p. tech. support mgr., 1994-96; cons. First Nat. Bank of Ctrl. Calif., Salinas, 1996-97; project mgr. EDS Corp., Burbank, 1997-98, customer group mgr. Charlotte, NC, 1998-99, bus. svcs. rep., 1999-2000, project mgr., 2000—02; installation project mgr. Jack Henry & Assocs., Inc., Charlotte, 2003—. Democrat. Avocations: swimming, bicycling, camping, knitting, sewing. Home: PO Box 481084 Charlotte NC 28269 E-mail: lcarino@jackhenry.com.

CARIOLA, ROBERT JOSEPH, artist; b. Bklyn., Mar. 24, 1927; Grad., Pratt Inst. Art Sch., 1954; student, Pratt Graphic Ctr., 1958-59. Instr. art La Salle Acad., Oakdale, N.Y., 1963-65. Instr. creative painting workshop Nat. Art League, Douglaston, Queens, N.Y.; instr. Art Workshop at Nassau County Mus. Fine Art Ctr., Roslyn, N.Y.; condr. art workshops in mixed media painting Bd. Continuing Edn. One-man shows include Long Beach Mus., N.Y., 1985, East Meadow Libr. Gallery, 1990, Merrick Symphony Performance Lobby of Hall, 1990; exhibited in group shows including Boston Mus. Printmakers Exhbn., 1962, Corcoran Gallery Art, Washington, 1963, Pa. Acad. Fine Arts, Phila., 1963, Vatican Pavilion-N.Y. World's Fair, 1964, Nat. Acad. Design, N.Y.C., 1970, Signature Gallery, Va., 1986, Cath. Mus. Arts and Antiquities, Olympic Towers, N.Y.C., 1995-96; represented in permanent collections Landing Gallery, Woodbury, 1990—, Soundview Gallery, Pt. Jefferson, N.Y., 1990—; contbr.: Illustrator Writer's Ann., 1958, Sign Mag., 1971, art mags.; executed murals in Sr. Citizen Ctr., Wantagh, N.Y., 1989, comty. rm. St. Johns Luth. Ch., Merrick, N.Y., 1992, also schs.; created, installed 4-sided Indian Monument dedicated to Meroke Tribe Indians-1643, Merrick, N.Y., 1993; painted murals and mosaics in 4 chapels; created metal, wood, and concrete sculptures, faceted stained glass windows St. Johns Cemetery Mausoleum, Queens, N.Y; created 3 large bronze and brass wall sculptures, 2 mosaics and 3 large etched glass windows and doors at St. Raymonds Cemetery Mausoleum, Bronx N.Y., pointed universe design on life sized horse casting, titled "Cosmic Dustin:, for Nassau County's "hourses of a Different Color" fund raising porject, installed at Wheatley Plaza in Greenvale, L.I.,N.Y.2003. Recipient Ann. Painting prize Hofstra, 1957, Purchase award Hofstra, 1957, Operation Democracy prize Locust Vally, N.Y., 1958, 1st prize for painting John Kennedy Cultural Ctr. Bankers Trust, 1971, Grumbacher Cash award Silvermine Artists Guild, New Canaan, Conn., 1976, Best in Show award Bayshore C. of C. Art Festival, 1979, 1st prize Long Beach (N.Y.) Mus., 1984; grnatee Tiffany Grants, 1965, 66, N.Y. State Creative Arts Program, 1988, Nassau County, 1989, Wantagh Creative Arts Program, 1992; subject of feature article in Equine Images, fall, 1991. Address: 1844 Gormley Ave Merrick NY 11566-3009

CARISTO-VERRILL, JANET ROSE, international management consultant; b. Quincy, Mass., Jan. 30, 1945; d. John J. and Adelaide Caristo; m. Richard M. Verrill, Mar. 31, 1984 (dec. Feb. 1995). BS, Boston U., 1968; diploma in social anthropology, Lady Margaret Hall, Oxford, Eng., 1974; M in Internat. Mgmt., Am. Grad. Sch. Internat. Mgmt., 1982. Social studies tchr. Boston, Pembroke & Cohasset Schs., Mass., 1969-81; summer planner, reunions MIT Alumni Office, Cambridge, 1973-76; pres. Macro Projects Internat., Wayland, Mass., 1984—. Advisor Govt. Can., 1985, Nepal, 1986, Nizhny Novgorod, 1994, Algeria, 1994, Bosnia, 1996, 97, Ctr. for Religious Dialogue, Sarajevo, 1999-2001, Montenegro, 2000, Kosovo, 2002, Habitat for Humanity, Belfast Unltd., 1994-96; guest spkr. energy conf. Govt. Turkey, Ankara, 1997; NGO del. UN Sci. & Tech. Commn., N.Y.C., 1993. Author: Civilian Military Cons. Corps, 1992,96; contbr. Macro Problems and World Projects, 1998. Filmmaker, vol Mother Theresa's Hosps., Calcutta, India, 1980; vol. U.S. Peace Corps, Nigeria, 1964—66, U.S./China People's Friendship, Cambridge, 1982—83; treas. Internat. Sunsat Energy Coun., 1986—; adv. com. MIT Dewey Libr., Cambridge, 1993—2000; mem. dispute resolution forum Harvard Law Sch., 2000—; guest White House Conf. Trade & Devel. No. Ireland, 1995; participant Friends Raoul Wallenberg Conf., Stockholm, 1997. Mem.: World Boston, English Spkg. Union, World Citizens Orgn. (dir. 2000—), Macro Engring. (pres. Boston chpt. 1985—), Internat. Assn. Macro-Engring. Soc.s (dir. 1996—2002), Brookline Bird Club, Oxford & Cambridge Club New Eng., United Oxford & Cambridge U. Club (London). Roman Catholic. Avocations: poetry, birdwatching, gardener, music, art and literature. Office: Macro Projects Internat Inc 174 Pelham Island Rd Wayland MA 01778-2513 E-mail: passingpeace@mediaone.net.

CARITHERS, JILL MARIE, speech pathology/audiology services professional; b. Peoria, Ill., Apr. 17, 1963; d. Kenneth R. and Dorothy L. Sanders; m. Don L. Carithers, June 15, 1985; children: Cody, Forrest. BS, U. Ctrl. Ark., 1985, MS, 1988. Speech pathologist Cherokee Elem. Sch., Hardy, Ark., 1985—. Speech pathologist, Hardy, 1989—; cons., 1989—; pub. spkr. for health seminars, 1989—. Mem.: Am. Speech and Hearing Assn. (clin. competence cert.). Baptist. Avocations: gardening, fly fishing, reading, outdoor activities. Office: Highland Pub Sch PO Box 419 Hardy AR 72542

CARITIS, STEVE NICK, obstetrician, gynecologist, educator; b. Steubenville, Ohio, Dec. 6, 1943; s. Nick P. Caritis. BA, W.Va. U., 1965, MD, 1969. Diplomate Am. Bd. Ob-Gyn. Resident U. Pitts., 1970-73; fellow Columbia U., N.Y.C., 1973-75; asst. prof. U. Pitts., 1975-81, assoc. prof., 1981-90, prof. ob-gyn., 1990—, co-dir. divsn. maternal and fetal medicine, 1975-91, dir. divsn. maternal and fetal medicine, 1991—. Mem. med. staff Magee Women's Hosp. Contbr. articles to profl. jours.; reviewer various jours. incl. New Eng. Jour. Medicine. NIH-NICHD grantee, 1986—. Mem. Soc. Gynecologic Investigation, Am. Gyn-Obstet. Soc., Soc. Maternal Fetal Medicine. Office: Magee Women's Hospital 300 Halket St Pittsburgh PA 15213-3180

CARIUS, JEFFREY RAPP, lawyer; b. Fukura, Japan, Aug. 29, 1949; s. Marvin Wilbur and Geraldine (Rapp) C.; m. Vicki Angia Williamson, June 2, 1973; children— Stephanie Lauren, Brian Timothy Marvin. B.A., U. Ill., 1971; J.D., Loyola U., New Orleans, 1975. Bar: Ill. 1975, Mo. 1995, U.S. Dist. Ct. (no. dist.) Ill. 1976, U.S. Ct. Appeals (7th cir.) 1976. Field atty. NLRB, Chgo., 1975-77; labor relations atty. Emerson Electric Co., St. Louis, 1977-83, sr. labor atty., 1983-90, asst. v.p. employee rels. & chief employment counsel. Served to capt. AUS, 1971-82. Mem. Ill. Bar Assn., Sigma Chi. Republican. Home: 14338 Willow Bend Park Apt 3 Town And Country MO 63017-8251 Office: Emerson Electric Co 8100 W Florissant Ave Saint Louis MO 63136-1494

CARIUS, ROBERT WILHELM, mathematics and science educator, retired naval officer; b. Peoria, Ill., Jan. 4, 1929; s. Henry Clarence and Mary Magdalen (Wilhelm) C.; m. Geraldine Mary Sullivan, Mar. 16, 1957; children: Patricia, Mary, Linda, Robert, Daniel, Sara. BS in Naval Sci, U.S. Naval Acad., 1951; BS in Aero. Engring, U.S. Naval Postgrad. Sch., 1958; MS in Nuclear Engring, Iowa State Coll., 1959. Commd. ensign USN, 1951, advanced through grades to rear adm., 1977, served with Fighter Squadron 74, 1953-56, served with U.S.S. Bennington, 1959-61, project mgr. U.S. AEC, 1964-65, served with Air Anti-Submarine Squadron 33, 1962-63, command officer Air Anti-Submarine Squadron 29, 1966-68, exec. officer U.S.S. Princeton, 1968-70, R & D br. head Dept. Navy, 1970-71, command officer U.S.S. New Orleans, 1971-73, mem. staff Anti-Submarine Wing Pacific, 1973-77, comdr. Anti-Submarine Wings Atlantic, Naval Air Sta., 1977-79, with aviation programs Dept. Navy, from 1979; instr. physics Ark. Coll., Batesville, 1983-85, asst. prof. physics, 1986—. Bd. govs. USO, Jacksonville. Mem. exec. bd. United Way of Jacksonville, N.E. Fla. coun. Boy Scouts Am.; pres. Independence County United Way. Decorated Legion of Merit, Air medal, Meritorious Service medal; recipient Spl. award United Way of Jacksonville, 1979 Mem. U.S. Naval Acad. Alumni Assn., Assn. Naval Aviation, Ret. Officers Assn., Ark. Hist. Soc., Batesville Symphony Assn., Naval Helicopter Assn., U.S. Naval Inst., Jacksonville C. of C. (gov.) Clubs: Rotary. Roman Catholic. Home: 2630 Antioch Rd Cave City AR 72521-9249 Office: Lyon Coll Batesville AR 72501 *Personal integrity and honesty to oneself have been key elements in my life's philosophy. Attempting to understand the people you work with and treating them as you prefer to be treated were other essential principles. Lastly, always do your very best in all endeavors, and you never have to look over your shoulder with regret.*

CARKIN, GARY BRYDEN, performing arts educator; b. York, Maine, Oct. 5, 1940; s. Laurence Earl and Beatrice Fillmore (Bryden) C.; m. Pachareeya Erawan, Jan. 1, 1961. BA, U. N.H., 1963; MA, U. N.Mex., 1977; PhD, Mich. State U., 1984. Actor Players' Theater of New Eng., Manchester, N.H., 1968-70; vis. prof. Thammasat U., Bangkok, Thailand, 1970-74; actor, tchr. U. N.Mex., Albuquerque, 1975-77; Mich. State U. Performing Arts Co., East Lansing, 1977-80, Fulbright scholar Thailand, 1980-81; prof. So. N.H. U., Manchester, 1982—. Vis. prof. Ramkhamhaeng U., Bangkok, 1981; theater dir. Manchester Youth Theater, 1986-91; property mgr. Carkin Properties, Manchester, 1991--. Author: How to Succeed in the USA, 1997. Avocations: travel, architecture, music, films. Home: 40 Cascade Cir Manchester NH 03103-6905 E-mail: g.carkin@snhu.edu.

CARL, JANET A. N, writing instructor, consultant; b. Omaha, Nebr., Feb. 24, 1948; d. Chauncey Howard and Marynelle Holmes Carl; m. Gregory R. Johnson, Nov. 20, 1952; children: William Theodore Carl Johnson, Nicholas John Carl Johnson. BA, U. Iowa, 1970, MA, 1973. Dean of students Hood Coll., Frederick, Md., 1973—76; assoc. dean of students Grinnell (Iowa) Coll., 1977—80; Iowa state rep. Iowa Gen. Assembly, Des Moines, 1981—86; dir. ct.-apptd. spl. advocate program Supreme Ct. State of Iowa, Des Moines, 1986—87; resource devel. dir. Mid-Iowa Comty. Action, Marshalltown, Iowa, 1987—2000; instr. writing lab. Grinnell Coll., 2000—. Office: Grinnell Coll Grinnell IA 50112

CARL, ROBERT E. retired marketing company executive; b. Sept. 1, 1927; s. Elmer T. Carl and Marion R. (Pack) C.; m. Linda Arlene Sutton, Aug. 30, 1967; children: Melanie Ruth, Robert Brady, Camber Carleen. BS, U. Kans., 1950; cert. in real estate, So. Meth. U., 1965; cert. in investment analysis, N.Y. Inst. Fin., 1967. V.p. sales promotion Riverside Press, Inc., Dallas, 1951-54; pres., COO Jones-Carl, Inc., Dallas, 1954-62; v.p. mktg. comms. Modern Am. Corp., Dallas, 1962-70; v.p. sales Dunn Properties of Tex., Inc., Dallas, 1970-71; sr. v.p. mktg. svcs. Vantage Cos., Dallas, 1971-84; pres. Mktg. Mgmt. Sys., Dallas, 1984-90; v.p. The Premium Group, Inc., 1990-92; mem. Dallas Cable TV Bd., 1981-83; v.p. mktg. Availent Mortgage Co., 2000—02. Co-founder Liberty Christian H.S., Dallas, 1995. Contbr. articles to profl. jours. Dir. comms. Rep. Party Dallas County; precinct chmn. Dallas County Grand Jury, election judge. Recipient Chevalier and Legion of Honor Degrees Internat. Supreme Coun. of Order of De Molay, 1957, Silver Anvil award Pub. Rels. Soc. Am., 1958, Eagle Scout with four palm awards. Mem. Sales and Mktg. Execs. Dallas (pres. 1976-77, Disting. Salesman's award 1954), S.W. Found. Free Enterprise (pres. 1975-76), Tex. Indsl. Devel. Coun., Nat. Assn. Corp. Real Estate Execs., Sales and Mktg. Execs. Internat. (sr. v.p.), Nat. Assn. Indsl. and Office Parks, Internat. Platform Assn., Dallas Advt. League, U. Kans. Alumni Assn. (life), Big D Toastmasters Club (pres. 1966), Press Club Dallas, Greater Dallas Pachyderm Club (chmn.), Park City Club (bd. govs. 1989-92), Masons (32d degree), Shriners, Dervish Club, Dallas Jr. C. of C. (bd. dirs.). Home: 4209 Gloster Rd Dallas TX 75220-3819 E-mail: rec4209@aol.com.

CARL, SUSAN MARIE, photographer, photojournalist; b. Ft. Hancock, N.J., Oct. 2, 1966; d. William Paul and Dolores Ruth Carl. BA, Coll.William and Mary, Williamsburg, VA, 1994; MA, U. Ga., Athens, 1997. Photojournalist U.S. Navy, Norfolk, Va., 1984—92; photojournalist U.S. Naval Reserves, Washington, 1992—2001; asst. archeologist U. Ga., Carthage, Tunisia, 1992—97; undergrad. asst. Coll. William and Mary, Williamsburg, 1992—94; grad. asst. U. Ga., Athens, 1995—97; photographer European Stars and Stripes, Darmstadt, DC, Germany, 1996—96, Action Press, Sarajevo, Bosnia-Herzegovina, 1997—98; programme mgr. Ind. Bur. for Humanitarian Issues, Islamabad, Pakistan, 1998; photo editor The European & Pacific Stars and Stripes, Washington D.C., DC, 1999—2001; vol. U.S. Peace Corps Island Hospice, Harare, Zimbabwe, 2001; graphics designer Ft. Wainwright Morale, Welfare and Recreation, Fairbanks, Alaska, 2002—. Consulting Photographer Internat. Com. Red Cross, Sarajevo, 1998—98. Petty Officer 1st Class U.S. Navy, 1984—92, Norfolk, VA. Named Military Photographer of Yr., U.S. Military and Nat. Press Photographers Assn., 1996. Avocation: Travel. Personal E-mail: SCARL49932@hotmail.com.

CARLBERG, JAMES EDWIN, lawyer; b. Jeffersonville, Ind., May 3, 1950; s. Dale Levan and Nanette (Prendergast) C.; m. Donna S. Funk, Oct. 28, 1950; children: Jason, Lindsay, Kelly. BS highest distinction, Ind U., 1972, JD cum laude, 1974. Bar: Ind. 1974, U.S. Dist. Ct. (no. and so. dists.) Ind. 1974. Ptnr. Klineman, Rose, Wolf & Wallack, Indpls., 1974-94, Bose, McKinner & Evans, Indpls., 1994—. Author: (with others) Indiana Continuing Legal Education Forum. Mem. ABA (secured creditors' sub com. of bankruptcy com., bus. and banking sect.), Ind. State Bar Assn., Indpls. Bar Assn. Office: Bose McKinney & Evans 2700 1st Indiana Pla Indianapolis IN 46204

CARLBERG, W. CHARLES, advertising executive; m. Gayle Carlberg. BA, U. Houston, 1965. Art dir. Lyle Metzdorf Advt., Houston, 1965-71; ptnr. Smith Smith Baldwin Carlberg, Houston, 1971-78; pres. Rives Smith Baldwin Carlberg/Young & Rubicam, Houston, 1978-86; CEO, pres. Rives Carlberg, Houston, 1986—. Office: Rives Carlberg 2800 Post Oak Blvd #3400 Houston TX 77056-6106

CARLE, HARRY LLOYD, social worker; b. Chgo., Oct. 26, 1927; s. Lloyd Benjamin and Clara Bell (Lee) C.; m. Elva Diana Ulrich, Dec. 29, 1951 (div. 1966); adopted children: Joseph Francis, Catherine Marie; m. Karlen Elizabeth Howe, Oct. 14, 1967 (dec. Feb. 1991); children: Kristen Elizabeth and Sylvia Ann (twins), Eric Lloyd; m. Diane Wyland Gambs, May 23, 1993. BSS, Seattle U., 1952; postgrad., U. Wash., 1952-54, MSW, 1966. LCSW Wash. Pacific N.W. regional dir. Collegiate Coun. UN, 1952-53; rep. indsl. placement and employer rels. State of Wash., Seattle, 1955-57; parole and probation officer Seattle and Tacoma, 1957-61; parole employment splst., 1961-63; vocat. rehab. officer, 1963-64; clin. social worker Western State Hosp., Ft. Steilacoom, Wash., 1964-66, US Penitentiary, McNeil Is., Wash., 1964-66; exec. dir. Snohomish County Cmty. Action Coun./Social Planning Coun., Everett, Wash., 1966-77; employment and edn. counselor Pierce County Jail Social Svc., Tacoma, 1979-81; dir. employment devel. clinic coord. vocat. program North Rehab. Facility King County Divsn. Alcoholism and Substance Abuse, Seattle, 1981-90; staff devel. cons. Counseling for Ind. Living, Newport, RI, 1992. Cmty. orgn. agy. mgmt. cons., 1968—92; cons. to pres. Geneal. Inst., Salt Lake City, 1974—78. Vol. Vis. Nurse Svc. Wash. Hospice and Home Care, Montlake Terrace, Wash., 1996-98; mem. social svc. project staff Pacific Luth. U., Tacoma, 1979-81. With USN, 1944-46. Named 1st honoree, Supt. O'Neill's Hall of Success, Iowa Tng. Sch. for Boys, Eldora, 1969; recipient scholarship, U.S. Office Vocat. Rehab., 1965—66. Mem. NASW, Seattle Geneal. Soc. (pres. 1974-76), Soc. Advancement Mgmt. (chpt. exec. v.p. 1970-71), Acad. Cert. Social Workers (ret. 1998), Henckel Family Nat. Assn., Seattle Japanese Garden Soc. (v.p. 1993-96), various hist. and geneal socs. in Pa. and Ill. Roman Catholic. Home: Poem Rising Garden 258 Two Crane Ln NW Poulsbo WA 98370-9700 E-mail: ecopsych@earthlink.net.

CARLEN, SISTER CLAUDIA, librarian, consultant; b. Detroit, July 24, 1906; d. Albert B. and Theresa Mary (Ternes) C. AB in Library Sci., U. Mich., 1928, MA in Library Sci., 1938; LHD (hon.), Marygrove Coll., 1981, Loyola U., Chgo., 1983, Sacred Heart Major Sem., 1989; LittD (hon.), Cath. U. of Am., 1983. Asst. libr. St. Mary Coll., Monroe, Mich., 1928-29, Marygrove Coll., Detroit, 1929-44, libr., 1944—68; on leave as index editor New Cath. Ency., 1963—67, Cath. Theol. Ency., 1968—70; libr. grad. div. Casa Santa Maria, N.Am. Coll., Rome, 1971—72; libr. St. John's Provincial Sem., Plymouth, Mich., 1972-80, libr. emeritus, 1980-82, scholar-in-residence, 1982-85, archivist, 1985-88; rschr. Bentley Hist. Libr., U. Mich., Ann Arbor, 1989-97. Supr. orgn. and servicing Community Ctr. Libraries staffed by vols.; bd. dirs. Corpus Instrumentorum, Inc., v.p., 1969-70; mem. instructional materials com. Mich. Curriculum Study; cons. McGraw Hill Ency. World Biography, 1968-72, World Book Ency., 1969-70; mem. working group on uniform headings for liturgical works Internat. Fedn. of Libr. Assns., 1972-75. Author: Guide to Encyclicals of the Roman Pontiffs, 1939, Guide to the Documents of Pius XII, 1951, Dictionary of Papal Pronouncements, 1958; editor: Papal Encyclicals, 1740-1981, 1981, Papal Pronouncements, 1991; editor: column At Your Service, Cath. Library World, 1950-52; Reference Book Rev. Sect., 1952-64, 66-72; Books for the Home column; monthly news release, Nat. Cath. Rural Life Conf., 1952-61; mem. adv. bd.: The Pope Speaks (quarterly periodical), 1953-88; contbr.: Catholic Bookman's Guide, 1961, Dictionary Western Chs, 1969, Ency. Dictionary of Religion, 1979, Translatio Studii, 1973, Intellectual Life on the Michigan Frontier, 1985; contbr.: Vatican Archives: An Inventory and Guide, 1997, Translatio Studii Festschrift. Trustee Marygrove Coll., Detroit, 1976-79, vice chmn. bd., 1977-79. Recipient Disting. Alumna award U. Mich. Sch. Libr. Sci., 1974, Domitilla award Marygrove Coll., 1991, Gabriel Richard award Mich. Cath. Libr. Assn., 1998. Mem. ALA (coun. 1958-61, 68-71), Cath. Libr. Assn. (chmn. com. membership 1946-49, chmn. Mich. unit 1952-54, chmn. coll. and univ. sect. 1954-56, chmn. publs. com. 1961-62, pres. 1965-67, Jerome award 1993), Mich. Libr. Assn. (chmn. coll. sect. 1956-57, chmn. recruiting com. 1959-60), Accademia Olubriense (Pietrabissara, Italy, charter), Am. Friends of Vatican Libr. (co-founder, v.p.), Phi Beta Kappa, Phi Kappa Phi, Beta Phi Mu. Home: 610 W Elm Ave #D208 Monroe MI 48162 *To form the habit of reading good books so that reading becomes a necessity in one's life is a sure means of continual development and growth; a means of attaining that poise of spirit and richness of mind that should mark every professional person; a means by which the mind acquires new light, the will new incentives, the heart new desires, and life new ideals.*

CARLEN, PETER LOUIS, neuroscientist educator, science administrator; b. Edmonton, Alta., July 22, 1943; m. 1970; 2 children. MD, U. Toronto, 1967. Intern Montreal (Que., Can.) Gen. Hosp., 1967-68, resident internal medicine, 1968-69; instr. neurophysiology, dept. zoology Hebrew U., Jerusalem, 1969-70; resident neurology U. Toronto, 1970-72; fellow neurophysiol. neurobiol. unit Hebrew U., Jerusalem, 1972-74; sr. physician, head neurol. program Addiction Rsch. Found. Clin. Inst., 1974-94; staff neurologist Toronto Western Hosp., U. Toronto, 1974; rsch. assoc. Playfair Neurosci. Unit U. Toronto, 1979-89, assoc. prof. dept. medicine and physiology, 1981-88, prof. dept. medicine & physiology, 1989—; dir. neurosci. unit Toronto Hosp., 1989-99. Fellow Can. Neurol. Soc., Am. Acad. Neurology, Am. Neurol. Assn.; mem. AAAS, Soc. Neurosci., Can. Physiol. Soc. Office: U Toronto -Toronto Western Hosp 399 Bathurst St Toronto ON Canada M5T 2S8

CARLENO, HARRY EUGENE, lawyer; b. Denver, Mar. 3, 1928; s. Benjamin Edward and Elizabeth Bess (De Rose) C.; m. Ann Marie Kraft, Sept. 14, 1957; children: Gregory S., Paul C., Jennifer A., Machelle L. BBA, U. Denver, 1951, LLB, 1955, JD, 1970. Bar: Colo. 1955, U.S. Dist. Ct. Colo. 1955, U.S. Ct. Appeals (10th cir.) 1959, U.S. Supreme Ct. 1959. Pres., atty. H.E. Carleno & Assoc., P.C., Englewood, Colo., 1955—80; atty. H.E. Carlino & Assocs. P.C., Littleton, Colo., 1980—. Mcpl. judge City of Wheat Ridge, Colo., 1970-77; dep. dist. atty. Arapahoe County, Littleton, 1968-78; owner, broker Eagle Real Esate Co, Denver, Colo., 1998—. Chmn. Dem. Com., Arapahoe County, 1958-60; chmn. Career Service Commn., Englewood, 1961-64; pres. Inter Faith Task Force Found., Englewood, 1986-88. Col. USAF, 1947-53. Recipient St. George award Denver Area council Boy Scouts Am., 1980. Mem. ABA (life), Res. Officers Assn. of U.S. (life), Ret. Officers Assn. (life), Fraternal Order of Eagles (life). Lodges: Kiwanis (local pres. 1966-67). Roman Catholic. Home and Office: 5471 S Sherman St Littleton CO 80121-1253 E-mail: hecarleno@msn.com.

CARLEONE, JOSEPH, business executive; b. Phila., Jan. 30, 1946; s. Frank Anthony and Amelia (Ciaccia) C.; m. Shirley Elizabeth Atwell, June 29, 1968; children: Gia Maria, Joan Maria. BS, Drexel U., 1968, MS, 1970, PhD, 1972. Civilian engring. trainee, mech. engr. Phila. Naval Shipyard, 1963-68; grad. asst. in applied mechanics Drexel U., Phila., 1968-72, postdoctoral rsch. assoc., 1972-73, NDEA fellow, 1968-71, adj. prof. mechanics, 1974-75, 77-82; chief rsch. engr. Dyna East Corp., Phila., 1973-82; chief scientist warhead tech. Aerojet Ordnance Co., Tustin, Calif., 1982-88; v.p., gen. mgr. warhead sys. divsn. GenCorp. Aerojet Precision Weapons, Tustin, Calif., 1988-89; v.p., dir. armament sys. Aerojet Electronics Sys. Divsn., Azuza, Calif., 1989-94; v.p. tactical def. and armament products Aerojet, Calif., 1994-97, v.p. ops., 1997-99, v.p., gen. mgr. remote sensing sys. and ops., 1999-2000; pres. Aerojet Fine Chems., LLC, 2000—; v.p. GenCorp, 2000—. Dir. Irvine Sensors Corp. Bd., 2003—. Editor: Tactical Missile Warheads, 1993; contbr. articles to profl. jours.; rschr. explosive and metal interaction, ballistics, projectile penetration, impact of plates. Mem. ASME, AIAA, NDIA, Sigma Xi, Tau Beta Pi, Pi Tau Sigma, Phi Kappa Phi. Home: 2112 Campton Cir Gold River CA 95670-8302 Office: Aerojet Fine Chems PO Box 1718 Rancho Cordova CA 95741

CARLESON, ROBERT BAZIL, public policy consultant, corporation executive; b. Long Beach, Calif., Feb. 21, 1931; s. Bazil Upton and Grace Reynolds (Wilhite) C.; m. Betty Jane Nichols, Jan. 31, 1954 (div.); children: Eric Robert, Mark Andrew, Susan Lynn; m. Susan A. Dower, Feb. 11, 1984. Student, U. Utah, 1949-51; BS, U. So. Calif., 1953, postgrad., 1956-58. Adminstrv. asst. City of Beverly Hills, Calif., 1956-57; asst. to city mgr. City of Claremont, Calif., 1957-58; sr. adminstrv. asst. to city mgr. City of Torrance, Calif., 1958-60; city mgr. City of San Dimas, Calif., 1960-64, Pico Rivera, Calif., 1964-68; chief dep. dir. Calif. Dept. Public Works, 1968-71; dir. Calif. Dept. Social Welfare, 1971-73; U.S. commr. welfare Washington, 1973-75; pres. Robert B. Carleson & Assocs., Sacramento, Calif. and Washington, 1975-81, chmn. Washington, 1987-93, 02—, San Diego, 1993-01; pres. Innovative Environ. Svcs. Ltd., Vancouver, B.C., Can., 1992; spl. asst. to U.S. pres. for policy devel. Washington, 1981-84; prin., dir. govt. rels. KMG Main Hurdman, Washington, 1984-87; dir. transition team Dept. HHS, Office of Pres.-Elect, 1980-81; spl. adviser Office of Policy Coordination; sr. policy advisor, chmn. welfare task force Reagan Campaign, 1980. Bd. dirs. Fed. Home Loan Bank of Atlanta, 1987-90, I.E.S., Ltd., Can., Transenviro Co., USA, Churchill Co., USA; adv. com. Fed. Home Loan Mortgage Corp., 1985-87; mem. strengthening family policy coun. Nat. Policy Forum, Washington, 1994. Eagle Scout qtr. master sea scout, 1948; lt. gov. Calif. Boys' State, 1948; adv. coun. gen. govt. Rep. Nat. Com., Washington, 1980-81; sr. fellow Free Congress Found., 1994—; chmn. Am. Civil Rights Union, 1998—. Officer USN, 1953-56, USNR, 1956-63. Mem.: Masons, Rotary (pres. 1964), Army & Navy (Washington), Capitol Hill, Fairfax Hunt. Home and Office: 175 Cameron Station Blvd Alexandria VA 22304 E-mail: rcarleson@aol.com.

CARLETON, DON EDWARD, history center administrator, educator, writer; b. Dallas, Jan. 22, 1947; s. Edward Preston and Wilma Jo (Smith) C.; m. Suzanne Marie Young, Jan. 2, 1974; children: Ian Alexander, Aunna Fleur. BS, U. Houston, 1969, MA, 1974, PhD, 1978. Tchr. Friendswood Ind. Sch. Dist., Tex., 1969-71; teaching fellow U. Houston, 1971-75; research asst. Southwest Ctr. for Urban Research, Houston, 1974-75; dir. Houston Met. Research Ctr., 1975-79, Barker History Ctr., Austin, 1979-91, Ctr. for am. History, U. Tex.,

Austin, 1991—. Urban adv. editor Handbook of Tex., Austin, 1983—95; sr. lectr. dept. history U. Tex., Austin, 1985—, dept. journalism, 1997—; J.R. Parten chair in Archives Am. History, 1989—; cons. Amon Carter Mus., Ft. Worth, 1983, Birmingham (Ala.) Pub. Libr., 1978. Editorial bd. Southwestern Hist. Quar., 1980-90; author: Who Shot the Bear?, 1984, Red Scare!, 1985, (Coral Tullis best book award Tex. Hist. Assn. 1986), "A Breed So Rare": The Life of J.R. Parten, Liberal Texas Oilman, 1896-1992, 1998 (Tex. Inst. Letters Book award 1998), Being Rapoport: Capitalist With a Conscience, 2002; editor: Focus on America Series, 1999-; oral hist., mem. bd. advs. Pioneers of Television Project, Acad. Television Arts and Scis., L.A., 1998-; contbr. articles to profl. jours. Recipient Presdl. Excellence award, U. Tex., Austin, 1982; grantee, Parten Found., 1982, O'Connor Found., 1982. Fellow: Tex. Inst. Letters, Tex. State Hist. Assn. (grantee 1983); mem.: Philos. Soc. Tex., U. Tex. Club, Headliners Club Austin. Democrat. Avocations: reading; travel. Office: U Tex Ctr Am History SRH 2-101 Austin TX 78713-7330 Business E-Mail: d.carleton@mail.utexas.edu.

CARLETON, JOSEPH GEORGE, JR., lawyer, state legislator; b. Bklyn., July 21, 1945; s. Joseph G. and Ellen (Gabriel) C. AB, Dartmouth Coll., 1969; JD, Boston U., 1972. Atty. Calderwood & Ouellette, Dover, N.H., 1972-79; pvt. practice Wells, Maine, 1979-83, 88—; atty., ptnr. Patterson Carleton & Mongue, Wells, 1983-88; mem. Maine Ho. of Reps., Augusta, 1990-98, asst. Rep. leader, 1994-96; commr. Gov.'s Blue Ribbon Commn. on Health, 2000, Maine Health Performance Coun., 2001—02. Chmn. Wells Site Rev. Bd., 1985-86; town meeting moderator Town of Wells, 1983—; mem. adv. bd. York County Tech. Coll., 1996—. Sgt. N.H. Air N.G., 1966-74. Mem. Wells C. of C. (pres. 1984), Elks, Masons. Republican. Avocations: golf, history, politics. Home and Office: PO Box 369 Wells ME 04090-0369 E-mail: atty@maine.rr.com.

CARLETON, WILLARD TRACY, retired finance educator; b. Boston, May 3, 1934; s. Frank Nagle and Margaret Lally (Parker) C.; married; children: James, Sarah, Leslie, Julia. AB, Dartmouth Coll., 1956, MBA, 1957, MA (hon.), 1971; MA in Econs., U. Wis., 1961, PhD in Econs., 1962. Acct. C.F. Rittenhouse & Co., Boston, 1956; mem. labs. staff Bell Telephone Labs., Inc., N.Y.C., 1957-58; teaching asst. econs. dept. U. Wis., 1958-59, research asst., 1959-61; economist Fed. Res. Bank St. Louis, 1961-63; asst. prof. fin. Grad. Sch. Bus. Adminstrn., NYU, 1963-65, assoc. prof., 1965-66; assoc. prof. quantitative methods and managerial econs. Sch. Bus., Northwestern U., 1966-67; assoc. prof. fin. and econs. Amos Tuck Sch. Bus. Adminstrn., Dartmouth Coll., 1967-70, prof. fin. and econs., 1970-73, Leon E. Williams prof. banking and fin., 1973-74; William R. Kenan Jr. prof. bus. adminstrn. U. N.C., Chapel Hill, 1974-84; Karl Eller prof. fin. U. Ariz., Tucson, 1984—99, Donald R. Diamond prof. fin., 1999—2001, prof. fin emeritus, 2001. Author: A Theory of Financial Analysis, 1966, Corporate Finance, 1985; contbr. articles to profl. jours. Trustee Coll. Retirement Equities Fund, N.Y.C., 1980—84, Tchrs. Ins. and Annuity Assn., N.Y.C., 1984—. Mem. Fin. Mgmt. Assn. (pres. 1977-78), Western. Fin. Assn. (bd. dirs. 1986-89), Am. Fin. Assn. (bd. dirs. 1973-75), Am. Econ. Assn., Am. Statis. Assn. Episcopalian. Avocations: fishing, reading, music. Home: 4915 N Camino Antonio Tucson AZ 85718-6005

CARLEY, CHARLES TEAM, JR., mechanical engineer; b. Greenville, Miss., Dec. 27, 1932; s. Charles Team and Ruby (McClendon) C.; m. Shirley Holland, May 28, 1955; children: Karen, Mary McClendon, Charles Team III, Holland. BS, Miss. State U., 1955; MS, Va. Poly. Inst., 1960; PhD, N.C. State U., 1965. Engr. Gen. Elec. Co., 1955; instr. Va. Poly. Inst., 1958-60; asst. prof. Miss. State U., 1960-61; Ford Found. fellow N.C. State U., 1961-64; assoc. prof. Miss. State U., 1964-68, prof., 1968-93, head mech. engring. dept., 1969-80, head mech. and nuclear engring. dept., 1981-90, prof., dept. head emeritus, 1993—; head Petroleum Engring., 1990-93; prin. C.T. Carley & Assoc., 1993—. Chmn. Miss. Tech. Adv. Bd. on Boiler and Pressure Vessel Safety, 1974-87; mem. ABET Engring. Accreditation Commn., 1981-86; mem. ABET Related Accreditation Commn., 1992-96, chmn., 1994-95; Fulbright sr. lectr. U. Buenos Aires, 1986, U. Catamarca, 1987. Chmn. Miss. Rep. Mcpl. Exec. Com., 1968-89. With USNR, 1955-58. Mem. ASME (v.p. region XI 1972-74, sr. v.p. edn. 1986-90, gov. 1990-92), Miss. Acad. Scis. (pres. 1976-77), Engrs. Coun. Miss. (pres. 1970-71), Sigma Xi, Omicron Delta Kappa, Phi Kappa Phi. Home: 213 Windsor Rd Starkville MS 39759-2137 E-mail: ctcarley@bellsouth.net.

CARLEY, DONALD MARTIN, lawyer; b. Mpls., Feb. 28, 1968; s. Harold Edwin and Mary Elizabeth Carley. BS, Coll. William and Mary, 1990; JD, Temple U., 1995. CPCU, Colo., 2001; bar: Calif. 1995, U.S. Dist. Ct. (no. dist.) Calif. 1995, U.S. Ct. Appeals (9th cir.) 1995, U.S. Dist. Ct. (ea. dist.) Calif. 1996, U.S. Dist. Ct. (so. dist.) Calif. 1997, U.S. Dist. Ct. (ctrl. dist.) Calif. 1999, U.S. Patent and Trademark Office 2001, U.S. Supreme Ct. 2002. Environ. claims rep. The PMA Group, Phila., 1990-92, CIGNA Property and Casualty, Phila., 1992-95; assoc. Gordon & Rees, LLP, San Francisco, 1995-97, Luce Forward Hamilton & Scripps LLP, San Francisco, 1997-98; ptnr. Sonnenschein Nath & Rosenthal, San Francisco, 1998—. Contbr. articles to profl. jours. Mem. ABA, CPCU Soc. (mem. Golden Gate chpt. 1995—, exec. com. mem. Golden Gate chpt. 1998—, bd. dirs. 2000—), Calif. Bar Assn., San Francisco Bar Assn., Barristers Club San Francisco (vice chair bridging the gap com. 1996, chair bridging the gap com. 1997, 98, bd. dirs. 1999—, pres. 2000—), Alpha Lambda Delta, Phi Eta Sigma. Avocations: cycling, travel, fly fishing, photography. Office: Sonnenschein Nath & Rosenthal 685 Market St Ste 6 San Francisco CA 94105-4202 Fax: 415-543-5472. E-mail: d3c@sonnenschein.com.

CARLEY, GEORGE H. judge; b. Jackson, Miss., Sept. 24, 1938; s. George L. Jr. and Dorothy (Holmes) C.; m. Sandra M. Lineberger, 1960; 1 child, George H. Jr. AB, U. Ga., 1960, LLB, 1962. Bar: Ga. 1961. Pvt. practice, Atlanta and Decatur, Ga., 1961-71; ptnr. McCurdy & Candler, Decatur, Ga., 1971-79; also spl. asst. atty. gen. Office. Atty. Gen.; judge Ct. Appeals Ga., 1979-89, chief judge, 1989-91, presiding judge, 1991-93; justice Supreme Ct. Ga., Atlanta, 1993—. Chmn. bd. visitors U. Ga. Law Sch., 1995-96. Bd. Visitors U. Ga. Law Sch.; past pres. U. Ga. Law Sch. Assn. Coun., 1989-90, active, 1986-91; trustee Ga. Legal History Found., Inc.; active Holy Trinity Episc. Ch., Decatur. Mem. ABA, State Bar Ga., Ga. Bar Found., Lawyers Club Atlanta, Old Warhorse Lawyers Club (pres. 1997-98), Joseph Henry Lumpkin Am. Inn of Ct. (pres. 1994-95), Pythagoras Lodge, Scottish Rite. Office: Supreme Court 244 Washington Street Atlanta GA 30334-9007*

CARLEY, KURT, actor; b. Greenville, Pa., Sept. 26, 1962; s. William Frederick and Eleanor Odessa (Scott) C. BFA in Theater cum laude, Point Park Coll., 1986. Actor Pitts. Playhouse Profl. Co., 1985-86, Portable Theater Co., Pitts., 1986; actor off-Broadway Little Shop of Horrors, N.Y.C., 1986-87; film actor Dominick & Eugene, Monkey Shines, Pitts., 1987. Creature movement specialist (films) Godzilla, 1997, Dungeons & Dragons, Meggiddo-Omega Code II, Underworld, 2003, (TV series) Special Unit 2, puppeteer (film) Lethal Weapon 4, 1998, motion capture performer (TV series) Starship Troopers, 1999—2000. Mem. Actors Equity Assn., Screen Actors Guild. Clubs: Drama (Pitts.). Address: 324 W Garfield Ave Glendale CA 91204 E-mail: Kcarley@earthlink.net.

CARLEY, MICHAEL JABARA, historian, director; b. Bklyn., Mar. 27, 1945; s. George Robert Carley, Virginia Jabara; m. Irina Borisovna Syrtsova. BA, George Washington U., 1967; MA, Queen's U., Kingston, Ont., Can., 1970, PhD, 1976. Dir. Aid to Scholarly Publs. Programme, Ottawa, Canada, 1985—98; cons. Policy Rsch. Secretariat, Govt. Can., Ottawa, 1999—2000; dir., prof. history U. Akron (Ohio) Press, 1999—. Author: 1939: The Alliance that Never Was and the Coming of World War II, 1999 (Three Year Major Research grant, Social Sciences and Humanities Research Council of Canada, 1995), Revolution and Intervention: The French Government and the Russian Civil War, 1917-1919, 1983 (Three Year Major Research grant, Social Sciences and Humanities Research Council of Canada, 1991), 1939: l'alliance de la dernière chance, une réinterprétation des origines de la Seconde Guerre mondiale, 2001 (grant-in-aid of publication, Aid to Scholarly Publications Programme, Canada, 2001); contbr. articles to profl. jours. Mem.: Hist. Soc. Office: U Akron Bierce Library 374B Akron OH 44325-1703 Office Fax: 330-972-8364.

CARLEY, MICHAEL JOHN, organization official, playwright, actor; b. Milton, Fla., Nov. 7, 1964; s. Michael John Carley and Constance Worthington; m. Barbara Wiechmann, Aug. 18, 1990 (div. 2002); 1 child, William Michael. BA, Hampshire Coll., Amherst, Mass., 1986; MFA, Columbia U., 1989. Pitching coach baseball team Hampshire Coll., 1990-93; playwright, actor, dir., freelance writer, N.Y.C., 1989—; UN non-govtl. orgn. rep. Vets. for Peace, Inc., Bklyn. and Washington, 1991—2001, project dir. Iraq water project Bklyn., 1999—2001; coord. Adult Aspergers Syndrome Support Group, N.Y.C., 2001—; exec. dir. GRASP Inc., 2003—. Author: (plays) Boris Simonov and the Last Frontier, 1992, Bo Calcullen Discovers the New World, and several others, 1995, In a Name, 1997, The Age of Belief, 1999; actor 1-man theatre piece The Idea of North (Glenn Gould), 1999. Avocations: American primitive-style guitarist, collector classical CDs, poker, surfing. . Fax: 718-622-6227. E-mail: mjcarley@aol.com.

CARLILE, CHRISTOPHER BLAKE, military officer, pilot; b. Paragould, Ark., June 22, 1962; s. Donald Gene and Jo Ann (Dinwiddie) C.; m. Sandra F. Pickett, Oct. 28, 1989; 1 child, Chelsea Brook. BS, Ark. State U., 1988; MBA, Embry-Riddle Coll., 1997; aviation officer course, Ft. Rucker, Ala., 1989, pilot, 1990; test pilot, Maintenance Coll., Ft. Eustis, Va., 1990. Commd. 2d lt. U.S. Army, 1988, advanced through grades to maj., 1999; exec. officer 1-145th Aviation Regiment Ft. Rucker, 1989; platoon leader 7-159th Aviation Regiment Stuttgart, Germany, 1990-92; prodn. control officer 7-159th Aviation Regiment Giebelstadt, Germany, 1992-93; co. comdr. A-3-158th Aviation Regiment Wiesbaden, Germany, 1993-95; exec. officer 1st Attack Tng. Bn. Ft. Knox, Ky., 1995-99; exec. officer B-101 101st AVN Rgt. 101st Airborne Divsn. Mem. Army Aviation Assn. of Am. (treas. 1989-96), Ducks Unltd. (Ky. bd.). Republican. Avocations: golf, hunting, fishing. E-mail: carlilec@campbell.army.mil.

CARLILE, JANET LOUISE, artist, educator; b. Denver, Apr. 26, 1942; d. Jessie Crawford and Alice Essie (Locker) Carlile. BFA, Cooper Union, 1966; MFA, Pratt Inst., 1971. Prof. Bklyn. Coll., CUNY, 1971—; prin., owner Red Mountain Gallery, Ouray, Colo., 2001—. Founder Incline Village (Nev.) Fine Arts Ctr., 1966—68; instr. Sch. Visual Arts, N.Y.C., 1968—70, Printmaking Workshop, N.Y.C., 1971, Scarsdale (N.Y.) Studio Workshop, 1971—73, SUNY-Stony Brook, L.I., 1976, Bard Winter Coll., Rhinebeck, NY, 1980; head printmaking, asst. dir. Bklyn. Mus. Art Sch., 1971—77; dir. Bklyn. Coll. Press, 1977—; cons. Woodstock (N.Y.) Sch. Art, 1980—84; judge Alpine Artists Show, Ouray, Colo., 1989; judge Landscape Painting Show Woodstock Art Assn., 1995; dir. Red Mountain Gallery, Ouray, Colo. One-woman shows include Blue Mountain Gallery, N.Y.C., 1980, Stetson U., Deland, Fla., 1995, Fairleigh Dickinson Coll., Teaneck, N.J., 1995, exhibited in group shows at Associated Am. Artists Gallery, N.Y., 1971—81, Bklyn. Mus., 1976, Ulster County Artists Show, N.Y. State Coun. Show, 1984, Alpine Artists Show Ouray County, 1987, IRT Bklyn. Mus. Sta. Sec. San Juan Vista Landowners Assn., Ridgway, Colo., 1980—86. Recipient Hirshorn Purchase prize, Soc. Am. Graphic Artists, 1969, Best of Show award, Alpine Artists Show Ouray County, 1987, Creative Incentive award, Rsch. Found., CUNY, 1992, 1996—, Pollack/Krasner Found. award, 2002—03; fellow, Pratt Inst., Bklyn., 1971; grantee NEA workshop, Colo. Coun. Arts; scholar full scholarship, Cooper Union, N.Y.C., 1962—66. Mem.: Ouray County Arts Assn. (pres. 1991—93). Avocation: Avocations: hiking, backpacking, skiing, yoga, rock climbing. Home: PO Box 1004 Ouray CO 81427-1004 Office: Brooklyn Coll Art Dept Bedford at Ave H Brooklyn NY 11210

CARLIN, BETTY, educator; b. N.Y.C. d. Samuel and Rose Sara (Bernstein) Grossberg; m. Arthur S. Carlin, July 18, 1953 (dec.); children: Lisa Anne Skinner, James Howard. BA, UCLA, 1952; MA, U. Calif., Berkeley, 1955. Educator L.A. Sch. Dist., 1952-55; owner Carlin's Shoes, L.A., 1952-68; educator Berkeley (Calif.) Sch. Dist., 1957-58; master tchr. spl. programs Calif. State Coll., Hayward, 1967-84; educator U. Calif., Berkeley, 1984-86; tchr. demonstrator C.V.U. Sch. Dist.; student tchr. supr. Calif. State U., Hayward. Co-owner Art-Car Corp., 1978-88. Creator ednl. videos for children Study in Characteristics of an Effective and Loving Mother, Children's Play as Related to Intelligence, An Eclectic Approach to Teaching Reading. Mem. Nat. Tchrs. Assn., Calif. Tchrs. Assn., Commonwealth Club, San Francisco Opera Guild. Avocations: swimming, opera, theater, gardening, vocal study.

CARLIN, CLAIR MYRON, lawyer; b. Sharon, Pa., Apr. 20, 1947; s. Charles William and Carolyn L. (Vukasich) C.; children: Eric Richard, Elizabeth Marie, Alexander Myron. BS in Econs., Ohio State U., 1969, JD, 1972. Bar: Ohio 1973, Pa. 1973, U.S. Dist. Ct. (so. dist.) Ohio 1973, U.S. Dist. Ct. (no. dist.) Ohio 1975, U.S. Supreme Ct. 1976, U.S. Ct. Claims, 1983, U.S. Tax Ct. 1985. Staff atty. Ohio Dept. Taxation, Columbus, 1972-73; asst. atty. City of Warren, Ohio, 1973-75; assoc. McLaughlin, DiBlasio & Harshman, Youngstown, Ohio, 1975-80; ptnr. McLaughlin, McNally & Carlin, Youngstown, 1980-98, Carlin & Vasvari, LLC, Poland, Ohio, 1998-2000, Clair M. Carlin, LLC, 2000—. Mem. editl. bd. Ohio Trial mag. Mem. Trumbull County Bicentennial Commn., Ohio, 1976; v.p. Svcs. for the Aging, Trumbull County, 1976-77; mem. Pres.' Club Ohio State U., Polit. Action Com. Maj. Ohio NG, 1972-82. Fellow Ohio State Bar Found.; mem. ATLA (bd. govs. 1996-2002, trustee PAC 1996-98), ABA, Ohio State Bar Assn. (negligence law com. 1991—), Ohio State Bar Coll., Mahoning County Bar Assn. (chmn. legal edn. com. 1985-86, counsel 1986-87, trustee 2000—, pres.-elect 2003—), Ohio Acad. Trial Lawyers (trustee 1988-92, polit. action com. chmn. 1991, exec. com. 1991-97, treas. 1992-93, sec. 1993-94, pres.-elect 1994-95, pres. 1995-96), Mahoning-Trumbull Acad. Trial Lawyers (pres. 1991), Ohio State U. Alumni Assn. (pres. Trumbull County chpt. 1985—), Cath. War Vets. (Ohio state commdr., Vet. of Yr. 1988), Rotary, Million Dollar Advocate Forum. Democrat. Roman Catholic. Home: 3524 Hunters Hl Poland OH 44514-5303 Office: Clair M Carlin LLC PO Box 5369 Youngstown OH 44514-0369 E-mail: cmc@carlin-law.com.

CARLIN, DENNIS J. lawyer; b. Chgo., Aug. 23, 1941; s. Herbert E. and Lillian (Schnelder) C.; m. Fern Carlin, Nov. 25, 1964; children: Gregory A., H. David, Stuart B. BBA, U. Wis., 1963; JD, DePaul U., 1967; LLM in Taxation, Georgetown U., 1971. Bar: Ill. 1967; CPA. Auditor Checkers, Simon & Rosner, Chgo., 1963-67; assoc. tax ct. litigation divsn. IRS, Washington, 1967-71; ptnr. Frankel, McKay, Orlikoff, Denten & Kostner, Chgo., 1971-77, Horwood & Carlin, Chgo., 1977-82, Gardner, Carton & Douglas, Chgo., 1982—, vice-chmn., 1998—2003. Contbr. articles to profl. jours. Mem. atty. div. Jewish United Fund; bd. dirs., exec. com. Coun. for Jewish Elderly. Mem. ABA, Am. Coll. Tax Counsel, Chgo. Bar Assn. (former chmn. fed. tax com.), Nat. Strategy Forum, NYU Inst. Fed. Taxation, DePaul U. Alumni Coun., Am. Israeli C. of C., Twin Orchard Country Club. Avocations: golf, skiing, reading, music, theatre. Office: Gardner Carton & Douglas LLC 191 N Wacker Dr Ste 3400 Chicago IL 60606-1698

CARLIN, DONALD WALTER, retired food products executive, consultant; b. Gary, Ind., Aug. 27, 1934; s. Walter Joseph and Mabel (Ebert) C.; m. Kathleen Susan McCone, Jan. 21, 1961; children: Michael Scott, Karen Mary, Mark Steven. BS in Engring, U. Notre Dame, 1956; LLB, U. Mich., 1959; grad., Advanced Mgmt. Program, Harvard U., 1978. Bar: Ind. 1959, Ill. 1960. Assoc. to ptnr. Soans, Anderson Luedeka & Fitch, Chgo., 1960-72; sr. atty. Kraft Inc., Glenview, Ill., 1972-73, v.p., asst. gen. counsel, 1974-79, sr. v.p., gen. counsel, 1979-81, sr. v.p., gen. counsel, sec., 1981-86, v.p., assoc. gen. counsel, 1986-89; v.p., dep. gen. counsel Kraft Gen. Foods, Northfield, Ill., 1989-92. Mem. bd. visitors Sch. Medicine, U. Calif.-Davis, 1990—. Mem. ABA (hon.; com. corp. law depts. sect. bus. law), Assn. Gen. Counsel (emeritus), Westmoreland Country Club (bd. dirs. 1989-94, pres. 1993-94), Notre Dame Club (Chgo.), Ironwood Country Club (pres. 2000-03, bd. dirs. 2000-03). Home and Office: 333 Regentwood Rd Northfield IL 60093-2762 also: 73-106 Galleria Ct Palm Desert CA 92260

CARLIN, HERBERT J. electrical engineering educator, researcher; b. N.Y.C., May 1, 1917; s. Louis Aaron and Shirley (Salzman) C.; children: Seth Andrew, Elliot Michael; m. Mariann J. Hartmann, June 29, 1975 B.E.E., Columbia Coll., 1938, M.E.E., 1950; PhD in Elec. Engring., Poly. Inst. N.Y., 1947. Engr. Westinghouse Corp., Newark, 1940-45; from asst. to assoc. prof. Poly. Inst. Bklyn., 1945-60, prof., head electrophysics, 1960-66; J. Preston Levis prof. engring. Cornell U., Ithaca, N.Y., 1966—, dir. elec. engring., 1966-75. Mem. adv. panel Nat. Bur. Standards, Boulder, Colo., 1967-70; mem. rev. com. Lehigh U., Bethlehem, Pa., 1966-74, U. Pa., Phila., 1979-82; vis. prof. Ecole Normale Superieure, Paris, 1964-67, MIT, Boston, 1973-74; vis. scientist Nat. Ctr. for Telecommunications, Issy Les Moulineaux, France, 1979-80; vis. lectr. U. Genoa, Italy, summer 1973, U. London, Dec. 1979, The Technion, Haifa, Israel, Mar. 1980, Tianjin U., China, summer 1982, Univ. Coll., Dublin, Ireland, summer 1983, Polytech. of Turin, Italy, summer 1985, 91, Fed. Polytech., Lausanne, Switzerland, summer 1992. Co-author: Wideband Circuit Design, 1997. Fellow NSF, 1964; recipient Outstanding Achievement award U.S. Air Force, 1965 Fellow IEEE (chmn. profl. group on circuit theory 1955-56, Centennial medal 1985) Home: 8 Highland Park Ln Ithaca NY 14850-1452 E-mail: hjc2@cornell.edu.

CARLIN, JOHN WILLIAM, archivist, former governor; b. Salina, Kans., Aug. 3, 1940; s. Jack W. and Hazel L. (Johnson) C.; m. Ramona Hawkinson, 1962 (div. 1980); children: John David, Lisa Marie; m. Lynn Lady, 1997. BS in Agr., Kans. State U., 1962, PhD (hon.), 1987. Farmer, dairyman, Smolan, Kans., 1962-79; mem. Kans. Ho. of Reps., 1971-79, speaker of ho., 1977-79; gov. State of Kans., Topeka, 1979-87; pres. Econ. Devel. Assocs., Inc., 1987-92; partner Carlin & Associates, Topeka, 1989-95; vice-chmn. Midwest Superconductivity, Inc., Lawrence, KS, 1990-94; partner Clark Publishing, Inc., Topeka, 1991-95; archivist of the U.S. Nat. Archives & Records Admin., Washington, 1995—. Vis. prof. pub. adminstrn. and internat. trade Wichita State U., 1987-88; chmn. Nat. Govs. Assn., 1984-85, Midwestern Govs. Conf., 1982-83. Democrat. Lutheran. Home: 18201 Allwood Ter Olney MD 20832-1716 Office: Nat Archives & Records Admin 7th & Pennsylvania Ave Washington DC 20408-0001 also: 8601 Adelphi Rd Rm 4200 College Park MD 20740-6002 E-mail: john.carlin@nara.gov.

CARLIN, PHYLLIS EVA SCOTT, education educator; d. L. and B. Scott; m. Charles J. Carlin; children: Laura, Sarah. PhD, So. Ill. U. English and speech tchr. Canton H.S., Canton, Mo., 1971—73; tchg. asst. So. Ill. U., Carbondale, 1974—76; prof. of communication U. of No. Iowa, Cedar Falls, 1976—. Guest editor Iowa Journal of Communication: Special Issue on Ethnography, Communication and Performance; contbr. articles to profl. jours. Recipient Cert. of Appreciation, Smithsonian Instn., 1997; grant, Iowa Humanities Bd., 1981—82, 1993, Grad. fellowship, So. Ill. U., 1973—74, Rising Star scholar, U. Iowa, 1994—. Mem.: Nat. Communication Assn. (sec. of interpretation divsn. 1987—88). Achievements include research in ethnography and oral history of rural life; narrative analysis of crisis discourse; cultural and life performance genres; designed new curriculum in communication in areas of cultural performance, ethnography, health communication, and discourse study.

CARLIN, SETH A. music educator, musician; b. N.Y.C., Feb. 8, 1945; s. Herbert Jacob Crlin and Esther Beth Carlin; m. Maryse Christiane Rodé, June 3, 1947; children: Tova Juliette, Daniel Guillaume. Licence de Concert Premier Nommé, Ecole Normale de Musique, Paris, 1965; BA cum laude, Harvard U., 1969; MS in Pnaio, Juilliard Sch., 1970. Asst. prof. music Hiram (Ohio) Coll., 1970—73; piano instr. Phillips Exeter (NH) Acad., 1973—79; prof. music, head piano program Washington U., St. Louis, 1979—. Piano soloist Friedenhaumer Kammerkonzerte, Berlin, 1999, St. Louis Symphony Orch., 2002; fortepiano soloist Philharmonia Baroque, San Francisco, 2000. Musician: (CD) Sonata and Bagatelles of Beethoven, 1990, Solo Fortepiano Music of Schubert, 1993, Four-hand Fortepiano Music of Schubert, 2001; performer: cycle of complete Schubert Fortepiano sonatas, Merkin Hall, NY, Marboro Music Festival, Newport Music Festival, Santa Fe Music Festival, Lincoln Ctr. Bd. trustees Westfield Ctr. for Keyboard Studies, 2000—. Recipient prize, Internat. Busani Piano Competition, 1973, CD Rec. of Mo. award, Alte Musik Actuelle mag., 2000; grantee, Nat. Endowment for Arts, 1989. Mem.: Coailtion for Environ., Sierra Club. Avocations: tennis, hiking, windsurfing. Office: Washington U Campus Box 1032 Saint Louis MO 63130

CARLIN, SYDNEY, state representative; b. Wichita, Kans., Nov. 20, 1944; m. John Carlin; 4 children. BS in Social Sci. City commr. City of Manhattan, Kans., 1993—96, mayor, 1996—97; state rep. Dist. 66, Kans., 2003—. Democrat. Roman Catholic. Office: 272-W State Capitol 300 SW 10th Ave Topeka KS 66612*

CARLINER, MICHAEL SIMON, economist, association executive; b. Balt., May 8, 1945; s. Morris Allen and Shirley (Flegman) C.; m. Asya Haroen, Oct. 23, 1976; children: Wayan, Melati. BS, U. Pa., 1966, postgrad., 1966-69. Pub. Harry Newspaper, Balt., 1969-71; sr. economist Dynamics Assocs., Cambridge, Mass., 1971-78; v.p. Regional Data Assocs., New Brunswick, N.J., 1978-82; sr. economist Chase Econometrics, Bala Cynwyd, Pa., 1982-84; staff v.p. for econs. Nat. Assn. Home Builders, Washington, 1984—. Home: 8607 Timber Hill Ln Potomac MD 20854-4240 Office: Nat Assn Home Builders 1201 15th St NW Washington DC 20005-2800

CARLING, FRANCIS, lawyer, mediator; b. N.Y.C., Nov. 2, 1945; s. James Andrew and Mary Amelia (Lorenzo) C.; m. Elisabeth Morse Kelley, Aug. 30, 1969 (div. Apr. 1979); 1 child, Duncan Campbell; m. Christina Ellen Black, Sept. 28, 1991 (div. Sept. 2000); children: Graham Black, Gillian Kirova. AB, Fordham U., 1967; JD, Yale U., 1970. Bar: Conn. 1970, U.S. Dist. Ct. Conn. 1971, N.Y. 1972, U.S. Dist. Ct. (so. and ea. dists.) N.Y. 1972, U.S. Ct. Appeals (2nd cir.) 1972, U.S. Supreme Ct. 1973, U.S. Dist. Ct. (no. dist.) Ohio 1978, U.S. Ct. Appeals (3d cir.) 1980, U.S. Dist. Ct. (we. dist.) N.Y. 1981, U.S. Ct. Appeals (6th cir.) 1986, U.S. Ct. Appeals (4th cir.) 1990. Staff atty. New Haven Legal Assistance Assn., 1970-72; assoc. Sullivan & Cromwell, N.Y.C., 1972-80, Winthrop, Stimson, Putnam & Roberts, N.Y.C., 1980-82, ptnr., 1982-97, Collazo Carling & Mish LLP, N.Y.C., 1997—. Author: Move Over: Students, Politics, Religion, 1969. Bd. dirs. Big Bros., Inc. N.Y., N.Y.C., 1974—, pres., 1993-95; v.p. Friends of Afghanistan, Inc., N.Y.C., 1985-90; bd. dirs. Vol. Cons. Group, Inc., N.Y.C., 1988-97. Mem. ABA, N.Y. State Bar Assn., Assn. Bar City N.Y., Union Club. Episcopalian. Avocation: music. Home: 205 E 17th St New York NY 10021-5431 Office: Collazo Carling & Mish LLP 747 3rd Ave New York NY 10017-2803 E-mail: fcarling@ccmlaw.com.

CARLINI, JAMES, management consultant; b. Berwyn, Ill., Aug. 27, 1954; s. Harvey Reno and Helen Dorothy (Stan) C.; m. Holly R. Haupin, Sept. 29, 1979. MusB, Roosevelt U., 1976, BS in Computer Sci., 1978; MBA in Mgmt. Info. Systems and Mktg., DePaul U., 1982. Info. systems designer Western Electric div. Bell Labs., Naperville, Ill., 1977-79; software engr. Motorola, Schaumburg, Ill., 1979-81; mgr. Ill. Bell, Chgo., 1981-83; dir. telecommunications and computer hardware cons. Arthur Young & Co., Chgo., 1983-86; pres. Carlini & Assocs., Inc., Hinsdale, Ill., 1986—. Adj. prof. Technol. Inst. Sch. Speech Northwestern U., Evanston, Ill., 1986—, grad. sch. bus. DePaul U., Chgo., 1986-89; dir. Teledata Hong Kong; mem. adv. bd. COMDEX. Editorial adv. bd. mem. Cabling Bus. Mag.; editl. columnist Eprairie.com; contbr. articles to profl. jours. Pres. Mental Health Bd., Berwyn, 1983. Recipient Northwestern U. Alumni Prof.'s award, 1995, Disting. Tchg. award Northwestern U., 1996. Mem. Assn. Cabling Profls. (dir. End User Coun., infrastructure cons., cabling facilities integrator, network cabling and applications integrator), Internat. Trade Assn., Data Processing Mgmt. Assn. (bd. dirs. 1988-96, Chgo. chpt. pres. 1994-96, Spkrs. award, Outstand Instrs. award 1993), Intelligent Bldg. Inst. (chmn. definitions com.), DAV (citation 1979), Federal Comms. Bar Assn. Roman Catholic. Avocations: yachting, golf. Office: Carlini & Assocs Inc 120 E Ogden Ave Ste 206 Hinsdale IL 60521-3546

CARLINI, PIERO ELISO, secondary school educator; b. Akron, Ohio, Feb. 13, 1961; s. Vincent Carlini and Filomena Berardi; m. Gilda Binayug Carlini, Aug. 7, 1997; 1 child, Giacomo. BA, UCLA, 1983; MA, Calif. State U., L.A., 1993. Tchr. Osaka (Japan) Coll. Fgn. Lang., 1989—90, Cambria English Inst., L.A., 1990—93, Fremont H.S., L.A., 1994—. Grantee NEA, 2002, Disney Corp., 2001, Mobile Corp., 1999. Mem.: TESOL. Home: 3140 Newton St 405-G Torrance CA 90505

CARLINO, GUY THOMAS, consulting company executive; b. N.Y.C., Sept. 2, 1928; s. Peter T. and Beatrice (Logerfo) C.; m. Berniece Ruth Horth, Sept. 28, 1952; children: Margaret M., Peter T., Sharon S., James C. Student, Columbia U., 1946-49. Pres. GTC Inc., 1993—. Bd. dirs. Am. State Corp., Am. State Bank, Hub States LLC, The Key Corp. Pres. Washington Twp. Sch. Found., Indpls., 1975, Indpls. Day Nursery Assn., 1982, Day Nursery Found, 1995. Sgt. U.S. Army, 1950-52. Mem. Indpls. Athletic Club, Gyro Club, Svc. Club, Contemporary Club. Office: GTC Inc 151 N Delaware St Indianapolis IN 46204-2599

CARLISLE, DALE L. lawyer; b. Walla Walla, Wash., Apr. 24, 1935; BA, U. Idaho, 1957; JD, George Washington U. School of Law, 1960. Judge advocate USAF, 1960—63; asst. U.S. atty. Wash. State (western dist.), 1964—66; with Gordon, Thomas, Honeywell, Malanca, Peterson & Daheim PLLC, Tacoma, 1966—; gen. counsel Levitt West, Inc., 1970—73; mng. ptnr. Gordon, Thomas, Honeywell, Malanca, Peterson & Daheim PLLC, Tacoma, 1990—2000, of counsel. Mem.: Wash. State Bar Assn. (pres.-elect 2000—01, pres. 2001—02, bd. govs. 1999—2002). Address: 1201 Pacific Ave Ste 2200 Tacoma WA 98402-4314 Mailing: PO Box 1157 Tacoma WA 98402*

CARLISLE, HENRY C. author; b. Sept. 14, 1926; BA, Stanford U., 1950, MA, 1952. Tradebook editor Alfred A. Knopf, 1954-59, Rinehart & Co., 1959-61. Author: Voyage to the First of December, 1972, The Land Where the Sun Dies, 1975, The Jonah Man, 1984, repub., 1999, (with Olga Andreyev Carlisle) The Idealists, 1999. Home: 1100 Union St San Francisco CA 94109-2019 E-mail: HCCarlisle@aol.com.

CARLISLE, JAMES PATTON, entrepreneur; b. Miami Beach, Fla., May 7, 1946; s. William Olin and Evelyn Obie (Ogden) C.; m. Laima Kirstina Launags; children: Alexandra Ji-Anne, Erika Li, Wendy Laubach, Scott Reidenbach. BA, Auburn U., 1969; MDiv, Emory U., 1976. Ordained to ministry Meth. Ch., 1975. Adminstrv. asst. Radney for Lt. Gov. Ala. campaign, 1969-70; asst. adminstr. Lee County Head Start, Auburn, Ala., 1970-72; assoc. pastor 10th St United Meth. Ch., Atlanta, 1974-76; dir. continuing edn. No. Ga. Ann. Conf. United Meth. Ch., Atlanta, 1975-78; program dir. Ctr. Profl. Devel. in Ministry, Lancaster, Pa., 1978-80; pres. Carlisle Leadership Group, 1989-99, The de Bono Group, 2000—; program master trainer Edward de Bono Thinking Methods, 2000—. Dir. Ctr. for Profl. Devel. in Ministry, Lancaster Theol. Sem., 1980—90; exec. dir. Ctr. for Creative Ch. Leadership, 1990; cons. on devel. of distributorships and trainers in S.Am. to APTT, global distbr. for Edward de Bono Thinking Methods ; distbr. Edward de Bono Thinking Methods, Mex., Argentina, Brazil, Colombia; dir. programs and continuing edn. events. Contbr. articles to profl. jours. Leader career planning events for clergy Uniting Ch. of Australia, Australia and N.Z.; elder N.Y. Ann. Conf. United Meth. Ch.; bd. dirs. Phila. Human Resources Planning Group; clergy mem. N.Y. Ann. Conf. of United Meth. Ch. Mem. OD Network Soc. Advancement Continuing Edn. for Ministry, Omicron Delta Kappa. Home and Office: 1722 Niblick Ave Lancaster PA 17602-4826 E-mail: jpc@debonogroup.com.

CARLISLE, KITTY, actress; b. New Orleans, Mar. 9, 1915; d. Joseph and Hortense (Holtzman) Couer; m. Aug. 11, 1946; children: Christopher, Catherine Stoeckle. Actress in field. Author: Kitty, 1988. Chmn. N.Y. State Coun. on the Arts, 1976—. Home: 32 E 64th St New York NY 10021-7359

CARLISLE, LILIAN MATAROSE BAKER (MRS. E. GRAFTON CARLISLE JR.), writer, lecturer; b. Meridian, Miss., Jan. 1, 1912; d. Joseph and Lilian (Flournoy) Baker; m. E. Grafton Carlisle, Jr., Jan. 9, 1933; children: Diana, Penelope. Student, Dickinson Coll., 1929-30, Pierce Coll. Bus. Adminstrn., 1930-31; BA, U. Vt., 1981, MA, 1986. Adminstrv. sec. RAF Ferry Command, Montreal, Can., 1942; exec. staff. mem. in charge collections, research Shelburne (Vt.) Mus., 1951-61; exec. sec. Burlington Area Community Health Study, 1963, coord., 1964; asst. coord. Vt. Mental Retardation Planning Project, 1965; project dir. 4-county Champlain Valley Medicare Alert, 1966; dir. publ. rels. Champlain Valley Agrl. Fair, 1968-77; lectr. U. Vt. Elder Hostel program, 1976-77. Mem. faculty Vacation Coll., 1980-83. Co-author: The Story of the Shelburne Museum, 1955, Profile of the Community, 1964, Environmental and Personal Health of the Community, 1964, Vermont Clock and Watchmakers, Silversmiths and Jewelers, 1970; also numerous catalogs on collections at Shelburne Mus.; editl. cons. Burlington Social Survey, 1967; editor: Historic Guide to Burlington Neighborhoods, 1991, vol. II, 1997, vol. III, 2003; contbr. articles to profl. jours. Pres., Burlington Comty. Coun. for Social Welfare, 1959-61, 1971-73; chmn. bd. Champlain Sr. Citizens, 1977-79, justice of peace, 1979-81; pres. Chittenden County Extension Adv. Com., 1977-78; chmn. publs. com. Vt. Bicentennial Commn., 1974-77; mem. Vt. Ho. of Reps., 1968-70. Recipient Community Coun. Disting. Citizen award, 1978, cert. of award for Excellence in Cmty. Svc. DAR, 1996. Mem. Vt. (trustee, chmn. mus. com. 1967), N.Y. (faculty seminar) Chittenden (pres. 1969-72, editor Heritage Series of 10 books about Chittenden County towns 1972-76) hist. socs., Vt. Old Cemetary Assn., Vt. Folklore So., League Vt. Writers (dir. 1962, v.p., pres. 1967-69), Am. Pen Women (pres. Green Mountain br. 1980-82), Order Women Legislators (pres. Vt. br. 1972-74), Meml. Soc. Vt. (pres. 1989-94), Zonta Club (pres. 1964-65), Chi Omega, Conglist. Home: 117 Lakeview Ter Burlington VT 05401-2901

CARLISLE, RICK, professional basketball coach; b. Ogdensburg, NY; m. Donna Carlisle. Attended, U. Maine; BA in Psychology, U. Va., 1984. Player Boston Celtics, 1984—87; asst. coach NJ Nets, 1992—94, Portland Trail Blazers, 1994—97, Ind. Pacers, 1997—2000; head coach Detroit Pistons, 2001—03, Ind. Pacers, 2003—. Named winner NBA Championship, 1985—86. Achievements include teams that have ranked no lower than 16th in the league in scoring and have ranked in the top-10 during four of those seasons. Avocations: golf, piano. Office: Ind Pacers 125 S Pennsylvania St Indianapolis IN 46204*

CARLISLE, RONALD DWIGHT, nursery owner; b. Bismarck, N.D., Oct. 28, 1940; m. Neva Carlisle, May 18, 1968. BS, Black Hills State Coll., 1966. Policy issue mgr. Provident Life Ins. Co., Bismarck, N.D., 1966-83; workers compensation commr. Bismarck, 1983-85; delivery driver Premium Beverage, Bismarck, 1985-86; owner trees N M Ore, Bismarck, 1986—; mem. N.D. Legislature. Chair Dist. 52-Dist. 30, Bismarck; del. Rep. State Conv., 1976, 78, 80, 82, 84, 86, 88, 90, 92, 94, 96, 98, 2000, 2002. With USN, 1958-62. Recipient Guardian of Small Bus. award NFIB, 1991. Mem. Am. Vets. (life), N.D. Nursery Assn., Elks, NRA. Address: PO Box 222 Bismarck ND 58502-0222

CARLISLE-FRANK, PAMELA L. researcher and writer, consultant; d. James E. and Barbara Carlisle; m. Joshua M. Frank, Mar. 13, 1988. BA with honors, U. Chgo., 1985, MA, 1986; PhD, U. Calif., Irvine, 1991. Rschr. The Hardiness Inst., Chgo., 1983-86, U. Chgo., 1983-86, U. Calif., Irvine, 1987-91, Eastern N.Mex. U., Portales, 1991-92; rsch. cons. Rsch. Inst. on Addictions, Buffalo, 1992; co-founder, pres. Found. Interdisciplinary Rsch./Edn. Promoting Animal Welfare, (FIREPAW), 1992—; self employed rsch. cons. San Francisco, NY, 1992—98; prof. Ea. N.Mex. U. Cons. Crisis Ctr., Clovis, N.Mex., 1991-92, Mental Health Resources, Clovis, 1992-93; adj. instr. Coll. San Mateo, Calif., 1997-98, Russell Sage Coll., Troy, N.Y., 1999; prof. Green Mountain Environ. Coll., 2000-01. Co-author: Addictive Behaviors in Women, 1994; contbr. articles to newspapers, mags., profl. jours. Vol. Homeless Teens, San Francisco, 1995—98. Regents fellow, 1998; U. Calif. Irvine rsch. fellow, 1990. Mem.: APA, Soc. for Study of Social Problems, Psychologists for Ethical Treatment of Animals, Am. Sociol. Assn. (sect. animals and soc.). Avocations: writing novels, hiking, painting. E-mail: firepaw@earthlink.net.

CARLO, WALDEMAR A. neonataologist; b. Mayaguez, P.R., May 20, 1952; s. Orlando and Nydia (Font) C.; m. Eugenia M. Lluch, May 14, 1977; children: Waldemar, Enrique, Julian, Maria. BS, U. P.R., Mayaguez, 1975; MD, U. P.R., San Juan, 1977. Diplomate Nat. Bd. Med. Examiners, in pediatrics and neonatal-perinatal medicine Am. Bd. Pediatrics; lic physician, Ohio, P.R., Ala. Pediatric intern and resident Univ. Children's Hosp./P.R. Med. Ctr., San Juan, 1977-80, chief resident in pediatrics, 1979-80; fellow in neonatology Rainbow Babies and Children's Hosp., Cleve., 1980-82; asst. prof. pediatrics Case Western Res. U. Sch. Medicine, Cleve., 1982-89, asst. prof. reproductive biology, 1984-91, assoc. prof. pediatrics, 1989-91; prof. pediatrics, dir. divsn. neonatology U. Ala. at Birmingham Med. Sch., 1991—; dir. newborn nurseries U. Ala. Med. Ctr. and The Children's Hosp. of Ala., 1991—. Author: New Therapies for Neonatal Respiratory Failure; mem. editorial bd. Pediatric Pulmonology, Jour. Neonatology; contbr. numerous articles toprofl. jours. Grantee NIH, 1996-, 96—, Ala. Dept. Health, 1991-92. Mem. AMA, Am. Acad. Pediatrics, Am. Thoracic Soc., Soc. for Pediatric Rsch., Latin Am. Pediatric Soc., So. Soc. for Pediatric Rsch., Am. Pediatric Soc., Jefferson County Pediatric Soc. Home: 1720 Indian Creek Dr Birmingham AL 35243-1700 Office: U Ala Med Ctr 525 New Hillman Bldg 619 19th St S Birmingham AL 35233-0001

CARLOCK, JOHN BRUCE, JR., English educator; b. Pitts., Sept. 21, 1925; s. John Bruce and Sydney Jane (Whiteside) C.; m. Ruth Olive McCardle, Oct. 19, 1948; children: Elizabeth Kehl, Rebecca Riley, John Bruce III, David Matthew (dec.). BA, Wesleyan U., 1951; PhD, U. S.C., 1973. Prof. English, Erskine Coll., Due West, SC, 1973—, chmn. dept. English. Dir. theatre studies Erskine Coll., Due West, 1973-91. Editor: (jour.) Voice of Sanity, 1988—. Bd. dirs. Upstate S.C. chpt. ACLU, Abbeville (S.C.) Opera House, pres., 1995-96. Served USAF, 1943—46, Maj. USAF, 1951—69, Vietnam. Decorated Bronze Star USAF, Air Force Commendation medal. Mem. MLA, Beta Theta Pi. Democrat. Avocations: reading, writing, speaking, orcharding. Home: Burning Tree Farm 247 Arborville Rd Donalds SC 29638 Office: Erskine Coll PO Box 458 Due West SC 29639

CARLOCK, MAHLON WALDO, financial consultant, former high school administrator; b. Plymouth, Ind., Sept. 17, 1926; s. Thorstine Clifford and Katheryn G. (Gephart) C.; m. Betty L. Dobbs, Aug. 27, 1954; children: Mahlon W. II, Rhena M., Shawn R. BS, Ind. U., 1951, MS, 1956. Tchr. jr. high Martinsville Schs. Corp., Brooklyn, Ind., 1952-53; tchr. high sch. Indpls. Pub. Schs., 1953-63, asst. to dean of boys, 1963-73, asst. dean of boys, 1973-75, bus. mgr., 1976-87; fin. cons. Indpls., 1987-93; property builder, owner. Lectr. on fin. and real estate; condr. seminars on estate planning and trust; income tax preparer. Sgt. U.S. Army, 1945-47. Mem. NEA (life), Indpls. Adminstrs., Ind. Bus. Edn. Assn., Indpls. Edn. Assn. (rep. 1958-63). Republican. Baptist. Avocation: investing in real estate. Home and Office: 9705 E Michigan St Indianapolis IN 46229-2564 *Personal philosophy: You must always feel that Christ is beside you in everything you do.*

CARLO-MELENDEZ, ARNALDO, mathematics educator; b. Mayaguez, P.R., Oct. 1, 1953; s. Asdrubal Ali and Herolida (Melendez) Carlo; divorced; 1 child, Arnaldo Ali. BA, U. S. Fla., 1975. Cert. math. tchr., grades 6-12, Fla. Math. tchr. U.S. Peace Corps., Washington, Montverde (Fla.) Acad. Mem. ASCD, Nat. Coun. Tchrs. Math., Phi Kappa Phi. Home: PO Box 560469 Montverde FL 34756-0469 E-mail: mva2math@hotmail.com.

CARLOTTI, RONALD JOHN, food scientist; b. Martins Ferry, Ohio, Sept. 20, 1942; s. John Peter and Mary Rose (Pilla) C.; m. Eileen Theresa Dorsey, May 17, 1969; children: Lori Ann, Christina Maria, Jennifer Ann, Theresa Maria. Student, Wheeling (W.Va.) Jesuit Coll., 1960-63; BS, Ohio State U., 1964; MS, W.Va. U., 1966, PhD, 1970; MM, Aquinas Coll., 1996. Postdoctoral fellow dept. biochemistry U. Iowa, Iowa City, 1971-72, asst. rsch. scientist dept. pediats., 1973-74; corp. nutritionist Kellogg Co., Battle Creek, Mich., 1974-77; mgr. nutrition/basic rsch. Frito Lay div. Pepsico, Dallas, 1977-82, prin. scientist new products, 1982-85; sr. rsch. scientist Amway Corp., Ada, Mich., 1985-89; dir. food sci. and tech. Country Home Bakers, Grand Rapids, Mich., 1990-93; pres. Carlotti and Assocs., Grand Rapids, 1994; pres., CEO Natura Inc., Lansing, Mich., 1995—2001, corp. sec., 2002—, bd. dirs., 2002—; regulatory affairs and devel. specialist Ranir/DCP Corp., Grand Rapids, Mich. Tech. rep. Snack Food Assn., Crystal City, Va., 1978-82, Grocery Mfrs. Am., Washington, 1975-77; nutritionist Am. Frozen Food Assn., Washington, 1990-93; vis. asst. prof. chemistry Grand Valley State U., Allendale, Mich., 2002; regulatory affairs and devel. specialist Ranir Corp., Grand Rapids, 2002—. Contbr. articles to profl. jours. Pres. Mary Immaculate Sch. Bd., Dallas, 1981-83. Recipient Lovable Spud award, Nat. Potato Promotion Bd., Denver, 1981. Mem. Am. Chem. Soc., Am. Assn. Cereal Chemists, Inst. Food Tech. Roman Catholic. Achievements include start-up of new biotechnology-based food and chemical ingredients company, development of patented taste-appealing shelf-stable blend of fruit juice and milk, development of first nutritionally improved (low fat/low calorie) prototype of Tostitos Baked tortilla chips, of new high potency dry dog food for Amway Corp., of a series of nutritionally improved fruit pies for diabetics, of a specially formulated pumpkin pie which will not allow for the growth of pathogenic bacteria innoculated after baking in testing required to verify that the product can be stored at ambient temperature for up to five days; initiation of tech. and regulatory functions for corporate products. Home: 6921 Maplecrest Dr SE Grand Rapids MI 49546-9208

CARLOTTI, STEPHEN JON, lawyer; b. Providence, Apr. 28, 1942; s. Albert Edward and Rose C.; m. Nancy Ann Arnold, Sept. 16, 1961; children: Stephen J., Cristina C. AB, Dartmouth Coll., 1963; LLB, Yale U., 1966. Bar: R.I. 1966, U.S. Ct. Mil. Appeals 1967, U.S. Ct. Appeals (9th cir.) 1969, U.S. Dist. Ct. R.I. 1970, U.S. Supreme Ct. 1972. Assoc. Hinckley, Allen, Salisbury & Parsons, Providence, 1966, 70-72; ptnr. Hinckley, Allen, & Snyder, Providence, 1972-89, 91, mng. ptnr., 1986-89, 92-96; with The Mut. Benefit Life Ins. Co., Newark, 1989-91. Chmn. Town Com., 1975-76; trustee Roger Williams U., 1978-93; chmn. Health Provider Svcs., R.I. Pub. Expenditures Coun. Capt. JAGC, U.S. Army, 1967-70. Mem. ABA, R.I. Bar Assn., R.I. Country Club, Univ. Club. Republican. Roman Catholic. Avocations: golf, sailing. Office: Hinckley Allen & Snyder 1500 Fleet Ctr Providence RI 02903-2319 E-mail: scarlotti@haslaw.com.

CARLS, ALICE CATHERINE, history educator; b. Mulhouse, France, June 14, 1950; came to U.S., 1977; d. Victor Adrien Clement and Lise Simone (Ebersolt) Maire; m. Stephen Douglas, June 25, 1977; children: Philip, Elizabeth, Paul. BA, Sorbonne U., Paris, 1970, MA, 1972, PhD, 1976. Asst. prof., polit. sci. Lambuth Coll., Jackson, 1985-88, asst. prof., history, polit. sci., 1988-92; asst. prof. history U. Tenn., Martin, 1992-96, chmn. dept. history, 1997-2000, assoc. prof. history, 1996-2001, prof. history, 2001—, chmn. long-range planning com. on Civil Rights Conf., 2001—. Ea. European corr. Ctr. Pub. Justice, Washington, 1981—97, mem. editl. bd., 1998—. Author: The Free City of Danzig in Crisis, 1938-1939, 1982; translator (Jan Kochanowski): A Life of One's Own, 1992; translator: (Wladyslaw Grzedzielski) The Polish Rider, 1991; translator: (Jozef M. Rostocki) Escaping Death, 1995, A Fly in My Soup, 1998; translator: (Jozef Wittlin) La Saga du patient fantassin, 2000; translator: Louis Loucheur, 1872-1931, Engineer, Statesman, Technocrat; translator: (Stephen D. Carls) Ingénieur, homme d'état, modernisateur de la France, 2000; translator: (Anna Frajlich) The Wind, Anew, Searchcs for Me, 2003; contbr. articles to profl. jours. Mem. Bicentennial Com., Ad-hoc Bicentennial Com., Jackson, 1987; alt. dir. Ad-hoc Com. Memories Life Bemis Jackson, 1991-92; dir. Ad-hoc Com. Polish Week, Sterling, Kans., 1982. Grantee Herbert Hoover Instn. for War, Revolution and Peace, 1984, Herbert Hoover Pub. Libr. 1979, Deutscher Akademischer Austausch Dienst 1975, French Ministry Fgn. Affairs 1973-75; recipient Internat. Scholar award U. Tenn., Martin, 1999. Cunningham award U. Tenn., Martin, 2002; featured scholar U. Tenn., Martin, 1999. Mem.: Am. Hist. Assn., Ctr. for Pub. Justice, So. Hist. Assn. (Simpson and Smith awards com. of the European history sect. 2001—, sec.-treas. European history sect. 2002—), Polish Inst. Arts and Sci., Am. Assn. for Advancement of Slavic Studies, Polish-Am. Hist. Assn. (exec. com. 1989—91, mem. editl. bd. 1991—93), UN Assn.-USA, Am. Hist. Assn., Pi Delta Phi, Phi Kappa Phi. Presbyterian.

CARLSEN, JAMES CALDWELL, musicologist, educator; b. Pasco, Wash., Feb. 11, 1927; s. Theodore N. and Eunice (Caldwell) C.; m. Mary Louisa Baird, May 1, 1949; children: Philip C., Douglas A., Susan A., Kristine L. BA, Whitworth Coll., 1950; MA, U. Wash., 1958; PhD, Northwestern U., 1962. Pub. sch. tchr., Almira, Wash., 1950-53; pub. sch. tchr. Portland, Oreg., 1953-54; mem. faculty Whitworth Coll., 1954-63, U. Conn., 1963-67; prof. music U. Wash., Seattle, 1967-92, head div. systematic musicology, 1968-92, ret., 1992, emeritus prof. music, 1992—. Rsch. assoc. Staatliches Institut für Musikforschung, West Berlin, Germany, 1973-74; adj. prof. psychology U. Wash., 1979-92; vis. lectr. Instituto Investigaciones Educativas, Buenos Aires, 1981, Ind. U., 1985, Centro de Investigacion en Educacion Musical del Collegium Musicum, Buenos Aires, 1994; vis. scholar U. Bergen, Norway, 1986; disting. vis. prof. music Aichi U. Edn., Japan, 1992; Housewright eminent scholar chair in music Fla. State U., 1998. Author: Melodic Perception, 1965; editor Jour. Research in Music Edn, 1978-81; assoc. editor Psychomusicology, 1980-01; cons. editor Jour. Music Perception and Cognition, Japan, 1998—. Condr. Spokane Symphonic Band, Wash., 1957-60; music dir. Walla Walla Choral Soc., 1997. Served with AUS, 1945-47. Danforth Tchr. Study grantee, 1960-61; grad. fellow Presbyn. Ch., 1961-62; Fulbright-Hays grantee, 1973-74; recipient Soc. Rsch. in Music Edn. Sr. Researcher award, 1994. Mem. AAUP, Music Educators Nat. Conf., Music Edn. rsch. Coun. (past chmn.), Coll. Music Soc., Soc. for Music Perception and Cognition, Internat. Soc. Music Edn. (chmn. rsch. commn. 1976-80), Internat. Soc. Music Edn. Rsch. Commn. Seminars (hon. life), Internat. Soc. Music Edn. (hon. life), Walla Walla Symphony Soc. (bd. dirs. 1997-2003). Home: 845 Fern Ct Walla Walla WA 99362-8857 E-mail: carlsen@wwics.com.

CARLSEN, JANET HAWS, retired insurance company owner, mayor; b. Bellingham, Wash., June 16, 1927; d. Lyle F. and Mary Elizabeth (Preble) Haws; m. Kenneth M. Carlsen, July 26, 1952; children: Stephanie L. Chambers, Scott Lyle, Sean Preble, Stacy K., Spencer J. Cert., Armstrong Bus. Sch., 1945; student, Golden Gate Coll., 1945-46. Office mgr. Cornwall Warehouse Co., Salt Lake City, 1950-55, Hansen's Ins., Newman, Calif., 1969-77; owner Carlsen Ins., Gustine, Calif., 1978-97, retired, 1997. Mem. city coun. City of Newman, 1980-82, mayor, 1982-94; bd. dirs. ARC, Stanislaus, Calif., 1982-83, Tosca, 1993-98; bd. dirs. Stanislaus County Area Agy. on Aging, 1995-2000, chairperson, 1996-99; bd. dirs. Calif. state com. TACC Commn. on Aging, 1996-98; grand marshal Newman Fall Festival, 1989; v.p. ctrl. divsn. League of Calif. Cities, 1989-90, pres. 1990, 91; bd. dirs. Sr. Opportunity Svc. Ctr., 1993-96, 97-98, Sr. Opportunity Svc. Program of Stanislaus County, 1995-96; chairperson Ctrl. Valley Opportunity Ctr., 1996-98; mem. Stanislaus County Vision Com., 1997-99; bd. dirs. Gt. Valley Ctr., 1997-99. Named Soroptimist Woman of Achievement, 1987, Soroptimist Woman of Distinction, 1988, Outstanding Woman, Stanislaus County Commn. for Women, 1989, Newman Rotary Club Citizen of Yr., 1993-94, Woman of Yr. Calif. State Assembly Dist. 26, 1994, Ambassador, City of Newman, 1997—, John T. Silver award Newman C. of C., 2000; recipient plaque Ctrl. Valley Opportunity Ctr., 2001. Mem. Booster Club (Newman) Soroptimist Club, Newman Women's Club, Newman Garden Club. Mem. Lds Ch. Home: 1215 Amy Dr Newman CA 95360-1003

CARLSEN, JOHN RICHARD, engineer; b. Palo Alto, Calif., June 16, 1970; Student, San Jose State U., 1988—91, Austin (Tex.) C.C., 1994—95; AA in Gen. Studies, DeAnza Coll., Cupertino, Calif., 1997, AA in Liberal Arts, 1998, AA in Tech. Comms., 1999, AA in Bus. Adminstrn. cum laude, 2000; AA in Acctg. cum laude, DeAnza Coll., 2000; BS in Computer Sci. cum laude, BBA cum laude, St. Edward's U., 2003. Engring. contractor Nolan K. Bushnell, Mountain View, Calif., 1988-89, Iguana Entertainment, Inc., Sunnyvale, 1991-93, sr. hardware engr., 1993-96; engring. contractor AAPPS Corp., Sunnyvale, Calif., 1989, Media Vision, Inc., Fremont, Calif., 1991-92; advanced layout engr. Altera Corp., San Jose, 1996—99; pres. Carlsen Comm., 1999—. Pres. Carlsen Electronic Rsch., Sunnyvale, 1988-93. Mem. IEEE, Soc. Tech. Comm., Math. Assn. Am., Am. Coun. Math. Achievements include design of interfaces and software tools for development of video games on Sony Playstation, Sega Saturn, Super Nintendo and Atari Jaguar; contributing designs for PC and Macintosh multimedia cards; creation of fully-custom CMOS integrated circuits, topological design rules, layout training program for college graduates. Home and Office: Carlsen Comm 13715 Cambourne Dr Pflugerville TX 78660-8857

CARLSEN, MARY BAIRD, clinical psychologist; b. Salt Lake City, Utah, Aug. 31, 1928; d. Jesse Hays and Susannah Amanda (Bragstad) Baird; m. James C. Carlsen, May 1, 1949; children: Philip, Douglas, Susan, Kristine. Student. St. Olaf Coll., 1946-47; BA, Whitworth Coll., 1950; MA, U. Conn., 1967; PhD, U. Wash., 1973. Profl. organist, piano tchr., Wash., Oreg., Ill., Conn., 1949-68; staff counselor Presbyn. Counseling Svc., Seattle, 1976-79; pvt. practice clin. psychologist, marriage therapist, cognitive, devel. psychology, career devel. Seattle, 1978-95; cons. creative aging Walla Walla, 1996—. Chmn. sr. adult adv. coun. Seattle Parks Dept., 1975-76; adv. bd. Northwest Ctr. for Creative Aging, 1995-98; mem. steering com. Quest Learning Inst., Walla Walla, Wash., 1997-2001, mem. faculty, 1997—; mem. nat. adv. bd. Ctr. for Creative Retirement, Asheville, N.C., 1998-2001. Author: Meaning-Making: Therapeutic Processes in Adult Development, 1988, Creative Aging: A Meaning-Making Perspective, 1991, 2d edit., 1996, Transformational Meaning-Making and the Practices of Career Counseling, 1991; contbr. chpts. to books and articles to profl. jours. Grantee PEO Rsch., 1972, U. Wash. Women's Guidance Ctr., 1972. Mem. APA, Am. Soc. Aging, Nat. Coun. on Aging.

CARLSEN, RUSSELL ARTHUR, county official; b. Cleve., Sept. 25, 1945; AS in Law Enforcement, Monterey Peninsula Coll., 1995; BA in Sociology, BA in History, U. Wash., 1977; MA in Mgmt., U. Redlands, 2001. Property mgr., Calif., 1974—86; housing mgr. Cmty. Devel. Commn. L.A. County, 1986-88; dep. city mgr. City of Fontana, Calif., 1988-91; mgmt. cons. Calif., 1991-95; city mgr. City of Big Bear Lake, Calif., 1995—2001; chief of staff legis. dist. 3 King County, Seattle, 2001—. Mgmt. cons. many orgns. With U.S. Army, 1969-71. Named Hon. Citizen San Juan Batista, 1993; recipient Key to the City City of Soledad, 1994. Mem. Internat. City Mgrs. Assn., Am. Soc. Pub. Adminstrn. (exec. bd. dirs. ethics sect.), Phi Alpha Alpha. Office: 516 3d Ave Rm 1200 Seattle WA 98104 E-mail: russellcarlsen@aol.com.

CARLSMITH, JAMES MERRILL, psychologist, educator; b. New Orleans, Apr. 12, 1936; s. Leonard Eldon and Hope (Snedden) C.; m. Lyn Kuckenberg, July 27, 1963; children— Christopher, Kimberly, Kevin. AB, Stanford U., 1958; PhD, Harvard U., 1963. Asst. prof. Yale U., 1962-64; from asst. prof. to prof. psychology Stanford U., 1964—, asso. dean grad. studies, 1972-75; fellow (Center for Advanced Study in Behavioral Scis.), 1975. Author: Social Psychology, 1970, Methods of Research In Social Psychology, 1976. Dir. Boys Town Center, 1980— . Office: Stanford U Dept Psychology Stanford CA 94305

CARLSMITH, ROGER SNEDDEN, chemistry and energy conservation researcher; b. N.Y.C., Oct. 2, 1925; s. Leonard Eldon and Hope (Snedden) C.; m. Thelma Kathleen Sutton, July 31, 1954; children: David, Nancy Lynn. AB in Chemistry cum laude, Harvard, 1948; MSCE, MIT, 1950. Rsch. engr. Oak Ridge (Tenn.) Nat. Lab., 1950-62, group leader, 1962-70, sect. mgr., 1970-78, prog. dir. conservation and renewable energy, 1978-94; ret., 1994. Mem. Gov.'s Energy Task Force, Tenn., 1972-74, adv. com. Fed. Power Commn., Washington, 1973; bd. dirs. Am. Coun. Energy Efficient Economy., Washington, Tenn. Citizens Wilderness Planning. Author: (book with others) World Energy Conference Survey of Energy Resourses, 1974. Sgt. USAF, 1943-46. Recipient Sadi Carnot medal for achievements in energy conservation rsch. Dept. Energy, 1996. Mem. AAAS, Sierra Club, The Wilderness Soc. Achievements include research and development of advanced technology for improved energy efficiency, alternative energy sources, environmental impacts of energy, energy and the economy. Home: 1052 W Outer Dr Oak Ridge TN 37830-8641 E-mail: carlsmith@worldnet.att.net.

CARLSON, ALLAN CONSTANTINE, historian; b. Des Moines, Iowa, May 7, 1949; s. Harry Bernard and Constance Ann Carlson; m. Elizabeth Cecelia Belin, July 1, 1972; children: Anders, Sarah-Eva, Anna, Miriam. AB, Augustana Coll., 1971; PhD in European History, Ohio U., 1978. Asst. dir. office for govtl. affairs Luth. Coun. in the USA, Washington, 1975-78; asst. to pres., history lectr. Gettysburg Coll., Pa., 1979-81; exec. v.p. The Rockford Inst., Ill., 1981-86, pres., 1986-97, The Howard Ctr. for Family, Religion & Soc., 1997—. Mem. Coun. on Families in Am., NYC, 1991—; cons. Family Rsch. Inst., Moscow, 1995—, US Dept. Justice, Washington, 1986-87, US Dept. Edn., Washington, 1986-88; gen. sec. World Congress Families in Prague, The Czech Republic, 1997, Geneva, Switzerland, 1999. Author:Family Questions, 1988, The Swedish Experiment in Family Politics, 1990, From Cottage to Work Station, 1993, The New Agrarian Mind, 2000, Person, Family & Society (in Russian), 2002, The 'American Way', 2003, The Family in America, 2003; co-author: The Family: Is it Just Another Lifestyle Choice?; contbr. articles to profl. jour. Commr. The Nat. Commn. on Children, Washington, 1988-93; adv. bd. project SHARE U.S. Dept. Health Human Svcs., Washington, 1983-85; leader Boy Scouts of Am., dist. chmn., 1995-96; bd. dir. Burpee Natural History Mus., vice chmn., 2003. NEH fellow Am. Enterprise Inst., 1979, Disting. fellow Family Policy Studies Family Rsch. Coun., Washington., 2002—; recipient George Washington Honor medal Freedoms Found. Valley Forge, 1985, 87. Mem. Phila. Soc. (1st v.p. 1986-87,2003-04), Rotary (pres. 1994-95), John Randolph Club (bd. dir., sec. 1993-95), Lutherans for Life (bd. dir. 1987-92), Phi Beta Kappa. Lutheran. Home: 1324 Camp Ave Rockford IL 61103-7104 Office: The Howard Center 934 N Main St Rockford IL 61103-7061 E-mail: allan@profam.org.

CARLSON, AMY L. lawyer; BSEE, Carnegie Mellon, 1986; MSEE, Rensselaer Poly. Inst., 1987; JD, MBA, U. So. Calif., 1991. Bar: Calif. 1995, DC 1994, U.S. Ct. Internat. Trade 1994, NY 1995, U.S. Patent and Trademark Office

2003. Design engr. III Interconnection Products Inc., Santa Ana, Calif., 1987-88; assoc. Dewey Ballantine, L.A., 1992, Washington, 1992-94, Preston, Gates, Ellis & Rouvelas Meeds, Washington, 1994-99, ptnr., 2000-01, Kilpatrick Stockton LLP, Washington, 2001—02. Mem. ABA, Women's Bar Assn. of DC, Women in Tech., Eta Kappa Nu, Tau Beta Pi. Office: Kilpatrick Stockton LLP Ste 900 607 14th St NW Washington DC 20005 E-mail: acarlson@kilpatrickstockton.com.

CARLSON, ANDREW RAYMOND, archivist; b. Ludington, Mich., Aug. 19, 1934; s. Louis Peter and Mable Pearl (Genter) C.; m. Linda Inara Volfarts, Sept. 5, 1959; children: Sharon Lee, Andrew Arthur. BA, Western Mich. U., 1960, MA, 1961; PhD, Mich. State U., 1970. Tchr. Galesburg (Mich.)-Augusta Schs., 1961-62, Kalamazoo (Mich) Pub. Schs., 1962-65, Portage (Mich.) Pub. Schs., 1962-65; asst. prof. Ea. Ky. U., Richmond, Ky., 1967-70, Ferris State U., Big Rapids, Mich., 1970-73, Western Mich. U., Kalamazoo, 1973-75; archivist Kalamazoo County, 1976—. Adj. prof. Western Mich. U., Kalamazoo, 1989—. Author: Anarchism in Germany, 1972, Germany Foreign Policy, 1970; (with others) Social Protest, Violence & Terror, 1982, Sozialprotest, Gewalt, Terror, 1982; contbr. articles to profl. jours. Adj. treas. Diabled Am. Vets., Allegan, Mich., 1976—; active Fontana Concert Soc. Sgt. U.S. Army, 1952-57. Mem. Am. Hist. Assn. (European sect.), So. Hist. Assn., Internat. Wissenschaftliche Korrespondenz, Internat. Labor & Workers History, German History Soc., German Studies Assn., Am. Philatelic Soc., German Philatelic Soc., Phi Gamma Mu, Phi Alpha Theta. Avocations: stamp collecting, post card collecting, book collecting. Office: Western Mich U Dept History Kalamazoo MI 49008-5020

CARLSON, ARNE HELGE, former governor; b. N.Y.C., Sept. 24, 1934; s. Helge William and Kerstin (Magnusson) C.; children by previous marriage: Arne H. Jr., Anne Davis; m. Susan Shepard, July 12, 1985; 1 child, Jessica Shepard. BA, Williams Coll., 1957; postgrad., U. Minn., 1957-58. Mem. advt. staff Control Data, Bloomington, Minn., 1962-64; councilman Mpls. City Council, 1965-67; ind. businessman Mpls., 1968-69; legislator Minn. Ho. Reps., St. Paul, 1970-78; state auditor State of Minn., St. Paul, 1978-90, gov., 1991-99; chmn. bd. Am. Express Funds, Mpls., 1999—. Bd. dirs. Minn. Land Exch. Bd., St. Paul; trustee Minn. State Bd. Investment, St. Paul, 1979-99. Bd. dirs. Exec. Coun., St. Paul, KidsFirst Scholarship Fund Minn., 1999—, Fairview Lakes Regional Health Care, 2002—; sec. Minn. Housing Fin. Agy., St. Paul, 1979-91; past pres. Pub. Employees Retirement Assn., St. Paul, 1985-88; adv. bd. mem. Nat. Heritage Acad., 2001—; mem. Nat. Gov.'s Assn., Midwest Gov.'s Assn., Great Lakes Govs.; mem. Nat. Ednl. Goals Panel of Nat. Gov.'s Assn. Bush Found. Leadership fellow, 1971; recipient Children's Champion award Minn. Children's Def. Fund, Nat. Audubon Soc. award, Small Bus. Guardian award Nat. Fedn. Ind. Businesses, 1994, Great Blue Heron award N.Am. Waterfront Mgmt. Plan/U.S. Fish & Wildlife Svc., 1995; named Rep. of Yr. Nat. Ripon Soc., 1993. Bd. dirs. Exec. Coun. St. Paul, sec. Minn. Housing Fin. Agy., St. Paul, 1979-91; past pres. Pub. Employees Retirement Assn., St. Paul, 1985-88; mem. Nat. Gov.'s Assn. (chmn. com. on human resources, mem. Nat. Ednl. Goals Panel), Rep. Gov.'s Assn., Midwest Gov.'s Assn., Great Lakes Govs. Republican. Avocations: reading, squash, university of minnesota basketball and football games. Home: 22005 Iden Ave N Forest Lake MN 55025-9329 Office: Am Express Funds 901 Marquette Ave Ste 2810 Minneapolis MN 55402-3268*

CARLSON, ARTHUR EUGENE, accounting educator; b. Whitewater, Wis., May 10, 1923; s. Paul Adolph and Dorothy Adeline (Cooper) C.; m. Lorraine June Bronson, Aug. 19, 1944; 1 child, George Arthur. EdB, U. Wis., Whitewater, 1943; MBA, Harvard U., 1947; PhD, Northwestern U., 1954. Instr. Ohio U., 1947-50; lectr. Northwestern U., 1950-52; from asst. prof. to prof. acctg. Washington U., St. Louis, 1952-88, prof. emeritus, 1988—. Vis. prof. U. Hawaii, 1963-64. Author: College Accounting, 1967, 7th edit., 1993, Accounting Essentials, 1973, 5th edit., 1991. Chmn. Robert Meml. Endowment Fund, University City, Mo., 1972-2003, trustee Police and Fire Pension Bd., 1979-88. Mem. Inst. Mgmt. Accts. (past pres.), Assn. Sys. Mgmt. (past pres., Disting. Svc. award 1973), Soc. Profs. Emeriti Washington U. (pres. 1995, disting. bus. alumni awards com. 1998—), Kiwanis (pres. 1969). Republican. Episcopalian. Avocations: bowling, gardening. Home: 801 S Skinker Blvd # 9A Saint Louis MO 63105-3228 E-mail: carlson@olin.wustl.edu.

CARLSON, BRUCE MARTIN, anatomist; b. Gary, Ind., July 11, 1938; s. Martin E. and Esther (Granquist) C.; m. Jean Ann Hyslop, Aug. 18, 1968; children: Martin, James. BA, Gustavus Adolphus Coll., 1959; MS, Cornell U., 1961; MD, PhD, U. Minn., 1986. Exchange scientist Inst. of Devel. Biology, Moscow, 1965-66; Fulbright fellow Hubrecht (Netherlands) Inst., 1973-74; Joshiah Macy scholar U. Helsinki, Finland, 1981-82; exchange scientist Inst. of Physiology, Prague, Czechoslovakia, 1971; asst. prof. of anatomy to prof. U. Mich., Ann Arbor, 1966—, prof. biology, 1979—, chmn. dept. anatomy and cell biology, 1988-2000, rsch. scientist Inst. Gerontology, 1989—, dir. Inst. Gerontology, 2000—. Fellow Fetzer Inst., Kalamazoo, Mich., 1990-96, trustee, 1998—; mem. study sects. NIH, 1986-90, Nat. Bd. Med. Examiners, 1994-96; NIH Fogerty fellow, U. Otago, Dunedin, New Zealand, 1999-00. Author: The Regeneration of Minced Muscles, 1972, Patten's Foundations of Embryology, 1974, 4th edit., 1981, 5th edit., 1988, 6th edit., 1996, Regeneration (in Russian), 1986, Human Embryology and Developmental Biology, 1994, 2d edit., 1999; editor: From Message to Mind, 1988, Regeneration and Transplantation, 1990, numerous others. Recipient Disting. Alumni award Gustavus Adolphus Coll., 1979, Newcomb-Cleveland prize AAAS, 1972, 650th Anniversary medal, Charles U., Prague. Fellow: AAAS, Russian Acad. Natural Scis.; mem.: Gerontol. Soc. Am., Internat. Soc. Devel. Biology, Soc. Devel. Biologists, Assn. of Anatomy, Cell Biology and Neurobiology Chairpersons (pres. 1995), Am. Soc. Ichthyologists and Herpetologists, Am. Soc. Zoologists (divsn. chmn. 1987—89), Am. Assn. Clin. Anatomists, Am. Assn. Anatomists (nominating com. 1991, exec. com. 1994, pres. 1997—99). Lutheran. Achievements include invention of techniques of free muscle transplantation. Home: 3838 Curlew Ln Ann Arbor MI 48103-9404 Office: U Mich Inst of Gerontology Ann Arbor MI 48109

CARLSON, BRUCE WILLIAM, diversified holding company executive; BS in Acctg., U. Buffalo, 1969. CPA, N.Y. Mgr. Arthur Andersen & Co., Rochester, N.Y., 1969-77; v.p. fin. Andco Inc., Buffalo, 1977-86; v.p., corp. contr. Delaware North Cos., Inc., Buffalo, 1986—. Mem. AICPA, Beta Gamma Sigma. Office: Delaware North Cos Inc 40 Fountain Plz Buffalo NY 14202 E-mail: bcarlson@dncinc.com.

CARLSON, CHARLES EDWARD, sportswriter; b. Washington, Sept. 2, 1957; s. Douglas Gordon and Ruth (McGuire) Carlson; m. Theresa Eileen Davis, Apr. 19, 1986; children: Brian, Patrick, Michael. BA in Journalism, Am. U., 1979. Sports editor The Enterprise, Lexington Park, Md., 1980—83; asst. sports editor Potomac News, Woodbridge, Va., 1983—84; writer Herald-Republic, Yakima, Wash., 1984—87, Herald & Rev., Decatur, Ill., 1987—90; columnist Post-Crescent, Appleton, Wis., 1990—2001; sports editor Citizen Patriot, Jackson, Mich., 2001—02; asst. sports editor Northwestern, Oshkosh, Wis., 2002—. Journalism tchr. Xavier H.S., Appleton, 2000 ; lectr. in field. Author: True Brew, 1993, Titletown Again, 1997, Puck, 1997. Named Sports Journalist of Yr., Thomson Corp., 2000, Columnist of Yr., Wis. Newspaper Assn., 2000. Avocations: golf, history, reading.

CARLSON, CHARLES EVANS, university official; b. Savanna, Ill., Aug. 25, 1941; s. Gustave Bert and Agnes Loretta (Johnson) C.; m. Nancy Jane Wahl, Aug. 10, 1963; children: Courtney E., Darrin C. BA, Carthage Coll., 1963; MA, U. Ill., 1965. Tchr. Polo (Ill.) Community High Sch., 1963-65; instr. history Ctrl. Mich. U., Mt. Pleasant, 1966-72, regional assoc. dir. Detroit campus, 1987—, coord. spl. projects, acad. advisor. Contbr. articles to profl. publs. Mem. Optimist Club. Avocation: golf. Office: Ctrl Mich U Cel North Mount Pleasant MI 48859-0001 E-mail: charles.e.carlson@cmich.edu.

CARLSON, CURTIS EUGENE, orthodontist, periodontist; b. Mar. 30, 1942; m. Dona M. Seely; children: Jennifer Ann, Gina Christine, Erik Alan. BA in Divisional Scis., Augustana Coll., 1965; BDS, DDS, U. Ill., 1969; cert. in periodontics, U. Wash., 1974, cert. in orthodontics, 1976. Dental intern Oak Knoll Navy Hosp., Oakland, Calif., 1969-70; dental officer USN, 1970-72; part-time dentist VA Hosp., Seattle, 1972-73; part-time periodontist Group Health Dental Coop., Seattle, 1973-76, part-time orthodontist, 1976-78; clin. instr. U. Wash., 1976; prin. Bellevue (Wash.) Orthodontic and Periodontic Clinic, 1976—; clin. instr., trainer Luxar Laser Corp., Bothell, Wash., 1992—. Presenter in field. Master of ceremonies Auctioneer Friendship Fair, Augustana Coll., 1965, orientation group leader, 1965, mem. field svcs. com. for high sch. recruitment, 1965. Fellow Am. Coll. Dentists; mem. ADA, Am. Acad. Periodontology, Am. Assn. Orthodontics, Western Soc. Periodontology (bd. dirs. 1984-85, 86, program chmn. 1986, v.p. 1988, pres. elect 1989, pres. 1990), Seattle King County Dental Soc. (grievance, ethics and pub. info. coms.), Wash. State Dental Assn., Wash. State Soc. Periodontists (program chmn., pres. elect 1987, pres. 1988, 89), Wash. Assn. Dental Specialists (com. rep. 1987, 88, 89), Wash. State Orthodontic Soc., Wash. State Soc. Periodontists, Pacific Coast Soc. Orthodontics, Omicron Kappa Upsilon (dental hon. fraternity), Pi Upsilon Gamma (social chmn. 1964, pres. 1965). Home: 16730 Shore Dr NW Seattle WA 98155-5634 Office: Bellevue Orthodontic/ Periodontic Clinic 1248 112th Ave NE Bellevue WA 98004-3712

CARLSON, CYNTHIA JOANNE, artist, educator; b. Chgo. d. Ivan Morris and Ruth (Holmes) C. BFA, Sch. Art Inst., Chgo., 1965; MFA, Pratt Inst., Bklyn., 1967. Instr. Phila. Coll. Art., 1967-72, U. Colo., Boulder, 1972-73; asst. prof. painting Phila. Coll. Art., 1973; assoc. prof. Phila Coll. Art., 1979-82; prof. Phila. Coll. Art., 1982-87, Queens Coll., CUNY, 1987—. One-person shows include Allen Meml. Art Mus., Oberlin, Ohio, 1980, Hudson River Mus., Yonkers, N.Y., 1981, Milw. Art Mus., 1982, Pam Adler Gallery, N.Y.C., 1983, Albright-Knox Art Gallery, Buffalo, 1985, Queens Mus., Flushing, N.Y., 1990, Charles More Gallery, Phila., 1990-96, AIR Gallery, N.Y.C., 1992, Neuberger Mus., Purchase, N.Y., 1999; exhibited in group shows The Contemporary Art Ctr., Cin., 1980, Whitney Mus. Art, N.Y.C., 1980, Hayden Art Gallery, MIT, Cambridge, 1981, Jacksonville (Fla.) Art Mus., 1982; represented in permanent collections Guggenheim Mus., N.Y.C., Bklyn. Mus. Art, Phila. Mus. Art, Richmond (Va.) Mus. Fine Arts, Denver Art Mus., Allen Meml. Art Mus., Oberlin; commns. include L.A. Metro Rail Sys., 1992-93, Criminal Justice Ctr., Phila., Dept. Arts and Culture, 1995. Grantee NEA, 1975, 78, 81, 87, Creative Artists Pub. Service, 1978. Home: 139 W 19th St New York NY 10011-4105 Office: CUNY Queens Coll Art Dept Klapper # 172 Flushing NY 11367-0904

CARLSON, DALE ARVID, university dean; b. Aberdeen, Wash., Jan. 10, 1925; s. Edwin C.G. and Anna A. (Anderson) C.; m. Jean M. Stanton, Nov. 11, 1948; children: Dale Ronald, Gail L. Carlson Manahan, Joan M. Carlson Lee, Gwen D. Carlson Lundgren. AA, Grays Harbor Coll., 1947; BSCE, U. Wash., 1950, MS, 1951; PhD, U. Wis., 1960. Registered profl. engr., Wash. Water engr. City of Aberdeen, 1951-55; asst. prof., assoc. prof., prof., chmn. dept. civil engring. U. Wash., Seattle, 1955-76, dean (Coll Engring.), 1976-80, dean emeritus, 1980 , dir. Valle Scandinavian Exch., 1980—2002; chmn. dept. civil engring. Seattle U., 1983-88, acting dean sci. and engring., 1990, dean sci. and engring., 1990-92. Vis. prof. Tech. U. Denmark, Copenhagen, 1970, Royal Coll. Agr., Uppsala, Sweden, 1976, 78 Contbr. articles to profl. jours. Exec. bd. Pacific N.W. Synod Luth. Ch. in Am., chmn. fin. com., 1980-84, treas., 1986-87, bd. edn., fin. com. Evang. Luth. Ch. in Am., 1987-91; v.p. Nat. Luth. Campus Ministry, 1988-91; treas. N.W. Washington synod Evang. Luth. Ch. in Am., 1996-2000, mem. synod candidacy com., 2001—; exec. bd. Nordic Heritage Mus., 1981-86; bd. dirs. Hearthstone Retirement Ctrs., 1984-93, Evergreen Safety Coun., 1980-86. With AUS, 1943-45. Named Outstanding Grad. Weatherwax High Sch., Aberdeen, 1972, Outstanding Grad. Grays Harbor Coll., 1947; guest of honor Soppeldagene, Trondheim, 1978 Mem. ASCE, Internat. Water Acad., Am. Soc. Engring. Educators, Am. Acad. Environ. Engring., Am. Water Works Assn., Am. Scandinavian Found., Swedish Am. C. of C. (bd. dirs. 1994-99), Norwegian Am. C. of C., Rainier Club, Rotary, Phi Beta Kappa, Sigma Xi, Chi Epsilon. Home: 9235 41st Ave NE Seattle WA 98115-3801 E-mail: dcarlson@engr.washington.edu.

CARLSON, DALE BICK, writer; b. N.Y.C., May 24, 1935; d. Edgar M. and Estelle (Cohen) Bick; children: Daniel, Hannah. BA, Wellesley Coll., 1957. Lic. wildlife rehabilitator. Founder, pres. Bick Pub. House, 1993—. Founder, pres. Bick Pub. House, 1993—. Author children's books, adult books, Perkins the Brain, 1964, The House of Perkins, 1965, Miss Maloo, 1966, The Brainstormers, 1966, Frankenstein, Counting Is Easy, 1969, Your Country, 1969, Arithmetic 1, 2, 3, 1969, The Electronic Teabowl, 1969, Warlord of the Genji, 1970, The Beggar King of China, 1971, The Mountain of Truth, 1972 (Spring Festival Honor book, named Am. Libr. Assn. Notable Book), Good Morning Danny, 1972, Hannah, 1972, The Human Apes, 1973 (named Am. Libr. Assn. Notable Book), Girls Are Equal Too, 1973; : 2d edit., 2000 (named Am. Library Assn. Notable Book), Baby Needs Shoes, 1974, Triple Boy, 1976, Where's Your Head?, 1971, The Plant People, 1977, The Wild Heart, 1977, The Shinning Pool, 1979, Lovingsex for Both Sexes, 1979, Boys Have Feelings Too, 1980, Call Me Amanda, 1981, Manners That Matter, 1982, The Frog People, 1982, Charlie the Hero, 1983—85, The Jenny Dean Science Fiction Mysteries, The Mystery of the Shining Children, The Mystery of the Hidden Trap, The Secret of the Third Eye, The James Budd Mysteries, The Mystery of Galaxy Games, The Mystery of Operation Brain, 1985, Miss Mary's Husbands, 1988, Basic Manuals in Wildlife Rehabilitation, 6 vols., 1993—94, Basic Manuals for Friends of the Disabled Series, 1995—96, Living With Disabilities, 1997, Wildlife Care for Birds and Mammals, 1997, Stop the Pain: Mediations for Teenagers, 1998 (N.Y. Pub. Libr. Best Books, 2000), Confessions of a Brain-Impaired Writer: A Memoir, 1998; Stop the Pain: Adult Meditations, 2000; editor: What Are You Doing With Your Life, 2001, In and Out of Your Mind: Teen Science, Human Bites, 2002, Who Said What? Philosophy Quotes for Teens, 2003. Mem. Authors League Am., Authors Guild. Address: 307 Neck Rd Madison CT 06443-2755 E-mail: bickpubhse@aol.com.

CARLSON, DAVID BRET, lawyer; b. Jamestown, N.Y., Aug. 16, 1918; s. David Albert and Gertrude (Johnson) C.; m. Jane Tapley, Apr. 12, 1947; children: Christopher Tapley, David Kurt, Nancy Berners-Lee. AB, Brown U., 1940; LL.B., Harvard U., 1947. Bar: N.Y. 1947, U.S. Supreme Ct. 1972. Assoc. Debevoise & Plimpton, N.Y.C., 1947-53, ptnr., 1953-87. Contbr. articles to profl. publs. Mem. ABA, N.Y. State Bar Assn., Bar Assn. City of N.Y. Home: PO Box 32 275 W Falmouth Hwy West Falmouth MA 02574

CARLSON, DAVID EMIL, physicist, researcher; b. Weymouth, Mass., Mar. 5, 1942; s. Emil Algot and Anne Alice (Salomaa) C.; m. Mary Ann Lewinski, June, 1966; children: Eric, Darcey. BS in Physics, Rensselaer Poly. Inst., 1963, PhD in Physics, Rutgers U., 1968. Research scientist U.S. Army Nuclear Effects Lab., Edgewood Arsenal, Md., 1968-69; head photovoltaic device research RCA Labs., Princeton, N.J., 1970-83; dep. gen. mgr., dir. research Solarex Thin Film Div., Newtown, Pa., 1983-86, gen. mgr., 1986-88, v.p., 1988-98; chief scientist BP Solar, 1999—. Contbr. articles to profl. jours.; patentee in field. Served to capt. Signal Corps U.S. Army, 1968-70, Vietnam. Decorated Bronze Star medal; recipient Ross Coffin Purdy award Am. Ceramic Soc., 1976, Outstanding Achievement award RCA Labs., 1973, 76, Walton Clark medal Franklin Inst., 1986, Karl W. Boer Solar Energy medal of merit U. Del. and Internat. Solar Energy Soc., 1995. Fellow IEEE (co-recipient Morris N. Liebmann award 1984, William R. Cherry award 1988); mem. Am. Phys. Soc., Am. Vacuum Soc., Sigma Xi. Achievements include inventor amorphous silicon solar cell, 1974. Home: 217 Yorkshire Dr Williamsburg VA 23185-3912 Office: BP Solar 3600 La Grange Pky Toano VA 23168-9348 *My career in science has resulted from a curiosity about the workings of nature and a desire to use the phenomena and materials of nature to benefit society.*

CARLSON, DEANNA LYNN, social worker; b. Burbank, Calif., Mar. 5, 1968; m. William Anthony Stacy. BA, Moody Bible Inst., 1990; MSW, Calif. State U., 1995. Program coord. Regional Ctr. Orange County, Orange, Calif., 1993-95; support group leader Padre Found., Orange, 1995-96; welfare policy assoc. Family Rsch. Coun., Washington, 1995, dir. cmty. outreach, 1996-2000, chmn. benevolence com., 1997-2000, adj. scholar, 2000—; ind. contractor, 2000—02; assoc. dir. Ctr. for Faith-based and Comty. Initiatives, Dept. Health and Human Svcs., Washington, 2002—. Author: The Welfare of My Neighbor, 1999; editor: (workbook) Applying the Principles Learned in The Welfare of My Neighbor, 1999. Mem. Alexandria Presbyn. Ch., 2002—. Recipient Soroptimist Youth Citizen award, 1986. Mem. Nat. Assn. Social Workers, N.Am. Asssn. Christians in Social Work (bd. dirs. 1999-2001). Avocations: reading, hiking, downhill skiing, travel.

CARLSON, DESIREE ANICE, pathologist; b. Clinton, Iowa, June 10, 1950; d. Donald Richard and Bernice Elfriede (Jacobs) C.; m. Helmut Gunther Rennke; stepchildren: Stephanie Rennke, Christianne Rennke. MD, Duke U., 1975. Diplomate in anat. and clin. pathology, blood banking and cytopathology Am. Bd. Pathology. Resident in pathology U. Wash., Seattle, 1975-76, N.E. Deaconess Hosp., Boston, 1976-77, Peter Bent Brigham Hosp., Boston, 1977-79; pathologist W. Roxbury VA Med. Ctr., Boston, 1979-82; med. dir. blood bank Univ. Hosp., Boston, 1982-90; assoc. chief pathology N.E. Meml. Hosp., Stoneham, Mass., 1990-93; chief pathology Brockton (Mass.) Hosp., 1993—; sec., treas. med. staff Brockton Hosp., 2001—02; v.p. Medical Staff Brooklyn Hosp., 2003—04. Asst. prof. pathology Boston U. Sch. Med., 1982—; cons. pathology Brigham and Women's Hosp., Boston, 1984-95; mem. adv. bd. ARC, Dedham, 1982-96. Contbr. articles to profl. jours., book chpts. Recipient Outstanding Contbd. Article award Med. Lab. Observer, 1988. Mem. Coll. Am. Pathologists (N.E. regional commr. 1991—), Am. Med. Women's Assn., Am. Assn. Blood Banks, Mass. Med. Soc. (coms.), Mass. Pathology Soc., N.E. Pathology Soc. (sec. 1996-98, treas. 1998-2000, pres.-elect 2000-01, pres. 2001-02, joint sponsored activities coord. 2002—). Republican. Methodist. Avocations: aerobic exercise, bicycling, hiking. Office: Brockton Hosp 680 Centre St Brockton MA 02302-3395 E-mail: dcarlson@brocktonhospital.org.

CARLSON, DEVON MCELVIN, architect, educator; b. Topeka, Dec. 1, 1917; s. Gustave Elvin and Gertrude M. (Swanson) C.; m. Mary E. Ackley, June 14, 1949; children: Mitchell Lans, Martha Sue, Judith Ann, Peter DeVon. BS in Architecture, U. Kans., 1941; BS in Archtl. Engring. with honors, U. Colo., 1947; MS in Architecture, Columbia U., 1949. Mem. faculty U. Colo., 1943-81, prof., chmn. dept. architecture and archtl. engring., 1959-62, dean Sch. Architecture, 1962-70, dean Coll. Environ. Design, 1970-71, dean emeritus, 1981—, mem. steering com. Creative Arts Program, 1959-80. Lectr. civic and profl. groups; past mem. Colo. Bd. Examiners Architects, pres., 1964-65. Co-author: An Approach to Architectural Design, 1950, Architecture/Colorado, 1966; contbr. articles to profl. jours. Past mem. Boulder Landmarks Bd.; advisor emeritus Nat. Trust for Hist. Preservation; mem. Colo. Hist. Preservation Rev. Bd., 1980-84, 85-93. Recipient Stearns award 1972, Disting. Alumnus award U. Kans., 1984; Columbia U. scholar, 1948. Fellow AIA (bd. dirs. Colo. chpt. 1966-67, pres. 1969, nat. scholarship com. chmn. 1977-78, mem. nat. com. on hist. resources 1978—, Silver medal Western Mountain region 1980, Carlson Lecture series established in his honor 1981); mem. Nat. Coun. Archtl. Registration Bds. (exam-devel. com. 1962-76, 87-93, chmn. 1975, editor Handbook 1976), Colo. Soc. Architects (pres. 1980), Assn. Coll. Schs. Architecture, Am. Soc. Engring. Edn. (past chmn. Colo. chpt.), Boulder C. of C., Rocky Mountain Liturg Art Assn., Hist. Boulder, Hist. Denver, Soc. Archtl. Historians, Scarab Club, Triangle Club, Rotary (bd. dirs.), Tau Beta Pi, Delta Phi Delta, Chi Epsilon. Address: 5472 White Pl Boulder CO 80303-1227

CARLSON, DONALD OTTO, magazine publisher, editor; b. Gary, Ind., Oct. 4, 1926; BA in Journalism, History, English, Ind. U., 1949. Spot news reporter Walla Walla (Wash.) Union Bulletin; mem. staff Inside Mich., Vance Pub. Corp., Chgo.; editor various, Chgo. and N.Y.C.; prin., owner CMN Assocs., Inc., Calif., 1964—. Editor, pub. Automated Builder, 1974—; author: Dictionary/Encyclopedia of Industrialized Housing, 1995, How to Start an Inner City Housing Plant, 1999, Shelter All Victims of Emergencies and Disasters, 2000, How and Why to Buy a Factory Built Home, 2001. Founder Automated Builders Consortium, 1993, ABC Saved shelter, 1999, ABC Home Buyers Mortage Movement, 2002. Recipient five nat. journalism awards; named Factory-Built Housing's Man of the 20th Century, Allen Newsletter, Indpls., 2000; charter mem. Hall of Fame, Modular Bldg. Inst., 2001. Mem. Soc. Profl. Journalists, Wood Truss Council Am. (hall of fame 1988), Wood Found. Inst. (co-founder 1980). E-mail: info@automatedbuilder.com.

CARLSON, DONNA, art association administrator, director; b. Grand Junction, Colo., Jan. 16, 1936; d. Vincent Grasso and Evalyn Eileen Holley; m. Leslie M. Carlson (div.). BA, U. Denver, 1956; MFA, U. S.D., 1957. Founder theater Thresholds, N.Y.C., 1962—69; dir. adminstrn. Art Dealers Assn. Am., N.Y.C. Mem.: Phi Beta Kappa. Office: Art Dealers Association America 575 Madison Ave New York NY 10022 Office Fax: 212-940-6484. E-mail: adaa@artdealers.org.

CARLSON, EDWARD C. anatomy educator; b. Iron Mountain, Mich., Feb. 22, 1942; s. Clarence H. and Rachel O. (Olsen) C.; m. Pam R. Carlson, 1995; children: Scott Edward, Susan Rebecca. BA, Bethel Coll., 1964; PhD, U. N.D., 1970. Spl. instr. dept. biology Bethel Coll., St. Paul, 1964-66; instr. anatomy U. Ariz., Tucson, 1970-72, asst. prof., 1972-77; assoc. prof. human anatomy U. Calif., Davis, 1977-81, prof., 1981—; chmn. dept. anatomy and cell biology U. N.D., Grand Forks, 1981—. Rsch. anatomist Calif. Primate Rsch. Ctr., Davis, 1982-85, rsch. affiliate, 1985—; co-dir. N.D. Diabetes Ocular Rsch. Ctr., Grand Forks, 1988—. Contbr. articles to profl. jours. Rsch. grantee Juvenile Diabetes Found., Am. Heart Assn., NIH, EPSCOR, NSF. Mem. Am. Assn. Anatomists, Am. Soc. for Investigative Pathology, Am. Soc. Cell Biology, Microcirculatory Soc. Avocations: running, fishing, skiing. Office: U ND Dept Anatomy & Cell Biol Grand Forks ND 58202

CARLSON, ELIZABETH BORDEN, historian, educator; b. Fall River, Mass., Oct. 5, 1937; d. Richard and Elizabeth McGinley Borden; m. William C. Badger, Sept. 14, 1957 (div. July 1974); children: Christopher C. Badger, Lisa A. Badger; m. Robert F. Carlson, May 5, 1985. Student, Radcliffe Coll., Cambridge, Mass., 1955—57; BA cum laude, Harvard U., 1975; MA with honors, U. Calif., Santa Barbara, 1983, PhD with honors, 1988. Assoc. and contbg. editor The Carlisle Gazette, Mass., 1975—80; head pub. relations Gregory Fossella Assocs., Boston, 1978—80; tchr. Westmont Coll., Santa Barbara, Calif., 1986—90; pres. The Ednl. Design Found., Norwich, Vt., 1991—. Contbr. Mem. Master Planning Com., Carlisle, Mass., 1974—78; Carlisle rep. Master Planning Com. of Greater Boston, 1978—80; bd. dirs. The Fenn Sch., Concord, Mass., 1969—73; pres. PTA, Carlisle, 1967—69. Mem.: Soc. of Archtl. Historians. Avocations: reading, birdwatching, tennis, swimming, skiing. Home: 502 Plaza Rubio Santa Barbara CA 93103 Office: The Ednl Design Found PO Box 25 66 Old Coach Rd Norwich VT 05055

CARLSON, GARY LEE, public relations executive, director, producer; b. Yakima, Wash., Oct. 15, 1954; s. Glenn Elmer and Helen Mary (McLean) Carlson. AA, Yakima Community Coll., 1975; BA in Communications, U. Wash., 1977. Dir. pub. affairs Sta. KCMU, Seattle, 1976-77; dir. programming and promotions Sta. KAPP-TV, Yakima, 1978-80; dir. promotions Sta. WBZ-TV, Boston, 1980-84; producer Sta. KCBS-TV, Los Angeles, 1985; dir. creative services Metromedia Producers, Los Angeles, 1985-86; dir. promotion publicity 20th Century Fox, Los Angeles, 1986—. Writer: (TV animation program) Bruno, the Kid, 1996; writer, co-prodr. (TV movie) Coaching a Murder, 1994; prodr., dir. M*A*S*H* 15th Ann. Campaign, 1987 (Internat. Film and TV Festival N.Y. award), The Fox Tradition, 1988 (Internat. Film and TV Festival N.Y. award, Clio finalist award 1988, Telly award 1988, B.P.M.E. award 1988); prodr., writer, dir. Consumer Reports, 1983 (Internat. Film and TV Festival N.Y. award, Houston Internat. Film and TV award). Mem. Broadcast Promotion and Mktg. Execs., Nat. Assn. TV Program Execs., Beta Theta Pi. Avocations: photography, scuba diving, history, traveling. Home: 1510 Rock Glen Ave Glendale CA 91205-2063 Office: 20th Century Fox Film Corp PO Box 900 Beverly Hills CA 90213-0900

CARLSON, GARY R. publishing executive; b. Ishpeming, Mich. s. James H. and Vivian M. (Maki) C.; m. Mardee G. Parkinson, Aug. 21, 1963 (div.Apr. 21, 1991); children: Bruce S., Robyn L.; m. Maryanne Koschier, June 25, 1994. BA Far Eastern Langs. and Lit., U. Mich., 1969. Sales rep. John Wiley and Sons, Ann Arbor, Mich., 1970-72, editor N.Y.C., 1972-80, pub., 1980-84; pres. SoftPress, Inc., Monroe, N.Y., 1984-86; v.p., dir. acquisitions W.H. Freeman and Co./Scientific Am. Books, N.Y.C., 1986-92; v.p., editor-in-chief Macmillan Coll. Pub., Inc., N.Y.C., 1992-94; v.p., editorial dir., publisher Wadsworth Pub. Co., Belmont, Calif., 1994-97; pub., exec. editor Brooks Cole Pub., 1998—2000; exec. editor Prentice-Hall, 2001—. Editor: (textbooks and trade books) General Chemistry by James B. Brady, 1975, Organic Chemistry by T.W.G. Solomons, 1976, Fundamentals of General, Organic and Biological Chemistry by John R. Holom, 1978, Basic Inorganic Chemistry by A. Cotton and G. Wilkinson, 1977; contbg. author: The Videodisc Book, 1984. With USAF, 1963-67, Taiwan. Mem. Am. Assn. Pubs.

CARLSON, GEORGE ARTHUR, artist; b. Elmhurst, Ill., July 3, 1940; s. William Emanuel and Mathilda Katherine (Jorgensen) C.; m. Pamela Gustavson Hatzenbiler, May 9, 1981; children: Solon Emil, Andra Sean, Erin Hatzenbiler

Vaughan, Eric Hatzenbiler. Student, Am. Acad. Art, Chgo., Art Inst. Chgo., U. Ariz.; DFA (hon.), U. Idaho. Lectr. 1st U.S./Soviet Art Summit, Tretyakov Mus., Moscow, 1989. One man exhbns. include Indpls. Mus. Art, 1979, 85, Smithsonian Inst., Washington, 1982, Southwest Mus., L.A., 1988, Autry Western Heritage Mus., 1993, Gilcrease Mus., Tulsa, 1994, Ft. Worth Zoo Art Gallery, 1995-96; one man shows include Saks Gallery, Colorado Springs, Colo., 1972, Kennedy Galleries, N.Y.C., 1976, Bishop Galleries, Scottsdale, Ariz., 1977, Stremmel Galleries, Reno, 1978, 81, Grand Cen. Galleries, N.Y.C., 1980, O'Grady Galleries, Chgo., 1977, 83, Gerald Peters Gallery, Santa Fe, N.Mex., 1977, 85, 88, 92, Gerald Peters Gallery, Dallas, 1987, Farber Gallery Fine Arts, Indpls., 1989, Kneeland Gallery, Sun Valley, Idaho, 1990, 93, 94, Fenn Galleries, 1993, The Art Spirit Gallery, 2001, Nicholas Gallery, Billings, Mont., 2002, Matthew -Chase Gallery, Santa Fe, 2002; featured in group exhbns. including Phoenix Art Mus., Denver Art Mus., Denver Natural History Mus., Penrose Library at U. Denver, Gillette Pub. Library, Wyoming, Nat. Acad. Western Art, Oklahoma City, 1973-87, The Peking Exhibit, Beijing, Peoples Republic of China, 1981, Artists of Am. Show, Denver, 1981-87, Nat. Sculpture Soc., N.Y.C., 1982-83, 86, 90, Mus. Western Art, Denver, 1985, Gilcrease Mus., Tulsa, 1985, Ft. Smith (Okla.) Art Ctr., 1986, Kyoto (Japan) World Expn. Hist. Cities, 1987, Sonoma County Mus., Santa Rosa, Calif., 1987, Western & Wildlife Mus., Jackson Hole, Wyo., 1988, Amerika Haus, Berlin, 1990, Nat. Acad. Design, N.Y.C., 1990, Hubbard Mus., Riudoso, N.Mex., 1990, Hakone Open-Air Mus.,Tokyo, 1991, Denver 7 Show Nat. Cowboy Hall of Fame, 1992, 93, others; represented in pub. and corp. collections including Indpls. Mus., Genesee Mus., Rochester, N.Y., Denver Pub. Library, Denver Natural History Mus., Los Angeles Athletic Club, Cherokee Nat. Hist. Soc., Chakota, Okla., Corning (N.Y.) Mus., Anshutz Collection, Denver, Outdoor Mus. Art, Denver, Rockwell Mus., Pitts., Bank of Am., Las Vegas, Boatmans Bankshare, Inc., St. Louis, Brownsville (Tex.) Nat. Bank, Mountain States Bank, Denver, Rocky Mountain Bank, Denver, Sierra Nev. Arts Mus., Reno, Nat. Cowboy Hall of Fame, Oklahoma City, Mobile Oil Corp.; represented in various pvt. corp. and mus. collections, including U.S. Embassy, Copenhagen, Tucson Mus. Art, Manville Corp., Denver, L.A. Athletic Club, Rockwell Internat., others; sculptures include Bill Cosby, 1979, Bill Harrah, 1981, Early Day Miner, Washington Park, Denver, 1980, Of One Heart, Genesee Country Mus., 1982, Of One Heart, Mus. of Outdoor Arts, Englewood, Colo., 1985, I'm the Drum, Bank Am., Las Vegas, 1987, The Greeting, Genesee Mus., 1988, Eiteljorg Mus., 1989, Paul Robeson Cen. State U., Wilberforce, Ohio, 1990, Phylicia Rashad, 1991, I'm the Drum, Colo. Springs Fine Arts Ctr., 1994, Old Blue, Amon Carter Mus., Ft. Worth, 1995, Ennis Cosby, 1997, Mane of Wind-Neck of Thunder, Kirkland, Wash., 1999; featured in various bibliographies and films. Served with USAR, 1963-69. Recipient gold medal Nat. Acad. Western Art, 1974, 78, 80, 85, 89, Prix de West, 1975, Silver medal, 1976, 81, 88, Robert Lougheed award, 1989, Gold medal, 1989; Merit award Western Rendezvous Show, 1983. Mem. Nat. Sculpture Soc., Nat. Acad. Western Art (Gold medal 1974, 78, 80, 85, (2) 1989, Best of Show 1975, Silver medal 1976, 81, 88). Address: PO Box 28 Harrison ID 83833-0028

CARLSON, GUSTAV GUNNAR, anthropology educator; b. Gwinn, Mich., Nov. 21, 1909; s. Axel Victor and Brita Christina (Mattson) C.; m. Edith Elizabeth Erickson, Nov. 15, 1933; children: Karen Elizabeth Carlson Ogden, Eric Gustav. AB, No. Mich. U., 1932; MA, U. Mich., 1934, PhD, 1940. Instr. anthropology U. Cin., 1936-40, asst. prof. anthropology, 1940-43, assoc. prof. anthropology, 1946-52, prof. anthropology, 1952-80, head dept. sociology & anthropology, 1961-69, head dept. anthropology, 1969-77, prof. emeritus, 1980—; chief ops. intelligence Office of War Info., 1943-46. Vis. prof. U. Yunnan, China, 1945; cons. in field. Rockefeller Found. fellow, 1933; recipient A.B. Cohen award Excellence in Univ. Tchg. U. Cin., 1961-62, Disting. Alumni award No. Mich. U., 1981. Mem. Phi Beta Kappa, Sigma Xi. Avocations: gardening, photography, bread baking.

CARLSON, HAROLD ERNEST, endocrinologist, educator; b. Staten Island, N.Y., May 17, 1943; s. Clarence Herbert and Edith Emilia (Anderson) C.; m. Gabrielle Arakelian, July 2, 1966; children: Gregory Allan, Jonathan Ernest. BS in Chemistry, Rensselaer Poly. Inst., 1964; MD, Cornell U., 1968. Diplomate Am. Bd. Med. Examiners, Am. Bd. Internal Medicine. Intern, then resident Barnes Hosp., St. Louis, 1968-70; clin. assoc. NIAMD, NIH, Bethesda, Md., 1970-72; fellow in metabolism Washington U. Sch. Medicine, St. Louis, 1972-74; asst. prof., then assoc. prof. medicine UCLA, 1974-82; assoc. prof., then prof. medicine U. Mo., Columbia, 1982-85; prof. medicine SUNY, Stony Brook, 1985—, chief endocrinology, 2002—, Northport (N.Y.) VA Med. Ctr., 1985-96. Editor: Endocrinology, 1983; editorial bd. Jour. Clin. Endocrinology and Metabolism, 1979-82; contbr. articles to profl. jours. Lt. comdr. USPHS, 1970-72. Grantee VA, 1974-92, March of Dimes, 1987-90. Fellow ACP; mem. Endocrine Soc., Western Soc. Clin. Investigation, Cen. Soc. Clin. Rsch. Achievements include many scientific contributions to pituitary gland physiology and diseases. Office: SUNY Stony Brook Dept Med Endocrinology HSC TI5-060 Stony Brook NY 11794-8154 E-mail: hcarlson@notes.cc.sunysb.edu.

CARLSON, JANET FRANCES, psychologist, educator; b. Newport, R.I., Oct. 3, 1957; d. Robert Carl and Alice Marion (Orina) Carlson; m. Kurt Francis Geisinger, Sept. 22, 1984. BS summa cum laude, Union Coll., Schenectady, 1979; MA in Clin. Psychology, Fordham U., 1982, PhD in Clin. Psychology, 1987. Lic. psychologist NY, cert. sch psychologist NY. Clin. psychology intern Conn. Valley Hosp., Middletown, Conn., 1983-84; rsch. fellow Schering-Plough Found., Bronx, N.Y., 1984-85; psychologist I Creedmoor Psychiat. Ctr., Queens Village, N.Y., 1985-86; psychologist Hallen Sch., Mamaroneck, N.Y., 1986-88; asst. prof. psychology Fordham U., Bronx, N.Y., 1988-89; asst. prof. sch. and applied psychology Fairfield (Conn.) U., 1989-93, dir. sch. and applied psychology programs, 1989-90; from asst. prof. counseling and psychol. svcs. to prof. SUNY, Oswego, 1993—2002, assoc. dean Sch. Edn., 1998-2001; prof. psychology, head dept. gen. academics Tex. A&M U., Galveston, 2002—. Cons. N.Y.C. Bd. Edn. Office Rsch., Evaluation and Assessment, 1988—92; vis. asst. prof. psychol. LeMoyne Coll., Syracuse, NY, 1992—93; dir. Office Tchg. Resources in Psychol., 2001—. Recipient Sugarfree scholarship, 1984—85; grantee Sigma Xi, 1984—85. Fellow: APA; mem.: NASP, N.Y. Assn. Sch. Psychologists, Northeastern Ednl. Rsch. Assn. (ed newsletter 1988—91, bd dirs. 1990—93, pres. 1995—96), N.Y. State Psychol. Assn., Eastern Psychol. Assn., Am. Ednl. Rsch. Assn., Psi Chi, Sigma Xi, Phi Kappa Phi (pres. 1995—96). Avocations: wildlife preservation, conservation issues.

CARLSON, JEANNIE ANN, writer; b. Bklyn., Jan. 13, 1955; d. Lloyd Arthur and Ruth Frances (Riley) C.; m. Kenneth D. Williams, May 15, 1976 (div. 1981); 1 child, Carl Philip; m. H. Daniel Hopkins, Dec. 16, 1987 (div. 1994); m. Timothy R. Burns, Mar. 21, 1998. BA, Randolph-Macon Woman's Coll., 1977. Mktg./editing rep. Harris Pub., White Plains, N.Y., 1982; adminstrv. asst. Ray Fried Assocs., Inc., Eastchester, N.Y., 1980-84; proofreader Nat. Pennysaver, Elmsford, N.Y., 1983-84; chief writer Profl. Resume and Writing Svc., St. Petersburg, Fla., 1984-87; exec. writer, pres. Viking Comm., Inc., 1987-98; v.p. comm. Technifax Svcs. Inc., St. Petersburg, 1998-2001, exec. v.p., 2001—. Staff corr. Tampa Bay Newpapers Inc., Largo, 1998—; feature writer Asbury News, Crestwood, N.Y., 1983-84; editl. asst. Children's Rights Am., Largo, Fla., 1984; pub. rels. coord. The Renaissance Cultural Ctr., Clearwater, Fla., 1985; com. mem. work area on commn. Pasadena Cmty. Ch., St. Petersburg, Fla., 1986-88, 2000—, Christian edn. bd. Our Savior Luth. Ch., St. Petersburg, 1991-93; edit. advisor Grief Recovery Ctrs., Fla., 1992; columnist Believer's Bay Online mag., St. Petersburg, 2000-02. Recipient Golden Poet award World of Poetry, 1985, 88, 89, 91, 92, Silver Poet award, 1986, 90, Recognition award Nat. Soc. Poets, 1979, poetry awards Internat. Publs., 1976-77, World of Poetry awards of merit, 1983 (2), 85, 87, 88 (2), 91, 92, Editor's Choice award Nat. Libr. Poetry, 1994, Woman of Yr. award ABI, 1995, 96, 97. Mem. City News Svc. (affiliate writer), Profl. Assn. Resume Writers, Phi Beta Gamma. Methodist. Avocations: theatre, culinary arts, music. Office: Technifax Svcs Inc PO Box 13667 Saint Petersburg FL 33733

CARLSON, JEFFERY JOHN, lawyer; b. Mpls., May 23, 1947; s. John Joseph and Sylvia Lorraine (Sandberg) C.; children: Erik John, Bryan Jeffery, Kimberly Anne. Student Augsburg Coll., 1965-66; BA summa cum laude, U. Minn., 1969, postgrad., 1970-71; JD, UCLA, 1974. Bar: Calif. 1974, U.S. Dist. Ct. (cen. dist.) Calif. 1974, U.S. Ct. Appeals (9th cir.) 1976. Teaching asst., rsch. asst. U. Minn., Mpls., 1970-71; assoc. Harwood & Adkinson, Newport Beach, Calif., 1974-77; assoc. Haight, Dickson, Brown & Bonesteel, Santa Monica, Calif., 1977-81, ptnr., 1981-88; sr. ptnr. Dickson, Carlson & Campillo, Santa Monica, 1988—; judge pro tem West Los Angeles Mcpl. Ct., 1981-83; arbitrator Panel of Arbitrators, Los Angeles, Orange and Ventura counties, 1980—; moderator, panel mem. program on recent devels. in tort practice; lectr. bus. law Calif. State U., Northridge, 1978. Author: Califorinia Tort Guide, 2d edit., (supplement to tort guide) California Continuing Education of the Bar, 2d. edit., 1990; cons. Punitive Damages and Restrictions on Recovery, of California Tort Damages Guide; contbr. articles to profl. jours. Mem. nominating com. Am. Soc. Pharmacy Law, pres. adv. com.; mem. ABA (vice-chmn. Com. on Toxic and Hazardous Substances and Environ. Law). Mem. So. Clif. Def. Counsel, Def. Research and Trial Lawyers Assn., Fedn. Ins. Corp. Counsel (chair pharm. litigation sect. 1995-96, mem. product liability adv. coun. 1995—), Phi Beta Kappa (James Harley Beal award 1987). Lutheran. Office: Dickson Carlson & Campillo 120 Broadway St Ste 300 Santa Monica CA 90401-2386

CARLSON, JENNIE PEASLACK, lawyer; b. Ft. Thomas, Ky., June 11, 1960; d. Roland A. and Shirley (Willen) Peaslack; m. Charles I. Michaels, Aug. 13, 1983 (div. May 1989); m. Richard A. Carlson, May 2, 1992. BA in English, Centre Coll., 1982; JD, Vanderbilt U., 1985. Bar: Ohio 1985. Atty. Taft, Stettinius & Hollister, Cin., 1985-91; sr. v.p., dep. gen. counsel Star Banc Corp., Cin., 1991—. Office: Firstar Corp 425 Walnut St Ste 9 Cincinnati OH 45202-3923 Home: 6425 Indian Hills Rd Minneapolis MN 55439-1160

CARLSON, JON GORDON, lawyer; b. Wakefield, Mich., June 25, 1943; s. John Edwin and Irene Anne (Erickson) C.; m. Jane McCann, June 17, 1965; children: Christine, Eric, Susan. BA, U. Ill., 1965, JD, 1967. Bar: Ill. 1967, Mo. 1990. Assoc. Edward F. O'Malley, East St. Louis, Ill., 1967-68, Kassly, Weihl & Bone, Belleville, Ill., 1968-70; ptnr. Kassly, Weihl, Bone, Becker & Carlson, Belleville, 1970-78, Chapman & Carlson, Ill., 1978-84, Talbert, Carlson & Mallon, Ill., 1985-86, Carlson & Alfeld, Edwardsville, Ill., 1986-87; prin. Jon G. Carlson & Assocs., P.C., Edwardsville, Ill., 1987-94, Carlson, Wendler & Assocs., P.C., Edwardsville, Ill., 1994-99, St. Louis, 1996-99, Carlson & Carlson, P.C., 1999—. Fellow Am. Bar Found.; mem. Ill. Trial Lawyers Assn. (pres. 1987-88), Mo. Trial Lawyers Assn. Trial Lawyers Am., Ill. Bar Assn., Mo. Bar Assn. Democrat. Avocations: flying (multi-engine instrument rated pilot), walking, hiking. Office: 90 Edwardsville Profl Park PO Box 527 Edwardsville IL 62025-0527

CARLSON, JULIA GAGE, poet, social worker; b. Winchester, Wash., May 15, 1948; d. Francis Elliott and Marguerite Moy; m. Peter Simeonides (div. 1980); 1 child, Alexandra Barnett. BA in Philosophy, Boston U., 1971; degree in ESL/linguistics, U. Toulouse, France, 1975; MSW, Lowry Cert., Boston U., 1991. Clin. coord. Bay Care Treatment Ctr., Boston, 1993—2000. Author: (book) 50 Poems, 2000, 50 Poems 1999-2001, 2002. Recipient Davis Kidd Poetry award, 2001. Avocations: gardening, reading, walking, dancing. E-mail: uberhuss@hotmail.com.

CARLSON, KATHLEEN, not-for-profit fundraiser, writer, journalist; b. San Nicholaas, Aruba, Netherlands Antilles, June 23, 1946; arrived in Milw., Wis., 1952; d. Arthur Hughborn Mendes and Wilhelmina Leanora (Hill) Bunyan; m. Vernon Marcus Carlson, Aug. 6, 1999; m. Roman Harry Januchowski, July 6, 1966 (dec. Sept. 1968); m. Timmons Wells, May 2, 1978 (div. Sept. 1996). BA in English, U. of Wis., 1972; MS in Journalism, Northwestern U., 1973; MA in English, U. of Wis., 1988. Cert. Resource Devel. Specialist Coun. for Resource Devel., DC, 1991, Cert. Fundraising Exec. Nat. Soc. of Fund Raising Executives, Alexandria, Va., 1996-1999. Compliance monitor, planner, grants, coord. Milw. County Exec., 1980—83; asst. admin. Sr. Citizens Svs. Inc., 1983—84; auditor Milw. County, 1984—87; prog. monitor Milw. Employment Training Inc., 1988; external programs spec. Waukesha County Tech. Coll., Pewaukee, 1989—91, devel. coord., 1991—. Wis. state coord. Coun. for Resource Devel., DC, 1992—96; mem. Wis. Mfg. Curriculum Consortium, Pewaukee, 1994—; region V dir. elect Coun. for Resource Devel., 1996—97, region V dir., 1998—99. Author: (poetry book) Deep Night, 1970; contbr. var. newsletters and jours., poetry book. Recipient Hon. Citation, Acad. Am. Poets, 1970—71; grantee Edit. Internship, Assn. for Edn. in Journalism, 1971, Reporting Internship, The Mil. Jour., 1970. Mem.: Coun. for Resource Devel. (2003 v.p. for Annual Nat. Conf. 2002—03), Minority Graphic Arts Orgn. Inc. (sec. 1983—), YWCA of Waukesha (sec. of bd. 1998—2000, chair, Diversity Task Force 1999—2004). Avocations: writing poetry and music, ballroom dancing, skiing. Office: Waukesha County Technical College 800 Main St Pewaukee WI 53072

CARLSON, KATHLEEN BUSSART, law librarian; b. Charlotte, NC, June 25, 1956; d. Dean Allyn and Joan (Parlette) Bussart; m. Gerald Mark Carlson, Aug. 15, 1987. BA in Polit. Sci., Ohio State U., 1977; JD, Capital U., 1980; MA in Libr. and Info. Sci., U. Iowa, 1986. Bar: Ohio 1980. Editor Lawyers Coop. Pub. Co., Rochester, N.Y., 1980-83; asst. state law libr. State of Wyo., Cheyenne, 1987-88, state law libr., 1988—. Mem. Bd. Adjustment, City of Cheyenne, 2001--; 2d v.p., bd. dirs. Wyo. coun. Girl Scouts U.S., Casper, 1990-92, 1st v.p., bd. dirs., 1993-96. Mem. Am. Assn. Law Librs. (indexing legal periodical lit. adv. com. 1993-96, chair 1994-96, scholarship com. 1996-98, citation format com. 1998-2000, 2002--, fair bus. practices com. 2000-02, exec. bd. 2003—, edn. com. State Ct. and County Law Librs. sect. 1991-92, sec.-treas. 1992-95, chair grants com. 1997-98 nominating com. 1998-99, co-chair membership com., chair edn. com. 2000-01), Western Pacific Assn. Law Librs. (pres. 1996-97, 2003—), Wyo. Libr. Assn. (sec. acad. and spl. librs. sect. 1990-92, pres. 1994-95), Bibliog. Ctr. for Rsch. (trustee 1991-95), Zonta (pres. local club 2002--), Kappa Delta, Beta Phi Mu. Avocations: arts and crafts, baking, travel. Home: 911 E 18th St Cheyenne WY 82001-4722 Office: State Law Libr 2301 Capitol Ave Cheyenne WY 82002-0001 E-mail: kcarls@state.wy.us.

CARLSON, KENNETH GEORGE, data processing executive; b. Duluth, Minn., Dec. 14, 1949; s. George Bernard and Laura Anna (Larson) C.; m. Stephanie Venn Petersen, Sept. 20, 1969; children: Laura, Anna. BSEE, U. Minn., 1972. Cert. in data processing; cert. systems profl. Systems programmer U. Minn. Computer Ctr., Mpls., 1969-74; dept. mgr. United Computing System, Kansas City, Mo., 1974-80; computer scientist Computer Scis. Corp., Falls Church, Va., 1980-82; pres., chmn. bd. LSS Data Sys., Mpls., 1982—86, 1987—2001, chmn. bd., chief tech. officer, CEO, 2001—; v.p. Minn. Supercomputer Ctr., Mpls., 1986-87, asst. to exec. v.p., 1987-90. Data processing advisor Johnson Community Coll., Overland Park, Kans., 1975-78; bd. dirs., chief fin. officer Superior Resources, Duluth, 1985—. Republican. Mem. United Ch. of Christ. Avocations: cross country skiing, downhill skiing, travel, running, bicycling. Office: LSS Data Systems 6423 City West Pkwy Eden Prairie MN 55344-3246

CARLSON, LAWRENCE ARVID, retired English language educator, real estate agent; b. San Diego, Dec. 29, 1935; s. Arvid Fritiof and Ruth Mathilda (Hedman) C.; m. Patricia Catherine Barlow, Sept. 8, 1963; children: Lawrence Stephen, Janine Catherine. BA in History, Roanoke Coll., 1957; MS in Edn., S.D. State U., 1962; MA in English, Calif. State U., Fullerton, 1966; grad., Realtor Inst., 2002. Cert. e-PRO Internet Profl. Tchr. Edison Jr. High Sch., L.A., 1962—63, Anaheim (Calif.) High Sch., 1963—66; prof. English Orange Coast Coll., Costa Mesa, Calif., 1966—2001; ret., 2001; instr. karate Orange Coast Coll., Costa Mesa, 1984—95. Sales assoc. Real Estate Offices, San Juan Capistrano, Calif., 1994—. Host, writer (ednl. TV show) Creative Writers Viewpoint, 1975. Horseback riding tour leader Rock Creek Pack Sta., Bishop, Calif., 1990-95; leader 4-H, Orange County, Calif., 1983-93; vol. Liberty Walk, Dana Point, Calif., 1997. Maj. USMCR, 1957-67. Recipient Excellence award Nat. Inst. Staff Orgnl. Devel., 1993. Mem. Nat. Assn. Realtors, Calif. Assn. Realtors, Orange County Assn. Realtors, Faculty Assn. Calif. C.C.'s. Democrat. Lutheran. Avocations: horseback riding, Karate, surfing. Home: PO Box 1266 Rancho Carrillo 10871 Verdugo Rd San Juan Capistrano CA 92693 Office: Ste A-102 32241 Camino Capistrano San Juan Capistrano CA 92675 Personal E-mail: ranchcarlson@earthlink.net. Business E-Mail: carlsons@larandpat.com.

CARLSON, LEROY THEODORE, JR., telecommunications industry executive; b. 1946; AB, Harvard U., 1968, MBA, 1971. Fin. analyst, mgr. fin. analysis and planning, mgr. acctg. Singer Corp., 1971-74; v.p. Telephone and Data Systems, Inc., 1974-78, exec. v.p., 1978-81, pres., 1981-86, pres., CEO, 1981—; chmn. bd. Am. Paging Sys., Inc., 1998. Chmn. bd. Am. Paging, Inc., TDS Telecomm., U.S. Cellular Corp., Am. Portable Telecom. Mem. U.S. Telephone Assn. (bd. dirs.), Nat. Rural Telecom. Assn. (bd. dirs.). Office: Telephone & Data Sys Inc 30 N La Salle St Ste 4000 Chicago IL 60602-2587

CARLSON, LINDA MARIE, language arts educator, consultant; b. St. Paul, Dec. 24, 1951; d. Kenneth Leroy Carlson and Margaret Berget. BS in English and Polit. Sci., U. Minn., Duluth, 1973, MEd in Rhetorical Theory, 1979; MBA, U. St. Thomas, 1987; postgrad., Rensselaer Poly. Inst., 1992—. Cert. Myers-Briggs Type Indicator adminstrn., cert. tchr., Minn. Tchr. English, curriculum leader Ind. Sch. Dist. 13, Columbia Heights, Minn., 1973-76, publs. advisor, coach, 1974-76; exec. asst. to provost Univ. Minn., Duluth, 1977-80; tech. editor EG and G (U.S. Dept. Energy), Idaho Falls, Idaho, 1980; tchr. English, gifted and talented Ind. Sch. Dist. 11, Coon Rapids, Minn., 1980—, lang. arts curriculum developer, 1981—, publs. advisor, 1982-84, learning styles cons., 1986—, assessment cons., 1989—. Performance assessment cons. Minn. State Dept. Edn., St. Paul, 1990-98; writing assessment cons. Minn. State Graduation Rule Pilot Site, St. Paul, 1994-98; lang. arts cons., curriculum design cons., multicultural cons. pvt. and pub. schs. Minn., 1987—. Mem. Minn. Arthritis Found., St. Paul, 1981-90, Commn. on Health and Healing, Mpls., 1984-86. Recipient Golden Apple Teaching award Ashland Oil Co., 1994; All-Univ. scholar Rensselaer Poly. Inst., 1992. Mem. NEA, ASCD, Am. Ednl. Rsch. Assn., Nat. Coun. for Tchrs. of English, Anoka-Hennepin Edn. Assn. (pub. rels. com. 1980-85), Coll. Compositional Comm. Avocations: jewelry making, hiking, white-water rafting, travel. Home: 11117 Cottonwood St NW Coon Rapids MN 55448-3385

CARLSON, LOREN MERLE, political science educator; b. Mitchell, SD, Nov. 2, 1923; s. Clarence A. and Edna M. (Rosenquist) C.; m. Verona Gladys Hole, Dec. 21, 1950; children: Catherine Ann, Bradley Reed, Nancy Jewel. BA, Yankton Coll., 1948; MA, U. Wis., 1952; JD, George Washington U., 1961. Bar: S.D. 1961, U.S. Supreme Ct. 1976. Asst. dir. Govt. Rsch. Bur., U. S.D., 1949-51; orgn. and methods examiner Dept. State, Washington, 1951-52; asst. dir. legis. rsch. State of S.D., 1953-55, dir., 1955-59, budget officer, 1963-68; rsch. asst. to U.S. Senator from S.D., 1959-60, adminstrv. asst., 1960-63; dir. statewide ednl. svcs. U. S.D., Vermillion, 1968-74, dean continuing edn., 1974, 1976—87, from assoc. prof. to prof. polit. sci., 1968—89, emeritus prof. polit. sci., 1989—; admin. asst. to US Rep. from SD, 1975—76; hwy. laws study dir. U. S.D. Law Sch., Vermillion, 1963; mng. editor U. S.D. Press, 1985-89, sr. editor, 1989-93. Chmn. Model Rural Devel. Commn., Dist. II, State of SD, 1972-74; chmn. Region VII Planning Commn. on Criminal Justice, S.D., 1969-74; vice-chmn. South East Coun. of Govts., 1989-90, chmn., 1993-97. Author: (with W.O. Farber and T.C. Geary) Government of South Dakota, 1979; contbr. articles profl. publs. Mem. Vermillion City Coun., 1980-90, 91-92, pres. 1982-90; mem. S.D. Humanities Found., 1989-97; mem. Vermillion Home Rule Task Force, 2002-03; bd. dirs. Vermillion Devel. Co., pres., 1987; mem. Vermillion Golf Course/Rsch. Market Analysis Study Rev. Com., 1993-94; mem. Vermillion Facilities Task Force, 1996-97; Rep. candidate State House of Reps., 1986; hon. life trustee U. S.D. Found., 1998. Named Outstanding Young Man Pierre Jaycees, 1959 Fellow: Nat. Univ. Continuing Edn. Assn.; mem.: Farber Found. (exec. bd. dirs. 1993—2001), Nat. Meml. Mt. Rushmore Soc., Spirit Mound Trust (v.p. 1984—2003), S.D. City Mgr. Assn. (hon.), Karl Mundt Found., S.D. Adult Edn. Assn. (chmn. 1973—74), ASPA, Pi Kappa Delta, Pi Sigma Alpha. Republican. Lutheran. Home: 229 Catalina Ave Vermillion SD 57069-3319 Office: U SD Dept Polit Sci Vermillion SD 57069 E-mail: lmcarlso@usd.edu.

CARLSON, MARVIN ALBERT, theater educator; b. Wichita, Kans., Sept. 15, 1935; s. Roy Edward and Gladys (Nelson) C.; m. Patricia Alene McElroy, Aug. 20, 1960; children— Geoffrey, Richard. BS, U. Kans., 1957, MA, 1959; PhD, Cornell U., 1961. Instr. speech and drama Cornell U., Ithaca, N.Y., 1961-62, asst. prof., 1962-66, assoc. prof. theatre arts, 1966-73, prof., 1973-79, chmn. dept., 1966-68, 73-78; dir. Cornell U. (Univ. Theatre), 1963-64, 65-66; prof. theatre and drama Ind. U., Bloomington, 1979-86, prof. comparative lit., 1984-86, disting. prof., 1986—; exec. officer PhD program in theatre Grad. Ctr. CUNY, 1986-95; Sidney E. Cohn chair in theatre CUNY, 1988—. Walker-Ames lectr. U. Wash., 1994. Author: Andre Antoine's Memories of the Theatre-Libre, 1964, The Theatre of the French Revolution, 1966, The French Stage in the Nineteenth Century, 1972, The German Stage in the Nineteenth Century, 1972, Goethe and the Weimar Theatre, 1978, The Italian Stage from Goldoni to D'Annunzio, 1981, Theories of the Theatre, 1984, The Italian Shakespearians, 1985, Places of Performance, 1989, Theatre Semiotics, 1990, Deathtraps, 1993, Performance, 1996, Voltaire and the Theatre of the Eighteenth Century, 1998, The Haunted Stage, 2001. Recipient George Jean Nathan award, 1994, ATHE Career Achievement award, 1995, Calloway prize, 2001; Guggenheim fellow, 1968, Ind. U. Soc. for Humanities fellow, 1993. Fellow Am. Theatre Assn.; mem. Am. Soc. Theatre Rsch. (Outstanding Achievement award 2000), Internat. Assn. Theatre Critics, Am. Theatre in Higher Edn., Internat. Fedn. Theatre Rsch., Nat. Theatre Conf. Home: 20 E 35th St New York NY 10016 Office: CUNY Grad Grad Ctr Program in Theatre 365 Fifth Ave New York NY 10016-4334 E-mail: mcarlson@gc.cuny.edu.

CARLSON, MARY SUSAN, lawyer; b. Lincoln, Nebr., Nov. 2, 1949; d. Arnold Emil Carlson and Mary Lloyd; m. Gerald P. Greiman, May 2, 1982; children: David Carlson Greiman, Nora Carlson Greiman. AA, Cottey Coll., 1970; BFA in Edn., U. Nebr., 1972, JD, 1976; postgrad., Notre Dame Law Sch., Tokyo, 1974. Bar: Nebr. 1977, D.C. 1979, U.S. Supreme Ct. 1986, Mo. 1987. Staff law clk. to presiding justice U.S. Ct. Appeals (8th cir.), St. Louis, 1976—78; assoc. Kilcullen, Smith & Heenan, Washington, 1978—79; vis. asst. prof. law Washington U., St. Louis, 1987—90, vis. assoc. prof., 1990—93; ptnr. Chackes, Carlson & Spritzer, LLP, St. Louis, 1995—; trial atty. Civil Divsn. U.S. Dept. Justice, Washington, 1980—86; with Guam land claims litigation/U.S. dept. Justice, Agana, 1981. Lectr. Sichuan U. Sch. Law, Chengdu, China, 1991; cert. neutral U.S. Dist. Ct. (ea. dist.) Mo., St. Louis, 1992—; arbitrator Am. Arbitration Assn., 1989—. Trustee St. Louis Met. Sewer Dist., 1994—97; del.-at-large nat. steering com. Nat. Women's Polit. Caucus, 1991—98; pres. ACLU Ea. Mo., 2000—, Mo. Nat. Women's Polit. Caucus, 1990—92, Mo. Nat. Abortion Rights Action League, 1994—98, PAC. Mem.: ATLA, ABA, Am. Arbitration Assn., Mound City Bar Assn., St. Louis Women's Bar Assn., Bar Assn. Met. St. Louis, Nebr. Bar Assn., D.C. Bar Assn., Mo. Bar Assn., Nat. Employment Lawyers Assn. Office: Chackes Carlson & Spritzer LLP 8390 Delmar Blvd Ste 218 Saint Louis MO 63124-2179 Office Fax: 314-872-7017. E-mail: scarlson@vccs-law.com.

CARLSON, MELINDA SUZANNE, librarian; b. LaPorte, Ind., Jan. 15, 1949; d. E. Stewart and Margaret S. Carlson. BA, Colo. Women's Coll., 1972; MAL, U. Denver, 1975. Media specialist Brown County Libr., Green Bay, Wis., 1975-78; audiovisual and interlibr. loan cons. Ea. Shore Regional Libr., Salisbury, Md., 1978-81; libr. cons. Washington, 1981-83; libr. ops. mgr. USA Today, Arlington, Va., 1983-90, rsch. analyst, 1990-93; mgr. news rsch. ABC News, Washington, 1993—. Cons. Newspaper Assn. of Am., Reston, Va., 1991-92. Mem.: ALA, Investigative Reporters and Editors, Spl. Librs. Assn. (broadcast chair news divsn. 1999—2002). Office: ABC News 1717 DeSales St NW Washington DC 20036-4407

CARLSON, MITCHELL LANS, international technical advisor; b. Boulder, Colo., Nov. 24, 1951; s. DeVon M. and Mary (Ackley) C. BA in History and Internat. Affairs, Lewis and Clark Coll., 1974; MA in Environ. Planning, UCLA, 1978; postgrad., U. Calif., Berkeley, 1978-80. Rsch. asst. Sch. Architecture and Urban Planning UCLA, 1977-78; project planner Calif. Energy Resource Conservation and Devel. Commn., Riverside, Calif., 1977-78, Vastu-Shilpa Found., Ahmedabad, India, 1978-79; with UNHCR, WFP, UNDP UNOps., 1974-92; chief tech. adviser UN (UNDP), Bahambang, Cambodia, 1992-95, Kigali, Rwanda, 1996-97, Sarajevo, 1998—2001, 2001—. Avocations: bicycling, photography, swimming, tennis. Home: 5472 White Pl Boulder CO 80303-1227 Office: UNOPS/RESS 405 Lexington Ave New York NY 10174 E-mail: mlcarlson838@yahoo.com.

CARLSON, NORMAN A. government official; b. Sioux City, Iowa, Aug. 10, 1933; s. Albert N. and Esther (Hollander) C.; m. Patricia Helen Musser, Sept. 8, 1956 (dec. Feb. 1994); children: Lucinda M., Gary N.; m. Phyllis J. Rohan, May 23, 1997. BA, Gustavus Adolphus Coll., 1955; MA, State U. Iowa, 1957, Princeton U., 1966. Parole officer Dept. Justice, U.S. Penitentiary, Leavenworth, Kan., 1957-58; casework supr. Fed. Correctional Inst., Ashland, Ky., 1958-60;

asst. supr. instl. programs Fed. Bur. Prisons, Dept. Justice, Washington, 1960-62, project officer, 1962-65, exec. asst. to dir., 1966-70; dir. Fed. Bur. Prisons, 1970-87; sr. fellow Hubert Humphrey Inst. Pub. Affairs, U. Minn., Mpls., 1987-88; prof. dept. sociology U. Minn., Mpls., 1988-98. Nat. Inst. Pub. Affairs fellow Princeton U., 1965-66; recipient Arthur S. Flemming award, 1972, Roger W. Jones award for exec. leadership, 1978, Atty. Gen.'s award for exceptional service, 1981 Mem. Am. Correctional Assn. (past pres., mem. exec. com., E.R. Cass award 1981) Home: 15745 W Vale Dr Goodyear AZ 85338-8757

CARLSON, ORVILLE JAMES (SKIP CARLSON), accountant, financial planner; b. Mpls., Sept. 20, 1944; s. Orville Harlan and Marguerite (Fleming) C.; m. Shirley A. Steele, Feb. 20, 1968; children: Orville J., Jr., Melissa. AA, U. Minn.; BS, St. Cloud (Minn.) State Coll. CPA. Minn. Staff acct. George M. Hansen, CPA, Mpls., 1972-75; sr. acct. J.K. Lasser & Co., CPA, Mpls., 1975-76, DeLaHunt Voto & Co., White Bear Lake, Minn., 1976—78; founder O.J. Carlson & Assoc., Anoka, 1978; founding ptnr. Wingad Carlson Cos., Anoka, Minn., 1984—; sr. mgr. corp. affairs Intuit, Inc., San Diego, 2000—02; sr. v.p. product devel. Trust File, Inc., Baton Rouge, 2003—. Tax com. fin. instns. and ins. from dist. 52A Minn. Ho. of Reps., 1995-97, Minn. Dept. Revenue, 1997-2000; bd. dirs., chmn. Family Life Ctr., Anoka, 1988—; sec.-treas. Flores do Mundo Inc., 1983; CFO, treas. Am.'s Floral Express, Inc., 1989—; CFO, sec.-treas. ParaBody, Inc., 1980—, LV ParaBody, 1994, The Equitable, 1994; nat. dir. Quicken Tax Freedom Project for Intuit, Inc. Chmn. Utility Adv. Bd., Anoka, 1975-84; treas. Anoka, Blaine, and Coon Rapids Outward Bound Found., Coon Rapids, Minn., 1984-86; bd. dirs. Anoka Bus. Assistance Network, Coon Rapids, 1985, Nat. Sports Ctr., Blaine, Minn., 1990; mem. charter commn. City of Fridley, 1987, Internal Audit Com. Anoka County, 1993—, chmn. Three Rivers Dist. Boy Scouts of Am., 1997-99. With U.S. Army, 1966-70. Mem. Nat. Soc. Pub. Accts., Minn. Assn. Pub. Accts., Nat. Assn. Tax Preparers, Inst. Cert. Fin. Planners, Minn. Assn. Life Underwriters, Anoka County C. of C. (bd. dirs., pres.), Soc. for Human Resource Mgmt., Mfrs. Alliance, Minn. Tech. CEO Roundtable. Mem. Evang. Free. Lodge: Rotary (Anoka, bd. dirs. 1979-85, pres. elect 1995). Home: 1032 Tesoro Ave San Marcos CA 92069 Office: Trust File Inc pO Box 64506 Baton Rouge LA 70896 Fax: 858-784-1382. E-mail: skip_carlson@intuit.com.

CARLSON, P(ATRICIA) M(CELROY), writer; b. Guatemala City, Guatemala, Feb. 3, 1940; (parents Am. citizens); d. James Benjamin and Alene (Jones) McElroy; m. M.A. Carlson, Aug. 20, 1960; children: Geoffrey, Richard. BA, Cornell U., 1961; MA, Cornell, 1966, PhD, 1974. Instr., lectr. psychology and human development Cornell U., Ithaca, N.Y., 1973-78. Mem. bd. dirs. Bloomington Restorations, Inc., 1982-84. Author: (with M. Potts, R. Cocking and C. Copple), Structure and Development in Child Language, 1979, Audition for Murder, 1985, Murder is Academic, 1985, Murder is Pathological, 1986, (with Richard Darlington) Behavioral Statistics, 1987, Murder Unrenovated, 1988, Rehearsal for Murder, 1988, Murder in the Dog Days, 1991, Murder Misread, 1991, Bad Blood, 1991, Gravestone, 1993, Bloodstream, 1995, Renowned Be Thy Grave, 1998, fourteen short stories. Chair Ithaca Environ. Commn., 1975-78; bd. dirs. Historic Ithaca, 1976-77. Mem. Mystery Writers Am. (bd. dirs. 1990-92, editor Mystery Writers Ann. 1993-96, 98-2000), Sisters in Crime (internat. sec. 1990 91, v.p. 1991-92, pres. 1992-93). Address: Vicky Bijur Literary Agy 333 W End Ave New York NY 10023-8128

CARLSON, RAYMOND HOWARD, retired military officer, prosecutor; b. Evergreen Park, Ill., June 19, 1951; s. Howard E. and Elizabeth J. (Lee) Carlson. BSChE, Purdue U., 1973; JD summa cum laude, Ind. U., 1981; LLM, U. Va., 1988; MA in Nat. Security and Strategy, USN War Coll., 1997. Bar: Ind. 1981, Fla. 1993. Commd. ensign USN, 1973, advanced through grades to comdr., 1990; with Navy Legal Office, Seattle, 1981-84, Subic Bay, Philippines, 1988-91, prof. jt. mil. ops., internat. law Mayport, Fla., 1997-2000; with Naval Sta., Rota, Spain, 1984-88; prin. legal advisor to comdr. Naval Base, Jacksonville, Fla., 1991-95; prof. jt. mil. ops., internat. law Naval War Coll., Newport, RI, 1995-97; asst. state atty. Duval County Courthouse, Jacksonville, 2000—. Mem.: Jacksonville Bar Assn., Judge Advs. Assn., Fed. Bar Assn. Office: State Attys Office Duval County Courthouse Jacksonville FL 32202-2484

CARLSON, RHONDA, writer, law educator; b. Moline, Ill., Aug. 23, 1946; d. Oliver W.O. and Edna M. Carlson; m. Edward J. Gac, Jan. 27, 1968. BA, U. Ill., 1968; JD, U. Calif., San Francisco, 1972; MLS, U. Calif., Berkeley, 1975. Cert. law libr. Law libr. U. Colo., Boulder, 1977-84; exec. Fred B. Rothman & Co., Littleton, Colo., 1984-93; pvt. practice writer, 1993—; prof. U. Denver Sch. Law, 1997—2000. Author: Introduction to Paralegalism, 1997, How to Attain Your HRMS Vision, 1999. Recipient cert. LeCordon Bleu Ecole de Cuisine, Paris, 1983. Mem. Am. Spaniel Club, Colo. Assn. Law Librs. (pres. 1981-82). Episcopalian. Home: 1946 Beacon Ct Boulder CO 80302-4946 E-mail: blkcocker@aol.com.

CARLSON, RICHARD GREGORY, accountant; b. Chgo., Aug. 24, 1949; s. Richard George and S. Diane (Russell) C.; m. Annette Claire Bonneville, Aug. 30, 1969 (div. May 1982); children: Scott Richard, Amy Kristin; m. Pamela Catherine Punzelt, Sept. 25, 1982. BBA, Western Mich. U., 1971. CPA, Ill. With Deloitte & Touche, Chgo., 1971—, ptnr., 1980—, dir. Chgo. real estate svc. ctr., 1980-91, mem. nat. real estate com., 1982-91, dirs. client svcs. and devel., 1985-88, mem. Chgo. exec. com., 1985-88, mng. ptnrs. adv. coun., 1986-88, nat. mng. ptnr. real estate constrn. and hospitality, 1989—, mng. dir. nat. real estate svcs., 1991—. Author: Real Estate Accounting and Reporting Handbook, 1995; editor Real Estate Accounting and Taxation Journal, 1991-93, Real Estate Strategies, 1991—; contbr. articles to profl. jours. Mem. MIT Real Estate Cir., 1995—; adv. bd. Ctr. Real Estate Studies Ind. U.; mem. bd. advisors Real Estate Fin. Jour., 1993—; bd. dirs. Western Mich. U. Found., 1986, mem. investment com., 1986-88, 91-97, mem. exec. com., 1988-97, vice-chmn., 1992-93, chmn. 1994-97; bd. dirs. Pin Oak Homeowners Assn., treas. 1982-86. With USAR, 1971-77. Recipient Disting. Acctg. Alumni award Western Mich. U., 1987, Disting. Alumni award 1993. Mem. AICPA, Am. Acctg. Assn. (Midwest regional steering com. 1983-87), Ill. Soc. CPAs, Internat. Coun. Shopping Ctrs., Western Mich. U. Alumni Assn. (bd. dirs. 1984-91, treas. 1984-86, pres. 1986-88), Nat. Assn. Real Estate Cos., Real Estate Roundtable. (bd. dirs. 1992—2001, pres. coun. 2001—), Nat. Coun. Real Estate Investment Fiduciaries (acctg. com. 1985—, pres. elect 1997, bd. dirs. 1993-99, pres. 1998-99),Urban Land Inst. (bd. trustees, 2002—); Plaza Club (Chgo.), Westmoreland Country Club (Wilmette, Ill., bd. dirs. 1988-92, treas. 1988-92), Ironwood Country Club (Palm Desert, Calif.). Republican. Office: Deloitte & Touche 2 Prudential Plz Chicago IL 60601

CARLSON, RICHARD WARNER, journalist, diplomat, federal agency administrator, broadcast executive; b. Boston, Feb. 10, 1941; adopted s. W.E. and Ruth Miriam (Rafuse) C.; m. Patricia Caroline Swanson; children: Tucker McNear, Buckley Peck. Student, U. Miss., 1961-62; LLD (hon.), Calif. Western U., 1988. Editl. asst. L.A. Times, 1962-63; writer, columnist UPI, San Francisco, Sacramento, 1963-66; investigative reporter, anchorman ABC-TV, San Francisco, 1966-71, anchorman, polit. editor L.A., 1971-75; anchorman Sta. KFMB-TV (CBS), San Diego, 1975-77; prodr., writer, dir. documentary films NBC-TV, Burbank, Calif., 1974; anchorman, host Carlson & Co., CBS-TV, San Diego, 1975-76; sr. v.p. Gt. Am. First Bank, San Diego, 1977-84; dir. USIA/Voice of Am., Washington, 1985-91; U.S. amb. to Republic Seychelles, 1991-92; pres., CEO Corp. for Pub. Broadcasting, 1992-97; CEO Kingworld Pub. TV, Washington, 1997-99; vice chmn. Found. for the Def. of Democracies, Washington, 2003—. Vice chmn. Found. for the Def. of Democracies; bd. dirs. Exec. Info. Svc., Radio Voyager, Inc.; pres. Gately-Carlson Cons.; lectr., cons. in field. Chmn. San Diego Coalition, 1980-81; gov. Scripps Meml. Hosps., La Jolla, 1981-90, Banff (Can.) TV Festival, 1996—, Am. Ctr. Children's TV, 1996—; mem. Calif. State Rep. Ctrl. Com., 1982-85; appointed Pres.'s Coun. Peace Corps, 1982-84; mem. La Jolla Planned Dist. Bd., 1982-84; bd. dirs. Sharp Hosp. Found., 1983—, Scripps Inst. Medicine and Sci., 1995—; mem. La Jolla Town Coun., 1983-85; mem. San Diego Crime Commn., 1984-85; trustee Fund for Am. Studies, 1988-91; mem. Rosalind Russell Arthritis Found., 1985-91; dir. Georgetown Club, 1995—. Recipient investigative reporting awards AP, 1968, 76, 77, awards news analysis, 1968, 69, 75, Nat. Headliners award, 1968, Emmy award best investigative reporting, 1977, Golden Mike award best documentary, 1972, investigative reporting, 1975, best commentary, 1975, George Foster Peabody award, 1976, L.A. Press Club Grand award, 1976, San Diego Press Club award, 1976, 77, 79, Friend of Lithuania award Knights of Lithuania, 1988, Jose Marti award Cuban Am. Polit. Soc., Miami, Fla., 1988, Broadcast Pioneer award, 1997. Mem. Nat. Press Club, Thunderbird Country Club (Rancho Mirage, Calif.), Mid-Ocean Club (Tuckerstown, Bermuda), Georgetown Club, Met. Club, Diplomatic and Consular Officers Retired, The Pilgrims (N.Y.C.), Am. Ambs. Episcopalian. Home: Tulip Hill 7718 Georgetown Pike Mc Lean VA 22102-1431

CARLSON, ROBERT CHARLES, financial advisor, writer; BS in Fin. Mgmt. with high honor, Clemson U., 1979; MS in Acctg., JD, U. Va., 1982. CPA Md.; bar: DC 1982. Law clk. US Dept. Justice, Washington, 1982, US Dept. Edn., Washington, 1982-83; editor Tax Savs. Report, Balt., 1983-85, Fin. Independence, Balt., 1983-85, Tax Wise Money (formerly Tax Avoidance Digest), Balt., 1985—97, Bob Carlson's Retirement Watch, 1991—; prin. R.C. Carlson Adv., Fairfax, Va., 1988-94; pres. Ctr. for Retirement Security, Inc., Fairfax, 1992—; mng. mem. Carlson Wealth Advisors, LLC. Mem. Va. Fiscal Alternative Commn., Richmond, 1989-91; trustee, vice chmn. Fairfax County, Va. Employees' Retirement System, 1992—, chmn. 1995—; trustee Va. Retirement Sys. Author: Tax Savings Through Short-Term Trusts, 1985, 199 Loopholes That Survived Tax Reform, 1987, How to Handle and Win a Federal Tax Appeal, 1988, Retirement Tax Guide, 1989, rev. 4th edit. 1994, How to Slash Your Mutual Fund Taxes, 1990, 2d rev. edit. 1991, Tax Wise Money Strategies, 1995, Estate Planning Strategies, 2d edit., 1998. Treas. 10th Dist. Rep. Com., Fairfax, 1988-92; treas. No. Va. Rep. Bus. Forum, Alexandria, 1990—, Atoka Country Supper Com., Springfield, Va., 1989-92; chmn. Fairfax Area Young Reps., Annandale, Va., 1989-91; treas. Wahlquist for Senate, 1988-94, Butler for Congress, 1992-94. Named one of Outstanding Young Men of Am., U.S. Jaycees, 1983. Mem. D.C. Bar Assn., Conservative Club, Phi Kappa Phi, Phi Gamma Sigma. Home and Office: PO Box 222070 Chantilly VA 20153-2070 E-mail: bcarlson@RetirementWatch.com.

CARLSON, ROBERT CODNER, industrial engineering educator; b. Granite Falls, Minn., Jan. 17, 1939; s. Robert Ledin and Ada Louise (Codner) C.; children: Brian William, Andrew Robert, Christina Louise. BSME, Cornell U., 1962; MS, Johns Hopkins U., 1963, PhD, 1976. Mem. tech. staff Bell Tel. Labs., Holmdel, N.J., 1962-70; asst. prof. Stanford (Calif.) U., Stanford, 1970-77, assoc. prof., 1977-82, prof. indsl. engring., 1982-2000, prof. mgmt. sci. & engring., 2000—. Program dir., lectr., cons. various spl. programs U.S., Japan, France, 1971—; cons. Japan Mgmt. Assn., Tokyo, 1990—, Boeing, L.A., 1998—, GKN Automotive, London, 1989—, Rockwell Internat., L.A., 1988—; vis. prof. U. Calif., Berkeley, 1987-88, Dartmouth Coll., Hanover, N.J., 1978-79; vis. faculty Internat. Mgmt. Inst., Geneva, 1984, 88. Contbr. articles to profl. jours. Recipient Maxwell Upson award in Mech. Engring. Cornell U., 1962; Bell Labs. Systems Engring. fellow, 1962-63, Bell Labs. Doctoral Support fellow, 1966-67. Mem. INFORMS (chmn. membership com. 1981-83), Inst. Indsl. Engrs., Am. Soc. Engring. Edn., Am. Prodn. and Inventory Control Soc. (bd. dirs. 1975-81), Confrerie des Chevaliers du Tastevin, Tau Beta Pi, Phi Kappa Phi, Pi Tau Sigma. Avocations: wine tasting, travelling. E-mail: r.c.carlson@stanford.edu.

CARLSON, ROBERT ERNEST, freelance writer, architect, lecturer; b. Denver, Dec. 6, 1924; s. Milton and Augustine Barbara (Walter) C.; m. Jane Frances Waters, June 14, 1952 (div. June 1971); children: Cristina, Bob, Douglas, Glenn, James. BS in Archtl. Engring., U. Colo., 1951. Registered architect, Colo. Architect H.D. Wagener & Assocs., Boulder, Colo., 1953-75; pvt. practice architect Denver, 1975-82; health and promotion cons. Alive & Well Cons., Denver, 1982-85; freelance writer Denver, 1985—. Mem. Colo. Gov.'s Coun. for Fitness, Denver, 1975—; state race walking chmn. U.S. Track & Field, Denver, 1983-97, master USA track and field ofcl., Denver, 1990—; bd. dirs. Colo. Found. for Phys. Fitness, Denver, 1987—; lectr. in field. Author: Health Walk, 1988, Walking for Health, Fitness and Sport, 1996, A History of L Company 86th Mountain Infantry, 2001. Vol. Colo. Heart Assn., 1985—, Better Air Campaign, 1986-87, Cystic Fibrosis, 1989-91, Multiple Sclerosis Soc., 1988-91, Qualife, 1989-95, March of Dimes, 1989, United Negro Coll. Fund, 1989, bd. trustees, 1990. With U.S. Army, 1943-45, ETO. Decorated Bronze Star; named One of Ten Most Prominent Walking Leaders in U.S.A., Rockport Walking Inst., 1989. Mem. Colo. Authors League (bd. dirs. 2002—), Philippides Track Club (walking chmn. 1981-85), Rocky Mountain Rd. Runners (v.p. 1983-84), Front Range Walkers Club (founder, pres. 1985—), Lions (bd. dirs. 1965-72). Episcopalian. Avocations: racewalking, skiing, cross-country skiing, orienteering. Home and Office: 2261 Glencoe St Denver CO 80207-3834 E-mail: BobCarlsonFrontRangeWalkers@att.net.

CARLSON, ROBERT JAMES, bishop; b. Mpls., June 30, 1944; s. Robert James and Jeanne Catherine (Dorgan) C.. BA, St. Paul Sem., 1964, MDiv, 1976; JCL, Catholic U. Am., 1979. Ordained priest Roman Catholic Ch., 1970. Asst. St. Raphael Ch., Crystal, 1970—72; assoc. St. Margaret Mary Ch., Golden Valley, 1972—73, adminstr., 1973—76; vice chancellor, dir. Vocation Office, 1976—79, dir., 1977; pastor St. Leonard of Port Maurice, Mpls., 1982—84; aux. bishop St. Paul and Mpls., Mpls., 1983—94, Archdiocese of St. Paul and Mpls., Mpls., 1984—94; apptd. coadjutor Bishop of Sioux Falls, SD, 1994—95, Sioux Falls, SD, 1995—. Author: Going All Out: An Invitation to Belong, 1985. Pres. Nat. Found. Cath. Youth Ministry, Washington, 1989—97; bd. govs. N.Am. Coll. Rome, 1997—2001; Sioux Falls Humane Soc., 2003—; Episcopal moderator Nat. Cath. Com. on Scouting, 1993—97, USA/Can. coun. Serra Internat., 1996—2001; bd. dirs. St. Paul Sem., 1993—2000, Mt. Angel Sem., Portland, Oreg., 1995—2001, St. John V. Coll. Sem., U. St. Thomas, St. Paul, 1997—2001, Hennich-Glennon Sem., St. Louis, 1998—2001. Recipient Friendship award, Knights and Ladies of St. Peter Claver, 1990, St. De LaSalle Meml. award, Cretin H.S. Alumni Assn., 1990, Humanitarian of Yr. award, S.D. Right to Life, 1998, Our Lady of Guadalupe medal, Inst. for Priestly Formation, 2003. Mem.: Canon Law Soc. Am., Serra Internat. (Dist. Svc. award 2002), Cosmopolitan Club of Sioux Falls (Disting. Svc. award 2002). Roman Catholic. Avocation: hunting. Office: The Chancery 523 N Duluth Ave Sioux Falls SD 57104-2714 E-mail: rcarlson@sfcatholic.org.

CARLSON, ROBERT MARSHALL, hospital professional services official; b. Jamestown, N.Y., Oct. 6, 1950; s. Marshall Lawrence and Alice (Christine) C.; m. Robin Shankey, May 29, 1987; children: Todd Marshall, Scott Thomas. BS, Bowling Green (Ohio) State U., 1972; postgrad. in pub. health, U. Utah, 1972; ME in Health Edn., U. Toledo, 1977. Planning analyst, then found. dir. Riverside Hosp., Toledo, 1975-78; hosp. planning coord. Med. Coll. Ohio, Toledo, 1978-80, asst. hosp. dir. for ambulatory programs, 1980-81; cons. P.M.S. (Planning & Mgmt. Services) Inc., Bloomington, Minn., 1981-82; dir. health tech. mktg., sr. cons. Ellerbe Cons. Group, Bloomington, 1983-85; mktg. dir. Ellerbe Assocs. Inc., Mpls., 1986; v.p. Ellerbe Assocs., 1987-89, Export USA Publs., Mpls., 1989-91; dir. physician svcs. HealthEast, St. Paul, 1991-95; exec. adminstr. OSF Med. Group, OSF Healthcare Systems, Peoria, Ill., 1995-99; dir. clin. svcs. Phycor, Inc., Nashville, 1999-2000; sr. assoc. Progressive Healthcare, Inc., Nashville, 2000—02; adminstr. Medicine Patient Care Ctrs., Vanderbilt U. Med. Ctr., Nashville, 2003—. Served to commdr., Med. Svc. Corps., USNR, 1972-98. Mem. Med. Group Mgmt. Assn., Am. Coll. Med. Practice Execs., Assn. Mil. Surgeons of U.S., Profl. Ski Instrs. Am., Res. Officers Assn., Phi Kappa Phi, Kappa Sigma. Lutheran. Office: Vanderbilt Univ Med Ctr 2568 TVC Nashville TN 37232-5999

CARLSON, ROBERT MICHAEL, artist; b. Bklyn., Nov. 19, 1952; s. Sidney Carlson and Vickey (Mihaloff) Woodward; m. Linda Schneider; m. Mary Elizabeth Fontaine, Feb. 24, 1984; 1 child, Nora. Student, CCNY, 1970-73; studied with Flora Mace and Joey Kirkpatrick, Pilchuck Glass Sch., 1981, studied with Dan Dailey, 1982. Teaching asst. Pilchuck Sch., Stanwood, Wash., 1986, 88, mem. faculty, 1989-90, 92, 95, Pratt Fine Arts Ctr., Seattle, 1988-90, Penland (N.C.) Sch. Crafts, 1994, Bild-Werk Sch., Germany, 1996-2000. Mem. artists adv. com. Pilchuck Sch., 1989, 90; vis. artist Calif. Coll. Arts and Crafts, Oakland, 1989, Calif. State U., Fullerton, 1991, blossom summer program Kent State U., Ohio, 1991, U. Ill., Urbana-Champaign, 1993, Toledo Mus. of Art Sch., 1994; visual-artist-in-residence Centrum Found., Port Townsend, Wash., 1992; prof. artist-in-residence Pilchuck Sch., Wash. One-man shows include Foster White Gallery, Seattle, 1987, 90, 92, The Glass Gallery, Bethesda, Md., 1988, Heller Gallery, N.Y.C., 1989, 95, Betsy Rosenfield Gallery, Chgo., 1991, 92, MIA Gallery, Seattle, 1994, Haratat Gall. Florida, 1998, William Traver Gall., Seattle, 2000, others; exhibited in group shows at Traver Gallery, Seattle, 1984, 89, Mindscape Gallery, Evanston, Ill., 1984, 86, Tucson Mus. Art., 1984 (Purchase award), 86 (Award of Merit), Hand and Spirit Gallery, Scottsdale, Ariz., 1985, 86, Craftsman Gallery, Scarsdale, N.Y., 1985, Robert Kidd Gallery, Birmingham, Mich., 1985, 88, Gazebo Gallery, Gatlinburg, Tenn., 1985, The Glass Gallery, Bethesda, Md., 1986 (Jurors award), 91, 92, 94, Artists Soc. Internat., San Francisco, 1987 (Critics Choice award), William Traver Gallery, Seattle, 1987, 90, 91, 92, Japan Glass Artcrafts Assn., Tokyo, 1987, Heller Gallery, 1988, 89, 90, 91, 93, 94, 95, 96, 97, Washington Sq. Ptnrs., 1988, Foster White Gallery, 1988, 90, Bellvue Art Mus., Wash., 1988, 91, 94, Am. Arts and Crafts Inc., San Francisco, 1989, Mus. Craft and Folk Art, San Francisco, 1989, Great Am. Gallery, Atlanta, 1989, Dorothy Weiss Gallery, San Francisco, 1989, Habitat Gallery, Farmington Hills, Mich., 1990, 93, Philabaum Gallery, Tucson, 1990, Greg Kucera Gallery, Seattle, 1990, Connell Gallery, Atlanta, 1990, Net Contents Gallery, Bainbridge Island, Wash., 1991, Seattle Tacoma Internat. Airport Installation, 1991, 95, Pratt Fine Arts Ctr., Seattle, 1991, Crystalex, Novy Bor, Czechoslovakia, 1991, Whatcom County Mus., Bellingham, Wash., 1992, Art Gallery West Australia, 1992, 1004 Gallery, Port Townsend, 1992, Bainbridge Island Arts Coun., 1992, MIA Gallery, 1993, Betsy Rosenfield Gallery, Chgo., 1993, Blue Spiral Gallery, Asheville, N.C., 1995, Huntington Mus., 1996, Salem Art Assn., 1996, Judy Yovens Gallery, Houston, 1997, Internat. Glass Art Exchange, Tucson, 1997, Habatat Gallery, Boca Raton, Fla., 1998, Habatat Gallery, Farmington Hills, Mich., 1998, Tampa (Fla.) Mus. Art, 1998, Traver Gall., 2001, Glass Gall., 2201, Habatat Gall., 2000, Glasmus., 2000, Kentucky Art & Luak Gall., 2000; represented in permanent collections Corning (N.Y.) Mus. Glass, Tucson Mus. Art, Toledo Mus. Art, Glasmuseum Frauenau, Germany, Glasmuseum Ebeltoft, Denmark, Valley Nat. Bank, Phoenix, Fountain Assocs., Portland, Oreg., Iceland Air Co., Reykjavik, Iceland, Crocker Banks, L.A., Davis Wright Tremain, Seattle, Meiwa Trading Co., Tokyo, Safeco Ins. Corp., Seattle, Crystalex Corp., L.A. County Mus. Art. Bd. dirs. Am. Craft Coun., 1996-99. Fellow Tucson Pima Arts Coun., 1987, NEA, 1990; John Hauberg fellow, 2000. Mem. Glass Art Soc. (conf. lectr. 1991, bd. dirs. 1992-94, v.p. 1993-94, pres. 1995-96). Office: PO Box 11590 Bainbridge Island WA 98110 E-mail: bobway@qwest.net.

CARLSON, ROBERT WELLS, physician, educator; b. Concord, Calif., Apr. 14, 1952; s. Robert L. Carlson and Mae E. Fox. BS in Biol. Sci., Stanford U., 1974, MD, 1978. Diplomate Am. Bd. Internal Medicine, Am. Bd. Med. Oncology. Intern Barnes Hosp., St. Louis, 1978-79, resident, 1979-80, Stanford (Calif.) Univ. Hosp., 1980-81; fellow Stanford U., 1981-83, clin. asst. prof., 1983-85, asst. prof., 1985-92, assoc. prof., 1992-97, prof., 1997—; assoc. chief for clin. affairs div. oncology, 1994-96. Exec. officer No. Calif. Oncology Group, Palo Alto, Calif., 1984-87, group chmn., 1987-91. Bd. dirs. Theatreworks, Palo Alto, 1994-99. Recipient Career Devel. award Am. Cancer Soc., 1987-90. Fellow ACP; mem. Am. Soc. Clin. Oncology, Am. Assn. Cancer Rsch. Office: Stanford U Oncology Day Care Clinic Stanford Med Ctr H0274 Stanford CA 94305

CARLSON, ROGER ALLAN, retired manufacturing executive, accountant; b. Mpls., Dec. 12, 1932; s. Carl Albert and Borghild Amanda (Anderson) Carlson; m. Lois Roberta Lehman, Aug. 20, 1955; children: Gene, Bradley. BBA, U. Minn., 1954. CPA Minn. Investment mgr. Mayo Found., Rochester, Minn., 1963-83; contr. Luth. Hosp. and Homes Soc., Fargo, ND, 1983-84; v.p., treas. Crenlo Inc., Rochester, 1984-94, also bd. dirs., part owner, 1984-99. Pres. Ability Bldg. Ctr., Rochester, 1974—75; bd. dirs. Samaritan Bethany, Inc., Rochester, 1991—95. Capt. U.S. Army, 1955—57. Mem.: AICPA, Minn. Soc. CPA's. Avocations: hunting, fishing, genealogy. Home (Summer): 4915 Sussex Pl Excelsior MN 55331-9217 Home: 14334 Harbour Landings Dr Fort Myers FL 33908-4906

CARLSON, ROGER DAVID, psychologist, clergyman, educator; b. Berkeley, Calif., Nov. 19, 1946; s. George Clarence and Elizabeth (Norris) C.; m. Ema T. Paviolo, June 11, 1977 (div. 1994); children: Erik Andreas Paviolo, Lucas Sven Paviolo, Justin Nikolaus Paviolo. AB, Calif. State U., Sacramento, 1968, MA, 1969; PhD, U. Oreg., 1972; cert. theol. studies, Pacific Sch. of Religion, 1994; MDiv, Pacific Sch. Religion, 1996. Ordained deacon, 1996, elder, 1998 United Meth. Ch.; lic. psychologist Pa., 1977, Calif., 2001, Oreg., 2002. Assoc. prof. psychology Lebanon Valley Coll., Annville, Pa., 1972-85; rsch. assoc. Eugene Pub. Schs., 1985-87; assoc. prof. edn. Williamette U., Salem, Oreg., 1987-88; assoc. prof. psychology Ea. Wash. U., 1991-92; adj. prof. Linfield Coll., 1993—; pastor Coburg (Oreg.) United Meth. Ch., 1992-94, Florence (Oreg.) United Meth. Ch., 1994—2001, Covenant United Meth. Ch., Reedsport, Oreg., 1995—99, 1st United Meth. Ch. of Stayton, Oreg., 2001—03, Bennett Chapel United Meth. Ch., Portland, Oreg., 2003—. Vis. scholar dept. history and philosophy of sci. Cambridge (Eng.) U., 1979-80; temporary sr. mem. Wolfson Coll.; vis. assoc. prof. psychology Whitman Coll., Walla Walla, Wash., 1988-89, 90-91, cons., 1989—; psychologist, pvt. practice, 1977-1985, 2001—. Author books, contbr. rsch. papers, jour. articles and book chpts. on numerous subjects in field. Mem. Friends Radio Sta. KPFA, v.p. 1969, pres. 1970; Wolfeboro Pioneer, Boy Scouts Am., 1959; co-founder, Pathways of Faith, Florence, Oreg., 1998; bd. dirs., Ecumenical Ministries Oreg., 2003—. Recipient Presdl. Sports award. Fellow Am. Coll. Heraldry; mem. APA, Oreg. Psychol. Assn., Am. Psychol. Soc., Am. Coll. Psychology, Soc. for Philosophy and Psychology (mem. exec. com. 1975-76), SAR, Airplane Owners and Pilots Assn., Sons Union Vets. Civil War, Am. Radio Relay League, Order of St. Luke, Psi Chi. Methodist. E-mail: rcarlson@linfield.edu.

CARLSON, RONALD LEE, lawyer, educator; b. Davenport, Iowa, Dec. 10, 1934; s. Arthur A. and Louise (Sehmann) C.; m. Mary Murphy, Apr. 10, 1965; children: Michael, Andrew. BA, Augustana Coll., 1956; JD (Clarion DeWitt Hardy law scholar), Northwestern U., 1959; LL.M. (E. Barrett Prettyman law scholar), Georgetown U., 1961. Bar: Ill. 1959, Iowa 1959, D.C. 1960, U.S. Supreme Ct. 1966. Mem. firm Betty, Neuman, McMahon, Hellstrom & Bittner, Davenport, Iowa, 1961-65; U.S. commr. So. Dist. Iowa, 1964-64; prof. law U. Iowa, Iowa City, 1965-73, Washington U., St. Louis, 1973-84; John Byrd Martin prof. law U. Ga., 1984-95, Fuller E. Callaway prof. law, 1995—. Vis. prof. Wayne State U., Detroit, 1974, Detroit, 1976—77, Detroit, 1979, U. Tex., 1978, St. Louis U., 1982—86, 1988, U. Iowa, 1986—87, 1996; cons. Legis. Com. Criminal Code Revision Iowa, 1969—73; lectr. Nat. Coll. State Judiciary, Reno, 1974, Nat. Coll. Dist. Attys., West Palm Beach, Fla., 1980, Chgo., 83, Inst. Cont. Legal Edn., Atlanta, 1990, 2000—02, Amelia Island, 2001, Nat. Pract. Inst., Kansas City, 1991, 93, 98, Omaha, 91, 96, 2001, Davenport, 00, Des Moines, 1991, Chgo., 91, San Francisco, 91, San Francisco, 96, St. Louis, 1992—93, St. Louis, 1997—98, St. Louis, 2000, Honolulu, 1992, 94, 96, 2001, New Orleans, 1992, 2001, 03, Seattle, 1992, Minn., 1992—97, 2001, 03, Boston, 1992, Houston, 92, Houston, 97, Cleve., 92, 97, 2001, Tampa, 1992, Miami, 92, San Diego, 93, L.A., 93, Phoenix, 93, 96, Detroit, 93, Portland, 93, Denver, 93, 95, Washington, 93, 97, Little Rock, 93, 97, 98, Newark, 94, Richmond, 94, Atlanta, 94, 95, 97, N.Y.C., 94, Birmingham, 95, Oklahoma City, 95, Nashville, 95, 2001, Salt Lake City, 1995, Charlotte, 98, Phila., 98, 2002, Las Vegas, 1998, Hartford, 2000, Columbus, 2000—02, Raleigh, 2001, Providence, 02; moderator Robert Vance Forum on The Bill of Rights, 1990—96, 2002—03; lectr. in field. Author (with M. Ladd): Cases on Evidence, 1972; author: (with J. Yeager) Criminal Law and Procedure, 1979; author: Criminal Law Advocacy, 1982, Successful Techniques for Civil Trials, 1983, rev. edit., 1992, Adjudication of Criminal Justice, 1986; author: (with M. Bright) Maine Objections at Trial, 1991, New Hampshire Objections at Trial, 1992, Oregon Objections at Trial, 1992; author: (with A. Montgomery and M. Bright) Minnesota Objections at Trial, 1992; author: (with R. Aronson and M. Bright) Washington Objections at Trial, 1992; author: Pocket Proof of Facts, 1993, Trial Handbook for Georgia Lawyers, 1993; author: (with J. Young, K. Curtis, and M. Bright) Virginia Objections at Trial, 1998; author: Criminal Justice Procedure, 1999; author: (with E. Imwinkelried, E. Kionka and K. Strachan) Evidence Teaching Materials for an Age of Science and Statues, 2002; author: (with M. Bright and E. Imwinkelried) Objections at Trial: A Concise Guide, 2002; author: (with E. Imwinkelried) Dynamics of Trial Practice: Problems and Materials, 2002. V.p. alumni bd. Augustana Coll., Rock Island, Ill., 1968. Recipient Roscoe Pound Found. Jacobson award, ATLA, 1987, Harrison Tweed award, Ali-Baba, 2000. Mem.: ABA, Fed. Ins. and Corp. Counsel, Am. Inns. of Ct., Fed. Practice Inst. (dir. 1980—83, dean 1985—89), Iowa Bar Assn., Fed. Bar Assn. (chmn. law sch. divsn. 1978—79, nat. coun. 1994—95, Earl W. Kintner award for disting. svc. 1992), Am. Assn. Law Schs. Republican. Home: 283 Skyline Pkwy Athens GA 30606-3842 Office: U Ga School of Law Sch of Law Athens GA 30602 E-mail: mlfield@arches.uga.edu. *Proper application of law provides the key to resolution of disputes: local, national, and international. As a teacher of law to judges, lawyers and students, it is my goal to educate in a manner which contributes to this needed resolution of conflict in a positive way.*

CARLSON, SCOTT HENERY, electrical engineer; b. DuBois, Pa., Jan. 29, 1964; s. John Donald and Laura Ann (Henery) C.; m. Nancy Marie Keelan, July 18, 1987 (div. 1989); m. Karen Louise Hasenplug, June 23, 1990; children: David Scott, Daniel Robert. AAS in Elec. Engring. Tech., Pa. State U., 1990, BS in Elec. Engring. Tech., 1994; A in Electronic Sys. Tech., C.C. Air Force, 2001. Quality engr. Quality Components Inc., St. Marys, Pa., 1990-91; lab. asst. Pa. State U., Middletown, 1992-94; field support engr. Eastman Kodak, Mechanicsburg, Pa., 1994-95; sr. test tech. Sechan Eletronics, Lititz, Pa., 1995-97; project engr. Bulova Techs. L.L.C., Lancaster, Pa., 1997-99; instr. electronics 211th Engring. Installation Sq. Lightning Force Acad. Pa. ANG, 1999—. Elec. tech. New Holland (Pa.) N.Am., 1995. Vol. firefighter Friendship Fire and Hose Co. No. 1, Elizabethtown, Pa., 1994—. Staff sgt. USAF, USNG, 1981-85, Pa. NG., 1992—. Mem. NRA, Air Force Sgts. Assn., IEEE, Am. Legion. Republican. Nazarene. Avocations: softball, hunting, fishing, walking, family activities. Office: 211th Engring Installation Squadron Lightning Force Acad Bldg 2-77 Fort Indiantown Gap Annville PA 17003-5120

CARLSON, SHAWN ERIC, physicist; b. San Francisco, Mar. 11, 1960; s. Devere Milfred Carlson Jr. and Beverly Ann Bennett; m. Michelle Lynn Tetreault, 1994; children: Katherine Joanne, Erik Philip. BS in Physics, Applied Math., U. Calif., Berkeley, 1981; MS in Physics, UCLA, 1983, PhD in Physics, 1989. V.p. R & D Flowgram Software Assocs., San Francisco, 1989-91; rsch. physicist, astrophysicist Lawrence Berkeley Labs., 1982-94; founder, exec. dir. Soc. Amateur Scientists, 1994—; co-founder Tinkers Guild Pubs., 1999; chief tech. officer Personal Genetics, 2000—01; ind. cons. sci. and tech., 1995—. Adj. prof. physics, San Diego State U., 1995—; sci. and tech. cons. CSICOP 1985—; vis. scholar Brown U., 2002--; speaker in field. Author: Satanism in America, 1989, Core Concepts in Physics, 1997, The Amateur Scientist-The Complete 20th Century Collection (CD-Rom), 2000, The Amateur Astronomer, 2000, The Amateur Biologist, 2001, Chasing Franklin's Kite, 2003; columnist Sci. Am. Mag., 1995-2001; columnist Humanist Mag., Buffalo, 1991-93; numerous radio and TV appearances. Investigator faith-healers, Satanism, religious miracles, astrology for Com. Scientific Examination of Religion, Buffalo, 1987, 89. Fellow MacArthur Found., 1999; named Headliner of Yr., San Diego Press Club, 2000; recipient San Diego State U. Svc. award, 2000. Mem. AAAS, Am. Astron. Soc., Nat. Assn. Sci. Writers, Sigma Xi. Office: Soc Amateur Scientists 5600 Post Rd Ste 114-341 East Greenwich RI 02818 E-mail: scarlson@sas.org.

CARLSON, SUZANNE OLIVE, architect; b. Worcester, Mass., Aug. 20, 1939; d. Sigfrid and Helga (Larson) C. BS, R.I. Sch. Design, 1963. Jr. ptnr. Dingnam-Fauteux & Partners, Worcester, 1969-70; ptnr. Richard Lamoureux Asso., Worcester, 1970-75, Herron & Carlson (AIA), Worcester, 1975-96; architect Edgecomb, Maine, 1997—. Guest lectr. Holy Cross Coll., 1969-70. Chmn. Worcester Hist. Commn., 1976-88; trustee Worcester Heritage Soc., 1982-88, Park Spirit of Worcester Inc., 1987—; v.p. Lincoln County Hist. Assn., 2001--; trustee Worcester Girls Inc. of Worcester, pres. 1989-92, 95-2002, sec. 1994-95; trustee Performing Arts Sch. Worcester, 1977-86, v.p. 1980-85; trustee Cultural Assembly Greater Worcester, 1981-86, v.p., 1982-83; pres. Edgecomb Hist. Soc., 1997—. Recipient European Honors Program grant Rome, Italy, 1961-62; recipient AIA School medal for excellence, 1963 Mem. AIA (exec. bd. Ctrl. Mass. chpt. 1969-71, sec.-treas. 1970-71, v.p. 1971-72, pres. 1972-73), Mass. Soc. Architects (exec. bd. 1972-74, v.p. 1975, pres. 1976), New Eng. Regional Coun. Architects (pres. 1977), New Eng. Antiquities Rsch. Assn. (membership chair 1982-84, 90-94, resource devel. chair 1994—, graphics dir. jours. 1982—, publs. chair 1995—, trustee 1990—). Home and Office: Suzanne O Carlson Architect 94 Cross Point Rd Edgecomb ME 04556-3208

CARLSON, TAMMI CLAIR, music educator, musician; b. Hillsdale, Mich., Aug. 26, 1961; d. Clarence Fred and Elaine Katherine Walters; m. Todd Harold Carlson, June 18, 1983; children: Caelyn Amber, Jenna Elizabeth. BA in Music, Valparaiso U., 1983; MusM in flute performance, Roosevelt U., Chgo., 2000. Free-lance performer, Ill., 1983—; flute instr., 1983—; music dir. St. Paul's Luth. Ch., Matteson, Ill., 1986—92; choir dir., music coord. Peace Luth. Ch., New Lenox, Ill., 1993—99; humanities and music instr. Moraine Valley C.C., Palos Hills, Ill., 2002—. Adjudicator, Ill., 1983—; mem. adj. faculty South Suburban C.C., South Holland, 1983—99, Moraine Valley C.C., Palos Hills, Ill., 1999—2002. Composer: Flute Method Book. Musician Peace Luth. Ch., New Lenox, 1997—2002. Mem.: Nat. Assn. Coll. Wind and Percussion Instrs., Nat. Flute Assn., Chgo. Flute Club, Sigma Alpha Iota (life; music dir. 1982—83, Sword of Honor 1983). Independent. Lutheran. Avocations: music, crafts, science fiction literature, hiking, home remodeling. Office: Moraine Valley C C 10900 S 88th Ave New Lenox IL 60451 E-mail: carlsont@morainevalley.edu.

CARLSON, THEODORE JOSHUA, lawyer, retired utility company executive; b. Hartford, Conn., Jan. 4, 1919; s. John and Hulda (Larson) C.; m. Jacqueline L. Coburn, Apr. 25, 1953; children: Stephanie, Christopher J., Victoria, Antoinette. AB, Montclair State U., 1940; JD, Columbia U., 1948, AM, 1951; postgrad., U. Chgo., 1942. Bar: N.Y. 1948. Assoc. Gould & Wilkie, N.Y.C., 1948-54, ptnr., 1954-96, sr. ptnr., 1970-96, of counsel, 1997—; dir. Central Hudson Gas & Electric Corp., Poughkeepsie, N.Y., 1968-89, chmn., prin. officer, 1975-89. Mem., chmn. fin. and audit com. N.Y. State Energy Rsch. Devel. Authority, 1980-88; dir. Empire State Electric Energy Rsch. Com., Edison Electric Inst., 1976-79; chmn. exec. com. Energy Assn. N.Y. State, 1976-77, 82-83, N.Y. Power Pool, 1977-78; dir., mem. exec. com. Mid-Hudson Pattern, Inc., Poughkeepsie, N.Y.; chmn. bd. dirs. Christian Herald Assn. and related cos., 1985-92. Author: A Design For Freedom. Pres. United Fund Rockville Centre, N.Y., 1966; chmn. adv. bd. Westchester County Salvation Army, 1977-80, State of N.Y., 1977-83; chmn. Greater N.Y. Adv. Bd., 1988-91; chmn. bd. trustees King's Coll., 1982-89. Capt. USAAF, 1942-46. Mem. ABA, N.Y. Bar Assn., Assn. of Bar of City of N.Y. (chmn. pub. utility sect. com. on post admissions-legal edn. 1970-73), Rotary (hon.). Office: Gould & Wilkie 1 Chase Manhattan Plz New York NY 10005-1401

CARLSON, THOMAS DAVID, lawyer; b. Mpls., Aug. 17, 1944; s. David W. and Grace M. (Laser) C.; m. Jane A. Gleeson; children: Amy A., Ryan T., Madeline Jane. BA, Colgate U., 1966; JD cum laude, U. Minn., 1969. Bar: Minn. 1969, U.S. Dist. Ct. Minn. 1969, U.S. Supreme Ct. 1973. Law clk. to Hon. Earl R. Larson U.S. Dist. Ct. (fed. dist.) Minn., Mpls., 1969-70; assoc. Best & Flanagan, Mpls., 1970-74, ptnr., 1974-91, Lindquist & Vennum, Mpls., 1991—. Bd. trustees Groves Acad.; asst. varsity hockey coach Edina H.S. Fellow Am. Coll. Trust & Estate Counsel; mem. ABA, Minn. State Bar Assn., Hennepin County Bar Assn., Mpls. Club, Minikahda Club, Colgate Silver Puck Club (bd. trustees), Spring Hill Golf Club, Colgate U. Alumni (bd. trustees). Office: Lindquist & Vennum 4200 IDS Ctr Minneapolis MN 55402

CARLSON, THOMAS JOSEPH, real estate developer, lawyer, mayor; b. St. Paul, Jan. 12, 1953; s. Delbert George and Shirley Lorraine (Willardson) C.; m. Chandler Elizabeth Campbell, July 15, 1973; 1 child, Thomas Chandler. BA, George Washington U., 1975; JD, U. Mo., Kansas City, 1979. Reporter Springfield (Mo.) News-Leader, 1975-76; editor Buffalo (Mo.) Reflex, 1976-77; assoc. Woolsey Fisher, Springfield, 1980-83; pvt. practice law Springfield, 1983-86; ptnr. Carlson & Clark, 1986-93, Carmichael, Carlson, Gardner & Clark, Springfield, 1993-94; mayor City of Springfield, 1987-93, 2001—; U.S. Bankruptcy trustee Springfield, 1982-98; pvt. practice, 1994-98. CEO, Resorts Mgmt., Inc., 1995—; bd. dirs. ITEC Attractions, Inc., Great So. Bancorp; lectr. in field. Contbr. articles to profl. jours. Mem. Springfield City Coun., 1983-87, 97—, Airport Bd. Springfield, 1994-97; chmn. Springfield-Branson Leadership Com., 1993—; bd. dirs. Mo. Cmty. Devel. Corp. Iniative, Mo. Commn. on Intergovernmental Cooperation; mem. bd. govs. S.W. Mo. State U., 2003—. Mem. Mo. Bar Assn. (Disting. Young Lawyer award 1989). Presbyterian. Office: 205 W Walnut Ste 200 Springfield MO 65806-2115

CARLSON, WALTER CARL, lawyer; b. Chgo., Sept. 14, 1953; s. LeRoy T. and Margaret (Deffenbaugh) C.; m. Debora M. DeHoyos, June 20, 1981; children: Amanda, Greta, Linnea. BA, Yale U., 1975; JD, Harvard U., 1978. Bar: Ill. 1978, U.S. Dist. Ct. (no. dist.) Ill. 1978, U.S. Supreme Ct. 1991. Law clk. to presiding justice U.S. Dist. Ct. No. Dist., Chgo., 1978-80; ptnr. Sidley, Austin, Brown & Wood, Chgo., 1980—, mem. exec. com., 2002—. Bd. dirs. Telephone and Data Sys., Inc., Chgo., mem. audit com. 1989-2001, chmn., 2002-; bd. dirs. U.S. Cellular Corp., 1989—, chmn. audit com. 1989-2001; bd. dirs. Aerial Comm., Inc., 1996-2000. Mem. Dist. 65 Sch. Bd., Evanston, Ill., 1993-2001, pres., 1997-2001. Mem. ABA, U.S. Supreme Ct. Hist. Soc., Am. Judicature Soc., Chgo. United. Office: Sidley Austin Brown & Wood Apt 605 425 W Surf St Chicago IL 60657-6139

CARLSON, WARREN ORE, civil engineer; b. Woodbine, Kans., Apr. 11, 1926; s. Percy Franklin and Olivia Luella (Gugler) C.; m. Lenna Nadine Norman, Nov. 27, 1948; children: Teri Ann, Donna Elaine, Diana Lynn, Tina Marie, Randall Warren. BS in Civil Engring., U. Colo., 1946. Registered profl. engr., Alta., Can. Project engr. Brown & Root Ltd., Calgary, Alta., 1960-62, Bechtel Inc., Paris and Holland, 1962-72; engring. cons. Booz-Allen-Hamilton, Algiers, Algeria, 1972-74; project mgr. Worley-Protech, London and Holland, 1974-80, PDO (Shell I.P.M.), Sultanate of Oman, 1980-82; cons. J.P. Kenny Ltd., London and Denmark, 1982-84; sr. tech. advisor Petroleum Ministry Govt. of Oman, 1984-86; cons. Randall Cons., Germany and Portugal, 1986-93; sr. project mgr. Oman-India gas pipelines Intec Engring. Inc., Houston, 1994-95; quality assurance coord. Kvaerner R.J. Brown, Houston, 1995—98; cons. on Baltic Oil Pipeline, Russia, 1998—99, Alaska-to-Chgo. gas pipeline, 2000—. Lt. (j.g.) USNR, 1943-46. Mem. ASME, Am. Soc. Civil Engrs. Republican. Avocations: photography, travel, geneology. Home: 960 Berry Ave Los Altos CA 94024-5531

CARLSON, WILLIAM CLIFFORD, retired defense company executive, retired naval officer; b. Detroit, Feb. 7, 1937; s. William and Marion Lucille Carlson; m. Jane Elder, Jan. 28, 1960 (div. Jne 1987); children: David, Scott, Jennifer Carlson-Burns; m. Linda Darlene Reid, June 6, 1991. BS in Edn., U. N.Mex., 1959; MS in Physics, U.S. Naval Postgrad. Sch., Monterey, Calif., 1965; MS equivalent, U.S. Naval War Coll., Newport, R.I., 1975. Commd. U.S. Navy, 1959, advanced through ranks to rear admiral, officer, 1959-92, mgr. ASW combat sys. Naval Sea Sys. Command, 1982-88, asst. dep. cmdr. Naval Sea Sys. Command, 1988-91, cmdr. Naval Undersea Warfare Ctr., 1991-92, ret., 1992; dir. advanced programs Scientific Atlanta Instrumentation Group, 1993-94; v.p. mktg. & sales Scientific Atlanta SPS Group, 1994-95; dir. surface ship ASW combat system programs Lockheed Martin, Syracuse, NY, 1995—2002. Mem. Acoustical Soc. Am., U.S. Naval Inst., U.S. Navy League, Surface Warfare Assn. Avocations: trout fishing, fly tying, skiing. Home: 3996 Pompey Hollow Rd Cazenovia NY 13035-9523 E-mail: wcarlso1@twcny.rr.com.

CARLSON, WILLIAM DWIGHT, college president emeritus; b. Denver, Nov. 5, 1928; m. Beverley Ann Bradshaw, 1950; children: Susan Elaine, Earl Dwight. DVM, Colo. State U., 1952, MS, 1956; PhD in Radiology and Radiation Biology, U. Colo., 1958. Prof., chmn. dept. radiology and radiation biology, founder Colo. State U., 1964-68, pres. rsch. found., 1964-68, acting dir., 1966-68; prof. radiation biology, adminstr. Am. studies U. Wyo., Laramie, 1968-79, pres., 1968-79, pres. emeritus, 1989—; affiliate prof. radiology, radiation biology Colo. State U., Fort Collins, 1968-80; CEO St. John's Hosp., Jackson Hole, Wyo., 1980-84; prin. vet. Cooperative State Research Service USDA, Washington, 1984-88, assoc./founding adminstr. Office Grants and Program Systems, 1984-94; acting and founding adminstr. Coop. State Rsch. Edn. and Ext. Svc. USDA, Washington, 1994-95; mem. USDA Nat. Agr. Research Com., 1985-95; joint coun. Food and Agr. Scis., 1985-95. Nat. cons. vet medicine to surgeon gen. USAF, 1970-75; trustee Wyo. Blue Shield/Blue Cross, 1976-85, chmn. bd. trustees, 1982-83; adv. dir. Wyo. Indsl. Devel. Corp., 1968-79; commr. Wyo. Western Interstate Commn. Higher Edn., 1968-79; mem. pres. coun. Land Grant Colls. and State Univs., 1968—; pres. coun. Western Athletic Conf., 1968-79; chmn. Assn. Western Univs., 1969, exec. com., 1970-79; regional adv. com. Inst. Internat. Edn., 1969-79; mem. scholarship com. Marathon Oil Co., 1977-79; mem. adv. bd. U.S. Army Gen. Command and Staff Coll., 1970-73. Author: Veterinary Radiology, 3d edit, 1978; editor procs. Internat. Symposium on the Effects of Ionizing Radiation of the Reproductive System, 1964; contbr. articles to profl. jours. Exec. com. Longs Peak council Boy Scouts Am., 1966-80, pres., 1974-76, v.p., North Central region, 1970-74; regional chmn. Nat. Eagle Scout Assn., 1975-80, Silver Beaver award, 1974; bd. dirs. U. Wyo. Found., 1968-79; bd. visitors Air U., Maxwell AFB, 1972-75; mem. Yellowstone Park Assn. Bd., 1974-86, mem. emeritus, 1986—, vice-chmn., 1976-83; mem. 4H Found. Bd., 1994-95; vol. interpretive divsn. Nat. Park Svc. Yellowstone Nat. Park, 1996—; vol. ct.-apptd. spl. advocate for abused children, 1997—. Named Outstanding Young Man of Yr. Colo. Jr. C. of C., 1960, Top Prof. Colo. State U., 1961, U.S. Vet. of Yr. Am. Animal Hosp. Assn., 1967, hon. alumni Colo. State U., 1971; recipient William E. Morgan award Colo. State U., 1989, Supervisory award Women's Action Taskforce, USDA, 1995, Group Honor award USDA, 1992. Fellow AAAS; mem. AVMA (trustee ins. trust 1985-87), Nat. Acad. Practice (emeritus mem., treas. 1988-96, coun. 1988-96, founding mem. vet. medicine acad. 1986—), Am. Coll. Vet. Radiology (founding, diplomate), Nuclear Medicine Soc. Am. (nat. trustee 1964-68), Wyo. Med. Soc., Am. Vet. Radiology Soc. (charter, pres. 1965), Laramie C. of C. (bd. dirs. 1968-79), Wyo. Hosp. Assn. (dir. 1982-84, sec.-treas. 1983), Nat. Cowboy Hall of Fame (hon. life mem.), Rotary (bd. dirs. 1965-84, 95-2000). Home: 210 Hollyhills Ln Denton TX 76205-8248 E-mail: bc@iglobal.net.

CARLSON ARONSON, MARILYN A. English language and education educator; b. Gothenburg, Nebr., July 24, 1938; d. Harold N. and Verma Elnora (Granlund) C.; m. Paul E. Carlson, July 31, 1959 (dec. Sept. 1988); 1 child, Andrea Joy; m. David L. Aronson, July 8, 1995. BS in Edn., English and Psychology, Sioux Falls Coll., 1960; MA in History, U. S.D., 1973, MA in English, 1992, EdD in Ednl. Adminstrn., 1997. Tchr. English and social scis. curriculum coord. Beresford (S.D.) Pub. Sch., 1960-78; tchr. English and social scis. Sioux Empire Coll., Hawarden, Iowa, 1979-85; instr. English and ESL, Midwest Inst. for Internat. Studies, Sioux Falls, S.D., 1985-89; asst. prof. English Augustana Coll., Sioux Falls, 1989-97, asst. prof. English and edn., 1997-2000; acad. affairs coord. acad. evaluation U. S.D., Vermillion, 2000—02; assoc. acad. dean Nat. Am. U., Sioux Falls, 2002—03, acad. dean, 2003—. Part time instr. psychology Northwestern Coll., 1985; part time instr. English and lit. Nat. Coll., 1985-88; part time instr. English and history Augustana Coll., 1986-89; presenter in field. Author: Visions of Light: Flannery O'Connor's Themes and Narrative Method, 1992, A Higher Education Perspective: Themes and Narrative Methods of Flannery O'Connor and Eudora Welty, 1997; Plains Goddesses: Heroines in Willa Cather's Prairie Novels, 1995; contbr. articles and revs. to profl. publs. including The Social Sci. Jour., others. Humanities Scholar evaluator Rainbow Project and Increasing Cultural Understanding Seminar, 2000; evaluator Profl. Devel. Conf. Native Am. Curriculum, Rapid City, S.Dak., 2001; mem. S.D. Humanities Coun., 2003—. Recipient Internat. Prof.'s Exch. award Sor Trondelag Coll., Trondheim, Norway, Jan. 1999; named Tchr. of Yr. Beresford (S.D.) Pub. Schs., 1976; S.D. Humanities scholar, 1993—; Bush mini-grantee, 1993, Internat. Studies grantee, 1994, 98, 99, S.D. Humanities Spkr.'s Bur. grantee, 1996—. Mem.: Delta Kappa Gamma. Home: 29615 469th Ave Beresford SD 57004-6457 Office: Nat Am U 2801 S Kiwanis Ave Sioux Falls SD 57105 E-mail: mcarlson@national.edu.

CARLSON-PICKERING, JANE, gifted education educator; b. Providence, Sept. 17, 1954; d. Arthur Julius and Laura Helen (Extovicz) Carlson; m. Allan Thomas Pickering, Nov. 2, 1980; children: Lauren, Taylor. BS in Art Edn., R.I. Coll., 1976, MEd in Art and Indsl. Arts Edn., 1983. Cert. elem. tchr., gifted edn. tchr., R.I. Profl. photographer Ted Pickering Studios, Warwick, R.I., 1973—; calligraphy tchr. Warwick Adult Edn., 1978; secondary tchr. graphics arts Warwick Sch. Dept., 1976-78, secondary tchr. gifted program, 1978-83; elem. gifted program coordinator and tchr. Chariho Sch. System, Wyoming, R.I., 1983-94, multiple intelligences program dir., tchr. M.I. Smart!, 1994—; computer coord. Chariho Elem. Schs., 1998—; multiple intelligence specialist Learning Network's Teachervision.com website, 2000-2001. Mem. Commr.'s Task Force on Vocat. and Indsl. Arts Edn., Providence, 1984-85, Commr.'s Task Force on Gifted and Talented Edn., 1991-92, Chariho K-12 Curriculum Coun., 1992—, tech. com., 1993—; aerial photographer for Aerovisions, 1988-92; adj. faculty R.I. Coll., 1996—; cons. R.I. Dept. Edn., 1996—; tchr. R.I. Found. Tchrs. in Tech. Program, 1998. Recipient First Pl. award photography Warwick Arts Found., 1984, Tchr. award Invent Am., 1991, Lunar Disc Program Tchr. Tng. Cert. NASA, 1991, Sci. Tchr. of Yr. award Amgen Biotech. Co., 2003; grantee R.I. Found. Tchrs. Tech. Pilot Program, 1997; R.I. Tchrs. in Tech. fellow, 1999-2003. Mem. NEA, ASCD, State Advs. Gifted Edn., Nat. Student Art Edn. Assn. Club (treas. 1971-72), Nat. Sci. Tchrs. Assn., Epsilon Pi Tau. Avocations: photography, golf, biking, travel. Home: 209 Blueberry Ln West Kingston RI 02892-1818 Office: Chariho Sch Dept Switch Rd Wood River Junction RI 02894 E-mail: jcpic@chariho.k12.ri.us., rif00227@ride.ri.net.

CARLSSON, BO AXEL VILHELM, economics educator; b. Ulricehamn, Sweden, July 22, 1942; s. Carl Axel Valentin and Dagmar Elisabet (Karlsson) C.; m. Glenda Joyce Bishop, Dec. 28, 1965; children: Eric, Mark, Amy. BA, Harvard U., 1968; MA, Stanford U., 1970, PhD, 1972; Docent, Uppsala U., Sweden, 1980. Sr. rsch. assoc. Indsl. Inst. Econ. and Social Rsch., Stockholm, 1972-84, dep. dir., 1977-81; Umstattd prof. indsl. econs. Case Western Res. U., Cleve., 1984-2000, de Windt prof. indsl. econs., 2000—, chmn. dept. econs., 1984-87, assoc. dean rsch. and grad. programs Weatherhead Sch. Mgmt., 1996—, dir. PhD programs and rsch., 2001—. Vis. scholar MIT, 1982; cons. World Bank, Washington, 1983-87, Swedish Fedn. Industries, Stockholm, 1984-89; min. of fin. Stockholm, 1993-94. Econ. Commn. for L.Am., 1996; project dir. Sweden's Tech. Sys., Stockholm, 1987—; mem. Indsl. and Sci. Coun., Nat. Bd. Tech. Devel., 1987-98; chair sci. adv. bd. Danish Rsch. Unit for Indsl. Dynamics, 1996—. Author: Technology and Industrial Structure, 1979, Industrial Subsidies, 1980, Swedish Industry Facing the 80s, 1981; editor: Industrial Dynamics, 1989, Technological Systems and Economic Performance, 1995, Technological Systems and Industrial Dynamics, 1997, Technological Systems in the Bio Industries: An International Study, 2002. Mem. Swedish cultural orgns. Mem. Europe Assn. Rsch. Indsl. Econs. (pres. 1983-85, exec. com.), Am. Econ. Assn., Ea. Econ. Assn. (bd. dirs. 1989-92), Internat. J.A. Schumpeter Soc. (prize selection com. 1988-90, 94-96), Assn. Christian Economists. Methodist. Home: 2708 Rochester Rd Cleveland OH 44122-2167 Office: Case Western Res Univ Weatherhead Sch Mgmt Dept Econs Cleveland OH 44106-7235 E-mail: Bo.Carlsson@cwru.edu.

CARLSTON, JOHN A. allergist; b. N.Y.C., Nov. 9, 1932; s. Ramon R. and Genevieve P. (Poss) C.; m. Jean L. Lawson, June 21, 1958; children: Ann, Kimberly, Susan. BS in Biology and Philosophy, Coll. of Holy Cross, 1954; MD, Yale U., 1958. Diplomate Am. Bd. Allergy and Immunology. Intern Akron (Ohio) Gen. Hosp., 1958-59, resident in internal medicine, 1959-61; fellow in allergy U. Pitts., 1961-62; instr. medicine in allergy U. Ill., Chgo., 1962-64; assoc. in medicine Northwestern U., Chgo., 1964-69; active staff in medicine Virginia Beach (Va.) Gen. Hosp., 1969—; assoc. prof. in medicine Eastern Va. Med. Sch., Norfolk, Va., 1974—. Bd. cert. Allergy, 1974, 77, 80, 83, 87, 93. Contbr. articles to profl. jours. Lt. col. U.S. Army Med. Corps, 1967-69. Fellow Am. Coll. Allergy and Immunology, Am. Acad. Allergy and Immunology; mem. Va. Allergy Assn., S.E. Allergy Assn., Va. Beach Med. Soc. (pres. 1976), Allergy Rehab. Found. (cons.). Republican. Episcopal. Avocations: Go, travel, skiing, golf, tennis. Office: Asthma and Allergy Specialists Ltd 1704 Sir William Osler Dr Virginia Beach VA 23454-3003

CARLTON, ALFRED PERSHING, JR., lawyer; b. Raleigh, N.C., Aug. 27, 1947; s. Alfred P. and Katherine (Singleton) C.; m. Blair Creech Carlton, Apr. 21, 2001; children: Mary Elizabeth, Troy Eugene. BSBA, U. N.C., 1969, JD, 1975; MPA, U. Dayton, 1973. Bar: N.C. 1975, U.S. Dist. Ct. (ea. dist.) N.C. 1975, U.S. Ct. Appeals (4th cir.) 1976, U.S. Supreme Ct. 1993. Pvt. practice, Raleigh, 1975-77; counsel N.C. Bankers Assn., Raleigh, 1977-79; sec., gen. counsel Bancshares N.C., Inc., Raleigh, 1979-82; adj. prof. law Campbell U., Buies Creek, N.C., 1979-82; ptnr. Sanford, Adams, McCullough & Beard, Raleigh, 1983-89; shareholder McNair & Sanford, Raleigh, 1990-95; ptnr. The Sanford Holshouser Law Firm, Raleigh, 1995—2001, Kilpatrick Stockton LLP, 2002—. Founding chmn. State Law Resources Inc., 1999—. Active City of Raleigh Hist. Properties and Hist. Dists. Commn., 1978-82; exec. bd. Occoneechee coun. Boy Scouts Am., 1983-94; trustee U. N.C. at Wilmington, 1997—; mem. Chief Justice's Commn. on Professionalism, 1998-2001. 1st lt. Med. Svc. Corps, USAF, 1970-73. Fellow Am. Bar Found.; mem. ABA (ho. of dels. 1987—, chmn. of the house 1996-98, bd. govs. 1996-98, chmn. standing com. on jud. independence 1998-2001, pres.-elect 2001—02, pres. 2002—), N.C. Bar Assn. (bd. govs. 1981-82, 92-95), Am. Law Inst., N.C. Legis. Rsch. Commn. (study com. on pub. financing 1985-88). Democrat. Episcopalian. Avocations: tennis, gardening. Office: Kilpatrick Stockton LLP 3737 Glenwood Ave Ste 400 Raleigh NC 27612 E-mail: acarlton@kilpatrick.com.

CARLTON, BUZZ (CLYDE GORDON CARLTON JR.), singer, songwriter, entertainer, recording artist; b. Richmond, Va., Aug. 8, 1962; Owner Milestone Records. Instr. music United Meth. Ch., Richmond, 1998—99. Performances include Nat. Anthem at Richmond Braves Baseball Game, 1989, 90, also TV, radio, and concerts; recorded song Freedom of Speech, 2001, album Blame It On the Blues, 2002. Vol. Salvation Army, Richmond, 1996—99. Mem.: Songwriters Guild, ASCAP. Democrat. Avocations: nature, psychology, philosophy. Office: Angel Prodn and Pub Co PO Box 8382 Richmond VA 23226-0382 E-mail: buzz@singerbuzz.com.

CARLTON, CAROLE GASSETT, medical/surgical nurse; b. Thomaston, Ga., Sept. 8, 1941; d. Oliver M. and Nan (Slaughter) Gassett; m. Frederick Michael Carlton, Apr. 22, 1967; children: Michelle Leigh, Andrea Lynne. AS, Ga. Southwestern Coll. Nursing, Americus, 1964, student, 1960-64. Cert. kidney transplant nurse, Reiki cert. Staff nurse Phoebe Putney Meml. Hosp., Albany, Ga., 1964-65; office nurse Albany, 1965-68; nurse, med.-surg unit St. Clare's Hosp., Schenectady, N.Y., 1982-83; nurse kidney transplant, open heart surgery SUNY Health Sci. Ctr., Syracuse, 1983-89; neurosurg. adolescent and pediatrics neonate and pediatric surgical unit Crouse Irving Meml. Hosp., Syracuse, 1989—. Avocations: horticulture, crafts and sewing, camping, reading. Home: 701 Hudson St Syracuse NY 13219-1007 E-mail: ccrn0805@aol.com.

CARLTON, CHARLES MERRITT, linguistics educator; b. Poultney, Vt., Dec. 12, 1928; s. Clarence Rann and Margaret Louise (Pennell) C.; m. Mary MacDonald, Aug. 31, 1957; children: David, John, Stephen. AB, U. Vt., 1950; MA, Middlebury Coll., 1951; PhD, U. Mich., 1963. Instr. Mich. State U., East Lansing, 1958-62; asst. prof. U. Mo., Columbia, 1962-66; prof. French and Romance linguistics U. Rochester, N.Y., 1966-99; ret.; asst. dir. NDEA French Inst., U. Vt., Burlington, summer 1964; lectr. U.S. State Dept Seminars, Brasov, Romania, summer 1972, U. Ky., Cluj, Romania, summer 1977; reader NEH, 1974—, dept edn. title VI programs, 1993. Fulbright lectr., 1971-72, Romania, 1986, Brazil. Author: Studies in Romance Lexicology, 1965, A Linguistic Analysis of a Collection of Late Latin Documents Composed in Ravenna Between A.D. 445-700: A Quantitative Approach, 1973, Romanian Poetry in English Translation: An Annotated Bibliography and Census (1740-1996), 1997; bibliographer: Romanian Language and Linguistics, 1973, 75-91, Comparative Romance Linguistics Newsletter; co-translator: (G. Doca) Acquisition Grammar of Romanian, 1995, (A. Marino) The Biography of the Idea of Literature, 1996; editor: Comparative Romance Linguistics newsletter, 1970-71. Fulbright fellow, Paris, 1950-51; fellow NSF, summer 1965, Nat. Def. Fgn. Lang., summer 1970; Fulbright grantee, 1974, 78, 82, 88, Romania, IREX grantee, 1982, 91. Mem.: UN Assn. Rochester, Soc. Romanian Studies, Romanian Studies Assn., Am. Romanian Acad., Am. Assn. Advancement Slavic Studies, Rennes-Rochester Sister City Com., Sigma Delta Pi. Home: 3 Thornfield Way Fairport NY 14450-3023 E-mail: charlesmcarlton6@cs.com.

CARLTON, DEAN, lawyer; b. Fort Worth, Nov. 4, 1928; s. Robert Ardine and Marjorie (Box) C.; m. Mary Ellen Williams, Sept. 9, 1949; children: Robert Mark, Scott Duane, Mary Ann. BS, Tex. A&M Coll., 1949; LLB, So. Methodist U., 1952. Bar: Tex. 1952, U.S. Supreme Ct 1968. Pvt. practice, Dallas, 1952-78; propr. The Carlton Firm, P.C., Dallas, 1970—, Fiedler, Akin, Frank & Carlton, P.A., Dallas, 1988—2002; gen. counsel Phoenix Telecom, 1997—2002. Mem. City of Richardson Bd. Adjustment, 1966-67, Tex. Water Code Adv. Com., 1968-70; co-founder, chmn. Dallas Martini Found. and Trust, 1970-85. Mem. ABA, Tex. Bar Assn., Tex. Aggie Bar Assn. (pres. 1974-75), Dallas Bar Assn., Richardson Bar Assn. (pres. 1968), Tex. A&M 12th Man Found. (exec. com. 1980-86, pres. 1985). Home: 1928 Holleman Dr W College Station TX 77840-6307

CARLTON, DENNIS WILLIAM, economics educator; b. Boston, Feb. 15, 1951; s. Jay and Mildred C.; m. Jane R. Berkowitz, 1971; children: Deborah, Rebecca, Daniel. BA summa cum laude, Harvard U., 1972; MS in Ops. Research, MIT, 1974, PhD in Econs., 1975. Instr. econs. MIT, Cambridge, Mass., 1975-76; asst. prof. econs. U. Chgo., 1976-79, assoc. prof., 1979-80; prof. U. Chgo. Law Sch., 1980-84, U. Chgo. Grad. Sch. Bus., 1984—; with Lexecon, Chgo., 1977—. Author: Market Behavior Under Uncertainty, 1984 (Outstanding Dissertation award 1984), (with J. Perloff) Modern Industrial

Organization, 1999; co-editor Jour. Law and Econs., 1980—. Recipient P.W.S. Andrews prize Jour. Indsl. Econs., 1979. Mem. Am. Econ. Assn., Econometric Soc., Phi Beta Kappa. Jewish. Office: Univ Chgo Grad Sch Business 1101 E 58th St Chicago IL 60637-1511

CARLTON, DIANE MICHELE, lawyer; b. L.A., Sept. 26, 1950; d. Thomas Neal and Fanny Jean (Crawford) Moon; m. Gregory Carlton, Sept. 12, 1969; children: Brendan, Dylan. BA in Spanish and Criminal Justice, U. Calif., Irvine, 1972; JD, U. Denver, 1976. Bar: Colo. 1977, U.S. Dist. Ct. Colo. 1977, U.S. Ct. Appeals (10th cir.) 1977. Pub. defender State of Colo., Denver, 1978—82; ptnr. Carlton & Jacobi, Denver, 1983—89; pvt. practice law Englewood, Colo., 1989—97; ptnr. Gutterman, Carlton & Heckenbach, 1997—2002, Heckenbach Carlton LLP, Lone Tree, Colo., 2002—. Judge City of Aurora, Colo., 1983-90. Fellow Am. Acad. Matrimonial Lawyers (Colo. pres. 2001); mem. ABA, Colo. Bar Assn., Arapahoe Bar Assn. (pres. 1997-98), Douglas/Elbert Bar Assn., Colo. Criminal Def. Bar Assn. Democrat. Avocations: reading, hiking, gardening, skiing. Home: 14063 E Fair Ave Centennial CO 80111-6008 E-mail: dcarlton@familylawcolorado.com.

CARLTON, DONALD MORRILL, research, development and engineering executive; b. Houston, July 20, 1937; s. Spencer William and Ruth (Morrill) C.; m. Elaine Yvonne Smith, Jan. 28, 1961; children: Donna Kay, Spencer Frank, Monica Elaine. BA, U. St. Thomas, Houston, 1958; PhD, U. Tex., Austin, 1962. Mem. staff, then group leader Sandia Corp., Albuquerque, 1962-65; with Tracor, Inc., Austin, 1965-69, asst. dir. research, 1968-69; pres., chmn. bd. Radian Corp., Austin, 1969-95; pres., CEO Radian Internat., LLC, Austin, 1996-98, ret., 1998. Chmn. adv. coun. Inst. Nuclear Power Ops., 1998; bd. dirs. Am. Elec. Power Co., Smith Barney Investment Series Trust, Nat. Instruments Corp., Temple-Inland, Crystatech Corp.; mem. mgmt. com. Signature Sci. Past chmn. natural sci. adv. coun. U. Tex., Austin, mem. Engring. Found. adv. coun., mem. adv. coun. Electric Power Rsch. Inst. Mem. Am. Chem. Soc., Tex. Taxpayers and Rsch. Assn. (past chmn.), Austin C. of C. (past dir.), Tex. C. of C. (past chmn.). Home: 403 N Weston Ln Austin TX 78733 Office: URS/RADIAN PO Box 201088 Austin TX 78720-1088

CARLTON, DOUG A. standards engineer; b. Lodi, Calif., June 22, 1962; s. Frank C. and Nancy N. Carlton. BSME, Rose-Hulman Inst. of Tech., 1984; MSME, U. Nev., 1999. Design engr. Square D Co., Peru, Ind., 1984-87; stds. engr. Click Bond, Inc., Carson City, Nev., 1992—. Advisor nat. aerospace stds. com. Aerospace Industries Assn., Washington, 1996-. Instr. Carson City Jr. Ski Program, 1994—; leader Awana; tchr. Sunday Sch.; counselor Ch. Camp. Mem. Soc. for Advancement of Materials and Process Engring. Avocations: running, hiking, skiing. E-mail: doug@clickbond.com.

CARLTON, MICHAEL, magazine editor; Editor Phila. Inquirer; exec. editor So. Living, Birmingham, 1999; editor Coastal Living, 1999—2001, Yankee Mag., Dublin, NH, 2001—. Dir. pub. rels. Island of Bermuda; travel editor Dallas Times Herald, Denver Post. Syndicated columnist: Wash. Post-L.A. Times. Recipient Lowell Thomas awards for travel writing. Office: Yankee Mag PO Box 520 1121 Main St Dublin NH 03444*

CARLTON, PAUL KENDALL, JR., physician, retired air force officer; b. Roswell, N.Mex., May 13, 1947; s. Paul Kendall and Helen C. (Sweat) C.; m. Dorothea Janice Prichard, July 5, 1969; children: Paul Kendall III, Christianne Joy, Stephanie Jill, Luke Jeffrey. BS, U.S. Air Force Acad., 1969; MD, U. Colo., Denver, 1973. Diplomate Am. Bd. Surgery. Commd. 2d lt. U.S. Air Force, 1969, advanced through grades to lt. gen., 1999; resident in surgery Wilford Hall Med. Ctr., San Antonio, 1973-78; comdr. USAF Hosp. Torrejon, Madrid, 1985-88, Scott Med. Ctr., Scott AFB, Ill., 1988-91; command surgeon Air Edn. and Tng. Command, San Antonio, 1991-94; comdr. Wilford Hall Med. Ctr., San Antonio, 1994-99, surgeon gen., 1999—2002. Decorated Air medal, Legion of Merit (2), Def. Disting. Svc. medal, Airman's medal. Fellow ACS (gov. 1992-96). Avocations: hunting, flying. Office: Tex A&M U Health Sci Ctr Homeland Security Dir College Station TX 77845 also: 7th Fl 301 Farrow St College Station TX 77840-7896 Fax: 979-458-7202.

CARLTON, TERRY SCOTT, chemist, educator; b. Peoria, Ill., Jan. 29, 1939; s. Daniel Cushman and Mabel (Smith) C.; m. Claudine Fields, 1960; children: Brian, David. BS, Duke U., 1960; PhD (NSF grad. fellow 1960-63), U. Calif., Berkeley, 1963. Mem. faculty Oberlin (Ohio) Coll., 1963—, prof. chemistry, 1976-2001, chmn. dept., 1980-83, prof. emeritus, 2001—. Vis. prof. chemistry U. N.C., Chapel Hill, 1976 Co-author: Composition, Reaction and Equilibrium, 1970. Home: 143 Kendal Dr Oberlin OH 44074-1906 Office: Oberlin Coll Dept Chemistry Oberlin OH 44074-1097 E-mail: terry.carlton@oberlin.edu.

CARLUCCI, JOSEPH P. lawyer; b. Port Chester, N.Y., Aug. 21, 1942; m. Elizabeth Smith; children: Susan Elizabeth, Kathleen Ann. B.S, in Econs., Georgetown U., 1964; JD, Fordham U., 1967. Bar: NY 1969. Ptnr. Pierro & Carlucci, Port Chester, N.Y., 1969-76; pvt. practice, Rye, N.Y., 1977-78; mng. ptnr. Cuddy & Feder & Worby LLP, White Plains, N.Y., 1979-99. Chief legis. counsel to N.Y. senator from Westchester County, 1971-73; chief counsel N.Y. State Select Com. on State's Economy, 1973-74. Co-founder, v.p. Rye Town-Port Chester Rep. Club, 1972; trustee Village of Port Chester, 1974-77; chmn. Port Chester Indsl. Devel. Agy., 1974-76; mem. Westchester County Econ. Devel. Coun., 1976-80, Narcotics Guidance Coun. Port Chester, 1970-74; chmn. Met. N.Y. YMCA Key Leaders Conf., 1984; mem. Parent's Coun., Wheaton Coll., 1986-87; bd. dirs. Port Chester YMCA, 1970-79, sec., 1972-77, v.p., 1978; mem. Port Chester Govt. Study Commn., 1971-73; commr. appraisal White Plains and Greenburgh Urban Renewal; counsel to South Shore Hotline, 1973-74; mem. Port Chester Pub. Employees Rels. Bd., 1973-77; mem. adv. bd. bd. dirs. Salvation Army, 1973-77; mem. adv. bd. Security Title and Guaranty Co., 1986-90; bd. dirs. Rye YMCA, 1979-87, pres., 1982-85, trustee, 1989—; trustee Rye Hist. Soc., 1979-83, 90-96, sec., 1980-81, v.p., 1982-83, 92-94, pres., 1994-96; interviewer alumni admissions program Georgetown U., 1988-96; bd. visitors Pace U. Sch. Law, 1990—; bd. dirs. Vol. Ctr. United Way Westchester County, 1991-97; mem. Westchester divsn. Cardinal's Com. for Laity, 1991-2001, vice chmn., 1992, chmn., 1993-95; mem. paralegal curriculum adv. com. SUNY Westchester C.C., 1994; bd. dirs. March of Dimes Birth Defects Found., 1994-96, Westchester Bus. Partnership, 1995-98, Westchester Partnership for Econ. Devel., 1996-97, Jacob Burns Film Ctr., Ind., 2000—; trustee Westchester Arts Coun., 2000—, Mercy Coll., 2002—. Recipient Golden R award Rennaissance Project, Inc., Gold Man award YMCA, 1985, Cmty. Svc. award Rotary Internat. Club, 1995. Mem. ABA (vice chmn. econs. of law practice com. on lawyering skills 1984-85), N.Y. State Bar Assn., Westchester County Bar Assn. (real property com. 1978-82), Port Chester-Rye Bar Assn. (sec. 1970-75, pres. 1976-77, bd. dirs. student assistance svcs. alcohol and drug abuse prevention program 1989-95, adv. bd. 1995—), Westchester C.C. Found. (bd. dirs. 1997—), Real Estate Fin. Assn. (bd. dirs. 2000-2003), Coveleigh Club (bd. govs. 1978-86, sec. 1979, v.p. 1980, pres. 1981-84), Georgetown U. Met. Club (bd. dirs. 1980-82), Hundred Club Westchester (bd. dirs.). Office: Cuddy & Feder LLP 90 Maple Ave White Plains NY 10601

CARLUCCI, MARIE ANN, nursing administrator, nurse; b. N.Y.C., Apr. 22, 1953; d. Clarence Hugh and Anna Rebecca (Mills) McNamee; m. Paul Pasquale Carlucci, Aug. 18, 1973; children: Christine, Patricia. Diploma in nursing, Mt. Vernon Hosp. Sch. Nursing, N.Y., 1974; BS in Behavioral Sci. summa cum laude, Mercy Coll., 1991; MPH, N.Y. Med. Coll., 1997. Cert. emergency nurse; cert. nurse adminstr.; lic. healthcare risk mgr.; cert. legal cons. Staff nurse Mt. Vernon (N.Y.) Hosp., 1974-82, Lawrence Hosp., Bronxville, N.Y., 1982-84, No. Westchester Hosp., Mt. Kisco, N.Y., 1984-91, asst. dir. nursing, mem. nurse mgmt. and ethics coms., 1991-94; asst. DON svcs. Ferncliff Manor, Yonkers, N.Y., 1994-95, dir. nursing svcs., 1995-97; dep. dir. nursing svcs. Taylor Care Ctr., Westchester, N.Y., 1997-2000; dir. residential svcs. Hillsborough (Fla.) Assn. for Retarded Citizens, 2000; dir. nursing Am. Retirement Corp., Sun City Center, Fla., 2000—01; med.-legal nurse cons., 2001—. Religious edn. tchr. St. John and St. Mary's Ch., Chappaqua, N.Y., 1984-99; campaign mgr. Com. to Elect Paul P. Carlucci, Chappaqua, 1990; mem. Surrogate Decision Making Com., N.Y. Commn. Quality Care for Mentally Disabled; mem. bd. trustees Field Home-Holy Comforter, 1995-99; guardian ad litem 13th Judical Cir., Tampa, Fla., 2000—; bd. adv. Hillsborough County Children's Svcs., 2002-. Mem.: Phi Gamma Mu, Psi Chi. Roman Catholic. Home: 3916 Appletree Dr Valrico FL 33594-4315

CARLYON, DIANE CLAIRE, nurse; b. Butte, Mont., Nov. 5, 1950; d. Roy and Claire Jenny (Madison) C.; (div.); children: Michael Wade Jr., Tammy Michelle. BSN, U. Tenn., 1987. Cert. std. first aid/CPR instr., ARC; cert. CPR instr., Am. Heart Assn. Staff nurse Oakland Naval Hosp., Calif., Kimberly Nurses, Memphis; staff nurse, staff nurse Meth. Cen. Hosp., Memphis; utilization mgmt. Qual-Med Health Plan, Bellevue, Wash.; utilization mgmt./quality assurance coord. Gen. Hosp. of Everett; IV infusion specialist Homedco, Redmond, Wash.; clin. field coord. Vis. Nurse's of N.W. Everett, Wash., 1991-95; infusion therapy coord. Vis. Nurses Svcs. of N.W., Seattle, 1995-2000, staff devel. specialist, 1998-2000; coord. infusion therapy Total Care, Inc., Charlotte, NC, 2000—01; dir. clin. svcs. Heartland Home Healthcare, Greensboro, NC, 2002—. Mem. adv. coun. Wellspring Adult Care; clin. mgr. Advanced Home Care, Greensboro, N.C., 2001-02. Mem. Meth. Hosp. Staff Adv. Bd., Assistance Impaired Nursing Students Com., Egyptian God of Leadership Soc., Snohomish County AIDS Task Force Consortium, 1991—, Ryan White Care Funds Planning Coun., Snohomish County AIDS Walk Com., 1994-97; bd. mem. AIDS Project Snohomish County, 1996—; task force Home Care of Wash., VRE. Mem. ANA, Tenn. Nurses Assn. (task force HIV), Wash. Nurses Assn., Intravenous Nurse Soc., Continuing Nursing Edn. (com.) Office: Heartland Home Healthcare 603-B Dolley Madison Rd Greensboro NC 27410 Home: Apt 2E 3988 Clubhouse Ct High Point NC 27265-8804

CARMACK, MILDRED JEAN, retired lawyer; b. Folsom, Calif., Sept. 3, 1938; d. Kermit Leroy Brown and Elsie Imogene (Johnston) Walker; m. Allan W. Carmack, 1957 (div. 1979); 1 child, Kerry Jean Carmack Garrett. Student, Linfield Coll., 1955-58; BA, U. Oreg., 1967, JD, 1969. Bar: Oreg. 1969, U.S. Dist. Ct. Oreg. 1980, U.S. Ct. Appeals (9th and fed. cirs.) 1980, U. S. Claims Ct. 1987. Law clk. to Hon. William McAllister Oreg. Supreme Ct., Salem, 1969-73, asst. to ct., 1976-80; asst. prof. U. Oreg. Law Sch., Eugene, 1973-76; assoc. Schwabe, Williamson & Wyatt, Portland, Oreg., 1980-83, ptnr., 1984-96, ret., 1996. Writer, lectr., legal educator, Oreg., 1969—; mem. exec. bd. Appellate sect. Oreg. State Bar, 1993-95. Contbr. articles to Oreg. Law Rev., 1967-70. Mem. citizen adv. com. State Coastal Planning Commn., Oreg., 1974-76, State Senate Judiciary Com., Oreg., 1984; mem. bd. visitors Law Sch. U. Oreg., 1992-95; mem. Oreg. Law Commn. Working Group on Conflict of Laws, 2000. Mem. Oreg. State Bar Assn., Order of Coif.

CARMACK, SHARON DEBARTOLO, genealogist, writer; b. Port Chester, N.Y., Oct. 17, 1956; d. Sal Bart and Mary Louise Fitzhugh; m. Stephen Harold Carmack; 1 child, Laurie. Bachelor's degree, Regis U., 1997. Cert. genealogist. Freelance writer, editor, Simla, Colo., 1997—; genealogist, 1985—. Cons. editor Newbury St. Press, New Eng. Hist. Geneal. Soc., Boston, 1998—; contract advisor Nat. Writers Union, N.Y.C., 2001—; spkr. in field. Author: The Ebetino and Vallarelli Family History, 1990, Italian-American Family History: A Guide to Researching and Writing About Your Ancestors, 1997, The Genealogy Sourcebook, 1997, A Genealogist's Guide to Discovering Your Female Ancestors, 1998, A Genealogist's Guide to Discovering Your Immigrant and Ethnic Ancestors, 2000, David and Charlotte Hawes (Buckner) Stuart of King George County, Virginia, 2001, My Wild Irish Rose: The Life of Rose (Norris) O'Connor Fitzhugh and her mother, Delia (Gordon) Norris, 2001, Organizing Your Family History Search, 1999, Your Guide to Cemetery Research, 2002, A Sense of Duty: The Life and Times of Jay Roscoe Rhoads and his wife, Mary Grace Rudolph, 2002, Italians in Transition, 2003; editor: Betterway Genealogy Books; contbg. editor: Family Tree Mag. Recipient Award of Merit, Fedn. Geneal. Socs., 1992, 2002; fellow, Utah Geneal. Assn., 1998. Mem.: New Eng. Hist. Geneal. Soc., Assn. Profl. Genealogists (Smallwood award 1990), Nat. Geneal. Soc., Nat. Writers Union (del. 2001), Jamestowne Soc. (life). Avocations: reading, family history. Home Fax: 719-541-2673. Personal E-mail: sdcarmack@juno.com. Business E-Mail: contact@sharoncarmack.com.

CARMAN, ANNE, management consultant; b. Kansas City, Mo., Mar. 17, 1942; d. Martin Albert and Areleta Laynelle (Burditt) Utterback; m. Robert G. Stevens, Dec. 30, 1989; children: James Powell Carman Jr., Christopher Tully Carman. BS in Edn., U. Mo., 1965, MA, 1968, PhD, 1983. Coord. women's studies U. Mo., Columbia, 1977-81, mgr. ann. giving, 1981-83; dir. ann. giving Found., So. Ill. U. Found., Carbondale, 1983-85, dir. major gifts, 1985-86, pres., 1986-88; mem. bus. adv. com. So. Ill. U., Carbondale, 1987-88, 91-97; v.p. Coun. for Advancement and Support Edn., Washington, 1988-90, The Aspen Inst., Washington, 1990-92, The Points of Light Found., Washington, 1993-96; sr. ptnr. Fin. Mgmt. Ptnrs., Annapolis, Md., 1992—. Bd. dirs. Greater D.C. Cares, 1993-97, Support Ctr. of Washington, 1993-2000. Avocations: sailing, hiking, bicycling, reading. Home and Office: Fin Mgmt Partners 1690 Coventry Pl Annapolis MD 21401-6422

CARMAN, ERNEST DAY, lawyer; b. Mpls. s. Ernest Clarke and Juanita Howland (Day) C.; children Eric, Brooke (dec.), Christiane, Dayna. BA, U. So. Calif.; MA, Stanford U.; Dr. ès Sci. Pol., U. Geneva, Switzerland; JD, U. San Francisco. Bar: Calif. 1957, U.S. Supreme Ct. 1973. Ptnr. Adams, Carman, Mansfield, Ball and Wenzel, 1959-65, Carman and Mansfield, 1965-70. Judge protem Santa Clara County Superior Ct., Orange County Superior Ct.; dir. various corps. Contbr. articles to profl. jours. Past chmn. Santa Clara County Dem. Cen. Com. Maj. USMCR. Mem. ABA, Calif. Employment Lawyers Assn. Office: 1 Corporate Plaza Dr Ste 110 Newport Beach CA 92660-7924 E-mail: eday99@earthlink.net.

CARMAN, GARY OLEN, child welfare company executive; b. Binghamton, N.Y., Oct. 27, 1935; s. George Earl and Ann (Bell) C.; m. Judith Florence Haight, Mar. 22, 1963; children: Virginia Eve, Monica Lou. BS, SUNY, Buffalo, 1962, MS, 1965; cert. in advanced study, Syracuse U., 1968, PhD, 1972; MSW, Fordham U., 2002. Tchr. Lakeshore Sch. Dist., Eden, N.Y., 1962-64, Gateway Treatment Ctr., Williamsville, N.Y., 1964-66; dir. Edn. Gateway Pub. Sch., Williamsville, N.Y., 1967-70; supr. Spl. Edn. North Syracuse (N.Y.) Pub. Schs., 1971-72; dir. spl. svcs. Yonkers (N.Y.) Pub. Schs., 1972-75; CEO Julia Dyckman Andrus Meml., Yonkers, 1975—2003. Mem. Coun. on Accreditation, Tex. Edn. Dept., Austin, 1971-72, N.Y. State Edn. Dept., 1973-74, Bd. Coop. Ednl. Svcs., North Westchester, Putnam, Yorktown Heights, N.Y., 1992. Author: Permanence & Family Support, 1988, Evaluation Criteria for Special Education in Residential Schools, 1991, Quality Indicators in Residential Treatment, 1994; contbr. articles to profl. jours. Chmn. bd. dirs. Salvation Army-Citadel Corp., Yonkers, 1977-88; mem. Mayor of Yonkers Blue Ribbon Task Force for selection of Bd. Edn., 1988-90; mem. Yonkers 2000 com., 1989-91; bd. dirs. YMCA, Yonkers, 1987-89, Nat. Commn. on Accreditation for Spl. Edn. Svcs., 1991—; bd. dirs. Alliance for Children and Families, 1997-2000; chair Westchester Behavioral Healthcare Network, 1996-98; governing bd. Internat. Coun. Exceptional Children, 1980-83. Recipient Nordlinger Child Welfare Leadership award, 1999; U.S. Office of Edn. fellow, 1966-67, 70-72, Paul Harris fellow Rotary Internat., 1988. Mem. Nat. Assn. Homes and Svcs. for Children (bd. dirs. 1984-87, pres. 1997), Child Welfare League of Am.), Internat. Inst. Edn. Spl. (bd. dirs. 1990—, chmn. internat. congress, chmn. Am. del. to internat. congress in Vienna 1992-96), Phi Kappa Phi. Avocations: golf, birdwatching, hi-power rifle competition, travel. Office: Carman Consulting 11 Timber Trail South Windsor CT 06074 E-mail: Goc63@aol.com.

CARMAN, GEORGE HENRY, retired physician; b. Albany, N.Y., Sept. 23, 1928; s. Simon Peter and Mary (Whish) C. BA, Cornell U., 1948, MD, 1951. Diplomate: Am. Bd. Internal Medicine, Am. Bd. Cardiovascular Disease. Intern, then asst. resident in medicine Barnes Hosp., St. Louis, 1951-53; asst. resident in medicine Salt Lake County Gen. Hosp., 1955-56; chief resident VA Hosp., Salt Lake City, 1956-57; fellow cardiovascular diseases U. Utah Coll. Medicine, 1957-60; pvt. practice cardiology and internal medicine Dallas, 1960-89; attending physician Baylor U. Med. Center, 1960-89; mem. clin. faculty U. Tex. Southwestern Med. Sch., Dallas, 1960-89, clin. prof. internal medicine, 1972-89; ret., 1989. Served to 1st lt. M.C. AUS, 1953-55. Fellow ACP (emeritus), Am. Coll. Cardiology (emeritus); mem. AAAS, Am. Heart Assn. (emeritus fellow coun. clin. cardiology), Cornell Club (N.Y.), Phi Beta Kappa, Alpha Omega Alpha. Episcopalian. Home: #19-D 3525 Turtle Creek Blvd Dallas TX 75219-5514

CARMAN, GREG, mechanical engineer, educator; b. Alexandria, Va., Mar. 15, 1959; s. William Charles and B. Faye Carman; 1 child, Cassidy. BS in Mech. Engring., Va. U. Tech., 1985; MS in Materials Engring., U. Ala., 1987; PhD in Mech. Engring., Va. U. Tech., 1991. Prof. mech. engring. UCLA, 1991—. Office: UCLA MAE Dept 38-137 M Eng IV Los Angeles CA 90009

CARMAN, GREGORY WRIGHT, federal judge; b. Farmingdale, N.Y., Jan. 31, 1937; s. Willis B. and Marjorie (Sosa) C. Exch. student, U. Paris, 1956-57; BA, St. Lawrence U., 1958; JD, St. John's U., 1961; Judge Adv. Gen. honors grad., U. Va. Law Sch., 1962. Bar: N.Y. 1961. Atty. Carman, Callahan & Sabino, Farmingdale, N.Y., 1964-83; councilman Town of Oyster Bay, N.Y., 1972-81; mem. 97th Congress from 3d Dist. N.Y., 1981-82; U.S. Congl. del. I.M.F. Cong., 1982; judge U.S. Ct. Internat. Trade, N.Y.C., 1983—, acting chief judge, 1991, now chief judge. Statutory mem. Jud. Conf. U.S., 1991. Capt. AUS, 1962-64. Fellow Am. Bar Found.; mem. ABA, N.Y. State Bar Assn. (cts. and cmty. com.), Nassau County Bar Assn., Nassau Lawyers Assn., St. John's Law Rev. Republican. Episcopalian. Office: US Ct Internat Trade 1 Federal Plz New York NY 10278-0001

CARMAN, ROBERT EUGENE, secondary school educator; b. Malden, Mo., July 21, 1940; s. Beauford Lav and Margaret Lav (Wiseman) C.; m. Betty Ann Robertson, July 1963 (div. 1968); m. Nada Joyce Shoemaker, Nov. 2, 1968; children: Jason Austin, Justin Aaron (dec.). BS in Edn., Southeast Mo. State Coll., 1962; MS in Combined Scis., U. Miss., 1966, cert., 1988. Cert. tchr., Mo. Tchr. math. Malden (Mo.) High Sch., 1962-67, Hazelwood Jr. High Sch., Florissant, Mo., 1967-72, supr. math., 1972-92, ret., 1992; early childhood and elem. edn. instr. U. Mo., St. Louis, 1993-95. Mid. level specialist SMILE Inst., St. Louis, 1989; cons. pub. schs., St. Louis, 1989-91, 96-99, St. Genevieve, Mo., 1990, Riverview Gardens Sch. Dist., St. Louis County, Mo., 1990, Mehlville, Mo., 1990-95, St. Charles, Mo., 1991, Wentzville, Mo., 1994, others, including Glencoe Pub. and Mimosa Pub., Milliken Pub.; program cons. Math. and Sci. Edn. Ctr., 1986-91. Author: Using Cooperative Techniques and Manipulatives to Teach Core Competence and Key Skills, 1989, Supermarket Math, 1993, Knowledge Works, 1996; editor books, software, manipulatives, articles, Math. Tchr., 1984-92. Named Hazelwood Jr. High Sch. Tchr. of Yr., 1992-93. Mem. ASCD, Math. Educators Greater St. Louis (bd. dirs. 1984-86, pres. 1988-89, newsletter editor 1986-88, Educator of Yr. 1991-92, chmn. student support spring conf. 1995, mem. chair 1996—, jour. com. 2002—), Mo. Coun. Tchrs. Math. (pres. 1992-93, exec. bd. 1988-90, chmn. jr. h.s. math. contest 1988-90, chair contest test writing, 1998—, gen. chmn. spring meeting 1991, Educator of Yr. 1991-92), Nat. Coun. Tchrs. Math. (chmn. student exhibit St. Louis Cen. Regional conf. 1988, chmn. mid grades conf. program 1991, chmn. workshop support Springfield Cen. Regional conf. 1995), Am. Philatelic Soc. Avocation: stamp collecting. Home: 3125 Matlock Dr Florissant MO 63031-1519 E-mail: bobcarman@aol.com.

CARMAN, SUSAN HUFERT, nurse coordinator; b. Detroit, Oct. 2, 1940; d. Theodore Louis and Margaret L. (O'Connor) Hufert; children: Amy E., Holly C., John T. BSN, Johns Hopkins U., 1964; MEd, Northeastern U., 1975; MS in Health Care Adminstrn., Simmons Coll., 1988. Instr. psychiat. nursing Salem (Mass.) Hosp. Sch. Nursing, 1975-78, Curry Coll., Milton, Mass., 1978-80; editor Beacon Comm. Corp., Acton, Mass., 1980-84; writer health promotion Honeywell Inc., Waltham, Mass., 1984-85; mgr. mental health unit Heritage Hosp., Somerville, Mass., 1986-87; specialist adult psychiatry Mass. Dept. Mental Health, Boston, 1987-93; clinician intensive clin. svcs. MHMA, Boston, 1994-96; dir. Arbour Counseling Svcs. Boston, 1996—. With SHC Assocs., Boston, 1993—; bd. dirs. Com. to End. Elder Homelessness, Boston, Mass., 1993-99, Dept. Social Svcs., Lowell, sec., 1982-92. Chair health planning com. Jamaica Plain (Mass.) Tree of Life/Arbol da Vida, 1994—2003; docent Arnold Arboretum, Boston, 1989—2000; founding mem. Boston Coalition for Promotion of Child and Adolescent Mental Health, 2000—; bd. dirs. First Steps/Health Families, Jamaica Plain, 1998—, Match-Up Interfaith, Boston, 2001—; chmn. Jamaic Plain Domestic Violence Provider Network, 2003—. Mem. ANA, Mass. Nurses Assn., Boston Coalition for Promotion of Child and Adolescent Mental Health, 2000—. Avocations: travel, reading, walking, classical music.

CARMEAN, JERRY RICHARD, broadcast engineer; b. Greenfield, Ohio, Apr. 2, 1938; s. Cloyde B. and Mary F. (Hedges) C.; m. Patricia H. Carmean; 1 child, Steven. BS in Edn., Ohio U., 1965, BS in Elec. Engring., 1984. Registered profl. engr., Ohio; lic. FCC gen. class radiotelephone operator. Tchr. New Philadelphia (Ohio) High Sch., 1965-66; broadcast engr. Ohio U. Telecommunications Ctr., Athens, 1966-81, dir. engring., 1981-92; pvt. broadcast engring. cons., 1992—. Cons. Sta. WLGN, Logan, Ohio, 1964-2000; tech. cons. Sta. 4VEH, Cap Hatien, Haiti. Served with U.S. Army, 1961-64. Mem. NSPE, Ohio Soc. Profl. Engrs., Antique Wireless Assn., Soc. Broadcast Engrs., Men for Missions Internat., Athens County (Ohio) Amateur Repeater Assn., The Planetary Soc., Rotary. Avocations: astronomy, photography, amateur radio, antiques. Home: 16341 Calico Ridge Rd Logan OH 43138-9416 Office: Sta WLGN Logan Broadcasting Co 1 Radio Ln Logan OH 43138-8762

CARMEN, IRA HARRIS, political scientist, educator; b. Boston, Dec. 3, 1934; s. Jacob and Lida (Rosenman) C.; m. Sandra Vineberg, Sept. 6, 1958 (div. June 1999); children: Gail Deborah, Amy Rebecca; m. Lawrence Lowell Putnam, Mar. 16, 2000. BA, U. N.H., 1957; MA, U. Mich., 1959, PhD, 1964. Asst. prof. Ball State U., 1963-66; assoc. prof. Coe Coll., 1966-68; prof. polit. sci. U. Ill., 1968—. Recombinant DNA adv. com. NIH, 1990-94; participant meetings on China-U.S. genetic engring. rsch. and policy rels., Beijing, 1991, European-U.S. human genetic experimentation and policy rels., London, Paris, Rome, 1995; program organizer Human Genome Orgn. internat. meeting, Heidelberg, 1996; vis. scholar Yale Law Sch., 1981; vis. lectr. Tamkang U., Taiwan, 1991. Author: Movies, Censorship, and the Law, 1966, Power and Balance, 1978, Cloning and the Constitution, 1985; co-prin. investigator Sociogenomics in Advanced Species, Consilience in Theory and Practice; contbr. articles to profl. jours. Sr. advisor Bush-Quayle Nat. Jewish Campaign Com., 1988; mem. Pres. George Bush's Inaugural Educators Adv. Com., 1989; guest del. Rep. Nat. Conv., 1992; mem. Rep. Nat. Com., Rep. Jewish Coalition, Straight Talk Am. Recipient Clarence Berdahl award U. Ill., 1980, 87, 90, All-Campus award for excellence in undergrad. teaching, 1980, William F. Prokasy award, 1995, Harriet and Charles Luckman award, 1995; grantee U. Ill. Mem. AAAS, Human Genome Orgn., Am. Soc. Gene Therapy, Assn. for Politics and Life Scis. (chmn. coun. 2000—), Phi Beta Kappa. Office: U Ill Dept Polit Sci Urbana IL 61801

CARMI, GIORA, illustrator; b. Kfar Malal, Israel, Sept. 17, 1944; s. Avraham and Miriam (Lozovick) C.; m. Avia Frenkel, May 19, 1965 (div. Jan. 1997); children: Ilil, Ore, Liane. Student, Bezalel Acad. Art and Design, Jerusalem, 1967-71; student art therapy, NYU, 2002—. Freelance graphic designer and illustrator, Israel, 1972-85; tchr. illustration Israel Inst. Tech., Tel Aviv, 1983-84, tchr. typography, 1983-84; freelance illustrator N.Y.C., 1985—. Bd. dirs. Israeli Assn. Graphic Designers, Tel Aviv, 1983-85, judge nat. design competitions, 1984. Designer & illustrator: many mags., newspapers and pvt. cos., 1972—85; author (and illustrator): And Shira Imagined, 1988, Night Farm, 1989, A Circle of Friends, 2003—; illustrator: over 40 books, 1972—, NY Times, —, Wall St. Jour., —; one-man shows include Galerie Roswitha Tittel, Cologne, Germany, 1998—. Lt. Israel mil., 1962-65. Recipient 1st pl. Simon Rockover award Am. Jewish Press Assn., 1988, 90, 1st pl. Sydney Taylor Book award Assn. Jewish Librs., 1991. Avocations: poetry, philosophy, music, literature. Home and Office: 530 W 113th St Apt 2A New York NY 10025 E-mail: giora.carmi@verizon.com.

CARMICAL, PHIL, editor; b. Dalton, Ga., Aug. 26, 1968; BA, Boston U., 1991; M, U. Chgo., 1997. Acquisitions editor Gulf Pub. Co., Houston, 1998—99, Pro2Net Corp., Austin, Tex., 1999—2001, Elsevier Sci. and Tech. Books, Austin, 2001—. Advisor Coun. Energy Advisors, 2002—. Editor: (book) Gas Migration (Medal of Achievement, Russian Acad. of Natural Sciences, 1999). Mem.: Shakespeare Oxford Soc., Assn. Authors and Pub., Austin Runners Club, Austin Triathletes, U.S. Triathlon. Independent. Episcopalian. Avocations: marathons and running, triathlon, shakespeare authorship question. Home: 8704 Cretys Cove Austin TX 78745 Office: Elsevier Sci and Tech Books PO Box 152046 Austin TX 78715-2046 Home Fax: 512-280-0558; Office Fax: 512-280-0558. Personal E-mail: pcarmical@austin.rr.com. E-mail: p.carmical@elsevier.com.

CARMICHAEL, ALEXANDER DOUGLAS, engineering educator; b. Sliema, Malta, July 19, 1929; s. Adam and Jane (Hamilton) G.; m. Rose Margaret Whittaker, Sept. 1, 1951; children— Gillian Ruth, Alison Rose, Peter Stewart. B.Sc., Plymouth Tech. Coll., London U., 1949; PhD, Cambridge U., 1958. Head aero. rsch. group Bristol-Siddely Engine Co., Bristol, England, 1958—60; chief engr. Dracone Developments Ltd., London, 1960-61; sr. project engr. No. Research and Engring. Corp., Cambridge, Mass, 1961-64; research fellow Imperial Coll. Sci. and Tech., London, 1964-68; tech. adv. English Electric Co. Ltd., Rugby, 1968-70; prof. power engring. MIT, 1970-96; prof. emeritus, 1996—. Fellow Soc. Naval Archs. and Marine Engrs. (v.p. N.E. region 1991-94), Whitworth Soc. (London). Home: 69 Otis St Newton MA 02460-1816 Office: MIT Dept Ocean Engring Cambridge MA 02139 E-mail: adcarmic@mit.edu.

CARMICHAEL, DAVID BURTON, physician; b. Santa Ana, Calif., Sept. 12, 1923; s. David Burton and Phyllis (Adams) C.; m. Ava Louise Smith, Dec. 26, 1944; children: Catherine Ann, Heather Sue, Linda L., Ava L. Student, Graceland U., 1940-42; BA, MD, U. Iowa, 1946; postgrad., Harvard U., 1949-50; LL.D. (hon.), Graceland U., Iowa, 1985. Diplomate: Am. Bd. Internal Medicine. Clin. and research fellow medicine Mass. Gen. Hosp., Boston, 1949-50; cons. cardiovascular diseases U.S. Naval Hosp., San Diego, Camp Pendleton, 1956-86, U.S. VA, 1960-82; chief dept. medicine Scripps Meml. Hosp., La Jolla, Calif., 1961-63, 65-67, chief staff, 1970-71. Clin. prof. medicine U. Calif. at San Diego, 1968—; pres. De Anza Lab. Corp., 1962-72, Carmichael-Carson Med.-Clin. Lab. Corp., 1962-75; sr. ptnr. Med. Clinic; founding med. dir. Cardiovascular Inst. Scripps Meml. Hosps., 1985-96; pres. Orange County Pioneer Coun., 1993-94; trustee GDE Systems, Inc., 1992-94. Contbr. articles to profl. jours. Trustee Millicent Rogers Mus., Taos, N.Mex., 1986—90, Graceland U., Iowa, 1987—, Rancho de las Golondrinas Mus., Santa Fe, 1989—. Rear adm. med. insp. gen. USNR. Decorated Legion of Merit; recipient Alumni Disting. Service award Graceland U., 1967. Fellow ACP (gov. So. Calif. region III 1972-76, Laureate award 1991), Am. Coll. Cardiology (dir., sec. 1975, trustee 1979-85, Disting. Fellow award 1994, Mastership 2001), Am. Coll. Chest Physicians; mem. AMA (chmn. specialty soc. and service delegation 1985-87, 93-96, mem. grad. med. edn. adv. com. 1983—89, chmn., 1985-87, chmn. sect. council on clin. cardiology, Disting. Svc. award 1997), Am. Heart Assn., San Diego County Heart Assn (pres. 1959-60), San Diego Biomed. Research Inst. (pres. 1958-59, 62-63, vice chmn. residency rev. com. internal medicine 1971-78), San Diego Soc. Internal Medicine (pres. 1959-61). Republican. Mem. Community Ch. of Christ. Home: 8333 Calle Del Cielo La Jolla CA 92037-3033 E-mail: ASCDBC@aol.com. *This country, with its Christian heritage, gives to the vast majority the opportunity to serve and often, the chance to excel. The guidance of parents and instructors should never be forgotten, nor should the sacrifices of those who have allowed us to preserve our freedom.*

CARMICHAEL, DAVID H. lawyer; b. Torrington, Wyo., Nov. 18, 1939; s. W.R. and Berniece Carmichael; m. Karen J. Carmichael, July 7, 1963; children: William, Kristin, Kara. BA, U. Wyo., 1964; JD, 1967. Bar: Wyo. 1967, Ariz. 1980, US Supreme Ct. 1972. Assoc. Kine & Tilker, Cheyenne, Wyo., 1967—68; ptnr. Hanes, Carmichael, Johnson, Gage & Speight, Cheyenne, 1970—76; pvt. practice law Cheyenne, 1976—77; ptnr. Carmichael & Statkus, Cheyenne, 1977—78, Carmichael, McNiff & Patton, Cheyenne, 1978; asst. city atty. City of Cheyenne, 1969—72; police commr., 1975; pvt. practice; chmn., spl. ad hoc com. Contingent Fees and Discovery Wyo. Sup. Ct., 1986; mem. staff Land and Water Law Rev., 1965—66; sr. editor, 1966—67; mem. Fair Employment Practices Commn., Wyo., 1970—74; mem. permanent rules com. Wyo. Supreme Ct., 1975—81; mem. Nat. Conf. Uniform State Laws, 1977—83. Mem.: Ariz. State Bar Assn., Wyo. State Bar Assn. (pres.-elect 1986—88), Wyo. Trial Lawyers Am., Assn. Trial Lawyers Am., Laramie County Bar Assn., Rocky Mountain region Nat. Parks Adv. Council (mem. 1976—78). Republican. Home: 10584 E Bella Vista Dr Scottsdale AZ 85258-5764 Office: PO Box 43 921 Evergreen St Cheyenne WY 82009-3216

CARMICHAEL, DAVID RICHARD, lawyer; BS, UCLA, 1964, JD, 1967. Bar: Calif. 1968. Assoc. Adams, Duque & Hazeltine, 1967-72; gen. counsel The Housing Group, Irvine, Calif., 1972-77; assoc. counsel Pacific Mut. Life Ins. Co., 1977-81, 2nd v.p., assoc. gen. counsel, 1981-89, v.p., investment counsel, 1989-92, sr. v.p., gen. counsel, 1992—. Office: Pacific Life Ins Co 700 Newport Center Dr Newport Beach CA 92660-6307

CARMICHAEL, DONALD SCOTT, lawyer, business executive; b. Toledo, Feb. 19, 1912; s. Grey Thornton and Edna Earle (Jaite) C.; m. Mary Glenn Dickinson, May 28, 1940; children: Mary Brooke McMurray, Pamela Hastings Keenan. AB, Harvard U., 1935, student Sch. Law, 1935-37; LLB, U. Mich., 1942. Bar: Ohio 1942. Staff dept. law City of Cleve., 1938-40; chief renegotiation br. Cleve. Ordnance Dist., War Dept., 1942-46; practiced in Cleve., 1946; asst. sec. Diamond Alkali Co., 1946-48, sec., 1948-57, gen. counsel, 1957-58; v.p.-gen. counsel Stouffer Corp., 1959-60, exec. v.p., 1960-64; practiced in Cleve., 1964-71; pres. Schrafft's divsn. Pet, Inc., N.Y.C., 1971-75, Sportsvc. Corp., Buffalo, 1975-80, Del. North Cos., Inc., Buffalo, 1980-89, vice chmn., 1989—; officer, dir. various corps.; dir., cons. Editor: F.D.R; Columnist, 1947; Contbr. to law revs. Mem. Cuyahoga County Charter Commn., 1959— ; chmn.; mem. Cleve. Met. Services Commn., 1957-59, President's Task Force on War Against Poverty, 1964; Del. Democratic Nat. Conv., 1960, 64; mem. Cuyahoga County Dem. Exec. Com.; Chmn. bd. trustees Cuyahoga County Hosps., 1958-64, Urban League, Karamu House. Mem. ABA, Ohio Bar Assn., Cleve. Bar Assn., Union Club Cleve., Chagrin Valley Hunt Club, Harvard Club N.Y.C., River Club N.Y.C., Buffalo Club, Phi Gamma Delta. Home: 11 Hardscrabble Rd Lyme NH 03768

CARMICHAEL, IAN STUART EDWARD, geologist, educator; b. London, Mar. 29, 1930; came to U.S., 1964; s. Edward Arnold and Jeanette (Montgomerie) C.; children by previous marriages: Deborah, Graham, Alistair, Anthea. BA, Cambridge U., Eng., 1954; PhD, Imperial Coll. Sci., London U., 1958. Lectr. geology Imperial Coll. Sci. and Tech., 1958-63; NSF sr. fgn. sci. fellow U. Chgo., 1964; mem. faculty U. Calif.-Berkeley, 1964—, prof. geology, 1967—, chmn. dept., 1972-76, 80-82, assoc. dean, 1976-78, 85-00, assoc. provost, 1986-2000, dir. Lawrence Hall of Sci., 1996—2003, acting dir. bot. garden, 1997—98; adj. prof. U. of Mich., 2002—. Author: Igneous Petrology, 1974; editor-in-chief Contbns. to Mineralogy and Petrology, 1973-90; contbr. numerous papers to profl. jours. Guggenheim fellow, 1992; recipient Arthur L. Day medal Geol. Soc. Am., 1991. Fellow Royal Soc. London, Mineral Soc. Am. (Roebling medal 1997), Mineral Soc. Gt. Britain (Schlumberger medal 1992), Am. Geophys. Union (Bowen award 1986), Geol. Soc. of London (Murchison medal 1995). Office: U Calif Berkeley Dept Earth/Planetary Sci Berkeley CA 94720-4767

CARMICHAEL, JAMES VINSON, JR., library and information science educator; b. Atlanta, Nov. 27, 1946; s. James Vinson and Frances Elizabeth (McDonald) C.; m. Karen Bryce Powers, June 18, 1969 (div. Sept. 1973). BA, Emory U., 1969, MLN, 1977; PhD, U. N.C., 1988. Inventory control clk. Lockheed Aircraft, Marietta, Ga., 1969, logistics asst., 1969-70; trust adminstrv. asst. Trust Co. Bank, Atlanta, 1970-76; ref., instrn. libr. Ga. Coll., Milledgeville, Ga., 1977-81; instr. U. N.C., Chapel Hill, 1988-89, Greensboro, 1988-89, asst. prof. libr., info. scis., 1989-95, assoc. prof. libr., info. sci., 1995-00, prof., 2000—. Editor: Daring To Find Our Names: The Search for Lesbigay Library History, 1998; contbr. articles to profl. jours. Recipient Louis Round Wilson award Southeasten Libr. Assn., 1988, Franklin M. Garrett award Atlanta Hist. Soc., 1990, Disting. Alumni award Univ. N.C., Chapel Hill, 1995, Edmund Pearson award 2001. Mem. ALA (chair libr. history round table 1995-96, mem. com. status of women 1993-96), N.C. Libr. Assn. (Ray Moore award 1992, 94, chair coll. and univ. sec., 2001—), Assn. Libr. and Info. Sci. Edn. Home: 2403 Cottage Pl Greensboro NC 27455-2912 E-mail: jim_carmichael@uncg.edu.

CARMICHAEL, JUDY LEA, record industry executive, concert jazz pianist; b. Lynwood, Calif., Nov. 27, 1952; d. John Alvin and Jeanne Pauline (Boock) Hohenstein. Student, Calif. State U., Long Beach, 1970-73, Calif. State U., Fullerton. Owner C&D Prodns., N.Y.C., 1989—. Chmn. jazz fellowships com. NEA, Washington, 1990-91; featured on Nat. Pub. Radio, Marian McPartland's Piano Jazz, 1990, Morning Edition Nat. Pub. Radio, also TV programs Entertainment Tonight, CBS, Sunday Morning with Charles Kuralt, 1993. Performed as pianist at Breda Jazz Festival, The Netherlands, 1986, Carnegie Hall, N.Y.C., 1988, 89, Rio de Janeiro, 1989, Peggy Guggenheim Mus., Venice, Italy, 1990, Am. Acad., Rome, 1990, 91, USIA Tour, Portugal, 1991, Spain, 1991, India, 1988, China, 1992, Singapore, 1994, S. Am., 1996, major U.S. tours 1993-95, also L.A., Zurich, Switzerland, Paris, Cannes, France; performer Stanford Symphony Pops with Skitch Henderson, 1997; author (music) Judy Carmichael's Complete Book of Stride Piano, 1987, You Can Play Stride Piano, 1996; prodr., artist (LP's) Jazz Piano, 1983, Two Handed Stride, 1980, (CD's) Trio, 1989, Old Friends, 1991, Pearls, 1985, ...And Basie Called Her Stride, 1993, Judy, 1994, Chops, 1995, PianoDisc, 1995, QRS piano rolls, 1996, (CD and player piano formats) High on Fats and Other Stuff, 1997; featured on CBS Sunday Morning with Charles Osgood, Entertainment Tonight, Prairie Home Companion, Nat. Pub. Radio's Morning Edit.; jazz editor Sheet Music mag., 1989-90; host, creator, prodr. Judy Carmichael's Jazz Inspired, Nat. Pub. Radio, 2000—, Pub. Radio Internat. on Sirius Satellite Network; stage show with Steve Ross 2000-2003 aboard QUII and throughout Europe and U.S.;contbr. numerous articles to profl. jours. NEA fellow, grantee; Grammy award nominee, 1980; chosen to be Steinway artist, 1986; nominated for Mac award Manhattan Assn. Cabarets and Clubs for Stage Show with Steve Ross, 1996. Avocations: golf, softball, tennis, skiing. E-mail: judy@judycarmichael.com.

CARMICHAEL, MARY ALICE, artist, genealogist; b. Colon, Panama, Nov. 28, 1936; came to U.S., 1937; d. Donald Croom and Mary Alice (Gatling) Beatty; m. James Donald Carmichael, Oct. 28, 1961; children: James Donald Jr., Beatty Payseur, Daniel Troy. BA, Howard Coll., 1960. Contbr. articles to profl. jours. Organizing mem. Ala. Men's Hall of Fame, 1988—, chair, 2002—; mem. Women's Com. of 100 of Birmingham, pres. 1989-91; steering com. Reynold's Hist. Soc., 1988—. Named one of Outstanding Young Women of Am., 1972-73. Mem. DAR (Outstanding Jr. Mem. award 1968, Most Outstanding Hist. Paper award 1988), Soc. Mayflower Descendants Ala. (gov. 1990-94, registrar 1985-94), Rotary (sec., helped initiate 1st heart pacemaker bank for the indigent in Bolivia). Presbyterian. Avocations: art, genealogy, photography, travel. Home: 2857 Canterbury Rd Birmingham AL 35223-1201

CARMICHAEL, PAUL LOUIS, ophthalmic surgeon; b. July 8, 1927; s. Louis and Christina Ciamaichela; m. Pauline Cecilia Lipsmire, Oct. 28, 1950; children: Paul Louis, Mary Catherine, John Michael, Kevin Anthony, Joseph William, Patricia Ann, Robert, Christopher. BS in Biology, Villanova U., 1945; MD, St. Louis U., 1949; MS in Medicine, U. Pa., 1954. Diplomate Am. Bd. Ophthalmology; cert. isotope methodology Hahnemann Med. Coll. Rotating intern St. Joseph's Hosp., Phila., 1949-50; resident in ophthalmology Phila. Gen. Hosp., 1952-54; asst. prof. ophthalmology Hahnemann Med. Coll., Phila., 1960-66, clin. assoc. prof. nuclear medicine, 1974-90. With radioactive isotope dept. Wills Eye Hosp., Phila., 1956-61, sr. asst. surgeon, 1961-65, assoc. surgeon, 1966-72, assoc. surgeon retinal svc., 1972-90; attending ophthalmologist Holy Redeemer Hosp., Meadowbrook, Pa., 1963-65; assoc. ophthalmologist Grand View Hosp., Sellersville, Pa., 1958-75; instr. opthalmology Grad. Sch. Medicine, U. Pa., 1956-63; clin. assoc. prof. ophthalmology Temple U., Phila., 1967-72; clin. assoc. prof. ophthalmology Thomas Jefferson U. Sch. Medicine, Phila., 1971-90; chief ophthalmology North Pa. Hosp., Lansdale, 1959-90, pres. staff, 1959; pres. Ophthalmic Assocs., Lansdale, 1969-90. Co-author: Nuclear Ophthalmology, 1976; contbr. chpts. to books, papers to profl. confs., articles to publs. in field. Pres. bd. dirs. North Pa. Symphony, 1976-78. Capt. M.C., U.S. Army, 1950-51. Named Outstanding Young Man of Yr., Lansdale Jaycees, 1959, Outstanding Young Man, State of Pa. Jaycees, 1960. Fellow ACS, Internat. Coll. Surgeons, Coll. Physicians Phila.; mem. AMA, Montgomery County Med. Soc., Pa. Med. Soc., Am. Acad. Ophthalmology, Pa. Acad. Ophthalmology, Assn. Rsch. in Ophthalmology, Inter-County Ophthalmol. Soc. (co-founder, pres. 1975-78), Ophthalmic Club Phila. (pres. 1964), Delaware Valley Ophthalmic Soc. (pres. 1985-89). Roman Catholic. Home: Box 680308 2567 Columbine Ct Park City UT 84068 E-mail: pplcsr@cs.com.

CARMICHAEL, RICHARD ARDEAN, marketing professional; b. Sigourney, Iowa, Jan. 2, 1930; children: Joseph, Laura, James, Janet, Jeanne, Cathy. Student, Wash. Jr. Coll., Iowa, 1949; D in Vet. Medicine, Iowa State U., 1955; student, Cambridge U., Eng., 1972. Owner, ptnr Speaker and Carmichael Vet. Clinic, Keota, Iowa, 1955-72; pres., gen. mgr. Maplehurst Ova Transplants, Inc., 1972-90; gen. mgr. Maplehurst Genetics Internat. Inc., 1990-97, 1997—2002. Contbr. articles to profl. jours. Recipient Award for Excellence Embryo Transfer Industry, 1988, The Tough Egg award Am. Embryo Transfer Assn., 1989. Mem. Iowa Vet. Med. Assn., Am. Vet. Med. Assn., Am. Assn. Bovine Practitioners, Internat. Embryo Transfer Soc. (com. chmn. 1974, bd. govs. 1975, sec., treas. 1976, pres. 1977, chmn. of workshop 1979, bd. dirs. 1982, v.p. 1982, pres, 1983, 84, govt. liaison and animal health and regulations com. chmn. 1983—), Soc. for Cryobiology, U.S. Animal Health Assn., Embryo Movement Symposium, Boy Scouts Am., Keota Cmty. Club, Knights of Columbus. Home: 32263 190th St Keota IA 52248-8551 E-mail: mapgen@lisco.com.

CARMICHAEL, RICHARD E. government official, financial manager, educator; b. Montclair, N.J., June 14, 1941; s. Charles Walter and Helen May C.; m. Inez K Alexander, Oct. 6, 1984; children: Gregory, Andrew. BS in Econ., Monmouth U., 1970; MBA in Fin., Pace U., 1972; PhD, Calif. Coast U., 1997. Divsnl. controller Mfrs. Hanover Corp., N.Y.C., 1972-82; v.p. market planning and rsch. Bank Am. Corp., San Francisco, 1982-84, 1st Interstate Bank Calif., L.A., 1984-88; ptnr. Findata Corp., Balt., 1988-91; budget mgr. dist. Md. U.S. Bankruptcy Ct., Balt., 1991-97; br. chief credit programs SBA, Washington, 1997-99; assoc. prof. Washington Coll., Chestertown, Md., 2000—01; Alex Lee prof. Lenoir-Rhyne Coll., Hickory, N.C., 2001—. Faculty assoc. Johns Hopkins U. Sch. Bus., Balt., 1991—99; asst prof. Newberry (S.C.) Coll., 1999—2000. Author: Evolution Economics, 1995, Politics & Economics in America, 1997. Rep. Methodist. Avocations: tennis, swimming. Home: 1323 Millrace Dr Conover NC 28613 E-mail: CarmichaelLR@lrc.edu.

CARMICHAEL, ROBERT WILLIAM, medical group administrator; b. Lansdale, Pa., Dec. 22, 1958; s. Paul Louis and Pauline Cecilia (Lipsmire) C.; m. Ruth Maria Avendano, July 22, 1983; children: Diana Christina, Anna Maria. BS in Econs., U. Pa., 1980; MBA, U. Miami, 1987. Treas. AIESEC, U.S., N.Y.C., 1980-81; asst. to contr. Comfamiliar Andi Fenalco, Barranquilla, Colombia, 1981-82; asst. to v.p. ops. ICN Pharms., Covina, Calif., 1982-83; fin. mgr. Paulmarc Systems, Lansdale, 1983-85; ops. mgr. Coopervision Info. Systems, Lansdale, 1985-86; bus. mgr. Ophthalmic Assocs., Lansdale, 1987-90; cons. Mass. Eye and Ear Infirmary, Boston, 1990-91, Carter Eye Ctr., Dallas, 1991-94, Ft. Lauderdale (Fla.) Eye Inst., 1995—96; pres. Sunrise Consulting, Inc., Plantation, Fla., 2001—; exec. dir. Greater Ft. Lauderdale Heart Group, 2001—. Ptnr. Poolside Cons., Lansdale, 1985—; founder, v.p. Profl. Ophthalmic Adminstrs., Phila., 1989—; bd. advisors AIESEC, Long Beach, Calif., 1983. Acct. Mary Mother of Redeemer Ch., Montgomeryville, Pa., 1988—; bd. dirs. North Penn Symphony Orch., Lansdale, 1989. Named Outstanding Young Man of Yr., Lansdale Jaycees, 1990. Republican. Roman Catholic. Avocations: basketball, reading, running. Office: Sunrise Consulting Inc 1844 Nob Hill Rd Ste 172 Plantation FL 33322-4851

CARMICHAEL, ROBERTA KAY, writer; b. Daytona Beach, Fla., Dec. 11, 1956; d. James Lawton and Barbara Kent Coward; m. Del Carmichael, July 5, 1974; 1 child, Joseph. Grad. H.S., Crescent City, Fla.; Breaking into Print Diploma, Long Ridge Writers Group, West Redding, Conn., 2000. Tchr. Kiddie Korner Nursery Sch., Crescent City, 1972—77; freelance writer Homosassa, Fla., 2000—. Contbr. articles to publs. Phys. therapy vol. Citrus Meml. Hosp., Inverness, Fla., 1992—93. Mem.: Pisgah Camping Club. Avocations: writing, reading, woodcarving, hiking, horseback riding. Home: 3610 S Springbreeze Way Homosassa FL 34448

CARMICHAEL, WILLIAM DANIEL, consultant, educator; b. Denver, Sept. 5, 1929; s. Fitzhugh Lee and Anna Devona (Sullivan) C.; m. Faith Young, June 21, 1958; children: Amy, Philip Fitzhugh, Daniel Owen. AB, Yale, 1950; MA, MPA, Princeton, 1952, PhD, 1959; BLitt (Rhodes scholar), U. Oxford (Eng.), 1955; LLD (hon.), U. W.I., 1989. Legislative analyst U.S. Bur. Budget, 1955-56, budget analyst, 1956-57; lectr. econs. and pub. affairs Princeton, 1957-60, asst. prof., 1960-62; dir. undergrad. program Woodrow Wilson Sch. Pub. and Internat. Affairs, 1958-62; prof. econ. policy, dean Grad. Sch. Bus. and Pub. Adminstrn., Cornell U., 1962-68; rep. Ford Found., Brazil, 1968-71, head, 1971-77, 1977-81, v.p. for developing country programs, 1981-89; exec. dir. Ea. European programs Inst. Internat. Edn., N.Y.C., 1989-93. Cons. on edn. and econ. devel., 1993—. Bd. dirs. Human Rights Watch, So. African Legal Svcs. and Edn. Program. Mem. Coun. on Fgn. Rels., Assn. Am. Rhodes Scholars, Phi Beta Kappa. Home and Office: 603 W Lyon Farm Dr Greenwich CT 06831-4363 E-mail: wdcarm@optonline.net.

CARMODY, ARTHUR RODERICK, JR., lawyer, director; b. Shreveport, La., Feb. 19, 1928; s. Arthur R. and Caroline (Gaughan) C.; m. Renee Aubry, Jan. 26, 1952 (div. 1980); children: Helen Bragg, Renee, Arthur Roderick, Patrick, Timothy, Mary, Virginia, Joseph; m. Mary Wells, Sept. 1, 1990. Grad. with honors, N.Mex. Mil. Inst.; BS, Fordham U., 1949; LLB, La. State U., 1952. Bar: La. 1952, U.S. Supreme Ct. 1971. Mem. firm Wilkinson, Carmody & Gilliam and its predecessors, Shreveport, 1952—. Bd. dirs. Kansas City So. Transport Co., Kansas City, Shreveport and Gulf Terminal Co., Shreveport Braves Baseball Club (Tex. League), Sta. KDAQ-FM Pub. Radio, pres., 1991, chmn., 1992, RED River Pub. Radio Network; mem. Shreveport Steamer (World Football League) Partnership; pres. Touchdown Club of Shreveport, 1960. Author: Legal Problems in the Development and Mining of Lignite, 1976; legal history columnist Shreveport Bar Review, 1995—; La. adv. editor The Insurance Bar, 1961—. Chmn. Met. Shreveport Zoning Bd. Appeals, 1959—72; pres. bd. trustees Jesuit H.S., 1976—82; chmn. bd. govs. Loyola Found., Shreveport, 1991—94; trustee Schumpert Med. Ctr., 1965—85; adv. bd. La. State U., Shreveport, 1982—86; mem. gov.'s ad hoc com. for preparation rules and regulations for mining and reclamation of lignite in State of La., Dept. Conservation, 1978—79; mem. select com. for rev. stds. juc. conduct Supreme Ct. La., 1994—; nat. bd. dirs. N.Mex. Mil. Inst., Roswell, 1967—68; bd. dirs. La. State U. Found., Baton Rouge, Agnew Day Sch., Shreveport, 1970—82, Ridgewood Montessori Sch., Christus Schumpert Health Sys. Found. 1st lt. USAR, 1948—50. Recipient Alumni Achievement award Fordham U., 1995; named Hon. Alumnus, elected to Ring of Honor Loyola Coll. Prep., 1993. Master: Am. Inns of Ct.; fellow: La. Bar Assn. (mem. com. on lawyer and judicial conduct 1996—), Am. Coll. of Trial Lawyers, La. Bar Found. (life); mem.: ABA, Mil. Order Stars and Bars, Crossed Saber Soc., Soc. for Civil War History, Soc. for Mil. History, U.S. Horse Cavalry Assn., North La. Civil War Round Table, Res. Officers Assn., La. Civil Svc. League, Soc. Hosp. Counsel, Rlwy. and Locomotive Hist. Soc., Kansas City So. Hist. Soc., Shreveport C. of C. (dir. 1968—70), Pub. Affairs Rsch. Coun., Nat. Legal Ctr. for the Pub. Interest, La. Assn. Bus. and Industry, Tarshar Soc., La. R.R. Assn. (exec. com. 1992—), Mid-Continent Oil and Gas Assn. (exec. com. 1984—), Am. Arbitration Assn. (panel arbitrators), Nat. Acad. Law and Medicine, La. Assn. Def. Counsel, Internat. Assn. Def. Counsel, Nat. Assn. R.R. Trial Counsel, Trial Attys. Am., Coll. Master Advocates and Barristers, La. Law Inst., Am. Judicature Soc., Univ. Assocs. of La. State U., Supreme Ct. of La. Hist. Soc., Scribes Soc., Nat. Soc. SAR (pres. Galvez chpt. 1997), Confederate Meml. Lit. Soc., La. Hist. Assn., North La. Hist. Soc., Federalist Soc., Fifth Fed. Cir. Bar Assn., U.S. Supreme Ct. Hist. Soc., Shreveport Bar Assn. (pres. 2003—), Fed. Bar Assn., Kappa Alpha Order, Sovereign Mil. Order of Malta, Phi Delta Phi. Home: 255 Forest Ave Shreveport LA 71104-4506 Office: Wilkinson Carmody & Gilliam 1700 Beck Bldg 400 Travis St Shreveport LA 71101-3108 E-mail: Acarmody@wcglawfirm.com.

CARMODY, JENNIFER LYNN, librarian; b. Livonia, Mich., Feb. 16, 1970; d. Donald Edward and Jean Marie Hansen; m. Cameron Anthony Carmody, Sept. 6, 1996. BA, U. Mich., 1992; M in Libr. and Info. Sci., Wayne State U., 1995. Youth svcs. libr. Garden City (Mich.) Pub. Libr., 1995; pub. svcs. libr. Otsego County Libr., Gaylord, Mich., 1996—98; reference libr. Lawrence Technol. U., Southfield, Mich., 1998; pub. svcs. libr. Monroe County C.C., Monroe, Mich., 1998—. Mem. adv. coun. Loex, Ypsilanti, Mich., 2000—. Scholar, Inst. for Info. Literacy, 1999. Mem.: AAUW, S.E. Mich. League of Librs. (at-large), Mich. Libr. Assn. (mem.-at-large reference divsn. 2001—), Assn. Coll. and Rsch. Librs., Am. Libr. Assn. Office: Monroe County C C 1555 S Raisinville Rd Monroe MI 48161 Fax: 734-384-4160.

CARMODY, RICHARD PATRICK, lawyer; b. Chgo., June 2, 1942; s. Thomas Francis and Margaret (Tully) C.; m. Alison Pierce Cutter, Dec. 27, 1968; children: Elizabeth Carmody Gonzalez, Emily Pierce Carmody. BA, U. Ill., 1964; JD, Vanderbilt U., 1975. Bar: Ala. 1975, U.S. Dist. Ct. (no., mid. and so. dists.) Ala. 1975, U.S. Ct. Appeals (11th cir.) 1985, U.S. Supreme Ct. 1988. Assoc. Lange, Simpson, Robinson & Somerville, Birmingham, Ala., 1975-81, ptnr., 1981—2002; chmn. exec. com. Lange, Simpson Robinson & Somerville, Birmingham, Ala., 1987-93; ptnr. Adams and Reese/Lange Simpson LLP, Birmingham, 2003—. Mem. Am. Bankruptcy Inst., Washington, 1985—, co-chair ethics com. 1999—; bd. dirs. Am. Bd. Cert., 2000—, mem. exec. com., 2001—; bd. cert. Bus. Bankruptcy Am. Bd. of Cert. Bd. dirs. Birmingham coun. Campfire Boys and Girls Inc., 1978-90, pres., 1983-85; bd. dirs. Ala. region NCCJ, 1995—, state chair, 2000-02; bd. dirs. St. Vincent's Hosp. Foudn., 2002—; active Leadership Birmingham, 1998—. Fellow Am. Coll. Bankruptcy, 1999—. Mem. Ala. Bar Assn. (chmn. bankruptcy and comml. law sect. 1985, exec. com. 1986-93), Greystone Golf & Country Club, Kiwanis. Roman Catholic. Avocations: golf, sports. Office: Adams & Reese LLP 2100 3d Ave N Ste 1100 Birmingham AL 35203 Business E-mail: richard.carmody@arlaw.com.

CARMODY, THOMAS JAMES, cardiologist; b. Chgo., 1949; MD, U. Autonoma, Guadalajara, 1975. Diplomate Am. Bd. Internal Medicine, Am. Bd. Cardiovascular Diseases. Intern Faculty of Medicine Meml. U. Newfoundland, St. John's, 1975-76; resident Good Samaritan Hosp., Dayton, 1976-79; asst. clin. prof. medicine Wright State U. Sch. Medicine, Dayton; with Good Samaritan Hosp., Dayton. Cardiovascular fellow Good Samaritan Hosp./Wright State U., 1982-84. Fellow: Am. Coll. Cardiology. Office: Ste 652 2200 Philadelphia Dr Dayton OH 45406-1830

CARMONA, JOSÉ ANTONIO, Spanish language educator, English language educator; b. Remedios, Las Villas, Cuba, Mar. 9, 1960; came to U.S., 1971; s. Felix and Maria Gloria (Reyes) C.; 1 child, Alberto José. BA, Drew U., 1983; MA, Columbia U., 1984, EdM, 1986, postgrad in Hispanic culture & lit. U.S., 1986—. Cert. Spanish tchr. K-12, N.J., ESL. Spl. edn. tchr. grades 5, 6. P.S. 121 N.Y. Bd. Edn., N.Y.C., 1984; ESL instr. Hispanic Inst. Rsch. & Devel., Paramus, N.J., 1985-86; adj. prof. of Spanish Bergen C.C., Paramus, 1985-87; instr. Spanish Drew U., Madison, N.J., 1987-91; ESL instr. Emerson Adult Edn. Program, Union City, N.J., 1988-89; adj. assoc. prof. Spanish County Coll. of Morris, Randolph, N.J., 1988; adj. prof. Spanish Coll. St. Elizabeth, Convent Station, N.J., 1990; instr., coord. ESL and Spanish Hudson County C.C., West N.Y., N.J., 1990-94, asst. prof. ESOL, modern lang. coord., 1994-96; supr. student tchrs. of Spanish William Paterson Coll., Wayne, N.J., 1996; assoc. prof. modern langs./EOSL Daytona Beach (Fla.) C.C., 1996—, chair dept. modern langs./ESL, 1999—. Case worker Angel Guardian Home, Bklyn., 1983; coord. Hispanic Leadership Program, St. Elizabeth Coll., Convent Station, 1989-90, Gov.'s Sch. on the Environ. Stockton State Coll., Pomona, N.J., 1989-93, co-dir. 1993; faculty adviser Hispanic House students, Drew U., Madison, 1987-91, acad. adviser and counselor to 1st and 2nd yr. students, other adminstrv. duties; freelance translator, 1985—; lectr. and or presenter at many nat. and internat. ednl. confs. Author: Adolescent Blues (poetry) 1992, Distinct Voices: A Multicultural Anthology for ESL Writers, 1996; co-author: Mixed Media: Authentic Reading for the Beginning ESL Student (text), 1993, Topics and Trends: First Authentic Readings for ESL Writers, 1994 (text), Exploremos: Spanish for the Community College Student, 2001; contbr. over 50 poems to Spanish and English mags, 1988—. Mem. Hispanic Affairs Adv. Com. Dept. Community Affairs, Trenton, N.J., 1989-91,community, Affirmative Action Com., Drew U., Madison, 1989-91; adv. bd. mem. Drew U. EOF program, Madison, 1990-95, Selective Svc. Bd., West N.Y., 1992-96; bd. dirs. Jose Marti Scholarship Fund, Union City, 1979—, Hudson County 4-Coll. Consortium, 1992, N.E. Fla. Tchrs. of English as 2d Lang., 2000—; bd. dirs. Magdalene, Inc., 2000-2001, pres. exec. bd., 2001—, Fla. Adult Edn. ESOL Task Force, 2002--. Recipient Hon. Literary Essay award Cuban Lions Club in Exile, Union City,1976, Outstanding Alumnus award N.J. Ednl. Opportunity Fund Profl. Assn., Newark, 1989, Golden Poet award World of Poetry, Calif., 1989, Frances B. Sellers award, Drew U. E.O.F. Alumni Assn., Madison, 1990. Mem. NEA (rev. panel bd. dirs. higher edn. jour. Thought and Action 1996-99, plaque for svc. to the jour. 1999), MLA, Fgn. Lang. Educators N.J., N.Y. Met. Assn. for Devl. Edn., TESOL (N.J. higher edn. rep. 1992-96, bd. dirs. 2002—), Hispanic Assn. for Higher Edn., Circulo Cultural Pan Am., Acad. Am. Poets, Trio (N.J. bd. dirs. 1991-92), Fla. Assn. Cmty. Colls., Sigma Delta Pi, Kappa Delta Pi,

Epsilon Omega Psi. Roman Catholic. Avocations: writing, reading, dancing. Home: 42 Ballenger Ln Palm Coast FL 32137-8852 Office: Daytona Beach CC 1200 Internat Speedway Blvd Daytona Beach FL 32120-2811 E-mail: carmonaja@cs.com., carmonj@dbcc.cc.fl.us.

CARMONA, RICHARD, surgeon general; b. N.Y.C., Nov. 22, 1949; m. Diana Sanchez; 4 children. BS, U. Calif., San Francisco, 1976, MD, 1979; MPH, U. Ariz., 1998. Prof. surgery U. Ariz., 1985—2002; surgeon gen., vice adm. USPHS, 2002—. With U.S. Army, 1967—70. Office: Office of Surgeon Gen 5600 Fishers Ln Rm 18-66 Rockville MD 20857

CARMONY, MARVIN DALE, linguist, educator; b. nr. Richmond, Ind., Feb. 27, 1923; s. Harry Edgar and Ellen (Brown) C.; m. Mary Joan Nicholson, May 31, 1947; children— Ronald Dee, Kathryn Lynn. Student, Valparaiso Tech. Inst., 1941-42, Olivet Nazarene U., 1947-49; AB, Ind. State U., 1950, MA, 1951; PhD, Ind. U., 1965. Radio operator Am. Airlines, Chgo., 1942-44; tchr. high schs. Pendleton and Shelbyville, Ind., 1953-59; from instr. English to assoc. prof. English and linguistics Ind. State U., Terre Haute, 1959-69, prof., 1969-88, assoc. dean Coll. Arts and Scis., 1970-86. Co-founder Ind. Place-Names Survey, 1968, dir., 1968-70; co-founder Ind. Names (now Hoosier Folklore), 1970, gen. editor, 1970-88. Author: (with D.F. Carmony) Indiana Dialects in Their Historical Setting, 1972, rev. edit., 1979, (with Ronald Baker) Indiana Place Names, 1975; also articles. Trustee Olivet Nazarene U., 1967-70, mem. alumni bd. dirs., 1995-2000. With U.S. Mcht. Marine, 1944-46; vet. USCG. Am. Council Learned Socs. fellow, 1964-65 Mem. Am. Dialect Soc. (adv. bd. publs. 1972-77, 82-86, pres. 1981-82), Soc. Wireless Pioneers, Am. Names Soc. (editorial bd. Names 1977-84), Linguistic Soc. Am., Nat. Soc. XVII Century Colonial Dames (Disting. Svc. award 1975), Phi Delta Lambda, Phi Delta Kappa, Sigma Tau Delta. Methodist. Home: 227 Madison Blvd Terre Haute IN 47803-1911

CARNAHAN, GEORGE RICHARD, business educator, consultant; b. Zanesville, Ohio, May 20, 1935; s. George Edwin and Anna Eloise (Beymer) C.; m. Mary Linn Burbage, June 14, 1958; children: Elizabeth, George, Glenn, John. BS, Juniata Coll., 1957; MBA, Miami U., Oxford, Ohio, 1962; PhD, Ohio State U., 1967. Prof. mgmt. No. Mich. U., Marquette, 1964-2001, dept. head, 1985-93. Bd. dir. Bay Mills C.C., Brimley, Mich., 1985—. Co-author: T.I.M.E. To Improve Management Effectiveness, 1986; also articles. Elder, deacon Presbyn. Ch., Marquette; Med. Care Access Coalition. Mem. Acad. Mgmt., Alpha Kappa Psi (v.p. 1983-87, pres. 1987-89). Democrat. Home: 1530 W Ridge St Apt 22 Marquette MI 49855-5703 E-mail: gcarnahan@tourvilles.com.

CARNAHAN, JEAN, former senator; m. Mel Carnahan (dec. Oct. 16, 2000); children: Randy (dec.), Russ, Robin, Tom. BA in Bus. and Pub. Admin., George Washington U. Senator State of Mo., 2001—02. Mem. armed svcs. com, small bus. and entrepreneurship com., gov. affairs com., commerce, sci. and transportation com., special com. aging, State of Mo.; co-founder Children in the Workplace; spkr. for domestic violence, cancer, osteoporosis, mental health, drug problems. Author: If Walls Could Talk, 1998, Christmas at the Mansion: Its Memories and Menus, 1999; contbr.: Vital Speeches of the Day, 1999, Will You Say a Few Words, 2000. Recipient Robert C. Goshorn award for pub. svc., State of Mo. Martin Luther King, Jr. Special Acheivement award, Child Adv. of Yr. award, Boys' and Girls' Town Mo., 1995, Citizen of Yr., March of Dimes, 1997, Woman of Yr., St. Louis Zonta Clubs Internat., 1999. Bd. mem. William Woods U. Democrat.

CARNAHAN, JOHN ANDERSON, lawyer; b. Cleve., May 8, 1930; s. Samuel Edwin and Penelope (Moulton) C.; m. Katherine A. Halter, June 14, 1958; children: Peter M., Allison E., Kristin A. BA, Duke U., 1953, JD, 1955. Bar: Ohio 1955. Pvt. practice, Columbus, Ohio, 1955-78; ptnr. Arter & Hadden, Columbus, 1978-99; in-house counsel The Excello Splty. Co., Cleve., 2000—. Lectr. Ohio Legal Ctr. Inst., 1969, 73-74. Editor Duke Law Jour., 1954-55; chmn. bd. editors Ohio Lawyer, 1986-91; contbr. articles to profl. jours. Chmn. UN Day, Columbus, 1960; pres. Capital City Young Republican Club, 1960; bd. dirs. Columbus Cancer Clinic, pres., 1978-81; bd. dirs. Columbus chpt. ARC, 1979-87; mem. governing bd. Hannah Neil Mission, Inc., 1974-78; chmn. Duke Alumni Admissions Adv. Com., 1965-79. Named one of Outstanding Young Men of Columbus, 1965. Fellow Am. Bar Found. (life, chmn. Ohio fellows 1988-95), Columbus Bar Found. (life); mem ABA (ho. of dels. 1984-95), Ohio State Bar Found. (trustee 1986-90), Nat. Conf. Bar Pres., Ohio State Bar Assn. (coun. of dels. 1965-67, exec. com. 1977-81, 82-85, pres.-elect 1982-83, pres. 1983-84, Ritter award for outstanding contbns. adminstrn. justice 1987), Columbus Bar Assn. (bd. govs. 1970-72, sec.-treas. 1974-75, pres. 1976-77, Professionalism award 1996), Kit Kat Club (past pres.). Presbyterian. Home and Office: 767 S 5th St Columbus OH 43206-2145 E-mail: jac5830@aol.com.

CARNAHAN, ORVILLE DARRELL, retired state legislator, retired college president; b. Elba, Idaho, Dec. 25, 1929; s. Marion Carlos and Leola Pearl (Putnam) C.; m. Colleen Arrott, Dec. 14, 1951; children: Karen, Jeanie, Orville Darrell, Carla. BS, Utah State U., 1958; M.Ed., U. Idaho, 1962, Ed.D., 1964. Vocat. dir., v.p. Yakima (Wash.) Valley Coll., Yakima, Wash., 1964-69; chancellor Eastern Iowa C.C. Dist., Davenport, 1969-71; pres. Highline Coll., Midway Wash., 1971-76; assoc. Utah Commr. for Higher Edn., Salt Lake City, 1976-78; pres. So. Utah U., Cedar City, 1978-81, Salt Lake C.C., Salt Lake City, 1981-90, pres. emeritus, 1990—; mem. Utah Ho. of Reps., 1993-99; ret., 1999. Cons. in field. Active Boy Scouts Am. Served with U.S. Army, 1952-54, Korea. Mem. Am. Vocat. Assn., NEA, Idaho Hist. Soc., Utah Hist. Soc., Alpha Tau Alpha, Phi Delta Kappa, Rotary Internat. Mem. Ch. of Jesus Christ of Latter-Day Saints. Home: 1653 Cornerstone Dr South Jordan UT 84095-5501 Office: Salt Lake Community Coll 4600 S Redwood Rd Salt Lake City UT 84123-3197

CARNAHAN, ROBERT PAUL, civil engineer, educator, researcher, consultant; b. Bradenton, Fla., July 22, 1936; s. Robert Dewey and Marion (Wilbur) C.; m. Geraldine Schott, July 30, 1938; children: Robert P. Jr., Christopher T., Sean P. BCE, U. Fla., 1959; MS in Sanitary Engring., U. N.C., 1964; PhD, Clemson U., 1973. Registered profl. engr., Fla., Va., Md. Commd. 2d lt. U.S. Army, 1959, advanced through grades to lt. col., 1975; co. comdr. 92d Engring. Battalion, Ft. Bragg, N.C., 1960-61; project officer U.S. Environ. Hygiene Agy., Edgewood Arsenal, Md., 1961-63; instr. Med. Field Service Sch., San Antonio, 1966-68; sr. environ. engr. 20th Pvt. Med. Unit, Socialist Republic of Vietnam, 1968-69; project officer U.S. Army Med. Research and Devel. Command, Washington, 1973-75; project devel. officer U.S. Army Material Devel. and Research Ctr., Ft. Belvior, Va., 1975-79; divsn. chief EPA br. U.S. Army Med. Bioengring. Rsch. and Devel. Lab, Frederick, Md., 1979-80. Adj. research prof. dept. of chemistry Am. U., 1976-77; adj. prof. dept. civil, mech. and environ. engring. George Washington U., 1979-80; asst. prof. dept. civil engring. and mechs. U. South Fla., 1980-84; assoc. prof. dept. civil engring. and mechs. U. South Fla., 1984-89, prof. dept. civil engring. & mechs., 1989-93, assoc. dean rsch. Coll. of Engring., 1993—. Contbr. numerous articles to profl. jours. Decorated Legion of Merit, Bronze Star with oak leaf cluster, Meritorious Service Medal with oak leaf cluster, Army Commendation medal with oak leaf cluster; recipient Silver medal for research and devel. Am. Def. Preparedness Assn., Rsch. award U.S. Dept. of Army Rsch., Comdr.'s award for tech. Meradcom. Mem. ASCE, Nat. Soc. Profl. Engrs., Am. Inst. Chem. Engrs., Am. Chem. Soc., Water Pollution Control Fedn., Am. Water Works Assn., N.A. Membrane Soc., Internat. Desalination Assn., Am. Desalting Assn. (Hall of Fame 1998), Fla. Engring. Soc., Internat. Assn. Water Pollution Research, Am. Acad. Environ. Engrs. (cert.), Sigma Xi, Chi Epsilon, Tau Beta Pi. Democrat. Roman Catholic. Home: 506 Terrace Hill Dr Tampa FL 33617-3850 Office: U South Fla Coll Engring Rsch Office 4202 E Fowler Ave Tampa FL 33620-8000 E-mail: carnahan@eng.usf.edu., gcarnahan@msn.com.

CARNALL, GEORGE HURSEY, II, lawyer, business executive; b. Ft. Smith, Ark., Feb. 19, 1947; s. George and Kathleen (Browne) C.; m. Janet Spaulding, Aug. 28, 1971; children: Clayton Wilson, Abigail Browne, Kevin Joseph. BS in Econs. and Bus. Adminstrn., Millikin U., Decatur, Ill., 1969; JD, Vanderbilt U., 1974. Bar: Tenn. 1974, U.S. Dist. Ct. (we. dist.) Tenn. 1974. Assoc. Arnoult & May, Memphis, 1974-76, Watson Cox & Arnoult, Memphis, 1976-79; gen. counsel S.M.R. Enterprises, Memphis, 1980-82, pres., 1982-87; pres. internat. divsn. Fantastic Sam's Internat., Inc., Memphis, 1987-91; pres. LP Svcs., Inc., Memphis, 1992-97, Mid South FS, Inc., Olive Branch, Miss., 1997—, Carnall Franchise Group, Memphis, 1991—. Contbr. articles to legal jours., mags., newspapers. Bd. dirs. Teen Challenge, Memphis, 1982-87. Served with U.S. Army, 1969-71. Mem. ABA, Tenn. Bar Assn., Memphis Bar Assn., Shelby Bar Assn. Mem. Assembly of God Ch. Home: 6155 Timber Oaks Dr Olive Branch MS 38654-6935 Office: Carnall Franchise Group 6155 Timber Oaks Olive Branch MS 38654

CARNASE, THOMAS PAUL, graphic designer, typographic consultant; b. Bronx, N.Y., Sept. 15, 1939; Assoc. B.F.A., N.Y.C. Community Coll., 1959. Assoc. designer Sudler & Hennessey, Inc., N.Y.C., 1959-64; pres., designer Bonder & Carnase Studio, Inc., N.Y.C., 1964-68; v.p., ptnr. Lubalin, Smith, Carnase, Inc., N.Y.C., 1969-79; pres. Carnase, Inc., N.Y.C., 1979—, Carnase Computer Typography, N.Y.C., 1979—, World Typeface Ctr., Inc., N.Y.C., 1981—. Mem. adv. com. N.Y.C. Community Coll., 1977— ; guest lectr./juror art dirs. clubs, schs., univs. throughout world Exhibited in group show Whitney Mus. Am. Art, N.Y.C.; editor Ligature jour., 1981— ; designer numerous typefaces; represented in permanent collection at Cooper Hewitt Nat. Design Mus. Recipient award of Excellence, Communication Arts mag.; cert. of Distinction Creativity mag. Mem. N.Y. Art Dirs. Club, N.Y. Type Dirs. Club, Soc. Publ. Designers, Am. Inst. Graphic Arts Office: Carnase Inc 21 Dorset Rd Scarsdale NY 10583

CARNEAL, GEORGE UPSHUR, lawyer; b. N.Y.C., May 31, 1935; AB, Princeton U., 1957; LLB, U. Va., 1961. Bar: Va. 1961, D.C. 1962. Law clk. to judge U.S. Ct. Appeals, D.C. Circuit, 1961-62; asso. firm Hogan & Hartson, Washington, 1962-68, partner, 1973—. Spl. asst. to sec. Dept. Transp., Washington, 1969-70; gen. counsel FAA, Washington, 1970-73; lectr. Georgetown U. Law Ctr., 1965-68; chmn. bd. trustees D.C. Bar Clients Security Trust Fund, 1973-78; gen. counsel Nat. Aeronautic Assn., 1984—. Decisions editor: Va. Law Rev, 1960-61; contbr. articles to legal jours. Bd. govs. Flight Safety Found., 1982-95; mem. exec. com. Princeton U. Alumni Coun., 1984-87; bd. dirs. Nat. Aviation Rsch. Inst., 2001-03. Mem. ABA, Fed. Bar Assn., Raven Soc., Order of Coif. Clubs: Princeton (pres. 1984-86), Aero (pres. 1982) (Washington), Metropolitan, Chevy Chase. Office: Hogan & Hartson 555 13th St NW Washington DC 20004-1161 E-mail: gucarneal@hhlaw.com.

CARNECCHIA, BALDO M., JR., lawyer; b. Hackensack, N.J., Sept. 2, 1947; s. Baldo M. Carnecchia and Cleo (Gerhart) Harper; children: Brian B., Justin W., Laura A. BS, Pa. State U., 1969; JD, Villanova U., 1972; LLM, Harvard U., 1973. Bar: Pa. 1972, U.S. Dist. Ct. (ea. dist.) Pa., U.S. Ct. Appeals (3d cir.) 1973, U.S. Supreme Ct. 1994. Legal writing asst. Boston U., 1973; assoc. Montgomery, McCracken, Walker & Rhoads, Phila., 1973-79, ptnr., 1979—. Adj. prof. law Villanova (Pa.) Law Sch.; mem. corp. exec. bd. Phila. Mus. of Art; mem. legal com. of Wharton/Spencer Stuart Directors Inst. Editor Villanova U. Law Rev., 1971-72. Mem. ABA, Pa. Bar Assn., Phila. Bar Assn. Clubs: Harvard, The Union League. Home: One Independence Place 241 S 6th St Unit 1608 Philadelphia PA 19106 Office: Montgomery McCracken Walker & Rhoads LLP 123 S Broad St Fl 24 Philadelphia PA 19109-1099 E-mail: baldo@mmwr.com.

CARNEIRO, MERVYN JOSEPH, mechanical engineer; b. Jabalpur, India, May 4, 1966; s. Felix Philip and Verona (Fernandes) C.; m. Smita Anne Maria Carneiro, Sept. 9, 1995; children, Ana Denise, Nikhil Felix. BS in Mech. Engring., Jabalpur U., 1989; MS, U. Wis., Milw., 1992. Cer. Engr.-in-tng., certify Assoc. Safety Professional. Design engr. Larsen and Toubro Ltd., Bombay, 1989-90; project engr. Safety Cons. Engrs., Schaumburg, Ill., 1992-95; process safety specialist Chilworth Tech., Monmouth Junction, N.J., 1995-2000; sr. process engr. Eli Lilly & Co., Lafayette, Ind., 2000—. Contbr. articles to profl. jours. Mem. Phi Kappa Phi. Office: Eli Lilly and Co 1650 Lilly Rd Lafayette IN 47909-1923 E-mail: m.carneiro@lilly.com.

CARNEIRO, ROBERT LEONARD, museum curator, anthropologist; b. N.Y.C., June 4, 1927; s. Anthony Mario and Serafina (Garrigo) C.; m. Barbara Ora Bode, Aug. 7, 1980; 1 child, Brett Rodrigo. BA, U. Mich., 1949, MA, 1952, PhD, 1957. Instr. anthropology U. Wis., Madison, 1956-57; asst. curator anthropology Am. Mus. Natural History, N.Y.C., 1957-63, assoc. curator anthropology, 1963-69, curator anthropology, 1969—. Ethnographic field work Kuikuru Indians, Brazil, 1953-54, 75, Amahuaca Indians, Peru, 1960-61, Yanomamo Indians, Venezuela, 1975; vis. prof. UCLA, 1968, Pa. State U., University Park, 1973, U. Victoria, B.C., 1977; adj. prof. anthropology Columbia U., 1992—. Author: The Chiefdom: Precursor of the State, 1981, The Muse of History and the Science of Culture, 2000, Evolutionism in Cultural Anthropology: A Critical History, 2003; editor: Herbert Spencer: The Evolution of Society, 1967; co-editor: Essays in the Science Culture, 1960, Leslie A. White: Ethnological Essays, 1987. Recipient Monks Meml. prize Inst. for Humane Studies, 1973. Fellow AAAS (chmn., nominating com. sect. H 1982-83), Am. Anthrop. Assn., N.Y. Acad. Scis. (vice chmn., chmn. anthropology sect. 1981-83, 83-85); mem. Nat. Acad. Scis. Achievements include formulation of one of the leading theories of the origin of the state. Office: Am Mus Natural History Central Pk W At 79th St W New York NY 10024 E-mail: carneiro@amnh.org.

CARNEIRO, RONALDO DOS SANTOS, surgeon; b. Rio de Janeiro, Mar. 17, 1946; m. Mary Alice Schuch; 3 children. BS, Cath. U. Rio Grande do Sul, Porto Alegre, Brazil, 1964; MD, Fed. U. Rio Grande do Sul, Porto Alegre, 1970. Diplomate Am. Bd. Plastic Surgery, Am. Bd. Surgery of the Hand; lic. physician, Brazil; lic. physician, surgeon, Pa., Calif. Intern Emergency Hosp. of Porto Alegre, Fla., 1968-69; preceptor dept. thoracic surgery Cath. U., Rio de Janeiro, 1969; preceptor in hand surgery Santa Casa Hosp., Rio de Janeiro, 1969; intern, resident Union Meml. Hosp., Balt., 1971-75, preceptor in hand surgery, 1975; resident in plastic surgery Allentown (Pa.) and Sacred Heart Hosp. Ctr., 1975; fellow in hand surgery dept. orthop. Jackson Meml. Hosp. and U. Miami (Fla.) Affiliated Hosps., 1977; maytag fellow in plastic surgery, fellow in exptl. microsurg U. Miami Sch. Medicine, 1978, assoc. prof. dept. orthop. and rehab., 1987, assoc. prof. clin. surgery, 1989-92; instr. hand surgery dept. orthop. Med. Sch. of U. Rio Grande do Sul, 1979-85; chief of hand surgery Hosp. Independencia, Porto Alegre, 1979-85; pvt. practice Western Hand Ctr., Downey, Calif., 1985-87; chief sect. hand surgery dept. plastic surgery Cleveland Clinic Naples, Fla., chmn. divsn. surgery, 2000—02, chief dept. hand surgery. Tchg. asst. lab. classes and rsch. Physiology Exptl. Inst., Med. Sch. Fed. U. of Rio Grande do Sul, 1967-68; with microsurgery lab. Union Meml. Hosp., Balt., 1974-75, U. Miami, 1978; instr. orthop. residents and med. students in hand surgery svc. dept. orthop. and rehab., U. Miami Sch. Medicine, 1987-91; vis. prof. Louisville Inst. Hand and Microsurgery, 1986; illustrious vis. prof. Sindicato Dos Medicos de Santa Maria, Brazil, 1989; internat. invited prof. IX Bolivian Nat. Meeting Orthop. and Traumatology, 1990, XVI Ecuadorian Nat. Meeting Orthop. and Traumatology, 1990, Venezuelan Nat. Meeting Hand Surgery, 1990, 1st Nat. Panamanian Congress, 1991, XVII Nat. Meeting Colombian Soc. Surgery of the Hand, 1990, XXV Regional Meeting So. Br. Brazilian Soc. Surgery of the Hand, 1st Ann. Internat. Meeting of Orthop. in Panama, 1992; cons. Children's Med. Svcs., Fla., 1987; presenter in field. Contbr. numerous articles to profl. jours. Named 1 of Best Drs. in Am., S.E. Region, 1996-97, 1998; rsch. grantee Biomatrix, Inc., U. Miami, 1987-88. Mem. Am. Soc. Surgery of the Hand, Brazilian Hand Soc. (pres. so. br. 1985), Brazilian Plastic Surgery Soc., Brazilian Soc. for Surgery of the Hand, Brazilian Med. Soc., Colombian Soc. Hand Surgery, Ecuadorian Soc. Orthop., Internat. Fedn. Socs. for Surgery of the Hand (com on infections of the hand), Venezuelan Soc. Hand Surgery, Fla. Hand Soc., Soc. Orthop. Surgeons De Santa Cruz De La Sierra Bolivia, S.Am. Hand Soc. (hon.). Office: Cleve Clinic Fla 6101 Pine Ridge Road Ext Naples FL 34119-3900 Office Fax: 941-348-4345.

CARNER, CHARLES ROBERT, JR., screenwriter, director; b. Chgo., Apr. 30, 1957; s. Charles Robert Carner Sr. and Barbara (Shields) Traeger. BA, Columbia Coll., 1978. Asst. to dir. TV show Dummy, Chgo., 1978; casting asst. film My Bodyguard, Chgo., 1979; story editor Tony Bill Prodns., Venice, Calif., 1979-81; screenwriter Fred Weintraub Prodns., Beverly Hills, Calif., 1981-82, Catalina Prodn. Group, Sherman Oaks, Calif., 1983-84, Trian Prodns./CBS-TV, Los Angeles, 1984-85; screenwriter, dir. Tristar Prodns., Los Angeles, 1985-89. Author: (screenplays) Seduced, 1985, Gymkata, 1985, Let's Get Harry, 1986, Blind Fury, 1988, Eyes of a Witness, 1991; writer, dir. TV series Midnight Caller, 1990, Reasonable Doubts, 1992, The Untouchables, 1993, TV movie A Killer Among Friends, 1992, One Woman's Courage, 1994, Vanishing Point, 1997, The Fixer, 1997, Who Killed Atlanta's Children?, 1999, Crossfire Trail, 2000, Crhsitmas Rush, 2002, Judas, 2003. Active East African Wildlife Soc., Kenya, Los Angeles, 1984—. Recipient Best Student Film award Chgo. Internat. Film Festival, 1978. Mem. NRA (life), Writers Guild Am., Sierra Club (life). Roman Catholic.

CARNER, GEORGE, foreign service executive, economic strategist; b. N.Y.C., Sept. 2, 1945; s. Joseph Carner Ribalta and Esther Cadefau; m. Michele Colette Delamotte, Apr. 20, 1968; children: Shawn L., Deric A. BA in Internat. Affairs, U. N.C., 1965; postgrad., Inst. Polit. Sci. La Sorbonne, Paris, 1966; MA in Internat. Affairs, George Washington U., 1971; student, Fgn. Svc. Inst., 1975. Internat. trade specialist U.S. Dept. Commerce, Washington, 1967-71; asst. program officer Agy. for Internat. Devel., Rabat, Morocco, 1971-75, dep. program officer Kabul, Afghanistan, 1976-79, program planning officer Manila, 1979-82, officer-in-charge India Washington, 1982-84, chief policy plan/eval. DP/AFR, 1984-86, dep. mission dir. Dakar, Senegal, 1986-88, mission dir. Tunis, Tunisia, 1988-91, Antan, Madagascar, 1991-94, Managua, Nicaragua, 1994-98, Guatemala City, Guatemala, 1998—2002; U.S. rep to OECD/DAC Paris, 2003—. Speaker, panelist Nat. Assn. of Schs. Pub. Affairs and Adminstrn., Honolulu and N.Y.C., 1981, 83, Harvard U., Boston, 1984. Contbr. articles to profl. jours. and procs. Recipient Superior Honor award Agency for Internat. Devel., Washington, 1978, Presdl. Meritorious Svc. awards The White House, 1987, 2000. Mem. Am. Fgn. Svcs. Assn., East-West Ctr., Rotary. Avocations: listening to jazz, art, scuba diving, nature walks. Address: Apartado de Correos 263 17200 Palafrugell, Girona Spain

CARNER, WILLIAM JOHN, banker; b. Springfield, Mo., Aug. 9, 1948; s. John Wilson and Willie Marie (Moore) C.; m. Dorothy Jean Edwards, June 12, 1976; children: Kimberly Jean, John Edwards Carner. AB, Drury Coll., 1970; MBA, U. Mo., 1972, PhD, 1989. Mktg. rep. 1st Nat. Bank Memphis, 1972-73; asst. br. mgr. Bank of Am., L.A., 1973-74; dir. mktg. Commerce Bank, Springfield, 1974-76; affiliate mktg. mgr. 1st Union Bancorp., St. Louis, 1976-78; pres. Carner & Assocs., Springfield, 1977—. Exec. v.p. Exch. Resources Ltd., Atlanta, 1992-94; pres. Carner Info. Resources, Inc., 1995—; instr. Drury Coll., 1975, 84-86, U. Mo., Columbia, 1986-88; asst. prof. S.W. Mo. State U., 1988-90; assoc. prof. St. Edwards U., 1991-96; adj. asst. prof. U. Tex., 1992—; bd. dirs. Ozark Pub. Telecom., Inc., 1982-88, sec., 1984-85, treas., 1985-86, vice chmn., 1986-87, chmn., 1987-88; sr. lectr. U. Tex., 1999—. Bd. dirs. Am. Cancer Soc., Greene County, Mo., 1974-82, crusade chmn., 1982-83, publicity chmn., 1974-78; bd. dirs. Springfield Muscular Dystrophy Assn., 1975-76, Greater Ozarks coun. Camp Fire Girls, 1980-81, Chameleon Puppet Theatre, 1988-89, Downtown Springfield Assn., 1989-90. Mem. Bank Mktg. Assn. (svc. mem. coun. 1985-88), Mo. Bankers Assn. (instr. Gen. Banking Sch.), Fin. Instns. Mktg. Assn. (chmn. svc. mem. com.), Drury Coll. Alumni Assn. (v.p. 1985-86, pres. 1986-87). Clubs: Hickory Hills Country, Univ. of Tex. Lodges: Masons, Shriners. Democrat. Mem. Christian Ch. (Disciples Of Christ). Home: 2910 Montebello Ct Austin TX 78746-6816 Office: PO Box 160757 Austin TX 78716-0757

CARNES, BRUCE ALFRED, gerontologist, researcher; b. Duncan, Okla., June 15, 1950; s. Mark Barnett and Donna Mae Carnes; m. Linda Lee Eigenberg, Dec. 5, 1948; children: Laurel, Rachael, Nathan. BS cum laude, U. Utah, 1973; MS, U. Houston, 1975; MA, PhD, U. Kans., 1980. From rsch. assoc. to biologist & biostatistician Argonne Nat. Lab., Argonne, Ill., 1980—88, biologist & biostatistician, 1988—99; sr. rsch. scientist Nat. Opinion Rsch. Ctr. U. Chgo., Chgo., 1999—. Rsch. assoc. Population Rsch. Ctr. Ctr. on Aging U. Chgo., Chgo., 1995—98; mem. com. Nat. Coun. Radiation Protection and Measurements Task Group on Interspecies Extrapolation, 1997—. Author: Quest for Immortality: Science at the Frontiers of Aging, 2001; co-author (with S. Jay Olshansky): A Journey Through the Interdisciplinary Landscape of Biodemography, 2003; contbr. articles to profl. jours. Named to Achievements Hall of Fame, Duncan, Okla., 2003; grantee, Found. Eviron. Edn., 1974, Dept. Energy, 1985—87, 1986—91, Social Security Adminstrn., 1994—95, NIH, 1999—, NASA, 1999—; scholar Athletic scholarship, 1968. Mem.: AAAS, Gerontological Soc. Am., Sigma Xi. Home: 10 S 567 Whittington Lane Naperville IL 60564 Office: Nat Opinion Rsch Ctr Univ Chgo 1155 E 60th St Chicago IL 60637 E-mail: bruce@src.uchicago.edu.

CARNES, BRUCE M. federal agency administrator; b. Xenia, Ohio, May 19, 1944; married; 2 children. BA, U. Colo., 1966; MA, U. Ind., 1969, PhD, 1971. Planning staff, program officer U.S. Dept. Health, Edn. & Welfare, Washington, 1976; with NEH, Washington, 1979-85; asst. Sec. of Edn., Washington, 1985-86; dep. undersec. Dept. Edn., Washington, 1986—; Chief Financial Officer & Dir Dept Energy, Mgt, Budget and Eval, Washington, 2001—. Office: Dept Energy Mgt Budget and Eval 1000 Independance Ave SW Washington DC 20585-0001

CARNES, EDWARD E. federal judge; b. Albertville, Ala., 1950; BS, U. Ala., Tuscaloosa, 1972; JD, Harvard U., 1975. Asst. Ala. atty. gen. Office Atty. Gen., 1975—92; cir. judge U.S. Ct. Appeals (11th cir.), Montgomery, Ala., 1992—. Office: US Courthouse Frank M Johnson Jr Fed Bldg 15 Lee St Ste 408 Montgomery AL 36104-4096 also: Elbert P Tuttle US Ct Appeals Bldg 56 Forsyth St NW Atlanta GA 30303*

CARNES, JAMES EDWARD, technology executive; b. Cumberland, Md., Sept. 27, 1939; s. Roy Clifton and Alta (Wigfield) C.; m. Nancy Louise Zolto, Nov. 27, 1977; 1 child, Gillian. BS in Engring. Sci., Pa. State U., 1961; MA in Elec. Engring., Princeton U., 1967, PhD in Elec. Engring., 1970; PhD (hon.), Thomas Edison State Coll., 1994, Kean U., 1998. Mem. tech. staff RCA Labs., Princeton, NJ, 1969-77; mgr. tech. application RCA Consumer Electronics, Indpls., 1977-80, dir. new products lab, 1980-82, div. v.p. engring., 1982-87; v.p. consumer electronics and info. scis. David Sarnoff Rsch. Ctr. (subs. SRI Internat.), Princeton, NJ, 1987-90, pres., COO, 1990-93, pres., CEO, 1993—2002, sr. advisor, 2002—; sr. v.p. SRI Internat., 1990-95; chmn. bd. Sensar, Inc., Princeton, NJ, 1992-2000, Orchid Biocomputer Inc., 1995-97, Sarnoff Digital Comm., Inc., 1996-97. Dir. Sarnoff Real Time Inc., Satif, Inc., Delsys Pharm. Corp., Orchid Biocomputer, Inc., Sarnoff Digital Comms., Nova Corp., SRI Internat., C-Cor.net; short course lectr. UCLA, 1978-81, Am. U. Washington, 1976, Ctrl. Poly. Inst., London, 1974. Contbr. articles to profl. jours. Campaign chmn. Princeton Area United Way, 1992, bd. dirs., 1992-94, 1st v.p., 1993-94; chmn. bd. trustees United Way Greater Mercer County, 1994-96; chmn. sci. adv. bd. Rider Coll., 1990-92; trustee Rider U., 1993-2002, Ind. Coll. Fund. N.J., 1990-96, Thomas Edison State Coll. Found., 1992—, Am. Boychoir Sch., 1995-2002, Regional Planning Partnership, 1997-2002; mem. bd . overseers N.J. Inst. Tech., 1993-98; co-chair Prosperity N.J., 2000-02. Lt. USN, 1961-65. Recipient David Sarnoff Outstanding Achievement award RCA, 1981, Engr. of Yr. award Ctrl. N.J. Engring. Coun., 1991, Humanitarian award NCCJ, 1994, Citizen of Yr. award Mercer County C. of C., 1996, N.J. Tech. Coun. High Tech. Hero award, 1999, N.J. Network Chmn.'s award, 2000; named to Jr. Achievement Bus. Hall of Fame, 1998, Am. Electronics Assn. N.J. High Tech Hall of Fame, 1999; Alumni fellow, 2003. Fellow IEEE (Centennial medal 1984, Region I award 1993); mem. Am. Electronics Assn., Nat. Acad. Engring., Pa. State U. Alumni Assn. (coun., exec. com., Outanding Engr. Alumnus award 1992, Pres. and Exec. dir. award 1995, Disting. Alumnus award 1996, v.p. 1997-99, pres. 1999-2001, alumni fellow 2003). Achievements include inventor in field. Avocations: flying, golf. Home: 117 Spencer Ln State College PA 16801 E-mail: jim.carnes@psualum.com.

CARNES, JOSEPH SYDNEY, clergyman; b. Memphis, Dec. 2, 1929; s. Samuel Leslye and Marion Rachel (Weaver) C.; m. Annie Frank Rutledge, June 22, 1952; children: Jane Ann, Joseph Sydney Jr., James Rutledge, John David. BS, Memphis State U., 1956; MDiv, Tex. Christian U., 1962, D Ministry, 1979. Ordained to ministry Christian Ch. (Disciples of Christ), 1949; cert. pastoral counselor Parkland Hosp., Dallas. Min. of membership 1st Christian Ch, Eugene, Oreg., 1962-65, sr. min. Nampa, Idaho, 1965-72, Lakeview Christian Ch., Dallas, 1972-81, Oak Cliff Christian Ch., Dallas, 1981—. Pres. Christian Chs. in Idaho, Boise, 1971. Co-author: Communion Meditations, 1966. Founding dir. Nampa Christian Housing, 1967; bd. dirs. Mercy Hosp., Nampa, 1968-72, Idaho Mental Health Dept., 1969-72. Col. Tex. State Guard, chief chaplains, 1972-94. Recipient Disting. Min. of Yr. award, Tex. Christian U., 2003. Mem. Mil. Chaplains Assn. U.S.A. (local pres. 1972—), Masons (33d

degree, chaplain 1988-95), Lions (local pres. 1981-82), Order Ea. Star. Republican. Avocations: fishing, hunting, world travel. Home: Wedgewood Twr Apt 615 2511 Wedglea Dr Dallas TX 75211-2041 Office: 1222 W Kiest Blvd Dallas TX 75224-3233

CARNES, JULIE ELIZABETH, judge; b. Atlanta, Oct. 31, 1950; m. Stephen S. Cowen. AB summa cum laude, U. Ga., 1972, JD magna cum laude, 1975. Bar: Ga. 1975. Law clk. to Hon. Lewis R. Morgan U.S. Ct. Appeals (5th cir.), 1975-77; spl. counsel U.S. Sentencing Commn., 1989, commr., 1990-96; asst. U.S. Atty. U.S. Dist. Ct. (no. dist.) Ga., Atlanta, 1978-90, judge, 1992—. Office: US Courthouse 75 Spring St SW Ste 2167 Atlanta GA 30303-3309

CARNES, LA ZETTA, educator; b. Dallas, Dec. 1, 1933; d. Clint Leo and Jimmie Lee Rosser C. BA, U. Dallas, 1969; MEd, East Tex. State U., 1978; postgrad., Richmond Coll., London, 1984, Tex. A&M U., 2000. Tchr. Mineral Wells (Tex.) Ind. Sch. Dist., 1969-71, St. Mary's, Sherman, Tex., 1972-73, Grayson County Jr. Coll., Sherman, Tex., 1986, Whitewright (Tex.) Ind. Sch. Dist., 1973-80, Bells (Tex.) Ind. Sch. Dist., 1973-95, Sherman Ind. Sch. Dist., 1998—. Author of poems. Mem. AAUW, United Daus. Confederacy, Tex. Ret. Assn., Grayson County Retired Sch. Personnel. Home: 1508 N Highland Ave Sherman TX 75092-3500

CARNES, LAURA, financial analyst; b. Jefferson, S.C., Aug. 13, 1936; d. John Howard and Lottie Lula (Killough) Carnes; m. John Beasley Benton (dec. 1970); m. Elton Edwin Wolfe, Jr., Apr. 2, 1972 (div. 1976); m. John Houston Hill, Oct. 3, 1990 (div. 1998); m. R. W. Briggs, Mar. 25, 2001. AD in Criminal Justice, U. S.C., AD in Liberal Arts, 1957, postgrad., 1998—; student, Lenoir Rhyne Coll., 1956. Cert. nursing asst., 1978. Credit clk. Sears Roebuck, Florence, SC, 1954-55; receptionist Pilot Life, Charlotte, NC, 1958-60, Am. Textile Mfrs. Inst., Charlotte, 1961-67; sec. Chas. T. Main Inc., Charlotte, 1961-67; treas., mgr. Chipper Svc., Lancaster, SC, 1967-68; credit mgr. Buensod divsn. Aeronca Inc., Pineville, NC, 1968-72; export internat. credit analyst Scovill Inc., Monroe, NC, 1972-87; bus. specialist broker CPI Assocs., Lancaster, 1987-88; internat. credit analyst John Deere Consumer Products, Inc., Charlotte, 1989—2001. Pres. Lancaster County Heart Assn., 1981; mem. Friends Andrew Jackson State Pk. Mem.: Nat. Assn. Credit Mgmt., Credit and Internat. Bus., Internat. Assn. Execs. Fin., Leaf and Petal Garden Club, Evening Garden Club (pres. 1981—83), Lancaster County Coun. Garden Clubs (pres. 1991—92), Am. Legion Aux. (Zone 2 v.p.). Democrat. Baptist. Avocations: reading, gardening, travel, swimming, public speaking. Home: 1832 Windsor Drive Lancaster SC 29720-1827

CARNESALE, ALBERT, academic administrator; b. Bronx, NY, July 2, 1936; m. Robin Gerber, Apr. 6, 2002; children: Keith, Kimberly. BME, Cooper Union, 1957; MS, Drexel U., 1961, LLD (hon.), 1993; PhD, N.C. State U., 1966, LLD (hon.), 1997; AM (hon.), Harvard U., 1979; ScD (hon.), N.J. Inst. Technology, 1984. Prof. N.C. State U., Raleigh, 1962—69, 1972—74; chief Def. Weapons Systems U.S. Arms Control and Disarmament Agy., Washington, 1969—72; prof. John F. Kennedy Sch. of Govt. Harvard U., Cambridge, Mass., 1974—97, acad. dean John F. Kennedy Sch. of Govt., 1981—91, dean John F. Kennedy Sch. of Govt., 1991—95, provost, Lucius N. Littauer Prof. Pub. Policy and Adminstrn., 1994—97; chancellor UCLA, 1997—. Author: Nuclear Power Issues and Choices: Report of the Nuclear Energy Policy Study Group, 1977, Living with Nuclear Weapons, 1983, Hawks, Doves and Owls: An Agenda for Avoiding Nuclear War, 1985, Superpower Arms Control: Setting the Record Straight, 1987, Fateful Visions: Avoiding Nuclear Catastrophe, 1988; co-author: New Nuclear Nations: Consequences for US Policy, 1993. Recipient Gano Dunn award Outstanding Profl. Achievement, Cooper Union, N.Y.C. Fellow: Am. Acad. Arts and Scis.; mem.: L.A. World Affairs Coun., Internat. Inst. for Strategic Studies, Coun. on Fgn. Rels. Office: UCLA Office of Chancellor 405 Hilgard Ave Los Angeles CA 90095-1405

CARNESI, KENNETH BRIAN, lawyer; b. N.Y.C., May 29, 1953; s. Frank and Angela (Dinardo) C.; m. Daria Mary Chmil, July 22, 1978; children: Kenneth Brian Jr., Katherine Elizabeth. BA, Bklyn. Coll., 1975; MPS, L.I. U., 1977; JD, N.Y. Law Sch., 1982. Bar: N.Y. 1983. Bank officer Chemical Bank, N.Y.C., 1978-82, counsel, 1982-84; ptnr. Carnesi & Assocs., Garden City, N.Y., 1984—; pres. Banfinanz Internat., Inc., N.Y.C., 1996—. Bd. dirs. The Prime Mint, Inc., N.Y.C., FAS Fragrances, Inc., N.Y.C., Granite State Mint, Inc., Amherst, N.H.. Contbr. articles to profl. jours. Recipient Elsberg award, N.Y. Law Sch., N.Y.C., 1982, Human Rights Jour. award, 1982, Businessman of Yr. award, U.S. Presdl. Bus. Commn., 2003. Mem. Nassau County Bar Assn., ABA, Am. Mgmt. Assn. Republican. Roman Catholic. Office: 1225 Franklin Ave Garden City NY 11530

CARNESOLTAS, ANA-MARIA, lawyer; b. Havana, Cuba, Feb. 9, 1948; came to U.S., 1962; d. Manuel Ramon and Zenaida de las Mercedes C.; 1 child, Caroline. BA, U. Calif., Santa Barbara, 1970; JD, Loyola U., L.A., 1978. Bar: Calif. 1978, Fla. 1979. Dep probation officer Probation Dept., Santa Barbara, Calif., 1970-73; personnel analyst Dept. Personnel, L.A., 1973-77; dep. dist. atty. Dist. Atty.'s Office, L.A., 1978-80; asst. U.S. atty. U.S. Atty.'s Office, Miami, Fla., 1980-82; pvt. practice law, Miami, 1982-83, Coral Gables, Fla., 1985-89; asst. city atty. City Atty.'s Office, Miami, 1983-85; judge Dade (Fla.) County Ct., 1989-93; pvt. practice, 1993—; lectr. YMCA, Miami, 1983-89; adj. prof. Fla. Internat. U.; prof. Miami-Dade C.C., 1989-92; hearing officer Dade County Pub. Schs., Miami, 1985-89; legal commentator Sta. TeleMiami, Fla., 1997—; legal commenrator WCMQ, Miami, 1993-97. Bd. dirs. Am. Heart Assn., M iami, 1983-86, YWCA, 1985-89, Alzheimer's Disease and Related Disorders Assn., 1987. Named Disting. Advocate, Loyola Law Sch., 1978. Mem. Nat. Assn. Women Judges (outreach com., task force on minority concerns, internat. community outreach com.), Conf. County Ct. Judges (edn. com., small claims com., civic proc. rules com.), Calif. Probation Parole and Corrections Assn. (v.p. 1972-73), Cuban Am. Attys. Council (sec. 1979-80), Cuban Am. Bar Assn. (dir. 1983, 88, sec. 1984), Dade County Bar Assn., ABA, Fla. Assn. Women Lawyers, Assn. Trial Lawyers Am., Fed. Bar Assn., Latin Bus. and Profl. Women's Club (pres. 1984-85, v.p.), Cuban Women's Club. Republican. Roman Catholic. Office: 1900 S Bayshore Dr Miami FL E-mail: amc4/aw@aol.com.

CARNEVALE, LOUIS, civil engineer, inventor; b. Rome, Sept. 16, 1954; s. Loreto and Josephine Carnevale; m. Elizabeth T. Wrobel, Sept. 27, 1991; children: Ingrid, Patrick, Joseph. BA in Liberal Arts magna cum laude, Coll. at Old Westbury, N.Y., 1984; BS in Civil Engring. cum laude, U. Buffalo, 1989. Profl. engr., N.Y., Ariz. Project mgr. Ea. Concrete Corp., Westhampton Beach, N.Y., 1989-91; civil engr. Suffolk County Water Authority, Oakdale, N.Y., 1991—. Author: How to Set Your VCR Clock, 1991; inventor detachable all terrain trailer. Cpl. USMC, 1977-81. Mem. Chi Epsilon. Avocations: camping, fishing, canoeing, hiking, running. Office: Suffolk County Water Authority Engine Dept PO Box 37 Oakdale NY 11769-0037 E-mail: lcarneva@suffolk.lib.ny.us.

CARNEY, ANDREA, public relations executive; BA in English Lit. and Journalism, U. N.H. With Franson & Assocs.; joined Infocom, 1984, Brodeur Worldwide, Boston, 1987, C.E.O. Began career in New England Newspapers and magazines. Mem. Brodeur Worldwide Global Bd. Avocations: family activities, outdoor activities. Office: Brodeur Worldwide 855 Boylston St Boston MA 02116-2622 Fax: 617-587-2828.

CARNEY, ANN VINCENT, retired secondary education educator; b. Slippery Rock, Pa., Feb. 17, 1933; d. Arthur Porter and Leila Felicia (Watson) Vincent; m. Charles Lucien Carney Jr., Dec. 15, 1954 (div. 1974); children: Adrienne Ann, Stephen Vincent. BS, Drexel Inst. Tech., 1955; MEd, U. Pitts., 1972. Cert. tchr., reading specialist, Pa. Tchr. English Allegheny Valley Sch. Dist., Springdale, Pa., 1957-62; reading specialist Gateway Sch. Dist., Monroeville, Pa., 1972-98. Mem. AAUW, Internat. Reading Assn., Keystone State Reading Assn., Three Rivers Reading Coun., Phi Kappa Phi, Omicron Nu. Republican. Avocations: reading, travel, needlework, cooking, gardening. Home: 4013 Impala Dr Pittsburgh PA 15239-2705

CARNEY, BRADFORD GEORGE YOST, lawyer, educator; b. Oct. 25, 1950; s. Blanchard Donald and Anne Carolyn (Yost) C.; m. Gail Elaine Hasson, Jan. 6, 1973: children: Jason Bradford, Brandon Burroughs. BA, Washington Coll., 1972; JD, U. Balt., 1976. Bar: Md. 1977, U.S. Dist. Ct. Md. 1978, U.S. Supreme Ct. 1982. Ptnr. Callahan, Calwell, Laudeman, Balt., 1982-87, Weinberg and Green, Balt., 1987-96; of counsel Royston, Mueller, McLean & Reid LLP, Towson, Md., 1996—. Asst. prof. law Villa Julie Coll., Stevenson, Md., 1983-97, assoc. prof., 1997—. Bd. trustees Boys' Latin Sch., Md., 1988-93. Mem. ABA, Nat. Assn. Criminal Def. Lawyers, Md. State Bar Assn., Md. Criminal Def. Attys. Assn., Balt. County Bar Assn., Balt. City Bar Assn., U. Balt. Alumni Assn. (bd. govs. 1984-87), Boys' Latin Sch. Alumni Assn. (bd. dirs. 1983-, pres. 1986-88). Home: 474 Five Farms Ln Lutherville Timonium MD 21093-2954 Office: Royston Mueller McLean & Reid LLP 102 W Pennsylvania Ave Towson MD 21204-4526 E-mail: bcarney@rmmr.com.

CARNEY, DANIEL L. program and financial management consultant; b. Taunton, Mass., June 12, 1947; s. Lawrence Vincent and Jeannette B. (Piche) C.; m. Patricia Anne Morse, Feb. 14, 1970; children: Michael Sean, Jennifer Lynn. BS, USCG Acad., 1969; MBA in Fin. Mgmt., George Washington U., 1976; postgrad., Def. Sys. Mgmt. Coll., 1991. Cert. govt. fin. mgr., 1996. With USCG, 1969-92, exec. officer group Sandy Hook, 1982-86, exec. officer supply ctr., 1986-89, project officer, chief of logistics, fleet renovation & modernization Washington, 1991-92; asst. program mgr. sys. to automate and integrate logistics Dept. Transp., Booz Allen & Hamilton, McLean, Va., 1992-93; bus. mgr. Navy extremely high frequency satellite program Dept. Def., Booz Allen & Hamilton, Crystal City, Va., 1993, fin. mgr. composite healthcare sys. Falls Church, Va., 1993-97; mem. team to replace fin. mgmt. info. sys. for U.S. Senate Booz Allen & Hamilton, Falls Church, Va., 1997-2000; team leader for the decennial census Bur. Census, 2000—; CFO St. Mary's County Md. Pub. Schs., 2000—. Fin. advisor USCG Credit Union, Boston, 1977-79. Lt. Arnold Vol. Fire Dept., Md., 1993—, treas., 1994—; basketball coach Our Lady of Perpetual Help, Highlands, N.J., 1983-88. Mem. Am. Soc. Mil. Comptrollers. Roman Catholic. Avocations: basketball, travel. Home: 22784 Avenmar Dr Leonardtown MD 20650- Office: PO Box 641 Moakley St Leonardtown MD 20650 E-mail: d.carney@mail.smcps.k12.mil.us.

CARNEY, DEBORAH LEAH TURNER, lawyer; b. Great Bend, Kans., Aug. 19, 1952; d. Harold Lee and Elizabeth Lura Turner; m. Thomas J.T. Carney, Mar. 20, 1976; children: Amber Blythe, Sonia Briana, Ross Dillon. BA in Human Biology, Stanford U., 1974; JD, U. Denver, 1976. Bar: Kans. 1977, U.S. Dist. Ct. Kans. 1977, U.S. Ct. Appeals (10th cir.) 1982, Colo. 1984, U.S. Dist. Ct. Colo. 1984, U.S. Supreme Ct. 1989, U.S. Claims Ct. 1990. With Turner & Boisseau, Great Bend, 1976-84, of counsel, 1984-93; assoc. Lutz & Oliver, Arvada, Colo., 1984-85; prin. Deborah Turner Carney, P.C., Golden and Lakewood, Colo., 1985-92; shareholder Carney Law Office, Golden, Colo., 1992-95, owner, 1995—. Author (newsletter) Profl. Solutions, 1984, (chpt.) Courtroom Handbook, 1998; editor Apple Law newsletter, 1984-86; contbr. articles to profl. jours. Pres. Canyon Area Residents for the Environment (C.A.R.E.), 1998. Mem. Colo. Trial Lawyers Assn., 1st Jud. Dist. Bar Assn. (Colo.), Genesee Daytime Bookclub (co-chair 1997-98), Kiwanis (bd. dirs. Denver club 1988-90, trustee 1990-92, sec. 1992-93). Republican. Avocations: horses, dancing, computers. Office: 21789 Cabrini Blvd Golden CO 80401-9488 E-mail: deb@carneylaw.net.

CARNEY, DENNIS JOSEPH, former steel company executive, consulting company executive; b. Charleroi, Pa., Mar. 19, 1921; s. Walter Augustus and Ann (Nandor) C.; m. Virginia M. Horvath, June 12, 1943 (dec. Jan. 1984); children— Colleen A., Dennis Joseph, Glenn P., Lynn C., Dianne V. BS in Metallurgy, Pa. State U., 1942; Sc.D., Mass. Inst. Tech., 1949. With U.S. Steel Corp., Pitts., 1942-74, gen. supt., 1963-65, v.p. long range planning, 1965-68, v.p. applied research, 1968-72, v.p. research, 1972-74; v.p. ops. Wheeling-Pitts. Steel Corp., 1974-75, exec. v.p., dir., 1975-76, pres., 1976-85, chief operating officer, 1976-77, chief exec. officer, 1977-85, chmn. bd., 1978-85; ret., 1985; pres. Intra-Continental Cons. Co, Fort Lauderdale, Fla., 1985—. Author: (with others) Gases in Metals, 1956. Bd. dirs. Wheeling (W.Va.) Club. Served to lt. (j.g.) USNR, 1943-46. Fellow Am. Soc. Metals (Grossmann award Pitts. chpt. 1959, trustee 1972—); mem. Am., Brit., Internat. iron and steel insts., Am. Inst. Mining, Metall. and Petroleum Engrs. (McKune award 1951, Benjamin F. Fairless award 1978), Am. Iron and Steel Engrs., Sigma Xi, Tau Beta Pi, Sigma Nu. Clubs: South Hills Country (Pitts.), Duquesne (Pitts.) (dir.); Laurel Valley Country, Fox Chapel Country. Home and Office: 3900 N Ocean Dr Apt 3C Fort Lauderdale FL 33308-5936

CARNEY, HORACE R., JR., performing arts educator; b. Nashville, May 31, 1941; s. Horace Richard and Sallie Edward Carney; m. Waymon Ann Edge, May 20, 1943; children: Meishawn Anita, Horace R. III; m. Sharon Marcena Carr, July 27, 1954; children: Ebonique, Zenas. BA in Music, Fisk U., Nashville, 1964; MA in Music Theory, Eastman Sch. Music, Rochester, N.Y., 1967; PhD in Music Theory, U. Iowa, 1981. Music theory instr., dir. coll. choir Talladega Coll., Ala., 1965—77, 1981—83; chmn. music dept., dir. choral activities Lincoln U., Pa., 1983—86; minister of music, dir. choral activities Sixth Ave. Bapt. Ch., Birmingham, Ala., 1986—90; chmn. dept. music Ala. A&M U., Huntsville, 1990—. Bd. dirs. AAMU-UAH Insvc. Bd., Huntsville, Ala., 1995—2001; ent. Birmingham, 1993—; dir., founder Horace R. Carney Jr. Chorale, 1989—. Mem. NAACP, Birmingham. With USAR, 1959. Grantee Title III grantee, Ala. A&M U., 1992—95, 1998—2000. Mem.: Tech. Inst. Music Edn. Baptist. Avocations: music, music arranging. Office: Alabama A&M Univ PO Box 1925 Huntsville AL 35762

CARNEY, JOHN C., JR., lieutenant governor; b. Claymont, Del. m. Tracey Quillen; children: Sam, James. BA in English, Dartmouth Coll., 1978; MPA, U. Del. Assoc. dir. Cath. Youth Orgn., Wilmington; staff asst. U.S. Senator Joseph R. Biden, 1986-89; dep. chief adminstrv. officer New Castle County, 1989-94, acting dir. pub. works; dep. chief of staff Gov. Carper, 1994-97; sec. of fin. State of Del., 1997-2000, lt. gov., 2000—. Bd. dirs. Cath. Youth Orgn. Democrat. Office: Tatnall Bldg Dover DE 19901*

CARNEY, JOSEPH BUCKINGHAM, lawyer; b. Greensburg, Ind., July 8, 1928; s. Edward O. and Grace Rebecca (Buckingham) C.; m. Constance J. Caylor, July 8, 1950; children: Elizabeth, Joseph Buckingham Jr., Julia, Sarah. AB, DePauw U., 1950; LLB, Harvard U., 1953. Bar: D.C. 1953, Ind. 1953, U.S. Dist. Ct. (so. dist.) Ind. 1953, U.S. Supreme Ct. 1957, U.S. Ct. Appeals (7th cir.) 1961; ind. cert. mediator. Assoc. Hogg, Peters & Leonard, Ft. Wayne, Ind., 1953-54, Baker & Daniels, Indpls., 1957-62, ptnr., 1962-95, mem. mgmt. com., 1993-94, sec., 1994, of counsel, 1996—. Mem. lawyers com. Nat. Ctr. State Cts., Williamsburg, Va., 1985—; assoc. Environ. Law Inst., Washington. Chmn. bd. dirs. Parkinson Awareness Assn. Ctrl. Ind., Inc.; past pres. Interfaith Homes, Inc., Indpls.; past chmn., elder Northwood Christian Ch., Indpls. 1st lt. U.S. Army, 1954-57. Recipient Disting. Alumni award DePauw U., 1984. Mem. ABA, Ind. Bar Assn., Indpls. Bar Assn., Am. Judicature Soc., 7th Cir. Bar Assn. (pres. 1983-84), Univ. Club, Columbia Club, Contemporary, Lawyers Club Indpls. (past pres.), Phi Eta Sigma, Phi Gamma Delta (bd. dirs. 1974-78, sec. 1976-78, pres. 1980-82), Phi Gamma Delta Ednl. Found. (bd. dirs., pres. 1996-98). Avocations: scuba diving, travel, photography. Office: Baker & Daniels 300 N Meridian St Ste 2700 Indianapolis IN 46204-1782

CARNEY, KAREN ROSE, music educator, pianist; b. Canton, Ohio, Dec. 9, 1940; d. Alex and Rose (Burky) Winkelman; 1 child, Miles. BMus, Baldwin-Wallace Coll., 1961; postgrad., Case Western Res. U., 1961; MA in Music Edn., Ohio State U., 1980, PhD in Music Edn., 1983. Cert. music tchr., N.C., Ohio. Accompanist, staff musician dance dept. Ohio State U., Columbus, 1983-85; asst. prof. N.C. Wesleyan Coll., Rocky Mount, 1985-87, U. S.D., Vermillion, 1987-88; pianist, spl. events Ohio State U., Columbus, 1988-90; lectr., choir accompanist Fayetteville (N.C.) State U., 1990-91; instr. performing arts Meth. Coll., Fayetteville, N.C., 1990-91; asst. prof. Lincoln U., Pa., 1991-93; assoc. prof. Paine Coll., Augusta, Ga., 1993-95, Winston-Salem (N.C.) State U., 1995-99; elem. music tchr. New Hanover County Schs., Wilmington, N.C., 1999-2000; lectr. U. Ctrl. Ark., Conway, 2000-01; music tchr. K-8 Franklin Local Schs., Duncan Falls, Ohio, 2001—. PRAXIS item writer Ednl. Testing Svc., Princeton, N.J., 1997; com. music edn. UNC/NCCC Articulation Agreement, Chapel Hill, N.C., 1997; clinician Nat. Group Piano Symposium, U. Okla., Norman, 1985; judge music contests, Ohio, N.C., S.D. Vol. tchr., performer Winston-Salem/Forsyth County Pub. Schs., 1997-99; vol. pianist Baltic (Ohio) Country Manor, 1992-2000, nursing and retirement homes, Winston-Salem, 1995-98; guest organist, pianist various chs., N.C. and Ohio. Rsch. grantee Lilly-Lincoln U., 1992; recipient Cert. of Recognition Winston-Salem State U. Friends of O'Kelly Libr., 1997. Mem.: Music Tchrs. Nat. Assn. (profl. cert. in piano), Nat. Assn. Music Edn., Coll. Music Soc., Am. Fedn. Musicians, Am. Mensa, Pi Kappa Lambda, Mu Phi Epsilon. Home: 53 Wilson Rd Roseville OH 43777-1067 E-mail: kcarney@columbus.rr.com.

CARNEY, KATE, actor, director, educator, playwright, storyteller; b. Rice Lake, Wis., Aug. 2, 1933; d. Rexford Hugh and Margot Caroline (Haanstad) C. BS, U. Wis., 1955; MA, Mt. Holyoke Coll., 1958; postgrad, Centre du Théâtre Nationale, Aix, France, 1970, Columbia U., Case Western U., 1957-63. Creative arts fellow U. Colo., 1963; actress performing in London, Paris, Istanbul, Ankara, Tel Aviv and Nicosia, 1970-72. Tchr., dir., Hunter Coll., Henry St. Playhouse, SUNY, 1972-77, Purchase, U. Calif.-Santa Cruz, 1977-80; assoc. prof. dept. theatre Smith Coll., Northampton, Mass., 1980-82, Bklyn. Coll., 1983-87; tchr. Ensemble Studio Theatre Inst., 1987, Brandeis U., 1989-92, Pine Manor Coll., 1993-96; condr. workshops for profls. in U.S. and abroad, Coll. of Charleston, 1989, Marymount Manhattan Coll., 1988; organizer, trainer La Mama theatre groups, Paris and Tel Aviv; bd. dirs. Bear Rep. Theatre, 1977-79; performed with Open Theater, 1965-67; seminarian with Jerzy Grotowski, 1975, 79; actress Off Off-Broadway! An Anthology with Kay Carney, N.Y.C., Boston, Chgo., San Francisco, Vancouver, Balt., Phila. and various U.S. colls., 1973—, Tongues, 1985, Camptown Ladies, 1986, Age of Englightenment, 1986, Vacancy, 1987, Taste of Honey, 1988, N.Y.C., And A Nightingale Sang, 1992, My Fair Lady, 1992, Boston, Washed Up Middle Aged Women, 1993, Dr. Owens-Adair, 1994, Two Boston Immigrants, 1995, Heroic Women You Can Talk To, 1996, Annie Sullivan, 1997, Mary Lyon of Mount Holyoke, Mary Antin, Russian Immigrant, 1998, Oral Report, 1999, Alternative Lifestyle, 2000, Three Peat, 2001, Mrs. Rachel Walker, Witness to the Revolution, 2000, The Greek Myths, 2003; dir. Mourning Pictures, Broadway and Lenox Arts Ctrs., 1974, A Pretty Passion, Interart Theatre, N.Y.C., 1982, Quilt Pieces, theatre of Open Eye, N.Y.C., 1983, Superwoman Bites the Dust, Playwright's Platform, Boston, 1984, The Mothers, Ubu Repertory Theatre, 1987, Airport, Theater at St. Peter's, 1988, A Good Time, Playwright's Horizons, 1988, Sleep Disturbances, Am. Renaissance Theatre, 1989, Man with the Killer Pen, New Dramatists, 1991, numerous others. Contbr. articles to profl. jours. Moratorium organizer, performer Angry Artists Against the War, 1966-70; mem. Performing Artist for Nuclear Disarmament, 1981—, St. Clements Arts in Religious Action Com, 1972-75, Nat. Storytelling Network, Women and Theatre Program; organizer Bay Area Women in Theatre Orgn., 1978-80; presenter nat. convs., mem. Assn. for Theatre in Higher Edn. Grantee SUNY Rsch. Found., 1976, Kosciuszko Found., 1979, Internat. Women Playwrights Conf., 1997, Winifred Found., 1997, English Speaking Union, 1997, Mass. Cultural Coun., 1997, Mass. Found. for Humanities, 2001. Mem. Actors Equity, AFTRA, SAG, Nat. Storytelling Network. Democrat. Unitarian Universalist. E-mail: carneyk@earthlink.net.

CARNEY, MICHAEL, orchestra leader; b. N.Y.C., Nov. 27, 1937; s. Edward M. and Jacqueline (Soutar) C.; m. Lisa Marshall, May 9, 1997. BA, Northwestern U., 1959. Securities analyst Butcher & Sherrerd Co., Phila., 1964-66; investment mgr. Barnes & Tucker Co., Haverford, Pa., 1966; orchestra leader Michael Carney Music, N.Y.C., 1970—. Mem. vis. com. Northwestern U. Sch. Music., Evanston, Ill., 1983—. Trustee Boys Club N.Y., 1981—. Mem.: River, Meadow, Bohemian. Republican. Home: 200 E 71st St New York NY 10021-5137 Office: 175 5th Ave New York NY 10010

CARNEY, RITA J. educational administrator; b. Hoboken, N.J., July 17, 1941; BA, Beaver Coll., Glenside, Pa., 1962; MA, Seton Hall U., South Orange, N.J., 1965; EdD, Columbia U., 1977; MA, Princeton Theol. Sem., 1980. Tchr. Latin and English, Phillipsburg (N.J.) Pub. Schs., 1962-65; guidance counselor Jefferson Twp. Pub. Schs., Oak Ridge, NJ, 1965-67; admin. asst. Supt./H.S. prin. Madison Twp. Pub. Schs., Old Bridge, NJ, 1967—70; program devel. N.J. Dept. Edn., Trenton, 1970—75; county supt. schs. Middlesex County, NJ, 1975—80; N.J. asst. commr. for rsch., planning and evaluation; assoc. v.p. for acad. adminstrn. Temple U., Phila.; asst. to pres., v.p. for acad. and student affairs Georgian Ct. Coll., Lakewood, NJ, 1990—2001. Lectr, presenter profl and ch related orgns; consult planning and orgn analysis. Pres. Diocesan Pastoral Coun., Trenton, Blessed Sacrament Parish Coun., Trenton, NJ, Hiltonia Civic Assn., Trenton; chmn. exec. com. Mercy Higher Edn. Colloquium, 1994—2000. Mem.: Soc Col and Univ Planning (state rep 1996—2000). Home: 32 N Avon Dr Jackson NJ 08527-3975 E-mail: ritacarney@care2.com.

CARNEY, ROBERT THOMAS, lawyer; b. Youngstown, Ohio, Mar. 28, 1947; s. Thomas P. and Mildred B. (Keeling) C.; m. Victoria L. Schrecengost, May 21, 1977; children: Brian, Michael. BS in Physics, Northwestern U., 1969; JD, Georgetown U., 1972. Bar: Ohio 1972, D.C. 1974, U.S. Ct. Appeals (fed. cir.), U.S. Ct. Fed. Claims, U.S. Tax Court, U.S. Patent and Trademark Office, U.S. Supreme Ct. Law clk. U.S. Dist. Ct., Cleve., 1972-73; trial atty. tax divsn U.S. Dept. Justice, Washington, 1973-79; ptnr. tax atty. Lee, Toomey & Kent, Washington, 1979-88, Dow, Lohnes & Albertson, Washington, 1988-90, Rogers & Wells, Washington, 1990-96; ptnr. Fulbright & Jaworski, Washington, 1996-98, Ernst & Young, Washington, 1998—. Adj. prof. Georgetown U. Law Sch., Washington, 1987—. Mem. Murdoch Inn of Ct. (master, sec.-treas.). Office: Ernst & Young 1225 Connecticut Ave NW Ste 700 Washington DC 20036-2621 E-mail: robert.carney@ey.com.

CARNEY, ROGER FRANCIS XAVIER, retired army officer; b. Bklyn., Oct. 20, 1933; s. Frank Clement and Clara Helen (Muller) C.; m. Linda Ann Bowlus, Aug. 11, 1963 (div. Mar. 1993); children: Kevin James, Stephen Jason, Brian Andrew. BS, Purdue U., 1960, MS in Indsl. Adminstrn., 1963; grad., U.S. Army Command and Gen. Staff Coll., 1975, U.S. Army War Coll., 1979; MA, U. Conn., 1992. Commd. 2d lt. U.S. Army, 1960, advanced through grades to lt. col., 1976; comdr. 583d Ordnance Co., Muenster, West Germany, 1969-72; R&D coord. Army Material Command Field Office, Kirtland AFB, N.mex., 1972-74; logistic staff officer CENTAG Signal Support GP (NATO), Seckenheim, West Germany, 1975-78; chief nuc. weapons logistic element G4 CENTAG (NATO), Seckenheim, 1978; comdr. 15th Ordnance Bn., Darmstadt, West Germany, 1978-80; prof. mil. sci. head dept. Worcester (Mass.) Poly. Inst., 1980-84; prof. mil. sci., head dept. Fitchburg (Mass.) State Coll., 1980-84, Nichols Coll., Dudley, Mass., 1982-84, dean student affairs, 1985-98, dir. Robert C. Fischer Inst. Mem. Worcester Com. Fgn. Rels., Worcester Econ. Club, Mil. Adv. Coun. Ctr. for Def. Info., bd. dirs. Ctrl. Mass. Coun. for Social Studies. Decorated Legion of Merit, Bronze Star, 2 Meritorious Svc. medals, Army Commendation medal. Mem. Assn. U.S. Army, Assn. Former Intelligence Officers, Am. Legion, DAV, Mil. Officers Assn. Am., U. Conn. Alumni Assn., Purdue Alumni Assn., Alpha Sigma Phi (pres. Purdue U. chpt. 1959-60), Pi Lambda Theta. Democrat. Home: 7 Thayer Pond Dr Apt 11 North Oxford MA 01537-1134 E-mail: carney@nichols.edu.

CARNEY, STEPHEN PATRICK, insurance company executive; b. Morristown, N.J., Aug. 14, 1950; s. Stephen M. and June K. Carney; m. Patricia Ann Davis, Oct. 29, 1989. BS, Coll. William & Mary, 1972, JD, 1980. Bar: Md. 1981. Law clk. to Hon. J. Calvitt Clarke, Jr. U.S. Dist. Ct. (ea. dist.) Va., Norfolk, 1980-81; labor assoc. Venable, Baetjer & Howard, Balt., 1981-84, assoc. real estate, 1984-88; gen. counsel, sec. Med. Mut. Liability Ins. Soc. Md., Hunt Valley, 1988-89, v.p., gen. counsel, sec., 1989-99, sr. v.p., gen. counsel, sec., 1999—. Bd. dirs. Med-Lantic Mgmt. Svcs. Inc., Health Liability Alliance; mem. Gov.'s Adv. Com. on Practice Parameters, Balt., 1993—. Bd. dirs. Md. chpt. March of Dimes, Balt., 1990—, mem. exec. com., chair pub. affairs com., 1993—. Recipient Alumni Svc. award Coll. William & Mary, 1998; named Pub. Affairs Com. Mem. of Yr. March of Dimes, White Plains, N.Y., 1998. Mem. ABA, Am. Corp. Counsel Assn., Physician Insurers Assn. Am. (legal sect.), Md. State Bar Assn., William & Mary Law Sch. Found. (bd. dirs., pres. 2003-). Avocations: sailing, golf, travel, classic cars. Office: Med Mut Liability Ins Soc Md 225 International Cir Hunt Valley MD 21030 E-mail: scarney@weinsuredocs.com.

CARNEY, T.J, lawyer; b. Denver, July 18, 1952; s. Thomas Joseph Carney and Patricia (Amack) Carney Calkins; m. Deborah Leah Turner, Mar. 20, 1976; children: Amber Blythe, Sonia Briana, Ross Dillon. BA in Econs., U. Notre Dame, Ind., 1974; JD, U. Denver, 1976. Bar: Colo. 1977, Kans. 1977, U.S. Dist. Ct. Colo. 1977, U.S. Dist. Ct. Kans. 1977, U.S. Ct. Ariz. 1995, U.S. Ct. Appeals (10th cir.) 1983. Legal asst. Turner & Hensley, Chartered, Great Bend, Kans., 1977; atty.-shareholder Turner and Boisseau, Chartered, Great Bend, 1977-84; atty., shareholder Bradley, Campbell, Carney & Madsen, Golden,

Colo., 1984-92, 95-97; atty.-shareholder Deborah T.J Carney, P.C., Lakewood and Golden, 1992-95; atty. officer Carney Law Office, Golden, Colo., 1997-99; spl. counsel Oliver & Kirven, P.C., Arvada, Colo., 1999; atty., shareholder Oliver and Carney, P.C., Arvada, 1999—. CLE instr. Nat. Inst. Trial Advocacy, 1st Jud. Bar Assn., Colo. Inc., Rocky Mountain Child Advocacy Tng. Inst.; cons. Vocat. Econs., Inc., 1998, others. Precinct com. Rep. Party, Jefferson County, Colo., 1988-94, 2000—, area capt., 1994-96, 2002—; bd. dirs. Jefferson County Libr. Found., 1999—, pres., 2002-03; area vice-chmn. West Area sch. accountability com. Jefferson R-1 Pub. Schs., 1985-89, fin. oversight com., 1987-88, textbook com., 1988-89; bd. dirs. Table Mountain Soccer Assn., 1985-92, treas., 1990-92. Mem. Colo. Bar Assn., Colo. Trial Lawyers Assn., Kansas Bar Assn., Kans. Trial Lawyers Assn., 1st Jud. Dist. Bar Assn. (trustee 1990-94, banquet com. chair 1996-98, award com. chair, 2003—), Phi Delta Phi (Province Grad. of Yr. 1977). Avocations: flying, martial arts, skiing, lacrosse, ballroom dancing. Office: Oliver and Carney PC 7903 Ralston Rd Arvada CO 80002-2435 Fax: 303-424-3629., 720-294-0480. E-mail: tjc@jeffcolawyers.net.

CARNEY, WILLIAM PATRICK, medical educator; b. Dillon, Mont., July 1, 1938; s. Thomas James and Helen Catherine (Ballard) C.; children: Christopher Patrick, Mark Daniel; m. Sharon Loreta Sonnek, Aug. 14, 1965. BA, St. Thomas U., Kenmore, Wash., 1960; BS, Western Mont. U., 1962; PhD, U. Mont., 1967; MPH, Johns Hopkins U., 1976. Cert. secondary tchr. in biol. scis. Rsch. assoc. Minot (N.D.) State U., 1967-69; commd. lt. USN, 1969, advanced through grades to capt., 1986; rsch. parasitologist Naval Med. Rsch. Inst., Bethesda, Md., 1969-70, 74-75; dir. parasitology dept. Naval Med. Rsch. Unit No. 2, Jakarta, Indonesia, 1970-74, dept. dir. Taipei, Taiwan, 1976-79, lab. and scientific dir. Jakarta, 1979-81; program mgr. Naval Med. Rsch. Devel. Command, Bethesda, 1981-84; lab. dir. Naval Bioscis. Lab., Oakland, Calif., 1984-87; prof., dir. grad. program Uniformed Svcs. U., Bethesda, 1987-91, ret., 1991; project mgr. schistosomasis rsch. project in Cairo Med. Svc. Corp. Internat., Arlington, Va., 1991-95; prof., dep. chair dept. preventive medicine Uniformed Svcs. U., Bethesda, Md., 1995—. Exec. com. bd. dirs. Gorgas Meml. Inst., Bethesda; cons. Vector Biology and Control Project, Arlington, 1989-94, Am. Inst. Biol. Scis., Washington, 1987—. Contbr. articles to profl. jours. Smokejumper USFS, 1962-64; adult leader Boy Scouts Am., Taipei, 1976-79. Decorated Legion of Merit. Mem. Am. Soc. Parasitologists, Am. Soc. Tropical Medicine and Hygiene, Helminthological Soc. Washington, Sigma Xi, Phi Sigma. Republican. Roman Catholic. Avocations: scuba diving, auto repair, carpentry, masonry, welding. Office: Uniformed Svcs U Dept Preventive Medicine 4301 Jones Bridge Rd Bethesda MD 20814-4712 E-mail: pcarney@usuhs.mil., pat-and-sharon@erols.com.

CARNEY NELSON, ELLEN B. elementary school educator; b. Soda Springs, Idaho, June 11, 1936; d. Clarence Lyle and Benda Gladys (Petersen) Burton; m. Earl J. Carney Jr., Mar. 17, 1954 (div. 1981); children: Dennis (dec.), Phyllis, Maureen, Wade, Gary; m. Lewis G. Nelson, June 7, 1996. BA in Edn., U. Ariz., 1972; MEd, U. Utah, 1976; postgrad., Idaho State U., 1990; student, U. Alaska, 1965, Brigham Young U., 1975. Cert. elem. tchr., Ariz., Idaho, Utah. Tchr. Kiddie Club Kindergarten, Ft. Walton Beach, Fla., 1967; substitute tchr. Tucson (Ariz.) Dist. Schs., 1971-72; tchr. Jordan Sch. Dist., Sandy, Utah, 1973-79; tchr., adminstr. Promised Horizons Pvt. Sch., Sandy, 1981; owner, operator Smart Start Preschool, Draper, Utah, 1978-81; tchr. Soda Springs Sch. Dist., 1981-90; grad. asst. Idaho State U., Pocatello, 1990-91; substitute tchr. Tooele Sch. Dist., 1991-95; tchr. Tooele Jr. H.S., 1996-2000, Grantsville Mdid. Sch., 2000-01. Sch. bicentennial chmn. South Jordan (Utah) Elem. Sch., 1976; mem. GEMS program devel. team Jordan Sch. Dist., 1976-79; owner Wayan (Idaho) Cash Store, 1985-90. Author: Dr. Ellis Kackley-Best Damn Doctor in the West, 1989, Flora Whittemore, 1990, The Mountain: Carriboo and Other Gold Camps in Idaho, 1990, Way Out in Grays Lake, 1992, The Oregon Trail: Ruts, Rogues and Reminiscences, 1993, River of Beaver, Stream of Gold, 1994, Historic Soda Springs: Oasis on the Oregon Trail, 1998, (plays) 200 Years Too Late, 1976; corr.: Soda Springs Sun, Idaho State Jour., 1983—; author: Mavericks in Calico, Powerful Mormon Women, 2003, Mavericks in Calico, 2003. Den mother, cub scout leader, fin. coun. Boy and Girl Scouts Am., Anchorage, 1965-66, Ft. Walton Beach, 1967-68, Sandy, 1973-75; neighborhood chmn. ARC, Sandy, 1979-80, hosp. vol., Tucson, 1970; bd. dirs. Caribou County Hist. Preservation Commn., Soda Springs, 1988-94; v.p. Caribou Hist. Soc., 2001--. Winner Bicentennial Contest Utah Edn. Assn., 1976. Mem. Lds Ch. Avocations: reading, writing, fishing, quiltmaking, handicrafts. Home: 23 Grays Lake Rd Wayan ID 83285

CARNICERO, JORGE EMILIO, aeronautical engineer, business executive; b. Buenos Aires, July 17, 1921; came to U.S., 1942, naturalized, 1950; s. Alberto and Ana (Sulimeau) C.; m. Jacqueline Joanne Damman, Feb. 22, 1946; children— Jacqueline Denise, Jorge Jay. Student, U. LaPlata, Argentina, 1939-41, Aero. Engr., Rensselaer Poly. Inst., 1945. Chief engr. Dodero Airlines, Argentina, 1945, Flota Aerea Mercante, Argentina, 1945-46; v.p. Air Carrier Svc. Corp., Washington, 1946, exec. v.p., 1947-55, chmn. bd. dirs., dir., 1955-88. Past chmn., bd. Dyncorp (formerly Calif. Ea. Aviation, then Dynalectron Corp.); pres., bd. dirs. Blue Cove, Inc., N.Y., Inter-Properties, Inc., Del., Trans-Am. Aero. Corp., Del., Round Hill Devel. Ltd., Jamaica. Bd. visitors Sch. Fgn. Service, Georgetown U., Washington; mem. council Rensselaer Poly. Inst., Troy, N.Y., adv. bd. mem. mech., aero. and mechanics dept.; bd. dirs. Internat. Eye Found., Washington. Fellow Royal Aero. Soc.; mem. Argentine-Am. C. of C. (bd. dirs.), Univ. Club, Met. Club, Congl. Country Club, Georgetown Club. Home: 3949 52nd St NW Washington DC 20016-1925 Office: 1313 Dolley Madison Blvd Mc Lean VA 22101-3926 E-mail: jccarjc@aol.com.

CARNICOM, GENE E. health services administrator; b. Miami, Fla., Nov. 13, 1944; s. Francis Eugene and Kathleen (Kitchens) C.; m. Sharon Boiseau Brown, 1966; m. Lillian Helen Baehr, Mar. 22, 1970; children: Patrick Dylan, Danielle Brooke; m. Clare Helminiak, Nov. 1, 1984; children: Whitney Alexis, Heath Britten, James Tiberius Kirk. BA in Social Welfare, San Diego State U., 1971, MSW, 1972; PhD, Southeastern U., 1981. Diplomate Am. Bd. Clin. Social Workers; lic. clin. social worker, Mont.; cert. ind. social worker. Commd. USPHS, 1974, advanced through grades to capt., 1980, ret., 2000; coord. Beach Area Free Clinic, San Diego, 1970-72; program cons. Balt. City Dept. Social Svc., 1973; chief social work Balt. City Jail, 1974-76; Hosp. social work dir. Pine Ridge Indian Health Svc. Hosp., SD, 1980 81; dir. mental health and social svc. USPHS Indian Health Svc. Hosp., Mescalero, N.Mex., 1981-84; alt. health resources coord. AK Native Med. Ctr., Anchorage, 1984-88; med. social worker IHS Ft. Peck Svc. Unit, Mont., 1988-89; dir. profl. svc. Parker Indian Hosp., Ariz., 1989—; social worker Ariz. Bapt. Children's Svc., Ariz., 2001—. Faculty U. Md., 1972-76, C.C. Balt., 1973-76, Morgan State U., 1974-76, Webster Coll., 1977-80, Oglala Sioux C.C., 1980-81, Park Coll., 1982-84, Golden Gate U., 1982-84, N.Mex. State U., 1982-84; steering com. Cmty. Congress San Diego, 1980-82; exec. dir. Retred, Inc., 1971-72. Contbr. articles to profl. jours. Bd. dirs. Innercity N.W. Neighborhood Corp., 1970-72; site selection task force cmty. corrections program Md. Dept. Corrections, 1973-74; grad. coun. Webster Coll., San Antonio, 1978-80; coord. child protection team Pine Ridge Indian Reservation, 1980-81, Mescalero Apache Indian Reservation, 1981-84, Alaska Aids Network; sr. leader 4-H; mem. La Paz County 4-H Leaders Coun., 1998-2001; comdr. Sierra Blanca CAP Cadet Squadron, 1982-84; coord. AIDS CRSU, 1992-2000; spl. edn. pals rep. Parker Unified Sch. Dist., 1993 98; coach Parker Little League, 1995-98, La Paz Youth Soccer League, 1993-99, pres. 1994-95; v.p. bd. dirs. La Paz Respite Found. 1997—, pres., 2000—; v.p. bd. dirs. Ariz. Coun. on Rural Disabilities, 1996-2002; parks and recreation com. Town of Parker, 1997—; disaster mental health vol., health and safety chair, supr. ARC, La Paz County, 2000-02, bd. dirs. ARC of Argona, 2002—; mem. Gov.'s Coun. on Devel. Disability, 2001--; chmn. legis. affairs com. Arc, Ariz., 1999—; treas. Parker Cmty. Child Abuse Prevention Coun., 1996—; advisor Oasis of La Paz County, 1998—; organist, lay leader Parker United Meth. Ch.; asst. coach Parker H.S. Varsity Soccer Team, 2002—. With USNR, 1962-68. Decorated Army Commendation medal; recipient Isolated Hardship Duty award USPHS, 1981, Hazardous Duty award, 1981, Commendation medal, 1989, Commendation award US Atty. Dist. of Ariz., 1998, Dirs. award for excellence PAIHS, 1998, Star of Ariz. award ARC-Ariz., 2001; named Man of Yr., Parker Area C. of C., 2000. Mem. NASW, APHA, Assn. Mil. Surgeons U.S., Am. Anthrop. Assn., Soc. Med. Anthropology, N.Am. Assn. Christians in Social Work, Am. Assn. Christian Counselors, History of Sci. Soc., Parker Area C. of C., Elks, Lions (sec., dir. zone chair,1995--), Mensa, Am. Legion. Democrat. Office: USPHS Indian Hosp RR 1 Box 12 Parker AZ 85344-9703 E-mail: carnicom@aol.com.

CARNIE, KAY C. artist, educator; b. NYC, June 8, 1942; d. James Ogden and Allegra MacCulloch Combes; m. Donald Ross Carnie, June 6, 1964; children: David, Michael. BA, Fla. So. Coll., 1964; MA, San Jose State U., 1988, MFA, 1993. Profl. artist, Cupertino, Calif., 1993—; instr. Palo Alto (Calif.) Art Ctr., 1996-99, San Mateo (Calif.) Cmty. Edn., 1999; tchr. Coll. of San Mateo, 2000—. Juror fine arts Santa Clara County Fair, San Jose, 1991, 97. Illustrator Painting Great Pictures from Photographs, 1999, Capturing Texture, 2002, illustrator, author Splash 4, 1996. Mem. Nat. Watercolor Soc. (signature), Midwest Watercolor Soc. (signature), Calif. Watercolor Assn. (signature), Watercolor West (juried mem.). Avocations: piano, photography, travel. Home and Office: 10439 Heney Creek Pl Cupertino CA 95014 E-mail: kccarnie@aol.com.

CARNIOL, PAUL J. plastic and reconstructive surgeon, otolaryngologist; b. N.Y.C., Sept. 26, 1951; s. David A. and Diane (Hadler) C.; m. Renie Rich, Jan. 3, 1976; children: Michael P., Alan R., Eric T. BA, NYU, 1972; MD, U. Pa., 1976. Diplomate Am. Bd. Otolaryngology, Am Bd. Facial Plastic and Reconstructive Surgery, Am. Bd. Cosmetic Surgery, Am. Bd. Med. Examiners. Resident in surgery U. Pa., Phila., 1976-77, resident in plastic and reconstructive surgery, 1981-83; resident in surgery North Shore U. Hosp., Manhasset, NY, 1977-78; resident in surgery and otolaryngology, clin. tchg. fellow Harvard Med. Sch., Boston, 1978-81; attending plastic surgeon, head and neck surgery Overlook Hosp., Summit, NJ, 1983—; clin. assoc. prof. U. Medicine and Dentistry of N.J., Newark. Cons. aesthetic, laser and reconstructive and plastic surgery; instr. courses on lasers in plastic surgery, facial rejuvenation, also numerous lectrs., TV presentations in field; chief sect. otolaryngology Overlook Hosp., 1992-97; police surgeon, New Providence, and Summit, N.J. Editor. Laser Skin Rejuvenation, 1998, Facial Rejuvenation, 2001; spl. editor: Am. Jour. Cosmetic Surgery, mem. editl. bd.: Jour. Cosmetic and Laser Therapy; contbr. articles to profl. jours. Interviewer for admissions com. U. Pa., Phila., 1987—. Recipient Community Svc. award Ciba-Geigy, Summit, 1978, Found. award NYU, 1972, Alumni Gold Medal award NYU, 1972. Fellow: ACS, Am. Acad. Cosmetic Surgery, Am. Acad. Facial Plastic and Reconstructive Surgery (v.p. R&D 1994—2003, dir. courses lasers, facial plastic surgery and cosmetic surgery 1996—98, care com., chmn. new tech. and surg. devices com. 1998—2000), Am. Acad. Otolaryngology, Nead and Neck Surgery; mem.: AMA, Union County Med. Soc. (planning com. 1986—89, pres. 2002—03, chmn. program com., exec. com., bd. dirs.), N.J. Acad. Otolaryngology (pres. 1993—96, 1997—), N.J. Med. Soc. (coun. on med. svcs.), Internat. Soc. Cosmetic Laser Surgery (v.p.), N.J. Acad. Medicine, Phi Beta Kappa. Avocations: golf, fishing, horseback riding, bicycling, Karate. Office: 33 Overlook Rd Ste 202 Summit NJ 07901-3562

CARNOCHAN, WALTER BLISS, retired humanities educator; b. N.Y.C., Dec. 20, 1930; s. Gouverneur Morris and Sibyll Baldwin (Bliss) C.; m. Nancy Powers Carter, June 25, 1955 (div. 1978); children— Lisa Powers, Sarah Bliss, Gouverneur Morris, Sibyll Carter; m. Brigitte Hoy Fields, Sept. 16, 1979. AB, Harvard, 1953, A.M., 1957, PhD, 1960. Asst. dean freshmen Harvard U., 1954-56; successively instr., asst. prof., assoc. prof., prof. English, Stanford (Calif.) U., 1960-94, prof. emeritus, 1994—, chmn. dept. English, 1971-73, dean grad. studies, 1975-80, vice provost, 1976-80, dir. Stanford Humanities Ctr., 1985-91, Anthony P. Meier Family prof. humanities, 1988-91, Richard W. Lyman prof. humanities, 1993-94, Richard W. Lyman prof. emeritus, 1994—, acting dir. Stanford Humanities Ctr., 1999. Mem. overseers com. to visit Harvard Coll, 1979-85, mem. bd. advisors Ehrenpreis Ctr. for Swift Studies, 1984—. Author: Lemuel Gulliver's Mirror for Man, 1968, Confinement and Flight: An Essay on English Literature of the 18th Century, 1977, Gibbon's Solitude: The Inward World of the Historian, 1987, The Battleground of the Curriculum: Liberal Education and American Experience, 1993, Momentary Bliss: An American Memoir, 1999. Trustee Mills Coll., 1978-85, Athenian Sch., 1975-88, Berkeley (Calif.) Art Mus., 1983-96, 98-2001. Home: 138 Cervantes Rd Portola Valley CA 94028-7725 E-mail: carnochan@stanford.edu.

CARNWATH, THOMAS HOWLAN, academic administrator; b. Plattsburgh, NY, Apr. 26, 1951; s. Samuel Wallace and Shirley Jane Howlan Carnwath; m. J. Babette Bauerle, Apr. 13, 1949; children: Emily Lueders, Theodore Harrison. BA, Albion Coll., 1969—73; MA, Widener U., 1991—93, MPA, 1995—97. Leadership Program EDUCAUSE, 2001. Assisant dir. of alumni rels. Albion Coll., Mich., 1973—75; asst. dir. of the ann. fund and govt. rels. Widener U., Chester, Pa., 1976—78, dir. of devel., 1978—79, Widener U. and Capital Projects, 1979—82; assist dean for devel. and alumni rels. Widener U. Sch. of Law, Wilmington, Del., 1982—87; dep. dir. for devel. and pub. rels. Hagley Mus. and Libr., Wilmington, 1987—89; asst. to the pres./asst. sec. to the bd. Widener U., Chester, 1990—2001, v.p. of info. tech. services, 1998—. Mem. Coun. for the Advancement and Support of Edn., Washington, 1973—98; chmn. Del. County C. of C., Media, Pa., 1985—86; dir. Nat. Soc. of Fundraising Executives - Brandywine Chpt., Wilmington, Del., 1985—89; mem. Am. Assn. of Museums, Washington, 1987—89, EDUCAUSE, Boulder, Colo., 1997—. Pres. The Savoy Co. of Phila., Phila., 1983—84; mem. The St. Andrew's Soc. of Phila., 1996—2003; dir. Del. County Transp. Mgmt. Assn., Media, 1993—2003. Mem.: Sigma Chi Frat. (life). Independent. Episcopalian. Home: 712 Cheltenham Rd Wilmington DE 19808 Office: Widener U One University Pl Chester PA 19013

CARO, EVELYN INGA ROUSE, writer; b. Monterey Park, Calif., June 2, 1956; d. Coburn Whitehead and Marcelaine (Ulvick) Rouse; m. Johnny Caro, Dec. 19, 1982; children: Jessica Lynn, Juan Abram, Matthew Jason, Ruben Emmanuel. Author: A Prelude to Summer, 1990, (novel) The Trial of Adam Smith, 1995 (play); contbr. poetry and articles to various publs. Elder 7th-day Adventist Ch., 1995—. Home: 9266 Valley View Ave Whittier CA 90603-1957 E-mail: thecaros6@aol.com.

CARO, IVOR, dermatologist; b. Johannesburg, June 2, 1946; came to U.S., 1975; s. Herbert and Rachel (Eisenstein) C.; m. Sheryl Helaine Marsden, Dec. 14, 1969; children: Howard Seth, Glen. MB, BCh, U. Witwatersrand, 1969. Diplomate, Am. Bd. Dermatology. Resident U. Witwatersrand, Johannesburg, 1971—74; fellow St. John's Hosp., London, 1974—76; asst. prof. U. N.C., Chapel Hill, 1975—78; pvt. practice Seattle, 1978—99; dir. internat. program dermatology Harvard Med. Sch., Boston, 1999—2003; dir. dermatol. clin. investigation unit Mass. Gen. Hosp./ Harvard Med. Sch., 2000—03; med. dir. dermatology Genentech, South San Francisco, 2003—. Clin. prof. U. Wash., Seattle, 1978-99; chief of dermatology, attending dermatologist Va. Mason Med. Ctr., Seattle, 1978-99. Contbr. to profl. publs. and textbooks. Fellow: Am. Acad. Dermatology; mem.: Pacific Dermatol. Soc., New Eng. Dermatol. Soc., Noah Worcester Dermatol. Soc. (sec., treas. 2000—), Seattle Dermatol. Soc. (pres. 1987—88). Office: Genentech 1 DNA Way MS 84 South San Francisco CA 94080

CARO, ROBERT ALLAN, author; b. NYC; s. Benjamin and Cele (Mendelow) C.; m. Ina Joan Sloshberg, June 9, 1957; 1 child, Chase Arthur. AB cum laude, Princeton U., 1957; DLitt (hon.), Merrimack Coll., 1983, L.I. U., 2003; LHD (hon.), New Sch. for Social Rsch., 1997. Reporter New Brunswick Home News, NJ, 1957-59, Newsday, Garden City, NY, 1960-66; Nieman fellow Harvard U., Cambridge, Mass., 1965-66. Historian, biographer, 1967—. Author: The Power Broker: Robert Moses and the Fall of New York, 1974 (Pulitzer prize for biography 1975, Francis Parkman prize Soc. Am. Historians 1975, Selected by Modern Libr. as 1 of 100 Best Nonfiction Books Written in English during the 20th Century), The Years of Lyndon Johnson: The Path to Power, 1982 (Nat. Book Critics award for biography 1983, Tex. Inst. Arts and Letters award for non-fiction 1983), The Years of Lyndon Johnson: Means of Ascent, 1990 (Nat. Book Critics Cir. award for biography 1991), The Years of Lyndon Johnson: Master of the Senate, 2002 (Nat. Book award for non-fiction 2002, Pulitzer prize for biography 2003, L.A. Times Book prize for biography 2003, Carl Sandburg Lit. award Chgo. Pub. Libr. Found. 2003). Bd. dir. Fund for City NY, NY Soc. Libr., Theatre for New Audience. Recipient Soc. of Silurians award, 1964, Deadline Club, 1964, 65, spl. citation NY chpt. AIA, 1975, H.L. Mencken prize Free Press Assn., 1983, award in lit. Am. Acad. and Inst. Arts and Letters, 1986, Lifetime Achievement in Arts award Guild Hall Acad. Arts, 1992, Pulitzer Prize for biography, 1975, 2003; co-recipient ann. polit. book award Washington Monthly, 1975, 83, 91. Fellow Soc. Am. Historians (Francis Parkman prize); mem. Authors Guild Am. (bd. dir. 1976—, pres. 1980-82), PEN Am. Ctr. (mem. exec. bd. 1986-88, v.p. 1989-92), Century Club. Office: Robert A Caro Inc 250 W 57th St Ste 2215 New York NY 10107-2209

CARO, WILLIAM ALLAN, physician, educator; b. Chgo., Aug. 16, 1934; s. Marcus Rayner and Adeline Beatrice (Cohen) Caro; m. Ruth Fruchtlander, June 15, 1959 (dec.); children: Mark Stephen, David Edward; m. Joan Peters, Oct. 18, 1997. Student, U. Mich., 1952-55; BS in Medicine, U. Ill., 1957, MD, 1959. Diplomate Am. Bd. Dermatology (bd. dirs. 1981-91, v.p. 1989-90, pres. 1990-91). Intern Cook County Hosp., Chgo., 1959-60; resident in internal medicine U. Ill. Rsch. and Edn1. Hosps., 1960-61; resident in dermatology Hosp. U. Pa., 1961-62, 64-66; Earl D. Osborne fellow dermal pathology Armed Forces Inst. Pathology, Washington, 1966-67; asst. in medicine U. Ill. Coll. Medicine, 1960-61; asst. instr. U. Pa. Med. Sch., 1961-62, 64-66; from asst. prof. to assoc. prof. dermatology Northwestern U. Med. Sch., 1967—81, prof., 1981—; pvt. practice specializing in dermatology Chgo., 1967—. Chief dermatology sect. MacDonald Army Hosp., Ft. Eustis, Va., 1962—64; attending physician Chgo. Wesley Meml. Hosp., 1969—72, Northwestern Meml. Hosp., 1972—, mem. med. exec. com., 1977—79; attending pathologist, cons. dermatologist VA Lakeside Hosp., Chgo.; cons. Rehab. Inst. Chgo., Mcpl. Tb Sanitarium Chgo., 1968—74. Mem. editl. bd. Curtis, 1975—; assoc. editor: Year Book Pathology and Clin. Pathology, 1977—80. Mem. medicine adv. bd. U. Ill. Coll. Medicine, 1988—; trustee Northwestern Meml. Hosp. Chgo., 1986—87, bd. dirs., 1988—91, Northwestern Meml. Corp., 1987—2000, mem. exec. com., 1988—91. Served as capt. M.C. USAR, 1962—64. Mem.: AMA, Dermatology Found. (Clark W. Finnerud award 2002), Pacific Dermatol. Assn., Internat. Soc. Dermatology, Am. Soc. Dermatopathology (pres.-elect 1995—96, bd. dirs. 1995—2000, pres. 1996—97), Am. Dermatol. Assn. (bd. dirs. 1993—98), Chgo. Dermatol. Soc. (pres. 1983 84, editor trans. 1971—73), Am. Acad. Dermatology (Gold award sci. exhibit 1970), U. Ill. Med. Alumni Assn. (exec. bd. 1977 80), Phi Kappa Phi, Alpha Omega Alpha. Office: 676 N Saint Clair St Ste 1840 Chicago IL 60611-2927

CAROFF, PHYLLIS M. social work educator; b. Bklyn., Feb. 22, 1924; d. Harry and Irene (Lesser) Friedman; m. Joseph Caroff, May 16, 1943; children— Michael, Peter. BA, Douglass Coll., 1944; MSW., N.Y. Sch. Social Work, 1947; D.S.W., Columbia U., 1969. Caseworker ARC, 1944-45; caseworker, student supr. Community Service Soc., N.Y.C., 1956-61; from lectr. to assoc. prof. Hunter Coll. Sch. Social Work, N.Y.C., 1961-76, prof., 1976-87; dir. Postmasters Program in Advanced Clin. Social Work, 1977-87; pvt. practice psychotherapy N.Y.C., 1964—. Cons. VA Hosp., N.Y.C., 1977-85, USPHS Hosp., S.I., 1974—; mem. adv. bd. Found. Thanatology, 1976—; mem. profl. adv. com. Grad. Program in Social Work, Inst. Health Professions, Mass. Gen. Hosp., 1980-86. Author: (with others) Before Addiction, 1973; editorial bd. Clin. Social Work Jour., 1972—, Jour. Gerontol. Social Work, 1978— ; editor: (with others) Social Work in Health Services: An Academic Practice Partnership, 1980, A New Model in Academic/Practice Partnership, 1985, Psychosocial Advances in Clinical Social Work, 1985. Mem. exec. com. of bd. Planned Parenthood N.Y.C., 1974-79, chmn. rsch. and evaluation com., 1974-77, bd. dirs., 1971-86. Named Disting. Practitioner, Nat. Acad. Practice in Social Work, 1983; NIMH fellow, 1964-65; various grants. Fellow Am. Orthopsychiat. Assn., N.Y. Acad. Medicine; mem. AAUP, Nat. Assn. Social Workers (chmn. clin. council 1981-84, mem. peer rev. adv. com. 1982-84), N.Y. State Soc. Clin. Social Work Psychotherapists. Home: 15 W 81st St New York NY 10024-6022

CAROLAN, DOUGLAS, wholesale company executive; BS, Western Mich. U., 1964. Store mgr. to dir. mktg. div. Nat. Tea Co., 1962-83; sr. v.p. Associated Wholesale Grocers, Inc., Kansas City, Kans., 1983-86, chief ops. officer, exec. v.p., sec., 1986—, CEO, pres., 1998—. Bd. dirs. UMB Bank, Food Mktg. Inst. Bd. dirs. Kans. City area food bank Harvesters. Office: Assoc Wholesale Grocers Inc PO Box 2932 Kansas City KS 66110-2932

CAROLAND, WILLIAM BOURNE, structural engineer; b. Clarksville, Tenn., July 9, 1929; s. Enoch Arden and Jennie Wimberly (Bourne) C.; m. Eloise Joyce Crickard, June 3, 1957; children: Richard Bradley, Jennifer Dorothy. Student, U. Tenn., 1947-52. Registered profl. engr., Ky., Tenn., Ind., Mich. Fla., W.Va. Survey party chief King & Clark Engrs., Clarksville, 1955-56, Michael Baker Jr., Inc., Jackson, Miss., 1956-57, asst. designer Charleston, W.Va., 1957-62, project supr. Louisville, 1962-63, designer Charleston, 1963-64; bridge designer Vogt, Ivers & Assocs., Cin., 1964-65; sr. structural engr. Brighton Engring., Frankfort, Ky., 1965-73; chief bridge engr. Beam, Longest & Neff, Indpls., 1973-79; with Am. Cons. Engrs., Lexington, Ky., 1979—, chief bridge engr., 1988—. Mem. Am. Cons. Engrs. Coun. Contbr. papers to profl. publs. With U.S. Army, 1952-55. Recipient Welded Steel Design award Lincoln Arc Welding Found., 1974, Welded Steel Design hon. mention, 1975, silver award 1999; Bridge Design award Prestressed Concrete Inst., 1977, 92, Grand Conceptor award Am. Consulting Engrs. Coun., 2001. Avocations: woodworking, photography. Home: 604 S Broadway St Georgetown KY 40324-1136 Office: Am Cons Engrs PLC 400 E Vine St Ste 100 Lexington KY 40507-1517 *When I was growing up my father always told me there is no such word as can't. Over the years I have come to agree with this. If we believe and work hard it can be done.*

CAROL ANN, artist, educator; Exhibited in group shows at World Fine Art's Gallery, N.Y.C., 2003, Agora Gallery, at Mali Villas Boas Galeria, Caribé Galeria de Arte, Centro Cultural de Suzano, Sao Paulo, Brazil, at Omma Center of Contemporary Art, Crete, Greece, Vera Simoes, Sao Paulo, Matiz Art Galeris, Escritorio de Arte Vera, exhibitions include Biennale Internazionale Dell'Arte Contemporanea, Florence, Italy, Ninth Fine Art's Gallery, V.I., international art competition Art Challenge, (award of merit, 2002). Home: 11736 Zenobia Loop Westminster CO 80031 Personal E-mail: artcarolann@aol.com.

CAROME, PATRICK JOSEPH, lawyer; b. Cleve., Nov. 20, 1957; s. Edward Francis and Jeanne Marie (Carrabine) C.; m. Elsie Elizabeth Orr, Oct. 7, 1989. BA, Boston Coll., Chestnut Hill, Mass., 1980; JD, Harvard U., 1983. Bar: Mass. 1984, D.C. 1985, U.S. Dist. Ct. D.C. 1985, U.S. Ct. Appeals (D.C. cir.) 1987, U.S. Supreme Ct. 1988, U.S. Ct. Appeals (4th cir.) 1989, U.S. Ct. Appeals (9th cir.) 1993, U.S. Ct. Appeals (10th cir.) 1999. Law clk. to Judge Milton Pollack, U.S. Dist. Ct. for So. Dist. N.Y., N.Y.C., 1983-84; staff atty. Washington Post, 1984-86; staff counsel select com. to investigate covert arms trans. U.S. Ho. of Reps., Washington, 1987; assoc. Wilmer, Cutler & Pickering, Washington, 1986-87, 88-90, ptnr., 1991—. Mem. ABA (vice chmn. com. on govt. info. and right to privacy com. adminstrv. law sect. 1988-90, chmn. 1990-94). Office: Wilmer Cutler & Pickering 2445 M St NW Ste 500 Washington DC 20037-1487

CARON, WILFRED RENE, retired lawyer; b. N.Y.C., July 23, 1931; s. Joseph Wilfred and Eva Caron; m. Anne Theresa Flanagan, AUg. 2, 1958. JD, St. John's U., 1956. Bar: N.Y. 1956, D.C. 1977, U.S. Dist. Ct. D.C. 1977, U.S. Dist. Ct. (no. dist.) N.Y. 1957, U.S. Dist. Ct. (so. and ea. dists.) N.Y. 1961, U.S. Ct. Appeals (2d cir.) 1965, U.S. Ct. Appeals (3d cir.) 1973, U.S. Ct. Appeals (5th cir.) 1977, U.S. Ct. Appeals (6th cir.) 1973, U.S. Ct. Appeals (8th cir.) 1975, U.S. Ct. Appeals (9th cir.) 1976, U.S. Ct. Appeals (D.C. cir.) 1975, U.S. Supreme Ct. 1961. Law clk. to chief judge N.Y. State Ct. Appeals, 1956-59; spl. asst. atty. gen. N.Y., 1959-60; assoc. Goldman & Drazen, 1960-64, Corner, Finn, Cuomo & Charles, N.Y.C., 1964-69; asst. gen. counsel Ronson Corp., Woodbridge, N.J., 1969-71; assoc. gen. counsel Securities Investor Protection Corp., Washington, 1972-80; gen. counsel U.S. Cath. Conf., Inc., Washington, 1980-87, Nat. Conf. Cath. Bishops, 1980-87, Cath. Telecom. Network Am., Inc., N.Y.C., 1981-88; ptnr. O'Connor & Hannan, Washington, 1987-88; sr. advisor Office of Policy Devel., U.S. Dept. of Justice, Washington, 1988-90; appellate counsel Travelers Ins. Co., 1990-92; ret., 1992. Contbr. articles to profl. jours. Adv. bd. St. Thomas More Inst. Legal Rsch., St. John's U. Sch. Law, N.Y.C., 1981-92; exec. bd. Ctr. for Ch.-State Studies, DePaul U. Law Coll., Chgo., 1982—. Served to 1st lt. U.S. Army, 1952-54, Korea. Mem.: ABA, D.C. Bar Assn., Am. Legion, VFW. Roman Catholic. Home: 44 Old Main Rd Little Compton RI 02837-1321

CARONE, GABRIELA ROXANA, philosophy educator, dancer; Lic. in Philosophy, U. Buenos Aires, 1989; PhD in Philosophy, King's Coll., U. London, London, 1995. Asst. prof. U. Buenos Aires, Buenos Aires, 1989—94, 2d rank, 1994—95; guest lectr. King's Coll. London, London, 1993—94; philosophy prof. U. Colo., Boulder, 1996—. Mem. exec. com. Argentine Soc. Ancient Philosophy, Buenos Aires, 1989—95. Author: The Notion of God in Plato's Timaeus; co-author: Platon: Timeo; mem. editl. com. Methexis, An Argentine Jour. Ancient Philosophy, Buenos Aires, 1989—96; contbr. articles (including leading articles) to profl. jours. (leading article), chapters to books. Recipient Brit. Coun. Award, Brit. Coun., 1992—95; CONICET fellow,

Argentina, 1989—92, NRC fellow, 1995—97, Faculty fellow, U. Colo., 2001, Laurance S. Rockefeller fellow, Ctr. for Human Values, Princeton U., 2003—04, vis. fellow (declined), Ctr. for Hellenic Studies, Harvard U., 2003—04, rsch. grantee, U. Colo., 1996, 1997, 1998, 2001—03. Address: Princeton U Univ Ctr Human Values 304 Louis Marx Hall Princeton NJ 08544-1006

CARONIS, GEORGE JOHN, insurance executive; b. Columbus, Ohio, Dec. 8, 1933; s. John George and Effie (Zarafonetis) C.; m. Shirley Ann Milburn, June 7, 1958; 1 child, Kevin M. BA, Ohio State U., 1955, MA, 1960. CLU; ChFC; chartered property and casualty underwriter; CFP. Asst. dean of men Ohio State U., Columbus, 1957-60; assoc. gen. agt. Tice Ins. Co., Columbus, 1960-74; v.p. pensions and estate planning Midland Mut. Life Ins. Co., Columbus, 1974-77; v.p. bus. devel. Bank One Trust Co., Columbus, 1977-79; v.p. fin. svcs. Kientz and Co., Columbus, 1979-82; dir. mktg. Nationwide Ins. Cos., Columbus, 1982-87; mktg. mgr. Aetna Life and Casualty Co., Columbus, 1987-89; v.p. advanced underwriting Western Res. Life Assurance Co., Clearwater, Fla., 1989-91, v.p. mktg., 1991—2001; sr. v.p. Asset Accumulation Group, Aegon U.S.A., 1994-98; exec. v.p. Aegon Equity Group, 1998—2001; registered prin. ProVise Mgmt. Group, LLC, 2002—. Bd. dirs. Mass. Fidelity Trust Co. 1st lt. U.S. Army, 1955-57. Recipient Thomas Arkle Clark award Alpha Tau Omega, 1955, Ralph D. Mershon award Ohio State U., 1990. Fellow Life Mgmt. Inst.; mem. Ohio State Alumni Assn. (nat. pres. 1983-85), Ohio State U. Found. (nominating com.), Nat. Assn. Life Underwriters, Am. Soc. CLUs and ChFCs. Home: 1371 River Oaks Ct Oldsmar FL 34677-4829 Office: Western Res Life Assurance 1371 River Oaks Ct Oldsmar FL 34677-4829

CAROOMPAS, CAROLE JEAN, artist, educator; b. Oregon City, Oreg., Nov. 14, 1946; d. John Thomas and Dorothy Lietta (Dirks) C. BA, Calif. State U., Fullerton, 1968; MFA in Painting, U. So. Calif., 1971. Instr. El Camino Coll., Torrance, Calif., 1971—72; vis. artist Calif. State U., Northridge, 1972—75; instr. Immaculate Heart Coll., L.A., 1973—76; vis. artist Calif. State U., Fullerton, 1976—78; instr. U. Calif., Irvine, 1976—80, Claremont (Calif.) Grad. Sch., 1976—79, Art Ctr. Coll. of Design, Pasadena, 1978—86, UCLA Extension, L.A., 1984—93; prof. fine arts Otis Coll. Art and Design, L.A., 1991—; vis. artist Anderson Ranch Art Ctr., Aspen, Colo., 1996, 98. One-woman shows include Jan Baum Art Gallery, L.A., 1978-82, Karl Bornstein Gallery, L.A., 1985, L.A. Contemporary Exhbns., 1989, U. Calif., Irvine, 1990, Sue Spaid Fine Art, L.A., 1992, 94, P.P.O.W., N.Y.C., 1994, Otis Coll. of Art and Design Art Gallery, 1997-98, Mark Moore Gallery, Santa Monica, 1997, 99, Mark Moore Gallery, 2000; exhibited in group shows at Pasadena Mus. Art, 1972, Whitney Mus. of Art, 1978, Mus. Modern Art, N.Y.C., 1976, L.A. County Mus., 1982, Corcoran Gallery of Art, 43rd Biennial Exhbn. of Contemporary Am. Painting, Washington, 1993, Under Contstrn. Armory Ctr. for Arts, Pasadena, 1995, UCLA Hammer Mus. of Art, L.A., 1996, Art Gallery, L.A., 1997, L.A. County Mus. Art, 1996, Beaver Coll., 1996, L.A. Mcpl. Art Gallery, 1997, UCLA Hammer Mus. Art, 2000, Calif. State U., Fullerton, 2001, San Jose Mus., 2002, Rosamund Felson Gallery, Santa Monica, Calif., 2003, Lewis and Clark Coll., Portland, Oreg., 2003; also a vocalist; recs. include 2 individual albums and inclusion in The Record: 13 Vocal Artists; contbr. articles to Paris Rev., Dreamworks, Whitewalls. Fellow Guggenheim Meml. fellow, 1995, Individual Artist's fellow, City of L.A. Cultural Affairs Dept., 2000; grantee NEA grantee, 1987, 1993, Faculty Devel. grantee, New Sch. Social Rsch., 1989, Support grantee, Esther and Adolph Gottlieb Found., 1993. Office: Otis Coll Art and Design 9045 Lincoln Blvd Los Angeles CA 90045-3505

CAROTHERS, A. J. scriptwriter; b. Houston, Oct. 22, 1931; s. A.J. and Vivian (Gibson) C.; m. Caryl Enid Volkman, Nov. 7, 1959; children: Cameron, Christopher, Andrew. BA, UCLA, 1954. Story editor Studio One, 1958; assoc. prodr. Playhouse 90 CBS TV, L.A., 1959-60; contract writer Walt Disney Prodns., Burbank, Calif., 1961-68; writer-prodr. Lorimar, Culver City, Calif., 1986-87. Guest lectr. UCLA; writer Music Ctr. Spotlight Awards, 1989-2003. Author: (screenplays) Miracle of the White Stallions, 1962, Emil and the Detectives, 1964, The Happiest Millionaire, 1967, Never a Dull Moment, 1968, Hero At Large, 1980, The Secret of My Success, 1987; (TV movies) The Making of a Male Model, 1984, Summer Girl, 1983, Forever, 1977, The Thief of Bagdad, 1978; creator, author, cons. (TV series) Nanny and the Professor, 1970-72; creator, writer (TV mini-series) Friends, 1979; creator, writer, exec. producer (TV series) Goodnight, Beantown, 1982-83, (mus. play) Busker Alley, 1994; writer (TV series) Studio One, 1958, My Three Sons, 1960-61, The Dupont Show, 1960-61, The Investigators, 1961, (TV spl.) Goldilocks, 1971. V.p. Fraternity of Friends, L.A., 1986—. With U.S. Army, 1954-56. Recipient Disting. Artists award, Club 100 of L.A. Music Ctr., 1990; Gold Lone Star award, Houston Film Festival, 1982; named Disting. Alumnus, KinKaid Sch., 1997. Mem. Motion Picture Acad. (writer's br. exec. com.), UCLA Theater Arts Alumni Assn. (bd. dirs. 1984-88). Home and Office: 1379 Midvale Ave Los Angeles CA 90024-6218

CAROTHERS, CHARLES OMSTED, retired orthopedic surgeon; b. Medina, N.Y., Aug. 2, 1923; s. Thomas Abbott and Helen Flavia (Olmsted) C.; children from a previous marriage: Thomas Abbott, Stephen Cole, Lisa Booker; m. Lucille Klau, June 20, 1971. BA, Williams Coll., 1944; MD, Harvard U., 1946; MS in Orthopedic Surgery, U. Tenn., 1954. Diplomate Am. Bd. Orthopedic Surgery. Intern Cin. Gen. Hosp., 1946-47; head bone research project Naval Med. Research Inst., Bethesda, Md., 1949; resident in gen. surgery U. Cin., 1949-51; resident in orthopedic surgery U. Tenn., 1951-54; practice medicine specializing in orthopedic surgery Cin., 1954-98; ret. Chief orthopedic sect. Bethesda Hosps., ret. 1988; mem. staff Univ. Med. Sch., Univ. Hosp. Cin. Pres., chief exec. officer Cin. Playhouse in the Park, 1974-88. Served with USN, 1949-51. Recipient Post-Corbett award for Contbn. to the arts, 1986. Mem. AMA, ACS, Am. Acad. Orthopedic Surgery, Clin. Orthopedic Soc., Mid-Am. Orthopedic Assn., Soc. Colonial Wars Ohio (dep. gov. 1979-82, gov. 1975-76), Wequetonsing Assn., Ocean Reef Club, Literary Club, Univ. Club, Losantiville Country Club, Cin. Country Club, Key Largo Anglers Club. Episcopalian. Home: 2737 Walsh Rd Cincinnati OH 45208

CAROTHERS, ROBERT LEE, academic administrator; b. Sewickley, Pa., Sept. 3, 1942; s. Robert Fleming and Mary (Skinner) C.; children: Robert Kennedy, Shelley Rye, Matthew K. Ruane. BS, Edinboro U., 1965; MA, Kent State U., 1966, PhD, 1969; JD, U. Akron, 1980. Bar: Pa. 1981. Prof. English, dean, v.p. Edinboro U., 1968-83; pres. S.W. State U., Marshall, Minn., 1983-86; chancellor Minn. State U. Sys., St. Paul, 1986-91; pres. U. R.I., Kingston, 1991—. Author: Freedom and Other Times, 1972; John Calvin's Favorite Son, 1980. Served with AUS, 1960-68. Avocation: fishing. Home: 56 Upper College Rd Kingston RI 02881-2022 Office: URI Office of the President Carlotti Administration Building 75 Lower College Rd Ste 7 Kingston RI 02881-1966

CAROVANO, JOHN MARTIN, not-for-profit administrator, conservationist; b. Tacoma, May 9, 1935; s. John and Elda C. (Martin) C.; m. Barbara Bevins, June 14, 1958; children: Kristen, Kathryn. BA, Pomona Coll., 1957, LL.D., 1979; MA, U. Calif. at Berkeley, 1961, PhD, 1965; LL.D., Hamilton Coll., 1974. Research asst., teaching fellow U. Calif. at Berkeley, 1959-63; instr. econs. Hamilton Coll., Clinton, N.Y., 1963-65, asst. prof., 1965-68, asso. prof., 1969-74, acting provost, 1971-72, provost, 1972-74, pres. coll., 1974-88; dir. N.Y. office The Nature Conservancy, 1988-94, planned giving officer, 1994—. Financial economist Office Tax Analysis, U.S. Dept. Treasury, Washington, 1968-69; chmn. N.Y. Com. of Selection, Rhodes Scholarship Trust, 1978-82; trustee Commn. on Ind. Colls. and Univs. N.Y., 1980-83 Mem. Democratic Com., Clinton, 1970-74. Served with AUS, 1957-58. Home: 26 St Agnes Ln Albany NY 12211-2058 Office: Nature Conservancy 415 River St Ste 4 Troy NY 12180-2896 E-mail: jcarovano@tnc.org.

CARP, DANIEL A. manufacturing company executive; b. Wytheville, Va. BBA in Quantitative Methods, Ohio U.; MBA, Rochester Inst. Tech.; MS in Mgmt., MIT. Stats. analyst Eastman Kodak Co., Rochester, NY, various postions in market rsch. and mgmt., gen. mgr. sales Kodak Can., gen. mgr. consumer electronics divsn., asst. gen. mgr. Latin Am. region, 1986-88, v.p., gen. mgr., 1988-90, gen. mgr. European Mktg. Cos., 1990, exec. v.p., asst. COO, 1995-97, pres., COO, 1997-2000, pres., CEO, 2000, chmn., pres., CEO, 2000—01, chmn., CEO, 2001—. Sloan fellow Sloan Sch. of Mgmt., MIT. Office: 343 State St Rochester NY 14650-0001

CARP, LARRY, lawyer; b. St. Louis, Jan. 26, 1926; s. Avery and Ruth C. Student, U. Mo., Columbia, 1944; cert., Sorbonne U., Paris, 1946; BA, Washington U., St. Louis, 1947; postgrad., Grad. Inst. Internat. Studies, Geneva, 1949; JD, Washington U., St. Louis, 1951. Bar: Mo. 1951, U.S. Dist. Ct. (ea. dist.) Mo. 1951. Mem. U.S. Dept. of State, Washington, 1951-53; mem. staff Senator Paul H. Douglas (Dem. Ill.), Washington, 1953-54; assoc. Fordyce, Mayne, Hartman, Renard, and Stribling, St. Louis, 1954-63; sole practice St. Louis, 1963-68; ptnr. Carp & Morris, St. Louis, 1968-90, Carp, Sexauer and Carr, St. Louis, 1990-94, Carp and Sexauer, St. Louis, 1994—. Assoc. counsel, acting chief counsel U.S. Senate Subcom. on Constitutional Rights, Washington, 1956; mem. St. Louis Regional U.S. Export Expansion Coun., 1964-74; mem. Mo. Commn. on Human Rights, 1966-78, vice chmn., 1977-78; vice chmn., bd. dirs. Pastoral Counselling Inst. for Greater St. Louis, 1964-91; mem. bd. trustees The Acad. Sci., St. Louis, 1984—, asst. treas., 1992-2003; mem. adv. bd. George Engelmann Math. and Science Inst., 1992-96; bd. dirs. St. Louis Ctr. for Internat. Rels., 1998—; legal advisor Image, Inc., St. Louis, 1998—; mem. cmty. adv. panel Double Helix (TV and Radio) Corp., 1999—. Co-author: (musicals) Pocahontas, The Pied Piper, Androcles; author: (musicals) For the Love of Adam, The Red Ribbon, Famous Last Words, GOD KNOWS!; contbr. articles to newspapers and mags. on subjects relating to immigration and nationality law. Mem. Common Cause, 1966-78, chmn. Mo. chpt., 1973-75; bd. dirs. Internat. Inst. of Metro St. Louis, 1980-86, English Speaking Union, St. Louis, 1985—, Mo. Prison Arts Program, 1999—; U.S. presdl. appointee as sr. adviser and U.S. pub. del. to UN 55th Gen. Assembly, 2000-2001. With U.S. Army, 1944-46, ETO. Decorated (2) Battle Stars; Rotary Internat. fellow Grad. Inst. Internat. Studies, Geneva, 1948-49; award for Outstanding Service in Recognition of Spl. Needs of Hispanic Community IMAGE, St. Louis, 1984; selected in immigration and naturalization law by his peers as one in Best Lawyers in Am., 1992— Fellow Am. Acad. Matrimonial Lawyers (cert.); mem. ABA (immigration law coord. com., chmn. immigration law com. gen. practice sect. 1981-86), Mo. Bar Assn., Bar Assn. Met. St. Louis (chmn. internat. law and trade com. 1973-79, chmn. immigration law com. 1989-92), Am. Immigration Lawyers Assn., St. Louis Ctr. for Internat. Rels. (bd. dirs. 1998—), UNA-USA Assn. (bd. dirs. St. Louis chpt. 1999—), Phi Delta Phi. Office: Carp and Sexauer Notary Pub 225 S Meramec Ave Ste 325 Saint Louis MO 63105-3511 Fax: 314-727-0308. E-mail: candslaw@earthlink.net.

CARPEL, EMMETT FRANKLIN, ophthalmologist, consultant; b. Phila. MD, Hahnemann U., 1968. Cert. Am. Acad. of Ophthalmology, 1976. Fellow U. Wash., Seattle, 1971—72, resident, 1972—75; staff Health Partners, Mpls., 1975—, Hennepin County Med. Ctr. HFA, Mpls., 1975—, Hennepin Faculty Assocs., Bloomington, Minn., 1975—. Cons. U. Minn., 1991. Contbr. articles. Capt. U.S. Army, 1969—71. Recipient Edn. Tchg. award, Group Health, 1993. Fellow: Am. Acad. Ophthalmology; mem.: Minn. Acad. Ophthalmology (bd. mem. 2000—), Royal Coll. Ophthalmologists. Achievements include patents for medical devices. Office: Health Partners 8600 Nicollet Ave So Bloomington MN 55420 Office Fax: 952-887-6677.

CARPENETI, WALTER L. judge; b. San Francisco, 1945; m. Anne Dose, 1969; children: Christian, Marianna, Lia, Bianca. AB in History with distinction, Stanford U., 1967; JD, U. Calif., Berkeley, 1970. Law clk. Justice John H. Dimond Alaska Supreme Ct., 1970-71; pvt. practice San Francisco, 1972-74; pub. defender Juneau, Alaska, 1974-78; pvt. practice, 1978-81; judge Alaska Superior Ct., Juneau, 1981-98, state supreme ct. justice, 1998—. Office: Alaska Supreme Ct PO Box 114100 Juneau AK 99811-4100

CARPENTER, AMY TACY, architect; b. Abington, Pa., July 20, 1970; d. Frederick John and Marlen Julia Livezey; m. Stephen M. Carpenter, Jan. 4, 1992; 1 child, Perry W. BArch, Temple U., 1993. Registered arch., Pa. Intern arch. Stevens Luchanko Arch., Glenside, Pa., 1991-94; project mgr. Mike Rosen & Assocs., Phila., 1994-97; exec. arch. The Martin Archtl. Group, Phila., 1997—2002; sr. arch. Wallace, Roberts & Todd, 2002—. Co-designer: Pavillion at Beaux Arts Ball, Phila., 1997 (1st pl. award Found. for Architecture/ELF-ATOCHEM). Mem. AIA, Nat. Assn. Archtl. Registration Bds. Avocations: swimming, travel. Office: Wallace, Roberts & Todd 260 S Broad St Philadelphia PA 19102

CARPENTER, ANGIE M. county legislator, small business owner, editor; b. Bay Shore, N.Y., Sept. 30, 1943; d. Joseph and Ida (Gullo) Linarello; m. Joe David Carpenter, Apr. 13, 1964; children: Richard, Robert. Student, Nassau C.C., 1962-63. Office mgr., graphic designer, typographer Merrick (N.Y.) Typographers and Maverick Pubs., 1966-76; founder, v.p. AC Typesetters and Printing, Inc., West Islip, N.Y., 1976-93. Editor, pub., co-founder West Islip Record, 1986-91; columnist The Graphic, The Beacon, 1985-87. Chmn. publicity com., trustee Babylon/West Islip Windmill Com., Inc., Babylon, N.Y., 1986—, ASK US, 1987-98; trustee West Islip After-Sch.-Care program, 1987-97, Our Lady of Consolation Geriatric Care Ctr.; vice chmn. West Islip Youth Enrichment Svcs., 1986-87; mem. govt. action coun. L.I. Assn., 1987; mem. recycling panel Town of Islip, 1987; chairperson TOI Blue Ribbon Com. on Recycling, 1987-88; trustee Suffolk County Vanderbilt Mus., 1990-93; vice chair Suffolk County Salvation Army Adv. Bd.; elected Suffolk County Legislator, 1993—. Mem. West Islip C. of C. (v.p., mchts. dir. 1982-84, pres. 1985, 86, 87, 88). Republican. Roman Catholic. Office: Office County Legislature 4 Udall Rd West Islip NY 11795-2341 E-mail: www.acarpent@suffolk.lib.ny.us.

CARPENTER, ARTHUR LLOYD, education educator; s. Arthur Betz and Mildred C. (Cunningham); m. Madeline Mae Daue, Aug. 1, 1953; children: Thomas Wayne, James Paul, Lee Arthur. BS, Ea. Mich. U., 1951; MS, Mich. State U., 1956; postgrad. studies, Wayne State U., 1957, U. Mic., 1958-66. Cert. elem., secondary tchr. (permanent), Mich. Tchr. Jefferson Consol. Schs., Monroe, Mich., 1951-53, Plymouth (Mich.) Comty. Schs., 1953-55; asst. prof. edn. U. No. Iowa, Cedar Falls, 1956-64; coord. instrnl. materials Wayne-Westland Comty. Sch., Wayne, Mich., 1964; asst. prof. edn. Ea. Mich. U., Ypsilanti, Mich., 1964-90. Cons. Iowa and Mich. schs., 1957-90, Fed. Correctional Prison, Milan, Mich., 1966; cons. with Nat. Coun. Accreditation of Tchr. Edn. Nebr. Wesleyan U., Lincoln, 1969. Film producer: 12 films for U. No. Iowa, 1957-64; Slide sets and F.S. 14 produced for U. No. Iowa, 1957-64; contbr. articles to 15 profl. publs.; photography reproduced in numerous mags.; book reviewer for several publishers. Recipient Red Balloon award Detroit Assn. Film Tchrs., 1970, 2d prize in Wayne Behling Meml. Photographic Contest, Ann Arbor, Mich., 1987. Mem. Wayne Hist. Soc. (bd. dirs., pres.), Mich. Bird Banders Assn. (pres.), Mich. Audubon Soc. (com. chmn.), Washtenaw Audubon Soc. (pres.), Mich. Natural Area Coun., Mich Photographic Hist. Soc. Home: 3646 S John Hix Rd Wayne MI 48184-1047

CARPENTER, BARRY KEITH, chemistry educator, researcher; b. Hastings, Sussex, U.K., Feb. 13, 1949; came to U.S., 1973; s. George Henry and Gladys Mable Carpenter. BSc with honors, Warwick U., Coventry, Eng., 1970; PhD, U. Coll., London, 1973. Postdoctoral fellow Yale U., New Haven, 1973-75; asst. prof. Cornell U., Ithaca, N.Y., 1975-81, assoc. prof., 1981-85, prof., 1985—, dept. chair, 2001—. Cons. Hoffman-La Roche, Inc., Nutley, N.J., 1985-97, Astra AB, Sodertalje, Sweden, 1989-95, Union Carbide, Linde divsn., Tarrytown, N.Y., 1991, Eastman Kodak Co., Rochester, N.Y., 1997—, Exxon Chem. Co., 1997, Bristol-Myers Squibb Co., 1998—, Archer-Daniels-Midland Co., 2000; R.A. Welch Found. lectr. Yale U., New Haven, 1989, Bergman lectr., 1992; Louis Jacob Bircher lectr. Vanderbilt U., Nashville, 1993; vis. prof. U. New South Wales, Sydney, Australia, 1997. Author: Determination of Organic Reaction Mechanisms, 1984; sr. editor Jour. Organic Chemistry, 1992-2000. NATO fellow, 1973, A.P. Sloan Found. fellow, 1980, J.S. Guggenheim Found. fellow, 1986; Av. Humboldt Found. grantee, 1990. Fellow AAAS; mem. Am. Chem. Soc. (Cope Scholar award 1997, James Flack Norris award 1999), Royal Soc. Chemistry. Office: Cornell U Dept Chemistry 328 Baker Lab Ithaca NY 14853-1301 E-mail: bkc1@cornell.edu.

CARPENTER, BETTY O. writer; b. Montreal, June 1, 1926; d. Harry and Dorothy (Schacher) Shmerling; m. David G. Ostroff, Apr. 6, 1946 (div. 1972); children: Jack Ostroff, Lucy Ostroff Harrow; m. Russell William Carpenter, Jr., Oct. 2, 1976 (dec.); stepchildren: Annette Marie Carpenter Freedman, Cynthia Carpenter Jefferson, Lori Carpenter Bembry. BA in Edn., Bklyn. Coll., 1947, MA in Edn., 1953; PhD in Adminstrn., NYU, 1973. Cert. sch. supt., prin., N.J., guidance counselor, elem. tchr., N.Y. Tchr. elem. grades N.Y.C. Pub. Schs. 54 and 139, Bklyn., 1946-54, 62; asst. prin. Pub. Sch. 139, Bklyn., 1962-67; pres. asst. prin. assoc. Ctrl. Office Bd. of Edn., N.Y.C., 1967-68, v.p. coun. suprs. and adminstrs., 1968-69, adminstrv. asst. pers., 1968-70; asst. supt. Plainfield (N.J.) Pub. Schs., 1970-74; supt. schs. Glen Rock (N.J.) Pub. Schs., 1974-84; ret. Author: Curriculum Handbook for Parents and Teachers, 1991, Tutoring for Pay, 1991, Musing, 1994, (book of poetry) The Brosh (Bionic Replacement of Species Humanoid), 1998, Lady of the Lake, 1999, Inherit the Rainbow, 2000, Art and Craftiness, 2001, Crystal Slopes, 2002, A Style of Their Own, 2002, Make Way for Pugsley, 2002. Trustee Glen Rock Libr. Bd., 1974-80, United Fund Bd., Glen Rock, 1975-77; vice chmn. Iredell County Bd. of Adjustment N.C., 1990-95; fellow mem. Lake Owners Gathered in Concern, N.C., 1985-88. Recipient Founders Day award NYU, 1973, Adminstrv. Leadership award NACEL, 1984. Mem. Soc. Children's Book Writers and Illustrators, Romance Writers Am., Nat. Writers Assn., Bergen County Supts. Assn. (pres.-elect), Nat. Scrabble Assn., Am. Contract Bridge League. Avocations: sculpture, golf, water aerobics, computers, bridge. Home: 11730 N 91 Pl Scottsdale AZ 85260-6866 E-mail: bcbcarp@aol.com.

CARPENTER, BILL, public relations executive; b. Fayettsville, NC, Oct. 14, 1965; s. William Arthur and Via Maria (Randall) C. Diploma, U. Bourgogne, Dijon, France, 1985; BA in History, Am. U., Washington, 1991. Mus. technician Nat. Mus. Am. History, Smithsonian Instn., Washington, 1987; press asst. Vietnam Vets. Am., Washington, 1987; editor Jour. Gospel Music, Washington, 1991-93; stringer Washington Post, People mag., Washington, 1992-98; freelance writer/critic various publs., 1992—; asst. entertainment press ssec. 1993 Clinton Inaugural, 1992-93; media dir. 30th Anniversary March on Washington, 1993; sr. publicist Carp Shank Entertainment Group, Washington, 1992-96; co-ptnr. Capital Entertainment, Washington, 1996—. Cons. Rhythm and BluesFound., Washington, 1993—, D.C Women's Coun., Washington, 1993-94. Contbg. writer: All Music Guide, 1992; contbr. articles to profl. jours.; radio host: The Music Jam, 2000—. Mem. NARAS, Gospel Music Assn. Address: Capital Entertainment Group 217 Seaton Pl N E Washington DC 20002

CARPENTER, CHARLES COLCOCK JONES, physician, educator; b. Savannah, Ga., Jan. 5, 1931; s. Charles Colcock Jones and Alexandra (Morrison) C.; m. Sally R. Fisher, Nov. 29, 1958; children— Charles Morrison, Murray Douglas, Andrew Fisher. AB, Princeton, 1952; MD, Johns Hopkins, 1956. Diplomate: Am. Bd. Internal Medicine (mem. bd. 1976—, chmn. exam. 1980—, chmn. 1983-84). Intern Johns Hopkins Hosp., 1956-57, resident, 1957-59, 61-62; practice medicine, specializing in infectious disease Balt., 1962-73; asst. prof. medicine Johns Hopkins, 1962-67, assoc. prof., 1967-69, prof., 1969-73; physician-in-chief Balt. City Hosps., 1969-73; prof., chmn. dept. medicine Case Western Res. Sch. Medicine, 1973-86; physician-in-chief Case Western Res. Univ. Hosp., 1973-85; prof. medicine Brown U., 1986—, dir. Internat. Health Inst., 1993—98. Dir. Cholera Research Program, Johns Hopkins Center Med. Research and Tng., Calcutta, India, 1962-64; chmn. cholera panel U.S.-Japan Coop. Med. Sci. Program, 1965-72; mem. U.S.-Japan Coop. Med. Sci. Program (U.S. del.), 1973—2000, chmn., 1990-2000; mem. adv. bd. Sch. Medicine Johns Hopkins U., 1982-97; mem. Nat. Adv. Coun. Allergy and Infectious Diseases, 1985-89; chmn. extramural cons. AIDS exec. com. NIH, 1986-87, nat. adv. com. for AIDS, NIH, 1992-93; chmn. adv. coun. AIDS Rsch., NIH, 1995-2000; dir. Lifespan/Tufts/Brown Ctr. for AIDS Rsch., 1998-. Trustee Internat. Ctr. for Infectious Disease Rsch., Bangladesh, 1979-83, Internat. Child Health Found., 1985-96, Miriam Hosp., 1992-97. Sr. asst. surgeon USPHS, 1959-61. Fellow ACP (master 1992), AAAS (chmn. med. scis. sect. 1994-96); mem. Inst. Medicine NAS, Am. Soc. Clin. Investigation, Assn. Am. Physicians (sec. 1975-81, councillor 1981-86, v.p. 1986-87, pres. 1987-88), Infectious Diseases Soc. Am. (Smadel medal 1991), Johns Hopkins Soc. Scholars, Johns Hopkins Med. and Surg. Assn. (pres. 1995-97), Order of the Sacred Treasure (Japan). Home: 12 Half Mile Rd Barrington RI 02806-4104

CARPENTER, CHARLES CONGDEN, zoologist, educator; b. Denison, Iowa, June 2, 1921; s. Harry Alonzo and Myrtle Ruth (Barber) C.; m. Mary F. Pitynski, Sept. 2, 1947; children— Janet Eleanor, Caryn Sue, Geoffrey Congden. BA, No. Mich. Coll. Edn., Marquette, 1943; postgrad., Tarleton State Coll., Stephenville, Tex., 1943-44, Stanford U., 1944, Wayne U., 1945; MS, U. Mich., 1947, PhD, 1951. Lab. asst. zoology No. Mich. Coll. Edn., 1941-43; teaching asst. zoology U. Mich., 1946; asst. herpetology and mammalogy Biol. Sta., summer 1948, teaching fellow zoology, 1947-51, instr. zoology, 1951-52; instr. U. Okla. Biol. Sta., Norman, summer 1952, U. Okla., 1953, asst. prof. zoology, 1953-59; assoc. prof. zoology, curator reptiles U. Okla. and, U. Okla. Biol. Sta., 1959-66, prof. zoology, curator reptiles, 1966-87, prof. emeritus zoology, curator emeritus reptiles and amphibians, 1988; rsch. assoc. in herpetology Dallas Zoo, 1980. Expdns. and field studies U. Mich. Paleontol. Expdn., Kans. and, Colo., 1947, Jackson Hole Research sta., Grand Teton Nat. Park, 1951, field trips throughout, Mexico and; S.W., U.S., 1979— ; Galapagos Islands Expdn., 1962; expdns. to islands of Gulf of Calif., 1964; invited scientist mem. Galapagos Internat. Sci. Project to Galapagos Islands, Ecuador and; Cocos Island, 1964— ; sec. Animal Research Council, Oklahoma City Zoo, 1972-74, 78—, chmn., 1980 Contbr. articles to profl. jours. Served with AUS, 1943-46. Recipient Disting. Alumni award No. Mich. U., 1972; Regents award U. Okla., 1980; numerous grants NSF; numerous grants N.Y. Zool. Soc.; numerous grants U. Okla. Alumni Devel. Fund; numerous grants U. Okla. Research Inst., 1951— Fellow Animal Behavior Soc. (sec. 1966-68), Okla. Acad. Sci. (pres. 1970, Outstanding Scientist award 1991), Herpetologist League (v.p. 1972-73, pres. 1974-75); mem. Am. Ornithologists Union, Am. Soc. Zoologists, Am. Inst. Biol. Sci., Ecol. Soc. Am., Am. Soc. Ichthyologists and Herpetologists, Wilson Ornithol. Soc., Southwestern Assn. Naturalists (bd. govs. 1965-68, pres. 1968-69, permanent sec. 1971-76, W. Frank Blair award 1987), Am. Soc. Mammalogists, Brit. Ecol. Soc., Soc. Study Amphibians and Reptiles, Explorers Club, Wilderness Soc., Nature Conservancy, Sigma Xi, Phi Kappa Phi, Phi Sigma. Home: 1218 Cruce St Norman OK 73069-4440 Office: U Okla Dept Zoology 730 Van Vleet Oval Norman OK 73019-6120

CARPENTER, CHARLES ELFORD, JR., lawyer; b. Greenville, S.C., Nov. 3, 1944; s. Charles Elford and Mary Charlotte (Campbell) C.; m. Nancy Townsend, June 8, 1968; children: Charlotte Elizabeth, John Morrison. BA, Furman U., 1966; JD, U. Va., 1969; MPA, U. S.C., 1976. Bar: Va. 1969, S.C. 1972, U.S. Dist. Ct. S.C. 1974, U.S. Ct. Appeals (4th cir.) 1978, U.S. Ct. Appeals (11th cir.) 1984, U.S. Supreme Ct. 1983. Assoc. Leatherwood, Walker, Todd & Mann, Greenville, 1969, Richardson, Plowden, Grier & Howser, Columbia, S.C., 1974-78; ptnr. Richardson, Plowden, Carpenter & Robinson, P.A., Columbia, S.C., 1978—. Mem. com. on grievances and discipline S.C. Supreme Ct., 1986-89, 1996; spkr. Law Seminars, Inc., Columbia, 1987, Outline for Post-Trial Practice, 1988, 89, 90; mem. S.C. Supreme Ct. Bd. Law Examiners, 1995-2001. Editor Appeal and Error, S.C. Jurisprudence; contbr. articles to legal jours. Mem. bd. visitors Presbyn. Coll., Clinton, S.C., 1983-87; trustee James H. Hammond Sch., Columbia, 1986-89, Trinity Presbytery; elder Eastminster Presbyn. Ch. Capt. U.S. Army, 1969-72. Fellow Am. Acad. Appellate Lawyers (bd. dirs.); mem. ABA (speaker appellate process program 1990, editor Appellate Practice Jour. 1989-2000, co-chair oral argument subcom. litigation sect., mem. task force on unreported opinions 1996—), S.C. Bar Assn. (mem. Richland County fee dispute com. 1984-88, speaker 1987, appellate practice, panel mem. proposed rules of appellate practicefor S.C. Bar ann. meeting 1989, mem. practice and procedure com., health and hosp. law subcom., appellate rules subcom., chmn. merit selection of judges subcom., alternative dispute resolution com. 1993—), Richland County Bar Assn., S.C. Def. Trial Attys. (chmn. amicus curiae com. 1981-85), Forest Lake Club, St. Andrews Soc., Tarantella Club, Columbia Ball Club, Torch Club (pres. 2000-01). Avocations: reading, hunting, tennis, fishing. Office: Richardson Plowden Carpenter & Robinson PA 1600 Marion St # 7788 Columbia SC 29201-2913

CARPENTER, CHARLES FRANCIS, lawyer; b. Raleigh, N.C., Apr. 3, 1957; s. William Lester and Mattie Frances (Wallace) C.; m. Heidi Ann Athanas, June 14, 1980. BA with honors, U. N.C., 1979, JD, 1982. Bar: N.C. 1982, U.S. Dist. Ct. (mid. dist.) N.C. 1982, U.S. Dist. Ct. (ea. dist.) N.C. 1986, U.S. Ct. Appeals (4th cir.) 1986, U.S. Dist. Ct. (we. dist.) N.C. 1988. Assoc. Newsom, Graham, Hedrick, Murray, Bryson & Kennon, Durham, N.C., 1982-87; ptnr. Newsom, Graham, Hedrick, Bryson & Kennon, Durham, 1988-93; pvt. practice Charles F. Carpenter, P.A., Durham, 1993-98; ptnr. Pulley, Watson, King & Lischer, PA, Durham, 1998—. Trustee N.C. Conf.

United Meth. Ch., 1993-2002; mem. exec. bd. Occoneechee Coun. Boy Scouts Am., 1988—. Mem. ABA, N.C. State Bar, N.C. Bar Assn., Durham County Bar Assn. (medico-legal com. 1994-2002, bd. dirs. 1998—), Order of the Old Well, Honorable Order of Ky. Colonels, Phi Beta Kappa. Democrat. Avocations: Karate, golf, softball, jogging, skiing. Home: 1325 Arnette Ave Durham NC 27707-1601 Office: 905 W Main St Ste 21 F Durham NC 27701-2076 E-mail: cfc@pwkl.com.

CARPENTER, DAVID ALLAN, lawyer; b. Cambridge, Mass., May 16, 1951; s. David Lawrence and Jane (Boucher) C.; m. Nancy Joan Surdyka, Apr. 29, 1973. BS in Bus. Adminstrn., Bucknell U., Lewisburg, Pa., 1972; MBA in Fin., Temple U., Phila., 1975; JD, Rutgers U., 1981. Banking officer Girard Bank, Phila., 1972-77, mng. ptnr., 1983-85, mng. ptnr. Mid Atlantic region, 1985-89, mng. ptnr. Atlantic region, 1989-92; nat. dir. litigation and claims svcs. Coopers & Lybrand, Phila., 1987-92, nat. dir. fin. adv. svcs. Boston, 1992-94; founding ptnr. Ptnrs. for Mkt. Leadership, Inc., Atlanta, 1995—; ptnr. Ptnrs. for Corp. Renewal, Phila., 1997—. Co-editor: Proving and Pricing Construction Claims, 1990, Environmental Dispute Handbook, 1991; contbr. articles to profl. jours., chpts. to books. Mem. Inst. Mgmt. Consultants, Turnaround Mgmt. Assn., Beta Gamma Sigma. Address: PO Box 903 Great Barrington MA 01230-0903 Office: Ptnrs for Mkt Leadership Inc 100 Galleria Pkwy SE Ste 400 Atlanta GA 30339-3122

CARPENTER, DAVID ERWIN, county planner; b. Appleton, Wis., Oct. 20, 1939; s. Erwin Carl and Othilia Mary (Killian) C.; m. Linda Louise Simkins, June 22, 1961 (div. Apr. 15 1983); children: Bradley John, Robert Anthony, Paige Elizabeth; m. Mary Starr (Davis) Griffin, May 18, 1991. BS, U. Wis., 1962, MS, 1979. Planner Wis. Dept. Devel., Madison, 1963-66, Fond du Lac County, Wis., 1966-68; supr. county planning Wis. Dept. Devel., Madison, 1968-69; assoc. dir. Southeastern Wis. Health Systems Agy., Milw., 1969-77; dir. planning St. Mary's Hosp. Med. Ctr., Madison, 1977-84; dir. mktg. St. Mary's Svcs., Madison, 1984-86; pres. David Carpenter Assocs., Madison, 1986-89; dir. planning Dodge County Planning and Devel., Juneau, Wis., 1989-95, exec. dir., 1995—. Author: Solid Waste Recycling Plan, 1991, Outdoor Recreation Plan, 1995. Pres. Wis. Soc. for Health Care Planning, 1982, pres. Charles E. Brown Archaeol. Soc., Madison, 1992-95; sec.-treas. Ice Age Park & Trail Found., Madison, 1990; vol. Columbus (Wis.) Downtown Devel. Corp., 1992; trustee Columbus United Meth. Ch., 1992—, pres. 1998—; mem. exec. com. Flyway Area Labor-Mgmt. Coun., Horicon, 1993-98; pres. Rock River Coalition, Watertown, 1995-97, chmn. comm. com., 1997-98; mem. Columbus Ad Hoc Econ. Devel. Com., 1994, Friends of Horicon Marsh Internat. Edn. Ctr., 1995—; vice chmn. Greater Columbus Recreation Commn., 1994-2002; mgr. Dodge County Heritage Preservation, Beaver Dam, 1991-97; vol. Columbus Main St. Program, 1992-95; docent Monona Terr. Cmty. and Conv. Ctr., Madison, 1999—; active City of Columbus Planning Commn., 2000—; bd. dirs. Columbus Area Aquatic Ctr., 2000—; mem. Skilaufers, Inc., 2001—, bd. dirs., 2002—, pres., 2003—; mem. Seth Peterson Cottage Conservancy Inc., 2002-03; vol. wis. Pub. TV, 2002—. Recipient Forward Wis. award, 1994, Elmer Kohlbeck Friend of Tourism award, 1995, Svc. award Rock River Coalition, 1998, Eileen Swiggum award for contbn. to Wis. archaeology, 2001. Mem. Am. Planning Assn., Wis. Archaeol. Soc., Charles E. Brown Archaeol. Soc., Olbrich Bot. Soc., League Am. Bicyclists, Wis. Hist. Soc., Western Pa. Conservancy, Phi Sigma Kappa. Avocations: archaeology, art, history, gardening, bicycling. Office: Dodge County Planning & Devel 127 E Oak St Juneau WI 53039-1329

CARPENTER, DAVID G. federal agency administrator; BA in Personnel Mgmt., Okla. State U., 1970; cert. Exec. Develop. Program, George Washington U., 1985. Former spl. agent U.S. Secret Svc., former spl. agt. in charge of presdl. protective divsn.; asst. sec. of state for diplomatic security U.S. Dept. of State, Washington, 1998—. Office: US Dept of State Bur of Diplomatic Security 2201 C St NW Washington DC 20520 Office Fax: 202-647-0953.

CARPENTER, DEE, publishing executive; Grad., Roanoke Coll. Pres. & pub. Virginian-Pilot, 2000—. Bd. dirs. Multiple Sclerosis Soc. of Hampton Roads. Mem. Va. Beach C. of C. Office: Virginian-Pilot 150 W Brambleton Ave Norfolk VA 23510

CARPENTER, DELBERT STANLEY, educational administration educator; b. Wichita Falls, Tex., May 18, 1950; s. Delbert Stanley Sr. and Nancy (Williams) S.; m. Noralyn Gray, July 13, 1973 (div. Mar. 1986); m. Janet Ann Stewart, July 15, 1989 (div. June 1993); m. Linda Jan Meerdink Evans, June 15, 1994; 1 child, Susanne Gray Carpenter; stepchildren: Robert Scott Evans, Peter Clark Evans. BS, Tarleton State U., 1972; MS, East Tex. State U., 1975; PhD, U. Ga., 1979. Actuarial technician A.S. Hansen, Inc., Dallas, 1972-74; grad. asst. cen. housing office East Tex. State U., Commerce, 1974-75; men's resident dir. Oglethorpe U., Atlanta, 1975-77; grad. asst. rsch., tchg., counseling and human devel. dept. U. Ga., Athens, 1977-79; dean students U. Ark., Monticello, 1979-81; asst. dir. devel. Tex. A&M U., College Station, 1982-84, from asst. prof. ednl. adminstrn. to assoc. prof., 1985-95, prof., 1995—. Mem. editl. bds. various profl. jours.; contbr. articles to profl. jours. Named Outstanding Doctoral Alumnus, Students Affairs Adminstrn. U. Ga., 1995, Disting. Tchg. award Assn. Former Students Coll. of Edn., 1996. Mem. Assn. for the Study Higher Edn. (exec. dir. 1987-98, Disting. Svc. award 1996), Am. Coll. Pers. Assocs. (Annuit Coeptis award 1995, Sr. Scholar 2000, chair 2001—), Nat. Assn. Student Pers. Adminstrn. (mem.-at-large nat. bd. 2001-2003), South Assn. for Coll. Student Affairs (Melvene Hardee award 1997), Alpha Phi Omega (pres., bd. dirs. 1986-90, Nat. Disting. Svc. award 1990, trustee endowment fund 1996—, chair 1997—), Alpha Chi. Avocations: golf, reading, travel. Home: 129 Mountain Laurel Way Bastrop TX 78602 E-mail: s-carpenter@tamu.edu.

CARPENTER, DERR ALVIN, landscape architect; b. Sunbury, Pa., Jan. 18, 1931; s. Alvin Witmer and Katharine (Rockefeller) C.; m. Helen Longden Hedge, Apr. 10, 1954; children: Mary Katharine Carpenter Denault, Melissa Sue Carpenter Sciumbata. BS, Pa. State U., 1953. Registered landscape architect. Chief landscape architect La. State Parks, Baton Rouge, 1955-58; asst. dir. City Parish Planning Com., Baton Rouge, 1958-62; chief planning and engring. Pa. State Parks, Harrisburg, 1962-67; pres. Derr A. Carpenter & Assocs., Camp Hill, Pa., 1967-73; v.p. Smith, Miller & Assocs. Inc., Camp Hill and Kingston, Pa., 1973-86, Rettew Assocs. Inc., Mechanicsburg and Lancaster, Pa., 1987-90; self employed landscape architect Mechanicsburg, 1990—. Lectr. Pa. State U., Harrisburg Area C.C., 1973-2003, Susquehanna U.; mem. legis. com. Pa. Recreation and Park Soc., University Park, 1982-90; bd. dirs. Pa. State Arts and Architecture Alumni Bd., University Park, 1985-95. Mem. Camp Hill Shade Tree Commn., 1968-87; councilman Tree of Life Luth. Ch., Linglestown, 1994-98, bldg. com., fellowship com., social ministry com.; bd. dirs. Park Adv. Bd., Cumberland County, Pa., 1978-84; bd. dirs. YMCA, Harrisburg, 1974-80, Capital Region Econ. Devel. Corp., 1988-93; chair Zoning Commn., 1989, Dauphin County Open Space Commn., 1989-92. With U.S. Army, 1953-55. Pa. State U. Alumni fellow, 1984 Fellow Am. Soc. Landscape Architects (trustee 1977-80, 1983, pres. chpt. 1973-77, nat. ethics com. chmn. 1984-87, dir. legislation 1968-90, Disting. Svc. award 1981, cert. appreciation 1984); mem. Susquehanna River Tri-State Assn. (pres. 1980 82, Leadership award 1982, bd. dirs.), Pa. Nursery Mktg. Adv. Coun. (chmn. 1976-77, bd. dirs. Outstanding Achievement award 1972), Pa. State Alumni Assn. of Harrisburg (pres. 1983-85, bd. dirs., Leadership award 1985). Lodges: Torch (bd. dirs. 1976-81), Rotary (bd. dirs. 1968-82), Masons. Republican. Lutheran. Avocations: gardening, hiking, reading, printing, massage. E-mail: laguy3@juno.com.

CARPENTER, EDMUND NELSON, II, retired lawyer; b. Phila., Jan. 27, 1921; s. Walter S. and Mary (Wootten) C.; m. Carroll Morgan, July 18, 1970; children: Mary W., Edmund Nelson III, Katherine R.R., Elizabeth Lea; stepchildren: John D. Gates, Ashley du Pont Gates. AB, Princeton U., 1943; LLB, Harvard U., 1948; LLD (hon.), Widener U., 1985, U. Del., 1999. Bar: Del. 1949, U.S. Supreme Ct. 1957. Assoc. Richards, Layton & Finger, Wilmington, Del., 1949-53, ptnr., 1953-78, dir., 1978-91, pres., 1982-85; retired, 1991. Dep. atty. gen. State of Del., 1953-54, spl. dep. atty., 1960-62; chmn. Del. Superior Ct. Jury Study Com., 1963-66, Del. Supreme Ct. Cts. Consol. Com., 1985-87; mem. Del. Gov.'s Commn. Law Enforcement and Adminstrn. Justice, 1969; chmn. Del. Supreme Ct. Adv. Com. on Profl. Fin. Accountability, 1974-75, Del. Jud. Nominating Commn., 1977-83, Del. Superior Ct. Study Com., 1991-92; mem. Long Range Cts. Planning Com., 1976-89, Del. Ct. Common Pleas Study Com., 1992, Del. Supreme Ct. Com. on Judicial Code of Conduct, 1991-93; co-chmn. Del. Justice Ctr. Com., 1994-97; mem. lawyers adv. com. U.S. Ct. Appeals (3d cir.) 1975-80, chmn., 1975-77; chmn. local rules com. U.S. Dist. Ct. Del., 1978-83, Del. Ct. on the Judiciary Rules Com., 1996-98; bd. dirs. Bank of Del., Barclay's Bank. Trustee Wilmington Med. Ctr., 1965—, U. Del., 1971-77, Princeton U., 1974-85, 86-91, Winterthur Mus., 1991-99, World Affairs Coun. Wilmington, 1968-80, Woodrow Wilson Found., 1985—, Lawrenceville Sch., 1953-74, trustee emeritus, 1974—; trustee Nat. Humanities Ctr., 1995-98; bd. dirs. Good Samaritan Inc., 1973—, pres., 1998—; mem. Del. Health Care Injury Ins. Study Commn., 1976-80. With U.S. Army, 1942-46, 50-52. Decorated Bronze Star, Soldier's medal, Chinese Order of the Flying Cloud with four battle stars; recipient 1st State Disting. Svc. award, Del. State Bar Assn., 1984, Josiah Marvel Cup award Del. State C. of C., 1990, Benjamin Franklin Disting. Pub. Svc. award Am. Philos. Soc., 1996, Professionalism award, Am. Inns of Ct., 2003, Caring Bowl award, U.S. Ct. Appeals, 2003. Fellow Am. Coll. Trial Lawyers, Am. Bar Found.; mem. ABA (ho. of dels. 1979-86), Del. State Bar Assn. (pres. 1971-72, Presdl. citation 1987), ATLA, Am. Judicature Soc. (bd. dirs. 1974-83, exec. com. 1978-80, v.p. 1980-81, pres. 1981-83, Justice award 1991). Home and Office: 600 Center Mill Rd Wilmington DE 19807-1502 E-mail: Nedcarp@aol.com.

CARPENTER, EDWARD KEARNEY, writer, editor; b. Atlanta, Mar. 17, 1932; s. Otto William and Katherine (Kearney) C.; m. Ruth Corn, Aug. 31, 1958 (div. Dec. 1977); m. Joanna Clapp, Mar. 18, 1986. BA, Haverford (Pa.) Coll., 1954; MA, U. Pa., Phila., 1958. Assoc. editor Indsl. Design Mag., N.Y.C., 1960-64; sr. editor Progressive Archiecture, N.Y.C., 1964-69; contbg. editor Design & Environ., N.Y.C., 1970-72, Environ. Design, N.Y.C., 1972-78; corr. at large Archtl. Forum, N.Y.C., 1972-75; editor Oyster River Press, Durham, N.H., 1991—. Cons. IBM, Poughkeepsie, N.Y., 1983. Author: The Best in Environmental Graphics, 1975, 37 Design and Environment Projects, 1976, Urban Design Case Studies, 1977, The Best in Exhibition Design, 1977, 78, 80, 82, 84, 86, 89, 91, 94, Design Case Studies, 1979, Design Review 25, 1979; writer, rschr.: Frommer's India on $5 and $10 a Day, 1976; contbr. articles to mags. and encys. Commr. Historic Dist. Commn., Durham, 1990-94. Sgt. U.S. Army, 1957-60, Korea. Mem. Nat. Audubon Soc. (life). Avocations: reading, sailing, skiing, canoeing, swimming.

CARPENTER, ELIZABETH JANE, communications executive; b. Cleve., Mar. 29, 1949; d. Robert E. and Joan Jaffe. BA, Western Coll., Oxford, Ohio, 1970. Pub. rels. asst. Lennen & Newell/Pacific, Honolulu, 1970-73; account exec. Marschalk Advt., Cleve., 1973-76; cons. Carpenter Advt. & Pub. Rels., Cleve., 1976-80; internat. pub. rels. mgr. Wang Labs., Inc., Boston, 1980-82, advt. mgr., 1982-87; mgr. worldwide comm. CSS Digital Equipment Corp., Merrimack, N.H., 1987-92, advt. mgr. U.S. Svcs. group, 1992-99; mktg. mgr. Logic Divsn. Avanti Corp., North Billerica, Mass., 2000—. Assoc. producer Am. Treasure, TV spl., 1986, The Entrepreneurs, TV spl., 1986-87; owner Carpenter Antiques, Dennis, Mass. Mem. Cape Cod Antiques Dealers Assn., Boston Advt. Club, Boston Club. Office: Avant! Corp 101 Billerica Ave North Billerica MA 01862

CARPENTER, FRANK CHARLES, JR., retired electronics engineer; b. L.A., June 1, 1917; s. Frank Charles and Isobel (Crump) C.; A.A., Pasadena City Coll., 1961; B.S. in Elec. Engring. cum laude, Calif. State U.-Long Beach, 1975, M.S. in Elec. Engring., 1981; m. Beatrice Josephine Jolly, Nov. 3, 1951; children, Robert Douglas, Gail Susan, Carol Ann. Self-employed design and mfgr. aircraft test equipment, Los Angeles, 1946-51; engr. Hoffman Electronics Corp., Los Angeles, 1951-56, sr. engr., 1956-59, project mgr., 1959-63; engr.-scientist McDonnell-Douglas Astronautics Corp., Huntington Beach, Calif., 1963-69, spacecraft telemetry, 1963-67, biomed. electronics, 1967-69, flight test instrumentation, 1969-76; lab. test engr. Northrop Corp., Hawthorne, Calif., 1976-82, spl. engr., 1982-83; mgr. transducer calibration lab. Northrop Corp., Pico-Rivera, Calif., 1983-86. Served with USNR, 1941-47. Mem. IEEE (life), Amateur Radio Relay League. Contbr. articles to profl. jours. Patentee transistor squelch circuit; helicaland whip antenna. Home: 2037 Balearic Dr Costa Mesa CA 92626-3514

CARPENTER, GENE BLAKELY, crystallography and chemistry educator; b. Evansville, Ind., Dec. 15, 1922; s. Leland A. and Juanita (Blakely) C.; m. Elizabeth E. Corkum, Apr. 15, 1949; children— Jonathan R., Anne E. BA, U. Louisville, 1944; MA, Harvard U., 1945, PhD, 1947. NRC fellow Calif. Inst. Tech., 1947-48, research fellow, 1948-49; instr. Brown U., 1949-52, asst. prof., 1952-56, asso. prof., 1956-63, prof., 1963-88, prof. emeritus, 1988—. Guggenheim fellow U. Leeds, Eng., 1956-57; vis. prof. U. Groningen, The Netherlands, 1963-64; Fulbright-Hayes lectr. U. Zagreb, Yugoslavia, 1971-72; vis. scientist Oak Ridge Nat. Lab., 1980, U. Göttingen, Fed. Republic of Germany, 1987, U. Canterbury, Christchurch, New Zealand, 1989. Author: Principles of Crystal Structure Determination, 1969; Contbr. articles to sci. jours. Mem. Am. Crystallographic Assn., Am. Chem. Soc. Home: 229 Medway St Apt 309 Providence RI 02906-5300 Office: Brown U Dept Chemistry Providence RI 02912-0001 E-mail: gene_carpenter@brown.edu.

CARPENTER, GEORGE ROBERT, artist; b. Boston, Dec. 13, 1928; s. George Gillis and Daisy Winifred Carpenter; m. Virgina A. forsyth, Oct. 14, 1966. One-man shows include Wilkes Coll., Wilkes-Barre, Pa., Rockport (Mass.) Art Assn., Red Piano Gallery, Hilton Head Island, S.C., quadrangle Gallery, Dallas, Hallway Gallery, Washington, Down East Gallery, Washington, Continental Galleries, Ontreal, Que., others; group shows include Acad. Artists Assn., Springfield, Mass., Anchorage Fine Arts Mus., Black Hills State Coll., Spearfish, S.C., cheyenne (Wyo.) Western Galleries, Copley Soc., Boston, Charles and Emma Frye Mus., Seattle, Mainstreams, Marietta, Ohio, Nat. Acad. of Design, N.Y., Rockport Art Assn., Salmagundi Club, N.Y., Wouthwestern Watercolor Soc., Dallas, others; represented in pub. and pvt. collections includingMerck Pharma., Miami U., Ohio, Mills coll., Oakland, Calif., Nat. Steamship Lines, Can., No. Trust Offices, Chgo., others. Mem. adv. bd. Coastal Conservation Assn., Maine, 1997—. Mem. Rockport Art Assn., Watercolor USA Honor Soc., Masons, Shriners, Lions. Avocation: fishing. Home: 74 Restview Ln Wells ME 04090 Office: George Carpenter Gallery Perkins Cove Ogunquit ME 03907

CARPENTER, GORDON RUSSELL, retired lawyer, banker; b. Denton, Tex., Feb. 6, 1920; s. Solomon Lafayette and Grace L. (Fowler) C.; m. Muriel E. James, Sept. 18, 1943 (dec.); m. Mary Alice Borah, Aug. 4, 1962. BS, North Tex. State U., 1940; postgrad., Georgetown U., 1941-42; LL.B., So. Meth. U., 1948. Bar: Tex. 1947, U.S. Supreme Ct. 1960. Announcer KDNT, Denton, Tex., 1940-41; spl. agent FBI, 1941-46; exec. sec. Southwestern Legal Found., Dallas, 1947-56; exec. dir., 1956-58; adminstv. asst. to dean Law Sch. So. Meth. U., 1951-58, asst. prof. law, 1956-68, pres. Law Alumni, 1959-60; trust officer 1st Nat. Bank, Dallas, 1958-60, v.p., 1960-79; v.p., sr. fin. planning officer InterfFirst Bank, Dallas, 1979-84. Pres. Law Alumni Assn., 1959. Bd. regents Tex. Sch. Trust Banking, 1981-82; bd. trustees Hatton W. Sumners Found., 1959—, exec. dir., 1985-95; chmn. North Tex. State U. Ednl. Found.; chmn. Luth. Med. Sys. Tex. Found., 1980-83; vice chmn. Farmers Br. Hosp. Authority, 1976-77. Recipient Pres.'s award State Bar Tex., 1963, Bd. Dirs. award, 1971, Gene Cavin award for excellence in con. legal edn., 1998, Disting. Law Alumni award So. Meth. U., 2001. Fellow Tex. Bar Found.; mem. ABA (chmn. publs. com. mineral and natural resources law sect. 1958-64), State Bar Tex. (chmn. cont. legal edn. com. 1952-54, 58-66, chmn. real estate, probate and trust law sect. 1964-65), Dallas Bar Assn. (dir. 1960-61, 65-66, chmn. centennial com. 1972-73), Dallas Bar Found. (trustee, sec.-treas.), Tex. Bankers Assn. (chmn. trust divsn. 1980-81), Soc. Former Spl. Agts. FBI (pres. 1963), Brookhaven Country Club, Masons, Delta Theta Phi. Republican. Presbyterian. Office: 325 N Saint Paul St Ste 3920 Dallas TX 75201-3821

CARPENTER, HOYLE DAMERON, music educator emeritus; b. Stockton, Calif., Aug. 8, 1909; s. William Horace and Mabel (Hanna) C.; m. Rose Mick, Feb. 24, 1968. MusB, U. Pacific, 1930; MusM, U. Rochester, 1932; PhD, U. Chgo., 1951-57; postgrad., U. Calif., Berkeley, 1949-50. Instr. Ft. Hays (Kans.) State Coll., 1942-44; asst. prof. Grinnell (Iowa) Coll., 1944-57; asst. prof. music Rowan U., Glassboro, N.J., 1957-60, assoc. prof., 1960-61, prof., 1961-76, prof. emeritus, 1976—. Author: Teaching Elementary Music Without a Supervisor, 1959, also edits. Holyoke's Instrumental Assistant, 1959, Crequillon Pisne me peult venir, 1962; also several poster sets on music, 1970; also articles; writer program notes for Hollybush Festival, Lenape Chamber Players, Craftsbury Chamber Players, 1980—, Allegro Soc.; book reviewer various jours.; original compositions string quartet, Pastorale for flute and strings, Organ Chorale Preludes, Quodlibet for oboe and piano, others. Treas. Gloucester County Mental Health Assn., 1963-68; committeeman Glassboro Dem. Com., 1964; v.p. Glassboro Dem. Club, 1964-66; bd. dirs. Glassboro Ctr. for the Arts, 1999--. Mem. AAUP, Am. Fedn. Tchrs., Am. Musicological Soc., Music Tchrs. Nat. Assn. (sec. Ea. divsn. 1962-64), Music Educators Nat. Conf., Renaissance Soc. Am., Am. Guild Organists, Internat. Musicological Soc., N.J. Music Tchrs. Assn. (pres. 1961-63), Pi Kappa Lambda. Home: 512 S Woodbury Rd Pitman NJ 08071-1636

CARPENTER, JAMES MICHAEL, curator; BS in Entomology, Mich. State U., 1977; PhD in Entomology, Cornell U., 1983. Assoc. curator Am. Mus. Natural History, N.Y.C., 1992—95, curator entomology, 1995—; fellow Smithsonian Instn., 1983—84. Adj. prof. dept. entomology Cornell U., 1995—; adj. prof. CCNY, 1996—. Fellow: Willi Hennig Soc. (editor 1988—90, coun. mem. 1994—96, 1998—, pres. 1996—98); mem.: Soc. Systematic Biologists (assoc. editor 1986—87, coun. mem. 1988—90), N.Y. Entomol. Soc. (editor 1993—98), Internat. Union for the Study of Social Insects, Internat. Soc. Hymenopterists (sec. 1988—92, pres.-elect 1995—96, pres. 1996 98), Am. Assn. for Zool. Nomenclature. Office: Am Mus Natural History Divsn Invertabrate Zoology Central Park West at 79th St New York NY 10024

CARPENTER, J.D. academic administrator; b. Logan, W.Va., June 9, 1967; s. Jean L. and Charles L. Carpenter; m. Lisa J. Barker, June 11, 1994. BS, W.Va. U., 1985—89, MS, 1989—91, EdD, 1998—2002; Edn. Specialist, Marshall U. Grad. Coll., 1998—2001. Resident dir. Concord Coll., Athens, W.Va., 1991—94; dir. of residence life Salem-Teikyo U., Salem, W.Va., 1995—95; dir. of campus life Bluefield State Coll., W.Va., 1995—2001; assoc. vp for ops./student devel. Mountain State U., Beckley, W.Va., 2001—. Membership coord. Region II - Nat. Assn. of Student Pers. Administrators, Washington, 1999—; naspa liaison W.Va. Assn. of Student Pers. Administrators, Beckley, W.Va., 2000—. Pres. Gamma Beta Phi Nat. Honor and Svc. Soc., Oak Ridge, Tenn., 1998—99; W. Va. state coord. Basset Hound Rescue of Old Dominion, Charlottesville, Va., 1998—2003; deacon Parkview Bapt. Ch., Bluefield, Va., 2002—03. Mem.: Nat. Assn. of Student Pers. Administrators (assoc.), W.Va. Assn. of Student Pers. Administrators (assoc.). Independent. Baptist. Avocations: camping, fishing, travel, photography. Office: Mountain State U PO Box 9003 Beckley WV 25802 Office Fax: 304-929-1571. E-mail: jd@mountainstate.edu.

CARPENTER, KENNETH JOHN, nutrition educator; b. London, May 17, 1923; came to U.S., 1977; s. James Frederick and Dorothy (George) C.; m. Daphne Holmes, June 22, 1944 (dec. 1974); 1 child, Roger Hugh; m. Antonina Pecoraro, June 18, 1977. BA, U. Cambridge, Eng., 1944, PhD, 1948, ScD, 1974. Mem. sci. staff Rowett Inst., Aberdeen, Scotland, 1948-56; lectr., then reader in nutrition U. Cambridge, 1956-77; prof. nutrition U. Calif., Berkeley, 1977-91. Author: History of Scurvy and Vitamin C, 1986, Protein and Energy, 1994, Beriberi, White Rice and Vitamin B, 2000; editor: Pellagra, 1982. Kellogg fellow Harvard U., 1955-56, Commonwealth fellow Cen. Food Tech. Rsch. Inst., Mysore, India, 1961, fellow Sidney Sussex Coll., Cambridge, U.K., 1961-77. Fellow Am. Inst. Nutritional Sci.(Atwater medal 1993, Hatch medal 1993); mem. History of Sci. Soc. Avocations: art history, gardening. Home: 6201 Rockwell St Oakland CA 94618-1350 Office: U Calif Dept Nutritional Sci Berkeley CA 94720-3104 E-mail: kcarp@uclink.berkeley.edu.

CARPENTER, KENNETH RUSSELL, international trading executive; b. Chgo., May 22, 1955; s. Kenneth and Margaret (Lucas) C.; 1 child, Matthew. AS in Aviation, Prairie State Coll., Chicago Heights, Ill., 1979. Respiratory therapist, Harvey, Ill., 1980-83; dir., owner, ptnr. Pulmonary Therapy Inc., Harvey, 1983—; v.p. Home Air Joliet Ltd., Harvey, 1984—; dir., owner Air Systems Internat. Export/Import Med. Equipment, Chicago Heights, 1981—, Air Systems, Ft. Lauderdale, 1991—, Home Ortho Ltd., Harvey, 1985—; pres., CEO Profl. Yacht Svcs., Inc., Chicago Heights, 1987-94; owner CLZ Exporting Inc., Chicago Heights, 1993-95; owner, CEO, Profl. Yacht Svcs., Chicago Heights, 1997—, Info. Plus Inc., Chicago Heights, 1997—. Acquisition and mgmt. of investment real estate KRLC, 1991—; dir. pub. rels. Lansing (Ill.) Med. Group, 1990; dir. pulmonary rehab. Cardio-Pulmonary Assocs., Munster, Ind., 1990—, CLZ Exporting, 1992—; maj. importer/exporter of durable med. oxygen equipment worldwide, KRLC Mktg., 1996—; founder Wilderness Trading Group, 2002. Pilot CAP, 1979-86. With USN, 1973-77. Mem. Am. Assn. Respiratory Therapy (cert.), Nat. Assn. Med. Equipment Suppliers, Ill. Assn. of Med. Equipment Suppliers, Am. Biog. Inst., Steger C. of C., Ill. C. of C. Avocations: flying, boating, computer programming. Home and Office: 23030 Miller Rd Steger IL 60475-5932

CARPENTER, LYNETTE, language educator; b. Houston, Dec. 31, 1951; d. Robert and Mary Jane Carpenter. BA, U. Tex., 1973; MA, Ind. U., 1974, PhD, 1979. Lectr. English U. Calif., L.A., 1979—80; asst. prof. English U. Cin., 1980—89, dir. women's studies, 1980—89; from asst. prof. to assoc. prof. Ohio Wesleyan U., Delaware, 1989—2001, prof., 2001—. Author (writing as D.B. Borton): (novels) Six Feet Under, 1991; author: (writing as Della Borton) Slow Dissolve, 2001; co-editor: Haunting the House of Fiction, 1991. Office: Dept English Ohio Wesleyan U Delaware OH 43015 E-mail: dbborton@delnet.net.

CARPENTER, MARGARET MARY, state legislator, information technology manager; b. Detroit, Aug. 3, 1950; m. C.A. Bryant, Jr. (dec. Mar. 1985); m. Dale Richard Carpenter, June 25, 1988; 1 child, Heather. BS, U. Ala., 1975; MEd, U. South Ala., 1989, postgrad., 1995. Cert. tchr. spl. edn., Ala. Kindergarten tchr. Gila Bend (Ariz.) Schs., 1976-77; tchr. 1st grade Dept. of Def. Overseas Schs., Okinawa, Japan, 1977-79; spl. edn. tchr. Selbyville (Del.) Middle Sch., 1980-81; dir. religious edn. Corpus Christi Ch., Mobile, Ala., 1990-93; spl. edn. tchr. Mobile County Schs., 1981-92; PhD asst. U. South Ala., Mobile, 1992-95; mgr. tng. and devel. Teledyne Continental Motors, Mobile, 1995—99; legislator State of N.C., 2000—02; internet bus. owner. Cons. Ala. Rsch. and Insvc. Ctr., Mobile, 1988-89; presenter papers at convs. Religion tchr. Corpus Christi Ch., Mobile, 1981-94. Mem. Coun. for Exceptional Children, Nat. Coun. for Children with Behavioral Disorders, Ala. Coun. for Children with Behavior Disorders, Kappa Delta Pi (Outstanding Student of the Yr. 1994). Roman Catholic. Avocations: golf, relaxation training, cross stitch. Home: PO Box 893 Waynesville NC 28786-0893

CARPENTER, MARGARET S. (MOLLY CARPENTER), artist, sculptor; b. Wilmington, Del., Jan. 21, 1960; d. Richard Paulett and Margaret Marvel Sanger; m. Samuel Preston Carpenter, Oct. 4, 1981; children: Benjamin Sanger, Margaret Paulett. Student, Pa. Acad. Fine Arts, Phila., 1978—79, Frudakis Acad. Fine Arts, 1978—81. Apprentice Charles Cropper Parks, Wilmington, 1977-80; sculptor, Salem, 1981—. One-woman shows include Gallery 50, Bridgeton, N.J., 1983, 86, 92, Gloucester C.C., 1988, Vineland Pub. Libr., 1988; exhibited in group shows, including Wilmington Christmas Shop Artists' Gallery, 1981-2000, Glassboro State Coll., 1989, Longwood Gardens, Kennett Square, Pa., 1993, Rockfeller Ctr., 1996, Independence Seaport Mus., Phila., 1996, The Coliseum, N.Y.C., 1996, Ronald McDonald House, 1996-98, Nat. Sculpture Soc., 1997, Catherine Lorillard Wolfe Art Club, Nat. Arts Club, N.Y.C, 1999, Del. Art Mus., 1999, Olympic Regional Devel. Assn., Mus., 2000, Goodwill Games Mus., 2000; represented in permanent collections Independence Seaport Mus., Du Pont Children's Hosp., Wilmington, 1989; commns. include Constl. Compass Rose, Del. Heritage Commn. for U.S. Constn. Bicentennial, Legis. Hall, Dover, 1987, bas relief sculpture to honor Judge Samuel Desimone, Bar Assns. Cumberland, Salem and Gloucester Counties, N.J., 2000; portrait sculptures include Vince Gioaya, Robert Kasey, Dr. Martin Luther King Jr.; designer rooms class Phila. Flower Show, 1990-2001. Bd. dirs. Salem County Arts Alliance, 1997—, v.p., 2000-02; mem. arts com. Salem County Cultural and Heritage Commn., 1998-2002; bd. dirs. Salem County Cultural and Heritage, 1998-2001. Recipient numerous best of show awards, award sculpture AIDS Del., 1998; creator of Achievement Award in Sculpture, Creative Grandparenting Del., 2000. Mem. Nat. Sculpture Soc. Home: 465 Kings Hwy Salem NJ 08079 E-mail: sculptor@mollycarpenter.com.

CARPENTER, MARK WARREN, social sciences educator; b. Long Beach, Calif., Nov. 11, 1949; s. Philip Benham and Nancy Anne (Banchor) C. BA in Comm., Calif. State U., Fullerton, 1974, MPA, 1977; MA in Behavioral Sci., Calif. State U., Dominguez Hills, 1982; MA in Edn., U. Calif., Riverside, 1994.

Life cert. tchr. cmty. coll. sociology; life cert. FCC. Editor, rsch. analyst, project coord. Govt. edn. Ctr., L.A., 1975-76; rsch. fellow Calif. State U., Dominguez Hills, 1980-81, mem. staff registrar's office Fullerton, 1984-87; tchg. asst. U. Calif., Riverside, 1987-88; lectr., mem. faculty dept. sociology Riverside C.C., 1989—. Founder, World Citizens Institute, 1986. Author/compiler: (ednl. directory) After Work in Los Angeles, 1976; author, editor: (gen. plan element) Torrance Energy Awareness Monograph, 1978. Sgt. U.S. Army, 1969-71, Vietnam. Mem. Am. Ednl. Rsch. Assn., Am. Soc. Pub. Adminstrn. (mem. higher edn. and govt. rels. com.), Sociology of Edn. Assn., Assn. Environ. Profls., Calif. Coop. Edn. Assn., Internat. Assn. Cognitive Edn., Internat. Platform Assn., Com. for Expanded Ednl. Opportunity, So. Calif. Assn. Govts., Mensa. Avocations: surfing, writing. Home: PO Box 8116 Moreno Valley CA 92552-8116 Office: Riverside C C 4800 Magnolia Ave Riverside CA 92506-1242 E-mail: markc@rccd.cc.ca.us.

CARPENTER, MARY CHAPIN, singer, songwriter; b. Princeton, N.J., 1958; d. Chapin and Mary Bowie. BA, Brown U., 1981, D (hon.), 1996. Owner GETAREALJOB Music and Why Walk Music. Albums Hometown Girl, 1987, State of the Heart, 1989, Shooting Straight in the Dark, 1990, Come On Come On, 1992, Stones in the Road, 1994, A Place in the World, 1996, Party Doll and Other Favorites, 1999, recs. CBS, 1987—. Named Top Female Vocalist by Country Music Assn., 1992, 1993, Acad. of Country Music Awards Top New Female Vocalist, 1990, Top Female Vocalist, 1993; recipient Grammy award for Best Female Country Vocal Performance for four consecutive years, 1992, 93, 94, 95, Country Album of the Yr., "Stones in the Road", 1995. Mem.: ASCAP. Office: Sony Music Entertainment Corp AGF Mgmt Ltd Clarysage 550 Madison Ave Fl 6 New York NY 10022-3211

CARPENTER, MICHAEL, financial services executive; b. London, Mar. 24, 1947; came to U.S., 1971; s. Walter and Kathleen Mary C.; m. Mary Aughton, Mar. 1, 1975; children— Nicholas James, Abigail Lee. B.Sc. with joint honors, U. Nottingham, Eng., 1968; MBA, Harvard U., 1973. Bus. analyst Mond div. Imperial Chem. Industries, Runcorn, Eng., 1968-71; cons., mgr. Boston Cons. Group, 1973-78, v.p., 1978-83, Gen. Electric Co., Fairfield, Conn., 1983-86; exec. v.p. Gen. Electric Credit Corp., Stamford, Conn., from 1986; also exec. v.p. GE Financial Services Inc.; joined Kidder Peabody & Co. Inc., 1989, chmn., pres., CEO, 1990-94; head life and annuity bus. Travelers Ins. Co., Hartford, 1994—; also exec. v.p. Travelers Group, Hartford, 1994—, vice chmn., chmn., CEO, pres. life and annuity; chmn., CEO Salomon Smith Barney, N.Y.C., Citigroup Global Investments, N.Y.C. Baker scholar Harvard Bus. Sch., 1973 Office: 399 Park Ave New York NY 10022

CARPENTER, MICHAEL H. lawyer; b. Huntington, W.Va., Mar. 3, 1953; BA, Ohio State U., 1974, JD, 1977. Bar: Ohio 1977. Former ptnr. Jones, Day, Reavis & Pogue, Columbus, Ohio; ptnr. Zeiger & Carpenter, Columbus, 1994—. Mem. Phi Beta Kappa, Order of Coif. Office: Zeiger & Carpenter 1600 Huntington Ctr 41 S High St Columbus OH 43215-6101

CARPENTER, MYRON ARTHUR, manufacturing company executive; b. Jacksonville, Ill., Nov. 12, 1938; s. Paul Floyd and Margaret Esther C.; m. JoAnn Fisher, June 22, 1963. BA in Acctg, U. Ill., 1960. C.P.A., Mo. Staff acct. Arthur Young & Co., St. Louis, 1960-67, audit mgr., 1967-71; controller Bank Bldg. & Equipment Corp., St. Louis, 1972-78; v.p., treas. Bank Bldg. & Equipment Corp. Am., St. Louis, 1978-82, v.p. fin., treas., 1982-83, sr. v.p., chief fin. officer, 1983-90; v.p. fin., adminstrn. Gemco, Inc., Collinsville, Ill., 1991—. Author: (with Neal W. Beckman) Purchasing for Profit, 1979. Served with U.S. Army, 1961. Mem. AICPA, Mo. Soc. CPAs, Delta Phi.

CARPENTER, NATHANIEL DENNARD, resident health services director; b. Phila., Feb. 2, 1959; s. Marvin Dennard and Rose Ann (Heath) Carpenter; m. Jennifer Jones, Mar. 24, 2001; 1 child from previous marriage, Natalie Deneen. Lic. practical nurse, James Martin Sch., Phila., 1982. Staff nurse Med. Coll. Pa., Phila., 1982-85; nursing coord. Hosp. Home Care Greater Phila., 1985-86; staff nurse Kimberly Quality Care, Phila., 1986-90; staff nurse ICU St. Agnes Med. Ctr., Phila., 1987-90; asst. resident health coord. Logan Sq. East, Phila., 1989-92, resident health coord., 1991-94; staff nurse New Ralston House, Phila., 1994—97. asst. primary instr. P&A nursing, 2003—. Author: Vital Signs, 1990. Vol. speaker Planned Parenthood, Phila., 1982-85. With USAF, 1976-77. Avocations: reading, sports. Home: 5209 Harlan St Philadelphia PA 19131-4022 Office: Logan Sq East 2 Franklin Town Blvd Philadelphia PA 19103-1238 E-mail: nuheart1@netzero.net.

CARPENTER, NOBLE OLDS, retired bank executive; b. Cleve., May 8, 1929; s. John W. and Maribel (Olds) C.; m. Ann Lindemann, Oct. 13, 1956 (dec. Aug. 1987); children: John L., Noble Olds, Robert W.; m. Sharon D. D'Atri, Aug. 11, 1990. AB cum laude, Princeton, 1951. Cert. comml. lender. Comml. Lending div. Am. Bankers Assn. Vice pres. Central Nat. Bank, Cleve., 1951-65; chmn., pres., chief exec. officer, dir. Central Trust Co. of Northeastern Ohio, N.A., Canton, 1965-91; dir. Bank One, Akron, Ohio, 1991-97. Mem. Internat. Exec. Svc. Corps.; dir. Mountain Lake Tree & Land Co., Ltd. Dep. sheriff Stark County; bd. dirs. Aultman Hosp. Devel. Found., Blue Coats, Inc., Greater Canton Partnership; trustee State Troopers of Ohio. Named outstanding Young Man of Year Jr. C. of C., 1965 Mem. Cleve. Pres. Orgn., Brookside Country Club. Home: 2503 Charing Cross NW Canton OH 44708-3221 E-mail: NC29@aol.com.

CARPENTER, NORMAN ROBLEE, retired lawyer; b. Cambridge, Mass., Aug. 26, 1932; s. Norman Roblee and Mary P. (Hannigan) C.; m. Janet (Gerhauser); children: Kevin D., Cynthia L., Kathryn Carpenter Nelson, Kim G. Powers, Jill Griffiths, Guy Griffiths. BA, Dartmouth Coll., 1953; JD, U. Mich., 1960. Bar: Minn. 1960. Assoc. Faegre & Benson, Mpls., 1960-67, ptnr., 1969-98; dep. atty. gen. State of Minn., St. Paul, 1967-69. Dir. Walter Judd Found., Mpls., 1963-70 Contbr. articles to profl. jours., short stories and poetry to lit. mags. Bd. regents Augsburg Coll., Mpls., 1970-82; chmn. bd. YMCA Camp Warren, Mpls., 1978-80, Charter Commn., City of St. Louis Park, Minn., 1965-67; trustee Plymouth Congl. Ch., Mpls., 1978-82; bd. dirs. Citizens League, Mpls., 1970-74, The Loft, 1994-2000; mem. Hennepin County Adv. Commn. on Chem. Dependency, 1977-79; vol. United Way, 1983-92. Capt. USMC, 1953-55. Mem. ABA, Minn. Bar Assn., Hennepin County Bar Assn., Dartmouth Coll. Alumni Coun., Minikahda Club. Republican. Home: 2223 Sherwood Ct Minnetonka MN 55305 *All I ask in life is my share of the ones.*

CARPENTER, PAMELA PRISCO, bank officer, foreign language educator; b. Norwood, Mass., July 12, 1958; d. Francis Joseph and Helene Louise (Swartz) Prisco; m. Charles Gilbert Carpenter, Oct. 18, 1981; children: Charles, Craig, Cameron. BA summa cum laude, Harvard U., 1980; grad. cert., U. Salamanca, Spain, 1980; postgrad., Boston State Coll., 1980-81. Cert. Spanish tchr., Mass.; lic. real estate sales assoc., Mass. V.p. global fin. instns. Fleet Nat. Bank, 1980—; bilingual edn. substitute tchr. Boston English H.S., 1979-80; grades K-2 Spanish tchr. IES Lang. Sch., Westwood, Mass., 1991-92; pvt. Spanish and French tutor. Pres. parent adv. bd. Mulberry Childcare and Pre-sch. Ctr., Norwood, 1991-94; mentor Bank of Boston/Hyde Park H.S. Partnership, 1990; sec. C.J. Prescott Elem. Sch. PTA, 1995-97. Radcliffe Club of Boston scholar, 1976. Mem. Phi Beta Kappa. Home: 549 Neponset St Norwood MA 02062-5201

CARPENTER, PAUL LYNN, cardiologist; b. Fairmont, Minn., Jan. 14, 1946; s. Orlo Earnest and Mae Elizabeth (Poulson) C.; m. Rhoda Ann Jordeth, Mar. 15, 1969; children: Amy Elizabeth, Emily Anne, Abigail Lynn. BSChE, U. Minn., 1968, MD, 1974. Diplomate Am. Bd. Internal Medicine. Chem. engr. 3M Co., St. Paul, 1968-69, USPHS, Cin., 1970-71; extern So. Bapt. Hosp., Ailoun, Jordan, 1975; resident in internal medicine Northwestern Hosp. U. Minn., Mpls., 1975-78, fellow in cardiology, 1978-80; invasive cardiologist Ctrl. Plains Clinic, Sioux Falls, S.D., 1980-81, North Ctrl. Heart, Ltd., Sioux Falls, 1981—; asst. clin. prof. dept. medicine U. S.D. Sch. Medicine, Sioux Falls, 1982-90, assoc. clin. prof. dept. medicine, 1990-98, clin. prof. medicine, 1998—. Chmn. cardiac care com. Mckennan Hosp., Sioux Falls, 1984-98, co-dir. cardiac catheterization lab., 1988—, dir. cardiac rehab., 1990—; pres. North Ctrl. Heart, Ltd., 1984-85. Girls basketball coach YMCA, Sioux Falls, 1987-96; girls coach Sioux Falls Soccer Assn., 1991-94; Sunday sch. tchr. Ctrl. Bapt. Ch., Sioux Falls, 1987-94. Fellow Am. Coll. Cardiology (gov. S.D. 1987-90), Am. Coll. Chest Physicians; mem. ACP, AMA, S.D. State Med. Assn., Christian Med. Soc. (life), Alpha Omega Alpha, Tau Beta Pi. Avocations: civil war and native american history, travel, sports, fishing. Office: No Ctrl Heart Ltd 4520 W 69th St Sioux Falls SD 57108 E-mail: paulcarpenter777@aol.com.

CARPENTER, PETER ROCKEFELLER, retired bank executive; b. Sunbury, Pa., Apr. 18, 1939; s. Alvin Witmer and Katharine (Rockefeller) C.; m. Janet Ross Buck, Aug. 24, 1963; children: Karen Louise Althaus, Jean Ellen Chronis, Peter Alvin. BA, Pa. State U., 1962. Mgr. dept. J.C. Penney Co., Menlo Park, NJ, 1964-67; ops. mgr. Allstate Ins. Co., Summit, NJ, 1967-73; adminstrv. mgr. Prudential Property & Casualty, Scottsdale, Ariz., 1973-75; v.p. Fortune Properties, Scottsdale, 1975-76; life underwriter Conn. Mutual Life, Phoenix, 1976-81; v.p. and dir. sales and mktg. No. Trust Bank, Phoenix, 1981-89; v.p. M&I Marshall & Ilsley Trust Co., 1989-94; dir. planned giving Luth. Social Svcs. of the S.W., 1994-95; v.p. trust dept. Founders Bank of Ariz., Scottsdale, 1995-96; v.p. dir. sales and mktg. Southwest Region Wells Fargo Pvt. Client Svcs., 1996-2000; ret. Mem. adv. bd. No. Ariz. U. Coll. Edn., 1997-2000. Sec. exec. bd. Samuel Gompers Rehab. Ctr., 1981-84, chmn. bd., 1984-91, bd. dirs. emeritus, 1998; divsn. chmn. Phoenix United Way, 1981, 82, 92, 86, 90; Rep. committeeman, Phoenix, 1978-86; bd. dirs. Scottsdale Boys and Girls Club, bd. govs., 1997-2000, sec.; bd. dirs. Scottsdale Cultural Coun. Adv., Herberger Theatre Ctr.; mem. adv. bd. Devereaux Ariz., 1998—; mem. support campaign Maricopa County C.C., 1997-2000. With USN, 1962-64. Mem. Pa. State U. Alumni Assn. (southwest region dir. 1979-86), SAR, Ariz. Club (bd. dirs., pres. 1999), U.S. Navy League, Kiwanis (Disting. pres., Disting. lt. gov.), Sigma Alpha Epsilon. Lutheran. Home: 33519 N 73d Pl Scottsdale AZ 85262-4277 E-mail: peterc631@aol.com.

CARPENTER, RICHARD NORRIS, retired lawyer; b. Cortland, N.Y., Feb. 14, 1937; s. Robert P. and Sylvia (Norris) C.; m. Elizabeth Bigbee, Aug. 1961 (div. June 1975); 1 child, Andrew Norris; m. Leslie Nordby, July, 1991. BA magna cum laude, Syracuse U., 1958; LLB, Yale U., 1962. Bar: N.Y. 1962, N.Mex. 1963, U.S. Dist. Ct. (no. dist.) N.Y., U.S. Dist. Ct. N.Mex., U.S. Ct. Appeals (D.C. and 10th cirs.), U.S. Supreme Ct. Assoc. Breed, Abbott & Morgan, N.Y.C., 1963—67, Bigbee Law Firm, Santa Fe, 1963—67, ptnr., 1967—78, Carpenter Law Firm, Santa Fe, 1997, Carpenter & Nixon, LLP, Santa Fe, 1997—2000; prin., owner Carpenter Law Firm, Santa Fe, 2000—02, ret., 2002. Spl. asst. atty. gen., State of N.Mex., 1963-74, 90-96; sec. Bokum Corp., Miami, Fla., 1969-70. Mem. adv. bd. Interstate Mining Compact, N.Mex., 1981-88; elder 1st Presbyn. Ch., Santa Fe, 1978-80, 86-89, trustee, 1975-77, pres., 1977; bd. dirs. Santa Fe Cmty. Coun., 1965-67, N.Mex. Edn. Asst. Found., 2003—; bd. trustees St. Vincent Hosp. Found., Santa Fe, 1980-82, Santa Fe Prep. Sch., 1981-84, pres., 1982-84, St. Vincent Hosp., 1980-86, 87-2001, chmn. 1985-86, 90-93, 98-2000; bd. dirs. Archdiocese Santa Fe Cath. Found., 2003—; bd. dirs. Santa Fe YMCA, 1964-69, pres., 1969; trustee Santa Fe Prep. Permanent Endowment Fund., 1987-90; bd. trustees, treas. Con Alma Health Found., 2002—; bd. regents N.Mex. Tech., 2003—. Rotary Found. fellow, Panjab U., Pakistan, 1959-60. Mem. N.Mex. Bar Assn., N.Y. State Bar Assn., The Best Lawyers of Am., Phi Beta Kappa, Pi Sigma Alpha, Phi Beta Phi. Home and Office: 1048 Bishops Lodge Rd Santa Fe NM 87501-1009 E-mail: rncarpenter@aol.com.

CARPENTER, ROBERT BRENT, lawyer; b. Newton, Mass., Feb. 9, 1949; s. Edward N. and Charlotte F. (Grant) C.; m. L. Deborah Gorchov, Mar. 25, 1978; children: Stephen Michael, Matthew Jeremy, Meredith Anne. AB, Bowdoin Coll., 1971; JD, Boston Coll., 1975; LLM, Temple U., 1977. Bar: Mass. 1975, U.S. Dist. Ct. Mass. 1977, U.S. Ct. Appeals (1st cir.) 1977, U.S. Supreme Ct. 1980, U.S. Ct. Appeals (fed. cir.) 2000. Teaching fellow, lectr. Temple U., Phila., 1975-77; shareholder, dir. Goldstein & Manello, P.C., Boston, 1977-99; ptnr. Schnader, Harrison, Goldstein & Manello, 2000—03, Seyfarth Shaw, 2003—. Contbr. articles to profl. jours. Mem. ABA, Mass. Bar Assn., Boston Bar Assn. Home: 1 Commonwealth Park Wellesley MA 02481-3213 Office: Seyfarth Shaw World Trade Ctr Two Seaport Lane ste 300 Boston MA 02210 E-mail: rcarpenter@seyfarth.com.

CARPENTER, RON D. music educator; b. Lyons, Kans., Oct. 22, 1966; life ptnr. Tim M. Outland. MusB in Edn., No. Ariz. U., 1985—90, M of Ednl. Leadership, 1995—97. Dir. of choirs Hendrix Jr. H.S., Chandler, 1993—; artistic dir. Phoenix Children's Chorus, 1993—. Day camp dir. U. of Miami Choral Camp, Coral Gables, 1999—. State officer Ariz. Music Educators Assn., Phoenix, 1998—2000. Mem.: Am. Choral Directors Assn. (standards com. 1999—2001, Invitation to perform at conv. 1998). Achievements include Bronze Certificate at the World Choral Olympics 2000. Avocations: travel, weight training. Office: Hendrix Junior High School 1550 W Summit Pl Chandler AZ 85224 Home Fax: 480-472-3396; Office Fax: 480-472-3396. Personal E-mail: azmisterc@aol.com. E-mail: azmisterc@aol.com.

CARPENTER, ROSALIE T. education educator, consultant; b. Braddock, Pa., Apr. 6, 1954; d. Frank William and Clara Zezzo Tigano; m. Stephen G. Carpenter, Jan. 7, 1978; children: Claire Elizabeth, George Wilson II. BA, Wesleyan U., 1976; MA, Marshall U., 1983; EdD, W.Va. U., 1994. Asst. prof. Fairmont (W.Va.) State Coll., 1995—96, Waynesburg (Pa.) Coll., 1996—2000; assoc. prof. Washington & Jefferson Coll., Washington, Pa., 2000—03. Cons. Ednl. Futures, Morgantown, W.Va., 1990—. Mem.: Coun. Exceptional Children, Nat. Assn. Edn. Young Children, Kappa Delta Epsilon (counselor). Avocations: walking, weightlifting, excerising. Fax: 724-250-3320. E-mail: rcarpenter@washjeff.edu.

CARPENTER, RUSSELL H., JR., lawyer; b. Providence, May 17, 1941; AB, Princeton U., 1963; BPhil in Politics, Oxford U., Eng., 1965; LLB, Yale U., 1968. Bar: D.C. 1968. Law clk. to Hon. David Bazelon U.S. Ct. Appeals (D.C. cir.), 1968-69; mem. Covington & Burling, Washington. Contbr. articles to profl. jours. Mem. Order Coif. Office: Covington & Burling PO Box 7566 1201 Pennsylvania Ave NW Washington DC 20004-2401 E-mail: rcarpenter@cov.com.

CARPENTER, SHEILA JANE, lawyer; b. Kyoto, Oct. 16, 1950; d. Chester Elwin and Betty (Boulger) C.; m. William Joseph McCarthy, May 26, 1973; 1 child, Diana Elizabeth. BA, Purdue U., 1972; JD, Yale U., 1975. Bar: Md. 1975, U.S. Dist. Ct. Md. 1976, D.C. 1977, U.S. Dist. Ct. D.C. 1978, U.S. Supreme Ct. 1980, U.S. Dist. Ct. (no. dist.) Ohio 1980, U.S. Claims Ct. 1982, U.S. Ct. Appeals (D.C. cir.) 1983, U.S. Ct. Appeals (4th and Fed. cirs.) 1984, U.S. Ct. Appeals (8th cir.) 2000. Assoc. Weinberg & Green, Balt., 1975-77, Sutherland, Asbill & Brennan, Washington, 1977-82, ptnr., 1982-96, Jorden Burt LLP, Washington, 1996—. Pub. svc. com. Sutherland, Asbill & Brennan, 1990-94, chair, 1990-92, chair litigation group Washington office, 1991-93; Web chair life, health and disability com. Def. Rsch. Inst., 2000—. Contbr. articles to profl. jours. Mem. ABA (mem. excess surplus lines and reins. com. TIPS sect., vice chmn. 1992-94, chair elect 1994-95, chair 1995-96, vice chair pub. regulation ins. commn. TIPS sect. 1995-2000), Am. Arbitration Assn. (arbitrator comml. panel), Md. Bar Assn., Phi Beta Kappa. Office: Jorden Burt LLP Ste 400E 1025 Thomas Jefferson St NW Washington DC 20007-5208 E-mail: sjc@wdc.jordenusa.com.

CARPENTER, STANLEY DEAN MACDONALD, military officer, educator; b. Raleigh, NC, Aug. 28, 1953; s. William Lester and Mattie Frances (Wallace) Carpenter; m. Jennifer Ann Wells, June 1, 1985 (div. Mar. 1998); children: Christopher Kenneth Wells, William Gerald Wells Wells, Samantha Theresa Wells. BA, U. of NC, 1975; MA in Lit., U. of St. Andrews, Scotland, 1978; PhD, Fla. State U., 1998; Diploma in Strategic Studies, US Naval War Coll., 2000. Real Estate Broker's Lic. NC State, 1987. Advanced through grades to capt. USN, 1979—; task leader Booz Allen & Hamilton, Inc., Arlington, Va., 1984—87; dep. program mgr. LSA, Inc., Arlington, 1988—90; grad. student/instr. Fla. State U., 1991—98; prof. of strategy/policy US Naval War Coll., 1998—, command historian, strategy/policy divsn. head, Coll. of Distance Edn. Adj. prof. of history Am. Mil. U., Manassas Pk., Va., 1996—, Salve Regina U., Newport, RI, 1999—. Author: (book) Mil. Leadership in the Br. Civil Wars: "The Genius of this Age", 2003; contbr. numerous articles in ency., conf. papers, and book reviews. Vol. Boy Scouts of Am., 1961, Portsmouth Cmty. Theater, RI, USS NC Hist. Detachment, Wilmington, NC, 1998—. Recipient Phi Alpha Theta, FSU Delta Chpt., 1992; grantee Clan Donald Ednl. and Charitable Trust scholarship, 1975—77, Richard C. Maguire scholarship, Rock Island Arsenal Hist. Soc., 1992—95, Henry J. Reilly Mem. Grad. scholarship, Res. Officers Assn. of the US, 1992—94. Fellow: Res. Officers Assn.; mem.: Navy League of the US, RI Employer Support to the Guard and Res., Naval Res. Assn., Royal United Services Inst., US Naval Inst., Triangle U. Security Inst., Fla. Conf. of Historians, Armed Forces Comm. and Electronics Assn., The Hist. Soc., Am. Hist. Assn. Avocations: cmty. theater, reenacting, scouts. Home: 2121 W Main Rd #101 Portsmouth RI 02871-1039 Office: US Naval War Coll 686 Cushing Rd Newport RI 02841

CARPENTER, TED GALEN, political scientist; b. Ladysmith, Wis., Oct. 1, 1947; s. Jay Dee and Magdalene (Stuner) C.; m. Barbara Lynette Bethke, May 11, 1968; children: Lara, Amber, Brian. BA, U. Wis., Milw., 1970, MA in History, 1971; PhD in History, U. Tex., 1980. Rsch. assoc. ideas and action project U. Tex., Austin, 1980-83; fgn. policy analyst Cato Inst., Washington, 1985-87, dir. foreign policy studies, 1987-95, v.p. def. and fgn. policy studies, 1996—. Cons. Profl. Mgmt. Resources, Austin, Tex., 1983-84. Author: A Search for Enemies: America's Alliances After the Cold War, 1992, Beyond NATO: Staying Out of Europe's Wars, 1994, The Captive Press: Foreign Policy Crises and the First Amendment, 1995, Peace & Freedom: Foreign Policy for a Constitutional Republic, 2002, Bad Neighbor Policy: Washington's Futile War on Drugs in Latin America, 2003; editor: Collective Defense or Strategic Independence: Alternative Strategies for the Future, 1989, NATO at 40: Confronting a Changing World, 1990, America Entangled: The Persian Gulf Crisis and Its Consequences, 1991, The Future of NATO, 1995, Delusions of Grandeur: The United Nations and Global Intervention, 1997, NATO's Empty Victory: A Postmortem on the Balkan War, 2000, NATO Enters the 21s Century, 2001; co-editor: The U.S.-South Korean Alliance; Time for a Change, 1992, NATO Enlargement: Illusions and Reality, 1998, China's Future: Constructive Partner or Emerging Threat?, 2000; meml. editl. bd.: Jour. Strategic Studies, meml. editl. adv. bd.: Mediterranean Quar.; contbr. articles to profl. jours. Mem.: Coun. on Fgn. Rels., Acad. Polit. Sci. Mem. Unitarian Ch. Office: Cato Institute 1000 Massachusetts Ave NW Washington DC 20001-5400 E-mail: tcarpenter@cato.org.

CARPENTER, THOMAS MILTON, lawyer; b. Lubbock, Tex., Feb. 15, 1952; s. Charles Loren and Mildred Elaine (McDonald) C.; m. Betty Kathryn Wilkins, Mar. 26, 1983; children: Matthew T., Mark L. BA, Hendrix Coll., 1974; JD, U. Ark.-Fayetteville, 1977. Bar: Ark. 1977, U.S. Dist. Ct. (ea. dist.) Ark. 1978, U.S. Ct. Appeals (8th cir.) 1980, U.S. Supreme Ct. 1981, U.S. Ct. Mil. Appeals 1985, USAF Ct. Mil. Rev. 1985; cert. criminal trial specialist, 1990-95, fellow in mcpl. law, Internat. Mcpl. Lawyer's Assn., 2000. Law clk. Ark. Supreme Ct., Little Rock, 1977-78; ptnr. Lessenberry & Carpenter, Little Rock, 1978-84; asst. city atty. Little Rock, 1984-90; chief comml. litigation divsn., city atty., 1991—. Coordinator Ark. Coalition Against the Death Penalty, 1978-83. Contbr. articles to profl. jours. Dist. commr. Boy Scouts Am., 1979; adminstrv. coun. Pulaski Heights Meth. Ch., Little Rock, 1982-85. Named Outstanding Asst. City Atty., Nat. Inst. Mcpl. Law Officers, 1991, Outstanding City Atty., Nat. Inst. Mcpl. Law Officers, 1994. Fellow Ark. Bar Assn. (exec. coun. 1991-94); mem. ABA, Nat. Bd. Trial Advocacy (bd. dirs. 1991—, v.p. 1995, pres.-elect 1996, pres. 1997-99), Ark. Bar Assn. (del. 1979-81, 83-85, tenured del., Golden Gavel award 1982, 1995), Assn. Trial Lawyers Am., Ark. City Atty.'s Assn. (pres. 1992-93), Pulaski County Bar Assn. Democrat. Office: Little Rock City Atty City Hall 500 W Markham St Ste 310 Little Rock AR 72201-1430 E-mail: tcarpenter@littlerock.state.ar.us.

CARPENTER, VIRGIE MAE, retired librarian; b. Pine Bluff, Ark., Oct. 3, 1934; d. William Clyde Clemons and Martha Pearl (Murdock) Jones; m. Bruce McKinley Tipton, Dec. 16, 1960 (dec. May 1979); m. Thomas F. Carpenter, Feb. 15, 1980. BS, Henderson State U., 1959; MLS, Tex. Woman's U., 1960. Tchr. Social Hill Elem. Sch., Malvern, Ark., 1956-59; libr. Malvern Jr. HS, 1960—2000; ret., 2000. Student Coun., Malvern, 1961-84. Sponsor Libr. Club, 1960—2000. Mem. NEA, Ark. Edn. Assn., Ark. Libr. Assn., Malvern Edn. Assn. Baptist. Avocations: reading, handicrafts, flower arranging. Home: 925 Clardy St Malvern AR 72104-4448

CARPENTER, WILL DOCKERY, chemical company executive; b. Moorhead, Miss., July 13, 1930; s. Horace Aubrey and Celeste (Brian) C.; m. Hellen E. Dodd, Mar. 26, 1960; children: Celeste, Bill. BS in Agronomy, Miss. State U., 1952; MS in Plant Physiology, Purdue U., 1956, PhD in Plant Physiology, 1958, DSc (hon.), 1999; grad. exec. program in bus. adminstrn., Columbia U., 1980. Research biochemist Monsanto Co., St. Louis, 1958-60, agrl. research chemist, 1960-61, staff agrl. devel., 1961-65; mgr. market devel. Monsanto Agrl. Div., St. Louis, 1965-71; dir. product devel. Monsanto Agrl. Products Co., St. Louis, 1971-77, dir. environ. ops., 1977-80, dir. environ. mgmt./environ. policy staff, 1980-84, gen. mgr. tech., 1984-86; v.p. technology Monsanto Agrl. Co., St. Louis, 1986-90, v.p., gen. mgr. new products, 1990-92; chmn., bd. dirs. Agridyne Techs. Inc. Served to capt. U.S. Army, 1952-54, Korea. Fellow Weed Sci. Soc. Am. (treas. 1975, pres. 1980); mem. Indsl. Biotech. Assn. (bd. dirs. 1986—), Chem. Mfrs. Assn. (chmn. environ. mgmt. com. 1982-84, chmn. chem. warfare disarmament com. Washington 1985—), North Cen. Weed Control Conf. (pres. 1977, hon. mem. 1982). Office: 456 Conway Meadows Dr Chesterfield MO 63017-9625 E-mail: wdchdc@aol.com.

CARPENTER, WILLIAM G. chemist, consultant; b. West Liberty, W.Va., May 7, 1931; s. Simon William Carpenter and Virginia Margaret Graham; m. Mary Jane Boyd; children: Daniel William, Michael Andrew. PhD, U. Md., College Park, MD, 1953—60. Program chmn. ACS Polymer Divsn., S. Orange, NJ, 1963—67. Contbr. articles to profl. jours. Mem.: Am. Chem. Soc. Home: 6 Hickory Knoll Place Hilton Head Island SC 29926 E-mail: williamgcarpent@aol.com.

CARPENTER, WILLIAM MORTON, English educator, writer; b. Cambridge, Mass., Oct. 31, 1940; s. James M. and Dorothy N. (Sauer) C.; m. Joanne Laventis, 1962 (div. 1987); 1 child, Matthew; m. Donna Gold; 1 child, Daniel. BA, Dartmouth Coll., 1962; PhD, U. Minn., 1967. Instr. U. Minn., Mpls., 1963-67; asst. prof. U. Chgo., 1967-72; mem. faculty dept. lit. Coll. of Atlantic, Bar Harbor, Maine, 1972—, faculty dean, 1983-89. Bd. dirs. Maine Acad. Coalition, Augusta. Author: The Hours of Morning, 1981, Rain, 1986, Speaking Fire at Stones, 1992, A Keeper of Sheep, 1994, Wooden Nickel, 2002. Recipient Neruda prize U. Okla., 1979, Contemporary Poetry award Assoc. Writing Program, 1981, Black Warrior Rev. prize U. Ala., 1984, Morse prize Northeastern U., 1985; NEA fellow, Venice, Italy, 1985, Inst. for Human Ecology fellow 1989—, Yaddo Ctr., fellow 1984, MacDowell Colony fellow, 1985. Office: Coll of Atlantic 105 Eden St Bar Harbor ME 04609-1105 E-mail: carpenter@acadia.net.

CARPENTER, WOODROW WILSON, enamel company executive, ceramic engineer; b. Snyder, Ill., Sept. 11, 1915; s. Marion Ernest and Margaretta (Fawver) Carpenter; m. Fay D. Turner, Nov. 24, 1939 (div. 1959); 1 child, Gay M. Caldwell; m. Irmgard K. Toberg, Sept. 3, 1960. BS in Ceramic Engring., U. Ill., 1939. Rsch. engr. Ingram Richardson Mfg. Co., Frankfort, Ind., 1939-54; dir. rsch. Barrows Porcelain Enamel Co., Cin., 1954-58; chmn. bd. Ceramic Coating Co., Newport, Ky., 1958-97; T Thompson Enamel, inc., Bellevue, Ky., 1997—. Founder mag. Glass On Metal, 1982. Lt. col. AUS, 1941-46, PTO Mem. Enamelist Soc. (founder). Avocations: magic, puzzles, golf. Home: PO Box 7 Cold Spring KY 41076 Office: 650 Colfax Ave Bellevue KY 41073-1621

CARPENTER-MASON, BEVERLY NADINE, quality assurance professional, medical/surgical nurse; b. Pitts., May 23, 1933; d. Frank Carpenter and Thelma Deresa (Williams) Carpenter Smith; m. Sherman Robert Robinson Jr., Dec. 26, 1953 (div. Jan. 1959); 1 child, Keith Michael Robinson; m. David Solomon Mason Jr., Sept. 10, 1960; 1 child, Tamara Nadina Mason. Grad., Shadyside Hosp. Sch. Nursing, Pitts.; BS, St. Joseph's Coll., North Windham, Maine, 1979; MS, So. Ill. U., 1981; PhD, Columbia Pacific U., 1995. RN Pa., DC, Fla., cert. PNP; state ombusman long term care North Pinellas Pasco County Long Term Care Ombudsman Coun. Staff nurse med. surgery, ob-gyn neonatology and pediat., Pa., N.Y., Wyo., Colo. and Washington, 1954-68; mgr. clinician dermatol. svcs. Malcolm Grow Med. Ctr., Camp Spring, Md., 1968-71; PNP Dept. Human Resources, Washington, 1971-73; asst. DON Glenn Dale Hosp., Md., 1973-81; nursing coord. medicaid divsn. Forest Haven Ctr., Laurel, Md., 1981-83, spl. asst. to supr. for med. svcs., 1983-84; spl. asst. to supt. for quality assurance Bur. Habilitation Svcs., Laurel, 1984-89; exec. asst. quality assurance coord. Mental Retardation Devel. Disabilities Adminstrn.,

Washington, 1989-91, also bd. dirs.; owner, prin. BCM Assocs., 1992—; coord. quality assurance health svcs. divsn. UPARC, Clearwater, Fla., 1993-94. Mem. exec. com. Am. Found. Edn. Healthcare Quality, 1995—97; bd. dirs. Dist. V, Fla. Dept. HHS, 1997—; cons.; lectr. in field. Author: (book) Quality Assurance: Toward a Paradigm of Universality, 1995; mem. editl. bd., case study editor: Am. Jour. Quality Assurance, 1985—; contbr. articles to profl. jours. Mem., star donor ARC Blood Dr., Washington, 1975—91; mem. health and human svcs. bd. Fla. Dept. Children and Families, 1997—2000, cons. Dist. XI, 1998; bd. dirs. Pinellas County (Fla.) Coun., Pinellas County WAGES Coalition, 1999; lay del. United Meth. Ch. Fla. Conf., 1998—; bd. dirs. North Pinellas divsn. Am. Cancer Soc., 2002—; bd. trustees, dir. Upper Pinellas Assn. for Retarded Citizens Bd./Found., 2002—; chair nominations com. Prince Georges Nat. Coun. Negro Women, Md., 1984—85; sec. Pipers Meadow Home Owners Assn., 1993—2001; mem. Long Term Care Fla. State Ombudsman Coun., 2000—. Named Woman of the Yr., 1990—96; recipient awards, Dept. Air Force and DC Govt., 1966—92, Della Foffia Gold medallion, Am. Acad. Pediat., 1972, John P. Lamb Jr. Meml. Lectureship award, E. Tenn. State U., 1988, Outstanding Svc. award, U.S. Congress Adv. Bd. Svc., 1991. Fellow: Am. Coll. Med. Quality (case study editor, mem. jour. editl. bd. 1985—, chmn. publs. com. 1987—, asst. treas. 1988—93, Svc. award 1999); mem.: NAFE, Am. Cancer Soc. (bd. dirs. North Pinellas divsn. 2002), Upper Pinellas Assn. Retarded Citizens (trustee 2002), Internat. Platform Assn., Healthcare Quality Inst., Assn. Retarded Citizens, Am. Bd. Quality Assurance and Utilizabetion Rev. Physicians (asst. treas. 1988—94, chair exam. com. 1990—93, chief proctor exam. com. 1995—97, Chmn. of the Yr. award 1992, presdl. citation, Calvin R. Openshaw Svc. award 1993), Am. Assn. Mental Retardation (conf. lectr. 1988), Top Ladies Distinction (1st v.p. 1986—91), Soroptimists Internat. (sec. Pinellas chpt. 1999, Achievement in Healthcare award 1997), Order Ea. Star (Achievement award Deborah chpt. 1991). Democrat. Avocations: studying languages, travel, reading, writing, collecting antiques. Fax: 727-787-5677 727-787-5677.

CARPENTIER, MARTHA C. English educator; b. Southampton, N.Y., Dec. 31, 1955; d. Ralph E. Carpentier and Sallie Blake; m. Donald E. Sherblom, Aug. 17, 1991; children: Lucien David, Zoe Marie. BA, Barnard Coll., N.Y.C., 1978; MA, Columbia U., N.Y.C., 1979; PhD, Fordham U., Bronx, 1989. Prof. Dept. of English, Seton Hall U., South Orange, NJ, 1989—, chair, 2000—. Author: (book of literary criticism) The Major Novels of Susan Glaspel, 2001, Ritual, Myth, and the Modernist Text, 1998. Mem.: The Virginia Woolf Soc., The James Joyce Soc., The Modernist Studies Assn., N.J. Coll. English Assn., MLA, Phi Kappa Phi. Office: Seton Hall University South Orange Ave South Orange NJ 07079

CARPENTIERI, SARAH C. neuropsychologist, researcher, clinical psychologist; b. Naples, Italy, Aug. 30, 1967; m. James F. Asbury. BBA/BA, U. Notre Dame, 1989; MS, U. Memphis, 1991, PhD, 1994. Lic. psychologist, neuropsychologist. Rschr. St. Jude Children's Hosp., Memphis, 1990—94; psychology intern Harvard Med. Sch. /Children's Hosp., Boston, 1994—95; neuropsychology post-doctoral fellow Harvard Med. Sch., 1995—97; instr., asst. psychology and neuropsychologist Harvard Med. Sch., Boston, 1997—; assoc. rsch. and neuropsychologist Children's Hosp., Boston, 1997—. Lead investigator pediatric brain tumor rsch. program Children's Hosp., Boston, 1998—; cons. Dana Farber Cancer Inst., Boston, 2001—. Contbr. articles to profl. jours. Fellow VanVleet, U. Memphis, 1993—94; grantee Rsch., Pitino Found., 1999—2000, Murphy Child's Trust, 1999—2000, S&S Found., 1997—2003. Mem.: APA, Nat. Acad. Neuropsychology, Internat. Neuropsychology Soc. Personal E-mail: sarah.carpentieri@carpenburymed.com.

CARPER, GERTRUDE ESTHER, artist, marina owner; b. Jamestown, N.Y., Apr. 13, 1921; d. Zenas Mills and Virgie (Lytton) Hanks; m. J. Dennis Carper, Apr. 5, 1942; children: David Hanks, John Michael Dennis, Michelle Kristen. Student violinist, Nat. Acad. Mus., 1931-41; diploma fine arts, Md. Inst. of Art, 1950; voice student, Frazier Gange, Peabody Inst. Music, 1952-55. Interior decorator O'Neill's (Importers), Balt., 1942-44; auditor Citizens Nat. Bank, Covington, Va., 1945-46; owner, developer Essex Yacht Harbour Marina, Balt., 1955—, owner, developer St. Michael's Sanctuary wildlife preserve, 1965—. Jewelry designer, 1987—; portrait artist, 1947—; exhibited one-woman shows Ferdinand Roten Gallery, Balt., 1963, Highfield Salon, Balt., 1967, Le Salon des Nations a Paris, 1985, Ducks and Geese of North Am., 1986, Series of Lighthouses, 1991; exhibited group shows Md. Inst. Alumni Show, 1964, Essex Libr., 1981, Hist. Preservation of Am., Hall of Fame, 1989, others; works included in collections including Prestige de la Peinture d'Aujourd'hos dans le Monde, 1990, Artists and Masters of the Twentieth Century, 1991; author: Expressions for Children, 1985, Fidere, 1993, Mentation, 1993; contbr. articles and poetry to ch. publs. and newspapers. Vol. tchr. of retarded persons, 1942—; leader Women's Circle at local Presbyn. chs., 1952-87, mem. 40 yrs. of choir svc. Mem. Md. Inst. Art Alumni Assn. (life), Grand Coun. World Parliament of Chivalry (Nobless of Humanity citation), Nat. Mus. Women in the Arts (charter, Washington). Avocations: raising orchids, reading, writing essays and poetry. Office: Essex Yacht Harbour Marina 500 Sandalwood Rd Baltimore MD 21221-5830

CARPER, N. GORDON, historian, educator; b. Bettsville, Ohio, May 10, 1935; s. Glenn and Cal Carper; m. Selma Joyce Bigham; children: Noel, Todd. BA, Heidelberg Coll., Tiffin, Ohio, 1960; MA, Fla. State U., 1961, PhD, 1964; postdoctoral, Harvard U., 1969. Asst. prof. history Muskingum Coll., New Concord, Ohio, 1963—65; assoc. prof. history Berry Coll., Mt. Berry, Ga., 1965—67, prof. history, chmn. social sci. dept., 1967—69, Dana prof. history, chmn. social sci. dept., 1969—75, Dana prof. history, 1975—. Cons. NEH, So. Regional Edn. Bd., Atlanta, Ga. Endowment for Humanities. Author (with Selma Carper): The Meaning of History: A Dictionary of Quotations, 1990; contbr. chapters to books. Chmn. Ga. com. NEH, Athens and Atlanta, Ga., 1978—80; co-dir. March of Dimes, Rome, Ga.; bd. dirs. Rome (Ga.) YMCA. Specialist 5th class U.S. Army, 1954—57. Recipient Gov.'s award in humanities, Gov. Ga., 1964, Leadership award, Ga. Ho. of Reps., 2000, Lifetime Achievement award, Coll. Bowl, Inc., 2002, Acad. Competition Fedn., 1999. Mem.: So. Hist. Assn., Am. Hist. Assn., Orgn. Am. Historians. Avocations: reading, travel, golf. Home: 200 Rollingwood Cir Rome GA 30165

CARPER, THOMAS RICHARD, senator, former governor; b. Beckley, W.Va., Jan. 23, 1947; s. Wallace Richard and Mary Jean (Patton) C.; m. Martha Stacy, Jan. 1, 1986; children: Christopher Thomas, Benjamin Michael. BA in Econs., Ohio State U., 1968; MBA, U. Del., 1975. Indsl. devel. specialist Del. div. Econ. Devel., Dover, 1975-76; state treas. State of Del., Dover, 1976-83; mem. 98th-102nd Congresses from Del., Washington, 1983-93; governor of Del., 1993-2001; U.S. senator from Del., 2001—; mem. banking, housing and urban affairs com., envt. and public works com., govtl. affairs com. Fund-raising chmn. Big Bros.-Big Sisters of Del., 1985, 93; hon. chair Del. Spl. Olympics, 1987—; bd. vice chair Jobs for America's Grads., 1996—. Lt. USN, 1968-73, capt. Res., 1973-91. Mem. Nat. Govs. Assn. (vice chmn. 1997-98, chmn. 1998-99). Democrat. Presbyterian. Office: US Senate 513 Dirksen Senate Office Bldg Washington DC 20510*

CARPER, WILLIAM BARCLAY, management educator; b. Winchester, Va., Apr. 3, 1946; s. Roy Silas and Evadnyr Joyce (Arthur) C.; m. Brenda Carol Campbell, Aug. 20, 1966 (div. Sept. 1994); children: Melissa Paige, Jonathan Barclay; m. Andrea Lynn Sikes, Mar. 15, 1997; 1 stepson, Christopher Paul Sikes. BA, U. Va., 1968; MBA, Coll. William & Mary, 1976; PhD, Va. Poly. Inst. and State U., 1979. Instr. Va. Poly. Inst. and State U., Blacksburg, 1976-79; asst. prof. Auburn (Ala.) U., 1979-81, George Mason U., Fairfax, Va., 1981-87; assoc. prof. mgmt. Ga. So. U., Statesboro, 1987 92, prof., 1992-95, dept. head., 1987-90, assoc. dean., 1989-95; dir. ctr. for mgmt. devel., 1993-94; dean Coll. U. West Fla. Coll. Bus., Pensacola, 1995-2000; prof. mgmt. U. West Fla., Pensacola, 1995—, assoc. v.p. for acad. affairs, 2000—03, dep. EEO/AA officer, 2000—03. Dir. small bus. programs George Mason Inst., 1983-85; pres. Strategic Mgmt. Systems, Inc., Statesboro and Pensacola, Fla., 1987—; cons. Nat. Health Advisors, Ltd., McLean, Va., 1983-95, Can. Mfrs. Inst., Washington, 1986-95; vis. prof. bus. Ecole Supérieure du Commerce Extérieur, Paris, 2001. Jour. reviewer Acad. Mgmt. Rev., Jour. Mgmt., Rev. Bus. and Econ. Rsch., Mgmt. Sci.; mem. editl. bd. Jour. Global Info. Mgmt., Jour. of Mktg. Theory and Practice; contbr. articles to profl. jours. USAFR advisor Montgomery County Composite Squadron CAP, Blacksburg, 1977-79; coach Youth League Soccer and Football, Auburn, Ala. and Vienna, Va., 1980-86; mem. exec. com. cub scouts Boy Scouts Am., Vienna, 1982-83; pres. Statesboro High Sch. Quarterback Club, 1991-92; mem. Leadership Pensacola, 1998-99. Pilot USAF, 1968—74. Decorated DFC, Air medal with 3 oak leaf clusters; recipient Disting. Faculty Mem. award George Mason U., 1984; grantee SBA, 1983-84, Commonwealth of Va., 1984-86, State of Ga., 1994-95. Mem. Acad. Mgmt. (dissertation award com.), Ea. Acad. Mgmt., So. Mgmt. Assn. (program com. 1981-82, bd. dirs. 1989 92, mem. teaching excellence com. 1992-94), Decision Scis. Inst. (program com. 1991-92, v.p., 2003—, bd. dirs., 2003—, Alpha Iota Delta liaison com. 2003—), S.E. Region Decision Scis. Inst. (program com. 1985-86, v.p. industry liaison 1986-87, v.p. planning and devel. 1987-88, sec. 1990-91, coun. mem. 1992-2003, coun. chair 1994-98, nominations com. 1996, program chair, 2003—), Inst. Mgmt. Sci. (editor Southeastern chpt. Proceedings Jour. 1987, coun. 1986—, program chmn. 1986-87, sec.-treas. 1987-88, v.p. 1988-89, pres. 1989-90, Disting. Svc. award 1992), So. Bus. Adminstrn. (bd. dirs. 1998-2000), Soc. Advancement Mgmt. (Disting. Svc. award 1985), Aircraft Owners and Pilots Assn., Mid-Day Optimist Club (membership dir. 1989-91, bd. dirs. 1989-91), 5 Flags Rotary, Leadership Pensacola, U. Va. Alumni Assn. (Pensacola chpt. treas. 1997—, bd. dirs. 1997—, pres. 1998-2000), Pensacola Navy Flying Club, Delta Sigma Phi, Beta Gamma Sigma (pres. chpt. 1995-2002), Phi Kappa Phi. Methodist. Avocations: scuba diving, golf, flying/air transport. Office: U West Fla Dept Mgmt Bldg 76 Pensacola FL 32514-5750

CARPINELLI, JOHN DOMINICK, computer engineering educator; b. Clifton, NJ, Sept. 12, 1961; s. Dominick D. and Nina (Nasissi) C. B Engring., Stevens Inst. Tech., 1983; M Engring., Rensselaer Poly. Inst., 1984, PhD, 1987. Spl. lectr. N.J. Inst. Tech., Newark, 1986-87, asst. prof. elec. and computer engring., 1987-93, assoc. dir. computer engring., 1992-94, dir. computer engring., 1994-96, assoc. prof. elec. and computer engring., 1993—. Tech. adv. bd. Cauldron Corp., Bethesda, Md., 1992—. Author: Computer Systems Organization and Architecture, 2001; contbr. articles to profl. jours. Mem. IEEE (sr.), IEEE Computer Soc., IEEE Edn. Soc., Am. Soc. Engring. Edn. Office: NJ Inst Tech University Heights Newark NJ 07102-1982

CARR, ANDREW, zoologist; B in Biology, PhD in Zoology. Joined Amersham Internat., 1987, mfg. dir., site dir., v.p. cell biology, 1997—98; v.p. sales and mktg. Amersham Bioscis., Uppsala, Sweden, 1998—2000, CEO, dir., 2000—. Office: Amersham Bioscis AB SE-751 84 Uppsala Sweden

CARR, BERNARD FRANCIS, hospital administrator; b. Wilkes Barre, Pa., July 13, 1919; s. John Daniel and Marjorie Veronica (Gallagher) C.; m. Mary Ann Reiss, Dec. 30, 1945; children: Bernard, Cathy, Irene, Patricia, Mary Ann. Grad., Rockland State Hosp. Sch. Nursing, 1942; BS, NYU, 1949; MBA in Hosp. Adminstrn., U. Chgo., 1951; student, Western State U. Coll. Law, 1981-82. R.N., Calif., Pa., Va.; lic. nursing home adminstr., Va.; lic. real estate agt., Calif.; lic. comml. aviator. Commd. USMCR, 1945; adminstrv. resident Ind. U. Med. Ctr., Indpls., 1950-51, adminstrv. asst., 1951-52, asst. adminstr., 1952-53; supt. Altoona (Pa.) Hosp., 1953-72; adminstr. South Coast Community Hosp., South Laguna, Calif., 1972-78, Bedford (Va.) County Meml. Hosp., 1978-79; exec. dir. South Coast Community Hosp. Found., 1976-77; dir., sec.-treas. Bedford Meml. Hosp. Found., 1978-79; regional mgr. Calif., Charter Med. Corp., Macon, Ga., 1978-81, div. mgr., 1981-84; adminstr., chief exec. officer Kellogg Psychiat (Charter Hosp.), Corona, Calif., 1981-82; pres., chief exec. officer New Riyadh (Saudi Arabia) Internat. Airport Hosp., 1980-81; assoc. dir. corporate quality assurance, dir. physician relations Charter Med. Corp., 1981-84. Committeman Hosp. Coun. So. Calif., 1981; coord. home nursing svc. Kimberly Quality Svc., Costa Mesa, Calif., 1992-96. Mem. Altoona Redevel. Authority, 1964-70, vice chmn., 1966-70; exec. com. Coordinating Council on Continuing Edn. in Health Care Systems, Pa. State U., 1971-73; mem. Blair County Child Welfare, Blair County Soc. for Crippled Children adv. bds., 1965-72; Blair County Human Devel. Task Force; mem. tech. adv. com. Altoona Community Renewal Program, 1971-73; fund raising chmn. Bedford area Piedmont div. Am. Heart Assn., 1978, White House Council on the Aged. Served at naval aviation cadet, 1943-45; cadet regimental comdr. Rensselaer Polytech. Inst., Chapel Hill, Glenview NAS, Pensacola, Fla. and Corpus Christi, Tex. 1st lt. USMCR, 1945-52. Fellow Am. Coll. Nursing Home Adminstrs., Am. Coll. Health Care Execs. (life); mem. Am. Hosp. Assn. (life, del. 1970—, mem. regional adv. bd., mem. council hosp. schs. nursing 1968-72), Calif. Hosp. Assn., Va. Hosp. Assn. (coms.), Hosp. Assn. Pa. (v.p. 1969-70, pres.-elect 1970-71, pres. 1971-72), Nat. League for Nursing (agy. rep. 1959—), Am. Health Care Assn., Va. Health Care Assn., Assn. Mental Health Adminstrs., Am. Pub. Health Assn., Hosp. Financial Mgmt. Assn., Nat. Council Community Hosps., Roanoke Area Hosp. Council, Laguna Beach C. of C. (dir.), VFW (Saddle Valley, El Toro chpt., life mem., quartermaster 2000—, post comr. 2001-02), Order of Cootie (life). Clubs: Rotarian (pres. elect Bedford 1979-80, pres. South-Laguna-Niguel 1976-77). Home: 31291 E 9th Dr Laguna Niguel CA 92677-2907 E-mail: boxiemary1@mindspring.com. *Throughout my career I've made it clear to my subordinates that I would never stand in the way of their career opportunities, even if I were hard pressed to replace them. Over the years this attitude became a trademark for me and has resulted in an eager supply of key associates. Each has learned a basic philosophy: "What you do is a reflection on you; what your adversaries do is a reflection on them."*

CARR, BESSIE, retired middle school educator; b. Nathalie, Va., Oct. 10, 1920; d. Henry C. and Sirlena (Ewell) C. BS, Elizabeth City Coll., N.C., 1942; MA, Columbia U. Tchrs. Coll., 1948, PhD, 1950, EdD, 1952. Cert. adminstr., supr., tchr. Prin. pub. sch., Halifax, Va., 1942-47, Nathalie-Halifax County, Va., 1947-51; prof. edn. So. U., Baton Rouge, 1952-53; supr. schs. Lackland Schs., Cin., 1953-54; prof. edn. Wilberforce U., Ohio, 1954-55; tchr. Leland Sch., Pittsfield, Mass., 1956-60; chair math. dept., tchr. Lakeland Mid. Sch., N.Y., 1961-83. Founder, organizer, sponsor 1st Math Bowl and Math Forum in area, 1970-76; founder Dr. Bessie Carr award Halifax County Sr. High Sch., 1962. Mem. Nat. Women's Hall of Fame. Mem. AAUW (auditor 1970-85), Delta Kappa Gamma (auditor internat. 1970-76), Assn. Suprs. of Math. (chair coordinating council 1976-80), Ret. Tchrs. Assn., Black Women Bus. and Profl. Assn. (charter mem. Senegal, Africa chpt.). Democrat. Avocations: travel, photography, souvenirs.

CARR, BOB, former congressman, lawyer; b. Janesville, Wis., Mar. 27, 1943; s. Milton Raymond and Edna (Blood) C.; m. Kathleen Smith; 1 child, Alexandra Anne; stepchildren: Jennifer McCloskey, Christopher McCloskey. BS, U. Wis., 1965, JD, 1968; postgrad., Mich. State U., 1968-69. Bar: Wis. 1968, Mich. 1969, U.S. Supreme Ct. 1973. Mem. staff of minority leader Mich. State Senate, 1968-69; adminstrv. asst. to atty. gen. State of Mich., Lansing, 1969-70, asst. atty. gen., 1970-72; counsel to spl. joint com. on legal edn. Mich. Legislature, Lansing, 1972; mem. 94th-96th, 98th-103rd Congresses from 6th (now 8th) Mich. Dist., Washington, 1975-80, 83; appropriations com., 1983-95; chmn. transp. subcom. appropriations, 1993-95; sr. v.p. The Jefferson Group, Inc., 1996-98, Henry J. Kaufman & Assocs., Washington, 1997-99, Carr Sherman Minjack, Washington, 1999—. Mgmt. cons., 1995—; sr. fellow UCLA Sch. Pub. Policy, 2000-2001; bd. dirs. World Wireless Comm. Mem. U.S. Assn. Former Mems. Congress (bd. dirs. 2001—). Democrat. Office: Ste 1200 815 Connecticut Ave NW Washington DC 20006-4004

CARR, BONNIE JEAN, professional ice skater; b. Chgo., Sept. 29, 1947; d. Nicholas and Agnes Marie (Moran) Musashe; m. James Bradley Carr, Dec. 8, 1984; children: Brittany Jean, James Bradley II, Brooke Anderson. BS, Northwestern U., 1969; JD (hon.), Loyola U., Chgo., 1978. Skater Adventures on Ice, Mpls., 1961; prin. skater Jamboree on Ice, Chgo., 1961-68; society editor The Free Press, Colorado Springs, Colo., 1969; prin. skater, publicist on tour, asst. lighting dir., tour ednl. tutor Holiday on Ice Internat., 1970-74; skating dir. William McFetridge Sports Ctr., Chgo., 1975-86; choreographer, prin. skater Ice Time, USA, Mundelein, Ill., 1975—. Skating coach St. Bronislava Athletic Club, Chgo., 1967-69; publicity dir. Amateur Skating Assn. Ill., Chgo., 1968; founder, dir. skating programs for blind, hearing impaired and mentally handicapped, Chgo., 1975-85; physical fitness advisor Exec. Health Seminars, Chgo., 1979; founder, dir. skating programs Fred Hutchinson Cancer Rsch. Ctr., Seattle, 1985-86; guest speaker Am. Cancer Soc., Columbia, S.C., 1973; conditioning coach Riverside Wellness and Fitness Ctr., Richmond, Va., 1989-91, Southampton Rec. Assn., Richmond, 1991-94; figure & speed skating coach Va. Spl. Olympics, 1991—. Recipient Key to City, Mobile, Ala., 1973, Service Recognition award Special Olympics, Chgo., 1984. Mem. Am. Guild Variety Artists, Am. Coun. on Exercise (cert. 1990-96). Roman Catholic. Avocations: writing, public speaking, choreography. Office: Ice Time USA 28800 N Gilmer Rd Mundelein IL 60060-9538 Home: 8 Fishing Point Elgin SC 29045-8636

CARR, CAROLYN KINDER, deputy director and chief curator; b. Providence, R.I. BA in Art History, Smith Coll.; MA in Art History, Oberlin Coll.; PhD in Art History, Case Western Reserve U. Instr. art history Kent (Ohio) State Univ., 1963-65, 67-68; art critic Akron (Ohio) Beacon Jour., 1968-73; chief curator Akron Art Mus., 1978=83; asst. dir. for collections Nat. Portrait Gallery, Washington, 1984-90, dep. dir., chief curator, 1991—. Vis. lectr. Akron U., Spring 1975, '76; organizer numerous art exhbitions Akron Art Mus., 1978-83, Nat. Portrait Gallery, 1984—. Contbr. articles to art publs. including Nat. Portrait Gallery, The Dictionary of Art, Am. Art, The Am. Art Jour., Dialogue, Currier Gallery of Art Bull.; author: art catalogs for exhibitions at Akron Art Mus., Chrysler Mus. of Art, Nat. Portrait Gallery and Smithsonian Instn. Office: Nat Portrait Ballery 750 9th St NW Box 37012 Washington DC 20013-7012 E-mail: carrc@npg.si.edu.

CARR, CHARLES F. orthopedist; b. Coronado, Calif., May 17, 1957; s. Robert Turner Carr and Marjorie (Carr) Dillon; m. Carol Anne LaCasse, May 7, 1985; children: Matthew, Daniel, Christopher. BA, Dartmouth Coll., 1979; MD, Dartmouth Med. Sch., 1981. Diplomate Am. Bd. Orthop. Surgery. Assoc. prof. Orthop. Surgery Dartmouth Med. Sch., Hanover, NH, 1989—. Head team physician Dartmouth Coll., Hanover, 1990—; dir. residency Dartmouth Hitchcock Med Ctr, Lebanon, NH, 1997—. Contbr. Office: Dept Orthopaedics Dartmouth-Hitchcock Med Ctr Lebanon NH 03756

CARR, CHARLES LOUIS, retired religious organization administrator; b. Rockport, Ind., Sept. 9, 1930; s. Louis E. and Loris B. (Lindsey) C.; m. Shirley R. Cron, Nov. 15, 1950; children: Kathleen Carr Wright, Charles Stephen, Jeffrey Louis, David Wayne. Student, Ind. State U., 1949-50, So. Bapt. Theol. Sem., 1965-67; BS, Oakland City U., 1978, DD, 1994. Ordained to ministry Gen. Assn. Gen. Bapts., 1957. Pastor East Oolitic Gen. Bapt. Ch., Bedford, Ind., 1959-63, Mt. Zion Gen. Bapt. Ch., Indpls., 1963-65, Hunsinger Lane Gen. Bapt. Ch., Louisville, 1965-67; missionary to Saipan Mariana Islands, 1967-73; exec. dir. Gen. Bapt. Fgn. Mission Soc., Poplar Bluff, Mo., 1973-96; ret., 1996; pastor Wyatt United Meth Ch., 1997—, Dogwood United Meth Ch., 1997—. Author: Seed, Soil and Seasons, 1988; contbr. articles to various publs. Home: 706 S 9th St Poplar Bluff MO 63901-5639 E-mail: carrsson@ims-1.com.

CARR, CLAUDIA, art gallery director, owner, artist; b. N.Y.C., June 7, 1948; d. Charles Robert and Geraldine Carr; m. Jacques Marcel Levy, Apr. 27, 1980; children: Maya, Julien. BA, Adelphi U., 1970; MA, SUNY, Buffalo, 1976. Artist, curator 22 Wooster Art Gallery, N.Y.C., 1977-84; assoc. dir. Sindin Gallery, N.Y.C., 1991-92; instr. art history Colgate U., Hamilton, N.Y., 1992-93, 94-95, asst. curator collections Picker Art Gallery, 1993-94; owner, dir. Claudia Carr Gallery, N.Y.C., 1996—; curator Jenny Okun at Show Walls, the Durst Orgn., 2002. Curator "Architectonics" The Durst Orgn., 2002. Painting exhbns. include 22 Wooster Gallery, 1978, 80, Provincetown Art Assn., 1984; author: (essay) Towards Abstraction, 1975, (catalogues) Harold Wallin: Anchorage Mus., 1999, Jason Stewart Spirals, 1999. Pres. Shuttleworth Artists Corp., N.Y., 1978-81. Recipient Regents award N.Y. State, 1966, 5 Towns Music and Art Sculpture award 5 Towns L.I., 1968. Mem. Soho Alliance. Office: Claudia Carr Gallery 478 W Broadway New York NY 10012-3168 E-mail: claudiacarr@nyc.rr.com.

CARR, CYNDA ANNETTE, elementary education educator; b. Harper, Kans., June 6, 1948; d. Don Edward and Raquel Ann (Daniels) C. BA, Wichita (Kans.) State U., 1974, MEd, 1980. Tchr. Unified Sch. Dist. 361, Anthony, Kans., 1974—. Steering com. Kans. Tchr. of Yr., 1995—; tchr. cons. Kans. Geographic Alliance, 1992—, Delta Kappa Gamma, 1981—, state editor, 1993—. Trainer Wheatbelt area coun. Girl Scouts U.S., Hutchinson, Kans., 1980—83, 1985—92, bd. dirs., 1987—91, active various coms. and task forces, neighborhood chmn. Anthony coun., 1985—91, troop leader, 1976—84, 1988—89; bd. dirs. Harper County chpt. Am. Cancer Soc., Anthony, 1986—98, Anthony United Way, 1987—89; mem. Leadership Harper County, 1994—95; activities counselor Camp Hope/Am. Cancer Soc., 1987; sponsor Kids for Saving Earth, 1991—98; mem. Soil Conservation Earth Team, 1992—; participant Golden Gift Leadership/Mgmt. Seminar, 1995; Young Careerist Anthony Bus. and Profl. Women's Club, 1976; Sunday sch. tchr., mem. choir 1st Congl. Ch., 1990—2001. Named Tchr. of Yr. Harper County Conservation Dist., 1992; recipient Silver Pen award Kans. Edn. Assn., 1987, Thanks Badge award Girl Scouts U.S., 1988, Contbn. to Conservation award Anthony Republican, 1992, Nat. Educator award Milken Family Found., 1994, Diana award Epsilon Sigma Alpha, 1985. Mem. Anthony Bus. and Profl. Women's Club. Avocations: calligraphy, collecting hippos. Home: 401 S Kansas Ave Anthony KS 67003-2624 Office: Anthony Elem Sch 215 S Springfield Ave Anthony KS 67003-2550

CARR, CYNTHIA, lawyer; b. San Antonio, Nov. 4, 1953; d. Robert Claude Carr and Alta Mae (Bletsch) Holmes; m. Marc Allan Wallman; children: Lydia Michael, Aidan Holmes. BA, Austin Coll., 1975; JD, Harvard U., 1984; LLM, NYU, 1990. Bar: N.Y. 1985, Conn. 1988. Coord. Cambodian sect. Internat. Rescue Com., Bangkok, Thailand, 1980-81; legal intern Mental Health Legal Advisers Com., Boston, 1982-83; assoc. White & Case, N.Y.C., 1984-87; assoc. gen. counsel, exec. dir. planned giving Yale U., New Haven, 1988-2000; gen. counsel Save the Children, Westport, Conn., 2000—. Vis. lectr. Yale U. Law Sch., New Haven, 1988-90. Vol. Peace Corps, West Africa, 1975-77, 79-80; bd. dirs. Yale Law Sch. Early Learning Ctr., 1990-95; trustee Yale U. Hong Kong Charitable Trust, 1997-2000, Oak Leaf Endowment Trust for Yale, 1997-2000. Mem. ABA (vice chair lifetime and charitable gift planning com. 2000—, probate and trust divsn. 2000-01), Conn. Bar Assn. (mem. charitable giving exempt orgns. subcom.), Trusts and Estates Mag. (charitable giving mini bd. mem. 1996-99), Jewish Found. New Haven (tax and legal com. 1999—), Conn. Planned Giving Group (bd. dirs. 2000-01). Home: 30 Hawley Rd Hamden CT 06517-2128 Office: Save the Children 54 Wilton Rd Westport CT 06880-3131 E-mail: ccarr@savechildren.org.

CARR, DANIEL BARRY, anesthesiologist, endocrinologist, medical researcher; b. N.Y.C., Apr. 6, 1948; s. Andrew Joseph and Florence (Glassman) C.; m. Justine M. Meehan, Nov. 11, 1978; children: Nora, Rebecca, Andrew. BA, Columbia U., 1968, MA, 1970, MD, 1976. Diplomate Am. Bd. Internal Medicine (subsplty. bds. Endocrinology and Metabolism, Anesthesiology, Pain Mgmt.). Intern Columbia-Presbyn. Med. Ctr., N.Y.C., 1976-78; resident med. svc. Mass. Gen. Hosp., Boston, 1978-79, endocrine fellow, 1979-82, staff physician endocrine unit, 1982-94, clin. assoc. physician, clin. rsch. ctr., 1982-84, fellow in anesthesiology, 1984-86, dir. analgesic peptide rsch. unit, 1986-94, staff physician anesthesia svc., co-dir. aneshesia pain unit, 1986-91, dir. divsn. pain mgmt., 1991-94; anesthetist, 1992-94; instr. medicine Harvard U. Med. Sch., 1982-84, asst.prof., 1984-88, assoc. prof., 1988-94; rsch. staff Shriners Burn Inst., Boston, 1986-94; Saltonstall prof. Pain Rsch. in anesthesia and medicine Tufts-New England Med. Ctr., 1994—. Co-chair acute and cancer pain mgmt. guideline panels Agy. for Health Care Policy and Rsch., U.S. Dept. HHS, 1990—94; vice chair rsch. dept. anesthesia New Eng. Med. Ctr., 1994—; pain rev. editor Cochrane collaboration rev. group Pain, Palliative and Supportive Care, 1998—; mem. Gov. Mass. Spl. Comm. Pain Mgmt., 1993—98; tech. expert Agy. Healthcare Rsch. and Quality, 1999—2002; chair pain outcomes expert com. JCAHO-AMA-NCQA, 2002—. Editor-in-chief IASP Pain: Clinical Updates, 1993—; mem. editl. bd. Clin. Jour. Pain, 1988—, Jour. Clin. Anesthesia, 1995—, Anesthesia and Analgesia, 1996-99, Acute Pain, 1998—, Jour. Pain, 1999—, Pain Medicine, 1999—; contbr. articles, rsch. reports, essays, revs. to profl. lib. Daland fellow Am. Philos. Soc., 1980-83. Mem. Am. Pain Soc. (bd. dirs. 1994-97), Am. Acad. Pain medicine (bd. dirs. 1995-98), France-Am. Pain Soc. (pres. 1996-98), Am. Soc. Anesthesiologists, Internat. Assn. for Study Pain (coun. 1996-99), Endocrine Soc., Soc. for Neurosci., Internat. Anesthesia Rsch. Soc., Assn. Univ. Anesthetists, Alpha Omega Alpha. Achievements include research on pain, analgesic peptides and stress responses; relationship between analgesia and clinical outcome; systematic reviews and guidelines for improved pain treatment in hospital, hospice and home care settings. Office: New Eng Med Ctr-Dept Anesthesia 750 Washington St Boston MA 02111-1526 E-mail: daniel.carr@tufts.edu.

CARR, DAVID J. lawyer; m. Sandra S. Carr; children: Jacob, Angela, Alex. BA summa cum laude, DePauw U., 1981; JD, Georgetown U., 1984. Bar: Ind., U.S. Dist. Ct. (so. dist.) Ind. 1984, U.S. Ct. Appeals (7th cir.) 1987, U.S. Supreme Ct. 1989. Assoc. Bingham Summers Welsh & Spilman, Indpls., 1984-90, Johnson Smith LLP, Indpls., 1990-92, ptnr., 1992—2001, Ice Miller, Indpls., 2001—. Contbr. articles to profl. publs. Coun. mem. Zionsville Town Coun., 1998—; bd. dirs. Zionsville Parks and Recreation Bd., 1996-98. Mem. ABA, Ind. State Bar Assn., Indpls. Bar Assn., Christian Legal Soc., Federalist Soc., Ct. Practice Inst. (diplomate), Delta Chi, Phi Beta Kappa. Office: Box 82001 One American Sq Indianapolis IN 46282-0002 E-mail: carr@icemiller.com.

CARR, DAVID TURNER, physician; b. Richmond, Va., Mar. 12, 1914; s. John Ernest and Mary Lela (King) Carr; m. Rosemary Rudow, June 18, 1948 (div. 1953); 1 child, Jennifer Anne Carr Oderkirk; m. Christine Nadeau, Dec. 27, 1979. Student, U. Richmond, 1931-33; MD, Med. Coll. Va., 1937; MS in Medicine, Mayo Grad. Sch. Medicine, 1947. Intern, then asst. resident Grady Hosp., Atlanta, 1937-39; resident chest diseases Bellevue Hosp., N.Y.C., 1940-41; fellow medicine Mayo Clinic, 1943-47, cons. medicine, 1947-79, chmn. dept. oncology, 1975; dir. Mayo Comprehensive Cancer Ctr., 1975; assoc. dir. Ctr. Cancer Control, 1976-79; prof. medicine Mayo Med. Sch., 1964-79, M.D. Anderson Hosp. and Tumor Inst., Tex. Med. Ctr., Houston, 1979-92; med.-legal cons., 1992—. Mem.-at-large bd. dirs. Am. Lung Assn., 1959—74, v.p., 1971—72; bd. dirs. Rochester Civic Theatre, 1951—70, pres., 1965—67; bd. dirs. at large Am. Cancer Soc., 1967—74, pres. Minn. divsn., 1974—75. Fellow: AAAS, ACP; mem.: Am. Thoracic Soc. (v.p. 1963—64), Internat. Assn. Study Lung Cancer (v.p. 1974—76, pres. 1976, treas. 1976—82), Ctrl. Soc. Clin. Rsch., Peruvian Atni-Tb Assn. (hon.), Rochester C. of C. (pres. 1959—60). Achievements include research in in pulmonary diseases. Home and Office: PO Box 9300 Rancho Santa Fe CA 92067

CARR, DAVIS HADEN, lawyer; b. Richmond, Va., July 21, 1940; s. Frederick and Bernice (Haden) Clifton; m. Judith A. Guerry, Aug. 1959 (div. Apr. 1979); children: Wendy, Judith Carr Stewart; m. Martha Cash, Feb. 12, 1983. BEE, U. Va., 1961; JD, Vanderbilt U., 1970. Bar: Tenn. 1970, Ky. 1989. Assoc. Boult, Cummings, Conners & Berry PLC, Nashville, 1970-74, ptnr., 1974—; mng. ptnr. Boult, Cummings, Conners & Berry, 1984-94, chmn., 1995-99. Active Leadership Nashville, 1977-78, chmn. alumni assn., 1978-79, bd. trustees 1997—, finance chair 2000-01; pres. Cumberland Museums, Nashville, 1978-80; bd. dirs. Greater Nashville Arts Found., 1991-97; bd. dirs. Jr. Achievement Mid. Tenn., 1991-99, chmn., 1995-97; trustee Vol. State Horsemen's Found., 1988-, Houghland Found., 1988—, The Bright Hour Trust, 2000— ; mem. bd. trustees, exec. com. Fisk U., 1996—, vice-chmn., 2000-2003; bd. dirs. Nashville Downtown Partnership, 1994-99, chmn., 1994-95, exec. com., 1997-99. Mem. ABA, Tenn. Bar Found., Tenn. Bar Assn., Nashville Bar Found., Nashville Bar Assn., Vanderbilt U. Law Alumni Assn. (bd. dirs.), Cumberland Club (pres. 1986-87), Belle Meade Country Club, Nashville Area C. of C. (gen. counsel, mem. exec. com. 1992-96, bd. govs.). Home: Martlesham Heath 1344 Carnton Ln Franklin TN 37064-3258 Office: Boult Cummings Conners & Berry PO Box 198062 Nashville TN 37219-8062 E-mail: dcarr@bccb.com.

CARR, EDWARD A. lawyer; b. Borger, Tex., July 31, 1962; AB with honors and distinction, Stanford U., 1984; JD, UCLA, 1987. Bar: Tex. 1988, D.C. 1989, U.S. Dist. Ct. (so. dist.) Tex. 1989, U.S. Ct. Appeals (5th cir.) 1989, U.S. Ct. Appeals (fed. cir.) 1989. Assoc. Vinson & Elkins, Houston, 1988-97, ptnr., 1997—. Lectr. in field. Contbr. articles to profl. jours., contbg. author: Business and Commercial Litigation in Federal Courts, 1998, Texas Legal Ethics in the American Legal Ethics Library, Cornell Law School, 1998; mem. UCLA Law Rev., 1985-87, mem. editl. bd., 1986-87. Fellow Tex. Bar Found. (life), Coll. State Bar Tex.; mem. ABA (sects. antitrust law, litigation), Am. Judicature Soc. (life), D.C. Bar, Fed. Bar Assn., State Bar Tex.(panel chair, dist. 4B5 grievance com. 2001-), Houston Bar Assn. Address: Vinson & Elkins LLP First City Tower 1001 Fannin St Ste 2300 Houston TX 77002-6760

CARR, EDWARD ALBERT, JR., medical educator, physician; b. Cranston, RI, Mar. 3, 1922; s. Edward Albert and Florence (Hodge) C.; m. Nancy Albosta, Dec. 27, 1952; children: Sharon L., Cynthia F. AB summa cum laude, Brown U., 1942; MD cum laude, Harvard, 1945. Rsch. fellow, instr. pharmacology Harvard Med. Sch., 1948-51; exch. fellow St. Bartholomew's Hosp., London, 1952-53; mem. faculty U. Mich. Med. Sch., Ann Arbor, 1953-74, prof. pharmacology, 1962-74, prof. internal medicine, 1967-74, dir. program investigative clin. pharmacology, 1962-74; mem. sr. staff Univ. Hosp., 1957-74; dir. Upjohn Ctr. Clin. Pharmacology, 1966-74; prof. medicine, prof. and chmn. dept. pharmacology Med. Sch., U. Louisville, 1974-76; prof. medicine, pharmacology and therapeutics Med. and Dental Sch., SUNY, Buffalo, 1976-92, emeritus prof. medicine, pharmacology and therapeutics, 1992—, chmn. dept. pharmacology and therapeutics, 1976-88. Mem. sr. staff, chmn. therapeutics com. Louisville Gen. Hosp., 1974-76; lectr. U. Helsinki, 1972, Autonomous U. Barcelona, 1974, Japan Med. Assn., 1977, Swedish Acad. Pharm. Sci., Stockholm, 1977, Esteve Found. Symposium, Mallorca, 1988; cons. Ann Arbor VA Hosp., 1954-74, Louisville VA Hosp., 1974-76, Buffalo VA Hosp., 1976-2002, Erie County Med. Ctr., 1978-92; hon. vis. prof. Prince Henry and Prince of Wales Hosp., Sydney, Australia, 1973. Co-author: Radioisotopes in Biology and Medicine, 1964; also articles. Mem. Nat. Joint Commn. on Prescription Drug Use, 1976-80; mem. coop. studies evaluation com. US VA, 1980-83; chmn. pharmacology com. Am. Inst. Biol. Sci., Walter Reed Army Inst. Rsch., 1985-86; vol. Niagara Hospice, 1992-2002, bd. dir., 1992-95, 1996-2002. Fellow ACP (emeritus); mem. Am. Thyroid Assn. (emeritus), Am. Soc. Pharmacology and Exptl. Therapeutics (emeritus) (exec. com. clin. pharmacology div. 1984-86), Am. Soc. Clin. Pharmacology and Therapeutics (emeritus, pres., 1974-75, Henry W. Elliott award 1981), Soc. Nuclear Medicine (emeritus), Ctrl. Soc. Clin. Rsch. (emeritus), Endocrine Soc. (emeritus), Phi Beta Kappa, Sigma Xi, Alpha Omega Alpha. Home: 2 Gothic Ledge Lockport NY 14094-9702

CARR, ELIZABETH DAVIS-JACKSON, municipal manager; b. Plymouth, N.C., May 13, 1932; d. Raleigh Sherman and Lillian Blanche (Davis) Jackson; m. Joseph Hargrove Bryan, Dec. 24, 1953; children: Joanna Davis, Peter-Michael. BA, East Carolina U., 1953; MA, Atlantic Christian Coll., 1955. Dir. Clinton (N.C.) C. of C., 1972-82; investments, venture capital Carr & Assocs., Inc., Atlantic Beach, N.C., 1985—; town mgr. Pine Knoll Shores, N.C., 1995—. Bd. dirs. First Citizens Bank & Trust, Clinton, 1982-84; mem. bd. realtors Carteret County, 1989-91. Democrat. Presbyterian. Avocations: reading, tennis, traveling.

CARR, GARY THOMAS, lawyer; b. El Reno, Okla., July 25, 1946; s. Thomas Clay and Bobbye Jean (Page) C.; m. Ann Elizabeth Smith, Jan. 5, 1985. AB, Washington U., St. Louis, 1968, BSCE, 1972, JD, 1975. Bar: Mo. 1975, U.S. Dist. Ct. (ea. and we. dists.) Mo. 1975, U.S. Ct. Appeals (8th cir.) 1977, U.S. Ct. Appeals (fed. cir.) 1980, U.S. Ct. Appeals (5th cir.) 1991. Jr. ptnr. Bryan, Cave, McPheeters & McRoberts, St. Louis, 1975-83, ptnr., 1984-99. Lectr. law Washington U., 1978-82, adj. prof., 1982-85; sec., dir. Bruton-Stroube Studios, Inc., 1978—. Trustee Parkview Subdiv. Assn., St. Louis, 1982-90, 2003—. 1st lt. U.S. Army, 1968-71, Vietnam. Mem. ABA, Mo. Bar Assn., St. Louis Bar Assn., Order of Coif. Avocations: woodworking, hunting, fishing, automobiles. Office: PO Box 3030 Saint Louis MO 63130-0430 E-mail: gtc10485@aol.com.

CARR, GEORGE FRANCIS, JR., lawyer; b. Bklyn., Feb. 11, 1939; s. George Francis and Edith Frances (Schaible) C.; m. Patricia Louise Shiels, Jan. 30, 1965; children: Frances Virginia, Anne McKenzie, Margaret Edith. BA, Georgetown U., 1961; LLB, Harvard U., 1964. Bar: Ohio 1964, U.S. Dist. Ct. Ohio 1964. Assoc. Kyte, Conlan, Wulsin & Vogeler, Cin., 1964-70, ptnr., 1970-78, Frost & Jacobs, Cin., 1978-82; sec., counsel Baldwin-United Corp., Cin., 1982-84, v.p., spl. counsel, 1984-85; sole practice Cin., 1985-86; ptnr. Douglas, Carr and Pettit, Milford, Ohio, 1987-88; staff v.p., assoc. gen. counsel Penn Cen. Corp., Cin., 1988-92, Gen. Cable Corp., Highland Heights, Ky., 1992-95, ret., 1995. Bd. dirs. Ctr. for Comprehensive Alcoholism Treatment, Cin., 1975-87, pres., 1980-83; bd. dirs. NCCJ, Cin., 1975-82. Served with U.S. Army, 1965—67. Avocations: farming, geology, hiking, physical fitness. Home: 7150 Ragland Rd # 4 Cincinnati OH 45244-3148

CARR, GERALD FRANCIS, German educator; b. Pitts., Dec. 29, 1930; s. James Patrick and Hannah (Sweeney) C.; m. Irmengard Rauch, June 12, 1965; children: Christopher, Gregory. BEd, Duquesne U., 1958; MA, U. Wis., 1960, PhD, 1968. Instr. in German Duquesne U., Pitts., 1960-62, asst. prof. German, 1964-68; tchg. asst. U. Wis., Madison, 1962-64; asst. prof. German Ea. Ill. U., Charleston, 1968-70, assoc. prof. German, 1970-75, prof. German, 1975-87, Calif. State U., Sacramento, 1987—. Co-editor: Linguistic Method: Essays in Honor of Herbert Penzl, 1979, The Signifying Animal: The Grammar of Language and Experience, 1980, Language Change, 1983, The Semiotic Bridge, 1989, On Germanic Linguistics, 1992, Insights in Germanic Linguistics I, 1995, Insights in Germanic Linguistics II, 1996, Semiotics Around the World, 1996, Essays for Irmengard Rauch, 1998, New Insights in Germanic Linguistics I, 1999, New Insights in Germanic Linguistics II, 2000, New Insights in Germanic Linguistics III, 2002; series editor: Studies in Old Germanic Languages and Literatures, assoc. editor: Interdisciplinary Jour. for Germanic Linguistics and Semiotic Analysis. Cpl. USMC, 1951-54. Dist. tchg. fellow U. Wis., 1966. Mem. MLA, Internat. Assn. for Semiotic Studies (co-dir. 5th congress 1994), Am. Coun. Tchrs. Fgn. Lang., Semiotic Soc. Am., Am. Assn. Tchrs. of German, Soc. German Philology, Calif. Fgn. Lang. Tchr. Assn., Semiotic Circle Calif., Kappa Phi Kappa, Delta Phi Alpha. Avocations: books, antiques. Office: Calif State U 6000 J St Sacramento CA 95819-2605

CARR, GERALD PAUL, former astronaut, retired business executive, former marine officer; b. Denver, Aug. 22, 1932; s. Thomas Ernest and Freda (Wright) C.; divorced; children: Jennifer, Jamee, Jeffrey, John, Jessica, Joshua; m. Patricia Musick, Sept. 14, 1979 BS in Mech. Engring., U. So. Calif., 1954; BS in Aero. Engring., U.S. Naval Postgrad. Sch., 1961; MS in Aero. Engring., Princeton U., 1962; DSc (hon.), St. Louis U., 1976. Registered profl. engr., Tex. Commd. 2d lt. USMC, 1954, advanced through grades to col., 1974, ret., 1975; jet fighter pilot U.S., Mediterranean, Far East, 1956-65; astronaut NASA, Houston, 1966-77; comdr. 3d Skylab Manned Mission, 1973-74; sr. v.p. CAMUS, Inc., Huntsville, Ark.; ret. Adv. bd. Nat. Space Soc., Space Dermatology Found., Eldorado Bank. Bd. trustees U. of the Ozarks. Recipient Group Achievement award NASA, 1971, Distinguished Service medal, 1974; Gold medal City of Chgo., 1974; Gold medal City of N.Y., 1974; Alumni Merit award U. So. Calif., 1974; Distinguished Eagle Scout award Boy Scouts Am., 1974; Robert J. Collier Trophy, 1974; Robert H. Goddard Meml. trophy, 1975; FAI Gold Space medal; others; inductee Astronaut Hall of Fame, 1997. Fellow Am. Astronautical Soc. (Flight Achievement award 1975); mem. NSPE, Marine Corps Assn., Marine Corps Aviation Assn., Soc. Exptl. Test Pilots, U. So. Calif. Alumni Assn., Tau Kappa Epsilon. Presbyterian. Home and Office: 1655 Madison 1200 Huntsville AR 72740-0919 E-mail: camus@madisoncounty.net.

CARR, GILBERT RANDLE, retired railroad executive; b. Rockford, Ill., Jan. 4, 1928; s. Audra Clifford and Marjorie (Lantz) C.; m. Marion Minnie Heinemann, Mar. 28, 1953; children: John W., James M. BS in Accounting and Mgmt, U. Ill., 1950. With Arthur Andersen & Co. (C.P.A.s), Chgo., 1950-57; with C.& N. W. Transp. Co., 1957-88, comptroller, 1967-79, v.p., comptroller, 1979-88. Served with AUS, 1946-47. Lutheran. Home: 1425 Linden Ave Park Ridge IL 60068-5545

CARR, GLADYS JUSTIN, publishing company executive, consultant, editor, writer; b. N.Y.C. d. Jack and Mollie (Marmor) Carr. BA, MA, Smith Coll.; postgrad., Cornell U. Sr. editor Prentice-Hall, Inc., Englewood Cliffs, N.J., 1969; exec. editor Cowles Comm., Inc., N.Y.C., 1969-71; editl. dir., editor-in-chief Am. Heritage Press, N.Y.C., 1971-75; sr. editor McGraw-Hill, Inc., N.Y.C., 1975-81, editor in chief, editorial dir., chmn. editorial bd., 1981-89, v.p., pub., 1988-89, HarperCollins Pubs., Inc., N.Y.C., 1989-2000; mng. dir. GJ Carr Assocs., N.Y.C., 2000—. Pub. and editor books by James Baldwin, Anthony Burgess, Erica Jong, Erma Bombeck, Philip Caputo, Brenda Maddox, Stuart Woods, Leon Uris, M.L. West, Ashley Montagu, Page Smith, Donald Spoto, Laurence Otis Graham, Albert Goldman, Joseph Persico, Jean Carper, Letty Pogrebin, William Novak, Bel Kaufman, John Davis, Leo Rosten, Phyllis Richman, Thomas Fleming, George Plimpton, Faith Popcorn, Lois Wyse, Ernest Lehman, Eric Severeid, Phyllis Chesler, Dwight Macdonald, Alan Jay Lerner, Sen. Fred Harris, Dan Kurzman, Nigel Hamilton, Beryl Bainbridge, others; pub. and editor autobiographies and memoirs by Anthony Quinn, David Schoenbrun, R.D. Laing, Ginger Rogers, Milton Berle, Shirley Temple Black, Dolly Parton, Joan Rivers, Mickey Mantle, others; pub. and editor biographies of W.B. Yeats, Laurence Olivier, Lillian Hellman, Dashiell Hammett, Robert E. Lee, Ulysses Grant, Truman Capote, F. Scott Fitzgerald, Sheilah Graham, Fiorello LaGuardia, Anthony Eden, George Patton, Field Marshall Bernard Montgomery, Edward R. Murrow, John Lennon, Elvis Presley, Marvin Gaye, Marilyn Monroe, Ingrid Bergman, Elaine and Willem de Kooning, Yitzhak Rabin, Ronald Reagan, John F. Kennedy, others; contbr. articles, revs. and poetry to profl. jours. Marjorie Hope Nicholson trustee fellow Smith Coll.; vis. Ford Found. fellow, Walter Francis Wilcox fellow Cornell U. Mem. PEN Am. Ctr., Women's Media Group, Phi Beta Kappa Clubs: Smith Coll. (N.Y.C.). Home and Office: 920 Park Ave New York NY 10028-0208 also: 1 Boulder Ln East Hampton NY 11937-1047

CARR, GLENNA DODSON, retired economics educator; b. Asheville, N.C., Jan. 7, 1927; d. Harry D. and Ruth (Gatling) Dodson; m. Thomas Deaderick Carr, May 20, 1961; 1 child, Susan Catherine. BS, James Madison U., Harrisonburg, Va., 1948; MS, Fla. State U., Tallahassee, 1951; EdD, U. Fla., 1959. Asst. prof. U. Fla., Gainesville, 1952—77, prof., 1977—2002; dir. U. Fla. Ctr. for Econ. Edn., Gainesville, 1977—2002, ret., 2002. Bd. dirs. Health Improvement Inc. Contbr. numerous articles to profl. jours. Democrat. Presbyterian. Avocation: tennis. Home: 1546 SW 35th Pl Gainesville FL 32608-3530 E-mail: gcarr@ufl.edu.

CARR, HAROLD NOFLET, investment corporation executive; b. Kansas City, Kans., Mar. 14, 1921; s. Noflet B. and Mildred (Addison) C.; m. Mary Elizabeth Smith, Aug. 5, 1944; children: Steven Addison, Hal Douglas, James Taylor, Scott Noflet. BS, Tex. A&M U., 1943; postgrad., Am. U., 1944-46. Asst. dir. route devel. Trans World Airlines, Inc., 1943-47; exec. v.p. Wis. Central Airlines, Inc., 1947-52; mem. firm McKinsey & Co., 1952-54; pres. North Central Airlines, Inc., Mpls., 1954-69, chmn. bd., 1965-79; chmn. Republic Airlines, Inc., 1979-84, chmn. exec. com., 1984-86; chmn. Carr and Assocs., 1986—. Professorial lectr. mgmr. engring. Am. U., 1952-62; mem. bd. nominations Nat. Aviation Hall of Fame; mem. exec. adv. coun. Nat. Register Prominent Americans and Internat. Notables, Minn. Aviation Hall of Fame. Trustee Tex. A&M Rsch. Found., Internat. Inst. for Effective Communication; mem. Pres.'s Coun. of Advisors, Tex. A&M U. Mem. Nat. Aero. Assn., World Bus. Coun., Am. Mgmt. Assn., nat. Trust Historic Preservation, Pine Beach Peninsula Assn., Am. Econ. Assn., Tex. A&M Former Students Assn., Beta Gamma Sigma. Clubs: Nat. Aviation, Aero (Washington), Minneapolis, Twelfth Man Found. (dir., Coll. Sta., Tex.), Tex. A&M Century, Racquet (Miami), Gull Lake Yacht (Brainerd, Minn.), Wings (N.Y.C.), Stearman Alumnus (Wichita, Kans.), Briarcrest Country. Episcopalian.

CARR, IRIS CONSTANTINE, artist, writer; b. Smyrna, Turkey, Aug. 4, 1922; d. John and Julia Kyrides Constantine (parents Greek citizens); m. Herman Edgar Carr Jr., 1947; 3 children. Diploma in dental nursing, Boston Sch. Dental Nursing, 1942; BA, Simmons Coll., 1970, postgrad., 1990-91, DeCordova Mus. Sch., 1986—. Anesthetist for oral surgeon, Boston, 1942-43; exec. med. sec. Boston Evening Clinic, 1943-44; lab. sec., dir. Boston Dispensary, 1944-45, Children's Hosp., Boston, 1944-47; editl. asst. Internat. Rsch. and Publs., 1947—; developed improved interlibr. loan svc. Wellesley Coll. Libr., 1964. Demonstrator watercolor technique Needham (Mass.) Arts Festival, 1996. One woman show at Needham Village Gallery, 1991, Needham Travel Svc. Bur., 1998-99; group shows include Mass. Med. Soc., 1999, Needham and Wellesley Art Assn., 1999, Needham Libr., 1999; contbr. articles to profl. publs.; contbg. editor Mass. Med. Soc. Alliance. Recipient over 14 awards for pastel, watercolor and oil paintings. Mem. Mass. Med. Soc. Alliance (pub. rels. com. 1985-94, contbg. editor 1995—), Dedham Art Assn. (featured artist), Wellesley Soc. Artists (bd. dirs., registration com. 1994—), Needham Art Assn. (bd. dirs., publicity com., pres. 1989-90, co-inaugurated 1st art gallery 1990), Nat. Mus. Women in Arts, Mus. Fine Arts, Boston. Democrat. Home: 14 Ingleside Rd Needham MA 02492-4239

CARR, JACK LESLIE, economics educator, economic consultant; b. Toronto, Ont., Can., Aug. 9, 1944; s. Meyer and Marion (Pinkus) C.; m. Honey Feldman, Dec. 27, 1965; children— Elana, Adam, David. B.Com., U. Toronto, 1965; M.A., U. Chgo., 1968, Ph.D., 1971. Asst. prof. econs. U. Toronto, 1968-73, assoc. prof., 1973-78, prof., 1978—, research assoc. Inst. Policy Analysis, 1968—, also assoc. chmn., dir. grad. studies; vis. assoc. prof. UCLA, 1975-76; econ. cons. Bell Can., Montreal, Que., 1968-70, Can. Bankers Assn., Toronto, 1980-84, Ont. Supreme Ct., Toronto, 1981, Can., Govt., Ottawa, Ont., 1977-79; econ. commentator on fed. budget CBC; econ. commentator TV and radio, Toronto, 1968-85. Author: Cents and Non Sense: The Economics of Canadian Policy Issues, 1972; Wage and Price Controls: Panacea for Inflation or Prescription for Disaster, 1976; Liability Rules and Insurance Markets, 1981; Tax-Based Income Policies: A Cure for Inflation, 1982. Woodrow Wilson Found. fellow, U. Chgo., 1965; Lily Honor fellow Eli Lily Fund, U. Chgo., 1965-68; Can. Council leave fellow, UCLA, 1975-76; Social Sci. and Humanities Research Council leave fellow U. Toronto, 1982-83. Mem. Am. Econ. Assn., Can. Econ. Assn., Can. Profs. for Peace in Middle East. Home: 163 Banbury Rd Don Mills ON Canada M3B 2L7 Office: U Toronto 150 St George St Toronto ON Canada M5S 1A1

CARR, JACQUELYN B. psychologist, educator; b. Oakland, Calif., Feb. 22, 1923; d. Frank G. and Betty (Kreiss) Corker; children: Terry, John, Richard, Linda, Michael, David. BA, U. Calif., Berkeley, 1958; MA, Stanford U., 1961; PhD, U. So. Calif., 1973. Lic. psychologist, Calif; lic. secondary tchr., Calif. Tchr. Hillsdale High Sch., San Mateo, Calif., 1958-69, Foothill Coll., Los Altos Hills, Calif., 1969—. Cons. Silicon Valley Companies, U.S. Air Force, Interpersonal Support Network, Santa Clara County Child Abuse Council, San Mateo County Suicide Prevention Inc.,Parental Stress Hotline, Hotel/Motel Owners Assn.; co-dir. Individual Study Ctr.; supr. Tchr. Edn.; adminstr. Peer Counseling Ctr.; led numerous workshops and confs. in field. Author: Learning is Living, 1970, Equal Partners: The Art of Creative Marriage, 1986, The Crisis in Intimacy, 1988, Communicating and Relating, 1984, 3d edit., 1991, Communicating with Myself: A Journal, 1984, 3d edit., 1991; contbr. articles to profl. jours. Vol. US Peace Corps., Sri Lanka, 1997. Mem. Mensa. Clubs: Commonwealth. Home: # 5-2G 390 N Winchester Blvd Santa Clara CA 95050-6563 Office: Foothill College 12345 El Monte Rd Los Altos CA 94022-4597

CARR, JAMES FRANCIS, lawyer; b. Buffalo, May 7, 1946; s. Maurice Kilner and Cecelia Francis (Harmon) C.; children: James Robert, Marguerite Louise. BS, USAF Acad., 1968; JD, George Washington U., 1971. Bar: D.C. 1972, Mich. 1972, Pa. 1972, U.S. Dist. Ct. D.C. 1972, U.S. Ct. Appeals (D.C. cir.) 1972, U.S. Supreme Ct. 1975, Colo. 1979, U.S. Dist. Ct. Colo. 1979, U.S. Ct. Appeals (10th cir.) 1979. Atty. Unity Ctr., Meadville, Pa., 1971-73; asst. pros. atty. Genesee County, Flint, Mich., 1973-79; sr. asst. atty. gen. State of Colo., Denver, 1979-82, 85—; assoc. Sumners, Miller & Clark, Denver, 1982-83, Miles & McManus, Denver, 1983-85. Mem. Colo. Bd. Law Examiners, 1992-02, coun. Licensure, Enforcement and Regulation; spkr. in field. Contbr. articles to profl. jours. Mem. Mich. Pub. Consultation Panel of Internat. Joint Commn., 1976-78; treas. Denver South High Sch. PTSA, 1988-91, pres., 1991-93; athletic dir. Most Precious Blood Sch., 1988-90; bd. dirs. Pioneer Jr. Hockey Assn., 1988-90. Mem. ABA (house of dels. 1997-2002, chmn. commn. on mental & physical disability law, 1998-2001, commn. on mental and phys. disability law 1995-2001, standing com. pub. edn., 2001-, tort and ins. practice sect., chmn. environ. law com. 1978-81, liaison jud. adminstrn. divsn. 1987-90, chmn. govt. liability com. 1988-89, 92-93, chmn. emerging issues com. 1996-97, sect. sec. 1997-99, TIPS coun. 1999-2002, mem. coun. govt. and pub. sector lawyers divsn. 1991-97, editor-in-chief The Brief 1981-87), ATLA, Denver Bar Assn. (chmn. pub. legal ednl. com. 1989-91, 99—, ABA del. 1997-2002, bd. trustees 2002—), Colo. Bar Assn. (chmn. health law sect. 1993-94, chmn. law edn. com. 1993-96, coun. licensure, enforcement and regulation, chmn. profl. discipline com. 1992-93, 98-99, program chmn. ann. meeting 1993-94, chair publs. com. 1995-97, chair elect 2003—). Democrat. Roman Catholic. Home: 10406 W Glasgow Ave Littleton CO 80127-3468 Office: Atty Gen Office 1525 Sherman St Fl 5 Denver CO 80203-1760 E-mail: jim.carr@state.co.us.

CARR, JAMES PATRICK, lawyer; b. Cheverly, Md., Apr. 13, 1950; s. Lawrence Edward Jr. and agnes (Dyer) C.; m. Mona L. Kyle, May 28, 1986; children: James P. Jr., Kristin, Kevin, Sean. BA, U. Notre Dame, 1972, JD, 1976. Bar: Md. 1976, Calif. 1977, U.S. Dist. Ct. (cen. dist.) Calif. 1977, U.S. Dist. Ct. (so. dist.) Calif. 1986. Assoc. Carr, Jordan et al, Washington, 1976-77; ptnr. Breidenbach, Swainston et al, L.A., 1977-84, Harney, Wolfe, Shaller & Carr, L.A., 1984-88, Carr & Shaller, L.A., 1988-89; pvt. practice law L.A., 1989—. Mem. Am. Bd. Trial Advs., Assn. Trial Lawyers Am., Consumer Attys. Calif., Consumer Attys. Assn. L.A. Democrat. Roman Catholic. Office: 11755 Wilshire Blvd Ste 1170 Los Angeles CA 90025-1539 E-mail: jpc@jpcarrlaw.com.

CARR, JAMES REVELL, museum executive, curator; b. Bryn Mawr, Pa., Aug. 11, 1939; s. Clinton DeWitt and Asta Marie (Knudsen) C.; m. Mary Elizabeth Bump, June 25, 1963 (div. Oct. 1986); children: James Revell III, George McKelvy; m. Barbara Palmer, Apr. 15, 1989. BA, Rutgers U., 1962; MA, U. Pa., 1969. Teaching asst. U. Pa., Phila., 1968-69; archeologist N.J. State Mus., Trenton, 1968-69; rsch. assoc. Mystic Seaport Mus. Inc., Mystic, Conn., 1969-70, chief curator, 1970-78, dir., 1978—, pres., 1988—. Pres. Internat. Congress Maritime Mus., Liverpool, Eng., 1984-87, Coun. Am. Maritime Mus., 1981-84; trustee Nat. Trust for Historic Preservation, Washington, 1983-92; accreditation commr. Am. Assn. Mus., Washington, 1988-94; chmn. Nat. Maritime Heritage Task Force, Washington, 1981-84. Author: Amerikanische Schiffsbuilder, 1976; contbr. chpts. to books, articles to profl. jours.; TV commentator Operation Sail, WBZ-TV, Boston, 1976, with Peter Jennings on ABC-TV, 1986, Columbus Celebration, Pub. Broadcast Sta., 1992. Corporator Lawrence and Meml. Hosp., New London, Conn., 1979-86; mem. vestry Calvary Ch., Stonington, Conn., 1978-81; mem., sec. Navy Adv. Com. Naval History. Lt. USNR, 1962-67. Mem. Am. Antiquarian Soc., Century Assn., Newcomen Soc. Avocations: running, skiing, sailing. Office: Egan Inst Maritime Studies 4 Winter St Nantucket MA 02554

CARR, KENNETH MONROE, naval officer; b. Mayfield, Ky., Mar. 17, 1925; s. Samuel Norman and Nancy Elmore (Monroe) C.; m. Mary Elizabeth Pace, June 10, 1949. Student, U. Louisville, 1944-45; BS, U.S. Naval Acad., 1949. Served as enlisted man U.S. Navy, 1943-45, commd. ensign, 1949; advanced through grades to vice adm., 1977; mem. commissioning crew U.S.S. Nautilus, 1954; comdg. officer U.S.S. Flasher, 1964-67, U.S.S. John Adams, 1967-68; mil. asst. to Dep. Sec. Def., 1973-77; comdr. submarine force Atlantic Fleet, Norfolk, Va., 1977-80; vice dir. Strategic Target Planning, Offutt AFB, Nebr., 1980-83; later dep. comdr. U.S. Atlantic Fleet, Norfolk, Va., 1983-85; commr. US Nuclear Regulatory Commn., 1986-89, chmn., 1989-91. Mem. bd. advisors MDM Svcs. Corp. Decorated D.S.M. (4), Legion of Merit (2). Mem. N.Y. Yacht Club, Army-Navy Country Club. Baptist. Home: 2322 Ft Scott Dr Arlington VA 22202-2207

CARR, LARRY DEAN, not-for-profit company executive; b. Mt. Vernon, Ill., Apr. 22, 1947; s. Jewell Dean and Mary Janet (Lawrence) C.; m. Jean Ann Swanson, May 12, 1973; 1 child, Lisa Diane. BS in Fin., U. Ill., 1969. CPCU. Analyst Allstate Ins. Co., Northbrook, Ill., 1970-75, controller Svc. Rev. Arlington Heights, Ill., 1975-76, regional controller Rochester, N.Y. and Murray Hill, N.J., 1976-80, exec. info. dir. Northbrook, 1980-82, dir. mktg., 1982-83; v.p. Crum and Forster Personal Ins. Co./U.S. Fire Ins. Co., Basking Ridge, N.J., 1983-84, sr. v.p., 1984-85, exec. v.p., 1985-86, chmn. bd. dirs., pres., CEO, 1986-90, also bd. dirs.; CEO Viking Inc. Co., 1986-90, Nat. Gen. Ins.Co., 1986-91; exec. v.p. Motors Ins. Corp., 1991; pres., CEO Presbyn. Ch. Found., 1993-99; pres., founding dir., chmn. bd. dirs. New Covenant Trust Co., N.A., 1997-99; pres. case mgmt. divsn. Concentra Managed Care, Inc., Waltham, Mass., 2000—02; COO Greater Boston Aid to the Blind, Inc., 2002—. Treas., bd. dirs. Somerset Hills YMCA, Basking Ridge, 1984-85; trustee Kent Place Sch., 1989-90; mem. adv. bd. Resource Ctr. for Women and Their Families, 1989-90; dir. Jarvie Commonweal Svc., 1994-99, Ky. Shakespeare Festival, 1997, Presbyn. Outlook Found., 2000— . Served with USAR, 1969-74. Mem. Pres.' Assn., Am. Mgmt. Assn., Delta Sigma Pi. Republican. Presbyterian. Avocations: swimming, skiing. E-mail: lcarr@gbab.org.

CARR, LAWRENCE EDWARD, JR., lawyer; b. Colorado Springs, Colo., Aug. 10, 1923; s. Lawrence Edward and Lelah R. (Rubert) C.; m. Agnes Isabel Dyer, Dec. 26, 1946; children— Mary Lee, James Patrick, Lawrence Edward III, Eileen Louise, Thomas Vincent. BS, U. Notre Dame, 1948, LL.B., 1949; LL.M., George Washington U., 1954. Bar: Colo. 1949, D.C. 1952, Md. 1961. With Travelers Ins. Co., 1949-51; practiced in Washington, 1952—; sr. ptnr. Carr Goodson, PC, Washington, 1984—2001, Carr Maloney, PC, 2001—. Mem. adv. coun. U. Notre Dame Coll. Law, 1985—. With USMCR, 1943-46, 51-52; col. Res.; ret. Fellow Am. Bar Found.; mem. ABA (ho. of dels. 1973-75), Bar Assn. D.C. (dir. 1969-71, pres. 1974-75), D.C. Def. Lawyers Assn. (pres. 1978-79), Bar Assn. D.C. Rsch. Found. (pres. 1985-86). Home: 111 Storm Haven Ct Stevensville MD 21666-3707 Office: Carr Maloney PC 1667 K St NW 11th Fl Washington DC 20006-1605 E-mail: lec@carmaloney.com.

CARR, LES, psychologist, educator; b. Bklyn., Mar. 7, 1935; s. Sam and Sara (Berman) Carr; children: Lincoln Damian, Sharon Rose, Lewis Wade, Faith Theresa. BA, NYU, 1957; MA, New Sch. for Social Rsch., N.Y.C., 1959; PhD, Vanderbilt U., 1963. Diplomate Am. Bd. Med. Psychotherapists (fellow); lic. psychologist, Calif.; cert. psychologist R.I. Rsch. and clin. intern Rockland State Hosp., N.Y.C. Dept. Mental Hygiene, 1958-59; cons. clin. psychologist to sr. clin. psychologist Ctrl. State Hosp., Nashville, 1962 64; sr. coord. psychol. svcs. U. R.I., Providence, 1963-68; prof., chmn. psychology dept., dean Summer Sch., Salve Regina Coll., Newport, R.I., 1966-70, v.p. acad. affairs, 1969-71; project dir. Newport Hosp., 1967-71; pres. Lewis U., Lockport, Ill., 1971-76; dean of faculty Columbia Pacific U., San Rafael, Calif., 1977—2000; pres. Columbia Commonwealth U., 2000—. Pres., dir. Elder 100 Plus, Inc., Somerset, Calif.; staff psychologist San Quentin State Prison, 1989—2000; former ednl. cons. to sultan and min. of edn., Oman; staff psychologist No. Calif. Women's Facility, 2000—03. Past chmn. R.I. Gov.'s Task Force on Mental Health Rehab.; chmn. bd. dirs. Sr. U., Richmond, Can.; mem. nat. adv. coun. Profl. Children's Sch., N.Y.C.; past chmn. adv. bd. dirs. Comprehensive Mental Health Ctr., Newport; past bd. dirs. Regional Ballet Soc., Joliet, Ill., R.I. Rehab. Assn.; past chmn. bd. trustees St. Mary's Acad., Nauvoo, Ill.; past mem. exec. com. R.I. Gov.'s Commn. on Vocat. Rehab. With U.S. Army, 1958. Mem. APA, Calif. Psychol. Assn. Home: 7900 Shenandoah Ln Somerset CA 95684-9597 Fax: 530 620-6427.

CARR, L(EWIS) CHARLES, clinical psychologist; b. Boston, Aug. 17, 1946; s. Lewis Chapman Carr and Mildred Anne Dodd; m. Joan Wood Carr, Aug. 5, 1967; children: Charles C., Jonathan E. BS in Biology, Gordon Coll., 1967; PhD in Psychology, Biola U., 1975. Diplomate Am. Bd. Med. Psychotherapists; cert. clin. psychology Am. Bd. Profl. Psychology. Pvt. practice, N.Y.C., 1975-86, Sandy Springs, Ga., 1986-89; sr. psychologist Hartford Hosp., Inst. of Living, Hartford, Conn., 1989-95; psychology sect. chmn. Mission Meml. Hosp/St. Joseph's Hosp. Health Sys., Ashville, N.C., 1995—. Cons. Western Carolina Sleep Ctr., Asheville, 1995—, GTE-Sylvania, Danvers, Mass., 1985. Mem. Am. Psychol. Assn., Nat. Register of Health Svc. Providers in Psychology, N.C. Psychol. Assn., Tokenake Club (Darien, Conn.). Presbyterian. Avocation: sailing. Office: 64 Merrimon Ave Asheville NC 28801-2323

CARR, MARCUS EUGENE, JR., internist; b. Greensboro, N.C., Mar. 9, 1949; s. Marcus Eugene and Alsie May (Barham) C.; m. Sarah Martin, Oct. 17, 1975 (div. June 1992); children: Joseph, Jonathan, Ashley, Mary, Katherine, Christian, Stephen; m. Sheryl L. Zekert, Nov. 1993. BS in Physics, Davidson Coll., 1971; PhD in Biomed. Engring., U. N.C., 1975, MD, 1979; postgrad, U.S. Army War Coll., 1999. Diplomate Am. Bd. Internal Medicine, Am. Bd. Hematology. Commd. 2nd lt. USAR, 1971, advanced through grades to capt., 1978; ret., 1979; intern N.C. Meml. Hosp., Chapel Hill, 1980-81, jr. resident internal medicine, 1981-82, sr. asst. resident in internal medicine, 1982-83, chief resident, 1983-84; asst. prof. medicine Med. Coll. Va., Richmond, 1985-91, asst. prof. pathology, 1988-91, assoc. prof. pathology, internal medicine, 1991—; founder, pres. Hemodyne, Inc., Richmond, Va., 1993—; comdr. U.S. Army Hosp., 1995—97, 2000—02. Mem. tissue and transfusion com., rsch. and devel. com., McGuire V.A. Med. Ctr., M-III med. curriculum com., admissions com. Sch. of Medicine, promotions com. dept. of pathology, Med. Coll. Va. Contbr. numerous articles and abstracts to profl. jours.; presenter many sci. seminars and meetings. inventor: internat. and nat. patents in field of hematology. Mem. Richmond Blood Club, Bon Air Bapt. Ch., Richmond. Recommd. maj. USAR M.C., 1987, advanced to lt. col., 1994, vet. Desert Storm. Recipient med. student rsch. fellowship, 1977; grantee: So. Med. Assn., 1983, Med. Coll. Va., 1985, A. D. Williams Faculty, 1985, VA Rsch. Adv. Group, 1985, '86. 88-91, Massey Ctr. Instl. grant 1987-88, Burroughs-Wellcome, 1989, 90-91, 92—. Fellow Am. Heart Assn., Am. Coll. Physicians, Am. Coll. Angiology, Internat. Coll. Angiology, Internat. Coll. Hematology; mem. Am. Coll. Physicians, Am. Soc. Hematology, Am. Fedn. Clin. Rsch. (coun. on thrombosis), Am. Heart Assn., Internat. Soc. Thrombosis and Haemostasis, Internat. Soc. Exptl. Hematology, Nat. Haemophelia Found., N.Y. Acad. Scis., Assn. Military Surgeons of U.S., So. Soc. Clin. Investigation, Am. Soc. Clin. Pathologists, Internat. Fibrinogen Rsch. Soc., Sigma Xi. Home: 2540 Swanhurst Dr Midlothian VA 23113-9612 Office: Med Coll Va PO Box 980230 Richmond VA 23298-0230

CARR, MARGARET, educator; b. St. Louis, Mar. 13, 1947; d. John William Henry and Dorothy Eugene Ryan Long; m. Douglas A. Ries Jr., June 7, 1969 (div. July 1979); children: Colleen Margaret, Kathryn Anne; m. Daniel Francis Carr, Sept. 25, 1982. AB cum laude, St. Louis U., 1969; MA in Tchg., Webster U., 1979. Life cert. tchr., Mo. Tchr. St. Timothy's, St. Louis, 1970-71, St. Peter's, St. Charles, 1972-73, Immocolata, St. Louis, 1971-72, 76-77; tchr., home tutor Spl. Sch. Dist., St. Louis, 1977-80; tchr. Our Lady of Sorrow Sch., St. Louis, 1980-84, United Ch. of Christ Sch., St. Louis, 1984-86, Mary Queen of Peace Sch., Webster Groves, Mo., 1987—. Author: Fort San Carlos, May 26, 1780, 1997, History of Mary Queen of Peace School, 1999. Recipient award and medal Am. citizenship VFW, 1998; named Tchr. of Yr., VFW, 2001. Mem. Mo. State Soc. U.S. Daus. of 1812 (state pres. 1998—, pres. St. Louis pioneer chpt. 1995-98), DAR Mo., Continental Soc. Daus. of Indian Wars (gov. Mo. soc. 1994-98, hon. gov. 1998—), New Eng. Women (state pres. 199—), Colonial Dames of the 17th Century (vice regen Margaret Allyn Wyatt chpt.), Colonial Dames of Am., Descs. of the Founders of Hartford, Sons and Daus. of the Pilgrims, Daus. of Union Vets., Delta Kappa Gamma (Beta Theta chpt. 1996—). Avocations: collection sewing tapes, antique costume jewelry, angels. Home: 17 S Maple Ave Webster Groves MO 63119-3021 Office: Mary Queen of Peace Sch 680 W Lockwood Ave Webster Groves MO 63119-3598

CARR, MARIE PINAK, book distribution company executive; b. Buffalo, June 17, 1954; d. Henry and Hildegard (Poech) Pinak; m. Richard Wallace Carr, Oct. 18, 1980; children: Katharine Marie, Ann Louise, Elizabeth Ashby. BS, Syracuse U., 1976. Cancer microbiologist Nat. Cancer Inst., Rockville, Md., 1976-78; mktg. specialist Precision Sci., Washington, 1978-80; art importer Dicmar Trading Co., Inc., Washington, 1981-83, book dist. Silver Spring, Md., 1983—. Bd. dir. CARE. Co-author: The Willard Hotel, 1986. Bd. dirs. Salvation Army Women's Aux., Washington, 1982—, pres., 1990-91; bd. dirs. Am. Cancer Soc., Washington, 1988-90; co-chmn. Nat. Cancer Ball, 1989, 90; active Jr. League Washington, 1987-90; bd. dirs. Achievement Rewards for College Students, 2000—; mem. exec. bd. CARE USA. Mem. Washington Club. Republican. Roman Catholic. Avocations: gardening, collecting textiles, tennis, travel. Office: Dicmar Trading Co Inc 4057 Highwood Ct NW Washington DC 20007-2131

CARR, M(ARY) L(OIS), mental health professional; b. Quincy, Fla., May 13, 1948; d. J.T. and Clara Drucilla (Sexton) C.; m. Daniel L. Groothuis, Sept. 16, 1967 (div. Sept. 1977); children: Gregory David, Kristen Lea. AA, Pensacola (Fla.) Jr. Coll., 1969; BS, U. South Fla., 1981; MS, Nova U., 1988. Developer, dir. resource ctr. Girls Club of Sarasota, Fla., 1981-83, assoc. dir., 1983, exec. dir., 1983-86, also bd. dirs.; pvt. practice, 1989-95, 1994-95; dir. Kids In Trauma, Phoenix, 1995—. Bd. dirs. Girls Club of Sarasota County Found., 1983-86, Sarasota County Youth Related Services Assn., 1983-85; creator, co-developer various Girls Club Programs; lectr. in field; dir. II Manatee Glens Corp., Bradenton, Fla., 1991-93. Writer children's advice column, Kila, 1982; co-writer TV program Girls In Motion, 1982-83; writer local TV pub. service announcement for Girls Club of Sarasota County, Coast Update, 1985; Contbr. articles on children to popular mags. Active Sarasota County Drug Task Force, 1983; asst. dir. Community Health Edn. Council, 1982-83, Women's Support Group, Venice, Fla., 1982, Sarasota County Driving Under the Influence Panel, 1987; evaluator, program com. mem. Big Brothers, Big Sisters of Sarasota County, 1985; co-founder Venice chpt. Students Against Drunk Driving,1984, fundraiser, 1986, advisor, 1987; mem. steering com. Resource co-chairperson project graduation Venice High Sch.; co-chmn. adv. bd. Make-A-Wish Found., Sarasota, 1988; client svcs. dir. Homeward Bound, Phoenix, 1998—. Mem. Phi Kappa Phi. Republican. Roman Catholic. Avocations: vol. work, travel. Home: 8088 E Via Del Valle Scottsdale AZ 85258-3003 E-mail: MLCarizona@aol.com.

CARR, MICHELE PAIGE, dental hygienist, educator; b. Queens, N.Y., Jan. 10, 1963; d. Michael Barry and Celia Barbara Zeitlin; m. John Joseph Carr, Aug. 31, 1986; children: Drew, Bailey. BS, Ohio State U., 1984, MA, 1993. Registered dental hygienist, 1984. Dental hygienist various dental offices, Columbus, Ohio, 1984—89; faculty coord. Nisonger Ctr., Columbus, 1989—96; asst. prof. dental hygiene Ohio State U., Columbus, 1996—. Contbr. Named Dental Hygiene Outstanding Instr., Ohio State U. Coll. of Dentistry, 1999; fellow Rsch. fellow, Am. Assn. Dental Schs./Warner Lambert, 1998; grantee, Ohio Devel. Disabilities Coun., 2001—. Mem.: Am. Dental Edn. Assn., Am. Dental Hygienists Assn., Am. Assn. of Dental Rsch., Ohio State U. Dental Hygiene Alumni Soc. (treas. 1999—), Sigma Phi Alpha. Avocation: tennis. Home: 1463 Harrison Rd SW Pataskala OH 43062 Office: Ohio State University 305 W 12th Ave #179 Columbus OH 43218-2357 Office Fax: 614-292-8013. Personal E-mail: carr.3@osu.edu. E-mail: carr.3@osu.edu.

CARR, OSCAR CLARK, III, lawyer; b. Apr. 9, 1951; s. Oscar Clark Carr Jr. and Billie (Fisher) Carr Houghton; m. Mary Leatherman, Aug. 4, 1973; children: Camilla Fisher, Oscar Clark V. BA in English with distinction, U. Va., 1973; JD with distinction, Emory U., 1976. Bar: Tenn. 1976, U.S. Dist. Ct. (we. dist.) Tenn. 1977, (no. dist.) Miss. 1977, U.S. Ct. Appeals (6th cir.) 1985, (5th cir.) 1995, U.S. Dist. Ct. (so. dist.) Miss. 2000; cert. mediator Tenn. Assoc. Glankler Brown, PLLC (formerly Glankler, Brown, et al, Memphis, 1976-82, ptnr., 1982—, chief mgr., 1998-00. Treas., vestryman St. John's Episcopal Ch., Memphis, 1988—91, sr. warden, 1991; mem. Commn. on Ministry Diocese of West Tenn., 1987—90; King of Carnival Memphis, 1994; bd. dirs. West Tenn. chpt. Juvenile Diabetes Found., 1998—, dir., 1998—2002; bd. dirs. Memphis Ballet Soc., 1980, Memphis-Shelby County Unit Am. Cancer Soc., Memphis Oral Sch. Deaf, 1988—91, Carnival Memphis. Recipient Living and Giving award, West Tenn. chpt. Juvenile Diabetes Rsch. Found., 2002. Mem. ABA, Tenn. Bar Assn. (we. dist. coun. environ. law 1992—), Memphis-Shelby County Bar Assn. (bd. dirs. 1985-87), Memphis Country Club (atty. 1997—). Office: Glankler Brown PLLC 1700 One Commerce Sq Memphis TN 38103 E-mail: ocarr@glankler.com.

CARR, PATRICIA ANN, community health nurse; b. Teaneck, N.J., Dec. 6, 1949; d. John O. and Elizabeth (Nestor) Olsen. Diploma, Mt. Sinai Hosp. Sch. Nursing, N.Y.C., 1970. RN, Ga., Fla.; AIDS cert. RN; cert. clin. rsch. coord. Asst. DON Taylor Meml. Hosp., Hawkinsville, Ga., 1979-81; staff nurse ICU Shands Teaching Hosp., Gainesville, Fla., 1981-82; staff nurse Venice Hosp., 1982-84; field nurse Fla. Home Health Svcs. Sarasota Inc., 1986-93; regulatory compliance coord. Fla. Home Health Svcs., Sarasota, 1993-96; program clin. coord. Cmty. AIDS Network, Inc., Sarasota, 1996-98; clin. studies coord. Infectious Diseases Assocs., Sarasota, 1998—. Contbr. articles to publs. Mem. APHA, Assn. Nurses in AIDS Care, Home Health Nurses Assn., Intravenous Nurses Soc., Assn. Practitioners in Infection Control, Assn. Clin. Rsch. Profls. Office: Infectious Diseases Assocs 1425 S Osprey Ave Ste 1 Sarasota FL 34239-2900 E-mail: paeoc@aol.com.

CARR, PAUL WALLACE, actor; b. New Orleans, Jan. 31, 1934; s. Edward Sidney and Elaine Grace Carr; children: Alexandra, Christina, Michael. Grad., Am. Theatre Wing, 1953. Actor, producing dir. L.A. Repertory Co., 1990—. Actor over 50 feature films, over 300 guest starring TV roles, over 100 stage prodns. Broadway, off-Broadway, L.A. and regional theatres. Recipient awards L.A. Weekly Newspaper, 1987, Dramalogue Mag., L.A., 1994. Democrat. Avocations: skiing, sailing, fishing.

CARR, RICHARD WILLIAM, federal program manager; b. Montgomery, Ala., Aug. 16, 1944; s. Walter Thomas Jr. and Maude Carr; m. Susan Lane Seckman, Sept. 30, 1967; 1 child, Richard II. AA in Computer Sci. and Elec. Engring., Miami-Dade Coll., 1972. Cert. Internet security specialist. Fed. computer/network sys. analyst Fed. Comms. Commn., Washington, 1972-79; fed. dir. info. tech. security Gen. Svcs. Adminstrn., Washington, 1979-85; fed. info. tech. project mgr. Dept. Justice, Washington, 1985-86; fed. info. tech. security program mgr. Dept. Energy, Germantown, Md., 1986-89, NASA, Washington, 1989—2002. Charter and founding mem. steering com. Forum of Incident Response and Security Teams, Washington, 1992-94; mem. Presdl. Com. on Nat. Security Telecomms. and Info. Sys. Security, Washington, 1986-94; mem. Presdl. Info. Infrastructure Task Force, Washington, 1993-96; mem. Nat. Security Policy Bd., Wash., 1993-96; mem. Sr. Fed. Adv. Coun. on Advanced Info. Tech. Security R&D Issues, Washington, 2000—. Recipient Unsung Hero of Computer Security award Fed. Computer week, Congress, OMB (Office of Mgmt. and Budget Exec. Office of the Pres.), NIST (Nat. Inst. of Standards and Tech.), 1991. Mem. Ops. Security Profls. Soc. Achievements include development of first computer incident handling team in fed. govt. Home: PO Box 35 104 Olde Point Ln Queenstown MD 21658-0035

CARR, RONALD EDWARD, ophthalmologist, educator; b. Newark, N.J., Sept. 17, 1932; s. Frank Edward and Mildred (Sasso) C.; m. Nancy May Gould, June 8, 1957; children: Peter Richardson, Jacqueline Marie, Timothy Edward. AB, Princeton U., 1954; MD, Johns Hopkins U., 1958; M.Sc., NYU, 1963. Intern Bellevue Hosp., N.Y.C., 1958-59; resident NYU Med. Ctr., N.Y.C., 1959-63; clin. assoc. NIH, Bethesda, Md., 1963-64, assoc. ophthalmologist, 1964-65; asst. prof. ophthalmology NYU Med. Ctr., 1965-67, assoc. prof., 1967-71, prof., 1971—. Author: Visual Electrodiagnosis, 1981, Electrodiagnostic Testing of the Visual System, 1990. Served to lt. comdr. USPHS, 1963. Recipient Knapp award AMA, 1966 Fellow Am. Acad. Ophthalmology, ACS; mem. Am Ophthal. Soc., N.Y. Ophthal Soc., Assn. Research in Ophthalmology Clubs: Princeton, Stone Horse Yacht. Republican. Episcopalian. Home: 130 E End Ave New York NY 10028-7553 Office: NYU Med Ctr 530 1st Ave New York NY 10016-6402 E-mail: nancycarr2@aol.com.

CARR, STEPHEN HOWARD, materials engineer, educator; b. Dayton, Ohio, Sept. 29, 1942; s. William Howard and Mary Elizabeth (Clement) C.; m. Virginia W. McMillan, June 24, 1967; children: Rosamond Elizabeth, Louisa Ruth. BS, U. Cin., 1965; MS, Case Western Res. U., 1967, PhD, 1970. Coop. engr. Inland divsn. GM, Dayton, 1960-65; asst. prof. materials sci. and engring. and chem. engring. Northwestern U., Evanston, Ill., 1970-73, assoc. prof., 1973-78, prof., 1978—, dir. Materials Rsch. Ctr., 1984-90, asst. dean engring., 1991-93, assoc. dean engring., 1993—. Cons. in field. Contbr. articles to profl. jours. Recipient Outstanding Alumni Achievement award U. Cin. Coll. Engring., 1993. Fellow Am. Soc. for Metals Internat., Am. Phys. Soc.; mem. AIChE, Soc. Automotive Engrs. (Ralph R. Teetor award 1980), Plastics Inst. Am. (Ednl. Svc. award 1975), Am. Chem. Soc., Soc. Plastics Engrs., Materials Rsch. Soc. Achievements include patents in plastics and textiles fields. Home: 2704 Harrison St Evanston IL 60201-1216 Office: Northwestern U 2145 Sheridan Rd Evanston IL 60208-0834

CARR, STEPHEN W. lawyer; b. Providence, Mar. 16, 1943; AB cum laude, Amherst Coll., 1965; JD cum laude, Harvard U., 1968. Bar: Mass. 1968. Law clk. to Hon. John Spaulding Mass. Supreme Judicial Ct., 1968-69; mem. Goodwin Procter, LLP, Boston. Mem.: ABA (bus. law sect.), Boston Bar Assn. Office: Goodwin Procter LLP Exchange Pl Boston MA 02109-2803

CARR, THOMAS A. real estate company executive; s. Oliver T. Carr, Jr. BA, Brown U.; MBA, Harvard U. Dir. Oliver Carr Co.; CFO CarrAmerica Realty Corp., 1993-95, pres., dir., 1993—, COO, 1995-97, CEO. Mem. Nat. Assn. Real Estate Investment Trusts, Young Pres. Orgn., Fed. City Coun., Internat. Devel. Rsch. Coun. Office: 1850 Kay St NW Washington DC 20006-2213

CARR, THOMAS ELDRIDGE, lawyer; b. Aug. 16, 1953; s. Peter Gordon and Margaret (Johnson) C.; children: Christopher Allen, Austin Thomas. BA, Tex. Tech. U., 1975, JD, 1977. Bar: Tex. 1978, U.S. Dist. Ct. (no. and we. dists.) Tex. 1978, U.S. Ct. Appeals (5th cir.) 1981, U.S. Supreme Ct. 1982. Assoc. Morgan, Gambill & Owen, Ft. Worth, 1978-81; ptnr. Morgan, Owen, & Carr, Ft. Worth, 1981-85, Quillin, Owen, Wilson & Carr, Ft. Worth, 1987-91, Owen & Carr, Ft. Worth, 1991-94, Taylor, Olson, Adkins, Sralla & Elam LLP, Ft. Worth, 1999—. Co-author: Of Counsel to Classrooms: A Resource Guide to Assist Attorneys and Teachers in Law Focused Education. Active Benbrook City Coun., Tex., 1984-86, Benbrook Park and Recreation Bd., 1981-84; mem. exec. bd. Longhorn coun. Boy Scouts Am., 1983-86; mem. Home Rule Charter Commn., Benbrook, 1983. Selected Outstanding Young Lawyer of Tarrant County, 1990. Mem. ABA (chmn. com.), Ft. Worth Tarrant County Young Lawyers Assn. (pres. 1983), State Bar Tex. (chmn. Sch. Law sect. 1991, bd. dirs. 1998-2001, Presdl. citation 2001), Tarrant county Bar Assn. (treas., sec. 1988), Tex. Young Lawyers Assn. (bd. dirs. 1984-86). Office: East Tower Ste 200 6000 Western Pl Fort Worth TX 76107

CARR, WALTER JAMES, JR., research physicist, consultant; b. Knob Noster, Mo., May 6, 1918; s. Walter James and Alice Frances (Koch) C.; m. Winifred Walker Schultz, Mar. 21, 1953; children: James Lawrence, Robert David. BSEE, U. Mo., Rolla, 1940; MEE, Stanford U., 1942; DSc in Physics, Carnegie-Mellon U., 1951. Engr. Westinghouse Electric R&D, Pitts., 1942-51, section mgr., 1951-57, adv. physicist, 1957-65, mgr. solid state theory, 1965-70, cons., 1970-85; cons., 1985—. Physicist Atomic Energy Establishment, Harwell, Eng., 1962. Author: AC Loss and Macroscopic Theory of Superconductors, 1983, 2d edit., 2001. Named to Acad. Elec. Engring., U. Mo., Rolla, 1981. Fellow Am. Phys. Soc., IEEE; mem. University Club. Avocation: tennis. Home: 1460 Jefferson Heights Rd Pittsburgh PA 15235-5220 E-mail: wjamescarrjr@worldnet.att.net.

CARR, WILLARD ZELLER, JR., lawyer; b. Richmond, Ind., Dec. 18, 1927; s. Willard Zeller and Susan (Brownell) C.; m. Margaret Paterson, Feb. 15, 1952; children: Clayton Paterson, Jeffrey Westcott. BS, Purdue U., 1948; JD, Ind. U., 1951. Bar: Calif. 1951, U.S. Supreme Ct. 1963. Ptnr. Gibson, Dunn & Crutcher, Los Angeles, 1952—. Mem. nat. panel arbitrators Am. Arbitration Assn.; former labor relations cons. State of Alaska; lectr. bd. visitors Southwestern U. Law Sch.; mem. adv. council Southwestern Legal Found., Internat. and Comparative Law Ctr. Trustee Calif. Adminstrv. Law Coll.; bd. dirs. Employers' Group, Calif. State Pks. Found., Los Angeles coun. Boy Scouts Am.; mem. Mayor's Econ. Devel. Policies Com.; past chmn. Pacific Legal Found.; past chmn. men's adv. com. Los Angeles County-USC Med. Ctr. Aux. for Recruitment, Edn. and Service; past chmn. bd. Wilshire Republican Club; past mem. Rep. State Central Com.; past mem. pres.'s coun. Calif. Mus. Sci. and Industry; mem. Nat. Def. Exec. Res., Los Angeles World Affairs Coun.; bd. dirs., sec. Los Angeles Police Meml. Found.; past chmn. Los Angeles sect. United Way; mem. adv. com. Los Angeles County Human Rels. Commn., past commr., Calif. State World Trade Commn.; Los Angeles chpt. ARC. Fellow Am. Bar Found.; mem. Internat. Bar. Assn. (past chmn. labor law com. of bus. law sect., past chmn. labor employment practice group), The Federalist Soc., Calif. Bar Assn., L.A. County Bar Assn., L.A. C. of C. (past chmn. 1991), Calif. C. of C. Home: 2185 Century Hl Los Angeles CA 90067-3516 Office: Gibson Dunn & Crutcher 333 S Grand Ave Ste 4400 Los Angeles CA 90071-3197 E-mail: wcarr@gibsondunn.com.

CARRA, ANDREW JOSEPH, advertising executive; b. Bklyn., July 30, 1943; s. Andrew Sylvester and Grace (Santoro) C.; m. Eileen Lynn Campbell, Aug. 6, 1966; children: Christopher Andrew, Allison Lynn, Courtney Lauren. BA, St. Bonaventure U., 1966. Asso. editor Sport Mag., Macfadden-Bartell, N.Y.C., 1967-71; mng. editor publs. div. Spencer Mktg. Services, N.Y.C., 1971-73; assoc. pub. Camping Jour. mag. Davis Pubs., N.Y.C., 1973-82; account supr. Robert Marston and Assocs., N.Y.C., 1982-83; v.p., dir. pub. relations Colarossi Griswold Inc., N.Y.C., 1983-84; pres. AC&R Pub. Relations, Inc., N.Y.C., 1984-86; dir. McCann-Erickson Inc., N.Y.C., 1987-96; creative dir. BBB Group Ltd., Hackensack, N.J., 1996—. Author: Complete Guide to Hiking and Backpacking, 1977, How to Go Camping, 1978; Contbr. chpts. to books, articles to periodicals. Mem. Outdoor Writers Assn., Am. Soc. Mag. Editors, Nat. Wildlife Fedn. Democrat. Roman Catholic. Home: 157 Fairfield Pl Fairfield CT 06824 Office: BBB Group Ltd 364 Summit Ave Hackensack NJ 07601-1413 E-mail: ajcarra@optonline.net.

CARRADINI, LAWRENCE, comparative biologist, science administrator; b. Astoria, N.Y., Apr. 18, 1953; s. George John and Florence (Camuti) C.; m. Susan Marie Peterson, Sept. 23, 1972 (divorced); 1 child, Daniel Lawrence. BS in Zoology, Columbia Pacific U., 1989, MS in Vertebrate Reproductive Physiology and Physiol. Ecology, 1992. From technician to lab. supr. Charles River Labs., Wilmington, Mass., 1978-91, rschr., 1991; sr. scientist, mgr. biol. labs. Mass. Health Rsch. Inst., Boston, 1992-96; chief labs. Mass. Biologic Labs., U. Mass. Med. Sch., Boston, 1996—. Chmn. Instnl. Animal Care and Use Com., State Lab. Inst./Orphan Biologics Inst./Mass. Dept. Pub. Health/Mass. Biologics Lab., 1995-96; apptd. to State DPGS task force on procurement practices; mem. Lake Survey, U. N.H., Salem, 1982-83; instr. Internat. Children's Vaccine Tng. Program; ex officio mem. instnl. animal care and use com. U. Mass. Med. Sch., 1997—. Mem. editl. bd. Internat. Jour. Advances in Contraceptive Delivery Systems; contbr. articles to Jour. Lab. Animal Sci., Jour. Am. Vet. Med. Assn.; author poetry: Burning Heads, 1996, Om I Am, 1999; contbr. poetry lit. mags. and Contemporary Foreign Literature, 2001. Officer, selectman apptd. mem. 208 Water Quality Study Com., Salem, N.H., 1981-82, chmn., selectman apptd. mem., 1982-83; mem. adv. bd. Internat. M.C. Chang Meml. Festschrift; pres. and chmn. bd. dirs., officer Lowell Celebrates Kerouac, Inc.; local organizer for Lowell reading UN Dialogue Among Nations Through Poetry, 2001. N.Y. State Regents scholar, 1971; hon. mention Richard A. Seffron Meml. Poetry award 1994. Mem. Soc. for Cryobiology, Nat. Am. Assn. Lab. Animal Sci., Am. Assn. Lab. Animal Sci. (New Eng. chpt., cert. nat. lab. animal technologist, item writer technician cert. examination program), Lab. Animal Mgmt. Assn., Internat. Platform Assn., N.Y. Acad. Scis. Democrat. Achievements include development of reliable method to cycle estrus in syrian hamsters; co-development of commercially available cryopreserved 1-cell mouse embryos for use in media assays; co-application of 1-cell technology toward development of commercially available cryopreserved, fertilized, pronuclear-staged mouse oocytes for DNA microinjection; development of central technical services group Massachusetts Biologic Laboratories. Home: PO Box 8797 Lowell MA 01853-8797 Office: 305 South St Boston MA 02130-3515

CARRAHER, CHARLES JACOB, JR., professional speaker; b. Sept. 22, 1922; s. Charles Jacob and Marcella Marie (Hager) C.; m. Joyce Ann Root, June 13, 1947; children: Cynthia A., Craig J. Grad. pub. schs., Norwood, Ohio. With Cin. Enquirer, 1937-72, office mgr., circulation mgr., admin. asst. to exec. v.p., 1947-66, dir. employee cmty. rels., 1966-72, corp. sec., 1969-72; exec. v.p., ptnr. Cin. Suburban Newspapers Inc., 1973-77; asst. dir. devel. Sta. WCET-TV, 1977-79; v.p. Garrett Computer Inc., 1979-81. Participant numerous symposia. Mem. bd., v.p. Cin. Conv. and Visitors Bur., 1966-72; mem. Cin. Manpower Planning Com., 1972; bd. dirs. Cen. Psychiat. Clinic, 1970-80, Mental Health Assn., 1970-72, Great Rivers coun. Girl Scouts U.S.A., 1969-74; v.p. bd. dirs. Neediest Kids of All, 1969-72; bd. dirs. Greater Cin. Urban League, 1971-74, 75-78. Lt. USAF, WWII, ETO. Decorated Air medal with cluster. Mem. Greater Cin. C. of C. (chmn. human resources devel. com. 1972), Beta Gamma Sigma. Republican. Home and Office: 10848 Lake Thames Dr Cincinnati OH 45242-3105

CARRANZA, CESAR AUGUSTO, surgeon; b. Trujillo, Peru, 1943; came to U.S., 1970; MD, Nat. U. Trujillo, 1970. Diplomate Am. Bd. Surgery. Intern Ellis Hosp., Schenectady, N.Y., 1971; resident St. Joseph Hosp., Balt., 1972-76; surgeon Norwegian Am. Hosp., Chgo., 1976—; pvt. practice, Palatine, Ill. Fellow ACS. Office: 41 S Brockway St Palatine IL 60067-0809 also: 3409 W Fullerton Ave Chicago IL 60647-2415

CARRASCO ALTAMIRANO, DIODORO, former federal official; b. Oaxaca, Mexico, Jan. 30, 1954; m. Clara Scherer Castillo; three children. Degree in Econs., Inst. Tech. Autónomo Mexico. Asst. dir. programming gen. dept. agro-indsl. devel. Dept. Agr. and Water Resources-SARH; gen. asst. dir. agro-indsl. planning gen. agro-indsl. coord. devel. dept. SARH; gen. asst. dir. for ino. and rsch. gen. dept. basic products and rural supply Dept. Commerce and Indsl. Devel. SECOFI, pvt. sec. to asst. sec. indsl. and comml. planning; sec. planning State Govt. Oaxaca; asst. govt. sec. Dept. of Interior, Govt. Mexico, Piso, 1999—2000; pres. Institucion Para La Vida Rural, 2000—. Fgn.

sec. bd. dirs. Coll. Nat. Economists, A.C.; v.p. Coll. Nat. Economists. Mem. Nat. Assn. Econs. SARH ANESARH (pres.), ANESARH (adv. coun.). Office: Rio Valsas No 57 Colonia Buenavista Colonia Uauhtem 06500 Mexico

CARRASQUEL-BELANDRIA, JOSE RAMON, language educator; b. Caracas, Venezuela, June 2, 1965; s. Jose Carrasquel-Hurtado and Maria Belandria-Belandria. PhD in romance linguistics, U. Wash., 1995. Spanish lectr. Stanford U., Calif., 1997—98; prof. No. Ill. U., DeKalb, 1999—. Editl. reviewer U. of Michigan-Dearborn, Fgn. Lang. Annals, Mich., 2001—; editl. cons. Houghton Mifflin Co., Boston, 2000—; faculty assoc. No. Ill. U., Ctr. for Latino and L. Am. Studies, 1999—. Contbr. conference (XVth Internat. Conf. on Hist. Linguistics in Melbourne, Australia, 2001); author: (articles) various profl. jours. (Internat. Conf. on Lang. Variation in Europe, in Barcelona, Spain, 2001, Fourth Hispanic Linguistics Symposium, 2002). Lobbyist Chgo. Chpt. of LGIRTF at Heartland Alliance, 1999—2000. Fellow Tchg. fellowship, U. Wash., 1990-1995, U. Oreg., 1988-1990; grantee Rsch. and Artistry award, Grad. Sch. at No. Ill. U., Summer 2002; scholar Study Abroad scholarship, Fundacion Gran Mariscal de Ayacucho, 1983-1988. Master: Phi Sigma Iota, Internat. Honor Soc. for Fgn. Languages (hon.; faculty adv. 1999); mem.: Am. Assn. of Tchrs., Spanish and Portuguese (assoc.), Linguistic Assn. of the S.W. (assoc.; conf. presenter 1995). Avocations: human/equal rights, education, internat. affairs, multiculturalism and diversity of all kinds, scholarships.

CARREAU, PIERRE, chemical engineering educator; b. Montreal, Que., Can., Nov. 14, 1939; married; 3 children. BSc, U. Montreal, 1963, MSc, 1965; PhD in Chem. Engring., U. Wis., 1968. Asst. chem. engr. Ecole Polytechnique, 1964—65; asst. prof. to assoc. prof. chem. engring. U. Montreal, 1968—80, chmn. dept., 1973—79, prof., 1980—; prof. chem. engring. Ecole Polytechnique, Montreal. Mem.: AIChemE, Soc. Petroleum Engrs., Soc. Rheology, Can. Soc. Chem. Engrs., Chem. Inst. Can.

CARREGAL, ENRIQUE J. anesthesiologist, educator; b. Spain, 1932; came to U.S., 1960; s. Enrique Alvarez and Manuela Carregal; m. Joan Markson Carregal, Jan. 19, 1960; children: James, Anthony. MD, U. Santiago, Santiago, Spain, 1955. Diplomate Am. Bd. Anesthesiology. Intern Hosp. Clinico Santiago, Spain, 1954-55; resident in Anesthesiology L.A. County-U. So. Calif. Med. Ctr., 1973-78, mem. staff Huntington Hosp., Pasadena, Calif., 1978—; clin. assoc. prof. U.So. Calif. Sch. Med., L.A., 1979—. Mem. AAAS, Internat. Assn. for Study of Pain. Office: Huntington Hosp 100 W California Blvd Pasadena CA 91105 E-mail: ecarregal@giovannella.com.

CARREGAL-FERREIRA, JORGE, software company executive; b. Lourenco Marques, Mozambique, Sept. 3, 1963; s. Angelo Franca and Susanna Else (Berrens) C.-F.; m. Maria Baur, Oct. 19, 1996; children: Victor, Marco. BS, U. Stuttgart, Germany, 1987, diploma in engring., 1992; Dr.Sc.Tech., Swiss Inst. Tech., Switzerland, 1996. Rsch. engr. Rolls-Royce, Derby, Eng., 1990; rsch. asst. Swiss Inst. Tech., Zurich, 1992-97; sales and svc. mgr. AEA Tech., Otterfing, Germany, 1997—, mgr. CFX-ops. Mem. AIAA, Verein Deutscher Ingenieure. Avocations: football, literature, architecture of the renaissance. Office: AEA Tech GmbH Staudenfeldweg 12 Otterfing Germany E-mail: jorge.ferreira@cfx-germany.com.

CARREKER, JOHN RUSSELL, retired agricultural engineer; b. Cook Springs, Ala., Aug. 15, 1908; s. John Robert and Cora Selina (Polk) C.; m. Helen Mackey Garrett, Feb. 10, 1934; children: Joan Louise, James Russell. BS, Ala. Poly. Inst. (now Auburn U.), 1930, MS, 1933. Agrl. engr. Civilian Conservation Corps, Dadeville, Ala., 1933-34, USDA-SCS, Anniston, Ala., 1935-38; rsch. agrl. engr. USDA-SCS & Agrl. Rsch. Svc., Watkinsville, Ga., 1938-58, rsch. lia. rep. Athens, Ga., 1958-61; rsch. leader USDA-Agrl. Rsch. Svc., Athens, 1961-73; ret., 1973. Author over 80 tech. papers on erosion control, irrigation and water mgmt. on farm land. Chmn. PTA, Athens, 1950; pres. Civitan Club, Athens, 1948, Residents Assn., Atlanta, 1986. Recipient Outstanding Alumnus award Auburn U., 1991. Fellow: Am. Soc. Agrl. Engrs. (emeritus, life mem., Soil and Water Engring. award 1970), Soil and Water Conservation Soc. (life); mem.: SAR.

CARREL, MARC LOUIS, lawyer, public affairs consultant; b. Buffalo, Aug. 31, 1967; s. Jerome D. and Judith E. (Fish) C. BA with distinction, U. Mich., 1988; JD, U. Pa., 1993. Bar: Calif., 1993, D.C., 1995. Staff asst. U.S. Senate Com. Agr., Nutrition, and Forestry, Washington, 1989, calender clk., 1989-90; assoc. cons. Office of Calif. State Assemblyman Richard Polanco, Sacramento, 1994; legis. cons. Office of Calif. State Senator Richard Polanco, Sacramento, 1994-96; counsel Calif. State Senate Dem. Caucus, Sacramento, 1995-96; legis. policy cons. to Calif. Assembly Spkr. Cruz M Bustamante, Sacramento, 1997, counsel, 1997-98; dep. issues dir. Jane Harman for Gov.of L.A., 1998; sr. cons. Office of Assemblymem. Cruz M. Bustamante, 1998; policy dir. Cruz M. Bustamante for Lt. Gov., 1998; transition dir. Office of Lt. Gov. Cruz M. Bustamante, 1998-99, sr. advisor to Lt. Gov., 1999-2000; sr. assoc. APCO Worldwide, Sacramento, 2000—02; dep. chief of staff Office of Assembly Majority Leader, 2002; asst. sec. of state, policy and planning Office of Calif. Sec. of State, Sacramento, 2003—. Mem. Legis. Task Force Land Use, Sacramento, 1995, L.A. Fiscal Crisis Working Group, Sacramento, 1995, Calif. Organized Investment Network Econ. Devel. Com., 1996; co-chair Ins. Reinvestment Task Force, Sacramento, 1995; mem. rural devel. strategic plan steering com. USDA, 1996-97; staff Gov.-Elect's Agr. Water Transition Task Force, 1998; coord. Gov.'s Emergency Freeze Assistance Task Force, 1999; mem. designee State Job Tng. Coord. Coun., 1999, Commn. Bldg. for 21st Century, 1999-2000; alternate State Lands Commn., 2000, Calif. World Trade Commn., 2003—; mem Voting Systems and Procedures Panel, 2003—; vice chair HAVA Steering Com., 2003; co-chair, sec. State's Ad Hoc Touch Screen Voting Task Force. Sec. Pa. Law Equal Justice, Phila., 1990-92; co-chair Young Leadership Divsn., Sacramento, 1996-97; trustee Jewish Fedn. Sacramento Region, 1996-97; mem. Jewish Cmty. Rels. Coun., Sacramento, 1997-2002, vice-chair, 1998-99, chair, 1999-2001; cofounder, sec. Jewish Civic Action Network, 1997-99; mem. Sacramento Police Adv. Com., 1999-2001; cofounder, bd. dirs. Capital Unity Coun., 1999—, Greater Sacramento Hate Crimes Task Force, 1999-2002; mem. Human Rights/Fair Housing Commn., Sacramento, 1999-2002; mem. facilities strategic planning com. Sacramento City Unified Sch. Dist., 2001-2002. Recipient U.S. Atty.'s Office Spl. Achievement award, Buffalo, 1991, William J. Branstrom Freshman prize, 1986, Vol. of Yr. award Jewish Fedn. of Sacramento Region, 2001. Mem. Am. Polit. Items Collectors, State Bar Calif., D.C. Bar, Sacramento Bar Assn., U. Mich. Alumni Assn., U. Pa. Law Alumni Soc. Avocation: collector of political paraphernalia. Office: Sec of States Office 1500 11th St 6th Fl Sacramento CA 95814

CARREL, MARIANNE EILEEN, music educator; b. Greenville, Pa., Aug. 28, 1957; d. Francis Raymond Cremi, Betty Hutton Cremi; m. Marion Lee Carrel. Student, Clarion U. Pa., 1975—76; BS, Edinboro U., 1979, MEd, 1985. Cert. elem. tchr. Ohio. Substitute tchr. Greenville and Reynolds Sch. Dists., Greenville, Pa., 1979—80; tchr. music Webster County Schs., Cowen, W.Va., 1980—84; grad. asst. Edinboro U., Edinboro, Pa., 1984—85; tchr. music Madison Local Schs., Madison, Ohio, 1985—86; tchr. music Geneva Area City Schs., Geneva, Ohio, 1986—. Sec. All-Am. Judges Assn., Ohio, 1989—. Named Assoc. of Yr., Am. Bus. Women's Assn., 2000-2001. Mem.: NEA, Internat. Double Reed Soc., Music Educators Nat. Conf., Ohio Edn. Assn., Kappa Delta Pi, Sigma Alpha Iota (life). Home: 4850 Boughner Rd Rock Creek OH 44084 Office: Geneva Area Schs 839 Sherman St Geneva OH 44041 Personal E-mail: mandmcarrel@direcway.com.

CARRELL, DANIEL ALLAN, lawyer; b. Louisville, Jan. 2, 1941; s. Elmer N. and Mary F. (Pfingst) C.; m. Janis M. Wilhelm, July 3, 1976; children: Mary Monroe, Courtney Adele. AB, Davidson Coll., 1963; BA, Oxford U., 1965, MA, 1969; JD, Stanford U., 1968. Bar: Va. 1972, U.S. Dist. Ct. (ea. dist.) Va. 1972, U.S. Ct. Appeals (4th cir.) 1975, U.S. Dist. Ct. (we. dist.) Va. 1985. Asst. prof. U.S. Mil. Acad., West Point, N.Y., 1968-71; assoc. Hunton & Williams, Richmond, Va., 1971-79, ptnr., 1979-95; prin. Carrell, Rice & Rigsby, Richmond, Va., 1996—. Hearing officer Commonwealth of Va., 2000—. Active Richmond Rep. Com., 1974—; co-counsel Dalton for Gov. campaign, Richmond, 1977; counsel Obenshain for Senate campaign, Richmond, 1978; treas. Va. Victory '92; state fin. chmn., fin. com., state ctrl. com. and budget com. Rep. Party Va., 1993-96; bd. dirs. Southampton Citizens Assn., 1985-2001; pres. Davidson Coll. Alumni Assn., 1987-88; trustee Davidson Coll., 1987-88; bd. dirs. Needle's Eye Ministries, 1986-90, adv. bd., 1990—, bd. dirs. U-Turn, Inc., 2001-; elder, trustee Stony Point Reformed Presbyn. Ch., 1993—; moderator James River Presbytery Presbyn. Ch. Am., 1998, 2001; chmn. com. constl. bus. Presbyn. Ch. Am., 2003—. Rhodes scholar, 1962; recipient Merit award Sports Illustrated Mag., 1963. Mem. ABA (chmn. exemption and Noerr Doctrine com. 1986-87, antitrust sect.), Va. Bar Assn. (chmn. young lawyers joint law-related edn. com. 1978-79, young lawyers fellow award 1980), Va. State Bar (chmn. com. on legal edn. and admission to bar 1984-91, bd. govs. sect. edn. lawyers 1992-99. dist. com. discipline 2001-03), Richmond Bar Assn., Christian Legal Soc., Westwood Club. Avocations: tennis, basketball, theatre, concerts. Home: 3724 Custis Rd Richmond VA 23225-1102 Office: Carrell Rice & Rigsby 7275 Glen Forest Dr Richmond VA 23226-3772 E-mail: lexrex3dac@aol.com.

CARRELL, HEATHER DEMARIS, school system administrator; b. Bryn Mawr, Pa., Jan. 4, 1951; d. Jeptha J. and J. Demaris (Affleck) C.; m. Peter F. Brazitis, June 27, 1981; children, Evan, Victoria. BA, Oberlin Coll., 1973; MEd, U. Wash., 1976, PhD, 1982. Cert. tchr., Wash. Head tchr., trainer Exptl. Edn. Unit U. Wash., Seattle, 1976-80, tchr. trainer, 1976-80, supr. early childhood and spl. edn. tchrs. in tng., 1980, coord. classrooms behavior disorders, 1980-81, coord. interdisciplinary tng., 1979-82, asst. prin., 1981-82, cons. Transition Rsch. Problems Handicapped Youth, 1986-88; self-employed cons., 1983-96; adminstr. North Kitsap Sch. Dist., Paulsbo, Wash., 1997—. Cons. North Kitsap Sch. Dist., Poulsbo, Wash., 1984; presenter edn. and spl. edn. various groups from U.S., Can., Australia, 1977-82; pres., co-founder Hansville (Wash.) Coop. Presch., 1982. 84-89; mem. diversity and multicultural advocacy team Wash. State Sch. Dirs. Assn.; rep. to U. Wash. Tchr. Profl. Edn. Adv. Bd., 1992-95; mem. WSSDA Fin. Task Force, 1994; mem. Intertribal Coun. Com. on Racism, North Kitsap, Wash., 1993-94. Author: (with others) The Experimental Education Training Program, 1977; contbr. articles to profl. publs. Commr. North Kitsap Dept. Parks and Recreation, 1983-84; dir. North Kitsap Sch. Bd., 1990-95, v.p., 1992-93, pres., 1993-95; trustee North Kitsap Tchr. of Yr. Found., 1989-90; bd. dirs. North Kitsap Juvenile Diversion Bd., 1987-91; co-founder, v.p. bd. dirs. Kitsap Cmty. Found., 1993-96. Bur. Edn. Handicapped fellow, 1974-75, 77-78.

CARRELL, TERRY EUGENE, manufacturing company executive; b. Monmouth, Ill., July 1, 1938; s. Roy Edwin and Caroline Hilma (Fillman) C.; m. Bonnie Lee Clements, July 11, 1964; children: Philip Edwin, Andrew David. AB, Monmouth Coll., 1961; MBA, Calif. State U., L.A., 1967; D of Bus. Adminstrn., U. So. Calif., 1970; AAS, Ivy Tech. State Coll., 1991. From sr. engr. to prin. engr. reconnaissance and comm. N.Am. Aviation, 1962-67; mgr. avionics analysis and techs. B-1 divsn. Rockwell Internat., 1967-73; dir. engring. Morse Controls divsn., 1973-74; gen. mgr. Morse Controls divsn. Incom Internat. Inc., 1974-78; pres. Morse Controls, 1978—82, Heim Bearings, 1982—85; gen. mgr. Stewart-Warner Corp., 1985-88; pres. Stewart Warner South Wind Corp., 1988-95, Stewart Warner Electronics Corp., 1991-95; pres., COO Nartron Corp., 1995-97; pres. Image Moulding and Frame, Inc., Image Arts, Inc., 1997-99, TECorp, Inc., 1997—, Best Weld, Inc., 1998—. Cons. in field; lectr. U. So. Calif., 1967-70. Contbr. articles to profl. jours; patentee in field. Active Hudson (Ohio) Econ. Devel. Com., 1979-82; bd. dirs., coun. commr. Boy Scouts Am., 1980-85, nat. coun., 1980-85; svc. rev. panel United Way of Summit County, 1980. NDEA fellow, 1961-63. Mem. Hudson C. of C. (trustee 1976-78), Boating Industry Assn. (chmn. steering task force 1974-85), Am. Boat and Yacht Coun. (dir. 1980-88). Office: 1315 W 18th St Anderson IN 46016-3800 E-mail: tcarrell@iquest.net.

CARREN, JEFFREY P. lawyer; b. Chgo., Oct. 8, 1946; AB with high honors, U. Ill., 1968; JD, Northwestern U., 1972. Bar: Ill. 1973, U.S. Dist. Ct. (no. dist.) Ill. 1973, U.S. Ct. Appeals (7th cir.) 1976, U.S. Supreme Ct. 1980. Formerly ptnr. Winston & Strawn, Chgo.; ptnr. Laner, Muchin, Dombrow, Becker, Levin & Tominberg Ltd., Chgo., 1994—. Editor notes and comments Northwestern U. Law Rev., 1971-72/ Edmund James scholar. Mem. ABA (tax and bus. sects.), Ill. State Bar Assn. (employee benefits sect.), Chgo. Bar Assn. (employee benefits com), Am. Arbitration Assn. (panel arbitrators), Phi Eta Sigma. Office: Laner Muchin et al 515 N State St Chicago IL 60610-4324 E-mail: jcarren@lmdblt.com.

CARRERA, VICTOR MANUEL, lawyer; b. Rio Grande City, Tex., Nov. 20, 1954; s. Eladio and Ines Olivia (Guerra) C. BS, U. Tex., 1975, BA with honors, 1976, JD, 1979. Bar: Tex. 1979, U.S. Dist. Ct. (so. dist.) Tex. 1980, U.S. Dist. Ct. (we. dist.) Tex. 1996, U.S. Dist. Ct. (no. dist.) Tex. 2001, U.S. Ct. Appeals (5th cir.) 1986; cert. civil trial law, personal injury trial law, civil appellate law, Tex. Assoc. Cardenas & Whitis, McAllen, Tex., 1979-80; briefing atty. U.S. Dist. Ct. (so. dist.) Tex., Brownsville, 1980-81; assoc. Keys, Russell & Seaman, Corpus Christi, Tex., 1981-84, Wood, Boykin, Wolter & Keys, Corpus Christi, 1984-86, ptnr., 1987-88; participating mem. Law Offices of Ramon Garcia, P.C., Edinburg, Tex., 1988-90; ptnr. Munoz, Hockema & Reed, McAllen, Tex., 1990-96, Reed & Carrera, Edinburg, Tex., 1997, Reed, Carrera & McLain, 1997—2003. Lectr. South Tex. Coll. Law, Houston, 1987, U. Houston, 1989-90, 96-99, State Bar Tex., 1992. Mng. editor: Tex. Internat. Law Jour., 1978—79. Recipient Outstanding Individual Contbn. Award Vol. Lawyers of Coastal Bend, 1985. Mem.: Hidalgo County Bar Assn. (lector - 2000, 2002) (lectr. 2000—02), Tex. Trial Lawyers Assn. (dir. 1991—96, lectr. 1993—94), Tex. Bar Assn. Democrat. Avocations: history, archaeology. Home: 5400 N 1st St Mcallen TX 78504-2211 Office: Reed Carrera & McLain PO Box 9702 Mcallen TX 78502-9702 also: Reed Carrera & McLain Bldg 101 1 Paseo del Prado Edinburg TX 78539 E-mail: vmcarrera@rcmlaw.com.

CARRERAS, FRANCISCO JOSÉ, retired university president, foundation executive; b. San Juan, P.R., May 13, 1932; s. Francisco and Antonia (Muriente) C.; m. Ana Elisa Carreras, Mar. 29, 1964; children: Inés María, María Soledad, Irene María, Marianne, Francisco José, María del Pilar. Student, Instituto Superior de Estudios Clásicos, Havana, Cuba, 1954-57; BA, Universidad Pontificia de Comillas, Santander, Spain, 1959; MA, Fordham U., 1960; PhD, Universidad Pontificia Gregoriana, Rome, 1966. Mem. faculty U. P.R., Rio Piedras Campus, 1962-69, acad. asst. to dir., 1967-69, dir. humanities dept., 1967-68; pres. Cath. U. P.R., Ponce, 1969-81; academician P.R. Acad. Arts and Scis., 1970; exec. dir. Angel Ramos Found., Inc., San Juan, P.R., 1984—; mem. P.R. State Commn. on Post-Secondary Edn., 1973. Dir. Banco Popular de P.R. Author: Filosofía de la Coordinación de José Vasconcelos, 1971, Incógnita y Revelación, 1981; also articles. Adv. Sociedad Puertorriqueña UNESCO, 1973; pres. P.R. Endowment for Humanities, 1977; bd. dirs. Angel Ramos Found., 1977; bd. dirs. Damas Hosp., 1978, P.R. Acad. Arts and Scis., 1980; adv. bd. dirs. Orgns. Universidades Católicas de América Latina, 1976. Recipient Pres.'s medal Ana G. Mendez Univ. Sys.-P.R., 2000. Mem. Fundación Puertorriqueña Humanidades (pres. 1977), Ponce Sales and Mktg. Execs. Assn., Alpha Phi Omega, Phi Delta Kappa. Clubs: Rotary, Lions. Roman Catholic. Home: 1 St C-16 Villas Del Pilar San Juan PR 00926 Office: Angel Ramos Found Inc PO Box 362408 San Juan PR 00936-2408 E-mail: fcarreras@far.org.

CARRERAS, JOSÉ, tenor; b. Barcelona, Dec. 5, 1947; s. Jose and Antonio C.; (married); children: Alberto, Julia. Doctor honoris causa, U. Barcelona, Spain, U. Sheffield and Loughborough, U.K., U. Mendeleyev, Russia, u. Camerino, Italy. Mus. dir. opening ceremonies Barcelona Olympics, 1992. Author: Singing from the Soul, 1991; profl. opera debut as Gennaro in Lucrezia Borgia, Liceo Opera House, Barcelona, 1970-71 season; appeared in La Bohème, Un Ballo In Maschera and I Lombardi alla Prima Crociata in Teatro Regio, Parma, Italy, 1972 season; Am. debut as Pinkerton in Madame Butterfly with N.Y.C. Opera, 1972; Met. Opera debut as Cavaradossi, Vienna Staatsoper with rigoletto at London's Royal Opera House with Traviata and at the N.Y. Metropolitan Opera House, Oper of Munich with Tosca, 1974, La Scala debut as Riccardo in Un Ballo In Maschera, 1975; appeared in film Don Carlos, 1980, TV Great Performances: West Side Story, 1985; other appearances throughout the world include Carnegie Hall, N.Y., Barbican and Royal Albert Hall, London, Salle Pleyel, Paris, Teatro Colón, Buenos Aires, Argentina, Covent Garden, London, Vienna Staatsoper, Easter Festival, Summer Festival, Salzburg, Aix en Provence, Edimburgh, Verona, Austria, Lyric Opera of Chgo., La Bohème San Francisco Opera, Musikverein and Konzerthaus, Vienna, Suntory Hall and NHK Hall Tokyo, others; recs. include Otello (Rossini), Un Ballo in Maschera, La Battaglia di Legnano, Il Corsaro, Un Giorno, I Due Fuscari, Simone Boccanegra, Macbeth, Don Carlo, Tosca, Thais, Aida, Cavalleria, Turandot, Pagliacci, Lucia di la mmermoor, Elisabetta d'Inghilterra, Amigos Para Siempre, Cabellé and Carreras in Paris, Hollywood Golden Classics, My Barcelona, With a Song in My Heart, Tenorissimi with Placido Domingo and Luciano Pavarotti, The Three Tenors, L.A. (also a PBS spl. and videotape); repertoire of over 60 operas include Andrea Chenier, La Bohème, Tosca, Werther, carmen, la Forza del Destino, I Pagliacci, L'Elisir d'Amore, Un Ballo in Maschera; leading role in operatic films for TV, Cinema, Video include La Bohème, I Lombardi, Andrea chnier, Turandot, Carmen, requiem (Verdi), Don Carlo, La Forza del Destino, Stiffelio, Fedora and jerusalem. Founder José Carreras Med. Rsch. Found.; pres. José Carreras Internat. Leukemia Found.; hon. mem. Leukemia Support Group; grand ofcl. Republic Italy; Goodwill Amb. UNESCO. Recipient Emmy Acad. TV, Grand Prix du Disque Acad. Paris, Luigi Illica prize, Grammy award, 1991, Sir Lawrence Olivier award, Gold medal N.Y. Spanish Inst., City Vienna, Fine Arts His Majesty the King of Spain, City of Barcelona, Autonomous Govt. Catalonia, Prince of Asturias award, 1991; honorary awardee Austrian Republic. Mem. Royal Acad. Music (hon.), European Soc. Medicine (hon.), Vienna Staatsoper (Kammersänger and lifetime hon. mem.) European Soc. Med.oncology (hon. patron); Commandeur des Arts et des Lettres and Chevalier dans l'Ordre de la Légion d'Honneur de la République Française, Gran Croce di Cavaliere, Albert Schweizer Music award,1996, Internat. award St. Boniface Gen. Hosp. Rsch. Found., 1996. Office: William Morris Agency care Dick Allen 151 S El Camino Dr Beverly Hills CA 90212-2775 also: Hoffamn Concerts Inc 1501 Broadway New York NY 10036-5601 also: Carreras Internat Leukemia Found Muntaner 383 2d 08021 Barcelona Spain Fax: 34 93 201 05 88. E-mail: fundacio@fcarreras.es.

CARRERE, CHARLES SCOTT, law educator, judge; b. Dublin, Ga., Sept. 26, 1937; 1 son, Daniel Austin. BA, U. Ga., 1959; LLB, Stetson U., 1961. Bar: Ga. 1960, Fla. 1961. Law clk. U.S. Dist. Judge, Orlando, Fla., 1962-63; asst. U.S. Atty. Middle Dist. Fla., 1963-66, 68-69, chief trial atty., 1965-66, 68-69; ptnr. Harrison, Greene, Mann, Rowe & Stanton, 1970-80; judge Pinellas County, Fla., 1980-96; vis. prof. law Stetson Coll. Law, 1997-98, Cumberland Law Sch., 1998-99. Recipient Jud. Appreciation award St. Petersburg Bar Assn., 1996, Alumnus of Yr. award Stetson Student Bar Assn., 1998. Mem. State Bar Ga., Fla. Bar, Phi Beta Kappa. Presbyterian. Address: PO Box 22034 Gateway Mall Sta Saint Petersburg FL 33742 Fax: 727-395-0444.

CARRES, LOUIS GEORGE, lawyer; b. Miami Beach, Fla., Aug. 14, 1943; s. Louis John and Helen (Davis) C.; m. Margaret Craig Good, July 10, 1983; children: Michele, Elliot. BA, Fla. Atlantic U., Boca Raton, 1965; JD, Stetson U., 1969. Bar: Fla. 1969, U.S. Dist. Ct. (so. dist.) Fla. 1971, U.S. Dist. Ct. (mid. dist.) Fla. 1974, U.S. Dist. Ct. (no. dist.) Fla. 1975, U.S. Ct. Appeals (5th cir.) 1973, U.S. Ct. Appeals (11th cir.) 1982, U.S. Supreme Ct. 1976. Staff atty. South Fla. Migrant Legal Svc.s, Delray Beach, 1969-71; mng. atty. Fla. Rural Legal Svcs. Delray Beach, 1971-73; chief appellate asst. Office of Pub. Defender, Tallahassee, Fla., 1977-80, asst., West Palm Beach, Fla., 1980— ; instr. bus. law Hillsborough Community Coll., Tampa, 1974. Mem. The Fla. Bar Assn. (appellate procedure rules com. 1987-91, criminal law sect. trial practice com. 1987-88), ABA, Palm Beach County Bar Assn. (mem. law reform com. 1971-72), Palm Beach Criminal Def. Assn., Am. Judicature Soc., Robert Bullington Law Soc. Democrat. Greek Orthodox. Home: 830 Palmetto St West Palm Beach FL 33405-3930 Office: Office of Pub Defender 6th Fl 421 3rd St Fl 6 West Palm Beach FL 33401-4203

CARREY, JIM, actor; b. Toronto, Ont., Can., Jan. 17, 1962; s. Percy and Kathleen Carrey; m. Melissa Womer, 1986 (div.); 1 child, Jane. Performances include (TV series) The Duck Factory, 1984, In Living Color, 1990-94; (TV films) Mike Hammer: Murder Takes All, 1989, Doing Time on Maple Drive, 1992; (films) Finders Keepers, 1984, Once Bitten, 1985, Peggy Sue Got Married, 1986, The Dead Pool, 1988, Earth Girls Are Easy, 1989, Pink Cadillac, 1989, High Strung, 1991, Ace Ventura: Pet Detective, 1993 (also screenwriter), The Mask, 1994, Dumb and Dumber, 1994 (MTV Movie awards), Batman Forever, 1995, Ace Ventura: When Nature Calls, 1995, The Mask's Revenge, 1996, Liar, Liar, 1996 (Blockbuster Entertainment award), The Cable Guy, 1996 (MTV Movie award), The Truman Show, 1997 (Golden Globe Best Performance award, MTV Movie award), Simon Birch, 1998, In My Life, 1998 (TV), Man on the Moon, 1999 (Golden Globe, 2000), Me, Myself and Irene, 3000, How the Grinch Stole Christmas, 2000, The Majestic, 2001, Bruce Almighty, 2003. Star on the Hollywood Walk of Fame, 2000. Office: UTA 9560 Wilshire Blvd Fl 5 Beverly Hills CA 90212-2401*

CARREY, NEIL, lawyer, educator; b. Bronx, N.Y., Nov. 19, 1942; s. David L. and Betty (Kurtzburg) C.; m. Karen Krysher, Apr. 9, 1980; children: Jana, Christopher; children by previous marriage: Scott, Douglas, Dana. BS in Econs., U. Pa., 1964; JD, Stanford U., 1967. Bar: Calif. 1968. Mem. firm, v.p. corp. DeCastro, West, Chodorow, Inc., L.A., 1967-97; of counsel Jenkens & Gilchrist, L.A., 1998—. Instr. program legal paraprofls., U. So. Calif., 1977-89; lectr. U. So. Calif. Dental Sch., 1987—, Employee Benefits Inst., Kansas City, Mo., 1996; legal cons. 33rd Dist. Calif. PTA, 1997—. Author: Nonqualified Defered Compensation Plans-The Wave of the Future, 1985. Treas. Nat. Little League, Santa Monica, Calif., 1984—85, pres., 1985—86, coach, 1990—95; referee, coach Am. Soccer Youth Orgn., 1989—95; officer Vista Del Mar Child Care Ctr., L.A., 1968—84; coach Bobby Sox Softball Team, Santa Monica, 1986—88, bd. dirs., 1988, umpire in chief, 1988; various positions The Santa Monica Youth Athletic Found., 1995—; dir. The Small Bus. Coun. of Am., 1995—, Santa Monica H.S. Booster Club, 1995—97; active various positions Santa Monica Police Activities League, 1995—; pres. Gail Dorin Music Found., 1994—; v.p. Sneaker Sisters, 1996—2001; pres. Santa Monica Jr. Rowing, 1997—2002; legal cons. 33d Dist. Calif. PTA, 1997—99; recreation and parks commr. City of Santa Monica, 1999—; sec. Santa Monica Lacers Club, 1999—2000; mem. U. Pa. Women's Sports Adv. Bd., 1998—; pres. Chris Carrey Charitable Found., 2000—; v.p. bd. Ivan and Sam Found., 2002—; active numerous coms. Santa Monica-Malibu Sch. Dist., 1983—; bd. dirs. Padres Contra el Cancer, 2001—03, v.p., 2002—03, pres., 2003—. Mem.: LWV (dir. 1997—), Children's Hosp. L.A. (adv. coun. 2001—), Children's Ctr. for Cancer and Blood Diseases, U. Pa. Alumni Soc. (pres. 1971—79, dir. 1979—87), Mountaingate Tennis Club, Alpha Kappa Psi (life). Jewish. Home: 616 23d St Santa Monica CA 90402-3130 Office: 12100 Wilshire Blvd Fl 15 Los Angeles CA 90025-7120 E-mail: ncarrey@aol.com., ncarrey@jenkens.com.

CARRICO, HARRY LEE, retired judge; b. Washington, Sept. 4, 1916; s. William Temple and Nellie Nadalia (Willett) C.; m. Betty Lou Peck, May 18, 1940 (dec. 1987); 1 child, Lucretia Ann; m. Lynn Brackenridge, July 1, 1994. Jr. cert., George Washington U., 1938, JD, 1942, LLD, 1987, U. Richmond, 1973, Coll. William & Mary, 1993. Bar: Va. 1941. With Rust & Rust, Fairfax, Va., 1941-43; trial justice Fairfax, Va., 1943-51; pvt. practice, 1951-56; judge 16th Jud. Cir., Va., 1956-61; justice Va. Supreme Ct., Richmond, 1961-81, chief justice, 1981—2003, sr. justice, 2003—. Chmn. bd dirs. Nat. Ctr. for State Cts., 1989-90. With USNR, 1945-46. Recipient Alumni Profl. Achievement award George Washington U., 1981. Mem. McNeill Law Soc., Conf. Chief Justices (bd. dirs. 1985-91, 1st v.p. 1987, pres.-elect. 1988, pres. 1989-90, co-chmn. nat. jud. coun. 1991-97), Order of Coif, Phi Delta Phi, Omicron Delta Kappa. Episcopalian. Office: Supreme Court of Va 100 N 9th St 4th Fl Richmond VA 23229-7610

CARRICO, VIRGIL NORMAN, physician; b. Cumberland, Md., Aug. 28, 1940; s. Virgil Norman and Lucille E. (Gnagy) C.; m. Nina Lois Lemper, Aug. 17, 1963; children: Pamela Beth Carrico-Miller, Sandra Kelly (dec.). BA, Wabash Coll., 1962; MD, Ind. U., 1966. Diplomate Am. Bd. Family Practice. Intern Marion County Gen. Hosp., Indpls., 1966-67; resident in family practice Akron (Ohio) City Hosp., 1970-72, chief resident in family practice, 1972, assoc. dir. family practice residency, 1972; chief family practice Bryan Cmty. Hosp., past chmn. bd. dirs. home health care; past mem. undergrad. med. edn. subcom. Med. Coll. Ohio, Toledo, past preceptor cmty. medicine, clin. asst. prof. family medicine, clin. prof. family medicine; past preceptor preventive medicine and family practice Ohio State U.; chief of staff Bryan Cmty. Hosp., 1977-78, preceptor Bryan Area Health Edn. Ctr., chmn. continuing med. edn. com.; med. dir. Bryan Area Health Edn. Ctr. Past pres., bd. dirs. Bryan Med. Group, Inc. Contbr. articles to profl. jours. Trustee YWCA, Bryan, Ohio, v.p., 1990-92; bd. dirs. United Fund, pres., 1990-92; bd. dirs. Jr. Achievement, 1981-83, Bryan Area Found. Capt. USAF, 1967-70. Fellow Am. Acad. Family Physicians (bylaw coms. 1989, 90, 91, 92, nat. chmn. 1993, chmn. patient care svcs. commn. 1988-89, chmn. mem. svcs. commn. 1989-90); mem. Soc. Tchrs. Family Medicine, Ohio Acad. Family Medicine, Am. Acad. Family Medicine, Williams County Med. Soc. (rpes. 1976-79, sec.-treas., v.p. 1980-83), Ohio

Acad. Family Physicians (del. to ho. of dels. 1972-85; pres. Fulton County chpt. 1973-85, chmn. resident affairs subcom., nominating com., student awards, fin. com., ref. com. of the ho. of dels.; treas. 1985-87, v.p. 1987-89, bd. dirs. 1983-92, pres.-elect 1990-91), Rotary Internat. Avocations: golf, traveling, reading. Office: Bryan Med Group 442 W High St Bryan OH 43506-1681

CARRIER, FRANCE, medical educator; b. Beauport, Que., Can., June 9, 1961; d. Philippe Carrier and Therese Pare; m. Steven I. Hirschfeld, June 9, 1950. PhD, U. Montreal, 1988. Postdoctoral fellow Biotechnology Rsch. Inst., Montreal, 1988—89; vis. assoc. NIH, Bethesda, Md., 1989—91; vis. scientist Nat. Cancer Inst. NIH, Bethesda, 1991—98; asst. prof. U. of Md., Balt., 1998—. Mem. Greenebaum Cancer Ctr., Balt.; instr. med. and grad. schs. Contbr. articles to profl. jours., chapters to books. Rsch. grantee (R01), NIH, 1999—2003, Rsch. grantee, Am. Cancer Soc., 2000—02, Rsch. grantee (STTR), NIH, 2001—02, Rsch. grantee, A-T Children's Project, 2003—, Internat. fellow, Human Frontier Sci. Program Orgn., 1990. Mem.: Am. Assn. for Cancer Rsch. (sponsor, Brigid Leventhal award 2002), N.Y. Acad. Scis., Cosmos Club (Elected mem. 1999). Achievements include patents for methods for determining the presence of functional p53 in mammalian cells; research in genotoxic stress-response, cancer progression, chromatin remodeling. Office: U Md 108 N Greene St Baltimore MD 21201-1503 Home Fax: 301-879-0776; Office Fax: 410-706-8297. Personal E-mail: fcarr001@umaryland.edu. Business E-Mail: fcarr001@umaryland.edu.

CARRIER, LYNNE THOMSON, journalist; b. Mar. 7, 1945; BA in Internat. Affairs, George Washington U., 1967. Reporter San Diego Tribune, 1977-86, dep. editor editl. page, 1987-91; politics and govt. writer San Diego Daily Transcript, 1992-96; contbg. editor San Diego Met. Mag., 1998—. Office: 211 Orange Ave Coronado CA 92118-1410 E-mail: lcarrier@cts.com.

CARRIER, RONALD EDWIN, academic administrator, director; b. Bluff City, Tenn., Aug. 18, 1932; s. James Murphy and Melissa (Miller) C.; m. Edith Marie Johnson, Sept. 7, 1955; children: Michael Lavon, Linda Lois Carrier Frazee, Jennine Marie. BS, Ea. Tenn. State U., 1955; MS in Econs., U. Ill., 1957, PhD in Econs., 1960. Assoc. prof. econs. U. Miss., Oxford, 1960-63; dir., prof. Bur. Bus. and Econ. Research, Memphis U., 1963-66, provost, v.p. acad. affairs, 1966-71; pres., chancellor James Madison U., Harrisonburg, Va., 1971—2002; pres. emeritus, 2002—; pres. Ctr. for Innovative Tech., Herndon, Va., 1986-87. Bd. visitors Va. State U., Sorensen Inst., Integic, Inc.; mem. adv. bd. Assn. Small Bus. Devel. Ctrs.; chancellor Romanian Am. U. Author: Plant Locations: A Theory and Explanations, 1968; contbr. articles and monographs to profl. publs. Mem. White House Conf. Balance Econ. Growth; mem. Va. Indsl. Facilities Study Commn., 1972-75; chmn. Va. Land Use Adv. Com., 1974-77, Va. Gov.'s Electricity Costs Commn., 1975—; mem. Va. Gov.'s Energy Resource Adv. Commn., 1975-76, Gov.'s Regulatory Reform Adv. Bd., 1983, Joint Subcom. to Study Coal Slurry Pipeline Feasibility, 1983, ethics com. Senate Va., 1999, Va. Higher Edn. Steering Commn., 2002. Earheart fellow 1958-60; recipient Ben Franklin award Memphis Printing Industry, 1966, faculty award East Tenn. State U., 1955, Disting. Svc. award Jr. C. of C., 1965, Virginian of Yr. award Va. Assn. Broadcasters, 1982; named Outstanding Virginian, FHA, 1990; cultural laureate Va.; named Outstanding Virginian FFA, 1991. Mem.: Sigma Phi Epsilon, Omicron Delta Gamma, Omicron Delta Kappa. Methodist. Home: PO Box 570 Basye VA 22810-0570 Office: James Madison U MSC 5760 Med Arts E Ste 2 Harrisonburg VA 22807

CARRIER, WARREN PENDLETON, retired university chancellor, writer; b. Cheviot, Ohio, July 3, 1918; s. Burly Warren and Prudence (Alfrey) C.; m. Marjorie Jane Regan, Apr. 3, 1947 (dec.); 1 child, Gregory Paul; m. Judy Lynn Hall, June 14, 1973; 1 son, Ethan Alfrey. Student, Wabash Coll., 1938-40; AB, Miami U., Oxford, Ohio, 1942; MA, Harvard U., 1948; PhD, Occidental Coll., 1962. Asst. prof. English U. Iowa, 1949-52; assoc. prof. Bard Coll., 1953-57; lit. faculty Bennington, 1955-58; vis. prof. Sweet Briar (Va.) Coll., 1958-60; prof. Deep Springs (Calif.) Coll., 1960-62, Portland (Oreg.) State U., 1962-64; prof., chmn. English dept. U. Mont., Missoula, 1964-68; assoc. dean. prof. English and comparative lit., chmn. comparative lit. Livingston Coll., Rutgers U., 1968-69; dean Coll. Arts and Letters, San Diego State U., 1969-72; v.p. acad. affairs U. Bridgeport, Conn., 1972-75; chancellor U. Wis., Platteville, 1975-82. Author: The Hunt, 1952, Bay of the Damned, 1957, Toward Montebello, 1966, Leave Your Sugar for the Cold Morning, 1977, The Diver, 1986, Death of a Chancellor, 1986, An Honorable Spy, 1992, Murder at the Strawberry Festival, 1993, An Ordinary Man, 1997, Death of a Poet, 1999, Justice at Christmas, 1999, Risking the Wind, 1999; founder Quar. Rev. of Lit.; editor: Guide to World Literature, 1980; co-editor: Reading Modern Poetry, 1955, 68, Literature from the World, 1981; assoc. editor: Western Rev., 1949-51; contbr. articles, poems, revs. to lit. mags. Mem. Jud. Commn. Wis. Vol., Am. Field Service attached to Brit. Army, India-Burma, 1944-45. Recipient award for poetry Nat. Endowment for Arts, 1972; Colladay prize for poetry, 1986 Mem. Nat. Coun. Tchrs. English, Royal Soc. Arts, Wis. Acad. Arts and Scis., Phi Beta Kappa. Home: 69 Colony Park Cir Galveston TX 77551-1737

CARRIERI, ARTHUR HELMUT, physicist, researcher; b. Phila., June 15, 1953; s. Phillip and Margot Carrieri. BA, Temple U., 1976; MS, Pa. State U., 1978. Sr. rsch. physicist U.S. Army Soldier and Biol.-Chem. Command, Aberdeen Proving Ground, Md., 1983—. Roman Catholic. Achievements include patents for infrared mueller matrix detection and ranging system, thermal luminescence sensor, chemical imaging sensor and laser beacon, earth monitoring satellite system, others. Avocation: scuba diving. Home: 3105 K Cardinal Way Abingdon MD 21009 Office: US Army SBCCOM Berger Lab E3549 5183 Blackhawk Rd Aberdeen Proving Ground MD 21010-5424 Office Fax: 410-436-5679. Business E-Mail: arthur.carrieri@us.army.mil.

CARRIGAN, DAVID OWEN, history educator; b. New Glasgow, N.S., Can., Nov. 30, 1933; s. Ronald and Marion Constance (Hoare) C.; m. Florence Catherine Nicholson, June 21, 1958; children: Nancy, Janet, David, Glen, Sharon, Douglas. BA, St. Francis Xavier U., 1954; MA, Boston U., 1955; PhD, U. Maine, 1966. Asst. prof. history St. Francis Xavier U., 1957-61, assoc. prof., 1961-67; assoc. prof. history Wilfred Laurier U., 1967-68; prin., dean arts Kings Coll., U. Western Ont., 1968-71; pres. St. Mary's U., Halifax, N.S., 1971-79, prof., 1979-99, prof. emeritus, 1999—. Author: Canadian Party Platforms, 1867-1968, 1968, Crime and Punishment in Canada: A History, 1991, Juvenile Delinquency in Canada a History, 1998; contbrs. articles to profl. jours. Former trustee Inst. Research on Public Policy; past mem. Can. Council; past bd. dirs. Can. Assn. for Treatment and Study of Families Mem.: Phi Kappa Phi. Office: St Mary's Univ Halifax NS Canada B3H 3C3

CARRIGAN, JIM R. arbitrator, mediator, retired judge; b. Mobridge, S.D., Aug. 24, 1929; s. Leo Michael and Mildred Ione (Jaycox) C.; m. Beverly Jean Halpin, June 2, 1956. Ph.B., JD, U. N.D., 1953; LL.M. in Taxation, NYU, 1956; LLD (hon.), U. Colo., 1989, Suffolk U., 1991, U. N.D., 1997. Bar: N.D. 1953, Colo. 1956. Asst. prof. law U. Denver, 1956-59; vis. assoc. prof. NYU Law Sch., 1958, U. Wash. Law Sch., 1959-60; Colo. jud. adminstr., 1960-61; prof. law U. Colo., 1961-67; partner firm Carrigan & Bragg (and predecessors), 1967-76; bd. regents U. Colo., 1975-76; justice Colo. Supreme Ct., 1976-79; judge U.S. Dist. Ct. Colo., 1979-95. Mem. Colo. Bd. Bar Examiners, 1969-71; lectr. Nat. Coll. State Judiciary, 1964-77, 95; bd. dirs. Nat. Inst. Trial Advocacy, 1971-73, 78—, chmn. bd. 1986-88, also mem. faculty, 1972—; adj. prof. law U. Colo, 1984, 1991—; bd. dirs. Denver Broncos Stadium Dist., 1996—. Editor-in-chief: N.D. Law Rev., 1952-53, Internat. Soc. Barristers Quar., 1972-79; editor: DICTA, 1957-59; contbr. articles to profl. jours. Bd. visitors U. N.D. Coll. Law, 1983-85. Recipient Disting. Svc. award Nat. Coll. State Judiciary, 1969, Outstanding Alumnus award U. N.D., 1973, Regent Emeritus award U. Colo., 1977, B'nai Brith Civil Rights award, 1986, Thomas More Outstanding Lawyer award Cath. Lawyers Guild, 1988, Oliphant Disting. Svc. award Nat. Inst. Trial Advocacy, 1993, Constl. Rights award Nat. Assn. Blacks in Criminal Justice (Colo. chpt.), 1992, Disting. Svc. award Colo. Bar Assn., 1994, Amicus Curiae award ATLA, 1994, Colo. Trial Lawyers Assn. Lifetime Achievement award, 2000. Fellow Colo. Bar Found., Boulder County Bar Found.; mem. ABA (action com. on tort system improvement 1985-87, TIPS sect. long range planning com., 1986-97; coun. 1987-91, task force on initiatives and referenda 1990-92, size of civil juries task force 1988-90, class actions task force 1995-97), Colo. Bar Assn., Boulder County Bar Assn., Denver Bar Assn., Cath. Lawyers Guild, Inns. of Ct., Internat. Soc. Barristers, Internat. Acad. Trial Lawyers (bd. dirs. 1995—), Fed. Judges Assn. (bd. dirs. 1985-89), Am. Judicature Soc. (bd. dirs. 1985-89), Tenth Circuit Dist. Judges Assn. (sec. 1991-92, v.p. 1992-93, pres. 1994-95), Order of Coif, Phi Beta Kappa. Roman Catholic. Office: Judicial Arbiter Group 1601 Blake St Ste 400 Denver CO 80202-1328 E-mail: carrigan2350@earthlink.net.

CARRIGG, JAMES A. retired utility company executive; b. 1933; Student, Union Coll., 1951-53; AAS in Electrical Engring. Tech., Broome C.C. From safety cadet to gen. mgr. N.Y. State Electric & Gas Corp., Ithaca, 1958-82, v.p. Binghamton, 1982-83, pres., dir., 1983-86, pres., COO, 1986-88, chmn., CEO, 1988-90, chmn., pres., CEO, 1991-96; ret., 1996. Bd. dirs. Energy East Corp., Security Mut. Life Ins. Co. N.Y. Bd. dirs. Broome County Cmty. Charities, Dr. G. Clifford and Florence B. Decker Found. Office: NY State Electric & Gas Corp PO Box 5224 Corporate Dr Binghamton NY 13902-5224

CARRIKER, ROBERT CHARLES, history educator; b. St. Louis, Aug. 18, 1940; s. Thomas B. and Vivian Ida (Spaunhorst) C.; m. Eleanor R. Gualdoni, Aug. 24, 1963; children: Thomas A., Robert M., Andrew J. BS, St. Louis U., 1962, AM, 1963; PhD, U. Okla., 1967. Asst. prof. Gonzaga U., Spokane, Wash., 1967-71, assoc. prof., 1972-76, prof. history, 1976—. Author: Fort Supply, Indian Territory, 1970, 90, The Kalispel People, 1973, Father Peter De Smet, 1995, 1998; editor: (with Eleanor R. Carriker) Army Wife on the Frontier, 1975, (with William L. Lang) Great River of the West, 1999; book rev. editor Columbia mag., 1987—.author, Am. looks West 2003 Mem. Wash. Lewis and Clark Trail Com., 1978-99; commr Wash. Maritime Bicentennial, Olympia, 1989-92; bd. dirs. Wash. Commn. for Humanities, Seattle, 1988-94. Burlington No. Found. scholar, 1985, 96; recipient Disting. Svc. award Lewis and Clark Trail Heritage Found., 1989. Mem. Wash. State Hist. Soc. (trustee 1981-90, v.p. 1993-2000), Western Hist. Assn., Phi Alpha Theta (councilor 1985-87). Roman Catholic. Avocations: travel, photography, cartography. Office: Gonzaga U 502 E Boone Ave Spokane WA 99258-0001 E-mail: CARRIKER@gonzaga.edu.

CARRILLO, ELISA ANNA, history educator, consultant; b. Bklyn. BA, St. Joseph's Coll., Bklyn., 1943; PhD, Fordham U., 1953. Mem. faculty dept. history Marymount Coll., Tarrytown, N.Y., 1945-2000, prof. emerita, 2000—. Cons. coll. proficiency exam program N.Y. State Edn. Dept., Albany, 1966-77; mem. Fulbright-Hays Nat. Screening Com., Italy, 1987-89; chair Columbia U. Faculty Seminar on Modern Italy, 1971-72, Marraro Prize Com., Am. Hist. Assn., 1976-80, 85-88; pres. N.Y. State Assn. European Historians, 1968-69; bd. dirs. Literacy Vols. of the Tarrytowns, 2001—. Author: Alcide de Gasperi: The Long Apprenticeship, 1965; contbr. chpts. to books. Recipient King award U.S. Cath. Hist. Soc., 1976. Mem. Soc. Italian Hist. Studies, Berkshire Conf. Women Historians, Am. Cath. Hist. Assn. Avocations: travel, music, theater.

CARRINGER, ROBERT, English language and film educator; b. Knoxville, Tenn., May 12, 1941; m. Sonia Raysor, Sept. 7, 1968. AB, U. Tenn., 1962; MA, Johns Hopkins, 1964; PhD, Ind. U., 1968. Asst. prof. English U. Ill., Urbana, 1970-76, assoc. prof. English, 1976-84, prof. English and film, 1985—, disting. prof., 1985. Author: Ernst Lubitsch, 1978 (Choice Outstanding Acad. Book award 1979), The Making of Citizen Kane, 1985, rev. edit., 1996, Magnificent Ambersons: A Reconstruction, 1993; editor: The Jazz Singer, 1979; contbr. articles to profl. jours.; prodr. laserdiscs. Mem. editl. bd.: Am. Studies, Quar. Rev. Film and Video, Cinema Jour. Recipient Instrnl. Tech. awards Amoco Corp., 1980, Apple Computer, 1988; Rsch. grantee NEH, 1986-87; fellow in cognitive psychology U. Ill., 1990-91; Getty scholar Getty Rsch. Inst., 1996-97. Mem.: MLA (chmn.film divsn. exec. com. 1981), Phi Beta Kappa, Phi Kappa Phi. Home: 50 County Rd 1675N Seymour IL 61875 Office: U Ill 608 S Wright St Urbana IL 61801 E-mail: fergus@uiuc.edu.

CARRINGTON, ARESE U. medical doctor, public health consultant; b. Lagos, Lagos, Nigeria, July 16, 1958; d. Elisha Noyoze Ukponmwan, Dora O. Ukponmwan; m. Walter C. Carrington, Feb. 18, 1995; 1 child, Temisan Oyowe. MBBS, U. Ibadan, Nigeria, 1980; MPH, Harvard U., 2000. Med. officer Nigerian Airport Authority, Ibadan, Nigeria, 1981—82; med. advisor Fan Milk Ltd., Ibadan, Nigeria, 1982—86; med. dir/ Health and Med. Svcs., Lagos, Nigeria, 1986—95; pvt. practice Ibadan and Lagos, Nigeria, 1981—97; assoc. dir. Harvard Sch. Pub. Health, AIDS Prevention Initiative Nigeria), Boston, 2000—02. Adv. bd. LYNX, Boston; mem. exec. bd. FATE. Contbr. articles. Mem. Wives of Heads of Diplomatic Missions, Lagos, Nigeria, 1995—97. Mem.: Am. Pub. Health Assn., Nigerian Med. Coun. Avocations: collecting and cataloguing African art, gardening, traveling. Office Fax: 617-432-5723. Personal E-mail: aresec@yahoo.com. Business E-Mail: acarring@hsph.harvard.edu.

CARRINGTON, GARY, psychologist; b. Cleveland, OH, Feb. 26, 1969; s. Marjorie Carrington; children: Gary, Imari, Inaya. BA, Morehouse Coll., Atlanta, GA, 1992; MA psychology, Kent State U, Kent, OH, 1995, PhD coun. psychology, 2003. Psychologist pvt. practice, Cleveland, Ohio; prof. Tri-C, Cleveland, Ohio. Cons. Diversified Consultants, Cleveland, Ohio. Mentor, 2000—03. Vol. Urban League, Cleveland, Ohio; tutor Project Learn, Cleveland, Ohio. Mem.: Am. Coun. Assoc. (assoc.), Am. Psychol. Assoc. (assoc.). Home: 3734 Silsby Rd University Heights OH 44118

CARRINGTON, MICHAEL DAVIS, criminal justice administrator, educator, consultant; b. South Bend, Ind., Mar. 9, 1938; s. Herman Lakin and Margaret (Davis) C.; m. Lynn Ogden, Feb. 8, 1958; children: Michael O. (dec.), Jill A., Elizabeth A., Gretchen L. BA, Ind. U., 1970; MALS, Valparaiso U., 1971. Parole officer State of Ind., South Bend, 1970-71; chief probation officer St. Joseph County, South Bend, 1971-74; dir. pub. safety City of South Bend, 1974-76, mayor's asst., 1976-80; adj. assoc. prof., dir. safety, security, police Ind. U., South Bend, 1979-94; presdl. appointment as U.S. Marshal Northern Dist. of Ind., South Bend, Ind., 1994—2002; ret. U.S. Marshall's Svc., 2002—. Cons. in pvt. security Pan Am. Games, Indpls., 1987; security advance agt. Olympic Torch Relay, Ind., 1984, Hands Across Am., Ind., 1986. Recipient Sagamore of Wabash award, 1984, 2002; named Ky. Col., 1984, Hon. Big. Brother of Yr., 1974, Disting. Alumnus award Coll. Arts and Scis., Ind. U., South Bend, 2002. Mem. Assn. of Threat Assessment Profls. Presbyterian. Avocations: travel, reading, walking, working. Office: Box 96 South Bend IN 46624 E-mail: mikecmarshal@netscape.net.

CARRINGTON, PAUL DEWITT, lawyer, educator; b. Dallas, June 12, 1931; s. Paul and Frances Ellen (DeWitt) C.; m. Bessie Meek, Aug., 1952; children: Clark DeWitt, Mary Carrington Coults, William James, Emily Carrington. BA, U. Tex., 1952; LLB, Harvard U., 1955. Bar: Tex. 1955, Ohio 1962, Mich. 1967. Practice, Dallas, 1955; teaching fellow Harvard U., 1957-58; asst. prof. law U. Wyo., 1958-60, Ind. U., 1960-62; assoc. prof. Ohio State U., 1962-65; prof. U. Mich., 1965-78; dean Duke U. Sch. Law, Durham, N.C., 1978-88, prof., 1978—. Reporter civil rules adv. com. Jud. Conf. of U.S., 1985-92. Author: (with Meador and Rosenberg) Justice on Appeal, 1977, (with Meador and Rosenberg) Appeals, 1994, (with Babcock) Civil Procedure, 1977, 3d edit., 1983, Stewards of Democracy, 1999. Mem. Ann Arbor (Mich.) Bd. Edn., 1970-73; pres. Pvt. Adjudication Ctr., Inc., 1988-94, chmn., 1995-2002. With U.S. Army, 1955-57. Guggenheim fellow, 1988-89. Fellow: Am. Acad. Appellate Lawyers, Am. Acad. Arts and Scis., Am. Bar Found.; mem.: ABA, Am. Law Inst. Episcopalian. Office: Duke U Sch Law Durham NC 27708-0362 E-mail: pdc@law.duke.edu.

CARRINGTON, VIRGINIA GAIL (VEE CARRINGTON), marketing professional, consultant; b. Dodge City, Kans., Apr. 20, 1949; d. Virgel Troy and Betty Lou (Rynerson) Fakes; Lynn Nugent Friesner, Aug. 4, 1971 (div. Feb. 1985); m. Paul Henry Carrington, Apr. 4, 1987. BA, Kans. Wesleyan, 1971; MS, U. Ill., 1972; MA, Kans. State U., 1978. Sci. cataloger Kans. State U. Libr., Manhattan, 1972-74, humanities bibliographer, 1974-78; dir. libr. devel. State Libr. Kans., Topeka, 1978-84; libr. network dir. Kans. Libr. Network, Topeka, 1982-84; edn. officer Pub. Libr. Assn. ALA, Chgo., 1984-86; pres. Carrington Cons., Waterbury, Conn., 1986-97; promotion coord. Assn. Coll. and Rsch. Librs. ALA, Middletown, Conn., 1997-01; pres. Carrington Cons. Assocs., Waterbury, Conn., 2001—. Mgr. mem. svcs. Mattatuck Mus., Waterbury, 1992-97. Asst. editor: Guide to Reference Books, 11th ed., 1994; asst. to editor: Guide to Reference Books Supplement to 10th ed., 1990. Mem. ALA (Continuing Libr. Edn. Network and Exch. Roundtable, Ind. Librs. Exch. Roundtable), Am. Soc. Assn. Execs., New England Libr. Assn. Democrat. Methodist. Avocations: travel, reading. Home: 130 Melbourne Ter Waterbury CT 06704-1843 Office: Carrington Co PO Box 392 Southington CT 06489 E-mail: veegeecee@yahoo.com.

CARRITHERS, JOSEPH EDWARD, english composition and literature educator; b. Red Bay, Ala., July 28, 1963; s. Edward Walden and Dessie Lee McClure. BA in Comm./Journalism, Miss. State U., Starkville, 1985, BA in English/History, 1987, MA in English, 1990, U. So. Calif., 1992, PhD in English, 2003. Reporter Comml. Dispatch, Columbus, Miss., 1985-88; mng. editor Starkville Daily News, 1988-90; asst. lectr. U. So. Calif., L.A., 1990-94; ESL instr. Don Martin Coll., Monterey Park, Calif., 1991; part-time prof. Mt. San Antonio Coll., Walnut, Calif., 1991-94; lectr. Woodbury U., Burbank, Calif., 1993-94; assoc. prof. English Fullerton (Calif.) Coll., 1994—. Mem. faculty senate Fullerton Coll. 1996-2002, pres. 1998-2001, mem. Planning and Consultative Coun., Fullerton Coll., 1997-2002, 2003—. Contbr. poetry to Forum; contbr. articles to Frontiers, Men's Fitness, Jour. Popular Film and TV. Mem. MLA, United Faculty, Nat. Coun. Tchrs. English, Am. Studies Assn., Gay and Lesbian Assn. Dist. Employees, Lambda Soc. (advisor). Office: Fullerton Coll 321 E Chapman Ave Fullerton CA 92832-2011

CARRO, CECILIA, political scientist, researcher; b. Buenos Aires, Argentina, Apr. 11, 1978; d. Daniel Hector Carro and Dina Esther Milovan de Carro. BA, Furman U., Greenville, S.C., 2000. Program rsch. asst. Inter-Am. Dialogue, Washington, 2001—02, program assoc., 2002—. Mem. Argentina 2020, Washington, 2003; rep. Centro de Estudiantes Lenguas Vivas, Buenos Aires, 1990—95; mem., student rep. Internat. Minority Coun. Furman U., Greenville, SC, 1997—2000. Iverson Brookes Academic Scholarship, Furman U., 1996—98, Howle Academic Scholarship, 1996—2000, Howes Academic Scholarship, 1999—2000. Mem.: Pi Sigma Alpha Nat. Polit. Sci. Honor Soc. Baptist. Avocations: pianist, swimming, crew. Office: Inter-Am Dialogue 1211 Connecticut Ave NW Ste 510 Washington DC 20036

CARROL, EDWARD NICHOLAS, psychologist; b. Newark, June 22, 1943; s. Wilfred and Ruth (Gluck) C.; m. Anne Marie McDonald, May 27, 1973 (div. May 1989); 1 child, Abbe Galen; m. Virginia Paisley Herbruck, Oct. 6, 1996. BA, Columbia U., 1965; MA, NYU, 1970, U. Del., 1975, PhD, 1979. Diplomate Am. Acad. Pain Mgmt. Dir. pain clinic VA Med. Ctr., Cleve., 1979—. *Dr. Carrol's professional focus has been in three main areas: the development of a four-drug regimen for the treatment of end-stage, metastatic cancer pain; the application of anti-convulsant medication to neuropathic, deafferentation, central pain syndromes; refinement of protocols for the electroanesthetic techniques of transcutaneous nerve stimulation and neuroprobe to the management of peripheral nerve injury, post-amputation stump pain, post-thoracotomy hyperesthesia, arthralgia and especially radicular pain.* Mem. Internat. Assn. Study of Pain, Midwest Pain Soc. Republican. Jewish. Avocations: dogs, classical and country music. Home: 21490 Claythorne Rd Shaker Heights OH 44122-1964 Office: VA Med Ctr Pain Clinic 10701 East Blvd Cleveland OH 44106-1702

CARROL, NORA, educational/communication company executive, artist; b. N.Y.C., Apr. 5, 1949; d. Herman Feingold and Mae Lieberman. MS, Syracuse U., 1991. Cert. online instr. Owner, pres. First Forward, Inc., Alexandria, Va., 1991-96, The First Forward Inst., Inc., McLean, Va., 1996—2001, CarroLearning, 2001—, Carrolart, 2002—. Assoc. prof. bus. and mgmt. U. Md. Univ. Coll., Adelphi, 1995—. Author: (profl. mag.) Severed Heads: Cues from the Distance-Learning Front, 2001, (trade mags.) Guilt By Omission: The Exclusion of Educational Level in Data Collection, 1989 (Tchg. Innovation grantee 1996, 98), Is Your Association Prepared for Change?, 1992, (newsletter) Talking the Language of Venture Capitalists, 1994; editor: (jour.) Ednl. Tech. and Soc., 1998; contbr. articles to profl. jours. Mem. acad. coun. Thomas Edison State Coll., 1998; mem. undergrad. programs adv. bd. U. Md. Univ. Coll., 1999 Mem. Assn. for Ednl. Comms. and Tech., Brit. Am. Bus. Assn., Arts Coun. Fairfax County, Md. Fedn. for the Arts. Office Fax: (703) 815-6179. E-mail: info@carrolearning.com.

CARROL, ROBERT KELTON, lawyer; b. Washington, Ind., Sept. 28, 1952; s. Louis Leon and Beatrice (Colbert) C. BA with distinction, So. Meth. U., 1974, JD, 1977. Bar: Tex. 1977, Calif. 1978, U.S. Dist. Ct. (no. and ea. dists.) Calif. 1978, U.S. Dist. Ct. (cen. and so. dists.) Calif. 1984, U.S. Ct. Appeals (9th cir.) 1978, U.S. Ct. Appeals (D.C. cir.) 1983, U.S. Supreme Ct. 1983. Assoc. Littler, Mendelson, Fastiff & Tichy, San Francisco, 1977-82, ptnr., 1982—. Contbr. articles to profl. publs. Vestry mem. St. Mary the Virgin Episc. Ch., San Francisco, 1982-85. Mem. ABA (labor law sect. 1977—, entertainment com. on devel. and sports law 1977—), State Bar Calif., State Bar Tex., Bar Assn. San Francisco, Phi Beta Kappa, Phi Delta Phi. Clubs: Lawyers' of San Francisco, Barristers of San Francisco.

CARROLL, ADELINE F. special education educator; b. Chester, Pa., June 30, 1949; d. Relda Cirilli; children: Colleen Dinae, Kathleen Marie Hagan, Michael Thomas, Richard Wallace. BS, West Chester U., 1971; Masters Degree, Calif. State U., Fullerton, 1998. Elem. tchr. Pa. Delco Sch. Dist., Aston, 1971—77; 2d grade tchr. St. Edwards Sch., Dana Point, Calif., 1986—94; 4th grade tchr. Carl Hankey Elem. Sch., Mission Viejo, Calif., 1994—97; resource specialist Aliso Viejo (Calif.) Mid. Sch., Aliso Viejo, 1997—; univ. lectr. Calif. State U., Fullerton, 1998—. Support provider BTSA, Alsio Viejo, 2001—; conf. presenter Dist. Profl. Devel. Acad., Aliso Viejo, 1998—; resource specialist assessors panel mem. Orange County Dept. of Edn., Costa Mesa, Calif., 2000—; conf. facilitator Calif. League of Mid. Schs., Maui, Hawaii, 2001, San Francisco, 02. Religious edn. tchr. St. Timothy's Ch., Laguna Niguel, Calif., 1986—88. Recipient Edn. award, Nat. Down Syndrome Congress, 1997. Roman Catholic. Home: 11 Rollins Pl Laguna Niguel CA 92677 Office: Aliso Viejo Mid Sch 111 Park Ave Aliso Viejo CA 92656 Personal E-mail: addiecarroll@cox.net.

CARROLL, AILEEN, retired librarian; b. Mason, Wis., Aug. 7, 1914; d. John P. and Mary (Noonan) C. BA, De Paul U., 1938; MA, Northwestern U., 1940; MLS, Rosary Coll., 1965. Tchr. Chgo. Pub. Schs., 1940-52; systems media dir., libr. organizer Cook County Pub. Schs., from 1952. Author and pub. of children's poetry. Vol. St. Vincent's Orphanage, Chgo., Sacred Heart Home for the Aged, Chgo. Recipient scholarship AAUW, 1991. Mem. AAUW (Western Springs, Ill.), LWV, Rep. Club of Oak Park, Art Group of Western Springs. Home: Western Springs, Ill. Died Dec. 10, 2001.

CARROLL, ARCHIE BENJAMIN, III, management educator; b. Jacksonville, Fla., Feb. 4, 1943; s. Archie Benjamin Jr. and Margaret Alice (Ives); m. Priscilla Dale Gossett, June 9, 1968; 1 child: Bradley. BS, Fla. State U., 1965, MBA, 1966, D Bus. Adminstrn., 1972. Asst. prof. Athens (Ala.) Coll., 1966-69; instr. Fla. State U., Tallahassee, 1969-72; prof. mgmt. U. Ga., Athens, 1972—, Robert W. Scherer prof. corp. pub. affairs, 1986—. Author: Business & Society, 1981, Business & Society: Ethics and Stakeholder Management, 5th edit., 2003; (with others) Management, 1980, Computers for Business, 1984; editor: Managing Corporate Social Responsibility, 1977; mem. editorial bd. Jour. of Mgmt., 1975-79, 2003—, U. Ga. Press, 1984-85; contbr. numerous articles to profl. jours. Named an Outstanding Young Man of Am., 1978; recipient Superior Teaching award U. Ga., 1982. Fellow So. Mgmt. Assn. (sec. 1975-77); mem. Acad. Mgmt. (div. chair 1976-77, mem. editorial bd. Acad. Mgmt. Rev. 1977-81), Beta Gamma Sigma (pres. U. Ga. chpt. 1981-82), Sigma Iota Epsilon. Avocations: golf, reading, writing. Office: U Ga Dept Mgmt Lumpkin St Athens GA 30602

CARROLL, BARRY JOSEPH, manufacturing and real estate executive; b. Highland Park, Ill., Jan. 22, 1944; s. Wallace Edward and Lelia (Holden) C.; m. Barbara Ann Pehrson, July 16, 1965; children: Megan, Sean, Deirdre, Colleen, Oona. Student, Boston Coll., 1961-63; AB, Shimer Coll., 1966; MBA, Harvard U., 1969. Lic. real estate broker, Ill. Account rep. Amerad Advt. Service, Chgo., summers 1966, 67; staff analyst Jamesbury Valve Co., Worcester, Mass., 1968; asst. to pres. Am. Gage & Machine Co., Elgin, Ill., 1969; pres. J.C. Deagan Co., Chgo., 1969-77; v.p. Internat. Metals & Machines, Des Plaines, 1977-92, also bd. dirs.; v.p. Katy Industries, Elgin, 1984-94, also bd. dirs.; pres. Katy Comm., Inc. (WIVS-AM, WXRD-FM, WAIT AM/FM), 1986-92, Sta. W45AJ-TV, Rockford, Ill., 1989-92. V.p., bd. dirs. Pehrson-Long Assocs., Real Estate

Mgmt., Am. Machine & Sci. Inc., CRL Inc., Carroll Internat. Corp. (chmn. 1992), GFS Holdings Co. Author: (monograph) Talking with Business, 1986; author of appendix/editor: What I Do Best: The Biography of Wallace Edward Carroll, 1992; editor/author: Private Means/Public Ends, 1987; author: Lake Forest, A Very Special Place, 1996; producer, dir. indsl. films, including In There Punching, 1965, Digging Lake County, 1999; dir./host (cable TV series) Area Arts, 2000—. Spl. asst. U.S. Sec. Edn., Washington, 1983-84; Presdl. Exch. exec., Washington, 1983-84; bd. govs. United Rep. Fund, Chgo., 1986-92; mem. Nat. Inst. Edn. Commn. Edn. and Tech., U.S. Dept. Edn., 1984-85; trustee Shimer Coll., 1970—, chmn. bd. trustees, 1975-78; trustee Barat Coll., Lake Forest, 1983—, life trustee, 1999—; trustee St. Xavier U., Chgo., 1988-94, Lake County Regional Sch. Bd., 1993—; bd. trustees Am. Ireland Fund, 1982-2001, sec., 1991-99; bd. dirs. Lake Forest Symphony, 1970—, Pageant of Peace/Nat. Christmas Tree, 1987-2000, Lake Forest Music Inst., 1991—, Roosevelt U., Chgo., 1996—, U. Ill. Eye Rsch. Inst., 1996—; bd. dirs. Chgo. Crime Commn., 1993—, treas., 1994-98; mem., chmn. Lake Forest Cultural Arts Commn., 1997—; chair adv. bd. Inst. Metro. Affairs Roosevelt U., 1998—. Shimer fellow Shimer Coll., Mt. Carroll, Ill., 1972, Shimer Hero award Shimer Coll., Waukegan, Ill., 1980, Dr. Letters, 1995. Mem. Woods Hole Oceanographic Inst. Assn., Ill. Mfrs. Assn. (bd. dirs. 1989—, treas. 1991-95), Assn. for Mfg. Tech. (bd. dirs. chmn. pub. affairs com. 1988-93), Onwentsia Club (Lake Forest), Chgo. Club, Met. Club (Washington), East Chop Beach Tennis and Yacht Clubs (Martha's Vineyard Island), Edgartown Yacht Club, Bath and Tennis Club (Palm Beach, Fla.), Soc. Colonial Wars in the State of Ill. (treas. 1988-94, gov. 1998-2000), Nat. Soc. Colonial Wars (dep. gov. gen. 2002—). Avocations: flying, sailing, skiing, scuba diving, photography. Office: Carroll Internat Corp 2340 Des Plaines Ave Des Plaines IL 60018-3212

CARROLL, BILLY PRICE, artist; b. Memphis, Nov. 27, 1920; d. Robert Ray and Olive (Thomas) Price; m. Robert Ray Hosmer, May 3, 1941 (div. Aug. 1948); 1 child, Nadia Jan Woodall; m. David Donald Carroll, Dec. 25, 1964. Student, Memphis Acad. Arts, 1939-40, Farnsworth Sch. Painting, 1949, 50-51, Accademia Delle Belle Arte, Florence, Italy, 1959; also pvt. study, various museums, Uffizi, Florence, Italy. Lectr., Chinese, Western painting; lectr. Fine Arts Mus., Little Rock, Ark., 1954, Brooks Art Gallery, 1957, 62, 63, 69, 77, National TV interview, tape, Taiwan 1969, interview, Taipei, 1969, Lynchburg Fine Arts Ctr., 1971, 83, Memphis State U. Gallery, 1987, Memphis U., Lecture Memphis Racquet Club, Gallery Eng. Speaking Union, 1990, Memphis Brooks Mus. Art, 1984, 91, Shainberg Gallery, Memphis, state conv. Nat. League Am. Pen Women. One-man shows include Fine Arts Mus., Little Rock, 1953, McCaughen and Burr Gallery Fine Arts, St. Louis, 1954, 64, 88, Brooks Meml. Art Gallery, Memphis, 1956, Greenville (Miss.) Art Assn., 1963, Hong Kong, 1968, Taiwan Nat. Art Center, Teipei, 1969, Mpls. Aquatennial Festival, 1970, Lynchburg Fine Arts Ctr., Va., 1971, 83, Memphis Brooks Mus. Art, 1984, Christian Bros. U. Art Gallery, 1993, Memphis Botanical Gardens, 2002, others; exhibited in group shows at Fla. Artists Group, 1952-53, 57-58, Brooks Meml. Art Gallery, 1953, 61, 66-67, Painting of Year Exhbn., Atlanta, 1955, Mo. Athletic Club, St. Louis Fine Arts Collection, 1954, 1st Hunter Ann., Chattanooga, 1960, Shainberg Gallery, 1987; represented in permanent collections Ga. Inst. Tech., Atlanta, Mo. Athletic Club, St. Louis, U. Tenn., Memphis, Memphis State U., United Chinese Bank, Hong Kong, Dr. Sun Yat Sen, 1st Pres. of China, City Hall Gallery of Memphis Mayor Wyeth Chandler, Portrait of Morrie Moss, major donor to Memphis Brooks Mus. Art, Christian Bros. U. Art Gallery, Judge Hu Anderson, Ct. Appeals, Jackson, Supreme Ct. Justice John Swepston, Memphis, Dean of Shelby County Jurists Judge Robert Hoffman, Memphis, Amherst Coll. Prof. Henry Steele Commager, Senator Howard Baker, Sr. Circuit Ct. Judge Harry Adams, Memphis, Circuit Ct. Judge Robert Hoffman, Memphis, two bishops of Tenn. Episcopal Diocese, Edmund P. Dandridge, Memphis, William E. Sanders, Knoxville, Mayor Elliott Shearer, Lynchburg, Va., Judge U.S. Bankruptcy Ct., Judge William Leffler U.S. Bankruptcy Ct., U.S. Circuit Judge Harry Wellford, Memphis, others, portrait Blanche Spain Christian Bros. U., 1993. Recipient Oil-first and Hon. award Tenn. Nat. League Am. Pen. Women, 1969, others; Jay Hambridge Found. fellow, 1954, Huntington Hartford Found. fellow, 1958. Mem. Memphis Brooks Mus. Art League. Home: 3232 W Lakewood Dr Memphis TN 38128 Fax: 901-377-3667.

CARROLL, BRENDA SANDIDGE, volunteer civic worker; b. Patuxent River Naval AB, Md., May 1, 1952; d. Ronald and Erma (McKay) Sandidge; m. Leo Elmer Carroll, Dec. 19, 1970; 1 child, Jennifer. BA, St. Mary's Coll. Md., 1989. Libr. acquisitions technician St. Mary's Coll., St. Mary's City, Md., 1989-95; ret., 1995. Vol. St. Mary's Caring, Lexington Park, Md., 1995—, St. Mary's County Literacy Coun., 1985—, St. Michael's Sch., 1977-83, St. Mary's County Hist. Preservation Com., 1986—; asst. food coord. Christmas in April, Hollywood, Md., 1991—; vol. Ridge Am. Legion Post 255; meal deliverer Meals on Wheels, St. Mary's County, Md., 1997—; vol. Office on Aging.

CARROLL, CHARLES A. manufacturing executive; Sales rep. Rubbermaid, 1971, pres., gen. mgr. housewares product divsn., 1990, pres., COO, 1993-99; pres., CEO Amana Appliances, 2000—. Office: Amana Appliances 2800 220th Trail Amana IA 52204

CARROLL, CHARLES E. electronics executive; CFO W.L. Gore & Assocs., Newark, Del., CEO, pres. Office: WL Gore & Assocs 555 Paper Mill Road Newark DE 19711*

CARROLL, CHARLES MICHAEL, music educator; b. Otterbein, Ind., Mar. 5, 1921; s. James William and Catherine Doretta (Bohan) C.; m. Mary Lipford Rosenbush, Sept. 4, 1951; children: Charles Michael, Mary Catherine, Theresa Jane, William Rosenbush. BM, Ind. U., Bloomington, 1949; MM, Fla. State U., Tallahassee, 1951, PhD, 1960. Asst. coordinator music services Ind. U., 1949-50; instr. music Fla. State U., 1950-53; concert mgr. symphony orchs. Toledo, Washington, Savannah, Ga., 1953-58; prof. music Pensacola (Fla.) Jr. Coll., 1960-64; prof. St. Petersburg (Fla.) Jr. Coll., 1964-89, chmn. communications dept. Music critic Tallahassee Democrat, 1950-53, St. Petersburg Evening Independent, 1976-86. Author: The Great Chess Automaton, 1975; contbr. articles to profl. jours., and encyclopaedias. Served to capt., AUS, 1942-46, ETO. Mem. Am. Symphony Orch. League (v.p. 1955-56), Am. Musicol. Soc. (nat. council 1974-77, chmn. chpt. 1974-76), Am. Soc. Eighteenth-Century Studies (exec. bd. region 1974-82, regional pres. 1979-80), Coll. Music Soc. (editor 1979-83, nat. council 1978-81, chmn. chpt. 1979-80), Société d'Etudes Philidoriennes (conseiller bibliographique 1988—). Home: 1701 80th St N Saint Petersburg FL 33710-3703

CARROLL, CHRISTOPHER DIXON, economics educator; b. Baton Rouge, La., Aug. 16, 1964; s. Sidney Lee Carroll and Elizabeth Blewer; m. Jennifer Elizabeth Manning, Aug. 8, 1998. PhD, MIT, 1990. Assoc. prof. Johns Hopkins U., 1999—2001, prof. econs., 2001—. Rsch. assoc. Nat. Bur. Econ. Rsch., Cambridge, 1995—. Sr. economist Coun. of Econ. Advisers, Washington, 1997—98. Recipient Samuelson award, TIAA-CREF, 1998; Sloan rsch. fellow, 1997. Home: 7363 Swan Point Way Columbia MD 21045 Office: Johns Hopkins University Department of Economics Baltimore MD 21218-2685 Home Fax: 410-516-7602; Office Fax: 410-516-6700. Business E-Mail: ccarroll@jhu.edu.

CARROLL, DAVID PAUL, social welfare administrator; b. N.Y.C., Nov. 22, 1935; s. Hugh Felix Carroll and Gertrude Jordan. BA in Physics, Cath. U. Am., Washington, 1958; M in Physics, Brown U., 1963; PhD in Sci. Edn., NYU, 1978. Data processing cons. Diocese Bklyn., 1965-68; founder, dir. Data Sys. Ctr. Archdiocese N.Y., N.Y.C., 1968-79, asst. to chancellor, 1979-82; dir. rsch. Pope John Paul II Ctr., N.Y.C., 1982-85; asst. to sec. gen. Cath. Near E. Welfare Assn., N.Y.C., 1985—. Adj. asst. prof. St. John's U., Jamaica, N.Y., 1978-86; adj. prof. NYU, 1981-97; mid. east advisor Holy See Permanent Mission to UN, N.Y.C., 1985—. Co-author: The Ethics of Nuclear Deterrence, 1991; contbr. over 70 articles to profl. publs. Co-chair Muslim/Roman Cath. Dialogue, N.Y.C., 1985—; treas. Bros. of Christian Schs. Found., Oak Brook, Ill., 1987—; bd. dirs. Future Millenium Found., Arlington, Va., 1996—, St. Thomas Aquinas Coll., Sparkill, N.Y., 1998—. Recipient Cross Pro Ecclescia Pro Pontifice Roman Cath. Pontiff, 1995. Mem. Cath. Acad. Scis. (founder, sec. 1987—), Equestrian Order Holy Sepulchre Jerusalem (knight comdr. with star 1987), Cath. Assn. Scientists & Engrs., Scholars Social Justice. Avocations: model railroading, canoeing, hiking, backpacking, classical music. Home: 367 Clermont Ave Brooklyn NY 11238 Office: Cath Near E Welfare Assn 1011 1st Ave Ste 1552 New York NY 10022 E-mail: bad@cnewa.org.

CARROLL, DAVID JOSEPH, stage manager; b. Stratford, N.J., July 9, 1979; s. David Ronald and Mary Jane (Popko) C. Student, Ctr. Talented Youth, 1991-92, ROGATE, 1991-92, Sch. Visual Arts, 1997—. Actor: (TV commls.) Rock & Roll Easter Eggs, 1989, British Knights, 1989, America's Funniest Home Videos, 1990, French Toast Clothes, 1990, Pizza Hut, 1990, Burger King, 1990, (films) Cadillac Man, 1989, Thank You and Goodnight, 1990; various commls., 2001-2003. Home: 30-75 34th St Apt 4D Astonia NY 11103-2432

CARROLL, DEIRDRE HOLDEN, psychiatric nurse practitioner, clinical researcher, educator; b. Lake Forest, Ill., Jan. 1, 1973; d. Barry Joseph and Barbara Pehrson Carroll. BSN, Boston Coll., Chestnut Hill, Mass., 1995; MSN, Yale U., 2000. Cert. psychiatric-mental health clinical nurse specialist, Conn., adult nurse practitioner, Conn., lic. advanced practice RN, Conn., RN Conn., Ill. Staff nurse Lake Forest Hosp., 1996, Rush North Shore Med. Ctr., Skokie, Ill., 1996—98, Ariaù (Brazil) Jungle Towers, 1998; clin. faculty Yale U. Sch. of Nursing, New Haven, 2002—, clin. preceptor. Co-investigator/clin. rsch., clin. faculty Yale U. Sch. Medicine, Child Study Ctr., New Haven, 2000—; psychiat. nurse practitioner Yale U. Sch. of Medicine, Child Study Ctr., New Haven, 2000—; co-investigator Rsch. Units in Pediatric Psychopharmacology, New Haven, 2000—; presenter in field. Contbr. articles to profl. jours. Mem. Am. Ireland Fund. Mem.: DAR, Coun. Fgn. Rels. Ill., Boston Coll. Nurses Assn., Ill. Nurses Assn., Conn. Nurses Assn., Am. Coll. of Nurse Practitioners, Internat. Soc. of Psychiatric-Mental Health Nurses, Irish-Georgian Soc., Landmarks Preservation Soc. Ill., Yale Alumnae Assn., Boston Coll. Alumni Assn., PA of Diving Instructors, USTA, Women's Athletic Club of Chgo., Yale Club of NYC, Sigma Theta Tau Internat. (named to Yale U. Honor Soc. 2001). Achievements include research in psychopharmacology and behavioral interventions or the treatment of children and adolecents with serious mental illness and developmental disorders. Avocations: international travel, classical piano, tennis/squash, photography, scuba diving. Home: 265 College St Apt 11d New Haven CT 06510 Office: Yale U Sch Medicine 230 South Frontage Rd OHM I 071 New Haven CT 06520-7900 Personal E-mail: deirdre.carroll@yale.edu. E-mail: deirdre.carroll@yale.edu.

CARROLL, EARL HAMBLIN, federal judge; b. Tucson, Mar. 26, 1925; s. John Vernon and Ruby (Wood) C.; m. Louise Rowlands, Nov. 1, 1952; children— Katherine Carroll Pearson, Margaret Anne BSBA, U. Ariz., 1948, LLB, 1951. Bar: Ariz., U.S. Ct. Appeals (9th and 10th cirs.), U.S. Ct. of Claims, U.S. Supreme Ct. Law clk. Ariz. Supreme Ct., Phoenix, 1951-52; assoc. Evans, Kitchel & Jenckes, Phoenix, 1952-56, ptnr., 1956-80; judge U.S. Dist. Ct. Ariz., Phoenix, 1980—, sr. judge, 1994—. Spl. counsel City of Tombstone, Ariz., 1962-65, Maricopa County, Phoenix, 1968-75, City of Tucson, 1974, City of Phoenix, 1979; designated mem. U.S. Fgn. Intelligence Surveillance Court by Chief Justice U.S. Supreme Ct., 1993-99; chief judge Alien Terrorist Removal Ct., 1996-01, 2001—. Mem. City of Phoenix Bd. of Adjustment, 1955-58; trustee Phoenix Elem. Sch. Bd., 1961-72; mem. Gov.'s Council on Intergovtl. Relations, Phoenix, 1970-73; mem. Ariz. Bd. Regents, 1978-80. Served with USNR, 1943-46; PTO Recipient Nat. Service awards Campfire, 1973, 75, Alumni Service award U. Ariz., 1980, Disting. Citizen award No. Ariz. U., Flagstaff, 1983, Bicentenial award Georgetown U., 1988, Disting. Citizen award U. Ariz., 1990, Sidney S. Woods Alumni Svc. award, 2000. Fellow Am. Coll. Trial Lawyers, Am. Bar Found.; mem. ABA, Ariz. Bar Assn., U. Ariz. Law Coll. Assn. (pres. 1975), Sigma Chi (Significant Sig award 1991), Phi Delta Phi. Democrat. Office: US Dist Ct US Courthouse Ste 521 401 W Washington SPC 48 Phoenix AZ 85003-2151

CARROLL, FRANCES LAVERNE, librarian, educator; b. Scammon, Kans., Dec. 6, 1925; d. Robert Allen and Truda Hilda (Flanagan) C. BS in Ed., Kans. State Tchrs. Coll., 1948; MA in Libr. Sci., U. Denver, 1956; postgrad., Western Res. U., 1957; PhD in Edn., U. Okla., 1970. Bookkeeper Baxter Springs Bank, Kans., 1944; tchr. English and journalism high sch. Caney, Kans., 1947-49; libr. Field Kindley Meml. HS, Coffeyville, Kans., 1949-54; librarian Coffeyville Jr. Coll., 1954-62; supr. elem. sch. libraries Coffeyville, 1957-62; asst. prof. library sci. U. Okla., Norman, 1962-67, assoc. prof., 1972-75, acting dir. sch. library sci., 1974-75, prof., 1975-86, emeritus, 1986—. Head library studies Nedlands Coll. Advanced Edn. (formerly Western Australian Secondary Tchrs. Coll.), Perth, 1977-81; guest lectr. Drexel Inst. Tech., Phila., 1964, U. London, 1972, Pahlavi U., Shiraz, Iran, 1976, Beijing Fgn. Studies U., 1992; dir. US Office Edn. Inst., 1966, 67, 69. Author: (with Mary Meacham) The Library at Mount Vernon, 1977, Exciting, Funny, Scary, Short, Different and Sad Books Kids Like, 1984, More Exciting, Funny, Scary, Short, Different and Sad Books Kids Like, 1992, (with Pat Beilke) Guidelines for the Planning and Organization of Sch. Libr. Media Ctr., 1979, Guidelines for Planning and Organization of Library Media Centers, 1990, Arabic translation, 1995, Recent Advances in Sch. Librarianship, 1981, (with John Harvey) Internationalizing Libr. Ed., 1987; nat. series editor: Reading for Young People, 1979-85; editor: (with Philip Schwartz) Biog. Directory of Nat. Librarians, 1989, Destination Discovery! Activities and Resources for Studying Columbus and Other Explorers, 1994, (with Susan Houck) Internat. Biog. Directory of Nat. Archivists, Documentalists and Librarians, 1996, (with John Harvey and Susan Houck) Internat. Librarianship, 2001; contbr. articles to profl. jour. US Office Edn. grantee, 1969 Mem. AAUW, AAUP, ALA, Okla. Student Libr. Assn. (state sponsor 1963-84), Okla. Libr. Assn., Internat. Rels. Round Table (chmn. membership 1970-74), Internat. Fedn. Libr. Assn. (chmn. sect. sch. libr. 1973-77), Delta Kappa Gamma, Phi Delta Kappa, Beta Phi Mu. Office: Sch Library & Info Studies 401 W Brooks St Norman OK 73019-6032

CARROLL, FRANK EDWARD, radiologist, researcher; b. Phila., Oct. 25, 1941; s. Frank Edward Sr. and Marie Elizabeth (Mullin) C.; m. Saramae Dorothy Dever, Sept. 4, 1965; children: Frank Leonard, Mark Edward. BS in Biology, St. Joseph's Coll., 1963; MD, Hahnemann Med. Coll., 1967. Diplomate Am. Bd. Radiology. Rsch. asst. Hahnemann Med. Coll. and Hosp., Phila., 1965-66; rotating intern U.S. Naval Regional Med. Ctr., Oakland, Calif., 1967-68; submarine med. officer U.S. Submarine Med. Sch., U.S. Naval Submarine Base, Gorton, Conn., 1968, SSBN 659 Will Rogers Polaris Nuclear Submarine, 1968-69; staff physician Armed Forces Staff Coll., Norfolk, Va., 1969-70; diagnostic radiology resident St. Mary's Hosp. and Med. Ctr., San Francisco, 1970-72; resident, fellow, rschr. U. Calif. San Francisco Sch. Medicine, 1972-73; asst. prof. diagnostic radiology Yale U. Sch. Medicine, New Haven, 1973-74; staff radiologist Broadway Hosp., Vallejo, Calif., 1974-75, Franklin (Pa.) Regional Med. Ctr., 1975-83; asst. prof. diagnostic radiology Vanderbilt U. Med. Ctr., Nashville, 1983-87, chief sect. pulmonary imaging, 1983—2000, assoc. dir. divsn. diagnostic radiology, 1984, dir. lab. radiologic rsch., 1984-85, assoc. prof. diagnostic radiology, 1987-94, dir. diagnostic radiology, 1985-89, assoc. prof. physics and astronomy, 1993-99, prof. diagnostic radiology, 1994—, prof. physics and astronomy, 1999—; founder Mxisystems, Inc., Nashville. Adj. asst. prof. diagnostic radiology Duke U. Med. Ctr., Durham, N.C., 1981-83; cons. in field; referee jours. in field, including Investigative Radiology, Acad. Radiology, Radiology, Chest, Jour. Applied Physiology, Archives of Internal Medicine, Am. Jour. Neuroradiology, others; grant reviewer NIH, Washington. Contbr. articles to profl. jours., chpts. to books. Bd. dirs. Nashville Opera, 1988-94, Franklin Emergency Ambulance Svc., 1975-83, St. Patrick's Sch. Bd., 1975-83; asst. scoutmaster Boy Scouts Am., Franklin, 1975-83, physician and merit badge counselor, Nashville, 1983—; pres. Am. Cancer Soc., Franklin, 1975-83; design prodn. vol. Cheekwood Fine Arts Mus., Nashville, 1995—. Lt. comdr. USNR, 1963-73. Fellow Am. Coll. Radiology, Am. Coll. Chest Physicians; mem. Am. Soc. Laser Medicine and Surgery, Soc. Photo-Optical Instrumentation Engrs., Soc. for Magnetic Resonance Imaging, Assn. Univ. Radiologists, Radiol. Soc. N.Am., Soc. thoracic Radiology, Tenn. Radiologic Soc., Mid. Tenn. Radiologic Soc. Achievements include production of pulsed, tunable, monochromatic X-rays by the free electron laser; dedicated tabletop laser synchrotron source monochromatic 3-D mammography without breast compression, k-edge imaging, phase contrast imaging, time-of flight imaging and protein crystallography; evaluation of lung water by magnetic resonance imaging. Home: 1216 Vintage Pl Nashville TN 37215-4707 Office: Vanderbilt U Med Ctr 1161 21st Ave S Nashville TN 37232-2675 E-mail: frank.carroll@vanderbilt.edu.

CARROLL, GEORGE JOSEPH, pathologist, educator; b. Gardner, Mass., Oct. 14, 1917; s. George Joseph and Kathryn (O'Hearn) C. BA, Clark U., Worcester, Mass., 1939; MD, George Washington U., 1944. Diplomate Am. Bd. Pathology. Intern Worchester City Hosp., 1944-45; resident in medicine Doctors Hosp., Washington, 1945-46; resident in pathology Sibley Hosp., Washington, 1948-49, VA Hosp., Washington, 1949-50; asst. pathologist D.C. Gen. Hosp., 1950-51, assoc. pathologist, 1951-52; pathologist Louise Obici Meml. Hosp., Suffolk, Va., 1952—, sec. med. staff, 1956-59, chief of staff, 1959-60, 67-69; pathologist Chowan Hosp., Edenton, N.C., 1952-71, Southampton Meml. Hosp., Franklin, Va., 1952—, Greensville Meml. Hosp., Emporia, Va., 1961—. Instr. pathology Georgetown U. Sch. Medicine, 1950-52; instr. bacteriology Am. U., Washington, 1950-51; assoc. clin. prof. pathology Med. Coll. Va., Richmond, 1968-70; clin. prof. pathology Va. Commonwealth U., 1970— ; prof. dept. pathology Eastern Va. Med. Sch., Norfolk, 1974— ; sec.-treas. Va. Bd. Medicine, 1967-86, treas., 1971-86. Contbr. articles to med. jours. Served with U.S. Army, 1946-48. Fellow ACP, Coll. Am. Pathologists, Am. Soc. Clin. Pathologists (bd. dirs. 1969—, pres. 1977—), Internat. Acad. Pathology; mem. AMA, So. Med. Assn. (Va. councilor 1965-70, pres. 1973-74), Med. Soc. Va., 4th dist. Med. Soc. (pres. 1968-70), Seaboard Med. Soc. (pres. 1957), George Washington Med. Soc., Tri-County Med. Soc. (pres. 1971-73), Am. Soc. Clin. Pharmacy Therapeutics, Va. Soc. Pathology (pres. 1973-74), Soc. Nuclear Medicine, Am. Assn. Blood Banks, Am. Cancer Soc. (bd. dirs. Va. div. 1955-62), Va. Med. Svc. Assn. (bd. dirs. 1960-71), Rotary. Home: 219 Northbrooke Ave Suffolk VA 23434-6647 Office: Obici Meml Hosp PO Box 1100 2800 Godwin Blvd Suffolk VA 23439-8038 Fax: 757-934-4398.

CARROLL, GREGORY JOSEPH, education educator; b. Fern Tree Gully, Victoria, Australia, May 26, 1962; s. Noel Patrick and Eileen Patricia Carroll; m. Karin Marie Staiti, Aug. 25, 1996; 1 child, Logan James Staiti. PhD, Monash U., Australia, 1999. Tchr. Hamilton HS, Australia, 1983—88, Munich Internat. Sch., Starnberg bei Percha, Germany, 1988—93, The Browning Sch., Manhattan, Utah, 1993—95, Am. Sch. of the Hague, Waasenar, Netherlands, 1994—95; environ. policy analyst Australian Conservation Found., Fitzroy, Australia, 1995—97; rsch. fellow Monash U., Clayton, Australia, 1996—98, lectr., 1998—99; asst. prof. Elmira Coll., 1999—2000, Salem State Coll., 2000—. Scholar Postgraduate award, Australian Govt., 1997—99. Mem.: Internat. Soc. for Environ. Ethics. Office: Salem State Coll 352 Lafayette St Salem MA 01970 Office Fax: 978-542-7215. E-mail: gcarroll@salemstate.edu

CARROLL, HARVEY FRANKLIN, chemistry and nutrition educator; b. New Haven, Aug. 25, 1939; AB, Hunter Coll., CUNY, 1961; PhD, Cornell U., 1969. Sr. chemist Uniroyal Chem., Naugatuck, Conn., 1968-69; prof. phys. scis. Kingsborough C.C./CUNY, Bklyn., 1969—2003, prof. emeritus, 2003—. Vis. prof. Hebrew U., Jerusalem, 1979-80. Mem. Am. Chem. Soc., Sigma Xi. E-mail: hcarroll@kbcc.cuny.edu.

CARROLL, HOWARD WILLIAM, lawyer, retired state senator; b. July 28, 1942; s. Barney M. and Lyla (Price) C.; m. Eda Stagman, Dec. 1, 1973; children: Jacqueline, Barbara. BBA, Roosevelt U., 1964; postgrad., Loyola U., 1964-65; JD, DePaul U., 1967. Bar: Ill. 1967. Staff atty. Chgo. Transit Authority, 1967-71; pvt. practice, 1971-74; ptnr. Carroll & Sain, Chgo., 1974—; mem. Ill. Senate, Springfield, 1973-99, asst. minority leader, 1993-99, chmn. appropriations com., 1977-93. Mem. Legis. Info. System Commn., Ill. Comprehensive Health Ins. Bd.; vice chmn. State Employees Suggestion Award Bd.; mem. fed. budget and taxation com. State-Fed. Assembly; mem. Assembly Com. on State's Legis. Fiscal Affairs and Oversight; prof. complemental faculty Rush U. Coll. Health Scis., Chgo.; lectr. in field. Mem. Ill. Ho. of Reps., 1971-72; chmn. fin. com. Chgo. and Cook County Dem. Crtl. Com., 1982-84, treas., 1984-2000; committeeman 50th Ward Dem. Orgn., 1980-2000; mem. platform com. Ill. Dem. Com., 1974—; former mem. youth adv. bd. Dem. Nat. Com.; del. nat. and Ill. Dem. convs.; v.p. Young Dem. Clubs Am., 1971-73, also former gen. counsel; mem. exec. bd. Atlantic Alliance Young Polit. Leaders, 1970-73; active numerous civic orgns.; mem. exec. com. Jewish Nat. Fund, 1977—; officer of and chair govt. affairs Jewish Fedn. Met. Chgo.; founder Howard W. Carroll Found. Recipient numerous awards, 1971, including cert. of appreciation Decalogue Soc. Lawyers, 1972, Hemophilia Found. Ill., 1988, City Colls. Chgo., 1992, Disting. Svc. award State of Israel Bonds, 1974, Self-Help Assn., 1986, citation for meritorious svc. DAV, 1986, Legislator of Yr. award Child Care Assn. Ill., 1988, Ill. Coun. on Long Term Care, 1988, Outstanding Legislator award Am. Acad. Ophthology, 1989, Legis. Advocacy award Ill. Coun. for Gifted, 1991, Founders medal Montay Coll., 1992; named Ill. Health Care Outstanding Legislator of Yr., 1995. Mem. Chgo. Bar Assn. (Disting. Lawyer and Legislator award 1974), Zionist Orgn. Chgo., Masons (32d degree), B'nai B'rith (bd. dirs. West Rogers Park, chmn. Anti-Defamation League 1978-80, mem. exec. com. and chmn. spl. events Greater Chgo. coun., bd. dirs. Budlong Woods chpt.) Home: 2929 W Albion Ave Chicago IL 60645-4203 Office: 7250 N Cicero Ave Lincolnwood IL 60712

CARROLL, IRWIN DIXON, engineer; b. Many, La., Nov. 6, 1934; s. Andrew Dixon and Elizabeth Margaret (Irwin) C.; m. Claudia Laverne Bratcher, June 27, 1958; children: Richard Irwin, Claudia Elizabeth. BS in Mech. Engring., So. Meth. U., 1957, MS in Elec. Engring., 1967. Registered profl. engr., Tex. Design engr. Tex. Instruments, Dallas, 1957-66, engring. supr., 1966-71, engring. mgr., 1971-75, ops. mgr., 1975-77, European div. mgr., 1977-79, mfg. ops. mgr., 1979-80, dept. mgr., 1980-85, George A. Greene Co., Campbell, Calif., 1985-86; cons. engr. Irwin Carroll Assocs., Dallas, 1986-88; dir. joint devel. programs, site mgr. Applied Materials, Inc., Austin, Tex., 1988—96. Tech. program dir. Semiconductor Equip. and Materials Inst., Dallas, 1983-85, speaker Zurich, Switzerland, 1986; mem. info. sys. adv. com. U.S. Dept. Commerce, 1990-96. Chmn. Zion Luth. Sch. Bd., Dallas, 1985-89; bd. dirs. Jr. Achievement of Ctrl. Tex., 1991-93, Japan-Am. Soc. of Austin, 1990-95, Austin Symphony Orch., 1994-97; pres. Austin Children's Mus., 1991-97; active Austin Choral Union, 1994-96; pres. Austin Cmty. Found., 1996-2001. Mem. ASME, Greater Austin C. of C. (bd. dirs. 1991-95), Rotary. Lutheran. Home: PO Box 923 Salado TX 76571-0923 Office: Design Tech Group Inc Electri-Chef 1215 Industrial Blvd Temple TX 76504

CARROLL, J. SPEED, lawyer, financial executive; b. Sherman, Tex., Apr. 23, 1936; s. Horace Bailey and Mary Joe (Durning) C.; m. Martha Coleman Huff, Apr. 12, 1957; 1 child, Charles Durning. BA, U. Tex., 1957; LLB cum laude, Harvard U., 1962. Bar: N.Y. 1964, U.S. Supreme Ct. 1971, Japan (fgn. legal cons.) 1993-95. Assoc. Cleary, Gottlieb, Steen & Hamilton, N.Y.C. and Paris, 1963-70, ptnr. N.Y.C., London, Tokyo, 1971-97, counsel, 1997—2002; mng. dir. Emerging Markets Partnership, Washington, 1997—. Cons. fgn. law Nagashima & Ohno, Tokyo, 1964-65; instr. Internat. Law Inst., Washington, 1973-83; bd. dirs. Mitsubishi Trust and Banking Corp., U.S.A., N.Y.C. Contbr. chapters to books and articles to profl. jours. Mem. Coun. on Fgn. Rels., N.Y.C., 1973—; trustee Parker Sch. Internat. and Comparative Law Columbia U., 1992—. Lt. USNR, 1957-59. Knox fellow Harvard U., 1962-63. Mem. Phi Beta Kappa. Office: Emerging Markets Partnership 2001 Pennsylvania Ave NW Washington DC 20006-1850

CARROLL, JAMES JOSEPH, lawyer; b. Cin., Aug. 1, 1946; s. John Daniel and Virgeal Catherine (Grever) C.; m. Marie Gemelli, May 7, 1977; children: Katharine, Emily. BBA, U. Cin., 1969; JD, No. Ky. U., 1978. Bar: Ohio 1978, U.S. Dist. Ct. (so. dist.) Ohio 1978, U.S. Tax Ct. 1979, U.S. Supreme Ct. 1979. Tax mgr. Main LaFrantz, Cin., 1974-77; sec., treas. R.E.S.C.O., Inc., Cin., 1977-80; owner, sec., treas. Sterling-Mead, Inc., Cin., 1980-87; pvt. practice Cin., 1987-88; of counsel Cors & Bassett, Cin., 1989—. Candidate Hamilton County auditor, 1974; treas. for various polit. candidates, Hamilton County, 1980, 82, 84; bd. dirs., past pres. Hyde Park Neighborhood Council, Cin., 1980-88; pres., trustee Neighborhood Improvement Corp., 1986-96; treas. Hamilton County Dem. Party, 1990-2001. Served with USAR, 1969-75. Mem. Cin. Bar Assn., Ohio Soc. CPAs, Cin. C. of C. (trustee Leadership Cin. alumni 1986-92, v.p. membership 1989-91), Bankers Club. Democrat. Roman Catholic. Office: Cors & Bassett 537 E Pete Rose Way Ste 400 Cincinnati OH 45202-3578 E-mail: jjc@corsbassett.com.

CARROLL, JAMES VINCENT, III, lawyer; b. Houston, Sept. 21, 1940; s. James Vincent and Adoline (Easley) C.; children: Mary Latham, James Vincent IV, David Carter. BBA, U. Tex., 1962, JD, 1964. Bar: Tex. 1965, D.C. 1983. Mem. Andrews & Kurth L.L.P. and predecessors, 1965-95; mng. ptnr. Washington, 1981-83; mng. shareholder Houston office of Littler, Mendelson, Fastiff,

P.C., 1995—; mem., firm-wide mgr. Comm. of Littler Mendelson P.C., 1995—98. Mem. U.S. del. 2d UN Conf. on Exploration and Peaceful Uses of Outer Space, 1982. Contbr. articles in field to profl. jours. Served with USCG, 1964-65, lt. comdr. USNR, 1965-69. Fellow Houston Bar Assn., ABA Found.; mem. NAM (labor law adv. com.), ABA (vice-chmn. oil com. natural resources sect. 1980-85, chmn. energy and natural resources litigation com. 1985-86, coun. mem. 1986-89), Tex. Bar Assn. (dir. labor law sect. 1974-76, chmn. fed. and state agy. subcom. com. on coordination with other state and fed. groups 1975-77), Houston Bar Assn. (founder and first chmn. labor and employment law sect. 1995-96, coun. mem. 1996-99), Tex. Assn. of Bus. (bd. dirs. 1986-89), U.S. C. of C. (labor law adv. com. 1984-87), East Tex. C. of C. (bd. dirs. 1984-87), U. Tex. Law Sch. Assn. (dir. 1980-83), Greater Houston Partnership (mem. govt. affairs coun. 1994-99), Houston Country Club, Tex. Home: 5130 Holly Terrace Dr Houston TX 77056-2100 Office: Littler Mendelson PC 1301 Mckinney St Ste 1900 Houston TX 77010-3029 E-mail: jcarroll@littler.com.

CARROLL, JOHN ARTHUR, musician, educator; b. Ottawa, Ill., Mar. 10, 1954; s. Ward Carroll and Mabel Lucille Anderson. MusB, Ind. U., 1976. Cert. performance Ind. U. Prin. trumpet Boston Opera Co., 1976; fourth/utility trumpet Detroit Symphony, 1977—79; prin. trumpet San Antonio (Tex.) Symphony, 1979—, Columbus (Ohio) Symphony, 1988; mem. music faculty St. Mary's U., San Antonio, 1989—, Our Lady of the Lake U., San Antonio, 1995—; prin. trumpet Sunriver (Oreg.) Music Festival, Cactus Pear Music Festival, San Antonio, 1997—; exec. dir. San Antonio Brass, Inc., 1998—. Composer: (viola quartet) Viola Quartet in B; musician (composer, sound engr.): (CD rec.) A Little Night Music. Bd. dirs. Winters Chamber Orch., San Antonio, 1989—91. Home: PO Box 100193 San Antonio TX 78201 Personal E-mail: tromba1@ix.netcom.com.

CARROLL, JOHN DOUGLAS, mathematical and statistical psychologist; b. Phila., Jan. 3, 1939; s. John Joseph and Nolie Fay (Godwin) C.; m. Sylvia Stevens Booma, Jan. 2, 1965; children: Gregory Alan, Steven Douglas. BS with honors, U. Fla., 1958; PhD, Princeton U., 1963. Research asst. dept. psychology Yale U., 1961-63; math.-statis. psychologist Bell Labs., Murray Hill, N.J., 1963-65, 66-89; bd. govs., prof. mgmt. and psychology Rutgers U., Newark, 1990—. Asst. prof. indsl. engrng. and ops. research NYU, 1965-66, adj. assoc. prof. stats., 1968-70; acting prof. psychology U. Calif.-San Diego, 1975-76; acting prof. social sci. U. Calif.-Irvine, 1975-76; adj. prof. stats. Baruch Coll., CUNY, 1971, adj. prof. mktg. U. Pa., 1978-79; Procter & Gamble adj. prof. of mktg. U. Pa., 1987-89; vis. rsch. prof. cognitive sci. U. Calif. Irvine, 1993. Contbr. numerous articles and chpts. to profl. publs.; author computer programs for multidimensional analysis of behavioral sci. data; assoc. editor: Psychometrika, 1973—, Jour. Exptl. Psychology, 1978-88; mem. editl. bd. Jour. Classification, 1984—, Jour. Mktg. Rsch., 1994—; editor Methodika, 1987-93. Ednl. Testing Service psychometric fellow, 1958-61; NIMH fellow, 1959-61 Fellow AAAS, APA (active Div. 5, pres.-elect 1990-91, pres. 1991-92, APA Disting. Sci. Contbn. award 1989), Am. Psychol. Soc. (William James fellow 1989), Am. Statis. Assn. (program chair stats. in mktg. sect. 1992, chair stats. in mktg. sect. 1993-94, mem. exec. com. 1991-95); mem. Psychometric Soc. (trustee 1971-77, 81-83, 84-87, 93-96, pres. 1975-76, mem. editl. coun. 1975-81), Classification Soc. N.Am. (governing coun. 1974-77, pres. 1980-83, bd. dirs. 1984-96), Internat. Fedn. Classification Socs. (rep. to coun. 1984—, v.p./pres.-elect 1995, pres. 1996—), Soc. Multivariate Exptl. Psychology (editl. adv. bd. 1980-81, pres. 1982-83), Ea. Psychol. assn., Psychonomic Soc., Soc. Math. Psychology, Am. Mktg. Assn., Assn. for Consumer Rsch., Soc. for Consumer Psychology, Inst. for Ops. Rsch. and Mgmt. Scis., Phi Beta Kappa, Sigma Xi, Beta Gamma Sigma. Home: 14 Forest Dr Warren NJ 07059-5802 Office: Rutgers U Grad Sch Mgmt Fac of Mgmt/Mgmt Edn Ctr 111 Washington St Newark NJ 07102-3027

CARROLL, JOHN SAWYER, newspaper editor; b. N.Y.C., Jan. 23, 1942; s. John Wallace and Margaret (Sawyer) C.; m. Kathleen Kirk, May 1, 1971 (div. Sept. 1982) children— Kathleen Louise, Margaret Adriane; m. Lee Huston Powell, Nov. 1985. BA, Haverford Coll., 1963. Reporter Providence Jour. - Bull., 1963-64; reporter Balt. Sun., 1966-72, 1967-69, Middle East, 1969, Washington Bur., 1969-72; city editor, met. editor Phila. Inquirer, 1973-79; exec. v.p., editor Lexington Herald-Leader, Ky., 1979-91; editor, sr. v.p. Balt. Sun, 1991-98; v.p. Times Mirror Co., 1998—2000; editor LA Times, 2000—, exec. v.p., 2000—. Bd. dirs. Am. Soc. Newspaper Editors, Pulitzer prize juror, 1987, 89, 94, Pulitzer prize bd., 1994—2003, chmn., 2002. Served with U.S. Army, 1964-66 Named Nat. Press Found. Editor of the Yr., 1998; Nieman fellow Harvard U., 1971-72; vis. journalist fellow Queen Elizbeth House, U. Oxford, 1988. Fellow: Am. Acad. of Arts and Sci. Office: Los Angeles Times 202 W First St Los Angeles CA 90012

CARROLL, JOSEPH GREGORY, pharmaceutical company executive; b. Phila., Nov. 1, 1948; s. Vincent P. Carroll and Eleanor (Kenny) Metz; m. Suzanne D. Lail, Aug. 25, 1973; children: Robert, Sean, Lindsay. BA, Cornell U., 1970; MA, Temple U., 1972; PhD, Cornell U., 1976. Sr. rsch. assoc. U. Cin., 1976-77; dir., registrar Sch. of Medicine U. Pa., Phila., 1977-83, lectr., adj. asst. prof. Sch. of Edn., 1978-83; assoc. prof., assoc. dean Pa. State U., University Park, 1983-89; dir. Bayer Inst. for Health Care Comm., West Haven, Conn., 1989—. External adv. bd. Sickle Cell Ctr., Children's Hosp., Phila., 1989-92; ednl. cons. div. oncology Children's Hosp., Phila., 1980-83, Nat. Bd. Med. Examiners, Phila., 1979-80; bd. dirs. Am. Acad. Physician and Patient. Nat. v.p. Golden Key Nat. Honor Soc., Pa. State U., 1984. With U.S. Army, 1970-76. Minority Health Careers grantee HHS, 1986-89. Mem. AAAS, Assn. Am. Med. Colls., Am. Ednl. Rsch. Assn., Am. Psychol. Assn., Sigma Xi, Phi Delta Kappa. Democrat. Roman Catholic. Home: 55 Madison Springs Dr Madison CT 06443-2419 Office: Bayer Corp 400 Morgan Ln West Haven CT 06516-4175

CARROLL, JOSEPH J(OHN), lawyer; b. N.Y.C., Sept. 18, 1936; s. James J. and M. Catherine (Molloy) C.; m. Barbara Ann Lediger, May 16, 1959; 1 child, Barbara Ann (dec.). BS, Manhattan Coll., 1958; LLB, St. John's U., 1963; LLM, NYU, 1968. Bar: N.Y. 1964, U.S. Supreme Ct. 1967. Ins. underwriter Atlantic Mut. Ins. Co., N.Y.C., 1959-63; pub. adminstrn. intern N.Y. State Housing Fin. Agy., N.Y.C., 1963-64, adminstrv. asst., 1964-67; assoc. Mudge, Rose, Guthrie, Alexander & Ferdon, N.Y.C., 1967-77, ptnr., 1977-95; of counsel Sullivan Donovan & Gentile, P.C., N.Y.C., 1995—. Mem. nat. coun. trustees Nat. Jewish Med. and Rsch. Ctr., Denver; trustee Manhattan Coll., N.Y.C., Queen of the Most Holy Rosary Parish, Roosevelt, N.Y. Mem.: ABA (health law sect.), Nat. Assn. Coll. and Univ. Attys., Am. Health Lawyers Assn., N.Y. State Bar Assn. (mcpl. health law sects.). E-mail: jjbacarroll@juno.com.

CARROLL, JULIAN MORTON, lawyer, former governor; b. Paducah, Ky., Apr. 16, 1931; s. Elvie B. and Eva (Heady) C.; m. Charlann Harting, July 22, 1951; children: Kenneth Morton, Iva Patrice, Bradley Harting, Ellyn Kriston. AA, Paducah Jr. Coll., 1952; AB, U. Ky., 1954, LLB, 1956. Bar: Ky. 1956. Ptnr. Emery & Carroll, Paducah, 1960-68; mem. Ky. Ho. of Reps., 1962-71, speaker, 1968-71; lt. gov. State of Ky., 1971-74, gov., 1974-79; of counsel Reed, Scent & Walton, Paducah, 1968-71; ptnr. Carroll & Assocs., Frankfort, Ky., 1980—. Chmn. Nat. Conf. Lt. Govs., 1974, Nat. Govs. Assn., 1978-79. Trustee Paducah Jr. Coll., Regency U. Lt. USAF, 1956-59. Recipient Minerva award U. Louisville, 1977, Man of Yr. award Advt. Club Louisville, 1978. Mem. ABA, Ky. Bar Assn., Franklin County Bar Assn., Optimist Club, Phi Delta. Democrat. Avocation: golf. Office: Carroll & Assocs 25 Fountain Pl Frankfort KY 40601-1942

CARROLL, KENT JEAN, retired naval officer; b. Newton, Iowa, Aug. 22, 1926; s. Lee A. and Mabel E. (McCormick) C.; m. Betty M. Harrington, Mar. 29, 1947; children: Craig, Debra Carroll Rollins, Lance S., Maureen Burt. BS in Naval Sci., U. Notre Dame, 1946; grad., U.S. Naval Postgrad. Sch., 1955, Naval War Coll., 1960, Army War Coll., 1965; BA in Internat. Affairs, George Washington U., 1965. Ensign USN, 1946, advanced through grades to vice adm., 1979; svc. in Korea and Vietnam; comdr. U.S.S. Sablefish, 1959-60, Submarine Divsn. 81, Divsn. 82, 1968-69, 69, U.S.S. Blue Ridge, 1970-72, Amphibious Squadron 10, 1972-73, Task Force 65, 1974-75, Naval Inshore Warfare Command, Atlantic Fleet, 1974-75, U.S. Naval Forces Marianas, 1975-77; dir. J-4 OJCS, Washington, 1977-81; comdr. Mil. Sealift Command, Washington, 1981-83. Decorated Navy D.S.M. with cluster, Def. D.S.M., Legion of Merit with 2 clusters; recipient John Paul Jones award Navy League, 1977; Presdl. citation for humanitarian svc., 1976, Rev. William Corby C.S.C. award U. Notre Dame, 1995. Mem. English Speaking Union (bd. dirs. 1999—). Home: Country Club NC 1600 Morganton Rd X 30 Pinehurst NC 28374-6862

CARROLL, KIM MARIE, nurse; b. Ottawa, Ill., Feb. 13, 1958; d. John J. and Charin E. (Reilley) Marmion; m. Thomas Christopher Carroll, Aug. 25, 1979; children: Christopher John, Meaghan Elizabeth, Sean Reilley. BSN, U. Denver, 1983; diploma, Copley Meml. Hosp. Sch. Nursing, Aurora, Ill., 1979. RN, Ill., Ind., Colo.; critical care practitioner. Staff nurse Penrose Hosp., Colorado Springs, Colo., 1979-83, asst. head nurse cardiac floor, 1983-84; asst. dir. nurses Big Meadows Nursing Home, Savanna, Ill., 1985-86, dir. nurses, 1986-88; clin. dir. Ind. Heart Physicians, Inc., Beech Grove, Ind., 1989-95; ambulatory care adminstr. The Gates Clinic, Denver, 1995-98; clin. mgr. Aurora Denver Cardiology Assoc., 1998—2002; triage nurse McKesson Health Solutions, Englewood, Colo., 2002—. Mem. Beta Sigma Phi (chpt. pres. 1988-89, rec. sec. 1991-92, treas. 1996-97), Sigma Theta Tau. Roman Catholic. Avocation: skiing. Home: 5293 S Cathay Way Aurora CO 80015-4859 Office: McKesson Health Solutions Harlequin Plz S Bldg Ste 106 7600 E Orchard Ave Englewood CO 80111

CARROLL, LINDA MARIE, vocologist; b. Sanford, Maine, July 29, 1956; d. Joseph Phillip C. and Julia Etta (Hollenbeck) Beals; m. William Riley, Nov. 1, 1998; 1 child, Jennifer Lassie Riley. MusB with distinction, BS with distinction, U. Maine, 1979; MS, Columbia U., 1993, MPhil, 1996, PhD, 2001. Cert. of clin. competence in speech-lang. pathology; cert. Lee Silverman Voice Treatment clinician. Voice tech., specialist Am. Inst. Voice & Ear Rsch., Phila., 1982-91; speech-lang. pathologist Lenox Hill Hosp., N.Y.C., 1993-95; instr. U. Iowa, Iowa City, 1995-96, Columbia U., N.Y.C., 1996-98; vocologist, speech pathologist Mt. Sinai Med. Ctr., N.Y.C., 1997—; asst. prof. NYU, 2000-01; asst. clin. prof. dept. otolayrngology Mt. Sinai Sch. Medicine, N.Y.C., 2002—. Guest faculty U. Maine, Orono, 1995; adj. lectr. Pace U., N.Y.C., 1996-2000; faculty mem. New Sch. Social Rsch., N.Y.C., 1994-99. Named Miss Maine, 1978; Carol N. Wilder fellow Columbia U., 1997-98; Feagin scholar U. Tulsa, 1998. Mem. Nat. Assn. Tchrs. Singing, N.Y. Singing Tchrs. Assn., Voice Found. Symposia, Pi Kappa Lambda, Mu Alpha Sigma. Avocations: cooking, entertaining. Home: Ste 1-B 424 W 49th St New York NY 10019-7290 Office: 5 E 98th St 1st Fl Ste 1653 New York NY 10029 E-mail: linda.carroll@mssm.edu.

CARROLL, LUCY ELLEN, choral director, music coordinator, educator; b. NYC, Oct. 11; d. Edward Joseph and Lucy Sophie (Czapszys) C. B in Music Edn., Temple U., 1968; MA, Trenton State Coll., 1973; D in Musical Arts, Combs Coll. Music, Phila., 1982. Cert. tchr. music, N.J., Pa., Nat. Cert., 1991. Tchr. music Log Coll. Jr. High Sch., Pa., 1968-72, Ind. (Pa.) High Sch., 1972-73, William Tennent High Sch., Warminster, Pa., 1973-98, dir. mus. theater, 1973-98; choir dir. St. John Bosco Parish Choir, 1999—2001; organist, dir. Carmelite Monastery, Phila., 1996—. Music coord. Centennial Schs., 1991-98; founder, dir. Madrigal Singers, Warminster, Pa., 1971-98; choral dir. Cabrini Coll., Radnor, Pa., 1974-77, First Day Singers, Phila., 1979-83, Combs Coll. Music, Phila., 1981-84, 87-88; choral adjudicator various Music festivals, 1973-98; theatre dir., Villa Joseph Marie (Holland), 1998-99; del. Internat. Arts Conf., Cambridge, Eng., 1992; adj. assoc. prof. Westminster Choir Coll., Princeton, 2002—; lectr. in field. Singer (operas Ambler Festival) Street Scene, 1970, Death of Bishop of Brindisi (premiere); (Robin Hood Dell) La Boheme; dir. (jazz theater piece N.Y.C.) Murder of Agamemnon, 1980, (drama) Power of Love (1705), 1986, (outdoor music theater) Vorspiel (Pa. Historic Commn. 1989); editor The Monastery Hymnal, 2002; columnist Polyphony mag., Adoremus Bulletin, 2002—; creator Churchmouse Squeaks cartoons, Monastery Mice cartoons; contbr. articles to profl. jours., and mags. Dir. Monastery Choir, Phila., 2001—. Recipient awards Writers of Future, 1985, 87, Andrew Ferraro award Combs Coll. Music, 1989, plaque for svc. to music Bucks County Commr., 1991, Disting. Citizen medal Southampton Twp., 1994, Harmony award Country Gentlemen Nat. Soc. for Preservation and Encouragement Barbershop Quartet Singing in Am., 1994; Scholar-In-Residence, Pa. Hist. and Museum Commn.; named Humanities Spkr. for 2000, Pa. Humanities Coun. Mem. Am. Choral Dirs. Assn., Sci. Fiction Fantasy Writers of Am., Am. Musicol. Soc., Am. Guild Organists, Organ Hist. Soc., Latin Liturgy Assn., Del. Valley Composers (choral cons. 1988-90), Hist. Soc. Pa., Smithsonian Assocs., Musical Fund Soc. of Phila., The Soc. for Am. Music, Pa. Music Educators Assn. (adv. bd. 1986-87, contbg. writer Spotlight on Tchg. Chorus 2003), Nat. ASsn. State Tchrs. of the Yr., Ephrata Cloister Assocs., Sigma Alpha Iota. Republican. Roman Catholic. Avocation: travel. Home: 712 High Ave Hatboro PA 19040-2418 E-mail: LucyCarroll@att.net.

CARROLL, MARIE-JEAN GREVE, retired educator, artist; b. Paterson, N.J., Dec. 19, 1930; d. William John and Charlotte Marie (Kranich) McGill; m. Theodore R. Greve, Nov. 4, 1950 (div. Oct. 1979); children: Richard W. Greve, Helen E. Greve Ficke, Theodore A. Greve; m. William P. Carroll, 1981 (div. 1989). BA in Art Edn., William Paterson Coll., Wayne, N.J., 1971; MA in Visual Art, 1976. Cert. art tchr., N.J. Art tchr. Pequannock (N.J.) Elem. Sch., 1971-72, Passaic Valley High Sch., Little Falls, N.J., 1972-77, 85-86, Ramapo High Sch., Franklin Lakes, NJ, 1986—2000; ret., 2000. Works exhibited at shows in Fla. galleries, 1983, Longboat Key Art Gallery, 1983,. 84, Manatee Art Gallery, 1984, Pike County Art Show, Milford, Pa., 1994, 95, 96, N.J. Printmakers Coun., Sommerville, Paterson Pub. Libr., 1998. Recipient art awards. Mem. NEA, Bergen County Edn. Assn., N.J. Edn. Assn., Nat. Art Edn. Assn. Avocations: poetry, swimming laps, golf.

CARROLL, MARSHALL ELLIOTT, architect; b. Durham, N.C., May 14, 1923; s. Dudley Dewitt and Eleanore (Elliott) C.; m. Dorothy Jane Grune, Mar. 28, 1953; married; children: Jane Dudley, Marshall Elliott, Frederick Grune. AB, Harvard Coll., 1943; student, Grad. Sch. Design, 1947-51. Assoc. G. Milton Small & Assos. (architects and engrs.), Raleigh, N.C., 1957-60; various positions to dep. exec. v.p. AIA, Washington, 1960-71; ptnr. Vincent G. Kling & Ptnrs., Phila., 1971-73; exec. asst. architect U.S. Capitol, 1973-89; ind. archtl. cons., 1989—. Mem. exec. com. US com. Internat. Coun. on Monuments and Sites, 1978-96, vice chmn., 1980-88, chmn., 1988-91, fellow, 1995, internat. v.p., mem. internat. exec. com., 1990-96; mem. Hist. Am. Bldg. Survey, Hist. Am. Engrng. Record, and Hist. Am. Landscape Survey, Found., 1996—, pres., 1996-99; mem. exec. com., chmn. com. on archtl. conservation Nat. Inst. for Conservation, 1975-85, vice chmn., 1983-85; lectr. Nantucket (Mass.) Preservation Inst., 1979-87; hist. preservation cons. for restoration of Arneri Palace, Korcula, Croatia, 1987—, for restoration of Tex. State Capitol, 1989-91, for restoration of Octagon House, Washington, DC, 1990-1997. Project dir. master plan for U.S. Capitol, 1976-81, U.S. Senate Office Sys. Rsch. Project, 1976-81, Thurgood Marshall Judiciary Office Bldg., Washington, 1986-89, restoration studies Russell and Dirksen Senate Office Bldgs., 1979-82, Capitol Hill Graphics Sys., 1977-81, Archtl. Graphic Stds., 6th, 7th, 8th edits., 1964-88. Pres. N.C. Symphony Soc., 1955-60; mem. exec. com. U.S. com. Internat. Ctr. for Conservation in Rome, 1973-89; alt. bd. dirs. Pennsylvania Ave. Devel. Corp., 1973-89; mem. Nat. Capitol Meml. Commn., 1973-89; alt. mem. U.S. Adv. Coun. on Hist. Preservation, 1973-89; mayor, chmn. governing bd. Village of Drummond, Md., 1976-77, treas., 1974-76; mem. gen. com. in charge Westtown Sch., Pa., 1993-2001; mem. D.C. Zoning Commn., 1987-89, D.C. Bd. Zoning Adjustment, 1987-89; mem. U.S. Commn. Fine Arts, Old Georgetown Bd., 1989-98, alt., 1998—; mem. Somerset Sch. Found., 1998-2001. Capt. USNR, 1944-46, 51-53. Fellow: AIA (chmn. com. on archtl. graphic stds. 1976—80, 1984—88, mem. com. on hist. resources 1981—89, Octagon restoration com. 1990—97); mem.: Assn. Preservation Tech. (pres. 1980—83). Democrat.

CARROLL, MARY COLVERT, corporate executive; b. Milw., June 5, 1940; d. Frederick Rolfing and Helen (McCall) Colvert; m. Andrew David Carroll; children: Sherri L. Oberg, Andrew David Carroll III. BA mgna cum laude, U. Miami, Fla., 1966. Bd. dirs. Phila. Suburban Corp., Bryn Mawr, 1979—; chmn. bd. Friends Independence Nat. Hist. Park, Phila., 1978-81; bd. dirs. Urban Affairs Coalition, Phila., 1979-90, advisor, 1990—; pres., founder Friends Conversation Hall, Phila., 1982-83; bd. dirs. Internat. House, Phila., 1982—98; chmn., founder Nat. Parks Mid-Atlantic Council, Phila., 1982—; vice chmn. bd. Nat. Parks and Conservation Assn., Washington, 1982-88; bd. dirs. Phila. First Econ. Devel. Coalition, 1983-90; chmn., founder, bd. dirs. Phila. Hospitality, Inc., 1998—2000; bd. dirs. World Affairs Council, Phila., 1984-88; bd. trustees Bryn Mawr (Pa.) Presbyn. Ch., 1984-90; mem. bd. advisors Independence Hall Assn., Phila., 1984-86; vice chair Phila. Hist. Preservation Corp., 1986-93; vice chmn. bd. Fort Mifflin on Del., Inc., Phila., 1986—2001; trustee William Penn Found., Phila., 1987-93. Hon. trade rep. of Nepal, 2002—. Bd. dirs. Met. YMCA, Preservation Action, 1993-97. Recipient Civic Environ. award Found for Architecture, 1983, Conservation Service award U.S. Dept. Interior, 1978, Friend of Nepal award Assn. Nepalis in the Americas, 2002. Mem. Merion Cricket Club. Republican. Presbyterian. Home and Office: 603 Winsford Rd Bryn Mawr PA 19010-3617

CARROLL, MARY PATRICIA, writer; b. Chgo., June 28, 1938; d. Anthony Bernard Carroll and Marie Cecilia Delaney. Student in writing, Columbia Coll., U. Fla.; BS in Humanities magna cum laude, Loyola U., Chgo., 1961, MSW, 1965; DSW, Smith Coll., 1970. Caseworker II Cook County Dept. Pub. Assistance, Chgo., 1961-64; sr. psychiat. social svc. worker Chgo. Bd. Health, Lower North Cmty. Mental Health Ctr., 1964—66; sch. social worker Sch. Dist. #81, Schiller Park, Ill., 1966—68; dist. dir. Family Svc. Assn. Greater Boston, 1970-73; program rep. United Cerebral Palsy Assns., N.Y.C., 1973-75; assoc. prof. George Williams Coll., 1975—77, Ind. U.-Purdue U., Indpls., 1977-81; assoc. prof., chmn. social work dept. U. Alaska, Anchorage, 1981-85; writer Mary P. Caroll Enterprises, 1985—. Contbr. articles, essays, short stories, poems to profl. and lit. publs. Recipient Hon. Mention award for fiction Writers Digest, 1987, for poetry, 1999; fellow VA Pub. Health, 1963-65, NIMH, 1968-70. Mem. Poetry Soc. of Va., Live Poets Soc., Amnesty Internat., Am. Acad. Poets, Nat. Com. to Preserve Social Security and Medicare. Democrat. Roman Catholic. Avocation: outdoor activities. E-mail: wnm4444@aol.com.

CARROLL, MICHAEL M. academic dean, mechanical engineering educator; b. Thurles, County Tipperary, Ireland, Dec. 8, 1936; came to U.S. 1960; s. Timothy and Catherine (Gleeson) C.; m. Carolyn F. Gahagan, Oct. 31, 1964; children— Patricia, Timothy J. BA, Univ. Coll., Galway, Ireland, 1958, MA, 1959; PhD, Brown U., 1965; DSc, Nat. U. Ireland, 1979, LLD (hon), 1992. Asst. prof. mech. engrng. U. Calif., Berkeley, 1965-69, assoc. prof., 1969-73, prof., 1973-83; Shell disting. chair Shell Cos. Found., 1983-88; dean George R. Brown Sch. Engrng., Burton J. and Ann McMurtry prof. engrng. Rice U., Houston, 1988-98, prof. engrng., 1998—. Bd. dirs. Daniel Industries Inc.; cons. TerraTek Labs., Salt Lake City, 1976-84, Thoratec Lab., Berkeley, Calif., 1976-84, Sci. Applications Internat., La Jolla, Calif., 1984—, JAG Industries, Trinidad, Calif., 1984—, Sandia Labs., Albuquerque, 1991—, Brit. Petroleum, Houston, 1991—, Adams Golf, 1998—. Contbr. articles to profl. jours.; mem. editorial bds. of tech. jours. Fellow ASME, Am. Acad. Mechanics (pres. 1994-95), Am. Acad. Arts and Scis.; mem. NAE, Am. Soc. Engrng. Edn. (gov. bd., deans coun. 1992—), Soc. Engrng. Sci. (bd. dirs., v.p., pres.), Sigma Xi. Roman Catholic. Avocations: crossword puzzles, golf, play writing. Home: 48 T Huxley Ln Missouri City TX 77459-1901 Office: Rice U Sch Computational & Applied Math PO Box 1892 MS 134 Houston TX 77251-1892

CARROLL, MICHAEL PATRICK, assemblyman; b. Fayetteville, N.C., Apr. 8, 1958; m. Sharon Carroll; children: Sean, James, Brian, Jane, Benjamin, Robert. BA, Johns Hopkins U., 1980; JD, Rutgers Newark Sch. of Law, 1983. Atty. pvt. practice, 1983—; assemblyman N.J. Gen. Assembly, 1995—. Rep. county com. Morris Twp., 1980—83, 1986—, chair, 1986. Mem. Morris County Young Reps., 1980—84. Mem.: Federalist Soc., Morris County Bar Assn., Friendly Sons of St. Patrick (youth soccer/hockey coach), Knights of Columbus. Republican. Roman Catholic. Office: 86 S St Ste A-3 Morristown NJ 07960 E-mail: AsmCarroll@njleg.org.

CARROLL, PHILIP JOSEPH, JR., engineering company executive; b. New Orleans, Sept. 24, 1937; s. Philip Joseph and Rosemary Agnes (McEntee) Carroll; m. Charlene Marie Phillips, Jan. 3, 1959; children: Phillip III, Kenneth, Bruce. BS in Physics, Loyola U., New Orleans, 1958; MS in Physics, Tulane U., 1961. Petroleum engr. Shell Oil Co., New Orleans, L.A., N.Y.C. and Midland, Tex., 1961—73; dir. energy conservation div. U.S. Dept. Commerce, Washington, 1973—74; exec. dir. Nat. Ind. Energy Conservation Coun., Washington, 1974; regional engr., mgr. so. exploration and prodn. Shell Oil Co., New Orleans, 1974—75, div. mgr. prodn., western exploration and prodn. Houston, 1975—78, gen. mgr. prodn., western ops., 1978—79, gen. mgr. plans and integration, 1979, v.p. pub. affairs, 1979—85; mng. dir. Shell Internat. Gas, Shell Internat. Petroleum Co., London, 1985—86; sr. v.p, adminstrn. Shell Oil Co., Houston, 1986—88, exec. v.p. adminstrn., 1988—93, pres., 1993—98, mem. bd. dirs., 1990; chmn., CEO Fluor Corp, Irvine, Calif., 1998—. Bd. dirs. Boise Cascade Corp. Trustee Com. for Econ. Devel., 1991—, Baylor Coll. Medicine, Boys & Girls Clubs of Am.; mem. Gov.'s Bus. Coun. (Tex.), Nat. Petroleum Coun., Conf. Bd., 1991—, Nat. Action Coun. for Minorities in Engrng., 1993—; adv. bd. mem. Salvation Army; bd. adminstrs. adv. bd. mem. Ctr. Bioenviron. Rsch. Tulane U.; bd. dirs. Am. Petroleum Inst., Am. Air Mus., Cen. Houston, Tex. Med. Ctr., Nat. Action Coun. for Minorities in Engrng. Master: 25 Yr. Club Petroleum Industry; mem.: Champions Golf Club, River Oaks Country Club, Tchefuncta Country Club (Covington, La.). Avocation: golf.

CARROLL, RAOUL LORD, lawyer, investment banker; b. Washington, Mar. 16, 1950; s. John Thomas and Gertrude Barbara (Jenkins) C.; m. Elizabeth Jane Coleman, Mar. 22, 1980; children: Alexandria Nicole, Christina Elizabeth. BS, Morgan State U., 1972; JD, St. Johns U., Jamaica, N.Y., 1975; postgrad., Georgetown U., 1980-81. Bar: N.Y. 1976, D.C. 1979, U.S. Dist. Ct. D.C. 1979, U.S. Supreme Ct. 1979, U.S. Dist. Ct. (so. and ea. dist.) N.Y. 1982. Asst. U.S. atty. Office U.S. Atty., Dept. Justice, Washington, 1979-80. Assoc. mem. U.S. Bd. Vets. Appeals, Washington, 1980-81; ptnr. Hart, Carroll & Chavers, Washington, 1981-86, Bishop, Cook, Purcell & Reynolds, Washington, 1986-89; gen. counsel U.S. Dept. Vets. Affairs, 1989-91; pres. Govt. Nat. Mortgage Assn., HUD, 1991-92; COO, M.R. Beal & Co., 1993-95; chmn. Christalex Ptnrs., Inc., 1995-2002, Am. Ctr. for Internat. Leadership, Balt.; trustee Christian Bros. Investment Svcs., Inc., N.Y.C., WINCOM, Inc., Century City, Calif., chmn. 1997—, pres. Pro-Banker Securities LLC, 2002—. Trustee The Enterprise Found., Columbia, Md. Capt. U.S. Army, 1975-79. Decorated Joint Service Commendation medal, Army Commendation medal; named Outstanding Young Man Am., U.S. Jaycees, 1979. Em. N.Y. State Bar Assn., D.C. Bar Assn., Washington Bar Assn., Asst. U.S. Attys. Assn., Omega Psi Phi. Republican. Baptist. Home: 7821 Morningside Dr NW Washington DC 20012-1448 Office: 1900 Ave of the Stars 5th Flr Los Angeles CA 90067

CARROLL, RAY DEAN, SR., veterinarian; b. Barry, Tex., Oct. 19, 1927; s. James William and Blanche Estelle (Jordan) C.; m. Lula Pearl Mayfield, June 6, 1957; children: James William, Ray Dean Jr. Assoc., Hillsboro Jr. Coll., 1948; BS in Animal Sci., Tex. A&M U., 1950, DVM, 1957. Vet. Carroll & Harpe Animal Hosp., Corsicana, Tex., 1957—; instr. Navarro Coll., Corsicana, 1970-95. Author: Beef Cattle Science Handbook, vol. 16, 1979. Mem. found. bd. Navarro Coll., 1985—, vice-chmn., trustee, 1990. With USN, 1945-46, 51-52. Mem. AVMA, Tex. Polled Hereford Assn. (pres. 1992-96), Navarro County Ext. Beef Commn. (chmn. 1960—). Democrat. Methodist. Home: 2203 Highland Cir Corsicana TX 75110-1611 Office: Carroll & Harper Animal Hosp 2508 W 2nd Ave Corsicana TX 75110-2520

CARROLL, ROBERT FRANKLIN, communications company executive; b. Bartow, Fla., June 18, 1931; s. Robert Franklin Sr. and Emma H. Carroll; m. Gwendolyn J. Carroll, Jan. 6, 1963; children: Tosca, Denise, Robert. BA in Biology, Fla. A&M U., 1958; MA in Pub. Adminstrn., Colo. U., 1962; postgrad., Yale U., 1969; D Humanities, Taiwan U., 1978. Cert. tchr., Fla., N.Y. Tchr. Union Acad., Bartow, 1958-60, asst. prin., 1960-61; asst. commr. N.Y.C. Human Resources Adminstrn., 1962-64, dep. commr., 1965-72; v.p. CCNY, N.Y.C., 1972-76; chief of staff U.S. Congressman Charles Rangel, Washington, 1976-81; chmn., CEO R.F. Carroll & Co., Inc., Washington, 1981—. Dep. commr. Presdl. Campaign of John Lindsay, 1972; asst. campaign mgr. Gubernatorial Campaign of Sen. Scott Kelley, Fla., 1961-62. Sgt. USAF, 1951-55, Korea. Recipient Pub. Adminstr. of Yr., U.S. Dept. HEW, 1965, Educator of Yr. award Cmty. Edn. Assn., 1973. Mem. Pub. Rels. Soc. Am. (bd. dirs. 1982-92), Mill River Country Club (sec. 1984—, Club Champion 1987, 89, 90), Alpha Phi Alpha. Democrat. Avocations: golf, reading, travel. Home: 37 Reynolds Rd Glen Cove NY 11542

CARROLL, ROBERT LYNN, biology educator, vertebrate paleontologist, museum curator; b. Kalamazoo, May 5, 1938; s. John Henry and Arvella Mae (Wickerham) Carroll; m. Helen Louise Swaim, June 22, 1961 (dec. Jan. 1972); 1 child, David Lynferd; m. Anna Di Turi, Sept. 26, 1987. BS, Mich. State U.,

1959; MA, Harvard U., 1961, PhD, 1963. NRC postdoctoral fellow McGill U., Montreal, Que., Can., 1962-63, asst. prof. zoology, 1964-69, assoc. prof. biology, 1969-74, prof. biology, 1974—, Strathcona prof. zoology, 1987—; curator vertebrate paleontology Redpath Mus., McGill U., 1965—, dir., 1985-90, 98-99, chmn. dept. biology, 1990-95. Vis prof biol Sir George Williams Univ, Montreal, 1965—66. Author: (book) Vertebrate Paleontology and Evolution, 1987, Patterns and Processes of Vertebrate Evolution, 1997; co-author: Paleontology - The History of Life, 1989; editor: Leposondyli, 1998; co-editor: Paleontology, The Evolutionary History of Amphibians, 2000; editor (assoc ed): Can Jour Earth Scis, 1984—93, Jour Vertebrate Paleontology, 1989—92; editor: (consulting ed) Trans Royal Soc Edinburgh: Earth Scis, 1993—; editor: (technical ed) Jour Paleontology, 2000—. Mem educ bd Linn Soc London, 1999—. Recipient Billings Medal for contbns to paleontology, Geological Asn Can; fellow NSF Postdoctoral, Brit Mus, London, 1963—64. Fellow: Linnean Soc, Royal Soc Can (Miller medal 2001); mem.: World Congress Herpetology (treas 1989—94), Am Soc Zoologists, Soc Vertebrate Paleontology (hon.; pres 1982—83), Paleontological Soc (Schuchert award 1978), Soc Study Evolution. Avocations: hiking, singing. Office: Redpath Mus/McGill Univ 859 Sherbrooke St W Montreal QC Canada H3A 2K6 E-mail: robertc@shared1.lan.mcgill.ca.

CARROLL, ROBERT W. retired business executive; b. Ossining, N.Y., May 29, 1923; s. John Francis and Catherine Veronica (Coyne) C.; m. Mary Bernardine Dugan, June 1, 1946; children: Kevin, Dennis, Terrence, Maura, Monica. Student, Sch. Commerce, NYU, 1952-56, Mgmt. Inst., 1957. With N.Y. Cen. R.R., 1942-68, asst. to sec., 1953-54, asst. sec., 1954-59, sec., 1959-68; sr. asst. sec. Penn Cen. Transp. Co., 1968-70, sec., 1971-76, also former v.p., sec., dir. several railroad, real estate, trucking and fin.-oriented subsidiaries, 1971-76; exec. dir. adminstrn. Law Offices La Brum and Doak, Phila., 1976-88; prin. Robert W. Carroll & Assoc., Mgmt. Cons., Radnor, Pa., 1989-93. Corp. sec. Pitts. and Lake Erie R.R. Co., 1959-79; v.p., sec., dir. Montour R.R. Co., Montour Land Co., Youngstown and So. Ry. Co., 1959-79; rep. Kissel Blake Orgn., Inc., 1983-89. Served with USCGR, 1942-46. Recipient Legion of Honor Chapel of the Four Chaplains, 1984. Mem. ABA (law office adminstrv. assoc. 1985-89), Internat. Assn. Legal Adminstrs. (bd. dirs 1987-88, v.p. 1987—, pres.-elect Phila. chapter 1988), VFW, Soc. Friendly Sons St. Patrick, Pa. Soc. K.C. (4), World Affairs Coun. Phila., Am. Soc. of Corp. Secs., Inc., Overbrook Golf Club (Bryn Mawr, Pa.). Home: 9 Ridgewood Rd Wayne PA 19087-3713

CARROLL, ROBERT WAYNE, mathematics educator; b. Chgo., May 10, 1930; s. Walter Scott and Dorothy (Le Monnier) C.; m. Berenice Jacobs, Sept. 7, 1957 (div. June 1974); children: David Leon, Malcolm Scott; m. Alice von Neumann, Sept. 1974 (div. Mar. 1977); m. Joan Miller, Jan. 1979. BS, U. Wis., 1952; PhD, U. Md., 1959. Aero. research scientist NASA, Cleve., 1952-54; NSF postdoctoral fellow, 1959-60; asst. prof. Rutgers U., 1960-63, assoc. prof., 1963-64; assoc. prof. math. U. Ill., Urbana, 1964-67, prof., 1967-97, prof. emeritus, 1997—. Author: Abstract Methods in Partial Differential Equations, 1969, Transmutation and Operator Differential Equations, 1979, Transmutation, Scattering Theory and Special Functions, 1982, Transmutation Theory and Applications, 1985, Mathematical Physics, 1988, Topics in Soliton Theory, 1991, Quantum Theory, Deformation and Integrability, 2000, Calculus Revisited, 2002; co-author: Singular and Degenerate Cachy Problems, 1976; assoc. editor Jour. Applicable Analysis, 1970—; contbr. over 180 articles to math. and physics jours. Served with U.S. Army, 1954-57. Mem. Am. Math. Soc., Am. Phys. Soc. Avocations: foreign languages, cello. Home: 1314 Brighton Dr Urbana IL 61801-6417 Office: Univ Ill Math Dept Urbana IL 61801

CARROLL, ROGER CLINTON, medical biology educator; b. Mt. Clemens, Mich., Sept. 28, 1947; s. Lee Stanley and Evelyn Marie (Badgett) C.; m. Andrea Kristine Skrec, Sept. 13, 1969; children: Brian Roger, Alicia Helene. BS, Cornell U., 1969, PhD, 1977. Rsch. assoc. U. Calif. San Diego, LaJolla, 1976-78, U. Okla. Health Sci. Ctr., Oklahoma City, 1978-79, asst. prof. dept. pathology, 1979-80, adj. asst. prof. dept. biochemistry, dept. physiology, 1980-84; assoc. prof. dept. med. genetics U. Tenn. Med. Ctr., Knoxville, 1984-90, prof. dept. med. genetics, 1990—, prof. dept. surgery, 1993-2000, prof. dept. anesthesiology, dir. anesthesiology rsch., 2000—. Asst. mem. Okla. Med. Rsch. Found. (Merrick award 1984), Oklahoma City, 1982-84; cons. Nat. Heart Lung and Blood Inst., 1985— (grantee 1980-90). Co-editor: (jour.) Seminars in Thrombosis and Hemostasis, vol. 1, 1995; contbr. articles to profl. jours., chpts. to books. Mem. Am. Heart Assn. (thrombosis coun., rsch. com. chmn., peer rev. com. chmn., Tenn. affiliate, grantee 1981-84, 1987—), Sigma Xi. Democrat. Roman Catholic. Avocations: swimming, gourmet cooking. Home: 706 Ala Dr Knoxville TN 37920-6364 Office: U Tenn Med Ctr Grad Sch Medicine 1924 Alcoa Hwy Knoxville TN 37920-1511

CARROLL, ROSEMARY FRANCES, historian, educator, lawyer; b. Providence, Oct. 15, 1935; d. Francis Edward and Katherine Loretta (Graham) C. AB, Brown U., 1957; MA, Wesleyan U., 1962; PhD, Rutgers U., 1968; JD, U. Iowa, 1983. Bar: Iowa 1983. Asst. prof. history Notre Dame Coll., N.Y.C., 1968-70; vis. asst. prof. history Denison U., Granville, Ohio, 1970-71; asst. prof. history Coe Coll., Cedar Rapids, Iowa, 1971-75, assoc. prof. history, 1975-84, prof. history, 1984—2000, chair dept. history, 1988—2000, affirmative action officer, 1973-98, prelaw advisor, 1988-98, rep. Truman Found., 1988, faculty rep. Rhodes Scholarship Trust, 1993-98, faculty rep. Brit. Marshal Scholarship, 1996-98, Henry and Margaret Hagg disting. prof. history, 2000—01, Henry and Margaret Hagg disting. prof. history emerita, 2001—. Contbr. articles to profl. jours. Vol. lawyer Legal Services Corp. Iowa, Cedar Rapids, 1984—2003, mem. adv. coun., 1985—2003. Olmsted fellow Hoover Presdl. Libr. Assn., 1987-92, Hoover grantee, 1992-94, NEH grantee, 1992-93. Mem. ABA, AAUP, AAUW, Iowa Bar Assn. (legal heritage com. 1988—), Linn County Bar Assn. (continuing legal edn. com. 1990-2002), Linn County Women Atty. (treas. 1990-91), Orgn. Am. Historians (membership com. 1978), So. Hist. Assn. (membership com. 1986-87, 88-89, 96-98), So. Assn. Womens Historians (pres. 1975-76, membership com. 1987-88, 89-90, 96-98), Phi Kappa Phi. Roman Catholic. Avocations: bicycling, swimming. E-mail: rfcarroll1@aol.com.

CARROLL, ROSSYE O'NEAL, college administrator; b. Corsicana, Tex., Sept. 27, 1929; s. Thearon Andrew and Elnora (Cook) C.; m. Neverro Jean Randle, June 6, 1958 (div. June 1982); children: Arnett, Brenda, Marvin, Stephen, Rossye Jr., Sheila, Vicky, Karen, Edwin; m. Bertha Lee Johnson, Aug. 23, 1982. BA, U. Nev., Las Vegas, 1982; AAS, C.C. of So. Nev., North Las Vegas, 1989. Cert. secondary edn. tchr., Nev. Instr. 523 Field Tng. Squadron USAF, Las Vegas, 1969-75, propulsion supt. 247th Field Maintenance, 1975-76, propulsion supt. 2d Field Maintenance Shreveport, La., 1976-78; supr. maintenance Meadows Mall, Las Vegas, 1978-79; substitute tchr. Clark County Sch. Dist., Las Vegas, 1979-84; asst. to dean for Nellis Zone continuing edn. C.C. of So. Nev., North Las Vegas, 1984—. Mem. choir 2d Bapt. Ch., Las Vegas, 1990—. Sr. master sgt. USAF, 1950-78. Recipient Air Force Commendation medal, 1975, Meritorious Svc. medal, 1978. Mem. AAUP, NEA, Nat. Coun. Instructional Adminstrs., Nev. Faculty Alliance. Democrat. Baptist. Avocations: guitar, choir, basketball. Home: PO Box 9856 Las Vegas NV 89191-0856 Office: C C So Nev 4475 England Ave Ste 217 Las Vegas NV 89191-6506 E-mail: rossyecarroll@ccsn.nevada.edu.

CARROLL, ROY, retired academic administrator; b. England, Arkansas, Dec. 8, 1929; m. Eleanor Kate Moorefield, 1953; children: Jane, Linda. BA cum laude, Ouachita Bapt. U., 1951; MA, Vanderbilt U., 1959, PhD, 1964. Math. tchr. Baker High Sch., Columbus, Ga., 1955; asst. prof. history and polit. sci. Mercer U., Macon, Ga., 1959-65; prof. history, chmn. dept. history and polit. sci. Armstrong State Coll., Savannah, Ga., 1965-69; prof. history, chmn. dept. history Appalachian State U., Boone, N.C., 1969-79; v.p. planning gen. adminstrn. U. N.C. System, 1979-90, 91-96, sr. v.p., v.p. acad. affairs, 1996-99, ret., 1999; interim chancellor U. N.C., Asheville, 1990-91. Mem. N.C. Justice Edn. and Tng. Standards Commn., 1979-90, chmn. Planning Com. of the Commn., 1981-88; mem. adv. bd. Inst. Transp. Rsch. and Edn., Rsch. Triangle Park, 1980—; bd. dirs. Western N.C. Devel. Assn., 1990-91, N.C. State Employees Credit Union, 1990-91, Rsch. Triangle Inst., 1996-2000; trustee Appalachian State U., 2000—. Contbr. articles to profl. jours. Inf. officer U.S. Army, 1951-53, Japan, Korea. Fulbright scholar, Eng., 1958-59. Home: 6811 Huntingridge Rd Chapel Hill NC 27517-8673 Office: U North Carolina Gen Adminstrn PO Box 2688 Chapel Hill NC 27515-2688 E-mail: rcl@ga.unc.edu.

CARROLL, STEPHEN DOUGLAS, chemist, researcher; b. Clarendon, Ark., Nov. 2, 1943; s. Albert Genson and Wilma Mae (Hill) C.; m. Nonnie Lee Dyer, June 8, 1991; children: Geoffrey Genson, Raymond Loyd. BA, Hendrix Coll., 1965; MS, U. Ark., 1970. Del. chemist Chicopee Mfg. Co., North Little Rock, Ark., 1969-73, Mgr. Quality Assurance, 1973-80; cons. self employed, Clarendon, Ark., 1980-82; rsch. asst. U. Ark., Marianna, 1982-87, rsch. specialist, 1987-98, rsch. assoc., 1998—. Mem. Am. Chem. Soc. Democrat. Methodist. Avocations: photography, writing, painting. Office: U Ark Highway 1 Byp Marianna AR 72360 E-mail: dcarroll@uark.edu.

CARROLL, TERENCE EVAN, professional society administrator; b. Berkley, Mich., Aug. 21, 1925; s. Philip Joseph Carroll and Effie Jeanette Grubb; m. Selma Wineberg, June 15, 1949 (div. Sept. 2019); children: David, Daniel, Julie; m. Sally Irene Aufrecht, Sept. 20, 1971. BA, Wayne State U., Detroit, 1949; MA, Columbia U., N.Y.C., 1950. Exec. v.p., CEO League Life Ins. Co., Detroit, 1960—71; exec. dir. Nat. Inst. on Rehab. and Health, Washington, 1971—87, Comprehensive Health Planning Coun., Detroit, 1987—93; pres. Nat. Assn. for Pub. Health Policy, Reston, Va., 1993—. Adj. assoc. prof. Wayne State U., Detroit, 1972—92. Cpl. Air Corps U.S. Army, 1943—46. Home: 11661 Charter Oak Ct Reston VA 20190 Office: Nat Assn Pub Health Policy 11661 Charter Oak Ct Reston VA 20190-4533

CARROLL, THOMAS LAWRENCE, JR., film and video producer; b. Kansas City, Mo., Apr. 3, 1931; s. Thomas Lawrence C. and Anna Alberta (Davis) Kelley; m. Carol Dieringer, May 4, 1997; children: Catherine Spencer, Cadence Beth, Thomas Leigh, Susan Davis. BA, U. N.C., 1953. Film prodn. assoc. Audio Prodns., Inc., N.Y.C., 1955-57; writer-dir. Paul Hance Prodns., Inc., N.Y.C., 1957-59; freelance writer, producer, dir. Norwalk, Conn., 1959-75; pres. In-sight Into Communication, Inc., Westport, Conn., 1975—. Dir. rsch. and writing U.S. Internat. Transp. Exposition, 1982, Internat. Trade Fairs, 1959, 60, 62. Prin. works include (documentaries) The American Navy in Vietnam, 1967, The Small Boat Navy, 1967, Tool Steel Today, 1974, Last Days of the Warrior, 1975, The Trestle at Ju'aymah, 1980, Introducing the Breed Air Bag, 1984, Safe Handling of Sulfuric Acid, 1985, The Saint Thomas Choir School, 1988, Introducing the Wadsworth Athaneum, 1988, Warehouse Operating Procedures, 1992, Sleep Better, Live Better, 1993, USS Houston, The Galloping Ghost, 1996, The UNIPOL Polyethylene Process, 2000, sales, tng. and corp. presentations. First student mgr. Sta. WUNC-FM, U. N.C., 1953. Home and Office: 22 Great Hill Rd Newtown CT 06470-1725

CARROLL, WARREN HASTY, retired historian; s. Herbert Allen and Gladys Harry Carroll; m. Anne Westhoff, June 7, 1967. BA, Bates Coll., 1953; MA, Columbia U., 1954, PhD, 1957; LLD (hon.), Christendom Coll., 1999. Instr. history Ind. U., Bloomington, Ind., 1957—58; asst. command historian Second AF Strategic Air Command, Barksdale AFB, La., 1958—59; legis. asst. Congressman John G. Schmitz, Washington, 1960—62; founder, pres. Christendom Coll., Front Royal, Va., 1975—85, prof. history, 1985—2002, ret., 2002. Bd. dirs. Christendom Ednl. Corp., Front Royal, Seton Sch., Manassas, Va., Aid to Ch. in Russia, Leesburg, Va. Author: 1917-Red Banners, White Mantle, 1981, Our Lady of Guadalupe and the Conquest of Darkness, 1983, History of Christendom, 1985, 1987, The Guillotine and the Cross, 1986; contbr. With Signal Corps. U.S. Army, 1955—57, Japan. Mem.: Fellowship of Cath. Scholars. Republican. Roman Cath. Avocation: writing. Home: 8061 Community Drive Manassas VA 20109 Office: Christendom College 134 Christendom Drive Front Royal VA 22630 E-mail: warren.h.carroll@trincomm.org.

CARROLL, WILLIAM, publishing company executive; Mgr., dir. Auto Book Press, Coda Publs.; dir., N.Mex. Books Coda Publs., Raton, N.Mex. Office: New Mex Books Coda Publs PO Box 71 Raton NM 87740-0071

CARROLL, WILLIAM KENNETH, law educator, psychologist, theologian; b. Oak Park, Ill., May 8, 1927; s. Ralph Thomas and Edith (Fay) C.; m. Frances Louise Forgue; children: Michele, Brian. BS in Edn., BA in Philosophy, Quincy Coll., Ill., 1950; MA, Duquesne U., 1964; STL, Catholic U., 1965; PhD, U. Strasbourg, France, 1968; JD, Northwestern U., 1972. Bar: Ill. 1972, U.S. Dist. Ct. (no. dist.) Ill 1972, U.S. Ct. Appeals (7th cir.) 1973; lic. clin. psychologist, Ill. Asst. editor Franciscan Press, Chgo., 1955-60; asst. prof. psychology and religion Carlow Coll., Pitts., 1962-65, Loyola U., Chgo., 1968-70; staff atty. Fed. Defender Program, Chgo., 1972-75; prof. law John Marshall Law Sch., Chgo., 1975—. Bd. dirs. Am. Inst. Adlerian Studies, 1982—; law reporter ABA Criminal Justice Mental Health Standards Project, 1981-83; cons. legal issues, Am. Psych. Assn.; standing com. on mental health law, Illinois. Author: (with Kosnik et al.) Human Sexuality, 1977; Eyewitness Testimony, Strategies and Tactics, 1984; contbg. author: By Reason of Insanity, 1983, Law for Illinois Psychologists, 1985, Law and Mental Health Professionals, 2002. Bd. dirs. Chgo. Sch. Profl. Psychology, 1978-82; mem. bd. advisors Ill. Sch. Profl. Psychology, 1985. Recipient Am. Juris award, 1970; U. Chgo. scholar, 1968-69. Fellow Inst. Social and Behavioral Pathology (chmn. 1987—); mem. ABA, AAUP, APA (Outstanding Contbn. to Psychology award 1998, com. on legal issues 1995—), Ill. Psychol. Assn., Cath. Theol. Soc. Am. Avocation: pvt. pilot. Office: John Marshall Law Sch 315 S Plymouth Ct Chicago IL 60604-3968 E-mail: 7carroll@jmls.edu.

CARROLL, WILLIAM MARION, financial services executive; b. Harrisburg, Oreg., May 7, 1932; s. Richard Eldon Carroll and Carolyn Flora (Williams) Bowles; m. Alma Louise Holmes; children: Kris, Karolyn, Mary. Student, Drake U., 1949-50; BCE, Oreg. State U., 1952; postgrad., US Corps Engrs, Anchorage, 1953, LaSalle U. Extension, Chgo., 1953-54. Civil engr., water resources U.S. Army CE, various locations, 1953-55; constrn. engr. U.S. Geol. Survey, Tacoma, 1956-58; owner, chief exec. officer Carroll Constrn. Co., Portland, Oreg., 1958-68; chmn., ptnr. Oakdell Cos., San Antonio, 1968-76; chmn., owner J C Corp., Bakersfield, Calif., 1972-75; owner, dir. Civic Savs. & Loan Assn., Irving, Tex., 1975-78; owner, CEO Metro Properties, Metro Fin., Dallas, 1977—; chmn., CEO The Seaford Group, Dallas, 1985—, Tri-Mark Constrn. Mgmt. Inc., Fla., Tex., Calif., 1984—. Dir. Property Solutions USA, Inc.; chmn. Tri Source In. Mem. ASCE, Am. Soc. Mil. Engrs., Nat. Asbestos Coun., Am. Geophys. Union, Am. Vets, Am. Legion, Alpha Tau Omega, Masons, Shriners. Republican. Avocations: golf, tennis, fishing. Home and Office: 9396 Huebner Rd Bldg B San Antonio TX 78240-1505 E-mail: bcmetro@juno.com.

CARRON, RONALD JOSEPH, electric power industry professional; b. North Dupo, Ill., Mar. 29, 1936; s. Albert Joseph Carron and Edith Cathrina Blais; m. Ellen C. Clark, July 6, 1936; children: Ronda Beth, Debra Ann, Ronald Joseph II. AS, Sr. N.C.O. Acad., Gunther AFB, Ala., 1989. Weldor A.O. Smith Corp., Granite City, Ill., 1963-75; power plant op. supr. Ctrl. Ill. Pub. Svc., Coffeen, 1977-93, ret., 1993. Adv. bd. Nat. SEC Counsel, Washington, 1988-93. Baseball coach Am. Legion Post 95, Vandalia, Ill., 1987. With USNR, 1953-79, USAFR, 1979-93. Republican. Roman Catholic. Avocations: fishing, hunting, playing guitar, kids home repair. Home: 31734 Shelton Dr Springfield LA 70462-8211

CARROTHERS, GERALD ARTHUR PATRICK, environmental and city planning educator; b. Saskatoon, Sask., Can., July 1, 1925; BArch, U. Man., Can., 1948, MArch, 1951; MCP, Harvard U., 1953; PhD, MIT, 1959. Lectr. architecture U. Man., Winnipeg, 1948-52; research asst. regional sci. Mass. Inst. Tech., Cambridge, 1953-56; asst. prof. town and regional planning U. Toronto, Ont., Can., 1956-60; assoc. prof. to prof. city planning U. Pa., Phila., 1960-67, chmn. dept. city planning, 1961-65; founding dir. Inst. Environ. Studies, 1965-67; prof. York U., Downsview, Ont., 1968—, founding dean faculty environ. studies, 1968-76. Chmn. U. Toronto-York U. Joint Program in Transp., 1971-78; adviser Central Mortgage and Housing Corp., Can., 1967-77; vis. prof. U. Nairobi, Kenya, 1978-80; mem. founding bd. dirs. Can. Urban Inst., 1988. Fellow World Acad. Art and Sci., Royal Archtl. Inst. Can., Can. Inst. Planners (founding editor Plan Can., 1959, councillor 1968-70); mem. Am. Inst. Cert. Planners (life), Regional Sci. Assn. (founding mem., founding editor Papers 1954, pres. 1970-71), Ont. Assn. Architects (life), Ont. Profl. Planners Inst. (founding registrar, founding bd. dirs. 1985). Home: 24 Bertmount Ave Toronto ON Canada M4M 2X9 Office: York U Fac Environ Studies 4700 Keele St Toronto ON Canada M4M 2X9

CARROW, LEON ALBERT, physician; b. Chgo., Jan. 18, 1924; s. Charles and Mollie (Sachs) C.; m. Joan Twaddell, June 21, 1974; children by previous marriage— Elizabeth, James. BS, U. Chgo., 1945, MD, 1947. Intern Cook County Hosp. and Chgo. Lying-in Hosp., 1947-48; resident Chgo. Wesley Meml. Hosp., Chgo. Maternity Center, 1949-51; sr. attending physician in obstetrics and gynecology Northwestern Meml. Hosp., 1954-91, sr. attending physician emeritus, 1991—, also past chief of staff. Asso. prof. obstetrics and gynecology Northwestern U. Med. Sch., 1967-73, prof. clin. obstetrics and gynecology, 1973-91, prof. emeritus, 1991—. Contbr. articles to profl. jours. Served with AUS, 1944-46; to capt. USAF, 1952-53. Fellow A.C.S.; mem. Ill., Chgo. med. socs., AMA, Chgo. Gynecology Soc., Am. Soc. Cytology, Central Assn. Obstetrics and Gynecology. Home: 566 Cedar St Winnetka IL 60093-2338

CARROW, MILTON MICHAEL, law educator; b. N.Y.C., Sept. 13, 1912; s. Samuel and Ethel (Berlin) Carrow; m. Betsey Wood Hall, Nov. 2, 1940 (div. 1968); children: David M, Thomas E, Deborah, James H, Emily W; m. Eve Wagner Cooper, Feb. 28, 1969 (div. 1986); m. Barbara M Barski, Nov. 2, 1996. AB, Syracuse U., 1933, postgrad., 1933-34; JD, Harvard U., 1937. Bar: NY 1938. Assoc. Legal Aid Soc., Rochester, N.Y., 1937-38, Lincoln Epworth & Nathan Sweedler, 1938-42, Emil Schlesinger, 1946-48; pvt. practice, 1948-53; ptnr. Lavine & Carrow, N.Y.C., 1953-59, Landis, Carrow, Benson & Tucker, N.Y.C., 1959-70, Carrow, Bernson, Hoeniger, Freitag & Abbey, 1970-73; dir. Ctr. for Adminstrv. Justice, ABA, 1973-77, Nat. Center for Adminstrv. Justice, Consortium of Univs. of Washington Met. Area, 1977-79; pres. Nat. Center for Adminstrv. Justice, 1979-82. Adj. asst. prof. Law Sch. NYU, 1964—68; cons. Nat. Adv. Com. Civil Disorders, 1967; mem. faculty appellate judges seminar Inst. Jud. Adminstrn., 1969—70; vis. prof. Nat. Law Ctr. George Washington U., 1973—80; adj. prof. Georgetown U., 1980—81, rsch. prof. pub. policy, 1983—; vice chmn. Weston Charter Comm., Conn., 1965—66; counsel UN We Believe, 1962—72; vis. intervenor XVIII Internat. Congress Adminstrv. Scis., Madrid, 1980; US rep. to standing com. law and sci. pub. adminstrn. Internat. Inst. Adminstrv. Scis., 1982; cons. Block Island Charter Commn., 1988—89. Author: (book) Background of Administrative Law, 1948, The Licensing Power in New York City, 1968; author: (with J D Nyhart) Law and Science in Collaboration, 1983; editor (with Robert Paul Churchill and Joseph J Cordes): Democracy, Social Values and Public Policy, 1998; contbr. articles to profl jours; editor: Working Paper series, Grad Program in Pub Policy, 1985—; Dir. Washington Cir. George Washington U., 1988—. With AUS, 1943—46. Mem.: ABA (chmn. sect. adminstrv. law 1971—72), Assn. Bar City NY (chmn. com. adminstrv. law 1964—67), Arts Club Washington (trustee, endowment com. 2001—). Home: 914 25th St NW Washington DC 20037-2101 Office: George Washington Univ 805 21st St NW Rm 602 Washington DC 20052-0001 E-mail: mcarrow@earthlink.net.

CARROW, ROBERT DUANE, lawyer, barrister; b. Marshall, Minn., Feb. 5, 1934; s. Meddie Joseph and Estelle Marie (Kough) C.; m. Jacqueline Mary Givens, Sept. 3, 1960; children: Leslie, Tamara, Amelia, Vanessa, Creighton, Jessica, Ramsey. Student, U. Colo., 1952; BA, U. Minn., 1956; JD, Stanford U., 1958. Bar: Calif. 1959, U.S. Supreme Ct. 1978, N.Y. 1983; barrister: Eng. 1981. Pvt. practice, Calif., 1959—; barrister London, 1981—. Judge pro tem Superior Ct. of Calif., San Francisco, 1992—. Bd. editors Minn. Law Rev., 1956-57. Mayor City of Novato, Calif., 1964-66. Fellow Ctr. Internat. Legal Studies, Soc. Advanced Legal Studies (assoc.); mem. ABA (accredited mediator), N.Y. Bar Assn., L.A. Bar Assn., San Francisco Bar Assn., Internat. Bar Assn., Chartered Inst. Arbitrators, Assn. Conflict Resolution, Honourable Soc. Mid. Inn of Ct. Office: Chambers 33 Bedford Row London WC1 England also: Goldstein & Musto 1 Embarcadero Ctr Ste 880 San Francisco CA 94111-3607 also: 7 Mount Lassen Dr Ste C134 San Rafael CA 94903-1170

CARRUTH, HAYDEN, poet; b. Waterbury, Conn., Aug. 3, 1921; s. Gorton Veeder and Margery Tracy Barrow (Dibb) C.; m. Sara Anderson, Mar. 14, 1943; 1 child, Martha Hamilton; m. Eleanore Ray, Nov. 29, 1952; m. Rose Marie Dorn, Oct. 28, 1961; 1 child, David Barrow II; m. Joe-Anne McLaughlin, Dec. 29, 1989. AB, U. N.C., 1943; MA, U. Chgo., 1948; LLD, New Eng. Coll., 1987, Syracuse U., 1993. Editor-in-chief Poetry mag., 1949-50; assoc. editor U. Chgo. Press, 1950-51; project adminstr. Intercultural Publs. Inc., N.Y.C., 1952-53; poetry editor Harper's mag., 1977—. Poet-in-residence Johnson State Coll., 1972-74; adj. prof. U. Vt., 1975-78; prof. English Syracuse (N.Y.) U., 1979-91, prof. emeritus, 1991—. Author: The Crow and the Heart, 1959, Journey to a Known Place, 1961, Norfolk Poems, 1962, Appendix A, 1963, North Winter, 1964, Nothing for Tigers, 1965, Contra Mortem, 1967, After the Stranger, 1965, For You, 1970, The Clay Hill Anthology, 1970, The Voice That Is Great Within Us, 1970, The Bird-Poem Book, 1970, From Snow and Rock, from Chaos, 1973, Dark World, 1973, The Bloomingdale Papers, 1975, Loneliness, 1976, Aura, 1977, Brothers, I Loved You All, 1978, Almanach du Printemprs Vivarois, 1979, Working Papers, 1982, The Mythology of Dark and Light, 1982, The Sleeping Beauty, 1982, If You Call This Cry a Song, 1983, Effluences from the Sacred Caves, 1983, Asphalt Georgics, 1985, Lighter than Air Craft, 1985, The Oldest Killed Lake in North America, 1985, The Selected Poetry of Hayden Carruth, 1986, Mother, 1986, Sitting In: Selected Writings on Jazz, Blues & Related Topics, 1986, Sonnets, 1989, Tell Me Again How the White Heron Rises and Flies Across the Nacreous River at Twilight Toward the Distant Island, 1989, Collected Shorter Poems, 1946-91, 92, Suicides and Jazzers, 1992, Collected Longer Poems, 1994, Selected Essays and Reviews, 1995, Scrambled Eggs and Whiskey, 1996, Reluctantly, 1998, Beside the Shadblow Tree, 1999, Faxes to William, 2000, Doctor Jazz, 2001; mem. editl. bd. Hudson Rev., 1971—. Sr. fellow N.Y. Found. Arts, 1993. Recipient Vachel Lindsay prize, 1954, Bess Hokin prize, 1956, Levinson prize, 1958, Ann. Poetry award Brandeis U., 1959, Harriet Monroe Poetry prize U. Chgo., 1960, Helen Bullis prize U. Seattle, 1962, Carl Sandburg prize, 1963, Emily Clark Balch prize, 1964, Gov.'s medal State of Vt., 1974, Shelley award Poetry Soc. Am., 1978, Lenore Marshall prize, 1979, Morton Zabel prize, 1968, Whiting Writers award, 1986, Sarah Josepha Hale award, 1988, Ruth Lilly Poetry prize, 1990, Nat. Book Critics Circle award in poetry, 1993, Lannan award for poetry, 1995, Nat. Book award for Poetry, 1996; fellow Bollingen Found., 1962, John Simon Meml. Guggenheim Found., 1965, 79, sr. fellow Nat. Endowment for Arts, 1988; grantee Nat. Found. on Arts and Humanities, 1967, 74. Home: RR 1 Box 128 Munnsville NY 13409-9549

CARRUTHERS, CLAUDELLE ANN, occupational and physical therapist; b. Chgo., Nov. 23; d. Veronica Josephine Walker; m. Philip J. Hannam. AA, Golden Valley Luth. Coll., Minn., 1981; BS in Occupational Therapy, U. Minn., 1984; M in Phys. Therapy, U. Iowa, 1991; PhD, U. Minn., 1995. Lic. occupational therapist, Iowa, phys. therapist, Iowa, Minn.; cert. occupational therapist, Minn. Dir., supr., occupational therapist Rehab. Specialists, Inc., Minnetonka, Minn., 1984-86; supr., occupational therapist St. Therese Home, Inc., Mpls., 1986-88; dir., supr., occupational therapist Allied Health Alternatives, Inc., Mpls., 1988-89; occupational therapist St. Luke's Hosp., Cedar Rapids, Iowa, 1989-91; occupational therapist, phys. therapist Fairview Riverside Med. Ctr., Mpls., 1991—; instr., rschr. U. Minn., 1992-95; prof. occupational and phys. therapy Coll. of St. Catherine, 1995—. Research in field of virtual reality, neurology/kinesiology; mem. adv. bd. occupational therapy program Anoka Tech. Coll., 1992—; mentor for occupational and phys. therapy students Coll. of St. Catherine's, St. Paul, 1992; mentor for occupational and phys. therapy and women athlete's of color U. Minn. Author publs. in field. Human rights commr. City of Plymouth, 1994-2003; mem. allocation panel United Way Mpls., 1992; mem. Minn. Zoo, 1986—. Recipiennt Vol. Basketball award Courage Ctr., Golden Valley, Minn., 1987, 89. Mem. Am. Phys. Therapy Assn. (student rep. 1981-83), Iowa Occupational Therapy Assn., Minn. Occupational Therapy Assn., Am. Occupational Therapy Assn., Occupational Therapy Minn.-Dak Assn. (panel presentor 1992), Glende Ski Club (2d v.p. 1987), Martin Luther King Tennis Club, Alpha Kappa Alpha. Avocations: doll collecting, stamp collecting, tennis, skiing, racquetball.

CARRUTHERS, PHILIP CHARLES, lawyer, public official; b. London, Dec. 8, 1953; s. J. Alex and Marie Carruthers. BA, U. Minn., 1975, JD, 1979. Bar: Minn. 1979, U.S. Dist. Ct. Minn. 1979, U.S. Ct. Appeals (8th cir.) 1979. Assoc. Nichols & Kruger, and predecessor firm, 1979-81; ptnr. Nichols, Starks, Carruthers and Kister, Mpls., 1982-84, Luther, Ballenthin & Carruthers, Mpls., 1985—92, Carruthers & Tallen, Mpls., 1992—93; pvt. practice Mpls., 1994—2000; pros. atty. City of Deephaven, Minn., 1979-2000, City of Woodland, Minn., 1980-2000; mem. Minn. Ho. of Reps., St. Paul, 1987-2000,

majority leader, 1993-96, spkr. of house, 1997-98; dir. prosecution divsn. Ramsey County Attys. Office, St. Paul, 2000—. Co-author: The Drinking Driver in Minnesota: Criminal and Civil Issues, 1982; note and comment editor Minn. Law Rev., 1978-79. Mem. Met. Coun. of Twin Cities Area, St. Paul, 1983-87. Mem. Minn. Trial Lawyers Assn. (bd. govs. 1982-86), Minn. State Bar Assn., Ramsey County Bar Assn. Democratic Farmer-Labor Party. Roman Catholic. Home: 6018 Halifax Pl Brooklyn Center MN 55429-2440 Office: 315 Government Ctr W 50 W Kellogg Blvd Saint Paul MN 55102-1657 E-mail: Phil.Carruthers@Co.Ramsey.mn.us.

CARRUTHERS, S. GEORGE, medical educator, physician; b. Londonderry, No. Ireland, Sept. 18, 1945; came to Can., 1977; s. Moses and Alice McKeague (Nicholl) C.; m. Gillian Margaret Devon, Oct. 4, 1969; children: Alison, David, Bruce, Michael. MB, BCh, Queen's U., Belfast, No. Ireland, 1969, MD, 1975. Diplomate Am. Bd. Internal Medicine, Am. Bd. Clin. Pharmacology (sec.-treas. 1996-98, chair 1998-2000). Intern Royal Victoria Hosp., Belfast, 1969-70; tchr. Belfast City Hosp./Queen's U. Belfast, 1970-75; Fogarty Internat. fellow NIH Kans. U. Med. Ctr., Kansas City, 1975-77; asst. prof. U. Hosp./U. Western Ont., London, Can., 1977-82, assoc. prof., 1982-87, prof. dept. medicine, 1987-88, 1995-2000, prof. dept. pharmacology and toxicology, 1987-88, 1995-2000; Carnegie and Rockefeller prof., head dept. medicine Dalhousie U., Halifax, N.S., Can., 1988-95; physician-in-chief Victoria Gen. Hosp., Halifax, 1988-91, pres. med. staff, 1992-93; chief medicine London Health Scis. Ctr., 1995—2000; dean faculty medicine and health scis. United Arab Emirates U., Al Ain, 2001—. Bd. commrs. Victoria Gen. Hosp., 1992-93; rep. Brit. Med. Assn., London, 1973-75; Richard Ivey prof., chmn. dept. medicine U. Western Ont., 1995-2001; pres. Foyle Coll. OBA, 1993-94; chmn. Cardio-Cerebrovascular Rsch. Adv. Coun.; bd. dirs. Heart and Stroke Found. Can., 1998-00 Co-author: Handbook of Clinical Pharmacology, 1978, 2d edit., 1983; co-editor: Melmon & Morelli's Textbook of Clinical Pharmacology, 4th edit., 2000. Fellow ACP (gov. Ont. 1998-2001), Royal Coll. Physicians Can., Royal Coll. Physicians (London and Glasgow), Am. Coll. Clin. Pharmacology; mem. Am. Soc. Clin. Pharmacology and Therapeutics (nominating com. 1989, v.p. 1991-92, awards com. 1992-98, sci. program com. 1995-2000, bd. dirs. 1997-2001, vice chmn. sci. program com. 1998-99, chmn. 1999-00), Can. Soc. for Clin. Pharmacology (pres. 1984-86, Piafsky Young Investigator award 1982, Disting. Achievement award 1992), Can. Hypertension Soc. (pres. 1990-91, bd. dirs. 1988-92, 99-2000, Disting. Svc. award 1995), Can. Assn. Profs. Medicine (pres. 1994-95), Can. Inst. Acad. Med., Brit. Pharm. Soc., West Haven G & C Club. Presbyterian. Avocations: travel, reading. Home and Office: United Arab Emirates Univ PO Box 17666 Fac Medicine Al Ain United Arab Emirates N6A 4G5 Fax: 971 3 767 2008. E-mail: carruthers@uaeu.ac.ae.

CARRUTHERS, THOMAS NEELY, lawyer; b. Columbia, Tenn., Oct. 11, 1928; s. Thomas Neely and Ellen Douglas (Everett) C.; m. Dale Gilder Jones, Feb. 7, 1959; children: Thomas Neely III, Virginia Carruthers Smith, Catherine Everett. AB, Princeton U., 1950; LLB, Yale U., 1955. Assoc. Bradley, Arant, Rose & White, Birmingham, Ala., 1955-63, ptnr., 1963—, chair exec. com. and mng. ptnr., 1990-95. Mem. editl. bd. Yale Law Jour., 1953-55. Trustee Children's Hosp. Ala., pres. 1996-97, Ala. Shakespeare Festival, Leadership Ala., pres. 1995-96, chmn., 1996-97; trustee Birmingham Mus. Art., chmn., 1995-2002; chmn. Gov.'s Tax Reform Task Force, 1991-92, exec. sec. devel. com., 1992-93; bd. dirs., dir. Comm. Found. Greater Birmingham, chmn., 1999-2002; bd. dirs. 2020 Birmingham Com., Ala. Dept. of Archives and History; bd. advisors Cumberland Law Sch., chmn., 1993-95; chancellor, Episcopal Diocese of Ala., 2003-; chmn. exec. com. Ala. Acad. Honor, 1999—; active Boy Scouts Am., Birmingham, exec. bd. Birmingham coun., silver beaver award, dist. Eagle Scout award. Recipient Thurmond Arnold Appellate Competition prize Yale U., 1954, Birmingham-So. Coll. medal Honor, 1992, award for pub. svc. Birmingham Bar, 1998, Brotherhood and Sisterhood award NCCJ, 2000, commendations: State Ala., Ala. Commn. Higher Edn., Jacksonville State U.; named Humanitarian of Yr., 1997. Fellow: Am. Bar Found.; mem.: ABA, Birmingham Bar Assn. (Outstanding Lawyer of Yr. award 2001), Ala. Bar Assn., Am. Law Inst., Am. Tax Policy Inst. (trustee), Am. Coll. Tax Counsel, So. Fed. Tax Inst. (pres. 1993—94, trustee, past chmn.), Internat. Bar Assn., Mountain Brook Club, Rotary (pres. 1992—93, Spain-Hickman award 2003). Episcopalian. Office: Bradley Arant Rose & White One Federal Pl 1819 5th Ave N Birmingham AL 35203

CARSCH, RUTH E. consulting librarian; b. London, May 3, 1945; came to U.S., 1949; d. Harry and Ellen Margot (Adler) C.; 1 child, Zachariah Robert. BA, CUNY, 1967; MS, Columbia U., 1968; cert. in Libr. Futures, U. Calif., Berkeley, Calif., 1997. Cert. libr., N.Y., Calif.; cert. info. sys. mgmt. U. Calif., Santa Cruz; cert. U. Calif. Berkeley Libr. Futures Inst. Reference libr. N.Y. Pub. Libr., 1968-70; tech. info. specialist Bechtel, Inc., San Francisco, 1972-75; rsch. assoc. Erick & Lavidge Mkt. Rsch. Assocs., San Francisco, 1980-86; instrnl. reference libr. San Mateo County C.C. Dist., 1987—; young adult/reference South San Francisco Pub. Libr., 1991—2002; reference libr. San Francisco Pub. Libr., San Francisco, 2001—. Cons. Port Authority N.Y. and N.J., 1982-84, Camp, Dresser, McKee Engrs., Boston, 1988, Met. Mus. Art, 1992, Calif. Conservation Corps., 1992, Haas Fund, 1995, Oregon Shakespeare, 1995, Oak Grove Sch. Dist., San Jose, Calif., 1998, Skidmore Owings Merrill, San Francisco, 2000. Mem. Art Librs. Soc., No. Calif. Architecture-Engring. Librs. Roundtable. Office: 1453 Rhode Island St San Francisco CA 94107-3248

CARSEY, MARCIA LEE PETERSON, television producer; b. South Weymouth, Mass., Nov. 21, 1944; d. John Edwin and Rebecca White (Simonds) Peterson; m. John Jay Carsey, Apr. 12, 1969; children: Rebecca Peterson, John Peterson. BA in English Lit., U. N.H., 1966. Exec. story editor Tomorrow Entertainment, L.A., 1971-74; sr. v.p. prime time series ABC-TV, L.A., 1978-81; founder Carsey Prodns., L.A., 1981; co-owner Carsey-Werner Co., 1982—; co-exec. producer TV series Oh Madeline, 1983; exec. producer The Cosby Show, 1984-92, A Different World, 1987-93, Roseanne, 1988-92, Chicken Soup, 1989-90, Grand, 1990, Davis Rules, 1991, You Bet Your Life, 1992-93, Frannie's Turn, 1992, Grace Under Fire, 1993, Cybill, 1995-97, 3rd Rock From The Sun, 1996—, Cosby, 1996—, Men Behaving Badly, 1996-97, Townies, 1996. Office: Carsey-Werner Prodns 4024 Radford Ave Bldg 3 Studio City CA 91604-2101

CARSOLA, ALFRED JAMES, oceanographer, geologist, educator; b. Los Angeles, Calif., June 6, 1919; s. Thomas and Margaret Rose Carsola; m. Joan Lorraine Breunig, June 21, 1947; children: Marie, Thomas, Timothy, Carol, Margaret, Catherine, Christopher, Paul. BS, UCLA, Los Angeles, CA, 1942; MS, U. of So. Calif., Los Angeles, CA, 1947; PhD, Scripps Instn. of Oceanography, LaJolla, CA, 1953. Oceanographer USN Electronics Lab., San Diego, Calif., 1947—60; scientist Lockheed Aircraft Corp., Burbank, Sunnyvale, Calif., 1960—75; rsch. scientist So. Calif. Coastal Rsch. Project, Los Angeles, Calif., 1971—72; lectr., adj. prof. San Diego State U., San Diego, Calif., 1956—59, 1976—82; lectr. U. of San Diego, San Diego, Calif., 1976—85; adj. prof. Grossmont Coll., El Cajon, Calif., 1974—92, San Diego Mesa Coll., San Diego, Calif., 1974—. Avocation: contract bridge. Home: 3569 Addison Street San Diego CA 92106

CARSON, BENJAMIN SOLOMON, neurosurgeon; b. Detroit, Sept. 18, 1951; s. Robert Solomon and Sonya (Copeland) C.; m. Lacena Rustin, July 6, 1975; children: Murray Nedlands, Benjamin Solomon Jr., Rhoeyce Harrington. BA, Yale U., 1973; MD, U. Mich., 1977; DSc (hon.), Gettysburg Coll., 1988, N.C. A&T, 1989, Andrews U., 1989, Sojourner-Douglas Coll., 1989, Shippenburg U., 1990, Jersey City State Coll., 1990, Southwestern Adventist Coll., 1992, U. Mass., Boston, 1992, Marygrove Coll., 1993, U. Detroit-Mercy, 1994, Spalding U., 1994, Western Md. Coll., 1994, Morgan State U., 1994, Long Island U., 1994, N.C. State U., 1994, Tuskegee U., 1995, Yale U., 1996, Del. State U., 1996, Med. U. South Africa, Medunsa, 1997, GMI Engring. and Mgmt. Inst., 1997, U. Del., 1997, Coll. William and Mary, 1998. Diplomate Am. Bd. Neurol. Surgery. Surg. intern Johns Hopkins Hosp., Balt., 1977-78, neurosurg. resident, 1978-82, chief resident, 1982-83; sr. registrar Sir Charles Gairdner Hosp., Perth, W. Australia, 1983-84; dir. pediatric neurosurgery Johns Hopkins Hosp., Balt., 1985—. Bd. dirs. Kellogg Co. Author: Pediatric Neurooncology, 1987, Achondroplasia, 1988, Gifted Hands, 1989; contbr. jour. articles. Mem. med. adv. bd. Children's Cancer Found., Balt., 1987—; hon. med. chmn. Md. Red Cross, Balt., 1987—. Recipient Am. Black Achievement award Ebony mag., Hollywood, Calif., 1988, Cum Laude award Am. Radiol. Soc., Chgo., 1982, Candle award Morehouse U., Atlanta, 1989; Paul Harris fellow Rotary Internat., 1988. Mem. Am. Assn. Neurol. Surgeons, Congress Neurol. Surgeons, AAAS, Pediatric Oncology Group, Nat. Med. Assn. Seventh Day Adventist. Office: Johns Hopkins Hosp 600 N Wolfe St #811 Baltimore MD 21287-0005

CARSON, BRAD ROGERS, congressman; b. Winslow, AZ., Mar. 11, 1967; m. Julie. Grad. with honors, Baylor U.; MA in politics, philosophy and econ., Oxford; grad., U. Okla. Coll. Law, 1994. Atty. pvt. practice; White House fellow, spl. asst. to Sec. Defense Spl. Projects, 1997-98; congressman second dist. Okla., 2001—. Vice-chair Congl. Native Am. Caucus. Mem. Phi Beta Kappa. Mem. Blue Dog Coalition, New Democrat Coalition; mem. First Baptist Ch. Claremore. Office: 317 Cannon House Office bldg Washington DC 20515-3602*

CARSON, CHARLES HENRY, microwave engineer; b. Malden, Mass., July 18, 1930; s. Philip Stanley and Margaret (Mitchell) C.; m. Olivia Rose Marie Barto, Apr. 23, 1967; children: Cynthia, Craig, Marcia, Claudia. Student, Northeastern U., Boston, 1956, postgrad., 1966. Devel. engr. microwave Raytheon, Bedford, Mass., 1953-56; sr. engr., dept. mgr. Airtron Inc., Cambridge, Mass., 1956-58; co-founder, v.p., dir. ops. Ferrotec Inc., Newton, Mass., 1958-70; dir. corp. mkt. planning MA/COM, Burlington, Mass., 1970-75; chmn., founder, chief exec. officer Carson Assocs., Inc., Milford, Mass., 1975—. Bd. dirs. Carson Assocs., Inc., Milford; co-founder, bd. dirs. Colonial Cablevision, Revere, Mass., 1976-86; co-founder, v.p. mktg., bd. dirs. Ferrotec Inc., Newton, 1958-70. Inventor in field; contbr. articles to profl. jours. Commr. Indsl. devel. Commn., Milford, 1968-70; minuteman Mass. Ind. Devel. Commn., 1969-73; bd. dirs. Order of St. Mary the Virgin, 1993. With USN, 1948-53. Mem. U.S. Polo Assn. (del. 1986-96), R.I. Tuna Tournament (bep. dir. 1973-77), Galilee Tuna Club (pres. 1976-77), Newport Polo Club (del. 1989-90). Avocations: polo, giant tuna fishing, sailing, shooting. Office: Carson Assocs Inc 5 Kellett Dr Milford MA 01757-4013

CARSON, CHRISTOPHER LEONARD, lawyer; b. Washington, Dec. 28, 1940; s. Leonard O. and Evelyn (Watters) C.; m. Cynthia Caffey, Dec. 27, 1963; 1 dau., Melissa Ann. AB, Duke U., 1962; JD, U. Mich., 1965. Bar: N.Y. 1965, Fla. 1968, Ga. 1970. Assoc. Olwine, Chase, O'Donnell & Weyher, N.Y.C., 1965-66; ptnr. Hansell & Post, Atlanta, 1969-89, Jones Day, Atlanta, 1989—. Contbg. author: Modern Real Estate Transactions; contbr. articles to legal publs. and mags. Bd. dirs., adv. coun. Atlanta Area Boy Scouts Am., 1974-80; bd. dirs. Young Life Urban Atlanta, 1983—. Lt. sr. grade USNR, 1960-69. Fellow Am. Coll. Coml. Fin. Lawyers; mem. ABA (Uniform Comml. Code Com., Subcoms. on Secured Transactions and Letter of Credit 1982-95), Southeastern Bankruptcy Law Inst. (dir. 1973—, pres. 1980-81, chmn. 1981-82), Atlanta Bar Bankruptcy Sect. (chmn. 1981-82), Ga. Bar Uniform Code Com. (chmn. 1984-87), Cherokee Club. Republican. Baptist. Avocations: running, reading, traveling. Office: Jones Day SunTrust Plz 303 Peachtree St NE Ste 3500 Atlanta GA 30308-3263 E-mail: clcarson@jonesday.com.

CARSON, CULLEY CLYDE, III, urologist, educator; b. Westerly, R.I., Feb. 25, 1945; s. Culley Clyde Jr. and Dorothy (Scarborough) C.; m. Mary Jo McDonald, Aug. 10, 1970; children: Culley Clyde IV, Hilary. BS, Trinity Coll., 1967; MD, George Washington U., 1971. Diplomate Am. Bd. Urology. Intern Dartmouth Med. Ctr., 1971-72, resident surgery, 1971-73; fellow urology Mayo Clinic, Rochester, Minn., 1975-78; instr. urology U. Minn. Mayo Med. Sch., Rochester, 1978; asst. prof. urology Duke U. Med. Ctr., Durham, N.C., 1978-84, assoc. prof., 1984-88, prof., 1988-93, Rhodes Disting. chair, 1993—; prof., chmn. urology U. N.C., Chapel Hill, 1993—, Rhoads disting. prof., 2000—. Chief urology Durham VA Hosp.; mem. new drug panel U.S. FDA; mem. exec. com. U.S. Pharmacopea. Author: Endourology, 1985, Atlas of Urologic Endoscopy, 1986, Impotence, 1992, 98, Complications of Invasive Procedures, 1995, Textbook of Erectile Dysfunction, 1999; editor-in-chief Mediguide to Urology, 1994—, Contemporary Urology, 1997—; contbr. chpts. to urol. texts. Maj. M.C., USAF, 1973-75. Recipient Calvin Klopp Rsch. award, 1971, Friedman rsch. prize, 1971, Cristol Mayo Alumni award, 1992, Jesse H. Neal award, 2001; named Command Flight Surgeon of Yr., USAF, 1974; Rsch. fellow Am. Heart Assn., 1969, O'Dea travel fellow, 1978. Fellow ACS, Am. Surg. Assn.; mem. AMA, AAAS, Am. Assn. Genitourinary Surgeons, Am. Urol. Assn., Internat. Soc. Urology, Am. Fertility Soc., Univ. Urol. Forum, N.Y. Acad. Scis., Mayo Alumni Assn., Gov.'s Club, Carolina Club, Trinity Club (Hartford), Sigma Xi, Psi Chi, Alpha Omega Alpha. Home: 2719 Spencer St Durham NC 27705-5720 Office: U NC Hosps Chapel Hill NC 27599-7235 E-mail: culleyccarson3@hotmail.com.

CARSON, ELLEN GODBEY, lawyer; b. Kingsport, Tenn., Apr. 30, 1955; d. Lewis Anderson and Doris Louise (Dempsey) C.; m. Robert Carson Godbey, June 2, 1979. BA summa cum laude, U. Tenn., Knoxville, 1976; JD cum laude, Harvard U., 1980. Consumer complaint specialist FTC, Boston, 1980; atty. civil rights divsn. HHS, Washington, 1980-81; assoc. Landis, Cohen, Rauh & Zelenko, Washington, 1981-87, Paul Johnson Alston & Hunt, Honolulu, 1987-91, Alston Hunt Floyd & Ing, Honolulu, 1991—. Mem. disciplinary bd. Hawaii Supreme Ct., 1990-95. Former pres., dir. D.C. Rape Crisis Ctr., Washington, Sex Abuse Treatment Ctr., Honolulu, Hale Kipa Youth Svcs., Honolulu; pres., trustee Ctrl. Union Ch., 1998-2002; past dir. Aloha United Way, Hawaii Women's Legal Found. Named Outstanding Woman Profl., YWCA, 1990; recipient Outstanding Svc. award Hawaii Women Lawyers, 1991. Mem. Am. Arbitration Assn. (arbitrator, mediator), Hawaii State Bar Assn. (pres., dir. 1995-1996, Pro Bono award 1989), Hawaii Women Lawyers (pres., dir. 1989-90, Women Lawyer of Yr. 1992, Disting. Svc. award 2000), Hawaii Justice Found. (v.p., dir. 1996-2002), Inst. Human Svcs. (pres., dir. 1996-2002). Avocations: scuba, quilting. Office: Alston Hunt Floyd & Ing 18th Fl Pacific Tower 1001 Bishop St Ste 1800 Honolulu HI 96813-3689 E-mail: ecarson@ahfi.com.

CARSON, GORDON BLOOM, retired engineering executive; b. High Bridge, NJ, Aug. 1, 1911; s. Whitfield R. and Emily (Bloom) C.; m. Beth Lacy, June 19, 1937 (dec. Mar. 1998); children: Richard Whitfield (dec. Oct. 2002), Emily Elizabeth (Mrs. Lee A. Duffus), Alice Lacy (Mrs. William P. Allman), Jeanne Helen (Mrs. Michael J. Gable). BSMechE, Case Inst. Tech., 1931, D Engring., 1957; MS, Yale U., 1932, ME, 1938; LLD, Rio Grande Coll., 1973. With Western Electric Co., 1930; instr. mech. engring. Case Inst. Tech., 1932-37, asst. prof., 1937-40, assoc. prof. indsl. engring. charge indsl. div., 1940-44; with Am. Shipbldg. Co., 1936; patent litigation, 1937; research engr., dir. research Cleve. Automatic Machine Co., 1939-44; asst. to gen. mgr. Selby Shoe Co., 1944, mgr. engring., 1945-49, sec. of corp., 1949-53; sec., dir. Pyrrole Products Co., 1948-53; dean engring. Ohio State U., Columbus, 1953-58, v.p. bus. and finance, treas., 1958-71; dir. Engring. Exptl. Sta., 1953-58, Accuray Corp., 1960-82, Cardinal Funds, Inc., 1962-98; exec. v.p. Albion (Mich.) Coll., 1971-76, exec. cons., 1976-77; asst. to chancellor, dir. fin. Northwood Inst., 1977-82; v.p. Mich. Molecular Inst., 1982-88; prin. Whitfield Robert Assocs., 1988—. Mem. adj. faculty Northwood U., 1984—; exec. cons. DeVos Grad. Sch. Mgmt., 1977—83. Editor: The Production Handbook, 1958; cons. editor, 1972—; Author of tech. papers engring. subjects. Trustee White Cross Hosp. Assn., 1960-71; bd. dirs. Orton Found., 1953-58, Cardinal Funds, 1966-98, bd. dirs. Goodwill Industries, 1959-67, 1st v.p., 1963-64; v.p. Ohio State U. Rsch. Found., 1958-71; v.p., chmn. adv. coun. Ctr. for Automation and Soc., U. Ga., 1969-71; chmn. tool and die com. 5th Regional War Labor Bd., 1943-45; chmn. Ohio state adv. com. for sci., tech. and specialized personnel SSS, 1965-70; pres. Larkin Parking Condo Assn., Inc., 1992—. Fellow ASME, AAAS, Inst. Indsl. Engrs. (pres. 1957-58); mem. Columbus Soc. Fin. Analysts (pres. 1974-75), Fin. Analysts Fedn. (bd. dirs. 1964-65), C. of C. (bd. dirs., treas. 1952-53), Am. Soc. Engring. Edn., Assn. Univs. for Rsch. in Astronomy (bd. dirs. 1958-71), Midwestern Univs. Rsch. Assn. (bd. dirs. 1958-71), U.S. Naval Inst., Nat. Soc. Profl. Engrs. (life), Romophos, Sphinx, Rotary (Paul Harris fellow), Sigma Xi (fin. com. 1975-89, nat. treas. 1979-89), Masons (32 deg.), Tau Beta Pi, Zeta Psi, Phi Eta Sigma, Alpha Pi Mu, Omicron Delta Epsilon. Office: Whitfield Robert Assocs 5413 Gardenbrook Dr Midland MI 48642-3402 Fax: 989-631-0925. *Integrity is as essential as health or intelligence. And it cannot be put on and taken off as can a garment. You either have it or you don't. Integrity must be nurtured, bolstered, and reaffirmed, lest the naturally corrupting influences of life destroy it. Without integrity, democracy cannot survive. Without it, government becomes a mutual looting society, with the citizens paying the bills. No society can be free unless a heavy majority of its citizens has integrity, and demands it on the part of all associates.*

CARSON, HAMPTON LAWRENCE, geneticist, educator; b. Phila., Nov. 5, 1914; s. Joseph and Edith (Bruen) C.; m. Meredith Shelton, Aug. 14, 1937; children: Joseph II, Edward Bruen. AB, U. Pa., 1936, PhD, 1943. Instr. U. Pa., 1938-42; faculty Washington U., St. Louis, 1943-70, prof. biology, 1956-70; prof. genetics U. Hawaii, 1971-85, emeritus, 1985—. Vis. prof. biology U. Sao Paulo, Brazil, 1951, 77. Author: Heredity and Human Life, 1963; Contbr. articles to profl. jours. Trustee B.P. Bishop Mus., Honolulu, 1982-88. Recipient medal for excellence in rsch. U. Hawaii, 1979, Leidy medal Acad. Natural Scis., Phila., 1985, Charles Reed Bishop medal Bishop Mus., Honolulu, 1992; Fulbright rsch. scholar zoology dept. U. Melbourne, Australia, 1961. Mem. Nat. Acad. Scis., Am. Acad. Arts and Scis., Genetics Soc. (pres. 1982), Soc. for Study Evolution (pres. 1971, George Gaylord Simpson award 1996), Am. Soc. Naturalists (pres. 1973), AAAS, Phi Beta Kappa, Sigma Xi. Office: Dept Cell & Molecular Biology U Hawaii at Manoa Honolulu HI 96822 E-mail: hampton@hawaii.edu. *As a life scientist, I study evolution with the tools of modern biology. Religious mysticism plays no role in either my scientific or philosophical thought. Each biological individual (man, mouse or fly) is unique in both genetic endowment and environmental experience. This fact is central to the ethics of a humanism that values each human life. The differences between us are mostly due to chance; some persons are more fortunate than others. Nevertheless, each has an equal right to be treated with dignity and forbearance.*

CARSON, JAY WILMER, pathologist, educator; b. Ki-Jang, Korea, Oct. 6, 1933; came to U.S., 1960; s. Han Kyu and Jin Chan (Son) Cha; m. Jennifer C. White, June 28, 1968 (dec. Aug. 1990); m. Teresa M. Alberda, July 14, 1995. MD, Seoul Nat. U., 1958. Diplomate Am. Bd. Pathology. Intern Bellevue Hosp. Ctr., N.Y.C., 1961-62; resident in pathology Albert Einstein Coll. Medicine, N.Y.C., 1963-66; fellow U. Montreal, Que., Can., 1967-68; chief anatomic pathology VA Hosp., Martinez, Calif., 1969-91; dir. cytopathology VA Med. Ctr., San Francisco, 1992-96; assoc. clin. prof. U. Calif. Med. Sch., San Francisco, 1992—. Aviation med. examiner FAA, Oklahoma City, 1987-96; assoc. clin. prof. U. Calif., Davis, 1985—; hosp. comdr. 347th Gen. Hosp., Sunnyvale, Calif., 1992-1993, 6253d Army Hosp., Santa Rosa, Calif., 1994-96. Patentee needle aspiration device. Mem. chmn.'s adv. bd. Nat. Rep. Com., Washington, 1995-96. Col. USAR, 1971-96. Decorated Order of Military Med. Merit, Meritorious Svc. Medal with one oakleaf cluster, Sr. Flight Surgeon Badge. Fellow Coll. Am. Pathologists; mem. Internat. Acad. Pathology, Assn. Mil. Surgeons U.S. (life), Res. Officers Assn. (life), U.S. Army War Coll. Alumni Assn. (life), Soc. U.S. Army Flight Surgeons (life). Avocations: skiing, sailing, music. Home: 1550 Sorrel Ct Walnut Creek CA 94598-4800 E-mail: jntcarson@astound.net.

CARSON, JEAN HOPKINS KESSEL, civic worker; b. Dayton, Ohio, Sept. 24, 1929; d. Arthur Vincent and Mary Helen (Hopkins) Kessel; m. John Gregg Carson, Feb. 1, 1951; children: James G., Elizabeth M., David R., Mary C. BS, Purdue U., 1952; diploma, Diocesan Theol. Sch., 1994. Trustee Episcopal Cmty. Svcs. Found., 1996—2003, Highland County Domestic Violence Task Force, 1991—2002; mem. Scott House Comn., 1990—96; founder, chmn. bd. trustees Samaritan Outreach Svcs. of Highland County, 1988—95; bus. mgr. Hillsboro chpt. Girl Scouts U.S., 1972—82; mem. Highland County Health Planning Coun., 1970—75; various activities with Scioto-Paint Valley Mental Health Ctr., Hillsboro Human Rels. Group, Ctrl. Ohio chpt. Am. Heart Assn., Highland County Mental Health Assn., St. Mary's Episcopal Ch., Hillsboro; mem. So. State C.C. Found. Bd.; various activities with Highland Dist. Hosp. Women's Aux., Episcopal Diocese of So. Ohio. Home: 5570 Holladay Rd Hillsboro OH 45133-7706

CARSON, JOHN, history educator; b. Bryn Mawr, Pa., Dec. 12, 1954; s. John and Patricia Kipping Carson. PhD, Princeton U., 1994. Asst. prof. U. Mich., Ann Arbor, 1998—. Fellow Post-doctoral Rsch. Fellowship, NSF-NATO, 1993-1994. Office: U Mich Dept of History 1029 Tisch Hall Ann Arbor MI 48109-1003 Office Fax: 734-647-4881. Personal E-mail: jscarson@umich.edu. E-mail: jscarson@umich.edu.

CARSON, JOHNNIE, ambassador; b. Chgo., Apr. 7, 1943; s. Dupree and Aretha (Rhodes) C.; m. Anne Diemer; Feb. 8, 1969; children: Elizabeth, Michael Dupree, Katherine Anne. BA, Drake U., 1965; MA in Internat. Rels., U. London, 1975. Tchr., vol. U.S. Peace Corps, Tanzania, 1965-68; fgn. svc. officer U.S. Dept. State, Washington, 1969—; polit. officer U.S. Embassy, Lagos, Nigeria, 1969-71; internat. rels. officer U.S. Dept. State, Washington, 1971-74; dep. chief of mission U.S. Embassy, Maputo, Mozambique, 1975-78; staff dir. fgn. affairs com. subcom. on Africa U.S. Ho. of Reps., Washington, 1979-82; dep. polit. counselor U.S. Embassy, Lisbon, Portugal, 1982-86, dep. chief of mission Gaborone, Botswana, 1986-90; Am. amb. Am. Embassy, Kampala, Uganda, 1991-94, Am. amb. to Zimbabwe Harare, 1995-97; prin. dep. asst. sec. for African Affairs Dept. of State, Washington, 1997-99, U.S. amb. to Kenya Nairobi, Kenya, 1999—. Contbr. to numerous Congl. Studies on Africa, also to book; author articles on Africa and refugees. Mem. NAACP, African Studies Assn. Baptist. Avocations: tennis, reading, cross country skiing, hiking, fishing. Address: Am Embassy Kenya Unit 64100 Box 1 Apo AE 09831-4100

CARSON, JOHNNY, television personality; b. Corning, Iowa, Oct. 23, 1925; s. Homer and Ruth (Hook) C.; m. Jody Wolcott, 1948 (div. 1963); children: Chris, Ricky, Cory; m. Joanne Copeland, Aug. 1963 (div.); m. Joanna Holland, 1972 (div. 1983); m. Alexis Maas, June 20, 1987. BA, U. Nebr., 1949. Announcer radio Sta. KFAB, Lincoln, Nebr., 1948; later at Sta. WOW, WOW-TV, Omaha; became announcer Sta. KNXT, Los Angeles, 1950. Co-chmn. Garden State Bank, Hawaiian Gardens, Calif. Started: TV show Carson's Cellar, 1951; next became writer for TV show, Red Skelton; emcee: TV quiz show Earn Your Vacation, 1954; star: TV quiz show The Johnny Carson Show, CBS, 1955; emcee: quiz show Who Do You Trust, ABC-TV, 1958-63; U.S. Steel Hour, Joys!, 1976; host: Tonight show, NBC-TV, 1962-92; performer, Las Vegas; pres. Carson Prodns.; author: Happiness Is a Dry Martini, 1965. Served with USNR, World War II. Recipient Entertainer of Yr. award AGVA, Presidential medal of Freedom, 1992, Kennedy Center Honor for Lifetime Achievement, 1993. Mem.: Friars (knight). Address: care NBC 6962 Wildlife Rd Malibu CA 90265-4309

CARSON, JUANITA ELAINE, biologist, educator; b. Ridge Spring, S.C., Dec. 5, 1940; d. James Padgett and Rosalind Vermelle (Scott) C.; m. Kenneth M. Chitwood, June 9, 1963 (div. Apr. 1983); children: Ami, Kira Susanne. AA, North Greenville Coll., 1960; BS in Biology, U. S.C., 1962; MS in Biology, Mich. State U., 1967; EdD in Sci. Edn., Temple U., 1977. Tchr. sci. Myrtle Beach (S.C.) High Sch., 1962-65, Richland County Schs., Columbia, S.C., 1965-68; coord. sci. & staff devel. Newton County Bd. Edn., Covington, Ga., 1977—97, adminstrv. asst. staff devel. evaluation, 1977—98; prof. edn. Wesleyan Coll., Macon, Ga., 1998—. Presenter in field. Fellow Temple U., Phila., 1974-77. Mem. Ga. Assn. Edn. Leaders, Ga. Staff Devel. Coun. (bd. dirs. 1988-91), Ga. Sci. Tchrs. Assn. (pres. 1980-82, Disting. Svc. award 1983), Met. Atlanta Tchr. Edn. Group (pres. 1987-88), Phi Delta Kappa. Democrat. Methodist. Avocations: running, hiking, travel. Home: 456 Adrian Pl Macon GA 31204-1702 Office: Wesleyan Coll 4760 Forsyth Ave Macon GA 31210

CARSON, JULIA M. congresswoman; b. Louisville, July 8, 1938; 2 children. Ed., Ind. U., 1960-62, St. Mary of the Woods, 1976-78. Mem. Ind. Ho. of Reps., Indpls., 1972-76, Ind. Senate, 1976-90, U.S. Congress from 7th Ind. dist. (formerly 10th), 1997—. Mem. fin. svcs. com., 1997—, Vets. Affairs com., 1997—. V.p. Greater Indpls. Prog. Com.; nat. Dem. committeewoman; trustee YMCA; bd. didrs. Pub. Svc. Acad. Recipient Woman of Yr. Ind. award, 1974, Outstanding Leadership award AKA, Humanitarian award Christian Theol. Sem. Mem. NAACP, Urban League, Nat. Coun. Negro Women. Democrat. Baptist. Office: 1535 Longworth HOB Washington DC 20515-1410*

CARSON, LEONARD ALLEN, lawyer; b. Lorain, Ohio, Nov. 6, 1940; s. Frank and Josephine (Sulewski) Guzewicz. BS in Bus. Adminstrn., U. Fla., 1963, JD, 1966. Bar: Fla. 1967. Staff acct. Peat, Marwick, Mitchell & Co., N.Y.C., 1963-64; mem. firm Kates and Ress, P.A., Miami, Fla., 1967-70; corp. counsel, asst. to exec. v.p. and treas. Cordis Corp., Miami, 1970-73; judge Indsl. Claims Ct., Ft. Lauderdale, Fla., 1973; mem. Fla. Indsl. Rels. Commn., Tallahassee, 1973-74, chmn., 1974-76, Fla. Pub. Employees Rels. Commn., Tallahassee, 1976-80; of counsel Seyfarth, Shaw, Fairweather & Geraldson, Tallahassee and Miami, 1980-83; pres. Carson & Adkins, Tallahassee, 1983—.

Mem. Fla. Law Revision Coun., 1976-77, Internat. Assn. Indsl. Accident Bds. and Commns., 1974-76 Served with USMCR, 1960-66. Mem. ABA, Am. Arbitration Assn. (nat. panel 1968-73). Clubs: Governors, Capital Tiger Bay. Republican. Roman Catholic. Home: 233 Rose Hill Dr N Tallahassee FL 32312-9022 Office: 2958 Wellington Cir Tallahassee FL 32309-6888 E-mail: guzewicz@aol.com.

CARSON, MARY SILVANO, career counselor, educator; b. Mass. d. Joseph and Alice V. Silvano; m. Paul E. Carson (dec.); children: Jan Ellen, Jeffrey Paul, Amy Jayne. BS, Simmons Coll., 1947; MA, U. Chgo., 1970, postgrad., 1971, 72, Ctr. Urban Studies, 1970, DePaul U., 1980. Cert. acad. counselor, Ill.; nat. cert. counselor. Mgr. S.W. Youth Opportunity Ctr., Dept. Labor, Chgo., 1964-68; careers counselor Gordon Tech. H.S., Chgo., 1971-74; dir. Career and Assessment Ctr., YMCA Coll., Chgo., 1974-81; project coord. Career Ctr., Loop Coll., Chgo., 1981-85; pvt. practice San Francisco, 1990—. Mem. adv. bd. City-Wide Coll. Career Ctr.; bd. dirs. Loop YWCA, Chgo., coord. employment project, 1985-87; ESL tchr., Greece, 1990. Mem. ACA, TESOL, Am. Ednl. Rsch. Assn., Nat. Career Devel. Assn., Internat. Counseling Assn., Internat. Lyceum (London), Browning Soc., World Coun., English Speaking Union, Met. Club, Commonwealth Club, Pi Lambda Theta (chpt. pres. 1975).

CARSON, MICHAEL, secondary school educator, music educator; b. Suffolk, Va., Jan. 15, 1960; s. James Lee and Mary Ann Carson; children: Chiquita Watford, Teneisha Faulks. MusM, Norfolk (Va.) State U., 1988, BS in Music Edn., 1982. Cert. tchr. instrumental music K-12. Band dir. John Yeates H.S. / Driver Intermediate, Suffolk, Va., 1982—90, Nansemond River H.S. / John Yeates Mid., Suffolk, 1990—99, Western Br. Mid. Sch., Chesapeake, Va., 1999—. Band leader, mgr. N-TREGUE, Chesapeake, 1994—. Musician local jazz-pop band. Mem.: Music Educators Nat. Conf. Office: Western Br Mid Sch 4201 Hawksley Dr Chesapeake VA 23321

CARSON, PAUL EUGENE, insurance examiner; b. Jan. 15, 1953; B in Bus. Adminstrn., Middle Tenn. State U., 1975; M in Accountancy, U. Mo., 1984. Legis. auditor Divsn. State Audit, Nashville, 1976-83; ins. examiner Tenn. Dept. Commerce and Ins., Nashville, 1987-94, Ariz. Dept. Ins., Phoenix, 1995—. Home: 200 Chapel Ave Nashville TN 37206-2410 E-mail: pecarson@aol.com., sofepaul@cs.com.

CARSON, REGINA E. healthcare administrator, geriatric specialist, pharmacist, educator; b. Washington; BS in Pharmacy, Howard U.; MBA in Mktg., MBA in Health Care Adminstrn., Loyola Coll., Balt., 1987. Asst. prof., asst. dir. pharmacy U. Md., Balt., 1986-88; asst. prof., coord. profl. practice Howard U., Washington, 1988-95; prin. Marrell Cons., Randallstown, Md., prin., mng. ptnr., 1993—; exec. dir. Sunrise Assisted Living, Fairfax, Va., 1997-99. Drug utilization rev. cons. Md. Pharmacy Assn., Balt., 1986—90; cons. pharmacist Baltimore county Adv. Coun. Drug Abuse, Towson, Md., 1984—86; edn. cons. ADWHE, Accra, Ghana, 1999; program evaluator Train Pharm., UMF-Cluj, Romania, 1999—2002. Bd. dirs. N.W. Hosp. Ctr. Aux., Randallstown, Joshua Johnson Coun., Balt. Mus. Art, Alzheimers Assn. Ctrl. Md.; trustee C.C. of Baltimore County, 1997—. Named Outstanding Alumni, Howard U. Coll. Pharmacy, 1992; recipient Gregor T. Popa medal, UMF-Iasi, Romania, 2000. Fellow: Am. Soc. Cons. Pharmacists; mem.: Nat. Assn. Retail Druggists (adv. com., long-term care com.), Nat. Pharm. Assn. (life, Outstanding Women in Pharmacy 1984), Am. Assn. Colls. Pharmacy, Nat. Assn. Health Svc. Execs. Avocation: Avocations: pharmacognosy, Windsor chairs, American art.

CARSON, RICHARD MCKEE, chemical engineer; b. Dayton, Ohio, June 6, 1912; s. George E. and Gertrude (Barthelemy) C.; children: Joan Roderer, Linda McCartan. BS in Chem. Engring., U. Dayton (Ohio), 1934. Registered profl. engr., Ohio. Rsch. chemist Dayton Mall Iron Co., 1934-45; pres. Carson-Saeks, Inc., Dayton, 1945-80, Carson & Saeks Cons. Assocs. Inc., Dayton, 1980—; sec.-treas. Cecile Baird, Inc., Hillsboro, Ohio. Mem. AAAS, Am. Chem. Soc. Achievements include 6 patents for clinical test procedures, reagents, and closet accessories. Home: 2310 Kershner Rd Dayton OH 45414-1214

CARSON, RICHARD TAYLOR, JR., economics educator; b. Jackson, Miss., Feb. 24, 1955; s. Richard Taylor and Alice Helen (Goldthwaite) C. BA, Miss. State U., 1977; MA, PhD, U. Calif., Berkeley, 1985. Staff mem. Resources for the Future, Washington, 1979-82; prof. U. Calif. San Diego, La Jolla, Calif., 1985—. Prin. Natural Resource Damage Assessment, Inc., La Jolla, Calif., 1990-2000. Author: Energy Oriented Input-Output Models, 1984, Using Surveys to Value Public Goods, 1989, A Contingent Valuation Study of Lost Passive Use Values Resulting From the Exxon Valdez Oil Spill, 1992. Grantee EPA, 1988, 89, 90, 95, Electric Power Rsch. Inst., 1988, 89, Alaska Dept. Fish and Game, 1987, Met. Water Dist., L.A., 1987, City of L.A., 1992, 93, NOAA,1991, 92, 93, 94, 95, Calif. Dept. Game and Fish, 1992, 95. Fellow Nat. Bur. Econ. Rsch. Office: U Calif San Diego Dept Econs La Jolla CA 92093

CARSON, ROBERT S. retired medical researcher; b. Weihsien, China, Jan. 17, 1925; arrived in U.S., 1927; s. Arthur L. Carson and Edith H. Scott; children: Sandra Steinberg, Susan Isaacs. BA, Reed Coll., 1948; MS, MD, U. Oreg., 1953. Diplomate Am. Bd. Neurology and Psychiatry, cert. acupuncturist N.Y. Intern U. Chgo. Med. Sch., 1953—54; resident N.Y. Hosp., N.Y.C., sr. staff, 1957—60; faculty Cornell Med. Sch., N.Y.C., 1960—73; dir. Acupuncture Ctr., North Attleboro, Mass., 1973—81. Sr. staff Fryer Rsch. Ctr., N.Y.C., 1981—99. With U.S. Army, 1946—47. Mem.: Physicians for Social Responsibility, Union of Concerned Scientists. Home: #B6 3 Woodstock Estates Dr Woodstock NY 12498

CARSON, ROBERT WILLIAM, lawyer; b. Port Huron, Mich., Nov. 26, 1948; s. Robert Y. and Cecilia E. (DeMars) C.; m. Pamela Jean French, May 3, 1974; children: Shayna, Keeley, Robbie. AA, St. Clair County Community Coll., 1968; BA, U. Mich., 1970; JD, U. Detroit, 1973. Bar: Mich. 1973. Assoc. Raymond L. Krell, Detroit, 1973-74, McIntosh, McColl, Carson, McName & Strickler (predecessor), Port Huron, 1975-77; ptnr. McIntosh, McColl, Allen, Carson, McNamee & Strickler and predecessor firms, Port Huron, 1977-79, sr. ptnr., 1979—. Bd. dirs. Guaranteed Tires, Inc., Port Huron. Campaign dir. St. Clair County March Dimes, Port Huron, 1978-80, chmn., 1980-82, bd. dirs. 1982—, legal liaison, 1984-85. Mem.: Port Huron Golf. Republican. Roman Catholic. Avocations: golf, basketball. Office: McIntosh McColl Carson McNamee & Strickler 3024 Commerce Dr Fort Gratiot MI 48059-3819

CARSON, SAMUEL GOODMAN, retired banker, company director; b. Glens Falls, N.Y., Oct. 6, 1913; s. Russell M.L. and Mary (Goodman) C.; m. Alice Williams, Oct. 14, 1939; children: Russell L., Frances Elizabeth (Mrs. Thomas E. Brady Jr.), Mary Goodman (Mrs. John A. Fedderke), Kathryn Williams (Mrs. Robert Richards), Samuel Goodman. BA magna cum laude, Dartmouth Coll., 1934. With Aetna Life Ins. Co., 1934-68; with Toledo Trust Co., 1967-84, exec. v.p., 1968, pres., 1969-84, chief exec. officer, 1970-84, chmn., 1976-84; chmn., dir. Toledo Trustcorp, Inc., 1976-84. Dir. Kiemle-Hankins Co., Plastic Technologies, Inc., Carson Assocs., Inc. Mem. Ottawa Hills Bd. Edn., 1954-64; pres. United Appeal Greater Toledo Area, 1969, campaign chmn., 1964; Bd. dirs., trustee Toledo chpt. ARC, 1950—, chmn., 1959-61; trustee Toledo Hosp., 1960—, v.p., 1963-65, pres., 1966-69; bd. dirs. Community Chest Greater Toledo, 1962-65, pres., 1965; pres. Boys' Club Toledo, 1961-64, trustee, 1957— ; trustee Toledo Mus. Art, 1967—, sec.-treas., 1969, v.p., 1973-78, pres., 1978-80. Recipient Service to Mankind award Sertoma Club Toledo, 1965, Man and Boy award Boys' Clubs Am., 1966, Pacemaker of Yr. award U. Toledo Coll. Bus. Adminstrn. Alumni Assn., 1969 Mem. Toledo Area C. of C. (trustee 1961-62, 73-76, pres. 1974-75), Phi Beta Kappa, Phi Gamma Delta. Clubs: Rotarian, Toledo Country, Toledo. Lodges: Rotary. Republican. Congregationalist. Office: 425 Madison Ave Toledo OH 43604-1229

CARSON, SOL KENT, artist, educator; b. Phila., June 7, 1917; s. Philip Pasach and Sarah Carson; m. Thelma Clearfield-Carson; 1 child, Kent Steven. Student, Zeckwer-Hahn Acad., Phila., Pa., 1937; BFA with hons., Temple U., 1944, BS with hons. in Edn., 1945, MEd in Fine Arts, 1946, student, 1957, NYU, 1958; PhD, U. Italy, 1960. Asst. Temple U., Phila., 1940—45, dir. dept. visual art, 1944—47, dir. dept. art Eckels Coll., 1946—55, prof., 1946—55; cons. art Bristol Twp. Sch. Dist., 1956—66; prof. art dept. Wis. State U., Superior, 1965; assoc. prof. art dept. Millerville State U., Lancaster, Pa., 1966—79. Mus. cons. U. Pa., 1945—46; art tchr. Phila. (Pa.) Bd. Edn., 1947—58. Scholar, Barnes Found. Mem.: NEA, AAUP, Pa. State Ednl. Assn., Artist Equity, Assn. Higher Edn., Phi Delta Kappa. Avocations: music, poetry. Home: 447 Alberto Way C128 Los Gatos CA 95032

CARSON, STEVEN DOUGLAS, science educator, biomedical researcher; b. Apr. 9, 1951; s. Harvey Arthur and Evelyn (Rule) C., Jr.; m. Sharon McLaren (div. 1985); 1 child, Shawn Kevin. BA, Rice U., 1973; PhD, U. Tex., Galveston, 1978. Asst. in chemistry EPA, Houston, 1972-73; rsch. asst. U. Tex. Med. Br., Galveston, Tex., 1973-78; rsch. assoc. Yale U., 1982, lectr., 1982-83; chemist pathology lab. VA, Denver, 1982-84; asst. prof. U. Colo. Sch. Medicine, Denver, 1982-88; assoc. prof. U. Nebr. Sch. Medicine, Omaha, 1988-93, prof., 1993—. Author rsch. papers, book chpt.; patentee in field. Recipient New Investigator award NIH, 1983, Rsch. Career Devel. award, 1988; fellow Robert Welch Found., 1970-72; grantee NSF, 1978-79, NIH, 1979-97. Mem. AAAS, Am. Soc. Biochemistry and Molecular Biology, Am. Soc. Human Genetics, N.Y. Acad. Sci., Am. Heart Assn., Internat. Soc. Thrombosis and Haemostasis. Home: 12817 Chandler St Omaha NE 68138-6017 E-mail: scarson@unmc.edu., 73632.3623@compuserve.com.

CARSON, STEVEN LEE, newspaper publisher; b. N.Y.C., Mar. 23, 1943; s. Harold and Mathilde (Seidel) C.; m. Yvonne DeDrozizhki, Aug. 8, 1971 (dec. Feb. 1980). BA, NYU, 1964, MA, 1965. Archivist, conf. dir. Nat. Archives, Washington, 1967-73; chmn. White House Conf. Pres. & Children, Washington, 1974; editor, writer Manuscript Soc. News, Washington, 1987—; conf. dir. The Manuscript Soc., 1974-80. Dir. history pavilion Hall of Fame Great Am., N.Y.C., 1964; editor Pres. Commn. Civil Disorders, Washington, 1968; mem. (charter) Hildene Robert Todd Lincoln estate; TV commentator; spkr.'s bur. agt. www.leadingauthorities.com.; bd. advisors U.S. Abraham Lincoln Bicentennial Commn., 2002—; spkr. in field. Author: Maximilien Robespierre, 1988; (plays) The Last Lincoln, Princess Alice; contbr. articles to profl. jours. Speechwriter The White House, U.S. Congress, Md. Ho. Dels., 1974—; historian Rock Creek Cemetery, Washington, 1997—. Recipient NYU Heights Daily News Alumni award, 1964, Archival medal, Republic of Korea, 1972, Internat. Psychohistory Assn. award, 1983, Lincoln Group of N.Y. award, 1988, 1992, Man of the Month award, Washington Bus. Jour., 1989, Surratt Soc. award, 1993, delivered ofcl. Lincoln Day Address, Ford's Theatre, Washington, 1996, Smithsonian lectr., 1999—; grantee, Md. Commn. Humanities, 1986, 1987, U.S. Dept. Interior, 1983, Ford Found. fellow, 1964, Johns Hopkins U, Chas Carroll Fulton fellow, 1965. Fellow: The Manuscript Soc.; mem.: Washington Ind. Writers, Nat. Writers Union, Nat. Press Club, NYU Soc. of the Torch, Abraham Lincoln Inst. (trustee 1997—), Lincoln Group D.C. (pres. 1985—88, Lincoln Recognition award 2003), Lincoln Forum (trustee 1997—), Lincoln Group III (trustee 1986—91), NYU Perstare et Praestare, NYU Hon. Soc. Avocation: collecting historic manuscripts & letters. Office: The Manuscript News 8811 Colesville Rd Ste 506 Silver Spring MD 20910-4332 E-mail: stevenlcarson@aol.com.

CARSON, THOMAS BODE, bank executive, consultant; b. Washington, May 30, 1932; s. Thomas D. and Margaret (Bode) C.; m. Anne Conover; 1 child, Natalie Ambrose. BA, Princeton U., 1954; MA, Georgetown U., 1998. V.p. Chase Manhattan Bank, N.Y.C., 1960-68; sr. ops. officer Inter-Am. Devel. Bank, Washington, 1969-89; cons. Washington, 1990—. Author: Beyond the American Dream: Work and Wealth in the 21st Century, 1998. 1st lt. U.S. Army, 1955-57. Fellow Woodrow Wilson Found., 1955. Mem. World Future Soc. (lectr.), Met. Club Washington, Chevy Chase Club, Knickerbocker Club, Phi Beta Kappa. Democrat. Episcopalian. Avocations: futurism, classical music. Home: 3323 Nebraska Ave NW Washington DC 20016

CARSON, THOMAS P. pediatric cardiologist; b. San Diego, May 14, 1951; BS, U. South Fla., 1974, MD, 1979. Diplomate in pediatrics and pediatric cardiology Am. Bd. Pediats. Intern, pediat. resident, fellow Emory U., 1979-84; pvt. practice Orlando, Fla., 1984—; chmn. dept. pediats. Fla. Hosp., 1999—2002. Pres. Orlando Metro divsn. Am. Heart Assn., 1992. Fellow Am. Coll. Cardiology, Am. Acad. Pediat. Office: 3813 Oakwater Cir Orlando FL 32806-6264

CARSON, TIMOTHY JOSEPH, lawyer; b. Darby, Pa., Feb. 17, 1949; s. Joseph Timothy and Marian (Maloney) C.; m. Janet Louise Duffy, May 30, 1975; children: Lindsey, Anne, Timothy J. BS in Econs., U. Pa., 1970; JD, Villanova Sch. Law, 1975. Bar: Pa. 1975, U.S. Ct. Claims 1976, U.S. Tax Ct. 1976. Assoc. Lentz, Riley, Cantor, Kilgore & Massey, Paoli, Pa., 1975-77, Townsend, Elliott & Munson, Phila., 1977; assoc. Saul, Ewing, Remick & Saul, Phila., 1977-81, ptnr. 1981—, chmn. dept. pub. fin., mem. policy com., 1994—; Mng. editor Villanova Law Rev., 1974-75; contbr. articles to profl. jours. and newsletters. Chmn. Tri-State Rep. Alliance, 1984—; mem. SBA Adv. Coun., Phila., 1982-85., Del. Valley Regional Planning Commn., 1996—; spl. advisor Pa. Ho. Local Govt. Com., 1985-88, Pa. Senate Intergovt. Affairs Com., 1989-93; chmn. fin. com. Rep. State Com. Pa., 1986-90, mem. leadership com. 1986-93; del. 1988, alt. del. 1992, Rep. Nat. Conv. Recipient Spl. awards and commendations U. Pa. Bd. Trustees, U.S. Navy and NASA, 1971, Rep. State Com. Pa., 1989, March of Dimes Birth Defects Found., 1990, commnr. Pa. Turnpike Commn., 2000; Fellow Am. Bar Found. (life), Pa. Bar Found., Phila. Bar Found. (trustee 1989-93, pres. 1992, Spl. award 1993, commnr. 1996-2001), Del. Valley Planning Commn. (chmn. 2000-01), Am. Coll. Bond Lawyers; mem. ABA, Phila. Bar Assn. (exec. com. young lawyers sect. 1981-84, bd. govs. 1997-99), Pa. Bar Assn. (bd. govs. 1979-82, 96—, chmn. young lawyers sect. 1980-81, ho. of dels. 1979—, del. 3d cir. jud. conf. 1979, chmn. commn. mcpl. fin. mcpl. law sect. 1984-87, chmn.'s award young lawyers sect. 1981, exec. officer, mem. bd. govs. 1997—, v.p. 2000-01, pres.-elect 2001-02, pres. 2002-03), Nat. Assn. Bond Lawyers, Pa. Assn. of Bond Lawyers (bd. dirs. 1988-90), Mcpl. Bond Club Phila. Republican. Roman Catholic. Clubs: Racquet (Phila.), U. Pa. Faculty, Merion Golf (Ardmore, Pa.). Office: Saul Ewing LLP Centre Sq W 1500 Market St 38th Fl Philadelphia PA 19102-2186*

CARSON, VIRGINIA HILL, oil and gas executive; b. L.A., Dec. 4, 1928; d. Percy Albert McCord and Flora May (Newking) Schultz; m. John Carson, Dec. 30, 1950 (dec.). BA in Internat. Rels., U. Calif., Berkeley, 1949; postgrad., Stanford U., 1948, UCLA, 1951. Gen. office worker UN, San Francisco, 1949; ind. oil and gas profl. U.S., Can., Cuba, 1953-73; supr., specialist, Sun Exploration & Prodn. Co. (named changed to Oryx Energy Co.), Dallas, 1978-83, profl. analyst, 1983-92; lit. rschr. and freelance editor, 1992—. Mem. Dallas Coun. World Affairs, 1984-2003, Dallas Mus. Fine Arts, 1984—; vol. North Tex. Taping and Radio for the Blind, 1992—. Nominated to pres.'s coun. Am. Inst. Mgmt., N.Y.C., 1974. Address: PO Box 12530 Dallas TX 75225-0530

CARSON, WALLACE PRESTON, JR., judge; b. Salem, Oreg., June 10, 1934; s. Wallace Preston and Edith (Bragg) C.; m. Gloria Stolk, June 24, 1956; children: Scott, Carol, Steven (dec. 1981). BA in Politics, Stanford U., 1956; JD, Willamette U., 1962. Bar: Oreg. 1962, U.S. Dist. Ct. Oreg. 1963, U.S. Ct. Appeals (9th cir.) 1968, U.S. Supreme Ct. 1971, U.S. Ct. Mil. Appeals 1977; lic. comml. pilot FAA. Pvt. practice law, Salem, Oreg., 1962-77; judge Marion County Cir. Ct., Salem, 1977-82; assoc. justice Oreg. Supreme Ct., Salem, 1982-92, state supreme ct. chief justice, 1992—. Mem. Oreg. Ho. of Reps., 1967-71, maj. leader, 1969-71; mem. Oreg. State Senate, 1971-77, minority floor leader, 1971-77; dir. Salem Area Community Council, 1967-70, pres., 1969-70; mem. Salem Planning Commn., 1966-72, pres., 1970-71; co-chmn. Marion County Mental Health Planning Com., 1965-69; mem. Salem Community Goals Com., 1965; Republican precinct commiteeman, 1963-66; mem. Marion County Rep. Central Exec. Com., 1963-66; com. predinct edn. Oreg. Rep. Central Com., 1965; vestryman, acolyte, Sunday Sch. tchr., youth coach St. Paul's Episcopal Ch., 1935— ; task force on cts. Oreg. Council Crime and Delinquency, 1968-69; trustee Willamette U., 1970— ; adv. bd. Cath. Ctr. Community Services, 1976-77; mem. comprehensive planning com. Mid-Willamette Valley Council of Govts., 1970-71; adv. com. Oreg. Coll. Edn. Tchr. Edn., 1971-75; pres. Willamette regional Oreg. Lung Assn., 1974-75, state dir., exec. com., 1975-77; pub. relations com. Williamette council Campfire Girls, 1976-77; criminal justice adv. bd. Chemeketa Community Coll., 1977-79; mem. Oreg. Mental Health Com., 1979-80; mem. subcom. Gov's Task Force Mental Health, 1980; you and govt. adv. com. Oreg. YMCA, 1981— . Served to col. USAFR, 1956-59. Recipient Salem Disting. Svc. award, 1968; recipient Good Fellow award Marion County Fire Svc., 1974, Minuteman award Oreg. N.G. Assn., 1980; fellow Eagleton Inst. Politics, Rutgers U., 1971 Mem. Marion County Bar Assn. (sec.-treas. 1965-67, dir. 1968-70), Oreg. Bar Assn., ABA, Willamette U. Coll. Law Alumni Assn. (v.p. 1968-70), Salem Art Assn., Oreg. Hist. Soc., Marion County Hist. Soc., Stanford U. Club (pres. Salem chpt. 1963-64), Delta Theta Phi. Office: Oregon Supreme Ct Supreme Ct Bldg 1163 State St Salem OR 97310-1331*

CARSON, WILLIAM CHARLES, sales and marketing executive; b. Palmyra, N.J., Nov. 9, 1924; s. William and Carrie (Forderer) C.; m. Jean Gingerich, Apr. 1, 1950; children: William Scott, Colleen Jean, Caroline Grace. BA, Gettysburg Coll., 1949. Sales rep. Nat. Sugar Refinery Co., Phila., 1949-60; account exec. Metal Edge Industries, Barrington, N.J., 1960-70, sales mgr., 1970-80; gen. mgr. Metal Edge div. Lydall, Inc., Hartford, Conn., 1980-83; mktg. and sales mgr. Mefco, North Wales, Pa., 1983-90; ret. Campaign chmn. United Way, Berkeley Heights, N.J., 1966, bd. dirs. Burlington County, N.J., 1985—, sec., bd. dirs. Moorestown, N.J., 1984—. Served to cpl. U.S. Army, 1943-45, ETO. Decorated Bronze Star with oak leaf cluster, Purple Heart, Combat Inf. badge. Mem. Am. Mgmt. Assn. (seminar chmn. 1972), Sales & Mktg. Execs. So. Jersey (v.p., bd. dirs. 1974-78), Am. Def. Preparedness Assn. (cons. 1984—, bd. dirs.), Def. Fire Protection Assn. (bd. advisors 1987—), Phi Kappa Psi (sec.). Republican. Avocation: golf. Home: 125 Somers Ct S Moorestown NJ 08057-3419

CARSON, WILLIAM MORRIS, manpower planning and development advisor; s. Edward Belmont and Frances Lucretia (Powell) C.; children: Lincoln Bruce Carson, Adrien Lee Allen, Anthony Lunt Carson, Karen Tracy Carson. BS, Columbia U., 1949; MA, Johns Hopkins U., 1951; postgrad., U. Chgo., 1955, London Sch. Econs., 1956; diploma in Arabic, Middle East Ctr. Arab Studies, 1969. Cairo corr. MBS, 1951-53; asst. prof. Mid. East Studies, SAIS, 1955-56; tng. officer U.S. AID, 1958-64; indsl. rels. staff analyst ARAMCO, Dhahran, Saudi Arabia, 1964-70; mgr. mgmt. deve. and tng. Saudi Arabian Airlines, Jeddah, 1970-72; chief tng. sect. UN Devel. Programme, N.Y.C., 1973-75; mgr. mgmt. devel. and tng. Sulvania Tng. Ops., Waltham, Mass., 1975-76; dir. tng. Ingersoll-Rand Constrn. Svcs., Winston-Salem, N.C., 1977-79; sr. advisor manpower planning and devel. Internat. Human Resources Devel. Corp., Boston, 1979-83; gen. mgr. ITECO divsn. Saudi Tng. Svcs., Riyadh, Saudi Arabia, 1983-84; mng. dir. Arab Resources Devel. Corp., Mass., 1984-87; mgr. Turkish tech. projects GE Internat. Svc. Corp., 1987-92; prin. Carson & Assocs., Balt., 1992-96, Nat. Manpower Strategies, 1997—. Cons. UN, Middle East Inst. fellow, Ford Found. area fellow. Co-author: International Manpower Planning: The Developing World, 1982; also articles. Recipient Outstanding Performance award AID. Fellow Royal Anthrop. Inst. Gt. Britain and No. Ireland, Inst. Comml. Mgmt.; mem. Ineamus Meloria Honor Soc. Address: 1908 C St Forest Grove OR 97116-2308 E-mail: tosca@prodigy.net.

CARSON, WILLIAM SCOTT, lawyer; b. Buffalo, Mar. 13, 1946; s. William Dana and Barbara Brenneman (Powell) C.; m. Elizabeth Karin Ellis, June 28, 1977; children— Bradley Robert, Karen Elizabeth. B.S., Brown U., 1969, A.B., 1969; J.D. with honors, George Washington U., 1973. Bar: Va. 1974, D.C. 1974, U.S. Patent and Trademark Office 1974, Colo. 1977, U.S. Ct. Appeals (D.C. cir.) 1982. Examiner, U.S. Patent Office, Arlington, Va., 1969-74; ptnr. Burton, Dorr and Carson, Denver, 1980-86, Dorr, Carson, Sloan & Peterson, 1987—. Mem. ABA, Colo. Bar Assn., Denver Bar Assn., Licensing Execs. Soc. Home: 101 Hudson St Denver CO 80220-5831 Office: Dorr Carson Sloan & Peterson 720 S Colorado Blvd Ste 1240 Denver CO 80246-1904

CARSTAIRS, SHARON, state legislator; b. Halifax, Nova Scotia, Apr. 26, 1942; d. Vivian and Harold Connolly; m. John Esdale Carstairs, 1966; children: Cathi, Jennie. BA in Polit. Sci. and History, Dalhousie U., 1962; MA in Teaching of History, Smith Coll., 1963; postgrad., Georgetown U., 1964, U. Calgary, 1968. Tchr. Dana Hall Sch. for Girls, Wellesley, Mass., 1963-65, Calgary (Alta.) Separate Sch. Bd., 1965-71; chmn. bd. referees Unemployment Ins. Commn., 1973-77; tchr. St. John's Ravenscourt Sch., Winnipeg, Man., 1978-81, St. Norbert (Man.) Collegiate, 1982-84; elected leader Liberal Party in Man., 1984; elected mem. Man. Legis. Assembly, River Heights, 1986—; elected leader Ofcl. Opposition, 1988-90; appointed to Senate, 1994—; appointed dep. leader of the govt. in the Senate, 1997-99; appointed leader, 2001—; appointed min. of health, 2002—; min. of justic and atty. gen. of Can., 1997—2002. Scriptwriter, narrator Calgary and Region Ednl. TV, 1967-69. Brownie leader, Halifax and Winnipeg; mem. Parks and Recreation Bd., City of Calgary; fund-raiser Manitoba Heart Found.; canvasser Can. Cancer Soc., Alta., Man., Alta. Soc. for the Mentally Retarded; vol. Man. Mus. of Man and Nature; bd. mem. Women and the Arts, Nursing Coun. Man.; campaign worker provincial elections, Nova Scotia, 1948, 52, 56, 60; exec. positions Dalhousie U. Liberal Club, Nova Scotia, 1958-62; nat. exec. Univ. Liberals, Nova Scotia, 1960-62, others; poll capt. Fed. elections, Alta. 1965, 68, 72, 74; exec. Alta. Women's Liberal Assn., 1965-68; sec. Liberal Party, Alta., 1968-70, v.p., 1972-74, pres., 1975-77, nat. exec. 1975-77; Calgary Regional v.p., Liberal Party Alta., 1970-72; mem. Fed. Campaign com., Alta. 1972, 74, Man. 1983—; candidate Provincial Liberal, Alta. 1975; poll worker Ft. Rouge Provincial constituency, Man., 1977, Ft. Garry Fed. constituency, Man., 1979-80; office mgr, Tuxedo Provincial constituency, Man., 1981; exec., River Heights Provincial constituency, Man., 1983—; mem. Man. Legislative Assembly 1986—; elected leader Official Opposition, Man., 1988-90. Recipient Dalhousie U. Entrance scholarship, Dalhousie U. scholarship, Smith Coll. Grad. fellowship. Mem. Winnipeg C. of C. Liberal Party Can.

CARSTARPHEN, EDWARD MORGAN, III, lawyer; b. Ancon, Panama Canal Zone, Oct. 25, 1957; s. Edward Morgan and Norlavine (Carson) C.; m. Celia LaRae Rawlings Buchalski, June 3, 1979 (div. Apr. 1990); 1 child, Lucy Catherine; m. Darleen Colton, Aug. 29, 1991; 1 child, Desirae Dixon Peters. BA cum laude, Vanderbilt U., 1979; JD, U. Tex., 1982. Bar: Tex. 1982, U.S. Dist. Ct. (so. dist.) Tex. 1983, U.S. Ct. Appeals (5th cir.) 1984, cert. in civil trial law Tex. Bd. Legal Specialization. Assoc. Holtzman & Urquhart, Houston, 1982-84; briefing atty. to chief justice Tex. State Ct. Appeals for 6th Dist., Texarkana, 1984-85; ptnr. Brockway & Carstarphen, Houston, 1985-86, Powers & Carstarphen, Houston, 1987; of counsel Woodard, Hall & Primm, P.C., Houston, 1988-91, ptnr., 1991—2001. Contbr. articles to profl. publs., chpt. to book. Fellow Tex. Bar Found.; mem. State Bar Tex., Phi Delta Phi. Office: Ellis Carstarphen Dougherty & Goldenthal PC 720 N Post Oak Rd Ste 330 Houston TX 77024

CARSTEN, ARLAND LEON, radiobiologist, researcher, educator, consultant; b. Hastings, Minn., Apr. 17, 1930; s. John Peter Carsten and Alfreda Victoria Rydeen; m. Marcia Carsten; 1 child, Stephanie. BS, Mankato (Minn.) State U., 1953; MS, PhD, U. Rochester, 1957. Diplomate Am. Bd. Health Physics. Rsch. assoc. in neurology Columbia U., N.Y.C., 1964—74; from asst. scientist to sr. scientist Broohaven Nat. Lab., Upton, NY, 1957—. From adj. rsch. assoc. prof. to prof. of pathology SUNY, Stony Brook, 1971—. Contbr. articles to profl. jours. Mem. and bd. dirs. Bellport Beach Property Owners Assn., East Patchogue, NY, 1966—. Staff sgt. U.S. Army, 1950—51. Recipient Bausch & Lomb Sci. award, 1948; fellow in radiol. physics, Atomic Energy Commn. Mem.: L.I. (N.Y.) Am. Nuclear Soc. (exec. bd.), Am. Nuc. Soc., Internat. Soc. Exptl. Hematology, Bioelectromagnetics Soc., Gentic Toxicology Assn., Environ. Mutagen Soc., Health Physics Soc., Radiation Rsch. Soc. (various). Avocations: golf, tennis, skiing, sailing, music. Office: Brookhaven Nat Lab Bldg 703M Upton NY 11973

CARSTEN, JACK CRAIG, venture capitalist; b. Cin., Aug. 24, 1941; s. John A. and Edith L. C.; m. Mary Ellis Jones, June 22, 1963; children: Scott, Elizabeth, Amy. BS in Physics, Duke U., 1963. Mktg. mgr. Tex. Instruments, Dallas, Houston, 1965-71, integrated circuits gen. mgr. Houston, 1971-75; v.p. sales and mktg. Intel Corp., Santa Clara, Calif., 1975-79, v.p., microcomputer gen. mgr., 1979-82, sr. v.p., components gen. mgr., 1982-87; gen. ptnr. U.S. Venture Ptnrs., Menlo Park, Calif., 1988-90; venture capitalist Tech. Investments, Los Altos, Calif., 1990-99, Horizon Ventures LLC, Los Altos, 2000—. Bd. dirs. Socket Comms., Inc., Comerica Bank-CA, and several privately held firms. Contbr. articles to profl.jours. Office: Horizon Ventures LLC 4 Main St Los Altos CA 94022-2998 E-mail: jack@carsten.com.

CARSTENS, CHARLENE B. composer, music educator; b. Chgo., Dec. 11, 1932; d. Sidney and Anne Donner Gross; m. Jay M. Brown, June 28, 1953 (div. Apr. 1976); children: Sharon Brown, Julie Brown; m. H. Paul Carstens, Oct. 17, 1986. BMus, Roosevelt U., Chgo., 1969; MMus, Roosevelt U., 1978. Mgr. R &

D grad. program libr. Northwestern U., Evanston, Ill., 1971—73; editor books, reports, papers Joan Masters, Inc., Chgo., 1976—77; founder, dir. The Music Sch., Springfield, Ill., 1978—81; faculty St. Martha's Sch., Sarasota, Fla., 1981—85, Manatee C.C., Sarasota, 1986—88; tchr. piano The Music Sch., Springfield, 1970—89; pvt. piano tchr. Chgo., Sarasota, 1970—89. Concert pianist various civic, music and ch. groups, various locations; lectr. in field; judge various piano competitions; rschr., dir. program of rare Am. civil war music City of Springfield, 1979; radio commentator Sunday Song, WSSR pub. radio, Springfield, 1978—80. Composer: Sing Along with Grandma Char, vols. I and II, 1991—92; author: Remembrances: Growing Up in Hollywood Park (Chicago, Ill.), 2002. Music dir. La Traviata Roman Cultural Soc., Springfield, 1981; chmn. Lincolnfest, Celebrity Corner City of Springfield, 1981; dir.75th anniversary show Sarasota Power Squadron, 1989; bd. dirs. Fla. West Coast Symphony Music Festival, Sarasota, 1987—89. Mem.: Sarasota Music Tchrs. Assn., Music Tchrs. Nat. Assn., Coll. Music Soc. Home: 7777 Calle Facil Sarasota FL 34238

CARSTENS, JANE ELLEN, retired library science educator; b. New Iberia, La., Apr. 19, 1922; d. Charles John and Marie Claudia (Blanchet) C. BA in Elem. Edn., U. Southwestern La., 1942; BS in LS, La. State U., 1945; MS in LS, Columbia U., 1955, DLS, 1975. Asst. libr. Hamilton Lab. sch. and instr. libr. sci. U. Southwestern La., Lafayette, 1942-54, asst. prof., 1954-65, assoc. prof., 1965-75; children's librarian/storyteller N.Y. Pub. Libr., N.Y.C., 1947, 48-49; vis. lectr. U. Minn., Mpls., 1955-56, summer 59, La. State U., Baton Rouge, summer 1958, State Coll. Iowa, Cedar Falls, summer 1963; prof. libr. sci. U. Southwestern La., Lafayette, 1975-94. Vis. lectr. Syracuse U., summers 1962, 64, U. Tex., Austin, summers 1976-86, 89. Trustee Our Lady of Wisdom Cath. Ch., 1995-2003. Named Tchr. of Yr., Amoco, 1982, Outstanding Alumna, U. Southwestern La., 1986; recipient Essae Culver Disting. Svc. award La. Libr. Assn., 1987, Alumni Faculty Excellence award Blue Key, 1990, Faculty Advisor of Yr. award U. Southwestern La. Student Govt. Assn., 1992, Point of Excellence award Kappa Delta Pi, 1992, Outstanding Tchr. award USL Found., 1994; Blue Key Faculty/Student Staff Directory dedicated to her, 1994-95. Mem. ALA, Assn. Libr. and Info. Sci. Edn., Assn. Libr. Svc. to Children (mem. Newbery award com. 1989-90), Am. Assn. Sch. Librs., La. Libr. Assn. (pres. 1959-60), Young Adult Libr. Svc. Assn., Lafayette Pub. Libr. Found., Univ. Women's Club, Phi Kappa Phi (pres. USL chpt. 1984-85), Delta Kappa Gamma (pres. Alpha chpt. 1988-90). Roman Catholic. Home: 214 Saint Joseph St Lafayette LA 70506-4535 also: ULL La Lafayette PO Box 40298 Lafayette LA 70504-0001

CARSTENSEN, EDWIN LORENZ, biomedical engineer, biophysicist; b. Oakdale, Nebr., Dec. 8, 1919; s. August Hans and Opal Lois (Norwood) C.; m. Pam McDonald, Aug. 1, 1947; children: Richard Lorenz, Allen Brent, Laura Lee, Loretta Dee, Christina Marie. BS, Nebr. State Tchrs. Coll., 1941; MS, Case Inst. Tech., 1947; PhD, U. Pa., 1955. Mem. sci. staff div. war rsch. Columbia U., 1942-45; head lab. sect. U.S. Navy Underwater Sound Reference Lab., Orlando, Fla., 1945-48; rsch. assoc. Moore Sch. Elec. Engring., U. Pa., 1948-55, asst. prof. elec. engring., 1955-56; prin. investigator U.S. Army Biol. Lab., Fort Detrick, Frederick, Md., 1956-61; assoc. prof. elec. engring. U. Rochester, 1961-73, prof., 1973-88, Arthur Gould Yates prof. engring., 1988-90, Arthur Gould Yates prof. engring. emeritus, 1990—, dir. biomed. engring., 1971-83, prof. biophysics, 1981-90, univ. mentor, 1982—, sr. scientist in elec. engring., 1990—. Dir. Rochester Ctr. for Biomed. Ultrasound, 1986-90. Author: Biological Effects of Transmission Line Fields, 1987; contbr. numerous articles to profl. pubs. Fellow Acoustical Soc. Am., IEEE, Am. Inst. Ultrasound in Medicine; mem. Biophys. Soc., Biomed. Engring. Soc., Nat. Acad. Engring. Democrat. Home: 103 Eastland Ave Rochester NY 14618-1027 Office: U Rochester Dept Elec/Computer Engring Rochester NY 14627 E-mail: ecarsten@rochester.rr.com.

CARSWELL, JANE TRIPLETT, retired family physician; b. Raeford, N.C., Feb. 26, 1932; d. Arthur Dula and Madeline Mapp (Warburton) C. Student, Flora Macdonald Coll., 1950-52; AB in Chemistry, U. N.C., 1954; MD, Med. Coll. Va., 1958. Diplomate Am. Bd. Family Practice. Resident Med. Coll. Va., Richmond, 1958-61; practice medicine specializing in family medicine Harlan, Ky., 1961-62, Lenoir, N.C., 1962—. Chmn. Lenoir Human Relations Com., N.C., 1962-64; vice-chmn. Caldwell County Council Status of Women, Lenoir, 1976-78 Mem. Caldwell County Med. Soc. (pres. 1965), N.C. Acad. Family Physicians (N.C. Family Physician of Yr. award 1983), N.C. Med. Soc., Am. Acad. Family Practice (Nat. Family Dr. of Yr. award 1984) Presbyterian. Avocations: wildflowers; hiking; backpacking; skiing; photography.

CARSWELL, LOIS MALAKOFF, botanical gardens executive, consultant; b. N.Y.C., Mar. 2, 1932; d. Arthur and Dora (Krechevsky) Malakoff; m. Donald Carswell, Oct. 12, 1957; children: Anne Carswell Tang, Alexander, Robert Ian. AB magna cum laude, Radcliffe Coll., 1953; cert. in bus. adminstrn., Harvard U. and Radcliffe Coll., 1954. Editor Dell Pub. Co., N.Y.C., 1954-56; publicist Ruth E. Pepper Co., N.Y.C., 1957-58; vol. Bklyn. Botanic Garden, 1964—, co-chmn. plant sales, 1967—, co-chmn. capital campaign, 1984-88, chmn. bd. dirs., 1989-98, chmn. emeritus, 1998—. Chmn. Coalition Living Mus. N.Y. State, N.Y.C., 1980—; cons. N.Y. State Natural Heritage Trust, 1982—. Office: Bklyn Botanic Garden 1000 Washington Ave Brooklyn NY 11225-1008 E-mail: loiscarswell@bbg.org.

CARTAINO, CAROL ANN, editor; b. N.Y.C., Dec. 7, 1944; d. Pietro Michael and Ann Wanda (Scotch) C.; 1 child, Clayton Collier-Cartaino. BA, Rutgers U., 1966; postgrad., NYU, 1967-68. Cert. English tchr., N.J. Prodn. editor trade book Prentice-Hall, Inc., Englewood Cliffs, N.J., 1966-68, from asst. to assoc. editor trade book, 1968-72, editor trade book, 1972-77; editor-in-chief Writer's Digest Books, Cin., 1978-86, freelance editor and collaborator, 1986—; editl. dir. Don Aslett, Inc., Pocatello, Idaho, 1987-93, Marsh Creek Press, Pocatello, Idaho, 1993—; assoc. Collier Assoc. Literary Agy., Seaman, Ohio, 1987-94; proprietor freelance editing and book cons. svc. White Oak Edits., 1987—; proprietor Carol Cartaino, Lit. Agt., 1994—. Speaker in field; instr. in writing So. State C.C., Hillsboro and Wilmington, Ohio, 1989—. Author: Keeping Work Simple, 1997, Get Organized, Get Published!, 2001. Vol. nurses aide Hackensack (N.J.) Hosp. State of N.J. scholar, 1962-66, Emerson (N.J.) PTA scholar, 1962. Roman Catholic. Avocations: hiking, photography, gardening, nature study. Home and Office: 2000 Flat Run Rd Seaman OH 45679-9412 E-mail: cartaino@aol.com.

CARTEN, FRANCIS NOEL, lawyer; b. Bryn Mawr, Pa., Dec. 25, 1935; s. Francis Patrick and Louise Cathleen (Leach) C. BS, U. Notre Dame, 1960; JD, Villanova U., 1964. Bar: Pa. 1967, N.Y. 1967, Conn. 1976. Assoc. Eyre, Mann & Lucas, N.Y.C., 1966-74; pvt. practice Danbury and Stamford, Conn., 1975-78, Stamford, 1985-88; patent counsel TIE/Comm., Inc., Shelton, Conn., 1978-79, Automation Industries, Inc., Greenwich, Conn., 1979-85; ptnr. Wyatt, Gerber & O'Rourke), LLP, Stamford, 1988—. With U.S. Army, 1954-56. Mem. N.Y. Intellectual Property Law Assn., Seawanhaka Corinthian Yacht Club (Oyster Bay, N.Y.). Republican. E-mail: fncarten@att.net.

CARTER, ANNA DEAN, volunteer; b. Lafayette, Tenn., June 21, 1935; d. Virgil Heston and Elsie Irene (Law) King; m. Billy Wilson Carter, Nov. 3, 1954; children: Billy Jr., Gerald, Debra. Grad. high sch., Lafayette, Tenn. Waitress Walgreen Drug, Lafayette, Tenn., 1951-54; factory Formfit Rogers, Lafayette, Tenn., 1955-56; substitute tchr. Macon County Schs., Lafayette, Tenn., 1958-59; factory True Loom Mfg. Co., Lafayette, Tenn., 1959-67; sch. sec. Macon County Schs., Lafayette, Tenn., 1968; bookkeeper Macon-Trousdale Coop., Lafayette, Tenn., 1968-98; retired, 1998. County commn. Macon County Govt., 1990—; E911 bd. dirs. Macon County, 1994—; mem. Tenn. Rural Health, Cookeville, 1998; sec. Macon County Health Coun., 1996—2001; v.p. Upper Culberland Health, 1998—; mem. Macon County Fair Bd., 1996—; active Macon County Job Svc., 1997—2002; mem. Macon Edn. Found., 1997—; bd. dirs. Tenn. Families First, 1998—. Named to, Board-Macon County Sports Hall of Fame, 2000. Mem.: Am. Assn. Retired People, Macon Sch. Health Advisory Bd., Macon County C. of C. (bd. dirs. 1998—2001, pres. 1999—), Sr. Citizens Orgn. (bd. dirs. 1999—), Historic Preservation Soc. (pres. 1996—). Baptist. Avocations: reading, needlework, photography, writing, walking. Home: 209 Donoho Ave Lafayette TN 37083-1404 E-mail: adcarter@nctc.com.

CARTER, ASHLEY HALE, physicist, educator; m. Eva Horvath Carter; children: Deborah Anne, Sarah Judith, Ashley Hale, Jr. AB, Harvard Coll., 1946; PhD, Brown U., 1963. Rsch. assoc. Woods Hole (Mass.) Oceanographic Instn., 1946—47; dept. head AT&T Bell Labs., Whippany, NJ, 1953—90; adj. prof. physics Drew U., Madison, NJ, 1975—, dir. Charles A. Dana Rsch. Inst. for Scientists Emeriti, 1999—. Author: (book) Classical and Statistical Thermodynamics, 2001. Lt. (j.g.) USN, 1943—46. Mem.: Acoustical Soc. Am., Am. Assn. Physics Tchrs., Am. Phys. Soc. Democrat. Avocations: literature, art, music, essay writing. Office: Drew U Hall of Scis 322 Madison NJ 07940 E-mail: acarter@drew.edu.

CARTER, BARRY EDWARD, lawyer, educator, administrator; b. L.A., Oct. 14, 1942; s. Byron Edward and Ethel Catherine (Turner) C.; m. Kathleen Anne Ambrose, May 17, 1987; children: Gregory Ambrose, Meghan Elisabeth. AB with great distinction, Stanford U., 1964; M.P.A., Princeton U., 1966; JD, Yale U., 1969. Bar: Calif. 1970, D.C. 1972. Program analyst Office of Sec. Def., Washington, 1969-70; mem. staff NSC, Washington, 1970-72; rsch. fellow Kennedy Sch., Harvard U., Cambridge, Mass., 1972; internat. affairs fellow Coun. on Fgn. Rels., 1972; assoc. Wilmer, Cutler & Pickering, Washington, 1973-75; sr. counsel Select Com. on Intelligence Activities, U.S. Senate, Washington, 1975; assoc. Morrison & Foerster, San Francisco, 1976-79; assoc. prof. law Georgetown U. Law Ctr., Washington, 1979-89, prof., 1989-93, 96—; exec. dir. Am. Soc. Internat. Law, Washington, 1992-93; acting undersec. for export adminstrn. U.S. Dept. Commerce, Washington, 1993-94, deputy undersec., 1994-96. Vis. prof. law Stanford U. Law Sch., 1990; bd. dirs. RWE Nukem, Inc., 1998—; chmn. adv. bd. Def. Budget Project, 1990—93; mem. UN Assn. Soviet-Am. Parallel Studies Project, 1976—87; adv. coun. Zurich Emerging Markets Solutions, 2001—. Author: International Economic Sanctions: Improving the Haphazard U.S. Legal Regime, 1988 (Am. Soc. Internat. Law Cert. of Merit 1989); co-author: International Law, 4th edit., 2003; co-editor: Internat. Law: Selected Documents, 2003—; contbr. articles to profl. jours. With U.S. Army, 1969-71. Mem.: ABA, Am. Soc. Internat. Law (hon. v.p. 1993—99, counselor 1999—2000), Coun. on Fgn. Rels., DC Bar Assn., Calif. Bar Assn., Am. Law Inst., Am. Bar Found., Phi Beta Kappa. Democrat. Roman Catholic. Home: 2922 45th St NW Washington DC 20016-3559 Office: Georgetown U Law Ctr 600 New Jersey Ave NW Washington DC 20001-2075 E-mail: carter@law.georgetown.edu.

CARTER, BECKY SUE, neonatal/perinatal nurse practitioner, consultant; b. Medina, Ohio, Feb. 1, 1961; d. Robert Gerald and Janet Marie Reich; m. Robin John Carter; children: Jennifer, Nicholas. M in Nursing, U. Wash., 1998. Lic. neonatal nurse practitioner-NCC. RN adult ICU U.S. Army Nurse Corps, Medina, 1983—89; neonatal intensive care RN Healthstaffers, Tacoma, 1989—91. Dir. program devel. cmty.-based lactation program, 1998. Author: Mother/Baby Care, 1996, (pamphlet) Down Syndrome, 1995. Vol. Wash. Spl. Olympics Assn., Gig Harbor, 1996—; vol. spkr. Health Edn. Class, Puyallup, Wash. Capt. U.S. Army, 1983—89. Recipient Svc. medal, U.S. Army, 1983, People's Choice award, Good Samaritan Hosp., 1996, 1998, People's Choice Elite Award, 1997. Mem.: Pacific N.W. Assn. Neonatal Nurses, Nat. Assn. Neonatal Nurses, Assn. Health Obstetric and Neonatal Nurses. Office: Children's Hosp 4800 Sand Point Way Seattle WA 98105 Office Fax: 425-261-3747. Personal E-mail: rjc@centurytel.net. Business E-Mail: Becky.Carter@providence.org.

CARTER, BRET ROBERT, lawyer; b. Muscatine, Iowa, Oct. 8, 1959; s. Burt Eugene and Mary Esther Carter; m. Hazel Mary Williams, Oct. 5, 1991. BS, Iowa State U., 1982; JD, Pepperdine U., 1987. Bar: Calif. 1987, U.S. Dist. Ct. (so. dist.) Calif., 1987, U.S. Dist. Ct. (cen., no. dists.) Calif., 1988, U.S. Dist. Ct. (ea. dist.) Calif., 1990, U.S. Ct. Appeals (9th cir.), 1993. Atty. Booth Mitchell & Strange, L.A., 1986-88, John T. Heaney, A Law Corp., L.A., 1988-93, Hart & Watters, L.A., 1993—. Contbr. articles to profl. jours. Mem. ARC, Santa Monica, Calif., City Hope-Bus. L.A. Recipient Young Lawyer award Achievement ABA, 1990. Mem. L.A. Venture Assn., Beverly Hills Bar Assn. (v.p. bd. govs. 1990-92), L.A. Bus. Property Coun. Avocations: hiking, biking. Office: Hart & Watters 12400 Wilshire Blvd Ste 500 Los Angeles CA 90025-1055

CARTER, BUTCH, professional basketball coach, former sports team executive; Grad., Ind. U. Player L.A. Lakers, 1980, Ind. Pacers, N.Y. Knicks, Phila. 76ers; coach Middletown (Ohio) H.S., 1986; asst. coach Long Beach (Calif.) State U., U. Dayton, 1989-91, Milw. Bucks, 1991-96, Toronto Raptors, 1997-98, head coach, 1998—. Named 1988 Ohio Coach of the Year, AP. Achievements include NBA record for most points scored in an overtime period, 1984. Office: Toronto Raptors 40 Bay St Ste 300 Toronto ON Canada M5J 2Y2

CARTER, CARLA CIFELLI, management consultant; b. Chicago Heights, Ill., June 2, 1949; d. John Louis and Irene Frances (Romandine) Cifelli. BA, Western Mich. U., 1971; MBA, Ariz. State U., 1985. Tchr. Limestone (Maine) High Sch., 1971-75; mgr. employment and tng. Chubb Life Ins., Concord, N.H., 1975-78; employee relations supr. TRW, Inc., Plainville, Conn., 1978-79; asst. dir. corp. tng. Cigna, Bloomfield, Conn., 1979-82; cons. to human resources dept. Sentry Ins. Co., Scottsdale, Ariz., 1983-84; asst. v.p. Bank of Am., Phoenix, 1984-87; pres. Carla Carter & Assocs., Inc., 1986—; employee devel. adminstr. City of Phoenix, 1987-90; dir. Am. Productivity and Quality Ctr., Houston, 1990-95. Sr. examiner Ariz. Quality Alliance, 1994-95; presenter in field. Author: Human Resources and the Total Quality Imperative, 1994, Understanding the Organization, 1982, The Responsive City, Am. Productivity and Quality Ctr., 1990, Seven Basic Tools, HR mag., 1992, Measuring and Improving the HR Function Continous Journey, 1993, Using TQM Principles to Develop Executives, Employment Relations Today, 1994, Making Measurement Work, 2000. Advisor Literary Vols., Phoenix, 1989; mem. tech. integrity coun. Ariz. Quality Alliance, 1996—. Mem. ASTD (govtl. affairs dir. 1988-89, comm. dir. 2000—), Am. Soc. Quality, Orgn. Devel. Network, Soc. Human Resource Mgmt., The Conf. Bd., LOMA Human Resources Forum, Ariz. Quality Alliance Avocations: reading, music, outdoor activities. Office: 6036 E Mountain View Rd Scottsdale AZ 85253

CARTER, CAROLYN HOUCHIN, advertising agency executive; b. Louisville, Nov. 2, 1952; d. Paul Clayton and Georgia (Houchin) C.; m. Jeffrey Starr, Dec. 8, 1988. BS in Journalism, Northwestern U., 1974, MS in Journalism, 1975. Asst. account exec. SSC&B Advt., Inc., N.Y.C., 1975-76, account exec., 1976-77, Grey Advt., Inc., N.Y.C., 1977-79, account supr., 1979-82, v.p., 1981-82, v.p., mgmt. supr., 1982-87, v.p., group mgmt. supr., 1985-87, sr. v.p., 1987-92, exec. v.p., 1992—2000; pres. Grey Worldwide Europe, Mid. East and Africa, 2000—02, Grey Global Group Europe, Mid. East, Africa, 2002—. Mem. Nat. Advt. Rev. Bd., 1983-87; mem. adv. bd. advt. history Smithsonian Nat. Mus. Am. History, 1988-94. Chmn. media advt. coun. March of Dimes, 1981-86; mem. U.S. coun. World Commn. Yr., 1983; active YMCA Acad. Women Achievers, 1992. Recipient Clairol Mentor award Clairol, Inc., 1991. Mem. Women in Comm. (pres. N.Y. chpt. 1982-83, N.Y. Matrix award in advt. 1988, Nat. Headliner award 1991), Internat. Women's Forum (bd. dirs. N.Y. chpt. 1994), Advt. Women N.Y. (bd. dirs. 1987-88). Office: Grey Global Group 777 3d Ave New York NY 10017-1401

CARTER, CAROLYN MARIE, social work executive; b. Takoma Park, Md., Oct. 27, 1954; d. Cecil Frederick and Carolyn (Middleton) Ellingwood; m. Warren Grover Carter Jr., May 16, 1975; adopted children: Timothy Allen Carter, Natasha Ashley McNeil Carter, Jade Tiara Carter, Andrew Julian Carter. BA, U. Md., 1976; MSW, U. Pa., 1985. Lic. cert. clin. social worker. Employment counselor Md. Job Svc., Crisfield, 1978-82; social worker Worcester County Dept. of Social Svcs., Snow Hill, Md., 1982-87; social work supr. Ea. Correctional Instn., Westover, Md., 1987—. Adj. instr. Univ. Md. Sch. Social Work and Community Planning, Balt., 1988—; instr. social work, sociology U. Md. Ea. Shore and Salisbury State U. Recipient Can Do Svc. award, Gov. of Md., 1990, Gov.'s citation for Svc. to Student Interns, 1993. Mem. Nat. Assoc. Acad. Cert. Social Workers. Democrat. Presbyterian. Avocations: travel, tennis. Office: Ea Correctional Inst 30420 Revels Neck Rd Westover MD 21890-3368

CARTER, CATHERINE LOUISE, elementary and middle school educator; b. Oakland, Calif., Mar. 31, 1947; d. Robert Collidge and Mae (Reidy) C. BA, Ohio Wesleyan U. Tchr. Barclay Elem. Sch., Cherry Hill, N.J., 1969-72, Malberg Elem. Sch., Cherry Hill, 1972-80, Beck Mid. Sch., Cherry Hill, 1980-89, 94-95, Carusi Jr. H.S., Cherry Hill, 1989—94, 1995—2002. Coord. Nat. Women's History Month Cherry Hill Jr. Schs., 1993-2002. Advisor Mother Earth and Friends Environ. Club, 1989-2000; mem. dist. Recycling Program Cherry Hill Pub. Schs., 1990-94, Womyn and Religion Untarian Universalist Ch. Cherry Hill, 1994—, Nat. Mus. Women Arts, 1996—, Women's Philharm., 1997—; sponser Childreach, 1997—. Mem. Nat. Ret. Tchr. Educators Assn., N.J. Ret. Tchr. Edn. Assn., Camden County Ret, Tchr. Edn. Assn., Cherry Hill Ret. Tchr. Edn. Assn., NOW,World Wildlife Fedn., Global Fund for Women, Planned Parenthood, Alice Paul Centenial Found., Seeking Edn. Equity and Diversity (study group 1994), Freedom from Hunger, Population Comms. Internat. Avocations: foreign travel, foreign films, arts, nature, jazz. Home: 10 Brookwood Dr Voorhees NJ 08043-4757

CARTER, CHARLENE ANN, psychologist; b. Marshall, Mich., Apr. 7, 1941; d. Charles V. F. and Eva L. (Hesling) Hampton.; m. Ross E. Carter, Jan. 15, 1966; children: Laura, Paul. BA in Psychology and Sociology, Albion Coll., 1962; MA in Clin. Psychology, Mich. State U., 1964, PhD in Clin. Psychology, 1968. Lic. psychologist, Wis. Clin. intern VA Hosp., Battle Creek, Mich., 1963-65, Psychol. Clinic, Mich. State U., East Lansing, 1965-66, Counseling Ctr., Mich. State U., East Lansing, 1966-68, asst. prof., 1968-69; clin. assoc. prof. dept. psychiatry and mental health sci. Med. Coll. Wis., Milw., 1983—; clin. asst. prof. dept. psychology U. Wis., Milw., 1993—; pvt. practice Bangor, Maine, 1971, Media, Pa., 1974-75, Milw., 1988—. Dir. clin. tng. Wis. Sch. for Girls, Oregon, Wis., 1969—70; staff psychologist The Counseling Ctr., Cmty. Mental Health Ctr., Bangor, Maine, 1971; mem. staff Aurora Psychiat. Hosp., 1989—, Waukesha Meml. Hosp., Waukesha, Wis., 1992—, Rogers Hosp., 2001—; psychologist cons. Office of Hearing and Appeals, Social Security Adminstrn., Milw., 1986—91; lectr. in field. Contbr. articles to profl. jours. USPHS fellow, 1962, 65, 66. Mem. APA. Office: Mayfair North Tower 2600 N Mayfair Rd Ste 320 Milwaukee WI 53226-1313

CARTER, CHERYL A. endoscopy nurse; b. Morgantown, W.Va., Apr. 11, 1960; d. Kenneth W. and Dorothy Eloise (Phillips) Smyth; m. James L. Carter, Oct. 15, 1988. BSN, W.Va. U., 1982. Staff nurse Ohio Valley Med. Ctr., Wheeling, W.Va., Riverside Meth. Hosp., Columbus, Ohio. Mem.: Soc. Gastroenterology Nurses and Assocs., Sigma Theta Tau. Home: 1974 Brittany Rd Columbus OH 43229-5706

CARTER, CHRIS, producer, director; b. Bellflower, Calif., Oct. 13, 1957; m. Dori Pierson Carter, 1989. Dir., exec. prodr., creator: The X-Files, 1993; author: The B.R.A.T. Patrol; composer: (films) In the Shadow of the Sun, 1980, (TV series) Rags to Riches, 1987; exec. prodr.(creator): Millenium, 1996; prodr.: (films) The X-Files, 1998; (TV series) Harsh Realm, 1999, Cameo by Night, 1987; co-author: Riptide, 2000. Named one of Time Mags. Most Influential Ams., 1997. Office: Broder Kurland Webb Uffner c/o Elliott Webb 9242 Beverly Blvd Ste 200 Beverly Hills CA 90210-3731

CARTER, COLIN ANDRE, education educator; b. Grande Prairie, Alberta, Can., Jan. 30, 1954; s. John Adley and Amy Janet (Flaten) Carter; m. Noreen Ann Roche; children: Dakota, Olesya. BA, U. Alberta, 1974, MSc, 1976; MA, U. Calif., Berkeley, 1978, PhD, 1980. Prof. U. Calif., Davis, 1986—. Cons. in field. Contbr. articles to profl. jours. Fellow: Am. Agrl. Econ. Assn. Avocation: golf. Office: Univ Calif One Shields Ave Davis CA 95616

CARTER, CRIS, retired professional football player, sportscaster; b. Middletown, Ohio, Nov. 25, 1965; Student, Ohio State U. With Phila. Eagles, 1987—89; wide receiver Minn. Vikings, 1990—2001; mem. Miami Dolphins, 2002; co-host Inside the NFL, 2002—. Named to Pro Bowl, 1993, The Sporting News NFL All-Pro team, 1994; recipient NFL Man of the Yr. award, 1999. Achievements include holding NFL single-season record for most pass receptions, 122, 1994.

CARTER, DALE WILLIAM, psychologist; b. Woodbury, N.J., Jan. 27, 1949; s. Charles Elmer and Dorothy Adele (Seibold) C. BS, Wake Forest U., 1971; MS, Radford U., 1976; PhD, U. Ga., 1982. Tchr. Gaston Day Sch., Gastonia, N.C., 1971-73, Charlotte (N.C.) Country Day Sch., 1973-74; psychologist Roanoke County Schs., Salem, Va., 1976-83, Gwinnett County Schs., Lawrenceville, Ga., 1983-94, coord. psychol. svcs., 1994—; pvt. practice Lilburn, Ga., 1985-93, Norcross, Ga., 1994—. Adj. prof. Mercer U., Atlanta, 1984-85; cons. N.E. Consulting Ctr., Lawrenceville, 1985-92; intern supervision Gwinnett County Schs., Lawrenceville, 1985—. Mem. APA (div. sch. psychology), Nat. Assn. Sch. Psychologists, Ga. Psychol. Assn., Ga. Assn. Sch. Psychologists, Beta Beta Beta, Kappa Delta Pi, Phi Kappa Phi. Home: 1300 Mountain Ivey Ct Sugar Hill GA 30518 Office: Gwinnett County Schs 52 Gwinnett Dr Lawrenceville GA 30045-5624

CARTER, DANITA M. writer, securities trader; d. Willie L. and Alline A. Carter. Series 7, Series 63 NASD/N.Y., 1997. Stock broker UBS Securities, N.Y.C., 1996—98, Prudential Securities, N.Y.C., 2000—01. Jewelry designer, N.Y.C., 1985—. Co-author: (novel) Revenge Is Best Served Cold, Talk of the Town, Unwrapped Packages. Recipient Gold Key award in Art, State of Ill., 1978. Avocations: tennis, skiing. Personal E-mail: pageturners@aol.com.

CARTER, DAVID EDWARD, communications executive, director; b. Nov. 24, 1942; s. Victor Byron and Lillie Elzena (Clarke) Carter; m. Linda Louise Gibson, May 31, 1969; children: Christa Ann, Lauren Louise. AB, U. Ky., 1965; MS, Ohio U., 1967; MBA, Syracuse U., 1995; SMM, Harvard U., 1995, OPM, 1998. Dir. advt. Wheeler & Williams Co., Ashland, 1965—66; instr. U. Ky., 1967—70; dir. comms. Ky. Electric Steel Co., Ashland, 1970—77; pres. David E. Carter Inc., Ashland, 1977—, Hollywood Ky. Corp. divsn. David E. Carter Inc., Sahland, Bangkok, Jakarta, Caracas, Hong Kong, 1996—; founder, CEO Interstate Data Inc., 1999—. Bd. dirs. Home Fed. Savs. & Loan Assn., Ashland, Decathlon Corp., Hanover Pub. Co.; exec. adv. bd. Ohio U. Sch. Bus.; adj. prof. Thammasat U., Bangkok, 1992—. Author: It's Not the Money — It's the Principle, 1975, Book of American Trade Marks, 11 vols., 1972—89, Designing Corporate Symbols, 1975, Corporate Identity Manuals, 1976, Letterheads, 7 vols., 1977—89, Ideas for Editors, 1977, Letterheads, 5 vols., 1979—89, American Corporate Identity, 5 vols., 1985—89, How to Improve Your Corporate Identity, 1986, Logos of Major American Companies, 1989, International Corporate Design Symbols, 1990, World Corporate Identity, 1990; writer, prodr.: TV series Sassafrass, 1987—88; prodr.: more than 12 sketches for The Johnny Carson Show, 1989—91 (2 Emmy awards, 91). Mem. alumni bd. dirs. U. Ky. Sch. Journalism; scoutmaster Tri-State Area coun. Boy Scouts Am., 1970—77, dist. commr., 1977—78. Named to Russell (Ky.) Hall of Fame, 2002; recipient dist. award of merit, Boy Scouts Am., 1975, Clio award, N.Y.C., 1980, Disting. Alumnus award, Ashland C.C., 1990, Ohio U. Sch. Journalism, 2002. Mem.: Am. Inst. Graphic Arts, Nat. Acad. TV Arts and Scis. (3 Emmy awards for writing TV programs 1990, 2 Emmy awards for producing pub. TV program 1990), NY Art Dirs. Club. Republican. Methodist. Avocations: sports collectibles, golf, photography. Home: 4727 Southern Hills Dr Ashland KY 41102-8213 also: 3225 W Gulf Dr Unit B301 Sanibel FL 33957-7700 Office: PO Box 2500 Ashland KY 41105-2500

CARTER, DAVID GEORGE, SR., university administrator; b. Dayton, Ohio, Oct. 25, 1942; s. Richard Walter and Esther Mae (Dunn) C.; children: Ehrika Aileen, Jessica Faye, David George Jr. BS, Cen. State U., 1965; MEd, Miami U., 1968; PhD, Ohio State U., 1971. Cert. elem. tchr., Ohio. Prin. Dayton Pub. Schs., 1969-70, supr., 1970-71, unit facilitator, dist. supt., 1971-73; asst. and assoc. prof. Pa. State U., State College, 1972-77; assoc. dean and prof. edn. U. Conn., Storrs, 1977-82, assoc. v.p. acad. affairs, 1982-88; pres. East Conn. State U., Willimantic, 1988—. Corporator Liberty Bank, 1999—, dir., 2000—, Marine Corps Univ. Mem., bd. of visitors, 1998, chair-elect, 2001. Contbr. articles to profl. jours. Bd. dirs. New England Regional Exch., Framingham, Mass., 1981-86, Haitian Health Found.; mem. Gov.'s Task Force on Jail and Prison Overcrowding; bd. visitors, Marine Corps U. Named Young Man of Yr. Dayton C. of C., 1973, Disting. Alumnus Ctrl. State U., Wilberforce, Ohio, 1988, Man of Yr., African Am. Affairs Commn., 2000—; inducted into Donald K. Anthony Achievement Hall of Fame Ctrl. State U., 1993; recipient Roy Wilkins Civil Rights award NAACP, 1994; 39th Americanism award Conn. Am. Legion, 1994; recipient Greater Hartford NAACP award of honor, 2001, Good Citizen award, Conn. Grand Lodge Order Sons of Italy in Am., 2001, Educator of Yr. award Greater Hartford Assn. of Negro Bus. and Profl. Woman's Club,

2003, Whitney M. Young Jr. Svc. award Urban Scouting Com. Conn. Rivers Coun. Boy Scouts Am., 2003. Mem. Nat. Orgn. Legal Problems of Edn. (bd. dirs. 1980-83), NCAA (chair pres.' commn. divsn. III 1995-97, pres.'s commn. 1991-97), Am. Ednl. Rsch. Orgn., Phi Delta Kappa, Pi Lambda Theta, Phi Kappa Phi, Sigma Pi Phi. Home: 9 Charles Ln Storrs Mansfield CT 06268-2308 Office: East Conn State U 83 Windham St Willimantic CT 06226-2211

CARTER, DENNIS R. music educator, band director, musician; b. Alton, Ill., Oct. 25, 1970; s. Sharrel L. and Shirley A. C.. BM in Music Edn., Millikin U., Decatur, Ill., 1993; A in Fine Arts in Music, Lewis and Clark C.C., Godfrey, Ill., 1990. Band dir. Mt. Pulaski Cmty. Sch. Dist., Mt. Pulaski, Ill., 1993—95, Triad Cmty. Unit Sch. Dist. No. 2, Troy, Ill., 1995—. Mem.: Am. Fedn. of Musicians, Ill. Grade Sch. Music Assn. (pres. 2001—), Madison County Band Directors Assn. (pres. 2002—), Ill. Music Educators Assn. (chmn. of jr. divsn. bands dist. VI 1999—2002). Home: 417 Washington East Alton IL 62024-1319 Office: Triad Mid Sch 9539 US Highway 40 Saint Jacob IL 62281 Office Fax: 618-644-9435. Personal E-mail: dcjazz1@charter.net. E-mail: dcarter@triad.madison.k12.il.us.

CARTER, DONALD PATTON, advertising executive; b. Richmond, Mo., July 30, 1927; s. R. D. and Lillian (Patton) Carter; m. Susan Virginia Wurst, Apr. 22, 1950 (dec. Apr. 1980); children: Jeffrey, Stephen, Carol; m. Carol Holzrichter, Dec. 27, 1983. Student, U. Louisville, 1945-46; BS, U. Mo., 1948; MBA, U. Pa., 1950. With Continental Color Press, Inc., Kansas City, Mo., 1950-52; pres. Nasco, Inc., Kansas City, Kans., 1953-54; from v.p. to pres. Biddle Co., Bloomington, Ill., 1955-68; pres. Post Keyes Gardner Inc., Chgo., 1968-78, also bd. dirs.; chmn., pres. Cunningham & Walsh Inc., Chgo., 1978-83, exec. v.p., 1978-83, also bd. dirs.; chmn. bd. dirs. Modu-line Industries, 1982-97. Instr. econs. and bus. adminstrn. Kansas City (Mo.) Jr. Coll., 1950—52; trustee Thomson-McKinnon Mut. Funds, 1983—96, PIMCO Multi-Mgr. Mut. Funds, 1996—. With USNR, 1945—47. Named Young of the Yr., Jr. C. of C., 1961. Mem.: Bob O'Link Golf Club, Knollwood Country Club, Phi Kappa Psi. Home: 434 Stable Ln Lake Forest IL 60045-2799

CARTER, E. GRAYDON, editor-in-chief; Co-founder, editor Spy, 1986—91; editor N.Y. Observer, 1991—92; editor-in-chief Vanity Fair Mag., N.Y.C., 1992—. Office: Conde Nast Publications Inc 4 Times Sq Fl 7 New York NY 10036-6522*

CARTER, EDWARD GRAYDON, editor; b. Canada, July 14, 1949; s. E.P. and Margaret Ellen Carter; m. Cynthia Williamson, July 6, 1975; 4 children. Student, Carleton U., U. Ottawa. Editor The Can. Rev., 1973—77; writer Time, 1978—83, Life, N.Y.C., 1983—86; founder, editor Spy, 1986—91; editor N.Y. Observer, 1991—92; hon. editor Harvard Lampoon, 1989; editor in chief Vanity Fair, N.Y.C., 1992—. Mem.: Washington (Conn.) Club. Avocation: fly fishing. Office: 4 Times Sq Fl 7 New York NY 10036-6522

CARTER, ELEANOR ELIZABETH, business manager; b. Durham, N.C., July 16, 1954; d. Joseph William Jr. and Sheila Dale (Swartz) C. BS in Social Work, N.C. State U., 1977. Field worker family planning Wake County Health Dept., Raleigh, N.C., 1975-76; sales rep. Bristol-Myers Products, N.C., 1977-80, regional adminstn. asst., 1980, regional trainer Washington, N.C., Va., 1980, sales adminstrn. mgr. corp. hdqrs. N.Y.C., 1980-81, dist. supr. Cin., 1981-82; account rep. Fuji Photo Film U.S.A., Inc., Cin., 1982-83, spl. account mgr. Chgo., 1983-90; nat. account mgr. Fuji Photo Film U.S.A., Itasca, Ill., 1991-97, v.p. nat. accounts, 1997—. Mem. NAFE, Alpha Kappa Delta. Presbyterian. Avocations: jogging, horseback riding, travel, dancing. Office: 850 Central Ave Hanover Park IL 60133-5422

CARTER, ELIZABETH WACKERMAN, retired mental health nurse; b. Charlestown, Ohio, Sept. 16, 1936; d. William W. and Grace L. (Lewis) Wackerman; m. James H. Carter, June 15, 1962. BSN, Case-Western Res., 1958; MS, Rutgers U., 1962; DPH, Columbia U., 1981. Staff nurse Univ. Hosps., Cleve., 1958-59, head nurse, 1959-60; supr. Montefiore Hosp. and Med. Ctr., N.Y.C., 1962-67; asst. prof. Adelphi U., Garden City, N.Y., 1967-71; program coord. ANA, N.Y.C., 1971-72; assoc. prof. Columbia U., N.Y.C., 1972-86; dep. exec. dir. N.Y. State Nurses Assn., Latham, 1986-98. Psychiat. nurse cons. divsn. psychiatry Montefiore Hosp. and Med. Ctr., Bronx, 1967-69; liaison mem. Nat. Adv. Mental Health Coun., NIMH, 1981-85; clin. cons. nursing dept. N.Y. State Psychiat. Inst., 1982-86; active mental health project N.Y. State Health Planning Commn. Health Adv. Coun., 1982-85; mem. nursing profl. devel. task force N.Y. State Office Mental Health, 1989-92; presenter in field. Contbr. articles to profl. jours. Chairperson com. on disaster health ARC, N.Y.C., 1982-85; bd. dirs. Raccoon Island Transp. Co., Lake Hopatcong, N.J. Recipient Amanda Silver Disting. Svc. award N.Y. Counties RN Assn., N.Y.C., 1990, Honorary Recognition award N.Y. Counties RN Assn., 1998; Alumni Rsch. grantee Case-Western Res. Sch. Nursing, Cleve., 1980; Rudin Rsch. scholar Columbia U. Sch. Nursing, N.Y.C., 1982-83. Mem. ANA (chairperson exec. com. coun. of specialists in psychiat. mental health nursing 1974-76, congress on nursing practice 1976-80, exec. com. divsn. psychiat. and mental health nursing practice 1980-84, com. of chairpersons 1980-83, chair com. on credentialing 1984-89, Psychiat. Nursing Recognition award 1987), N.Y. State Nurses Assn. (chairperson psychiat. conf. group 1978-82, coun. certification 1978-82), Am. Psychiat. Nurses Assn. (award for excellence in leadership 1998); others. Address: 1000 Riverside Dr Apt B302 Palmetto FL 34221-5040

CARTER, ELLIOTT COOK, JR., composer; b. N.Y.C., Dec. 11, 1908; s. Elliott Cook and Florence (Chambers) Carter; m. Helen Frost-Jones, July 6, 1939; 1 child, David. AB, Harvard U., 1930, AM, 1932, MusD (hon.), 1970, New Eng. Conservatory Music, 1961, Swarthmore Coll., 1956, Princeton U., 1967, Boston U., 1970, Yale U., 1970, Oberlin Coll., 1970, Cambridge (Eng.) U., 1983. Music dir. George Balanchine's Ballet Caravan, 1936—40; tchr. St. John's Coll., Annapolis, Md., 1940—42; cons. O.W.I., 1943—44; tchr. Greek and math.; tchr. music theory and composition Peabody Conservatory, Balt., 1946—48; dir., pres. Am. sect., Internat. Soc. Contemporary Music, 1946—52; assoc. prof. music Columbia U., N.Y.C., 1948—50, Queen's Coll., N.Y.C., 1955—56; tchr. Am. studies Salzburg (Austria) Seminars, 1958; lectr. music seminar Princeton (N.J.) U., 1959—60; prof. of composition Yale U., New Haven, 1960—62; Am. del. East-West Encounter, Tokyo, 1962; composer in residence Am. Acad. in Rome, 1963, 1967, Am. Sch., West Berlin, 1964; prof. of composition Julliard Sch. Music, N.Y.C., 1967—84; Andrew D. White Prof.-at-Large Cornell U., Ithaca, NY, 1967—68. Composer: (symphonies/orchestral) Symphony, Suite from Pocahontas, 1939 (Juilliard pub. award, 1940), Symphony No. 1, 1942, Holiday Overture, 1944 (1st prize Ind. Music Publishers Contest, 1945), Suite, From the Minotaur, 1947, Elegy, 1952, Variations for Orchestra, 1954—55, Double Concerto (Sibelius medal, 1961, Critics' Cir. award, 1961), Piano Concerto, 1964—65, Concerto for Orchestra, 1968—69, A Symphony of Three Orchestras, 1976, Penthode, 1984—85, A Celebration of Some 100 x 150 Notes, 1986, Oboe Concerto, 1988, Remembrance, 1988, Anniversary, 1989, Violin Concerto, 1990 (Grammy award Best Contemporary Composition, 1994), Allegro Scorrevole, 1996 (Prince Rainier Found. Music award, 1998), Clarinet Concerto, 1997, (symphony) Sum fluxae pretium spei, 1996, Asko Concerto, 2000, Cello Concerto, 2000 (commissioned by the Chgo. Symphony Orch.), Boston Concerto, 2002 (commissioned by Boston Symphony), (chamber/instrumental) Canonic Suite, 1939 (BMI pub. prize, 1945), Pastoral, 1940, Elegy, 1941, Piano Sonata No. 1, 1945—46, Woodwind Quintet, 1948, Cello Sonata, 1948, Eight Études and a Fantasy, 1949—50, Eight Pieces for Four Timpani/Recitative and Improvisation, 1950—66, String Quartet No. 1, 1950—51 (1st prize Internat. Quartet Competition, Liège, Belgium, 1953), Sonata, 1952, String Quartet No. 2, 1959 (Pulitzer prize for music, 1960, Critics'Cir. award, UNESCO award, Naumburg award, 1956), String Quartet No. 3, 1971 (Pulitzer prize for music, 1973), Canon for Three: In Memoriam Igor Stravinsky, 1971, Duo, 1973—74, Brass Quintet, 1974, A Fantasy About Purcell's Fantasia Upon One Note, 1974, Birthday Fanfare for Sir William Glock's 70th, 1978, Night Fantasies, 1980, Triple Duo, 1982—83, Changes, 1983, Canon for Four: Homage to William, 1984, Esprit rude/Esprit doux, 1984, Riconoscenza per Goffredo Petrassi, 1984, String Quartet No. 4, 1986, Enchanted Preludes, 1988, 1994, Con Leggerezza Pensosa (Omaggio a Italo Calvino), 1990, Scrivo in Vento, 1991, Quintet for Piano and Winds, 1991, Trilogy for Harp and Oboe, 1992, Gra for clarinet alone, 1993, Figment for cello alone, 1994, Fragment for string quartet, 1994, esprit rude/esprit doux II, 1995, String Quartet No. 5, 1995, more than 90 for piano, A Six-Letter Letter (for Paul Sacher's 90th Birthday) for English Horn alone, 1996, Luimen, 1997, Quintet for Piano and String Quartet, 1997, Tempo e tempi, 1999, Luimen, 1998, (vocal, choral) My Love is in a Light Attire, 1928, Tarantella, 1936, Harvest Home, To Music, Let's Be Gay, Heart Not So Heavy As Mine, Tell Me Where is Fancy Bred?, The Defense of Corinth, 1941, Three Poems of Robert Frost, 1943, The Difference, The Harmony of Morning, 1944, Musicians Wrestle Everywhere, 1945, Emblems, 1947, A Mirror on which to Dwell, 1975, Syringa, 1978, In Sleep, In Thunder, 1981, Of Challenge and Of Love, 1995, Two Diversions for piano, 1999, (statement) Remembering Aaron, for violin alone, 1999, (fantasy) Remembering Roger for violin alone, 1999, Rhapsodic Musings for violin alone, 2000, (ballet) Pocahontas, 1936, The Minotaur, 1947, (opera) What Next?, 1998, (incidental music) Philocetes, 1931, Mostellaria, 1936. Trustee Am. Acad. in Rome. Named Commandeur dans l'Ordre des Arts et des Lettres, France, 1987, Commendatore in the Order of Merit of the Republic of Italy, 1991; recipient Am. Composers' Alliance prize, 1943, Acad.-Inst. award in Music, Am. Acad. and Inst. of Arts and Letters, 1950, Guggenheim fellowships, 1945, 1950, Prix de Rome, 1953, Harvard Glee Club medal, 1967, Gold medal, Am. Acad. and Inst. of Arts and Letters, 1971, Handel medallion, 1978, Ernst von Siemens Musik-Preis, Munich, 1985, MacDowell medal, 1983, George Peabody medal, 1984, Nat. Medal of Arts, Nat. Endowment for the Arts, 1985. Mem.: Acad. Santa Cecilia (Rome), Acad. der Kunste (Berlin), Am. Composers Alliance (bd. dirs. 1939—52, treas. 1949—50), Am. Acad. Arts and Scis., Nat. Inst. Arts and Letters, Internat. Soc. Contemporary Music (bd. dirs. 1946—52, pres. U.S. sect. 1952), League Composers (bd. dirs. 1939—52). Address: Boosey & Hawkes Inc 35 E 21st St New York NY 10010-6212

CARTER, EMILY ANN, physical chemist, researcher, educator; b. Los Gatos, Calif., Nov. 28, 1960; d. David and Rebecca (Blumberg) C.; m. Bruce E. Koel, 1994; 1 child, Adam. BS in Chemistry, U. Calif., Berkeley, 1982; PhD in Chemistry, Calif. Inst. Tech., 1987. Postdoctoral rsch. assoc. U. Colo., Boulder, 1987-88; asst. prof., physical chemistry UCLA, 1988-92, assoc. prof., 1992-94, prof., 1994—2002, prof. chemistry and materials sci. and engring., 2002—. Mem. Def. Sci. Study Group, 1996-97; vis. scholar in physics Harvard U., 1999; cons. Inst. for Def. Analysis, 1998-, Los Alamos Nat. Lab., 2000-, mem. theoretical divsn. rev. com., 2000-; vis. scholar in aeronautics Calif. Inst. Tech., 2001; UCLA dir. modeling and simulation Calif. Nano Systems Inst.; McDowell lectr. U. B.C., 2002. Mem. editl. bd. Jour. Phys. Chemistry, 1995-2000, Surface Sci., 1994-99, Ency. Chem. Physics and Phys. Chemistry 1996-2001, Chem. Phys. Letters, 1998-2003, Phys. Chem. Comm., 1998-2002, Chem. Phys. Chem., 2000-, Jour. Chem. Phys., 2000-02, Modeling and Simulation in Materials Sci. and Engring., 2001—, SIAM jour., 2001-; guest editor Jour. Phys. Chem., 1999-2000; contbr. numerous articles to tech. jours; given over 225 invited lectures. Recipient rsch. innovation recognition awards Union Carbide Co., 1990, 91, New Faculty award Camille and Henry Dreyfus Found., 1988, Hanson-Dow award for excellence in tchg., 1998, others; NSF Presdl. Young Investigator award, 1988, Dreyfus Tchr. Scholar award, 1992, Alfred P. Sloan fellow, 1993, Internat. Acad. of Quantum Molecular Sci. medal, 1993, Exxon faculty fellow, 1993, Glen T. Seaborg Rsch. award, 1993, Herbert Newby McCoy Rsch. award, 1993, Peter Mark Meml. award Am Vacuum Soc., 1995, Dr. Lee vis. rsch. fellow Oxford U., 1996, UCLA Hanson-Dow award, 1998, UCLA Dean's Recognition award for rsch., 2002. Fellow AAAS, Am. Vacuum Soc., Am. Phys. Soc., Inst. of Physics; mem. Am. Chem. Soc., Material Rsch. Soc., Sigma Xi, Phi Beta Kappa. Democrat. Jewish. Avocations: theater, films, cooking, reading, tennis. Office: U California Dept Chem Box 951569 Los Angeles CA 90095-1569 E-mail: eac@chem.ucla.edu.

CARTER, ERIC, state representative; b. Feb. 19, 1972; m. Heather, Aug. 21, 1993; 3 children. AB in Phys. Sci., Harvard Coll., 1994; student, Cambridge U., U. Miami, 1994—96; JD, U. Mo., 1997. Atty.; mem. Kans. Ho. of Reps., 2003—. Adv. coun. fin. Blue Valley Bd. Edn. Mem.: Harvard Club, Rotary. Republican. Avocations: Judo, running, triathlons. Office: 427-S State Capitol 300 SW10th Ave Topeka KS 66612 Home: 14340 Mackey Overland Park KS 66223*

CARTER, FRANCES MOORE, educator, writer, foundation executive; b. Washington; d. Joel Presley and Ora Emma Moore; m. Richard Dunn Carter, July 2, 1949 (dec. 1992); children: Karen Anne, Marcia Lee, Richard Dunn Jr. BA in English, Coll. of William and Mary, 1947; MA in Arts and Humanities, West Chester U., 1972; EdD in Edn. and Adminstrn., U. Pa., 1978. Cert. elem. and secondary tchr., secondary prin., curriculum and instrn. supr., supt., Pa. Elem. tchr. Chester-Upland Sch. Dist., Chester, Pa., 1968-69; tchr. in English and humanities Marple Newtown Sch. Dist., Newtown Square, Pa., 1969-78; adj. prof., English and edn. Villanova U., Pa., 1978-79; adj. prof. English and edn. St. Joseph's U., Phila., 1978-79; dir. career edn. Del. County Intermediate Unit, Media, Pa., 1979-83; dir. industry-edn. Del. County Partnership for Econ. Devel., Media, Pa., 1979-83; exec. dir. Chester Edn. Found., Pa., 1989-90; assoc. Career Solutions Planning Group, Paoli, Pa., 1990-93; pres. MicroGraph, Inc., Broomall, Pa., 1993-95, Drexel U. Founds., Phila., 1999—. Commr. Accrediting Commn. for Career Schs. and Colls. of Tech., Washington, 1990-94; bd. mem., exec. com., chair rev. com. Pa. State Bd. Pvt. Licensed Schs., Harrisburg, 1987-95; mem. Phila. Regional Labor Task Force, 1989-92; writer Drexel U. Found. Author: (curriculum series) Employability and Life Skills Training, 1982, (book) Delaware County Job Planning Guide, 1982, Delaware County Training Resource Guide, 1983, Meeting the Challenge of Change, 1988; scriptwriter Cable TV series Solving the Job Puzzle, 1983; writer Drexel U. Found. Charter Schs., 1999—. Chmn. bus./industry com. Partnership for Econ. Devel., Media, 1988-90; founder, dir. Clearinghouse for Edn./Industry, Delaware County, Pa., 1983-89; bd. mem., mem. exec. com., Resource Ctr. for Human Svc., Phila., 1986-92, Leadership, Inc., Phila., Class of 1986-87; elder Presbyn. Ch. (USA), 1968—; bd. dir. Girl Scouts of Del. County, Media, 1985-90, Girls Coalition S.E. Pa., sec., pres., 1983—; clk. of session Swarthmore (Pa.) Presbyn. Ch., 1993— elder, 1968—; mem. adv. bd. Pa. State U. (Lima campus), 1988—. Recipient Athena award Del. County C. of C., 1990, Educator of Yr. award, Nat. Assn. for Industry/Edn. Cooperation, 1989, Woman of Distinction award, Del. County Women's Commn., 1989, Disting. Svc. award, Del. County Coun., Media, 1988, Exemplary Achievement award Del. County Coun., 1984. Mem. Del. County Press Club (bd. dirs., chair comm. day 1987—), Phi Delta Kappa, Pi Lambda Theta, Mortarboard, Pi Beta Phi. Presbyterian. Avocations: reading, piano, theatre, sailing, travel. Home and Office: 77 S Rolling Rd Springfield PA 19064-2415

CARTER, FRANCES TUNNELL (FRAN CARTER), fraternal organization administrator; b. Springville, Miss. d. David Atmond and Mary Annie (McCutcheon) Tunnell; m. John T. Carter; children: Wayne, Nell Branum. BS, U. So. Miss., 1946; MS, U. Tenn., 1948; EdD, U. Ill., 1954. Elem. sch. tchr., Thaxton, Miss., 1942-43, Cumberland, Miss., 1943-44; tchr. high sch. home econs. Randolph, Miss., 1944-45, Maben, Miss., 1946-47; instr. Wood Coll., Mathiston, Miss., 1948, East Central Jr. Coll., Decatur, Miss., 1948-49; prof. home econs. Clarke Coll., Newton, Miss., 1950-56; prof. Samford U., Birmingham, Ala., 1956-84; editor, children and youth projects and resources Woman's Missionary Union, Birmingham, 1983-85; pres. CarterCraft, Inc., Birmingham, 1985-89; nat. exec. dir. Kappa Delta Epsilon, Birmingham, 1987—. Vis. prof. Hong Kong Bapt. U., 1965-66, Anhui Normal U., People's Republic of China, 1987; tchr. workshops in China, 1988, 90, 92, 95, 97, 2000; tchr. workshops in Indonesia, 1993; lectr. in symposium at invitation of Russian Edn. Ministry, Moscow, 1994, U. Nanjing, People's Republic of China, 1997; curriculum writer Bapt. Brotherhood Commn., 1986-90; writer N.Am. Mission Bd., 1995-98. Author: Sammy in the Country, 1960, Tween-Age Ambassador, 1970, Ching Fu and Jim, 1978; co-author: Sharing Times Seven, 1977, also short stories, articles; feature writer: Crusader Mag., 1986-95, The Current, 1987—; editor 103 Rosie Stories, 2001. Tchr. Sunday sch. Bapt. Ch., Birmingham, 1980—; mem., lt. col. CAP, 1968—, bd. dirs. Aerospace Edn. Ala. Wing, 1991-94, dir. pub. affairs region S.E., 1994-95; v.p. Women's Civic Club of Birmingham, 1997—; placement officer ESL Sch., 1995-98, pres., 1982-83, Test of English as a Fgn. Lang. tchr., 1998--. Recipient Career Achievement award Profl. Fraternity Assn., 1988, Outstanding Alumnae award Wood Coll., 1992, Outstanding award Kappa Delta Pi, 1992, Brewer award for Aerospace Edn. Southeast region CAP, 1994, Vol. of Yr. award Nat. Profl. Fraternity Assn., 1999; elected Birmingham's Woman of Yr., 1977, Birmingham's Vol. of Yr., 1980, Silver rep. Dist. 6 Ala. Nat. Silver Haired Congress, 1996—; named Ala. Silver Haired Legislator Dist. 55 Jefferson County, 1994-97, cert. Rosie the Riveter reunion, Little White House, Warm Springs, Ga., 1997. Mem. AARP (local pres. 1988-89, asst. state dir. 1989-93, Nat. Cmty. award 1992), Birmingham's Women C. of C. (pres. 1975-76), Nat. League of Am. Pen Women (3rd v.p. 1988-90, nat. pres. 1994-96), Ala. League of Pen Women (pres. 1970-72), Birmingham League of Am. Pen Women (pres. 1968-70, 76-78), Ala. Writers Conclave (pres. 1978-79), Ala. State Poetry Soc. (pres. 1979-82), Ala. Federated Women's Clubs (dist. dir. 1988-90, Outstanding Woman of Ala. Club award 1988), Freedoms Found. Valley Forge (pres. Birmingham Area chpt. 1990-91), Nat. Fellowship Bapt. Educators (sec. 1987-93), Birmingham Bus. and Profl. Club (pres. 1986-87), Am. Rosie the Riveter Assn. Inc. (founder, pres. 1998—), Kappa Delta Epsilon (nat. pres. 1980-85, co-dir. ESL Sch. 1994-98), Alpha Delta Kappa, Delta Kappa Gamma, Phi Delta Kappa (Nat. Profl. Fraternity Assn. award 1999, cert. emeritus 2000). Home and Office: 2561 Rocky Ridge Rd Birmingham AL 35243-4442 E-mail: fran.carter@juno.com.

CARTER, FRANK MOULTON, physician; b. Phila., Apr. 21, 1958; s. Frank Moulton and Esther Louise (Ruggiero) C. BA, U. Va., 1980; MD, Temple U., 1994. Resident in gen. surgery U. Mass., Worcester, 1984-89; fellow in colon and rectal surgery U. Toronto, 1989-90; pvt. practice, Wyomissing, Pa., 1990—. Republican. Office: Berkshire Surgical Assoc 301 S 7th Ave Ste 315 West Reading PA 19611-1451

CARTER, GENE, judge; b. Milbridge, Maine, Nov. 1, 1935; s. K.W. and S. Loreta (Beal) C.; m. Judith Ann Kittredge, June 24, 1961; children: Matthew G., Mark G. BA, U. Maine, 1958, LLD (hon.), 1985; LLB, NYU, 1961. Bar: Maine 1962. Ptnr. Rudman, Winchell, Carter & Buckley (and predecessors), Bangor, Maine, 1965-80; assoc. justice Maine Supreme Jud. Ct., 1980-83; judge U.S. Dist. Ct. Maine, 1983-89, 1996—2003, chief judge, 1989-96, sr. dist. judge, 2003—. Chmn. adv. com. on rules of civil procedure Maine Supreme Jud. Ct., 1976-80. Chmn. Bangor Housing Authority, 1970-77. Mem. Am. Trial Lawyers Assn., Internat. Soc. Barristers, Am. Coll. Trial Lawyers. Office: US Dist Ct 156 Federal St Portland ME 04101-4152

CARTER, GENE RAYMOND, professional association executive; b. Staunton, Va. BA, Va. State U.; MA, Boston U.; EdD, Columbia U., 1973; LLD (hon.), Va. State U.; LittD, Old Dominion U. Various teaching and ednl. adminstrv. pos., 1960-92; exec. dir. ASCD, 1992—. Cons. various colls. and univs. Trustee Va. Wesleyan Coll.; bd. dirs. Norfolk So. Corp.; mem. adv. bd. Edn. Commn. of the States. Recipient Brotherhood citation Nat. Conf. of Christians and Jews, 1985, Presdl. citation Nat. Assn. Equal Oppty. in Higher Edn., 1985, Outstanding Sch. Supt. in Va. in 1985 award John F. Kennedy Ctr. for the Performing Arts, 1985, Nat. Supt. of the Yr. award Am. Assn. Sch. Adminstrs., 1988, Annual Leadership for Learning award Am. Assn. Sch. Adminstrs., 1990, Disting. Alumni award Teacher's Coll. Columbia U., 1991. Office: ASCD 1703 N Beauregard St Alexandria VA 22311-1714 Home: 10910 Chatham Ridge Way Spotsylvania VA 22553 E-mail: gcarter@ascd.org.

CARTER, GEORGE EDWARD, education educator; b. Leominster, Mass., Sept. 16, 1934; s. Lester Earl and Anita (Bourque) C.; m. Carmen Ophelia Vazquez-Carter, Nov. 13, 1955 (wid. Sept. 1980); children: Lydia M. Carter-Zimmer, David Edward Carter, Russell George, Douglas Anthony; m. Betty K. Tonsing-Carter, Aug. 27, 1983; children: Eva Y Tonsing-Carter, Joseph Tonsing-Carter. BA, Calif. State U., Sacramento, 1961, MA, 1962; PhD, U. Oreg., 1970. Cert. tchr. Calif. Assoc. prof. U. Wis., LaCrosse, 1970-80; prof., scholar-in-residence UCLA, Calif. Polytech Pomona, U. Santa Clara, 1980-82; prof. Nat. U. of Lesotho, Roma, Lesotho, Africa, 1982-85; project coord. Acad. for Ednl. Devel., Maseru, Lesotho, 1985-88; prof., dir. acad. devel. Rhodes U., Grahamstown, S. Africa, 1988-93. Adj. prof. Ind.-Purdue U., Ft. Wayne, 1993—94, Ft. Wayne, 1997—. U. S.C., Columbia, 1994—96, Wartburg Coll., Waverly, Iowa, 1997; cons. UN Devel. Program, Maseru, 1990—92, U.S. Agy. for Internat. Devel., 1988—90. Editor: Black Abolitionist Papers Project, 1982, Exploration in Ethnic Studies Jour., 1978-80. Fellow NEH, Yale U., 1973-74, Nat. Hist. Publs. Comm., Dartmouth Coll., 1968-69; Fulbright scholar Nat. U. Lesotho, 1982-85; rsch. grantee Rhodes U., Grahamstown, S. Africa, 1989-92. Mem.: Nat. Assn. for Interdisciplinary Ethnic Studies (sec.-treas. 1975—81, pres. 1982), Assn. for Documentary Editing (nominating com. 1978), Anti-Slavery Internat., Am. Studies Assn. Democrat. Mem. Soc. Of Friends. Avocations: trout fishing, camping, biking, hiking, hunting. Home: 1301 Pemberton Dr Fort Wayne IN 46805 Office: Indiana-Purdue Univ Fort Wayne IN 46805 E-mail: mtzebra@aol.com.

CARTER, GORDON THOMAS, lawyer; b. Birmingham, Ala., Sept. 20, 1956; s. George Gordon and Mildred Orene (Davis) C. BA, U. Ala.; JD, Cumberland Sch. of Law. Law clk. Ala. Civil Appeals Ct., Montgomery, 1981-82; asst. gen. counsel Alfa Mut. Ins. Co., Alfa Corp., Montgomery, 1982—2000, v.p., assoc. gen. counsel, 2000—. Legal advisor Montgomery Advt. Fedn. Mem. ABA, Ala. State Bar, Montgomery County Bar Assn., Sons Confederate Vets., Toastmasters (treas. Montgomery chpt. 1986, pres. 1987), Sunrise Exch. Club (pres. 1991), Phi Alpha Theta, Phi Alpha Delta, Phi Kappa Psi. Republican. Presbyterian. Avocations: reading, biking, swimming, genealogy. Home: 8537 Plantation Ridge Rd Montgomery AL 36116-6652 Office: Alfa Mut Ins Co 2108 E South Blvd Montgomery AL 36116-2015

CARTER, HAROLD LLOYD, secondary education educator; s. Gustavus and Vennie (Carroll) C. BS, Columbia U., 1960; MA, Ohio State U., 1976. Cert. tchr., Ohio. Legal stenographer, law dept. The Port of N.Y. Authority, N.Y.C., 1954-59; legal stenographer Calif. State Atty. Gens. Office, San Francisco, 1963; history tchr. Buckeye Youth Ctr. Sch., Columbus, Ohio, 1969—, chmn. history dept., 1972-76; history tchr. Circleville (Ohio) Youth Ctr. Sch., 1993-94, Scioto Juvenile Correctional Ctr. Sch., Delaware, Ohio, 1994-98, Riverview Juvenile Correctional Facility, 2000; ret., 2000. Tutor Columbus Pub. Sch., 1976. Author: The African Heritage in Human Biological and Cultural History: From Pre-Historic Times and Early Civilizations to the 21st Century, 2003. Vol. ACLU, L.A., 1965; So. Episc. Diocese of Ohio del. Nat. Conf. on Race, Atlanta, 1981; trustee, cmty. rels. com., pers. com. Neighborhood House, Columbus, 1982-88 (Commemoration plaque 1988). Sgt. U.S. Army, 1950-53. Mem. NEA, Ohio Edn. Assn., Nat. Coun. Social Studies, World History Assn., Ohio Valley World History Assn., Ohio Acad. History, Ohio State U. Alumni Assn., Columbia Club of N.Y., Alpha Phi Alpha (nat. asst. v.p. 1958-59). Democrat. Episcopalian. Avocations: music, swimming, collecting black history and culture documentaries, history research. Home: 4671 Owens Dr Dayton OH 45406-1342 E-mail: lclloyd@sbcglobal.net.

CARTER, HARRIET VANESSA, marketing professional, aide; b. N.Y.C. d. Gerard Frederick and Eugenia Carter. BA in Spanish magna cum laude, Tulane U., 1969; MEd in Spanish, U. Ill., 1974; postgrad., U. D'Aix en Provence, France, 1972, U. Nice, 1974, U. Montreal, 1979, U. Vienna, 1980. Tchr. Spanish King Philip Jr. HS, West Hartford, Conn., 1971-76, Irvington (N.Y.) HS, 1976-77, Closter (N.J.) Village Sch., 1977-78; tchr. Spanish, coord. acad. awards program Benjamin Sch., North Palm Beach, Fla., 1978-81; asst. to clin. dean., pub. rels. and med. residency coord. Am. U. Caribbean Sch. Medicine, Miami, Fla., 1981-84; asst. dir. admissions Ross U. Sch. Medicine, N.Y.C., 1984; coord. ednl. tng., asst. to pres. United Schs. of Am., Miami, 1985-86; pub. rels. specialist edn., medicine, polit. govt., travel, 1986—; coord. divsn. Latino studies Fla. Internat. U., Miami, 1987-88, promotions cons. in broadcasting, 1989-90, TV prodr., exec. asst. to program dir., 1990-91; TV prodr., co-host series Volunteer Miami Sta. WLRN-TV, 1991-92; congl. aide, 1993—. Tchg. asst. Spanish U. Ill., Urbana, 1970—71; instr. med. Spanish Mt. Sinai Hosp., Hartford, 1973, U. Conn. Med. Sch., Farmington, 1974; pub. rels. mgr. Voyager mag., Lake Park, Fla., 1981—82. Founder, editor (newsletter) Focus on Multi-Cultural Happenings, 1975—76; editor: (newsletter) Am. Univ. Caribbean Sch. Medicine, 1981—84; contbr. articles to profl. jours. Pub. rels. and comm. com. Leadership Miami, 1989—; vol. Miracle Telethon, Miami Children's Hosp., 1986; active Jerry Lewis Labor Day Telethon, 1989, 1993—95; with auction Sta. WLRN-TV, Miami, 1990—94; with vol.-a-thon United Way Dade County, Sta. WPLG-TV, 1991; guide So. Gov.'s Conf., Miami, 1985; participant Nat. Women's Leadership Summit, Washington, 2002; Hispanic leadership tng. program Cuban-Am. Nat. Coun., Miami, 1988; vol. Rep. Nat. Conv., San Diego, 1996; invitee, attendee George W. Bush Presdl. Inauguration, 2001; invitee, attended Jeb Bush Gubernatorial Inauguration, 2003; vol. Rep. Gov.'s Assn. Ann. Conf., Miami, 1997; mem. steering com. Jeb Bush for Gov., 1998; alt. committeewoman exec. com. Rep. Party Miami-Dade County, 2001—; active Greater Miami Ambs. Corps., 1985—92, Coun. Internat. Vis. Greater Miami. Recipient Recognition award, U.S. Ho. of Reps., 1991, cert. of merit for commitment to cmty. svc., Pres. of U.S., 1991; fellow, U. Ill.,

1969—70; scholar, Govt. of Austria, 1980. Mem.: AAUW (co-chmn. women 1980—81), NATAS, Phi Beta Kappa, Phi Delta Kappa. Avocations: travel, swimming, theater, tennis, reading. Office: 9357 Fontainebleau Blvd Ste 202 Miami FL 33172-4275

CARTER, HARRY ROBERT, fire protection consultant; b. Neptune, N.J., July 29, 1947; s. Harry Barringer and Stella (Napiorkowski) C.; m. Jacalyn Roberta Miller, Apr. 29, 1972; children: Ellen, Kathleen, Todd. AA, Brookdale Coll., 1971; BA, Thomas Edison State Coll., 1975; BS magna cum laude, Jersey City State Coll., 1976; MA, Rutgers U., 1979; PhD, Western States U., 1984. Fire fighter Rahway (N.J.) Fire Dept., 1972-73, Newark (N.J.) Fire Dept., 1972-77, fire capt., 1977-90, battalion fire chief, 1990-97, dep. to divsn., 1997-99, ret., 1999. Assoc. prof., Mercer County Coll., West Windsor, N.J., 1999—; adj. prof. Ocean County Coll., Toms River, N.J., 1977-81; pres. Carter Fire Protection, Inc., Adelphia, N.J., 1980—; fire marshal N.J. Army Nat. Guard, 1981-91. Author: Management in the Fire Service, 1989, Managing Fire Service Finances, 1989, Understanding Fire Behavior, 1995, Strategic Planning and Fire Protection, 1996, Tactics in Fire Department Management, 1997, Firefighting Strategy and Tactics, 1998, Management in the Fire Service, 3d edit., 1998, It's All About Me, 2002; contbr. articles to profl. jours. Vol. firefighter, officer Howell Twp. Fire Co. # 1, Adelphia, NJ, 1971—, tng. officer, 1978—91, fire chief, 1991; fire commr. fire dist. # 2 Howell Twp. Bd. Fire Commrs. Mem. ISFSI (bd. dirs. 1989-2001, pres. bd. dirs. 1999), N.J. Soc. Fire Instrs. (bd. dirs. 1978-80, pres. 1980-82), Nat. Fire Protection Assn. (adv. coun. 1975-90), Internat. Assn. Fire Chiefs (scholarship 1975-76), Internat. Assn. Fire Fighters, Wall-Spring Lake Lodge F & AM, VFW, Am. Legion, Optimist Internat. Republican. Lutheran. Avocations: military music, playing the tuba, poetry, collecting military medals. Home: PO Box 100 Adelphia NJ 07710-0100

CARTER, HENRIETTA MCKEE, educator; d. Horace Adolphus and Thelma Henrietta McKee; m. William Grandvil Carter (dec. Dec. 1993); children: Darius Grandvil, Grandvil Elliott, Jonathan Grandvil. BS in biology, Northeastern Univ., 1959; MM in voice, New Eng. Conservatory, 1964; MS in edn., National Univ., 1988. Dir. music Walnut Hill Sch., Natick, Mass., 1964-68; instr. voice and music theory Inner City Inst., L.A., 1972-74; instr. voice Univ. So. Calif. Preparatory Sch. of Arts, L.A., 1970-74; rsch. fellow Univ. Ghana, Legon, Accra, Ghana, 1974-75; prof. voice, music Golden West Coll., Huntington Beach, Calif., 1976—, chair music and dance, 1993-98, chair performing arts, 1998—. Pvt. voice studio, Huntington Beach, Calif., 1976—, Rossmoor, Calif., 1999—, voice cons., Southern Calif., 1976—, pvt. voice studio, Legon Accra, Ghana, 1974-75, voice cons., 1974-75; prof. soprano soloist for recitals, TV, radio and others; study abroad instr., Florence, 2002. Bd. dirs. Scout Trail Homeowners Assn., 1992. Recipient Woman of Yr. award Northeastern Univ., 1959; recipient numerous fellowships. Mem. Music Assn. Calif. C.C. (v.p. 1980-81), Music Tchr.'s Assn. Calif., Music Tchr.'s Nat. Assn., Nat. Assn. Tchrs. of Singing, Soc. for Ethnomusicology, Delta Sigma Theta. Democrat. Avocations: photography, theatre and concerts, reading. Office: Golden West Coll 15744 Golden West St Huntington Beach CA 92647

CARTER, HENRY MOORE, JR., retired foundation executive; b. Portsmouth, Va., Mar. 10, 1932; s. Henry and Debbie (McCoy) C.; m. Martha Rhea Greene, Aug. 21, 1954; 1 dau., Ann Clair. BA, Randolph-Macon Coll., 1953; MA, Vanderbilt U., 1954. Tchr. English, Norfolk County Public Schs., Portsmouth, 1954-59, head dept. English, 1957-59; headmaster Bollingbrook Sch., Petersburg, Va., 1959-66; dir. public relations Randolph-Macon Coll., Ashland, Va., 1966-68; dir. Randolph-Macon Fund, 1968-69, dir. devel., 1969-77; pres. Winston-Salem (N.C.) Found., 1977-97. Pastmem. adv. com. Kate B. Reynolds Trust for Poor and Needy; former chair bd. dirs. N.C. Ctr. for Nonprofits; former sec. Winston-Salem Campaign Coordinating Com. Past chmn., bd. dirs. coord. com. Winston-Salem Crime Stoppers; past chmn. Emergency Loan Fund; past mem. adv. bd. Mary Baldwin Coll.; past chmn. Southeastern Coun. Founds., N.C. Assn. Cmty. Founds; former sec.-treas. Twin City Devel. Corp; past chmn. bd. Forsyth Common Vision Coun.; chmn. bd. dirs. Old Salem Inc.; past bd. dirs. Crosby Scholars Cmty. Partnership, Hospice Found., Forsyth Tech. Coll. Found.; pres. Waccamaw Cmty. Found. Carnegie fellow, 1953-54. Mem. Litchfield Country Club, Rotary. Republican. Methodist. Office: 860 W 5th St Winston Salem NC 27101-2506 E-mail: Grants1sc@aol.com.

CARTER, HERBERT EDMUND, former university official; b. Mooresville, Ind., Sept. 25, 1910; s. George Benjamin and Edna (Pidgeon) C.; m. Elizabeth Winifred DeWees, Aug. 30, 1933; children— Anne Winsett, Jean Elizabeth. AB, DePauw U., 1930, ScD, 1952; AM, U. Ill., 1931, PhD, 1934, ScD, 1974, U. Ind., 1974, U. Ariz., 1984; LHD, Thomas Jefferson U., 1975. Instr. chemistry U. Ill., 1933-35, asso., 1935-37, asst. prof., 1937-43, asso. prof., 1943-45, prof., 1945-71, acting dean grad. coll., 1963-64, head dept. chemistry and chem. engring., 1954-67, vice chancellor for acad. affairs, 1967-71; coordinator interdisciplinary programs U. Ariz., Tucson, 1971-77, head dept. biochemistry, 1977-81; rsch. fellow Office Arid Lands Studies, 1981—, spl. asst. to v.p. rsch., 1984-90, coord. interdisciplinary programs, 1987-90. Mem. Pres.'s Com. on Nat. Medal of Sci., 1963-66; mem. nat. sci. bd. NSF, 1963-76, chmn., 1970-74; mem. Citizens Commn. Sci., Law and Food Supply.; Mem. exec. com. div. chemistry and chem. tech. NRC, 1949-55, 57-68 Mem. editorial bd. Bio Chem. Preparations; editor-in-chief, Vol. I.; contbr. to tech. publs. Trustee Assn. Univs. for Argonne, 1980-83, Nutrition Found., 1972-85. Awarded Rector Scholarship, Rector Fellowship DePauw U.; Eli Lilly & Co., Annual award ($1,000 and bronze medal to biochemist under 35 years of age showing promise in research), 1943; Am. Oil Chemists Soc. award in lipid chemistry, 1966 Mem. Am. Chem. Soc. (dir., asso. editor Bio-Chemistry 1961-67, William H. Nichols medal N.Y. sect., also Spencer award Kansas City sect. 1969), Am. Inst. Nutrition (sec. 1945-47), Am. Soc. Biol. Chemists (editorial bd. 1951-60, editorial com. 1963-66, pres. 1956-57), Nat. Acad. Scis. (chmn. section biochemistry 1963-66, mem. council 1966-69), Blue Key, Phi Beta Kappa, Sigma Xi, Phi Eta Sigma, Lambda Chi Alpha, Gamma Alpha, Alpha Chi Sigma. Democrat. Presbyterian. E-mail: hcarter@earthlink.net.

CARTER, HODDING, III, (WILLIAM HODDING CARTER), foundation executive, former journalist, public official and educator; b. New Orleans, Apr. 7, 1935; s. William Hodding and Betty Brunhilde (Werlein) C.; m. Margaret A. Wolfe, June 21, 1957 (div. 1978); children: Catherine Ainsworth, Elizabeth Fearn, William Hodding IV, Margaret Lorraine; m. Patricia M. Derian, 1978. BA, Princeton U., 1957; LLD (hon.), Stetson Coll., 1980, Kenyon Coll., 1984; LittD (hon.), Tusculum Coll., 1983; LLD (hon.), George Washington U., 1986, N.Y. Inst. Tech., 1987; LHD (hon.), U. Maine, 1985, U. San Diego, 1991, Millsaps Coll., 1998. Reporter Delta Democrat-Times, Greenville, Miss., 1959-62, mng. editor, 1962-66, editor, pub., 1966-77; asst. sec. state for pub. affairs, dept. spokesman Dept. State, Washington, 1977-80; vis. prof. Am. U., 1980; anchorman and chief corr. Inside Story, PBS, 1981-84; chief corr., exec. editor Capitol Jour., PBS, 1985-86; pres. MainStreet TV Prodn. Co., 1985-95; Knight chair in pub. affairs journalism U. Md., 1995-98; pres., CEO, John S. and James L. Knight Found., 1998—. Vis. prof. Duke U., 1990; op. ed. columnist Wall St. Jour., 1980-91. Author: The South Strikes Back, 1959, The Reagan Years, 1988; contbr. to books, newspapers and mags.; commentator on TV and radio; columnist Newspaper Enterprise Assn., 1992-95. Co-chmn. Young Dem. Clubs Miss., 1965-68; founding mem. Loyal Dems. of Miss., 1968; mem. Charter Commn. Dem. Party, 1973-74; del. Dem. Conv., 1968, 72, 76, Dem. Mini Conv., Kansas City, Mo., 1974; mem. campaign staff Johnson for Pres., 1964, Carter for Pres., 1976; mem. exec. com. So. Regional Coun., 1969-75, Miss. Dem. Party, 1976-79; trustee Princeton U., 1983-98; dir. Dreyfus Corp. Funds; bd. dirs. Century Found., Found. for the Mid South, Enterprise Corp. of the Delta, Ind. Sector; former chmn. adv. bd. Pew Ctr. for Civic Journalism; former chmn. Action Coun. for Peace in the Balkans. Recipient Editl. award, Soc. Profl. Journalists, 1961, Disting. Achievement award, U. So. Calif. Sch. Journalism, 1972, 4 Emmy awards for pub. affairs TV, 1984—85, Edward R. Murrow award for best fgn. documentary, 1984; fellow Nieman fellow, Harvard U., 1965—66. Mem.: Nat. Press Club, Coun. Fgn. Rels., Tarratine Club. Episcopalian. E-mail: carter@knightfdn.org.

CARTER, JAINE M(ARIE), human resources specialist, director; b. Chgo., Oct. 29, 1946; d. Bruno and Louise Kucinski; m. James Dudley Carter, Apr. 8, 1970; children: Paul, Todd. BS, Northwestern U., 1968; PhD, Walden U., 1988. Mgmt. cons. to bus., 1964—69; chmn. bd. Pers. Devel., Inc., Palatine, Ill., 1969—; dir. women's divsn. Lake Forest (Ill.) Coll. Advanced Mgmt. Inst., 1970—. Writer, lectr., tchr., cons. mgmt. devel. programs; faculty AMA; speaker weekly cable TV series Life Skills; pres. bd. dirs. Family Renewal Inst., 1991—96. Author: (book) How to Train for Supervisors, 1969, Career Planning Workshop for Women, 1975, Training Techniques That Bring About Positive Behavioral Change, 1976, Assertive Management Role Plays, 1976, Understanding the Female Employee, 1976, Rx for Women in Business, 1976, New Directions Needed in Management Training Programs, 1980, The Burnout of Retirement, 1983, Successfully Working with People, 1984, Assertiveness Training for Supervisors, 1985, Successfully Managing People, 1986, The New Success, 1986, Employee Assistance Program Handbook, 1988, Stay Out of Your Own Way-And Get the Job You Want, 1989, He Works/She Works-Successful Strategies for Working Couples, 1996; columnist: Scripps- Howard News Svc., Balancing Work and Family, 1996—; moderator, content expert (TV spl.) Commitment to Quality, Nat. Tech. U., 1989; author: (TV series) Executive Communications, 1988 prodr.: (TV series) Relationships, 1992; creator, prodr., host (TV series) Choices, 1992, 1993, host (radio talk show), 1992—96, columnist Scripps-Howard News Svc. He Works/She Works, 1996—, co-host (radio talk show) Your Own Business!, 1993—97. Mem.: Pres.'s Forum (exec.dir.), SAG, Am. Mgmt. Assn., AGVA, AFTRA. *People can only be free when they are able to take personal responsibility for their actions, turn their back on the expectations of others, and confidently pursue their own unlimited realities.*

CARTER, JAMES, mayor, educator, tax consultant, real estate agent; b. Woodland, Ga., July 6, 1944; s. Jim and Mae (Bell) Carter; children: Willie B., Isabell Huff, Millie Blount, Laura Taylor. BS, Albany State U., 1966; postgrad., Ga. State U., 1966-68, U. Ga., 1988-92. Cert. tchr., Ga. Tchr. Ctrl. H.S., Talbotton, Ga., 1966—; real estate agt. Woodland, Ga., 1980—; mayor City of Woodland, 1981—; tax cons., 1966—. Mem. Joint Ctr. for Polit. Studies, Washington, 1984—99, Ga. Rural Water, Barnesville, 1984—99, Nat. Conf. Black Mayors, Atlanta, 1984—99; pres. vocat. adv. bd., 2003; v.p. Dem. Com., 2002; bd. dirs. Mcpl. Gas Authority, Atlanta, 1999, Rural Devel., Columbus, Ga., 1984—, West. Ga. Sch. to Work. Named Man of the Century, Citizens of Woodland, 1984; recipient Outstanding Citizen award, Ga. Mcpl. Assn., 1995, Adams County, 1998, Am. award, Montel Williams, 1999, award, St. Jude's Children's Hosp., 1999—2003, Cmty. Svc. award, Delta Sigma Theta Sorority, Inc., 2000, Educator's award, 2003. Mem. NAACP (Cmty. Svc. award 2000), Ga. Fin. Assn., Ga. Mcpl. Clks., Internat. Clks. (dep. clk.). Democrat. Avocations: basketball, football, baseball, golf, tennis. Home: PO Box 148 Woodland GA 31836-0148 Office: City of Woodland PO Box 187 Woodland GA 31836-0187

CARTER, JAMES CLARENCE, university administrator; b. N.Y.C., Aug. 1, 1927; s. James Clarence and Elizabeth (Dillon) C. BS in Physics, Spring Hill Coll., 1952; MS in Physics, Fordham U., 1953; STL in Theology, Woodstock Coll., 1959; PhD in Physics, Cath. U. Am., 1956. Ordained priest Roman Cath. Ch., 1958. Instr., asst. prof. Physics Loyola U., New Orleans, 1960-67, assoc. prof. of Physics, 1967—, v.p., 1970-74, pres., 1974-95, chancellor, 1995-2001; pastor Immaculate Conception Parish, New Orleans, 2001—. Bd. dirs. Met. Area Com.; mem. higher edn. facilities com. State La., 1971-73, Am. Council's Commn. on Leadership in Higher Edn., 1975-78; bd. trustees Loyola U. Chgo., 1981-90; chmn. Mayor's Com. Ednl. Uses CATV, 1972. Contbr. articles to profl. jours. Mem. adv. com. New Orleans Pub. Library for the NEH Grant, 1975; bd. dirs. Greater New Orleans Area United Way, 1976-82, La. Ednl. TV Authority, 1977-83; bd. trustees Regis U., 1980-90, 94—, U. San Francisco, 1991-2000, St. Joseph's U., 1993—. Recipient Torch of Liberty award Anti-Defamation League of B'nai B'rith, 1983. Mem. Palmes Academiques, So. Assn. of Colls. and Schs. (exec. council of the commn. on colls.), Am. Phys. Soc., Am. Assn. Physics Tchrs., Assn. Jesuit Colls. and Univs. (chmn. acad. v.p. conf. 1971-74, chmn. 1991-94, exec. dir. 1996), Nat. Assn. Ind. Colls. and Univs. (bd. dirs. 1977-82), Am. Council Edn., Sigma Xi. Office: Jesuit Ch 130 Baronne St New Orleans LA 70112

CARTER, JAMES FOLGER, obstetrician-gynecologist, educator, consultant; b. Kingstree, S.C., Aug. 29, 1949; s. Almer Burnis and Mary Emma (Folger) C.; m. Deborah Josephine Cook, May 24, 1975; children: Jared Cook, Chad Michael Folger, Todd Joseph. BS, U. S.C., 1971, MD, 1975. Cert. in ob-gyn. Intern Richland Meml. Hosp., Columbia, 1975-76; resident in ob-gyn. Naval Regional Med. Ctr., San Diego, 1977-81; chief ob-gyn. Georgetown (S.C.) Meml. Hosp., 1990-92; with Charleston (S.C.) Meml. Hosp., VA Hosp., St. Francis Hosp. Assoc. prof. ob-gyn. Med. U. S.C., Charleston, 1992—; tchr. advanced laparoscopic surgery, Charleston, 1992—. Author tchg. monograph; contbr. articles to med. jours. Bd. dirs. Tarahall Home for Boys, Georgetown County, 1995. Fellow ACOG, Assn. Advanced Laparoscopic Surgery, South Atlantic Assn. of Obstetricians and Gynecologists; mem. AMA, Soc. Laparoscopic Surgeons, Am. Fertility Soc., S.C. Med. Assn. Office: Med U SC Dept Ob-gyn 171 Ashley Ave Dept Ob Charleston SC 29425-0001 E-mail: carterja@musc.edu.

CARTER, JAMES H. judge; b. Waverly, Iowa, Jan. 18, 1935; s. Harvey J. and Althea (Dominick) C.; m. Jeanne E. Carter, Aug. 1965; children: Carol, James. BA, U. Iowa, 1956, JD, 1960. Law clk. to judge U.S. Dist. Ct. 1960-62; assoc. Shuttleworth & Ingersoll, Cedar Rapids, Iowa, 1962-73; judge 6th Jud. Dist., 1973-76, Iowa Ct. Appeals, 1976-82; justice Iowa Supreme Ct., Des Moines, 1982—. Office: Supreme Court Iowa Judicial Branch Bldg 111 E Court Ave Des Moines IA 50319 E-mail: James.carter@jb.state.us.*

CARTER, JAMES HAL, JR., lawyer; b. Ames, Iowa, Sept. 25, 1943; s. James H. Sr. and Louise (Benge) Carter; m. Theresa Carter; children: Janet, Faith, Katherine. BA, Yale U., 1965, LLB, 1969. Bar: N.Y. 1971, U.S. Ct. Appeals (2d cir.) 1971, U.S. Dist. Ct. (so. dist.) N.Y. 1972, U.S. Dist. Ct. (ea. dist.) N.Y. 1975, U.S. Supreme Ct. 1976, U.S. Ct. Internat. Trade 1980, U.S. Dist. Ct. Conn. 1981, U.S. Ct. Appeals (1st and 5th cirs.) 1984, U.S. Ct. Appeals (fed. cir.) 1988, U.S. Ct. Appeals (3d cir.) 1990, U.S. Dist. Ct. (no. dist.) N.Y. 1992, U.S. Dist. Ct. (we. dist.) Mich. 1992. Law clk. U.S. Ct. Appeals (2d cir.), 1969-70; with Sullivan & Cromwell, N.Y.C., 1970—77, ptnr., 1977—. Lectr. internat. comml. arbitration Practicing Law Inst. Corr. editor: Internat. Legal Materials; contbr. articles to profl. jours. Bd. dirs. Am. Bar Found. Fulbright scholar, Cambridge (Eng.) U., 1965—66. Mem.: ABA (past chair internat. law and practice sect., former co-chmn. internat. comml. arbitration com.), Am. Arbitration Assn. (bd. dirs., chmn. exec. com.), Coun. Fgn. Rels., Assn. Bar City N.Y. (former chmn. internat. affairs coun.), N.Y. State Bar Assn. (former chmn. internat. dispute resolution com.), Am. Law Inst., Am. Soc. Internat. Law (pres.-elect), U.S. Coun. Internat. Bus. (mem. com. arbitration). Office: Sullivan and Cromwell 125 Broad St 32d Fl New York NY 10004-2498 E-mail: carterj@sullcrom.com.

CARTER, JAMES HARVEY, psychiatrist, educator; b. Maysville, N.C., May 11, 1934; s. Thomas and Irene (Barber) C.; m. Jettie Lucille Strayhorn, Aug. 21, 1957 (dec. Sept. 1987); 1 child, James Harvey; m. Elsie Richardson, Aug. 26, 1988; 1 child, Saunia McDonald-Wilson. BS, N.C. Ctrl. U., Durham, 1956; MD, Howard U., 1966; MDiv, Shaw U., 2000. Diplomate Am. Bd. Psychiatry and Neurology, Am. Bd. Forensic Examiners. Rotating intern Walter Reed Army Hosp., Washington, 1967; resident in gen. adult psychiatry Dorothea Dix/Duke Med. Ctr., Raleigh-Durham, N.C., 1969-70; assoc. dept. psychiatry Duke U., Durham, 1971-74, asst. prof., 1974-78, assoc. prof., 1978-83, prof., 1983—; sr. psychiatrist Dept. Correction, Raleigh, 1974—. Lectr. N.C. Found. for Alcohol and Drug Studies, U. N.C., Wilmington, 1989-95. Editor Epikrisis. Bd. dirs. Gov.'s Inst. on Alcohol and Substance Abuse, 1992-94; co-founder Drug Action of Wake County, Raleigh. Served to Col. M.C., U.S. Army, 1958-94. Decorated Order of Mil. Merit; recipient Profl. Designation A, U.S. Army Surg. Gen., 1985, Order of the Oak Leaf Pine Gov.'s award, 1999, Salomon Carter Fuller award, Am. Psychiatric Assn., 2003; E.Y. Williams clin. scholar, 1994; Josiah Macy Faculty fellow, 1970-74; Falk fellow, 1971-72. Fellow Am. Psychiat. Assn. (life, vice chair com. on chronic mental illness), Orthopsychiat. Assn.; mem. AMA, Alpha Kappa Mu, Alpha Omega Alpha. Achievements include founding of various drug awareness programs. Office: Duke U Med Ctr PO Box 3106 Durham NC 27715-3106 Fax: 919-681-7504. E-mail: carte049@mc.duke.edu.

CARTER, JAMES W. electronics executive; BS, MIT, 1967, MS, 1968. With Raytheon Co., 1968—, v.p., dep. of network centric systems, 1991—, v.p., 1990—. Mem.: Air Force Assn., Am. def. Preparedness Assn., Assn. U.S. Army. Office: Raytheon Co 1001 Boston Post Rd Marlborough MA 01752*

CARTER, JANE FOSTER, agriculture industry executive; b. Stockton, Calif., Jan. 14, 1927; d. Chester William and Bertha Emily Foster; m. Robert Buffington Carter, Feb. 25, 1952 (dec. Dec. 1994); children: Ann Claire Carter Palmer, Benjamin Foster; m. Frank Anthony Bauman, Aug. 15, 1998 (div. Aug. 2003). BA, Stanford U., 1948; MS, NYU, 1949. Pres. Colusa (Calif.) Properties, Inc., 1953—; owner Carter Land and Livestock, Colusa, 1965—; pres. Sartain Mut. Water Co., Inc., 1992—2003, Carter Mut. Water Co. Inc., 2003—, J&B Rice Farms, Inc., Colusa, 1996—. Sec./treas. Carter Farms, Inc., Colusa, 1975—94, pres., 1994—2002; bd. dirs. Colusa Bean Growers, Inc., 1996—2002, sec., 1998—2002. Author: If the Walls Could Talk, Colusa's Architectural Heritage, 1988; author, editor: Colusa County Survey and Plan for the Arts, 1981, 82, 83, Implementing the Colusa County Arts Plan, 1984, 85, 86. Adv. mem. Calif. Gov.'s Commn. on Agr., Sacramento, 1979—82, Calif. Rep. Ctrl. Com., 1976—94; trustee Calif. Hist. Soc., 1979—89, regional v.p., 1984—89; mem. Calif. Reclamation Bd., 1982—96, sec., 1986—96; mem. Calif. Hist. Resources Commn., 1994—2001, vice chair, 1996—97, chair, 1997—99; mem. Colusa Heritage Preservation Com., 1976—2000, chmn., 1977—83, vice chmn., 1983—91, sec., 1997—2000; bd. dirs. Colusa Cmty. Theatre Found., 1980—99; trustee Calif. Preservation Found., 1989—95; del. Rep. Nat. Conv., Kans. City, Mo., 1976, Detroit, 1980, Dallas, 1984; bd. dirs. The English-Spkg. Union of the U.S., N.Y.C., 1995—2001, English-Spkg. Union, San Francisco, 1992—, pres., 1993—95, v.p., 1995—; bd. dirs. Leland Stanford Mansion Found., Sacramento, 1992—; bd. dirs. Colusa County br. Am. Cancer Soc., 1960—86, chmn., 1964—86. Recipient award of Merit for Historic Preservation Calif. Hist. Soc., 1989, Design award Calif. Preservation Found., 1990, Pres.'s award, 2001, Citizens award English-Speaking Union U.S., 2002. Mem. Sacramento River Water Contractors Assn. (sec. 1992-2003, exec. com. 1974-2003), Francisca Club, Kappa Alpha Theta. Episcopalian. Avocations: travel, art, hist. preservation. Home and Office: 4746 River Rd Colusa CA 95932-4200

CARTER, JANICE JOENE, telecommunications executive; b. Portland, Oreg., Apr. 17, 1948; d. William George and Charline Betty (Gilbert) P. Student, U. Calif., Berkeley, 1964, U. Portland, 1966-67, U. Colo., Boulder, 1967-68; BA in Math, U. Guam, 1970; MBA, Golden Gate U., 1998. Computer programmer Ga.-Pacific Co., Portland, 1972-74; systems analyst ProData, Seattle, 1974-79; systems analyst, mgr. Pacific Northwest Bell, Seattle, 1979-80; data ctr. mgr. Austin Co., Renton, Wash., 1980-83; in bus. devel. Wright-Runstad, Seattle, 1983-84; system adminstr. Hewlett-Packard, Bellevue, Wash., 1984; corp. telecomms. dir. Nordstrom, Inc., Seattle, 1984-96; global telecomm. mgr. Hewlett-Packard Co., Palo Alto, Calif., 1996 98; dir. info. tech. 20th Century Fox, L.A., 1998-2000; regional sales dir. AT&T, L.A., 2000—02; prin. cons. Carter Comms., Marina del Ray, Calif., 2000—. Ski instr. Alpental, Snoqualmie Pass, Wash., 1984-87; bd. dirs. Educationally Gifted Children, Mercer Island, Wash., 1978-80; mem. curriculum com. Mercer Island Sch. Bd., 1992-95; adult literacy tutor. Mem.: Century City C. of C. Avocations: roller blading, french, travel, opera theater, dancing and singing. Office: 4314 Marina City Dr #726C Marina Del Rey CA 90292

CARTER, JARED, poet; b. Elwood, Ind., Jan. 10, 1939; s. Robert Alton and Cleva Lois (Hackett) C.; m. Diane Haston, June 21, 1979; 1 child, Selene. BA, Goddard Coll., 1969. Writer-in-residence Knightstown (Ind.) H.S., 1977, Purdue U., West Lafayette, Ind., 1983, 86; vis. writer U. Hamburg, Germany, 1986. Panelist for lit. Nat. Endowment for the Arts, Washington, 1985, 86. Author: Work, for the Night is Coming, 1981, After the Rain, 1993, Les Barricades Mystérieuses, 1999. Recipient Walt Whitman award Acad. Am. Poets, N.Y., 1980, New Writers award Great Lakes Colls. Assn., Phila., 1982, Gov.'s Arts award, Indpls., 1985, New Letters Literary award U. Mo., Kansas City, 1992, The Poets' prize Nicholas Roerich Mus., N.Y., 1995, Rainmaker award Zone 3 mag., 2002; Bridgman fellow Bread Loaf Writer's Conf., Middlebury, Vt., 1981, Literary fellow Nat. Endowment for the Arts, Washington, 1981, 91, John Simon Guggenheim Found. fellow, N.Y., 1983. Home: 1220 N State Ave Indianapolis IN 46201-1162 E-mail: jaredrcarter@hotmail.com.

CARTER, JASON WAYNE, music educator; b. Forest City, N.C., Jan. 9, 1974; s. Thomas H. Carter and Judith M. Horney; m. Judith M. Horney; 1 child, Debra A. Woodruff. MusB in Music Edn., U. N.C., Greensboro, 1996. Band dir. North Davidson Mid. Sch., Lexington, NC, 1997—. Grantee, Lexington Furniture Industries, 1997. Mem.: N.C. Music Educators Assn., Internat. Trombone Assn. Avocations: computers, RPGs. Office: North Davidson Mid Sch 333 Critcher Dr Lexington NC 27295 E-mail: ndmsband@yahoo.com.

CARTER, JEAN GORDON, lawyer; b. Fort Belvoir, Va., July 30, 1955; d. Thomas Laney and Cleone (Hunter) Gordon; m. Michael L. Carter, Sept. 17, 1977; children: Christina Jean, William Gordon. BS magna cum laude with honors in Accountancy, Wake Forest U., 1977; JD with high honors, Duke U., 1983. Bar: N.C. 1983; CPA; bd. cert. specialist in estates. Acct. Arthur Andersen & Co., Charlotte, N.C., 1977-80; atty. Moore & Van Allen, Raleigh, N.C., 1983-90; ptnr. Hunton & Williams, Raleigh, N.C., 1990—. Mem. Am. Coll. Trusts and Estates Coun., N.C. Bar Assn., Wake County Estate Coun. (pres. 1991-92), Order of Coif, Phi Beta Kappa. Democrat. Presbyterian. Avocation: reading. Home: 3913 Stratford Ct Raleigh NC 27609-6351 Office: Hunton & Williams 1 Hannover Sq Ste 1400 Raleigh NC 27601-2947 E-mail: jcarter@hunton.com.

CARTER, JEANIE, performing company executive; b. Decatur, Ill., May 16, 1950; children: James L. Cook, Abigail G. Cook;; 1 child, Sarah E. Mason. B in music, Millikin U., 1972. Cons. Hewitt Assoc., Lincolnshire, Ill., 1989—2000; owner, dir Bel Canto Studios, Grayslake, Ill., 2001—; vocal instr. Willow Creek Arts Ctr., S. Barrington, Ill., 2003—. Voice lessons Clare Kittner, Northbrook, Ill., 1972—85, Willow Creek Arts Ctr., 2002—03; voice lessons vocal dept. Northeastern Ill. U., Chgo., 2003—. Composer: Footprints, 2002. Soprano soloist 1st Presbyn. Ch., Libertyville, Ill., 1972—92; vocal ministry Willow Creek Cmty. Ch., South Barrington, 2002—. Mem.: Music Tchr's. Nat. Assn. Avocation: attend classical and contemporary concerts. Office: Bel Canto Studios Inc 250 Lexington Ln Grayslake IL 60030-3742 Office Fax: 847-548-6716. E-mail: jeaniecarter@belcantostudios.com.

CARTER, JEANNE WILMOT, lawyer, publisher; b. Iowa City, Iowa, Oct. 25, 1950; d. John Robert and Adelaide Wilmot (Briggs) Carter; m. Daniel Halpern, Dec. 31, 1982; 1 child, Lily Wilmot. BA cum laude, Barnard Coll., N.Y.C., 1973; MFA, Columbia U., 1977; JD, Yeshiva U., N.Y.C., 1986. Bar: N.Y. 1987. Assoc. Raoul Lionel Felder, P.C., N.Y.C., 1986—; pres., co-owner, dir. Ecco Press, Hopewell, N.J., 1992—. Author: Dirt Angel, 1997, Tales from the Rain Forest, 1997; editor: On Music, 1994; contbr. articles to profl. jours. and books including Reading the Fights, N.Am. Rev., O'Henry Prize Stories 1986, Antaeus, Antioch Rev., Arts and Entertainment Law Jour., Ont. Rev., Denver Quar., Jour. Blacks in Higher Edn., others. Bd. dirs. Nat. Poetry Series, 1981—, AIDS Helping Hand, N.Y.C., 1987-95, Planned Parenthood of Mercer County, 1998—; vol. litigator Womanspace, Princeton, N.J., 1994; mem. Jr. League of N.Y.C., 1980-91. N.Y. Found. of the Arts fellow, 1989. Mem. ABA, N.Y. State Bar Assn.

CARTER, JIMMY (JAMES EARL CARTER JR.), 39th President of the United States; b. Plains, Ga., Oct. 1, 1924; s. James Earl and Lillian (Gordy) C.; m. Rosalynn Smith, July 7, 1946; children: John William, James Earl III, Donnel Jeffrey, Amy Lynn. Student, Ga. Southwestern Coll., 1941-42, Ga. Inst. Tech., 1942-43; BS, U.S. Naval Acad., 1946 (class of 1947); postgrad., Union Coll., 1952-53; LLD (hon.), Morris Brown Coll., 1972, Morehouse Coll., 1972, U. Notre Dame, 1977, Emory U., 1979, Kwansei Gakuin U., Japan, 1981, Ga. Southwestern Coll., 1981, N.Y. Law Sch., 1985, Bates Coll., 1985, Centre Coll., 1987, Creighton U., 1987; DEng (hon.), Ga. Inst. Tech., 1979; PhD (hon.), Weizmann Inst. Sci., 1980, Tel Aviv U., 1983, Haifa U., 1987; DHL (hon.), Cen. Conn. State U., 1985. Farmer, warehouseman, Plains, Ga., 1953-77; mem. Ga. Senate, 1963-67; gov. State of Ga., Atlanta, 1971-75; President of United States, 1977-81; disting. prof. Emory U., Atlanta, 1982—. Leader internat. observer teams Panama, 1989, Nicaragua, 1990, Dominican Republic, 1990, Haiti, 1990; host peace negotiations Ethiopia, 1989 Author: Why Not the Best?, 1975, A Government as Good as Its People, 1977, Keeping Faith/Memoirs of a President, 1982, Negotiation: The Alternative to Hostility, 1984, The Blood of Abraham, 1985, (with Rosalynn Carter) Everything to Gain: Making the Most of the Rest of Your Life, 1987, An Outdoor Journal, 1988, Turning Point: A Candidate, A State, and a Nation Come of Age, 1992, Talking Peace: A Vision

for the Next Generation, 1993, Always a Reckoning, 1995, Living Faith, 1996, Sources of Strength: Meditations on Scripture for a Living Faith, 1997, The Virtues of Aging, 1998, An Hour Before Daylight: Memoirs of Rural Boyhood, 2001, Christmas in Plains: Memories, 2001. Mem. Sumter County (Ga.) Sch. Bd., 1955-62, chmn., 1960-62; mem. Americus and Sumter County Hosp. Authority, 1956-70; mem. Sumter County (Ga.) Library Bd., 1961; chmn. congl. campaign com. Dem. Nat. Com., 1974; founder Carter Ctr. Emory U., 1982; bd. dirs. Habitat for Humanity, 1984-87; chmn. bd. trustees Carter Ctr., Inc., 1986—, Carter-Menil Human Rights Found., 1986—, Global 2000 Inc., 1986—; chmn. Coun. of Freely-Elected Heads of Govt., 1986—; chmn. Coun. Internat. Negotiation Network, 1991—. Served to lt. USN, 1946-53. Recipient Gold medal Internat. Inst. Human Rights, 1979, Internat. Mediation medal Am. Arbitration Assn., 1979, Martin Luther King Jr. Nonviolent Peace prize, 1979, Internat. Human Rights award Synagogue Coun. Am., 1979, Conservationist of Yr. award, 1979, Harry S. Truman Pub. Svc. award, 1981, Ansel Adams Conservation award Wilderness Soc., 1982, Disting. Svc. award So. Bapt. Conv., 1982, Human Rights award Internat. League for Human Rights, 1983, World Meth. Peace award, 1985, Albert Schweitzer prize for Humanitarianism, 1987, Edwin C. Whitehead award Nat. Ctr. for Health Edn., 1989, Jefferson award Am. Inst. Pub. Svc., 1990, Phila. Liberty medal, 1990, Spirit of Am. award Nat. Coun. for Social Studies, 1990, Physicians for Social Responsibility award, 1991, Aristotle prize Alexander S. Onassis Found., 1991, Félix Houphouet-Boigny Peace prize UNESCO, 1995, Nobel Peace prize, 2002. Democrat. Office: Carter Ctr 1 Copenhill 453 Freedom Pkwy NE Atlanta GA 30307-1406*

CARTER, JOHN BOYD, JR., oil operator, bank executive; b. Ft. Worth, Oct. 19, 1924; s. John Boyd and Enlie (Corder) C.; m. Susie Ann Browne, Feb. 9, 1946 (div. Dec. 1968); children: Catherine Browne Malone, John Mason; m. Winifred Trimble Runnells, Feb. 23, 1970 (div. Jan. 1987); m. Elizabeth Langston Bayless, Apr. 29, 1987. Student, Kemper Mil. Sch., 1941-43, U. Tex., 1943-46, Babson Coll., 1946-47. Mortgage loan supr. Am. Gen. Investment Corp., 1947; ind. oil operator, 1948-49; sec., treas. Tex. Fund, Inc., 1949-52, mem. investment adv. bd., 1951-58; pres. Tex. Fund Rsch. and Mgmt. Assocs., 1950-52; ind. oil operator and fin. cons., 1952-58; Southwestern rep. Lehman Bros., 1959-65, gen. ptnr., 1965-77, mng. dir., 1970-77; sr. v.p., dir. Pogo Producing Co., 1977-80, former chmn. bd. dirs. Houston Nat. Bank; dir. Sterling Bank. Chmn. bd. dirs. B.C.M. Tech., Inc.; pres., bd. dirs. High Prairie Ranch Co.; adv. bd. Technas Ventures, Austin, Tex. Trustee Baylor Coll. Medicine, Howard Florey Inst., Melbourne, Australia. Bd. dirs. Robert Kleberg Found., Pvt. Enterprise Rsch. Corp. Tex. A&M U., Tex. State Hist. Soc. Mem. Houston Country Club, U.S. Seniors Golf Assn., Bayou Club, Pilgrims Club (N.Y.C.), Brook Club (N.Y.C.), Sigma Alpha Epsilon. Home: 5422 John Dreaper Dr Houston TX 77056-4231 Office: 5757 Memorial Dr Houston TX 77007-8011

CARTER, JOHN DALE, organizational development coordinator; b. Tuskegee, Ala., Apr. 9, 1944; s. Arthur L. and Ann (Bargyh) C.; m. Veronica Louise Helen Hopper, Oct. 12, 1986; children: Annelise Grace, Hopper Carter. AB, Ind. U., 1965, MS, 1967; PhD (NDEA fellow), Case Western Res. U., 1974. Dir. student affairs Dental Sch. Case Western Res. U., Cleve., 1974-75, asst. prof. applied behavioral sci., 1974-90, asst. dean orgn. devel. and student affairs, 1975-78; pres. John D. Carter and Assocs., Inc., Cleve., 1969—; ptnr. Portsmouth Cons. Group, 1984—. Chmn. bd. Gestalt Inst. Cleve., 1974-80, chmn. orgn. and systems devel. program, 1980—, program dir., fin. dir. 1981-86, dir. corp. svcs., 1989-95, dean of faculty, 1992-96; pres. Orgn. and Systems Devel. Ctr., 1996—; mem. exec. bd. Nat. Tng. Labs., 1975-78; faculty Am. U., 1980-90, 94-96; mem. Nat. Tng. Labs., 1976—; bd. dirs. Behavioral Sci. Found., Cleve., Orgn. Devel. Network, 1999—; exec. bd. Fielding Inst., 1987-89; preceptor Shri Ram Chandra Mission, Sahag Marg Meditation, 1993—; Gestalt Inst. Cleve., 1996—; bd. mem. ODN Orgn. Devel. Network, 1999—. Author: Counselling the Helping Relationship, 1975, Managing the Merger Integration Process, 1986, Institutionalizing Change, 1995. Hon. fellow Gestalt Inst. Cleve., 1999. Fellow Gestalt Inst. of Cleve. (hon.); mem. Internat. Assn. Applied Social Scientists (cert. cons. Internat.), Kappa Alpha Psi (pres. Alpha chpt. 1964-65), Alpha Phi Omega. Home and Office: 2232 Harcourt Dr Cleveland OH 44106-4622

CARTER, JOHN DOUGLAS, lawyer; b. Pendleton, Oreg, Feb. 6, 1946; s. Douglas Toner and Carmen Lucile (Cecil) C.; m. Diane Louise Werthen, Aug. 15, 1970 (div. 1977); m. Linda Louise Levy, Aug. 5, 1977; children: Courtney, Douglas, Christopher. AB, Stanford U.; LLB, JD, Harvard U. Bar: Calif. Law clk to Hon. J.F. Kilkenny US Ct. Appeals (9th cir.), San Francisco, 1971-72; from assoc. to ptnr. Thelen, Marrin, Johnson & Bridges, San Francisco, 1972-82; chief litigation counsel Bechtel Power Corp., San Francisco, 1982-86; from asst. gen. counsel to gen. counsel, sr. v.p. Bechtel Group, Inc., San Francisco, 1986-97, exec. v.p., 1997—2002; pres. Bechtel Enterprises, San Francisco, 1992-97; pres. N.Am. Bechtel Group Inc., San Francisco, 1997; pres. Europe, Africa, Mid. East, S.W. Asia Bechtel Group, Inc., London, 1997-98; prin. Goldschmidt Imeson Carter, Portland, Oreg., from 2002. CFO, sr. officer pub. rels., internal audit Legis. Office, 1988-92; mem. chmn. leadership coun. Bechtel Group, Inc., 1996-2002; exec. sponsor Telecomms., Indsl., Water, Civil Inst., exec. sponsor corp. svc., 2001-02; bd. dir. Bechtel Group, Inc., Bechtel Enterprises, Inc.,retired 2003; Goldschmidt Imeson Carter, Portland, Oreg., 2003-; N.W. Natural Gas Co., London & Continental Rys. Editor: Construction Litigation: Representing the Contractor, 1986, 2d edit., 1992, Dow Jones Handbook of Joint Venturing, 1988, Construction Litigation Formbook, 1990, Construction Disputes: Representing the Contractor, 3d edit., 2001. Mem. ABA, Calif. Bar Assn., San Francisco Bar Assn., Internat. Bar Assn., San Francisco C. of C. (bd. dirs. 1988-92), Olympic Club, Crosswater Club, Bankers Club, Chmn.'s Club. Home: Atherton, Calif. Deceased.

CARTER, JOHN FRANCIS, II, lawyer; b. Washington, Dec. 21, 1939; s. John F. and Majorie (Thomas) C.; children: J. F. III, Marion; m. Catherine Dulany Turner, 2000. AB, Princeton U., 1963; JD, U. Tex., 1970. Bar: Tex. 1970, U.S. Supreme Ct. 1977. Analyst Rotan Mosle, Houston, 1967-68; ptnr. Hutcheson & Grundy, Houston, 1970-90, mng. ptnr., 1990-94; sr. counsel Akin, Gump, Strauss, Hauer & Feld, Houston, 1996-98; atty. pvt. practice, Houston, 1998—. Mem. State Bar Grievance Commn., Houston, 1976-79; internat. sr. advisor to dep. sec. U.S. Dept. Energy, 1994-96. Co-author: Incorporation in Texas, 1980. Chmn. Tex. Arts Alliance, 1981-82, Mcpl. Art Commn., Houston, 1988-90; pres. Arts Coun., Houston, 1983-84; chmn., sec. Harris County Dem. Party, Tex., 1988-90; mem. host com. Econ. Summit, Houston, 1989-90. Capt. U.S. Army, 1963-67, Vietnam. Mem. ABA (com. chair 1987-94), Houston Club, Tejas Breakfast Club, Univ. Cottage Club, Princeton Club N.Y., Phi Delta Phi. Avocations: music, ballet, history. Office: The Carter Law Office 3417 Milam St Houston TX 77002-9531 E-mail: jackcarter@aol.com.

CARTER, JOHN LOYD, lawyer; b. Clayton, N.Mex., Oct. 2, 1948; s. John Allen and Ruth (Laughlin) C.; m. Dorel Susan Payne, Sept. 20, 1975; children: Matthew, Caroline, Susan. BA, So. Meth. U., 1970, JD cum laude, 1973. Bar: Tex. 1973, U.S. Ct. Appeals (5th and 11th cirs.) 1975, U.S. Supreme Ct. 1976, U.S. Dist. Ct. (so. dist.) Tex. 1974, U.S. Dist. Ct. (no. dist.) Tex. 1978, U.S. Dist. Ct. (ea. dist.) Tex. 1985, U.S.Dist. Ct. (we. dist.) Tex. 1999. Assoc. Vinson & Elkins, Houston, 1973-80, ptnr., 1980—. Fellow Am. Coll. Trial Lawyers, Am. Bar Found., Tex. Bar Found., Houston Bar Found. Office: Vinson & Elkins 2300 First City Tower Houston TX 77002-6760 E-mail: jcarter@velaw.com.

CARTER, JOHN MACK, publishing company executive; b. Murray, Ky., Feb. 28, 1928; s. William Z. and Martha (Stevenson) C.; m. Sharlyn Emily Reaves, Aug. 30, 1948; children: Jonna Lyn, John Mack II. Student, Murray State Coll., 1944-46, LL.D., 1971; B.J., U. Mo., 1948, MA, 1949; LL.D., St. John's U., 1983. Reporter Murray Ledger & Times, 1945; asst. editor Better Homes & Gardens mag., 1949-51; mng. editor Household mag., Topeka, 1953-57, editor, 1957-58; exec. editor Together mag., 1958-59; editor Am. Home mag., 1959-61; editor-in-chief McCall's mag., 1961-65; v.p. McCall Corp., N.Y.C., 1962-65; editor-in-chief Ladies Home Jour., 1965-74, pub., 1967-70; pres., chief operating officer Downe Communications Inc., 1972-73, chmn. bd., editor-in chief, 1973-77; pres. Am. Home Pub. Co., 1974-75; editor-in-chief Good Housekeeping mag., N.Y.C., 1975-95; dir. new mag. devel. Hearst Corp., N.Y.C., 1980—; pres. Hearst Mag. Enterprises. Bd. dirs. Future Homemakers Am., Am. Cancer Soc., Christian Ch. Found., Religion in Am. Life, Am. Bible Soc., Nat. Ctr. for Voluntary Action, Guideposts Mag. Served as lt. (j.g.) USNR, 1951-53. Recipient Walter Williams award for writing, 1949, Honor award for disting. service in journalism U. Mo., 1979, Faith and Freedom award Religious Heritage of Am., 1980, Quality of Life award for media Am. Lung Assn., 1986; named one of 10 Outstanding Men of Yr., U.S. Jr. C. of C., 1963, Pub. of Yr., Brandeis U., 1977, Headliner of Yr., Women in Communications, Inc., 1978, to Ky. Journalism Hall of Fame, 1983, Pub. of Yr., Mag. Pubs. Am., 1990. Mem. Kentuckians of N.Y. (pres.), Am. Soc. Mag. Editors (pres., inducted into Hall of Fame 2000), Sigma Delta Chi (pres. N.Y. chpt.). Office: Hearst Corp 959 8th Ave New York NY 10019-3795

CARTER, JOHN RICE, congressman; b. Houston, Nov. 6, 1941; s. John James and Elizabeth (Rice) C.; m. Erika Theodora Van Bruegel, June 15, 1968; children— Gilianne, John, Theodore, Danielle. B.A., Tex. Tech U., 1964; J.D., U. Tex.-Austin, 1969. Bar: Tex. 1969. Legis. counsel Tex. Legis. Council, Austin, 1969-72; pvt. practice, Round Rock, Tex., 1973-81; dist. judge Tex. Dist. 277, Georgetown, 1981—2002, mem, U.S. Ho. of Reps. from 31st Tex. dist., 2003-; counsel Agr. Com., Tex. Ho. of Reps., 1973; city judge, Round Rock, 1978-80. Chmn. Planning Com. Round Rock, 1975-78. Mem. Williamson County Bar Assn. (pres. 1976), Round Rock Jaycees (pres. 1975, Jaycee of Yr. 1975). Republican. Lutheran. Club: Rotary. Home: RR 2 Box 200 Round Rock TX 78664-9807 Office: 408 Cannon Ho Office Bldg Washington DC 20515-4331*

CARTER, JOHN ROBERT, physician; b. Buffalo, Apr. 21, 1917; s. John Harvey and Gertrude Ann (Buckpitt) C.; m. Adelaide Briggs, May 8, 1943; children— Marilyn Anne, Jeanne Catherine. BS, Hamilton Coll., 1939; MD, U. Rochester, 1943. Diplomate: Nat. Bd. Med. Examiners. Intern State U. Iowa, 1943-44, resident, 1944-48, asst. dept. pathology, 1944, from instr. to asso. prof., 1944-55, prof., 1955-59; prof., chmn. dept. pathology and oncology U. Kans. Med. Center, 1960-66; prof. pathology dept. orthopedics Case Western Res. U., Cleve., 1981—2001, dir. Inst. Pathology, chmn. dept. pathology, 1966-81; prof. emeritus, 1987—; ret., 1995. Cons. VA Hosp., U.S. Army Hosp., U.S. Penitentiary, Watkins Meml. Hosp.; Past chmn. pathology study sect. NIH; mem. pathology tng. grant com. Nat. Inst. Gen. Med. Scis.; mem. pathology adv. council Central VA Office; mem. sci. adv. bd. Armed Forces Inst. Pathology.; Bd. dirs. Univs. Asso. Research and Edn. Pathology; past pres. Mem. editorial bd.: Am. Jour. Pathology. Served to lt. USNR, 1946-48. Mem. AMA, AAAS, Cleve. Acad. Medicine, Path. Soc. Gt. Britain and Ireland, Am. Assn. Pathologists and Bacteriologists (past pres.), Internat. Acad. Pathology, Am. Soc. Clin. Pathology, Am. Soc. Exptl. Pathology, Am. Soc. Investigative Pathology, Coll. Am. Pathologists, Soc. Exptl. Biology, AAUP, Central Soc. Clin. Research, Phi Beta Kappa, Sigma Xi, Alpha Omega Alpha. Home: 36570 Ridge Rd Willoughby OH 44094-4106

CARTER, JOHN ROBERT, music educator; b. Kentfield, Calif., Dec. 7, 1950; s. Robert Ditson Carter and Nancy Pearl Ballou; m. Linda June Barnshaw, June 5, 1955; children: Andrew, Elizabeth, Robert, Carolyn. MusB, Chapman U., Orange, Calif., 1974; MusM, Westminster Choir Coll., Princeton, N.J., 1977. Cert. vocal performance Temple U., 1998. Music dir. Royal Oak First United Meth. Ch., Mich., 1977—79; instr. Empire Elem. Sch., Calif., 1982—84, Modesto Jr. Coll., Calif., 1983—84; prof. Columbia Coll., Sonora, Calif., 1984—. Adjudicator Music in the Parks, Douglasville, Pa., 1992—; tenor soloist. Editor: (newsletter) Nat. Assn. Tchrs. of Singing, 2000. Bd. pres. Sonora Bach Festival, Calif., 1985—88, bd. mem., 1997—2000. Mem.: Am. Choral Dirs. Assn., Nat. Assn. of Tchrs. of Singing. Avocations: reading, hiking, movies. Office: Columbia Coll 11600 Columbia Coll Dr Sonora CA 95370

CARTER, JOHN SWAIN, museum administrator, consultant; b. Exeter, N.H., May 11, 1950; s. John F. C. and Ethel Mae Carter; m. Karin Carter, Aug. 8, 1978; 1 child, Elsbeth. BS in Psychology, U. Mass., 1973; MA in History of Tech., U. Del., 1979. Editor The Am. Neptune, Salem, Mass., 1979-82; curator Peabody Mus. Salem, 1979-82; dir. Maine Maritime Mus., Bath, 1982-89; pres. Phila. Maritime Mus., 1989-96, Independence Seaport Mus., 1996—. Vice chmn. Internat. Congress Maritime Mus., Oslo, 1987-93; dir. Phila. City Sail, Springside Sch. (v.p. 1996-98), Cushing Acad., 1999— Herreshoff Marine Mus., 1991—, Merchant's Fund, 1995—, Pa. Fedn. Mus., 1997—. Author: Wood Book, 1980, (catalogs) Am. Traders, Maritime Arts, 1982. Mem. Am. Assn. Mus. (mem. coun. 1987-90), Coun. Am. Maritime Mus. (pres. 1986-90), Mus. Coun. Phila. (pres. 1991-93), Bostonian Soc., Union League, Corinthian Yacht Club, Phila. Cricket Club, Phila. Club, N.Y. Yacht Club, Crusing Club of Am., Edgartown Yacht Club, Royal Bermuda Yacht Club, Club Odd Volumes. Office: Independence Seaport 211 S Columbus Blvd Philadelphia PA 19106-3199

CARTER, JOHN THOMAS, retired educational administrator, writer; b. Mantee, Miss., Dec. 16, 1921; s. John Franklin and Mattie (George) C.; m. Frances Tunnell, Mar. 16, 1946; children: John W., Nell Carter Branum. Student, Clarke Coll., 1940-42, Miss. State U., 1942-45, BS, 1947; MS, U. Tenn., 1948; EdD, U. Ill., 1954. Cert. tchr. Tchr., prin. Maben Consol. Sch., Miss., 1946-47; faculty Wood Jr. Coll., Mathiston, Miss., 1947-48; faculty, farm supt. Clarke Coll., Newton, Miss., 1948-56; faculty, dean Sch. Edn. Samford U., Birmingham, Ala., 1956-87. Guest prof. Anhui Normal U., China, 1987, U. Ala. Birmingham, 1987-88; guest cons. to edn. sys. in China, Indonesia, and Russia, 1988, 90, 91, 92, 93, 94, 95, 97, 2000. Author 6 books for children and youth, 1958-75, including East is West, 1965; Witness in Israel, 1969, Sharing Times Seven, 1971. Regional dir. Aerospace Edn. CAP, 1970-84, 94. Served with U.S. Army, 1942-45, NATOUSA, ETO. Recipient Brewer award CAP, 1977, Crown Circle award Nat. Congress Aerospace Edn., 1983. Mem. ASCD, Assn. Tchr. Educators (pres. 1970-71), Assn. Colls. for Tchr. Edn. (exec. bd. 1983-86), Fellowship Bapt. Educators (nat. coord. 1988-2000, exec. dir. 2000—), Kiwanis, Kappa Delta Pi (treas. 1980-87), Phi Delta Kappa (v.p. 1982-83). Republican. Baptist. Avocations: flying, travel. Home: 2561 Rocky Ridge Rd Birmingham AL 35243-4442 Office: Samford U 800 Lakeshore Dr Birmingham AL 35229-0002

CARTER, JOSEPH CARLYLE, JR., lawyer; b. Mayfield, Ky., June 3, 1927; s. Joseph Carlyle and Cynthia Elizabeth (Stokes) Carter; m. Dianne C. Dinwiddie, July 14, 1949; children: Joseph Carlyle, Hugh D., William H., Henry S., Dianne C. BA, U. Va., 1948, LLB, 1951. Bar: Va. 1951. Assoc. firm Hunton & Williams, Richmond, Va., 1951-58, ptnr., 1958-93, mng. ptnr., 1972-82, sr. counsel, 1993—. Chmn. Richmond Pub. Libr. Bd., 1967—77, mem., 1980—85; vice-chmn. Richard City Sch. Bd., 1990—94; trustee Colonial Williamsburg Found., 1977—93, Assn. Preservation Va. Antiquities, Med. Coll. Va. Found., 1976—99, pres., 1984—87; trustee U. Va. Law Sch. Found., 1985—99, pres., 1988—98; elder, trustee 2d Presbyn. Ch., Richmond. Recipient Algernon Sidney Sullivan award, 1948, Good Govt. award, Richmond First Club, 1994. Mem.: ABA, Am. Judicature Soc., Am. Law Inst., Richmond Bar Assn., Va. Bar Assn., Newcomen Soc., Country Club Va. (Richmond), Commonwealth Club (Richmond). Presbyterian. Home: 5102 Harlan Cir Richmond VA 23226-1637 Office: Hunton & Williams 951 E Byrd St Richmond VA 23219-4074

CARTER, JUDITH ROCKWELL, real estate broker; b. Belle Plaine, Iowa, Jan. 12, 1939; d. Gilbert Pearl and Marian Alberta (Hoffman) Rockwell; m. John Wesley Carter Jr., Nov. 22, 1959; children: Rebecca Rockwell Carter Stone, Roberta Roxianne Carter Sheda. Student, Coe Coll., 1957-60, St. Lukes Nursing Sch. With reservation dept. United Air Lines, Omaha, Cedar Rapids, Iowa, 1959-66; owner Black Angus Farm, Belle Plaine, 1966-76; salesperson Valley Sales, Belle Plaine, 1976-80; owner Carter Realty, Belle Plaine, 1980—. Pres. Iowa Meth. Found., Des Moines, 1990-91. Mem. Conf. Coun. Fin. and Adminstrn. Iowa Meth., Des Moines, 1976-84; pres. Belle Plaine Devel. Commn., 1986-88; mem. Christ United Meth. Adminstrv. Bd., 1989-92, 1996-2001; mem. Belle Plaine Improvement Corp., 1986—; mayor City of Belle Plaine, Iowa, 1999—. Mem. Benton County Bd. Realtors, Belle Plaine C. of C. (exec. bd. dirs. 1990-93), Rotary (pres. 1992).

CARTER, JULIA MARIE, secondary education educator; b. Topeka, May 2, 1958; d. Jack Earnest and Bonita Aileen (Hatfield) Estes; m. Dan W. Carter; children: John-Thomas, Jessica Raye. BA, Ouachita Bapt. U., 1982; MBA, U. Phoenix, 2003. Cert. tchr. K-12, Ark., Fla., Md., Va., Pa., Mich., Ohio, Iowa. Tchr. French Dunbar Jr. High, Little Rock, 1989-91; tchr. Mt. Vernon (Ark.) Schs., 1991; tchr. French Cathedral Sch., Little Rock, 1991-92; tchr. St. Mark's Episcopal Sch., Oakland Park, Fla., 1992-93; tchr. French Miramar (Fla.) High Sch., 1993-96, Benjamin Franklin Sch., 1996—98, West Village Acad., 1999—2000, Detroit Public Sch., 2000—01, Bettendorf (Iowa) Pub. Schs., 2001—, Davenport (Iowa) Pub. Schs., 2003—. Owner Carter's Ednl. Svcs.; author, presenter in field. Vol. Chicot Elem., Little Rock, 1989-90, Silver Lake Mid. Sch., North Lauderdale, Fla., 1992-93, Miramar High Sch., 1993-95; mem. Ednl. Materials Equality Com., Little Rock, 1990-91. Fullbright scholar, 1989. Mem. Am. Assn. Tchrs. French (Prof. du Laureat 1989, 92), Am. Fedn. Tchrs. Democrat. Methodist. Avocations: traveling, historic research, writing.

CARTER, KAREN D. management professional; m. Eldridge M. Carter, June 1997; 1 child, Donovan. AB in Chemistry with honors, Coll. of Holy Cross, 1989; MBA, Ohio State U., 1993. Chem. analyst Kellogg Co., Battle Creek, Mich., 1989-90; quality profl. Abbott Labs., Columbus, Ohio, 1990-92, product leader project assurance, 1992-95, sr. quality engr., 1995-97, supr. mfg. North Chicago, Ill., 1997-98, mgr. regulatory and good mfg. practices compliance, 1998—2002, mgr. quality assurance, 2001—02, account mgr., 2002—. Sunday sch. tchr., dir. ch. nursery Waukegan Comty. Ch., Ill., 2001—. Mem. Am. Soc. Quality (cert. quality auditor, cert. quality engr., mem. diversity com. 1996—). Avocations: volleyball, jogging.

CARTER, KIMBERLY FERREN, nursing educator; b. Wheeling, W.Va., July 15, 1963; d. Donald Ray and Nan Shaw Ferren; m. Gregory Lawrence Carter; children: Leanna, Brandon. Diploma, Ohio Valley Gen. Hosp. Sch. Nursing, Wheeling, W.Va., 1984; BSN, Radford U., 1986; MSN, U. Va., 1987, PhD, 1997. Cert. breast health facilitator Am. Cancer Soc.; RN; cert. 2nd Degree Reiki practitioner. Pub. health nurse educator Cen. Shenandoah Health Dist., Staunton, Va., 1987—88; nursing edn. specialist edn. and health promotion Kennestone Regional Health Care Sys., Marietta, Ga., 1988—90; asst. prof. nursing West Ga. Coll., Carrollton, Ga., 1990—92; from instr. to asst. to assoc. prof. Radford U., Va., 1992—. Bd. dir. Salem Rsch. Inst.; bd. rev. Advances in Nursing Sci., Fredericksburg, 1999—; rsch. cons. VA Med. Ctr., Salem, 1997—2002. Contbr. profl. stds. document; author: (book) Documenting health assessment findings: an applications module, 1995, Instructor's Guide and Test Bank for Sims, 1995. Mem. Roanoke Valley Task Force on Homelessness, Roanoke, 1996—. Recipient Am. Cancer Soc. award for Outstanding Svc. and Commitment to Breast Cancer Detection, 1999; grantee curriculum devel. grant, Helene Fuld Health Trust, 2001—03, faculty seed grantee, Radford U., 1999, faculty rsch. grantee, 1997. Mem.: Phi Kappa Phi, Sigma Theta Tau (corr. sec. 1996—2000, 2002—). Office: Radford U Box 6964 Radford VA 24142 Office Fax: 540-831-7716. Business E-Mail: kcarter@radford.edu.

CARTER, L. PHILIP, neurosurgeon, consultant; b. St. Louis, Feb. 26, 1939; s. Russell G. and Dorothy Ruth (Zerweck) Carter; m. Marcia L. Carlson, Aug. 26, 1960 (div. Apr. 1989); children: Kristin, Melinda, Chad Philip; m. Colleen L. Harrington, Oct. 20, 1990. MD, Washington U., St. Louis, 1964. Active staff Barrow Neurol. Inst., Phoenix, 1976-88, dir. microsurg. lab., 1978-88, chief cerebral vascular surgery, 1983-88; prof. neurosurgery, chief neurosurg. svcs. Coll. Medicine U. Ariz., Tucson, 1988-93; prof., chmn. dept. neurosurgery U. Okla. Health Sci. Ctr., Oklahoma City, 1993-96; clin. prof. neurosurgery Coll. Medicine, U. Ariz., Tucson, 1997—; pvt. practice, 1997—. Chief of surgery Eldorado Hosp., Tucson, 2001—; med. cons. Flowtronics, Inc., Phoenix, 1980—; vis. prof. Japan Neurosurg. Soc., Kyoto, 1983; cons Ariz. Head Injury Found., 1988—93, Ariz. Epilepsy Found., 1973—75. Editor: Neurovascular Surgery, 1994; co-editor: Cerebral Revascularization for Stroke, 1985; contbr. Capt. USAF, 1965—67. Fellow, Internat. Coll. Surgeons, 1973; grantee, Ariz. Disease Control for Study of Treatment of Stroke, 1986. Fellow: ACS, Am. Heart Assn.; mem.: Ariz. Neurosurg. Soc. (sec.-treas. 1985—91, pres. elect 2003), We. Neurosurg. Soc. (program chmn. 1990, 1995, v.p. 2001), Rocky Mountain Neurosurg. Soc., Soc. Neurol. Surgeons, Am. Assn. Neurol. Surgeons. Republican. Achievements include patents for describing equipment for measuring cortical blood flow; a design of new instruments for osseus dissection and microsurgery. Home: 4981 N Avenida De Castilla Tucson AZ 85718-6073 *Anything we learn about the human brain helps us understand our existence.*

CARTER, LAURA LEE, academic librarian, psychotherapist; b. Iowa City, Apr. 9, 1955; d. Jack L. and Martha Ann (Shelton) C.; m. William Douglas Rolfe, Oct. 1, 1994. BA in East Asia Studies magna cum laude, U. Colo., 1977; M of Librarianship, U. Washington, 1979; grad. FALCON program, Cornell U., 1983; tng. in Chinese lang., Stanford Ctr., Taipei, Taiwan, 1983-84; MA in Third World History, U. Colo., 1988; MA in Transpersonal Counseling Psychol., Naropa Inst., Boulder, Colo., 1995. Internat. documents libr., asst. libr. Documents Divsn. Marriott Libr., U. Utah, Salt Lake City, 1979-82; original cataloger Norlin Libr., U. Colo., Boulder, 1986-89; internat. documents libr., asst. prof. Govt. Publs. Libr., U. Colo., Boulder, 1989-94; documents libr., asst. prof. Colo. State U., Ft. Collins, 1995-98; gen. ref. libr. Regis U., Denver, 1998—. Part-time instr. Chinese and Japanese history dept history U. No. Colo., Greeley, 1987; invited participant/libr. collection devel. tour S.E. Asia, China and Japan, 1982; judge Most Notable Documents sect. Libr. Jour., 1994; organizer programs and confs.; lectr. and presenter in field. Contbr. book revs. to profl. publs., articles to periodicals. Participant Boulder County Big Sisters Program, 1992. Co-recipient READEX/GODORT/ALA Catherine Reynolds award, 1991, Univ. Colo. Program grant, 1990-91; Japan Found. Libr. Support grantee U. Utah, 1980-81; Nat. Resource fellow for Chinese lang. study Cornell U., 1982-83; tuition scholar Inter-Univ. Program for Advanced Chinese Lang. Studies, 1983-84. Mem. ALA (coord. internat. documents task force 1992-93, program chmn. internat. documents task force 1991). Avocations: gardening, hiking, biking, cooking. Home: 920 Deborah Dr Loveland CO 80537 E-mail: lcarter@regis.edu.

CARTER, LINDA WHITEHEAD, oncology nurse, educator, consultant, researcher; b. Bluefield, W.Va., Dec. 20, 1941; d. Lee Joseph and Kathleen (Witherspoon) Whitehead; m. J. Stephen Carter, Mar. 11, 1961; children: Paul Scott, Kristin Hope. Student, Westmoreland Coll., Youngwood, Pa., 1980-83, St. Vincent Coll., Latrobe, Pa., 1984-85; BSN, Carlow Coll., Pitts., 1986; MSN, U. Pitts., 1992. RN, Pa.; cert. advanced oncology nurse; clin. nurse specialist. Oncology staff nurse Westmoreland Hosp., Greensburg, Pa., 1986-93, facilitator support group, 1988-93, oncology educator, 1990-93; clin. nurse specialist Magee Women's Hosp., Pitts., 1993-94; homecare nurse, 1996—; home care nurse U. Pitts. Med. Ctr. Home Care, Pitts., 1996-99; case mgr., 1996—. Faculty Carlow Coll. Divsn. Nursing, Pitts., 1993-97; grad. asst. Pitts. Cancer Inst., 1990; grad. clin. nurse specialist Allegheny Gen. Hosp., Pitts., 1991-92; nurse of hope Am. Cancer Soc., 1987, mem. pub. edn. com. Westmoreland Unit, 1987-88, mem. nursing edn. com., 1987-94, mem. profl. edn. com., 1990-93, bd. dirs., 1989-97. Mem. editl. rev. bd. Oncology Nursing Forum, 1994-98. Named Vol. of Yr., Am. Cancer Soc., 1988, Pa. Div. scholar, 1987, Nat. scholar, 1989-91. Mem. ANA, Pa. Nurses Assn., Nat. League for Nursing, Oncology Nursing Soc. (nominating com. Greater Pitts. chpt. 1990-91, newsletter com. 1992-93, chair awards com. 1997-2001, Found. liaison com. chair), Internat. Soc. Nurses in Cancer Care, Sigma Theta Tau. Home: 2922 Bryer Ridge Ct Export PA 15632-9393

CARTER, LUTHER FREDRICK, university president; b. Kenova, W.Va., May 30, 1950; s. Luther and Elaine (Jones) C.; m. Theresa Siskind, Dec. 18, 1975 (div. 1988); 1 child, Bryan; m. Florence Roach, Feb. 29, 1992; 1 child, Luke. BA, U. Ctrl. Fla., 1972; MPA, U. S.C., 1976, PhD in Polit. Sci., 1979; LHD (hon.), U. Charleston, 1992, Lander U., 1998, The Citadel, 2000. Assoc. prof. polit. sci. Coll. of Charleston, S.C., 1981-85, chmn. dept. polit. sci., 1985-87; sr. exec. asst. to gov. State of S.C., Columbia, 1987-91; exec. dir. S.C. Budget and Control Bd., Columbia, 1991-99; pres. Francis Marion U., Florence, S.C., 1999—. Rsch. fellow Nat. Def. U., 1983-84; mem. Pres. Com. on White House Fellowships, 2000—; chief of staff to Gov. of S.C. sabbatical, 2003. Author: Personnel: Managing Human Resources, 1985; editor: Government in the Palmetto State, 1983, Mobilization and the National Defense, 1985, Government in the Palmetto State: Toward the 21st Century, 1993. Active S.C. Humanities Coun., Columbia, 1988-94; trustee Winthrop U., Rock Hill, S.C., 1989-93, S.C. Ednl. TV Endowment, 2000—. 1st lt. USMC, col. USMCR. Rsch. fellow Nat. Def. U., 1983-84. Mem. Am. Polit. Sci. Assn., So. Polit. Sci. Assn., Am. Soc. for Pub. Adminstrn., Southeastern Conf. on Pub. Adminstrn. (chmn. 1984, Pugliese award 1987). Roman Catholic. Home and Office: Francis Marion U 4822 E Palmetto St Florence SC 29506-4530 E-mail: lcarter@fmarion.edu.

CARTER, MAE RIEDY, retired academic official, consultant; b. Berkeley, Calif., May 20, 1921; d. Carl Joseph and Avis Blanche (Rodehaver) Riedy; m. Robert C. Carter, Aug. 19, 1944; children: Catherine, Christin Ann. BS, U. Calif., Berkeley, 1943. Ednl. adviser, then program specialist div. continuing edn. U. Del., Newark, 1968-78; asst. provost women's affairs, exec. dir. status of women Office Women's Affairs, U. Del., 1978-86; mem. adv. bd. Rockefeller Family Grant Project, 1979-83. Regional v.p. Del. PTA, 1960-62; pres. Friends Newark Free Library, 1968-69, mem. fiscal planning com. Newark Spl. Sch. Dist., 1972. Author: Research on Seeing and Evaluating People, 1982, (with Geis and Butler) Seeing and Evaluating People, 1982, revised, 1986, (with Haslett and Geis) The Organizational Woman: Power and Paradox, 1992, also papers and reports in field. Recipient Outstanding Svc. award Women's Coordinating Coun., 1977, 79, Spl. Recognition award Nat. U. Extension Assn., 1977, award for credit programs, 1971, Creative Programming award, 1971, medal of distinction U. Del., 1998; AAUW grantee, 1968; Fulbright grantee, 1976; named to Del. Women Hall of Fame, 1995. Mem. AAUW (past br. pres.), LWV, NOW, Women's Legal Def. Fund, Nat. Women's Polit. Caucus. Democrat. Home: 604 Dallam Rd Newark DE 19711-3110

CARTER, MARY ANDREWS, paralegal; b. Greenville, S.C., Sept. 27, 1958; d. Harold M. Andrews and Mary Nancy Dollar; m. Donald P. Carter, Aug. 1, 1982 (div. Sept. 27, 1986); children: Christina Marie, Jason Paul. Diploma in paralegal, Greenville Tech., 1988. Paralegal Alan. O Campbell, P.E., Inc., Sullivan's Island, SC, 1995—99; pvt. practice, 1999—2001; paralegal Campbell, Schneider & Assocs., John's Island, SC, 2001— Mem. adv. coun. Clark Acad., Charleston, 1998—2000; guardian, litem State of S.C., Charleston, 1999—2001. Office: Campbell Schneider and Assocs 3690 Bohicket Rd Ste 1D Johns Island SC 29455

CARTER, MICHAEL ALLEN, nursing educator; b. Springfield, Mo., Feb. 13, 1947; s. William Franklin and Mary Alyne Kelly; m. Sarah Ann Jennings, July 4, 1969; 1 child, Elizabeth Ruth. BS in Nursing, U. Ark., 1969, MS in Nursing, 1973; D of Nursing Sci., Boston U., 1979. Cert. family nurse practitioner. Instr. U. Ark., Little Rock, 1972-73; nurse practitioner VA Hosp., Bedford, Mass., 1974-75; asst. prof. Boston U., 1975-76, U. Colo., Denver, 1976-79, assoc. prof., 1979-82; prof., coll. dean U. Tenn., Memphis, 1982-2000, univ. disting. prof., 2000—. Chmn. Vis. Nurses Assn., Memphis. 1st lt. Nurse Corps, U.S. Army, 1969-71. Named Vol. of Yr. Salvation Army, Denver, 1978; recipient Better Life award Tenn. Health Care Assn., 1988. Fellow Am. Acad. Nursing; mem. Nat. Acads. Practice (Disting. practitioner). Home: 369 Belmont Acres Cir Tumbling Shoals AR 72581 Office: U Tenn Coll Nursing 877 Madison Ave Memphis TN 38103-3408 E-mail: mcarter@utmem.edu

CARTER, MICHELLE C. music educator; b. Hattiesburg, Miss., Feb. 3, 1964; d. Clayton Charlie and Perlene West Creel; m. Gerald E. Jr., Aug. 8, 1987 (div. June 1998); children: Grant, Jordan. AA in Music, Jones County Jr. Coll., Ellisville, Miss., 1984; B.Music Edn., U. So. Miss., 1987. With Daniel, Coker, Horton & Bell Law Firm, Jackson, Miss., 1987—88; sec. Broadmoor Bapt. Ch., Jackson, 1988—89; piano tchr. Jackson and Ovett, Miss., 1989—94; dir. South Jones Mid./H.S., Ellisville, 1995—98; choral dir. Petal Sch. Dist., Miss., 1998—. Pianist First Bapt. Ch., Ellisville, 1991—94, 1995—2000, Laurel, 2000—; mus. dir., accompanist Laurel Little Theatre, 1999—, Hattiesburg Civic Lite Opera, 1999—; staff accompanist Showchoir Camps of Am., Millikin U., Decatur, Ill., 2000—. Named Tchr. of the Wk., Future Educators of Am., Petal, Miss., 2003. Mem.: Miss. Music Educators Assn. (dist. V chair 2001—03), Am. Choral Dirs. Assn., Miss. Profl. Educators. Republican. Baptist. Avocations: gardening, reading.

CARTER, NANETTE CAROLYN, artist; b. Columbus, Ohio, Jan. 30, 1954; d. Matthew Gameliel and Frances (Hill) C. BA, Oberlin Coll., 1976; MFA, Pratt Inst. of Art, 1978. Tchr. art Dwight Englewood Prep Sch., Englewood, NJ, 1978-87; profl. artist, 1987-92, CCNY, 1992-93; vis. lectr., one woman shows Pratt Inst. of Art, Bklyn., 2001—. Artist-in-residence Triangle Workshop, Pine Plains, NYC, 1991. One-woman shows include Ericson Gallery, NYC, 1983, G.R. N'Namdi Gallery, Detroit, 1984, 86, 92-2002, Birmingham, Mich., 1989, 92, 96, 99, Chgo., 1999-2002, Cinque Gallery, NYC, 1985, Montclair (NJ) Art Mus., 1988, Jersey City (NJ) Mus., 1990, June Kelly Gallery, NYC, 1990, 94, 97, 2000, Southampton (NY) Coll., 1991, Franklin Marshall Coll., Lancaster, Pa., 1992, Kebede Fine Arts, LA, 1992, Sande Webster Gallery, Phila., 1993, 95, 97, 99, Alitash Kebede, LA, 1995, Hodges-Taylor Gallery, Charlotte, NC, 1997; exhibited in group shows at Bklyn. Mus., 1981, Newark Mus., 1985, Pa. Acad. Fine Arts, Phila., 1986, Clocktower Gallery, NYC, 1986, Associated Am. Artists Gallery, NYC, 1986, Wennigger Gallery Boston, 1987, Kenkelaba Gallery, NYC, 1987, Fashion Moda Gallery, Bronx, NY, 1988, Studio Mus. in Harlem, NY, 1988, Louisa McIntosh Gallery, Atlanta, 1990, Sande Webster Gallery, 1990, East Hampton Ctr. for Contemporary Art, NY, 1990, Space Gallery, Cleve., 1991, Mary Ryan Gallery, NYC, 1991, New Visions Gallery, Ithaca, NY, 1991, Bennington (Vt.) Coll., 1991, The Rifle Gallery, Columbus, Ohio, 1991, Bristol-Myers Squibb Co., Princeton, NJ, 1992, The Nat. Mus. of Woman in the Arts, Washington, 1992, The Paine Webber Art Gallery, NYC, 1993, Mus. Art, R.I. Sch. of Design, Providence, 1994, 98, Pratt's Inst.'s Manhattan Ctr., NYC, 1995, Skoto Gallery, NYC, 1995, Phila. Mus. Art, 1996, Wayne State U., Detroit, 1996, Pitts. Ctr. for Arts, 1996, W.Va. Wesleyan Coll., Buckhannon, 1996, Yale U. Art Gallery, New Haven, 1996, Spelman Coll. Mus. Fine Art, Atlanta, 1996, Rush Art, NYC, 1997, The Schomburg Ctr., NYC, 1998, Louis Ross Gallery, NYC, 1998, Nabisco, East Hanover, NJ, 1998, The Parish Art Mus., Southampton, NY, 1998, Elise Goodheart Gallery, Sea Harbor, NY, 1998, RI Sch. Design, Providence, 1998, Arlene Bujese Gallery, East Hampton, NY, 1999, Nat. Arts Club, NYC, 1999, Concordia Coll., Ann Arbor, Mich., 2000, Ark. Arts Ctr., Little Rock, 2000, and numerous others; represented in permanent collections Planned Parenthood, NYC, Jane Zimmerli Art Mus., Rutgers U., New Brunswick, NJ, Jersey City Mus., Libr. of Congress, Washington, ARCO, Phila., Reader's Digest, Pleasantville, NY, Schomburg Libr., NYC, Salomon Bros., NYC, Newark Mus., Herbert Johnson Mu., Art, Cornell U., Ithaca, NY, Studio Mus. Harlem, NY, MCI Telecomm., Chgo., Times Mirror, NYC, AT&T, NJ, IBM, Stamford, Conn., Lang Comm., Randolph, Vt., Merck Pharm. Co., Phila., Johnson & Johnson, Inc., New Brunswick, Pepsi-Cola, NYC, Motown Corp., L.P., LA, Am. Express, Mpls., Mus. Art RI Sch. Design, Providence, Yale Gallery of Art, New Haven, Conn., USA Assurance, San Antonio, Tex., Nextel Corp., LA, GE, Fairfield, Conn., Cochran Found., La Grange, Ga., Rutgers Grad. Sch. Mgmt., Newark, ARCO, Phila., Magic Johnson Enterprises, LA, Nissho Iwai Am. Corp., NYC, Pa. Acad. Fine Arts, Phila., Lucent Tech., Basking Ridge, NJ, Butler Inst. Am. Art, Youngstown, Ohio, Conkling Gallery, Minn. State Univ., Mankato, MN, 2002; Group shows: Jacktilton Gallery, NYC; Exhibit A Gallery, NYC; Pfizer Incorp., NYC, 2002; and numerous others. Grantee Nat. Endowment for Arts, 1981, The Jerome Found., 1981, NJ Coun. on Arts, 1985, NY Found. for Arts, 1990, The Pollock-Krasner Found., 1994, Wheeler Found., NYC, 1996, Fellowship, Lower East Side Printshop, NYC, 1997, Fellowship, Brandywine Workshop, Philadelphia, 1999

CARTER, NEVILLE LOUIS, geophysicist, educator; b. Los Angeles, Aug. 21, 1934; s. Herman Louis and Maribelle (Sheller) C.; m. Susan Ruth Orton, Aug. 1, 1987; children from previous marriage: James Neville, Lindsay Louis, Jenifer June. AB, Pomona Coll., 1956; MA, UCLA, 1958, PhD, 1963; postgrad. (Fulbright fellow), U. Oslo, Norway, 1958-59. Research assoc. Inst. Geophysics, UCLA, 1963; research geologist Shell Devel. Co., Houston, 1963-66; assoc. prof. geology and geophysics Yale U., New Haven, 1966-71; prof. geophysics SUNY-Stony Brook, 1971-78; prof., head dept. geophysics, faculty assoc. Ctr. for Tectonophysics, Tex. A&M U., College Station, 1978-83, dir., 1984-89; faculty assoc. Geodynamics Rsch. Inst., Tex. A&M U., 1984-96; prof. emeritus geology and geophysics Tex. A&M U., 1996—. Author, editor numerous publs. in field. Mem. Am. Geophys. Union (pres. tectonophysics sect. 1974-76), Sigma Xi. Home: PO Box 1442 Crescent City CA 95531-1442

CARTER, NICHOLAS CARTER, education educator; b. Akron, Ohio, July 10, 1968; s. Judith Elaine and Clairmont Parks Carter. PhD, MIT, 1986—99. Rsch. asst. prof. U. of Ill., Urbana-Champaign, 1999—. Author: (textbook) Schaum's Outline of Computer Architecture. Mem.: ACM, IEEE. Achievements include patents for the design of memory systems for multiprocessor computers (2). Office: U of Ill Urbana-Champaign 1308 W Main St Urbana IL 61801

CARTER, PAMELA LYNN, former state attorney general; b. South Haven, Mich., Aug. 20, 1949; d. Roscoe Hollis and Dorothy Elizabeth (Hadley) Fanning; m. Michael Anthony Carter, Aug. 26, 1971; children: Michael Anthony Jr., Marcya Alicia. BA cum laude, U. Detroit, 1971; MSW, U. Mich., 1973; JD, Ind. U., 1984. Bar: Ind. 1984, U.S. Dist. Ct. (no. dist.) Ind. 1984, U.S. Dist. Ct. (so. dist.) Ind. 1984. Rsch. analyst, treatment dir. U. Mich. Sch. Pub. Health and UAW, Detroit, 1973—75; exec. dir. Mental Health Ctr. for Women and Children, Detroit, 1975—77; consumer litigation atty. UAW-Gen. Motors Legal Svcs., Indpls., 1983—87; securities atty. Sec. of State, Indpls., 1987—89; Gov.'s exec. asst. for health and human svcs. Gov.'s Office, Indpls., 1989—91, dep. chief of staff to Gov., 1991—92; with Baker & Daniels, 1992—93; atty. gen. State of Ind., Indpls., 1993—96; ptnr. Johnson & Smith, 1996—97; v.p., gen. mgr. Europe, Mid. East & Africa Cummins Engine Co., Inc., Columbus, Ind., 1998—. Author (numerous poems). Active Jr. League, Indpls., Dem. Precinct, Indpls., Cath. Social Svcs., Indpls. Named Breakthrough Woman of the Year, 1989; named one of Outstanding Young Woman of America, 1977; recipient Outstanding Svc. award, Ind. Perinatal Assn., 1991, Cmty. Svc. Coun. Ctrl. Ind., 1991, Non-profl. Healthcare award, Family Health Conf. Bd. Dirs., 1991, award for excellence, Women of the Rainbow, 1991. Mem.: Ind. Bar Assn., Nat. Bar Assn., Coalition of 100 Black Women. Democrat. Avocations: gardening, hiking, travel, reading. Office: VP, Global Sales & Marketing Cummins Engine Co Inc 500 Jackson St Columbus IN 47201*

CARTER, PAUL, food products executive; BA, U. Ala. Exec. Foster Farms, Livingston, Calif., 1979—86, head poultry divsn., 1998—2000, COO, 2000—01, pres., CEO, 2001—. Bd. dirs. Nat. Chicken Coun., vice chmn., bd. dirs. Office: Foster Farms PO Box 457 Livingston CA 95334*

CARTER, PAUL EDWARD, publishing company executive; b. Spokane, Wash., July 7, 1925; s. Richard Bert and Lula Selena (Jones) C.; m. Helen Barbara Crosby, Nov. 2, 1950; children: Nancy, Thomas, Richard, Robert. BA in English and Journalism, Wash. State U., 1949. Advt. mgr. The Spokesman-Rev. and Spokane Daily Chronicle, 1949-87; advt. dir. Hobbs Daily News-Sun, N.Mex., 1987-91; western sales mgr. Geiger Slike, Lewiston, Maine, 1983—. Cons. various daily newspapers. Editor numerous ch., coll., club pubs., 1948-98. Pres. Inland Empire coun. Boy Scouts Am., Spokane, 1971-73; divsn. chmn. United Way of Spokane County, 1955-68; pres. adv. bd. Spokane City U., 1977-83; bishopric LDS Ch., mem. high coun., young men's program leader, Sunday sch. supt., Elders Quorum pres., High Priest quorum leader, scoutmaster, explorer scout adviser. 1st lt. USAAF, WWII, 1943-46, USAF, Korea, 1950-52. Recipient Ramsey Oppenheim award Advt. Assn. of the West, 1962, Silver Beaver award Boy Scouts Am., 1973, Demolay Legion of Honor, 1955, Don Dirstine award Spokane Jr. C. of C., 1950, Disting. Svc. award Spokane Ctrl. Lions Club, 1958, 60 Yrs. Svc. Recognition award Boy Scouts Am., 1997. Mem. Internat. Newspaper Advt. Execs. (dist. dir. 1989-92), Pacific N.W. Newspaper Advt. Execs. (pres. 1973-74), Soc. Profl. Journalists (pres. Coll. chpt.), Am. Press Inst. (del. 1958), SAR (pres. Salt Lake City chpt. 1997-98, pres. Utah Soc. 1999-2000), Spokane Advt. Club (pres. 1961-62, Advt. Man of the Yr. 1962, hon. life), Hobbs Rotary (pres. 1991-92, Rotarian of the Yr. 1989-90). Republican. Mem. Lds Ch. Avocations: writing, computers, golf, rocks and minerals, church work. Home: 760 E Three Fountains #109 Murray UT 84107-5257

CARTER, PAUL RICHARD, physician; b. St. Louis, Apr. 14, 1922; s. Paul William and Lily Edith (Kreutzer) C.; m. Lenora Martha Parker, Dec. 24, 1944; children: Richard Brian, Janet Carol Becker. BA in English and History, Union Coll., 1944; MD, Loma Linda U., 1947. Diplomate Am. Bd. Gen. Surgery & Thoracic Surgery. Intern L.A. County Gen. Hosp., 1947-49, surg. resident, 1949-52, 54-56, head physician surgery, 1957-67; resident in chest surgery Olive View Sanitarium, 1956-57; chief of surgery Rancho Los Amigo Hosp., Downey, Calif., 1967-69; prof. of surgery Loma Linda (Calif.) U., 1960-98; clin. prof. surgery U. Calif., Irvine, 1960-95; pvt. practice surgery Covina, Calif., 1960-94. Chief thoracic surgery Pettis VA Hosp., Loma Linda, 1978-94. Author about 100 articles and book chpts. in field; co-author: History of the Pacific Coast Surgical Association, 2 vols., 1982, 88. Capt. USAMC, 1952-54, Korea. Recipient Fulbright scholarship, Oxford, 1959; named to editorial bd., Annals of Thoracic Surgery for 11 yrs. Fellow. ACS (recorder, sec., treas., pres. So. Calif. chpt. 1989, gov. 1991, exec. com. bd. govs. 1993-97); mem. Pacific Coast Surgical Assn. (v.p. 1987—, historian 1989-98), Am. Assn. Thoracic Surgery, Soc. Thoracic Surgeons, Western Surgical Assn., Societe Internat. Chirurgie, Coll. Chest Physicians, Gen. Thoracic Surgical Club, Internat. Soc. Diseases of the Esophagus. Republican. Avocations: travel, medical history, writing. Home: 10316 Wellside Hill Ave Las Vegas NV 89145

CARTER, QUINCY, football player; b. Oct. 13, 1977; Degree in edn., U. Ga. Football player Dallas Cowboys, 2001—. Office: Dallas Cowboys Cowboys Ctr One Cowboys Pkwy Irving TX 75063

CARTER, RICHARD, publisher, writer; b. N.Y.C., Jan. 24, 1918; s. Samuel J. and Alice (Kulka) C.; m. Gladys Chasins, Oct. 20, 1945; children— Nancy Jane, John Andrew. BA, Coll. City N.Y., 1938. Music editor Billboard mag., 1940-46; staff organizer N.Y. Newspaper Guild, 1946-47; writer N.Y. Daily Mirror, 1947-49, N.Y. Daily Compass, 1949-52; pres. Millwood Publs., Inc., 1971-80; columnist The Racing Times, 1991-92, Daily Racing Form, 1992—. Author, contbr. mags., 1952— ; Author: The Man Who Rocked the Boat, 1956, The Doctor Business, 1958, The Gentle Legions, 1961, Your Food and Your Health, 1964, Breakthrough: The Saga of Jonas Salk, 1966, Superswine, 1967, (with Curt Flood) The Way It Is, 1971, (under pseudonym Tom Ainslie) The Compleat Horseplayer, 1966, Ainslie's Jockey Book, 1967, Ainslie's Complete Guide to Thoroughbred Racing, 1968, The Handicapper's Handbook, 1969, Theory and Practice of Handicapping, 1969, Ainslie's Complete Guide to Harness Racing, 1970, Ainslie's Complete Hoyle, 1975, Ainslie's Encyclopedia of Thoroughbred Handicapping, 1978, How to Gamble in a Casino, 1979, (with Bonnie Ledbetter) The Body Language of Horses, 1980. Served with USAAF, 1942-45, PTO. Recipient George Polk Meml. award, 1952 Mem. Authors Guild, Nat. Assn. Sci. Writers, Nat. Turf Writers Assn. Address: 32 Pyngyp Rd Stony Point NY 10980-3649 E-mail: lmc12345@aol.com.

CARTER, RICHARD BONNER, application developer; b. Lancaster, S.C., Dec. 11, 1946; s. Samuel Hazel and Sue Simpson (McCain) C.; m. Patricia Joann Phillips, June 14, 1969; children: Jennifer Carter Duffie, Courtney Ann, Richard Bonner, II. BA in Math., Erskine, 1969. Programmer Springs Mills, Lancaster, 1969-77, systems analyst, 1977-83; systems specialist Springs Industries, Lancaster, 1983—2001, sr. software engr., 2001—. Youth leader Unity Assoc. Reformed Presbyn. Ch., Lancaster, 1973—, deacon, Lancaster, 1974-95, elder, 1996—; unit commr. Boy Scouts Am., Lancaster, 1990—, com. chmn. Troop 69, 1972—; vice chmn. Buford Sch. Improvement Coun., Lancaster, 1998-2002. Avocations: woodworking, picture framing, furniture refinishing. Home: 3474 Unity Church Rd Lancaster SC 29720-8388 Office: Springs Industries PO Box 111 Lancaster SC 29721-0111 E-mail: richard.carter@springs.com

CARTER, RICHARD DUANE, business educator; s. Herbert Duane and Edith Irene (Richardson) C.; m. Nancy Jean Cannell, Sept. 3, 1955; 1 child, Erich Richardson. AB, Coll. William and Mary; MBA, Columbia U.; PhD, UCLA, 1968. Sr. advisor, dir. Taiwan Metal Industries Devel. Ctr. (under auspices of ILO), 1966-67; dir. UNDP, cons. svcs., Taiwan, 1966-67; chief exec. officer Human Resources Inst., Baton Rouge, La., 1968-70; liaison advisor Internat. Inst. Applied Systems Analysis, Vienna, Austria, 1975; U.S. rep., dir. indsl. mgmt. and cons. svcs. program UN Indsl. Devel. Orgn., Vienna, 1970-75; mem. East West Trade and Mgmt. Commn., 1973-75; sr. advisor, dir. Korean Inst. Sci. and Tech. (under auspices of UN), Seoul, 1974-75; dean Sch. Bus. Quinnipiac Coll., Hamden, Conn., 1977-80; chmn. bd. TCG Industries, Inc., N.Y.C., 1980—; prof. mgmt., program coord. Fairfield (Conn.) U., 1980-84; founder, mng. dir. Internat. Mgmt. Consortium, Vienna, Westport and Millerton, N.Y., 1975—; assoc. mem. Seminar on Orgn. and Mgmt. Columbia U., 1975-89, vice-chmn. Seminar on Orgn. and Mgmt., 1976-89, chmn. rsch. and publ. com. Seminar on Orgn. and Mgmt., 1983-89; mng. dir. Wainwright & Ramsey Securities, Inc., N.Y.C., 1985—. Mem. editorial bd. Indian Adminstrv. and Mgmt. Rev., New Delhi, 1974-76; author: Management: In Perspective and Practice, 1970, The Future Challenges of Management Education, 1981; also numerous articles and revs. Trustee Dingletown Community Ch., Greenwich, Conn., 1978-87; mem. adv. coun. Calif. Coll. Tech., L.A., 1978—. Recipient Disting. Alumni medallion (Olde Guarde), Coll. William and Mary, 2001. Fellow Internat. Acad. Mgmt.; mem. Acad. Mgmt., Am. Mgmt. Assns. (pres.'s council, dir. 1976-77), N.Am. Soc. Corp. Planning, N.Am. Mgmt. Coun. (bd. dirs. 1983-87), Soc. Internat. Orgn. Devel., Mensa, Triple Nine Soc., Explorers Club, Sharon (Conn.) Country Club, Beta Gamma Sigma. *Success depends upon the art of optimizing the skills of confrontation, accommodation and cooperation.*

CARTER, ROBERTA ECCLESTON, therapist, counselor; b. Pitts. d. Robert E. and Emily B. (Bucar) Carter; divorced; children: David Michael Kiewlich, Daniel Michael Kiewlich. Student, Edinboro State U., 1962-63; BS, California State U. Pa., 1966; MEd, U. Pitts., 1969; MA, Rosebridge Grad. Sch., 1987. Tchr. Bethel Park Sch. Dist., Pa., 1966-69; writer, media asst. Field Ednl. Pub., San Francisco, 1969-70; educator, counselor, specialist Alameda Unified Sch. Dist., Calif., 1970—. Master trainer Calif. State Dept. Edn., Sacramento, 1984—; personal growth cons., Alameda, 1983—. Author: People, Places and Products, 1970, Teaching/Learning Units, 1969; co-author: Teacher's Manual Let's Read, 1968. Mem. AAUW, NEA, Calif. Fedn. Bus. and Profl. Women (legis. chair Alameda br. 1984-85, membership chair 1985), Calif. Edn. Assn., Alameda Edn. Assn., Charter Planetary Soc., Oakland Mus., Exploratorium, Big Bros of East Bay, Alameda C. of C. (svc. awsard 1985). Avocations: aerobics, gardening, travel. Home: 1516 Eastshore Dr Alameda CA 94501-3118

CARTER, RONALD MARTIN, SR., pharmaceutical company executive; b. Chgo., Nov. 18, 1925; s. Jack Edward and Anna (Press) C.; m. Joy Wolf, Nov. 14, 1946; children: Ronald M. Jr., Craig Alan. Student, U. Ill., 1942-43, 45-46. Sales mgr. Preston Labs., Inc., Chgo., 1948-52; v.p. Myers-Carter Labs., Inc., Phoenix, 1952-69, pres., 1969-75, Carter-Glogau Labs., Inc., Glendale, Ariz., 1975-86, Steris Labs., Inc., Phoenix, 1987—, The Pharmikon Co., 1987—. Cons. Internat. Exec. Service Corp., Stamford, Conn., 1985—. Served as cpl. U.S. Army, 1943-45. Mem. Drug, Chem. Allied Trades, Generic Pharm. Industry Assn., Nat. Assn. Pharm. Mfrs., Nat. Pharm. Alliance (pres. 1983-84). Clubs: Arizona, Plaza (Phoenix). Democrat. Jewish. Avocations: hunting, fishing. Home: 5707 N 40th St Phoenix AZ 85018-1108 E-mail: roncar@cox.net.

CARTER, ROSALYNN SMITH, wife of former President of United States; b. Plains, Ga., Aug. 18, 1927; d. Edgar and Allie (Murray) Smith; m. James Earl Carter, Jr., July 7, 1946; children: John William, James Earl III, Donnel Jeffrey, Amy Lynn. Grad., Ga. Southwestern Coll.; DHL (hon.), Morehouse Coll., 1980; LLD (hon.), U. Notre Dame, 1987. Disting. fellow Inst. Women's Studies Emory U., Atlanta, 1990—. Vice chair, bd. trustees The Carter Ctr., chair Mental Health Task Force Carter Ctr.; pres., bd. dirs. Rosalynn Carter Inst. of Ga. Southwestern State U.; co-founder Every Child by Two Campaign for Early Immunization. Author: First Lady from Plains, 1984, (with Jimmy Carter) Everything to Gain: Making the Most of the Rest of Your Life, 1987, Helping Yourself Help Others: A Book for Caregivers, 1994, Helping Someone With Mental Illness: A Compassionate Guide for Family, Friends and Caregivers, 1998. Bd. advisors Habitat for Humanity; mem. Ga. Gov.'s Commn. to Improve Svcs. for Mentally and Emotionally Handicapped, 1971; hon. chmn. Pres.'s Commn. on Mental Health, 1977-78. Recipient Presdl. Citation APA, 1982, Nathan S. Kline medal of merit Internat. Com. Against Mental Illness, 1984, Disting. Alumnus award Am. Assn. State Colls. and Univs., 1987, Dorothea Dix award Mental Illness Found., 1988, Dean's award Columbia U. Coll. Physicians and Surgeons, 1991, Notre Dame award for internat. humanitarian svc., 1992, Eleanor Roosevelt Living World award Peace Links, 1992, Nat. Caring award, The Caring Inst., 1995, Kiwanis World Svc. medal, Kiwanis Internat. Found., 1995, Jefferson award Am. Inst. for Pub. Svc., 1996, Into the Light award Nat. Mental Health Assn., 1997, Presdl. Medal of Freedom, 1999; named Nat. Women's Hall of Fame, 2001. Hon. fellow Am. Psychiat. Assn. Democrat.

CARTER, SALLY PACKLETT, elementary education educator; b. Clovis, N.Mex., May 15, 1948; d. Charles Everett and Marion Jamie Gee; m. Leonard Gene Carter, Mar. 7, 1969; 1 child, Dale Lee. BS in Edn., Ctrl. Mo. State U., 1969, MS in Edn., 1981. Cert. vocat. home econs. grades 7-12, elem. edn. grades K-6, Mo., K-8 elem. edn., home econs. grades 7-12, Ariz., EA/sci., nat. bd. cert. tchr. Home econ. tchr. Deepwater (Mo.) High Sch., 1969-71; tchr. grade 7 Deepwater (Mo.) Sch., 1971-73; tchr. grades 1 and 2 Davis R-12, Clinton, Mo., 1974-80; tchr. grade 5 Southeast Elem., Clinton, 1980-96; substitute tchr. Mesa, Ariz., 1996-97; tchr. grade 6 Fountain Hills (Ariz.) Middle Sch., 1997—. Mem. Mo. State Tchrs. (pres. ctrl. dist. 1989-90), Clinton Tchrs. Assn. (pres. 1985, 90, 92), Ariz. Edn. Assn., VFW Ladies Aux. Post 1894, Delta Kappa Gamma (1st v.p. Mu. chpt. 1992-94, pres. Mu. chpt. 1994-96, Alpha Epsilon chpt. 1996—, 1st v.p. 2002—), Phi Kappa Phi. Avocations: reading, fishing, cooking, sewing. Home: 6316 E Quartz St Mesa AZ 85215-0943

CARTER, SARALEE LESSMAN, immunologist, microbiologist; b. Chgo., Feb. 19, 1951; d. Julius A. and Ida (Oiring) Lessman; B.A., National Coll., 1971; m. John B. Carter, Oct. 7, 1979; children: Robert Oiring, Mollie. Supr. lab. immunology Weiss Meml. Hosp., Chgo., 1973-80; lab. immunology supr. Henrotin Hosp., Chgo., 1980-84; tech. dir. Lexington Med. Labs., West Columbia, S.C., 1984—; mem. nat. workshop faculty Am. Soc. Clin. Pathologists; clin. instr. faculty Med. U. S.C. Mem. Am. Soc. Clin. Pathologists (subspecialty cert. in microbiology and immunology, cert. med. technologist). Researcher Legionnaires Disease and mycoplasma pneumonia World Soc. Pathologists, Jerusalem, Israel, 1980. Contbr. articles to profl. jours.; Mem. Rep. Senoritorial Inner Circle, co-chmn. S.C. Young Profls. for George Bush. Office: 110 Medical Ln E Ste 100 West Columbia SC 29169-4817

CARTER, STEVE, state attorney general; b. Lafayette, Ind. BA in Econs-.(hon.), Harvard U., 1976; JD, MBA, Ind. U. Chief city-county atty. Indpls.-Marion County; atty. gen. State of Ind., 2001—; chief of staff Former Mayor Stephen Goldsmith Ind.; legis. counsel Ind. State Senate; chief of staff, agrl. asst. Ind. Lt. Gov. John Mutz. Republican. Office: Ind Govt Ctr S 5th Fl 302 W Washington St Indianapolis IN 46204*

CARTER, SYLVIA, journalist; b. Keokuk, Iowa; d. Charles Sylvester and Frances Elizabeth (Smith) C. B of Journalism, U. Mo., 1968. Intern Quincy (Ill.) Herald-Whig, 1966, Detroit Free Press, 1967; reporter The N.Y. Daily News, 1968-70; successively gen. assignment reporter, edn. reporter, food writer, restaurant critic, food columnist Newsday, Melville, N.Y., 1970—; food writer, restaurant critic N.Y. Newsday, N.Y.C., 1985-95; founder, editor Kidsday Newsday, Melville. Author: Eats: The Best Little Restaurants in New York, 1988, Eats N.Y.C.: A Guide to the Best, Cheapest, Most Interesting Restaurants in Brooklyn, Queens and Manhattan, 1995; contbr. to Family Circle and other publs. Trustee Anne O'Hare McCormick Scholarship Fund, N.Y.C., 1988—. Recipient Feature Writing award U. Mo., 2000. Mem. Newswomen's Club N.Y. (pres. 1990-92, bd. dirs., Front Page award 1982). Democrat. Presbyterian. Avocations: reading, collectibles, hiking, music, cooking. Home: 111 Waverly Pl New York NY 10011-9142 also: 46 Crescent Bow Ridge NY 11961-2915 Office: Newsday 235 Pinelawn Rd Melville NY 11747-4250 E-mail: sylvia.carter@newsday.com.

CARTER, TAMERA LYNNETTE, clinical nurse specialist; b. Camden, Tenn., July 10, 1960; d. Joseph David and Delana Janet (Jordan) Rayburn; m. Barry Lynn Carter, Dec. 11, 1981; children: Shanna Lynn, Kyla Shea. BSN, SUNY, Albany, 1988; MSN, Murray State U., 1997. RN, Tenn., Ky.; cert. clin. specialist in med./surg. nursing ANCC. Staff nurse Three Rivers Hosp., Waverly, Tenn., 1981 85; office mgr., inservice dir. Tri County Quality Home Health, Camden, 1985-93; health scis. tchr. Humphreys County Dept. Edn., Waverly, 1993-94; staff nurse Jackson (Tenn.) Madison County Gen., 1994-95; risk mgmt. dir. Camden Gen. Hosp., 1995-97, performance improvement dir., 1995—, case mgmt. dir., 1997—, jr. vol. coord., 1999—. CPR instr.Am. Heart Assn., ARC, 1990—; ACLS instr. Am. Heart Assn., 1999—; advisor Bd. Tenn. Nutrition and Consumers Edn. Program, Camden, 1996—; adv. coun. Humphrey's County Health Occupations Students of Am., 1997—98, Benton County Health Occupations Students Am., 1999—, mem. adv. bd., 2000, Benton County Vocat. Ctr., 2000—. Adult vol. leader 4-H, Camden, 1984—; water safety instr., 1990—; mem. allocations com. United Way, Camden, 1994—96; mem. cmty. adv. panel E.I. DuPont, New Johnsonville, Tenn., 1995—; pres. Leadership Benton County, 1999—2000. Mem. Camden Quarterback Club (sec. 2001-02), Apples to Apples (charter, pres. 1997—), U.

TennMartin Nursing Honor Soc. (charter mem.), Sigma Theta Tau (Delta Epsilon and Pi Tau chpts.). Avocations: swimming, reading, traveling. Home: 184 Camden Bay Rd Camden TN 38320-7140 Office: Camden Gen Hosp 175 Hospital Dr Camden TN 38320-1617

CARTER, T(HOMAS) BARTON, law educator; b. Dallas, Aug. 6, 1949; s. Sydney Hobart and Josephine (Wren) C.; m. Eleonore Dorothy Alexander, June 3, 1978 (div. 1988); 1 child, Richard Alexander. BA in Psychology, Yale U., 1971; JD, U. Pa., 1974; MS in Mass Communication, Boston U., 1978. Bar: Mass. 1974, U.S. Dist. Ct. Mass. 1975, U.S. Ct. Appeals (1st cir.) 1975. Asst. prof. law Boston U., 1979-85, assoc. prof., 1985-96, prof., 1996—; pvt. practice Boston, 1974—. Pres. Tanist Broadcasting Corp., Boston, 1981—2001. Co-author: The First Amendment and the Fourth Estate, 1985, 8th edit., 2000, The First Amendment and the Fifth Estate, 1986, 6th edit., 2003, Mass Communications Law in a Nutshell, 1988, 5th edit., 2000. Mem. ABA, Assn. for Edn. in Journalism and Mass Comm. (clk. 1981-82, asst. head 1982-83, head 1983-84), Broadcast Edn. Assn. (chair law and policy divsn. 1989-90), Fed. Comm. Bar Assn., Univ. Club. Avocation: bridge. Home: 109 Commonwealth Ave Apt 6 Boston MA 02116-2345 Office: Boston U 640 Commonwealth Ave Boston MA 02215-2422 E-mail: comlaw@bu.edu.

CARTER, THOMAS SMITH, JR., retired rail transportation executive; b. Dallas, June 6, 1921; s. Thomas S. and Mattie (Dowell) C.; m. Janet R. Hostetter, July 3, 1946 (dec. 1981); children: Diane Carter Petersen, Charles T., Carol Carter Koehler. BSCE, So. Meth. U., 1944; MS in Engring. Mgmt., Kans. U., 1991. Registered profl. engr., Mo., Kans., Okla., Tex., La., Ark. With Mo. Kans. Tex. R.R., 1946-54, chief engr., 1954-61, v.p. ops., 1961-66; v.p. Kansas City So. Rlwy. Co., La. and Ark. Rlwy. Co., 1966-74; pres. Kansas City So. Rlwy. Co., 1973-86, chmn. bd., 1981-91; pres. La. and Ark. Rlwy. Co., 1974-86, chmn. bd., 1981-91, CEO, 1981-91; ret., 1991. With U.S. Corps of Engrs., 1944-46. Fellow ASCE; mem. NSPE, Am. Rlwy. Engring. and Maintenance Assn. (life), Hide-A-Way Lake Club. Home: 131 Clubview Dr Lindale TX 75771-5054

CARTER, TYRONE, writer; b. Chgo., Oct. 24, 1961; s. Josephine Foster; 3 children. Grad., Manley H.S., Chgo. Recreational asst. YMCA, Chgo., 1975—79; with U.S. Army, 1979—83; mail handler U.S. Post Office, Chgo., 1985—86; security guard Burns Security, Oakland, 1987—89; gun sealer Zenith Co., Chgo., 1989—92; pres. T.C. Prodn., Chgo., 1994—, CHI-Track Records, Chgo., 1994—. Cmty. rep. local sch. coun. Orr H.S., Chgo., 2000—. Avocations: writing, basketball. Home: 1307 N Lorel Chicago IL 60651

CARTER, VINCE, professional basketball player; b. Jan. 26, 1977; Grad., U. N.C., 2001. Forward Toronto (Can.) Raptors, 1998—. Established Embassy of Hope Found. Named mem., 1995 USA Basketball Jr. Tam, World Championships, Goodwill Amb., Big Bros./Big Sisters Am.; named to NCAA Tournament All-East Regional Team, 1997, 1998, Schick All-Rookie 1st Team; recipient Schick Rookie of Yr. award, 1998—99. Office: c/o Toronto Raptors 40 Bay St Ste 400 Toronto ON Canada M5J 2X2

CARTER, WILFRED WILSON, financial executive, controller; b. Providence, Feb. 22, 1923; s. Leo and Florence (Wilson) C.; m. Elsa Aulisio, June 17, 1950; children— Linda J., Donald J., Paul J., Gregory J. AA, Roger Williams Coll., 1951; student, Bryant Coll., 1958-62. Sec., tax mgr. Nicholson File Co., East Providence, 1940-73; controller Columbia Chase Corp. (name changed to Chase Corp.), Braintree, Mass., 1973-84, v.p. fin., controller, 1984-88, CEO, pres., treas., CFO, 1988-91, chmn. bd. dirs., CEO, treas., 1991-93, chmn. bd. dirs., 1993-94; ret., 1994. Vestryman All Saints Meml. Ch., Providence, R.I., 1968-76, 94-2000, treas., 1968-76. With USAAF, 1942-46. Mem. Tax Exec. Inst. Episcopalian (vestryman 1968-76, 94-2000, treas. 1968-76). Home: 40 Kennedy Blvd Lincoln RI 02865-3602

CARTER, WILLIAM ALLEN, sales executive, insurance company executive; b. Princess Anne, Md., Jan. 23, 1919; s. Orman Dallas and Mary Letitia (Porter) C.; m. Ann Whitmore, Apr. 12, 1943; children: William W. (dec.), Melinda Carter Luedtke, Richard B. BA, St. John's Coll., 1940; AA (hon.), Del. Tech. and C.C., Dover, 1993; PhD, Berne U., 1998. Commd. ensign U.S. Navy Acad., 1941; released to reserve duty USN, 1946; sales mgr. Houston-White Co., Millsboro, Del., 1946-58; dist. agent Northwestern Mutual Life Ins. Co., Millsboro, Del., 1958-84, emeritus agent, 1984—; sec., treas. Hub of Sussex, Inc., Millsboro, Del., 1965-82. Commr. Town of Millsboro, Del., 1953-62, pres. of commn., 1957-62; mem. Del. Gov.'s State Goals Commn., 1961-65, chmn. com. pub. edn.; mem. Del. Indsl. Bldg. Commn., 1962-69, chmn. 1965-69; founding chmn. Del. Higher Edn. Scholarship Coun., 1963-68; rep. Del. State Na.t Com. Support Pub. Schs., Washington, 1964-69; founding mem. bd. dirs. Rsch. for Better Schs., Inc., Phila., 1965-75, state bd. trustees Del. Tech. and C.C., sec., 1966-69, chmn., 1973-83; chmn. feasibility study com. Del. State C.C., 1965-66; mem. state bd. trustees Del. Tech. and C.C. Ednl. Found., 1967—; mem. Del. Higher Edn. Commn., 1993—, Del. Com. Pub. Health, 1995—, bd. trustees Del. Inst. Med. Edn. and Rsch. Comdr. USNR, 1953. Decorated Silver Star, Order of the Great Patriotic War 1st class USSR, Del. Order of the 1st State Gov. of Del. Mem. Sussex Pines Country Club, Masons, Shriners. Democrat. Episcopalian. Home and Office: 227 Morris St Millsboro DE 19966-0248

CARTER, WILLIAM GERALD, non-profit corporation executive; b. Bethany, Mo., Jan. 12, 1929; s. William Young and Leah Genevieve (Cover) C.; m. Geralyn Gail Finlay, July 22, 1951; children: Kathryn Carter Gee, Karen Carter Winn, William Ralph. BSc, U. Mo., 1950. Assoc. editor Nat. Livestock Prodr., Chgo., 1950-51; comm. specialist Farmland Industries, Kansas City, Mo., 1953-54; advt. dir. MFA Oil Co., Columbia, Mo., 1954-58; ptnr. Neds & Wardlow Advt. Agy., Springfield, Mo., 1958-68; chmn., pres. Tri-State Pharm Co., Oklahoma City, 1968-81; real estate broker W.G. Carter Real Estate, Oklahoma City & Foster City, Calif., 1981-96; founder, chmn. Am. Acad. Vols. in Edn., Foster City, Calif., 1994-2000. Spl. agent intelligence U.S. Army, 1951-53. Named Young Man of Yr., C. of C., Springfield, 1964. Mem. Optimist Internat. (mem. various coms. 1981-89, v.p., bd. dirs. 1984, chair coms. 1985-87, v.p. Optimist Vols. for Youth, Inc. 1992-99). Republican. Methodist. Avocations: reading, writing. Home and Office: 1909 NW Quail Trl Lees Summit MO 64081-1614

CARTER, WILLIAM HAROLD, SR., physicist, researcher, electrical engineer; b. Houston, Nov. 17, 1938; s. William Henry and Fannie Augusta (Simpson) Carter; children: William Harold Jr., Elizabeth Lee. BSEE, U. Tex., 1962, MSEE, 1963, PhD, 1966. Rsch. asst. U. Tex., Austin, 1962-66; program dir. Office of R&D, CIA, Washington, 1966—69; rsch. assoc. U. Rochester, N.Y., 1969-70; rsch. physicist Naval Rsch. Lab., Washington, 1971-93; prof. U. Nebr., Lincoln, 1981-82; instr. Johns Hopkin's U., Balt., 1989-93; program dir. NSF, Arlington, Va., 1993—95. Vis. rsch. fellow U. Reading, Eng., 1976-77; vis. scientist applied physics lab. Johns Hopkin's U., Columbia, Md., 1991-92. Contbr. articles to profl. jours. Cellist Alexandria (Va.) Symphony, 1979-88, Georgetown Symphony, 1981—. Capt. U.S. Army, 1967-69. Fellow Optical Soc. Am. (topical editor jour. 2000—), Internat. Soc. for Optical Engring. (chmn. tech. coun. 1980-82, chmn. pub. com. 1981-83, chmn. fellows com. 1986); mem. IEEE (sr., conf. chmn. 1988), Am. Phys. Soc., Cosmos Club, Sigma Xi, Tau Beta Pi, Eta Kappa Nu. Achievements include co-discovery of the quasi-homogeneous source model; research in optical coherence, in applications of speckle phenomena, and in processing images and data from optical sensors. Home: 8301 Cherry Valley Ln Alexandria VA 22309-2117

CARTER, WILLIAM JOSEPH, lawyer; b. Balt., Sept. 1, 1949; s. Henry Merle and Florence (Rogan) C.; m. Monica Anne Urlock, July 17, 1976. BS in Psychology, Va. Poly. Inst., 1971; JD, Coll. William and Mary, 1974. Bar: Va. 1974, Pa. 1974, Md. 1980, D.C. 1980, U.S. Dist. Ct. D.C. 1981, U.S. Dist. Ct. Md. 1983, U.S. Dist. Ct. (ea. dist.) Va. 1985, U.S. Ct. Claims 1977, U.S. Tax Ct. 1977, U.S. Ct. Mil. Appeals 1975, U.S. Ct. Appeals (D.C. and 4th cirs.) 1979, U.S. Ct. Appeals (fed. cir.) 1982, U.S. Ct. Appeals (6th cir.) 1988, U.S. Ct. Appeals (3d and 5th cirs.) 1992, U.S. Ct. Appeals (11th cir.) 2002, U.S. Supreme Ct. 1977. Commd. 2d lt. U.S. Army, 1971, advanced through grades to capt., 1974, served with JAGC, 1971-79, resigned, 1979; assoc. Carr, Jordan, Coyne & Savits, Washington, 1979-84; shareholder Carr, Goodson & Lee, P.C., 1984-95, Carr Goodson Lee & Warner Profl. Corp., Washington, 1996-98, Carr Goodson Warner Profl. Corp., Washington, 1999-2000, Carr Goodson, P.C., Washington, 2000—01, Carr Maloney, P.C., Washington, 2001—. Mem. Deans adv. roundtable Coll. Arts and Scis., Va. Poly. Inst. Author: Appellate Practice Handbook for Maryland, Virginia and District of Columbia, 1996; editor: Appellate Practice Manual for the District of Columbia Court of Appeals, 1992. Mem.: ABA, D.C. Bar Assn. (cts. and adminstrn. of justice sect., ct. rules com., chair 1998—2001), Counselors, Bar Assn. D.C., Rotary (pres. Olney, Md. chpt. 1999—2000). Episcopalian. Avocations: ice hockey, tennis, music, scuba diving, skiing. Office: Carr Maloney PC Ste 1100 1667 K St NW Washington DC 20006

CARTER, WILLIAM WALTON, physicist, researcher; b. Pensacola, Fla., Nov. 7, 1921; s. Eugene Hudson and Nannie (Ledyard) C.; m. Elizabeth Jean Dedick, June 11, 1945; children— Carolyn A., Susan J., Judith J., Paul W. BS, Carnegie Inst. Tech., 1943; MS, Calif. Inst. Tech., 1948, PhD, 1949. Atomic and thermonuclear weapon R&D group leader weapons physics group, weapons div. Los Alamos Sci. Lab., 1949-59, project leader 1st thermonuclear weapon to enter regular nat. stockpile, also mem. joint working com.; chief scientist Army Missile Command, Redstone Arsenal, 1959-67; asst. dir. nuclear programs, def. research and engring. Office Sec. Def., Washington, 1967-71; assoc. dir. Harry Diamond Labs. U.S. Army, 1971-74, tech. dir., 1975-84, also chmn. staff devel. council; sr. scientist Pacific-Sierra Rsch., Arlington, Va., 1984-94; scientific cons. nuclear treaty monitoring, 1994—. Designer, deployer instruments to verify nuclear treaties; chmn. steering com. Huntsville Rsch. Inst. Served to lt. USNR, 1944-46. Asso. fellow AIAA; mem. AAAS, Am. Phys. Soc., Am. Def. Preparedness Assn., Am. Inst. Physics, Assn. U.S. Army. Achievements include design of air samplers for worldwide network of sensors to monitor non-proliferation and nuclear test ban treaties.; installation first unit in Turkmenistan, 1994. Home: 1124 Ormond Ct Mc Lean VA 22101-2960

CARTER, YVONNE BREAUX, retired librarian; b. Crowley, La., Aug. 3, 1922; d. Valentin D. and Annie H. (Oertling) Breaux; m. Walter R. Carter, Apr. 23, 1943. BS in Edn. with high distinction, U. Southwestern La., 1943; BS in Libr. Sci., George Peabody Coll. Tchrs., 1950, MA, 1960, EdS, 1966. Cert. tchr. and libr., D.C. Tchr., libr. Vermillion Parish Sch. Bd., Abbeville, La.; prin. Sardis (Tenn.) H.S., 1944—45; tchr. Calcasieu Parish, Lake Charles, La., 1942-43; libr. U.S. Office of Edn., 1967-76; adminstrv. libr. U.S. Dept. Edn., Washington, 1976-93. Asst. prof. Northwestern State U., Natchitoches, La., 1964-65, U. Southwestern La., 1966-67. Mem. Lafayette Pub. Libr. Found. Bd. Kappa Kappa Iota scholar, Delta Kappa Gamma Epsilon scholar. Mem.: DAR (regent Galvez chpt. 1998—), AAUW, ALA, North La. Hist. Assn., La. Libr. Assn., Am. Assn. Sch. Librs., Women in Arts, Attakapas Hist. Assn., Women's Club Lafayette, Beta Phi Mu, Delta Kappa Gamma, Alpha Beta Alpha, Kappa Delta Pi.

CARTER, ZACHARY W. lawyer; BA, Cornell U., 1972; JD, NYU, 1975. Bar: N.Y., U.S. Dist Ct. (ea. dist.) N.Y., U.S. Dist. Ct. (so. dist.) N.Y., U.S. Ct. Appeals (2d cir.), U.S. Supreme Ct. Asst. U.S. atty. U.S. Dist. Ct. (ea. dist.) N.Y., 1975-80; mem. Patterson, Belknap, Webb & Tyler, 1980-81; exec. asst. dist. atty. King County Dist. Atty's. Office, Bklyn., 1982-87; exec. asst. to dep. chief adminstrv. judge N.Y. City Cts., 1987; judge criminal ct. City of N.Y., 1987-91; U.S. magistrate judge E.D.N.Y., 1991-93; U.S. atty. ea. dist. N.Y. U.S. Dept. Justice, Bklyn., 1993-99; ptnr. Dorsey & Whitney, N.Y.C., 1999—. Mem. N.Y. Bar Assn. (chmn. Mayor's adv. com. on jud. selection). Office: Dorsey & Whitney LLP 250 Park Ave New York NY 10177-0001 E-mail: carter.zachary@dorseylaw.com.

CARTER-CRAM, KIMBERLY KAY, French language educator; b. Cleve., Sept. 26, 1968; d. Jonathan and Kay Lorraine Hosac Carter; m. Michael William Cram, May 26, 1991; 2 children. PhD, UCLA, 2000. Asst. prof. French, Idaho State U., Pocatello, 1996—. Contbr. articles to profl. publs., including Ency. of Life Writing, 2001. Mem. MLA, NOW, Idaho State U. Profl. Women (former bd. dirs.), Amnesty Internat. Democrat. Office: Idaho State U Campus Box 8203 Pocatello ID 83209-8203

CARTER-WOMMACK, BARBARA, retired educator; b. Decatur, Ga., Apr. 10, 1937; d. Robert Leonidas and Ruth Inez (Boyles) C.; m. Hines Lawrence Wommack, Mar. 21, 1974; 1 child, Beth. AB, LaGrange Coll., 1959; MEd, U. Ga., 1966, EdD, 1969. Ednl. asst. Brookhaven Meth. Ch., Atlanta, 1959-60; tchr. elem. DeKalb County Bd. Edn., Doraville, Ga., 1960-65; grad. tchg. asst. U. Ga., Athens, 1965-68; prof. reading Western Carolina U., Cullowhee, N.C., 1968-70, Ga. So. Coll., Statesboro, 1970-74; prof. Ga. Southwestern Coll., Americus, 1975-88; instrl. coord. Thomas Elem. Sch., Warner Robins, Ga., 1988-93; cons. So. Assn. Colls. and Schs., Atlanta, 1993-97; ret., 1997. Mem. Internat. Reading Assn. (Reading Tchr. Yr. S.W. Ga. Coun. 1976, Annette Hopson svc. award 1988, Ga. Hall of Fame 1994), Delta Kappa Gamma. Methodist. Avocations: gardening, travel, reading. Home: 424 Meadowlark Dr Albany GA 31707-3145

CARTHAY, R. JON, hand model, actor; b. Ellenville, N.Y., July 26, 1948; s. Alexander F. and Edith C.; m. Jane Brem, June 14, 1980. BA, Long Island U., 1971. Lic. pvt. pilot. Photographer's asst., 1977; profl. hand model Ford Models, Inc., N.Y.C., 1980—. Actor Tranum Robertson Hughes, Inc, 1987-97, J. Michael Bloom, Inc., 1987-97. Author: New York Modelline, 1996; hands featured in ads for AmEx, Diners Club, Black Label, Absolut Vodka, Ernest and Julio Gallo, Remy Martin, Citibank, Freixenet, Tylenol, Carlsberg Beer, Pepsi, Schweppes, TDK, Ford, Bulova, Piaget, Dunkin Donuts, numerous others. Named Most Photographed Hands in the World Tranum Robertson Hughes, Inc., 1997. Mem. Am. Fedn. TV and Radio Artists, Screen Actors Guild. Avocations: flying, sailing. Office: N Y Modelline 339 E 58th St Apt 7H New York NY 10022-2268 E-mail: jcarthay@yahoo.com.

CARTIER, BRIAN EVANS, association executive; b. Providence, Apr. 12, 1950; s. Clarence Joseph and Mary Anna (Evans) C. BA, R.I. Coll., 1972; MEd, Springfield (Mass.) Coll., 1973. Exec. dir. Arthritis Found. Conn., Hartford, 1976-78, dep. exec. dir. N.Y. chpt. N.Y.C., 1979; exec. dir. Found. for Chiropractic Edn. and Rsch., Arlington, Va., 1979-90, Nat. Ct. Reporters Assn., 1990-98; CEO Nat. Assn. Coll. Stores, Oberlin, Ohio, 1998—. Mem. Am. Mgmt. Assn. (cert. assn. exec.), Am. Soc. Assn. Execs., Greater Washington Soc. Assn. Execs., U.S. C. of C. Republican. Roman Catholic. Office: NACS 500 E Lorain St Oberlin OH 44074-1238

CARTIER, CHARLES ERNEST, alcohol and drug abuse services professional; b. Chgo., Aug. 4, 1931; s. Charles E. and Kathryn (Hanlon) C.; m. JoAnne Murphy, July 12, 1958; children: Kevin, Julia, Theresa, Carol. BS in Commerce, DePaul U., 1953. Nat. cert. alcohol, drug and addictions counselor. Program asst. Alcoholism Svcs. of Cleve. (Ohio), Inc., 1983-84; community liaison coord. Merrick Hall Adolescent Chem. Dependency Program, Cleve., 1984-86; instr. D.W.I. Counter Attack Project Cleve. (Ohio) State Univ., 1984-92; clin. supr. Fresh Start, Inc., Cleve., 1986-91; rehab. therapist alcohol treatment program VA Med. Ctr., Brecksville, Ohio, 1991—. Lectr. Cuya Hoga Community Coll., Sch. of Mental Health Tech., Cleve., 1987—; bd. mem., v.p. Exodus, Inc. Treatment Program, 1986-90. Sgt. U.S. Army, 1953-55. Mem. Nat. Assn. Alcoholism and Drug Abuse Counselors, Ohio Assn. Alcoholism and Drug Abuse Counselors (sec. 1986-91, Hinkle Meml. award for Outstanding Work in the Field of Alcoholism Counseling 1990, Superior Performance award 1997). Roman Catholic. Avocations: race walking, editorial writing. Home: 9049 Roosevelt Dr Northfield OH 44067-1222

CARTIER, RUDOLPH HENRI, JR., lawyer, legal educator; b. Yonkers, N.Y., Oct. 8, 1947; s. Rudolph Henri and Edith Edna (Hartling) C.; m. Linda Clair Truzzolino, Jan. 24, 1970 (div. July 1980); m. Mary Anne Lavorata, Aug. 16, 1980; children: Laura Anne, Stephen Robert. BA, LaSalle Coll., 1969; JD, St. John's U., Jamaica, N.Y., 1975. Bar: N.Y. 1976, U.S. Dist. Ct. (ea. and so. dists.) N.Y. 1976, U.S. Supreme Ct. 1982. Asst. dist. atty. Suffolk County Dist. Atty.'s Office, Riverhead, N.Y., 1975-77; sole practice, Selden, N.Y., 1977-82; ptnr. Rogers & Cartier, P.C., Patchogue, N.Y., 1982— ; gen. counsel Suffolk County Assn. Mcpl. Employees; asst. prof. Suffolk County Community Coll., Selden, N.Y., 1978-84, paralegal adv. bd.; spl. asst. dist. atty., Village of Head of the Harbor, 1985—. Atty., mem. steering com. Smithtown Citizens for Edn., N.Y., 1983—. Mem. N.Y. State Bar Assn. (criminal discovery and correctional services coms.), Suffolk County Bar Assn. (fee dispute resolution and criminal law coms.), Suffolk County Criminal Assn., L.I. Indsl. Relations Research Assn. Republican. Roman Catholic. Home: 11 Peace Ln East Setauket NY 11733-1957 Office: Rogers and Cartier PC 180 E Main St Patchogue NY 11772-3171 also: 900 Ellison Ave Westbury NY 11590-5142

CARTLEDGE, RAYMOND EUGENE, retired paper company executive; b. Pensacola, Fla., June 12, 1929; s. Raymond H. and Meddie (Brookins) C.; m. Gale Perry, June 30, 1962; children: John R., Perri Ann, Susan R. BS, U. Ala., 1952; postgrad., Harvard Bus. Sch., 1970. With Procter & Gamble Co., 1955-56; with Union Camp Corp., Wayne, N.J., 1956-70, 80-94, pres., COO, 1983-86, chmn., pres., CEO, 1986-94; pres., CEO Clevepak Corp., White Plains, N.Y., 1971-79; chmn. Savannah Foods, 1996-97. Past chmn. Am. Paper Inst., solid waste task force; trustee Am. Enterprise Inst.; trustee, life councillor The Conf. Bd.; bd. dirs. Blountint, Chase Brass Industries, Delta Airlines, The Sun Co., Grafton Internat., Formica, Inc.; past chmn. Inst. Paper Sci. and Tech., Nat. Coun. Paper Industry for Air and Stream Improvement, internat. bus. com. Am. Forest & Paper Assn. Served with U.S. Army Airborne Infantry, 1952-55. Office: #235 15 Lake St Savannah GA 31411-2913

CARTLIDGE, EDWARD SUTTERLEY, mechanical engineer; b. Trenton, N.J., Feb. 5, 1945; s. Leon James and Agnes Jean (Cinkay) C.; m. Marilyn Spinuzza, July 21, 1979. BS in Marine Engring., U.S. Mcht. Marine Acad., 1968; MSME, N.J. Inst. Tech., 1971; MBA, Temple U., 1982; MA, Biblical Theol. Sem., 2001. Registered profl. engr., Pa., Ill., Del., Md., N.J., Va., Wis., Calif., Fla. Marine engr. Seatrain Lines, 1968-69; performance engr. Foster Wheeler Corp., Livingston, N.J., 1969-71; cons. engr. Fluor, Sargent & Lundy, and Kuljian Corp., 1971-75; chief engr. Gimpel Corp., Langhorne, Pa., 1976-79; sr. R&D engr. Yarway Corp., Blue Bell, Pa., 1979-82; sr. project process engr. and power utilities supr. Merck & Co., Inc., West Point, Pa., 1982-91; sr. project mgr. Conmec, Inc., Bethlehem, Pa., 1992-93, Edward S. Cartlidge, PE and Assocs., Brandon, Fla., 1993—2000; mgr. facilities engring. Cardinal Health, Inc., Softgel Pharm. Mfg., St. Petersburg, Fla., 2000—. Cons. Pharm., Polymer, Utilities, Semiconductor, Steel Fab., Gideon; Christian fin. counselor, lectr., seminar leader. Bd. dirs. Grand Old Gospel Fellowship. Served to comdr. USNR, 1968-91. Mem. NSPE (chpt. pres.), ASME, ASHRAE, Fla. Engring. Soc., Internat. Soc. Pharm. Engrs., Pa. Soc. Profl. Engrs. (Young Engr. of Yr. 1990), Naval Res. Assn., Nat. Fire Prevention Assn., Gideons Internat. (v.p.). Home: 901 Stratford Manor Dr Brandon FL 33510-2810 E-mail: ed.cartlidge@cardinal.com.

CARTMAN, SHIRLEY ELEISE, retired music educator; b. Chgo., June 27, 1931; d. Johnny Theophilus Cartman and Hattie Lee Marshall. BS in Music Edn., U. Ill., 1950—53; M in Bus. Mgmt. and Supervision, Ctrl. Mich. U., 1977—78. Cert. tchg. cert. Wash., 1960, provisional tchg. cert. Gary Cmty. Sch. Corp., 1966, life tchg. cert. Ga. Dept. Edn., 1987. 4th grade tchr. Clover Park Sch. Dist., Tacoma, 1960—64; strings tchr. Gary (Wash.) Cmty. Sch. Co-op., 1965—70; music tchr. Prince Georges C.C., Camp Springs, Md., 1973—74; orch. tchr. Dekalb County Bd. of Edn., Decatur, Ga., 1989—91; string ensemble prof. Spelman Coll., Atlanta, 1998—99; music conservatory directress Chapel Hill Harvester Ch., Decatur, Ga., 1992—96; strings instr. New Birth Missionary Bap. Ch. Faith Acad. Sc., Decatur, Ga., 1997—2000. Talent coord. for talented Youth of Gary, Ind., 1968—70; cons. "Jackson Five" Steel Town Record C., Gary, 1967—68; mgr. New Generation Band, New Experience Bank, Decatur, 1985—87; first lady of gospel violin various churches throughout Atlanta area, 2000—01; pt. time strings instr. DeKalb County (Ga.) Bd. Edn., 2000—01; creator, designer The Cartman Fun Music Curriculum Greenforest McCalep Early Learning Ctr., Decatur, Ga. Musician (profl. entertainer): Shelia Carr, 1970; musician: (songwriter) (songs) Lonely Heart, 1968 (Sung by the Jackson Five, 1972); author: (children's short story collection) Stolen Key, 1974, A Teacher Remembers the Jacksons, 1987, 4 children's music books; designer and creator (songs books and teaching aids) The Cartman Fun Music Method, 2002; author: tiny-tot music books for children. SP4 U.S. Army, 1974—75, Fort Mead, Md. Mem.: NAACP (life; ACT-SO chairperson 2000—02, Plaque for Svc. as ACT-SO chairperson 2000—01). Democrat. Avocation: travel. Home: 3945 Johns Hopkins Ct Decatur GA 30034 Office: Cartman Music Studio 3945 Johns Hopkins Ct Decatur GA 30034 Office Fax: 678-418-0166.

CARTNICK, EDWARD NATHANIEL, obstetrician-gynecologist; b. Garfield, N.J., 1914; AB, Harvard U.; MD, Tufts U., 1940. Intern Kings County Hosp., N.Y.C., 1940-42, resident, 1946-49; dir. gyn oncology Nassau County Med. Ctr., Uniondale, N.Y.; dir. Ob-gyn Mercy Hosp., Rockville Center, N.Y. Served to maj. M.C., U.S. Army, 1942-46. Mem. AMA, ACS (bd. govs.), Am. Coll. Ob-Gyn.

CARTON, GARY L. performing arts association administrator; s. Herbert A. and Gwendolyn T. Carton; m. Shirley A. Gergen, Dec. 28, 1974; 1 child, Theresa I. Coor. BA, S.W. State U., Marshall, Minn., 1967—71; MA, U. Wash., Seattle, 1974. Tech. dir., instr. S.W. State U., Marshall, Minn., 1974—75; designer, asst. prof. Emporia State U., Emporia, Kans., 1975—78; theatre dir., asst. prof. U. N.D., Grand Forks, 1978—88; facility dir. CAM-PLEX, Gillette, Wyo., 1990—97; dir. performing arts ctr. Kirtland C.C., Roscommon, Mich., 1998—. Chmn. Performing Arts Adv. Com., Roscommon. State Arts grantee, Minn. Arts Coun., 1967-1974, ND State Arts Coun., 1978-1988, Wyo. Arts Coun., 1990-1997, Mich. Coun. Arts and Cultural Affairs, 1998- 2003. Mem.: Mich. Non-profit Presenters, Mich. Assn. of Cmty. Arts Agencies (regional dir. 2001—03), Artserve, USITT, Houghton Lake Playhouse Com. Home: 10353 Chase Bridge Rd Roscommon MI 48653 Office: Kirtland C C 10775 N St Helen Rd Roscommon MI 48653 Home Fax: 989-275-8745; Office Fax: 989-275-8745. Personal E-mail: cartong@kirtland.edu.

CARTON, LONNIE CAMING, educational psychologist; b. Balt. d. Daniel and Shirley (Cooper) Caming; m. Edwin B. Carton; children: Evan, Deborah, Paula. BS, Johns Hopkins U.; MS, U. Md.; PhD, Pa. State U. Tchr. Laurel (Md.) H.S.; instr. Pa. State U., State College, Temple U., Phila.; newspaper columnist Delaware County Times, Chester, Pa.; instr., then asst. prof. Tufts U., Medford, Mass., 1964-80; learning sys. cons. Tufts New Eng. Med. Ctr., Boston, 1968-73. Broadcast journalist CBS Radio, N.Y.C., 1974—; family support sys. cons. Boston Ptnrs. in Edn., 1985—; ind. cons., lectr., workshop leader in field; guest appearances of various radio and TV shows; family lit. cons. Mass. Dept. Edn., 2001—; cons., dir. teen and family resources Warm 2 Kids, Inc., 2003—. Author: Mommies, 1960, Daddies, 1963, Raise Your Kids Right, 1980, No is a Love Word, 1992, (cassette tapes) Parenting Preschoolers from the Park Bench, 1999; sr. editor Edn. Today, Boston, 1992-98; broadcast journalist Voice of Am., 1995-98; contbr. articles to profl. pubs. Grantee Gannet Found., U.S. Dept. Edn., Mass. Dept. Edn., U.S. Dept. Hwy. Safety, Mass. Gov.'s Alliance Against Drugs; recipient Nat. Media award APA, 1978, 80, San Francisco State Broadcast Media award, 1983, Contbn. to Lives of Children award UNICEF, Margaret Sanger Soc. award Planned Parenthood, 1985, Don Bosco Friend of Youth award Salesian Soc., awards from Mass. Psychol. Assn., Nat. Commn. Against Drunk Driving, Gabriel Broadcaster's and Allied Communicators, Mass. Soc. Against Cruelty to Children, 1988; named to One Hundred Most Remarkable Women in Mass., Boston Woman's Mag., 1989, Freedoms Found., George Washington medal for pub. comms., 1998. Avocations: tennis, spectator football, reading. Office: The Learning Ctr PO Box 204 New Town MA 02456-0204

CART-ROGERS, KATHERINE COOPER, emergency nurse, nurse consultant; b. Jacksonville, Tex., Aug. 7, 1948; d. Raymond Jesse and June (Walker) Cooper; m. Frank E. Rogers, Sept. 25, 1981; 1 child, Natalie Christine Cart. Med. Technologist, St. Mary's, Galveston, Tex., 1967; BS in Nursing, Stephen F. Austin U., Nacogdoches, Tex., 1989; MA in Mgmt., Regent U., Virginia Beach, Va., 1995. Cert. emergency nurse, TNCC instr., ENPC instr., legal nurse cons. Pharmacology-toxicology researcher U. Tex. Med. Br., Galveston, 1967-68, Ohio State U., Columbus, 1968-72; physicians asst., lab. supr. Newborn Meml. Hosp., Jacksonville, 1975-78; lab. mgr. East Tex. Med. Ctr., Rusk, 1978-87; lab. supr. Nacogdoches Meml. Hosp., 1987-89, emergency rm. nurse, 1989-91; emergency rm. chrge nurse Kingwood (Tex.) Pla. Hosp., 1991-92; nursing cons. Thorstenson Eye Clinic, Nacogdoches, Tex., 1991-92; dir. surg. svcs. Thorstenson Ambulatory Surgery Ctr., Nacogdoches, Tex., 1992-93; dir. Emergency/Trauma Svcs., ETMC-Jacksonville, 1992—2002; surgery dir. Thorstenson Ambulatory Surgery Ctr., Nacogdoches, 2002—; dir.

Emergency/Trauma Svcs., Palestine Regional Med. Ctr., 2002—. Mem. Emergency Nurses Assn., Tex. Trauma Coords., Tex. Regional Adv. Coun. for Trauma Area G. Home: Rte 3 Box 2 Rusk TX 75785-9503 E-mail: katbalou@attglobal.net.

CARTWRIGHT, ALTON STUART, electrical manufacturing company executive; b. Casper, Wyo., Oct. 7, 1922; s. Alton Stuart and Blanche Susan (Harper) C.; m. Adelaide Frances Igoe, Dec. 22, 1951; children: Stuart Andrew, Matthew Alton, David Francis, Patrick Harper. BS in Elec. Engring, Oreg. State U., 1944; grad., Advanced Mgmt. Program, Harvard U., 1969. Registered profl. engr., Mass. With Gen. Electric Co., 1946-85; with Can. Gen. Electric Co. Ltd., 1970-85, exec. v.p., 1972, pres., 1972-77, chmn. bd., chief exec. officer, 1977-85, also dir. Sr. mem. Conf. Bd. Served to 1st lt. AUS, 1942-46. Mem. No. Lake George Yacht Club, John's Island Club (Vero Beach, Fla.), Sigma Alpha Epsilon. Home: 676 Ocean Rd Vero Beach FL 32963-3516

CARTWRIGHT, BILL, professional basketball coach; b. Lodi, Calif., July 30, 1957; m. Sheri Cartwright; children: Justin, Jason, James, Kristin. student, MA in Orgnl. Devel. and Human Resources, U. San Francisco. Basketball player Chgo. Bulls, NBA World Championships; asst. coach Chgo. Bulls, 1996, head coach, 2001—. Named One time NBA All-Star, 1980, 3 time All Am. Player of Yr., WCC's 50 Greatest Student-Athletes of All-Time; named to NBA Ea. Conf. All-Star Team, 1980; recipient NBA All-Rookie Team honors, 3 time West Coast Conf. Player of Yr. . Achievements include Dons all-time leading scorer; helped the Bulls win 55 victories in each of his final five seasons in Chicago including the first back-to-back 60+ win seasons in Bulls history, 1990-92. Office: United Ctr 1901 W Madison St Chicago IL 60612

CARTWRIGHT, BRIAN GRANT, lawyer; b. Seattle, May 29, 1947; s. John Brydonne and Helen Ruth (Engman) C.; m. Jean Claudia Libby, Jan. 5, 1975; children: Grant, Eliot, Bryce. BS, Yale U., 1967; PhD, U. Chgo., 1971; JD, Harvard U., 1980. Bar: D.C. 1981, U.S. Dist. Ct. D.C. 1981, U.S. Ct. Appeals (D.C. cir.) 1981, Calif. 1984. Law clk. U.S. Ct. Appeals (D.C. cir.), Washington, 1980-81, U.S. Supreme Ct., Washington, 1981-82; assoc. Latham & Watkins, L.A., 1982-88, ptnr., 1988—, mem. exec. com., 1994-98; lectr. U. Calif., Los Angeles, 1999—. Mem. Los Angeles County Bar Assn. (mem. exec. com., bus. and corps. law sect. 1992-99). Office: Latham & Watkins 633 W 5th St Ste 3800 Los Angeles CA 90071-2007

CARTWRIGHT, KEITH ALLEN, literature educator; b. Murray, Ky., Feb. 22, 1960; s. Joseph Cartwright, Pamela Cartwright; m. Amanda Gross, Dec. 22, 1989; children: Jesse, Maya. BA, U. South, 1982; MA, U. Ark., 1990; PhD, Ind. U., 1997. Ext. agt. Fisheries U.S. Peace Corps, Dagana, Senegal, 1983—85; staff U.S. Fish and Wildlife Svc., N.Y.C., 1986—87; instr. Selma U., Selma, Ala., 1990—91, Coastal Ga. C.C., Brunswick, 1993—97; lectr. Coll. of Bahamas, Nassau, 1997—98, Murray State U., Murray, Ky., 1998—99; asst. prof. Roanoke Coll., Roanoke, Va., 1999—. Author (poetry): Saint-Louis, 1997, Junkanoo, 2000; author: Reading Africa into American Literature, 2002. Fellow Poetry fellow, Va. Commn. for Arts, 2002. Santeria. Avocations: fishing, gardening, kayaking. Home: 200 Pico Rd Buchanan VA 24066 Office: English Dept Roanoke College Salem VA 24153

CARTWRIGHT, KEROS, hydrogeologist, researcher; b. L.A., July 25, 1934; s. Eugene Ewing and Charlotte Lucy (Searle) C.; m. Sharon Miller, July 5, 1955 (dec.); children: Sylvia, Jennifer; m. Jennifer Elizabeth Moberley, Mar. 9, 1962 (div. Sept. 1988); children: David, Bridget; m. Madalene Rose Tierney, Feb. 16, 1990. AB in Geology, U. Calif., 1959; MS in Geology, U. Nev., 1961; PhD in Geology, U. Ill., 1973. Cert. profl. geologist, profl. hydrologist. Hydrogeologist Humboldt River Rsch. Project, Winnemucca, Nev., 1959-61, Ill. State Geol. Survey, Champaign, 1961-2000, head hydrogeology and geophysics sect., 1975-84, prin. scientist and head gen. and environ. geology group, 1984-88, prin. rsch. scientist, 1988-99, chief scientist emeritus, 1999—; adj. prof. geology No. Ill. U., DeKalb, 1979—, U. Ill., Urbana, 1985—. Cons. pvt. practice in hydrogeology, N.Am. and Europe, 1968—, U.S. Environ. Protection Agy. Sci. Adv. Bd., Washington, 1983—, Savannah River Site Environ. Adv., Aiken, S.C., 1988—. Mem. editorial bd. Elsevier Sci. Publ. Jour. of Hydrology, 1982-85; contbr. articles to profl. jours. Named Disting. Lectr. Assn. Groundwater-Water Scientists and Engrs., 1987; recipient Cert. Appreciation U.S. Environ. Protection Agy., 1988. Fellow: Geol. Soc. Am. (officer hydrogeology sect. 1975—78, mem. editl. bd. Jour. Water Resources Rsch. 1975—81, chmn. 1978—79, Bull. 1981—83, mem. governing coun. 1993—97, chmn. publs. com., Birdsall disting. lectr. 1987—88, George B. Maxey Disting. Svc. award 1991), Explorers Club; mem.: ASTM (vice chmn. subcom. D-14 1984—88), Internat. Assn. Hydrogeologists (U.S. com. 1985—89), Am.Water Resources Assn., Am. Geophys. Union (assoc. editor 1975—81), Am. Inst. Hydrology (mem. editl. bd. Jour. Hydrol. Sci. and Tech. 1985—). Avocation: farming. Office: Ill Geol Survey 615 E Peabody Dr Champaign IL 61820-6918 Fax: 217-687-4172. E-mail: redoaks@soltec.net.

CARTWRIGHT, PETER, electronics company executive; b. 1930; m. June Cartwright; 4 children. BS, Princeton U.; MS in engring., Columbia U. Engr. Gibbs and Hill Archtl. Engring., 1979—84; pres., CEO, founder, chmn. Calpine, San Jose, Calif., 1984—. Officer civil engring. corps. USN. Office: Calpine 50 W San Fernando St Ste 500 San Jose CA 95113-2433*

CARTWRIGHT, PHILLIP AUGUST, management consultant; b. Springfield, Ill., Dec. 29, 1953; s. Thomas Hume and Miriam (Beyer) C.; m. Blanche Victoria Baumann (div. Jan. 1987); m. Virginia L. Martin, Aug. 1, 1987. BA, Tex. Christian U., 1975, MA, 1976; MS, U. Ill., 1980, PhD, 1982. Asst. assoc. prof. econs. U. Ga., Athens, 1982-87; v.p. econmetric analysis A.C. Nielsen, Northbrook, Ill., 1987-93, v.p. analytics Paris, 1993-96; sr. mgr. Ernst & Young Global Client Cons., Paris, 1996-2000; prin. Andersen Bus. Cons., Paris, 2000—. Assoc., chair com. U. Bus. and Econ. Rsch., 1985--87; mem. Kellogg Found., Interdisciplinary Task Force Project on the Economy, 1985-87. Contbr. articles to profl. jours. Fellowship U. of Ill., 1982. Mem. Am. Statis. Assn. (chair sect. govt. stats. 1990, chair com. on govt. stats. 1989), Am. Econ. Assn., European Soc. for Opinion and Mktg. Rsch., Strategic Mgmt. Soc.

CARTWRIGHT, TALULA ELIZABETH, writing and leadership educator, consultant; b. Asheville, N.C., Oct. 25, 1947; d. Ralph and Sarah Helen (Medford) C.; m. Edwin Byram Crabtree, May 23, 1976 (div. Sept. 1984); children: Charity, Baxter; m. Richard Thomas England, Apr. 27, 1986; 1 child, Isaac. BA, U. N.C., 1971, MEd, 1974, EdD, 1988. Instr. McDowell Tech. Inst., Marion, N.C., 1972-73, Guilford Tech. C.C., Jamestown, N.C., 1973-89, Guilford Coll., Greensboro, N.C., 1982-87, U. N.C.-Greensboro, 1982-87, N.C. A&T State U., Greensboro, 1984-85. With Communication Assocs., Lenoir, Shelby, Asheboro, Greensboro, 1981—; dean continuing edn. Caldwell C.C., Lenoir, N.C., 1989-92; v.p. acad. programs Cleve. C.C., 1992-95; sr. faculty and program mgr. Ctr. for Creative Leadership, Greensboro, N.C., 1996—; bd. dirs Carolinas Quality Consortium, 1993-95, N.C. Quality Coun., 1994-95; chmn. bd. dirs. Cleve. Abuse Prevention Coun., 1993-95. Tchr. of Yr. award Guilford Tech. C.C. Edn. Assn., 1982, Edn. Honor Roll award 1989; winner Human Rights Writing Contest, 1988, 89. Mem. NCAE (pres. local unit 1988-89, chmn. higher edn. commn. 1989-90, 92-95), Am. Assn. Women in C.C., Women's Adminstrs. in N.C. (exec. bd. 1995).

CARTY, DONALD J. former airline company executive; Grad., Queen's U., Kingston, Ont., Harvard U. With Air Canada, Canadian Pacific Rwy.; gen. mgr. Montcel Distbrs. unit Celanese Can. Ltd., Montreal; sr. v.p. fin. Americana Hotels; v.p. profit improvement, v.p. ops. rsch. American Airlines, sr. v.p., controller, sr. v.p. airline planning, 1987-89; exec. v.p. fin. and planning AMR and Am. Airlines, DFW Airport, Tex., 1989-95; pres. AMR Airline Group and Am. Airlines, Inc., DFW Airport, Tex., 1995-98; pres., CEO CP Air; chmn., pres., CEO AMR Corp., Ft. Worth, 1998—2002, chmn., CEO, 2002—03. Bd. dirs. Dell computer Corp., Sears, Roebuck & Co. Bd. trustees Queen's U. Fax: 817-967-4162.*

CARTY, HEIDI MARLENE, educator, researcher; b. Salt Lake City, July 19, 1967; d. Richard Eathel Coon and Sharon (Pitcher) Smith; m. Shawn Patrick Carty. BS in Psychology with honors cum laude, Loyola U., 1992, MA in Rsch. Methodology and Stats., 1994, PhD in Rsch. Methodology and Stats., 1998. Rsch. asst. Loyola U. Med. Ctr., Maywood, Ill., 1993, Loyola U., Chgo., 1993-94, grad. asst. statis. computing, 1992-94; statis. cons. Iota, Inc., Chgo., 1993-95; grad. asst. rsch. methodology Loyola U., Chgo., 1994-96; statis. cons. U. San Diego, 1996-98; asst. prof. rsch. Hofstra U., Hempstead, N.Y., 1998-99; asst. dir. stud. rsch. and information Univ. Calif. San Diego, San Diego, 1999—. Part-time lectr. Loyola U., Chgo., 1992-96; lectr. biology dept. U. San Diego, 1998—; test reviewer Buros Inst. Mental Measures, 2002—; prof. U. Phoenix Online, 2002—. Contbr. articles to profl. jours. Recipient grad. assistantship Loyola U., 1992-94, 94-96; scholar Nat. AMBUCS, 1991. Fellow Am. Ednl. Rsch. Assn.; mem. APA, Am. Ednl. Rsch. Assn., Assn. for Instnl. Rsch., Calif. Assn. for Instnsl. Rsch., Psi Chi (pres.), Alpha Epsilon Delta, Sigma Xi. Avocations: sailing, reading, jogging, movies, theater. Office: UCSD 9500 Gilman Dr La Jolla CA 92093-5004

CARTY, JOHN WESLEY, lawyer; b. Lansing, N.C., Oct. 29, 1923; s. John Arthur and Bertha (Eller) C.; m. Doris Frances Barnes, June 27, 1948; children: Dixie Lynne, John Jeffrey. BA, Buena Vista Coll., 1950; JD, Drake U., 1952. Bar: Iowa 1952, U.S. Dist. Ct. (so. dist.) Iowa 1952, U.S. Ct. Appeals (8th cir.) 1965. Assoc. Pryor, Hale, Plock, Riley & Jones, Burlington, Iowa, 1952-54; ptnr. Carty & Jones, Des Moines, 1960-75; pvt. practice Winfield, Iowa, 1955—. Bd. dirs. Farmers Nat. Bank, Winfield, Iowa, pres., chmn. 1984—; pres. Oxidex, Inc., Winfield, 1971—; broker, dir Winfield Realty Co., 1956-98; pres., chmn. Winfield Health Care & Retirement Ctr., 1972-77; dir., sec., treas. Satellite Mill, Inc., 1961-63. Co-author: Business Law & The Cooperative, 1962; assoc. editor Drake U. Law Rev., 1951-52. City atty. City of Winfield, Iowa, 1954-89, City of Wayland, Iowa, 1962-70; mem. Henry County Conservation Bd., Mt. Pleasant, Iowa, 1972-74; chmn. Henry County Compensation Commn., 1987-92; sec. S.E. Iowa Planning Coun., 1973-74; mem. Gov.'s Heartland Leadership Coun., Iowa, 2003; dir. S.E. Iowa Health Care Coun., Ft. Madison, 1974-76; mem. Iowa Archaeol. Soc., 1991—; mem. commn. eminent domain Henry County, 1993-98; mem. Gov.'s Heartland Leadership Coun., Iowa, 2003. With combat infantry U.S. Army, 1944-46, ETO. Decorated Combat Infantryman's badge, Bronze star; recipient Spl. award Bur. Nat. Affairs, 1952, Annual award Greene County Conservation Bd., 1987. Mem. Henry County Bar Assn. (pres. 1961-62), S.E. Iowa Bar Assn. (pres. 1962), Iowa State Bar Assn., Hawkeye Archeol. Soc., Am. Legion, VFW, Masons, Phi Alpha Delta. Presbyterian. Home: 1586 Oasis Ave Mount Union IA 52644-9506 Office: Carty Law Office Farmers Nat Bank Bldg Winfield IA 52659

CARTY, MARY ELLEN, psychologist; b. N.Y.C., Aug. 7, 1958; d. Walter Vincent and Sally Rita (Clarke) C. BA, Coll. of New Rochelle, 1980, MS, 1991; PsychD, Yeshiva U., 1997. Cert. sch. psychologist, N.Y.; lic. psychologist., N.Y. Grad. asst. Coll. of New Rochelle, N.Y., 1989-90, rsch. asst., 1990-91; sch. psychologist intern Pawling (N.Y.) Ctrl. Sch. Dist., 1990-91; sch. psychologist Pawling Jr./Sr. H.S., 1991-93, Clarkstown H.S. South, West Nyack, N.Y., 1993-94; behavior specialist, psychologist Esperanza Ctr., N.Y.C., 1993-96; clin. psychology intern, postdoctoral fellow Ctr. Preventive Psychiatry, 1996-98; program psychologist So. Westchester Bd. Coop. Ednl. Svcs., Harrison, 1998—2002; sch. psychologist Rye Neck Middle/H.S., Mamaroneck, NY, 2002—. Cons. acad. counselor Iona Coll., New Rochelle, N.Y., 1990-94, 96-97. Vol. English tchr. Immaculate Conception H.S., Jamaica, 1983—85, 1983—85; mem. grad. sch. adv. bd. Coll. of New Rochelle, 1999—, mem. bd. dir. alumni assn., 2001—; co-pres. alumni assn. Ferkauf Grad. Sch. Psychology, Yeshiva U., 2000—; dir. Alumni Assn. Coll. of New Rochelle, 2001—; trustee, mem. ch. coun. St. Pius X Ch., Jamaica, 1983—85. Recipient Ursula Laurus citation, 2000; Empire Challenger fellow N.Y. State Edn. Dept., 1988-89. Mem.: APA, NY Assn. Sch. Psychologists (Ted Bernstein award 1996), Ferkauf Alumni Assn. Yeshiva U. (co-pres. Grad. Sch. Psychology 2000—), Psi Chi. Democrat. Roman Catholic. Avocations: cycling, meditation, travel. Home: 434 N High St Mount Vernon NY 10552-3103 Office: Rye Neck Union Free Sch Dist 300 Hornridge Rd Mamaroneck NY 10543 E-mail: carty434@netscape.net.

CARTY, RAYMOND WESLEY, academic administrator; b. Carlinville, Ill., Jan. 26, 1956; m. Elaine Smith, Apr. 21, 1979; children: Brooke Angelyn, Devan Alicia. AA, Hannibal-LaGrange (Mo.) Coll., 1977; BS, S.W. Bapt. U., 1979; MA, Liberty U., 1990. Registered social worker, Ill. Youth therapist Macoupin County Mental Health Ctr., Ill., 1979-84; assoc. dir. admissions Hannibal-LaGrange Coll., 1984—, assoc. dean of admissions, 1987-95, dean of enrollment mgmt., 1995-98, v.p. for enrollment mgmt., 1998—. Mem. Mo. Assn. Coll. Admissions Counselors, Ill. Assn. Coll. Admission Counselors. Baptist. Avocations: music, antique automobiles. Office: Hannibal-LaGrange Coll 2300 Palmyra Rd Hannibal MO 63401-1919 Home: 219 Humming bird lane Hannibal MO 63401-3615 E-mail: rcarty@hlg.edu.

CARUANA, JOAN, educator, psychotherapist, nurse; b. Bklyn., Dec. 11, 1941; d. Gaetano and Fanny Caruana. BS, Boston Coll., 1964; MA, NYU, 1975; grad., Psychoanalytic Psychotherapy Study Ctr., 1992. RN, N.Y.; cert. clin. specialist in adult psychiat. mental health nursing, psychiat. nurse practitioner. Instr. St. Vincent's Hosp. Sch. Nursing, N.Y.C., 1965-99; psychotherapist N.Y.C., 1987—. Mem. St. Vincent's Hosp. Sch. Nursing Alumnae Assn. (editor newsletter 1978—, pres. 1998—). Office: 153 Waverly Pl 5th Fl New York NY 10014-3872

CARUCCI, JOHN A. physician; b. Lyndhurst, NJ, Dec. 17, 1963; s. John Joseph and Dorothy Ann Carucci; m. Ingrid Helena Olhoffer, Aug. 21, 1999. BA, Columbia U., 1981—85; MS, New York U., 1985—87; MD, PhD, SUNY, 1994. Cert. dermatology Am. Bd. of Dermatology, 1998, Mohs Micrographic Surgery Am. Coll. of Mohs Micrographic Surgery and Cutaneous Oncology, 2000. Dir., mohs micrographic and dermatologic surgery Cornell-New York Presbyn. Hosp., New York, 2001—. Contr. author to profl. jours. including the Journal of the American Academy of Dermatology (Presdl. Citation from the Am. Acad. of Dermatology, 2001); contbr. textbook. Dermatologist Investigator Rsch. fellowship, Dermatology Found., 1998—99. Mem.: Internat. Transplant Skin Cancer Collaborative (bd. of dirs. 2001—). Catholic. Avocations: guitar, musical composition, running, weight training. Office: New York Presbyterian Hospital 525 East 68 th Street New York NY 10021

CARUCCIO, LORRAINE G. research scientist; b. Teancek, NJ, Jan. 11, 1959; d. Carmine J. and Patricia E. Caruccio. PhD, Rutgers U., 1995; BS in Med. Tech., Fairleigh Dickinson U., 1982. Specialist in Blood Banking NIH, 2001, Medical Tech. (ASCP) Am. Soc. of Clin. Pathologists, Ill., 1982. Staff scientist NIH, Bethesda, Md., 2001—; postdoctoral fellow NY Med. Coll., Valhalla, NY, 1995—99. Contemporary ensemble St. Jane's de Chantal, Bethesda, Md., 2001—. Mem.: Am. Assn. of Blood Banks, Am. Assn. for Cancer Rsch. Independent. Christian. Avocations: singing, dancing, swimming, animals art. Home: 645 Elmcroft Blvd Apt 13306 Rockville MD 20850 Office: Nat Inst of Health 9000 Rockville Pike Bethesda MD 20892-1184 E-mail: lcaruccio@mail.cc.nih.gov.

CARUS, MILTON BLOUKE, publisher children's periodicals; b. Chgo., June 15, 1927; s. Edward H. and Dorothy (Blouke) C.; m. Marianne Sondermann, Mar. 3, 1951; children: Andre, Christine, Inga. BS in Elec. Engring, Calif. Inst. Tech., 1949; postgrad., Mexico City Coll., summer 1949, U. Freiburg, Germany, 1949-51, Sorbonne U., Paris, 1951. Devel. engr. Carus Chem. Co., Inc., LaSalle, Ill., 1951—55, asst. gen. mgr., 1955—61, exec. v.p., 1961—64, chmn., CEO, 1964—90, Carus Corp., Peru, 1990—; editor Open Ct. Pub. Co., 1962—67, pub., pres., 1967—88, pub., 1988—89, sr. cons., 1989—; pub. Cricket mag., 1973—89; sr. cons. Cricket mag. group, 1989—2000, chmn., 2000—. Treas. Bookbird Internat. Bd. Books Young People, 1994-1996. Chmn. Ill. Valley Cmty. Coll. Com., 1965-67; pres. Internat. Baccalaureat N.Am. Inc., 1977, chmn., 1980-89; mem. IBO Coun., Geneva, 1977-94; co-trustee Hegeler Inst., 1968-89, chmn., 1989-; mem. employment and tng. com. U.S. Chamber, 1981-85; mem. Nat. Coun. on Ednl. Rsch. Nat. Inst. Edn., Dept. Edn., 1982-85, vice chmn., 1983-85; trustee Parliament of World's Religious, 1988—; mem. Ill. Gov.'s Task Force on Sch.-to-Work, 1994-96. Mem. Ill. Valley Indsl. Assn. (pres. 1970—), Chem. Mfrs. Assn. (dir. 1977-80), Ill. Mfrs. Assn. (dir. 1972-77, 1988-99, chmn. edn. com. 1988—), LaSalle County Hist. Soc. (dir. 1979-85), Phila Soc., Ill. State C. of C. (edn. com. 1973-75). Office: Carus Corp Hdqrs 315 5th St Peru IL 61354-2859

CARUSO, AILEEN SMITH, managed care consultant; b. Albany, N.Y., July 25, 1949; d. Robert Vincent and Mary (Prince) Smith; 1 child, Patrick Michael. AAS in nursing, Russell Sage Jr. Coll., Albany, 1970; BSBA cum laude, Coll. St. Rose, 1994. Cert. case mgr., adminstr. Physician Practice Mgmt. (CAPPM); RN N.Y. Staff nurse neuro and thoracic surgery units VA Hosp., 1970-71; staff nurse family practice Milton F. Gipstein, MD, Schenctady, N.Y., 1971-74; psychiat. nurse Peter F. Andrus, MD, Albany, 1977-81; coll. health nurse State U. N.Y., Albany, 1979-82; orthopedic staff nurse Rosa Road Orthopedics, Schenectady, 1980-82; coll. health nurse Union Coll., Schenectady, 1982-87; customer svc. rep. Empire Blue Cross, Albany, 1987-88; fin. planner N.Y. Life Ins., Albany, 1988-89; sr. mgr. Corp. Health Demensions, Troy, N.Y., 1989-94, dir. implementation and tng., 1994-96, dir. implementation and corp. case mgmt., 1996, v.p. implementation, 1997, v.p. ops., 1998-99; dir. clin. ops. U.S. Oncology Network, 1999—. Mem. adv. bd. Amgen, MGI Pharma; advisor Gen. Elec. Corp. R&D Safety Com., Schenectady, 1992-94; chmn. profl. devel. Northeast N.Y. Health Promotion, Albany, 1994-99; com. chair Schenectady Health Coalition, 1993-95; edn. and by laws com., com. chair govt. affairs Am. Occupational Health Nurses, Albany, 1994-99; cert. adminstr. physician practice mgmt.; cons. for healthcare for bus., 2003—. Co-author: Occupational Health Services Administrative/Patient Management Manual. Pres. Ch. Women, St. George's Episcopal Ch., 1994-97, mem. exec. bd. dirs., 1989-97, sr. vestryman, mem. exec. search com., 1998-99, also lector; chmn. worksite program N.E. N.Y. Tobacco-Free Coalition, 1993-94; co-mgr. The Bookshop at St. Georges, 1993-95; mem. Futures Charity Golf Tournament; mem. USON Exec. Leadership/Clin. Leadership Coun., mem. exec. b., 2002—; co-chair Cancer Survivors Day, 2001-02; mem. reimbursement com. Uson Clin. Leadership Coun.; mem. Nat. Patient Advocate Found.; co-chair N.Y. state task force Patient Advocate Found. Recipient Rector's Recognition award St. George's Ch., 1991. Mem. Am. Assn. Occupl. Health Nurses (chair govtl. affairs com.), Capital Dist. Occupl. Health Nurses (nominating com.), Schenectady County Health Promotion Consortium, Health Promotion Coun. of N.E. N.Y., Oncology Nurses Soc., Schenectady County Bus. and Profl. Women, Capital Dist. Case Mgmt. Assn. (nominating com.), Am. Acad. Physician Practice Mgmt., Alpha Sigma Lambda. Avocations: racquetball, boating, reading, golf. Home: 1156 Spearhead Dr Scotia NY 12302-3122 Office: US Oncology/Hematology 1003 Loudon Rd Latham NY 12110

CARUSO, DANIEL F. lawyer, judge, former state legislator; b. Greenwich, Conn., Dec. 12, 1957; s. Frederick A. Caruso and Ruth Collins. BA, U. Conn., 1980; JD, U. Vt., 1983. Bar: Conn. 1983, U.S. Dist. Ct. Conn. 1984. Atty. Paul M. Tymniak & Assocs., Fairfield, Conn., 1984-88; sole practice Fairfield, 1988-97; mem. Conn. Gen. Assembly, Hartford, 1989-94, asst. house minority leader, 1992-94, ranking mem. gen. law com., 1991; judge of probate Probate Dist. of Fairfield, 1995—; adminstrv. judge Probate Dist. of New Cannan, 2001, Probate Dist. of Greenwich, 2002; atty. Owen, Schine & Nicola, P.C., Fairfield, Conn., 1997—. Co-chmn. House Rep. Policy Group on Drug Control Strategy; mem. gen. law com. Conn. Gen. Assembly, 1991-94, mem. judiciary com., 1989-94, mem. regulation rev. com., 1989-94. Mem., advisor Nat. Heritage Trust Adv. Bd., 1990-91; treas. Town of Fairfield, 1993-95, mem. bd. fin., 1985-89; del. Rep. Nat. conv., Houston, 1992. Mem. Kiwanis, Eagle Scouts Am., Pi Sigma Alpha, Phi Alpha Theta, Alpha Phi Omega. Roman Catholic. Home: 160 Fairfield Woods Rd Apt 61 Fairfield CT 06432-3348 Office: 53 Sherman St Fairfield CT 06430-5821

CARUSO, FRANK S. pharmaceutical executive; b. Hartford, Conn., Aug. 29, 1936; s. Frank J. and Victoria V. (Villara) Caruso; m. Lucy R. Magazzu, Aug. 14, 1955 (div. Jan. 1970); children: Patricia, Andrea, Frank, Jr.; m. Patricia H. Went, Feb. 13, 1993. BS, Trinity Coll., 1958; MS in Pharmacology, U. Rochester, 1961, PhD in Pharmacology, 1963. Dir. clin. rsch. analgesics Bristol Labs., Syracuse, NY, 1974—80; dir. clin. pharmacology Revlong Health Care Group, NY, 1980—85; v.p. R&D Roberts Pharms., Eatontown, NJ, 1985—92; exec. v.p. R&D Algos Pharms., Neptune, NJ, 1994—2000; pres. Caruso Pharm. Consultation Svcs., 2000—. Achievements include patents for in pharmaceutical products. Avocations: boating, fishing. Home and Office: 900 Ocean Drive Apt 1202 Cape May NJ 08204

CARUSO, GUY, federal agency administrator; Bachelor's, master's, U. Conn.; M in Pub. Affairs, Harvard U. Sr. econ. analyst CIA; dir. office market analysis in Office Internat. Affairs Dept. Energy, Washington, with Office Energy Emergencies and Internat. Affairs then Office Domestic and Internat. Energy Policy, 1986—93; dir. Office Non-member Countries Internat. Energy Agy., Paris, 1993—98; exec. dir. strategic energy initiative Ctr. Strategic and Internat. Studies Dept. Energy, Washington, 1998—2002, adminstr. Energy Info. Adminstrn., 2002—; head oil industry div. Internat. Energy Agy. Office: Dept Energy EI-1 Energy Info Adminstrn 1000 Independent Ave SW Washington DC 20585-0001

CARUSO, MARK JOHN, lawyer; b. L.A., Apr. 27, 1957; s. John Mondella and Joyce Dorothy C.; m. Judy F. Velarde, Aug. 15, 1987. BS cum laude, Pepperdine U., 1979, JD cum laude, 1982. Bar: Calif. 1982, N.Mex. 1987, U.S. Dist. Ct. (ctrl. dist.) Calif. 1982, U.S. Dist. Ct. N.Mex. 1987, U.S. Dist. Ct. (no. and so. dists.) Calif. 1995, U.S. Ct. Appeals (9th cir.) 1983, U.S. Ct. Appeals (10th cir.) 1987. Law clk. Fed. Trade Commn., L.A., 1981-82; pvt. practice, Burbank, Calif., 1982—, Albuquerque, 1987—. Mem. N.Mex. Ho. of Reps., 1990-94, mem. labor com., consumer and pub. affairs com., workers compensation oversight interim com., ct. correction and justice interim com., jud. com., labor com., workers compensation oversight com.; lobbyist Nat. Right to Work Com., 1984-86. Col., aide de camp to gov. State of N. Mex., 1987; chmn. N. Mex. Mcpl. Boundary Commn., 1988—; del. Rep. Nat. Conv., 1988, 92; lectr. breast implant litigation, Fen Phen diet drug litigation; Sandoval county chmn. George Bush for Pres., 1988; campaign mgr. Boulter for U.S. Congress, Tex., 1983-84. Recipient platinum award N.Mex. Free Enterprise Adv., 1986. Mem. ATLA, Breast Implant Litigation Group, Consumer Attys. of Calif., Albuquerque Hispano C. of C., Greater Albuquerque C. of C. Office: 4302 Carlisle Blvd NE Albuquerque NM 87107-4811 Fax: 505-883-5012. E-mail: mark@carusolaw.com.

CARUSO, NICHOLAS DOMINIC, protective services official; b. Wilmington, Del., Feb. 2, 1957; s. Nicholas Anthony and Philomena Marie (Pelaia) C. BA in Polit. Sci., U. Del., 1985; MA in Liberal Arts, Widener U., 1991. Sr. analyst Bank of N.Y., Newark, 1985-89; police officer Wilmington Police Dept., 1989— With U.S. Army, 1975-78, USN, 1979-83. Mem. Nat. Intelligence Study Ctr., Internat. Assn. of Stategic Studies, Acad. of Polit. Sci. Democrat. Roman Catholic. Avocations: book collecting, creative writing. Home: 909 W 21st St Wilmington DE 19802-3820 Office: Wilmington Police Dept 300 N Walnut St Fl 2 Wilmington DE 19801-3989 E-mail: nicholas.caruso@verizon.net.

CARUSO, VICTOR GUY, investment banker; b. Cleve., Jan. 20, 1948; s. Joseph Carl and Constance Christine (Dimitri) C.; m. Bonnie L. Kephart, July 21, 1973 (div. Jan. 1989); children: Nicholas Michael, Meredith Anne; m. Jeannine G. Smith, Oct. 5, 1991; children: Joseph Richard, Alessandra Maria. BS, Miami U., Oxford, Ohio, 1970; MBA, U. Chgo., 1972. CPA, Minn., N.Y. Fin. analyst Ford Motor Co., Detroit, 1972-74; asst. v.p. First Chgo. Corp., 1974-80; v.p., treas. N.W. Bancorp, Mpls., 1980-82; v.p. Chem. Bank, N.Y.C., 1982-83; sr. v.p. Lehman Bros., N.Y.C., 1983-92; mng. dir. Bear Stearns & Co., N.Y.C., 1992-95; sr. mng. dir. Seneca Fin. Group., Greenwich, Conn., 1996-97; investment banking ptnr. Gordian Group LLC, N.Y.C., 1998—. Mem. AICPA, N.Y. Soc. CPAs, Am. Fin. Assn., Am. Bankruptcy Inst., Turnaround Mgmt. Assn., Darien Country Club, U. Chgo. Club. Republican. Roman Catholic. Home: 20 Carleton St Greenwich CT 06830-4626

CARVAJAL, ARTHUR GONZALEZ, editor, lawyer; b. San Antonio, Dec. 14, 1962; s. Arthur Carrillo Carvajal and Maria Antonia Gonzalez Berumen. BA, St. Mary's U., San Antonio, 1985; JD, U. Notre Dame, 1988. Bar: Ill. 1989, Tex. 1998. Assoc. Kralovec, Marquard, Doyle & Gibbons, Chartered, Chgo., 1989-93, Robert S. Fritzshall & Assocs., Chgo., 1995-96; sr. legal editor Dearborn Fin. Pub., Inc., Chgo., 1997—. Pro bono counsel Chgo. Vol. Legal Svcs., 1990. Mem. Tex. Bar Assn., Chgo. Bar Assn., Lambda Chi Alpha. Roman Catholic. Office: Dearborn Fin Pub Inc 30 S Wacker Dr Ste 2500 Chicago IL 60606-7481 Fax: 312-577-2458. E-mail: carvajal@dearborn.com.

CARVAJAL, JORGE ARMANDO, endocrinologist, internist; b. Chiscas, Boyaca, Colombia, Dec. 20, 1935; came to U.S., 1963; s. Julio and Natividad (Caicedo) C.; m. Carlota Mellonunes Ribeiro, Sept. 5, 1965; children: Jorge Jr., Fernando, Eduardo. MD, U. Nacional Fac. Medicine, Bogota, Colombia, 1963. Diplomate Am. Bd. Internal Medicine, Am. Bd. Endocrinology. Resident Hosp.

San Jose, Bogota, 1962-63; intern Meth. Hosp., Peoria, Ill., 1963-64; resident in medicine Meml. Hosp., Detroit, 1964-65, Mt. Sinai Hosp., Mpls., 1965-66, VA Med. Ctr., Long Beach, Calif., 1966-67, fellow in endocrinology L.A., 1967-69; asst. prof. U. Rosario, Bogota, 1969-72; fellow in metabolism U. Calif.-Davis, Sacramento, 1972-73; staff endocrinologist Kaiser-Permanente Hosp., Sacramento, 1973-75; staff physician VA Med. Ctr., Long Beach, Calif., 1975-76; pvt. practice Anaheim, Calif., 1976—. Staff Anaheim Meml. Hosp., 1976—. Fellow Am. Coll. Endocrinology. Democrat. Roman Catholic. Avocations: boating, jogging, reading. Home: 16562 Grimaud Ln Huntington Beach CA 92649-1828 Office: 1211 W La Palma Ave Ste 702 Anaheim CA 92801-2814 Fax: 562-592-4666. E-mail: jorcarv@aol.com.

CARVALHO, JOHN JOSEPH, IV, molecular geneticist, philosopher of science; b. Providence, Aug. 10, 1973; s. John Joseph and Eva (Petrella) C. AS Chemistry/Philosophy, BS in Biology, U. Dallas, 1996; PhD in Genetics, Washington U., St. Louis, 1998, PhD in Molecular Genetics, 2003. Cert. radiation safety specialist. Chemist John B. O'hara Program, Dallas, 1992; asst. lab. instr. U. Dallas, 1993, lab. instr., 1994, dir. of labs., 1995-96; geneticist, population biologist Nat. Marine Fisheries Svc., Charlston, S.C., 1994; molecular biologist Baylor Coll. Medicine, Houston, 1995-96; rsch. geneticist Washington U., St. Louis, 1996—; pres., CEO Scikron Corp.; rsch. virologist/geneticist Harvard Med. Sch., 2003—. Mem. Ctr. for Theology and Natural Scis., Berkeley, 1998—; Inst. on Religion in an Age of Sci., N.H., 2000—. Author: Towards a Comprehensive Evolutionary Synthesis, 1999, Towards a Comprehensive Philosophy of Biology, 2000; editor-in-chief: Scikron: Online Chronicle of Scis.; mem. editl. bd. Cons-ciencias: Portuguese Jour. of Consciousness Studies, 2002--; assoc. editor Cons-Sciencias; contbr. articles to profl. jours. Recipient Nev. Scholar's award, 1992, rsch. award Med. U. S.C., 1994, 200 Eminent Scientists award, Cambridge, Eng., 2000. Mem. AAAS, Am. Soc. Microbiology, N.Y. Acad. Scis. (Scholarship award 1999), Genetics Soc. Am. (congl. liaison com. 1999), Internat. Philosophy of Biology Soc., Am. Cath. Philos. Assn., European Soc. for Evolutionary Biology, Internat. Soc. History, Philosophy and Social Studies of Biology, Philosophy of Sci. Assn. Chgo., Philosophy of Sci. Assn. Roman Catholic. Avocations: world travel, violinist, tutor, cross country sports, writing. Home: 4961 Laclede Ave Apt 409 Saint Louis MO 63108-1430

CARVALHO, JOSEPH, III, museum and library executive; b. Kinston, N.C., Aug. 28, 1953; s. Jose Jr. and Janine M. (Gagnon) C.; m. Gayle Elizabeth Conklin, Oct. 16, 1976; children: Alyssa Gayle, Michael Armand. BA, Westfield State Coll., 1975; MA, Coll. William and Mary, 1977; M in Libr. and Info. Sci., U. R.I., 1984. Instr. Westfield (Mass.) State Coll., 1976; genealogy and local history libr. Springfield (Mass.) Libr. Sys., 1977—, supr. genealogy and local history libr. and archives, 1977—; dir. History Mus. Conn. Valley Hist. Mus., Springfield, 1986-94; pres., exec. dir. Springfield Libr. and Mus. Assn., 1994—. Dir. Inst. for Mass. Studies, Westfield State Coll., 1990. Author: Black Families of Hampden County, Mass.: 1650-1855, 1984; editor: Guide to the History of Massachusetts, 1988; assoc. editor: Labor in Massachusetts, 1990; assoc. editor Hist. Jour. Mass., 1978—; exec. prodr. (video documentary) Springfield Duryea: America's First Successful Gasoline-Powered Automobile, 1993. Trustee Josiah Day House Mus., West Springfield, 1986-94; bd. dirs. Urban League Greater Springfield, 1992—; v.p. Indian Motorcycle Mus., Springfield, 1996—; founder, bd. dirs. Springfield Bus. Improvement Dist., 1998—. Recipient Commendation, Am. Assn. for State and Local History, 1989, Excellence in Programming award Cable TV Endowment, Springfield, 1991, 92, 93, Video Hist. Documentary award New Eng. Hist. Assn., Providence, 1993. Mem. Nat. Geneal. Soc. (book rev. editor Nat. Geneal. Soc. Quarterly 1987-95, Nat. award for advancing geneal. rsch. publs. 1996), Am. Assn. Mus., Acad. Cert. Archivists (cert. archivist), Assn. Profl. Genealogists (regional trustee 1992-96), New Eng. Mus. Assn. Avocations: fishing, chess, guitar, scuba diving. Office: Springfield Libr & Mus Assn 220 State St Springfield MA 01103 E-mail: president@spfldlibmus.org.

CARVALHO, JULIE ANN, psychologist; b. Washington, Apr. 11, 1940; d. Daniel Henry and Elizabeth Cecilia (Gardiner) Schmidt; children: Alan R., Dennis M., Melanie D., Celeste A., Joshua E. BA with high honors, U. Md., 1962, postgrad., 1962-63, 68-73; MA, George Washington U., 1966; postgrad., Va. Poly. Inst., 1979-88; doctoral studies in curriculum and insruction, Argosy U., 2003—. Social sci. rsch. analyst Mental Health Study Ctr., NIMH, Adelphi, Md., 1963-67; edn. and tng. analyst Computer Applications, Inc., Silver Spring, Md., 1967-68; edn. program specialist, program analyst Nat. Ctr. for Ednl. R&D, U.S. Office of Edn., Washington, 1969-73; equal opportunity specialist Office of Sec., HEW, Washington, 1973-77; legis. program, civil rights analyst Office for Civil Rights Dept. Health and Human Svcs., Washington, 1977-85; ind. cons.; propsal evaluator Fed. Programs DHUD, DHHS, 1980—. Adj. lectr. No. Va. C.C., George Mason U., Montgomery Coll., Strayer Park U. Coll., Shepherd Coll., Germanna Coll., U. Md. U. Coll., Va. Internat. U., Prince William Hosp., Fairfax County Pub. Schs., Fairfax County Dept. Social Svcs., all Washington area, 1986—; proposal evaluator HUD, HHS, 1989—. Contbr. articles to profl. jours. Bd. dirs. Child Care Ctrs., 1970-76, HEW Employees Assn., 1973-78; mem. steering com. Alliance for Child Care, 1975-80; tchr. seminars for single-parent and spiritual groups. Mem.: ASPA (condr. panels 1975, 1991), APA (panel condr. 1969—75, editor Bull. of Peace Psychology 1991—97, divsn. 48), Federally Employed Women (nat. editor 1975—79), Psychologists Soc. Responsibility (cons.), Capitol Area Social Psychologists Assn. (conf. chmn. 1985, 1993), Fairfax County Assn. for the Gifted (pres. 1980), Phi Alpha Theta, Psi Chi, Alpha Sigma Lambda (hon.). Home and Office: PO Box 11500 Alexandria VA 22312-0500 E-mail: visionaries@pocketmail.com.

CARVER, DAVID HAROLD, physician, educator; b. Boston, Apr. 18, 1930; s. Elias and Lottie (Jaffe) C.; m. Patricia Jo Nair, Aug. 2, 1963; children: Randolph Nair, Rebecca Lynn, Leslie Allison. AB magna cum laude, Harvard U., 1951; MD, Duke U., 1955. Intern Johns Hopkins Hosp., 1955-56; rsch. fellow pediatrics Clevc. Met. Hosp., 1956-58; jr. asst. resident Children's Hosp. Med. Center, Boston, 1958-59, sr. asst. resident, 1959-60, chief resident, 1960-61, USPHS spl. rsch. fellow Harvard Med. Sch., 1961-63; asst. prof. pediatrics Albert Einstein Coll. Medicine, 1963-66; from assoc. prof. to prof. pediatrics Johns Hopkins U. Med. Sch., 1966-76; prof. pediatrics U. Toronto Med. Sch., 1976-88; physician-in-chief Hosp. Sick Children, Toronto, 1976-86; chmn. dept. pediatrics U. Toronto, 1976-86; prof., chmn. dept. pediatrics Robert Wood Johnson Med. Sch., New Brunswick, N.J., 1988-2001, prof. pediat., assoc. dean faculty affairs Piscataway, NJ, 2001—. Mem. study sect. USPHS Ctr. Disease Control, 1971-73; mem. provincial research grants rev. com. Ont. Ministry Health, 1977-83, chmn., 1981-83 Assoc. editor: Textbook of Pediatrics, 14th edit., 1968, 15th edit., 1972, 16th edit., 1977; mem. editl. bd. Pediatrics, 1973-79. With USPHS, 1956-58. Recipient Schaffer award clin. teaching Johns Hopkins U. Med. Sch., 1973, Bain award for clin. teaching Hosp. Sick Children, 1978, Kennedy Sr. scholar, 1966-73 Mem. Am. Acad. Pediatrics (com. on infectious diseases 1973-79), Infectious Disease Soc. Am., Am. Soc. Virology, Internat. Soc. Interferon Research, Canadian Infectious Disease Soc., Am. Soc. Microbiology, Soc. Pediatric Research, Am. Pediatric Soc., Can. Pediatric Soc., Harvard Club Princeton. Home: 220 Sayre Dr Princeton NJ 08540-5852 E-mail: carver@umdnj.edu.

CARVER, DOROTHY LEE ESKEW (MRS. JOHN JAMES CARVER), retired secondary education educator; b. Brady, Tex., July 10, 1926; d. Clyde Albert and A. Maurine (Meadows) Eskew; m. John James Carver, Feb. 26, 1944; children: John James, Sheila Carver Bentley, Chuck, David. Student, So. Oreg. Coll., 1942-43, Coll. Eastern Utah, 1965-67; BA, U. Utah, Hayward, 1968; MA, Cal. State Coll. at Hayward, 1970; postgrad., Mills Coll., 1971. Instr. Rutherford Bus. Coll., Dallas, 1944-45; sec. Adolph Coors Co., Golden, Colo., 1945-47; instr. English Coll. Eastern Utah, Price, 1968-69; instr. speech Modesto (Calif.) Jr. Coll., 1970-71; instr. personal devel. men and women Heald Bus. Colls., Oakland, Calif., 1972-74, dean curricula Walnut Creek, Calif., 1974-86; instr. Diablo Valley Coll., Pleasant Hill, Calif., 1986-87, Contra Costa Christian H.S., 50 1992; ret., 1992. Communications cons. Oakland Army Base, Crocker Bank, U.S. Steel, I. Magnin, Artec Internat.; presenter in field. Author: Developing Listening Skills. Mem. Gov.'s Conf. on Higher Edn. in Utah, 1968; mem. finance com. Coll. Eastern Utah, 1967-69; active various cmty. drives; bd. dirs. Opportunity Ctr., Symphony of the Mountain; pres. adv. bd. Walnut Creek Srs., 1998—. Mem. AAUW, Bus. and Profl. Womens Club, Nat. Assn. Deans and Women Adminstrs., Delta Kappa Gamma. Episcopalian (supt. Sunday Sch. 1967-69). Clubs: Soroptimist Internat. (pres. Walnut Creek 1979-80, sec., founder region 1978-80); Order Eastern Star. Home: 20 Coronado Ct Walnut Creek CA 94596-5801

CARVER, GEORGE ALLEN, JR., retired lawyer; b. Washington, Nov. 8, 1940; s. George Allen and Barbara Ellen (Bristol) C.; m. Joan Page, Dec. 13, 1964; children: George Allen III, Robert William. BS, U.S. Mil. Acad., 1964; JD, U. Va., 1972. Bar: Va. 1972, D.C. 1978, U.S. Ct. Appeals (D.C. cir.) 1979, U.S. Ct. Appeals (9th cir.) 1986, U.S. Ct. Appeals (4th cir.) 1988. Trial atty. gen. crimes sect. Criminal divsn. U.S. Dept. Justice, Washington, 1972-76, trial atty. pub. integrity sect., 1976-81, dir. conflicts of interest crimes br., pub. integrity sect., 1981-88, dep. chief fraud sect., 1988-92, prin. dep. chief fraud sect., 1992-95, sr. counsel to chief asset forfeiture/money laundering sect., 1995-96, dep. chief, sr. counsel to the chief, 1996-2000; ret., 2000. Capt. inf. U.S. Army, 1964-69. Decorated Silver Star, Bronze Star, Purple Heart. Avocations: photography, fishing, boating, walking, reading. Home: 6049 Makely Dr Fairfax Station VA 22039-1324

CARVER, JOAN SACKNITZ, academic administrator; b. Spokane, Wash., Jan. 22, 1931; d. Weldon and Mabel (Swanson) S.; m. Jay Randall Carver, June 25, 1955; 1 child, James Randall (dec.). BA, Barnard Coll., 1953; MA, U. N.C., 1957; PhD, U. Fla., 1965. Exec. sec. Iranian del. to UN, N.Y.C., 1953-55; tchr. Lake Shore Jr. High Sch., Jacksonville, Fla., 1956-57; office mgr. Bartram Sch., Jacksonville, 1957-58; from asst. to assoc. prof. Jacksonville U., 1958-60, 63-75, prof., 1975—, chmn. div. social scis., 1982-83, dean Coll. Arts and Scis., 1983-2000, dir. Taft Seminars in Practical Politics, 1968-78, v.p. acad. affairs, 2000—01. Instr. employee seminars City of Jacksonville, 1969-82; evaluator ABT Assocs., Boston, 1975; mem. reaffirmation coms. So. Assn. Colls., Atlanta, 1983-99. Contbr. articles to profl. jours., chpts. to books. Sec., bd. dirs. Jacksonville Cmty. Coun., Inc., 1976-80; commr. 1st Appellate dist. Jud. Nominating Commn., Tallahassee, 1983-87; commr. Jacksonville Mayor's Com. on Status of Women, 1984-88; bd. trustees St. John's Country Day Sch., Orange Park, Fla., 1984-95, pres., 1993-95; chair career opportunities subcom. Def. Adv. Com. on Women in Svc., Washington, 1991-93; bd. dirs. Fla. Humanities Coun., 1993-97, Meninak Bd., 1998-2000; bd. dirs. N.E. Fla. LWV, 1999-2000. Recipient Prof. of Yr. award Jacksonville, U., 1972, EVE award for achievement in edn. Fla. Times Union, Jacksonville, 1982; nominated Jacksonville U. Woman of Yr., 2000; Seven Coll. Conf. nat. scholar Barnard Coll., 1949-53; grad. fellow U. Fla., 1960-63, Integritas Vitae award, Jacksonville U., 2002. Mem. Fla. Polit. Sci. Assn. (pres. 1975-76), Am. Soc. for Pub. Adminstrn. (pres. N.E. Fla. chpt. 1987-88), Women's Caucus for Polit. Sci.-South (pres. 1981-82), So. Polit. Sci. Assn. (membership chmn. 1983-91, rec. sec. 1993-94), Jacksonville Women's Network (pres. 1987-90), Phi Beta Kappa. Democrat. Episcopalian. Avocations: swimming, reading, gardening. Home: 46 15th St Jacksonville FL 32233-5722 Office: Jacksonville U 2800 University Blvd N Jacksonville FL 32211-3394 E-mail: jcarver@ju.edu.

CARVER, JOAN WILLSON, publishing executive, artist; b. St. Paul; d. Stuart Van Vranken and Marie (Carlson) Willson; m. Norman F. Carver Jr., Aug. 15, 1953; children: Norman III, Cristina. BA, Smith Coll., 1950; postgrad., Yale U.:Sch. Architecture:, 1950-53. Architect Larson Playter Architects, Eau Claire, Wis., 1953, John W. King Assocs. Architects, Tokyo, 1954-55; designer Norman F. Carver Jr. Architect, Kalamazoo, 1958-78; v.p., treas. Documan Press Ltd., Kalamazoo, 1979—; editor World Architecture Calendars, 1982—; artist Joan Willson Carver Porcelains and Glass, Kalamazoo, 1981—. Instr. ceramics and glass Kalamazoo Inst. of Arts, 1983—. Exhibited in group shows at Wichita (Kans.) Art Mus., Kalamazoo Art Ctr., Battle Creek (Mich.) Art Mus., Circle Gallery, Mich. Potters Assn., Six 17 Gallery, The Clay Studio, Lizards and Mice Gallery, Holland Area Arts Ctr., Dumont Gallery, 1997, Wearley Studio Gallery, 1997, 98, Kalamazoo Arts. Coun., 1999, 2001, 03, Acorn, 2000; co-founder, editor Perspecta-Yale Achitecture Jour. Sustainer Kalamazoo Jr. League, 1971—; chmn. Kalamazoo Dental Clinic, 1972; bd. dirs. Kalamazoo Symphony Orch., 1975-78. Mem. Kalamazoo Inst. Arts (bd. dirs. 1966-73, 78-84, pres. bd. dirs. 1970-73, chmn. exhbns. 1967-73, 78-87, scholarship com. 1980—, edn. com. 1985—), Jr. League of Kalamazoo. Clubs: Service of Kalamazoo (pres. 1969-70), Current Events (Kalamazoo) (pres. 1982-83, treas. 1986-87). Episcopalian. Office: Documan Press Ltd 3201 Lorraine Ave Kalamazoo MI 49008-2003

CARVER, JOHN H. medical science organization administrator; b. Buffalo, Dec. 27, 1965; s. Robert L. Carver and Katherine E. Smith; stepfather, Gerald J. Smith; m. Paula D. Deinhart, Oct. 18, 1992; children: Madeline Haase, Charles John. BS in Bus./Mgmt. Econs., SUNY, Buffalo, 1988; C.M.R. in Sci. and Medicine, Bus. Healthcare, Cert. Med. Representative Inst., 1997; postgrad., St. Bonaventure U., 2001, MS in Exec. and Profl. Leadership, 2002; MBA in Internat. Bus .Adminstrn., Beijing Inst. Tech., 2001. Forms products broker Moore Bus. Products, Amherst, N.Y., 1990-92; med. liaison, ctrl. nervous sys. specialist Solvay Pharms., Inc., Marietta, Ga., 1992-97; founding mgr. Med. Sci. Liaison Programs, Forest Labs., Inc., N.Y.C., 1997—2001, sr. ctrl. area mgr., 2001—. Adj. instr. in pharmacology Lake Erie Coll. Osteo. Medicine, Erie, Pa., 1996-98; bd. dirs. Westfield Devel. Corp., N.Y., 2001-2002. Avocations: yacht racing, flying sail planes, downhill skiing, mountain biking, photography, archery. Office: Forest Labs Inc 909 Third Ave New York NY 10022-4731 E-mail: John.Carver@FRX.com.

CARVER, JUANITA ASH, plastic company executive; b. Apr. 8, 1929; d. Willard H. and Golda M. Ashe; children: Daniel Charles, Robin Lewis, Scott Alan. Student, Ariz. State U., 1948, 72, Mira Mar Coll., 1994. Cons. MOBIUS, 1983—. Pres. Carver Corp., Phoenix, 1977—. Patentee latch hook rug Yarner, Pressure Lift; author series of children's stories. Bd. dirs. Scottsdale Meml. Hosp. Aux., 1964-65, now assoc. Republican. Methodist.

CARVER, KATHRYN LOUISE, music educator; b. Seattle, Feb. 5, 1944; d. Leon Cooper and Rubye Lee Jones; m. Larry Kinsler, Oct. 4, 1968 (div. Jan. 1993); children: Curtis Leon Kinsler, Tony McQueen Kinsler; m. Harold Leo Carver, Nov. 5, 1994. BA, Seattle U., 1968; MEd, Coppin State Coll., Balt., 1979; Dr.Sacred Music (hon.), Va. Sem. and Coll., Lynchburg, Va., 1992. Sec. devel. office Seattle U., 1963—66; counselor Upward Bound project U. Wash., Seattle, 1964—66; sec. Balt. City Pub. Schs., 1968—69, sch. social worker, 1969—71; counselor Coppin State Coll., Balt., 1972—79, acting dir. vets. affairs, 1972—74, dir. acad. advisement, 1979—82, assoc. dir. acad. advisement and counseling, 1982—84; sr. student svcs. specialist U. of D.C., Washington, 1984—86; placement dir. Balt. Urban League, 1986—87, counselor, 1991; coop. edn. coord. Coppin State Coll., 1987—89; tng. specialist Md. New Directions, Balt., 1989—90; owner/instr. Kinsler Acad. Music, Balt., 1991—. Musician Mt. Pleasant Bapt. Ch., Balt., 1968—83, Balt., 1985—89, instr., 1985—90; minister of music Christian Life Fellowship Bapt. Ch., Balt., 1983—85; assoc. prof. Essex C.C., Balt., 1986—87; asst. minister of music Good Shepherd Bapt. Ch., Balt., 2000; minister of music Sharon Bapt. Ch., Balt., 1989—2000; musician St. Paul Bapt. Ch., Balt., 2000—01, Hymns of Balt., 1989—, Joseph L. Russ Funderal Home, 1991—, Ebenezer Bapt. Ch., 2001—; judge Omega Psi Phi, 2001—; exec. bd. Hampton U. Music Guild, 2003—. Dir. choirs Missionary Bapt. Conv. of Md., Balt., 1989—, dir. children's choir, 1989—95, dir. The Voices, 1991—93, dir. Minister's Wives and Widows Internat. chorus, 1996; dir. George L. Crawley Lenten Fellowship Choir, 1999—2001. Named Woman of the Yr., Md. Assn. of Christian Women in Edn., 1978—79, Grad. of the Yr., Coppin State Coll., 1979, Alumni of the Yr., Seattle U., 1990, Outstanding Preacher's Kid, Missionary Bapt. Conv. Md., 2003, Outstanding Musician, Missionary Bapt. Conv., 1994. Mem.: Music Tchrs. Nat. Assn., Music Guild of Balt. (sec. 2003—), Delta Sigma Theta. Democrat. Baptist. Avocations: interior decorating, singing, liturgical dance. Home: 3612 Laguna Ct Randallstown MD 21133 Office: Kinsler Acad Music 1911 Harlem Ave Baltimore MD 21217

CARVER, KENDALL LYNN, insurance company executive; b. Spencer, Iowa, Nov. 4, 1936; s. Marion and Letha G.; m. Carol Lee Spiers, July 1, 1961; children: Merrian, Kendra, Lee, Christine. BS, U. Iowa, 1958. Rep. field sales Washington Nat. Ins. Co., Evanston, Ill., 1958-73, regional dir., 1974-77, pres., 1977—, CEO, 1978-94; mng. dir. Kendall Carver and Assocs. LLC, 1996-98; chmn. fin. com. First Benefit Ins. Co. of Phoenix, 1996-98; also bd. dirs. First Benefit Inst. Co. of Phoenix, 1997; founder, pres., CEO Confirmation-Plus LLC, 1998—. Bd. dirs. Life Ins. Coun. N.Y., chmn., 1991; chmn. bd. dirs. Security Adminstrs. Inc., Binghamton, N.Y., 1999-2001; bd. dirs., mem. exec. com. Gt. Am. Life Ins. Co. N.Y., 1999-2001; founder, chmn. Exec. Men's Group, 2001-03; cons. to ins. industry. Bd. dirs., mem. exec. com. Great Am. Life Ins. Co. of N.Y., 1999. Fellow Life Mgmt. Inst.; mem. Am. Coll. Life Underwriters. Republican.

CARVER, NORMAN FRANCIS, JR., architect, photographer; b. Jan. 27, 1928; m. Joan Willson, Aug. 15, 1953; children: Norman F. III, Cristina. Grad., Yale. Practice architecture, Kalamazoo; prof. advanced photography Kalamazoo Inst. Arts, 1971-86. Vis. lectr., critic Carnegie Inst. Tech., Mich. State U., Yale U., MIT, So. Ill. U.; guest lectr. King Faisal U., Saudi Arabia, 1981. Exhibited photography U.S. and abroad; photographs published in Aperture, House Beautiful, Horizon, others; author: Form and Space of Japanese Architecture, 1955, 2d edit., 1993, Silent Cities of Mexico and the Maya, 1966, rev. edit., 1986, Italian Hilltowns, 1979, rev. edit., 1995, Iberian Villages - Spain and Portugal, 1981, Japanese Folkhouses, 1984, rev. edit., 2003, North African Villages, 1989, Greek Island Villages, 2001. Recipient Fulbright awards to Japan, 1953-54, 64, silver medal Archtl. League, 1962, award Archtl. Record, 1960, 61, 62, Robert Hastings award Mich. Soc. Architects, 1987. Home: 3201 Lorraine Ave Kalamazoo MI 49008-2003

CARVER, RITA, fundraising consultant; b. Minden, Nebr. d. Jess Albert and Marguerite Florence Ford; m. Rodney A. Carver, July 9, 1971 (div. June 1999); children: David Christopher, Heather Michelle. BS in Comm., Dallas Bapt. U., 1976; MA in human scis., Our Lady of the Lake, 2000. Freelance writer, 1976—82; account exec. Walvoord, Killian, McCabe, Dallas, 1982—86; sr. v.p. Resource Devel., Inc., Plano, Tex., 1986—2001; pres. R-Designs Inc., Plano, 2001—. Instr. Resource Inst., Springfield, Mo., 1986-99. Creative dir.: Portraits of Hope, 1996; editor: He Leadeth Me, 1999. Vol. Collin County Children's Adv. Ctr., Plano, 1999—. Named Outstanding Young Women of Am., 1980, Most Stressed Out Bus. Traveler, Rosewood Hotel and Resorts, 1994. Mem. AAUW, NAFE, Sierra Club, Plano C. of C. Methodist. Avocations: scuba diving, writing, dancing, traveling. Office: R-Designs Inc 752 Nicklaus Dr Plano TX 75025

CARVER, TODD B. corporate lawyer, law professor; b. Dayton, Ohio, Oct. 25, 1958; s. Ellis B. and Patricia L. (Boggs) C.; m. Deborah K. Tucker, June 21, 1980; children: Edwin, Brittany. BA in Polit. Sci. cum laude, Wright State U., 1987; JD magna cum laude, U. Dayton Sch. Law, 1991. Investigator Smith & Schnacke Attys., Dayton, 1978-81, paralegal, 1981-84; litigation paralegal NCR Corp., Dayton, 1984-91, atty., 1991-92; sr. atty. NCR Corp., Dayton, 1992—98; v.p., chief legal counsel teradata divsn. NCR Corp., Dayton, 2000—; prof. law U. Dayton Sch. Law, 1996—; sr. atty. U.S. West, Inc., Denver, 1998—2000. Legal, civic lectr., hist. researcher. Editor U. Dayton Law Rev., 1990-91; contbr. articles to profl. jours. including Harvard Bus. Rev. Cmty. adv. coun. Bank One of Dayton, 1986-92; active Boy Scouts Am., Dayton, 1970—; chmn. local bd. Selective Svc. Commn., Dayton, 1982-2000; pres. St. Anne's Hill Hist. Soc., Dayton, 1983-84, Dayton Area Coun. Hist. Neighborhoods, 1985-87; pres. Preservation Dayton, Inc., 1987-89, trustee, 1991-98; exec. com. Dayton Neighborhood Leadership Inst., 1991-98, preservation com. Montgomery County Hist. Soc., 1990-98, U. Dayton Sch. Law, v.p., bd. dirs. westernlands and lifestyles program, 1994—. Named one of Outstanding Young Men Am., U.S. Jaycees, 1982, Moot Ct. Top Oralist, Law Rev., 1989-90; recipient Founder's award Boy Scouts Am., 1984, Cmty. Svc. award City of Dayton, 1987, Cmty. Preservation award, 1985, 5 awards Am. Jurisprudence Soc., 1989-91, 2 awards of excellence Judge Walter Rice Moot Ct. Competition, Lawyers' Lawyer award U. Dayton Sch. Law, 1991. Mem. Optimists (bd. dirs. 1984-86). Republican. Methodist. Avocations: chuckwagon cooking, music, history, literature, horseback riding. Home: 9638 Collett Road Waynesville OH 45068 Office: NCR Corp Teradata Divsn Law Group 1700 S Patterson Blvd Dayton OH 45479

CARVETTE, ANTHONY M. construction executive; V.p. fin., assoc. pub. N.Y. Mag.; contr. Harper's Mag.; acct. Peat Marwick & Mitchell; exec. v.p., COO Georgette Klinger; pres., COO Structure Tone Orgn., N.Y.C. Office: Structure Tone Orgn 770 Broadway 9th Fl New York NY 10003*

CARVOTTA, CRYSTAL CHAMPAIGNE, nursing administrator, consultant; b. Stoneham, Mass., Mar. 21, 1972; d. Edward Anthony and Lillian Jay Carvotta. BSN, Boston Coll., 1995; M in Mgmt./Healthcare Adminstrn., Cambridge Coll., 2003. Cert. case mgr. Commn. for Case Mgr. Certification, 1998, case mgmt. adminstr. The Ctr. for Case Mgmt., Inc., 2001; rehab. RN, Rehab. Nursing Certification Bd., 2001. Pres., founder Negotiation Specialists, Inc., Arlington, Mass., 1998—. Mem.: Am. Assn. Managed Care Nurses, Assn. Rehab. Nurses, Mass. Nurses Assn., Case Mgmt. Soc. Am. Independent. Avocations: reading, travel, life-long learning, cooking, home improvement. Office: Negotiation Specialists Inc PO Box 315 Arlington MA 02476 Home Fax: 781-316-1786; Office Fax: 781-316-1786. Personal E-mail: crystalcarvotta@negotiationspecialists.com. E-mail: crystalcarvotta@negotiationspecialists.com.

CARWELL, GLORIA JEAN, writer; b. Snow Hill, NC, Feb. 25, 1962; d. James Earl Whifield Sr. and Mary Magalene Whitfield. Attended, Fayetteville State U., 1982, Wayne Cmty. Coll., 1982. Writer lyrics. Mem.: 4-H Club. Democrat. Baptist. Avocations: writing, softball, volleyball, kickball. Home: 2476 NC Hwy 87 So Broadway NC 27505 also: P O Box 1114 Broadway NC 27505

CARWELL, HATTIE VIRGINIA, health physicist; b. Bklyn., July 17, 1948; d. George and Fannie (Tunstall) C. BS in Chemistry/Biology, Bennett Coll., 1970; MS in Radiation Sci., Rutgers U., 1971; postgrad., U. Calif., Berkeley, 1973-75. Rsch. asst. Thomas Jefferson U. Hosp., Phila., 1970-72; health physicist AEC, Upton, N.Y., 1972-73, Energy Rsch. Adminstrn., Oakland, Calif., 1973-80; internat. nuclear safeguards insp. and group leader Internat. Atomic Energy Agy., Vienna, Austria, 1980-85; health physicist U.S. Dept. Energy, Oakland, Calif., 1985-90, program mgr. for high energy and nuclear programs, 1990-91, program mgr. Berkeley, Calif., 1991-93, ops. br. chief, 1993-94, ops. team head, 1994—. Asst. environ. survey team leader Dept. Energy, Washington, 1987; lectr. U. Calif.-Berkeley, Stanford U., Cabrillo Coll., Can. Coll., Tougaloo Coll; dir. Mus. African Am. Tech. Sci. Village. Author: Blacks In Science: Astrophysicist to Zoologist, 1977, In Pursuit of Excellence: Dr. Warren Henry - World Class Scientist, 1998, Solar Cooker Design Training Guide, 1996; contbr. sci. articles to profl. jours. Co-founder, chmn. Devel. Fund for Black Students in Sci. and Tech., Washington, 1983—; dir., co-founder Mus. African Am. Tech. Sci. Village, 2000—; bd. dirs. Nat. Inventors Hall of Fame Found., 2001—03; treas. Nat. Coun. Black Scientists and Engrs., 2001—03; regional dir., mem. Nat. Tech. Assn., Washington, 1977—80. Named inductee, Black Coll. Hall of Fame, 1991, included in exhibit, The African Am. Presence in Physics, 1999; recipient Fed. Cmty. Svc. award, 1977, Elijah McCoy award, 1989, vol. recognition, Dept. Energy, 1990, Disting. Alumni award, 1992, Image award, Bennett Coll., 1997, Inspiring Scientist award, Jr. Arts and Sci. Ctr. of Oakland, 2002. Mem.: NAACP (life), No. Calif. Coun. Black Profl. Engrs. (pres. 1986, 1987, sec. 1988, pres. 1994, 1995, sec. 1996—99, pres. 2000—03), Inst. Materials Mgmt. (treas. Vienna chpt. 1985), Nat. Health Physics Soc., Nat. Tech. Assn. (James C. Jones Humanitarian award 2000). Avocations: writing, travel. Home: 4622 Meldon Ave Oakland CA 94619-2646

CARWILE, BILLY PRICE, computer engineer, civilian military employee; b. Richmond, Va., June 24, 1948; s. Willie Price and Elva Laura Carwile; m. Bonnie Beth Carwile, Feb. 10, 1973; children: Tamilyn, Christopher. BS in Computer Sci., Campbell U., 2002. Enlisted 1st sgt. U.S. Army, 1996; gunner's mate Coastal divs. 11 and 13 Swift Boats - Rivers and canals of the Mekong Delta, Vietnam, 1970; gunner's mate USS Concord, AFS-5 U.S.N., Norfolk, Va., 1971—73; comm. sgt. 2d Ranger bn. U.S. Army, Ft. Lewis, Wash., 1976—79, comm. sgt. A Co., 1st bn., 7th. spl. forces group Ft. Bragg, NC, 1984—88, intelligence sgt. A Co., 1st bn., 7th spl. forces group, 1989—90, ops. sgt. A Co., 3rd bn., 7th spl. forces group, 1990—96, first sgt. HSC, 3rd bn., 7th spl. forces group, 1996—97, sr. instr. E Co., 1st bn., spl. warfare tng. group, 1997—99, comm. specialist John F. Kennedy Spl. Warfare Ctr., 1999—2002; computer ops. mgr., civilian contractor Army Spl. Ops. Mission Support Ctr., Ft. Bragg, NC, 2002—. Avocations: writing, computers, motorcycling. Home: 2604 Quail Forest Dr Fayetteville NC 28306-9121 Personal E-mail: bcarwile@nc.rr.com.

CARY, ANN HAGAN, nurse, educator, health facility administrator; b. Tulsa, Apr. 28, 1950; d. John Joseph and Jewel M. (Rynberk) Hagan; m. Robert Durkin Cary, Sept. 3, 1976; children (2). BSN, La. State U., 1972; MPH, Tulane Sch. Pub. Health, 1974; PhD in Edn., Cath. U. Am., 1983; student Exec. Leadership Program, Harvard U., 2000. RN, Va. Project dir., home care adminstr. Cath. U., Washington, 1984-89, project dir., continuity of care program, 1989-90; prof., assoc. dean students, alumni devel. Sch. of Nursing La. State U. Med. Ctr., New Orleans, 1990 95; primary care fellow USPHS, 1994—; coord. doctoral program George Mason U., Fairfax, Va., 1995-98; scholar-in-residence Am. Nurses Credentialing Ctr., 1998—, dir. Inst. for Rsch. Edn., cons., 2000—03; ind. cons., 2003—. Rschr. in field. Author more than 50 publs. on pub. health leadership, policy, rsch. Vice chair Nat. Fund for Med. Edn., 1999—. Named Outstanding Pub. Health Nurse Educator in Va., 1998, Outstanding Nurse in Va., 1999, Disting. Practitioner, Nat. Academies of Practice, 2001. Mem. ANA (past chair congress on nursing practice and econs.), APHA (chmn. legis. com.), Assn. Cmty. Health Nursing Educators (pres. 1991-93), Primary Care Fellowship Soc. (pres. 1998-99), Sigma Theta Tau. Home and Office: 7313 S View Ct Fairfax Station VA 22039-2929 E-mail: ncary1950@aol.com.

CARY, ARLENE D. retired hotel company sales executive; b. Chgo., Dec. 19, 1930; d. Seymour S. and Shirley L. (Land) C.; student U. Wis., 1949-52; BA, U. Miami, 1953; m. Elliot D. Hagle, Dec. 30, 1972 (div.). Pub. rels. acct. exec. Robert Howe & Co., 1953-55; sales mgr. Martin B. Iger & Co., 1955-57; sales mgr., gen. mgr. Sorrento Hotel, Miami Beach, Fla., 1957-59; gen. mgr. Mayflower Hotel, Manomet, Mass., 1959-60; with Aristocrat Inns of Am., 1960-72, v.p. mktg., McCormick Center Hotel, Chgo., 1972-93; ret. 1993. Active Nat. Women's Polit. Caucus, Internat. Orgn. Women Execs., membership promotion chmn., 1979-80, bd. dirs., 1980-81. Recipient Disting. Salesman award Sales and Mktg. Execs. Internat., 1977. Mem. Profl. Conv. Mgmt. Assn., Internat. Assn. Exposition Magmt., Hospitality Sales and Mktg. Assn. Internat., Meeting Planners Internat., Am. Soc. Assn. Execs., N.Y. Soc. Assn. Execs., Chgo. Soc. Assn. Execs., Ind. Hotel Alliance (sec. 1986—). Jewish. Home: 6007 N Sheridan Rd Apt 18H Chicago IL 60660-3063

CARY, PHILLIP SCOTT, philosphy educator; b. Buffalo, N.Y., June 10, 1958; s. Gene Leonard and Janice McDonald C.; m. Nancy Ruth Hazle, Sept. 17, 1983, children: Jonathan David, Christopher Nathan, Jacob Paul. BA, Washington Univ., St. Louis, Mo., 1980; MA, Yale U., New Haven, Ct., 1989; PhD, Yale U., 1994. Ennis fellow in the humanities Core Humanities Prog., Villanova (Pa.) U., 1994-97; Barbieri fellow in the humanities Villanova U., 1997-98; asst. prof. philosophy Eastern U., St. Davids, Pa., 1998-2001, dir. philosophy prog., 1999—, assoc. prof., 2001—; scholar in residence Templeton Honors Coll., St. Davids, 2000—. Author: Augustine's Invention of the Inner Self, 2000, (lecture tape series) Augustine Philosopher and Saint, 1997, Philosophy and Religion in the West, 1999. Mem. Am. Philosophical Assn., Am. Acad. Religion, Soc. Christian Philosophers. Office: Eastern U 1300 Eagle Rd Saint Davids PA 19087 E-mail: pcary@eastern.edu.

CARY, WILLIAM STERLING, retired church executive; b. Plainfield, N.J., Aug. 10, 1927; s. Andrew and Sadie C.; m. Marie B. Phillips; children: Yvonne, Denise, Sterling, Patricia. BA, Morehouse Coll., 1949, also D.D.; MDiv, Union Theol. Sem., 1952; LL.D., Bishop Coll.; D.D., Elmhurst Coll.; L.H.D., Allen U., Ill. Coll.; MDiv, Union Theol. Sem. Ordained to ministry Baptist Ch., 1948; pastor Butler Meml. Presbyn. Ch., Youngstown, Ohio, 1953-55, Interdenominational Ch. of Open Door, Bklyn., 1955-58, Grace Congl. Ch., N.Y.C., 1958-68; area min. Met. and Suffolk assns. N.Y. Conf. United Ch. Christ, 1968-75; pres. Nat. Coun. Chs., N.Y.C., 1972-75; conf. min. Ill. Conf. United Ch. Christ, 1974—94, conf. min. emeritus, 2001. Chmn. United Ch. Christ Council Conf. Execs., Council Religious Leaders Met. Chgo., 1986-92; mem. governing bd. Nat. Council Chs.; mem. rep. consultation on ch. union United Ch. of Christ; mem. exec. council United Ch. of Christ; mem. Council on Ecumenism, Ch. World Service, Pres.'s Adv. Com. Vietnam Refugees; lectr. in field. Named One of 100 Most Influential Blacks in Am. for 1974-75 Ebony mag. Address: 206 Le Moyne Pkwy Oak Park IL 60302-1122

CARYL, NAOMI, artist; b. N.Y.C., June 27, 1931; d. Joseph Herman and Jennie (Berman) Hirshhorn. Student, Feagin Sch. Drama & Radio, 1951-52. Artist, composer, actor, producer, L.A., 1962—. One-woman shows include Ankrum Gallery, L.A., 1962, 69, 71, 72, 75, 83, 87, Zara Gallery, San Francisco, 1973, Lighthouse Gallery, Fla., 1989, Foster Harmon Gallery, Sarasota, Fla., 1991, Jerry Soloman Gallery, L.A., 1997; composer Spoon River Anthology, 1963 (Emmy nomination 1969), Mirror Image, 1995, others; author (plays) Nobody Safe Here, 1981 (new play award L.A. Weekly 1981, S.T.A.G.E. award 1997), The Start of The Blues, 1987, The Dressing Room, 1988, others. Co-chair, producer The S.T.A.G.E. Benefit, L.A., 1986—. Recipient L.A. Beautiful award Cactus Garden, 1989, Crystal Apple award AIDS Project, L.A., 1991, The Spirit of Hope award, 1999. Mem. ASCAP, SAG, Am. Fedn. TV and Radio Artists, Equity, Dramatists Guild, Theatre West. Avocations: gardening, reverend, personalized weddings. Home and Office: 2071 Castilian Dr Los Angeles CA 90068-2608

CASAD, ROBERT CLAIR, legal educator; b. Council Grove, Kans., Dec. 8, 1929; s. Clair L. and Eula Imogene (Compton) C.; m. Sally Ann McKeighan, Aug. 20, 1955; children: Benjamin Nathan, Joseph Story, Robert Clair, Madeleine Imogene. AB, U. Kans., 1950, MA, 1952; JD with honors, U. Mich., 1957; SJD, Harvard U., 1979. Bar: Kans. 1957, Minn. 1958, U.S. Dist. Ct. Kans. 1957; U.S. Ct. Appeals (10th cir.) 1985. Instr. law U. Mich., Ann Arbor, 1957-58; assoc. firm Streater & Murphy, Winona, Minn., 1958-59; asst. prof. law U. Kans., Lawrence, 1959-62, assoc. prof., 1962-64, prof., 1964-81, John H. and John M. Kane prof. law, 1981-97; John H. and John M. Kane prof. law emeritus, 1997. Vis. prof. UCLA, 1969—70, U. Ill., 1973—74, U. Calif., Hastings, 1979—80, U. Colo., 1982, U. Vienna, 1986, U. Mich., 1986, U. Valladolid, 1988, Chuo U., 1992, U. Salamanca, 1995, Emory U., 2001—02. Author: Jurisdiction and Forum Selection, 1988, 2nd edit., 1999, Jurisdiction in Civil Actions, 1983, 2d edit., 1991, (with Richman) 3d edit., 1998, Expropriation Procedures in Central America and Panama, 1975, (with others) Kansas Appellate Practice, 1978, Civil Judgment Recognition and the Integration of Multiple State Associations, 1982, Res Judicata in a Nutshell, 1976; (with Fink and Simon) Civil Procedure: Cases and Materials, 2d edit., 1989, (with Gard) Kansas Code of Civil Procedure Annotated, 3rd edit., 1997, (with Clermont) Res Judicata: A Handbook on its Theory, Doctrine and Practice, 2001; contbr. numerous articles to legal jours. Mem. civil code adv. com. Kans. Jud. Coun. 1st lt. USAF, 1952-53. Recipient Coblentz prize Sch. Law, U. Mich., 1957, Rice prize U. Kans. Law Sch., 1976, 83, 84, 88, 89, medal Dana Fund for Internat. and Comparative Legal Studies, 1981, Balfour Jeffrey Rsch. prize U. Kans., 1984; Ford fellow, 1965-66, fellow in law Harvard U., 1965-66, OAS fellow, 1976, NEH fellow, summer 1978; grantee Dana Fund for Internat. and Comparative Legal Studies. Mem. Am. Law Inst., ABA, Kans. Bar Assn., Order of Coif. Democrat. Home: 1130 Emery Rd Lawrence KS 66044-2515 E-mail: casad@ku.edu, crobkan@cs.com.

CASADESUS, PENELOPE ANN, advertising executive, film producer; b. Calcutta, India, Sept. 20, 1940; came to U.S., 1980; d. Francis John and Betty (Walker) Copeland; m. Jean-Claude Casadesus, Jan. 20, 1960; children: Caroline, Sebastian. Gen. Cert. of Edn., Godolphin Sch., Eng. Head of prodn. S.S.C.B. Lintas, Paris, 1975—78, Grey-France, Paris, 1978—80, Grey Worldwide, N.Y.C., 1980, exec. producer Internat. Health and Beauty divsn., 1991—, sr. v.p., group prodr. Ind. film producer, 1984—. Author, producer (screenplays) Transvaal Episode, The Cuckoo.

CASADY, DOROTHEA JANE, artist, educator, sculptor; b. Dallas, Feb. 23, 1910; d. James O. and Edna Louise (Bradley) Stevenson; children: Richard R. Casady II, Christopher Bradley Casady. Diploma, Snow Fraelik Sch. Indsl. Design, Chgo., 1921; studied with Nan Sheets, Oklahoma City, 1925; BFA, U. Okla., 1929; student, Bistrram Sch. Art, Taos, N.Mex., 1931, Julian Academe, Paris, 1934; MFA in Painting, U. Okla., 1943. Cert. art tchr. Art tchr. Classen H.S., Oklahoma City, 1932, 1935; head art dept. Oklahoma City U., 1938-43; prof. Sch. Art U. So. Calif., 1945-48; staff designer Artisan House Inc., 1972—. Art tchr. U.S. Army Ednl. Program, Fort Sill, Okla., 1944; past art tchr. extension courses UCLA. One-woman shows include Oklahoma City U., 1939, 85, Okla. YWCA, 1939, Tulsa Jr. League, 1940, Okla. Aart Assn., 1941, Gutzon Borglum Studio, Brekenridge Park, San Antonio, 1945, Oklahoma City U., 1985; joint exhbn. (with Edna B. Stevenson) Celebrations Gallery, Taos, 1988; group exhbns. include U.S. Collegiate Art Exhibit, Washington, 1931, Kansas City Art Inst., 1933, Philbrook Mus., Tulsa, 1941, Kansas City Art Inst., 1942, Arsuna Sch., Santa Fe, 1943, L.A. Art Mus., 1945, 46, Ankrum Gallery, L.A., 1960, 80, others; prin. works include 8x8 WPA mural Classen H.S., now in Mcpl. Art Gallery, mural Lib. Wilson Elem. Sch., Oklahoma City, Tryptich alter piece St. Michael's and All Saints Episcopal Ch., Lindsay, Okla., mural State Capitol, Oklahoma State, Office Home Econs., Seven Sculptors Exhbn., Fine Arts Bldg., L.A. Bd. mem. Craft and Folk Art Mus.; mem. Folkarit Coun. Fellow The McDowell Colony; mem. Women Painters of the West, Assn. Okla. Artists, Calif. Designers Coun. Assn., L.A. Art Assn., Bead Soc. (founder, past pres., chair bd. dirs. 1995—), Kappa Pi, Delta Delta Delta (nat. dir. art activities 1934-39). Home: 734 Brooktree Rd Pacific Palisades CA 90272-3901

CASAGRANDA, ROBERT CHARLES, industrial engineer; b. Iron River, Mich., Oct. 8, 1939; s. Charles Casagranda and Lillian Otto Seppi; m. Sheila Adele Mikkola, Nov. 24, 1961; children: Gregory Charles, Wendy Jean, Jodi Marie, Renee Lynn. AA, Cerritos Coll., 1974. Sr. planner McDonnell Douglas, Long Beach, Calif., 1966-72; parts planner N. Am. Rockwell, El Segundo, Calif., 1972; quality analyst White Sunstrand, Belvidere, Ill., 1972-78; supr. Ares Inc., Port Clinton, Ohio, 1978-81; mgr. MFG. Systems-Ex-Cell-O, Rockford, Ill., 1981-84; mfg. con. Ingersoll Engrs., Rockford, 1984-88; project engr. Ingersoll Milling Machine Co., Rockford, 1988-90; sr. ptnr., owner, cons. The Mfg. Cons. Group, Inc., Rockford, 1990—. With U.S. Army, 1958-60. Mem. Soc. Mfg. Engrs., Soc. Mfg. Technologists. Home: 5450 Tam Oshanter Dr Rockford IL 61107-3764 Office: The Mfg Cons Group Inc 5450 Tam Oshanter Dr Rockford IL 61107-3764 E mail: rcc-mcg@juno.com.

CASAGRANDE, PETER JOSEPH, humanities and English educator; b. Delabole, Pa., Dec. 19, 1938; s. Anthony F. and Alvera S. Casagrande; m. Pamela Mills, Mar. 3, 1961; children: Teresa, Antonia, Peter, Vincent, Elizabeth. BA, Gettysburg Coll., 1960; MA, Ind. U., 1962, PhD, 1967. Prof. English and humanities U. Kans., Lawrence, 1967—, assoc. dean humanities, 1991-2000. Chair Kans. Humanities Coun., 1991-93. Author: Unity in Hardy's Novels, 1982, Hardy's Influence on the Modern Novel, 1987, "Tess of the d'Urbervilles", 1992. Capt. U.S. Army, 1964-66. NEH fellow, 1972-73. Mem. MLA. Avocations: dressage, pleasure riding, hunting, gardening, cooking. Office: Univ Kans Lawrence KS 66066

CASAGRANDE, VIVIEN ALICE, neuroscientist, researcher; d. Arthur and Erna Casagrande; m. James Andrew McKanna, Nov. 30, 1975; children: James Arthur McKanna, Paul Grayson McKanna. PhD, Duke U., 1967—72. Rsch. asst. Arthur D. Little Inc., Cambridge, Mass., 1965—67; USPHS predoctoral fellow Duke U., 1970—73; rsch. asst. dept. anatomy U. Wis., Madison, 1973—75; asst. prof. dept. anatomy and psychology Vanderbilt U., Nashville, 1975—80, assoc. prof. depts. cell biology and psychology, 1980—86, prof. depts. cell and devel. biology, psychology and ophthalmology and visual scis., 1986—. Cons. NIH, Bethesda, Md., 1995—98. Recipient The Charles Judson Herrick award, Am. Assn. Anatomists, 1981. Mem.: Soc. for Neurosci. Achievements include research in the role of parallel pathways in vision. Office: Vanderbilt Medl Sch B2323 Med Ctr North Nashville TN 37232-2175 Office Fax: 615-343-4539. E-mail: vivien.casagrande@vanderbilt.edu.

CASALE, ALFRED STANLEY, thoracic and cardiovascular surgeon; b. Passaic, N.J., Nov. 28, 1955; s. Alfred Stanley and Regina Josephine (Cembor) C.; m. Mary Louise Cavell, Aug. 1, 1976; 1 child, Katherine. BA, Johns Hopkins U., 1976, MD, 1980. Diplomate Am. Bd. Surgery, Am. Bd. Thoracic Surgery; cert. Surg. Critical Care. Intern Johns Hopkins U., Balt., 1980-81, resident in surgery, 1981-85, resident in thoracic surgery, 1985-88, asst. prof., 1988-90; surgeon Mid Atlantic Surg. Assocs., Morristown, N.J., 1990-2000, ptnr., 1993—2000; chief cardiac surgery U. Hosp., UMD N.J., Newark, 2000—01; dir. cardiothoracic surgery Geisinger Wyoming Valley Med. Ctr., Wilkes-Barre, Pa., 2001—; co-dir. Heart Inst., Geisinger Health Sys., Danville, PR, 2002—. Assoc. chief cardiac surgery Atlantic Health Sys., Florham Park, NJ; chief cardiac surgery Gen. Hosp. Ctr., Passaic, NJ, 2000; mem. cardiovasc. health adv. panel N.J. Dept. Health, Trenton; assoc. prof. N.J. Med. Sch., UMD N.J., 2000—01. Contbr. articles to profl. jours. Dir. Madison YMCA, N.J., 1990-96, Am. Heart Assn., Morristown, 1990—, Kirby Child Care Ctr., Madison, 1992-96. Fellow Am. Coll. Surgeons, Am. Coll. Cardiology, Am. Coll. Chest Physicians; mem. Assn. Acad. Surgery (Resident Rsch. award 1984), Internat. Soc. Heart Transplantation, Soc. Thoracic Surgery. Avocations: skiing, tennis, fishing, shooting. Office: Geisinger Wyo Valley Med Ctr 1000 E Mountain Blvd Wilkes Barre PA 18711 E-mail: al@casale.org., ascasale@geisinger.edu.

CASALE, THOMAS BRUCE, medical educator; b. Chgo., Apr. 21, 1951; m. Jean M. Casale; 1 son, Jeffrey G. BS cum laude, U. Ill., 1973; MD, Chgo. Med. Sch., 1977. Diplomate Am. Bd. Internal Medicine, Am. Bd. Allergy and Immunology. Resident in internal medicine Baylor Coll. Medicine, Houston, 1977-80; med. staff fellow lab. clin. investigation NIAID, NIH, Bethesda, Md., 1980-84; from asst. prof. to prof. internal medicine U. Iowa, Iowa City, 1984-94, prof. internal medicine, 1994-96; dir. Nebr. Med. Rsch. Inst., 1996-99; adj. prof. pediatrics Coll. Medicine U. Nebr., 1996—; clin. prof. medicine Creighton U., Omaha, 1997-99, prof., asst. chair dept. medicine, dir. clin. rsch., 1999—, chief allergy/immunology, 2001—. Chief med. staff fellow lab. clin. investigation, NIAID, NIH, Bethesda, 1982-83; attending physician VA Med. Ctr., Iowa City, 1984-96, staff physician, 1986-96, clin. investigator, 1991-96; asst. dir. tchg. allergy/immunology divsn. dept. internal medicine U. Iowa, Iowa City, 1989-92, acting dir., 1992, dir., 1993-96, faculty inerdisciplinary immunology grad. degree program U. Iowa, 1993-96; bd. dirs. Am. Bd. Allergy and Immunology, Am. Acad. Allergy, Asthma and Immunology; reviewer over 15 profl. and sci. jours. Contbr. over 200 articles to profl. publs.; mem. editl. bd. Jour. Allergy Clin. Immunology, 1988-93, clin. asthma revs., 1996-99, Allergy & Clinical Immunology Internat., 1997—; editor Respiratory Digest, 1999—, Ann. Allergy, Asthma & Immunology, 1999—. Mem. asthma technical adv. group Am. Lung Assn., 1989-96. Lt. commdr. USPHS, 1980-83, USPHS Res., 1983—. Recipient Dr. John J. Sheinin Rsch. award Chgo. Med. Sch., 1977, Clin. Investigator VA, 1991-96, Am. Soc. Clin. Investigation, 1992, grantee NIH, 1986 91, 87-90, 92-93, 93-94, VA Merit Rev., 1986-89, 89-92, 92-96, Environ. Health Sci. Core Ctr., 1990-96, Novartis Pharms., 1997—, Sepracor, Inc., 1997, Immune Tolerance Network, 2003—, others. Fellow ACP, Am. Acad. Allergy Immunology (cutaneous allergy com. 1985-90, postgrad. edn. com. 1988-91, chmn. 1989-90, program com. dermatologic diseases sect. 1988-93, sec. 1989-90, vice chmn. 1990-91, chmn. 1991-92, prof. edn. coun. 1998—, chair 1998—, sec. 1993-95, vice chair 1995—, chmn. bronchoalveolar lavage com. 1991-95, 98—, others), Am. Coll. Allergy Immunology (profl. allergy/immunology edn. com. 1989-94); mem. Am. Acad. Allergy Asthma Immunology (bd. dirs. 2001—), Am. Fedn. Clin. Rsch., Am. Thoracic Soc. (sec. allergy immunology and inflammation scientific assembly 1990-91, chair-elect 1991-93, chair program com. 1992-93, chair 1993-95, long-range planning and policy com. sci. assembly on allergy immunology and inflammation 1991-96, sci. conf. com. 1991-93, bd. dirs. 1993-95, chair asthma adv. com. 1995-99), Am. Bd. Allergy and Immunology (bd. dirs. 1999—), Iowa Soc. Allergy Immunology (pres. 1987-89), Am. Assn. Immunologists, Midwest Sect. Am. Fedn. Clin. Rsch., Ctrl. Soc. Clin. Rsch., Am. Soc. Clin. Invest., Am. Lung Assn. (mem. rsch. coordinating com. 1996-99), European Respiratory Soc. Office: Creighton U Dept Medicine 601 N 30th St Ste 5850 Omaha NE 68131-2137 Fax: 402-280-4115. E-mail: tbcasale@creighton.edu.

CASALS, ROSEMARY, retired professional tennis player; b. San Francisco, Sept. 16, 1948; Profl. tennis player, 1968—; nat. championships and major tournaments include U.S. Open singles (finalist), 1970, 71, U.S. Open doubles, 1967, 71, 74, 82, U.S. Open mixed doubles, 1975, Wimbledon doubles, 1967, 68, 70, 71, 73, Wimbledon mixed doubles, 1971, 73, finalist with Dick Stockton, 1976, Italian doubles, 1967, 70, Family Circle Cup (winner), 1973, Wightman Cup, 1967, 76-81, Bridgeston doubles championships (finalist), 1975, Spalding mixed doubles, 1976, 77, U.S. Tennis Assn. Atlanta doubles, 1976, Fedn. Cup, 1967, 76-81; winner 1st Virginia Slims tournament, 1970; 3d place Virginia Slims Championships, 1976, 4th place, 1977, 78; winner Murjani-WTA championship, 1980; Fla. Fed. Open doubles, 1980; pres. sports promotion co. Sportswoman, Inc., Sausalito, Calif., 1981—; Virginia Slims Legends Tour, 1995—. Mem. Los Angeles Strings team, World Team Tennis, 1975-77; founder Women's Sports Legends Inc. Virginia Slims Event tennis winner, 1986, doubles winner (with Martina Navratilova), 1988, 89; inducted in to Internat. Tennis Hall of Fame, Newport, R.I., 1996. Mem. Women's Internat. Tennis Assn. (bd. dirs.). Office: Sportswoman Inc PO Box 537 Sausalito CA 94966-0537 E-mail: sportswonn@aol.com.

CASALS-ARIET, JORDI, physician; b. Viladrau, Girona, Spain, May 15, 1911; came to U.S., 1936, naturalized, 1946; s. Martin and Margarida (Ariet) Casals-A.; m. Ellen Evelyn Brock, Dec. 6, 1941; 1 dau., Christina. B.Ciencias, Instituto Nacional, Barcelona, Spain, 1928; Licenciado en Medicina y Cirurgia con Grado, U. Barcelona, 1934. Intern Med. Sch. Hosp., Barcelona, 1934-36; research asso. Cornell U. Med. Coll., N.Y.C., 1936-38; asso. Rockefeller Inst. Med. Research, N.Y.C., 1938-52; mem. staff Rockefeller Found., N.Y.C., 1952-74; prof. epidemiology Yale U., 1964-81, prof. emeritus, 1981—; vis. prof. dept. neurology Mt. Sinai Sch. Medicine, N.Y.C., 1981-84, professorial lectr. dept. neurology, 1984—. Contbr. articles to profl. jours. Served with Spanish Army, 1933. Recipient Kimble Methodology award Am. Pub. Health Assn., 1969 Fellow Am. Soc. Tropical Medicine and Hygiene (Taylor award 1968), Royal Soc. Tropical Medicine and Hygiene (hon.); mem. Soc. Exptl. Biology and Medicine, Harvey Soc., AAAS, N.Y. Acad. Medicine, N.Y. Acad Scis., French Soc. Microbiology (hon.), Internat. Com. on Taxonomy of Viruses (life). Home: 25 Claremont Ave New York NY 10027-6802 Office: One Gustave L Levy Pl New York NY 10029

CASANOVA, ALDO JOHN, sculptor; b. San Francisco, Feb. 8, 1929; s. Felice and Teresa (Papini) C.; children: Aviva, Liana, Anabelle. BA, San Francisco State U., 1950, MA, 1951; PhD, Ohio State U., 1957. Asst. prof. art San Francisco State U., 1951-53; asst. prof. Antioch (Ohio) Coll., 1956-58; asst. prof. art Tyler Sch. Art, Temple U., Phila., 1961-64, Tyler Sch. Art, Temple U. (Italy campus), Rome, 1968-70; prof. art Scripps Coll., Claremont, Calif., 1966—, chmn. art dept., 1971-73; vis. prof. SUNY, 1981; faculty mem. Skowhegan Sch. Painting and Sculpture, Maine, summers 1973-74. One-man shows include Esther Robles Gallery, L.A., 1967, Santa Barbara (Calif.) Mus., 1967, Calif. Inst. Tech., 1972, Carl Schlosberg Fine Arts, L.A., 1977, SUNY, 1981, Casanova Retrospective Williamson Galleries, Claremont Colls., Calif. 2002; represented in permanent collections Whitney Mus., San Francisco Mus. Art, San Diego Mus. Sculpture Garden, Hirshhorn Collection, Cornell U., Columbus (Ohio) Mus., UCLA Sculpture Garden, Calif. Inst. Tech., Pasadena, Univ. Judaism, L.A., Air and Space Mus., Washington, Collection of Nat. Acad. of Design, N.Y.C., 1993, Robert Feldmuth Meml. Commn., W.M. Keck Sci. Ctr., Claremont, Calif., 1995, Orange County Mus., Calif., 1996, Rancho Santa Ana Botanic Gardens, Claremont, Calif. Recipient Prix-de-Rome Am. Acad. in Rome, 1958-61; Louis Comfort Tiffany award, 1970 Fellow: Am. Acad. in Rome; mem.: NAD, Nat. Sculpture Soc., Sculptors' Guild. Democrat. Roman Catholic. Office: Scripps Coll Art Dept Claremont CA 91711

CASARELLA, WILLIAM JOSEPH, physician; b. Dunmore, Pa., Nov. 17, 1937; s. Rocco F. and Madeline M. Casarella; m. Carolyn A. Hughes, June 18, 1966; children: Jennifer, Gregory. BA, Yale U., 1959; MD, Harvard U., 1963. Intern U. Pa. Hosp., 1963—64; resident in medicine Boston City Hosp., 1966—67; resident in radiology Columbia U.-Presbyn. Med. Center, 1967—70, attending radiologist, 1970—81; prof. radiology Columbia U. Coll. Physicians and Surgeons, N.Y.C., 1977—81; chmn. dept. radiology Emory U., Atlanta, 1981—; exec. assoc. dean Emory U. Sch. Medicine, Atlanta, 1986—; pres. Am. Bd. Radiology, 1998—99. Contbr. articles to med. jours. Nat. bd. dirs. Am. Cancer Soc. Served to capt. Med. Corps U.S. Army, 1964—66. Fellow: Am. Coll. Radiology; mem.: Soc. Chmn. Acad. Radiology Depts. (sec.-treas. 1989—, pres.-elect 1991), Am. Roentgen Ray Soc. (exec. coun. 1988—), Soc. Cardiac Angiography, N.Y. Roentgen Soc., Ea. Radiol. Soc., Assn. Univ. Radiologists, N.Am. Soc. Cardiac Angiography, Radiol. Soc. N.Am., Am. Heart Assn., Soc. Cardiovasc. Radiology (pres. 1979). Office: Emory Univ 69 Butler St Bldg 103 Atlanta GA 30322-0001

CASAS, WALTER MARIO DE LAS, writer; b. Feb. 3, 1947; s. Mario C. Everardo de las C. and Aracelia Vivó. BA cum laude, Iona Coll., 1970; MA, Hunter Coll., 1977. Writer, 1968—; tchr. secondary schs., NY, 1970-96. Author: La niñez que dilata, 1986, Libido, 1989, Tributes, 1993, Discourse, 1999. Recipient Americanism medal Am. Legion, N.Y.C., 1965. Mem. Am. Assn. Tchrs. Spanish & Portuguese. Home: 323 Dahill Rd Apt 1A Brooklyn NY 11218-3848 E-mail: delascasis2@netzero.net.

CASASENT, DAVID PAUL, electrical engineering educator, data processing executive; b. Washington, Dec. 8, 1942; s. Harold Kane and Delta (Fletchall) C.; m. Paula Timko; children: Candace, Erin, Maureen, Tod, Jon. BSEE, U. Ill., Urbana, 1964, MS, 1965, PhD, 1969. Prof. elec. engring. Carnegie Mellon U., Pitts., 1969—; pres. Unicorn Systems, Inc., Pitts., 1983—. Dir. Ctr. for Optical Data Processing, Pitts. Editor: Optical Data Processing, 1978; contbr. more than 600 articles to tech. jours. Recipient Thomas K. Benedict award AIAA, 1979; named George Westinghouse prof. Carnegie-Mellon U., 1980. Fellow IEEE (local pres. 1971-72, Barry Carlton award 1976), Optical Soc. Am. (local pres. 1975-77), Soc. Photo-Optical Instrumentation Engrs. (gov. 1982-85, 87-90, pres. 1993, exec. bd.), Internat. Neural Network Soc. (gov. 1992-95, 1998-00, pres. 1999). Republican. Roman Catholic. Avocations: travel, basketball, volleyball. Home: 133 Woodland Farms Rd Pittsburgh PA 15238-2021 Office: Carnegie Mellon U Dept Elec & Computer Engring Pittsburgh PA 15213-3890

CASATI, FABIO, engineer; b. Como, Italy, Jan. 28, 1971; s. Giulio Casati and Antonia Zocca. PhD, Politecnico di Milano, Milan, Italy, 1998. Engineer, Italy, 1996, cert. engr. With Hewlett-Packard, Palo Alto, Calif., 1998—, now rsch. scientist. Chmn. numerous internat. confs. on web applications. Author: (book) Web Services, 2003. Recipient Best Software Application award, Rotary Club Como, 1994. Office: Hewlett-Packard 1501 Page Mill Rd MS 1142 Palo Alto CA 94304 E-mail: fabio.casati@hp.com.

CASAZZA, JOHN ANDREW, electrical engineer, business executive, educator; b. Bklyn., Jan. 3, 1924; s. John Andrew and Jean (Granata) C.; m. Madeline Russo, Apr. 24, 1949; children: John Anthony, Joan Bernadette Casazza Fram. Student, Cooper Union, 1941-43; BEE, Cornell U., 1945. Registered profl. engr., N.J. Successively system planning and devel. engr., gen. mgr. planning and rsch., v.p. planning and rsch. Pub. Svc. Electric & Gas Co., Newark, 1946-77; v.p. Stone & Webster Mgmt. Cons., N.Y.C., 1977-79; pres. Casazza, Schultz & Assocs., Inc., Arlington, Va., 1979-90; chmn. bd. CSA Energy Cons., 1991-97; pres. Am. Edn. Inst., 1994—. Mem. energy engring. bd. NRC, 1988—94; mem. rsch. adv. com. Elec. Power Rsch. Inst., Palo Alto, Calif., 1976—77; mem. U.S. Energy Assn. World Energy Conf., 1983—92; bd. dirs. Ga. Sys. Ops. Co. Contbr. numerous articles to profl. publs. Pub. trustee N.J. Marine Scis. Consortium, 1973-79; treas. N.J. Energy Rsch. Inst., 1977; mem. N.J. Gov.'s Panel on Solar Energy, 1975-77. Ensign USN, 1943-45. Fellow IEEE (life, chmn. energy policy com. 1981-82, chmn. environ. quality com. 1984-85, U.S. activities bd. citation of honor 1985, Herman Halperin award 1990, U.S. activities bd. dirs. VII profl. leadership award 1992); mem. Internat. Conf. on Large High Voltage Electric Sys. (Exec. com. U.S. nat. com. 1974 93, Atwood assoc. 1986—, spl. citation 1982, Philip Sporn award 1994). Springfield Golf and Country Club. Roman Catholic. Avocations: golf, writing. Office: Am Edn Inst 8208 Donset Dr Springfield VA 22152-1810

CASAZZA, MARTHA ELLEN, developmental education educator; b. Providence, R.I., Feb. 9, 1947; d. H. Nord and Judith (Clarke) Kitchen; m. Lawrence J. Casazza, June 21, 1968; children: Christopher Lawrence, Justin Clarke. BA, Western Coll. for Women, 1968; MEd, Loyola U., Chgo., 1978, EdD, 1988. Reading instr. Triton Coll., River Grove, Ill., 1980-83; learning assistance counselor Loyola U., 1984; dir. learning ctr. Kendall Coll., Evanston, Ill., 1985-91; asst. prof. Nat.-Louis U., Chgo., 1991—, assoc. prof., 1992-99, prof., 1999—2002, dean Coll. Arts and Scis., 2002—. Co-author: Learning Assistance and Developmental Education, 1997, Learning and Development, 2000; mem. editl. bd. Jour. Devel. Edn., contbr. articles to profl. jours. Lilly grantee, 1992. Fellow: Am. Coun. Devel. Edn. Assns. (charter); mem.: Nat. Coll. Learning Ctr. assn. (past pres. coun. 1989, pres. 1990, co-editor Learning Assistance Rev.), Nat. Assn. Devel. Edn. (newsletter editor 1987—93, pres. 1999, chair nat. cert. bd. 2000), Internat. Reading Assn. (manuscript reviewer 1990—, adult edn. columnist Reading Today), Am. Ednl. Rsch. Found. Avocations: reading, travel. Office: Nat Louis U 122 S Michigan Ave Chicago IL 60603-3200 E-mail: vivamamma@aol.com., mcasazza@nl.edu.

CASAZZA, PETER GEORGE, mathematician, educator; b. Albany, N.Y., June 28, 1945; s. Edward Francis Bunting (Stepfather); m. Janet Crandell Crandell, July 4, 1986; 1 child, Perry Edward. PhD, U. Iowa, 1972. Prof. math. U. Mo., Columbia, 1983—. Contbr. articles to profl. jours. Mem.: SIAM, SPIE, Math. Assn. Am., Am. Math. Soc. Office: Univ Mo Dept Math Math Sciences Building Columbia MO 65211-4100 Home Fax: 573-882-1869; Office Fax: 573-882-1869. Personal E-mail: pete@math.missouri.edu. E-mail: pete@math.missouri.edu.

CASBY, ROBERT WILLIAM, lawyer; b. Norwood, Mass., Aug. 18, 1951; s. William M. Casby and Charlotte Rita (Rice) Warnock; m. Patricia Alice Myers, Jan. 6, 1979; children: James Myers, Michael Robert. BA magna cum laude, Boston Coll., 1975; JD, Suffolk U., 1982. Bar: Mass. 1982, U.S. Dist. Ct. Mass. 1983, U.S. Ct. Appeals (1st cir.) 1993, U.S. Supreme Ct. 1993. Assoc. Sugarman & Sugarman, P.C., Boston, 1982-87, ptnr., 1987—. Lectr. in field. Editor, bd. dirs. Suffolk Law Rev., 1981-82. With USMC, 1969-71. Fellow Mass. Bar Found., Am. Coll. Trial Lawyers, Internat. Acad. Trial Lawyers; mem. ATLA, Mass. Bar Assn. (lectr. 1987—), Mass. Acad. Trial Attys. (lectr. 1987—, bd. govs. 1995—), Am. Bd. Trial Advocates (pres. Mass. chpt. 1998-99, nat. bd. dirs.), Suffolk Law Alumni Assn. (bd. dirs. 1992-97). Office: Sugarman & Sugarman PC One Beacon St Boston MA 02108 E-mail: rcasby@sugarman.com.

CASCAVAL, RADU CRISTIAN, education educator; s. Alexandru and Aneta Cascaval; m. Raluca Ioana Brumariu, May 25, 1996; 1 child, Andrea Joanna. BS, U. of Iasi, 1990—95; PhD, U. of Memphis, 1996—2000. Postdoctoral fellow U. of Mo., Columbia, Mo., 2000—03; asst. prof. U. of Colo. at Colo. Springs, Colo. Springs, 2003—. Office: Department of Mathematics University of Colorado Springs Colorado Springs CO 80933 Office Fax: 719-262-3605. E-mail: radu@math.uccs.edu.

CASCIANI, SANTA, Italian studies educator; b. L'Aquila, Italy, Aug. 1, 1954; arrived in US, 1969; d. Evangelista and Giannina Casciani. BA, St. John Fisher Coll., 1987; MA, Ohio State U., 1989; PhD, U. Wis., 1994. Asst. prof. Italian Pa. State U., State College, 1995-99; dir. Bishop Pilla Program in Italian Am. Studies, assoc. prof. Italian John Carroll U., University Heights, 1999—. Author, critic: (book) The Fiore and the detto d'Amore: a Late 13th Century Italian Translation of the Roman De La Rose, Attributable to Dante, 2000, Communications in the Middle Ages. Fellow Gladys Krieble Delmas/Am. Coun. Learned Socs., 1998-99. Roman Catholic. Office: John Carroll U 20700 N Park Blvd University Heights OH 44118 E-mail: scasciani@jcu.edu.

CASCIANO, DANIEL ANTHONY, biologist, educator; b. Buffalo, Mar. 1, 1941; s. Frederick James and Rose Ann C.; m. Gertrude Ann Tara, Aug. 22, 1964; children: Anne, Jonathan. BS, Canisius Coll., 1962; PhD, Purdue U., 1971. Rsch. asst. Roswell Park Meml. Inst., Buffalo, 1963-64; rsch. asst. dept. biol. scis. Purdue U., Lafayette, Ind., 1965-66, tchg. asst., 1969, rsch. trainee, 1966-71; postdoctoral investigator U. Tenn., Oak Ridge Nat. Labs., 1971-73; rsch. biologist Nat. Ctr. Toxicol. Rsch., Jefferson, Ark., 1973—, program dir. divsn. mutagenesis rsch., 1976-78, dir. divsn. genetic toxicology, 1979-97; assoc. prof. dept. biochemistry and molecular biology U. Ark. for Med. Scis., Little Rock, 1974-90, prof. dept. biochemistry and molecular biology, 1990—; trainee NIH, 1966-71; dir. divsn. genetic and reproductive toxicology Nat. Ctr. Toxicol. Rsch., 1997-99, dep. dir. for rsch., 1999-2000, acting dir., 1999-2000, dir., 2000—. Contbr. articles to profl. jours. Mem. Tissue Culture Assn., Environ. Mutagen Soc., AAAS, Beta Beta Beta Home: 47 Marcella Dr Margeux Pl Little Rock AR 72223-9172 Office: FDA Nat Ctr Toxicological Rsch Jefferson AR 72079 E-mail: dcasciano@nctr.fda.gov.

CASCIANO, JOHN P. executive; b. Phila. m. Patricia M Simmons; 1 child, John. BS in Langs. cum laude, Georgetown U., 1965, MA in Polit. Sci., 1972; grad. (disting.), Squadron Officer Sch., 1973, Air Command and Staff Coll., 1979; grad., NATO Def. Coll., Rome, 1983; grad. program in nat. security, Harvard U., 1991, grad. program nat./internat. security, 1994; CAPSTONE grad., Nat. Def. U., 1992; grad. jt. flag officer warfighting, Maxwell AFB, Ala., 1995. Commd. 2d lt. USAF, 1965, advanced through grades to maj. gen., 1995, chief intelligence divsn. Air Def. Command, intelligence watch officer, analyst, briefer, chief br. Nakhon Phanom Royal AFB, Thailand, 1969-70, intelligence plans and programs officer, tng./career devel. Washington, 1970-74; asst. prof. polit. sci., squadron faculty officer, dir. Air Force Acad. Assembly, USAF Acad., Colorado Springs, Colo., 1974-78; chief intelligence plans and policy divsn., dep. dir. plans Hdqrs. Strategic Air Command, Offutt AFB, Nebr., 1979-83; chief intelligence plans and programs br. Hdqrs. U.S. European Command, Stuttgart-Vaihingen, Germany, 1983-87; dir. warning and assessments Air Force Intelligence Agy., Washington, 1987-88; dir. policy, plans and programs, asst. chief of staff intelligence Hdqrs. USAF, Washington, 1988-91; dep. chief staff intelligence Hdqrs. Tactical Air Command, then Air Combat Combat, Langley AFB, Va., 1991-93; dir. plans and requirements, asst. chief staff intelligence Hdqrs. USAF, Washington, 1993-94; cmdr. Air Intelligence Agy., dir Jt. Command Ctrl. Warfare Ctr., Kelly AFB, Tex., 1994-96; dir. intelligence, surveillance, reconnaisance Hdqrs. USAF, Washington, 1997-99; sr. v.p. enterprise security Litton/TASC, Chantilly, Va., 1999-2001; group sr. v.p. Secure Bus. Solutions SAIC, McLean, Va., 2001—. Decorated Legion of Merit, Meritorious Serv Medal with 2 bronze oak leaf clusters, Republic of Vietnam Gallantry Cross with Palm, Air Force Outstanding Unit Award with V Device, Ordre Nat du Mèrite with Rank of Officer, others. Office: Sci Applications Internat Corp 8301 Greensboro Dr Ste 390 Mc Lean VA 22102 E-mail: cascianoj@saic.com

CASCORBI, HELMUT FREIMUND, anesthesiologist, educator; b. Berlin, July 13, 1933; came to U.S., 1958; s. Gisbert and Isa (Ruckert) C.; m. Ann M. Morgan, Aug. 7, 1965; children: Alicia Maria, Kathryn Ann. MD, U. Munich, W. Ger., 1957; PhD, U. Md., 1962. Prof., chmn. dept. anesthesiology Case Western Res. U., Cleve., 1980-2000. Mem. Am. Soc. Anesthesiologists, AMA, Assn. Univ. Anesthetists, Am. Soc. Pharmacology and Exptl. Therapeutics Home: 2844 Fairmount Blvd Cleveland OH 44118-4059 Office: Univ Hosps of Cleve 11100 Euclid Ave Cleveland OH 44106-1736 E-mail: helmut.cascorbi@uhms.com.

CASE, COLLEEN MAE, computer graphics educator; b. Aurora, Ill, Nov. 3, 1952; d. Harry Sherman Jr. and JoAnne Mae (Rife) C.; children: William Matt, Thomas Wesley, Corey Isaac. BS, U. Wis., LaCrosse, 1981; MLS, Ea. Mich. U., 1991. Cert. computer sci. tchr., Mich. Systems analyst Midwest Regional Tech-Unisys Corp., Okemos, Mich., 1981-88; computer educator UAW/Ford Computer Learning Ctr., Wixom, Mich., 1989-95; video prodr. Creative Media Consultants, Livonia, Mich., 1990-95; assoc. prof. computer graphics tech. Schoolcraft Coll., Livonia, 1996—. Tech. editor Course Technologies and other publ., 1996—. Mem. Assn. Computing Machinery SIGGRAPH (S2001 educators program chair, dir. for edn., dir. for edn. 2003—). E-mail: ccase@schoolcraft.cc.mi.us., colleen_case@siggraph.org.

CASE, DAVID KNOWLTON, management consultant; b. Worcester, Mass., Mar. 26, 1938; s. Frederic Howard and Frances Mary (Knowlton) C.; m. Caroline Porter Richards, Feb. 2, 1974; children— Elizabeth, Sarah BA, Yale U., 1961; grad. mktg. mgmt. program, Harvard U., 1973. Pub. rels. rep. U.S. Steel Corp., Pitts., 1962-66; comms. dir. John Hancock Ins. Co., Boston, 1966-70; asst. v.p. Shawmut Bank, Boston, 1970-76; devel. dir. Boston Ctr. for the Arts, 1977; dir. Plimoth Plantation, Plymouth, Mass., 1977-90, pres., CEO, 1990-96; owner, CEO Case Consulting, Norwell, Mass., 1997—; ptnr. Case & Mann, Osterville, Mass., 2000—. Bd. assocs. ARTS/Boston, 1988—; pres. emeritus, hon. dir. English-Speaking Union, Boston; pres. emeritus, dir. Plymouth County Devel. Coun., 1988—; mem. adv. bd. S.E. Mass. Am. Automobile Assn., 1988—; mem. adv. bd. trustees Jordan Hosp., Plymouth; mem. external rels. com. Milton Acad. Recipient Golden Coin award Bank Mktg. Assn., 1973, Nat. award Bus. Com. Arts, N.Y., 1975, Leadership award Soc. Mayflower Descendants, 1994, Jackson Bowl award Milton Acad., 1995, Silver medal SAR, 1996, Lifetime Achievement award Mass. Office Travel and Tourism, 1997. Mem. Am. Assn. Mus., New Eng. Mus. Assn., Colonial Soc., Soc. Colonial Wars in Commonwealth of Mass., Yale Club (Boston and N.Y.), Harvard Club (Boston), The Beach Club (Centerville, Mass.). Republican. Episcopalian. Home and Office: 378 River St Norwell MA 02061-2205 also: PO Box 361 205 Seapuit Rd Osterville MA 02655-1819

CASE, DAVID LEON, lawyer; b. Lansing, Mich., Sept. 22, 1948; s. Harlow Hoyt and Barbara Jean (Denman) C.; m. Cynthia Lou Rhinehart, Jan. 28, 1968; children: Beau, Ryan, Kimberly, Darren, Stephanie. BS with distinction, Ariz. State U., 1970, JD cum laude, 1973. Bar: Calif. 1973, U.S. Dist. Ct. (cen. dist.) Calif. 1973, U.S. Tax Ct. 1974, Ariz. 1976, U.S. Supreme Ct. 1997. Assoc. Willis, Butler & Scheifly, Los Angeles, 1973-75; from assoc. to mem. Ryley, Carlock & Applewhite, Phoenix, 1975—. Fellow Ariz. Bar Found., Am. Coll. Trust and Estate Counsel; mem. ABA (tax sect., corp. sect., probate and trust sect.), Ariz. Bar Assn., Ctrl. Ariz. Estate Planning Coun. (bd. dirs., pres. 1988-89), Beta Gamma Sigma. Republican. Presbyterian. Avocations: guitar, sports. Office: Ryley Carlock & Applewhite PO Box 634 Phoenix AZ 85001-0634 E-mail: dcase@rcalaw.com.

CASE, DAVID RANDALL, trade association executive; b. Indpls., Sept. 23, 1950; s. Kenneth Sothern and Shirley (Bernat) C.; m. Ellen M. Case, Sept. 1, 1973; children: Benjamin, Daniel, Meredith. AB, Amherst Coll., 1972; LLM, Cambridge U., 1974; JD, U. Mich., 1976. Atty. Jones Day Reavis & Pogue, Washington, 1977-79, Crowell & Moring, Washington, 1979-89; gen. counsel Environ. Tech. Coun., Washington, 1989-97, exec. dir., 1997—. Mem. editl. adv. bd. Environ. Law Reporter, Washington, 1995—. Co-author: All About Environmental Auditing, 1996. Mem. The University Club. Home: 5502 Pollard Rd Bethesda MD 20816-3328 Office: Environ Tech Coun 734 15th St NW Ste 720 Washington DC 20005-1013

CASE, DOUGLAS MANNING, lawyer; b. Cleve., Jan. 3, 1947; s. Manning Eugene and Ernestine (Bryan) Case; m. Marilyn Cooper, Aug. 23, 1969. BA, U. Pa., 1969; JD, MBA, Columbia U., 1973. Bar: N.Y. 1974, N.J. 1975, Calif. 1980, Ohio 1991, Fla. 2000. Assoc. Brown & Wood, N.Y.C., 1973-77; corp. counsel PepsiCo Inc., Purchase, NY, Irvine, Calif., 1977—83, Nabisco Brands Inc., N.Y.C., East Hanover, N.J. and London, 1983-89; asst. gen. counsel Chiquita Brands Internat., Inc., Cin., 1989-92; prin. Douglas M. Case Law Offices, Cin., Vero Beach, Fla., 1993—. Lectr. numerous seminars. Contbr. articles to profl. jours. Chmn. Olde Colonial Dist.; active Morris-Sussex area coun. Boy Scouts Am., 1986—88; sec., trustee Marble Scholarship Com., N.Y.C., 1983—88; trustee Cin. Opera Guild, 1994—99, pres., 1997—98, chmn. 1998—99, hon. trustee, 1999—; bd. dirs., mem. exec. com. Cin. Opera Assn., 1997—98. Mem.: ABA, Quality in Law (chmn. 1996—98), Cin. Bar Assn. (continuing legal edn. chair internat. law com. 1994—96, chair solo and small firm practitioners com. 1995—97, sec. 1996—97, vice chair 1997—98, chair 1998—2000), Fla. Bar Assn., Internat. Bar Assn., Munich Sister City Assn. Greater Cin. (chmn. econ. devel. com. 1995—96), Kenwood Country Club, Columbia Bus. Sch. Club (N.Y.C.) (pres., bd. dirs. 1974—79), Morris County Golf Club, Met. Club (N.Y.C.), Lawyers Club Cin. (mem. exec. com. 1995—2000, treas. 1996, sec. 1997, 2d v.p. 1998, 1st v.p. 1999, pres. 2000). Avocation: golf. Office: 501 Bay Dr Vero Beach FL 32963-2163 E-mail: dcaselaw@bellsouth.net.

CASE, ED, congressman; b. Hilo, Hawaii, Sept. 27, 1952; m. Audrey Case; children: David, Megan, James, David. BA, Williams Coll., 1975; JD, U. Calif., 1981. Aide to U.S. Rep. Spark Matsunaga from Hawaii, Washington, 1975—78; clk. to Hon. William Richardson Hawaii Supreme Ct.; clk. Hawaii State. Dept. Labor; from assoc. to mng. ptnr. Carlsmith Ball, Honolulu; mem. Hawaii Ho. of Reps., 1994—2002, majority leader, 1999—2000; mem. from 2d Hawaii dist. U.S. Ho. of Reps., Washington, 2002—, mem. edn. and workforce com., agr. com., small bus. com. Mem. Manoa Neighborhood Bd., Honolulu, 1985—89. Named Legislator of Yr., Honolulu Weekly, 1995, Small Bus. Hawaii, 2000, New Economy Legislator of Yr., Hawaii Tech. and Trade Assn., 2000. Office: 128 Cannon HOB Washington DC 20515 also: 5104 Prince Kuhio Fed Bldg Honolulu HI 96850*

CASE, ELDON DARREL, materials science educator; b. Logan, Kans., Aug. 23, 1949; s. Eldon George and Ila Marie (Lewis) C.; m. Linda Lee Lubken, Aug. 29, 1975 (div. Mar. 1993); 1 child, Carl Allen; m. Rebecca J. Ervin, 1996. BA in Physics and Math., U. Colo., 1971; MA in Physics, U. No. Colo., 1975; PhD in Materials Sci., Iowa State U., 1980. Rsch. asst. dept. materials sci. Iowa State U., Ames, 1976-80; NRC postdoctoral assoc. Nat. Bur. Standards, Gaithersburg, Md., 1980-82; rsch. engr. in materials sci. and mining engring. U. Calif., Berkeley, 1982-85; asst. prof. metallurgy, mechanics and materials sci. Mich. State U., East Lansing, 1985-88, assoc. prof., 1988-99, prof., 1999—. Cons. Indsl. Tech. Inst., Ann Arbor, Mich., 1990, Westinghouse, West Mifflin, Pa., 1991-92; judge Nat. Am. Indian Sci. and Engring. Fair, 1993-2001; grand awards judge Internat. Sci. and Engring. Fair, 2000; mem. internat. sci. com. ACUN-3 Advanced Composites, Sydney, Australia, 2000-01. Assoc. editor Jour.of Applied Ceramics Tech., 2003—; contbr. over 110 articles to profl. jours. including Jour. Materials Sci., Materials Sci. Engring., Applied Physics Letters. Speaker to sch. groups Okemos (Mich.) Pub. Schs., 1986-90; asst. with middle-sch. activities Episcopal Ch., East Lansing, 1988-92; judge Nat. Am. Indian Sci. and Engring. Fair, 1993-2001. Recipient Tchr.-Scholar award Mich. State U., 1989, Withrow Excellence in Tchg. award Engring. Coll. Mich. State U., 1993, 95, 98; Regents scholar U. Colo., 1967-71; NRC postdoctoral assoc., 1980-82; grantee NASA, 1987, NSF, 1987-90, Mich. State U., 1989, AFOSR, 2001--. Fellow Am. Ceramic Soc.; mem. AAUP, ASM (chair advanced joining tech. com. 1999—, tech. programming bd. for joining critical tech. sector 1999—), Nat. Inst. Ceramic Engrs., The Metall. Soc. (sec. structural materials div. 1988-91, chair non-metall. com. 1988-91), Sigma xi; fellow Am. Ceramic Soc. (pres. Mich. sect. 1998—, officer nominating com. engring. ceramics divsn., internat. sci. adv. com. for ACUN-3 advanced composites symposium Sydney, Australia, 2000-01). Democrat. Achievements include first neutron scattering study from microcracks in a polycrystalline ceramic; statistical analysis of water drop impact damage cracks in infrared windows; microwave sintering and joining of ceramics and ceramic composites; adhesion studies of diamond thin-films on brittle substrates; thermal-shock and thermal fatigue studies on ceramics and ceramic composites, microwave sintering and joining of ceramics. Home: 4469 Fairlane Dr Okemos MI 48864-2407 Office: Materials Sci and Mechanics Sci Dept East Lansing MI 48824 E-mail: casee@egr.msu.edu.

CASE, GERARD RAMON, drafting technologist, paleontologist; b. Bklyn., Dec. 22, 1931; s. James Sanford and Adele Elizabeth (Harris) C. Student BFA program, Pratt Inst., Bklyn., 1955-59. Cert. comml. artist and draftsman. Pvt. practice advt. and art, N.Y.C., 1955-72, Ultra Cooling Corp., N.Y.C., 1972-85; drafting technician Engring. div. Dept. of Pub. Works, Hackensack, N.J., 1986—; rsch. assoc. The Carnegie Mus. of Natural History, Pitts., Mich. State U. Mus., East Lansing; field assoc. dept. entomology The Am. Mus. of Natural History, N.Y.C. Author: Fossil Shark-Fish Remains of North America, 1967, Fossils Illustrated, 1968, Handbook of Fossil Collecting, 1972, Fossil Sharks: A Pictorial Review, 1973, Pictorial Guide to Fossils, 1982; contbr. over 100 articles to profl. jours. With USN, 1951-55. Recipient Harrell L. Strimple award Paleontol. Soc., 1992; Rsch. grantee Griffis Found./Am. Littoral Soc., 1976-86. Mem. AAAS, Internat. Platform Asssn., Am. Littoral Soc., Soc. Vertebrate Palaeontology, Paleontol. Soc., Am. Legion, Korean War Vets. Soc., Soc. Col. Wars, Hereditary Order 1st Families Mass. (life), Sons of the Revolution (life). Republican. Baptist. Achievements include research in genera and species of fossil remains; discovery of insects in amber, new genera and species of fossil fish, and a new order of fossil fishes, the Iniopterygians.

CASE, HADLEY, oil company executive; b. N.Y.C., Mar. 28, 1909; s. Walter Summerhayes and Mary Soule (Hadley) C.; m. Julie Marguerite Ill, June 8, 1935 (dec. Mar. 1975); children: Mary C. Durham, Julie Anne, Rosalie C. Clark, Deborah Joan; m. Elizabeth M. McCabe, Nov., 1975. Student, Kent (Conn.) Sch., 1924-29, Antioch Coll., 1929-33; DSc (hon.), DS (hon.), Antioch U., 1991. Geol. field work, Australia, 1933-34, 1935-36; with geol. dept. Case, Pomeroy & Co., Inc., N.Y.C., 1936-39, v.p., 1939-41, pres., 1941-83, CEO, 1983-93, chmn. bd., 1983-99, chmn. emeritus, 1999—; also bd. dirs.; pres., CEO Felmont Oil Corp., 1952-84; chmn. of bd., CEO Felmont Oil Corp. (merger Felmont and Homestake Mining Co.), 1972-84; dir. Homestake Mining Co., 1984-95, Brown Bros. Harriman Trust Co. Fla., 1986-93. Trustee Antioch U., 1987-93, Kent Sch., 1959-75, Brewster Acad., 1956-63, Boys' and Girls' Camps, Inc., Boston, 1971-76; trustee Hosp. St. Barnabas, Newark, 1942-59, pres. bd. trustees, 1949-52; bd. dirs. Greenwich Boys Club Assn., 1957-73, hon. mem., 1974—; trustee Naples (Fla.) Community Hosp., 1985-91; bd. dirs. Naples Philharm. Ctr. for Arts, 1988—; dir. The Conservancy, Naples, 1985-91; chancellor Kent Sch., 1985—, trustee, 1986—. Mem. Am. Inst. Mining and Metall. Engrs., Am. Petroleum Inst., Ind. Petroleum Assn. Am. (past v.p., dir.) Office: Case Pomeroy & Co Inc 529 5th Ave Fl 16 New York NY 10017-4684

CASE, JAMES HEBARD, lawyer; b. Lihue, Hawaii, Apr. 10, 1920; s. Adrial Hebard and Elizabeth (McConnell) C.; m. Suzanne Catherine Espenett, Sept. 18, 1948; children: Edward E., John H., Suzanne D., Russell L., Elisabeth C. Marguleas, Bradford Case. AB, Williams Coll., 1941; JD, Harvard U., 1949. Bar: Hawaii 1949, U.S. Supreme Ct. 1985. Assoc. Pratt, Tavares & Cassidy, Honolulu, 1949-51, Carlsmith & Carlsmith, Hilo, Hawaii, 1951-59; ptnr. Carlsmith Ball, Honolulu, 1959—2002, of counsel, 2002—. Bd. dirs. ML Resources, Honolulu. Trustee Hanahauoli Sch., Honolulu, 1970-82, Cen. Union Ch., Honolulu, 1984-88, Arcadia Retirement Residence, Honolulu, 1985-91. Lt. comdr. USNR, 1943-46, PTO. Mem. ABA, Hawaii Bar Assn., Hawaii Yacht Racing Assn. (bd. dirs. 1994-2000). Clubs: Pacific (bd. dirs. 1978-82); Kaneohe Yacht (Honolulu). Republican. Congregationalist. Avocations: sailing, tennis. Home: 3757 Round Top Dr Honolulu HI 96822-5043 Office: Carlsmith Ball PO Box 656 Honolulu HI 96809-0656 E-mail: jhc@carlsmith.com.

CASE, KAREN ANN, lawyer; b. Milw., Apr. 7, 1944; d. Alfred F. and Hilda M. (Tomich) Case. BS, Marquette U., 1963, JD, 1966; LLM, NYU, 1973. Bar: Wis. 1966, U.S. Ct. Claims 1973, U.S. Tax Ct. 1973. Ptnr. Meldman, Case & Weine, Milw., 1973-85, Meldman, Case & Weine divsn. Mulcahy & Wherry, S.C., 1985-87; Sec. of Revenue State of Wis., 1987-88; ptnr. Case & Drinka, S.C., Milw., 1989-91, Case, Drinka & Diel, S.C., Milw., 1991-97, CoVac, 1997—. Lectr. U. Wis., Milw., 1974-78; guest lectr. Marquette U. Law Sch., 1975-78; dir. WBBC, 1998—. Contbr. articles to legal jours. Mem. gov.'s Commn. on Taliesin, 1988, gov.'s Econ. Adv. Commn., 1989-91, pres.'s coun. Alverno Coll., 1988-94, nat. coun., 1998-2000; bd. dirs. WBCC, 1998—. Fellow Wis. Bar Found. (dir. 1977-90, treas. 1980-90); mem. ABA, Milw. Assn. Women Lawyers (founding mem., bd. dirs. 1975-78, 81-82), Milw. Bar Assn. (bd. dirs. 1985-87, law office mgmt. chair 1992-93), State Bar Wis. (bd. govs. 1981-85, 87-90, dir. taxation sect. 1981-87, vice chmn. 1986-87, 90-91, chmn. 1991-92), Am. Acad. Matrimonial Lawyers (bd. dirs. 1988-90), Nat. Assn. Women Lawyers (Wis. del. 1982-83), Milw. Rose Soc. (pres. 1981, dir. 1981-83), Friends of Boerner Bot. Gardens (founding mem., pres. 1984-90), Profl. Dimensions Club (dir. 1985-87), Tempo Club (sec. 1984-85). Home: 2212 Harbour Ct Longboat Key FL 34228-4174 Office: CoVac 9803 W Meadow Park Dr Hales Corners WI 53130-2261 *Delegate tasks for responsibility and accountability. then spend the resulting freed time nourishing your soul. Resign yourself to the fact that the tasks will not be completed as you would have but they will be done, sometimes with more creativity. Give credit and praise always.*

CASE, KENNETH MYRON, physics educator; b. N.Y.C., Sept. 23, 1923; SB, Harvard U., 1945, MS, 1946, PhD, 1948. Rsch. assoc. Lawrence Radiation Lab., 1949-50, U. Rochester, 1950-51; prof. U. Mich., 1951-69, Rockefeller U., 1969-88, prof. emeritus, 1988—. Adj. prof. Inst. Nonlinear Studies, U. Calif., San Diego, 1988—, vis. prof., 1981-82, Lawrence Radiation Lab., 1956, 61, MIT, 1963-64; scientist Los Alamos Sci. Lab., 1944-45; mem. Inst. Adv. Study, Princeton, 1948-50, 56-57, 70-88; cons. Rand Corp., Ramo-Woolridge Corp., La Jolla Inst. & Phys. Dynamics. Recipient Guggenheim fellow, 1963. Fellow Am. Phys. Soc.; mem. Nat. Acad. Scis. Home: 1429 Calle Altura La Jolla CA 92037-7802

CASE, MANNING EUGENE, JR., retired food products executive; b. Sioux City, Iowa, Mar. 19, 1916; s. Manning Eugene and Loretta (Seims) C.; m. Ernestine Bryan, July 26, 1941; children: Douglas Manning, Randall Bryan. AB, Western Res. U., 1938, JD, 1941. Bar: Ohio 1941. Asst. counsel B.F. Goodrich Co., Akron, 1941-52; sec., treas., gen counsel, dir. Perfection Industries, 1952-55; sec. Hupp Corp., 1955-57; v.p. service and fin. M&M Candies div. Mars Inc., 1957-60; asst. treas. Standard Brands Inc., N.Y.C., 1961-62, treas., 1962-68, v.p., treas., 1968-77, v.p., chief fin. officer, 1977-78, sr. v.p., chief fin. officer, 1978-80, sr. v.p. human resources, 1980-81, Nabisco Brands, Inc., Parsippany, N.J., 1981-82, sr. v.p., 1983-84. Served to col., JAGC U.S. Army, 1942-46. Mem. ABA, Phi Beta Kappa, Delta Sigma Rho, Omicron Delta Kappa, Beta Theta Pi, Phi Delta Phi. Clubs: Met., N.Y. Athletic, Royal Palm Yacht and Country, Delray Beach. Home: 1717 Homewood Blvd Apt 100 Delray Beach FL 33445-6892

CASE, RICHARD PAUL, electronics executive; b. Akron, Ohio, May 13, 1935; s. Charles Robert and Barbara (Ebinger) C.; m. Virginia Carolyn Quallich, Sept 1, 1956; children: Duane, Ralph, Glenn, Ellen, Sarah, Eileen, Katherine, Melinda. BSEE, Case Inst. Tech., Cleve., 1956; MSEE, Syracuse U., 1985. Registered profl. engr., Conn. Tech. engr., then sr. programmer IBM, 1956-65, mgr. programming ctr., 1965-66, dir. systems architecture, 1966-71, dir. advanced systems, 1971-75, cons. to dir. rsch. Thomas J. Watson Rsch. Ctr. Yorktown Heights, N.Y., 1975-77, dir. advanced systems devel. Data Processing Product Group, 1977-78, dir. tech. ops. for System Products Div., 1979-81, v.p. devel. ops. Gen. Tech. Div. White Plains, N.Y., 1981-82, dir. product lab. Endicott, N.Y., 1983, v.p. for devel. Systems Tech. Div., 1983-84, dir. tech. pers. devel., 1984-86, dir. univ. rels. and tech. programs, 1986-87, dir. systems analysis, 1987-91, dir. tech. strategy devel. Armonk, N.Y., 1991-97; commr. Pres.'s Commn. on Critical Infrastructure Protection, Washington, 1997-98; ind. computer cons., 1998—. Panelist Nat. Computer Conf., Anaheim, Calif., 1975, Comp-Con, Washington, 1975, 4th IEEE Careers Conf., 1985, NRC Panel on Reliability, Integrity and Privacy in Telecommunications, 1985-86, TECH-WORLD Symposium, Washington, 1987, Ann. Jud. Conf. 2d Jud. Cir. U.S., Bolton Landing, N.Y., 1989, 2d Nat. Conf. on Ct. Mgmt., Phoenix, 1990; participant in Air Force Studies Bd. Workshop on Software Devel. and Procurement, Woods Hole, Mass., 1976; mem. sponsors adv. com. Ctr. for Integrated Systems, Stanford U., 1980-84; mem. adv. com. Office of Tech. Assessment, Congress of U.S., 1983; keynote speaker Conf. on Automation and Robotics, Pa. State U., 1983, Symposium on Bus. and the Creative Process, AIESEC, R.I., 1985, Computer Integrated Mfg. and Communications, Anaheim, Calif., 1985; speaker numerous symposiums and confs.; ind. computer cons., 1998—. Chmn. editorial bd. Systems Programming Series, 1975—; contbr. articles to profl. jours. Chmn. evaluation PFG Com., Met. N.Y. Synod, Luth. Ch. in Am., 1973-77; bd. dirs., treas. Mid-Hudson Philharm. Orch., 1974-77; bd. dirs. Binghamton Symphony Orch., 1983-84, Greenwich Symphony Orch., 1989—; trustee Wagner Coll., S.I., N.Y., 1982-88, Nat. Tech. U., 1984-88; trustee, chmn. exec. com. Computer Mus., Boston, 1989—; bd. dirs. nat. judge Nat. Math. Counts Found., 1992—. Recipient Outstanding Invention award IBM, 1965, award for excellence in principles of mgmt. and quantative methods Inst. Certification of Computer Profls., 1976. Fellow IEEE (various offices); mem. Assn. for Computing Machinery, Sigma Xi (assoc.), Tau Kappa Alpha, Tau Beta Pi, Eta Kappa Nu. Office: 40 Bush Ave Greenwich CT 06830-7067 E-mail: case004@attglobal.net.

CASE, STEPHEN M. media and entertainment company executive; b. Honolulu, Aug. 21, 1958; m. Joanne Case (div.); 3 children. BA in Polit. Sci., Williams Coll., 1980. With mktg. dept. Procter & Gamble, 1980—82; mng. new pizza devel. Pizza Hut divsn. PepsiCo, 1982—83; with Control Video, 1983—85, Quantum Computer Svcs., 1985—92; CEO America Online, 1992—2001, chmn., 1995—2001, AOL Time Warner, N.Y.C., 2001—. Named Named Entrepreneur of Yr., Inc. Mag., 1994. Avocation: reading political science and social history. Office: AOL Time Warner 75 Rockefeller Plz New York NY 10019-9302

CASE, STEPHEN SHEVLIN, lawyer; b. Mpls., Nov. 16, 1943; s. George Price and Helen (Beckwith) C.; m. Judy Elizabeth Everett, Apr. 5, 1969 (div. Feb. 1979); children: Mackenzie Beckwith, Julia Lee; m. Pamela Ellen Earl, Apr. 29, 1981 (div. 1991); m. Monica Ann Triano, July 18, 1999. BA, Washington and Lee U., 1966, LLB with honors, 1969. Bar: Ariz. 1969, Colo., 2001, U.S. Tax Ct. 1970, U.S. Ct. Appeals (9th cir.) 1984. Assoc., Fennemore, Craig, von Ammon & Udall, Phoenix, 1969-73; majority atty. (Rep.) Ariz. State Senate, 1973; trust counsel First Interstate Bank of Ariz., Phoenix, 1973-76; ptnr. Norris & Case, P.C., Sun City, Ariz., 1976-85, Case & Bennett, Sun City and Scottsdale, Ariz., 1985-95, Case, Siler & Church, PLC, Sun City and Scottsdale, Ariz., 1995—; instr. Golden Gate U., Phoenix, 1983-87; lectr. in field. Bd. dirs. Cen. Ariz. Estate Planning Coun., 1978-81, Am. Humanics at Ariz. State U., 2000—; mem. bd. adjustment Town of Paradise Valley, Ariz. 1987-91, Lukes Men of St. Lukes Hosp., 1976—, pres. 1981-82; bd. dirs. ARC

(ctrl. Ariz. chpt.) 1992-98, 2002-, vice chmn., 1995-96, chmn., 1996-98, biomed. region 1998-, chmn. 2001-). Fellow Am. Coll. Trust and Estate Counsel; mem. ABA, State Bar Ariz. (chmn. sect. real property, probate and trust law 1981-82, exec. coun. 2002-, chmn. sect. taxation 1983-84, disciplinary hearing com. 1989-96, chmn. 1994-96), Delta Theta Phi, Rotary (dir. Sun City Found. 1977-81, 95—98, chmn. 1996—98). Contbr. articles to profl. jours. Avocations: trout fishing, skiing, backpacking. Office: 5725 N Scottsdale Rd Ste 195C Scottsdale AZ 85250-5908 E-mail: stephen_s_case@prodigy.net. *Notable cases include: Estate of R.H. Black, 85-2 USTC Sect. 13, 628, 765 F2d 862 (1985, 9th cir.), reversing long-standing tax law construction which held that transfer of jointly held assets to a joint revocable trust severs the joint tenancy and creates community property.*

CASE, THOMAS LOUIS, lawyer; b. Dallas, June 14, 1947; s. Donald L. and Ellen (Hanson) C.; m. Bonnie Nally, July 8, 1972. BA, Vanderbilt U., 1969, JD, 1972; cert. civil trial law, Tex. Bd. Legal Specialization. Bar: Tex. 1972, U.S. Dist. Ct. (no. dist.) Tex. 1973, U.S. Dist. Ct. (we. and ea. dists.) Tex. 1978, U.S. Dist. Ct. (so. dist.) Tex. 1979, U.S. Dist. Ct. (ea. dist.) Ark. 1981, U.S. Ct. Appeals (5th cir.) 1977, U.S. Supreme Ct. 1978, U.S. Ct. Appeals (8th cir.) 1984, U.S. Ct. Appeals (11th cir.) 1981. Assoc. Johnson, Bromberg, Leeds & Riggs, Dallas, 1972-77; ptnr. Bickel & Case, Dallas, 1977-84, St. Claire & Case, Dallas, 1984-93, Thomas L. Case & Assocs., P.C., Dallas, 1993-2000; shareholder Case Carter Salyers & Henry, Dallas, 2000—01; ptnr. Bell, Nunnally & Martin, Dallas, 2002—. Mem. ABA, Tex. Bar Assn., Tex. Assn. Def. Coun., Dallas Assn. of Def. Counsel, Dallas Bar Assn. Office: Bell Nunnally & Martin 3232 McKinney Ave Ste 1400 Dallas TX 75204 E-mail: tomc@bellnunnally.com.

CASEBEER, DOUGLAS KELLEY, artist, ceramist, consultant; b. Joplin, Mo., Nov. 1, 1956; s. Charles William and Sue (Dalby) C.; nm. Susan Roscoe, Dec. 22, 1979; children: Emily Clara, Logan Oliver. Student, U. Okla., 1974-76, Mo. Western Stat Coll., 1977-78; BFA in Ceramics, Wichita State U., 1980; MFA in Ceramics, Alfred U., 1982. Dir. ceramics and sculpture program, instr., resident artist Anderson Ranch Arts Ctr., Snowmass Village, Colo., 1985—, program dir. artist-in-residency program, 1987—, dir. programs, 1995-97. Tchg. asst. advanced pottery and kilns N.Y. State Coll. Ceramics, Alfred U., 1980-82; instr. ceramics Jamaica Sch. Art, Kingston, 1984; ceramic cons. UN Indsl. Devel. Orgn., Vienna, Austria, 1982-85, German Agy. for Tech. Cooperation, Eschborn, 1985, Govt. of Nepal, Kathmandu, 1985, USIS, Washington, 1993, Hui Noeau Visual Arts Ctr., Makawao, Maui, Hawaii, 1998; prof. ceramics U. Ga., Cortona, Italy, 1993; mem. nat. adv. bd. Aspen Ednl. Rsch. Found., Woody Creek, Colo., 1998—; co-leader, instr. Gobardia project Potters to Nepal, ceramics study tour, Deohkuri, Dang Dist., Nepal, 1993-00; condr. workshops, lectr., vis. artist, 1983—; co-leader, instr. cermaics study tour Potters to Nepal Gobardiya Project Anderson Ranch Arts Ctr., Deohkuri, Dang Dist., Nepal, 1993-2001. Exhibited in numerous group shows, 1978—, latest being Foothills Art Ctr., Golden, Colo., 1995, 98, Auckland (New Zealand) Studio Potters, 1996, 2000, U. So. Colo., Pueblo, 1996, Taller Huara-Huara, Santiago, Chile, 1996, Daniel Arvizu Gallery, Santa Ana, Calif., 1996, Mus. Nebr., Kearney, 1996, S.E. Ind. U., New Albany, 1997, Grosvenor Gallery, Kingston, Jamaica, 1997, Coll. of Ozarks, Point Lookout, Mo., 1997, Roundtree Art Ctr., Denver, 1997, Contemporary Artifacts Gallery, Brea, Ky., 1997, Greenwich House Pottery, N.Y.C., 1997, 98, 99, Adelson Gallery, Aspen, Colo., 1998, Evelyn Siegel Gallery, Ft. Worth, 1998, 2000, Ching-Tao Fang Ceramics Gallery, Kaohsiung, Taiwan, 1998, Odyssey Gallery, Asheville, N.C., 1999, Islip Art Mus., New Islip, N.Y., 1999, Yoyokaku Gallery, Karatsu-Chi, Saga, Japan, 1999, Gallery Ichibankan, Fukuoka, Japan, 1999, Andrews U., Beriens Springs, Mich., 2000, Hibberd/McGrath Gallery, Breckenridge, Colo., 2000, Signature Gallery, Atlanta, 2000, Nassau County Mus. Art, Nassau, N.Y., 2000, Kreeger Pottery Gallery, Harwich, Mass., 2000, Pub. Libr. Charlotte (N.C.), 2001, Archie Bray Found., Helena, Mont., 2001, Indigo Gallery, Kathmandu, 2001, Blue Spiral Gallery, Asheville, N.C., numerous others; represented in permanent collections Islip Art Mus., Contemporary Ceramics Arts Inst., Taipei, Taiwan, Auckland Art Mus., Jamaica Nat. Gallery, Stetson U., Bemidji (Minn.) State U., Eccelson Harrison Mus. Art, Utah State U., Logan, N.Y. State Coll. Ceramics, Alfred U., Topeka Pub. Libr., also pvt. and corp. collections; work reviewed in newspapers and mags. Mem. Am. Craft Coun., Coll. Art Assn., Nat. Coun. on Edn. Ceramic Arts, Colo. Artist Craftsmen Assn. (bd. dirs. 1990-91). Achievements include development variety of kilns in U.S. and Caribbean; research on glazes and clay bodies in relation to demands of final project; discovered and developed 5 clays and variety of basic minerals for manufacture of ceramic products, 3 stoneware and 2 earthenware clays, 3 varieties of silica, dolomite, limestones, gypsum, haematite, steatite, and prophyry granites for feldspars. Office: Anderson Ranch Arts Ctr PO Box 5598 5263 Owl Creek Rd Snowmass Village CO 81615 E-mail: dcasebeer@andersonranch.org.

CASEBEER, WILLIAM D. adult education educator; b. Claremore, Okla., Oct. 25, 1969; s. James William and Mary Belle Casebeer; m. Adrianne Waldman, Apr. 8, 1995. PhD in Cognitive Sci. and Philosophy, U. of Calif., 2001. Chief ninth air force briefing team Ctrl. Air Forces, Shaw AFB, 1993—95; asst. prof. philosophy U.S. Air Force Acad., Colo. Springs, 2001—. Author: (book) Natural Ethical Facts: Evolution, Connectionism, and Moral Cognition, 2003 (Best Dissertation at U. of Calif., 2001). Officer in charge Big Bros. Big Sisters, USAF Acad., Colo., 2002—03. Maj. USAF, 1996—2003. Multiple grants to rsch. nat. security issues, Inst. for Nat. Security Studies, 1996, 1997, 2002, 2003. Fellow: Soc. for Empirical Ethics (assoc.; bd. dirs. 2002—03). Achievements include research in Neural mechanisms of moral cognition. Office: USAF Acad 2354 Fairchild Dr Ste 1A10 U S A F Academy CO 80840 E-mail: william.casebeer@usafa.af.mil.

CASEBOLT, JAMES R. psychologist, educator; s. James R. and Mary Alice Casebolt; m. C. Elizabeth Boring, Nov. 7, 1987; children: Bryon S., Megan T. BA, Alderson-Broaddus Coll., Philippi, WV, 1989; MA, U. NC, 1991, PhD, 1994. Asst. prof. psychology Danville (Va.) C.C., 1993—96, Ohio U., St. Clairsville, 1996—. Mem. appraisal commn. Unitarian Universalist Assn., Boston, 2001—. Mem.: APA (webmaster 2002, mem. divsn. psychology of religion), Soc. Personality and Social Psychology, Am. Psychol. Soc., Religious Rsch. Assn., Soc. Sci. Study Religion. Office: Ohio University Eastern Campus 45425 National Road Saint Clairsville OH 43950 Office Fax: 740-695-7076. E-mail: casebolt@ohio.edu.

CASEBOLT, JAMES STANTON, lawyer; b. Denver, Apr. 27, 1950; s. Stanton Taylor and Josephine Almira (Cole) C.; m. Joanne Ruth Tuthill, June 10, 1972; children— Matthew, Zachary. B.A. magna cum laude, Colo. Coll., 1972; J.D., U. Colo., 1975. Bar: Colo. 1975, U.S. Dist. Ct. Colo. 1975, U.S. Ct. Appeals (10th cir.) 1983. Assoc. Younge & Hockensmith, P.C., Grand Junction, Colo., 1975-78, dir., sec., 1978—, sr. litigation ptnr., 1984—. Author: Civil Jury Selection Procedure and Pattern Voir Dire. Mem. adv. bd. Salvation Army Grand Junction; trustee Presbytery Western Colo., 1982-85, chmn., 1984-85; cubmaster Boy Scouts Am., Grand Junction, 1984-87. Mem. ABA, Colo. Bar Assn. (litigation council 1982-85), Mesa County Bar Assn. (sec.-treas. 1980-83, bd. dirs.), Colo. Def. Lawyers, Phi Beta Kappa. Address: Younge & Hockensmith 743 Horizon Ct Ste 200 Grand Junction CO 81506-8716 Home: 5601 Northwood Dr Evergreen CO 80439-5520

CASEI, NEDDA, mezzo-soprano; b. Balt. d. Howard Thomas and Lyda Marie (Graupman) Casey; m. John A. Wiles, Jr., 1971 (div. 1979); m. Samuel Strasbourger, 1983 (dec. 1987). Cert., Mozarteum, Salzburg, Austria, 1959; B in Performing Arts Adminstrn. magna cum laude, Fordham U., 1982; studied voice with, William P. Herman, N.Y.C., Vittorio Piccinini, Milan, Italy, Loretta Corelli, N.Y.C.; also student piano, langs., modern dance, ballet. Tchr. master classes, lectr. univs. and festivals. Judge vocal competitions for Met. Opera, Fulbright Scholarship, Rosa Ponselle Internat. Competition, Savannah Festival, George London Found. Competition, First Internat. Vocal Competition, Baku, Azerbaijan, and others; vis. prof. Aichi Prefectural U. Fine Arts and Music, Nagoya, Japan; guest prof. Flaine Festival/Paris Conservatory, Haut Savoie, France, Mannes Coll. Music, New Sch. Social Rsch., N.Y.C., Internat. Vocal Arts Inst., Tel Aviv; pvt. tchr. Operatic debut Theatre Royal de la Monnaie, Brussels, 1960, with La Scala, Milan, Met. Opera, N.Y.C., 1964, Theatre Royal de la Monnaie, Brussels (with La Scala); operatic performances at Met. Opera, 1964-86, Basel Stadttheater, Gran Liceo, Barcelona, Teatro Carlo Fenice, Genova, San Remo Festival, Trieste Opera, Opera du Rhin, Strasbourg, Salzburg Festspielhaus, Teatro San Carlo, Naples, Chgo. Lyric Opera, Bogota Opera, Caracas Opera, Pitts. Opera, Vancouver Opera, Cape Town Opera, Brno Opera, Bratislava Opera, Kosice Opera, Prague Opera, Miami Opera, Houston Opera, San Diego Opera, Hartford Opera, Phila. Opera, Toledo Opera, Dayton Opera, Memphis Opera, Mobile Opera, Los Angeles Opera, Boston Opera, N.J. Opera, Taipei Opera, Opera of Mexico City; performances in numerous mus. festivals, concerts, recitals and operatic guest appearances in Europe, South Africa, Cen. Am., S.Am., Can., U.S., Far East, Middle East and Australia, inclucing Detroit Symphony, Cin. Orch., Toronto Symphony. Liepzig Gewandhaus, Philharm. Bruxelles, Phila. Orch., NY Philharm.; performed on radio and TV in Holland, Belgium, Leipzig, Japan, U.S., German Dem. Republic, Fed. Republic of Germany, Hong Kong, Singapore; performed at White House, Washington; made various recs. Supraphon, Everest, Nonesuch, Concert Hall, Vanguard, CETRA, VAI, others; contbr. articles to profl. jours.; guest editor Opera Quar. Coord. mus. events and benefits for Internat. Ctr. for Disabled, Morningside Home, Aging in Am. Gerontol. Acad.; mem. adv. bd. Fordham U at Lincoln Ctr., 1984—; bd. dirs. Theatre for a New Audience, Am. Coun. for Arts, Nat. Cultural Alliance, Songs of Love; mem. Career Transition for Dancers Nat. Adv. Bd. Recipient Outstanding Young Singers award, 1959, Martha Baird Rockefeller Found. award, 1962, 1964, Woman of Achievement award, 1969, Cmty. Leaders and Noteworthy Americans, 1975—76, Outstanding Achievement award on behalf of Arts and Edn., Opera Music Theater Internat. and Children's Emergency Med. Fund, 2000, Outstanding Lifetime Achievement award, Licia Albanese/Puccini Found., 2001, Extraordinary Women award, 2000, honors at, 100 Year Verdi Celebration by Met. Opera. Mem. AFTRA, Actors Equity, Am. Guild Mus. Artists (nat. pres. 1983-93, chmn. Emergency Relief Fund 1983-94), Nat. Assn. Tchrs. Singing (bd. govs.), N.Y. Singing Tchrs. Assn., Assn. Music Tchrs. League, The Players, James Beard Found. E-mail: neddanewyork@nyc.rr.com., neddanagoya@guitar.ocn.ne.jp.

CASEIRAS, JO ANN STRIGA, artist, educator; b. Bklyn., Dec. 17, 1950; d. Michael Striga and Stella Mary Lango; m. Frank Caseiras, May 21, 1983; children: Michael Allen, Kevin Frank, Amanda Beth, Robert Anthony. BFA, St. John's U., Jamaica, N.Y., 1972; MFA, SUNY, New Paltz, 1975. Tchr. continuing edn. SUNY, New Paltz, 1974-75, prof. Buffalo, 1976-78; tchr. Marlboro (N.Y.) Elem. Continuing Edn., 1980-82; parent advocate Rondout Valley Ctrl. Sch. Dist., Accord, N.Y., 1992-97, tchr. program for the handicapped, 1999—. Exhibited in shows at Reavin Gallery, New Paltz, N.Y., 1976, Benjamin's Works of Art, Buffalo, 1977, Art Zone 208, New Paltz, 1979, Mamaroneck Artists Guild, White Plains, N.Y., 1979, Womanart Gallery, N.Y.C., Schenectady (N.Y.) Mus., 1980, New Rochelle (N.Y.) Art Assn., 1994, Heritage Art Gallery, Poughkeepsie, N.Y., 1995, St. John's U., Jamaica, N.Y., 1996, Heritage Gallery, Rhinebeck, N.Y., 1997, Highland (N.Y.) Cultural Art Ctr., 1996-98, Coffey Gallery, Kingston, N.Y., 1998, Woodstock (N.Y.) Art Assn., 1995—, First Union Bank, New Paltz, 2000, Marbletown Arts Assn., 2002, Marbletown Tricentennial Exhbn., 2003. Recipient Mortimer L. Medrich Meml. award, 1979. Mem. Woodstock Art Assn., Art Soc. Kingston, Downs Syndrome Assn. Democrat. Roman Catholic. Avocations: sports, swimming, piano, photography. E-mail: jstrigacaseiras@aol.com.

CASELLA, ANTHONY JOHN, cardiologist; b. N.Y.C., Mar. 8, 1945; s. Anthony Daniel and Benedetta Ann Casella; m. Kathleen Ann Barrs, Aug. 31, 1986; children: Daniel Edward, Eric Michael;1 child from previous marriage, Joseph Anthony. BA, NYU, 1966; MD, N.Y. Med. Coll., 1970. Diplomate Am. Bd. Internal Medicine. Intern, resident N.Y. Hosp.-Meml. Hosp., 1970-73; fellow cardiology Columbia-Presbyn. Med. Ctr., N.Y.C., 1975-77; cardiologist Diagnostic and Clin. Cardiology PA, West Orange, NJ, 1977—. Cardiologist St. Barnabas Med. Ctr., Livingston, NJ, 1977—, Clara Maass Med. Ctr., Belleville, NJ, 1977—; assoc. St. Michaels Med. Ctr., Newark, 1984—. Mem.: AMA, Essex County Med. Soc., Alpha Omega Alpha. Republican. Roman Catholic. Office: Diagnostic and Clin Cardiology PA 769 Northfield Ave West Orange NJ 07052-1198

CASELLA, MARGARET MARY, artist, photographer; b. Bklyn. d. John August and Ann Elizabeth (Krajci) Butkovsky; m. Anthony Joseph Casella, Nov. 23, 1961; children: Paul Joseph, David John, Gregory Anthony. Cert. in Merchandising, Tobe-Coburn Sch., N.Y.C., 1961; BFA, L.I. U., 1982, MFA, 1984. Lectr. in field. Photographer: (book) Garbage or Art?, 1990 (Gold award Photo Design Mag. 1990); exhibited in solo exhbns. Midtown Y Photography Gallery, N.Y.C., 1991, Grand Ctrl. Terminal, N.Y.C., 1991, Ctr. for Photography at Woodstock, N.Y., 2000, Hort. Soc. N.Y./Webster Gallery, 2000, Elaine Benson Gallery, Bridgehampton, N.Y., others; group shows include U. Tex. at Arlington, Deutser Art Gallery, Houston, Heckscher Mus., Huntington, N.Y., Konica Plz., Tokyo, Firehouse Gallery, Garden City, N.Y., The Visual Club, N.Y.C., Hillwood Art Mus., Greenvale, N.Y.; works in permanent collections of Mus. for Photography, Branschweig, Germany, Yergeau Musee Internat. d'Art, Montreal, Fine Art Mus. of L.I., Hempstead, N.Y., Houston fotofest Permanent Archives, Houston. Founder, dir. Art Upstairs Gallery, East Williston, 1983-91; mem. adv. bd. C.W. Post Campus Sch. of Visual and Performing Arts. Named to Women's Roll of Honor, Town of North Hempstead, NY, 2003. Avocation: gardening. Studio: Casella Photography 889 Broadway New York NY 10003-1212

CASELLA, PETER F(IORE), patent and licensing executive; b. June 5, 1922; s. Fiore Peter and Lucy (Grimaldi) C.; m. Marjorie Eloise Enos, March 9, 1946 (dec. Aug. 1989); children: William Peter, Susan Elaine, Richard Mark. BChE, Poly. U., Bklyn., 1943; student in chemistry, St. John's U., N.Y.C., 1940. Registered to practice by the U.S. Patent and Trademark Office, Can. Patent and Trademark Offices. Head patent sect. Hooker Electrochem. Co., Niagara Falls, N.Y., 1943-54; mgr. patent dept. Occidental Chem. Corp. (formerly Hooker Chem. Corp.), Niagara Falls, N.Y., 1954-64, dir. patents and licensing, 1964-81, asst. sec., 1966-81, ret., 1981. Pres. TFA Products, Inc., Houston, Intra Gene Internat., Inc., Lewiston, N.Y., 1981-92; chmn. bd. In Vitro Internat., Inc., Linthicum, Md., 1983-86; cons. patents and licensing, Lewiston, N.Y., 1981—; Dept. Commerce del. on patents and licensing exchange, USSR, 1973, 90, Poland and German Dem. Rep., 1976. Editor: Drafting the Patent Application, 1957. Mem. Lewiston Bd. Edn., 1968-70. With AUS, 1944-46, Mediterranean Theater of Operation. Recipient Centennial citation Poly. U., Bklyn., 1955, Golden Jubilee Soc., 1993. Mem. ACS, AIChE, Assn. Corp. Patent Counsel (emeritus, exec. com. 1974-77, charter mem.), N.Y. Intellectual Property Law Assn. (Niagara Frontier chpt. pres. 1973-74, founder award 1974), Licensing Exec. Soc. (v.p. 1976-77, Trustees award 1977), Chartered Inst. Patent Agts. Gt. Britain (emeritus), Patent and Trademark Inst. Can., Internat. Patent and Trademark Assn. (emeritus), U.S. Trademark Assn., Nat. Assn. Mfrs. (patent com.), Mfg. Chemists Assn., Pacific Indsl. Property Assn., U.S. Patent Office Soc. (assoc.), U.S. Trademark Office Soc. (assoc.), Chemists Club (emeritus N.Y.C. chpt.), Niagara Club (Niagara Falls pres. 1973-74).

CASELLA, RUSSELL CARL, physicist; b. Framingham, Mass., Nov. 6, 1929; s. Rosario and Lena Casella; m. Marilyn Smith, Jan. 27, 1952; children: Sheryl M., Cynthia L. Conturie. BS in Physics, MIT, 1951, MS in Physics, 1953; PhD in Physics, U. Ill., 1956. Physicist Cambridge (Mass.) AF Rsch. Ctr., 1951-52; teaching and rsch. asst. physics dept. U. Ill., Urbana, 1953-55, rsch. fellow physics dept., 1955-56, rsch. assoc. physics dept., 1956-58; theoretical physicist IBM T.J. Watson Rsch. Ctr., Yorktown Heights, N.Y., 1958-65, Nat. Inst. Standards and Tech., Gaithersburg, Md., 1965-95. Contbr. articles to profl. jours. Recipient Silver medal U.S. Dept. Commerce, 1973. Mem. Am. Phys. Soc., Sigma Xi. Achievements include development of theory of condensed-matter and of elementary-particle physics; research in (broken) symmetries; neutron scattering; Bose condensation of excitons; tests of time reversal and CPT symmetries in Kaon physics; neutrino scattering; topology in neutron interferometry; high-temperature superconductivity; hydrogen in metals; quark-parton-sea content of the nucleon in deep-inelastic electroweak scattering. Home: 1485 Dunster Ln Potomac MD 20854-6107

CASELLAS, JOACHIM, art gallery executive; b. Gerona, Spain, Aug. 1, 1927; came to U.S., 1954; s. Juan and Dolores Farres (Carrera) C.; m. Elizabeth Reed Brannon, Mar. 17, 1952 (dec. Dec. 1984); m. Janice Mary Bezverkov, May 29, 1990 (dec. Apr. 2002). BA, Gerona Coll., 1948; MA, Sacred Heart Coll., 1953. Curator Mus. Provincial, Gerona, Spain, 1952; art appraiser Feist Co., N.Y.C., 1952-68, Mahan Co., New Orleans, 1968-72; pres. Casell Gallery, New Orleans, 1972—. One-man shows include Ft. Walton (Fla.) Beach Mus. Art, 1987. Mem. Ocean Springs Yacht Club. Republican. Episcopalian. Avocations: photography, plants, travel, antiques, boating. Home: 107 Shearwater Dr Ocean Springs MS 39564-4828 Office: Casell Gallery 818 Royal St New Orleans LA 70116-3115 Personal E-mail: joaquin_cas@msn.com.

CASELLAS, SALVADOR E. judge; b. 1935; BS in Fgn. Svc. cum laude, Georgetown U., 1957; LLB magna cum laude, U. P.R., 1960; LLM, Harvard U., 1961. Ptnr. Fiddler, Gonzalez & Rodriguez, 1962-72, 77-94; judge U.S. Dist. Ct. P.R., San Juan, 1994—. Mem. P.R. Acad. Jurisprudence, P.R. Commn. on Bicentennial of U.S. Constn., 1987-89; aide to Sec. of U.S. Army, 1985-89, emeritus, 1990—. Dir. Alliance for Drug Free P.R., 1993-94. 1st lt. U.S. Army, 1961-62, Res., JAGC, 1963-67. Recipient Comdrs. medal Second U.S. Army, 1990, P.R. Nat. Guard medal, 1990. Mem. ABA, Am. Bar Found., P.R. Bar Assn., P.R. Bar Assn. Found., Caparra Country Club, Banker's Club. Office: US Dist Ct PR US Courthouse 150 Ave Carlos Chardon # 111 San Juan PR 00918-1703

CASEMAN, AUSTIN BERT, civil engineering educator; b. Feb. 13, 1922; s. Artie B. and Winnie (Yergensen) C.; m. Susan Louise Burleson, Nov. 9, 1946; 1 child, Cathy Anne. BS in Civil Engring., Utah State U., 1947, MS in Civil Engring., 1948; SC.D. in Civil Engring., MIT, 1961. Registered profl. engr., Ga. Instr. then asst. prof. civil engring. Wash. State U., 1948—56; assoc. prof. civil engring. Ga. Inst. Tech., Atlanta, 1956—62, prof., 1962—87, prof. emeritus, 1987—. With City Planning Commn., Logan, Utah, 1948; structural engr. Boeing Aircraft, Seattle, 1951, U.S. Army C.E., Walla Walla, Wash., 1952, Douglas Aircraft, Long Beach, Calif., 1953, Lockheed Aircraft, Marietta, Ga., 1956. 1st lt. U.S. Army, 1943—46. Decorated Bronze Star, Combat Infantry badge; Faculty fellow, NSF, 1957—59. Mem.: ASCE, Am. Concrete Inst., Phi Kappa Phi, Sigma Tau, Chi Epsilon, Sigma Xi, Blue Key, Pi Kappa Alpha. Mem. Lds Ch. Home: 2136 Kodiak Dr NE Atlanta GA 30345-4150

CASEY, AMY L. communications educator, film producer; b. NJ, June 27, 1974; d. Francis P. and Anne C. Loeber. BA in English, Comm., Le Moyne Coll., Syracuse, NY, 1996; MA in TV, Radio, Film Prodn., Syracuse U., 1998. Lectr., instr. of record SUNY, New Paltz, 1999—2000; asst. prof. Pine Manor Coll., Chestnut Hill, Mass., 2001—. Tchg. asst. Syracuse U., 1997—98; freelance film prodr. Blind Id Prodns., Boston, 2002—, Spiritmantis Prodns., Dorchester, Mass., 2002—. Prodr.: (films) Consequences Before Dawn, Four and Little Brother. Mem.: Chronicle Higher Edn. (assoc.). Home: 717 Watertown St Newtonville MA 02460 Office: Pine Manor Coll 400 Heath St Chestnut Hill MA 02467 Personal E-mail: amylcasey@hotmail.com. E-mail: caseya@pmc.edu.

CASEY, BERNARD J. lawyer; b. June 4, 1942; s. Andrew J. and Theresa (Lennon) C.; m. Kathleen A. Wall; children: Brendan, B. John. AB, Providence Coll., 1964; JD, Catholic U., 1967. Bar: R.I. 1967, D.C. 1971, Calif. 2003, U.S. Supreme Ct. 1972, U.S. Cir. Ct. (D.C. cir., 4th cir., 6th cir.). Assoc. Gall, Lane & Powell, Washington, 1971-76, ptnr., 1976, Reed Smith LLP, Washington, 1976—. Bd. dirs. Cath. Charities, 1994-99, chmn., 1997-98. Served to capt. AUS, 1967-71. Decorated Bronze Star medal. Mem. ABA (litigation com.), Barristers, Lawyers Club, Univ. Club (bd. govs. 1989-97, pres. 1990-92), Chevy Chase Country Club. Roman Catholic. Home: 4700 Connecticut Ave NW Apt 607 Washington DC 20008-5613 Office: Reed Smith LLP East Tower 1301 K St NW Ste 1100 Washington DC 20005-3317

CASEY, BONNIE MAE, artist, educator; b. Chgo., Ill., Aug. 1, 1932; d. Edward Frances Kusch, Bessie Elaine (Moulding) Kusch; m. George Daniel Casey, Feb. 21, 1953; children: Cheryl Ann, Stuart Evan, Charles Alan. Student, Am. Acad. Art, Chgo., Harper Jr. Coll., Schamburg, Ill. Instr. Village Art Sch., Skokie, Ill., 1965—80, Art Barn, Elk Grove Village, Ill., 1978—83, Mountain Artists Guild, Prescott, Ariz., 1985—2000, Pima Coll., Green Valley, Ariz. Bd. dirs. Southwestern Artists Assn.; mem. visual arts com. Prescott Fine Arts Assn., 1995—2003; bd. dirs. Prescott Arts and Humanities, 1986—99; tchr. Vaison la Romaine, France, San Mignel del Allende, Mexico; instr. in field; organizer, arts curator Open Space Alliance, 2001. Contbr. articles to Fine Art Collector mag., Wine and Dine mag.; prin. works include painting 9-11-01, 2001, logo design, Arts and Humanities Coun., Prescott, Town of Chino Valley, Ariz., mural design, History of Chino Valley, one-woman shows include Mitchell Mus., Trinidad, Colo., 1992, 50 Yr. Art Retrospective, 2003, exhibited in group shows at Phippen Mus. Named Curator of Yr., Prescott Fine Arts Assn.; recipient Grumbacher Gold medal, 1992, 1996, Gov.'s award nominee, Ariz. Commn. on Arts; featured artist 50 Yrs. of Art Retrospective, Prescott Fine Arts Gallery, 2003. Mem.: Southwestern Artists Assn., Western Acad. Women Artists (historian), Oil Painters Am., Phippen Mus., Prescott Art Docents (docent auditor 1996—2003). Avocation: travel. Home: 3380 N Yuma Dr Chino Valley AZ 86323

CASEY, BRIAN LEE, music educator; b. Central City, Nebr., Jan. 13, 1964; s. Gerald Wayne and Bettye Ritchie Casey. BA in Music Edn., Harding U., 1984; MusM, U. Del., 2001. Music tchr. Christian Schs. of Beaumont, Beaumont, Tex., 1985—87, Boyd-Buchanan Sch., Chattanooga, 1987—88; loan adjustor, report specialist Delaware Trust Co./Meridian Bank, Wilmington, Del., 1988—93; tech. coord. CoreStates Bank, Phila., 1993—98; dir. of bands McKean H.S., Wilmington, 2000—01; instr. of music, dir. bands and choruses Highland (Kans.) C.C., 2001—. Clinician-instrumental music Oreg. Trail League, Axtell, Kans., 2002; dir. Newark (Del.) Cmty. Band, 1999—2001, Cecil County Choral Soc., Elkton, Md., 2000—01. Composer: (songs) (hymns) Into Our Hands Hymnal, 2000; contbr. articles to Image and Worship Leader mags. Mem. Atchison Cmty. Orch., Atchison, 2002—; instrumentalist A-town Brass Ensemble, Atchison, 2002—; mem. Kansas City Wind Symphony, Philharmonia Orch., Liberty Symphony Orch.; vocalist First Christian Ch. Praise Team, Atchison, Kans., 2002—. Mem.: Am. Choral Dirs. Assn., Coll. Band Dirs. Nat. Assn., Am. Fedn. Musicians. Avocation: bicycling, hiking, racquetball, travel, audiophilia. Home: 1100 Kansas Ave Atchison KS 66002 Office: Highland Cmty Coll 606 W Main Highland KS 66035

CASEY, EDWARD DENNIS, newspaper editor; b. Binghamton, N.Y., Apr. 16, 1931; s. Edwin John and Agnes Mary (Casey) C.; m. E. Jacqueline Wilson, July 13, 1957; children: Daniel, Jeanne, Edward, John. BA, St. Bonaventure U., 1952; postgrad., Armed Forces Pub. Information Sch., 1953, Syracuse U. Grad. Sch. Journalism, 1954. News editor Sun-Bull., Binghamton, 1960-65; editor Daily Advance, Dover, N.J., 1965-71; exec. editor Capital-Gazette Newspapers, Annapolis, Md., 1971—. Vice pres. Community Chest of Anne Arundel County.; bd. dirs. Annapolis Symphony Orch.; pres. Annapolis/Bywater Boys and Girls Club. With U.S. Army, 1952-54. Recipient Pub. Service award A.P., 1964, Nat. Headliners award, 1965 Mem. AP Mng. Editors Assn., Am. Soc. Newspaper Editors, KC, Sigma Delta Chi. Roman Catholic. Home: 1517 Riverdale Dr Annapolis MD 21401-5839 Office: The Capital 2000 Capital Dr Annapolis MD 21401-3157

CASEY, EDWARD PAUL, manufacturing company executive; b. Boston, Feb. 23, 1930; s. Edward J. and Virginia (Paul) C.; m. Patricia Pinkham, June 23, 1950 (dec. Nov. 1996); children: Patricia Estes Casey Shepherd, Tyler Casey White, Jennifer Paul Casey Lowden, Sheila Pinkham Casey McManus, Virginia Louise Casey Pettengill; m. Mary Ann Patton, Mar. 28, 1998. AB, Yale U., 1952; MBA, Harvard Coll., 1955. With Davidson Rubber Co., Dover, N.H., 1950-65; COO McCord Corp., Detroit, 1965-78, pres., 1965-78, COO Ex-Cell-O Corp., Troy, Mich., 1978-81, CEO, pres., 1981-86, chmn., 1983-86; vice chmn. Textron Inc., 1986-87; pres. E. Paul Casey Assocs., 1987-89; mng. gen. ptnr. Metapoint Ptnrs., Peabody, Mass., 1989-97, chmn., 1997—. Trustee Henry Ford Health Care Sys., Detroit; pres. Hobe Sound Cmty. Chest, Fla. Mem. Chief Execs. Orgn., Harvard Bus. Sch. Club So. Fla., N.Y. Yacht Club (N.Y.C.), Yondotega Club (Detroit), Ea. Yacht Club (Marblehead, Mass.), Jupiter Island Club, Hobe Sound Yacht Club (Jupiter Island, Fla.). Home: 330 S Beach Rd Hobe Sound FL 33455-2606

CASEY, ELLEN PATRICIA, obstetric and gynecological nurse; b. Cambridge, Mass., Nov. 10, 1960; d. John Michael and Ellen Louise (Clark) O'Connor. BSN, Boston Coll., 1982. Staff nurse med. surgery The Cambridge Hosp., 1982-85, staff nurse ob-gyn. and newborn nursery, 1985-86, staff nurse

ICU, 1986-87, staff nurse ob-gyn. NBN, 1987—. CPR instr. The Cambridge Hosp., 1983—, unit preceptor, 1987—; instr. neonatal resuscitation program, 1992. Mem. Mass. Nurses' Assn. Avocations: cross stitch, travel. Home: 66 Dow Ave Arlington MA 02476-7106

CASEY, GAVIN, former stock exchange executive; b. 1947; Various positions to dep. chief exec. County Nat. West Bank, from 1972; fin. dir. Smith New Court, 1989-94, COO, 1994; chief adminstrv. officer for internat. equities Merrill Lynch, 1994-96; chief exec. The Stock Exch., London, 1996—2000; non-exec. dir. & chmn. several companies, 2001—.*

CASEY, GENEVIEVE M. librarian, educator; b. Mpls., July 13, 1916; d. Eugene James and Cecelia (Malerich) C. BS, Coll. St. Catherine, St. Paul, 1937; MA, U. Mich., 1956. Mem. staff Detroit Pub. Library, 1937-46, 48-61, chief extension dept., 1948-61; Mich. State librarian Lansing, 1961-67; prof. library scis. Wayne State U., 1967-83. Fulbright prof. U. Brasilia, 1979; librarian U.S. Army Libraries, ETO, 1946-47; scholar in residence U. Mo. Sch. Library and Informational Sci., 1985. Author: Library Service to the Aging, 1983, Father Clem Kern, Conscience of Detroit, 1989. Named Mich. Librarian of Yr. 1978. Mem. ALA (pres. Assn. Hosp. and Instn. Libraries 1961-62, pres. library edn. div. 1970-72), Pub. Library Assn. (pres. 1976-78), Mich. Library Assn., Am. Assn. Library Schs. (pres. 1979) Address: 1121 Torrey Rd Grosse Pointe MI 48236-2358

CASEY, GEORGE EDWARD, JR., construction executive; b. Cohasset, Mass., July 15, 1946; s. George Edward and Dorothea Evelyn (Oliver) C.; m. Linda Lauraine Bail, Aug. 24, 1974; children: Peter, Matthew. BS in Environ. Engring., Rensselaer Poly. Inst., 1968; MBA, U. Pa., 1974. V.p. Charter Adv. Co., Jacksonville, Fla., 1974-76; owner, mgr. Casey & Co., Brunswick, Maine, 1976-79; project mgr. Toll Bros., Inc., Huntingdon Valley, Pa., 1979-81, v.p., 1981-84, sr. v.p., 1984-89; v.p. Realen Homes, Berwyn, Pa., 1989-91, sr. v.p., chief fin. officer, 1992-95; pres., CEO Zaring Homes, Inc., Cin., 1995-98, also bd. dirs.; pres. South Fla. ops. Arvida, Weston, 1998—2003, pres. Mid Atlantic ops., 2003—. Bd. dirs. Robertson Bros. Builders, Inc., BuildIQ, McStain Enterprises, Inc. Trustee Am. Boychoir Sch., Princeton, NJ, 1986-88, Fla. Edn. Found., 2000-03, chmn. ULI Rsrch. Neighborhood coun., 1999-2002. Lt. USN, 1968-72, Vietnam. Decorated Bronze Star. Mem. Urban Land Inst., Wharton Real Estate Ctr., Patroons Rensselaer, Weston Hills Country Club, Lauderdale Yacht Club, Beta Gamma Sigma. Republican. Avocations: ocean sailboat racing, skiing, golfing, traveling. Home: 3619 English Gardens Charlotte NC 28226 Office: Arvida 517 S Sharon Amity Rd Ste 100 Charlotte NC 28211

CASEY, GEORGE W. military career officer; b. Japan, July 22, 1948; BS in Internat. Rels., Georgetown U., 1970; MA in Internat. Rels., U. Denver. Commd. 2nd lt. U.S. Army, 1970, advanced through grades to lt. gen., 1996, various positions, 1970-82, exec. officer 1st Battalion, 10th Infantry, 4th Divsn., 1982-84, sec. gen. staff 4th Infantry Divsn., 1984-85, comdr. 1st Battalion, 10th Infantry, 4th Divsn., 1985-87; congl. program coord. Office of the Chief of Legis. Liaison, Washington, 1988-89; spl. ast. to Chief of Staff U.S. Army, Washington, 1989-91, chief of staff 1st Cavalry Divsn. Ft. Hood, Tex., 1991-93, comdr. 3rd Brigade, 1st Cavalry Divsn., 1993-95; asst. chief of staff G-3 (ops.), V Corps. U.S. Army Europe, 1995; chief of staff V Corps. U.S. Army Europe and Seventh Army, Germany, 1995-96, asst. divsn. comdr. 1st Armored Divsn., 1996-97; asst. dep. dir. politico-mil. affairs J-5 The Joint Staff, Washington, 1997-99; comdg. gen. U.S. Army Europe, 1st Armored Divsn., 1999—2001; dir. for strategic plans, policy Joint Staff, Washington, 2001—03, dir., 2003—. Decorated Legion of Merit with 2 oak leaf clusters, Def. Meritorious Svc. medal, Meritorious Svc. medal, Army Commendation medal with oak leaf cluster, Army Achievement medal with oak leaf cluster. Office: OCJCS 9999 Joint Staff Rm 2D844 Washington DC 20318-9999*

CASEY, GERARD WILLIAM, retired food products company executive, lawyer; b. N.Y.C., Nov. 12, 1942; s. William Gerard and Bridget (Carmody) C.; children: Jennifer, William, Thomas, Andrew, Patrick. BS in History, Fordham Coll., 1963; MA in History, NYU, 1966; JD, Fordham U., 1967. Bar: N.Y. 1969. Criminal investigator U.S. Army, U.S., Korea, 1967-69; v.p., gen. counsel Pepsi Cola Co., PepsiCo, Inc., Puchase, NY, 1969—2001. Mem. Friendly Sons of St. Patrick, White Plains, 1987—; dir., chmn. bd. mgrs. Lincoln Hall Sch., Lincolndale, N.Y., 1988-91. Mem. ABA, N.Y. State Bar Assn., Am. Corp. Counsel Assn., Vets. Foreign Wars. Roman Catholic.

CASEY, H(ORACE) CRAIG, JR., electrical engineering educator; b. Houston, Dec. 4, 1934; s. H.c. and Mae (Walls) C.; m. Jean Anne Merritt, June 14, 1960 (div. 1983); children: Anne, Michael; m. Jacqueline Lucas, Jan. 22, 1983. BSEE, Okla. State U., 1957; MSEE, Stanford U., 1959, PhD, 1964. Devel. engr. Hewlett-Packard, Palo Alto, Calif., 1957-62; mem. tech. staff Bell Labs., Murray Hill, N.J., 1964-79; chmn. dept. elec. engring. Duke U., Durham, N.C., 1979-94, prof. elec. engring., 1979—. Mem. Dept. of Def. Adv. Group Electron Devices, Washington, 1975-79; bd. dirs. Acme Elec., 1984-91. Author: Heterostructure Lasers, 1978, Devices for Integrated Circuits: Silicon and III-V Compounds, 1999. Fellow IEEE (pres. Electron Devices Soc. 1988-89, editor centennial issue Trans. on Electron Devices 1984); mem. Am. Phys. Soc. Office: Duke U Dept Elec Engring Durham NC 27706 E-mail: hcc@ee.duke.edu.

CASEY, JAMES B. librarian; b. Syracuse, NY, June 29, 1950; s. John Joseph and Louise (Countryman) C.; m. Diane Dates, Nov. 16, 1984; children: Nathan, Jeremy. MLS, SUNY, Geneseo, 1973; MA, Cleve. State U., 1979; PhD, Case Western Res. U., 1985. Head librarian Ohio Hist. Soc., Columbus, 1983-84; dir. Pickaway County Pub. Libr., Circleville, Ohio, 1984-92, Oak Lawn (Ill.) Libr., 1992—. Editor: Libby Prison Autograph Book, 1984. Grant rev. com. Ill. State Libr. Constrn., 1999—. Recipient Heath Lit. award, Am. Numis. Assn., 1980, Heath Literary award, Am. Numismatic Assn., 1980. Mem. ALA (mem. coun. 1996—), Ill. Libr. Assn. (pub. policy com. 2001—). Avocation: numismatics. Home: 9717 Parkside Ave Oak Lawn IL 60453-3657 Office: Oak Lawn Libr 9427 Raymond Ave Oak Lawn IL 60453-2405 E-mail: drjbc92@lib.oak-lawn.il.us.

CASEY, JAMES FRANCIS, management consultant; b. Boston, May 22, 1935; s. James Francis and Elizabeth Mary (MacNeil) C.; m. Margaret Ann Flaherty, Jan. 22, 1977. Sales mgr. Xerox Corp., Stamford, Conn., 1963-79; dir. product mktg. Computervision Corp., Bedford, Mass., 1979-82; v.p. CTX Corp., Sunnyvale, Calif., 1982-83; sr. mktg. exec. Hewlett-Packard Corp., Palo Alto, Calif., 1983-86; group mgr. Digital Equipment Corp., Maynard, Mass., 1986-92; mng. ptnr. Synergy Cons., Los Altos, Calif., 1992—; mem., dir., mem. exec. com. Agincourt Capital Plc. Dublin, 1997-2000; pres., bd. dirs. Mcpl. Utility Dist., State of Tex., 1998—. Cons. numerous clients, including IBM, Hewlett-Packard Co., Ceridian, Lexis-Nexis, E-Commerce Group, Reed Elsevier Plc. Group, others. Patron San Francisco Opera Co., 1982-99, San Francisco Orch., 1982-91; Friend Boston Symphony Orch., 1976-81; contbr. Austin Symphony Orch. Mem. Am. Mgmt. Assn. (bd. dirs. 1962-65), Am. Electronic Assn. (mktg. com. chmn. 1989-91), Hill Country Intergroup Assn. (chmn. bd. overseers), Del. Valley Reprographic Soc. (v.p.1965-69), Jr. C. of C. (pres. Phila. chpt. 1965-66). Home and Office: 10123 Treasure Island Dr Austin TX 78730-3559 Fax: 512-346-6024. E-mail: jcasey@austin.rr.com.

CASEY, JOHN ALEXANDER, lawyer; b. Wisconsin Rapids, Wis., Apr. 7, 1945; s. Samuel Alexander and Ardean A. AB, Stanford U., 1967; JD, U. Mich., 1970. Ptnr. Quarles & Brady, Milw., 1970—. Office: Quarles & Brady 411 E Wisconsin Ave Ste 2040 Milwaukee WI 53202-4497 E-mail: jac@quarles.com.

CASEY, JOHN DUDLEY, writer, English language educator; b. Worcester, Mass., Jan. 18, 1939; s. Joseph Edward and Constance (Dudley) C.; m. Jane Barnes, June 10, 1967 (div. 1980); children: Maud, Nell; m. Rosamond Pinchot Pittman, June 27, 1982; children: Clare, Julia. BA, Harvard U., 1962, LLB, 1965; MFA, U. Iowa, 1968. Prof. English U. Va., Charlottesville, 1972-92, U. Iowa, 1998, U. Va., 1999—. Lit. executor Estate of Breece D'J Pancake, 1979—; resident scholar Am. Acad. in Rome, 1990-91. Author: An American Romance, 1977 (runner up Ernest Hemingway award 1977), Testimony and Demeanor, 1979 (Friends Am. Lit. award 1980), Spartina, 1989 (Nat. Book award 1989), Supper at the Black Pearl, 1995, The Half-life of Happiness, 1998; co-translator: You're an Animal, Viskovitz (By A. Boffa), 2002; contbr. stories (O. Henry award 1989), essays maj. nat. mags. including New Yorker, Esquire. With USAR, 1959-60. Guggenheim fellow, 1979-80, Nat. Endowment for Arts fellow, 1983, resident Am. Acad. in Rome, 1990-91; grantee Strauss living AAAL, 1992-97. Mem. PEN. Avocation: rowing. Office: U Va Dept English Bryan Hall Charlottesville VA 22903-3289 also: Michael Carlisle Carlisle & Co 24 E 64th St New York NY 10021-7201

CASEY, JOHN FREDERICK, lawyer; b. Martinsville, Ohio, May 19, 1939; s. Raymond J. and Esther E. (Read) C.; m. Karen S. Bollenbacher, Sept. 2, 1978. BS, Ohio State U., 1961, JD, 1965. Bar: Ohio, 1965, U.S. Dist. Ct. (so. dist.) Ohio 1967, D.C. 1981, U.S. Tax Ct. 1967. Ptnr. Means, Bichimer & Burkholder, Columbus, Ohio, 1965-70, Chamblin, Snyder & Casey, Columbus, 1971-75; pvt. practice Columbus, 1976-83, 91-93; ptnr., shareholder Wiles, Doucher, Van Buren, Boyle & Casey, Columbus, 1984-85; ptnr. Thompson, Hine & Flory, Columbus, 1986-88, Casey & Christensen, Columbus, 1989, Casey, McFadden & Winner, Columbus, 1990, Harris, McClellan, Binau & Cox, Columbus, 1994; prin. John F. Casey, A Legal Profl. Assn., 1994—. Adv. coun. mem. U.S. Small Bus. Adminstrn., Columbus, 1985-93. Mem. gov.'s Ohio Farmland Preservation Task Force, 1996-97. Mem. Ohio State Bar Assn. (bd. govs. 1990-99, emeritus 2000, estate planning, trust, and probate law sect.), Fin. Planning Assn. Ctrl. Ohio (founding trustee 2000), Columbus Bar Found., Ohio State U. Coll. Law (nat. coun.), Greater Columbus C. of C. Avocations: gardening, golf. Home: 207 E Whittier St Columbus OH 43206-2638 Office: Lucas Predergast Albright Gibson & Newman 600 S High St Columbus OH 43215-5656

CASEY, KAREN ANNE, banker; b. Bklyn., Oct. 5, 1955; d. Stanley Joseph and Helen Katherine (Kosowski) Mozeleski; m. Dennis Joseph Casey, May 14, 1977; children: Christopher Sean, Erin Michelle. BBA, Baruch Coll., CUNY, 1977. CPA, N.Y., CFP. Jr. acct. Coopers & Lybrand, N.Y.C., 1977-78, sr. acct., 1978-79, supr., 1979-81; asst. fin. contr. Gulf Internat. Bank, N.Y.C., 1981-82, fin. contr., 1982; v.p., fin. contr. Allied Irish Banks plc, N.Y.C., 1982-87, sr. v.p., fin. contr., 1988-89, sr. v.p. mgmt. support svcs., 1989-92, sr. v.p., CFO, 1992-94, sr. v.p., head pvt. fin. svcs., 1994-2001, sr. v.p., head retail and bus. banking, 2001—. Bank rep. to Inst. Cert. Fin. Planners, 1991—. Mem. AICPA. Roman Catholic. Avocations: gardening, golf, tennis, reading. Office: Allied Irish Banks Plc 405 Park Ave New York NY 10022-4405

CASEY, KATHLEEN HEIRICH, lawyer, educator; AB, Radcliffe Coll., 1959; JD, St. John's U., 1974. Bar: N.Y. 1975, U.S. Dist. Ct. (so. and ea. dists.) N.Y. 1975, U.S. Ct. Appeals (2d cir.) 1975, U.S. Supreme Ct. 1976, Calif. 1989, U.S. Dist. Ct. (no. dist.) Calif. 1989, U.S. Ct. Appeals (9th cir.) 1989. Asst. corp. counsel N.Y.C. Law Dept., 1974-76; appellate counsel Div. Criminal Justice, N.Y.C., 1976-77; asst. atty. gen. N.Y. Law Dept., 1977-78; prin. law clk. N.Y. State Supreme Ct., N.Y.C., 1978-81; assoc. Colton, Weissberg, Hartnick, Yamin & Sheresky, N.Y.C., 1981-83, Milbank, Tweed, Hadley & McCloy, N.Y.C., 1983-86; pvt. practice, N.Y.C., 1986—, Orinda, Calif., 1989—; adj. faculty N.Y. Law Sch., N.Y.C., 1983-85; mem. family dispute resolution and comml. panels Am. Arbitration Assn., N.Y.C., 1984—, Nat. Assn. Securities Dealers, 1989—. Contbr. articles to profl. jours. Nassau County committeewoman, 1972-79, 81-87; mem. law com. Nassau County Democratic Party, 1977-81, Navy League of U.S., N.Y. Council, 1980. Fellow Am. Acad. Matrimonial Law; mem. ABA, Calif. Bar Assn., Queen's Bench, N.Y. Women's Bar Assn. (officer 1985—), N.Y. State Bar Assn., Assn. of Bar of City of N.Y., N.Y.C. Lawyers Assn. Office: 120 Village Sq Ste 64 Orinda CA 94563-2502

CASEY, KENNETH LYMAN, neurologist; b. Ogden, Utah, Apr. 16, 1935; s. Kenneth Lafayette and Lyzena (Payne) C.; m. Jean Louise Madsen, June 21, 1958; children— Tena Jeanette, Kenneth Lyman, Teresa Louise. BA, Whitman Coll., Walla Walla, Wash., 1957; MD with honors, U. Wash., Seattle, 1961. Diplomate Am. Bd. Neurology and Psychiatry. Intern in medicine Cornell U. Med. Center-N.Y. Hosp., 1961-62; USPHS officer lab. neurophysiology NIMH, 1962-64; fellow in psychology McGill U., Montreal, Que., Can., 1964-66; mem. faculty U. Mich. Med. Sch., Ann Arbor, 1966—, prof. neurology and physiology, 1978—; resident in neurology U. Mich Hosp., 1971-74; chief neurology svc. VA Med. Center, Ann Arbor, 1979—2002, cons. in neurology, 2002—. Sci. bd. dirs. Nat. Inst. Dental Rsch., 1984-88; sci. adv. com. Santa Fe Neurol. Inst., 1984—. Assoc. editor Clin. Jour. Pain, 1984—, Pain, 1991—; editor-in-chief Am. Pain Soc. Jour. Pain Forum, 1991-99; contbr. articles to profl. jours., chpts. to books. Grantee, NIH, 1966—; Spl. fellow, 1964—66, Bristol-Myers rsch. grantee, 1988—93. Fellow Am. Acad. Neurology; mem. Am. Physiol. Soc., Am. Acad. Neurology, Am. Neurol. Assn., Soc. Neurosci., Am. Pain Soc. (pres. 1984-85, F.W.L. Kerr Basic Sci. Rsch. award and lecture 1998), Wayne County Med. Soc. (Rhoades lectr. and medalist 2002), Internat. Assn. Study Pain, Phi Beta Kappa, Sigma Xi, Alpha Omega Alpha (J.J. Bonica disting. lectr. and awardee 1991). Unitarian Universalist. Achievements include named lectureship established in his honor by Pfizer Co. in 2002. Home: 2775 Heatherway St Ann Arbor MI 48104-2852 Office: VA Med Ctr Neurology Svc 2215 Fuller Rd Ann Arbor MI 48105-2300 E-mail: kencasey@umich.edu.

CASEY, MICHEAL WILLIAM, portfolio manager; b. Indpls., Oct. 4, 1955; s. Robert Ellsworth and Mildred Jane (Holland) C.; m. Christine McCarthy, Apr. 11, 1991 (div. Sept. 1997); children: Kathleen Maura, Thomas Robert, James Patrick. AB, Ind. U., 1978; MS, London Sch. Econs., 1985; PhD, New Sch. Social Rsch., 1996. Translator U. Graz, Austria, 1978-80; tchr. math. Peace Corps, Sierra Leone, 1981-83; economist McCarthy, Crisanti & Matthei, N.Y.C., 1986—90; internat. economist Maria Ramierz, Inc., N.Y.C., 1990—96; portfolio mgr. Federated Investors, N.Y.C., 1996—2002; pres. Discretionary Global Mgmt., N.Y.C., 2002—. Mem. Am. Econ. Assn., Ea. Econ. Assn., Internat. Economists Club N.Y. E-mail: mikecasey@rcn.com.

CASEY, PATRICIA CAROLYN, retired social worker; b. Roseburg, Oreg., Aug. 27, 1936; d. Clarence Wayne and Mary Elizabeth (Frederick) Park; m. John Joseph Casey, Aug. 4, 1956 (div. 1980); children: Kathleen, Brian; m. Mark Preston Siegel, Mar. 14, 1987. BA in Social Work, San Francisco State U., 1962; MSW, Portland State U., 1989. Caseworker Santa Clara County Welfare, San Jose, Calif., 1962-63; community svc. worker Mid Willamette Valley Community Action Agy., Salem, Oreg., 1974-78; asst. dir. Marion Polk Yamhill Coun. on Aging, Salem, 1978-83; teen mother program dir. YWCA, Salem, 1984-87; counselor Clackamas Family Ct. Svc., Oregon City, Oreg., 1987-88; social work intern VA Hosp., Portland, Oreg., 1988, Oreg. Health Scis. U., Portland, 1988-89; med. social worker Salem Hosp., 1989—2001; ret., 2001. Commr. Polk County Welfare Dept., Dallas, Oreg., 1964-67; planning coun. MWV Manpower Consortium, Salem, 1975-83. Producer: (TV program) Sr. Citizens Today, 1980-81; prodn. coord.: (documentary films) Special Special, 1981, Conspiracy of Silence, 1981. Commr. Marion-Polk Boundary Commn., Salem, 1977-81; mem. Oreg. Women's Polit. Caucus, Salem, 1987—. Named Outstanding Young Woman of Am. of 1968, Oreg. Med. Social Worker of Yr., 1998, Oreg. Hosp. Social Svc. Dirs. Assn. Mem. Nat. Assn. Social Workers, City Club. Democrat. Unitarian Universalist. Home: 482 Ewald Ave SE Salem OR 97302-4700 E-mail: marknpat@open.org.

CASEY, PATRICK ANTHONY, lawyer; b. Apr. 20, 1944; s. Ivanhoe and Eutimia (Casados) C.; m. Gail Marie Johns, Aug. 1, 1970; children: Christopher Gaelen, Matthew Colin. BA, N.Mex. State U., 1970; JD, U. Ariz., 1973. Bar: N.Mex. 1973, Ariz. 1973, U.S. Dist. Ct. N.Mex. 1973, U.S. Ct. Appeals (10th cir.) 1979, U.S. Supreme Ct. 1980, U.S. Dist. Ct. Ariz. 1999. Assoc. Bachicha & Casey, Santa Fe, 1973-76; Patrick A. Casey, P.A. Santa Fe, 1976—. Bd. dirs. Santa Fe Sch. Arts and Crafts, 1974, Santa Fe Animal Shelter, 1975-81, Cath. Charities of Santa Fe, 1979-82, Old Santa Fe Assn., 1979-88, Santa Fe Fiesta Coun., 1982—; bd. dirs. United Way, 1986-89, N.Mex. State U. Found., 1985-93. With USN, 1961—67. Mem.: VFW, Vietnam Vets. of Am., Am. Legion, Hispanic Bar Assn., Bar Assn. 1st Jud. Dist. (pres. 1980), N.Mex. Trial Lawyers Assn. (dir. 1977—79, treas. 1979—83, pres. 1983—84, dir. 1985—, treas. 2000—01), Western Trial Lawyers Assn. (gov. 1987—90, bd. dirs. 1988—91, officer 1990—95, pres. 1996—97, treas. 2000—), ABA, ATLA (state del. 1988—89, bd. govs. 1990—91, 1993—95), B.P.O. Elks. Office: 1421 Luisa St Ste P Santa Fe NM 87505-4073

CASEY, PAUL ARNOLD, writer, composer, photographer, producer, director; b. Inglewood, Calif., Dec. 10, 1934; s. Paul Franklyn and Orilee Corinne (Gray) C. AA, BA, UCLA. Pres., genetics cons. CSCA Internat., Sun Valley, Calif.; pres., tech. advisor Solenz Corp., Wilmington, Del. Dramaturg L.A. Playwrights Group, 1996; dir., CEO L.A. Playwrights Group. Author poetry: Songs of Youth, 1951; writer TV show Lassie, 1969; photographer wildlife: Girl Scouts Calendar, 1995; developer breed of cat: Calif. Spangled, 1971-86; inventor power lens, 1967; prodr. (theatrical) Original Sins; dir.: (film and theatrical prodn.) Smoke Screen; playwright: Anna & Ylenna; playwright Jewel Box Theatre Ctr. for Performing Arts, 1998-02. With USN, 1953-54. Recipient Nat. Humane Soc. award, 1965; U.S. Govt. scholar, 1954. Mem. L.A. Playwrights Group (gen. sec. 1995-96, bd. dirs. 1998-99). Avocations: wildlife photography, astronomy, archaeology, natural power systems technology. Office: CSCA International PO Box 368 Sun Valley CA 91353-0368

CASEY, PAULA JEAN, former prosecutor; b. Charleston, Ark., Feb. 16, 1951; d. Arthur Clinton and Mildred Aleene (Underwood) C.; m. Gilbert Louis Glover II, Mar. 13, 1981. BA, Ea. Cen. (Okla.) U., 1973; JD, U. Ark., 1977. Staff atty. Ctrl. Ark. Legal Services, Hot Springs, Ark., 1977-79; dep. pub. defender 6th Jud. Dist. Pub. Defender, Little Rock, 1979; clinic supr. U. Ark. at Little Rock Law Sch., 1979-81, asst. prof., 1981-84, assoc. prof., 1984-92, prof., 1992-93, assoc. dean, 1986-90; legis. dir., chief counsel U.S. Senator Dale Bumpers, 1990-92; lobbyist Ark. Bar Assn., 1993; U.S. atty. Ea. Dist. Ark., 1993—2001; prof. law U. Ark. at Little Rock Law Sch., 2001—. Cons. for juvenile affairs 6th Jud. Dist. Judges, Ark., 1987. Author, editor: Poverty Law Practice Manual, 1985. Sec. Pulaski County Dem. Com., Little Rock, 1984-89; mem. Ark. Dem. Com., 1984-89; mem. Juvenile Adv. Group, Little Rock, 1985-89; mem. Gov.'s Task Force on Juvenile Cts., Ark., 1987; chmn. Ark. Dem. Jud. Com., 1987; bd. dirs. Ctrl. Ark. Legal Svcs., Little Rock, 1986-89. Named One of Top 100 Women in Ark., Ark. Bus. Pubs., 1996, 98, 99; recipient Gale Pettus Pontz award U. Ark.-Fayetteville Law Sch. Women Students Assn., 1994, award of merit Organized Crime Drug Enforcement Task Force, 1997. Fellow Ark. Bar Found. (bd. dirs.); mem. Ark. Bar Assn. (del. 1986-90), Am. Inns Ct., Overton Am. Inns of Ct., 8th Cir. Ct. Appeals (fed. adv. comm. 2001-05). Democrat. Office: U Ark at Little Rock Sch Law 1201 McMath Blvd Little Rock AR 72202 E-mail: pjcasey@ualr.edu.

CASEY, REBECCA LYNN, music educator; b. Bluffton, Ohio, Jan. 28, 1963; d. Lloyd Charles and Marjorie Ann Harnishfeger; m. Clayton James Casey, May 14, 1988; 1 child, Leah Erin. BMusic in Piano Performance/Music Edn., Ohio No. U., Ada, 1985; MMusic in Piano, U. Cin., 1987, DMUsical Arts in Piano, 1997. Nat. cert. tchr. music. Music instr. Findlay (Ohio) City Schs., 1988-92; instr. music Ohio No. U., 1994-97, asst. prof. music, 1997—. Mem. Coll. Music Soc., Ohio Music Tchrs. Assn., Music Tchrs. Nat. Assn. Home: 548 Hefner Dr Lima OH 45801-3861 E-mail: r-casey@onu.edu.

CASEY, RITA JO ANN, nursing administrator; b. Paulsboro, N.J., Nov. 19, 1942; d. George John and Louise Elizabeth (De Santis) Centofanti; m. Robert Joseph Casey, June 5, 1965; children: Joseph, Thomas. Diploma, Woman's Med. Coll. Hosp., 1963; BSN, Holy Family Coll., 1985. RN Pa. Staff nurse Woman's Med. Coll. Hosp., Phila., 1963-68; sch. nurse Bensalem (Pa.) Sch. Dist., 1979-83; dir. health svcs. Holy Family Coll., Phila., 1983—. Sec. HFC Student Svcs. Mid. States Evaluation Com., Phila., 1991-92, 2000—; mem. HFC Cmty. Svc. Adv. Bd., 1991—; mem. HFC Strategic Planning Com., Phila., 1993; CPR instr. ARC, 1991—, first aid instr., 2000—. Chartered orgn. rep. Boy Scouts Am., 1976—; pres. Bensalem H.S. Football Booster Club, 1988-89; sec. Bensalem Meml. Day Parade Com., 1989-94; chmn. Phila. Archdiocesan Cath. Com. Scouting, 1992—; co-founder Bensalem Tricentennial Commemorative Hist. Trail, 1993. Mem. Am. Coll. Health Assocs., Nat. Assn. Sch. Nurses, Nat. Athletic Trainers Assn., Southeast Coll. Health Nurses Assn., Med. Coll. Pa. Sch. Nursing Alumni Assn. (banquet chair 1963-94). Roman Catholic. Avocations: reading, boating, fishing, crocheting, needlepoint. Home: 2370 Ogden Ave Bensalem PA 19020-5211 Office: Holy Family U Grant & Frankford Aves Philadelphia PA 19114

CASEY, ROBERT FITZGERALD, lawyer, educator; b. Chgo., Sept. 28, 1943; s. John Francis and Gertrude Bernice (Fitzgerald) C. BA, Notre Dame U., 1964, MBA, 1987; MS in Edn., No. Ill. U., 1968; JD, DePaul U., 1974, LLM, 1980. Bar: Ill. 1975, Ind. 1976, Fla. 1977, U.S. Tax Ct. 1981, U.S. Ct. Claims 1982, U.S. Ct. Mil. Appeals 1982, U.S. Supreme Ct. 1982. Pvt. practice, 1975—; counselor Consolidated HS Dist. 230, guidance dir., dean students, ret., 2002; atty. USNR, 1981—2001; ret., 2001. Blue/gold liaison officer U.S. Naval Acad. Lt. comdr. JAGC USNR. Mem. Ill. Bar Assn., Ind. Bar Assn., Notre Dame Club (Chgo.), Phi Alpha Delta. Roman Catholic. Home: 403 Country Club Dr Mchenry IL 60050-5677 Office: PO Box 11354 1210 White Oak Dr South Bend IN 46634-0354 Fax: 574-287-9872.

CASEY, ROBERT REISCH, lawyer; b. New Orleans, May 19, 1946; s. Robert Taylor Casey and Merlyn Lucille (Reisch) Weilbaecher. BBA in Acctg. magna cum laude, U. Notre Dame, 1968; JD, Tulane U., 1971; LLM in Taxation, NYU, 1973. Bar: La. 1971. Ptnr. Jones, Walker, Waechter, Poitevent, Carrere and Denegre, Baton Rouge, 1971—. Mem. bd. editors Tulane Law Rev., 1970-71. Mem. ABA (chmn. partnership com. tax sect. 1982-84, mem. coun. 1985-88, sec. 1988-90, vice chmn. 1989-91), Order of Coif, Beta Gamma Sigma, Beta Alpha Psi. Avocations: golf, French horn. E-mail: rcasey@joneswalker.com.

CASEY, ROGER NEAL, English language educator, director, actor, academic administrator; b. Spartanburg, S.C., Feb. 28, 1961; s. Ruskin Winfred and Barbara Nell (Lawson) C. BA, Furman U., 1983; MA, Fla. State U., 1988, PhD, 1991. Instr. English Fla. State U., Tallahassee, 1986-91; prof. English Birmingham (Ala.)-So. Coll., 1991—2000; dean of faculty Rollins Coll., Winter Park, Fla., 2000—. Actor, dir. Birmingham Festival Theatre, 1992-99; dir. Associated Colls. of the South Summer Tchrs. Workshop, 1993-2000, mem. coun. of deans, 2000—. Artistic dir. Off-St. Players Theatre, Inc., Tallahassee, 1987-91; prodr. Tallahassee Playwright Festival, Tallahassee, 1987-88; actor Off-St. Players Tallahassee, 1987-91; author: Textual Vehicles, 1997; contbr. articles to profl. jours. Recipient Best Actor award Tallahassee Theatre, 1989, Meritorious Teaching award Fla. State U., 1989, Leadership 3-M, 1992-93; Rotary scholar Furman U., 1979-83, Pipkin scholar, 1982-83; Mid. East travel fellow Patillo Found., 1985; grantee Ala. Humanities Found., 1992-94; Kellogg Nat. Leadership Fellowship, 1994-97; Excellence in Teaching award Birmingham So. Coll., 1993. Mem. MLA, Am. Coun. Acad. Deans, Kellogg Fellows Leadership Alliance, Phi Beta Kappa. Democrat. Avocations: travel, antique collecting, cars. Office: 1000 Holt Ave Winter Park FL 35254

CASEY, SUE (SUZANNE MARGUERITE PHILIPS), actress, real estate broker; b. L.A., Apr. 8, 1926; d. Burke Dewey and Mildred Louise (Hansen) Philips; children: Colleen O'Shaughnessy, John Joseph Durant III, Christopher Kent Durant, Diane M. Kelly; m. Jack Hoffmann (div.); stepchildren: Joy Hoffmann Molloy, Kristen Hoffmann Blutman. Student, UCLA Extension, 1972-75. Lic. real estate broker and saleswoman, Calif. With Coldwell Banker/Jon Douglas Co., Beverly Hills, Calif. Appeared in numerous movies, including swimming in 5 Esther Williams films, singing and dancing in over 20 films, Goldwyn Girl, 1945-47; Star Is Born, Surf Terror, 1965, Catalina Caper, 1967, Happy Ending, Secrets of Monte Carlo, The Family Jewels, Marriage Young Stockbroker, The Big Circus, The Errand Boy, Two Weeks in Another Town, Paint Your Wagon, Camelot, Evil Speak, 1981, Swamp Country, Ladies Man, Lucky Lady, Annie Get Your Gun, Show Boat, Carpetbaggers, Rear Window, Breakfast at Tiffany's, The Scarf, Main Event, Brady Bunch Sequel, 1996, American Beauty, 1999; appeared in TV shows, including Hunter, Hotel, Hart to Hart, White Shadow, Sunny Valley, Lucy, Gunsmoke, Arnie, Marcus Welby, Sky Terror, Dallas, Days of Our Lives, Unsolved Mysteries, Rosie O'Neill, Haggerty, Emergency, California Fever, I Love Lucy, Farmer's Daughter, Beverly Hillbillies, Delta House, Bodies of Evidence, The Faculty, Divorce Court, Colgate Comedy Shows, Carol Burnett Shows, Red Skelton Show, Roy Bolger Show, All Star Revues, Bob Hope Specials, Ann Southern Show, Family Medical Center, Red Shoe Diaries, What Love Sees, Boy Meets World, 1997, Diagnosis Murder, 1999; has appeared in over 200 TV commls.; stage appearances include Picnic, Goodnight Ladies. Ball chmn. The Footlighters, Inc., 1971-73, 93-94, press chmn., 1972-73, pres., 1982-83, 98-99, parliamentarian, 1983-94, 99-00,02-03, hospitality chmn., 1992-93. Named Ms. Sr. Am. of L.A., 1993. Mem. AFTRA, SAG, Actors Equity Assn. Office: Coldwell Banker 301 N Canon Dr Beverly Hills CA 90210-4722 E-mail: caseysue@aol.com.

CASEY, THOMAS CLARK, trust company executive, investment advisor; b. Akron, Ohio, Dec. 17, 1929; s. Thomas W. and Portia (Clark) C.; m. Tanya Seely, July 2, 1958 (dec.); children: Tate, Doug, John, Gary, Brad, Nina, Mimi,

Tom W.; m. Suzanne Rhodes, Apr. 5, 1997. BA, Bowdoin Coll.; MBA, Stanford U.; cert. fin. svcs. counselor, Northwestern U. Sales rep. Acushnet Co., New Bedford, Mass., 1953-55, Reeves Rubber Co., San Clemente, Calif., 1957-59; gen. mgr. Polymer Corp., Santa Ana, Calif., 1959-61; from trust officer to pres. 1st Am. Trust Co., Santa Ana, 1965-95; registered investment advisor, 1995—. Bd. dir. First Am. Trust F.S.B., 1999—. Trustee Bowdoin Coll., 1989—2001; bd. dirs. Hoag Meml. Hosp., 1982- 95; chmn. Orange County com. So. Calif. Bldg. Fund, 1986—94; co-chmn. capital expenditure rev. com. United Way, 1982—; chair bd. dirs. Hoag Hosp. Found., 1995—99; bd. dirs. Newport Ctr. Assn., 1976—2002, pres., 1979; trustee Newport-Mesa Unified Sch. Dist., 1969—77, pres., 1975—77; bd. dirs. Orange County Bar Found., 1995—2001; bd. dirs., mem. exec. com. Alzheimers Assn. Orange County, 2000—. Named Outstanding Vol. of Yr., Orange County, Calif., 2003. Mem.: Orange County Soc. Investment Mgrs., Calif. Bankers Assn., L.A. Soc. Fin. Analysts, Soc. Preservation New Eng. Antiquities. Avocations: golf, skiing, snorkeling, travel. Office: Ste 1100 620 Newport Ctr Dr Newport Beach CA 92660-8011

CASEY, THOMAS JEFFERSON, business executive, investment banker, venture capitalist, environmental entrepreneur; Student, U.S. Naval Acad., 1964—65; MBA, Harvard U., 1970; postgrad., U. London/Am. U., 1997—. Pres./COO New Eng. Furniture Group, Boston, 1968-71; chmn./CEO Commonwealth Industries, Inc., N.Y.C., 1971-75; pres./gen. mgr. Damson Oil Corp. AMEX, N.Y.C. and Houston, 1975-80; founder/chmn./CEO The Sovereign Group, Ltd., N.Y.C., 1980-90; chmn., CEO Quantum Renewable Energy, N.Y.C., 1991—. Guest lectr. Wharton Grad. Sch. Bus. Adminstrn.; former mem faculty internat. mgmt. Northeastern U. Sch. Mgmt. and Adminstrn., Boston; sr. fin./investment advisor to several Fortun 500 cos., sovereign fgn. govts. and internat. fin. instns. Avocations: golf, tennis, sailing, skiing, flying. Office: Quantum Renewable Energy Inc 730 5th Ave Ste 900 New York NY 10019-4105

CASEY, THOMAS WARREN, graphic design company executive, architect; b. Columbus, Ohio, Dec. 9, 1942; s. Warren Vale and Martha Elizabeth (Greene) C.; m. Susan Henrietta Davis, Oct. 1, 1966. BArch, Ohio State U., 1966. Registered architect, N.Y. Draftsman Skidmore Owings & Merrill, Chgo., 1964-66; architect U.S. Peace Corps, Tanzania, 1966-69; designer Brooks Barr Graeber & White, Austin, Tex., 1969-71, Hardy Holzman Pfeiffer, N.Y.C., 1971-73; design dir. Paul Arthur & Assoc., N.Y.C., 1973-74; designer Page, Artibrio & Resen, N.Y.C., 1974-79; ptnr. Greenboam & Casey Assocs., Inc., N.Y.C., 1979-94, The Casey Group, New Canaan, Conn., 1994—. Con. Conn. Trust for Hist. Preservation, 1995, U.S. Gen. Svc. Adminstrn., 1996, juror Print Casebook Awards, N.Y.C., 1988, Hotel Sales & Mktg. Assoc., N.Y.C., 1987-90, Soc. Environ. Graphic Design 1997 Design Awards; adj. prof. N.J. Sch. of Architecture, Newark, 1980-82; guest lectr. Harvard U., Boston, 1982, U. Cin., 1990. Pres. Friends of New Canaan Libr., 1998—2001. Recipient Print Casebook 7 award, 1987. Mem.: AIA (hist. resources com. Acad. of Architecture for Health), Soc. Environ. Graphic Design (bd. dirs. 1985—90, 1996—99, pres. 1988—89), Am. Assn. Airport Execs. (assoc.; N.E. chpt.), Conn. Trust for Hist. Preservation, S.W. Pks. and Monuments Assn. (life), Gridiron Club of New Canaan, Dutch Treat Club. Democrat. Fax: (203) 966-0250. E-mail: tscasey@webquill.com.

CASEY-BEICH, MICHEAL LOUANNA, theater director, artist; b. Bloomington, Ill., Oct. 9, 1950; d. David George and Anne Lee (Williamson) Casey; m. Otto Gerkin Beich II, Dec. 24, 1977 (div. Mar. 10, 1991); children: Otto Gerkin III, Rossie Anne, Oscar Casey. Grad. H.S., Bloomington, 1969. Dir. The Rock of Praisers and ROPpp Events, Biblelympics, 1996, 2000, 2004, ROPp-pELTON Summr Tennis, 2003—, other ROPppELTON events. Avocations: cello, ballet, gardening, harp. Home: 1107 E Jefferson St Bloomington IL 61701-4144 Office: Authentic ROPpp Art Galleries Studio 1107 E Jefferson St Bloomington IL 61701-4144 *Psalm 144: "Blessed be the Lord my strength, which teacheth my hands to war, and my fingers to fight".*

CASH, ALAN SHERWIN, electronics assembly specialist; b. Chgo., Oct. 28, 1938; s. Edward A. and Mildred M. Cash; m. Carole M. Hoffman, July 31, 1966; children: Susan, Jody. BS in Indsl. Engring., U. Ill., 1961; MBA, Northwestern U., 1969. Registered profl. engr., Calif.; cert. electrostatic discharge engr. and technician; cert. IRCA provisional auditor, Internat. Register Cert. Auditors. Sr. process engr. Cook Electric Co., Morton Grove, Ill., 1973-75; sr. indsl. engr. Motorola, Carol Stream, Ill., 1975-77; supr. indsl. engring. def. sys. divsn. Northrop Grumman, Rolling Meadows, Ill., 1977-80, mgr. tech. svcs. def. sys. divsn., 1980-84, mgr. advance mfg. tech. def. sys. divsn., 1984-86, mgr. tng. ctr. def. sys. divsn., 1986-95; ops. program engr., 1995—; category C instr., examiner, ISO 9000 lead assessor Dept. Def., electrostatic discharge site coord., 1997—. Mem. Nat. Soldering Std. Working Coms., 1990-93, mem. IPC J-stds. coms.-001, 002, 003, 004, 005, 006, 1990—, mem. IPC Term and Definitions Com. Mem. Nat. Assn. Radio and Telecomm. Engrs. (cert. engr., technician), Inst. Indsl. Engring. (pres. North Suburban Ill. chpt. 1982-83, program chmn. Dist. 8, 1984—, spouses program chmn. 1992 internat. conv., Midwest chpt. ESD assoc. libr. chmn., pres. 1998, treas. 2000), Inst. Indsl. Engrs., Assn. Old Crows, U. Ill. Alumni Assn., Northwestern U. Alumni Assn., Northwestern Club Chgo., ESD Assn. (Midwest chpt.). Office: Northrop Grumman ESSS-DSD 600 Hicks Rd Rolling Meadows IL 60008-1098

CASH, DEAN W. military career officer; b. N.J., Dec. 28, 1946; m. Dee Cash; children: Mindy, Caitlin. Grad., Kearney State Coll., 1971; Masters Degree, Va. Poly. Inst., 1979; grad., Command and Gen. Staff Coll., 1986, Indsl. Coll. Armed Forces, 1992. Commd. officer U.S. Army Infantry, 1971, advanced through grades to maj. gen., airborne inf. platoon leader 1st Bn., 60th Inf., weapons platoon leader, co. exec. officer Bn. S-1/Bn. S-2, co. comdr., S-3 tng. officer 3d Inf. Regiment Ft. Myer, Va., with Spl. Warfare Ctr. Ft. Bragg, N.C., with 82d Airborne Divsn., divsn. G-3 plans officer, dep. G-3, exec. officer 1/505th; with U.S. Army Europe (USAREUR) Staff, 1986-89; comdr. 4th Bn., 8th Inf. U.S. Army, Sandhofen, Germany, 1989; infantry sys. team chief Dept. of the Army; comdr. 2d Brigate, 1st Armored Divsn. U.S. Army, Baumholder, Germany, 1993, comdr. ops. group Combat Maneuver Tng. Ctr. Hohenfels, Germany, asst. divsn. comdr. for maneuver of the 4th Inf. Divsn. Ft. Hood, Tex., 1996 97, comdg. gen. Nat. Tng. Ctr. and Ft. Irwin, 1997-98, comdr. U.S. Army Alaska, 1998-2000; dir. joint experimentation J9 U.S. Atlantic Command, Norfolk, 2000—. Decorated Legion of Merit, Bronze Star, Meritorious Svc. medal, Army Commendation medal, S.W. Asia Svc. medal, Armed Forces Expeditionary medal. Office: US Atlantic Command Jt Experimentation J9 Norfolk VA 23511-3488

CASH, DEANNA GAIL, retired nursing educator; b. Coatesville, Pa., Nov. 28, 1940; Diploma, Jackson Meml. Hosp., 1961; BS, Fla. State U., 1964; MN, UCLA, 1968; EdD, Nova U., Ft. Lauderdale, Fla., 1983. Staff and relief charge nurse Naples (Fla.) Comty. Hosp., 1961-62; staff nurse Glendale (Calif.) Comty. Hosp., 1964-65; instr. Knapp Coll. Nursing, Santa Barbara, Calif., 1965-66; staff nurse, team leader Kaiser Found. Hosp., Bellflower, Calif., 1968-69; prof. nursing El Camino Coll., Torrance, Calif., 1969-96, ret., 1996. Coord., instr. Internat. RN Rev. course, L.A., 1974-76; mentor statewide nursing program, Long Beach, Calif., 1981-88; clin. performance in nursing exam. evaluator Western Performance Assessment Ctr., Long Beach, 1981-96. Mem. ANA.

CASH, JEFFREY MARC, commercial artist, photographer; b. Bklyn., Jan. 17, 1961; s. Murray and Dorothy Cash; m. Cindy Michele Kannett, May 15, 1988; children: Stephanie, Taylor. At, LI U., 1980, Sullivan Cmty. Coll., 1981. Owner C. Cash Distbg., Monticello, NY, 1988—; artist-owner Art Studio of Jeff Cash, 1990—, JC Designs, 1990—. Artist on campus Mt. St. Mary Coll. Prints, paintings and illustrated guides. Contr. fundraiser art Am. Cancer Soc., Kingston, NY, 2003—. Recipient fine art and photography prizes, Orange County Fair, 2002. Mem.: Catskill Art Soc., Middletown Art Group, Orange County Art Fedn. Avocations: music, writing. Home: PO Box 390 Kiamesha Lake NY 12751

CASH, LAVERNE (CYNTHIA CASH), physicist; b. Statesville, N.C., Oct. 7, 1956; d. William J. and Martha Lee (Stroud) C. BS, Appalachian State U., 1979; MS, Clemson U., 1982; AA, Mitchell C.C., 1976; PhD, Johns Hopkins U., 1999. Physicist U.S. Army Material Systems Analysis Activity, Aberdeen Proving Ground, Md., 1984-88; rsch. physicist U.S. Army Edgewood Rsch., Devel. and Engring. Ctr., Aberdeen Proving Ground, 1988—. Contbr. articles to profl. publs. Mem. Oak Grove Bapt. Ch, Bel Air, Md., singer in choir, sound engr., numerous others. Mem. Am. Phys. Soc., Sigma Phi Sigma, Pi Mu Epsilon, Phi Theta Kappa, Gamma Beta Phi. Baptist. Home: 100 Drexel Dr Bel Air MD 21014-2002 E-mail: lavernecash@yahoo.com.

CASH, RODERICK WILLIAM, JR., lawyer; b. N.Y.C., June 13, 1949; s. Roderick William and Fannie (Pisciotta) C.; m. Paulis Neila Waber, June 24, 1978; 1 child, Mason Roderick. B.A., Wesleyan U., 1971; J.D., Am. U., Washington, 1974. Bar: D.C. 1975, U.S. Dist. Ct. D.C. 1976, U.S. Ct. Appeals (Fed. cir.) 1976, U.S. Ct. Customs and Patent Appeals 1977, U.S. Customs Ct. 1978, U.S. Supreme Ct. 1978, U.S. Ct. Claims 1980, U.S. Tax Ct. 1980, N.Y. 1981. Atty., U.S. Customs Service, Dept. Treasury, Washington, 1975-77; ptnr. Cash & Cash, Washington, 1977-85; assoc. O'Connell & Kittrell, Washington, 1985-86; pres. Roderick Cash, Inc., 1986—; panelist Sta. WYCB Med. Malpractice Today, 1982, Sec., Dupont Circle Neighborhood Ecology Corp., Washington, 1976. Mem. Assn. Trial Lawyers Am., D.C. Bar Assn., Assn. Trial Attys. D.C., Assn. of Plaintiffs Trial Attys. (bd. govs. 1983—). Club: Univ. (Washington). Home: 3915 Huntington St NW Washington DC 20015-1913 Office: O'Connell & Kittrell 1710 Rhode Island Ave NW Washington DC 20036-3007

CASHDOLLAR, CHARLES DAVID, history educator; b. Pitts., Oct. 24, 1943; s. Chester Leroy and Grace Eleanor (Magee) C.; m. Donna Evans, Aug. 24, 1968. BS, Indiana U. of Pa., 1965; MA, U. Pa., 1966, PhD, 1969. Fellow U. Pa., Phila., 1965-68, instr. history, 1969; asst. prof. history Indiana U. of Pa., 1969-74, assoc. prof. history, 1974-77, prof. history, 1977-94, univ. prof. history, 1994—, dir. liberal studies, 1987-93. Author: The Transformation of Theology, 1830-1890: Positivism and Protestant Thought in Britain and America, 1989, A Spiritual Home: Life in British and American Reformed Congregations, 1830-1915, 2000; contbr. articles to profl. jours. Am. Coun. Learned Socs. Rsch. fellow, 1995-96. Mem. Am. Hist. Assn., Pa. Hist. Assn. (book review editor 1977-87, coun. mem. 1986—, sec. 1993—), Am. Soc. of Ch. History, Orgn. Am. Historians. Democrat. Presbyterian. Avocation: music. Home: 215 Church St Indiana PA 15701-2124 Office: Indiana Univ of Pa Dept History Indiana PA 15705-0001

CASHEN, HENRY CHRISTOPHER, II, lawyer, former government official; b. June 25, 1939; s. Raymond and Catherine C.; m. Leslie Renchard, June 28, 1967 (div. 1982); children: Raymond II, Hayley Holloway, Henry Christopher III; m. Diana Knowles Pryor, June 4, 1988. AB, Brown U., 1961; grad., U. Mich. Law Sch., 1963. Bar: Mich. 1964, U.S. Supreme Ct. 1969. Mem. firm Dickinson, Wright, McKean & Cudlip, Detroit, 1964-69; dep. counsel to Pres. U.S., Washington, 1969-70, dep. asst. to, 1970-73; mem. firm Dickstein, Shapiro & Morin (and predecessor), Washington, 1973—. Mem. Barristers Soc., D.C. Mich. bar assns., Fed. Nat. Mortgage Assn. (bd. dirs. 1985-91), Country Club of Detroit, The Brook, Met. Club, Chevy Chase Club, Psi Upsilon Phi Delta Phi. Republican. Roman Catholic. Office: 2101 L St NW Washington DC 20037-1526 E-mail: cashenh@dsmo.com.

CASHMAN, GIDEON, lawyer; b. N.Y.C., Sept. 10, 1929; s. Abba Morris and Rachel (Cashman) Cashman; m. Kathryn Batchelder, 1985; children: Adam Parker, Lindsey Avril, Emily Parker Hyle. AB, NYU, 1951; JD, Columbia U., 1954. Bar: D.C. 1954, N.Y. 1954. Asst. counsel Waterfront Commn. N.Y., 1954-55; asst. U.S. atty. criminal divsn. So. Dist. Ct. N.Y., 1958-61, chief criminal apls., 1959-61; assoc. Christy Perkins & Christy, N.Y.C., 1961-63; sr. ptnr. Pryor, Cashman, Sherman & Flynn LLP, N.Y.C., 1963—. Lectr. trial tactics Practicing Law Inst.; bd. dirs. Irvington Inst. for Med. Rsch. Trustee Friars Found., Heart Rsch. Found., Eugene O'Neill Teatre Ctr. 1st lt. U.S. Army, judge advocate Gen.'s Corps, 1955-58. Mem. ABA, N.Y. State Bar Assn., Assn. Bar City N.Y., N.Y. County Lawyers Assn., Friars Club (N.Y.C.). Jewish. Home: 812 Park Ave New York NY 10021-2759 Office: 410 Park Ave New York NY 10022-4441

CASHMAN, MICHAEL RICHARD, small business owner; b. Owatonna, Minn., Sept. 26, 1926; s. Michael Richard and Mary (Quinn) C.; m. Antje Katrin Paulus, Jan. 22, 1972 (div. 1983); children: Janice Katrin, Joshua Paulus, Nina Carolin. BS, U.S. Mcht. Marine Acad., 1947; BA, U. Minn., 1951; MBA, Harvard U., 1953. Regional mgr. Air Products & Chems., Inc., Allentown, Pa., 1959-64, then pres. so. div. Washington, 1964-68; mng. dir. Air Products & Chems., Inc. Europe, Brussels, 1968-72; internat. v.p. Airco Indsl. Gasses, Brussels, 1972-79; pres. Continental Elevator Co., Denver, 1979-81; assoc. Moore & Co., Denver, 1981-84; prin. Cashman & Co., Denver, 1984—. Committeeman Denver Rep. Com., 1986—, congl. candidate, 1988; chmn. "Two Forks or Dust" Ad Hoc Citizens Com.. Lt. (j.g.) USN, 1953-55. Mem. Bldg. Owners and Mgrs. Assn., Colo. Harvard Bus. Sch. Club, Am. Rights Union, Royal Golf de Belgique, Belgian Shooting Club, Rotary, Soc. St. George, Phi Beta Kappa. Avocations: skiing, golf, sailing, guitar, opera. Home: 2512 S University Blvd Apt 802 Denver CO 80210-6152

CASHMAN, SUZANNE BOYER, health services administrator, educator; b. Phila., Apr. 14, 1947; d. Vincent Saul and Ethel (Wolf) Boyer; m. Daniel Cashman, Jan. 16, 1971; children: Adam, Rebecca, David. BA, Tufts U., 1969; MS, Cornell U., 1973; ScD, Harvard U., 1980. Sr. analyst Urban Sys. Rsch., Cambridge, Mass., 1979-82; cons. Mass. Dept. Pub. Health, Boston, 1982-83; spl. asst. to v.p. Brigham and Women's Hosp., Boston, 1983-85; assoc. dir. rsch. Boston U. Office Spl. Projects, 1985-89; asst. prof. Boston U. Sch. Pub. Health, 1985-96; evaluator Cmty. Oriented Primary Care, Boston, 1989-91; assoc. dir. Ctr. for Cmty. Responsive Care, Boston, 1991-97; pub. health cons. U. Mass. Med. Ctr., Worcester, 1998; assoc. prof. dept. family medicine, cmty. health Med. Sch. U. Mass., Worcester, 1999—, asst. dir. preventive medicine residency, 1999—. Cons. Acad. Health Ctrs., Derby, Conn., Columbia, SC, Atlanta, Balt., 1995—97; conf. planner New Eng. Rural Health Roundtable. Co-editor: Community Oriented Primary Care, 1998; contbr. articles to profl. jours. Mem. leadership tng. program., sec. alumni orgn. com. NCCJ, Boston, 1995—2002; sec. bd. exec. com., conf. planner Cmty.-Campus Partnerships for Health and New England Rural Health Roundtable; bd. mem. Assn. Tchrs. of Preventive Medicine; mem. bd. dirs. Cmty. Ptnrs., Inc. Mem. APHA, New Eng. Pub. Health Assn., Assn. Tchrs. Preventive Medicine (conf. planner, bd. dirs.). Avocations: ballet dancing, sewing, cooking, jogging, gardening. Home: 17 Calvin Rd Newtonville MA 02460-2104 Office: U Mass Med Ctr Dept Family Medicine 55 Lake Ave N Worcester MA 01655-0002 E-mail: suzanne.cashman@umassmed.edu.

CASHMAN, TYRONE MCNALLY, philosophy educator, consultant; b. Mpls., Minn., Feb. 13, 1938; s. Edwin James and Mary McNally Cashman. BA, MA, St. Louis U.; PhD, Columbia U., 1964—74. Dir. wind energy devel. Office Gov. Calif., Sacramento, 1977—79; pres. Am. Wind Energy Assn., Washington, 1979—81, Point Found., San Rafael, Calif., 1994—96, Solar Economy Inst., Mill Valley, Calif., 1982—2003; adj. faculty U. San Francisco, 2003—. Cons. New Energy Found., Tokyo, 1993—95. Author: (articles) Whole Earth Magazine. D-Liberal. Roman Catholic. Avocation: hiking.

CASHMORE, ANTHONY, biologist, educator; BS, U. Auckland, New Zealand, 1962, MS, 1963, PhD, 1966. Postdoctoral rschr. MRC Lab. Molecular Biology U. Cambridge, England; postdoctoral rschr. U. Calif., Berkely; mem. faculty Rockefeller U., N.Y.C.; Robert I. Williams prof. biology and dir. Plant Sci. Inst. U. Pa., Phila. Contbr. articles to profl. jours.; mem. editl. bd. Plant Molecular Biology, The Plant Jour. Mem.: NAS. Office: Dept Biology U Pa 105 Mudd Bldg Philadelphia PA 19104*

CASIDA, JOHN EDWARD, entomology educator; b. Phoenix, Dec. 22, 1929; s. Lester Earl and Ruth (Barnes) Casida; m. Katherine Faustine Monson, June 16, 1956; children: Mark Earl, Eric Gerhard. BS, U. Wis., 1951, MS, 1952, PhD, 1954; D (hon.), U. Buenos Aires, 1997. Research asst. U. Wis., 1951-53, mem. faculty, 1954-63, prof. entomology, 1959-63, U. Calif.-Berkeley, 1964—; scholar-in-residence Bellagio Study and Conf. Center, Rockefeller Found., Lake Como, Italy, 1978. Messenger lectr. Cornell U., 1985; Sterling B. Hendricks lectr. USDA and Am. Chem. Soc., 1992; dir. Environ. Chemistry and Toxicology Lab., U. Calif., Berkeley, 1964—; William Muriece Hoskins chair in chem. and molecular entomology U. Calif., Berkeley, 1996—, faculty rsch. lectr., 1998; lectr. in sci. Third World Acad. Scis., Buenos Aires, 1997. Author: rsch. publs. With USAF, 1953. Named Jeffery lectr., U. New South Wales, Australia, 1983; recipient medal, 7th Internat. Congress Plant Protection, Paris, 1970, Disting. Svc. award, USDA, 1988, Wolf prize in Agrl., 1993, Koro-Sho prize, Pesticide Sci. Soc. Japan, 1995; fellow Haight traveling fellow, 1958—59, Guggenheim fellow, 1970—71. Fellow: Entomol. Soc. (Bussart Meml. award 1989); mem.: NAS, Soc. Environ. Toxicology and Chemistry (Founder's award 1994), Am. Chem. Soc. (Internat. award rsch. pesticide chemistry 1970, Spencer award in agrl. and food chemistry 1978), Soc. Toxicology (hon.), Royal Soc. UK (fgn). Home: 1570 La Vereda Rd Berkeley CA 94708-2036

CASIDA, KATI, artist; b. Viroqua, Wis., Mar. 28, 1931; d. Gerhard Aniel and Eloise Margaret (Nedland) Monson; m. John Edward Casida, Jne 16, 1956; children: Mark Earl, Eric Gerhard. BS in Art Edn., U. Wis., 1953. Tchr. art Beaver Dam (Wis.) Schs., 1954-55, Upsala Coll., East Orange, N.J., 1955-56, Spring Harbor Sch., Madison, Wis., 1960, Adult Vocat. Sch., Madison, 1961; freelance artist, sculptor Berkeley, Calif., 1963—. Founder Nordic 5 Arts, San Francisco Bay area, 1993X. Sculpture commns. include pub. art, Oakland, Calif., Viroqua, Wis., San Francisco, Palo Alto, Calif., Dallas, Brea, Calif., Santa Clara, Calif.; invitational solo sculpture exhbn. Gallery 555, Oakland Mus., 2002-2003; contbr. articles to Hellenic Jour., 1974—. Recipient Pub. Art Sculpture award Divsn. Cultural Arts, City of Oakland, Calif., 1992. Mem. Internat. Sculpture, Pacific Rim Sculpture Group, Calif. Soc. Printmakers, Headlands for Arts, Nat. Mus. Women in Arts, Kala-Printmakers, Greek Cypriots No. Calif. Avocations: greek folk dancing, travel, photography. Home: 1570 La Vereda Rd Berkeley CA 94708-2036

CASILLAS, MARK, lawyer; b. Santa Monica, Calif., July 8, 1953; s. Rudolph and Elvia C.; m. Natalia Settembrini, June 2, 1984. BA in History, Loyola U., L.A., 1976; JD, Harvard U., 1979. Bar: N.Y. 1982, Calif. 1983. Clk. to chief judge U.S. Ct. Appeals (10th cir.), Santa Fe, 1979-80; assoc. Breed, Abbott & Morgan, N.Y.C., 1980-82; counsel Bank of Am. Nat. Trust and Savs. Assn., San Francisco, 1982-84; assoc. Lillick & Charles, San Francisco, 1984-87, ptnr., 1988-95, Russin & Vecchi LLP, San Francisco, 1995-96; of counsel LeBoeuf, Lamb, Greene & MacRae, LLP, San Francisco, 1997-2000; atty. Wilson Sonsini Goodrich & Rosati, Palo Alto, Calif., 2000—. Counsel Internat. Bankers Assn. in Calif., L.A., 1984-89, 94-97. Co-author: California Limited Liability Company: Forms and Practice Manual, 1994; mng. editor Harvard Civil Rights-Civil Liberties Law Rev., 1978-79. Mem. ABA (apptd. mem. airfin. subcom. 1991—), N.Y. Bar Assn., Calif. Bar Assn. (vice-chmn. fin. instn. com. 1987-88), Internat. Bar Assn., The Japan Soc., Bankers Club (bd. dirs. 1996—, pres. 2003-). Avocations: skiing, travel. Office: Wilson Sonsini Goodrich & Rosati 650 Page Mill Rd Palo Alto CA 94304 E-mail: mcasillas@wsgr.com.

CASINI, JANE SLOAN, wholesale distribution executive; b. Richmond, Va., Sept. 22, 1947; d. James Turner and Jane Patrick (Coleman) Sloan; m. Mauro Casini (div.). Student, Villa Mercede, Florence, Italy. Owner, Richmond and Washington; retailer; leather salesman. Bd. dirs. Va. Home for Boys, Richmond, 1991. Home: 5621 Cary St Rd Richmond VA 23226 Office: Jane Casini 5407 Lakeside Ave Richmond VA 23228

CASKIE, WILLIAM WIRT, accountant, securities broker; b. N.Y.C., May 9, 1945; s. John Minor and Rosa Maria (Marchese) C.; BS in Physics, Georgetown U., 1967; MBA in Ops. Research, NYU, 1970; BS magna cum laude in Acctg., Golden Gate U., 1976. Tchr. math. N.Y.C. pub. schs., 1968-71; statistician Fed. Res. Bank of San Francisco, 1972-74; pvt. practice acctg., L.A., 1977— ; registered rep. Fin. Network Investment Corp., 1986-92, H.D. Vest Fin. Svcs., 1993—. Mem. Inland Soc. Tax Cons., Nat. Assn. Enrolled Agts., Calif. Soc. Enrolled Agts., Mensa, H.D. Vest Fin. Svcs. Home and Office: 3121 S Barrington Ave Apt 4 Los Angeles CA 90066-1185

CASLER, FREDERICK CLAIR, SR., academic administrator, law enforcement educator; b. Corry, Pa., Mar. 7, 1946; s. Clair O. and Helen M. (Church) C.; m. Janice L. Newrick, Nov. 26, 1983; 1 child, Frederick Clair Jr. AA, Miami-Dade Jr. Coll., 1970; BGS, Rollins Coll., 1975, MS in Criminal Justice, 1979; cert., Kissimmee Police Acad., 1974, 88; PhD in Bus. Adminstrn., Fla. Christian U., 2002. Cert. tchr., Fla. Tchr. criminal justice Orange County Schs., Orlando, Fla.; tchr., work experience coord. Osceola County Schs., Kissimmee, Fla., dep. sheriff, dep. sheriff sgt. res.; police-sch. liaison officer Kissimmee Police Dept./Osceola County Schs.; vocat. adult and community education tchr. Kissimmee Police Acad./Osceola Dist. Schs.; coord., dep. dir. Kissimmee Criminal Justice Acad.; dep. dir. Criminal Justice Acad. Adviser various youth orgns. including SADD, Just Say No Club; cubmaster Boy Scouts Am.; res. dep. sheriff, sgt. Osceola County Sheriff's Office; mem. Osceola County Rep. Exec. Com. Mem.: AARP, NEA, AFL-CIO, NRA (life), U.S. Army-Vets Assn., Law Enforcement Officers Christ, U.S. Dep. Sheriff's Assn., Fla. Sheriff's Assn., Am. Fedn. Tchrs., Am. Criminal Justice Assn., Internat. Conf. Police Chaplains, Fla. Peace Officers Assn., Fla. Criminal Justice Tng. Officers Assn., Osceola County Tchrs. Assn., Fla. Tchrs. Assn., Fla. Assn. Sch. Resource Officers, Nat. Assn. Chiefs of Police, Am. Soc. Law Enforcement Trainers, Internat. Conf. of Police Officers, Am. Fedn. of Police, Son Vets. Fgn. Wars, U.S. Army Vietnam-Era Vets. Assn. (assoc.), Police Acad. Alumni Assn., Am. Police Hall of Fame, Sons Confederate Vets., Sons the Am. Legion, Law Enforcement Officers for Christ, Am. Assn. Christian Counselors, Fla. Police Benevolent Assn., Sons Union Vets. Civil War, Sons VFW of the U.S., Kiwanis (dir.), Moose, Scottish Rite, Shriners, Am. Legion (pst comdr. 1973), Masons, Elks, York Rite, Alpha Omega Epsilon (chpt. pres. 1996), Lambda Alpha Epsilon.

CASNER, TRUMAN SNELL, lawyer; b. Balt., Oct. 9, 1933; s. A. James and Margaret (Snell) Casner; m. Elizabeth Lyons, June 12, 1954 (dec. Aug. 1997); children: Richard Dana, Elizabeth Anne, Abigail Lee; m. Cynthia Ferris Evans, May 29, 1999. BA cum laude, Princeton U., 1955; LLB cum laude, Harvard U., 1958. Bar: Mass. 1958. Law clk. to Chief Justice Raymond Wilkins, Mass. Supreme Judicial Ct., 1958-59; assoc. firm Ropes & Gray, Boston, 1959-68, partner, 1968—, mng. ptnr., 1994-99. Bd. dirs. State St. Corp., State St. Bank and Trust Co. Active Belmont Town Meeting, 1971—95; trustee, exec. com. Belmont Hill Sch., 1966—94, pres., 1985—89, chmn., 1989—2001; sec., trustee, mem. exec. com. Pine Manor Coll., 1973—79; overseer, trustee Boston Mus. Sci., 1981—; trustee Old Dartmouth Hist. Soc. (New Bedford Whaling Mus.), 2000—. Mem.: Am. Law Inst., Tavern Club, Cruising Club of Am., Kittansett Club, Comml. Club of Boston, New Bedford Yacht Club. Episcopalian. Home: 54 Fairgreen Pl Chestnut Hill MA 02467-2710 Office: Ropes & Gray One International Pl Boston MA 02110 E-mail: tcasner@ropesgray.com.

CASO, ADOLPH, publishing company executive; b. Mirabella, Avellino, Italy, Jan. 7, 1934; came to U.S., 1947; s. Raffaele and Prisca (DeLuca) C.; m. Margaret; children: Richard Anthony, Robert Ralph, Liana Cristina. BA, Northeastern U., 1957; AM, Harvard U., 1965. Dir. binlingual edn. Waltham (Mass.) Pub. Schs., 1964-83; pres., editor Branden Pub. Co. Inc., Boston, 1983—. Author: The Straw Obelisk, 1973, Lives of Italian Americans, 1976, Water and Life, 1979, America's Italian Founding Fathers, 1984, Bilingual Two Language Battery of Tests, 1985, Mass Media vs. The Italian Americans, 1986, Issues in Foreign Language and Bilingual Education, 1987, Pages and Windows, 1991; (with Joseph Kinney) Young Rocky--The Life of Rocky Castellani, 1983; co-author: Tuskegee Airmen; contbg. editor: Dante in the 20th Century, 1985; editor: On Crimes and Punishments (Cesare Beccaria), 1985, Romeo and Juliet*Original Text, 1992, Straw Obelisk, 2d edit., 1995, We, The People, 1995, Kaso English to Italian Dictionary, 2003, others. Pres. PTA, Newton, Mass., 1965, Waltham Overseas Studies, 1966-69; founder, pres. Dante U. Found., Boston, 1976—. With Signal Corps, U.S. Army, 1957-62; col. U.S. Army Res., 1963-87. Decorated cavaliere Republic of Italy; Fulbright scholar, 1966; Tchg. fellow Harvard U., Cambridge, Mass., 1964. Mem. Sons of Italy (commr.). Roman Catholic. Avocations: music, art, swimming, walking, italian cuisine. Office: PO Box 81294 Wellesley MA 02481-0003 E-mail: Braden@Braden.com.

CASON, JUNE MACNABB, musician, educator, arts administrator, fundraiser; b. Phila., June 21, 1930; d. Vernon C. and Eleanor (Scarlet) Macnabb; m. Roger Lee Cason, June 12, 1952; children: David Alan, Diane Louise, Nancy Lynn. Student, Eastman Sch. Music, Rochester, N.Y., 1948-52; grad., U. Houston, 1969; postgrad., U. Pa., 1984. Dir. youth chorus St. John's Episcopal Ch., Charleston, W.Va., 1956-63; soloist ch. and music groups Charleston, 1957-63; founder, dir. music summer camp Episcopal Diocese W.Va., 1961-62; founder, gen. mgr., soloist Minikin Opera Co., Wilmington, Del., 1972-87; faculty Wilmington Music Sch., 1973-77; mem. Del. Pro Musica, Wilmington,

1973-77, chmn., 1975-77; dir. music Immanuel Episcopal Ch., Wilmington, 1973-75; instr. music Albert Einstein Acad., Wilmington, 1975-76; v.p. Resource Ctr. for Performing Arts, 1982-86; chmn. Music Consortium New Castle County, 1982-84; devel. dir. Opera Del., 1988-92; trainer, cons. Nonprofit Mgmt. Devel. Ctr., LaSalle U., 1989—; dir. devel. arts and humanities U. Del., 1992-99, MacIntyre Assocs., 1998—. Soloist Christ Ch. Cathedral, Houston, 1963-71, Gilbert and Sullivan Soc., Houston, 1970; pvt. tchr. voice, Houston, 1965-71, Wilmington, Del., 1971-92; tchr. voice San Jacinto Coll., Pasadena, Tex., 1969-71; pres. Del. Classical Showcase, 2001—. Contbr. articles to profl. jours. Pres. Friends of Mt. Harmon, Inc., 2002—. Recipient Theta Eta award U. Rochester, 1952. Mem. Assn. Fundraising Profls. (pres. Brandywine chpt. 1999-2000), Met. Opera Guild, Caesar Rodney Rotary Club, Sigma Alpha Iota (Sword of Honor 1971). Republican. Home and Office: 1125 Grinnell Rd Wilmington DE 19803-5125 E-mail: jcason@udel.edu.

CASON, MARILYNN JEAN, technological institute official, lawyer; b. Denver, May 18, 1943; d. Eugene Martin and Evelyn Lucille (Clark) C.; married. BA in Polit. Sci., Stanford U., 1965; JD, U. Mich., 1969; MBA, Roosevelt U., 1977. Bar: Colo. 1969, Ill. 1973. Assoc. Dawson, Nagel, Sherman & Howard, Denver, 1969-73; atty. Kraft, Inc., Glenview, Ill., 1973-75; corp. counsel Johnson Products Co., Inc., Chgo., 1975-86, v.p., 1977-86, mng. dir. Lagos, Nigeria, 1980-83, v.p. internat. Chgo., 1986-88; v.p., gen. counsel DeVry, Inc., Chgo., 1989-96; sr. v.p. gen. counsel, corp. sec., 1996—. Trustee Arthritis Found., Atlanta, 1993—96, Chgo. Symphony Orch., 1997—2003; bd. dirs. Ill. chpt. Arthritis Found., Chgo., 1979—, chmn., 1991—93; bd. dirs. Internat. House, Chgo., 1986—92, Interfaith House, Chgo., 1996—2002, Ill. Humanities Coun., Chgo., 1987—96, chmn., 1993—96. Mem. ABA, Nat. Bar Assn., Cook County Bar Assn. (pres. community law project 1986-88). Clubs: Stanford (Chgo.) (pres. 1985-87). Home: 3108 Colfax St Evanston IL 60201-1842 Office: DeVry Inc 1 Tower Ln Ste 1000 Oakbrook Terrace IL 60181-4663 E-mail: mcason@devry.com.

CASON, NICA VIRGINIA, nursing educator; b. Edna, Tex. 1 child, Cynthia Diane. Diploma, Lillie Jolly Sch. Nursing, 1965; BSN, U. Tex. Med. Br., Galveston, 1967; MSN, U. So. Miss., 1981. RN, Miss. Pub. health nurse Miss. State Dept. Health, Pascagoula, 1978; nursing instr. Miss. Gulf Coast Community Coll.-Jackson County Campus, Gautier, 1981-84, chair ADN program, 1984—. Col. USAFR, ret. Mem. NOADN, Nat. League Nursing, Sigma Theta Tau, Phi Kappa Phi.

CASON, ROGER LEE, retired chemical company executive, educator, consultant; b. Madison, Wis., Aug. 13, 1930; s. Hulsey and Eloise (Boeker) C.; m. June Ely Macnabb, June 12, 1952; children: David Allan, Diane Louise, Nancy Lynn. BSME with high distinction, U. Rochester, 1951, MS, 1952; MBA, U. Del., 1977, MA in Liberal Studies, 1998. Registered profl. engr., Del. With E.I. DuPont de Nemours & Co., various locations, 1955-92, sr. mech. engr., prodn. supr., mech. supr. Houston, 1963-70, staff bus. analyst Wilmington, Del., 1971-75, bus. analysis mgr., 1975-83, prin. cons., 1983-92; cons. to for profit, non-profit orgns., 1993—. Contbr. articles to profl. jours. Treas. Del. Chamber Music Festival, 2000—. Served with C.E.C., USN, 1952-55. Mem.: Wilmington Power Squadron (comdr. 1988—89, 1995—96, sr. navigator), Nat. Model R.R. Assn. (dir. mid-eastern region 2001—, Master Model Railroader), Tau Beta Pi, Phi Beta Kappa, Sigma Xi (assoc.), Beta Gamma Sigma. Republican. Episcopalian. Home and Office: 1125 Grinnell Rd Wilmington DE 19803-5125

CASPAR, DONALD L.D. biophysics and structural biology educator; b. Ithaca, N.Y., Jan. 8, 1927; s. Caspar V. and Blanche (Dvorak) C.; m. Gwladys Williams, Dec. 20, 1962; children: Emma, David. BA in Physics, Cornell U., 1950; PhD in Biophysics, Yale U., 1955. Postdoctoral fellow Calif. Inst. Tech., 1954-55, MRC Lab. Molecular Biology, Cambridge, Eng., 1955-56; instr. biophysics Yale U., New Haven, 1956-58, asst. prof., 1958-59; rsch. assoc. Harvard U., Cambridge, Mass., 1962-63; lectr. Harvard Med. Sch., Boston, 1963-73; rsch. assoc. in pathology Children's Hosp. Med. Ctr., Boston, 1959-73; prof. of physics, rsch. prof. of structural biology Rosenstiel Basic Med. Scis. Rsch. Ctr., Brandeis U., Waltham, Mass., 1972-94, acting dir., 1987-88; prof. biol. scis. Inst. Molecular Biophysics Fla. State U., 1994—. Mem. biophysics and biophys. chem. study sect. NIH, 1969—73; guest rsch. assoc. in biology Brookhaven Nat. Lab., 1973—, chmn. biology dept. vis. com., 1974—77, mem., 1996—99, mem. neutron users adv. com. biology dept., 1980—81, 1991—97, mem. adv. com. scanning transmission electron microscope facilty, 1985—96, mem. program adv. com. high flux beam reactor physics dept., 1992—97, Haworth disting. scientist, 1994—96; mem. nat. laser users facility steering com. Lab. Laser Energetics U. Rochester, NY, 1981—84; mem. sci. adv. com. European Molecular Biology Lab., Heidelberg, Germany, 1976—81; mem. sic. adv. com. structural biology ctr. Argonne Nat. Lab., 1989—94; mem. adv. bd. Nat. Ctr. Macromolecular Imaging Baylor Coll. Medicine, 1995—2000; mem. editl. com. Ann. Revs. Biophysics and Bioengring., 1970—73; vis. prof. Inst. Molecular Biophysics Fla. State U., 1994; rsch. fellow Japan Soc. Promotion Sci. Inst. Molecular Biology Nagoya U., 1984. Contbr. articles, rsch. papers to profl. publs. Grantee NIH, 1969-88, 2001—, NSF, 1983-86, Guggenheim fellowship, 1994; recipient Outstanding Investigator award Nat. Cancer Inst., 1988-2002. Fellow Am. Acad. Arts and Scis., Biophys. Soc. (pres. 1991-92, nat. lectr. 1985, charter fellow 1999); mem. NAS, Am. Crystallographic Assn. (Fankuchen award 1992). Achievements include research in structural biology of viruses, membranes and protein adaptability. Home: 911 Gardenia Dr Tallahassee FL 32312-3001 Office: Fla State U Inst Molecular Biophysics Tallahassee FL 32306-4380

CASPAR, GEORGE J., III, lawyer; b. 1933; BS, Ohio State U, 1954; LLB, U. Mich., 1957; LLM, NYU, 1958. Bar: Mich. 1957, NY 1962, Conn. 1987. Assoc. White & Case, 1962—65; asst. gen counsel Heublein Inc., Farmington, Conn., 1965—69, sec., gen. counsel, 1972—84, sr. v.p., 1969—71, sec., gen. counsel, 1971—72, v.p., sec., gen. counsel, 1972—84, sr. v.p., 1983—86; assoc. gen. counsel, corp. sec. Travelers Corp., Hartford, Conn., 1986—. Office: Travelers Corp 1 Tower Sq Hartford CT 06183-0001

CASPER, BARRY MICHAEL, physics educator; b. Knoxville, Tenn., Jan. 21, 1939; s. Barry and Florence (Becker) C.; m. Nancy Carolyn Peterson, Aug. 25, 1979; children: Daniel Casper, Benjamin Casper, Michael Casper, Aaron Syverson, Jay Syverson, Kaarin Madigan. BA, Swarthmore Coll., 1960; PhD in Physics, Cornell U., 1966. From asst. prof. to prof. physics Carleton Coll., Northfield, Minn., 1966—; rsch. fellow Stanford U., Calif., Minn., 1973-74, Harvard U., Cambridge, Mass., 1975-76, U. Minn., Mpls., 1976-77, MIT, Cambridge, Mass., 1980-81, U. Calif., San Diego, 1992-93. Policy advisor to U.S. Sen. Paul Wellstone, 1991. Co-author: Revolutions in Physics, 1972, Powerline: First Battle of America's Energy War, 1981; author: Lost in Washington: Finding the Way Back to Democracy in America, 2000. Dir. Nuclear War Graphics Project, Northfield, 1981-89, Minn. Nuclear Weapons Freeze Campaign, 1983-84 Recipient Pub. Citizen award Minn. Pub. Interest Research Group, 1984 Mem. Am. Phys. Soc. (nat. council 1980-83; Forum on Physics and Soc. prize 1984), Fedn. Am. Scientists (nat. council 1970-74, 80-84, 91-95). Home: 100 Nevada St Northfield MN 55057-2341 Office: Carleton College Dept Physics Northfield MN 55057 E-mail: mcasper@carleton.edu.

CASPER, CHARLES B. lawyer; b. Boise, Idaho, June 9, 1952; s. John Blaine and Joyce Lucile (Mercer) C.; m. Brenda Cheryl Bowers, Aug. 28, 1976; children: Timothy L., Jonathan B. BA, Yale U., 1974; JD, U. Va., 1977; MDiv, Princeton Theol. Sem., 1985. Bar: Utah 1977, U.S. Dist. Ct. Utah 1977, U.S. Ct. Appeals (10th cir.) 1978, U.S. Supreme Ct. 1982, Pa. 1985, U.S. Dist. Ct. (ea. dist.) Pa. 1989, U.S. Ct. Appeals (3d cir.) 1989, U.S. Dist. Ct. N.J. 1990, N.J. 1990. Assoc. Fabian & Clendenin, Salt Lake City, 1977-82, shareholder, 1982; assoc. pastor Arch St. United Meth. Ch., Phila., 1985-89; assoc. Montgomery, McCracken, Walker & Rhoads, LLP, Phila., 1989-92, ptnr., 1992—, vice chmn. litigation dept., 1996-98, 2002—. Bd. dirs. Ptnrs. Sacred Places, 1999-2003, chmn., 2003—, Evangelical Svcs. for the Aging Found., 1996-99, United Meth. Neighborhood Svcs., Phila., 1987-93, Parent-Infant Ctr., Phila., 1990-93; com. chair Utah Heritage Found., Salt Lake City, 1979-82; nat. bd. Emergency Food and Shelter Program, 1988-98, chair, 1998—, Phila. (Pa.) bd. Recipient Svc. award Utah Heritage Found., 1982. Mem. ABA, Utah State Bar Assn., N.J. Bar Assn., Pa. Bar Assn., Phila. Bar Assn. Republican. Office: Montgomery McCracken Walker and Rhoads LLP 123 S Broad St Fl 24 Philadelphia PA 19109-1099

CASPER, COREY, physician, researcher; m. Therese S. Casper. BA, Wesleyan U., Middletown, Conn.; MPH, U. Wash., Seattle, Wash.; MD, Cornell U., N.Y. Internal Medicine Am. Bd. of Internal Medicine. Acting instr. of medicine U. Wash., Seattle, 2003—. Office: UW Virology Rsch Clinic 600 Broadway Ste 400 Seattle WA 98122

CASPER, GERHARD, former academic administrator, law educator; b. Hamburg, Germany, Dec. 25, 1937; s. Heinrich and Hertha C.; m. Regina Koschel, Dec. 26, 1964; 1 child, Hanna. LL.M., Yale U., 1962; Dr.iur., U. Freiburg, Germany, 1964; hon. degree, Yale U., 2000, Uppsala U., 2000; legal state exam, U. Frieburg, U. Hamburg, 1961. Asst. prof. polit. sci. U. Calif., Berkeley, 1964—66; assoc. prof. law and polit. sci. U. Chgo., 1966—69, prof., 1969—76, Max Pam prof. law, 1976—80, William B. Graham prof. law, 1980—87, William B. Graham Disting. Svc. prof. law, 1987—92, dean law sch., 1979—87, provost, 1989—92; prof. law Stanford (Calif.) U., 1992—2000, pres. emeritus, 1992—2000; Peter and Helen Bing prof., 2000—. Vis. prof. law Cath. U., Louvain, Belgium, 1970, U. Munich, 1988, 91. Author: Realism and Political Theory in American Legal Thought, 1967, (with Richard A. Posner) The Workload of the Supreme Court, 1976; co-editor: The Supreme Ct. Rev., 1977-91, Separating Power, 1997. Successor, trustee Yale U., 2000—; bd. dirs. Am. Acad. in Berlin, 2000—. Fellow Am. Acad. Arts and Scis.; mem. Internat. Acad. Comparative Law, Am. Bar Found. (bd. dirs. 1979-87), Coun. Fgn. Rels., Am. Law Inst. (coun. 1980—), Oliver Wendell Holmes Devise (permanent com. 1985-93), Am. Philos. Soc., The Trilateral Commn., 1998—. E-mail: gcasper@stanford.edu.

CASPER, MARIE LENORE, middle school educator; b. Honesdale, Pa., Mar. 26, 1954; d. Frank J. and Ellenore L. (Austin) Shedlock; m. Gerald Joseph Casper, Oct. 9, 1976 (dec. Oct. 1998); children: Julia Anne, Jennifer Marie. BA, Marywood Coll., 1976; masters equivalency cert., State of Pa., 1982. Cert. elem. and secondary social studies tchr., Pa. Substitute tchr. Western Wayne Sch. Dist., South Canaan, Pa., 1976-81, secondary and elem. tchr., 1981-86, chpt. 1 math. specialist, 1986-90, middle sch. social studies tchr., 1990—; social studies tchr. Wallenpaupack Area Sch. Dist., Hawley, Pa., 1980-81. Coord. Western Wayne Middle Sch., WWII commemorative com. Contbr. articles to profl. jours. Active PTA Wilson Sch., Western Wayne Mid. Sch. Mem. NEA, Pa. State Edn. Assn., Pa. Mid. Sch. Assn., Waymart Hist. Soc., Western Wayne Edn. Assn., Wayne County Hist. Soc., Smithsonian Instn., Audubon Soc., Nat. Geog. Soc., Platform Assn., Am. Legion Aux. (life). Republican. Roman Catholic. Avocations: piano and vocal music, needlecraft, reading, antiques, genealogy. Home: PO Box 31 Lake Quinn Rd South Canaan PA 18459-0031 Office: Western Wayne Mid Sch RR 8 Box 8170 Lake Ariel PA 18436-9802

CASPER, RICHARD HENRY, lawyer; b. Chgo., Nov. 4, 1950; s. Edson Lee and Dorothy Ellen (Klemp) C.; m. Betty Gene Ward, Aug. 26, 1972; children: Terrance, Laura, Russell, Jeremy. AB, Bowdoin Coll., 1972; JD, Northwestern U., 1975. Bar: Wis. 1975, U.S. Dist. Ct. (ea. dist.) Wis. 1975. Assoc. Foley & Lardner, Milw., 1975-82, ptnr., 1982—. James Bowdoin scholar Bowdoin Coll, 1972. Mem. Wis. Bar Assn., Milw. Bar Assn., Order of the Coif. Office: Foley & Lardner Firstar 777 E Wisconsin Ave Milwaukee WI 53202-5367 E-mail: rcasper@foleylaw.com.

CASPERSEN, FINN MICHAEL WESTBY, diversified financial services company executive; b. N.Y.C., Oct. 27, 1941; s. Olaus Westby and Freda Caspersen; m. Barbara Caspersen, June 17, 1967. BA With honors in Econs., Brown U., 1963; LLB cum laude, Harvard U., 1966; DHL (hon.), Johns Hopkins U., 1999; various hon. degrees. Assoc. Dewey, Ballantine, Bushby, Palmer & Wood, N.Y.C., 1969-72; chmn. bd., chief exec. officer, mem. exec. com. Beneficial Corp., Wilmington, Del., 1976-98; chmn. bd. dirs., CEO Knickerbocker LLC. Past bd. dirs., mem. exec. com. Beneficial Nat. Bank; chmn. bd. dirs. Beneficial Bank, Plc; bd. advisors Inst. Law and Econs., U. Pa.; past chmn. Coalition for Better Transp.; past co-chair Prosperity N.J.; pres. emeritus U.S. Equestrian Team; chmn. internat. coun. Hosp. for Spl. Surgery. Emeritus trustee Brown U.; chmn. Save Ellis Island; moderator, bd. dirs. Shelter Harbor Fire Dist.; pres. O.W. Caspersen Found.; trustee BGCN Life Camp Inc.; chmn. bd. trustees Peddie Sch., Hightstown, N.J.; former chmn. bd. trust Gladstone Equestrian Assn. Inc.; bd. dirs. Drumthwacket Found.; charter mem. Partnership for N.J., New Brunswick; bd. dirs. Coalition of Svc. Industries, Inc., Washington, 1982-95, vice chair, 1995; chmn. World Pair Championship, 1993; chmn. Princeton World Cup Regatta, 20002; chmn., CEO Princeton Internat. Regatta Assn.; mem. corp. Cardigan Mountain Sch.; mem. exec. com. Harvard Resources Com.; trustee BGCN Life Camp Inc., John Carter Libr.; chmn. dean's adv. com. Harvard Law Sch.; past dir. Clay Math. Inst. Lt. USCG, 1966-69. Recipient Pres.'s medal Johns Hopkins U., Ethics in Bus. award BBB, 1992, Gov.'s award Alexander Hamilton Econ. Devel., 1997, President's medal Brown U., 1997, Brightest Star award Boys and Girls Clubs Newark, Inc., 1997, Humanities Citizen of Yr. award N.J. Coun. for Humanities, 1999; named Civic Leader of Yr., YMCA, 1982, Citizen of Yr., Morristown Meml. Hosp., 1993. Mem. Am. Fin. Svcs. Assn. (bd. dirs., chmn. govt. affairs com., chmn. membership com., adminstrn. com., past chmn.), Fla. Bar Assn., N.Y. Bar Assn., Harvard Club, Knickerbocker Club, Univ. Club, Wilmington Club, Shelter Harbor Golf Club (founder, chmn.). Office: Knickerbocker LLC 240 Main St Gladstone NJ 07934-2057

CASPERSEN, R(ALPH) FREDERICK, lawyer; b. Mpls., Dec. 8, 1942; s. Ralph Bernhard and Mary Jane (Schmitt) C.; m. Patricia Niemi. A.D., Harvard U., 1964; J.D., Stanford U., 1971. Bar: Calif. 1972, U.S. Dist. Ct. (no. dist.) Calif. 1972, U.S. Tax Ct. 1974. Assoc. Farella, Braun & Martel, San Francisco, 1971-77, ptnr., 1977— . Served to lt. USNR, 1964-68; Vietnam. Mem. ABA, Calif. State Bar, Bar Assn. San Francisco. Republican. Club: Commercial. Lodge: Elks. Office: Farella Braun & Martel 235 Montgomery St Ste 3000 San Francisco CA 94104-2902

CASPY, BARBARA JANE, social worker; b. N.Y., Jan. 11, 1945; d. Harold Brooks Mandel and Lillian (Metzger) Rost; m. Avram Caspy, Apr. 24, 1966; children: Nick Walker, Karen Caspy Nielsen. BA, Bklyn. Coll., 1966; MSW, Rutgers U., 1984. Lic. clin. social worker, Nev. Family counselor Family Svc. Agy. Princeton, N.J., 1984; pvt. practice clin. social work Princeton, 1985-87; social worker Trenton (N.J.) Psychiat. Hosp., 1987-89; clin. social worker So. Nev. Adult Mental Health Svcs., Las Vegas, Nev., 1989-92, Apogee, Inc., Las Vegas, 1992-96, So. Nev. Adult Mental Health Svcs., Las Vegas, 1996—. Social work cons. Family Infant Resource Ctr., Princeton, 1985-88; group facilitator Rutgers Med. Sch. Sexuality Seminar, Piscataway, N.J., 1984-87. Mem. Nat. Assn. Social Workers (diplomate clin. social work), Nat. Rifle Assn. (life). Avocation: hiking.

CASS, DAVID, economist, educator; b. Honolulu, Jan. 19, 1937; s. Phil and Muriel (Dranga) C.; m. Janice Vernon, Sept. 14, 1959 (div. July 1983); children— Stephen, Lisa B. AB, U. Oreg., 1958; PhD in Econs. and Stats., Stanford U., 1965; D (hon.), U. Geneva, 1994. From asst. to assoc. prof. Yale U., New Haven, 1964-70; prof. econs. Carnegie-Mellon U., Pitts., 1970—74, U. Pa., Phila., 1974-88, Paul F. and E. Warren Shafer Miller prof. econs., 1988—, dir. Ctr. for Analytic Rsch. in Econs. and the Social Scis. Prof. econs. European Union Inst., Italy, 1996—97. Contbr. articles to profl. jours.; co-editor: Selected Readings in Macroeconomics from Econometrica, 1974; The Hamiltonian Approach to Economics, 1976 1st lt. USAR, 1959-65 Guggenheim fellow, 1970-71; recipient Morgan prize U. Chgo., 1976; Sherman Fairchild Disting. Scholar Calif. Inst. Tech., 1978-79; NSF grantee, 1971-91. Fellow AAAS, Am. Econ. Assn., Econometric Soc., Am. Acad. Arts and Scis.; mem. Phi Beta Kappa Office: Univ Pa 435 McNeil/6297 3451 Walnut St Philadelphia PA 19104

CASS, MARY LOUISE, librarian; b. Jersey City, N.J., May 27, 1956; d. Eugene Louis and Catherine (Reynolds) Cass; m. Edward John Skillin, Dec. 2, 2000. BA in History, Rutgers U., 1978, MLS, 1979. Cataloguer Fairleigh Dickinson U., Madison, N.J., 1979-81; mgr. Montclair (N.J.) Pub. Libr., 1982-96, br. dir., 1996—. Bibliographer: (book) Suicide, 1991. Treas. Upper Mountain Gardens Bd., Montclair, 1998-2003. Mem. ALA (pres. cmty. info. sect. 1991-92). Democrat. Roman Catholic. Home: 29 Upper Mountain Ave Montclair NJ 07042-1919 Office: Montclair Pub Libr 185 Bellevue Ave Montclair NJ 07043

CASS, ROBERT MICHAEL, lawyer, consultant; b. Carlisle, Pa., July 5, 1945; s. Robert Lau and Norma Jean (McCaleb) C.; m. Patricia Ann Garber, Aug. 12, 1967 (dec. Jan. 1999); children: Charles McCaleb, David Lau. BA, Pa. State U., 1967; JD, Temple U., 1971. Bar: N.Y. 1974; cert. arbitrator AIDA Reins. and Ins. Arbitration Soc. Benefit examiner Social Security Adminstrn., Phila., 1967-68; mktg. rep. Employers Comml. Union Ins. Co., Phila., 1968-70; asst. sec. Nat. Reins. Corp., N.Y.C., 1970-77; asst. v.p. Skandia Am. Reins. Corp., N.Y.C., 1977-80; mgr. Allstate Reins. divsn., South Barrington, Ill., 1980-86, R.K. Carvill, Inc., Chgo., 1986-87; pres. R. M. Cass Assocs., Chgo., 1987—. V.p. Assurance Alliance, Inc., Crystal Lake, Ill., 1989; lectr. Ins. Sch. Chgo., Coll. of Ins. N.Y., U. Wis., Am. Inst. for Chartered Property Casualty Underwriters. Author: (with others) Reinsurance Contract Wording, Reinsurance Practices, 2d edit.; editor, reviewer: (with others) The Legal Environment of Insurance, 4th edit. Mem. ABA (tort and ins. practice sect., past chair com. on excess, surplus lines and reins. law, standing com. on professionalism, standing com. on emerging issues, com. on long range planning, past chmn. internat. com., liaison to ABA Ctrl. & East European Law Initiative, chair 3rd Chinese-Am. law seminar, Guangzhou, China, 1999, chair 4th Chinese-Am. law seminar Beijing and Shanghai 2001, dispute resolution sect., past chair com. large complex case arbitration), Soc. CPCUs (past chair risk mgmt. sect. com., mem. excess, surplus and splty. lines sect. com., reinsurance sect. com., past officer Chgo. N.W. suburban chpt.), Am. Arbitration Assn. (panel neutrals), Assn. Ind. Reins. Cons. (pres.), Internat. Assn. Ins. Receivers (publs. com., past chair membership com.), Fellows of Am. Bar Found., N.Y. State Bar Assn., Assn. Internat. de Droit des Assurances, Ill. Captive and Alternative Risk Funding Ins. Assn. (pres. bd. dirs.), Coalition Alternative Risk Funding Mechanisms (bd. dirs.). Home: 330 N Jefferson Ct #1705 Chicago IL 60661-1212 Office: PO Box 543460 Chicago IL 60654-3460 E-mail: mikecassre@aol.com.

CASS, RONALD ANDREW, dean; b. Washington, Aug. 12, 1949; s. Millard and Ruth Claire (Marx) C.; m. Valerie Christina Swanson, Aug. 24, 1969; children: Laura Rebecca, Alexander Stephan. BA with high distinction, U. Va., 1970; JD with honors, U. Chgo., 1973. Bar: Md. 1973, D.C. 1974, U.S. Dist. Ct. D.C. 1974, U.S. Ct. Appeals (D.C. cir.) 1974, U.S. Supreme Ct. 1977, Va. 1979. Law clk. to chief judge U.S. Ct. Appeals (3d cir.), Wilmington, Del., 1973-74; assoc. Arent, Fox, Kintner, Plotkin & Kahn, Washington, 1974-76; asst. prof. law U. Va. Sch. Law, Charlottesville, 1976-81; assoc. prof. law Boston U., 1981-83, prof., 1983-95; dean Boston U. Law Sch., 1990—; Melville Madison Bigelow prof. Boston U., 1995—; legal advisor Office Plans and Policy, FCC, Washington, 1987-88; mem. U.S. Internat. Trade Commn., Washington, 1988-90, vice chmn., 1989-90. Cons. comm. program Aspen (Colo.) Inst., 1977-78, Admisntrv. Conf. U.S. Washington, 1980-87, Helsell, Fetterman, Martin, Todd & Hokanson, Seattle, 1984-85, Assn. Trial Lawyers Am., Phila., 1985-87, UN Conf. Trade and Devel., Geneva, 1991, U.S. Dept. Justice, 1998, Microsoft Corp., 1998-; spl. cons. Nat. Econ. Rsch. Assn., Cambridge, Mass., 1990-94; arbitrator Biogen v. Schering-Plough, 1999-2000, Telesia Sistemas v. Lucent Tech., 2000-2002, UPS v. Canada, 2001-; adj. scholar Am. Enterprise Inst., Washington, 1993-; sr. fellow Internat. Ctr. Econ. Rsch., Turin, 1996-97, 99-2002; sesquicentennial assoc. Ctr. Advanced Studies U. Va. Law Sch., 1980-81; mem. nat. adv. bd. Case Western Res. U. Sch. Law, 1996-97; disting. lectr. U. Francisco Marroquin, Guatemala City, 1996, IMADEC Internat. Bus. Sch., Vienna, 2000, U. Aix en Provence, 2002, Boston U. London Program, 2002. Author: Revolution in the Wasteland: Value and Diversity in Television, 1981, (with Colin S. Diver) Administrative Law: Cases and Materials, 1987, (with Colin S. Diver and Jack M. Beermann) Administrative Law: Cases and Materials, 2nd edit., 1994, 3d edit., 1998, 4th edit., 2002, (with John R. Haring) International Trade in Telecommunications, 1998, The Rule of Law in America, 2001; contbr. articles and essays to profl. jours., also chpts. to books. Bd. dirs. Northwestern Va. Health Systems Agy., Culpeper, 1980; bd. govs. Sightsavers Internat., Washington, 1989-91; bd. dirs. Telecomm. Policy Rsch. Conf., Washington, 1989-91, sec.-treas. 1989-90, vice chmn., 1991-92; bd. dirs. New Eng. Legal Found., 1994-2002, New England Coun., 1995-; bd. overseers Boston Bar Found., 1992-94, Supreme Jud. Ct. Hist. Soc., 1997-2000; sr. Europe Discussion Group, Ctr. for Strategic and Internat. Studies, 1989-96; bd. advisors George Mason U. Law Sch. Law & Econs. Ctr., 1996-99, Inst. Dem. Comm., Boston, 1991-92, Fundación de la Commn. Social, Madrid, 1995-, IMADEC Internat. Bus. Sch., Vienna, 1999-2001, Legal Issues in Econ. Integration, Amsterdam, 2000-. Fellow Am. Bar Found.; mem. ABA (adminstrv. law and regulatory practice sect., coun. 1993-95, chair 1998-99, legal edn. and admission bar sect., review commn. 1994-95, ho. of dels. 2000-02), Am. Law Inst., Am. Law Deans Assn. (bd. dirs. 1995—, pres. 1995-97), Mont Pelerin Soc., Boston Bar Assn. (coun. 1992-95), Adminstrv. Conf. U.S. (pub. mem. 1990-95, govt. mem. 1988-90), Transatlantic Policy Network (U.S. Working Group), Spring Valley C. C., Order of Coif, Phi Beta Kappa, Bay Club, Federalist Soc., Internat. Law (exec. com. 2001-). Republican. Jewish. Home: 250 Hammond Pond Pkwy #205 S Chestnut Hill MA 02467-1517 Office: Boston U Sch Law 765 Commonwealth Ave Boston MA 02215-1401

CASSADY, DANIEL BENNET, music educator; b. Des Moines, Iowa, Mar. 14, 1951; s. James Neal and Inez Bardella Cassady; m. Lori Janine Becker, July 29, 1988; children: Nathan, Megan; m. Dixie Lee Miller, Aug. 2, 1975 (div. July 31, 1985); 1 child, Michael. MusB, The U. of Iowa, 1973, MA, 1984. Cert. Tchr. State of Iowa, 1973, lic. Iowa Bd. Ednl. Examiners, 73. Band dir. Graettinger Cmty. Sch., Graettinger, Iowa, 1973—76, Hawley Elem. Sch., Fort Dodge, Iowa, 1976—77, Ft. Dodge Sr. H.S., Fort Dodge, Iowa, 1976—95; dir. of bands Iowa Ctrl. C.C., Fort Dodge, Iowa, 1995—, instr. humanities, 1995—. Guest dir. Reggie Schive Summer Jazz Camps, Storm Lake and Okoboji, Iowa, 1982—, Southwestern C.C. Summer Jazz Camps, Creston, Iowa, 1985—97. Musician: (albums) Brass Transit, 1998. Orch. mgr., trombonist, arranger Ft. Dodge Civic Glee Club, Fort Dodge, 1976; active various capacities Karl L. King Mcpl. Band, 1977, bd. dir., 1977. Recipient Excellence award, Nat. Inst. for Staff and Orgnl. Devel. U. of Tex., Austin, 1999. Mem.: NEA, Iowa H.S. Music Assn. (adjudicator 1979—), Music Educators Nat. Conf. (north ctrl. rep. 1996—2000), Iowa Bandmasters Assn. (county chmn. jazz com. 1973, county chmn.coll. affairs com. 1973), Iowa Alliance for Arts Edn., Internat. Trombone Assn., Internat. Jazz Educators Assn., Am. Sch. Band Directors Assn. (sgt. at arms 1997). Methodist. Avocations: billiards, jazz, motorcycling. Home: 1801 Lainson Avenue Fort Dodge IA 50501-8531 Office: Iowa Central Community College 330 Avenue M Fort Dodge IA 50501 Office Fax: 515-576-7724. E-mail: cassady@triton.iccc.cc.ia.us.

CASSADY, JAMES ROBERT, oncologist, educator; b. L.A., Nov. 16, 1938; s. George Edward and Margaret Elizabeth (Cabañas) C.; m. Deborah Joan Bacon, July 28, 1962; children: Kristin Deborah, Robert Sean. BA, U. So. Calif., 1959; MD, Harvard Med. Sch., 1963. Diplomate Am. Bd. Radiology. Intern King County Hosp., Seattle, 1963-64; resident Columbia Presbyn. Med. Ctr., N.Y.C., 1964-67; fellow, instr. Stanford (Calif.) Med. Ctr., 1969-71; asst. prof. radiation therapy Joint Ctr. for Radiation Therapy Harvard Med. Sch., Boston, 1971-75, assoc. prof. radiation therapy, 1975-82, prof. radiation therapy, 1982-84; prof., head dept. radiation oncology U. Ariz. Coll. Medicine, Tucson, 1984-95; chmn. dept. radiation oncology Lahey Clinic, Burlington, Mass., 1995—. Hosp. appointments include VA Hosp., Tucson, 1985-95, El Dorado Hosp. and Med. Ctr., 1985-95, R.W. Bliss Army Comm. Hosp., Ft. Huachuca, Ariz., 1986-95, Tucson Gen. Hosp., 1987-95; lectr. in field. Contbr. articles to profl. jours. Surgeon USPHS, 1967-69. Mem. Am. Coll. Radiology, Am. Soc. Therapeutic Radiologist, Am. Coll. Radiation Oncology (v.p. 1993-94, pres. 1994-95, chmn. bd. dirs. 1995-96, gold medal 1997), Soc. Clin. Oncology, Soc. Pediatric Radiology, Pima County Med. Soc., Am. Bd. Radiology (writer examiner, oral bd. examiner), Am. Soc. Therapeutic Radiology and Oncology (chmn. workforce com. 1998—), Phi Beta Kappa, Phi Kappa Phi, Alpha Epsilon Delta. Avocations: stained glass, hiking, bonsai, caudiciform plants.

CASSADY, MARSH G. writer, editor; b. Johnstown, Pa., June 12, 1936; s. Clarence L. and Hazel B. Cassady; m. Pat J. Mizer (dec. Feb. 1978); children: Kathi, Kim, David, Beth, Heather BA, Otterbein Coll., 1958; MA, Kent State U., 1967, PhD, 1972. Staff writer The Daily Reporter, Dover, Ohio, 1960-63;

tchr. Garaway, Sugar Creek, Ohio, 1963-64, Cen. H.S., New Philadelphia, Ohio, 1964-66; instr. Kent (Ohio) State U., 1967-72; asst. prof. Montclair (N.J.) State U., 1972-75; author, editor, 1975—. Author: Oral Interpretation: Make Yourself Clear, 1974, 76, Theatre: A View of Life, 1982, Melinda: A Survivor, 1987, Love Theme with Variations, 1989, Alternate Casts, 1990 (Lambda Lit. Award finalist), Pervertd Proverbs, 1992, The Music of Tree Limbs, 1993 (Cicada Press Haiku Chapbook award), The Book of Monologues for Aspiring Actors, 1994, (novel) Light, 1994, The Theatre: An Introduction, 1996, Funny Business, 1996, (play) Vampire Wedding, 1998, (with John Anderson) The Newhall Incident, 1999 (San Diego Book award for nonfiction), The Diversity of American Theatre, 2001, (electronic book) Ice Cold Moon, 2001, Brass Pony, 2002, others, also plays, short stories; host: (radio show) On Location, 1975-77; editl. advisor Buckeye Country mag., 1975-80; book rev. editor: Hill Courier and Lambda Book Report, 1990s; fiction and drama editor Crazyquilt Quar., 1986-98, Davids' Place Jour., 1996; co-pub., editor Los Hombres Press, 1990-98; freelance editor Quill Driver Books/Word Dancer Press, 1999—; columnist, Viernes; acquisitions/copy editor The Fiction Works, 2000—; actor: Trumpet: The Land, New Philadelphia, 1970, 77-79. Faculty grantee Montclair State U., 1975. Avocations: reading, music, theater, bridge. Home: MCD R-03 PO Box 439016 San Diego CA 92143 E-mail: gary@telnor.net.

CASSAR, GEORGE HARRIS, historian, educator; b. Sherbrooke, Que., Can., Oct. 31, 1938; arrived in U.S., 1996; s. Michael and Nazareth Cassar; m. Mary Louise Breutzman, May 11, 1984; children: Alexandra, Michael, Jarrod. BA, U. N.B., Fredericton, 1962, MA, 1963; PhD, McGill U., Montreal, Que., Can., 1968. Lectr. No. Mich. U., Marquette, 1966—68; asst. prof. Ea. Mich. U., Ypsilanti, 1968—72, assoc. prof., 1972—77, prof., 1977—. Author: The French and the Dardanelles, 1971, Kitchener: Architect of Victory, 1977, The Tragedy of Sir John French, 1985, Beyond Courage, 1985, Asquith as War Leader, 1994, The Forgotten Front, 1998; co-author: A Survey of Western Civilization, World History. Republican. Lutheran. Office: Dept History Ea Mich Univ Ypsilanti MI 48197

CASSARA, FRANK, artist, printmaker; b. Partinico, Italy, Mar. 13, 1913; came to U.S., 1913, naturalized, 1936; s. Gaspare and Rosalia (Savarino) C.; m. Gretchen Jean Grathwohl, Dec. 28, 1946; children: Christina, Francesca. Student, U. Iowa, summer 1956, Atelier 17, Paris, summer 1958; MS in Design, U. Mich., 1954. Supr. easel painting sect. WPA, 1937; instr. Detroit Sch. Art, 1935-36, Soc. Arts and Crafts, Detroit, 1946-47; prof. U. Mich., Ann Arbor, after 1947, now prof. emeritus. Instr. Nat. Music Camp, Interlochen, Mich., summers 1948-49 Illustrated manuscript published in Artists Proof, A Collectors Edition, 1963; one-man shows include: U. Man., Can., Winnipeg, Flint (Mich.) Inst. Arts, Toledo Mus., 1983, Kalamazoo Art Ctr., U. Maine, Orono, U. Ill., Urbana, U. Oreg., Corvallis, U. Nebr., Lincoln; group shows include: 7th Internat. Prints, Chgo. Art Inst., Mus. Palace Legion of Honor, San Francisco, Gallerie Nees Morphes, Athens, Greece, Bklyn. Mus., Achenbach Found. Graphic Arts, San Francisco, Okla. Art Ctr., Oklahoma City, Internat. Conf. Hand Papermakers, Boston, 1980, Internat. Papermakers, Birmingham Art Assn., Ella Sharp Mus. and Slusser Gallery; represented in permanent collections at Bibliotecque Nationale, Paris, Stadelijk Mus., The Netherlands, Libr. of Congress, USIA Agy., Nat. Mus. Am. Art, Smithsonian Instn., Washington; mural executed East Detroit Post Office, 1939, Sandusky (Mich.) Post Office, 1941, Lansing (Mich.) Water Conditioning Plant, 1941, renovated, 1989, Palio, Ann Arbor, 1996. Served with U.S. Army, 1942-46. Decorated 2 Bronze Stars.; Grantee Rackham Research Found., U. Mich., 1957-61, 68; Recipient over 50 awards in National and regional exhibitions. Mem. Ann Arbor Art Assn. (past pres., dir. 1954-62), Nat. Acad. Design. Achievements include being the innovator of two white grounds for etching.

CASSARO, JAMES P. musicologist; b. Buffalo, Mar. 29, 1954; BA in Music, SUNY, 1978, MLS, 1980; MA in Musicology, Cornell U., N.Y., 1993. Sound rec., reference libr. SUNY Music Libr., Buffalo, 1980; music av cataloger North Tex. State U., Denton, 1980—83; asst music libr. Cornell U., Ithaca, NY, 1983—99; head Theodore M. Finney music libr. U. of Pitts., 1999—. Editor: (critical music edit.) J.B. Lully, Ballet des Saisons; author: (bio-bibliography) Gaetano Donizetti: A Guide to Research, (technical report) Planning & Caring for Audio Facilities, Space Utilization in Music Libraries. Program com., co-chair; mktg. com., mem.; devel. com., mem. Renaissance & Baroque Soc., Pitts., 2000. Mem.: Soc. of Dance History Scholars, Internat. Assn. of Music Libraries (cataloguing commn., chair 1991—99, program com., mem. 2002), Soc. for 17th Century Music, Soc. for Am. Music (devel. com., chair 1999—2000), Am. Musicological Soc. (co-editor newsletter 2002), ALA, Music Libr. Assn. (pres. 2001—03). Liberal. Roman Catholic. Office: U of Pitts Music Libr B30 Music Bldg Pittsburgh PA 15260 Office Fax: 412-624-4180.

CASSEL, CHRISTINE KAREN, physician; b. Mpls., Sept. 14, 1945; d. Charles Moore and Virginia Julia (Anderson) Cassel. AB, U. Chgo., 1967; MD, U. Mass., 1976. Diplomate Am. Bd. Internal Medicine (chmn. 1998-99). Intern, resident in internal medicine Children's Hosp., San Francisco, 1976—78; fellow in bioethics Inst. Health Policy Studies, U. Calif., San Francisco, 1978—79; fellow geriatrics Portland (Oreg.) VA Hosp., 1979—81; asst. prof. medicine and public health U. Oreg. Health Scis. U., 1981—83; asst. prof. geriatrics and medicine Mt. Sinai Med. Ctr., N.Y.C., 1983—85; prof. medicine, prof. pub. policy U. Chgo., 1985—95, chief gen. internal medicine, 1985—95; chmn. and prof. geriatrics and medicine Mt. Sinai, 1995—2001; dean sch. of medicine Oreg. Heatlh and Sci. U., 2001—02. Author: Ethical Dimensions in the Health Professions, 1981, Geriatric Medicine: Principles and Practice, 1984, 1990, Nuclear Weapons and Nuclear War: A Sourcebook for Health Professionals, 1984. Bd. dirs., chmn. Greenwall Found. Fellow Hastings Ctr. fellow, 1991—92, Ctr. Advanced Study in Behavioral Sci. fellow, 1991—92; scholar Henry J. Kaiser Family Found. faculty scholar, 1982—85. Fellow: ACP (regent 1989—97, pres. 1997—98), Am. Geriatrics Soc.; mem.: Am. Soc. Law and Medicine (bd. dirs.), Soc. Health and Human Values (pres. 1986), Physicians for Social Responsibility (dir. 1983—, pres. 1988—), Inst. of Medicine of NAS. Office: ABIM Found 510 Walnut St Philadelphia PA 19105 E-mail: casselc@abim.org.

CASSEL, DOUGLASS WATTS, JR., lawyer, educator, journalist; b. Balt., Aug. 29, 1948; s. Douglass Watts and Vivian Elizabeth (Keller) C.; m. Joan Ellen Steinman, June 1, 1974 (div. 1986); children: Jennifer Lynn, Amanda Hilary; m. Beatriz Cervantes, Sept. 10, 1988; 1 child, Magdalena Maria. BA, Yale Coll., 1969; JD, Harvard Law Sch., 1972. Bar: Md. 1972, D.C. 1973, Ill. 1976. Writer, rschr. Ralph Nader's Congress Project, Washington, 1972; lawyer USNR, Great Lakes Naval Base, Ill., 1973-76; from atty. to gen. counsel BPI, Chgo., 1976-91; journalist Chgo. Reader, 1989; exec. dir. DePaul U. Coll. Law Internat. Human Rights Law Inst., Chgo., 1990-98; dir. Northwestern U. Sch. Law Ctr. for Internat. Human Rights, Chgo., 1998—. Legal advisor UN Truth Commn. for El Salvador, N.Y.C., 1992-93; human rights cons. U.S. Dept. State, Washington, 1997—; commentator WBEZ, Chgo., 1994—; pres., bd. dirs. Justice Studies Ctr. of the Ams., 2000—; pres. Due Process of Law Found., 2000—. Mem. ABA, Am. Soc. Internat. Law. Democrat. Roman Catholic. Avocation: swimming. Office: Northwestern U Sch Law 357 E Chicago Ave Chicago IL 60611-3059

CASSEL, JOHN ELDEN, accountant; b. Verden, Okla., Apr. 24, 1934; s. Elbert Emry and Erma Ruth (McDowell) C.; m. Mary Lou Malcom, June 3, 1953; children— John Elden, James Edward, Jerald Eugene. Plant mgr., also asst. gen. mgr. Baker and Taylor Co., Oklahoma City, 1966-71; paymaster, office mgr. Robberson Steel Co., Oklahoma City, 1971-76; pvt. investor, 1976—. Democrat. Methodist. Home: 2332 NW 118th St Oklahoma City OK 73120-7404

CASSEL, JOHN MICHAEL, plastic surgeon; b. Miami, Mar. 25, 1948; m. Robyn Cassel, July 12, 1987; children: (twins) Adrienne and Brandon. BS, U. Miami, 1972, MD, 1978. Diplomate Am. Bd. Plastic Surgery. Gen. surg. intern U. Va., Charlottesville, 1978-79, gen. surg. resident, 1979-80, Cedars-Sinai Med. Ctr., L.A., 1980-81; jr. resident in plastic surgery U. Miami Sch. Medicine, 1981-82, sr. resident in plastic surgery, 1982-83; microsurgery and hand surgery fellow Ralph K. Davies Med. Ctr., San Francisco, 1984; pvt. practice plastic surgery Miami, 1985—. Clin. assoc. prof. plastic surgery U. Miami Sch. Medicine, 1984—. Fellow Am. Coll. Surgeons; mem. Am. Soc. Plastic & Reconstructive Surgeons, Am. Soc. Aesthetic Plastic Surgeons. Avocations: sculpture, stained glass, gem, jewelry design & fabrication. Office: 8950 N Kendall Dr Ste 106 Miami FL 33176-2131

CASSELL, ERIC JONATHAN, physician; b. N.Y.C., Aug. 29, 1928; s. Hyman William and Anne (Lake) Goldstein; m. Joan M. Fishman, Oct. 17, 1957 (div. 1987); children: Justine, Stephen; m. Patricia M. Owens, May 26, 1990. BA, Queens Coll., 1950; MA, Columbia U., 1950; MD, NYU, 1954; DHL (hon.), Med. Coll. Pa., 1985. Intern 3d med. divsn. Bellevue Hosp., N.Y.C., 1954—55, asst. resident 3d med. divsn., 1955—56, physician 3d, 4th med. divsn., 1965—66; USPHS trainee in infectious diseases Weill Med. Coll., Cornell U., N.Y.C., 1959—61; clin. prof. pub. health Cornell U., N.Y.C., 1971—; attending physician French Hosp., N.Y.C., 1961—74; assoc. attending physician Mt. Sinai (N.Y.) Hosp., 1966—71; assoc. dir. ambulatory care Community Med., Mt. Sinai, 1966—68; attending physician N.Y. Presbyn. Hosp., 1984—; asst. resident 3d med. divsn. Bellevue Hosp., N.Y.C., 1958—59. Clin. assoc. prof. medicine NYU, 1965—66, Mt. Sinai Hosp., 1966—71; bd. dirs. Hasting's Ctr., Garrison, NY, 1975—; commr. Nat. Bioethics Adv. Commn., 1997—2001; vis. investigator Meml. Sloan Kettering Cancer Ctr., 1999—. Author: Healer's Art, 1976, Place of Humanities in Medicine, 1984, Talking with Patients (2 vols.), 1985, The Nature of Suffering, 1991, Doctoring: The Nature of Primary Care Medicine, 1997; editor: Changing Values in Medicine, 1979. Capt. M.C. U.S. Army, 1956—58. Master: ACP; fellow: N.Y. Acad. Medicine; mem.: Inst. of Medicine of NAS. Democrat. Jewish. Avocations: woodworking, metalworking. E-mail: eric@ericcassel.com.

CASSELL, LUCILLE RICHARDSON, small business owner; b. Sikeston, Mo., Feb. 23, 1958; d. Glen and Cenia (McCaster) Richardson; m. Arthur Earl Cassell, Apr. 12, 1986; children: Christopher Glen, Bryan Mitchell, David Arthur, Aaron Lamar. AA in Edn., S.E. Mo. State U., 1980; deaconess lic., Green Meml. Bible Inst.-Coll., Sikeston, 1982; B in Bus. Mgmt., Frederick Taylor U., 1997. Shoe packer Wohl Shoe Co., Sikeston, 1980-84; sales clk. J.C. Penney, Sikeston, 1984-85; bookeeper, teller Bank of Sikeston, 1985-86; computer operator Sta. KBSI-TV, Cape Girardeau, Mo., 1986-89; data clk. Falcon Cable TV, Sikeston, 1989-90; owner, mgr. Wee=Care Daycare Ctr., Charleston, 1990-99; pres. CBD Enterprises, Inc., Charleston, 1999—; tchr. kindergarten Sikeston (Mo.) Pub. Schs., 2000, Charleston (Mo.) Pub. Schs., 2001. Author: (poem) The Best That I Can Be, 1995; patented disposable diapers, adult diapers; patentee in field. Participant walk-a-thons Cystic Fibrosis Found., Charleston, 1992; leader Kid's Beat Program, Opportunity COGIC Drill Team; youth drill team; presentation History of Fancy Bottom Diapers Sikeston Local Libr., Cape Girardeau Pub. Lib., Charleston Pub. Lib.; vol. Delta Med. Ctr., Sikeston, 1990; Sunday sch. tchr. Green Meml. Ch., Sikeston, Mo., 1985—86, Opportunity Ch., Charleston. Mem. Ch. of God in Christ. Avocations: reading, volleyball, music, bowling. Home: PO Box 284 Charleston MO 63834-0284 Fax: 573-683-2152. E-mail: cbdenterprises@ldd.net.

CASSELL, ROBERT HOLLAND, internist, oncologist; b. Nashville, June 11, 1948; MD, Duke U., 1979. Diplomate Am. Bd. Internal Medicine, Am. Bd. Oncology. Intern, then resident medicine Grady Meml. Hosp., Emory U., Atlanta, 1979-82, fellow in hematology and oncology, 1982-84; pvt. practice Bond Clin., Winter Haven, Fla., 1984—; with staff Winter Haven Hosp., 1984—. Mem. ACP, AMA, Am. Soc. Clin. Oncology. Office: Bond Clinic 500 E Central Ave Winter Haven FL 33880-3094

CASSELL, SAMUEL JAMES, basketball player; b. Balt., Md., Nov. 18, 1969; Grad., Dunbar H.S., Balt., San Jacinto Coll., 1993. Basketball player Houston Rockets, 1994-96, Pheonix Suns, 1996, Dallas Mavericks, 1996-97, N.J. Nets, East Rutherford, 1997-99, Milw. Bucks, Houston; co-owner shoe store, Houston. Mem. NBA championship team, 1994,95; won Fleer Shoot-Around during the 1996 All-Star Weekend, San Antonio, Tex; named NBA Player of Week from Apr. 6-12, 1998. Office: Milw Bucks 1001 N 4th St Milwaukee WI 53203-1314

CASSELL, WILLIAM COMYN, retired college president; b. Vallejo, Calif., Oct. 8, 1933; s. Comyn R. and Emily E. (Duckwith) C.; m. Jeanne Taylor, Dec. 27, 1955; children: Paul, Susan, David. BA, Pomona Coll., 1956; MA, Claremont Grad. Sch., 1969; LHD (hon.), Lakeland Coll., 1977; LLD, William Penn Coll.; D in Bus. Adminstn., Won Kwang U.; MBA, DLitt, Heidelberg Coll. Broker Hornblower and Weeks, Inc., Orange, Calif., 1958-64; asst. to treas. Claremont (Calif.) Coll., 1964-65; dir. income trusts and bequests Calif. Inst. Tech., Pasadena, 1965-69; dir. devel. and pub. relations Menninger Found., Topeka, 1969-70; dir. devel. U. Denver, 1970-74; pres. Coll. of Idaho, Caldwell, 1974-80, Heidelberg Coll., Tiffin, Ohio, 1980-96, pres. emeritus, 1996—. Cons. Ford Found., Phelps-Stokes Fund, Congress of No. Marianas Islands, numerous colls. and govt. agys., 1983—; hon. royal consul gen. Nepal; bd. dirs. Fifth-Third Bank No. Ohio. Author: The Case for Deferred Giving, 1966, Deferred Giving Programs: Administration and Promotion, 1972; editorial adv. bd.: Ednl. Record. Mem. Parks and Recreation Commn., Claremont, 1967-69, City Council, Bow Mar, Colo., 1967-69; mem. adv. bd. Salvation Army, Caldwell,, Western Electric Fund; trustee Caldwell Meml. Hosp., chmn., 1976; mem. Idaho newspaper carrier scholarship selection com.; mem. Missions on Am. Mgmt. and Ednl. Techniques to Indonesia and Jamaica; mission leader Thailand on Edn. and Mgmt.; mem. White House Adv. Com. on Libr. and Tech., White House Conf.; mem. Ohio Higher Edn. Facilities Commn., Depository Libr. Commn. of U.S.; adv. com. chmn. bd. Western Ind. Coll. Funds; bd. dirs. Tiffin YMCA; vice-chmn. Ketchum/Sun Valley Transit Authority; jr. warden St. Thomas Episcopal Ch.; chair adv. bd. Minn. Pub. Radio of Wood River Valley, 2000—; sec., bd. dirs. The Arts Found. for the Wood River Valley. Capt. USAR, 1957-58. Recipient Brakeley award for Outstanding Coll. Devel. Am. Alumni Coun., 1968, Nat. Fund Raising Coun. award, 1969; named Outstanding Young Man of Yr., Claremont, Calif., 1967, an Idaho Disting. Citizen, 1977, hon. VIP Sta. KIDO, Boise, Citizen of Yr. City of Tiffin, 1991. Mem. Coun. for Advancement of Support of Edn., Caldwell C. of C. (exec. bd. dir.), Tiffin C. of c. (bd. dirs., v.p.), Internat. Assn. Univ. Pres. (exec. com.), World Bus. Coun., North Cen. Accreditation Assn. (commr.), Am. Coun. on Edn. (commn. internat. edn.), Rotary (fellows selection com. dist., Citizen of Yr., Tiffin, Ohio 1991), Ketchum Sun Valley Rotary Club (mem. internat. projects com. Rotary dist.). Home: PO Box 1688 Sun Valley ID 83353-1688

CASSELL, WILLIAM WALTER, retired accounting operations consultant; b. Chgo., Apr. 10, 1917; s. Charles F. and E. Margaret (Jackson) C.; m. Rosamond Mary Fisher, May 13, 1944; children: Anne, Gerald, Douglas, Mary. Student, U. Wash., 1936-38, Syracuse U., 1943-44; grad., Am. Inst. Banking, 1957, Grad. Sch. Savs. Banking, 1965, Savs. Banks Mgmt. Devel. Program, U. Mass., 1970. Officer's asst. Syracuse (N.Y.) Savs. Bank, 1959-66, treas., 1966-71, v.p., 1971-75, sr. v.p., controller, 1975-77, exec. v.p., 1977-83, cons., 1983, also dir.; dir. State Bank of Chittenango, 1963-73, 83—, Credit Bur. Syracuse, 1976-83, Consumer Credit Counseling Service, 1979-83. Chmn. bd. dirs. State Bank of Chittenango, 1993—, SBC Fin. Corp., 1993—. Bd. dirs. Syracuse Symphony Orch., 1979-81, Opera Theater of Syracuse, 1982-84; pres. Madison County Hist. Soc., 1982-84. Served with U.S. Army, 1941 45, ETO. Decorated Bronze Star Mem. Am. Inst. Banking, Fin. Execs. Inst. (pres. Syracuse chpt. 1971-72). Clubs: Men's Garden of Am, Monarch of Syracuse. Republican. Methodist. Home: 131 W Genesee St Chittenango NY 13037-1501 *To find happiness in little things each day; to be all I am capable of being, judged within the framework of my own real values and to make others glad I came this way— this is the measure of a life worthwhile: contentment, not complacency.*

CASSELLA, DENNIS GENE, retired county official; b. Pratt, Kans., Oct. 24, 1946; s. Barney Joseph and Norma Jeanne Cassella. AA, Sacramento C.C., 1970; BA in History/Polit. Sci., U. Calif., Davis, 1971; MPA, East Tex. State U., 1975. City pers. dir. City of Texarkana, Ark., 1971—75; dir. adminstrv. svcs. Ark. Dept. Local Svcs., Little Rock, 1975—76; dir. gen. svcs. County of Nevada, Calif., 1977—2002; ret., 2002. Dir. emergency svcs. County of Nevada, 1988—; sr. adj. prof. Golden Gate U., Sacramento, 1979—. Mem. Nevada City (Calif.) Police Cmty. Rels. Commn., 1991—93, Nevada City Bicentennial of the Constn. Commn., 1986—; commr. Grass Valley (Calif.) Pers. Com., 2003—. Mem. Nevada County Libr. Found. (pres. 1998-99), Gold Country Lions (pres. 1987), Am. Soc. for Pub. Adminstrn. Home: 205 Cypress Hill Dr Grass Valley CA 95945 E-mail: henryv@nccn.net.

CASSELLA, WILLIAM NATHAN, JR., retired organization executive; b. Alton, Ill., July 14, 1920; s. William Nathan and Martha (Stanly) C.; m. Margaret Powers Crowley, June 22, 1946 (dec. Nov. 1987); children: John Woodson, Stephen Rowan, Mark Crowley, William Kent. AB, U. Ill., 1942; MS, Syracuse U., 1943; A.M., Harvard, 1951, PhD, 1953. Research asst. Pub. Adminstrn. Clearing House, Washington, 1946; instr., then asst. prof. polit. sci. U. Mo., 1948-54; with Nat. Mcpl. League, 1953-90, exec. dir., 1969-85, project coord., 1985-90; sr. assoc. Inst. Pub. Adminstrn., 1988—. Rsch. assoc. Govt. Affairs Found., 1954-57; vis. assoc. prof. pub. adminstrn. Columbia, 1957; sr. rsch. assoc. Columbia (Met. Region Program), 1957-61; mem. adv. com. state and local govt. stats. Bur. Census, 1962-65, chmn., 1963-65; mem. area devel. adv. bd. Com. Econ. Devel., 1964-66; cons. Adv. Commn. Intergovtl. Rels., 1967-89. Author: Constitutional Aspects of Metropolitan Government, 1961, also articles; contbg. editor Nat. Civic Rev., 1954-85, chmn. editorial bd., 1969-85. Mem. Greenburgh (N.Y.) Bd. Edn., 1961-64; mem. Westchester County Planning Bd., 1962-97, vice chmn., 1967-72, chmn., 1973-97, Hudson River Valley Greenway Compact Commn., 1997—, Conservation Adv. Bd., Dobbs Ferry, N.Y., 1997—; bd. dirs. Westchester County Indsl. Devel. Agy., 1976-83; trustee Pub. Adminstrn. Service, 1969-76; governing bd. Governmental Affairs Inst., 1969-76. Served to lt. USNR, 1943-46. Mem. Am. Polit. Sci. Assn., Am. Soc. Pub. Adminstrn., Govtl. Rsch. Assn., Internat. City/County Mgmt. Assn., Nat. Acad. Pub. Adminstrn., Regional Plan Assn. N.Y., Phi Beta Kappa, Alpha Kappa Lambda, Delta Sigma Pi, Omicron Delta Kappa, Pi Alpha Alpha. Episcopalian. Home: 100 Buena Vista Dr Dobbs Ferry NY 10522-3521 Office: Inst Pub Adminstrn 411 Lafayette St New York NY 10003-7032 E-mail: wncassella@aol.com.

CASSELMAN, BARRY, political correspondent, nonprofit administrator, author; b. Erie, Pa., May 24, 1942; s. Hyman Lawrence and Pauline (Masiroff) C. BA with honors, U. Pa., 1964; postgrad., U. Madrid, 1966-67; MFA, U. Iowa, 1969. Editor Harcourt Brace & World, N.Y.C., 1970; editor, pub. Appleseeds newspaper, Chaska, Minn., 1972-73, Many Corners newspaper, Mpls., 1973-86; pres. Preludium News Svc., Mpls., 1986—. Polit. corr. Rothenberg Polit. Report, Weekly Standard, Utne Reader, Washington Times; lectr. Cunard Lines, 1988—; radio commentator Sta. WCCO-AM, Mpls., Voice of America; TV commentator CONUS All News Channel. Author: Language, A Magical Enterprise, The Body, 1978, Among Dreams, 1985, (poetry) The Rippling Water Sleeve, 1969, Equilibrium Fingers, 1977, The Boat of the Blue Rose, 2002. Exec. dir. Internat. Conf. Found., Mpls., 1990—. Office: Internat Conf Found 1107 Hazeltine Blvd Ste 505 Chaska MN 55318 E-mail: barcass@mr.net.

CASSELMAN, FREDERICK LEE, computer artist; b. Columbus, Ohio, Jan. 5, 1940; s. Carroll Dean Casselman and Marjory Evelyn Howard; m. Carol Esther Puffer, Nov. 23, 1968; children: Amy, Aaron. BEE, Ohio State U., 1963, MSEE, 1965. Sr. engr. GTE Corp., Needham, Mass., 1966-94. Exhibited in one-man shows at Boston Cyberarts Festival, 1999, Chelsea (Mass.) Waterfront Gallery, 2000, Sonoma Mus. Visual Art, 2002, Ctrl. Wyo. Coll., 2002; author website The Earth Echo Project, 1996—; artist on-line-exhbn. Digital Americana, Orlando Mus. Art, 1998. Publicity dir. Framingham (Mass.) Cultural Coun., 1996-2001; vol. Mass. Correctional Instn., Framingham, 1999—. Home: 48 Florissant Ave Framingham MA 01701-4224 E-mail: fred@earthecho.com.

CASSELMAN, WILLIAM E., II, lawyer; b. Washington, Pa., July 8, 1941; s. William E. and Lucy (Bobbs) C.; m. Mia Kang, June 15, 1993; children: Katharine Carr, Lee Wilson. BA, Claremont-McKenna Coll., 1963; postgrad., U. Madrid, 1963-64; JD, George Washington U., 1968. Bar: Va. 1968, D.C. 1972, U.S. Supreme Ct. 1975. Legis. asst. to Robert McClory U.S. Ho. of Reps., 1965-68; staff asst. Office of Pres., 1969, dep. spl. asst. to Pres., 1969-71, counsel to Pres., 1974-75; gen. counsel Gen. Svcs. Adminstrn., 1971-73; legal counsel to Vice Pres. U.S., 1973-74; ptnr. Ambrose & Casselman, P.C., 1975-79; pvt. practice Washington, 1979-82; ptnr. Dorsey & Whitney, 1982-84, Popham, Haik, Schnobrich & Kaufman, Ltd., Washington, 1985-93; of counsel Stairs Dillenbeck Finley & Rendon, N.Y.C., 1993—; pvt. practice Washington, Va., 1993—. Mem. adminstrv. conf. U.S., 1971-73; adv. mem. Nat. Conf. Commrs. on Uniform State Laws, 1975; mem. Gerald R. Ford Commemorative Com., 1977-82; bd. dirs. gen. counsel, mem. fin. com., fellow Georgetown U. Ctr. for Internat. Bus. and Trade (formerly Nat. Ctr. Export-Import Studies), 1983-93. Recipient Disting. Alumni Achievement award George Washington U., 1975. Mem. ABA, Fed. Bar Assn. (chmn. gen. counsels com. 1973-74, nat. coun. 1974-79, Disting. Svc. commendation 1974), George Washington Law Assn. (bd. dirs. 1976-81), Nat. Trust for Hist. Preservation (mem. com. on legal svcs. 1978-80), Delta Theta Phi, Theta Chi. Republican.

CASSELS, MARTHA BEASLEY, realtor, developer; b. Greenwood, S.C., Oct. 22, 1932; d. Hugh Alton and Ora Faith (Mitchell) Beasley; m. Marion Carlyle Crenshaw, Jr., June 25, 1953 (div. 1979); children: Marion Carlyle III, William Frank, Hugh Charles, Faith Byrd; m. Samuel Jones Cassels, III, Oct. 6, 1979 (div. 1999). BA, Converse Coll., 1953. Cert. residential specialist Realtors Nat. Mktg. Inst., 1979. Tchr. Carr Jr. H.S., Durham, N.C., 1953-55, 1st Congl. Pre Sch., Branford, Conn., 1964-66; dir. Barfield Kindergarten, Durham, 1966-68, Duke Meml. Pre Sch., Durham, 1968-74; sec. corp. Bob Gunter Realty, Inc., Durham, 1972-77; owner Crenshaw Co., Inc., Durham, 1977-79, Cassels Real Estate, Montgomery, Ala., 1980—. Pres. Hampton Killingsworth, Inc. 1990—, Montgomery Area Bd. Realtors, Ala. Bd. Realtors, 1979—, Nat. Bd. Realtors, Chgo., 1974—. Mem. County Bd. Edn., Durham, 1972—79; patron theatre dept. Ala. State U., Montgomery, 1994—; active Montgomery Zoo; bd. dirs. Scott and Zelda Fitzgerald Mus., Montgomery, 1986—, sponsor statewide lit. contest for high schs. and colls. Named Top Prodr., Montgomery Area Bd. Realtors, 1981; recipient Top Residential award Montgomery Area Bd. Realtors, 1982, 10 Consecutive Yrs. of Multi Millions award Montgomery Area Bd. Realtors, 1990. Mem.: YMCA, AAUW, Greater Montgomery Home Builder Assn., Prattville C. of C., Montgomery Area C. of C., C.E.O. Roundtable, Jr. Twentieth Century Club, Mobile Yacht Club. Episcopalian. Avocations: reading, swimming, sailing. Office: Cassels Real Estate 623 S Perry St Montgomery AL 36104-5890 E-mail: sales@casselsrealestate.com.

CASSENS, NICHOLAS, JR., ceramics engineer; b. Sigourney, Iowa, Sept. 8, 1948; s. Nicholas and Wanda Fern (Lancaster) C.; m. Linda Joyce Morrow, Aug. 30, 1969; 1 son, Randall Scott. BS in Ceramic Engring., BSChemE, Iowa State U., 1971; MS in Material Sci. and Engring., U. Calif., Berkeley, 1979. Jr. rsch. engr. Nat. Refractories and Minerals Corp., Livermore, Calif., 1971-72, rsch. engr., 1972-74, sr. rsch. engr., 1974—77, staff rsch. engr., 1977-84, sr. staff rsch. engr., 1984—2002; sr. mgr. product devel. Refractory and Advanced Specialties Inc., Stockton, Calif., 2003—. Mem. Am. Ceramic Soc. Democrat. Achievements include patentee in field U.S., Australia, S.Am., Japan, Europe. Home: 4082 Suffolk Way Pleasanton CA 94588-4117 Office: 818 McCloy Ave Rough and Ready Island Stockton CA 94550

CASSENS, PATRICK, mathematician, educator; b. Litchfield, Ill., Oct. 21, 1938; s. Eldor Dietrich and Iola Henry Cassens; m. Barbara A Arunski, Dec. 29, 1962; children: Edward G., Mary A. BS, Saint Louis U., 1960, MS, 1962, PhD, 1966. Instr. to asst. prof. U. Mo., St. Louis, 1964—68; asst. prof. to assoc. prof. State U. NY Coll. at Oswego, 1968—76, assoc. dean arts and scis., 1973—76; v.p. academic affairs Siena Coll., Loudonville, NY, 1977—79; v.p. academic affairs, prof. U. Central Okla., Edmond, 1979—83; v.p. academic affairs Dakota State U., Madison, SD, 1985—86; prof. of math. Mo. Southern State U., Joplin, 1988—. Internet course developer Mo. Southern State U., 1999—. Contbr. articles. Pres. Rotary Club, Edmond, 1984—85, Webb City/Carl Junction, Mo., 1997—98. Grantee Post Doctoral grant, Math. Assn. of Am., 1966. Mem.: Math. Assn. of Am., Am. Math. Soc., Rotary Club, Soc. of the Sigma Xi. Avocations: jogging, opera, music, reading, family. Office: Mo So State Coll 3950 E Newman Rd Joplin MO 64801 E-mail: cassens-p@mail.mssu.edu.

CASSENS, SUSAN FORGET, artist; b. Ft. Pierce, Fla., May 11, 1956; m. Steven Dale Cassens, Mar. 4, 1979; children: Christopher, Michael, Scott. AA, U. Fla., 1976; BA in Edn. with honors, Fla. Atlantic U., 1978. Tchr. Garden City Elem., Ft. Pierce, 1978-79; owner Brush Strokes Art Gallery, Ft. Pierce, 1993-95; co-owner Indian River Crafters Guild, Ft. Pierce, 1995; pub., mfr. Somerset Greetings USA, 1998. Bd. mem. St. Lucie County Cultural Affairs Coun., Ft. Pierce, 1993-97, chmn., 1996-97. Cover artist: Cracker Cuisine, 1993; exhbns. include A.E. Backus Gallery and Mus., Ft. Pierce, Treasure Coast Art Gallery, Ft. Pierce. Chpt. sec. P.E.O. chpt. R., Ft. Pierce, 1987, chpt. pres.,

1989; bd. dir. A.E. Backus Art Gallery and Mus., Mainstreet (Ft. Pierce) Inc., St. Lucie Hist. Soc.; chair St. Lucie Mural Soc., Ft. Pierce, 1994. Mem. Nat. Mus. Women in Arts (charter), Heathcote Bot. Gardens (charter). Presbyterian. Avocations: antiques, art books, travel. Office: PO Box 593 Fort Pierce FL 34954-0593

CASSERLY, JAMES LUND, lawyer; b. Norfolk, Va., Dec. 26, 1951; s. James Robert and Patricia (Lund) C.; m. Kathleen Ann Flynn, Apr. 25, 1981; 1 child Laura Flynn. AB magna cum laude, Tufts Coll., 1973; JD, Columbia U., 1976. Bar: D.C. 1976, U.S. Dist. Ct. D.C. 1980, U.S. Ct. Appeals (D.C. cir.) 1981. Law clk. to trial judges U.S. Ct. Fed. Claims, Washington, 1976-77; law clk. to judge Marion Bennett U.S. Ct. Appeals Fed. Cir., Washington, 1977-78; assoc. Wilkinson, Cragun & Barker, Washington, 1978-82, Squire Sanders & Dempsey, Washington, 1982-85, ptnr., 1985-94; sr. legal advisor to Commr. Susan Ness FCC, Washington, 1994-99; ptnr. Mintz Levin Cohn Ferris Glovsky & Popeo PC, Washington, 1999—2002, Willkie Farr & Gallagher, Washington, 2003—. Home: 2839 Allendale Pl NW Washington DC 20008 Office: Willkie Farr & Gallagher 1875 K St NW Washington DC 20006-1238 E-mail: jcasserly@willkie.com.

CASSERS, DANIEL LEE, forester, educator; b. Dixon, Ill., Dec. 15, 1946; s. Ludwig P. and Ethel A. Cassens; m. Victoria Jean Vinkovich. BS, U. Ill., 1968; MS, U. Calif., 1969; PhD, U. Wis., 1973. Wood technologist U.S. Forest Products Lab., Madison, Wis., 1970—73; ext. specialist La. State U., Baton Rouge, 1973—77; prof. Purdue U., W. Lafayette, La., 1977—; prin., owner Cassers Trees, W. Lafayette, 1980—. Mem.: Soc. Wood Sci. and Tech., Forest Products Rsch. Soc. Avocations: tree management, tree growing, sawmilling. Home: 601 N 400 West West Lafayette IN 47906 Office: Purdue Univ Dept Forestry and Natural Resources 1200 Forest Prod B West Lafayette IN 47907 Fax: 765-494-3643. E-mail: dcassers@fnr.purdue.edu.

CASSIDAY, BENJAMIN BUCKLES, III, lawyer; b. Honolulu, Sept. 6, 1950; s. Benjamin B. Jr. and Barbara (Dennison) C.; m. Maile Burgundy, May 8, 1996. BS, Stanford U., 1973; JD, Boston Coll., 1977. Bar: Colo. 1977, Hawaii 1980, U.S. Ct. Appeals (9th cir.) 1982. State pub. defender Pub. Defender's Office, Littleton, Colo., 1977-80; pvt. practice Honolulu, 1981-82, 88—, 1st dep. Fed. Pub. Defender's Office, Honolulu, 1982-87. Lawyer rep. 9th Cir., 1993-95. Mem. Am. Bd. Criminal Lawyers, Hawaii Assns. Criminal Def. Lawyers (bd. dirs.). Avocations: poker, pool. Home: 5699 Kalanianaole Hwy Honolulu HI 96821-2303 Office: Law Office of Ben Cassiday 841 Bishop St Ste 2201 Honolulu HI 96813-3921 E-mail: bencassiday@hotmail.com.

CASSIDY, BARRY ALLEN, physician assistant, clinical medical ethicist; b. Chgo., Aug. 28, 1947; s. Frank Thomas and Ann Marie (Panek) C.; m. JoAnn DeRue (div.); m. Robyn G. Lacher (div.); children: Colleen Conarchy, Jason Lacher, Nathaniel Austin; m. Barbie A. Cassidy. Cert. physician assoc., Duke U., 1971; BS, Univ. State N.Y., Albany, 1992; PhD, Union Inst., 1995. Cert. physician asst. Physician assoc. Med. Offices of T.C. Rozema, MD, Waukegan, Ill., 1971—73; instr. in healthcare sci. Sch. Medicine George Washington U., Washington, 1973—75; med. cons. Medicolegal Rsch., Washington, 1975—79; CEO, dir. health svcs. Occucare, Inc., Research Triangle Park, NC, 1979—81; v.p. Coastal Group, Inc., Durham, NC, 1981—82; exec. v.p. So. Emergency Med. Assocs., Research Triangle Park, 1982—83; physician asst. Ariz. Heart Inst., Phoenix, 1983—86; pres. West Health Corp., Phoenix, 1986—87; thoracic and cardiovascular surgery physician asst. Mayo Clinic, Scottsdale, Ariz., 1987—96; assoc. prof., assoc. dir. physician asst. program Coll. Allied Health Scis. Midwe. U., Glendale, Ariz., 1996—99, dir. physician asst. program, 1998—2002, prof. health sci., 1999—2002, assoc. dean Coll. Health Scis., 1999—2002; exec. dir. Ariz. Med. Bd., 2002—. Adj. faculty S.W. Ctr. for Osteo. Med. Edn. and Health Scis., 1995-96; chmn. Joint Bd. Regulation Physician Assts., 1998, pres., 2002—; exec. dir., Ariz. Med. Bd., 2002—. Mem. editl. bd. Physician Assts. in Primary Care, 1985-88; inventor break-away catheter sys. Advisor on allied health Ill. Med. Soc., Chgo., 1972; advisor Gov.'s Health Licensure Commn., State of Ill., Chgo., 1972. Sgt. USAF, 1965-69. Mem. Ariz. Med. Assn., Ariz. Acad. Physician Assts., Am. Acad. Physician Assts. (chmn. jud. affairs com., v.p. 1974). Jewish. Home: 6630 E Lafayette Blvd Scottsdale AZ 85251-3134 Office: Ariz Med Bd 9545 E Double Tree Ranch Rd Scottsdale AZ 85258 E-mail: bcassidy@azmdboard.org.

CASSIDY, CATHERINE, editor-in-chief; Exec. editor Prevention Mag., N.Y.C., 1997—2001, editor-in-chief, 2001—. Office: Prevention Mag 733 3d Ave New York NY 10017

CASSIDY, DAVID MICHAEL, lawyer; b. Amityville, N.Y., May 31, 1954; s. Paul Francis and Theresa Alice (Britts) C.; children: Daniel B., Caitlin E. BA, SUNY, Stony Brook, 1981; JD, St. John's U., Jamaica, N.Y., 1985. Bar: N.Y. 1986. Assoc. Rivkin Radler LLP, Uniondale, NY, 1985-92, ptnr., 1992—. Mem. Suffolk County Bar Assn., L.I. Assn. Office: Rivkin Radler LLP Eab Plz Uniondale NY 11556-0001

CASSIDY, DONALD L. investment analyst; b. Cambridge, Mass., June 25, 1945; s. Francis Joseph and Ethel Dorothy (Lange) C. BS in Econs., U. Pa., 1967. Asst. to pres. Spear & Staff, Inc., Wellesley, Mass., 1973-74; sr. analyst Arthur D. Little Decision Resources, Cambridge, 1974-86; sr. research analyst Boettcher & Co., Inc., Denver, 1986, v.p., 1987-89; sr. analyst, mgr. closed-end funds svcs. Lipper Inc., Denver, 1990-95, mgr. money flows analysis, 1999—. Author: Plugging Into Utilities, 1993, It's When You Sell That Counts, 1996, 30 Strategies for High-Profit Investment Success, 1997, When the Dow Breaks, 1999, Trading on Volume, 2001. Umpire Little League Baseball, 1970-96; chmn. bd. dirs. Citizens for Ltd. Taxation, Boston, 1978-84, author, drafter tax-limitation initiative ballot question, 1980. Served with U.S. Army, 1968-70. Mem. Am. Assn. Individual Investors, Nat. Spkrs. Bur., Denver Soc. Securities Analysts. Libertarian. E-mail: don.cassidy@Lipper.Reuters.com.

CASSIDY, EDWARD Q. lawyer; b. Pekin, Ill., July 15, 1951; s. Clement James and Patricia Quinn Cassidy; m. Michele A. Cohn, Oct. 30, 1982. JD, Hamline U., 1981. Ptnr. Felhaber, Larson, Fenlon & Vogt, St. Paul, 1994—. Office: Felhaber Larson Fenlon & Vogt 2100 World Trade Ctr Saint Paul MN 55105

CASSIDY, ESTHER CHRISTMAS, retired government official; b. Upper Marlboro, Md., Aug. 5, 1933; d. Donelson and Esther Christmas; divorced; children: William Keeling, Carroll Cassidy Drewyer, Daniel Clark. BA, Manhattanville Coll., 1955. Phys. scientist, R&D Nat. Bur. Standards, Gaithersburg, Md., 1955-73; sci. advisor U.S. Congressman Teno Roncalio, Washington, 1973-74; asst. dir. congl. affairs Energy R&D Adminstrn. Dept. Energy, Washington, 1974-78; dir. congl. and legis. affairs Nat. Inst. Stds. and Tech., Gaithersburg, 1978-98; ret., 1998. Contbr. articles to profl. jours. Mem. IEEE (sr.). Avocations: horse racing, golf.

CASSIDY, EUGENE PATRICK, pathologist; b. N.Y.C., July 21, 1940; s. Eugene Zachary and Anita Hilda (Corsi) C.; m. Hollis Elizabeth Ward, Sept. 25, 1965; 1 child, Meredith. BA, Williams Coll., 1962; MD, Yale U., 1966. Diplomate Am. Bd. Pathology. Intern Yale-New Haven Hosp., Conn., 1966-67; resident then fellow in pathology and lab. medicine Yale U. Med. Ctr., 1967-70; dir. pathology Appalachian Lab. for Occupational Respiratory Disease, Morgantown, Wis., 1970-72; pathologist Clarkson Hosp., Omaha, 1972-78, Scripps Hosp., Encinitas, Calif., 1978-84; dir. pathology Marshalltown (Iowa) Med. and Surgical Ctr., 1984—. Asst. prof. W.Va. U. Sch. Medicine, Morgantown, 1970-72, U. Nebr. Sch. Medicine, Omaha, 1974-78. Contbr. articles to profl. jours. Served with USPHS, 1970-72. Fellow Internat. Acad. Pathology, Coll. Am. Pathologists, Am. Soc. Clin. Pathologists; mem. AMA, Am. Assn. Blood Banks. Republican. Avocations: music, architecture. Home: 505 Craig Cir Marshalltown IA 50158-6303 Office: Marshalltown Med & Surg Ctr 3 S Fouth Ave Marshalltown IA 50158-2924

CASSIDY, FREDERICK, psychiatrist; b. N.Y., Feb. 17, 1960; BA, Columbia Coll., 1982; MD, Vanderbilt U., 1988. Rsch. asst. Coll. of Physicians and Surgeons, N.Y.C., 1982—84; resident Duke U. Med. Ctr., Durham, NC. Recipient Robbins Guze award, Am. Psycopathological Assn., 2001. Office: Duke Univ Box 3414 Duke Univ Med Ctr Durham NC 27712

CASSIDY, JACK, academic administrator, educator; b. Phila., Mar. 12, 1941; married; 2 children. BA in English, Gettysburg Coll., Phila., 1962; MEd in Secondary Edn., Temple U., Phila., 1965, PhD in Ednl. Psychology, 1975. Tchr. Hawaii Dept. Pub. Instrn., Island Kauai, Lihue, 1965-69; instr. Temple U., 1970-71; reading supr. Newark (Del.) Sch. Dist., 1972-78; prof. Millersville (Pa.) U., 1981-98; asst. dean Coll. Edn. Tex. A&M Univ., Corpus Christi, 1998—. Spl. cons. Ednl. Testing Svc., 1977-93. Sr. author: Basic Life Skills, Macmillan Lit. Series, Read-Reason-Write, Scribner Reading Series; contbr. articles to profl. jours. Coach Community Swim Teams, Kapaa, Hawaii, 1967-68. Mem. Internat. Reading Assn. (legis. com. 1975-76, dir. 1976-79, pres. 1982-83), Diamond State Reading Assn. (pres. 1974-75), Nat. Coun. Tchrs. English, Assn. for Supervision and Curriculum Devel., Nat. Coun. Accreditation Tchr. Edn. (exec. bd. 1986-88, chmn. 1988-89, 1997-2000), Coll. Reading Assn. (dir. 1994-97, pres. 1999-2000), Phi Delta Kappa. Home: 322 Santa Monica Pl Corpus Christi TX 78411-1612 Office: Early Childhood Devel Ctr Tex A&M Univ 6300 Ocean Dr Corpus Christi TX 78412-5503 E-mail: jcassidy@falcon.tamucc.edu.

CASSIDY, JAMES MARK, construction company executive; b. Evanston, Ill., June 22, 1942; s. James Michael and Mary Ellen (Munroe) C.; m. Bonnie Marie Bercker, Aug. 1, 1964 (div. Dec. 1981); children: Micaela Marie, Elizabeth Ann, Daniel James; m. Patricia Margaret Mary Murphy, Sept. 15, 1984. BA, St. Mary's Coll., 1963. Estimator Cassidy Bros., Inc., Rosemont, Ill., 1963-65, project mgr., 1965-67, v.p., 1967-71, exec. v.p., 1971-77, pres., 1978—. Trustee Plasterer's Health & Welfare Trust, 1971-92; chmn. labor liaison com. Laborers Internat. Union N.Am. and Assn. Wall and Ceiling Industries, 1982-85, chmn. labor-mgmt. group, 1985-88; chmn. Chicagoland Assn. Wall and Ceiling Contractors' Carpenters Union Negotiating Team, 1983—; trustee, vice chmn. laborers dist. coun. Chgo. and Vicinity Laborers-Employers Cooperation and Edn. Trust Fund, 1999—. Area fund leader Constrn. Industry Salute to Boy Scouts Am., 1975; mem. president's coun. St. Mary's Coll. With U.S. Army, 1963-64, N.G., 1964-69. Mem. Chgo. Plastering Inst., Builder Uppers Club (pres. 1973-74), Chicagoland Assn. Wall and Ceiling Contractors (pres. 1976-79), Great Lakes Coun., Internat. Assn. Wall and Ceiling Contractors (chmn. 1977), Constrn. Employers Assn. Chgo. (bd. dirs. 1976—, pres.-elect 1989-90, pres. 1991-93, chmn. com. labor-mgmt. rels. 1983-93), Chicagoland Safety Coun. (bd. dirs. 1988-92), Joint Conf. Bd. Cook County (chmn. 1996-97, 98-99), Assn. Wall and Ceiling Industries Internat. (bd. dirs. 1978-81, 88-89, fin. v.p. 1990, 2d v.p. 1991, pres.-elect 1992, pres. 1993), Park Ridge County Club (Ill.) (bd. dirs. 1994-97), Eagle Creek Country Club (Naples, Fla.).

CASSIDY, JOHN FRANCIS, JR., industrial technology executive; b. Troy, N.Y., Nov. 26, 1943; s. John F. Sr. and Beverly A. (Blowers) C.; m. Paulina C. DiBacco, July 24, 1965; children: Rachel, Sean. BEE, Rensselaer Poly. Inst., 1965, MEE, 1967, PhD, 1969. Various R & D mgmt. positions GM, 1969-81; with control systems R & D GE Corp. R & D Labs., 1981-89; corp. dir. tech. mgmt. United Techs. Corp., 1989-92; dir. United Techs. Rsch. Ctr., 1992-93, v.p., 1993-98; sr. v.p. sci. and tech. United Techs. Corp., Hartford, Conn., 1998—; mem. corp. Draper Labs., 2000—. Vice chair bd. dirs. Rensselaer at Hartford. Mem. IEEE (sr.), Soc. Automotive Engrs. (sr.), Conn. Acad. Sci. and Engring. Office: United Techs Rsch Ctr MS 129-04 411 Silver Ln East Hartford CT 06118-1127 E-mail: cassidjf@utrc.utc.com.

CASSIDY, JOHN HAROLD, lawyer; b. St. Louis, June 18, 1925; s. John Harold and Jennie (Phillips) C.; m. Marjorie Blair, Nov. 26, 1947; children: Patricia, John, Brian. AB, Washington U., 1949, JD, 1951. Bar: Mo. 1951, U.S. Dist. Ct. (ea. dist.) Mo. 1951, U.S. Ct. Appeals (8th crct.) 1951, U.S. Supreme Ct. 1955. Atty. U.S. Govt., St. Louis, 1951-56; pvt. practice St. Louis, 1956-59; atty. Crown Zellerbach Corp., San Francisco, 1959-61, Ralston Purina Co., St. Louis, 1961-89, v.p., 1975-85, v.p., sec., sr. counsel, 1985-89. Served with U.S. Mcht. Marine, 1943-45. Mem.: ABA, Am. Soc. Corp. Secs., St. Louis Bar Assn., Mo. Bar Assn. Republican.

CASSIDY, JOHN JOSEPH, hydraulic and hydrologic engineer; b. Gebo, Wyo., June 21, 1930; s. Valentine Patrick and Johannah Elizabeth (Johnson) C.; m. Alice Willman, Mar. 15, 1953; children: Val Patrick, Jon Allan, Debra Kay. BSCE, Mont. State U., Bozeman, 1952, MSCE, 1960; PhD, U. Iowa, 1964. Registered profl. engr., Mont., Calif., Wash., Idaho, Wyo., Nebr., N.Y., Ariz. Hwy. engr. U.S. Bur. Pub. Rds., Missoula, Mont., 1951-52; design engr. Mont. State Water Bd., Helena, 1954-58; instr. civil engring. Mont. State U., Bozeman, 1958-60; rsch. asst. in hydraulics U. Iowa, Iowa City, 1960-63; prof., chmn. civil engring. U. Mo., columbia, 1963-74; dir. Wash. Water Resources Ctr. Wash. State U., Pullman, 1979-81; chief hydrologic engr. Bechtel Corp., San Francisco, 1974-79, 81-85, mgr. hydraulics and hydrology, 1985-94, mgr. hydraulics and geotechnical svcs., 1994-95; ret., 1995. Cons. dam safety Hydro Que., Montreal, 1993-94; cons. water resources Wyo. State Engrs. Office, Cheyenne, 1990-2001; cons. dam design MK Corp., Boise, Idaho, 1980-81; cons. hydrology Gomez and Cajon, Bogota, Colombia, 1980-81; commn. Binacional de Yacryeta, Buenos Aires, Argentina, 1994-96, Hidroestudios, Bogota, Columbia, 1995-97, Consutoria Colombiana, 1998 Co-author: Hydrology for Engineers and Planners, 1974, Small and Mini Hydropower Systems, 1984, Engineering Hydraulics, 1988, 98, Design of Hydropower Systems, 1989. Chmn. fin. com. Walnut Creek (Calif.) United Meth. Ch., 1990-92. Served to cpl. U.S. Army, 1952-54. Recipient Ray K. Linsley award for hydrology Am. Inst. Hydrology, 2001; Bechtel fellow, 1987; named to Disting. Engring. Alumni Acad., U. Iowa, 2002. Fellow ASCE (hon., Hunter Rouse Hydraulic Engring. award 1988, Hydraulic Structures medal 1996); mem. NAE, Internat. Assn. Hydraulic Rsch., U.S. Soc. on Dams (dir. 1987-95), Internat. Commn. on Large Dams (com. chmn. 1987-96). Republican. Methodist. Avocations: woodworking, fly fishing. Home: 2884 Saklan Indian Dr Walnut Creek CA 94595 E-mail: JCassidys@aol.com.

CASSIDY, JOHN LEMONT, retired engineering executive; b. Springfield, Mass., Jan. 2, 1934; s. Elbridge Floyd and Marion (Arent) C.; m. Katherine Helen Carollo, Feb. 9, 1954 (div. Apr. 1970); children: Debbie M. Batliner, Sheryl A. Batliner, Dennis M.; m. Jane Frances Wahlmeier, Nov. 21, 1974; children: Armon J. Scheetz, Carla A. Luffman, Monica L. Scheetz. BS in Physics, U. Mo., Kansas City, 1969. V.p. mfg. Hisonic, Inc., Olathe, Kans., 1969-83; v.p. Unimark, Inc., Overland Park, Kans., 1984—2001. Pres. Unimark Svc. Co., 1988-93; sr. judge Am. Water Ski Assn., 1975-80. Mem., U.S. Leadership Coun. Spl. Olympics Internat., 2003—; Alpine/nordic ski coach Spl. Olympics Kans., chmn. winter games, 1990—95, bd. dirs., 1998—; nordic ski coach Team USA Spl. Olympics World Winter Games, 2001; chmn. bd. dirs. Spl. Olympics Kans., 2002—. With USMC, 1953—56. Recipient Outstanding Svc. award, Mo-Kan Ski Club, 1979, Disting. Svc. award, Kans. Spl. Olympics, 1990, SGMA Kans. Heroes award, 2001. Mem. U.S. Recreational Ski Assn. (chmn. bd. dirs. 1985-88, Slim Davis award for outsdanding svc. 1988), Kansas City Ski Club (bd. dirs. 1980-85, 92-94, pres. 1983-84), Mensa, Clockwinders Optimist Club. Republican. Avocations: golf, snow and water skiing, scuba diving, volunteer activities. Home: 15942 Linden St Overland Park KS 66085 E-mail: jjcassidy21@juno.com.

CASSIDY, KEVIN ANDREW, retired engineering company executive; b. N.Y.C., May 20, 1931; s. Joseph Aloyisius and Norine Beatrice (Mangan) C.; m. Mary Elizabeth Hennessey, Jan. 16, 1954; children: Kevin Andrew Jr., Mark Robert, Karen Marie, Richard Joseph. BCE, Manhattan Coll., 1953. Registered profl. engr., N.J. Engr. Standard Oil (Ind.), Whiting, Ind., 1953-59; project engr. Foster Wheeler, N.Y.C., 1959-69; project mgr. Foster Wheeler Energy Corp., Livingston, N.J., 1969-78, div. v.p., 1978-82; dir. Foster Wheeler Energy Ltd., Reading, Eng., 1982-96, Hytech, Moscow, 1989-94; v.p. Foster Wheeler Internat. Corp., Perryville, N.J., 1985-96. Dir. Foster Wheeler Eastern Private Ltd., Singapore. Served with U.S. Army, 1954-56. Republican. Roman Catholic. Avocations: golf, skiing.

CASSIDY, RICHARD ARTHUR, environmental engineer, governmental water resources specialist; b. Manchester, N.H., Nov. 15, 1944; s. Arthur Joseph and Alice Ethuliette (Gregoire) C.; m. Judith Diane Maine, Aug. 14, 1971; children: Matthew, Amanda, Michael. BA, St. Anselm Coll., 1966; MS, U. N.H., 1969, Tufts U., 1972. Field biologist Pub. Svc. Co. N.H., Manchester, 1968; jr. san. engr. Mass. Divsn. Water Pollution Control, Boston, 1968-69; aquatic biologist Normandeau Assocs., Bedford, N.H., 1969-70; hydraulic engr. New Eng. divsn. U.S. Army Civil Engrs., Waltham, Mass., 1972-77; engr. northwestern divsn. Portland (Oreg.) dist. U.S. Army Civil Engrs., 1977-81, supr., environ. engr., 1981-99, environ. engr. northwestern divsn., 2000—03; ptnr. Am. Voyageur Enterprises, Beaverton, Oreg., 2003—. Interpretive guide, 2003—; cons. water resources specialist, 2003—. Contbr. articles to books and profl. jours. Den leader Pack 164 and 598 Columbia Pacific coun. Cub Scouts Am., Beaverton, Oreg., 1982-83, Webelos leader, 1984-85, 90-91, troop 764 committeeman, 1985-87, asst. scoutmaster, 1992, scoutmaster, 1993-94, troop 598 scoutmaster, 1995-2001, Cascade Pacific coun. Boy Scouts Am., 1985-87 (Silver Beaver award 2003); mem. Planning Commn. Hudson, N.H., 1976-77. Recipient commendation for exemplary performance Mo.-Miss. flood, 1973, commendation for litigation defense, 1986, commendation for mgmt. activities, 1987, 1991, Comdr.'s award for civilian svc., 1997, Achievement medal for civilian svc., 2000, Silver Beaver award, Boy Scouts Am., 2003. Mem. Am. Inst. Hydrology (cert., profl. ethics com. 1986, v.p. Oreg. sect. 1987-89, pres. Oreg. sect. 1990-92, nat. treas. 1995-2000), Internat. Tng. in Comm. (pres. West Way Club 1989-90), Nat. Assn. for Interpretation (cert.). Home: 7655 SW Belmont Dr Beaverton OR 97008-6335 Office: Am Voyageur Enterprises 7655 SW Belmont Dr Beaverton OR 97008 E-mail: cassidy@historytoursnw.com.

CASSIDY, ROBERT CHARLES, JR., lawyer; b. Beaumont, Tex., May 16, 1946; s. Robert Charles and Peggy (Timken) C.; m. Leslie Fleming Iben, Sept. 2, 1949; children: Robert Charles III, Thomas Reinhard, Leslie Anne Vallandingham. BA, Johns Hopkins U., 1968; JD, U. Pa., 1973; LLM, Georgetown U., 1977. Bar: Pa. 1973, U.S. Dist. Ct. D.C. 1975, U.S. Ct. Appeals (D.C. cir.) 1975, U.S. Ct. Internat. Trade 1982, U.S. Ct. Appeals (fed. cir.) 1982. Asst. counsel Office of Legis. Counsel U.S. Senate, 1973-75, internat. trade counsel Com. on Fin., 1975-79; gen. counsel Office of U.S. Trade Rep., Exec. Office of Pres., Washington, 1979-81; ptnr. Kaye, Scholer, Fierman, Hays & Handler, Washington, 1982-83, Wilmer, Cutler & Pickering, Washington, 1983—, internat. practice group leader, 1995-2000, trade group leader, 1985—2001. Bd. dirs. Cordell Hull Inst., 1999—. With U.S. Army, 1968—70. Mem.: ABA (chmn. internat. trade law com. 1986—89), Am. Soc. Internat. Law., D.C. Bar Assn. Office: Wilmer Cutler & Pickering 2445 M St NW Washington DC 20037-1487 E-mail: Robert.Cassidy@wilmer.com.

CASSIDY, SAMUEL H. lawyer, lieutenant governor, state legislator, humanities educator; children: Rachael, Sarah, Samuel H. IV. BA, U. Okla., 1972; JD, U. Tulsa, 1975; postgrad., Harvard U., 1991. Bar: Okla., 1975, U.S. Supreme Ct. 1977, U.S. Ct. Appeals (10th cir.), 1977, Colo. 1982. Pvt. practice law, 1975—; mem. Colo. State Senate, 1991-94; lt. gov. State of Colo., 1994-95; pres. Jefferson Econ. Coun., 1995-97; pres., CEO Colo. Assn. Commerce and Industry, 1997-2000; chair dept. bus. ethics and legal studies U. Denver, 2001—. Bd. dirs. Capital Reporter; instr. U. Tulsa, 1978-81, Tulsa Jr. Coll., 1979; owner High Country Title Co.; developer of residential and commercial real estate, pres. Sam Cassidy, Inc. oil and gas exploration and production co., mem. agriculture and natural resources com., 1991-92, state, mil. and vet. affairs com., 1991-92, local govt. com. 1991, legal svcs. com. 1991-92, hwy. legis. review com. 1991-93, nat. hazards mitigation coun., 1992-93, appropriations com., 1993, judiciary com., 1993; pres. Econ. Devel. Coun. of Colo., 1997-98; exec. com. legis coun., 1993-94, senate svcs. com. 1993; elected Senate Minority Leader, 1993-94, exec. com. Colo. Gen. Assembly; sr. fellow U. Denver, 1997—. Bd. dirs. Colo. DLC, 1993-95, Leadership Jefferson County, Rocky Flats Local Impacts Initiative, dir.; chmn. bd. Arts Comm., Inc. Named Outstanding Legislator for 1991 Colo. Bankers Assn., ACLU Outstanding Legis. 1994; recipient Outsatnding Legis. Efforts award Colo. Counties, Guardian of Small Bus. award, NFIB, 1992, 94; fellow Gates Found., 1991, U. Denver sr. fellow. Mem. Colo. Bar Assn. (bd. gov. 1993-94), S.W. Colo. Bar Assn., Nat. Conf. State Legis. (Colo. rep., task force on state-tribe rels.), Rotary (hon. mem., sustaining Paul Harris fellow), Club 20 (bd. dirs.), San Juan Forum (chmn., bd. dirs.). Avocations: fine art photography, skiing, fishing. Home: # 128 2800 S University Blvd Denver CO 80210 E-mail: scassidy@du.edu. *Leaders must nurture the positive. They must identify and promote issues which concern the whole community and the future of their grandchildren. They cannot indulge themselves in the profits of the politics of division. This is a vision which is hard to sell next November but which clearly distinguishes leaders from politicians.*

CASSIDY, TERRENCE PATRICK, JR., engineering consultant; b. Honolulu, May 21, 1964; s. Terrence Patrick Sr. and Geraldine C. BS Marine Engring., U.S. Merchant Marine Acad., 1987. 3d asst. engr. Crowley Maritime, Ft. Lauderdale, Fla., 1987-89; 2d asst. engr. D2-Meba-Amo, Dania, Fla., 1989-91, 1st asst. engr., 1991-92; project engr. Spectec Gen., Irvine, Calif., 1991; sr. project engr., corp. sec. Impact Engring., Inc., Ft. Lauderdale, 1992-97; v.p. Impact Engring. Inc., Ft. Lauderdale, 1995-97, also bd. dirs.; corp. sec. Impact Engring. Equipment, Inc., Ft. Lauderdale, 1993-97, v.p., 1995-97; CFO, Qualtair, Inc., Seattle, 1994-95; owner, bd. dirs. TC Internat., Ft. Lauderdale, Fla., 1994—2001; sr. analyst Reliability Maintenance Svcs., Inc., Ft. Lauderdale, 1998-2000; chief oper. officer Qualtair Inc., Mill Creek, Wash., 2000-01, CEO, 2001. Dir. internat. ops. TRA Internat. Group, LLC, 2001—. Lt. USNR. Mem. Soc. Naval Architects and Marine Engrs. Republican. Roman Catholic. Avocations: photography, skiing, boating, rollerblading. Office: TRA Internat Group 1511 E Commercial Blvd # 2 Fort Lauderdale FL 33334

CASSIDY, WILLIAM ARTHUR, geology and planetary science educator; b. N.Y.C., Jan. 3, 1928; s. John and Nellie (Briel) C.; m. Beverly J. Griffith, Aug. 29, 1959; children: Shauna Lynne, Laura Dawn, Brian John. BS in Geology, U. N. Mex., 1952; PhD in Geochemistry, Pa. State U., 1961. Seismic computer Superior Oil Co. of Calif., Midland, Tex., 1952-53; research scientist Lamont Geol. Obs., Palisades, N.Y., 1961-67; assoc. prof. geology and planetary sci. U. Pitts., 1968-80, prof., 1981-98, prof. emeritus, 1998—. Trustee Univ. Space Research Assn., Columbia, Md., 1975-82, chmn., 1978-79; chmn. meteorite working group Lunar and Planetary Sci. Inst., Houston, 1977-83 Author: Meteorites, Ice and Antarctica, 2003; contbr. articles to profl. jours. Served with USNR, 1945-46. Recipient Antarctic Svc. medal NSF, 1978; Fulbright student, 1953-54; grantee NSF, NASA. Mem. Am. Geophys. Union, Meteoritical Soc. (Barringer award 1995), Antarctican Soc. (Washington). Office: U Pitts 200 Space Research Coordination Ctr Pittsburgh PA 15260-3303 E-mail: ansmet@pitt.edu.

CASSILL, HERBERT CARROLL, artist; b. Percival, Iowa, Dec. 24, 1928; s. Howard Earl and Mary Elizabeth (Glosser) C.; m. Jean Kuniko Kubota, Aug. 23, 1951; children: Sarah Eden, J. Aaron. Student, Purdue U., 1944-45; B.F.A., State U. Iowa, 1948, M.F.A., 1950. Instr. printmaking State U. Iowa, Iowa City, 1953-57; prof., head dept. printmaking Cleve. Inst. Art, 1957-91, prof. emeritus, 1991—. One man shows include Oakland (Calif.) Art Mus., Ohio State U., Columbus, Cleve. Inst. Art, U. Wis., William Busta Gallery, 1990, 93, 96, 2001; group shows include Library of Congress, Washington, Bklyn. Art Mus., Bradford Internat. Invitational, 1984; represented in permanent collections, Mus. Modern Art, N.Y.C., Cleve. Mus. Art, Oakland Art Mus., San Francisco Art Mus., and others. Tiffany fellow printmaking, 1953 Home: 3084 Coleridge Rd Cleveland OH 44118-3556 Office: 11141 East Blvd Cleveland OH 44106-1710

CASSIMATIS, PETER JOHN, economics educator; b. Greece, Jan. 30, 1928; came to U.S., 1946, naturalized, 1946; s. John G. and Coula N. (Lourantos) C.; m. Margaret Ann Nell, Nov. 30, 1958; 1 son, Gregory. BCE, CUNY, 1953, MBA, 1961; PhD, New Sch. Social Research, 1967. Registered profl. engr., N.Y.; cert. cost analyst. Project mgr. several mgmt. and engring. cons. firms, 1953-64; prof. econs. and finance Fairleigh Dickinson U., Teaneck, N.J., 1964-99, emeritus prof. econs. and finance, 1999—. Vis. prof. Center for Planning and Econ. Research, Athens, Greece, 1972-73 Author: Economics of the Construction Industry, 1970, Construction and Economic Development, 1975, The Construciton Industry in Greece, 1976, Engineering Economics, 1988, Managerial Economics, 1996; contbr. articles to profl. jours. Served with AUS, 1946-47. Research fellow Found. Econ. Edn., 1970 Mem. Am. Econ. Assn., Eastern Econ. Assn., Nat. Assn. Bus. Economists, Acad. Internat. Bus., World Future Soc., Fin. Mgmt. Assn. Home: 19 Lorraine Dr Eastchester NY 10709-2008 Office: Fairleigh Dickinson U Economics Dept Teaneck NJ 07666

CASSIN, SANDRA JANE, social worker; b. Rochester, N.Y., July 3, 1952; d. Richard and Shirley Kalpin; m. John Cassin; 1 child, Brian. BS in Social Work & Psychology, SUNY, Brockport, 1993; MSW, SUNY, Buffalo, 1994. Cert. social worker, N.Y. Trainee in debriefings and defusings Internat. Critical

Incident Stress Found., Inc., 1996; team leader Monroe County Critical Incident Stress Mgmt. Team, 1998—. Mem. planning com., participation organizer Foodlink, Rochester, N.Y., 1991-93; program dir. Student Social Work Orgn., Brockport, N.Y., 1992-93; intern Park Ridge Chem. Dependency, Rochester, 1992-93, Rochester Psychiat. Ctr., 1993-94; therapist DePaul 2000--. Recipient Life Long Learning award Spencerport Parent U., 1995, Spl. Svc. award Emergency Comms. Dept. Rochester/Monroe County, N.Y., 2003. Mem. NASW, Phi Alpha (sec. 1993), Psi Chi. Avocations: research and advocacy in mental health and health care, reading and crafts. Home: 11 Rene Dr Spencerport NY 14559-1619 E-mail: jcassin1@rochester.rr.com.

CASSINELLI, JOSEPH PATRICK, astronomy educator; b. Cin., Aug. 23, 1940; s. Herbert John and Louise Margaret (Schlottman) C.; m. Mary LeFever; children: Joseph Michael, Carolyn Marie, Mary Kathleen. BS in Physics, Xavier U., 1962; MS in Physics, U. Ariz., 1965; PhD in Astronomy, U. Wash., 1970. Research asst. Kitt Peak Nat. Obs., Tucson, 1963-65; research engr. Boeing Co., Seattle, 1965-66; postdoctoral research assoc. Joint Inst. for Lab. Astrophysics, Boulder, Colo., 1970-72; postdoctoral fellow U. Wis., Madison, 1972-73, asst. prof., 1973-77, assoc. prof., 1977-81, prof., 1981—, chmn. astronomy dept., 1986-89. Vis. scientist Space Astronomy Lab., Utrecht, the Netherlands, 1975-76, Space Telescope Sci. Inst., 1991, High Altitude Obs., 1998; Donders chair U. Utrecht, 1985; sr. vis. fellow dept. physics and astronomy U. Glasgow, Scotland, 1998. Co-author: Introduction to Stellar Winds, 1999. Langley Abbot research fellow Harvard Smithsonian Ctr. for Astrophysics, 1981; Fulbright research fellow Sonnenborgh Obs., 1986. Mem. Am. Astron. Soc., Internat. Astron. Union. Roman Catholic. Home: 1520 Chandler St Madison WI 53711-2210 Office: U Wis Astronomy Dept 475 N Charter St Madison WI 53706-1582 E-mail: cassinelli@astro.wisc.edu.

CASSISI, NICHOLAS JOHN, otolaryngologist, dean; b. Portage, Pa., Mar. 2, 1935; s. Nicolo and Mary (Bonarrigo) C.; m. Elayne Ersay, Dec. 7, 1957; children: Jeffrey E., Nicole M. Cassisi Pope, Christopher M. BA, Case Western Res. U., 1957, DDS, 1961; MD, U. Miami, 1965. Diplomate Am. Bd. Otolarngology (assoc. examiner, sr. examiner 1993-99). Intern Jackson Meml. Hosp., Miami, Fla., 1965-66, asst. resident in gen. surgery, 1966-67; rsch. fellow Washington U., St. Louis, 1967-68; resident in otolaryngology Barnes Hosp., St. Louis, 1968-71; asst. clin. prof. U. Louisville Sch. Medicine, 1971-72; chief otolaryngology Ireland Army Hosp., Ft. Knox, Ky., 1971-73; joint appointments oral surgery U. Fla., Gainesville, 1973-91, assoc. prof. surgery divsn. otolaryngology Coll. Medicine, 1973-77, prof. surgery, chief divsn. otolaryngology Coll. Medicine, 1977-91, prof., chmn. otolaryngology Coll. Medicine, 1991-2000, sr. assoc. dean clin. affairs Coll. Medicine, 1997—; chief staff Shands/U. Fla. and Shands/AGH, Gainesville, 1998-2000. Coord. editor: Practical Reviews in Otolaryngology - Head and Neck Surgery, 1992-98; editor: Management of Head and Neck Cancer: A Multidisciplinary Approach, 1993; co-author: A Handbook of Physicians, 4th edit., 1995, Otolaryngology, 1996. Lt. col. U.S. Army, 1971-73. Mem. NCAA, Southeastern Conf. of NCAA, Accrediation Coun. Grad. Med. Edn. (chmn. residency rev. com. 1995-2001), Am. Soc. Head and Neck Surgery. Home: 3105 SW 5th Ct Gainesville FL 32601-9043 Office: U Fla Coll Medicine Dean's Office 1600 SW Archer Rd Rm M107 Gainesville FL 32610-0192 Fax: 352-392-6241.

CASSMAN, MARVIN, biochemist; b. Chgo., Apr. 4, 1936; s. Harry and Anna (Singer) C.; m. Alice M. Baker, June 24, 1972. BA, U. Chgo., 1954, BS, 1957, MS, 1959; PhD, Albert Einstein Coll. Medicine, 1965. Postdoctoral fellow U. Calif., Berkeley, 1965-67, asst. prof. Santa Barbara, 1967-75; adminstr. Nat. Inst. Gen. Med. Sci. NIH, Bethesda, Md., 1975-78, sect. chief, 1978-84, program dir., 1984-89, dep. dir., 1989-93, acting dir., 1993-96, dir., 1996—2001; exec. dir. Inst. for Quantitative Biomedical Rsch., U. Calif., San Francisco, 2001—. Mem. staff subcom. in sci., rsch. and tech. U.S Ho. of Reps., Washington, 1982-83; sr. policy analyst Office Sci. and Tech. Policy The White House, Washington, 1985-86. Recipient Sr. Exec. Svc. award USPHS, 1987, Pres. Meritorious award, 1991. Jewish. Avocations: music, racquetball. Home: 5608 Beam Ct Bethesda MD 20817-6303 Office: U Calif 513 Parnassus Ave Rm 5115 San Francisco CA 94143-0400

CASSO, RAMIRO PAUL, retired family physician, college official; b. Laredo, Tex., Aug. 4, 1922; s. Francisco Margarito and Josefa (Villarreal) C.; m. Emma Laurel, July 18, 1949; children: Thelma Casso Morales, Lydia Casso Tummel, Sylvia Casso Filoteo, Daniel, David. BSME, Tex. A&M U., 1943; BA in Chemistry, Baylor U., 1952; MD, U. Tex., Dallas, 1956. Diplomate Am. Bd. Family Practice. Hydraulic engr. Internat. Boundary and Water Commn., Laredo, 1948-50; tchr. math. Martin H.S., Laredo, 1946-48; med. intern Robert B. Green Hosp., San Antonio, 1956-57; pvt. practice McAllen, Tex., 1957—95; ret., 1995; v.p. instnl. advancement South Tex. C.C., Hidalgo-Starr County C.C. Dist., McAllen, 1995—2002. Adj. prof. Tex. A&M U. Health Sci. Ctr., 1999—; bd. dirs. McAllen Mcpl. Hosp./McAllen Med. Ctr. Hosp., 1975-85; founder, bd. dirs. Hidalgo County Health Care Corp., 1975-85; mem. nat. adv. bd. health rsch. facilities NIH, Washington, 1964-67; participant White House Confs. on Food and Food Nutrition and Health, Washington, 1965-69; spkr. on pub. health and primary care issues pertaining to South Tex. and U.S.-Mex. borderlands; presenter Hispanic health issues position Tex. Minority Health Conf., Houston, 1999. Mem. McAllen Ind. Sch. Dist. Sch. Bd., 1959-65; mem., v.p. Tex. Bd. Health, Austin, 1977-81, 91-97; mem. Texas Human (Employment) Rights Commn., Austin, 1983-87; established charity clinic for farm workers United Farmworkers, McAllen, 1970; bd. dirs. Area Health Edn. Ctr., 1997-98; pres., bd. dirs. El Milagro Clinic Bd., 1998—; founder El Milagro Primary Care Clinic, McAllen, Tex., 2000. Capt. anti-aircraft arty. U.S. Army, 1943-46. Named McAllen Man of Yr., McAllen C. of C., 1996, Notable Rio Grande Valley Hispanic, U. Tex.-PanAm., Edinburg, 1999, 100 Outstanding Hispanic-Ams. in Tex. in 20th Century Latino Monthly Mag., 2000; recipient Bishop Medeiros Golden Deeds award Tex. AFL-CIO and United Farmworkers, 1970, yearly award Hidalgo County Women's Polit. Caucus, 1991, Disting. Citizen award League United L.Am. Citizens, 1997, Living Legend award South Tex. C.C., 2002, Golden Trowel Maconic award City of Rio Grande and McAllen Tex. Lodges, 2003; Dr. Ramiro R. Casso S.T.C.C. Nursing and Allied Health Ctr. bldg. named in his honor, 2001. Fellow Am. Acad. Family Physicians; mem. AMA (life), Tex. Med. Assn. (life). Democrat. Baptist. Avocations: travel, reading, hunting, fishing. Office: Tex A&M Univ Health Sci Ctr 901 E Vermont Mcallen TX 78501

CASSON, ALAN GRAHAM, thoracic surgeon, researcher; b. Birmingham, Eng., Apr. 22, 1958; arrived in Can., 1981; m. Sharon Margaret Coffey; 1 child, Angela. MB ChB, Manchester U., Eng., 1981; MSc, Meml. U., St. John's, Nfld., Can., 1986. Asst. prof. surgery and oncology U. Western Ont., Can., 1991-93; asst. prof. surgery, program dir. thoracic surgery U. Toronto, Can., 1994-97; prof. thoracic surgery U. of Warwick, England, 1997-98; cons. thoracic surgery Heartlands Hosp., Birmingham, England, 1997-98; prof. surgery, head divsn. thoracic surgery Dalhousie U., Halifax, Canada, 1998—. Author: Oncogene Activation in Esophageal Cancer, 1992, Key Topics in Thoracic Surgery, 1999; mem. editl. bd. Jour. Surg. Oncology, Diseases of the Esophagus; contbr. chpts. to surg. textbooks and articles to profl. jours. Fellow Royal Coll. Surgeons Can., Am. Coll. Chest Physicians (young investigator award 1993), Am. Coll. Surgeons; mem. Internat. Soc. for Diseases of the Esophagus, Am. Assn. Cancer Rsch., Soc. Thoracic Surgeons. Avocations: fly fishing, squash, sailing. Office: Divsn Thoracic Surg 1278 Twr Rd Victoria Bldg 7-008 Halifax NS Canada B3H 2Y9 E-mail: thoracic@dal.ca.

CASSON, IRA RICHARD, neurologist; b. Bklyn., Apr. 6, 1949; s. Walter William and Gloria Casson; m. Susan Barbara Casson, June 10, 1972; children: Joshua, Benjamin. BA cum laude, Cornell U., 1971; MD, NYU, 1975. Diplomate Am. Bd. Pryoh & Neurology. Intern Long Island Jewish Hosp., NY, 1975-76; resident NYU Med. Ctr., N.Y.C., 1976-79; chief neurology Queens Hosp. Ctr., Jamaica, N.Y., 1979-81; pvt. practice neurology Forest Hills, N.Y., 1981—. Attending neurologist L.I. Jewish Hosp., New Hyde Park, N.Y., 1980—; chief neurology Parkway Hosp., Forest Hills, 1988—; instr. neurology NYU Sch. Medicine, N.Y.C., 1980—; asst. prof. clin. neurology Albert Einstein Coll. Medicine, Bronx, N.Y., 1990—; neurol. cons. NFL, N.Y.C., 1993—, N.Y. Jets Football Team, N.Y.C., 1993—, N.Y. Islanders Hockey Team, Uniondale, N.Y., 1996—. Contbr. articles to profl. jours. Mem. AMA, Am. Acad. Neurology, Med. Soc. State N.y., Queens County Med. Soc., Phi Beta Kappa. Office: 11203 Queens Blvd Forest Hills NY 11375-5550

CASSON, RICHARD FREDERICK, lawyer, travel bureau executive; b. Boston, Apr. 11, 1939; s. Louis H. and Beatrix S. C. AB, Colby Coll., 1960; JD, U. Chgo., 1963. Bar: Ill. 1963, Mass. 1964. Ptnr. Casson & Casson, Boston, 1967-68; assoc. counsel, corp. sec. Bankers Leasing Corp., 1968-75; asst. gen. counsel, corp. sec. Commonwealth Planning Corp., 1975-76; assoc. gen. counsel, asst. sec. Prudential Capital Corp., 1976-92; pres. Autumn Crest Corp., 1991-98; v.p. Casseden Corp. Asst. innkeeper Jackson House Inn, Woodstock, Vt. Capt. JAGC U.S. Army, 1964-67. Decorated Bronze Star. Jewish. Home and Office: 6648 John Smith Ln Hayes VA 23072 E-mail: rich0439@3bubbas.com.

CAST, ALICIA DEANNE, social sciences educator; d. Larry and Beverly Cast. PhD, Wash. State U., 1998. Postdoctoral fellow Ind. U., Bloomington, 1998—2000; asst. prof. Iowa State U., Ames, 2000—. Contbr. articles to profl. jours.

CAST, ANITA HURSH, small business owner; b. Columbus, Ohio, July 11, 1939; d. Charles Walter and Hulda Marie (Ramsey) Hursh; m. William R. Cast, Apr. 1, 1961; children: Jennifer, Carter, Meghan. BA, DePauw U., 1961. Ptnr. Cast Hursh and Assocs., Ft. Wayne, Ind., 1982—; pianist Words and Music, Ft. Wayne, 1983—; owner Anita Cast's Wearable Art, Ft. Wayne, 1986—. Bd. dirs. Fort Wayne Philharmonic, Indpls. Internat. Violin Competition; exec. com. Arts United; past pres. Exec. Com. Ind. U. Friends of Music; pres. Ind. Endowment for the Arts. Bd. dirs., pres. Am. Symphony Orch. League, vol., v.p., 1985—86; commr. Ind. Gov.'s Mansion Commn., 1987, Ind. Arts Commn., 1979—87; bd. dirs. Ft. Wayne Philharm., pres., 1977—79; mem. Mayor's Bicentennial Exec. Bd., 1989—94, Ind. Cultural Congress Hon. Com.; active Ft. Wayne's Celebrate 2000 Com.; v.p. adv. bd., exec. com., bd. dirs. Leadership Ft. Wayne, Ft. Wayne; bd. dirs. WBNI Nat. Pub. Radio, Ft. Wayne; chmn. bd. dirs. Fine Arts Found., Ft. Wayne, 1988; pres. bd. dirs. Ind. Endowment Arts; chmn. bd. dirs. Arts United Greater Ft. Wayne, 1988—90; bd. dirs. Arts United; pres., bd. dirs. Ind. U. Friends Music, 1995—97, past pres. exec. com.; v.p. adv. bd. Leadership Ft. Wayne; pres. Met. YMCA, Ft. Wayne, 1986—. Lily Endowment Leadership fellow; named Miss Indiana. Mem.: Duodecimo Club, Quest Club. Republican. Episcopalian. Avocations: music, cooking, golf, hiking, reading. Home and Office: Anita Cast Wearable Art 4401 Taylor St Fort Wayne IN 46804-1913

CASTAGNA, WILLIAM JOHN, federal judge; Student, U. Pa., 1941-43; LLB, JD, U. Fla., 1949. Bar: Fla. 1949. Ptnr. MacKenzie, Castagna, Bennison & Gardner, 1970-79; judge U.S. Dist. Judge (mid. dist.) Fla., 1979—, now sr. judge. Democrat.

CASTAGNOLA, GEORGE JOSEPH, JR., lawyer, mediator, secondary education educator; b. Scotia, Calif., July 6, 1950; s. George Joseph and Olga Esther Castagnola; m. Sandra Annette Castagnola, June 7, 1975; children: George Joseph III, Laura, Joseph. Grad., U. San Francisco, 1974; JD, N.W. Calif. U., Sacramento, 1990, D Juridical Sci., 1992. BAr: Calif. 1990. Tchr. El Molino H.S., Forestville, Calif., 1977—; charter boat capt. Castagnola Fishing, Petaluma, Calif., 1971—; prof. law N.W. Calif. U., 1990—; atty., mediator Law and Mediation Office of George Castagnola, Petaluma, Calif., 1990—. Cpl. USMCR, 1968-74. Mem. Calif. Bar Assn., Sonoma County Bar Assn., Calif. Tchrs. Assn., Golden Gate Sport Fishing Assn. Roman Catholic. Avocations: weightlifting, fishing. Home and Office: 802 Wine Ct Petaluma CA 94954-7420

CASTALDI, DAVID LAWRENCE, healthcare company executive; b. Logansport, Ind., Jan. 27, 1940; s. Lawrence J. and Ruth (Speitel) C.; m. Judith A. Pille, June 18, 1966; children: Valerie A., Maria C. BBA maxima cum laude, U. Notre Dame, 1962; MBA with high distinction, Harvard U., 1966. Sec., dir. Mid-West Spring Mfg. Co., Inc., Chgo., 1961-71; with Baxter-Travenol Labs., Inc., 1971-87, exec. v.p. Artificial Organs divsn., 1976-77, pres. hyland therapeutics divsn. Glendale, Calif., 1977-87; founder, pres., CEO, bd. dirs. BioSurface Tech., Inc., Cambridge, Mass., 1987-94. Bd. dirs. Biolink Corp., Middleboro, Mass., chmn. bd. dirs., 1995-98, CEO, 1996-98; founder, chmn., bd. dirs. Cadent Med. Corp., Bedford, Mass., 1996-2000, CEO, 1998-1999; chancellor Roman Cath. Archdiocese Boston, 2001; bd. dirs. Cytomatrix, Woburn, Mass., Tissue Regeneration Inc., Medford, Mass., Harbus Investors, Inc., St. Petersburg, Fla., Nabi Biopharms, Boca Raton, Fla., Embrex Inc., Durham, N.C. Mem. bd. of transplantation svcs. ARC, 1988-90, nat. skin adv. coun., 1990-92; mem. gov.'s biotech. subcom., 1991; bd. trustees St. John's Sem., Brighton, Mass., Voice of the Faithful Inc., With U.S. Army, 1962-64. Republican. Roman Catholic.

CASTALDI, FRANK JAMES, environmental engineer, consultant; b. Elizabeth, N.J., May 24, 1947; s. Frank James and Anita (Arditi) C.; m. Keerocha Srithavatch, July 2, 1981; 1 child, Ann Elizabeth. BS in Civil Engring., N.J. Inst. Tech., 1969; ME in Environ. Engring., Manhattan Coll., Bronx, N.Y., 1971; PhD in Civil (Environ.) Engring., U. Tex., 1976. Registered profl. engr., Tex. Engr. Alexander Potter Assocs., N.Y.C., 1969; rsch. assoc. Manhattan Coll., 1969-71; design engr. Buck, Seifert and Jost Engrs., Englewood Cliffs, N.J., 1971-72; rsch. asst. U. Tex., Austin, 1972-76; project mgr., engr. Engring. Sci., Inc., Austin, 1976-84; sr. staff engr., group leader Radian Internat. LLC, Austin, 1986-90, prin. engr., 1990-2000; project mgr. URS Corp., Austin, 2000—. Chmn. Synfuels Wastewater Biotreatment Workshop Morgantown (W.Va.) Energy Tech. Ctr., 1983. Contbg. author: Applied Biotechnology for Site Remediation, 1994, Microbial Processes for Bioremediation, 1995, Standard Handbook of Hazardous Waste Treatment and Disposal, 1997; patentee in field. Mem. ASCE, Water Environ. Fedn., Internat. Water Assn. Roman Catholic. Avocation: numismatics. Office: URS Corp PO Box 201088 Austin TX 78720-1088 E-mail: frank_castaldi@urscorp.com.

CASTAÑEDA, JAMES AGUSTIN, Spanish language educator, university golf coach; b. Bklyn., Apr. 2, 1933; s. Ciro Castañeda and Edna May Sincock; m. Terrill Lynn McCauley, Sept. 14, 1957; 1 child, Christopher James; m. Clara Luz Gutiérrez, Dec. 9, 1991. BA summa cum laude, Drew U., 1954; MA, Yale U., 1955, PhD, 1958; Certificat d'Aptitude à l'Enseignement du Français à l'Etranger, Université Paris, 1957; postgrad., Universidad de Madrid, 1957—; student summer inst. tchrs. fgn. langs., Purdue U., 1959. Asst. to assoc. prof. Spanish and French Hanover (Ind.) Coll., 1958-61; asst. prof. Spanish Rice U., Houston, 1961-63, assoc. prof. Spanish, 1963-67, prof. Spanish, 1967—. Vis. prof. Spanish U. So. Calif., 1959, U. N.C., 1962, 68, Western N.Mex. U., 1970; Florence Purington vis. prof. Mt. Holyoke Coll., 1976-77; prof. summer program Hispanic studies in Spain Rice U., 1979, 82, 83-90, head freshman baseball coach, 1962-67, asst. varsity coach, 1962-83, chmn. dept. Classics, Italian, Portuguese, Russian and Spanish, 1964-72, moderator television series, 1964-67, 68-69, head golf coach, 1983-98; lectr., dir., adviser and sponsor numerous acad. and other coms. in field. Author: A Critical Edition of Lope de Vega's "Las paces de los reyes, y Judía de Toledo", 1962, introducción, edición, 1971, Agustín Moreto, 1974, Mira de Amescua, 1977, El esclavo del demonio, 1980; contbr. numerous articles to profl. jours. Chmn. interview team in Europe Kent Fellowship Program, 1968; active Internat. Good Neighbor Coun. Rose Meml. scholar Drew U., 1950-54, Varsity Club scholar, Alumni Assn. Meml. scholar, Fulbright scholar Université de Paris, 1956-57, scholar Instituto de Cultura Hispánica, 1971; Danforth fellow Yale U., 1954-58, teaching fellow 1958—; named Miembro Titular, Instituto de Cultura Hispánica de Madrid, 1972, Hon. Master Will Rice Coll., 1976, Spanish Tchr. of Yr. and Fgn. Lang. Tchr. of Yr., Tex. Fgn. Lang. Tchrs.' Assn., 1982; recipient Drew U. Alumni Achievement award in Humanities, 1973, Will Rice Coll. James St. Fulton Svc. award 1973, Bklyn. Cadets Alumni Assn. Achievement award, 1976, Spanish Heritage award 1982, Disting. Svc. award Assn. Rice Alumni, 2000; named to Drew U. Athletics Hall of Fame, 1997. Mem. Am. Assn. Spanish and Portugese (numerous coms. and offices), Am. Assn. Tchrs. French, Am. Coun. Tchrs. Fgn. Langs. (del. affiliate assembly, 1970-75), S. Ctrl. Modern Lang. Assn. (various coms. and offices), Houston Area Tchrs. Fgn. Langs. (various coms. and offices), Modern Lang. Assn. (various coms. and offices), Inst. Hispanic Culture Houston (founding mem. 1966, numerous other coms. and offices), Sigma Delta Pi (hon. pres. 1998). Office: Rice Univ 6100 Main St Houston TX 77005-1892 E-mail: spangolf@rice.edu.

CASTANEDA, JORGE G. former government official, political scientist; b. Mexico City, May 24, 1953; BA, Princeton U.; PhD, U. Paris. Prof. internat. affairs Nat. Autonomous U. Mex., 1978—; sec. fgn. rels. Mexico, 2000—03; chmn. latin amer. studies & pol. sci. NYU, 1997—. Author: Utopia Unarmed: The Latin American Left after the Cold War, 1993, The Mexican Shock, 1995, Companero, The Life and Death of Che Guevera, 1997; co-author (with Robert Pastor): Limits to Friendship: The United States and Mexico, 1988. Office Fax: (+525) 254-5549.*

CASTANO, GREGORY JOSEPH, lawyer; b. Kearny, NJ, Feb. 17, 1929; s. Nicholas and Marianna (Prestinaci) C.; m. June Dwyer, Oct. 15, 1966; children: Gregory, Christopher, John, Timothy. BS, Seton Hall U., 1950; JD, Fordham U., 1953; LLM, NYU, 1956. Bar: NJ 1956, US Ct. Appeals (3d cir.) 1957, US Supreme Ct. 1959, US Tax Ct. 1974, NY 1985. Sports writer Newark Star-Ledger, 1946—53; pvt. practice Harrison, NJ, 1959—78; atty. Bd. Adjustment, Harrison, 1978; judge Superior Ct. N.J., Jersey City, 1978—85; ptnr. Tompkins, McGuire & Wachenfeld, Newark, 1985—88, Waters, McPherson & McNeill, Secaucus, NJ, 1988—2002, Castano Quigley LLC, West Caldwell, NJ, 2002—. Asst. atty. Town of Harrison, 1959-64; asst. prosecutor County of Hudson, NJ, 1963-71; atty. Town of West New York, NJ, 1977-78, Town of Kearny, NJ, 1999—, Harrison Redevel. Agy., 1997—; adj. prof. Seton Hall U. Sch. Law, Newark, 1988—; master com. to computerize criminal cts. Essex County; mediator US Dist. Ct., Superior Ct. Tax assessor Town of Harrison, 1964-78, del. NJ Constl. Conv., 1964; mem. juvenile conf. com. Twp. West Caldwell, NJ, 1977-78; trustee Caldwell (NJ) Coll., 1985-91, chmn. acad. affairs com. bd. trustees, 1987-91; chmn. County Govt. Transition Com., Hudson County, 1987-88; mem. Hudson County Community Coll. Blue Ribbon Task Force, 1992-93. With US Army, 1953-55. Named Man of Yr., Kearny Jaycees, 1963, Alumnus of Yr., Dorf Feature Service, 1987, Caldwell Coll., 2003, Pres. Award. Fellow Am. Bar Found.; mem. ABA, NJ Bar Assn., Hudson County Bar Assn. (Justice medallion 1985), Essex County Bar Assn., West Hudson Bar Assn. (pres. 1977-78), Assn. Fed. Bar NJ, Essex Fells Country Club. Home: 19 Sunset Rd West Caldwell NJ 07006-6540 Office: Castano Quigley LLC 1120 Bloomfield Ave W Caldwell NJ 07007

CASTBERG, EILEEN SUE, construction company owner; b. Santa Monica, Calif., Mar. 12, 1946; d. George Leonard and Irma (Loretta) Conroy; m. David Christopher Castberg, Oct. 27, 1967; children: Eric, Christopher. Grad. high sch., U. High Sch., L.A., 1964; certificate, Anthony Schs., 1990. Lic. real estate agt., Calif. Exec., co-founder Advanced Connector Telesis, Inc., Santa Ana, Calif., 1986-87; exec. Western Energy Engrs., Inc., Costa Mesa, Calif., 1987-89; owner Dave Castberg and Assocs., Inc., Ramona, Calif., 1989—; sales assoc. Ramona and Country Estates Realty, Keller Williams Realty, 1999—2002, Coldwell Banker Assoc. Realty, 2002—. Cons. Watt Asset Mgmt., Santa Monica, 1990-91. Mem. choir Ramona Luth. Ch.; 3d v.p. Holy Cross Luth. Ch. Women's League, Cypress, Calif., 1983; pres., bd. dirs., sec. San Diego Country Estates Timeshare, past pres. Internmountain Republican Women's Fed.; nat. awards chair San Diego County Fedn. Republican Women, 1994—. Mem. San Diego Bd. Realtors, Ramona Real Estate Assn. (bd. dirs.), Intermountain Rep. Women's Fedn. (past pres.), Ramona Christian Women's Club, San Vicente Valley Club (pres. 2000-01). Republican. Avocations: statuary painting, singing, gardening, decorating, reading.

CASTEEL, DIANN BROWN, principal; b. Greeneville, Tenn., Dec. 16, 1953; d. Harold James Brown and Clara Ruth (Phillips) Johnston; m. Everette Kenneth Casteel, Oct. 7, 1972; children: Trisha DiAnn, Mary Camille, Cheyenne James. BS, East Tenn. State U., 1973, MA, 1976, EdD, 1994. Cert. tchr., Tenn. Tchr. Greene County Bd. Edn., Greeneville, 1973-90; dir. Project Choice, Greeneville-Greene County Ctr. for Tech., 1990-91; tchr. Doak Sch., Tusculum Sta., Tenn., 1992-2000; asst. prin. Chuckey (Tenn.) Elem. Sch., Greene County Bd. Edn., 2001—03, Chuckey Elem. Sch., Greene County Bd. Edn., Mohawk, Tenn., 2000—01, Doak Elem. Sch., Greeneville, 2003—. Founder Iowa-Tenn. Student Exch. Program, Dayton and Greeneville, 1986—87; asst. prof. edn. Tusculum Coll., Greenville, Guidance and Assessment for Single Parent/Displaced Homemaker Program, 1989—90. Founder, conor Hay Relief Program, Tenn., 1986-87; leader 4-H Club, Baileyton Elem. Sch., 1985-88; mem. Ottway United Meth. Ch., Greenville, 1985-92; v.p. Ottway United Meth. Women, Greeneville, pres., 1976; mem. women's group study exch. to India, Rotary Internat., 1989; mem. 1st Christian Ch., Greenville, Tenn., 1992—. Recipient Horse of Yr. award Appalachian Horse Show Assn., 1967, Outstanding Citizen award Ruritan Nat., 1986, 4-H Emerald Club Leader award, 1987, DIANA award Epsilon Sigma Alpha, 1990, Book of Golden Deeds award Greeneville (Tenn.) Exchange Club, 1992. Mem. NEA, Greene County Edn. Assn., East Tenn. Edn. Assn., Tenn. Edn. Assn., Internat. Platform Assn., U.S.S.S. Greenville, Inc., Kappa Delta Pi, Phi Delta Kappa. Democrat. Avocations: horses, creative cooking, reading, swimming. Home: 2545 Flatwoods Rd Greeneville TN 37745-8582 Office: Doak Elem Sch 70 West St Greeneville TN 37743

CASTEEN, JOHN THOMAS, III, university president; b. Portsmouth, Va., Dec. 11, 1943; s. John Thomas and Naomi Irene (Anderson) C.; children: John Thomas IV, Elizabeth, Lars. BA with high honors, U. Va., 1965, MA, 1966, PhD, 1970; LLD, Shenandoah Coll. and Conservatory Music, 1984; DHL, Bentley Coll., 1992; hon. degree, Piedmont (Va.) C.C., 1992; DPA, Bridgewater Coll., 1993; D honoris causa, U. Athens, Greece, 1996; DHL (hon.), Transylvania U., 1999. Asst. prof. English U. Calif., Berkeley, 1970—75; assoc. prof., dean admissions U. Va., Charlottesville, 1975—82; adj. prof. Va. Commonwealth U., Richmond, 1982—85; prof. English, pres. U. Conn., Storrs, 1985—90; pres. U. Va., 1990—, George M. Kaufman presdl. prof. of English, 1990—. Bd. dirs. NCAA, Wachovia, Inc., Sallie Mae, Ctrl. Va.'s Pub. Broadcasting; mem. Assn. Acad. Health Ctrs.' Coun. Health Scis. and Univ.; mem. com. Nat. Inst. on Alcohol Abuse and Alcoholism and Misuse on Coll. Campuses; chair Coun. for Higher Edn. Accreditation, 2000—. Author: 16 Stories, 1981; contbr. articles to various publs.; mem. editl. adv. bd. The Presidency. Sec. edn. Commonwealth of Va., Richmond, 1982-85; trustee Mariner's Mus., 1990—, Coll. Entrance Exam Bd., N.Y.C., 1980-90, chmn. 1986-88; mem. So. Regional Edn. Bd., 1982-85. New Eng. Bd. of Higher Edn., 1986-90; mem. nat. adv. com. Nat. Domestic Violence Media Campaign, 1992—, dir. Am. Coun. on Edn., 1993-96. Recipient Outstanding Virginian award, 1993, Gold medal award Nat. Inst. Social Scis., 1998. Mem. Assn. Am. Univs. (exec. com.), So. Assn. Colls. and Schs. (chair commn. on colls. 1995-97, pres.-elect 1997, pres. 1998), Assn. Governing Bds. Colls. and Schs. (coun. of pres. 1992—), Keswick Club, Farmington County Club, Commonwealth Club (Richmond), Phi Beta Kappa. Episcopalian. Office: P O Box 400224 Charlottesville VA 22904 E-mail: jtc@virginia.edu.

CASTEL, JEAN GABRIEL, lawyer; b. Nice, France, Sept. 17, 1928; s. Charles A. and Simone (Ricour de Quinsac) C. Lic., U. Paris, 1948; JD, U. Mich., 1953; SJD, Harvard U., 1957; LLD (hon.), Aix-Marseille, France, 1988. Created queen's counsel. From asst. prof. to assoc. prof. law McGill U., 1954-57; now prof. emeritus law Osgoode Hall Law Sch., York U., Toronto, Canada; counsel Shibley Righton, Toronto, Canada. Author: International Law as Interpreted and Applied in Canada, 1978, Canadian Criminal Law: International and Transnational Aspects, 1981, Extraterritoriality in International Trade, 1988, The Canadian Law and Practice of International Trade, 1991, 2d edit., 1997, Canadian Conflict of Laws, 5th edit., 2002; editor: Can. Bar Rev., 1957-83. Mem. spl. group for settlement of disputes under Can.-U.S. Free Trade Agreement, 1989-93. Served with French Resistance, 1943-45. Decorated officer Order of Can., officier Ordre Nat. du Merite, chevalier Légion d'Honneur, Order of Ont.; recipient medal Law Soc. Upper Can., John Read medal Internat. Law. Fellow Acad. Arts and Scis., Royal Soc. Can.; mem. Can. Bar Assn. (hon.), Internat. Acad. Comparative Law (assoc.). E-mail: jgcastel@sympatico.ca.

CASTEL, NICO, tenor, educator; b. Lisbon, Portugal, Aug. 1, 1935; s. Felix and Margalitt (Castel) Kalinhoff; 1 child, Alexandra. BA, Temple U., 1952. Artist in residence Mannes Coll. of Music, N.Y.C., 1980—. Instr. diction and langs. Mannes Coll. Music, Manhattan Sch. Music, Juilliard Sch. Music, Internat. Vocal Arts Inst., Tel Aviv, Finnish Nat. Opera, Helsinki, Aspen Festival, Colo.; diction coach Met. Opera; stage dir. opera; adj. faculty Boston U. Author: The Nico Castel Book of Ladino Songs, A Singers' Manual of Spanish Lyric Diction, The Complete Puccini, Verdi, Mozart Libretti with phonetics and translation; Debuts include, N.Y. City Opera, 1965, Metropolitan Opera, 1970; permanent artist, Metropolitan Opera; extensive concert tours,

U.S., S.Am., Europe; tchr. master classes in multilingual diction and style. With U.S. Army, 1952-54. Mem. Am. Guild Mus. Artists. Democrat. Jewish. Home: 214 W 92nd St Apt 77E New York NY 10025-7455 Office: c/o Met Opera Lincoln Ctr New York NY 10023

CASTEL, P. KEVIN, lawyer; b. N.Y.C., Aug. 5, 1950; s. Peter A. and Mildred (Cronin) C.; m. Patricia A.; 2 children. BS, St. John's U., Jamaica, N.Y., 1972, JD, 1975. Bar: N.Y. 1976, U.S. Dist. Ct. (so. and ea. dists.) N.Y. 1976, U.S. Ct. Appeals (2nd cir.) 1979, U.S. Supreme Ct. 1983, U.S. Ct. Appeals (fed. cir.), 1986, U.S. Ct. Appeals (10th cir.), 1988, U.S. Ct. Appeals (3rd cir.) 1989, U.S. Ct. Appeals (4th cir.) 1991, U.S. Ct. Appeals (7th cir.) 1995, U.S. Ct. Appeals (11th cir.) 1997. Law clk. to judge U.S. Dist. Ct. (so. dist.) N.Y., 1975-77; assoc. Cahill Gordon & Reindel, N.Y.C., 1977-83, ptnr., 1983—; nominated by Pres. George W. Bush for U.S. Dist. Judge (so dist.) N.Y., 2003. Mem. departmental disciplinary com. appellate divsn. 1st dept., 1987—93, hearing panel chair, 1991—93, mem. policy com., 1997—2002. Articles editor St. John's Law Rev., 1974-75. Mem. mayor's panel Martin Luther King Jr. Inst. for Law and Social Justice, 1987—89; nat. chmn. ann. giving campaign St. John's U., 1994—95; bd. dirs. The Legal Aid Soc., 2000—. Recipient Pres.'s medal St. John's U., 2000. Fellow: N.Y. Bar Found., Am. Bar Found.; mem.: N.Y. County Lawyers Assn., Fed. Bar Coun. (pres. 2000—02, sec. 1983—85, trustee 1985—93, 1997—, chmn. publs. com. 1984—95, chmn. program com. 1995—98, v.p. 1988—90), Assn. Bar City of N.Y. (com. profl. and jud. ethics 1994—97, coun. on jud. adminstrn. 1997—), N.Y. State Bar Assn. (com. on cts. of appellate jurisdiction 1979—86, com. fed. cts. of appellate jurisdiction 1979—86, com. fed. cts. 1986—89, chmn. com. fed practice 1989—91, exec. vice chmn. comml. and fed. litig. sect. 1991—92, chmn. 1993—94, ho. of dels. 1994—95), St. John's U. Law Sch. Alumni Assn. (bd. dirs. 1991—, v.p. 1998—), Supreme Ct. Hist. Soc. Office: Cahill Gordon & Reindel 80 Pine St Fl 17 New York NY 10005-1790

CASTELE, THEODORE JOHN, radiologist; b. New Castle, Pa., Feb. 1, 1928; s. Theodore Robert and Anne Mercedes (McNavish) C.; m. Jean Marie Willse, Oct. 20, 1951; children: Robert, Ann Marie, Richard, Mary Kathryn, Thomas, Daniel, John. BS, Case Western Res. U., 1951, MD, 1957. Diplomate Am. Bd. Radiology, 1962. Intern then resident U. Hosps. Cleve., 1957-61, fellow, 1961-62; dir. of radiology Luth. Med. Ctr., Cleve., 1968-75, 77-89, chief of staff, 1975-81; pres. Med. Ctr. Radiologists, Inc., Cleve., 1978-95; v.p. med. and copr. devel. Health Cleve. Inc., 1989-91; chmn. Lakeshore Radiology Inc., Cleve., 1991-96, emeritus chmn., 1996—. Med. editor sta. WEWS-TV-ABC, Cleve., 1975-99; chmn. bd. Med. Cons. Imaging Co., Cleve., 1981-97; asst. clin. prof. radiology Case Western Res. U., chmn. dean's tech. coun. Sch. Medicine, 1996—, chmn. vis. com. Cleve. Health Scis. Libr., chmn. campaign for future of acad. medicine, 1998—. Exec. editor Prime mag., 2000—. Chmn. Southwestern dist. Greater Cleve. coun. Boy Scouts Am., 1969, 73; mem. bd. med. cons. Cleve. Police Dept., pres., 1988-90; trustee Comty. Dialysis Ctr., chmn. 1997-99, chmn. emeritus, 2000—; active Luth. Med. Ctr. Found., chmn. bd. trustees, 1969-75, pres., 1988-90; trustee Case Western Res. U., Blue Cross/Blue Shield Ohio, Greater Cleve. Hosp. Assn., Fairview Health, Luth. Med. Ctr., 1975-80, Fairview Hosp. Found.; bd. trustees Fairview Luth. Hosp. Found., 1999—, No. Ohio Lung Assn.; chmn. Health Mus. Cleve., 1996—, Humility of Mary Healthcare Sys., 1995-98; dir. Coun. Pub. Reps. for NIH, 1999-2001. With USN, 1946-47. Recipient Order of Merit award Boy Scouts Am., 1971, Silver Beaver award, 1972, Nat. Disting. Eagle Scout award, 1984, Frances Payne Bolton Sch. of Nursing Disting. Svc. award, 1990, Outstanding Philanthropist award Nat. Soc. of Fundraising Execs., 1991, Alumnus of the Yr. award Dept. Radiology of Case Western Res. U., 1996, LMC Found. Women's Bd. award, 1996, Luth. Hosp. award Fairview Health Sys. Bd., 1996, Midwest Nursing Rsch. Soc. Media award, 1998, Lamplighter Humanitarian award 2001; named Knight of the Equestrian, Order of the Holy Sepulchre of Jerusalem, 1993—; recipient Magis award St. Ignatius H.S.; named to Med. Hall of Fame, Case Western Res. U., Cleve. Mag., 1999, No. Ohio Italian-Am. Found., 1999. Fellow Am. Coll. Radiology; mem. AMA (Physician Spkr. Gold award 1978, 80, Silver 1979, Bronze 1978, Benjamin Rush award 1989, Golden Achievement award Golden Age Ctrs., 1996, chmn. Ohio del. 1987-96), Ohio State Med. Assn. (5th dist. councilor 1977-79, Spl. award 1979, Disting. Svc. award 1997), Cleve. Radiol. Soc. (pres. 1969-70), Cleve. Med. Libr. Assn. (pres. 1996, 97-98), Case Western Res. U. Med. Alumni Assn. (pres. 1971-72, 91-92, Disting. Svc. award 1987, Spl. Trustees award 1997, Univ. medal 1998), Cleve. Acad. Medicine (pres. 1974-75, Disting. Mem. award 1990, Disting. Svc. award 1984, Spl. Honor award and portrait 1998), Ohio State Radiol. Soc. (Silver award 1990). Home: 18869 Canyon Rd Cleveland OH 44126-1703 Office: Case Western Reserve University School of Medicine Cleveland OH 44106

CASTELLANI, LAWRENCE P. automotive company executive; From stock boy to CEO Tops Friendly markets, Buffalo; pres. support svcs. for S.Am. stores Royal Ahold NV; CEO Advance Auto, Roanoke, Va., 2000—. Office: Advance Holding Corp 5673 Airport Rd NW Roanoke VA 24012*

CASTELLANI, VICTOR, foreign language and literature educator; b. Feb. 14, 1947; s. Anthony Joseph and Frances Agnes (Pajer) Castellani; m. Cheryl Ann Beauford; children: Stephen Beauford, Julia Beauford. BA in Greek and Latin, Fordham Coll., 1968; PhD in Classics, Princeton U., 1971. Adj. instr. Fordham U., Bronx, NY, 1970—71; instr. U. Denver, 1971—72, asst. prof., 1972—80, assoc. prof., 1980—, dir. classical studies, 1973—, chmn. dept. langs. and lits., 1981—85, 1989—98. Coll./univ. educators adv. coun. Denver Ctr. Theatre Co., Denver, 1993—; cons. on wine to Oxford English Dictionary; leader Denver Wine Symposia, 1980—. Contbg. editor: Rocky Mountain Wine Guide, 1983—85; contbr. articles, revs. and papers to profl. jours., books and confs. Dem. precinct committeeman, Denver, 1980—82. Recipient Book award, Columbia Tchrs. Coll., N.Y.C., 1968; NDEA Title IV and Princeton U. nat. fellow, 1968—71, Colo. Humanities Program project planning grantee, Denver, 1984, ACLS Travel grantee, 1990, 1994, NEH grantee, 1992. Mem.: ProRiesling Verein (Trier, Germany), Rocky Mountain MLA (pres. 1984), Classical Assn. Mid. West and South, Pacific Ancient and Modern Lang. Assn., Am. Classical League, Am. Philological Assn., Archaeol. Inst. Am., Am. Numismatic Assn. Democrat. Roman Catholic. Home: 1901 S High St Denver CO 80210-3313 Office: Univ Denver Dept Fgn Langs And Lits Denver CO 80208-0001 E-mail: vcastell@du.edu.

CASTELLANO, CHRISTINE MARIE, lawyer; b. Jacksonville, Fla., Jan. 10, 1966; d. James Todd and Constance Marie (Wallis) Drylie; m. Ralph Castellano, Sept. 15, 1997. BA summa cum laude, U. Colo., 1987; JD cum laude, U. Mich., 1990. Bar: Colo. 1990, Ill. 1991, U.S. Dist. Ct. Colo. 1991, U.S. Dist. Ct. (no. dist.) Ill. 1991, U.S. Dist. Ct. (ctrl. dist.) Ill. 1994, U.S. Ct. Appeals (10th cir.) 1991, U.S. Ct. Appeals (7th cir.) 1993, U.S. Supreme Ct. 1995. Clk. to chief judge Sherman G. Finesilver U.S. Dist. Ct. Colo., Denver, 1990-91; income ptnr. McDermott, Will & Emery, Chgo., 1991-96; ops. atty. Corn Products divsn. of CPC Internat. Inc., Summit-Argo, Ill., 1996-97; atty. Corn Products Internat., Inc., 1998—2002, counsel, U.S. and Can., 2002—. Adminstr. Family Law Project, Ann Arbor, Mich., 1988-91; judge Julius H. Miner Moot Ct., Northwestern U. Sch. Law, 1993-95, Northwestern U. Sch. Law Negotiation Competition, 1992-94. Writer newspaper The Res Gestae, 1987-90; editor yearbook The Quadrangle, 1988-90; contbg. editor Jour. of Law Reform, 1988-90. Vol. Lincoln Park Homeless Shelter, Chgo., 1991-92, Chgo. Cares, 1993-96; co. coord. Youth Motivation Program, 1991-96. Recipient Negligence Sect. award Mich. Bar Assn., 1990; Carl B. Gussin Meml. prize U. Mich., 1991; scholar Elk's, 1983-84, faculty U. Colo., 1983-84; U. Colo. grantee, 1987. Mem. ABA, Colo. Bar Assn., Ill. Bar Assn., Denver Bar Assn. (vol. teen ct. 1991), Chgo. Bar Assn., Chgo. Coun. Laywers, Women Law Students Assn., U. Colo. Alumni Assn., U. Mich. Alumni Assn., Moot Ct., Mortar Bd., Phi Beta Kappa, Pi Sigma Alpha. Avocations: photography, ice skating, camping, hiking. Office: Corn Products Internat 5 Westbrook Corporate Ctr Westchester IL 60154

CASTELLANO, JOSEPH ANTHONY, retired chemist, management consulting firm executive; b. N.Y.C., Oct. 28, 1937; s. Joseph and Marie Antoinette (Gallo) C.; m. Rosalie Ann Fantaci, Aug. 28, 1960; children: Joseph, Thomas, Laura. BS in Chemistry, CCNY, 1959; MS in Chemistry, Poly. Inst. N.Y., 1964, PhD in Chemistry, 1969. Cert. profl. chemist; cert. community coll. instr. Research chemist Witco Chem. Co., Paterson, N.J., 1959-62; sr. research chemist Thiokol Chem. Corp., Denville, N.J., 1962-65; mem. tech. staff, project mgr. RCA Labs., Princeton, N.J., 1965-73; chmn., CEO Princeton Materials Sci., 1973-75; ops. mgr. Fairchild Camera and Inst. Corp., Palo Alto, Calif., 1975-77; mgr. ops. Kylex, Mt. View, Calif., 1977-78; pres. Stanford Resources, San Jose, Calif., 1978—2002. Cons. scientist Princeton U., 1970-72; lectr. Rutgers U., Kent State U., SUNY-Binghamton, NASA Research Ctr., USAF Materials Lab., Office Naval Research, IBM Research Ctrs., RCA Labs., Motorola and various profl. and trade assns. Author: Handbook of Display Technology, 1992; publisher: Electronic Display World, The Electronic Display Industry Svc.; contbr. articles to profl. jours.; patents in field. Recipient RCA Doctoral Study award 1966, RCA Labs. Outstanding Achievement award, 1967, R&D Mag. IR-100 award, 1968, David Sarnoff Team award in Sci., 1969, PATCA award for Guidance and Exceptional Svc., 1983, Svc. cert. Soc. Motion Picture Scientists and Engrs., 1989, Spl. Recognition award Soc. Info. Display, 2000, 24 Yr. Svc. award iSuppli Corp., 2002. Fellow Am. Inst. Chemists; mem. AAAS, Am. Chem. Soc., Am. Assn. Advancement Sci., N.Y. Acad. Sci., Royal Chem. Soc., Soc. Info. Display, Profl. and Tech. Cons. Assn., Soc. Tech. Comm., N.Y. Acad. Sci., Sigma Xi. Roman Catholic. Home: 7017 Elmsdale Dr San Jose CA 95120-3225 E-mail: drjcast@aol.com.

CASTELLANO, JOSEPH P. assistant principal; b. Bklyn., May 16, 1956; s. Philip and Helen Castellano; m. Mary C. McHale, July 13, 1985. BA (with hons.), U. Va., 1978; MA, Columbia U., 1983; PhD, CUNY, 1992. Tchr., asst. prin. St. Francis Prep. Sch., Fresh Meadows, NY, 1983—. Grantee Edn. grant, United Fedn. Tchrs., 1995. Mem.: ASCD, MLA, Nat. Coun. Tchrs. English. Avocations: cooking, walking, travel. Office: St Francis Prep Sch 6100 Francis Lewis Blvd Fresh Meadows NY 11365

CASTELLANO, MICHAEL ANGELO, research forester; b. Bklyn., June 26, 1956; s. Biagio and Mildred Anne (Cucco) C.; m. Elizabeth Marie Phillips, July 14, 1979; children: Nicholas Aaron, Daniel Robert Feller, Kelly Marie, Katlyn Morgan. AAS, Paul Smiths Coll., 1978; BS, Oreg. State U., 1982, MS, 1984, PhD, 1988. Forest technician Weyerhauser Co., Columbus, Miss., 1979; forester trainee USDA Forest Svc., Pacific N.W., Corvallis, Oreg., 1980-84, forester, 1984-87, rsch. forester, 1987—. Cons. CSIRO, Div. of Forestry, Australia, 1988-95, Spanish-Am. Binational Prog., Barcelona, 1987, 91. Author: Key to Hypogeous Fungi, 1989, (agr. handbook) Mycorrhizae, 1989, Handbook to Strategy I Fungal Species, 1999; contbr. articles to profl. jours. Bishop LSD Ch. Named one of Outstanding Young Men, Am. JayCees, 1984. Mem. Soc. Am. Foresters, N.Am. Truffling Soc. (advisor), Soil Ecology Soc., Mycol. Soc. of Am. (nomenclature 1986), Sigma Xi. Avocations: genealogy, baseball, computers, stamps, literature. Home: 1835 NW Garfield Ave Corvallis OR 97330-2535 Office: USDA Forest Svc 3200 SW Jefferson Way Corvallis OR 97331-4401 E-mail: michael.castellano@orst.edu.

CASTELLANOS, JESUS ANTONIO, U.S. magistrate judge; b. 1942; BA, Inter-Am. U., San German, P.R., 1963; LLB, Inter-Am. U., Hato Rey, P.R., 1968. Bar: P.R. 1970, U.S. Dist. Ct. P.R. 1976, U.S. Ct. Appeals P.R. 1982, U.S. Ct. Internat. Trade 1983. Atty., mgmt. asst. legal dept. Office Gen. Counsel, P.R. Water Resources Authority, Santurce, 1963-71; in-house counsel Commonwealth Resources Mgmt. Corp., Hato Rey, 1973-74; assoc. Francis, Doval, Colorado & Carlo, Hato Rey, 1974-76; legis. asst. to Hon. Jorge Luis Cordova, U.S. Ho. of Reps., 1976; asst. U.S. atty. U.S. Dept. Justice, Old San Juan, 1976; legis. asst. to Hon. Baltasar Corrada del Rio, U.S. Ho. of Reps., 1977-80; magistrate judge for P.R., U.S. Magistrate Ct., San Juan, 1980—. Lectr. Legal Aid Clinic, U. P.R. Law Sch., 1974-76. Mem. P.R. Bar Assn. Office: Ruiz-Nazario Fed Bldg 150 Ave Carlos Chardon # 181 San Juan PR 00918-1703

CASTELLANOS, JULIO J. banker; b. Havana, Cuba, Mar. 7, 1910; came to U.S., 1960, naturalized, 1967; s. Manuel de Jesus and Virginia (Justiniani) C.; B of Arts and Letters, De La Salle Coll., Havana, 1927; JD, Tulane U., 1933; DCL, U. Havana, 1934; student Fed. Res. System Examiner's Sch., 1964-65; m. Irene Machado, Dec. 27, 1976; children: Julio J., Maria, Ana Maria, Carlos. Bar: Cuba 1934. Tax commr. City of Havana, from 1934; sr. ptnr. Lopez Munoz & Castellanos, Havana; sec. gen. Banco de la Construccion, Havana, 1959-60; analyst Morgan Guaranty Trust Co. N.Y., N.Y.C., 1960-63; examiner Fed. Res. Bank N.Y., N.Y.C., 1963-66; v.p. Marine Midland Bank, N.Y.C., 1966-71; founder, organizer, sr. v.p., mgr. First Wis. Internat. Bank, N.Y.C., 1971-76; pres. Pan Am. Nat. Bank, Union City, N.J., from 1976; exec. rep. Banco de Intercambio Regional, N.Y.C., 1976-80; pres. Banco del Estado Holding Co. Inc., Atlanta, 1982-84; adviser Banco de Reservas de la Republica Dominicana, N.Y.C., 1982-84; N.Y.C. rep. Banco del Estado, Bogota, Colombia, 1978-84; N.Y. rep. Banco Hipotecario Dominicano, 1983-85; banking cons. law firm Reid & Priest, 1983-86; v.p. BHD Corp., real estate investments, 1984-86; pres., chief cons. Castellanos Cons. Group Inc., 1984—; v.p. IDOSA N.Y. Inc., 1984-85. Bd. dirs. Colombian-Am. Assn. Pan Am. Soc. of U.S., 1984-85. Recipient retirement recognition diploma First Wis. Internat. Bank, 1976, pub. recognition diploma Dr. Guillermo Belt, former Mayor Havana, 1979. Mem. Havana Bar Assn. (del. in exile 1994). Republican. Address: 510 E 85th St New York NY 10028-7430

CASTELLANOS-BRANDON, ALBA G. secondary school educator; b. Vedado, Cuba, Oct. 12, 1957; d. Jesus René Castellanos Gomez and Ana Maria Brandon Merino. AA and AS, William Rainey Harper Coll., 1979; BA in Edn., U. Ill., Chgo., 1987; MA in Edn., Roosevelt U., 2001. Tchr. various dists. to River Trails Dist. #26, Mt. Prospect, Ill., 1988—2001; tchr. William R. Harper Coll., Palatine, Ill., 1985—, Schaumburg (Ill.) Twp. Dist. #54, 2001—. Mem. multicultural com., Schaumburg, Ill., 2001—. Author: (novels) Images of Winter, 1993, (manuscripts) various, including Resolving the Misconceptions of LD Labeling in the Reading Domain, 1999. Avocation: reading, writing, arts, crafts, outdoor sports.

CASTELLI, ALEXANDER GERARD, accountant; b. N.Y.C., May 3, 1929; s. Gerard and Carmela (Canzoneri) C.; m. Michelina Castelli, Jan. 8, 1961; children— Gerard, Alexander, JoAnn. BS, N.Y. U., 1958. C.P.A., N.Y., Md., 1970. Chief accountant Daitch Crystal Dairies, Inc., Bronx, N.Y., 1965-68; asst. controller Alexander's, Inc., N.Y.C., 1968-70; v.p., treas. Bond Stores, Inc., N.Y.C., 1970-73; v.p. fin. McBrides, Inc., Washington, 1973-77; mng. ptnr. Castelli & Catudal, P.A., 1977—. Bd. advisers Nat. Bank of Washington. Served with CIC AUS, 1951-53. Recipient Founder's Day award NYU, 1958 Mem. Am. Inst. CPA's, N.Y. State Soc. CPA's, Beta Gamma Sigma. Roman Catholic. Home: 10009 Gainsborough Rd Rockville MD 20854-4276 Office: 7925 Glenbrook Rd Bethesda MD 20814-2441 E-mail: agcast@aol.com.

CASTELLINI, CLATEO, retired medical technology company executive; b. 1935; BA in Econs., Bocconi U., Milan, Italy, 1958; postgrad., Harvard U., 1973. With Lepetit, S.A. (became subs. Dow Chem. 1965), 1959-77; various mgmt. positions Becton Dickinson & Co., Franklin Lakes, N.J., 1978-89, pres. med. sector, 1989-94, chmn. bd. dirs., 1994-99, ret., 1999—. Office: Becton Dickinson & Co 1 Becton Dr Franklin Lakes NJ 07417-1880

CASTELLINO, RONALD AUGUSTUS DIETRICH, radiologist, educator; b. N.Y.C., Feb. 18, 1938; s. Leonard Vincent and Henrietta Wilhelmina (Geffken) C.; m. Joyce Cuneo, Jan. 26, 1963; children: Jeffrey Charles, Robin Leonard, Anthony James. Student, Creighton U., Omaha, 1955-58, MD, 1962. Diplomate: Am. Bd. Radiology. Rotating intern Highland Alameda County Hosp., Oakland, Calif., 1962-63; USPHS/Peace Corps physician Brazil, 1963-65; resident in diagnostic radiology Stanford U. Hosp., 1965-68, chief resident, 1967-68; asst. prof. radiology Stanford U. Med. Sch., 1968-74, assoc. prof., 1974-81, prof., 1981-93, chief diagnostic oncologic radiology, 1970-89, chief CT body scanning, 1979-89, dir. div. diagnostic radiology and assoc. chmn. dept. radiology, 1981-86, acting chmn. dept. diagnostic radiology and nuclear medicine, 1986-89, prof. emeritus, 1993—; chair dept. radiology, Carroll and Milton Petrie chair Meml. Sloan Kettering Cancer Ctr., N.Y.C., 1990-98; prof. radiology Cornell Med. Sch., 1994-98, chief med. officer R-2 tech., 1998—. Mem. U.S. Cancer del., People's Republic China, 1977 Co-editor: Pediatric Oncologic Radiology, 1977; assoc. editor; Lymphology, 1973-97, Investigative Radiology, 1985-94, Academic Radiology, 1994-97, Radiology, 1986-94, Postgrad. Radiology, 1986-98; contbr. numerous rsch. papers to profl. jours., chpts. to books. Recipient T.F. Eckstrom Fund award, 1978; Guggenheim fellow, 1974-75 Mem.: N.Y. Acad. Medicine, N.Y. Roentgen Soc., Calif. Acad. Medicine, N.Am. Soc. Lymphology (charter), Soc. Cancer Imaging (charter), Soc. Thoracic Radiology (charter), Calif. Radiol. Soc., Calif. Med. Assn. (adv. panel sect. radiology 1972—89), Western Angiography Soc. (charter), Internat. Cancer Imaging Soc. (charter), Am. Roentgen Ray Soc., Soc. Cardiovascular and Interventional Radiology (charter), Radiol. Soc. N.Am., Assn. Univ. Radiologists (exec. com. 1981—85), Am. Coll. Radiology, Internat. Soc. Lymphology (exec. com. 1975—85), Am. Soc. Therapeutic Radiation Oncologists (hon.), Alpha Omega Alpha. Office: R-2 Tech 1195 W Fremont Ave Sunnyvale CA 94087 E-mail: rcastellino@r2tech.com.

CASTEN, RICHARD FRANCIS, physicist; b. N.Y.C., Nov. 1, 1941; s. Daniel F. and Constance Mary (Bell) C.; m. Jo Ann Daly, June 6, 1964. BS magna cum laude, Coll. of the Holy Cross, 1963; PhD, Yale U., 1967. Postdoctoral fellow Niels Bohr Inst., Copenhagen, 1967-69, Los Alamos (N.Mex.) Sci. Lab., 1969-71; asst. scientist Brookhaven Nat. Lab., Upton, N.Y., 1971-73, assoc. scientist, 1973-76, scientist, 1977-81, sr. scientist, 1981-96, group leader nuclear structure group, 1981-96; prof. physics, dir. A.W. Wright Nuclear Structure Lab. Yale U., New Haven, Conn., 1995—. Chmn. N.Am. steering com. for Isospin Lab. Radioactive Beam Facility, 1989-2002, co-chmn. RIA steering com., 2002-03, mem. nuc. sci. advis. comn., Nuc. Sci. Adv. Com., 1998-2000, chmn. 2002-03; guest prof. U. Cologne, Germany, 1985—; mem. panel on basic nuclear data NAS, 1990-92; mem. long-range plan working group Nuclear Sci. Adv. Com., 1989, 95, 2001; mem. subcom. on implementation of long-range plan, 1991; mem. spl. emphasis panel NSF, 1993; U.S. rep. Megasci. Forum for Nuclear Physics, Subpanel on Intense Beams and Target Sys., 1997, 98; co-chair writing panel for Columbus White Paper on sci. opportunities with an advanced ISOL facility, 1997; chair ISAC/TRIUMF rev. com., 1997; mem. Can. NSERC com. on subatomic physics, 1999-2001; mem. panel internat. rev. of standing and potential of physics rsch. in U.K.; co-convenor 1995 TUNL Town Meeting on Nuc. Structure and 2000 Rare Isotope Accelerator (RIA) Workshop; numerous other nat. and internat. coms.; co-organizer four internat. confs. on nuc. physics; adv. coms. for many internat. confs.; spkr. in field. Author: Nuclear Structure from a Simple Perspective, 1990, rev. edit., 2000; co-author, co-editor: Algebraic Approaches to Nuclear Structure, 1993; mem. editl. bd. (Jours.) Nuclear Physics News Internat., Internat. Jour. Modern Physics, Modern Physics Letters, assoc. editor Phys. Rev. C, 2001—; contbr. Pres. Jo Ann and Richard Casten, Ltd., 1973—. Danforth fellow, 1963-67; recipient Sr. Alexander von Humboldt prize, 1983; honoree Internat. Nuclear Structure Conf., Jackson, Wyo., 2002. Fellow AAAS, Am. Phys. Soc. (exec. com. divsn. nuclear physics 1991-93, chmn. task force to rev. jour. Phys. Rev. C 1995), Sigma Xi. Achievements include discovery of O(6) symmetry of IBA model and other experimental verifications of the IBA including extensive study of 168-Er and 196-Pt; invention of symmetry triangle of the IBA known as the Casten Triangle; co-inventor of consistent Q formalism; research in evolution of nuclear structure with nucleon number, valence p-n interaction, NpNn scheme and P-factor, quenching of the N=20 and Z=64 shell gaps, fragility of magicity; generalization of the Federman-Pittel mechanism for the onset of deformation in nuclei; radioactive nuclear beams, Q-invariants, application of Landau theory to equilibrium structure of nuclei; development of signatures of nuclear structure, ARC method of complete spectroscopy; first to use of the GRID technique for nuclear structure studies, evidence for large hexadecapole deformations in odd-A nuclei, extensive tests of Coriolis mixing in nuclei; discovery of empirical examples of E (5) and X (5) critical point symmetries for nuclear phase transition regions; co-discovery of new evidence for multi-phonon states in nuclei, global correlations of nuclear observables; co-discovery of anharmonic vibrator and tripartite correlations of nuclear observables. Office: Yale Univ Wright Nuc Structure PO Box 208124 New Haven CT 06520-8124 E-mail: rick@riviera.physics.yale.edu.

CASTENSCHIOLD, RENÉ, engineering company executive, author, consultant; b. Mt. Kisco, N.Y., Feb. 7, 1923; s. Tage and Juno (Hagemeister) Castenschiold; m. Martha Naomi Stinson, Dec. 14, 1947; children: Gail F., Frederick T., Lynn Castenschiold Jones. BEE, Pratt Inst., 1944. Registered profl. engr., N.Y., N.J., Pa., profl. planner, N.J. Test engr. (Manhattan Project) GE, Pittsfield, Mass., 1944-45, design engr. Schenectady, 1946-47; sr. product engr. Am. Transformer Co., Newark, 1947-50; design engr. Automatic Switch Co., Florham Park, N.J., 1951-57, chief customer engr., 1957-74, exec. engring. mgr., 1974-85; pres. LCR Cons. Engrs. P.A., Green Village, N.J., 1986—. Lectr. N.J. Inst. Tech., Newark, 1967—79; adviser Underwriters Labs., Inc., Melville, NY, 1973—85; chmn. U.S. Tech. Adv. Group; U.S. del. Internat. Electrotech. Commn., Geneva, 1981—90. Contbr. articles and papers to profl. jours., chapters to books. Chmn. Bd. of Adjustment, Harding Twp., 1975—77, Planning Bd., Harding Twp., 1982—85; dir. Civil Def., 1966—70; trustee Wash. Assn. N.J., Morristown, 1984—93, sec., 1985—88, v.p., 1989—92, pres., 1992—93; trustee Morristown Meml. Health Found., Inc., 1995—; co-chmn. Jefferson Soc. Morristown Meml. Hosp., 1995—98; vestryman Episcopal Ch., 1991—94. Named Disting. Alumni Bd. Visitors, Pratt Inst., 1979; recipient Disting. Svc. award, Morristown Nat. Hist. Park, 1993, Achievement award, Wash. Assn. N.J., 1995, listed in Danmarks Adel Aarbog, 1923—. Fellow: IEEE (stds. bd. 1983—85, Achievement award 1988, Richard Harold Kaufmann award 1990, Industry Applications Mag. prize article award 2002); mem.: NSPE, Nat. Forensic Ctr., Nat. Elec. Safety Found. (workplace safety com.), Can. Stds. Assn., N.J. Christmas Tree Growers' Assn., Internat. Platform Assn., Nat. Fire Protection Assn., Am. Cons. Engrs. Coun., Cons. Engring. Splty. Bds. (bd. cert. diplomate), Nat. Acad. Forensic Engrs., Internat. Assn. Elec. Insps., Nat. Elec. Mfrs. Assn. (chmn. automatic transfer switch com. 1982—88, James H. McGraw award 1986), Instrument Soc. Am., Danish Am. Soc., Morristown (N.J.) Club, Skytop Club (Pa.). Republican. Achievements include patents in field; research in promulgation of numerous nat. and internat. elec. stds. Avocations: swimming, tree farming, photography, hiking, antique cars. Home: PO Box 154 Lees Hill Rd New Vernon NJ 07976 Office: LCR Cons Engrs PA PO Box 2 Green Village NJ 07935-0002

CASTER, ANDREW IAN, ophthalmologist; b. Coral Gables, Fla., Oct. 30, 1954; s. Milton and Carolyn (Teperson) C.; m. Jacqueline Jacobs, Oct. 15, 1989; children: Bryce, Jocelyn Lilly. AB, Harvard Coll., 1976; MD, Harvard Med. Sch., 1980. Diplomate Am. Bd. Ophthalmology. Resident UCLA Jules Stein Eye Inst., L.A., 1981-84; intern Wadsworth VA Hosp., Los Angeles, 1980-81; resident UCLA Jules Stein Eye Inst., Los Angeles, 1981-84; med. dir. Caster Eye Ctr., Beverly Hills, Calif., 1986—. Author: The Eye Laser Miracle, 1997. Fellow ACS, Am. Acad. Ophthalmology, Calif. Assn. Ophthalmology (asst. v.p. 1992); mem. Am. Soc. Cataract and Refractive Surgeons. Avocations: tennis, skiing, travel, photography. Office: Caster Eye Ctr 9100 Wilshire Blvd Ste 265E Beverly Hills CA 90212-3482 E-mail: acaster@castervision.com.

CASTILE, RAND (JESSE RANDOLPH III), retired museum director; b. NC, July 15, 1938; s. Jesse Randolph II and Pauline Virginia (Simmons) C.; m. Sondra Meadow Myers, 1960; children: Leath Willow, Heather Rain. BA, Drew U., Madison, N.J., 1960; diploma, Urasenke Tea Ceremony, Kyoto, Japan, 1967; LHD (hon.), Drew U., 1992. With ARTnews, NYC, 1963-65; dir. edn. Japan Soc., NYC, 1967-71, dir. performing arts, 1981-86, dir. Japan House Gallery, 1971-86; dir. Asian Art Mus., San Francisco, 1986-94, dir. emeritus, 1994—. Vis. com. Met. Mus. Art, 1974-99; sec., mem. US-Japan Cultural and Ednl. Conf., 1972-86; mem. Maine Art Commn., 1997-2001, vis. com. Arian Art, Mus. Fine Arts, Boston, 2000—; sr. adv. Sherman E. Lee Inst. Japanese Art, 2000-2002; mem. North Atlantic Cultural Coun., 2002—. Author: The Way of Tea, 1971, 79; (exhbn. catalogue) Japanese Art Now: Tadaaki Kuwayama & Rikuro Okamoto, 1980, other catalogues; editor: Japanese Art Exhibitions with Catalogue in US, 1980; contbr. articles to profl. jour. Panelist Calif. Arts Coun., 1986-91; bd. dir. West-East Coun. Cathedral Ch. of St. John the Devine, 1977-86, AAM/ICOM, 1982-85, Japan Soc. No. Calif., 1986-95, San Francisco Bay Area Dance Coalition, 1986-88, Rock and Roll Mus., San Francisco, 1988-89, U. San Francisco Ctr. for Pacific Rim, 1989-95, Seoul-San Francisco Sister City Com., 1987-93, Nat. Maritime Mus., San Francisco, 1989-93; mem. internat. adv. com. Ctr. for Internat. Contemporary Arts, 1989-95; chair co-chair gov. State Calif. awards for Art and Philanthropy, 1990-94, others; chmn. Eastport Area Millenium Festival, 1997-2000; mem. vis. com. Mus. Fine Arts, Boston. Fulbright-Hayes fellow, 1966-67; recipient Mayor's award of Honor for Arts and Culture, NYC, 1982, Plowshares Humanitarian award, 1990, Harry Mattin award Eastport Area C. of C., 2000. Mem. Assn. Art Mus. Dirs. (emeritus), Am. Assn. Mus. (bd. dirs. Internat. coun. 1982-86), Mus. Trustee Assn. (adv. coun. of dirs. 1989-95), Am. Fedn. Arts (nat. exhbn. com. 1980-95), Acad. Lacquer Rsch. Tokyo (Am. sec. 1977-86), Japan Soc. No. Calif. (bd. dir. 1986-95, mem. collections com. Farnsworth Mus. 2000—), Can.-Am. Cultural Bd., Century Assn., St. Croix Country Club (bd. dirs. 2001—), Herring Cove Golf Club.

CASTILLO, JOSEPHINE, small business owner, educator; b. Brownsville, Tex., Oct. 14, 1950; d. Douglas Ernest and Mary Castillo. Home econs. edn., Tex. Women's U., 1973. Tchr. CVAE Brownsville (Tex.) Independent Sch. Dist., 1973—74; tchr. Houston, 1974—79; home economist Microwave Oven Ctr., Houston, 1979—86, Club Party, Houston, 1986—87, Landlock Seafood, Houston, 1987—88; family consumer scis. tchr. Houston Independent Sch. Dist., 1988—. Mem.: FCST Houston, FCSTAT. Democrat. Roman Catholic. Avocations: crafts, sewing, cooking, reading mystery books. Home: 17515 Canton Forest Richmond TX 77469 Office: Southwest Dem Promotions PO Box 940755 Houston TX 77094-7755 Office Fax: 281-491-5595. Business E-Mail: jcastillo@teacher.esc4.com.

CASTILLO, LEANNE MARLOW, artist, nurse; b. Lone Rock, Iowa, July 24, 1933; d. Lemuel Jess Marlow and Ida Mary Kollasch; m. Jozef Bednarz, July 6, 1953 (div. Jan. 1977); children: Barbara Goecke, Katherine Rike, Jan Christensen, John Bednarz, Angie Curell, Theresa Gerdis, Mary Palmer, Margaret Shellenberg, Rob Michael, Tom Bednarz, Sandra Lamoreux, Sharon Bednarz; m. Cruz Castillo, July 14, 1983 (dec. Sept. 1987). Cert. in comml. design, Art Instrn. Inc., 1953; degree in nursing, Iowa Lakes C.C., 1980. LPN, Iowa. Staff nurse Algona (Iowa) Good Samaritan Home, 1980-83; charge nurse Westview Care Ctr., Britt, Iowa, 1983—86, 1987—2003; staff nurse Pinal County Nursing Ctr., Florence, Ariz., 1986-87. Artist over 50 oil paintings Britt Hobo Kings and Queens, 1988—. Chair Britt Hobo Days Art Show, 1988-97, 2000-01. Mem. Portrait Soc. Am., Iowa Artists, North Iowa Artist's League. Democrat. Roman Catholic. Home: Castillo Art Studio 545 1st St SE Britt IA 50423-2002

CASTILLO, LUIS ANTONIO DONATO, professional baseball player; b. San Pedro de Macoris, Dominican Republic, Sept. 12, 1975; Infielder Fla. Marlins, Miami, 1996—. Office: Fla Marlins Pro Player Stadium 2267 Dan Morino Blvd Opa Locka FL 33028 Fax: 305-626-7428.

CASTILLO, MARIO ENRIQUE, artist, educator; b. Rio Bravo, Mexico, Sept. 19, 1945; came to U.S., 1955, naturalized, 1965; s. Manuel Castillo and Maria Enriquez de Allen. Cert., Ill. Inst. Design, 1964; BFA, Sch. of Art Inst., Chgo., 1969; MFA, Calif. Inst. Arts, 1972; postgrad., U. So. Calif., 1969-70, Pasadena City Coll., 1977, Calif. State U., L.A., 1980-81, Calif. State U., Dominguez Hills, 1986-88, East L.A. City Coll., 1982, Nat. U., Inglewood, Calif., 1990, Columbia Coll., Chicago, Il, 1996. Designer J.M. Pateros Studios, Inc., Chgo., 1965, Lukas & Assocs., Chgo., 1966; instr. Pilsen Settlement House, Chgo., 1967; comml. artist Chgo. Bd. Edn., 1968; instr. United Christian Cmty. Svc., Chgo., 1968-69; mural dir. Halsted Urban Progress Ctr., 1968, Dept. Human Resources, Chgo., 1969, McHenry Coll., Crystal Lake, Ill., 1992, No. Ill. U., DeKalb, 1993, Joliet Jr. Coll., Ill., 1994, Coll. of Lake County, Grayslake, Ill., 1994, U. Guadalajara, Ocotian, Mex., 1995, SAIC & Lincoln Park Cultural Ctr., Chgo., 1996, Bemis Found., Omaha, 1996, Triton Coll., River Grove, Ill., 1997; tchg. asst. Calif. Inst. Arts, Valencia, 1970-72, instr., 1972-73, Santa Monica (Calif.) City Coll., 1973; mem. faculty dept. art U. Ill., Champaign, 1973-76; comml. artist L.A., 1977; instr. art Immaculate Heart Coll., Hollywood, Calif., 1979-80, Pacific Asian Consortium in Edn., 1980-81, E.C.F. Art Ctr., L.A., 1986-90, L.A. Unified Sch. Dist., 1986-90, Instituto Comercial Artistico, Maywood, Calif., 1987, Lexicon Sch. Languages, 1987-88, Plaza de la Raza, 1989-90; mem. faculty art dept. Columbia Coll., Chgo., 1990—. Panelist at Northeastern Ill. U., Chgo., 1974, Coll. Art Assn., Chgo., 1975, Columbia Coll., Chgo., 1992, 94, 96, Chgo. Artist Coalition, 1993, Nat. Assn. Chicano Studies, Chgo., 1994, 96, Suburban Fine Arts Ctr., Highland Park, Ill., 1995, U. Guadalajara, Jalisco, 1995; presenter workshop Human Rights Portfolio, Chgo., 1994, Chgo., 1995; guest lectr. Galeria J.M. Velazco, Mexico City, 1975, Centro de la Causa, Chgo., 1975, Latino Cultural House, Champaign, 1975, U. Ill., Champaign, 1975, 76, Corpus Christi (Tex.) State U., 1978, McHenry County Coll., 1991, 92, Northwestern U., 1991, Columbia Coll., Montebello Sch. Dist., 1990, No. Ill. U., DeKalb, 1993, Triton Coll., River Grove, Ill., 1993, 94, Prospectus Gallery, Chgo., 1993, Joliet (Ill.) Jr. Coll., 1994, St. Cloud (Minn.) State U., 1994, MacMurry Coll., Jacksonville, Ill., 1994, Coll. of Lake County, 1994, Nat.-Louis U., Chgo., 1995, Melrose Park (Ill.) Pub. Libr., 1995, Mobil Art Gallery, Jacksonville, Ill., 1994, Northeastern U., Chgo., 1995, Harold Washington Libr., Chgo., 1995, Munster Ind. Cultural Ctr., 1995, U. Guadalajara, Ocotlan, Jalisco, 1995, 96, CCC Art Gallery, Chgo., 1995, Winnetka (Ill.) Cultural House, 1995, No. Ill. U., DeKalb, 1995, U. Guadalajara, La Barranca Campus, 1996, Lincoln Park Cultural Ctr., Chgo., 1996, Triton Coll., River Grove, 1996, 97; art juror Weisman Scholarship CCC, Chgo., 1993, Old Town Art Fair, Chgo., 1994, Hokin Gallery CCC, Chgo., 1995, Weisman Best of Show, Chgo., 1996; curator art exhibitions U. Ill., Champaign, 1975, Columbia Coll., Chgo., 1994, 95, Triton Coll., 1995, No. Ind. Arts Assn., Munster, 1995, 11th Street Art Gallery CCC, 1995, Hokin Ctr. Gallery, Columbia Coll., 1996; interior designer El Mercado Co., L.A. 1981-83; regular performer musical program Noches Rancheras, East L.A., Calif., 1981-83; cons. in field. One-man shows include Scholarship and Guidance Assn., Chgo., 1968, Calif. Inst. of the Arts, Burbank, 1971, Valencia, Calif., 1972, Latino Cultural House, U. Ill., Champaign, 1976, Inst. for Hispanic Cultural Studies, Santa Monica, Calif., 1989, Orlando Gallery, Sherman Oaks, Calif., 1989, Sangre De Cristo Arts and Conf. Ctr., Pueblo, Colo., 1991, Prospectus Gallery, Chgo., 1991, 93, McHenry County Art Gallery, 1991, No. Ill. U. Art Gallery, DeKalb, 1993, Atwood Art Ctr., St. Cloud U., 1994, MacMurry Coll., Jacksonville, Ill., 1994; numerous group shows including Fresno Art Mus., Calif., 1991, San Francisco Art Mus., 1991, San Francisco Mus. of Modern Art, 1991, Albuquerque Mus., 1991, Denver Art Mus., 1991, 93, Expo, 1993, San Antonio Mus. of Art, 1993, Nat. Mus. of Am. Art, 1993, Chgo., 1993, 94, Chgo. Latino Film Festival, 1994, Las Artes Galeria, Omaha, 1994, Open Windows Gallery, Chgo., 1994, S. Suburban Coll., South Holland, Ill., 1994, Columbia Coll., Chgo., 1994, 95, J.R. Shapiro Gallery, Oak Park, 1994, Cath. Theol. Union, Chgo., 1995, John Linsey Dallery, Oak Park, 1995, Hokin Gallery CCC, Chgo., 1995, Oak Park Art League, 1995, Pilsen Artist to Artist, Chgo., 1996, Prospectus Gallery, Chgo., 1998, CCC Faculty Exhbn., Chgo., 1996, Richard Love Gallery, Chgo., 1996, La Llorona Gallery, Chgo., 1997, Prospectus Art Gallery, Chgo., 1997, Mexican Fine Arts Ctr. Mus., 1997, Chgo. Hist. Soc., 1996, 97, Mus. Contemporary Art, Chgo., 1996, 97, numerous others film screenings U.S., Europe, and Mexico; commd. muralist in public locations and pvt. residences; represented in permannet collections: Sara Lee Corp., Chgo., Mexican Mus. of Fine Arts, Chgo., San Francisco Mus. of Art, San Francisco Mus. of Contempory Art, Tucson Mus. of Art, Latino Inst., Chgo., Columbia Coll., Chgo., Bell Telephone Co., Chgo., Lake Meadows Assn., Chgo., Scholarship and Guidance Assn., Chgo., City of Chgo., San Antonio Art Mus., Guadalupe Cultural Arts Ctr., Denver, Evergreen State Coll., Olympia, Wash., Chgo. Humanities and Art Coun., Denver, Ariztlan, Inc., Phoenix, Mira, Chgo., Centro Cultural de La Raza, San Diego, San Diego Art Mus, Albuquerque Mus., San Francisco Art Mus., San Diego Mus. Contemporary Art, Denver Art Mus., Mex. Mus., San Francisco, Portland Art Mus., Nat. Mus. Am. Art, Washington, numerous group exhibitions include: Norris Gallery Cultural Arts Ctr., 1997, Instituto Cultural Puertoriqueno, 1998, Chgo. Atheneum, Schaumburg, 1998, Ill. State Museum, 1999, Guadalupe Cultural Ctr., 2000; also numerous pvt. collections. Contbr. articles to numerous publications. Active contributor to cultural organizations. Recipient numerous awards includ ing nat. gold medal, gold keys and certs. Scholastic Mag., 1963-65, cert. of merit N.Y. Times, 1965, 1st Prize award, Chgo. Police Dept., 1964, 1st Prize award Chgo. Assn. Commerce & Industry, 1965, 1st Pl. award U. Ill. Chgo. LASP design competition, 1st prize Maldef Art Competition, 1989, 1st pl. ESDC's Archtl. Relief Design Competition for New Homes in Chgo., 1992; artist to represent Midwest in nat. workshop, UCLA, 1988, artist to represent Latino culture in Spanish TV comml., 1989, 1st prize Homewood (Ill.) C. of C., 1967, 1st prize Fiesta del Quinto Sol, Chgo., 1974, 1st prize Mus. Sci. and Industry, Chgo., 1975, 1st prize for 18th St. banner design, Chgo., 1994; Am. Film Inst. grantee, 1972; Oakley fellow U. So. Calif., 1969-70; Scholarship and Guidance Assn. grantee, 1965-68, Ford Found. grantee, 1975; named Artist of Yr., Latino Inst., 1991. Achievements include rsch. in Perceptualism (the phenomena of after-images and optical illusions in paintings to create the feeling of the 4th dimension and alterations in color perception, visual investigations into discovering peculiar ways of presenting the human condition on this planet using superimposed layers of different states of realities and warping images and space so as to turn them "up-side-down"; composing numerous songs. Home: 10101 S Avenue M Chicago IL 60617-5925 Office: Columbia Coll Dept Art & Design 600 S Michigan Ave Chicago IL 60605-1900 E-mail: mcastillo@colum.edu., mario@mariocastillousa.com.

CASTLE, EMERY NEAL, agricultural and resource economist, educator; b. Eureka, Kans., Apr. 13, 1923; s. Sidney James and Josie May (Tucker) C.; m. Merab Eunice Weber (dec.), Jan. 20, 1946; 1 child, Cheryl Diana Delozier; m. Betty Thompson, Mar. 18, 2000. BS, Kans. State U., 1948, MS, 1950; PhD, Iowa State U., 1952, LHD (hon.), 1997. Agrl. economist Fed. Res. Bank of Kansas City, 1952-54; from asst. prof. to prof. dept. agrl. econs. Oreg. State U., Corvallis, 1954-65, dean faculty, 1965-66, prof., head dept. agrl. econs., 1966-72, dean Grad. Sch., 1972-76, Alumni disting. prof., 1970, prof. univ. grad. faculty econs., 1986—, dir. rural studies program, 2001—03; v.p., sr. fellow Resources for the Future, Washington, 1976-79, pres., 1979-86. Vice-chmn. Environ. Quality Commn. Oreg., 1988-95; pres. Acad. for Lifelong Learning, Oreg. State U., 2002-03. Editor: The Changing American Countryside: Rural People and Places, 1995; mem. editl. bd. Land Econs., 1969—. Recipient Alumni Disting. Service award Kans. State U., 1976; Disting. Service award Oreg. State U., 1984 Fellow AAAS, Am. Assn. Agrl. Economists (pres. 1972-73), Am. Acad. Arts and Scis. Home: 1112 NW Solar Pl Corvallis OR 97330-3640 Office: Oreg State U 227 Ballard Corvallis OR 97331

CASTLE, GRACE ELEANOR, legal investigator; b. Waldport, Oreg., Feb. 13, 1943; d. James Everett and Ethel Grace (Smith) Elting; m. Terry Lynn Castle, Feb. 3, 1962; children: Nancy Kae Castle Cary, Tari Ann Castle Utterback. Cert. legal investigator. Investigator, paralegal William A. Barton, PC, Newport, Oreg., 1987-89; owner, operator Castle Investigations, Newport, 1989-96; exec. mng. dir., innocence project coord. Paul J. Ciolino and Assoc., LLC, Palatine, Ill., 1996—2002; with Cluesonline LLC, Eugene, Oreg., 2002—. Co-host N.Am. Conf. on Wrongful Conviction Investigations, 2001. Co-author, editor: Advanced Forensic Civil Investigations, 1997, Advanced Forensic Criminal Defense Investigations, 2000; co-author: Corporate Investigations, 2002; editor The Legal Investigator Mag., 1993-98, Nat Assn. Profl. Process Servers, 1994-99, Cluesonline, 2000—, PI Mag., 2002—; contbr. articles to profl. jours. Mem. Oreg. Assn. Licensed Investigators (pres. 1991-92), Huguenot Hist. Soc., New Paltz, NY, Aux. VFW (pres. post #732 1965). Avocations: historical research and writing, photography. Office: Cluesonline LLC PO Box 2981 Eugene OR 97402 E-mail: gecastle@cluesonline.com.

CASTLE, HOWARD BLAINE, retired religious organization administrator; b. Toledo, July 15, 1935; s. Russell Wesley and Letha Belle (Hobbs) C.; m. Patricia Ann Haverty, Aug. 12, 1957; 1 child Kevin Blaine. AB, Marion Coll., 1958; postgrad., Valparaiso U., 1960. Pastor The Wesleyan Ch., Valparaiso, Ind., 1958-60, Toronto, Ohio, 1963-69; assoc. pastor Northridge Wesleyan Ch., Dayton, Ohio, 1960-63; exec. dir. gen. dept. youth Wesleyan Ch. Hdqrs., Marion, Ind., 1968-72, dir. field ministries gen. dept. Sunday schs., 1972-74, exec. dir. curriculum, 1980-81; mng. editor WIN Mag., Marion, Ind., 1969-72; asst. gen. sec. Gen. Dept. of Local Ch. Edn., Marion, Ind., 1974-80; gen. dir. estate planning Wesleyan Ch. Internat Ctr., Indpls., 1982—2002, ret., 2002. Editor Ohio dist. The Wesleyan Ch., Columbus, 1961-69; gen. conf. del. The Wesleyan Ch., Anderson, Ind., 1968, Greensboro, N.C., 2000. Writer: Curriculum-Religious Adult Student/Teacher, 1982—, Light from the Word, 1982—. Mem. Christian Holiness Partnership, Christian Stewardship Assn., Christian Mgmt. Assn. Mem. Wesleyan Ch. Avocations: music, reading. E-mail: castleh@wesleyan.org. *Life's choices impact more than any other factor the measure of our success and achievements. Circumstances cannot defeat one who chooses to rise above them by acting in accord with his choice.*

CASTLE, JAMES CAMERON, information systems executive; b. Peoria, Ill., Nov. 4, 1936; s. Charles Cameron and Betty Evelyn (Shaw) C.; m. Dorothy Patricia Gorbandt, June 7, 1958; children: James Charles, Patricia Elizabeth. BS, U.S. Mil. Acad., 1958; MSEE, U. Pa., Phila., 1963, PhD, 1966. Pres., chief exec. officer Honeywell Bull Network Info. Svcs., S.A., Paris, 1975-78; gen. mgr. GE, Daytona Beach, Fla., 1978-80; v.p. ops. Honeywell, Inc., Billerica, Mass., 1980-82; exec. v.p. Memorex Corp., Santa Clara, Calif., 1982-84; pres. TGB Info. Systems, Inc., N.Y.C., 1984-87; chmn., pres., chief exec. officer Infotron Systems Corp., Cherry Hill, N.J., 1987-91; CEO Teradata Corp., El Segundo, Calif., 1991-92; chmn., chief exec. officer USCS Internat., Sacramento, 1992—; pres., CEO Castle Info. Techs., El Segundo, 2000—. Bd. dirs. ADC Telecomms., Mpls., PMI Group, Inc., San Francisco, S.W. Water Co., West Covina; pres. Chief Exec. Orgn., Bethesda, Md.; trustee West Point (N.Y.) Assn. Grads. 1st lt. U.S. Army, 1958-61. Mem. World Presidents Orgn.

CASTLE, JANICE MORRIS, medical association administrator; b. Rocky Mount, Va., July 21, 1956; d. Brady Lee and Lena Love Morris. AAS, Va. Western Community Coll., 1976; BSN, Radford U., 1990; MBA, Francis Marion U., 2002. RN, Va.; cert. med.-surg. nursing. Asst. head nurse ICU Community Hosp. Roanoke (Va.) Valley, acting head nurse ICU, head nurse chronic respiratory unit, nursing resource coord.; dir. clin. computer svcs. Carilion Health Systems, Roanoke, Va., 1990-95; exec. dir., healthcare mgmt. cons. Superior Cons., Co., Inc., 1995-97; dir. clin. computers McLeod Regional Med. Ctr., Florence, S.C., 1997-99; chief info. officer, asst. v.p. McLeod Health, Florence, 1999—. Mem. NAFE, Va. Lung Assn. (bd. dirs. Roanoke Region, pres. 1991-93), Sigma Theta Tau. E-mail: jcastle@mcleodhealth.org.

CASTLE, JOHN KROB, merchant banker; b. Cedar Rapids, Iowa, Dec. 22, 1940; s. Clyo F. and Emma (Krob) C.; m. Marianne Sherman, Sept. 20, 1969; children: William Sherman, John Sherman, James Sherman, David Alexander. SB, MIT, 1963; MBA with high distinction, Harvard U., 1965; LHD (hon.), N.Y. Med. Coll., 1988. Assoc. Donaldson, Lufkin & Jenrette, Inc., N.Y.C., 1965-68, v.p., 1968-71, exec. v.p., 1971-73, mng. dir., 1973-80, chief operating officer, 1979-84, pres., 1980-86, chief exec. officer, 1985-86; pres., chief exec. officer Branford Castle, Inc., N.Y.C., 1986—; also founder, chmn., CEO Castle Harlan, Inc., N.Y.C., 1987—, also founder, chmn., chief exec. officer, 1987; chmn., gen. ptnr. Castle Harlan Ptnrs. II, III and IV. Bd. dirs. Morton's Restaurant Group, Inc., Marie Callender's, AdobeAir, Inc., Am. Achievement Corp., Advanced Accessory Sys., LLC. Author: Financial Executives Handbook: Dividend Policy and Equity Financing, 1970, The Strategy of Corporate Financing: Packaging a Merger of Acquisition, 1971, Acquisition and Merger Negotiation Strategy, 1971; co-pub. Castle Connolly Guide, 1994, 1995, 1997—2003, Parent's Helper, 1996. With N.Y. Med. Coll., chmn. bd., 1979-90; mem. corp. MIT, 1987-2000; mem. vis. com. dept. econs; trustee The Whitehead Inst. for Biomed. Rsch., N.Y. Presbyn. Hosp.; chmn. Rhodes Scholar Selection Com., N.Y. State, 1986-90, Columbia-Presbyn. Health Sci. Adv. Coun.; endowed Castle Krob Fellowship for grad. study in econs. MIT, Castle Krob Fund for rsch. support at N.Y. Med. Coll., Castle Krob Devel. Chair in econs. MIT, John K. Castle Pubs. Fund on Ethics, Politics and Econs., Yale U. Mem. Links Club, Met. Club, Harvard Club, N.Y. Yacht Club, Palm Beach Polo Club, Doubles Ltd., Club Collette. Home: 1095 N Ocean Blvd Palm Beach FL 33480-3230 Office: Castle Harlan Inc 150 E 58th St New York NY 10155-0002 E-mail: jcastle@castleharlan.com.

CASTLE, JOSEPH LANKTREE, II, energy company executive, consultant; b. Germantown, Pa., July 25, 1932; s. George Scott and Frances (Murphy) C.; m. Sally Buckman Watson, May 4, 1957; children: Sallie Buckman Harder, Joseph Lanktree III, Kathryn Lanktree Van Blarcom. AB in English, Princeton U., 1954. V.p. Phila. Nat. Bank, 1954-66; ptnr. Butcher & Sherrerd, Phila., 1966-72; cons. Joseph L. Castle Assocs., Gladwyne, Pa., 1972-74; trustee The Reading Co., Blue Bell, Pa., 1974-80; CEO, Castle Energy Corp., Radnor, Pa., 1981—. Bd. dirs. Comcast Corp., Charming Shoppes, Bensalem, Pa. Capt. U.S. Army, 1955-59. Republican. Presbyterian. Avocations: golf, fly fishing. Home: 1790 Aloha Ln Gladwyne PA 19035-1031 Office: Castle Energy Corp 100 Matsonford Rd Radnor PA 19080-0001

CASTLE, JOYCE M, mezzo soprano; b. Beaumont, Tex., Jan. 17, 1939; d. George Malicky and Ethel Lucille Reed; m. Wendell Castle (div.); m. Bruce Brewer (div.). BFA in voice/theatre, U Kans., 1961; MA, Eastman Sch. Music, 1966. Principal artist N.Y.C. Opera, 1983—, Met. Opera, N.Y.C., 1985—, Chgo. Lyric Opera, Seattle Opera Co., Santa Fe Opera, opera cos. throughout U.S., Europe, Tel Aviv, Japan, Brazil. Artist in residence U. Kans., 2001—. Singer: (Operas) (world premiere) Dream of Valentino by D. Argento, Central Park by Michael Torke, (N.Am. premiere) The Handmaid's Tale, (albums) (by G. C. Menotti) The Medium, The Consul, (by L. Bernstein) Candide (Grammy Best Opera Recording, 1986). Mem.: AGMA, Actors Equity, Mu Phi Epsilon. Office: U Kans Dept of Music and Dance Murphy Hall Lawrence KS 66045

CASTLE, MICHAEL N. congressman; b. Wilmington, Del., July 2, 1939; s. J. Manderson and Louisa B. Castle. BA, Hamilton Coll., 1961; JD, Georgetown U., 1964. Bar: Del. 1964, D.C. 1964. Assoc. firm Connolly Bove and Lodge, Wilmington, 1964-73; mem. Del. Ho. of Reps., 1967-69, Del. State Senate, 1969-77; ptnr. firm Connolly Bove and Lodge, 1973-75; dept. atty. gen. State of Del., 1965-66; ptnr. firm Schnee and Castle (P.A.), 1975-80; lt. gov. State of Del., Wilmington, 1981-85; prin. Michael N. Castle (P.A.), 1981—; gov. State of Del., 1985-93; mem. Congress from Del. (at large), 1993—; mem. edn. and workforce com., intelligence com.; chmn. subcom. Edn. Reform, chmn. tech. and tactical intelligence. Mem. Del. Ho. of Reps., 1966-67, Del. State Senate, 1968-76, minority leader, 1976 Bd. dirs. Boys Club of Wilmington. Mem. Del. State Bar Assn., ABA, Council State Govts., Nat. Gov.'s Assn., Rep. Gov.'s Assn., Southern Gov.'s Assn. Republican. Roman Catholic. Office: US Ho of Reps 1233 Longworth Bldg Washington DC 20515-0801*

CASTLEBERRY, ARLINE ALRICK, architect; b. Mpls., Sept. 19, 1919; d. Bannona Gerhardt and Meta Emily (Veit) Alrick; m. Donald Montgomery Castleberry, Dec. 25, 1941; children: Karen, Marvin. B in Interior Architecture, U. Minn., 1941; postgrad., U. Tex., 1947-48. Designer, draftsman Elizabeth & Winston Close, Architects, Mpls., 1940-41, Northwest Airlines, Mpls., 1942-43, Cerny & Assocs., Mpls., 1944-46; archtl. draftsman Dominick and Van Benscotten, Washington, 1946-47; ptnr. Castleberry & Davis Bldg. Designers, Burlingame, Calif., 1960-65; prin. Burlingame, 1965-90; ret. Recipient Smith Coll. scholarship. Mem. AIA, Am. Inst. Bldg. Designers (chpt. pres. 1971-72), Commaisini, Alpha Alpha Gamma, Chi Omega. Democrat. Lutheran. Home and Office: 1311 Parrott Dr San Mateo CA 94402-3630 E-mail: dcac6@juno.com.

CASTLEBERRY, CRATA LEE, librarian; b. Jonesboro, Ark., Sept. 1, 1951; d. William Rex and Crata (Walker) C.; m. Dallas D. Miles (div. Dec. 1983); 1 child, Caroline Miles. BA, U. Ark., 1973; MS in Libr. Sci., U. So. Calif., 1982. Savs. mgr. Glendale Fed. Savs. & Loan, Canoga Pk., Calif., 1978-81; reference asst. Ark. State Libr., Little Rock, 1982-83; rsch. libr. U. Ark., Little Rock, 1983-93; libr. U.S. Cts. Br. Libr., Little Rock, 1993—. Office: US Cts Br Libr 600 W Capitol Ave Ste 224 Little Rock AR 72201-3329

CASTLEBERRY, W. THOMAS, financial company executive; b. Tuscon, Ariz., Aug. 3, 1937; s. Wayne Texas and Dorothy (Roby) C.; m. Jean Ann Mrocek, Oct. 24, 1972; children: Melanie, Mark, Kelly, Cheryl, Nicole, Matthew. BS, U. Calif., Davis, 1960. Cons. Touche Ross, San Francisco, 1967-69; sr. v.p. Crocker Nat. Bank, 1969-72; sr. v.p. $D Ramada Inns, Phoenix, 1972-78; v.p. EDS, Phoenix, 1978-80; chmn. CEO Anasazi, Phoenix, 1980-83, 87-93; sr. v.p. VISA, Phoenix, 1983-87, FDC, Phoenix, 1993-95; vice chmn., CEO Rezsolutions, Phoenix, 1996—99; chmn. bd. & CEO Eldorado Computing, Inc., Phoenix, 2000—. Capt. U.S. Army, 1960-61, with USNG, 1961-72. Mem. Phoenix Boys and Girls Clubs. Office: Eldorado Computing Inc 5353 N 16th St Ste 400 Phoenix AZ 85016

CASTLEMAN, ALBERT WELFORD, JR., physical chemist, educator; b. Richmond, Va., Jan. 7, 1936; s. Albert W. and Mildred L. Castleman; m. Heide Gisela Engel, Mar. 10, 1976; children: Sharon Beth, Robert Gill, Clifton Carl. BChemE, Rensselaer Poly. Inst., 1957; MS, Poly. Inst. Bklyn., 1963, PhD, 1969; PhD (hon.), U. Innsbruck, Austria, 1987. Leader chemistry rsch. group Brookhaven Nat. Lab., 1958-75; adj. prof. atmospheric chemistry depts. earth and space sci. and mechanics SUNY, Stony Brook, 1973-75; prof. chemistry, CIRES fellow U. Colo., Boulder, 1975-82; prof. chemistry Pa. State U., University Park, 1982—, Evan Pugh prof. chemistry, 1986—, adv. bd. Particulate Materials Ctr., 1987-94, mem. Ctr. for Materials Physics, 1993—, Eberly disting. chair in sci., 1999—, prof. physics, 1999; adv. bd. Ctr. for Nanoscale Sys. Materials Va. Commonwealth U., 1992—. Vis. prof. Physics Inst., Leopold-Franzens U., Innsbruck, Austria, 1981, 84, 99; mem. rev. com. chem. physics programs, Oak Ridge Nat. Lab., 1979, adv. com. to lab. dir. chem. physics programs, Health and Safety Divsn., 1987-90, chmn., 1990, mem. Dept. Energy rev. com. for chem. physics and radiol. physics program, 1985, Fulbright guest prof., 1990; adv. to Dept. Energy on chem. physics pertaining to energy related environ. programs, 1980; mem. ad hoc. panel on atmospheric chemistry Com. on Atmospheric Scis., NRC, NAD, 1980; mem. rev. com. for radiol. and environ. rsch. divsn. Argonne Univs. Assn. Argonne Nat. Lab., 1977-81, chemistry divsn., Argonne, 1988; mem. various rev. and adv. coms. Nat. Ctr. for Atmospheric Rsch., U.S. Dept. Energy U.S. Nuc. Regulatory Commn.; cons. Mfg. Chemists Assn., 1975-80, nuc. divsn. Oak Ridge Nat. Lab., 1976-86, E.I. Dupont de Nemours, 1989—; chmn. subcom. on ions, aerosols and radioactivity Internat. Commn. Atmospheric Electricity, 1976-80; sr. scientist von Humboldt awardee Tech. Hochschule Darmstadt, 1987, Philipps U., Marburg, Germany, 1988, U. Wuerzburg, 1998; bd. dirs. chem. sci. and tech. NRC-NAS, 2001—. Mem. editl. bd. Jour. Phys. Chemistry, 1985-88, 2000—, sr. editor, 1988-98; mem. editl. bd. Jour. Am. Chem. Soc., 2002—, Chem. Phys. Letters, 1995—, Jour. Cluster Sci., Internat. Jour. Mass Spectrometry and Ion Proc., 1987-90, Jour. Chem. Physics, 1985-87, Jour. Atmospheric Chemistry, 1982-94, Aerosol Sci. and Tech., 1982-86, Advances in Chem. Physics, 1995—, Nano Letters, 2000—, Springer Series in Chem. Physics, 2003—, Chem. Physics, 2003—; co-editor, mem. editl. bd. Zeitschrift fer Physick D., 1987-90; mem. chem. physics editl. adv. bd. Rsch. Trends; contbr. articles to profl. jours. Recipient Sr. Scientist Alexander von Humboldt award, 1986, Sr. Scientist Fulbright award, 1990, Wilhelm-Jost-Meml. Lecture award, 2000; Sherman Fairchild Disting. scholar, Calif. Inst. Tech., 1977; NSF Creativity Award grantee, 1985-87; Japanese Soc. for Promotion Sci. fellow, 1983, 97, Fellow AAAS, Am. Acad. Arts and Scis.,, Am. Phys. Soc., N.Y. Acad. Scis.; mem. Nat. Acad. Scis., Am. Chem. Soc. (Creative Advances in Environ. Sci. and Tech. award 1988), Am. Geophys. Union, Am. Assn. Aerosol Rsch., Deutsche Bunsen-Gesellschaft Soc., N.Y. Acad. Scis., Materials Rsch. Soc., Sigma Xi, Phi Lambda Upsilon. Home: 425 Hillcrest Ave State College PA 16803-3419 Office: Pa State U Dept Chemistry 152 Davey Lab University Park PA 16802-6300

CASTLEMAN, BREAUX BALLARD, health management company executive; b. Louisville, Aug. 19, 1940; s. John Pryor and Mary Jane (Ballard) Castleman; m. Sue Ann Foreman (div. 1995); children: Matthew B., Shea B.; m. Patricia Templin Castleman, 2002. BA in Econs., Yale U., 1962; postgrad., NYU, 1963. Mgmt. trainee Bankers Trust Co., N.Y.C., 1963-65; mng. dir. Castleman and Co., Houston, 1965-71; dir. program planning, econ. U.S. Dept. HUD, Ft. Worth, Dallas, 1971-73; v.p., office mgr. Booz Allen and Hamilton, Dallas, Houston, 1973-85; mng. dir. Castleman Group, Houston, 1985-87; CEO Kelsey-Seybold Clinic, P.A., Houston, 1987-95; pres. physician resources divsn. Caremark Internat., Inc., 1994-96; pres. Scripps Clinic, La Jolla, Calif., 1996-99; CEO Physia Corp., Houston, 2000—; pres., CEO Syntiro Healthcare Svcs., Inc., Englewood Cliffs, NJ, 2001—. Contbr. articles to profl. jours. Candidate state legislature, Houston, 1968. Mem. Am. Med. Group Assn. (bd. dirs. 1996-99), Planning Forum (chmn. 1985-86), Yale Club N.Y., Presidio Golf Club.

CASTLEMAN, LOUIS SAMUEL, metallurgist, educator; b. St. Johnsbury, Vt., Nov. 24, 1918; s. Max and Fannie (Svetkey) C.; m. Mildred Blanche Rubin, Jan. 25, 1948; children— Michael Z., David A., Steven J., Daniel J. BS, Mass. Inst. Tech., 1939, D.Sc., 1950. Plant metallurgist Sunbeam Electric Mfg. Co., Evansville, Ind., 1939-41; sr. scientist, supr., acting sect. mgr. Westinghouse Atomic Power Div., Pitts., 1950-54; metall. specialist Gen. Telephone & Electronics Labs., Inc., Bayside, N.Y., 1954-64; prof. phys. metallurgy Poly. U., N.Y., 1964-89, prof. emeritus, 1989—. Cons. phys. metallurgy. With AUS, 1941-46; lt. col. Ret. Recipient Distinguished Tchr. award Poly. Inst. N.Y., 1975 Fellow AAAS; mem. Am. Soc. Metals (chpt. chmn. 1963-64), Am. Inst. Mining, Metall. and Petroleum Engrs., Am. Phys. Soc., Metal Sci. Club N.Y. (pres. 1973-74), Sigma Xi. Democrat. Jewish religion. Home: 120 Morris Ave Apt C5 Rockville Centre NY 11570-4240 Office: 6 Metrotech Ctr Brooklyn NY 11201-3840 E-mail: lcastlem@optonline.net.

CASTLEYOUNG, BRENDA, social worker, mental health nurse; b. Toronto, June 18, 1942; came to US, 1964; d. Mervyn William and Ruth Vera Young; m. Sylvanus B. Jones, Sept. 9, 1999; children: Stephen M. Castagnola, Gregory J. Castagnola, Thomas M. Castagnola. RN, Toronto E. Gen. Hosp., 1960; BSPA, St. Joseph's Coll., 1980; MSW, U. Md., 1983; PhD, 1992. RN. Nurse Syosset (N.Y.) Gen. Hosp., 1964-69; RN/LCSW Anne Arundel Gen. Hosp., Annapolis, Md., 1970-90; nurse, clin. specialist, social worker Crofton (Md.) Counselling Ctr., 1983-90; RN/CS-P, LCSW-C, LCWS, PRD Arundel Mental Health Profls.,

1988—; Spectrum Behavioral Health Profls., 1990—. Author: Child Sexual Abuse and Subsequent Adolescent Behavioral Patterns, 1992, poems. Fellow U. Md. Hosp.; mem. ANA, NASW. Home: 2982 W Friends Rd Annapolis MD 21401 Office: # 303 49 Old Solomons Is Annapolis MD 21401 Fax: (410) 573-1972.

CASTLOO, SHIRLEY ANNETTE, government official, retired civilian military employee; b. Gilmer, Tex, Sept. 18, 1943; d. John and Thula Runette (Clark) C. AS, Kilgore Coll., Tex., 1971; student, E. Tex. State U., 1971, Tex. Woman's U., Denton, 1972. Owner restaurant, Biloxi, Miss., 1967-68; emergency rm. supr. Gilmer Hosp., Tex., 1968-70; asst. nursing supr. Care Inn Nursing Home, Gladwater, Tex., 1970-71; nurses aide Bapt. Hosp., Beaumont, Tex., 1972-74; tng. specialist Tex. Air Nat. Guard, Nederland, 1974, vehicle maintenance supr., 1973-77, graphic arts specialist, 1977-84; engring. asst. US Postal Svc., Beaumont, Tex., 1984-94, carrier tech., 1974-97, supr. customer svc., 1997—2000; officer in charge U.S. Postal Svc., Winnie, Tex., 2001—02; acting mgr. Tobe Hahn Sta., 2002—03. With USAF, 1962-66. Recipient Air Res. Forces Meritorious Svc. award, 1975, 79, 83, 87, Meritorious Svc. medal, 1995, Lone Star Disting. Svc. Medal, 1995, Tex. Faithful Svc. awd., 1983, Air Force Achievement medal, 1990. Democrat. Baptist. Avocations: music, painting, bowling, travel. Home: 13912 Santa Fe Trl Hamshire TX 77622-9007 Office: US Post Office 5815 Walden Rd Beaumont TX 77707-5501 E-mail: scastloo@aol.com.

CASTNER, DEBORAH A. librarian; b. Kingston, Pa., Jan. 15, 1957; d. Robert D. and Dorothy F. O'Malley; children: Jennifer, Kyle. BS in Elem. Edn., Coll. Misericordia, Dallas, Pa., 1978; MEd in Classroom Tech., Wilkes U., Wilkes-Barre, Pa., 2002. Tchr. 6th to 8th grade Holy Child Sch., Plymouth, Pa., 1988—2000; libr. Wyoming Valley West, Plymouth, Pa., 2000—; bookseller Barnes & Noble, Wilkes-Barre, Pa., 1999—. Mem.: NEA, Pa. State Edn. Assn. Home: 13 Willow St Plymouth PA 18651

CASTNER JR. THEODORE G. education educator; b. Orange, NJ, USA, June 17, 1930; s. Theodore Grant and Anna W. Castner; m. Emily Knapp Shirley, Aug. 5, 1967; children: Mary S Castner, Timothy Hardy Castner. Bach. Engr. Physics, Cornell U., Ithaca N.Y., 1948—53; M.S. Physics, U. of Illinois, 1955, PhD. Physics, U. Illinois, 1958. Rsch. specialist Gen. Electric Rsch Lab, Schenectady, NY, 1958—63; prof. of physics U. of Rochester, Rochester, NY, 1963—91; program dir. Nat. Sci. Found., Washington D.C., 1990—91; adj. prof. of physics U. of Mass. Lowell, Lowell, Mass., 1994—. Cons. Solar Energy Rsch. Institute, Golden, Colo., 1980. Author: (article) Current Contents, 1982. Recipient Guggenheim Fellowship, Guggenheim Found., 1969—70. Fellow: Am. Physical Soc. Protestant. Achievements include research involving major contributions to both experimental and theoretical results, to understanding physics of the Metal - Insulator Transition in doped semiconductors. Avocations: skiing, music, sailing, bicycling. Home: 71 Hayden Road Hollis NH 03049

CASTON, J(ESSE) DOUGLAS, medical educator; b. Ellenboro, N.C., June 16, 1932; s. Lemuel Joseph and Myrtice Elizabeth (Vassey) C.; m. Marry Ann Keeter, June 1, 1958; children: John Andrew, Elizabeth Anne, Mary Susan. AB, Lenoir Rhyne Coll., 1954; MA, U. N.C., 1958; PhD, Brown U., 1961. Fellow Carnegie Instn., Washington, Balt., 1961-62; asst. prof. anatomy Case Western Res. U., Cleve., 1962-71, assoc. prof., 1971-76, prof., 1976-98, co-dir. Devel. Biology Ctr., 1971-77, prof. emeritus, 1999—. Cons. Diamond Shamrock Corp., Cleve., 1975-77; coordinator Core Acad. Program, Sch. Medicine, 1985-94. Patentee folate assay, methotrexate assay; contbr. numerous articles to sci. jours., 1962— . Served with AUS, 1954-56. Fellow H.W. Wilson, 1956; grantee USPHS, 1963—, Cancer Soc., 1963—. Mem. Am. Chem. Soc., AAAS, Am. Soc. Zoologists and Developmental Biologists, Biophys. Soc., Soc. Cell Biology, Am. Assn. Anatomists Episcopalian.

CASTOR, CAROL JEAN, artist, teacher; b. Bend, Oreg., Feb. 3, 1944; d. Keith and Lena (Morara) Morrison; 1 child, William Franklin. BFA, U. Okla., 1967; postgrad., U. Tulsa, summer 1976, Art Student's League of N.Y., N.Y.C., summer 1984. Benedictine Oblate with Osage Monastery, Sand Spring, Okla. Dir. art dept. Jefferson Jr. High Sch., Oklahoma City, 1967-68; art instr. Vinita (Okla.) High Sch., 1976-80; profl. artist specializing in commd. portraiture Carol Castor Art Studio, Vinita, 1980—, profl. portrait artist: also paints Native Ams., cowboys, Americana and sacred subjects, 1980—; maintains art studio Vinnie Ream Cultural Ctr. Bd. dirs. Craig Gen. Hosp.; artist-in-residence mural project Vinita Pub. Sch. Alternative Sch., 1998, landscape project, 2000, Sculpture Park Garden, 2001, Collage, 2003; artist-in-residence Vinita Pub. Schs. Arts Experience, 1998-99, 2001-03. Represented in permanent collections at Vinita Pub. Libr., Craig Gen. Hosp., Vinita, 1st Nat. Bank & Trust, Vinita, Cowgirl Hall of Fame and Western Heritage Ctr., Ft. Worth, Okla. Hall of Fame, Oklahoma City, Okla. U. Med. Sch., Oklahoma City, Oklahoma U. Law Sch., Norman, Okla. U. Pharmacy Sch., Oklahoma City, Columbia Presbyterian Med. Ctr., N.Y., Nat. Cmty. Pharmacists Assn., Alexandria, Va.; featured in 2nd edit. of American Artists: An Illustrated Survey of Leading Contemporaries; portraits represented by Grand Ctrl. Galleries, N.Y.; artist cover illustration Oklahoma's Guide to Grand Lake, P.E.O Record, 2003; contbr. illustration to Labor of Love: The Life and Times of Vinnie Ream; cover artist for Mar.-Apr. 2003 issue P.E.O. Record. Mem. Mayor's Adv. Com., Vinita, 1972-74; mem. bldg. com. Vinita Pub. Libr., 1974-75; charter mem. Vinita chpt. Okla. Alliance for Mentally Ill, 1986—; organizer, mem. com. Young Life, Vinita, 1987-89; mem. com. for chronically and mentally ill Vinita Day Ctr. Inc., 1987—; organizer Ea. Trails Art Assn., 1972-84, chmn. Art Invitational '98, '99, '00, '01, Vinita; bd. dirs. Craig Gen. Hosp., 1995—; chmn. Med. Svcs. Corp., 1998-2000, Attuck Alternative Acad., 2002; mem. Benedictine Oblate of Osage Monastery. Recipient Cmty. Svc. award Vinita C. of C., 1984, named to Hall of Fame, 1993. Mem. AAUW (pres. Vinita chpt. 1972-74, Best banner award nat. conv. 1979, Women of Achievement award 1985, pres. Vinnie Ream Cultural Ctr. Found. 2000-02; bd. dirs.), P.E.O., Am. Soc. Portrait Artists. Democrat. Roman Catholic. Avocations: song writing, reading, piano, writing, poetry. Home: 121 Jennie Ln PO Box 411 Vinita OK 74301 E-mail: castorart@junct.com.

CASTOR, CHRISTINA PELAYO, critical care nurse; b. St. Louis, June 3, 1956; d. Jacobo E. and Abundia L. (Pelayo) C. AS in Nursing, Ind. U., Gary, 1980; BSN, Purdue U., Hammond, Ind., 1983, MS in Nursing, 1984; MD, U. Santo Tomas, Manila, The Philippines, 1989. RN, Calif., Ill., Ind., Mich.; CEN; cert. ACLS, PALS; mobile intensive care; cert. trauma nurse, emergency nursing pediat. cours; emergency commns. RN. Staff nurse/charge nurse Our Lady of Mercy Hosp., Dyer, Ind., 1980-85, 86, 87; office nurse Conrado P. Castor MD, Munster, Ind., 1984-90; staff nurse Humana Hosp., Hoffman Estates, Ill., 1990; staff nurse/charge nurse emergency rm. St. Margaret Mercy Hosp., Hammond, Ind., 1990—; pres., CEO, CDC Bus. Inc., 2000—. Mem. Emergency Nurse's Assn. Office: CDC Bus Inc PO Box 602 Schererville IN 46375 E-mail: cpcastor@mail.com.

CASTOR, JON STUART, electronics company executive; b. Lynchburg, Va., Dec. 15, 1951; s. William Stuart and Marilyn (Hughes) Castor; m. Stephanie Lum Castor, Jan. 7, 1989; 1 child, David Jon. BA, Northwestern U., 1973; MBA, Stanford U., 1975. Mgmt. cons., Menlo Park, Calif., 1981-96; pres., CFO TeraLogic, Inc., 1996—2000, CEO, 2000—02; sr. v.p., gen. mgr. Oak Tech. Inc., Sunnyvale, 2002—. Dir. Midwest Consumer Adv. Bd. to FTC, 1971-73; v.p., bd. dirs. San Mateo coun. Boy Scouts Am., 1991-93; bd. dirs. Pacific Skyline coun. Boy Scouts Am., 1994-2003; trustee Coyote Point Mus. Environ. Edn., San Mateo, 1992-95. Achievements include patents in field. Office: Oak Tech TeraLogic Group 1390 Kifer Rd Sunnyvale CA 94086

CASTOR, WILBUR WRIGHT, futurist, writer, consultant, playwright, actor; b. Harrison Twp., Pa., Feb. 3, 1932; s. Wilbur Wright and Margaret (Grubbs) C.; m. Donna Ruth Schwartz, Feb. 9, 1963; children: Amy, Julia, Marnie. BA, St. Vincent Studies, 1959; PhD, Calif. U. Advanced Studies, 1990. Sales rep. IBM, Pitts. and Cleve., 1959-62; v.p. data processing ops. Honeywell, Waltham, Mass., 1962-80; pres., chief exec. officer Aviation Simulation Tech., Lexington, Mass., 1980-82; sr. v.p. Xerox Corp., El Segundo, Calif., 1982-89; freelance cons., 1989—. Author: (play) Un Certaine Soirire, 1958, (mus. comedy) Breaking Up, 1960, (stage play) This is Your Wife, 1997, (book) The Information Age and the New Productivity, 1990, (play) This is Your Wife, 1997, (ballet) Animal Crackers, 2003; contbr. articles to profl. jours. Mem. Presdl. Rep. Task Force; pres., bd. dirs. Internat. Acad., Santa Barbara, Olendorf Found.; chmn. bd. dirs. Marymount Coll., 1999—; bd. dirs. Ryan Bld. Group, 2003—, SAVE, Ryan Bldg. Group. Served to capt. USN, 1953-58, with USAFR, 1958-76. Recipient Disting. Alumnus of Yr. award St. Vincent Coll., 1990. Mem. The Strategy Bd., U. Denver "Netthink", World Future Soc., Aircraft Owners and Pilots Assn., U.S. Senators Club. Avocations: flying, scuba diving, music, reading, writing. Home: 19 Georgeff Rd Rolling Hills Estates CA 90274-5272

CASTORA, JOSEPH CHARLES, history educator; b. N.Y.C., Nov. 20, 1946; s. Charles Carlo and Clara Mary (Toto) C. BA with hons., Manhattan Coll., 1968; MA, NYU, 1973, MPhil, 1979, PhD, 1990. Shipping coord. Amax, Inc., N.Y.C., 1969-83; adj. asst. prof. Manhattan Coll., N.Y.C., 1991—2002, vis. asst. prof., 2002—; adj. asst. prof. Yeshiva U., N.Y.C., 1992. Recipient scholarship NYU, 1973-74, Lane Cooper fellowship, 1983-84. Mem. Am. Hist. Assn., Medieval Acad. Am., Am. Cath. Hist. Assn., Am. Classical League, Phi Alpha Theta. Roman Catholic. Avocations: classical music, opera. Home: 96-01 24th Ave East Elmhurst NY 11369 Office: Manhattan Coll Manhattan Coll Pkwy Bronx NY 10471 E-mail: joseph.castora@manhattan.edu.

CASTORENA, MARIA ANCELITA, writer; b. Del Rio, Tex., Dec. 28, 1945; d. Manuel and Isabel Castorena; m. James P. Dean, Sept. 11, 1971 (div. Oct. 1981); children: Rodolfo, Augustus, Sheila M., James J. Student, Syracuse U., 1985. Author, pub. Castorena Pubs., Syracuse, NY, 1991; sec. Corcoran High Sch., 1984; telemarketer Nat. Childrens Orgns., Houston, 1987. Author: Cuenhos Hispanas, 1991, Como Uma Piedrn, 1991, Chicano Art, 1991. Activist Tent City, Pasadena, Tex., 1982; pres., co-founder Advocates Women Poverty, Syracuse, 1983. Conservative. Roman Catholic. Avocations: doll collecting, gardening, birdwatching. Home: PO Box 34076 San Antonio TX 78265-4076

CASTORINO, SUE, communications executive; b. Columbus, Ohio, May 5, 1953; m. Randy Minkoff, Oct. 23, 1983. BS in Speech, Northwestern U., Evanston, Ill., 1975. Grad. fellow Ohio Gov.'s Sch., Columbus, 1975; producer, community affairs Sta. WBBM-TV, Chgo., 1975; news anchor, reporter Sta. WBBM, Chgo., 1981-86; news reporter Sta. WHTH-AM/FM, Newark, Ohio, 1975; news anchor, reporter Sta. WERE, Cleve., 1975-78, Sta. WWWE, Cleve., 1978-81; founder, pres. Sue Castorino: The Speaking Specialists, Chgo., 1986—. Leader media and presentation skills seminars; pvt. voice coach; active internat. exec. comm. tng. in media, crisis and issue mgmt.; lectr. in field. Author: North Shore Mag., 1987—92. Recipient Golden Gavel award, Chgo. Soc. Assn. Execs., 1991, various news reporting awards, AP. UPI, Chgo., 1981—86. Avocations: sports, film, accomplished pianist. Office: The Speaking Specialists Ste 2602 435 N Michigan Ave Fl 2602 Chicago IL 60611-4001

CASTORO, ROSEMARIE, sculptor; b. Bklyn., Mar. 1, 1939; d. Michael Peter and Camille C. Student in painting, Mus. Modern Art, N.Y.C., 1955-56; BFA cum laude, Pratt Inst., Bklyn., 1963. Tchr. Sch. Visual Arts, N.Y.C., 1971, Hunter Coll., N.Y.C., 1972, Calif. State U., Fresno, 1973, Syracuse (N.Y.) U., 1975, U. Colo., Boulder, 1977, Stockton State U., N.J., 1983, Boston Mus. Sch., 1983, Am. U., Corciano, Italy, 2000. Lectr. art Boston Mus. Sch. Art, 1971, 80, New Sch. Social Rsch., N.Y.C., 1972, 73, Phila. Coll. Art, 1974, Atlanta Coll. Art, 1974, Rome Art Assn., N.Y. State, 1975, Syracuse (N.Y.) U., 1975, U. Calif., Berkeley, 1976, Suzuki-Walker, Sausalito, Calif., 1976, Art Inst. Sch., Chgo., 1980, Pratt Inst., N.Y.C., 1982, 95, C.W. Post, L.I., N.Y., 1984, San Jose (Calif.) U., 1984, 85, N.J. Ctr. for Visual Arts, Summit, 1989, Ecole Nat. Superieure des Beaux-Arts, Paris, 1995. Solo shows include Tibor de Nagy Gallery, N.Y.C., 1971, 72, 73, 75, 76, 78, 81, 83, 85, 89, Hal Bromm Gallery, N.Y.C., 1976, 78, 79, 80, 83, 87, 91-92, 97, 2002, Julian Pretto, N.Y.C., 1978, 79, Marion Deson, Chgo., 1981, Am. Ctr., Paris, 1983, Eaton/Shoen Gallery, San Francisco, 1984, 86, Newark Mus., 1991, Arnaud Lefebvre Gallery, Paris, 1993, 95, 97, 98, 99, 2003, Stella R Graphics, Paris, 1993, Eaton Fine Arts, West Palm Beach, Fla., 2000; group shows include Bklyn. Mus., 1963, Tibor de Nagy Gallery, 1966, Stable Gallery, 1966, Dwan Gallery, N.Y.C., 1968, 69, Richard Feigen Gallery, N.Y.C., 1968, Paula Cooper Gallery, N.Y.C., 1969, 71, Vancouver (B.C., Can.) Art Gallery, 1970, Stadtische Kunsthalle, Dusseldorf, Germany, 1970, Allen Art Mus., Oberlin, Ohio, 1970, Hundred Acres Gallery, N.Y.C., 1970, 112 Greene St Gallery, N.Y.C., 1971, 72, Richard Gray Gallery, Chgo., 1972, Storm King Art Gallery, Mountainville, N.Y., 1972, 74, 75, Grapestake Gallery, San Francisco, 1975, 76, Moore Coll. Art, Phila., 1977, John Weber Gallery, N.Y.C., 1977, Hal Bromm Gallery, 1977, 81, 82, 85, 86, 87, Indpls. Mus. Art, 1978, Whitney Mus. Am. Art, N.Y.C., 1978, Nancy Lurie Gallery, Chgo., 1978, Smithsonian Instn., Washington, 1980, Hunter Mus. Art, Chatanooga, Tenn., 1980, Banco Gallery, Brescia, Italy, 1980, Hirshhorn Mus. and Sculpture Garden, Washington, 1981, Pratt Inst. Art Gallery, Bklyn., 1981, Eaton/Shoen Gallery, 1982, Maier Mus. Art, Lynchburgh, Va., 1983, 90, Laguna Gloria Art Mus., Austin, Tex., 1985, Mus. Modern Art, N.Y.C., 1985, Newark Mus., 1987, Marvin Seline Gallery, Houston, 1990, Jan Baum Gallery, L.A., 1990, Stellar Graphics, Paris, 1992, Galerie Arnaud Lefebvre, Paris, 1993, 95-96, 2001, 2003, Henry St. Settlement, N.Y.C., 1993, Athenaeum Music & Arts Libr., La Jolla, Calif., 1995, Beaumanoir, Le Leslay, France, 1995, and many, many others; commns. include Battery Park City, N.Y.C., 1978, GSA, Topeka, Kans., 1979, Am. Ctr., Paris, 1983, Athena Found., L.I., N.Y., 1986, Woodstock '94, Saugerties, N.Y., 1994, and others; permanent collections include Allen Art Mus., Oberlin, Ohio, Boca Raton (Fla.) Mus., Bank of Am., Calif., Chase Manhattan Bank, N.A., GSA, Washington, Mus. Modern Art, N.Y.C., Newark Mus., Univ. Art Mus., U. Calif., Berkeley, U. Mass., Woodward Found., Washington, and others. Treas. HIV-Arts, N.Y.C., 1994-2003. Guggenheim fellow, 1971; grantee Woodward Found., 1970, CAPS, 1972, 74, NEA, 1974-75, 84-85, Tiffany Found., 1977, Pollock-Krasner Found., 1989-90, 97-98. Home: 151 Spring St # 6 New York NY 10012-3850 E-mail: rcastoro@earthlink.net.

CASTRATARO, BARBARA ANN, lawyer; b. Bethpage, N.Y., Apr. 25, 1958; d. Vincent James and Theresa (Chiarini) C. BA in Music, L.I. U., 1984; JD, N.Y. Law Sch., 1989. Bar. N.Y. 1990, U.S. Dist. Ct. (so. dist.) N.Y. 1990. Music dir. CBS Network, N.Y.C., 1979-81, exec. ops., 1985-88; music dir. NBC Network/Score Prodns., N.Y.C. and L.A., 1983-84, Score Prodns./ABC Network, N.Y.C. and L.A., 1980-84; assoc. Donald Frank Esq., N.Y.C., 1989-93, Law Offices of Joel C. Bender, White Plains, N.Y., 1993-99, Bender, Jenson, Silverstein & Castrataro, LLP, White Plains, 1999-2000; pvt. practice Law Offices of Barbara A. Castrataro, Chappaqua, N.Y., 2000—. Lectr. on divorce and separation parenting; founder Castrataro Artist Mgmt., 1997-99; adj. faculty mem. Berkeley Coll., White Plains, N.Y. Recipient 3 Emmy nominations N.Y. Acad. TV Arts and Sci., 1979, 82-83. Mem. N.Y. State Bar Assn., Womens Bar Assn. Avocations: sailing, gourmet cooking, gardening. Office: PO Box 132 Chappaqua NY 10514 E-mail: cambac233@aol.com.

CASTREJON, ELIZABETH BLACKWELL, artist; b. East Orange, N.J., Feb. 10, 1935; d. William Thomas and Helen Williams (Hardy) Blackwell; m. Jose Castrejon Rodriguez, Oct. 20, 1957 (div. July 1984); children: Jose, Pedro. BFA, Syracuse U., 1956, U. Ams., 1957. Asst. mgr. Monte de Tacxo, Mexico, 1970-74; corp. interior designer Posados de Mexico, Mexico City, 1974-80, Krystal Hotels, Mexico City, 1980-85; interior designer Wesloh Designs, Costa Mesa, Calif., 1985-87, Barbara Swartz Interiors, Westlake Village, Calif., 1987, Interior Form & Function, Camarillo, Calif., 1987-92; owner Castrejon Originals, Westlake Village, 1992—. Mem. Am. Soc. Interior Design, Calif. Coun. Interior Design, Conejo Assn. Interior Designs. Republican. Home: 1111 Via Colinas Westlake Village CA 91362-5056

CASTRIOTTA, RICHARD J. medical educator, physician; b. Winchester, Mass., Dec. 21, 1945; s. Louis and Mary Castriotta; m. Laura Gillespie, Feb. 19, 1983; 1 child, Gabrielle. AB, Holly Cross Coll., 1967; MD, U. Bologna, Italy, 1974. Diplomate internal medicine Am. Bd. Internal Medicine, 1978, pulmonary disease Am. Bd. Internal Medicine, 1980, sleep medicine Am. Bd. Sleep Medicine, 1989. Rsch. asst. Mass. Gen. Hosp., Boston, 1967—74; med. resident Hosp. St. Raphael, New Haven, 1974—78; pulmonary fellow U. Conn. Health Ctr., Farmington, 1978—80; asst. prof. of medicine and pathology U. of Conn. Sch. of Medicine, Farmington, Conn., 1981—92; assoc. profesor clin. medicine U. Conn. Sch. Medicine, Farmington, 1992—95; dir. pulmonary medicine Mt. Sinai Hosp., Hartford, Conn., 1981—85, dir. Sleep Disorders Ctr., 1983—95, asst. chief medicine, 1991—95, interim chief medicine, 1992—93; med. dir. Meml. Hermann Hosp. Sleep Disorders Ctr., Houston, 1995—; assoc. prof. internal medicine U. Tex. Med. Sch., Houston, 1995—2002, prof. internal medicine, 2002—, assoc. dir. divsn. pulmonary, critical care and sleep medicine, 2003—. Dir. Hartford Health Dept. Chest Clinic (for Tb), 1981—94; med. dir. Pulmonary Physiology Lab. Mt. Sinai Hosp., Hartford, 1981—95, med. dir. Blood Gas Lab., 1981—92, med. dir. respiratory therapy dept., 1981—95, chmn. ethics com., 1986—95, med. dir. ICU, 1991—92; mem. Sch. Medicine. coun. U. Conn. Health Ctr., Farmington, 1992—95; chmn. tb elimination adv. com. State Conn., Hartford, 1992—95; chmn. sleep medicine sect. Conn. Thoracic Soc., 1992—95; chmn. ethics meeting group Conn. Hosp. Assn., Wallingford, 1993—95; chmn. ethics com. St. Francis Hosp. and Med. Ctr., Hartford, 1995—95; med. adv. com. Blue Cross and Blue Shield Tex., Richardson, 1996—; faculty senate U. Tex. Med. Sch., Houston; sleep fellowship program dir. U. Tex. Health Sci. Ctr., Houston; chmn. futility rev. com. Meml. Hermann Hosp., Houston. Mem. Conn. Opera, Hartford, 1994—95. Fellow: Am. Coll. Chest Physicians, Am. Acad. Sleep Medicine (sleep network steering comittee 1999—); mem.: So. Sleep Soc. (sec.-treas. 2001—), Am. Thoracic Soc. Home: 2406 Reba Dr Houston TX 77019 Office: Univ Tex Med Sch Ste 1266 6431 Fannin Houston TX 77030 Office Fax: 713-500-6824. Personal E-mail: castriotta@sbcglobal.net. E-mail: richard.j.castriotta@uth.tmc.edu.

CASTRO, CHARLES EDWARD, chemist, consultant; b. Santa Clara, Calif., Nov. 17, 1931; s. Albert Joseph Castro and Ora Castro (Acronico); m. Ruth Scriver Wade, June 19, 1970; m. Johanna Maria Felber (div.); children: Lony Christine Avina-Castro, Albert Joseph, Ann Mary Crowell-Castro, Karl Thomas, Hans Michael, Claire Mary Karney-Castro, Mark Teilhard. AB, San Jose State Coll., 1953; PhD in Chemistry, U. Calif., Davis, 1957. Quality control chemist Economics Laboratories Inc., Santa Clara, Calif., 1952—53; asst. in chemistry U. of Calif., Davis, Calif., 1953—57; rsch. chemist, organic chemistry Shell Devel. Co., Emeryville, Calif., 1957—60; chemist and prof. U. of Calif., Riverside, 1960—95, chemist and prof. emeritus, 1995—; chem. cons., expert witness Chem. & Environ. Consulting, Laguna Beach, Calif., 1996—. Acting dir. environ. toxicology U. of Calif., Riverside, Calif., 1993—94; mem. Malathion Health Adv. Com./Cal EPA, Calif., 1992, Lab. Regulatory Reform Task Force/CalEPA, Calif., 1994. Author (and researcher): (chemical research) Chemical,Biochemical and Biological Journals of the American Chemical Society and others/Book Chapters/Patents. Program chair/chair/past chair San Gorgonio Sect. Am. Chem. Soc., Riverside, Calif., 1991—93. Fulbright scholar in chemistry, US Govt., U. Heidelberg, Germany, 1953—54. Mem.: Am. Chem. Soc. (life). Achievements include discovery of The Castro Reaction(s); development of A Theory of Hemeprotein Reactivity; research in Mechanistic Transition Metal- Organic Redox Chemistry; Biodehalogenation; discovery of Plant Protection with Inorganic Ions; Ozone Generation from Bio-molecules; development of Site Reactivity Probes for the Environment. Avocations: running, skiing, hiking. Office: Chemical & Environmental Consulting 1090 Madison Place Laguna Beach CA 92651-2841 Office Fax: 949-494-0180. E-mail: cecastro@ccasceccon.com.

CASTRO, CYNTHIA M, clinical psychologist, researcher; BA, Stanford U., 1988—92; PhD, SDSU/UCSD Joint Ph.D. Program, 1992—97. Lic. psychologist Calif., 2000. Rsch. assoc. Stanford U., 1999—. Mem.: Soc. of Behavioral Medicine. Office: Stanford University SCRDP 730 Welch Road Suite B Palo Alto CA 94304-1583

CASTRO, FEINBERG ROSA, education educator; b. NYC; d. Antonio Castro y Garcia and Violeta de Llano Castro; m. Alfred Feinberg, June 29, 1968; m. Stephen Jones, Feb. 8, 1959 (div. 1965); 1 child, Lincoln Jones. BA, Fla. State U., 1960, MS, 1968; PhD, U. Miami, 1977. Cert. tchr. and adminstr., Fla. Pub. sch. tchr./adminstr. Gadsden, Leon and Dade Counties, Fla., 1960-72; rsch. prof. U. Miami Sch. Edn., 1973-90; assoc. prof. Fla. Internat. U. Coll. Edn., 1990—2003. Staff mem. Race Desegregation Consulting Ctr., 1973-90; dir. Nat. Origin Desegration Assistance Ctr., 1973-90, Bilingual Edn. Tng. Program for Adminstr., 1973-90, Inst. for Cultural Innovation, 1973-90; mem. F.L. Post-Secondary Edn. Planning Commn.; mem. Dade County Sch. Bd., 1986-96; bd. dir. South East Fla. Libr. Info. Ctr. Freenet. Contbr. chpts. to books and articles to profl. jour. Bd. dirs. Ctyr. for Applied Linguistics, 1991—96. Mem. Spanish Am. League Against Discrimination (adv. coun.), NOW, Nat. Conf. Puerto Rican Women, Coalition of Hispanic Am. Women. Democrat. Office: Founds Dept Coll Edn Fla Internat Univ Miami FL 33199-0001

CASTRO, IDA L. state official, former federal official; d. Ezequiel and Aurora Castro; 1 child, Isamar. BA, U. P.R.; 1972; MA, Rutgers U., 1978, JD, 1982; PhD (hon.), St. Joseph's Coll., West Hartford, Conn., 2000. Assoc. prof. Rutgers Inst. Mgmt. & Labor Relations, 1976—83; asst. dep. pub. advocate State of NJ, 1986—87; dir. of labor relations C.U.N.Y., 1988—90; with New York Health and Hospitals Corp., 1990—94; acting dep. solicitor Nat. Ops.; dep. asst. sec. workers' comp. Employment Stds. Adminstrn. U.S. Dept. Labor, Washington, 1994—98, acting dir. Women's Bur., 1996-98; chair, CEO, gen. coun. Equal Employment Opportunity Commn., Washington, 1998—2001; comm. NJ Dept. of Personnel, Trenton, NJ, 2002. Tchr. labor law Rutgers U., N.J.; dir. job tng. and job devel. programs, P.R. and N.J.; union rep. as labor lawyer; active Hostos C.C., South Bronx; active numerous labor, women's and Hispanic orgns. Mem., dir. manpower mayor's cabinet Municipality of Carolina, P.R.; founder, co-chair Hispanic Women's Com. of N.J.; dep. campaign mgr. Mayor Dinkins campaign, N.Y.C.; sen. adv. & dir. Dem. Nat. Comm. Women Vote Ctr., 2001-2002. Democrat. Mailing: NJ Dept Personnel PO Box 317 Trenton NJ 08625 Office: 44 S Clinton Ave Trenton NJ 08625

CASTRO, JAN GARDEN, writer, arts consultant, educator; b. St. Louis, June 8, 1945; d. Harold and Estelle (Fischer) Garden; 1 child, Jomo Jemal. Student, Cornell U., 1963-65; BA, U. Wis., 1967; pub. cert., Radcliffe Coll., 1967; MA in Tchg., Washington U., St. Louis, 1974, MA, 1994. Life cert. tchr. secondary English, speech, drama and social studies, Mo. Tchr., writer, St. Louis, 1970—; dir. Big River Assn., St. Louis, 1975-85; adj. prof. humanities Lindenwood Coll., 1980—. Co-founder, dir. Duff's Poetry Series, St. Louis, 1975-81; founder, dir. River Styx P.M. Series, St. Louis, 1981-83; arts cons. Harris-Stowe State Coll., 1986-87; vis. scholar Am. Acad. in Rome, summer 2000. Contbg. author: rev. books San Francisco Rev. Books, 1982—85, Am. Book Rev., 1990—93, Mo. Rev., 1991, New Letters, 1993, 1996, Tampa Rev., 1994—2000, The Nation, Am. Poetry Rev., Sculpture Mag., 1997—; author: (poetry) Mandala of the Five Senses, 1975, The Art and Life of Georgia O'Keeffe, 1985, 1995, Memories and Memoirs...Contemporary Missouri Authors, 2000, (poetry) The Last Frontier, 2001—, Sonia DeLaunay: La Moderne, 2002—; editor: (jours.) River Styx mag., 1975—86; co-editor: (essays) Margaret Atwood: Vision and Forms, 1988; co-prodr.(TV host, co-prodr.): (shows) The Writers Cir., Double Helix, 1987—89; contbg. editor: (jours.) Sculpture Mag. Seeking St. Louis, Voices from a River City, 1670—2000. Mem. University City Arts and Letters Commn., Mo., 1983-84. NEH fellow UCLA, 1988, Johns Hopkins U., 1991, Camargo Found. fellow (Cassis, France), 1996; recipient Arts and Letters award St. Louis Mag., 1985, Editor's award and editor during G.E. Younger Writers award to River Styx Mag., Coord. Coun. for Lit. Mags., 1986, Arts award Mandrake Soc. Charity Ball, 1988, Leadership award YWCA St. Louis, 1988. Mem. MLA, CAA, PEN Am. Ctr., Nat. Coalition Ind. Scholars, Margaret Atwood Soc. (founder). Home: 7420 Cornell Ave Saint Louis MO 63130-2914 Office: LCIE Coll Lindenwood U Saint Charles MO 63301 E-mail: jan_g_castro@mail.com.

CASTRO, JOSEPH ARMAND, music director, pianist, composer, orchestrator; b. Miami, Ariz., Aug. 15, 1927; s. John Loya and Lucy (Sanchez) C.; m. Loretta Faith Haddad, Oct. 21, 1966; children: John Joseph, James Ernest. Student, San Jose State Coll., 1944-47. Mus. dir. Herb Jeffries, Hollywood, Calif., 1952, June Christy, Hollywood, 1959-63, Anita O'Day, Hollywood, 1963-65, Tony Martin, Hollywood, 1962-64, Tropicana Hotel, Las Vegas, Nev., 1980-97, Desert Inn, Las Vegas, 1992-93; orch. leader Mocambo Night Club, Hollywood, 1952-54; soloist Joe Castro Trio, L.A., N.Y.C., Honolulu, 1952-65, Sands Hotel, Desert Inn, Las Vegas, 1975-80; mus. dir. Folies Bergere, 1980-89; with Joe Castro Trio with Loretta Castro, 1995—. Co-founder JoDo Inc., 1964, Clover Records, 1964. Recs. include (in 1950s) Zoot Sims, Oscar Pettiford, Lucky Thompson, Ron Jefferson, Sonny Truitt, Doris Duke's Farms, Falon Cair Beverly Hills, L.A., Cool School with June Christy, 1960, Anita O'Day Sings Rodgers and Hart, 1961, Lush Life, 1966, Groove-Funk-Soul, Mood Jazz, Atlantic Records, Ballads for Night People with June Christy, Road Show with Stan Kenton Orch., Best of June Christy Jazz Series, Spotlight on June Christy, Anita O'Day, Verve Records, Billy May Swing Rodgers & Hart, also albums with Teddy Edwards, Stan Kenton, Jimmy Borges with Joe Castro Trio, 1990,

Loretta Castro with Joe Castro Trio, 1990; command performance, Queen Elizabeth II, London Palladium, 1989, Concerts with Jimmy Borges and Honolulu Symphony Pops Concerts, 1991; jazz concert (with Nigel Kennedy) Honolulu Symphony, 1990; jazz-fest, Kailua-Kona, Hawaii, 1990. With U.S. Army, 1946-47. Roman Catholic. Home: 2812 Colanthe Ave Las Vegas NV 89102-2026 Fax: 702-878-9588.

CASTRO, LEONARD EDWARD, lawyer; b. L.A., Mar. 18, 1934; s. Emil Galvez and Lily (Meyerholtz) C.; 1 son, Stephen Paul. A.B., UCLA, 1959, J.D., 1962. Bar: Calif. 1963, U.S. Supreme Ct. 1970. Assoc. Musick, Peeler & Garrett, Los Angeles, 1962-68, ptnr., 1968— . Mem. ABA, Los Angeles County Bar Assn.Bd. editors, note and comment editor: UCLA Law Review, 1961-62. Contbd. chpts. to books. Panelist, spkr., various legal edn. programs. Office: Musick Peeler & Garrett 1 Wilshire Blvd Ste 2000 Los Angeles CA 90017-3876

CASTRO, MARIA GRACIELA, medical educator, geneticist, researcher; b. Buenos Aires, Mar. 2, 1955; d. Nestor Antonio Castro and Maria Esther Rodriquez; m. Pedro Ricardo Lowenstein, Jan. 12, 1988; 1 child, Elijah David Lowenstein. BSc 1st class in Chemistry, Nat. U. La Plata, Argentina, 1979, MSc in Biochemistry, 1981, PhD in Biochemistry, 1986. Fogarty postdoctoral fellow Lab. Neurochem. & Neuroimmunol. Nat. Inst. Child Health and Human Devel. NIH, Bethesda, Md., 1986-88; sr. rsch. fellow Lab. Molecular Endocrinology Dept. Biochemistry and Physiology U. Reading, England, 1988-90; lectr. dept. molecular and life scis. U. Abertay, Dundee, Scotland, 1991-92; lectr. in neurosci., dept. physiology U. Wales Coll. Cardiff, 1991-95; sr. lectr. medicine Sch. Medicine U. Manchester, England, 1995-98, prof. molecular medicine, 1998—, dir. molecular medicine and gene therapy unit, 1996— Expert Women in Sci. Tech., Sheffield, England, 1996—; neurosci. panel Wellcome Trust, England, 1999—; co-dir. dept. molecular medicine Cedar-Sinai Med. Ctr., 2001—; co-dir. bd. govs. Gene Therapeutics Rsch. Inst., Cedars Sinai Med. Ctr., 2001—; prof. medicine UCLA, 2002—. Mem. editl. bd.: Jour. Endocrinology, Jour. Molecular Endocrinology, Current Gene Therapy, Gene Therapy, Pituitary, 2000, Neuro Molecular Medicine, 2001—; contbr. articles to profl. jours. Rsch. grantee, Brit. Heart Found., 1997, Med. Rsch. Coun., 1998, Biotechnology and Biol. Rsch. Coun., 1999—2000, Wellcome Trust, 1999, NIH, 2003—. Mem.: NIH, Nat. Inst. Neurol. Disorders and Stroke (mem. study sect., grant award), Internat. Soc. Nerovirology (founding mem.), Soc. Neuroscience, Endocrine Soc., Am. Gene Therapy Assn. Achievements include patents in field; research in program development of gene therapy for chronic neurological diseases and brain cancer. Fax: 310-423-7308. E-mail: castromg@cshs.org.

CASTRO, MARIO, medical educator, health facility administrator; b. Mantanzas, Cuba, Sept. 14, 1964; came to U.S., 1965; s. Moises Angel and Margot Julia (Madruga) C.; m. Marianne Castro, Oct. 1, 1988. BA, MD, U. Mo., 1988; MPH, St. Louis U., 1998. Instr. medicine Mayo Grad. Sch. Medicine, Rochester, Minn., 1991—94; dir. PFT lab. Asthma Ctr., asst. prof. medicine Sch. Medicine Washington U., St. Louis, 1994—2001, assoc. prof. medicine, 2002—. Chmn. com. asthma Am. Lung Assn., St. Louis, 1997—, bd. dirs. ea. Mo. chpt., St. Louis, 1997—. Burgher Family Endowed fellow, 1993-94, Am. Coll. Chest Physicians fellow, 1995; recipient Travel award Soc. Leukocyte Biology, 1992, Midwest Trainee award Am. Fedn. Clin. Rsch., 1993. Mem. Am. Thoracic Soc. (mem. program com.), Am. Med. Soc., Am. Coll. Physicians (mem. program com.). Roman Catholic. Office: Washington U Sch Medicine Box 8052 660 S Euclid Ave Saint Louis MO 63110-1010

CASTRO, MARY MCDERMOTT, language educator; b. East Liverpool, Ohio, Apr. 13, 1952; d. Elizabeth Costello and Elizabeth Costello McDermott; 1 child, Sarah Elizabeth. BA, Seton Hill, 1974; MA, Ohio U., 1976. Spanish tchr. Mercyhurst Prep. Sch., Erie, Pa., 1976—78; lectr. in spanish U. of Minn., Duluth, Minn., 1979; tchg. asst. in english U. of Pitts., 1979; tchg. asst. in spanish U. of N.C., Chapel Hill, 1980—83; lectr. in spanish N.C. State U., Raleigh, NC, 1984—90, U. of N.C., Charlotte, 1990—. Dir. of spanish lang. & culture in costa rica program U. of N.C., Charlotte, 1993—, sigma delta pi advisor, 1995—2003; instr. English Instituto Anglo-Mexicano, Jalapa, Mexico, 1982. Named Outstanding Tchr., N.C. Gen. Assembly, 1994, 1996. Mem.: The Fgn. Lang. Assn. of N.C., The Am. Coun. on the Tchg. of Fgn. Langs., The Am. Assn. of Tchrs. of Spanish and Portuguese, The Assn. of Academic Programming in L.Am. and the Caribbean, N.C. State U. Acad. of Outstanding Tchhs. (life), Phi Beta Delta (pres. 1994—95), Sigma Delta Pi. Avocation: dog breeding. Home: 6435 Schubert Place Charlotte NC 28227-1019 Office: University of North Carolina-Charlotte 9201 University City Blvd Charlotte NC 28223-0001 Personal E-mail: marysec88@aol.com.

CASTRO, RAUL HECTOR, lawyer, former ambassador, former governor; b. Cananea, Mexico, June 12, 1916; came to U.S., 1926, naturalized, 1939; s. Francisco D. and Rosario (Acosta) C.; m. Patricia M. Norris, Nov. 13, 1954; children— Mary Pat, Beth. BA, Ariz. State Coll., 1939; JD, U. Ariz., 1949; LL.D. (hon.), No. Ariz. U., 1966, Ariz. State U., 1972, U. Autonoma de Guadalajara, Mex. Bar: Ariz. bar 1949. Fgn. service clk. Dept. State, Agua Prieta, Mexico, 1941-46; instr. Spanish U. Ariz., 1946-49; practiced in Tucson, 1949-51; dep. county atty. Pima County, Ariz., 1951-54; county atty., 1954-58; judge Superior Ct., Tucson, 1958-64, Juvenile Ct., Tucson, 1961-64; U.S. ambassador to El Salvador, 1964-68, to Bolivia, La Paz, 1968-69; practice internat. law Tucson, 1969-74, Phoenix, 1980—; gov., 1975-77; U.S. ambassador to, 1977-80; operator Castro Pony Farm, 1954-64. Pres. Pima County Tb and Health Assn., Tucson Youth Bd., Ariz. Horseman's Assn.; Bd. dirs. Tucson chpt. A.R.C., Tucson council Boy Scouts Am., Tucson YMCA, Nat. Council Christians and Jews, YWCA Camp; Bd. Mem. Ariz. N.G., 1935-39. Recipient Outstanding Naturalized Citizen award Pima County Bar Assn., 1964, Outstanding Am. Citizen award D.A.R., 1964; Pub. Service award U. Ariz., 1966; John F. Kennedy medal Kennedy U., Buenos Aires. Mem. Am. Fgn. Service Assn., Am. Judicature Soc., Inter-Am. Bar Assn., Ariz. Bar Assn., Pima County Bar Assn., Nat. Council Crime and Deliquency (bd. dirs.), Assn. Trial Lawyers Am., Council Am. Ambassadors, Nat. Assn. Trial Judges, Nat. Council Juvenile Ct. Judges, Fed. Bar Assn., Nat. Lawyers Club, Phi Alpha Delta. Clubs: Rotarian. Democrat. Roman Catholic.

CASTRO, STEPHANIE L. business management educator; b. San Antonio, Tex., Mar. 8, 1968; d. Reuben Riley and Mary Jaquelyn Loeffler; m. Erik Ricardo Castro, Aug. 21, 1993; 1 child, Cole Anthony. BBA, Fla. Internat. U., 1993; PhD, U. Miami, 1998. Asst. prof. La. State U., Baton Rouge, 1998—2000; vis. asst. prof. U. Miami, 2000—02; asst. prof. Fla. Atlantic U., 2002—. Mem.: APA, Acad. Mgmt., Soc. Indsl. Orgnl. Psychologists. Home: 17411 SW 61st Ct Fort Lauderdale FL 33331-1715

CASTRO, TERESA JACIRA, small business owner; b. Chgo., July 18, 1956; d. Jene Paul and June Edith (Aleff) Harper; m. Oscar Armando Rodriguez (div. 1981); 1 child, Avelina; m. Jorge Castro (div. 1993); 1 child, Pablo. AA in Opera, Fleming Coll., Florence, Italy, 1975; BA in Spanish and Portuguese cum laude, U. N.Mex., 1979; M Info. Tech., Am. Intercontinental U., 2001. Adminstrv. asst. Latin Am. Inst., Albuquerque, 1981-83; law office mgr. Camacho & Hinkle, San Francisco, 1983; owner, founder, pres. Access Word Processing, San Francisco and Viña del Mar, Chile, 1983-95; tech. translator Red de Television Universitaria (RTU), Santiago, Chile, 1990-95; freelance computer and word processing systems analyst; pers. banker Chase Manhattan Bank, Santiago, 1993-94; owner, operator Receptive Tourism and Interpreting Svc., Santiago, 1994-95; pres. Salsapower.com, Inc., 2000—. Tech. translator and simultaneous interpreter specializing in engring., fin. and legal matters, Miami, Fla., 1995—; owner, Accent Translations, 1999—; instr. Salsa-Casino Dance Studios, Miami, 1997-98; dir. Absolute Salsa Dance Studio, 1999—. Vol. notary pub. People With AIDS/ARC, 1985-91, The AIDS Found./Shanti Project, San Francisco, 1986-90; chairperson bilingual adv. bd. Buena Vista Sch., San Francisco, 1986; bd. dirs. Escola Nova de Samba, San Francisco, 1987; vol. working on reunification searches for adoptees and birth parents, Calif., N.Y., Latin Am.; tchr. Spanish law enforcement pers. San Francisco Police Acad., 1988-89, Spanish for med. pers. Kaiser Permanente Med. Ctr., San Francisco, 1988-89. Mem. NAFE, Nat. Assn. Photoshop Profls., Toastmasters Internat. Avocations: dancing samba, salsa, teaching children's dance classes.

CASTRO-KLAREN, SARA, Latin American literature educator; b. Arequipa, Sabandia, Peru, June 9, 1942; d. José Andrés and Zoila Rosa (Rivas) Castro-Valdivia; m. Peter F. Klaren, Sept. 3, 1962; 1 child, Alexandra. BA, UCLA, 1962, MA, 1965, PhD, 1968. Asst. prof. Dartmouth Coll., No. Hampshire, N.H., 1970-84; chief Hispanic div. Lib. of Congress Fed. Govt., Washington, 1984-86; prof. Latin Am. lit. Johns Hopkins U., Balt., 1986—. Dir. program Latin Am. Studies, JHU. Author: El Mundo Magico de J.M. Arquedas, Lima, 1973, Mario Vargas Llosa, Analisis Introductorio, Lima, 1988, Escritura Sujeto y Transgresión, Mexico, 1989, Understanding Mario Vargas Llosa, U. S.C., 1990, Women's Writing in Latin America, 1991, Latin American Women's Narrative: Practices and Theoretical Perspectives, 2003. Fellow Woodrow Wilson Ctr. for Scholars, Washington, 1977-78. Mem. MLA, AAUP, Latin Am. Studies Assn., Ibero-americana, Soc. Hispanists, Am. Assn. Colls. and Univs. Avocation: gardening. Home: 9438 Rabbit Hill Road Great Falls VA 22066

CASTRONOVO, DAVID, humanities educator, writer; b. Bklyn., Oct. 30, 1945; s. Anthony John and Doris Loretta (Oliver) C. BA, Bklyn. Coll., 1967; MA, Columbia U., 1968, PhD, 1975. Reader Columbia U., N.Y.C., 1969; adj. asst. prof. Bklyn. Coll., 1972-76, Pace U., N.Y.C., 1976-79, asst. prof., 1979-86, assoc. prof., 1986-88, prof. English, 1988—. Author: Edmund Wilson, 1984 (N.Y. Times Notable Book 1985), Thornton Wilder, 1986, The English Gentleman, 1987, The American Gentleman, 1991, (with Janet Groth) From the Uncollected Edmund Wilson, 1995; (with Steven Goldleaf) Richard Yates, 1996, Edmund Wilson Revisited, 1998, (with Janet Groth) Edmund Wilson, The Man in Letters, 2001; contbr. Colliers Ency., N.Y.C., 1987, Ency. of World Lit. in the 20th Century, N.Y.C., 1980, Dictionary of Literary Biography, Modern American Critics 1920-1955, 1988, Critical Essays on Thornton Wilder, Ency. Am. Lit., 1999, Thornton Wilder: New Essays, 1999, Scribner's Encyclopedia of American Lives, 2000; reviewer and essayist (jours.) America, Commonweal, New Eng. Rev., The Forward, Shofar. Fellow Columbia U., 1967-71. Mem. PEN, MLA, Princeton Club of N.Y. Democrat. Roman Catholic. Avocations: trout fishing, art history, water color painting. Home: 1619 3d Ave New York NY 10128-3459 E-mail: davidcastronovo@aol.com.

CASTRONOVO, THOMAS PAUL, architect, consultant; b. Chgo., Apr. 7, 1932; s. Paul Thomas and Nancy (Racina) C. Student, U. Akron, 1949-51; BArch, Ohio State U., 1955. Registered architect, Ohio, Calif., Colo., Fla. Intern architect E.J. Guran, Architect, Akron, Ohio, 1957-58, A.W. Petersen, Architect, Akron, 1958-60; pres., owner Thomas P. Castronovo, Architect, Akron, 1960—. Chmn. Akron Urban Design and Fine Arts Commn.; mem. Akron Civic Design Awards Com., 1972, Akron Regional Devel. Bd., 1983-87. 1st lt. USAF, 1955-57. Mem. AIA (bd. dirs. Akron chpt. 1987-90), Architects Soc. Ohio, Pi Kappa Epsilon (Akron U. chpt., pres. alumni 1982-84, mem. Hall of Fame 1982). Avocations: tennis, skiing, gardening, cooking, boating. Office: 1175 N Main St Akron OH 44310-1047

CASTURO, DON JAMES, venture capitalist; b. McKeesport, Pa., Nov. 9, 1942; s. Charles and Elizabeth B. (Barno) C.; m. Judith K. Erkman, Aug. 22, 1964; children: Don J.E., Christian D.E. BA, Mich. State U., 1964; MBA, U. So. Calif., 1966. Participant mgmt. devel. program Mellon Bank, Pitts., 1966-67, investment rschr., 1967-69, asst. invesment officer, 1969-71, investment officer, 1971-73, asst. v.p., 1973-82; v.p. mgr. Venture Capital Investments, 1982-88; gen. ptnr. Point Venture Ptnrs., Pitts. Bd. dirs. GALT Technologies, Inc., Tri Foods, Inc., Lloyd's Food Products, Inc., Network Data Corp., Creativators, Inc., Meretek Diagnostics, Southdown Trading, Inc., The Steak-umm Co., SpaElegance.com., Inc. Co-chmn. enrichment program Mich. State U.; bd. dirs. Upper St. Clair Athletic Assn. Mem. Pitts. Soc. Fin. Analysts (past pres., chmn. exec. com., dir.), Assn. for Investment Mgmt. and Rsch. (chartered fin. analyst), Nat. Venture Capital Assn., Pitts. Venture Capital Assn. (founding mem., past pres., bd. dirs.), Sigma Nu. Republican. Orthodox Catholic. Home: 2339 Morton Rd Pittsburgh PA 15241-3301 Office: Point Venture Ptnrs Ste 400 130 7th St Pittsburgh PA 15222-3409

CASWELL, DOROTHY ANN COTTRELL, arts administrator; b. N.Y.C., Dec. 18, 1938; d. Donald Peery and Eleanor Hildaborg (Westberg) Cottrell; m. Allen Edward Caswell, Oct. 24, 1959; children: David Alan, Bruce Leland. Student, Carleton Coll., Northfield, MN., 1956-59; AB in Psych., George Wash. U., 1960-61; postgrad. in vocal performance, SUNY, Oneonta, 1971-76. Sec. U.S. Fgn. Service, Tunis, Tunisia, 1959-61; mng. dir. Glimmerglass Opera, Inc., Cooperstown, N.Y., 1975-78; exec. dir. Upper Catskill Community Council on the Arts, Oneonta, N.Y., 1978-80; devel. officer Catskill Arts Consortium, Oneonta, 1981-83; devel. cons. Otsego Urban Rural Self-Devel. Assocs., Inc., Oneonta, 1982-83; co-founder, pres. Catskill Choral Soc., 1970-76, 81-84; assoc. producer Orpheus Theatre, Inc., Oneonta, 1984-91; voice tchr. Oneonta, 1984—; ptnr., co-owner OnStage Prodn. Svcs., 1991—. Cons., arts adminstrv. Dorothy Caswell Assocs., Oneonta, 1981—; past pres., mem. sub-area coun. Health Sys. Agy. NE, NY, mem. planning adv. group, rev. adv. Actor(film series Susquehanna Stories): WSKG-TV Pub. TV, 1990—. Mem. chorus Glimmerglass Opera, Cooperstown, 1974—; mem. mil. acad. selection com. Congressman Sherwood Boehlert, NY, 1993—; mem. Otsego County Health Planning Adv. Coun. Otsego Publ Health Partnership; bd. dirs. Otsego County Tourism Bur., 1987—90, Oneonta Downtown Coalition, 1982—84. Recipient Honored for Outstanding Performance and Svcs. to Cmty., SUNY, 1975. Democrat. Avocations: painting, performing arts, gardening, swimming.

CASWELL, HERBERT HALL, JR., retired biology educator; b. Marblehead, Mass., May 21, 1923; s. Herbert Hall and Grace (Parker) C.; m. Ethel Claire Preble, Mar. 28, 1948; children: Hal, Martha, William, Edward, Thomas, Michael. BS, Harvard U., 1948; MS, UCLA, 1950; Ph.D, Cornell U., 1956. Prof. biology Eastern Mich. U., Ypsilanti, 1955-88, prof. emeritus, 1988, head dept. biology, 1974-88. Served to 1st lt. U.S. Army, 1942-46. Mem. Ecol. Soc. Am., Assn. Field Ornithol., Am. Inst. Biol. Scis., Sigma Xi. Home: 952 Sheridan St Ypsilanti MI 48197-2713 E-mail: eccaswell@prodigy.net.

CASWELL, LINDA KAY, insurance agency executive; b. Canton, Ohio, Sept. 29, 1952; d. Lloyd Norman and Eva Mae (Clark) C. Grad. high sch., Canton, Ohio. Office mgr., sec. Harold Dickinson Architect, Canton, 1970-73; dist. mgr., sec., clk. Met. Life Ins., Canton, 1973-80, office mgr., 1980-86; brokerage assoc. Met. Brokerage, Canton, 1986-89; owner, pres. Golden Horizons Ins. Agy., Canton, 1987—. Avocations: cards, fishing, golden retreivers. Office: Golden Horizons Ins Agy 5874 Fulton Dr NW Canton OH 44718-1735

CASWELL, RANDALL SMITH, physicist; b. Eugene, Oreg., Feb. 7, 1924; s. Albert Edward and M. Constance (Edwards) C.; m. Jean M. Miller, June 14, 1945; children: William Edward (dec.), Virginia Lee, Anne Marden, Ellen Sue, Wendy Jean (dec.), Julia Constance. SB, MIT, 1947, PhD in Physics, 1951. Assoc. prof. physics U. Ky., 1950-52; rschr. particle solid state physics Oak Ridge Nat. Lab., 1952; physicist neutron physics Nat. Bur. Standards, 1952-69; dep. dir. Ctr. Radiation Rsch., 1969-78, chief nuclear radiation divsn., 1978-85; chief ionizing radiation divsn. Nat. Inst. Standards & Tech., Gaithersburg, Md., 1985-94, ret., 1994. Adj. prof. physics Am. U. 1957-71; mem. Nat. Coun. Radiation Protection & Measurements, 1967-91; chmn. neutron measurements sect. Adv. Com. Standards Ionizing Radiation Measurement, Bur. Internat. des Poids et Mesures, 1969-89; mem. Internat. Commn. Radiation Units & Measurement, 1975-2002, sec., 1979-2002; chmn. sci. panel Com. Interagy. Radiation Rsch. and Policy Coord. Office Sci. and Tech. Policy, 1984-94. Assoc. editor Radiation Rsch., 1977-80. Fellow Am. Physics Soc.; mem. Radiation Rsch. Soc. Office: Nat Inst of Stds Tech Physics Rm C229 Radiation Physics Bldg 245 Gaithersburg MD 20899-0001

CASWELL, SALLY ELLEN, artist, art educator; b. Brockton, Mass., Nov. 1, 1941; d. Sherman Clarke Sr. and Eleanor Catherine Caswell; m. Carl Lewis Hayter, 1962 (div. June 1973); children: Dana Ward Hayter, Royce Evan Hayter; m. Leonard Linhares, Aug. 1976 (div. Aug. 1987). BFA, Mass. Coll. Art, Boston, 1965; MAT equivalency, R.I. Coll., 1978; MFA disting. thesis, U. Mass., 1990. Cert. lifetime tchr., R.I. Tchr. art-ceramics Johnston (R.I.) H.S., 1972-80, 83-84; tchr. painting, watercolor Attleboro (Mass.) Mus., 1980-83; tchr. advanced watercolor, drawing, design R.I. Sch. Design, Providence, 1986-94; adj. asst. prof. art C.C. R.I., Warwick, 1987—, dir. Knight Campus Art Gallery, 1995-99; tchr. watercolor, spl. studies The Chautauqua (N.Y.) Instn., 1996—; fine artist, illustrator Swansea, Mass., 1965—. Mem. arts festival com. Wickford (R.I.) Art Assn., 1982-83; mem. exec. bd. Pawtucket (R.I.) Arts Coun., 1986-88; mem. exec. bd. Nat. Mus. Women in Arts, R.I. chpt., 1997-99; art lectr. Fall River (Mass.) Art Assn., 1996-2000; contbg. artist fundraising raffle R.I. Watercolor Soc., Pawtucket, 1997; tchr. watercolor and art history workshop, Florence and Siena, Italy, 2000; represented by The Gallery at Caterpillar Hill, Sedgwick, Maine. One-person shows include Bierstadt Gallery, New Bedford, Mass., 1990, Gallery 401, Providence, 1991, Windsor Gallery, Providence, 1991, South County Art Ctr., Wakefield, R.I., 1993, Wickford Art Assn. Gallery, 1993, 2002, South County Art Assn., Kingston, R.I., 1993, C.C. R.I., Lincoln, 1993, Nicole Saul-Kogut Gallery, Providence, 1994, 95, Pawtucket, 1995, Winds of March Gallery, Chautauqua, 1996, Providence Art Club, 1997, Spencer Gallery, Wickford, R.I., 1998, Dodge House Gallery, Providence Art Club, 2000, 2002, The Summer Gallery, Chautauqua, N.Y., 2001, others; exhibited in group shows at Japan/Am. Exch. Exhbn., R.I. Watercolor Soc., Pawtucket, Tokyo, Saku City, Japan, 1986, Bristol (R.I.) Art Mus. Invitational, 1986, Art of N.E. U.S.A. Exhbn., Silvermine Galleries, New Canaan, Conn., 1988, U. Mass., Dartmouth, 1990, South Wharf Gallery, Nantucket, Mass., 1980-90, Hera Gallery, Wakefield, 1992, Cornwall Gallery, Jamaica Plain, Mass., 1992, South County Ctr. for Arts, Kingston, 1993, Woods-Gerry Gallery, R.I. Sch. Design, Providence, 1987-93, Mass. Coll. Art Tower Bldg. Alumni Gallery, Boston, 1993, Copley Soc. Boston, 1993-2002, C.C. R.I. Galleries, 1987—, Nicole Saul-Kogut Gallery, Pawtucket, 1989-96, Providence Art Club, 1996, Fall River Art Assn., 1996, Cape Cod Art Assn., 1997, R.I. Watercolor Soc., 1997, Providence Art Club, 1997, Wickford Art Assn., 1997-2002, Attleboro Museum, 1998, R.I. Econ. Devel. Corp., 1999—, Providence Art Club, 2000, Gallery by the Sea, Plymouth, Mass., 2000, 2001, Grimshaw-Gudewicz Gallery Bristol Comty. Coll., Fall River, Mass., Bush Gallery, Providence, 2001, Newport Art Mus., 2002, 03, others; represented in permanent collections at U.S. Naval War Coll. Mus., Newport; also corp. collections; illustrator: An Anniversary Collection, 1984-1988: Winning Poems From the Pawtucket Arts Coun. Annual Poetry Competition, 1988, The Watchman. A Novel by G.R. Conrad, 1972, Objective Drawing Techniques-New Approaches to Perspective in Interior Space by Calvin Burnett, 1966. Supt. Sunday Sch. Ch. of the Mediator, Unitarian-Universalist, Providence, 1967; tchr. ESL Adult Sch., Warren, R.I., 1968-69. Recipient awards Providence Watercolor Club, 1981, 82, Fall River Art Assn., 1983, Bristol Art Mus., 1983, New Haven Paint and Clay Club, All Eng. and N.Y. Show, 1983, Providence Art Club Open Painting Exhbn., 1985, R.I. Watercolor Soc., 1989, Duxbury Art Complex Mus., All New Eng. Exhbn., 1989, Am. Artist Mag., 1990, Wickford Art Assn., 1994, Providence Art Club Abstract/Representational Exhbn., 1996, Greater Fall River Art Assn., Ann. Regional Show, 1996, 2002. Mem. Wickford Art Assn. (program chair, juror), R.I. Watercolor Soc., Providence Art Club, Copley Soc. (Copley Artist), 19 on Paper. Avocations: cross-country skiing, sailing, art history, writing. Home: 611 Warren Ave Swansea MA 02777-3332 E-mail: Caswellart@comcast.net

CASWELL, WILLIAM STEPHEN, JR., civil engineer; b. South Kingston, R.I., Feb. 2, 1962; s. William Stephen Caswell and Shirley Frances (Mason) Farrell; m. Joy Lynne Russo, Aug. 4, 1984; children: William Stephen III, Benjamin Perry. Registered profl. engr., N.H. Civil engr. N.H. Dept. Transp., Concord, 1984-89, CAD/D applications engr., 1989—. Planning bd. Boscawen (N.H.) Planning Bd., 1996—. Mem. R.I. Geneal. Soc., N.H. Hist. Soc., Conn. Soc. Genealogists. Baptist. Avocations: genealogy, hiking. Home: 3 Buxton Pl Boscawen NH 03303-1219 Office: NH Dept Transp PO Box 483 Concord NH 03302-0483

CATA, ISABELLE MARIE GROS, foreign language educator; b. Boulogne Billancourt, France, Jan. 27, 1961; arrived in U.S., 1984; d. Claude Raoul and Ginette (Naudin-Spagnol) G. BA in English/Spanish, U. Paris III, 1982; MA in French, U. So. Calif., 1987, PhD in French, 1993. Asst. prof. Grand Valley State U., Allendale, Mich., 1993-99, assoc. prof. French, 1999—. Contbr. articles to profl. jours. Josephine de Karman fellow, 1991-92; Grand Valley State U. summer rsch. grantee, 1993, Circle Tchg. grantee, 1997-98, 98-99, 99-2000, 2000—. Mem.: MLA, Conseil Internat. d'Etudes Francophones, Women in French, Assn. Victor Segalan, Pi Delta Phi. Buddhist. Avocations: reading, yoga, dancing. Home: 501 Pleasant St SE Grand Rapids MI 49503 Office: Grand Valley State Univ 1 Campus Dr Allendale MI 49401 E-mail: catai@gvsu.edu.

CATACOSINOS, WILLIAM JAMES, utility company executive; b. N.Y.C., Apr. 12, 1930; s. James and Penelope (Paleologos) C.; m. Florence Maken, Oct. 16, 1955; children: William, James. BS, NYU, 1951; MBA, 1952, PhD, 1962. Asst. editor 20th Century-Fox, N.Y.C., 1951-52; asst. dir. bus. mgmt. and adminstrn. Brookhaven Nat. Lab., Upton, NY, 1956-69; pres. Applied Digital Data Sys., Inc., Hauppauge, NY, 1969-77, chmn., CEO, 1977-82, Market Span Corp. formerly L.I. Lighting Co., Hicksville, NY, 1984-98, also bd. dirs.; chmn., pres., CEO TNP Enterprises, Inc., Fort Worth, Tex. Adj. asst. prof. NYU, 1962-64; chmn. bd. Corometrics Med., 1968-74; bd. dirs. Atlantic Bank N.Y.; adv. com., policy com. on strategic planning, bd. dirs. Edison Electric Inst., 1990-95. Bd. dirs. L.I. Assn., New N.Y. Alliance, Brookhaven Town Indsl. Commn., 1956-77, Am. Cancer Soc. Suffolk County chpt., 1969-77, Stony Brook Found., 1978-85; trustee Poly. Inst. N.Y., 1981-85; nat. chmn. Am. Soc. Prevention Cruelty to Children, 1981-83. With USN, 1952-56.

CATALANO, CARL PHILIP, small business owner; b. Chgo., May 13, 1953; s. Philip Thomas and Arlene Margret (Hora) C.; m. Maria Rosa Diaz, Feb. 14, 1983. AS, Miami (Fla.) Dade Community Coll., 1984, AA, 1985; student, Am. Inst. Med. Law, 1986; BS in Audio Engring., Kennedy-Western U., 1993, PhD in Mgmt. Info. Sys., 2002. Cert. TV and radio broadcaster FCC, Nat. Radio Inst. (NRI), 1993. Drummer Queens Kidds, Miami and Ft. Lauderdale, Fla., 1970-74; show drummer Kickin, Fla., 1974-76; producer I.J.E. Distbrs. Inc., Hollywood, Fla., 1976-79; coordinator, v.p., case mgr., computer engr. Catalano Registry Inc., Hialeah, Fla., 1979—; owner, prodr. Soundtrack Rec., Hialeah, 1986-96, Studio-K Prodns., Miramar, Fla., 1996—; computer programmer, arranger Final Chpt. Inc., 1988-89. Stage and location gripper Channels 1 and 2, Miami, 1984-85; free-lance programmer drum computer, photographer, Miami and Hialeah, 1983—; musician various studios, Fla., 1983—. Appeared in (TV show) Miami Vice, 1985; (film) Mean Season, 1985. Mem. Am. Fedn. Musicians, Nat. Drum Assn., Am. Bd. Risk Mgmt. Profls. (diplomate). Home: 2522 SW 180th Ave Miramar FL 33029-5191 E-mail: studiok9@aol.com., groovemaster@studio-k9.com.

CATALANO, GERALD, accountant; b. Chgo., Jan. 17, 1949; s. Frank and Virginia (Kreiman) C.; m. Mary L. Billings, July 4, 1970; children: James, Maria, Gina. BSBA, Roosevelt U., 1971. CPA, Ill. Jr. acct. Drebin, Lindquist and Gervasio, Chgo., 1971, Leaf, Dahl and Co., Ltd., Chgo., 1971-77, prin., 1978-80, ptnr., 1980-82; prin. Gerald Catalano, CPA, Chgo., 1982-83; ptnr. Barbakoff, Catalano & Assocs., Chgo., 1983-87; pres. Barbakoff, Catalano & Caboor Ltd., Chgo., 1993—. V.p. Tri-City Oil, Inc., Addison, Ill., 1983-93; treas. Uncle Andy's, Inc., 1991-94; corp. officer Bionic Auto Parts, Inc.; bd. dirs. EDT, Inc., treas., 1993—; ptnr. PetCatMouse Publ., 1996—; owner IEP Record Group, 1996—, dir. United Community Lisle, IL, 2001-. Pres. Young Dems., Roosevelt U., 1967-71; trustee U. Ill. Russo Scholarship Fund, 1989 ; dir. Elmhurst Jaycees, 1976. Mem. AICPA, ASCAP (assoc.), NARAS (assoc.), Ill. CPA Soc., Theosophical Soc. Roman Catholic. Office: 1 S 376 Summit Ave Oakbrook Terrace IL 60181 E-mail: jerryc@catboor.com.

CATALANO, JAMES ANTHONY, social worker, consultant; b. Lackawanna, N.Y., Nov. 5, 1954; s. George and Frances (McGowan) C. BA, Canisius Coll., 1977, BA, 1992; MS, Columbia U., 1985, PhD in Social Work, 2000; MDiv, Weston Jesuit Sch. Theology, Cambridge, Mass., 1994, ThM, 1995, MA in Ednl. Psychology, 1999. Cert. social worker, N.Y.; diploma clin. social work NASW, 1991. Caseworker Neighborhood Info. Ctr., Buffalo, N.Y., 1975-79; dir. Youth Svcs. Program Lincoln Community Ctr., Buffalo, N.Y., 1979-80; psychiatric social worker, discharge planner Bry-Lin Hosp., Buffalo, N.Y., 1981; social worker Cath. Charities of Western N.Y., Buffalo, N.Y., 1987-89; asst. to the dir. Inst. of Faith and Justice Canisius Coll., Buffalo, N.Y., 1989-90; pvt. practice Buffalo, N.Y., 1989—. Spkr. on San Salvador Diocese of Buffalo, 1990—91; workshop leader Buffalo Traditional H.S., Buffalo City H.S. East Campus, 1988—89; asst. prof. social work Fordham U., 2001—03. Relief worker Jesuit Refugee Svcs., San Salvador, El Salvador, 1985; chmn. Site Selection Com. for Resdl. Care Facilities, Buffalo, 1979—81; advisor to chmn. Pub. Svc. Commn. of N.Y., 1979—81; com. mem. Dem. Orgn. Erie County, Buffalo, 1978—81. Recipient Vol. Svc. award VA, Syracuse, N.Y., 1982. Mem. NASW. Home and Office: 50 Glenwood Ave Jersey City NJ 07306-4606

CATALANO, LOUIS WILLIAM, JR., neurologist; b. Bklyn., Apr. 20, 1942; s. Louis William and Aileen (Bobb) C.; m. Diana Catalano; children: Louis William III, Jamea Elizabeth, Adriana Louise. BS cum laude, U. Pitts., 1963, MD, 1967. Diplomate Am. Bd. Psychiatry and Neurology, Am. Bd. Electroencephalography, Am. Bd. Pain Medicine, Am. Bd. Med. Examiners. Intern Presbyn.-St. Luke's Hosp., Chgo., 1967-68; rsch. assoc. NIH, Bethesda, Md., 1968-70; fellow neurology The Neurol. Inst., N.Y.C., 1970-73; clin. asst., prof. neurology U. Pitts. Sch. Med., 1973—; pvt. practice Greensburg, Pa., 1973—. Staff Latrobe (Pa.) Area Hosp., 1973—, Westmoreland Regional Hosp., Greensburg, 1973—, Indiana (Pa.) Hosp., 1983—; cons. Jeannette (Pa.) Mercy Hosp., 1984—, Frick Cmty. Health Ctr., Mt. Pleasant, Pa., 1991—, Torrance (Pa.) State Hosp., 2000—; mem. med. bd. Epilepsy Found. Western/Ctrl. Pa.; lectr. in field. Contbr. articles to profl. jours. Pres. Neurol. Inst. We. Pa. Spl. fellow Columbia U., NIH, 1970-73, epilepsy minifellow, Bowman Gray Sch. Medicine, Winston-Salem, N.C., 1988. Fellow: Am. Acad. Neurology, Royal Soc. Medicine; mem.: AMA, European Fedn. Neurol. Socs., Pitts. Neurosci. Soc., Latrobe Acad. Medicine, Westmoreland County Med. Soc., World Fedn. Neurology, Pa. Med. Soc., Am. Sleep Disorders Assn., Am. Acad. Clin. Neurphysiology, Am. Soc. Neuroimaging, Am. Med. Electroencephalographic Assn., Am. Acad. Pain Mgmt., Alpha Omega Alpha, Sigma Xi. Avocations: sport fishing, scuba diving, skiing, travel. Office: Cen Med Arts RD 7 Old Rte 30 Frye Farm Rd Greensburg PA 15601

CATALANO, RICHARD, retired educational association administrator; b. Pitts., Apr. 19, 1934; s. Michael Joseph and Roma Agnes Catalano. BA, Bowdoin Coll., Brunswick, 1955; MA, Fletcher Sch., Medford, Mass., 1958; LLB, JD, George Washington Univ., Washington, 1963. Sec. bd. trustees City Univ. of N.Y., N.Y., 1976—78, vice chancellor, 1976—84; assoc. v.p. employee & labor rels. Office of Pres., Oakland, Calif., 1984—90; deputy dir. San Francisco Mus. Modern Art, San Francisco, 1990—92; ret. Cons. labor rels., San Francisco, 1992—96. Mem.: San Francisco Zen Ctr. (bd. dir.). Avocations: music, tennis, history, travel. Home: 2180 post St San Francisco CA 94115

CATALANO, ROBERT ANTHONY, ophthalmologist, physician, hospital administrator, writer; b. Albany, N.Y., Nov. 24, 1956; s. Anthony Joseph and Ida Santa (Mussolino) C.; m. Madeline Faye Kalmer, Aug. 6, 1978; children: Christopher, Ruth, Thomas, Matthew. BS, Union Coll., Schenectady, 1978; MD, U. Va., 1982; MBA, Rensselaer Poly. Inst., 1992. Resident in ophthalmology Albany Med. Coll., 1983-86, vice-chmn. dept. ophthalmology, 1989-90, acting chmn., 1990-91; fellow in pediatric ophthalmology Wills Eye Hosp., Phila., 1986-87; v.p. med. affairs Olean (N.Y.) Gen. Hosp., 1991-93, COO, 1994-95, pres., CEO, 1995—2001; med. dir. Albany Med. Ctr. Hosp., 2001—. Bd. dirs. Westlink Corp. Author: Atlas of Ocular Motility, 1989, Ocular Emergencies, 1992, Pediatric Ophthalmology: A Text/Atlas, 1994, When Autism Strikes, 1998; contbr. articles to profl. jours. Recipient Nat. Found. award March of Dimes Found., 1978, Robert D. Reinecke award Albany Med. Coll., 1985, Shannon award U. Va., 1982; Heed Found. fellow, 1986, Forty Under Forty award, 1993. Mem.: So. Tier Healthcare Network (bd. dirs. 1994—2001, chmn. 2001), Western N.Y. Hosp. Assn. (bd. dirs. 1992—95, 1999—2001, treas. 2001), Am. Coll. Healthcare Execs., Am. Coll. Physician Execs., Acad. Ophthalmology, Alpha Omega Alpha. Roman Catholic. Office: Albany Med Ctr S Clin Campus Mail Code 201 Albany NY 12208-3499

CATALDI, PATRICIA LEE, surgeon; b. Glastonbury, Conn., Sept. 7, 1945; d. George Anthony Cataldi and Frances Mary (Thurz) Scorso. MD, Hahnemann U., 1977. Diplomate Am. Bd. Surgery. Gen. surgeon St. Jude's Hosp., St. Lucia, W.I., 1982-87, St. Anne's Hosp., Brunapeg, Zimbabwe, 1988—00, McDowell ARH Hosp., McDowell, Ky., 2000—02, Three River Med. Ctr., Louisa, Ky., 2003—. Mem. Assn. of Sisters, Bros., Priests, Physicians, Assn. Women Surgeons, Ky. Med. Assn. Roman Catholic. Home: Apt B 1358 Gene Wilson Blvd Louisa KY 41230-9681 Office: TRM Plz Ste 103 PO Box 30 Louisa KY 41230 E-mail: pcataldi@hotmail.com.

CATALDO, LOUIS, retired protective services official; b. East Boston, Mass., June 11, 1920; m. Lora G. Cataldo, June 14, 1947; children: Steven, Michael, Louis G. Grad., FBI Nat. Acad., 1955. Dir. Bur. Criminal Investigation Barnstable County Sheriff's Dept., Barnstable, Mass., 1948—74, chief dep. sheriff, 1960—74; dir. Barnstable County Police Acad., 1960—74; chief police Dennis, Mass., 1974—76. Intelligence officer Barnstable County Civil Def., 1960—. Author: (book) Judgement Seat, 1992, (booklet) Cape Cod Trivia, 1987, Distinguished Cataldo Family, 1997. Pres. Cape Cod United Fund, 1971—73; chmn. Barnstable Hist. Commn., 1969—; founder, pres. Tales of Cape Cod, Inc., 1949—; co-chmn. Barnstable Civil War Centennial Com., 1961—66; coord. Nat. Bicentennial Commn., Barnstable, 1973—74; founding dir. Cape Cod YMCA, 1966; founder Donald G. Trayser Mus., 1960—; sec. Old Indian Ch. Meeting House Authority, Mashpee, 1968—74; Chmn. James Otis Jr. Com., 1991; chmn. Iyanough Meml. Com., 1991, Mercy Otis Warren Com., 2001; Bd. dirs. Cape Cod United Fund, 1962—73, Cape Cod Com. on Alcoholism, 1964—74; bd. dirs. Old Indian Ch. Meeting House Authority, Mashpee, 1959—74. With USN, 1939—45. Named B'nai B'rith Citizen of Yr., 1974, Hon. Dep. Sec. State Mass., 1974. Mem.: Cape Cod Investigators Assn. (coord. 1970—73), Mass Dep. Sheriffs Assn., Nat. Sheriffs Assn., Mass. Police Tng. Officers Assn. (pres. 1972—76), Internat. Assn. for Identification (regional v.p. 1972—74, Lifetime Achievement award New Eng. chpt. 2001, Presdl. Lifetime Achievement award 2001), VFW. Home: PO Box 191 Barnstable MA 02630

CATALFO, ALFRED, JR., (ALFIO CATALFO), lawyer; b. Lawrence, Mass., Jan. 31, 1920; s. Alfio and Vincenza (Amato) C.; m. Caroline Joanne Mosca (dec. Apr. 1968); children: Alfred Thomas, Carol Joanne, Gina Marie; m. Gail Varney, 1988. BA, U. N.H., 1945, MA in History, 1952; LLB, Boston U., 1947, JD (hon.), 1969; postgrad., Suffolk U. Sch. Law, 1955-56, Am. Law Inst., N.Y.C., 1959. Bar: N.H. 1947, U.S. Dist. Ct. 1948, U.S. Ct. Appeals 1978, U.S. Supreme Ct. 1979. Pvt. practice, Dover, N.H., 1948—; ptnr. Catalfo Law Firm, Dover, 1980—; county atty. Strafford County, Dover, N.H., 1949-50, 55-56; bd. immigration appeals U.S. Dept. Justice, 1953—; football coach Berwick Acad., South Berwick, Maine, 1944, Mission Catholic H.S., Roxbury, Mass., 1945-46. Author: Laws of Divorces, Marriages, and Separations in New Hampshire, 1962, History of the Town of Rollinsford, 1623-1973, 1973. Pres. Young Dems. of Dover, 1953-55; 1st vice-chmn. Young Dems., N.H., 1954-56; mem. Strafford County Dem. Com., 1948-75; vice-chmn. N.H. Dem. Com., 1954-56, 1st chmn., 1956-58, chmn. spl. activities, 1958-60; del. Dem. Nat. Conv., 1956-60, 76; chmn. N.H. Dem. Conv., 1958, conv. dir., 1960; mem. Dem. state exec. com., 1960-70; Dem. nominee for U.S. Senate, 1962; vice-chmn. Dover Cath. Sch. Com., 1969-71; mem. Dover Bd. Adjustment, 1960-65; apptd. lt. commdr. N.H. Govs. Mil. Staff. Pilot U.S. Naval Air Corp., lt. commdr. USNR, 1942-44. Recipient keys to cities of Dover, Somersworth, Concord, Berlin, Manchester and Rochester N.H., 6 nat. plaques DAV, 3 disting. svc. awards Am. Legion, Am. Legion Life Membership award, spl. recognition award Berwick Acad., 1985. Mem. ABA, N.H. Bar Assn., Strafford County Bar Assn. (v.p. 1966-67, pres. 1968-69), Assn. Trial Lawyers Am., N.Y. State Trial Lawyers Assn., Mass. Trial Lawyers Assn., N.H. Trial Lawyers Assn., Tex. Trial Lawyers Assn., Nat. Assn. Criminal Def. Lawyers, N.H. Assn. Criminal Def. Lawyers, Am. Judicature Soc., Phi Delta Phi, DAV (judge adv. N.H. dept. 1950-68, 72—; comdr. chpt. 1953-54, comdr. N.H. 1956-57), Am. Legion (life, chmn. state conv. 1967, 77, 84), Navy League, N.H. Hist. Soc., Dover Hist. Soc., Rollinsford Hist. Soc., Eagles Club, Sons of Italy, Lions, Elks, K.C. (grand knight 1975-77), Moose, Lebanese Club. Clubs: Eagles (Somersworth, N.H.), Sons of Italy (Portsmouth, N.H.). Lodges: Lions, Elks, K.C. (grand knight 1975-77), Moose, Lebanese (Dover). Home: 20 Arch St Dover NH 03820-3602 Office: 450 Central Ave Dover NH 03820-3451

CATALFO, BETTY MARIE, health service executive, nutritionist; b. N.Y.C., Nov. 2, 1942; d. Lawrence Santo and Gemma (Patrone) Lorefice; children—Anthony, Lawrence, Donna Marie. Grad. Newtown High Sch., Elmhurst, N.Y., 1958. Sec., clk. ABC-TV, N.Y.C., 1957-60; founder, lectr., nutritionist Weight Watchers, Manhasset, N.Y., 1964-75; founder, pres. Every-Bodys Diet, Inc. dba Stay Slim, Queens, N.Y., 1976—; dir. in-home program N.Y. State Dept. Health, N.Y.C., 1985—; founder, pres. Delitegul Diet Foods, Inc., 1988—; lectr. in field. Author: 101 Stay-Slim Recipes, 1983, Get Slim and Stay Slim Diet Cook Book, rev. ed., 1987, Diet Revolution, 1991, Holiday Cookbook, 1992, Fat Counts in Fast Food Spots, 1992, Choose to Loose!, 1993, You Are Not Alone, 1993, Eating Out, 1994, Change or Select, 1994, Calories Do Count!, 1994, Fat Free Receipes, 1994; author, dir., producer: (video) Dancersize for Overweight, 1986, Get Slim and Stay Slim Diet Cook Book, Eating Right for Your Life, Hello It's Me and I'm Slim, (videos) Stay Slim Line Dancing, 1989, Stay Slim Food Facts, 1989, Help Me Before I Give In, 1990, A New Year A New You!, 1991, Relax and Meditate, 1991, Come Shop with Me, 1991, Change or Accept, 1993, The Bag Lady, 1993, Sneak Eater, 1993, Sins That Every Dieter Makes, 1994, Stay Slim from Start to Finish, 1994, Here's Some Helpful Diet Tips, 1994, What Every Smart Dieter Knows, 1994, Mirror Mirror on the Wall, 1994, Weight Management Techniques, 1995; author, editor: (video) Eating Right For Life, 1985, Isometric Techniques for Weight Reduction, Dance Your Calories A-Weigh; author, producer: (video) Eating Habits, 1986—; (video) Isometric Techniques for Weight Reduction, 1986, Patience Is a Virtue When Weight Loss is the Goal, 1986, Slow Down you Eat to Fast, 1994, Always Giving Never Receiving, 1994, Relax and Don't You Worry, 1994; producer, dir.: (video) Positive and Negative Diet Forces, 1987, (video) Hello It's Me and I'm Thin, 1987, (video) Dance Your Calories A-Weigh, 1987, (video) Positive and Negative Diet Forces, 1987. Sponsor, lectr. St. Pauls Ctr., Bklyn., 1981—, Throgs Neck Assn. Retarded Children, Bronx, 1985—; active ARC, LWV, Am. Italian Assn., United Way Greenwich, Council Chs. and Synagogues, Heart Assn., N.Y. Meals on Wheels, 1985—, Health Assn. Fairfield County, Food Svcs. for Homeless People, 1993, 94, 95; chairperson, sponsor Battered Women, 1994—. Named Woman of Yr., Bayside Womens Club, N.Y., 1983, O, PK Woman of Yr., 1986—, Woman of Yr. Richmond Boys Club, 1987, Woman of Yr. Bronx Press Club Assn., 1987; recipient Merit award for Svc. Cath. Archdiocese of Bklyn., 1985, Merit award Svcs. Cath. Archdioces of Bklyn. and Queens, 1992, 93, 94, Community Service award Sr. Citizens Sacred Heart League Bklyn./Queens Archdiocese. N.Y. State Nutritional Guidance for Children Nat. Assn. Scis. Mem. Nat. C. of C. for Women (Woman of Yr. 1987, 90), Pres.'s Coun. on Nutrition, Roundtable for Women in Food Service, Bus. and Profl. Women's Club, Pres. Council for Phys. Fitness, Nat. Assn. Female Execs., Assn. for Fitness in Bus. Inc., Nat. Assn. Female Bus. Owners. Democrat. Roman Catholic. Club: Mothers Sacred Heart Sch. (chairperson 1979-82). Avocations: reading; travel, golf, family. Home: 21422 27th Ave Flushing NY 11360-2608 also: 58 Riverview Ct Greenwich CT 06831-4127 Office: 10005 101st Ave Ozone Park NY 11416-2601

CATALFOMO, PHILIP, retired university dean; b. Providence, Dec. 27, 1931; s. Antonio and Frances (Di Giuseppe) C.; m. Magdalena Wettstein, Jan. 8, 1962; children— Kristina, Anthony Werner. BS, Providence Coll., 1953, U. Conn., 1958; MS, U. Wash., Seattle, 1960, PhD, 1962. Mem. faculty Oreg. State U., 1963-75, prof. pharmacognosy, 1966-75, head dept., 1966-75; prof. pharmacognosy, dean Sch. Pharmacy, U. Mont., Missoula, 1975-86; dean coll. health scis. U. Wyo., Laramie, 1986-91; ret., 1991. Author research articles fungal metabolism. Served with AUS, 1953-55. Gustavus A. Pfeiffer Meml. research fellow, 1969-70 Home: 81800 Old Hwy # 93 Dayton MT 59914

CATALONA, WILLIAM, surgeon, urologist, educator, researcher; b. Cleve., Nov. 14, 1942; s. William and Lucille Evelyn Catalona; m. Janet Pauline Flenner; 1 child, Alexander Paul. BS, Otterbein Coll., 1964; MD, Yale U., 1968. Diplomate Am. Bd. Urology. Intern in surgery Yale-New Haven Hosp., 1968-69; resident in surgery U. Calif., San Francisco, 1969-70; clin. assoc. surgery br. Nat. Cancer Inst., Bethesda, Md., 1970-72; resident in urology Johns Hopkins U. Hosp., Balt., 1972-76; assoc. prof. urology Washington U. Sch. Medicine, St. Louis, 1976-82, prof., 1982—, chief urology, 1984-99; prof. urology Northwestern U. Feinberg Sch. of Medicine. Dir. clin. prostate cancer program Robert H. Lurie Comperhensive Cancer Ctr.; cons. Am. Cancer Soc., Nat. Kidney Found. Contbr. numerous articles to med. jours., including New Eng. Jour. Medicine, Jour. AMA, Am. Jour. Human Genetics. Mem. Am. Urol. Assn. (Gold Cystoscope award 1986, Eugene Fuller medal 1998, Hugh Hampton Young award), Am. Assn. Genitourinary Surgeons (Barringer medal 1999, Keyes medal, 2003), Soc. Urologic Oncology (founding, pres. 1994-95), Clin. Soc. Genitourinary Surgeons, Johns Hopkins Soc. Scholars, St. Louis Acad. Sci., 2003. Achievements include introduction of prostate specific antigen test for prostate cancer screening; developed free PSA blood test for increasing accuracy of PSA; identified chromosomal regions statistically linked to familial prostate cancer; a pioneer nerve-sparing radical prostatectomy for prostate cancer. Office: Northwestern U Feinberg Sch Medicine Dept Urology 675 N St Clair St Ste 20-150 Chicago IL 60611 Fax: 312-695-1482. E-mail: wcatalona@nmff.org.

CATALYUREK, UMIT VEYSEL, computer engineer, researcher; b. Uskudar, Turkey, May 12, 1970; s. Osman and Hayriye Catalyurek; m. Gamze Ugan, Dec. 10, 1970; 1 child, Kaan. BS in Computer Engring., Bilkent U., Ankara, Turkey, 1992, MS in Computer Engring., 1994; PhD in Computer Engring., Bilkent U., 2000. Rsch. asst. Bilkent U., 1992-99; rsch. assoc. Johns Hopkins Med. Instn., Balt., 1999—2001; asst. prof. Ohio State U., Columbus, 2001—. Cons. DAG Elektronik Ltd., Ankara, 1992—99. Scholar Bilkent U., 1987-99. Office: Ohio State Univ Dept Biomed Informatics 3019 Graves Hall/333 W 10th Ave Columbus OH 43210 E-mail: catalyurek.1@osu.edu.

CATANELLO, IGNATIUS ANTHONY, bishop; b. Bklyn., July 23, 1938; Student, Cathedral Prep. Sem.; BA, St. Francis Coll., Bklyn.; STB, Cath. U. Washington; MA, MS, St. John's U., LLD (hon.), 1989; PhD, LLD, NYU. Ordained priest Roman Cath. Ch. 1966. With St. Rita's, L.I., NY, 1966—76, St. Helen's, Howard Beach, NY, 1976—81, St. Ann's, Flushing, NY, 1981—86, O.L.O. Angles, Bay Ridge, NY, 1987—88; titular bishop Diocese of Deulto, 1994—; auxiliary bishop Diocese Bklyn., 1994—. Adj. prof. St. John's U.; bd. govs. Maj. Sem., Huntington, NY; co-chair Roman Cath.-Islamic Dialogue; vicar for evangelization Roman Cath. Diocese of Bklyn.; regional bishop Queens South; chair convocation on crime Religious Leaders of N.Y.C.; established bilateral com. Cath. and Ea. Orthodox. Editor: Cath.-Jewish Guidelines for Diocese of Bklyn. Episcopal liaison Nat. Holy Name Soc. Recipient Builder of Brotherhood award, Nat. Conf. on Christians and Jews, Disting. Svc. award, State of N.Y. Mem.: AAUW, Religious Edn. Assn., Cath. Biblical Assn. Office: 75 Greene Ave PO Box C Brooklyn NY 11202-3604*

CATANESE, ANTHONY JAMES, academic administrator; b. New Brunswick, N.J., Oct. 18, 1942; s. Anthony James and Josephine Marlene (Barone) C.; m. Sara Jean Phillips, Oct. 23, 1968; children: Mark Anthony, Michael Scott, Mark Alexander. BA, Rutgers U., 1963; M in Urban Planning, NYU, 1965; PhD, U. Wis., 1968. Asst. prof. city planning Ga. Inst. Tech., Atlanta, 1967-78, assoc. prof., 1968-73, chmn. doctoral studies com., 1970-73; James A. Ryder prof. transp. and planning, dir. Ryder program in transp. U. Miami, Coral Gables, Fla., 1973-75; dean Sch. Architecture and Urban Planning U. Wis., Milw., 1975-82; prof. architecture and urban planning, provost Pratt Inst., N.Y.C., 1982-84; dean Coll. Architecture, U. Fla., Gainesville, 1984-89; pres. Fla. Atlantic U., Boca Raton, 1989—2002, pres., prof., 1990—2002; pres. Fla. Inst. Tech., Melbourne, 2002—. Sr. Fulbright prof., Colombia, 1971-72; sr. cons. State of Wis., 1965-67, sr. planner State of N.J., 1963-67; pres. A. J. Catanese & Assocs., Inc., 1967—; mem. pres. commn. NCAA, 1991-93. Author: Scientific Methods of Urban Analysis, 1972, New Perspectives on Urban Transportatio Research, 1972, Systematic Planning-Theory and Applications, 1970, Planners and Local Politics: Impossible Dreams, 1973, Urban Transportation in South Florida, 1974, Personality, Politics and Planning, 1978, Introduction to Urban Planning, 1979, Introduction to Architecture, 1979, The Politics of Planning and Development, 1984, Urban Planning, 1988; contbr. articles to profl. jours. Chmn. Mid. DeKalb County Dem. Party, 1969-71, mem. 5th Congl. Dist. Dem. caucus, 1971; aide-de-camp Gov.'s Office, State of Ga., 1971-72; mem. Ga. Dunes Studies Commn., 1972-73; bd. dirs. Archtl. Rsch. Ctrs. Consortium, 1976—; mem. Urban Policy Task Force, Carter presdl. campaign, 1976, 80; pres. Park West Redevel. Corp., 1976-78; chmn. Milw. City Plan Commn., 1978-82; bd. dirs. Goals for Milw. 2000, 1978-82, Environ. Edn. Found. Fla.; chmn. Gainesville (Fla.) Planning Bd., 1986-89. With USAR, 1961-63. Recipient fellowships State of N.J. Act of 1927, 1962-63, Werner Hegemann Found., 1963-65, Wis. Alumni Rsch. Found., 1965-68, Richard King Mellon Trust, 1966-67, Ford Found., 1967, Nat. Endowment Arts, 1980. Mem. Am. Inst. Planners (bd. govs., v.p. 1971-74), Am. Inst. Cert. Planners (mem. exec. com. 1971-74), Am. Planning Assn., Transp. Rsch. Bd., Regional Sci. Assn., Am. Acad. Polit. and Social Scis., Assn. Coll. Schs. Planning, Heritage Club, Wycliff Club, Tower Club. Office: Fla Inst Tech 150 W University Blvd Melbourne FL 32901

CATANIA, A(NTHONY) CHARLES, psychology educator; b. N.Y.C., June 22, 1936; s. Charles John and Elizabeth (Lattarulo) C.; m. Constance J. Britt, Feb. 10, 1962; children: William John, Kenneth Charles. BA in Psychology with highest honors, Columbia U., 1957, MA, 1958; PhD (NSF fellow), Harvard U., 1961. Postdoctoral research fellow Harvard U., 1961-62; sr. pharmacologist Smith, Kline & French Labs., Phila., 1962-64; asst. prof. NYU, 1964-66, asso. prof., 1966-69, prof., chmn. dept. psychology, 1969-73; prof. dept. psychology U. Md. Baltimore County, Catonsville, 1973—, program dir. master's track in applied behavior analysis; mem. psychobiology com. NSF, 1982-85. Vis. prof. Keio U., Tokyo, 1992. Author: Learning, 1979, 4th edit., 1998; co-author: (with E. Shimoff and B.A. Matthews) Behavior on a Disk, 1989; editor: Contemporary Research in Operant Behavior, 1968; co-editor: (with T.A. Brigham) Handbook of Applied Behavior Analysis, 1978, (with S. Harnad) The Selection of Behavior: The Operant Behaviorism of B.F. Skinner, 1988, (with P.N. Hineline) Variations and Selections, 1996, (with V.G. Laties) B.F. Skinner's Cumulative Record, definitive edit., 1999; editor: Jour. Exptl. Analysis Behavior, 1966-69, rev. editor, 1969-76, 83-91; assoc. editor: Behavioral and Brain Scis., 1980—; mem. bd. editors various jours.; contbr. articles to profl. jours.; contbr. chpts. to textbooks. Recipient James McKeen Cattell Sabbatical award, 1986-87, Outstanding Sci. Contbns. to Psychology award Md. Psychol. Assn., 1993, Outstanding Contbr. Behavior Analysis award No. Calif. Assn. Behavior Analysis, 1990; NSF grantee, 1965-67, 74-79, 82-88, USPHS grantee, 1967-73, 79-83; Fulbright sr. rsch. fellow, Wales, Bangor, 1986-87. Fellow APA (pres. divsn. 25 1976-79, 96-98, Don Hake award divsn. 25); mem. Assn. Behavior Analysis (pres. 1982-83, chair publ. bd. 1992-95, pres. Md. chpt. 2001-02), Ea. Psychol. Assn. (dir. 1979-82), Soc. Exptl. Analysis of Behavior (pres. 1966-67, 81-83, v.p. 2003—), Lang. Origins Soc. (program chair 1996). Home: 10545 Rivulet Row Columbia MD 21044-2420 Office: U Md Baltimore County Dept Psychology Baltimore MD 21250-0001 E-mail: catania@umbc.edu.

CATANZARO, DANIEL FRANK, molecular biologist, educator; b. Sydney, Australia, Apr. 4, 1957; came to U.S., 1990; m. Cathy L. Budman; 2 children. BA in Biol. Scis. with honors, Macquarie U., 1978; PhD in Physiology and Molecular Biology, U. Sydney, 1986; MBA, Columbia U., 2000. Vis. rsch. biochemist U. Calif., San Francisco, 1985; lectr. in eukaryotic molecular genetics U. Sydney, 1986-90; asst. prof. physiology in medicine Cornell U. Med. Coll., 1990-95; assoc. prof. Weill Med. Coll., Cornell U., N.Y.C., 1995-99, assoc. prof. physiology in cardiothoracic surgery, 1999—. Dep. editor basic sci. Am. Jour. Hypertension, 1999-2001; co-exec. editor Am. Jour. Hypertension, 2002-; contbr. articles and revs. to profl. jours. Postgrad. scholar U. Sydney Faculty of Medicine, 1979-81; recipient investigatorship award Am. Heart Assn., 1995. Fellow AHA High Blood Pressure Rsch. Coun.; mem. Endocrine Soc., Am. Soc. Hypertension (Young Scholars award 1993). Office: Cornell U Weill Med Coll Cardiovascular Ctr A-863 1300 York Ave New York NY 10021-4805

CATCHI, (CATHERINE OELAND CHILDS), artist; b. Phila., Aug. 27, 1920; d. William Henry Harrison and Catherine Stuart (Oeland) C.; widow; children: Diane Childs Willis Neuse, Heather Childs Willis Sargent, Charles Everett Willis III. Student, Briarcliff Jr. Coll., 1937. Artist-in-residence Friends Acad., Locust Valley, N.Y., 1984, Vt. Studio Ctr., Johnson, 2002—03. One woman shows include Galerie di Arte Spinetti, Florence, Italy, 1973, Coin di Arte Galleria, Genoa, Italy, 1974, Rosenberg Mus., Galveston, Tex., 1977, Galerie Beck, Homberg, Germany, 1978, Internat. Mus., McAllen, Tex., 1984, Art Mus., Wichita Falls, Tex., 1985, Longview (Tex.) Art Mus., 1987, Elliott Mus., Hutchinson Island, Stuart, Fla., 1990, Country Art Gallery, Locust Valley, N.Y., 1991, Kiya Galerie Konoha, Tokyo, 1995, Shelter Rock Gallery, Manhasset, N.Y., 1995, others; group shows include Riverside Mus., N.Y.C., 1973-76; represented in permanent collection Jane Voorhees Zimmerli Mus., Rutgers U., Rosenberg Found., Hofstra U., also pvt. collections; illustrations included in Internat. Sculpture Symposium book. Recipient Grumbacher award Guild Hall Mus., 1963, 1st prize Riverside Mus., 1973-76, Robert J. Newhouse Meml. award, 1987, Emily Lowe award, 1989; grantee Dr. Maury Leibovitz Art Award, 1986. Mem. Nat. Assn. Women Artists (pres. 1981-85), N.Y. Soc. Women Artists (pres. 1985-87), Artists Equity N.Y. (bd. dirs. 1988-89). Avocations: rug hooking, gardening. Home: 2 Gristmill Ln Manhasset NY 11030-1108

CATCHINGS, TAMIKA, professional basketball player; b. Stratford, N.J., July 21, 1979; d. Harvey Catchings. Profl. basketball player Ind. Fever, 2001—. Mem. USA Jr. World Championship Qualifying Team, 1996, USA Basketball Jr. World Championship Team, 1997. Named Naismith All-Am., Atlanta Tip-Off Club, 1999, Naismith Player of Yr., 2000, Nat. Player of Yr., Associated Press, U.S. Basketball Writers Assn. (USBWA), Kodak/WBCA, 2000, All-Am. 1st team selection, Kodak/WBCA, All-Am. 2nd team, Associated Press, 1998, Nat. Rookie of Yr., Sporting News, 1998, 3 time All-Southeastern Conf. 1s team selection, 1998—2000, All-Southeastern Conf. 2nd team, 2001, Southeastern Conf. Newcomer of Yr., Associated Press, Freshman of Yr., Women's Basketball Jour., Southeastern Conf., 1998, All-Freshman 1st team, All-Southeastern Conf., All-Freshman 1st team, 1998, 4 time Parade Mag. All-Am., Gatorade Cir. Champions, Southwest Region, 1997, Tex. Player of Yr., 1997; named to All-Final Four teams, CNAA, 1998, 2000; recipient Gold medal, FIBA Jr. World Championship, 1997, Southeastern Conf. All- Tournament honors, 1998—2000, Gold medal, R. William Jones Cup, 1998, All-Am., Sports Illustrated, Sporting News, 1999, 2000. Office: 125 S Pennsylvania St Indianapolis IN 46204 Office Fax: 317-917-2899.

CATCHINGS, YVONNE PARKS, artist, educator; d. Andrew Walter and Hattie Marie (Brookins) Parks; m. James A.A. Catchings, May 30, 1960 (dec.), children: Andrea Yvonne Hunt Warner, Wanda Elaine Hunt McLean, James Albert A. AB in Art, Spelman Coll., 1955; MA in Art Edn., Columbia U., 1958; MA in Mus. Practice, PhD in Edn., U. Mich., 1970; MA, Wayne State U., 1994. Cert. art therapist. Tchr. art Atlanta Bd. Edn., 1955—59; instr. in art Spelman Coll., 1956—57; tchr. art Detroit Bd. Edn., 1959—75, art specialist, 1976—77, reading specialist, 1987—. Asst. prof. art Valdosta State Coll., 1987—88; lectr. Marygrove Coll., 1970—72. One-woman shows include Black Artist South, Huntsville (Ala.) Mus., 1978, exhibited in group shows at Forever Free: Art by African Am. Women 1862-1980, traveling show, 1981, Westbeth Art Gallery, NY, 1993, N.C.A. Mich-Gallery, 1993; author: You Ain't Free Yet Notes From a Black Woman, 1976; subject of: American Negro Art by Cedric Dover, 1960, Black Artist on Vol. 2 by Samella Lewis, 1970, Black Personalities of Detroit, 1975, Builders of Detroit by Anne Russell, 1978, The Art of Black American Women by Robert Henkes, 1993; author: Gumbo Ya Ya: Anthology of Contemporary African American Women Artists, 1995. Trustee Afro Am. Mus., 1970—72; program chmn. Nat. Aux. to Nat. Dental Assn., 1966, chmn. art and craft, 1976; chmn. reception com. United Negro Coll. Fund, Detroit, 1980. Recipient Fulbright Hayes grant for study, Zimbabwe, 1982, Spirit of Detroit award, Detroit Common Coun., 1978, Mayor's award of Merit, City of Detroit, 1980, James D. Parks Art award, Nat. Conf. Art, 1979. Mem.: Am. Art Therapy Assn., Mich. Art Therapist Assn., Your Heritage House Mus., Nat. Conf. Artists, Nat. Art Edn. Assn., Carrousels Club, Links Club, Smart Set Club, Moles Club, Delta Sigma Theta (chmn. Founders Day 1965, nat. chmn. heritage and archives, mem. nat. exec. bd.), Phi Delta Kappa. Home: 1306 Joliet Pl Detroit MI 48207-2834

CATCHPOLE, HUBERT RALPH, physiologist; b. London, May 13, 1906; came to U.S., 1930; m. Robin Jane Miller, Dec. 28, 1973. BA, Cambridge U., 1928; PhD, U. Calif., Berkeley, 1933. Prof. pathology U. Ill., Chgo., 1950-73, prof. histology, 1973—; vis. prof. humanities Rush U., Chgo., 1973—. Contbr. over 150 articles to profl. jours. With USN, 1942—46 USNR, 1942—46. Commonwealth fellow, 1941-42. Mem. Am. Soc. Physiology, Am. Soc. Anatomy, Am. Soc. Endocrinology, Brit. Soc. Endocrinology, The Chgo. Lit. Club. Democrat. Home: 110 W Oak St Chicago IL 60610-2814 Office: U Ill at Chgo 808 S Paulina St Dept Oral Biology Chicago IL 60612

CATE, FRED HARRISON, law educator, lawyer; b. McRae, Ga., May 20, 1963; s. Robert L. and Dorothy W. C.; m. Beth E. Orlowski. AB, Stanford (Calif.) U., 1984, JD, 1987. Bar: Calif. 1987, U.S. Dist. Ct. Calif. 1987, U.S. Ct. Appeals (9th cir.) 1987, D.C. 1988, D.C. Ct. Appeals 1998, Ind. 1998, U.S. Supreme Ct. 2002. Assoc. Debevoise & Plimpton, Washington, 1987-90; assoc. prof. Sch. of Law Ind. U., Bloomington, 1990-96, prof., 1996—2003, Disting. prof., 2003—; sr. counsel Ice Miller, 1997-2001. Sr. fellow Annenberg Washington Program in Comm. Policy Studies, Washington, 1990—96; of

counsel Fields & Dir., Washington, 1990—94; dir. Inst. on Info. and Comml. Law Ind. U., 1997—2002, dir. Ctr. Applied Cybersecurity, 2003—; sr. policy advisor Hunton A. Williams Ctr. for Info. Policy Leadership, 2001—. Author: (with others) Death and Organ Donation, 1991, Privacy in the Information Age, 1997, The Internet and the First Amendment, 1998, Mass Media Law, 6th edit, 2000, Privacy in Perspective, 2001; faculty advisor Fed. Comm. Law Jour., 1993—; contbr. articles to profl. jours. Bd. dirs. Nat. History Day, 1989-2000. Mem. Phi Beta Kappa Fellows (bd. dirs.), Phi Beta Kappa (senator). Home: 2928 Olcott Blvd Bloomington IN 47401-2400 Office: Ind U School of Law 211 S Indiana Ave Bloomington IN 47405-7001 E-mail: fcate@indiana.edu.

CATE, PHILLIP DENNIS, art museum director emeritus; b. Washington, Oct. 19, 1944; s. Phillip Harding and Catherine (Watson) C.; m. Lynn Gumpert; children from previous marriage: Phillip Isaac, Anthony David. BA, Rutgers U., 1967; MA, Ariz. State U., 1970. Asst. to dir. Pa. Acad. Fine Arts, Phila., 1967-68; instr. Phila. Coll. Art, Phila., 1969-70; dir. University Art Gallery Rutgers U., New Brunswick, NJ, 1970-82, dir. Zimmerli Art Mus. (formerly University Art Gallery), 1983—2002, supr. curatorial and acad. activities Zimmerli ARt Mus., 2002—. Author: (exhbn. catalogues) The Color Revolution: Color Lithography in France, 1978, The Circle of Toulouse-Lautrec, 1985, The Eiffel Tower a Tour de Force, 1989, From PIssarro to Picasso: Color Etching in France, 1992, The Spirit of Montmarte: Cabarets, Humor and the Avant-garde, 1875-1905, 1996, Prints Abound: Paris in the 1890's, 2000. Mem. Assn. Art Mus. Dirs., Print Coun. Am., le Comité nat. de la gravure française. Home: 85 John St New York NY 10038 Office: Rutgers U Jane Voorhees Zimmerli Mus George & Hamilton Sts New Brunswick NJ 10001

CATELL, ROBERT BARRY, gas utility executive; b. Bklyn., Feb. 1, 1937; s. Joseph Daniel and Belle (Mishkind) Cicatelli; m. Joan Kathryn Weigand, June 25, 1971; children: Laura Anne, Erica Anne; children by previous marriage: Robert Edward, Carla Ann, Donna Theresa. BME, CCNY, 1958, MME, 1964. Registered profl. engr. Asst. v.p. Bklyn. Union Gas Co., 1974-78, v.p., 1978-82, sr. v.p., 1982-84, exec. v.p., 1984-86, exec. v.p., COO, 1986-90, pres., COO, 1990-91, pres., CEO, 1991-96; chmn., CEO Key Span Energy Corp. (formerly Bklyn. Union Gas Co.), 1996—. Trustee Independence Savs. Bank, Bklyn., 1984—, Gas. Rsch. Inst., 1992; mem. regional adv. com. Chase Bank; chmn. N.Y. State Energy Assn., L.I. Assn. Mem. N.Y. Serda Bd.; chmn. N.Y.C. Partnership; mem. N.Y. State Bus. Coun., vice chmn. Mem. Am. Gas Assn., Soc. Gas Lighting. Avocations: swimming; golf; tennis. Office: Key Span Corp One Metrotech Ctr Brooklyn NY 11201

CATER, JUDY JERSTAD, librarian; b. San Francisco, Jan. 20, 1951; d. Theodore S. and Estelle E. (Christian) Jerstad; m. Jack E. Cater, Nov. 24, 1973; children: Joanne Jerstad, Jennifer Jerstad. AB, Mount Holyoke Coll., 1973; MS, Simmons Coll., 1974; MA, U. San Diego, 1984. Cert. libr., libr. tech., supr. chief adminstrv. officer. Cataloging libr. Palomar Coll., San Marcos, Calif., 1975-76, fine arts, evening reference libr., 1976-77, acquisitions libr., 1977-86, media svcs., acquisitions libr., 1988-90, dir. libr. media ctr., 1986-88, 90-92, media svcs. libr., 1993-97, acquisitions libr., 1997—. Cons., manuscript asst. Presidio Army Mus., Calif. Hist. Soc., San Francisco, 1974-75; rschr. Charles H. Brown Archaeol. Site, San Diego, 1977. Pres. Mount Holyoke Club of San Diego, 1982-86. Recipient Girl Scouts of San Diego and Imperial Counties Disting. Leader award, 1990, Faculty Svc. award Palomar Coll., 1990, NISOD Excellence award, 1991. Mem. ALA, Calif. Libr. Assn. (sec. treas. 1986, membership chair 1987, minority scholarship com. 1991-93, awards and scholarships com. 1993—), Calif. Tchrs. Assn. (pres. Palomar Coll. chpt. 1979-80), Faculty Assn. Calif. Cmty. Colls. Avocations: mystery fiction, needlepoint. Office: Palomar Coll Libr 1140 W Mission Rd San Marcos CA 92069-1415 E-mail: jcater@palomar.edu.

CATES, CORAL J. HANSEN, nurse practitioner, respiratory therapist; b. Seattle, June 5, 1950; d. Raymond Leland and Rosalie (Van Deman) H. Cert. in respiratory therapy, Seattle Cen. Coll., 1975; BS in Nursing summa cum laude, Seattle U., 1987; M in Psychosocial Nursing magna cum laude, U. Wash., 1990. Registered respiratory therapist, Wash.; RN, Wash.; advanced RN practitioner with prescriptive authority; cert. clin. specialist in adult mental health/psychiat. nursing. Respiratory therapist Cura-Care Inc., Modesto, Calif., 1975-84, Northwest Hosp., Seattle, 1984-88; critical care and rehab. nurse University Hosp., Seattle, 1986-87; psychiat. nurse jail psychiat. health Seattle Dept. Pub. Health, 1991; psychiat. nurse Minerth-Meier Psychiat. Unit, Seattle, 1991-97; pvt. practice psychotherapy/counseling adult mental health Seattle, 1991-97; nursing home surveyor, bdg. home licensor, instl. nurse cons., quality improvement specialist Dept. Aging and Adult Svcs., Wash., 1997-2000; psychiat. nurse practitioner with presciptive authority Greater Lakes Mental Health Care, Lakewood, Wash., 2001—. Contbr. letters to profl. jours. Profl. Nurse Traineeship grantee NIH, 1988-89. Mem. ANA, Assn. Advanced Practice Psychiat. Nurses, DAR, Sigma Theta Tau. Avocations: writing short stories, travel, running, collage.

CATES, DENNIS LYNN, education educator; b. Dallas, Nov. 25, 1946; s. Robert N. and Wanda June (Boyd) C.; m. Sue Anne Sadler, Aug. 9, 1975. BA, Tex. Tech U., 1968, MEd, 1976, EdD, 1986; MA, Sul Ross State U., 1981. Cert. secondary edn. tchr., deficient vision, learning disabilities, mental retardation, supervision, mid-mgmt., orientation and mobility instr. Tchr. Eagle Pass (Tex.) Ind. Sch. Dist., Beeville (Tex.) Ind. Sch. Dist., Levelland (Tex.) Ind. Sch. Dist.; tchg. asst. Tex. Tech. U., Lubbock; asst. prof. West Tex. State U., Canyon, 1986-89, U. S.C., Columbia, 1989-95, dir. Ctr. for Excellence in Spl. Edn. Tech., 1992-93; assoc. prof. Cameron U., Lawton, Okla., 1995-2000, prof., 2000—. Presenter numerous profl. confs.; field reviewer edn. jours. and pubs. Contbr. articles to profl. jours. Sgt. USAF, 1969-73. Grantee Consultation Tchrs. grant, 1981—82. Mem.: AAUP, ASCD, Assn. Tchr. Edn., Assn. Edn. and Rehab. for Blind and Visually Impaired (chmn. Divsn. 3 1998—2000, past chmn. 2000—02, newsletter editor Divsn. 3), Am. Coun. for Rural Spl. Edn. (chmn.-elect 2000—02, chmn. 2002—03, past chmn. 2003—, 2003—, bd. dirs., chmn. commn. com., past chmn. 2003—), Coun. for Exceptional Children (pres. Okla. chpt. 2001—02, treas. Okla. subdivsn. devel. disabilities divsn. 2001—, past pres. 2002—03, past pres. Okla. chpt. 2002—03, past pres. 2002—03), Am. Ednl. Rsch. Assn., Internat. Assn. Spl. Edn., Am. Assn. Mental Retardation, Nat. Coun. Geog. Edn., Nat. Coun. for Social Studies, Phi Delta Kappa. Office: Cameron U Dept Edn Lawton OK 73505 E-mail: dennisc@cameron.edu.

CATES, EDWARD WILLIAM, writer, publisher; b. Manchester, N.H., Mar. 11, 1952; s. William and Helen Mary Cates. BA in English, Boston U., 1974; postgrad., Simmons Coll., 1978, Harvard U., 1980-84. Social worker Somerville (Mass.) Cmty. Corp.; sec. Harvard U. Bus. Sch., Boston; geriatric counselor Boston Family Svcs., 1976-80. Part-time therapist, lectr.; former reporter N.E. Human Rights Network News. Author: (poetry) Geopolitics, 1979, (with Charles Dvorak) Remember Your Dreams, 1980; translator: The Gypsy's Bible: Selected Poems of Julian Tuwim, 1989; editor: Small Moon: International and New England Poets 1974-1979. Fellow Mass. Found. for Arts and Humanities, 1979, Mass. Cultural Coun., 1985, 87. Mem. New Eng. Poetry Club. Home: 1050 Auburn St Manchester NH 03103

CATES, GILBERT, film, theater, television producer and director; b. N.Y.C., June 6, 1934; s. Nathan and Nina (Peltzman) Katz; m. Jane Betty Dubin, Feb. 9, 1957 (div.); children: Melissa Beth, Jonathan Michael, David Sawyer, Gilbert Lewis; m. Judith Reichman, Jan. 25, 1987; stepchildren: Ronit Reichman, Anat Reichman. BS, Syracuse U., 1955, MA, 1965. Prof. theatre, film and TV UCLA, 1990—, dean, 1990-99; with Cates-Doty Prodns., Inc.; prodr. dir. Geffen Playhouse, L.A., 1995—. Com. mem. 1 drama dept. Syracuse U., 1969-73. TV prodr., dir. Haggis Baggis, 1959, Camouflage, 1961-62, Internat. Showtime, 1962-64, Hootenanny, 1962, To All My Friends on Shore, 1972, The Affair, 1974, After the Fall, 1974, Johnny, We Hardly Knew Ye, 1977, The Kid From Nowhere, 1982, Country Gold, 1982, Faerie Tale Theatre, 1982, Hobson's Choice, 1983, Consenting Adult, 1984, Child's Cry?, 1986, Fatal Judgement, 1988, One More Time, 1988, Muffin Man, 1989, Call Me Anna, 1990, Absolute Strangers, 1991, Overruled, 1992, Confessions-Two Faces of Evil, 1994, Innocent Victims, 1995, A Death in the Family - Masterpice Theatre, 2001, Collected Stories-PBS, 2002; film prodr., dir.: The Painting, 1962, Rings Aroung the World, 1967, I Never Sang for My Father, 1970, Summer Wishes, Winter Dreams, 1973, Dragonfly, 1976, The Promise, 1978, The Last Married Couple in America, 1979, O God, Book II, 1980, Backfire, 1986; theatrical prodr.: You Know I Can't Hear You When the Water's Running, 1967, I Never Sang for My Father, 1968, The Chinese and Doctor Fish, 1970, Solitaire-Double Solitaire, 1971; dir.: Voices, 1972, Tricks of the Trade, 1980; prodr.: Ann. Acad. Awards, 1990-1995, 1997-99, 2001, 2003, To Life, America Celebrates Israel's 50th (CBS-TV), 1998, America Celebrates Ford's Theater (ABC-TV), 1999, 2000, 02, 03. Bd. dirs. Israeli Cancer Rsch. Fund, 1992-94. Recipient Best Short Film award Internat. Film Importers and Distbrs., 1962, Chancellor'smedal Syracuse U., 1974, Emmy award, 1991, Star on Hollywood Walk of Fame, 1994, Jimmy Doolittle award L.A. Theater, 1998, Best Prodn. Ovation award, 1999, Lifetime Dirs. Achievement award Caucus of Prodrs., Writers and Dirs., 1998, Arents award Syracuse U., 2003. Mem. Dirs. Guild Am. (hon. life award 1990, v.p. Ea. region 1965, Western region 1980—, pres. 1983-87, Robert B. Aldrich award 1989, nat. sec.-tras. 1997—), Acad. Motion Picture Arts and Scis. (bd. govs., chmn. bd. dirs. 1985-94), Women in Film (bd. dirs. 1993-94. v.p. 2003), League N.Y. Theatres, Friars Club (gov. 1980—). Office: 10920 Wilshire Blvd Ste 820 Los Angeles CA 90024-6510 *Craft is freedom.*

CATES, JO ANN, library administrator, writer; b. Ft. Worth, June 25, 1958; d. Charles Kimbrough and Lydia Joe (Sachse) C.; m. Joseph Daniel Frank, Oct. 28, 1989; children: Jacob Abraham Frank, Dec. 9, 1993, Mabel Rose Frank, Sept. 2, 1996. BS in Journalism, Boston U., 1980; MLS, Simmons Coll., 1984. Advt. asst. Boston Phoenix, 1978-79; med. serials asst. Mass. Gen. Hosp., Boston, 1979-80; editorial asst. Exceptional Parent Mag., Boston, 1980-81; libr. reference asst. Lesley Coll., Cambridge, Mass., 1981-84; head reference libr. Lamont Libr., Harvard U., Cambridge, Mass., 1984-85; chief libr. Poynter Inst. for Media Studies, St. Petersburg, Fla., 1985-91; head transp. libr. Northwestern U., Evanston, Ill., 1991-94; regional rsch. mgr. Ctr. for Bus. Knowledge Ernst & Young, 1997—2001; libr. dir. Columbia Coll., Chicago, Ill., 2001—. Tchr. News Libr. and Newsroom Seminars Poynter Inst., 1990-91; mem. Harvard Com. on Instrn. Libr. Use, 1984, mem. adv. com. on book and serial budgets, 1991-94; cons. journalism orgns. Calif., Fla., Mass., 1984—; book reviewer Libr. Jour., Choice, 1985-2000, Am. Reference Book Annual, 1993—; knowledge mgmt. column editor B&F Divsn. Bull., 1999-2000. Author: Journalism: A Guide to the Reference Literature, 1990, 2d edit., 1997; editor Transp. Divsn. Bull., 1992-94; mem. editorial bd. Footnotes, 1991-94; contbr. articles to profl. jours. Mem. Transp. Rsch. Bd. Info. Svcs. Com., 1991-94; media intern Dem. Nat. Com., Boston, 1979-80. Scholar Women in Comm., 1976-78; Trustee scholar Boston U., 1978-80; Simmons Coll. grantee, 1982-84. Mem. Spl. Librs. Assn., Assn. for Edn. in Journalism and Mass Comm., Suncoast Info. Specialists (pres. 1990-91). Am. Libr. Assoc. Avocations: gourmet cooking, collecting books. Home: 540 Hinman Ave Apt 4 Evanston IL 60202-3081

CATES, SUE SADLER, educational diagnostician; b. Ft. Worth, Aug. 7, 1947; d. Randall and Mary Jo (Merkt) Sadler; m. Dennis Lynn Cates, Aug. 9, 1975. BA, Baylor U., 1970; MEd, Sul Ross State U., 1977. Cert. tchr., counselor, ednl. diagnostician, Tex. Tchr. spl. edn. Eagle Pass (Tex.) Ind. Sch. Dist., 1974-76, Beeville (Tex.) Ind. Sch. Dist., 1976-80; supr., ednl. diagnostician Sinton (Tex.) Ind. Sch. Dist., 1980-81; counselor, diagnostician Snyder (Tex.) Ind. Sch. Dist., 1981-86; ednl. diagnostician Pampa (Tex.) Ind. Sch. Dist., 1987-89; elem. counselor Richland County Sch. Dist., Columbia, S.C., 1989-95; ednl. diagnostician Wichita Falls (Tex.) Ind. Sch. Dist., 1995-97, Graham (Tex.) Ind. Sch. Dist., 1997-98, Carrollton-Farmers Branch (Tex.) Ind. Sch. Dist., 1998-2000, Cedar Hill Ind. Sch. Dist., 2000-01, Arlington (Tex.) Ind. Sch. Dist., 2001—02, Ft. Worth (Tex.) Can! Acad. Charter Sch., 2002—, Ft. Worth Can! Acad. Charter Sch., 2002, Van Zandt/Rains County SSA-Edgewood ISD, 2003—. Bd. dirs. Scurry County Sheltered Workshop, 1981-85, Tex. Assn. Children with Learning Disabilities, 1976-77, 81-83; coach Tex. Spl. Olympics, Beeville, amd Sinton, 1978-81; mem. sanctuary choir Floral Heights United Meth. Ch., Wichita Falls, 1995-98, Stephen min., 1992-2003; tchr. Sunday sch., youth coordinator, various other positions. Mem. Tex. Ednl. Diagnosticians' Assn., Council Exceptional Children, Council Ednl. Diagnosticians, Assn. Supervision and Devel., Nat. Assn. Workshop Dirs., NEA, Tex. State Tchrs. Assn., Tex. Classroom Tchrs. Assn., Am. Assn. Counseling and Devel., Tex. Assn. Counseling and Devel., Tex. Ednl. Diagnosticians Assn., AAUW, Phi Delta Kappa, Zeta Phi Eta. Avocations: swimming, coin collecting, travel, singing, jewelry. Home: 4402 York St Wichita Falls TX 76309-4014 Office: Edgewood Ind Sch Dist Van Zandt/Rains County SSA PO Box 727 Edgewood TX 75117

CATHCART, DAVID ARTHUR, lawyer; b. Pasadena, Calif., June 1, 1940; s. Arthur James and Martelle C.; m. Janet Eileen Farley, June 19, 1973; children: Sarah Emily, Rebecca Eileen. BA with gt. distinction, Stanford U., 1961; MA, Harvard U., 1966, LLB cum laude, 1967. Bar: Calif. 1968, U.S. Dist. Ct. (cen. dist.) Calif. 1969, U.S. Dist. Ct. (so., no. dists.) 1975, U.S. Dist. Ct. (ea. dist.) 1979, U.S. Ct. Appeals (9th cir.) 1975, U.S. Supreme Ct. 1979. Assoc. Gibson, Dunn & Crutcher LLP, L.A., 1968-70, 72-75, ptnr., 1975—. Legis. asst. U.S. Senate, Washington, 1971-72; mem. NLRB Adv. Com., 1994-98. Editor-in-chief: Employment Discrimination Law Five-Year Cumulative Supplement, 1989, Employment-At-Will: A 1989 State-By-State Survey, 1990; co-author: California Employment Litigation Practice Guide, 2001; contbr. chpts. to legal texts, articles to profl. jours. Bd. dirs. Western Ctr. on Law and Poverty, LA, 1985-88, US-South Africa Leadership Devel. Program, 1992—, Employers Group, 2000-03. Woodrow Wilson fellow, 1961-62, Danforth fellow, 1961-64. Fellow Coll. of Labor and Employment Lawyers; mem. ABA (mem. coun. 1997—, mgmt. co-chmn. equal employment opportunity law com., 1994-96, sect. labor and employment law, co-chmn. employment and labor rels. law com., 1985-88, litigation sect., class action task force 2002-03), LA County Bar Assn. (chmn. labor & employment law sect. 1991-92), Am. Employment Law Coun. (chmn. 1993—), Chancery Club, City Club on Bunker Hill, Harvard Club NYC, Phi Beta Kappa. Office: Gibson Dunn & Crutcher LLP 333 S Grand Ave Los Angeles CA 90071-3197

CATHCART, HAROLD ROBERT, hospital administrator; b. Odebolt, Iowa, Mar. 9, 1924; s. Chatham Silas and Martha M. (Wells) C.; m. Tressa Bolt, July 20, 1951; 1 child, Tressa Ann. Student, Drake U., 1941-43; BA, State U. Iowa, 1947; D.H.A., U. Toronto, Can., 1948. Fellow W.K. Kellogg Found., 1948-49; mem. staff Pa. Hosp., Phila., 1949-91, v.p., 1960-70, pres., 1970-91. Cons. Lomax Health Sys., Chalfort, Pa.; bd. trustees Waverly Heights Ltd., Gladwyne, Pa.; adj. prof. health care sys. Associated Faculty of U. Pa.; Hunter Group. Bd. dirs. Am. Medico-Legal Found. Served with U.S. Army, 1943-46. Recipient Health Care award B'nai B'rith, 1988. Mem. Am. Hosp. Assn. (chmn. council of nursing 1967-68, council on manpower and edn. 1969-71, trustee 1972-74, chmn. bd. trustees 1976, speaker ho. dels. 1977, Disting. Service award medal 1983), Am. Coll. Health care Execs. (Gold medal 1986), Hosp. Assn. Pa. (pres. 1967-68, Disting. Service award 1977), Delaware Valley Hosp. Council, Greater Phila. Partnership. Home: Villa # 62 1400 Waverly Rd Gladwyne PA 19035-1254 Fax: 215-893-4714. E-mail: hrcathcart@att.net.

CATHCART, ROBERT STEPHEN, mass media consultant; b. LA, Jan. 30, 1923; s. Stephen Joseph and Martha (Morley) C.; m. Dolores June Hawley, July 1, 1944; children: Linda L., Stephen P. AB, U. Redlands, 1944, MA, 1947; PhD, Northwestern U., 1953. Teaching fellow U. Redlands, 1946-47; instr. Purdue U., 1947-49; teaching fellow Northwestern U., 1949-51; instr. U. Md., 1953-55; prof. rhetorical theory Calif. State U. at Los Angeles, 1955-68; chmn. dept. communication Queens Coll., 1968-72; prof. communication theory, 1972-88; prof. emeritus Queens Coll., 1988—. Cons. USN Officer Tng. Corps., U.S. Army Ordnance Ctr., Carnation Co.; mem. Pres.'s Adv. Commn. of Scholars, 1967; sr. visitor in philosophy Oxford (Eng.) U., 1966; dir. Casa Dolores, Study Ctr. of the Popular Arts of Mex.; vis. prof. Sophia U., Tokyo, 1974, U. Oreg., 1986, 89. Author: (with M. Laser and F. Marcus) Ideas and Issues, 1963, (with J. Dahl and Laser) Student, School and Society, 1964, Post Communication, 1966, rev. edit., 1983, (with L. Samovar) Small Group Communication, 1970, rev. edit., 1995, (with G. Gumpert) Inter/Media-Interpersonal Communication in a Media World, 1979, rev. edit., 1988, Television Stereotypes of Three Nations: France, U.S. and Japan, 1988, (with Susan Drucker) American Heroes in a Media Age, 1994. Bd. dirs. Casa Dolores Ctr. for Study of Mexican Arts & Crafts, Cathcart Millennium Found. Lt. USNR, 1943—46, lt. USNR, 1951—53. Home: 829 Hot Springs Rd Montecito CA 93108-1108 Office: Queens Coll Flushing NY 11367 Fax: 805-565-0357. E-mail: rscathcart@cox.net.

CATHELL, DALE ROBERTS, judge; b. Berlin, Md., July 30, 1937; s. Dale Parsons Cathell and Charlotte Robert (Hocker) Terrell; m. Charlotte M. Kerbin; children: Kelly Ann, Dale Kerbin, William Howard. Student, U. Md., 1962-64; LLB, U. Balt., 1967; cert., Nat. Jud. Coll., 1983. Bar: Md. 1967. Atty. City of Ocean City, Md., 1970-76; assoc. judge Md. Dist. Ct., Worcester County, 1980-81; judge Md. Cir. Ct., Worcester County, 1981-89, Ct. Spl. Appeals, 1st Appellate Cir., 1989-97, Ct. Appeals, 1997—. Adj. prof. law U. Balt., 1997—; mem. family and domestic rels. law com. Md. Jud. Conf., 1995-97, past mem. exec. com.; instr. WOR-WIC C.C., 1973, Salisbury State U., 1978. Mem. Pub. Service Commn. Adv. Panel, Md., 1970, charity revision com. Mayor City Council, Ocean City, 1970; mem. Worcester County Shoreline Com., Md., 1971; mem. charter revision com. City of Ocean City, 1973, mem. utility consumer adv. panel, 1978; creator Alt. Com. Service Program, Md., 1980—; organizer Legal Intern Program Pub. Schs., Worcester County, 1981—. Served with USAF, 1955-59. Mem. Md. Bar Assn. (jud. appointment com. 1970), Worcester County Bar Assn. (pres. 1970), Balt. City Bar Assn. Democrat. Episcopalian. Office: Ct Appeals Md Robert C Murphy Cts Apl Bld 361 Rowe Blvd Annapolis MD 21401-1672 also: PO Box 4306 Salisbury MD 21803-4306

CATHEY, MARY ELLEN JACKSON, religious studies educator; b. Florence, S.C., Jan. 12, 1926; d. John William and Mary Ellen (Heinrich) Jackson; m. Henry Marcellus Cathey, May 31, 1958; children: Mary Emily Cathey Ewell, Henry Marcellus Jr. AB, Winthrop Coll., 1947; MRE, Presbyn. Sch. Christian Edn., Richmond, Va., 1953. Cert. Christian educator. Tchr. English, drama Jenkins Jr. High Sch., Spartanburg, S.C., 1947-51; dir. Christian edn. First Presbyn. Ch., Anderson, S.C., 1953-56, Bethesda (Md.) Presbyn. Ch., 1956-59; organizer, dir. Co-op Nursery Sch., Bethesda Presbyn. Ch., 1967-70; dir. Christian edn. Potomac Presbyn. Ch., Potomac, Md., 1977-83, Bethesda Presbyn. Ch., 1983-85, Nat. Presbyn. Ch., Washington, 1985-88; freelance cons. and educator Nat. Capital Presbytery, Washington, 1988—. Edn. cons. Covenant Presbyn. Ch., Arlington, Va., 1987, First Presbyn. Ch., Arlington, 1989-91, Lewinsville Presbyn. Ch., McLean, 1990; elder Nat. Presbyn. Ch., 1990—; elder commr. Gen. Assy., Presbyn. Ch., Milw., 1992. Author hymn text: God Almighty, God Eternal, 1956, others, numerous poems; co-author: Confirmation Guidebook, 1988, The Circle of Wholeness, 1991. Mem. Nat. Leadership Ctr., Washington, 1999—2000; mem. pres.;s adv. coun. Union Sem.-Presbyn. Sch. Christian Edn., Richmond, Va.; pub. trustee Washington Theol. Consortium; elder Presbyn. Ch. USA, copmmr. gen. assembly, 1992. Recipient Sparkler Award Presbyn. Sch. of Christian Edn. Alumni/ae Coun., 1991. Mem. Hymn Soc. U.S. and Can., Presbyn. Writers' Guild, Presbyn. Assn. Musicians, Assn. Presbyn. Ch. Educators, Nat. Capital Presbytery Educators. Avocations: travel, theatre, music, dancing, writing. Home and Office: 1817 Bart Dr Silver Spring MD 20905-4418

CATHEY, PATRICE ANTOINETTE, secondary school educator, director; b. Buffalo, Oct. 13, 1954; d. Eulis Merle and Ruth Houston Cathey; children: Jonathan Eulis Barr, Patrick Jason Barr, Stephan James Barr. BA, Canisius Coll., 1995—98, EdM, 2000—02; PhD, Walden U., 2002—. Cert. of Interior Design J.R. Powers Sch., 1982. Founder/dir. Poetically Speaking Poetry Workshops For Children, Buffalo, 1995—, Ethics and Etiquette, Buffalo, 1996—; writers in edn. instr. Just Buffalo Lit. Ctr., 1996—2000; tchr. St. John Christian Acad., Buffalo, 1997—2000; academic coord. Upward Bound of Buffalo State Coll., 2000—01; dir. Liberty Partnerships Program, Buffalo, 2001—. Comm. coord. B.E.A.M.-Buffalo-Area Engring. Awareness for Minorities, 1996—; founder/pub. Onya Pub., Buffalo, 1998—; dir. of mentoring/tutoring Liberty Partnerships Program, Buffalo, 2001—. Writer: poetry Perhaps Virginia (written form) (Internat. Soc. of Poetry, 2000); actor: (performance poetry) A Woman of Her Words (Performance of Critical Acclaim Awards, 1998); performer (poetry on cd) Perhaps Virginia (Internat. Soc. of Poetry). Mem. Cmty. Sch. #53, Buffalo, 2001—02; vol. Darwin Martin Ho., Buffalo, 2002, Albright Knox Art Gallery, Buffalo. Recipient Distingushed Alumni Award, The Buffalo Sem., 2002, Uncrowned Queens, African Am. Women Cmty. Builders of Western N.Y., 2001; scholar Academic Scholarship, Women's Bus. Soc. of Amherst, 1997. Mem.: Internat. Soc. of Poets, Poetry Soc. of Am., The Acad. of Am. Poets, Women in Higher Edn., Nat. Assn. of U. Women, Nat. Assn. of Black Sch. Educators, AEEE, The Jr. League of Buffalo, Alpha Kappa Alpha Sorority. Office: Liberty Partnerships Program 1300 Elmwood Avenue-CLL-E103 Buffalo NY 14222 Office Fax: 716-878-4015. Personal E-mail: patricecathey@yahoo.com. E-mail: catheypc@buffalostate.edu.

CATHEY, WADE THOMAS, retired electrical engineering educator; b. Greer, S.C., Nov. 26, 1937; s. Wade Thomas Sr. and Ruby Evelyn (Waters) C.; children: Susan Elaine, Cheryl Ann. BS, U. S.C., 1959, MS, 1961; PhD, Yale U., 1963. Group scientist Rockwell Internat., Anaheim, Calif., 1962-68; from assoc. prof. to prof. elec. engring. U. Colo., Denver, 1968-85, chmn. dept. elec. engring. and computer sci., 1984-85, chmn. faculty senate, 1982-83, prof. Boulder, 1985-97, rsch. prof., 1997—2003, ret., 2003. Pres. CDM Optics, 1996—; dir. NSF Ctr. Optoelectronic Computing Sys., Boulder, 1987-93; cons. in field, 1968—. Author: Optical Information Processing and Holography, 1978; contbr. articles to profl. jours.; inventor in field. Fellow Croft, U. Colo., 1982, Faculty, U. Colo., 1972-73. Fellow IEEE, Optical Soc. Am. (topical editor 1977-79, 87-90), Soc. Photo-Optic Instrumentation Engrs. Achievements include extend focal depth and passive ranging in imaging systems, rsch. on matching image acquisiton and signal processing systems. Home: 248 Alpine Way Boulder CO 80304-0406 Office: U Colo Dept Elec Engring Boulder CO 80309-0425 also: CDM Optics Inc 4001 Discovery Dr Ste 2110 Boulder CO 80303 E-mail: tomc@cdm-optics.com.

CATHEY-GIBSON, SHARON SUE RINN, school principal, college administrator; b. Reed City, Mich., June 11, 1940; d. Sherwood and Ellen (Hutson) Rinn.; children: Joel A., Julie A.; Sharon Sue Rinn Cathey-Gibson, Aug. 27, 1996; m. Warren Gibson, Aug. 27, 1996. BA in Edn., San Francisco State U., 1962; postgrad., U. Mich., 1972-74, U. Calif., 1975-77; MA in Edn., U. Nev., 1988, EdD in Curriculum and Instrn., 1991. Tchr. Laguna Salada Union Sch. Dist., Pacifica, Calif., 1962-64, Redwood City (Calif.) Sch. Dist., 1964-66, Lapeer (Mich.) Sch. Dist., 1970-74; tchr., choral dir. Pine Middle Sch., Reno, 1978-84; tchr. Washoe County Sch. Dist., Reno, 1985—, adminstrv. elem. edn. cons., 1991-92; adminstrv. cons. Nev. State Dept. Elem. Edn., Carson City, 1990—; prin. Anderson Elem. Sch., Reno, 1992—, Elizabeth Lenz Elem. Sch., 1994, Libby Booth Sch., Reno, 1994-97; prof., adminstr. Sierra Nev. Coll., 1994—2002, adminstr., 1997—2002, ret., 2002; asst. prof. U. Nev., Reno, 2002—, cons. for literacy, 2001—03; cons., ptnr., editl. staff Superior Edn. and Leadership Inc. Adminstr. Sierra Advocates for Family Equity; statewide exec. dir. tchr. edn. Thompson Learning Ctr., Reno, 1987—89, diagnostician, 1987—89; asst. U. Nev., 1988—90; cons. Nev. State Be. Elem. Edn., 1990, Computer Users Educators of No. Nev.; adminstr., prof. and coord. sch. based programs, dir. tchr. edn. dept. Sierra Nev. Coll.; CASA worker; cons., editor Superior Learning & Leadership Corp.; presenter in field; ptnr. Superior Learning Co. Adminstr. Sierra Advocates for Family Equity. Recipient Celebrate Literacy award, Internat. Reading Assn., 2003; grantee, Nev. ESSA, 1977. Mem.: AAUW (pres. 1976—78), Nev. Assn. Coll. Tchrs. Edn., Nat. Coun. Tchrs. English, Nat. Reading Assn., Internat. Reading Assn. (state pres. 1992, local pres. 1993—94, Literacy award 1995, Celebrate Literacy award 2003), Washoe County Tchrs. Assn., Kiwanis (Reno Sunrisers chpt. sec. 1995—98, pres. 2001—02), Kappa Delta Epsilon (adviser), Delta Kappa Gamma (state pres. 1989—91), Phi Kappa Phi. Republican. Episcopalian. Avocations: music, art, swimming. Home: 2550 Comstock Dr Reno NV 89512-1347

CATHOU, RENATA EGONE, chemist, consultant; b. Milan, June 21, 1935; d. Egon and Stella Mary Egone; m. Pierre-Yves Cathou, June 21, 1959. BS, MIT, 1957, PhD, 1963. Fellow, rsch. assoc. in chemistry MIT, Cambridge, 1962-65, rsch. assoc. Harvard U. Med. Sch., Cambridge, 1965-69, instr., 1969-70; rsch. assoc. Mass. Gen. Hosp., 1965-69, instr., 1969-70; asst. prof. dept. biochemistry Sch. Medicine, Tufts U., 1970-73, assoc. prof., 1973-78, prof., 1978-81; pres. Tech. Evaluations, Lexington, Mass., 1983-2000; sr. cons. SRC Assocs., Park Ridge, N.J., 1984-93. Sr. investigator Arthritis Found., 1970-75; vis. prof. dept. chemistry UCLA, 1976-77; mem. adv. panel NSF, 1974-75; mem. bd. sci. counselors Nat. Cancer Inst., 1979-83; ind. cons. and writer. Mem. editl. bd. Immunochemistry, 1972-75; contbr. chpts. to books and articles to profl. jours. MIT Company Founders citation, 1989; NIH predoctoral fellow, 1958-62; grantee Am. Heart Assn., 1969-81, USPHS, 1970-81. Mem. AAAS, Am. Soc. for Biochemistry and Molecular Biology, Am. Assn. Immunologists, U.S. Power Squadron (past dist. lt. comdr.), Charles River Squadron (past comdr.), Circumnavigators Club. Avocations: photography, opera, fine arts.

CATINO, DONALD, physician; b. Newark; s. George and Alice May (Thompson) C.; divorced; children: Jennifer, Donald, Laurie, Anthony. BA, Princeton U., 1956-60; MD, Cornell U., 1964. Diplomate in internal medicine and geriatrics Am. Bd. Internal Medicine, cert. med. dir. in long term med. care, Coll. Acupuncture and Neuromuscular Therapy. Intern Bellevue Hosp., Cornell U., N.Y.C., 1964-65; fellow in pathology N.Y. Hosp., N.Y.C., 1965-66; resident in internal medicine Boston City Hosp./Harvard U., 1968-70, Mary Hitchcock Hosp./Dartmouth, Hanover, N.H., 1970-71; chief internal medicine Hosp. Albert Schweitzer, Haiti, 1971-73; pvt. practice internal medicine, New London, NH, 1973—. Contbr. articles to profl. jours. Trustee Coun. on Aging, New London, 1992. Capt. M.C., U.S. Army, 1966-68, Viet Nam. Recipient Pathology prize Cornell Med. Sch., 1962. Fellow ACP, Am. Assn. Med. Acupuncturists (cert. acupuncture), Am. Assn. Integrative Medicine; mem. AMA, Am. Geriatrics Soc., Am. Acad. Med. Acupuncturists, N.H. Med. Soc., Merrimack County Med. Soc., Am. Osler Soc., Am. Med. Dirs. Assn. Avocations: triathlons, marathons, Karate, trekking. Office: 276 Newport Rd New London NH 03257

CATLETT, RICHARD H., JR., retired lawyer; b. Boston, May 1, 1921; s. Richard Henry and Martha Barton (Taylor) Catlett; m. Marion Frances Buckey, Apr. 3, 1948 (dec. Sept. 1967); children: Ross C. Rose, Richard H. III, Thomas Y., Maria C. Eldredge; m. Barbara Ann L'Orange, May 1, 1969. BSEE, Va. Mil. Inst., 1943; LLB, U. Richmond, 1952. Engr. C&P Tel. Co., Richmond, Va., 1946-47, Catlett-Johnson Corp., Richmond, Va., 1947-50; assoc., ptnr. Christian & Barton, Richmond, Va., 1952-76; ptnr. McGuire Woods LLP, Richmond, Va., 1976-91; ret., 1991. Bd. dirs. Ga. Pacific Corp., gen. counsel, sec., 1969—90; gen. counsel Signet Banking Corp. (now First Union Corp.), Richmond, 1985—89; adj. asst. prof. law U. Richmond, 1990—93. Chmn. City of Richmond Personnel Bd., 1971—80; dir. Westminster-Canterbury Ho., Richmond, 1985—89, chmn., 1987—89; mem. vestry St. James Episc. Ch., Richmond, 1954—75. 1st lt. U.S. Army, 1943—46, ETO. Mem.: ABA, Va. State Bar Assn. (chmn. bus. law sect. 1972—73), Va. State Bar (chmn. bus. law sect. 1971—72), Commonwealth Club (Richmond), Country Club Va. (dir. 1966—69, 1971—74). Home: 300 N Ridge Rd Richmond VA 23229 E-mail: rcatlett@mcguirewoods.com.

CATLETT, S. GRAHAM, lawyer; b. Little Rock, Ark., Aug. 12, 1952; s. G. G. and Betty H. (Hubach) C.; m. Meredith Polk, June 29, 1974. B.B.A., U. Ark., 1974, J.D., 1977. Bar: Ark. 1977, U.S. Dist. Ct. Ark. 1977, U.S. Ct. Appeals (8th cir.) 1977, U.S. Tax Ct. 1977. Ptnr. Catlett, Yancey & Stodola PLC, Little Rock, 1977—; mng. ptnr. Catlett Tower Partnership, Little Rock, 1986—; pres. Quality Products Moscow, 1990-2002, Catlett, Inc., Little Rock, 1989—; lectr. continuing Legal Edn., 1982—. Mem. ABA, AICPA, Ark. Bar Assn., Ark. Soc. CPAs, Democrat. Presbyterian. Home: 323 Center St Ste 1800 Little Rock AR 72201-2607 Office: Catlett Stubblefield Bonds & Fleming 1800 Tower Bldg Little Rock AR 72201 E-mail: gcatlett@catlaw.com.

CATLEY-CARLSON, MARGARET, not-for-profit developer; b. Nelson, B.C., Oct. 6, 1942; d. George Lorne and Helen Margaret Catley; m. Stanley F. Carlson, Oct. 30, 1970. BA with honors, U. B.C., 1966; postgrad., Inst. Internat. Relations, U. W.I., St. Augustine, Trinidad and Tobago, 1970; LLD (hon.), U. Regina, 1985; LittD (hon.), St. Mary's U., 1985. Joined Dept. External Affairs., Canada, 1966; with Dept. External Affairs, Canada, 1970-74, asst. under-sec., 1981-82; 2d sec. Can. High Commn., Colombo, Sri Lanka, 1968, econ. counsellor London, 1975-77; v.p. Can. Internat. Devel. Agy., 1978, sr. v.p., acting pres., 1979-80, pres., 1983-89; asst. sec. gen. UN; dep. exec. dir. ops. UNICEF, 1981-83; dep. min. Health and Welfare Country Can., 1989-92; pres. Population Coun., N.Y.C., 1993-99. Chair Global Water Partnership; chmn. water resource adv. com. Group Suez, Paris; chmn. change devel. and mgmt. team CGIAR, Washington, 2001; vice-chair Internat. Devel. Rsch. Ctr., Ottawa; chmn. Ctr. Agr. Rsch. Dry Areas, Syria; mem. 2020 vision policy global food policy Internat. Food Policy Rsch. Inst., Washington; with Libr. Alexandria, Egypt, Inter-Am. Dialogue, Washington; clin. prof. Tulane U., New Orleans. Fellow, Ryerson Poly. Inst. Concordia U., 1986, Mt. St. Vincent U., 1990, U. B.C., 1994, U. Calgary, 1994, Carleton U., 1995. Home: 249 E 48th St Apt 8A New York NY 10017

CATLIN, AVERY, engineering and computer science educator, writer; b. N.Y.C., Jan. 29, 1924; s. Randolph and Hannah (White) C.; m. Edith J. Reed, Sept. 7, 1946; children: Avery W., Edith R., Beverly L., Frederic F. B.E.E., U. Va., 1947, MA, 1949, PhD, 1960. Assoc. prof. elec. engring. and materials sci. U. Va., 1960-67, prof., 1967-82, univ. prof. computer sci., 1982-94, assoc. dean engring., 1967-74, exec. v.p., 1974-82, prof. emeritus, 1994—. Office: U Va Thornton Hall Charlottesville VA 22903-2442

CATLIN, FRANCIS IRVING, physician; b. Hartford, Conn., Dec. 6, 1925; s. Robert Irving and Frances Rose (Maleski) C.; m. Rebecca Vaughan Graham, June 11, 1948; children: Robert, Andrew, Martha. AA, Princeton U., 1949; MD, Johns Hopkins U., 1948, DSc, 1959. Diplomate: Am. Bd. Otolaryngology. Intern Union Meml. Hosp., Balt., 1948-49; resident in otolaryngology Johns Hopkins Hosp., Balt., 1950, 52-54; from instr. to assoc. prof. Johns Hopkins U. Med. Sch., Balt., 1956-72; prof. otorhinolaryngology and communicative scis. Baylor U. Med. Sch., Houston, 1972-91, prof. emeritus, 1991—. Chief otolaryngology svc. Tex. Children's Hosp., 1972-91, emeritus staff, 1991—, mem. credentials com., 1989—. Contbr. articles to med. jours. Capt. M.C. USAF, 1950-52. Fellow Am. Otol. Soc.; mem. AMA, ASTM (F29 com. on anesthesia and respiratory equipment 1989—)Tex. Med. Soc., Am. Acad. Otolaryngology, Am. Coun. Otolaryngology, Am. Laryngological, Rhinological and Otol. Soc., Am. Speech and Hearing Assn. (life). Republican. Episcopalian. Home: 13307 Queensbury Ln Houston TX 77079-6013

CATLIN, ROBERT THOMAS, city planning consultant; b. Rockford, Mich., Feb. 4, 1926; s. Clyde Dwight Catlin and Leone Clair Fitch; m. Joyce Annette Teepe, June 24, 1950; children: Richard Mason, Cynthia Catlin Hurd. Student, Western Mich. Coll., 1944-45, 46-47; BS in Urban Planning, Mich. State U., 1950. Lic. city planner, N.J. Asst. planning dir. City Planning Dept., Grand Rapids, Mich., 1950-52; ptnr. Bagby & Catlin Cons., Montclair, N.J., 1952-60; pres., chmn. bd. Robert Catlin & Assocs., Denville, N.J., 1960-91, ret., 1991. Mem. Gov.'s Tech. Adv. Com., 1953. Prepared over 100 master plans for cities in U.S. and Asia. First chmn. Planning Bd., Rockaway, N.J., 1954. With USN, PTO, 1944-46. Mem. N.J. Soc. Consulting Planners (founder), Am. Inst. Cert. Planners, VFW, Am. Legion. Republican. Avocations: golf, tennis, world travel, woodworking. Home: 25 Laurelwood Dr Rockaway NJ 07866-2510

CATO, GLORIA MAXINE, retired secondary education educator, school program administrator; b. Covington, La., Mar. 22, 1942; d. Dan and Roxieana (Washington) Smith; widowed; 1 child, Mark. BS, Southern U., 1965; MS, Pepperdine U., 1974. Tchr. Los Angeles Unified Sch. Dist., 1965-81, counselor, magnet program coordinator, 1981—, PUSH for Excellence program coordinator, 1978-80, student activities coordinator, 1982-84, coll. advisor, 1984-85, personnel specialist, tchr. advisor, 1986-87, asst. prin., 1992—99; ret., 1999. Edn./counselor cons. L.A. Unified Sch. Dist. Trustee L.A. Ednl. Alliance Restructuring Now. Recipient Community-Sch. Service award City of Los Angeles, 1978; named to Top Ladies of Distinction, 1992. Charter mem. NEA, Nat. Assn. Biology Tchrs. (finalist Tchrs. award 1978), Magnet Coordinator Assn., Los Angeles Counselors Assn.; mem. United Tchrs. Los Angeles, Associated Adminstrs. L.A., Assn. Calif. Sch. Adminstrs., Asst. Prin. Secondary Counseling Svcs. Orgn., Phi Delta Kappa, Alpha Kappa Alpha (Mu Beta Omega chpt.). Democrat. Baptist. Home: 3661 Kensley Dr Inglewood CA 90305-2230

CATOE, BETTE LORRINA, physician, health educator; b. Apr. 7, 1926; d. John Booker and Laura Beola (Adams) C.; m. Warren J. Strudwick, Sept. 17, 1949; children: Laura Christina, Warren J., William J. BS cum laude, Howard U., 1948, MD, 1951. Intern Freedmen's Hosp., Washington, 1951-52; pediat. resident Howard U./Freedman's Hosp., 1952-55, practice medicine specializing in pediatrics, 1956—2003, ret., 2003; instr. bacteriology Howard U., 1955-57; mem. staff Providence Hosp., Columbia Hosp., Howard U. Hosp., Wash., Hosp. Ctr.; sch. health officer Dept. Health, Washington, 1960-64; clin. instr. Howard U., 1956-58; health cons., 2003—. Mem. D.C. Health Planning Adv. Coun., 1967-77, chmn. 1973-77; chmn. D.C. Devel. Disabilities Adv. Coun., 1970-74; mem. D.C. Mayor's Commn. on Food and Nutrition, 1971-72, Mayor's Commn. on Maternal and Child Health, 1978-84, appt. vice chmn. Pub. Benefit Corp., 1997-2001; mem. D.C. Commn. Jud. Tenure and Disabilities, 1977-2001, chmn. Bd. Public Benefit Corp. of D.C., 1998-2001; bd. govs. St. Alban's Sch., 1978-84; bd. dirs. D.C. Health and Welfare Coun., 1968-73, pres., 1973-74; del. Democratic Nat. Conv., 1976; bd. dirs. Met. Washington Health and Welfare Coun., 1970-72, Parent Coun. of Washington, 1974-75, Met. Med. Founds., Inc., Silver Spring YMCA, 1977-80, Kingsburg Ctr., 1997-99; mem., chair emergency med. com. Mayor's Health Policy Coun., 1998-2001. Mem.: NAACP, AMA, Women's Aux. Medico-Chirurg. Soc., Assn. Comprehensive Health Planners (dir. 1975—77), Urban League, Am. Med. Women's Assn., Nat. Med. Assn. (chmn. pediat. sect. 1981—83), D.C. Chirurg. Soc. (trustee 1996—99, nominating com. 2000—03, jud. legis. com. 2001—03), Women's Nat. Dem., Jack and Jill Am., Carrousels Club (nat. v.p. 1986—88, nat. pres. 1988—90), Links Club, Century Club of Nat. Assn. Negro Bus. and Profl. Women's Clubs (pres. 1985—89), Alpha Kappa Alpha. Home and Office: 1748 Sycamore St NW Washington DC 20012-1031

CATOLINE-ACKERMAN, PAULINE DESSIE, small business owner; b. Ft. Worth, Dec. 17, 1937; d. Byron Hillis and Dessie Elizabeth (Plumlee) Doggett; children: Sherry Lou, Brenda Lynn; m. Donald Ralph Ackerman, Feb. 19, 1993. BA in Bus. Mgmt. (labor rels. specialty), Hiram Coll., 1989. Sec. Gen. Am. Life Ins. Co., Ft. Worth, 1956-57, Kelly Girl Svcs., Youngstown, Ohio, 1965-69; legal sec. Burgstaller, Schwartz & Moore, Youngstown, 1962-65, Green, Schiavoni, Murphy & Haines, Youngstown, 1969-71, Flask & Policy, Youngstown, 1971-83; sec. Western Res. Care System, Youngstown, 1983-87, exec. sec., 1987-90; owner, mgr. Pauline's Place, Youngstown, 1993—; legal sec. Henderson, Covington, Stein, Donchess & Messenger Law Firm, 1993-94; exec. adminstrv. asst. to pres. CEO, sr. v.p. Internat. Renaissance Developers, Youngstown, 1994-96; adminstrv. asst. to v.p. and client svc. mgr. Bank One Investment Mgmt. & Trust Group, Youngstown, 1996—2000; admin. assoc. regional divsn. Am. Heart Assn., Youngstown, 2000—01; owner, mgr. Paulines Pl., 2001—; staff Kelly Svcs., Youngstown, Ohio, 2001—. Pres. PTA, Cottage Hills, Ill., 1968-69, brownie and scout leader, 1968-69. Mem. Mahoning County Legal Secs. Assn. (v.p. 1973-74, editor monthly booklet 1974-75), Exec. Link, Missionary Group Club. Democrat. Methodist. Avocations: oil painting, reading poetry, tennis, swimming, horseback riding. Home: 3961 Cannon Rd Youngstown OH 44515-4604

CATSIMATIDIS, JOHN ANDREAS, retail chain executive, airline executive; b. Nissiros, Greece, Sept. 7, 1948; came to U.S., 1949, naturalized, 1950; s. Andreas John and Despina (Emmanulides) C. BS in Engring., NYU, 1970. Chmn., chief exec. officer Red Apple Cos. (Gristedes, Red Apple stores), N.Y.C. and Ft. Lauderdale, Fla., 1970—, United Refining Inc., Warren, Pa., 1986-94, Gristedes Foods. Chmn., CEO Sloan's Supermarket, N.Y.C. Recipient Humanitarian award NCCJ, 1978, Am. Jewish Com., 1982, Nat. Kidney Assn., 1986; Entrepreneurship award NYU Bus. Sch., 1987. Mem. Westside C. of C. (vice chmn. 1975—). Clubs: New York Univ., Wings, Young Men Philanthrapic League, N.Y. Athletic. Office: Red Apple Group 823 11th Ave New York NY 10019-3557

CATTANEO, JACQUELYN ANNETTE KAMMERER, artist, educator; b. Gallup, N.Mex., June 1, 1944; d. Ralph John and Gladys Agnes (O'Sullivan) Kammer; m. John Leo Cattaneo, Apr. 25, 1964; children: John Auro, Paul Anthony. Student, Tex. Woman's U., 1962-64. Portrait artist, tchr., Gallup, N.Mex., 1972. Coord. Works Progress Adminstrn. art project renovation McKinley County, Gallup, Octavia Fellin Performing Arts wing dedication, Gallup Pub. Libr.; formation com. mem. Multi-Modal/Multi-Cultural Ctr. for Gallup; exch. with Soviet Women's Com. USSR Women Artists del., Moscow, Kiev, Leningrad, 1990; Women Artists del. and exch., Jerusalem, Tel Aviv, Cairo, Israel; mem. Artists Del. to Prague, Vienna and Budapest; mem. Women Artists Del. to Egypt, Israel and Italy, 1992, artist del., Brazil, 1994, Greece, Crete, Turkey, Spain, 1996, N.S. and Ont., N.B., PEI, Can., 2000. One-woman shows include Gallup Pub. Libr., 1963, 66, 77, 78, 81, 87, Gallup Lovelace Med. Clinic, Santa Fe Sta. Open House, 1981, Gallery 20, Farmington, N.Mex., 1985—, Red Mesa Art Gallery, 1989, Soviet Retrospect Carol's Art & Antiques Gallery, Liverpool, N.Y., 1992, 97, N.Mex. State Capitol Bldg., Santa Fe, 1992, Lt. Govt. Casey Luna-Office Complex, Women Artists N.Mex. Mus. Fine Arts, Carlsbad, 1992, Rio Rancho Country Club, N.Mex., 1995; exhibited in group shows including Navajo Nation Libr. Invitational, 1978, Santa Fe Festival of the Arts Invitational, 1979, N.Mex. State Fair, 1978, 79, 80, Catharine Lorrilard Wolfe, N.Y.C., 1980, 81, 84, 85, 86, 87, 88, 89, 90, 91, 92, 4th ann. exhbn. Salmagundi Club, 1984, 90, 98, 3d ann. Palm Beach Internat., New Orleans, 1984, Fine Arts Ctr., Taos, 1984, The Best and the Brightest O'Brien's Art Emporium, Scottsdale, Ariz., 1986, Gov.'s Gallery, 1989, N.Mex. State Capitol, Santa Fe, 1987, Pastel Soc. West Coast Ann. Exhbn., Sacramento Ctr. for Arts, Calif., 1986-90, gov.'s invitational Magnifico Fest. of the Arts, Albuquerque, 1991, Assn. pour la Promotion du Patrimone Artistique Française, Paris Nat. Mus. of the Arts for Women, Washington, 1991, Artists of N.Mex., Internat. Nexus '92 Fine Art Exhbn., Trammell Corw Pavillion, Dallas, Carlsbad (N.Mex.) Mus. Fine Art; represented in permanent collections Zuni Arts and Crafts Ednl. Bldg., U. N.Mex., C.J. Wiemar Collection, McKinley Manor, Gov.'s Office, State Capitol Bldg., Santa Fe, Hist. El Rancho Hotel, Gallup, Sunwest Bank, Fine Arts Ctr., Taos, Armand Hammer Pvt. Collection, Wilcox Canyon Collections, Sadona, Ariz., Galaria Impi, Netherlands, Woods Art and Antiques, Liverpool, N.Y., Stewarts Fine Art, Taos, N.Mex., Rehoboth McKinley Christian Hosp. & Sacred Heart Cathedral, Gallup, NM. Mem. Dora Cox del. to Soviet Union-U.S. Exch., 1990. Recipient Cert. of Recognition for Contbn. and Participation Assn. pour la Patrinome du Artistique Français, 1991, N.Mex. State Senate 14th Legislature Session Meml. # 101 for Artistic Achievements award, 1992, Award of Merit, Pastel Soc. West Coast Ann. Membership Exhbn., 1998, award N.Mex. State Ho. Reps. for Artistic Achievement, 2001, Holbein award for excellence in painting Pastel Soc. West Coast Internat. Juried Exhbn.; honored for preservation of WPA Dept. Edn. N.Mex. State Ho. of Reps., 2001. Mem. Internat. Fine Arts Guild, Am. Portrait Soc. (cert.), Oil Painters of Am., Pastel Soc. of West Coast (cert., Hobein award, award of excellence mem.'s show 1999), Mus. N.Mex. Found., N.Mex. Archtl. Found., Mus. Women in the Arts, Fechin Inst., Artists' Co-op (co-chair), Gallup C. of C., Gallup Area Arts and Crafts Coun. (nat. and internat. artist of distinction award 1997), Am. Portrait Soc. Am., Pastel Soc. N.Mex., Catharine Lorillard Wolfe Art Club of N.Y.C. (oil and pastel juried membership), Oil Painters of Am., Pastel Soc. N.Mex., Soroptomists (Internat. Woman of Distinction 1990), Salmagundi Art Club. Address: 210 E Green St Gallup NM 87301-6130 E-mail: cattaneo@cnetco.com.

CATTANEO, MICHAEL S. heating and cooling company executive; b. Detroit, May 30, 1948; s. Alex and Bernadine (Krause) C.; m. Nancy Lucille Horsch, Sept. 6, 1969; children: Michael Alex, Jason Ryan. Cert., Lawrence Inst. Tech., 1970, Macomb Coll., 1977. Service tech. Reliable Heating and Cooling, Detroit, 1965-69; service supr. Artic Air Inc., Detroit, 1969-77; supt. Kropf Service Inc., Detroit, 1977-78; owner Greater Detroit Heating and Cooling, Inc., 1978—, J.B. Air Conditioning Inc., 1978—. Mech., tech. educator, Career Prep. Ctr., Warren, Mich., 1982-83; tech advisor Macomb Prosecutor's Office div. consumer fraud, Mt. Clemens, Mich., 1985—; pres. Catt Enterprises Real Estate and Investments; mng. ptnr. B.P.C. Group Investments LLC; v.p. Reit Air Mgmt. Inc.v.p. Catt Air Ballancing Inc. Named Republican of Yr., Mich., 2000, Republican Businessman of Yr., 2002. Mem. Italian Cultural Ctr. (Warren), Ams. Italian Origin, Mich. Italian C. of C. Republican. Roman Catholic. Avocations: fishing, hunting, competitive shooting, golf, NASCAR racing. Office: Greater Detroit Heating and Cooling Inc 31485 Groesbeck Ste B Fraser MI 48026-1961 E-mail: catt8484@aol.com.

CATTANI, LUIS CARLOS, manufacturing engineer; b. Rosario, Santa Fe, Argentina, Oct. 14, 1962; came to U.S., 1987; s. Carlos Candido and Margarita Dora (Rebola) C.; m. Maria Andrea Marañon, Jan. 7, 1989. BSME, Cath. U. of Cordoba, Argentina, 1987; MSME, U. Detroit, 1989, DEng, 1993. Project engr. Modern Automation Specialties, Detroit, 1988-90; computer integrated mfg. mgr. Uni Boring Co. Inc., Howell, Mich., 1990-95, program mgr., 1996-99, mgr. internat. ops., 2000—01, mgr. Ford and internat. programs, 2001—. Co-author (book) Advances in Control and Dynamic Systems, 1991; contbr. articles to profl. pubs. Mem. IEEE, ASME (assoc.), Robotics Internat., Computer and Automated Systems Assn., Soc. Mfg. Engrs. (chmn. Detroit chpt. 1991). Roman Catholic. Avocations: golf, soccer. Office: Uni Boring Co Inc 7261 Commerce Blvd Canton MI 48187-4287

CATTELL, HEATHER BIRKETT, psychologist; b. Carlisle, eng., Dec. 16, 1936; came to U.S., 1958; d. Wilfred B. and Anne Birkett; m. Russel B. Shields, June 10, 1958 (div. 1968); children: Vaughn, Gary, Heather Luanne; m. Raymond B. Cattell, May 9, 1981. BA, U. Hawaii, 1974, MA, 1977, PhD, 1979. Lic. clin. psychologist, Hawaii. Dir. rsch. Salvation Army, Honolulu, 1979-81; pvt. practice Honolulu, 1981—. Lectr., workshop leader, U.S., Australia, Can., and United Kingdom, 1989—. Author: The 16PF: Personality in Depth, 1989, The Cattell Comprehensive Personality Inventory, 1998. Mem. Phi Beta Kappa.

CATTERALL, MARLENE, Canadian legislator; b. Ottawa, Ont., Can., Mar. 1, 1939; d. Paul and Isobel Petzold; m. Ron Catterall, July 14, 1962; children: Karen, Chris, Cheryl. Ed., Carleton U. Alderman City of Ottawa, 1976-85; coun. mem. Regional Municipality Ottawa-Carleton, 1976-85; mem. from Ottawa West Ho. of Commons, 1988-97, apptd. parliamentary sec. to pres. of treasury bd., 1993, mem. from Ottawa W., Nepean, 1997—. Apptd. dep. govt. whip, 1994; apptd. chief gov. whip, 2001; mem. Procedure and House Affairs Com. Mem. coun. women Friends of Can. Mus. Civilization. Liberal. Roman Catholic. Office: House of Commons Rm 451-S Centre Block Ottawa ON Canada K1A 0A6 E-mail: cattem@parl.gc.ca.

CATTERALL, WILLIAM A. pharmacology, neurobiology educator; b. Providence, Oct. 12, 1946; s. William V. and Alice (Aldred) C.; m. Nancy Sharples; children: W. Douglas, Elizabeth R. BA in Chemistry, Brown U., 1968; PhD in Physiol. Chemistry, Johns Hopkins U., 1972. Postdoctoral research fellow Lab. of Biochem. Genetics NIH, Bethesda, Md., 1972-76, staff scientist, 1976-77; assoc. prof. dept. pharmacology U. Wash., Seattle, 1977-82, prof., 1982—, chmn. dept. pharmacology, 1984—, chmn. interdisciplinary com. on neurobiology, 1986—. Editor Molecular Pharmacology, 1986-90; contbr. numerous articles to profl. jours. and textbooks. Recipient Young Scientist award Passano Found., 1981, Jacob Javits Neurosci award, NIH, 1984, 91, Basic Sci. Prize award Am. Heart Assn., 1992; numerous grants. Mem. Nat. Acad. Sci., Inst. of Medicine, Am. Acad. Arts and Sci., Am. Soc. Pharmacology and Exptl. Therapeutics, Soc. for Neurosci., Am. Soc. Biol. Chemists, Neurosci. Rsch. Program. Avocations: sailing, skiing. Office: Univ Wash Dept Pharmacology PO Box 357280 Seattle WA 98195-7280

CATTERLIN, CINDY LOU, English educator; b. Linton, Ind., Nov. 20, 1958; d. Ralph Lloyd and Betty Lou Miller; m. Davey Lee Catterlin Jr., July 3, 1982; children: Davey Lee III, Melissa Joy. BS summa cum laude, Ind. State U., 1980, MS, 1981. Cert. advanced profl. tchr. Music tchr. Kossouth St. Bapt. Sch., Lafayette, Ind., 1981-82; pvt. instrumental music instr. Beckley, W.Va., 1986-94; bd. dir. Raleigh County Bd. Edn., Beckley, 1994-95; tchr. English Heritage Christian Acad., Englewood, Fla., 1997—, also bd. dirs., choir dir. Pianist Calvary Bapt. Ch., Englewood, 1995—, boys and girls Awana dir., 1995—. Mem. Am. Assn. Christian Schs. Avocations: sewing, music. Home: 620 N Elm St Englewood FL 34223-2753 Office: Heritage Christian Acad 75 Pine St Englewood FL 34223-3925

CATTERTON, MARIANNE ROSE, occupational therapist; b. St. Paul, Feb. 3, 1922; d. Melvin Joseph and Katherine Marion (Bole) Maas; m. Elmer John Wood, Jan. 16, 1943 (dec.); m. Robert Lee Catterton, Nov. 20, 1951 (div. 1981); children: Jenifer Ann Dawson, Cynthia Lea Uthus. Student, Carleton Coll., 1939-41, U. Md., 1941-42; BA in English, U. Wis., 1944; MA in Counseling Psychology, Bowie State Coll., 1980; postgrad., No. Ariz. U., 1987-91. Registered occupl. therapist, Occupl. Therapy Cert. Bd. Occupl. therapist VA, N.Y.C., 1946-50; cons. occupl. therapist Fondo del Seguro del Estado, PR, 1950-51; dir. rehab. therapies Spring Grove State Hosp., Catonsville, Md., 1953-56; occupl. therapist Anne Arundel County Health Dept., Annapolis, Md., 1967-78; dir. occupl. therapy Ea. Shore Hosp. Ctr., Cambridge, Md., 1979-85; cons. occupl. therapist Kachina Point Health Ctr., Sedona, Ariz., 1986. Regional chmn. Conf. on revising Psychiat. Occupl. Therapy Edn., 1958-59; instr. report writing Anne Arundel C.C., Annapolis, 1974-78. Editor: Am. Jour. Occupl. Therapy, 1962—67. Active Md. Mental Health Assn., 1959—60; mem. task force on occupl. therapy edn. Md. Dept. Health, 1971—72; chmn. Anne Arundel Gov. Com. on Employment of Handicapped, 1959—63; gov.'s com. to study vocat. rehab. Md., 1960; com. mem. Annapolis Youth Ctr., 1976—78; curator Dorchester County Heritage Mus., Cambridge, 1982—83; citizen interviewer Sedona Acad. Forum, 1993, 1994; vol. Respite Care, 1994—98, Verde Valley Caregivers, 1993—; ministerial search com. Unitarian Ch. Anne Arundel County, 1962; v.p., officer Unitarian-Universalist Fellowship Flagstaff, 1988—93, v.p., 1993—97; co-moderator, founder Unitarian-Universalist Fellowship Sedona, 1994—96, pres., 1997—98, co-pres., 2001—03. Mem.: Dorchester County Mental Health Assn. (pres. 1981—84), Md. Occupl. Therapy Assn. (del. 1953—59), Am. Occupl. Therapy Assn. (chmn. history com. 1958—61), P.R. Occupl. Therapy Assn. (co-founder 1950), Sedona Muses, Nature Conservancy, Zero Population Growth, Ret. Officers Assn., Pathfinder Internat., Air Force Assn. (Barry Goldwater chpt., sec. 1991—92, 1994—), Newcomers (Sedona, pres. 1986), Severn Town Club (treas. 1965, sec. 1971—72, 1994—95), Toastmasters, Internat. Club (Annapolis, publicity chmn. 1966), Delta Delta Delta. Republican. Home: 415 Windsong Dr Sedona AZ 86336-3745

CATTO, BONNIE A. classicist, educator; b. Boston, Apr. 19, 1951; d. H. Harold and Lina Dixon (Turner) MacNeill; m. Alistair J. Catto. AB, Mt. Holyoke Coll., 1973; MA, U. Pa., 1976, PhD, 1981. Vis. instr. classics U. Mass., Amherst, 1978; asst. prof. classics Mt. Holyoke Coll., S. Hadley, Mass., 1978-87, assoc. prof., 1987-88; vis. assoc. prof. classics Middlebury (Vt.) Coll., 1988-89; assoc. prof. Assumption Coll., Worcester, Mass., 1989-97, prof., 1997—, chair fgn. lang. dept., 2000—02. Author: Lucretius: Selections from De Rerum Natura, 1998; contbr. articles to profl. jours.; mem. editl. bd. New Eng. Classical Jour., 1993-99, 2002—. Mem. Am. Philological Assn., Am. Classical League, Archaeol. Inst. Am., Classical Assn. New Eng. (pres. 1997-98, pres.-elect 1996-97, past pres. 1998-99, chmn. Edward Phinney fellowship 1998-2000), Classical Assn. Mass., Pioneer Valley Classical Assn. (pres. 1987-88), Phi Beta Kappa, Omicron Delta Kappa, Eta Sigma Phi. Avocations: cello, golf, biking, piano. Office: Assumption Coll 500 Salisbury St Worcester MA 01609

CATTO, HENRY EDWARD, former government official, former ambassador; b. Dallas, Dec. 6, 1930; s. Henry Edward and Maurine (Halsell) C.; m. Jessica Oveta Hobby, Feb. 15, 1958; children: Heather, John, William, Elizabeth. BA, Williams Coll., 1952; JD (hon.), U. Aberdeen, 1990. Ptnr. Catto & Catto, San Antonio, 1955—2003, ret., 2003; dep. rep. Orgn. Am. States, Washington, 1969-71; ambassador to El Salvador, 1971-73; U.S. chief protocol White House, Washington, 1974-76; ambassador to UN, Geneva, 1976-77; asst. sec. def. Pentagon, Washington, 1981-83; vice chmn. H & C Communications, 1983-89; amb. to U.K., 1989-91; dir. U.S. Info. Agy., Washington, 1991-93; adj. prof. U. Tex., San Antonio, 1993—. Mem. Coun. on Fgn. Rels., N.Y.C., 1973; vice chmn. The Aspen Inst. 1993—; chmn. Atlantic Coun. U.S., 1999—. Mem. Metro Club (Washington). Republican. Office: 200 Navarro San Antonio TX 78205

CATTRALL, KIM, actress; b. Liverpool, Eng., Aug. 21, 1956; Student, London Acad. Music and Dramatic Art, Banff Sch. Fine Arts, Alta., Can.; grad., Am. Acad. Dramatic Arts, N.Y.C. Actor: (films) Crossroads, 2002, The Devil and Daniel Webster, 2001, 15 Minutes, 2001; (TV films) Sex and the Matrix, 2000, 36 Hours to Die, 1999; (films) Baby Geniuses, 1999, Modern Vampires, 1998; (TV series) Sex and the City, 1998— (SAG award, 2001, Golden Globe award, 2002, Women in Film Lucy award, 1999); (TV films) Creature, 1998, Invasion, 1997; (films) Exception to the Rule, 1997, Where Truth Lies, 1996; (TV films) Every Woman's Dream, 1996; (films) Unforgettable, 1996, Live Nude Girls, 1995; (TV films) The Heidi Chronicles, 1995; (films) Above Suspicion, 1995; (TV films) OP Center, 1995, Two Golden Balls, 1994, Running Delilah, 1994; (films) Breaking Point, 1993; (TV series) Angel Falls, 1993; (TV miniseries) Wild Palms, 1993; (TV films) Double Vision, 1992, Miracle in the Wilderness, 1992; (films) Split Second, 1992, Star Trek VI: The Undiscovered Country, 1991, Bonfire of the Vanities, 1990, Honeymoon Academy, 1990, La Famiglia Buonanotte, 1989, The Return of the Musketeers, 1989, Midnight Crossing, 1988, Palais Royale, 1988, Masquerade, 1988, Mannequin, 1987, Big Trouble in Little China, 1986, Hold-Up, 1985, City Limits, 1985, Turk 182!, 1985; (TV films) Sins of the Past, 1984; (films) Police

Academy, 1984, Porky's, 1982, Ticket to Heaven, 1981, Tribute, 1980, Rosebud, 1975, others, (various TV guest appearances). Office: c/o Jeffrey Witjas William Morris Agy 151 El Camino Dr Beverly Hills CA 90212*

CATULLO, DORIS JANE, sculptor; b. Phila., Aug. 17, 1929; d. Charles J. and Jane M. (Karsner) Corrigan; m. Albert Catullo, May 18, 1949 (dec. Sept. 6, 1993); 1 child, Jayne-Leslie; m. Frank Riggenbach, May 20, 1995. Student, No. Va. C.C., Mary Washington Coll., Corcoran Sch. Art, Washington, Art League Sch., Alexandria, Va., 1986-87, Biani and Cacia Art Foundry, Pietrasanta, Italy, 1988, Bruno Cacciatori Marble Studio, 1988, Scottsdale (Ariz.) Artist Sch., 1989-90, Loveland Acad. Fine Arts, Loveland, Colo., 1996. Sculptor, 1986—. Sculptor: (bronze bas relief) Aaron Burr (at site of birth) Newark, N.J., 1997, (5 foot bronze ballerina) Attitude (lobby Concert Hall) George Mason U., 1993, (bust) Gen. Lewis B. Hershey (Selective Svc. hdqts.) Washington, William Ford Bldg., William Ford NPWA, Alexandria Park, Alexandria, Va., Norman Hamilton Bldg., Washington, Md.; exhbns. include Arts Club of Washington, 1988, Art League Gallery, Alexandria, Va., 1988, 89, Allied Artists of Am. 78th ann. exhibit, Nat. Arts Club, .Y.C., 1991, Nat. Acad. Design, N.Y., 1994, Nat. Sculpture Soc. "Making Faces", Americas Tower, N.Y.C., 1996; solo show Campbell House, Southern Pines, N.C., 2000. Recipient Elaine and Albert Ominsky award for Portraiture Knickerbocker Artists N.Y., 1992, Traditional Sculpture Catherine Lorrilard Wolfe award, 1993, Elected Signature Artist award Knickerbocker Artist Internat., 1993, Award of Excellence Art League, Alexandria, Va., 1988, 89. Mem. Nat. Sculpture Soc., Knickerbocker Artist Internat., Pen and Brush N.Y. Home: 7 Piney Pt Whispering Pines NC 28327-9475

CATUZZI, J(EROME) P(RIMO), JR., lawyer; b. N.Y.C., Aug. 23, 1938, s. J.P. Sr. and Ida (Ghezzi) C.; m. Chantal Mauricette Marais, Nov. 10, 1979; children: Daniella Firenze, Vanessa Carmen, Lee. BA, Columbia U., 1958; JD, Georgetown U., 1961; LLM in Internat. Law, NYU, 1963; PhD in Internat. Bus., La Salle U., 1998. Bar: N.Y., D.C., Asesor Legal, Spain 1973. Assoc. Baker & McKenzie, N.Y.C. and Chgo., 1963-65; gen. counsel, exec. v.p. Royal Bus. Fund Corp. (Amex), N.Y.C., 1965-72; exec. v.p., gen. counsel Holmes Protection, Inc. (Amex); internat. counsel, mng. dir. Occidental S.A., Madrid and Geneva, 1972-84; counsel U.S. Consulate, Costa del Sol, Spain, Sotogrande, S.A.; U.S. gen. counsel Soparind S.A., N.Y.C. and Paris, 1984-86; resident U.S. ptnr. Berlioz, Ferry, David, Lutz & Rochefort, N.Y.C., 1986-88; resident prin. J.P. Catuzzi, Jr. & Assocs., N.Y.C., 1989—; internat. counsel Colina la Ropa, S.A.; Mexico, 1987. Adj. prof. law and fin. C.W. Post campus Long Island U., N.Y.C., 1985—; nat. lectr. Internat. Bus. Network, N.Y.C. and Santa Monica, Calif., 1980-84; internat. cons. Eums Pharma, S.A., Geneva, Switzerland, Magellan, GmbH, MNG Industries, GmbH, Fed. Republic Germany, GEFI Holdings, Ltd., Gibraltar, ChartHouse Holdings, Ltd., Ireland, Galia, Ltd., Lausanne, Switzerland,, Centro Geotecnico, S.R.L., Rome, Geosaf, Inc., Montreal, Can., Hanover Trust House, Ltd., Ireland; internat. coun. Chropi, S.A., Greece, Igos Comm., S.A., Paris, Ireland, Lenzburg Capital Corp, Calgary, Alta., Can.; gen. internat. counsel Centrum European Securities, Ltd., Geneva, Switzerland; int. counsel golden Hat Resources, Inc., Vancouver, B.C., Canada; gen. counsel Orbis Capital Investment, Ltd., Dublin, Irelandm South Winds, LLC, Isle of Man; cons. Fond D'aide au Devel. NGO Econ. and Social Coun. UN, Geneva, N.Y.C., 1999—; pres. Ingenicard Trust, Zug, Switzerland, KI-Int. Mgmt. Group, London; internat. legal advisor, Europena Econ. Devel. Coun., 2003. Legis. cons. to Gov. Rockefeller div. human rights State of N.Y., Albany, 1968-70; mem. legal com. N.Y. County Rep. Party, 1967-72. Mem. Confrerie des Chevalier du Tastevin (N.Y.C.) (chevalier 1985—), Knights of Malta. Roman Catholic. E-mail: ilmaestro7@hotmail.com.

CATZ, BORIS, endocrinologist, educator; b. Troyanov, Russia, Feb. 15, 1923; came to U.S., 1950, naturalized, 1955; s. Jacobo and Esther (Galbmilion) C.; m. Rebecca Schechter; children: Judith, Dinah, Sarah Lea, Robert. BS, Nat. U. Mex., 1941, MD, 1947; MS in Medicine, U. So. Calif., 1951. Intern Gen. Hosp., Mexico City, Mex., 1945-46; prof. sch. medicine U. Mex., 1947-48; instr. medicine U. So. Calif., 1952-54, asst. clin. prof., 1954-59, 1959-83, clin. prof., 1983—; pvt. practice L.A., 1951-55, Beverly Hills, Calif., 1957—. Chief Thyroid Clinic L.A. County Gen. Hosp., 1955-70; sr. cons. thyroid clin. U. So. Calif., L.A. Med. Ctr., 1970—; clin. chief endocrinology Cedars-Sinai Med. Ctr., 1983-87. Author: Thyroid Case Studies, 1975, 2d edit., 1981; contbr. numerous articles on thyroidology to med. jours. Capt. U.S. Army, 1955-57. Rsch. fellow medicine U. So. Calif., 1949-51; Boris Catz lectureship in his honor Thyroid Rsch. Endowment Fund, Cedars Sinai Med. Ctr., 1985. Fellow ACP, Am. Coll. Nuclear Medicine (pres. elect 1982), Royal Soc. Medicine, Am. Thyroid Assn. (Disting. Svc. award 2001); mem. AMA, AAAS, Cedars Sinai Med. Ctr. Soc. History of Medicine (chmn.), L.A. County Med. Assn., Calif. Med. Assn., Endocrine Soc., Am. Thyroid Assn., Soc. Exptl. Biology and Medicine, Western Soc. Clin. Rsch., Am. Fedn. Clin. Rsch., Soc. Nuclear Medicine, So. Calif. Soc. Nuclear Medicine, N.Y. Acad. Scis., L.A. Soc. Internal Medicine, Collegium Salerni, Cedar Sinai Soc. History Medicine, B'nai B'rith Club, The Profl. Man's Club (past pres.), Phi Lambda Kappa. Home: 300 S El Camino Dr Beverly Hills CA 90212-4212 Office: 435 N Roxbury Dr Beverly Hills CA 90210-5027

CAUCHON, MARTIN, Canadian government official; Lic. in Civil Law, U. Ottawa, 1984; MI in Internat. Law, U. Exeter, 1990. Practiced civil and comml. law, 1985-93; mem. Parliament. Govt. of Can., Ottawa, 1993—, pres. Liberal Party Can., 1993-95, vice. chmn. standing com. pub. accts., 1994, chmn. Can.-France Inter-Parliamentary Assn., 1994-95, mem. standing com. human resources devel., 1994-96, sec. state responsible for Can. econ. devel., 1996—2002, mgr. Can.-Quebec infrastructure works agreement, cmty. futures program, min. of nat. revenue, 1999—2002, min. of justice & attorney gen., 2002—, min. with polit. responsibility for Que., 2002—. Liberal Party Can. Office: Justice Canada East Meml Bldg 4th fl 284 Wellington St K1A 0H8 Ottawa ON Canada also: Rm 312 West Block House of Commons Ottawa ON Canada K1A 0A6

CAUDILL, SAMUEL JEFFERSON, architect; b. Tulsa, June 5, 1922; s. Samuel Jefferson and Maymie Starling (Boulware) C.; m. Joy Maxwell, May 31, 1952; children: Jody Caudill Cardamone, Julie Hertzberg, Samuel Boone, Robert Maxwell, Anne Goertzen BArch, Cornell U., Ithaca, N.Y., 1946. Registered architect Colo., Calif., Idaho, Ariz. Prin. architect Samuel J. Caudill, Jr., Aspen, Colo., 1954-59, Caudill Assocs. Architects, Aspen, 1959-80; pres. Caudill Gustafson & Assocs. Architects, PC, Aspen, 1980-87, Caudill Gustafson Ross & Assocs., Architects, P.C., Aspen, 1987-92; pres., CEO Caudill Gustafson & Assocs., Architects, P.C., Aspen, 1992—. Mem. Pitkin County Planning and Zoning Commn., Colo., 1955-58; mem. outdoor edn. com. Colo. Dept. Edn., 1966-68; chmn. Pitkin County Bd. Appeals, 1970; mem. Colo. Water Quality Control Commn., 1977-80. Wildlife rep. adv. bd. Bur. Land Mgmt. Dept. Interior, Grand Junction, Colo., 1969-75, 80-85; chmn. citizens adv. com. Colo. Hwy. Dept. for I-70 through Glenwood Canyon, 1975-92; chmn. Colo. Wildlife Commn., 1978-79. Recipient Outstanding Pub. Service Bur. Land Mgmt., 1975; named to Aspen (Colo.) Hall of Fame, 1998. Fellow AIA (Community Svc. award 1976, Architect of Yr. award 1992, mem. emeritus 1995); mem. Colo. Soc. Architects (pres. 1983), Colo. Coun. on Arts and Humanities, Aspen C. of C. (pres. 1956-57), Masons, Shriners (Denver). Home: 1055 Stage Rd Aspen CO 81611-1096 Office: Caudill Gustafson & Assocs Architects PC 234 E Hopkins Ave Aspen CO 81611-1938

CAUDILL, TOM HOLDEN, governmental policy and analysis executive; b. St. Augustine, Fla., June 21, 1945; s. Julian Terrill and Alta Jane (Holden) C.; 1 child, Mara Julia. BA in History, East Tenn. State U., 1967, MA in Internat. Rels., 1977; MA in Mgmt. Sci., Webster U., 1980. Instr. English as second lang., polit. sci., mgmt. sci. U.S. Peace Corps, Loei, Thailand, 1970-73; instr. English as second lang., polit. sci., mgmt. sci. Steed Coll., Johnson City, Tenn., 1973-76; instr. Internat. Ctr. U. Tex., Austin, 1976-77; tng. specialist Air Tng. Command USAF, Lackland AFB, Tex., 1977-80, tng. specialist Logistics Command Wright-Patterson AFB, Ohio, 1980-81, logistics mgmt. specialist, 1981-85, chief, policy and procedures Internat. Logistics Ctr., 1985-88, chief policy and analysis, 1986—, chief plans and devel., 1988; dir. Arabian programs Internat. Logistics Ctr., 1991-95; exec. fellow Woodrow Wilson Sch. Govt. Princeton U., 1995-96; dep. dir. internat. programs Air Force Security Assistance Ctr., 1996; chief prodn. policy Hdqtrs. Air Force Material Command, Wright Patterson AFB, Ohio, 1997-99; dir. ops. mgmt. Air Force Security Assistance Ctr., Wright Patterson AFB, Ohio, 1999-2000, dir. case mgmt., 2000—. Vis. instr. English as a second lang., polit. sci., mgmt. sci. Antioch Coll., Yellow Springs, Ohio, 1986—; asst. dep. plans policy mgmt. systems, 1988, dir. plans and policy, 1988, tech. lead integrated logistics support, acquisition logistics div., 1988—, instr. mgmt. sci. Author: Textbook in Logistics 1988, Policy Regulations/Procedural Instructions 1986—; contbr. articles to profl. jours., 1987—. Adminstr. Refugee Assistance Program, Greene County, Ohio, 1981-84, AFS chpt. v.p.; Scoutmaster Buckeye Trails coun. Girl Scout U.S., Yellow Springs, 1982-86; active Dayton (Ohio) Coun. on World Affairs, 1984—; pres. local chpt. Am. Field Svc., Greene County, 1988—. Mem LWV (fin. chm. Greene county chpt. 1987—). Democratic. Methodist. Avocations: traveling, scouting, reading, profl. rsch. writing. Home: 3009 Highlander Dr Beavercreek OH 45432 Office: Global Mgmt Air Force Security Assistance Ctr Wright Patterson Afb OH 45433 E-mail: Tom.Caudill@wpafb.af.mil.

CAUDILL, WILLIAM HOWARD, lawyer; b. Memphis, Mar. 18, 1951; s. John W. Caudill and Elizabeth (Rivers) Stayton; m. Chris Looney, Sept. 2, 1978; children: Lucy L., W. Christopher. BSBA, U. Ark., 1973; M in Pub. Acctg., U. Tex., 1977, JD, 1978. Bar: Tex. 1978, U.S. Dist. Ct. (so. dist.) Tex. 1978, U.S. Tax Ct. 1978, U.S. Claims Ct. 1978, U.S. Ct. Appeals (5th cir.) 1978; CPA. Ptnr. Fulbright & Jaworski, LLP, Houston, 1986—; pres. Meml. Endowment Fund, 1995—. Mem. Tex. Quarter Dollar Coin Design Com., 2002-03; mem. vestry St. John the Divine Episc. Ch., Houston, 1982-86, 89-93; coun. del. Episcopal Diocese of Tex., 2003. Mem. ABA (chair spl. projects subcom., vice chair partnership com. 2000-03, tax sect. 1994-98, chair CLE subcom., 1998-2000), State Bar Tex. (bd. dirs. taxation sect. 1987-92, chair-elect 1990, chair 1991-92, dir. tax course 1986-87). Avocations: fishing, music, golf. Office: Fulbright & Jaworski LLP 1301 Mckinney St Ste 5100 Houston TX 77010-3031

CAUDRON, JOHN ARMAND, accident reconstructionist, forensic examiner; b. Compton, Calif., Sept. 26, 1944; s. Armand Robert and Evelyn Emma (Hoyt) C.; m. Marily Edith Fairfield, Mar. 16, 1968; children: Melita, Rochelle. AA, Ventura Coll., 1965; BA, Calif. State U., Fullerton, 1967; postgrad., U. Nev., 1975-78; MS, U. So. Calif., 1980. Dist. rep. GM, Reno, 1969-75; mgr. Snyder Rsch. Lab., Reno, 1976-78, v.p. El Monte, Calif., 1978-82, pres., 1982—; prin. Fire and Accident Reconstruction, Walnut, Calif., 1985—. Pub. accident reconstrn. newsletter. With U.S. Army, 1967-69. Fellow Am. Bd. Forensic Examiners (bd. cert.); mem. ASCE, NSPE, Am. Soc. Safety Engrs., Nat. Fire Protection Assn., Geol. Soc. Am., Firearms Rsch. and Identification Assn. (pres. 1978—), Am. Soc. Metals, Nat. Safety Coun., Nat. Assn. Profl. Accident Reconstruction Specialists. Republican. Baptist. Avocations: hiking, traveling, photography. Office: Fire & Accident Reconstruction PO Box 620 Wrightwood CA 92397-0620 Fax: (760) 249-1098. E-mail: m1892@earthlink.net.

CAUGHFIELD, LANCE ERIC, lawyer; b. Abilene, Tex., Jan. 14, 1970; s. Dwight A. and Alice M. Caughfield; m. Adrienne Helenne Rigsby, May 22, 1993. BA i n Comm., BA in Polit. Sci., Abilene Christian U., 1993; JD, U. Tex., 1996. Bar: Tex. 1996, U.S. Cir. Ct. (5th cir.) Tex. 2001. Intern Supreme Ct. Tex., Austin, 1995; assoc. Fletcher & Springer, LLP, Dallas, 1996—. Articles editor Tex. Intellectual Property Law Jour., 1996; contbr. articles to profl. jours. Mem. Abilene Christian U. Alumni Assn. (dir. 1993-2001, bd. dirs.). Republican. Mem. Church of Christ. Avocations: woodworking, militaria, scuba diving. Office: Fletcher & Springer LLP 8750 N CentralExpy 16th Floor Dallas TX 75231 Fax: 214-987-9866. E-mail: lance@fletchspring.com.

CAUGHLIN, STEPHENIE JANE, organic farmer; b. McAllen, Tex., July 23, 1948; d. James Daniel and Betty Jane (Warnock) C. BA in Family Econs., San Diego State U., 1972, MEd, 1973; M in Psychology, U.S. Internat. U., San Diego, 1979. Cert. secondary life tchr. Owner, mgr. Minute Maid Svc., San Diego, 1970-75; prin. Rainbow Fin. Svc., San Diego, 1975-78; tchr. San Diego Unified Sch. Dist., 1973-80; mortgage broker Santa Fe Mortgage Co., San Diego, 1984-88; owner, sec. Nationwide Metals Corp.; owner, gen. mgr. Seabreeze Organic Farm, 1984—. Sec. Arroyo Sorrento Assn., Del Mar, Calif., 1978—. Co-founder Slow Foods San Diego Convivium, treas. Mem. Greenpeace Nature Conservancy, DAR, Sierra Club, Jobs Daus. Republican. Avocations: horseback riding, swimming, skiing, gardening. Home and Office: 3909 Arroyo Sorrento Rd San Diego CA 92130-2610 E-mail: seabreezed@sbcglobal.net.

CAULFIELD, JEROME JOSEPH, lawyer; b. Phila., Aug. 9, 1949; s. Charles Patrick and Pauline Gertrude (Riley) C.; m. Rosita Noyes Murray, Aug. 4, 1973; children: Andrew, Alexandra. BS in Fgn. Svc., Georgetown U., 1971; JD, Am. U., 1974; LLM, NYU, 1977. Bar: N.Y. 1976, U.S. Tax Ct. 1980, U.S. Dist. Ct. (so. dist.) N.Y. 1986. Assoc. Carter, Ledyard & Milburn, N.Y.C., 1978-83, ptnr., 1984-99, mng. ptnr., 1999—2003, mem. exec. com., 2003—. Contbr. articles to profl. jours. Bd. dirs. Impact on Hunger Inc., 1984-86. Mem. ABA, N.Y. State Bar Assn., Assn. of Bar of City of N.Y. Roman Catholic. Home: 35 Stanwich Rd Greenwich CT 06830-4842 Office: Carter Ledyard & Milburn 2 Wall St Fl 13 New York NY 10005-2072 E-mail: caulfield@clm.com.

CAULFIELD, JOAN, director, educator; b. St. Joseph, Mo., July 17, 1943; d. Joseph A. and Jane (Lisenby) Caulfield; m. Alan Warne, Sept. 7, 1996. BS in Edn. cum laude, U. Mo., 1963, MA in Spanish, 1965, PhD, 1978; postgrad. (Mexican Govt. scholar), Nat. U. Mexico, 1962-63. TV tchr. Spanish Kansas City (Mo.) pub. schs., 1963-68; tchr. Spanish, French Bingham Jr. High Schs., Kansas City, 1968-78; asst. prin. S.E. High Sch., Kansas City, 1984; prin. Nowlin Jr. High Sch., Independence, Mo., 1984-86, Lincoln Coll. Preparatory Acad., Kansas City, Mo., 1986-88; asst. supt. Kansas City, 1988-89; part-time instr. U. Mo.-Kansas City; dir. English Inst. Rockhurst Coll., summers 1972-75; coord. sch. coll. rels. Rockhurst U., 1989-2001, chmn. edn. dept.; adj. prof. St. Louis U.; pres., CEO The Brain Inc., 2001—. Mem. nat. steering com. Brain-Based Learning Network, facilitator; assessor dept. elem. and secondary edn. State Mo.; mem. women's coun. bd. U. Mo.-Kansas City, 1994—; pres., CEO The Brain Inc.; vis. social scientist Midwest Rsch. Inst. Contbr. articles to profl. jours. Co-Author: Inciting Learning: a Guirde to Brain Compatible Instr. Active Sister City Commn., Kansas City, 1980—, Kans.' Quality Performance Assessment Team, Metro-Vision Task Force; ofcl. translator to mayor on trip to Seville, Spaine, 1969; bd. dirs. Kansas City chpt. NCCJ, Expo '92 World's Fair, Seville, Spain, translator 1992, St. Theresa's Acad., 1991-94, Kansas City Acad. of Learning; selected leadership training Greater Mo.; trainer Harmony in a World of Difference, 1989-93; task force C. of C. bd. dirs. Girls to Women; edn. alumni bd. U. Mo., Kansas City; del. leader Spain People to People Internat., 1997; trustee Kansas City Pub. Libr. mem. mayor's commn., Kansas City. Named Outstanding Secondary Educator, 1973. Mem.: MLA (contbr. jour.), ASCD, Mo. Mid. Sch. Assn. (contbr. jour.), Am. Assn. Tchrs. Spanish and Portuguese, Nat. Assn. Secondary Sch. Prins., Magnet Sch. Am. (contbr. jour.), Friends of Art, Friends of Seville, Sigma Delta Pi, Phi Kappa Phi, Delta Kappa Gamma (state scholar 1977—78, contbr. jour. Bull.), Phi Delta Kappa, Phi Sigma Iota, Kappa Delta Pi. Presbyterian. Home: 431 W 70th St Kansas City MO 64113-2022 E-mail: joancaulfield@prodigy.net.

CAULFIELD, PATRICK FRANCIS, physician; b. Moycullen, Ireland, Oct. 4, 1944, came to U.S., 1968; s. James and Margaret Ann (Kyne) C.; m. Lois Sawyer, Jan. 1, 1970; children: Brian, Heather, Christopher. BA, St. Anselm Coll., Manchester, N.H., 1974; MD, U. N.Mex., 1978. Diplomate Am. Bd. Family Practice. Family practice inern Med. Ctr. Hosp. Vt., Burlington, 1978-79, resident in family practice, 1979-81; attending physician Nat. Health Svc. Corps, Tulsa, 1981-84, Coll. Hwy. Family Practice, Southwick, Mass., 1984-85; asst. prof. Albany (N.Y.) Med. Coll., 1985-91, assoc. prof., 1991-99, interim chmn. dept. family practice, 1993-97, prof., 1999; chief profl. svcs. 364th Field Hosp., Albany, 1996—. Med. dir. Guildcare, Albany, 1995-2000, Eden Park Nursing Home, Albany, 1986-87. Mem. Am. Acad. Family Practice (chmn. Albany chpt. 1999-2001), N.Y. State Acad. Family Practice (vice chair geriatrics 1996-98), Assn. Mil. Surgeons U.S., Soc. Tchrs. Family Medicine. Democrat. Roman Catholic. Avocations: walking, cycling. Office: Capital Care Family Practice 2524 Rte 9 W Ravena NY 12143 E-mail: pcaulfie@capcare.com.

CAUNA, NIKOLAJS, physician, medical educator, scientist; b. Riga, Latvia, Apr. 4, 1914; came to U.S., 1961; s. Nikolajs and Marija (Manika) C.; m. Dzidra Priede, June 23, 1942. MD, U. Latvia, 1942; M.Sc., U. Durham (Eng.), 1954, D.Sc., 1961. Lectr. anatomy U. Latvia, Riga, 1942-44; gen. practice medicine Sarsted and Eschershausen, West Germany, 1944-46; acting chmn. anatomy dept. Baltic U., Hamburg, Germany, 1946-48; lectr. anatomy Med. Sch. U. Durham (Eng.), 1948-57, reader, 1958-61; prof. anatomy Sch. Medicine U. Pitts., 1961-84, chmn., 1975-83, prof. emeritus, 1984—. Mem. editorial bd. Anat. Record, 1969-91, Histology and Histopathology, 1985-90; contbr. articles to profl. jours. Recipient Golden Apple award (tchr. of year) U. Pitts., 1964, 67, 73; research grantee Royal Soc. Eng., 1958-60; USPHS grantee, 1962-82; Am. Cancer Inst. grantee, 1961. Mem. AAAS, Anat. Soc. Gt. Britain and Ireland, Am. Assn. Anatomists, Royal Micros. Soc., Anatomische Gesellschaft, Histochem. Soc., Am. Soc. Cell Biology, Internat. Assn. for Study Pain. Achievements include research in normal and pathol. sensory receptor organs, in autonomic control mechanism, in devel. and evolution of sense organs and limbs. Home: 5850 Meridian Rd Apt 311C Gibsonia PA 15044-4811

CAUSEY, ROBERT LOUIS, philosopher, educator, consultant; b. Los Angeles, Apr. 13, 1941; s. Robert Vester and Gertrude (Bloom) C.; m. Sandra Lee Shliff, Jan. 25, 1964; children— Britt Ann, Diane Sue. BS, Calif. Inst. Tech., 1963; PhD, U. Calif., Berkeley, 1967. Asst. prof. dept. philosophy U. Tex., Austin, 1967-73, asso. prof., 1973-79, prof., 1979—, chmn. dept. philosophy, 1980-88; co-founder, assoc. dir. U. Tex. Artificial Intelligence Lab., 1984-97. Cons. NSF, 1979-81; spkr. numerous confs., univs., broadcasts; cons. to U.S. Army and various pvt. corps. and univs. Author: Supplement to Logic, Sets, and Recursion, 2002, Logic, Sets, and Recursion, 1994, rev. edit., 2001, Unity of Science, 1977; co-author: Introduction to Artificial Intelligence and Expert Systems, Video-Course, 1988; contbr. articles and revs. to philos. and sci. jours.; author various ednl. and exptl. computer programs. NSF fellow, NSF grantee, 1973-74, 79-81; U. Tex. Rsch. Inst. grantee, 1979; rsch. scientist, U.S. Army Rsch. Office grantee, 1984-89; U. Tex. Dean's fellow, 1997. Mem.: Assn. Computing Machinery, Am. Assn. Artificial Intelligence, Philosophy of Sci. Assn. (bd. govs. 1980—81), Am. Philos. Assn. (mem. com. on computer use in philosophy 1994—97, rev. editor electronic newsletter on philosophy and computers 1996—2001). Achievements include development of new system for automated defeasible reasoning. Office: Univ Tex Dept of Philosophy Waggener Hall # 316 Austin TX 78712

CAUTHEN, CHARLES EDWARD, JR., retail executive, business consultant; b. Columbia, S.C., Oct. 26, 1931; s. Charles Edward and Rachel (Macaulay) C.; m. Hazel Electa Peery, June 13, 1959; children: Portia Cauthen White, Rachel Cauthen Rohrer, Sara Cauthen Landfear, Sidney Cauthen Bullard. BA, Wofford Coll., 1952; cert. Charlotte Meml. Hosp., Sch. Hosp. Adminstrn., 1956; MS in Bus. Adminstrn. and Labor Mgmt., PhD in Bus. Adminstrn., Kennedy-Western U., 1986; LLD, Montreat-Anderson Coll., 1991. Asst. adminstr. Union Meml. Hosp., Monroe, N.C., 1956-58; adminstr. Lowrance Hosp., Inc., Mooresville, N.C., 1958-61; v.p., mgr. Va. Acme Market, Bluefield, W.Va., 1961-68; v.p. Acme Markets and A-Mart Stores (now Acme Markets of Tazewell, Va., Inc.), North Tazewell, Va., 1965-87; adminstr. Lowrance Hosp., Inc., Mooresville, N.C., 1958-61; v.p., mgr. Va. Acme Market, Bluefield, W.Va., 1961-68; v.p. Acme Markets and A-Mart Stores (now Acme Markets of tazewell, Va., Inc.), North Tazewell, Va., 1965-87, exec. v.p., 1968-71, pres., 1971-87; provost King Coll., Bristol, Tenn., 1987—92, pres., 1987—92, Doran Devel. Corp., 1971-87, Big A Market, Inc., 1981-87. Cons. in field, 1992—2000. Author: Evaluation of the Small Company for Strategic Planning, Merger or Acquisition, 1987. Deacon, elder, trustee Westminster Presbyn. Ch., Bluefield, W.Va.; mem. Internat. Adv. Coun. Han Nam U., Korea, 1991; mem. exec. bd., 1992-2001; bd. dirs. Internat. Inst. Christian Studies, 1993-97, Tenn. Inst. for Pub. Policy, 1994-2001. Served to 1st lt. AUS, 1952-54. Mem. W.Va. Assn. Retail Grocers (v.p., dir. 1968-82), Va. Food Dealers Assn. (dir. 1978), Bluefield Sales Exec. Club (dir. 1965-67), Rotary (bd. dirs. 1966). Republican. Home and Office: 100 Muirfield Williamsburg VA 23188

CAUTHEN, KENNETH, theological educator; b. Milner, Ga., Mar. 10, 1930; s. John Wilfred and Beulah Harris C.; m. Eloise Nelson, Dec. 19, 1954 (div. Aug. 1984); children: Paul, Nancy, Melissa; m. Gloria Hoyer Fish, Oct. 13, 1984. AB, Mercer U., 1950; BDiv, Yale Divinity Sch., 1953; MA, Emory U., 1955; PhD, Vanderbilt U., 1959. Pastor Locust Grove (Ga.) Bapt. Ch., 1953-55; prof. Christian ethics Mercer U., Macon, Ga., 1957-61; prof. theology Crozer Theol. Sem., Chester, Pa., 1961-70, Colgate-Rochester/Crozer Theol. Sem., Rochester, N.Y., 1970-92, prof. theology emeritus, 1992—. Author: The Impact of American Religious Liberalism, 1962, The Triumph of Suffering Love, 1966, Christian Biopolitics, 1971, The Ethics of Enjoyment, 1975, Process Ethics, 1984, Systematic Theology, 1986, The Passion for Equality, 1987, Theological Biology, 1991, Toward A New Modernism, 1997, The Many Faces of Evil, 1997, The Ethics of Assisted Death, 1999, The Ethics of Belief, 2001, Rejoicing in Lifes "Melissa Moments", 2002, I Don't Care What the Bible Says, 2003. Am. Assn. Theol. Schs. grantee, 1971, Assn. Theol. Schs. grantee, 1990; Ford fellow, 1955-57, Postdoctoral fellow Advanced Study Sci. and Theology, Meadville Theol. Sem., 1966-67. Home: 46 Azalea Rd Rochester NY 14620 E-mail: kenc@frontiernet.net.

CAUTHORNE-BURNETTE, TAMERA DIANNE, family nurse practitioner, healthcare consultant; b. Richmond, Va., Apr. 13, 1961; d. Robert Francis Cauthorne and Lois Avery (Lloyd) Cumashot; m. William Nichols Burnette, Dec. 3, 1983. BSN, U. Va., 1983; postgrad., Med. U. S.C., 1988; MSN, Old Dominion U., 1993, grad. cert. in women's studies, 1994; postgrad., Univ. Coll., Oxford (Eng.) U., 1996. RN, Va.; family nurse practitioner. Staff nurse, charge nurse gynecology-oncology unit U. Va. Med. Ctr., Charlottesville, 1983, staff nurse, charge nurse high-risk labor and delivery, ICU, 1984-85; staff nurse, charge nurse, preceptor med. ICU Med. U. S.C., 1985-87, staff nurse ICU, 1988; staff nurse, charge nurse med.-surg. ICU, progressive care Stuart Cir. Hosp., Richmond, Va., 1988-90; staff nurse pediat. and neonatal ICU Childrens' Hosp. of the King's Dau., Norfolk, Va., 1990, staff nurse, team leader neonatal ICU, 1990-91; pvt. health care cons., 1993—; with Delmar Pub., 1994—; pres. The Foxmont Co., LLC, 1995—; with Sussex Ctrl. Health Ctr., 1995; men's responsibility clinic coord. Planned Parenthood, 1996; chief nurse practitioner med. svcs. Va. League Planned Parenthood, 1997-99; pvt. practice Air Park Med., Ashland, Va., 1999-2001; with James Jones and Assocs. Ob-gyn., 2001. Cons. Old Dominion U. Coll. Health Sci., Sch. Nursing, 1993—, undergrad. clin. facility, 1994—; condr. analysis of Russian and Ukrainian health care system; breast self-exam instr. Am. Cancer Soc., 1982—; presenter at profl. confs.; mng. mem. The Foxmont Co., L.L.C.; mem. adj. faculty Sch. Nursing U. Va., 1996; primary med. provider Va. League Planned Parenthood, 1997; mem. clin. faculty sch. of nursing Va. Commonwealth U., 1999, assoc. prof., 2001. Contbg. author A Quick Reference for Health Assessment, 1997, Clin. Companion to Health Assessment and Physical Examination, 1998; contbr. articles to profl. jours. Vol. Ronald McDonald House, 1980-83; docent Spoleto Festival USA, 1984-92, MacArthur Meml. Mus., 1991; vol. receptionist info. ctr. Gibbes Art Gallery, 1987-89; vol. ARC Blood Donation Ctr., 1986-92; mem. coun. U. Va. Coll. of Health Scis.; mem. adv. coun. U. Va. Sch. Nursing, 1997—; chmn. Va. Nurses PAC, 2002. Named Vol. of Yr., U. Va. Sch. Nursing. Fellow Internat. Pedagogical Acad./Moswoc. Order of Omega Nat. Honor Soc., Raven Honor Soc. U. Va., Sorenson Inst. Polit. Leadership U. Va.; mem. AACN, DAR, AAUW, Va. Coalition for Nurse Practitioners, U. Va. Sch. Nursing Alumnae Assn. (pres., CEO 1994—, adv. coun. 1997—), Jr. League Va. (chair state pub. affairs com.), Virginians Patient Choice Coalition, Jr. League Norfolk and Virginia Beach (state pub. affairs vice chmn./lobbyist 1995), Daus. of Confederacy, Carolina Art Assn., S.C. Hist. Soc., Confederate Meml. Lit. Soc., U. Va. Coll. Health Scis. Coun., Alpha Delta Pi (chmn. nat. panhellenic rels. com., nat. by-laws and resolutions com.), Sigma Theta Tau. Avocations: riding, raising and showing thoroughbred racing horses, collecting sporting art, foxhunting.

CAVA, MICHAEL PATRICK, chemist, educator; b. Bklyn., Feb. 13, 1926; s. Michael R. and Catherine (Lombardo) C.; m. Esther Laden, June 11, 1951; 1 son, John M.; m. Armelle Laden-Guinard, Dec. 21, 1998. BS, Harvard U., 1946; MS, U. Mich., 1948, PhD, 1951. Postdoctoral fellow Harvard, 1951-53; from asst. prof. to prof. Ohio State U., 1953-65; prof. Wayne State U., Detroit, 1965-69; prof. chemistry U. Pa., Phila., 1969-85; prof. U. Ala., Tuscaloosa, 1985—. Mem. study sect. NIH, 1987-91. Author: (with M.J. Mitchell) Cyclobutadiene and Related Compounds, 1967; also numerous articles. Alfred P. Sloan Found. fellow. Mem. Am. Chem. Soc. Achievements include research on organic sulphur, selenium and tellurium compounds; organic condrs., benzocyclobutenes, natural products chemistry. Home: 440 Northshore Dr Tuscaloosa AL 35406-2012 Office: U Ala Dept Chemistry PO Box 870336 Tuscaloosa AL 35487-0001

CAVAGLIERI, GIORGIO, architect; b. Venice, Italy, Aug. 1, 1911; came to U.S., 1939, naturalized, 1943; s. Gino and Margherita (Maroni) C.; m. Norma Sanford, Jan. 31, 1942. D. Archtl. Engring, Sup. Sch. Engring., Milan, Italy, 1932; student spl. city planning, Sup. Sch. Architecture, Rome, 1934. Apprenticeship N.Y. office R. Candela, Balt. offices J.O. Chertkof, also; Benjamin Franklin, architect, prior to World War II; propr. own firm N.Y.C., 1946—; adj. prof. Sch. Architecture, Pratt Inst., 1956-69. Trustee Nat. Inst. Archtl. Edn., chmn. trustees, 1957-60; academician NAD. *Drafted in 1935 during the Ethiopian war, was sent as a lieutenant of Air Force Engineers, to supervise construction of the Airport of El-Adem 16Km. South of Tobruk, Lybia. Dismissed in 1938 from the position of Instructor and lecturer at the Architectural and Engineering faculties of the Superior School of Engineering (Politecnico) of Milan, when anti-semitic laws were established in Italy, decided to emigrate to the U.S. Drafted in the U.S. Army Corps of Engineers in 1943. Landing in Normandy in the European campaign was decorated with five Battle Stars and a Bronze Star.* Prin. works in Milan, prior to World War II; prin. works include in the U.S., Fenton Hall reconstrn. Fredonia (N.Y.) Coll., Astor Library restoration and conversion to N.Y. Pub. Theatre, N.Y. Shakespeare Festival, Jefferson Market Courthouse restoration and conversion to N.Y. Pub. Library, Branch Library, Riverdale, N.Y., N.Y. Pub. Library main bldg. Periodical Dept., Pub. Sch. 32, S.I., Kip's Bay br. library; assoc. architect Pension Bldg./Nat. Mus. Bldg. Arts, Washington; architect-in-charge Rosary Hall, U.S. Mil. Acad. Mus.; Eldridge St. Synagogue restoration, N.Y.C.; Chapel of the Good Shepherd reconstrn., Roosevelt Island, N.Y. Served with C.E. AUS, 1943-45. Decorated Bronze Star; recipient Honor award A.I.A., 1968, House Improvement award, 1961; Bard award, spl. citation City Club N.Y., 1968; Illuminated scroll Municipal Art Soc. N.Y., 1966; Clients award N.Y. State Assn. Architects, 1964; Gold medal honor architecture Archtl. League N.Y., 1956; winner 1st prize nat. competition auditorium Rome, 1935, 3d prize competition city hosp. Cuneo, Italy., 1938, hon. mention Armed Forces bldgs. Rome World's Fair, 1938, 3d prize N.Y.C. Bd. Edn. archtl. competition for modernization Bronx Jr. High Sch., 1967; certificate of merit for excellence in design N.Y. State Assn. Architects, 1976; 1st honor award ALA/AIA, 1976; Sidney L. Strauss Meml. N.Y. Soc. Architects, 1977; recipient award Excellence in Design N.Y.C. Art Commn., 1992, Design award for Preservation Gen. Svcs. Admnistrn., 1992; Outstanding Cert. for Competition N.Y.C. Bd. Edn., 1997, Lucy Moses award N.Y. Landmark Conservancy, 2002, Bronze medal Fine Art Fedn. N.Y., 2002. Fellow AIA (pres. N.Y. chpt. 1970-71, Disting. Architecture award 1985, Honor award 1986, Presdl. citation 1990, Medal of Honor N.Y. chpt. 1990); mem. Mcpl. Art Soc. N.Y. (pres. 1963-65, 4th Annual Preservation award 1992), Archtl. League N.Y. (v.p. 1961-63), Am. Soc. Interior Designers (v.p. 1984-85, 87-88, medal 1985), Fine Arts Fedn. N.Y. (pres. 1970-72, 74-76, 2000-01, Centennial Yr. honoree 1995), N.Y. Coun. Arts and Govt., N.Y.C. Victorian Soc. (Outstanding in Preservation award 1986). Democrat. Home: 75 Central Park W New York NY 10023-6011 Office: 250 W 57th St Ste 2511 New York NY 10107

CAVAGNA, ANTONINO FORTUNATO, management consultant; b. Brescia, Italy, Aug. 5, 1938; s. Enos and Agnese C.; m. Gerlinde Irene Patzak, Dec. 11, 1967; children: Marc, Elsa, Thomas. Degree in economy, Parma U., Italy, 1963; M, INSEAD, Paris, 1973; postgrad., Harvard U., 2002. Budget mgr. Edison Chimica, Milan, Italy, 1960-65; mgr. long range planning Nestle, Milan, Italy, 1967-68; cons. A.T. Kearney, Milan, Italy, 1969-70; mgr. P.M.M.C Co., Milan, Italy, 1970-74; mng. dir. Agrifull Group, Rome, Italy, 1975-77; gen. mgr. IRCA Group, Treviso, Italy, 1978-81; CEO Marelli Motori, Arzignano, Italy, 1993-97, Marzoli Inc., Palazzolo, Italy, 1987-99. Pres. Industries Province Vicenza, 1997-98. Co-author: Incentivazione E Finanziamento Innovazione, 1981, Fusioni E Acquisizioni, 1992; contbr. artilces to profl. jours. Pres. Lyons Club, Jebino, 1985. Lt. Italian Mil., 1964-65. Named Hon. Knight of Italian Republic, Pres. of Italian Republic, 1997. Mem. Journalist Assn. Avocations: swimming, water polo, soccer. Home: Via Privata San Vigilio 1 25049 Iseo (Brescia) Italy

CAVALIERE, TERRI ANGELA, neonatal nurse practitioner; b. Bklyn. d. Antonio and Anna (Bonica) Salerno; m. Anthony J. Cavaliere, Dec. 11, 1982. BSN, Hunter Coll., 1970; MS, U. Calif., San Francisco, 1973. RN, N.Y.; cert. neonatal nurse practitioner. Staff nurse King's County Hosp., Bklyn., 1970-72, U. Calif.-San Francisco Moffett Hosp., 1973-74, sr. staff nurse, 1974-75; asst. head nurse NICU-North Shore U. Hosp., Manhasset, N.Y., 1976-77; clin. nurse specialist Winthrop U. Hosp., Mineola, N.Y., 1977-80; neonatal practitioner North Shore U. Hosp., Manhasset, 1982—; clin. preceptor grad. program in nursing SUNY, Stony Brook, 1988—, Adelphi U., Garden City, N.Y., 1984-93, Columbia U., 1995-96. Mem. NCC test com. for neonatal nurse practitioner cert. exam 1990—; faculty/cons. nurse practitioner program Harlem Hosp., N.Y.C., 1991-94; clin. preceptor grad. program in Nursing Adelphi U., Garden City, N.Y., 1984-90, asst. adj. prof. Sch . Continuing Edn. in Nursing, 1978-80, asst. clin. prof, perinatal nurse clinician program, 1976-77; asst. adj. prof. Sch. Continuing Edn. in Nursing Adelphi U.; clin. asst. prof. Sch. Nursing Neonatal Nurse Practitioner, Program SUNY, Stony Brook, 1994—; ednl. Ednl. book reviewer: Nurse's Book Club, 1984; videotape reviewer Am. Jour. Nursing, 1985, manuscript reviewer W.B. Saunders Nursing Texts, 1990—91, Neonatal Network, 1991—; contbr. articles to profl. jours, to textbooks. Recipient Diana Dolgin Nurse of Yr. award March of Dimes, 1992, N.Y. State Nurse of Distinction Continuing Edn. grant, 1995. Mem. N.Y. State Nurses Assn. (coun. on ethical practice in nursing 1987-91), Nat. Assn. Neonatal Nurses (chair NNP edn. stds. task force 1999-2002), L.I. Assn. Neonatal Nurses (pres. 1994-95, past pres., Disting. Svc. award 2002), Nurse Practitioner Forum North Shore Health Sys. (chair 1999), N.Y. State Perinatal Assn., Patient Care Svcs. Ethics Com. North Shore U. Hosp. Manhasset (co-chair 2000). Office: North Shore Univ Hosp 300 Community Dr Manhasset NY 11030-3801

CAVALLARO, JOSEPH JOHN, retired microbiologist; b. Lawrence, Mass., Mar. 18, 1932; s. John and Salvatrice (Zappala) C.; m. Margaret Hare, Aug. 24, 1964; children: Theresa Margaret, Sandra Marie; m. Kathleen Frances Kraus, Dec. 2, 1972; children: Elizabeth Camille, Danielle Kay, Gina Kathleen. BS, Tufts U., 1952; MS, U. Mass., 1954; PhD, U. Mich., 1966. Pub. health sanitarian Hartford (Conn.) Health Dept., 1954-55, 57-61; tchg. asssoc. dept. microbiology U. Mass., Amherst, 1961-62; rsch. virologist Med. Rsch. Labs. Charles Pfizer & Co., Groton, Conn., 1966-67; rsch. assoc. dept. epidemiology Sch. Pub. Health U. Mich., Ann Arbor, 1967-70; microbiology, diagnostic immunology tng. br. Ctrs. for Disease Control, Atlanta, 1971-86, rsch. microbiologist anaerobic bacteria br., 1986-2000; ret., 2000. Lectr. resident pathologists Grady Meml. Hosp., Atlanta, 1975; asst. prof. pathology Morehouse Sch. Medicine, 1982-85, clin. assoc. prof., 1986-97; adj. asst. prof. pathology and lab. medicine Emory U. Sch. of Medicine, 1985-2000; cons. Pan Am. Health Orgn., Colombia and Brazil, 1976-77, WHO, 2003. Prin. author/co-author over 12 lab manuals; contbr. over 30 articles to profl. jours., 3 chpts. to books. Served with M.C., AUS, 1955-57. Registered specialist microbiologist Nat. Registry Microbiologist, Am. Acad. Microbiologist. Fellow Am. Acad. Microbiology; mem. Am. Soc. Microbiology, Am. Assn. Immunologists, N.Y. Acad. Sci., KC, Sigma Xi. Democrat. Home: 1325 Balsam Dr Decatur GA 30033-2905 E-mail: cavallaro@mindspring.com.

CAVALLARO, MARY CAROLINE, retired physics educator; b. Everett, Mass., Feb. 2, 1932; d. Joseph and Domenica Cavallaro. BS, Simmons Coll., 1954, MS, 1956; EdD, Ind. U., 1972; postgrad., Tufts U., 1980-81. Inst. math. and physics Sweet Briar (Va.) Coll., 1955-56; instr. physics Simmons Coll., Boston, 1956-58, Randolph-Macon Woman's Coll., Lynchburg, Va., 1958-59; lectr. Boston U., 1960-61; asst. prof. physics Framingham (Mass.) State Coll., 1961-63; prof. physics Salem (Mass.) State Coll., 1963-94; ret., 1994. Cons. Introductory Phys. Scis. group Edn. Devel. Ctr., Newton, 1966; asst. to dean grad. studies Salem State Coll., 1971-78, coord. pre-engring. program, 1980-89, coord. secondary edn. program, 1989-91; vis. scholar Harvard U. Grad. Sch. Edn., Cambridge, Mass., 1989-90. Grantee, NSF, 1962. Mem.: MTA, NEA, AAUW, Am. Inst. Physics, Am. Assn. Physics Tchrs., Am. Phys. Soc., Ind. U. Alumnae Assn., Simmons Coll. Alumnae Assn., Pi Lambda Theta. Avocations: travel, reading, swimming. Home: 14 Winford Way Medford MA 02155-1526

CAVALLINI, DONNA FRANCESCA, law librarian; b. St. Louis, Nov. 3, 1962; d. Giovanni Iader and Yolanda Marie (Boveri) Cavallini; m. Jeffrey Alan Mills, Jan. 13, 1986 (div. Nov. 1991); m. Gregory Joseph Kern, Aug. 31, 2000. BA, Washington U., St. Louis, 1983; JD, St. Louis U., 1990. Ref. libr. Huey, Guilday, Kuersteiner & Tucker, P.A., Tallahassee, 1988-91; libr. program adminstr. Office of the Atty. Gen., Tallahassee, 1991-96; ref. libr. Kilpatrick Stockton, LLP, Atlanta, 1996-99, mgr. competitive knowledge, 1999—. Fla. State Ct. and County Law Librs. scholar, 1992; recipient Davis Productivity award Fla. Taxwatch Inc., 1994. Mem. Am. Assn. Law Librs., Soc. Competitive Intelligence Profls. Home: 1961 Dorset Dr Fort Collins CO 80526 Office: 1100 W Peachtree St NW Ste 2800 Atlanta GA 30309-3609

CAVALLO, JO ANN, Italian language educator; b. Summit, N.J., May 21, 1959; d. Joseph Anthony and Jacqueline Amelia (Toth) C.; children: Maria Cristina, Alberto Joseph. Student, U. Florence, Italy, 1979-80, U. Valencia, Spain, 1980; BA, Rutgers U., 1981; student, Inst. French Studies, Avignon, 1982; MA, Yale U., 1984, PhD, 1987. Instr. dept. Italian Yale U., New Haven, 1983-86, instr. dept. Spanish, 1986-87, instr. Sch. Music, 1986-87; asst. prof. U. Wash., Seattle, 1987-88; assoc. prof. of Italian Columbia U., N.Y.C., 1988—. Mem. sci. com. Boiardo Quincentennial Celebration, Italy, 1993-94; founder and program dir. Columbia U. Summer Program in Scandiano, Italy, 1995—. Author: Boiardo's Orlando Innamorato: An Ethics of Desire, 1993; co-editor: Fortune and Romance: Boiardo in America, 1998; adapter: Orlando Innamorato for young readers, 2001. Recipient scholarship Nat. Italian Am. Found., Washington, 1986, fellowship grant Columbia U. Coun. for Rsch. in the Humanities, 1989, 90. Mem. MLA, Am. Assn. for Tchrs. of Italian, Am. Assn. of Italian Studies, Renaissance Soc. Am., Phi Beta Kappa. Roman Catholic. Home: 733 Buchanan St Toms River NJ 08753-7207 Office: Columbia Univ Italian Dept 1130 Amsterdam Ave Hamilton Hall Rm 514 New York NY 10027

CAVALLO, TITO, physician; b. São Paulo, Brazil, Feb. 9, 1936; came to U.S., 1968; s. Fiore and Carmen (Martin); m. Anita Hahn, Jan. 28, 1966; children: Alexander, Charles. MD, U. São Paulo, 1963; MA (hon.), Brown U., R.I., 1987. Diplomate Am. Bd. Anatomic Pathology. Instr. pathology U. São Paulo, 1964-68; resident, chief resident Peter Bent Brigham/Mallory Inst., Boston, 1968-72; instr. pathology Harvard Med. Sch., Boston, 1971-72, Boston U., 1971-72; asst. instr. pathology Mallory Inst., Boston, 1971-72; assoc. prof. U. Pitts., Penn., 1972-77; prof. U. Tex., Galveston, 1977-86, Brown U., Providence, 1986-91, U. Cin., 1991—. Mem. study sects. NIH, Bethesda, 1974-95; trustee, bd. dirs. Acad. Pathology Assocs., Cin., 1991—; bd. dirs. Kidney Found., Cin., 1995—; trustee Med. Ctr. U. Cin., 1998—. Grantee Health Svc. Rsch. Found., Pitts., 1973-75, NIH, Bethesda, 1975-95. Mem. Internat. Acad. Pathology, Am. Assn. for Investigative Pathology, Am. Soc. Nephrology, Am. Soc. Transplant. Office: U Cin 231 Albert Sabin Way Cincinnati OH 45267-0329 E-mail: tito.cavallo@uc.edu

CAVALUZZI, ANTHONY DAVID, English studies educator; b. Newark, Jan. 6, 1952; s. Anthony Rudolf and Elaine Fannie (Quigley) C. BA in English, Montclair State Coll., 1973, MA in English, 1977; cert. in African studies, U. Nairobi, Kenya, 1977; ABD in English Edn., NYU, 1981; cert. humanities Birkbeck Coll., U. London, 1976. Tchr. English West Side High Sch., Newark, 1973-79; instr. English Middlesex County Coll., Edison, N.J., 1979-81; prof. English Adirondack C.C., Queensbury, N.Y., 1982—. Adj. instr. English Rutgers U., Newark, 1979-81. Contbr. articles to cultural mags. Mem. Am.-Italian Hist. Assn., African Lit. Assn., N.Y. African Studies Assn. (treas.). Home: 639 Gansevoort Rd South Glens Falls NY 12803-5231 Office: Adirondack C C Bay Rd Queensbury NY 12804 E-mail: cavaluza@acc.sunyacc.edu.

CAVANAGH, CARROLL JOHN, business advisor, lawyer, art services consultant; b. N.Y.C., Nov. 11, 1943; s. Carroll and Mona (Schmid) C.; m. Valerie Ives Mixter (div.); children: Dorothy, Carroll III; m. Candida N. Smith, June 22, 1991; children: Hudson Nicholas, Gabriel Herald. BA, Yale U., 1964; JD cum laude, U. Pa., 1970; cert., Hague (The Netherlands) Acad. Internat. Law, 1969. Bar: D.C. 1979, Conn. 1970, N.Y. 1970. Assoc. Sullivan & Cromwell, N.Y.C., 1970-79; sec., gen. counsel Nat. Gallery of Art, Washington, 1979-85, trustee's coun., 1984-95; prin. asst. Paul Mellon, Upperville, Va., 1985-96; pres. Belvedere Found., 1993—. Lt. USNR, 1964-71. Mem.: Irish Georgian Soc. (head N.Y. chpt.), Metropolitan (Washington), Union (N.Y.C.). Home: 156 W 13th St New York NY 10011-7908 Office: One State St Plz Ste 2920 New York NY 10004 E-mail: carrolljcavanagh@aol.com.

CAVANAGH, DENIS, physician, educator; MB, ChB, U. Glasgow, Scotland, 1952. Diplomate: Am. Bd. Obstetrics and Gynecology. Former prof. gynecology and obstetrics, chmn. dept. St. Louis U. Sch. Medicine, 1966-77; prof. obstetrics, gynecology, dir. gynecologic oncology U. South Fla. Coll. Medicine, 1977—. Fellow ACS, ACOG, Am. Gyn-Ob Soc., Royal Coll. Obstetricians and Gynecologists; mem. South Atlantic Assn. Obstetricians and Gynecologists, Soc. Gynecol. Oncologists, Soc. Pelvic Surgeons. Home and Office: 8701 Midnight Pass Rd #206A Sarasota FL 34242

CAVANAGH, GERALD FRANCIS, business educator; b. Cleve., Sept. 13, 1931; s. Gerald Francis and Margaret Mildred (Gilmore) C. BS in Engring., Case Western Res. U., 1953; MBA, St. Louis U., 1958, Licentiate in Philosophy, 1959, MEd, 1960; Licentiate in Theology, Loyola U., Chgo., 1965; D in Bus. Adminstrn., Mich. State U., 1970; PhD, LHD (hon.), Loyola U., Balt., 1989, Siena Heights U., 1998. Ordained Jesuit Cath. priest, 1964. Assoc. prof. Wayne State U., Detroit, 1970-79; chair bus. ethics Santa Clara (Calif.) U., 1979-80; prof. U. Detroit, 1980-86; Gasson chair Boston Coll., 1986-87; acad. v.p. U. Detroit Mercy, 1989-92, provost, chancellor, 1992-95, chair bus. ethics, 1995—. Trustee Fordham U., N.Y.C., 1974-80, Xavier U., Cin., 1981-84, Santa Clara U., 1991-2003, Holy Cross, Mass., 2001—; bd. chair U. Detroit, 1975-77; presenter in field. Author: Blacks in the Industrial World: Issues for the Manager, 1972, The Businessperson in Search of Values, 1976, American Business Values in Transition, 1976, Ethical Dilemmas in the Modern Corporation, 1988, American Business Values with International Perspectives, 4th rev. edit., 1998; contbr. articles to profl. jours. Mem. bd. ethics City of Detroit, 1994-2000. Mem. Internat. Assn. for Bus. and Soc., Acad. Mgmt. (Sumner Marcus award 1990), Soc. for Bus. Ethics, Theta Tau, Blue Key, Alpha Phi Omega (advisor), Beta Gamma Sigma, Tau Kappa Alpha, Alpha Sigma Nu. Office: Univ Detroit Mercy Lansing-Reilly Hall PO Box 19900 Detroit MI 48219-0900 E-mail: cavanagf@udmercy.edu.

CAVANAGH, HARRISON DWIGHT, ophthalmic surgeon, medical educator; b. Atlanta, July 22, 1940; s. William Edwards and Marie Corrine (Logue) C.; m. Lynn Ayres Gantt, Dec. 27, 1964; 1 dau., Catherine DuVal. AB, Johns Hopkins U., 1962, MD (Joseph Collins scholar 1963-65), 1965; PhD in Biology, Harvard U., 1972. Life diplomate Am. Bd. Ophthalmology. Intern Johns Hopkins Hosp., 1965-66, resident in ophthalmology, 1969-73; fellow corneal surgery Mass. Eye and Ear Infirmary, Boston, 1973-75; instr. ophthalmology Johns Hopkins Med. Sch., 1969-73; asst. prof. Harvard U. Med. Sch., 1975-76; mem. faculty Emory U., 1976-87, F. Phinizy Calhoun prof. ophthalmology, chmn. dept., 1978-87; prof. Georgetown U., Washington, 1987-91; Disting. Univ. prof., vice chmn. dept. ophthalmology U. Tex. Southwestern Med. Ctr., Dallas, 1991-95, W. Maxwell Thomas chair prof., 1995—; med. dir., assoc. dean clin. svcs. Zale Lipsky U. Hosp./U. Tex. Southwestern Med. Ctr. Vis. prof. Georgetown U., 1986-87; cons., chmn. visual scis. study sect A NIH, 1980-84; Heed Found. scholar, 1973-74; sci. adv. panel Nat. Soc. Prevention Blindness, Knights Templar Found.; civilian cons. USAF, 1983-86, USN, Bethesda Naval Hosp., 1989-91; mem. neuroscis. behavior study sect. NIH, 1989-93; organizing com. 3rd-4th Internat. Conf. on Confocal Microscopy and 4th-5th Internat. Conf. on 3D Image Processing in Microscopy, 1991—. Editor-in-chief Jour. Cornea, 1989-96, Eye and Contact Lens Jour., 2002-2007; mem. editorial bd. Jour. Scanning, Bioimaging Jour.; contbr. articles to profl. jours. Recipient Heed Found. award, 1981, 2d Joseph Koplowitz lectr. Georgetown U., 1983, 14th Waldert lectr. U. Rochester, 1987, 5th Morton B. Sarver lectr. U. Calif., Berkeley, 1991, George Nissel lectr. Brit. Contact Lens Assn., 1997; 21st James McDonald lectr., Loyola U. Chicago, 1998, 3d Maxwell Boschner lectr., U. Toronto; recipient Sr. Scientific Investigators award Rsch. to Prevent Blindness, Inc., 1996. Fellow ACS, Internat. Coll. Surgeons, Am. Acad. Ophthalmology (hon., assoc. sect. govt. rels. and rsch. 1979-83, Honor Recognition award 1982, Whitney Sampson lectr. 1997, Sr. Achievement award 1999), Am. Acad. Optometry (hon.), Royal Microscopy Soc., Royal Soc. Medicine; mem. Contact Lens Assn. Ophthalmologists Am. (pres. 1987, 20th Conrad Behrens medal lectr. 1989, Honor Recognition award 1988), Castroviejo Soc. Corneal Surgeons (pres. 1988-90, Honor Recognition award 1987, 96), Keratorefractive Soc. (bd. dirs.), Internat. Eye Found. Eye Surgeons, New Eng. Ophthal. Soc., Assn. Rsch. in Vision and Ophthalmology (exec. sec.-treas. 1981-86, Honor Recognition award 1987), South-Ctrl. Eyebank Assn. (pres. 1997), Eye Bank Assn. Am. (bd. dirs. 1997-99, R. Townley Paton, M.D. award 2000), Johns Hopkins Club, Park Cities Club, Harvard Club (Dallas, N.Y.), Order of St. John (U.S., U.K.), Phi Beta Kappa. Republican. Episcopalian. Home: 27 Lakeside Park Dallas TX 75225-8110 Office: U Tex Southwestern Med Ctr Dept Ophthalmology 5323 Harry Hines Blvd Dallas TX 75390-9057

CAVANAGH, JOHN CHARLES, advertising agency executive; b. San Francisco, Dec. 19, 1932; s. John Timothy and Alicia Louise (McDowell) C.; m. Mary Ann Anding, Apr. 10, 1959; children: Karen, Brad. Student, U. Hawaii, 1950; BS, U. San Francisco, 1954. Pub. rels. rep. Kaiser Industries Corp., Oakland, Calif., 1956-58; pub. rels. mgr. Kaiser Cement & Gypsum Corp., Oakland, Calif., 1958-63; pub. relations dir. Fawcett-McDermott Assos. Inc., Honolulu, 1964-66, ops. v.p., 1966-69, exec. v.p., 1969-73, pres., dir., 1973-75, Fawcett McDermott Cavanagh Inc., Honolulu, 1975-87, Fawcett McDermott Cavanagh Calif., Inc., San Francisco, 1975-87; pres. The Cavanagh Group/Advt. Inc., Santa Rosa, Calif., 1987—2001. 1st. lt. 740th Guided Missile Bn. AUS, 1954-56. Named Advt. Man of Yr. Honolulu Advt. Fedn., 1985. Mem. Pub. Rels. Soc. Am. (accredited, v.p. 1970, pres. Hawaii chpt. 1971), Advt. Agy. Assn. Hawaii (pres. 1973), Am. Assn. Advt. Agys. (chmn. Hawaii coun. 1980-81), Affiliated Advt. Agys. Internat. (chmn. 1984-85), Outrigger Canoe Club. Home: 3750 St Andrews Dr Santa Rosa CA 95403-0945

CAVANAGH, MICHAEL FRANCIS, state supreme court justice; b. Detroit, Oct. 21, 1940; s. Sylvester J. and Mary Irene (Timmins) C.; m. Patricia E. Ferriss, Apr. 30, 1966; children: Jane Elizabeth, Michael F., Megan Kathleen BA, U. Detroit, 1962, JD, 1966. Bar: Mich. 1966. Law clk. to judge Ct. Appeals, Detroit, 1966-67; atty. City of Lansing, Mich., 1967-69; ptnr. Farhat, Story, et al., Lansing, Mich., 1969-73; judge 54-A Dist. Ct., Lansing, 1973-75, Mich. Ct. Appeals, Lansing, 1975-82; justice Supreme Ct., Lansing, 1983—, chief justice, 1991-94; Supreme Ct. liaison Mich. Indian Tribal Cts./Mich. State Cts. Supervising justice Sentencing Guidelines Com., Lansing, 1983-94, Mich. Jud. Inst., Lansing, 1986-94, 2001-03; bd. dirs. Thomas M. Cooley Law Sch., 1979-88; chair Mich. Justice Project, 1994-95, Nat. Interbranch Conf., Mpls., 1994-95. Bd. dirs. Am. Heart Assn. Mich., 1982—, chmn. bd. Am. Heart Assn. Mich., Lathrup Village, 1984-85; bd. dirs. YMCA, Lansing, 1978. Mem. ABA, Fed. Bar Assn., Ingham County Bar Assn., Inst. Jud. Adminstrn. (hon.), Inc. Soc. of Irish/Am. Lawyers (pres. 1987-88). Democrat. Roman Catholic. Avocations: jogging, racquetball, fishing. Office: Mich Supreme Ct PO Box 30052 925 W Ottawa St Lansing MI 48933-1067

CAVANAGH, PETER ROBERT, academic administrator, department chairman, science educator, researcher; b. Wolverhampton, Staffordshire, Eng., July 31, 1947; came to U.S., 1972; s. John Joseph and Dorothy Ann (Stokes) C.; m. Magda Margalova, Dec. 21, 1968 (div. 1979); 1 child, Sasha; m. Ann Elizabeth Vandervelde, Apr. 18, 1981; children: Drew, Chris, Jennifer. BEd, U. Nottingham, Loughborough Coll., 1968; PhD, U. London, Royal Free Hosp. Sch. Med., 1972. Rsch. asst. Royal Free Hosp. Sch. Med., London, 1968-72; asst. prof. Pa. State U., University Park, 1972-75, assoc. prof., 1975-81, prof. biomechanics, 1981—86, prof. locomotion studies, 1986—2002, dir. Ctr. Locomotion Studies, 1986—2002, prof. biobehavioral health, 1989—2002, rsch. dir. Diabetic Foot Clinc, 1989—2002; prof. medicine Pa. State U. Coll. Med., Hershey, 1993—2002; prof. orthopaedic surgery and rehabilitation Pa. State U., 1994—2002, disting. prof. kinesiology, medicine, orthopedics & rehabilitation and biobehavioral health, 1993—2002; v.p. rsch. DIApedia LLC, State Coll., Pa., 1999—; rsch. dir. Diabetic Foot Clinic, Milton S. Hershey Med. Ctr., Hershey, 1993—2002; Virginia Lois Kennedy chmn. biomedical engring. dept. & acad. dir. Diabetic Foot Care Program Cleveland Clinic Found., 2002—. Vis. prof. U. Dept. Med., Manchester Royal Infirmary, U. Manchester, United Kingdom, 1990-91; cons. U.S. Olympic Com., Colorado Springs, Colo., 1984-90, NASA, Houston, 1986—, various athletic shoe and biomedical cos., U.S., Japan, Germany, 1978—; expert witness for patent and trademark, diabetic foot, foot injury, footwear and footprints; trustee Mus. Contemporary Art, Cleveland, 2003-. Author: The Running Shoe Book, 1980; co-author: Biomechanics and Physiology of Cycling, 1978, The Biomechanics of Distance Running, 1990, The Foot in Diabetes: A Bibliography, various edn. 1992, 2000, The Foot in Diabetes, 2nd and 34d edn., 1994, 2000; mem. edtl. bd. Posture and Gait, Foot & Ankle Internat., 1994—, Internat. Journ. Lower Extremity Wounds, 2001-. Mem. Internat. Soc. Biomechanics (pres. 1995-97, Muybridge medal 1987), Am. College Sports Medicine (fellow 1983, trustee 1987-90, Wolffe lectr. 1987, Citation award 1997, Dill lectr. 2001), Am. Soc. Biomechanics (pres. 1986-87, Borelli award 1994), Am. Diabetes Assn. (chmn. foot coun. 1997-99, Pecoraro lectr. 2002), Aerospace Med. Assn., Orthopedic Rsch. Soc., European Assn. Study Diabetes, Am. Soc. Bone and Mineral Rsch., Am. Orthopaedic Foot and Ankle Soc. (hon.), Melpomene Inst. Adv. Bd., IOC Olympic Acad. Sport Sci. Avocations: running, music, flying. Office: Cleveland Clinic Found 9500 Euclid Ave ND20 Cleveland OH 44195

CAVANAGH, RICHARD EDWARD, research policy organization executive; b. Buffalo, June 15, 1946; s. Joseph John and Mary Celeste (Stack) C.; m. Patricia Sypher, 1995; 1 child. BA, Wesleyan U., Middletown, Conn., 1968; MBA, Harvard U., 1970. Assoc. McKinsey & Co. Inc., Washington, 1970-77, ptnr., 1980-88; exec. dir. fed. cash mgmt. U.S. Office Mgmt. and Budget, Washington, 1977-79; exec. dean Kennedy Sch. Govt. Harvard U., Cambridge, Mass., 1988-95; pres., CEO The Conference Board, Inc., N.Y.C., 1995—. Cons. Carter-Mondale Presdl. Transition, 1976-77; domestic coord. Pres.' Reorgn. Project, The White House, Washington, 1978-79; mem. exec. com. Pres.' Pvt. Sector Survey on Cost Control, Grace Commn., 1982-83. Co-author: (with Donald K. Clifford Jr.) The Winning Performance: How America's High-Growth Midsize Companies Succeed, 1985, 2d edit., 1988 (pub. in 11 fgn. langs.). Mem. bd. judges Dively Award, Harvard U., 1984-94; trustee Ctr. for Excellence in Govt., 1985, 96—, Drucker Found., 1998-2002, Ednl. Testing Svc., 1997—, vice chair, 2002-; trustee Wesleyan U., 1988-2000, vice chair, 1997-2000; trustee, dir. Black Rock Mut. Funds, 1994—; dir. Fremont Group, 1997—, The Guardian Ins., 1998—, Arch Chems., Inc., 1996—, Airplanes Group and Aircraft Fin. Trust, 1999—. With U.S. Army, 1968. Recipient Presdl. commendation, 1979, 80, 83; John Reilly Knox fellow, 1969, Clark fellow, 1969. Mem. Am. Soc. Pub. Adminstrn., Acad. Polit. Sci., Coun. on Fgn. Rels., Raimond Duy Baird Assn., Wesleyan U. Alumni Assn. (chmn. 1985-87), Met. Club (D.C.), Harvard Club (N.Y.C., Boston), Siwanoy Country Club (Bronxville, N.Y.), The Links (N.Y.C.), Beta Theta Pi. Democrat. Roman Catholic. Office: The Conference Board Inc 845 3rd Ave New York NY 10022-6600

CAVANAGH-MCKEE, KATHRYN, nurse; b. N.Y.C., July 11, 1938; d. Arthur James and Ethel (Adrian) Cavanagh; div.; children: Victoria, Carolyn. BA magna cum laude, Hunter Coll., CUNY, 1985; BSN, Hunter-Bellevue Sch. Nursing, 1988. RN, N.Y. Med.-surg. nurse N.Y. Hosp., N.Y.C., 1989-90; emergency room intern St. Luke's Hosp., N.Y.C., 1990-91; nurse emergency dept. A.O. Fox Meml. Hosp., Oneonta, N.Y., 1991-93; emergency dept. asst. nurse care coord. St. Francis Hosp., Jersey City, 1994-95; staff nurse student health svcs. NYU, N.Y.C., 1995-98; sr. staff nurse, IV team NYU Med. Ctr., N.Y.C., 1998—. Mem. Sigma Theta Tau. Home: Apt MG 530 E 23rd St New York NY 10010-5022 E-mail: Cavank02@endeavor.med.nyu.edu.

CAVANAUGH, CHARLES DAVIS, computer scientist, educator; b. Tyler, Tex., Aug. 9, 1973; s. C.J. and Bonita Cavanaugh. AA, Tyler Jr. Coll., 1993; BS, U. Tex., Tyler, 1995, MS, 1997; PhD, U. Tex., Arlington, 2000. Cert. tchr. secondary edn. Tex. Rsch. asst. U. Tex., Tyler, 1996—97, asst. instr. computer sci. Arlington, 1998, grad. rsch. asst., 1997—2000; intern Naval Surface Warfare Ctr., Dahlgren, Va., 1998; asst. prof. computer sci. U. Mo., Rolla, 2000—01; asst. prof. Ctr. Advanced Computer Studies U. La., Lafayette, 2002—. Presenter confs. in field. Contbr. articles to profl. jours. Mem.: Assn. Computing Machinery (v.p. U. Tex. Tyler student chpt. 1996—97, sec. 1996), IEEE Computer Soc., Epsilon Delta Pi, Alpha Chi, Kappa Delta Pi, Phi Theta Kappa, Tau Beta Pi (life). Home: 13020 CR 2220 Whitehouse TX 75791 Personal E-mail: c.d.cavanaugh@att.net.

CAVANAUGH, DAVID K. clinical psychologist; b. Holland Patent, N.Y., July 8, 1929; s. Charles H. and Clara A. (Stannard) C.; m. Maxine Cornell, Feb. 8, 1953; children: David Charles, Carolyn Jeanne Clair. BA, Colgate U., 1951; MS, Pa. State U., 1953; PhD, U. Buffalo, 1957. Licensed psychologist, N.Y. Staff psychologist Polk State Sch., Pa., 1953-54; chief psychologist Buffalo Psychiatric Ctr., N.Y., 1958-74, pvt. practice, 1974—. Cons. psychologist Attica Correctional Facility, N.Y., 1958-74, Niagara County, Lockport, N.Y., 1969-73,

N.Y. State Office Vocat. Rehab., 1974-85. Lt. col. USAFR, 1953-74. Mem. Psychol. Assn. of Western N.Y. Avocations: snorkling, travel, tennis. Home and Office: 161 Sweet Briar Rd Tonawanda NY 14150-7511

CAVANAUGH, JAMES HENRY, medical corporate executive, former government official; b. Orange, N.J., Mar. 3, 1937; s. James H. and Madeline Rachel (McFerren) C.; m. Esther Sally Musselman, Jan. 20, 1962; children: Elizabeth Anne, Michael Patrick. BS, Fairleigh Dickinson U., 1959; MA, U. Iowa, 1961, PhD, 1964. Asst. adminstr. Princeton (N.J.) Hosp., 1961-62; asst. prof. hosp. and health care adminstrn. U. Iowa, 1964-66; spl. asst. to surgeon gen. USPHS, 1966-67, dir. office comprehensive health planning, 1967-68; dep. asst. sec. health and sci. affairs HEW, 1969-71; staff asst. for health affairs Pres. Nixon, The White House, 1971-73, asst. dir. domestic council, 1973-74, dep. dir., 1974-75; dep. chief White House staff for Pres. Ford, 1975-76; v.p. corp. devel. Allergan Pharms., Irvine, Calif., 1977-78, sr. v.p. sci. and planning, 1978-81; spl. cons. to Pres. Reagan, 1981; pres. Allergan Internat., 1981-82, SmithKline BioSci. Labs., 1983-85, Smith Kline & French Labs. US, Phila., 1985-01, HealthCare Investment Corp. Founding bd. dirs. Marine Nat. Bank, Santa Ana Calif., Nat. Venture Capital Assn.; bd. dirs. MedImmune, Inc., Shire Pharms. Group, PLC, Diversa Corp., Versicor, Inc., 3-Dimensional Pharms., Inc. Mem. Pres.'s Export Council, 1981-85; bd. dirs. Proprietary Assn., 1980-82; trustee Nat. Com. for Quality Health Care, nat. chmn. 1988; trustee emeritus Calif. Coll. Medicine; mem. nat. adv. com. Am. Refugee Com. Recipient Disting. Alumnus award U. Iowa Coll. Medicine, Disting. Alumni Achievement award U. Iowa. Mem. Am. Hosp. Assn. (hon.), Pharm. Mfrs. Assn. (bd. dirs. 1986-88), Union League Club (Phila.), Nassau Club. Episcopalian (vestryman). Home: 554 Dorset Rd Devon PA 19333-1845 Office: HealthCare Ventures LLC 44 Nassau St Princeton NJ 08542-4506

CAVANAUGH, JOHN JOSEPH, JR., lawyer; b. Albany, N.Y., June 14, 1936; s. John J. Sr. and Jane A. (McKeon) C.; m. Judith A. Myers, Sept. 5, 1964. BA cum laude, Siena Coll., 1958; JD, Albany Law Sch., 1961. Bar: N.Y. 1961, U.S. Dist. Ct. (no. dist.) N.Y. 1961, U.S. Supreme Ct. 1967. Assoc. Donohue & Bohl, Albany, 1961-64, Arthur J. Harvey, Albany, 1964-67; pvt. practice Albany, 1967—. Ind. counsel Rosenblum & Sarachan, Albany, 1978-87. Assoc. editor Albany Law Rev., 1961. Cpl. U.S. Army, 1956-63. Mem. N.Y. State Bar Assn., Albany County Bar Assn., Capital Dist. Trial Lawyers Assn., Am. Arbitration Assn. (arbitrator), Am. Legion, K.C. Avocations: reading, tennis, travel, coin collector. Home: 28 Bancroft St Albany NY 12208-1615 Office: 210 Delaware Ave Delmar NY 12054-1221

CAVANAUGH, KENNETH CLINTON, retired housing consultant; b. Fremont, Mich., Apr. 30, 1916; s. Frank Michael and Buryll Marie (Preston) C.; m. Barbara Blythe Boling, Feb. 24, 1979; children from previous marriage: Patricia Ann, James Lee, John Thomas. BS in Forestry, Mich. State U., 1939. County supr. Farm Security Adminstrn., USDA, Kalamazoo, 1939-43; community mgr. PHA, Willow Run, Mich., 1946-49, dir. fiscal mgmt. Washington, 1949-55, dir. elderly housing Housing & Home Fin. Agy., 1955-57, reg. dir. San Juan, P.R., 1957-58; dir. housing programs HUD, Washington, 1958-73; controller/dep. dir. San Francisco Housing Authority, 1973-78; pres. Ken C. Cavanaugh & Assocs., pvt. internat. housing and community devel. cons., Vista, Calif., 1978—; fin. finder Merrill Lynch-Huntoon Paige Co., San Francisco, 1979-81, Western Pacific Fin. Co., Newport Beach, Calif., 1981-83; gen. ptnr. The Knolls, Rogers, Ark., 1980-89. Exec. dir. Arlington (Va.) Youth Found., 1950-58; advisor Salvation Army adv. bd., Honolulu, 1985-88. Served to capt. USN, 1943-46, USNR, 1946-73. Recipient Superior Svc. award, Pub. Housing Adminstrn., 1956. Mem. Nat. Assn. Housing & Redevel. Ofcls., Ret. Officers Assn., Res. Officers Assn., Naval Res. Assn., Shadowridge Golf Club (Vista), Elks, Masons. Avocations: golf, travel. Home and Office: PO Box 749 Vista CA 92085-0749 E-mail: BlytheCav@aol.com.

CAVANAUGH, MARGARET ANNE, chemist; b. Dayton, Ohio, July 17, 1947; m. Joseph C. Cavanaugh. BS in Chemistry, U. Pitts., 1968; PhD in Phys. Inorganic Chemistry, Cath. U. Am., 1973. Asst. prof. chemistry and physics St. Mary's Coll., Notre Dame, Ind., 1975-79, assoc. prof., 1979-86, prof., chair, 1981-82, 85-89, acting dept. chair, 1981-82, 85-86; program officer chemistry divsn. NSF, Arlington, Va., 1989-91, program dir. chemistry divsn., 1991-2000, staff assoc. for env., Office of Dir., 2000—. Vis. asst. prof., rsch. assoc. chemistry U. New Orleans, 1973-75; vis. scientist UOP, Inc., 1983; test devel. com. for advanced placement exam. in chemistry The Coll. Bd., 1988-91; lectr. Am. U., 1991, George Wash. U., 1990-92. Trustee U. Dayton, 1990-99. Fellow Am. Inst. Chemists; mem. Am. Chem. Soc. (councilor 1984-90, women chemists com. 1982-88, chair 1988, meetings and expositions com. 1985-87, nominations and elections com. 1987-95, sec. com. on edn. assn. 1991-95, coun. com. pub. rels. chair 1994 96, com. on sci. 1997—, chair 2002—, C&EN adv. bd. 1998—, award for encouraging women into careers in chem. scis. 1995), Internat. Union Pure and Applied Chemistry, Sigma Xi, Iota Sigma Pi (editor 1981-87, v.p. 1987-90, pres. 1990-93, immediate past pres. 1993-96). Achievements include research in synthesis and reactions of transition metal compounds, particularly those containing metal clusters, unusual oxidation states, or proton interactions. Office: NSF Directors Office Rm 1205 Arlington VA 22230-0001 E-mail: mcavanau@nsf.gov.

CAVANAUGH, MICHAEL EVERETT, lawyer, arbitrator, mediator; b. Seattle, Dec. 23, 1946; s. Wilbur R. Cavanaugh and Gladys E. (Herring) Barber; m. Susan P. Heckman, Sept. 7, 1968. AB, U. Calif., Berkeley, 1973; JD, U. Wash., 1976. Bar: Wash. 1976, U.S. Dist. Ct. (we. dist.) Wash. 1977, U.S. Ct. Appeals (9th cir.) 1977, U.S. Dist. Ct. (ea. dist.) Wash. 1978. Staff atty. U.S. Ct. of Appeals (9th crct.) Calif., San Francisco, 1976-77; from assoc. to ptnr. Preston & Thorgrimson, Seattle, 1981-85; ptnr. Bogle & Gates, Seattle, 1985-97, assoc., 1977-81, ptnr., 1985-97; propr. Michael E. Cavanaugh, J.D., Arbitration and Mediation, Seattle, 1997—. Contbg. author: Employment Discrimination Law, 3d edit., 1995. Avocations: sailing, creative writing, music. Office: 1420 5th Ave # 2200 Seattle WA 98101-1346 E-mail: mec@cavanaugh-adr.com.

CAVANAUGH, TOM RICHARD, artist, antiques dealer, retired art educator; b. Danville, Ill., July 19, 1923; s. Harry William and Hazel (Brown) C. B.F.A., U. Ill., 1947, M.F.A. (McLellan fellow), 1950. Art and ednl. dir. Springfield (Ill.) Art Assn., 1947-49; mem. faculty Kansas City Art Inst., 1952-55, Washington U. Sch. Art, St. Louis, 1955-56; emeritus prof. painting and drawing La. State U., Baton Rouge, 1957-83, ret., 1983. Owner, dir. The Bay Street Studio, Boothbay Harbor, Maine, 1950—, gallery g Art & Antiques. One man shows, Chapellier Gallery, N.Y.C., 1963, La. State U., 1963, 78, Griffith-Menard Gallery, Baton Rouge, 1986, Gallery of Art, 2003; group shows include, Met. Mus. Art, 1950, Whitney Mus., 1951-58, Corcoran biennials, 1959, 61, Nelson Gallery Art, 1952, Joslyn Mus. Art, 1954, Mulvane Art Mus., 1955, Kans. State Coll., 1956, New Orleans Mus., 1959, Ark. Arts Center, 1961; represented in permanent collections, Mead Corp., N.Y.C., Joslyn Mus. Art, New Orleans Mus.; executed mural Govt. Bldg., Baton Rouge; publication: Outstanding Educators of America, 1975. Served with U.S. Army, 1943-45. Fulbright fellow Italy, 1956-57; McDowell Colony fellow, 1973 Mem. Assoc. Antique Dealers Am. (exec. bd. dirs.). Office: 6 Bay St Boothbay Harbor ME 04538-2142 Home: 8155 Gulf Blvd Navarre FL 32566-7115

CAVANAUGH, WILLIAM, III, electric utility company executive; b. New Orleans, 1939; Grad., Tulane U., 1961. Sr. v.p. Mid. South Utilities (now Entergy Corp.), New Orleans, Mid. South Utilities System Svcs. Inc.; pres., chief exec. officer System Energy Resources Inc., Jackson, Miss., also bd. dirs.; chmn., pres. and CEO Progress Energy Inc., Raleigh, NC. Dir. Atomic Indsl. Forum, Am. Nuclear Energy Coun., Trustmark Corp., Trustmark Nat. Bank. Office: Progress Energy Inc 411 Fayetteville Street Mall Raleigh NC 27601-1748

CAVARNOS, CONSTANTINE PETER, writer; b. Boston, Oct. 19, 1918; s. Peter (Panagiotes) John and Irene (Maistrou) C. AB magna cum laude, Harvard U., 1942, AM, 1947, PhD, 1948. Tchg. asst. in philosophy Harvard U., Radcliffe Coll., 1945-46; teaching fellow in philosophy Harvard U., Cambridge, Mass., 1946-47; teaching asst. in philosophy Tufts U., Wellesley (Mass.) Coll., 1948-49; asst. prof. philosophy U. N.C., Chapel Hill, 1949-54; assoc. prof., prof. philosophy and Byzantine art Greek Orthodox Sch. Theology, Brookline, Mass., 1954-56; vis. assoc. prof. philosophy Wheaton Coll., Norton, Mass., 1965-67, Clark U., Worcester, Mass., 1967-68; pres. Inst. for Byzantine and Modern Greek Studies, Belmont, Mass., 1969—. Adj. prof. philosophy and Byzantine art Hellenic Coll., Brookline, 1978-82. Author: A Dialogue Between Bergson, Aristotle and Philologos, 1949, Byzantine Sacred Art, 1957, Anchored in God, 1959, Man and the Universe in American Philosophy, 1959, Symbols and Proofs of Immortality, 1964, Modern Greek Philosophers on the Human Soul, 1967, 2d edit., 1987, Byzantine Thought and Art, 1968, Modern Greek Thought, 1969, The Holy Mountain, 1973, Plato's Theory of Fine Art, 1973, 2d edit., 1998, The Classical Theory of Relations, 1975, Plato's View of Man, 1975, Orthodox Iconography, 1977, Japanese edit., 1999, A Dialogue on G.E. Moore's Ethical Philosophy, 1979, Paths and Means to Holiness, 1980, Modern Orthodox Saints, Vols. I-XIV, 1971-2000, St. Nectarios of Aegina, 1981, 2d edit., 1988, 95, The Future Life According to Orthodox Teaching, 1984, The Educational Theory of Benjamin Lesvos, 1984, Meetings with Kontoglou, 1985, Bysanttilainen Taide, 1987, The Goodness of God and the Self-Willed Wickedness of Man, 1987, St. Methodia of Kimolos, 1987, Smoking and the Orthodox Christian, 1988, Fasting and Science, 1988, The Hellenic-Christian Philosophical Tradition, 1989, New Library, Vol. 1, 1989, Vol. 2, 1992, Vol. 3, 1995, Vol. 4, 2002, Immortality of the Soul, 1993, Guide to Byzantine Iconography, Vol. I, 1993, Vol. II, 2001, Pythagoras on the Fine Arts as Therapy, 1994, Biological Evolutionism, 1994, 2d edit., 1997, Orthodox Christian Terminology, 1994, Cultural and Educational Continuity of Greece, 1995, To Haigion Oros (Greek version of The Holy Mountain 1973), 2000; editor: Greek Language and Culture: Their Vitality and Importance Today, 1995, Byzantine Churches of Thessaloniki, 1995, He Hiera Byzantine Techne, 1995, Spiritual Beauty, 1996, The Concept of Christian Love, 1996, The Seven Sages of Ancient Greece, 1996, Ecumenism Examined, 1996, Victories of Orthodoxy, 1997, Nikai tes Orthodoxias (Greek version of Victories of Orthodoxy), 2002, St. Nectarios' Study on Holy Icons, 1997, Byzantine Chant, 1998, Fine Arts as Therapy, 1998, St. Photios The Great: Philosopher and Theologian, 1998, Dostoievsky's Philosophy of Man, 1998, Koncepti i Dashurise Kristiane, 1998, The Hellenic Heritage, 1999, St. Gregory of Nyssa on the Human Soul, 2000, Plutarch's Advice on Keeping Well, 2001, Photios Kontoglou peri Byzantines Eikonographias kai Mousikes, 2001, Aristotle's Theory of the Fine Arts, 2001, Holiness: Man's Supreme Destiny, 2001, The Priest as Spiritual Father, 2002, Psychopheleis Didachai tou Photiou Kontoglou, 2003, Orthodoxy and Philosophy, 2003; editor, Sacred Catechism of the Orthodox Church, 2003. Sheldon Traveling fellow in philosophy, Harvard/Athens-Paris-Cambridge (Eng.)-Oxford, 1947-48, Fulbright Rsch. scholar U. Athens, 1957-59; recipient Archon of the Oecumenical Patriarchate, Constantinople, 1979, Ann. Faculty award Hellenic Coll., 1986, The Florovsky Theol. prize Ctr. for Traditionalist Orthodox Studies, 1992. Mem. Am. Philos. Assn., Metaphysical Soc. Am. (past treas. 1949), Am. Soc. Aesthetics, Internat. Inst. Arts & Letters, Revista Soc. Argentina Philosophy, Plomaritan Soc. Boston (past pres.), Ctr. Estudios Bizantinos Neohelénicos Fotios Malleros U. Chile (hon.). Greek Orthodox. Avocations: music, restoration of icons, walking. Office: Inst Byzantine & Greek Studies 115 Gilbert Rd Belmont MA 02478-2200 Fax: 617-876-3600.

CAVAROCCHI, NICHOLAS GUY, public relations executive; b. Phila., May 6, 1939; s. Joseph and Christine Iezzoni Cavarocchi; m. Bridget V McAuliffe, May 2, 1964; children: Nicholas Lane, Douglas Joseph. BS, La Salle U., 1961; MBA, Am. U., 1972. Grants mgr. NIH, Bethesda, Md., 1964-69; budget officer Health Svcs. and Mental Health Adminstrn., Washington, 1969-71; exec. v.p. Georgetown U. Cmty. Health Plan, Washington, 1971-74; profl. staff com. on appropriations U.S. Ho. of Reps., 1974-79; assoc. exec. dir. group health Group health Assn., Washington, 1979; sr. ptnr. Cavarocchi Ruscio Dennis Assocs., Washington, 1980—. Home: PO Box 617 Oakland MD 21550-4617 E-mail: ncavarocchi@dc-crd.com.

CAVAT, IRMA, artist, educator; b. Bklyn. children: Karina Cavat-Gore, Nika Cavat-Hoffman. Student, NYU, 1956, Alexander Archipenko Sch., Woodstock, N.Y., 1959, New Sch. for Social Rsch., N.Y.C., 1960-62. Prof. art U. Calif., Santa Barbara, 1964-91. One-woman shows include Pollock Fine Art, Summerland, Calif., 2002, Gallery Sistina, Rome, 1961, 63, Santa Barbara Mus. Art, 1966, Phoenix Art Mus., 1967, Kennedy Gallery, N.Y.C., 1972, 74, 78, Arwin Galleries, Detroit, 1982, 84, 87, Feingarten Gallery, L.A., 1991, Cline Gallery, Santa Fe, 1995, Fielding Inst., Santa Barbara, Calif., 1996, Arts and Letters Gallery, Santa Barbara, 1999, others. Fulbright fellow, Rome, 1957-59. Avocations: poetry, travel. Office: Univ of California Dept Art Santa Barbara CA 93106

CAVAZOS, ANA A. librarian; b. L.A., Mar. 30, 1963; d. Alfonso and Lidia Gloria Aguirre; m. Fred Cavazos, May 22, 1982; children: Cassandra Lee, Cassandra Lee, Melissa Lizzette. BA, U. Tex., Brownsville, 1995, cert. in elem. early childhood edn., cert. in elem. self contained grades 1-8, cert. in elem. English grades 1-8, U. Tex., Brownsville, 1996, learning resources endorsement, 1999. Libr. asst. San Benito (Tex.) Ctrl. Ind. Sch. Dist., 1987—92, computer lab. mgr., 1992—94, tchr. grade 2, 1994—2003, libr., 1997—. Tech. rep. elem. and middle sch., 1997—. Author poetry. Sponsor Girl Scout, 1999—2000. Avocations: reading, writing, walking. Home: 26762 Kornegay Rd San Benito TX 78586 Office: San Benito CISD 2901 Shafer Rd San Benito TX 78586

CAVE, KENT R. national park ranger; b. Elkin, NC, Oct. 6, 1952; s. John Marvin and Bessie Irene (Dezern) C.; m. Annette Gail Pruitt, May 28, 1983; children: John Carlton, Jacob Reuben, Benjamin Pruitt. BA, Appalachian State U., 1974, student, 1974-76, U. Tenn., 1976-80. Editorial asst. Papers of Andrew Johnson, Knoxville, 1976-80; park ranger Blue Ridge Pkwy, Asheville, NC, 1975-77; Pk. ranger Gt. Smoky Mountains Nat. Pk., Gatlinburg, Tenn., 1980-83, Andrew Johnson Nat. Hist. Site, Greeneville, Tenn., 1984-87, chief Pk. ranger, 1987-88, Ft. Pulaski Nat. Monument, Savannah, Ga., 1988-97; info. officer NPS E. Region Incident Mgmt. Team, 1994—; staff Pk. ranger, resource edn. at. Smoky Mountains Nat. Pk., Gatlinburg, Tenn., 1997—. Active Bull St. Bapt. Ch., Savannah, Ga., 1992-97, dir. Royal Ambassador youth group, 1993-97; active 1st Bapt. Ch., Gatlinburg, Tenn., 1997—, mem. missions com., 1998-2000. Hilton Smith fellow U. Tenn., 1980. Mem. Nat. Park Svc. Employees and Alumni Assn. (life), Savannah Fed. Exec. Assn. (pres. 1991), Nat. Assn. Interpretation, Appalachian Studies Assn., Great Smoky Mountains Assn. (life). Avocations: woodworking, hiking, photography, Am. history, early 20th century naval history. Office: Gt Smoky Mountains Nat Park Resource Education 107 Park Headquarters Rd Gatlinburg TN 37738-4102 E-mail: kent_cave@nps.gov.

CAVENEE, WEBSTER K. director; Dir., prof. Ludwig Inst. for Cancer Rsch. U. Calif., LaJolla, 1991—. Office: Ludwig Inst 9500 Gilman Dr La Jolla CA 92093-0660 E-mail: wcavenee@ucsd.edu.

CAVENEY, WILLIAM JOHN, former pharmaceutical company executive, lawyer; b. Wheeling, W Va., Aug. 5, 1944; s. James Joseph and Esther Virginia (Ackermann) Caveney; m. Margaret Carol Serota, Sept. 18, 1971; children: Ryan Benjamin, Christine Joanna. AB cum laude, W.Va. U., 1966; JD, Vanderbilt U., 1969; LLM in Taxation, NYU, 1977. Advanced Profl. Cert. in Fin., Grad. Sch. Bus. Adminstrn., 1979; bar: N.Y. 1972, U.S. Supreme Ct. 1976. Tax mgr. Arthur Andersen & Co., N.Y.C., 1969—73; tax atty. Texaco, Inc., N.Y.C., 1973—76; mgr. tax planning Norton Simon, Inc., N.Y.C., 1976—78; dir. tax planning Warner-Lambert Co., Morris Plains, NJ, 1978—79; corporate tax counsel, mem. tax planning com. Pfizer, Inc. (formerly Warner-Lambert), 1979—2000. Former mem. Township Com., mayor, Millburn-Short Hills, NJ; lectr. Taxation and Internat. Fin., CPA, NY; trustee Free Pub. Libr., Millburn, NJ. Contbr. articles to profl. jours. Mem.: World Trade Inst., Tax Execs. Inst. (chmn. internat. tax steering com.), N.Y. State Soc. CPA's, N.Y State Bar Assn. (mem. exec. com. tax sec.), ABA (com. fgn. activities of U.S. taxpayers), AICPA, Short Hills Assn. (council mem., auditor), Zoning Bd. Adjustment, Millburn, Hist. Preservation Commn., Millburn, Cora Hartshorn Arboretum, Short Hills, N.J., Club of Millburn, Short Hills (trustee rep.). Home: 1499 Folkstone Ct Ann Arbor MI 48105-2847

CAVENY, LEONARD HUGH, mechanical engineer, aerospace scientist, consultant; b. Atlanta, Oct. 30, 1934; s. Elmer Leonard and Dorothy (Franklin) C.; m. Joyce Rodal, Apr. 10, 1957; children: Polly J., Rebecca R., Teresa L., Leslie Y., Susan C. BME, Ga. Inst. Tech., 1956, MSME, 1960; PhD in Mech. Engring., U. Ala., 1969. Registered profl. engr. Ala., 1965. Supr. aerothermodynamics Thiokol Chem. Corp., Huntsville, Ala., 1960-67; sr. tech. staff Princeton (N.J.) U., 1969-80; program mgr. Air Force Office Sci. Rsch., Washington, 1980-85; dep. dir. sci. and tech. Strategic Defense Initiative Orgn., Washington, 1985-93; dir. sci. & tech. Ballistic Missile Defense Orgn., Washington, 1993-97. Mem. Com. on Thermionic Rsch. and Tech. NRC, 2000—01, mem. com. to review NASA's pioneering revolutionary tech., 2002—, chair Air Force propulsiton proposal rev. panel, 2004—; cons. in field; nat. rsch. coun. Air Force Propulsion Proposal Review Panel, 2003—. Editor: Orbit-Raising and Maneuvering Propulsion, 1984; inventor in field. Lt. (j.g.) USN, 1956-59. Recipient Yuri Gagarin medal, Moscow, 1993. Fellow AIAA (chair elec. propulsion tech. com. 1984-86, chair Princeton sect. 1974-75, tech. chair internat. elec. propulsion conf. 1985, editorial adv. bd. 1988—, Wyld Propulsion medal 1997); mem. The Combustion Inst. Avocations: photography, construction, tennis. Home: 13715 Piscataway Dr Fort Washington MD 20744-6635 E-mail: lhcaveny@cs.com.

CAVERLY, ROBERT, adult education educator; PhD, The Johns Hopkins U., 1979—83. Prof. Villanova U., 1997—. Author: (research) IEEE Transactions on Microwave Theory and Techniques. Recipient Dow Outstanding Young Faculty Mem., ASEE, 1987. Mem.: IEEE. Office: Villanova U 800 Lancaster Ave Villanova PA 19085

CAVERT, HENRY MEAD, physician, retired educator; b. Mpls, Mar. 30, 1922; s. William Lane and Mary (Mead) C.; m. June Lorraine Sederstrom, Jan. 27, 1946; children: John Mead (dec.), Harlan McCrea, Winston Peter. BS in Agrl. Biochemistry, U. Minn., 1942, MD, 1951, PhD in Physiology, 1952. Postdoctoral research fellow Am. Heart Assn., 1951-54, faculty U. Minn. Med. Sch., 1953-92, assoc. dean, 1964-92, prof. physiology, 1967-92, prin. investigator Gen. Clin. Rsch. Ctr., 1978-92, prof. emeritus, 1992—. Nat. Heart Inst. spl. rsch. fellow, vis. prof. biochemistry U. Edinburgh, Scotland, 1961-62; established investigator Am. Heart Assn., 1954-57; mem. program project com. B, Nat. Heart Inst., 1966-69; cons. Nat. Heart and Lung Inst., 1969-92. Author: (with A.J. Carlson and V. Johnson) Machinery of the Body, 5th edit., 1961; also numerous articles. Mem. met. bd. dir. YMCA, Mpls., 1968-70, mem. endowment com., 1988—; mem. bd. mgmt. U. Minn. YMCA, 1955-57, 77-83, 84-90, chmn., 1968-70, chmn. capital campaign endowment, 1992-95, chmn. capital bldg. campaign, 1998-99; mem. bd. parish edn. Am. Luth. Ch., 1958-72, Luth. Health Care Bangladesh, 1994—; trustee Minn. Med. Found., 1958-92, chmn. scholarship and loan com., 1960-68, chmn. honors and awards com., 1970-76, mem. spl. grants com., 1981—, chmn. student fin. aid com., 1984-92, active 1992—, mem. planned giving com., 1991—. Recipient Harold S. Diehl award, 2001. Mem. AMA, Assn. Am. Med. Coll. (chmn. com. student aspects internat. med. edn. 1966-68, steering com. group on student affairs 1967-68, com. internat. rels. med. edn. 1968-75), Am. Physiol. Soc., Minn. Acad. Medicine (pres.-elect 1989-90, pres. 1990-91), Minn. Med. Alumni Soc. (bd. dir. 1992-98), Minn. Med. Assn. (pres. award 1988, mem. various coms.), Sigma Xi, Phi Lambda Upsilon, Alpha Omega Alpha, Gamma Sigma Delta, Alpha Zeta. Home: 2250 Luther Pl Condo #106 Saint Paul MN 55108

CAVES, RICHARD EARL, economist, educator; b. Akron, Ohio, Nov. 1, 1931; s. Earl Leroy and Verna Louise (Jobes) C. AB, Oberlin Coll., 1953; MA, Harvard, 1956, PhD (Wells prize 1958), 1958; D of Econ. Sci., U. London, 1999. Asst. prof., asso. prof. econs. U. Calif. at Berkeley, 1957-62; prof. econs. Harvard, 1962—, chmn. dept. econs., 1966-69. Cons. Council Econ. Advisers, 1961; dep. to spl. asst. to Pres. U.S. for fgn. trade policy, 1961; cons. Treasury Dept., 1961-62, Bur. Budget, 1963-64; mem. White House Task Force on Fgn. Econ. Policy. Author: (with R.H. Holton) The Canadian Economy: Prospect and Retrospect, 1959, Trade and Economic Structure, 1960, Air Transport and Its Regulators, 1962, American Industry: Structure, Conduct, Performance, 1964, (with J.S. Bain, J. Margolis) Northern California's Water Industry, 1966, (with others) Britain's Economic Prospects, 1968, (with G.L. Reuber) Capital Transfers and Economic Policy: Canada, 1951-62, 1971, (with R.W. Jones) World Trade and Payments, 1973, (with M.J. Roberts) Regulating the Product: Quality and Variety, 1974, (with M. Uekusa) Industrial Organization in Japan, 1976, (with M.E. Porter and M. Spence) Competition in the Open Economy: A Model Applied to Canada, 1980, (with others) Britain's Economic Performance, 1980, Multinational Enterprise and Economic Analysis, 1982, (with others) The Australian Economy: A View from the North, 1984, (with S.W. Davies) Britain's Productivity Gap, 1987, (with D.R. Barton) Efficiency in U.S. Manufacturing Industries, 1990, (with others) Industrial Efficiency in Six Nations, 1992, Creative Industries: Contracts Between Art and Commerce, 2000; contbr. numerous articles to profl. jours. Recipient Henderson prize Harvard Law Sch., 1967, Kenan Enterprise award, 1990; Ford Found. fellow, 1959-60 Fellow Am. Acad. Arts and Scis.; mem. Am. Econ. Assn. Home: 24 Agassiz St Cambridge MA 02140-2802

CAVIGLI, HENRY JAMES, petroleum engineer; b. Colfax, Calif., Mar. 14, 1914; s. Giovanni and Angelina (Giachi) C.; m. Ruth Loree Denton, June 11, 1942; children: Henry James Jr., Robert D., Paul R., Loree Ann McIntire. BS in Petroleum Engring., U. Calif., Berkeley, 1937, MS in Mech. Engring., 1947. Sr. engr. Chevron Corp., Rio Vista, Calif., 1954-57, supt. No. Calif., 1958-69, mgr. non operated joint ventures LaHabra, Calif., 1970-76; cons. Cavigli & Mee, petroleum cons., Sacramento, Calif., 1976—. Author: Escapades in the Blue, 1996. Mem. sch. bd. Rio Vista High Sch., 1962-67. Maj. USAF, 1942-47. Decorated Bronze Star with 4 oak leaf clusters. Mem. Soc. Petroleum Engrs., Petroleum Prodn. Pioneers, Calif. Conservation Commn. Oil Producers (chmn. 1971-72), Sutter Club, C. of C., Lion, Sigma Xi, Theta Tau Epsilon. Republican. Roman Catholic. Achievements include research in mech. sampling-field oil tanks, determination of minimum chem., productivity index of pumping wells, rotating piston pressure recorder. Home: 6271 Eichler St Sacramento CA 95831-1864 Office: Cavigli & Mee PO Box 22815 Sacramento CA 95822-0815

CAVILEER, DENISE MARIE, poet; b. Point Pleasant, N.J., Nov. 21, 1973; d. Joseph G. and MaryLou Cooley; m. Matthew Patrick Cavileer; children: Kristina, Sarah, A.J. Cert. child devel. presch. tchr. Va., 1992. Tchr. in home day care, Chesapeake, Va., 1993—98. Contbr. anthology, other anthologies. Nominee Poet of the Year, 2002; recipient Achievement award, Poetry.com, 2001. Avocations: being with my children, writing, singing, music. Personal E-mail: Lyricalgirlpoet@aol.com.

CAVILEER, SHARON E. writer, public relations executive, consultant; b. Washington, Apr. 27, 1949; d. Douglas Richards and Grace Elizabeth Cavileer; m. Peter L. D'Alessandro; children: Jessica Flaherty, Rachel Pullen. BA in English, Kent State U., 1970, postgrad., George Mason U. Account exec. E.G. White & Assocs., Vienna, Va., 1983—85, Stackig, McLean, Va., 1985—88; pres. Cavileer & Co., Clifton, Va., 1987—; pub. rels. mgr. Prince William County Park Authority, Manassas, Va., 1992—99. Press officer The Freedom Mus., Manassas, 1999—; media relations staff Spotlight on the Arts, Fairfax, 1992; dir. Fairfax City Auto Dealers Assn., 1992—; lectr. in field. Author: Virginia Curiosities, 2002; contbr., articles to profl. jours. Mem.: Greater Manassas C. of C., Ctrl. Fairfax C. of C., Soc. Am. Travel Writers (Phoenix con. 2001—). Republican. Presbyterian. Office: Cavileer & Co 12950 Clifton Creek Dr Clifton VA 20124

CAVILL, RONALD WILLIAM, financial planner; b. Escanaba, Mich., July 8, 1944; s. Robert Hugh and Lorraine (Kondory) Cavill. BA, U. Md., 1971. Cert. financial planner. Regional v.p. Am. Gen. Corp., Houston, 1973-75; pres. Corp. Benefit Cons., Inc., Denver, 1975-80, Cavill and Co., Washington, Denver, 1980—; dir. Internat. Downshifters Inst., Golden, Colo., 1996—. Bd. advisors Tax Mgmt. Fin. Planning (BNA), Washington, 1985—88. Pres. Jefferson County Assn. Retarded Citizens, Denver, 1977; bd. dirs. Celebrate Colo. Artists, 1999—, treas., 2003—; bd. dirs. Inst. Sci. and Pub. Policy, Washington, 1997—99, Good Shepherd Life Care Ctr., Silver Spring, Md., 1985, Ronald McDonald Ho., Washington, 1989—96; chmn. Nat. Inst. Fin. Issues and Svcs. Elders, 1991—96; chair audit com. Wireless Tech. Rsch., LLC, Washington, 1995—; bd. dirs. Nat. Coun. Aging, 1991—99, treas., 1995—99. Mem.: Internat. Assn. Fin. Planning (v.p. nat. capital chpt. 1984—86). E-mail: RWCavill@aol.com.

CAVIN, EDWARD SCOTT, economist, consultant; b. Pontiac, Mich., May 12, 1953; s. George E. and Margaret L. (Weihe) C.; m. Eleanor E. Smith, May 22, 1976; 1 child, Marion E. BA in Econs., Mich. State U., 1975; AM in Econs., U. Mich., 1979, PhD in Econs., 1980. Sr. economist Math. Policy Rsch., Princeton, N.J., 1980-86; sr. rsch. assoc. Manpower Demonstration Rsch. Corp., N.Y.C., 1984; sr. analyst Ctr. for Naval Analyses, Alexandria, Va., 1987—. Cons. Office

Tech. Assessment, Washington, 1986. Contbg. editor Jour. Policy Analysis and Mgmt., 1983-85; assoc. editor Evaluation Rev., 1986-89; also articles. Grad. fellow NSF, 1975; recipient DoD Exceptional Svc. award, 2001, S.W. Asia Civilian Svc. medal, 1992. Mem. Mil. Ops. Rsch. Soc. Avocation: computer repair. Office: Ctr for Naval Analyses 4825 Mark Center Dr Alexandria VA 22311-1850

CAVIN, KRISTINE SMITH, lawyer; b. Decatur, Ga., Mar. 26, 1969; d. Richard Theodore and Sherri (Nash) Smith; m. James Michael Cavin, May 13, 1995. BA, Furman U., 1991; JD, Calif. Western Sch. Law, 1995. Bar: Ga. 1995. Legal asst. Smith & Jenkins, P.C., Atlanta, 1991-92; intern child abuse and domestic violence unit San Diego City Atty.'s Office, 1995; assoc. Smith, Ronick & Corbin, L.L.C., Atlanta, 1995—. Mem. ABA, Nat. Assn. Women Lawyers, Nat. Assn. Profl. Mortgage Women, Mortgage Bankers Assn. (assoc.), Ga. Bar Assn., Ga. Assn. for Women Lawyers, Ga. Real Estate Closing Attys. Assn. (sec. 1997—), Atlanta Bar Assn. Avocations: gourmet cooking, wine, gardening. Office: Smith Ronick & Corbin LLC 750 Hammond Dr NE Bldg 11 Atlanta GA 30328-5532 E-mail: kristinecavin@closingattorney.com.

CAVIN, SUSAN ELIZABETH, sociologist, writer; b. Trion, Ga., Mar. 18, 1948; d. John Charles and Mary (Risk) C.; 1 child, Julian Samuel Cavin-Zeidenstein. BA, Vanderbilt U., 1970; MA, Rutgers U., 1973, PhD, 1978. Teaching asst., sociology Rutgers U., Newark, N.J., 1970-75; typesetter SoHo News, N.Y.C., 1976; asst. prof. sociology Green Mountain Coll., Poultney, Vt., 1979-83; lectr. women's studies Rutger's U., New Brunswick, 1984-91, asst. dir. women's studies, 1988-91; project dir. women in engring. sci. tech. program, 1991-97; rsch. scientist N.Y.C. Dept. Health, 1999; lectr. women's studies Rutgers U., Newark, 1999—2000; dir. evaluation Annenberg Grant, 2002—. Cons. Gov.'s Study Commn. on Discrimination, Trenton, NJ, 1992; adj. asst. prof. sociology NYU, 1990—97, assoc. prof., 1998—; regional technician N.Y. Regional Census Ctr., Census 2000, 2000. Author: Lesbian Origins, 1985, poetry book, 1973, (cd-rom) Alice in Techiland, 1997; founding editor: (newspapers) Radical Chick, 1992-95, Big Apple Dyke News (B.A.D. News), 1981-88, Green Mountain Dyke News, 1980, (jour.) Tribad, 1977-79. Named Outstanding Tchr. of Yr., Green Mountain Coll., Poultney, 1982-83, winner Declamation awards, Ga. High Sch. Assn., 1965-66; winner fiction prize N.Y.C. Gay Ctr. Ann. Writing Contest, 2002-03; tchg. fellow Rutgers U., 2000—. Mem. Nat. Writers Union, Am. Sociol. Assn., Nat. Women's Studies Assn., N.Y. Acad. Scis. Democrat. Avocations: writing, poetry.

CAVIOR, WARREN JOSEPH, communications executive; b. Boston, Sept. 18, 1929; s. Joel H. and Shirley (Miller) C.; m. Mariko Sanjo, Oct. 12, 1969; children— Mayu, Samuel. AB cum laude, Harvard, 1951; MA, Columbia, 1952; postgrad., Oxford U., 1952-53. Asso. editor Forbes Mag., 1956-59; pres. Wall Street Consultants, Inc., N.Y.C., 1959-62, Warren J. Cavior & Co., N.Y.C., 1962-67; chmn. bd. Universal Communications Inc., N.Y.C., 1967-74; exec. v.p. Rogers, Cowan & Taplinger, Inc., N.Y.C., 1974-76; sr. v.p. Rogers & Cowan, Inc., N.Y.C., 1976-81; pres. Cavior Orgn., Inc., 1981—; chmn. The Am. Depositary Receipt Assn., 1993—; treas., dir. Wako Internat. Corp., 1962-67. Adv. bd.: Present Tense Mag. Chmn. Cavior Found., 1968— . Mem. Am. C. of C. in Japan. Office: 2 Fifth Ave New York NY 10011 E-mail: caviorg@aol.com.

CAVNAR, MARGARET MARY (PEGGY CAVNAR), business executive, former state legislator, nurse, consultant; b. Buffalo, July 29, 1945; d. James John and Margaret Mary Nightengale; m. Samuel M. Cavnar, 1977 (div. 2000); children: Heather Anne Hicks, Heide Lynn Gibson. BSN, D'Youville Coll., 1967; MBA, Nat. U., 1991. Utilization rev. coord. South Nev. Meml. Hosp., Las Vegas, 1975-77. Pres. PS Computer Svc., Las Vegas, 1978—86; bd. mem. Nev. Eye Bank, 1987—89, exec. dir., 1990—91; dir. health fairs Centel & Ch13TV, 1991—94; bd. dirs. Bridge Counseling Assocs., 1992—2000, pres., 1994—95; healing touch practitioner, 1994—; 1st v.p. bd. dirs. Nev. Alternative Medicine Assocs., 1997—2000; clin. rsch. coord. dept. and neurology U. Nev. Sch. Medicine, 2000—. Mem. Clark County Rep. Ctrl. Com., 1977-87, Nev. Rep. Ctrl. Com., 1978-80; mem. Nev. Assembly, 1979-81; Rep. nominee for Nev. Senate, 1980, for Congress from Nev. 1st dist., 1982, 84; bd. dirs., treas. Nev. Med. Fed. Credit Union; v.p. Cmty. Youth Activities Found., Inc., Civic Assn. Am.; mem. utilization rev. bd. Easter Seals; trustee Nev. Sch. Arts, 1980-87; nat. advisor Project Prayer, 1978-2000; co-chmn. PRIDE com., 1983-2000, tax limitation com., 1983, personal property tax elimination com., 1979-82, self-help against food tax elimination denial com., 1980; mem. nat. bd. dirs., co-chmn. Nev. Pres. Reagan's Citizens for Tax Reform Com., 1985-88; mem. Nev. Profl. Stds. Rev. Orgn., 1984; co-chmn. People Against Tax Hikes, 1983-84; bd. dirs. Nev. Eye Bank, 1988-90. Mem. Nev. Order Women Legislators (charter, parliamentarian 1980—), Cosmopolitanly Hers Info. (pres.), Sigma Theta Tau.

CAVNAR, SAMUEL MELMON, writer, publisher, activist; b. Denver, Nov. 10, 1925; s. Samuel Edward and Helen Anita (Johnston) C.; m. Peggy Nightengale, Aug. 14, 1977; children by previous marriage: Dona Cavnar Hambly, Judy Cavnar Bentrim; children: Heather Anne Hicks, Heide Lynn Gibson. Student pub. schs., Denver. Dist. mgr. U.S. C. of C., various locations, 1953-58; owner Cavnar & Assocs.; mgmt. cons. Washington, Las Vegas, Nev., 1958—, Denver, Reseda, Calif., 1958—; v.p. Lenz Assoc. Advt., Inc., Van Nuys, Calif., 1960—. Dist. mgr. Western States Nu-Orm Plans, Inc., L.A., 1947-52; cons. to arch. and contractor 1st U.S. Missile Site, Wyo., 1957-58; prin. organizer Westway Corp. and subsidiaries, So. Calif. Devel. Co., 1958—; chmn. bd. Boy Sponsors Inc., Denver, 1957-59; pres. Continental Am. Video Network Assn. Registry, Inc., Hollywood, Calif., 1967—; pres. United Sales Am., Las Vegas and Denver, 1969—; sr. mgmt. cons. Broadcast Mgmt. Cons. Svc., Hollywood, Las Vegas, Denver, Washington, 1970—; pres., dir., exec. com. Am. Ctr. for Edn., 1968—; pub. Nat. Ind., Washington, 1970—, Nat. Rep. Statesman, Washington, 1969—, Nat. Labor Reform Leader, 1970—, Nat. Conservative Statesman, 1975—; owner Ran Vac Pub., Las Vegas and L.A., 1976—; ptnr. P.S. Computer Svcs., Las Vegas, 1978—, C & A Mgmt., Las Vegas, 1978—, Westway Internat., 1983—, Internet Cons., 1997—, Affiliate Internet Presentations, Inc., 1997—; lectr. in field; spl. cons. various U.S. senators, congressmen, 1952—. Author: Run, Big Sam, Run, 1976, The Girls on Top, 1978, Big Brother Bureaucracy, The Cause and Cure, 1977, Kiddieland West, 1980, Games Politicians Play: How to Clean Up Their Act, 1981, A Very C.H.I.C. President, 1981, How to Clean Up Our Act, 1982, Assassination By Suicide, 1984, How to Get Limited Government, Limited Taxes, 1985, Tax Reform or Bust, 1985, At Last: Real Tax Reform, 1986, On the Road to a Real Balanced Budget, 1989, It's Time for Term Limitation, 1990, Clinton's "Investments": Just More Taxes, 1993, Hillary-Billary's New Road to Socialism, 1993, The Cause and the New Cure, 1995, Messin' with My Mind and Body, 1995, Reaction to Messin with My Mind, 1996, Millennium 5000 Chronicles, 1998, 99, 5th edit., 2003, The Ranvac Understandings, 2000, Stroke of Good Luck—Messin' with My Mind 7 Years Later, 2001, Living in the Future Now, 2001, Chronicles for 2003. Nat. gen. chmn. Operation Houseclean, 1966-81; nat. candidate chmn. Citizens Com. to Elect Rep. Legislators, 1966, 68, 70, 72-74, 85—; mem. Calif. and L.A. County Rep. Cen. Coms., 1964-70; nat. gen. chmn. Project Prayer, 1962—; exec. dir. Project Alert, 1961—; nat. chmn. Nat. Labor Reform Com., 1969—; sustaining mem. Rep. Nat. Com., 1964—; Western states chmn. and nat. co-chmn. Am. Taxpayers Army, 1959—; area II chmn. Calif. Gov.'s Welfare Reform Com., 1970; chmn. Com. Law and Order in Am., 1975; mem. Nev. State Rep. Com., 1972—; mem. Clark County Rep. Com., 1972—; bd. dirs. Conservative Caucus, Las Vegas, 1974, 76, 82, 92, Rep. candidate for U.S. Senate from Nev., 1976, 82, 92, U.S. Congress from 1st dist. Nev., 1998; Rep. nominee for U.S. Congress from 30th dist. Calif., 1968, 70; nat. chmn. Return Pueblo Crew, 1968, Citizens League for Labor Reform, 1984—; nat. co-chmn. U.S. Taxpayers Forces, 1985—; pres., trustee Cmty. Youth Activities Found., 1977—; nat. chmn. Operation Bus Stop, 1970—, P.R.I.D.E. Com., 1981—, Positivics Program, 1982—; co-chmn. Question 8 Com., 1980-82, S.H.A.F.T.E.D. Tax Repeal Com., 1982 C.H.I.C. Polit. Edn. Com., 1977—, People Against Tax Hikes Com., 1983—; bd. dirs., Nev. co-chmn. Pres. Reagan's Citizens's Com. for Tax Reform, 1985-86; nat. chmn. Term Limitation Com., 1988—; nat. chmn. Combined Coms. for Rep.'s Contract with Am., 1994—; chmn. Citizen's to Return Barloon and Daliberti, 1995—, New Nurses project, 2003—. With USN, 1942-45, USAF, 1950-53, Korea; comdr. USCG Aux., 1959-60. Recipient Silver medal SAR. Mem. Am. Legion (comdr. 1947-48, mem. nat. conv. disting. guest com. 1947-52), DAV, VFW, Am. Security Coun. (nat. adviser 1966—), U.S. C. of C. (sr. mem. rep. 1986—). Home: 6681-B Bubbling Brook Dr Las Vegas NV 89107-1135 Office: 1615 H St NW Washington DC 20062-0001

CAW, THOMAS WILLIAM, retired publisher and editor; b. Zanesville, Ohio, Nov. 21, 1929; s. William Hooper and Hazel Lavern Caw; m. Margaret Jane Derry, Dec. 26, 1951; children: Melanie Jane Caw Woods, Thomas Shepherd. Grad., Mergenthaler Linotype Sch., N.Y.C., 1950. Linotype operator The Pataskala (Ohio) Standard, 1950-76, editor, pub., co-owner, 1955-65, editor, pub., owner, 1965-96. Advisor, mem. com. Bicentennial book People Make the Difference, 1976; creator, bd. dirs. Pataskala Lost Arts Festival, 1972-75. Mem. Pataskala Planning Commn., 1965; mem. Pataskala Zoning Bd., 1967; bd. dirs. Licking County Red Cross, Newark, Ohio, 1977; mem. commn. Licking Meml. Hosp., Newark, 1977—; mem. exec. com. Boy scouts Am., Licking County, 1978-79; poll worker, pres. judge Licking County Bd. Elections, 1997—; mem. Comprehensive Planning com., Pataskala, 1998—; mem. adv. bd. YMCA, 1999. Cpl. USMC, 1951-53. Recipient Order of Merit award Licking County Boy scouts, 1980, Licking County Citizen of Yr. award, 1995, Cmty. Svc. award Masons, 1995, Paul S. Noblitt Sch. Bell award, 1982, Rotary Four Way Test award, 1998, numerous others. Mem. Ohio Newspaper Assn., Nat. Newspaper Assn., Soc. Profl. Journalists, Lions Club (bd. dirs., treas., sec., pres.), Pataskala C. of C. (charter mem., bd. dirs., Outstanding Citizen 1976). Seventh-day Adventist. Avocations: golf, reading, walking. Home: PO Box 1394 Pataskala OH 43062-1394

CAWLEY, CHARLES M. banker; Grad., Georgetown U. Chmn., CEO MBNA Am. Bank N.A., Wilmington, Del., 2002—. Pres., dir. MBNA Corp., 1985—; bd. dirs. MasterCard Internat. Exec. com. bd. dirs. Am. Quality Found.; bd. regents Georgetown U. Office: MBNA America Bank NA 1100 King St Wilmington DE 19884-0001*

CAWLEY, JOSEPH DOUGLAS, retired reading educator; b. Savannah, Ga., Dec. 12, 1929; s. Henry Hughes and Bertha (Platt) C.; m. Grace Ashliman, June 21, 1951; children: Lorraine Cawley Gaufin, Carolyn Nielsen; m. Jacqueline Boss, May 22, 1987. BS, Brigham Young U., 1954; MS, U. Utah, 1961, PhD, 1970. Cert. elem. tchr., Utah, Ga. Tchr. Dekalb County Sch. Dist., Atlanta, Salt Lake City Sch. Dist.; asst. prof. edn. Adams State Coll., Alamoso, Colo.; prof., chmn. reading dept. Met. State Coll., Denver, prof. emeritus, 2001—. Author: Handbook for Experiential Education, 1988, From Alsace to South Carolina Jonas Beard, 1730-1796, Patriot, Statesman, 2002, From Herrstein to South Carolina Reverend John Nicholas Martin, 2003. Mem. CCIRA (past pres., Pres. award), Kappa Delta Pi (Outstanding Counselor award), Phi Delta Kappa.

CAWLEY, LEO PATRICK, pathologist, immunologist; b. Oklahoma City, Aug. 11, 1922; s. Pat Bernard and Mary Elizabeth (Forbes) C.; m. Joan Mae Wood, June 20, 1948; children: Kevin Patrick, Karin Patricia, Kary Forbes. BS in Chemistry, Okla. State U., 1948; MD, Okla. Sch. Medicine, 1952. Diplomate Am. Bd. Pathology, Am. Bd. Nuclear Medicine, Am. Bd. Allergy and Immunology, Am. Bd. Med. Lab. Immunology, Am. Bd. Pathology in immunopathology. Intern Wesley Med. Ctr., Wichita, 1952-53, resident in pathology, 1953-54, Wayne County Gen. Hosp., Eloise, Mich., 1954-56, chief resident in pathology, 1956-57; clin. pathologist, asst. dir. lab. Wesley Med. Ctr., Wichita, Kans., 1957-69, dir. sci., 1965-86, dir. labs., 1969-77, dir. clin. immunology, 1979-86; med. dir. Roche Biomed. Lab., Wichita, Kans., 1979-86; dir. clin. labs. Vetazyme Corp., Tempe, Ariz., 1988—. Pres. Kilcawley Enterprises, 1986—. Author: Electrophoresis/Immunoelectric Phoresis, 1969; editor series Lab Med Little Brown, 1965-81; contbr. 210 articles to profl. jours. Pfc. USM, 1942-45. Fellow Am. Soc. Clin. pathologist (bd. dirs. 1968, Disting. Svc. award 1980, Dist. Pathology edn. award, 1998), Coll. Am. Pathologist; mem. AAAS, ACS, Am. Assn. Clin. Chemists, Alpha Pi Mu, Phi Lambda Upsilon, Alpha Omega Alpha. Avocations: reading, history. Office: KilCawley Enterprises 7135 E Main St Scottsdale AZ 85251-4315

CAWNS, ALBERT EDWARD, computer systems consultant; b. Houston, Apr. 3, 1937; s. Harry William and Blanche Ophelia (Bays) C.; m. Sheila Mathie Climie, June 24, 1961; children: Elizabeth Carrick, Jennifer Kathryn. AB in Math., Drury Coll., Springfield, Mo., 1958; BS in Mech. Engring., U. Mo., Rolla, 1959, MS in Computer Sci., 1984; M Engring. Adminstrn., Washington U., St. Louis, 1965. Engr. White Rodgers Co., St. Louis, 1959-62, McDonnell Aircraft Co., St. Louis, 1962-64; v.p. Thomas Inc., St. Louis, 1964-82; pres. Talos Co., St. Louis, 1982—. Adj. faculty Webster U., St. Louis, 1986-91, asst. prof. math. and computer sci., dir., M.S. in Comp. Sci. Prog., 1991—, assoc. prof. math. and computer sci., 1995—, chairperson math and computer sci. dept., 1999—. Moderator Southeast Mo. Presbytery, 1971; mem. Gen. Assembly Mission Bd., Presbyn. Ch. U.S.A., 1973; trustee Westminster Presbyn. Ch., St. Louis, 1976; pres. alumni adv. coun. Sch. Engring., Washington U., St. Louis, 1990-92. Cpl. USMCR, 1954-62. Home: 7391 Stratford Ave Saint Louis MO 63130-4138 Office: Talos Co PO Box 3069 Saint Louis MO 63130-0469

CAWOOD, ALBERT MCLAURIN (HAP CAWOOD), retired newspaper editor; b. Harlan, Ky., Nov. 10, 1939; s. Frank Finley and C. Eugene (Barwick) C.; m. Sonia Barreiro, July 3, 1965; children: Romy Lanier, Shuly Xochitl. BA in English, Union Coll., 1962; MA in Journalism, Ohio State U., 1966. Asst. city editor Dayton (Ohio) Daily News, 1966, editorial writer, 1966-82, editorial page editor, 1982-99; ret., 1999. Vol. Peace Corps., Sierra Leone, 1962-64; chmn. Ohio Com. on Crime and Delinquency, 1969-70; bd. mem. Engring. Sci. Found., Dayton, Ohio, 2003—. Recipient Disting. Svc. award for Editorial Writing, Nat. Soc. Profl. Journalists, 1968, Walker Stone award for Editorial Writing, Scripps-Howard Found., 1984; named to Union Coll. Bus. and Profl. Hall of Fame. Mem. Am. Soc. Newspaper Editors, Nat. Conf. Editl. Writers, Engrs. Club Dayton (pres. 2003—). Democrat. Home: 211 S Winter St Yellow Springs OH 45387-1730

CAWOOD, JENNY LIND, social worker, poet; b. Harlan, Ky, Aug. 15, 1940; d. James Abram and Lillian Greer Cawood; m. Hartwell Lynn Chenault, Mar. 1966 (div. 1986); children: James Cawood Chenault, Henry Brian Chenault. BA in Speech, Abilene Christian U., 1962; MSW, U. Louisville, 1966. LCSW Va. Dir. social work Battey State Hosp., Rome, Ga., 1967—68; clin. social worker Child and Family Svcs., Monroe, Mich., 1974—78; oncology social worker The Toledo Hosp., 1978—79; clin. social worker Ide Cmty. Mental Health, Toledo, 1979—80, Cmty. Mental Health Ctr. West, Toledo, 1980—84; unit social worker St. Albans Hosp., Radford, Va., 1984—85; clin. social worker Human Affairs Internat., Raleigh, NC, 1988. Episcopal Church. Avocations: writing poetry, doing poetry readings, managing rental properties. Home: 1210 Canterbury Dr Abilene TX 79602

CAWS, MARY ANN, French language and comparative literature educator, critic; b. Wilmington, NC, Sept. 10, 1933; d. Harmon Chadbourn and Margaret Devereux (Lippitt) Rorison; m. Peter Caws, June 2, 1956 (div. 1987); children: Hilary, Matthew. BA, Bryn Mawr Coll., 1954; MA, Yale U., 1956; PhD, U. Kans., 1962; D.Humane Letters, Union Coll., 1983. Asst. instr. Romance Langs. U. Kans., Lawrence, Kans., 1957-62, asst. editor Univ. press, 1957-58, vis. asst. prof., spring 1963; lectr. Barnard Coll. Columbia U., NYC, 1962-63; mem. faculty Sarah Lawrence Coll., Bronxville, NY, 1963-64, Hunter Coll. CUNY, NYC, 1966-88; prof. Grad. Sch. CUNY, NYC, 1969-88, exec. officer comparative lit. program Grad. Sch., 1977-79, exec. officer French program Grad. Sch., 1979-86, Disting. prof. French and comparative lit. Grad. Sch., 1983—, prof. English, 1985—, Disting. prof. French, comparative lit., English Grad. Sch., 1987—. Phi Beta Kappa vis. scholar, 1982-83; dir. NIH summer seminars for coll. tchrs., 1978, 85; mem. faculty Sch. of Criticism and Theory, Dartmouth U., 1988, Sch. Visual Arts, 1993; professeur associé Université de Paris VII, 1993-94; co-chair Henri Peyre Inst. for the Humanities, 1980-1996, French Inst., 1997-2002; lectr. NY Coun. for Humanities, 1992-96. Author: Surrealism and the Literary Imagination, 1966, The Poetry of Dada and Surrealism, 1970, The Inner Theatre of Recent French Poetry, 1972, The Presence of René Char, 1976, René Char, 1977, The Surrealist Voice of Robert Desnos, 1977, La Main de Pierre Reverdy, 1979, The Eye in the Text, Essays on Perception, Mannerist to Modern, 1981, André Breton, 1982, 96, The Metapoetics of the Passage, Architextures in Surrealism and After, 1982, Yves Bonnefoy, 1984, Reading Frames in Modern Fiction, 1988, Edmond Jabès, 1988, The Art of Interference: Stressed Readings in Visual and Verbal Texts, 1989, Women of Bloomsbury, 1991, Robert Motherwell: What Art Holds, 1996, Carrington and Lytton: Alone Together, 1996, The Surrealist Look: An Erotics of Encounter, 1997, Picasso's Weeping Woman: The Life and Art of Dora Maar, 2000, Virginia Woolf: Illustrated Life, 2002, Robert Motherwell with Pen and Brush, 2003, Marcel Proust: Illustrated Life, 2003; co-author: Bloomsbury and France: Art and Friends, 1999; editor: Dada-Surrealism, 1972, co-editor, 1980-2002, Le Siècle éclaté, 1974-78, About French Poetry from Dada to Tel Quel, 1974, Selected Poetry Prose of Stéphane Mallarmé, 1982, Selected Poems of St.-John Perse, 1983, Writing in a Modern Temper, 1984, Textual Analysis, 1986, Perspectives on Perception: Philosophy, Art, and Literature, 1989, City Images, 1992, Joseph Cornell's Theater of the Mind: Selected Diaries, Letters and Files, 1994, Manifesto: A Century of Isms, 2001, Mallarme in Prose, 2001, Surrealist Painters and Poets, 2001, Surrealist Love Poems, 2002, Vita Sackville-West: Selected Writings, 2002; co-editor: Selected Poems of René Char, 1992, Contre-Courants: Les femmes s'écrivent à travers les siècles, 1994, Écritures de femmes: Nouvelles Cartographies, 1996; translator: Poems of René Char, 1976, Approximate Man and other Writings of Tristan Tzara, 1975, Mad Love, 1987, The Secret Art of Antonin Artaud, 1998, Ostinato, 2002; co-translator: Poems of André Breton, 1984, Communicating Vessels, 1990, Break of Day, 1999; chief editor Harper Collins World Reader, 1994, Manifesto: A Century of isms, 2001, Surrealist Painters and Poets, 2001, Mallarmé in Prose, 2001; contbr. articles to profl. jours. Decorated officier Palmes Académiques, France; fellow Guggenheim Found., 1972-73 NEH, 1979-80, Fulbright traveling fellow, 1972-73, Rockefeller Found. fellow, 1994; Getty scholar, 1990. Mem. MLA (exec. coun. 1973-77, v.p. 1982-83, pres. 1983-84), Am. Assn. Tchrs. French, Assn. for Study Dada and Surrealism (pres. 1982-86), Internat. Assn. Philosophy and Lit. (exec. bd. 1982—, chmn. 1984), Acad. Lit. Studies (pres. 1985), Am. Comparative Lit. Assn. (exec. com. 1981, v.p. 1986—, pres. 1989-91). Home: 140 E 81st St New York NY 10028-1805 Office: CUNY Grad Ctr 365 Fifth Ave New York NY 10016

CAWS, PETER JAMES, philosopher, educator; b. Southall, Eng., May 25, 1931; came to U.S., 1953; naturalized, 1995; s. Geoffrey Tulloh and Olive (Budden) C.; m. Mary Ann Rorison (div.); children: Hilary, Matthew; m. Nancy Breslin, Nov. 28, 1987; 1 child, Elisabeth. BS, U. London, 1952; MA, Yale U., 1954, PhD, 1956. Instr. natural sci. Mich. State U., 1956-57; asst. prof. philosophy U. Kans., 1957-60, assoc. prof., 1960-62, chmn. dept., 1961-62, Rose Morgan vis. prof., 1963; vis. prof. U. Costa Rica, 1961; exec. assoc. Carnegie Corp. N.Y., 1962-65, cons., 1965-67; prof. philosophy Hunter Coll., N.Y.C., 1965-82, chmn. dept., 1965-67; exec. officer Ph.D. program in philosophy CUNY, 1967-70, 81-82; Univ. prof. philosophy George Washington U., 1982—, dir. PhD Program in Human Scis., 1991-93; vis. prof. NYU, spring 1982, U.Md., spring 1985; tchr. New Sch. Social Research, 1965-67; mem. adv. bd. Learning Corp. of Am., 1968-74. Vis. scholar U. Kent, Canterbury, Eng., 1993-94; lectr. Smithsonian Resident Assocs. Program, 1988-95; mem. Coun. Philos. Studies, 1965-71; bd. dirs. Coordinating Coun. Lit. Mags., 1969-70; mem. Scientists Inst. for Pub. Info., 1967-94, treas., 1969-72, fellow, 1972-94, dir., 1975-80, vice chmn., 1975-79; mem. editl. bd. Environment, 1972-78; mem. bd. advisers, history of physics program Am. Inst. Physics, 1966-75; mem. NRC, 1967-70, Assembly Behavioral and Social Scis., 1973-77; nat. lectr. Sigma Xi, 1975-77; dir. Bicentennial Symposium of Philosophy; cons. in humanities LWV, 1978; vis. scholar Phi Beta Kappa, 1983-84; 1st Philip Morris Disting. lectr. in bus. and soc. Baruch Coll., N.Y.C., 1986; sr. fellow Christina River Inst., 2001—. Author: The Philosophy of Science, Systematic Account, 1965, Science and the Theory of Value, 1967, Sartre, 1979, Structuralism: A Philosophy for the Human Sciences, 1997, Yorick's World: Science and the Knowing Subject, 1993, The Capital Connection, 1993, Ethics from Experience, 1996; editor: Two Centuries of Philosophy in America, 1980, The Causes of Quarrel: Essays on Peace, War and Thomas Hobbes, 1989; mem. editl. bd. Jour. Enterprise Mgmt., 1976-81, Philosophy Documentation Ctr., mem. cmty. adv. bd. The News Jour., Wilmington, Del., 1998—2001. Recipient Pres.'s medal Grad. Sch., CUNY, 1978; Am. Council Learned Socs. fellow Paris, 1972-73; Rockefeller Found. humanities fellow, 1979-80 Fellow AAAS (v.p. 1967); mem. Am. Philos. Assn. (dir., chmn. com. on internat. coop. 1974-84), Fedn. Internat. des Socs. de Philosophie (commn. on policy 1979-88, comité dir. 1978-88), Philosophy of Sci. Assn. (del.), Soc. Gen. Systems Rsch. (pres. 1966-67), Soc. Am. de Philosophie de Langue Française (v.p. 1989-92, pres. 1992-94), Elizabethan Club, Washington Philosophy Club (pres. 1988-89), Phi Beta Kappa (hon. Alpha chpt. D.C.). Home: 237 Cheltenham Rd Newark DE 19711-3617 Office: George Washington U Dept Philosophy Washington DC 20052-0001 E-mail: pcaws@gwu.edu.

CAWTHON, FRANK H. retired construction company executive; b. Kissimmee, Fla., Apr. 3, 1930; s. Benjamin Hill and Eva Elizabeth (Mullins) C.; m. Mary Elizabeth Dickert, July 10, 1959; 1 child, Frank H. Grad. high sch. Asst. sec.-treas. Orange Belt Truck & Tractor, Orlando, Fla., 1948-52, Murdock Constrn. Co., Inc., Orlando, 1954-59; sec.-treas. Amick Constrn. Co., Inc., Orlando, 1959-90; ret., 1990. Bd. dirs. Amick Constrn. Co., Inc. Bd. dirs. Conway Little League, Orlando, 1977. With U.S. Army, 1952-54. Mem. Cen. Fla. Rd. Bldrs. Assn. Democrat. Lutheran. Avocations: oil painting, gardening, fishing. Home: 391 Brushwood Ln Casselberry FL 32708-4955 Office: Amick Constrn Co 401 Ferguson Dr Orlando FL 32805-1009

CAWTHON, TONY W. social sciences educator; b. Lexington, Tenn., Apr. 18, 1959; s. Thelma Jane Page and John Paul Page, Jr.(Stepfather). BA in Psychology/Sociology, U. Tenn., 1981, MA in Sociology, 1983; PhD, Miss. State U., 1995. Asst. dir. residence life Miss. State U., Starkville, 1984—91; dir. residential life Clemson (S.C.) U., 1991—95, assoc. prof., 1996—. Co-editor: (spl. issue So. Assn. Coll. Student Affairs jour.) Community Found. Sec. AID Upstate, Greenville, SC, 2000—03; pres. Anderson (S.C.) Free Clinic, 2002—02. Mem.: Soiree. Office: Clemson Univ 313 Tillman Hall Box 340710 Clemson SC 29634-0710 Office Fax: 864-656-1322. Personal E-mail: cawthot@clemson.edu. E-mail: cawthot@clemson.edu.

CAWVEY, CLARENCE EUGENE, retired physician; b. Du Quoin, Ill., May 16, 1929; s. Clarence Eli and Lois Jane (Matheny) C.; m. Paulina Isabel Hincke, Sept. 12, 1953 (dec. Apr. 1973); children: Janet Edna, William Clarence, Paulina Ann, Jean Hincke; 1 stepchild, Douglas Lance Hester; m. Linda Mae Rice, Jan. 26, 1974. BA, Yale U., 1951; MD, U. Chgo., 1955. Diplomate Am. Bd. Family Practice. Intern Cook County Hosp., 1955-56; resident in psychiatry Brook Army Hosp., 1956-57; ptnr. Pickneyville (Ill.) Med. Group, 1958-98; ret., 1998. Clin. asst. prof. Med. Sch. So. Ill. U., Springfield, 1976-2000, adv. com. continuing med. edn., 1977-2000; exec. com. Ctrl. Ill. Profl. Rev. Orgn., Champaign, 1988-2002; bd. dirs., chmn. First Nat. Bank, Pinckneyville. Founding mem., pres. Perry County Health Dept., Pinckneyville, 1970. Capt. U.S. Army, 1956-58. Fellow Am. Acad. Family Physicians; mem. AMA, Ill. State Med. Soc. (del. 1960-70), Perry County Med. Soc. Republican. Methodist. Avocations: skiing, photography, travel, gardening. Home: 204 W Laurel St Pinckneyville IL 62274-1019

CAYEA, DONALD JOSEPH, lawyer; b. Bklyn., Mar. 3, 1948; s. Glendon Vernon and Marie Nicola (Gesualdo) C. BA, L.I. U., 1969; JD, Western New Eng. Coll., 1975. Bar: N.Y. 1976, U.S. Dist. Ct. (so. and ea. dists.) N.Y. 1978, D.C. 1979, U.S. Supreme Ct. 1979. Prin. Donald J. Cayea & Assoc., N.Y.C., 1976—; ptnr. Kroll & Tract, N.Y.C., 1988-90, Levitan, Frieland & Cayea, N.Y.C., 1990-94, Klepner & Cayea, N.Y.C., 1994-98, Brand, Cayea & Brand, LLC, N.Y.C., 1998—2002, Gallet, Dreyer & Berkey, LLP, N.Y.C., 2002—; gen. counsel Entertainment USA, 1990—. Lectr. Paralegal Inst., NYU, 1984—, adult edn. program Nassau County Bar Assn., Mineola, N.Y., 1978-79; panelist trial advocacy program Cardozo Law Sch., Yeshiva U., N.Y.C., 1984—; spkr. Ft. Lauderdale (Fla.) Film Festival, 1989, 90, Coun. on Mgmt. Worker's Compensation Update, N.Y.C., 1995, 96; guest panelist Property Loss Rsch. Bur., Washington, 1989, Chgo., 1991. Prodr.: (video) Dahmer, the Secret Life, 1993, (off Broadway) West Side Stories, Theatre Arielle, N.Y.C., 1993, Conversations with My Daughter; exec. prodr. (film) The Hunt for CM24, 1997; prodr. (theatre) The Remarkable Thing About Star Dust, Mother Lode, 1999, (off-Broadway) Panache, 2000. Pres. Seascape Condominium, Westhampton Beach, N.Y., 1986-92; sponsor Richmond Roller Hocker Assn., Staten Island, N.Y., 1984-89; mem. Pres.'s Coun., L.I. Univ. Served in U.S. Army, 1970-71. Mem. ABA (editor TIPS publ. editorial bd. 1990-93), Assn. Trial Lawyers Am., N.Y. State Bar Assn., Internat. Bar Assn., Assn. of Bar of City of N.Y., New York County Lawyers Assn., Phi Epsilon Pi. Office: 845 3d Ave 8th Fl New York NY 10022

CAYETANO, BENJAMIN JEROME, former governor, former state senator and representative; b. Honolulu, Nov. 14, 1939; s. Bonifacio Marcos and Eleanor (Infante) C.; m. Vicky Tiu, 1997; children: Brandon, Janeen, Samantha, Cayetano, Marissa, William Liu. BA, UCLA, 1968; JD, Loyola U., 1971; LLD (hon.), U. Philippines, 1995; D in Pub. Svc. (hon.), Loyola Marymount U., 1998. Bar: Hawaii 1971. Practiced in, Honolulu, 1971-86; mem. Hawaii Ho. of Reps., 1975-78, Hawaii Senate, 1979-86; lt. gov. State of Hawaii, 1986-94, gov., 1994—2002. Adv. U. Hawaii Law Rev., 1982-84 Mem. bd. regents Chaminade U., 1980-83; chmn. Western Gov.'s Assn., 1999. Recipient UCLA Alumni award for excellence in pub. svc., 1993, UCLA Medal, 1995, Disting. Leadership award, UCLA John E. Anderson Sch. of Mgmt., 1995, Leadership award Harvard Found., 1996, Edward A. Dickson Alumnus of Yr. award UCLA, 1998, Disting. Alumnus of Yr., Loyola Law Sch., 2002. Democrat. E-mail: gov@gov.state.hi.us.*

CAYNE, BERNARD STANLEY, editor; b. N.Y.C., Nov. 8, 1924; m. Helen M. Burgard, Apr. 11, 1953; children— Claudia Elizabeth, Douglas Andrew. Student, Cornell U., 1940-42; BS, Moravian Coll., 1945; postgrad., U. Pa., 1945-46; research fellow, Harvard U., 1953-55; MA, Columbia U., 1947. Head sci. dept. Adelphi Acad., 1946-47; instr. Bklyn. Coll., 1947-49; tchr. N.Y.C. Pub. Schs., 1948-49; head sci. sect., test devel. dept. Ednl. Testing Service, Princeton, N.J., 1949-53; dir. research Boston U. Coll. Basic Studies, 1953-54; sr. sci. editor Ginn & Co., Boston, 1955-61; v.p. Crowell-Collier Ednl. Corp., N.Y.C., 1961-68; exec. editor Collier's Ency., 1963-68, Collier's Ency. Yearbook, 1963-68; editor-in-chief Merit Students Ency., 1961-69, asst. editorial dir. corp., 1963-68; mng. editor, sch. div. Macmillan Co., 1968-69; editor-in-chief Ency. Americana, Danbury, Conn., 1969-90; v.p., editorial dir. Grolier, Inc., Danbury, 1980-90; creative dir. The Readfern Group, Newtown, Conn., 1990—. Chmn. bd. editors: Harvard Edn. Rev, 1954. Fellow AAAS, Am. Psychol. Soc.; mem. N.Y. Acad. Scis., Am. Ednl. Rsch. Assn., Phi Delta Kappa. Home: 8 Old Green Rd Sandy Hook CT 06482-1043 Office: The Readfern Group 100 Acre Wood PO Box 3431 Newtown CT 06470-3431

CAYNE, JAMES E. investment banker; b. 1934; With Bonn Bush Mach, 1954-66, Lebenthal and Co., 1966-69; pres., past sr. mng. dir. Bear Stearns and Co. Inc., also bd. dirs., CEO, pres., 1993—. Office: Bear Stearns & Co Inc 245 Park Ave Fl 9A New York NY 10167-0002

CAYSON, JOYCE SCALLORN, editor, small business owner; b. Sardis, Miss., May 16, 1952; d. Lance Leon and Clara Lou Scallorn; m. Royce Lee Cayson, Aug. 31, 1998. Adv. bd. Night Town Records, Golden, Miss., 1995—; editor R J Pub. Co, Vina, Ala., 1999—. Author: (book) The Coming: The Bible's Identity of So Called UFOs (pseudonym: Jamie Lance), Fables In The Fold (pseudonym: Jamie Lance). Office: R J Publishing Co 11142 County Hwy 13 Vina AL 35593 E-mail: joyce@rjpublishing.net.

CAYTAS, IVO GEORGE, lawyer; b. Plovdiv, Bulgaria, Feb. 3, 1958; s. George I. and Hilda (Plankl) Kaitasow. MA in Diplomacy, U. St Gallen, Switzerland, 1982, PhD in Law, 1984, PhD in Fin., 1986; LLM, Yale U., 1986. Bar: D.C. 1997, U.S. Ct. Internat. Trade, U.S. Claims Ct., U.S. Tax Ct., U.S. Dist. Ct. (so. and ea. dists.) N.Y. 1992, (no. and ctrl. dists.) Calif. 1992, U.S. Ct. Appeals (1st-11th cirs., fed. and D.C. cir.), U.S. Supreme Ct. 1996. Asst. to chmn. IMAG Corp., Vienna, Austria, 1979-80; ptnr. Caytas & Cie, St. Gallen, 1984-89, CCCC, St. Gallen, 1989-91; mng. dir. Swissconsult Corp., N.Y.C., 1990-91; pres., gen. counsel Swiss Am. Group Inc., N.Y.C., 1991-95; ptnr. Caytas & Assocs., 1996—. Bd. dirs. The London Ct. of Internat. Abritration. Author: Investment Banking, 1988, Global Political Risk, Modern Financial Instruments, 1992, Transnational Legal Practice, 1992; contbr. articles to profl. publs. Fellow Swiss Nat. Sci. Found., 1985, 88, Max Planck Inst., 1987; recipient Walther-Hug Found. award, 1984. Mem. ABA (sect. of internat. law and practice, internat. investment com., internat. taxation com.), Assn. of Bar of City of N.Y. (com. on govt. ethics), Calif. Bar Assn. (internat. law com., task force on internat. legal svcs.), Yale Club. Roman Catholic. Office: 146 W 57th St New York NY 10019-3301

CAYTON, MARY EVELYN, minister; b. Morgantown, W. Va., July 7, 1926; d. Adam Johnson and Dorothy Ena (Bigler) Cayton. Student, Internat. Bible Coll., San Antonio, Tex., 1955. Ordained minister Full Gospel Denomination, 1958. Clk. First Nat. Bank, Morgantown, 1945-51; founder, pastor Morgantown Revival Ctr., 1956-92; staff, controller's office W.Va. U., Morgantown, 1951-55, '58-84. Chmn. Morgantown Revival Ctr. Assn., 1956—. Home and Office: 1702 Tyrone Rd Morgantown WV 26508-5902 *I have found through life that "With Man some things are possible", but "With God nothing is impossible".*

CAZA, BRIAN PATRICK, political scientist, educator; b. San Antonio, Mar. 4, 1969; s. Allen Patrick and Helen Jimenez Caza. BA with honors, Northwestern U., Evanston, Ill., 1991; postgrad., U. Chgo., 2003—. Tchr. Ecole d'Humanite, Hasliberg-Goldern, Switzerland, 1996—98; lectr. U. of Chgo., 1999—2001, preceptor com. on internat. rels., 2000—02; asst. prof. Georgetown Coll., Georgetown, Ky., 2002—. Recipient Grodzins Prize Lectureship, Dept. of Polit. Sci., The U. of Chgo., 2000—01; fellow Grad. fellow, NSF, 1991—94. Mem.: Soc. for Utopian Studies, Midwest Polit. Sci. Assn., Am. Polit. Sci. Assn., Sierra Club, Nat. Parks Conservation Assn. Avocations: mountaineering, travel, photography, rock climbing, hiking. Home: 102 N Lafayette Dr Georgetown KY 40324 Office: Georgetown College 400 East College St Georgetown KY 40324 E-mail: brian_caza@georgetowncollege.edu.

CAZALAS, MARY REBECCA WILLIAMS, lawyer, nurse; b. Atlanta, Nov. 11, 1927; d. George Edgar and Mary Annie (Slappey) Williams; m. Albert Joseph Cazalas (dec.). *Her great-great-grandfather, General John Coffee, fought in the Battle of New Orleans. His son,Peter Coffee married Mary Donelson, who was niece of Mrs. Andrew Jackson. Their son, Major John A. Coffee, served in the Civil War. His daughter, Mary Stevens Coffee, married Dr. John George Slappey, prominent physician at Jeffersonville, Georgia. His grandfather was Hans (John) George Slappey, who fought in the Revolution, and his father was Robert Rutherford Slappey. His daughter, Mary Annie Slappey, married George Edgar Wiliams. His mother was Sarah Cobb of Kosiesco, Mississippi. He graduated from Mercer University and was Chief Dispatcher of Central of Georgia Railroad.* BS in Pre-medicine, Oglethorpe U., Atlanta, 1954; MS in Anatomy, Emory U., 1960; JD, Loyola U., 1967, Loyola U., New Orleans, 1967. RN, Ga.; Bar: La. 1967, U.S. Dist. Ct. (ea. dist.) La. 1967, U.S. Ct. Appeals (5th cir.) 1972, U.S. Supreme Ct. 1975, U.S. Ct. Appeals (fed. cir.) 1999. Gen. duty nurse, 1948-68; instr. maternity nursing St. Josephs Infirmary Sch. Nursing, Atlanta, 1954-59; med. rschr. in urology Tulane U. Sch. Medicine, New Orleans, 1961-65; legal rschr. for presiding judge La. Ct. Appeals (4th cir.), New Orleans, 1965-71; pvt. practice New Orleans, 1967-71; asst. U.S. atty., 1971-79; sr. trial atty. Equal Employment Opportunity Commn., New Orleans, 1979-84; owner Cazalas Apts., New Orleans, 1962—. Lectr. in field. Contbr. articles to profl. jours. Bd. advisors Loyola U. Sch. Law, New Orleans, 1974, v.p. adv. bd., 1975; active New Orleans Drug Abuse Adv. Com., 1976-80; task force Area Agy. on Aging, 1976-80, pres. coun. Loyola U., 1978—; adv. bd. Odyssey House, Inc., New Orleans, 1973; chmn. womens com. Fed. Exec. Bd., 1974; bd. dirs. Bethlehem House of Bread, 1975-79. Named Hon. La. State Senator, 1974; recipient Superior Performance award U.S. Dept. Justice, 1974, Cert. Appreciation Fed. Exec. Bd., 1975-78, Rev. E.A. Doyle award, 1976, Commendation for tchg. Guam Legislature, 1977, Career Achievement award Mt. de Sales Acad., 1995. Mem. Am. Judicature Soc., La. Sate Bar Assn., Fed. Bus. Assn. (v.p. 1976—, pres. 1976-78, bd. dirs. 1972-75), Fed. Bar Assn. (1st v.p. 1973, pres. New Orleans chpt. 1974-75, nat. coun. 1974-79), Assn. Women Lawyers, Nat. Health Lawyers Assn., DAR, Bus. and Profl. Womens Club, Am. Heart Assn., Emory Alumni Assn., Oglethorpe U. Alumni Assn., Loyola U. Alumni Assn. (bd. dirs. 1974-75, 77, v.p. 1976), Jefferson Parish Hist. Soc., Sierra Club, Zonta, Leconte Hon. Sci. Soc., Phi Delta Delta (merged with Phi Alpha Delta pres. 1970-72, bd. dirs., vice justice 1974-75), Alpha Epsilon Delta, Phi Sigma. Democrat.

CAZALOT, CLARENCE P., JR., oil industry executive; BS in Geology, La. State. U. Various positions with Texaco, 1972—2000, v.p., 1999—2000; pres., CEO Marathon Oil, 2000—. Mem. bd. advisors Maguire Energy Inst.; bd. dirs. Baker Hughes, US-Saudi Arabian Bus. Coun. Trustee Spindletop Charities; bd. dirs. Sam Houston Area Coun. Boy Scouts Am. Mem.: NAM (bd. dirs.), Am. Petroleum Inst. (bd. dirs.), All-American Wildcatters, Nat. Petroleum Coun., Am. Assn. Petroleum Geologists. Office: Marathon Oil 5555 San Felipe Rd Houston TX 77056

CAZAN, MATTHEW JOHN, political science educator; b. Beclean, Romania, Mar. 10, 1912; s. John and Marie (Sipos) C.; m. Sylvia Marie Buday, July 14, 1935; 1 child, Matthew John George. Student, U. Bucharest Law Sch., Youngstown Coll., Georgetown U. Sch. Fgn. Svc. Lectr. Georgetown U., Washington, 1942-44; spl. lectr. Indsl. Coll. Armed Forces, 1947; assoc. in Romanian, Georgetown U. Inst. Langs. and Linguistics, 1949—. Lectr. polit. sci. and econs. Sch. Fgn. Svc., 1943-57; lectr. The Inst. Fgn. Svc. Officer Preparation, 1953— ; lectr. polit. sci. George Washington U., 1963—; spl. employee U.S. Dept. Justice, 1947-60, FBI, 1963-94, ret., 1994; internat. claims analyst Fgn. Claims Settlement Commn., 1960-63. Chmn. Labarca youth guidance com. Va. Gov.'s Conf. on Youth. Mem. AAUP, Am. Polit. Sci. Assn., Am. Soc. Internat. Law, Conf. Dem. Theory, Pi Gamma Mu. Home: 6369 Lakeview Dr Lake Barcroft Estates Falls Church VA 22041

CAZAVAN, LARRY O. television executive; b. Cin., Aug. 21, 1945; s. Norman A. and Lily A. (Shafer) C.; m. Karen E. Cranor (div.); children: Kimberly, Kelly. BFA, U. Cin., 1967; MCP, Vanderbilt U., 1999. Registered state lobbyist. Dir. Sta. WCPO-TV, Cin., 1967, Sta. KMBC-TV, Kansas City, Mo., 1967—70, program dir., 1970—71; asst. program dir. Sta. WLS-TV, Chgo., 1972; program dir. Sta. WXYZ-TV, Detroit, 1972—75, Sta. WISH-TV, Indpls., 1975—78, mgr. Sta. KITV-TV, Honolulu, 1978—85; program mgr. Sta. WTSP-TV, Tampa, Fla., 1985—91; sta. mgr. Sta. WATE-TV, Knoxville, Tenn., 1991—95; v.p. ops. Sta. WNAB-TV, Nashville, 1995—97; exec. v.p. Fla. Assn. Broadcasters, Tallahassee, 1997—99, Barcazmor Consulting, 1999—; sales mgr. Sta. WHDF-TV, Huntsville, Ala., 2002. Exec. producer: (syndicated TV show) Hot Fudge, 1973. Pres. Hawaii chpt. Muscular Dystrophy Assn., Honolulu, 1984; sec., treas. Christmas Toy Network, Tampa, 1986-91; bd. dirs. St. Petersburg Urban League, 1986-90, Operation PAR, St. Petersburg, 1986—. With USNR, 1963-67. Recipient Silver medal N.Y. Film Festival, 1982, 84, Bronze medal N.Y. Film Festival, 1984. Mem. Nat. Assn. TV Program Execs. (Iris award 1980, 83). Avocations: flying, golf. Home: 2013 Flagstone Dr Apt 1006 Madison AL 35758 E-mail: loc821@aol.com.

CAZDEN, COURTNEY B(ORDEN), education educator; b. Chgo., Nov. 30, 1925; d. John and Courtney (Letts) Borden; m. Norman Cazden (div. 1971); children: Elizabeth, Joanna. BA, Radcliffe Coll., 1946; MEd, U. Ill., 1953; EdD, Harvard U., 1965. Elem. tchr. pub. schs., N.Y., Conn., Calif., 1947-49, 54-61, 74-75; asst. prof. edn. Harvard U., Cambridge, Mass., 1965-68, assoc. prof., 1968-71, prof., 1971-95, Charles William Eliot prof. emerita, 1996—. Vis. prof. U. N.Mex. summer 1980, U. Alaska, Fairbanks, summer 1982, U. Auckland, N.Z., spring 1983, Bread Loaf Sch. of English, Vt., 1986—; chairperson bd. trustees Ctr. Applied Linguistics, Washington, 1981-85. Author: Child Language and Education, 1972, Classroom Discourse: The Language of Teaching and Learning, 2d edit., 2001, Whole Language plus Essays on Literacy in the US and New Zealand, 1992; co-editor: Functions of Language in the Classroom, 1972, English Plus: Issues in Bilingual Education, 1990; editor: Language in Early Childhood Education, rev. edit., 1981. Trustee Highland Ednl. and Rsch. Ctr., New Market, Tenn., 1982-84; bd. dirs. Feminist Press, Old Westbury, N.Y., 1982-84; clk. New Eng. regional office Am. Friends Svc. Com., Cambridge, 1989-92. Recipient Alumna Recognition award Radcliffe Coll., 1988; fellow Ctr. Advanced Study in Behavioral Scis., Stanford, Calif., 1978-79; Fulbright research fellow, New Zealand, 1987. Mem. Nat. Acad. Edn., Coun. on Anthropology and Edn. (pres. 1981, George & Louise Spindler award 1994), Am. Assn. Applied Linguistics (pres. 1985), Nat. Conf. on Rsch. in English (pres. 1993-94), Am. Ednl. Rsch. Assn. (exec. com. 1981-84, award for disting. contbns. to ednl. rsch. 1986). Mem. Soc. Of Friends. Office: Harvard U Grad Sch Edn Appian Way Cambridge MA 02138

CAZEAUX, ISABELLE ANNE MARIE, retired musicology educator; b. N.Y.C., Feb. 24, 1926; d. François and Marie-Anne (Fort) C. BA magna cum laude, Hunter Coll., 1945; MA in Musicology, Smith Coll., 1946; MS in Libr. Sci., Columbia U., 1959, PhD in Musicology, 1961. Licence d'Enseignement, Ecole Normale de Musique, Paris, 1950; Première Médaille, Conservatoire Nat. de Musique, Paris, 1950. Sr. music catalogue, head sect. music and phonorecords cataloging N.Y. Pub. Libr., N.Y.C., 1957-63; mem. faculty Manhattan Sch. Music, N.Y.C., 1969-82, Bryn Mawr Coll., Pa., 1963-92, chmn. dept., 1978-92, prof., 1972-92, Alice Carter Dickerman prof. emeritus music, 1992—. Vis. prof. Douglass Coll. Rutgers U., New Brunswick, N.J., 1978. Author: French Music in the 15th and 16th Centuries, 1975; editor: The Chansons of Claudin de Sermisy, 1974; translator: The Memoirs of Philippe de Commynes, 1969, 2d vol., 1973; contbr. articles to profl. jours. Recipient Libby van Arsdale prize Hunter Coll., 1945; fellow Smith Coll., 1945-46, Inst. Internat. Edn., 1948-50; Martha Baird Rockefeller Fund grantee, 1971-72, Herman Goldman Found. grantee, 1980. Mem. Am. Musicol. Soc. (coun. 1968-70, com. on status of women 1974-76), Music Libr. Assn., Soc. Française de Musicologie, Internat. Musicol. Soc. Roman Catholic. Avocations: opera, concerts. Home: 415 E 72nd St New York NY 10021-4412

CAZEL, HUGH ALLEN, industrial engineer, educator; b. Asheville, N.C., Aug. 6, 1923; s. Fred Augustus and Agnes (Petrie) C.; m. Edna Faye Hawkins, Sept. 2, 1944; children: Audre Elizabeth, Hugh Petrie, Susan Margaret, Steven Sidney. BS in Indsl. Engring., N.C. State U., 1948, M in Indsl. Engring., 1972. Registered profl. engr., N.C., Ga. Svc. mgr. Cazel Auto Svc. Co., Asheville, 1948-51; sales rep. Snap-On Tools Corp., Kenosha, Wis., 1951; estimator, cost acct. Std. Designers, Inc., Asheville, 1951-52; designer Robotyper Corp., Hendersonville, N.C., 1952-53; engr. Western Electric Co., Burlington, N.C., 1953-74; alt. rep. configuration mgmt. subcom. Electronic Industries Assn., 1970-72; mgr. engring. BellSouth Telephone Co., Atlanta, 1974-79; ret., 1979; ptnr. Engring. Unltd., 1963—. Instr. math. Elon Coll., 1956-59; instr. engring. graphics and design Ga. Inst. Tech., 1977-87, ret., 1987; instr. constrn. blue print reading DeKalb C.C., 1981-87; project engr. Dept. Def. Election poll worker, 1960-93. Re. candidate N.C. Ho. of Reps., 1964; mem. Dekalb County (Ga.) Adv. Com., 1979-82; dir. Glendale Townhouses Assn., chmn, 1979-80; mem. adminstrv. bd. 1st United Meth. Ch., Decatur, 1976-86; interviewer Decatur Emergency Assistance Ministry, 1990-92; lay mem. Ea. N.C. Ann. Conf. United Meth. Ch., 1965-73; vol. Dept. Vets. Affairs Med. Ctr., Durham, N.C., 1993-97, ambulance driver chpt. 20 Disabled Am. Vets., Guilford County; active Muir's Chapel United Meth. Ch., 2002—. With AUS, 1943-46, ETO. Mem. NSPE, AAAS, Am. Inst. Indsl. Engrs. (pres. Raleigh, N.C. chpt. 1963-64), Profl. Engrs. N.C. (pres. North Piedmont chpt. 1972-73, state bd. dirs. 1970-73), Ga. Profl. Engrs. in Industry (chmn. 1976), Ga. Soc. Profl. Engrs. (energy com. 1979-86, Ga. Engr. of Yr. in Industry 1976), Tel. Pioneers Am. (life, pres. Dixie chpt. 1991-92), Rep. Club, Odd Fellows, Rotary, Lions (local sec. 1991—2003). Achievements include patent for ultra low frequency sound generator for deep sea, 1972. Home: 801 Meadowood St Apt 24 Greensboro NC 27409-2831

CAZIER, BARRY JAMES, electrical engineer, software developer; b. Phoenix, May 10, 1943; s. James Henry and Dorothy Marie (Lynton) C.; m. Susan Arline Shewey, June 13, 1964 (dec. July 1979); children: Suzanne, Bryan; m. Illene D. Miller, Dec. 19, 1994. Student, Colo. Sch. Mines, 1961-62; BSEE, U. Colo., 1965; student advanced bus. adminstrn., Ariz. State U., 1974-77. Mfg. mgmt. Gen. Electric, Richland, Wash., 1965-66, Warren, Ohio, 1966-67, system engr. Schenectady, N.Y., 1967-69; project mgr. Honeywell, Phoenix, 1970-80, dir. field ops., 1980-85, program mgr., 1985-99. Prin. Cazier Software Designs, Scottsdale, Ariz., 1985—. Adv. Jr. Achievement, Phoenix, 1972. Mem.: IBM PC Users (Phoenix). Avocations: music, jogging, camping, fishing, reading. Home: 8508 E Via Montoya Scottsdale AZ 85255-4936 E-mail: bjcazier@yahoo.com.

CEASOR, AUGUSTA CASEY, medical technologist, microbiologist, research scientist; b. Birmingham, Ala., Feb. 22, 1943; d. Augustus and Willie Mae (Stubbs) C. AS, SUNY, 1981; BS, So. Ill. U., 1981. Cert. clin. lab. scientist Nat. Cert. Agy. Lab. asst. Mt. Sinai Hosp., Miami Beach, Fla., 1967-68; lab. technician Coordinated Lab. Svcs., Jamaica, N.Y., 1969-71; med. technician Andrew Radar U.S. Army Health Clinic, Ft. Myer, Va., 1972-76; med. technologist Armed Forces Inst. Pathology, Washington, 1976-91, Dept. Army, Mil. Dist. Wash., Ft. Myer, Va., 1991-97; ret. Dept. of Army, 1997; cons. clin. lab. sci., 1997—. Dept. asst. Webster U., Ocala, Fla., 1999; sci. fair judge Am. Soc. Microbiology, Washington, 1988—97; high sch. sci. mentor Minority Women in Sci., 1989—; spkr. to profl. groups; records mgr. Marion County Govt., 2000—01. Mem. editl. bd. Metroscope Newsletter, 1985-98, editor, 1989-98; tech. asst. Mycobacteriology Rsch., 1985-90. Active minority alumni scholarship com. So. Ill. U., Carbondale, 1981—; mem. Montgomery Knolls Cmty. Assn., Silver Spring, Md., 1983-96, v.p., chmn. safety and environ. com., 1984-85. Recipient Cert. of Meritorious Svc., 1991, Performance award, 1987, 89, 93, 95-97. Fellow: Alpha Mu Tau (scholarship com. 1995—97); mem.: Fla. Soc. for Clin. Lab. Sci. (dir. Dist. II 2000—, chair membership devel. com.), Capital Area Soc. for Clin. Lab. Sci. (pres.-elect 1995—96, pres. 1996—97, past pres. 1997—98), D.C. Soc. Med. Tech. (profl. and pub. rels. chair 1985—86, program com. chair 1986—87, pres. 1987—88, microbiology chair 1988—89, awards chair 1988—98, profl. and pub. rels. chair 1992—93, Past Pres. award 1988, Svc. award 1989, Mem. of Yr. 1989—90, Disting. Svc. award 1991, Profl. Achievement award in Microbiology 1994), Am. Bd. Bioanalysis, Internat. Soc. Clin. Lab. Tech. (cert. gen. supr.), Am. Soc. Med. Tech. (mem. Region II Coun. 1986—93, Region II microbiology chair 1988—89, Region II mem. chair 1990—93, mem. Region II Coun. 1996—97, Cert. of Recognition 1990), Am. Soc. Clin. Lab. Sci. (minority forum sec. 1994—96, forum scholarship com. 1996—, chair forum scholarship com. 1997—, editor The Forum newsletter 2002—, Omicron Sigma award 1987—97, 2001, 2002), Roman Catholic. Achievements include research in unique toxin of mycobacterium ulcerans. E-mail: acaseyc@hotmail.com.

CEBALLOS, JACQUI MICHOT, feminist activist, organizer, administrator; b. Mamou, La., Sept. 8, 1925; d. Louis Joseph Michot and Marie Adele Domás; m. Alvaro Ceballos, Jan. 3, 1951; children: Douglas, Denis, Michele, Janine. BA in Edn.-Music, U. La., 1946. Founder, pres. Teatro de la Opera, Bogota, Colombia, 1960—64; pres. NOW, N.Y.C., 1971—72, v.p. east region, 1972—73; co-founder Nat. Women's Polit. Caucus, 1973—74; pres. Ceballos Phillips Corp., N.Y.C., 1973—75; co-founder, exec. dir. Women's Forum, N.Y.C., 1992—; founder, pres. Vet. Feminists Am., N.Y.C., 1992—. Founder, pres. Acadiana Women's Polit. Caucus, 1967—71; co-founder La. Women's Polit. Caucus, 1997—. Prodr. New Feminist Theatre, N.Y.C., 1968—70; pres. New Yorkers for Women in Pub. Office, 1972—. Democrat. Avocations: opera, concerts, art, reading. Office: Vet Feminists Am #225D 220 Doucet Rd Lafayette LA 70503-3471

CECCHETTI, STEPHEN GIOVANNI, economics educator; b. Berkeley, Calif., Aug. 18, 1956; s. Giovanni A. and Ruth Elizabeth (Schwabacher) C.; m. Ruth M. Charney, Sept. 6, 1986; children: Daniel A., Ethan B. SB in Econs., MIT, 1977; MA in Econs., U. Calif., Berkeley, 1979, PhD in Econs., 1982. Rsch. assoc. Nat. Bur. Econ. Rsch., 1986—2003; prof. econs. Ohio State U., Columbus, 1987—2002; exec. v.p., dir. rsch. Fed. Res. Bank, 1997—99; prof. internat. econs. and fin. Brandeis U., Waltham, Mass., 2003—. Rsch. assoc. fellow Nat. Bur. Econ. Rsch., 1986—; cons. Fed. Res. Banks, Fed. Res. Bd., Fgn. Ctrl. Banks. Editor Jour. Money Credit and Banking, 1992-2001; referee and editl. bd. dirs. numerous profl. jours.; contbr. articles to profl. jours., chpts. to books and Fin. Times. Office: Graduate Sch of Internat Econ and FIn Brandeis Univ Mail Stop 32 Waltham MA 02454-9110 E-mail: steve@cecchetti.net.

CECCHINI, PENELOPE CRAWFORD, piano educator; b. Kokomo, Ind., Oct. 8, 1943; d. Maurice Sinclair and Grace Anne (Gasho) Crawford; m. Andrea Angelo Giovanni Cecchini, Oct. 9, 1976. MusB Piano Performance magna cum laude, Butler U., 1965; MusM in Piano Performance, Mich. State U., 1966, diploma advanced grad. study, 1969; postgrad., Aspen Inst., 1966; pvt. study with Orazio Frugoni, Cetona, Tuscany, Italy, 1987, 93. Grad. asst. Mich. State U., East Lansing, 1965-66; prof. piano, coord. keyboard divsn. dept. music-theatre arts U. Wis., Eau Claire, 1966—2002. Grantee U. Wis., 1969-70, 87, 93. Mem. Music Tchrs. Nat. Assn., Wis. Music Tchrs. Assn., Sigma Alpha Iota, Phi Kappa Phi, Pi Kappa Lambda. Office: U Wis Dept Music and Theatre Arts Eau Claire WI 54701

CECCOLA, RUSS, game strategy guide writer; b. Phila., Aug. 29, 1966; s. Philip John and Irma Theresa (Bogash) C. BEE, Villanova U., 1988. Engr. PECO Energy Co., Phila., 1988-98; software engr. Lockheed Martin, King of Prussia, Pa., 2001—02; reviewer, strategy guide, author, screenwriter West Conshohocken, Pa., 1999—. Author: Phantasmagoria Official Player's Guide, 1995, William Shatner's TekWar-The Official Strategy Guide, 1995, WarGames-Exclusive Strategy Guide, 1998, Juggernaut: Prima's Official Strategy Guide, 1999, Tomba! 2 The Evil Swine Return: Prima's Official Strategy Guide, 2000, Crazy Taxi: Prima's Official Strategy Guide, 2000, Heroes of Might and Magic III: The Shadow of Death: Prima's Official Strategy Guide, 2000, Smuggler's Run: Prima's Official Strategy Guide, 2000. Republican. Roman Catholic. Avocations: computer/video games, comic books, movies, horror, star trek. Home: 121 Merion Ave West Conshohocken PA 19428-2839 E-mail: RCCola666@aol.com.

CECELIC, JERONE CHARLES, lawyer; b. Dayton, Ohio, June 3, 1958; s. John Jerone and Edna Bernadine (Kelch) C.; m. Elizabeth Ann Kurtzhals, June 13, 1981. B in Indsl. Engring, Ga. Inst. Tech., 1980; JD, Duke U., 1986. Bar: N.C. 1986, U.S. Dist. Ct. (mid. dist.) N.C. 1986. Commd. 2d lt. U.S. Army, 1980, advanced through grades to capt., 1984, task force judge advocate Multinat. Force, 1987, trial counsel, 1987-89, region judge advocate, 1989-91, atty., 1991-92; assoc. Howrey & Simon, Washington, 1992-97; asst. v.p. corp. integrity HCA. Mem. ABA. Office: HCA Ethics and Compliance Dept 1 Park Plz Bldg Nashville TN 37203-1548 E-mail: jerone.cecelic@hcahealthcare.com.

CECH, JOSEPH HAROLD, retired chemical engineer; b. Flint, Mich., Oct. 8, 1951; s. Joseph Jr. and Margaret Luella (Taphouse) C. BS in Chem. Engring., Mich. Tech. U., 1978. Trainee Menasha Corp., North Bend, Oreg., 1978-79, project engr. molded products div. Watertown, Wis., 1979-84, plastic devel. engr., 1984-86, composite engr., coordinator, 1986-90, sr. process engr., 1990-92, process material supr., 1992-97, material/process mgr., 1996-97; tech./environ. mgr. Applied Molded Products Corp., Watertown, 1998—2001; ret., 2001—. With USN, 1971-75. Mem. Mensa, Soc. Plastic Engrs., Am. Inst. Chem. Engrs., Nat. Geog. Soc., Watertown Conservation Club. Methodist.

CECH, THOMAS ROBERT, chemistry and biochemistry educator; b. Chgo., Dec. 8, 1947; m. Carol Lynn Martinson; children: Allison E., Jennifer N. BA in Chemistry, Grinnell Coll., 1970; PhD in Chem., U. Calif., Berkeley, 1975; DSc (hon.), Grinnell Coll., 1987, U. Chgo., 1991, Drury Coll., 1994, Colo. Coll., 1999, U. Md., Baltimore County, 2000, Williams Coll., 2000, Charles U., Prague, 2002. Postdoctoral fellow dept. biology MIT, Cambridge, Mass., 1975—77; from asst. prof. to assoc. prof. chemistry U. Colo., Boulder, 1978—83, prof. chemistry and biochemistry also molecular cellular and devel. biology, 1983—, disting. prof., 1990—; rsch. prof. Am. Cancer Soc., 1987—; investigator Howard Hughes Med. Inst., 1988—99, pres., 2000—. Co-chmn. Nucleic Acids Gordon Conf., 1984; Phillips disting. visitor Haverford Coll., 1984; Vivian Ernst meml. lectr. Brandeis U., 1984; Cynthia Chan meml. lectr. U. Calif., Berkeley; mem. Welch Found. Symposium, 1985; Danforth lectr. Grinnell Coll., 1986; Pfizer lectr. Harvard U., 1986; Hastings lectr., 92; Verna and Marrs McLean lectr. Baylor Coll. Medicine, 1987; Harvey lectr., 87; Mayer lectr. MIT, 1987; HHMI lectr., 89; T.Y. Shen lectr., 94; Martin D. Kamen disting. lectureship U. Calif., San Diego, 1988; Alfred Burger lectr. U. Va., 1988; Berzelius lectr. Karolinska Inst., 1988; Osamu Hayaishi lectr. Internat. Union Biochemistry, Prague, 1988; Beckman lectr. U. Utah, 1989; Max Tishler lectr. Merck, 1989; Abbott vis. scholar U. Chgo., 1989; Herriott lectr. Johns Hopkins U., 1990; J.T. Baker lectr., 90; G.N. Lewis lectr. U. Calif., Berkeley, 1990; Sonneborn lectr. Ind. U., 1991; Sternbach lectr. Yale U., 1991; W. Pauli lectr., Zurich, 92; Carter-Wallace lectr. Princeton U., 1992; Stetten lectr. NIH, 1992; Dauben lectr. U. Wash., 1992; Marker lectr. U. Md., 1993; Hirschmann lectr. Oberlin Coll., 1993; Beach lectr. Purdue U., 1993; Abe White lectr. Syntex, 1993; Robbins lectr. Pomona Coll., 1994; Bren lectr. U. Calif., Irvine, 1994; Wawzonek lectr. U. Iowa, 1994; Sumner lectr. Cornell U., 1994; Steenbock lectr. U. Wis., 1995; Murachi lectr. FAOB Congress, Sydney, 1995; Streck award lectr. U. Nebr., 1996; Gardner-Davern lectr. U. Utah, 1996; Priestley lectr. Pa. State U., 1996; Beckman lectr. Calif. Inst. Tech., 1996; Lemieux lectr. U. Alta., Canada, 1997; Hogg Award lectr. M.D. Anderson Cancer Ctr., 1997; DeCoursey Nobel lectr. Trinity U., 1998; Tschirgi lectr. U. Calif., San Diego, 1998; Boxer Meml. lectr. Robert Wood Johnson Med. Sch., 1998; Thomas lectr. U. Mo., 1999; Bachmann Meml. lectr. U. Mich., 1999; DuPont-Marshall lectr. U. Pa., 1999; Feodor Lynen lectr. Mosbach Germany,

2001; The Morgenthaler lectureship Case Wetern Res. U., 2001; Tercentenary Silliman lectr. Yale U., 2001; Nathans lectr. Johns Hopkins U., 2002; Tishler Prize lectr. Harvard U., 2002; Furlaud Disting. lectr. The Rockefeller U., 2002; non-resident fellow Salk Inst., 1999. Assoc. editor Cell, 1986—87, RNA Jour., mem. editl. bd. Genes and Devel.; contbg. editor: Sci. mag., 1999. Trustee Grinnell Coll. Named Westerner of Yr., Denver Post, 1986; named to Esquire Mag. Register, 1985; recipient medal, Am. Inst. Chemists, 1970, Rsch. Career Devel. award, Nat. Cancer Inst., 1980—85, Young Sci. award, Passano Found., 1984, Harrison Howe award, 1984, Pfizer award, 1985, U.S. Steel award, NAS, 1987, V.D. Mattia award, 1987, Louisa Gross Horowitz prize, Columbia U., 1988, Newcombe-Cleveland award, AAAS, 1988, Heineken prize, Royal Netherlands Acad. Arts and Scis., 1988, Gairdner Found. Internat. award, 1988, Lasker Basic Med. Rsch. award, 1988, Rosenstiel award, Brandeis U., 1989, Warren Triennial prize, 1989, Nobel Prize in chemistry, 1989, Hopkins medal, Brit. Biochem. Soc., 1992, Feodor Lynen medal, 1995, Nat. Sci. medal, 1995, Mike Hogg award, M.D. Anderson, 1997, Wright prize, Harvey Mudd Coll., 1998, Gregor Mendel medal, Acad. Sci. Czech Republic, 2002; fellow, NSF, 1970—75, Pub. Health Svc.; rsch. fellow, Nat. Cancer Inst., 1975—77, Guggenheim fellow, 1985—86. Mem.: NAS, AAAS, RNA Soc. (v.p. 1993—96), European Molecular Biology Orgn., Am. Philos. Soc., Am. Acad. Arts and Scis., Am. Soc. Biochem. Molecular Biology, Inst. Medicine. Office: Howard Hughes Med Inst 4000 Jones Bridge Rd Chevy Chase MD 20815-6789 Fax: (301) 215-8558. E-mail: president@hhmi.org.

CECI, JESSE ARTHUR, violinist; b. Phila., Feb. 2, 1924; s. Luigi Concezio and Catherine Marie (Marotta) C.; m. Catherine Annette Stevens, Aug. 5, 1979. BS, Juilliard Sch. Music, 1951; license de concert, L'Ecole Normale de Musique, Paris, 1954; MusM, Manhattan Sch. Music, 1971. Assoc. concertmaster New Orleans Philharm. Orch., 1953-54; violinist Boston Symphony Orch., 1954-59, N.Y. Philharm. Orch., N.Y., 1959-62, Esterhazy Orch., N.Y.C., 1962-68; concertmaster Denver Symphony Orch., 1974-89, Colo. Symphony Orch., 1989-95. Over 50 performances of 22 major works; mem. Zimbler Sinfonietta, Boston, 1957-59; participant Marlboro Festival Chamber Orch. Vt., summmers 1960-62, 65, Marlboro Festival Chamber Orch. European-Israeli tour, 1965, Grand Teton Festival, Wyo., 1972, with Denver Duo, 1975—, N.Mex. Festival, Taos, 1980, Carmel (Calif.) Bach Festival, 1987—, Whistler (B.C., Can.) Mozart Festival, 1989-90, Bear Valley (Calif.) Festival, 1995—, Mendocino (Calif.) Festival, 1996—; mem. faculty Congress of Strings, Dallas, 1985, N.Y. Coll. Music, 1961-71, NYU, 1971-74, U. Colo., 1975-79; guest mem. faculty Univ. Denver, 1986; mem., assoc. concertmaster Casals Festival Orch., San Juan, P.R., 1963-77; violinist Cleve. Orch. fgn. tours, 1967, 73, 78, Cin. Symphony Orch. world tour, 1966; 1st violinist N.Y. String Quartet in-residence at U. Maine, Orono, summer 1969; guest violinist Fla. West Coast Symphony, Sarasota, 1993-98; concertmaster Minn. Orch., summers 1970-71, Denver Chamber Orch., 1985-90; guest concertmaster Pitts. Symphony Orch., Pitts., L.A., 1988, mem. N.Y. Philharmonia Chamber Ensemble in-residence at Hopkins Ctr., Dartmouth U., summer 1973; recitalist, Paris, 1963, Amsterdam, 1963, recitalist Carnegie Recital Hall, N.Y.C., 1963, Town Hall, N.Y.C., 1968, 70, Alice Tully Hall, N.Y.C., 1972; fgn. tour Pitts. Symphony Orch., 1989; soloist Royal Chamber Orch. Japan, 1997-98, appointment to concert master position of the Royal Chamber Orchestra and the Royal Metropolitan Orchestra of Japan, 1999—. Cpl. U.S. Army, 1943-46, PTO. Fulbright fellow Paris, 1951-52 Democrat. Roman Catholic. Office: Colo Symphony Orch 1031 13th St Denver CO 80204-2156

CECI, LOUIS J. former state supreme court justice; b. N.Y.C., Sept. 10, 1927; s. Louis and Filomena C.; m. Shirley; children— Joseph, Geraldine, David; children by previous marriage: Kristin (dec.), Remy, Louis. Ph.B., Marquette U., 1951, JD, 1954. Bar: Wis. 1954, U.S. Dist. Ct. (ea. dist.) Wis. 1954, U.S. Dist. Ct. (we. dist.) Wis. 1987; cert. appellant cons., cert. civil mediator. Sole practice, Milw., 1954-58, 63-68; asst. city atty. City of Milw., 1958-63; mem. Wis. Assembly, Madison, 1965-66; judge Milw. County Ct., 1968-73, Milw. Circuit Ct., 1973-82; justice Wis. Supreme Ct., Madison, 1982-93, retired, 1993; res. judge State of Wis., 1993—. Lectr. Wis. Jud. Confs., 1970-79 Lectr. Badger Boys State, Ripon, Wis., 1961, 1982-84; asst. dist. commr. Boy Scouts Am., 1962. Recipient Wis. Civic Recognition PLAV, Milw., 1970; recipient Community Improvement Pompeii Men's Club, Milw., 1971, Good Govt. Milw Jaycees, 1973, Community-Judiciary Pompeii Men's Club, 1982 Mem. ABA, Wis. Bar Assn., Dane County Bar Assn., Milw. County Bar Assn., Waukesha County Bar Assn., Am. Legion (comdr. 1962-63). E-mail: appeal301@aol.com.

CECIL, ALEX THOMSON, travel executive; b. Birmingham, Ala., May 5, 1930; s. Alex Thomson and Martha (Lamar) C.; m. Jennifer Brown, Dec. 2, 1962 (div. 1976); children: Thurston, Lila; m. Jacqueline Bottger, May 10, 1980 (div. 1997); children: Julia, Caroline; m. E. Ritter, May 5, 1997; 1 child, Henry. Student, Ohio State U., 1950-52. Chmn., CEO, owner Auto-Europe, Inc., N.Y.C., 1953—97; chmn. Cognoscenti Health Inst., Orlando, Fla., 1999—. E-mail: acecil@europe.com.

CECIL, CHARLES HARKLESS, artist, educator; b. Kansas City, Mo., May 12, 1945; s. Charles F. and Alice (Harkless) C.; m. Isabelle Claude Jeanne Touren, Dec. 30, 1982; 1 dau., Charlotte Alice Marcelle. BA, Haverford Coll., 1967; postgrad., Yale U., 1967-69. Co-dir. Studio Cecil-Graves, Florence, Italy, 1983-91; dir. Charles H. Cecil Studios, Florence, 1991—; instr. Villa Schifanoia, Grad. Studio Fine Arts, Florence, 1983-87. Exhibited in group shows at N.A.D., N.Y.C., 1979, 80, Dallas, 1983; represented in permanent collections at: Portrait Gallery, Haverford Coll., Pa., West Bend Gallery Fine Arts, Wis; executed: portrait Dr. Jonathon Rhodes for Am. Philos. Soc.; 10th Anniversary Exhibit of Charles H. Cecil Studios, London, 2001. NDEA grantee, 1967-69; Elizabeth Greenshields Found. grantee, 1970-73; John F. Stacey Found. grantee, 1980; R.H. Ives Gammell Studios Trust grantee, 1986-2001; recipient Julius T. Hallgarten First prize for oil painting, 1979, Benjamin Altman Second prize for landscape 155 Ann. Exhbn. Nat. Acad. Design, 1980 Home: Via Pandolfini 21 50122 Florence Italy Office: Charles H Cecil Studios Borgo San Frediano 68 50124 Florence Italy E-mail: cecilstudios@dada.it.

CECIL, DAVID ROLF, mathematician, educator; b. Tulsa, July 12, 1935; s. Neil McKinley and Ola Ethel (Turner) C.; m. Betty Lou Poe, June 14, 1958; 1 child, Eric Alan. Student (Pitts. Plate Glass Co. scholar), Carnegie Inst. Tech., 1954-55; BA, U. Tulsa, 1958; postgrad (fellow), Tulane U., 1958-59; MS, Okla. State U., 1960, PhD, 1962. Grad. teaching asst. Okla. State U., 1959-62; sr. research mathematician Atlantic Refining Co., 1962; asst. prof., then assoc. prof. math. North Tex. State U., Denton, 1962-69; prof. math. Butler U., Indpls., 1969-70, Tex. A&M U., Kingsville, 1970—, chmn. dept., 1980-85, asst. dean coll. arts and scis., 2000—. Cons. Edn. Service Ctr. Region II, 1979-80, Air Force Office Sci. Rsch., Wilford Hall Med. Ctr., Tex., 1988-90; organizer Kingsville Computer Club, 1980; mem. credit com. Kingsville Area Educators Fed. Credit Union, 1979— Contbr. articles to math. jours. Faculty fellow North Tex. State U., 1968-69; Faculty fellow Tex. A&I U., 1971-73 Fellow Tex. Acad. Scis. (v.p. 1999, pres. 2001-2002); mem. Assn. for Computing Machinery, Am. Statistical Assn., Sigma Xi. Clubs: Kingsville Radio (pres. 1974). Methodist. Office: Tex A&M U Office of Dean Arts & Scis Kingsville TX 78363 E-mail: d-cecil@tamuk.edu.

CECIL, DONALD, retired investment company executive; b. N.Y.C., Jan. 3, 1927; s. Leopold and Viola C.; m. Jane Grossman, Mar. 5, 1953; children: Alec, Leslie (twins). BS in Applied Econs., Yale U., 1947. Sr. instl. rsch. analyst Eastman Dillon Union Securities, N.Y.C., 1961-63; from dir. instl. rsch. to sr. v.p. Shearson Hamill, Inc., N.Y.C., 1963-70; pres. Shearson Hamill Mgmt. Co., 1966-70; founding ptnr. Cumberland Assocs., N.Y.C., 1970-82; ret., 1982. Trustee 45 Merrill Lynch domestic, global and offshore mutual funds and trusts, 1977-99; bd. dirs. Rycote Adv. Panel, Geneva, Switzerland, Grey Global Group, 1978-87; chmn. valuation bd. Biotech. Investments, Ltd., London, 1986-99; dep. chmn. Internat. Biotech. Trust Ltd., London, 1994-2001; chmn. dirs. svc. com., Investment Com. Inst., Washington, 1996-2000. Chmn. Bd. Transp., Westchester County, White Plains, N.Y., 1978—; vice-chmn. bd. trustees SUNY Purchase Coll. Found., 1987—; sponsor I Have a Dream Found., Mt. Vernon, N.Y., 1987—; chmn. bd. Friends of Neuberger Mus., Purchase, 1989-91; sponsor Jandon Scholars Program Westchester County, 1999—; dir., treas. Ctr. for Ednl. Innovation/Pub. Edn. Assn. Mem. Chartered Fin. Analysts (cert.), N.Y. Econ. Club, N.Y. Soc. Security Analysts. Avocations: theater, travel, tennis. Office: Cumberland Assocs Rm 3803 1114 Avenue Of The Americas New York NY 10036-7703

CECIL, KIM MARIA, radiologist, educator; d. Joseph Fredrick and Betty Lou Cecil. BS, Ky. Wesleyan Coll., Owensboro, 1988; MS, Vanderbilt U., Nashville, 1991; PhD, Vanderbilt U., 1993. Asst. prof. of radiology and pediat. Cin. Children's Hosp. Med. Ctr., 1998—. Contbr. NIH grantee, 2001—. Mem.: Internat. Soc. for Magnetic Resonance in Medicine, Am. Soc. for Neuroradiology. Achievements include research in Discoveries in medicine using magnetic resonance imaging techniques. Office: Cincinnati Children's Hospital 3333 Burnet Ave Cincinnati OH 45229

CECIL, LOUIS ANTON, retired mathematics educator; b. Oak Park, Ill., Dec. 19, 1940; m. Joan Rose Johnson, Dec. 15, 1962; children: Sutton Roberta, Cecil, Smith. BS, U. Minn., 1969. Cert. life tchr. secondary math., Wis. Insp. Honeywell, Mpls., 1959-65; math. educator Sheboygan (Wis.) Area Sch. Dist., 1969-99; ret., 1999. Track coach North H.S., Sheboygan, 1981-99. Bd. dirs. Sheboygan Symphony Orch., 2000-02. Named Melvin Jones fellow Lions Club Internat., 1992. Mem. Sheboygan Evening Lions (pres. 1978-79, zone chmn. Lions. Multiple Dist. 27B-1 1981-82, region chmn. 1984-87, Leo chmn. 1993-97, state Leo chmn. 1995-97, dist. sec.-treas. 1998-99), Elks Lodge #299. Democrat. Methodist. Avocations: participation in arts, golf, camping. Home: 1922 N 2nd St Sheboygan WI 53081-2916

CECIL, MAXINE, critical care nurse; b. Healdton, Okla., Sept. 25, 1921; d. James Albert and Clara (Phelps) Metz; children: Harold E. Seals, James Michael Seals, David Ray Smith. LPN, Seventh Day Adventist Hosp., Ardmore, Okla., 1954; ADN cum laude, No. Okla. Coll., Tonkawa, Okla., 1979. RN, Okla. LPN Seventh Day Adventist Hosp., Ardmore, 1953-66; LPN, charge nurse at nursing homes Ardmore, 1966-74; LPN and RN Johnston Meml. Hosp., Tishomingo, Okla., 1974-80; RN Meml. Hosp. So. Okla., Ardmore, Okla., 1980-84; charge nurse Love County Med. Ctr., Marietta, Okla., 1988-90; charge nurse, RN Lakeland Manor, Inc., Ardmore, 1982—; nurse Meml. Convalescent Home, Ardmore, 1990—, ret., 2003—. Pres. LPN Assn for Carter, Love, Johnston and Marshall Counties, 1963-70; mem. state bd. LPNs, 1968. Instr. first aid ARC, Ardmore, 1960-62; pathfinder dir. Seventh Day Adventist Ch., Ardmore.

CEDAR, PAUL ARNOLD, church executive, minister; b. Mpls., Nov. 4, 1938; s. Carl Benjamin and Bernice M. (Peterson) C.; m. Jean Helen Lier, Aug. 25, 1959; children: Daniel Paul, Mark John, Deborah Jean. BS, No. State Coll., Aberdeen, S.D., 1960; MDiv, No. Bap. Theol. Sem., 1968, Calif. State U., Fullerton, 1971; DMin, Am. Baptist Sem. of the West, 1973. Ordained to ministry Evang. Free Ch. of Am., 1966. Youth for Christ, crusade dir. Billy Graham Evang. Assn., Leighton Ford Team, 1960-65; pastor Evang. Free Ch., Naperville, Ill., 1965-67, Yorba Linda, Calif., 1969-73; exec. pastor 1st Presbyn. Ch. Hollywood, Calif., 1975-81; sr. pastor Lake Ave. Congl. Ch., Pasadena, Calif., 1981-90; pres. Evang. Free Ch. Am., Mpls., 1990-96; chmn., CEO Mission Am., 1995—. Guest dean Billy Graham Sch. Evangelism, Mpls., 1983-2002; vis. prof. Fuller Theol. Sem., Pasadena, Talbot Theol. Sem., La Habra, Calif., Trinity Div. Sch., Deerfield, Ill. Author: How to Make Love Your Motive, 1977, Becoming a Lover, 1978, Seven Keys to Maximum Communication, 1980, Sharing the Good Life, 1980, Communicators Commentary, 1983, Strength in Servant Leadership, 1987, Mastering the Pastoral Role, 1991, Where Is Hope?, 1992, A Life of Prayer, 1998. Mem. Nat. Prayer Com. Mem. Christian TV and Film Commn., Internat. Students, Worldwide Leadership Coun., Caleb Ministries, Leadership Renewal Ctr., John M. Perkins Found., Revival Prayer Fellowship, Barnabas Internat., Pioneer Clubs. Mem. Evangelist Free Ch. Of Am. Avocations: athletics, music, writing, carpentry. Office: 77564 Country Club Dr # A Palm Desert CA 92211-0484 E-mail: PaulC@missionamerica.org. *I am convinced that when all of life is over, only one thing will matter ultimately-fufilling the will of God.*

CEDARBAUM, MIRIAM GOLDMAN, federal judge; b. N.Y.C., 1929; d. Louis Albert and Sarah (Shapiro) Goldman; married; 2 children. BA, Barnard Coll., 1950; LLB, Columbia U., 1953. Bar: N.Y. 1954, U.S. Dist. Ct. (so. dist.) N.Y. 1956, U.S. Ct. Appeals (2d cir.) 1956, U.S. Ct. Claims 1958, U.S. Supreme Ct. 1958, U.S. Dist. Ct. (ea. dist.) N.Y. 1980, U.S. Ct. Appeals (5th and 11th cirs.) 1981. Law clk. to judge Edward Jordan Dimock U.S. Dist. Ct. (so. dist.) N.Y., 1953-54, asst. U.S. atty., 1954-57; atty. Dept. Justice, Washington, 1958-59; part-time cons. to law firms in litig. matters, 1959-62; 1st asst. counsel N.Y. State Moreland Act Commn., 1963-64; assoc. counsel Mus. Modern Art, N.Y.C., 1965-79; assoc. litig. dept. Davis, Polk & Wardwell, N.Y.C., 1979-83, sr. atty., 1983-86; acting village justice Village of Scarsdale, NY, 1978—82, village justice, 1982-86; judge U.S. Dist. Ct. (so. dist.) N.Y., 1986-98, sr. judge, 1998—. Mem. com. defender svcs. Jud. Conf. U.S., 1993—99; bd. vis. Columbia Law Sch.; trustee Barnard Coll. Contbr. articles to profl. jours. Recipient Medal of Distinction Barnard Coll., 1991; James Kent scholar. Mem. ABA (chmn. com. on pictorial graphic sculptural and choreographic works 1979-81, copyright com. fed. practice and procedure 1983-84), Am. Law Inst., N.Y. State Bar Assn. (chmn. com. on fed. legis. 1978-80, com. on dist., city, village, and town cts. 1983-84), Assn. of Bar of City of N.Y. (com. on copyright and lit. property 1982-84, com. on the Bicentennial 1988-92), Fed. Bar Coun., Copyright Soc. U.S.A. (trustee, exec. com. 1979-82), Supreme Ct. Hist. Soc. Jewish. Office: US Dist Ct US Courthouse 500 Pearl St Rm 1330 New York NY 10007-1312

CEDEL, MELINDA IRENE, music educator, violinist; b. Ft. Worth, July 31, 1957; d. Albert and Emilia Florence (Sylvester) C. Student, N.C. Sch. Arts, 1974-77; MusB Edn., U. S.C., 1979. Cert. tchr., S.C. Tchr. music Charleston (S.C.) County Pub. Schs., 1979—92. Pvt. tchr. music, 1983—; concertmaster Brunswick (Ga.) Civic Orch., 1993-97, pers. mgr., 1995-96. Performed with Florence Symphony, Columbia Philharm., S.C. Chamber Orch., Augusta Symphony, Jacksonville Symphony Orch., Savannah (Ga.) Symphony, Hilton Head (S.C.) Symphony, Jacksonville Summer Symphonetta, Valdosta (Ga.) Symphony Orch.; musician Charleston Symphony, 1979-92, Charleston Symphony Chamber Orch., Long Bay (S.C.) Symphony; musician, mgr. Charlestowne String Quartet, 1983-92; condr. Charleston County Prep. Orch., 1983-84; performer Piccolo Spoleto, 1980-91; co-dir. Charleston County Strolling Strings. Bd. dirs. Brunswick Cmty. Concert Assn. Mem. Am. Fedn. Musicians, Am. String Tchrs. Assn., Brunswick Cmty. Concert Assn., Mensa, Kappa Phi Kappa. Avocations: sailing, water sports, reading, travel, tennis. Home: 220 Five Pounds Rd Saint Simons GA 31522-1903

CEDERBERG, JAMES, physics educator; b. Oberlin, Kans., Mar. 16, 1939; s. J. Walter and Edith E. (Glad) C.; m. Judith Ness, June 10, 1967; children: Anna Sook, Rachel Eun. BA, U. Kans., 1959; MA, Harvard U., 1960, PhD, 1963. Lectr., rsch. assoc. Harvard U., Cambridge, Mass., 1963-64; asst. prof. St. Olaf Coll., Northfield, Minn., 1964-68, assoc. prof., 1968-80, prof., 1980—, Grace A. Whittier prof. sci., 1992—. Councilor Coun. on Undergrad. Rsch., 1985-91, 92-95, pres. physics coun., 1985-88. Recipient Distinguished Service Citation awd., Am. Assn. of Physics Teachers, 1993. Fellow: Am. Phys. Soc. (Undergraduate Rsch. prize 2002); mem.: Am. Assn. Physics Tchrs. (mem. coun. on undergraduate rsch.). Lutheran. Office: St Olaf Coll 1520 Saint Olaf Ave Northfield MN 55057-1098 Fax: 507-646-3968. E-mail: ceder@stolaf.edu.

CEDERING, SIV, poet, writer; b. Overkalix, Sweden, Feb. 5, 1939; came to U.S., 1953, naturalized, 1958; d. Hilding and Elvy (Wikstrom) C.; children: Lisa, Lora, David. Artist Elaine Benson Gallery, Bridgehampton, NY, 1991—98, Loveland Mus., Loveland, Colo., 1992, East End Arts Coun. Gallery, Riverhead, NY, 1992, Clayton-Liberatori Gallery, Bridgehampton, NY, 1991, Guild Hall Mus., East Hampton, NY, 2001, Hutchin Gallery, Green Vale, NY, 1993, Peconic Gallery, Riverheard, NY, 1993, East New Mex. Univ., Portales, N.Mex., 1992. Lectr. U. Mass., Amherst, 1973; cons. Coordinating Council Lit. Mags., 1972-75 Author: (poems and photographs) Cup of Cold Water, 1973, Letters from the Island, 1973; (poems) Letters from Helge, 1974, Two Swedish Poets, Gost Friberg and Goran Palm (transl. from Swedish), 1974, Mother Is, 1975, The Juggler, 1977, How to Eat a Fortune Cookie, 1977, Color Poems, 1978, Letters From the Floating World: New and Selected Poems, 1984, The Blue Horse, 1979; (children's poems) Leken i Grishuset, 1980 (books transl. into Japanese, Swedish); editor, translator: Det Blommande Trädet (The Flowering Tree, collection Am. Indian and Eskimo lyrics), 1973, You and I and the World, Poems by Werner Aspenström, 1980; poems and prose published in several periodicals, including, Harper's, New Republic, Partisan Rev., Paris Rev., Quar. Rev. Lit., others, exhibited photography, Modernage Galleries, NYC, 1973. Recipient William Marion Reedy award Poetry Soc. Am., 1970, John Masefield Narrative Poetry award, 1969; Annapolis Fine Arts Festival poetry prize Md. Fine Arts Council, 1968; Photography prize Sat. Rev., 1970; Borestone Mountain Poetry award, 1974; Pushcart prize, 1977; Emily Dickinson award, 1978; NY State Council on Arts fellow, 1974; Swedish Writers Union stipend, 1979 Mem. Poetry Soc. Am. Home: PO Box 89 Sagaponack NY 11962-0089

CEDILLO, GILBERT A. state senator; BA in Sociology, UCLA, 1979; JD, People's Coll. Law, 1983. Subst. tchr.; law clk. ACLU; counselor Pasadena City Coll.; dir. Campaign for Dignity and Civic Participation; field rep. L.A. Mayor Tom Bradley, 1982—83; with local 660 Svc. Employees Internat. Union, 1985, gen mgr. local 660, 1991—96; cand. dist. 46 Calif. State Assembly, 1998, mem. dist. 46, 1998—2002; mem. dist. 22 Calif. State Senate, Sacramento, 2002—. Mem. Budget and Fiscal Review Com., Bus. and Professions Com., Govt. Orgn. Com., Housing and Cmty. Devel. Com., Judiciary Com.; chair Revenue and Taxation Com. Democrat. Mailing: State Capitol Rm 3048 Sacramento CA 95814 Office: 617 S Olive St Ste 710 Los Angeles CA 90014*

CEDOLINI, ANTHONY JOHN, psychologist; b. Rochester, N.Y., Sept. 19, 1942; s. Peter Ross and Mary J. (Anthony) C.; m. Clare Marie De Rose, Aug. 16, 1964; children: Maria A., Antonia C., Peter E. Student, U. San Francisco, 1960-62; BA, San Jose State U., 1965, MS, 1968; PhD in Ednl. Pscyhology, Columbia Pacific U., 1983. Lic. ednl. psychologist, sch. adminstr., marriage, family, child counselor, sch psychologist, sch. counselor, social worker, Calif.; Lic. real estate broker, Calif. Mng. ptnr. Cienega Valley Vineyards and DeRose Winery (formerly Almaden Vineyards) and Comml. Shopping Ctrs., 1968—; coord. psychol. svcs. Oak Grove Sch. Dist., San Jose, Calif., 1968-81, asst. dir. pupil svcs., 1977-81, dir. pupil svcs., 1981-83; pvt. practice, ednl. psychologist Ednl. Assocs., San Jose, 1983—. Co-dir. Biofeedback Inst. of Santa Clara County, San Jose, 1976-83; ptnr. in Cypress Ctr.-Ednl. Psychologists and Consultancy, 1978-84; cons., program auditor for Calif. State Dept. Edn.; instr. U. Calif., Santa Cruz and LaVerne Coll. Ext. courses; guest spkr. San Jose State U.; lectr., workshop presenter in field. Author: Occupational Stress and Job Burnout, 1982, A Parents Guide to School Readiness, 1971, The Effect of Affect, 1975; contbr. articles to profl. jours. and newspapers. Founder, bd. dirs. Lyceum of Santa Clara County, 1971—, Graham Owners Club of Calif. Avocations: collecting antique furniture and coins, stained glass, wine making, classic cars, wood carvings. Home and Office: 1183 Nikulina Ct San Jose CA 95120-5441 E-mail: tonyced@pacbell.net.

CEDRASCHI, TULLIO, investment management company executive; b. Zurich, Switzerland, Oct. 4, 1938; s. Guido and Ida (Colombara) C. Degree in Civil Engring., Coll. Tech., Zurich, 1960; MBA, McGill U., 1968. Civil engr., project mgr. Conrad Zschokke, Zurich, 1960-61, Bur. D'Etudes Quoniam, Paris, 1961-63, BBR Switzerland and Can., 1963-65, R. R. Nicolet and Assocs., Montreal, 1968—, gen. mgr. CN investment divsn., 1973-77, pres., CEO, 1977—. Bd. dirs. Toronto Stock Exch., Western Oil Sands Inc., Freehold Resources Ltd., Helix Investments. Bd. govs. McGill U., Nat. Theatre Sch. Mem. Montreal Soc. Fin. Analysts, Hillside Tennis Club. Avocations: tennis, skiing. Home: # 605 2600 ave Pierre-Dupuy Habitat 67 Cite du Havre Montreal QC Canada H3C 3R6 Office: CN Investment Divsn Ste 1515 PO Box 11002 5 Pl Ville Marie Montreal QC Canada H3C 4T2 also: Canadian National Railways 935 de la Gauchetiere St W Montreal QC Canada H3C 3N4

CEDRONE, LOUIS ROBERT, JR., critic; b. Balt., June 25, 1923; s. Louis and Lucia (Mazzola) C.; m. Nancy Nelson, Sept. 11, 1954; children— Linda, David. BS, U. Md., 1951. With Balt. Evening Sun, 1951-92, drama-film critic, 1963-92, ret., 1992; corr. Variety, 1957-77, 82-85; TV show cablevision Critics Corner, 1982-85. Swimming instr. ARC, 1961-68. Served with inf. AUS, 1943-45. Decorated Purple Heart with oak leaf cluster, Bronze Star. Mem. Sigma Nu, Omicron Delta Kappa, Pi Delta Epsilon. Home: 9 Muirfield Ct Lutherville Timonium MD 21093-3905

CEFALO, ROBERT CHARLES, obstetrician, gynecologist; b. Boston, 1933; MD, Tufts U., 1959. Diplomate Am. Bd. Ob-Gyn. Intern Chelsea Naval Hosp., Boston, 1959—60; resident in ob.-gyn. U.S. Naval Hosp., Oakland, Calif., 1961—64; prof. dept. ob-gyn. Med. Sch. U. N.C., Chapel Hill. Mem.: SGI, AMA, ACOG. Office: U NC Med Sch 214 Macnider Chapel Hill NC 27599-0001

CEFALU, CHARLES A. medical educator; b. New Orleans, La., Jan. 30, 1951; s. Nicholas V. and Mary Ann Cefalu; m. Aug. 11, 1984; children: Sarah, Charles Jr., John N., Michael J., Gregory J. BS in Zoology, Southeastern La. U., 1971; MD, La. State U., 1974; MS in Epidemiology, Bowman Gray Sch. Medicine, 1992. Diplomate Am. Bd. Family Practice, added qualifications in geriatric medicine. Rotating intern Earl K. Long Meml. Hosp., Baton Rouge, 1975, family medicine resident, 1976-77, asst. dir. Sixth Dist. Family Residency Program, 1978-79, dir. Sixth Dist. Family Medicine Residency Tng. Program, 1979-81; asst. prof. medicine Tulane U. Sch. Medicine, New Orleans, 1981-85; pvt. practice Kentwood Med. Clinic, 1985-89; full-time emergency physician Coastal Emergency Svcs., 1989-90; geriatric medicine fellow Bowman Gray Sch. Medicine, Winston-Salem, N.C., 1990-92; assoc. prof., dir. geriatrics dept. family medicine Georgetown U. Sch. Medicine, Washington, 1992-97; prof., assoc. chmn. geriatrics program dept. family medicine La. State U. Med. Ctr., New Orleans, 1997—; med. dir. geriactric medicine Med. Ctr of La., New Orleans, 2000—. Part-time assoc. Kentwood (La.) Med. Clinic, 1975-86; active staff E.S. Pike Meml. Hosp., Kentwood, 1975-89; med. dir. Baton Rouge Long-Term Care Facility, Baton Rouge, 1978-79; instr. family medicine La. State U. Sch. Medicine, New Orleans, 1978, asst. prof. family medicine, 1978-81; med. supr. Baton Rouge Area Substance Abuse Clinic, 1978-81; project dir. for geriatrics La. State U. Med. Ctr., New Orleans, 1979-81; med. dir. Lallie Kemp State Hosp., Independence, La., 1981-85, coord. alcohol and drug abuse unit, 1981-82, chmn. quality assurance com., 1981-85, dir. continuing med. edn., 1981-85, dir. emergency medicine, 1981-82; acting med. dir. State La. Dept. Health and Human Resources, 1983-84; asst. med. dir. Pike Meml. Hosp., Kentwood, 1985-89; geriatrics cons. Carroll Manor Nursing Home, Hyattsville, Md., 1992-97, clin. dir., 1996-97; active provisional staff Providence Hosp., Washington, 1993-97, chief geriatrics, 1993-97; dir. Georgetown U./Providence Hosp. Geriatric Medicine Fellowship, 1994-97; mem. long term care coun. Am. Hosp. Assn., 1996-2000; presenter in field. Physician reviewer Am. Family Physician, 1993, Jour. Family Practice, 1995—; mem. adv. editl. bd. Annals of Long-term Care, 1999—; contbr. chpts. to books and articles to profl. jours. Fellow: Am. Geriatrics Soc. (bd. dirs. 1999—2002, co-chmn.coun. State affiliated 1999—2002), Am. Acad. Family Physicians; mem.: AMA (Physicians Recognition award 1981—94, 1996—2000, Geriatrics Recognition award 2002—), La. Acad. Family Physicians, Am. Med. Dirs. Assn. Republican. Roman Catholic. Avocation: fishing. Home: 1070 Old River Rd Slidell LA 70461-2701 Office: LSUMC Dept Family Medicine 1542 Tulane Ave New Orleans LA 70112-2825 E-mail: ccefal@lsuhsc.edu.

CEHELSKA, OLGA M. musicologist, music therapist; b. Austria, Apr. 6, 1946; d. George Michael and Veronica Bronislava (Drozdowska) C. BMus magna cum laude, Temple U., 1968; MusM, U. Miami, 1978; MSc, Am. Coll. Holistic Health, 1995; PhD holistic nutrition, Clayton Coll. Natural Health, 1999. Cert. Music Educator, N.J.; Cert. Flight Instr., FAA; Cert. Music Therapist Nat. Assn. Music Therapy. Tchr. music Phila. Pub. Sch. System, 1967-71; flight instr. Tamiami Airport, Homestead Airport, Homestead, Fla., 1973-74, Fulton County Airport, Atlanta, Ga., 1974-75; intern activity therapy Ga. Mental Health Inst., Atlanta, 1974; dir. activity therapy Met. Psychiat. Ctr., Atlanta, 1974-75; coord. adult psychiat. day treatment North Dekalb Cmty. Mental Health Ctr., 1975-80; piano instr., 1980—; CEO Cehelska Piano Studio, 1991—; flight instr. Norfolk Airport, Va., 2000—. Musician Young Audiences of Va., Norfolk, 1990-95, cons. Dekalb County Day Program, 1975-80, Nutritional Wellness, Va. Beach, 2000—. Contbr. articles to profl. jours. Mem. Ukrainian Women's League of Am., Ukrainian Scouting, Ukrainian Dancers of Miami, Ukrainian Am. Club of Miami, Nat. Assn. Music Therapy, Aircraft Owners and Pilots Assn., Nat. Assn. Flight Instr., Sigma Alpha Iota Alumni, Tidewater Music Tchrs. Forum, Music Tchrs. Nat. Assn., Va. Music Tchrs. Assn. Ukrainian Catholic. Avocation: traditional ukrainian music on bandura. Office: Cehelska Piano Studio/Nutr Wellness 2313 Beach Haven Dr Unit 103 Virginia Beach VA 23451-1263 E-mail: omcstudio@msn.com.

CEJAS, PAUL L. diplomat, executive; b. Havana, Cuba, Jan. 4, 1943; BBA in Acctg., U. Miami, 1969; PhD (hon.), Fla. Internat. U., 1988. CPA. Amb. to Belgium U.S. Dept. of State, 1998—; chmn., CEO PLC Investments, Inc. Founder, chmn., CEO CareFlorida Health Systems, Inc. Former chmn. Dade County Sch. Bd.; apptd. by Gov. Chiles to bd. regents State of Fla. U., 1994; chmn. Post-Summit Com. for the 1994 Hemispheric Summit of the Americas; chmn. Fla. Partnership of the Americas, 1994-97; rep. to U.S. Delegation to the Gen. Assembly of the Orgn. of Am. States, 1996, others. Office: 27 Blvd de Regent Box 002 Psc 82 Apo AE 09710-0082

ČEJKA, JIŘI, b. Roudnice, N.L., Czech Republic, Sept. 2, 1929; s. Josef and Božena (Roudnická) C.; m. Marie Sedláčková, July 26, 1958; children: Jiří, Jan. MSc, Inst. Chem. Tech., Prague, Czechoslovakia, 1961, PhD, 1970; DSc, Acad. of Scis. of Czech Republic, 1994. Rsch. chemist Reagencia, Kralupy, Czechoslovakia, 1954-59, Glazura, Roudnice, 1959-72; head rsch. chem. divsn. Nat. Mus.-Natural History Mus., Prague, 1972-93, scientist, 1972-88, sr. rsch. scientist, 1988—, dir., 1991-2001, dir. emeritus, 2001—. Author: Secondary Uranium Minerals, 1990; editor Acta Mus. Nat. Pragae, Hist. Natur., 1974-93; regional editor Czech Republic Art and Archaeology Tech. Abstracts, The Getty Conservation Inst., Marina del Rey, Calif., 1988-94; contbr. articles to profl. jours. Mem.: Internat. Mineralogical Assn., Commn. on New Minerals and Mineral Names (a new mineral named cejkaite to honor contributions to uranium mineralogy 1999), European Crystallographic Assn., Junák Assn. of Scouts and Guides of Czech Republic (award 1947, 1987, 1990, 1992, 1999, 2002), Crystallographic Soc., Slovak Chem. Soc., Czech Chem. Soc., Confederation Polit. Prisoners Czech Republic (award 1998), Scout History Assn., Scouts' Velen Fanderlik Troop (troop leader 1999—2001, award 1999). Achievements include patents in field. Avocations: classical music, jazz, fine arts, philosophy of the world scout movement. Home: Michálkova 1672 413 01 Roudnice N.L. Czech Republic Office: Nat Scis Mus of Nat Mus Václavské náměstí 68 115 79 Prague 1 Czech Republic E-mail: jiri_.cejka@tiscali.cz.

CEKAUSKAS, CYNTHIA DANUTE, social worker; b. Detroit, Mar. 24, 1954; d. Vladas Algimantas and Isabel Gana (Stasiulis) Cekauskas; m. Randall Dean Voelker, Mar. 20, 2000. BA in Sociology, Madonna Coll., Livonia, Mich., 1976; MSW, U. Mich., 1979. Lic. clin. social worker La., Fla. Psychiat. social worker Charity Hosp. New Orleans, 1982-84; social worker child and adolescent svc. DePaul Hosp., New Orleans, 1986-87; social worker, family adv. program mgr. Army Cmty. Svcs., Friedberg, Germany, 1988-89; social worker, family adv. program mgr., chmn. family adv. case mgmt. team Cmty. Counseling Ctr., Camp Zama, Japan, 1989-90; social worker, exceptional family mem. program mgr. Army Cmty. Svcs., Bamberg, Germany, 1990-91, alt. family adv., on-call crisis counselor Desert Storm, 1990-91; social worker, family advocacy rep., head dept. family adv. Naval Med. Clinic, New Orleans, 1991-96; social worker, family advocacy program mgr. Army Cmty. Svcs., Augsburg, Germany, 1997-98, Wiesbaden, Germany, 1998-2000; social worker, case mgr. Navy Family Advocacy Ctr., Norfolk, Va., 2000-01; social worker, family advocacy program mgr. U.S. Army Garrison Family Support Ctr., Miami, Fla., 2002—. Presenter Child Abuse Prevention Bad Nauheim Elem. Sch., 1988—89. Contbr. Hosp. corpsman USN, 1979—82. Recipient Customer Svc. award, Giessen Mil. Cmty., 1988—89, Friend Bad Nauheim Elem. Sch. award, 1989, Commendation for Exceptional Svc., Cam Zama, 1991, Scroll of Appreciation for Desert Storm/Desert Shield, Bamberg, Germany, 1990—91, Outstanding Performance award, 1993—94, Presdl. Sports award for racewalking, 1996, Presdl. Sports award for aerobic dance, 1996, Presdl. Sports award for weight tng., 1996, Presdl. Sports award for endurance walking, 1996, 15 Yrs. Fed. Svc. cert. of recognition, U.S. Govt., 2002, Cold War cert. of recognition, 1999. Mem.: NOW, NASW, Acad. Cert. Social Workers, Sierra Club, Nat. Orgn. Victim Assistance, People for Ethical Treatment Animals, German Am. Social Club Greater Miami. Democrat. Roman Catholic. Office: US Army Garrison Miami Family Support Ctr 3511 NW 91st Ave Miami FL 33172-1217

CELANO, PETER J., JR., lawyer; b. Camden, N.J., Apr. 2, 1956; s. Peter J. and Dorothy (Lopez) C.; m. Mary Beth Kramer, Mar. 31, 1984; children: Peter III, William, John. BS, Villanova U., Pa., 1978, JD, 1981. N.J. 1981, Pa. 1981, U.S. Dist. Ct. (ea. dist.) Pa., U.S. Dist. Ct. N.J., U.S. Ct. Appeals (3d cir.). Sr. assoc. Law Office of Joel Feldscher, Cherry Hill, N.J., 1984-87; ptnr. Law Office Celano & Kramer, Woodbury, N.J., 1987—. Pres., Wenonah (N.J.) Bd. Edn. Mem. Gloucester Cty. Bar Assn., Assn. Trial Lawyers Am., Woodbury Country Club. Avocations: golf, swimming, boating, skiing. Office: Celano & Kramer 903 N Broad St Woodbury NJ 08096-3598 E-mail: CelanoKramer@comcast.net.

CELEDONIA, BAILA HANDELMAN, lawyer; b. Bklyn., Jan. 8, 1945; s. Herman and Ida (Rubin) Handelman; m. Arthur Celedonia, Sept. 5, 1966; children: Miriam D., Loren E. BA, Carnegie Inst. Tech., 1965; JD summa cum laude, Bklyn. Law Sch., 1975. Bar: N.Y. 1976, U.S. Dist. Ct. (so. dist.) N.Y. 1976, U.S. Dist. Ct. (ea. dist.) N.Y. 1980, U.S. Ct. Appeals (9th, 10th and 11th cirs.) 1989, U.S. Supreme Ct. 1988. Law clk. U.S. Dist. Ct. (so. dist.) N.Y., N.Y.C., 1975-77; assoc. Cowan, Liebowitz & Latman, P.C., N.Y.C., 1977-82, ptnr., 1983—. Adj. prof. Bklyn. (N.Y.) Law Sch., 1987—88; 1st v.p. Am. Intellectual Property Law Edn. Found., 2001—. Mng. editor Bklyn. Law Rev., 1974-75. Trustee Bklyn. Law Sch., 1984-86. Mem. ABA, Am. Intellectual Property Law Assn. (sec. 1997-2000), Assn. Bar City N.Y., N.Y. State Bar Assn., Internat. Trademark Assn. (bd. dirs. 1990-92), Practicing Law Inst. (intellectual property adv. com. 1997—). Jewish. Home: 35 Prospect Park W Brooklyn NY 11215-2370 Office: Cowan Liebowitz & Latman PC 1133 Avenue Of The Americas New York NY 10036-6710 E-mail: bhc@cll.com.

CELELLA, KAREN ANN, music teacher, author; b. Altoona, Pa., Aug. 16, 1954; d. Alfred Richard and Anna Irene (Harpster) Gerhard; m. Philip Gregory Celella, Sept. 6, 1976 (div.); m. Kelly Ann, Philip Richard. AA, Nassau C.C., Uniondale, N.Y., 1972-74; BA, L.I. U., Brookville, N.Y., 1974-76. Nat. cert. musician. Sales Brandells, Garden City, N.Y., 1972-74, Wordsworth Books, Garden City, 1974-77; ind. music tchr. piano, organ, keyboard, theory, Suffolk County, N.Y., 1972—; tchr. Erol Piano Studio, Coram, 1976-79, Frank & Camille's Studio, Port Jefferson, N.Y., 1982-84, K.C. Studio, Coram, 1979—. Adjudicator Music Educators Nat. Conf., 1993—, Am. Coll. Musicians, Nat. Guild Piano Tchrs., 1998—. Author: KAC Music Assignment Journal, 1995—, also articles; presenter workshops. With USCG auxiliary. Named to Piano Guild Hall of Fame, 2001, Nat. Honor Roll, Nat. Piano Playing Auditions, 1988—. Mem. Suffolk Piano Tchrs. Forum (treas. 1990-96, pres. 1996—2000, v.p. 2000—02, bd. dir., 2002—), Am. Coll. Musicians (cert. tchr.), Music Educators Nat. Conf., Music Tchrs. Nat. Assn., Suffolk County Music Educators Assn., Aircraft Owners and Pilots Assn., U.S. Coast Guard Aux. Avocations: art (cut mat board designs), flying, computers. Home: 20 Summercress Ln Coram NY 11727-2617 Office: KC Studio 20 Summercress Ln Coram NY 11727-2617 E-mail: KCelella2@aol.com.

CELENTO, FLORENCE M. librarian; b. Phila., May 2, 1934; d. Dennis and Dorothy Rose Haggerty; m. Joseph Stephen Celento, Jr., Dec. 17, 1953 (dec. Dec. 1996); children: Christine, Elizabeth, Dennis, Marysusan, Stephanie, Joseph, Emily. BA, Washington & Jefferson Coll., 1983. Cert. libr., Pa. Asst. libr. Chartiers Houston Libr., Houston, Pa., 1980-89; customer svc. rep. United Airlines, Dulles, Va., 1989-90; sec., treas. Celento Assoc. Archs., Houston, Pa., 1990-96; mem. staff Canonsburg (Pa.) Libr., 1999—2001, Peters Twp. Pub. Libr., McMurray, Pa., 2001—. Vol. Rep. Councilman, McMurray, Pa., 1996. Avocations: reading, walking, traveling, needlework. Home: 403 Scott Ln Venetia PA 15367-1121 Office: Peters Twp Pub Libr 616 E McMurray Mc Murray PA 15317-1312

CELESIA, GASTONE GUGLIELMO, neurologist, neurophysiologist, researcher; b. Genoa, Italy, Nov. 22, 1933; came to U.S., 1959, naturalized, 1970; s. Raffaele Amadeo and Ottavia (Tortrino) C.; m. Linda Irene Pike, Aug. 1, 1964; children— Gloria, Laura MD, U. Genoa, 1959; MS, McGill U., Montreal, 1965. Diplomate Am. Bd. Psychiatry and Neurology in Neurology, Am. Bd. Psychiatry and Neurology in Clin. Neurophysiology. Intern Madison Gen. Hosp., Wis., 1960; fellow neurophysiology U. Wis., Madison, 1960-62, asst. prof. neurology, 1966-69, assoc. prof., 1970-73, prof., 1974-79, 1979-83; resident in neurology Montreal Neurol. Inst./McGill U., Montreal, Que., Can., 1962-66; chief neurology service VA Hosp., Madison, 1979-83; chmn. dept. neurology Loyola U., Chgo., 1983-99. Editor in chief: Electroenceph. Clin. Neurophysiol., 1988-99; contbr. articles to profl. jours. Fellow Am. Acad. Neurology; mem. AMA, Am. EEG Soc., Am. Acad. Clin. Neurophysiology (pres. 1993-95), Am. Neurol. Assn., Ctrl. Assn. EEG, Wis. Neurol. Soc. Wis. Med. Alumni Assn., Wis. Neurol. Soc. (pres. 1975-76), Soc. Neurosci., Am. Epilepsy Soc., N.Y. Acad. Scis. AAAS, Royal Soc. Medicine, Am. Soc. Exptl. Med. Therapeutics. Office: Loyola Univ-Chgo Dept Neurology 2160 S 1st Ave Maywood IL 60153-3304 E-mail: gcelesi@lumc.edu.

CELESTE, ARDELLA HAZEL, retired writer; b. Lenoir City, Tenn., May 18, 1929; d. James Edgar and Hazel Della Benson; m. Anthony Celeste, Dec. 29, 1950 (div. July 27, 1973); children: Joanne, Anthony, Christopher, Craig, Michael. Writer Writers Digest Book Club, Cincinnati, Ohio, 2002—02. Writer, Perrysburg, Ohio, 1978—; writing instr. U. Toledo, 1982—83. Contbr. articles to profl. jours. Contbr. Wood County Jefferson Meeting, Wood County, Ohio, 1989—89. Recipient Cert. Participation, Judge Kurfess & Brian Ballard, Co-Chairman, 1989. Avocations: traveling, garage sales, walking, reading. Home: 201Trinity Court Perrysburg OH 43551-3184 Personal E-mail: emerald@wcnet.org.

CELESTE, RICHARD F. academic administrator, former ambassador, former governor; b. Cleve., Nov. 11, 1937; s. Frank C.; m. Dagmar Braun, 1962; children: Eric, Christopher, Gabriella, Noelle, Natalie, Stephen BA in History magna cum laude, Yale U., 1959; Ph.B. in Politics, Oxford U., 1962. Staff liaison officer Peace Corps, 1963, dir., 1979-81; spl. asst. to U.S. amb. to India, 1963-67; mem. Ohio Ho. of Reps., Columbus, 1970-74, majority whip, 1972-74; lt. gov. State of Ohio, Columbus, 1974-79, gov., 1983-91; mng. ptnr. Celeste & Sabety, Ltd., Columbus, Ohio; amb. to India New Delhi, 1997—2001; co-chair, Homeland Security Proj. The Century Found., 2002—; pres. Colorado Coll., 2002—. Mem. Ohio Dem. Exec. Com. Rhodes scholar Oxford U., Eng. Mem. Am. Soc. Pub. Adminstrn., Italian Sons and Daus. Am. Methodist. Office: Office Pres Colorado Coll 14 E Cache La Poudre St Colorado Springs CO 80903*

CELIA, GEORGE, composer, writer; b. Ragusa, Italy, Mar. 17, 1921; came to U.S., 1923; s. Giorgio Giuseppe and Lucia Giovanna (Sola) C.; m. Rosemary Fern Walker, Apr. 26, 1958; 1 child, Georgene Fern. Student, Northwestern U., 1944-48, U. Chgo., 1968. Personnel mgr., asst. contr. Consolidated Radio Products Co., Chgo., 1949-55; office mgr., chief acct., contr., treas. Gulbransen Piano & Organ Co., Melrose Park, Ill., 1955-70; owner George Celia U. & Libr., 1971, Life Mgr. Co., Richardson, Tex., 1971-73, Get Organized Co., Richardson, 1973-97, Ultimate You, George Celia Creative Enterprises, Richardson, 1986-97, Midland, 1998—, Celia Ingram Comm. Spl. feature writer Chgo. (Ill.) Tribune, 1954. Composer (processional): The Triumph of Ideals, 1945; composer: March of the Nations-UN song, 1945, Fight Boys Fight Sport Song, 1945, Song of the Returning Soldier, 1945, Rispetto, 1989, Student's Procession on the Shoulder's of Giants, 2000, The Gladness, 2001, AnniMETsary Song, 2003; author: Focus Books, 1971, Ultimate You, 1989, Personal Magna Carta, 1989, The Triumph of Ideals, 1997, Love Affair with Every Day, 1997, Musikgarten & Art, 2000, Incredible Galleries, 2000, The Unstilled Quills, 2001, Keyboard Extravaganza, 2002, Historic Letter to Louisa, 2003; author: (travel and autobiog. drama scenes) Roman Britain, 1992, Columbus 500th, Genoa Maternal Relatives Reunion, 1992, Rome, Paternal Relatives Reunion, 1992, Scafati (bordering Pompeii) Maternal Roots, 1992, Awed by Ragusa, Beautiful Sicilian City Scene, 1992, Ode to the Statue of Liberty and to the Marseillaise, 1992. Treas. City Coun. Campaign, Richardson, 1987. Mem.: Alpha Kappa Psi. Republican. Methodist. Avocations: composer, author, photographer, sports. Home: 3208 Whitney Dr Midland TX 79705-6246

CELL, GILLIAN TOWNSEND, historian, educator; b. Birkenhead, Cheshire, Eng., June 5, 1937; came to U.S., 1962; d. Thomas Edmund and Doris Abigail (Clark) Townsend; m. John Whitson Cell, Oct. 19, 1962 (dec.); children: Thomas K., Katherine A., John D. BA, U. Liverpool, Eng., 1959, PhD, 1964. Instr. U. N.C., Chapel Hill, 1965-66, asst. prof., 1966-70, assoc. prof., 1970-78, prof., 1978-91, affirmative action officer, 1981-83, chmn. dept. history, 1983-85, dean Coll. Arts and Scis., 1985-91; provost Lafayette Coll., 1991-93, Coll. of William and Mary, 1993—. Author: English Enterprise in Newfoundland; 1577-1660, 1969; editor: Newfoundland Discovered, 1982. Office: Coll William and Mary Office of Provost PO Box 8795 Williamsburg VA 23187-8795

CELLI, BARTOLOME ROMULO, internist; b. Valencia, Venezuela, Dec. 17, 1946; came to U.S., 1970; s. Romulo and Dinorah (Croquer) C.; m. Doris Cruz; children: Doris Lucia, Natalia Dinorah Maria Gabriela, Romulo Alberto. BS, La Salle U., Caracas, Venezuela, 1964; MD, Cen. U., Caracas, 1971. Diplomate Am. Bd. Internal Medicine, Am. Bd. Pulmonary Diseases, Am. Bd. Critical Care Medicine. Intern St. Vincent Hosp., Worcester, Mass., 1971-72; resident Boston City Hosp., 1972-75; mem. pulmonary medicine staff Boston U. Med. Ctr., 1975-77; chief pulmonary and intensive care units Coromoto Hosp., Maracaibo, Venezuela, 1977-82; staff physician Boston City and Univ. Hosp., 1982—. Adj. asst. prof. Boston U. Sch. Med., 1982, assoc. prof., 1988—; prof. medicine Tufts U., Boston, 1995—; dir. pulmonary physiology Boston City and Univ. Hosp., 1983—; chief pulmonary sect. Boston V.A. Med. Ctr., 1987-94; chief pulmonary/critical care sect. St. Elizabeth's Med. Ctr. Contbr. articles to med. jours. Recognition award AMA, 1983. Fellow Am. Coll. Chest Physicians; mem. Am. Thoracic Soc., Am. Fedn. Clin. Research, Am. Physiol. Soc. Roman Catholic. Office: 31 River Glen Rd Wellesley MA 02481-1626 E-mail: bcelli@cchcs.org.

CELLIERS, PETER JOUBERT, public relations specialist; b. Vogelfontein, S. Africa, 1920; s. Bartilimy and Elsie Blanche (Goldberg) Celliers; m. Helen Rassaby, Sept. 10, 1949; children: Gordon A.J., Jennifer A.J. Editor, to 1959; cons. to fgn. govts., internat. corps. Peter J. Celliers Co., N.Y.C., 1958-68; chief fgn. press svcs. Olympic Organizing Com., Mexico, 1968; dir. for N.Am., Mexican Nat. Tourist Coun., 1962-72; owner Ellis Assocs., N.Y.C., 1969-91. Tech. adviser internat. market devel. to UN, hotels, carriers, govts.; ret. Mem. Soc. Am. Travel Writers (founder). Home and Office: 240 Garth Rd Scarsdale NY 10583-3962

CELLUCCI, ARGEO PAUL, ambassador, former governor; b. Marlboro, Mass., Apr. 24, 1948; s. Argeo R. and Priscilla Rose C.; m. Janet Garnett, 1971; children: Kate, Anne. BS, Boston Coll., 1970, JD, 1973. Atty. Kittredge, Cellucci and Moreira, Hudson, Mass., 1973-90; mem. Hudson charter commn. Hudson, 1970-71; selectman, 1971-77; state rep. Third Middlesex Dist., Mass., 1977-84; state senator Middlesex and Worcester Dists., Mass., 1985-90; lt. gov. State of Mass., 1991-97, gov., 1997—2001; Am. amb. to Canada, 2001—. Capt. USAR, served in USAR 1970-1978. Recipient Haskins and Fells Found. award, 1969. Mem. ABA, Mass. Bar Assn., Elks, Sons of Italy. Republican. Roman Catholic. Office: Embsy USA 490 Sussex Dr Ottawa ON K1N1 1G8 Canada E-mail: reference@usembassycanada.gov.*

CELLURA, A(NGELE) RAYMOND, psychologist; b. Rochester, N.Y., Dec. 22, 1932; s. Raymond Anthony and Helen (Balistrere) C.; children: Jon, Jane, Todd. BA, St. Francis Coll., 1957; MS, L.I. U., 1960, SUNY, New Paltz, 1960; EdD, U. Rochester, 1965. Lic. psychologist, Mass., Ga. Psychologist City Sch. Dist., Rochester, 1961-63; sr. clin. psychologist N.Y. State Dept. Mental Hygeine, 1964-65; asst. dir. cmty. mental health rsch. tng. program Washington U., St. Louis, 1964-65, asst. prof. Grad. Inst. Edn., 1964-65; head dept. human devel. U. Mass., Amherst, 1965-68; assoc. prof. psychology R.I. Coll., Providence, 1968-70; pres. EDPSI, Inc., Sharon, Mass., 1970-89; psychologist IV, S.C. Dept. Mental Health, Columbia, 1989-91; med. cons. disability determination S.C. Divsn. Voc. Rehab., 1991-93; prin. Behavior Consults, Hartwell Ga., 1993—, Abbeville, S.C., 1993—. Mental health cons. Head Start program Ctrl. Savannah River Area-Econ. Opportunity Authority, Augusta, Ga., 1998-2000; trainee postdoctoral program in psychopharmacology U. Ga.-Ga. State U., 1999-2000; chief psychology svcs. Ga. Regional Hosp. at Augusta, 2002-, dir. Psychosocial Treatment Svcs. East Ctrl. Reg. Hosp., Augusta, Ga., 2003-. Contbr. articles to profl. jours. including Am. Edn. Rsch. Jour. and Am. Jour. Mental Deficiency. Mem. AAAS, Am. Psychol. Assn., N.Y. Acad. Scis. Achievements include development first head start teacher training program at U. Mass., Amherst, 1966, introduced mental health consultation programs at Deerfield Academy, Eaglebrook school, Lincoln Academy, Wheeler Academy, Providence Country Day School, 1965-67; development of need potential for acad. achievement questionnaire. Office: Behavior Consults 2418 Cedar Springs Rd Abbeville SC 29620-9803 E-mail: arcellura@wctel.net.

CELMER, VIRGINIA, psychologist; b. Detroit, June 26, 1945; d. Charles and Stella (Kopicko) C. BA in English, Marygrove Coll., 1968; MA in Theol. Studies, St. Louis U., 1977; PhD in Counseling Psychology, Tex. Tech. U., 1986. Lic. psychologist; lic. chem. dependency counselor; cert. diplomate in managed mental health care; bd. cert. alcohol and drug counselor level III diplomate; internat. cert. alcoholism and drug abuse counselor, cert. group psychotherapist; cert. sex addicion therapist level II. Chaplain Mercy Ctr. for Health Care Svcs., Aurora, Ill., 1977-81; grad. asst. counselor U. Counseling Ctr., Tex. Tech. U., Lubbock, 1982-86, pre-doctoral intern in counseling psychology, 1985-86; post-doctoral intern Consultation Ctr., San Antonio, 1986-89, staff psychologist, 1989-90; pvt. practice psychologist San Antonio, 1989—. Instr. dept. psychology Tex. Tech. U., Lubbock, 1981-85, Oblate Sch. Theology, San Antonio, 1989-90. Contbr. articles to profl. jours. Mem. APA, Tex. Psychol. Assn., Bexar County Psychol. Assn., Am. Group Psychotherapy Assn., San Antonio Group Psychotherapy Assn., Nat. Assn. Alcoholism and Drug Abuse Counselors, Tex. Assn. Alcoholism and Drug Abuse Counselors. Office: 5440 Babcock Rd Ste 110 San Antonio TX 78240-3946

CELMINS, VIJA, artist, photographer; b. Riga, Latvia, 1939; U.S. Student, Yale U.; MFA, UCLA, 1965. One-woman shows include Whitney Mus. Am. Art, N.Y.C., 1993, Represented in permanent collections Sheldon Meml. Art Gallery and Sculpture Garden, U. Nebr., Lincoln, F.M. Hall Collection. Office: 745 5th Ave Fl 4 New York NY 10151-0099

CELORIE, DENNIS JAY, not-for-profit executive; b. Eugene, Oreg., Mar. 26, 1939; s. Francis Emmett and Mildred Maxine C.; m. Linda Lou Celorie, Aug. 24, 1974; 1 child, Lyndsie. BA in Speech, Pacific U., 1963. Program dir. KWFS Radio, Eugene, 1963-68; pres., gen. mgr. Linn Broadcasting, Sweet Home, Oreg., 1968-70; asst. prof. Lane C.C., Eugene, 1970-74; dir. devel. Oreg. Easter Seal Soc., Portland, 1974-80; exec. dir. Ga. Easter Seal Soc., Atlanta, 1980-87; pres., CEO Easter Seal-Southwest Fla., Sarasota, 1987—2001; pres. Inspirit Enterprises, Tallevast, 2001—. Vice chair Human Svcs. Planning Assn., Sarasota, 1989-94; bd. trustees Commn. Accreditation Rehab. Facilities, Tucson, 1998—; spkr. in field. Chair Oreg. Govs., Salem, 1976-78; bd. dirs. Workforce Devel. Bd., Sarasota, 1997-2001; chair Fla. Rehab. Coun. on Handicapped, Tallahassee, 1999-2000, Occupl. Access Opportunity Commn., Tallahassee, 2000—. Recipient Voice of Experience award Pacific U., 1962, Regional Svc. to Mankind award Sertoma Internat., 1996. Mem. Fla. Rehab. Facilities (bd. dirs. 1989, Michael Gillman award 1992), Easter Seal Leadership Assn. (treas. 1993), Easter Seal S.E. CEO's (chair 1996). Republican. Roman Catholic. Avocations: disabled sailing, disabled golf. Home: 1367 Georgetowne Cir Sarasota FL 34232 Office: Inspirit Enterprises PO Box 197 Tallevast FL 34270 E-mail: dcelorie@aol.com.

CELOTTA, ROBERT JAMES, physicist; b. N.Y.C., Nov. 18, 1943; s. Bart and Agnes Margaret (Comerford) C.; m. Beverly Kay Lauter, Nov. 20, 1966; children: Jennifer Ann, Daniel Wayne. BS in Physics, CCNY, 1964; PhD in Physics, NYU, 1969. Rsch. asst. IBM Watson Lab., N.Y.C., 1963-64; rsch. asst. dept. physics NYU, N.Y.C., 1964-69, instr., 1966-69; postdoctoral rsch. assoc. Joint Inst. Lab. Astrophysics, Boulder, Colo., 1969-71; physicist Nat. Inst. Standards and Tech., Gaithersburg, Md., 1971-86, fellow, 1987—. Mem. gen. com. Internat. Conf. on Physics of Electron and Atom Collisions, 1985—89; participant NSF-Nat. Coun. for Sci. and Tech. U.S.-L.Am. Coop. Sci. Program, 1984—86, U.S.-Spain Sci. Program, 1985—88, U.S.-Yugoslav Coop. Rsch. Program, 1978—87; vice chair Gordon Conf. on Magnetic Nanostructures, 1997—99, chair, 2000—02; mem. com. on emerging micro and nano technologies NRC, 2002—. Series editor Methods of Exptl. Physics, 1981-95, Exptl. Methods in Phys. Scis., 1995—; mem. editl. bd. Rev. Sci. Instruments, 1982-85, vice chair Davisson-Germer Prize Com., 1990-91, chair, 1992-93, adv. com. Conf. on Magnetics and Magnetic Materials, 1996-97; contbr. articles to Phys. Rev. Letters, Science, Phys. Rev., Jour. Vaccum Sci. Tech., Jour. Applied Physics, Applied Physics Letters, Revs. Sci. Instruments, Sci., Jour. Physics, Jour. Magnetism and Magnetic Materials, Jour. Chem. Physics, numerous others; contbr. to conf. procs. Recipient Disting. Young Scientist award Md. Acad. Scis., 1978, Edward V. Condon award U.S. Dept. Commerce, 1980, IR-100 award R & D Mag., 1980, 85, Fed. Lab. Consortium award Excellence in Tech. Transfer, 1988, William P. Slichter award Nat. Inst. Stds. and Tech., 1992, Alumni Achievement award NYU, 1997. Fellow: AAAS (Centennial spkr. 1998—99), Washington Acad. Sci. (Outstanding and Disting. Career in Sci. award 1994), Am. Vacuum Soc. (Gaede-Langmuir prize 1994), Am. Phys. Soc. (exec. com. topical group on instrumentation and measurement scis. 2000—, mem. McGrody prize com. 2000—02). Achievements include patents for Absorbed Current Electron Polarization Detectors; Apparatus and Methods for Electron Spin Polarization Detection; Laser Controlled Nanolithography; developed photodetachment spectroscopy method for electron affinity measurement; pioneering measurements in polarized electron scattering from atoms and surfaces, scanning tunneling microscopy, surface magnetism and laser controlled atom deposition; developed the GaAs polarized electron source, the diffuse low energy polarization detector, and the technique of scanning electron microscopy with polarization analysis (SEMPA). Office: NIST B206 Metrology Bldg Gaithersburg MD 20899-8412 E-mail: Robert.Celotta@nist.gov.

CEMBER, M. NATHAN, lawyer, speaker; b. N.Y.C., July 18, 1928; s. Arthur and Lilly (Schuster) C.; m. Esther Weissman, June 29, 1952; children: Richard, Mark, William. LLB, Bklyn. Law Sch., 1950, LLM, 1955. Bar: N.Y. 1951, U.S. Dist. Ct. (so. dist.) N.Y. 1960, U.S. Supreme Ct. 1967. House counsel Tenax, Inc., N.Y.C., 1953-66, Cember & Cember PC, Nyack, N.Y., 1966—. Chmn. Rockland County Com. for Soviet Jewry, N.Y., 1975; pres. Congregation Sons of Israel, Nyack, 1964-65. With U.S. Army, 1950-52, Korea. Mem. N.Y. State Bar Assn., Rockland County Bar Assn., Comml. Law League, B'nai B'rith (v.p. dist. 1 1982-85, pres. 1985-86, internat. v.p. 1990-92). Democrat. Office: Cember & Cember PC 10 S Broadway Nyack NY 10960-3119 E-mail: bignat28@aol.com.

CENARRUSA, PETE T. retired state official; b. Carey, Idaho, Dec. 16, 1917; s. Joseph and Ramona (Gardoqui) C.; m. Freda B. Coates, Oct. 25, 1947; 1 son, Joe Earl (dec.). BS in Agr., U. Idaho, 1940. Tchr. high sch., Cambridge, Idaho, 1940-41, Carey and Glenns Ferry, Idaho, 1946; tchr. vocat. agr. VA, Blaine County, Idaho, 1946-51; farmer, woolgrower, nr. Carey, 1946-95; mem. Idaho Ho. of Reps., 1951-67, speaker, 1963-67; sec. state of Idaho, 1967—90, 1991—2002. Mem. Idaho Bd. Land Commrs., Idaho Bd. Examiners; pres. Idaho Flying Legislators, 1953-63; chmn. Idaho Legis. Council, 1964—, Idaho Govt. Reorgn. Com.; Idaho del. Council State Govts., 1963— Elected ofcl., mem. BLM Adv. Coun., Boise Dist.; Rep. administr. Hall of Fame, 1978; sr. mem. State Bd. Land Commrs., 1967-96; dean Nations Secs. of State, 1967—. Maj. USMCR, 1942-46, 52-58. Named Hon. Farmer Future Farmers Am., 1955; inductee Agrl. Hall of Fame, 1973, Idaho Athletic Hall of Fame, 1976, Basque Hall of Fame, 1983, Idaho Hall of Fame, 1998; recipient Am. Century award for Idaho Washington Times Found. Mem. Blaine County Livestock Mktg. Assn., Idaho Wool Growers Assn. (chmn. 1954), Carey C. of C. (pres. 1952), U. Idaho Alumni Assn., Gamma Sigma Delta, Tau Kappa Epsilon. Republican. Achievements include serving longer than any constitutional official elected in Idaho concluding with 50 years on 12/1/00.*

CENDES, ZOLTAN JOSEPH, electrical engineer, educator; b. Feffernitz, Austria, May 16, 1946; arrived in U.S., 1960; s. Joseph and Madeline Cendes; m. Marie E. Cendes; children: Linda, Patrick, Yvette. BS in Engring., U. Mich., 1968; MS in Engring., McGill U., 1970, PhD, 1972. Assoc. McGill U., Montreal, Canada, 1973—74; engr. Gen. Electric Co., Schenectady, NY, 1974—80; assoc. prof. McGill U., 1980—81; prof. Carnegie Mellon U., Pitts., 1982—96; prin., owner Ansoft Corp., Pitts., 1984—. Fellow: IEEE. Office: Ansoft Corp 4 Station Street Pittsburgh PA 15219

CENICEROS, MACIEL HECTOR ALFONSO, business systems executive, consultant; b. Fed. Dist., Mex., Sept. 28, 1966; s. Flores Hector Ceniceros and Miranda Rosalia Maciel. Degree in Acctg., Univ. ISEC, Mexico City, 1995. Gen. mgr. SSE, Mexico City, 1990—. Mktg. mgr. Video Tech. mag., 2003. Author: Unforgettable Adventure, 1999, The Last Journey, 2001, Looking for Paradise, 2001, A Second for Eternity, 2001, Simon's Mountain, 2002. Home: Tlacoquemecatl 102-202 del Valle DF 03200 Mexico City Mexico Office: Tokio 701-D Portales 03300 Mexico DF Mexico

CENKNER, WILLIAM, religion educator, academic administrator; b. Cleve., Oct. 25, 1930; s. Joseph Paul and Sophia (Gladis) C. BA, Providence Coll., 1954; STB, Dominican Faculty, Washington, 1956, STL, 1959; PhD, Fordham U., 1969. Ordained priest Roman Cath. Ch., 1958. Lectr. Aquinas Coll. High Sch., Columbus, Ohio, 1959-64, St. Charles Coll., Columbus, 1962-64; asst. prof. religion Marist Coll., Poughkeepsie, N.Y., 1964-65, Cath. U. Am., Washington, 1969-73, assoc. prof., 1973-83, prof., 1983—, dean Sch. Religious Studies, 1985-93, Katharine M. Drexel prof. religious studies, 1998—2002, prof. emeritus, 2002—; scholar-in-residence Barry U., 2002—. Mem. exec. com. Am. Conf. on Religious Movements, Washington, 1988-98. Author: The Hindu Personality in Education, 1976, A Tradition of Teachers: Sankara and Jagadgurus Today, 1983; editor: The Religious Quest, 1983, The Multicultural Church, 1995, Evil and the Response of World Religions, 1996. Chmn. Faiths in the World Com., Washington, 1985-93. Rsch. grantee Chauncy Stillman Found., India, 1969, C. VanderLinde Found., India, 1979, Nanzan Inst. Religion and Culture, Japan, 1983. Mem. Am. Acad. Religion, Cath. Acad. Scis. in U.S., Assn. Asian Studies, Am. Oriental Soc., Coll. Theology Soc. (pres. 1978-80), Internat. Assn. History of Religions. Roman Catholic.

CENSER, JACK RICHARD, history educator; b. Memphis, Dec. 8, 1946; s. Joseph B. and Dorothy Theresa (Jiedel) C.; m. Emily Jane Turner, May 23, 1976; children: Marjorie, Joel. BA, Duke U., 1968; MA, Johns Hopkins U., 1971, PhD, 1973. Asst. prof. history Coll. of Charleston, S.C., 1974-77; from asst. prof. to full prof. George Mason U., Fairfax, Va., 1977—, chmn. dept. history, 1995—. Asst. dir. Urban Studies Program, Coll. Charleston, 1974-77. Author: Prelude to Power, 1976, the Press in the Age of Enlightenment, 1994, Liberty, Equality, Fraternity: Exploring the French Revolution, 2001; editor: Press in Pre-Revolution France, 1986. Fellow Ctr. for Met. Planning Johns Hopkins U., Balt., 1973-74, Am. Coun. Learned Socs., N.Y., 1989-90, Max Planck Inst., 1986, 89; Mellon fellow U. Pitts., 1978-89; grantee NEH, 1977, 98. Mem. Am. Hist. Assn. (chair Gershoy prize com. 2000-01), Soc. for French Hist. Studies (mem. program com., 1978, 1979, 1980, 1989, 1999, prize com. 1978, 80, 89, v.p. 1989). Democrat. Jewish. Home: 4122 Lenox Dr Fairfax VA 22032-1111

CENSITS, RICHARD JOHN, retired business executive; b. Allentown, Pa., May 20, 1937; s. Stephen A. and Theresa M. Censits; m. Linda A. Malin, June 21, 1958; children: Debra, Mark, David. BS in Econs., U. Pa., 1958; MBA, Lehigh U., 1964. Sr. auditor Arthur Andersen & Co., 1958-62; mgr. acctg. Air Products & Chems., 1962-64; contr. Hamilton Watch Co., Lancaster, Pa., 1964-69; v.p., contr. IU Internat., Phila., 1969-75; v.p., CFO Campbell Soup Co., Camden, N.J., 1975-86; CEO, chmn. MedQuist Inc., Marlton, NJ, 1986—95; bus. cons., 1995—2002; ret., 2002. Bd. dirs. First Fla. Bank; trustee NCH Healthcare Sys. Mem.: The Club at Pelican Bay. Home: 688 Annemore Ln Naples FL 34108-7520 E-mail: r.censits@worldnet.att.net.

CENTAFONT, LUCY ANN ALEXANDER, occupational therapy consultant; b. Anchorage, Alaska, Apr. 6, 1953; d. Robert C. and Lucy Ann (Morgan) Alexander; m. Richard A. Centafont, May 13, 1978; children: Ryan Alan, Jeffrey Richard, Lauren Ann. BS in Occupational Therapy, Temple U., 1977, MS, 1987; BS in Health Edn., Slippery Rock U., 1975. Occupational therapy cons. Bucks County Assn. for Retarded Citizens, Doylestown, Pa.; dir. occupational therapy Community Found. for Human Devel., Sellersville, Pa.; chief occupational therapy Rolling Hill Hosp., Elkins Park, Pa.; pvt. practice occupational therapy cons. Southampton, Pa. Mem. Am. Occupational Therapy Assn., Pa. Occupational Therapy Assn. (developmental disabilities spl. interest group, adminstrv. spl. interest group).

CENTENO, GRISSELLE, industrial engineer; d. Gamaliel Centeno and Carmen Maria Rodriguez; m. Ismael Acevedo, Nov. 21, 1998. PhD, U. of Ctrl. Fla., Orlando, FL, 1994—98, MS in Indsl. Engring., 1992—94; BS in Indsl. Engring., U. of PR, Mayaguez, Mayaguez, Puerto Rico, 1987—92. Asst. prof. U. of South Fla., Tampa, Fla., 2000—; vis. asst. prof. U. of Ctrl. Fla., Orlando, Fla., 1998—2000; indsl. engr. Lucent Technologies, Orlando, 1992—98. Advisor Soc. of Hispanic and Profl. Engineers, Tampa, Fla., 2001—; co-pi Stars Program, Tampa, Fla., 2002—; prin. investigator Ctr. for Urban Transp. Rsch., Tampa, Fla., 2001—. Author article. As. Fellow Lucent Tech. Rsch. Award, Lucent Tech., 1992-1998. Office: University of South Florida 4202 E Fowler Ave ENB118 Tampa FL 33620 Office Fax: 813-974-5953. E-mail: gcenteno@eng.usf.edu.

CENTENO-DAINTY, SONIA MARGARITA, artist; b. Arecibo, P.R., Mar. 4, 1948; arrived in U.S., 1960; d. Eugenio Centeno Faria and Carmen Maria Valencia Franco; m. James Albert Dainty, Jan. 17, 1970; 1 child, James William Dainty. Student journalism and art schs. Educator Boys & Girls Club, N.Y.C.; real estate realtor N.Y.C.; owner constrn. co. Produced portraits and landscapes for pvt. collections. Republican. Roman Catholic. Avocations: gardening, travel, sewing, photography. Home: 348 Old Dutch Hollow Rd Monroe NY 10950

CENTNER, CHARLES WILLIAM, lawyer, educator; b. Battle Creek, Mich., July 4, 1915; s. Charles William and Lucy Irene (Patterson) C.; m. Evi Rohr, Dec. 22, 1956; children: Charles Patterson, David William, Geoffrey Christopher. AB, U. Chgo., 1936, AM, 1938, 39, PhD, 1941; JD, Detroit Coll. Law, 1970; LLB, LaSalle Extension U., 1965. Bar: Mich. 1970. Asst. prof. U. N.D., 1940-41, Tulane U., New Orleans, 1941-42; liaison officer for Latin Am., Dept. State at Lend-Lease Adminstrn., 1942; assoc. dir. Western Hemisphere divsn. Nat. Fgn. Trade Coun., N.Y., 1946-52; exec. Ford Motor Co., Detroit, 1952-57, Chrysler Corp. and Chrysler Internat. S.A., Detroit and Geneva, Switzerland, 1957-70. Adj. prof. Pace U., N.Y.C., 1950-52, Wayne State U., Detroit, 1971-78, U. Detroit, 1970-72, Wayne County C.C., 1970-2001. Author: Great Britian and Chile, 1810-1914, 1941. Lt. comdr. USNR, 1942-45, Res., 1945-75. Mem. ABA, State Bar Mich., Oakland County Bar Assn., Masons. Republican. Episcopalian. Home: 936 Harcourt Rd Grosse Pointe Park MI 48230-1874

CENTO, WILLIAM FRANCIS, retired newspaper editor; b. St. Louis, Mar. 20, 1932; s. Frank and Augusta (Albietz) C.; m. Vera Ann Shaide, May 16, 1964. BS, St. Louis U., 1954. Gen. assignment reporter East St. Louis (Ill.) Jour., 1954-56; suburban editor Globe-Democrat, St. Louis, 1956-61; copyeditor Post-Dispatch, St. Louis, 1961-62; make-up editor Pioneer Press, St. Paul, 1962-65, wire editor, 1965-67, Sunday editor, 1967-73; graphics editor Pioneer Press & Dispatch, St. Paul, 1974-77; mng. editor St. Paul Dispatch, 1977-84; assoc. editor Pioneer Press, St. Paul, 1984-90. Owner Give Me Rewrite, West St. Paul, 1990—; editor, pub. Letter from Minn., West St. Paul, 1995—. Editor: Fifty and Feisty APME: 1933 to 1983, 1983. Recipient numerous awards including Twin Cities Newspaper Guild Page 1 award Makeup 1st pl. award, 1969, 71, 74, 2d pl., 1971, 72, Award of Appreciation, AP Mng. Editors Assn., 1983. Mem. Soc. Profl. Journalists, AP Mng. Editors Assn. (bd. dirs. 1982-88). Roman Catholic. Avocations: painting, graphic design. Home and Office: 111 Imperial Dr W Apt 103 West Saint Paul MN 55118-2249 E-mail: mnletter@aol.com.

CENTOFANTI, JOSEPH, accountant; b. Watervliet, N.Y., Oct. 2, 1965; s. Anthony Joseph and Mary Ann (Sutton) C. AS in Mgmt., BS in Acctg., Bentley Coll., 1987. CPA, Conn.; cert. Govt. Fin. Mgr.; cert. Fraud Examiner. Staff acct. Pannell Kerr Forster, Hartford, Conn., 1987-88, sr. acct., 1988-91, Kostin, Ruffkess and Co., Farmington, Conn., 1991-92, supr., 1992-95, mgr., 1995-99, dir. govt. svcs., 2000-01; ptnr. Kostin Ruffkess & Co. LLC, Farmington, 2001—. Author: Audit Manual; contbr. articles to profl. jours. Treas. New Britain (Conn.) Jaycees, 1991-97, pres., 1993-95, v.p. membership, 1995-97; treas. Greater New Britain Art Alliance, 2001-. Mem.: AICPA, Conn. Soc. CPAs (chair govtl. acctg. and auditing com. 2002—03), Assn. Govt. Accts., Assn. Cert. Fraud Examiners (v.p. and tng. dir.), Govt. Fin. Officers Assn. (spl. rev. com.). Home: 205 Merigold Dr New Britain CT 06053-1445 Office: Kostin Ruffkess & Co LLC Pond View Corp Ctr 76 Batterson Park Rd Farmington CT 06032-2515 E-mail: jcentofanti@kostin.com.

CENZER, DOUGLAS ALFRED, mathematician, educator; b. Detroit, Nov. 15, 1947; s. Alfred Vitold and Hattie (Czaczkowski) C.; m. Pamela Scharstein, June 21, 1970; children: Michael, Meredith. BS in Math., Mich. State U., 1968; PhD in Math., U. Mich., 1972. Asst. prof. U. Fla., Gainesville, 1972-77, assoc. prof., 1977-87, prof., 1987—. Vis. assoc. prof. math. North Tex. State U., Denton, 1981-82; mem. Math. Sci. Rsch. Inst., Berkeley, 1989-90. Contbr. articles to profl. jours. Scholar Ford Motor Co. Fund, 1965-68; NSF fellow, 1968-72; NSF grantee, 1974-77. Mem. Am. Math. Soc., Assn. for Symbolic Logic (chair membership com. 2001—, assoc. editor Arch. Math. Logic 2002—), Pi Mu Epsilon, Phi Beta Kappa (chpt. v.p. 1991-92, pres. 1992—). Avocation: tennis. Office: U Fla Dept Math PO Box 118105 Gainesville FL 32611-8105

CEO, BARBARA ANN, speech-language pathologist, educator; b. Scranton, Pa., Oct. 2, 1948; d. Anthony J. and Emilia M. (Weber) Sieborowski; children: F. Avery, David A., Brian J. BA, New Coll. of U. So. Fla., 1970; tchr. cert., Toronto Tchrs. Coll., Ont., Can., 1973; MS, Columbia U., 1979. Cert. Clin. Competence-Speech Lang. Pathology. Stipend trainee Bklyn. VA Med. Ctr., NY, 1978-79; home health provider Lexington Sch. for Deaf, Queens, NY, 1980-81; N.E. coord. Human Unity found., 1981-82; rep. A.L. Williams Corp., Ft. Lauderdale, Fla., 1982-84; dir. Help for Sr., NYC, 1985-89; speech-lang. pathologist Manatee County Sch. Bd., Sarasota, Fla., 1990-91, Sarasota County Sch. Bd., 1991-92, Easter Seals of S.W. Fla., Sarasota, Fla., 1992-95, Lakeside Terrace S.W. Fla., Sarasota, Fla., 1995-96, Fla. Ear and Sinus Ctr., Sarasota, Fla., 1996-97; pvt. practice Sarasota, Fla., 1997—. Mem. alumni grants com. New Coll. of U. South Fla., 1993—. Bd. dir. PTA, Southside Sch., Sarasota, 1992-93. Recipient Legion of Honor, Chapel of the Four Chaplains, 1982. Mem. Am. Speech-Lang.-Hearing Assn., Fla. Speech and Hearing Assn. (early intervention com. 1992-94), Fla. Speech-Lang. Assn. (pub. info. and mktg. com. 1992—), Suncoast Speech and Hearing Assn. (founding mem., sec. 1993-94, treas. 1994-95, v.p. 1995-96, pres. 1996-97). Avocation: ballroom dancing. Office: Aim Therapy 2831 Ringling Blvd Ste 220F Sarasota FL 34237-5354

CEPEDA, CLAUDIO, psychiatrist; b. Moniquira, Boyaca, Colombia, June 2, 1942; came to U.S, 1970; s. Santos and Zoila Abril C.; m. Rosalba Cepeda, Dec. 24, 1966; children: Rene, Adrian, Joe. MD, U. Nacional, Bogota, Colombia, 1968; gen. psychiatrist, Ypsilanti Regional Psychiat., 1974, Am. Bd. Psychiatry & Neurology, 1976; psychoanalyst, Detroit Psychoanalytic Inst., 1979. Dir. acute svcs. Yorkwood Ctr., Ypsilanti, Mich., 1974-84; fellow in child and adolescent psychiatry U. Mich., Ann Arbor, 1984; med. dir. Charter Rio Grande Hosp., Laredo, Tex., 1984-87; dir. acute svcs. S.W. Mental Health Ctr., San Antonio, 1987—. Clin. faculty dept. psychiatry U. Tex., San Antonio, 1987—. Author: Concise Guide to the Psychiatric Interview of Children and Adolescents, 2000. Named Outstanding Tchr. Child Psychiatry Residents, 1991, 2000, Outstanding Child and Adolescent Psychiatry Faculty, Child and Adolescent Fellows, 1996; recipient Excellence in Tchg. award Gen. Psychiat. Residents, 1995. Fellow: Am. Acad. Child and Adolescent Psychiatry, Am. Acad. Psychoanalysts; mem.: APA, Tex. Soc. Child and Adolescent Psychiatry. Avocation: numismatics-art. Home: 911 Serene Meadow San Antonio TX 78258-1931 Office: SW Psychiat Physicians 8535 Tom Slick San Antonio TX 78229-3367

CEPEDA, ORLANDO, retired professional baseball player; b. Ponce, P.R., Sept. 17, 1937; m. Miriam Cepeda; children: Orlando Jr., Hector, Malcolm, Ali Manuel. 1st baseman San Francisco Giants, 1958—66, St. Louis Cardinals, 1966—69, Atlanta Braves, 1969—72, Oakland Athletics, Calif., 1972, Boston Red Sox, 1973, Kansas City Royals, 1974; cmty. rep. San Francisco Giants, 1990—. Named Rookie of Yr. San Francisco Giants, 1958, Comeback Player of Yr., St. Louis Cardinals, 1966, Nat. League Most Valuable Player, 1967; named to Sports Hall of Fame, P.R., 1993, Baseball Hall of Fame, 1999; recipient Designated Hitter of Yr. award, 1973. Achievements include being lifetime .297 hitter with 379 home runs; making 1,364 RBIs; appearing in 3 World Series games; being an 11-time All-Star; hitting over .300 9 times in career. Office: c/o San Francisco Giants 3 Com Park San Francisco CA 94124-3904

CEPIELIK, ELIZABETH LINDBERG, educator; b. Syracuse, N.Y., Sept. 18, 1941; d. Herman Elroy and Kathryn Emily (Karl) Lindberg; m. Michael A. Zemel, Apr. 22, 1967 (div. Jan. 1973); 1 child, Molly; m. Martin Joseph Cepielik, Mar. 10, 1973; children: Jeffrey, Kristina, Julie. AA, Stephens Coll., Columbia, Mo., 1961; BA, San Jose State Coll., 1963; postgrad., Calif. State U., L.A., 1963-67. Tchr. Humphreys Ave. Sch., L.A., 1963-71; math. specialist Non-Pub. Schs. Program, L.A., 1971-84; tchr. Sheridan Street Sch., L.A., 1984—2003; receptionist Weight Watchers, Arcadia, Calif., 1987—. Editor News of Polonia. Vol. Sta. KPCC, Pasadena, Calif., 1988-94. Mem.: DAR, Swedish Am. Ctrl. Assn. (auditor 1987—90, sec. 1989—), Polish Nat. Alliance (sec. lodge 1980—, sec. coun. 1983—93, treas. Woman's divsn. 1992—93), Polish Am. Congress (sec. 1990—93, auditor, bd. dirs. 2001—), Skandia (auditor, sec. Pasadena lodge 1983—), Stephens Coll. Alumnae Club (pres. Pasadena chpt. 1967—68), Swedish Am. Women's Club. Republican. Presbyterian. E-mail: polishnews@earthlink.net.

CEPPOS, JEROME MERLE, newspaper editor; b. Washington, Oct. 14, 1946; s. Harry and Florence (Epstein) C.; m. Karen E. Feingold, Mar. 7, 1982; children: Matthew, Robin. BS in Journalism, U. Md., 1969; postgrad., Knight-Ridder Exec. Leadership Program, 1989-90. Reporter, asst. city editor, night city editor Rochester (N.Y.) Democrat & Chronicle, 1969-72; from asst. city editor, to nat. editor, to asst. mng. editor The Miami (Fla.) Herald, 1972-81; assoc. editor San Jose (Calif.) Mercury News, 1981, mng. editor, 1983-94, exec. editor, sr. v.p., 1995-99; v.p. news Knight Ridder, 1999—. Bd. visitors Coll. Journalism, U. Md.; pres. Accrediting Coun. on Edn. in Journalism and Mass Comm. Mem. AP Mng. Editors (immediate past pres.), Am. Soc. Newspaper Editors, Calif. Soc. Newspaper Editors (former mem. bd. dirs., past pres.), Soc. Profl. Journalists, Assn. for Edn. in Journalism and Mass Comm., No. Calif. Cancer Ctr. (bd. trustees), Silicon Valley Capital Club. Office: Knight Ridder 50 W San Fernando St San Jose CA 95113-2429 E-mail: jceppos@knightridder.com.

CERA, LEE MARIE, veterinarian; b. Chgo., June 24, 1950; d. Ernest Joseph and Gloria (Bonet) Cera BS, St. Xavier Coll., 1971; BA, U. Ill., 1973, DVM, 1975; PhD in Pathology, U. Chgo., 1992. Clin. veterinarian U. Chgo., 1975-78; chief lab. services Office Animal Care, U. Chgo., 1978-80, dir., 1980-91; dir. lab. animal medicine Pathology Assocs. Inc., Chgo., 1991-93; asst. dean comparative medicine, dir. lab. animal medicine Loyola U. Chgo., 1993—. Dir. program Davis Vet. Pathology Found., Sayre, Pa., 1977—; adv. Lincoln Park Zoo, Chgo., 1978—; cons. Orland Park Small Animal Hosp., 1980— Contbr. articles to profl. jours. Recipient Pfizer award Pfizer Drug Co., 1974, Humane Soc. award, Lake County, 1974, Vet. Pathology award C.L. Davis, 1986, Honored Alumni award St. Xavier award, 1995; Cancer Soc. fellow, 1991-92. Mem. AVMA, Midwest Vet. Pathology Assn., C.L. Davis Found. for Vet. Pathology (Service award 1981), Am. Soc. Lab. Animal Practitioners, Assn. Wildlife Veterinarians Roman Catholic. Avocations: dressange, siberian huskies, wildlife pathology, wilderness camping, pet therapy, sailing. Office: Loyola U Stritch Sch of Medicine 2160 S 1st Ave Maywood IL 60153-5590

CERE, RONALD CARL, languages educator, consultant, researcher; b. N.Y.C., Oct. 22, 1947; s. Mindie Anthony and Edvige Clelia (Ruggero) C. BA, CUNY, 1968; MA, Queens Coll., 1969; PhD, NYU, 1974. Asst. prof. SUNY, Old Westbury, 1974-77, U. Ill., Urbana, 1977-80, U. Nebr., Lincoln, 1980-83, Gettysburg (Pa.) Coll., 1983-85; prof. Ea. Mich. U., Ypsilanti, 1985-90, 1990—. Cons. Trinity Dynamics, N.J., Harcourt Brace Jovanovich, Harper & Collins, D.C. Heath, Prentice-Hall, Random House, Scott Foresman Pub. Cos., 1985—; speaker, presenter in field. Author: Los Fabulistas, 1969, Exito Comercial, 3d edit., 2001; contbr. Recipient James C. Healy award NYU, 1974. Mem. MLA, ASTD, Am. Assn. Tchrs. Spanish and Portuguese (dir. career svcs.), Am.Coun. Teaching Fgn. Langs., Soc. for Intercultural Edn., Tng. and Rsch., Southern Conf. Lang. Teaching (bd. advisors). Home: 2245 Glencoe Hills Dr Apt 7 Ann Arbor MI 48108-3017 Office: Ea Mich U Dept Fgn Langs 219 Alexander Hall Ypsilanti MI 48197-2255 E-mail: fla_cere@online.emich.edu.

CEREGHINO, JAMES JOSEPH, health facility administrator, neurologist; b. Portland, Oreg., Oct. 27, 1937; s. Joseph Thomas and Amelia E. (Arata) C. BS, Portland State Coll., 1959; MD, U. Oreg., 1964; MS in Neurophysiology, Linfield U., 1971. Intern Good Samaritan Hosp., Portland, 1964-65; resident Good Samaritan Hosp. and Med. Ctr., Portland, 1965-68; rotating resident in neuropathology Sch. of Medicine U. Wash., 1967; rotating resident in child neurology U. Calif. Med. Ctr., San Francisco, 1968; rotating resident in psychiatry Med. Sch. U. Oreg., 1968; nerol. cons. pub. health svc.-health svcs. and mental health adminstrn.-neurol. and sensory disease control program HEW, Rockville, Md., 1968-70, staff neuroglogist epilepsy br. NIH Bethesda, Md., 1970-85; chief epilepsy br. convulsive, devel. and neuromuscular disorders program Nat. Inst. Neurol. Disorders and Stroke, Bethesda, Md., 1985-93; dir. rsch. Epilepsy Ctr. Oreg. Health Scis. U., Portland, 1993—. Prof. dept. neurology Oreg. Health Scis. U., 1993—; attending neurologist VA Med. Ctr., Portland, 1993—; devel. coun. Neurol. Sci. Inst., 1998—, brain net coun., 2000—; spkr. in field. Editor-in-chief Epilepsia, 1986-94, emeritus, 1994-97, supplements editor, 1994-97; contbr. articles to profl. jours. Capt. USPHS, ret. Fellow: Am. Clin. Neurophysiology Soc. (pub. rels. com. 1980—81); mem.: Neurological Scis. Inst. (development coun. 1998—, brain net coun. 2000—), Alzheimer's Assn. Oreg. (rsch. com. 2000—), Alzheimer's Rsch. Alliance Oreg. (exec. coun. 1994—2000, chmn. rsch. awards com. 1995—2001), World Fedn. Neurology (epidemiology rsch. group 1978—), Epilepsy Found. Oreg. (sec. 1993—97, region 9 rep. to Epilepsy Found. Am. 1996—, pres. 1997—99, v.p. 2001—02), Uniformed Svcs. Orgn. Neurologists (chmn. awards com. 1984—85), Med. Soc. D.C. (sect. neurology and neurol. surgery 1971—94), Internat. League Against Epilepsy (edn. com., coun. mem. 1985—94), Epilepsy Internat. (libr. devel. com. 1981, chmn. 1981—85), Epilepsy Found. of Am. (profl. adv. bd. Washington chpt. 1969—93, speaker's bur. 1972—93, v.p. 1973—75, region IX rep. to EFA profl. adv. bd. 1996—), Am. Neurologic Assn., Am. Epilepsy Soc. (membership com. 1970—74, chmn. 1975—77, chmn. edn. com. 1978—80, constn. com. 1980—81, dir. continuing med. edn. 1981—83, 1st v.p. 1982—82, pres. 1983—84, v.p. to ILAE 1985—86, coun. 1985—94), Am. Acad. Neurology, U. Oreg. Med. Sch. Alumni Assn. Office: Oreg Health Scis Univ Epilepsy Ctr CDW-3 3181 SW Sam Jackson Park Rd Portland OR 97239-3011 E-mail: cereghin@ohsu.edu.

CERF, VINTON GRAY, telecommunications company executive; b. New Haven, June 23, 1943; s. Vinton Thruston and Muriel (Gray) C.; m. Sigrid L. Thorstenberg, Sept. 10, 1966; children: David, Bennett. BS, Stanford U., 1965; MS in Computer Sci., UCLA, 1970, PhD in Computer Sci., 1972; PhD (hon.), Capitol Coll., Gettysburg Coll., U. Balearic Islands, U. Lulea, Swiss Fed. Inst. Tech.; PhD (hon.), George Mason U., U. Twente, U. Rovira and Virgili. Sys. engr. IBM Corp., 1965-67; prin. programmer UCLA, 1967-72; asst. prof. elec. engring. and computer sci. Stanford (Calif.) U., 1972-76; sr. programmer Jacobi Sys. Corp., Santa Monica, Calif., 1968-70; program mgr. info. processing techniques office Def. Advanced Rsch. Projects Agy., U.S. Dept. Def., Arlington, Va., 1976-81, prin. scientist, 1981-82; dir. sys. devel. MCI Comm. Corp., 1982-83; v.p. engring. MCI Digital Info. Svcs. Co., Washington, 1983-86; v.p. Corp. for Nat. Rsch. Initiatives, Reston, Va., 1986-94; sr. v.p. technology strategy MCI, Ashburn, Va., 1994—. Author: A Practical View of Communication Protocols, 1979. Named to Datamation Hall of Fame, 1989; recipient Kilby award, 1995, Silver medal Internat. Telecomms. Union, 1995, Industry Legend award Computer and Comms. Industries Assn., 1996, NEC Computer and Comm. prize, 1996, Computer Networks and Smithsonian Leadership award, 1996, Nat. Medal of Tech., 1997, Charles Stark Draper award, 2001, Prince of Asturias award, 2002; Marconi fellow, 1998. Fellow IEEE (Kobayashi award 1992, Alexander Graham Bell award 1997), AAAS, Assn. Computing Machinery (chmn. SIG Comm. 1987-91, coun. 1990-92, Software award), Internat. Fedn. Info. Processing, Internet Activities Bd. (chmn. 1979-82, 89-91), Internet Soc. (pioneer mem., trustee 1992-2002, pres. 1992-95, v.p. chpts. 1996-97, chmn. 1998-99); mem. Nat. Acad. Engrs., Sigma Xi. Office: MCI Data Svcs Divsn 2100 Reston Pkwy Rm 6002 Reston VA 20191-1244 E-mail: vinton.g.cerf@mci.com. *My entire working career has been focused on science and technology, in many forms—teaching, research, engineering management. The trait I have come to admire most among technical colleagues is absolute honesty in reporting or assessing results—blemishes and failures as well as successes.*

CERIANI, PETER JOHN, medical association administrator; b. Boston, Apr. 30, 1956; s. Raymond John and Madelyn Marcia (Finnegan) C.; m. Sheryl A. Flomenhoft, July 12, 1998. BA in Biology, Holy Cross Coll., 1978; MBA in Healthcare Mgmt. with honors, Boston U., 1980. Dir. patient bus. affairs U. Mass. Med. Sch. Group Practice Plan, Worcester, 1980-82, dir. bus. ops., 1982-87, dir. bus. and computer ops., 1987-90; adminstr. joint program in neonatology Harvard Med. Sch., Boston, 1990-92; clinic administrator Joslin Diabetes Ctr., Inc., 1992-96; exec. adminstr. RIH Med. Found., 1997—2000; COO U. Medicine Found., Brown Med. Sch., Providence, 2000—. Mgmt. cons. faculty practice plans and teaching hosps., 1987—; chmn. IDX Northeast Region Users Group, 1987-89. Mem. Healthcare Fin. Mgmt. Assn. (advanced), Am. Coll. Med. Group Adminstrs. (nominee), Assn. Am. Med. Colls., Adminstrs. of Internal Medicine, Med. Group Mgmt. Assn., Mass. Hosp. Assn., Mass. Pub. Health Assn., Holy Cross Club Greater Boston (exec. sec. 1983-90, v.p. 1989-90, pres. 1990-91, scholarship trustee 1991-93, scholarship chmn. 1993). Avocations: sailing, classical music, cars, water skiing. Home: 2 Earle Rd Wellesley MA 02481-2448 Office: RI Hosp-Dept Medicine 593 Eddy St Providence RI 02903-4923

CERINI, KENNETH RUSSELL, accountant; b. Flushing, N.Y., Aug. 19, 1964; s. Martin L. and Dolores R. (Rio) C.; m. Bonnie Anne Alexander, June 1, 1990; children: Kelli-Anne, Arielle Nicole, Erik Jason. BA, LIU, 1986. CPA, N.Y.; CFP. Mgr. Ernst & Young, Melville, NY, 1986—93; ptnr. Cerini and Assocs., LLP, CPAs, Islandia, NY, 1993—; mem. Cerini and Assocs. Consulting Group, LLC, Islandia, 1996—, Cerini and Assocs. Monarch Valuation Group, LLC, Islandia, 2002—. Writer, L.I. Bus. News. Treas. Make-a-Wish Found. Suffolk County, Inc., Northport, N.Y., 1990-92; sec./treas. Mus. of Universe, 1997—; mem. adv. bd. Friends of Karen, 2001—. Recipient L.I. 40 Under 40 award, 2001, Class of 2001 award L.I. chpt. Multiple Sclerosis Soc. Mem. AICPA, Am. Bd. Forensic Acctg. (diplomat), Assn. Fundraising Profls., N.Y. State Soc. CPAs (Suffolk County chpt. chmn. govt. and not-for-profti com. 1997-98, bd. dirs. 1998—, sec. 2001, treas. 2002), Internat. Bd. CFP, Not-for-Profit Acctg. and Tax Exempt Orgn. (tech. com. 1996—, healthcare tech. com. 2002—), Delta Mu Delta. Avocations: music, sports, collecting sports memorabilia. Home: 35 Locust Dr Nesconset NY 11767-2704 E-mail: Kenc@Ceriniandassociates.com.

CERIO, MILISSA BAUSCH, social worker; b. Binghamton, N.Y., July 10, 1959; d. Charles E. Bausch and Theresa M. (Benton) McKerrow; m. Charles P. Cerio, July 28, 1984; 1 child, Charles James. BSW, Lock Haven State Coll., 1981; MSW, Marywood Coll., Scranton, Pa., 1982. Cert. social worker. Child care worker Elmira (N.Y.) Glove House, Inc., 1982-83, asst. group home supr., 1983-84, sch. social worker, 1984-87; social worker alcohol rehab. unit New Dawn Alcohol Rehab. Unit, Elmira, 1987-90, clin. coord. alcohol rehab. unit, 1990-92; pvt. practice clin. social worker Clin. Social Work and Counseling Svcs. of The FingerLakes, Elmira, 1990—. Profl. advisor Depression and Bipolar Support Alliance of the Finger Lakes, 1997—. Mem. coms. Jr. League Elmira, 1986-91. Mem. NASW. Avocations: antiques, reading, family activities. Home: 808 W 3rd St Elmira NY 14905-2117 Office: Clin Social Work and Counseling Svcs Finger Lakes 963 Walnut St Elmira NY 14901-1831

CERISOLA Y WEBER, PEDRO, secretary of communications and transportation for Mexico; b. Mexico City, Mar. 13, 1949; Studied architecture, Nat. Autonomous U. Mex., Mexico City, Iberoam. U.; studied bus. adminstrn., IPADE. Various positions including opers. dir., dir. planning, regional sales mgr. Teléfonos de Mex., S.A. de C.V.; dir. bur. civil aeronautics Sec. Comms. and Transp.; founder, gen. mgr. Aerovías de Mex., 1988; gen. mgr. projects and planning Mexico City Internat. Airport Aeropuertos y Servicios; comml. asst. dir. Aeronaves de Mex., S.A. de C.V., dir. opers.; gen. coord. electoral campaign Pres. Vicente Fox; advisor to Pres. transition staff Govt. of Mex., sec. comms. and transp., 2000—. Office: Ave Universidad-Xola Cuerpo "C" 2ndo pis Colonia Narvarte 03028 Mexico City Mexico*

CERKEVITCH, TARAS JOSEPH, psychologist, consultant; b. Munich, July 26, 1948; came to U.S., 1951; s. Konstantin Tarasevitch Jakowliw-Cerkevitch and Eva Maria Brejzek; children: Angela, Christina. BA, CUNY, 1970; MA, U. So. Miss., 1972, PhD, 1974. Instr. U. So. Miss., Hattiesburg, 1971-73, U. So. Ala., Mobile, 1973-82; psychologist Searcy Hosp., Mt. Vernon, Ala., 1973-79; pvt. practice clin. psychologist McLean, Va., 1974—. Cons. Social Security Disability, Fairfax, Va., 1985—; prodr. radio program WEBR 94.5 Cable FM, Fairfax, 2000—. Author series Transitional Analysis for Physicians, 1975; contbr. articles to profl. jours., newspapers. Sunday sch. instr. St. Luke Serbian Orthodox Ch., McLean, 1984-88, St. Mark Orthodox Ch., Bethesda, Md., 1988-93; reader, subdeacon St. Elijah Orthodox Cmty., Arlington, Va., 1994—. Mem. Am. Bd. Profl. Disability Cons. (pres. 1988—, editor newsletter 1988—,

author dir. 1990—), Psi Chi. Avocations: singing, composing, piano, painting. Home: 1703 Westmoreland St Mc Lean VA 22101 Office: ABPDC 1350 Beverly Rd # 155-327 Mc Lean VA 22101 E-mail: abpdc@erols.com.

CERMAK, JACK EDWARD, engineer, educator; b. Hastings, Colo., Sept. 8, 1922; s. Joseph and Helen (Herman) C.; m. Helen Jane Carlson, Dec. 17, 1949; children: Douglas Karl, Jonathan Joel. BS, Colo. State U., 1947, MS, 1948; PhD, Cornell U., 1959; NATO postdoctoral fellow, Cambridge U., Eng., 1961-62. Mem. faculty Colo. State U., Ft. Collins, 1947—, prof. charge fluid mechanics and wind engring. program, also dir. Fluid Dynamics and Diffusion Lab., 1960-85, univ. disting. prof., 1986—, chmn. engring. sci. maj. program, 1963-72; pres., dir. Colo. State U. (Research Found.), 1965-72; pres. Cermak Peterka Petersen Inc., 1982—. Cons. in field; mem. bd. mems. Univ. Corp. Atmospheric Research, 1966-67; pres., chmn. 10th Midwestern Mechanics Conf., 1966-67; dir. summer inst. fluid mechanics NSF, 1963, 65, 68, 72; chmn. 2d U.S. Nat. Conf. Wind Engring. Research, 1975, 5th Internat. Conf. Wind Engring., 1979; founding mem., pres. Wind Engring. Research Council, Inc., 1979-85; co-chmn. U.S.-Japan Seminar Lab. Simulation of Stratified Shear Flows; co-dir. NATO Advanced Study Inst., 1993; mem. Colo. Gov.'s Sci. and Tech. Adv. Council, Com. on Army Basic Research, NRC, 1979-83. Mem. editl. adv. bd. Indsl. Aerodynamics Abstracts, Mechanics Rsch. Comms., Internat. Jour. Wind Engring.; mem. inernat. editl. bd. Wind and Structures; contbr. articles to profl. jours. Fellow AAAS, AIAA (assoc.), ASCE (hon.; chmn. engring. mechanics divsn. 1965, chmn. wind effects com. structural divsn. 1991, Erenst E. Howard award, 2002, Jack E. Cermak medal established 2002), Am. Acad. Mechanics; mem. ASME (Freeman scholar 1974, disting. lectr. 1987-89), ASHRAE (mem. com. flow around bldgs.), NSPE (Outstanding Profl Achievement award), Air and Waste Mgmt. Assn., Am. Soc. Engring. Edn. (chmn. mechanics divsn., Sr. Rsch. award 1987), Nat. Acad. Engring. (chmn. com. natural disasters, chmn. panel on wind engring. rsch.), Internat. Assn. Wind Engring. (chmn. bd. 1975-79, regional sec. N.Am. and S.Am. 1983—), Am. Meteorol. soc., Am. Geophys. Union, Instn. Civil engrs. (Scruton lectr. 1995), N.Y. Acad. Scis., Rotary, Sigma Xi (nat. lectr. 1976-77), Chi Epsilon (nat. honor). Home: 407 E Prospect Rd Fort Collins CO 80525-1058 E-mail: jecermak@lamar.colostate.edu. *My thoughts and actions have been influenced always by a belief and an awareness that man, the near environment, and the far reaches of the universe are influenced by common natural laws. I believe that the order found in natural events, as revealed by scientific investigation, can someday become manifest in the behavior of man. Ultimately, through persistent and directed effort, I am confident that man will integrate religion, science, and technology to achieve harmony of man with man, and man with the environment. For the most part, my achievements and contributions to society can be attributed to the motivation and direction stemming from these convictions.*

CERMELE, CHARLES, vocalist, performing arts administrator; b. Morristown, NJ, Dec. 10, 1958; s. Michael Archangel and Phyllis Belsante C.; life ptnr. Christopher G. Moore. BA in Drama magna cum laude, Tufts U., Medford, MA, 1980; MA in Am. Popular Song, NYU, NYC, 2003. Singer: (recording) Look In My Eyes (Bistro Award for Outstanding Rec., 1995); prodr.: (recording) Look In My Eyes; singer: (recording) Ask Me Again; prodr.: (recording) Ask Me Again. Recipient Bistro Award for Outstanding Male Vocalist, Backstage Mag., 1993, Award for Outstanding Male Vocalist, Manhattan Assn. Cabarets and Clubs, 1998. Mem.: Actor's Equity Assn.

CERNICA, JOHN N. engineering educator, civil engineer, consultant; b. Calvaser, Romania, May 14, 1932; arrived in U.S., 1945; s. John and Mary Cernica; m. Mary Patricia Marinelli, June 25, 1959; children: Kathy, Jude, Alice, Johanna, Patricia, Sarah. BE, Youngstown (Ohio) State U., 1954; MS in engring., Carnegie Mellon U., Pitts., 1955, PhD in engring., 1957. Registered Ohio, Tex., Fla., Ga., Ind., Iowa, DC, Ky., Md., Mich., NY, NJ, Miss., Pa., SC, Tenn., Va., W. Va., Nat. Cert. Prof. civil engring. Youngstown State U., 1958—, dept. head civil engring.; owner J.N. Cernica & Assoc., Cons. Engrs., Youngstown, Ohio. Panelist Nat. Sci. Found.; examiner Ohio Bd. Registration Profl. Engrs. and Surveyors. Author: (textbooks) Fundamentals of Reinforced Concrete, 1964, Strength of Materials, 1 edit., 1966, (Textbooks) Strength of Materials, Spanish edit., 1968, (textbooks) Strength of Materials, 2 edit., 1977, Strength of Materials, Chinese edit., 1982, Geotech. Engring., 1982, Soil Mechanics, 1994, Found. Design, 1994; contbr. scientific papers, articles to profl. jours. Recipient Ohio's Outstanding Engr., 1964, Man of the Yr. award, 1970, Outstanding Civil Engr., 1981, Disting. Prof. award, Youngstown State U. Mem.: Mahoning County Soc. of Profl. Engrs., Nat. Soc. of Profl. Engrs., Am. Soc. of Engring. Edn., Am. Concrete Inst., Am. Soc. of Civil Engrs., Sigma Tau, Sigma Xi, Phi Kappa Phi, Tau Beta Pi. Mailing: 611 Plymouth Dr Youngstown OH 44512

CERNUGEL, WILLIAM JOHN, consumer products and special retail executive; b. Joliet, Ill., Nov. 19, 1942; m. Laurie M. Kusnik, Apr. 22, 1967; children: Debra, James, David. BS, No. Ill. U., 1964. CPA, Ill. Sr. supr. KPMG LLP, Chgo., 1964-70; asst. corp. contr. Alberto-Culver Co., Melrose Park, Ill., 1970-71, corp. contr., 1972—74, v.p., contr., 1974-82, v.p. fin., 1982-93, sr. v.p. fin., 1993-2000, sr. v.p., CFO, 2000—. Mem. bd. govs., treas. Gottlieb Meml. Hosp., Melrose Park; assoc. mem. bd. advisors Coll. Bus., No. Ill. U. Mem. AICPA, Am. Mgmt. Assn. (fin. coun.), Inst. Mgmt. Accts., Ill. Soc. CPAs, Fin. Exec. Internat., Lions. Home: 8111 Lake Ridge Dr Burr Ridge IL 60527-5977 Office: Alberto-Culver Co 2525 Armitage Ave Melrose Park IL 60160-1163

CERNY, JOSEPH, III, chemistry educator, scientific laboratory administrator, university dean and official; b. Montgomery, Ala., Apr. 24, 1936; s. Joseph and Olaette Genette (Jury) C.; m. Barbara Ann Nedelka, June 13, 1959 (div. Nov. 1982); children: Keith Joseph, Mark Evan; m. 2d Susan Dinkelspiel Stern, Nov. 12, 1983. BS in Chem. Engring., U. Miss.-Oxford, 1957; postgrad. Fulbright scholar, U. Manchester, Eng., 1957-58; PhD in Nuclear Chemistry, U. Calif.-Berkeley, 1961; PhD in Physics (hon.), U. Jyväskylä, Finland, 1990. Asst. prof. chemistry U. Calif., Berkeley, 1961-67, assoc. prof., 1967-71, prof., 1971—, chmn. dept. chemistry, 1975-79, head nuclear sci. div., 1979-84, assoc. dir. Lawrence Berkeley Lab., 1979-84, dean grad. div., 1985-2000, provost for research, 1986-94, vice chancellor for rsch., 1994-2000. Mem. Nat. Acad. Scis. Physics Commn., chair nuclear physics panel, 1983-86; mem. NASA Adv. Coun., Univ. Rels. Task Force, 1991-93, NRC Study of Rsch. Doctorates, 1992-95. Editor: Nuclear Reactions and Spectroscopy, 4 vols., 1974; contbr. numerous articles to field to profl. jours. Served with U.S. Army, 1962-63. Recipient E.O. Lawrence award AEC, 1974, A. von Humboldt sr. scientist award, 1985; named to U. Miss. Alumni Hall of Fame, 1988. Fellow AAAS, Am. Phys. Soc.; mem. Am. Chem. Soc. (Nuclear Chemistry award 1984), Assn. Grad. Schs. (v.p., pres. 1992-94). Democrat. Home: 860 Keeler Ave Berkeley CA 94708-1324 Office: Lawrence Berkeley Nat Lab Univ Calif Bldg 88 Berkeley CA 94720 E-mail: jcerny@uclink4.berkeley.edu.

CERNY, JOSEPH CHARLES, urologist, educator; b. Apr. 20, 1930; s. Joseph James and Mary (Turek) C.; m. Patti Bobette Pickens, Nov. 10, 1962; children: Joseph Charles, Rebecca Anne. BA, Knox Coll., 1952; MD, Yale U., 1956. Diplomate Am. Bd. Urology. Intern U. Mich. Hosp., Ann Arbor, 1956-57, resident, 1957-62; practice medicine specializing in urology Ann Arbor and Detroit, 1962—. Instr. surgery (urology) U. Mich., Ann Arbor, 1962-64, asst. prof., 1964-66, assoc. prof., 1961-77, clin. prof., 1971—; chmn. dept. urology Henry Ford Hosp., Detroit, 1971—, chmn. emeritus urology Henry Ford Hosp., 1998; pres. Resistors, Inc., Chgo., 1960—; cons. St. Joseph Hosp., Ann Arbor, 1973—; chief urology sect., dept. surgery Ann Arbor VA Hosp., 1999—; mem. instnl. rev. bd. for rsch. U. Mich. Med. Sch., 2001. Mem. editl. bd. Am. Jour. Kidney Diseases, 1988—; contbr. articles to profl. jours., chpts. to books. Bd. dirs., trustee Nat. Kidney Found. Mich., Ann Arbor, 1988—, chmn. urology coun., 1987—, exec. com., 1987—, pres., 1988—, emeritus trustee, 1997; bd. dirs. Ann Arbor Amateur Hockey Assn., 1980-83; pres. PTO, Ann Arbor Pub. Schs., 1980; chmn. capital campaign Nat. Kidney Found. Mich., 2002. Lt. USNR, 1956-76. Recipient Disting. Svc. award Transplantation Soc. Mich., 1982, Disting. Svc. award Nat. Kidney Found. Mich., 1993, Champion of Hope award Nat. Kidney Found., 1997, Disting. Career award Henry Ford Hosp. Alumni, 2000. Fellow ACS (pres.-elect Mich. br. 1984-85, pres. 1985—); mem. Am. Acad. Med. Dirs., Am. Coll. Physician Execs., Internat. Soc. Urology, Am. Urol. Assn. (pres. Mich. br. 1980-81, pres. North Cen. sect. 1985-86, manpower com. 1987-88, 90-92, jud. rev. com. 1987-91, tech. exhibits 1987-88, fiscal affairs rev. commn. 1985-89, audit commn. 1992-96, chmn. 1995, exec. commn. 1993—, bd. dirs. 1994—, work force com., publs. com. 1995—, chmn. publs. com. 1999, Best Sci. Exhibit award 1978, Best Sci. Films award 1980, 82, audio-visual com. 1994—, program rev. com. 1994—, urology work force com. 1995—, jud. and ethics com. 1997—), Transplantation Soc. Mich. (pres. Mich. 1983-85), Am. Assn. Transplant Surgeons, Endocrine Surgeons, Soc. Univ. Urologists, Am. Assn. Urologic Oncology, Am. Fertilitiy Soc., Am. Coll. Physician Execs., Am. Acad. Med. Dirs., S.W. Oncology Group, Barton Hills Country Club, Ann Arbor Racquet Club. Avocations: tennis, fishing, civil war. Home: 2800 Fairlane St Ann Arbor MI 48104-4110 Office: U Mich Health Sys Sect Urology Dept Surgery 1500 E Medical Center Dr Ann Arbor MI 48109-0005 E-mail: jocerny@umich.edu.

CERNY, LOUIS THOMAS, civil engineer, railway engineering consultant; b. Berwyn, Ill., Mar. 7, 1942; s. Thomas Alois and Rosalia Patricia (Havranek) C.; m. Lana Sally Taylor, June 6, 1964; children— Leonard, David BSCE, U. Ill., 1964, MS, 1965. Registered profl. engr., Ill., Miss. Rsch. asst. U. Ill., Urbana, 1964-65; various engring. positions Elgin, Joliet & Eastern Ry., Joliet, Ill., 1965-75; v.p., chief engr. Columbus & Greenville Ry., Miss., 1975-78; v.p. ops. Erie Western Ry., Huntington, Ind., 1978-79; exec. dir. Am. Ry Engring. Assn., Washington, 1979-94. Exec. dir. engring. divsn. Assn. Am. Railroads, 1979-97, cons., 1997—; leader engring. dels. to China, 1983, 84. Contbr. articles to profl. jours.; patentee in field Mem. Am. Railway Engring. and Maint.-of-Way Assn. Unitarian Universalist. Avocations: travel; photography; hiking; astronomy.

CERNY, RONALD NEAL, business executive; b. Passaic, NJ, Jan. 6, 1952; s. Anthony F. and Rosemarie (Litchenberger) C.; m. Alida Vangolen, Jan. 19, 1974; children: Kimberly, Corinne, Douglas. BSME, Lafayette Coll., 1973; MBA, Villanova U., 1994. From rsch. engr. to product mgr. Johns Manville Corp., Denver, 1973—83; sales mgr. Specialty Glass Corp., Willow Grove, Pa., 1983-86; from mktg. mgr. to dir. ops. Johnson Matthey, Inc., West Chester, Pa., 1986—93; gen. mgr. J.M. Ney Co., Bloomfield, Conn., 1993-95, pres., 1995—2002; pres. and CEO Am. Electronic Components, Inc., Elkhart, Ind., 2003—. Patentee in joint assembly, high-temperature conduit vent, improved slurry processing. Mem. ASME. Avocations: skiing, golf. Office: Am Electronic Components Inc 23590 County Rd 6 Elkhart IN 46514

CERNY, WILLIAM, retired education educator, musician; b. N.Y.C., Dec. 27, 1928; s. Karl Otto Cerny and Mathra Rossler; m. Mary Ann Cunningham, June 26, 1954; children: Elaine, Jean, Mary, Carol. BA magna cum laude, Yale Univ., New Haven, Conn., 1951; MusB, Yale Sch. of Music, New Haven, Conn., 1952, MusM, 1954. Profl. accompanist freelance, N.Y., 1954—59; assoc. prof. Eastman Sch. of Music, Rochester, NY, 1959—72; prof. Univ. Notre Dame, South Bend, Ind., 1972—2000. Chmn., music dept. Notre Dame Univ., South Bend, Ind., 1972—81; evaluator Nat Assoc. of Sch., Washington, 1980—95; classical music concerts of music, throughout U.S.A. Musician (concert panist and chamber musician): (concerts in scores) coll. and univ., 1965—96; musician: (eplorations into paino lit.) weekly 1/2 hr. NPR Program, 1981—. Seaman USNR, 1948—57. Mem.: Phi Beta Kappa. Independent. Cath. Achievements include formed Wilmare Rec., Inc., classical CD's 110, Cd's made availabe to Col. and Univ. throughout USA and abroad; a contbn. to ednl. cmty. Avocations: carpentry, sailing, fishing. Home: 2918 Caroline St South Bend IN 46614

CEROKE, CLARENCE JOHN, engineer, consultant; b. Chgo., Dec. 1, 1921; s. Paul Anthony and Anne (Krieger) C.; m. Violet Marie Lobonc, Sept. 21, 1947; children: Paul, Donald, Robert, Marie, Louise, Karen. BS in mech. Engring., Ill. Inst. Tech., 1943. Reg. profl. engr., Ill. Supr. product devel. U.S.I. Clearing, Chgo., 1969-74; engr. Panduit Corp., Tinley Park, Ill., 1974-75; design engr. Interlake Steel, Chgo., 1975-76; mgr. engring. AFL Industries, West Chicago, 1976-77; design engr. Castle Engring., Chgo., 1977-80; supr. Dreis and Krump, Chgo., 1980-81; project engr. Epstein Process Engring., Chgo., 1981-83; cons. engr. Beacon Engring., Homewood, Ill., 1983-84; engr. Espo Engring., Canton, Ohio, 1984—. Owner Beacon Engring., Homewood, 1978—. Patentee in field; author books. Pres. St. Kilians Holy Name Soc., Chgo., 1960; coach Little League Baseball, Chgo., 1959. With USN, 1943-44. Mem. Mt. Carmel Alumni Assn., Pi Tau Sigma, Hall-Fame Racquet Club. Roman Catholic. Avocations: tennis, contract bridge, in plant safety and environmental research. Home: 755 Wood St Crown Point IN 46307-4910 Office: Beacon 755 Wood St Crown Point IN 46307-4910

CERRA, FRANK BERNARD, dean; b. Oneonta, N.Y., Feb. 13, 1943; m. Kathie Krieger; children: Josh, Christa, Nicole. BA in Biology, SUNY, Binghamton, 1965; MD, Northwestern U., 1969. Diplomate Nat. Bd. Med. Examiners, Am. Bd. Surgery. Intern, resident in surgery Buffalo Gen. Hosp., 1969—74; staff surgeon U. Minn. Hosp. Clinic, Mpls.; prof. U. Minn. Med. Sch., 1981—, dean, prof. surgery, 1995—96, sr. v.p. health scis., 1996—. Clin. asst. instr. surgery SUNY, Buffalo, 1969—75, asst. prof., 1975—80, assoc. prof. surgery and biophysics, 1980; interim head surgery U. Minn., 1994—95, dean med. sch., 1995—96, provost acad. health ctr., 1996—; rsch. asst. pharmacology Upstate Med. Ctr., 1963—64; rsch. asst. transplantation Northwestern U., 1967—69; rsch. assoc. immunology and cardiovasc. rsch. labs. Buffalo Gen. Hosp., 1972—73, SUNY, Buffalo, 1974—75; dir. surg. critical care, dir. nutrition support svcs. U. Minn. Hosp. and Clinic; vis. lectr. in exptl. surgery Harvard U., 1991; vis. prof. Rush Presbyn.-St. Lukes Med. Ctr., 1991. Editor: Perspective in Critical Care, 1988—91, Critical Care Outlook, 1988—90, Critical Care Medicine, 1990—; mem. editl. bd.: Drug Intelligence & Clin. Pharmacy Panel on Critical Care, 1982—87, Nutrition, 1982—, Critical Care Medicine, 1983—, Circulatory Shock, 1987—93, Jour. Parenteral and Enternal Nutrition, 1987—93, Am. Jour. Surgery, 1987—, Shock, 1993—, Current Opinion in Gen. Surgery, 1992—, Jour. Critical Care Nutrition, —; contbr. articles to profl. jours. Mem. acute care com. Found. for Health Care Evaluation, 1983—86; adv. group Minn. Emerging Infections Program, 1995—. Recipient Owen Wangensteen award, 1987, Therapeutic Frontiers Rsch. award, Am. Coll. Clin. Pharmacy, 1990, Disting. Investigator award, Am. Coll. Critical Care Medicine, 1993; Clark Found. fellow, 1965—69, Kellogg Nutrition fellow, 1987—89, Surg. Infection Soc. Rsch. fellow, 1988—90, Soc. Critical Care Medicine Lilly Rsch. fellow, 1990—93, Svc. award fellow, NIH, 1994—96, United Health Found. Rsch. Tng. grantee, 1972—73. Fellow: ACS (chmn. pre-postoperative care com. 1985—87), Coll. Critical Care Medicine, Am. Coll. Nutrition; mem.: AAAS, AMA, Hennepin County Med. Soc., Am. Soc. Home Care Physicians, Am. Soc. for Artificial Internal Organs (membership com. 1994—95), Internat. Assn. for the Surgery Trauma and Surg. Intensive Care, Soc. Internat. Surgery, Shock Soc., Surg. Biology Club, St. Paul Surg. Soc., Assn. for Surg. Edn., Am. Assn. for the Surgery Trauma, Ctrl. Surg. Assn., Soc. Univ. Surgeons (exec. coun. 1984—85), Assn. Internat. Anesthesistes-Reanimateurs D'Expression, Assn. for Acad. Surgery, Soc. Critical Care Medicine (treas. 1990, pres. 1991—92), Am. Soc. Parenteral and Enteral Nutrition (bd. govs. 1987—88), Soc. for Surgery the Alimentary Tract, Soc. Parenteral Alimentation. Achievements include patents pending for for the prevention of catabolism, nutrition support of immune function. Office: 420 Delaware St SE # 501 Minneapolis MN 55455-0374 also: U Minn Health & Scis Ctr 410 Ch RC 426 Church St SE Minneapolis MN 55455 Fax: 612-625-5000.*

CERRITOS, RONALD, professional soccer player; b. San Salvador, El Salvador, Jan. 3, 1975; Forward San Jose Earthquakes (formerly San Jose Clash), 1997—; mem. All-Star West team, 1997. Named Honda's MVP, 1998. Office: c/o San Jose Earthquakes 3550 Stevens Creek Blvd Ste 100 San Jose CA 95117-1031

CERULLO, RUDY MICHAEL, II, psychology, theology educator, minister; b. Phila., Feb. 25, 1952; s. Rudy and Edith Elizabeth (Cullen) C.; m. Kathleen Marie Evans, June 10, 1993. BA, Oral Roberts U., Tulsa, 1973; MDiv, Fuller Theol. Sem., Pasadena, Calif., 1976, ThM, 1984; DMin, ThD, So. Calif. Theol. Sem., 1990; PhD, Vision Internat. U., Ramona, Calif., 1996; DDiv, Kingsway Theol. Sem., Des Moines, 1989. Ordained to ministry Assemblies of God, 1977; cert. pastoral counselor. Assoc. pastor Orange (Calif.) Covenant Ch., First Presbyn. Ch., Alhambra, Calif., Tri-City Assembly Ch., Covina, Calif., Woodland Hills (Calif.) Neighborhood Ch., Palm View Assembly of God Ch., Whittier, Calif., En Agape Christian Fellowship Ch., Alta Loma, Calif.; psychiat. hosp. program dir., clinician in pvt. practice Brea (Calif.) Hosp. Neuropsychiat. Ctr., Terrace Plaza Med. Ctr., Baldwin Park, Calif., Manor West Hosp., L.A., Buena Park (Calif.) Med. Ctr., Agape Counseling and Therapy Svcs., Anaheim; prof. theology So. Calif. Coll., Costa Mesa, Calif., 1979-83; prof. psychology/theology, acad. dean So. Calif. Theol. Sem., Stanton, 1989-92, Trinity Coll. of Grad. Studies, Orange, 1989-92; sr. pastor Harmony Christian Fellowship Ch., Anza, Calif., 1994-96, Agape Christian Fellowship Church, Larned, Kans., 2002—. Pastor Discipleship Regency Christian Ctr., Downey, Calif., 1996-99; prof. psychology/theology, psychology dept. dir. Vision Internat. U., Pomona, 1991-99, Calif. Union U., Fullerton, 1991-99, Calif. Grad. Sch. Theology, Rosemead, 1991-99, New Hope U., Stanton, 1996-99, Ctrl. U., Palos Verdes, Calif., 1991-99; missionary to Republic of Korea, 1996-98; mem. faculty Benjamin U., Buena Park, Calif., 1998-99; ch. Mason Bible Coll., Pomona, 1998-99. Assoc. pastor New Gethsemane Ch. of God in Christ, Pomona, Calif., 1998—99; sr. pastor New Covenant Ch., Larned, Kans., 1999—2002; sr. pastor, exec. dir. Agape, Christian Fellowship Ch. and Counseling Ctr., Larned, 2002—. Named Disting. counselor in field of Psychiat. Hosp. Devel., U.S. Pubs., Inc., 1990. Fellow: ACA (student cert. sponsor 1988—). Republican. Avocations: renaissance faire actor, antique collecting. Address: 501 Kansas St Larned KS 67550-3030

CERVANTES, LUIS AUGUSTO, neurosurgeon; b. Torreon, Mex., Mar. 5, 1953; came to U.S., 1976; s. Luis Augusto and Gloria (Galindo) C.; m. Joann Frances Emanuele, Feb. 10, 1979; children: Luis III, Sara, Francis, Nicolas, Juan Carlos, Maria Teresa. MD, Nat. U. Mex., 1976. Intern Suburban Hosp., Bethesda, Md., 1977-78; resident in surgery Washington Hosp. Ctr., 1978-79; resident in neurology George Washington U., Washington, 1979-80, resident in neurosurgery, 1980-84; chief neurosurgery sect. dept. surgery Meml. Hosp. Burlington County, Mount Holly, N.J., 1992—. Cons. in neurosurgery Deborah Heart and Lung Ctr., Browns Mills, N.J., 1999—. Fellow ACS, Internat. Coll. Surgeons; mem. Am. Assn. Neurol. Surgeons, Congress Neurol. Surgeons. Roman Catholic. Avocation: golf. Office: 110 Marter Ave Ste 309 Moorestown NJ 08057-3124

CERVONE, LAUREEN AVERY, educational consultant, researcher; b. N.Y.C., Sept. 8, 1957; d. Guy William and Irma Landman Avery; children: Jason Anthony, Eric William. BS, Cornell U., 1978; MEd, RI Coll., 2000. Curriculum specialist RI Dept. Edn., Providence, 1992—97; ind. cons., 1995—; ednl. rschr. Brown U., Providence, 1997—. Author: Addressing the Leadership Challenges Faced by Principals, 2002. Office: Edn Alliance at Brown U 222 Richmond St Providence RI 02903 E-mail: laureen_cervone@brown.edu.

CESA, MICHAEL PETER, cardiologist, consultant; b. N.Y.C., Sept. 4, 1946; s. John J. and Catherine R. Cesa; m. Barbara A. Perrelli, June 21, 1969; children: Christopher, Thomas, Gregory, Meredith. BS, Manhattan Coll., 1968; MD, SUNY, Bklyn., 1972. Diplomate Am. Bd. Internal Medicine, Am. Bd. Cardiovasc. Disease. Intern dept. medicine Kings County Hosp., Bklyn., 1972-72, med. resident dept. medicine, 1973-75, cardiology fellow dept. medicine, 1975-77; clin. asst. prof. medicine SUNY, Stony Brook, 1994—; pres. med. staff St. Johns Episcopal Hosp., Smithtown, N.Y., 1984, 2000chief cardiology, 1997—2000; COO North Suffolk Cardiology Assocs., Stony Brook, 1984—, pres., 2000—. Fellow Am. Heart Assn. (coun. on clin. cardiology), Am. Coll. Cardiology, Am. Coll. Chest Physicians; mem. Am. Soc. Nuc. Cardiology (cert.). Roman Catholic. Avocations: collecting toy trains, baseball cards, hi fi stereos, sports. Office: North Suffolk Cardiology 2500 Nesconset Hwy Ste 1 Stony Brook NY 11790-2561

CESAR, KAMALA, dancer, educator; b. Bklyn., Dec. 9, 1948; d. Bruno Gonzales Cesar and Mary Kariwahawe Papnieau; m. Thomas Watson Buckner, Mar. 16, 1992; children: Robin, Paul, Tuy, Rana, Meera, Kiran. BA in Conservation of Natural Resources, U. Calif., Berkeley, 1976. Exec. dir., bd. dirs. The Balasaraswati Sch. of Music and Dance, N.Y.C., 1985—89; artistic and exec. dir. Lotus Fine Arts Prodns. Inc., N.Y.C., 1989—, also bd. dirs. Artistic dir., performer (videotape) Bharata Natyam, The Sacred Dance of India, 1991. Named Am. Indian of Yr., Thunderbird Am. Indian Dancers, N.Y.C., 2002; recipient Ethnic Dance award, Dance Giant Steps, Inc., Bklyn., 1996; Folk Arts Apprentice, Nat. Endowment for the Arts, 1986. Democrat. Buddhist. Avocation: carnatic vocals. Office: Lotus Music and Dance Studios 109 W 27th St 8th Fl New York NY 10001 Fax: 212-675-7191. Business E-Mail: info@lotusarts.com.

CESARANI, SAL, fashion designer; b. N.Y.C., Sept. 25, 1941; Student, High Sch. of Fashion Industries, Fashion Inst. Tech., N.Y.C. Sportswear designer Bobbie Brooks, 1963-64; fashion coord. men's wear Paul Stuart, 1964-69; merchandising dir. men's and women's apparel Ralph Lauren/Polo, 1969-73, Country Britches, 1973-75, collection S. Blacker, 1976(Cesarani est. 1977), collection Jaymar Ruby, 1979, collection Pulliman/Spencer, 1984-86, collection Hartmarx (SJC Concepts est. 1979-93), 1986-87. Commd. by U.S. Olympic Com. to design ceremonial uniforms of the Winter Olympics, 1980; lic. to W. Seitchek and Sons, Phila., 1995-97, lic. to Salvatore J. Cesarani, Italy, 1997—, lic. in Japan for Men's Apparel Collection, 1979—, lic. to Men's Furnishing & Acess in Japan, 1979, lic. Childrenswear, 1992, lic. in Japan Eyewear, 1992, lic. in Japan Leather Bays, 1992; tchr. Parson Continuing Edn., Parson Sch. Design. Vol. NYU Med. Ctrs. Vol. Corp. Recipient Coty award, 1974, 75, 82. Mem. Coun. Fashion Designers Am. Home and Office: care SJC Concepts 201 E 79th St New York NY 10021-0830

CESARIO, ROBERT CHARLES, franchise executive, consultant; b. Chgo., Apr. 6, 1941; s. Valentino A. and Mary Ethel (Kenny) C.; m. Susan Kay DePoutee; children: Jeffrey, Bradley. BS in Gen. Edn., Northwestern U., 1975; postgrad. in bus. adminstrn., DePaul U., 1975. Mgr. fin. ops. Midas Internat. Corp., Chgo., 1968-73; dir. staff ops. Am. Hosp. Supply Corp., McGaw Park, Ill., 1973-76; v.p. Car X Svc. Sys. Inc., Chgo., 1976-78, v.p. oil svcs., 1983-84; v.p. Chicken Unltd. Enterprises Inc., Chgo., 1978-83; pres. Growth Strategies, Inc., 1984-87; pres., CEO Lube Pro's Internat., Inc., 1987—. With USMC, 1960-62. Office: Lube Pros Internat Inc 1630 W Colonial Pkwy Palatine IL 60067-1209

CESARIO, ROBERT JAMES, music educator, performer; b. Wauwatosa, Wis., June 23, 1951; s. James and Virginia (Morrone) C.; m. Sandra Kay Block, May 29, 1976; children: Anthony Robert, Anastasia Louise. BFA, U. Wis., Milw., 1974, MusM, 1978; MA, NE Mo. State U., 1977; ArtsD, U. No. Colo., 1990. Temp. asst. instr. NE Mo. State U., Kirksville, 1975-77; dir. instrumental music Mayville (N.D.) State Coll., 1978-79; dir. bands N.Mex. Highlands U., Las Vegas, 1979-82; dir. univ. bands Panhandle State U., Goodwell, Okla., 1982-83; mem. faculty, dir. instrumental music Rogers State Coll., Claremore, Okla., 1983-90; adminstr., curriculum coord. for music Tulsa Pub. Schs., 1990-98; dir. of bands Rice U., Houston, 1998—2002, Huntsville (Tex.) HS, 2002—. Conducting asst. U. No. Colo., Greeley, 1981-82; performer Tulsa Philharmonic, Okla. Sinfonia, Starlight Concert Band; soloist with various high sch. bands, coll. orchs. Composer: (music for band) Penache, 1987. Bd. dirs. Claremore Community Concerts Assn., 1983-91, pres., 1985-88. Mem. Internat. Assn. Jazz Educators, Music Educators Nat. Conf., Coll. Music Soc., Coll. Band Dirs. Nat. Assn. (condr. nat. conducting symposium 1983, 84, nat. conv. 1985), Okla. Music Educators Assn. (condr. honor jazz ensemble 1985, 88, honor concert band 1989), Nat. Band Assn., World Assn. Symphonic Bands and Ensembles (sec. 2002—), Tex. Bandmasters Assn., Tex. Music Educators Assn., Western Athletic Conf. Band Dirs. Assn., Phi Beta Mu. Democrat. Roman Catholic. Avocations: racquetball, microcomputers. Home: 3511 Southdown Dr Pearland TX 77584-2367 Office: Huntsville HS 441 FM2821 E Huntsville TX 77320

CESARIO, SANDRA KAY, women's health nurse, educator, researcher; b. Racine, Wis., May 3, 1955; d. Harold J. and Bernice (Ittner) Block; m. Robert J. Cesario, May 29, 1976; children: Tony, Anna. RN, St. Luke's Hosp., Racine, Wis., 1976; BSN, Ft. Hayes State U., Hays, Kans., 1985; MS, U. Okla., 1989; PhD, Tex. Woman's U., 1999. Nursery charge nurse Kirksville (Mo.) Osteopathic Hosp., 1976-77; staff nurse NICU St. Joseph's Hosp., Milw., 1977-78; ob staff nurse N. Colo. Med. Ctr., Greeley, 1981-82; ob nursing instr. Luna Vo-Tech., Las Vegas, N.Mex., 1980-81; ob insvc. coord. Guymon (Okla.) Meml. Hosp., 1983; coord. ob nurse residency prog. Indian Health Svc., Oklahoma City, 1989-92; clin. asst. prof. U. Okla., 1992-99; asst. prof., dir. rsch. Tex. Woman's U., 1999—. Adj. clin. faculty Langston U., 1994; NCLEX item writer. Mem. editl. bd. Jour. Nursing Theory Constrn. and Testing, Jour. Obstet., Gynecol. and Neonatal Nursing. Mem. Assn. Womens Health Obstetrics and Neonatal Nursing (chair practice com. 1999-2002, chair adv. panel

childbearing and newborn 2003—), Tex. Nurses Assn. (dist. 9 sec., 2001-2003), Okla. Nurses Found. (bd. dir. 1997-99), Am. Nurses Assn., Midwest Nursing Rsch. Soc., So. Nursing Rsch. Soc., Sigma Theta Tau (v.p. chpt. 2000-02, pres. elect 2003-).

CESARIO, THOMAS CHARLES, dean; b. Kenosha, Wis., June 19, 1940; BS, U. Wis., 1961, MD, 1965. Resident in internal medicine Harvard U., 1965-67; fellow Harvard and U. Calif., Irvine, 1969-72; dean med. sch. U. Calif., Irvine, 1994—. Office: U Calif Coll Medicine 252 Irvine Hall Irvine CA 92697-3950

CESNIK, JAMES MICHAEL, union official, newspaperman, printer, consultant; b. Marshfield, Wis., Oct. 6, 1935; s. Ignatius Anthony and Mary Catherine (Bayuk) C.; m. Elizabeth Louise Havlik, Aug. 1, 1959 (div. 1987); children: Margaret Mary, Sarah Elizabeth, Michael Ignatius; m. Barbara E. Nelson, Jan. 1, 1990. BA, St. John's U., Collegeville, Minn., 1958. Reporter, Rice Lake (Wis.) Chronotype, 1958; reporter, copy, makeup and layout editor Mpls. Star & Tribune, 1958-64; internat. rep., asso. dir. rsch. and info., dir. rsch. and info. Newspaper Guild, CWA,AFL-CIO/CLC, Washington, 1965-75; editor Guild Reporter, 1973-93; v.p. Internat. Labor Press Assn., Washington, 1973-79, pres., 1980-82; sec.-treas. Internat. Labor Comm. Assn., Washington, 1984-87; editor Internat. Labor Comm. Assn. Reporter, Washington, 1983-84; sec.-treas. JBTM Enterprises Inc., Winchester, Va., 1989-91, 2002—, pres., 1991—2001, Signet Screen Printing and Embroidery, Winchester, Va., 1993—2001; ptnr. TJC LLC, Winchester, Va., 1999—. Elijah P. Lovejoy lectr. So. Ill. U., Carbondale, 1970; cons., 1993—; publs. cons., Falls Church, Va., 1993—. Mem. Falls Church (Va.) Democratic Com., 1970-84; founding mem. Falls Church Com. on Status of Women, 1975-76; pres. Montessori Sch. No. Va., 1970. Mem. Slovenian Heritage Com. Washington, Slovenian Choral Soc. Washington, Am. Slovenian Cath. Union, Soc. for Slovene Studies. Roman Catholic. E-mail: jim@cesnik.com.

CETIN, ANTON, artist; b. Bojana, Croatia, Sept. 18, 1936; arrived in Can., 1968, naturalized, 1973; s. Tomo and Terezija (Grcic) C.; m. Milka Katalenic, Dec. 16, 1962; 1 child, Dawn Antonia. Diploma, Sch. Applied Arts, Zagreb, 1959; master diploma, Acad. Fine Arts, Zagreb, 1964. One-man shows include Art Gallery Hamilton, 1978, Galeria Juan Martin, Mexico City, 1979, Ullman Galleries, Chgo., 1983, Mus. Arts and Crafts, Zagreb, 1986, Beverly Gordon Gallery, Dallas, 1987, Nat. and Univ. Libr., Zagreb, 1988, Oberhausmuseum, Passau, Germany, 1990, Sony Plaza Art Gallery, Tokyo, 1991, Gallery 7, Hong Kong, 1993, Museo del Chopo, Mexico City, 1993, Salas Nactionales de Cultura-Palais de Glace, Buenos Aires, Argentina, 1994, Museo Mcpl. de Arte J.C. Castagnino, Mar del Plata, Argentina, 1995, Mus. and Gallery Ctr., Zagreb, 1996, City Mus. Vara[009e]din, Croatia, 1998, Art Gallery, Split, Croatia, 1998, Gallery Fine Arts & Waldinger Gallery, Osijek, Croatia, 2000, Herman Hesse Mus., Calw, Germany, 2000, Mercedes Zentrum, Stuttgart, Germany, 2000-01, Gallery Anton Cetin, Cazma, Croatia, 2001, State Archives and Gallery Kortil, Rijeka, Croatia, 2002, Gallery HKZ-Hrvatsko slovo, Zagreb, Croatia, 2003, Multicultural Gallery, Halifax, Can., 2003, Gallery Ministry of Fin., Zagreb, Croatia, 2003; group exhbns. include Mus. Modern Art, Crakow, Poland, 1972, Brockton Art Ctr., 1974, Nat. Libr. France, 1978, 2d Cabo Frio Internat. Print Biennial, Brazil, 1985, Del Bello Gallery, Toronto, 1986, 87, 89, 90, Crespano del Grappa, Italy, 1988, Nat. Libr. Can., 1990, Art Asia, 1993, Olympic Games, Atlanta, 1996, Shenzhen Fine Art Inst., Shenzhen Mus. Modern Art, Shanghai, 2000, Point K Galerie, Nice, France, 2001, Círculo del Arte, Barcelona, Spain, 2002, Six Stories, Multicultural Gallery, Halifax, Can., 2003, others; represented in permanent collections at nat. librs. France, Croatia, Can., U.N., Japan and Salas Nacionales-Palais de Glace, Buenos Aires, Museo del Chopo, Mexico City, Vatican, Italy, Mus. Arts and Crafts, Gallery Klovicevi dvori, Zagreb, Croatia, Can. Cultural Ctr., France, Circulo del Arte, Barcelona, Spain, Gallery Anton Cetin, Cazma, Croatia, others; author: Eve and the Moon, 1975; co-author: Amerika Croatan America, 1988. Named Artist of Yr., Can. Croatian Artists Soc., 1986; honored for outstanding merits in the field of culture, govt. of Croatia, 1995 Home: PH3 5 Greystone Walk Dr Scarborough ON Canada M1K 5J5 E-mail: acetineve@aol.com.

CETRULO, JERRY, artist, sculptor; b. Jersey City, N.J., Sept. 10, 1941; s. Gerardo Cetrulo and Eva Augustine; m. Renate Cetrulo, 1961 (div.); children: Michael, Mark, Heidi; m. Barbara Cetrulo, Aug. 2, 1998. Customer engr. IBM, Cranford, N.J., 1967-99; ret., 1999; instr. Am. Woodcarving Sch., Wayne, N.J., 1992—. With U.S. Army, 1959-62. Avocations: woodcarving, painting. Home: 18 Cayuga Ave Rockaway NJ 07866-1012 Office: Am Woodcarving Sch 21 Pompton Plains Xrd Wayne NJ 07470-6326 E-mail: njcarver@optonline.net.

CETTEL, JUDITH HAPNER, artist, secondary school educator; b. Langley, Va., Aug. 28, 1945; d. Francis S. and Mary Louise (Ellers) Hapner. BFA, Miami U., Oxford, Ohio, 1967, MEd, 1972; student, La Varenne Cooking Sch., Paris, 1976, Alliance Francais, 1976. Cert. tchr. art K-12, Ohio. Artist WMUB TV, Miami U., Oxford, Fla., 1966-67; grad. tchg. asst. Miami U., Oxford, Fla., 1971-72; graphic designer, asst. to editor Miami U. Dept. Alumni Affairs, Oxford, Fla., 1967-69; tchr. art Mason HS, Ohio, 1969—; chair dept. fine arts K-12 Mason City Sch., Mason, Ohio, 1980—99; ptnr. Life Style Designs, Cin., 1978—; chair visual arts dept., K-12 Mason City Sch., Mason, Ohio, 1999—. Graphic designer/advt. dir. Hurrah! Gourmet Kitchenware and Cooking Sch., Cin., 1973—80; freelance fine artist, Cin., 1967—; mem. crisis intervention team Mason City Sch., Mason, Ohio, 1993—95, mem. faculty adv. bd., 1994—96, coord. curriculum fine arts, 1995—99, mem. bldg. design team, 1994, Mason, 99, mem. fine arts coun., 1998—; commd. artist Big Pig Gig, Cin., 1999—2000. Artist murals in various comml. and residential settings, 1982—; represented in pvt. collections, Ohio, Ohio, N.H., N.J., N.C., Va.; featured in article Arts and Activities Mag., 1994. Mem., vol. Mt. Adams Civic Assn., Cin., 1976—, Mt. Adams Garden Club; adv. coun. mem. Assn. for Advancement of Arts in Edn., 1995-98, mem. long range planning team, 1996—; mem. planning team Vis. Artists' Alliance. Recipient Golden Apple award Mason City Schs., 1988, Shining Star award, 1995, 96, Contemporary Design award Homerama-Cin. Home Builders Assn., 1980, Martha Holden Jennings Master Tchr. award, 2002; Arts in Edn. grantee Ohio Arts Coun., 1987; grantee Arts Connection Pilot Sch., 1996—, Harvard Inst. for Sch. Leadership, 2001. Mem. NEA, Ohio Edn. Assn., Mason Edn. Assn., Nat. Art Edn. Assn., Ohio Art Edn. Assn., S.W. Ohio Art Edn. Assn., Assn. Advancement Arts Edn. Avocations: scuba diving, cooking, travel, historic restoration, painting murals and large canvases. Office: 1224 Ida St Cincinnati OH 45202

CEYER, SYLVIA T. chemistry educator; Grad. summa cum laude, Hope Coll., Holland, Mich.; PhD, U. Calif., Berkeley. Postdoctoral fellow Nat. Bur. Standards; faculty mem. dept. chemistry MIT, Cambridge, Mass., 1981—, J.C. Sheehan prof. chemistry. Recipient Recognition award for young scholars AAUW Ednl. Found., 1988, Nobel Laureate Signature awd. for Graduate Education in Chemistry, Am. Chemical Soc., 1993. Fellow NAS (chmn. chemistry sect.), Am. Phys. Soc., Am. Acad. Arts and Scis. Office: MIT 6-217 Dept Chemistry 77 Mass Ave Dept Cambridge MA 02139-4307

CHA, SE DO, internist; b. Seoul, Korea, Dec. 17, 1942; came to U.S., 1966, naturalized, 1977; s. Young Sun and Hee Joo (Chang) C.; m. Elsa Jane Greene, Dec. 21, 1974; 1 child, Elizabeth. MD, Yon Sei U., 1966. Diplomate Am. Bd. Internal Medicine. Intern Presbyn.-U. Pa. Med. Ctr., Phila., 1966-67; resident in medicine Harrisburg (Pa.) Hosp., 1967-70; chief resident in medicine Roger Williams Gen. Hosp., Providence, 1970-71, cardiologist, 1973-75; fellow in cardiology Deborah Heart and Lung Center, Browns Mills, N.J., 1971-73, cardiologist, 1975—, asst. dir. adult cardiac catheterization lab., 1975-86, dir., 1987—. Clin. asst. prof. U. Medicine and Dentistry N.J., 198-20037; instr. Brown U., Providence, 1973-75. Contbr. articles to profl. jours. Fellow ACP, Soc. for Cardiac Angiography; mem. AMA, Fedn. Clin. Rsch., Am. Heart Assn. Office: Deborah Heart and Lung Ctr Trenton Rd Browns Mills NJ 08015

CHA, SOYOUNG STEPHEN, mechanical engineer, educator; b. Inchon, Korea, June 25, 1944; arrived in U.S., 1974; s. Sang O. and Sook S. (Lee) C.; m. Young W. Park, Sept. 4, 1974. BS, Seoul (Korea) Nat. U., 1969; MS, Mich. State U., 1976; PhD, U. Mich., 1980. Project rsch. engr. Northrop corp., Rsch. Triangle Park, N.C., 1979-84; prof., dir. opto-mech. lab. U. Ill., Chgo., 1984—. Spkr. in field; co-chair Beijing Optical Diagnostics Symposium, 2002. Editor numerous procs. vols., Optics Lasers in Engineering; contbr. more than 130 articles to profl. jours. Dept. of Energy fellow, 1987, NASA fellow, 1994, USAF fellow, 1996. Fellow Internat. Soc. Optical Engring. (conf. chair, co-chair 1991—), ASME (tech. com. 1983-87), Am. Soc. Aeronautics and Astronautics (tech. com. 1994-97, 1998—), Visualization Soc. Japan (conf. co-chair 1998, 2002). Methodist. Achievements include patent for holographic velocimetry.

CHABAN, LAWRENCE RICHARD, lawyer; b. Pitts., Apr. 8, 1955; s. Donald W. and June H. (Klee) Chaban; children: Matthew A., Micah R. BA, U. Pitts., 1977, JD, 1980. Bar: Pa. 1980, U.S. Dist. Ct. (we. dist.) Pa. 1980, U.S. Ct. Appeals (3rd cir.) 1981, U.S. Ct. Appeals (4th cir.) 1984, U.S. Ct. Appeals (6th cir.) 1993. Compensation atty. Dist. 5 United Mine Workers Am., Pitts., 1980-81; with Yablonski, Costello & Leckie, P.C., Washington, Pa., 1980—2003; sole practitioner Pitts., 2003—. Mem. ABA, Nat. Employment Lawyers Assn., Pa. Bar Assn., Allegheny County Bar Assn., Order of Coif, Pa. Trial Lawyers Assn., Nat. Orgn. Social Security Claimant's Reps. Democrat. Jewish. Avocations: miniature gaming, golf. Home: 111 Overlook Dr Pittsburgh PA 15216-1434 Office: 825 Grant Bldg 310 Grant St Pittsburgh PA 15219 Office Fax: 412-434-7795. E-mail: lchaban@lydonschubert.com.

CHABOT, ELLIOT CHARLES, lawyer; b. Anniston, Ala., Mar. 29, 1955; s. Herbert L. and Aleen (Kerwin) C.; m. Christine H. Swan, July 3, 1998. BA with honors, U. Md., 1977; JD, George Washington U., 1980. Bar: D.C. 1980, U.S. Dist. Ct. D.C. 1981, U.S. Ct. Fed. Claims 1981, U.S. Ct. Internat. Trade 1981, U.S. Tax Ct. 1981, U.S. Ct. Appeals Armed Forces 1981, U.S. Temporary Emergency Ct. Appeals 1981, U.S. Ct. Appeals (D.C. cir.) 1981, U.S. Ct. Appeals (4th, 5th, 8th, 9th, 10th, 11th, fed. cirs.) 1982, U.S. Ct. Appeals (7th cir.) 1983. Applications analyst, atty., House Info. Systems U.S. Ho. of Reps., Washington, 1980-81, project leader integrated law revision and retrieval project, 1981-89, legal support project leader House Info. Sys., 1989-95, webmaster internet law libr., 1994-99, legal sys. team leader House Info. Resources, 1995—. Bd. dirs. Am. Revenue Assn., Rockford, Iowa, 1983—87, Threshold Services, Inc., Silver Spring, Md., 1984—89; v.p. Banor Housing Inc., Kensington, Md., 1987—88, Kensington, 1990—2001, Kensington, 2003—. Columnist Aspen Hill Gazette, 1987-96. Pres. Aspen Hill (Md.) Civic Assn., 1985—95, dir., 1995—2000; adv. com. Aspen Hill Libr., 1972, 1986—2001; sec. Friends Aspen Hill Libr., 1994—96, dir., 1996—; mem. exec. com. Allied Civic Group, Silver Spring, 1987—89, corr. sec., 1992—94; mem. Dist. 21 [illegible] Kensington Vol. Fire Dept., 1989; mem. Greater Layhill Community Night Com., 1989, Aspen Hill Master Plan Citizens Adv. com., 1990—94, Wheaton Action Group, 1990—95; chmn. Wheaton Woods Recreation Ctr. Adv. Com., 1990; mem. Bauer Drive Community Ctr. Adv. Com., 1992—; rec. sec. Dist. 19 Dem. Club, Montgomery County, 1983—86, 2d v.p., 1986—89, 1st v.p., 1989—92; sec. Montgomery County Dem. Party, 1994—, chmn. rules com., 1994—, chmn. Internet Svcs. com., 1995—2002, mem. ballot questions adv. com., 1988—90, 1998—2002; vice chmn. precint orgn. com. of the party opers. task force, 1991—92; area coord. Dist. 19, 1992—94, chmn. Precinct 13-43, 1987—92, treas. Precinct 13-45, 1978—85; campaign chmn. Dist. 19 Democratic Team, 1989—90; dir. dist. 3 Montgomery Citizens Polit. Action Com., 1991—92; sec. Montgomery County United Democrats, 1997—2002; mem. Md. State Dem. Ctrl. Com., 1994—, alt. mem. exec. com., 2002—, mem. rules com., 2003—; vice chmn. homeless com. Temple Shalom, Chevy Chase, Md., 1992—93; pres. Parkland Community Sch. Coun., Aspen Hill, 1983—87, 1994—96, v.p., 1971—73, mem. coun., 1970—74, 1982—96; chmn. community svcs. com. Greater Wheaton (Md.) Citizens Adv. Bd., 1986—92; chmn. Ga. Ave. Men's Shelter Adv. Bd., Aspen Hill, 1989—96, Community Edn. Devel. subcom. of Citizens Adv. com. to the Interagency Coordinating Bd. for Community Use of Ednl. Facilities and Svcs., 1985—88; dist. 3 v.p. Montgomery County Civic Fedn., 1990—91; exec. com. Robert E. Peary High Sch. PTA, Aspen Hill, 1972—73, Montgomery County Coun. com. on re-use of Peary High Sch., 1986, task force to examine the regional dist. act, 1991; corr. sec. Area 2 adv. coun. Montgomery County Pub. Schs., 1972—74, adv. com. spl. edn. programs, 1974; commr. Gov.'s Commn. on Student Affairs, Md., 1976—77; legal and acctg. div. steering com. Washington Israel Bonds, 1984—86; chmn. Kensington/Wheaton Human Svcs. Area Plan Adv. Group, 1988; sec. Robert E. Peary H.S. Alumni Assn., Aspen Hill, Md., 2001—. Recipient George Washington award, George Washington U., 1980, Donald R. Spivak award Montgomery County Interagency Coordinating Bd. Community Use of Edn. Facilities and Services, 1987, Total Quality Team award Chief Adminstrv. Officer of U.S. Ho. of Reps., 1996; named One of Outstanding Young Men, U.S. C. of C., 1982, Ky. Col. Hon. Order Ky. Cols., 1967, Citizen of Yr. Greater Wheaton Citizen's Adv. Bd., 1990, One of the Federal 100 Federal Computer Week, 1994. Mem. ABA, FBA, Internat. Law Inst. (mem. faculty legis. drafting 2000—), George Washington U. Law Alumni Assn. (pres. Capitol Hill chpt. 1987-89, sec. 1985-87), Phi Alpha Delta (clk. Jay chpt. 1979-80), Omicron Delta Kappa. Home: 3501 Beret Ln Aspen Hill MD 20906-3029 Office: US Congress House Info Resources H2-641 Ford Ho Office Bldg Washington DC 20515-6165 E-mail: elliotchabot@abanet.org.

CHABOT, HERBERT L. judge; b. N.Y.C., July 17, 1931; s. Meyer and Esther (Mogilansky) C.; m. Aleen Carol Kerwin, June 16, 1951; children: Elliot C., Donald J., Lewis A., Nancy Jo. BA, CCNY, 1952; LLB, Columbia U., 1957; LLM, Georgetown U., 1964. Bar: N.Y. 1958. Staff counsel Am. Jewish Congress, 1957-60; law clk. U.S. Tax Ct., Washington, 1961-65, judge, 1978—, judge sr. status, 2001—. Atty. Joint Congl. Com. Taxation, 1965—78. Del. Md. Constl. Conv., 1967-68. With U.S. Army, 1953-55. Mem. ABA, Fed. Bar Assn. Office: US Tax Ct 400 2nd St NW Washington DC 20217-0002

CHABOT, STEVEN J. congressman; b. Cin., Jan. 22, 1953; s. Gerard Joseph and Doris Leona (Tilly) C.; m. Donna Daly, June 22; children: Erica, Randy. BA, Coll. William & Mary, 1975; JD, Salmon P. Chase Coll. of Law, 1978. Bar: Ohio; cert. tchr., Ohio. Tchr. St. Joseph Sch., Cin., 1975-76; atty. Cin., 1978-95; mem. city coun. City of Cin., 1985-90; commr. Hamilton County, Ohio, 1990-94; mem. U.S. Congress from 1st Ohio Dist., Washington, 1995—; internat. rels., judiciary, sm. bus. coms. Mem. internat. rels. with Africa, internat. econ. policy & trade, comml. & adminstrv. law, crime, procurement, exports & bus. opportunities coms. Republican. Roman Catholic. Avocations: reading, spending time with family. Office: US House Reps 129 Cannon Bldg Washington DC 20515-3501*

CHABRA, ANAND, public health physician, epidemiologist; b. Bukit Mertajam, Malaysia, May 16, 1966; s. Harbans L. and Lilly Chabra; m. Michelle E.D. Chabra, Mar. 25, 1995; children: Isaac, David. BA, Stanford U., 1988; MD, U. Wash., 1993; MPH, U. Calif., Berkeley, 1995. Diplomate Am. Bd. Pub. Health and Gen. Preventive Medicine. Pediatric intern U. Calif., San Francisco, 1993-94, resident preventive medicine Berkeley, 1994-96; med. epidemiologist Calif. Maternal and Child Health, Berkeley, 1996-99; maternal, child and adolescent health dir. San Mateo (Calif.) County, 1999—. Mem. adv. com. U. Calif. Berkeley/U. Calif. San Francisco Preventive Medicine, 1994-96, 98—; mem. exec. com. MCAH Action, 2000—, treas., 2000-03, pres., 2003—; mem. Adolescent Health Collaborative, 1999—. Contbr. articles to profl. jours. Program svcs. com. mem. March of Dimes, San Francisco, 1999—. Fellow: Am. Coll. Preventive Medicine; mem.: APHA, Calif. Pub. Health Assn., Calif. Med. Assn., Am. Assn. Pub. Health Physicians, Christian Med. Assn., Calif. Acad. Preventive Medicine (dir. 1997—2000), CityMatch, Stanford Alumni Assn. Office: San Mateo County Health Svcs Agy 225 37th Ave Rm 300 San Mateo CA 94403-4324 E-mail: achabra@co.sanmateo.ca.us.

CHABRAJA, NICHOLAS D. b. Gary, Ind., Nov. 6, 1942; BA, Northwestern U., 1964, JD, 1967. Bar: Ind. 1967, Ill. 1968. Ptnr. Jenner & Block, Chgo., 1968-97; sr. v.p., gen. counsel Gen. Dynamics Corp., 1993-94, exec. v.p., bd. dirs., 1994-97. Spl. counsel to Ho. of Reps. re-Impeachment Trial of Judge Harry E. Claiborne before U.S. Senate, 1986. Fellow Am. Coll. Trial Lawyers; mem. ABA, Ill. Bar Assn., Chgo. Bar Assn. Office: General Dynamics Corp 3190 Fairview Park Dr Ste 1 Falls Church VA 22042-4523

CHABROW, PENN BENJAMIN, lawyer; b. Phila., Feb. 16, 1939; s. Benjamin Penn and Annette (Shapiro) Chabrow; m. Sheila Sue Steinberg, June 18, 1961; children: Michael Penn, Carolyn Debra, Frederick Penn. BS, Muhlenberg Coll., 1959; JD, George Washington U., 1962, LLM in Taxation, 1968; postgrad. in econs., Harvard U. Bar: Va. 1963, D.C. 1964, U.S. Ct. Appeals (D.C. cir.) 1964, U.S. Tax Ct. 1964, U.S. Supreme Ct. 1966, Fla. 1972, U.S. Ct. Claims 1974, U.S. Ct. Appeals (5th and 11th cirs.) 1981, bd. cert. tax atty. Fla. tax law specialist IRS, Washington, 1961—67; tax counsel C. of C. U.S., Washington, 1967—74; pvt. practice Miami, 1974—; shareholder Wampler, Buchanan, Walker, Chabrow & Banciella, PA, Miami, 1993—. Pres. Forum Realty Co., Phila., Pure Poultry Enterprises, Inc., Miami, Heartland Farms of Fla., Inc.; lectr. fed. taxation Barry U. Grad. Schl. of Bus., 1977—81. Contbr. articles to profl. jours. Founding dir. The Dan Marino Found., Inc., The Melissa Inst. for Violence Prevention and Treatment, Inc., Elier Dacal Found., Inc. Fellow: Am. Coll. Tax Counsel; mem.: ABA, D.C. Bar Assn., Va. Bar Assn., Fed. Bar Assn., Fla Bar Assn., Muhlenberg Coll. Internat. Vis. Com., Phi Sigma Tau, Phi Alpha Delta. Office: SunTrust Internat Ctr 1 SE Third Ave Ste 1700 Miami FL 33131

CHACE, WILLIAM MURDOUGH, former university administrator; b. Newport News, Va., Sept. 3, 1938; s. William Emerson and Grace Elizabeth (Murdough) Chace; m. JoAn Elizabeth Johnstone, Sept. 5, 1964; children: William Johnstone, Katherine Elizabeth. BA in English, Haverford Coll., 1961; MA in English, U. Calif., Berkeley, 1963; PhD in English, U. Calif., 1968; LLD (hon.), Amherst Coll., 1990, William Coll., 1992. Instr. Stillman Coll., Tuscaloosa, Ala., 1963—64; teaching asst. U. Calif., Berkeley, 1964—66, acting instr., 1967—68; asst. prof. English Stanford U., 1968—74, assoc. prof., 1974—80, prof., 1980, assoc. dean Sch. Humanities and Scis., 1981—85, vice provost for acad. planning and devel., 1985—88; pres. Wesleyan U., Middletown, Conn., 1988—94, Emory U., Atlanta, 1994—2003. Dir. Sun Trust Banks; cons. Hewlett-Packard, Hallmark Cards, Inc., Hawaiian Ednl. Fund, Midwestern Mgmt. Assn.; vis. prof. The Coll. Aboard the Delta Queen, 1979, 80, 82, The Coll. in Western Europe and Brit. Isles, 1985; lectr. to libr. assocs. Stanford U., 1976; lectr. 6th Internat. James Joyce Symposium, Dublin, 1977, MLAL Ann. Conv., 1977, 78, Tufts Symposium, 1978, English Conf. U. Calif., Berkeley, 1979, Eighth Internat. James Joyce Symposium, Dublin, 1982, IBM Internat. Bus. and Acad. Conf., Monte Carlo, 1984, Ezra Pound Centennial Colloquium, San Jose State U., 1985, Ann. Meeting of Assn. of Grad. Liberal Studies Programs, St. Louis, 1986, Chico State U., La. State U., 1987, U. Utah Sch. Medicine Pub. Lecture series, 1987, No. Calif. Sci. Meeting Am. Coll. Physicians, Monterey, Calif., 1987, 13th Internat. James Joyce Symposium, 1992; presenter Joyce and History conf. Yale U., 1990; spkr. Fleur Cowles Flair Symposium, U. Tex., Austin, 2000. Author: James Joyce: A Collection of Critical Essays, 1973, The Political Identities of Ezra Pound and T.S. Eliot, 1973, Lionel Trilling: Criticism and Politics, 1980; co-author: Graham Greene: A Revaluation, 1990; co-editor: Justice Denied: The Black Man in White America, 1970, An Introduction to Literature, 1985; co-editor: (with JoAn E. Chace) Making It New, 1972, contbr. articles to profl. jours.*

CHACHANIDZE-MARGOLIN, LIA LEON, mathematician, educator, physicist, researcher; b. Tbilisi, Georgia, Feb. 26, 1964; d. Leon Samson and Kate Michael (Shadinova) Chachanidze; m. Richard Miron Margolin, Oct. 2, 2001; m. Vladimir Albert Muradov, Sept. 14, 1996 (div. May 2000); 1 child, John Muradov. BS, Tbilisi State U., 1983, MS, 1985; PhD, Moscow State U., 1994. Sr. rschr. Georgian Acad. Sci., 1985—2001; prof. math. and physics Tbilisi State U., 1986—99; prof. math. K. Gibbs Coll., N.Y.C., 2002—. Vis. scientist Rice U., Houston, 2000—01; cons. UNESKO, Georgia, 1995—2001. Author: Algebra and Geometry, 1994; contbr. articles to profl. jours. Grantee, J. Soros Found., Georgia, 1995, UNESKO, Georgia, 1998. Mem.: Am. Math. Soc., N.Y. Acad. Sci. Avocations: piano, writing, poetry. Home: 927 Willow Ave Hoboken NJ 07030 Office: Katharine Gibbs Coll 50 W 40th St New York NY 10138

CHACHOLIADES, MILTIADES, economics educator; b. Omodos, Limassol, Cyprus, June 22, 1937; came to U.S. 1962; s. Panagis Themistokli and Hariclea (Miltiadou) C.; m. Mary Modenos, Dec. 30, 1962; children: Lea, Marina, Linda. BA, Sch. Bus. & Econs., Athens, 1961; PhD, MIT, 1965. Asst. prof. NYU, 1965-68; vis. assoc. prof. UCLA, 1970; assoc. prof. econs. Ga. State U., Atlanta, 1968-71, prof. econs., 1971-73, rsch. prof. econs., 1973-87, chmn. dept. econs., 1986-89, prof. econs., 1989-93, prof. emeritus, 1995—; prof. econs. U. Cyprus, Nicosia, 1993—2000, rector, 1995-99. Author: The Pure Theory of International Trade, 1973, Brit. edit. 1974, Internat. Monetary Theory and Policy, 1978, internat. student edit., 1978, International Trade Theory and Policy, 1978, internat. student edit., 1978, Principles of International Economics, 1981, Spanish edit., 1982, Malaysian edit. 1988, Microeconomics, 1986, Greek edit., 1989, Microeconomics: Instructors Manual, 1986, internat. econs. edit., 1990, International Economics: Instructors Manual, 1990; contbr. articles to profl. jours.; editorial advisor Greek Econ. Rev. Athens Sch. fellow, Am. Hellenic Ednl. and Welfare Fund fellow, 1962-64, MIT Sloan rsch. assistantship, 1962-63, econs. fellow, 1963-64, others. Mem. Royal Econ. Soc., Ea. Econ. Assn., Greek Econ. Assn., So. Econ. Assn., Am. Econ. Assn. Office: 5219 Forest Spring Dr Dunwoody GA 30338

CHACKO, GEORGE KUTTICKAL, systems science educator, consultant; b. Trivandrum, India, July 1, 1930; came to U.S., 1953. s. Geevarghese Kuttickal and Thankamma (Mathew) C.; m. Yo Yee, Aug. 10, 1957; children: Rajah Yee, Ashia Yo Chacko Lance. MA in Econs. and Polit. Philosophy, Madras U., India, 1950; postgrad., St. Xavier's Coll., Calcutta, India, 1950-52; B in Commerce, Calcutta U., 1952; cert. postgrad. tng., Indian Stat. Inst., Calcutta, 1951; postgrad., Princeton U., 1953-54; PhD in Econometrics, New Sch. for Social Rsch./New School U., N.Y.C., 1959; postdoctoral, UCLA, 1961. Asst. editor Indian Fin., Calcutta, 1951-53; comml. corr. Times of India, 1953; dir. mktg. and mgmt. rsch. Royal Metal Mfg. Co., N.Y.C., 1958-60; mgr. dept. ops. rsch. Hughes Semicondr. div., Newport Beach, Calif., 1960-61; cons., 1961-62; ops. research staff cons. Union Carbide Corp., N.Y.C., 1962-63; mem. tech. staff Research Analysis Corp., McLean, Va., 1963-65, MITRE Corp., Arlington, Va., 1965-67; sr. staff scientist TRW Systems Group, Washington, 1967-70; asst. in rsch. Princeton U., 1953—54; cons. def. systems, computer, space, tech. systems and internat. devel. systems, assoc. in math. test devel. Ednl. Testing Service, Princeton, N.J., 1955-57; asst. prof. bus. adminstrn. UCLA, 1961-62; lectr. Dept. Agr. Grad. Sch., 1965-67; asst. professorial lectr. George Washington U., 1965-68; professorial lectr. Am. U., 1967-70, adj. prof., 1970; vis. prof. def. systems Mgmt. Coll., Ft. Belvoir, Va., 1972-73; vis. prof. U. So. Calif., 1970-71, prof. systems mgmt., 1971-83, prof. systems sci., 1983-94, prof. emeritus, 1994; prof. mgmt. U. Pertanian/U. Putra, Malaysia, 1996—2000; prin. investigator IRPA project U. Pertanian, Malaysia, 1996-97; prof. U. Putra, Malaysia, 1997—; prof. tech. mgmt. Malaysian Grad. Sch. Mgmt., 1997—; founder, chmn. Joint MIT-MGSM Pan-Asian Program in Mgmt. of Tech., 1997—2000; prof. mgmt. tech. Multimedia U., Selangor, 2001—; chmn. Centre of Excellence of Mgmt. Tech., 2001—02, sr. advisor, 2002—; sr. consultant to Profitera Corp. Malaysian Govt. Multimedia Development Corp. R&D Project: Electronic Enhancement of Receivables Realization, 2002—; consultant ptnr. Natl. Info. Tech. Coun., Govt. of Malaysia, 2003—; chmn., CEO George Chacko Mgmt. Sdn. Bhd., Kuala Lumpur, Washington D.C., 2003—. Sr. Fulbright prof. Nat. Chengchi U., Taipei, 1983-84, sr. Fulbright rsch. prof., 1984-85; prin. investigator and program dir. Tech. Transfer Project, Taiwan Nat. Sci. Coun., 1984-85; disting. fgn. expert lectr. Taiwan Ministry Econ. Affairs, 1986; sr. vis. rsch. prof. Taiwan Nat. Sci. Coun. Nat. Chengchi U., Taipei, 1988-89; sr. vis. rsch. prof. Dah-Yeh Inst. Tech., Dah-Tsuen, Chang-Hwa, Taiwan, 1993-94; vis. prof. Nat. Chengchi U., Taipei, 1993-94; v.p. program devel. Systems and Telecom. Corp., Potomac, Md., 1987-90; chief sci. cons. RJO Enterprises, Lanham, Md., 1988-89; cons. Med. Svcs. Corp. Internat., vector biology and control project U.S. Agy. for Internat. Devel., 1991; guest lectr. Tech. Univs. Tokyo, Taipei, Singapore, Dubai, Cairo, Warsaw, Budapest, Prague, Bergen, Stockholm, Helsinki, Berlin, Madras, Bombay, London, 1992, Yokohoma, Taipei, Hong Kong, Kuala Lampur, Madras, Bombay, Alexandria, Jerusalem, Cairo, Paris, London, 1993-94, Madrid, Bologna, Milan, Monte Carlo, Amsterdam, Vienna, Austria, Kuala Lampur, Bangkok, 1994; Bogta, Quito, Lima, Santiago, Buenos Aires, Rio De Janeiro, Johannesburg, Kuala Lumpur, 1996; USIA sponsored U.S. sci. emissary to Egypt, Burma, India, Singapore, 1987; USIA sponsored U.S. expert on tech. transfer and military conversion 1st Internat. Conf. on Reconstrn. of Soviet Republics, Hannover, Germany, 1992; keynote speaker 2d annual conf. on mgmt. edn. in China, Taipei, Taiwan, 1989, world conf. on transition to advanced market economies, Warsaw, Poland, 1992, annual conv. Indian Inst. Indsl. Engring., Hyderabad, India, 1993, First Sino-South Africa Bilateral Symposium on Tech. Devel., Taipei, 1994, First Asia-Pacific Convention on Bus. mgmt. Edn., Kuala Lumpur, 1996, Annual Conf. of Malaysian Soc. of Ops. Rsch. and Mgmt. Scis, 1997; keynote spkr. Portland Intl. Conf. on Mgmt. of Engring. and Tech., 2003; mem. internat. adv. com. on restructuring strategies for electronics info. industry Asian Inst. Tech. Workshop, 1994, Technological Forecasting and Social Change, 1996—; mem. First Convention on Bus. and Mgmt. Edn., Kuala Lumpur, 1996, mem. Asian-Pacific Conf. on Mgmt. Sci.,

Malaysia, 1997. Author: 31 books in field including Applied Statistics in Decision Making, 1971, Computer Aided Decision Making, 1972, Systems Approach to Public and Private Sector Problems, 1976, Operations Research Approach to Problem Formation and Solution, 1976, Management Information systems, 1979, Trade Drain Interperative of Technology Transfer: U.S. Taiwan Concomitant Coalistions, 1985, Robotics/Artificial Intelligence/Productivity U.S.-Japan Concomitant Coalitions, 1986, Technology Management: Applications to Corporate Markets and Military Missions, 1988, The Systems Approach to Problem-Solving: From Corporate Markets to National Missions, 1989, Toward Expanding Exports Through Technology Transfer: IBM Taiwan Concomitant Coalitions, 1989, Dynamic Program Management: From Defense Experience to Commercial Application, 1989, Decision-Making Under Uncertainty: An Applied Statistics Approach, 1991, Operations Research/Management Science: Case Studies in Decision Making Under Structured Uncertainty, 1993, Invoking Intercessory Prayer Power: Mediating Modern-day Miracles, 1997, Targeting Strategies for Continuous Competitiveness: 33 Corporate, Country, and Cross-Country Applications for Information Technology (IT) Industry, 1988, Half-Indian, Half-Chinese, and All American, 1998, Synergizing Invention and Innovation for Missions and Markets: 31 Corporate, Country and Cross Country Applications in Integrating Technology and Territory within and Between Corporations and Countries, 1999, Survival Strategies of Hitech Corporations: Applicable Insights from 20th Century Eminent Executive Narratives, 1999; columnist: The Sunday Star, 1998-2003, Bus. Times, 2003, Asian Beacon, 2003—; contbr. articles to profl. pubs.; editor, contbr. 25 books including The Recognition of Systems in Health Services, 1969, Reducing the Cost of Space Transportation, 1969, Systems Approach to Environmental Pollution, 1972, National Organization of Health Services-U.S., USSR, China, Europe, 1979, Educational Innovation in Health Services-U.S., Europe, Middle East, Africa, 1979, Management Education in the Republic of China: Second Annual Conference, 1989, Expert Systems: 1st World Congress Proceedings, 1991, Transition to Advanced Market Economics: Internat. Conf. Proceedings, 1992, Industrial Engineering Interfaces: Indian Nat. Conf. Proceedings, 1993, Technological Development: 1st Sino-South Africa Bilateral Symposium Proceedings, 1994, Lenten Daily Devotions, 1996, Asia Pacific Convention on Dynamism and Invention in Management Education Proceedings, 1996, Foundations of Game Theory, 1997; guest editor Jour. Rsch. Comm. Studies, 1978-79; assoc. editor Internat. Jour. Forecasting, 1982-85; mem. internat. editl. bd. Malaysian Jour. Mgmt. Scis., 1996-98. Active Nat. Presbyn. Ch., Washington, 1967-84, mem. ch. coun., 1969-71, mem. chancel choir, 1967-84, co-dean ch. family camp, 1977, coord. life abundant discovery groups, 1979; chmn. worship com. Taipei Internat. Ch., 1984, founder, dir. Intercessory Prayer Power, 1984, mem. adult choir, 1983-85, 88-89, 93-96, chmn. membership com., 1985, chmn. stewardship and fin. com., 1985, chmn. com. Christian edn., 1988, Sunday Sch. supt., 1989, adult Sunday sch. leader, 1993; adult Sunday Sch. leader 4th Presbyn. Ch., Bethesda, Md., 1986-87, mem. sanctuary choir, 1985—; participant 9th Internat. Ch. Mus. Festival, Coventry Cathedral, 1992; mem. Men's Ensemble, 1986-93; mem. Ministry Com. Men of 4th Rep. to Session, 1990—; founder, dir. Prayer Power Partnership, 1990—; adult Sunday sch. leader Kuala Lumpur Internat. Ch., 1996—; mem. internat. adv. bd. Technol. Forecasting and Social Change, 1996—; charter mem. IndUS Entrepreneurs, Malaysian chpt. 2002—. Recipient Gold medal Inter-Collegiate Extempore Debate in Malayalam U. Travancore, Trivandrum, India, 1945, 1st pl. Yogic Exercises Competition U. Travancore, 1946, Jr. Lectureship prize Physics Soc. U. Coll., 1946, 1st prize Inter-Varsity Debating Team Madras, 1949, NSF internat. sci. lectures award, 1982, USIA citation for invaluable contbr. to America's pub. diplomacy, 1992, Commendation for 2 books on U.S. - Taiwan Technology Transfer by Presidential Palace, Taipei, 1993; Coll. scholar St. Xavier's Coll., 1950-52; Inst. fellow Indian Stat. Inst., 1951, S.E. Asia Club fellow Princeton U., 1953-54, Univ. fellow UCLA, 1961. Fellow AAAS (nat. coun. 1968-73, chmn. or co-chmn. symposia 1971, 72, 74, 76, 77, 78), Am. Astronautical Soc. (v.p. publs. 1969-71, editor Tech. Newsletter 1968-72, mng. editor Jour. Astronautical Scis. 1969-75); mem. Ops. Rsch. Soc. Am. (vice chmn. com. of representation on AAAS 1972-78, nat. coun. tech. sect. on health 1966-68, editor Tech. Newsletter on Health 1966-73), Washington Ops. Rsch. Coun. (trustee 1967-69, chmn. tech. colloquia 1967-68, editor Tech. Newsletter 1967-68, Banquet chmn. 1992-93), Inst. Mgmt. Scis. (rep. to Internat. Inst. for Applied Systems Analysis in Vienna, Austria 1976-77, session chmn. Athens, Greece 1977, Atlanta 1977), World Future Soc. (editl. bd. publs. 1970-71), N.Y. Acad. Scis., Soc. Scientific Mgmt. and Ops. Rsch. (Egypt, 1st hon. fgn. mem.), Inst. for Ops. Rsch. and the Mgmt. Scis. (founding, INFORMS 1994); Kiwanis (charter 1st v.p., Life-time Hickson fellow 1995), Costa Mesa North Club (charter 1st v.p., dir.), Friendship Heights Club (charter pres., dir., Outstanding Svc. award 1972-73, Life award), Bethesda Club (disting. divsn. one svc. award, 1968, 70, capital dist. chmn. 1967, 69-70, 71-72, inter divsn. chmn. Green Candle of Hope Dinner, 1965-82), Capital dist. Found. 1982, Taipei-Keystone Club (disting. dir., spl. rep. of internat. pres. and counselor to dist. of Republic of China 1983-86, Pioneer Premier Project award Asia-Pacific conf. 1986, Legion of Honor 1985), Bethesda Club (dir. 1967-69, 95, chmn. internat. rels. 1991—, chmn. hon. com. 1992—, numerous coms. 1966—). Democrat. Office: U So Calif Inst Safety And Sys Mgmt Los Angeles CA 90089-0001 *As one who was privileged to be born into a Christian family tracing itself to the founding in the year 52 of the Mar Thoma Syrian Church in Southwest India by Thomas the Doubting Disciple of Jesus Christ, I look upon the exciting encounters I have had with new ideas (such as Theory of Games) and new professions (such as Operations Research) as precious talents over which I exercise stewardship by enjoying excellence of effort and exposition toward a better tomorrow at home and abroad, as an Indian-American blest with a most supportive family.*

CHACKO, SAMUEL, association official; came to U.S., 1970; s. Chanda Pillai and Sosamma (Cheriyan) C.; m. Omana Chellimalayil George, May 21, 1979; children: Roshen Samuel, Renee Susan. BA in Econs., U. Kerala, 1963, MA in History, 1966, MA in Polit. Sci., 1968; BA in Social Sci., Olivet Nazarene U., Kankakee, Ill., 1971; MA in Comm., Govs. State U., 1974; postgrad., U. Ill., Chgo., 1981—86. Cert. in gerontology, cmty. nutrition. Dir. dept. aging Kankakee Land Community Action Agy., 1972—76; head sr. citizens dept. Oakland-Livingston Human Svcs. Agy., Pontiac, Mich., 1976—78; dir. Benton Harbor (Mich.) Area Parks and Recreation Bd., 1978—79; program analyst Ill. Migrant Coun., Chgo., 1980—84; dir. energy svcs. Community and Econ. Devel. Assn. Cook County, Inc., Chgo., 1985—2001; v.p. Cmty. and Econ. Devel. Assn. Cook County, Inc., Chgo., 2001—. Mem. Ill. State Commerce Commn. Task Force on Rewriting Utility Svc. Rules, 1995—, Ill. State Energy Assistance Program Working Group, 1991-93. Bd. dirs. NAACP, 1973-76; bd. dirs., Ea. Ill. U. Parents Club, 2000-. Mem.: Lions Club Internat. Office: Cmty and Econ Devel Assn Cook Cty Inc 208 S Lasalle St Ste 850 Chicago IL 60604-1000

CHACON, MICHAEL ERNEST, computer company executive; b. L.A., Feb. 14, 1954; s. Ernest Richard and Teresa Marie (Venegas) Chacon; m. Virginia Marie Chacon; children: Mylan Graham, Aubrie Sarah, Christina Nabseth, Caitlyn Nabseth, Julia Anna. Student, Pierce Coll., 1972-74, Boise State U., 1980-82; BSBA, U. Phoenix, 1997, postgrad., 2002—. Sys. cons. MEC & Assocs., Riverside, Calif., 1986-91; regional mgr. Inacom Corp., Garden Grove, Calif., 1991-97; chief tech. officer, chief tng. officer Ascolta Tng. Co., Irvine, Calif., 1997-2000; prin. architect Netigy Corp., San Jose, Calif., 2000—01; solutions arch. ePresence, Westboro, Mass., 2002—03; v.p. product devel. Conpressus, Inc., Washington, 2003—. Cons. in field; lectr. Microsoft Corp., Bellvue, Wash., 1990—92; instr. Irvine Valley Coll. Author: (book) Understanding Networks, 1991, Windows 2000 Accelerated Study Guide, 2000; columnist: Microsoft Cert. Profl. Mag.; contbr. articles to profl. jours. Mem.: 3Com Adv. Coun. (pres. tech. adv. bd. 1986—92), L.A. World Affairs Coun., Lake Elsinore Sportsman Assn. Avocations: songwriting/composing, rocketry, shooting, photography. E-mail: mechacon@cox.net.

CHADBOURNE, JOHN FREDERICK, JR., engineering executive; b. Detroit, Oct. 10, 1948; s. John Frederick and Wilhelmina (Williams) C.; m. Deborah Ann Bennett, Aug. 13, 1968. BSChemE, U. Fla., 1970, MS in Engring., 1971, PhD in Environ. Engring., 1977. Staff cons. environ. sci. and engring. U. Fla., Gainesville, 1971-74; proprietor Environ. Cons. Svcs., Orlando, Fla., 1974-77; corp. environ. mgr. Lafarge Corp., Dallas, 1977-87, dir. environment and indsl. hygiene, 1992-94; v.p. tech. and regulatory affairs Systech Environ. Corp., Dallas, 1987-92; pres. Chadbourne Environment and Safety Programs Inc., Dallas, 1994—. Vis. prof. environ. engring. So. Meth. U., 1997—. Author (book chpt.) Burning Hazardous Waste in Cement Kilns, 1989, 97. Mem. AAAS, AIChE, Air and Waste Mgmt. Assn. (com. chair 1977-97), N.Y. Acad. Scis. Achievements include having secured permits to replace fosssil fuel with hazardous waste on many cement kilns. Office: CESP Inc 13106 Roaring Springs Ln Dallas TX 75240-5643 E-mail: john.chadbourne@essroc.com.

CHADBURN, AMY, pathologist; b. Springhill, Oreg., Apr. 17, 1957; BS, Oreg. State U., 1979; MD, Stanford Med. Sch., 1983. Asst. prof. Commna U., N.Y.C., 1989—94, Cornell U., N.Y.C., 1994—; assoc. prof. Cornell U. Will Med. Sch.; asst. attending pathologist Presbyn. Hosp. Columbia campus, N.Y.C., 1989—94, N.Y. Presbyn. Hosp., 1994—; assoc. attending pathologist Cornell campus, 1994—. Pathologist AMC, Washington, 2001—. Named Best Dr. N.Y.C., Castle Connelly; recipient Arthur Purdy Stout award, Arthur Purdy Stout Soc., 1992. Mem.: Am. Soc. Clinical Pathologists, Soc. Human Pathology, U.S. and Canadian Acad. Pathology. Avocation: running. Office: NY Presbyn Hosp Canell Campus 525 E 68th St New York NY 10021

CHADSEY, HAROLD A. astronomer; s. Harold E. and Delores G. Chadsey; m. Carol Ellen Cooper, Nov. 9, 1991. BS, Centenary Coll., 1982; MS, Am. U., 1995; PhD, Kennedy-Western U., 2001. Astronomer U.S. Naval Obs., Miami, Fla., 1985—89, Washington, 1989—. GPS timinig Precise Time & Time Interval, 1993—; timing and clock adviser USCG, Alexandria, Va., 1989—; atomic frequency stds., 1995—. Author: An Automated Quality Control System for Cesium Frequency Standards, 2001. Judge H.S. Sci. Fairs D.C. Pub. Schs., Washington, 1991—2002, Fairfax County Pub. Schs., 1998—; mentor H.S. students Dept. of the Navy, U.S. Naval Obs., 2002—. Named Safety Rep., Naval Dist. Washington, 2002. Mem.: No. Va. Radio Control (pres. 1997), Quantico Flying Club, El Karubah Shrine. Avocations: building and flying remote control airplanes, private pilot.

CHADWICK, BRUCE PERCY, political scientist, consultant; b. Palo Alto, Calif., Sept. 11, 1968; s. George Brierley and Andrea Elsie (Herzog) Chadwick. BA, Pomona Coll., Claremont, Calif., 1990; MA, Columbia U., N.Y.C., 1992, MPh, 1997; PhD, 2000. Project cons. Inst. Pro-Natura, Rio de Janeiro, 1996—98; vis. scholar Inst. for Study of Religion, Rio de Janeiro, 1998—99; team leader knowledge techs. Winrock Internat., Washington, 1999—2003; asst. prof. Columbia U. Sch. Internat. Affairs and Earth Inst., 2003—. Rapporteur Brazil Seminar Columbia U., N.Y.C., 1992—94, electronic resources advisor, 1996—98; tech. advisor Tijuca Environ. Planning Com., Rio de Janeiro, 1999. Named Fellow, Nat. Sci. Found., Washington, 1991; recipient Fellowship award, Inst. for Study of World Politics, Vis. Scholar fellowship, Rio de Janeiro, Rockefeller Found., 1995. Mem.: Soc. for Internat. Devel., Internat. Soc. for Ecological Econs., Am. Polit. Sci. Assn. Achievements include research in linking democracy and more effective, sustainable development; developed models for information technology services to alleviate poverty and raise environmental awareness among the poor. Home: 1545 18th St NW Washington DC 20036 Office: SIPA 420 W 118th St New York NY 10027

CHADWICK, CYDNEY MARIE, writer, art projects executive; b. Oakland, Calif. MA, Kootenay Sch. of Writing, Vancouver, B.C., Can., 1996. Exec. dir. Syntax Projects for Arts, Penngrove, Calif., 1990—; writer Penngrove, Calif., 1993—. Author: Enemy Clothing, 1993 The Gift Horse's Mouth, 1994, Oeuvres, 1995, Persistent Disturbances, 1995, Interims, 1997, Inside the Hours, 1998, Benched, 2000. Office: AVEC PO Box 1059 Penngrove CA 94951-1059

CHADWICK, DEREK JAMES, foundation administrator; b. Carshalton, Surrey, Eng., Feb. 9, 1948; s. Dennis Edmund and Ida (Kay) Chadwick; m. Susan Reid, Dec. 20, 1980 (dec. May 15, 2002); children: Andrew John, Frederick Mark. BA in Chemistry, Oxford U., 1969, BSc, 1970, MA, D Philosophy, Oxford U., 1972. ICI fellow Cambridge U., 1972-73; Prize fellow Magdalen Coll., Oxford U., 1973-77; Royal Soc. European exch. fellow Eidgenössische Technische Hochschule, Zurich, Switzerland, 1975-77; lectr., sr. lectr., reader Liverpool U., 1977-88; vis. prof. U. Alsace, Mulhouse, France, 1988; dir. The Ciba Found. (now named The Novartis Found.), London, 1988—. Coun. mem. Louis Jeantet Found., Geneva, 1988-98, Assn. Med. Rsch. Charities, London, 1991-2000; vice-chmn., 1994-2000; coun. mem. Cou. Ctrl. Lab. of Rsch. Couns., 2002--; mem. steering com. Scientists Inst. for Pub. Info., N.Y.C., 1989-96; vis. prof. U. Trondheim, Norway, 1996—. Editor 50 books; author 100 papers and chpts. in sci. jours. and books. Fellow Royal Soc. Chemistry; mem. Am. Chem. Soc., Worshipful Soc. Apothecaries London, Hague Club Dirs. European Founds. (sec. 1993-97). Avocations: music, gardening, skiing. Office: The Novartis Found 41 Portland Pl London W1B 1BN England E-mail: dchadwick@novartisfound.org.uk.

CHADWICK, JOHN EDWIN, financial consultant; b. Mpls., Feb. 6, 1957; s. Edwin Bazley and Roberta Mae (Brown) Chadwick; m. Patti E. Anderson, June 20, 1997; 2 children. BA, Gustavus Adolphus Coll., St. Peter, Minn., 1979; cert., Am. Coll., Bryn Mawr, Pa., 1989. CFP. Feed ingredient merchandiser Pillsbury Co., Mpls., 1979-81; pres. Chadwick Co., Bloomington, Minn., 1982-84; v.p. sales Red Wing (Minn.) Bus. Sys., 1984-85; fin. counselor CIGNA, Mpls., 1985-88; prin. Chadwick Group, Inc., Bloomington, 1989—. Bd. trustees Gustavus Adolphus Coll., 2000, chair investment com. Lutheran. Avocations: hunting, water-skiing, fishing. Office: Chadwick Group Inc 9905 N 45th Ave N Plymouth MN 55442

CHADWICK, ROBERT, lawyer, judge; b. Jackson, Miss., Apr. 5, 1924; s. Hudson and Annie (Eley) C.; m. Helen Faye Josey, Apr. 5, 1953; children: Robert Hudson, Celia, Dan, Lea Ann, Robin. BA, Auburn U., 1950; JD, Miss. Coll., 1957; postgrad., U. So. Calif., 1973, 75-76. Bar: Miss. 1963, U.S. Supreme Ct. 1970, U.S. Ct. Mil. Appeals 1975, Ky. 1980, U.S. Dist Ct. (ea. dist.) Ky. 1987. Chief regulation staff div. pesticide regulation USDA, Washington, 1965-70; atty., ecologist div. enforcement EPA, Washington, 1970-75, chmn. com. pesticide misuse rev., 1975-79; asst. gen. counsel Presdl. Clemency Bd. White House Dept. Justice, Washington, 1975; pvt. practice law Frankfort, Ky., 1980-82, 83—; law judge parole bd. Corrections Cabinet, Frankfort, 1982-83; asst. dir. div. hazardous materials Ky. Dept. Natural Resources and Environ. Protection, Frankfort, 1983—. Chmn. bd. Exis, Inc.; staff atty., gen. counsel Ky. Cabinet for Human Resources, 1989-90. Pres. PTA Oxon Hill (Md.) Jr. High Sch., 1974, Frankfort Audubon Soc., 1981-83. Cpl. U.S. Army, 1943-45. Mem. ABA, Nat. Assn. Adminstrv. Law Judges, Miss. State Bar Assn., Ky. State Bar Assn., Franklin County Bar Assn., VFW, Masons. Home and Office: 16 Ryswick Ln Frankfort KY 40601-3848

CHADWICK, WILLIAM JORDAN, lawyer; b. N.Y.C., Apr. 21, 1948; s. William Leroy and Mildred (Jordan) C.; B.A., St. Lawrence U., 1970; J.D., Vanderbilt U., 1973. Bar: Calif. 1973. Assoc. Paul, Hastings, Janofsky & Walker, Los Angeles, 1973-74, ptnr., 1977— ; atty advisor for tax policy U.S. Treasury Dept., Washington, 1974-75; spl. asst. to adminstr. Pension and Welfare Benefit Programs, U.S. Dept. Labor, Washington, 1975-76, adminstr., 1976-77; dir. Westam. Packaging, Los Angeles, Fin. Select Seminars, Inc., Santa Barbara, Calif., Prudential-Bache Broadcasting. Author: The Annotated Fiduciary, 1978; Regulation of Employee Benefits, 1978. Contbr. articles to profl. jours. Trustee St. Lawrence U., Canton, N.Y., 1977-83; bd. dirs. Internat. Found. Employee Benefits Plans, Brookfield, Wis., 1980-83. Served to 1st lt. U.S. Army, 1966-73. Recipient Spl. Achievement award U.S. Dept. Treasury, 1975, U.S. Dept. Labor, 1976, Sec's Spl. Commendation award U.S. Dept. Labor, 1977. Mem. ABA, Calif. Bar Assn., D.C. Bar Assn. Home: 901 Enchanted Way Pacific Palisades CA 90272-2824 Office: Paul Hastings Jonofsky & Walker 555 S Flower St Los Angeles CA 90071-2300

CHAFE, WALLACE LESEUR, linguist, educator; b. Cambridge, Mass., Sept. 3, 1927; s. Albert J. and Nathalie (Amback) C.; m. Mary Elizabeth Butterworth, June 23, 1951 (div. 1980); children— Christopher, Douglas, Stephen; m. Marianne Mithun, Jan. 25, 1985 BA, Yale U., 1950, MA, 1956, PhD, 1958. Asst. prof. U. Buffalo, 1958-59; linguist Bur. Am. Ethnology, Smithsonian Instn., 1959-62; mem. faculty U. Calif.-Berkeley, 1962-86, prof. linguistics, 1967-86, U. Calif., Santa Barbara, 1986-91, prof. emeritus, 1991—, rsch. prof., 2003—. Author: Seneca Thanksgiving Rituals, 1961, Seneca Morphology and Dictionary, 1967, Meaning and the Structure of Language, 1970, The Pear Stories, 1980, Evidentiality, 1986, Discourse, Consciousness, and Time, 1994. Served with USNR, 1945-46. Mem. Linguistic Soc. Am., Am. Psychol. Assn., Am. Anthrop. Assn., Am. Psychol. Soc. Office: Univ Calif Dept Linguistics Santa Barbara CA 93106 E-mail: chafe@linguistics.ucsb.edu.

CHAFE, WILLIAM HENRY, history educator; b. Boston, Jan. 28, 1942; s. William Robinson and Elsie (Crabtree) C., m. Lorna Jane Waterhouse, July 12, 1964; children: Christopher Robert, Jennifer Elizabeth. AB, Harvard U., 1962; AM, Columbia U., 1966, PhD, 1971. Instr. Columbia Grammar Sch., N.Y.C., 1963-65, Vassar Coll., Poughkeepsie, N.Y., 1970-71; asst. prof. Duke U., Durham, N.C., 1971-74, assoc. prof., 1974-79, prof., 1979—, Alice Mary Baldwin prof. history, 1988—, acad. dir. Ctr. for Rsch. on Women, 1987-89, co-dir. Duke Oral History Program, 1974-82, sr. rsch. assoc. Duke Ctr. for Documentary Studies, chair, history dept., 1990-95, dean Faculty Arts and Scis., 1995—, vice provost undergrad. edn., 1999—. Author: The American Woman, 1972, Women and Equality, 1977, Civilities and Civil Rights, 1980 (R.F. Kennedy book award 1981), The Unfinished Journey, 1986, A History of Our Time, 1986, The Paradox of Change, 1991, Never Stop Running, 1993 (Sidney Hillman Found. book award 1994), The Road to Equality, 1994, Remembering Jim Crow, 2002 (Lillian Smith award, 2003). NEH fellow, 1974 75, 84-85, Rockefeller Found. fellow, 1978, Guggenheim fellow, 1989-90; grantee Nat. Humanities Ctr., Rsch. Triangle Pk., N.C., 1981-82, Ctr. for Advanced Study, Palo Alto, Calif., 1989-90. Fellow Soc. Am. Historians; mem. Am. Hist. Assn. (chmn. nominating com., 1987-88), Orgn. Am. Historians (co-chmn. program com. 1981-82, chair nominating com. 1991, exec. bd. 1993-96, pres. 1998-99), Am. Studies Assn., So. Hist. Assn. Avocations: sailing, tennis. Office: Duke U 104 Allen PO Box 90046 Durham NC 27708-0046

CHAFEE, INGRID ROBERTA HOOVER COLEMAN, French language educator; b. Evanston, Ill., Dec. 12, 1934; d. Richard Thomas and Ingrid (Krogvig) Hoover; m. Samuel Henry Coleman III, Sept. 10, 1958 (wid. Oct. 1974); children: Robert D., Charles E.; m. Nathaniel Chafee, July 8, 1989. AB, Western Coll. of Miami, Oxford, 1956; MA, U. Va., 1959; PhD, Emory U., 1980. Part-time instr. Ga. State U., Atlanta, 1976-81; asst. prof. Morehouse Coll., Atlanta, 1981-83, 1990-95, assoc. prof., 1995—, acting chair dept. modern fgn. langs., 2000. Tech. writer, trainer Am. Software, Inc., Atlanta, 1984-90; coord. European Program, Morehouse Ctr. for Internat. Studies, Atlanta, 1994-96; jour. referee Jour. of Assn. for W. Ga. Coll., 1996—. Contbr. articles to profl. jours. Coord. prisoner of conscience coms., Amnesty Internat., Atlanta, 1983-87. Mem. MLA, South Atlantic Modern Lang. Assn., Am. Assn. Tchrs. of French, Phi Beta Kappa. Democrat. Avocations: writing, listening to music, history, film, theatre, swimming, sailing. Home: 476 Princeton Way NE Atlanta GA 30307-1131 Office: Morehouse Coll Dept Modern Fgn Langs 830 Westview Dr SW Atlanta GA 30314-3773 E-mail: ingridcc@aol.com., Ichafee@morehouse.edu.

CHAFEE, LINCOLN, senator; b. Warwick, R.I., Mar. 26; m. Stephanie Chafee; three children. BA in Classics, Brown U., 1975; postgrad., Mont. State U. Farrier various harness racktracks; planner Gen. Dynamics, Quonset Point, R.I., 1983; exec. dir. N.E. Corridor Initiative; del. R.I. Constnl. Conv., 1985; mem. Warwick City Coun.; mayor City of Warwick, 1992; R.I. senator U.S. Senate, 1999—, mem. com. on environment and pub. works, chmn. subcom. on superfund, com. fgn. rels., chmn. subcom. near ea. and south Asian affairs, banking, housing and urban affairs com. Republican. Office: US Senate 141A Russell Senate Office Washington DC 20510-0001 also: Unit 1100 170 Westminster St Providence RI 02903-2104

CHAFEL, JUDITH ANN, educator; b. Rochester, N.Y., Apr. 8, 1945; d. James Arthur and Florence Joan (Santangelo) C. AB, Vassar Coll., 1967; MSEd, Wheelock Coll, 1971; PhD, U. Ill., 1979. Cert. elem. tchr., Mass., N.J., N.Y. Tchr. Spruce St. Sch., Lakewood, N.J., 1972-74, Sodus (N.Y.) Primary Sch., 1974-76; grad. research and teaching asst. U. Ill., Urbana, 1976-79; vis. asst. prof. U. Tex., Austin, 1979-80; asst. prof. dept. curriculum and instrn. Ind. U., Bloomington, 1980-86, assoc. prof., 1986—2001, prof., 2001—; profl. staff mem. com. on ways and means U.S. Ho. Reps., Washington, 1989-90. Adj. assoc. prof. philanthropic studies Ctr. on Philanthropy, 1991-2001; reviewer Hist. Publs. and Records Commn., Nat. Archives, Washington, 1979, Little, Brown and Co., Boston, 1982-84, Office for Ednl. Rsch. and Improvement, U.S. Dept. Edn., 1991, 93. Mem. editorial adv. bd. Early Child Devel. and Care, 1985—, Youth and Soc., 1995—, Jour. of Poverty: Innovations on Social, Political and Economic Inequalities, 1998—; cons. editor Early Childhood Rsch. Quar., 1988-91, 92-95; contbr. editor Am. Jour. of Orthopsychiatry, 2000—; reviewer and contbr. articles to profl. jours. Proffitt Endowment grantee, Ind. U., 1982, 88, 1998, Ctr. on Philanthropy grantee, 1991, Spencer Found. grantee for young scholars, 1985, 98; Congl. Sci. fellow Soc. Rsch. in Child Devel., 1989. Mem. Soc. Rsch. in Child Devel. (program com. 1986, 92), Am. Ednl. Rsch. Assn. (program com. 1984, 86, 87, 91, 92, 94, 96-99, 2002, nominations com. 1986, 88, chair 1993-95, mem.-at-large spl. interest group on early edn. and child devel. 1991-93), Nat. Assn. Edn. Young Children (reviewer 1980—), Assn. Childhood Edn. Internat. (pub. com. 1982-84, bull. and pamphlets rev. editor jour. 1982-84, rsch. com. 1984-88). Office: Ind U Sch Edn 3214 Education Bldg Bloomington IN 47405

CHAFETZ, SAMUEL DAVID, lawyer; b. Memphis, Mar. 6, 1945; m. Patricia S. Shandel, Aug. 20, 1967. BA, U. Mich., 1967; JD, Harvard U., 1970. Bar: N.Y. 1971, Tenn. 1973. Assoc. Wachtell Lipton Rosen & Katz, N.Y.C., 1970—73; from assoc. to ptnr. Ireland Gibson Reams Henderson & Chafetz, Memphis, 1973—77; ptnr. Waring Cox PLC, Memphis, 1977—2000, Baker, Donelson, Bearman & Caldwell, Memphis, 2001—. Mem. Memphis Shelby County Bar Assn. (chmn. securities sect. 1998-99). Office: Baker Donelson Bearman & Caldwell 165 Madison Ave # 2100 Memphis TN 38103

CHAFFEE, KEVIN ST. CLAIR, writer; b. Erie, Pa., June 2, 1952; s. Clair Edgar and Madelyn R. (von Lindenberg-Bruder) C. Student, U. Nice, France, 1973; AB, MA in History, Georgetown U., 1974; postgrad., U. Bologna, Italy, 1975; MA in Internat. Rels., Johns Hopkins U., 1977. Researcher Washington bur. Balt. Sun, 1973; asst. to press sec. Rep. Marc L. Marks, Washington, 1976-77; asst. to pres. Internat. Mgmt. Resources Corp., Washington, 1978-79; editor, asst. pub. Encore mag., Washington, 1979-80, City Life mag., Washington, 1980-81; editorial cons., bus. mgr. Almanac Am. Politics, Washington, 1981-83; speechwriter, cons. Office of Pub. Affairs HUD, Washington, 1984-89; asst. features editor Washington Times, 1991—. Cons. Arab Republic Egypt, Washington, 1979-80, Ctr. for Pub. Integrity, Washington, 1990-94; cons. pub. rels. Congl. Quar., Inc., Washington, 1990-91, Citizens Rsch. Found., L.A., 1989; mng. editor, editl. cons. Campaigns and Elections Jour., Washington, 1980; pub. rels., editl. cons. Washington Bur. Quotidien de Paris, 1982-85; exec. producer Election Night 1986 Coverage C-Span Cable Network, Campaign Rsch. Ctr., Washington, 1990-91. Author: 50 Maps of Washington, D.C., 1991, Saving for a Rainy Day; How Congress Turns Campaign Cash into Golden Parachutes, 1990, 94; asst. features editor, social editor Metrotimes sect. of Washington Times, 1991—; contbr. articles, editorials to Town and Country, George and other mags. and newspapers. Bd. dirs. Source Theatre, Washington, 1982-90, Montesquieu Found., Paris, 1988-92; fundraiser Dance Theatre Harlem, 1989; cons. Paul Schrader Prodns., N.Y., 1999-2000. Avocations: cycling, theater, dance, travel. Home: 1536 15th St NW Washington DC 20005-1913 E-mail: kchaffee@washingtontimes.com.

CHAFFEE, PAUL CHARLES, newspaper editor; b. Racine, Wis., Aug. 10, 1947; s. Raymond Russell and Ellen Mary (Tiles) C.; m. Bonnie Louise Burmeister, Aug. 9, 1969. BA in Journalism, U. Minn., 1969. Reporter Grand Rapids (Mich.) Press, 1969-79, asst. met. editor, 1979-81; met. editor Saginaw (Mich.) News, 1981-88, editor, 1988—. Founding mem. adv. bd. dept. journalism Ctrl. Mich. U., Mt. Pleasant, 1987—; past mem. Hispanic adv. bd. dept. journalism Mich. State U.; past pres. bd. dirs. Mich. AP Editl. Assn.; past bd. dirs. Mid Am. Press Inst. Bd. dirs. Salvation Army, Saginaw, 1986—, St. Charles (Mich.) Cmty. Schs. Found., 1994—, Westlund Child Guidance Clinic, 1995-99, Saginaw Bay Symphony, 1996—; mem. Leadership Saginaw Steering Bd.; mem. steering com. Bridge Ctr. Racial Harmony. Mem.: Nat. Assn. Hispanic Journalists, Soc. Profl. Journalists, Am. Soc. Newspaper Editors, Saginaw Country Club. Avocations: gardening, horses. Office: Saginaw News 203 S Washington Ave Saginaw MI 48607-1283

CHAFFEE, PAUL DAVID, city official; b. Kansas City, Mo., Mar. 8, 1953; m. Marsha R. Isaacson; children: Ashley, Jennifer. BS in Econs., Kans. State U., 1975, M Regional and Cmty. Planning, 1982. Planning intern Wichita (Kans.) Urban Renewal Agy., 1976; coord. human resources City of Dodge City, Kans., 1977-78, asst. planner, 1978-86, dir. planning, 1986-88; city planner City of Shawnee, Kans., 1988-94, dir. planning, 1994—. Mem. hist. adv. bd. Johnson County Mus., Shawnee, 1993—; mem. growth tech. forecast com. Mid-Am. Regional Coun., Kansas City, Mo., 1994—; mem. peripheral transp. com. Johnson County, Olathe, 1997—. Bd. dirs. Dodge City Area Arts Coun., 1978-81; bd. edn. United Sch. Dist. 443, Dodge City, 1985-88. Mem. Am. Inst. Cert. Planners, Am. Planning Assn. Lutheran. Home: 14409 W 72nd St Shawnee Mission KS 66216 Office: City of Shawnee 11110 Johnson Dr Shawnee KS 66203-2799

CHAFFIN, CEAN, producer; Prodr.: (films, with Steve Golia) The Game, 1997, Fight Club, 1999. Recipient Grammy award Best Music Video-Short Form, 1995, 1996. Office: Anonymous Content 8522 National Blvd Ste 101 Culver City CA 90232-2454

CHAFFIN, TOM, writer; b. Atlanta, Nov. 21, 1952; s. James T. Sr. and Martha B. Chaffin; m. Lena Margareta Larsson, Aug. 13, 1988. BA in English, Ga. State U., 1977; MA in Am. Civilization, NYU, 1982; PhD in U.S. History, Emory U., 1995. Rschr. Esquire Mag., N.Y.C., 1980-81; freelance mag. San Francisco and Paris, 1981-85; dir. Emory Oral History Project/Emory U., 1996—; lectr. Emory U., 2001—. Vis. lectr. U. Ga., 2000-01; corr. Pacific News Svc., San Francisco, 1983-86. Author: Fatal Glory: Narciso López and the First Clandestine U.S. War Against Cuba, 1996, Pathfinder: John Charles Frémont and the Course of American Empire, 2002; contbr. articles to profl. jours., mags. and newspapers. Fellow Huntington Libr., Emory U. Democrat. Avocations: hiking, birdwatching. Office: Dept History Emory U Atlanta GA 30322

CHAFFIN, VERNER FRANKLIN, lawyer, educator; b. Martin, Ga., Sept. 26, 1918; s. Emory Franklin and Mabel Lea (Verner) C.; m. Corinne Ethel Tison, July 17, 1943; children— Ethel, Verner Franklin, Mary Davis, John Edwards. AB, U. Ga., LLB, 1942; JSD, Yale, 1961. Bar: Ga. bar 1942, Ala. bar 1953, U.S. Supreme Ct. bar 1965. Atty. Dept. Justice, 1946-47; mem. faculty U. Ala., 1947—57, U. Ga., Athens, 1957—, prof. law, 1954-69, Fuller E. Callaway prof., 1969—89, Fuller E. Callaway prof. emeritus, 1989—; mem. nat. labor panel Am. Arbitration Assn., 1957—89, mem. pub. employment disputes settlement panel, 1969—89; mem. panel arbitrators Fed. Mediation and Conciliation Service, 1973—89. Trustee Inst. Continuing Legal Edn. Ga., 1969-76 Author: Georgia Annotations to the Restatement (Second) Trusts, 1970, Studies in the Georgia Law of Decedents' Estates and Future Interests, 1979, The Rule Against Perpetuities in Georgia, 1984; Contbr. numerous articles to legal jours. Mem. permanent jud. commn. Gen. Assembly, Presbyn. Ch. U.S.A., 1972-75; elder 1st Presbyn. Ch., Athens, 1966-71, 74-79, 96-98; pres. Athens chpt. Am. Cancer Soc., 1968-69, Athens Community Concert Assn., 1966-67; with USN; Lt. Cmdr. USNR. Sterling fellow Yale, 1950-51 Fellow Am. Coll. Trust & Estate Council (life), Lawyers Found. GA (life); mem. Am. Law Inst., ABA, Internat. Acad. Law and Sci.,Pres. Athens Historical Soc., Western Circuit, Ga., Am. bar assns., Ga. Hist. Soc., Athens-Clarke Heritage Found., Blue Key, Sphinx, Order of Coif, Phi Beta Kappa, Phi Kappa Phi, Phi Delta Phi, Omicron Delta Kappa, Sigma Nu. Clubs: Athens City, Yale club Ga. Home: 510 Riverview Rd Athens GA 30606-4830 Office: University of Georgia Law School Athens GA 30602

CHAFKIN, RITA M. physician, dermatologist; b. N.Y.C., Apr. 11, 1929; d. Joseph and Dora (Winslow) Melnick; m. Samuel Chafkin, June 29, 1952; children: Elise Ceil Perkins, Marc David Chafkin (dec.). BA, NYU, 1949; MD, NYU Med. Sch., 1953; cert. in dermatology, NYU Postgrad. Med. Sch., 1957. Diplomate Am. Acad. Dermatology, 1959. Intern in internal medicine Kings County Hosp., Bklyn., 1953-54; dermatology resident Bellevue Hosp., N.Y.C., 1954-55; postgrad. trainee NYU Postgrad. Med. Sch., 1955-56, fellow in dermatology, 1956-57; precepteeship with Dr. Marion Sulzberger; pvt. practice dermatology, 1958-94; assoc. clin. prof. dermatology U. Calif., Davis, 1975-97. Clinic dir. dermatology Stanislavs County Med. Ctr., Modesto, 1958-97. Artist in mixed media. Bd. dirs. Stanislaus County Med. Ctr. Found., 1982-97, pres. 1984-85. Recipient Tchr. of the Yr. award Stanislaus County Med. Ctr., Modesto, 1988, Founder's Dinner honoree, 1992. Fellow Am. Acad. Dermatology; mem. AMA, Calif. Med. Soc., San Francisco Dermatology Soc., Stanislaus County Med. Soc. (pres. 1983-84), Pacific Dermatology Assn. (fin. com. 1959—). Jewish.

CHAGALL, DAVID, journalist, writer; b. Phila., Nov. 22, 1930; s. Harry and Ida (Coopersmith) C.; m. Juneau Joan Alsin, Nov. 15, 1957. Student, Swarthmore Center Coll., 1948-49; BA, Pa. State U., 1952; postgrad., Sorbonne, U. Paris, 1953-54. Social caseworker State of Pa., Phila., 1955-57; sci. editor Jour. I.E.E., 1959-61; pub. relations staff A.E.I.-Hotpoint Ltd., London, 1961-62; mktg. research assoc. Chilton Co., Phila., 1962-63; mktg. research project dir. Haug Assos., Inc. (Roper Orgn.), Los Angeles, 1964-74; research cons. Haug Assos., 1976-79; investigative reporter for nat. mags., 1975—. Host TV series The Last Hour, 1994—. Author: Diary of a Deaf Mute, 1960, The Century God Slept, 1963, The Spieler for the Holy Spirit, 1972, The New Kingmakers, 1981, The Sunshine Road, 1988, Surviving the Media Jungle, 1996, Target, 2000; contbr.: Television Today, 1981, The Media and Morality, 1999; pub.: Inside Campaigning, 1983; syndicated column, articles, revs., stories and poetry to mags., jours., newspapers; contbg. editor: TV Guide, L.A. Mag.; editor (website): www.lasthour.com, 2002--, www.lasthour.org. Apptd. to Selective Svc. Bd., 1991, apptd. chmn., 1999; bd. dirs. Chosen Prophetic Ministries, 1991. Recipient U. Wis. Poetry prize, 1971; nominee Nat. Book award in fiction, 1972, Pulitzer prize in letters, 1973, Disting Health Journalism award, 1978; Presdl. Achievement award, 1982; Carnegie Trust grantee, 1964 Home: PO Box 85 Agoura Hills CA 91376-0085 E-mail: Dchagall@aol.com.

CHAGANTI, RAJU S. geneticist, educator, researcher; b. Samalkot, Andhra, India, Mar. 12, 1933; came to U.S., 1960. s. Sanyasi Raju and Seetasiromani (Vallury) C.; m. Seeta Ramam Kurada, Aug. 20, 1966; children: Seeta, Sara. BS with honors, Andhra U., 1954, MS, 1955; PhD, Harvard U., 1964. Diplomate Am. Bd. Med. Genetics. Mem. Med. Rsch. Coun. Radiobiology Unit, Harwell, Berks, U.K., 1967-71; rsch. assoc. N.Y. Blood Ctr., N.Y.C., 1971-73, assoc. investigator, 1973-76; asst. prof. Meml. Sloan-Kettering Cancer Ctr., N.Y.C., 1976-83, assoc. prof., 1983-87, prof., 1987—, William E. Snee chair, 1995—. Profl. assoc. N.Y. Hosp., N.Y.C., 1979—; founder, bd. dirs. Cancer Genetics, Inc., Cambridge. Editor: Genetics in Clinical Oncology, 1985; contbr. articles to profl. jours. Recipient research awards NIH, Nat. Cancer Inst., 1979—. Fellow AAAS, Am. Coll. Med. Genetics; mem. Am. Soc. Human Genetics, Harvey Soc. Achievements include research in the genetic basis of cancer development. Home: 325 E 79th St Apt 15C New York NY 10021-0900 Office: Meml Sloan-Kettering Cancer Ctr 1275 York Ave New York NY 10021-6094

CHAGNON, LUCILLE TESSIER, workforce development and literacy specialist; b. Gardner, Mass., June 1, 1936; d. Fred G. Tessier and Alfreda C. (Ross) Noel; m. Richard J. Chagnon, Sept. 16, 1978; children: Daniel, David. BMus, Rivier Coll., Nashua, N.H.; cert. in human resource mgmt. and cmty. devel., Inst. Cultural Affairs, Chgo., 1969; MEd, Boston Coll., 1972. Educator, N.H., 1960-73; internat. cons. Inst. Cultural Affairs, Chgo., 1973-79; staff tng. dir. CO-MHAR, Inc., Phila., 1979-81; pres., owner Chagnon Assocs., Collingswood, N.J., 1981-86; prin. Sacred Heart Sch., Camden, N.J., 1986-87; founder, dir. Lifeline Literacy Project, 1988-94; literacy and developmental learning specialist Rutgers U., Camden, 1989-99; coord. work readiness, Workforce Devel. Inst. Drexel U., Phila., 1999-2000. Adj. grad. faculty dept. counseling psychology Temple U. Sch. Edn., Phila., 1985—90; sr. project staff Right Assocs., Phila., 1982—91, 2001—. Author (with Richard J. Chagnon): The Best is Yet to Be: A Pre-Retirement Program, 1985; author: Easy Reader, Learner, Writer, 1994, Voice Hidden, Voice Heard: A Reading and Writing Anthology, 1998, You, Yes YOU, Can Teach Someone to Read, 2004. Bd. dirs. Camden County Literacy Vols. of Am., 1987—91, Handicapped Advocates for Ind. Living, 1987—; mem. Collingswood (N.J.) Bd. Edn., 1985—89. Mem.: ASCD, Internat. Reading Assn., Internat. Alliance for Learning, Inst. Cultural Affairs, Brain-Based Edn. Network, Nat. Learning Found. (adv. bd. 1997—). Home and Office: 408 River Rd Wilmington DE 19809-2731 Fax: 302-762-0285. E-mail: lifeline248@aol.com.

CHAGULA, PAUL MACHIYA, technology company executive, trade consultant; b. Dar es Salaam, Tanzania, July 16, 1969; s. Wilbert Kumalija and Jane (Ubwe) C.; m. Aug. 1, 1993; 1 child, James M. Student, Westchester Bus. Inst., White Plains, N.Y., 1988-90. Troubleshooting asst., operational mgr. Bloomingdale's Inc., White Plains, 1990-91; pres. PC Courier Svc., Mt. Vernon, N.Y., 1991—; co-founder, v.p. J&P Cleaning Svc., Mt. Vernon, 1994—; founder, chmn., CEO, Tangible Techs. Internat. Inc., Bronx, N.Y., 1997—. Cons. Tanzania C. of C., Dar es Salaam, 1994-96; copy cons. Kinko's Inc., Mt. Kisco, N.Y. Advisor Tanzania Am. Assocs., N.Y.C., 1992-93, Chama Cha Mapinduzi, revolutionary party, Dar es Salaam, 1994, Govt. of Tanzania, N.Y.C., 1996. Avocations: consulting, advising, writing. Home: 56 Sheridan Ave Apt 4C Mount Vernon NY 10552-2525 Office: Apt 4C 56 Sheridan Ave Mount Vernon NY 10552-2525 E-mail: chagula@hotmail.com.

CHAHINE, MOUSTAFA TOUFIC, atmospheric scientist; b. Beirut, Jan. 1, 1935; s. Toufic M. and Hind S. (Tabbara) C.; m. Marina Bandak, Dec. 9, 1960; children: Tony T., Steve S. BS, U. Wash., 1956, MS, 1957; PhD, U. Calif., Berkeley, 1960. With Jet Propulsion Lab., Calif. Inst. Tech., Pasadena, 1960—, mgr. planetary atmospheres sect., 1975—, sr. research scientist, mgr. earth and space scis. div., 1978-84, chief scientist, 1984—2001. Vis. scientist MIT, 1969-70; vis. prof. Am. U., Beirut, 1971-72; regent's lectr. UCLA, 1989-90; mem. NASA Space and Earth Sci. Adv. Com., 1982-85; mem. climate rsch. com. Nat. Acad. Scis., 1985-88, bd. dirs. atmospheric scis. and climate, 1988—; chmn. sci. steering group Global Energy and Water Cycle Experiment World Meteorol. Orgn., 1988-99; cons. U.S. Navy, 1972-76 Contbr. articles to profl. jours. Recipient medal for exceptional sci. achievements NASA, 1969, NASA Outstanding Leadership medal, 1984, William T. Pecora award, 1989, Jule G. Charney award, 1991, Losey Atmospheric Scis. award AIAA, 1993, NASA Exceptional Achievement medal, 2000, William Nordberg medal Com. on Space Rsch./COSPAR, 2002. Fellow AAAS, Am. Geophys. Union, Am. Phys. Soc., Royal Soc., Am. Meteorol. Soc.; mem. Internat. Acad. Astronautics, Sigma Xi. Office: 4800 Oak Grove Dr Pasadena CA 91109-8001

CHAHINIAN, A(RAM) PHILIPPE, oncologist; b. Paris, June 21, 1942; came to U.S., 1974; m. Marjorie Ellen; 1 child, Michael J. B., Buffon Coll., Paris, 1960; MD, Paris U., 1969. Diplomate Am. Bd. Internal Medicine, Am. Bd. Med. Oncology. Intern, resident Paris Univ. Hosps., France, 1968-74; fellow noeplastic diseases Mt. Sinai Sch. Medicine, N.Y.C., 1971-76, asst. prof., 1976-79, assoc. prof., 1980-88; prof. clin. medicine Coll. Physicians and Surgeons Columbia U., N.Y.C., 1990-92; prof. dept. medicine Mt. Sinai Sch. Medicine, N.Y.C., 1995—, prof., 1995—. Adj. prof. dept. neoplastic diseases Mt. Sinai Sch. Medicine, N.Y.C., 1992-95. Author: Lung Cancer, 1976; author (with others) of books; contbr. articles to profl. jours. Lt. Med. Corps, French Army, 1970. Rsch. grantee Nat. Cancer Inst., 1984. Fellow Am. Coll. Physicians; mem. Am. Soc. Clin. Oncology, Am. Assn. Cancer Rsch., Am. Fedn. Clin. Rsch., N.Y. Acad. Scis. Achievements include research in treatment of various cancers including lung cancer, asbestos related cancers, and mesothelioma by transplantation of human cancers into mice. Office: Mt Sinai Sch of Medicine Dept NeoPlastic 1 Gustave L Levy Pl New York NY 10029-6500

CHAI, TOBY C. urologic surgeon, research scientist; b. Taipei, Taiwan, Oct. 5, 1964; BA, Johns Hopkins U., 1989; MD, Ind. U., Indpls., 1989. Lic. urology Am. Bd. of Urology. Asst. prof. U. of Md. Sch. of Medicine, Balt., 1997—2002, assoc. prof., 2002—. Recipient Young Investigator award, Soc. for Basic Urologic Rsch., 2001, Basic Rsch. Essay Winner, Soc. for Urodynamics and Female Urology, 2001, Pfizer Internat. Cardura Competitive award, Pfizer Co., 2001, Dornier Rsch. scholarship, Am. Found. for Urologic Diseases, 1995—97; grantee, NIH, 2001, Mentored Clinician-Scientist Career Devel. award, 1996—2001, 2002. Fellow: ACS. Office: U MD Divsn Urology S8D18 22 S Greene St Baltimore MD 21201 Office Fax: 410-328-0595.

CHAI, WINBERG, political science educator; b. Shanghai, Oct. 16, 1932; came to U.S., 1951, naturalized, 1973; s. Ch'u and Mei-en (Tsao) C.; m. Carolyn Everett, Mar. 17, 1966 (dec. 1996); children: Maria May-lee, Jeffrey Tien-yu. Student, Hartwick Coll., 1951-53, LittD, 2002; BA, Wittenberg U., 1955; MA, New Sch. Social Rsch., 1958; PhD, NYU, 1968; DHL, Wittenberg U., 1997; DL, Hartwick Coll., 2002. Lectr. New Sch. Social Rsch., 1957-61; vis. asst. prof. Drew U., 1961-62; asst. prof. Fairleigh Dickinson U., 1962-65, U. Redlands, 1965-68, assoc. prof., 1969-73, chmn. dept., 1970-73; prof., chmn. Asian studies CCNY, 1973-79; disting. prof. polit. sci., v.p. acad. affairs, spl. asst. to pres. U. S.D., Vermillion, 1979-82; prof. polit. sci., dir. internat. programs U. Wyo., Laramie, 1988—. Hmn. Third World Conf. Found., Inc., Chgo., 1982—; pres. Wang Yu-fa Found., Taiwan, 1989—. Author: (with Ch'u Chai) The Story of Chinese Philosophy, 1961, The Changing Society of China, 1962, rev. edit., 1969, The New Politics of Communist China, 1972, The Search for a New China, 1975; editor: Essential Works of Chinese Communism, 1969, (with James C. Hsiung) Asia in the U.S. Foreign Policy, 1981, (with James C. Hsiung) U.S. Asian Relations: The National Security Paradox, 1983, (with Carolyn Chai) Beyond China's Crisis, 1989, In Search of Peace in the Middle East, 1991, (with Cal Clark) Political Stability and Economic Growth, 1994, China Mainland and Taiwan, 1994, revised edit. 1996, Hong Kong Under China, 1998; co-translator: (with Ch'u Chai) A Treasury of Chinese Literature, 1965; co-author (with May-Lee-Chai) The Girl from Purple Mountain, 2001; contbg. editor: Encyclopedia of Modern Asia, 2003. Haynes Found. fellow, 1967, 68; Ford Found. humanities grantee, 1968, 69, Pacific Cultural Found. grantee, 1978, 86, NSF grantee, 1970, Hubert Eaton Meml. Fund grantee, 1972-73, Field Found. grantee, 1973, 75, Henry Luce Found. grantee, 1978, 80, S.D. Humanities Com. grantee, 1980, Pacific Culture Fund grantee, 1987, 90-91. Mem. AAAS, AAUP, NAACP, Am. Polit. Sci. Assn., Am. Assn. Chinese Studies (pres.1978 80), N.Y. Acad. Scis., Internat. Studies Assn. Democrat. Home: 1071 Granito Dr Laramie WY 82072-5045 Office: PO Box 4098 Laramie WY 82071-4098 E-mail: WinbergChai@aol.com. *Born in China and educated in the United States, I feel privileged to have experienced two rich cultures. My goals include promoting better understanding of all cultures and peoples.*

CHAI, XIN-SHENG, research scientist; s. Junhai Chai and Qiongliang Mao; m. Qiuping Zhang, Sept. 25, 1958; 1 child, Chengran. PhD, Royal Inst. of Tech., Stockholm, 1996. Lic. engr. Shanghai, 1982. Sr. scientist Inst. Paper and Tech. Ga. Inst. Tech., Atlanta, 1996—. Scientist. Recipient Best Rsch. Paper award, TAPPI, 1997. Achievements include research in Analytical and environmental chemistry.

CHAIDARUN, SUSHELA SONGTANIN, endocrinologist, researcher; b. Sawankaloke, Sukhothai, Thailand, Apr. 13, 1963; arrived in U.S., 1994; d. Kittisak and Kanitha Songtanin; m. Sumet Chaidarun; children: Arthur Nachapon, Leo Pirapon, Tricia Tanyawan. MD, Chulalongkorn U., Bangkok, 1988; PhD, U. Birmingham, Eng., 1994; postgrad., Harvard U., 1994—98. Bd. certified internal medicine Am. Bd. Internat. Medicine. Postdoctoral rsch. fellow Mass. Gen. Hosp./ Harvard Med. Sch., Boston, 1994—98; med. resident internal medicine St. Vincent Hosp./Worcester Med. Ctr., U Mass. Med. Sch., Worcester, 1998—2001; endocrine clin. fellow U. Va. Health Sys., Charlottesville, 2001—03. Rsch. fellow /assoc. Harvard Med. Sch., Boston, 1994—98. Contbr. articles to profl. jours. Grantee Travel grant, Am. Endocrine Soc./Women in Endocrinology, 1996. Mem.: AMA, ACP (Med. Jeopardy Championship award Mass. chpt. 2000), Am. Endocrine Soc. Avocations: travel, swimming, cooking, piano, music. Office: Univ Va Health Sys Dept Medicine PO Box 801408 450 Ray C Hunt Dr Charlottesville VA 22908 Office Fax: 434-243-9143. Personal E-mail: schaidarun@hotmail.com. Business E-Mail: sc7vj@virginia.edu.

CHAIFETZ, DAVID HARVEY, lawyer; b. Worcester, Mass., Nov. 6, 1942; s. Harry and Gertrude (Katz) C.; m. Edith Jakubs; children: Rosalyn, Pamela, Matthew. BS in Bus. Adminstrn., Clark U., 1965; JD, Boston Coll., 1968. Bar: Mich. 1968, U.S. Dist. Ct. (ea. dist.) Mich. 1968, U.S. Supreme Ct., 1995. Staff atty. Chrysler Corp., Highland Park, Mich., 1968-75; div. atty. Union Carbide Corp., N.Y.C., 1975-77, sr. div. atty., 1978-81, group counsel Danbury, Conn., 1981-85, asst. gen. counsel, 1985-92; gen. counsel Union Carbide Indsl. Gases Inc., Danbury, 1988-92; v.p., gen. counsel, sec. Praxair, Inc., Danbury, 1992—; mem. Town of Fairfield (Conn.) Police and Fire Retirement Bd., 2000—. Bd. dirs. Conn. Legal Svcs., Middlebury, 1991-92, 97—, Conn. Yankee Coun. Trustee U.S. China Legal Coop. Fund, 1998—2002. Mem. ABA, Conn. Bus. and Industry Assn. (bd. dirs. 1999—), Corporate Bar Assn. (chmn. pro bono com. 1990-93), Westchester-Fairfield Corp. Counsel Assn. (pres. 1988-89, bd. dirs. 1984-90), Coun. of Chief Legal Officers (conf. bd. 1997—). Avocations: golf, travel. Office: Praxair Inc # MI-535 39 Old Ridgebury Rd # Mi-535 Danbury CT 06810-5103

CHAIKEN, BERNARD HENRY, internist, gastroenterologist; b. Bklyn., Oct. 14, 1927; s. Max and Esther (Golland) C.; m. Mildred Gilbert, Dec. 5, 1950; children: Barry Glenn, Caryl Joy Gordon. Student, NYU, 1944-45; MD, U. Tex., Dallas, 1949. Diplomate Am. Bd. Internal Medicine, subspecialty Bd. Gastroenterology. Intern Boston City Hosp., 1949-50; resident physician Cushing VA Hosp., Framingham, Mass., 1950-51, Phila. VA Hosp., 1953-54; staff physician VA Hosp. Dallas, 1954-55, VA Hosp., East Orange, N.J., 1955-56; attending physician Overlook Hosp., Summit, N.J., 1956—, St. Barnabas Med. Ctr., Livingston, N.J., 1956—. Vis. fellow Hosp. of U. Pa., Phila., 1954; clin. instr. Southwestern Med. Sch., U. Tex., Dallas, 1954-55; clin. asst. prof. medicine Seton Hall Coll. Medicine, Jersey City, 1956-58. Contbr. articles to med. jours. Capt. U.S. Army M.C., 1951-53. Fellow ACP, Am. Coll. Gastroenterology (Best Clin. Vignette Paper and Poster Presentation 1995); mem. Am. Soc. Internal Medicine, Am. Gastroenterol. Assn., Med. Soc. N.J., N.J. Gastroenterol. Soc. (pres. 1964-65). Avocation: collecting early american folk art. Home: 12 Taylor Rd Short Hills NJ 07078-2226 Office: 58 Chatham Rd Short Hills NJ 07078-2321

CHAIKIN, MARY CARRIE, psychology librarian; b. Balt., Oct. 8, 1947; d. John Jr. and Mary (Fratta) Moscato; m. Philip Chaikin, Dec. 29, 1974; 1 child, Carrie Marie. BA, U. Balt., 1969; MLS, Rutgers U., 1981. Libr. Balt. City Hosp. Med. Libr., 1966-74; interlibr. loan tech. U. Ky. Med. Libr., Lexington, 1974-75; catalog libr. Ortho Pharms., Raritan, N.J., 1980-81; asst. psychiat. libr. Carrier Found., Belle Meade, N.J., 1981-83; asst. plasma physics libr. Princeton U., 1983-84, psychology libr., 1984—. Mem. Spl. Librs. Assn. (career guidance chair Princeton Trenton chpt. 1990-91, 92-93), Assn. Mental Health Librs. Home: 121 Wilshire Dr Belle Mead NJ 08502-5539 Office: Princeton U Psychology Libr Green Hall Princeton NJ 08540

CHAIKLIN, HARRIS, retired social work educator; b. Bridgeport, Conn., June 27, 1926; s. David and Victoria (Spector) C.; m. Sharon Udren, June 5, 1955; children: Seth, Matthew, Martha, Nina. BA with distinction, U. Conn., Storrs, 1950; MA in Sociology, U. Conn., 1952; MS in Social Work, U. Wis., 1953; postgrad. in Sociology, NYU, 1953-55; PhD, Yale U., 1961. Lic. social worker, Md., Acad. Cert. Social Workers. Psychiat. social worker, caseworker Jewish Bd. of Guardians, N.Y.C., 1953-56; caseworker Jewish Family Svc., New Haven, Conn., 1958-59; instr. sociology U. Conn., 1959-60; asst. prof. Smith Coll., Northampton, Mass., 1960-62, U. Md., Balt., 1962-64, assoc. prof., 1964-71, prof., 1971-97, asst. dean Informatics, 1990-97, prof. emeritus, 1998; caseworker Jewish Family and Children's Svc., Balt., 1963-76; pvt. practice, 1977—. Caseworker John F. Kennedy Inst. Family Ctr., 1984-86; clin. assoc. prof. psychiatry U. Md. Med. Sch., 1974—; assoc. John F. Kennedy Inst. for Handicapped Children; vis. prof. Haifa U., 1976-77, 80-81, 86-87, Morgan State U., 1977-78; tchr. U. Calif, Berkeley, U. Conn. Sch. Social Work, Hartford Coll., U. Mass., U. Vt., others. Editor: Marian Chace: Her Papers, 1975, Inventory of Research, 1963-65; (with others) Aides for Research Teachers: I-IV, 1969; (with Ralph Segalman) Symbolic Interaction and Social Welfare, 1979; contbr. articles to profl. jours.; mem. editl. bds. Recipient Harry Greenstein award Balt. Associated Jewish Charities, 1986, Md. Higher Edn. Assn. award of Merit, 1991; named Commonwealth Fund fellow, Yale U., 1956-58, Sr. Fulbright Hays lectr., Haifa U., 1976-77. Mem. NASW (Social Worker of Yr., Md. 1973, Social Work Pioneer 2001), Am. Sociol. Assn., Am. Orthopsychiat. Assn., Coun. on Social Work Edn. Home: 5173 Phantom Ct Columbia MD 21044-1318 E-mail: hchaikli@comcast.net., hchaikli@erols.com.

CHAIM, LINDA SUSAN, special education administrator; b. Detroit, May 20, 1950; d. Donald J. and Shirley R. (Dennis) McCarthy; 1 child, Jeremy Chaim. B Edn. and Psychology, Concordia U., Montreal, Que., Can., 1978; MEd in Psychology, McGill U., 1992; cert. in Autism Spectium Disorders, U. Vt. Adolescent clin. tchr., team leader McGill-Montreal Children's Hosp. Learning Ctr., 1976—; clin. tchr., cons. team leader Lansdowne Ctr., Montreal, 1982—; dir. student svcs. Vanguard Intercultural Sch., Montreal, 1986—; dir. student support svcs. Franklin West Supervisory Union, Fairfax, Vt., 1994-96; spl. edn. adminstr. Franklin N.W. Supervisory Union, 1996—. Mem. adv. bd. for behaviorally challenged children Vt. Dept. Edn., Montpelier, 1995—96; dir., founder, advisor camp for spl. needs Camp Sitara, Montreal; cons., cook Camp Tournesol, Montreal; mem. Vt. Rural Autism project U. Vt., Montpelier, 1997—; mem. exec. bd. Northwestern Counselling and Support Svcs., 2002. Mem. rev. panel devel. disabilities State of Vt. Human Rights Commn., 2002—; active Scouts Can., 1989—93; mem. exec. bd. dirs. Vt. Parents and Info. Ctr., 1997—. Recipient Spl. Edn. Adminstr. of Yr., State of Vt., 2000—01, Cmty. Partnership award on behalf of children with devel. disabilities Franklin and Grand Isle County, State Autism Task Force, 2000—01. Mem. Coun. for Exceptional Children, Assn. Mediators Families Que., Assn. Camps Que. Avocations: cooking for large groups, camping, writing children's books. Office: Franklin NW Supervisory 21 Church St Swanton VT 05488-1434

CHAIN, BOBBY LEE, electrical contractor, former mayor; b. Hattiesburg, Miss., Sept. 19, 1929; s. Zollie Lee and Grace (Sellers) C.; ; m. Betty Sue Green, June 30, 1967; children: Robin Ann, Laura Grace, Bobby Lee, John Webster. BS, U. So. Miss., Hattiesburg, 1957; DBA (hon.), William Carey Coll., Hattiesburg, 1983. Chief electrician Miss. Power & Light Co., Natchez, 1950-53; asst. to gen. supt. atomic energy plant Allegany Electric Co., Oak Ridge, 1954-55; owner, chmn. bd. Chain Electric Co., Hattiesburg, 1955, Chain Lighting & Appliance Co., Hattiesburg, 1960; owner, pres. Chainco, Inc., oil properties, Hattiesburg, 1974—. Adv. dir. Deposit Guaranty Nat. Bank, Jackson, 1965-2000, Am. South Bank, 2000-01; mem. Interstate Oil Compact Commn., 1972—; mem. nat. adv. coun. SBA, 1966-67; bd. dirs. Miss. Econ. Coun., 1991-93; mayor city of Hattiesburg, 1980-85. Past mem., past pres. Miss. Trustees Instns. Higher Learning; past mem. and pres. So. Regional Edn. Bd., Mississippians for Quality Edn.; past chmn. Commn. on Efficiency in Govt., Miss. Econ. Coun.; mem. Miss. State Workforce Devel. Coun.; chmn. Pearl River County Dist. Workforce Coun.; past bd. dirs. Pub. Edn. Forum of Miss., chmn. Advanced Tech. Ctr., Pearl River Coll.; mem. commissioning com. USS John C. Stennis CVN-74 Aircraft Carrier, 1995; bd. dirs. Armed Forces Mus., Camp Shelloy, Miss. With U.S. Army, 1950—51, Korea. Recipient Disting. Svc. award U. So. Miss., 1976, Hub award, 1979, Continuous Outstanding Svc. award, 1980, Liberty Bell award Forrest County Bar Assn., 1980, Svc. to Edn. award Phi Delta Kappa, 1980, Disting. Citizen award Pine Burr Area Coun. Boy Scouts Am., 1995; named to U. So. Miss., Miss. Bus. Hall of Fame, 1994; Bobby L. Chain Tech. Ctr. named in his honor; Bobby L. Chain Hattiesburg Mcpl. Airport named in his honor; Paul Harris fellow Rotary Internat., 1990. Mem. Newcomen Soc. N.Am., U. So. Miss. Alumni Assn. (Outstanding Svc. award 1972, Sales and Mktg. Man of Yr. award 1981), Hattiesburg C. of C. (past dir.), Miss. Bus. Roundtable, Kiwanis, Hattiesburg Country Club (past pres.), U. So. Miss. Century Club, Shriners, Omicron Delta Kappa, Beta Gamma Sigma. Baptist. Home: 312 6th Ave Hattiesburg MS 39401-4294 Office: PO Box 2058 Hattiesburg MS 39403-2058 E-mail: blc@bchain.com.

CHAIRES, ROBERT HAROLD, JR., law educator; b. South Bend, Ind., July 22, 1948; s. Robert Harold and Betty Teresa (Cross) Chaires; children: Nicole, William. BS, Loyola U., Chgo., 1974; MCJ, U. Colo., 1978, PhD, 1995; JD, U. Denver, 1982. Bar: Colo. 1983, U.S. Dist. Ct. Colo. 1983. Officer Denver Police Dept., 1975—81; ptnr. Lentz & Chaires, Denver, 1983—90; asst. prof. U. Nev., Reno, 1991—. Legal access atty. Colo. Dept. Corrections, 1988—91; adj. prof. Met. State Coll., Denver, 1986—. Author: (column) Streets, 1983—85; contbr. ; co-editor: Star Trek: Visions of Law and Justice. Mem. The Brotherhood, Denver, 1975—. With U.S. Army, 1965—69. Recipient 11 commendation awards, Denver Police Dept. Mem.: ATLA, ABA, Police Involved in Grad. Studies (charter), Soc. Colo. Attys. in Law Enforcement (charter), Am. Soc. Pub. Adminstrn., Am. Motorcyclist Assn., U.S. Parachute Assn. (jumpmaster award). Office: U Nev Dept Criminal Justice 214 Reno NV 89557-0001

CHAIRSELL, CHRISTINE, academic administrator; children: T., Tyler. EdD, MA in polit. sci., BA in polit. sci., U. Nev. Las Vegas. Acting pres. Nev. State Coll., 2002; assoc. vice chancellor U. & CC Sys. Nev.; assoc. vice pres. Computing Svc.; dean spl. programs CC So. Nev.; dir. environ. edn. U. Nev. Las

Vegas, faculty polit. sci. dept. Pres. Aqua Vision, 1992—94; mem. Leadership Las Vegas Class, 1993. Recipient women of achievement edn., Las Vegas Chamber Commerce, 1993. Office: NV State Coll 1125 Dawson Ave Henderson NV 89015

CHAISON, GARY N. labor relations educator, researcher; b. Bklyn., Oct. 21, 1943; s. Alfred A. Chaison, B. Chaison Ada; m. Joanne D. Danaher. BA, City Coll. N.Y., 1965, MBA, 1966; PhD, SUNY, Buffalo., 1972. Asst. to assoc. prof. U. New Brunswick, Fredericton, Canada, 1972—81; prof. Clark U., Worcester, Mass., 1981—. Author: When Unions Merge, 1986, Union Mergers in Hard Times, 1996, Unions and Legitimacy, 2002. Grantee Rsch. grant, Can. Dept. Labor, 1977, 1979, 1983, Can. Coun., 1975—77; scholar, Can. Dept. Labor, 1975. Mem.: Acad. Mgmt., Can. Indsl. Rels. Assn., Internat. Indsl. Rels. Assn., Indsl. Rels. Rsch. Assn. Jewish. Avocations: photography, cooking, sailing. Office: Clark Univ 950 Main St Worcester MA 01610

CHAISSON, ERIC JOSEPH, astrophysicist, science administrator, educator; b. Lowell, Mass., Oct. 26, 1946; m. Lola Judith Eachus; children: Megan Lyra, Paul Cygnus, Bridget Aquila. BS cum laude, U. Mass., Lowell, 1968; AM, Harvard U., 1969, PhD, 1972. NAS/NRC post-doctoral fellow Smithsonian Astrophys. Observatory, 1972-74; rsch. assoc. Harvard Coll. Observatory, 1972-74; staff mem. Harvard-Smithsonian Ctr. for Astrophysics, 1974-82; asst. prof. Harvard U., 1974-79, assoc. prof., 1979-82; prof. of astronomy and physics Haverford Coll., 1982-86; sr. rsch. physicist MIT Lincoln Lab., 1986-87; sr. scientist, dir. ednl. programs Space Telescope Sci. Inst., Balt., 1987-92; adj. prof. physics and astronomy Johns Hopkins U., 1987-92; assoc. dir. Johns Hopkins U. Space Grant Coll., 1987-92; dir. Wright Ctr. for Sci. Edn., Tufts U., Medford, Mass., 1992—; prof. physics and astronomy, prof. edn. Tufts U., Medford, 1992—; co-dir. MIT Space Grant Consortium, 1992—. Non-resident tutor Mather House Harvard Coll., 1979-82, Quincy House Harvard Coll., 1986-87; assoc. Harvard Coll. Observatory, 1986—; Shapley vis. prof., Amer. Astron. Soc., 1979-83; adj. prof. Wellesley Coll., 1986-87; mem. sci. adv. com. Hayden Planetarium, Boston Mus. Sci., 1975-82; bd. overseers Boston Mus. Sci., 2001—; mem. com. on acad. studies Harvard Astronomy Dept., 1975-82, chmn., 1978-82; mem. com. on pub. edn. Harvard-Smithsonian Ctr. for Astrophysics, chmn., 1978-82; mem. users' com. Nat. Radio Astronomy Observatory, 1978-81; mem. sci. working group on extra-terrestrial intelligence NASA, 1979-90; mem. Bowdoin Prize com. Harvard U., 1979-82; mem. panel NAS, 1988-90; mem. adv. com. NSF, 1989; nat. lectr. Phi Beta Kappa, 1995-96; lectr. in field. Author: Cosmic Dawn: The Origins of Matter and Life, 1981 (Phi Beta Kappa award 1981, Am. Inst. Physics-U.S. Steel Found. award 1981, Nat. Book award finalist 1982), La Relativita, 1983, The Life Era: Cosmic Selection and Conscious Evolution, 1987, Relatively Speaking: Black Holes, Relativity and the Fate of the Universe, 1988, Universe: An Evolutionary Approach to Astronomy, 1988, (with Steve McMillan) Astronomy Today, 1993, 96, 99, 2002, (with George B. Field) The Invisible Universe: Probing the Frontiers of Astrophysics, 1985, The Hubble Wars: Astrophysics Meets Astropolitics in the Two-Billion Struggle Over the Hubble Space Telescope, 1994 (Am. Inst. Physics award 1995), (with Steve McMillan) Astronomy: A Beginner's Guide to the Universe, 1995, 98, 2001, (with T. Kim) The 13th Labor: Improving Science Education, 1999, Cosmic Evolution: The Rise of Complexity in Nature, 2001; mem. editl. bd. Zygon: The Jour. Religion and Sci., 1982—; bd. editors World Futures: The Jour. Gen. Evolution, 1986—; contbg. editor Air and Space Mag.; sci. advisor PBS "Search for Solutions"; co-writer PBS "Starfinder"; co-writer (IMAX movie) Cosmic Voyage, 1992-94. Bd. dirs. Found. for the Future, 1997—; mem. bd. overseers Boston Mus. Sci., 2001—. Capt. U.S. Air Force, 1969-73. Rsch. fellow Alfred P. Sloan Found., 1976-79; recipient Bok prize Harvard U., 1977, Smith-Weld prize, Harvard U., 1978, Hubble Space Telescope Project cert. Merit NASA, 1993. Mem. AAAS, Am. Inst. Physics (com. on pub. edn. and info. 1981-83, book award 1981, 95), Am. Astron. Soc. (edn. adv. bd. 1985-89, Harlow Shapley vis. prof. 1979-83), Am. Assn. Physics Tchrs., Internat. Astron. Union, Internat. Union Radio Sci., Fedn. Am. Scientists, Authors Guild, Authors League of Am., Emerson Soc., Thoreau Soc. Achievements include research on the origins and evolution of material systems throughout the universe. Home: 77 Walden St Concord MA 01742-2508 Office: Tufts U Wright Ctr for Sci Edn 4 Colby St Medford MA 02155-6013 E-mail: eric.chaisson@tufts.edu.

CHAIT, ANDREA MELINDA, school psychologist; b. Buffalo, May 7, 1970; d. Marvin and Rochelle (Benatovich) C. BS in Health Edn., Ithaca (N.Y.) Coll., 1992; MEd in Spl. Edn., U. Fla., 1995, MA in Edn., 2001, PhD in Sch. Psychology, 2002. Nat. cert. sch. psychologist. Substitute tchr. Cortland (N.Y.) H.S., 1992; tchrs. aid, substitute Stanley G. Falk, Cheektowaga, N.Y., 1993; pvt. spl. edn. tutor Buffalo and Gainesville, 1992—99; behavioral disorders tchr. Paul D. West Middle Sch., East Point, Ga., 1995-96; chair discipline com. spl. edn. dept. Paul P. West Middle Sch., East Point, Ga., 1995—; grad. tchg. asst. U. Fla., 1998-99; sch. psychologist internal sub. Browar Co. Pub. Schs., 2001—02. Adj. mem. faculty Santa Fe C.C., 2000—; clin. coord. LEAP program Kennedy Krieger Inst., 2002—. Vol. Task Force for Battered Women, Ithaca, 1991, Human Rights Orgn., Gainesville, 1993-94. Mem. APA, Nat. Assn. Sch. Psychologists, Pi Lambda Theta, Kappa Delta Pi, Phi Kappa Phi. Jewish. Avocations: reading, drawing, game development. Home: 1600 Trebor Ct Lutherville MD 21093

CHAIT, ARNOLD, retired radiologist; b. N.Y.C., Jan. 20, 1930; s. Irving and Tillie (Newman) C.; m. Joan Lois Oppenheim, Mar. 14, 1965; children: Andrea, Elizabeth, Caroline. BA, NYU, 1951; MD, U. Utrecht, Netherlands, 1957; MA (hon.), U. Pa., 1971. Diplomate: Am. Bd. Radiology. Intern Kings County Hosp., Bklyn., 1958; resident in pathology Manhattan Vets. Hosp., N.Y.C., 1959; radiology Kings County Hosp., 1959-62; instr. radiology SUNY, Bklyn., 1962-64, asst. prof. radiology, 1964-67, assoc. prof., 1967; asst. prof. radiology U. Pa., Phila., 1967-70, assoc. prof., 1970-74, prof., 1974-76, clin. prof., 1976-98; chief vascular radiology Hosp. U. Pa., 1969-76, dir. dept. radiology Grad. Hosp., 1976-88, pres. med. staff, 1981-83; prof. radiology Allegheny U. of the Health Scis., 1997-99. Cons. radiology Bklyn. VA Hosp., 1962-67, Phila. VA Hosp., 1969-76, Phila. Naval Hosp., 1975-76 Contbr. articles to profl. jours. Fellow Coll. Physicians Phila., Am. Coll. Radiology; mem. Pa., Phila County med. socs., Am., Roentgen Ray Soc., Phila. Roentgen Ray Soc. (pres. 1983-84), Radiol. Soc. N. Am., N.Y. Roentgen Soc., AAAS, Assn. U. Radiologists, Soc. Cardiovascular Radiology Am. Heart Assn. (council on cardiovascular radiology), Soc. Uroradiology, Soc. Cardiovascular and Interventional Radiology. Home: 835 Chauncey Rd Narberth PA 19072-1303 E-mail: achait2000@yahoo.com.

CHAIT, FAY KLEIN, health administrator; b. Chgo., Jan. 12, 1929; d. Victor and Rose (Begun) Magid; m. Jerome G. Klein, June 27, 1948 (div. 1970); children: Leslie Susan Janik, Debra Lynne Maslov; m. Manuel Chait, Aug. 28, 1994. BA in English, UCLA, 1961; MA in Pub. Adminstrn., U. So. Calif., 1971. Cert. health adminstrn. Supr. social workers L.A. County, 1961-65; program specialist Econ. and Youth Opportunity Agy., L.A., 1965-69; sr. health planner Model Cities, L.A., 1971-72; dir. prepaid health plan Westland Health Svcs., L.A., 1972-74; exec. dir. Coastal Region Health Consortium, L.A., 1974-76; grants and legis. cons. Jewish Fed. Council of L.A., 1976-79; planning coun. Jewish Fed. Coun. of So. Fla., Palm Beach to Miami, 1979-82; adminstrv. dir. program in kidney diseases Dept. Medicine UCLA, 1982-84; exec. dir. west coast Israel Cancer Rsch. Fund, L.A., 1984-94; cons. to non-profit orgns. Santa Monica, 1994—. Cons. Arthritis Found., L.A., 1984, Bus. Action Ctr., L.A., 1982, Vis. Nurses Assn., L.A., 1982. Charter mem. L.A. County Mus. of Art, Mus. of Contemporary Art; cons. L.A. Mcpl. Art Gallery, 1979; mem. UCLA/Armand Hammer Mus. Fellow U.S. Pub. Health, U. So. Calif., 1970-71. Mem. APHA, UCLA Alumni Assn. (life), U. So. Calif. Alumni Assn. (life).

CHAIT, MAXWELL MANI, physician; b. Linz, Austria, Nov. 7, 1947; came to the U.S., 1953; s. Morris and Eva (Lederman) C.; m. Lynne Robin Milstein C.; children: Alanna Rose, Daniel Lawrence, Michael Paul. BA magna cum laude, U. Utah, Salt Lake City, 1969; BS cum laude, U. Calif., San Francisco, 1969, MD, 1972. Diplomate Am. Bd. Internal Medicine, 1975, Am. Bd. Gastroenterology, 1977; lic. N.Y., Utah. Intern st. medicine U. So. Calif. Med. Ctr., L.A. County, 1972-73; resident in medicine Cornell Coop. Hosps., North Shore U. Hosp., Manhasset, N.Y., 1973-75; fellow GI Cornell Coop. Hosps., Meml. Sloan-Kettering Cancer Ctr., N.Y.C., 1975-77; attending physician White Plains (N.Y.) Hosp., 1977—; asst. attending physician Columbia Presbyn. Med. Ctr., N.Y., 1993—; asst. clin. prof. medicine Coll. Physicians & Surgeons of Columbia U., 1993—. Bd. dirs. Bd. Jewish Edn. Greater N.Y.; bd. trustees Crohn's & Colitis Found., 2000—; lectr. in field. Pres. Westchester Assn. of Hebrew Schs., 1992-94; former mem. bd. trustees Temple Israel of White Plains; coach baseball, softball, basketball Scarsdale Recreation Dept. Fellow Am. Coll. Gastroenterology, Am. Coll. Physicians; mem. Am. Gastroenterological Assn., Am. Soc. Gastrointestinal Endoscopy, N.Y. Acad. Gastroenterology, N.Y. Soc. Gastrointestinal Endoscopy, Westchester Acad. Medicine, Crohn and Colitis Found. of Am. (CMAC com.). Office: Hartsdale Med Group 180 E Hartsdale Ave Hartsdale NY 10530-3544 E-mail: mdgi77@aol.com.

CHAITIN, GILBERT D. humanities educator, researcher; s. Nathan and Sabina (Dauer) Chaitin; m. D. Joy Gellerman; 1 child, Sharon N. AB in Philosophy, Princeton U., 1962, MA in Romance Lang., 1965, PhD, 1969. Prof. Ind. U., Bloomington, 1966—. Vis. prof. U. Bordeaux, France, 1970—71; dir. study abroad Ind.-Purdue U., Strasbourg, France, 1993—94; dir. acad. program Ind.-Mich.-Wis. U., France, 2002—03. Author: The Unhappy Few, 1972, Romantic Revolutions, 1990, Rhetoric and Cultures in Lacan, 1996. Fellow, Mellon Found., 1972, NEH, 1999—2000. Office: Ind Univ 1020 E Kirkwood Ave Bloomington IN 47405 Business E-Mail: chaitin@indiana.edu.

CHAITMAN, HELEN DAVIS, lawyer; b. N.Y.C., July 5, 1941; d. Philip and Miriam (Pfeffer) D.; m. Edmund Chaitman, Feb. 29, 1964 (div. 1978); children: Jennifer, Alison; m. George B. Gelman, Oct. 21, 1979. AB cum laude, Bryn Mawr Coll., 1963; JD, Rutgers U., 1976. Bar: N.J., 1976, N.Y. 1978, U.S. Dist. Ct. N.J. 1976, U.S. Dist. Ct. (so. and ea. dists.) 1978, U.S. Supreme Ct. 1981, Ct. Fed. Claims 2001, U.S. Ct. Appeals (8th cir.) 2002. Assoc. Paul, Weiss, Rifkind, Wharton & Garrison, N.Y.C., 1977-82; ptnr. Wilentz, Goldman & Spitzer, Woodbridge, N.J., 1983-87, Ross & Hardies, Somerset, N.J., 1987-99, Wolf Haldenstein Adler Freeman & Herz LLP, N.Y.C., 1999—2002. Author: The Law of Lender Liability, 1990; contbg. author: Commercial Damages, 1985; editor Emerging Theories of Lender Liability, 1985-87. Mem.: ABA (chmn. comml. fin. svcs. com. 1994—97, sect. bus. law), Pub. Law Inst., Am. Law Inst. (sustaining mem. 1992—2003). Home: The Farm 115 Fairview Rd Frenchtown NJ 08825-3013 Office: Phillips Niza LLP 666 Fifth Ave New York NY 10103-0084 also: 45 Essex St Hackensack NJ 07601 E-mail: hchaitman@phillipsnizer.com.

CHAJET, CLIVE, brand and corporate image consultant; b. London, Feb. 27, 1937; came to U.S., 1950, naturalized, 1964; s. Henry W. and Anne (Kravis) C.; m. Bonnie Sue Loeb, Mar. 20, 1966; children: Lisa Ellen, Lori Menschell. BA, Columbia U., 1959. Acct. exec. Fuller, Smith & Rose, N.Y.C., 1960-63; designer Milprint, N.Y.C., 1963-65; exec. Gould Assocs., N.Y.C., 1965-72; founder Chajet Design Group, N.Y.C., 1972-83; chmn. Lippincott & Margulies, Inc., N.Y.C., 1983-96, Chajet Consultancy, 1997—. Bd. dirs. Triac Cos., Inc., Sr. Bridge Family Co., Inc. Author: Image by Design, 1991, From Corporate Vision to Corporate Reality, 1991, 2d edit., 1997. Trustee Town Sch., N.Y.C., 1980—83; bd. dirs. 92d St. YMHA, 1997—, Jewish Communal Fund, Am. Jewish Congress. Mem. Package Designers Coun. (pres. 1980-82), University Club. Jewish. Home: 1035 Fifth Ave New York NY 10028-0135 Office: Chajet Consultancy LLC 575 Madison Ave Fl 10 New York NY 10022-2511 E-mail: thechaj@aol.com.

CHAKKO, SIMON C. cardiologist, educator; b. Kerala, India, Sept. 30, 1950; came to U.S., 1975; MB, BS, St. John's Med. Coll., Bangalore, India, 1974. Diplomate Am. Bd. Internal Medicine; sub-splty. cardiovasc. diseases. Intern St. Martha's Hosp. St. John's Med. Coll., 1973-74, resident, 1974-75; intern Jersey City (N.J.) Med. Ctr., 1976-77, resident, 1977-78, fellow in cardiology, 1978-79, Temple U. Hosp., Phila., 1979-81, clin. instr., 1979-81; from asst. prof. to assoc. prof. U. Va., Charlottesville, 1981-88; assoc. prof. clin. medicine U. Miami, Fla., 1988-92, assoc. prof. medicine, 1992-98, prof. medicine, 1998—. Assoc. chief cardiology VA Med. Ctr., Salem, Va., 1981-87, chief, 1987-88, chief coronary care unit, Miami, 1988-89, chief non-invasive cardiac labs., 1989-97, cheif cardiology sect., 1997—; attending staff physician divsn. cardiology Jackson Meml. Hosp., Miami, 1988—, U. Miami Hosps. and Clinics, 1988—. Contbr. chpts. to books and articles to profl. jours.; referee reviewer: Am. Heart Jour., Chest, Jour. Am. Coll. Cardiology Clin. Cardiology. Mem. community leadership club U. Miami United Way Campaign, 1989, 90, 91. Recipient Physicians Recognition award AMA, 1982—. Fellow Am. Coll. Cardiology, ACP; mem. Am. Fedn. for Clin. Rsch., AM. Soc. Echocardiography, Am. Heart Assn. Scientific Coun. on Clin. Cardiology. Home: 12641 SW 103 Ct Miami FL 33176-4767 Office: VA Med Ctr 111-A Cardiology Miami FL 33176

CHAKRABARTI, JAI, internist, cardiologist; b. Calcutta, India, 1962; MD, Calcutta Med. Coll., 1985. Cert. in internal medicine and cardiovasc. disease. Intern Med. Coll. Hosps. Calcutta, 1985-86, resident in internal medicine, 1986-87, RK Mission Hosp., Calcutta, 1987-88; med. officer divsn. cardiology Medinova Diagnostic Svcs., Calcutta, 1988-90; rsch. fellow cardiovascular and interventional radiology Brigham & Women's Hosp./Harvard Med. Sch., Boston, 1990-92; resident in internal medicine Boston VA Med. Ctr./Boston U. Sch. Med., 1992-95; fellow in cardiology Baystate Med. Ctr./Tufts U. Sch. Medicine, Springfield, Mass., 1995—; attending cardiologist William W. Backus HOsp., Norwich, Conn., 1999—. Coord. web site Internat. Nuclear Disarmament and Peace Issues, www.mytholysis.com. Contbr. articles to profl. jours. Office: William W Backus Hosp Norwich CT 06360

CHAKRABARTI, SUBRATA KUMAR, marine research engineer; b. Calcutta, India, Feb. 3, 1941; came to U.S., 1964, naturalized, 1981; s. Asutosh and Shefali C.; m. Prakriti Bhaduri, July 23, 1967; children: Sumita, Prabal. BSME, Jadavpur U., Calcutta, India, 1963; MSME, U. Colo., 1965, PhD, 1968. Registered profl. engr., Ill. Asst. engr. Kuljian Corp., Calcutta, 1963-64, Simon Carves Ltd., Calcutta, 1964; instr. engring. U. Colo., Boulder, 1965-66; hydrodynamicist CB&I Tech. Svcs. Co. (formerly Chgo. Bridge and Iron Co.), Plainfield, Ill., 1968-70, head analytical group, 1970-79, dir. marine rsch., 1979-95, dir structural devel., 1995-96; pres. Offshore Structure Analysis, Inc., Plainfield, 1996—. Vis. prof. U.S. Naval Acad., Annapolis, Md., 1986, 88, Indian Inst. Tech., Madras, 1996; presenter in field. Author: Hydrodynamics of Offshore Structures, 1987, Nonlinear Methods in Offshore Engineering, 1990, Offshore Structure Modeling, 1994, Theory and Practice of Hydrodynamics and Vibration, 2002; editor: Fluid Structure Interaction in Offshore Engineering, 1994, Fluid Structure Interaction, 2001, Fluid Structure Interaction II, 2003; tech. editor Applied Ocean Rsch., 1998—, mem. editl. bd., Marine Structures, Topics in Engring., Advances in Fluid Mechanics series, assoc. editor Energy Resources Tech., 1983—86; contbr. articles, chapters to books. Recipient Jadavpur U. Gold medal, 1963; U. Colo. fellow, 1968; named Outstanding New Citizen, 1981. Fellow AAAS, ASCE (publ. com. waterway divsn., James R. Cross Gold medal 1974, Freeman scholar 1979), ASME (exec. com., editor jour. offshore mechanics and arctic engring. divsn. 1986-96, chmn. divsn., 1987-88, awards com. 1983—, tech. session devloper, chmn. 1983—, chmn. tech. program com. 1988-89, tech. program chair, 2004, Ralph James award 1984, co-editor proc. internat. symposium, Offshore Mechanics and Arctic Engring. achievement award 1990, Ten Paper award 1991, Disting. Svcs. award 1998), NAS (com., design group, marine structures group 1989-91, chmn. 1992-95), Nat. Acad. Engring., Sigma Xi. Achievements include patents in field. Office: Offshore Structure Analysis Inc 13613 Capista Dr Plainfield IL 60544-7966 E-mail: chakrab@aol.com.

CHAKRABARTI, SUPRIYA, space astrophysicist; b. Howrah, India, June 22, 1953; came to U.S., 1975; s. Chiraranjan and Ranu Chakrabarti; m. Joanne Soljack, Dec. 17, 1983; children: Misha, Robin. BE, U. Calcutta, India, 1975; MS, U. Calif., Berkeley, 1980, PhD, 1982. Sr. fellow U. Calif., Berkeley, 1983-92; assoc. prof. astron. dept. Boston U., 1992-96, prof., 1996—, dir. Ctr. for Space Physics, 1997—. Mem. Ultraviolet/Visible and Gravitational Astrophysics Mgmt. Ops. Working Group, NASA, 1992-95. Author: (ency.) Remote Sensing of the Upper Atmosphere, 1991; guest editor Optical Engring., 1993; editor conf. procs. in field. Dir. community svc. Rotaract Club Howrah, 1974-75. Mem. Am. Geophys. Union (life), Am. Inst. Physics, Am. Astron. Soc. Achievements include research in space instrumentation, planetary atmosphere and ionosphere, astrophysical plasma. Office: Boston U Ctr for Space Physics 725 Commonwealth Ave Boston MA 02215-1401 E-mail: supc@bu.edu.

CHAKRABARTY, ANANDA MOHAN, microbiologist; b. Sainthia, India, Apr. 4, 1938; arrived in U.S., 1965; s. Satya Dos and Sasthi Bala (Mukherjee) Chakrabarty; m. Krishna Chakraverty, May 26, 1965; children: Kaberi, Asit. BSc, St. Xavier's Coll., 1958; MSc, U. Calcutta, India, 1960, PhD, 1965. Sr. rsch. officer U. Calcutta, 1964-65; rsch. assoc. biochemistry U. Ill., Urbana, 1965-71, prof. dept. microbiology Med. Ctr., 1979-89, disting. prof., 1989—; mem. staff GE R&D Ctr., Schenectady, NY, 1971-79. Editor: (book) Genetic Engineering, 1977, Biodegradation and Detoxification of Environmental Pollutants, 1982. Named Scientist of Yr., Indsl. Rsch. Mag., 1975; recipient Inventor of the Yr. award, Patent Lawyers' Assn., 1982, Pub. Affairs award, Am. Chem. Soc., 1984, Disting. Scientist award, EPA, 1985, Merit award, NIH, 1986, Pasteur award, 1991, Proctor & Gamble award, 1995; scholar, U. Ill., 1989. Mem.: Am. Soc. Biol. Chemists, Am. Soc. Microbiology. Home: 206 E Julia Dr Villa Park IL 60181-3340 Office: U Ill Med Ctr Dept Microbiology M/C 790 835 S Wolcott Ave Chicago IL 60612-7340 Business E-Mail: pseudomo@uic.edu.

CHAKRABORTY, JOANA, physiology educator, research center administrator; b. Calcutta, W. Bengal, India, June 1, 1934; came to U.S., 1962; d. Mohadev and Nilima Mukherjee; m. Ajit Chakraborty; 1 child, Mellary. BS, Sci. Coll., Calcutta, 1954, MS, 1956; PhD, Inst. of Nuclear Physics, Calcutta, 1962. Rsch. asst. Inst. of Nuclear Physics, Calcutta, 1960-62; postdoctoral asst. Iowa State U., Ames, 1962-63; lectr. Inst. of Nuclear Physics, Calcutta, 1964-69; Ford found. fellow Harbor Gen. UCLA Med. Ctr., 1969-70; dir. Electron Microscopy Lab. Med. Coll., Toledo, Ohio, 1970-89; asst. prof. Med. Coll. Ohio, Toledo, 1972-75, assoc. prof., 1975-82, prof., 1982—, interim chmn., 1991-94. Spkr. in field. Author: Chemical Exposure and Toxic Responses, 1997, also chpts., revs. and abstracts; contbr. numerous articles to profl. jours. Recipient World AIDS Found. award; recipient many extramural rsch. grants including NIH rsch. grant awards. Mem. AAAS, Am. Soc. Cell Biology, Electron Microscopy Soc. of Am., Am. Soc. of Andrology, Soc. Study of Reprodn., N.Y. Acad. Sci., Internat. AIDS Soc. Office: Med Coll of Ohio 3035 Arlington Ave Toledo OH 43614-2570 E-mail: jchakraborty@meo.edu.

CHAKRABORTY, UDAY KUMAR, computer scientist, educator; s. Sakti Pada and Sikha C.; m. Mandira Chattopadhyay, June 17, 1989; 1 child, Uttara. BE in Electronics, Jadavpur U., India, 1985, ME in Computer Sci., 1987, PhD in Computer Sci., 1994. Sr. rsch. assoc. Computer-Aided Design Ctr., Calcutta, India, 1986-88; vis. scientist Carnegie-Mellon U., Pitts., 1987; sys. engr. CMC Ltd., Calcutta, 1988-90; lectr. Jadavpur U., Calcutta, 1990-93, reader, 1993—2000; guest rschr. GMD, St. Augustin, Germany, 1995, 96, rschr., 1998—99; asst. prof. U. Mo., St. Louis, 2001—. Reviewer rsch. articles to various profl. jours. and confs. Author: Software and Systems: An Introduction, 1995; guest editor Jour. Sys. Arch. Info. Sci.; contbr. articles to profl. jours. Recipient Career Award for Young Tchrs., AICTE/Govt. of India, 1996; UNIDO fellow, Vienna, 1987, Commonwealth Scholarship Commn. scholar, London, 1992. Mem. editorial bd. Jour. of Computing and Info. Tech. Hindu. Office: U Mo St Louis 328 CCB Math Computer Dept 8001 Natural Bridge Saint Louis MO 63121 Fax: 314-516-5400. E-mail: uday@cs.umsl.edu.

CHAKRAPANI, J(AYATHEERTHA), information technologist; b. Bangalore, Karnataka, India, Mar. 27, 1962; parents H.G. and Malathi Chakrapani; m. Saroja Sitaram. B in Engring., Bangalore U., 1984, M in Engring., 1987; PhD, U. Bristol, Eng., 1995. Actuate Certification 2000, Web Securities and Devel. 2000, Visual C++ 1998, C++ 1997. Scientist/engr. Nat. Aero. Labs., Bangalore, 1987—92; Commonwealth scholar U. Bristol, 1992—95; scientist/asst. dir. Nat. Aero. Labs., 1995—98; sr. software engr. Spike Techs. India, Bangalore, 1998—99; project leader Menon Info. Tech., Bangalore, 1999; info. technologist Actuate Corp., Iselin, NJ, 1999—. Contbr. articles to profl. jours. Home: 1203 Woodhaven Drive Edison NJ 08817 Home Fax: 707-222-3725. Personal E-mail: jchakrapani@yahoo.com.

CHAKRAVARTI, ARNAB, physician, researcher; b. Bethlehem, Pa., Oct. 3, 1968; s. Kalidas and Anita Chakravarti; m. Kimberly Denise Chakravarti, Oct. 24, 1998. BA, Duke U., 1990; MD, U. Va., 1995. Resident in medicine Mass. Gen. Hosp., Harvard Med. Sch., Boston, 1996-99, chief resident in radiation oncology, 1999-2000, asst. radiation oncologist, 2000—. Mem. prostate cancer rsch. com. Radiation Therapy Oncology Group, 1999—; voting mem. neuro-oncology spore com. Dana-Farber Harvard Cancer Ctr., Boston, 2000—; voting mem. instnl. review bd. Dana-Farber/Ptnrs. Cancer Ctr., Harvard Med. Sch., 2000—. Contbr. articles to profl. jours. Pres. Linc of Duke U., Durham, N.C., 1989-90. Mem. AMA, AAAS, Am. Assn. Cancer Rsch. (Glaxo-Wellcome Rsch. award 2000, Novartis Rsch. award 2001), Am. Soc. Therapeutic Radiology Oncology (Nat. Resident Rsch. award 1999), Mass. Med. Soc. Avocations: meteorology, music, tennis, baseball, travel. Office: Mass Gen Hosp Dept Radiation Oncology Cox Basement Boston MA 02114 E-mail: achakravarti@partners.org.

CHAKRAVARTY, SREEJIT, computer engineer, researcher; b. Shillong, India, May 12, 1958; came to U.S., 1981; s. Sunil Kumar and Maya (Bhattacharjee) C.; m. Kohinoor Ganguly, Jan. 28, 1988; children: Ayush, Suhail. B in Electronic Engring., Brila Inst. Tech. Sci., Pilani, India, 1980; MS in Computer Sci., SUNY, Stonybrook, 1983; PhD in Computer Sci., SUNY, Albany, 1986. Devel. engr. Tata Electric Co., Mumbai, India, 1980-81; asst. prof. SUNY, Buffalo, 1986-92, assoc. prof., 1992-98; sr. design engr. Intel Corp., Santa Clara, Calif., 1997—. Rsch. asst. SUNY, Stoneybrook, 1981-83, Albany, 1983-86; vis. rschr. Tima Labs., Grenoble, France, 1990; vis. faculty U. Ill., Urbana, 1994. Author: Introduction to IDDR Testing, 1997; contbr. articles to profl. jours. Grantee NSF, 1989, 92. Fellow IEEE (steering com. 1992—, gen. chair symposium 1995); mem. N.Y. Acad. Sci., Assn. Computing Machinery, Sigma Xi. Achievements include development of a variety of methodologies and computer algotithms which are used to develop computer-aided tools to test and verify integrated circuits after manufacturing. Home: 1833 Grant Rd Mountain View CA 94040-3216 Office: SC12-604 Intel Corp 3600 Juliette Ln Santa Clara CA 95054-1540

CHALAM, KAKARLA VENKATA, physician, educator; b. Pedamuttevi, India, Aug. 1, 1959; s. Kasturi C., m. Aruna Potla, June 3, 1982; 1 child, Sandeep. BS, Loyola Coll., 1972; MD, Guntur (India) Med. Sch., 1978; MS, Postgrad. Inst., Chandigarh, India, 1983. Diplomate Am. Bd. Ophthalmology. Asst. instr. U. Tex. Southwestern Med. Sch., Dallas, 1992-94; asst. prof. U. S.C. Sch. Medicine, Columbia, 1994-97, assoc. prof., 1998—2000, program dir., 1994-2000; assoc. chmn. U. Fla. Sch. Medicine, Jacksonville, 2000—. Sect. editor Ocular Pharmacology, 1997-2000. Fellow Royal Coll. Surgeons Edinburgh. Republican. Avocations: photography, classical music, technical writing, table tennis. Address: 580 W 8th St Jacksonville FL 32209-6511 Fax: 904-224-9391. E-mail: kvchalam@aol.com.

CHALCRAFT, ELENA MARIE, actor, singer; b. Bklyn., Oct. 14, 1959; d. James Abdou and Vivian (Trovato) Edwards; m. Rory Charles Chalcraft, Aug. 1, 1992; 1 child, Christopher Aston. BA in Speech, English and Theater Arts, Shippensburg State Coll., 1981; MFA in Acting, Va. Commonwealth U., 1984. Human resources analyst APA, Washington, 1985-98; music dir. Our Lady Queen of Peace Ch., Arlington, Va., 1992-98; soprano Philomusica Chamber Choir, 1999—; ind. kitchen cons. The Pampered Chef, 1999—; soprano St. Bartholomew Choir, 2000—01. Actor, singer (plays): Man of La Mancha, 1988, Ben, 1989-90, Maryland Renaissance Festival, 1987-91, Ziggy, 1992, The Snow Queen, 1994; actor: (play) Broadway Bound, 1993, (tng. film) GAO, 1990; dramaturg (play) Ballets Russes and Drood, 1993. Mem. liturgy com. Our Lady Queen of Peace Ch., 1995-98. Roman Catholic. Avocations: reading, writing children's books, piano, cross-stitch, crosswords. E-mail: emcrcc@worldnet.att.net.

CHALEFF, CARL THOMAS, brokerage house executive; b. Inpls., Nov. 21, 1945; s. Boris Carl and Betty J. (Miller) C.; m. Carolyn F. Heath, Apr. 26, 1970 (div. Apr. 1985); children: Fritz, Eric; m. Darlene Finkel, Dec. 13, 1987. BS in Econs., Purdue U., 1969; MBA in Fin., Xavier U., 1976. Asst. v.p. Am. Can Corp., N.Y.C., 1969-70, sales mgr. Cin., 1970-73; account exec. Merrill Lynch, Cin., 1973-76; v.p. Oppenheimer, Chgo., 1976-81; assoc. dir. Bear Stearns & Co., Chgo., 1981-88; ptnr., mng. dir. CIBC Oppenheimer, 1988—. Pres. bd. dirs. Nat. Kidney Found. of Ill.; exec. com. U. Chgo. Childrens Hosp., Boy Scouts Am., 1992-94; former bd. dirs. AIDS Care, bd. dir. Adler Planetarium & Mus., Chgo., bd. dir., Jobs for Youth. Mem. Chgo. Bond Club, Am. Arbitration

Assn., Nat. Bd. Arbitrators, East Bank Club, Rainbows (bd. dirs. 1984-96), Met. Club, Chgo. Mercantile Exch. Club, Chgo. Yacht Club, Ctr. for Excellence in Edn. (bd. dirs. 1990-92), Chgo. Filmmakers (bd. dirs. 1986-98). Avocations: sailing, skiing, tennis. Home: 55 W Goethe St Chicago IL 60610-7406 Personal E-mail: chaleff@21stcentury.net. Business E-Mail: carl.chaleff@us.cibc.com.

CHALFANT, WILLIAM YOUNG, lawyer, author, historian; b. Hutchinson, Kans., Oct. 3, 1928; s. Claude Edward and Junia Maurine (Young) C.; m. Martha Ann Wallbillich, June 30, 1956; children: William David, Kristin. AB, U. Kans., 1950; JD, U. Mich., 1956. Bar: Kans. 1956, U.S. Ct. Appeals (10th cir.), U.S. Supreme Ct. Ptnr. Branine, Chalfant & Hill, Hutchinson, 1956—. Bd. dirs. First Nat. Bank, Hutchinson; mem. Kans. State Bd. of Law Examiners, 1966—92, chmn., 1986—92; mem. constnl. law drafting com. Nat. Conf. of Bar Examiners, 1974—85. Author: Cheyennes and Horse Soldiers, 1989, Dangerous Passage, 1993, Without Quarter, 1991, Cheyennes at Dark Water Creek, 1997. Drive chmn. Reno County Cmty. Chest, Hutchinson, 1957-58l bd. dirs. Reno County Red Cross, Hutchinson, 1960-64; dist. commr. Boy Scouts Am., 1965-75. Capt. USMC, 1950-53. Recipient Gold award Santa Fe Nat. Hist. Trail/Nat. Park Svc., 1995. Mem. ABA, Kans. Bar Assn., Santa Fe Trail Assn. (bd. dirs., award of merit 1995), Western History Assn. (chmn. fin. com.). Avocations: history, writing. Home: 1007 W 95th Ave Hutchinson KS 67502-8325 Office: Branine Chalfant & Hill 418 First Nat Ctr Hutchinson KS 67501

CHALFANT-ALLEN, LINDA KAY, retired Spanish language educator; b. New Kensington, Pa., Oct. 9, 1943; d. Fred and Evelyn V. (Peters) C.; m. Charles V. Utley, Sr., Jan. 26, 1963 (div.); children: Charles V. Utley, Yvette Melissa Utley; m. Simon Allen, Feb. 13, 1998. BA in Child Study, Vassar Coll., 1965; MS in Spanish and Linguistics, Georgetown U., 1971. Cert. tchr., N.Y., D.C. Bilingual rsch. asst. Georgetown U., Washington, 1966-71; curriculum writer D.C. Pub. Schs., 1969-70, 91; asst. prof., rsch. assoc. U. D.C., 1982-85; asst. to dir. Latin for Modern Sch., McLean, Va., 1968-94; tchr. D.C. Pub. Schs., 1965-95, ret., 1995; freelance cons., editor, 1961—; bilingual legal sec. Wilkinson, Barker, Knauer & Quinn, Washington, 1996-97; legal sec. Thelen Reid & Priest, 1998-2000. Proposal review panelist Nat. Endowment for Humanities, Washington, 1984, 87, 89, U.S. Dept. Edn., Washington, 1986. Founder, 1st pres. Fgn. Lang. Action Group, Washington, 1978-79; Sunday sch. tchr., Washington, 1972-93. Recipient Grad. Study fellowship King Juan Carlos Found., Spain, 1994, Travel grant Spain '92 Found., 1994. Roman Catholic. Avocations: travel, reading, bowling, baking, exercise, crochet. E-mail: lindachalfant@msn.com.

CHALFEN, JUDITH RESNICK, community activist; b. Boston, June 26, 1925; d. Abram and Rose (Pollen) Resnick; m. Melvin Harold Chalfen, Dec. 18, 1949; children: Robert Noah, Daniel, Andrew David. BA, Smith Coll., Northampton, Mass., 1947. Traffic/music libe Radio Sta. WOR, N.Y.C., 1947-49; announcer, editor Lowell Broadcasting Coun., WGBH-FM, Boston, 1950-52; co-founder, treas. Action for Childrens TV, Newton, Mass., 1968-74; co-founder, dir. Newton Arts Ctr, 1976-78; real estate broker Melvin Cline, Realtors, Newton Highlands, Mass., 1978-87. Co-founder, actress Everyman Theatre, 1959-61. Co-chmn. Cultural Affairs Commn., Newton, 1975-77; pres. Underwood Sch. PTA, Newton, 1963-64; mem. Ward 7 Dem. City Com., Newton, 1957-80; bd. govs Newton Arts Ctr., 1978—; docent Newton Free Libr., 1991—. Avocations: reading, travel, theatre/mus. going, modern dance, gardening. Home: 22 Hyde Ave Newton MA 02458-2311

CHALK, JOHN ALLEN, SR., lawyer; b. Lexington, Tenn., Jan. 16, 1937; AA, Freed-Hardeman Coll., 1956; BS, Tenn. Tech. U., 1962, MA, 1967; JD, U. Tex., 1973. Bar: Tex. 1973, D.C. 1977; ordained to ministry Ch. of Christ, 1956. Pastor chs., Dayton, Ohio, 1956-60, Cookeville, Tenn., 1960-66, Abilene, Tex., 1966-71; assoc. Rhodes and Seamster, Abilene, 1973-74, Rhodes and Doscher, Abilene, 1974; ptnr. Rhodes, Doscher, Chalk and Heatherly, Abilene, 1975-78; gen. counsel La Jet, Inc., Abilene, 1978-84, also v.p., sec; exec. v.p. Dabney Corp., Dallas, 1984-86; pres. Dabney Capital, Dallas, 1984-86; assoc. Gandy, Michener, Swindle, Whitaker & Pratt, Ft. Worth, 1986, ptnr., 1987-93, Michener Larimore Swindle Whitaker Flowers Sawyer Reynolds & Chalk, Ft. Worth, 1993-2000, Whitaker Chalk Swindle & Sawyer LLP, Ft. Worth, 2000—. Pres. Equity, Inc., 1982-90; bd. dirs. Osteo. Health Sys. Tex., Inc.; mem. strategic alliances com. for edn. Nat. Ct. Reporters Assn., 1994-95; cert. master mediator Dispute Resolution Svcs. Tarrant County, Tex.; Tex. court-approved mediator; mem. panel of comml. and employment neutrals Am. Arbitration Assn.; contract mediator EEOC, Dallas, 1999-2001. Author: The Praying Christ, 1964, Three American Revolutions, 1970, Jesus' Church, 1970, The Christian Family, 1973, Great Biblical Doctrines, 1973, The Devil, You Say!, 1974; author numerous articles on U.S. Dept. Edn. fed. student fin. assistance, domestic and internat. arbitration and mediation, also articles on religion; presenter in fields. Trustee Abilene Regional Mental Health Retardation Ctr., 1978—80, Christian Scholarship Found., Inc., Atlanta, 1980, chmn. bd., 1992—93; chmn. Ailene Bicentennial Com., 1975—76; mem. nat. adv. coun. Am. United for Separation of Ch. and State, 1979—82, pres. bd. trustees, 1981—82; mem. nat. devel. coun. Abilene Christian U.; featured spkr. radio and TV programs Herald of Truth, 1966—69; trustee Osteo. Health Care Found., Inc., Ft. Worth, 1987—96, sec.-treas., 1990—91, sr. v.p., pres.-elect, 1991—92, pres., 1992—93; mem. Strategy for 2000, City of Ft. Worth, 1995—2000; bd. dirs. Health Care of Tex., Inc., 1987—2003. Fellow Tex. Bar Found. (life), Chartered Inst. Arbitrators London (chartered arbitrator), Tarrant County Bar Found. (founding, life); mem. ABA (acting assoc. editor, mem. editl. bd. Family Adv. 1977-78), FBA, Coll. State Bar Tex. (maintaining), Am. Health Lawyers Assn. (disput resolution svc. panel of neutrals), Am. Arbitration Assn. (panel arbitrators and mediators), Internat. Ctrs. for Arbitration (panel arbitrators and mediators), London Ct. Internat. Arbitrators, Tex. Assn. Mediators, Tarrant County Assn. Mediators, Tex. Ct.-Approved Mediators, State Bar Tex., Ft. Worth Bar Assn., Nat. Arbitration Forum (panel of neutrals), London Ct. Internat. Arbitration. Home: 3601 Verde Vista Ct W Aledo TX 76008-3679 Office: Whitaker Chalk Swindle & Sawyer 3500 City Ctr II Fort Worth TX 76102-4186 E-mail: jchalk@whitakerchalk.com.

CHALKER, RONALD FRANKLIN, lawyer, educator; b. Atlanta, Oct. 18, 1957; s. Nolan Franklin and Beverly Jean (Granger) C.; m. Brenda Elise Wright, June 13, 1981; children: Jessica Elise, Hannah Nichole, Jordan Annette. BS, Ga. So. U., 1979; JD, Woodrow Wilson Coll. Law, 1982. Bar: Ga. 1982, U.S. Dist. Ct. (no. dist.) Ga. 1982, U.S. Ct. Appeals (11th cir.) 1989. Assoc. Brooks & Brock, Marietta, Ga., 1983-85; ptnr. Hogan, Casey, Chalker & Cooper, Marietta, 1985-87, Robert A. Falanga, P.C., Atlanta, 1988-90, Falanga, Barrow & Chalker, Atlanta, 1991-94, Falanga & Chalker, Atlanta, 1995—. Adj. prof. law So. Poly. U., Marietta, 1989—. Contbr. articles to profl. jours. Mem. ABA, ATLA, Ga. Trial Lawyers Assn., Atlanta Bar Assn., Cobb County Bar Assn., Kiwanis (pres. Marietta Club 1992-93, Pres.'s award 1989). Republican. Avocations: golf, skiing. Office: Falanga & Chalker 1820 The Exchange NW Ste 400 Atlanta GA 30339-2018 E-mail: ronchalker@mindspring.com.

CHALKLEY, JACQUELINE ANN, retail company executive; b. Benson, Minn., Jan. 3, 1946; d. Vincent Otto and Dorothy Mildred (Alsaker) Kaehler; m. C. Wayne Callaway. BA in Art History cum laude, Brown U., 1967; MA, Columbia U., 1968; postgrad. in Contemporary Art, New Sch. for Social Rsch., N.Y.C., 1968-70; postgrad. in Ceramics, U. Md., 1970-72. Art tchr. Summit (N.J.) High Sch., 1968-70, Rockville (Md.) High Sch., 1970-74; adj. prof. ceramics Montgomery Coll., Rockville, 1974-78; owner Jackie Chalkley at Foxhall Square, Washington, 1978-99, Jackie Chalkley at Willard Collection, Washington, 1986-99, Jackie Chalkley at Chevy Chase Plz., Washington, 1989-99; retail and product devel. cons., 1999—. Juror Rhinebeck Craft Fair, 1981, New Eng. Buyers Market, Boston, 1982, Craft Art '82, Richmond, Va. Craft Show, 1983, Smithsonian Crafts Exhbn. '83, Smithsonian Instn. Women's Com. Craft Show, 1984, Annie Albers fashion show at Renwick Gallery, 1984, Morristown Craft Fair, 1984, Washington Craft Show, 1986, Potomac Craftsmen's Guild Show, 1987, Harrisburg Arts Festival, 1987, Ceramic Guild Washington, 1987, Washington Guild Goldsmiths, 1987, 18th Bienniel Exhbn. Creative Crafts Coun., 1988, Art Balt., 2003, others; appointee screening com. Piedmont Craftsman's Guild, Winston-Salem, N.C., 1983-86, D.C. Commn. Arts, 1983-85; mem. hon. com. Brandeis Art Exhbn., 1984; mem. hon. com. various exhbns. and fundraisers Textile Mus., 1984-86. Featured in Ceramics Monthly, 1994, Women's Wear Daily, 1995. Mem. hon. com. 2d Ann. 34th St. Art Fair, John Eaton Sch., 1985; mem. benefit com. Washington Charitable Fund, 1989; hon. bd. trustees D.C. chpt. Design Industries Found. for AIDS, 1989, 90; mem. auction ann. benefit com. Washington Project for Arts, 1989, 90, benefit com. Source Theater, 1993, benefit com. Corcoran Mus. Jazz Evening, 1993, hon. com. Lab Sch. Wash., 1992, hon. benefit com. Arena Stage Living Theater, 1997, 98; sponsor Wearable Art Fashion Show, Renwick Mus., 1993; juried Smithsonian Craft Show, 1994; hon. chmn. Friends of the Corcoran Mus. Benefit, 1999-2000, mem. exec. com., 2001-02; mem. benefit com. Living Stage & Arena Theatre, 1997, 98, 99; chmn. Craft Leaders Caucus Day 2000; mem. nat. resource bd. James Renwick Alliance of Renwick Mus., 2000-03, gala exec, com. Rincones Dance Theater, 2001—; mem. Hon. Com. for Aid to Artisans D.C. event at Cambodian Embassy, 2003. Appeared on cover of Forecast Mag., 1978; recipient Best Taste in Washington award Washingtonian Mag., 1982, 1st Ann. Outstanding Accessories Merchandising award Accessories Mag., 1985; named one of 23 People to Watch in 1983, Washingtonian Mag., 1982; her apt. chosen as Residential Interior of Yr., Am. Soc. Interior Designers, 1985, 92; her store named 1986 Comml. Interior of Yr., Am. Soc. Interior Designers; nat. award for logo design Am. Corp. Identity, 1988, 91 Mem. Am. Craft Coun., Washington Fashion Group, James Renwick Craft Leaders Caucus, Friends of the Corcoran Gallery of Art, Washington Performing Arts Soc. (impresario coun.). Avocations: travel, food, modern dance, visual arts, swimming. Office: Jackie Chalkley 2130 Cathedral Ave NW Washington DC 20008-1502

CHALLA, PRATAP, ophthalmologist, researcher; MD, U. of Fla., Gainesville, 1993; BS, U. of Fla., 1989. Asst. prof. of ophthalmology Duke U. Eye Ctr., Durham, NC, 2000—. Residency program dir. Duke U. Eye Ctr., Durham, NC, 2001—. Mem.: Am. Glaucoma Soc., Am. Acad. of Ophthalmology. Achievements include patents for method of treating disorders of the eye; pressure Project; studies of glaucoma genetics. Office: Duke Univ Eye Ctr Erwin Road Box 3802 Durham NC 27710 E-mail: pratapc60@hotmail.com.

CHALLONER, DAVID REYNOLDS, university official, physician; b. Appleton, Wis., Jan. 31, 1935; s. Reynolds Ray and Marion (Below) C.; m. Jacklyn Davnes Anderson, Aug. 30, 1958; children: David Harvey, Laura Reynolds, Britt-Davnes. BS cum laude, Lawrence Coll., Appleton, 1956; postgrad., Cambridge (Eng.) U., 1958; MD cum laude, Harvard, 1961. Resident in internal medicine Columbia Presbyn. Hosp., N.Y.C., 1961—63; research assoc. Nat. Heart Inst., Bethesda, Md., 1963—65; chief med. resident and endocrinology research fellow U. Wash., Seattle, 1965—67; prof. medicine, asst. chmn. dept. Ind. U. Sch. Medicine, Indpls., 1967—75; vis. scholar Inst. Medicine, Nat. Acad. Sci., 1974; dean St. Louis U. Sch. Medicine, 1975—82; v.p. health affairs U. Fla., Gainesville, 1982—98; dir. Inst. for Sci. and Health Policy U. Fla., Gainesville, Fla., 1998—2002. Chmn. pres.'s com. on nat. med. sci. NIH, 1988-91, mem. dirs. adv. com., 1990-96; mem. com. sci., engring. pub. policy NAS, 1993-97; cons. Eli Lilly & co., NIH; mem. NAS Nat. Rsch. Coun. governing bd., 1997—; foreign sec. NAS, Inst. Med., 1998—. Served to lt. codr. USPHS, 1963—65. Recipient Harvard Med. Alumni award, 1961, Dr. William Beaumont award AMA, 1982, Disting. Alumnus award Lawrence U., 1987. Fellow AAAS; mem. Inst. of Medicine (fgn. sec. 1998—), Am. Fedn. Clin. Rsch.pres. 1975), Inst. Medicine, Nat. Acad. Sci., Am. Soc. Clin. Investigation, Endocrine Soc., Am. Diabetes Assn., Assn. Am. Physicians, Boylston Soc., Am. Clin. and Climatol. Assn., Phi Beta Kappa, Alpha Omega Alpha, Beta Theta Pi. Clubs: Racquet (St. Louis); Cosmos (Washington). Home: 2715 NW 22nd Dr Gainesville FL 32605-2975 Office: U Fla PO Box 103204 Gainesville FL 32610-3204

CHALMERS, DAVID B. petroleum executive; b. Denver, Nov. 17, 1924; s. David Twiggs and Dorrit (Bay) C.; 1 child, David B. BA, Dartmouth Coll., 1947; A.M.P., Harvard U., 1966. Various positions Bay Petroleum Co., Denver, 1951-55; various positions Tenneco Oil Co., Houston, 1955-67; v.p. Occidental Petroleum Corp., Houston, 1967-68; pres. Can. Occidental Petroleum Ltd., 1968-73; pres., chief exec. officer Petrogas Processing Ltd., 1968-73; officer Cansulex Ltd., 1968-73; chmn., chief exec. officer, dir. Coral Petroleum, Inc. and subs., Houston, 1973—. Served to lt. USMC, 1943-45, 49-50, Korea Mem. Am. Petroleum Inst., Petroleum Club of Houston, Lochinvar Golf Club, Houston Racquet Club, Denver Country Club, Houston Club. Republican. Episcopalian. Home: 5600 San Felipe St Unit 4 Houston TX 77056-2617 Office: Coral Oil and Gas Inc 909 Texas St Unit 202 Houston TX 77002-3197 E-mail: coraloil@aol.com.

CHALMERS, JON D. director; s. Margaret Strong and Fred Gaskin. BA, U. of Ala., 1994; MEd, Harvard U., 1998. Asst. dir. Program for Rural Services and Rsch., Univ. of Ala., Tuscaloosa, 1998—2001, dir., 2001—. Episcopalian. Avocations: hiking, appalachian trail, travel. Office: U of Ala Rural Svcs Box 870372 Tuscaloosa AL 35487 Office Fax: 205-348-2412. E-mail: jon.chalmers@ua.edu.

CHALSTY, JOHN STEELE, investment banker; b. Port Elizabeth, Republic of South Africa, Nov. 7, 1933; came to U.S., 1955, naturalized, 1964; s. Frederick H. and Sarah S. (Lamprecht) C.; m. Jennifer Blomefield, Feb. 16, 1957; children: Susan Chalsty Neely, Deborah Ann. B.Sc. in Chemistry and Physics, U. Witwatersrand, 1952, B.Sc. with honors in Chemistry, 1953, M.Sc., 1954; MBA (Baker scholar), Harvard U., 1957. With Exxon Corp., N.Y.C., 1957-69; dir. Donaldson, Lufkin & Jenrette, Inc., N.Y.C., 1969-2000, chmn., 1986—. Bd. dirs. Occidental Petroleum Corp.; chmn. N.Y. Econ. Devel. Corp. Bd. dirs. Teagle Found. Inc., 1974—, chmn., 1997—; trustee Columbia U., St. Barnabas Med. Ctr.; pres. Lincoln Ctr. Theater; bd. dirs. Am. Ballet Theater, N.Y. Philharm. Mem. Short Hills (N.J.) Club, Harvard Club, Univ. Club (N.Y.C).

CHALUPNIK, STEVEN ANDREW, music educator; b. Chgo., Oct. 30, 1965; s. Raymond and Barbara Chalupnik. BA, Western Ill. U., Macomb, Ill., 1989. Music and drama dir. Music on The Move, Brookfield, Ill., 1990—91, Cathedral of St. Raymond Sch., Joliet, Ill., 1991—. Prin. bassist West Suburban Symphony Orch., Hinsdale, Ill., 1990—, Wheaton Symphony Orch., Wheaton, Ill., 1991—; bassist Knox-Galesburg Symphony, Galesburg, Ill., 1987—89; prin. bassist Monmouth Civic Orch., Monmouth, Ill., 1988—88; bassist Quincy Symphony Orch., Quincy, Ill., 1987—89, SW Symphony Orch., Oak Lawn, Ill., 2002—02. Bd. dir. West Suburban Symphony Orch., Hinsdale, Ill., 1994—98. Mem.: Nat. Assn. of Pastoral Musicians (assoc.), Music Educators Nat. Conf. (assoc.), Ill. Music Educators Assn. (assoc.), Alpha Phi Omega (assoc.). Home: 430 W Madeline St Joliet IL 60436 Office: Cathedral of St Raymond School 713 W Douglas St Joliet IL 60435 Personal E-mail: lunartunes@attbi.com.

CHAMBERLAIN, ADRIAN RAMOND, transportation engineer; b. Detroit, Nov. 11, 1929; s. Adrian and Leila (Swisher) C.; m. Melanie F. Stevens, May 19, 1979; children: Curtis (dec.), Tracy, Thomas (dec.). BS, Mich. State U., 1951, D Engring., 1971; MS, Wash. State U., 1952; PhD, Colo. State U., 1955; LittD, Denver U., 1974. Registered profl. engr., Colo. lic. real estate broker, Colo., 1981-91. Rsch. engr. Phillips Petroleum Co., 1955; rsch. coord., civil engr. Colo. State U., 1956-57, chief civil engr. sect., 1957-61, acting dean engring., 1959-61, v.p., 1960-66, exec. v.p., treas., governing bd., 1966-69, pres., 1969-80; chmn. bd. dirs. Univ. Nat. Bank, 1964-69, dir., 1964-74; pres., dir. Mitchell & Co., Inc., 1981-85; exec. v.p. Simons, Li & Assocs., Inc., 1985-87; pres., CEO, Chemagnetics, Inc., Ft. Collins, Colo., 1987-89; exec. dir. Colo. Dept. Hwys., Denver, 1987-91, Colo. Dept. Transp., 1991-94; v.p. engring. cons. firm Parsons Brinckerhoff, Denver, 1998—. Chmn. NSF Commn. Weather Modification, 1964-66; mem. Nat. Air Quality Criteria Adv. Com., 1967-70; vice chmn. rsch. and tech. coord. com. Fed. Hwy Admiinstrn. of Transp. Rsch. Bd., NRC, 1991-94. Colo. commr. Western Interstate Commn. on Higher Edn., 1974-78; pres. State Bd. Agr. Sys., 1978-80; trustee Cystic Fibrosis Found., 1971-84; bd. trustees Univ. Corp. for Atmospheric Rsch., 1967-72, 74-81, chmn. bd. trustees, 1977-79; pres. Black Mountain Ranch, Inc., 1969-85; bd. dirs. Nat. Ctr. for Higher Edn. Mgmt. Sys., 1975-80, chmn. bd. dirs., 1977-78; bd. visitors Air U., USAF, 1973-76, chmn., 1975-76; exec. com. Nat. Assn. State Univs. and Land Grant Colls., 1976-80, pres.-elect, 1978-79, chmn., 1979-80; mem. adv. coun. to dir. NSF, 1978-81; chmn. Ft. Collins-Loveland Airport Authority, 1983-86; bd. dirs. Synergetics Internat. Inc., 1987-90; mem. exec. com. strategic hwy. rsch. commn. Transp. Rsch. Bd. NRC, 1989-93, chmn. strategic transp. rsch. study hwy. safety, 1989-90, exec. com., 1991-96, vice-chmn., 1992, chmn., 1993; mem. Gov.'s Cabinet, State of Colo., 1987-94; mem. Info. Mgmt. Commn., 1988-93. Fulbright student U. Grenoble, 1955-56 Mem. ASCE, Am. Assn. State Hwy. and Transp. Ofcls. (policy com. 1987-92, v.p. 1990-91, pres. 1991-92, bd. dirs. 1992-94, chmn. standing com. on adminstrn. 1993-94), Am. Trucking Assn. (v.p. for freight policy 1994-98, mng. dir. found. 1998), Order of Aztec Eagle, Mex., Sigma Xi, Tau Beta Pi, Phi Kappa Phi, Chi Epsilon. Home: 124 Idlewild Ln Winter Park CO 80482 Office: Parsons Brinckerhoff 1660 Lincoln St Ste 2100 Denver CO 80264-2001

CHAMBERLAIN, BARBARA KAYE, small business owner, communications executive; b. Lewiston, Idaho, Nov. 6, 1962; d. William Arthur and Gladys Marie (Humphrey) Greene; m. Dean Andrew Chamberlain, Sept. 13, 1986 (div.); children: Kathleen Marie, Laura Kaye; m. Daniel Eric Pocklington, Apr. 11, 1998. BA in English cum laude, BA in Linguistics cum laude, Wash. State U., 1984; MPA, Ea. Wash. U., 2002. Temp. sec. various svcs., Spokane, Wash., 1984-86; office mgr. Futurepast, Spokane, 1986-87; dir. mktg. and prodn. Futurepast: The History Co., Melior Publs., Spokane, 1987-88, v.p., 1988-89; founder, owner PageWorksInk, Coeur d'Alene, Idaho, 1989—; mem. dist. 2 Idaho State Ho. of Reps., 1990-92; mem. Idaho State Senate, 1992-94; dir. comm. and pub. affairs Wash. State U., Spokane, 1998—. Adj. faculty North Idaho Coll., 1995. Author North Idaho's Centennial, 1990; editor Washington Songs and Lore, 1988. Bd. dirs. Mus. North Idaho Coeur d'Alene, 1990-91, Ct. Apptd. Spl. advocates, 1993-96; trustee North Idaho Coll., 1996—2001, chair, 2001, pres. 2002-; bd. dirs. Spokane Pub. Rels. Coun., 1999—2001. Named Child Advocate Legislator of Yr., Idaho Alliance for Children, Youth and Families, 1993. Democrat. Office: 601 W First Ave Spokane WA 99201-3899

CHAMBERLAIN, CHARLES JAMES, railroad labor union executive; b. Ashton, Ill., Aug. 7, 1921; s. Charles Hubert and Katherine (Reitz) C.; m. Joyce Lois Swanson, June 27, 1942; children: Richard B., Charles M. Student pub. schs. With signal dept. C. & N.-W. Ry., 1938-57; grand lodge rep. Brotherhood of R.R. Signalmen, 1957-61, sec.-treas., 1961-67, pres., 1967—. Appointed Labor mem. by Pres. Carter to U.S. R.R. Retirement Bd., Chgo., 1977, reappointed, 1979-84, reappointed by Pres. Reagan, 1986-89, reappointed by Pres. Bush, 1989-92, ret. 1992; arbitrator Nat. Mediation Bd., 1996. Alderman DeKalb (Ill.) City Coun., 1949-57; pres. 4 Colonies Condo Assn., Crystal Lake, Ill., 1987—; chmn. St. John's Luth. Ch., Algonquin, Ill., 1990-91, 94—. Mem. Ry. Labor Execs. Assn. (chmn. 1970—) Home: 740 St Andrews Ln Apt 33 Crystal Lake IL 60014-7043

CHAMBERLAIN, DANIEL ROBERT, college president; b. Mexico, Mo., Aug. 22, 1932; s. Ray Willis and Marianne Elizabeth (Horine) C.; m. Joyce F. Books, June 22, 1952; children: Rodney, Mark, Anthony, Priscilla, Aletha, Cynthia, Marianne. BA, Upland Coll., 1953; MA, Calif. State U., Los Angeles, 1957; postgrad., UCLA, 1958-59; D.Ed., U. So. Calif., 1967; DHL (hon.), Huntington Coll., 2000, Houghton Coll., 2001. Tchr., adminstr. Western Pilgrim Schs., El Monte, Calif., 1953-59; tchr. English and history Pasadena (Calif.) City Schs., 1959-63; chmn. div. profl. studies, acting pres. Upland Coll., 1963-65; asst. univ. dean for univ. wide activities SUNY, Albany, 1965-68; dean of coll. Messiah Coll., Grantham, Pa., 1968-76; pres. Houghton (N.Y.) Coll., 1976—. Lectr. on higher edn. and social scis. in People's Republic of China, 1984, 87, 88, 89. Pres. Calif. youth Wesleyan Ch., 1954-66; chmn. bd. dirs. Mile High Camp, Barton Flats, Calif., 1959-65; pres. men's commn. Christian Holiness Assn., 1975-80; bd. dirs. Commn. Ind. Colls. and Univs.; chmn. Ind. Coll. Fund, N.Y., Western N.Y. Consortium Higher Edn., 1976—; mem. gen. bd. adminstrn. Wesleyan Ch., 1988-92, 2000—; chmn. Western N.Y. Consortium Higher Edn., 1991-93; bd. dirs. N.Y. State Commn. on Ind. Colls. and Univs., 1994-97. Named One of 50 Most Outstanding Alumni, Calif. State U., L.A., 1997. Mem. Christian Coll. Consortium (chmn.), Council of Mennonite Coll. Deans (chmn.), Am. Assn. Higher Edn., Middle States Assn. Schs. and Colls. (evaluator, team chmn.), Wesleyan Edn. Council (chmn.), Lions, Phi Delta Kappa. Republican. Office: Houghton Coll Office of Pres Houghton NY 14744 E-mail: daniel.chamberlain@houghton.edu.

CHAMBERLAIN, DOUGLAS REGINALD, lawyer; b. Burlington, Vt., Sept. 8, 1951; s. Reginald B. and Ethelda B. (Towle) C.; m. Linda J. Canfield, Sept. 11, 1982; children: Samuel Douglas, Sarah Riley. AB, Harvard U., 1973; JD, Columbia U., 1976. Bar: N.H. 1976, U.S. Dist. Ct. N.H. 1976. Assoc. Wiggin & Nourie, Manchester, N.H., 1976-81, ptnr., 1982-91, chmn. corp. dept., 1987-93; shareholder Wiggin & Nourie, P.A., Manchester, 1992—2002; mem. Sulloway & Hollis, P.L.L.C., Concord, NH, 2002—. N.H. Minimum CLE (bd. mem. 1992—, chmn. 1997—). Bd. dirs. N.H. Performing Arts Ctr., Manchester, 1981-89; mem. Mayor's Child Care Comn., 1988-92; mem. vestry Grace Episcopal Ch., 1995-98, jr. warden, 1999-2002, sr. warden, 2002—; mem. Constn. and Canons Com., Episcopal Diocese of N.H., 1999—, chair, 2002--. Mem. ABA (employee benefits com. 1982—, taxation sect.), N.H. Employee Benefits Coun. (pres. 1983-84, bd. dirs., sec. 1997-2000, v.p. 2000-01, pres. 2001-03), N.H. Med. Group Mgmt. Assn., Human Resources Assn. Greater Concord (bd. dirs., sec. 2003—), N.H. Bar Assn. (com. on ethics 1981-86, chmn. 1986-88, chmn. group ins. pension plan com. 1984-85, continuing legal edn. com. 1988-98, legis. com. 1996—, lawyer dispute resolution com. 1988-90, tax sect., vice chair, 2001-03, chair 2003--, bus. law sect.). Republican. Office: Sulloway & Hollis PLLC PO Box 1256 Concord NH 03302-1256 E-mail: dchamberlain@sulloway.com.

CHAMBERLAIN, JAMES ROBERT, lawyer; b. Cedar Rapids, Iowa, Nov. 13, 1949; s. Robert Glenn and Jane Helen (Newlin) C.; m. Marsha Lois Gurland, June 23, 1971; children: Jonathan J., Zachary T., Seth A., Jeremy D. BA, U. Wis., 1971, MS, 1973; JD, So. Meth. U., 1976. Bar: Tex. 1976, U.S. Dist. Ct. (no. dist.) Tex. 1978. Atty. trade regulation div. FTC, Dallas, 1976-80; sr. counsel antitrust div. Westinghouse Electric Corp., Pitts., 1980-92, asst. gen. counsel antitrust and Thermo King, 1992-95; v.p. and gen. counsel Thermo King Corp., Mpls., 1995—; asst. gen. counsel Ingersoll-Rand Co., Mpls., 2000—. Adj. prof. antitrust law Duquesne U., 1986-92, William Mitchell Coll. of Law, 2000. Editor Human Rights Jour., 1975-76. Home: 6604 Limerick Dr Minneapolis MN 55439-1260 Office: Thermo King Corp 314 W 90th St Minneapolis MN 55420-3693 E-mail: jim_chamberlain@thermoking.com.

CHAMBERLAIN, JOHN LOOMIS, III, retired pediatrician, educator; b. Balt., July 18, 1930; s. John Loomis Jr. and Marie (Brosius) C.; m. Eleanor Fulton, 1956 (div. Apr. 1976); m. Amelie Marie Chamberlain, Apr. 29, 1977; children: Carolyn, Allison, John Loomis IV. BA, Amherst Coll., 1953; MD, U. Va., 1957. Pediatrician Lexington (Ky.) Clinic, 1962-66; asst. prof. pediat. U. Ky. Sch. Medicine, Lexington, 1962-66; clin. prof. child health and devel. George Washington Sch. Medicine, Washington, 1966—; pediatrician Office of Drs. Howard, Daisley and Ong, Washington, 1966-70; pvt. practice, 1970—90; ret., 1992. Chmn. med. staff Children's Hosp., 1976-79. Editor-in-chief Clin. Proceedings, 1979-84; mem. editl. rev. bd. Contemporary Pediat., 1984-87, Pediat. in Review, 1985-88. Col. U.S. Army, 1991-93. Decorated Army Commendation medal, Meritorious Svc. medal U.S. Army. Fellow Am. Acad. Pediat. (v.p. Washington chpt. 1985-88); mem. Vis. Nurse Assn. (med. adv. bd. 1972-89), D.C. Med. Soc. (exec. bd. 1988-89), U. Va. Med. Alumni Assn. (pres. 1992-93), Rotary, Cosmos Club. Republican. Episcopalian. Avocations: tennis, self education. Home: 4321 Westover Pl NW Washington DC 20016-5553

CHAMBERLAIN, JOSEPH MILES, astronomer, educator; b. Peoria, Ill., July 26, 1923; s. Maurice Silloway and Roberta (Miles) C.; m. Paula Bruninga, Dec. 12, 1945; children: Janet Ann, Susan Louise, Barbara Jean. BS, U.S. Mcht. Marine Acad., 1944; BA, Bradley U., 1947; AM, Tchrs. Coll. Columbia, 1950, EdD, 1962. Instr. Columbia Jr. High Sch., Peoria, 1943; instr. nav. War Shipping Adminstrn., 1944-45; boys sec. YMCA, Peoria, 1946-47; instr. U.S. Mcht. Marine Acad., Kings Point, N.Y., 1947-50, asst. prof., 1950-52; asst. curator Am. Museum-Hayden Planetarium, N.Y.C., 1952-53, gen. mgr., chief astronomer, 1953-56, chmn., 1956-64; asst. dir. Am. Mus. Natural History, 1964-68; dir. Adler Planetarium, Chgo., 1968-91, pres., 1977-91, ret., 1991. Prof. astronomy Northwestern U., 1968-78; professorial lectr. U. Chgo., 1968-71; led eclipse expdns. to Atlantic Ocean, 1972, 73, 94, Mexico, 1970, Can., 1954, 79, Ceylon, 1955, Pacific Ocean, 1977, 91, astro-geodetic expdns. to Can., 1956, 57, Greenland, 1958; dean coun. of sci. staff Am. Mus. Nat. History, 1960-62. Co-author: Planets, Stars and Space, 1957; author: Time and the Stars, 1964; also articles on popular astronomy. Active Boy Scouts Am., Met. Chgo. YMCA; trustee Lakeview Mus. Arts & Scis., Peoria, 1993—; bd. dirs. Heartland Water Resources Coun., 1995-98. Lt. USNR, 1945-46; staff Naval Res. Officers Sch. 1953-54, N.Y.C. Mem. Am. Astron. Soc., Internat. Astron. Union, Internat. Planetarium Dirs. Conf. (vice chmn. 1968-77, chmn. 1977-87), Am. Polar Soc., Am. Assn. Museums (mem. council 1965-77, v.p. 1971-74, pres. 1974-75),

Mus. Trustee Assn. (bd. dirs. 1996-98), Peoria Hist. Soc. (trustee 1993-96), Ill. Valley Yacht Club, Univ. Club (Chgo.). Republican. Presbyn. (elder). Home: 5424 W Flagstone Dr Peoria IL 61615-9466

CHAMBERLAIN, KATHLEEN PATRICIA, humanities educator, writer; b. Cleve., Jan. 13, 1947; d. James Frederick and Ada Mae (Crowl) Egan; m. David John Chamberlain, Dec. 27, 1969 (div. May 1974); 1 child, David John Chamberlain Jr. BS in Edn., Ohio State U., 1969; MA in History, U. Colo., 1992; PhD in History, U. N.Mex., 1998. Freelance writer, 1969—74; mng. editor jour., 1974—84; tng. mgr. Am. Water Worker Assn., Denver, 1984—92; asst. prof. Castleton (Vt.) State Coll., 1998—2001, Ea. Mich. U., Ypsilanti, 2001—. Author: Under Sacred Ground, A History of Navajo Oil, 1922-1982, 2000. Susan Topham grant, Charles Redd Ctr., Brigham Young U., 1999—2000. Mem.: Orgn. Am. Historians, Am. Hist. Assn., Mich. Inst. Arts and Letters, Western History Assn., Phi Alpha Theta. Democrat. Mem. Christian Ch. Office: Ea Mich Univ Dept History 701 Pray Harrold Hall Ypsilanti MI 48197

CHAMBERLAIN, KENT CLAIR, business owner, poet; b. Abilene, Kans., Jan. 22, 1943; s. Clarence Edward Jr. and Lucille Michelle (Barkyoumb) C. Student, Merritt Davis Coll. of Bus., So. Oreg. U. Owner Aquarius Enterprises. Author: Ship Bound for Where, Winter's Bird; contbr. poems to profl. publs.; appeared in GRIT and CAPPER's, No. Stars and AIM. Recipient 1st Pl. Quar. award United Amateur Press Assn. of Am., trophy Am. Poets Fellowship Soc. Mem. AARP, Oreg. State Poetry Assn. (life). Democrat. Home: 625 Holly St Ashland OR 97520

CHAMBERLAIN, MARIAM KENOSIAN, economist; b. Chelsea, Mass., Apr. 24, 1918; d. Avack and Zabel (Mazmanian) Kenosian; m. Neil W. Chamberlain, June 27, 1942 (div. 1967). AB, Radcliffe Coll., 1939; PhD, Harvard U., 1950; D in Humanities, U. Ariz., 1985; D in Human Letters, Rensselaer Polytechnic Inst., Troy, N.Y., 1989. Instr. Conn. Coll., New London, 1949-52; cons. U.S. Intelligence Agy., Washington, 1953; lectr. Columbia U., N.Y.C., 1954-56; from program asst. to program officer Ford Found., N.Y.C., 1956-60 66-82; rsch. assoc. Yale U., 1960-66; from pres. to founding pres. Nat. Coun. Rsch. on Women, N.Y.C., 1982—. Bd. mem. Feminist Press, N.Y.C., 1982, Women's Interart Ctr., N.Y.C., 1990, Inst. Women's Policy Rsch., Washington, 1991—, Internat. Assn. for Feminist Econ., 2002—, Network of East-West Women, 1999—. Editor Women in Academe, 1988. Bd. mem. Women's Equity Action League, Washington, 1982-90; sec. treas. U.S. Coun. UN Internat. Rsch. and Training Inst. for Advancement of Women, N.Y.C., 1989—. Mem. AAUW, Am Econ. Assn., Internat. Assn. for Feminist Econs. (bd. dirs. 2002—), Network of East-West Women, Women and Founds. Corp. Philanthropy, Harvard Club of N.Y.C., Cosmopolitan Club. Home: 60 Sutton Pl S New York NY 10022-4168 Office: National Coun Rsch Women 11 Hanover Sq New York NY 10005-6508

CHAMBERLAIN, MARY, retired academic administrator, translator; b. Media, Pa., Mar. 26, 1928; d. Lloyd William Chamberlain, Sr. and Marie Gertrude Meloney. BA in Chemistry, Rosemont Coll., 1949; MS in French, Georgetown U., 1957, PhD in Linguistics and Spanish, 1965. Bus. office asst. Dunbarton Coll., Washington, 1950—58; prof. Spanish U. Md. Overseas, Torrejon Airbase, Spain, 1959—61; asst. edn. adviser USAF, Torrejon Airbase, Spain, 1959—61; asst. rschr. Bantu lang. Georgetown U., Washington, 1961—62; prof. Spanish and French Howard U., Washington, 1961—62; chief trainee selection Orgn. Am. States, Washington, 1962—89; ret. Translator: (chronicles) New Norcia Studies No. 9, 2001, New Norcia Studies No. 10, 2002. Roman Catholic. Avocations: music, opera, translations. Home: Apt 1013 2601 Woodley Pl Washington DC 20008

CHAMBERLAIN, MICHAEL ALLEN, marketing professional, consultant; b. Auburn, N.Y., Mar. 22, 1956; s. Demart Carl and Marie Jane. BA, SUNY, Stony Brook, 1978; AAS, Onondaga C.C., 1984; MBA, Syracuse U., 1985. Dir. East Timor Human Rights Com., N.Y.C., 1978-85; sr. auditor Xerox Corp., Rochester, N.Y., 1985-89, contr. Syracuse, N.Y., 1989-92, strategy mgr. Rochester, N.Y., 1993-96, mktg. exec., 1996-98; v.p. Cayuga County Econ. Devel. Coun., NY, 1998-99; exec. dir. N.Y. Agr. Devel. Corp., 1999—2001; prin. Develop. Svcs. Assocs., 2001—. Pres. Auburn Astros, 1992-95. Treas. Humanitarian Project, Washington D.C., 1985-97, chair Leadership Cayuga, 1989-94. Recipient Outstanding Student award Wall St. Jour., 1984, Key to City, City of Auburn, 1995. Avocations: backpacking, travelling. Home: 133 South St Auburn NY 13021-4811

CHAMBERLAIN, NEIL CORNELIUS WOLVERTON, economist, emeritus educator; b. Charlotte, N.C., May 18, 1915; s. Henry Bryan and Elizabeth (Wolverton) C.; m. Mariam Kenosian, June 27, 1942 (div. June 1967); m. Harriet Feigenbaum, Aug. 9, 1968. AB, Western Res. U., 1937, MA, 1939; PhD, Ohio State U., 1942. Rsch. fellow Brookings Instn., 1941-42; rsch. dir. Labor and Mgmt. Ctr., Yale, 1946-49, asst. dir., 1949-54; asst. prof. econs. Yale, 1947-49, assoc. prof., 1949-54, prof. econs., 1959-67, Columbia, 1954-59, 67-80, Armand G. Erpf prof. of modern corp., 1969-80, prof. emeritus, 1981—. Dir. program in Econ. Devel. and Adminstrn. Ford Found., 1957-60 Author: Collective Bargaining Procedures, 1944, The Union Challenge to Management Control, 1948, Management in Motion, 1950, Collective Bargaining, 1951, rev., 1965, 3d edit., 1986, Social Responsibility and Strikes, 1953, The Impact of Strikes, 1954, A General Theory of Economic Process, 1955, Labor, 1958, Source-book on Labor, 1958, The Firm: Micro- Economic Planning and Action, 1962, The West in a World Without War, 1963, The Labor Sector, 1965, rev., 1971, 80, Private and Public Planning, 1965, Enterprise and Environment, 1968, Beyond Malthus, 1970, The Place of Business in America's Future: A Study in Social Values, 1973, The Limits of Corporate Responsibility, 1973, Remaking American Values: Challenge to a Business Society, 1977, Forces of Change in Western Europe, 1980, Social Strategy and Corporate Structure, 1982, Intellectual Odyssey: An Economist's Ideological Journey, 1996; editor: Contemporary Economic Issues, 1969, rev., 1978, Business and the Cities, 1970; co-editor: Cases on Labor Relations, 1949, A Decade of Industrial Relations Research, 1958, Frontiers of Collective Bargaining, 1968; mem. editorial bd., editorial cons.: Mgmt. Internat, 1960-70; bd. editors: Am. Econ. Rev, 1957-59. Bd. dirs. Salzburg Seminar in Am. Studies, 1957-78; trustee Columbia Jour. World Bus., 1969-72, 75-80. Served from ensign to lt. USNR, 1942-46. Mem.: Indsl. Rels. Rsch. Assn. (exec. bd. 1955—58, pres. 1967, Lifetime Achievement award 2003), Am. Econ. Assn., Phi Beta Kappa. Home: 49 W 24th St New York NY 10010-3206

CHAMBERLAIN, OWEN, nuclear physicist; b. San Francisco, July 10, 1920; m. Babette Copper, 1943 (div. 1978); 4 children; m. June Steingart, 1980 (dec.); m. Senta Pugh, 1998. AB (Cramer fellow), Dartmouth Coll., 1941; PhD, U. Chgo., 1949. Instr. physics U. Calif., Berkeley, 1948—50, asst. prof., 1950—54, assoc. prof., 1954—58, prof., 1958—89, prof. emeritus, 1989—; civilian physicist Manhattan Dist., Berkeley, Los Alamos, 1942—46. Recipient Nobel prize (with Emilio Segre) in Physics, for discovery of anti-proton, 1959, The Berkeley citation, U. Calif., 1989, Loeb lectr., Harvard U., 1959; fellow Guggenheim, 1957—58. Fellow: Am. Acad. Arts and Scis., Am. Phys. Soc.; mem.: NAS, Berkeley Fellows. Office: U Calif Phys Dept Berkeley CA 94720-0001

CHAMBERLAIN, ROBERT GLENN, retired tool manfacturing executive; b. Cedar Rapids, Iowa, Feb. 17, 1926; s. Glenn Arlie and Ora Margarite (Castle) C.; m. Jane Helen Newlin, June 13, 1946; children: Carole, James, Sue, Patricia, Tracey. BSM.E., Iowa State U., 1949; postgrad., U. Wis.Milw. With Link-Belt Speeder, Cedar Rapids, 1949-54, Giddings & Lewis, Fond du Lac, Wis., 1954-83, group v.p. indsl. products, 1980-82, exec. v.p. machine tools, 1982-83, ret., 1983. Pioneer numerical control programmer, 1954-59. Mem. PTO; v.p. Bay Lakes coun. Boy Scouts Am., Menasha, Wis., 1982-89, exploring chmn. in sch., Dallas, 1981, exploring chmn. Area 1 NC region, Oak Brook, Ill., 1977; bd. dirs. Evergreen Retirement Cmty., 1989-94. With USNR, 1944-46. Recipient Silver Beaver award Boy Scouts Am., 1974, Silver Antelope award, 1983. Mem. Masons. Home: W2728 Oakwood Beach Rd Markesan WI 53946-8904

CHAMBERLAIN, THOMAS EUGENE, mechanical engineer; b. Hammonton, N.J., Dec. 14, 1939; s. Thomas Morton and Eugenia Dobas Chamberlain; m. Mary Agnes Chamberlain, Oct. 22, 1966; 1 child, Thomas Charles. BS in Aero. Engring., Boston U., 1961; MS in Aeronautics and Astronautics, MIT, 1966; PhD in Mech. Engring., U. Calif., Berkeley., 1972. Aerodynamicist The Boeing Co., Seattle, 1961-63; physicist Physics Internat., San Leandro, Calif., 1966-68; rsch. scientist TRW, Inc., Redondo Beach, Calif., 1972-78; cons. Jet Propulsion Lab., Byron Jackson, others, 1978-95; prin. engr./scientist The Boeing Co., Long Beach, Calif., 1995—2002. Ind. rschr. in human behavior, psychology, social psychology, econs., 1982—. Contbr. articles to profl. publs., including Sci., Aerospace and Electronic Sytems Mag. (co-author Best Article 1976 Sci.); presenter numerous internat. confs. Mem. AAAS, AIAA, ASME, Am. Econ. Assn., Soc. Math. Psychology, Western. Econ. Assn. Internat., Econometric Soc., European Union Studies Assn., Internat. Atlantic Econ. Soc., Soc. for Advancement Behavioral Econ., Boston U. Alumni Assn., MIT Alumni Assn. Home and Office: 843 W 24th St # 2 San Pedro CA 90731 E-mail: tomchamb@ix.netcom.com.

CHAMBERLAIN, WILLARD THOMAS, retired metals company executive; b. New Haven, Nov. 22, 1928; s. Thomas Huntington and Alice Irene (Daley) C.; m. Harriet Halbert Keck, Nov. 20, 1965; children: Huntington Wilson, Amy Thatcher. B.E., Yale U., 1950; postgrad., Ill. Inst. Tech., 1951-53. With Armour Research Found., Chgo., 1951-53; asst. to tech. mgr. Anaconda Brass div. Anaconda Corp., Waterbury, Conn., 1953-56, tech. supr., 1956-60, metall. mgr. Torrington, Conn., 1960-61, mgr. devel. Waterbury, 1961-62, lab. mgr., 1962-64, mgr. research-tech. ctr., 1964-67, mgr. Valley Mills, 1967, Ansonia, 1967-70, mgr. prodn. planning, 1970-71, v.p. mfg., 1971-72, exec. v.p. Brass div., 1972-74, pres., 1974-80, Anaconda Industries, 1980; sr. v.p. Atlantic Richfield Co., 1980-82; pres. Arco Metals Co., 1982-85; sr. v.p. corp. affairs Atlantic Richfield Co., 1985-87; sr. v.p. govt. and pub. affairs ARCO, 1987-89. Mem. So. Calif. bus. com. Econ. Literacy Council Adv. of Calif. Mem. exec. bd. Waterbury Republican Town Com., 1964-70; commr. Waterbury Bd. Fin., 1966-67, chmn. charter revision com., 1966-67; mem. exec. bd. Mattatuck council Boy Scouts Am., 1965-72, Waterbury Assn. for Retarded Children, 1965-66; co-chmn. Clergy-Industry Conf., 1965-66; campaign chmn. Valley United Fund, 1970-71; bd. dirs. United Way, Central Naugatuck Valley, 1974, The Banking Ctr., 1974-81, Western Conn. Indsl. Council, 1974-81, Calif. State U. Found., Found. for Am. Communications, Los Angeles Arts Council; trustee Calif. Mus. Found., Harvey Mudd Coll.; bd. trustees Greater Los Angeles Partnership for the Homeless; bd. dirs. L.A. Habitat for Humanity. Recipient Outstanding Civic Leader award, 1967. Mem. Copper Devel. Assn., Aluminum Assn. (dir.), Am. Soc. Metals, Yale Engring. Assn., Greater Waterbury C. of C. (bd. dirs. 1974), Alliance Aging Rsch. (bd. dirs.), Am. Petroleum Inst. (emerging issues task force), Brookings Instn. (coun. mem.), Calif. State U. Found. (bd. dirs., compensation planning com., chmn. investment com.), Calif. State U. Bus. Assocs., Constl. Rights Found. (bus. adv. coun.), Econ. Literacy Coun. Adv. Calif. (so. Calif. bus. com.), Found. Am. Communications (dir.), Hugh O'Brian Youth Found., Math. Engring. and Sci. Achievement (industry adv. bd.), Nat. Action Coun. for Minorities in Engring., Nat. Minority Supplier Devel. Coun. (bd. dirs.), Nat. Wetlands Policy Forum, Nat. Wildlife Fedn. (vice chmn. corp. conservation coun.), Vols. of Am., L.A., Town Hall, U.S. C. of C., World Affairs Coun., Univ. Club L.A., Yale Club, So. Calif. Presbyterian. Home: 7115 Hawarden Dr Riverside CA 92506 E-mail: wtc91107@yahoo.com.

CHAMBERLAIN, WILLIAM EDWIN, JR., management consultant; b. St. Louis, June 8, 1951; s. William Edwin Sr. and Grace (Salisbury) C. AA in Bus. Mgmt., Mesa (Ariz.) Community Coll., 1983; BBA, U. Phoenix, 1988. Tng. and human resources devel. specialist Motorola, Inc., Phoenix, 1979-87; pres., seminar speaker Chamberlain Cons. Svcs., Reno, Nev., 1987—. Curator, dir. ops. U.S. Wolf Refuge. Mem. Network for Profl. Devel. Avocations: wildlife preservation and management, hiking, backpacking, tennis, basketball, racquetball. *Personal philosophy: Better people make better workers and better workers make better people. A company's workforce is often its biggest investment, therefore efforts to develop its workers will often bring the biggest returns.*

CHAMBERLAND, MARC A. mathematician, educator; b. Shawinigan, Que., Can., Aug. 22, 1964; arrived in U.S., 1997; s. André J. and Denise G. Chamberland; m. Marion Weber, Apr. 30, 1994; children: Jacob, Lucas, Julia. B in Math., U. Waterloo, Can., 1988, M in Math., 1990, PhD, 1995. Postdoctoral fellow McMaster U., Hamilton, Canada, 1995—97; asst. prof. Grinnell (Iowa) Coll., 1997—. Co-organizer Internat. Conf. on the Collatz Problem and Related Topics Katholische Univ., Eichstätt, Germany, 1999. Contbr. articles to profl. jours. Natural Scis. and Engring. Rsch. Coun. Can. grad. fellow, U. Waterloo, Natural Scis. and Engring. Rsch. Coun. Can. postdoctoral fellow, McMaster U., 1995—97, Harris fellow, Grinnell Coll., 2001—02. Office: Grinnell Coll 1116 8th Ave Grinnell IA 50112

CHAMBERLIN, ANN, novelist, playwright; b. Salt Lake City, Mar. 28, 1954; d. R. Eliot and F. Elizabeth (Maud) C.; m. Curt F. Setzer, Sept. 14, 1978; children: Eliot, Harris. BA, U. Utah, Salt Lake City, 1978. Author: (novels) The Virgin and the Tower, 1979, Tamar, 1994, Sofia, 1996 (best fgn. historical Affaire de Coeur mag.), The Sultan's Daughter, 1997 (best fgn. historical, best all-round historical), The Reign of the Favored Woman, 1998, Leaving Eden, 1999, The Merlin of St. Gilles Well, 1999 (Best Fantasy Novel of Yr., Booklist), The Merlin of the Oak Wood, 2001 (Best Fantasy Novel or Yr., VOYA); (plays) To Life (winner Utah Playwriting Competition), Faerie Tale (winner Utah Playwriting Competition), Ex Cathedra (winner Utah Playwriting Competition), Shadow Play, Acting Heads of State (1st choice finalist category Albalt Play Search 1993), Someone Like No Other (finalist Cleve Pub. Theatre's Festival of New Plays 1994), The Piper Must Be Paid (semi-finalist Shiras Inst./Mildred and Albert Panowski award 1994), Every Woman Blues (finalist Shenandoah Playwrights Retreat 1995, Dayton's Futurefest 1995), Simoom (finalist Jane Chambers Playwriting award 1995), Jihad (Best New Play of Yr. Off-Off Broadway Review 1996). Mem. Romance Writers Am., Dramatists Guild, Novelists, Inc., Sci. Fiction Writers Am. Avocations: gardening, cooking, folk dancing. Home: PO Box 711114 Salt Lake City UT 84171-1114 E-mail: setzers@msn.com.

CHAMBERLIN, DONALD DEAN, computer engineer; b. San Jose, Calif., Dec. 21, 1944; BS, Harvey Mudd Coll., 1966; PhD in Elec. Engring., Stanford U., 1971. Rsch. staff mem. IBM, San Jose, Calif., 1971—. Adj. prof. Santa Clara U., 1992-95. Author: Using the New DB2: IBM's Object-Relational Database System, 1996, A Complete Guide to DB2 Universal Database, 1998; contbr. articles to profl. jours. Fellow Assn. Computing Machinery; mem. Nat. Acad. Engring., Inst. Elec. & Electronics Engrs. Office: Almaden Research Ctr IBM 650 Harry Rd San Jose CA 95120-6001 Fax: 408-927-3215. E-mail: chamberlin@almaden.ibm.com.

CHAMBERLIN, EDWARD ROBERT, career officer, educator; b. Boston, May 16, 1944; s. Joseph King and Ruth Louise (Cooper) C.; m. Sandra Jean Stratton, June 10, 1972; children: Jill, Courtney, Katherine, Rebecca. BBA, U. Wis., 1966; MBA, Harvard U., 1973. Commd. ensign USN, 1966, advanced through grades to rear adm., 1993; head data processing dept. Naval Air Sta., Jacksonville, Fla., 1973-75; supply officer USS Little Rock, Gaeta, Italy, 1976; instr. Navy Supply Corps Sch., Athens, Ga., 1976-79; weapons policy officer Aviation Supply Office, USN, Phila., 1980-82; supply officer USS Nimitz, Norfolk, Va., 1983-84; with Stock Point ADP Replacement project office Naval Supply Systems Command, Washington, 1985-88; asst. chief of staff logistics Naval Air Force Pacific, Coronado, Calif., 1989-90; exec. asst., asst. sec. of def. Office of Sec. of Def., Washington, 1991-92; COO Def. Logistics Agy., Alexandria, Va., 1997—; pres., CEO, NISH, Vienna, Va., 2000—. Pres. Parent Tchrs. Student Orgn., Churchville, Pa., 1982, 83; elder 1st United Presbyn. Ch., Dale City, Va., 1993, 94; mem. Pres.'s Com. Purchase From Blind and Disabled, Washington, 1998—; vol. Naval Credit Union, Vienna, Va., 1997-99; bd. dirs. Westminster/Ingleside Retirement Cmtys., 2001—. Decorated Def. Superior Svc. (2), Legion of Merit (2), Def. Disting. Svc. medal. Avocations: swimming, jogging, biking. Office: NISH 2235 Cedar Ln Vienna VA 22182-5200 E-mail: bchamberlin@nish.org.

CHAMBERLIN, JOAN MARY, school system administrator; b. Cleve., May 30, 1955; d. John A. and Patricia Irene (Mirous) Chesney; m. Alexis Lee Chamberlin, Apr. 24, 1976; children: Matthew James, Sarah Marie, Michael Alexis. BS in Edn., Kent State U., 1976, MED, 1992, EdS, 1996. Cert. asst. supt., prin., tchr. Ohio. Elem. tchr. Cleve. Diocese, 1976-78; mid. sch. tchr. Garfield Heights (Ohio) City Schs., 1978-79, elem. tchr., 1989-93, computer tchr., 1994-95, adult edn. dir., 1994-98, unit prin., 1998, Ednl. Mgmt. Info. Sys. dir., 1994—2003, asst. prin., 1993-98, pupil svcs. dir., 1998—2003, asst. supt., 2003—. Adminstrv. leader Alternative Juvenile Program, 1998-2003. Adminstrv. leader Garfield Heights Youth, Family and Teen Svcs., 1997-98; mem., officer St. Nick and St. Vincent De Paul, Garfield Heights, 1994—. Kurdziel grantee Henry and Kathryn Kurdziel Found., 1993-94; Ohio Classrm. Mgmt. grantee, 1997-98. Mem. ASCD, East Side Adult Edn. Roundtable. Roman Catholic. Avocations: piano playing, choir, swimming, camping, crafts. Home: 6404 Hathaway Rd Garfield Heights OH 44125 Office: Garfield Heights City Schs 5640 Briarcliff Dr Garfield Heights OH 44125 E-mail: jmchamberlin@garfield-heights.k12.oh.us.

CHAMBERLIN, JOHN STEPHEN, investor, former cosmetics company executive; b. Boston, July 29, 1928; s. Stephen Henry and Olive Helen (McGrath) C.; m. Mary Katherine Leahy, Oct. 9, 1954; children— Mary Katherine, Patricia Ann, Carol Lynn, John Stephen Jr., Liane Helen, Mark Joseph. AB cum laude, Harvard U., 1950, MBA, 1953. Lamp salesman Gen. Electric Co., N.Y.C., 1954-57, mgmt. cons., 1957-60, mgr. product planning TV receiver dept. Syracuse, N.Y., 1960-63, mgr. mktg., gen. mgr. radio receiver dept. Utica, N.Y., 1963-70; exec. v.p., dir. Lenox Inc., Trenton, N.J., 1970-71; v.p., gen. mgr. housewares div. Gen. Electric Co., Bridgeport, Conn., 1971-74, v.p., gen. mgr. housewares and audio div., 1974-76; pres., chief exec. officer, dir. Lenox Inc., Lawrenceville, N.J., 1976-81, chmn., chief exec. officer, 1981-85; pres., chief operating officer Avon Products, Inc., N.Y.C., 1985-88; pvt. investor Princeton, N.J., 1988—. Bd. dirs. Health South Corp.; sr. advisor Mancuso & Co., 1992—98. Trustee Med. Ctr. at Princeton, vice chmn. 1995, chmn., 2002; trustee Woodrow Wilson Nat. Fellowship Found. Mem. Bedens Brook Club, Harvard Club N.Y.C., Nassau. Home: 182 Fairway Dr Princeton NJ 08540-2410

CHAMBERLIN, MICHAEL JOHN, biochemistry educator; b. Chgo., June 7, 1937; s. John Windsor and Marian (McMichael) C.; m. Caroline Marie Kane, Jan. 31, 1981. AB, Harvard U., 1959; PhD, Stanford U., 1963. Asst. prof. virology U. Calif., Berkeley, 1963—67, assoc. prof. molecular biology, 1967—71, assoc. prof. biochemistry, 1971—73; prof., 1973—99, U. Calif., Berkeley, 1973, vice chmn. dept. biochemistry, 1983—88, prof. biochemistry and molecular biology, 1989; emeritus prof., 1999. Mem. physiol. chemistry study sect. NIH, 1970-74, molecular biology study sect., 1980-84; mem. study sect. Am. Heart Assn., 1983-86. Mem. editorial bd. Jour. Biol. Chemistry, 1975-78, Biochemistry, 1993—; contbr. articles to profl. jours. Recipient Charles Pfizer award Am. Chem. Soc., 1974. Mem. NAS, AAAS, Am. Acad. Arts and Scis., Am. Soc. Biochemistry and Molecular Biology, Am. Soc. Microbiology, Am. Acad. Microbiology, Phi Beta Kappa, Sigma Xi. Office: U Calif Dept Molecular/Cell Biology 401 Barker Hall Berkeley CA 94720-3208 E-mail: mar-lin@socrates.berkeley.edu.

CHAMBERLIN, MICHAEL MEADE, lawyer; b. Omaha; s. Cecil Meade and Helen Gail (Russell) C. AB in Econs., Princeton U., 1972; JD, George Washington U., 1975. Bar: N.Y. 1976. Assoc. Shearman & Sterling, N.Y.C., 1975-83, ptnr., 1984-93; CEO, exec. dir. EMTA, 1994—. Avocations: conservation, running, choral music, skiing, flying. E-mail: mchamb@emta.org.

CHAMBERLIN, RALPH VARY, physicist, educator; b. Albuquerque, Apr. 22, 1956; s. Richard Eliot and Frances Elizabeth Chamberlin; m. Ute Elisabeth Chamberlin, July 23, 1988; children: Christopher Eliot, Richard Martin, Thomas Bernhard. BS, U. Utah, 1978; MS, UCLA, 1979, PhD, 1984. Rsch. investigator U. Pa., Phila., 1984-86; from asst. prof. to assoc. prof. Ariz. State U., Tempe, 1986-2000, prof., 2000—. Vis. assoc. prof. Technische Hochschule Darmstadt, Germany, 1993. Contbr. articles to profl. jours. Recipient Rsch. prize, Alexander von Humboldt Found., 2001. Mem. AAAS, Am. Phys. Soc., Sigma Xi. Achievements include invention of vertical cantilever non-contact force microscope. Office: Ariz State U Box 871504 Tempe AZ 85287-1504

CHAMBERLIN-DAVIS, ANN ELIZABETH, artist, writer; b. Plainfield, N.J., May 10, 1955; d. Earl Martin and Mary Helen Chamberlin; m. Steven Joseph Davis, Aug. 7, 1993. Student, Whitney Mus. Ind. Study, N.Y.C., 1975; BA, Rutgers U., 1977. Artist, author, linguist, Highland Park, N.J., 1986—. Author: (novels) The Writer, 1993, May Nancy, 1995, Her Other Life, 1997; (short story) Slum City Memoirs, 1972. Pub. spkr. The Club, New Brunswick, N.J., 1986-93. Grantee N.J. State Coun. Arts, 1981. Avocations: painting, writing, russian language, poetry, music. Home: 29 S Adelaide Ave Apt 1 Highland Park NJ 08904

CHAMBERS, ANNE COX, newspaper executive, former diplomat; b. Dayton, Ohio; Student, Finch Coll., N.Y.C.; D in Pub. Svc. (hon.), Wesleyan Coll., 1982; DHL (hon.), Spelman Coll., 1983; LLD (hon.), Oglethorpe U., 1983; DHL (hon.), Brenau Coll., 1989; LLD (hon.), Clark Atlanta U., 1989. Chmn. bd. Atlanta Jour.-Constn.; Am. amb. to Belgium, 1977-81. Bd. dirs. Cox Enterprises, Inc. Bd. dirs. Atlanta Arts Alliance, High Mus. Art, Cmtys. in Schs., MacDowell Colony, Forward Arts Found., Emory Mus. Art and Archaeology, N.Y. Bot. Garden, Coun. Am. Ambs., Chmn.'s Coun., Met. Mus. Art, Fr.-Am. Found.; trustee Mus. Modern Art, Carter Ctr.; mem. internat. coun. Mus. Modern Art; mem. nat. com. Whitney Mus. Am. Art. Decorated Legion of Hon. (France). Mem. Coun. Fgn. Rels. Office: 6205 Peachtree Dunwoody Rd Atlanta GA 30328

CHAMBERS, AUDLEY C. music historian, educator, researcher; s. H. Chambers and Chambers P.. Diploma in structural engring., South London Coll. Structural Engring., 1973—80; BSc in music edn., Oakwood Coll., 1981—86; MA in music history, Ohio State U., 1986—88; PhD, Northwestern U., 1989—99. Vocal/choral K-12 (music edn.) Dept. Edn., 1986, vocal/choral (music edn.) North Am. Divsn. Office Edn., 1986. Grad. tchg. assoc. Ohio State U., Columbus, Ohio, 1986—88; asst. prof. (music and black studies) Coll. Wooster, Wooster, Ohio, 1988—89; grad. tchg. assoc. Northwestern U., Evanston, Ill., 1989—94; vis. instr. music Columbia Coll., Chicago, 1990—90; asst. prof. music history and lit. Oakwood Coll., Huntsville, Ala., 1994—2000, assoc. prof. music history and lit., 2000—. Freelance music critic Huntsville Times, Ala., 1999—2000; freelance music critic Decature Concert Assn./ Dectur Daily, Ala., 2000—. Contbr. audio cassette; musician: (Oakwood Coll. video cassette) Oakwood College: A Centennial of Service. Bd. mem. Huntsville Youth Symphony Orch., 1995—98. Grantee Faculty Retraining Grant, UNCF, 1999. Mem.: Hymn Soc., Soc. Am. Music, Internat. Adventist Music Soc., Ctr. Black Music Rsch., Am. Musicological Soc., Coll. Music Soc. Achievements include research in Frederic H. Cowen (1852-1935): Reception History of His songs for voice and Piano. Avocations: fell walking, hiking, camping, badminton, gourmet vegan cuisine.

CHAMBERS, CAROL TOBEY, elementary school educator; b. L.A., July 17, 1947; d. Joseph Richard and Jean Doris (Neal) Tobey; m. Joseph Price Chambers, June 8, 1973; 1 child, Ryan Leigh. Student, Ohio State U., 1965-67; BS in Edn., George Peabody Coll. Tchrs., 1969; postgrad., U. Tenn., 1971, Belmont U., 1971, 88, 96, Tenn. State U., 1980-83, Vanderbilt U., 1986, 92, Trevecca Coll., 1978, 89, 90, Tenn. Arts Acad., 1989, 94-96; arts seminar, workshop, Coll. of Santa Fe, 1997. Cert. tchr. elem. edn., K-12 art, Tenn. Tchr. 4th grade Metro-Nashville Pub. Sch., Nashville, 1969-70, tchr. art, music, 1970-71; tchr. 5th grade Harding Acad., Nashville, 1971-75, tchr. art K-8, 1977-2000, tchr. art K-5, 2000—, chmn. fine arts com. Presenter workshops Mid-So. Assn. Ind. Schs., Nashville, 1971—75; vis. com. Oak Hill Sch. So. Assn. Colls. and Schs., Nashville, 1990; vis. com. St. Bernard Acad., 1991; chair planning com. Harding Acad., Nashville, 1992—94, mem. 25th ann. com., chmn. fine arts com.; fine arts chair St. Cecilia Acad. Parents Club, Nashville, 1991—93, mem. Parents Club; co-founder Art Tchrs. Guild, Nashville; organizer Youth Art Month Exhibit, Nashville, 1992—. V.p. in charge of art Children's Internat. Edn. Ctr., Nashville, 1985-90; mem. edn. coun. Frist Fine Arts Ctr.; mem. Cheekwood Fine Arts Ctr. and Bot. Gardens, Nashville, 1987—; prodr. parent's seminar 1st Bapt. Ch., 1986; charter mem. Frist Mus. for Visual Arts. Recipient C. of C. award for best spl. project/display for Artworks 9, 2000; Outstanding Tchr. of Humanities grantee Tenn. Humanities Couns., 1988; named Tenn. Elem. Art Tchr. of Yr., Tenn. Art Edn. Assn., 2001. Mem. Nat. Art Edn. Assn., Tenn. Art Edn. Assn., Nat. Mus. Women in the Arts (charter). Baptist. Avocations: watercolor and calligraphy, traveling, singing, piano. Home: 722 Starlit Rd Nashville TN 37205-1210 Office: 170 Windsor Dr Nashville TN 37205-3719 E-mail: chambersc@hardingacademy.org.

CHAMBERS, CAROLYN SILVA, communications company executive; b. Portland, Oreg., Sept. 15, 1931; d. Julio and Elizabeth (McDonnell) Silva; widowed; children: William, Scott, Elizabeth, Silva, Clark. BBA, U. Oreg. V.p., treas. Liberty Comm., Inc., Eugene, Oreg., 1960-83; pres. Chambers Comm. Corp., Eugene, 1983-95, chmn., 1996—; chmn., CEO, bd. dirs. Chambers Constrn. Co., 1986—. Bd. dirs., dep. chair bd. Fed. Res. Bank, San Francisco, 1982-92; bd. dirs. Portland Gen. Corp.; bd. dirs. U.S. Bancorp. Mem. Sacred Heart Med. Found., 1980—, Sacred Heart Gov. Bd., 1987-92, Sacred Heart Health Svcs. Bd., 1993-95, PeaceHealth Bd., 1995—; mem. U. Oreg. Found., 1980—, pres., 1992-93; chair U. Oreg. Found., The Campaign for Oreg., 1988-89; pres., bd. dirs. Eugene Arts Found.; bd. dirs., pres., dir. search com. Eugene Symphony; mem. adv. bd. Eugene Hearing and Speech Ctr., Alton Baker Park Commn., Pleasant Hill Sch. Bd.; chmn., pres., treas. Civic Theatre, Very Little Theatre; negotiator, treas., bd. dirs., mem. thrift shop Jr. League of Oreg. Recipient Webfoot award U. Oreg., 1986, U. Oreg. Pres.'s medal, 1991, Disting. Svc. award, 1992, Pioneer award, 1983, Woman Who Made a Difference award Internat. Women's Forum, 1989, U. Oreg. Found. Disting. Alumni award, 1995, Tom McCall awrd Oreg. Assn. Broadcasters, 1995, Disting. Alumni award U. Oreg., 1995, Outstanding Philanthropist award Oreg. chpt. Nat. Soc. Fund Raising Execs., 1994. Mem. Nat. Cable TV Assn. (mem. fin. com., chmn. election and by-laws com., chmn. awards com., bd. dirs. 1987-89, Vanguard award for Leadership 1982), Pacific Northwest Cable Comm. Assn. (conv. chmn., pres.), Oreg. Cable TV Assn. (v.p., pres., chmn. edn. com., conv. chmn., Pres.'s award 1986), Calif. Cable TV Assn. (bd. dirs., conv. chmn., conv. panelist), Women in Cable (charter mem., treas., v.p., pres., recipient star of cable recognition), Wash. State Cable Comm. Assn., Idaho Cable TV Assn., Community Antenna TV Assn., Cable TV Pioneers, Eugene C. of C. (first citizen award, 1985). Home: PO Box 640 Pleasant Hill OR 97455-0640 Office: Chambers Comm Corp PO Box 7009 Eugene OR 97401-0009

CHAMBERS, CHARLES MACKAY, university president; b. Hampton, Va., June 22, 1941; s. Charles McKay and Ruth Ellanora (Wallach) C.; m. Barbara Mae Fromm, June 9, 1962; children: Charles M., Catherine M., Christina M., Carleton M. BS, U. Ala., 1962, MS, 1963, PhD, 1964; JD, George Washington U., 1976. Bar: Va. 1977, D.C. 1978, U.S. Patent and Trademark Office, 1978, U.S. Supreme Ct. 1980, U.S. Dist. Ct. D.C. 1985, U.S. Ct. Appeals (D.C. cir.) 1987, U.S. Dist. Ct. (ea. dist.) Va. 1988, U.S. Ct. Appeals D.C., 1987, U.S. Ct. Appeals (4th cir.) 1990, Mich. 1994; cert. comml. pilot, multiengine, land and instrument. Aerospace engr. NASA, Huntsville, Ala., 1962-63; rsch., teaching asst. U. Ala. Rsch. Inst., Huntsville, Ala., 1963-64; research fellow NASA, Cambridge, Mass., 1964-65; assoc. prof. U. Ala., Tuscaloosa, 1965-69; mng. dir. Univ. Assocs., Washington, 1969-72; prof., assoc. dean George Washington U., Washington, 1972-77; v.p., gen. counsel Council on Postsecondary Accreditation, Washington, 1977-83; exec. dir. Am. Inst. Biol. Sci., Washington, 1983-87; pres. Am. Found. Biol. Scis., Washington, 1987-93, Lawrence Tech. U., Southfield, Mich., 1993—. Cons., evaluator, accreditation rev. coun. commn. on instns. of higher edn. Noth Ctrl. Assn. Colls. and Schs., Chgo.; bd. dirs. Automation Alley, Mich., Internat. Sci. and Engring. Fair 2000, Mich. Sci. and Math. Alliance, 2000—. Author: (with others) Understanding Accreditation, 1983; pub. BioScience; contbr. chpts. to books. Mem. Diocesan Adv. Coun., Arlington, Va., 1978-84, Fairfax County (Va.) Dem. Com., 1979-95; judge No. Va. Sci. Fair, 1976—; trustee, sec. Southeastern U., Washington, 1983-87; trustee BIOSIS, Inc., Phila. and London, 1991-93; mem. Oakland County (Mich.) Workforce Devel. Bd., 1996—; bd. dirs. Automation Alley, 1999—. Recipient Olive Branch award Editors and Writers Com., N.Y.C., 1986, Citizenship award Am. Legion, 1959; postdoctoral fellow Nat. Sci. Found., 1964. Fellow AAAS; mem. ABA, AAUP, Am. Assn. Univ. Adminstrs. (pres. 1984-85), Engring. and Sci. Devel. Found. (bd. dirs., pres. 1996-2000, fellow Engring. Soc. 1997), Am. Coun. Edn. (bus. and higher edn. forum), Soc. Automotive Engrs., Nat. Soc. Black Engrs. (hon.), ESD-The Engring. Soc. (bd. dirs. 1999—), Circumnavigators Club, Econ. Club of Detroit (bd. dirs.), Detroit Athletic Club, Cosmos Club, Phi Beta Kappa, Sigma Xi, Tau Beta Pi. Roman Catholic. Avocation: flying. Office: Lawrence Tech U 21000 W 10 Mile Rd Ste M351 Southfield MI 48075-1058 E-mail: mail@charleschambers.com.

CHAMBERS, CLARICE LORRAINE, clergy, educational consultant; b. Ossining, N.Y., Oct. 7, 1938; d. Willie and Louise (McDonald) Cross (dec.); m. Albert W. Chambers, June 9, 1962; children: Albert W., Cheryl L. Fultz. Diploma, Manna Bible Inst., Phila.; BS in Bibl. Studies, Trinity Coll. of Bible, Newburgh, Ind., 1983; MA in Bibl. Theology, Internat. Bible Inst. and Sem., Orlando, Fla., 1986. Ordained to ministry Pentecostal Ch., 1977. Master data specialist Naval Supply Dept., Phila., 1957-65; dir. tng., tchr. Opportunities Indsl. Ctr., Harrisburg, Pa., 1969-72; pub. info. asst. Pa. Dept. Revenue, Harrisburg, 1972-79; pastor Antioch Tabernacle United Holy Ch. of Am., Harrisburg, 1979—. Fin. sec. United Holy Ch. of Am., Greensboro, N.C., 1978-92, treas. no. dist., Linden, N.J., 1992-96; screening team La. Dept. Edn., Baton Rouge, 1995. Mem. Harrisburg Sch. Bd., 1975-2001; pres. Pa. Sch. Bds. Assn., New Cumberland, 1992; bd. dirs. Nat. Sch. Bds. Assn., Alexandria, Va., 1993-2002, pres., 2000; trustee Shippensburg (Pa.) U., 1989-96. Recipient Cmty. Sv. award Ctrl. Pa. chpt. Nat. Assn. Black Accts., 1984, Harrisburg chpt. Black United Fund. Pa., 1989, Outstanding Leadership award Greater Harrisburg NAACP, 1987, Svc. award Coun. of Pub. Edn., 1995. Democrat. Avocations: singing, reading. Home: 140 Sylvan Ter Harrisburg PA 17104-1079 Office: Antioch Tabernacle UHC of Am 1920 North St Harrisburg PA 17103-1631 E-mail: pastor.c@att.net.

CHAMBERS, CLYTIA MONTLLOR, public relations consultant; b. Rochester, N.Y., Oct. 23, 1922; d. Anthony and Marie (Bambace) Capraro; m. Joseph John Montllor, July 2, 1941 (div. 1958); children: Michele, Thomas, Clytia; m. Robert Chambers, May 28, 1965. BA, Barnard Coll., N.Y.C., 1942; Licence en droit, Faculte de Droit, U. Lyon, France, 1948; MA, Howard U., Washington, 1958. Assoc. dir. dept. rsch. Coun. for Fin. Aid to Edn., N.Y.C., 1958-60; asst. to v.p. indsl. rels. Sinclair Oil Corp., N.Y.C., 1961-65; writer pub. rels. dept. Am. Oil Co., Chgo., 1965-67; dir. editorial svcs., v.p. Hill & Knowlton Inc., N.Y.C., 1967-77, sr. v.p., dir. spl. svcs. L.A., 1977-90, sr. cons., 1990—. Cons. and trustee Children's Inst. Internat., L.A., 1988-93. Co-author: The News Twisters, 1971; editor: Critical Issues in Public Relations, 1975. Mem.: Calif. Rare Fruit Growers (editor Fruit Gardener 1979—2000, editor emerita 2000—). Home: 11439 Laurelcrest Dr Studio City CA 91604-3872 E-mail: clytia@sbcglobal.net.

CHAMBERS, CURTIS ALLEN, clergyman, church communications executive; b. Damascus, Ohio, Sept. 24, 1924; s. Binford Vincent and Margaret Esther (Patterson) C.; m. Anna June Winn, Aug. 26, 1946; children: David Lloyd, Curtis Allen II, Deborah Ann, Charles Cloyde. Th.B., Malone Coll., 1946; AB, Ind. Wesleyan U., 1947; B.D., Asbury Theol. Sem., 1950; postgrad., Oberlin Grad. Sch. Theology, 1951-53; S.T.M., Temple U., 1955, S.T.D., 1960; D.D. (hon.), Lebanon Valley Coll., 1967. Ordained to ministry Evang. United Brethren Ch., 1954. Pastor 1st Ch., Cleve., 1951-53, Rockville Ch., Harrisburg, Pa., 1953-59; editor adult publs. Evang. United Brethren Ch., 1959-65; assoc. editor Ch. and Home mag., Dayton, Ohio, 1963-66, editor, 1967-69; asst. editorial dir. Together and Christian Advocate, Meth. Pub. House, Park Ridge, Ill., 1969; editor Together mag., 1969-73; acting editorial dir. gen. periodicals United Meth. Ch., 1971-72, editorial dir., 1972-73; gen. sec. United Meth. Communications, 1973-84; gen. mgr. Alternate View Network, 1984-85; minister edn. and communication First United Meth. Ch., Shreveport, La., 1985-87, minister pastoral care and communication, 1987-88; minister program and communication St. Paul's United Meth. Ch., Monroe, La., 1988-90; religious communication cons. Nashville, 1990—; assoc. pastor Andrew Price United Meth. Ch., Nashville, 1991-94. Book editor Evang. United Brethren Ch., 1965-68; co-editor Plan of Union, United Meth. Ch., 1965-68, Plan of Union, United Meth. Ch. (Book of Discipline), 1968, chmn. staff com. long range planning, 1969-72, mem. commn. on ch. union, 1965-68; dir. radio-TV relations gen. confs. Evang. United Brethren Ch., 1958, 62, 66, United Meth. Ch., 1966, 68; Chmn. commn. on edn. media Nat. Council Chs., 1965-66, chmn. com. on audio visual and broadcast edn., 1962-65, exec. com. broadcasting and film commn., chmn. communications commn., 1975-78, v.p., 1975-78; chmn. Religious Communications Congress, 1980; named 1 of 12 editors sent to Middle East on fact-finding trip, 1969 Contbr. articles to religious lit. Served as capt. (chaplain) CAP, 1960-65. Recipient Distinguished Alumni award Malone Coll., 1967, Alumni of Year, 1978, Distinguished Alumni award Goshen High Sch. Alumni Assn., 1992; named to Communicators Hall of Fame United Met. Assn. Communicators, 1992. Mem. Aircraft Owners and Pilots Assn., United Meth. Assn. Communicators (v.p. 1968-72, Communicators' Hall of Fame 1992), World Assn. Christian Communications (central com., chmn. Jour. editorial bd. 1975-82, chmn. periodical devel. com., exec. com., sec. 1978-82), Asso. Ch. Press (hon. life), Religious Pub. Relations Council. Clubs: Chgo. Press (Dayton), Torch (Dayton). Home: 120 Saddle Tree Ct Hermitage TN 37076-1372 *When I was young I thought that anything was possible for me and that I had a long, long time to achieve it. With maturity I have come to a recognition of mortality, finitude, a limitation of time and opportunity. Thus my life has taught me three things: 1) Choose the best. Life is too precious to squander it on the second rate. 2) Live for others. The quality of one's life is enhanced rather than diminished as one shares himself/herself with others. 3) Fulfill your dreams. Tomorrow may never come; act now so that life's opportunities may not be lost forever.*

CHAMBERS, DAVID LEE, music educator; b. Kansas City, KS, Feb. 11, 1962; s. Robert Sterling and Ruth Lavaun Chambers; m. Donna Gilda Mannino, July 18, 1998; 1 child, Marie Nicole. MusB instrumental, U of Ctrl. OK, Edmond, OK, 1984, MusM vocal, 1990. Cert. music tchr.K-12 Assoc. of Christian Sch. Serving line worker/ delivery driver Crystal's Pizza and Spaghetti, Oklahoma City, 1979—84, 1986—87; mail clk. OK Dept. of Trans., Oklahoma City, 1987—88, OK Employment Security Commn., Oklahoma City, 1984—90; min. of music Oak Grove Bapt. Ch., Midwest City, Okla., 1987—90; music prof. Bapt. Bible Coll. East, Hyde Pk., Mass., 1990—94; tchr. Frederick Christian Acad., Frederick, Md., 1994—99, Mt. Calvary Christian Sch., Elizabethtown, Pa., 1999—2002. Choir mem., vocal and instrumental soloist Mt. Calvary Ch., Elizabethtown, Pa., 1999—2002; music dir. People's Bapt. Ch., Frederick, Md., 1995—99. Mem.: Music Ed. Nat. Conf., PA music Ed. Assoc. Republican. Bible Ch. Avocations: composing and arranging, reading, tennis, bowling. Home: 549 Mountainview Rd Middletown PA 17057 Office: Mt Calvery Christian School 629 Holly St Elizabethtown PA 17022

CHAMBERS, DONALD ARTHUR, biochemistry and molecular medicine educator; b. N.Y.C., Sept. 24, 1936; AB, Columbia U., 1959, PhD, 1972. Rsch. biochemist dept. surgery Harvard Med. Sch./Mass. Gen. Hosp., Boston, 1961-66; rsch. fellow in hematology dept. surgery Harvard Med. Sch./Beth Israel Hosp., Boston, 1967-68; faculty fellow in chem. biology Columbia U., N.Y.C., 1969-71; asst. rsch. biochemist Ctr. for Med. Genetics dept. medicine U. Calif. Med. Ctr., San Francisco, 1972-74, lectr. in biochemistry and biophysics, 1972-74, asst. prof. molecular biology and biochemistry, 1974-75; asst. prof. biol. chemistry and dermatology U. Mich., Ann Arbor, 1975-79, assoc. prof. biol. chemistry, 1979; prof. molecular biology U. Ill., Chgo., 1979—, prof. biol. chemistry, 1980—, rsch. prof. dermatology, 1981—, prof. biol. psychiatry, 1996. Assoc. mem. Dental Rsch. Inst. U. Mich., 1978-79, adj. rsch. investigator Dept. Biol. Chemistry, 1979—; dir. Ctr. for Molecular Biology of Oral Disease, U. Ill., Chgo., 1979—, interim head dept. biochemistry, 1985, head dept. biochemistry, 1986—; vis. scholar Green Coll., Oxford U., 1989-93, hon. vis. fellow, 1993—; sr. rsch. assoc. Wellcome Unit History of Medicine, Oxford. 2000--; fellow Honors Coll., 1985—, Phi Kappa Phi lectr., 1991, Sigma Xi lectr., 2001; nat. action com. Am. Assn. Dental Rsch., 1981—; study sect. rev. NIH, 1983-86, 92, 98—. Mem. editl. bd.: Perspectives in Biology and Medicine. Recipient James Howard McGregor prize Columbia U., 1971; named Inventor of Yr., U. Ill., 1990; fellow in hematology NIH, 1967-68, fellow in chem. biology, 1969-71; Rsch. grantee NIH, Am. Cancer Soc., Office of Naval Rsch.,1986—, Helene Curtis, Inc., 1988—, Tng. grantee NIH-NIGMS, 1975-79, NIH-NIAMDD, 1976-79, 77-80, NIH-NIDR-NIAMDD, 1980—, NIH-NCI, 1982-88, NIH-NIDCR, 2003-, NIH-NIAID, 2003-. Mem. AAAS, Am. Assn. Med. Colls., Am. Assn. Immunology, Am. Chem. Soc., Am. Fedn. Clin. Rsch., Am. Soc. Biol. Chemistry, Am. Soc. Cell Biology, Am. Soc. Microbiology, Internat. Assn. Dental Rsch. (com. on rsch. progress 1982-85, chmn. 1984-85, chmn. grad. tng. forum com. exptl. pathology sect. 1983), Assn. Dept. Chmn. Biol. Chemistry, Chgo. Assn. Immunologists, N.Y. Acad. Scis. (organizer meeting The Double Helix, 40 Yrs. 1993), Royal Soc. Medicine, Soc. Investigative Dermatology, Oxford Med. Alumni Assn. (N.Am. rep. 2000—), Green Coll. Oxford Soc. (N.Am. rep. 2000—), Athenaeum Club London, Phi Kappa Phi, Sigma Xi (NIDCR 1998, spl. emphisii panel), Sigma Xi (pres.-elect 2000, pres. 2001), Oxford Med. Alumni (N.Am Sec. 2001-). Achievements include patents (U.S., Can.) for method of determining periodontal disease, (with other) method of quantifying aspartate amino transferase in periodontal disease; research in role of cyclic nucleotides, prostaglandins, hormones and other regulatory factors in the regulation of cell function, proliferation and differentiation, in molecular medicine in neural-immune interactions, the regulatory mechanisms of host-microbial interactions, in the history and devel. of concepts in the bio-med. scis. Office: U Ill Coll Med Dept Biochemistry 1819 W Polk St # C 536 Chicago IL 60612-7331 also: Ctr Molecular Biol Oral Diseases 801 S Paulina St # C 860 Chicago IL 60612-7210 E-mail: donc@uic.edu.

CHAMBERS, ELENORA STRASEL, artist; b. Strassel, Oreg. d. Augustine George and Frieda Rose (Westermann) Strasel; m. Edward Lucas Chambers, Oct. 9, 1954; children: Robert, Margaret L. BA, Marylhurst (Oreg.) Univ., 1942; student, Portland Art Mus. Sch., U. Miami, Fla., Fla. Internat. U. One person shows include Mirell Gallery, Coconut grove, Fla., 1961, Miami Mus. Modern Art, 1965, 80 Washington Sq. E., N.Y.C., 1983; Kendall Campus Art Gall., Miami, 1992, group exhbns. include Ringling Mus. Sarasota, Fla., 1956, Norton Gallery, West Palm Beach, 1956, Lowe Art Mus., Miami (award winner), 1957, 1976, Soc. of Four Arts, Palm Beach, 1958, 61, 62, 65, 67, 72, 74, 77, 81, Ft. Lauderdale Mus. Arts (award winner), 1964, 65, Profl. Women Artists, Lowe Art Mus., Miami, 1976, Mus. of Arts and Scis., Daytona Beach, Fla., 1979, Met. Dade County Coun. of Arts and scis., Miami, 1979, Lowe Levinson Gallery, Miami Beach, 1981, North Miami Mus. and Art Ctr., 1987, Metro-Dade Cultural Ctr., Miami, 1990, Mus. Contemporary Art, 1995, House Art Gallery, N.Y., 1996, Ambrosino Gallery, Miami, 1997, Ambrosino Gallery, Miami, 1998, Robert Hittel, Ft. Lauderdale, 1998, Dorsch Gallery, Miami, 1999, Kendall Campus Art Gallery, Miami, 2000, Snitzer Gallery, Miami, 2002; works in permanent collections Miami Mus. Modern Art, Hopkins-Easton Assocs., Omni Internat., many pvt. collections. Recipient Beaux Art award Lowe Art Mus., 1957, Hortt Meml. award Ft. Lauderdale Mus. Arts, 1964, Atwater Kent award 29th Ann. Exhbn. Contemporary Am. Paintings, Soc. Four Arts, 1967, 39th Ann. exhbn., 1977. Home: 5790 SW 51st Ter Miami FL 33155-6324

CHAMBERS, GLENN DARRELL, wildlife photographer, artist; b. Butler, Mo., June 14, 1936; s. E. Glenn and Fern M. (Woods) C.; m. Marilyn Janell Henry, Aug. 29, 1959 (div. Jan. 1980); children: James D. (dec.), Russell G., Lindell C.; m. Jeannie Bay Erwin, Feb. 27, 1980; stepchildren: Robert Roemer, Matthew Roemer. BS, Ctrl. Mo. State U., 1958; MA, U. Mo.-Columbia, 1961; DSc (hon.) (hon.), Ctrl. Mo. State U., 2001. Area mgr. Mo. Dept. Conservation, Jefferson City, 1961-62, research biologist, 1962-69, biologist, photographer, 1969-79; regional dir. Ducks Unltd., Columbia, Mo., 1979-83, wildlife photographer, 1984-88; pres. Niska Art, Inc., Columbia, Mo., 1984—, Paddlefoot Prodns., Inc., 1994—. Motion picture specialist Mo. Dept. Conservation, 1988-95; exec. v.p. Mo. Bird Obs., 1988; freelance cinematographer, 1995—. Films include: (with Charles and Elizabeth Schwartz) Return of the Wild Turkey (2d place award Outdoor Writers Assn. Am.), 1971, The Show-Me Hunter (2d place award Outdoor Writers Assn. Am.), 1972, Wild Chorus: The Story of the Canada Goose (1st place award Outdoor Writers Assn. Am.), 1974, (Best Motion Picture award Wildlife Soc.), 1974; More Than Trees: Ecology of the Forest (2d place award Forestry Film Festival, 1st place award Outdoor Writers Assn. Am.), 1977, It's Your Choice, 1990 (Teddy Roosevelt award Mich. Outdoor Writers Assn.), Forests for the Future, 1991 (Teddy Roosevelt award Mich. Outdoor Writers Assn.), Back to the Wild, 1998 (3 TV Emmy awards); prodr. Otter Chaos, Nat. Geog. TV, 2000; tech. articles to Jour. Wildlife Mgmt., 1961-77; winner 1984-85 Mo. Waterfowl Stamp Design Contest; recipient TV Emmy award for Best Non-News Feature Glenn and the Geese, 1990, Where Eagles Soar, 1995 (2d Place award Assn. for Conservation Info.), Furbearers of Mo., 1997. Dist. chmn. Boonslick Dist. Boy Scouts Am., 2001—. Mem.: Mo. Conservation Heritage Found. (bd. dirs. 1990—), Conservation Fedn. Mo. (bd. dirs. 1998—, Conservationist of Yr. award 2001, Lifetime Achievement award 2002), Wildlife Soc. (E. Sidney Stephens award 1990). Democrat. Baptist. Home: 807 Cornell Columbia MO 65203-1828

CHAMBERS, HENRY CARROLL, realty broker; b. Beaufort, S.C., July 23, 1928; m. Elizabeth Lee Brewer (dec. 2003). BSCE, Clemson U., 1949. From ptnr. to v.p. Burton Block Co., 1952-65; pres., gen. mgr. Burton Block & Concrete Co., Inc., 1965-81; pres. Deerfield Sand & Mining Co., Inc., 1958-74, 1963-73, Chambers-Cleckley, Inc., 1967-74, Hilton Head Concrete, Inc., 1970-74, South Atlantic Leasing Corp., 1961-74; v.p. MSC, Inc., 1981-84; broker Beaufort Realty Co., 1982—; sec.-treas. Brays Island Plantation Co., 1987-91. Mayor City of Beaufort, 1969-91; chmn. Beaufort County Devel. Bd., 1958-63; pres., campaign chmn. Beaufort County United Fund, 1960-63, bd. dirs., 1963; ruling elder First Presbyterian Ch. Beaufort; nat. alumni coun. rep., bd. visitors, pres. statewide adv. com. Clemson U.; mem. Hist. Beaufort Found., 1969-82, Gov.'s Beautification and Cmty. Improvement Bd., 1971-74; chmn. Beaufort dist. Boy Scouts Am., 1959-60, pres. Coastal Carolina coun., 1968-69; pres., chmn. bd. Beaufort Acad., 1967-75 Officer USAR, Korean War. Named Beaufort Young Man of Yr., Beaufort Jaycees, 1961, Boss of Yr., 1969; recipient Rotary Bowl for civic svc. Rotary Club, Beaufort, 1970, Pub. Svc. award Nat. Trust for Hist. Preservation, 1978; Silver Beaver award Boy Scouts Am., Silver Antelope award; Disting. Svc. Key, Boys Clubs Am. Mem. AIA (hon. nat. and S.C. chpt.), SCV, SAR, Am. Soc. Landscape Architects (honor award 1987), Concrete Masonry Assn., Soc. Am. Mil. Engrs., Am. Concrete Inst., S.C. Asphalt Pavement Assn. (past bd. dirs.), S.C. Concrete Masonry Assn. (past pres. and bd. dirs.), S.C. Hist. Soc. (bd. curators, 1st v.p.), Jamestowne Soc., Beaufort County C. of C. (past bd. dirs.), Nat. Sorjourners, Beaufort Coun. Navy League, First Families S.C., Jamestowne Soc. First Families, Hugenots Soc., Sertoma Club (bd. dirs. Beaufort 1956-58, charter pres.), Masons, Scottish Rite, York Rite. Office: 210 Carteret St Beaufort SC 29902-5524

CHAMBERS, HENRY GEORGE, orthopedic surgeon; b. Portsmouth, Va., June 22, 1956; s. Walter Charles and Teresa Frances (Fernandez) C.; m. Jill Annette Swanson, June 10, 1978; children: Sean Michael, Reid Christopher. BA summa cum laude in Biochemistry, U. Colo., 1978; MD, Tulane U. Sch. Medicine, 1982. Diplomate Am. Bd. Orthop. Surgery. Commd. 2d lt. U.S. Army, 1978, advanced through grades to maj., 1988; intern Fitzsimmons Army Med. Ctr., Aurora, Colo., 1982-83; orthopaedic surgery resident Brooke Army Med. Ctr., Ft. Sam Houston, Tex., 1983-87, chief resident, 1986-87, staff orthopaedic surgeon to asst. residency program dir., 1987-89, asst. chief surgeon orthopaedic surgery svc., 1990-92; staff orthopaedic surgeon DeWitt Army Hosp., Ft. Belvoir, Va., 1987; pediatric orthopaedic fellow San Diego Children's Hosp., 1989-90; asst. prof. surgery Uniformed Svcs. U. Health Scis., Bethesda, Md., 1987—; asst. program dir. Brooke Army Med. Ctr. Orthopaedic Surgery, 1987-92; assoc. prof. U. Calif.-San Diego Med. Ctr., 1989—; pvt. practice San Diego, 1992—; chmn. dept. orthopedic surgery San Diego Children's Hosp., 1997—2001, chief of staff-elect, 2001—; med. dir. Motion Analysis Lab. Co-author: Long Distance Runner's Guide to Training, 1983, The Pediatric Spine—Principles and Practice, 2000, Fractures in Children, 2001; contbr. various articles to profl. jours. Physician St. Vincent de Paul Clinic for Homeless, San Diego, 1989—; v.p. United Cerebral Palsy. Recipient Comdrs. award for outstanding rsch., Brooke Army Med. Ctr., 1987. Fellow: Am. Orthop. Assn., We. Orthop. Assn., Am. Acad. Orthop. Surgeons, Orthop. Rsch. Soc., Am. Acad. Pediats., Acad. Cerebral Palsy Devel. Medicine (treas.), Pediat. Orthop. Soc. N.Am., Acad. Orthop. Soc.; mem.: Union Concerned Scientist, Physicians for Social Responsibility, Handgun Control, Phi Beta Kappa. Democrat. Unitarian Universalist. Avocations: weight lifting, golf, bicycling. Home: 5458 Sandburg Ave San Diego CA 92122-4128 E-mail: hchambers@chsd.org.

CHAMBERS, IMOGENE KLUTTS, school system administrator, financial consultant; b. Paden, Okla., Aug. 6, 1928; d. Odes and Lillie (Southard) Klutts; m. Richard Lee Chambers, May 27, 1949. BA, East Ctrl. State U., 1948; MS, Okla. State U., 1974, EdD, 1980. High sch. math. tchr. Marlow (Okla.) Sch. Dist., 1948-49; with Bartlesville (Okla.) Sch. Dist., 1950-94; asst. supt. bus. affairs, treas. Ind. Sch. Dist. 30, 1977-87, treas., 1985-94; fin. acctg. cons. Okla. State Dept. Edn., 1987-92; dir. Plz. Bank, Bartlesville, 1984-93. Adv. dir. Bank Okla., 1994-96. Treas. Okla. Schs. Ins. Assn., 1982—97, adminstr., 1993—97; bd. dirs. Mutual Girls Club, 1981—. Mem. Okla. Assn. Sch. Bus. Ofcls., Assn. Sch. Bus. Ofcls. Internat., Okla. Ret. Educators Assn., Washington County Ret. Educators Assn., Okla. State U. Alumni Assn., East Ctrl. U. Alumni Assn. (bd. dirs. 1994-96). Democrat. Methodist. Home: 911 SE Greystone Pl Bartlesville OK 74006-5141 E-mail: ikcgene@bartnet.net.

CHAMBERS, JACK ALLEN, educator; b. Hamilton, Ohio; s. Glen S. and H. Edna C.; m. Ruth Coe, 1957; children: Melissa Ann, Wendy Colleen. AB, U. Miami, 1954; MA, U. Cin., 1955; PhD, Mich. State U. Dir. computer ctr. Mansfield (Pa.) U., 1972-74; dir. computing and comms. Calif. State U., Fresno, 1974-86, Duquesne U., Pitts., 1986-89; exec. dir. computing and comms. Loyola Coll., Balt., 1989-90; planning and info. rsch. ctr. mgr. Fla. C.C., Jacksonville, 1990-99, inter. dir. Assessment and Cert. Ctrs., 1999-2000, dir. program devel. for instrnl. tech., 2000—. Co-author: (with others) (book) Computer Assisted Instruction: Its Use in the Classroom, 1983; (chpt.) Motivating Students for Lifetime Learning in New Directions in Education and Training Technology, 1985; author: chpt. in Facilitating Academic Software Development, 1988; editor: (books) Selected Papers Fifth InternatConference on College Teaching and Learning, 1994, Sixth Conference, 1995, Seventh Conference, 1996, Eighth Conference, 1997, Ninth Conference, 1998, Tenth Conference, 1999, Eleventh Conference, 2000, Twelfth Conference, 2001, Thirteenth Conference, 2002, Fourteenth Conference, 2003. Grantee: James McKeen Cattell Fund, Calif. State Dept. Edn., Calif. State Univ. System, NSF, FIPSE. Office: Fla CC at Jacksonville 501 W State St Jacksonville FL 32202-4086 E-mail: jchamber@fccj.edu.

CHAMBERS, JERRY RAY, school system administrator; b. St. Joseph, Mo., Oct. 1, 1947; s. Ray Linden and Betty Allene (Roach) C.; m. Jacqueline Kaye Thomas, Feb. 11, 1967; children: Sandra Kaye, Jennifer Lynn. AS, Mo. Western State Coll., 1967; BA, U. Mo., Kansas City, 1969, MA in Edn. Adminstrn. and History, 1971; postgrad., U. Madras, India, 1974; PhD in Edn. Adminstrn., U. Mo., Kansas City, 1986. Tchr. Lillis High Sch., Kansas City, Mo., 1969; high sch. tchr. Sch. Dist. St. Joseph, Mo., 1969-80, dir. media svcs., 1980-90; supt. schs. Sch. Dist. Washington, Mo., 1990-2001, Wolf Br. Sch. Dist., Swansea, Ill., 2001—. Coun. pres. ITV Kansas City Pub. TV, 1981-90; assessor Mo. Prin. Assess Ctr., DESE, Jefferson City, Mo., 1987-90; bd. dirs. 353 Econ. Devel. Corp. Washington, 1991-2000, Network Ednl. Devel., St. Louis, 1993-96; exec. com. Coop. Sch. Dists. St. Louis. Author: Missouri Students Tune IN, 1987, History of Missouri Instructional Television, 1986, Beyond the Bullet Hole, 1988. Bd. dirs. Regional Bluffs Libr., St. Joseph, 1989, United Fund, Washington, 1992-95; campaign co-chmn. Earnings Tax Com., St. Joseph, 1988; chmn. edn. divsn. United Way, St. Joseph, 1986-89, bd. dirs. 1992; bd. dirs. Tri-County Fine Arts Ctr., 1992-97. Recipient Alumni Achievement award U. Mo., Kansas City, 1988, Disting. Alumni award Mo. Western State Coll., 1990, Disting. Leadership award Nat. Assn. Com. Leadership, 1988, Key to City award City of St. Joseph Mayor, 1990, Mo. Supt. of Yr. award, 1999, Pearce award 1999; Fulbright scholar, 1974. Mem. Am. Assn. Sch. Adminstrs., Ill. Assn. Sch. Adminstrs., Lions Club (Washington chpt., 1990-2003, St. Joseph Host Club pres. 1989-90, chmn., exec. com. Cooperating Sch. Dists. Greater St Louis, 1996-98, pres. CSD 1999-2000). Avocations: basketball, tennis, reading, model railroading, nostalgia, baseball. Home: 2 Winchester Ct Washington MO 63090-5314 Office: School Dist Wolf Br 410 Huntwood Rd Swansea IL 62226

CHAMBERS, JOAN LOUISE, retired librarian, retired dean; b. Denver, Mar. 22, 1937; d. Joseph Harvey and Clara Elizabeth (Carleton) Baker; m. Donald Ray Chambers, Aug. 17, 1958 BA in English Lit., U. No. Colo., Greeley, 1958; MS in L.S., U. Calif.-Berkeley, 1970; MS in Systems Mgmt., U. So. Calif., 1985; cert., Coll. for Fin. Planning, 1989. Libr. U. Nev., Reno, 1970-79; asst. univ. libr. U. Calif., San Diego, 1979-81, univ. libr. Riverside, 1981-85; dean librs., prof. Colo. State U., Ft. Collins, 1985-97, emeritus dean and prof., 1997—. Mgmt. intern Duke U. Libr., Durham, N.C., 1978-79; sr. fellow UCLA Summer, 1982; cons. tng. program Assn. of Rsch. Libraries, Washington, 1981; libr. cons. Calif. State U., Sacramento, 1982-83, U. Wyo., 1985-86, 94-95, U. Nebr., 1991-92, Calif. State U. System, 1993-94, Univ. No. Ariz., 1994-95. Contbr. articles to profl. jours., chpts. to books. Bd. dirs. Consumers Union, 1996—. U. Calif. instl. improvement grantee, 1980-81; State of Nev. grantee, 1976, ARL grantee, 1983-84. Mem.: PEO, Colo. Mountain Club, Phi Kappa

Phi, Kappa Delta Phi, Phi Lambda Theta, Beta Phi Mu. Avocations: hiking, snow shoeing, skiing, cycling, tennis. Home and Office: PO Box 1477 Edwards CO 81632-1477 E-mail: chambers@vail.net.

CHAMBERS, JOE CARROLL, physician, consultant, educator; b. Bristol, Va., Aug. 12, 1932; s. Joseph Lemuel and Anna Chambers; m. Ruth Gwen Renfro Aycock, Dec. 20, 1956 (div. Apr. 1971); m. Bettye Anne Terry, Dec. 9, 1972; 1 child, Cynthia Anne. Student, East Tenn. State U., 1952; MD, U. Tenn., Memphis, 1956; MPH, U. N.C., 1962. Diplomate Am. Bd. Preventive Medicine. Intern Mid-States Bapt. Hosp., Nashville, 1957; health officer Tenn. Dept. Pub. Health, Johnson City, 1957-58; gen. asst. surgeon USPHS, Montgomery, Ala., 1958-60; dep. health officer, then health officer Jefferson County Health Dept., Birmingham, Ala., 1960-68; coord. regional med. program Med. U. S.C., Charleston, 1968; dir. Appalachian Regional Ctr. for Healing Arts, Johnson City, 1969-71; health dir. S.C. Dept. Health, Myrtle Beach, 1971-73, Aiken, S.C., 1974, Charleston, 1975-96; cons. Carealliance Health Svcs., Charleston, 1996—; clin. assoc. prof. preventive medicine and epidemiology Med. U. S.C., 1973—. Adj. prof. Sch. Pub. Health U. S.C., 1977—; exec. dir. Tri-County Project Care, 2001—. Pres. S.C. chpt. Am. Lung Assn., Columbia, 1989-91; mem. Preservation Soc. Charleston, 1972—; mem. Mayor's Task Force on Homeless, Charleston, 1985—; mem. stroke task force Am. Heart Assn., Columbia, S.C., 1998—. Mem. APHA, S.C. Pub. Health Assn. (pres. 1987-88, Hayne medal), So. Health Assn. (pres. 1985-86), Carolina Yacht Club, Delta Omega. Presbyterian. Avocations: culinary arts, music, sketching. Home: 35 State St Charleston SC 29401-2811 Office: Roper St Francis Healthcare 316 Calhoun St Charleston SC 29401-1113 E-mail: joe.chambers@ropersaintfrancis.org.

CHAMBERS, JOHN T. computer company executive; m. Elaine Chambers; 2 children. BS, BA, JD, W.Va. U.; MBA, Ind. U. Sr. v.p. worldwide ops. Cisco Sys., Inc., San Jose, Calif., 1991-94, exec. v.p., 1994-95, pres., CEO, 1995—. Bd. dirs. Clarify, Inc., San Jose, Arbor Software, Sunnyvale, Calif. Office: Cisco Sys Inc 170 W Tasman Dr Bldg 10 San Jose CA 95134-1706 E-mail: jochambe@cisco.com.

CHAMBERS, JOHN WHITECLAY, II, history educator; b. West Chester, Pa., Aug. 6, 1936; s. John McCausland and Le-Arie P. Chambers; m. Dorothy Roman, 1958; children: John Bret, Jeffrey Mark, Michael Adam; m. Amy Russo Piro, 1982; 1 child, Tacy Elizabeth. Reporter Pasadena (Calif.) Ind. Star-News, 1958-60, San Rafael (Calif.) Ind.-Jour., 1960-61; news and documentary writer/prodr. KRON-TV, San Francisco, 1961-65; asst. prof. history Barnard Coll., Columbia U., N.Y.C., 1972-82, Rutgers U., New Brunswick, N.J., 1982-87, assoc. prof., 1987-93, prof., 1993—2002, disting. prof., 2002—, dept. chair, 1997-98. Fulbright lectr. U. Rome, spring 1982; project dir. Rutgers Ctr. Hist. Analysis, 1993-95; vis. lectr. U. Tokyo, 1997. Author: Three Generals on War, 1973, Draftees or Volunteers, 1975, The Eagle and the Dove: The Peace Movement and U.S. Foreign Policy, 1900-1922, 1976, 2d edit., 1991, The Tyranny of Change: America in the Progressive Era, 1890-1920, 1980, 3d edit., 2000; author: (with Warren Susman) American History Reading Lists, 3 vols., 1983; author: To Raise an Army: The Draft Comes to Modern America, 1987 (Best Book award Soc. Mil. History, 1988, Best Book on Mil. History, 1987); author: (with Charles C. Moskos) The New Conscientious Objection: From Sacred to Secular Resistance, 1993; author: (with David Culbert) World War II Film and History, 1996; author: (with G. Kurt Piehler) Major Problems in American Military History, 1998; editor in chief Oxford Co. to Am. Mil. History, 1999 (Disting. Ref. Book award Soc. Mil. History, 2001). NEH grantee, 1974; humanities fellow Rockefeller Found., 1981-82, vis. fellow Inst. Advanced Study, Princeton, 1995-96. Mem.: Soc. Mil. History, Orgn. Am. Historians, Am. Hist. Assn., Peace History Soc. (pres. 1975—77). Office: Rutgers U 16 Seminary Pl New Brunswick NJ 08901-1108 E-mail: chamber@rci.rutgers.edu.

CHAMBERS, JOHNNIE LOIS (TUCKER CHAMBERS), elementary school educator, rancher; b. Crocket County, Tex., Sept. 28, 1929; d. Robert Leo and Lois K. (Slaughter) Tucker; m. R. Boyd Chambers; children: Theresa A., Glyn Robert, Boyd James, John Trox. BEd, Sul Ross State U., Alpine, Tex., 1971. Tchr. 1st and 2d grades Candelaria (Tex.) Elem. Sch., 1971-73; head tchr. K-8 Ruidosa (Tex.) Elem. Sch., 1973-77, Presidio Ind. Sch. Dist. at Candelaria Elem. Sch., 1977-91, tchr. 2d and 3d grades, 1991-93, tchr. pre-kindergarten, kindergarten and 1st grade, 1993-98, acting prin. Candelaria Elem. and Jr. High, 1995-98, head tchr. pre-K to 8th grades, 1996-98, tchr. pre-K, kindergarten, 1st and 2d grades, 1996—99, ret., 1999; tchr. Redford (Tex.) Elem. Sch., 2001—, tchr. pre-K-6, 2001—01. Mem. sight-base decision making, Presidio, 1991-94; mem. Chihuahuan Desert Rsch. Inst., Alpine, 1982-94. Leader Boy Scouts Am., Ruidosa and Candelaria, 1973-91, Cub Scout leader, 1973-91; chpt. mem. Sheriffs Assn. Tex., Austin, 1980; bd. dirs. Big Bend Regional Hosp. Dist., 2001—; mem. Ctr. for Big Bend Studies. Recipient awards Boy Scouts Am., 1969, 83, winner Litter Gitter award, 1994-95. Mem. Tex. State Tchrs. Assn., Tex. Fedn. Rep. Women, The Archaeol. Conservancy, Phi Alpha Theta. Avocations: hiking, camping, anthropologic digs, cave exploring, cooking. Home: 99 Retirement Cir Marfa TX 79843 E-mail: johnnieltc@brooksdata.net.

CHAMBERS, JUDITH TARNPOLL, speech pathologist, audiologist; b. Newark, Mar. 17, 1940; d. Morris and Grace Annette (Lambeck) Tarnpoll; m. John Darby Chambers, May 29, 1977; 1 child, Joshua. BA, Rutgers U., 1964; MA, Columbia U., 1966. Cert. audiologist, N.Y., Conn. Speech and lang. therapist League Sch., Bklyn., 1967; lang. therapist BOCES, Elmsford, N.Y., 1968-70; chief audiologist Royal Victoria Hosp., Montreal, Que., Can., 1972-76; ind. dispensing audiologist Bridgeport, Conn., 1977-92; speech and lang. pathologist Symphony Rehab. Svcs. Inc., 1994-98, Fla. Hearing Care Ctrs., 1999—, Hearx Ltd., 2000-2001; pvt. practice, 2001—; speech-lang. pathologist Manor Care, Boca Raton, Fla., 2002—. Mem. Am. Speech-Lang.-Hearing Assn., Acad. Dispensing Audiologists, Am. Acad. Audiology (charter mem.). E-mail: judyc@gate.net.

CHAMBERS, JULIUS LEVONNE, lawyer; b. Montgomery County, N.C., Oct. 6, 1936; BA, N.C. Cen. U., 1958; MA, U. Mich., 1959; LLB, U. N.C., 1962; LLM, Columbia U., 1963. Bar: N.C. 1962, N.Y. 1986. Ptnr. Chambers, Ferguson, Stein, Chambers, Adkins, Gresham & Sumter, Charlotte, NC, 1964-84; dir., counsel NAACP Legal Def. and Ednl. Fund, N.Y.C., 1984-92; chancellor N.C. Ctrl. U., Durham, 1993-2000; with Ferguson, Stein, Wallas, Adkins, Gresham & Sumter, Charlotte, 2000—. Former trustee N.J. State Bd. Higher Edn.; former bd. visitors Harvard U., Columbia U. Law Sch.; former trustee U. Pa., mem. bd. overseers Law Sch.; former bd. dirs. Children's Def. Fund, Legal Aid Soc. N.Y. Mem. ABA (bd. editors ABA jour.), N.C. Bar Assn., Mecklenburg County Bar Assn., N.Y. State Bar Assn., Assn. of Bar of City of N.Y., Nat. Bar Assn., Assn. Black Lawyers N.C., Order of Coif, Order of Golden Fleece, Phi Alpha Theta. Office: Ferguson Stein Wallas Adkins Gresham & Sumter 741 Kenilworth Ave Ste 300 Charlotte NC 28204

CHAMBERS, KENTON LEE, botany educator; b. Sept. 27, 1929; s. Maynard Macy and Edna Georgia (Miller) C.; m. Henrietta Laing, June 21, 1958; children: Elaine Patricia, David Macy. AB with highest honors, Whittier Coll., 1950; PhD (NSF fellow), Stanford U., 1955. Instr. biol. scis. Stanford (Calif.) U., 1954-55; instr. botany, asst. prof. Yale U., New Haven, Conn., 1956-60; assoc. prof., prof. botany Oreg. State U., Corvallis, 1960-90, prof. emeritus, 1991—. Curator Herbarium, 1960-90; program dir. systematic biology NSF, Washington, 1967-68. Contbr. articles in field to profl. jours. Fellow AAAS; mem. Bot. Soc. Am. (Merit award 1990), Am. Soc. Plant Taxonomists, Am. Inst. Biol. Scis., Calif. Bot. Soc. Home: 4761 SW Hollyhock Cir Corvallis OR 97333-1245 Office: Oreg State U Herbarium Botany Dept Corvallis OR 97331-2902 E-mail: chamberk@science.oregonstate.edu

CHAMBERS, LETITIA PEARL CAROLINE, consulting firm executive; b. Alva, Okla., Feb. 1, 1943; d. E. Wade and Anita (Sims) Chambers; m. Stephen Morelock, May 1964 (div. 1970); 1 child, Melissa. BA, U. Okla., 1965; MS, Okla. State U., 1971, EdD, 1973. Tchr. Oklahoma City Pub. Schs., 1965-70, adminstr., 1973-74; dir. fed. programs N.Mex. State Edn. Agy., Santa Fe, 1974-75; sr. analyst US Senate Budget Com., Washington, 1976-77; minority staff dir. US Senate Spl. Com. on Aging, Washington, 1978; staff dir. US Senate Com. on Labor & Human Resources, Washington, 1979-81; pres. Chambers Assocs., Inc. (a subsidiary of Navigant Consulting), Washington, 1982—; U.S. rep. to the UN gen. assembly 51st Session, N.Y.C., 1996. Pres. Coalition of Publicly Traded Partnerships, Washington, 1987—; dir. Adams Nat. Bank, Washington, 1989-94; dir. Stratego Investments, Prague, Cech Republic, 1997-2000. Author various senate reports, policy studies. Chief budget adv. Clinton/Gore Transition, 1992—93; trustee Inst. Am. Indian Arts and Culture, Santa Fe, 1997—; Elder Chevy Chase (Md.) Presbyn. Ch., 1986—89; bd. visitors U. Okla., 1995—2002; bd. dirs., chair IAIA Found.; bd. dirs. Internat. Shakespeare Guild, 1998—. Recipient Disting. Alumni award U. Okla., 1998. Mem. Coun. for Excellence in Govt. (bd. dirs.), Cosmos Club. Avocation: landscape gardening. Office: Chambers Assocs Inc 805 15th St NW Ste 500 Washington DC 20005-2265 Home: 2022 Foothills Rd Santa Fe NM 87505 E-mail: lchambers@navigantconsulting.com.

CHAMBERS, LINDA DIANNE THOMPSON, social worker; b. Mexia, Tex., Apr. 21, 1953; d. Lee and Essie Mae (Hopes) Thompson; m. George Edward Chambers, Nov. 30, 1978; 1 child, Brandon. AS cum laude, Navarro Coll., 1974; B in Social Work magna cum laude, Tex. Women's U., 1976; cert. gerontology and Human Svcs. Mgmt., Sam Houston U., 1982; M in Social Work, U. Tex., Arlington, 1990. Lic. marriage and family therapist, social worker-advanced practitioner; cert family life educator; registered sex offender treatment provider. Mem. social work staff Dept. Human Res., Ft. Worth, 1975, Children's Med. Ctr., Dallas, 1976, Mexia State Sch., Tex., 1976-93, Methodist Home, Waco, Tex., 1993-96, Tex. Dept. Health, Waco, Tex., 1996—, Parkview Regional Hosp., 1996—; mem. social work staff geripsychiatric program Limestone Med. Ctr., 2001—. Pres. Raven Exquisites, Mexia, 1983-84, sec.-treas., 1984-85; pres., bd. dirs., Limestone County Child Welfare Bd., Hospice, Inc., Limestone County unit Am. Cancer Soc. Bd. dirs. Gibbs Meml. Libr., Teen Pregnancy Prevention Coun., Childcare Mgmt. Svcs.; vol. McLennan County Pub. Health Dist. AIDS Clinic, Ctr. for Action Against Sexual Assault, Family Abuse Ctr.; coord. founder Limestone County Teen Parent Program; co-founder Limestone County Parenting Coalition; mem. Limestone County Youth Adv. Com, Limestone County Parenting Coalition (co-founder); PTO sec. Ctrl. Tex. Literacy Coalition, 1992—; mem. Tex. Hist. Found., Nat. Mus. Women in the Arts, 1985—. Recipient numerous awards for scholarship and profl. excellence. Fellow Internat. Biog. Assn. (dep. bd. gov., life); mem. NAFE, AAUW, Am. Sociol. Soc. (sec. 1975-76), Tex. Dem. Women, Univ. Women's Assn., Am. Childhood Edn. Internat., Nat. Assn. Social Workers, Am. Assn. Mental Retardation, Nat. Assn. Future Women, Am. Soc. Profl. and Exec. Women, Nat. Assn. Negro Bus. and Profl. Women's Clubs, Tex. Woman's U. Nat. Alumni Assn., Mortar Bd. Honor Soc. (sec.-treas. 1975-76), Tex. Soc. Clin. Social Workers, Internat. Platform Assn., Internat. Assn. Bus. and Profl. Women, Am. Biog. Assn. (dep. bd. govs.), Nat. Mus. Women Arts, Los Amigos, Phi Theta Kappa, Alpha Kappa Delta, Alpha Delta Mu, Young Dems. Avocations: reading, gardening, gourmet cooking. Home: 102 Harding Mexia TX 76667

CHAMBERS, LOIS IRENE, insurance automation consultant; b. Omaha, Nov. 24, 1935; d. Edward J. and Evelyn B. (Davidson) Morrison; m. Peter A. Mscichowski, Aug. 16, 1952 (div. 1980); 1 child, Peter Edward; m. Frederick G. Chambers, Apr. 17, 1981. Clk. Gross-Wilson Ins. Agy., Portland, Oreg., 1955-57; sec., bookkeeper Reed-Paulsen Ins. Agy., Portland, 1957-58; office mgr., asst. sec., agt. Don Biggs & Assocs., Vancouver, Wash., 1958-88, v.p. ops., 1988-89, automation mgr., 1989-91, mktg. mgr., 1991-94; automation cons. Antiques and Collectables, Chambers & Assocs., Tualatin, Oreg., 1985—; sys. mgr. Contractors Ins. Svcs., Inc., 1997-2000. Chmn. adv. com. Clark C.C., Vancouver, 1985-93, mem. adv. com., 1993-94. Mem. citizens com. task force City of Vancouver, 1976-78, mem. Block Grant rev. task force, 1978—. Mem. Ins. Women of S.W. Wash. (pres. 1978, Ins. Woman of Yr. 1979), Nat. Assn. Ins. Women, Nat. Users Agena Sys. (charter; pres. 1987-89), Soroptimist Internat. (Vancouver; pres. 1979-80). Democrat. Roman Catholic. Office: Chambers & Assocs 8770 SW Umatilla St Tualatin OR 97062-6340 E-mail: fchamb8026@aol.com.

CHAMBERS, MARJORIE BELL, historian; b. N.Y.C., Mar. 11, 1923; d. Kenneth Carter and Katherine (Totman) Bell; m. William Hyland Chambers, Aug. 8, 1945; children: Lee Chambers-Schiller, William Bell, Leslie Chambers Trujillo, Kenneth Carter. AB cum laude, Mt. Holyoke Coll., South Hadley, Mass., 1943; MA, Cornell U., 1948; PhD, U. N.Mex., 1974; LLD honoris causa, Ctrl. Mich. U., 1977; LHD (hon.), Wilson Coll., 1980, Northern Michigan U., 1982. Staff asst. Am. Assn. UN, League of Nations Assn., N.Y.C., 1944-45; program specialist dept. rural sociology Cornell U., Ithaca, N.Y., 1945-46, rsch. asst. dept. speech and drama, 1946-48; substitute tchr. Los Alamos (N.Mex.) Pub. Schs., 1962-65; project historian U.S. AEC, Los Alamos, 1965-69; adj. prof. U. N.Mex., Los Alamos, 1970-76, 84-85; pres. Colo. Women's Coll., Denver, 1976-78; dean Union Inst. and U. Grad. Sch. Interdisciplinary Arts and Scis., Cin., 1979—82, mem. core faculty Grad. Sch., 1979—; interim pres. Colby-Sawyer Coll., New London, N.H., 1985-86. Vis. prof. Cameron U., Lawton, Okla., 1974; commr., vice-chair N.Mex. Commn. on Higher Edn., Santa Fe, 1987-91; dir. N.Mex. Endowment for Humanities, 1995-2002, sec.-treas. 2001-2002; mem. bd. dirs. Coun. Ind. Colls. and Univs., Santa Fe, 1991-2001; rep. Los Alamos County Labor Mgmt. Bd.; lectr. U. N.Mex., Albuquerque, 1986. Contbr. articles to profl. jours. Coun. treas. Sangre de Cristo Girl Scouts Am., 2002; chair Los Alamos County Coun., 1976, councilor, 1975-76, 79; Rep.candidate N.Mex. 3d Congl. Dist., 1982, lt. gov. N.Mex., 1986; chair Sec. of Navy's Advisor Bd. on Edn. and Tng., Washington and Pensacola, Fla., 1981-89; chair Citizen Bd. of U.S. Army Command and Gen. Staff Coll., Fort Leavenworth, Kans., 1989-1992; acting chair, vice-chair adminstrn. Pres. Carter's Com. for Women, Washington, 1977-80; chair Pres. Ford's Nat. Adv. Bd. on Women's Ednl. Programs, Washington, Los Alamos County Pers. Bd., 1985-90, mem. bd., 1983-90; mem. nat. adv. coun . U.S. SBA, 1990-92; mem. Los Alamos and N.Mex. Rep. Ctrl. com., 1982—; trustee Colby-Sawyer Coll., New London, N.H., 1980-89; pub. mem. U.S. Dept. State Fgn. Svc. selection bd., 1978; mem. U.S. del. UN Conf. Women, Copenhagen, 1980; bd. dirs. N.Mex. Endowment for the Humanities, 1997—. Recipient Teresa d'Avila award Coll. St. Teresa, Winona, Minn., 1978, Disting. Woman award U. N.Mex. Alumni Assn., Albuquerque, 1990, N.Mex. Disting. Pub. Svc. award Gov. and Awards Coun., Albuquerque, 1991, Zia award U. N.Mex. Alumni Assn., 2001; named Outstanding N.Mex. Woman Gov. and Com. on Status of Women, Albuquerque, 1988, 89, Lifetime Achievement award, 2003. Mem. AAUW (life, U.S. rep. coun. 1973-75, nat. pres. 1975-79, pres. Edn. Found.), DAR, Bus. and Profl. Women (Los Alamos parliamentarian and dist. parliamentarian 1991-93), Nat. Women's Polit. Caucus (gov. bd. conv., keynoter, vice-chair Rep. caucus 1971-89), Internat. Women's Forum (founding mem. Colo. forum), N.Mex. Hist. Soc. (pres.), Los Alamos Hist. Soc. (pres., Sangre de Cristo Girl Scouts "Woman of Distinction" 1996). Presbyterian. Avocations: figure skating, skiing, swimming, painting, public speaking.

CHAMBERS, MORTIMER HARDIN, JR., retired history educator; b. Saginaw, Mich., Jan. 9, 1927; s. Mortimer Hardin Chambers and Helen Elizabeth Bishop; m. Marcia Gail Hamilton, June 11, 1949 (div. July 1, 1970); children: Pamela, Julia, Blake; m. Catherine Mary Perry, Jan. 12, 1973. AB, Harvard U., 1949, PhD, 1954; MA, Oxford (Eng.) U., 1955. Instr. Harvard U., Cambridge, Mass., 1954—55; asst. prof. U. Chgo., 1955—58; from asst. prof. to prof. UCLA, 1958—2000. Author: Aristoteles, Staat der Athener, 1990, Georg Busolt: His Career in His Letters, 1990; co-author: Aristotle's History of Athenian Democracy, 1962. Sgt. U.S. Army, 1944—46. Rhodes scholar, 1949, Fulbright fellow, 1974. Mem.: Am. Philol. Assn. Democrat. Avocations: book collecting, travel. Office: Dept History UCLA 405 Hilgard Ave Los Angeles CA 90095

CHAMBERS, RAY WAYNE, security and loss control consultant; b. Cascade, W.Va., June 22, 1931; s. Robert and Mildred Ethel (Starrett) C.; m. Joan Roberta Tilley, Apr. 7, 1952; children: Rebecca H. Frase, Bonita I. Knight, Diana L. Sobalvarro. Cert. protection profl., mgmt. cons. Enlisted U.S. Army, 1949, advanced through grades to lt. col., 1971, sgt.-maj. tank battalion, 1952-53, 1956-60, 62-65, 67-70, intelligence battalion ops. officer, 1966-67, dep. chief staff ops., intelligence command, ret., 1973; v.p. loss prevention Little Gen. Store div. Gen. Host Corp., Tampa, Fla., 1973-84; pres. Assets Protection Systems Assocs., Inc., Largo, Fla., 1985—. Loss control cons. JRB Investigations Inc., Largo, 1986-87. Contbr. articles to profl. jours.. Bd. dirs. Del Prado Imperial Assn., Largo, chmn. neighborhood watch com., 1983-88. Decorated Bronze Star, Legion of Merit. Mem. Am. Soc. Indsl. Security (chmn. 1975-76, cert. 1976), Internat. Assn. Profl. Security Cons. (exec. dir. 1990-93), Retail Grocers Assn. Fla. (chmn. crime prevention 1983-85), Pinellas Assn. Pvt. Investigators (pres. 1986), Fla. Crime Prevention Officers Assn., Nat. Assn. Convenience Stores, Internat. Found. for Protection Officers, Assn. Counter Intelligence Corps Vets, Inst. Mgmt. Cons. Republican. Avocations: swimming, historial studies. Home and Office: Assets Protection Sys Assoc Inc 11113 Bella Loma Dr Largo FL 33774-4622

CHAMBERS, RICHARD LEON, retired Turkish language and civilization educator; b. Brundidge, Ala., Sept. 27, 1929; s. Cody Leon and Eunice Gertrude (Logan) Chambers. BS in History, U. Ala., Tuscaloosa, 1950, MA in History, 1955; BS in Fgn. Svc., Georgetown U., 1951; MA in History and Oriental Studies, Princeton U., 1958, PhD in Near Ea. Studies, 1968. Lectr. history Am. U. in Cairo, 1958-59; asst. in instrn. Princeton (N.J.) U., 1960; instr. history St. Lawrence U., Canton, N.Y., 1960-62; instr. Turkish lang. and civilization U. Chgo., 1962-65, asst. prof., 1965-71, assoc. prof., 1971-95, dir. Ctr. for Mid. Ea. Studies, 1979-85, assoc. prof. emeritus, dir. devel. Ctr. for Mid. Ea. Studies, 1995—2000. Co-founder, dir. Am. Rsch. Inst. in Turkey-Bosphorus U. summer Turkish lang. program, Istanbul, 1982-88; pres. Am. Rsch. Inst. in Turkey, Chgo. and Phila., 1985-88. Co-editor: Beginnings of Modernization in the Middle East: The 19th Century, 1968, Contemporary Turkish Short Stories, 1977; contbr. articles to profl. jours. and Ency. Brit. Recipient edn. award Am.-Turkish Coun., Washington, 1997, Svc. award Mid. East Studies Assn., 1998; fellow German Acad. Exch. Svc., Munich, 1951-52, Ford Found., Princeton, 1955-57, rsch. fellow Am. Rsch. Inst. in Turkey, Istanbul, 1965. Mem.: Turkish Studies Assn. (sec./treas. 1997—99), Am. Assn. Tchrs. Turkic Langs., Mid. East Studies Assn. N.Am., Internat. Assn. Mid. Ea. Studies, Am. Oriental Soc., Am. Hist. Soc. Avocations: travel, reading, gardening, antiques. Home: 1243 Westmoreland Ave Montgomery AL 36106-2017 Office: U Chgo Ctr for Mid Eastern Studies 5828 S University Ave Chicago IL 60637-1515 E-mail: rlc3@mailstation.com.

CHAMBERS, ROBERT HUNTER, III, college president, American studies educator, consultant; b. Winston-Salem, N.C., Oct. 24, 1939; s. Robert Hunter and Hildred (MacDonald) C.; m. Alice Louise Grant, Aug. 18, 1962 (div. 1995); children: Lisa, Grant. AB, Duke U., 1962; B.D., Yale U., 1965; PhD, Brown U., 1969. Asst. prof., dean Davenport Coll. Yale U., New Haven, 1969-74; vis. fellow Clare Coll., Cambridge U., Eng., 1972-73; prof., dean Coll. Arts and Scis. Bucknell U., Lewisburg, Pa., 1975-84; vis. scholar Doshisha U., Kyoto, 1982; pres., prof. English Western Md. Coll., Westminster, 1984—2000; sr. cons. Marts & Lundy, Inc., Gainesville, Fla., 2001—. Founding dir. Wellway Ctrs., Inc., Ft. Worth, 1984—88, WMC Devel. Corp., 1985—88; presdl. chmn. Centennial Conf., Md. and Pa., 1986, 1998—99; mem. segmental adv. com. State Bd. Higher Edn., Annapolis, Md., 1985—88; mem. internat. adv. coun. U. Buckingham, England; mem. cmty. bd. Carroll Co. Health Svcs., Inc., 1988—2000; assoc. fellow Davenport Coll., Yale U. Author, editor: Twentieth Century Interpretations of All the King's Men, 1977. Contbr. articles to profl. jours. Bd. dirs. Ind. Coll. Fund of Md., Balt.,1984—; mem. coun. on grad. edn. Brown U., 1989; mem. City of Westminster Mayoral Task Force, 1990; co-chair spl. gifts Am. Heart Assn.; mem. task force on assessment Nat. Assn. Ind. Colls. and Univs., 1991-92, mem. commn. on state rels., 1992-95; mem. Gov.'s Edn. Policy Transition Team, 1994-95; mem. Md. Citizens for Arts; bd. dir. Coun. of Ind. Colls., 1997—. Rockefeller Brothers fellow, 1962-63; Nat. Endowment for the Humanities grantee, 1978, U.S.-Japan Friendship Commn. grantee, 1982; recipient Balt. Regional Coun. Govts. award, 1989. Mem.: NCAA (pres. coun. 1999—2000), MLA, Internat. Assn. Univ. Presidents, Coun. on Econ. Edn. in Md. (trustee 1), Am. Studies Assn., Md. Ind. Coll. and Univ. Assn. (bd. dirs. 1984—2000, exec. com. 1985—88, 1991—2000, budget com. 1985—89, 1991, chair 1994—98), Mid. States Assn. Colls. and Schs. (commr. 1985—91, exec. com. 1986—91, vice chair 1987—89, chair 1990), Higher Edn. Commn., The Japan Soc., Nat. Assn. Ind. Colls. and Univs. (policy com. 1998—2000), Center Club, Yale Club, Rotary (hon. 1990), Phi Beta Kappa Assocs., Phi Beta Kappa. Avocations: running, reading, traveling. Office: Marts & Lundy Inc 10440 SW 52d Rd Gainesville FL 32608 E-mail: robertgam@netline.com, changers@martsandlundy.com.

CHAMBERS, ROBERT WILLIAM, financial company executive; b. Atlanta, Apr. 4, 1943; s. Robert William Chambers and Mary Emily (Martin) Nalley; m. Wendy Ann Treneer, Dec. 28, 1967 (div. 1979); 1 child, Robert William III. AB, Princeton U., 1965; MA, Indiana U., 1970, PhD, 1974. Assoc. instr. Ind. U., Bloomington, 1970-73; instr. Kans. State U., Manhattan, 1973-74; gen. mgr. Standard Collective Products Inc., Atlanta, 1974-75; mgr. sales, ops. Disposable Plastic Systems Inc., Marietta, Ga., 1975-77; asst. v.p., account exec. instl. sales Robinson-Humphrey Co. Inc., Atlanta, 1977-80; columnist, fin. reporter Atlanta Journal, 1980-81; account exec. Hill and Knowlton (J. Walter Thompson Group), Atlanta, 1981-83; sr. v.p., sales mgr. ea. divsn. Colonial Investment Svcs. Inc., Boston, 1983-90; sr. fin. cons. The Gwent Group, Atlanta, 1990-92; v.p., treas. Rabun Gap Film Corp., Atlanta, 1993—; dir. Bus. Svcs. Div. Porraro and Assocs., Atlanta, 1993-95; mgr. accts. divsn. Atlanta Rsch. and Trading, 1994-95; regional mktg. dir. Stephens, Inc., Atlanta, 1996-97; fin. reporter Atlanta-Jour.-Constn., 1997-99; COO The Resource Ctr., Atlanta, 2000; CEO Chambers Capital Adv., 2002—. Ga. correspondent The Economist, London, 1978-83, 99-2000; Am. Bankers Assn. fellowship, 1998. Chair bd. Oglethorpe U. Art Mus., 1998—. Mem.: Internat. Bus. Brokers Assn. (cert. bus. intermediary 2003), The Author's Guild, Soc. Colonial Wars, Nine O'Clocks Club (Atlanta), Piedmont Driving Club. Episcopalian. Home: 335 Franklin Rd NE Atlanta GA 30342-2711 Office Fax: 404-255-7644. E-mail: robcha@bellsouth.net.

CHAMBERS, RONALD D. book publishing executive; b. N.Y.C., Oct. 7, 1943; s. Burl W. and Blanche E. C.; m. Louise Callahan, June 10, 1966; children: Lalie Elizabeth, Richard Callahan. BA History, Coll. William and Mary, 1966; MA cum laude Latin Am. History, Univ. de las Ams., Mex., 1972. Sales rep. Coll. divsn. Prentice Hall, 1973-75, acquisitions editor edn. Coll. divsn., 1975-77; sr. acquisitions editor the Free Press Macmillan, 1977-80; editor in chief Praeger Publ., 1980-86, editor in chief, gen. mgr., 1986-93; v.p., edit. dir. Greenwood Pub. Group, 1993; dir. Naval Inst. Press, 1994. With USMC, 1967-70, Vietnam. Decorated Bronze Star. Office: Naval Inst Press 291 Wood Rd Annapolis MD 21402-5034 E-mail: rchambers@usni.org.

CHAMBERS, THOMAS EDWARD, college president, psychologist; b. Cleve., Aug. 1, 1934; s. James Clyde and Mary Celestine (Malone) C. BA, U. Notre Dame, 1956, MA, 1962, PhD, 1976; MA, Holy Cross Coll., 1961. Lic. counselor, Ohio, La. Dir. student residences U. Notre Dame, Ind., 1969-73, dir. student activities, 1973-74, asst. v.p. student affairs, 1974-76; v.p. acad. affairs Ursuline Coll., Cleve., 1976-87; pres. Our Lady of Holy Cross Coll., New Orleans, 1987—. Founder Internat. Student Leadership Inst., 1968; mem. exec. com. Sta. WLAE-TV, New Orleans, 1987—; pres. Willwoods Cmty., 2003—. Editor: For Leaders Only, 1975. Mem. exec. com. Met. Area Com., New Orleans, 1987—; trustee Gilmour Acad., Cleve., 1978—, United Way; chmn. Boy Scouts Am.; bd. dirs. King's Coll., Wilkes-Barre, Pa., 1989—, St. Joseph Sem. Coll., Will Woods Cmty., New Orleans, 1998—. Recipient Nat. League Nursing award of Ohio Nat. League Nursing, 1986, Trustee award Cathedral High Sch., 1987. Mem. Am. Psychol. Assn., Am. Cath. Colls. and Univs., Plimsoll Club, Internat. House Club. Roman Catholic. Office: Our Lady of Holy Cross Coll 4123 Woodland Dr New Orleans LA 70131-7337

CHAMBERS, TIMOTHY EDWARD, philosopher, educator; b. Milw., May 4, 1971; s. Charles Hoy Chambers and Patricia Ann Moriarty. BA, BS, U. Conn., 1993; MA, Tufts U., 1995; postgrad., Brown U., 1995—. Instr. Brown U., Providence, 2000—. Adj. instr. U. R.I., Kingston, 2000—, R.I. Coll., Providence, 2000—. Contbr. articles to profl. jours. Younger Scholars grantee NEH, 1988; Univ. scholar U. Conn., 1992-93; Tchg. fellow Brown U., 1998—, Dissertation fellow, 1999, Tchg. fellow Harvard U., 2001. Mem. Am. Philos. Assn., Sigma Pi Sigma. Avocations: logic, mathematics, chess, hangul. Home: 154 Taber Ave Providence RI 02906 Office: Brown U Dept Philosophy Box 1918 Providence RI 02912 E-mail: wellwisher68@hotmail.com.

CHAMBERS, WILLIAM EDMOND, telephone techician, writer; b. Brooklyn, NY, Oct 9, 1943; s. William Robert and Julia Mary (Lynch) Chambers; m. Marie Antoinette Kaczanowska, Aug. 29, 1964. Attended HS, Haaren, NYC, 1957—61; diploma HS equivalency, Stevens Inst. of Tech., Hoboken, NJ, 1961. Cert. merit United Way of Tri-State, 1980. Truck drivers helper M&M Transp., Queens, NY, 1961—62; constn. laborer Roman Stone Construction Co., Brooklyn, NY, 1962—65; tel. tech. NY Tel/Verizon, Manhattan, NYC, NY,

1965—91. Dir. MWA, NY, NY, 1970—74. Author: (novels) Death Toll, 1976, The Redemption Factor, 1980, (short stories) Don't Kill a Karate Fighter; If I Quench Thee; A Better Way; One Up; Daddy's Little Girl; Night Service; Above Reproach; The Rationalist; Another Night to Remember, 1976—2002, (poem) An Ode to Freedom, 2000; author: (editor) (columns) Vital Signs; Bloodlines. Nominee Brooke Russell Astor Award, 2002; recipient leadership CWA, City of Hope, 1986, Couple of the Yr., Seneca Club/ Dem. Party, 1998, Seneca Club/ Dem., 2001, 2002, 2003. Mem.: Sisters in Crime, Pvt. Eye Writers of Am., Mystery Writers of America (hon.; N.Y. chpt. pres. 1995—97, exec. v.p. 2000—02). Democrat. Roman Catholic. Achievements include Novels, stories, and articles influenced political reps. to aquire fund for new library. Avocations: history, reading, weightlifting, collecting books, politics. Home: 65 Meserole Ave Brooklyn NY 11222

CHAMBERS-STEINBERG, WANDA, researcher; d. Abraham, Sr. and Lessie Dickey; m. George, III Steinberg. BS in Chemistry, Howard U., Washington, DC; MS in Chemistry, Am. U., Washington, DC; post grad., Touro U., Calif. Program and mgmt. analyst Office of Rsch.; mgmt. analyst Nat. Inst. of Edn.; mgmt. assoc. Toys R Us; grad. asst. U. of Md.; rsch. assoc. Bell Labs., 1982; rsch. asst. Howard U., 1983; program officer, rsch. analyst Office of Rsch. and Ednl. Improvement, 2003; program mgr. U.S. Energy Dept., Washington, 2003—. Nat. sci. fair judge local schs., Washington, 1987—2001; vol. Cancer-.org, 2001, Vol. Match, 2001—03; tutor local schs. Washington; co-coord. GED program local orgn., Md., 1990—93. Recipient Performance awards, U.S. Dept. of Edn., 1990—2002, Sec. Innovation Team award, 1997; fellow MARC Scholar, NSF, 1981—83; scholar Nat. Competitive Scholar, Howard U., 1979—83. Mem.: Am. Chem. Soc. (corr.), APHA (corr.), Am. Math. Soc. (corr.), Am. Assn. for the Advancnement of Sci. (corr.), N.Y. Acad. of Scis. (corr.).

CHAMBLISS, PRINCE CAESAR, JR., lawyer; b. Birmingham, Ala., Oct. 3, 1948; s. Prince Caesar and Marguerite (Pearson) C.; m. Patricia Toney, Dec. 26, 1971; children: Patience Brandyn. Student Wesleyan U., Middletown, Conn., 1966-68; BA, U. Ala., Birmingham, 1969-71; JD, Harvard U., 1974. Bar: Ala. 1974, Tenn. 1976. Spl. asst. to pres. U. Ala., Birmingham, 1974-75; law clk. to Judge U.S. Dist. Ct. (no. dist.) Ala. Birmingham, 1975-76; assoc. firm Armstrong, Allen, Braden, Goodman, McBride & Prewitt, Memphis, 1976-81, ptnr., 1981—; sec., treas. Tenn. Bd. Law Examiners, 1988-92, v.p., 1992—. Bd. dirs. ARC Memphis chpt., 1st vice chmn., 1988-89; trustee Miles Coll. Sch. Law, Birmingham, 1982-88. Recipient Community Service award Jud. Council Nat. Bar Assn., 1982; named Boss of Yr., Memphis Legal Secs. Assn., 1984. Mem. ABA, Memphis Bar Assn. (dir. 1983-85, pres. 1997-98), Fed. Bar Assn. (pres. Mid-South chpt. 1984-85), Nat. Bar Assn., Tenn. Bar Assn. (sec. 1995-97), Ala. Bar Assn, Memphis Council for Internat. Visitors (bd. dirs. 1983—). Home: 1917 Miller Farms Rd Memphis TN 38138-2752 Office: Armstrong Allen Braden Goodman McBride & Prewitt 80 Monroe Ave Memphis TN 38103-2481

CHAMBLISS, SAXBY, senator; b. Warrenton, N.C., Nov. 10, 1943; m. Julianne Chambliss; 2 children. BA in Bus. Adminstrn., U. Ga., 1966; JD, U. Tenn., 1968. Atty., 1968—95; mem. U.S. Congress from 8th Ga. dist., 1995—2002, mem. agriculture com., armed svcs. com., 1996—2002; U.S. senator Georgia, 2003—. Mem. forestry, resource conservation & rsch. com., chmn. gen. farm commodities and risk mgmt. subcom. Republican. Office: Off of Senator Chambliss US Senate Washington DC 20510

CHAMEIDES, STEVEN B. lawyer; b. N.Y.C., Sept. 6, 1946; s. Robert and Belle (Karpen) C.; m. Sandra R. Fetterman. BSE in Math. and Naval Architecture, U. Mich., 1967, JD, 1970. Bar: N.Y. 1971, U.S. Supreme Ct. 1975, D.C. 1976. Assoc. Haight, Gardner, Poor & Havens, N.Y.C., 1970-76, Arent, Fox, Kinter, Plotkin & Kahn, Washington, 1976-79; ptnr. Becker & Chameides, Washington, 1979-84, Chameides & Goldstein, Washington, 1985-89, Foley & Lardner, Washington, 1989—. Dir. Transglobe Container Svc., Inc., Washington. Mem. Mid-Atlantic Cancer Rsch. Found., Washington, Internat. Found. Thrombosis Rsch., United Jewish Appeal Fedn., Washington. Lt. JAGC, USN, 1971-74. Mem. ABA, Maritime Law Assn., Soc. of Naval Archs. Avocations: sailing, flying. Office: Foley & Lardner Washington Harbour 3000 K St NW Fl 5 Washington DC 20007-5109 E-mail: schawmeides@foleylaw.com.

CHAMINGS, PATRICIA ANN, nurse, educator; b. Lakeland, Fla., June 21, 1940; d. Roy John and Esther Delilah (O'Steen) C. Diploma, Orange Meml. Hosp., 1961; BSN, U. Fla., 1964, M of Nursing, 1965; PhD, George Peabody Coll., 1978. Cert. nurse adminstr. advanced. Dir., assoc. prof. grad. program Vanderbilt U., Nashville, 1976-84; asst. dean Emory U., Atlanta, 1984-85; prof. U. N.C., Greensboro, 1985—, dean, 1985-90, dir. anesthesia edn. project, 1989-92. Bd. trustees Wesley Long Cmty. Hosp., 1989-97; bd. dirs. N.C. Ctr. for Nursing, Health Svc. Ministry, N.C. Commn. on Mental Health, Devel. Disabilities and Substance Abuse Svcs., Wesley Long Cmty. Health Found. Named N.C. Nurse Educator of Yr., 1988; advanced nurse tng. grantee USPHS, 1989-92. Fellow Am. acad. Nursing; mem. Sigma Theta Tau Internat.

CHAMIS, CHRISTOS CONSTANTINOS, aerospace scientist, educator; b. Sotira, Greece, May 16, 1930; arrived in U.S., 1948; s. Constantinos and Anastasia (Kyriakos) C.; m. Alice Yanosko, Aug. 20, 1966; children: Chrysanthie, Anna-Lisa, Constantinos. BS in Civil Engring., Cleve. State U., 1960; MS, Case Western Res. U., 1962, PhD, 1967. Draftsman, designer Cons. Engring., Cleve., 1955-60; tech. asst. Case Western Res. U., Cleve., 1960-62, rsch. assoc., 1964-68; rsch. mathematician B.F. Goodrich, Brecksville, Ohio, 1962-64; aerospace engr. Glenn Rsch. Ctr. NASA, Cleve., 1968-78, sr. rsch. engr., 1978-86, sr. aerospace scientist, 1986—. Cons. Lawrence Livermore Labs., Calif., 1974-79; adj. prof. Cleve. State U., 1968—, Akron U., 1980—, Case Western Res. U., 1984—. Editor: Composites Analysis/Design, 1975, Test Methods and Design Allowables for Composites, 1979, 89; mem. editl. bd. Jour. Composites Rsch. and Tech., Reinforced Plastics and Composites, Internat. Jour. Damage Mechanics, Theoretical and Applied Fracture Mechanics; contbr. numerous articles to sci. jours.; patentee in field for Intraply Hybrid Composites and Exoskeletal Engine Concepts; rschr. in hygrothermal composite micromechanics, computational composite mechanics-computer codes, high-temperature composite structures, structural tailoring of engine structures, computational simulation of progressive fracture, engine structures computational simulations, computational simulation/tailoring of coupled multi-discipline problems, and probabilistic structural analysis. Served with USMC, 1952-53. Fellow ASME, AIAA (assoc. editor 1986-88), ASCE, ASTM, Soc. Advancement Materials and Process Engring., Soc. Automotive Engrs.; mem. Soc. Exptl. Mechanics, Am. Soc. Metals, Am. Soc. Composites, Soc. Engring. Sci., Am. Ceramic Soc., Sigma Xi, Dodoni Club, Hellenic U. Club. Home: 24534 Framingham Dr Cleveland OH 44145-4902 E-mail: christos.c.chamis@nasa.gov.

CHAMNESS, CHARLES MORRIS, professional society administrator; b. Bloomington, Ind., Nov. 15, 1962; s. Dale L. and Luanne C.; m. Briget Polichene, Aug. 26, 1989; children: Charles, Sarah, Robert, Joseph. BA, Ind. U. Dep. asst. sec. pub. affairs U.S. Dept. HUD, 1991—92; dir. Office of Pub. Affairs, Fed. Housing Fin. Bd., Washington, 1992-95; v.p.pub. affairs Nat. Assn. of Mut. Ins. Cos., Indpls., 1995—2003; pres. Nat. Assn. Mut. Ins. Cos., 2003—. Sec. bd. Assurance Ptnrs. Bank, Indpls., 1998—. Pres. Friends of Holliday Park, Indpls., 1999. Mem. Pub. Rels. Soc. Am. (chmn. pub. affairs conf. 2002). Office: Nat Assn of Mutual Ins Co 3601 Vincennes Rd Indianapolis IN 46268

CHAMORRO, JUAN PABLO, financial analyst, business development executive; b. Zaragoza, Aragon, Spain, Feb. 14, 1967; s. Angel and Fiorella Angela Chamorro; m. Kristin L. Andersen, Apr. 19, 1997; one child: Clara V. Chamorro, Oct. 14, 1999. BBA, U. Mass., 1989; MBA, Columbia U., 1993. Fin. assoc. United Technologies, Pratt & Whitney, East Hartford, Conn., 1989-91; equity rsch. assoc. J.P. Morgan Investment Mgmt., NYC, 1992; sr. fin. analyst AlliedSignal Inc., Morristown, NJ, 1993-94; regional mgr. AlliedSignal Fluro-chems. Europe B.V., Amersfoort, Netherlands, 1994-95; product mgr. Allied-Signal Europe, Heverlee, Belgium, 1995-96; industry mktg. mgr. AlliedSignal, Inc., Morristown, NJ, 1996-98; mgr. finance Pharmacia & Upjohn, Peapack, NJ, 1999-2000; dir. finance and bus. analysis Pharmacia Corp., Bridgewater, NJ, 2000—02, dir. finance, bus. devel., and R&D Peapack, NJ, 2003; dir. portfolio mgmt. Pfizer, Inc., Morris Plains, NJ, 2003—. Mem. Fin. Mgmt. Assn. Roman Catholic. Avocations: travel, tennis, history, reading. Home: 16 Collinwood Rd Maplewood NJ 07040-1002 Office: Pfizer Inc 201 Tabor Road Morris Plains NJ 07950

CHAMOT, DENNIS, research organization executive; b. Bklyn., June 5, 1943; s. Joe and Sarah C.; m. Judith Ornstein, May 19, 1974; children: Jonathan, Joshua. BS in Chemistry, MS in Chemistry, Poly. Inst. Bklyn., 1964; PhD in Chemistry, U. Ill., 1969; MBA, U. Pa., 1974. Rsch. chemist E.I. duPont de Nemours and Co., Wilmington, Del., 1969-73; asst. to exec. sec. coun. unions for profl. employees AFL-CIO, Washington, 1974-77, asst. dir. dept. for profl. employees, 1977-84, assoc. dir. dept., 1984-90, exec. asst. to pres. dept., 1990-94; assoc. exec. dir. Commn. on Engring. and Tech. Sys., NRC, Washington, 1994—2000, Divsn. on Engring. and Phys. Sciences, NRC, 2001—. Mem. com. on computer aided mfg., assembly of engring. NRC, 1980-81, mem. com. on edn. and utilization of engr., 1982-85, mem. panel on tech. and women's employment, 1984-86, mem. commn. on engring. and tech. sys., 1985-92, mem. com. on rev. of info. sys. modernization of IRS, 1990-94, mem. coordinating coun. for edn., 1991-92, mem. com. to study impact of info. tech. on performance of svc. activities, 1991-93, mem. nat. com. on sci. edn. stds. and assessment, 1992-94, mem. com. on internat. stds., conformity assessment and U.S. trade policy, 1993-95, acting dir. bd. on infrastructure and constructed environ., 1994-95, acting dir. bd. on engring. edn., 1995; mem. pub. understanding of sci. adv. com. NSF, 1977-79, chmn. informal sci. edn. oversight com., 1985-86, mem. adv. coun., 1984-89; mem. adj. faculty George Mason U., Fairfax, Va., 1983, 84; adj. asst. prof. Univ. Coll. U. Md., College Park, 1993—; mem. external rev. com. Nat. Inst. Occupl. Safety and Health; mem. adv. panel on info. tech., automation and the workplace Office Tech. Assessment, U.S. Congress, 1982-84; mem. nat. adv. com. for tng. in new tech. Work in Am. Inst., 1985-87; mem. rev. panel Ctr. on Edn. Quality of Workforce, U.S. Dept. Edn., 1990; provider testimony various congl. hearings, 1982, 83, 87; participant, presenter numerous profl. confs. and symposia, most recently tech. summit Berkeley Round Table on Internat. Economy, San Francisco, 1993, presdl. colloquium on chem. rsch. environ. in next century, Washington, 1994, Symposium on Restructuring, Retooling, Reinventing Employment in Chemistry, 1997. Contbr. many articles to profl. publs. Recipient Charles Gordon award Chem. Soc. Washington, 1986; travel grantee Swedish Inst., 1984; Mary E. Switzer meml. scholar Nat. Rehab. Assn., 1969; Fellow AAAS; mem. Am. Chem. Soc. (councilor 1975—, soc. com. on profl. rels. 1988-89, chmn. subcom. on career support and mem. assistance 1990-91, chmn. subcom. on career support 1989, cons. 1992-93, chmn. com. on Project Seed 1992-94, chmn. divsn. profl. rels. 1982, chmn. mem. adv. bd. 1973, mem. com. on econ. status 1978-86, mem. task force on occupl. health and safety 1987-94, Henry Hill award 1992, chmn. coun. com. on econ. and profl. affairs, 2001-02, mem. coun. policy com., 2001-02; bd. dirs., 2002—), Soc. for Occupl. and Environ. Health (sec.-treas. 1978-82, plaque 1982), Sigma Xi, Phi Kappa Phi, Phi Lambda Upsilon. Office: NRC 500 Fifth St, NW Washington DC 20001

CHAMOUN-NICOLAS, HABIB, business development consultant; b. Nueva Rosita, Coahuila, Mexico, Nov. 17, 1959; s. Habib Chamoun and Maria Elena Nicolas; m. Marcela Guerra Farah de Chamoun, Jan. 14, 1989; children: Habib Chamoun-Farah, Emile Chamoun-Farah, Antoine Chamoun-Farah, Marcelle Chamoun-Farah. BS in Chem. Engring., Monterrey (Mexico) Inst. Tech., 1982; MSc in Chem. Engring., U. Tex., 1985, PhD, 1988. Registered profl. engr., Tex., 1992. Bus. devel. dir. Surfchem, Austin, 1988—89; postdoctoral staff Elf Aquitaine, Pau, France, 1989—90; mktg. coord., process engr. Brown and Root Braun, Houston, 1990—94; bus. devel. dir. Escala Internat., Monterrey, 1994—95; bus. devel. mgr. ICA Fluor Daniel, Mexico City, 1995—96; mktg. assoc. Irvine, Calif., Greenville, SC, 1996—97; founder, gen. dir. Global Azez, Monterrey, 1998—, Houston, 1998—. Author: (book) Business Development, Deal-guide for a Faultless Negotiation, 2003, Robust Negotiations-How to Obtain Great Deals? It is not a Coincidence, 2003; contbr. articles to profl. jours. Mem.: Am. C. of C. Roman Catholic. Achievements include research in how Mexicans negotiate; development of negotiation mindset model; sales methodology tailored to Mexican clients. Avocations: swimming, travel. Office: 4414 Pine Breeze Dr Kingwood TX 77345 Personal E-mail: glazez@kingwoodcable.net. E-mail: glazez@intercable.net.

CHAMPA, JOHN JOSEPH, telecommunications engineer, consultant; b. Columbus, Ohio, Oct. 16, 1944; s. Antonio John and Helen Catherine (Izzie) C.; children: Lea Christine Kuhn, Susan Catherine Muscat, Rebecca Lynn Champa-McLaughlin, Patrick John C.; m. Karen Lynn Feder, Sept. 27, 2002. BA, Ohio State U., Columbus, 1974; MA, Cen. Mich U., Mt. Pleasant, 1975; MS, Columbia Pacific U., San Rafael, Calif., 1985, PhD, 1986. Cert. telecom. engr.; FCC lic. amateur radio operator. Mem. U.S. police Fed. Protective Svc., Nashville & Columbus, 1972-74; safety engr. Borden Corp., Columbus, 1974-76; plant safety engr. Buckeye Steel Castings, Columbus, 1976-80; divsn. safety engr. Cooper Energy Svcs., Mount Vernon, Ohio, 1980-82; sr. safety engr. Goodyear Atomic Corp., Piketon, Ohio, 1982-83; corp. safety engr. Unisys Corp., Detroit, 1984-88; mgr., chief engr. Unisys Worldwide Videoconferencing, Detroit, 1988-94; dir. Multimedia Comms. Svcs., Plymouth, Mich., 1994—; exec. v.p. Radio Amateur Satellite Corp., Washington, 1988—91; adj. prof. Franklin U., Columbus, 1979; chmn. high speed digital and multimedia working group Technology Task Force, ARRL, 2002—. Inventor: Digital Video Switch for Videoconferencing, 1992; author: CD-ROM Unisys Multimedia and Video Conferencing Solutions, Videoconferencing Skills, 2002; co-author: Am. Nat. Stds. Inst. (ANSI) Z241 Std.; contbr. articles to profl. jours. Capt. Mil. Police Corps U.S. Army, 1967-71. Mem.: VFW (past post comdr., past trustee), NRA, Union Concerned Scientists, Nat. Parks Conservation Assn., Mich. Sheriffs' Assn., Nat. Geog. Soc., Nature Conservancy Mich. Chpt.-Gt. Lakes Soc., Nat. Assn. Radio and Telecom. Engrs., Internat. Teleconf. Assn. (bd. dirs. 1993—99, exec. com. 1996—97), Gun Owners Am., Jews for Preservation Gun Ownership (charter mem.), Nat. Space Soc., Safari Club Internat., Right to Keep and Bear Arms (citizens com.), World Wildlife Fund, Upper Peninsula Bear Houndsman Assn., Nat. Arbor Day Found., Nat. Wildlife Fedn., Sons of Italy Found., Am. Hiking Soc., Am. Canoe Assn., Great Lakes Paddlers Assn., Mich. Bear Hunters Assn., Livingston County Amateur Radio Club (past program dir.), Am. Radio Relay League (chmn. high-speed digital networks and multimedia working group), Sierra Club (Novi chpt.), Mich. United Conservation Clubs. Avocations: hunting, cartography, camping, amateur radio. Office: Unisys Corp Bldg 1 41100 Plymouth Rd 2d Fl Plymouth MI 48170-1892 E-mail: john.champa@unisys.com., K80CL@arrl.net.

CHAMPAGNE, CECILE BELISLE, nursing educator, maternal/child health nurse; b. Worcester, Mass., Jan. 7, 1941; d. Alfred N. and Blanche (Poissant) B.; m. Raymond W. Champagne, Jr., Aug. 20, 1967; 1 child, Robert Raymond. BS, Salve Regina Coll., Newport, R.I., 1962; MS, Boston U., 1964; DNSc, Widener U., Chester, Pa., 1992. Instr. Salve Regina Coll., Newport, R.I.; asst. prof. Wilkes Coll., Wilkes-Barre, Pa., Coll. Misericordia, Dallas, Pa.; assoc. prof. East Stroudsburg (Pa.) U. Active N.E. program svcs. com. March of Dimes. Mem. Sigma Theta Tau, Kappa Gamma Pi. Home: 117 Donny Dr Taylor PA 18517-9707

CHAMPAGNE, DUANE WILLARD, sociology educator; b. Belcourt, N.D., May 18, 1951; m. Carole Goldberg; children: Talya, Gabe, Demelza. BA in Math., N.D. State U., 1973, MA in Sociology, 1975; PhD in Sociology, Harvard U., 1982. Teaching fellow Harvard U., Cambridge, Mass., 1981-82, rsch. fellow, 1982-83; asst. prof. U. Wis., Milw., 1983-84, UCLA, 1984-91, assoc. prof., 1991-97, prof., 1997—. Publs. dir. Am. Indian Studies Ctr., UCLA, 1986-87, assoc. dir., 1990, acting dir., 1991, dir., 1991-02, affiliate faculty UCLA Native Nations Law and Policy Ctr., 2003—; adminstrv. co-head interdepartmental program for Am. Indian studies UCLA, 1992-93; mem. grad. rsch. fellowship panel NSF, 1990-92, minority fellowship com. ASA; cons. Energy Resources Co., 1982, No. Cheyenne Tribe, 1983, Realis Pictures, Inc., 1989-90, Sta. KCET-TV, L.A., 1990, 92, Salem Press, 1992, Book Prodns. Systems, 1993, Readers Digest, 1993, Rattlesnake Prodns., 1993. Author: American Indian Societies, 1989, Social Order and Political Change, 1992, The ACCIP Community Service Report: A Second Century of Dishonor-Federal Inequities and California Indians, 2002; editor: Native American Studies in Higher Education: Models for Collaboration Between Indigenous Nations, 2002, Special Issues on Indigenous Issues: Hagar, International Social Science Review, 2001, Native North American Almanac, 1994, Native North American Almanac, 2d edit., 2001, Chronology of Native North American, 1994; co-author: Native America: Portrait of the Peoples, 1994, A Second Century of Dishonor: Federal Inequities and California Tribes, 1996, Service Delivery for Native American Children in Los Angeles County, 1996; editor: Native Am. Studies Assn. Newsletter, 1991—92; co-editor: Native American Activism: Alcatraz to the Longest Walk, 1997, Contemporary Native American Cultural Issues, 1999; book rev. editor: Am. Indian Culture and Rsch. Jour., 1984—86; editor, 1986—2002; series editor: Contemporary American Indian Issues, 1998—; editor: The Native North American Almanac, 2d edit., 2001, Native American Studies in Higher Education, 2002; contbr. Mem. city of L.A. Cmty. Action Bd., 1993, L.A. County/City Am. Indian Commn., 1992-2000, chair, 1993, 95-97, 2000-2002, sec., 2002-, v. chair, 1997-2000; mem. subcom. for cultural and econ. devel. L.A. City/County Native Am. Commn., 1992-93; bd. dirs. Ctr. for Improvement of Child Caring, 1993—, Greater L.A. Am. Indian Culture Ctr., Inc., 1993, Incorporator, 1993; bd. trustees Southwest Mus., 1994-97, Nat. Mus. Am. Indian, 1998—; Master of Coll. of Humanities and Social Sci., N.D. State U., 1996. Recipient L.A. Sr. Health Peer Counseling Cmty. Vol. Cert. of Recognition, 1996; Writer of Yr. award Cir. Native Writers and Storytellers, 1999; honoree Nat. Ctr. Am. Indian Enterprise, 1999; grantee Rockefeller Found., 1982-83, U. Wis. Grad Sch. Rsch. Com., 1984-85, Wis. Dept. Edn., 1984-85, 87-88, 88-89, NSF, 1985-88, 88-89, Nat. Endowment for Arts, 1987-88, 91-92, NRC, 1988-89, Nat. Sci. Coun., 1989-90, John D. and Catherine T. MacArthur Found., 1990-91, Hayes Found., 1990-91, 92-93, Calif. Coun. for Humanities, 1991-92, Ford Found., 1990-92, Gale Rsch. Inc., 1991-93, 93-95, Rockwell Corp., 1991-93, GTE, 1992-93, Kellog Found., 1997-2000, Pequot Mus. and Rsch. Ctr., 1997-2002, So. Calif. Indian Ctr., 1998; Fund for the Improvement of Post Secondary Edn., 1998-2003, Nat. Endowment for Humanities, 2002—, Dept. Justice, 2001—; Am. Indian scholar, 1973-75, 80-82, Minority fellow Am. Sociol. Assn., 1975-78, RIAS Seminar fellow, 1976-77; Rockefeller Postdoctoral fellow, 1982-83, NSF fellow, 1985-88, Postdoctoral fellow Ford Found., 1988-89. Avocations: chess, jogging. Home: 2152 Balsam Ave Los Angeles CA 90025 Office: UCLA Native Nations Law and Policy Ctr Dept Sociology 264 Haines Hall Los Angeles CA 90095-1551 E-mail: champagn@ucla.edu.

CHAMPE, PAMELA CHAMBERS, biochemistry educator, writer; b. Oakland, Calif., Aug. 29, 1945; d. Robert Leroy and Leah June (Musser) Chambers; m. Sewell Preston Champe, June 28, 1969 (dec.); stepchildren: Mark Adrian, Sewell Peter. BA, Stanford U., 1967; MS, Purdue U., 1969; PhD, Rutgers U., 1971; instr. Rutgers Med. Sch., Piscataway, N.J., 1974-76; asst. prof. Robert Wood Johnson Med. Sch. U. Medicine and Dentistry N.J., Piscataway, 1977-84, assoc. prof. Robert Wood Johnson Med. Sch., 1984-96; prof. emeritus Robert Wood Johnson Med. Sch., 1996—. Lectr. several med. schs. and tng. programs. Co-editor: Gene Families of Collagen and Other Proteins, 1980; co-author: Biochemistry (Lippincott's Illus. Revs.), 1987, 2nd edit., 1994; co-author, co-editor: Pharmacology (Lippincott's Illus. Revs.), 2nd edit. 1997, Microbiology (Lippincott's Illus. Revs.), 2001. Health and Human Svcs. grantee, 1988-94; recipient Nat. award Basic Sci. Educator of the Yr., 1995. Mem. AAAS, Assn. Am. Med. Colls., N.Y. Acad. Scis., Alpha Omega Alpha. Avocation: malachology. Office: U Medicine and Dentistry NJ Robert Wood Johnson Med Sch 675 Hoes Ln Piscataway NJ 08854-5627

CHAMPEY, ELAINE, science and technology research coordinator; b. Amityville, N.Y., Sept. 1, 1950; d. Chris Strum-Arden and Celia Strum; m. Michael Champey, June 20, 1976; children: Christine Anne, Michael Edward, Lauren Marie. BA in Polit. Sci., St. John's U., 1971, postgrad., 1974-76; M in Liberal Scis., SUNY, Stony Brook, 1993. Permanent cert. in chemistry, biology, gen. sci. Rsch. technician dept. pharmacology SUNY, Stonybrook, 1977-80; pvt. piano instr. Smithtown, N.Y., 1980-96; substitute tchr. St. Anthony's H.S. Smithtown Sch. Dist., 1991-96, tchr., 1996—; adj. prof SUNY, Albany, 1999—. Cons. Dept. Edn. Grant, 1999; technician tissue culture Procs. of NAS, 1978, technician biochem. assays, 1980; mentor finalists Siemens-Westinghouse Sci. Competition, 1999, 2000, 02. Named Tchr. of Merit, Intel Sci. Talent Search, 1998-2002; recipient Commendation for finalist Internat. Sci. and Engring. Fair, 2000, Recognition award N.Y. Sci. Talent Search, 1998, 99, 2000, 2001, 2002; First Robotic Advisor, 2001-2003; Recognition award Jr. Scis. and Humanities Symposium, 2001. Mem. N.Y. State Tchr. Union, Smithtown Parent Tchr. Assn., Smithtown Sch. Dist. Tchr. Ctr. (vice chair 1996-2001, mini-grantee 1998), Smithtown H.S. Industry Adv. Bd. (exec. bd., com. chair 1996-2003), Suffolk County Sci. Tchrs. Assn. (historian 1999-2000). Avocations: playing piano, singing. E-mail: echampey@juno.com.

CHAMPINE, GEORGE A. computer scientist; b. Fairmont, Minn., May 16, 1934; s. A. Floyd and C. Genevieve (Northway) C.; m. Barbara Joan Nelson, Mar. 17, 1956; children: Renee, Mark, Lisa. BS in Physics, U. Minn., 1956, MS in Physics, 1959, PhD, 1975. Dir. rsch. Sperry Univac, St. Paul, 1979; v.p. engring. Exxon Enterprises, Florham Pk., N.J., 1980-81; dir. tech. Digital Equipment Corp. (acquired by Compaq Computer Corp.), Maynard, Mass., 1981—. Adj. prof. U. Tex., Austin, 1984-86, MIT, Cambridge, Mass., 1986-88, U. Mass., Lowell, 1987-92. Author: Computer Technology, 1978, Distributed Computing, 1980, MIT Project Athena, 1991. Mem. IEEE Computer Soc., I.T. Alumni Soc. U. Minn. (past pres.). Methodist. Avocations: photography, music, genealogy, jogging. Home: 2A Strawberry Ln Hudson MA 01749

CHAMPION, DAVID, music educator; b. Pittsburgh, Pa., June 14, 1937; m. Janice Ann Champion; children: David Eric Camesi, Erica Ann. BS, Juilliard Sch., New York, NY, 1961; MA, Columbia U, New York, NY, 1965. Music prof. Ca State U Dominguez Hills, Carson, Calif., 1969—. Author: (book) 18th Century Conducting. Mem.: Am. Musicological Soc., Coll. Music Soc., Am. Fedn. of Musicians, Locals 47 & 802, Mu Phi Epsilon (faculty advisor 1976). Home: 229 15th St Manhattan Beach CA 90266 Personal E-mail: david@thechampions.com.

CHAMPION, HALE (CHARLES HALE CHAMPION), political science educator, former public official; b. Coldwater, Mich., Aug. 27, 1922; s. Paul Upham and Ruth Emma (Hungerford) C.; m. Marie Ozine Tifft, Aug. 21, 1952; children: Thomas Paul, Katherine Marie. BA, Stanford U., 1952. Journalist UPI, Milw. Jour., Sacramento Bee, San Francisco Chronicle, Reporter mag., 1946-49, 52-58; legis. asst. to Congressman Andrew J. Biemiller of Wis., 1950; press and exec. sec. to Gov. Edmund G. Brown of Calif., 1958-60, dir. fin. State of Calif., 1961-66; dir. Boston Redevel. Authority, 1968-69; v.p. fin., planning and ops. U. Minn., Mpls., 1969-71; v.p. fin. Harvard U., Cambridge, Mass., 1971-76, exec. dean John F. Kennedy Sch. Govt., 1980-87; undersec. HEW, Washington, 1977-79; chief of staff to Gov. Michael S. Dukakis of Mass., Boston, 1987-88; lectr. John F. Kennedy Sch. Govt. Harvard U., 1989-91. Mem. Presdl. Task Force Reorgn. Fed. Govt., 1966-67, Presdl. Task Force Role of Univ. in Urban Affairs, 1967-68; chmn. Mass. Joint Legis.-Exec. Com. Fed. Base Conversion, 1973-74; chmn. Presdl. Commn. on Nat. Health Ins., 1977-78. Bd. dirs. Kaiser Family Found., 1984-92, chmn., 1989-92; bd. dirs. Ctr. for Study of Social Policy, 1986—, chmn., 1998—. Served with AUS, 1942-46. Nieman fellow Harvard U., 1956-57; fellow John F. Kennedy Inst. Politics, 1967 Mem. Nat. Acad. Pub. Adminstrn. (trustee 1980-86). Democrat. Office: Harvard Univ John F Kennedy Sch Govt 79 Jfk St Cambridge MA 02138-5801

CHAMPION, HELENA MARGARET, pharmaceutical executive; b. Durban, South Africa, July 1, 1950; d. Antoon and Helena Marie Meeuwissen; m. Alfred Timothy Champion, Sept. 23, 1972 (div. 1983); 1 child, Ian Champion. BS, Natal U., Durban, 1971; BS with honors, Rhodes U., Grahamstown, South Africa, 1972; MS, U. Guelph, Ont., Can., 1981; MBA, Northeastern U., Boston, 1985. Lab. instr., supr. Capilano C.C., North Vancouver, Can., 1976-78; sr. scientist, project mgr. Millipore Corp., Bedford, Mass., 1980-85; pres., CEO Bed and Breakfast Inc., Newton, Mass., 1985-91; sr. scientist Baxter Lytening Systems Inc., Danvers, Mass., 1992-93; sr. project engr. Amicon (divsn. of Millipore Corp.), Danvers, 1994-95; diagnostic unit mgr. Genzyme Corp., Cambridge, Mass., 1996-98; quality assurance mgr. Biogen Inc., Cambridge, 1998—2001; GMP mgr. Cambridge Isotope Labs., Inc., Andover, Mass., 2001—. Patentee in field. Mem. ACS, Parenteral Drug Assn. Avocations: skiing, mountain biking, tennis, music, reading.

CHAMPION, HERMAN DANIEL, JR., college dean; b. Water Valley, Miss., Feb. 24, 1942; s. Herman Daniel and Louise Elizabeth (Vines) C.; m. Lily Ruth Shoemake, Jan. 30, 1942; children: Tara Elizabeth, Lori Alyson. BA, Miss. Coll., 1963; MDiv, New Orleans Bapt. Theol. Sem., 1966; MA, La. State U.,

1968, PhD, 1980. Pastor Beech Grove Bapt. Ch., Pattison, Miss., 1962-65, Calvary Bapt. Ch., Smithdale, Miss., 1966-68; chmn. comm. arts dept. Carson-Newman Coll., Jefferson City, Tenn., 1976-90, chmn. divsn. humanities, 1983-90; v.p. for acad. affairs, acad. dean Limestone Coll., Gaffney, S.C., 1990-91, 92-95, interim pres., 1991-92; dean gen. studies Bapt. Coll. Health Scis., Memphis, 1995—. Contbr. chpt. to book. Speaker various civic orgns. and chs., Tenn., Va., S.C., Miss., N.C., Ark. Mem. Speech Communication Assn., Assn. for Communication Adminstrs., So. Speech Communication Assn., Pi Kappa Delta. Democrat. Baptist. Avocations: woodworking, preaching. Home: 2860 Stage Park Dr Memphis TN 38134-4457 E-mail: dan.champion@bchs.edu.

CHAMPION, MICHAEL EDWARD, physician assistant, clinical perfusionist; b. Oroville, Calif., Jan. 30, 1954; s. Robert Joseph and Shirley Anne (Rowland) C.; m. Marie S. Sittner, Oct. 8. 1990. AS, Cuyahoga C.C., 1980; BS, USNY, Albany, 1983; MEd, Boston U., 1986; M of Med. Sci., St. Francis Coll., 1996; postgrad., U. London, 1999, Nova Southeastern U. clin. perfusionist ABCVP. Enlisted U.S. Army, 1972, advanced through grades to maj., 1994; ret., 1994; aviation medicine physician asst., 1980-87; chief physician asst./perfusionist Letterman Army Med. Ctr., 1989-91; founding physician asst./perfusionist Madigan Army Med. Ctr., 1991-94; cardiac surgery mgr., chief physician asst/perfusionist Mercy Med. Ctr., Janesville, Wis., 1994-96; dir. cardiac svcs. Hutchinson (Kans.) Hosp., 1996-98; v.p. projects Champion Constrn., Inc., Wichita, Kans., 1997—; sr. physician asst./perfusionist Hays (Kans.) Med. Ctr., 1998—2002; chief perfusionist Wilford Hall Med. Ctr., San Antonio, 2001—. Clin. instr. U.S. Army Physician Asst. Program, 1981-84, U.S. Army Adult Nurse Practitioner Program, 1982; EMS instr. Fayetteville Tech. Inst., 1983; instr. MEDEX program U. Washington, 1992-95, MMS programs St. Francis Coll., Loretto, Pa., 1996—; CEO Champion and Assocs., LLC; organizer Surg. Physician Asst. course, Jamaica, 1995; CEO Operational Med. Solutions, LLC, 2002—. Contbr. articles to profl. jours. Treas. Rock County Rep. Party, Janesville, 1994; mem. Red Cross, Am. Cancer Soc., EAA Young Eagles Program. Mem. Am. Acad. Physician Assts. (rsch. rev. com. 1984, profl. and continuing edn. com. 1988, vets. caucus bd. dirs. 1989-91, vets. caucus pres. 1991-92, chmn. pilots assn. 1995, chmn. vets. caucus awards 1992-95, jud. affairs com. 1994, vice chmn. surg. congress 1994-96, chmn. 1996-97, Outstanding Svc. award 1989), Wis. Acad. Physician Assts. (chair legis. com., sec. 1995, pres.-elect 1996), Soc. Army Physician Assts. (life, chief del. 1983-84, v.p. 1984-85, pres. 1985-86, 98-99), Assn. Physician Assts. in Cardiovasc. Surgery, Assn. Mil. Surgeons of U.S. (life, Physician Asst. ot Yr. 1992), Am. Soc. Extracorporeal Tech., Am. Heart Assn., Am. Acad. Med. Adminstrs., Am. Coll. Cardiovasc. Adminstrs., Assn. Physician Assts. i Anesthesia (founder 2003). Republican. Roman Catholic. Avocation: private pilot. Home: 1322 Walkers Way San Antonio TX 78216-7709

CHAMPION, NORMA JEAN, communications educator, state legislator; b. Oklahoma City, Jan. 21, 1933; d. Aubra Dell (dec.) and Beuleah Beatrice (Flanagan) Black; m. Richard Gordon Champion, Oct. 3, 1953 (dec.); children: Jeffrey Bruce, Ashley Brooke. BA in Religious Edn., Cen. Bible Coll., Springfield, Mo., 1971; MA in Comm., S.W. Mo. State U., 1978; PhD in Tech., U. Okla., 1986. Producer, hostess The Children's Hour, Sta. KYTV-TV, NBC, Springfield, 1957-86; asst. prof. Cen. Bible Coll., 1968-84; prof. broadcasting Evangel U., Springfield, 1978—; mem. Springfield City Coun., 1987-92, Mo. Ho. of Reps., Jefferson City, 1993—2002, Mo. Senate, 2003—. Adj. faculty Assemblies of God Theol. Sem., Springfield, 1987—, pres. coun.; bd. dirs. Global U.; mem. Commn. on Higher Edn., Assemblies of God, 1998—; frequent lectr. to svc. clubs, edn. seminars; seminar spkr. Internat. Pentecostal Press Assn. World Conf., Singapore, 1989; announcer various TV commls. Contbr. numerous articles to religious publs. Mem. bd Mo. Access to Higher Edn. Trust, 1990—, Boys & Girls Town of Mo.; regional rep. Muscular Dystrophy Assn.; mem. adv. bd. Chameleon Puppet Theater, 1987; mem. exec. bd. Univ. Child Care Ctr., 1987; hon. chmn. fund raising Salvation Army, 1986; also numerous other bds., hon. chairmanships.; judge Springfield City Schs. Recipient commendation resolution Mo. Ho. of Reps., 1988; numerous award for The Children's Hour; Aunt Norma Day named in her honor City of Springfield, 1976. Mem. Nat. Broadcast Edn. Assn., Mo. Broadcast Edn. Assn., Nat. League Cities, Mo. Mcpl. League (human resource com. 1989, intergovtl. rels. com. 1990), Nat. Assn. Telecom. Officers and Advisors, PTA (life). Republican. Mem. Assemblies of God Ch. Avocations: gardening, reading, interior decoration. Home: 3609 S Broadway Ave Springfield MO 65807-4505 Office: Evangel Univ 1111 N Glenstone Ave Springfield MO 65802-2125 E-mail: mchampio@servics.state.mo.us.

CHAMPION, SARA STEWART, lawyer; b. Boston, Apr. 1, 1942; d. William Julius Champion and Mary Stewart Cunningham; m. Wayne L. Kinsey, Dec. 12, 1964 (div. Feb. 1971); m. John Q. Adams, Apr. 25, 1998 (div. Oct. 2000). BA, Duke U., 1963; MA, U. Calif., Davis, 1974; JD cum laude, N.Y. Law Sch., 1992. Bar: N.Y. 1992, Conn. 1992. Rsch. analyst Nat. Security Agy., Ft. Meade, Md., 1963-65; instr. Russian Def. Lang. Inst., Monterey, Calif., 1970-72; claims rep. Social Security Adminstrn., San Francisco, 1974-78, claims rep., ops. supr. N.Y.C., 1978-87; office adminstr. Bachelder Law Offices, N.Y.C., 1987-97, assoc., 1992-97, ptnr., 1997—2002, Vedder, Price, Kaufman and Kammholz, N.Y.C., 2002—. Mem.: DAR, New England Soc., Soc. Mayflower Descs., Silver Spring Country Club (Ridgefield, Conn.), Univ. Club, Wianno Yacht Club (Osterville, Mass.). Avocation: genealogy. Office: Vedder Price Kaufman & Kammholz 805 3d Ave New York NY 10022 E-mail: schampion@vedderprice.com.

CHAMPLIN, CHARLES DAVENPORT, television host, book critic, writer; b. Hammondsport, N.Y., Mar. 23, 1926; s. Francis Malburn and Katherine Marietta (Masson) C.; m. Margaret Frances Derby, Sept. 11, 1948; children: Charles Jr., Katherine, John, Judith, Susan, Nancy. AB cum laude, Harvard U., 1947. Reporter Life mag., N.Y.C., 1948-49, corr. Chgo., 1949-52, asst. editor, 1954-59; corr. Denver, 1952-54, Time mag., L.A., 1959-62, London, 1962-65; arts editor, columnist L.A. Times, 1965-91, prin. film critic, 1967-80, book critic, 1981-82. Host-commentator Ste. KCET-TV, L.A., ETV Network, Z Channel Cable TV, Bravo Channel, 1969-96; adj. prof. Loyola-Marymount U., L.A., 1969-86; adj. prof. U. So. Calif., 1986-96. Author: (with C. Sava) How to Swim Well, 1960, The Flicks, 1977, The Movies Grow Up, 1981, Back There Where the Past Was, 1989, George Lucas: The Creative Impulse, 1992, enlarged, 1997, John Frankenheimer: A Conversation, 1995, Woody Allen at Work, 1995, Hollywood's Revolutionary Decade, 1998, Tony's World, 1999, My Friend, You Are Legally Blind, 2001; contbr. numerous articles to mags. and publs. Bd. dirs. Am. Cinemateque; trustee L.A. Film Tchrs. Assn. With U.S. Army, 1944-46, ETO. Decorated Purple Heart; recipient Order Arts and Letters, France, 1977 Mem. PEN, Nat. Book Critics Cir., L.A. Film Critics Assn., Authors Guild, Overseas Press Club. Democrat. Home: 2169 Linda Flora Dr Los Angeles CA 90077-1408 E-mail: champc@aol.com.

CHAMPLIN, STEVEN M. management consultant; b. Providence, R.I., June 4, 1951; s. Arthur and Julia Munger C.; m. Mary E. Cahill. BA, Wesleyan U., Middleton, Conn., 1974, MA, 1976; MDiv, Yale Divinity Sch., 1980. Dir. of Washington office Vietnam Vets. of Am., Washington, 1978-81; adminstrv. asst., legis. dir. Office of Congressman David Bonior, Washington, 1981-87; exec. flr. asst. House Majority Whip, Washington, 1987-91; exec. dir. Ho. Dem. Caucus, Washington, 1991-93; v.p., treas. bd. dirs. The Duberstein Group, Inc., Washington, 1993—. Co-author: (with David E. Bonior, Timothy S. Kelly) The Vietnam Veteran, A History of Neglect, 1984. Democrat. Office: The Duberstein Group Inc 2100 Pennsylvania Ave NW Washington DC 20037-3202 E-mail: schamplin@dubersteingroup.com.

CHAMPLIN, WILLIAM GLEN, clinical microbiologist-immunologist; b. Rogers, Ark., Sept. 10, 1923; s. Glen and Anna Champlin; m. Helen Elizabeth Garner, Feb. 2, 1951; 1 child, Steven. BS, N.E. Okla. State U., 1948; MS, U. Ark., 1965, PhD, 1971. Lab. dir. VA Med. Ctr., Fayetteville, Ark., 1955-65, clin. microbiologist, lab. dir., 1965-80, cons. ANL Med. Lab. Wash. Regional Med. Ctr., 1965-90; edn. coord. Antaeus Inst. Sch. Med. Tech., 1980-90; vis. prof. microbiology U. Ark., 1978-85. With U.S. Army, 1943-45. Mem. Am. Acad. Microbiology, Am. Soc. Clin. Pathologists, Sigma Xi.

CHAMPNEY, RAYMOND JOSEPH, advertising and marketing executive, consultant; b. NYC, Aug. 6, 1940; s. Raymond Joseph and Florence (McConnell) C.; m. Anne Kelly, Jan. 10, 1976. Student, CCNY, 1961-63, NYU, 1965. With BBDO Advt., N.Y.C., 1964-66, McCann Erickson Advt., 1966-68, Clinton E. Frank Advt., 1968-71, Norman Craig & Kummel Advt., 1971-73, Doyle Dane Bernbach Advt., 1973-74, Guest Pub. Co., 1974-77, Bozell & Jacobs Advt., 1977-79; sr. v.p. Weekley & Assocs., 1980-84, pres. Weekley & Champney Advt., 1984-86; pres., chief exec. officer Champney and Assoc. Advt., Dallas, 1986-92; pres. Champney Publicidad S.A. de C.V., Mexico City, 1987-92, Champney Fulfillment, 1987-92, RJC Internat., Bedford, Tex., 1992—. Dir. gen. Osama Al Madany/RJC Internat., Saudi Arabia, 1994—97; tab facilitator RJC Enterprises LLC-Cons., 2001. Served with U.S. Army, 1959-61. Mem. Sales Mktg. Execs., Dallas Ad League, Am. Mgmt. Assn., Presidents Assn.,. Am. Soc. Travel Agts., Hotel Sales and Mktg. Assn., Better Bus. Bur., Dallas C. of C., HEB C. of C. Home: 2300 Marshfield Dr Bedford TX 76021-7300 Office: PO Box 1072 Bedford TX 76095-1072 E-mail: raymond@rjcenter.com.

CHAMPOUILLON, DAVID CHARLES, music educator, musician; b. Kew Gardens, N.Y., Mar. 27, 1959; s. Emil Robert Champouillon and Roberta Maria Van der Peyl; m. Teresa Marie Roybal; children: Luke, Rick, Roberta. AAS in Music, Onondaga C.C., 1979; BMus in Studio Music and Jazz, U. Miami, 1987; MA in Music, Ea. Ill. U., 1988; DA in Music, U. No. Colo., 1998. Assoc. instr. trumpet and jazz studies Ea. Ill. U., Charleston, 1987—88; instr. trumpet U. Utah, Salt Lake City, 1992—95; assoc. instr. jazz studies U. No. Colo., Greeley, 1995—96; instr. music U. Pa., Kutztown, Pa., 1997—98; asst. prof. music Roanoke Coll., Salem, Va., 1998—99; assoc. prof. trumpet, brass and jazz studies East Tenn. State U., Johnson City, 2000—. Brass reviewer Oxford U. Press, 2002—. Musician: Syracuse Symphony Orch., 1999, Ash-Lawn Highland Opera, 1999, Johnson City Symphony Orch., 2002, Kingsport Symphony Orch, 2002, Lehigh Valley Chamber Orch., Pa. Sinfonia Orch., Greeley Philharmonic Orch., Utah Chamber Orch., Ballet West, Utah Opera, Salty Lake City Symphony Orch., USAF Band of the Golden Gate, (CD recording) UNC Jazz Lab - Alive XV, 1997, Syracuse Symphony, 2000. With USAF, 1979—83. Fellow, U. No. Colo., 1995. Mem.: Internat. Assn. Jazz Educators, Internat. Musician's Union, Musical Educator's Nat. Conf., Internat. Trumpet Guild. Home: 513D Pilgrim Ct Johnson City TN 37601 Office: East Tenn State Univ Dept Music Box 70661 Johnson City TN Home Fax: 423-439-7088; Office Fax: 423-439-7088. Business E-Mail: champoui@etsu.edu.

CHAMPY, WILLIAM, JR., mathematician, educator, researcher, scientist, writer, biologist, chemist, inventor, physicist; b. Orangeburg, S.C., July 23, 1949; s. Buster and Mamie (Brown) Champy. BS in Profl. Chemistry, S.C. State Coll., 1977, MEd, 1985, postgrad.; cert. prodn. operator, Orangeburg-Calhoun Tech. Coll., Orangeburg, S.C., 1990; cert. computer operator, Orangeburg-Calhoun Tech. Coll., 1997. Cert. critical needs tchr. in sci. and math.; lic. bus driver, S.C., armed security guard, small bus. owner, operator. Mgr., owner Champy's Night Club, Orangeburg, S.C., 1968-84; tchr. chemistry, physics, sci. Quinas H.S., Augusta, Ga., 1980; instr. math. Orangeburg-Calhoun Tech. Coll., Orangeburg, S.C., 1985-87; tchr. math Branchville (S.C.) H.S., 1987; coord. devel. lab., math instr. Denmark (S.C.) Tech. Coll., 1989-90; lab. mgr., adminstr., instr. biology/chemistry and physics lab. Voorhees Coll., Denmark, SC, 1991-92; math instr. Midlands Tech. Coll., Columbia, S.C., 1994; security officer Security Force, Inc., 1992-94, Spartan Security, 1995-96, Pinkerton, Inc., 1988—, Sizemore Security, Columbia, 1996—; rsch. asst. dept. energy, divsn. ecology S.C. State U., Orangeburg, unit mgr. dormatory, student svc. program coord. I, 1999—; with U.S. Census, 2000. Truck driver, laborer City of Columbia, 1980; edgefiler, tool sharpener Utica Tool Co., Inc., Orangeburg, 1982; security officer Wells Fargo, Orangeburg, 1990-92, Security Force, Inc., 1992-94, others; substitute tchr., bus driver Orangeburg Sch. Dist. # 5, 1988—; freelance personal income tax preparer, 1998—; coord. Swapop Tutoring Program S.C. State U./NASA, Orangeburg, 1998—; press operator, blademaker Frigidaire Corp., Orangeburg, 1998—; saw operator, laborer, inspector N.Am. Container, Orangeburg, 1996. Holder 20 copyrights, 2 patents in field. Census enumerator, summer 1990; custodian, maint., set-up helper Episcopal Ch. of the Redeemer, 1997; field rep. U.S. Census Bur., 1997; security officer Am. Security, Inc. Mem. AAAS, ACS, NAACP, Nat. Assn. Physics Students, Nat. Inst. Sci., Am. Mgmt. Assn., S.C. State U. Nat. Alumni Assn., S.C. Tech. Edn. Assn., Nat. Inst. Sci., Nat. Soc. Black Engrs., Nat. Assn. Black Engrs., Ernest E. Just Sci. Club, Chem Phi Chem Chemistry Club, Masons (sec.), Phi Delta Kappa, Omega Psi Phi. Avocations: pocket billiards, reading, fishing, hunting, checkers. Home and Office: PO Box 2669 Orangeburg SC 29116 E-mail: wchampy@scsu.edu.

CHAN, ALBERT W. cardiologist; MD, U. Toronto, 1994; MS in Clin. Epidemiology, Harvard U., 1999. Diplomate Am. Bd. Interventional Cardiology, Am. Bd. Cardiovascular Medicine, Am. Bd. Internal Medicine, lic. physician La., Ohio, Med. Coun. Can. Resident U. Toronto, 1994—97; fellow in cardiology U. B.C., Vancouver, 1997—2000; interventional fellow dept. cardiovascular medicine The Cleve. Clinic Found., 2000—02; assoc. dir. cardiac catheterization lab., mem. staff interventional cardiology Ochsner Clinic Found., New Orleans, 2002—. Presenter in field. Contbr. articles to profl. jours. Mem.: ACP, Can. Med. Assn., Can. Cardiovascular Soc., Am. Coll. Cardiology, Am. Heart Assn. (sci. coun.). Avocations: music, jogging, skiing, travel. Office: Ochsner Clinic Found 1514 Jefferson Hwy New Orleans LA 70121 Office Fax: 504-842-5387. Business E-Mail: achan@ochsner.org.

CHAN, BUDDY TAK-BIU, investment company executive; b. Hong Kong, Oct. 1, 1961; s. Peter P.F. and Vivian P.K. (Chan) Chan; children: Christina Akie, Catherine Yoshie, Cary Toshiki. Diploma, Oxford Coll. Applied Sci., Eng., 1984; BSc, DSc, Pacific Western U., 1986. Founder, dir. Buddy Electronics & Systems Ltd., Hong Kong, 1979—; exec. dir. Peter Chan (Secs.) Ltd., Hong Kong, 1983—; gen. mgr. Pacific Essential Ltd., Hong Kong, 1987-92, dir., 1987—; editor Hong Kong Economist Newspaper Ltd., 1987-92; mng. dir. Concord Securities Ltd., Hong Kong, 1987—; mgr. Essential Projects Corp., U.S., 1988-92, Essential Tech. Ltd., Can., 1988—. Bd. dirs. Pacific Essential Ltd., Buddy Electronics & Sys. Ltd., Concord Securities Ltd., Essential Tech. Ltd., Hong Kong Economist Newspaper Ltd. Author: Application of Robotic Technology in Rehabilitation Medicine, A Restaurant Served by Robots--A Feasibility Study, The Illustrated Encyclopedia of Robotic Technology, The Share Registration Program--An Advance Approach. Recipient cert. Dir. of the Assn. for Mgmt. Excellence, U.S., 1989, Internat. Bus. Inst., U.S., 1989, Hong Kong Productivity Coun., 1988, Japan Found. and Japan Assn. Internat. Edn., 1987, Stock Exch. of Hong Kong Ltd., 1987, Hallmark Medallion, World Decoration of Excellence, 1989, Leader in Sci. award Am. Biog. Inst., 1989, Award of Honor, Internat. Civil Aviation Orgn., 1979; fellow Oxford Coll. Applied Sci., 1984. Fellow Internat. Biog. Assn. UK; mem. Robotic Internat. (sr.), Soc. Mfg. Engrs. USA (sr.), Nat. Svc. Robot Assn. USA (charter), Hong Kong Inst. Fishery (exec. com.), N.Y. Acad. Scis. (sustaining), Am. Biog. Inst. Rsch. Assn. (dep. gov. 1989-90), ASME, German Assn. Engrs., French Soc. Mech. Engrs., Robotic Soc. Am., Japan Indsl. Robot Assn., Robotics Soc. Japan, Engring. Mgmt. Soc., IEEE, Inst. Sci. Tech. UK, Laser Soc. Japan, ABI Rsch. Bd. Advisers. Avocations: aeronautical science, criminology, horseback riding, tennis. Office: 2119 Turnberry Ln Coquitlam BC Canada V3E 3N3 E-mail: buddyc@telus.net.

CHAN, CARLYLE HUNG-LUN, psychiatrist, educator; b. Clarksdale, Miss., July 4, 1949; s. Henry Howe and Jennie (Wong) C.; m. Patricia Meyer, June 18, 1977; children: Christopher, Diana. BS, U. Wis., 1971; MD, Med. Coll. Wis., 1975. Diplomate Am. Bd. Psychiatry and Neurology. Resident in psychiatry U. Chgo., 1975-78; postdoctoral fellow R.W. Johnson clin. scholar Yale U. Sch. Medicine, 1978-80; asst. prof. Med. Coll. Wis., Milw., 1980-86, assoc. prof., 1986-98; prof. Med. Coll. of Wis., Milw., 1998—; dir. residency edn. Med. Coll. Wis., Milw., 1987—, prof., 1998—, vice chair edn. and informatics, 1997—, dir. continuing med. edn., 1990—; dir. catchment area Milw. County Mental Health Complex, 1981-82; chief psychiatrist Psychiatrist Ctr., Columbia Hosp., Milw., 1982-87; dir. continuing med. edn. Soc. Tchg. Scholars, 1994. Dir. course annual psychiat. conf., 1982—; dir. Door County (Wis.) Summer Inst., 1987—. Asst. editor Asian-Am. Psychiatry Newsletter, Washington, 1983-84; assoc. editor Asian Psychiatry Newsletter, 1991-94; contbr. articles to profl. jours. Bd. dirs. Planning Council for Mental Health and Social Service, 1983—. Jr. Faculty Devel. award NIMH, 1983-85; Community Devel. award Apple Computer Co., Milw., 1984. Fellow Am. Psychiat. Assn.; mem. Am. Coll. Psychiatrists, Wis. Psychiat. Assn. (pres. Milw. chpt. 1990-91, chair edn. com. 1995—), Assn. Acad. Psychiatry (regional coord. 1987—, regional coord. dir. 1993-96, treas. 1996—), Am. Assn. Dirs. Psychiat. Residency Tng. (sec. 1994-95, pres.-elect 1995, pres. 1996, treas. 1990-92, program com. chair 1993-94), Orgn. Program Dirs. Assns. (sec.-treas.), Wis. State Med. Soc., Milw. County Med. Soc. Med. Coll. of Wis., Soc. Teaching Scholars. Avocations: tennis, golf, running. Office: Med Coll Wis Dept Psychiatry 8701 W Watertown Plank Rd Milwaukee WI 53226-3548 E-mail: cchan@mcw.edu.

CHAN, DANIEL SIU-KWONG, psychologist; b. Swatow, China, June 6, 1952; came to U.S., 1973; s. Hon-Kwong and Suet-Hing (Wong) C.; m. Rosario Arroyo, Dec. 14, 1985; children: Nathaniel Arroyo, Jennifer Arroyo. BA, Buena Vista Coll., 1977; MS, U. La Verne, 1980; PhD, U.S. Internat. U., 1984. Diplomate psychopharmacology; lic. psychologist, Calif. Dir. outreach program Chinese Cmty. Ch., San Diego, 1980-81; exec. dir. Chinese Social Svc. Ctr., San Diego, 1981-82; rehab. counselor Asian Rehab. Svcs., Inc., L.A., 1982-84; program dir. Hawthorne (Calif.) Cmty. Group Home, 1984-86; psychologist Pacific Clinics, Pasadena, Calif., 1986-89, Fairview Devel. Ctr., Costa Mesa, Calif., 1989—; pvt. practice San Gabriel Valley, Calif., 1989—. Cons. psychologist Ingleside Hosp., Rosemead, Calif., 1991—95, Garfield Med. Ctr., Monterey Park, 1993—99, Asian Youth Ctr., Rosemead, 1993—96, Rosemead, 2000—, Allied Physicians Calif., San Gabriel, 1993—, Project SHINE, Inc., Downey, Calif., 1982—88. Mem.. APA, Am. Coll. Advanced Practice Psychologists, Internat. Coll. Prescribing Psychologists, Prescribing Psychologists Register. Republican. Presbyterian. Avocations: classical music, reading, traveling. Home: 11107 Mcvine Ave Sunland CA 91040-2121 Office: 100 W Clary Ave San Gabriel CA 91776 Fax: 818-352-6262.

CHAN, DAVID HAN-SENG, equity analyst, portfolio manager; b. N.Y.C., Mar. 17, 1962; s. Kam F. and Lau C. C.; m. Jeannie Park, Sept. 29, 1990; children: Ella Park-Chan, Ryan Park-Chan. Student, Juilliard Pre-Coll., 1973-79, Am. Film Inst., 1983-84; BS, Harvard U., 1983; MBA, Columbia U., 1989. CFA. Filmmaker Weatherbird Film Prodns., N.Y.C., 1983-87; mgmt. cons. Boston Consulting Group, N.Y.C., 1989-92; exec. v.p. Jennison Assocs. LLC, N.Y.C., 1992—, also portfolio mgr. Filmmaker Passing It On, 1985. Mem. N.Y. Soc. Security Analysts, Beta Gamma Sigma. Office: Jennison Assocs LLC 466 Lexington Ave New York NY 10017-3140

CHAN, DAVID RONALD, tax specialist, lawyer; b. L.A., Aug. 3, 1948; s. David Yew and Anna May (Wong) Chan; m. Mary Anne Chan, June 21, 1980; children: Eric, Christina. AB in Econs., UCLA, 1969, MS in Bus. Adminstrn., 1970, JD, 1973. Bar: Calif. 1973, U.S. Tax Ct. 1974, U.S. Ct. Appeals (9th cir.) 1974, U.S. Dist. Ct. (ctrl. dist.) Calif. 1980. Acct. Oxnard Celery Distbrs., L.A., 1968-73, Touche Ross & Co., L.A., 1970; tax prin. Kenneth Leventhal & Co. (name now E&Y Kenneth Leventhal Real Estate Group), L.A., 1973—. Contbr. chpts. to books and articles to profl. jours. Founder, dir. Chinese Hist. Soc. So. Calif., L.A., 1975—; mem. spkrs. bur. L.A. 200 Bicentennial, L.A., 1981; spkr. Project Follow Through, L.A., 1981, EY Tax Forum, UCLA Real Estate Forecast, Merril Lynch Symposium, Calif. CPA Soc. Recipient Forbes Gold medal Calif. Soc. CPAs, L.A., 1970, Elijah Watt Sells cert. AICPA, L.A., 1970, cert. recognition Chinese Hist. Soc. So. Calif., L.A., 1985. Mem. So. Calif. Chinese Lawyers Assn., L.A. County Bar Assn., Chinese Am. CPAs So. Calif., Asian Bus. League, Chinese For Affirmative Action. Republican. Avocations: chinese cuisine, sports memorabilia, philately. Office: E&Y Kenneth Leventhal Real Estate Group Ste 1800 2049 Century Park E Los Angeles CA 90067-3119 E-mail: david.chan02@ey.com.

CHAN, JANET, publishing executive; children: Jack, Laura. Sr. editor Glamour Mag.; exec. dir. Good Housekeeping, Redbook; v.p., editor Parenting Mag., 1996—. Editl. dir. Time Inc.'s Parenting Group including Baby Talk, Family Life and Healthy Pregnancy. Office: The Parenting Group Inc 530 Fifth Ave 4th Fl New York NY 10036

CHAN, JENNIE M. retired music educator; b. Lebanon, Pa., Aug. 30, 1937; d. Yee S. and Lila L. Chan. BS, West Chester State U., 1959; M of Music, U. Mich., 1961. Cert. tchr. Mass. Tchr. string music Wayne (Mich.) Pub. Schs., 1961-64, Wyandotte (Mich.) Pub. Schs., 1964, Kans. State U., Ft. Hayes, 1964-66, Luther Coll., Decorah, Iowa, 1966-68, Medford (Mass.) Pub. Schs., 1974-76, Brookline (Mass.) Pub. Schs., 1976—2000, ret., 2000. Coord. March String Fest, Brookline, 1983—; dir. Bay State String Camp, Hanson, Mass., 1986—, Bornoff String Workshop, Hanson, 1986—. Mem.: Brookline Educators Assn., Mass. Music Educators Assn., Music Educators Nat. Conf., Am. String Tchrs. (pres. Mass. chpt. 1998—2000), Found. for Advancement of String Edn. (pres. 1978—), Sigma Alpha Iota. Home: 27 Trinity Ter Newton Center MA 02459-1923 Office: Found for Advancement of String Edn Inc PO Box 610215 Newton MA 02461-0215

CHAN, LAI LEE, lawyer; b. Jan. 18, 1969; BA, NYU, 1991, JD, 1994. Bar: N.Y. 1997, U.S. Dist. Ct. (so. and ea. dists.) N.Y. 1997. Assoc. Law Offices Richard S. Missan, N.Y.C., 1994-97; pvt. practice N.Y.C., 1997—. Office: Ste 15D 404 E 76th St New York NY 10021

CHAN, LAWRENCE SIU-YUNG, dermatologist, educator; b. Hong Kong, Dec. 10, 1949; came to U.S., 1975; s. Cheong-Yin Chan and Chun-Fun Wu. AA, Montgomery Coll., Takoma Park, Md., 1978; student, Messiah Coll., Grantham, Pa., 1978-79; BS, BS, MIT, 1981; MD, U. Pa., 1985. Diplomate Am. Bd. Dermatology, Nat. Bd. Med. Examiners. Intern Rutgers Med. Sch., Camden, N.J., 1986-87; resident U. Mich., Ann Arbor, 1987-91; asst. prof. Wayne State U., Detroit, 1991-93, Northwestern U., Chgo., 1993—2002, dir. immunodermatology divsn., 1993—2002; assoc. prof. U. Ill., 2002—, dir. immunology rsch., 2002—. Adj. lectr. U. Mich., 1991-93. Editor: (sci. textbook) Animal Models of Human Inflammatory Skin Disease, 2003. Recipient Clin. Investigator award, NIH, Bethesda, 1996; grantee Merit Rev., VA Rsch. Com., 1996; Small Project, High-risk Project and Rsch. Project grantee, NIH, 2001. Fellow Am. Acad. Dermatology; mem. Soc. Investigative Dermatology, Ctrl. Soc. Investigative Dermatology (chmn. 1995), Dermatology Found. (Career Devel. award 1993), Am. Assn. Immunologists, Am. Soc. Investigative Pathology, Alpha Omega Alpha. Achievements include identification of a novel skin basement membrane component, generation of an animal model of atopic dermatitis, generation of an animal model of an autoimmune hairloss disorder alopecia areata. Office: U Ill Dept Dermatology 808 S Wood Chicago IL 60612-3010 E-mail: larrycha@uic.edu.

CHAN, LOIS MAI, library and information science educator; b. Nanking, China, July 30, 1934; came to U.S., 1956; d. Kar K. and Sau N. Mark; m. Shung Kai Chan, June 22, 1963; children: Jennifer M., Stephen Y. AB, Nat. Taiwan U., Taipei, 1956; MA, Fla. State U., 1958, MS, 1960; PhD, U. Ky., 1970. Asst. order libr. Purdue U., Lafayette, Ind., 1960-61, asst. cataloger, 1961-63; serials acquisition libr. Northwestern U., Evanston, Ill., 1963-64; asst. libr. Lake Forest U., Ill., 1964-66; serials cataloger U. Ky., Lexington, 1966-67, asst. prof. libr. sci., 1970-74, assoc. prof., 1974-80, prof., 1980—. Vis. lectr. U. Minn., Mpls., summer 1979, U. Hawaii, Honolulu, summer 1982; project cons. Online Computer Library Ctr., Dublin, Ohio, 1983-86, U. Mich., Ann Arbor, 1988-89; chmn. Decimal Classification Editorial Policy Com., Washington, 1986-91. Author: Cataloging and Classification: An Introduction, 1981, 2d edit., 1994, Library of Congress Subject Headings, 1981, 3d edit., 1995, A Guide to the Library of Congress Classification, 5th edit., 1999; co-author: Thesauri Used in Online Databases, 1988, Dewey Decimal Classification: A Practical Guide, 1994, 2d edit., 1996. Recipient Gt. Tchr. award U. Ky. Alumni Assn., 1990, Disting. Svc. award Chinese-Am. Librs. Assn., 1992, Disting. Alumni award Fla. State U. Sch. Libr. and Info. Studies, 1996, Excellence in Tchg. award U. Ky. Coll. Comm. and Info. Studies, 2001. Mem. ALA (Margaret Mann citation 1989). Mem. Christian Ch. (Disciples Of Christ). Office: U Ky Sch Libr And Info Sci Lexington KY 40506-0039

CHAN, LO-YI CHEUNG YUEN, architect; b. Canton, China, Dec. 1, 1932; came to U.S., 1942, naturalized, 1954; s. Wing tsit and Wai hing (Lei) C.; m. Mildred Wu, Sept. 1, 1957; children: Christopher, Leighton, Leicia. BA, Dartmouth Coll., 1954; MArch, Harvard U., 1959, postgrad. (Appleton fellow), 1959-60. Asso. firm I. M. Pei & Partners, N.Y.C., 1960-65; practice architecture N.Y.C., 1965—. Adj. asst. prof. architecture Columbia, 1963-67; vis. critic Coll. Architecture, Cornell U., 1965-68, Harvard U., 1976, 78, 80, Mass. Inst. Tech., 1977; panelist Am. Arbitration Assn., 1972-80. Bd. dirs. Parks Council, N.Y.C., 1971-85, pres., 1974; trustee Cmty. Svc. Soc., N.Y.C., 1977-86, Henry St. Settlement, 1980-99, Lingnan Found., 1986—, chmn., 1990—, mem. N.Y.C.

Art Commn., 1992-97, Berkshire Sch., 1992—; active N.Y. State Coun. Arts, 1993-96; bd. dirs. Berkshire Taconic Cmty. Found., 2000—. With AUS, 1955-57. Nat. Endowment for Arts Design fellow, 1975-76 Fellow AIA (corp.); mem. Phi Beta Kappa. Home and Office: 270 Riverside Dr New York NY 10025 E-mail: chanfaia@aol.com.

CHAN, PHILIP, dermatologist, retired army officer; b. Oceanside, N.Y., Oct. 14, 1946; s. Walter O. and Ann (Yee) C. BA, Harvard U., 1968; MD, Columbia U., 1972. Diplomate Am. Bd. Dermatology. Commd. capt. U.S. Army, 1973, advanced through grades to col., 1987; dermatologist Martin Army Cmty. Hosp., Ft. Benning, Ga., 1995-98; retired U.S. Army, 1998. Adj. asst. prof. Uniformed Svcs. U. Health Scis., 1995—97; part-time instr. Rankin Arts Ctr., Columbus State U. Editor (govt. pub.) Procs. of Vesicant Workshop, 1987; conbtr. articles to profl. jours. Fellow Am. Acad. Dermatology; mem. AMA, Mensa, Assn. of Mil. Dermatologists. Avocation: teaching Reiki. Home: 6300 Milgen Rd #1285 Columbus GA 31907-5962

CHAN, RAYMOND, Canadian government minister; b. Hong Kong, Oct. 25, 1951; m. Maureen Chan, 1975; 2 children. B Applied Sci. in Engring. Physics, U. B.C., Vancouver, Can., 1977. Owner, operator restaurant, 1974-89; engr. TRIUMF Rsch. Ctr., U. B.C., 1977-93; mem. Parliament of Can., Ottawa, 1993—2000; Sec. of State (Asia-Pacific), 1993—2001; pres. Global Bus. Develop. Inc.; dir. Heart and Stroke Found. of BC. Apptd. spl. amb., 2002; dir. BC chpt. Can./China Bus Coun. also: # 221-4940 No 3 Rd Richmond BC Canada V6X 3A5 Office: SFU at Harbour Ctr 515 West Hastings St Ste 2600 Vancouver BC Canada V6B 5K3

CHAN, SHU-PARK, electrical engineering educator; b. Canton, China, Oct. 10, 1929; came to U.S., 1951, naturalized, 1965; s. Chi-Tong and Shui-Ying (Mok) C.; m. Stella Yok-Sing Lam, Dec. 28, 1956; children: Charlene Li-Hsiang, Yau-Gene. BEE, Va. Mil. Inst., 1955; MEE, U. Ill., 1957, PhD, 1963. Instr. elec. engring. and math. Va. Mil. Inst., 1957-59; instr. elec. engring. U. Ill., 1960-61, rsch. assoc., 1961-62, asst. prof. math., 1962-63; assoc. prof. elec. engring. U. Santa Clara, 1963-68, prof., 1968-92, chmn. elec. engring. and computer sci. dept., 1969-84; Nicholson Family Chair prof. Santa Clara U., 1987-92, prof. emeritus, 1992—, acting dean Sch. Engring., 1987-88; founder, pres. Internat. Technol. U., Santa Clara, 1994—, pres. Chu Hai Coll., Hong Kong, 1995-96. Prin. investigator NSF, NASA; Univ. fellow U. Ill., 1959-60; vis. spl. chair prof. elec. engring. dept. Nat. Taiwan U., 1973-74; spl. lectr. Acad. Sci., Peking, China, summer 1980; hon. prof. elec. engring. dept. U. Hong Kong, 1980-81; hon. prof. Anhuei U., China, 1982; spl. chair Tamkang U., Taipei, Taiwan, 1981; apptd. mem. J. William Fulbright Fgn. Scholarship Bd., 1991-93; founder, pres. Internat. Tech. U. Found., 1994—. Author: introductory Topological Analysis of Electrical Networks, 1969, (with others) Analysis of Linear Networks and Systems—A Matrix-Oriented Approach with Computer Applications, 1972, (with E. Moustakas) Introduction to the Applications of the Operational Amplifier, 1974; editor: Network Topology and Its Engineering Applications, 1975, Graph Theory and Applications, 1982. Chmn. bd., pres. Acad. Cultural Co., Santa Clara; founder, pres. China Exptl. U. Found., 1985—; chmn. Santa Clara County Bicentennial Chinese Festival Com.; pres. Chinese Arts and Culture Inst., 1976—; trustee Inst. Sino-Am. Studies, San Jose, Calif., 1971-76, West Valley-Mission C.C. Dist., Calif., 1988. Recipient Disting. Elec. Engring. Alumnus award U. Ill., 1983, 1991 Rschr. of Yr. award Sch. Engring., Santa Clara U., 1992, Courvoisier Leadership award in Edn., 1994; named Engr. of Yr. in Engring. Edn. San Francisco session AIAA, 1994, Chinese Am. Pioneer award Orgn. Chinese Ams., San Francisco, 1996; Hon. Prof. award S. China Normal U., Guangzhou, China, 1997—, Educator of Yr. award Chinese Consol. Benevolent Assn. and Chinese Consol. Women's Assn., 1999, Mayor's awrd City of San Francisco, 1999. Fellow IEEE (past chmn. circuit theory group San Francisco sect., chmn. asilomar conf. circuits and sys. 1970); mem. Am. Soc. Engring. Edn., Chineses Alumni Assn. U. Santa Clara (pres.), U. Santa Clara Faculty Club (pres. 1971-72), Sigma Xi, Tau Beta Pi, Eta Kappa Nu, Pi Mu Epsilon, Phi Kappa Phi. Home: 2085 Denise Dr Santa Clara CA 95050-4557 E-mail: spchan@itu.edu. *I would like to attribute my personal success to the teaching of my father, the late General of the Army Chi-Tong Chan, who taught me the Four Principles of Goodness: Set a good goal in mind; acquire a good wealth of knowledge; exercise good self-discipline; and perform only good deeds.*

CHAN, SUNNEY IGNATIUS, chemist, educator; b. San Francisco, Oct. 5, 1936; s. Sun and Hip-For (Lai) C.; m. Irene Yuk-Hing Tam, July 11, 1964; 1 son, Michael Kenneth. BS in Chem. Engring, U. Calif. at Berkeley, 1957, PhD in Chemistry, 1960. Asst. prof. chemistry U. Calif., Riverside, 1961—63; mem. faculty Calif. Inst. Tech., 1963—, prof. chem. physics, 1968—92, prof. biophys. chemistry, 1976—92, George Grant Hoag prof. biophys. chemistry, 1992—2001, exec. officer for chemistry, 1977—80, 1989—94, master student houses, 1980—83, chmn. faculty, 1987—89; dir. Inst. of Chemistry, Academia Sinica, Taipei, Taiwan, 1997—99; disting. rsch. fellow Inst. Chemistry Acad. Sinica, Taipei, 1997—; v.p. Academia Sinica, Taipei, Taiwan, 1999—2003; George Grant Hoag prof. biophys. chemistry emeritus Calif. Inst. Tech., 2002—. R.T. Major lectr. U. Conn., 1998; Wilson T.S. Wang Disting. Internat. prof. Chinese U. Hong Kong, 1993; Reilly lectr. U. Notre Dame, 1973-74; Chan Meml. lectr. U. Calif., Berkeley, 1984; cons. in field. Author numerous articles in field. Guggenheim fellow, 1968-69; Sloan fellow, 1965-67; NSF Postdoctoral fellow, 1960-61; Fogarty fellow NIH, 1986. Mem. AAAS, Academia Sinica, Am. Chem. Soc., Chinese Am. Chem. Soc. (chmn. bd. 1988-97), Am. Phys. Soc., Am. Soc. Biochemistry and Molecular Biology, Biophys. Soc., Biophysical Soc. Taiwan (pres. 1998-2001), So. Calif. Chinese Engrs. and Scientists Assn. (Progress award 1971), Chinese Collegiate Colleagues So. Calif. (v.p. 1970-71, pres. 1971-72), Chinese Am. Faculty Assn. (pres. 1988, Achievement award 1991, Disting. Svc. award 2000), Phi Beta Kappa, Sigma Xi, Tau Beta Pi, Alpha Chi Sigma, Phi Tau Phi (pres. 1981-83). Home: 327 Camino Del Sol South Pasadena CA 91030-4107 Office: Calif Inst Tech Chem Dept Pasadena CA 91125-0001 E-mail: chans@its.caltech.edu., chans@chem.sinica.edu.tw.

CHAN, THOMAS TAK-WAH, lawyer; b. Kowloon, Hong Kong, 1950; BA magna cum laude, U. Wis., Whitewater, 1973; JD, U. Wis., 1979. Bar: Wis. 1979, Minn. 1983, Calif. 1987. Judicial intern Wis. Supreme Ct., 1978; atty. Wausau (Wis.) Ins., 1979-82; staff atty. CPT Corp., Eden Prairie, Minn., 1982-84; gen. counsel Lee Data Corp., Eden Prairie, 1984-85; dep. gen. counsel Ashton-Tate Corp., Torrance, Calif., 1985-87; pres. Chan Law Group LC, L.A., 1987—. Mem. adv. bd. SBA Export Devel. Ctr., 1992-2000; founder Bus. Software Alliance, Washington, 1987; mem. industry sector adv. com. and U.S. trade rep., U.S. Dept. Commerce, 1988-91; founder Asian Pacific Am. Coord. Com., 1996; bd. dirs. Asian Pacific Am. Legal Ctr., 2002—. Bd. dirs. Torrance Meml. Med. Ctr. Found., 2000—. Mem. Asian Pacific Am. Bar Assn. (founder, dir. 1998-00), Wis. Bar Assn., Calif. Bar Assn. (lectr. 1988) Computer Law Assn., So. Calif. Chinese Lawyers Assn. (gov. 1990-92) Export Mgrs. Assn. So. Calif. (dir. 1990-92), S.Bay Chinese Am. C. of C. (founder, dir. 1997—, pres. 2003—), S.Bay Chinese Culture Ctr. (dir. 1998-01), Cause (dir. 1994-97, chmn. 1995-96), Phi Kappa Phi. Avocations: skiing, hiking, tai chi. Office: Chan Law Group LC Ste 1880 1055 W Seventh St Los Angeles CA 90017 E-mail: thelaw@chanlaw.com.

CHAN, WAI-YEE, geneticist, educator; b. Canton, China, Apr. 28, 1950; arrived in U.S., 1974; s. Kui and Fung-Hing (Wong) Chan; m. May-Fong Sheung, Sept. 3, 1976; children: Connie Hai-Yee, Joanne Hai-Wei, Victor Hai-Yue, Amanda Hai-Pui, Bessie Hai-Lui. BSc with first class honors, Chinese U. of Hong Kong, 1974; PhD, U. Fla., 1977. Tchg. asst. dept. biochemistry and molecular biology U. Fla., Gainesville, 1974-77; rsch. assoc. U. Okla., Oklahoma City, 1978-79, asst. prof. dept. pediats., 1979-82, assoc. prof., 1982-89, asst. prof. dept. biochemistry and molecular biology, 1979-82, assoc. prof., 1982-89; prof. dept. pediats., biochemistry, molecular biology and cell biology Georgetown U., Washington, 1989—. Staff affiliate pediat. endocrine metabolism and genetic svc. Okla. Children's Meml. Hosp., Oklahoma City, 1979—89, dir. Clin. Trace Metal Diagnostic Lab., 1979—85, asst. sci. dir. Biochem. Genetics and Metabolic Screening Lab., 1980—87; co-dir. State of Okla. Tchg. Hosp., 1982—87. Editor: 2 books and monograph, Jour. Endocrine Genetics, Jour. Am. Coll. Nutrition, Jour. Current Molecular Medicine; contbr. articles to profl. jours. Assoc. mem. Okla. Med. Rsch. Found., Oklahoma City, 1987—89. Recipient Okla. Med. Rsch. Found. Merrick award, 1988; fellow NATO, 1979; scholar, Chinese U. Hong Kong, 1972—74, 1973—74. Mem.: Am. Coll. Nutrition, Endocrine Soc., Am. Assn. Immunology, Soc. Pediat. Rsch., Am. Soc. Cell Biology, Am. Soc. Human Genetics, Am. Soc. Biochem. Molecular Biology, Am. Inst. Nutrition. Achievements include patents for for application of pregnancy-specific glycoproteins; development of of in-vitro diagnostic method for Wilson's Disease. Home: 10708 Butterfly Ct North Potomac MD 20878-4209 Office: LCG NICHD NIH Bldg 49 Rm 2A08 49 Convent Dr MSC 4429 Bethesda MD 20892-4429 E-mail: chanwy@mail.nih.gov.

CHAN, WING-CHUNG, pathologist, educator; b. Hong Kong, Oct. 11, 1947; came to U.S., 1975; s. Kwok-Ping and Yuet-Wah (Ching) C.; m. Angelina H. Li, May 16, 1981; children: Eric J., Jason E. MBBS, U. Hong Kong, 1973, MD, 1988. Diplomate in anat. pathology, clin. pathology and hematology Am. Bd. Pathology. Resident in pathology U. Chgo., 1975-79, rsch. assoc. in immunology, 1979-80; asst. prof. pathology Emory U. Sch. Medicine, Atlanta, 1980-86, assoc. prof., 1986-91; prof. pathology U. Nebr. Med. Ctr., Omaha, 1991—. Mem. editorial bd. Am. Jour. Clin. Pathology, 1990—; assoc. editor Am. Jour. Pathology, 2000—; contbr. chpts. to books, numerous articles to profl. jours. Mem. U.S. and Can. Acad. Pathology, Hematopathology Soc. (charter), Am. Soc. Hematology, Am. Assn. Immunologists. Achievements include research in the lymphoproliferative disorder involving large granular lymphocytes; study of myeloperoxidase gene expression in health and in leukemic conditions; study of retroviral gene sequences in lymphomas and leukemias; study on lineage and clonality of Hodgkin's disease and gene expression pattern of non-Hodgkin's lymphoma. Home: 10617 Castelar St Omaha NE 68124-1841 Office: 983135 Nebr Med Ctr Omaha NE 68198-3135

CHAN, YING KIT, artist, educator; s. Man and Kit Chun Chan; m. Julie Tallent, Dec. 24, 1987; children: Yi, Tian. Diploma in social sci., Hong Kong Bapt. Coll., 1975; BFA in Art, U. Okla., 1981; MFA in Art, U. Cin., 1983. Vis. asst. prof. art W.Va. U., Morgantown, 1983—84; head of studio program, prof. art dept. fine arts U. Louisville, 1984—. Mem. substantive change com. So. Assn. Colls. and Schs., 1987; mem. rev. panel NEA/Rockefeller Founds. New Art Forms Grants, 1990; pres. Founds. in Art: Theory and Edn., 1995—97; program chair of studio sessions Joint Conf. of S.E. Coll. Art Conf. / Mid-Am. Coll. Art Assn., Louisville, 2000; mem. profl. practices com. Coll. Art Assn. of Am., N.Y.C., 2003—. One-man shows include Lee Foto Gallery, Toronto, Can., Taipei (Taiwan) Mus.Art. Recipient Urban Coun. Fine Arts award, Hong Kong Mus. Art, 1977; Individual Artist's fellow, Nat. Endowment for the Arts/So. Arts Fedn., 1992, Al Smith Individual Artist's fellow, Ky. Arts Coun., 1994, 2002. Office: U Louisville Dept Fine Arts Louisville KY 40292

CHAN, YIUMO, biochemist; b. Hong Kong, June 25, 1967; s. Man and Kwok-ying Chan; m. Mei-hua Chen, Dec. 19, 2001. BS in Chemistry, U. Chgo., 1989, PhD of Devel. Biology, 1995. Postdoctoral fellow Harvard Med. Sch., Boston, 1995—2001; staff scientist Geisinger Hosp., Danville, Pa., 2001—. Adv. Coun. Healthcare Berson Lehrman Group, N.Y.C., 2001—; mem. Sci. Adv. Bd., Arlington, Va., 2002—. Co-author: Principles of Molecular Medicine, 1998; contbr. Mem.: ACLU, AAAS, N.Y. Acad. Scis., Am. Soc. Human Genetics (mentorship program), Amnesty Internat. Democrat. Achievements include discovery of genetic basis of an inherited skin blistering disease, Weber-Cockayne Epidermolysis Bullose Simplex; research in understanding the molecular mechanism of muscular dystrophy. Avocations: reading, travel, art, numismatics, philately. Office: Geisinger Hosp Weis Ctr for Rsch 100 N Academy Ave MC 26-11 Danville PA 17822

CHANCE, BETH L. statistician, educator, statistician, researcher; m. Frank Chance, July 17, 1993. BS, Harvey Mudd, 1990; PhD, Cornell U., 1994. Asst. prof. U. of the Pacific, Stockton, Calif., 1994—99; assoc. prof. Calif. Poly. State U., San Luis Obispo, 1999—. Editor: STATS Mag. Mem.: Math. Assn. Am. (Am. Statis. Assn./Math. Assn. Am. joint com. 1999—), Am. Statis. Assn. (exec. com. 1999—2001, Waller Edn. award 2002).

CHANCE, BRITTON, biophysics and physical chemistry educator emeritus; b. Wilkes Barre, Pa., July 24, 1913; s. Edwin M. and Eleanor (Kent) Chance; m. Jane Earle, Mar. 4, 1938 (div.); children: Eleanor, Britton; m. Lilian Streeter Lucas, Nov. 1956 (div.); children: Margaret, Lilian, Benjamin, Samuel;children: Jan, Peterstepchildren: Ann Lucas, Gerald B. Lucas, A. Brooke Lucas, William C. Lucas. BS, MS, U. Pa., 1936, PhD (E.R. Johnson Found. fellow), 1940; PhD, U. Cambridge, 1942, DSc, 1952; MD (hon.), Karolinska Inst., Stockholm, 1962, U. Buenos Aires; DSc (hon.), Med. Coll. Ohio, 1974, Semmelweis U., Budapest, 1976; MD (hon.), Hahnemann Coll. and Hosp., 1977; DSc (hon.), U. Pa., 1985, U. Helsinki, 1990; MD (hon.), U. Dusseldorf, Fed. Republic Germany, U. Buenos Aires, 1993, U. Copenhagen, 1995, U. Degli Studi Di Roma "Tor Vergata", 1997. Acting dir. E.R. Johnson Found. U. Pa., Phila., 1940—41, dir., 1949—83, asst. prof. biophysics and phys. biochemistry, 1941—49, prof. biophysics and phys. biochemistry, grad. group of biophysics, 1947—49, chmn. dept. biophysics and phys. biochemistry, 1949—75, Eldridge Reeves Johnson prof. biophysics, dept. biophysics, 1964—75, prof. biochemistry and biophysics, 1975—83, Eldridge Reeves Johnson univ. prof. emeritus of biochemistry, biophysics and phys. biochemistry, 1983—92; Eldridge Reeves Johnson univ. prof. emeritus of biochemistry and biophysics and phys. biochemistry, and radiol. physics Sch. Medicine, U. Pa., 1992—; pres. Med. Diagnostic Rsch. Found., Phila., 1998—. Cons. NSF, 1952—55; mem. adv. coun. Nat. Inst. Alcohol Abuse and Alcoholism, 1971—75; mem. Pres.'s Sci. Adv. com., 1959—60; mem. molecular control working group Nat. Cancer Inst., 1973—; dir. Inst. Structural and Functional Studies, Univ. City Sci. Ctr., Phila., 1982—90, Inst. Biophys. and Biomed. Rsch., 1990—; numerous lectureships, including Presdl. lectr. U. Pa., 1975; Julius L. Jackson Meml. lectr. Wayne State U., 1976; Da Costa orator Phila. County Med. Coll., 1976; Harvey lectr., 54; Phillips lectr., 55, 65; Pepper lectr., 57; Herter lectr. NYU, 1968; Redfearn lectr., 70; Troy C. Daniels lectr. U. Calif.-San Francisco, 1984; Pendergrass lectr. U. Pa., 1991. Author (with F.C. Williams, V. Hughes, E.F. McNichol, David Sayre): Waveforms, 1949; author: (with R.I. Hulsizer, E.F. McNichol, F.C. Williams) Electronic Time Measurements, 1949; author: Energy-Linked Functions of Mitochondria, 1964; author: (with Q.H. Gibson, R. Eisenhardt, K.K. Lonberg-Holm) Rapid Mixing and Sampling Techniques in Biochemistry, 1964; author: (with R.W. Estabrook, J.R. Williamson) Control of Energy Metabolism, 1965; author: (with R.W. Estabrook, T. Yonetani) Hemes and Hemoproteins, 1966; author: (with others) Probes of Structure and Function of Macromolecules and Enzymes, 1971; author: Alcohol and Aldehyde, 1974, 1977, Tunneling in Biological System, 1979; reviewer articles Advances in Enzymology, Vol. 12, 1951, vol. 17, 1956, Ann. Rev. Biochemistry, 1952, 1970, 1976, The Enzymes, Vol. II, Part 1, 1952, vol. XIII, 1976, Ann. Rev. Plant Physiology, 1958, 1968, bd. editors Physiol. Revs., 1951—54, FEBS Letters, 1973—75, BBA Revs., 1972—, Photobiochemistry and Photobiophysics, 1979—, contbr. articles to Am., Brit., Swedish, German and Japanese jours., —. Recipient Paul Lewis award for enzyme chemistry, 1950, Pres.'s cert. of merit for svcs., 1941—45, Pres.'s cert. of merit for svcs. staff mem. Radiation Lab. of MIT, 1950, Genootschapps medal, Dutch Acad. Scis., 1965, Heineken medal, 1970, Keilin medal, Brit. Biochem. Soc., 1966, Pa. award for excellence in life scis., 1968, Nichols award, N.Y. sect., Am. Chem. Soc., 1970, award, Phila. sect., 1969, Gairdner award, 1972, Post Congress Festschrift, Stockholm, 1974, Semmelweis medal, 1974, Nat. medal of Sci., 1974, Benjamin Franklin medal, Am. Philos. Soc., 1990, Christopher Columbus Discovery award in biomed. rsch., NIH, 1992; fellow Guggenheim, Stockholm, 1946—48, Overseas, Churchill Coll., 1966; scholar exch. to USSR, 1963. Fellow: AAAS, IEEE (Morlock award 1961, Phila. sect. award 1984), Am. Inst. Chemists, Am. Phys. Soc.; mem.: NAS, Harvey Soc., Royal Soc. London (fgn. mem.), Argentine Nat. Acad. Sci., Max-Planck Gesellschaft für Forerung der Wissenschaften (fgn. mem.), Acad. Leopoldina (Germany), Bavarian Acad. Scis., Royal Acad. Arts and Scis. (Sweden), Royal Swedish Acad. Scis., Swedish Biochem. Soc., Biophys. Soc. (coun. 1959—62), Soc. for Neurosci., Am. Inst. Physics, Soc. Gen. Physiologists (coun. 1957—60), Soc. Magnetic Resonance in Medicine (Gold medal 1988), Am. Acad. Orthopaedic Surgeons (Elizabeth Winston Lanier award 1981, Kappa Delta award 1986), Am. Physiol. Soc., Am. Acad. Arts and Scis., Am. Philos. Soc. (v.p. 1984—90), Am. Soc. Biol. Chemists (Sober lectr. 1984), Biochem. Soc. Eng., Royal Soc. Arts, Am. Chem. Soc., Internat. Union Pure and Applied Biophysics (pres. 1972—75), St. Anthony Club, Corinthian Yacht Club (Phila.), Tau Beta Pi, Sigma Xi. Achievements include patents in field of automatic steering devices, fast spectrophotometers, radar range and bombing devices, nuclear magnetic resonance photonmigration in tissues, optical imaging; Gold medal (yachting) 1952 Olympics. Office: U Pa Dept Biochemistry/Biophys 250 Anatomy Chemistry Philadelphia PA 19104-6059 E-mail: chance@mail.mcd.upenn.edu.*

CHANCE, F. EARLAYNE, artist; b. Austin, Tex., Oct. 29, 1942; d. (stepfather) Alford B. and Ermer Grace Hess; father: Earl J. Lee Summerrow; m. Kenneth D. Chance; children: Michael, Gregory A. Student, S.W. Tex. State U., 1961—63, U. Tex., Austin, 1963—64. Greenberg Pub. Co., Chester, NY, 1994-2002, Salmagundi Art Club Non-Mems. Show, 1994, Irving (Tex.) Art Ctr., 1994, Hill Country Art Found., Ingram, Tex., 2000, 01-03, S.W. Classic Invitational, Kerrville, Tex., 2000, Galleries across the Southwest, 1995-. Mem. Hays County Women's Polit. Caucus, San Marcos, Tex., 1989-96. Recipient Best of Show award PBS Sta. KLRU-TV, 1996. Mem. DAR, Daus. Republic of Tex., Kerrville C. of C. Methodist. Avocations: travel, photography. Office: Chance Studio 220 Oak Hills Dr Kerrville TX 78028 Fax: (830) 896-2063. E-mail: echance@ktc.com.

CHANCE, GRAHAM WILFRID, retired pediatrician, emeritus educator; b. Birmingham, Eng., May 9, 1933; arrived in Can., 1970; s. Wilfrid Joseph and Edith (Rumsey) C.; m. Mary Eugenia Lewis, Mar. 25, 1961; children: Valerie Mary, Andrea Jane, Christine Anne. MB ChB, U. Birmingham, Eng., 1956. Diplomate in child health. Tng. positions various hosps., England, 1956-64; lectr. U. Birmingham, 1965-67, sr. lectr., 1967-70; assoc. prof. U. Toronto, 1970-78, prof., 1978-79, U. Western Ont., London, Can., 1979-96. Cons. pediatrician United Birmingham Hosps., 1967-70; dir. neonatal intensive care unit Hosp. for Sick Children, Toronto, 1970-78; chair divsn. neonatal/perinatal medicine U. Western Ont. and St. Joseph's Health Ctr., London, Ont., 1979-96. Editr: Textbook of Perinatal Medicine, 1975; contbr. articles to profl. jours.; author govt. publs. Vol. chair Can. Inst. Child Health, 1994-99; served on numerous nat., provincial, local bds. and coms. for profl. socs., govts. and ednl. instns. Capt.Royal Army, 1957-59, Malaya and Singapore. Recipient Sisters of St. Joseph award for excellence, London, Can., 1995, Dean's award U. Western Ont., 1996, Graham Chance award Can. Inst. Child Health; Mary Crosse meml. lectr. U. Birmingham, 1981; Martha May Elliott Forum lectr. APHA, 1982, others. Fellow Royal Coll. Physicians (London), Royal Coll. Physicians (Can.), Can. Pediatric Soc., Am. Acad. Pediatrics, Westminster Inst. Ethics and Human Values; mem. Sirmoor Club. Anglican. Avocations: child health advocacy, classical music, gardening. Office: Can Inst Child Health 384 Bank St Ste 300 Ottawa ON Canada K2P 1Y4 E-mail: cich@cich.ca.

CHANCE, JANE, English literature educator; b. Neosho, Mo., Oct. 26, 1945; d. Donald William and Julia (Mile) C.; m. Dennis Carl Nitzsche, June, 1966 (div. Mar. 1969); 1 child, Therese; m. Paolo Passaro, Apr. 30, 1981,(div. May 2002); children: Antony Damian, Joseph Sebastian. BA in English with honors and highest distinction, Purdue U., 1967; AM in English, U. Ill., 1968, PhD in English, 1971. Lectr. U. Saskatchewan, Can., 1971-72, asst. prof., 1972-73; asst. prof. English, Rice U., Houston, 1973-77, assoc. prof., 1977-80, prof., 1980—; hon. rsch. fellow U. Coll. U. London, 1977-78. Sec., Scientia, 1982-83, acting dir., 1983-84; dir. NEH Summer Seminar for Coll. Tchrs. on Chaucer and Mythography, 1985, NEH Inst. for Coll. Tchrs. on Medieval Women, 1997; pres., founder TEAMS, 1986-89; founder, dir. med. studies program Rice U., 1986-92; founding mem. Rice U. Commn. on Women, 1986-88; resident Rockefeller Found., Bellagio, Italy, 1988; mem. Sch. Hist. Studies Inst. for Advanced Study, Princeton U., 1988-89; vis. rsch. fellow Inst. for Advanced Studies in Humanities, U. Edinburgh, summer, 1994; Eccles fellow Humanities Ctr., U. Utah, 1994-95; plenary spkr. Rocky Mountain Med. and Renaissance Assn., 1995; 2d annual lectr. on Italian archaeology Friends of Archaeology U. St. Thomas/Fedn. Italian Assns., Houston, 1997; semi-plenary spkr. 4th annual meeting Internat. Soc. for the Classical Tradition, 1998; plenary spkr. Medieval Studies Forum, Fu Jen Cath. U., Taipei, Taiwan, 2000, Tex. Medieval Assn., Baylor U., Waco, 2000. Author: The Genius Figure in Antiquity and the Middle Ages, 1975, Tolkien's Art: A Mythology for England, 1979, rev. edit., 2001, Japanese edit., 2003, Woman as Hero in Old English Literature, 1986, The Lord of the Rings: The Mythology of Power, 1992, rev. edit., 2001, Japanese edit., 2003, Medieval Mythography: From Roman North Africa to the School of Chártres, AD 433-1177 (South Ctrl. MLA book prize 1994), The Mythographic Chaucer: The Fabulation of Sexual Politics, 1995, Medieval Mythography, vol. 2: From the School of Chartres to the Court at Avignon, 1177-1350, 2000; translator: Christine de Pizan's Letter of Othea to Hector, 1990; editor: The Mythographic Art: Classical Fable and the Rise of the Vernacular in Early France and England, 1990, Medievalism in the Twentieth Century, Studies in Medievalism, vol. 2:2, 1983, The Inklings and Others, vol. 3:3, 1990, Gender and Text in the Later Middle Ages, 1996, The Assembly of Gods, 1999, Tolkien the Medievalist, 2002; co-editor: Mapping the Cosmos, 1985, Approaches to Teaching Sir Gawain, 1986; gen. editor Focus Libr. Medieval Women, 1988—, Boydell & Brewer Libr. of Medieval Women, 1997—; series editor: Greenwood Guides to Historic Events in the Medieval World, 2001—, Praeger Series on the Middle Ages, 2003—; mem. editl. bd. Coll. Lit. Bd. dirs. Rice U. Press, 1981-88. NEH fellow, 1977-78, Guggenheim fellow, 1980-81, ACLS Travel grantee, 1982, Mellon leave Rice U., 1988, Disting. Faculty Tchg. fellow, 1995, Ctr. for Study Cultures fellow, 1998, NEH Fellow, St. Louis Univ. Ctr. for Med. Studies, 2003, Mellon Fellow, Pope Pius Vatican Film Libr., 2003; recipient Women's Ctr. IMPACT award Rice U., 1998. Mem. AAUP (Rice U. chpt. sec., treas. 1975-76), MLA, Scientia (acting dir. 1983-84, sec. 1982-83), Internat. Soc. Classical Tradition, Internat. Neo-Latin Soc. Avocations: book collecting, photography, travel. Office: Rice U Dept English MS 30 PO Box 1892 Houston TX 77251-1892 E-mail: jchance@rice.edu.

CHANCE, KENNETH BERNARD, endodontist, educator, university official; b. N.Y.C., Dec. 8, 1953; s. George E. and Janie L. (Bolles).; m. Sharon Lee Lewis, July 11, 1981; children: Kenneth Bernard, Dana Marie, Christopher, Jacquelyn. BS, Fordham U., 1975; DDS, Case Western Res. U., 1979; Cert. in Endodontics, U. Medicine and Dentistry N.J., 1982. Asst. attending Jamaica Hosp., Queens, N.Y., 1981-87; chief endodontics Kings County Med. Ctr., Bklyn., 1982-91; assoc. prof. endodontics U. Medicine and Dentistry N.J., 1987; also dir. external affairs N.J. Dental Sch.; asst. attending North Ctrl. Bronx (N.Y.) Hosp., 1983-91, Kingsbrook Jewish Med. Ctr., 1986-92; asst. dean external affairs and urban resource devel. N.J. Dental Sch., 1989-97; cons. Harlem Hosp., N.Y.C., 1982-90; health policy advisor to U.S. Senator Frank Lautenberg of N.J., 1991—99; dir. health policy program The Joint Ctr. Polit. and Econ. Studies, 1993-94; acting chmn. dept. endodontics N.J. Dental Sch., 1994-97; fed. rels. adv. com. U. Medicine and Dentistry N.J., 1994-97; dean, prof. endodontics Meharry Med. Coll. Sch. Dentistry, 1997-2000; prof., dir. divsn. endodontics U. Ky., Lexington, 2000—. Min. of music, sr. organist Sharon Bapt. Ch., Bronx, 1983; mem. healthcare task force Congl. Black Caucus, 1994-2001. Recipient Dr. Paul F. Sherwood award for excellence in endodontics Case Western Res. U. Dental Sch., 1979, Cmty. Svc. award U. Medicine and Dentistry N.J., 1997, Tenn. Outstanding Achievement award, 1998, Outstanding Academician award U. Medicine and Dentistry N.J., 1999; Found. grant award U. Medicine and Dentistry N.J., 1984, Exceptional Merit award, 1985, Excellence award, 1990, Disting. Practioner award Nat. Acad. Practice Denistry, 2001; fellow Nat. Dental Leadership Devel. PEW, 1991, Robert Wood Johnson Health Policy, 1991, Pierre Fauchard Acad., 1996. Fellow Am. Coll. Dentists, Internat. Coll. Dentists; mem. ADA, Internat. Assn. Dental Rsch., Am. Dental Edn. Assn. (chair minority affairs sect. 2003), Am. Assn. Dental Schs., Nat. Dental Assn., Am. Assn. Endodontists, Greater Met. Dental Soc. N.Y. (pres.-elect 1986-87, v.p. 1984-86), Ky. Assn. Endodontists, Omicron Kappa Upsilon. Home: 344 Princess Arch Lane Lexington KY 40511 E-mail: kbchan2@pop.uky.edu.

CHANCE, KENNETH DONALD, engineer; b. Denver, July 27, 1948; s. John Jefferson and Evelyn Pauline (Jacobs) C. AA, Red Rocks Coll., Golden, Colo., 1982. Stationery operating engr. EG&G Rocky Flats, Golden, 1980—.

CHANCE, TRUETT LAMAR, retired secondary school educator; b. Liberty Hill, Tex., Aug. 23, 1913; s. Edgar Lee and Edith Alma Chance; 1 child, Trudy Jo Kinnison. BS, Southwestern Tex. State Tchrs. Coll., 1936; MEd, U. Tex., 1942, PhD, 1970. Tchr., supr. various schs., 1945—92; ret., 1992. With U.S. Army. Democrat. Avocation: gardening. Home: 7202 Westboro Pl San Antonio TX 78229

CHANCELLOR, VAN, professional basketball coach; b. Louisville, Miss. m. Betty Chancellor; children: John, renee. Student, East Ctrl. Jr. Coll., Decatur, Miss.; B.Math. and Phys. Edn., Miss. State U., 1965, MEd, 1974. Head coach boys' basketball Noxapater (Miss.) H.S.; head coach women's basketball U. Miss., Oxford; head coach, gen. mgr. Houston Comets, 1997-99. Three time WNBA champions. Office: Houston Comets Two Greenway Plz #400 Houston TX 77046-3865

CHANCELLOR, WILLIAM JOSEPH, agricultural engineering educator; b. Alexandria, Va., Aug. 25, 1931; s. John Miller and Caroline (Sedlacek) C.; m. Nongkarn Bodhiprasart, Dec. 13, 1960; 1 child, Marisa Kuakul BS in Agr., BSME, U. Wis., 1954; MS in Agrl. Engring., Cornell U., 1956, PhD, 1957. Registered profl. agrl. engr., Calif. Prof. agrl. engring. U. California.-Davis, 1957-94; prof. emeritus. Vis. prof. agrl. engring. U. Malaya, Kuala Lumpur, Malaysia, 1962-63; UNESCO cons. Punjab Agrl. U., 1976 Contbr. articles to profl. jours.; patentee transmission, planters, dryer, 1961-73 East/West Ctr. sr. Fellow, Honolulu, 1976 Fellow Am. Soc. Agrl. Engrs. (Kishida Internat. award 1984); mem. Soc. Automotive Engrs., Sigma Xi: found. mem. Asian Assoc. for Agrl. Engring. Office: Univ of California Dept Biol & Agrl Engineering Davis CA 95616 E-mail: wjchancellor@ucdavis.edu.

CHANDAN, JIT S. management consultant, educator; b. Jahania Mandi, India, Mar. 29, 1937; arrived in U.S., 1963; s. Gurdit Singh and Bhanwan Bai; m. Sundesh K. Chandan, July 21, 1968; children: Sunjit S. Chawla, Upjeet K. MS, Sheffield U., U.K., 1963, Columbia U., 1965, PE, 1966; MBA, Baruch Coll., 1972; PhD, Delhi U., India, 1977. Cert. 1st class colliery mgr. cert. Ministry of Fuel and Power, U.K. Asst. prof. N.Y. Inst. Tech., 1966—72; prof. Medgar Evers Coll. CUNY, 1977—. Author: Management Concepts and Strategies, 1998, Statistics for Business and Economics, 1997, Organizational Behavior, 1994. Chair edn. and rsch. coms. Soc. Indian Academics of Am., N.Y.C., 1990—; gen. sec. Internat. Punjabi Soc., N.Y.C., 1972—92. Fellow King George VI Meml. fellowship, English Speaking Union, 1963—64. Mem.: Acad. Mgmt. Avocations: photography, travel, spiritual understanding. Home: 137-74 75 Rd Flushing NY 11367 Office: Medgar Evers Coll CUNY 1650 Bedford Ave Brooklyn NY 11225

CHANDAN, KAMLESH C. information technology executive, researcher; b. Pune, Maharashtra, India, Sept. 2, 1975; s. Chandrakant J. and Varsha C. Chandan; m. Divya K. Raichura, Jan. 21, 2001. BE in Computer Engring., Pune Inst. Computer Tech., India, 1997; MS (Entrepreneurship) in Computer Sci., U. So. Calif., 2000. Founder, CEO Chandan Computers, Pune, 1994—98; rsch. asst. U. So. Calif., L.A., 1998—2000; analyst developer Goldman Sachs & Co., N.Y.C., 2000—. Tutor, adminstr. Media Touch, Pune, 1997—98; cons. We-bCAD. Mem.: AAAS, Assn. Computing Machinery, NY Acad. Sci., IEEE, Rotary (Paul Harris fellow 2001). Home: 377 S Harrison St #13M East Orange NJ 07018 Office: Chandan Inc 337 S Harrison St #13M East Orange NJ 07018 Personal E-mail: kamlesh@chandangroup.com.

CHANDER, ANUPAM, lawyer; b. Punjab, India, Apr. 15, 1967; s. Harish and Yash (Garg) C. AB, Harvard U., 1989; JD, Yale U., 1992. Bar: N.Y. 1993. Clk. to Judge W. Norris U.S. Ct. Appeals (9th cir.), L.A., 1992-93; clk. to Chief Judge Newman U.S. Ct. Appeals (2d cir.), Hartford, Conn., 1993-94; assoc. Cleary, Gottlieb, Steen & Hamilton, N.Y.C., 1994-99; assoc. prof. law Ariz. State U., Tempe, 1999-00; prof. U. Calif., Davis, 2000—. Contbg. author: UNHCR Human Rights Manual, 1998. Co-dir. South Asian Youth Action, N.Y.C., 1998-99. Mem. Assn. Bar City N.Y. (human rights com. 1997-99). Avocation: reading. Office: U Calif Sch Law 400 Mrak Hall Dr Davis CA 95616-5201 E-mail: anupam@post.harvard.edu.

CHANDER, SUBHASH, educator; b. Hoshiarpur, India; BTech, Indian Inst. of Tech., 1968; MS, U. Calif., Berkeley, 1970, PhD, 1973. Asst. rsch. engr., lectr. U. Calif., Berkeley, 1973-74, vis. assoc. prof., 1981-83; asst. prof. Indian Inst. of Tech., Kanpur, India, 1974-81; assoc. prof. Pa. State U., University Park, 1983-89, prof., 1989—. Mem. Am. Chem. Soc., Soc. for Mining, Metallurgy and Exploration Engrs. (Arthur F. Taggart award 1992, Disting. Mem. 1997). Office: Pa State U 123 Hosler University Park PA 16802 E-mail: sxc14@psu.edu.

CHANDLER, ALBERT BENJAMIN, III, state attorney general; b. Sept. 12, 1959; m. Jennifer Chandler; children: Lucie Brasher, Albert Benjamin IV, Russell Branham. BA in History with distinction, U. Ky., JD, 1986. Bar: Ky. 1986. Assoc. Brown, Todd & Heyburn, Lexington, Ky., Reeves & Graddy, Versailles, Ky.; auditor State of Ky., 1991—94, atty. gen., 1995—. Recipient Achievement of Yr. award, Assn. Govt. Accts., 1993—94. Mem.: ABA, Woodford County Bar Assn., Ky. Bar Assn. (named Outstanding Young Lawyer 1993). Democrat. Presbyterian. Office: Office of Atty Gen Ste 118 Capitol Bldg Frankfort KY 40601-2831*

CHANDLER, ALFRED DUPONT, JR., historian, educator; b. Guyencourt, Del., Sept. 15, 1918; s. Alfred Dupont and Carol (Ramsay) C.; m. Fay Martin, Jan. 8, 1944; children: Alpine Douglass Chandler Bird, Mary Morris Chandler Watt, Alfred Dupont III, Howard Martin. AB, Harvard U., 1940, AM, 1947, PhD, 1952, LLD (hon.), 1995; PhD (hon.), U. Leuven, Belgium, 1976, U. Antwerp, 1979; LHD (hon.), Babson Coll., 1982, Ohio State U., 1987; LLD (hon.), York U., Can., 1988, New England Coll., 1992; LLD (hon.), U. Del., 2002; DBA (hon.), Northeastern U., 2002. Research assoc. MIT, 1950-51, from instr. to prof., 1951-63; prof. history Johns Hopkins U., 1963-71, chmn. dept., 1966-70, dir. Center for Study Recent Am. History, 1964-71; Straus prof. bus. history Harvard U. Bus. Sch., 1971-89, prof. emeritus, 1989—. Vis. fellow All Souls Coll., Oxford U., 1975; vis. prof. European Inst. Advanced Studies in Mgmt., Brussels, 1979; Walker-Ames vis. prof. U. Wash., 1981; cons. U.S. Naval War Coll., 1954; mem. Nat. Adv. Council on Edn. Professions Devel., 1970-71; chmn. adv. hist. com. U.S. AEC (renamed ERDA 1974), 1969-77. Author: Henry Varnum Poor, 1956, Strategy and Structure (Newcomen award 1964), 1962, Giant Enterprise, 1964, The Railroads, 1965; co-author (with Stephen Salsbury): Pierre S. duPont, 1971; author: The Visible Hand (Pulitzer and Bancroft prizes for 1978); co-author (with Herman Daems): Managerial Hierarchies, 1980; co-author: (with Richard Tedlow) The Coming of Managerial Capitalism, 1985; author: Scale and Scope, 1990, Inventing the Electronic Century, 2001; editor: Papers of Dwight D. Eisenhower, 5 vols., 1970; co-editor: Big Business and The Wealth of Nations, 1997, The Dynamic Firm, 1998, A Nation Transformed by Information, 2000; editor (asst.): The Letters of Theodore Roosevelt, 4 vols., 1954; subject of The Essential Alfred Chandler, 1988. Trustee Park Sch., Brookline, Mass., 1957-63, chmn. bd., 1961-63; trustee Brookline Pub. Libr., 1959-63, Roland Park Sch., Balt., 1964-70, Johns Hopkins U., 1971-81, Eleutherian Mills-Hagley Found., 1981-95, hon. trustee, 1995—. Lt. comdr. USNR, 1940-45. Recipient Pulitzer prize for history, 1978, Bancroft prize, 1978, award, Assn. Am. Pubs., 1991, Melamed prize, 1992; grantee rsch. fellowship, Harvard U., 1955, Guggenheim fellow, 1958—59. Mem. Am. Acad. Arts and Scis., Econ. History Assn. (trustee 1966-70, pres. 1971-72), Orgn. Am. Historians (exec. bd. 1969-72), Soc. for History Tech. (exec. coun. 1972-75), Am. Hist. Assn. (Scholarly Distinction award 1997), Soc. Am. Historians, Mass. Hist. Soc. (coun. 1977-83), Bus. History Conf. (pres. 1977-78, Life Time Achievement award 2002), Am. Antiquarian Soc., Am. Philos. Soc., Brit. Acad., Japan Acad., Acad. Mgmt. (Scholarly Contbn. to Mgmt. award 1985), St. Botolph Club (Boston), Nantucket Yacht Club (Mass.). Episcopalian.

CHANDLER, ALICE, higher education consultant, university president; b. Bklyn., May 29, 1931; d. Samuel and Jenny (Meller) Kogan; m. Horace Chandler, June 10, 1954; children: Seth, Donald, Barnard C. AB, Columbia U., 1951, MA, 1953, PhD, 1960; LHD, Kean U., 1997, Ramapo Coll., 2001. Instr. Skidmore Coll., 1953-54; lectr. Columbia U. Barnard Coll., 1954-55, Hunter Coll., CUNY, 1956-57; from instr. to prof. CCNY, 1961-76, v.p. instl. advancement, 1974-76, v.p. acad. affairs, 1974-76, provost, 1976-79, acting pres., 1979-80; pres. SUNY Coll., New Paltz, 1980-96; interim pres. Ramapo Coll., 2000-2001. Cons. in higher edn., 1996—; bd. dirs. Mohonk Mountain House, N.J. Coun. Humanities. Author: The Prose Spectrum: A Rhetoric and Reader, 1968, The Theme of War, 1969, A Dream of Order, 1970, The Rationale of Rhetoric, 1970, The Rationale of the Essay, 1971, From Smollett to James, 1980, Foreign Student Policy: England, France, and West Germany, 1985, Obligation or Opportunity: Foreign Student Policy in Six Major Receiving Countries, 1989, Access, Inclusion and Equity: Imperatives for America's Campuses, 1997, Public Higher Education and the Public Good: Public Policy at the Crossroads, 1998, Paying the Bill for International Education: Programs, Purposes, and Possibilities at the Millenium, 1999. Lizette Fisher fellow. Mem. Lotos, Phi Beta Kappa.

CHANDLER, ARTHUR BLEAKLEY, pathologist, educator; b. Augusta, Ga., Sept. 11, 1926; s. Clemmons Quillian and Mary Isabella (Bleakley) Chandler; m. Jane Stoughton Downing, Sept. 2, 1953; children: Arthur Bleakley, John Downing. Student, U. Ga., 1943-44; MD, Med. Coll. Ga., 1948. Diplomate Am. Bd. Pathology. Intern Baylor U. Hosp., Dallas, 1948-49; resident in pathology, NIH trainee in cancer dept. pathology Med. Coll. Ga., 1950-51, asst. in pathology, 1949-50, mem. faculty, 1949—, prof. pathology, 1962-2000, chmn. dept., 1975-2000, emeritus prof., emeritus chmn., 2001—. Com. mem. Nat. Heart, Lung and Blood Inst., 1969—93. Mem. editl. bd. Haemostatis, 1975—83, Pathology Rsch. and Practice, 1987—2001; contbr. chapters to books, articles to profl. jours. Trustee Young Mens Libr. Assn. Fund, 1962—72, Historic Augusta, Inc., 1966—69, Augusta-Richmond County Mus., 1965—87, Dan Printup Meml. Trust, 1985—2000, Acad. Richmond County, 1984—. Officer AUS Med. Corps, 1951—53. Fellow Commonwealth Fund, Norway, 1963—64. Mem.: AMA, Sch. Medicine Alumni Assn. Med. Coll. Ga. (pres. 1996—97), Richmond County Med. Soc. (trustee 1984—2002, sec. 1987, v.p. 1988), Med. Assn. Ga., Ga. Heart Assn., Ga. Assn. Pathologists (pres. 1984—85), Am. Heart Assn. (chmn. coun. on thrombosis 1978—80, chmn. com. on coronary lesions and myocardial infarctions 1980—82, fellow coun. arteriosclerosis), Am. Soc. Hematology, Am. Assn. Pathologists, Coll. Am. Pathologists, Am. Assn. History Medicine, Internat. Soc. for History of Medicine, Internat. Soc. Thrombosis and Haemostasis, Internat. Acad. Pathology, Alpha Omega Alpha. Episcopalian. Home: 803 Milledge Rd Augusta GA 30904-4351 Office: Med Coll Ga Dept Pathology Augusta GA 30912

CHANDLER, AUSTIN GRACE, psychologist; BA in Psychology with honors, Columbia U., 1970, MA, 1972; PhD, Fordham U., 1982; postgrad. in Bus., U. N.C., Greensboro, 1990. Lic., clin. psychologist. Corp. cons. Farr Assocs., 1983-85; mem. adj. faculty, founder, dir. coll. counseling ctr. Greensboro Coll., 1985-92; founder, pres. Allied Counseling and Consulting Enterprises, 1992—; chief psychologist Evergreens Sr. Health Care Facilities, NC, 1997—2001; psychology cons. Therapeutic Alternatives, Inc., NC, 2002—03. Mem. adj. faculty U. N.C., Greensboro; bd. dirs. Ashley Industries. Author: (with Jack Bornstein) Food is Killing You, 1997; contbr. articles to profl. jours. Bd. dirs. N.C. Aging and Mental Health Coalition. Recipient Psychologist of Yr. award N.C. Chiropractic Assn. Mem. APA, N.C. Psychol. Assn., Prescription Privileges for Psychologists Register (charter), Sigma Xi. Avocations: oil painting, writing, following the stock market, snow skiing. Office: Allied Counseling & Consulting Enterprises 8200 Crows Nest Ln Greensboro NC 27455-9294 Fax: 336-643-6850. E-mail: askaustin1@msn.com.

CHANDLER, BRUCE FREDERICK, internist; b. Bohemia, Pa., Mar. 26, 1926; s. Frederick Arthur and Minnie Flora (Burkhardt) C.; m. Janice Evelyn Piper, Aug. 14, 1954; children: Barbara, Betty, Karen, Paul, June. Student, Pa. State U., 1942-44; MD, Temple U., 1948. Diplomate Am. Bd. Internal Medicine, cert. internal medicine, subsplty. pulmonary disease. Commd. med. officer U.S. Army, 1948, advanced through grades to col., 1967; intern Temple U. Hosp., Phila., 1948-49; chief psychiatry 7th Field Hosp., Trieste, Italy, 1950; resident Walter Reed Gen. Hosp., Washington, 1949-53; renal dialysis clinician Peter Bent Brigham Hosp., Boston, 1953; battalion surgeon 2d Div. Artillery, Korea, 1953-54; chief renal dialysis unit 45th Evacuation Hosp. and Tokyo Army Hosp., Korea, Japan, 1954-55; various assignments Walter Reed Gen. Hosp., Fitzsimons Gen. Hosp., Letterman Gen. Hosp., 1955-70; comdg. officer 45th Field Hosp., Vicenza, Italy, 1958-62; pvt. practice internist Ridgecrest (Calif.) Med. Clinic, 1970-76; chief med. svc. and out-patients VA Hosps., Walla Walla, Spokane, Wash., 1976-82; med. cons. Social Security Adminstrn., Spokane, Wash., 1983-87; ret., 1987. Lectr. in field of pulmonary disease. Panel mem. TV shows, 1964-70; contbr. articles to profl. jours. Decorated Legion of Merit; recipient Outstanding Med. Student Gold melad Temple U., 1948. Fellow ACP, Am. Coll. Chest Physicians; mem. AMA, Am. Thoracic Soc., N.Y. Acad. Scis., So. European Task Force U.S. Army Med. Dental Soc. (pres. 2000, founder 1958-62), Alpha Omega Alpha (alumnus). Republican. Methodist. Avocations: photography, travel, fishing, collecting books (especially by jules verne and agatha christie). Home: 6496 N Callisch Ave Fresno CA 93710-3902

CHANDLER, CHRISTOPHER MARK (CHRIS CHANDLER), professional football player; b. Everett, Wash., Oct. 12, 1965; Degree in econ., Wash. State U., 1988. Quarterback Indpls. Colts, 1988—89, Tampa Bay Buccaneers, 1990—91, Phoenix Cardinals, 1991—93, L.A. Rams, 1994, Houston Oilers, 1995—96, Atlanta Falcons, 1997—2001, Chicago Bears, 2002—; NFC conf. champions, 1998—99; lost Superbowl 33 to Denver Broncos, 1999; mem. Pro Bowl team, 1997. Office: Halas Hall 1000 Football Drive Lake Forest IL 60045

CHANDLER, DAVID, scientist, educator; b. Bklyn., Oct. 15, 1944; SB, MIT, 1966; PhD, Harvard U., 1969. Research assoc. U. Calif., San Diego, 1969-70; from asst. prof. to prof. U. Ill., Urbana, 1970-83; prof. U.Pa., Phila., 1983-85, U. Calif., Berkeley, 1986—. Vis. prof. Columbia U., N.Y.C., 1977-78; vis. scientist IBM Corp., Yorktown Heights, N.Y., 1978, Oak Ridge Nat. Lab., 1979; cons. Los Alamos Nat. Labs., 1987-90; Miller rsch. prof., 1991; dir. de recherche Ecole Normale Superieure de Lyon, France, fall 1992; Christensen vis. fellow Oxford U., winter 1993, Hinshelwood lectr., 1993; Kolthoff lectr. U. Minn, 1994; faculty chemist Lawrence Berkeley Nat. Lab., 1996—, Miller rsch. prof., 1999-2000; Mulliken lectr. U. Chgo.; Lennard-Jones lectr. Royal Chem. Soc., Eng., 2001. Editor Chem. Physics, 1985—; mem. editl. bd. Jour. Statis. Physics, 1976-78, 94-96, Jour. Chem. Physics, 1978-80, Chem. Physics Letters, 1980-82, 91-2001, Molecular Physics, 1980-87, Theoretica Chimica Acta, 1988-89, Jour. Phys. Chemistry, 1987-92, Procs. NAS, 2001-02, Phys. Rev. E, 1995-2001, Adv. Chem. Phys., 1995—; mem. editl. adv. bd. PhysChemComm, 1999—. Proceedings Nat. Acad. Sci., 2000-01; author books in field; contbr. articles to profl. jours. Recipient Bourke medal, Faraday divsn. Royal Chem. Soc., Eng., 1985, Hirschfelder Theoretical Chemistry prize, U. Wis., 1998, Humboldt Rsch. award, 1999; fellow, Alfred P. Sloane Found., 1972—74, vis. fellow, Merton Coll., Oxford, 2001. Fellow AAAS, Am. Phys. Soc.; mem. NAS, Am. Acad. Arts and Scis., Am. Chem. Soc. (chmn. divsn. theoretical chemistry 1984, chmn. divsn. phys. chemistry 1990, Joel Henry Hildebrand award 1989, Theoretical Chemistry award 1996). Avocations: tennis, piano. Office: Dept Chem 1460 U Calif Berkeley Berkeley CA 94720-1460 E-mail: chandler@cchem.berkeley.edu.

CHANDLER, DAVID LESLIE, engineer; b. Kansas City, Mo., Oct. 15, 1955; s. Paul Leslie and Paula Del (Wolf) C.; m. Susan Juanita Higgason, may 14, 1977; children: Deborah Juanita, Jonathan Leslie. BSEE, DeVry Inst., Phoenix, 1976. Bench tech. Stoner Comms., Cucamonga, Calif., 1976-77; R&D engr. Safetron Systems, Cucamonga, 1977—79; electronic engr. Climet Instruments Co., Redlands, Calif., 1979-84, engring. mgr., 1984—. Patentee in field. Mem. Inst. Environ. Scis., Parenteral Drug Assn. Republican. Avocations: guitar, harmonica, bluegrass and folk music. Office: Climet Instruments Co 1320 W Colton Ave Redlands CA 92374-4524

CHANDLER, EDWARD WILLIAM, communication systems engineer, electrical engineer, electrical engineering educator; b. Milw., Oct. 10, 1953; s. Donald Harold and Helen Aliedia (Wonders) C.; m. Christine Anne Wohl, June 13, 1987; children: Rebecca Marie, Marcella Anne, Mary Elizabeth, Andrew Donald. BS, U. Wis., Milw., 1975; MSEE, Ill. Inst. Tech., 1978; PhD, Purdue U., 1985. Registered profl. engr., Wis. Electronics engr. Comms. and Electronics divsn. Motorola Inc., Schaumburg, Ill., 1976-77; instr. elec. engring. Milw. Sch. Engring., 1977-79, asst. prof., 1979-80, assoc. prof., 1982-84, prof., 1992—, acting head electronic comms. engring. tech. program, 1978-79, head, 1979-80, dir. elec. engring. program, 1982-84, dir. MS in Engring. program, 1992-2001; asst. prof. elec. engring. Marquette U., Milw., 1984-86; sr. engr. Titan Corp. (formerly Govt Sys. divsn. M/A-COM, Inc.), San Diego, 1986-88, mem. tech. staff, 1988-92, engring. cons. Comms. Products divsn., 1992—. Lectr. U. Wis., Milw., part-time 1979-83; invited lectr. Czech Tech. U., 1997, 98, Tech. U. Budapest, 1998, Fachhoschchule, Lübeck, Germany, 2000; grad. instr. rsch. Purdue U., West Lafayette, Ind., 1980-82; rsch. cons. Naval Ocean Systems Ctr., San Diego, 1986. Contbr. articles to profl. jours. David Ross summer grantee, 1981; faculty rsch. grantee Milw. Sch. Engring., 1983; recipient Outstanding Tchr. award Marquette U. Coll. Engring., 1986, Titan Most Valuable Performer award, 1990, Noel Amherd Tech. Performer award, 1991. Mem. IEEE (sr., newsletter editor Milw. sect. 1985-86), Am. Soc. Engring. Edn., Armed Forces Comms. and Electronics Assn., Air Force Assn., Triangle, Sigma Xi, Tau Beta Pi, Eta Kappa Nu. Home: 7030 N Range Line Rd Glendale WI 53209-2621 Office: Milw Sch Engring 1025 N Broadway Milwaukee WI 53202-3109 E-mail: chandler@msoe.edu.

CHANDLER, E(DWIN) RUSSELL, clergyman, writer; b. L.A., Sept. 9, 1932; s. Edwin Russell Sr. and Mary Elizabeth (Smith) C.; m. Sandra Lynn Swisher, Aug. 24, 1957 (div. 1977); children— Heather, Holly, Timothy John; m. Marjorie Lee Moore, Dec. 21, 1978; 3 stepchildren Student, Stanford U., 1950-52; BS in Bus. Adminstrn., UCLA, 1952-55; postgrad., U. So. Calif. Grad. Sch. Religion, 1955, New Coll., Edinburgh, Scotland, 1955-56; M.Div., Princeton Theol. Sem., 1958; grad., Washington Journalism Ctr., 1967. Ordained to ministry Presbyterian Ch., 1958. Asst. pastor 1st Presbyn. Ch., Concord, Calif., 1958-61; pastor Escalon Presbyn. Ch., Calif., 1961-66; reporter Modesto Bee, Calif., 1966-67; religion editor Washington Star, 1968-69; news editor Christianity Today, Washington, 1969-72; reporter Sonora Daily Union Dem., Calif., 1972-73; religion writer L.A. Times, 1974-92; interim pastor 1st Presbyn. Ch., Columbia, Calif., 1995-96. Author: The Kennedy Explosion, 1972, Budgets, Bedrooms and Boredom, 1976; co-author: Your Family--Frenzy or Fun?, 1977, The Overcomers, 1978, Understanding the New Age, 1988 (Silver Angel award 1989, Wilbur award 1989), Racing Toward 2001, 1992, Doomsday, 1993, Feeding the Flock, 1998; contbr. articles to profl. jours. Recipient Arthur West award United Methodist Communications Council, 1978, Faith and Freedom award Religious Heritage of Am., 1993; co-recipient Silver Angel award, Religion in Media, 1985 Mem. Religion Newswriters Assn. (pres. 1982-84, co-founder ann. Chandler award 2003, James O. Supple Meml. award, 1976, 1984, 86, John M. Templeton Reporter of Yr. award 1984, 87, 89), Phi Delta Theta Republican. Avocations: travel, beekeeping, birdwatching. also: 14304 Lake Vista Dr Sonora CA 95370-9692 E-mail: erchandler@aol.com.

CHANDLER, ELISABETH GORDON (MRS. LACI DE GERENDAY), sculptor, harpist; b. St. Louis, June 10, 1913; d. Henry Brace and Sara Ellen (Sallee) Gordon; m. Robert Kirkland Chandler, May 27, 1946 (dec.); m. Laci de Gerenday, May 12, 1979 (dec.). Grad., Lenox Sch., 1931; pvt. study sculpture and harp; LHD (hon.), St. Joseph Coll., 2001. Mem. Mildred Dilling Harp Ensemble, 1934-45; prof. sculpture Lyme Acad. Fine Arts, 1976—, chair sculpture dept. Exhibited sculpture NAD, Nat. Sculpture Soc., Allied Artists Am., Nat. Arts Club, Pen and Brush, Lyme Art Assn., Mattatuck Mus., Catherine Lorillard Wolfe Art Club, Am. Artists Profl. League, Hudson Valley Art Assn., USIA, 1976-78, Lyme Art Ctr., 1979, retrospective exhbn. Lyme Acad. Fine Arts, 1987, Madison Gallery, 1987, Old State House, Hartford, Conn., 1989, Mellon Art Ctr., Wallingford, Conn., 1989, Fairfield U. Walsh Gallery, 1991, Brit. Mus., London, Am. Medallic Sculptors Assn. Traveling Exhbn., 1994, Slater Mus. Cropsey Found., 1995, Nat. Sculpture Exhbn. Lyme Acad. Fine Arts, 1995-96, Lever House, N.Y.C., 1996, America's Tower, 1996-98, Hillsdale (Mich.) Coll., 1997, Nat. Acad. Mus., N.Y.C., 1998; represented in permanent collections Aircraft Carrier USS Forrestal, Gov. Dummer Acad., James Forrestal Rsch. Ctr. of Princeton U., Lenox Sch., James L. Collins Parochial Sch., Tex., Storm King Art Ctr., Columbia U., Pace U., White Plains, N.Y., St. Patrick's Cathedral, N.Y.C., McAuley Ctr., St. Joseph's Coll., West Hartford, Conn., Nat. Acad. Mus.; designed and executed Brookgreen Gardens medal, Forrestal Meml. Medal, Timoschenko Medal for Applied Mechanics, Benjamin Franklin Medal, Albert A. Michelson Medal, Jonathan Edwards Medal, Shafto Broadcasting Award Medal, Enrichment of Life medal Soc. Medallists, Adlai Stevenson bronze bust for Woodrow Wilson Sch. of Princeton U., 250 Ann. George Washington medal,Owen R. Cheatham bronze bust for Ga. Pacific Bldg., Atlanta, Messiah Coll., Grantham, Pa., Adlai E. Stevenson High Sch., Ill., Queen Anne's County Courthouse Square, Md., Our Lady Mercy Hosp., N.Y.C., Albert A. Michelson bust in Hall of Fame for Great Americans, pvt. collections. Active mus. therapy divsn. Am. Theatre Wing, 1942-45; trustee The Lenox Sch., 1953-55; chmn. Associated Taxpayers Old Lyme, 1969-72; trustee Brookgreen Gardens, S.C., 1989-97; founder, life trustee Lyme Acad., Coll. Fine Arts, 1976, prof. sculpture, 1976—. Recipient 1st prize Bklyn. War Meml. competition, 1945, 1st prize sculpture Catherine Lorillard Wolfe Art Club, 1951, 58, 63, Gold medal, 1969, Founders prize Pen & Brush, 1954, 76, 78, Gold medal, 1957, 61, 63, 69, 74, 76, Am. Heritage award, 1968, Solo Show award, 1961, 69, 75, Thomas R. Proctor prize NAD, 1956, Dessie Greer prize, 1960, 79, 85, Sculpture prize Nat. Arts Club, 1959, 60, 62, Gold medal, 1971, Gold medal Am. Artists Profl. League, 1960, 69, 73, 75, prize, 1981, Anna Hyatt Huntington prize, 1970, 76, Harriet Mayer Meml. prize, 1961, Gold medal Hudson Valley Art Assn., 1956, 69, 74, Mrs. John Newington award, 1976, 78, Lindsey Morris Meml. prize Allied Artists Am., 1973, Gold medal, 1982, Sculpture prize Acad. Artists, 1974, Sydney Taylor Meml. prize Knickerbocker Artists, 1975, New Netherlands DAR Bicentennial medal, 1976, Pietro Montana Meml. prize Hudson Valley Art Assn., 1995, Citation, State of Conn., 1995, Govs. Arts award Conn. Commn. on the Arts, 2000, Gari Melchers award Artist's Fellowship, 2002; named Citizen of Yr., Town of Old Lyme, Conn., 1985. Fellow: Internat. Inst. Arts and Letters, Am. Artists Profl. League, Nat. Sculpture Soc. (coun. 1976—85, Tallix Foundry award 1979, John Spring Founders award 1986, John Cavanaugh Meml. prize 1991, Silver medal, citation 1992, Herbert Adams Meml. medal for svc. to Am. sculpture); mem.: NAD (academician), Conn. Comm. for the Arts (Govs. medal 2000), Am. Profl. Artists League, Coun. Am. Artists Socs., Lyme Art Assn. (pres. 1973—75), Catherine Lorillard Wolf Art Club, Pen and Brush, Am. Medallic Art Soc., Allied Artists Am., Nat. Arts Club, Fedn. Internat. de la Medaille. Home: 2 Mill Pond Ln Old Lyme CT 06371-1118 Fax: 860-434-8725.

CHANDLER, FAY MARTIN, artist; b. Norfolk, Va., Sept. 15, 1922; d. Howard Gresham and Alpine Douglas (Gatling) Martin; m. Alfred Dupont Chandler Jr., Jan. 8, 1944; children: Alpine C. Bird, Mary C. Watt, Alfred D. III, Howard Martin. BA, Sweetbriar Coll., 1943; MFA, Md. Inst. Coll. Art, Balt., 1967. Coord., dir. Fell's Point Gallery Md. Inst. Coll. Art, 1968-73; fellow Va. Ctr. Creative Arts, Sweetbriar, 1993. Bd. dirs. Md. Inst. Alumni Coun., Nantucket Island Sch. Design and Arts, Mass., Boston Ctr. for the Arts; hon. bd. dirs. Mass. Vol. Lawyers for the Arts; founder, bd. dirs. The Art Connection, Boston; arts in edn. adv. coun. Harvard Grad. Sch. Edn., mem. coun. for the Arts at MIT. One-woman shows include Kenneth Taylor Little Gallery, Nantucket, 1973, 76, Fells Point Gallery, Balt., 1974, 76, Mills Gallery, Boston, 1974-88, Main St. Gallery, Nantucket, 1977, Ensign-Sibley Gallery, Nantucket, 1978, Sibley Gallery, Nantucket, 1980-85, Billiard Room Gallery, Cambridge, Mass., 1980, Helen Shlien Gallery, Boston, 1980, Bodley Gallery, N.Y.C., 1980, St. Botolph Club, Boston, 1982, Stebbins Gallery, Cambridge, Mass., 1987, Bentley Coll., Waltham, Mass., 1987, Columbia (Md.) Ctr. for the Arts, 1987, Babcock Gallery Sweet Briar Coll., Va., 1993, Wenham (Mass.) Mus., 1993, Nantucket Island Sch. Design Gallery, 1994, Boston Ctr. For the Arts, 1995, Children's Mus., Boston, 1996, Decker Gallery/Md. Inst. Art, 1997, Stenbaum Krauss Gallery, N.Y.C., 1997, Sacramento St. Gallery, Cambridge, Mass., 2002, Revolving Mus., Lowell, Mass.; exhibited in group shows. Bd. dirs. Friends of Art-Sweetbriar Coll., 2001—. Papers and slides chosen to be preserved Schlesinger Libr., Radcliffe Coll., Cambridge, Mass. Mem. Cambridge Art Assn. (bd. dirs.). Avocations: train trips, mystery books, philosophy. Home: 1010 Memorial Dr Apt 17E Cambridge MA 02138-4857 Studio: Engine House Studios 444 Western Ave Boston MA 02135-1016 E-mail: fay@dougwatt.com.

CHANDLER, GENE G. state legislator; s. Earle Walter and Flora (Giles) C.; m. Nancy Katherine Sheehan, 1969; children: Erik, Justin. Student, N.H. Coll., 1965-66, Olivet Coll., 1966-67. Selectman Town of Bartlett, N.H., 1974—; owner Bartlett (N.H.) Land and Timber Co., 1975—; rep N.H. Ho. of Reps., Dist. 1, Manchester, 1983—; spkr. of Ho., chmn. Rules Com., 2000—. Chmn. pub. works and hwys. coms., mem. rules com., N.H. Ho. of Reps.; former moderator Bartlett Town and Sch. Dist.; former mem. N.H. Saco Watershed Commn.; former chmn. Regional Ambulance Svc. Former co-chmn. Carroll County (N.H.) Rep. Com.; pres. Attitash Ski Edn. Found., 1984—; dir. Mt. Washington Valley Ski Edn. Found., 1983—; mem. Mt. Washington Commn. Mem. Bd. Realtors. Republican. Address: General Delivery Bartlett NH 03812-9999

CHANDLER, GEORGE FRANCIS, III, lawyer, naval architect; b. Winthrop, Mass., Dec. 15, 1940; s. George Francis Jr. and Phyllis (McKay) C.; children: Heather Suzanne, George Francis IV. BSME, Va. Poly. Inst., 1963; JD, Suffolk U., 1972. Bar: Mass. 1972, N.Y. 1973, N.J. 1978, U.S. Dist. Ct. Mass. 1972,

U.S. Dist. Ct. (so. dist.) N.Y. 1973, U.S. Dist. Ct. (ea. dist.) N.Y. 1977, U.S. Dist. Ct. (so. dist.) Tex. 1990), U.S. Dist. Ct. N.J. 1977, U.S. Ct. Appeals (2d cir.) 1973, U.S. Supreme Ct. 1977, U.S. Ct. Appeals (4th cir.) 1978, U.S. Ct. Appeals (11th cir.) 1983, U.S. Ct. Appeals (1st cir.) 1984, U.S. Ct. Appeals (5th cir.) 1992 ; profl. engr., Mass. Naval architect Dept. BuShips USN, Boston, 1958-63, 67-72; assoc. Bigham, Englar, Jones & Houston, N.Y.C., 1972-78; ptnr. Hill, Rivkins & Hayden LLP (and predecessor firm), N.Y.C., 1978—. U.S. rep. to UNCITRAL for Electronic Commerce, 1991-96, rep. for transport law, 2001—; mem. joint work group UNCITRAL/CMI, 1995-96; del. Comite Maritime Internat., 1990, 98, 2001, CMI subcom. on H/V Rules, 1995-99, CMI steering commn. on transport law, 1997—; titulary mem. CMI Subcom. on Electronic B/L. Contbr. articles to profl. jours. Pres., founder Spl. Edn. PTA, Maplewood, N.J., 1984-87. Lt. USNR, 1963-67. Mem. ABA, Soc. Naval Archs. (chmn. N.Y. sect. 1986-87), Maritime Law Assn. (proctor, bd. dirs. 1993-96, chmn. com. on carriage of goods 1991-95, chmn. subcom. on electronic contracts of carriage 1990-91, chmn. electronic comm. com. 1995-99), Houston Maritime Arbitrators Assn. (founder, chmn., bd. dirs. 1998—). Office: Hill Rivkins & Hayden LLP Ste 1515 712 Main St Houston TX 77002-3209

CHANDLER, HARRIETTE LEVY, state legislator, management consultant, educator; b. Balt., Dec. 20, 1937; d. Lester and Reba K. Levy; m. Burton Chandler, July 12, 1959; children: Frank Levy, Victoria Jane, Edward Lee. BA, Wellesley Coll., 1959; MA, Clark U., 1963, PhD, 1973; MBA, Simmons Coll., 1983; PhD in Pub. Adminstrn. (hon.), Worcester State Coll., 1998. High sch. history tchr. Worcester (Mass.) Pub. Schs., 1959-61; polit. sci. prof. Clark U., Worcester, 1973-77; prof. polit. sci. Tufts U., Medford, Mass., 1977-78; exec. dir. nat women's com. Brandeis U., Waltham, Mass., 1978-81; cons. Prime Computer, Natick, Mass., 1983-84; mgr. documentation tng. Adelie Corp., Cambridge, Mass., 1984-85, mgr. mktg. svcs., 1985-87, prin., 1987-89; dir. communication Open Software Found., Cambridge, 1989; mgmt. cons. Chandler Assocs., 1990—. Chair joint com. on pub. svc. Mass. Senate, 2002—. Author: (book) U.S. Soviet Relations During World War II, 1982. Chmn. com. on shareholder responsibility Clark U., 1982—86; mem. Worcester Sch. Com., 1992—94, vice chmn., 1994, Mass. Comm. on Common Core of Learning, 1994; chmn. bd. trustees Worcester Meml. Auditorium, 1987—89; founding mem. Worcester Women's Polit. Caucus, 1985, Worcester Com. Fgn. Rels.; mem. Worcester Econs. Club; incorporator YWCA, Greater Worcester Cmty. Found., Worcester Art Mus.; past pres. Jewish Healthcare Ctr.; state rep. 13th Worcester Dist., Mass. Legislature, 1995—2000, chair joint com. on health care, 1996—2000, state sen., 2001—, chair fed. fin. asst., Worcester Dist.; vice chair health care Assembly on Fed. Issues, Nat. Coun. State Legislatures, 1998—99; mem. Dem. State Com., 1999—2002; co-chair Ctrl. Mass. Legis. Caucus; chair joint com. on housing and urban devel. 13th Worcester Dist., Mass., chmn. pub. svc., 2002, chmn. housing and urban devel., 2003; vice chmn. transp., 2003; mem. joint com. on health care, long term debt, pub. safety, energy, and counties, 2003—; mem. steering com. Reforming States Group. Jewish. Avocations: walking, swimming, knitting, reading. Home: 97 Aylesbury Rd Worcester MA 01609-1314 Office: Rm 578 State House Boston MA 02133

CHANDLER, HUBERT THOMAS, former army officer; b. Charleston, W.Va., Dec. 8, 1933; s. Hubert Paris and Eleanor Lee (Gay) C.; m. Mary Frances Ritter, June 4, 1955; 1 son, Thomas Ritter. Student, Morris Harvey Coll., Charleston, 1951-52, U. Louisville, 1952-53; D.D.S., Balt. Coll. Dental Surgery, 1957; grad., Army War Coll., 1974. Diplomate: Am. Bd. Prosthodontics. Commd. Dental Corps U.S. Army, 1957, advanced through grades to maj. gen., dep. to chief Dental Corps, 1975-78, dep. comdr. Med. Command, dental surgeon, 1979-82, asst. surgeon gen., chief Dental Corps, 1982-86, dir. personnel Med. Dept., 1983-85; assoc. dean for profl. devel. Dental Sch., U. Md., Balt., 1988-92. Exec. com. Transatlantic council Boy Scouts Am., 1980-82; chmn. trust fund Girl Scouts Europe, 1981-82; pres. European Assn. Rod and Gun Clubs, 1981-82, Am. German Friendship Club, Heidelberg, W. Ger., 1981-82. Decorated D.S.M., Bronze Star, Meritorious Service medal, Army Commendation medal Fellow Am. Coll. Prosthodontists; mem. ADA. Office: 1714 Besley Rd Vienna VA 22182-2004 E-mail: htchandler@earthlink.net.

CHANDLER, J. HAROLD, insurance company executive; b. 1949; MBA, U. S.C. With Citizens & So. Nat. Bank S.C., Columbia, 1972-88, Citizens & So. Nat. Bank, Atlanta, 1988-91, NationsBank Corp., Atlanta, Washington, 1992-93; pres., CEO, chmn. Provident Companies, Inc., Chattanooga, 1993-99; chmn., pres., CEO UNUMProvident Corp. (formed by merger of UNUM & Provident Cos. in 1999), Chattanooga, 1999—2003. Bd. dirs. AmSouth Bancorporation, Herman Miller, Inc., Healthsource, Inc.

CHANDLER, JAMES BARTON, international education consultant; b. Conway Springs, Kans., May 27, 1922; s. James Perry and Bessie May (Stone) C.; m. Madeleine Racoux, July 27, 1946; children: Paul A., Peter R., Michele A. Chandler Dore. AB, U. Kans., 1947, MA, 1949; postgrad., U. Mich., 1950—54. Asst. prof., fgn. student advisor Ea. Mich. U., 1953-55, 57-58; lang. edn. advisor Okla. A&M/Ethiopia, 1955-57, U. Mich./Laos, 1958-60; tchr. edn., advisor U.S. AID-Laos, Vientiane, Laos, 1960-61, edn. div. chief, 1961-63, asst. dir. manpower, industry, pub. administrn., 1965-69, deputy mission dir., 1969-73; higher edn. advisor U.S. AID-Tunisia, Tunis, Tunisia, 1963-65; dir. Office of Edn. AID, Washington, 1973-76, assoc. asst. adminstr., 1976-77; dir. Internat. Bur. Edn. UNESCO, Geneva, 1977-83; cons. Ann Arbor, 1983-88; St. Louis, 1989—. With Rotary, Vientiane, Laos, 1966-73, sec. 1968-69. Capt. U.S. Army, 1943-47, ETO. Decorated Bronze Star, 1945; recipient Meritorious Honor award AID, 1973, Disting. Career Svc. award, 1977, Cert. Appreciation Pres. Gerald Ford, 1975, Letter Appreciation Dir. Gen. UNESCO, Geneva, 1983; S.L. Whitcomb fellow U. Kansas, 1948-49; fellow Ford Found., 1951-52. Mem. AAUP, Am. Acad. Social and Polit. Sci., Am. Fgn. Svc. Assn., NRA, Nat. Icarian Soc., Nat. Assn. Scholars, Nat. Parks and Conservation Assn., Am. Assn. Retired Persons, Nat. Wildlife Fedn., Archaeol. Inst. Am., Ind. Rights Found., Comparative and Internat. Edn. Soc., Diplomatic and Consular Officers Ret. (regional corr.), Nat. Assn. Ret. Fed. Employees (pres. Ann Arbor chpt. 1986-89, v.p. St. Louis chpt. 1989-90, pres. 1991-93, bd. dirs. 1992-93), Mo. Hist. Soc., Richmond Heights Srs. (v.p., pres.), Smithsonian Assocs., World Affairs Coun., Wilson Ctr. Assn., Nature Conservancy, Assn. Former Internat. Civil Servants, VFW, Am. Legion, 4th Cavalry Assn., Austrian Soc. of St. Louis, Soc. Francaise St. Louis (bd. dirs., v.p., pres., sec., sgt.-at.-arms), Ctr. for Internat. Understanding., Alliance Francaise, St. Louis-Lyon Sister Cities Com., Rotary (bd. dirs., officer 1992-2001, mid-County chpt. 2001—), St. Louis Discussion Club, Great Decisions Discussion Group, UN Assn. U.S.A., Phi Beta Kappa, Pi Delta Phi, Phi Kappa Phi. Roman Catholic. Avocations: bowling, bridge, billiards, oil painting, writing memoirs, stamps and coins. Home and Office: 7449 Rupert Ave Richmond Heights MO 63117

CHANDLER, JAMES JOHN, surgeon, educator; b. Dayton, Ohio, Nov. 13, 1932; s. James Kapp and Margaret Bertha (Paulson) Chandler; m. Fleur Elizabeth Varney, July 23, 1955; 1 child, Jennifer Hauge. AB, Dartmouth Coll., 1954, diploma in medicine, 1955; MD cum laude, U. Mich., 1957. Diplomate Am. Bd. Surgery. Intern Harvard Surg. Svc., Boston City Hosp., 1957-58, jr. asst. resident, 1958; resident, chief resident in surgery, clin. fellow Am. Cancer Soc. U. Oreg. Hosps., Portland, 1961-64, instr. surgery, 1964; courtesy staff, chmn. surgery Med. Ctr. at Princeton, NJ, 1972—92, pres. med. and dental staff, 1993-94; clin. prof. surgery U. Medicine and Dentistry N.J.-Robert Wood Johnson Med. Sch., Piscataway, 1976—; active staff Robert Wood Johnson U. Hosp., New Brunswick, NJ, 2000—. Cons. in surgery Princeton U.; trustee Med. Ctr. Princeton, 1993—94. Contbr. chapters to books, articles to profl. jours. Bd. dirs. Trinity Counseling Svc., 1968—, chmn., 1968—72; pres. Princeton Day Sch. PTA, 1976—78, trustee, 1976—81; mem. alumni coun. Dartmouth Med. Sch., 1981—86, Dartmouth Coll., 1983—86; active All Sts. Episcopal Ch., Princeton, 1965—. Lt. USN, 1958—60, served to lt. comdr. USNR, 1960—61. Fellow: ACS (pres. N.J. chpt. 1976—77, gov. 1981—87), Soc. Surg. Oncology, Am. Coll. Chest Physicians; mem.: AMA, Soc. Internat. Surgery, Soc. Surg. Alimentary Tract, Collegium Internationale Chirurgiae Digestivae, Med. Soc. N.J. (sec., chmn. surgery sect. 1967—69), Soc. Surgeons N.J., Am. Soc. Clin. Oncology, Gatineau Fish and Game Club, Bedens Brook Club, Nassau Gun Club (pres. 2001—02), Alpha Omega Alpha. Home: 95 Russell Rd Princeton NJ 08540-6729 Office: 1 Robert Wood Johnson Pl New Brunswick NJ 08903-0019 E-mail: chandljj@umdnj.edu.

CHANDLER, JAMES PHILLIP, law educator; b. Bakersfield, Calif., Aug. 15, 1938; s. Isaac and Lillie Mae Chandler; m. Elizabeth Thompson (div.); children: James P. IV, Elizabeth Lynne, Ruth Rebekah, Isaac II, Aaron Daniel Pushkin, David Martin Thompson. BA, U. Calif., Berkeley, 1962; JD, U. Calif., Davis, 1970; LLM, Harvard U., 1971; LLD (hon.), La Academia Mexicana de Derecho Internacional, 1988. Bar: D.C. 1976, Pa. 1978, U.S. Dist. Ct. D.C., U.S. Ct. Appeals (1st, 3d, 4th and 7th cirs.), U.S. Dist. Ct. Md., U.S. Dist. Ct. (ea. dist.) Pa., U.S. Supreme Ct. Grad. fellow Harvard U., Cambridge, Mass., 1970—71; fellow Acad. Engring. of the NAS, Washington, 1971; faculty fellow engring. dept. Stanford U., Calif., 1972; disting. vis. prof. law U. Miss., Oxford, 1975; prof. law and dir. Computers in Law Inst. George Washington U. Nat. Law Ctr., Washington, 1977—93; mng. prin. The Chandler Law Firm, Chartered, Washington, 1979—; pres., bd. dirs. Nat. Intellectual Property Law Inst., Washington, 1993—. Vis. scholar Harvard U., Cambridge, 1984; cons. U.S. Gen. Acctg. Office, Washington, 1973—82, Computer Application in the Cts., Md. Ct. of Appeals, Adminstrv. Office of the Cts., Annapolis, 1974—76; mem. Nat. Infrastructure Assurance Coun., Washington, 1999. Contbr. Bd. dirs. Sarah's Cir., Washington, 1999—2002. Mem.: Computer Law Assn. Am. (bd. dirs. 1972—82), Army-Navy. Avocation: racquetball. Home: 10621 River Rd Potomac MD 20854 Office: Nat Intellectual Property Law Inst 1815 Pennsylvania Ave NW #300 Washington DC 20006

CHANDLER, JOHN WESLEY, educational consultant; b. Mars Hill, N.C., Sept. 5, 1923; s. Baxter Harrison and Mamie (McIntosh) C.; m. Florence Gordon, Aug. 25, 1948; children: Alison, John, Jennifer, Patricia. Student, Mars Hill Coll., 1941-43; AB, Wake Forest Coll., 1945, L.H.D. (hon.); B.D., Duke U., 1952, PhD, 1954; LL.D., Hamilton Coll., 1968, Colgate U., 1968, Williams Coll., 1973, Amherst Coll., 1974, Wesleyan U., 1978, North Adams State Coll., 1983; L.H.D., Wake Forest U., 1968, Trinity Coll., 1982, Middlebury Coll., 1983, Bates Coll., 1983, Beaver Coll., Duke U., 2002. Instr. philosophy Wake Forest Coll., 1948-51, asst. prof., 1954-55; asst. prof. religion Williams Coll., 1955-60, assoc. prof., chmn. dept., 1960-65, Cluett prof. religion, 1965-68, acting provost, 1965-66, dean faculty, 1966-68; pres. Hamilton Coll., Clinton, N.Y., 1968-73, Williams Coll., Williamstown, Mass., 1973-85, Assn. Am. Colls., Washington, 1985-90; ednl. cons. Korn/Ferry Internat., Washington, 1990-91, Acad. Search Cons. Svc., Washington, 1992—. Contbg. author: Miscellany of American Religion, 1963, Masterpieces of Religious Literature, 1963, also jour. articles and revs. Trustee Williams Coll., 1969-72; bd. visitors Wake Forest Coll., 1971-77, 79-91; bd. dirs. Williamstown Theatre Festival, 1973-85, Sterling and Francine Clark Art Inst., 1973-85; pres. New Eng. Assn. Schs. and Colls., 1977-78, Assn. Ind. Colls. and Univs. Mass., 1977-79; chmn. New Eng. Colls. Fund, 1978; trustee Duke U., 1985-94, chmn., 1993-94; trustee Randolph-Macon Woman's Coll., 1985-88, Phillips Collection, 1997-2001; dir. Value Line Funds, 1991—. Fulbright fellow India, 1963; Kent fellow. Mem. Phi Beta Kappa. Mem. United Ch. of Christ. Clubs: Williams; Cosmos (Washington). Office: Williams Coll Oakley Ctr Williamstown MA 01267 E-mail: John.W.Chandler@williams.edu.

CHANDLER, KENT, JR., lawyer; b. Chgo., Jan. 10, 1920; s. Kent and Grace Emeret (Tuttle) C.; m. Frances Robertson, June 19, 1948; children: Gail, Robertson Kent. BA, Yale U., 1942; JD, U. Mich., 1949. Bar: Ill. 1949, U.S. Dist. Ct. (no. dist.) Ill. 1949, U.S. Ct. Appeals (7th cir.) 1955, U.S. Ct. Claims 1958. Assoc. Wilson & McIlvaine, Chgo., 1949-56, ptnr., 1957-94, spl. counsel to firm, 1994-98; of counsel Bell Jones & Quinlisk, Chgo., 1998—. Bd. dirs. No. Trust Bank, Lake Forest, Ill., 1969-90, A.B. Dick Co., 1971-79, Internat. Crane Found., 1988—. Mem. zoning bd. appeals City of Lake Forest, Ill., 1953-63, chmn., 1963-67, mem. plan commn., 1955-69, chmn., 1969-70, pres. bd. local improvements, 1970-73, mayor, 1970-73, mem. bd. fire and police commn., 1975-82, chmn., 1982-84. Served to maj. USMCR, 1941-46. Mem. ABA, Ill. State Bar Assn., Chgo. Bar Assn., Lake County Bar Assn., Lawyers Club Chgo. (pres. 1985-86), Univ. Club, Onwentsia Club (Lake Forest), Old Elm Club (Highland Park, Ill.). Republican. Presbyterian. Office: 200 W Adams St Ste 2600 Chicago IL 60606-5233

CHANDLER, KIMBERLEY LYNN, educational administrator; b. Waynesboro, Va., Sept. 28, 1961; d. Alden Hugh and Cecille Frances (Brooks) C. BA in Elem. Edn., Coll. William and Mary, 1984, MA in Edn./Gifted Edn., 1992, postgrad. Lic. educator, Va. Tchr. Fredericksburg (Va.) Pub. Schs., 1984-87, Henrico County Pub. Schs., Richmond, Va., 1987-98; gifted edn. resource specialist Hanover County Pub. Schs., Richmond, Va., 1998-2000; supr. enrichment programs, coord. of sci. K-12 Amherst County Pub. Schs., Va., 2000—03; cert. curriculum cons. Ctr. for Gifted Edn., 2002—; panel reviewer Jacob K. Javits Grant Program, U.S. Dept. Edn., 2002; postdoctoral fellow, curriculum coord. Ctr. for Gifted Edn. Coll. of William and Mary, Williamsburg, Va., 2003—. Summer sch. coord. Henrico County Pub. Schs., 1996, 97, staff devel. presenter, 1996, 97; curriculum cons. Coll. of William and Mary, Williamsburg, Va., 1996; presenter in field.; mem. gifted edn. staff devel. talent bank, mem. tchr. stds. com. Va. Dept. Edn.; mem. peer coaching program, Prin.'s Acad.; sch. renewal planning team facilitator Hanover County Pub. Schs.; mem. adj. faculty U. Va., 2001—; instr. Casenex, Inc.; participant David L. Clark Grad. Student Seminar, 2003. Author: (curriculum unit) Literary Reflections, 1992; author: (with others) Aiming for Excellence-Gifted Program Standards: Annotations to the NAGC Pre-K-Grade 12 Gifted Program Standards, ERIC Research Report, 2002, (book review) Gifted and Talented International; editor (newsletter): Va. Assn. for the Gifted, 1999—. Vol. Hanover Humane Soc., 1994—, Habitat for Humanity Global Village Program, Nicaragua Disaster Relief Mission Team, 1999, Brazil VBS Mission Team, 2000; mem. Habitat for Humanity Global Village Team to South Africa, 2001. Recipient Doctoral Student award Nat. Assn. for Gifted Children, 2002, Hollingworth Rsch. award, 2003; grantee Henrico Edn. Found., 1997, Henrico Gifted Adv. Coun., 1997, Pntrs. in Arts grantee Richmond Arts Coun., 1996, Hanover Edn. Found., 1999, Coll. William and Mary, 2003; postdoctoral fellow Ctr. Gifted Edn., Coll. William and Mary, 2003—. Mem.: Va. Assn. for the Gifted (ex officio bd. dirs.), Va. Soc. for Tech. in Edn., Hanover County Prins. Acad., Nat. Assn. for Gifted Children (sec./treas. technol. divsn. 1997—99, sec./treas. profl. devel. divsn. 1997—99, chair profl. devel. divsn. 2003—, Harry Passow Classroom Tchr. scholarship 1997, Outstanding Curriculum award 2000, Doctoral Student award 2002, Hollingworth award 2003), Delta Kappa Gamma, Kappa Delta Pi (chpt. sec.). Home: 11444 New Farrington Ct Glen Allen VA 23059-1629 Office: Coll William and Mary Ctr for Gifted Edn PO Box 8795 Williamsburg VA 23187-8795 E-mail: kchan11444@aol.com.

CHANDLER, LAWRENCE BRADFORD, JR., lawyer; b. New Bedford, Mass., June 20, 1942; s. Lawrence Bradford and Anne (Crane) C.; m. Madeleine Bibeau, Sept. 7, 1963 (div. June 1984); children: Dawn, Colleen, Brad. BS in Bus. Adminstrn., Boston Coll., 1963; LLB, U. Va., 1966, JD, 1970. Bar: Mass. 1966, U.S. Supreme Ct. 1967, Va. 1970, W.Va. 1993; diplomate Nat. Bd. Trial Advocacy; advocate Am. Bd. Trial Advocates. Ptnr. Chandler, Franklin & O'Bryan, Charlottesville, Va., 1971—. Pres. Western Va. Chpt., 1992-93. Capt. U.S. Army, 1967-71. Mem.: ATLA (chair state dels. 1993—94, exec. com. 1993—94, bd. govs. 1995—2001), ABA, Am. Assn. Profl. Liability Attys., Am. Soc. on Law, Medicine and Ethics, Am. Coll. Legal Medicine, Charlottesville Bar Assn., Nat. Bd. Trial Advocacy (bd. examiners), Am. Bd. Trial Advs. (pres. Va. chpt.), Va. Trial Lawyers Assn. (pres. 1985—86), Assn. U.S. Army (pres. 1971—73). Roman Catholic. Home: 1445 Old Ballard Rd Charlottesville VA 22901-9469 Office: Chandler Franklin & O'Bryan PO Box 6747 Charlottesville VA 22906-6747 E-mail: goofyc@mindspring.com.

CHANDLER, MARCIA SHAW BARNARD, farmer; b. Arlington, Mass., Aug. 22, 1934; d. John Alden and Grace Winifred (Copeland) Barnard; m. Samuel Butler Chandler, Aug. 31, 1952 (dec. 1986); children: Shawn Chandler Seddinger, Mark Thurmond, Matthew Butler. BA, Francis Marion Univ., Florence, S.C., 1976; MEd, U. S.C., 1985. Resource person United Cerebral Palsy of S.C., Dillon, 1976-79; instr. English Horry-Georgetown Tech. Coll., Conway, S.C., 1980-81; farm owner, mgr. Dillon; drama critic Dillon (S.C.) Herald, 1986—. Author: (with others) Best of Old Farmer's Almanac, First 200 Years, 1991, A Primer for the New Millennium, 1999; cover artist So. Bell Telephone Directory, 1988; artist Dillon County Lib., 1998. Bd. dirs., publicist, pres. Dillon County Theatre, Inc., 1985—; publicist, bd. dirs., artist MacArthur Ave. Players, Dillon, 1990—; bd. dirs. Friends of Francis Marion U., 1985-95; pres. Dillon Area Arts Coun., 1980-85, Jr. Charity League of Dillon, 1960-75; nat. poetry judge DAR, 1982; Dunbar libr. com., Dillon County, 1999. Recipient Honorable Commendation for civic involvement S.C. Ho. Reps., Mar. 22, 1990. Mem. Cousteau Soc., Ctr. Environ. Edn., Internat. Fund Animal Welfare, World Wildlife Fund, Nature Conservancy, Sea Shepherd Conservation Soc., Humane Soc. U.S. Avocations: snorkeling, animal welfare activities, theater, travel. Home: 309 E Reaves Ave Dillon SC 29536-1919 E-mail: marciacani@aol.com.

CHANDLER, MARGARET MCNEILL, home economist, educator; b. Laurens, S.C., Feb. 22, 1955; d. William S. and Mary Ann (Wharton) McNeill; children: Keri Lee, Travis McNeill; m. Thomas B. Chandler. BS, Lander U., 1977; MEd, Converse Coll., 1991. Cert. tchr., S.C. Social worker Laurens County DSS, 1978; tchr. Laurens Dist. 55 H.S., 1978—. Pianist, choir dir. Waterloo United Meth. Ch. Mem. NEA, S.C. Edn. Assn., Laurens County Edn. Assn. Methodist. Avocations: cooking, painting, staining, sewing, bookkeeping/management consulting. Home: 40 Sesame St Laurens SC 29360-8936 Office: Laurens Dist 55 HS 5058 Hwy 76 W Laurens SC 29360-9378 E-mail: m0mc@charter.net.

CHANDLER, MARGUERITE NELLA, real estate corporation executive; b. New Brunswick, N.J., May 16, 1943; d. Edward A. and Marguerite (Moore) C.; m. Ronald Wilson, May 30, 1964 (div. Nov. 1973); children: Mark, Adam; m. Richmond Shreve, Nov. 22, 1979; 1 child, Laura. BS in Acctg., Syracuse U., 1964; MS in Polit. Mgmt., George Washington U., 1988. Tax acct. Peat Marwick Mitchell, Providence, 1964; grant adminstr., psychology dept. Brown U., Providence, 1965; intern in devel. cons. Washington, 1973-75; prin., tng. cons. M. Chandler Assocs., 1975-76; mgmt. cons. Edmar Corp., Bound Brook, N.J., 1976-78, pres., chief exec. officer, 1978-90, pres., 1991—. Peace Corps vol., 1966-68; established Food Bank Network of Somerset County, 1982, pres., 1982-85; established Worldworks Found., Inc., 1983; founder PeopleCare Ctr., 1984, pres., 1984-86; bd. dirs. N.J. Coun. for Arts, 1986-87; pres. bd. trustees N.J. Coun. of Chs., 1985-90; bd. dirs. United Way Somerset Valley, 1984-91, gen. campaign chmn., 1985-86; recorder Blue Ribbon Com. on Ending Hunger in N.J., 1984-86; vol. Somerset Community Action Program, 1969-71, Missionaries of Charity, Calcutta, India, 1981; treas. Somerset County Day Care Assn., 1969-71; mem. N.J. Gov.'s Task Force on Pub./Pvt. Sector Initiatives, 1986-91; Dem. candidate for U.S. Congress Dist. 12, 1990; mem. adv. bd. US-USSR Youth Exch., Ptnrs. in Peacemaking, The Giraffe Project; mem. Gov.'s Adv. Coun. on Solid Waste Mgmt., 1991-92; chairperson numerous fund-raising events to combat world hunger; established Heritage Trail Assn. of Somerset County, pres. 1994—97, chmn. bd. dirs. Friends Retirement Inc., 1996—02. Named Woman of Yr., Women's Resource Ctr. Somerset County, 1983, Citizen of Yr., Somerset County C. of C., 1985, N.J. Chpt. Nat. Assn. Soc. Workers, 1986, Bus. and Profl. Women's Club, 1987, Person of Decade, Courier-News, 1989, Bus. Person of Yr., Bus. for Ctrl. N.J. mag., 1993; recipient People's Champion award Somerset Family Planning Svc., 1985, Disting. Svc. award N.J. Speech-Lang.-Hearing Assn., 1986, N.J. Women of Achievement award Douglass Coll. and N.J. Fedn. Women's Clubs, 1986, Brotherhood award Cen. Jersey chpt. Nat. Conf. Christians and Jews, 1986, Presdl. End Hunger award, 1987, Somerset Alliance for the Future Quality of Life award, 1996. Mem. Assn. N.J. Recyclers (pres. 1991-93), Somerset C. of C. (chmn. bd. 1989-90, chmn. strategic planning cultural and heritage com., tourism coun.), World Bus. Acad. (bd. dirs. 1988-89), Rotary (pres. Bound Brook-Middlesex club 1993-94), Regional Plan Assn. (bd. dirs. 1994-96), Heritage Trail Assn. Somerset County (founder, pres. 1994-99), Crossroads of the Am. Revolution Assn. (pres. 2001—). Mem. Soc. Of Friends. Avocation: quilting. Home: PO Box 250 Cape May Point NJ 08212 Office: PO Box 710 Bound Brook NJ 08805-0710

CHANDLER, MARSHA, academic administrator, professor; BA, CCNY, 1965; PhD, UNC Chapel Hill, 1972. Prof. political econ. Univ. Toronto, 1977-96, dean arts and sci., 1990-97; sr. vice chancellor U. Calif., San Diego, MA, 1996—. Vis. scholar Harvard U., Boston, 1995-96. Co-author: Trade and Transmissions, 1990, The Political Economy of Business Bailouts, 2 vols., 1986, The Politics of Canadian Public Policy, 1983, Public Policy and Provincial Politics, 1979, Adjusting to Trade: A Comparative Perspective, 1988; contbr. articles to profl. jours. Fellow, Royal Soc. of Canada, mem., Dept. of Political Sci., Faculty of Law, bd. dirs. San Diego Opera, Mingei Mus. of Internatl. Folk Art, UCSD Found. Bd. and the Charter 100, adv. com. on Fed. Judicial Appts., bd. of Canadian Inst. for Adv. Rsch.; trustee, Art Gall. of Ontario, Mt. SInai Hosp., Huntsman Marine Sci. Ctr., Ontario Lightwave, Laser Rsch. Ctr. Office: U Calif 9500 Gilman Dr La Jolla CA 92093-5004

CHANDLER, MELANIE LYNN, surgical technologist, paralegal; b. Hammond, Ind., Oct. 11, 1967; d. Michael Edward and Mary Josephine Simkins; children: Courtney, Brian, Lindsey. Student paralegal studies, Calumet Coll. St. Joseph, 2001. Cert. surgical technologist. Cert. nurses aide Resthaven Christian Svs., South Holland, Ill., 1996—98; gastrointestinal lab technician Adv. Trinity Hosp., Chicago, Ill., 1998—2000, cert. surg. technologist, 1997—; paralegal Barry Sherman & Assocs., Hammond, Ind., 2002—. Latex allergy liason Adv. Trinity Hosp., Chgo., 1999—. Mem.: Calumet Coll. Paralegal Club (sec., treas. 2002). Office: Barry Sherman & Assocs 6920 Hohman Ave Hammond IN 46320 Personal E-mail: melaniechandler@aol.com.

CHANDLER, NETTIE JOHNSON, artist; b. Christian County, Ky., Nov. 15, 1912; d. Sol James amd Georgia Bell (Davis) Johnson; m. Percy Scott Chandler, Oct. 14, 1944. Student, Watkins Inst., Nashville, 1937-45, 53-56, Harris Sch. Art, 1937, Oklahoma City U., 1952, Coll. William and Mary, 1957-58; AS cum laude, Thomas Nelson C.C., Hampton, Va., 1983. Bookkeeper Keach Furiture Co., Hopkinsville, Ky., 1929-32; office sec., bookkeeper Baus Mfg. Co., Hopkinsville, 1933-35; bookkeeper Castner Knott Co., Nashville, 1936-39; sec., artist, editor Young South page' Baptist & Reflector, Nashville, 1939-45; real estate saleswoman Grinnell Realty, Nashville, 1950-51; typist Griffiss AFB, Rome, N.Y., 1952-53; sec., artist Tenn. State Libr., Nashville, 1953-56; tech. illustrator NASA, Hampton, 1956-72. Comml. artist, until 1972; fine art painter, 1973—. Represented in permanent collections Va. Air and Space Mus., 1999—. Vol. ARC, Nashville, 1985-86. Recipient awards for art including 2nd place Watkins Inst., 1955, 1st place Parthenon, Nashville, 1956, 1st place Watkins Inst., 1956, 1st place (3 times) Tenn. State Fair, 1985-96, Best of Show, Watkins Inst., 1986, 3rd place Watkins Inst., 1987, 2nd place for miniatures Tenn. Art League (3 times), 1988-92, 3d place Tenn. Art League, 1989, Best of Show, Tenn. Art League, 1990, 2nd place for graphics Tenn. Art League, 1996, Best of Show, Gallery Eight WDCN TV, 1997, Daily Press Newport News, Va. Snapshot award, 1983. Mem. Am., Tenn. Art League (leader Monday Painters 1984-98). Republican. Baptist. Avocations: travel, walking, gardening, writing, designing. Home: 404 Deer Lake Dr Nashville TN 37221-2108

CHANDLER, RICHARD GATES, lawyer; b. Stockton, Calif., July 6, 1952; s. Kensal Roberts and Barbara (Gates) Chandler; m. Heidi Pankoke, Oct. 22, 1994. BA, Lawrence U., 1974; JD, U. Chgo., 1977. Bar: Wis. 1977. Assoc. Minahan & Peterson SC, Milw., 1979—84; legis. counsel to State Rep. Tommy G. Thompson, Wis. Assembly, Madison, 1985—86; legis. asst. Congressman Robert W. Kasten, Jr., Washington, 1977—78; budget dir. State of Wis., 1987—2001; sec. Dept. Revenue, Madison, Wis., 2001—03; public policy cons. Chandler Cons. LLC, Madison, 2003—. Mem.: Phi Beta Kappa. Republican. Methodist. Home: 810 Ottawa Trail Madison WI 53711-2941

CHANDLER, ROBERT CHARLES, healthcare consultant; b. Birmingham, Ala., Apr. 15, 1945; s. Coleman Duke and Myrtle (Cleveland) C.; m. Linda Watson, May 17, 1997; children: Jason Charles, Jonathan Robert. BS in Pharmacy, Samford U., 1968; MS in Hosp. and Health Adminstrn., U. Ala.-Birmingham, 1972. Registered pharmacist. Pharmacy intern Carraway Meth. Hosp., Birmingham, 1968-69; chief pharmacist Holy Family Hosp., Birmingham, 1969-70; v.p. Ft. Sanders Med. Ctr., Knoxville, Tenn., 1971-78; sr. v.p. Bapt. Med. Ctrs., Birmingham, 1978-79; exec. v.p. Princeton, 1979-85; pres. E. Tenn. Bapt. Hosp., Knoxville, 1985-90, The Bapt. Health Sys. East Tenn., Knoxville, 1986-90; ptnr. Ward Howell Internat., Atlanta, 1991-98, TMP Worldwide, Atlanta, 1998-99; sr. v.p., global practice leader Healthcare and Pharms., Stratford Group, Atlanta, 2000—01; exec. v.p., nat. practice leader for healthcare and life scis. DHR Internat., Atlanta, 2002—. Bd. dirs. Am. Healthcare Sys. San Diego, 1988-90; chmn. bd. dirs. SunHealth Care Plans Tenn., 1986-88; bd. dirs. Ala. Quality Assurance Found., Birmingham, 1984-85, Ala. Med. Rev., Birmingham, 1980-84; mem. adv. bd. Blue Cross/Blue Shield, Birmingham, 1983-85; mem. liaison com. Jefferson County Med. Soc., Birmingham, 1984-85; various faculty appts. U. Ala., Birmingham, Emory U. Sch.

Medicine, Atlanta; divsn. chmn. United Way, Birmingham, 1984; bd. dirs. United Way Greater Knoxville, 1987-88, Knoxville Opera Co., 1988; Sunday sch. tchr. Dawson Bapt. Ch., Birmingham; deacon chmn. 1st Bapt. Ch., Knoxville, 1988-90. Recipient Cert. Appreciation, Tenn. Gov. Ray Blanton, 1978, Disting. Svc. award Tenn. Com. on Employment of Handicapped, 1978, Award of Excellence Ala. Pub. Rels. Coun., 1979. Fellow Am. Coll. Hosp. Adminstrs.; mem. Birmingham Regional Hosp. Coun. (pres.-elect 1985), Hosp. Alliance Tenn. (pres. 1987-88), Ala. Hosp. Assn. (trustee 1984-85), Birmingham C. of C. (chmn. health svcs. com. 1980), The Club (Birmingham), Rotary (mem. group study exch. 1977). Office: DHR International 100 Galleria Pkwy Ste 1150 Atlanta GA 30339

CHANDLER, ROBERT LESLIE, public relations executive; b. Phila., Mar. 3, 1948; s. Joel Leslie and Evelyn Laney (DeLaney) C.; m. Pamela Lin Gemmel, Sept. 22, 2002. AS, Atlantic C.C., 1969; BS, Bowling Green State U., 1971; MS, Ohio U., 1972; MBA in Hosp. Adminstrn., Wagner Coll., 1980. Dir. pub. rels. Athens Mental Health Ctr., Ohio, 1972; internal comms. editor, pub. affairs dept. Owens-Corning Fiberglas Corp., Toledo, 1972-74; dir. cmty. rels. Wyandotte Gen. Hosp., Mich., 1974-76; v.p. asst. adminstr. mktg./pub. affairs Meth. Hosp., Bklyn., 1976-82; exec. v.p. Burson-Marsteller Pub. Rels., N.Y.C., 1982-95; pres. Chandler-Chicco Agy., 1995. Mem. budget com. United Way Mich., 1975-76; bd. dirs. N.Y. chpt. Am. Heart Assn. Am. Heart Assn. N.J./N.Y. State scholar, 1969. Mem. Pub. Rels. Soc. Am., Am. Soc. Health Care Mktg. and Planning, Am. Coll. Healthcare Execs. (assoc. mem.), Sigma Delta Chi, Kappa Tau Alpha. Office: Chandler Chicco Agy 450 W 15th St Ste 700 New York NY 10011-7014

CHANDLER, RONALD JAY, lawyer; b. Springfield, Mo., Jan. 15, 1949; s. Jack Dempsey and Esta Lee (Cravens) C.; m. Patricia Ann Meyer, June 17, 1973; 1 child, Mary Coday. BA, Mo. So. State Coll., 1975; JD, U. Tulsa, 1979. Bar: Okla. 1979, U.S. Dist. Ct. (no. dist.) Okla. 1980, U.S. Ct. Appeals (10th cir.) 1981. Asst. dist. atty. Office of Dist. Atty., Tulsa, 1979-80; ptnr. Chandler & Cantrell, Tulsa, 1980; atty. Cities Svc. Co., Tulsa, 1980-82; assoc. Prichard, Norman & Wohlgemuth, Tulsa, 1982-84; ptnr. Norman, Wohlgemuth & Thompson, Tulsa, 1984-89, Norman Wohlgemuth Chandler & Dowdell, Tulsa, 1989—. Instr. Tulsa Jr. Coll., 1980-83, 86; vis. asst. prof. Univ. Ctr., U. Okla., Tulsa, 1990-97. With U.S. Army, 1968-70. Mem. ABA, Okla. Bar Assn., Tulsa County Bar Assn., Summit Club, Tulsa So. Tennis Club, Phi Alpha Delta. Republican. Episcopalian. Avocations: sailing, tennis, reading. Office: Norman Wohlgemuth Chandler & Dowdell 2900 Mid-Continent Tower Tulsa OK 74103

CHANDLER, WILLIAM HENRY, lawyer; b. Heminway, SC, May 5, 1948; s. William Jackson and Margaret Eloise (Nelson) C.; m. Ann Rodgers Tomlinson, July 31, 1982; children: Jared Witherspoon Nelson, Martha Elizabeth Hartman, Ann Paisley Snowden. AB, U. S.C., 1970, JD, 1973. Bar: S.C. 1973, U.S. Dist. Ct. (we. dist.) La. 1975, U.S. Dist. Ct. S.C. 1973, U.S. Ct. Mil. Appeals 1974. Ptnr. Chandler & Ruffin, Hemingway, S.C., 1978-84, Askins, Chandler, Ruffin & Askins, Hemingway, S.C., 1984—. Instr. bus. law Williamsburg Tech. Coll., Kingstree, S.C., 1978-79, instr. state and local govt., 2002. Vice chmn. Williamsburg County Bd. Trustees, 1979—84, Williamsburg County Devel. Bd.; chmn. The Continuum of Care for Emotionally Disturbed Children, Williamsburg County Planning Commn., 2001—; mem. State Hist. Records Adv. Bd.; pres. Williamsburg Co. Forest Landowners Assn.; chmn. Williamsburg Co. Planning Commn.; supt. ch. sch. First Presbyn. Ch., Bossier City, La., 1975—77; law spkr. Presbytery of the Pines Presbyn. Ch. U.S., Bossier City, 1976—77; ruling elder Indiantown Presbyn. Ch., Hemingway, 1980—; bd. dirs. Francis Marion Coll. Found., Williamsburg County Farm Bur.; vice chmn. Pee Dee Heritage Found.; bd. dirs. Williamsburg Regional Hosp. Found., Lake City Mus.; atty. Town of Stuckey, SC, 1979—. Col. USAF. Mem. ABA, SAR, Am. Legion, S.C. Geneal. Soc., S.C. Libr. Soc., French Higuenot Soc., S.C. Hist. Soc., Williamsburg County Bar Assn., Williamsburg County Hist. Soc. (pres.), Three Rivers Hist. Soc. (pres.), St. Andrews Soc., Charleston Preservation Soc., Lions, Masons (Hemingway), Williamsburg Hometown C.C. (bd. dirs.), Hog Crawl Hunting Club, Wilson Lake Fishing Club, Phi Eta Sigma, Omicron Delta Kappa, Phi Delta Phi. Home: 1949 Henry Rd Hemingway SC 29554 Office: PO Box 10 Hemingway SC 29554

CHANDLER, WILLIAM KNOX, physiologist; b. Chgo., Oct. 13, 1933; s. William Knox and Margaret Belle (Colston) C.; m. Caroline Hardee Teague, June 6, 1957; children— William Knox, Janet Colston, Caroline Louise, Margaret Teague. AB, U. Louisville, 1955, MD, 1959. Postdoctoral fellow Physiol. Lab., Cambridge, Eng., 1962-65; staff asso. Lab. Biophysics, Nat. Inst. Neurol. Diseases and Blindness, Bethesda, Md., 1965-66; asso. prof. physiology Yale U. Sch. Medicine, 1966-72, prof., 1973—. Editor Physiol. Revs, 1968-74, Jour. Physiology, 1974-81, Jour. Gen. Physiology, 1990—. Served with USPHS, 1959-61, 65-66. Mem. NAS, Biophys. Soc., Physiol. Soc., Soc. Gen. Physiologists. Democrat. Home: 594 County Rd Guilford CT 06437-1035 Office: 333 Cedar St New Haven CT 06510-3206 E-mail: knox.chandler@yale.edu.

CHANDO, THEODORE JOHN, research scientist; s. Marion May and Edward Stephen Chando. BS, Rutgers Coll., 1970; MBA, Monmouth U., 1985. Rsch. assoc. E. R. Squibb & Sons Inc., New Brunswick, NJ, 1970—72; biochemist Carter-Wallace Inc., Cranbury, 1980—87; sr. rsch. scientist Bristol-Myers Squibb Inc., Princeton, 1987—. Contbr. articles to profl. jours. Mem.: Am. Assn. Pharm. Scientists, Internat. Soc. Study Xenobiotics. Achievements include research in Studied the biotransformation of numerous xenobiotics, including pravastatin, irbesartan and atazanavir; Performed drug metabolism and toxicology studies on numerous drug candidates; Presented scientific work at national meetings (ASMS, ISSX, AAPS). Avocations: canoeist, naturalist. Office: Bristol-Myers Squibb Inc Rte 206 & Provinceline Rd Princeton NJ 08543 Office Fax: 609-252-6802. E-mail: chandot@bms.com.

CHANDOLA, ANOOP C. educator, writer; b. Pauri, India, Dec. 24, 1937; came to U.S., 1959; s. Satya Prasad and Kishori Devi (Ghildyal) C.; m. Sudha Nautiyal, July 14, 1963; 1 child, Varn. BA, Allahabad Univ., 1954; MA, Lucknow U., India, 1956, U. Calif., Berkeley, 1961; PhD, U. Chgo., 1966. Tutor, lectr. S.V. Patel Univ., Vallabh Vidyanagar, India, 1956-58; lectr. MS Univ. of Baroda, India, 1958-59; asst. prof. U. Ariz., Tucson, 1963-66, assoc. prof., 1967-71, prof. comparative lit. and religions, 1971—. Vis. assoc. prof. U. Calif., Berkeley, summers 1967, 68; vis. prof. U. Tex., 1972, U. Wis., 1973. Author: Folk Drumming in the Himalayas, 1977, Situation to Sentence, 1979, (book)Discovering Brides, 2000, The Second Highest World War, 2002. Ford Found. scholar, U. Chgo., 1961; NSF grantee, 1973. Mem. Assn. for Asian Studies, Am. Anthrop. Assn., Linguistic Soc. Am., Linguistic Soc. India. Hindu. Avocations: yoga exercises, lecturing on hinduism. Home: 6041 N Culebra Tucson AZ 85718

CHANDOR, STEBBINS BRYANT, pathologist; b. Boston, Dec. 18, 1933; s. Kendall Stebbins Bryant and Dorothy (Burrage) C.; m. Mary Carolyn White, May 30, 1959; children: Stebbins Bryant Jr., Charlotte White. BA, Princeton U., 1955; MD, Cornell U., 1960. Diplomate Am. Bd. Pathology. Intern Bellevue Hosp., N.Y.C., 1960-61, resident, 1965-66, Stanford U. Med. Ctr., Palo Alto, Calif., 1962-65; instr. Cornell U., Ithaca, N.Y., 1966; asst. prof. U. So. Calif. Med. Ctr., Los Angeles, 1969-73, assoc. prof., 1974-76, SUNY, Stony Brook, 1976-80; prof., chmn. dept. pathology Marshall U. Sch. Medicine, Huntington, W.Va., 1981-91, assoc. dean for clin. affairs, 1990-91; prof., vice chmn. Sch. Medicine U. So. Calif., L.A., 1991—; pathologist Tripler Army Med Ctr, Honolulu, 1966-69; dir. immunopathology U. So. Calif., Los Angeles County Med. Ctr., 1969-76; dir. clin. lab. Univ. Hosp., Stony Brook, N.Y., 1978-80; dir. JMMS Labs., Huntington, W.Va., 1981-91; dir. labs. U. So. Calif. U. Hosp., L.A., 1991—. Contbr. articles to profl. jours. Pres. San Marino Tennis Found., 1975; governing bd. U. Pathol. Consortium, 1999—. Served to maj. USAR, 1966-69. Decorated Army Commendation medal; recipient Physicians Recognition award AMA, 1983, 86, 89, 93, 99. Fellow Am. Assn. Med. Coll. (exec. coun. 1998—), Am. Soc. Clin. Pathologists (deputy commn. 1993-98, continuing edn., bd. dirs. 1990-96, chair by-law com., 1993-96, chmn. pathology group, 1993-98, v.p. 1997-98, pres. 1999-2000), Coll. Am. Pathologists (state commr. I&A program 1987-91, dist. commr. 1991-99); mem. Calif. Soc. Pathologists (sec.-treas. 1974-75, pres. elect. 1975-76), Assn. Am. Pathologists, W.Va. Assn. Pathologists (pres. 1985-86), Assoc. Pathol. Chmn. Acad. Clin. Lab. Physicians and Scientists (rep. CAS 1991—, adminstrv. bd. 1997—), exec. coun. Am. Assn. Med. Colls. 1998-2000, L.A. Acad. Medicine, Princeton Club, Valley Club (v.p. 1975, bd. dirs. 1993), City Club (v.p. 1988-89, pres. 1989-90), San Gabriel Country Club, Valley Hunt Club, Valley Club of Montecito. Republican. Episcopalian. Home: Apt A 985 S Orange Grove Blvd Pasadena CA 91105-1727 Office: 2011 Zonal Ave Los Angeles CA 90033-1034 E-mail: sbcmcc@aol.com., chandor@usc.edu. *Have fun and make life enjoyable for those around you.*

CHANDRA, ABHIJIT, engineering educator; b. Calcutta, India, Jan. 4, 1957; came to U.S., 1980; s. Ramesh Kumar and Sandhya (Dey) C.; m. Dolly Day, June 4, 1984; children: Koushik, Shoma. B of Tech. with honors, Indian Inst. Tech., Kharagpur, India, 1978; MS, U. N.B., Fredericton, Can., 1980; PhD, Cornell U., 1983. Sr. rsch. engr. GM Rsch. Labs., Warren, Mich., 1983-85; asst. prof. U. Ariz., Tucson, 1985-89, assoc. prof. engring., 1989-95; prof. Mich. Tech. U., Houghton, 1995-99; Engel prof. Iowa State U., Ames, 1999—. Cons. Goodyear Tire and Rubber Co., Akron, Ohio, 1988-89, Advanced Ceramic Rsch., Tucson, 1990-95, ALCOA, Pitts., 1990-95, Thermoanalytics Inc., 1999-2001. Author: Boundary Element Methods in Manufacturing, 1997; guest editor Internat. Jour. Solid Structures, 1994; contbr. over 80 articles to profl. jours. Alexander von Humboldt fellow, 1991; recipient Presdl. Young Investigator award NSF, 1987, Arc Welding Achievement award J. F. Lincoln Arc Welding Found., 1989. Fellow ASME (sec. So. Ariz. sect. 1988-89); mem. SME (Outstanding Paper award 1999), Sigma Xi. Avocations: swimming, skiing, tennis, gardening, fiction writing. E-mail: achandra@iastate.edu.

CHANDRA, PRAMOD, art history educator; b. Varanasi, India, Nov. 2, 1930; came to U.S., 1964; s. Moti and Shanti (Devi) C.; m. Mary Carmen Lynn, 1981; children: Abhijit, Sasanka. BS, Georgetown U., 1951; PhD, U. Bombay, 1964. Asst. curator Prince of Wales Mus. of Western India, Bombay, 1954-60, curator art and archaeol. sects., 1960-64; assoc. prof. U. Chgo., 1964-71, prof., 1971-80; George P. Bickford prof. Indian and South Asian art Harvard U., Cambridge, Mass., 1980—. Founder, dir. Ctr. for Art and Archaeology, Am. Inst. Indian Studies, 1965-71; founder, pres. Am. Com. South Asian Art, 1963-71; hon. advisor on archaeology and mus. Govt. of Madhya Pradesh, India; hon. advisor Govt. of Chattisgarh, 2000--; guest curator Sculpture of India exhbn. Nat. Gallery Art, Washington, 1985. Author: Bundi Painting, 1959, Stone Sculpture in the Allahabad Museum, 1971, Studies in Indian Temple Architecture, 1974, The Cleveland Tuti-nama and the Origins of Mughal Painting, 1976, On the Study of Indian Art, 1983, Sculpture of India 3000 BC-1300 AD, 1985 Recipient Bharat Kala Bhavan award Banaras Hindu U., India; grantee NEH, 1976-80. E-mail: pchandra@fas.harvard.edu.

CHANDRA, VINAY, entrepreneur; b. Opelika, Ala., Mar. 12, 1970; s. Sajjan G and Uma Chandra; m. Nandini Palaniswamy, Jan. 25, 1998. BSEE, BA in Math., Boston U., Boston, MA, 1992. Exec. dir. Orr Cee Electronics, Ltd., Bangalore, India, 1993—94; mng. dir. Reinig Lighting Ltd., Bangalore, India, 1994—96; CTO & COO Sweet Light, Nuernberg, Germany, 1996—2000; pres. Resourcis Info. Svcs, Inc., Atlanta, 2000—. Office: Resourcis Info Svcs Inc 1050 Crown Pointe Pky Ste 1460 Atlanta GA 30338 Office Fax: 770-234-4194. E-mail: vinay@resourcis.com.

CHANDRAMOULI, RAMAMURTI, electrical engineer; b. Oct. 2, 1947; s. Ramamurti and Rajalakshmi (Ramamurti) Krishnamurti; m. Ranjani, Dec. 4, 1980; children: Suhasini, Akila. BSc, Mysore U., 1965, BE, 1970; MEE, Pratt Inst., 1972; PhD, Oreg. State U., 1978. Instr. Oreg. State U., Corvallis, 1978; sr. engr. R & D group, tech. staff spacecraft datasys. sect. Jet Propulsion Lab., Pasadena, Calif., 1978-81; staff engr., design automotive group Am. Microsys. Inc., Santa Clara, Calif., 1982-83; staff software engr. corp. computer-aided design Intel, Santa Clara, 1983-86; project leader computer-aided design Sun Microsys., Mountain View, Calif., 1986-93; tech. mktg. engr. Mentor Graphics, San Jose, Calif., 1993-95; dir. Bist Products Logicvision, San Jose, 1995-98; product line mgr. test products Synopsys, Mountain View, 1998—. Adj. lectr. Calif. State U., Fullerton, 1987—. Sec. South India Cultural Assn., L.A., 1980-81; bd. dirs. Am. Assn. East Indians. Mem. IEEE, IEEE Computer Soc., Sigma Xi, Eta Kappa Nu. Home: 12167 Terrence Ave Saratoga CA 95070-3346 Office: Synopsys 700 E Middlefield Rd Mountain View CA 94043-4033

CHANDRAMOULI, SRINIVASAN (CHANDRA CHANDRAMOULI), management and systems consultant; came to U.S., 1978; s. Veda and Padmavathi Srinivasan; m. Janaki Chandramouli. BS in Math. and Physics, Ferguson Coll., Pune, India, 1973; postgrad., Indian Inst. Tech., New Delhi, 1973-74; MBA in Mktg. and Gen. Mgmt., Indian Inst. Mgmt., Ahmedabad, 1976; MBA in Fin. and Acctg., U. Chgo., 1980. CPA, Ill. Cons. Hindustan Petroleum Corp. Ltd., Bombay, India, 1975; fin. mgr. prodn. Associated Cement Cos., Bombay, 1976-77; cons., researcher The World Bank, Washington, 1979-80; v.p. Am. Mgmt. Systems Inc., Chgo., 1980-99; ptnr. Deloitte Cons., 1999—. Vis. faculty mem. K.C. Coll. Mgmt. U. Bombay, 1976-77. Gen. sec. Jawahar Mitra Mandal, Pune, 1970-74. Fellow Inst. Profl. Acctg. U. Chgo., 1979-80; Open Merit and Nat. Merit scholar Govt. of India U. Poona, 1969-73. Mem. Am. Inst. CPA's, Ill. CPA Soc., Beta Gamma Sigma. Republican. Hindu. Avocations: bridge, chess, tennis. Home: 16118 E Prentice Pl Centennial CO 80015-4172 Office: Deloitte Cons 2868 Prospect Park Dr Suite 400 Sacramento CA 95670

CHANDRAN, LATHA, pediatrician, educator; d. Viswanatha Kurup and Meenakshi Amma; m. Prem Chandran, Nov. 2, 1985; children: Anand, Ashok. MBBS, Kerala U., India, 1984, DGO, 1987; MPH, Johns Hopkins U., 2001. Diplomate Am. Bd. of Pediat., 1992, Am. Bd. of Adolescent Medicine, 1999. Divsn. chief gen. pediat. and adolescent medicine SUNY, Stony Brook, NY, 1995—. Assoc. prof. clin. pediat. U. N.Y., Stony Brook, 1997—. Named Woman of Yr. in Medicine2, Town of Brookhaven, Office of Women's Svcs., 2002. Mem.: Ambulatory Pediat. Assn. (co-chair faculty develop. spl. interest group 2002), Am. Acad. Pediat. Office: Dept Pediatrics HSC T11-080 SUNY at Stony Brook Stony Brook NY 11794-8111 Office Fax: 631-444-6045.

CHANDRANKUNNEL, MATHEW MICHAEL, priest, educator; b. Poonjar, Kerala, India, Feb. 9, 1933; arrived in U.S., 1989; s. Michael Michael Chandrankunnel and Anna Chacko Aikarakunnel. B of Commerce, Sacred Heart Cochin, Kerala, 1955; PhB, Papal Sem., Poona, Mumbai, 1961, ThM, 1965; M of Commerce, Sacred Heart Cochin, Kerala, 1967. Cert. income tax U.S. Prof. commerce St. Thomas Coll., Kerala, 1967—88; rector minor sem. Kashmir Diocese, Jammu, India, 1988—89; Cath. chaplain St. Clare Hosp., N.Y.C., 1990, Englewood Hosp., NJ, 1990—. Author: (book) Cost Accounting, 1981. Avocation: reading. Office: Englewood Hosp Chaplain's Office 350 Engle St Englewood NJ 07631

CHANDRAS, KANANUR V. psychology educator; b. Bangalore, India, Jan. 1, 1935; s. K. and Parvathamma Veerabhadraiah; children: Tara, Kiran, Sunil. BS, Mysore U., Karnataka, India, 1958; MA, Hindu U., 1958; MS, PhD, Southern Ill. U., 1962, 1968; MS, Valdosta State U., 1978, EdS, 1979. Lic. counselor, Ga.; cert. criminal justice specialist; nat. cert. counselor. Prof. edn. McGill U., Montreal, Can., 1968-71; prof. counseling psychology, head dept. Ft. Valley (Ga.) State U., 1972—. Vis. prof. edn. U. Northern Iowa, Cedar Falls, Fla. A&M U., Tallahassee. Author 13 books; contbr. articles to profl. jours.; editl. bd. Jour. Counselor Edn. & Supervision, 1992—, Counseling and Devel. Jour. Recipient numerous awards and honors; Can. Coun. grantee. Mem. AAUP, Am. Counseling Assn., Am. Sch. Counselors Assn., Am. Mental Health Counselors Assn., Assn. Counselor Edn. and Supervision, Mental Health Counselor Assn., Adult Devel. Aging & Counseling Interest Network (chair), Ga. Mental Health Counseling Assn., Internat. Assn. Addictions and Offender Counselors. Office: Ft Valley State U Fort Valley GA 31030 E-mail: chandrak@mail.fvsu.edu.

CHANDRASEKAR, KRISHNAMURTI, economics educator; b. Vellore, Tamil Nadu, India, May 25, 1935; came to U.S., 1959; s. Sattanamjeri Krishnamurti and Kamakshi Sundaradhikshadar; m. Suseela Nagarajan. BA with honors, St. Joseph's Coll., Trichy, Tamil Nadu, India, 1954; MA, Madras (India) U., 1956; PhD, New Sch. Social Rsch., N.Y.C., 1969; cert. urban econs., MIT, 1974. Asst. prof. econs. SUNY, New Paltz, 1964-69; prof. econs. N.Y. Inst. Tech., N.Y.C., 1969—, chair Sch. of Mgmt., 1991, dean Sch. of Mgmt., 1995—96. Vis. prof. Census Bus., U.S. Dept. Commerce, Washington, 1979-80, cons., 1982-87. Pres. Bharathi Soc. N.Am., N.Y.C., 1981-82; trustee Carnatic Music Assn., N.Y.C., 1988-89. Mem. Am. Econ. Assn., AAUP. Home: 5 Westminster Dr Montville NJ 07045-9654 Office: NY Inst Tech 1855 Broadway New York NY 10023-7692

CHANDRASEKARAN, BALAKRISHNAN, computer and information science educator; b. Lalgudi, Tamil Nadu, India, June 20, 1942; came to U.S., 1963; s. Srinivasan and Nagamani Balakrishnan; m. Sandra Mamrak, Oct. 21, 1978; 1 child, Mallika. B in Engring., Madras U., Karaikudi, India, 1963; PhD, U. Pa., 1967. Devel. engr. Smith Kline Instruments, Phila., 1964-65; rsch. specialist Philco-Ford Corp., Blue Bell, Pa., 1967-69; asst. prof. computer and info. sci. Ohio State U., Columbus, 1969-71, assoc. prof., 1971-77, prof., 1977-95; sr. rsch. scientist, 1995—; dir. Lab. for Artificial Intelligence Rsch., Columbus, 1983—. Co-chmn. Symposium on Potentials and Limitations of Mech. Intelligence, Anaheim, Calif., 1971; chmn. Norbert Wiener Symposium, Boston, 1974; sci. dir. Summer Sch. on Computer Program Testing, SOGESTA, Urbino, Italy, 1981; vis. scientist Lawrence Livermore Nat. Lab., Livermore, Calif., summer 1981, cons. fall 1981; vis. scientist MIT Computer Sci. Lab., 1983; dir. NIH Artificial Intelligence in Medicine Workshop, 1984; organizer panel discussion on artificial intelligence and engring. ASME, 1985; vis. scholar Stanford U., 1990-91; keynote spkr. World Congress on Expert Sys., Mexico City, 1998, Internat. Conf. on Diagrammic Reasoning, Callaway Gardens, Ga., 2002. Editor: Diagrammatic Reasoning, 1995; co-editor Computer Program Testing, 1981; editor ACM Sigart Spl. Issue on Structure, Function, and Behavior, 1985; assoc. editor Artificial Intelligence in Engring., 1986—; mem. bd. editors Internat. Jour. Pattern Recognition & Artificial Intelligence, Med. Expert Systems, Artificial Intelligence in Engring.; assoc. editor Internat. Jour. Human-Computer Interactions, 1996—. Recipient Outstanding Paper award Pattern Recognition Soc., 1976; Moore fellow U. Pa., 1964-67. Fellow IEEE (editor-in-chief Expert Jour. 1990-94), Am. Assn. for Artificial Intelligence (chmn. workshops on diagrammatic reasoning 1992), Assn. for Computing Machinery; mem. Sys. Man and Cybernetics Soc. IEEE (v.p. 1974-75, pattern recognition com. 1969-72, assoc. editor Trans. 1973—, guest editor spl. issue on distributed program solving 1981). Democrat. Avocation: travel. Home: 2053 Iuka Ave Columbus OH 43201-1415 Office: Ohio State U Dept Computer and Info Sci 2015 Neil Ave Columbus OH 43210-1210 E-mail: chandra@cis.ohio-state.edu.

CHANDRASEKHAR, SUJANA S. surgeon, otologist/neurotologist; 3 children. BS cum laude, City Coll. N.Y., 1984; MD, Mt. Sinai Sch. Medicine, N.Y.C., 1986. Intern, residency otolaryngology NYU Med. Ctr., 1986—92; fellow in otolaryngology/neurology Ho. Ear Inst., La., 1993; from asst. to assoc. prof. UMDNJ-N.J. Med. Sch., Newark, 1994—2001, dir. otology/neurotology, 2001—; assoc. prof. otolaryngology Mt. Sinai Sch. Medicine, N.Y.C., 2001—. Dir. otology/neurotology Mt. Sinai Med. Ctr., N.Y.C., 2001—, dir. cochlear implant program, 2001—. Recipient Honor award, AMA, 2000, Am. Acad. Otolaryngology-Head and Neck Surgery, 2002. Office: Mount Sinai School-Medicine 8th Fl Box 1191 5 East 98th St New York NY 10029 Office Fax: 212-427-4088.

CHANDY, MAMMEN G. surgeon; b. Bangalore, India, Sept. 14, 1941; s. George and Mary (Mammen) C.; m. Laila Abraham, June 7, 1971. MBBS, Christian Med. Coll.-Madras U., India, 1963, MS, 1970. Diplomate Am. Bd. Surgery. Intern Christian Med. Coll.-Madras U., Vellore, India, 1964-65; resident in surgery Boston City Hosp., 1971-74, SUNY, Stony Brook, 1974-76; fellow in surgery Penin Hosp. Ctr.-SUNY, Stony Brook, 1976-77, USAF Med. Ctr., 1979-89; pvt. practice Oroville Calif. Mem. staff Oroville Cmty. Hosp. Fellow ACS. Republican. Office: MD FACS 2721 Olive Hwy Ste 4 Oroville CA 95966-6115

CHANDY, RAJESH K. business educator; b. Ernakulam, India, Oct. 2, 1969; came to U.S., 1990; s. Koshy and Rachel Chandy; m. Pattana Thaivanich, Mar. 2, 1996. B in Engring., Madurai Kamaraj U., Madurai, India, 1990; MBA, U. Okla., 1992; PhD, U. So. Calif., 1996. Vis. asst. prof. UCLA, 1996-97; asst. prof. bus., Melcher Faculty fellow U. Houston, 1997-2000; asst. prof. U. Minn., 2000—. Contbr. articles to profl. jours. Named Young Scholar, Mktg. Sci. Inst., 2003; recipient Alden Clayton award, 1995; grantee, Inst. Study Bus. Mkts., 1995. Mem. Am. Mktg. Assn. (Harold H. Maynard award for contbn. to mktg. theory and thought 2000), Acad. Mktg. Sci. (Mary Kay award 1998), Inst. Mgmt. Scis., Acad. Mgmt. Avocations: travel, reading. Office: U Minn 3-150 Carlson Sch of Mgmt 327 19th Ave S Minneapolis MN 55455 E-mail: rchandy@csom.umn.edu.

CHANEN, STEVEN ROBERT, lawyer; b. Phoenix, May 15, 1953; s. Herman and Lois Marion (Boshes) C. Student, UCLA, 1971-73; BS in Mass Communications, Ariz. State U., 1975, JD, 1979. Bar: Ariz. 1980, U.S. Dist. Ct. Ariz. 1980, U.S. Ct. Appeals (9th cir.) 1980, Calif. 1981, U.S. Dist. Ct. (no. dist.) Calif. 1982. Ptnr. Wentworth & Lundin, Phoenix, 1980-86, of counsel, 1986-87; pres. Chanen Constrn. Co., Inc., 1991—. Appointed bd. dirs. Ariz. Gov.'s Commn. on Motion Pictures and TV, 1986, chmn., 1990; fin. intermediary, chmn. bd. dirs. S.R. Chanen and Co, Inc.; pres. Media Tech. Capital Corp., 1987-91; bd. dirs. ILX, Inc.; pres., bd. dirs. Electronic Mail Sys. Inc. Bd. dirs. Anytown, Am., Phoenix, 1986—, COMPAS, Inc., Phoenix, 1986-92, Ariz. Sci. Ctr., Phoenix, 1987—, Mus. Theater Ariz., Phoenix, 1988-89, Ariz. Politically Interested Citizens; pres. bd. dirs. Cmty. Forum, Phoenix; bd. dirs. Phoenix Children's Hosp., Nat. Conf., Maricopa County C.C. Dist. Found. (pres.). Recipient J. Leonard Amdur Man of the Year award, Herberger Humanitarian of Yr. award, Ariz. Humane Soc., 2000, Leader of Distinction award, Anti-Defamation League. Mem. ABA (forum com. entertainment and sports industries 1981—), Ariz. Bar Assn., Calif. Bar Assn., Maricopa County Bar Assn., Assn. Trial Lawyers Am. Republican. Jewish. Office: 3300 N 3rd Ave Phoenix AZ 85013-4304

CHANES, JEROME ALAN, non-profit organization administrator, public affairs analyst; b. N.Y.C., Mar. 29, 1943; s. Manuel S. and Berta (Gottlieb) C.; m. Eva Fogelman, June 19, 1988. BA, Yeshiva U., 1964, MSW, 1974; postgrad., Columbia U., 1966-68, Brandeis U., 1974-76. Nat. affairs dir. Nat. Jewish Community Rels. Adv. Coun., N.Y.C., 1983-96; assoc. dir. Nat. Found. Jewish Culture, N.Y.C., 1996—2001. Adj. prof. sociology, Barnard Coll., N.Y.C., 2000—, Stern Coll., N.Y.C., 2002—; adj. prof. Jewish communal issues Wurzweiler Sch. Social Work, Yeshiva U., N.Y.C., 1990—; adj. prof. Jewish sociology, Azrieli Grad. Sch. Yeshiwa U., 2003—; rsch. fellow Ctr. for Jewish Studies, CUNY Grad. Ctr.; founding chmn. Project Ezra. Author: Antisemitism in America Today, 1995, A Profile of the American Jewish Community, 1998, Dark Side of History: Antisemitism through the Ages, 1999, A Primer on the American Jewish Community, 2000, Antisemitism: A Reference Guide; contbr. articles to profl. jours., chpts. to books. Benjamin Hornstein fellow, 1974. Mem. PEN. Home: 60 Riverside Dr Apt 11G New York NY 10024-6170 E-mail: jchanes@barnard.edu.

CHANEY, BRADFORD WILLIAM, educational research consultant; b. LA, Sept. 4, 1953; s. Robert H. and Lorna M. (Forbes) C.; m. Heidi Suzanne Heath, Mar. 14, 1987; children: Nathan Richard, Carl Edward. BA in Polit. Sci. and Math., U. Calif., Riverside, 1975; MA in Polit. Sci., U. Rochester, 1978, PhD in Polit. Sci., 1981. Asst. prof. polit. sci. Washington Coll., Chestertown, Md., 1981-82; sr. policy analyst Applied Mgmt. Scis., Silver Spring, Md., 1983-86; sr. study dir. Westat, Rockville, Md., 1986—. Trustee Roberts Wesleyan Coll., Rochester, N.Y., 1988-92. Contbr. articles to Ednl. Evaluation and Policy Analysis. Mem. Am. Ednl. Rsch. Assn. Republican. Achievements include research in areas of mathematics and science education, policy evaluation, and other education related areas. Office: Westat 1650 Research Blvd Rockville MD 20850-3195 E-mail: BradChaney@westat.com.

CHANEY, DON, professional basketball coach; b. Baton Rouge, Mar. 22, 1946;. U. Houston, Houston, TX. Player Boston Celtics, Boston, 1968-75, Los Angeles Clippers, Los Angeles, CA, 1976-77, Boston Celtics, Boston, 1978-80; asst. coach Detroit Pistons, Detroit, 1980-83, San Diego, Los Angeles Clippers, 1983-85; head coach Los Angeles Clippers, Los Angeles, CA, 1985-87; asst. coach Atlanta Hawks, Atlanta, 1987-88; head coach Houston Rockets, Houston, 1988-92, Detroit Pistons, Auburn Hills, Mich., 1993-95; asst. coach N.Y. Knicks, 1996—, head coach, 2001—. Named Coach of Year NBA, 1991. Office: NY Knicks Two Pennsylvania Plz New York NY 10121

CHANEY, SHARON HENDERSON, secondary education educator, consultant; b. Fayetteville, Tenn., July 16, 1948; d. Eugene Wilson and Avis Marie (Tomerlin) Henderson; m. Carl William Chaney, Dec. 26, 1970; children: Daniel Eugene, Carl David. BA, Belmont U., Nashville, 1970; MA in Edn., Austin Peay State U., Clarksville, Tenn., 1975; EdD, Vanderbilt U., 1991. Cert. tchr. English and Latin, secondary prin., Tenn.; cert. Nat. Bd. Profl. Tchg. Stds., 1999. Tchr. English and French, Springfield (Tenn.) H.S., 1971-76; tchr. English, Latin and French, Goodlettsville (Tenn.) H.S., 1983-86; tchr. advanced placement English and writing Hunters Lane Comprehensive H.S., Nashville, 1986—2002, internat. baccalaureate coord., 1999—. Adj. faculty Peabody/Vanderbilt U., Nashville, 1990-95, Belmont U., 1987-96; mem. writing assessment scoring com. State of Tenn., Nashville, 1994—; mem. adv. coun. on tchr. edn./cert. State Bd. Edn., Nashville, 1995—; cons., reader, table leader, presenter Coll. Bd. So. Regional Office, Atlanta, 1995—; facilitator trainee Nat. Bd. for Profl. Tchg. Standards, 1997, state mentor, 2000—; manuscript reviewer English Jour., 1993—. Contbr. articles to profl. jours. Pianist, Inglewood Bapt. Ch., Nashville, 1990-95; mem. choir First Bapt. Ch., Downtown, Nashville, 1995—. Recipient Milken Found. Nat. Educator award, 1999; named Tchr. of Yr., Springfield H.S., 1976, Goodlettsville H.S., 1986, Hunters Lane H.S., 1990-91, Metro Secondary Tchr. of Yr., Met. Pub. Schs., Nashville, 1991, Career Ladder III, State of Tenn., 1986—. Mem.: Nashville Coun. Tchrs. English (pres., newsletter editor), Tenn. Coun. Tchrs. English (bd. dirs., pres. 1997—98, Award for Excellence in Tchg. English 1994), Nat. Coun. Tchrs. English (local arrangements conv. chmn. 1997—98, mem. resolution com. 2003, High Sch. Tchr. of Excellence award 2001), Alpha Delta Kappa (state rec. sec. 1998—2000, assoc. chair secondary sect. steering com. 2000—, chpt. pres., state membership com.), Delta Kappa Gamma (chpt. pres., Golden Gift Leadership Mgmt. Sem. 1997, Distinctive Svc. to Edn. award 2000). Avocations: swimming, piano, travel, reading, writing. Home: 4315 Grandville Blvd Nashville TN 37207-1021 E-mail: drschaney@juno.com.

CHANEY, VERNE EDWARD, JR., surgeon, foundation executive, educator; b. Kansas City, Mo., July 16, 1923; s. Verne Edward and Adelaide (Hafner) C.; divorced; children: Christopher Edward, Steven Wood. BS, Va. Mil. Inst., 1951; MD, Johns Hopkins U., 1948, M.P.H., 1972; DSc (hon.), U. N.C., 2002. Diplomate: Am. Bd. Surgery, Am. Bd. Thoracic and Cardiac Surgery. Intern surgery Johns Hopkins U. Hosp., 1948-49, asst. resident 1949-50, instr. anatomy, 1950-53; surg. resident N.C. Meml. Hosp., Chapel Hill, 1953-56; chief of surgery Albert Schweitzer Hosp., Deschappeles, Haiti, 1956-58; practice medicine specializing in thoracic surgery Monterey, Calif., 1958-61; pres. and founder Intermed Internat. Inc. (formerly Thomas A. Dooley Found.-INTERMED, Inc.), N.Y.C., 1961—; clin. prof. surgery U. Miami, 1976—, clin. prof. epidemiology and pub. health, 1977—; founder, pres. INTERMED, Geneva, 1976—. Patentee in field. Served from pvt. to capt. M.C. U.S. Army, 1944, 50-52. Decorated Silver Star medal; decorated Bronze Star medal with V, Purple Heart U.S., Croix de Guerre France, Order of Million Elephants Laos; recipient Disting. Svc. award Sch. Medicine U. North Carolina, 1991. Fellow ACS, Am. Coll. Chest Physicians; mem. N.Y. State Med. Soc., N.Y. Acad. Medicine, Am. Pub. Health Assn., Internat. Health Soc. (pres. 1987-88), Nathan A. Womack Surg. Soc., Internat. Soc. Surgeons, Nat. Soc. Fund Raising Execs., Explorers Club. Clubs: N.Y. Athletic, Sky, West Side Tennis. Republican. Episcopalian. Home: 530 E 72nd St Apt 16E New York NY 10021-4863 Office: Dooley Found Intermed 420 Lexington Ave Rm 2331 New York NY 10170-2332

CHANEY, VINCENT VERLANDO, b. Elkins, W. Va., June 12, 1913; s. Thomas H. and Anna Gertrude (Merge) Chaney; m. Caroline O'Neale, Feb. 5, 1939; 1 child, Malcolm L.;1 child, Michael Thomas. BA, W. Va. U., 1936; JD, 1938. Bar: W. Va. 1938, US Dist. Ct. (so. dist.) 1938, US Dist. Ct. (no. dist.)/W. Va. 1938, US Ct. Apls. (4th cir.). Assoc. Kay, Casto & Amos, 1938—50; ptnr. Kay Casto & Chaney, Charleston, W.Va., from 1950; sec., gen. counsel, dir. Ray Resources Corp., Charleston, W.Va., 1969—75, Mountaineer Gas Co., Charleston, from 1984; dir. Allegheny & western Energy Corp., Charleston, from 1981; mem. inspection teams USIA, Venezuela, 1971, 1974, 1976, 1976, US Internat. Comm. Agy., Hong Kong, China, 1978. 1st. lt. to lt. col. AUS, 1941—46. Fellow Am. Bar Found. Mem.: W. Va. Law Rev. (mem. 1936—38), Order of Coif, W. Va. U. Alumni Assn. (exec. council 1965—72, pres. 1971—72), Am. Arbitration Assn. (panel from 1972), Am. Law Inst., Am. Judicature Soc., Kanawha County Bar Assn., W. Va. State Bar (bd. gov. 1956—62, pres. 1962—63), W. Va. Bar Assn., ABA, W. Va. U. Coll. Law (vis. com. 1980—84), Kanawha Valley Dental Health Found. (mem. 1965—70), Charleston Area Med. Ctr. (trustee from 1972, chmn. bd. 1975—78), Sunrise Ctr. and Mus. (bd. dir. 1972—74), Edgewood Country, Phi Beta Kappa. Democrat. Home: Charleston, W.Va. Died 1997.

CHANEY, WILLIAM ALBERT, historian, educator; b. Arcadia, Calif., Dec. 23, 1922; s. Horace Pierce and Esther (Bowen) C. AB, U. Calif., Berkeley, 1943, PhD, 1961. Mem. faculty Lawrence U., Appleton, Wis., 1952-99, George McKendree Steele prof. Western culture, 1966-99, Steele prof. emeritus, 1999—, chmn. dept. history, 1968-71, 95-96. Vis. prof. Mich. State U., summer 1958. Author: The Cult of Kingship in Anglo-Saxon England: The Transition from Paganism to Christianity, 1970, reprinted 1999; contbr. articles to profl. jours. and encys. Jr. fellow Harvard Soc. Fellows, 1949-52; grantee Am. Council Learned Socs., 1966-67. Fellow Royal Soc. Arts; mem. MLA, AAUP, Am. Hist. Assn., Mediaeval Acad. Am., Am. Soc. Ch. History, Conf. Brit. Studies, Archeol. Inst. Am. Episcopalian. Home: 215 E Kimball St Appleton WI 54911-5720 Office: Lawrence Univ Dept History Appleton WI 54912

CHANG, ALFRED EDWARD, surgeon; b. Hornell, N.Y., 1950; MD, Harvard U., 1974. Diplomate Am. Bd. Surgery. Intern Duke U. Med. Ctr., Durham, N.C., 1974-75, resident in surgery, 1975-76, Hosp. U. Pa., Phila., 1979-82; fellow in surg. oncology Nat. Cancer Inst., Bethesda, Md., 1976-79; mem. staff U. Mich. Med. Ctr., Ann Arbor, 1988—. Prof. U. Mich., 1992—. Fellow ACS; mem. Am. Assn. Immunologists, Am. Assn. Cancer Rsch., am. Soc. Clin. Oncology, Soc. Surg. Oncology. Office: U Mich Med Ctr 3302 Cancer Ctr 1500 E Medical Center Dr Ann Arbor MI 48109-0005

CHANG, CHAWNSHANG, science educator, laboratory administrator; b. Taichung, Taiwan, Nov. 26, 1955; came to U.S., 1980; s. Su-In Chang and Tsu-Hon Chang-Ko; m. Amly Liu, June 12, 1980; children: Eugene, Philip. BS, Nat. Taiwan U., Taipei, 1974-78; PhD, U. Chgo., 1985. Asst. prof. prostate cancer/male hormone action U. Chgo., 1988-90; asst. prof. U. Wis., Madison, 1990—93, assoc. prof., 1993-96, prof., 1996—97; George Whipple prof. U. Rochester, N.Y., 1997—. Patentee androgen receptor gene; contbr. articles to profl. publs. Chairperson Taiwanese Student Assn., U. Chgo., 1984-85. Lt. Taiwanese Army, 1978-80. Andrew Mellon Found. fellow, 1989-90; recipient Jr. Faculty award Am. Cancer Soc., Atlanta, 1990—, Pres. award Taiwan Urology Assn., 1999, Pres. award Taiwan Osteoporesis Assn., 1999. Fellow Japan Archology Soc. (hon.); mem. Am. Assn. for Cancer Rsch., The Endocrine Soc. (Ayerst Travel award 1988). Avocations: table tennis, volleyball, music, swimming. Home: 19 Sandy Ln Pittsford NY 14534-1078 Office: U Rochester Dept Urology 601 Elmwood Ave Rochester NY 14642 E-mail: chang@urmc.rochester.edu.

CHANG, CHRIS C.N. physician, pediatric surgeon; b. Taiwan, China, June 20, 1943; s. Shu-Ming and Yu-Bow (Chow) C.; m. Rose Lee Chang, Mar. 4, 1972; children: Lynda, Steven. MD, Nat. Taiwan U., 1969. Intern Nat. Taiwan Univ. Hosp., 1968-69, resident in surgery, 1970-72, Albert Einstein Med. Ctr., Phila., 1972-76; resident in pediat. surgery St. Christopher's Hosp. for Children, Phila., 1976-78; dir. pediat. surgery Lehigh Valley Hosp., Allentown, Pa., 1993—. Fellow ACS, Internat. Coll. Surgeons, Am. Acad. Pediats.; mem. Am. Pediat. Surg. Assn. Office: Chop Specialty Care Ctr LV 2545 Schoenersville Rd Bethlehem PA 18017-7300 Fax: 484-884-3300.

CHANG, CLARENCE DAYTON, retired chemist; b. Tianjin, China, Mar. 8, 1933; came to U.S., 1939; s. Hsueh Tseng and Lucy Chang; m. Cheryl Schucker, June 28, 1958 (div. 1987); 1 child, Christopher E.; m. Elizabeth C. O'Donoghue, June 28, 1987; 1 child, Stephen D. AB, Harvard U., 1954. Project chemist Weyerhaeuser Co., Longview, Wash., 1954-55, Sugar Rsch. Found., N.Y.C., 1955-61; supr. M.W. Kellogg Co., Piscataway, N.J., 1961-70; sr. rsch. chemist Mobil R & D Corp., Princeton, N.J., 1970-74, rsch. assoc., 1974-81, rsch. scientist, 1981-84, sr. scientist, 1984-95, Mobil Tech. Co., Paulsboro, N.J., 1995-2000. Author: Hydrocarbons from Methanol, 1983; editor: Methane Conversion, 1988; also articles; over 200 U.S. patents in field. Pem. Catalysis Soc. (excellence in catalysis award 1984), Am. Chem. Soc. (E.V. Murphree award 1992), Chinese-Am. Chem. Soc. (bd. dirs. 1993), N.Am. Catalysis Soc. (E.J. Houdry award 1999). E-mail: cdchang@nji.com.

CHANG, DANIEL PAN YIH, environmental engineering educator; b. Shanghai, Mar. 25, 1947; m. Pauline Amber Wong, Aug. 23, 1969; 2 children. BS, Calif. Tech. Inst., 1968, MS, 1969, PhD, 1973. Asst. prof. U. Calif., Davis, 1973-81, assoc. prof., 1981-87, prof., 1987—, vice-chairperson, 1991-93, chairperson, 1998—, Ray B. Krone prof. engring. Appointed mem. rsch. screening com. Calif. Air Resources Bd., Sacramento, 1980-84; reviewer Innovative Clean Air Tech., 1990—. Contbr. over 120 articles to profl. jours. 2d lt. USAF, 1973. Grantee U.S. EPA, Calif. Air Resources Bd., NSF, Calif. Competitive Tech. Program, Calif. Dept. Commerce, 1991-92, Nat. Inst. Environ. Health Scis., Dept. Def. Mem. Air and Waste Mgmt. Assn. (bd. dirs. Mother Lode chpt. 1989-92), Am. Chem. Soc., Sigma Xi. Office: U Calif Dept Civil & Environ Engrs Davis CA 95616

CHANG, DARWIN RAY, civil engineer; b. Jukao, Kiangsu, China, Aug. 1, 1917; came to U.S., 1945, naturalized, 1962; s. Wey and Susan (Hsiong) C.; m. Yen Ma, Dec. 23, 1961; children: Gordon, Susan, Martha, Leslie. BS, Chiao Tung U., Shanghai, China, 1940; MCE, Cornell U., 1946. Structural engr. Borsari Tank Corp., N.Y.C., 1951; project engr. Ebasco Internat. Corp., N.Y.C. 1956-60; prin. engr. Pub. Svc. Electric and Gas Co., Newark, 1960-80; mktg. mgr. Lehigh Utility Assos., Inc., South Plainfield, N.J., 1981-83; pres. D and Y Chang Enterprises Inc.; 1980—. Bd. visitors Drew U. Mem. N.J. Soc. Profl. Engrs., Chinese Inst. Engrs., Cornell Club of N.Y., Rotary. Presbyterian. Contbr. articles on esthetic transmission structures to trade mags. Home: 108 Green Ave Madison NJ 07940-2534 Office: 24 Main St Madison NJ 07940-1818

CHANG, DAVID, orthopaedic surgeon; b. Pontiac, Mich., Oct. 29, 1970; s. Victor F. S. and Mary Chu Chang; m. Marisol Fernandez Loresto, Feb. 14, 2000; children: Trinity, Christian. BA, MA, Boston U., 1988—92; MD, Pa. State U., Hershey, Pa., 1992—96. Intern LAC + USC, Los Angeles, Calif., 1996—97; resident San Francisco Orthopaedic Residency Program, San Francisco, 1998—2002; sports med. phys. Calif. State U., Dominguez Hills, Calif., 2002—03. Faculty rep. Pa. State U. Coll. Medicine, Hershey, Pa., 1995—96; student interviewer Boston U., Boston, 1991—92. V.p. Am. Med. Student Assn., Hershey, 1994—95. Recipient Undergraduate Rsch. award, Boston U., 1992, Cancer Fedn. award, 1992, Golden Key, National Honor Soc., 1992. Mem.: Calif. Orthopaedic Assn., Am. Acad. of Orthopaedic Surgeons, Alpha Epsilon Delta (pres. 1990—91).

CHANG, EDWARD H. computer company executive; b. Taipei, Taiwan, Jan. 10, 1958; came to U.S., 1975; s. James T. and Yu-Chin Chang. BA, U. Hawaii, 1981. Cert. Inst. for Cert. Bus. Counselor. Mktg. dir. Prometheus World Enterprise, Santa Ana, Calif., 1983-88; gen. mgr. Trans PC, Inc., Norwalk, Calif., 1989-91; v.p. consumer products Microtome, Inc., St. Louis, 1992-95; exec. dir. Lotus Profl., L.A., Calif., 1996—. Exec. dir. EKM Computer, Inc., Buena Park, Calif., 1997-99, LPS Telemgmt., L.A., 1995—. Bd. dirs. Vairotsana Found., pres., 1996-98. Buddhist. Achievements include co-patent for system and apparatus for electronic communication. Office: Lotus Profl Media Tower II Rm 411 1600 Taft Ave Los Angeles CA 90028-3706 E-mail: edward8888@aol.com.

CHANG, FENIA I-FEN, music educator, pianist; arrived in U.S., 1984; d. Kwong-Fu and Yun-Ying Chang; m. Yin Eugene Shen, Oct. 7, 2000; 1 child, Warren Shen. MusB, Julliard Sch., NYC, 1987, MusM, 1989; Mus D, U. Md., Coll. Pk., 1996. Staff accompanist Julliard Sch., NYC, 1985—89; instr. of piano Soo-Chow U., Taipei, Taiwan, 1990—91; tchg. asst. U. Md., Coll. Pk., 1992—96; asst. prof. piano Washington Bible Coll., Lanham, Md., 1995—96, Taipei City Normal Coll., Taiwan, 1997—2001, Tex. A&M U., Commerce, 2002—. Mem. competition jury Taipei City Piano Competition, Taiwan, 1997, 2000, Taiwan Nat. Piano Competition, 1997, 99, 2001, Hunt Country Keyboard Festival, Commerce, Tex., 2003—. Recipient 1st prize, Elizabeth Davis Internat. Competition, 1984, LI Piano Competition, 1985, 2nd prize, Frinna Awerbuch Competition, 1989. Mem.: Hunt Country Music Tchrs. Assn. (v.p. 2002—), Friday Morning Music Club. Office: Tex A&M Univ-Commerce PO Box 3011 Commerce TX 75429-3011 E-mail: feniac@hotmail.com.

CHANG, GAIL CATHRYN MAY, music educator; b. Hamilton, Can., Mar. 31, 1951; d. Dean Ralston and Beatrice May Gordon; m. Brad Hsien-Ming Chang, Nov. 11, 1971; children: Kevin Da-An, Brian Da-Hir, Karen Da-An. MusB, Ariz. State U, 1969—73, MusM, 1974—76. Music tchr. Cartwright Elem. Sch., Phoenix, 1992—99; music instr. Maricopa Coll., Avondale, Ariz., 1997—2000; piano instr. A-Z Sch. For The Arts, Phoenix, 1999—2002. Nat. com. Composition MENC Benchmarks, 1997—. Composer numerous musical compositions. Master: Autistic Tchr. Nat. Assn. (assoc.); mem.: Music Educators Nat. Conf., Am. String Tchr. Assn. (assoc.). Christian. Home: 2008 N 57 Drive Phoenix AZ 85035 Office: 2008 N 57 Drive Phoenix AZ 85035

CHANG, GENE HSIN, economics educator, humanities educator; b. Shanghai, Feb. 22, 1952; came to U.S., 1982. s. Huaisheng Chang and Jiahui Huang; m. Kathryn Jinmei Chang, Aug. 12, 1985; children: Elaine, Emily. BA, Fudan U., Shanghai, 1982; MA, U. Calif., Berkeley, 1984; PhD, U. Mich., 1989. Asst. prof. U. Toledo, 1989-92, assoc. prof., 1995—2003, prof., 2003—, dir. Asian Studies Inst., 1997—. Vis. prof. Fudan U., China. Editor: China Economic Reform, 1991; co-editor China Econ. Rev., 1997—; contbr. articles to profl. jours., chpts. to books. Wheeler fellow U. Calif., Berkeley, 1983-84, Rackham fellow U. Mich., Ann Arbor, 1988-89 Mem. Am. Econ. Assn., Assn. Asian Studies, Assn. for Comparative Econ. Studies, Chinese Economist Soc. (bd. dirs. 1985-88, pres. 1990-91). Avocations: ping-pong, reading.

CHANG, HEEWON, education educator, Electronic Journal Editor; b. Seoul, Korea (South), Aug. 1, 1959; d. Chin Ho Chang, Eui Sook Cho; m. Klaus Ernst Manfred Volpert; children: Hannah Volpert, Peter Volpert. Ph. D. in Anthropology and Education, University of Oregon, Eugene, Oregon, 1984—89, M. A. in Anthropology and Education, 1982—84; B. A. in Education, Yonsei University, Seoul, Korea, 1978—82. Instr. U. of Oreg., Eugene, Oreg., 1987; pvt. practice Wayne, Pa., 1990—98; instr. Ursinus Coll., Collegeville, Pa., 1994; asst. prof. Eastern U., St. Davids, Pa., 1997—. Director, The M. Ed. in Multicultural Education Program Eastern University, St. Davids, PA, 1999—2002; Korean Language & Culture Consultant self-employed, Wayne, PA, 1990—98. Author: (Book) Adolescent Life and Ethos: An Ethnography of a US High School, 1992; editor-in-chief: Electronic Mag. of Multicultural Edn., 1998—; contbr. articles to profl. jours. Elder Bryn Mawr Presbyterian Church, Bryn Mawr, PA, 1999—2002. Mem.: The Pa. Assn. Colls. and Tchr. Educators, Am. Ednl. Rsch. Assn., Am. Anthrop. Assn. (com. chmn. 1999—2002), Kappa Delta Pi. Presbyterian. Avocation: singing, ice skating, traveling, reading, and cooking. Office: Eastern University 1300 Eagle Road Saint Davids PA 19087 Business E-Mail: hchang@eastern.edu.

CHANG, HELEN CHUNG-HUNG HSIANG, piano pedagogy specialist; b. Shanghai, July 20, 1937; d. Shou-Tsu Edward and Chen-Tze Kiang Hsiang; m. Nai Lin Chang; children: Tai Deborah, Huan Justina, Lan Samantha, Ling Patricia. BA cum laude, Mt. Mercy Coll., Cedar Rapids, Iowa, 1960; BMus cum laude, Lawrence U., 1980; postgrad. in pedagogical study, Am. Suzuki Inst., Stevens Point, Wis., 1972, 83, 88-89. Cert. tchr. Music Tchrs. Nat. Assn., Wis. Music Tchr. Assn., Suzuki Assn. of the Ams. Co-chair Fox Valley Keyboard Tchrs., Appleton, Wis., 1981-82, chair, 1982-83, treas., 1996-97; recital chair Suzuki Edn. Assn. of the Fox Valley, Appleton, 1984-96. Judge regional competitions Wis. Music Tchrs. Assn., 1988-97, state competition, 1994, 95, others, coach numerous students. Mem. Northeast Wis. Chinese Assn. (Chinese lang. instr. 1972-76), Wis. Music Tchrs. Assn (award of excellence 1981, 94, 99, 2003), Music Tchr. Nat. Assn., Suzuki Assn. of the Ams., Suzuki Assn. of Wis.

CHANG, HENRY C. library administrator; b. Canton, China, Sept. 15, 1941; came to U.S., 1964, naturalized, 1973; s. Ih-ming and Lily (Lin) C.; m. Marjorie Li, Oct. 29, 1966; 1 dau., Michelle. LL.B., Nat. Chengchi U., 1962; MA, U. Mo., 1966; MA in L.S, U. Minn., 1968; PhD, 1974. Reader advisor Braille Inst. Am., Los Angeles, 1965-67; reference librarian U. Minn., Mpls., 1968-70, instr., librarian, 1970-72, asst. head govt. document div., 1972-74; library dir., lectr. in social scis. U. of the V.I., St. Croix, 1974-75; dir. div. libraries, museums and archeol. services, 1975-88; dir. V.I. Library Tng. Inst., 1975-76; coordinator, chmn. V.I. State Hist. Records Adv. Bd., 1976-88; pres., libr. cons., 1988-89; dir. libr. svcs. Braille Inst. Am., L.A., 1990—. Chmn. microfilm com. ACURIL, 1977-88; coordinator V.I. Gov.'s Library Adv. Council, 1975-87; mem. V.I. Bicentennial Commn., 1975-77, Ft. Frederik Commn., 1975-76; mem. adv. com. on research tng. Caribbean Research Inst., 1974-75; coordinator Library Conf., 1977-87; project dir. cultural heritage project Nat. Endowment for Humanities, 1979-83; chmn. nat. collection devel. com. nat. libr. svcs. Libr. of Congress, 1998, chmn. western conf. group, 2001--. Author: A Bibliography of Presidential Commissions, Committees, Councils, Panels and Task Forces, 1961-72, 1973, Taiwan Democraphy, 1964-71: A Selected Annotated Bibliography of Government Documents, 1973, A Selected Annotated Bibliography of Caribbean Bibliographies in English, 1975, A Survey of the Use of Microfilms in the Caribbean, 1978, Long-Range Program for Library Development, 1978, Institute for Training in Library Management and Communications Skill, 1979; contbr. numerous articles and book revs. on libr. sci. to profl. jours. Chmn. bd. dirs. Eden Found. for People with Disabilities, 1995-98. 2d lt. Taiwan Army, 1962-63. Recipient Libr. Adminstrs. Devel. Program fellowship award, 1972, Cert. of Appreciation, Govt. V.I., 1985, Eden Found., 1999, L.A. Internat. Lions Club award, 1992, 95, Driver Safety award, 1993, Cert. of Achievement, Braille Inst., 2001; named Mem. Staff of Yr., Coll. V.I., 1974-75; Nat. Commn. on Librs. and Info. Sci. grantee. Mem. ALA (counselor 1980-84), AAUP, Asian Pacific ALA (chmn. fin. com. 1993-96), Population Assn. Am., Am. Sociol. Assn., Chinese Am. Profl. Soc. Home: 3713 Lowry Rd Los Angeles CA 90027-1437 Office: Braille Inst Am 741 N Vermont Ave Los Angeles CA 90029-3594

CHANG, HIANG-CHU AUSILIA, education educator, researcher; b. Yong-Goang, South Korea, Dec. 10, 1945; arrived in Italy, 1964; d. Yoon-Hwan and Ok-Nim (Kim) C. BA, U. Auxilium, Turin, Italy, 1969, MA, 1972; PhD, U. Auxilium, Rome, 1980. Prof. didactics Pontifical Faculty Scis. of Edn., Turin, Rome, 1975—, prof. comparative edn., 1980—, vice-dir., 1989-95, 98—, dir. Inst. of Edn., 1987-93. Cons. exptl. lycées, Turin, Rome, Montecatini, Italy, 1982-92; cons. Nat. Com. of Salesian Schs., Rome, 1990-95, Com. for Salesian Schs. of Europe, 1992—, Internt. Found. Nova Spes, Rome, 1998—. Author: Comparative Education as Educational Discipline, 1982, Interdisciplinarity and Discovery Method in School, 1983, (with M. Checchin) Intercultural Education, 1996; co-editor: Women and Humanization of Culture at the Threshold of the Third Millenium. The Way of Education, 1998. Mem. Cath. Ctr. Univ. Profs. Edn., Comparative Edn. Socs. in Europe, Internat. Office of Cath. Edn. Office: Pontifical Fac Scis of Edn Auxilium Rome 00166 Italy E-mail: achang@pfse-auxilium.org.

CHANG, HOU-MIN, science educator, researcher; b. Chiayi, Taiwan, China, Aug. 29, 1938; s. Li-Sho and Lee-Fun Chang; m. Anne Han-ming chu Chang, Mar. 19, 1966; children: Lisa, Christopher. B of Agr., Nat. Taiwan U., Taipei, 1962; MS, U. Wash., 1966, PhD, 1968. Rsch. asst. U. Wash., Seattle, 1965—68; postdoctoral fellow NC State U., Raleigh, 1968—69, asst. prof., 1969—73, prof., 1977—90, R.B. Roberston disting. prof., 1990—; sci. specialist, vis. Weyerhaeuser Co., Seattle, 1976. Vis. prof. U. of Tokyo, Tokyo, 1981, Kyoto U., Kyoto, 1998; vis. sr. rschr. Taiwan Forestry Rsch. Inst., Taipei, Taiwan, 2002. Author: of more than 140 sci. and tech. articles. Recipient Sigma Xi Rsch. award, Sigma Xi, 1974, Alumni Outstanding Rsch. award, NC State U., 1985, Tech. award, TAPPI, 1992. Fellow: Internat. Acad. Wood Sci. (bd. dirs. 2002—, fellow 1983); mem.: TAPPI (bd. dirs. 1999—2002, fellow 1999). Achievements include patents for holder of 8 US patents. Home: 3410 Redbud Lane Raleigh NC 27607 Office: Department of Wood and Paper Science North Carolina State University Raleigh NC 27695 Office Fax: 919-515-6302.

CHANG, IRIS SHUN-RU, writer; b. Princeton, N.J., Mar. 28, 1968; d. Shau-Jin and Ying-Ying Chang; m. Bretton Lee Douglas, Aug. 17, 1991. BS in Journalism, U. Ill., 1989; MA in Writing, Johns Hopkins U., 1991; Doctorate (hon.), Coll. Wooster, 2002. Author: (books) Thread of the Silkworm, 1995, The Rape of Nanking, 1997 (N.Y. Times Bestseller, N.Y. Times Notable Book, Bookman Rev. Syndicate Best Books of 1997), The Chinese in America: A Narrative History, 2003. Recipient Peace and Internat. Coop. award John D. and Catherine T. MacArthur Found., 1992, Nat. Woman of Yr. award Orgn. Chinese Am. Women, 1998; rsch. grantee NSF, 1993, Harry Truman Presdl. Libr., 1993. Mem. Com. of One Hundred. Home and Office: PO Box 641104 San Jose CA 95164-1104

CHANG, ISABELLE C. librarian, educator, writer; b. Boston, Feb. 20, 1924; d. Que Wah Chin and June Hall; m. Min Chueh Chang, May 28, 1948; children: Francis Hugh, Claudia, Pamela. BS in Lib. Sci., Simmons Coll., 1946; MA in English, Clark U., 1967; MA in Psychology, Anna Maria Coll., 1982. Lib. trustee Shrewsbury (Mass.) Pub. Lib., 1958-59, 65-68, lib. dir., 1959-64; tchr. English, audio visual and media coord., librarian Shrewsbury (Mass.) Schs., 1964-91, guidance counselor, 1980-91. Author: What's Cooking at Changs, 1959, Chinese Fairy Tales, 1965, Tales from Old China, 1969, Gourmet on the Go, 1970, The Magic Pole, 1977, Spag: The American Dream, 1992, Artemas Ward, 2002. Shrewsbury Town Rep., 1997—. Recipient award for Disting. Writing Chandler Greene, 1966. Mem. ALA (life), NEA (life), AAAS (life), AARP (dir. 1995—), Nat. Acad. Scis. (life), Mass. Tchrs. Assn. (life), Shrewsbury Hist. Soc. (life), Worcester Art Mus. (life). Home: 15 Fiske St Shrewsbury MA 01545-2721 E-mail: isabellechang@aol.com.

CHANG, I-SHIH, aerospace engineer; b. Taipei, Taiwan, Dec. 2, 1945; came to U.S., 1968; s. I.H. and T.C. Chang; m. O.J. Chang, May 25, 1974; children: Anna, Brandon Degree in mech. engring., Taipei Inst. of Tech., 1965; MS, U. Kans., 1969; PhD, U. Ill., 1973. Scientist assoc.-rsch. Lockheed Missiles & Space, Huntsville, Ala., 1973-76; mem. tech. staff Rockwell Internat., Anaheim, Calif., 1976-77, The Aerospace Corp., El Segundo, Calif., 1977-80, engring. specialist, 1980-90, sr. engring. specialist, 1990-91, disting. engr., 1991—. Contbr. articles to profl. jours. Fellow AIAA (assoc.); mem. Phi Kappa phi. Democrat. Home: 890 S Calle Venado Anaheim CA 92807-5004 Office: The Aerospace Corp M4/967 2350 E El Segundo Blvd El Segundo CA 90245-4691 E-mail: i-shih.chang@aero.org.

CHANG, JACK CHE-MAN, imaging materials and media administrator; b. Shanghai, Nov. 19, 1941; came to U.S., 1958; s. Tse-Liang and Ho-Chen (Tyen) C.; m. Elizabeth P. Ng; children: Clara, Anthony. BA, Asbury Coll., 1961; MS, U. Ill., 1963, PhD, 1966. Rsch. chemist Eastman Kodak, Rochester, N.Y., 1967-73, lab. head, 1973-78, asst. dir. analytical scis. div., 1978-81, asst. dir. electrophotography divsn., 1981-84, mgr. advanced tech. devel. copy products, 1984-85, dir. chemistry Kodak rsch. labs. div., 1985-86, dir. corp. rsch. labs. divns., 1986-93, dir. photosci. rsch. divsn., 1993-96, v.p., assoc. dir. R&D, imaging materials and media, 1996-99, v.p., asst. dir. R&D, 1999—. Patentee in field. Mem. Am. Chem. Soc., Electrochem. Soc., Chinese Am. Chem. Soc. (bd. dirs. 1989-92). Home: 1198 Fox Holw Webster NY 14580-9150 Office: Eastman Kodak Co Imaging Materials And Media Rochester NY 14650-0001

CHANG, JAE CHAN, hematologist, oncologist, educator; b. Aug. 29, 1941; arrived in U.S., 1965; s. Tae Whan and Kap Hee (Lee) Chang; m. Sue Young Chung, Dec. 4, 1965; children: Sung-Jin, Sung-Ju, Sung-Hoon. MD, Seoul (Korea) Nat. U., 1965. Diplomate Am. Bd. Internal Medicine, Hematology, Med. Oncology, Am. Bd. Pathology (Hematology). Intern Ellis Hosp., Schenectady, NY, 1965—66; resident Harrisburg (Pa.) Hosp., 1966—69, fellow in nuclear medicine, 1969—70; fellow in hematology and oncology, instr. U. Rochester, 1970—72; chief hematology sect. VA Hosp., Dayton, Ohio, 1972—75; hematopathologist, co-dir. hematology lab. Good Samaritan Hosp., Dayton, 1975—2002, dir. oncology unit, 1976—2001, chief hematology and oncology sect., 1976—2003; clin. prof. medicine U. Calif., Irvine, Calif., 2003—; dir. hematology and oncology fellowship program Chao Family Comprehensive Cancer Ctr., U. Calif., Irvine, 2003—. Asst. clin. prof. Ohio State U., Columbus, 1972—75; assoc. clin. prof. Wright State U., Dayton, 1975—80, clin. prof., 1980—99, prof., 1999—2003, co-dir. hematology and med. oncology fellowship program, 1993—98; cons. hematology VA Hosp.; adv. com. Greater Dayton Area chpt. Leukemia Soc. Am., 1977; trustee Montgomery County Soc. Cancer Control, Dayton, 1976—85, Dayton Area Cancer Assn., 1985—88, Cmty. Blood Ctr., 1982—86, Hipple Cancer Rsch. Crt., 1999—2002. Contbr. articles to profl. jours., columns in newspapers.

Recipient Med. Econ. Essay Competition award, 1990, Wright State U. Acad. of Medicine award, 1985, Laureate award, APC-ASIM Ohio Chpt., 2001, Spl. Commendation, Ohio Senate, 2002. Fellow: ACP; mem.: AAAS, Montgomery Med. Soc. (dir. 1990—93), Dayton Soc. Internal Medicine (pres. 1989), Am. Soc. Clin. Oncologists, Am. Soc. Hematology. Home: 230 City Blvd W #303 Orange CA 92868 Office: UCI Med Ctr Div Hematology/ Oncology Chao Family Comp Cancer Ctr 101 The City Dr Orange CA 92868 E-mail: jaec@uci.edu.

CHANG, JANICE MAY, lawyer, naturopathic doctor, psychologist; b. Loma Linda, Calif., May 24, 1970; d. Belden Shiu-Wah (dec.) and Sylvia (Tan) C. BA, cert. paralegal studies, Calif. State U., San Bernardino, 1990, cert. creative writing, 1991; JD, LaSalle U., 1993; D in Naturopathy, Clayton Sch. Natural Healing, 1993; DFA in Creative Writing: Poetry, Am. Internat. U., 1999; MD in Alternative Medicines, Open Internat. U., 2001; DPsychology, Calif. Coast U., 2002; LLM in Taxation, Wash. Sch. of Law, 2003. Cert. bd. cert. alternative med. practitioner Am. Alternative Med. Assn.; Notary Pub. Calif. Victim/witness contact clk.-paralegal Dist. Atty.'s Office Victim/Witness Assistance Program, San Bernardino, Calif., 1990; gen. counsel JMC Enterprises, Inc., Riverside, Calif., 1993—; law prof. LaSalle U., Mandeville, La., 1994-97; corp. counsel, CFO, JDS Assocs., Inc., Loma Linda, 1998-99; corp. counsel, CFO DJS, L.P., Loma Linda, 1998-99; trust officer/trust svcs. Southeastern Calif. Conf. Seventh-Day Adventists, Riverside, 1998—; CFO/mgr. Stanberden Properties, 2001—. Spkr. graduation ceremony/conv. Internat. U., Las Vegas, 1998. Contbr. poetry to anthologies, including Am. Poetry Anthology, 1987-90, The Pacific Rev., 1991, The Piquant, 1991, River of Dreams, 1994, Reflections of Light, 1994, Musings, 1994 (Honorable Mention award 1994), Treasured Poems of America, 1994, Windows of the Soul, 1995, Best Poems of 1995 (Celebrating Excellence award 1995, Inspirations award 1995), Am. Poetry Annual, 1996, 99, Best New Poems of 1996, Interludes, 1996, Meditations, 1996, Perspectives, 1996 (Honorable Mention award 1996), Keepsakes, 1997 (Honorable Mention award 1997), Best Poems of 1997, Poetic Voices of America, 1997, The Isle of View, 1997, The Other Side of Midnight, 1997, Treasures, 1998, Best Poems of 1998, Writingscapes: Insights & Approaches to Creative Writing, 1998, Mirrors, 1999 (Pres.'s Lit. Excellence award), Pieces of the Heart, 2000, The Silence Within, 2001, Nature's Echoes, 2001, The Best Poems and Poets of 2001, The Best Poems and Poets of 2002; Theatre of the Mind, Noble House, 2003, contbr. to Internat. Libr. Photography: Tapestry of Dreams, 1999, Mystical Seasons, 1999, Candid Captures, 2001, The Mirror's Reflection, 2003. Vol. Health Fair Expo La Sierra U., 1988, 1989, Path of the Just Tree Project, 1998; vol. first aid, CPR, other classes ARC, 1994—; sponsor Student Employment Recognition Banquet La Sierra U., Riverside, Calif., 1999—2003. Recipient Poet of Merit award, Am. Poetry Assn., San Francisco, 1989, Golden Poet award, World of Poetry, Washington, 1989, Publisher's Choice award, Watermark Press, 1990, Editor's Choice award, The Nat. Libr. Poetry, 1990—97, Pres.'s award for lit. excellence, Iliad Press, 1995—99, Editor's Choice award, Poetry.com, 2002. Fellow Am. Coll. Internat. Physicians; mem. ACA, APA, ATLA, Nat. Bar Assn., Nat. Notary Assn., Brit. Guild Drugless Practitioners (life). Republican. Seventh-Day Adventist. Avocations: poetry writing, photography, music, drama, literature, numismatics. Home: 1025 Crestbrook Dr Riverside CA 92506-5662 Office: Southeastern Calif Conf 7th-Day Adventists PO Box 8050 11330 Pierce St Riverside CA 92515-8050 E-mail: changjm@secc-sda.org.

CHANG, JEANNETTE, publishing executive; BS, CCNY. Advt. sales rep. Cosmopolitan mag. Hearst Mags., N.Y.C., 1973-77, fashion advt. mgr., 1977-79; dir. fashion mktg. Bazaar mag. Hearst Mags., N.Y.C., 1979-84; assoc. pub. Harper's Bazaar mag. Hearst Mags., N.Y.C., 1984-94, v.p., 1992-94, v.p., pub., 1994—2000; sr. v.p., internat. pub. dir. Hearst Mags., Intl., 2000—. Spkr. in field. Active City Meals on Wheels, Meml. Sloan Kettering Found., Susan G. Komen Breast Cancer Found. Named to YWCA Acad. of Women Achievers, 1992. Mem. Fashion Group Internat. (bd. dirs., chair cosmetic exec. women's com.). Office: Mearst Mags Intl 959 8th Ave Rm 306 New York NY 10019-3737*

CHANG, JEFFREY CHAI, dentist, educator, researcher; b. Canton, China, Dec. 19, 1946; came to U.S., 1967; s. Po Wing and Wai Ming (Chan) C.; m. Frances Fuhnan Liang; children: Sheila Sai, Kenneth Kiu. BA with honors, Northeastern U., 1971; DDS, Georgetown U., 1976; MS in Dentistry, U. Tex. Dental Br., Houston, 1996. Commd. 2d lt. U.S. Army, 1976, advanced through grades to maj.; gen. dental officer Dental Corps Ft. Bliss, Tex., 1976-79; officer-in-charge Dental Clinic U.S. Army, Pusan, Korea, 1979-80, asst. chief clinician dental activity Ft. Momouth, N.J., 1980-83, chief dental emergency svc. dental activity Ft. Hood, Tex., 1983—85, resigned, 1985; clin. asst. prof. Dental Sch. U. Calif., San Francisco, 1985-88; clin. asst. prof. NYU Coll. Dentistry, N.Y.C., 1988-90; asst. prof. U. Tex. Dental Br., 1990-92, assoc. prof., 1992—. Cons. VA Med. Ctr., San Francisco, 1987-88, St. Barnabas Hosp., Bronx, N.Y., 1988-90, VA Med. Ctr., Houston, 1993—, ADA Coun. on Sci. Affairs, 1996—; scientist Houston Biomaterials Rsch. Ctr., 1996—. Contbr. 40 articles, 20 abstracts to profl. jours. Col. USAR, 1996—. Master Acad. Gen. Dentistry; fellow Am. Coll. Dentists, Acad. Dentistry Internat., Internat. Coll. Dentists; mem. ADA, Am. Assn. Dental Rsch., Internat. Assn. Dental Rsch., Chinese Am. Drs. Assn. (bd. dirs. 1994-2001), Am. Legion, Omicron Kappa Upsilon, Delta Sigma Delta. Avocations: soccer, stamps, contemporary music, photography, hi-fi systems. Home: 4123 Custer Creek Dr Missouri City TX 77459-1545 E-mail: drjeffchang@hotmail.com.

CHANG, JENGHWA, biomedical and electrical engineer, medical physicist; b. Taipei, June 18, 1962; came to U.S., 1989; s. Tsen-Ming Chang and Yu-Jeng Huang; m. Shiaoching Gong. BS in Control Engring., Nat. Chiao-Tung U., Hsinchu, Taiwan, 1984, MS in Comm. Engring., 1986; MS in Elec. Engring., Poly. U. N.Y., 1991, PhD in Elec. Engring., 1995, MS in Computer Sci., 2000. Cert. med. dosimetrist, med. physicist. Rsch. and tchg. asst. Nat. Chiao-Tung U., Hsinchu, Taiwan, 1984-86; rsch. asst. Academia Sinica, Taipei, 1988-89, N.Y. Hosp.-Cornell Med. Ctr., N.Y.C., 1991-93; rsch. asst. prof. SUNY Health Sci. Ctr., Bklyn., 1993-98; clin. med. physicist Rahway (N.J.) Hosp., 1994-97, Peninsula Hosp. Ctr., Far Rockaway, N.Y., 1996-97; asst. attending physicist and asst. mem. Meml. Sloan-Kettering Cancer Ctr., N.Y.C., 1997—. Contbr. chpt. to book, over 20 articles to profl. jours. Scholar for Spl. Tech. Chinese Min. Edn. Affairs, 1985, 86; named Excellent Officer award Chinese Marine Corps, 1988. Mem. IEEE, Am. Assn. Physicists in Medicine, AAAS, Radiol. and Med. Physics Soc. N.Y., Am. Soc. for Therapeutic Radiology Oncology. Achievements include pioneering in reconstructing tomographic images of biological tissues from scattered light source and verification of intensity modulated beam for radiation treatment of cancers using electronic portal imaging devices. Office: Meml Sloan-Kettering Cancer Ctr Dept Med Physics 1275 York Ave New York NY 10021-6094 E-mail: changj@mskcc.org.

CHANG, JIE (JAY CHANG), power electronics and control specialist; b. Laian, China, Nov. 6, 1962; came to U.S., 1988; s. Shaoju and Bing (Cheng) Zhang; 1 child, Jiajia. MSEE, U. Calgary, Can., 1985, PhD in Elec. Engring., 1988. Sr. rsch. & devel. engr. Elec. South, Inc., Greensboro, N.C., 1988-89, v.p. engring., 1989-90; sr. rsch. & devel. engr. Westinghouse Elec. Co., Tampa, Fla., 1990-92; leader, prin. engr. Reliance Elec Rsch. Ctr., Rockwell Internat. Co., Euclid, Ohio, 1992-93, sr. prin. engr., 1993-95; sr. scientist, team leader Rockwell Sci. Ctr., Rockwell Internat. Co., Thousand Oaks, Calif., 1996-98, prin. scientist, mgr. dept. control and power tech., 1999—. Mem. Rockwell Tech. panel on power electronics. Inventor in field. Tchr., vol. Thousand Oaks Chinses Sch., 1996—. Mem. IEEE (sr.). Avocations: swimming, basketball, ping pong, camping, calligraphy. Home: 1640 Meadowglen Ct Thousand Oaks CA 91320-3470 Office: Rockwell Sci Ctr 1049 Camino Dos Rios Thousand Oaks CA 91360-2362 Fax: 805-373-4383. Business E-Mail: jiechang@ieee.org.

CHANG, JOHNNY W. dancer; b. People's Republic of China; Grad., Beijing Dance Acad. Ballet Co., 1979. Prin. dancer Beijing Dance Acad. Ballet Co., 1981—84, Central Ballet of China, 1984—92, Royal Winnipeg Ballet, 1992—99, resident guest artist, ballet master, 1999—. Guest prin. artist Beijing Dance Acad. Ballet Co., 1986—92. Dancer (ballets) The Sleeping Beauty, Giselle, Don Quixote, Swan Lake, The Nutcracker, Raymonda, La Fille Mal Gardée, Coppélia, La Sylphide, The Afternoon of the Faun, Allegro Brillante, Scotch Symphony, Dracula, Miroirs, Romeo and Juliet, Four Last Songs. Recipient Bronze medal, 2d Internat. Ballet Competition, 1982, Second prize, 4th World Ballet Competition, Osaka, Japan, 1984, Bronze medal, 5th Moscow Internat. Ballet Competition, 1985, Highest Honour award, 1st Nat. Ballet Competition, Beijing, China, 1985. Office: Royal Winnipeg Ballet 380 Graham Ave Winnipeg MB Canada R3C 4K2

CHANG, JONATHAN LEE, orthopedist, educator; b. Lebanon, Pa., Feb. 22, 1959; s. Timothy Scott and Annabelle (Yee) C. Ed., U. Mich., 1980; MD, Duke U., 1984. Intern in surgery U. Va., Charlottesville, 1984-85, resident in surgery, 1985-86, resident in orthopedics, 1986-90; fellow in sports medicine Ky. Sports Medicine, Lexington, 1991; pvt. practice Pacific Orthopaedic Med. Group, Monterey Park, Calif., 1991—. Clin. asst. prof. U. So. Calif., L.A., 1994—; clin. asst. prof. We. U. Health Scis., 1996—; physician U.S. Olympic Com., 1999; apptd. Indsl. Med. Coun. by Gov. Calif. Editl. bd. Jour. Musculoskeletal Medicine, 1993—; manuscript reviewer Medicine and Sci. in Sports and Exercise, 1996—; contbr. articles to profl. jours. Mem. Am. Orthopedic Soc. for Sports Medicine, James Smithson Soc., Calif. Med. Assn., Am. Acad. Orthop. Surgeons, Am. Coll. Sports Medicine, Los Angeles County Med. Assn., Olympic Sports Medicine Soc. (U.S. Olympic Com.), McCue Soc., Asian Am. Med. Assn., Western Orthopaedic Assn., Calif. Orthopaedic Assn. Avocations: distance running, weight lifting, skiing, scuba diving, numismatics. Office: Pacific Orthopedic Med Group 500 N Garfield Ave Ste 204 Monterey Park CA 91754-1242

CHANG, KATHRYN JINMEI, accountant; b. Shanghai, People's Republic of China, Jan. 21, 1962; came to U.S., 1985; d. Rui-chang Jiao and Fu-ying Pan; m. Gene H. Chang, Aug. 12, 1985; children: Elaine A., Emily G. BA in Finance, Fudan U., 1984; MA in Applied Econs., Ea. Mich. U., 1989; BBA in Acctg., U. Toledo, 1993. CPA. Fin. analyst Shanghai Acad. Social Scis., 1984-85; cost acct., asst. contr. Bay Compressor Svcs., Toledo, 1993-96; fin. analyst Dana Corp, Maumee, Ohio, 1996-98, internat. acct. Toledo, 1998—. Mem. AICPAs, Ohio Soc. CPAs. Office: Dana Corp PO Box 1000 Toledo OH 43697-1000

CHANG, KUK WON, humanities educator, researcher; b. Yesan, Chungnam, Korea, Apr. 15, 1938; arrived in U.S., 1999; parents Hyun Tae Chang and Dae Jae Lee; m. Yeon Sook Lee, May 15, 1982; children: Sang Eun, Sang Young. BA, Seoul Nat. U., 1961, MA, 1967; AM, Duke U., 1971; PhD, Dr. Habil, Muenster U., 1980. Dir. Aram Inst. for Ancient Studies, Anyang, Republic of Korea, 1981—2001; pres. Korean Soc. for Ancient Near Ea. Studies, Seoul, 1983—; prof. Hansei U., Kunpo, 1990—2001. Vis. scholar Cornell U., Ithaca, NY, 1985—87; rsch. scholar Duke U., Durham, NC, 1991—2002; sec. gen. United Cultural Conv., Raleigh, NC, 2001—; sr. fellow Inst. for Interdisciplinary Studies, Pasadena, Calif., 1997—; advisor to dir. gen. Internat. Biog. Ctr., Cambridge, England, 2001—. Contbr. articles to profl. jours. 1st lt. Korean Army, 1963—67. Address: Apt A 110 Misty Woods Cir Chapel Hill NC 27514-2497 E-mail: kwpchang@han-mail.net.

CHANG, LAN SAMANTHA, writer, educator; b. Appleton, Wis., Jan. 18, 1965; d. Nai Lin and Helen Chung-Hung (Hsiang) Chang. BA, Yale U., 1987; MPA, Harvard U., 1991; MFA, U. Iowa, 1993. Tchg., writing fellow U. Iowa, Iowa City, 1991—93; Stegner fellow Stanford U., Calif., 1993—95, Jones lectr., 1995—98; Hodder fellow Princeton U., NJ, 1999—2000; Radcliffe fellow Harvard U., Cambridge, Mass., 2000—01, Briggs-Copeland lectr., 2002—; vis. assoc. prof. U. Iowa, Iowa City, 2001—02. MFA faculty Warren Wilson Coll., Asheville, NC, 2000—. Actor: Hunger: A Novella and Stories, 1998; author: short stories. Nat Endowment for the Arts grantee, 1998. Home: 34 Parker St Apt 6 Cambridge MA 02138-2200 Office: Harvard Univ 12 Quincy St Cambridge MA 02138

CHANG, LENG KAR, interior designer; b. Ipoh, Perak, Malaysia, Aug. 31, 1973; arrived in U.S., 1997; MA, Savannah Coll. Art and Design, 1999; cert., Visionary Designing, 2001. Interior designer Innervision Design Cons., Kuala Lumpur, Malaysia, 1994—96, Winsonart Design and Contracts, Paya Lebah, Singapore, 1997—98, Ai Group, Atlanta, 2000—. Contbr. (design) Residential Product and Interior Design, Home Max, 1997. Named Monroe Curus Propes fellow, Savannah Coll. Art and Design, 1998, Internat. and Regional winner, Interior Design Educators Coun. Student Design Competition, 1999; scholar, Savannah Coll. Art and Design, 1998. Home: 3659 Lantern Crest Cove Scottdale GA 30079 Office: Ai Group 3424 Peachtree Rd NE Ste 1600 Atlanta GA 30326 Fax: 404-266-9935. Personal E-mail: lengkar@hotmail.com. Business E-Mail: lchang@aigroupdesign.com.

CHANG, LING WEI, consulting services executive; b. Taiwan, China, July 27, 1960; arrived in U.S., 1976; d. Thomas T.P. and Hou Hsin (Wang) C. BE, Cooper Union, 1982; MS, Syracuse U., 1989. Engr. Data Systems div. IBM Corp., Poughkeepsie, N.Y., 1982-85, sys. engr. U.S. mktg. and svcs. N.Y.C., 1985-90; adv. mktg. rep. N.Y. gov. br. IBM U.S., N.Y.C., 1991-92; acct. mgr. N.Y. Pub. Svcs. IBM N.Am., N.Y.C., 1993-94; br. mgr. LEXIS-NEXIS, N.Y.C., 1994-95; nat. account mgr. Computer Assocs. Internat. Inc., N.Y.C., 1996-99; acct. prin. Compaq Profl. Svcs., N.Y.C., 1999-2000, dir. N.Y./N.J. area, 2000—01; client prin. Hewlett-Packard Svcs., 2002—. Vol. City Hosp. Ctr. at Elmhurst, N.Y., 1978; jr. judge Nat. Energy Found., 1979-82; bd. mgrs. Queens Ctr. Pla. Condominium, 1990-92. Mem.: Exec. Women's Golf Assn. (sponsorship chair, Big Apple chpt.), Eta Kappa Nu, Tau Beta Pi. Avocations: piano, golf, skiing, tennis. Home: 87-08 Justice Ave Apt 10D Elmhurst NY 11373-4580 Office: Hewlett-Packard Co 2 Penn Plz Fl 8 New York NY 10121-0899 E-mail: ling.chang@hp.com.

CHANG, LYDIA LIANG-HWA, social worker, educator; b. Wuhan, Hubei, China, Sept. 25, 1929; came to U.S., 1960; d. Shu-Tze Yu-Rou and Jian-Bung (Young) C.; m. Norman Stock, Aug. 20, 1998; children: Elizabeth Shu-Mei L. Ip, George Shu-Ang Lee. Diploma in Spanish and Lit., U. Sorbonne, Paris, 1959; MSW, NYU, 1963; cert. in advanced social work, Columbia U., N.Y.C., 1977, PhD in Social Work, 1980. Cert. social worker, cert. sch. bilingual social worker, N.Y. Supr. Cath. Charities, N.Y.C., 1969-71; dir. mental health cons. ctr. Univ. Settlement, N.Y.C., 1971-73; psychotherapist Luth. Med. Ctr., Bklyn., 1974-78; assoc. prof. U. Cin., 1978-80; asst. prof. Borough of Manhattan C.C., N.Y.C., 1983-86; bilingual sch. social worker N.Y.C. Bd. Edn., 1987-98, instr. for staff devel. program, 1991-98; psychotherapist Western Queens (N.Y.) Consultation Ctr., 1998—. Govt. ofcl.; cmty. sch. bd. treas. Dist. 30 N.Y.C. Bd. Edn., 1999—; cons. Cath. Social Svc. Bur., Cin., 1978-80; faculty advisor Borough of Manhattan C.C., 1983-86. Contbr. articles and poetry to various publs. Mem. adv. bd. Pub. Sys. of Schs., Cin., 1978-80, Orange County Asian Am. orgn., Goshen, N.Y., 1980-82; treas. U.S.-China Ednl. Fund, Hastins-on-Hudson, N.Y., 1994—; mem. Asian-Am. Dem. Assn., Queens, 1993—, Am. Voters Assn., Queens, 1986—; founder of the Shu-Tze Chang and Jian-Bung Young Chang Ednl. scholarship fund, China, 1996. Mem. NASW, Nat. Assn. Sch. Social Workers, Columbia Alumni Assn., Nankai Alumni Assn. (v.p. 1991-94). Episcopalian. Avocations: flute, tai-chi-chuang, swimming, reading. Home: 77-11 35th Ave Apt 2P Jackson Heights NY 11372

CHANG, MABEL LI, economist, educator; b. Hong Kong, May 26; came to U.S., 1946; d. H.C. and Y.C. Li; m. T. Timothy Chang, Nov. 23, 1957; 1 child, Robert Timothy. BA, Nat. Ctrl. U., Chungking, China, 1945, Manhattanville Coll. Sacred Heart, 1948; MA, NYU, 1948, PhD, 1956. English tchr. to exec. staff Yu Fung Mills, Chungking, 1944-45; asst. to chief acct. United China Relief, Chungking, 1945-46; head Claver index project Cath. Interracial Coun. N.Y., 1948-60; lectr. Bernard Baruch Sch. Bus. Adminstrn. CUNY, 1960-65; from instr. to prof. social scis. Bronx C.C., 1962-92, vol. rsch. work, 1992—; prof. emerita CUNY, 1992—. Author: Exercises in Microeconomics, 1976, Workbook in Microeconomics, 1978, Basic Concepts in Microeconomics, 1991; co-author: Economics for Hong Kong, 1970. Vol. Chinese Christian Fellowship, N.Y.C., 1950—, Sch. Social Work Ret. Faculty Sch. Initiative, Columbia U., 1993-98. Fellow United Bd. for Christian Higher Edn. in Asia, 1955-56, Found. for Econ. Edn., 1967; grantee GE Found. and U. Chgo., 1964. Mem. Chinese Am. Scholars Assn. (bd. dirs. 1991—), Asian Am. Higher Edn. Coun. (bd. dirs. 1991—), Am. Econ. Assn. (com. on the status of women in econ. profession) Avocation: communication with people. Home: 501 W 123rd St Apt 5C New York NY 10027 Office: Bronx CC of CUNY University Ave and 181st St Bronx NY 10453

CHANG, MARIAN S. filmmaker, composer; b. Atlanta, Aug. 19, 1958; d. C. H. Joseph and C. S. (Chun) Chang. MusB, Harvard U., 1981; MFA in Filmmaking, Columbia U., 1994. Composer, dir., choreographer Exptl. Theatre, Dance, Boston, 1981-88; composer for modern dance co. Performing Arts Ensemble, Boston, 1986-88; co-dir., choreographer, performer Theatre S., Boston, 1987-88; prodr., dir., writer, sound designer, composer N.Y.C., 1991—. Founder, prodr. Shy Artists Prodns., Boston, N.Y.C., 1988—94. Recipient 1st prize, Kansas City Music Scholarship Competition, 1976, Nino Cerruti Film award, 1995; grantee, N.Y. Coun. Humanities, 1998; Mass. Artists fellow in choreography, 1987, Mass. Artists fellow in music composition, 1988. Home: 220 E 27th St Apt 7 New York NY 10016-9234

CHANG, MICHAEL, tennis player; b. Hoboken, N.J., Feb. 22, 1972; s. Joe and Betty Chang. Round of 16 U.S. Open, N.Y.C., 1988, 89, 91, 94, Wimbledon, London, 1989, 90, quarterfinalist, 1994; champion French Open, Paris, 1989, quarterfinalist, 1990, 91, finalist, 1995; semifinalist Australian Open, Melbourne, 1995, finalist, 1996, U.S. Open, N.Y.C., 1996; champion Infiniti Open, L.A., 1996, Legg Mason Tennis Classic, Washington, 1996, Newsweek Champions Cup, Indian Wells, Calif., 1996. Other tournaments include: semifinalist WCT Scottsdale (Ariz.) Open, 1987, champion Transamerica Open, San Francisco, 1988; semifinalist Volvo Tennis Indoor, Memphis, 1989, semifinalist, 1991; finalist Volvo Tennis L.A., 1989, 90, 93; champion Silk Cuts Championships, Wembley, Eng., 1989; semifinalist Sovran Bank Classic, Washington, 1990; champion Player's Ltd. Internat. Can. Open, Toronto, 1990, semifinalist Suntory Japan Open, Tokyo, 1991, 92; semifinalist Open de la Ville de Paris, 1991, 94; finalist Compaq Grand Slam Cup, Munich, 1991, 92; champion Diet Pepsi Indoor Challenge, Birmingham, Eng., 1991; semifinalist Thriftway ATP Championships, Cin., 1992, champion, 1993, 94, finalist, 1995; semifinalist Waldbaum's Hamlet Cup, L.I., N.Y., 1992; semifinalist Seiko Super Tennis, Tokyo, 1992, finalist, 1994, champion, 1995; semifinalist European Cmty. Championships, Antwerp, Belgium, 1992; finalist Salem Open, Hong Kong, 1992, champion, 1994, 95, champion, Osaka, 1993, champion, Kuala Lumpur, 1993, champion, Beijing, 1993, 94, 95; champion Volvo Tennis/San Francisco, 1992; champion Newsweek Champions Cup, Indian Wells, Calif., 1992, semifinalist, 1993; champion Lipton Internat. Players Championships, Key Biscayne, Fla., 1992; semifinalist Kroger St. Jude Internat., Memphis, 1993, finalist, 1998; Ford Australian Open, Melbourne, 1997, U.S. Open, N.Y.C., 1997; champion Indonesian Open, Jakarta, 1993; finalist Japan Open, Tokyo, 1994, semifinalist, 1995; champion Indonesian Men's Open, Jakarta, 1994; champion Comcast U.S. Indoor, Phila., 1994, finalist, 1995; champion AT&T Challenge, Atlanta, 1994, 95, Infiniti Open, L.A., 1996, U.S. Men's Clay Ct. Championships, 1997, Salem Open, Hong Kong, 1997, Legg Mason Tennis Classic, Washington, 1996, 97, Kroger St. Jude, 1997, Newsweek Champions Cup, Indian Wells, Calif., 1996, 97; finalist Sybase Open, San Jose, Calif., 1995, semifinalist, 1996, 1998; finalist ATP World Tour Championships, Frankfurt, Germany, 1995; mem. U.S. Davis Cup Squad, 1989-91; semifinalist du Maurier Open, Montreal, Canada, 1997; semifinalist Great Amer. Insurance ATP Championship, Cincinnati, Oh., 1997; semifinalist Heineken Open, Rosmalen, The Netherlands, 1997. Achievements include being the youngest player to win USTA Boys' Nat. Championships, 1987; youngest male to advance to semifinals of Super Series tournament, 1987; youngest male to win match at U.S. Open, 1987; youngest male to win match at Wimbledon, 1988; youngest player to win Super Series tournament, 1988; youngest player to be named to U.S. Davis Cup Squad, 1989; youngest male Grand Slam Champion in Open Era, 1989; youngest ever French Open Champion, 1989; first Am. since Tony Trabert to win French Open, 1989. Address: Advantage Internat 1751 Pinnacle Dr Ste 1500 Mc Lean VA 22102-3833

CHANG, MONA MEI-HSUAN, computer programmer, analyst; b. N.Y.C., Sept. 7, 1962; d. Meng-Hsiu and Lydia Chia-Hwa (Chu) C. BA in Computer Sci. and Biochemistry, Columbia U., 1985, MA in Med. Informatics, 1997, MPhil in Med. Informatics, 1999. Data mgr. N.Y. Hosp., Cornell U. Med. Ctr., N.Y.C., 1990—92, computer programmer analyst, 1992—96; trainee in med. informatics Nat. Libr. Medicine, Columbia U., N.Y.C., 1999—2001; rsch. data coord. Meml. Sloan-Kettering Cancer Ctr., N.Y.C., 2002—. Mem. Cancer and Leukemia Group B (chmn. computer com. for data mgrs. 1990-92), Iota Sigma Pi. Avocations: chinese butterfly harp, chinese watercolor painting, tennis. Home: 549 W 123rd St Apt 19F New York NY 10027-5041 E-mail: mmc60@columbia.edu.

CHANG, NELSON LIANG AN, electrical engineer, researcher; b. Raleigh, N.C., Sept. 8, 1970; s. Ching Ming and Birdie S.C. Chang. BSE magna cum laude, Princeton U., 1992; MS, U. Calif., Berkeley, 1994, PhD, 1999. Rsch. asst. Princeton U., 1991-92; grad. student instr. U. Calif., Berkeley, 1992, rsch. asst., 1993-99; rsch. scientist Hewlett-Packard Labs., Palo Alto, Calif., 2000—. Nat. Merit scholar, 1988; Air Force Lab. grad. fellow, 1993. Mem. IEEE, IEEE Signal Processing Soc., Assn. for Computing Machinery, Tau Beta Pi. Avocations: songwriting, roller hockey, volleyball. E-mail: nlachang@hpl.hp.com., nlachang@yahoo.com.

CHANG, PARRIS HSU-CHENG, law-maker, political science educator, writer; b. Chikou, Chiayi, Taiwan, Dec. 30, 1936; came to U.S., 1961; s. Chao and Liu (Chen) C.; m. Shirley Hsiu-chu Lin, Aug. 3, 1963; children: Yvette, Elaine, Bohdan. BA, Nat. Taiwan U., 1959; MA, U. Wash., 1963; postgrad., Pa. State U., 1963-64; PhD, Columbia U., 1969, cert. Asian studies, 1966. Research polit. scientist U. Mich., Ann Arbor, 1969-70; asst. prof. polit. sci. Pa. State U., University Park, 1970-72; vis. fellow Australian Nat. U., Canberra, 1978; vis. scholar Inst. Sino-Soviet Studies, George Washington U., Washington, 1979; assoc. prof. polit. sci. Pa. State U., University Park, 1972-76, prof., 1976-97, dir. Ctr. for East Asian Studies, 1989-93; mem. Legis. Yuan Parliament, Taiwan, Republic of China, 1993—; prof. emeritus polit. sci., 1997—. Cons. The Rand Corp., Santa Monica, Calif., 1975-82, BDM, Vienna, Va., 1975—, Voice of Am., Washington, 1982—, Dept. State, 1983-84, Titan Sys., Vienna, 1985—; assoc. China coun. Asia Soc., N.Y.C., 1976—; vis. prof. Columbia U., summer 1985, Sch. Internat. Studies, JFK Spl. Warfare Ctr., Ft. Bragg, N.C., 1985-86, Tokyo U. Fgn. Studies, 1986-87; pres. steering com. unrepresented Nations and Peoples Orgn., The Hague, 1993—; pres. Taiwan Inst. for Polit. Econ. and Strategic Studies, 1994—. Author: Radicals and Radical Ideology in China's Cultural Revolution, 1973, Power and Policy in China, 1975, 3d edit. 1990, Elite Conflict in the Post-Mao China, 1981, 2d edit. 1983; co-author, co-editor: If China Crosses the Taiwan Strait, 1993, Chinese View of Future Warfare: Taiwan's Response, 1998; columnist Newsweek, 1985-87. Fellow Fulbright Council Internat. Exchange of Scholars, 1977; research grantee Social Sci. Research Council, 1972; travel grantee Internat. Research Exchange Council, 1982, 85 Fellow Japan Soc. for Promotion of Sci.; mem. Assn. Asian Studies (pres. Mid-Atlantic region 1976-77), Inter-Univ. Seminar on Armed Forces and Soc., Am. Polit. Sci. Assn. Office: 3-2 Chingtao E Rd Taipei Taiwan Fax: 886 2 2391 3760. E-mail: tipess@ms14.hinet.net.

CHANG, REN FANG, physicist, researcher; b. Nanking, China, Jan. 14, 1938; came to U.S., 1962; s. C.F. and T.S. (Wong) Ch.; m. Elizabeth Anne Brabson, Apr. 27, 1968. BS, Taiwan U., 1960; PhD, U. Md., 1968. Rsch. assoc. U. Md., College Park, 1968-70, asst. prof., 1970-77, sr. rsch. assoc., 1977-78; physicist Nat. Inst. Standards and Tech., Gaithersburg, Md., 1978—. Recipient Apollo Achievement award NASA, 1969. Office: Nat Inst Standards And Tech Gaithersburg MD 20899-8364 E-mail: renchang@nist.gov.

CHANG, RODNEY EIU JOON, artist, dentist; b. Honolulu, Nov. 26, 1945; s. Alfred Koon Bo and Mary Yet Moi (Char) C.; m. Erlinda C. Feliciano, Dec. 4, 1987; children: Bronson York, Houston Travis, Rochelle Jessica. BA in Zoology, U. Hawaii, 1968; AA in Art, Triton Coll., 1972; DDS, Loyola U., 1972; MS in Edn., U. So. Calif., 1974; MA in Painting and Drawing, U. No. Ill., 1975; MA in Community Leadership, Cen. Mich. U., 1976; BA in Psychology, Hawaii Pacific U., 1977; MA in Psychology of Counseling, U. No. Colo., 1980; PhD in Art Psychology, The Union Inst., 1980; MA in Computer Art, Columbia Pacific U., 1989. Pvt. practice dentist, Honolulu, 1975—; dir. SOHO too Gallery and Loft, Honolulu, 1985-89; freelance artist Honolulu, 1982—; curator Webfelt Mus. of Early Cyberart, Honolulu, 1996—, East Hawaii Cultural Ctr. Internat. Cybernet World Tour, Honolulu, 2002; curator/artist India's 1st Internat. Art Exhbn., Calcutta, 1999. Founder Pygoya Internat. Art Group, 1990—, Art Cap Group, Slap Caps Co., Honolulu, 1993, Ctr. Cyberspace.com, eobituary.com; columnist Milk Cap News; dir. ann. Honolulu City Hall

Hawaiian Computer Art Exhbn., 1990-92; speaker on art psychology and computer art, also numerous TV and radio interviews; dir. centerofcyberspace-.com, 2000. Author: Mental Evolution and Art, 1980, Rodney Chang: Computer Artist, 1988, Commentaries on the Psychology of Art, 1980; host (radio show) Disco Doc Hour, Sta. KISA; one-man shows include Honolulu Acad. Arts, 1986, Shanghai State Art Mus., People's Republic of China, 1988, Retrospective Exhbn. 1967-87, Ramsay Gallery, Honolulu, 1987, Visual Encounters Gallery, Denver, 1987, The Bronx Mus. of the Arts, N.Y.C., 1987, Nishi Noho Gallery, N.Y.C., 1987, Eastern Wash. U. Gallery of Art, 1988, Salon de la Jeune Peinture, Paris, 1989, Holter Art Mus., Mont., 1989, Las Vegas Art Mus., 1990, Forum Art Sch. Gütershoh, Fed. Republic of Germany, 1990, Siggraph-Dallas, 1990, Tartu State Art Mus., Estonia/USSR, 1990, U. Oregon Continuation Ctr., Portland, 1991—, Kauai Art Mus., Hawaii, 1993, RC Gallery of Computer Art, Honolulu, 1994, Archtl. Design of the Pygoya Home Mus., 1994; conceived, produced 1st milk cap art exhbn., Arts of Paradise Gallery, Waikiki Beach, 1993; organizer, artist 1st internat. digital art exhbn., Bombay, India; founder New York Net Gallery.com; featured artist Indian 1st Internat. Digital Art Exhbn., Calcutta, 1999. Judge Jr. Miss Contest, Honolulu, 1981. Served to capt., U.S. Army, 1973-74. Mem. ADA, Hawaii Dental Assn., Assn. of Honolulu Artists (pres. 1989, v.p. 1999), Nat. Computer Graphics, Acad. Gen. Dentistry, Hawaii Space Soc., Bernice Bishop Mus. Honolulu. Roman Catholic. Achievements include publication and issue of world's first pre-paid long distance telephone cards as signed and numbered, limited edition fine art prints, Pygoya Webmuseum of Cyberart on Internet, 1997; dir. Internet Programs, Las Vegas Art Mus., eobituary.com. and centerofcyberspace.com., 2000, lifeportraits.org, centerofcyberculture.com, others. Office: 2119 N King St Ste 206 Honolulu HI 96819-4550 E-mail: pygoya@pixi.com.

CHANG, SAM SHIFENG, meteorologist; b. Shanghai, Jan. 15, 1938; s. Yu Qing Zhang and Xing Lin Zhou; m. Rui Lian Chang, July 15, 1964; children: Hong Gao, Heather. BS, Nanjing U., 1959, MS, 1962; PhD, U. Wash., 1988. Asst. prof. Nanjing U., China, 1976-79; vis. scholar U. Wis., Madison, 1979-81; vis. scientist NCAR, Boulder, Colo., 1981-82, Oreg. State U., Corvallis, 1982; rsch. asst. U. Wash., Seattle, 1983-88; rsch. assoc. U. Chgo., 1988-89; meteorologist Air Force Rsch. Lab., Lexington, Mass., 1989-99, Army Rsch. Lab., Adelphi, Md., 1999— Invited lectr. Nagoya U., Japan, 1996. Author: Cumulus Dynamics, 1965; contbr. articles to profl. jours. Mem. Am. Geophys. Union, Am. Meteorol. Soc., European Geophys. Soc., Sci. Rsch. Soc., Sigma Xi. Avocations: ping pong, basketball. Home: Apt 1213 9727 Mt Pisgah Rd Silver Spring MD 20903 Office: Army Rsch Lab 2800 Powder Mill Rd Adelphi MD 20783-1197 E-mail: schang@arl.army.mil.

CHANG, SHIRLEY LIN (HSIU-CHU CHANG), librarian, educator; b. Chia-yi, Taiwan, June 22, 1937; came to U.S., 1962; naturalized, 1977. d. Tzu-kun and Ying (Chang) Lin; m. Parris H. Chang, Aug. 3, 1963; children: Yvette Y., Elaine Y., Bohdan P. BA, Nat. Taiwan U., Taipei, 1960; postgrad., U. Wasn., 1962-63; MLS, Columbia U., 1967; MA, Pa. State U., 1988. Libr. asst. Yale U., New Haven, 1964-67; asst. ref. libr. Pa. State U., University Park, 1971-75; cataloguer Australian Nat. U., Canberra, 1978; catalog/ref. libr. Lock Haven U., 1979—, asst. prof., 1982-88, assoc. prof., 1988—. Reference libr., reference catalog/desk coord. Lock Haven U., Pa. Author: Taiwan's Brain Drain and Its Reversal, 1999. Mem. ALA, Chinese-Am. Librs. Assn. (chmn. awards com. 1982-83), Asian/Pacific Am. Librs. Assn., Assn. for Asian Studies, Pa. Libr. Assn., Phi Beta Delta Honor Soc. Home: 1221 Edwards St State College PA 16801 Office: Lock Haven U Stevenson Libr Lock Haven PA 17745 E-mail: schang@lhup.edu.

CHANG, SIDNEY H. (SIDNEY H. CHANG), history educator; b. Wuchang, China, Jan. 1, 1934; PhD, U. Wis., 1967. Postdoctoral fellow Harvard U., Boston, 1969-70; prof. history Calif. State U., Fresno, 1996—2002, prof. emeritus history, 2002—. Home: Cedar And Shaw Fresno CA 93740-0001 Office: Calif State U Dept History Fresno CA 93710 E-mail: schang@csufresno.edu.

CHANG, STANLEY F. gastroenterologist; b. Aug. 22, 1945; m. Cathy Chang, Mar. 27, 1973; children: George, Elaine. AB, Dartmouth Coll., Hanover, N.H., 1966; MD, Mt. Sinai Sch. Medicine, N.Y.C., 1970. Diplomate Am Bd. Diagnostic Radiology, Am. Bd. Internal Medicine, subspeciality Bd. Gastroenterology. Resident Harvard Med. Sch.-Beth Israel Hosp., Boston, 1971-74; instr. U. Mich., Ann Arbor, 1974-75, asst. prof., 1977-78; resident U. Chgo., 1975-76; fellow Yale-New Haven Hosp., 1976-77; pvt. practice Fresno, Calif., 1978—. Fellow ACP, Am. Coll. Gastroenterology. Office: 688 Medical Center Dr E Clovis CA 93611-6807

CHANG, STEVE, internet security company executive; BS in Applied Math., Fu-Zen Cath. Univ., Taiwan; MS in Computer Sci., Lehigh U. Engr. Hewlett Packard; founder Asia Tek, Inc., Taiwan; founder, CEO Trend Micro, Calif., 1988—. Named in FORTUNE Mag., 1996; recipient Innovator of Yr. award, EDN Asia Mag., 1996, Stars of Asia award, Bus. Week Mag., 1997, 1998. Office: Trend Micro Inc Odakyy So Tower 10th Fl 2-2-1 Yoyogi Shibuya-ku Tokyo 1S1-8583 Japan

CHANG, STEVEN DANIEL, neurosurgeon; b. Honolulu, June 25, 1968; s. Hing Dat Sum and Lorene Mary (Anastasi) C.; m. Helen Hsin-I, July 6, 1996. BS in Biology, BA in Econs., Stanford U., 1989, MD, 1993. Pres. BMI, Inc., Honolulu, 1986—; asst. prof. dept. neurosurgery Stanford (Calif.) U., 1999—. Mem. AMA, NASD, Honolulu Bd. Realtors, Am. Assn. Neurol. Surgeons, Congress Neurol. Surgeons, Calif. Assn. Neurol. Surgeons. Republican. Roman Catholic. Avocation: medical-legal issues. Office: 300 Pasteur Dr Stanford CA 94305

CHANG, SYLVIA TAN, health facility administrator, educator; b. Bandung, Indonesia, Dec. 18, 1940; came to U.S., 1963. d. Philip Harry and Lydia Shui-Yu (Ou) Tan; m. Belden Shiu-Wah Chang, Aug. 30, 1964 (dec. Aug. 1997); children: Donald Steven, Janice May. Diploma in nursing, Rumah Sakit Advent, Indonesia, 1960; BS, Philippine Union Coll., 1962; MS, Loma Linda (Calif.) U., 1967; PhD, Columbia Pacific U., 1987. Cert. RN, PHN, ACLS, BLS instr., cmty. first aid instr., IV, TPN, blood withdrawal. Head nurse Rumah Sakit Advent, Bandung, Indonesia, 1960-61; critical care, spl. duty and medicine nurse, team leader White Meml. Med. Ctr., L.A., 1963-64; nursing coord. Loma Linda U. Med. Ctr., 1964-66; team leader, critical care nurse, relief head nurse Pomona (Calif.) Valley Hosp. Med. Ctr., 1966-67; evening supr. Loma Linda U. Med. Ctr., 1967-69, night supr., 1969-79, adminstrv. supr., 1979-94; sr. faculty Columbia Pacific U., San Rafael, Calif., 1986-94; dir. health svc. La Sierra U., Riverside, Calif., 1988—. Site coord. Health Fair Expo La Sierra U., 1988-89; adv. coun. Family Planning Clinic, Riverside, 1988-94; blood and bone marrow drive coord. La Sierra U., 1988—. Counselor Pathfinder Club Campus Hill Ch., Loma Linda, 1979-85, crafts instr., 1979-85, music dir., 1979-85; asst. organist U. Ch., 1982-88. Named one of Women of Achievement YWCA, Greater Riverside C. of C., The Press Enterprise, 1991, 2000, Safety Coord. of Yr. La Sierra U., 1995. Mem. Am. Coll. Health Assn., Pacific Coast Coll. Health Assn., Adventist Student Pers. Assn., Sigma Theta Tau. Republican. Seventh-day Adventist. Avocations: music, travel, collecting coins, shells and jade carvings. Home: 1025 Crestbrook Dr Riverside CA 92506-5662 Office: 4700 Pierce St Riverside CA 92515-8247 E-mail: schang@lasierra.edu.

CHANG, TED T. chemist; b. Tainan, Taiwan, Oct. 6, 1935; arrived in U.S., 1961; s. Shei-huei and Ou-chiu Chang; m. Kay H. Hsu, Jan. 10, 1960; children: Grace, Susan, Diana. BS, Nat. Taiwan U., Taipei, 1957; MS, U. Va., 1963, PhD, 1965; postgrad., Calif. Inst. Tech., 1965—66. Lectr. Nat. Cheng-Kung U., Tainan, 1959—61; rsch. chemist Am. Cyanamid, Stamford, Conn., 1966—71, prin. rsch. scientist, 1979—86; group leader Wyeth Labs., Radnor, Pa., 1971—79; assoc. rsch. fellow Am. Cyanamid/Cytec, Stamford, 1986—92; rsch. fellow Cytec Industries, Stamford, 1992—. Tech. expert to China UN, 1984. Contbr. more than 50 articles to profl. publs. Mem.: Chinese Am. Soc. Mass Spectrometry (pres. 1981—98, hon. permanent pres. 1998), Am. Soc. Mass Spectrometry, Am. Chem. Soc. (mem. U.S. delegation to Sino-Japan conf. 1987). Achievements include research in mass spectrometry, polymer analysis, electrochemistry, colorimetry and atomic absorption spectroscopy; introduced tandem analytical techniques of TGA-GC-MS and TLC-FAB-MS. Home: 157 Dogwood Ln Stamford CT 06903 Office: Cytec Industries 1937 W Main St Stamford CT 06904 E-mail: ted.chang@cytec.com.

CHANG, THOMAS MING SWI, medical scientist, biotechnologist; b. Swatow, Kwantang, China, Apr. 8, 1933; arrived in Can., 1952; m. Lancy Yuk Lan Jin, June 21, 1958; children: Harvey, Victor, Christine, Sandra. BSc, McGill U., Montreal, Que., Can., 1957, MD, CM, 1961, PhD, 1965. Intern Montreal Gen. Hosp., 1961-62; rsch. fellow depts. physiology and chemistry McGill U., 1962-65, asst. prof. physiology, 1966-69, assoc. prof., 1969-72, prof. physiology, 1972—, dir. artificial organs rsch. unit, 1975-79, prof. medicine, 1975—, dir. artificial cells and organs rsch. ctr., 1979—, assoc. dept. chem. engring., 1985—, assoc. dept. chemistry, 1986—2001, prof. biomed. engring., 1990—, dir. MSSS-FRSQ rsch. group (d'equipe) on blood substitute in transfusion medicine, 2002—; lab. and clin. rschr. med. scis., biotech., biomed. engring. Montreal, 1962—. Mem. staff Royal Victoria Hosp.; hon. mem. staff Montreal Chinese Hosp., 1970—; cons. Montreal Children's Hosp., 1979—, Med. Rsch. Coun. fellow, 1962-65, scholar, 1965-68, career investigator, 1968-99; hon. prof. Nankai U., 1983—. Inventor artificial cells and blood substitutes; author: Artificial Cells, 1972, Biomedical Application of Immobilized Enzymes and Proteins, Vols. I and II, 1977, Artificial Kidney, Artificial Liver and Artificial Cells, 1978, Hemoperfusion-Kidney and Liver Supports and Detoxification, 1980, Hemoperfusion, 1981, Past, Present and Future of Artificial Organs, 1983, Microencapsulation and Artificial Cells, 1984, Hemoperfusion and Artificial Organs, 1985, Blood Substitutes, 1988, Blood Substitutes and Oxygen Carriers, 1993, Blood Substitutes: Principles, Methods, Products & Clinical Trials, Vol. I, 1997, II, 1998; editor-in-chief Artificial Cells, Blood Substitutes and Biotechnology; sect. editor Internat. Jour. Artificial Organs, 1977—, Trans. Am. Soc. Artificial Organs, 1977-2001; assoc. editor BioTechnology Ann. Rev., 1995—; mem. editl. bd. Jour. Biomaterial Med. Devel. and Orgn., 1972-87, Jour. Membrane Sci., 1975-92, Jour. Bioengring., 1975-79, Jour. Enzyme and Microbial Tech., 1978-86. Recipient Decorated officer, Order of Can., 1992—, Can. 125th Confereration medal, 1993, Queen Elizabeth Jubilee medal, 2002. Fellow Royal Coll. Physicians Can., Royal Soc. Can.; mem. Internat. Soc. Artificial Organs (trustee 1982-87, 89-92, congress pres. 1991, pres. 1994-96, immediate past pres. 1996-98), Can. Soc. Artificial Organs (pres. 1980-82), Internat. Soc. Artificial Cells, Blood Substitutes and Immobilization Biotech. (hon. pres. 1990—, hon. congress pres. 1994, 97, 2001), Internat. Symposium Blood Substitutes (hon. pres. 2003), Internat. Soc. Microencapsulations (hon.). Office: McGill U Artificial Organs Rsch Ctr 3655 Drummond St Rm 1006 Montreal QC Canada H3G 1Y6 E-mail: artcell.med@mcgill.ca.

CHANG, WALTER TUCK, SR., drafting and AutoCAD educator, real estate agent, national defense instructor; b. Honolulu, Feb. 16, 1920; s. Awai Abner and Clara Pa'a auao (Fairman) C.; m. Rita AnaMarie Yee Chang, Aug. 16, 1950 (div. June 1959); children: Walter Tuck Jr., Nani; m. Mercedes Arroyo Chang, June 15, 1961 (div. June 1973); m. Evelyn Show Chiao Huang, Aug. 25, 1973. BA in Indsl. Arts with honors, Tchr.'s credential, San Jose State U., 1945; postgrad. in trade and industry adminstrn., U. Calif., Berkeley, 1949-55; MA in Edn. and Adminstrn., San Francisco State U., 1959; postgrad. in elem. sch. adminstrn. and supv. of practice tchrs., U. Hawaii, 1959-64; postgrad. in indsl. arts and vocat. edn., U. Md., 1967-68. Gen. secondary credential, Calif., spl. subject supervision vocat. class A, spl. subject supervision vocat. class C1, spl. secondary life diploma in indsl. arts, secondary sch. adminstrn., supervision secondary sch. tchrs., Calif., spl. secondary life diploma in trade industry; profl. secondary cert. in indsl. arts, Hawaii. Drafting apprenticeship engring. and estimation dept. Hawaiian Elec. Co., Honolulu, 1937-39; journeyman machinist, leadman, nat. war manpower job instr. Joshua Henry Iron Works, Sunnyvale, Calif., 1942-45; vocat. instr. San Jose State U., 1942-45; automotive machinist Garden City Sales and Svc. Co., San Jose, Calif., 1945-46; journeyman machinist Oliver M. Johnson Machine Shop, San Jose, Calif., 1946; machinist Food Machine Corp., San Jose, Calif., 1946; machinist, tool maker Ames Aeronautical Lab., Moffett Field, Calif., 1946-51; adult evening vocat. instr. Leland Evening H.S., San Jose, 1951; vocat. inst., supr., driver edn., tng. John Swett Union H.S., Crockett, Calif., 1951-59; journeyman machinist Oliver United Filters Inc., Oakland, Calif., 1952-53; vocat. dir., night prin. John Swett Union H.S., Crockett, Calif., 1952-59; indsl. arts, English, World Hist. instr. McKinley H.S., Honolulu, 1959-62; indsl. arts metal works instr. Kailua H.S., Oahu, 1962; indsl. arts tchr. edn. instr., supr. indsl. arts student tchrs. U. Hawaii Coll. Edn. Manoa Campus, Honolulu, 1962-64; drafting instr. archtl. engring., electronics and metals tech., auto-cad, supr. driver edn. tng. Kamehameha Schs., Honolulu, 1964-90. Built over 1,000 engines for liberty, cargo steam ships, minesweepers during WWII, 1942-45. Author: Getting Started With the Calipro, 1965, The Kidjel Ratio Concept in Designing and Drafting. Hawaiian musician entertainer ARC, San Francisco Bay Area, 1942-49; Sunday Sch. tchr. Hayward (Calif.) Missionary Bapt. Ch., 1958-59, Missionary Bapt. Chs. on Oahu, Hawaii, 1960—; v.p. PTA of New Keolu Elem. Sch., 1961-62, v.p. monthly meetings; designed and built 3 chs. and 2 parsonages, Calif. and Hawaii; support Missionary Bapt. Chs. and Missions, U.S., Can., South Am., The Philippines, Japan, China, India, Africa, Russia, Jerusalem, 1958—. Recipient Nat. Merit Honor Soc. award, 1938, Best Auto-CAD Architecture in Hawaii award Sausilito Software, 1985, Nat. Hon. Edn. Fraternity award Phi Delta Kappa, 1962, award Solid Wood Poi Pounder, Best Designed 4 Million Dollar Indsl. Arts Complex in Hawaii award Kamehameha Schs.; named Most Outstanding Alumni in field of edn., Kamahameha Alumni Assn., Honolulu, 1984. Mem. Oahu Indsl. Arts Tchrs. Assn. (exec. bd. 1959, v.p. in charge of monthly workshops 1960, pres. 1961), Epsilon Pi Tau, Kappa Delta Pi. Avocations: photography, raising gold fish, travel, reading books, sports. Home: 94-1015 Uke'e Pl Waipahu HI 96797-4272

CHANG, WILLIAM SHEN CHIE, electrical engineering educator; b. Nantung, Jiangsu, China, Apr. 4, 1931; s. Tung Wu and Phoebe Y.S. (Chow) C.; m. Margaret Huachen Kwei, Nov. 26, 1955; children: Helen Nai-yee, Hugh Nai hun, Hedy Nai-lin. BSE, U. Mich., 1952, MSE, 1953; PhD, Brown U., 1957. Lectr., rsch. assoc. in elec. engring. Stanford (Calif.) U., 1957-59; asst. prof. elec. engring. Ohio State U., 1959-62, assoc. prof., 1962-65; prof. dept. elec. engring. Washington U., St. Louis, 1965—79, chmn. dept., 1965-71, dir. Applied Electronic Scis. Lab., 1971-79, Samuel Sachs prof. elec. engring., 1976-79; prof. dept. elec. and computer engring. U. Calif., San Diego, 1979—, chmn. dept., 1993-96. Author: Principles of Quantum Electronics, 1969, RF Photonic Technology in Optical Fiber Links, 2002; Contbr. articles to profl. jours. Fellow Am. Optical Soc., IEEE; mem. Am. Phys. Soc. Achievements include research on quantum electronics and guided wave optics. Home: 12676 Caminito Radiante San Diego CA 92130 Office: U Calif San Diego MS-0407 Dept Elec/Computer Engring La Jolla CA 92093-0407 E-mail: wchang@ucsd.edu.

CHANG, WILLIAM ZHI-MING, physicist, researcher; b. Shanghai, June 6, 1955; s. Yinfang Chang and Shanlin Chen; m. Sandra Schlachter, Aug., 1987; 1 child, Caroline Dagmar. BS, U. So. Calif., 1984, MS, 1985, PhD, 1992. Rsch. assoc. U. So. Calif., L.A., 1992-93; rsch. scientist Max Planck Soc. x-ray optics group Friedrich-Schiller U., Jena, Germany, 1993-96; sr. scientist advanced rsch. and applications corp. Aracor, Sunnyvale, Calif., 1996—. Contbr. articles to profl. jours. and books. Disting. scholar Microbeam Analysis Soc., San Jose, Calif., 1991, Boston, 1992. Mem. Optical Soc. Am. Achievements include patents in field. Avocations: opera, calligraphy. Home: 8592 Peachtree Ave Newark CA 94560-3342 Office: Aracor 425 Lakeside Dr Sunnyvale CA 94085-4716 E-mail: chang@aracor.com.

CHANG, WINSTON WEN-TSUEN, economist, educator; b. I-lan, Taiwan, Aug. 1, 1939; came to the U.S., 1963; s. Tsan-chin and Sheu-feng (Chen) C.; m. Shanyong Kuo, June 11, 1966; children: David, Jacqueline. BA, Nat. Taiwan U., 1962; MA, U. Rochester, 1966, PhD, 1968. Asst. prof. econs. SUNY, Buffalo, 1967-70, assoc. prof. econs., 1970-78, prof. econs., 1978—, dir. undergrad. program in econs., 1999—2000. Dir. Ph.D. program in econs. dept. econs. SUNY, Buffalo, 1991; project specialist Chinese U. Devel. Project U.S. Nat. Acad. Scis., 1987, 89, 90. Contbr. articles to profl. jours., chpts. to books. NSF grantee, 1969. Mem. Am. Econs. Assn.

CHANG, WON, economist; b. Seoul, Republic of Korea, Jan. 7, 1969; s. Charlie H.J. Chang and Moon Sook Uhm. BA, NYU, 1992; PhD, Columbia U., 1999. Cons. The World Bank, Washington, 1997—2000; internat. economist U.S. Dept. Treasury, Washington. Contbr. articles to profl. jours. Achievements include research in Regional Integration Impact and Analysis. Office: US Dept Treasury 1500 Pennsylvania Ave NW Washington DC 20220 Office Fax: 202-622-1731. Personal E-mail: wchang_264@msn.com. E-mail: won.chang@do.treas.gov.

CHANG, WUNG, business advisor, researcher, lecturer; b. Kangke Pyongbuk, Republic of Korea, Apr. 24, 1942; came to U.S., 1973; s. Jae Sun and Key Bok (Yoo) C.; m. Han Jin Yang, Nov. 14, 1970; children: Min, Won. MPA, Yon-Sei U., 1971; PhD in Bus. Mgmt., Union U., 1983. Editor-in-chief Korea Photo Times, Seoul, 1970-73; sec.-gen. Wum Found., L.A., 1986-87; sr. analyst Pacific Rsch. Inst., L.A., 1988-92; advisor Korea Travel News, Seoul, 1988-93; contr. US Top Capital Corp., LA, 1991—2000. Vice chmn. Mid-Wilshire Tng. Ctr. divsn. Adult and Career Edn., L.A. Unified Sch. Dist. Adv. Coun., 1994—96; vol. lectr. The Korean Sr. Citizens Assn. of San Fernando Valley Coll., 1995—96; co-chmn. Internat. Rsch. Inst. Govt. and Pub. Adminstrn., L.A., 1995—99; commentator Radio Korea, USA, 1997—2000; sr. advisor So. Calif.-Korean Fedn. Coun. of No. Korea, 1998—2001; adv. mem. So. Calif.-Korean Assn. of Pyung-An-Book-Do Province, 1999—; sr. adv. Hypnosis Career Coll., 2002—. Mem. Rep. Presdl. Adv. Commn., Washington, 1991; active Rep. Senatorial Com., Washington, 1991; nat. campaign advisor Rep. Senatorial Inner Circle, Washington, 1995—; chmn. bd. dirs. Kang I. Lee Found., Inc., 2002—. Capt. Korean Army, 1966-70. Recipient Presdl. Order of Merit, 1991, Rep. Presdl. Task Force Wall of Honor, 1992, Rep. Senatorial medal of freedom, 2002. Avocations: fishing, swimming, music, baseball. Home: 7625 Radford Ave North Hollywood CA 91605-2858

CHANG, YA-TING, pianist, music educator, educator; b. Taipei, Taiwan, July 15, 1974; d. Ken-Hu Chang and Li-Ying Shih; m. Peter I. Sirotin, Sept. 8, 2000. MusB, Peabody Inst., John Hopkins U., MusM, 1998. Pianist Mendelssohn Piano Trio, Rockville, Md., 1997—; piano instr. Columbia Union Coll., Takoma Park, Md., 2001—03; piano and chamber music instr. Messiah Coll., Pa., 2003—. Office: Mendelssohn Piano Trio 2507 Lindley Overlook Rockville MD 20850 Personal E-mail: yating@mendelssohnpianotrio.com. E-mail: mpt@mendelssohnpianotrio.com.

CHANG, YI-SHIH JOSHUA, health researcher; b. Che-Ding, Taiwan, Sept. 13, 1961; s. Te-Chi and Tung-Hua (Lee) C.; m. Hui-Yu Victoria Hsaio, Aug. 11, 1990. BS, Nat. Tsing-Hua U., 1984; MS, U. Mo., 1992. Therapeutic recreation specialist Mid-Mo. Mental Health Ctr., Columbia, 1991; lab. asst. U. Mo., Columbia, 1992-93; rsch. analyst Mid-Mo. Mental Health Ctr., 1993-98; dir. analytic and evaluative svcs. Mo. Patient Care Review Found., Jefferson City, 1998-99, rsch. assoc., 1999—. Mem. Nat. Assn. Healthcare Quality. Avocations: computing, table tennis, traveling, card games. Office: Mo Patient Care Review Found 3425 Constitution Ct Ste E Jefferson City MO 65109-5753 E-mail: joshua@mpcrf.org., joshuachang@juno.com.

CHANG, YONGBIN, physicist; b. Peixian, Jiangsu, China, Jan. 3, 1965; s. Jingxiang and Xianzhen (Zhai) C.; m. Yaqin Chen, Jan. 1, 1990; 1 child, Lisa. BS, Nat. U. Def. Tech., Changsha, China, 1985; MS, Inst. Plasma Physics, Hefei, China, 1988, PhD, 1997. Asst. prof. Inst. Plasma Physics, Chinese Acad. Sci., Hefei, 1988-95, assoc. prof., 1995-96; vis. scientist Eindhoven (The Netherlands) U. Tech., 1996-97; rsch. asst. U. North Tex., Denton, 1997—. Contbr. articles to profl. jours. Pres. Chinese Students and Scholars, Denton, 1997. Mem. AAAS, Am. Physics Soc., Sigma Xi. Home: 5863 Carmel Way Union City CA 94587-5170 Office: U North Tex PO Box 311427 Denton TX 76203 E-mail: yc0010@jove.acs.unt.edu.

CHANG, YOON IL, nuclear engineer; b. Seoul, Korea, Apr. 12, 1942; came to U.S., 1965; s. Paul Kun and In Sil (Hahn) C.; m. Ok Ja Kim, Dec. 19, 1966; children: Alice, Dennis, Eugene. BS in Nuclear Engring., Seoul Nat. U., 1964; ME, Tex. A & M U., 1967; PhD, U. Mich., 1971; MBA, U. Chgo., 1983. Mgr. spl. projects Nuclear Assurance Corp., Atlanta, 1971-74; asst. nuclear engr. Argonne (Ill.) Nat. Lab., 1974-76, group leader, 1976-77, sect. head, 1977-78, assoc. divsn. dir., 1978-84, gen. mgr. IFR program, 1984-94, dep. assoc. lab. dir. for engring. rsch., 1994—98, assoc. lab. dir. for engring. rsch., 1998—2002, interim lab. dir., 1999—2001, assoc. lab. dir. at large, 2002—. Recipient E. O. Lawrence award U.S. Dept. Energy, 1994. Fellow Am. Nuclear Soc. (Walker Cisler award 1997—). Home: 2020 Palmer Dr Naperville IL 60564-5664 Office: Argonne Nat Lab 9700 Cass Ave Argonne IL 60439-4803

CHANG-DIAZ, FRANKLIN R. astronaut; b. San José, Costa Rica, Apr. 5, 1950; s. RamÓn A. Chang-Morales and Maria Eugenia Diaz De Chang; m. Peggy Marguerite Doncaster; 4 children. BSc in Mech. Engring., U. Conn., 1973; PhD in Applied Plasma Physics, MIT, 1977; PhD (hon.), U. National de Costa Rica; DSc (hon.), U. Santiago de Chile, U. Conn.; LLD (hon.), Babson Coll. Mem. technical staff Charles Stark Draper Lab. MIT, Mass., 1978—81; astronaut NASA, Houston, 1981—. Vis. scientist plasma fusion ctr. MIT, Mass., 1983—93; adj. prof. physics Rice U., Houston, U. Houston, Houston; dir. advanced space propulsion lab. Johnson Space Ctr. NASA, Houston, 1993—; presenter in field; founder Astronaut Sci. Colloquium Program, 1987—; founder, dir. Astronaut Sci. Support Group, 1987—89; astronaut Space Shuttle Columbia, 1986, Space Shuttle Atlantis, 1989, 92, Wake Shield Facility, Space Habitation Module 2, 1994, U.S. Microgravity Payload, 1996, Discovery, 1998. Named Hon. Citizen, Govt. Costa Rica, 1995; recipient Liberty medal, Pres. Ronald Reagan, 1986, Cross of Venezuelan AF, Pres. Jaime Lusinchi, 1988. Avocations: music, glider planes, soccer, scuba diving, hiking. Office: Astronaut Office CB NASA Johnson Space Center Houston TX 77058

CHANG-MOTA, ROBERTO, electrical engineer; b. Caracas, Venezuela, Dec. 28, 1935; came to US, 1948; s. Roberto W. and Mary C. (Mota) Chang; m. Alicia Santamaria-Gonzales, May 4, 1968; children: Roberto Ignacio, Roxana Ivette, Ricardo Ignacio. DEE, U. Cen. Venezuela, 1960; MS, U. Ill., 1962; AR, Harvard U., 1970; PhD, UCLA, 1983. Dir. sch. engring., prof. Ctrl. U., Caracas, 1964-69; pro., dean Simon Bolivar U., Caracas, 1971-77; pres. Colegio de Ingenicros de Venezuela, Caracas, 1974-79; dir. Venezuelan Power Co., Caracas, 1974-79; pres. Latin Am. Orgn. Engring., Quito, Ecuador, 1977-79, Corporoil, Caracas, 1981-85, Audio Interface Corp., Caracas, 1983-96; v.p. ESCA Corp., Caracas, 1991-95; pres. 3R Corp., Caracas, 1995—; CEO, pres. Cositel Corp., 2002—, SSS Corp., 2002—; pres. 35 Corp., 2002, Inti Corp., Caracas. Spl. cons. Venezuelan Navy and Army, 1971-75, Venezuelan Congress, 1989-96; mem. tech. com. Venezuelan Supreme Election Coun., 1971-81, exec. dir., 1981-82, gen. dir., 1982-97; gen. dir. Consejo Nacional Electoral, 1991-98; cons. Ministry of Interior, 1990; v.p. Electronic Cir. Corp., 1991-2000; trustee Simon Bolivar U., 1985-98; bd. dirs. Sistemas y Procesos Automatizados, SEPAI Corp. Gen. dir. Nat. Election Coun., 1985-99; pres. Sistemas Electorales y Procesos Automatizados, 2001. Mem. IEEE, Am. Soc. Engring. Edn., Venezuelan Soc. Elec. and Mech. Engring. (pres. 1972-73), Instn. Elec. Engrs., Puerto Azul Club, Playa Pintada Club, Caracas Racquet Club. Roman Catholic. Home: 7861 SW 180th St Miami FL 33157-6216 also: Prados del Este Calle Colon Quinta Cumana Caracas 1080 Venezuela

CHANIN, JEFFREY, lawyer; b. Bklyn., Oct. 10, 1940; s. Louis and Julia (Levine) C.; m. Elizabeth Ann, June 15, 1963 (div. 1983); children: Joseph Robert, Jane Louise; m. Kristin Blaire, Dec. 17, 1983. AB, Bklyn. Coll., 1962; JD, Harvard U., 1965. Bar: Calif. 1966, U.S. Supreme Ct. 1967. Assoc. and ptnr. Statman, Treister & Glatt, L.A., 1965-77, of counsel, 1979-82; sr. v.p. and dir. Daylin Inc., L.A., 1977-79; pres. Handy Dan/Angels, L.A., 1978-79; exec. v.p. Wickes Cos., Inc., Santa Monica, Calif., 1982-84, also bd. dirs.; pres. Chamin & Co., 1984-87; mng. dir. Drexel Burnham Lambert Mdse., 1987—. Office: 131 S Rodeo Dr Beverly Hills CA 90212-2402

CHANIN, MICHAEL HENRY, lawyer; b. Atlanta, Nov. 11, 1943; s. Henry and Herma Irene (Blumenthal) C.; m. Margaret L. Jennings, June 15, 1968; children: Herma Louise, Richard Henry, Patrick Jennings. AB, U. N.C., 1965; JD, Emory U., 1968. Bar: Ga. 1968, D.C. 1981. Dir. So. Ctr. for Studies in Pub. Policy, Atlanta, 1968-69; asst. and acting legal officer 1st Coast Guard Dist., Boston, 1969-72; atty. Powell, Goldstein Frazer & Murphy, Atlanta, 1972-77; spl. asst. to sec. U.S. Dept. Commerce, Washington, 1977-78; dep. asst. to pres. The White House, Washington, 1978-81; ptnr. Powell, Goldstein, Frazer & Murphy, Washington, 1981—. Served to lt. USCGR, 1969-72. Mem. ABA, D.C. Bar Assn., State Bar Ga. Democrat. Office: Powell Goldstein Frazer & Murphy 1001 Pennsylvania Ave NW Fl 6 Washington DC 20004-2505

CHANIN, ROBERT HOWARD, lawyer; b. Bklyn., Dec. 24, 1934; s. Frank and Irene (Goldfein) C.; m. Rhoda Paley, June 9, 1957; children: Jeffrey, Stacy, Lisa. BA, Bklyn. Coll., 1956; LLB, Yale U., 1959; MA, Columbia U., 1961. Bar: N.Y. 1959, D.C. 1969. Instr. in psychology New Haven Coll., 1956-59;

staff atty. Law Sch. Columbia U., N.Y.C., 1959-62; assoc. Kaye, Scholer, Fierman, Hays & Handler, N.Y.C., 1962-68; gen. counsel NEA, Washington, 1968—, gen. counsel, dep. exec. dir., 1973-80. Profl. lectr. George Washington U. Law Sch., Washington, 1973-80; mem. Bredhoff & Kaiser, P.L.L.C., Washington, 1980—; trustee NEA Ins. Trust, Washington, 1975—. Author: The Law and Practice of Teacher Negotiations, 1970, The Law and Practice of Teacher Negotiations, 1974; contbr. articles to profl. jours. Mem. Nat. Orgn. Lawyers for Edn. Assn. (pres. 1969—). Office: Bredhoff & Kaiser PLLC 805 15th St NW Ste 1000 Washington DC 20005-2286

CHANNING, CAROL, actress; b. Seattle, Jan. 31, 1921; d. George Channing and Adelaide (Glaser) C.; m. Charles F. Lowe, Sept. 5, 1956 (div.); 1 son, Channing George. Student, Bennington Coll. Actress: (Broadway prodns.) No for an Answer, 1941, Let's Face It, 1941, Proof Through the Night, 1942, So Proudly We Hail, Lend an Ear, 1948 (Theatre World award, Critic's Circle award), Gentlemen Prefer Blondes, 1949, 51-53, Wonderful Town, 1953, Pygmalian, 1953, The Vamp, 1955, Show Business, 1959, Show Girl, 1961, George Burns-Carol Channing Musical Revue, 1962, The Millionairess, 1963, Hello Dolly, 1964-67, also 3 revivals (Tony award for Best Actress, N.Y. Drama Critics Cir. award for Best Actress), Carol Channing and Her Ten Stout-Hearted Men, 1970 (London Critics award), Four on a Garden, 1971, In Cabarets, 1972, Festival at Ford's, 1972, Carol Channing and Her Gentlemen Who Prefer Blondes Revue, 1972, Jerry's Girls, 1984-85, Legends, 1986, (theatre tours) Lorelei, 1973-75, Carol's Broadway Revue; (films) First Travelling Saleslady, 1956, Thoroughly Modern Millie, 1967 (Golden Globe award as Best Supporting Actress 1967), Skidoo, 1968, Shinbone Alley (voice), 1971, Sgt. Peppers Lonely Hearts Club Band, 1978, Happily Ever After (voice), 1990, Hans Christian Andersen's Thumbelina (voice), 1994, The Line King: Al Hirschfeld, 1996, others; (TV prodns.) Svengali and the Blonde, Three Men on a Horse, Crescendo; (TV appearences) The Love Boat, 1977, Alice in Wonderland, 1985, Where's Waldo? (voice), 1991, Addams Family (voice), 1992, The Magic School Bus (voice), 1994, Homo Heights, 1998; autobiography: Just Lucky I Guess, 2002 Recipient Best Night Club Act award, 1957, 64, Spl. Tony award, 1968, Theatre World award for Bronze medallion City of N.Y., 1978, Lifetime Achievement Tony award, 1995. Christian Scientist. Office: William Morris Agy 1 William Morris Pl Beverly Hills CA 90212

CHANNING, LAURENCE, graphics artist; b. Boston, May 13, 1942; s. Laurence Minot and Mary (Carter) C.; m. Barbara Lawrence, Sept. 1961 (div. 1968); children: David, Katharine, Edward; m. Susan Rose Channing, June 13, 1970; 1 child, Haley. BFA, MFA, Yale U., 1968. Exhbn. and graphics designer Wadsworth Atheneum, Hartford, Conn., 1967-70, Kimbell Art Mus., Ft. Worth, Tex., 1970-72; pub. designer Worcester (Mass.) Art Mus., 1972-75; exghn. graphics designer Isabella Stewart Gardner Mus., Boston, 1973-78, The Bostonian Soc., 1974-80; graphic designer Phila. Mus. Art, 1982-85; head of pubs. The Cleve. Mus. of Art, 1985—. One-man shows include William Busta Gallery, Cleve., 1991-92, 94-95, 97; exhibited in group shows at Addison Gallery Am. Art, Andover, Mass., 1998, Riffe Gallery, Columbus, New Work, The Bonfoey Co., Cleve., 1999, Cleve. Ctr. for Contemporary Art, 1999, Spheris Gallery, NYC, 2000; commns. include Univ. Print Club, 1998, Print Club of Cleve., 2001; represented in collections Addison Gallery Am. Art, Cleve. Mus. Art. Mem. vis. com. on the arts Groton (Mass.) Sch., 1998—. Ohio Arts Coun. fellow, 1990, 98, 2003; recipient Pub. awards Am. Assn. Mus., 1983-89, 93, 97-98, Print Regional awards Print Mag., 1983, 89, Cleve. Arts prize Women's City Club Cleve., 2000. Home: 3069 Scarborough Rd Cleveland Heights OH 44118 Office: The Cleveland Museum of Art 11150 E Boulevard Cleveland OH 44106 E-mail: lchanning@clevelandart.org.

CHANOCK, ROBERT MERRITT, pediatrician; b. Chgo., July 8, 1924; married; two children. BS, U. Chgo., 1945, MD, 1947, DSc (hon.), 1977. NRC fellow Children's Hosp., Cin., 1950—52; asst. prof. rsch. pediat. Coll. Medicine, U. Cin., 1954—56; asst. prof. epidemiology Sch. Hygiene and Pub. Health, Johns Hopkins U., 1956—57; surgeon USPHS, 1957—59, head respiratory viruses sect., 1959—61; chief lab. infectious diseases Nat. Inst. Allergy and Infectious Diseases, NIH, Bethesda, Md., 1968—. Nat. Found. Infantile Paralysis fellow, 1951—52; sr. rsch. fellow USPHS, 1956—57; virologist Children's Hosp. D.C., 1957—; mem. Internat. Nomenclature Com. Myxoviruses, 7th and 8th Internat. Microbiol. Congress, Armed Forces Epidemiology Bd., Com. Acute Respiratory Disease, 1960—62; assoc. mem. Com. Influenza, 1963—74; dir. Internat. Ref. Ctr. Lab. Mycroplasms, WHO, 1962; mem. Internat. Com. Nomenclature Bacteria, 1966; clin. prof. Georgetown U., 1970—71; mem. nominating com. NAS, 1979—80; mem. sci. rev. com. Scripps Clin. and Rsch. Found., 1986—89. Recipient E. Mead Johnson award pediatric rsch., 1964, Squibb Gorgas medal, Assn. Mil. Surgeons, 1972, Robert Koch medal, Fed. Republic of Germany, 1981, Virol prize, ICT Internat., 1990, Bristol-Myers Squibb award, Albert B. Sabin Gold medal. Mem. NAS, Soc. Pediat. Rsch., Am. Soc. Microbiology, Am. Epidemiol. Soc., Am. Epidemiology, Am. Pediat. Soc., Am. Soc. Clin. Investigation, Soc. Exptl. Biology and Medicine, Assn. Am. Physicians, Royal Danish Acad. Scis. (fgn. mem.). Office: NIH Inst Allergy Infectious Diseases Lab Infectious Diseases 7 Center Dr Rm 100 Bethesda MD 20817

CHAO, ALEXANDER WU, physicist, educator; s. Tu-Hong and Roung Chao; m. Patricia Wen-I Yang, May 29, 1973; children: Clifford, Laura. PhD, SUNY, Stony Brook, 1974. Postdoctoral rschr. Stanford (Calif.) Linear Accelerator Ctr., 1974—76, exptl. physicist, 1976—82, group leader, 1982—84; divsn. head Superconducting Super Collider Conceptual Design Group, Berkeley, Calif., 1984—89; sr. scientist, assoc. project mgr. Superconducting Super Collider Lab., Dallas, 1989—93; prof. physics Stanford (Calif.) U., 1993—. Fellow: Am. Phys. Soc.; mem.: Academia Sinica Taiwan (academician). Office: Stanford Linear Accelerator Center Mail Stop 26 PO Box 20450 Stanford CA 94309 E-mail: achao@slac.stanford.edu.

CHAO, BEI TSE, mechanical engineering educator; b. Soochow, China, Dec. 18, 1918; arrived in U.S., 1948, naturalized, 1962; s. Tse Yu and Yin T. (Yao) C.; m. May Kiang, Feb. 7, 1948; children: Clara, Fred Roberto. BS in Elec. Engring. with highest honor, Nat. Chiao-Tung U., China, 1939; PhD (Boxer Indemnity scholar), Victoria U., Manchester, Eng., 1947. Asst. engr. tool and gage div. Central Machine Works, Kunming, China, 1939-41, asso. engr., 1941-43, mgr. tool and gage div., 1943-45; research asst. U. Ill., Urbana, 1948-50, asst. prof. dept. mech. engring., 1951-53, assoc. prof., 1953-55, prof., 1955-87, prof. emeritus, 1987—, head thermal sci. div., 1971-75, head dept. mech. and indsl. engring., 1975-87; assoc. mem. U. Ill. (Center for Advanced Study), 1963-64. Cons. to industry and govtl. agys., 1950-94; vis. Russell S. Springer prof. mech. engring. U. Calif., Berkeley, 1973; mem. reviewing staff Zentralblatt für Mathematik, Berlin, 1970-82; mem. U.S. Engring. Edn. Del. to Visit People's Republic of China, 1978; mem. adv. screening com. in engring. Fulbright-Hays Awards Program, 1979-81, chmn., 1980, 81; mem. com. U.S. Army basic sci. rsch. NRC, 1980-83; Prince disting. lectr. Ariz. State U., 1984; bd. dirs. Aircraft Gear Corp., 1989-94. Author: Advanced Heat Transfer, 1969; tech. editor Jour. Heat Transfer, 1975-81; mem. adv. edit. bd. Numerical Heat Transfer, 1977-95; mem. hon. edit. bd. Internat. Jour. Heat and Mass Transfer, 1987-97, Internat. Comm. in Heat and Mass Transfer, 1987-97; contbr. numerous articles on mech. engring. to profl. jours. Recipient Outstanding Tchr. award Ill. Mech. Engring. Alumni, 1978, Max Jakob Meml. award ASME/Am. Inst. Chem. Engring., 1983; Tau Beta Pi Daniel C. Drucker eminent faculty award, 1985; Univ. scholar, 1985 Fellow AAAS, ASME (hon.; Blackall award 1957, Heat Transfer award 1971, William T. Ennor Mfg. Tech. award 1992), Am. Soc. Engring. Edn. (Outstanding Tchr. award 1975, Western Electric Fund award 1973, Ralph Coats Roe award 1975, Benjamin Garver Lamme award 1984, Centennial Medallion 1993); mem. Nat. Acad. Engring., Academia Sinica, Chiao-Tung U. Alumni Assn. (pres. Midwest sect. 1975-76), Tau Beta Pi, Pi Tau Sigma (hon.). Home: 101 W Windsor Rd Apt 6103 Urbana IL 61802-6663 Office: Univ Ill 264 Mech Engring Bldg 1206 W Green St Urbana IL 61801-2906 E-mail: btmchao@hotmail.com.

CHAO, ELAINE L. secretary of labor; d. James S.C. and Ruth M.L. (Chu) C.; m. Mitch McConnell, 1993. AB, Mt. Holyoke Coll., 1975; MBA, Harvard U., 1979; LLD (hon.), Villanova U., 1989, Sacred Heart U., 1991; DLD (hon.), St. John's U., 1991; DHL (hon.), Niagara U., 1992, Goucher Coll., 1996, U. Louisville, 1996; DHum (hon.), Drexel U., 1992, St. John's U., 1991, Thomas More Coll., 1994, Ky. Wesleyan Coll., 1998; D Arts and Letters (hon.), Miami-Dade C.C., 2001; DPA (hon.), Campbellsville U., 2002; D Pub. Svcs. (hon.), DePauw U., 2002; LLD (hon.), St. Marys Coll., 2002. Assoc. Gulf Oil Corp., Pitts., summer 1978; sr. lending officer Citicorp, NA, N.Y.C., 1979-83; v.p. capital markets group BankAmerica, San Francisco, 1984-86; dep. maritime adminstr. U.S. Dept. Transp., Washington, 1986-88; chmn. Fed. Maritime Commn., Washington, 1988; dep. sec. U.S. Dept. Transp., Washington, 1989-91; pres. United Way Am., Alexandria, Va., 1992-96; sr. editor, disting. fellow The Heritage Found., Washington; sec. U.S. Dept. Labor, Washington, 2001—. White House fellow, 1983-84; adj. asst. prof. Grad. Sch. Bus. Adminstrn., St. John's U., 1984. Recipient Young Achiever award Nat. Coun. Women U.S., Inc., 1986; Eisenhower Fellow Assn. fellow, 1984; named. one of 10 Outstanding Women of Am., 1988. Mem. Coun. on Fgn. Rels., Inc., Am. Coun. Young Polit. Leaders (bd. dirs. 1989), Harvard Bus. Sch. (vis. com. 1989, Outstanding Alumni award 1993), Harvard Club. Republican. Office: Dept Labor Off of Sec 200 Constitution Ave NW Washington DC 20210

CHAO, GEORGIA, biostatistician; b. Taipei, Taiwan, Nov. 26, 1964; arrived in U.S., 1993; m. Jonathan Cooperman, Nov. 24, 1995. BBA in Indsl. Mgmt. Sci., Nat. Chengkung U., Tainan, Taiwan, 1990; MS in Stats., Temple U., 2000. Biostatistician Premier Rsch., Phila., 2000—. Mem.: Am. Statis. Assn. Home: 1028 Hartranft Ave Fort Washington PA 19034 E-mail: chiaochi2000@yahoo.com.

CHAO, JAMES LEE, chemist, educator; b. Lafayette, Ind., Sept. 4, 1954; s. Tai Siang and Hsiang Lin (Lee) Chao; m. Juliana Meimei Ma, Apr. 4, 1992; 1 child, Jamie. BS in Chemistry, U. Ill., 1975, MS in Chemistry, 1976; PhD in Chemistry, U. Calif., Berkeley, 1980. Applications scientist IBM Instruments, Inc., Danbury, Conn., 1980-87; vis. assoc. prof. dept. chemistry Duke U., Durham, N.C., 1986-87, adj. asst. prof. dept. chemistry, 1987-91, adj. assoc. prof., 1992-2000, adj. prof., 2000—; adv. scientist Materials Engring. Lab., IBM, Research Triangle Park, N.C., 1987-2000, program mgr. for strategic IP licensing, 2000—02, IBM alphaworks emerging tech. strategist, 2002—. Cons. Lab. for Laser Energetics, U. Rochester, N.Y., 1979-80; postdoctoral fellow Lab. for Chem. Biodynamics, Lawrence Berkeley Lab., 1980; referee Applied Spectroscopy, 1982—, Applied Physics Letters, Jour. Applied Physics, 1989—; grant referee N.C. Biotech. Ctr., 1991—. Contbr. articles to profl. jours. Edmund James scholar, 1972-75, Dow Chem. scholar, 1977. Fellow N.Y. Acad. Scis., Am. Inst. Chemists; mem. ASTM, Am. Chem. Soc. (chmn. N.C. sect. 1991, councilor 1993—, mem. internat. activities com. 1998-2001, assoc. mem. patents and related matters 2002-, editl. bd. ACS Job Spectrum 2002-, Marcus E. Hobbs svc. award 1995), Soc. for Applied Spectroscopy, Coblentz Soc., Triangle Coun. Engring. and Sci. Socs. (treas. 1992-94), Sigma Xi. Achievements include development of step scan implementation for FT-IR spectrometers to study photothermal and time-resolved spectroscopies; stds. project authority for IBM environmental gaseous corrosion testing. Home: 7424 Ridgefield Dr Durham NC 27713-9503 Office: IBM Corp Dept WUVA/667 PO Box 12195 RTP Durham NC 27709

CHAO, JAMES MIN-TZU, architect; b. Dairen, China, Feb. 27, 1940; came to U.S., 1949; naturalized, 1962; m. Kirsti Helena Lehtonen, May 15, 1968. BArch, U. Calif., Berkeley, 1965. Registered arch., Calif., Ariz., Colo., Ill., N.Mex.; cert. instr. real estate, Calif. Intermediate draftsman Spencer, Lee & Busse, Archs., San Francisco, 1966-67; asst. to pres. Import Plus Inc., Santa Clara, Calif., 1967-69; job capt. Hammaberg and Herman, Archs., Oakland, Calif., 1969-71; project mgr. B A Premises Corp., San Francisco, 1971-79; constrn. mgr. The Straw Hat Restaurant Corp., San Francisco, 1979-81, mem. sr. mgmt., dir. real estate and constrn., 1981-87; mem. mktg. com. Straw Hat Coop. Corp., San Francisco, 1988-91; pvt. practice Berkeley, 1987—; dir. real estate Papillon Devel. Inc., 1998—. Pres. Food Svc. Cons. Inc., 1987-89; pres., CEO Stratsac, Inc., 1987-92; prin. arch. Alpha Cons. Group Inc., 1991-98; v.p. Intersyn Industries Calif., 1993-99; nat. tng. dir. Excel Telecom., Inc., 1995-99; CEO Nuts and Bolts Books, 1997—; lectr. comml. real estate site analysis and selection for profl. real estate seminars; coord. minority vending program, solar application program Bank of Am.; guest faculty mem. N.W. Ctr. for Profl. Edn.; mem. Nat. Coun. Archtl. Registration Bds., 1998—. Author: The Street-Smart Restaurant Development Handbook, 1996; patentee tidal electric generating system; author 1st comprehensive consumer orientated performance specification for remote banking transaction. Patron charter mem. Asian Art Mus., San Francisco, 2002—. Mem. Encinal Yacht Club (bd. dirs. 1977-78). Republican.

CHAO, JASON, family physician, educator; b. Chgo., July 18, 1955; s. Jen-Hung and Julia (Yu) C.; m. Betsy Charlene Wolf, July 27, 1984; 1 child, Elysa Wolf Chao. BS, Northwestern U., 1977, MD, 1979; MS, Case Western Res. U., 1984. Registerd physician, Ohio; diplomate Am. Bd. Family Practice. Resident family practice U. Iowa Hosps. and Clinics, Iowa City, 1979-82; fellow family medicine Case Western Res. U., Robert Wood Johnson Faculty Devel., Cleve., 1982-84; asst. prof. Case Western Res. U., Cleve., 1984-93, assoc. prof., 1993—. Attending physician U. Hosps. of Cleve., Ohio, 1984—, med. dir. dept. family practice, 1991-95; trustee Ohio Group Against Smoking Pollution, 1986-89; exec. com. Clin. Sci. Program, Case Western Res. U. Med. Sch., Cleve., 1990-92; assoc. med. dir. QualChoice Health Plan, 1995-97, med. dir., 1997-99; curriculum dir. Year 1-2 primary care track Case Western Res. U. Med. sch., Cleve., 1999—, predoctoral divsn. dir. dept. family medicine, 2000—. Author: (computer instrnl. materials) MED-CAPS Diagnostic Problem Cases, 1989; contbr. articles to profl. jours. Vol. physician Cleve. (Ohio) Free Med. Clinic, 1982—; bd. dirs. Chinese Student and Alumni Svcs., 1984-86; systems operator Family Medicine Area of Cleve. Freenet, 1985-99; mem. all-star volleyball team Euclid Ch. League, Cleve., 1988, 89, 91, 95, 96, 97, 98, 99, 2000, 2002. Recipient Community Svc. award Northwestern U. Med. Sch., Chgo., 1979, grant for predoctoral tng. in family medicine USPHS, 1987-90, 2001—. Fellow Am. Acad. Family Physicians; mem. Ohio Acad. Family Physicians (rsch. advisor 1987-93, Merit award 1988), Cleve. Acad. Family Physicians, Soc. Tchrs. Family Medicine, N.Am. Primary Care Rsch. Group, Physicians for Social Responsibility (treas. NEO chpt. 1984-2000, pres. NEO chpt. 2000—), Chinese Am. Med. Soc. Methodist. Avocations: computers, volleyball, downhill skiing. Office: 11100 Euclid Ave Cleveland OH 44106-1736

CHAO, MARSHALL, chemist; b. Changsha, Hunan, China, Nov. 20, 1924; came to U.S., 1955, s. Heng-ti and Hwei-yng C.; m. Patricia Hu, July 20, 1968; 1 dau., Anita A. BS, Nat. Central U., Nanking, China, 1947; MS, U. Ill., 1958, PhD, 1961. Tech. asst. Taiwan Fertilizer Co., Taipei, 1949-55; research chemist Dow Chem. Co., Midland, Mich., 1960-72, research specialist, 1973-80; research leader Dow chem. Co., Midland, Mich., 1980-86; sr. assoc. Omni Tech Internat., Ltd., Midland, 1986—. Author: Taiwan Fertilizers, 1951; editor newsletter Midland Chinese Christian Fellowship, 1987-94; contbr. articles to profl. jours.; patentee in field. Mem. Ch. Council Grace Bapt. Ch., Taipei, 1951-55; deacon 1st Baptist Ch., Midland, 1974-76. Univ. fellow U. Ill., 1957-60 Fellow Am. Inst. Chemists; mem. Am. Chem. Soc., Electrochem. Soc. (sect. chmn. 1973-74, 83-84, councilor 1974-76, 85—, vice chmn. 1964-65), Soc. Electroanalytical chemistry (charter), N.Y. Acad. Scis., Mensa, Sigma Xi, Phi Lambda Upsilon Clubs: Midland Chinese (chmn. 1975-76), Tittabawassee Toastmasters (sec.-treas. 1976-77). Home: 1206 Evamar Dr Midland MI 48640-7213 Office: Omni Tech Internat Ltd 2715 Ashman St Midland MI 48640-4449 *A man's intrinsic worth is measured by the good he has done his fellow men. As for outward signs of success, such as recognition or rewards, he should much rather have people wondering why he didn't get them than have people wondering why he got them at all.*

CHAO, TSAI CHUNG, physician, residency program director; b. Hangzhou, Zhejiang, China, Oct. 13, 1944; came to U.S., 1981; s. Chi Chang and Chi Hsiao (Sun) C.; m. Hsian Fang Hsiang; children: Charlene, James. Diploma, Zhejiang Med. U., 1969; MD, SUNY, N.Y.C., 1993. Diplomate Am. Bd. Phys. Medicine and Rehab. Ind. Med. Examiners, Am. Acad. Pain Mgmt. Surg. intern Xiaoshan County Hosp., Xiaoshan City, China, 1969-70; gen. practitioner Xiaoshan Coal & Iron Mining, 1970-72; surg. ho. physician Linpu People's Hosp., Xiaoshan City, 1972-74; surg. resident Zhejiang Med. U., Hangzhou City, 1974-80; surg. oncology fellow Hangzhou Cancer Inst., 1980; asst. prof., staff surgeon Zhejiang Med. U., Hangzhou City, 1980-81; instr. S. Baylo U., Garden Grove, Calif., 1984-86, SAMRA U. Oriental Medicine, L.A., 1985-86; surg. resident Interfaith Med. Ctr., Bklyn., 1986-88; rehab. medicine resident SUNY Downstate Med. Ctr., Bklyn., 1988-91, clinic asst. prof., attending physician, 1991-97, dir. rehab. med. residency program, 1997—. Course dir. continuing med. edn. program in med. acupuncture SUNY Downstate Med. Ctr. Contbr. articles to profl. jours. Fellow Am. Acad. Phys. Med. and Rehab.; mem. AMA, Am. Congress Rehab. Medicine, Am. Acad. Med. Acupunture, Am. Coll. Occupl. and Environ. Medicine, N.Y. Acad. Scis. Home: 330 E 38th St Apt 37N New York NY 10016-2782 Office: SUNY Health Sci Ctr PO Box 30 Brooklyn NY 11203-0030

CHAO, YONG-SHENG, physicist; b. Hexian, Anhui, China, Oct. 6, 1936; came to U.S., 1981; s. De-Yi and Wangshi Chao; m. Feng-Liu Chao, Apr. 8, 1967; children: Yi, Lei, Ying. BA, MS, Tsinghua U., Beijing, 1960; PhD, MIT, 1985. Dir. radiation lab. Atomic Energy Inst. Academia, Sinica, Beijing, 1960-80; vis. scientist, rsch. fellow MIT, Cambridge, 1981-85; rsch. assoc. Mass. Gen. Hosp./Harvard U. Med. Sch., Cambridge, 1985-89; sr. rsch. scientist Sci. Rsch. Assocs., Inc., Glastonbury, Conn., 1989-92; pres. Advaned Optical Techs., Inc., East Hartford, Conn., 1992—. Contbr. articles to profl. jours. Recipient Nat. prize Chinese Cen. Govt., 1978. Achievements include patents for three-dimensional x-ray imaging; novel high performace projection displays for high resolution projection displays for digital cinemas; electronic control of light beam direction in free space; electrooptical switching for fiberoptic communications, others; hand-held six dimensional pointing device for realtime control of computers and digital tvs. Office: 156 River Rd Ste H Willington CT 06279

CHAPDELAINE, PERRY ANTHONY, JR., public health and preventive medicine physician, educator; b. Mason City, Iowa, Feb. 23, 1950; s. Perry Anthony Sr. and Ruby Elizabeth (McCurley) C.; m. Catherine Joan Tidwell, May 22, 1981; 1 child, Rachel Maria. BA in Sociology, St. Ambrose U., 1972; MD, Meharry Med. Coll., 1989, MSPH, 1992. Diplomate Am. Bd. Preventive Medicine; registered land surveyor, Tenn., 1976-86. CEO, pres. AC Projects Inc., Franklin, Tenn., 1974-86; epidemiologist Meharry Med. Coll., Nashville, 1992-95, asst. prof., 1993—95, 2001—03, dir. preventive medicine residency program, 1995; chief med. physician City of Nashville, Metro Health Dept., 1995-2000; pvt. cons. practice, 2000—. Cons. St. Thomas Hosp. Clin. Ethics Ctr., Nashville, 1993-98, Nashville Prevention Mktg. Initiative, 1994-96; med. dir. Samaritan Recovery Cmty., Nashville, 1993-95; mem. Access Med Plus Peer Rev. Com., Nashville, 1996-2000. Co-editor: The John W. Campbell Letters, 1985 (Hugo award nominee 1986). Mem. Alpha Chi, Alpha Omega Alpha. Avocations: writing, photography, dulcimer, hiking. Home: 7111 Sweetgum Rd Fairview TN 37062-9384 Office: Preventive Medicine and Wellness Ctr 1415 Robinson Rd Old Hickory TN 37138 E-mail: docanthony1@yahoo.com.

CHAPEL, ROBERT CLYDE, stage director, theater educator; b. June 25, 1945; married. BA in TV, U. Mich., 1967, MA in Theatre, 1968, PhD in Theatre, 1974. Asst. prof. dept. theatre U. Ala., Ala., 1974-75; profl. actor LA, 1975-77; dir. devel. Force Ten Prod., LA, 1977-78; v.p. prodn. Trans-Atlantic Enterprises, LA, 1978-81; actor, dir. LA, 1981-83; dir. BFA mus. theatre program U. Mich., Mich., 1983-84; coordinating dir. MFA mus. theatre program Tisch Sch. of Arts NYU, NYC, 1984—86; co-prodr. Shubert Archives Series Lyceum Theatre, NYC, 1984-86; artistic dir. Music Theatre North, Potsdam, NY, 1986; freelance dir. NYC, 1986—88; dir. mus. theatre program San Diego State U., San Diego, 1988-90; prof., chair dept. drama U. Va., Va., 1990—; mng. dir. Heritage Repertory Theatre, Charlottesville, Va., 1990-94, prodr., artistic dir., 1995—; exec. dir. Va. Film Festival, Va., 1996—2000. Chmn. pres. commn. on fine arts and performing arts U. Va., 1998-2001. Mem. SAG, AFTRA, Assn. for Theatre in Higher Edn., Nat. Assn. Schs. of Theatre, Actors Equity Assn., Soc. Stage Dirs. and Choreographers. Home: 1029 Hazel St Charlottesville VA 22902-4904 E-mail: rcc2u@virginia.edu.

CHAPEL, SUNNY, research scientist; b. Seoul, Republic of Korea, Sept. 12, 1968; d. ChinSuk Kim; m. Steven E. Chapel, Mar. 2, 1967; 1 child, Stanley E. BS in Pharmacy, Seoul Nat. U., 1992, MS in Bioanalytical Chemistry, 1995; MS in Stats., U. Iowa, 2000, PhD in Pharmacokinetics, 2001. Lic. pharmacist Korea, 1992. Rsch. asst. U. Iowa, Iowa City, 1995—2001; rsch. scientist Aventis Pharmaceuticals, Inc, Bridgewater, NJ, 2002—. Recipient Grad. rsch. award, AAPS, 2001. Office: Aventis Pharmaceuticals Inc Mail Stop 303B 1041 Route 202/206 Bridgewater NJ 08807 Office Fax: 908-231-5932. Personal E-mail: sunnychapel@earthlink.net. E-mail: sunny.chapel@aventis.com.

CHAPELLE, SUZANNE ELLERY GREENE, history educator; b. Phila., Sept. 21, 1942; d. John Channing and Jessie Horn (Myers) Ellery; m. Michael Thomas Greene, Sept. 15, 1972 (dec. 1973); 1 child, Jennifer; m. Francis Oberlin Chapelle, Apr. 14, 1984 (dec. 1999). BA, Harvard U., 1964; MA, Johns Hopkins U., 1966, PhD, 1970. Asst. prof. Am. history Towson State U., Balt., 1969-71; assoc. prof. Am. history Morgan State U., Balt., 1971-75, prof., 1975—. Author: Books for Pleasure, 1976, Baltimore: An Illustrated History, 1980, 2d rev. edit., 2000; sr. author: Maryland: A History of its People, 1986; revisions author: A Child's History of the World, 1994, African American Leaders of Maryland, 2000, The Maryland Adventure, 2001; mem. publs. bd. Md. Hist. Soc. Bd. dirs. Md. Interfaith Coalition for the Environment, 1997-2001, v.p., 1999-2001; bd. dirs. Md. Conservation Coun., 1999-2000, Irvine Nature Ctr., 2001—. Mem. Am. Hist. Assn., Am. Studies Assn. (mem. exec. bd. Chesapeake chpt. 1988-90), Popular Culture Assn. (bd. dirs. 1980-82), Orgn. Am. Historians, Md. Hist. Soc. (publs. com. 1998—), Mid-Atlantic Popular Culture Assn. (pres. 1977-80), Balt. County League Environ. Voters (exec. bd. 1992-96), Episcopal Diocese of Md. Com. on the Environ. (sec. 1994—), Ruxton-Riderwood Assn. (bd. govs. 1987-91), The Johns Hopkins Club, The Harvard-Radcliffe Club Md. Episcopalian. Home: 6021 Lakeview Rd Baltimore MD 21210-1033 Office: Morgan State U Hist Dept Baltimore MD 21251-0001 E-mail: schapelle@moac.morgan.edu., suechapelle@hotmail.com.

CHAPIN, DEBORAH, artist; b. Ft. Collins, Colo., Jan. 15, 1954; d. Wallace Everett and Nancy Arlene (Jones) Chapin; m. Calvin Lee Keeler, May 25, 1979 (div. Sept. 1987). BS in Biology, Mary Washington Coll./U. Va., 1976; postgrad. French studies, USDA, Washington, 1990-92; master classes, Nat. Acad., 1999, acad. atelier, 2002. One-woman shows include Grand Central Galleries, 1984, Greenwich (Conn.) Workshop Galleries, 1987, Audubon Naturalist Soc., 1992, 94-95, 2002, Nat. Arts Club, Gregg Gallery, N.Y., 1998, 2003, Palette and Chisel, Chgo., 2002; group shows include Balt. Museum of Art, 1980, Greenwich Workshop Galleries, 1983-85, Mystic (Conn.) Seaport Museum, 1984-87, Md. Hist. Museum, Balt., 1989, Catharine Lorillard Exhbn., 1982-83, 94, Colo. Hist. Mus., 1988, 90, R.J. Schafter Mus., Mystic, Conn., 1992, Salmagundi Open, N.Y.C., 1996, Louvre-Salon de Soc. Nat. des Beaux Arts, Paris, 1999-2001, Grand Palais, Salon des Ind., Paris, 1993-94, others; participant Arts-in-Embassies program, exhibited in Am. Embassies in Abu Dhabi, Quito, Ecuador, Sanaa, Yemen, Bogota, Colombia, Baku, Azerbaijan. Mem. Nat. Arts Club, Artists Fellowship, Calif. Art Club, Artists of Am., Soc. Nat. Soc. des Beaux Arts, Am. Artists Profl. League (artist fellow), So. Vt. Art Ctr., Nat. Acad. Profl. Plein Air Painters. Avocations: hiking, swimming, still and video photography. E-mail: nhstudios@nhstudios.com.

CHAPIN, DWIGHT ALLAN, columnist, writer; b. Lewiston, Idaho, June 16, 1938; s. Don Merle and Lucille Verna (Walker) C.; m. Susan Enid Fisk, Feb. 14, 1963 (div. 1973); children— Carla, Adam; m. Ellen Gonzalez, Aug. 10, 1983 BA, U. Idaho, 1960; MS in Journalism, Columbia U., 1961. Reporter Lewiston Morning Tribune, Idaho, 1956-62; reporter, editor Vancouver Columbian, Wash., 1962-65; sportswriter Seattle Post-Intelligencer, 1965-67, Los Angeles Times, 1967-77; columnist San Francisco Examiner, 1977-2000, San Francisco Chronicle, 2000—. Co-author: Wizard of Westwood, 1973; contbr. numerous articles to popular mags. Served with USNG, 1962-68 Recipient Sports Writing award AP, Calif./Nev., 1968-69; Baseball Writing award Am. Assn. Coll. Baseball Coaches Mem. Sigma Delta Chi (sports writing award Wash. state 1964, 65, 66) Democrat. Avocation: trading card and sports memorabilia collecting. Office: San Francisco Chronicle 901 Mission St San Francisco CA 94103-2988 E-mail: dchapin@sfchronicle.com.

CHAPIN, JUNE ROEDIGER, education educator; b. Chgo., May 19, 1931; d. Henry and Stephanie L. (Palke) Roediger; m. Ned Chapin, June 12, 1954; children: Suzanne, Elaine. BA in Liberal Arts, U. Chgo., 1952, MA in Social Sci., 1954; EdD in Edn., Stanford U., 1963. Tchr. credentials, Calif., Ill. Tchr. Chgo. (Ill.) Pub. Schs., 1954-56, Redwood City (Calif.) Schs., 1956-60, San Francisco (Calif.) State U., 1963-65, U. Santa Clara, Calif., 1965-67; prof. edn. Coll. Notre Dame (now Notre Dame de Namur U.), Belmont, Calif., 1967—. Author, co-author twelve books. Recipient Hilda Taba award Calif. State Social Studies Coun., 1976. Mem. Am. Sociol. Assn., Am. Ednl. Rsch. Assn., Nat.

Coun. for the Social Studies, Social Sci. Edn. Consortium, Phi Delta Kappa. Avocations: swimming, stamp collecting. Home: 1190 Bellair Way Menlo Park CA 94025-6611 E-mail: JuneChapin@aol.com.

CHAPIN, MARY Q. television personality, arbitrator, mediator, writer, performing artist; b. Shepherdstown, W.VA., May 5, 1933; d. Guy Estil and Anne Mildred (Jones) Quisenberry; m. Edward John Chapin Jr.; children: John Edward, Susan Q. (dec.). SUNY Regent's Degree, 1985; AAS, SUNY, Binghamton, BS, 1991. Pers. adminstr. Mohawk Valley Psychiatric Ctr., Utica, N.Y., 1976-89; arbitrator Am. Arbitration Assn., N.Y.C., 1989-99; pres. Dispute Resolution Internat., New Hartford, N.Y., 1993—; neutral chair NYSDOL Office of Labor Mgmt., Albany, N.Y., 1993—. Mem. adv. coun. on safety and security in N.Y. State schs. N.Y. State Dept. Edn., Albany, 1995-97; founder, mem., bd. dirs. Forum on Conflict and Concensus, 1993-941 chair Mohawk Valley Women's History Project, 1998—. Author: Woman's Suffrage: A Dream of Full Citizenship; author, performer An Afternoon with Susan B. Anthony; host weekly TV show. Pres. Utica/Rome Metro League of Women Voters, 1992-97; coord. Com. on Met. Orgn., 1995-97; coord. of multicultural commn. League of Women Voters Edn. Fund, 1997; trustee amerita Mohawk Valley Cmty. Coll., 1996-2002; Utica C. of C., 1995-98. Recipient Found. award The Found. of SUNY at Binghamton, 1992, Recognition award NYS League of Women Voters, 1995, 97, Recognition award U.S. LWV Edn. Fund, 1998, Labor Mgmt. award Office of Mental Health, 1988, Conservator of Women's History award NOW, 2002. Mem. AAUW, Central N.Y. Futurist, Bd. Neighborhood Ctr. Home and Office: 56 Woodbrooke Rd New Hartford NY 13413-4805

CHAPIN, MARYAN FOX, civic worker; b. Easton, Pa., Apr. 26, 1933; d. Louis Rodman and Mary Catherine (Cannon) Fox; m. Richard Chapin, Nov. 3, 1956; children: Aldus Higgins II, Margery Rodman, Marya Marsh, Richard Dickinson. AB, Vassar Coll., 1954. Contr. Chapin's Market, Cambridge, 1986-88. Trustee Longy Sch. Music, 1974-75; pres. founding bd. trustees New Sch. Music, 1976-77; bd. dirs. Young Audiences of Mass., 1976-83, chairman, 1980-82; adv. bd. Wheelock Coll. Family Theatre, 1985-92; treas. Richards Libr., Georgetown, Maine; trustee Bowdoin Summer Music Festival, 1994-2003, chmn., 1997-99. Bd. dir. Lark Soc. for Chamber Music, 1997—; Maine Arts Commr., 2001-2003. Mem.: New Eng. Conservatory (bd overseers 1987—92), Vincent Club (bd. mgrs. 1961—67). Home: 13 Knubble Rd Georgetown ME 04548

CHAPIN, NANCY LOUISE GILBERT, librarian; b. Norfolk, Va., Nov. 3, 1938; d. Oscar Linwood Jr. and Mary Margaret (Nicholls) Gilbert; m. Neil McKay Chapin, Sept. 9, 2000. BA, Greensboro Coll., 1961; MLS, U. North Carolina, 1968. Libr. Va. Beach (Va.) Pub. Libr., 1968, U.S. Army, Worms, Crailsheim and Mannheim, Germany, 1968-74, Pentagon Libr., Washington, 1974-80, U.S. Army Mil. History Inst., Carlisle Barracks, Pa., 1980-2000, ret., 2000. Mem. Mid-Atlantic Region Archives Conf. Avocations: travel, reading, photography.

CHAPIN, RICHARD, arbitrator; b. Boston, Dec. 25, 1923; s. Vinton and Elizabeth (Higgins) C.; m. Maryan Gainor Fox, Nov. 3, 1956; children: Aldus Higgins II, Margery Rodman, Marya Chapin Lundgren, Richard Dickinson. SB, Harvard U., 1944, MBA, 1949; LLD (hon.), Emerson Coll., 1972. Asst. to treas. Anderson, Davis & Platt, Inc., 1946; journeyman machinist Yale & Towne Co., 1947; various adminstrn. and instnl. positions Harvard Grad. Sch. Bus. Adminstrn., 1949-67; pres. Emerson Coll., Boston, 1967-75. Dir. Norton Co., 1974-90; exec. dir. Cheswick Ctr., 1976-84, dir., 1984-95; bd. dirs. Advanced Mech. Tech., Inc.; hon. dir. Alden Yachts, Inc., Nickerson Lumber Co.; bd. advisors Venture Capital Fund Am.; arbitrator N.Y. Stock Exch., Nat. Assn. Security Dealers. Trustee Bigelow Found., Riggs Cove Found.; vice chmn. Bigelow Lab. Ocean Sci. Served with USNR, 1942-46. Mem.: N.Y. Yacht, Harvard, Tavern, St. Botolph. Home: 13 Knubble Rd Georgetown ME 04548-9410 Office: 13 Story St Ste #35 Cambridge MA 02138-4927 E-mail: rchapin440@aol.com.

CHAPIN, RICHARD EARL, retired librarian; b. Danville, Ill., Apr. 29, 1925; s. Harry W. and Lula May (Briggs) C.; m. Eleanor Jane Lang, Aug. 15, 1949; children: Robert Lang, David Brian, Rebecca Anne. AB, Wabash Coll., 1948; MS, U. Ill., 1949, PhD, 1954; LHD (hon.), Wabash Coll., 1991. Reference asst. Fla. State U., 1949-50; libr. asst. U. Ill., 1950-53, vis. prof., 1957; asst. dir., asst. prof. Sch. Libr. Sci., U. Okla., 1953-55; assoc. libr., assoc. prof. Mich. State U., East Lansing, 1955-59, dir. librs., prof. journalism, 1959-89, dir. librs. emeritus, prof. emeritus, 1989—; libr. advisor United Arab Emirates U., 1989-92. Dir. Mich. State U. Press, 1986-90; cons. to govts., founds., colls., and univs.; bd. dirs. Ctr. for Rsch. Librs., 1978-83; bd. dirs. OCLC Users' Coun., 1980-83, pres., 1983. Contbr. articles to libr. periodicals and encys. Mem. East Lansing Human Relations Commn., 1966-69, chmn., 1969; mem. East Lansing Bd. Edn., 1970-74, 75, pres., 1973-74; bd. dirs. W.B. and Candace Thoman Found., 1991—. Served to lt. (j.g.) USNR, 1943-46. Mem. ALA, Mich. Library Assn. (pres. 1967), Assn. Research Libraries (bd. dirs. 1984-87), Blue Key, Sigma Chi, Phi Kappa Phi Home: 2539 Koala Dr East Lansing MI 48823-7211 E-mail: chapinR@msu.edu.

CHAPIN, SCHUYLER GARRISON, cultural affairs executive, university dean; b. N.Y.C., Feb. 13, 1923; s. L.H. Paul and Leila H. (Burden) C.; m. Elizabeth Steinway, Mar. 15, 1947 (dec. 1993); children: Henry Burden, Theodore Steinway, Samuel Garrison, Miles Whitworth; m. Catia Zoullas Mortimer, Sept. 15, 1995. Student, Longy Sch. Music, 1940-41; LHD (hon.), NYU, 1974, Hobart/William Smith Coll., 1974, Hofstra Coll., 1999; DLitt (hon.), Emerson Coll., 1976; MusD (hon.), Mannes Coll., New Sch., 1990, Curtis Inst. Music, 2000. Spot salesman NBC-TV, N.Y.C., 1947-51; gen. mgr. Tex and Jinx McCary Enterprises, N.Y.C., 1951-53; booking dir. Judson, O'Neill & Judd divsn. Columbia Artists Mgmt., 1953-59; dir. masterworks to v.p. creative svcs. Columbia Records divsn. CBS, 1959-63; v.p. programming Lincoln Center for the Performing Arts, 1964-69; exec. producer Amberson Enterprises, N.Y.C., 1969-71; acting gen. mgr. Met. Opera, N.Y.C., 1972-73, gen. mgr., 1973-75; dean faculty arts Columbia U., 1976-87, dean emeritus, 1987—; v.p. worldwide concert and artist activities Steinway & Sons, N.Y.C., 1990-92; commr. of cultural affairs City of N.Y., 1994—2002. Cons. Carnegie Hall Corp., 1979-87. Author: (autobiography) Musical Chairs, 1977, Leonard Bernstein: Notes from a Friend, 1992, Sopranos, Mezzos, Tenors, Bassos and Other Friends, 1995. Past chmn. Bagby Music Lovers Found.; past chmn., trustee Am. Symphony Orch. League, 1985-92; trustee Naumburg Found., 1949, Richard Tucker Found., 1975-92, Am. Inst. for Verdi Studies, 1975, Bklyn. Philharm., 1978-92, Lenox Music Theatre Group, 1984, Lincoln Ctr. Theatre, 1985-94, 2001—, Carnegie Hall Soc., 1987-94, 2001—, Curtis Inst. Music, 1986-92, Pres.'s Com. on Arts and Humanities, 1982-90, Redwood Libr. and Athenaeum, 1990-96; chmn., exec. com. Franklin and Eleanor Roosevelt Inst., 1982—. Decorated chevalier Legion of Honor (France); recipient N.Y. State Conspicuous service cross, 1951, Christopher award, 1971, Emmy awards 1972, 76, 80, Gold Medal Nat. Arts Club, 1983. Fellow Am. Acad. Arts & Scis. Clubs: Century Assn. (N.Y.C.), Knickerbocker. Home: 655 Park Ave New York NY 10021-5937 *Throughout my career, and indeed my life, I have been fortunate to make my avocation my vocation. I've worked in, around, about and for the arts in a variety of ways. That, I hope, has brought as much happiness to others as it has to me. I have been privileged to be part of what a poet once called the Arts: the Signature of Man.*

CHAPIN, SUZANNE PHILLIPS, retired psychologist; b. Syracuse, N.Y., Aug. 9, 1930; d. Harold Bridge and Charlotte Virginia (Warner) Phillips; m. Richard Hilton Chapin, June 13, 1953 (div. 1964); children: Bruce Phillips Chapin, Linda Chapin Fry. BA, Syracuse U., 1952; MA, Columbia U., 1965. Statis. asst. Syracuse Bd. of Edn., 1952-53; psychol. examiner Stamford (Conn.) Pub. Schs., 1965-68, psychologist Head Start program, 1967-68; psychologist Southbury (Conn.) Tng. Sch., 1968-74, Onondaga Assn. for the Retarded, Syracuse, 1974, Harlem Valley Psychiatric Ctr., Wingdale, N.Y., 1974-93, Mid-Hudson Psychiat. Ctr., New Hampton, 1993; ret., 1993. Mem.: Nature Conservancy, LWV. Democrat. Avocations: biking, kayaking, golf, hiking, travel. Home: 10 S Bearwood Dr Palmyra VA 22963-2834 *Human beings suffer the vices of greed and prejudice, bringing wars and pollution which now threaten our continued existence on planet Earth. I fervently hope reason will prevail to both reduce population growth and control its vices.*

CHAPIN, THEODORE STEINWAY, entertainment company executive; b. N.Y.C., Sept. 7, 1950; s. Schuyler Garrison and Elizabeth (Steinway) C.; m. JoAnna Chapin, June 2, 1978; children: Anika, Zoe. BA, Conn. Coll., 1972. Assoc. Pangloss Prodns., N.Y.C., 1972-75; musical dir. Nat. Theatre of Deaf, Waterford, Conn., 1976-77; producer Musical Theatre Lab, N.Y.C., Washington, 1978-80; exec. dir. Rodgers & Hammerstein, N.Y.C., 1981-92; pres., exec. dir. The Rodgers & Hammerstein Orgn., N.Y.C., 1993—. Producer Smithsonian/Doubleday Series, Washington, 1981-87; panelist NEA/Opera Musical Theatre, Washington, 1985-89; mem. adminstrv. and nominating coms. Tony Award, 1986—. Home: 450 West End Ave New York NY 10024 Office: Rodgers & Hammerstein 1065 Ave Of The Americas # 2400 New York NY 10018-2506

CHAPLIN, HARVEY, wine and liquor wholesale executive; b. Bklyn., 1929; Chmn., CEO So. Wine Spirits of Am., Miami, 1994—. Office: Southern Wine & Spirits 1600 NW 163rd St Miami FL 33169-5672*

CHAPLIN, HUGH, JR., physician, educator; b. N.Y.C., Feb. 4, 1923; m. Alice Dougherty, June 16, 1945; 4 children; m. Lee Nelken Robins, Aug. 5, 1998. AB, Princeton U., 1943; MD, Columbia U., 1947. Diplomate Am. Bd. Internal Medicine, Nat. Bd. Med. Examiners. Intern Mass. Gen. Hosp., Boston, 1947-48, resident, 1948-50; fellow in hematology Brit. Postgrad. Med. Sch., London, 1951-53; physician in charge Clin. Center Blood Bank, NIH, Bethesda, Md., 1953-55; Commonwealth Fund fellow Wright Fleming Inst. Microbiology, London, 1962-63, Josiah Macy Faculty scholar, 1975-76. Instr. in medicine Washington U. Sch. Medicine, St. Louis, 1955-56, asst. prof. medicine and preventive medicine, 1956-62, asso. dean, chmn. admissions com., 1957-62, asso. prof., 1963-65, prof., 1965, William B. Kountz prof. preventive medicine, 1965-83; dir. IWJ Inst. of Rehab., St. Louis, 1964-72; prof. pathology, dir. Barnes Hosp. Blood Bank, St. Louis, 1983-91; emeritus prof. pathology and medicine, 1991—; mem. Am. Standards Com. for Blood Transfusion Equipment; mem. subcom. on transfusion problems NRC, 1959-62, mem. com. on blood and transfusion problems, 1963-67; chmn. ad hoc blood program research com. ARC, 1967-73, bd. govs., 1978-84 Assoc. editor Transfusion, 1960-98; contbg. editor Vox Sanguinis, 1960-79. Served with USNR, 1942-45. Mem. Am. Fedn. Clin. Research, Central Soc. Clin. Research, Am. Soc. Clin. Investigation, Assn. Am. Physicians, Am., Internat. socs. hematology, Brit. Med. Research Soc., Brit. Royal Soc. Medicine, Am. Assn. Blood Banks (sci. program com. 1959-60, Emily Cooley award 1968, Morton Grove-Rasmussen award 1985), Phi Beta Kappa, Alpha Omega Alpha, Sigma Xi. Office: Washington U Sch Medicine Box 8118 4949 Barnes Hospital Plz Saint Louis MO 63110-1003

CHAPLIN, PEGGY LOUIE, lawyer; b. Guantanamo Bay Naval Base, Cuba, Nov. 22, 1940; d. Raymond Gerard Fannon and Joan Marie (Carguil) Boyce. BS, Johns Hopkins U., 1971; JD, U. Md., 1973; LLM in Internat. Comml. Law, Georgetown U., 1983. Bar: Md. 1973, U.S. Dist. Ct. Md. 1973, U.S. Ct. Internat. Trade 1975, U.S. Ct. Appeals (fed. cir.) 1986, (D.C. cir.) 1988, U.S. Supreme Ct. 2003. V.p. Vanguard Shipping & Import, Balt., 1972-77, F.W. Myers & Co., Inc., Balt., 1977-84; assoc. Ober, Kaler, Grimes & Shriver, Balt., 1984-91, ptnr., 1992-97, Sandler, Travis & Rosenberg, P.A., Balt., 1997—. Chair Johns Hopkins U. Inst. of Policy Studies com. Logistics and the Economy, 1996-99. Contbr. articles to bar jours. Mem. Gov.'s Commn. World Trade Efforts, 1984, Balt. City Wage Commn., 1986-90, Md. Trade Policy Com., 1986; chair 2d Ann. Md. Internat. Trade Conf.; chair air cargo devel. com. BWI Econ. Devel. Coun., 1993-96. Mem.: NAFTA (chpt. 19 roster), Assn. Transp. Law, Logistics and Policy (newsletter editor Import/Export Regulation), Am. Assn. Exporters and Importers, Am. Arbitration Assn. (panelist), Md. Internat. Trade Assn. (pres. 1984—86), Women's Bar Assn. Md. (pres. 1977—78), Md. State Bar Assn. (chair internat. comml. law sect. 1991—92), Md. C. of C. (chmn. internat. trade com. 1984—97). Office: Sandler Travis & Rosenberg PA 111 S Calvert St Ste 2700 Baltimore MD 21202-6143 E-mail: pchaplin@strtrade.com.

CHAPLIN, STEPHEN MICHAEL, retired diplomat; b. Charleston, S.C., Dec. 28, 1940; s. George and Esta Lillian (Solomon) C.; m. Carol Joan McCloskey, Feb. 1, 1969; children: Christopher D., Jonathan B. BA, Kenyon Coll., 1962; MA, UCLA, 1966. Chief policy divsn. U.S. Info. Agy., Washington, 1980-82; counselor pub. affairs Am. Embassy, Lisbon, 1982-86; chief fgn. svc. personnel U.S. Info. Agy., Washington, 1986-87; exec. asst. to dir. and dep. dir. U.S. Info. Agy. Washington, 1986-87; counselor for pub. affairs Am. Embassy, Caracas, Venezuela, 1990-94; dir. office inter-Am. affairs U.S. Info. Agy., Washington, 1995-97, staff dir. resource mgmt. com., 1997-99; ret., 1999. Dir. Mexican Area studies course Fgn. Svc. Inst., Washington, 2000—. Mem. editl. bd. Fgn. Svc. Jour., 1980-82. 1st lt. USAF, 1962-65. Mem. Am. Fgn. Svc. Assn. (bd. dirs. 1980-82), Diplomatic and Consular Officers Retired, Inter-Am. Dialogue, Washington Inst. Fgn. Affairs. Jewish. Avocations: photography, travel, collecting folk art. Home: 7018 Hector Rd Mc Lean VA 22101-2113

CHAPMAN, ALLEN D. music educator; b. Offfumwa, Iowa, May 25, 1949; s. Everett Winfield and Ina Shepard Chapman; m. Sandra L. Dye, June 22, 1974; 1 child, Anne Winfield. BA, Iowa Wesleyan Coll., 1971; MA, Truman State U., 1984. Choral dir. Moravia (Iowa) Schs., 1971—73, LDF Schs., Le Grand, Iowa, 1973—78, Ft. Madison (Iowa) HS, 1978—. Dir., trustee Iowa Wesleyan Coll., Mt. Pleasant, Iowa, 1985—91; nat. HS chair Am. Choral Dirs. Assn., Lawton, Okla., 1988—98; state choral chair Iowa HS Music Assn., Boone, 1992—96. Dir. city wide prodn., 1988—95; sister city commr. Sister Cities Internat., 1998—. Recipient Tchr. of Yr., FMEA, 1989, Amb. of Yr., City of Madison (Iowa), 1991, McCowen award, Iowa Choral Dirs. Assn., 2001. Mem.: Ft. Madison Edn. Assn., Music Educators Nat. Conf., Am. Choral Dirs. Assn. (convention chair). Avocation: travel. Home: 1209 Ave C Fort Madison IA 52627 Office: Ft Madison Schs 20th St B Fort Madison IA 52627 E-mail: allencha@interlinklc.net.

CHAPMAN, ALLEN FLOYD, management educator, college dean; b. Dawson, N.Mex., Apr. 14, 1930; s. Thomas and Velma (Sylva) C.; m. Ann Bunker; children: Margaret Ann, Nancy Elizabeth. BS, U. Colo., 1951; D Bus. Adminstrn., Harvard U., 1965; MBS, Hartford Grad. Ctr., 1982. Commd. ensign USN, 1951, advanced through grades to lt., resigned, 1960; rsch. assoc. Harvard U., Boston, 1961-63; dean grad. sch. bus. C.W. Post Ctr., L.I. U., Greenvale, N.Y., 1963-77; prof. mgmt. Hartford (Conn.) Grad. Ctr., 1977-96, dean Sch. of Mgmt., 1977-79, 81-84, 87-89; prof. mgmt. Sch. Mgmt. Rensselaer at Hartford, 1996—. Pres., founder various pvt. corps., N.Y., Conn., 1965—; cons. to various corps. and depts. and agys. of U.S. Govt. Patentee in field. Recipient Cert. for Patriotic Civilian Svc. U.S. Army, 1973. Home: 64 Great Hl Pond Rd Portland CT 06480-1315

CHAPMAN, ALVAH HERMAN, JR., newspaper executive; b. Columbus, Ga., Mar. 21, 1921; s. Alvah Herman and Wyline (Page) C.; m. Betty Bateman, Mar. 22, 1943; children: Dale Page Chapman Webb, Chris Ann Chapman Hilton. BS, The Citadel, 1942, hon. degree, 1971, Barry U., 1985, Fla. Internat. U., 1988, U. Miami, Coral Gables, Fla., 1989, U. Notre Dame, 1991. Bus. mgr. Columbus Ledger, 1945-53; exec. v.p., gen. mgr. St. Petersburg (Fla.) Times, 1953-57; pres., pub. Morning News and Evening Press, Savannah, Ga., 1957-60; exec. Knight-Ridder Newspapers, Inc., Miami, Fla., 1960-89, exec. com., 1960-2000; dir. Knight Ridder, 1962-2000; exec. v.p. Knight-Ridder Newspapers, Inc., 1967-73, pres., 1973-82, CEO, 1976-88, chmn., 1982-89, dir., chmn. exec. com., 1984-95; v.p., gen. mgr. Miami Herald, 1962-70, pres., 1970-82. Lectr. Am. Press Insts., Columbia; vice chmn., exec. com. Miami Coalition for Safe & Drug-Free Cmty.; mem. Pres.'s Drug Adv. Coun., 1989-92; chmn. emeritus Fla. Internat. U. Found.; bd. trustees Fla. Internat. U. 2001-2002; trustee John S. and James L. Knight Found., 1971-2002. Mem. Pres.'s Drug Adv. Coun., 1989—92; chmn. emeritus Fla. Internat. U. Found.; founding chmn. Cmty. Anti-Drug Coalitions Am.; chmn. We Will Rebuild, 1992—93, Gov.'s Commn. on Homeless, 1992—94; founding chmn. Cmty. Partnership for Homeless, Inc., 1993—; mem. State's Commn. on the Homeless, 2000; bd. dirs. ARC Greater Miami and the Keys, 2001—. Maj. USAAF, World War II. Decorated D.F.C. with 2 oak leaf clusters, Air medal with 5 clusters U.S., Croix de Guerre; named one of 5 Outstanding Young Men in Ga., 1951, Outstanding Young Man, Columbus Jr. C. of C., 1952, Dade County's Outstanding Citizen of 1968-69, Brigham Young U. Internat. Businessman of Yr., 1984; recpient Citadel Palmetto award, 1985, Isaiah Thomas award Rochester Inst. Tech., 1986, Joseph Wharton Statesman award, 1988, United Negro Coll. Fund's Disting. Svc. award, 1988, The Miami Herald Spirit of Excellence Lifetime Achievement award, 1989, Anne Ackerman Disting. Floridian award, 1991, LeRoy Collins Lifetime Achievement award Leadership Fla., 1992, United Way Dorothy Shula award for Volunteerism, 1994, Salvation Army Red Shield award, 1994, ARC Humanitarian of Yr. award, 1994, Health Found. of South Fla. Concern award 1995, Drum Maj. of Justice award Miami-Dade C. C., 1996, Spirit of Martin Luther King Jr. Parade & Festivities Dinner Com. award, 1996, Citizen of Yr. award Gray Panthers North Dade, 1996, Resolution State Fla., 1996, Named Hon. Dir. Fla. C. of C., 1997, Lifetime Achievement award Cmty. Anti-Drug Coalitions Am., 1999, Ellis Island medals of honor, 2000, Pontifical medal Benemerenti, 2000, Fla. Meml. Coll. Cmty. Leadership award, 2001, Pillar award Fla. Internat. U., 2001; named to South Fla. Bus. Hall of Fame, 2000; Alvah H. Chapman, Jr. Grad. Sch. Bus., Fla. Internat. U., named 2001; Cmty. Partnership for Homeless's Betty and Alvah Chapman, Jr. Ctr. named 2002; ; 1st recipient Cmty. Partnership for Homeless's Alvah H. Chapman, Jr. Humanitarian award, 2002; 1st recipient Corp. Citizenship award, Nat. Coalition for Homeless, 2002. Mem. Newspaper Assn. Am., Am. Newspaper Pub. Assn. (chmn., pres. 1986-87), So. Newspapers Pubs. Assn. (pres. 1976), Arland D. Williams Soc. at the Citadel (inducted 2002). Methodist. Home: Grove Harbour 1690 S Bayshore Ln # 10ab Miami FL 33133-4073 Office: Knight Ridder Inc One Herald Plz Miami FL 33132-1693

CHAPMAN, ANTHONY BRADLEY, psychiatrist; b. Salem, Mass., June 22, 1938; s. Anthony Bredick and Gladys Gwendolyn (Poole) C.; m. Ella Mueller, Aug. 30, 1963; children: Bradley, Jeffrey. BS with honors, Northeastern U., 1961; MD, Stanford U., 1966. Diplomate Am. Bd. Psychiatry and Neurology. Rsch. asst. Harvard Med. Sch., Boston, 1957-61; intern Case-Western Res. U., Cleve., 1966-67; resident Johns Hopkins Hosp., Balt., 1967-69, fellow in behavioral medicine, 1967-69; fellow in child psychiatry U. Pa., Phila., 1969-71; pvt. practice Alexandria, Va., 1973—. Dir. Attention Disorder Ctr. No. Va., Alexandria, 1991—; guest lectr. Children and Adults with Attention Deficit Disorder, Arlington, Va., 1990-96. Editor Hyperactive Child Newsletter, 1974-78. Maj. U.S. Army, 1971—73. Recipient Outstanding Tchr. award Am. Acad. Family Practice, 1976-81. Mem. Am. Med. Soc., Am. Psychiat. Electrophysiology Assn., Va. Med. Soc., Alexandria Med. Soc., Attention Deficit Disorders Profls. No. Va. (pres. 1990-92). Avocations: jazz, Brazilian music, tennis, skiing. Office: 2059 Huntington Ave Ste 108 Alexandria VA 22303-1602 E-mail: brad_chapman@msn.com.

CHAPMAN, CAROLYN, broadcasting director; b. Portsmouth, Ohio, Feb. 4, 1933; d. Roger Donald and Flowery Alice (Callaway) Carr; diploma Portsmouth Interstate Bus. Coll., 1954, S. Ohio Manpower Tng. Ctr., 1965; m. Edward J. Chapman, May 13, 1966; children— Cheryl, Roger, Lisa, Mark, Edmond, Sean. Dep. probation officer Scioto County Juvenile Ct., Portsmouth, 1960-63; coder II, Aid for Aged, Ohio Dept. Pub. Welfare, Columbus, 1964; clk. typist II, Bur. Vital Stats., Dept. Health, Columbus, 1964, clk.-stenographer II, CD Div., 1966; clk.-stenographer ABC, Los Angeles, 1967, ops. coordinator, 1968-72, assoc. dir., on-air dir., 1972— ; cons. in video tape and TV prodn.; mem. negotiating com. Teamsters Union, Los Angeles, 1970. Ch. sec. Findlay St. Meth. Ch., Portsmouth, 1959-63, chmn. women's day program, 1962, chmn. commn. on missions, 1959-62, del. ann. conf., Cleve., 1963, sec. ofcl. bd., 1959-62; pres. local chpt. Ohio Republican Council, 1959-62, mem. state bd., 1962, del. from Scioto County to State Rep. Conv., Ohio, 1962; mem. film editing com. Social Health and Hygiene Assn., 1961-62; tribute com. for Tribute to Dorothy Arzner, 1975; Los Angeles Jr. C. of C., 1977. Mem. ABC Employees Assn. (pres. Hollywood branch, 1971-73), Dirs. Guild Am. (council 1981-83). Address: PO Box 43025 Los Angeles CA 90043-0025

CHAPMAN, CLIFFORD KENNETH, music educator; b. Meadeville, Pa., Apr. 8, 1950; s. Richard Wesley and Annice Blanche Chapman; m. Laurie Ann Nickson, Dec. 27, 1969 (div. Sept. 1984); 1 child, Victoria Ann; m. Kathleen Girard Chapman, June 27, 1986; 1 child, Kristen Elizabeth. MusB, performer's cert., SUNY, Fredonia, 1972, MusM, 1973. Grad. tchg. asst. SUNY, Fredonia, 1972—73; instr. Ea. Mich. U., Ypsilanti, 1973—76; tchr. Marlette (Mich.) Cmty. Schs., 1976—77, Clarkston (Mich.) Cmty. Schs., 1977—, fine arts coord., 1980—. Mem.: Music Educators Nat. Conf., Nat. Band Assn. (state chair), Am. Sch. Band Dirs. Assn. (Mich. chpt.), Mich. Competing Band Assn., Mich. Sch. Band and Orch. Assn. (dist. 4 and state pre., Band Tchr. of the Yr. Dist. 4), Phi Mu Alpha Sinfonia, Kappa Kappa Psi (hon.). Office: Clarkston HS 6093 Flemings Lake Rd Clarkston MI 48346

CHAPMAN, DAVID ARTHUR, education educator; b. New York, NY, USA, Aug. 27, 1960; s. Peter Francis and Pauline Greenberg Chapman; m. Kathleen Rence Ferguson, June 1, 1985; children: Matthew Ferguson, Emma Rames. BA., Swarthmore Coll., 1982; MS., U. of Rochester, 1990, PhD., 1992. Assoc. prof. of fin. and econ. U. of Tex., Austin, Tex., 1999—, asst. prof. of fin. and econ., 1992—99; visting asst. prof. U. of Rochester, Rochester, NY, 1995—96. Assoc. editor jour. of fin. Am. Fin. Assn., 2000—, mem. nominating com., 2002. Author: (articles) Econometrica, 1998, Jour. of Fin., 1998; co-author, 2000. Mem.: Am. Econ. Assn., Econ. Soc., Am. Fin. Assn.

CHAPMAN, DENNIS EARL, social services administrator; b. Louisville, Dec. 15, 1952; s. Earl and Rosa Lee Chapman; m. Patricia Chapman, Aug. 17, 1976; children: Crishelle, Benjamin, Anna, Andrew. BS, Tenn. Temple U., 1975. Adminstr. Morningside Christian Sch., Sioux City, Iowa, 1985—2001; assoc. exec. dir. devel. City Union Mission, Kansas City, 2001—. Editor: The Light mag., 2001. Mem.: Profl. Photographers Assn., Rotary.

CHAPMAN, EDGAR LEON, literature educator; b. Bloomfied, Mo., Sept. 23, 1936; s. Evert Leon Chapman and Iva Otelia Coburn; m. Margaret Lee Sullivan, Feb. 24, 1945 (div. Dec. 1992); children: Benjamin Patrick, Terrence Leon. BA in English, William Jewell Coll., 1957; MA in English, Brown U., 1960, PhD in English, 1964. From instr. English to prof. Bradley U., Peoria, Ill., 1963—97, prof. English, 1997—2002, ret., 2002. Author: The Magic Labrynth of Philip Jo Sue Farmer, 1984, The Road to Castle Mount, 1999. Sgt. Reserves USAF, 1964—67. Mem.: Assn. Literacy Scholars and Critics, Robert Penn Warren Cir., Internat. Assn. Fantastic in the Herds. Home: 400 Circuit Court East Peoria IL 61611

CHAPMAN, GARY H. artist, educator; BS in Indsl. Arts, BA in Art, Berea Coll., 1984; MFA in Painting and Drawing, Cranbrook Acad. Art, 1986. Lectr. Birmingham Mus. Art, Montgomery Mus. Fine Arts, Vanderbilt U., Nashville, Fla. State U., Tallahassee, U. Ga., Athens; vis. artist lectr. Wimbledon Sch. Art, London, Kent Inst. Art and Design, Canterbury, England, Carmarthenshire (Wales) Coll. Tech. and Art, U. Ulster, Belfast, Northern Ireland. One-man shows include Blue Spiral 1 Gallery, Asheville, N.C., U. Miami The New Gallery, Coral Gables, Fla., U. Ga., The Main Gallery, Sch. Art, Athens, U. Cin., The Aranoff Ctr. DAAP Gallery U. Art Mus., U. Southwestern La., Lafayette, Montgomery (Ala.) Mus. Fine Arts, exhibited in group shows at Birmingham (Ala.) Mus. Art, Southeastern Ctr. Contemporary Art, Winston-Salem, N.C., Cummer Mus. Art, Jacksonville, Fla., Huntsville (Ala.) Mus. Art, Hunter Mus. Am. Art, Chattanooga, Columbus (Ga.) Mus. Art, Alexandria (La.) Mus. Art, Represented in permanent collections Huntsville Mus. Art, Birmingham Mus. Art, Montgomery Mus. Fine Arts, Mobile (Ala.) Mus. Art, Fla. State U. Mus. Art, Tallahassee, pvt. collections. Fellow grantee, Ala. State Coun. on the Arts, 1994—95, faculty rsch. grantee, U. Ala., Birmingham, 1991, 1993, 1997, 1998. Office: c/o Blue Spiral One 38 Biltmore Ave Asheville NC 28801-3625

CHAPMAN, GILBERT BRYANT, physicist; b. Uniontown, Ala., July 8, 1935; s. Gilbert Bryant and Annie Lillie (Stallworth) C.; m. Loretta Woodward, June 5, 1960 (dec. Sept. 1994); children: Annie L., Bernice M., Cedric N., David O., Ernest P., Frances Q.H., Gilbert Bryant III; m. Betty J. Chapman, June 27, 1999. BS in Math. and Chemistry, Baldwin Wallace Coll., Berea, Ohio, 1968; MS in Physics, Cleve. State U., 1973; MBA, Mich. State U., 1990; postgrad., Kent State U., Ohio, 1974-76, U. Windsor, Ont., Can., 2001—. Phys. sci. technician NASA-Lewis Rsch. Ctr., Cleve., 1953-68, emission spectroscopist, 1968-75, materials engr., 1975-77; sr. rsch. engr. Ford Motor Co., Redford Twp., Mich., 1977-83, project engr., 1983-86; adv. materials testing specialist Chrysler Corp., Highland Park, Mich., 1986-89, adv. materials specialist Madison Heights, Mich., 1989-91, advanced materials and product exec. 1991-95, advanced materials cons., 1995-98; sr. mgr. advanced materials and product devel. DaimlerChrylser Corp., Rochester Hills, Mich., 1998—. Chmn auto. com. '87 Soc. Mfg. Engrs. Composites Group, Dearborn, 1987, chair bd.

1996; chmn. ind. adv. bd. NDE/Ctr., Iowa State U., Ames, 1989, 90; served as mem. indsl. adv. bd. Inst. for Mfg. Rsch., Wayne State U., Ctrl. State U., U. Tex.-Pan Am., U. Mich.-Dearborn, Oakland U., Rochester, Mich.; chair Internat. Symposium on Automotive Tech. and Automation Materials Conf., 1996, 98, Automotive Composites Consortium, 1996. Contbr. articles to profl. jours., chapters to books. Lay leader, elder SDA Ch. of Southfield, Mich., 1983-95; elder SDA Ch. of Farmington Hills, Mich., 2000--; trustee Mt. Vernon Acad., Ohio, 1972-76; lay adv. coun. Ohio Conf. SDA, 1974-77. With USAF, 1959—61. Recipient Group Achievement award, NASA Lewis Rsch. Ctr., 1970, Apollo Achievement award, 1968, Mayor Archer's Proclamation, Motor City Youth Fedn., 1994, Spirit of Detroit award Detroit City Coun., 1994; named one of Best and Brightest Profls., Dollars and Sense Mag., 1993, Black Engr. of Yr. and Career Achievement award U.S. Black Engr. and Info. Tech. mag., 1999. Fellow Am. Soc. Nondestructive Testing (cert. level III 6 NDT methods); mem. ASM (polymer composites program com. 1986), ASTM, IEEE, SAE (award for excellence in oral presentation), Am. Chem. Soc., Am. Phys. Soc., Am. Soc. for Composites, Can. Assn. Physicists, Engring. Soc. Detroit (sci. com., ASM/ESD Best Paper award 1993), Fedn. of Analytical Chemists, Nat. Tech. Assn. (Cleve. program com.), Soc. for Applied Spectroscopy (Cleve. vice chair, sec.), Soc. Mfg. Engrs. (chaired CMA adv. bd.), Soc. Physics Students (pres.). Achievements include patents for infrared inspection method for friction welds in thermoplastics and advanced vehicle concepts; development of low-frequency ultrasonic inspection methods for polymer composites and adhesive bond joints; co-development of D.C. arc method of determining work functions of refractory alloys, spectrochemical analysis of microgram-size samples. Home and Office: Advanced Transp Techs 38671 Greenbrook Ct Farmington Hills MI 48331-2979 Office Fax: 519-253-3000 ext. 2672., 519-971-3611. Personal E-mail: gbchapman2@aol.com. *The persistant pursuit of moral and ethical values, faith and the concomitant virtues while seeking to serve more effectively, can lead to a successful and satisfying life.*

CHAPMAN, GILBERT WHIPPLE, JR., publishing company executive; b. N.Y.C., July 1, 1933; s. Gilbert W. and Katherin (Bright) C.; m. Judith Coste, June 14, 1956; 1 child, Gilbert W. III BA, Yale U., 1956. Pub. McGraw-Hill, Inc., N.Y.C., 1958-72; exec. v.p., dir. Morgan Grampain, Inc., N.Y.C., 1971-75; pres. Pub. Group Esquire Inc., N.Y.C., 1975-78; pres., dir. Diversion Communications, Inc., N.Y.C., 1978-85, Kalo Communications, Inc., N.Y.C., 1985-91; pub. U.S. Banker Mag., 1985-91; chmn., CEO Cemark, Inc., 1991—. Trustee Village of Mill Neck, 1993—2000, Choate Sch., Wallingford, Conn., 1986—91, Pomfret Sch., 1980—86; bd. dirs. Planned Parenthood of Nassau County, 1985—2002, Planned Parenthood of Nassau County Found., 2000—, Cmty. Hosp. of Glen Cove, 1986—90, North Shore U. Hosp., 1990—94. Mem.: Piping Rock Club (pres. 2000—), Racquet and Tennis Club. Republican. Episcopalian. Home: Factory Pond Rd Locust Valley NY 11560-1405 Office: 13531 E Boundary Rd Midlothian VA 23112-3953

CHAPMAN, HOPE HORAN, psychologist; b. Chgo., Feb. 13, 1954; d. Theodore George and Idelle (Poll) H.; m. Stuart G. Chapman, Dec. 4, 1983. BS, U. Ill., 1976; MA, No. Ill. U., 1979; cert. lawyer's asst. program, Roosevelt U., Chgo., 1996, 97; student, Ballet Russe Sch., 1999—2002. Lic. pharmacy technician, Ill.; diplomate Am. Bd. Disability Analysts. Psychologist Glenwood (Iowa) State Hosp. Sch., 1979-83, Gov. Samuel H. Shapiro Devel. Ctr., Kankakee, Ill., 1985-86, dir. staff tng. and devel. Glenkirk, 1988-90; clin. assoc. Bennett & Assocs., 1990-91; psychologist Singer Mental Health & Devel. Ctr., Rockford, Ill., 1992-93; forensic psychologist Elgin (Ill.) Mental Health Ctr., 1993-94. Contbr. papers to profl. confs., articles to jours. Active Omaha Symphonic Chorus, 1981-83; mem. Omaha Pub. Schs. Citizens Adv. Com., 1980-81; mem. edn. com. Anti-Defamation League, 1980-85, chmn. com. anti-Semitism and Jewish youth, 1983; commr. youth commn. Village of Hoffman Estates, Ill., 1988-94; vice chmn. oversight com. Vogelei Teen Ctr., 1988-94; commr. Environ. Commn., Village of Hoffman Estates, 1994-2000, chmn. Schaumburg Twp. Mental Health Bd., 1993-94; election judge Cook County, 1992—; judge's asst. Cook County Cir. Ct., 1996—, mem chmn.Chicagoland chpt. U.S. Amateur Ballroom Dancers Assn. 2003. Scholar State of Ill. Fellow Am. Coll. Forensic Examiners; mem. APA, Midwest Psychol. Assn., Am. Bd. Disability Analysts, Ill. Paralegal Assn., Phi Kappa Phi, Psi Chi. Jewish.

CHAPMAN, HOWARD REED, city and county transportation engineer, consultant; b. Dayton, Ohio, Aug. 3, 1946; s. Roy Howard and Elvira Evelyn (Riccio) C.; m. Rosemary O'Donohue, Dec. 7, 1968 (div. 2003); children: Lara, Amy, Jennifer, Gregory. BSCE, Va. Mil. Inst., 1968; ME, U. S.C., 1970. Reg. profl. engr., S.C., Fla. Engr. Va. Dept. Hwys., Richmond, 1968; project engr. Wilbur Smith & Assocs., Columbia, S.C., 1968-70; asst. dir. Charleston (S.C.) Dept. Traffic and Transp., 1970-71, dir., 1971-77, 78-99; city engr., chief transp. divsn. City of Boca Raton, Fla., 1977-78. Exec. dir. CARTA, 1999—, dep. to mayor, coord. Hurricane Recovery, 1989-91; emergency preparedness coord. City of Charleston, 1990—; cons. Charleston County, Town of Mt. Pleasant, S.C., S.C. Downtown Devel. Assn., State Main St. Program; guest lectr. U. S.C., Clemson U., Coll. of Charleston; chmn. Charleston County transp. com., 1999—. Mem. exec. com. Palmetto Safety Coun., 1974-81, treas., 1982-83, v.p., 1984-85, pres., 1985-88; mem. Washington Light Infantry, 1995—. Lt. USAF, 1968-70; ret. Res., 1970—. Mem. ASCE, NSPE, Inst. Transp. Engrs. (sec.-treas. so. sect. 1983-84, v.p. 1984-85, pres. 1985-86, M.J. Hensley Outstanding Individual Activity award, so. sect. 1982, Transp. Engr. of Yr. S.C. divsn. 1983, Herman J. Hoose Disting. Svc. award, so. sect. 1989), Transp. Assn. S.C. (Leadership award 2003), Nat. Safety Coun. (bd. dirs. 2001—), Kappa Alpha, Tau Bet Pi. Roman Catholic. Office: 36 John St Charleston SC 29403

CHAPMAN, HUGH MCMASTER, banker; b. Spartanburg, S.C., Sept. 11, 1932; s. James Alfred and Martha (Marshall) Chapman; m. Anne Allston Morrson, Dec. 27, 1958 (dec. Mar. 1993); children: Anne Allston, Rachel Buchanan, Mary Morrison; m. Janis Guzzle, Aug. 17, 2001. BSBA, U. N.C., 1955. With Citizens & So. Nat. Bank S.C., 1958-91, pres., 1971-74, chmn. bd., 1974-91; pres. Citizens & So. Corp., Atlanta, 1986-91; vice chmn. C&S/Sovran Corp., 1990-91; chmn. Nations Bank S., 1992-97; ret., 1997. Bd. dirs. Inman Mills., West Point Stevens, Williams Cos. Trustee East Lake Cmty. Fedn., Duke Endowment. 1st lt. USAF, 1955-57. Office: Bank of Am Plz 600 Peachtree St Fl 55 Atlanta GA 30308-2265

CHAPMAN, JAMES ALBION, novelist, publisher; b. Oakland, Calif., Nov. 10, 1955; s. David Duane and Esther June (Stormont) C. BA in English, U. Calif., Berkeley, 1978. Pub. Fugue State Press, N.Y.C., 1992—. Author: Our Plague: A Film from New York, 1993, The Walls Collide as You Expand, 1993, Glass: Pray the Electrons Back to Sand, 1995, In Candyland it's Cool to Feed on Your Friends, 1997, Daughter! I Forbid Your Recurring Dream!, 2000, Stet,2004; contbr. works to Jacob's Ladder, Central Park, N.W. Rev., Appearances, Global City Rev., Jour. of Experimental Fiction, Cambridge Rev., others. Office: Fugue State Press PO Box 80 New York NY 10276-0080 E-mail: jim@fuguestatepress.com.

CHAPMAN, JAMES L. (JIM CHAPMAN), former congressman, lawyer; b. Washington, Mar. 8, 1945; BBA, U. Tex.; JD, So. Meth. U. Dist. atty., Tex., 1977-85; mem. 99th-104th Congresses from 1st Tex. dist., Washington, 1985-96; mem. appropriations com.; ptnr. Arter & Hadden, Washington, 1996-99, Bracewell & Patterson, Washington, 1999—. Democrat. Home: 2691 Marcey Rd Arlington VA 22207-5231 Office: Bracewell & Patterson 2000 K St NW Ste 500 Washington DC 20006-1872 Fax: 202-223-1225. E-mail: jcchapman@bracepatt.com.*

CHAPMAN, JANET CARTER GOODRICH (MRS. JOHN WILLIAM CHAPMAN), economist, educator; b. Bklyn., May 26, 1922; d. Carter and Florence (Nielsen) Goodrich; m. John William Chapman, Feb. 10, 1943; 1 child, Hazel Perry. BA, Swarthmore Coll., 1943; MA, Columbia U., 1951, PhD, 1963; D Econs (hon.), Cracow Acad. Econs., 1990. Analyst Nat. War Labor Bd., Phila., 1943; economist Bd. of Govs. Fed. Res. System, 1945-46; cons. econs. dept. RAND Corp., Santa Monica, Calif., 1949-69; assoc. prof. U. Pitts., 1964-67, prof. econs., 1967-92, prof. emeritus, 1992—, chair econs. dept., 1978-85; chmn. com. Russian and East European studies, 1965-83, dir. Russian and East European studies, 1970-83. Vis. lectr. econs. Swarthmore Coll., 1962-63; vis. fellow Australian Nat. U., 1964; organizer and participant Con. The Polish Economy in the Year 2000, U. Pitts., 1987. Author: Real Wages in Soviet Russia Since 1928, 1963, Wage Variation in Soviet Industry: The Impact of the 1956-60 Wage Reform, 1970; contbr.: Economic Trends in the Soviet Union, 1963, The Soviet Economy: A Book of Readings, 1966, 70, The Socialist Price Mechanism, 1977, Women in Russia, 1977, Industrial Labor in the USSR, 1979, Income Inequality, 1979, Economic Reforms and Welfare Systems in the USSR, Poland and Hungary, 1991, In Search of Flexibility: The New Soviet Labour Market, 1991. Hannah Leedom fellow, 1946-47; Garth fellow, 1946-47; Russian Inst. grant, 1947-48; N.Y. State fellow AAUW, 1948-49; Am. Coun. Learned Socs. grant for Soviet studies, 1973; NSF res. grant, 1973-74; Nat. Coun. for Soviet and East European Rsch. grant, 1982-83; Internat. Rsch. and Exchs. Bd. sr. scholar travel grantee, 1985 Mem. AAUW (fellowship com. 1974-78), Am. Econ. Assn., Assn. Advancement Slavic Studies (dir. 1974-79), Assn. for Comparative Econ. Studies (exec. com. 1976-79, pres. 1983), Phi Beta Kappa. Home: 8 Shipcarpenter Sq Lewes DE 19958-1246

CHAPMAN, JOHN ANDREW, retired chamber of commerce executive; b. Evanston, Ill., Oct. 12, 1928; s. Roger Edington and Margaret Holloway (Morgan) Chapman; m. Betsy Miller, June 23, 1951; children: Andrew K., Jean M., Margaret(dec.), Peter S. BS, Northwestern U., 1950, Cert. Nat. Inst. Orgn. Mgmt. Asst. dir. pub. rels. Northwestern U., Evanston, 1950-54; asst. mgr. Joliet (Ill.) Assn. Commerce, 1954-57; mgr. Twin Cities Area C. of C., Benton Harbor/St. Joseph, Mich., 1957-67; pres. Muskegon Area Devel. Coun. and C. of C., Mich., 1967-74, Charleston (W.Va.) C. of C., 1974-94; mng. dir. Kanawha Pastoral Counseling Ctr., 1994-98; ret., 1998. Former chmn. Berrien County (Mich.) Planning Commn.; past treas. Tri-Cap, Inc.; mem. emeritus Salvation Army, Charleston; dir., past pres. Kanawha County Pub. Safety Coun.; dir., sec. Good News Mountaineer Garage; former mem. Cmty. Coun. Charleston Job Corps; past chmn. Charleston Police Civilian Rev. Bd.; mem. U.S. Atty. Heavy Metal Task Force; past vestryman St. John's, St. Edward's and St. Gregory's Episcopal Ch.; past warden St. Augustine's Episcopal Ch.; former bd. dirs. Charleston Symphony; bd. dirs. Charleston Renaissance Corp.; past v.p. Southwestern br. Mich. Children's Aid Soc.; past sec. Bishop Whittemore Found.; past treas. W.Va. Taxpayers Assn.; pres. Charleston Leadership Coun. Pub. Safety; past vice-chair W.Va. Regional Cmty. Policing; vice-chair Eisenhower Math.-Sci. Consortium; dir., v.p. Craik-Patton House, Inc. Mem.: Cert. C. of C. Exec., So. Assn. C. of C. Execs. (past pres., sec.), Am. C. of C. Execs. (bd. dirs.), Mich. C. of C. Execs. (past pres.), W.Va. C. of C. Execs. (past pres.), Anvil Club, Rotary. Republican. Home: 209 Ashby Ave Charleston WV 25314-1009 E-mail: john.and.betsy@juno.com.

CHAPMAN, JOHN DONALD, research biophysicist; b. Estevan, Canada, Feb. 18, 1941; s. Elmer Henderson and Alice Gertrude (Phillips) C.; m. Ann Elizabeth Chapman, June 15, 1963 (div. June 1989); children: Marlyss Dawn, Derek John, Lee Ann, Robert Charles; m. Beverly Ann Chapman, Nov. 10, 1989. BS, U. Saskatchewan, 1963, MS, 1965; PhD, Pa. State U., 1967. Rsch. scientist Atomic Energy Can., Pinawa, 1968-77; assoc. prof. Cross Cancer Inst., Edmonton, Can., 1977-84; prof. Univ. Alberta, Edmonton, Can., 1984-90; sr. scientist Fox Chase Cancer Ctr., Phila., 1990—. Adj. prof. U. Pa., Phila., 1990— Nat. Cancer Inst. Can. fellow, 1963-64; postdoctoral fellow Nat. Rsch. Coun. Can., 1967-68; recipient 6th Milford Schultz award, Harvard Med. Sch., 1983. Mem. AAAS, Am. Soc. Therapeutic Radiology and Oncology, European Soc. Therapeutic Radiology and Oncology, Radiation Rsch. Soc. (8th Rsch. award 1979), Soc. Nuclear Medicine. Presbyterian. Office: Fox Chase Cancer Ctr 7701 Burholme Ave Philadelphia PA 19111-2497 E-mail: jd_chapman@fccc.edu.

CHAPMAN, JOHN STEPHEN, retired internist, medical administrator; b. L.A., Aug. 13, 1927; s. Nathaniel Dabney and Barbara Brotherhood (Burns) C.; m. Mary Jo Becker, Feb. 22, 1955; children: Catherine, Stephen, Beth, Carol, Dan, Michael, Mary Kay. AB, Washington and Lee U., 1950; MD, U. Va., 1954. Intern U. Iowa, Iowa City, 1954-55, resident, 1955-58; pvt. practice Dubuque (Iowa) Internal Medicine, 1958-96, ret., 1996; assoc. med. dir. Healthcorp, managed care co., Dubuque, 1996—. Med. dir. Dubuque Ambulance, 1974-82; co-med. dir. Hospice of Dubuque, 1993—. Pres. Finley Hosp. Found., 2000—, bd. dirs., 1993—2001, Dubuque Mus. Art, 1997—, v.p. bd. trustees, 2001—, pres. bd. dirs., 2003—; bd. dirs. Hospice of Dubuque, 1985—97, VNA Found., Dubuque, 1985—91. Named Internist of Yr., Am. Soc. Internal Medicine, Iowa, 1986. Fellow ACP (Laureate award 1988); mem. AMA, Iowa Med. Soc., Iowa Clin. Med. Soc. (pres. 1983-85), Dubuque County Med. Soc. (pres. 1978-79), Dubuque Golf and Country Club. Avocations: drawing, cartooning, woodwork. Home: 435 Moore Hts Dubuque IA 52003-7708

CHAPMAN, JUDITH COSTE, charitable institution volunteer administrator; b. St. Louis, Nov. 22, 1934; d. Felix Wilkins Coste and Dorothy (Cramer) Coste Gale; m. Gilbert Whipple Chapman Jr., June 14, 1956; 1 child, Gilbert Whipple III. BA, Sarah Lawrence Coll., 1956. Mgr. North Country Garden Club of L.I., N.Y., 1975-78, 2d v.p., 1981-83, treas., 1983-86, pres., 1989-91; bd. dirs. Raynham Hall Mus., Oyster Bay, N.Y., 1991-94, treas., 1994-99, v.p., 1999—. Bd. dirs. North Shore Wildlife Sanctuary, Mill Neck, N.Y., 1988—, pres., 1991—. Co-chair Jane B. Francke Sanctuary, Brookville, N.Y., 1977—; bd. dirs. Planned Parenthood Nassau County, 1972-76, pres.'s adv. com., 1977-94. Recipient Medal of Merit, Garden Club of Am., 1994. Episcopalian. Home: 121 Factory Pond Rd Locust Valley NY 11560-1415

CHAPMAN, KENNETH MAYNARD, science administrator; b. Corinth, Ky., Sept. 30, 1938; s. Leonard N. and Rachel (Howard) C.; m. Patricia L. Gross Barnhill, July 15, 1960 (div. May 1976); children: Kenneth L., Karen L.; m. Virginia L. Robinson, June 4, 1976; stepchildren: Stephen E. Howell, Michael A. Howell. AAS in Chem. Tech., Ohio Coll. Applied Sci., Cin., 1958; BS in Chem. Engring., MIT, 1961; MA in Adult Edn., George Washington U., Washington, 1969. Acting head chem. tech. Ohio Coll. Applied Sci., Cin., 1961—63; head chem. engring. tech. Temple U., Phila., 1963—67; asst. edn. sec. for 2-yr. colls. Am. Chem. Soc., Washington, 1967—69, assoc. dir. chem. tech. project Berkeley, Calif., 1969—72, mgr. spl. programs Washington, 1973—82, head R&D in edn., 1982—90, spl. asst. to dir., 1990—99, head tech. resources/edn., 1993—99; ret., 1999; v.p. Computer-Based Instrnl. Sys., San Antonio, 1972—73; prin. ptnr. Cardinal Workforce Developers LLC, 2001—; cons. ACS Coll. Chemistry Consultants Svc., 1999—; pres. CWD Informatics, Inc., 2002—. Co-author: The Chemical Technicians Handbook, 1973; co-author/editor: (book series) Modern Chemical Technology, 1973; co-author: Foundations for Excellence in the C.P.I., 1997; co-author/editor: (booklet) Gaining the Competitive Edge, 1993. Mem. Triangle Coalition for Sci. and Tech. Edn. (bd. dirs. 1985-99, sec.-treas. 1990-97), Nat. Vo-Tech Honor Soc. (bd. dirs. 1998-2001). E-mail: kmc97@aol.com.

CHAPMAN, LEWIS DUANE, economist; b. Sept. 3, 1940; s. Lewis Ray and Alice Louise (Fullerton) Chapman; m. Mary Jane Angelacos, Aug. 16, 1961 (div. 1998); children: Erin Marie, Amy Nicole; m. Josephine Carol Crossley, Feb. 22, 1991 (div. 1998). BA, Mich. State U., 1961; PhD, U. Calif., Berkeley, 1969. Economist Oak Ridge (Tenn.) Nat. Lab., 1969—71; asst. prof. dept. applied econs. and mgmt. Cornell U., Ithaca, NY, 1971—76, assoc. prof., 1976—82, prof., 1982—, coord. Climate Change Rsch. Program, 1993—97. Leader, industry and the urban environ. U.S. AID, 1991—95. Author: Energy Resources and Energy Corporations, 1983, Environmental Economics, Theory, Application and Policy, 2000; contbr. over 170 articles to profl. jours. Mem. task force on regional transmission Nat. Gov.'s Assn., 2001—02; mem. pub. info. adv. bd. Tompkins County Legislature. Scholar, Fulbright Found., U. Natal, South Africa and U. Zimbabwe, 1991. Mem.: NAS (mem. nuc. power panel 1976—80, mem. electric power panel 1986, mem. U.S.-Czechoslovakia agr. and environ. panel 1986—87), Internat. Soc. Ecol. Econs., N.E. Assn. Agrl. and Resource Economists, Western Econ. Assn. Internat., Assn. Environ. and Resource Economists, Internat. Assn. Energy Economists, Am. Econ. Assn. Avocations: hiking, tennis, travel, snow shoeing. Office: Cornell U 246 Warren Hall Ithaca NY 14853-7801

CHAPMAN, LOREN J. psychology educator; b. Muncie, Ind., Jan. 5, 1927; s. Herbert L. and Lurana Gertrude (Treff) C.; m. Jean Marilyn Paulsen, June 6, 1953; children: Nancy, Laurence. AB cum laude, Harvard U., 1948; MS, Northwestern U., 1952, PhD, 1954. USPHS postdoctorate research fellow U. Chgo., 1954-56, instr., asst. prof., 1956-59; assoc. prof. U. Ky., Lexington, 1959-62; from assoc. prof. to prof. Southern Ill. U., Carbondale, 1962-67; prof. U. Wis., Madison, 1966-93, NIMH rsch. scientist, 1988-93; prof. emeritus, 1994—. Author: Disordered Thought in Schizophrenia, 1973; contbr. over 100 articles to profl. jours. Recipient Disting. Scientist award Soc. for Sci. Clin. Psychology, 1992; NIMH research grantee, 1952-97. Fellow AAAS, APA (Disting. Sci. award for application of psychology 1999); mem. Am. Psychopathol. Assn., Soc. Rsch. Psychopathology (pres. 1989, Joseph Zubin award 1992), Am. Psychol. Soc. (William James fellow 1995). Home: 129 Richland Ln Madison WI 53705-4834 Office: Univ Wis Dept Psychology 1202 W Johnson St Madison WI 53706-1611

CHAPMAN, MICHAEL WILLIAM, orthopedist, educator; b. Newberry, Mich., Nov. 29, 1937; m. Elizabeth Casady; adopted sons: Mark, Craig. AA, Am. River Coll., Sacramento, Calif., 1957; BA, U. Calif., Davis, 1958; BS, U. Calif., San Francisco, 1959, MD, 1962. Diplomate Am. Bd. Orthopaedic Surgery (ad hoc appeal com. 1986, site visitor 1986, certification renewal com. 1985-88, certification renewal com. chmn. 1986-88). Intern San Francisco Gen. Hosp., 1962-63, asst. chief orthopaedic surgery svc., 1971-79, acting chief orthopaedic surgery svc., 1972-73; resident in orthopaedic surgery U. Calif., San Francisco, 1963-67, asst. prof. dept. orthopaedic surgery, Sch. Medicine, 1971-76, assoc. prof. dept. orthopaedic surgery, Sch. Medicine, 1976-79; resident in orthopaedic surgery U. Calif. Hosps., San Francisco, 1963-64, Samuel Merritt Hosp., Oakland, Calif., 1964, Highland-Alameda County Hosp., Oakland, 1965, Children's Hosp. of the East Bay, Oakland, 1966, Shriners Hosp., Honolulu, 1966-67; fellow Nat. Orthopaedic Hosp., London, 1967-68; chmn. dept. orthopaedic surgery U. Calif., Davis, Sacramento, 1979-99, prof. dept. orthopaedic surgery, 1981-2000, David Linn chair orthopaedic surgery, 1998-2001, prof. emeritus, 2000—. Panelist Calif. Crippled Children Svcs. Panel in Orthopaedic Surgery; cons. VA Hospital, Martinez, Calif.; co-chmn. Zimmer Trauma Panel, 1983-84; vis. prof. Fresno Valley Med. Ctr., 1975, Dept. Orthopaedics, U. Calif., Davis, 1976, U. Hawaii, Honolulu, 1977; vis. prof., cons. to Surgeon Gen. U.S. Army, Europe, 1978; vis. prof. U. Basel, Switzerland, 1979, Phoenix Orthopaedic Residency Program, 1979, Stanford U., 1981, U. Hawaii, 1982, U. So. Calif., L.A., 1984, SUNY, Buffalo, 1985, U. Utah, 1985, U. Iowa Coll. Medicine, 1987, Duke U. Sch. Medicine, 1988, U. Calif. Irvine, Div. Orthopaedics, 1990, U. S.C., 1990, Mass. Gen. Hosp., Harvard U., 1990, Boston U., 1994, Stanford U., 1995, Med. Coll. Pa., 1996, numerous others; also guest lectr. numerous instns.; insp. for residency rev. com. ad hoc appeal com. Accreditation coun. for Grad. Med. Specialist Site, 1983-86. Editor: (with M. Madison) Operative Orthopaedics, 1988 (Best New Book in Clin. Medicine Assn. Am. Pubs.); contbr. numerous articles and numerous abstracts to profl. jours.; presenter exhibits, audiovisual programs, some 500 other presentations; cons. editor Skiing Mag., 1973-77; mem. bd. assoc. editors Clin. Orthopaedics and Related Rsch., 1982-85, Internat. Med. Soc. Paraplegia, 1972-80; reviewer Jour. Bone and Joint Surgery, 1980-85, trustee, 1995-03, sec. to bd. trustees, 1999, chmn. bd. trustees, 2000; past reviewer New Eng. Jour. Medicine; patentee in field. With U.S. Army, 1968-70. Decorated Army Commendation medal; recipient Outstanding Tchg. award U. Calif., San Francisco, 1972, Outstanding Tchr. award U. Calif., Davis, 1984, 93; named One of Best 100 Doctors Am., Good Housekeeping Mag.; Fogarty Sr. Internat. fellow NIH, 1978-79, 80-81; grantee Johnson & Johnson, 1983-84, Zimmer Inc., 1983-85, 85-86, 87-90, Interpore Internat., 1985-86, 89-90, Collagen Inc., 1985-86, 88-89, Upjohn Inc., 1985-86, Orthopaedic Rsch. and Edn. Found., 1988-89. Mem. AMA (Physicians Recognition award 1989-96), ACS, Am. Acad. Orthopaedic Surgeons (bd. dirs. 1982-83, numerous coms., Zimmer award for Disting. Contbn. to Orthop. Surgery, 2002), Am. Orthopaedic Assn. (bd. dirs. 1985-86, pres. 1990-91, various coms.), Internat. Orthopaedic Assn., Assn. for Study of Internal Fixation (N.Am. chpt.), Internat. Soc. Orthopaedic Surgery and Traumatology, Internat. Soc. for Fracture Repair, Brit. Orthopaedic Assn., South African Orthopaedic Assn. (hon.), Am. Acad. Orthopaedic Surgeons, Am. Assn. for Surgery of Trauma, Am. Bd. Med. Spltys., Assn. Am. Med. Colls., Leroy C. Abbott Orthopaedic Soc., Austrian Trauma Assn., Paul R. Lipscomb Soc., Northwestern Med. Assn., Orthopaedic Rsch. Soc., Orthopaedic Trauma Assn., Sierra Club, U. Calif. San Francisco Alumni Assn., Western Orthopaedic Assn., Houston Orthopaedic Assn. (hon.), Calif. Med. Assn., Calif. Orthopaedic Assn., Sacramento-El Dorado Med. Soc., Wilson Interurban Orthopaedic Soc., Alpha Omega Alpha. Avocations: skiing, mountaineering, backpacking, tennis, bicycling. Office: U Calif-Davis Sch Med Dept Orthopedics 4860 Y St Ste 3800 Sacramento CA 95817-2307

CHAPMAN, MORRIS HINES, denominational executive; b. Kosciusko, Miss. m. Jodi Francis; 2 children. Grad., Miss. Coll.; MDiv, D of Ministry, Southwestern Bapt. Theol. Sem.; hon. doctorates, S.W. Bapt. U., Miss. Coll. Pastor 1st Bapt. Ch., Albuquerque, 1974-79, Wichita Falls, Tex., 1979-92; pres. So. Bapt. Conv., 1990-92, pres., CEO, exec. com., 1992—. Pres., CEO, exec. com., 1992—; pres. pastor's conf. So. Bapt. Conv., 1986, preacher Conv. Sermon, Las Vegas, 1989. Author: Faith: Taking God at His Word, The Wedding Collection. Office: Executive Committee Southern Baptist Convention 901 Commerce St Nashville TN 37203-3620

CHAPMAN, ORVILLE LAMAR, chemist, educator; b. New London, Conn., June 26, 1932; s. Orville Carmen and Mabel Elnora (Tyree) C.; m. Faye Newton Morrow, Aug. 20, 1955 (div. 1980); children: Kenneth, Kevin; m. Susan Elizabeth Parker, June 15, 1981. BS, Va. Poly. Inst., 1954; PhD, Cornell U., 1957. Instr. chemistry Iowa State U., 1957-59, asst. prof., 1959-62, assoc. prof., 1962-65, Prof. chemistry, 1965-74; prof. chemistry UCLA, 1974—. Cons. Mobil Chem. Co., 1964—98. Recipient NYAS award, 1974, Founders prize, Tex. Instruments, George and Freda Halpern award in phothchemstry, N.Y. Acad. Scis., 1978, Outstanding Patent of Yr. award, Mobil Corp., 1992, Best USe of Info. Tech. in Edn. and Academia award, Computer World/Smithsonian Instn. Mem. Am. Chem. Soc. (award in pure chemistry 1968, Arthur C. Cope award 1978, Midwest award 1978, Havinga medal 1982, McCoy award UCLA, 1985). Home: 1213 Roscomare Rd Los Angeles CA 90077-2202 Office: UCLA Dept Chemistry 405 Hilgard Ave Los Angeles CA 90095-9000 E-mail: chapman@chem.ucla.edu.

CHAPMAN, PETER HERBERT, investment company executive; b. Stockton, Calif., Mar. 6, 1953; s. Duff Gordon and Emalee (Sala) C.; m. Diane Chapman Clark; children: Charlotte Moseley, Alexander Clark. BA, Columbia U., 1977. V.p. Salomon Bros., Inc., N.Y.C., 1977-86, The First Boston Corp., N.Y.C., 1986—90; sr. vp. Bessemer Group, Inc., N.Y.C., 1991-92; exec. dir. CIBC Oppenheimer Corp., N.Y.C., 1993-99; chmn. PH Chapman Advisors, LLC, N.Y.C., 1999—; mng. dir. Chapman, Downing, Keesee & Co. LLC, NYC, 2002—. Bd. dirs. C.D. Stimson Co., Seattle, 1988-92. Bd. dirs. Am. Internat. Sch., Florence, Italy, 1982-94. Mem. Soc. Calif. Pioneers, The Links Club, Racquet and Tennis Club, Piping Rock Club, Knickerbocker Club. Republican. Home: 923 Fifth Ave New York NY 10021-2649

CHAPMAN, PHILIP LAWRENCE, lawyer; b. Jersey City, Apr. 24, 1935; s. Norman and Gertrude Chapman; m. Vera Friedman, June 14, 1959; 1 child, Avery S. BA in History, Princeton U., 1957; LLB, Harvard U., 1966. Bar: N.J., 1961. Assoc. Hellring, Lindeman & Landau, Newark, 1961-68, Hannoch Weisman, Newark, 1968-70, ptnr., 1970-80, Klein Chapman, Clifton, NJ, 1981-93, Chapman, Kessler, Peduto & Saffer, LLC, Clifton and Roseland, NJ, 1993—2003, Lum, Danzis, Drasco & Positan, LLC, Roseland, NJ, 2003—. Mem. 3 person com. to revise N.J.'s non-profit corp. law, 1979-83. Lectr. Inst. Continuing Legal Edn., New Brunswick, N.J., 1983—. With U.S. Army, 1960-61. Mem. N.J. State Bar Assn. (trustee corp. and bus. law sect. 1979—), Basking Ridge Country Club. Democrat. Jewish. Avocations: golf, reading. Office: Lum Danzis Drasco & Positan LLC 103 Eisenhower Pkwy Roseland NJ 07068

CHAPMAN, RICHARD GRADY, engineer; b. Greer, S.C., Oct. 25, 1937; s. Richard Grady Sr. and Mary Idell (Davis) C.; m. Eleanor Raye Kernells, Oct. 13, 1956 (div. Apr. 1978); children: Abby Leigh, Pamela Kathryn, Robert Pope; m. Georgia Ann Burke, Apr. 7, 1978. BS in Engring., U. Nebr., 1974; MS in Geoenviron. Engring., Shippensburg U., 1984. Registered profl. engr., Terr. of Guam. Commd. 2d lt. U.S. Army, 1959, advanced through grades to col., 1984, aviation officer, 1966-71, engr. officer, 1971-89, ret., 1989; designer Coleman & Townes Architects and Engrs., Greenwood, S.C., 1960-66; rsch. engr. U. N.Mex., Albuquerque, 1990-97; cons. engr. Colorado Springs, Colo., 1997-99; gen. mgr. LB-B Assocs. O&M Contract, Ft. Carson, 1999—. Co-chair U.S.-Japan environ. com. U.S. Forces Japan, Tokyo, 1980-83; chief of facilities U.S. Army, Europe, Heidelberg, Germany, 1984-86; comdr. Kwajalein Missile Range, Marshall Islands, 1986-88; CINCPAC rep. to pres. Marshall Islands.

Author: (tng. program) Hazardous Waste Management Course for BLM, 1990, (books) Energy Master Plan, 1994, NORAD's Cheyenne Mountain, 1996; co-author manual: Combat Air Base Planning Principles, 1991. Dir. Regional Water Dist., El Paso County, Colo., 1994-98, Regional Fire Dist., el Paso County, 1994-98; vice chmn. County-Wide Policy Plan, El Paso County, 1994-98; guide, v.p. Visually Impaired and Blind Skiers of Colorado Springs, 1998—. Recipient Resolution award Parliament, Republic of Marshall Islands, 1988, Bd. Commrs. El Paso County, 1998, plaque Visually Impaired and Blind Skiers of Colorado Springs, 1998. Fellow: Am. Soc. Mil. Engrs. (pres. 1977—78, cert. 1985); mem.: Disting. Flying Cross Soc., Ret. Officers Assn. Baptist. Avocations: skiing, flying, scuba diving, art, travel. Home and Office: 11365 N Placita Alameda Dorada Tucson AZ 85757 E-mail: springsengr@aol.com.

CHAPMAN, RICHARD LEROY, public policy researcher; b. Yankton, SD, Feb. 4, 1932; s. Raymond Young and Vera Everette (Trimble) C.; m. Marilyn Jean Nicholson, Aug. 14, 1955; children: Catherine Ruth Hoff, Robert Matthew, Michael David, Stephen Raymond, Amy Jean Johnson. BS, S.D. State U., 1954; postgrad., Cambridge (Eng.) U., 1954-55; MPA, Syracuse U., 1958, PhD, 1967. With Office of Sec. of Def., 1958-59, 61-63; dep. dir. rsch. S.D. Legis. Rsch. Coun., 1959-60; mem. staff Bur. of the Budget, Exec. Office of Pres., Washington, 1960-61; profl. staff mem. com. govt. ops. U.S. Ho. of Reps., Washington, 1966; program dir. NIH, Bethesda, Md., 1967-68; sr. rsch. assoc. Nat. Acad. Pub. Adminstrn., Washington, 1968-72, dep. exec. dir., 1973-76, v.p., dir. rsch., 1976-82; sr. rsch. scientist Denver Rsch. Inst., 1982-86; mem. adv. com. Denver Rsch. Inst. U. Denver, 1984-86; ptnr. Milliken Chapman Rsch. Group Inc., Denver, 1986-88; v.p. Chapman Rsch. Group, Inc., Littleton, 1988-98. Cons. U.S. Office Pers. Mgmt., Washington, 1977-81, Denver, 1986-98; cons. CIA, Washington, 1979, 80, 81, Arthur S. Fleming Awards, Washington, 1977-81; exec. staff dir., cons. U.S. Congressman Frank Denholm; lectr. on sci., tech., govt. and pub. mgmt. Author: (with Fred Grissom) Mining the Nation's Braintrust, 1992; contbr. over 70 articles and revs. to profl. jours. and congl. staff reports. Mem. aerospace com. Colo. Commn. Higher Edn., Denver, 1982-83; chmn. rules com. U. Denver Senate, 1984-85; bd. dirs. S.E. Englewood Water Dist., Littleton, 1984-88, pres. 1986-88; mem. strategic planning com. Mission Hills Bapt. Ch., 1986, bd. dirs. Lay Action Ministry Program, 1988-96, chmn. 1992-96; established Vera and Raymond Chapman Scholarship Fund, S.D. State U.; mem. Fairfax County Rep. Ctrl. Com., Va., 1969-71, Fairfax County Com. of 100, 1979-82. With U.S. Army, 1955-57, Korea, capt. Res. Syracuse U. Maxwell Sch. fellow, 1957-58, 63-64, Brookings Inst. fellow, 1964-65. Mem. Tech. Transfer Soc. (bd. dirs. 1987-95, Pres.'s award 1991, founder Colo. chpt., Thomas Jefferson award 1996), Fed. Lab. Consortium (nat. adv. com. 1989-98), S.D. State U. Found. (bd. dirs. 1992-98, vice chmn. 1994-96, chmn. bd. 1996-98), Southglen Country Club, Masons, KT, Order of DeMolay (Cross of Honor 1982), Rotary (fellow Internat. Found. 1954-55, Paul Harris fellow 1989). Republican. Avocations: hunting, fishing, golf, reading, gardening. *Treat all of life as an opportunity to learn and to contribute. As one enriches the lives of others, you receive great satisfaction and returns that cannot be imagined.*

CHAPMAN, ROBERT FOSTER, judge; b. Inman, S.C., Apr. 24, 1926; s. James Alfred and Martha (Marshall) Chapman; m. Mary Winston Gwathmey, Dec. 21, 1951 (dec. Sept. 1998); children: Edward, Foster, Winston; m. Mary Vail St. Georges, Sept. 30, 2000. BS, U. S.C., 1945, LLB, 1949, LLD (hon.), 1986, Coll. Charleston, 1999. Bar: S.C. 1949. Assoc. firm Butler & Moore, Spartanburg, 1949—51; partner firm Butler, Chapman & Morgan, Spartanburg, 1953—71; U.S. dist. judge for S.C., 1971—81; U.S. cir. judge, 1981—. Chmn. S.C. Rep. Party, 1961—63. Lt. USNR, 1943—46, lt. USNR, 1951—53. Recipient Nat. Patriot's award, Congl. Medal of Honor Soc., 1985. Fellow: Am. Coll. Trial Lawyers. Presbyterian. Home: PO Box 1043 Camden SC 29020-1043

CHAPMAN, ROBERT GALBRAITH, retired hematologist, administrator; b. Colorado Springs, Colo., Sept. 29, 1926; s. Edward Northrop and Janet Galbraith (Johnson) Chapman; m. Virginia Irene Potts, July 6, 1956; children: Lucia Tully, Sarah Northrop Bohrer, Robert Bostwick. Student, Westminster Coll., 1944-45; BA, Yale U., 1947; MD, Harvard U., 1951; MS, U. Colo., 1958. Diplomate Am. Bd. Internal Medicine and Pathology; lic. physician, Colo., Calif. Intern Hartford (Conn.) Hosp., 1951-52; resident in medicine U. Colo. Med. Ctr., Denver, 1955-58; fellow in hematology U. Wash., Seattle, 1958-60; chief resident in medicine U. Colo., Denver, 1957-58, instr. medicine, 1960-62, asst. prof. medicine, 1962-68, assoc. prof., 1968-91; chief staff VA Hosp., Denver, 1968-70; dir. Belle Bonfils Meml. Blood Ctr., Denver, 1977-91, retired, 1991. Regionalization com. Am. Blood Commn., Washington, 1985-87, Co-lo.sickle cell com., Denver, 1978-91, gov.'s AIDS Coun., 1987-88; trustee Coun. Community Blood Ctrs., v.p., 1979-81, pres., 1989-91, rsch. inst. bd. Palo Alto Med. Found., 1991-97. Contbr. articles to profl. jours. Treas. Carmel Valley Village Improvement Com., 1995—. Capt. USAF, 1953-55. USPHS fellow, 1958-60. Fellow ACP; mem. Am. Assn. Blood Banks, Mayflower Soc., Denver Med. Soc., Colo. Med. Soc., Western Soc. Clin. Rsch., Am. Radio Relay League, Alpha Omega Alpha. Mem. United Ch. Christ. Avocations: amateur radio, computers, investments, genealogy. Home: 47 La Rancheria Carmel Valley CA 93924-9424 E-mail: drrob@redshift.com.

CHAPMAN, ROBERT JAMES, clinical psychiatrist, educator; b. Delaware, Ohio, July 10, 1936; s. Edward Samuel and Frances Mae (Stephenson) C.; m. Janice Holmes, June 18, 1960; children: Steven Holmes, Scott Edward, Erik Wellington. AB, Oberlin Coll., 1958; MD, Ohio State U., 1963. Diplomate Am. Bd. Psychiatry and Neurology. Instr., fellow, USPHS U. Rochester (N.Y.) Sch. Med., 1968-69; asst. prof. clin. psychiatry Dartmouth Med. Sch., Hanover, N.H., 1969-79, asst. prof. cmty. and family med., 1976-79, assoc. prof. clin. psychiatry, 1980-94, adj. assoc. prof. psychiatry, 1994—2002, adj. assoc. prof. psycyhiatry emeritus, 2003—. Dir. Robert Wood Johnson Primary Care/Physician Mgr. residency program Dartmouth Med. Sch., Hanover, N.H., 1977-79, dir. Fellowship Program in Rural Cmty. Psychiatry, 1979-81, dir. Comprehensive Alcoholism Svcs. program, 1973-75; dir. Mt. Ascutney Psy-chiat. Assocs., Windsor, Vt., 1984-94; dir. Choate Psychiat. Assocs., New London, N.H., 1995-99. Contbr. chpts. to books, articles to profl. jours. Mem. steering com. Upper Valley Health Care Coalition, White River Junction, Vt./Lebanon, N.H., 1984-86; mem. Area Health Planning Coun., N.H., 1977-80; bd. dirs. Planned Parenthood Assn. Upper Valley, Lebanon, 1970-78; chmn. profl. adv. com. Hanover Vis. Nurse Svc., 1979-80; bd. dirs. Hanover (N.H.) Conservation Coun., 2003—. Sr. asst. surgeon with USPHS, 1964-66, with Peace Corps, Nigeria. Fellow Am. Psychiat. Assn. (disting. life); mem. AMA, AAAS, N.H. Psychiat. Soc. (pres. 1983-84, chmn. ethics com. 1985-86), Physicians for Social Responsibility, Global Health Coun., Physicians for Human Rights, Internat. Physicians for Prevention of Nuclear War, Human Rights Watch, Amnesty Internat., Union Concerned Scientists. Avocations: camping, canoeing, photography, wilderness travel. Home: 33 Rip Rd Hanover NH 03755-1616

CHAPMAN, ROBERT LEE, III, fund administrator, real estate developer; b. Jacksonville, Fla., Dec. 14, 1946; s. Robert Lee Jr. and Elisabeth (Trotter) C.; m. Vicky Lee Patton, July 19, 1945; children: Margaret Patton, Robert Lee IV, Anna Elisabeth, Charlotte Elisabeth. BA, Duke U., 1971. Gen. mgr. Sta. WDBS-FM, Durham, N.C., 1971; dir. media ctr. Duke U., Durham, 1972-73; pres. Chapman Patton & Assocs., Durham, 1974-75, Learning Resources Network, Durham, 1975-90, Southlake Devel. Group, Clermont, Fla., 1990—2002, Southlake Utilities, Inc., Clermont, 1990—2002; mng. dir. The TND Fund, LLC, Durham, N.C., 1999—. Bd. dirs. Broadcasting Found. Am., N.Y.C., 1980-82, Coun. Entrepreneurial Devel., Research Triangle Park, N.C., 1982-86; cons. interactive tech., Burroughs Wellcome Co. and Glaxo, Inc., Research Triangle Park, 1982-86; coord. USA-USSR Summer Arts Festival; juror, Kammerer Meml. Filmmaking prize, Duke U., 1984-89. Editor: Arts Festival Planning Guide, 1974; exec. producer over 100 films and videos. Coord., Durham Bicentennial Commn., 1975-76; bd. dirs. Ctrl. Park Sch. for Children, 2001—, Historic Preservation Soc. of Durham, 2002—, Carolina Cinema Corp., Durham, 1978-82, Friends of Duke U. Arts Mus., Durham, 1986-89, Nat. Town Builders Assn.; chmn. N.C. Smart Growth Alliance, Chapel Hill; trustee, Duke Sch. for Children, Durham, 1986-90. Mem. Samuel Cook Soc. (Duke U.), Order of Red Friars, Sigma Nu. Avocations: travel, jogging, backpacking. Home: 2525 Lanier Pl Durham NC 27705-5005 Office: 310 1/2 W Franklin St Chapel Hill NC 27514 E-mail: bob@tndfund.com.

CHAPMAN, ROGER STEVENS, JR., construction company executive; b. Hartford, Conn., Dec. 3, 1927; s. Roger Stevens Chapman, Katherine Marie (Willetts) Chapman; m. Viola Mohl, Feb. 7, 1959; children: David, Ellen. BCE, Cornell U., 1949; MS in Mgmt., Rensselaer Poly. Inst., 1970. Registered Profl. engr. Field engr. A.S. Wikstrom, Inc., Skaneateles, NY, 1949—54; project engr. Savin Constrn. Co., East Hartford, Conn., 1954—58; mgr. project Merritt-Chapman & Scott Corp., N.Y.C., 1958—62; supt., chief estimator, v.p. C.W. Blakeslee & Sons, Inc., New Haven, 1962—76; v.p., dir. Blakeslee Arpaia Chapman, Inc., Branford, Conn., 1976—86, pres., 1986—. V.p., dir. BAC Marine, Inc., Branford, 1977—. Bd. dirs. Sou;theastern Conn. Better Bus. Bur., 1980—86. With U.S. Army, 1951—53. Fellow: ASCE; mem.: Conn. Constrn. Industries (bd. dirs., chmn. 1991—94), Conn. Rd. Builders Assn. (v.p. 1985—88, pres. 1988—91), Am. Rd. and Transp. Builders Assn. (bd. dirs. 1988—99, pres. contractors divsn. 1993—94), Am. Arbitration Assn. Republican. Episcopalian. Achievements include patents for in field. Office: Blakeslee Arpaia Chapman Inc 200 N Branford Rd Branford CT 06405-2846

CHAPMAN, RONALD THOMAS, musician, educator; b. Bklyn., Dec. 16, 1933; s. William Leon and Rosamond (Walker) C.; m. Joyce Elaine Chase, Dec. 1966 (dec. May 1973); adopted child, Debra Anne (dec. July 1992); m. Virginia Marie Knochenhauer, Feb. 14, 1975 (dec. July 1989); stepchildren: Suzanne, Michael. BS cum laude, CUNY, 1982; MA in Teaching, Lehman Coll., 1983; PhD in Music in Higher Edn., NYU, 1989. Cert. tchr. music, N.Y., tchr. Spanish, N.Y. Toured with Leonard dePaur Infantry Chorus, 1953-55; mem. trio The Versatones, U.S. and Can., 1955-59; vocalist, 1978—; asst. dir. men's choir Kingsborough Community Coll., 1980-82; asst. to dir. mixed chorus Lehman Coll., CUNY, 1982-83; instr. voice NYU, N.Y.C., 1986—; instr. computer music for music teachers N.Y. Inst. Tech., N.Y.C., 1987; music tchr. Hempstead Sch. Dist., 2002—. Pvt. instr. voice, piano, guitar, computerized music, music theory, sight singing and music lit., 1980—; substitute tchr. Hempstead (N.Y.) Sch. Dist., 1983-85, 2002—, mem. faculty, 1988-89, tchr. adult edn., ESL, 1993—, tchr. group piano, group voice in continuing adult edn. program, 1993—, substitute music tchr., 2002-03; instr. voice NYU, 1986—; bd. dirs. Cultural Environ, Queens, N.Y.; adjudicator N.Y. Singing Tchrs. Assn., 1995. Performed in Spain, Japan, Thailand, The Philippines, Eng., Jamaica, Can., Vietnam, P.R., Fed. Republic of Germany, Laos, Portugal and U.S. including N.Y.C., Atlanta and Miami; TV appearances on Johnny Carson Show, Arthur Godfrey Talent Scouts, Gary Moore Show, Tex and Jinx Falkenburg Show, many others; rec. artist for Columbia Records, RCA Records, Island in the Sun soundtrack; appeared in Broadway play Kwamina; appearing nightly Fox Hollow, 1978-93, Caterer/Restaurant, Woodbury, N.Y., 1978—; starred in Playboy Club and Hotel Chain, 1960-67, (movies) Rueda de Sospechosos, 1963, (revue) The Ronnie Chapman Show, 1968-69; debuted by singing and accompanying himself on piano a medley of Broadway Show Tunes and Internat. Art Songs in various langs. Carnegie Hall, 1991, 92, 93, 94, 95, 96; Cafe Trilussa, 1996-97, J. DeCarlos Restaurant, Huntington, N.Y., 1998—. Bd. dirs. Cultural Environment, Queens, N.Y., 1978—; apptd. dep. gov. Am. Biog. Inst. Rsch. Assn., 1992. Mem. Internat. Assn. for Rsch. in Singing (rsch. assoc. Found. for Rsch. Singing), Nat. Assn. Tchrs. of Singing, N.Y. Singing Tchrs. Assn., N.Y. State Sch. Music Assn. (cert. to adjucate "Voice"), Internat. Assn. Jazz Educators, Chopin Found. N.Y., Am. Assn. Choral Dirs., Music Educators Nat. Conf., Music Tchrs. Nat. Assn., Assoc. Music Tchrs. League N.Y., Internat. Platform Assn., Am. Choral Dirs. Assn., Phi Delta Kappa (v.p. programs NYU chpt. 1988-89), Pi Kappa Lambda, Kappa Delta Pi (chpt. 3d v.p. 1994—). Achievements include being awarded a design patent for invention of a portable back rest/supporter, 1993. Home and Office: 108 Glenmore Ave Hempstead NY 11550-6630 E-mail: drchapman@ronchainc.com.

CHAPMAN, RUSSELL LEONARD, botany educator; b. Bklyn., May 30, 1946; s. Russell Hood and Helen C.; m. Melanie Anne Chapman, June 28, 1969; children: Christopher John, Timothy Sean. BA, Dartmouth Coll., 1968; MS, U. Calif., Davis, 1970, PhD, 1973. NSF grad. fellow dept. botany U. Calif., Davis, 1971-73; asst. prof. dept. botany and plant biology La. State U., Baton Rouge, 1973-77, assoc. prof. dept. botany, 1977-83, prof. dept. botany, 1983—95, prof. dept. biol. sci., 1995—, assoc. dean Coll. of Arts and Scis., 1979-83, assoc. dean Coll. of Basic Scis., 1983-84, chmn. dept. botany, 1988-94, assoc. vice chancellor Office of Rsch. and Econ. Devel., 1994-96, interim exec. dir. Ctr. for Coastal, Energy and Environ. Res, 1995-96, exec. dir. Ctr. for Coastal, Energy and Environ. Resources, 1996-2001, dean Sch. of the Coast and Environment, 2001—, adj. prof. dept. oceanography and coastal scis. Mem. editl. bd.: Jour. of Phycology, Algologia, Molecular Phylogenetics and Evolution; assoc. editor Am. Jour. of Botany, 1995—; author book chpts. in field; contbr. articles to profl. jours. Bd. dirs. Baton Rouge Earth Day, Inc., 1990-92; mem. Found. for Hist. La., Baton Rouge, 1973—; trustee Johnston Sci. Found., 2000- (bd.dirs. 2001-). Recipient Outstanding Undergrad. Teaching award Amoco Found., Inc., 1978, Disting. Faculty award La. State U. Alumni Fedn., Baton Rouge, 1981; Paul Harris fellow, 2000. Fellow Linnean Soc. London; mem. Phycol. Soc. Am. (sec., v.p., pres. 1985-90, bd. trustees 1994—), Botanical Soc. Am. (chmn. phycol. sect. 1983-85, fin. adv. com. 2000—), British Phycol. Soc., Internat. Phycol. Soc. (exec. coun. 2001—), Internat. Soc. for Evolutionary Protistology, Willie Hennig Soc., La. Soc. Electron Microscopy (treas., pres. 1976-80), Environ. Rsch. Consortium La. (bd. trustees 1998—, pres. 1999-2000, sec.-treas. 2000-01), Phi Kappa Phi, Sigma Xi, Omicron Delta Kappa. Episcopalian. Home: 6920 Bayou Paul Rd Saint Gabriel LA 70776-5602 Office: La State U Sch Coast & Environ 1002 R Energy Coast and Environ Bldg Baton Rouge LA 70803-4110 E-mail: chapman@lsu.edu.

CHAPMAN, SAMUEL GREELEY, political science educator, criminologist; b. Atlanta, Sept. 29, 1929; s. Calvin C. and Jane (Greeley) C.; m. Patricia Hepfer, June 19, 1949 (dec. Dec. 1978); children: Lynn Randall, Deborah Jane; m. Carolyn Hughes, June 1, 1991. AB, U. Calif.-Berkeley, 1951, MA, 1959. Officer Police Dept., Berkeley, 1951-56; police cons. Pub. Adminstrn. Service, Chgo., 1956-59; asst. prof. Sch. Police Adminstrn., Mich. State U., East Lansing, 1959-63; police chief Multnomah County, Portland, Oreg., 1963-66; asst. dir. Pres.'s Commn. on Law Enforcement and Adminstrn. of Justice, Nat. Crime Commn., Washington, 1966-67; prof. dept. polit. sci. U. Okla., Norman, 1967-91; prof. emeritus, 1991—; chmn. athletic council U. Okla., 1971-72, 79-80. Adj. prof. criminal justice U. Nev., Reno, 1995—; assoc.'s disting. lectr., 1985-86. Author: Dogs in Police Work, 1960, The Police Heritage in England and America, 1962, Police Patrol Readings, 1964, rev. edit., 1970, Perspectives on Police Assaults in the South Central United States, 1974, Short of Merger, 1976, Police Murders and Effective Countermeasures, 1976, Police Dogs in North America, 1979, 2d. edit., 1990, Cops, Killers and Staying Alive: The Murder of Police Officers in America, 1986; Murdered On Duty: The Killing of Police Officers in America, 1998; contbr. chpts. to books, articles to profl. jours. Mem. Norman City Council, 1972-83, mayor pro-tem, 1975-76, 79-80, 81-83. Recipient Amoco Found. award, 1986. Mem. Nev. Hist. Soc. (docent), Alpha Delta Phi. Republican. Home and Office: 680 Kane Ct Reno NV 89512-1354 E-mail: sgchapman@charter.net.

CHAPMAN, SARA ELEANOR, French historian; b. Weatherford, Okla., June 14, 1967; d. Charles Wayne and Sarabelle J. Chapman. BA with honors, Okla. State U., 1989; PhD, Georgetown U., 1997. Asst. prof. history Oakland U., Rochester, Mich., 1997—2003, assoc. prof., 2003—. Vol. Rec. for Blind and Dyslexic, Troy, Mich., 1999—2003. Mem.: Soc. French Hist. Studies. Office: Dept History Oakland U 366 O'Dowd Hall Rochester MI 48309 E-mail: chapman@oakland.edu.

CHAPMAN, SUE TURNER, artist; b. Albany, Sept. 25, 1927; d. Charles and Isabel (Fite) T.; m. Robert Joseph Chapman, Oct. 4, 1954 (div. 1968); 1 child, Paul. Scorer auto races, 1947-68; staff artist Indpls. Blueprint, 1960-61; prodn. artist Pinarie Lithographing, Louisville, 1968-70; art dir. Humana, Louisville, 1970-77; dir. Floyd County Mus., New Albany, Ind., 1980-82; working backside thoroughbred race horses, 1979-86; freelance comml. artist, 1983—. Presenter in field. One-woman shows, Ind., Ky., S.C., N.Y., 1977—, including Ctr. for Creative Arts, Indpls., 1999, Mill Cottage Gallery, Rensselaerville, N.Y.; artist cover Anvil mag., 1998, CD cover Corydon Dulcimer Soc., 2002. Recipient 1st place watercolor Womans Club Louisville, 1981, merit award, Best of Show award Ind. Heritage Arts, Brown County Art Gallery, Nashville, 1991, merit award Southside Art League, Indpls., 1996, 1st place sr. exhbn. Brown County Art Guild, 2000. Democrat. Avocations: camping, photography, gardening. Home: 1244 S Whiskey Run Ranch Rd Milltown IN 47145-7302

CHAPMAN, WES, dancer, performing company executive; b. Union Springs, Ala. Studies with Emily Caruso, Dame Sonia Arova, Thorsutowski. Mem. State of Ala. Ballet, Am. Ballet Theatre, 1984-87, soloist, 1987-89, prin. dancer, 1989-93, 95-96, Bavarian Nat. Ballet, Munich, Germany, 1993-95; artistic dir. Ala. Ballet, Birmingham, Ala., 1996—. Solo La Bayadere, The Nutcracker, Raymonda, Romeo and Juliet; leading roles include Ballet Imperial, La Bayadere, Donizetti Variations, The Leaves Are Fading, Les Rendezvous, Les Sylphides, Symphonie Condertante, Theme and Variations, The Nutcracker, Romeo and Juliet, The Sleeping Beauty, Swan Lake, La Sylphide, Onegin, Taming of the Shrew, A Midsummer Nights Dream, Don Q., Giselle, Grass, Brief Fling, Symphonic Variations, Sinfonietta, Coppelia, Paquita; featured roles Birthday Offering, Drink to Me Only With Thine Eyes, Etudes, Great Galloping Gottschalk, In the Upper Room; created leading role Bruch Violin Concerto No. 1. Recipient Prix d'Excellence de Dance and Duane Dushion award, ASFA, 1983, Disting. career Award, Soc. for the Fine Arts, U. of Ala., 1998. Office: Alabama Ballet 2026 1st Ave S Birmingham AL 35233

CHAPMAN, WILLIAM, baritone; b. Los Angeles; s. William Cloud and Augusta Jane (Kiel) C.; m. Irene Veronica Meyer, Sept. 15, 1957; children—Alexa Maria, Teren Cloud. BA in Drama, U. So. Calif. Propr. vocal studio, Los Angeles, 1967—. Mem. faculty U.S. Internat. U. Performing Arts Sch., San Diego, 1971-86; mem. extension faculty UCLA. Leading baritone N.Y.C. Opera, 1956—, also other opera houses, U.S. and Europe; opened Spoleto Festival as Macbeth in Macbeth, 1957; leading performer: Menotti's Maria Golovin as produced by David Merrick, Broadway, Frank Loesser's Greenwillow, Alvin Theater, (original prodn.) Candide, Martin Beck Theater; Broadway appearances as Charlie in Shenandoan, 1978-79, also in N.Y.C. Center revival of South Pacific; appeared as Frank Maurrant for N.Y.C. Opera, also PBS-TV; TV appearances on Wonderful World of Disney; Columnist: Notes for the Singing Actor, Voice Mag.; appearing as Cecil B. DeMille in 1996-97 Nat. Touring Co. of Sunset Blvd. Rockefeller grantee; recipient DramaLogue award for performance, 1992, various certs. of appreciation. Mem. Screen Actors Guild, Actors Equity, Am. Guild Variety Artists, AFTRA. E-mail: icy1@pacbell.net.

CHAPNICK, DAVID B. lawyer; b. N.Y.C., Apr. 24, 1939; s. H.M. and G. (Kraft) C.; m. Elaine Schlozman, Dec. 25, 1966; children: Adam Lawrence, Melissa Rachel. AB with honors, Union Coll., 1959; LLB, NYU, 1962. Bar: N.Y. 1963. Law clk. to Hon. Warren E. Burger U.S. Ct. Appeals (D.C. cir.), Washington, 1962-63; pvt. practice N.Y.C., 1963-67; assoc. Simpson Thacher & Bartlett, N.Y.C., 1967-69, ptnr., 1970—2000, of counsel, 2001—. Trustee Union Coll., Schenectady, N.Y., 1991—, vice chmn., 1995-96, chmn., 1998-02. Mem. N.Y. State Bar Assn., Assn. Bar City N.Y. Office: Simpson Thacher & Bartlett 425 Lexington Ave New York NY 10017-3954

CHAPOTON, JOHN EDGAR, lawyer, government official; b. Galveston, Tex., May 18, 1936; s. Otis Byron and Grace Donaldson (Wayman) C.; m. Sarah Eastham, Jan. 5, 1963; children: John Edgar Jr., Clare Eastham. Student, Washington and Lee U., 1954-55; BBA with honors, U. Tex., 1958, LLB with honors, 1960. Bar: Tex. 1960, D.C. 1985. Assoc. Andrews, Kurth, Campbell & Jones, Houston, 1961-69; with Dept. Treasury, Washington, 1969-72, 81-84, tax legis. counsel, 1970-72, asst. sec. for tax policy, 1981-84; ptnr. Vinson & Elkins, Houston, 1972-81, mng. ptnr. Washington, 1984—2000; ptnr. Brown Investment Adv. & Trust Co., 2001—. Chmn. law firms div. United Way Capital Area, Washington, 1988-90; bd. dirs. Boys and Girls Clubs Greater Washington, 1990—, Meridian Internat. Ctr., 2001—. Recipient Achievement award Tax Soc. NYU, 1984. Fellow Am. Coll. Tax Counsel; mem. ABA (sect. taxation, vice chair govt. rels.), Tex. State Bar Assn., D.C. Bar Assn., Am. Law Inst. Republican. Episcopalian. Avocation: golf. Office: Brown Investment Advisory Inc 1737 H St NW Washington DC 20006 Home: 18 W Kirke St Chevy Chase MD 20815

CHAPP, JEFFREY A, education educator, artist; s. August Anthony Chapp and Barbara VanDuyne; m. Belena S Skievaski; 1 child, Dylan. BS, Appalachian State U., 1973—80; MA, Purdue U., 1981—83; MFA, U. of Del., 1986—88. Asst. prof. Lincoln U., Pa., 1995—2000, assoc. prof., chair, 2000—02, assoc. prof., visual arts program coord., 2002—. Panelist Divsn. of the Arts/Del. State Arts Coun., Wilmington, Del., 1998, Mid-Atlantic Arts Found., Balt., 1992. Exhibitions include 2000 Internat. Cone Box Show (Purchase award, 2000), New Ceramic Works, Archon, N.Y.C., Phila. Clay Regional (hon. mention), Clay Cup III, SIU Museum (pres.'s Purchase award), Carbondale, Ill., Clay USA, Radford U. (award of excellence), Va., Crafts Nat. II Upton Hall Gallery, Buffalo, NY. Artistic v.p. Del. Ctr. for the Creative Arts (DCCA), Wilmington, 1989—90. Grantee Profl. Devel. grant, U. of Del., 1988; Academic fellowship, 1987, Assoc. Level Summer fellowship, Ind. Arts Commn., 1984, Faculty Devel. Grant, Lincoln U., 1998—99, Individual Artist fellowship, Del. State Arts Coun., 1989—90. Mem.: Coll. Arts Assn. Unitarian. Office: Lincoln University 1570 Baltimore Pike Lincoln University PA 19352-0999 E-mail: jchapp@lu.lincoln.edu.

CHAPPARS, TIMOTHY STEPHEN, lawyer; b. Cin., July 23, 1952; s. Gregory S. and Helen (Maragos) C.; m. Laurie A. Kress, Dec. 24, 1986 (div. Sept. 1987); m. Laurie A. Kress, Apr. 18, 1990; children: Alexander T., Jake A. BS, Duke U., 1974; JD, U. Cin., 1978. Assoc. Cox & Chappars, Xenia, Ohio, 1978-94, Bryant Law Office, Wilmington, Ohio, 1981—. Trial atty. Pub. Defender's Office, Clinton County, Wilmington, 1978-88; lectr. So. State Jr. Coll., Wilmington, 1982. Mem. Ohio Bar Assn., Am. Trial Lawyers Acad., Ohio Acad. Trial Lawyers. Methodist. Avocations: tennis, piano, hiking, cycling, skiing. Home: 2025 Winding Brook Way Xenia OH 45385-9382 Office: PO Box 280 Xenia OH 45385-0280

CHAPPELEAR, STEPHEN ERIC, lawyer; b. Columbus, Ohio, Dec. 25, 1952; s. Thornton White and Phyllis Evelyn (Williams) C.; m. Sharon Sue Starr, June 8, 1974; children: Katherine Sue, Christopher Charles. BA, Ohio State U., 1974, JD, 1977. Bar: Ohio 1977, U.S. Dist. Ct. (so. dist.) Ohio, U.S. Dist. Ct. (no. dist.) Ohio, U.S. Dist. Ct. (ea. dist.) Wis., U.S. Tax Ct., U.S. Ct. Appeals (6th cir.). Assoc. Emens, Hurd, Kegler & Ritter, Columbus, 1977-82, prin., 1983—2001, Kegler Brown Hill & Ritter, Columbus; ptnr. Hahn, Loeser & Parks, Columbus, 2001—. Mem. exec. coun. Nat. Conf. Bar Pres., 1997-2000; pres. Met. Bar Caucus, 2001-02. Author: The Complete Book of Jury Verdicts II, Franklin County, Ohio, 1985-91, The Complete Book of Franklin County Jury Verdicts, 1990, So What's Your Case Reaaly Worth?: A Decade of Jury Trial Verdicts, 1995; editor jour. Bar Briefs, 1986-88; contbr. articles to profl. jour. Fellow Ohio State Bar Found. (trustee), Columbus Bar Found.; mem. ABA (litig. sect., trial practice com., trial and ins. practice sects. com. on trial techniques and comml. torts) Ohio State Bar Assn. (bd. gov., coun. dels., former chair fed. cts. and practice com., litigation sect., bd. gov., pres. 2002-03), Columbus Bar Assn. (bd. govs., pres. 1995-96), Am. Inns of Ct. (Franklin chpt. pres. 1994-95), Million Dollar Adv. Forum, Lawyers Club of Columbus, New Albany Country Club. Avocations: sports, movies, theater, writing. Office: Hahn Loeser & Parks 21 E State St Ste 1050 Columbus OH 43215-4213 E-mail: sechappelear@hahnlaw.com.

CHAPPELL, ANNETTE M. higher education consultant, minister; b. Washington, Oct. 31, 1939; d. Joseph John and Annette B. (Harley) C.; m. Brian Thomas Flower, Sept. 3, 1960 (div. Mar. 1983); m. Frank Joseph Sanders, Apr. 8, 1985 (dec. Dec. 1995). BA in English, U. Md., 1962, MA, 1964, PhD, 1970; MDiv, Gen. Theol. Sem., 2003. Lectr. European div. U. Md., Eng., 1965-66, instr. English, 1966-69; asst. prof. English Towson (Md.) U., 1969-72, assoc. prof., 1972-79, prof., 1979—99, spl. asst. to pres., affirmative action officer, 1974-77; dean humanistic, social and managerial studies Towson (Md.) State U., 1977-82, dean Coll. Liberal Arts, 1982-95, assoc. v.p. acad. affairs, 1995-99; ind. cons., 1999—; rector Ch. of the Resurrection, Balt., 2003—. Contbr. articles to profl. jours. and book revs. to Ms Mag., Balt. Sun. Lay reader, chalicist All Saints Episcopal Ch., Reisterstown, Md., 1973-2003; pres. Baltimore County Commn. for Women, 1977-79; bd. dirs. Baltimore County Sexual Assault and Domestic Violence Center, 1978-83, pres., 1980-82. Mem. AAUP, MLA, Am. Assn. Higher Edn., Council Colls. Arts and Scis. (bd. dirs. 1984-86), Exec. Women's Council Md. (1st v.p. 1980, pres. 1981) E-mail: achappall@towson.edu.

CHAPPELL, CHARLES FRANKLIN, meteorologist, consultant; b. St. Louis, Dec. 7, 1927; s. Hubert Guy and Wilma Halle (Lindsey) C.; m. Doris Mae Kennedy, Aug. 4, 1951; children— Christa Ann, Susan Lynne, Deborah Louise BS, Washington U., St. Louis, 1949; postgrad., St. Louis U., 1952-54; MS, Colo. State U., 1967, PhD, 1971. Flight data engr. McDonnell Aircraft Co., St. Louis, 1950-55; weather forecaster U.S. Weather Bur., Kansas City, Mo., 1956-67; research assoc. Colo. State U., Ft. Collins, 1967-70; assoc. prof. Utah State U., Logan, 1970-72; research meteorologist NOAA, Boulder, Colo., 1972-79, research dir., 1979-87; head applied sci. group Nat. Ctr. for Atmospheric Research, Boulder, 1988-89, sr. scientist coop. program for operational meteorology edn. and tng., 1989-94; meteolologist cons., Boulder, 1995—. Cons. meteorologist Midwest Weather Service, Kansas City, Mo., 1958-60 Assoc. editor Jour. Atmospheric Sci., 1984-87; contbr. articles to prof. jours. (Best Sci. Paper award in NOAA-Environ. Research Labs. 1981). Served as seaman 1st class USN, 1945-46 Recipient silver medal Dept. Commerce, 1957 Fellow Am. Meteorol. Soc.; mem. Nat. Weather Assn., Weather Modification Assn., Am. Geophys. Union, Phi Kappa Phi. Avocations: hiking, painting, gardening, piano. Home and Office: 3110 Heidelberg Dr Boulder CO 80305-7010 E-mail: chapmo@msn.com. *You can always accomplish more than you think, so do it.*

CHAPPELL, DAVID FRANKLIN, lawyer; b. St. Louis, Mo, Apr. 18, 1943; married; children: Libbey Paige, Wade Garrett. BA in Polit. Sci., U. Tex., 1964, JD with honors, 1968. Bar: Tex., US Ct. Appeals (5th, 9th, and 11th cir.); cert. civil trial law, Tex. Bd. Legal Specialization, 1978. Ptnr. Chappell, Hill & Lowrance, LLP, Ft. Worth. Mem. task force on delay Supreme Ct. Tex., 1985, spl. master US Dist. Ct. (no. dist.) Tex., Ft. Worth; mem. Ft. Worth City Coun., 1989-93; chair nat. adv. coun. US SBA, 1998-2000, chair, Ft. Worth Day Resource Ctr., 2003. Editorial bd. The Texas Lawyer, 1985-86. V.p., gen. counsel Tarrant County Arts Coun., 1980-86; vice chmn. City of Ft. Worth Human Rels. Com.; chair Area Ambulance Authority, 1994-98; chair adv. bd. U. Tex. at Arlington-Ft. Worth, 2001. Fellow Tex. Bar Found. (chmn. bd. trustees 1987-88); mem. Am. Bar Found., Tex. Bar Assn. (bd. dir. 1982-86, chmn. bd. 1984-85, chmn. health law sect. 1985-86, spl. com. to revise grievance process), ABA (editor Practice TIPS 1980, sec., exec. council of Tort and Ins. Practice Sect. 1983-87, chmn. Young Lawyers Div. 1978), Am. Judicature Soc. (exec. com, bd. dir. 1979), Tex. Young Lawyers Assn. (sec. 1976), Ft. Worth and Tarrant County Young Lawyers Assn. (pres. 1974, Outstanding Young Lawyer award 1979). Office: Chappell Hill & Lowrance LLP 400 City Center Tower I 201 Main St Fort Worth TX 76102-4140 E-mail: chappell@cmlaw.com.

CHAPPELL, FRED DAVIS, English language educator, poet; b. Canton, N.C., May 28, 1936; s. James Taylor and Anne Mae (Davis) C.; m. Susan Nicholls, Aug. 2, 1959; 1 son, Christopher Heath. BA, Duke U., 1961, MA, 1964; LittD, U. N.C., Asheville, 1989, Spring Hill Coll., 1991. Prof. English U. N.C., Greensboro, 1964—. Adv. editor Skyhook, 1958-59, Red Clay Reader, 1964-65, Greensboro Rev., 1964—, Ga. Rev., 1990—. Author: It Is Time, Lord, 1963, The Inkling, 1965, Dagon, 1968, The World Between the Eyes, 1971, The Gaudy Place, 1972, Midquest, 1981, Moments of Light, 1982, Castle Tzingal, 1984, I Am One of You Forever, 1985, Source, 1985, The Fred Chappell Reader, 1988, First and Last Words, 1989, Brighten the Corner Where You Are, 1989, More Shapes Than One, 1992, C, 1993, Plow Naked, 1993, Spring Garden: New and Selected Poems, 1995, Farewell, I'm Bound To Leave You, 1996, A Way of Happening, 1998, Look Back All the Green Valley, 1999, Family Gathering, 2000. Recipient Roanoke-Chowan Poetry prize N.C. Lit. Assn., 1979, Prix de Meilleur des Lettres Etrangers, 1973, N.C. award in lit. State of N.C., 1987, Bollingen prize for poetry, 1985, World Fantasy award World Fantasy Assn., 1992, 94, T.S. Eliot prize Ingersoll Found., 1993, Aiken Taylor Poetry award, 1996, Irene Lenore Heasley prize, 1999, SEBA Novel award, 2000, Eminescu medal for poetry, 2001; N.C. Poet Laureate, 1997-2002; NDEA fellow, 1961-63; Rockefeller grantee, 1967-68, grantee Nat. Acad. Arts and Letters, 1968. Mem.: Order of the Longleaf Pine. Democrat. Avocations: books, wine, mischief. Office: U NC English Dept Greensboro NC 27412-0001

CHAPPELL, JOHN CHARLES, lawyer; b. Minden, Nebr., Jan. 28, 1935; s. Charles Arthur and Eletta Hope (Pattison) C.; m. Joyce Joan Dawson, Sept. 1, 1957; children: Laura, Pamela, James, Allegra. BS in Edn., U. Nebr., 1956; JD, NYU, 1960. Bar: N.Y. 1960. Summer assoc. firm Dewey Ballantine, N.Y.C., 1959, assoc., 1960-68; ptnr. Dewey Ballantine LLP, N.Y.C., 1968-00, of counsel, 2000—. Served to 1st lt. U.S. Army, 1957. Root-Tilden scholar NYU, 1956 Mem.: Assn. Bar City N.Y. Home: 2 Galloping Hill Cir Holmdel NJ 07733-1848 Office: Dewey Ballantine LLP 1301 Ave Of The Americas New York NY 10019-6022

CHAPPELL, KATHLEEN DIANE, fundraising executive; b. Scott AFB, Ill., Feb. 4, 1953; d. John E. and Edith F. Chappell. AB in Social Scis., Shimer Coll., 1976; MBA, So. Ill. U., Edwardsville, 1981. Grad. admissions officer So. Ill. U., Edwardsville, 1976-78, staff asst., 1978-85, staff asst. Edwardsville Found., 1985-87, dir. ann. giving Edwardsville Found., 1987-91; dir. fin. devel. ARC, St. Louis, Mo., 1991-94; dir. devel. comm. The Nature Conservancy, Chgo., 1994-98; asst. dean devel. Ill. Inst. Tech., Chgo., 1998—. Bd. dirs. Friends of the Chicago River; vol. Pullman Civic Orgn. Mem. Nat. Soc. Fundraising Profls., Coun. Advancement and Support of Edn. Avocation: birding. Home: 11348 S Saint Lawrence Ave Chicago IL 60628-5112 Office: Ill Inst Tech 3301 S Dearborn St Chicago IL 60616 E-mail: chappell@iit.edu.

CHAPPELL, MILES LINWOOD, JR., art history educator; b. Norfolk, Va., June 6, 1939; s. Miles Linwood Sr. and Melrose Clarice (Debnam) C.; m. Marcial Cassada, July 23, 1966; children: Ashley, Oliver, Picot. BS in Chemistry, Coll. William and Mary, 1960; PhD in Art History, U. N.C., 1971. Prof. art history dept. art and art history Coll. William and Mary, Williamsburg, Va., 1971—; chair dept. Chancellor prof. art history Coll. William and Mary, 1987; artistic adv. bd. Interlochen Ctr. for Arts. Author: Cristofano Allori, 1984, Lodovico Cigoli, Disegni, 1992, The Fine Art of Drawing, 1993; co-author: Disegni dei Toscani, 1979, Lodovico Cigoli, tra manierismo e barocco, 1992, Renascence of the Florentine Baroque in "Dialoghi di storia dell'arte", 1998, The Artistic Education of Maria de'MEdici, 2003; formulator and co-author: Form, Function and Finesse: Drawings from the Herman Found., 1983; asst. editor: Studies in Iconography, 1978-80; adv. editor: Eighteenth-Century Life, 1980-84, 85—; contbr. articles on Renaissance, Baroque and Am. art to profl. jours. Mem. internat. survey of Jewish monuments, U. Ill., 1978. Harvard U. Ctr. for Italian Renaissance Studies fellow, Florence, 1980; Cité Internat. des Arts, 1995; recipient numerous rsch. grants. Mem. Kunsthistorisches Institut Florence, Phi Beta Kappa (Alpha chpt. award for scholarship 1987, v.p. 1992-93). Avocations: drawing, painting, music. Home: 139 Ridings Cv Williamsburg VA 23185-3903 Office: Coll William & Mary Dept Art History Williamsburg VA 23187 E-mail: mlchap@wm.edu.

CHAPPELL, MILTON LEROY, lawyer; b. Accra, Ghana, Mar. 25, 1951; (parents Am. citizens); s. Derwood Lee and Helen Jean (Freeman) C.; m. Margot Cecelia Shields, Dec. 18, 1972; children: Marton Gerald, Monet Louise. BA summa cum laude, Columbia Union Coll., 1973; JD, Cath. U., 1976; diploma, Nat. Inst. Trial Advocacy, Boulder, Colo., 1978; cert., U. Miami, 1982. Bar: Md. 1976, D.C. 1977, U.S. Ct. Appeals (4th, 5th, 9th and D.C. cirs.) 1977, U.S. Dist. Ct. D.C. 1978, U.S. Ct. Appeals (6th cir.) 1979, U.S. Supreme Ct. 1980, U.S. Ct. Appeals (11th cir.) 1981, U.S. Dist. Ct. Md. 1982, U.S. Ct. Appeals (7th cir.) 1988, U.S. Dist. Ct. (no. dist.) Calif., 1990, U.S. Ct. Appeals (3rd cir.) 2000. Sole practice, Silver Spring, Md., 1976—; staff atty. Nat. Right to Work Legal Def. Found., Springfield, Va., 1976—. Lectr. Columbia Union Coll., Takoma Park, Md., 1976-77; legal cons. JNA Elem. Sch., Takoma Park, 1980-83; gen. counsel Playgrounds Unltd., Inc., 1988-2000, Internat. Play Equipment Mfrs. Assn., Inc., 1995—, Park Dreams Internat., Ltd., 2000—; participant play settings subcom. recreation access adv. com. U.S. Archtl. and Transp. Barriers Compliance Bd., 1993-94. Contbr. to Ohio No. U. Law Rev., Govt. Union Rev., Calif. Pub. Employee Rels. Mem. Hillandale Civic Assn., Silver Spring, 1980—; legal cons., bd. dirs. Silver Spring Seventh-day Adventist Ch., 1976-84, Takoma Park.; participant U.S. Arch. and Trans. Barriers Compliance Bd., Recreation Access Adv. Com., Play Settings subcom., 1993-94. Mem. ABA, Md. Bar Assn. D.C. Bar Assn. Home: 10321 Royal Rd Silver Spring MD 20903-1616 Office: Nat Right to Work Legal Def Found 8001 Braddock Rd # 600 Springfield VA 22151-2110 E-mail: mlc@nrtw.org.

CHAPPELL, WALLACE, performing company executive; b. Dallas, Aug. 8, 1941; BA, Dartmouth Coll., 1963; MFA, U. Hawaii, 1965; postgrad., U. Minn. Staff dir. L.A. Music Ctr. Mark Taper Forum, 1969—75; assoc. artistic dir. Alliance Theatre, Atlanta, 1975—78; artistic dir. Repertory Theatre of St. Louis, 1980—83; dir. Hancher Auditorium, U. Iowa, 1986—2001; exec. dir. Am. Ballet Theatre, N.Y.C., 2001—. Cons., spkr., panelist, advisor, site visitor various orgns, including Nat. Endowment for Arts, Lila Wallace-Reader's Digest Fund, Assn. Performing Arts Presenters. Bd. dirs. Dance/USA. Mem.: Stage Soc. Dirs. and Choreographers, Internat. Soc. Performing Arts (pres. 1993—95). Office: Am Ballet Theatre 890 Broadway New York NY 10003

CHAPPELL, WILLARD RAY, physics educator, environmental scientist; b. Boulder, Colo., Feb. 27, 1938; s. Willard Bruce and Mildred Mary (Weaver) C.; m. Juanita June Benetin, Mar. 5, 1981; children: Ginger Ferguson, Robert Ferguson. BA in Math., U. Colo., 1962, PhD in Physics, 1965; A.M. in Physics, Harvard U., 1963. Postdoctoral research assoc. Smithsonian Astrophys. Obs., Cambridge, Mass., 1965-66; postdoctoral research assoc. Lawrence Livermore Lab., Calif., 1966-67; asst. prof. physics U. Colo., Boulder, 1967-70, assoc. prof., 1970-73, prof., 1973-76, prof. physics, dir. Ctr. for Environ. Scis. Denver, 1976—. Chmn. Dept. Energy Oil Shale Task Force, 1978 83; mem. adv. com. to dir. on health scis. Los Alamos Nat. Lab.; mem. Colo. Gov.'s Sci. Adv. Com., 1974-76, chmn., 1975-76 Author: Transport and Biological Effects of Molybdenum in the Environment, 1975 Served with U.S. Army, 1956-58 NSF fellow, 1962-65; grantee Fleishman Found., 1969-71, NSF, 1971-76, EPA, 1975-79, Dept. Energy, 1976-83, U.S. Bur. Mines, 1979-81 Mem. Am. Phys. Soc., AAAS, Soc. Environ. Geochemistry and Health (exec. com. 1981-83, 86-88, sec./treas. 1988—), Phi Beta Kappa Democrat. Office: U Colo Environ Scis PO Box 173364 Denver CO 80217-3364

CHAPPIDI, PRASAD V. neurologist; b. Cuddapah, India, Aug. 14, 1957; came to U.S., 1992; s. Venkatrami Reddi and Savitri Chappidi; m. Nivedita Chappidi; children: Rohit, Nidhi. MB, BS Bchir, Kurnool Med. Coll., 1980; MD in Ophthalmology, All India Inst. Med. Scis., New Delhi, 1984. Bd. cert. in neurology. Intern Govt. Gen. Hosp., Kurnpool, 1981; resident in ophthalmology All India Inst. Med. Scis., New Delhi, 1984; pvt. practice in ophathlmology Cuddapah, 1984-92; resident, fellow Wayne State U., Detroit, 1994-98; neurologist Chgo., 1998—. Mem. AMA, Am. Acad. Neurology. Office: 5600 W Addison Set 206 Chicago IL 60634

CHAPPLE, MICHAEL JOSEPH, marketing professional, security firm executive; s. Joseph William and Grace B. Chapple; m. Renee Krystine Kolessar, June 10, 2000; children: Richard Joseph, Matthew Wiliam. BS, U. Notre Dame; MS, U. Idaho. CISSP (ISC)2, 2001, MCDBA Microsoft, 1999, MCSE Microsoft, 1999, CCNA Cisco, 1999. Chief info. officer Brand Inst., Inc., Miami, Fla., 2001—03, exec. v.p., 2003—. Author: (book) CISSP Training Guide, GSEC Prep Guide, TICSA Training Guide, Designing Windows 2000 Directory Services. Capt. USAF, 1997—2001. Mem.: Am. Mktg. Assn. Office: Brand Institute Inc 12th Fl 200 SE 1st St Miami FL 33131 Personal E-mail: mike@chapple.org. E-mail: mchapple@brandinstitute.com.

CHAPPLE, THOMAS LESLIE, lawyer; b. Canandaigua, N.Y., Nov. 28, 1947; s. Howard Leslie and Elizabeth Chapple; m. Shelly Smith, July 17, 1982; children: Adam Roger, Hannah Elizabeth. BA, Cornell U., 1970; JD, Albany Law Sch., 1973. Bar: N.Y. 1974, U.S. Supreme Ct. 1981, Va. 1992. Atty. assoc. Nixon, Hargrave, Devans & Doyle, Rochester, N.Y., 1973-76; sec., asst. gen. counsel Gannett Co., Inc., Arlington, Va., 1977-79, assoc. gen. counsel., sec. Rochester, N.Y., 1979-81, v.p., assoc. gen. counsel, sec., 1981-91, gen. counsel, sec., 1991-95, sr. v.p., gen. counsel, sec., 1995—2003, sr. v.p., chief adminstv. officer, gen. counsel, 2003—. Sec. The Gannett Found., 1983-89. Mem. ABA, Assn. Corp. Counsel, N.Y. State Bar Assn., Sigma Pi Republican. Methodist. Office: Gannett Co Inc 7950 Jones Branch Dr Mc Lean VA 22107

CHAPUT, CHARLES J. archbishop; b. Concordia, Kans., Sept. 26, 1944; Student, St. Fidelis Coll., Capuchin Coll., Cath. U., U. San Francisco. Ordained priest Roman Cath. Ch., 1970, consecrated bishop 1988. Bishop, Rapid City, SD, 1988—97; archbishop Denver, 1997—. Office: Cath Pastoral Ctr 1300 S Steele St Denver CO 80210-2526*

CHAPUT, EUGENE MICHAEL, advertising executive; b. San Francisco, July 5, 1941; s. Eugene Rene and Lucille Marie (Longuy) C.; m. Susan Mary Oliphant, Dec. 18, 1965; children: J. Michael, E. John, Thomas Patrick. BS, U. So. Calif., 1963, MBA, 1965. Sr. media planner Young & Rubicam, San Francisco, 1965-69; v.p., dir. mktg. svcs. Grey Advertising, San Francisco, 1969-78; v.p., mgmt. supr. Hoefer, Dieterich & Brown, San Francisco, 1978-79; v.p. Young & Rubicam, San Francisco, 1979-2000; pres., CEO One-Off Products Group (OOP Groop), 2000—. Patentee: inflatable portable sofa, 1996, electronic self defense weapon disguised as personal accessory, 1999; copyright holder parent-child bonding exercise program; contbr. to numerous creative advertising concepts. Coach Little League Baseball, Youth Soccer, Portola Valley, Calif., 1973-86; chmn. Portola Valley Parks and Recreation, 1978-83. Recipient numerous advt. awards, 1985—; named first honoree Top of the Dial award, No. Calif. Broadcasters Assn., 1995. Mem. San Francisco Olympic Club (physical fitness commr. 1982-87, Weight Lifting record 1998, 2000, 03). Avocations: physical fitness, skiing, tennis, motorcycling. E-mail: genechaput@earthlink.net.

CHAR, PATRICIA HELEN, lawyer; b. Honolulu, Mar. 23, 1952; d. Lincoln S. and Daisy Char; m. Thomas W. Bingham, Mar. 20, 1982; children: Matthew Thomas Bingham, James Nathan Bingham. BA, Northwestern U., 1974; JD, Georgetown U., 1977. Bar: Wash. 1977, U.S. Dist. Ct. (we. dist.) Wash. 1977, U.S. Dist. Ct. (ea. dist.) Wash. 1982, U.S. Ct. Appeals (9th cir.) 1981, U.S. Supreme Ct. 1984. Assoc. Bogle & Gates, Seattle, 1977-84; ptnr., mem. Bogle & Gates PLLC, Seattle, 1984-99; of counsel Garvey, Schubert & Barer, Seattle, 1999-2000; ptnr. Preston Gates & Ellis LLP, Seattle, 2000—. Author: Ownership By a Fiduciary, 1997. Trustee YWCA, Seattle-King County-Snohomish County; vol. King County Big Sisters, United Way of King County, Seattle, 1987-90, Guardian Ad Litem Program, Seattle, 1987-93. Fellow Am. Coll. Trust and Estate Counsel; mem. ABA, Wash. State Bar Assn. (co-author chpts. 3 and 4 Wash. Civil Procedure Deskbook 1992). Office: Preston Gates & Ellis LLP 925 4th Ave #2900 Seattle WA 98104-1158 E-mail: pchar@prestongates.com.

CHAR, VERNON FOOK LEONG, lawyer; b. Honolulu, Dec. 15, 1934; s. Charles A. and Annie (Ching) C.; m. Evelyn Lau, June 14, 1958; children: Richard, Daniel, Douglas, Charles, Elizabeth. BA, U. Hawaii, 1956; LLB, Harvard U., 1959. Bar: Hawaii 1959. Dep. atty. gen. Office of Atty. Gen., Honolulu, 1959-60, 62-65; ptnr. Damon Key Char & Bocken, Honolulu, 1965-89, Char, Sakamoto, Ishii, Lum & Ching, Honolulu, 1989—. Chmn. Hawaii Ethics Commn., Honolulu, 1968-75, Hawaii Bicentennial Com., 1986-91. Mem. ABA (bd. govs. 1991-94), Hawaii Bar Assn. (pres. 1985), U. Hawaii Alumni Assn. (pres. 1989-90). Home: 351 Anonia St Honolulu HI 96821-2052 Office: Char Sakamoto Ishii Lum & Ching Davies Pacific Ctr 841 Bishop St Ste 850 Honolulu HI 96813-3957 E-mail: vflchar@lawcslc.com.

CHARAN, NIRMAL B. pulmonologist, educator; b. Ranikhet, U.P., India, Dec. 7, 1946; arrived in U.S., 1977; s. Isaac A. Charan and Salomi Singh; m. Lalita Clive, June 20, 1973; children: Ankur, Neev; m. Paula Carvalho, Jan. 16, 1999. MBBS, Christian Med. Coll., 1968, MD, 1974. Diplomate Am. Bd. Internal Medicine, Pulmonary Medicine. Chief Pulmonary/Critical Care VA Med. Ctr., Boise, Idaho, 1980—. Prof. Medicine U. Wash., Seattle, 1988—. Contbr. . Treas. John Butler Lung Found., Boise, 1994—. Fellow: ACP, Am. Coll. Chest Physicians (gov.); mem.: Am. Thoracic Soc. (pres. Idaho chpt.). Avocations: photography, travel. Home: 722 Harcourt Rd Boise ID 83702 Office: VA Med Ctr 500 W Fort St Boise ID 83702

CHARANIA, BARKAT, real estate consultant; b. Ahmedabad, Gujrat, India, June 27, 1941; came to U.S., 1961; s. Ismail and Zenabai Charania; m. Jerilyn Lee Scott, Apr. 10, 1962 (div. May 1970); children: Sultana, Ramzan, Kalvin, Kevin, Stephen; m. Maher Kurani, Oct. 11, 1970; children: Munira, Rahim, Munira Moon. Student, Alpena (Mich.) Community Coll., 1961-62, U. Calif., L.A., 1962-63, U. Pa., 1965-68, Lincoln Tech. Sch., 1983. Cert. comml. investment mem.; cert. hotel adminstr. Pres. Eurindus, Inc., Cherry Hill, N.J., 1965-83, Airline Inn, Inc., Atlanta, 1980-83; owner B.C. Investments & Realty Co., Atlanta, 1985—; pres. Southern Inn, Inc., Chattanooga, 1987—; owner B.C. Hospitality Mgmt. Co., Atlanta, 1987—; pres. Trident Devel. Corp., Charleston, S.C., 1989—, BJM Hospitality, Inc., 1993—, ICI Long Distance Inc., 1995—, Universal Connect Corp., 1995—; CEO, CRM Ventures, LLC, 1997—, RBM Properties, LLC, 2000—; sr. assocs. Marcus & Millichap, Atlanta, 1996-97; CEO Charania Bros., LLC, 1999—, 786 Investments, LLC, 2003—, Small Axe, Inc., 2003—. Cons. Pattni Holdings, Atlanta, 1984—, Esmail Internat., Inc., Atlanta, 1986—, Harbour Enterprise, Chattanooga, 1987—, Shin Inc., Chattanooga, 1987—, ABC Inc., Chattanooga, 1988—. Ga. coord. Agakhan Found. U.S.A., Atlanta, 1988; chmn. Southeastern Enterprising People's Assn., 1990, 91. Mem. Atlanta Bd. Realtors, Nat. Assn. Realtors, Realtor Nat. Mktg. Inst., Comml. Investment Real Estate Coun., Edn. Inst., Internat. Real Estate Inst., Ismaili Commerce Club (v.p. Atlanta chpt. 1982), S.E. Region (chmn. Agakhan econ. planning bd. for U.S.A.), Internat. Real Estate Fedn. Republican. Avocations: reading, travel, swimming, tennis. Home and Office: 3000 Edmonton Green Ct Alpharetta GA 30022 Fax: 770-667-5939. E-mail: bcharania@hotmail.com. *People don't care how much you know until they know how much you care...about them. How far you go in life depends on your being tender with the young, compassionate with the aged, sympathetic with the striving, and tolerant of the weak and the strong. Because someday in life you will have all of these.*

CHARAP, STANLEY HARVEY, electrical engineering educator; b. N.Y.C., Apr. 21, 1932; s. William and Esther Charap; m. Marilyn Novick, Aug. 7, 1955; children: Joshua David, Lawrence Gordon. BS in Physics, Bklyn. Coll., 1953; PhD in Physics, Rutgers U., 1959. Mem. rsch. staff IBM T.J. Watson Rsch. Ctr., Yorktown Heights, N.Y., 1958-64; rsch. scientist Rsch. div. Am.-Standard Inc., Piscataway, N.J., 1964, supr. solid state physics, 1965-66, mgr. physics and electronics, 1966-68; assoc. prof. elec. and computer engring. Carnegie Mellon U., Pitts., 1968-71, prof., 1971-96; prof. emeritus, 1997—; assoc. head dept. Carnegie Mellon U., Pitts., 1980-85, acting head dept., 1981-82, vice chmn. faculty senate, 1972-73, chmn. faculty senate, 1986-87, assoc. dir. Data Storage Systems Ctr., 1990-96. Cons. Westinghouse Rsch. Ctr., Pitts., 1969-84; mem. tech. staff Bell Labs., Whippany, N.J., summer 1973; sr. vis. fellow U. Wales, Cardiff, spring 1976; vis. scientist Control Data Corp., Mpls., summer 1987. Editor: Physics of Magnetism, 1964; contbr. to Magnetism & Metallurgy, 1969; contbr. over 60 tech. articles to profl. jours. V.p. Sch. Advanced Jewish Studies, Pitts., 1989-91. Recipient Tech. Achievement award Nat. Storage Industry Consortium, 1998. Fellow IEEE (fellow com. 1997-99, Millennium medal 2000); mem. IEEE Magnetics Soc. (sec.-treas. 1987-88, v.p. 1989-90, pres. 1991-92, past pres. 1993-94, editor-in-chief IEEE Trans. on Magnetics 1982-86, editl. bd. IEEE Press 1989-91, IEEE Tech. activities bd., liaison coun. 1993, gen. chmn. Joint INTERMAG-MMM conf. 1994, Disting. Lectr. 1996, Achievement award 1998), Am. Inst. Physics, Conf. on Magnetism and Magnetic Materials (treas. 1981-83, gen. chmn. 1986). Office: Carnegie Mellon U Dept Elec-Computer Engring 5000 Forbes Ave Pittsburgh PA 15213-3890 E-mail: s.charap@ieee.org.

CHARBONEAU, JOSEPH WILLIAM, radiologist, medical educator; b. Dubuque, Iowa, Sept. 7, 1947; s. Wilfred James and Leone Virginia Charboneau; m. Catherine Ann Baird, Dec. 29, 1973; children: Nicholas Tanner, Benjamin Tyler, Laurie Baird. B.S., U. of Wis., Platteville, 1967—71; M.D., U. of Wis. Med. Sch., Madison, 1972—76. Diplomate Am. Bd. of Radiology, 1980. Resident in diagnostic radiology Mayo Grad. Sch. of Medicine, 1976—80; instr. in radiology Mayo Med. Sch., Rochester, Minn., 1980—81, asst. prof. of radiology, 1981—85, assoc. prof. of radiology Rochster, Minn., 1986—91, prof. of radiology Rochester, Minn., 1991—. Mem. adv. com. NAS, Washington, 1997—99; sr. assoc. cons. Mayo Clinic, Rochester, Minn., 1980—83; staff cons. Mayo Grad. Sch. of Medicine, 1983. Editor: (textbook) Diagnostic Ultrasound; assistant editor (book) Mayo Clinic Family Health Book; contbr. articles to profl. jours. Founder Stuff for Life - Youth Leadership Program, Rochester, Minn., 1985—90. Recipient Carman award for Excellence in Clincal Radiology, Radiology Dept., 2001, Profl. Accomplishment award, U. of Wis. - Platteville, 2000, John S. Dunn award, Sr. Lectureship, U. of Tex. MD Anderson Cancer Ctr., 2002. Fellow: Soc. of Radiologists in Ultrasound; mem.: AMA, Soc. of GI Radiologists, Am. Roentgen Ray Soc., Radiol. Soc. of North Am., Am. Coll. of Radiology. Office: Mayo Clinic 200 First St SW Rochester MN 55905-0002

CHARCHAFLIEH, JEAN, physician, educator; b. Aleppo, Syria, June 22, 1959; MD, Aleppo Med. Sch., 1983. Diplomate Am. Bd. Anesthesiology, Am. Bd. Critical Care Medicine. Intern Stritch Sch. Medicine Loyola U., Maywood, Ill., 1988-89, resident in anesthesiology Stritch Sch. Medicine, 1989-92, attending physician in anesthesiology Med. Ctr., 1992-93; rsch. fellow in anesthesiology Mass. Gen. Hosp., Boston, 1985-88; fellow in critical care medicine Meml. Sloan Kettering Cancer Ctr., N.Y.C., 1993-94; fellow in neuroanesthesiology SUNY Health Sci. Ctr., 1994-95; attending physician in anesthesiology Kings County Hosp., Bklyn., 1995—, L.I. Coll. Hosp., 1995—, U. Hosp. Bklyn., 1995—; asst. prof. anesthesiology SUNY Health Sci. Ctr., Bklyn., 1995—. Mem. AMA, AAAS, N.Y. Acad. Scis., Am. Soc. Anesthesiology, Soc. Neurosurgical Anesthesia and Critical Care, Am. Soc. Critical Care Anesthesiologists, Soc. Critical Care Medicine. Office: SUNY Health Sci Ctr Anes Box 6 450 Clarkson Ave Brooklyn NY 11203-2056

CHAREN, SOLOMON, psychologist; b. Cleve. m. Thelma June Golden. BA, Western Res. U.; MA, U. Pitts.; PhD, Cath. U. Am. Pvt. practice psychology, Kensington, Md., 1950-77; dir. child guidance clinic Jewish Social Svc., Rockville, Md., 1967-77 (ret. 1977); chief psychologist Jewish Social Svc. Agy., Rockville, 1955-77. Contbr. numerous articles to profl. jours. With U.S. Army, 1943-46. Mem. APA, Ea. Psychol. Assn., Md. Psychol. Assn., D.C. Psychol. Assn. Avocation: golf. Home: 8736 Preston Pl Chevy Chase MD 20815-5739

CHARENDOFF, MARK STUART, educator; b. Toronto, Aug. 21, 1963; s. Nathan and Lillian (Zaid) C.; m. Susan Frances Cohen, Sept. 7, 1992. B Hebrew Letters, Darche Noam Coll., Jerusalem, 1985. Ordained rabbi, 1986. Asst. regional dir. B'nai B'rith Youth Orgn., Toronto, 1986—88, cons., 1994—95; dir. Judaic Cultural Devel. Jewish Cmty. Ctr. Toronto, 1988—94; program cons. Charles R. Bronfman Found., Montreal, Canada, 1992—95; dir. Jewish Ednl. Svcs. Jewish Cmty. Ctrs. Assn. N.Am., N.Y.C., 1994—98; v.p. Andrea and Charles Bronfman Philanthropies, N.Y.C., 1998—2002; pres. Jewish Funders Network, N.Y.C., 2002—. Mem. adv. bd. Washington Inst. for Jewish Leadership and Values, 1996—, Nat. Ctr. for Hebrew Lang., 1997—; chmn. Forum Jewish Educators, N.Y.C., 1990-93. Editor: Jewish Education and the Jewish Community Center, 1974. Bd. dirs. Coalition for Advancement Jewish Education, 1997—, Edah, 1999—. Jewish. Avocations: sailing, biking, travel. Office: Jewish Funders Network 300 7th Ave 18th Fl New York NY 10001

CHARETTE, CECILE M. music educator; b. Lowell, Mass., Oct. 15, 1920; d. Arthur Joseph and Eva Marie (Croteau) C. MusB, U. Montreal, 1956, MusM, 1962; postgrad., Boston U., 1965-67. Joined Order of Holy Cross, 1939. Prof. music Basile Moreau Coll., St. Laurent, Canada, 1946—62, Notre Dame Coll., Manchester, NH, 1962—2002; pvt. music instr. Goffstown, NH. Choir dir., dir. operas, 1974-78. Mem. Nat. Assn. Tchrs. Singing (N.H. gov. 1978-84), Metro. Opera Guild, Nat. Music Tchrs. Roman Catholic. E-mail: cecilecha@aol.com.

CHARETTE, SHARON JULIETTE, library administrator; b. Woonsocket, RI, Apr. 24, 1956; d. Roland Alfred Lionel and Juliette Cecile (Lavoie) C. BA in French and English, R.I. Coll., 1978; MLS, U. R.I., 1981; cert. in computer info. systems, Bryant Coll., 1989; student, RISD, 1989-91. Asst. serials Wheaton Coll., Norton, Mass., 1978—79, catalog asst., 1979—82, libr. acquisitions, 1982—86; dir. libr. New Eng. Inst. Tech., Warwick, RI, 1986—. Seamstress, designer, craftsman, 1976—. Chair Franco Am. com. R.I. Heritage Commn., Providence, 1987-90, treas., 1982-87; costume designer Kaleidoscope Theatre, 2003—. Mem. ALA, New England Libr. Assn., R.I. Libr. Assn., No. R.I. Coun. of Arts, Theatre Works (costume designer 2001—, web mgr. 2002—), Mensa, TechACCESS of R.I. (bd. dirs., corr. sec. 1992-98, 2003—, chair 1998-2003, web mgr. 2002—). Avocations: jewelry design, historical costume reproduction, computers, music, theatre. Home: 147 Greenville Rd North Smithfield RI 02896-7422 Office: New Eng Inst Tech 2500 Post Rd Warwick RI 02886-2244 E-mail: scharette3@cox.net.

CHAREWICZ, DAVID MICHAEL, photographer; b. Chgo., Feb. 17, 1932; s. Michael and Stella (Pietrzak) C.; student DePaul U., 1957, Northwestern U., 1952; MA in Photography, Profl. Photographers Am. Inc., 1986; m. Catherine Uccello, Nov. 8, 1952; children: Michael, Karen, Daniel. Trainee, Merill Chase, Chgo., 1950-51; dark room technician Maurice Seymour, Chgo., 1951-52; photographer Oscar & Assos., Chgo., 1955-63; owner Dave Chare Photography, Park Ridge, Ill., 1963—; pres., owner C&C Duplicating, Inc., 1978-93. Pres. Oakton Parent Tchr. Club, 1968-69, del. dist. 64 caucus, 1970, 73; mem. centennial photo com., Park Ridge, Ill., 1973; mem. sponsoring com. Park Ridge Men's Prayer Breakfast 1982—. Served with AUS, 1952-54. Mem. Am. Soc. Photographers, Profl. Photographers Assn., Midstate Indsl. Photographers Assn. (treas. 1981, pres. 1984-85). Home: 739 N Northwest Hwy Park Ridge IL 60068-2541 Office: 739 N Northwest Hwy Park Ridge IL 60068-2541

CHARFOOS, LAWRENCE SELIG, lawyer; b. Detroit, Dec. 7, 1935; s. Samuel and Charlotte (Salkin) C.; m. Jane Emerson. Student, U. Mich., 1953-56; LLB, Wayne State U., 1959. Bar: Mich. 1959, Ill. 1965. Pvt. practice, Detroit, 1960-63; pres., ptnr. Charfoos & Christensen PC, Detroit, 1967—; theatrical producer, legitimate theater mgr. Chgo., 1963-67. Cons. med.-legal problems Mich. Med. Soc., Mich. Hosp. Coun., ATLA; US cts. com. State Bar Mich.; lead counsel N.W. Airlines, 1999. Author: The Medical Malpractice Case: A Complete Handbook, 1974, Daughters at Risk, 1981, Personal Injury Practice, Technique and Technology, 1986; contbr. articles to profl. jours. Trustee Lawrence S. Charfoos Found. Elected to Inner Circle of Advocates, 1973 Mem. ABA, Mich. Bar Assn., Detroit Bar Assn. (past dir.), Am. Bd. Profl. Liability Attys. (founder, past pres.), Internat. Acad. Trial Lawyers, Plaintiff's Steering Com./Breast Implant Cases. Office: 5510 Woodward Ave Detroit MI 48202-3804

CHARI, KRISHNAN, research scientist; b. Madras, India, Aug. 15, 1958; s. Ranga Sadagopa and Saroja (Parthasarathy) C.; m. Laxmi Chakravarty, Nov. 5, 1988; children: Sindhuja, Priyakrit. B Tech., U. Madras, 1980; MS, Columbia U., 1982; PhD, Rensselaer Poly. Inst., 1985. Rsch. scientist Kodak Rsch. Labs., Rochester, N.Y., 1985-89, sr. rsch. scientist, 1989-94, rsch. assoc., 1994—. Lectr. in field. Contbr. articles to profl. publs.; patentee in field. Mem. Am. Chem. Soc. Home: 39 Canterbury Trl Fairport NY 14450-8783 E-mail: krishnan.chari@kodak.com.

CHARIS, BARBARA, nutritionist, consultant, health researcher; b. Pitts., Feb. 26, 1934; d. Robert Edward and Clara L. Wakefield; m. Roger S. Markle, May 19, 1956 (div. July 1980); children: Mitchell, Tarri, Heidi, David. Student, Pa. State U., 1951-53, U. Pitts., 1954, Harbor Coll., Wilmington, Calif., 1966; M. in Holistic Health Sci., Columbia Pacific U., San Rafael, Calif., 1982. Dir., cons. Charis Holistic Ctr., North Hollywood, Calif., 1982—. Host (radio show) The Health Beat, L.A., 1988-89; producer (TV show) Sharing from the Heart, L.A., 1996-97; author: Sharing from the Heart, 1995. Mem. Nat. Health Fedn., Vegetarian Soc. (v.p. 1982-83), Book Publicists So. Calif. Avocations: poetry, songwriting, lecturing, spiritual counseling, running (L.A. Marathon 1994, 99). Home and Office: Charis Holistic Ctr 6227 Morse Ave North Hollywood CA 91606-2948

CHARKA, SATYA NARAYANA, language educator, dance director; b. Hyderabad, A.P., India, Aug. 1, 1941; s. Daniah and Sandamma Charka; m. Varalaxmis Charka, Nov. 15, 1987 (div. Feb. 10, 2000). Diploma in Kathak dance, Govt. Coll. Music and Dance, Hyderabad, 1957—62; BA, Vivek Vardhni Coll., Hyderabad, 1965; diploma in choreography, Natya Inst., New Delhi, India, 1965—69. Dance dir. Children's Little Theater, New Delhi, 1966—68; artist, mem. staff S & D Divsn. Indian Ministry, New Delhi, 1969—70, NIR-Natya Inst., New Delhi, 1970—72; leader-cultural del. S.N Acad., New Delhi, Japan, 1972—73; dir. dance ICCR Indian Externa Ministry, Fiji Islands, 1976—79; tchr. dance dept. edn. B-I-D-I New South Wales, Sydney, 1980—81. Guest artist Sheli Nat. Folkloric Festivals, Sydney, 1976—80; artist, dir. Indian Dance Dance Ctr. Bodenwieser, Sydney, Australia, 1980—81; dir., prodr. East-West Sch. Dance, Monroe, NY, 1981—; founder, dir. Internat. Indian Dance Ctr., Queens, NY, 2002—; dancer presentations, competitions, India, Sydney; dir. cultural promotion. Named Best Classical Dance, India, 1961, Cultural Amb., Japan, 1974; recipient Merit award, India, 1965, cert. presentation, Sydney, 1977. Mem.: Arya Samaj N.Y., Yoga Soc. N.Y. Home: East-West Sch Dance 13 Sapphire Rd Monroe NY 10950 Fax: 845-774-7368. E-mail: charkaon@hotmail.com.

CHARLA, LEONARD FRANCIS, lawyer; b. New Rochelle, NY, May 4, 1940; s. Leonard A. and Mary L. Charla; m. Kathleen Gerace, Feb. 3, 1968 (div. Dec. 1988); children: Larisa, Christopher; m. Elizabeth A. Du Mouchelle, Aug. 27, 1993. BA, Iona Coll., 1962; JD, Cath. U., 1965; LLM, George Washington U., 1971. Bar: D.C. 1967, N.J. 1970, Mich. 1971. Tech. writer IRS, Washington, 1966-67; atty. adv. ICC, 1967, atty., 1968-69; mgmt. intern HEW, 1967-68; atty. Bowes & Millner, Transp. Cons., Newark, 1969-71; atty. legal staff GM, Detroit, 1971-85, sr. counsel, 1985-87, asst. gen. counsel, 1987-89; sr. v.p. Clean Sites Inc., Alexandria, Va., 1989-90; shareholder Butzel Long, Detroit, 1990—. Mem. faculty Coll. Creative Studies, Detroit, 1978-89, adj. asst. prof., 1982-89; faculty art U. Mich., 1980, 84-89, adj. asst. prof. 1988-89. Author: Never Cooked Before/Gotta Cook Now!, 1999. Bd. dirs. Gt. Lakes Performing Artists Assocs., 1983-85; bd. dirs. Mich. Assn. Cmty. Arts Agys., 1983-89, 92-93, vice-chair, 1986-88, chair, 1988-89; bd. govs. Cath. U. Am. Alumni, 1982-2002, v.p., 1993-99; active Info. Network Superfund Settlements, 1988—; bd. regents Cath. U. Am., 1992-2002, Birmingham Bloomfield Art Assn., 1987-88, 94-95; bd. dirs. Friends Modern Art, Detroit Inst. Arts, 1996—, v.p., 1998—; bd. dirs. Art Ctr. Mt. Clemens, Mich., 1997 , chair facilities com., 2001-, v.p. 2001-. Fellow N.Y. State Regents, 1962; scholar Cath. U. Law Sch., 1962-65. Mem. ABA, Nat. Spkrs. Assn., Mich. State Bar Assn. (arts com. entertainment and sports sect. 1979-87, chmn., 1980-81, 92—). Office: Butzel Long 100 Bloomfield Pkwy Ste 200 Bloomfield Hills MI 48304 E-mail: charla@butzel.com.

CHARLES, ALLAN G. physician, educator; b. N.Y.C., Nov. 15, 1928; s. Harry G. and Alice (Grotzky) C.; m. Phyllis V. J. Vail, June 28, 1957; children: Della Marie, Aaron Joseph, David Jonathan. AB cum laude, NYU, 1948, MD, 1952. Diplomate: Am. Bd. Obstetrics and Gynecology. Intern Phila. Gen. Hosp., 1952-53; resident in obstetrics and gynecology Mt. Sinai Hosp., N.Y.C., 1955-57, Michael Reese Hosp., Chgo., 1957-60, clin. asst., 1960-61, assoc. attending physician, 1961-69, attending physician, 1969—; co-dir. Michael Reese Hosp. (Rh-Investigative Clinic), 1963—, vice-chmn. dept. obstetrics and gynecology, 1971, pres. staff, 1978, bd. dirs., 1981-84; chief obstetrics and gynecology Michael Reese Hosp., 1990-99; chmn. rsch. and edn. found. Michael Reese Hosp. Med. Staff, 1996-2000; pvt. practice specializing in office gynecology Chgo., 1960—. Courtesy staff Chgo. Lying-In-Hosp.; clin. asst. prof. ob-gyn. U. Ill. Coll. Medicine, Chgo., 1960-64, Chgo. Med. Sch., 1964-72; clin. prof. Pritzker Sch. Medicine, U. Chgo., 1972-84; attending physician Northwestern Meml. Hosp., 1984-90; prof. clin. ob-gyn. Northwestern U., 1983; clin. prof. ob-gyn. U. Ill. Coll. Medicine, 1991. Author: Rh Iso Immunization and Erythroblastosis Fetalis, 1969; Contbr. articles to profl. jours. Fellow Am. Coll. Obstetricians and Gynecologists, Internat. Coll. Surgeons (chmn. Am. sect. obs. and gynec. 1979-83, sec., asst. treas. Am. sect.), Central Assn. Obstetricians and Gynecologists; mem. AMA, Ill., Chgo. med. socs., Chgo. Gynecol. Soc. (v.p. 1980—, sec. 1988-90, pres.-elect, 1992, pres. 1993-94). Achievements include developing substitute for uterine tube, Rh-sensitization. Home: 1150 N Lake Shore Dr Apt 22GH Chicago IL 60611 Office: 55 E Washington St Fl 37 Chicago IL 60602-2103 E-mail: agcobg@aol.com.

CHARLES, BERTRAM, radio broadcasting executive; b. Boston, Jan. 26, 1918; s. Jacob H. and Annie L. (Kanter) Fein; m. Alberta Marie Carpenter, Sept. 4, 1948; children— Meredith Ann Trapp, Blair Carpenter Adams. Student, NYU, 1935-38. Reporter Bklyn. Daily Eagle, 1938-39, N.Y. Post, 1939-40; news and sports announcer Sta. WAOV, Vincennes, Ind., 1945; sportscaster Sta. WIRE, Indpls., 1945; dir. sports and pub. service Sta. WAKR, Akron, Ohio, 1946-48; program and sports dir. Sta. WVKO-AM-FM, Columbus, Ohio, 1948-49, sta. mgr., 1949-53, v.p., 1953-71, pres., gen. mgr., 1971-82, ret. Trustee Columbus Zoo, Opera/Columbus, Upper Arlington Rotary Club; patron Columbus Art Gallery; past pres., chmn. bd. Charity Newsies; chmn. artistic com. Columbus Opera. Served with U.S. Army, 1941-42, USAF, 1942-45; vice chmn. Upper Arlington Cultural Arts Commn. Named Columbus Father of Year, 1961; Paul Harris fellow Rotary Internat. Mem. Columbus Better Bus. Bur. (past dir.), Ohio Radio and TV Execs. (pres. 1957), Columbus Radio Broadcasters, Ohio Assn. Broadcasters (past dir.), Soc. Profl. Journalists (dir.), Ohio Sportscasters Assn. (past dir.), Nat. Football Found. Hall of Fame, Columbus Advt. Fedn. Clubs: York Temple Country, Maennerchor, Rotary (bd. dirs.), Agonis, Probus (pres.), Torch (pres.), Capital. Home: 2548 W Lane Ave Columbus OH 43221-3657 E-mail: Treb12618@webtv.net. *Although I've prayed to God as if everything depended upon Him, I've worked all my life as if everything depended upon me.*

CHARLES, BLANCHE, retired elementary education educator; b. Spartanburg, S.C., Aug. 7, 1912; d. Franklin Grady and Alice Floride (Hatchette) C. BA, Humboldt State U., 1934. Tchr. Mt. Signal and El Centro schs., 1934—48, Calexico (Calif.) Unified Sch. Dist., 1958-94; libr. Calexico Pub. Lib., 1948—59; ret., 1994. Elem. sch. named in her honor, 1987. Mem. NEA, ACT, Calif. Tchrs. Assn., DAR, Nat. Soc. Daus. of Confederacy, Delta Kappa Gamma. Avocations: gardening, reading. Home: 37133 Hwy 94 Space 3 Boulevard CA 91905-9524

CHARLES, CHERYL, non-profit and business executive; b. Seattle, Nov. 4, 1947; d. Tom E. Charles and Irene D. (Brown) Shelver; m. Robert E. Samples, Sept. 15, 1973; 1 child, Stician M. BA, U. Ariz., 1969; MA, Ariz. State U., 1971; PhD, U. Wash., 1982. Lic. secondary edn. Tchr. Phoenix Union H.S., 1969-71; staff assoc. Social Sci. Edn. Consortium, Boulder, Colo., 1971-72; social studies dept. chmn. Trevor Browne H.S., Phoenix, 1972-73; asst. dir. Essentia: Environ. Studies for Urban Youth, Olympia, Wash., 1973-75; nat. dir. Project Learning Tree, Tiburon, Calif. & Boulder, Colo., 1976-84; exec. dir. Project Wild, Boulder, 1981-93; pres. Sol y Sombra Found., Santa Fe, 1991-2000; exec. dir. Ctr. for Study of Cmty., Santa Fe, 1993-2000; COO The Santa Fe Group, 1996—2001; owner Hawksong Assocs. Prin. investigator MacArthur Found., Chgo., 1993-94, Bradley Found., Milw., 1995-99, Ednl. Found. Am., Westport, Conn., 1995-2000; project dir. McCune Found., Santa Fe, N.Mex., 1995-97; sr. dir. BITS, The Fin. Svcs. Roundtable, 1997—. Co-author: The Whole School Book, 1977; editor: Project Wild Elementary and Secondary Guide, 1983-92, Project Wild Aquatic Guide, 1987-92; co-editor, designer Windstar Jour., 1987-90. Mem. nat. adv. com. U. Mich. Coll. Engring., East Lansing, Mich., 1990-93, nat. judge Duke Youth Challenge, 1994; bd advisors Aspen (Colo.) Global Change Inst., 1990—; bd. trustees Hispanic Culture Found., Albuquerque, 1995-98; pres. bd. trustees Windstar Land Conservancy, 1996-2000; chair bd. trustees Windstar Found., 1995-2001. Recipient Leadership award U.S. Forest Svc., internat. region, 1985, L.B. Sharp award excellence in outdoor/environ. edn., 1993, Gold medal Pres. Environ. and Conservation Challenge award, Washington, 1991; named Profl. of Yr. Western Assn. Fish/Wildlife Agys., 1991. Mem. N.Am. Assn. Environ. Edn., Nat. Coun. Social Studies, N.Mex. First Town Hall, No. N.Mex. Grant Makers. Avocations: writing, horseback riding, dancing, cooking, reading. Office: 3 N Chamisa Dr Ste 2 Santa Fe NM 87508-9463

CHARLES, CORY ANNE, television guest booking director; b. Bklyn., Oct. 3, 1965; d. John Thomas and Anne Jane Azumbrado; m. Nick Charles, Oct. 4, 1997; 1 stepchild, Katie. BA in Comms., L.I. U., 1987; MA in Polit. Sci., U. Calif., Santa Barbara, 1988. Asst. dir. rsch. McLaughlin Group, Washington, 1989-90; rschr., editl. prodr. CNN, Atlanta, 1990-98; dir. internat. guest booking CNNI, Atlanta, 1998—; copy person N.Y. Daily News, 1986. Bd. dirs. Mt. Paran-Northside Neighborhood Assn., Atlanta, 2000-02. Fellow German Marshall Fund, 2001. Mem. Coun. on Fgn. Rels. Avocations: travel, reading, cooking, photography, animals, architecture. Office: CNN 1 CNN Center Atlanta GA 30303 E-mail: Cory.Charles@turner.com.

CHARLES, GEORGE P. religious studies educator; b. Pengugtali, Nelson Island, Alaska, Feb. 13, 1941; s. Nicholas Ayaginar and Elena Charles; m. Nancy Jean Furlow, Aug. 6, 1999. AA in Electronics Tech., U. Alaska, 1971; BA, Alaska Pacific U., 1991; MA, PhD, U. Calif., Santa Barbara, 2000. Asst. prof. dept. Alaska native and rural devel. Coll. Rural Alaska, Anchorage, 2002—; asst. prof. Alaska native studies U. Alaska, Fairbanks, 1999—2002. Carving yupiaq transformation masks & yupiaq graphic art; actor: (films) Legend of Spirit Dog; voice actor : On Deadly Ground; 13th Warrior. With U.S. Navy, 1965—69, Vietnam. Recipient Dennis Demmert Appreciatioin and Recognition award, Native Am. Bus. Leaders and Rural Student Svcs., 2002; fellow Grad. Opportunities fellow, U. Calif. Santa Barbara, 1994—98, Rowney fellow, 1995—96, Dissertation fellow, Ctr. Advanced Study, Oslo, Norway, 1998—99, Allaway fellow, U. Calif. Santa Barbara, 1998—99, Affirmative Action Dissertation fellow, 1998—99, Michaelson fellow, 1998—99. Mem.: SAG (assoc.). Achievements include research in Yupiaq Narrative from Family Stories. Avocation: yupiaq graphic art and carving. Office: Danrd/Cra 2221 E No Lights Blvd # 213 Anchorage AK 99508 Office Fax: 907-279-2716. E-mail: ffgpc@uaf.edu.

CHARLES, GERARD, performing company executive, choreographer; b. Folkstone, Eng. m. Catherine Yoshimura; 1 child, Max. Student, Royal Ballet Sch. Ballet master BalletMet, Les Grands Ballets Canadiens; profl. dancer Milw. Ballet, Ballet Internat., London; assoc. artistic dir. BalletMet Columbus, artistic dir., 2001—. Choreographer, tchr., restager of works internationally in field. Choreographer The Sleeping Beauty, Coppelia; artistic dir. : Cinderella. Choreographic fellow, Nat. Endowment for Arts. Office: BalletMet Columbus 322 Mount Vernon Ave Columbus OH 43215 Office Fax: 614-229-4858.

CHARLES, ISABEL, university administrator; b. Bklyn., Mar. 10, 1926; d. James Patrick and Isabel (Roney) C. BA, Manhattan Coll., 1954; MA, U. Notre Dame, 1960, PhD, 1965; postgrad., U. Mich., 1968-69. Chmn. dept. English Bishop Watterson High Sch., Columbus, Ohio, 1954-59, St. Mary of the Springs Acad., Columbus, 1959-62; asst. prof. English Ohio Dominican Coll., Columbus, 1965-68, acad. dean, exec. v.p., 1969-73; asst. dean Coll. Arts and Letters, U. Notre Dame, 1973-75, acting dean, 1975, dean, 1976-82, asst. provost, 1982-87, assoc. provost, 1987-95; assoc. provost emerita U. Notre Dame, 1995—. Contbr. articles to profl. jours. Mem. MLA, Assn. Am. Colls. Home: 1802 Stonehedge Ln South Bend IN 46614-6341

CHARLES, JOEL, forensic audio and video tape analyst, voice identification consultant; b. Phila., Jan. 12, 1914; s. Samuel William and Minnie (Fink) Blumenstein; m. Lillian DuBowe, May 31, 1938 (div. 1964); children: Mark Blumenstein, Richard Blumenstein; m. Nancy Sher, Oct. 24, 1988. BSChemE, Drexel U., 1938. Pres. The Charles Agy., Phila., 1938-42, 45-64; physicist Naval Air Exptl. Station, Phila., 1942-45; pres. The Dento-Med. Tapes, Upper Darby, Pa., 1957-73, Associated TV Prodns., Inc., Phila., 1948-52, Computerized Electronic Edn., Upper Darby, Pa., 1969-73; dir. continuing edn., media instructional methodology Pa. Coll. of Podiatric Medicine, Phila., 1973-77; pvt. practice Plantation, Fla., 1977-96, Coral Springs, Fla., 1996—2001, Boynton Beach, Fla., 2001—. Expert witness on tape recordings; lectr. Tex. Criminal Def. Lawyers Inst., La. Pub. Def. Criminal Lit. Seminar, Broward Criminal Def. Lawyers Assn., Dade Criminal Def. Lawyers Assn., Phoenix Pub. Defenders, Dade Fed. Pub. Defenders, Fla. Investigators Assn. Contbr. articles to profl. jours. Mem. NACDL (assoc.), Nat. Forensic Ctr., Internat. Assn. for Forensic Phonetics, Am. Fedn. Musicians, Am. Dialect Soc., Audio Engring. Soc. (chmn. forensic tape com.). Achievements include development of early rapid form of computerized voice identification, designed first high-speed portable audio cassette duplicator. Home and Office: 1505 Siena Ln Boynton Beach FL 33436 E-mail: jayceco@aol.com.

CHARLES, JOSEPH, JR., state legislator; b. Jersey City, Jan. 6, 1944; BA, Rutgers U., 1965, JD, 1969. Law clk. N.J. Supreme Ct., 1969-70; dep. atty. gen. State of N.J., 1970-71; mem. N.J. Gen. Assembly, Dist. 31, 1981—; atty. Ashley & Charles, Newark. Asst. majority leader N.J. Gen. Assembly, 1990-91, assoc. minority leader, 1992-93, chmn. assembly black caucus. Democrat. Address: PO Box E Jersey City NJ 07304-0905 Office: Dem Assembly Office State House Annex Trenton NJ 08625*

CHARLES, LYN ELLEN, marketing executive, commercial artist, photograph; b. Little Falls, N.Y., Sept. 1, 1951; d. Searle and Barbara Charles. BA, U. Conn., 1973; grad., Art Instrn. Schs. Inc., 1976. Rsch. asst. Conn. State U., New Britain, 1974; comml. artist Conn. C.C., Hartford, 1978; market rschr. Karen Assocs., Simsbury, Conn., 1981; market rsch. operator Consumer Surveys Telemarketing, Inc., Dedham, Mass., 1981-87; receptionist, file clk. Jobpro Temp. Svcs., 1987-88; field rep. Actnow, Westhampton Beach, N.Y., 1987-88; with Inventory Control Co., South Hackensack, N.J., 1988-98, Fred Meyer Vanguard Mktg. Svcs., Portland, Oreg., 1997, Regional Inventory Specialists, 1997. Artist, vol. Farmington Valley Arts, Avon, Conn., 1982-84; freelance artist West Hartford Art League, 1978-81, Northwestern Conn. Art Assn., 1979-81, Wadsworth Atheneum, 1980-82. Vol. med. receptionist Hosp. and Clin. Info. Desk, U. Conn. Health Ctr., 1975, 76-78, Office Cultural Affairs, Pub. Survey to Select Artist for Art Work at Coliseum, Hartford Civic Ctr., 1979; mem. Childreach Sponsorship of PLAN Internat. USA, 1992—, Corvallis Arts Ctr., 1995—; vol. Cmty. Outreach, Inc., 1999. Recipient Alice Collins Dunham prize, 69th Ann. Exhbn. of Conn. Acad. Fine Arts, 1980; named Duchess of Bedfordshire, Eng., Cromwell Estate and Covent Garden, 1990. Mem. Christian Ch. Avocations: hiking, swimming, ballet, bicycling, horseback riding. E-mail: bycsfc@aol.com.

CHARLES, MICHAEL HARRISON, architectural interior designer; b. Feb. 8, 1952; s. Melvin Mowrer and Sylvia Ann (Cookus) C. BA, U. Fla., 1976; AS, Fla. Jr. Coll., 1982. Lic. interior designer, Fla. Ptnr., v.p. St. Johns Lighting Design, St. Augustine, Fla., 1978-81; archtl. interior designer KBJ Architects, Inc., Jacksonville, Fla., 1982-86; owner Michael H. Charles Assocs.-Comml./Resdl. Interior Design, N.Y., Fla., 1988—; dir. interior design DeWolff Ptnrship. Architects, Rochester, N.Y., 1986-88. Cons. in field, St. Augustine, Fla., 1984—. Featured in: Interior Designers of the U.S.A., 1991. Mem.: ASID (bd. dirs. upstate N.Y., Can. East chpt. 1996—99), Soc. of the Cin., English Speaking Union, Coun. Qualification Resdl. Interior Designers (nat. bd. dirs.), Internat. Interior Deisgn Assn., Interior Design Soc. (nat. bd. dirs. 1995), Order of St. Maurice and St. Lazarus, Pa. Soc. Sons of Revolution, St. George's Soc. N.Y. (bd. dirs.), Nat. Soc. Sons of Am. Colonists (v.p. gen. 2001, gov. Fla. chpt.), Pilgrims of the U.S., Soc. Sons St. George Phila., Order Stars and Bars (N.Y. comdr.), Nat. Soc. Descendants of Colonial Govs., Nat. Soc. CAR (chpt. organizing pres. 1963, sr. Fla. officer 1985—86), St. David's Soc. N.Y., St. Andrew's Soc. N.Y., St. Nicholas Soc., Huguenot Soc. Am. (life; coun. mem.), Order Ams. Armorial Ancestery (life), Flagon and Trencher (life), Descs. of Early Quakers (life), Soc. Colonial Wars (coun. mem.), Colonial Soc. of the Acorn, SAR (v.p. Fla. chpt. 1982—86, N.Y. chpt. bd.), Colonial Soc. Pa., Gen. Soc. War 1812 (Fla. State pres. 1993—98), Nat. Soc. Sons and Daus. of Pilgrims, Descendants of Colonial Clergy, Am. Priory Venerable Order St. John Jerusalem, Lansdowne Club (London), Knights Templar, The Ch. Club N.Y., Ponte Vedra (Fla.) Club, Sovereign Mil. Order of Temple of Jerusalem (grand officier), Masons (32 degree). Republican. Episcopalian. Avocations: boating, genealogy. also: 18 Carrera St Saint Augustine FL 32084-3622 Office: 420E 58th St Apt 5B New York NY 10022-2346 E-mail: design@mhcharles.com.

CHARLES, RAY (RAY CHARLES ROBINSON), musician, singer, composer; b. Albany, Ga., Sept. 23, 1930; s. Bailey and Areatha Robinson; 9 children. Student music at sch. for blind, St. Augustine, Fla. TV appearances Ray Charles' 50 Years in Music, Uh-Huh!, 1991; TV advertising, 1992—. Musician: played with bands in south, organized trio, played on TV in Seattle, formed own band, 1954; musician: (rec. artist) Atlantic Records, 1952—59, ABC-Paramount, 1959—65, Tangerine Records, 1965—73, Crossover Records Co., 1973—; musician: numerous TV, concert appearances, (albums) Message from the People, Volcanic Action of My Soul, Renaissance, Porgy and Bess, Brother Ray is At It Again, Rockin' With Ray, Friendship, Do I Ever Cross Your Mind, The Genius After Hours, From the Pages of My Mind, 1986, Just Between Us, 1988, Greatest Country and Western Hits, 1988, Genius + Soul = Jazz, 1991, (with Willie Nelson) Seven Spanish Angels and Other Hits, Goin' Down Slow, The Real Ray Charles, 1986, Wish You Were Here Tonight, Would You Believe, 1990, (with Milt Jackson) Soul Brothers Soul Meeting, 1989, Birth of a Legend, 1992, The Session Vol. 2, 1992, My World, 1993, Blues and Jazz, 1994, Strong Love Affair, 1996, and others; performer: sang in We Are the World, 1985; appear in films : Blues for Lovers, 1966; Blues Brothers, 1980; Limit Up, 1989; Spy Hard, 1996. Established (Ray Charles) Robinson Foundation. Named number 1 male singer, 16th Internat. Jazz Critics Poll, 1968, into the Rock and Roll Hall of Fame, 1986, 1986; named to Playboy Jazz and Pop Hall of Fame, Songwriters Hall of Fame; recipient New Star award down beat Critics poll, 1958, 1961—64, Image award, NAACP, 12 Grammy awards, Grammy Lifetime Achievement award, 1987, best soul/R & B artist, Down Beat critics poll, 1984, hon. life chmn. Rhythm and Blues Hall of Fame, gold records include Ray Charles' Greatest Hits, 1962, Modern Sounds in Country and Western Music, Vol. 1 1962, Vol. 2, 1963, Ray Charles: A Man and His Soul, 1967, Leadership awd., NAFEO, 1991, Lifetime Achievement award, Ebony Mag., 1993. Address: care Ray Charles Entertainment 2107 W Washington Blvd Los Angeles CA 90018-1536*

CHARLES, ROBERT BRUCE, lawyer; b. Portsmouth, Va., Aug. 23, 1960; s. Roland Wilbur Charles Jr. and Doris Anne (Hassell) Babineau; m. Marina Timasheff, Oct. 16, 1988; children: Nicholas Westcote, Sophia Anne. AB, Dartmouth Coll., 1982; MA, Oxford U., 1984; JD, Columbia U., 1987. Bar: N.Y. 1989, Conn. 1989, Maine 1990. Law clk. to judge U.S. Ct. Appeals (9th cir.), Seattle, 1987-88; assoc. Kramer, Levin et al, N.Y.C., 1988-91, Weil, Gotshal & Manges, N.Y.C., 1991-92, Washington, 1993-95; dep. assoc. dir. office of policy devel The White House, Washington, 1992-93; chief staff, chief counsel nat. security, internat. affairs and criminal justice subcommittee U.S. Ho. of Reps., Washington, 1995-99; chief staffer Speaker's Task Force on Drug Free Am., 1997-99; prof. govt. and cyberlaw Harvard U. Extension Sch., 1998—2001; pres. The Charles Group, 1999—. Summer assoc. The White House, Washington, 1982-84, Supreme Ct. India, 1985. Contbr. articles to profl. jours., chpts. to books. Active Coun. on Fgn. Rels. Theodore Roosevelt Assn. Officer USNR, 1998—. Keasbey scholar, Phila. 1982, Tony Patino fellow Columbia U., 1984; recipient Petra T. Shattuck Disting. Tchg. award Harvard U., 2000. Republican. Avocations: distance running, hiking, writing. E-mail: RCharlesZZ@aol.com.

CHARLES, WALTER, actor; b. East Stroudsburg, Pa., Apr. 4, 1945; s. Theodore Edmund and Catherine Alexandra (Carstensen) Jacobsen. MusB, Boston U., 1968. Appeared in Broadway shows La Cage Aux Folles, Aspects of Love, Me & My Girl, Cats, Sweeney Todd, Grease, Knickerbocker Holiday, Call Me Madam, A Christmas Carol, Sunset Boulevard (Can. co.), Kiss Me Kate, Boys from Syracuse, Big River, others; off Broadway, Wit, The Immigrant; films: A Fine Mess, Weeds, Fletch Lives, Prancer, TV programs Cagney & Lacey, Kate & Allie, Law & Order, The Street, 1981 Tony Awards, PBS Great Performances, 1983 Grammy awards, All My Children, others, also various nat. tours, regional and stock theatrical prodns., commls. and voice-overs. Recipient Best Actor in Musical award Bay Area Drama Critics, 1984.

CHARLES-KAY, JOY, not-for-profit fundraiser; d. Melvin and Ernestine (Pryor) Charles; m. Bryan Samuel Kay, June 6, 1987; children: Justine Lydia Kay, Christian Samuel Kay. BA, Rutgers Coll., New Brunswick, NJ, 1984; MA, Montclair (N.J.)State U., 1993. Asst. dir. donor rels. and stewardship Kent Pl. Sch., Summit, NJ, 2000—01, mgr. found. rels., 1999—2000; dir. of devel. Family Connections, Inc., Orange, NJ, 2001—. Bd. dirs. African Globe Theatre, Newark, 2000—02. Mem.: Kent Pl. Sch. Alumnae Bd. (assoc.; mem. 1992—94), Jack and Jill of Am., Inc. (assoc.; vice pres., program dir. North Jersey chpt. 2000—02). United Methodist. Avocations: travel, reading, volunteering. Office Fax: 973-673-5782. E-mail: info@familyconnectionsnj.com.

CHARLESWORTH, ARTHUR THOMAS, mathematics and computer science educator; b. Gainesville, Fla., Nov. 8, 1944; s. Arthur Riggs and Martha Jean (Hamilton) C.; m. Josephine Ann Owenby, Sept. 10, 1966; 1 child, Jonathan David. BS in Math., Stetson U., 1966; AM in Math., Duke U., 1968, PhD in Math., 1974; MS in Computer Sci., U. Va., 1983. Trajectory analysis engr. Apollo support dept. GE, Daytona Bch., Fla., 1966-67; instr. Jacksonville (Fla.) U., 1968-69, Randolph-Macon Coll., Ashland, Va., 1969-71; asst. prof. Queens Coll., Charlotte, N.C., 1974-76, U. Richmond, Va., 1976-82, assoc. prof., 1982-89, prof., 1989—. Sec. astronomy, math., physics sect. Va. Acad. Sci., 1977-78, chmn., 1978-79; treas. Md., D.C., Va. sect. Math. Assn. Am., 1980-82. Contbr. articles to profl. jours. Chmn. Trinity Meth. Comsn. on Missions, Richmond, 1981. Research grantee NASA Langley Rsch. Ctr., Hampton, Va., 1987, 88, 89, 90, 91, 92. Mem. IEEE, Assn. Computing Machinery, Omicron Delta Kappa, Sigma Xi. Avocations: hiking, rock collecting. Office: U Richmond Dept Math/Computer Sci Richmond VA 23173

CHARLETON, MARGARET ANN, child care administrator, consultant; b. Calif., Aug. 3, 1947; d. Arthur Mitchell and Isabelle Margaret (Esser) C.; (div. Sept. 1985). AA in Liberal Arts, Orange Coast Coll., 1968; BA in Psychology, Chapman U., 1984. Head tchr. Presbyn. Ch. of the Master, Mission Viejo, Calif., 1977-81; child care program adminstr. Crystal Stairs, Inc., L.A., 1981—2001. Mem. adv. bd. Children's Home Soc., Santa Ana, Calif., 1982-83; cons. Calif. Sch. Age Consortium, Costa Mesa, 1987, Calif. State Dept. of Edn., 1988, trainer preschool edn. program Sesame Street PBS, 1994-96; lectr. in field; presenter Western Regional Child Care Food Program Conf., San Francisco, 1997, Save the Children Conf., Atlanta, Ga., 1998, 10th Ann. Child Care Food Program Sponsor's Conf., 2001. Contbr. articles to profl. jours. Mem. South Orange County Community Svc., Mission Viejo, 1983—; liaison Family Svcs.-Marine Base, El Toro, Calif., 1989—; mem. adv. bd. Dept. Social Svc., 1997—. Recipient Plaque of Recognition, Vietnamese Community of Orange County, 1984. Mem. NAFE. Roman Catholic. Avocations: sailing, skiing, traveling, wine. Office: Child Nutrition Program So Calif 7777 Alvarado Rd Ste 700 La Mesa CA 91941

CHARLEY, NANCY JEAN, communications professional; b. LaCrosse, Wis., Jan. 6, 1956; A in Bus. Adminstrn., Midway Coll., 1992, A in Computer Info. Systems, 1993, BBA, 1994, MBA, Regis U., 2001. Cert. health unit coord., project mgr. profl. 2003. Office mgr. for neurologist, Lexington, Ky., 1985-88; health unit coord. acute care hosp., Lexington, 1979-91, health unit coord. trainer, 1992-93, coord. order comms., order mgmt. trainer mgmt. info. system, 1988-95; system support analyst Mgmt. Info. Systems, 1994-96, sys. support analyst, patient auditor, trainer, 1996-97; clin. informatics analyst Ctrl. Bapt. Hosp., Lexington, 1997-98; application analyst for home health Appalachian Regional Healthcare, Lexington, 1998-2000; clin. analyst Shriners Hosps. for Children, Lexington, 2000—. Freelance cons.; presenter in healthcare/mgmt. Contbg. author: Health Unit Coordinating Expanding the Scope of Practice, 1999. Named Ky. Col., 1989. Mem. Nat. Assn. Health Unit Coords. (support cons. 1990, edn. bd. 1990-95, chmn. continuing edn. com. 1991-93, mem. several ad hoc coms.), Project Mgmt. Inst., Midway Coll. Alumnae Assn. Avocations: tai chi, swedish massage, ice skating, dance, water activities. Office: Shriners Healthcare for Children 1900 Richmond Rd Lexington KY 40502

CHARLIE, WAYNE ALEXANDER, civil engineering educator; b. Toronto, Ont., Can., Mar. 4, 1945; s. Jack C. and Ellen A. (Whittingham) C.; m. Deanna Durnford, Sept. 21, 1984. BSCE, BA in Social Scis., Mich. State U., 1971, MSCE, 1972, PhDCE, 1975. Registered profl. engineer, Maine, Colo. Vol. U.S. Peace Corps., Ethiopia, 1966-68; asst. prof. U. Maine, Orono, 1975-76, Colo. State U., Ft. Collins, 1976-82, assoc. prof., 1982-90, prof., 1990—. Fulbright prof. Univ. Khartoum, Sudan, 1980; vis. prof. U. Auckland, New Zealand, 1983-84, Cornell U., Ithaca N.Y., 1983-84, 93-94; cons. Tasman Paper Co., Kawerau, New Zealand, 1984-85, Bur. Reclamation, Denver, Colo., 1981, D'Appolonia Cons. Engrs., Denver, 1980, Climax (Colo.) Molybdenum Co., 1978, Soil Testing Svc., Green Bay, Wis., 1990—, U. Fla., Gainesville, 1990—; geotech. program leader, 1987—. Contbr. 45 articles to profl. jours. Rsch. grantee NSF, 1978—. Fellow ASCE; mem. Soc. Explosives Engrs., Internat. Soc. Soil Mechanics and Found. Engrs., Phi Kappa Phi, Sigma Xi. Achievements include research/patentee on explosive and earthquake induced liquefaction of soil. Office: Colo State U Dept Civil Engring A319 Erc Fort Collins CO 80523-1372 E-mail: wcharlie@engr.colostate.edu.

CHARLIP, RALPH BLAIR, military officer, health facility administrator; b. Detroit, July 16, 1952; s. Jack Edward and Dorothea (Steinman) Charlip; m. Cynthia Lanell Sallas, May 23, 1987. BA, U. Ariz., 1976, MPA, 1977. Commd. 2nd lt. USAF, 1978, advanced through grades to lt. col., 1994; squadron comdr. USAF Regional Hosp., Langley AFB, Va., 1978-79, dir. patient adminstrn., 1979-80, plant mgr., 1980-81; dir. med. resource mgmt. USAF Clinic Andersen, Andersen AFB, 1981-82; dir. patient adminstrn. Malcolm Grow USAF Med. Ctr., Andrews AFB, Md., 1983-84; intern Data Systems Design Ctr., Gunter AFB, Ala., 1984-85; health policy devel. officer USAF Hdqs., Bolling AFB, DC, 1985-89; dir. patient adminstrn. USAF Med. Ctr., Wright-Patterson AFB, Ohio, 1989-92; assoc. dir. med. svcs. Air Nat. Guard Hqrs., Andrews AFB, 1992-94; dir. plans integration and mktg. Dept. Def. Health Svcs. Region VII, Ft. Bliss, Tex., 1994-96; comdr. 423 Clinic, Upwood, England, 1996-97; adminstr. aerospace med. Armstrong Lab., Brooks AFB, Tex., 1997; dep. comdr. 59 Med. Support Group, Lackland AFB, Tex., 1997-99; assoc. adminstr. 59 Med. Wing, Lackland AFB, 1999-2000; dir. health adminstrn. ctr. VA, Denver, 2000—. Author: (book) Your Health Benefits, 1989. Fellow: Am. Acad. Med. Adminstrs., Am. Coll. Healthcare Execs. Office: VA HAC 300 S Jackson St Ste 444 Denver CO 80209-3134

CHARLOT JR, JOSEPH LEONCE, preventive medicine physician; b. Bkyln., Oct. 19, 1967; s. Joseph Leonce and Marie Andree Charlot; m. Denise Michelle Johnson, July 11, 1967. BA, Rutgers U., 1986—90; MD, UMDNJ-Robert Wood Johnson Med. Sch., 1990—95; MPH, UMDNJ-Rutgers Sch. of Pub. Health, 1991—93. Med. Rev. Officer Med. Rev. Officer Certification Coun., Ill. State, 2001, Advanced Cardiac Life Support Am. Heart Assn., Ill. State, 2002, Basic Life Support Am. Heart Assn., Ill. State, 2002, Preventive Medicine Am. Bd. of Preventive Medicine, Ill. State, 2003; Prison Religious Vol. Prison Fellowship, Va. State, 1999. Resident physician U. of Md. Med. Sys., Balt., 1995—97, Trover Clinic, Madisonville, Ky., 1997—98; locum tenens occupl. medicine physician Concentra Med. Centers, Richmond, Va., 1999—2000; resident physician Ft. Wayne Med. Found., Ft. Wayne, Ind., 2000—00; med. dir. Cmty. Occupl. Medicine, Elkhart, Ind., 2001—02; plant occupl. medicine physician Damiler Chrysler Kokomo Transmission Plant, Kokomo, Ind. Prison religious vol. Prison Fellowship, Richmond, Va., 1999—2000; religious vol. Kokomo Rescue Mission, Kokomo, Ind., 2003—03; physician vol. Kokomo Cmty. Health Initative, 2002—03. Fellow Rsch. Fellowship, Robert Wood Johnson Med. Sch., 1991. Mem.: APHA (assoc.), Am. Coll. of Occupl. and Environ. Medicine (assoc.), AMA (assoc.), Am. Coll. of Preventive Medicine (assoc.), Christian Med. and Dental Associations (assoc.). Avocations: basketball, reading, computer programming, bicycling, weightlifting. Office: Damiler Chrysler Kokomo Transmission 2401 South Reed Rd Kokomo IN 46904 Office Fax: 765-454-1745.

CHARLTON, BETTY JO, retired state legislator; b. Reno County, Kans., June 15, 1923; d. Joseph and Elma (Johnson) Canning; BA, U. Kans., 1970, MA, 1976; m. Robert Sansom Charlton, Feb. 24, 1946 (dec. 1984); children: John Robert, Richard Bruce. Asst. instr. polit. sci. and western civilization U. Kans., Lawrence, 1970-73; legis. adminstrv. svcs. employee State of Kans., Topeka, 1977-78, legis. aide gov's. office, 1979; mem. Kans. Ho. of Reps., 1980-95, ret., 1995.

CHARLTON, CATHERINE MARIE, musician, composer; b. Charlottesville, Va., 1974; d. Jeannette S. and James P. Charlton. BS, Cornell U. Composer (musician): (albums) River Dawn: Piano Meditations (Top 3, Worldwide New Age Radio Charts, 2002), Jeweled Rain (3rd Pl. Best Solo Instrumental Album, JPFolks Nat. Music Awards, 2001), Strange Attractors. Recipient Top Ten Coll. Women, GLAMOUR Mag., 1994, Nat. Arts Laureate, Tau Beta Pi Engring. Honor Soc., 1994, Woman of Distinction, Seven Lakes Girl Scout Coun., 1995; grantee Artist Fellow, Jazz Performance, Del. Divsn. of the Arts, 2002, Artist Fellow, Solo Recital, 2000.

CHARLTON, GORDON RANDOLPH, physicist; b. Newport News, Va., Aug. 30, 1937; s. George Randolph and Sarah Louise (Harper) C. BSc, Ohio State U., 1957; MSc in Physics, W.Va. U., 1960; PhD in Physics, U. Md., 1966, M of Gen. Adminstrn. in Applied Mgmt., 1996. Charge de recherches Ecole Poly. Lab., Paris, 1966-69; asst. physicist high energy physics div. Argonne (Ill.) Nat. Lab., 1969-72; rsch. assoc. Stanford (Calif.) Linear Accelerator Ctr., 1972-73; rsch. fellow physics dept. U. Toronto (Ont., Can.), 1973-75; sr. physicist divsn. high energy physics Office of Sci., U.S. Dept. Energy, Washington, 1975-99; cons., 2000—. Contbr. articles to Phys. Rev., Phys. Rev. Letters, Physics Letters. Mem. Am. Phys. Soc., U.S. Croquet Assn. Office: PO Box 20545 Bradenton FL 34204-0545 E-mail: gordon.charlton@pobox.com.

CHARLTON, JENNIFER J, music educator; b. Great Falls, Mont., Jan. 3, 1968; d. Paul Leroy Carlson and Nadine Phylis Carlton; m. Vince Dale Charlton, July 14, 1990. BE, Mont. State U., 1990. Music tchr. pvt. instr., 1992—. Ch. musician Valley Bapt. Ch., Huntley, Mont., 1990—; accompaniment for local music festival Billings, Mont., 1996—2002.

CHARLTON, JESSE MELVIN, JR., management educator, lawyer; b. Livonia, La., May 12, 1916; s. Jesse Melvin and Anna Lela (Medlin) C.; m. Mary Camp, Oct. 4, 1941; children: Jesse Melvin, Frances Anne. BS, La. State U., 1937, MBA, 1938; JD, Harvard U., 1951. Bar: U.S. Ct. Mil. Appeals 1952, U.S. Supreme Ct 1963, D.C. 1951. Instr. U. Ala., 1938-40; commd. 2d lt., inf. U.S. Army, 1940; advanced through grades to col. U.S. Army (Judge Adv. Gen.'s Corps), 1962; dep. comdr. Judge Adv. Gen. Sch., Charlottesville, Va., 1962-64; ret., 1964; mem. faculty U. New Orleans Coll. Bus., 1964-81, prof. mgmt., 1971-81, prof. emeritus, 1981—; asst. dean coll. bus. U. New Orleans, 1967-71, dean grad. sch., 1978-80. Author handbook; co-editor: Statistical Abstract of Louisiana, 5th edit, 1974. Decorated Bronze Star. Mem. D.C. Bar Assn. Republican.

CHARLTON, JOHN KIPP, pediatrician; b. Omaha, Jan. 26, 1937; s. George Paul and Mildred (Kipp) C.; m. Susan S. Young, Aug. 15, 1959; children: Paul, Cynthia, Daphne, Gregory. AB, Amherst Coll., 1958; MD, Cornell U., 1962. Intern Ohio State U. Hosp., Columbus, 1962-63; resident in pediatrics Children's Hosp., Dallas, 1966-68, chief resident in pediatrics, 1968-69, fellow in nephrology U. Tex. Southwestern Med. Sch., Dallas, 1969-70; pvt. practice medicine specializing in pediatrics, Phoenix, from 1970; chmn. dept. pediatrics Maricopa Med. Ctr., Phoenix, 1971-78, 84-93, pres. med. staff, 1991; med. dir., bd. dirs. Crisis Nursery, Inc., 1977—. Clin. assoc. prof. pediat. U. Ariz. Coll Medicine, asst. dean for student affairs, 2000—. Author articles and book revs. in field. Pres. Maricopa County Child Abuse Coun., 1977-81; bd. dirs. Florence Crittenton Svcs., 1980-83, Ariz. Children's Found., 1987-91; mem. Gov.'s Coun. on Children, Youth and Families, 1984-86. Officer M.C., USAF, 1963-65. Recipient Hon. Kachina award for volunteerism, 1980, Jefferson award for volunteerism, 1980, Horace Steel Child Advocacy award, 1993; named Clin. Sci. Educator of Yr., U. Ariz., 1997, 99, 2000, 2001. Mem. Am. Acad. Pediatrics, Ariz. Pediatric Soc., Maricopa County Pediatric Soc. (past pres.). Home: 6230 E Exeter Blvd Scottsdale AZ 85251-3060 Office: Maricopa Med Ctr 2601 E Roosevelt St Phoenix AZ 85008-4973 E-mail: kipp.charlton@hcs.maricopa.gov.

CHARLTON, MICHAEL R, physician, researcher; b. London, May 27, 1962; s. Warwick M and Marilyn L Charlton; m. Fiona M Simpson, Sept. 2, 1989; children: Henry W, Sophie K, William M. M.B., B.S., U. of London, 1981—86. Diplomate U. of London, 1986, Bd. Cert. in Gastroenterology and Hepatology Am. Bd. of Internal Medicine, 1995, Bd. Cert. in Internal Medicine Am. Bd. of Internal Medicine, 1992. Cons. Mayo Clinic, Rochester, Minn., 1995—, assoc. prof. of medicine, 2000—. Mem. NIH Liver Transplant Database Steering Com., 1995—2003, United Network of Organ Sharing Sci. Adv. Com., 1998—2000; assoc. med. dir. for liver transplantation Mayo Clinic, 2001—, chair for transplant rsch., 2003—. Contbr. articles to profl. jours., chapters to books; mem. editl. bd. Hepatology, 2002—03, assoc. editor Clin. Gastroenterology and Hepatology, 2003—. Recipient Alpha Omega Alpha, Med. Honor Soc., 1994, Young Investigator award, Am. Soc. of Transplant Physicians, 1998, Clin. Sci. Investigator award, Am. Transplant Congress, 2002, Sci. Presentation prize, ACP, 1994; Clin. Assoc. Physician grant, NIH, 1995—98. Mem.: AMA, Internat. Liver Transplant Soc., Am. Assn. for the Study of Liver Diseases, Am. Gastroenterology Assn. Achievements include research in liver disease; invention of method for measuring viral turnover in vivo; first to predict outcomes in liver transplant recipients. Avocations: travel, literature, hiking. Office: Mayo Clinic CH-10 200 FIrst St SW Rochester MN 55905 Office Fax: 5078-266-2810.

CHARLWOOD, KEVIN EDWARD, mathematician, educator; s. Reginald Edward Charlwood. BS, Carroll Coll., Wis., 1986; MS, Univ. Minn., 1988; PhD, U. of Wis., Milw., 1994. Asst. prof. of math. St. Leo Coll., Saint Leo, Fla., 1995—97, Washburn U., Topeka, 1997—, 2003—. Mem.: Young Mathematician's Network (mng. editor Concerns of Young Mathematicians 1995—), Math. Assn. of Am., Am. Math. Soc., Phi Kappa Phi, Kappa Mu Epsilon. Office: Washburn University 1700 SW College Avenue Topeka KS 66621

CHARM, JOEL BARRY, consulting consultant executive; BA in Chemistry, U. Mass., 1965; MS in Radiation Biology/Environ. Health, U. Mich., 1967; cert. advanced mgmt. program, Columbia U., 1977. With Dow Chem. Co., Midland, Mich., 1968-73, radiation safety officer, 1968-73, chief indsl. hygienist dept. chem. prodn., 1970-72, rsch. specialist in indsl. hygiene, 1972-73; corp. mgr. indsl. hygiene Miles Labs., Elkhart, Ind., 1973-75; mgr. occupl. health and toxicology Allied Corp., Morristown, N.J., 1975-77, dir. corp. product safety and integrity, 1977-96, dir. occupl. health and product safety, 1996-97; leader Product Stewardship Ctr. of Excellence, 1996-97; pres. Charm HS&E Internat., Inc., Randolph, N.J., 1998—. Spkr., lectr. on ISO-14000 toxic substances control, indsl. hygiene, OSHA, radiation, pollution control at univs., profl. meetings; chmn. U.S. Tech. Adv. Group on ISO-14000. Author profl. reports and papers. NIH fellow, 1967. Mem. ASTM (tec.sec. air sampling methodology and occupl. safety and health criteria), Am. Acad. Indsl. Hygiene (diplomate), Am. Indsl. Hygiene Assn. (chmn. com. product safety and health), Ind. Indsl. Hygiene Soc. (bd. dirs.), Mich. Indsl. Hygiene Soc. (bd. dirs. 1969-70), Health Physics Soc., Am. Soc. Safety Engrs. (profl.) N.J. Indsl. Hygiene Soc. Office: Charm HS&E Internat 15 Springhill Rd Randolph NJ 07869-4324 E-mail: jcharm@optonline.net.

CHARNAS, FRAN ELKA, theatre director, educator, author; b. Cleve. d. Morris and Zelda (Wymor) C. BFA in Theatre, Ohio U., 1968; MA in Theatre, Emerson Coll., 1981. Producer, dir. East Cleveland (Ohio) Music Theatre, 1972-74; mem. faculty Boston Conservatory, 1980—; adminstrv. dir. Summer Inst. in Mus. Theatre, Boston, 1984, grad. thesis project dir., 1992—. Presenter and cons. in field. Author, dir., choreographer (mus.) The All Night Strut, 1975—, (TV spl.), 1988; dir. (mus.) Party of One, 1989, (opera) Look What A Wonder Jesus Has Done, 1990; co-author, dir. (mus.) Sheboppin, 1987; dir. various plays and mus. including The Wheel, 2002; author, dir. In the Groove, 1998. Mem. New Eng. Theatre Conf., New Opera Musical Theatre Initiative. Avocations: antiques, travel. Office: The Boston Conservatory 8 Fenway Boston MA 02215-4099

CHARNAS, MICHAEL (MANNIE CHARNAS), investment company executive; b. Cleve., Sept. 24, 1947; s. Max and Eleanor (Gross) C.; m. Mimi F. Stein, June 10, 1990; 1 child from previous marriage, Matthew; 1 child, Max. BBA, Ohio State U., 1969, MBA, 1971. Page Ohio Ho. of Reps., 1969; mem. Ohio Staters, Inc., 1969; fin. analyst Addressograph-Multigraph, Inc., Cleve., 1971-73; asst. to pres., dir. planning and budget 1st Nat. Supermarkets, Inc. (Pick-N-Pay), Cleve., 1975-78, asst. to pres., v.p. planning and budgets, 1978-79, sr. v.p. fin., adminstr., 1979-81, sr. v.p., CFO, adminstrv. officer Hartford, Conn., 1981-86; founder Charnas Mktg. and Investment Co., 1986—; pres., owner Indsl. Pallet and Packaging Co., Beachwood, Ohio, 1986-94; regional v.p. Pallet Pallet, Inc. (formerly Indsl. Pallet and Packaging Co.), Toronto, 1995-97; co-owner Samm Properties and Samm Mgmt. Svcs., Ltd., 1998—; owner, operator Self Storage Facilities, Ohio. Bd. dirs. Gorman-Lavelle Corp.; owner/CEO Pallet Distbrs., Inc., 1999-2001; fin. adv. bd. Gooey Industries, 2000-03; v.p., owner PMC Investment Group, 2003-; franchisee of Qdoba Mexican Grill Restaurants, Cen. Ill. Jewish. Avocations: tennis, reading, collecting modern classic cars. Office: 23811 Chagrin Blvd Ste 160 Cleveland OH 44122-5715 E-mail: bizwiz924@cs.com.

CHARNEY, CRAIG RUSSELL, pollster, political scientist; b. N.Y.C., Oct. 27, 1956; s. Roy L. and Lena (London) Charney. BA, Brandeis U., Waltham, Mass., 1977; MPhil, Oxford U., 1979; DEA, Sorbonne U., Paris, 1986; MPhil, Yale U., 1989, PhD, 2000. Polit. reporter The Star, Johannesburg, 1980-81; assoc. editor Mgmt. Mag., Johannesburg, 1982-83; instr. polit. sci. Yale U., New Haven, 1989-90; rschr., trainer Local 1199, N.Y.C., 1990; rsch. fellow Wits U., Johannesburg, 1991-92; ptnr. Rsch. Initiatives, Johannesburg, 1992-93; pollster South African Broadcasting Corp., 1994-95; sr. analyst Penn & Schoen Assocs., N.Y.C., 1996-97; pres. Charney Rsch., N.Y.C., 1997—; sr. rsch. fellow Milano Sch. of Pub. Policy New Sch. U., N.Y.C., 2002—. Contbr. articles to profl jours, newspapers and mags. Mem. N.Y. County Dem. Com.; Bd. dirs. Headstart Bloomingdale Family Program. Mem.: Am. Assn. Polit. Cons., Nat. Writers Union, Am. Polit. Sci. Assn. Office: Charney Rsch 2nd Fl 5 W 102nd St Fl 2 New York NY 10025-4778

CHARNEY, DENNIS S. psychiatrist; b. N.Y.C., Mar. 31, 1951; s. Joseph Louis and Charlotte Marilyn (Landman) C.; m. Andrea Robin Orson, May 28, 1972; children: Allison, Meredith, Lauren, Alexander, Danielle. BA, Rutgers Coll., 1973; MD, Pa. State U., 1977. Chief resident Clin. Neuroscience Res. Unit, New Haven, 1980-81, chief, 1983-88; assoc. chief biol. sci. Conn. mental Health Ctr., New Haven, 1981-82; asst. prof. Yale U. Sch. Medicine, New Haven, 1981-85, assoc. prof., 1985—2000; dir. Affective Disorders Clinic, New Haven, 1981-83; chief psychiatry svc. West Haven (Conn.) VA Med. Ctr., 1988—2000; chief, mood & anxiety disorders res. prog. Nat. Inst. Mental Health, 2000—, chief, experimental therapeutics & pathophysiology, 2000—. Mem. exec. com. Conn. Mental Health Ctr., 1984-88, Yale Clin. Rsch. Ctr.; residency selection com. Yale U. Dept. Psychiatry, 1984-88; cons. in field; mem. adv. bd. OCD Found, Inc., 1988; mem. scientific adv. bd. Neurogen, Inc., 1988. Mem. editorial bd. Jour. Affective Disorders, Jour. Anxiety Disorders; rev. numerous profl. jours. including Jour. Am. Med. Assn., Am. Jour. Psychiatry, Jour. Clin. Psychiatry; contbr. articles to profl. jours. Mem. Am. Assn. for the Advancement Sci., Am. Coll. Neuropsychopharmacology, Nat. Inst. Mental Health (mem. small grant rev. bd.), Am. Coll. Neuropsychopharmacology, Inst. Medicine, Soc. for Neuroscience, Am. Psychiatric Assn., Soc. Biol. Psychiatry, Conn. Psychiatry Soc. Democrat. Jewish. Office: Nat Inst Mental Health 10 Center Dr Rm 4N-222 MSC 1381 Bethesda MD 20892-1381

CHARNEY, EVAN, pediatrician, educator; b. N.Y.C., Feb. 24, 1933; BA, Cornell U., 1954; MD, Albert Einstein Coll. Medicine, 1960. Intern, resident Strong Meml. Hosp, N.Y.S., 1960—63; from asst. to assoc. prof. pediat. Strong Meml Hosp., U. Rochester, NY, 1963—75; prof. pediat., chief pediat. dept. Sinai Hosp. Balt., Johns Hopkins U., 1975—87; prof., chmn. dept. pediat. U. Mass. Med. Ctr., Worcester, 1987—98, prof. dept. pediat., 1987—. 1st lt. Ordnance Corps U.S. Army, 1954—56. Recipient Armstrong award, Ambulatory Pediatric Assn., 1982; scholar Markle, Acad. Medicine, 1968—73. Fellow: Inst. Medicine NAS; mem.: Am. Acad. Pediat. Home: 32 Rivers Edge Rd East Falmouth MA 02536-5454 Office: U Mass Med Sch Worcester Found Campus 222 Maple Ave Shrewsbury MA 01545

CHARNEY, JONATHAN ISA, law educator, lawyer; b. NYC, Oct. 29, 1943; s. Wolfe R. and Rita Dorothy (Greenfield) Charney; m. Sharon Renee Lehman, June 12, 1966; children: Tamar, Adam, Noah. BA, NYU, 1965; JD, U. Wis., 1968. Bar: Wis. 1968, Tenn 1974, NY 1980, US Supreme Ct. 1971. Atty., Land and Natural Resources div. Dept. Justice, Washington, 1968—71; atty., chief marine resources sect., 1972; asst. prof. law Vanderbilt U., Nashville, 1972—75; assoc. prof., 1978—. Cons. in field; vis. prof. U. Pa., 1989. Contbr. articles. Mem.: Order of Coif, Internat. Boundary Rsch. Unit (mem. bd. adv. 1993—), Assn. Am. Law Sch. (chmn. internat. law sect. 1985), Am. Jour. Internat. Law (bd. editors 1986—, editor in chief 1998—), Am. Soc. Internat. Law (exec. council 1982—85, v.p. 1994—96), Am. Law Inst., Coun. Fgn. Rels., Am. Br. Internat. Law Assn. (chair com. on formation of internat. law 1986—90), ABA (chair internat. law sect. internat. ct. com. 1988—89, dep. vice chair sect. on internat. law, pub. internat. law div. 1988—90), Wis. Law Rev. (bd. editors 1966—68), Ocean Develop. and Internat. Law (bd. editors 1985—, editor in chief 1998—), Marine Policy Ctr. (sr. advisors com. 1987—96, chair 1991—96), Woods Hole Oceanographic Inst. Office: Vanderbilt University Law School 131 21st Avenue South Nashville TN 37203-1181

CHARNEY, JONATHAN ZACHARY, neurologist; b. Bklyn., Dec. 20, 1942; s. Morris and Nettie Charney; children: Samuel, Aaron. BA, Franklin and Marshall Coll., 1963; MD, N.Y. Med. Coll., 1969. Diplomate Am. Bd. Psychiatry and Neurology, Nat. Bd. Med. Examiners. Intern Meth. Hosp., Houston, 1969-70; resident in neurology Baylor Coll. Medicine, Houston, 1970-71, Neurol. Inst., Presbyn. Hosp., N.Y.C., 1971-73; pvt. practice N.Y.C., 1975—; asst. attending Mt. Sinai Hosp., N.Y.C., 1975—. Lectr. neurology Cath. Med. Coll., Seoul, Korea, 1973-74; instr. neurology U. Hawaii, Honolulu, 1974-75; asst. prof. neurology Mt. Sinai Coll. Medicine, N.Y.C., 1975-77, asst. clin. prof. neurology, 1977—. Contbr. articles to profl. jours. With U.S. Army, 1973-75. Fellow N.Y. Acad. Medicine, Am. Heart Assn. (stroke coun.); mem. AMA, Acad. Neurology, N.Y. State Med. Soc., N.Y. County Med. Soc., Assn. Rsch. in Nervous and Mental Disorders. Office: 1111 Park Ave # 1H New York NY 10128-1234

CHARNEY, LENA LONDON, property manager, poet; b. Simyatycze, Poland, Jan. 26, 1919; d. Moysei Isaakovitch and Emma (London) Barengoits; m. Roy L. Charney, Nov. 10, 1955 (dec. 1972); 1 child, Craig Russell. BA cum laude, Hunter Coll., 1941; MA, Clark U., 1942; postgrad., Columbia U. Cert. tchr. N.Y., adminstr. Owner, mgr. London's Studio Apts., 1959—. Millinery designer Sanjour Studio, 1937, 1939—41, Lenblac Millinery, 1938; sec. to mgr. N.Y.C. Office Ins. Field, 1945; saleswoman Bonwit-Teller, Lane Bryant, Arnold Constable, 1947—49; tchr., prin. St. Basil's Acad. Garisson, NY, 1968—73; substitute tchr. various sch. dists., NY, 1974—82; Sunday sch. tchr. Temple Beth Am, Yorktown Heights, NY. Featured poet Evening of Poetry, Mt. Pleasant Libr., Pleasantville, N.Y.; contbr. articles and poetry to profl. jours. and lit. jours.; asst. editor: Ins. Weekly, 1946. Charter mem., rec. sec., bd. dirs. Lakeland Jewish Ctr., Mohegan Lake, Sunday sch. tchr.; dir., tchr. Workmen's Cir. Yiddish Sch., Shrub Oak, NY; active Hudson Valley Hosp. Ctr. Aux., U.S. Holocaust Mus., Greenpeace, Amnesty Internat., ACLU, Am. Found. Blind, Anti-Defamation League, Gen. Israel Orphans Home Girls, Mohegan Lake Vol. Fire Assn., Mohegan Lake Vol. Ambulance Corps, Nat. Yiddish Book Ctr., Lighthouse, Rec. for Blind, Jewish Braille Inst., Am. Printing Ho. for Blind, Eye Bank Sight Restoration, Glaucoma Rsch.; mem. Westchester Arts Coun.; active United Jewish Appeal-Fedn. Telethon; chmn. eye rschl. project, chmn. Am. affairs, chmn. Zionist affairs, v.p. edn., pres. Aviva chpt. Hadassah; active World Jewish Congress, Union Couns. Soviet Jews; rec. sec. Mohegan Lake (N.Y.) Resort Owners Assn.; v.p. Mohegan Lake Improvement Corp.; v.p. publicity nat. women's com. Brandeis U. Named Outstanding Sr. of the Yr., Compound Sr. Citizens Club, Woman of the Yr., Aviva Hadassah. Mem.: Poetry Soc. Am., Acad. Am. Poets, Hudson Valley Writers Ctr., Nat. Writers Union, Acad. Polit. Sci., Am. Hist. Assn. Avocations: swimming, walking, dancing, movies, travel. Home: PO Box 145 Mohegan Lake NY 10547-0145

CHARNEY, MELVIN, artist, architect, educator; b. Montreal, Que., Can., Aug. 28, 1935; s. H. and F. (Cassack) C.; m. Ann Korsower, May 29, 1960; 1 child, Dara Alexandra. BArch, McGill U., Montreal, 1958; MArch, Yale U., 1959. Prin. Melvin Charney, Architect, Montreal, 1964—; prof. U. Montreal, 1964-95. Mem. architects com. Am. Acad. Arts and Scis., Boston, 1968-69; co-dir. task force on housing Govt. of Can., Ottawa, 1970-71; mem. adv. com. Can. Centre for Architecture, Montreal, 1983-89; founding bd. dirs. Conseil des Arts et des Lettres, Quebec, 1994-97; invited prof. to numerous univs. One-man shows include Harvard U., 1977, Art Gallery of Ont., Toronto, 1978, Musee d'Art Contemporain, Montreal, 1979, P.S.1, N.Y.C., 1979, Can. Cultural Ctrs., Paris and Brussels, 1980, Mus. Contemporary Art, Chgo., 1982, Richard Gray Gallery, Chgo., 1982, 49th Parallel, Centre for Can. Contemporary Art, N.Y.C., 1982, 87, Agnes Etherington Art Centre, Kingston, Ont., 1983, represented Can. at the 42nd Venice Biennale, 1986, Renè Blouin Gallery, Montreal, 1987, 88, Ctr. for Can. Art, N.Y., 1987, Sable-Castelli Gallery, Toronto, 1988, 91, 92, 93, 95, 97, 99, 2001, maj. retrospective Can. Centre for Architecture, Montreal, 1991-92, de Beyrie Gallery, Paris, 1994, Israel Mus., Jerusalem, 1996, Power Plant Gallery Contemporary Art, Toronto, 1995, Franc Basse-Normandie, Caen, France, 1997, Fondation pour l'architecture, Brussels, 1997; Can. Pavilion, 7th Venice Biennale of Architecture, 2000, major retrospective Musée d'art Contemporain de Montréal, 2002; exhibited in group shows at Montreal Mus. Fine Arts, 1972, 83, Musee d'Art Moderne de la Ville de Paris, 1973, Institut d'Art Contemporain, Montreal, 1975, 76, XXI Olympic Games, Montreal, 1976, John Weber Gallery, N.Y., 1979, Max Protetch Gallery, N.Y.C., 1979, Los Angeles Inst. Contemporary Art, 1980, Vancouver Art Gallery, 1980, Centre George Pompidou, 1980, Musee du Que., 1981, 83, 85, 89, 91, 98, Akademie der Kunst, Berlin, 1983, Kunstverein, Stuttgart, 1983, Mus. Contemporary Art, Chgo., 1984, Internationalen Bauausstellung, Berlin, 1984, 17th Trianale di Milano, 1985, Centre internat. d'art contemporain, Montreal, 1985, 96, Musee d'art Contemporain de Montreal, 1987, 92, 99, 2000, Power Plant, Contemporary Art at Harbourfront, Toronto, 1988, The Canadian Ctr. Architecture,

Montreal, 1989, 99, 00, Musee du Quebec, 1989, 91, Nat. Mus. Contemporary Art, Seoul, South Korea, 1990, Mus. des Jacobins, Morlaix, France, 1991, Canadian Pavilion, V Biennale di Architettura, Venice, 1991, Passages, Ctr. d'art contemporain, Troyes, France, 1992, Musèe nat. d'art moderne, Paris, 1994, Ctr. Cultura Contemporania, Barcelona, 1994, Royal Festival Hall Galleries, London, 1995, Manchester City Art Gallery, 1995, Marlborough-Chelsea Gallery, N.Y., 1998, Espaid'art Contemporani de Castello, Spain, 2000, Bibliotheque Nat. de France, Paris, 2000, Concordia U. Art Gallery, 2001, Centre nationale de la photographie, Paris, 2002, others; sculpture commns. The Can. Tribute to Human Rights, Ottawa, 1986, Urban Sculpture Garden for Can. Ctr. Architecture, Montreal, 1987, Place Berri, Montreal, 1991; represented in permanent collections Nat. Gallery Can., Ottawa, Can. Coun. Art Bank, Ottawa, Art Gallery Ont., Toronto, Musee d'art contemporain, Montreal, Can. Ctr. Architecture, Montreal, Mus. Contemporary Art, Chgo., IBM Collection, Chgo., Fonds Nat. d'Art Contemporain, Paris, Musee du Quebec, Montreal Mus. Fine Arts, Frac Basse Normandie, France, Art Gallery Hamilton, Israel Mus., Jerusalem; contbr. articles to profl. jours. Recipient Arts award Minister des Affaires Culturelles, 1967, research award Humanities and Social Scis. Coun., 1971, Berlin Arts award Deutcher Akademischer Austanschdienst, 1982, Sr. Arts award Can. Coun., 1983, 87, 96, Prix du Que. in visual arts, 1996, Lynch-Stanton award to disting. artists Can. Coun., 1997, Arts award Couseil Arts et Letters du Que., 2000. Mem. Royal Can. Acad., Ras. des Artists du Que, Royal Architectural Inst. of Can. Home: 3620 Marlowe Ave Montreal QC Canada H4A 3L7

CHARNEY, NATALIE J. behavioral health services administrator, researcher; d. Frances E and Leon A Seidman; m. David Charney (dec.); 1 child, Melissa D Jonassen. BA, U. Pa., 1988, MA, MSEd, U. Pa., 1991. Bd. Cert. Med. Psychotherapist/Psychodiagnostician Am. Bd. of Med. Psychotherapists & Psychodiagnosticians, 1991, Cert. Cognitive Behavioral Therapist Nat. Assn. of Cognitive Behavioral Therapists, 1996. Rsch. and adminstrv. assoc./acting dir., psychoendocrinology in psychiatry Hosp. of the U. of Pa, Philadelphia, Pa., 1972—82; cognitive therapist Pvt. Practice, Philadelphia, Pa., 1991—; asst. adminstr. Phila. Mental Health Clinic, Philadelphia, Pa., 1983—85; adminstr., sect. of geriatric psychiatry Hosp. of the U. of Pa, Philadelphia, Pa., 1985—93; dir., family based mental health services Dr. Warren E. Smith CMH/MR/SA Centers, Philadelphia, Pa., 1993—95, divsn. dir., mental health services, 1995—96; divsn. mgr., mental health services/vocat. rehab. programs Phila. OIC, Philadelphia, Pa., 1998; dir. of admissions, adult outpatient behavioral health services and rsch. Cmty. Coun. for MH/MR, Inc., Philadelphia, Pa., 1998—; faculty appointment-clinical assoc. in psychiatry U. of Pa, Med. Sch., Philadelphia, Pa., 1992—; staff therapist, ctr. for cognitive therapy U. of Pa, Philadelphia, Pa., 1992—. Presenter at several seminars, workshops, and nat. confs. Mem. editl. bd. The Medical Psychotherapist; contbr. articles to profl. jours. Recipient Cert. of Gratitude, Sled Toys for Tots, 1994. Mem.: Nat. Assn. of Cognitive-Behavioral Therapists, Am. Bd. of Med. Psychotherapists & Psychodiagnosticians, Gerontol. Soc. of Am. (rsch. edn. and practice com. & pvt. sector task force 1989—92), APA (assoc.), Phila. Coalition of Cmty. Care Providers (mental health directors com. & children's mental health com. 1995—2003), Pa. Cmty. Providers Assn. (family-home based subcommittee & mental health com. 1993—96). Office: Cmty Council for MH/MR Inc 4900 Wyalusing Ave Philadelphia PA 19131 E-mail: nataliecharney@lycos.com.

CHARNEY, SHARON RENEE, artist; b. Pitts., Aug. 20, 1943; d. Jacob Eliazer and Leah Lehman; m. Jonathan Isa Charney, June 12, 1966; children: Tamar, Adam, Noah. BFA, Carnegie Mellon U., 1965; MS, U. Wis., 1967; postgrad., Nashville State Tech. Inst., 1986-89. Art tchr. Middleton (Wis.) State Graded Schs., 1967-68, Cheekwood Mus. Art, Nashville, 1973-76, 90, The Harpeth Hall Sch., Nashville, 1979-86, art dept. chairperson, 1981-86; art instr. Nashville Sch. of Art, Watkins Inst., 1986-88, Metro Parks and Recreation, Nashville, 1990-95; artist, 1972—. Guest spkr. Vol. State C.C., Gallatin, Tenn., 2000, Tenn. Technol. Inst., Cookeville, Tenn., 1998, Cumberland U., Lebanon, Tenn., 2001; evaluation com. So. Assn. of Colls. and Schs., Franklin, 1984; workshop sect. leader Ind. Schs. of Nashville Area, 1982. Exhibited in solo shows at Wis. Ctr., Madison, 1967, Univ. Club of Nashville, 1977, Bookstar, Nashville, 1993, Greater Vision Gallery, Nashville, 1994, Metro Courthouse, Nashville, 1996, Vanderbilt U. Med. Ctr., Nashville, 1998-99, Local Color Gallery, Nashville, 1999, Tenn. State Mus. at Tenn. Performing Arts Ctr., Nashville, 2001, Nashville Internat. Airport, 2003-2004, others. Event artist Family and Children's Svcs., Nashville, 2000, 2001; mem. steering com. Nashville C. of C., 1998, 1999; tchr. West End Synagogue, 1987—97. Named Best of Show, WDCN Channel 8, 1994, Featured Artist for Season, Humanities Outreach of Tenn., 1996—97; recipient Merit award, Renaissance Ctr., 2000. Mem.: Visual Arts Alliance of Nashville (dir. exhbns. in govt. spaces 1995—2002, bd. dirs. 1997—2002). Avocations: jewelry making, hiking.

CHARNIN, JADE HOBSON, magazine executive; b. N.Y.C., Mar. 12, 1945; d. John Louis Campo and Elizabeth (Anne) Stanton); m. David Alan Hobson-,Dec. 30 (div. 1972); m. Martin Charnin, Dec. 18, 1984. BA, NYU, 1967. Asst. editor Glamour mag., N.Y.C., 1970; accessory editor Vogue mag., N.Y.C., 1970-78, fashion editor, 1978-81, fashion dir., 1981-86, creative dir. fashion, 1987-88; v.p., dir. creative svcs for fashion and design group Revlon Inc., 1988; exec. creative dir. Mirabella Mag., 1988-94; fashion dir. N.Y. Mag., 1994-98; freelance journalist, 1999—. Pres. Growing things (landscape design co.), 2002—; cons. editor Self mag., N.Y.C., 1979—81. Costume coord. for off-Broadways shows Upstairs at Oneals, 1981, Laughing Matters, 1989, Martin Charnin, the Hits and the M.S.'s, 1990. Mem.: ASPCA, Hort. Soc. N.Y. (bd. dirs.), Am. Hort. Soc., Assn. Profl. Landscape Designers, Humane Soc. N.Y. (bd. dirs.), Wilton Garden Club (bd. dirs.). Avocations: gardening, opera, ballet, theater, skiing. E-mail: jadehobson@aol.com.

CHARNIN, MARTIN, theatrical director, lyricist, producer; b. N.Y.C., Nov. 24, 1934; s. William and Birdie (Blakeman) C.; m. Lynn Ross, Mar. 2, 1958 (div.); 1 son, Randy; m. Genii Prior, Jan. 8, 1962 (div.); 1 dau., Sasha; m. Jade Hobson, Dec. 1985. BA, Cooper Union, 1955. Acting stage debut West Side Story, 1957; also appeared in The Girls Against the Boys, 1959; writer: lyrics and sketches Fallout Revue, 1959; lyricist: revue Pieces of Eight, 1959, Little Revue, 1960, Hot Spot (Broadway), 1963, Zenda, 1963, Mata Hari, 1967; lyricist, dir. Ballad for a Firing Squad, 1968; lyricist: Two by Two, 1970; conceived and directed: revue Nash at Nine (Broadway), 1973; dir.: revue Music! Music!, 1974; lyricist, dir., creator: Annie (Tony award for lyrics), 1977 (2 Drama Desk awards for lyrics and direction); dir. 4 nat. cos., 1978, also London prodn., 1978; dir. Bar Mitzvah Boy, London, 1978; lyricist: I Remember Mama, 1979; lyricist, dir., co-book writer The First (2 Tony nominations), 1981; lyricist: TV spl. Feathertop, 1961, Jackie Gleason Show, 1961; conceived and produced: TV spl. the Women in the Life of a Man, 1970 (2 Emmy awards); conceived, produced, directed and wrote TV spls. George M, 1970, Jack Lemmon in 'S Wonderful, 'S Marvelous, 'S Gershwin (2 Emmy awards), 1972 (Peabody award for Broadcasting), Jack Lemmon in Get Happy— The Music of Harold Arlen, 1973, Dames at Sea, 1972, Cole Porter in Paris, 1973, Annie and the Hoods, 1974, The Annie Xmas Show, 1977, C'mon Saturday, 1977; author: TV spls. The Giraffe Who Sounded Like Ol' Blue Eyes, 1976, Annie: A Theatre Memoir, 1977; dir. On the Swing Shift, A Backer's Audition, 1983; creator, writer, dir. Upstairs at the O'Neals, 1983; dir. Jokers at Goodspeed, 1986, An Evening of Neil Simon at the Public Theater, 1986; creator, writer, dir. The No-Frills Revue, 1987; dir. Cafe Crown at the Public Theater, 1988, Cafe Crown on Broadway, 1989, Laughing Matters, Off Broadway Sid Caeser and Co., Annie 2, 1990, N.Y. premiere Jules Feiffers Carnal Knowledge, 1991; lyrics and dir. Annie Warbucks at Goodspeed, Mata Hari, N.Y., 1996; producer N.Y. Shakespeare Festival Evenings for Joseph Papp, 1990, 91; one show Rainbow and Stars, N.Y.C.; lyrics, co-writer, dir. Winchell, 1991; lyrics, dir. Galileo, 1992, Annie Warbucks, 1993; dir. Loose Lips Revue, 1995, Can Can, rev. 1995; dir. Jeanne, Montreal, 1996; dir. Annie revival, Sydney, Australia, 2000. Office: care Richard Ticktin 1345 Avenue Of The Americas New York NY 10105-0302

CHARNOV, BRUCE HIRSCHL, management educator, chaplain, rabbi; b. Grand Rapids, Mich., Nov. 16, 1946; s. Abraham and Winona Belle (Fuller) C.; m. Naomi Charnov, Aug. 20, 1971 (div. Mar. 1984); children: Miryam Esther, Aharon Chayim, Jessica Lauren. BA, U. Mich., 1968; MA, Jewish Theol. Sem. Am., 1971; MBA, Fairleigh Dickinson U., 1982; PhD, U.S. Internat. U., 1976; JD, Hofstra U., 1990. Ordained rabbi, 1972; bar: N.Y., U.S. Dist. Ct. (ea. and so. dists.) N.Y. 1991. V.p. Yankelovich, Skelly & White, Inc., N.Y.C., 1977-80; rabbi, sch. prin. Mountain Jewish Ctr., Warren, NJ, 1980-86; prof. mgmt. Fairleigh Dickinson U., Teaneck, NJ, 1980—81; asst. prof. mgmt. and gen. bus. Hofstra U., Hempstead, NY, 1980-90; assoc. Proskauer Rose Goetz & Mendelsohn, N.Y.C., summer 1989; assoc. dept. litigation Fulbright & Jaworski, N.Y.C., 1990-92; assoc. prof. mgmt. and gen. bus. Hofstra U., 1993—; chairperson mgmt., entrepreneurship and gen. bus. dept. Frank G. Zarb Sch. of Bus./Hofstra U., 1997—2003. Author: From Autogiro to Gyroplane: The Amazing Survival of an Aviation Technology, 2003; co-author: (with Dr. Patrick Montana) Management, 1987, 3d edit., 2000, Greek edit., 1995, Portuguese edit., 1997, (with Dr. Ellen Weisbord and Jonathan Lindsey) Managing People in Today's Law Firm: The Human Resources Key to Survival, 1995; co-editor: (with Dr. George Roukis and Dr. Hugh Conway) Global Corporate Intelligence, 1990, From Autogiro to Gyroplane: The Amazing Story of an Aviation Technology, 2003; contbr. articles to profl. jours. Capt. USNR, 1990-98, ret., Jewish chaplain, 1972-77, res., 1977-98. Mem. N.Y. Bar Assn., Rabbinical Assembly, Naval Inst., Naval Res. Assn., Naval Enlisted Res. Assn., Res. Officers Assn., N.Y. Naval Militia, Popular Rotorcraft Assn. Avocations: chess, military history (ancient and medieval), Autogiro/gyrocopter flying and history. Office: Hofstra Univ 134 Hofstra Hempstead NY 11549-1340 E-mail: mgbbhc@hofstra.edu.

CHAROCHAK, DALE MICHAEL, airport executive; b. Pitts., Apr. 18, 1955; s. Michael and Alice (Nazak) C.; m. Kathleen Gallagher. BS in Biochemistry, U. Pitts., 1977. Contr. County Controller's Office, Pitts., 1977-80; contract supr. Dept. Aviation, Pitts., 1980-84, chief property adminstr., 1984-91; chief contract adminstr. Pitts. Internat. Airport, 1991-96, mgr. of compliance, 1996—2000, program mgr., 2000—. Former Dem. committeeman Moon, Pa., 1982-98, sch. bd. dir., legis. rep., 1983-85; bd. trustees Montour (Pa.) Football Orgn., 1979-81; Pa. state commr. Am. Wallyball Assn.; asst. scoutmaster Boy Scouts Am., Montour; softball coach Montour Girls; bd. dirs., co-chmn., Robinson Twp. Parks & Recreation, head girls softball coach. Mem. Am. Assn. Airport Execs. (bd. dirs. acad. com.), Pitts. Aero Club. Byzantine Catholic. Avocations: basketball, softball, wallyball, photography. Home: 502 Hidden Ct Mc Kees Rocks PA 15136-4004 Office: Pitts Internat Airport PO Box 12370 Ste 4000 Pittsburgh PA 15231-0370 E-mail: dcharochak@pitairport.com.

CHAROENWONGSE, CHINDARAT, pianist, educator, school administrator; b. Bangkok, Aug. 18, 1968; d. Vivat and Yuwadee Charoenwongse; m. George Grover Shaw, Sept. 25, 1999. BFA, Chulalongkorn U., Bangkok, 1989; M of Music Edn., U. Rochester, 1993; D of Musical Arts in Piano Performance, and Pedagogy, U. Okla., 1998. Instr. piano Chulalongkorn U., Bangkok, 1989-90; instr, lectr. piano Kasetsart U., Bangkok, 1990-91; exec. sec., adminstrv. asst. Johnson Electric Indsl. (Thailand) ltd., Bangkok, 1989-91; dir. piano dept. Chintakarn Music Inst., Bangkok, 1997-98; pianist, instr., dir. In Tune Music Co. Inc., Oklahoma City, 1999—; asst. prof. piano U. Ctrl. Okla., 2000—. Clinician, workshop presenter and cons., Alfred Publs., Bangkok, 1998, Chintakarn Music Inst., 1993, 97-98, 2000—, Hal Leonard Publs., Bangkok, 2000—; guest lectr. Chulalongkorn U., Bangkok, 1998, 2000—, Srinakharinwirot U., Prasanmitr Campus, 2000. Contbr. articles to profl. jours. Pianist Outreach Mission Com., Norman, Okla., 1996-97, 1999, St. John's Episcopal Ch., Norman, 1996-97. Fulbright scholar, 1991-93, Marjorie Martin Caylor scholar, U. Okla., Norman, 1994-96, Martha Boucher scholar, U. Okla., Norman, 1996-97; rsch. grantee U. Okla., Norman, 1997. Mem. Music Tchrs. Nat. Assn., Okla. Music Tchrs. Assn., Ctrl. Okla. Music tchrs. Assn. (co-chmn. notification com. 1998-2003), Phi Kappa Phi, Sigma Alpha Iota (sec. corr. com. 1996-97). Episcopalian. Avocations: travel, reading, musical performances, theater, opera. Office: U Ctrl Okla Sch Music 100 N Univ Dr Edmond OK 73034

CHARON, KENNETH ARNOLD, JR., artist; b. St. Albans, NY, July 26, 1954; s. Kenneth Arnold Sr. and Carol Oddo Charon; m. Nella P. Andrews Seriphine, Sept. 1984 (div. 1991); children: Roy Maxime, Nicole Anne; m. Rebecca L. Rosen, Aug. 2003. Student, Am. Coll. Switzerland, Leysin, 1972—74, Calif. Coll. Arts and Crafts, 1974—75, Academie Julian, Paris, 1976—77. Studio artist, Paris, 1978—83, Kurtistown, Hawaii, 1984—; exhibits installer East Hawaii Cultural Ctr., Hilo, 1990—. Artist in schs. Big Island (Hawaii) Dept. Edn., 1986—; founded Summit Session Art Expdn., 1989; invited to USSR for art exhibits, 90. Represented in permanent collection : V.P. Al Gore; exhibitions include 1st Schaefer Portrait Challenge, Maui Arts and Cultural Ctr., Kahului, Hawaii, 2003. Dir. Big Island Art Guild, Hilo, 1986—88, East Hawaii Cultural Ctr., Big Island, 1998—2000; co-chmn. Hawaii Green Party, Big Island, 2001—02. Recipient Painting prize, East Hawaii Cultural Ctr., 2001. Green Party. Avocations: homestead orchard, hiking, art history. Home: PO Box 742 Kurtistown HI 96760 E-mail: artfarm@aloha.net.

CHAROS, EVANGELOS NIKOLAOU, economics educator; b. Larnaca, Cyprus, Sept. 13, 1953; s. Nicos Demetriou Charos and Alexandra Charou; m. Maryann Andrews, Oct. 2, 1976; children: Nikolas, Alexandra, Melanie. Bs in Math., U. N.H., 1975, MA in Econs., 1978, PhD in Econs., 1984. Instr. Nasson Coll., Springvale, Maine, 1980—83; asst. prof. Merrimack Coll., North Andover, Mass., 1983—88, assoc. prof. econs., 1988—94, prof. econs., 1994—, chmn. econs. dept., 2001—. Asst. dir. computer svcs. U. N.H., Durham, 1976-80. Asst. editor, data base mgr. Internat. Bus. Conditions Digest, 1980-83. Mem. Am. Econ. Assn., Northeast Bus. & Econs. Assn., Internat. Assn. Bus. Forecasters, Omicron Delta Epsilon. Greek Orthodox. Home: 1 Center Dr Dover NH 03820-4646 E-mail: evangelosc@aol.com., evangelos.charos@merrimack.edu.

CHARPAK, GEORGES, physicist, nuclear scientist; b. Dabrovica, Poland, Aug. 1, 1924;, naturalized, France, 1946; s. Maurice and Anna (Szapiro) C.; m. Dominique Vidal, 1953; children: Yves, Nathalie, Serge. BSc in Engring., Ecole des Mines de Paris, 1948; PhD in Physics, Collège de France, 1954; doctorate (hon.), U. Geneva, 1977, U. Thessalonica, Greece, 1993, Vrije Univ. Brussels, 1994, U. Coimbra, Portugal, 1994, U. Ottawa, Can., 1995, U. Rio de Janeiro, 1996. Lic. civil mining engr. Prof. Centre Nation de la Recherche Scientifique, 1948-59, Centre Européen pour la Recherche Nucléaire, Geneva, 1959—; rschr. Cern Lab. for Particle Physics, Geneva. Joliot-Curie prof. Ecole Supérieure de Physique et Chimie de la Ville de Paris, 1984—. Contbr. articles to profl. jours. With French Army, prisoner of war, Dachau. Decorated chevalier Legion of Honor, Mil. Cross 39-45, Croix de Guerre (France), Officer Nat. Order of Merit; recipient Paul Ricard prize French Soc. Physics, 1980, High Energy and Particle Physics prize, 1989, Nobel prize for physics, 1992. Mem. NAS (fgn. assoc.), French Acad. Scis. (Commissariat prize of Atomic Energy 1984), Austrian Acad. Scis. (hon.), Russian Acad. Scis. (fgn.), Lisboa Acad. Scis. (corr.), French Acad. Medicine (nat. corr. mem.). Achievements include invention of multiwire proportional chambers, drift chambers, diverse types of flash chambers without photography; development of particle detectors in high energy physics, installations for biological research using Beta-ray imagery; new fast gaseous detector adapted to accelerators to be constructed; research in in nuclear structure by reactions. Home: 2 rue de Poissy 75005 Paris France Office: CERN Lab for Particle Physics CH 1211 Geneva Switzerland

CHARPENTIER, GAIL WIGUTOW, private school executive director; b. N.Y.C., Mar. 10, 1946; d. Jacob M. and Ethel (Israel) Wigutow; m. Peter Jon Charpentier; children: Elisabeth Marie, Matthew Kyle. BA, CUNY, 1967; MA, New Sch. Social Research, N.Y.C., 1976; PhD, LaSalle U., 2002. Lic. social worker; cert. adminstr. of spl. edn. Tchr. Spl. Service Pub. Sch., Bronx, N.Y., 1967-73; adminstr. Boston City Hosp., 1973-76; dir. Monson Devel. Ctr., Palmer, Mass., 1976; residential dir. Kolburne Sch., New Marlboro, Mass., 1976-79; exec. dir. Berkshire Meadows, Housatonic, Mass., 1979—. Rschr. Nat. Opinion Rsch. Ctr., N.Y.C. and Boston, 1973-76; trainer residential child care, Mass., 1978—; mem. human rights bd. Oakdale Found., Great Barrington, 1980-90. Recipient Community Criminal Justice award Justice Resource Inst., 1984. Mem. NAFE, Am. Assn. Mental Retardation, Mass. Assn. Approved Pvt. Schs. (bd. dirs. 1982-84, ins. trustee 1984-87, svc. award 1982), New Eng. Assn. for Child Care, Rotary, Berkshire Profl. Women, Hop Brook Club (pres.). Avocations: skiing, tennis, sailing, bass fishing, golf. Home: Orchard House PO Box 406 Tyringham MA 01264-0406 Office: Berkshire Meadows 249 N Plain Rd Housatonic MA 01236-9736 E-mail: gcharpentier@jri.org.

CHARPENTIER, KEITH LIONEL, school system administrator; b. Attleboro, Mass., Mar. 6, 1959; s. David L. and Matilda (Marchand) C. AS, Mitchell Coll., 1980; BS, Plymouth State Coll., 1982, MEd in Guidance and Counseling, 1992, cert. advanced studies adminstrn./supr., 1999. Cert. phys. edn. and health sci. tchr., N.H.; cert. reality therapist; cert. guidance dir., N.H.; rsch. for better tchg. cert. observing and analyzing tchrs. Health, sci. tchr. SAU #23 Sch. System, Woodsville, N.H., 1982-84; counselor F.L. Chamberlain Sch., Lyman, N.H., 1984-86; spl. edn. tchr. Blue Mt. Union Sch., Wells River, Vt., 1985-86; dean of students, counselor Pike (N.H.) Sch. Inc., 1986-93; guidence counselor New Found Mid. Sch., Bristol, N.H., 1993-98, dean students, vice prin., 1998—. Instr. assoc. level Crisis Prevention Inst., Brookfield, Wis., 1989—, Drug/Alcohol Edn., Meredith, N.H., 1988—. Life Skills Edn., Granville, Ohio, 1987—; pvt. provider outpatient counseling Divsn. Children, Youth and Families, Dept. Health and Human Svcs., State of N.H., 1992—. Vol. firefighter, capt. Haverhill Corner Fire Dept. Recipient Mitchell Coll. Athletic Trainers award, 1980. Mem. ASCD, ACA, Nat. Athletic Trainers Assn., Nat. Mid. Sch. Assn., N.H. Assn. of Sch. Principals, Nat. Assn. of Secondary Sch. Principals, Phi Delta Kappa. Avocations: sports, coaching, skiing, fishing, hunting, photography, gardening. Home: 214 Rockcreek Dr North Haverhill NH 03774

CHARPIE, ROBERT ALAN, physicist, researcher; b. Cleve., Sept. 9, 1925; s. Leonard Asbury and Dorothy (McLean) C.; m. Elizabeth Downs, July 12, 1947; children: Richard Alan, Carol Elizabeth, David Wayne, John Robert. BS with honors, Carnegie Inst. Tech., 1948, MS, 1949, D.Sc. in Theoretical Physics, 1950; D.H.L., Denison U., 1965; D.Sc., Alderson-Broaddus Coll., 1967; LL.D., Marietta Coll., 1975; D.Sc., Boston Coll., 1982. With Westinghouse Electric Corp., 1947-50; with Oak Ridge Nat. Lab., 1950-51, tech. asst. to research dir., 1952-54, asst. research dir., 1954-58, dir. reactor divsn., 1958-61; mgr. adv. devel. Union Carbide Corp., 1961-63, gen. mgr. devel. dept., 1963-64, dir. tech., 1964-66, pres. electronics divsn., 1966-68; pres. Bell & Howell Co., Chgo., 1968-69, Cabot Corp., Boston, 1969-86, also. bd. dirs., chmn. Waltham, Mass., 1986-88, Ampersand Ventures, Wellesley, Mass., 1988—. Trustee Mitre Corp., Boston, 1966-82, chmn., 1972-82; sec. gen. adv. com. AEC, 1959-63; mem. Nat. Sci. Bd., 1969-76; sci. sec., editor-in-chief proc., also asst. U.S. mem. 7 nation adv. com. 1st Internat. Conf. Peaceful Uses Atomic Energy, 1955; coordinator U.S. fusion research exhibit, 2d Conf., 1958; chmn. invention and innovation panel U.S. Dept. Commerce, 1965-67. Gen. editor: Internat. Monograph Series on Nuclear Energy, 1955-60; editor: Progress Series in Nuclear Energy, 1955-60, Jour. Nuclear Energy, 1955-60. Mem. Oak Ridge Bd. Edn., 1957-61; pres. Byram Hills Central Sch. Dist., 1966-68; trustee Carnegie Inst. Tech., 1962—. Recipient Alumni Merit award Carnegie Inst. Tech., 1957 Fellow Am. Phys. Soc., Am. Nuclear Soc. (dir.), mem. N.Y. Acad. Sci., Nat. Acad. Engring., Sigma Xi, Tau Beta Pi, Phi Mu Epsilon. Office: Ampersand Ventures 55 William St Ste 240 Wellesley MA 02481-4003

CHARRIEZ, BLANCA NOELIA, social worker; b. Bayamon, P.R., Sept. 27, 1947; d. Luis and Juanita (Robles) C.; m. William F. Quinn, 1995. Student, Barnard Coll., 1965-66; BA, Brandeis U., 1969; MS in Social Svcs., Boston U., 1971. Lic. ind. clin. social worker, Mass., N.Mex. Group worker Roxbury (Mass.) Comprehensive Cmty. Health Ctr., 1971—72; counselor-lectr. Herbert Lehman Coll., CUNY, Bronx, 1972-75; social worker Family Svc. Assn. Greater Boston, 1975-79; family svcs. coord. follow through prog. Cambridge (Mass.) Sch. Dept., 1979-81; counselor Boston U. Counseling Ctr., 1982-86; project dir. Hispanic mentoring program Boston U., 1984-86; sr. counselor U. Mich. Counseling Ctr., Ann Arbor, 1987-88; sr. clin. social worker Boston U. Counseling Ctr., 1989-95; therapist Raton (N.Mex.) Mental Health Clinic, 1995—; pvt. practice, 1996—. Grantee, Hispanic, Asian and Native-Am. Ministries, United Meth. Ch., 1984-86. Mem. NASW (diplomate, com. on racial and ethnic affairs Mass. chpt. 1990-95), APA, Bus. and Profl. Women. Democrat. Avocations: travel, journal writing. Home: 545 Rio Grande Ave Raton NM 87740-3950 Office: Raton Mental Health 220 4th Ave Raton NM 87740-3907 Office Fax: 505-445-2225.

CHARRIEZ, LASTON SAMUEL, marketing professional, director; b. Santo Domingo, Dominican Republic, Sept. 8, 1964; s. Samuel and Iraida Charriez; m. Angie Charriez, Mar. 31, 1990; children: Kenneth George, Nicolle Kamille. BS in Mgmt./Mktg., Purdue U. Krannert Sch. of Mgmt., West Lafayette, Ind., 1985—85, MS in Mgmt. /Mktg., 1987. Asst. brand mgr. Procter & Gamble PR, San Juan, 1987—90; brand mgr./mktg. mgr. Procter & Gamble Ctrl. Am., Guatemala City, Guatemala, 1990—94; mktg. mgr. health care Procter & Gamble, Mex. City, Mexico, 1994—95; mktg. mgr./mktg. dir. paper & food and beverage Procter & Gamble PR, San Juan, 1996—99; mktg. dir. Latin Am. tissue & towel Procter & Gamble L.Am., Caracas, Venezuela, 1999—2000; mktg. dir. N. Am. charmin & puffs Procter & Gamble N.Am. Family Care, Cin., 2000—. Bd. mem. Greater Cin. Hispanic Chamber of Commerce, Cincinnati, Ohio, 2000—; Procter & Gamble rep. US Hispanic C. of C., Washington a, 2002—. Scholar Full Scholarship, PR Econ. Devel. Dept., 1985-1987. Independent. Avocations: mountain biker, long distance runner. Office: Procter & Gamble Family Care 6105 Center Hill Ave Cincinnati OH 45244

CHARRON, HELENE KAY SHETLER, retired nursing educator; b. West Bloomfield, N.Y., Nov. 17, 1937; d. Ellis John and Helene Esther (Moore) Shetler; m. Ronald W. Charron, July 1964; children: Michele Gefell, Andrea Hagen. Diploma, Rochester State Hosp. Sch., N.Y., 1958; BS in Nursing, U. Rochester, 1964, MS in Nursing Edn., 1965. Staff nurse Strong Meml. Hosp., Rochester, 1958-60; head nurse Monroe Community Hosp., Rochester, 1961-63; coord. psychiat. nursing Monroe Community Coll., 1965-87; mental hygiene staff devel. specialist Rochester Psychiat. Ctr., 1982-83; chairperson dept. nursing Monroe Community Coll., Rochester, 1987-95; ptnr. Initiatives in Nursing Edn., West Bloomfield, N.Y., 1995—. Cons., lectr. on integration of Computer Assisted Instruction in nursing curricula and hosp. staff devel. Writer numerous instructional computer programs, ancillaries, test banks, videotapes and games in field. Office: 9148 Dugway Rd West Bloomfield NY 14585-0196

CHARRON, JOSEPH L. bishop; b. Redfield, SD, Dec. 30, 1939; Ordained priest Roman Cath. Ch. 1967. Asst. theology prof. St. John's U., Collegeville, Minn., 1970—76; asst. gen. sec. U.S. Catholic Conf., 1976—79; assoc. gen. sec. Nat. Conf. Cath. Bishops, 1976—79; Kansas City Provincial dir. CPPS, 1979—87; aux. bishop Diocese of St. Paul/Mpls., 1990—93; bishop Diocese of Des Moines, 1994—. Admin. comm. Nat. Conf. Cath. Bishops/U.S. Cath. Conf. Mem.: Cath. Theol. Soc. Am., Soc. Precious Blood. Roman Catholic. Office: Chancery 601 Grand Ave Des Moines IA 50309*

CHARRON, PAUL RICHARD, apparel company executive; b. Schenectady, N.Y., Aug. 24, 1942; s. Richard Armand and Helen Marie (Barringer) C.; m. Kathy Lyn Herdt, June 29, 1974; children: Bradley, Ashley. BA, U. Notre Dame, 1964; MBA, Harvard U., 1971. Brand mgr. Procter & Gamble Corp., Cin., 1971-78; category mgr. Gen. Foods Corp., White Plains, N.Y., 1978-81; sr. v.p. sales, mktg. Cannon Mills Co., N.Y. and N.C., 1981-83; pres., chief operating officer Atwater Group, Inc., St. Paul, 1983-87; pres., chief oper. officer Brown & Bigelow, St. Paul, 1983-87; exec. v.p. VF Corp., Wyomissing, Pa., 1988-94; chmn., CEO Liz Claiborne Inc., N.Y.C., 1994—. Lt. USN, 1964-69, Vietnam. Decorated Meritorious Service medal. Office: Liz Claiborne Inc 1441 Broadway Fl 22 New York NY 10018-2088*

CHARRY, MICHAEL R(ONALD), musician, conductor; b. N.Y.C., Aug. 28, 1933; s. Harold Paul and Sylvia C.; m. Jane Thoms, Mar. 31, 1956; children: Stephen Walter, Barbara. Student, Oberlin Conservatory Music, 1950-52; BS, Juilliard Sch. Music, 1955, MS in Orch. Conducting, 1956; studies with, Jean Morel, Pierre Monteux, Hans Schmidt-Isserstedt, George Szell. Competition artistic advisor New Internat. Music Festival, Seoul, Republic of Korea, 1999—2001, artistic dir., 2001—02. Mem. faculty Mannes Coll. Music, 1988-99, head, orch. conducting, 1989-99, music dir. Mannes Coll. Music Orch., 1989-99; chmn. Music Consortium of Nashville, 1977-79, Nashville Inst. Arts, 1979-80. Condr., pianist, José Limón Modern Dance Co. tours, Europe, 1957, South and Central Am., 1960, Far East, 1963; asst. condr., prin. oboist, R.I. Philharmonic, 1960-61; music dir., condr., Canton Symphony Orch., 1961-74; apprentice condr., Cleve. Orch., 1961-65, asst. condr., 1965-72; music dir., condr., Nashville Symphony Orch., 1976-82, Peninsula Music Festival, 1978-82; guest condr. concerts, operas, U.S. and Europe; assoc. prof. orchestral conducting, dir. orchestral activities, Syracuse U. (N.Y.), 1983-85; prof., mus. dir. orchestral and opera programs Boston U. Sch. Music, 1984-87; contbr. Sony Classical Masterworks Heritage CDs, The Revised New Grove Dict. of Music and Musicians. With U.S. Army, 1958-60. Fulbright scholar, 1956-57; Martha Baird Rockefeller grantee, 1975, Elizabeth Ring Mather and William Gwinn

Mather Fund grantee, 1991, 94, 97; recipient Alice M. Ditson award Columbia U., 1981, Spl. Merit award Tenn. Arts Commn., 1982. Mem. Am. Symphony Orch. League, Condrs. Guild (bd. dirs. 1983-95, 1st v.p. 1989-91, pres. 1991-93).

CHARSKY, THOMAS ROBERT, elementary education educator; b. Binghamton, N.Y., Feb. 20, 1952; s. Matthew J. and Margaret L. (Katusak) C. BM, Cath. U. Am., 1974, MM, 1986. Cert. music tchr., N.J. Vocal music tchr. Clifton (N.J.) Bd. Edn., 1981—. Adj. prof. music William Paterson U., Wayne, NJ, 2001—. Recipient Gov.'s Tchr. Recognition award; named Passaic County Tchr. of Yr., 1988-89. Mem.: NEA, Clifton Tchrs. Assn. (pres., Educator of Yr. 1993), N.N.J. Orff-Schulwerk Assn. (membership sec., treas., v.p., pres.), Am. Orff-Schulwerk Assn. (nat. trustee, region V rep.), N.J. Music Educators Assn., Music Educator Nat. Conf., N.J. Edn. Assn., Phi Mu Alpha. Home: 54 Beverly Hill Rd Clifton NJ 07012-1402

CHARTERS, ALEXANDER NATHANIEL, retired adult education educator; b. Verdant Valley, Alta., Can., Aug. 22, 1916; came to U.S., 1948, naturalized, 1957. s. Alexander Allen and Louisa Magdalena (Kern) C.; m. Margaret Anne MacNaughton, Mar. 29, 1952; children: A. William, David W., John C., Louisa A. Vike. BA, U. B.C., 1938; PhD, U. Chgo., 1948. Tchr. pub. schs., Fernie, B.C., 1939-41, Vancouver, 1941-42; asst. to dean Univ. Coll., Syracuse U., 1948-50, asst. dean, 1950-52, dean, 1952-64, asst. prof. Sch. Edn., 1950-54, assoc. prof., 1954-59, prof., 1959-83, prof. emeritus, 1983—, area chmn. for adult edn., 1950-80, univ. v.p. for continuing edn., 1964-73. Vis. faculty U. Chgo., 1958; UNESCO del. Internat. Conf. on Adult Edn., UNESCO, 1972; observer, del., Tokyo, 1972, Paris, 1985; coord. US participation pvt. sector CONFINTEA V, Hamburg, also observer and U.S. del., 1997, mem. U.S. del. team, 1997; cons. UNESCO Inst. for Edn., 1998; mem. standing com. 5th World Conf. on History of Adult Edn., 1991; mem. steering com. Internat. Assocs., 1991—; chmn. program com. Internat. Conf. Rethinking Adult Edn. for Devel., Ljubljana, Slovenia, 1993; adv. S. Rodriguez U., Caracas, Venezuela, 1994; external examiner adult edn. U. Madras, 1996; presenter edn. conf., Jena, Germany, 1996; cons. in adult edn. Inst. Pedagogida Rural, Venezuela, 1998; founding cons. Academic Inst. Educators of Adults, 1998; cons. to field. Author numerous books and publs. Mem. bd. Ctr. Study Liberal Edn. Adults, 1957-67, chmn., 1964-65; mem. Internat. Coun. for Adult Edn. (hon. 1998); founding mem., treas. Internat. Congress U. Adult Edn., 1962-67; mem. N.Y. State Adv. Bd. on Continuing Higher Edn.; chmn. Galaxy Conf. Adult Edn. Orgns., 1969; chmn. priorities com. Cmty. Chest and Coun.; trustee Chautauqua Inst., 1960-69; bd. mem. Laubach Literacy Internat., 1965-70, sec., 1967-70; trustee Ctrl. N.Y. UN Assn., Syracuse World Affairs Edn. Orgns.; mem. U.S. Nat. Com. UNESCO, presenter 5th world assembly, Cairo, 1994; bd. visitors U. Pitts., Washington U., St. Louis; founding mem., bd. dirs. Coalition Adult Edn. Orgn., 1964-82; exec. bd. dirs. Westminster Manor Ctr.; bd. dirs., treas. Vandercamp Conf. and Recreation Ctr., 1991-95, Ctrl. N.Y. Presbytery Conf. Ctr., 1991; clk. of session, elder Park Ctrl. Presbyn. Ch. With Royal Can. Naval Vol. Res., 1942-45. Recipient William Pearson Tolley medal for disting. leadership in adult edn. Syracuse U., 1986, Lifetime Achievement award Ctrl. N.Y. Coalition on Adult and Cont. Edn.; Alexander Charters Libr. Resources for Educators of Adults named for him Syracuse U., 1998. Mem. Assn. Continuing Higher Edn. (pres. 1947-48, Leadership citation 1973), Am. Assn. Adult Continuing Edn. (Pioneer award 1980), Nat. U. Continuing Edn. Assn. (pres. 1965-66, Bitner award 1973, Alexander N. Charters award 1999), Internat. Coun. Adult Edn. (founder 1972, chair documentation 1974, coord. confs., mem. Internat. Adult and Continuing Edn. Hall of Fame 1996, Scroll of Appreciation 1990), Internat. Soc. Comparative Adult Edn. (founding pres. 1992), Acad. Inst. Educators of Adults (founding cons. 1998), Ctrl. N.Y. Coalition on Adult and Continuing Edn. (lifetime achievement award 1998), Rotary (internat. Paul Harris fellow 1992), Beta Theta Pi. Home: 216 Lockwood Rd Syracuse NY 13214-2035 E-mail: ancharte@mailbox.syr.edu.

CHARTERS, ANN, biographer, editor, educator; b. Bridgeport, Conn., Nov. 10, 1936; d. Nathan and Kate Danberg; m. Samuel B. Charters, Mar. 14, 1959; children: Mallay, Nora Lili. AB, U. Calif.-Berkeley, 1957; MA, Columbia U., 1960, PhD, 1965. Mem. faculty Colby Jr. Coll., New London, NH, 1961—63; lectr. Columbia U., 1965—66; asst. prof. Am. lit. N.Y.C. Community Coll., 1967-70; assoc. dean of the coll. Brown U., 1989-90; prof. Am. lit. U. Conn., Storrs, 1974—. Author: Nobody—Life and Times of Bert Williams, 1967, Kerouac, 1973, 2d edit., 1986, I Love—Story of Vladimir Mayakovsky and Lili Brik, 1979, The Story and Its Writer, 6th edit., 2002, The Beats: Literary Bohemians in Post-War America, 1983, Beats and Company: A Portrait of a Literary Generation, 1986, The Viking Portable Beat Reader, 1992, Major Writers of Short Fiction, 1993, The Viking Portable Jack Kerouac Reader, 1995, Selected Letters of Jack Kerouac, 1995, (with Samuel Charters) Literature and Its Writers, 1997; author intro. Penguin Classic edit. Three Lives and Q.E.D. (Gertrude Stein), On the Road (Jack Kerouac), Selected Letters of Jack Kerouac, vol. 2, 1999, The American Short Story and Its Writer, 1999, (with Samuel Charters) Blues Faces, 2000, Beat Down to Your Soul, 2000, The Portable Sixties Reader, 2003. Office: U Conn Dept English PO Box U-25 Storrs Mansfield CT 06269-0001 E-mail: acharters@uconn.edu.

CHARTERS, KAREN ANN ELLIOTT, critical care nurse, health facility administrator; b. Chelsea, Mass., Apr. 3, 1946; d. Albert Charles and Hazelle Marie (Kraus) Elliott; m. Byron James Charters, Feb. 4, 1972. Diploma, Grace New Haven Sch. Nursing, New Haven, Conn., 1967; student, So. Conn. State Coll., 1968, U. New Haven, 1974; BS in Healthcare Adminstrn., St. Leo Coll., 1999. Cert. CCRN. Asst. head nurse Yale New Haven (Conn.) Hosp., 1972-76; staff nurse critical care unit Hosp. Corp. Am., 1982—; relief clin. coord. Cmty. Hosp. of New Port Richey, Fla., 1987—, nursing supr., 1997—. Mem. AACN (bd. dirs. Gulf Coast chpt. 1990-91, 96-97, treas. 1991-93), Am. Heart Assn. (past bd. dirs.). Home: 7519 Clanton Trail Hudson FL 34667 Office: Cmty Hosp New Port Richey 5637 Marine Pkwy New Port Richey FL 34652

CHARTIER, KIRK LEE FREUND, business services executive; b. Chgo., July 27, 1963; s. George William Freund, Imogene Rasmussen; m. Michele Renee Chartier; children: Max children: Kate. BSCE with highest distinction, Worcester Poly. Inst., Mass., 1986; BA in Econs., Coll. of the Holy Cross, Worcester, 1986; MBA, Syracuse Un., 1996. Cert. mgmt. acct. 2001, instrument flight rating 1988, lic. comml. airline pilot 1988. Auditor GE Co., Fairfield, Conn., 1996—97; strategy dir. RCA, Inc., Irvine, Calif., 1997—98; sr. dir. Answerthink, Inc., Atlanta, 1998—2002; SVP cons. Commerce Quest, Tampa, Fla., 2002—. Examiner Malcolm Baldrige Nat. Quality Award, Washington, 1996—99. Lt. col. USMC, 1981—. Decorated Air Medal, Navy Commendation Medal (3); recipient Silver Medal---Leadership, Naval Assn., 1994. Mem.: Marine Corps Rse. Officer's Assn. (life). Republican. Episcopalian. Home: 2879 Normandy Dr NW Atlanta GA 30305 Personal E-mail: kirk_chartier@hotmail.com.

CHARTIER, TIMOTHY P. mathematician, educator; s. Myron R. and Janet A. Chartier; m. Tanya R. Harman, Aug. 20, 1994; 1 child, Noah L. PhD in Applied Math., U. of Colo., Boulder, 2001; student, with Marcel Marceau, Marc Bauman, San Francisco. Cert. Sun Java Academic faculty Sun Microsystems, 2000. Summer intern Lawrence Livermore Nat. Lab., Livermore, Calif., 1998—2000. Mime and puppeteer (perform/teach at international levels) Mime-ation (mime)/ Inanimates (puppets). Recipient Student and New PhD paper award, Copper Mountain Conf. on Iterative Methods, 2002, AMS Project NExT Fellow, Math. Assn. of Am., 2002-2003; fellow Preparing Future Faculty fellow, U. of Colo., 1998—2001; grantee R & D of spectral AMGe, Lawrence Livermore Nat. Lab., 2002; Phi Kappa Phi fellow, Western Mich. U. Chpt., 1993. Mem.: Math. Assn. of Am., Soc. of Applied Mathematicians. Avocations: juggling, unicycling, trail running, cycling. Office: University of Washington Box 354350 Seattle WA 98195 Personal E-mail: timchartier@hotmail.com.

CHARTIER, VERNON LEE, electrical engineer; b. Feb. 14, 1939; s. Raymond Earl and Margaret Clara (Winegar) C.; m. Lois Marie Schwartz, May 20, 1967; 1 child, Neal Raymond. BSEE, BS in Bus., U. Colo., 1963. Registered profl. engr., Pa.; cert. electromagnetic compatibility engr. Rsch. engr., cons. Westinghouse Electric Co., East Pitts., Pa., 1963-75; prin. engr. high voltage phenomena Bonneville Power Adminstrn., Vancouver, Wash., 1975-95; power sys. EMC cons. Portland, 1995—. Contbr. articles to profl. jours. Fellow IEEE (fellow com. 1993-96, Herman Halperin Transmission and Distbn. award 1995, 3d Millennium medal 2000, chmn. Herman Halperin Transmission & Distbn. Award com.); mem. Power Engring. Soc. of IEEE (chmn. transmission and distbn. com. 1987-88, chmn. fellows com. 1990-92), Internat. Conf. Large High Voltage Electric Sys. (Attwood Assoc. award 1999), Chartier Family Assn. Baptist. Home and Office: 13095 SW Glenn Ct Beaverton OR 97008-5664 E-mail: vlchartier@ieee.org.

CHARTOFF, ROBERT IRWIN, film producer; b. N.Y.C. s. William and Bessie Chartoff; children: Jenifer, William, Julie, Charley, Miranda. AB, Union Coll., 1955; LLB, Columbia U., 1958. Producer: numerous films including Double Trouble, 1967, Point Blank, 1967, The Split, 1968, Leo the Last, 1969, They Shoot Horses Don't They, 1969, The Strawberry Statement, 1970, The Gang That Couldn't Shoot Straight, 1971, The New Centurions, 1972, The Mechanic, 1972, Up the Sandbox, 1972, Busting, 1974, Peeper, 1975, The Gambler, 1975, Rocky, 1976 (Acad. award for best picture), Nickelodeon, 1976, New York, New York, 1977, Valentino, 1977, Comes A Horseman, 1978, Uncle Joe Shannon, 1978, Rocky II, 1979, Raging Bull, 1980, True Confessions, 1981, Rocky III, 1982, The Right Stuff, 1983, Rocky IV, 1985, Beer, 1986, Rocky V, 1990, Straight Talk, 1992. Office: Chartoff Prodns Inc 1250 6th St Ste 101 Santa Monica CA 90401-1612 E-mail: chartoffprod@cs.com.

CHARTON, MARVIN, chemist, educator; b. Bklyn., May 1, 1931; s. William and Elsie (Halpern) C.; m. Barbara Israel, Aug. 28, 1955; children— Michael, Sarah, Deborah. BS, CCNY, 1953; MA, Bklyn. Coll., 1956; PhD, Stevens Inst. Tech., 1962. Instr. chemistry Pratt Inst., Bklyn., 1956-61, asst. prof., 1961-64, asso. prof., 1964-67, prof., 1967—, chmn. dept., 1969—. Vis. prof. Polymer Rsch. Inst., Poly. U., Bklyn., 1985—. Editor: Advances in Quantitative Structure Property Relationships Vol. 1, 1996, Advances in Quantitative Structure Property Relationships Vol. 2, 1999, Advances in Quantitative Structure Property Relationships Vol. 3, 2002; co-editor: Topics in Current Chemistry, vol. 114, 1983; contbr. articles to profl. jours.; mem. editl. bd.: Quantitative Structure, Activity Relationships. Fellow AAAS, Intrasci. Rsch. Found.; mem. Am. Chem. Soc., Internat. Group for Correlation Analysis in Chemistry, Internat. QSAR Soc., Royal Chem. Soc. London, N.Y. Acad. Scis., Sigma Xi. Home: 1 Grace Ct Brooklyn NY 11201-4195 E-mail: mcharton@pratt.edu.

CHARTRAND, ROBERT LEE, information scientist; b. Kansas City, Mo., Mar. 6, 1928; s. Joseph Sterling, Jr. and Isabel Christine (Doherty) C.; m. Eleanor Salmon, Oct. 9, 1967; children: Leslie, Kevin; stepchildren: James, Jennifer. BA, U. Mo., Kansas City, 1948, MA, 1949; postgrad., La. State U., 1949-50, U. Mo., 1956. Staff Whatsoever Circle Community House, 1950; supr. phys. recreation welfare dept. City of Kansas City, Mo., 1951, chief rec. supr., 1956; mem. tech. staff Nat. Photo Intelligence Ctr., 1959; Mem. tech. staff Thompson-Ramo-Wooldridge (TRW), Denver and Canoga Park, Calif., 1959-61; with fed. system div. IBM Corp., Bethesda, Md., 1961-64, mgr. advanced systems mktg., 1964; mgr. applications devel. Planning Research Corp., Washington, 1964-66; specialist in info. sci. Congressional Research Service, Library of Congress, Washington, 1966-77, sr. specialist in info. policy and tech., 1977-88, sr. fellow in info. policy and tech., 1988-90. Fulbright-Hays lectr., 1968, UN lectr., 1979; cons. Pres.'s Commn. on Population Growth and Am. Future, 1970-71, U.S. Commn. Civil Rights, 1972-78, George Washington U., 1975-77, UNESCO, 1977, Exec. Office of Pres., 1977-82, Office of Tech. Assessment, 1979-89, NAS, 1981-83, Nat. Acad. Pub. Adminstrn. Sr. Res. Assoc., 1995—, sr. cons. Global Disaster Info. Network, 1997-2001, IRS, 1985-86, Dept. Energy, 1986, Fed. Election Com., 1976-77, U.S. Dept. Commerce, 1985-88, GSA, 1983, 86, 92-96, OMB, 1995-97, Fed. Emergency Mgmt. Agy., 1986-88, NASA, 1993, Carnegie Commn. on Sci., Tech. and Govt., 1993-94, NLM, 1994-95, Turner Edn. Svcs., 1994-96, inSite Learning, Inc., 2001-02, World Future Soc., 1997—, Nat. Reconnaissance Office, 2002; adj. fellow Ctr. for Strategic and Internat. Studies, 1990-95, sr. assoc., 2003—, Disaster Mgmt. Ptnrs., 2002; mem. STI bd. NAS/NRC, 1990-91, mapping sci. com., 1990-93; mem. adv. coun. Nat. Inst. Urban Search and Rescue, 1991—; mem. Extreme Info. Infrastructure (XII) Technical Working Group, 1999—; adj. prof. Am. U., 1974-78; lectr. U.S. Info. Agy., 1977; sr. lectr. UN Devel. Program, 1979; vis. prof. UCLA, 1982, U. Pitts., 1989, 1991-2001 mem. adv. bd. coll. info. studies U. Md., 1999—; lectr. Internat. Coll., 2000-01, Fla. Gulf Coast U., 2000-02; spl. advisor Open Systems Conf. Bd., 1990-94, Internat. Green Cross, 1993-94; mem. program adv. bd. Govt. Tech. Leadership Inst., 1998-2000; mem. adv. com. US-CSC, 1973-80, White House Conf. on Libr. and Info. Svcs., 1979-80; adv. NSF, 1977-79; mem. planning panel for toxicology and environment NLM, 1991-92; mem. adv. panel Dept. State, 1978-84; NLM, 1985-86, 91-92; mem. adv. bd. Chem. Abstracts Svc., 1979-84, Info. Inst., 1983-86, Econ. Devel. Found., 1985-90, Ency. Libr. and Info. Sci., 1986—, Internat. Design for Extreme Environments Assembly, 1991-95, Partnership for Intergovtl. Innovation (Pi2), 2000—, Internat. Energy Mgmt. & Engr. Soc., 1993, 94-96, S.W. Fla. Emergency Adv. Bd., 1993-99, Collier County Disaster Recovery Coalition Com., 1995-99, Collier County Pub. Safety Com., 1999-2000, Greater Naples Leadership Alumni Coun., 1999-2001; mem. bd. visitors FEMA Emergency Mgmt. Inst., 1987-89; proj. devel. cons. U. Mo., Kansas City, 1985-89, White House Conf. Libr. and Info. Svc., 1990-91; spl. cons. U. Mo. Sys., 1991, 93; nat. bd. dirs. Alliance of Info. and Referral Sys, 1994-98; bd. govs. Naples Inst., 1994-97, Internat. Coun. for Computer Commns., 1994—, sr. adv. Stennis Ctr. Pub. Svc., 1998-2000. Author: Systems Technology Applied to Social and Community Problems, 1971, Computers and Political Campaigning, 1972, (with others) State Legislature Use of Information Technology, 1978, Opportunities for the Use of Information Resources and Advanced Technologies in Congress, 1993; also congl. studies; editor, contbg. author: Information Support, Program Budgeting and the Congress, 1968; editor, contbg. author: Computers in the Service of Society, 1972, Critical Issues in the Information Age, 1991; editor: Hope for the Cities: A Systems Approach to Human Needs, 1971; co-editr, contbg. author: Information Technology Serving Society, 1979, Strategies and Systems for Disaster Survival, 1989; editorial bd.: Law and Computer Tech, 1968-82, The Information Society, 1979—, Hazard, 1979-95, Futures Res. Quar., 1987—, Am. Fedn. Info. Processing Socs. Washington Report, 1989-90; editorial adviser: Rutgers Jour. Computers and the Law, 1970-72, ASK, 1987-86, ASIS Bull., 1979-91, cons. editor: Info. Storage and Retrieval, 1969-74, SIAM News, 1976-79; contbr. articles to profl. jours. Trustee Windham Coll., 1974-76, Engring. Info., 1980-83, Capital Children's Mus., 1982-86; vice chmn. Friends of Montgomery County Libr., 1984-87; cons. advisor Smithsonian Inst., 1986-90; bd. dirs. Friends of Libr. Collier County, Fla., 1991—, v.p., 1993-95, pres.-elect, 1994, pres., 1995-96, exec. com., 1997-2000; mem. Leadership Collier Masters, 1996-97, class chmn., 1997-98, mem. adv. com., 1997-99; mem. MPA adv. com. Fla. Gulf Coast U., 1997-98, mem. external rels. coun., 1999—. With U.S. Naval Intelligence, 1952-59. Decorated Cavaliere Ufficiale Italy; named to Govt. Computer News Hall of Fame, 1988; recipient Interagy. Com. on ADP award, 1976, Test of Time award, 1979, Alumni Achievement award, U. Mo., Kansas City, 1984, Internat. Emergency Mgmt. and Engring Soc. Life Achievement award, 1993, Libr. of Congress award for Superior Svc., 1988, Cert. of Appreciation, Congl. Rsch. Svc., 1988, Outstanding Svc. award, 1994. Fellow AAAS (sect. chmn. 1983-84); mem. Am. Soc. Info. Sci. and Tech. (cons. editor bull. 1974-90), cert. appreciation 1976, award of merit 1985, Pioneer award 1988, 99), Nat. Coun. on World Affairs, Naval Intelligence Profls., Cosmos Club, Kenwood Golf and Country Club, Naples Bath and Tennis Club. Unitarian Universalist. Home: 5101 River Rd Apt 1402 Bethesda MD 20816-1570 E-mail: rlchartrand@prodigy.net. *If there is to be a future, every effort must be expended by technologists and humanitarians alike to meld their philosophies and pragmatic undertakings. The global dimensions and impacts of mankind's major initiatives are inextricably related, and the ancients were prescient in their avowal that "where there is no vision, the people perish."*

CHARWAT, ANDREW FRANCISZEK, engineering educator; b. Poland, Feb. 10, 1925; came to U.S., 1945; s. Franciszek and Wanda (Niec) C.; m. Halina M. Stieglitz, Aug. 18, 1948 (dec.); 1 child, Danuta K. Charwat McCall. M Engring., Stevens Inst. Tech., 1948; PhD, U. Calif., Berkeley, 1952. Aerodynamicist Propulsion Research Corp., Los Angeles, 1952-53; designer Northrup Aircraft Corp., Los Angeles, 1953-55; prof., dept. mech. and aerospace engring. UCLA, 1955-92, prof. emeritus, 1992—. Cons. to numerous industry and govt. agys., 1955—; expert witness various legal cases; dir. Univ. Study Ctr., Lyon and Grenoble, France, 1986-88. Contbr. over 80 articles and research papers. Guggenheim fellow, 1962. E-mail: acharwat@ucla.edu.

CHARY, ERIKA M. music educator; b. Vienna, Feb. 8, 1923; came to the U.S., 1967; d. Ignaz Weiner and Mariska Gonda-Weiner; m. Henry Heinz Chary, Nov. 3, 1945. Assoc. in Piano Performing, Royal Coll. Music, London, 1949; Licentiate in Piano Tchg., Royal Acad. Music, 1952; tchg. diploma, U. London, 1953. Founder, dir. Young Artists Peninsula Music Festival; adjudicator piano competitions, Calif., Europe. Recipient Golden Order of Merit, Austrian Govt., 1996. Mem. European Piano Tchrs. Assn. (spkr., performer), Nat. Music Tchrs. Assn., Calif. Music Tchrs. Assn., Calif. Assn. Profl. Music Tchrs. Home: 6931 Vallon Dr Palos Verdes Estates CA 90275-5307

CHARYK, JOSEPH VINCENT, retired satellite telecommunications executive; b. Canmore, Alta., Can., Sept. 9, 1920; came to U.S., 1942, naturalized, 1948; s. John and Anna (Dorosh) C.; m. Edwina Elizabeth Rhodes, Aug. 18, 1945; children: William R., J. John, Christopher E., Diane E. B.Sc., U. Alta., 1942, LL.D., 1964; MS, Calif. Inst. Tech., 1943, PhD, 1946; D.Engring. (hon.), U. Bologna, 1974. Sect. chief Jet Propulsion Lab., Calif. Inst. Tech., 1945-46, instr. aeros., 1945-46; asst. prof. aeros. Princeton (N.J.) U., 1946-49, assoc. prof., 1949-55; dir. aerophysics and chemistry lab., missile systems div. Lockheed Aircraft Corp., 1955-56; dir. aero. lab. Aeronutronic Systems, Inc. subs. Ford Motor Co., 1956-58, gen. mgr. space tech. div., 1958-59; asst. sec. for research and devel. USAF, 1959, under sec., 1960-63, dir. nat. reconnaissance office, 1961—63; pres. Communications Satellite Corp., 1963-79, chief exec. officer, 1979-85, chmn., 1983-85, Draper Labs., 1987-90. Recipient Lloyd V. Berkner Space Utilization award, 1967, Disting. Aviation Aerospace Svc. award, 1973, Gugliemo Marconi Internat. award, 1974, TV Arts and Scis. Directorate award, 1974, Theodore Von Karman award, 1977, Goddard Astronautics award, 1978, award Computer and Comm. Found., 1985, Nat. Medal of Tech., 1987, Arthur C. Clarke award, 1992, Disting. Alumni award U. Alta., 1993. Fellow AIAA, IEEE; mem. Nat. Acad. Engring., Internat. Acad. Astronautics, Nat. Space Club, Chevy Chase Country Club, Gulf Stream Golf Club, Gulf Stream Bath and Tennis Club, Sigma Xi. Home: 790 Andrews Ave Apt A302 Delray Beach FL 33483-7257*

CHARYN, JEROME, novelist; b. N.Y.C., May 13, 1937; s. Sam Charyn and Fannie Paley. BA, Columbia Coll., 1959. Lectr. creative writing Princeton U., N.J., 1981-86; vis. dist. prof. City U. N.Y., N.Y.C., 1988-89; prof. film studies Am. U. Paris, France, 1995—. Author: Citizen Sidel, 1997, Death of a Tango King, 1998, The Dark Lady from Belorusse, 1998, The Black Swan, 2000, Ping-pong or the Art of Staying Alive, 2001, Hurricane Lady, 2001, Bronx Boy, 2002, Gangsters and Gold Diggers, 2003. Named Guggenheim fellow, 1982; recipient Comdr. des Arts et des Lettres France Govt, 2002. Democrat. Avocation: tournament table tennis. Office: Am Univ Paris 31 ave Bosquet Paris France 75007 E-mail: jeromecharyn@aol.com.

CHASALOW, ERIC DAVID, composer, educator; b. Newark, May 25, 1955; s. Ivan and Carolyn Chasalow; m. Barbara Anne Cassidy, July 12, 1998; 1 child, Simon. Student, New Eng. Conservatory Music, 1975—76; BA, Bates Coll., 1977; MA, Columbia U., 1979, DMA, 1985. Exec. dir. Guild of Composers, N.Y.C., 1982—85, Assn. for Classical Music, N.Y.C., 1988—90; asst. prof. music Brandeis U., Waltham, Mass., 1990—96, assoc. prof. music, 1996—2001, prof. music, 2001—, chair of music, 1996—2002. Dir. Brandeis Electro-Acoustic Music Studio, Waltham, 1990—; bd. advisors Auros Group for New Music, Boston, 1996—; adv. bd. mem. Aaron Copland Soc., Cortlandt Manor, NY, 1998—; music com. mem. Boston CyberArts Festival, Boston, 1998—; music editor Agni, Boston, 1999—. Composer: (orchestra and tape) Dream Songs, (piano trio) Yes, I Really Did, (soprano and string quartet) Five Simic Songs, (electric guitar and tape) 'Scuse Me, (flute and piano) To The Edge and Back (Pappoutsaki Flute Competition commn., 1997), (computer generated) Portrait of The Artist, Left to His Own Devices, (piano sonata) A Loose Translation, (soprano and piano) Pass it On, (trumpet and tape) Out of Joint, (computer generated) And it flew upside-down, (flute, violin, piano) Lo Schermo, (chamber ensemble) In The Works, (computer generated) The Fury of Rainstorms, This Way Out, (piano solo) Little Word, (horn solo) Winding Up, (string quartet) First Quartet, (percussion and tape) Fast Forward, (chamber orchestra) Leaping to Conclusions, (piano solo) Groundwork, (flute and tape) Over The Edge, (piano and tape) Due (Cinta)mani, (soprano and tape) The Furies, (soprano and piano) Triptych, (cello and tape) Hanging in the Balance, (flute, violin, viola, cello) Returning to the Point, (piano trio) Two From Three, (chorus) Words, (solo flute) Falling Forward, (improvisers and tape) Reverses, (horn, percussion, tape) Verses and Fragments, (solo flute) Anti-Chambers, (harp and tape) What is Danced.(and what is not), (computer generated) Clapping Game, (bass clarinet and tape) In a Manner of Speaking, (computer generated) Crossing Boundaries (Bates Coll. Millenial Commn., 2000), (flute, clarinet, violin, cello, tape) Suspicious Motives (Boston Musica Viva millenial commn., 1999), (computer generated) Seven Variations on Three Spaces; co-author (with Barbara Cassidy): The Video Archive of Electro-Acoustic Music. Named Young American's Art Song Competition winner, G. Schirmer Music Publishers, 1995; recipient First Prize, Wash. Sq. Contemporary Music Series Competition, 1988, first prize, Internat. Soc. for Contemporary Music, U.S. Sect., 1989, 1994, Nat. New Publications prize, Nat. Flute Assn., 1993, Acad. Music award, Am. Acad. Arts Letters, 2003; fellow, John Simon Guggenheim Found., 1986, N.Y. Found. for the Arts, 1986; grantee, Fromm Found. For Music at Harvard U., 1993, 2001; Composer's fellow, Nat. Endowment for the Arts, 1983, Charles Ives fellow, Am. Acad. Arts & Letters, 1986. Mem.: ASCAP, Am. Music Ctr., Internat. Computer Music Assn., Soc. for Electro-Acoustic Music in the U.S., Electronic Music Found. Achievements include Left to His Own Devices, CD on New World Records, 2003; Over the Edge, CD on New World Records, 1993; other music on SEAMUS, ICMC, InterSound Net Records, and RRRecords. Avocations: asian antiques, mycology, cooking. Office: Brandeis Univ Slosberg Music Center MS 051 Waltham MA 02454-9110 Office Fax: 781-736-3320. E-mail: chasalow@brandeis.edu.

CHASANOW, HOWARD STUART, retired judge, mediator; b. Washington, Apr. 3, 1937; 1 child from previous marriage, Andrea; m. Deborah Hovis Koss, May 15, 11983. BA, U. Md., 1959, JD, 1961; LLM, Harvard U., 1962. Bar: Md. 1961, U.S. Supreme Ct. 1965. Asst. states atty. Prince George County, Upper Marlboro, Md., 1963-64, dep. states atty., 1964-67; judge Dist. Ct., Upper Marlboro, 1971-77, 7th Jud. Cir., 1977-90, Ct. Appeals of Md., 1990-99, ret., 1999. Lectr. Sch. Law U. Md., Balt., 1973—, Nat. Jud. Coll., Reno, 1980—, Am. Acad. Jud. Edn., 1984—; chmn. adv. bd. Sentencing Guidelines, Md., 1982-90, chmn. jud. adminstrn. sect., 1982-84; mem. Md. Commn. on Criminal Sentencing Policy, 1996—; mem. standing com. on rules of practice and procedure Ct. Appeals, 1985-90; mem. govs. task force to Revise Criminal Code, 1992—. Contbr. law rev. articles. Served with USAF, 1968-69. Office: Ct Appeals Md Prince George County Courthouse PO Box 399 Upper Marlboro MD 20773-0399

CHASE, CHEVY (CORNELIUS CRANE CHASE), comedian, actor, author; b. Woodstock, NY, Oct. 8, 1943; s. Edward Tinsley and Cathalene Crane (Widdoes) C.; m. Jayni Chase, 1982; children: Cydney Cathalene, Caley Leigh, Emily Evelyn. BA in English, Bard Coll., 1967; CCS, Inst. Audio Rsch., 1970. Artist MGM Records, 1968; writer for Mad mag., 1969; actor in his first film The Groove Tube, 1967-71; writer, actor Gt. Am. Dream Machine, 1971; dir., writer, actor, Nat. Lampoon Theatre Co., 1972-74, performing in Nat. Lampoon's Lemmings, off Broadway and on nat. tour; launched his career as a writer, actor in Sat. Night Live TV show, 1975-76; appeared on TV in Paul Simon Spl., host of The Chevy Chase Show, 1993; appeared in films Foul Play, 1978, Oh Heavenly Dog, 1980, Caddyshack in 1980, Caddyshack II in 1988, Seems Like Old Times, 1981, Under the Rainbow, 1981, Modern Problems, 1981, Vacation, 1983, Deal of the Century, 1983, Fletch, 1984 and Fletch Lives 1989, European Vacation, 1985, Spies Like Us, 1985, Follow That Bird, 1985, The Three Amigos, 1986, Funny Farm, 1988, The Couch Trip, 1988, Christmas Vacation, 1989, Nothing But Trouble, 1991, LA Story, 1991, Memoirs of an Invisible Man, 1992, Hero, 1992, Last Action Hero, 1993, Cops and Robbersons, 1994, Man of the House, 1995, National Lampoon's Vegas Vacation, 1997, Snow Day, 1999; he made appearances in Last Action Hero and Orange County. Recipient award for best script in comedy variety spl. Writers Guild, award best supporting actor in comedy variety series Nat. Acad. TV Arts and Sci.; won two Emmy Awards for Saturday Night Live and a third Emmy for co-writing The Paul Simon Special; hon. by Harvard Univ. Hasty Pudding Theatrical Group, 1992. Mem. Am. Fedn. Musicians, Stage Actors Guild, Actors Equity, AFTRA. Democrat. Office: Cornelius Prods PO Box 257 Bedford NY 10506-0257

CHASE, CLINTON IRVIN, psychologist, educator, business executive; b. Aug. 14, 1927; m. Patricia Cronenberger; 1 child. BS in Psychology with honors, U. Idaho, 1950, MS in Adminstrn., 1951; PhD in Ednl. Psychology, U. Calif.-Berkeley, 1958. Asst. to dean students Wash. State U., 1951-52; sch. psychologist Piedmont Pub. Schs., Calif., 1957-58; asst. prof. ednl. psychology Idaho State U., 1958-61, Miami U., Oxford, 1961-62, Ind. U., Bloomington, 1962-64, assoc. prof., 1964-68, prof., 1968-95; prof. emeritus Indiana U., Bloomington, 1995—; assoc. dir. Bur. Evaluative Studies and Testing Ind. U., Bloomington, 1962-70, dir., 1970-89, chmn. dept. ednl. psychology, 1970-74; dir. Ind. Testing and Evaluation Svc., Bloomington, 1976-87, Ind. Ctr. for Evaluation, 1988-94; owner, mgr. Ind. Testing and Evaluation Svc., 1990—. Author: (with H. Glenn Ludlow) Readings in Educational and Psychological Measurement, 1966, Elementary Statistical Procedures, 1967, 3d edit., 1984, Measurement for Educational Evaluation, 1974, 2d edit., 1978; (with L.C. Jacobs) Developing and Using Tests Effectively, 1992, Contemporary Assessment for Educators, 1999; contbr. more than 120 articles to profl. jours. Served with USN, 1945-46; to capt. USAF, 1952-55. Named Ky. Col., 1998. Fellow Am. Psychol. Assn., Am. Ednl. Research Assn., Nat. Council on Measurement in Edn., Phi Beta Kappa, Kappa Delta Pi E-mail: chase@indiana.edu. *The careful establishment of objectives, and the persistant pursuit of objectives, are the primary ingredients of achievement.*

CHASE, COCHRANE, advertising agency executive; b. Berwyn, Ill., Feb. 6, 1932; s. Henry Cochrane and Roselyn (Scott) C.; m. Janis Valeria Kueber, June 19, 1954; children— Katherine Ann, Anthony Scott, Lisa Marie. BA, Wesleyan U., 1954. With steel warehousing div. Jessop Steel Co., Broadview, Ill., 1956-62, mgr. sales, 1961-62; with Jessop Steel Calif., Santa Fe Springs, 1963-64; asst. mgr. market research Ducommun Metals & Supply Co., Los Angeles, 1964-65; v.p. Newport Advt. Inc., Newport Beach, Calif., 1965; pres. Cochrane Chase, Livingston & Co., Inc., Irvine, Calif., 1966, chmn. bd., chief exec. officer, 1966-88; chmn. emeritus AC&R/CCL, Irvine, Calif., 1988-89. Co-author: Marketing Problem Solver, 1973, Newport Financial Planner, 1985. Served with USNR, 1954-56. Home: 2162 Papaya Dr La Habra CA 90631-7917

CHASE, DORIS TOTTEN, sculptor, video artist, filmmaker; b. Seattle, 1923; d. William Phelps and Helen (Feeley) Totten; m. Elmo Chase, Oct. 20, 1943 (div. 1972); children: Gregary Totten, Randall Jarvis Totten. Student, U. Wash., 1941-43. Lectr. tours for USIA in S.Am., 1975, Europe, 1978, India, 1972, Australia, 1986, Eastern Europe, 1987, Ireland, England, France; vis. lectr., presenter U. Colo., Boulder, Mary Mount Coll., N.Y., the Kitchen Ctr. for Film & Video, Nat. Film Bd. of Can., Toronto, N.Y. Grad. Sch.; artist-in-residence Pilchuck Glass Sch., 1999. One-woman shows include Ruth White Gallery, N.Y.C., 1967, 69, 70, Fountain Gallery, Portland, Oreg., 1970, U. Wash. Henry Gallery, 1971, 77, 98, Wadsworth Athenum, Hartford, Conn., 1973, Hirshhorn Mus., Washington, 1974, 77, Anthology Film Archives, N.Y.C., 1975, 80, 83, Donnell Libr., N.Y.C., 1976, 79, 83, 92, Performing Arts Mus. at Lincoln Ctr., 1976, Mus. Modern Art, N.Y.C., 1978, 80, 87, 93, 98, High Mus., Atlanta, 1978, Herbert Johnson Mus., 1982, A.I.R. Gallery, N.Y.C., 1983-85, Art in Embassies, USIS, 1984-88, Inst. Contemporary Art, London, 1989, Woodside/Braseth Gallery, 1990, 92, 94, John F. Kennedy Ctr., 1990, Seattle Arts Mus., 1990, 92, 95, 99, 2002, Mus. N.W. Art La Conner Wash., 1995; circulating exhibit Western Mus. Assn., 1970-71, Am. Inst. Archs., Seattle, 1994, Friesen Gallery, Seattle, 1997, 98, 99, 2001; represented in permanent collections Finch Coll. Mus., N.Y.C., Mus. Modern Art, N.Y.C., Seattle Art Mus., Ashai Shimbum, Tokyo, Georges Pompidou Ctr., Paris, Battelle Inst., Mus. Fine Arts Boston, Milw. Art Inst., Art Inst. Chgo., Mus. Fine Arts Houston, Frye Art Mus., Seattle, Nat. Collection Fine Arts, Smithsonian Instn., Washington, Wadsworth Athenum, N.C. Mus. Art, Raleigh, Mus. Modern Art, Kobe, Japan, Pa. Acad. Art, Phila., Portland Art Mus., Vancouver (B.C.) Art Gallery, Montgomery (Ala.) Mus. Fine Art, Hudson River Mus., N.Y.C., Tacoma Art Mus.; works represented in archival collections Ctr. for Film and Theatre Rsch., U. Wis., Madison, U. Wash., Seattle, UCLA Film Archives, Lincoln Ctr. Performing Arts Libr., N.Y.C., Pompideau, Paris, Archieves of Am. Art Smithsonian Instn., Washington; executed monumental kinetic sculpture Kerry Park, Seattle, Lake Park, 1976, Anderson, Ind., Expo '70, Osaka, Japan, Sculpture Park, Atlanta, Met. Mus. Art, N.Y.C., Montgomery Mus. Fine Arts, monumental bronze sculpture installed, Seattle Ctr., 1999; multi-media sculpture for 4 ballets, Opera Assn. Seattle; included in Sculpture in Park program N.Y.C., Playground of Tomorrow ABC-TV, L.A.; prodr., dir. (film and video) Doris Chase Dance Series, 1971-80, Concept Series, 1980-85, By Herself Series: Table for One (with Geraldine Page), 1985; prodr. (with Jennie Ventris) Glass Curtain, 1984(with Anne Jackson) Dear Papa, 1986, (with Luise Rainer) A Dancer, 1987, (with Priscilla Pointer) Still Frame, 1988, (with Joan Plowright) Sophie, 1989, The Chelsea, 1994, Danse de colour, 2002. Recipient honors and awards at numerous festivals in U.S. and fgn. countries; grantee Nat. Endowment for Arts, Am. Film Inst., 1988, N.Y. State Coun. for Arts, Mich. Arts Coun., Seattle Art Commn., 1992, Jerusalem Film Festival, 1987, Berlin Film Festival, 1985, 87, Athens Film Festival, 1995, London Film Festival, 1986, Am. Film Inst. Festival, 1987, 94, Retirement Rsch. Found., 1994, Lockwood Found., Herzman Family Found., Seattle Center Found., NEA, N.Y. State Coun. for Arts; subject of documentary Doris Chase: Portrait of the Artist, PBS, 1985; subject of book and video: Artist in Motion, 1993; subject of documentary Doris Chase: Circle at the Center, PBS, 1999; Doris Chase Day proclaimed by Mayor and City Coun. Seattle; recipient Wash. Gov.'s Art award, 1992; honored at N.Y. Pub. Libr. and N.Y. Film Video Coun., 2003. Mem. Actors Studio (writer, dirs. wing 1986). Achievements include all work in film and video being in collection and archives of Mus. Modern Art, N.Y.C.; established Doris Totten Chase scholarship fund U. Washington, 2002.

CHASE, EMERY JOHN, JR., nuclear engineer, researcher; b. St. Albans, Vt., Dec. 27, 1943; s. Emery J. and Rita M. (Tatro) C.; m. Eleanora M. Fitzwilliam, June 3, 1995; children: Emery J. III, Kenneth D., Heather M. BS, U.S. Mil. Acad., West Point, N.Y., 1965; MS in Nuclear Engring., MIT, 1967; MS in Bus. Adminstrn., U. No. Colo., 1978. Registered profl. engr., Colo., Va. Commd. 2d lt. U.S. Army, 1965-92, advanced through grades to col.; asst. prof. physics USAF Acad., Colorado Springs, Colo., 1972-75; analyst, engr. Engr. Sch., Ft. Belvoir, Va., 1977-78; spl. asst. nuclear Office of Sec. of Def., Washington, 1978-81; comdr. Engr. Battalian, Darmstadt, Germany, 1981-84; asst. corps engr. Vth U.S. Corps, Frankfurt, Germany, 1983-84; rsch. asst. testing Def. Nuclear Agy., Washington, 1984-86, dir. nuclear assessments and applications, 1986-89; exec. asst. OSD Office of Sec. of Def., Washington, 1989-92; dir. Ctr. for Verification Rsch./SAIC, Newington, Va., 1992-99, Treat Reduction Support Ctr./SAIC, Herndon, Va., 1999; dep. ops. mgr. SAIC, McLean, Va., 1999—. Lectr. Inter-Am. Def. Coll., Ft. McNair, 1988-92. AEC fellow, 1965, Sr. Ofcls. in Nat. Security award Harvard U., Boston, 1988. Mem. NSPE, Soc. Mil. Engrs., Arms Control Assn., Alumni Assn. U.S. Mil. Acad., MIT Alumni Assn., Harvard U. Alumni Assn. Avocation: reading. Home: 3701 Del Mar Dr Woodbridge VA 22193-1719 Office: Sci Applications Internat Corp 1710 Goodridge Dr # Md16-2 Mc Lean VA 22102-3701

CHASE, ERIC LEWIS, lawyer; b. Princeton, N.J., Sept. 21, 1946; s. Harold William and Bernice Mae (Fadden) C.; m. Jamie Campbell, Dec. 29, 1979; children: Eric Campbell, Kathryn Dianne, John Harold. BA, Princeton U., 1968; JD cum laude, U. Minn., 1974. Bar: N.J. 1974, D.C. 1975, U.S. Ct. Appeals (3d cir.) 1979, U.S. Supreme Ct. 1981, U.S. Claims Ct. 1982, U.S. Tax Ct. 1982, N.Y. 1983, U.S. Ct. Appeals (2d cir.) 1988, U.S. Ct. Appeals (6th cir.) 2003. Trial atty. FCC, 1974-78; asst. U.S. atty. Dist. N.J., Newark, 1978-80; ptnr. Margolis Chase, Verona, N.J., 1980-90, Hannoch Weisman, Roseland, N.J., 1990-93, Bressler, Amery & Ross, Florham Park, N.J., 1993—. Prof. law of war Marine Corps Command and Staff Coll., Quantico, Va., 1990-99. Author: Automobile Dealers and the Law, 1994, 7th edit., 2000; contbr. articles on law and mil. to profl. publs., including N.Y. Times, Washington Post, Newsweek mag. With USMC, 1968-71; col. Res., ret. Mem. ABA (mem. task force on internat. criminal ct.), N.J. State Bar Assn. (franchise com 1997—, co-chair franchise com. 1999-2001). Office: Bressler Amery & Ross 325 Columbia Tpke Ste 8 Florham Park NJ 07932-1212 E-mail: echase@bressler.com.

CHASE, HELEN LOUISE, banker; b. Waukegan, Ill., Sept. 29, 1943; d. David William and Ruth Virginia (Sawyer) C. BA, U. Ill., 1965. Sec., exec. sec. Foote, Cone and Belding, Chgo., 1965-66; various positions Continental Bank (now Bank Am.), Chgo., 1966-73; internat. banking officer Continental Bank, Chgo., 1973-76, 2nd v.p., 1976-77, Brazil rep. Sao Paulo, 1977-80; 2nd v.p., sect. head Far East group Continental Bank Internat., N.Y.C., 1980-81; 2nd v.p. internat. div. Continental Bank, Chgo., 1981-83; v.p. N.Am. Union Trust Bank (Signet Bank), Balt., 1983-84; v.p., mgr. internat. ops. Signet Bank (now First Union), Balt., 1984-89; v.p. internat. dept. Meridian Bank (now First Union), Lancaster, Pa., 1989-92; v.p. mgr. internat. ops. Meridian Bank, Lancaster, Pa., 1992-94; pvt. practice internat. fin. cons., 1994-95; v.p., mgr. internat. divsn., v.p. internat. trade fin. Compass Bank, Birmingham, Ala., 1995—. Avocations: art, music, active sports. Fax: (205) 297-3996. E-mail: helen.chase@compassbnk.com.

CHASE, J. SCOTT, Lawyer (corporate); b. Houston, Tex, Mar. 14, 1946; s. Donald Lloyd and Jean Lou (Gamache) Chase; m. Jance Dahrling Chase, Nov. 22, 1968 (div.); 1 child, Jeffrey. BA Polit. Sci., U. Houston, 1968, JD, 1971. Bar: Tex. 1973, US Dist. Ct. Tex. 1978, US Dist. Ct. Mil. Appeals 1978. Assoc. counsel Campbell Taggart, Inc., Dallas, 1973—76; staff atty. Dr. Pepper Co., Dallas, 1976—, asst. sec., 1977—. Served USAR, 1971—73. Mem.: Dallas Assn. Young Lawyers (pres. 1982), Dallas Bar Assn. (dir. 1982, chmn. corp. counsel sect. 1981—82). Office: PO Box PO Box 225086 Dallas TX 75222-5086

CHASE, J. VINCENT, shopping center executive, justice of the peace; b. N.Y.C., Nov. 5, 1949; m. Addie Lee Pickus, Sept. 3, 1983. BS, U. Bridgeport, 1972. Pers. adminstr. Ins. Svcs. Office, N.Y.C., 1972-77; gen. mgr. pers. John Wiley & Sons, N.Y.C., 1977-79; pers. dir. CitiCorp, N.Y.C., 1979-83; pres., owner Colonial Square Shopping Ctr., Stratford, Conn., 1983—; mem. Conn. Ho. of Reps., Hartford, 1980-96, dep. minority leader, 1990-96; asst. treas. Conn. Office of the State Treasurer, Hartford, 1997-98; chief investigator U.S. Ho. of Reps., Washington, 1998—. Bd. dirs. Union Cemeetery Assn; bd. trustees Stratford Libr. Assn.; Stratford Rep. Town Com.; candidate for U.S. Ho. or Reps. from 3d Dist. Conn., 1990. Recipient Outstanding Svc. award Stratford Tenants' Coun., 1982, Man of Yr. award Stratford Civitan Club, 1983, Alumnus of Yr. award U. Bridgeport, 1990, Legislator of Yr. award Conn. Profl. Ins. Agts. Assn., 1991, Legislator of Yr. award Conn. Assn. Optometrists, 1993, Legislator of Yr. award Conn. Chiropractic Assn., 1994, Legislator of Yr. award Conn. Adoption Coun., 1996, Legislator of Yr. award U.S. Humane Soc., 1997. Mem. U. Bridgeport Alumni Assn. (bd. dirs.), Washington D.C.-Conn. Soc., Masons, Scottish Rite. Congregationalist.

CHASE, JAMES KELLER, retired artist, museum director, educator, b. Logansport, Ind., May 18, 1927; s. James Howard and Agnes (Keller) C.; m. Marcelle Pierard, Dec. 29, 1969; 1 son, Henrik Clovis. BS, Ball State U., Muncie, Ind., 1952, doctoral fellow, 1972-74; MA, Mich. State U., 1963. Art supr. Chili (Ind.) schs., 1952-53, Sturgis (Mich.) schs., 1953-57; asst. prof. Western Mich. U., 1957-60; tchr. edn. TV on camera Central Mich. U., 1960-65; prof., chmn. fine arts dept. Northwood U., Midland, Mich., 1964-74; dir. Saginaw (Mich.) Mus., 1975-77, Ariz. Capitol Mus., Phoenix, 1978-81, McPherson Coll., 1982-87; art instr. Maricopa County, 1982-89; ret., 1989. Vis. prof. Western Mich. U., Saginaw Valley U., Delta Coll., Saginaw, Johns Hopkins U. at Ariz. State U.; mem. Mich. Higher Edn. Commn., 1967, Mich. Creativity Com., 1966; bd. dirs. Midland Ctr. Arts, 1967-71, Thompson Draw, Tonto Nat. Forest. Author: Nine Fine, 1977; contbr. articles to edn. jours., newspapers, mags.; exhibiting artist state, regional and nat. shows. Pres. Sands East II Homeowners Assn., 1987-89, sec., 1989-96; vol. ct. vis. guardianship rev. project Ariz. Superior Ct., 1994—. Mem. Am. Assn. Museums, Ariz. Adminstrs. Assn., Central Ariz. Museums Assn., Ariz. Hist. Assn. Home: PO Box 3411 Carefree AZ 85377 *Creating, sharing and understanding art and beauty adds truth and vibrance to life.*

CHASE, JAMES RICHARD, retired college president; b. Oxnard, Calif., Oct. 7, 1930; s. James Warren and Nina Marie (Fiscus) C.; m. Mary Corinne Sutherland, Dec. 16, 1950; children: Kenneth Richard, Jennifer Corinne. B. Theology, Biola Coll., 1951; BA, Pepperdine U., 1953, MA, 1954; PhD, Cornell U., 1961. Instr. Biola Coll., La Mirada, Calif., 1953-57, prof., chmn. dept. humanities, 1959-65, v.p. acad. affairs, 1965-70, pres., 1970-82, Wheaton (Ill.) Coll., 1982-93, pres. emeritus, 1993—. Teaching asst. Cornell Univ., Ithaca, N.Y., 1957-59; bd. dirs. World Christian Tng. Ctr., 1970-82; bd. dirs. Christian Coll. Coalition, 1977-79, chmn. bd., 1977-79; bd. dirs. Mission Aviation Fellowship, 1975-81, chmn. bd., 1978-81; bd. dirs. Western Coll. Assn., 1980-82 Mem. Nat. Assn. Ind. Colls. and Univs. (dir. 1980), Assn. Ind. Calif. Colls. and Univs. (mem. exec. com. 1978-82), Am. Assn. Bible Colls. (dir. 1974-80), Nat. Assn. Intercollegiate Athletics (pres. adv. com. 1976-82), Nat. Assn. Evangelicals (exec. com. 1984-92), We. Assn. Schs. and Colls. (sr. commn. 1981-82), Am. Assn. Pres. Ind. Colls. and Univs. (dir. 1980-85, v.p. 1982-85), Speech Communication Assn., Christian Coll. Consortium (chmn. 1986), Coalition (chmn. 1976), Fedn. Ind. Ill. Colls. and Univs. (exec. com., chmn. bd. 1989-91). Baptist.

CHASE, JOHN DAVID, university dean, physician; b. Detroit, Sept. 24, 1920; s. Clyde Harrison and Bonnie Lucille (Fogas) Chase; 1 child, Robert Winslow. AB, Wabash (Ind.) Coll., 1942; MD, Western Res. U., 1945. Diplomate Am. Bd. Internal Medicine. Intern Detroit Receiving Hosp., 1945—46; resident in internal medicine Wayne State U. Hosp., 1948—52; teaching fellow Nat. Heart Inst., 1952; with VA, 1952—78, dep. asso. chief med. dir. academic affairs, 1970—73; chief med. service VA Hosp., Tacoma, 1973—74; chief med. dir. VA Central Office, Washington, 1974—78; assoc. dean clin. affairs U. Wash. Sch. Med., Seattle, 1978—81, dean Sch. Medicine, 1981—82, dean emeritus, 1983—. Mem. nat. adv. coun. Heart and Lung Inst., 1968—70, Regional Med. Programs, 1970—73, Nat. Libr. Medicine, 1972—73; mem. Nat. Adv. Coun. VA Edn., 1973, Nat. Adv. Coun. Health Svcs. Planning and Resources, 1976, Fed. Coordinating Coun. Sci., Engring. and Tech., 1976—78, Nat. Adv. Coun. Health Planning and Devel., 1976—; bd. govs. Armed Forces Inst. Pathology, 1976—78. With M.C. USNR, 1946—48. Recipient Disting. Svc. award, Wayne State U. Med. Sch., 1976. Fellow: ACP, Am. Coll. Chest Physicians; mem.: AMA (ho. dels.), Am. Hosp. Assn. (trustee 1976—78), Assn. Mil. Surgeons U.S., Inst. Medicine. Home: 112 Frederick Rd Fredericksburg TX 78624

CHASE, JONATHON B. law school dean, educator; b. Orange, N.J., June 6, 1939; s. David Boyd and Lillian (Reuben) C.; m. Nancy Markey, June 25, 1961; children— Tamara, Adam, Rebecca, Eli. B.A., Williams Coll., Williamstown, Mass., 1961; LL.B. cum laude, Columbia U., 1964. Bar: N.Y. 1964, Colo. 1969, U.S. Dist. Ct. (D.C. dist.), U.S. Dist. Ct. Colo., U.S. Ct. Appeals (10th cir.), U.S. Supreme Ct. Asst. prof. law Boston U., 1965-66; prof. law U. Colo., Boulder, 1966-82; exec. dir. Colo. Rural Legal Services, 1969-72; dean, prof. Sch. of Law, Vt. Law Sch., South Royalton, 1982—. Contbr. articles to profl. jours. Bd. dirs. Colo. br. ACLU, 1975-82, ACLU, Vt., 1982—, Vt. Planned Parenthood, 1982-84, Vt. Legal Aid, 1984—. Mem. ABA, Vt. Bar Assn. Democrat. Jewish. Home: PO Box 684 Norwich VT 05055-0684

CHASE, MARILYN, journalist; b. L.A. AB in English, Stanford U., 1971; MA in Journalism, U. Calif., Berkeley, 1973. Reporter Wall St. Jour., San Francisco, 1978—94, health columnist, 1994—99, sr. spl. writer health and medicine, 1999—. Author: (book) The Barbary Plague: The Black Death in Victorian San Francisco, 2003. Office: Wall St Jour 201 California St Ste 1350 San Francisco CA 94111-5022

CHASE, NICHOLAS JOSEPH, lawyer, educator; b. Windsor, Conn., Jan. 9, 1913; s. Michael and Lucy A. (Sinisgalli) C.; m. F. Louise Dooley, Dec. 27, 1936; children: Stephen Edward, Mary Ann, Michael Dooley, Clare Lucia, Martha Louise. AB in Philosophy, Cath. U. Am., 1933, AM in Politics, 1934, postgrad., 1935-36; Columbian fellow, Brookings Instn., 1934-35; JD magna cum laude, Georgetown U. Law Sch., 1940. Bar: D.C. 1939, U.S. Ct. Appeals 1940, U.S. Ct. Claims 1940, U.S. Supreme Ct. 1943, Md. 1950, U.S. Mil. Ct. Appeals, 1949-65, U.S. Emergency Ct. Appeals, 1952-62. Pvt. practice, Washington, 1939—; adminstrv. asst. Pub. Works Admin., 1935-40; atty. Leahy & Hughes, Washington, 1940-47; prof. law Cath. U. Am., 1943-45; gen. coun. Chevy Chase Village, Md., 1943-48; prof. law Georgetown U., Washington, 1946-66; prin. Chase & Williams, Washington, 1948-52, Chase & McChesney, Washington, 1952-62, Chase & Colton, Washington, 1962-65. Mem. adv. com. Fed. Rules of Criminal Prodedure for U.S. Cts., 1940-49; mem. com. on Rules for Mcpl. and Superior Cts., 1943-63; mem. D.C. Coun. Law Enforcement, 1950-59; judge moot ct. Georgetown U., 1959-66, Prettyman Criminal Law Clinic, 1956-66; arbitrator Am. Arbitration Assn., 1970—, trial specialist, 1940-65; mem. Jud. Conf. D.C. Cir., 1952-62; def. counsel U.S. Dist. Ct. for D.C., 1941-66. Author: Federal and Washington, D.C. Relations, 1801-1933, publs. on Adams Meml., Miscellaneous Essays: 1994, Essays of Prof. Anon, 1997-98, Washington Adams Memorial and Centennial of Cath. U. Am., Moments: 1913-98; assoc. editor Washington D.C. Bar Jour., 1951-59. Pres. Plaintiffs Trial Lawyers Assn., Washington, 1958-62; past chm. bd. trustees Hawthorne Sch., Washington, 1969-74; adminstr. 1st dist. Columbia Bar Assn. CLE Inst., 1960-61; bd. dirs. Rehoboth Art League, 1949-58. Fellow Columbian, Cath. U. Am., 1933—36. Mem. ABA, Bar Assn. D.C. (1st v.p., bd. dirs. 1958-63), Georgetown Alumni Assn. (mem. bd. govs. 1958-62), Cath. U. Am. Alumni (pres. 1952-54), Columbia Hist. Soc. (chmn. memls. and plaques com.), Congrl. Country Club (parliamentarian 1956-70), Nat. Press Club, Counsellors Club (founder), St. Thomas More Legal Soc. (pres. Washington chpt. 1968-70), Touchdown Club (Washington, founder), John Carroll Soc. (founder), Kenwood Country Club, Rehoboth Country Club, Pi Epsilon (Nat. Journalism), Blue Key (nat. extra curricula), Phi Delta Phi (nat. legal). Home: 5205 Oakland Rd Chevy Chase MD 20815-6640 E-mail: njchase@webtv.net.

CHASE, NORMA, lawyer; b. Evergreen Park, Ill., Dec. 30, 1952; d. Harry and Joan (Sirutis) C. AB, U. Pitts., 1972; JD, Duquesne U., 1978. Bar: Pa. 1978, U.S. Dist. Ct. (fed. dist.) 1978, U.S. Ct. Appeals (3rd cir.) 1983, U.S. Supreme Ct. 1984. Pvt. practice, Pitts., 1978—. Contbr. articles to Word Perfect for the Law Office, 1995. Mem. Pa. Bar Assn. (atty. discipline study com. 1991-97, client security fund study com. 1991-94, vice chair latter com. 1991-93, chmn. 1993-94, vice-chair plain English com. 1998—, mem. coun. of solo and small firm practice sect. 1998—; editor coun. newsletter 2000—, appellate advocacy com. 2003-). Democrat. Avocations: reading, writing, computing, hiking. Office: 220 Grant St Pittsburgh PA 15219-2123 E-mail: normac@genericlawyer.com.

CHASE, PEARLINE, adult education educator; b. Lake Providence, La., Jan. 25, 1949; d. Willie and Rebecca (Thompson) C. BS in Liberal Studies and Math., So. U., 1970; MS in Math. Edn., La. Tech. U., 1977; EdM in Adminstrn. Planning Social Policy, Harvard U., 1984, EdD, 1987. Tchr. Caddo Parish Schs., Shreveport, La., 1970-78, East Carroll Parish Schs., Lake Providence, La., 1980-81; program coord., staff asst. Harvard U., Cambridge, Mass., 1983-84; exec. asst. to pres. Ky. State U., 1985-86, assoc. v.p. acad. affairs, 1986-87, v.p. student affairs, 1987-88; dir. bd. programs and policy analysis City Colls. Chgo., 1988-89; v.p. acad. affairs Paul Quinn Coll., Dallas, 1990-92; cons. Wilmington Inst., Dallas, 1992-96; prof. math. DeVry inst. Tech., Irving, Tex., 1996—. Teaching fellow U. Okla., Norman, 1981-83; fellow Congl. Black Caucus, Washington, 98th Congress, U.S. Ho. of Reps., Woodrow Wilson fellow; T.H. Harris scholar. Mem. Nat. Coun. Tchrs. Math., Nat. Assn. Devel. Educators, Alpha Kappa Alpha. Office: DeVry IUniv 4800 Regent Blvd Irving TX 75063-2439 E-mail: pchase@dal.devry.edu.

CHASE, ROBERT ARTHUR, surgeon, educator; b. Keene, N.H., Jan. 6, 1923; s. Albert Henry and Georgia Beulah (Bump) Chase; m. Ann Crosby Parker, Feb. 3, 1946; children: Deborah Lee, Nancy Jo, Robert N. BS cum laude, U. N.H., 1945, DSc (hon.), 1993; MD, Yale, 1947. Diplomate Am. Bd. Surgery, Am. Bd. Plastic Surgery. Intern New Haven Hosp., 1947—48, asst. resident, 1949—50, sr. resident surgery, 1952—53, chief resident surgeon, 1953—54; mem. faculty Yale Sch. Medicine, 1948—54, 1959—62, asst. prof. surgery, 1959—62; mem. faculty U. Pitts., 1957—59, resident plastic surgeon, also teaching fellow, 1957—59; attending surgeon VA Hosp., W. Haven, Conn., 1959—62, Grace New Haven Community Hosp., 1959—63; prof., chmn. dept. surgery Stanford Sch. Medicine, 1963—74, Emile Holman prof. surgery, 1972—; prof. surgery U. Pa., 1974—77; attending surgeon Pa. Hosp., Hosp. U. Pa., Grad. Hosp., Phila., 1974—77; pres., dir. Nat. Bd. Med. Examiners, Phila., 1974—77; prof. anatomy Stanford (Calif.) U., 1977—. Cons. plastic surgery Christian Med. Coll. and Hosp., Vellore, India, 1962; cons. to surgeon gen. USAF, 1970—; Benjamin K. Rank prof. Australasian Coll. Surgeons, 1974. Author: Atlas of Hand Surgey; editor: Videosurgery, 1974—; mem. editl. bd.: Med. Alert Communication, —; contbr. articles to profl. jours. Mem. bd. overseers Dartmouth Med. Sch., 1998-; mem. found. bd. U. N.H., 1998-. Maj. M.C. AUS, 1949—57. Recipient Francis Gilman Blake award, Yale Sch. Medicine, 1962, Henry J. Kaiser award, Stanford U. Sch. Medicine, 1978, 1979, 1984, 1986, 1990, 1993, Calif. Golden Apple award, 1991, Albion William Hewlett award, 1992, Pettee award, U. N.H., 1998. Fellow: ACS, Australasian Coll. Surgeons (hon.); mem.: AMA, NAS, Halsted Soc., Am.. Soc. Most Venerable Order Hosp., St. John of Jerusalem, Inst. Medicine (exec. com. 1976, coun. 1986—), Soc. Univ. Surgeons, Found. Am. Soc. Plastic and Reconstructive Surgery (dir.), Am. Cancer Soc. (clin. fellowship com.), James IV Assn. Surgeons, Pacific Coast Surg. Soc., Western Surg. Assn., Soc. Clin. Surgery, Plastic Surgery Rsch. Coun., Am. Assn. Surgery Trauma, Am. Soc. Cleft Palate Rehab., Am. Soc. Surgery Hand (pres.), Conn. Med. Soc., Santa Clara County Med. Soc., Am. Surg. Assn., San Francisco Surg. Soc., Calif. Acad. Medicine (pres.), Am. Soc. Clin. Anatomists (hon.; pres.), South African Soc. Plastic and Reconstructive Surgery (hon.), South African Soc. Surgery Hand (hon.), Am. Assn. Plastic Surgery (hon.), Am. Assn. Clin. Anatomists (hon.; pres.), Am. Assn. Plastic Surgeons (hon.), Sigma Xi, Phi Beta Kappa. Home: 69 Pearce Mitchell Pl Stanford CA 94305 Office: Stanford U Div Anatomy 269 Campus Dr Stanford CA 94305-5102 E-mail: rchase6880@aol.com.

CHASE, ROBERT F. educational association executive; BA, Providence Coll.; MA, Western Conn. State Coll. Social studies tchr. middle sch., Danbury, Conn.; pres. NEA, Washington, 1996—. Exec. bd. Nat. Coun. for the Accreditation Tchr. Edn., Nat. Found. for the Improvement Edn., Nat. Bd. Profl. Tchg. Stds. With U.S. Army, 1968-70. Mem. NEA Danbury (negotiations chair, v.p., pres.), Conn. Edn. Assn. (v.p., pres.). Office: NEA 1201 16th St NW Washington DC 20036-3290

CHASE, SANDRA LEE, clinical pharmacist, consultant; b. Oak Park, Ill., July 31, 1959; d. William Warren and Charlene Lois (Johnson) Chase; m. Christopher Paul Bloch, Sept. 8, 1984; children: Kyle Thaddeus Bloch, Matthew William Bloch. Student, Mich. State U., 1977-80; BS in Pharmacy, U. Mich., 1983, PharmD, 1984. Lic. pharmacist Del., Mich., Pa.; cert. leader arthritis found. YMCA Aquatic Program. Rsch. asst. U. Mich., Ann Arbor, 1980-81; pharmacy intern Three Rivers (Mich.) Hosp., 1981, Cmty. Pharmacy, Ann Arbor, 1980-83; pharmacy intern, grad. intern St. Francis Hosp., Wilmington, Del., 1982-83; resident in hosp. pharmacy Thomas Jefferson U. Hosp., Phila., 1984-85, clin. pharmacist in cardiopulmonary medicine, 1985-89; sr. med. info. coord. ICI Pharms. Group, Wilmington, Del., 1989-92; clin. pharmacist Thomas Jefferson U. Hosp., Phila., 1989-93, clin. pharmacist drug use policy and clin. svcs., 1993-98; clin. pharmacy specialist Spectrum Health, Grand Rapids, Mich., 1999—. Adj. asst. prof. clin. pharmacy Temple U. Coll. Pharmacy, 1990—98, Ferris State U. Coll. Pharmacy, 1999—; clin. instr. in pharmacy practice Phila. Coll. Pharmacy and Sci., 1985—87, clin. asst. prof., 1987—88, clin. assoc. prof., 1988—98; instr. clin. care cardiopulmonary medicine in nursing Episcopal Hosp., Phila., 1986—88, Thomas Jefferson U. Hosp., Phila., 1985—91, Our Lady of Lourdes Med. Ctr., Camden, NJ, 1988—91; coord., prof. pharmacology and drug therapeutic for advanced nursing practice course Sch. Nursing Ctr. Profl. Devel., U. Pa., Phila., 1994—2001; mem. Pa. Osteoporosis Soc. Bd., 1996—98; presenter in field. Mem. editl. bd. : RN, referee: ; contbg. editor; mem. editl. bd. : Med. Econs., referee: AHFS Drug Info., Am. Druggist, Am. Jour. Hosp. Pharmacy, Nursing 96 Drug Handbook, Nursing 97 Drug Handbook, Pharmacotherapy, Annals of Pharmacotherapy, U. Hosp. Consortium Monographs; contbr. articles to profl. jours. Mem. adv. bd. Nursing Mothers Network; cert. leader aquatic program Arthritis Found. YMCA, 2000—; chmn. Coll. Pharmacy Alumni Soc., 2000—, bd. dirs., 1991—97, 1999—. Fellow, Mich. Pharmacists Assn., 2001. Mem.: Am. Heart Assn., Aerobics and Fitness Assn. Am., Western Mich. Soc. Health-Sys. Pharmacists (bd. dirs. 1998—2000), Pediat. and Adult Asthma Network West Mich., Mich. Soc. Health Sys. Pharmacists (chair edn. com. 2000—), Mich. Pharm. Assn. (mem. exec. bd. 2002—), Del. Pharm. Soc. (conv. com. 1990—94, ACPE com. 1990—94), Nat. Headache Found., Am. Diabetes Assn., Am. Pharm. Assn., Am. Soc. Health Sys. Pharmacists, Am. Coll. Clin. Pharmacy, Rho Chi Pharm. Soc. Republican. Lutheran. Avocations: aerobics, waterskiing, cross-country skiing, gardening. Office: Spectrum Health Dept Pharmacy 100 Michigan St NE Grand Rapids MI 49503-2560 E-mail: Sandra.Chase@spectrum-health.org.

CHASE, THOMAS NEWELL, neurologist, researcher, educator; b. Westfield, N.J., May 23, 1932; s. Newell Adams and Gudrun Margarethe (Eskesen) C.; 1 child, Thomas Newell. BS, MIT, 1954; postgrad., Columbia U., 1957-58; MD,

Yale U., 1962; postgrad., Harvard U., 1963-66. Engr. Singer Mfg. Co., Bridgeport, Conn., 1954-55; technician Columbia U. Coll. Phys. and Surgs., 1957-58; intern in internal medicine Yale-New Haven Med. Center, 1962-63; asst. resident in neurology Mass. Gen. Hosp., Boston, 1963-64, resident, 1965-66; fellow in neuropathology Harvard U. Med. Sch., 1964-65; guest worker NIMH, Bethesda, Md., 1966-68, chief unit on neurology, 1968-70, chief sect. exptl. therapeutics, 1970-74; chief lab. of neuropharmacology Nat. Inst. Neurol. and Communicative Disorders and Stroke, Bethesda, 1974-76, dir. intramural research, 1974-83, chief pharmacology sect., 1976—, chief exptl. therapeutics br., 1983—. Mem. sci. adv. bd. Nat. Parkinson Found.; mem. adv. bd. Nat. Ataxia Found., Astra-Zenica. Assoc. editor Jour. Psychiatry and Neurosci.; mem. editl. bd. Progress in Neuro-Psychopharmacology, Movement Disorders, Drug Devel. Rsch., Parkinsonian and Related Disorders, Contemporary Neurology, Current Treatment Options in Neurology, Jour. Neural Transmission, Neurotoxicology Rsch., Neurodegenerative Diseases; contbr. articles to med. jours. Served with Signal Corps U.S. Army, 1955-57. Recipient Winternitz prize in pathology, 1960, Ramsay prize for clin. medicine, 1961, diploma of recognition of merit for humanitarian svcs. Govt. of Bolivia, 1974, USPHS Meritorious Svc. medal, 1978, 96, USPHS Outstanding Svc. medal, 1991, Springer prize for Parkinson's disease rsch., 1994; summer fellow, 1960; USPHS summer fellow, 1961; Nat. Inst. Neurol. Diseases and Blindness spl. fellow, 1966-68. Fellow Am. Coll. Neuro-Psychopharmacology, mem. Am. Neurol. Assn., Am. Acad. Neurology, Am. Soc. Exptl. Neurotherapeutics (pres. 1997-2001), Soc. Neurosci., Internat. Soc. Neurochemistry, Am. Soc. Neurochemistry, Assn. for Rsch. in Nervous and Mental Disease, Internat. Brain Rsch. Orgn., Internat. Basal Ganglia Soc., World Fedn. Neurology, Movement Disorder Soc. Office: NINDS 9000 Rockville Pike Rm 5c103 Bethesda MD 20892-0001

CHASE, WILLIAM ROBERT, television executive; b. Mt. Vernon, N.Y., Mar. 8, 1951; s. Irving Warren and Muriel Ada Chase. BA, Queens Coll., 1974; MS, Bklyn. Coll., 1976. Scenic and lighting dir. Bklyn. Coll. of CUNY, 1974-76; freelance lighting dir. N.Y.C., 1974—; unit prodn. mgr. various TV prodn. cos., 1983-87; prodn. mgr. Sta. WNET-TV/PBS, N.Y., 1979-87; dir. prodn. mgmt. Sta. WNET-TV, N.Y., 1987-88; dir. east coast prodn. HBO, Inc., N.Y.C., 1988-90, v.p. prodn., east coast, 1990—. Instr. Bklyn. Coll., 1976-85, N.Y. Inst. Tech., 1982-85. Assoc. producer Roanoak, 1985; unit prodn. mgr: (TV shows, mini-series, spls.) Kennedy, 1983, Finnegan Begin Again, 1984, Murder of Mary Phagan, 1987; line producer (TV series) Pee-Wee's Playhouse, 1986. Mem. Dirs. Guild Am., Nat. Acad. TV Arts and Scis. Avocations: photography, computers.

CHASEMAN, JOEL, communications consultant; b. Feb. 18, 1926; m. Marlene Meyerson, Sept. 11, 1955; children: Martha Hope, Joanne Amy. BA, Cornell U., 1948. CEO Post-Newsweek Stas., Washington, 1973-90; chmn. NATAS, 1980-82; dir. Advt. Coun., 1986-90; prin. Chaseman Enterprises Internat., 1990—. Chmn. Advanced TV Test Ctr., 1987—93; CEO NevadaVision, Inc., 1990—2001, Hobby Craft Interactive Network, 1999—; chmn. adv. bd. Nearware Networks, 2001—; adv. bd. Coun. Pub. Integrity, 2003—; mem. adv. bd. Ctr. for Pub. Integrity, 2003—. Trustee Mus. Broadcasting, 1988. Mem. Assn. Maximun Svc. Telecasters (chmn. 1988-91), Nat. Assn. Broadcasters (bd. dirs. 1988-90). E-mail: joechase@wdn.com.

CHASEN, SYLVAN HERBERT, computer applications consultant, investment advisor; b. Richmond, Va., May 19, 1926; s. Nathan and Hanna (Pass) C.; m. Catherine Hudlow, Mar. 25, 1946; children: Deborah Wyatt, Dianne Lipsey, Jane Morrison, Susan Mazur.. Student, Va. Poly. Inst., 1943-44; BS in Engring, B. Chem. Engring., Ga. Inst. Tech., 1946; MS, Emory U., 1951. Math. instr. Ga. Inst. Tech., Atlanta, 1946-50; head computer facility Naval Air Test Ctr., Patuxent, Md., 1951-58; dir. advanced computing CAD and interactive graphics Lockheed-Ga. Co., Marietta, 1958-87; pres. Center CAD/CAM Tech., Inc. Cons. Author: Geometric Principles and Procedures for Computer Graphics Applications, 1978, The Guide for the Evaluation and Implementation of CAD/CAM Systems, 1980, 2d edit., 1983. Served as ensign USN, 1944-46. Recipient Outstanding Contbns. award Gov. Md., 1957; recipient Disting. Contbns. award Soc. Mfg. Engrs., 1982 Mem. ASME, Soc. Mfg. Engrs., SIGGRAPH, NCGA Home: 760 Starlight Ct NE Atlanta GA 30342-2826

CHASEY, JACQUELINE, lawyer; Bar: N.J. 1983, N.Y. 1984. Formerly counsel Bertelsmann, Inc.; sr. counsel Bertelsman, Inc., 1990-93, v.p. legal affairs, 1994—2002, sr. v.p. legal affairs, 2002—. Office: Bertelsmann Inc 1540 Broadway New York NY 10036-4039

CHASNOFF, JULES, retired lawyer; b. St. Louis, July 15, 1927; s. Jacob and Julia Linenthal C.; m. Martha Slay, Aug. 21, 1949; children: David M., Paul E., Richard A. AB, Washington U., St. Louis, 1949; LLB, Harvard U., 1952. Bar: Mo. 1952, U.S. Dist. Ct. (ea. dist.) Mo. 1953, U.S. Ct. Claims 1960. Assoc. Tucker & Chasnoff, St. Louis, 1952-54, Grand, Peper, Martin & Roudebush and predecessors, St. Louis, 1954-59, Lowenhaupt & Chasnoff, St. Louis, 1959-63, ptnr., 1963-2001, ret., 2001. Mem. ABA, Mo. Bar Assn., Met. St. Louis Bar Assn., Am. Judicature Soc. Jewish. E-mail: julescha@swbell.net.

CHASON, JACOB (LEON CHASON), retired neuropathologist; b. Monroe, Mich., May 12, 1915; s. Ben and Ida (Beiser) C.; m. Helen Pelok, May 19, 1942; children: Steven, Ellen, David. AB, U. Mich., 1937, MD, 1940. Intern Wayne County Gen. Hosp., 1940-41, resident, 1941-42, 46-49, asst. pathologist, 1949-50; fellow in neuropathology Mayo Clinic, 1952; dir. lab. VA Hosp., Allen Park, Mich., 1950-52; asst. prof. neuropathology Wayne State U., 1952-54, asso. prof., 1954-57, prof., 1958-86, chmn. dept. pathology, 1964-78, assoc. dean Sch. Medicine, 1970-72; neuropathologist Henry Ford Hosp., Detroit, 1978-88, cons., 1989-90. Cons. in field. Contbr. articles to profl. publs. With U.S. Army, 1942-46. NIH sr. fellow, 1959-60; grantee, 1961-63 Mem. Am. Assn. Neuropathologists, Am. Soc. Clin. Pathologists, Coll. Am. Pathologists, Internat. Acad. Pathology, Am. Acad. Neurology. Home: Apt 103A 7831 Park Ln Dallas TX 75225-2041

CHASSAY, ROGER PAUL, JR., engineering executive; b. Chgo., Aug. 30, 1938; children: Cynthia, Terri, Donald, Dean, Paul, Brett. BS, La. State U., 1961; postgrad., Ohio State U., 1962. F8U-3 fighter wing designer, Dallas, 1958; aerospace engr. Saturn & Skylab Programs Office NASA/Marshall Space Flight Ctr., New Orleans & Huntsville, Ala., 1964-74, SPAR project mgr. Huntsville, 1974-77, mgr. integration/ test office Microgravity Projects Office, 1977-82; mgr. expt. carriers office Microgravity Projects Office, NASA/Marshall Space Flight Ctr., Huntsville, 1982-86, dep. mgr. Microgravity Projects Office, 1986-88; mgr. space sta./advanced projects office Microgravity Projects Office NASA/Marshall Space Flight Ctr., Huntsville, 1988-94, project mgr. lightning detection from earth orbit, 1995-98, asst. program mgr. Gravity Probe B, 1999—2002. Chmn. orbiter motion subcom. NASA, 1984-86, ctr. rep. flight assignments working group, Huntsville and Washington, 1985-86, chmn. internat. space sta. microgravity requirements integration group, Huntsville, 1990-94. Author: Application of Mathematics to the XB70 Bomber, 1963, Low-g Measurements by NASA, 1986, Processing Materials in Space: History and Future, 1987, (chpt.) Low Gravity Materials Experiments in Space Sta., 1989, Cooperation Between NASA and ESA for the First Microgravity Materials Science Glovebox, 1992, Microgravity Glovebox Program, 1998; author, editor: (NASA movie) Space Processing Applications Rocket Project, 1979. Sr. arbitrator Better Bus. Bur., Huntsville, 1987-97; pres. Holy Spirit Ch. Coun., Huntsville, 1982, N.E. Ala. Ch. Coun., Huntsville, 1984-85; scoutmaster Boy Scouts Am., Dayton, Ohio, 1963; clarinetist Huntsville Concert Band, 1987-91, 93—; pole vaulting All Am., Masters Track and Field, 2000-01. Capt. USAF, 1961-64. Assoc. fellow AIAA. Achievements include management of test program for world's largest turbojet engine, management of first successful levitation experiments in space, management of first materials science glovebox in space, management of first commercial product made in space (monodisperse latex spheres), management of first nuclear detector and beryllium experiments in space, management of first and second lightning detection instruments in space. Office: NASA Marshall Space Flight Ctr SD 31/53 Huntsville AL 35812

CHASSE, EMILY SCHUDER, librarian, educator, storyteller; b. Paducah, Ky., June 10, 1953; d. Charles Bernard and Ann (Sidwell) Schuder; m. William Chasse, Aug. 30, 1980; 1 child, Sarah Ann Schuder Chasse. Student, Iowa State U., 1972-74; BA in Elem. Edn., Antioch Coll., 1976; MLS, U. R.I., 1979. Cert. tchr., Conn. Child care worker Walker Home & Sch., Needham, Mass., 1975-78; children's libr. Plainville (Conn.) Pub. Libr., 1979-82; part-time instr. in children's lit. Manchester (Conn.) Community Coll., 1981-83; asst. curriculum lab. libr. Cen. Conn. State U., New Britain, 1982-89, libr. on-line search svcs., 1989—. Freelance storyteller, 1980—. Contbr. articles to profl. jours. Mem. ALA, Conn. Libr. Assn., Conn. Storytelling Assn., Hither & Yon Storytellers. Democrat. Mem. Soc. Of Friends. Office: Cen Conn State U Burritt Libr 1615 Stanley St New Britain CT 06053-2439

CHASSMAN, KAREN MOSS, educational administrator; b. Bklyn., Aug. 18, 1946; d. Bernard and Esther (Steier) Kahn; m. Robert Moss (div. 1973); 1 child, Jeff; m. Richard Chassman, Oct. 31, 1992 (dec. Feb. 1994). BA, Hunter Coll., 1967; MS in Edn., Bklyn. Coll., 1969, advanced cert. in lang. arts, 1978. Tchr. nursery, kindergarten and grades 1-6 Common Branches, 1967-78; sales rep., real estate broker various cos., 1978-91; dir., owner The Reading Improvement Ctr., East Islip, N.Y., 1991—. Mem. Islip C. of C., Islip Rotary (ednl. scholar 1992—). Avocations: aerobic exercise, antiques, travel. Office: Reading Improvement Ctr 2545 Middle Country Rd Centereach NY 11720 Address: 234 E Main St East Islip NY 11730 Office: Reading Improvement Ctr 268 East Main St East Islip NY 11730

CHASSMAN, LEONARD FREDRIC, labor union administrator, retired; b. Detroit, Sept. 30, 1935; s. Joachim and Lillian (Abrams) C.; m. Phyllis Perlman, Aug. 25, 1957; children: Mark, Cheryl, Gregory. BA, UCLA, 1957. Rep. AFTRA, Los Angeles, 1959-63, Screen Actors Guild, Los Angeles, 1963-65; staff exec. Writers Guild Am., West, Inc., Los Angeles, 1965-77, exec. dir., 1978-82; nat. exec. sec. Screen Extras Guild Inc., 1982-84; Hollywood exec. dir. Screen Actors Guild Inc., 1984-01, trustee Screen Actors Guild producers pension and health funds; bd. dirs. Entertainment Industry Found. Pres. Hollywood Entertainment Labor Coun. Bd. dirs. L.A. Pvt. Industry Coun. E-mail: Lchassman930@aol.com.

CHASTAIN, BRANDI DENISE, professional soccer player; b. San Jose, Calif., July 21, 1968; Mem. U.S. Women's Soccer Team, 1996; asst. coach women's soccer team Santa Clara U. Mem. Shiroke Serena, Japan, 1993. Recipient Gold medal, Olympic Games, 1996. Achievements include mem. championship team U.S. Olympic Festival; CONCACAF Championship, N.Y., 1993. Office: c/o Santa Clara U Athletics Dept 500 El Camino Real Santa Clara CA 95050-4345 also: US Soccer Fedn 1801 S Prairie Ave # 1811 Chicago IL 60616-1319

CHASTAIN, KENNETH DUANE, retired foreign language educator; b. Salem, Ind., July 20, 1934; s. Lloyd Lionel and Cristal Louise (Hoke) C.; m. Mary Janice McFadden, June 14, 1959; children: Kevin Duane, Brian Duane, Michael Allen. BS, Ind. U., 1956; MA, Ball State U., 1962; PhD, Purdue U., 1968. Tchr. Seymour HS, Ind., 1956-62, Columbus HS, Ind., 1962-64; grad. instr., prof. Purdue U., Lafayette, Ind., 1964-72; prof. Asbury Coll., Wilmore, Ky., 1972-73, U. Va., Charlottesville, Va., 1973-95, prof. emeritus, 1995—. Author: Developing S-L Skills, 1988, Imaginate, 1991, Spanish Grammar in Review, 1993, Exploraciones en la Literatura Hispanica, 1993, The Money Chase: Counting the Cost, 2000, Social Security and More: Comments on Government, 2001, English as a Communication System, 2001. With U.S. Army, 1957-58. Recipient Florence Steiner Leadership in Fgn. Lang. Edn. award Am. Coun. Teaching Fgn. Langs., 1989. Avocations: exercise, gardening, nature, travel. Home: 2674 Bakers Chapel Church Rd Big Sandy TN 38221-5318 E-mail: jkchas@compu.net.

CHASTAIN, MARK ALAN, dermatologist, otolaryngologist, educator; b. Columbus, Ga., Aug. 2, 1968; s. Joseph B. and Dorothea M. Chastain; m. Jennifer Buckley, Feb. 15, 2001; 1 child, Austin Joseph. BA, Emory U., 1990; MD, Tulane U., 1996. Diplomate Am. Bd. Dermatology, 2000. Intern Tulan & Charity Hosps., 1996—97, resident, 1997—2000; prin., owner Chastain Properties, Columbus, 1990—; asst. prof. dermatology and otolaryngology Med. Sch. Tulane U., New Orleans, 2001—02, clin. asst. prof. dermatology and otolaryngology, 2002—. Cons. Dermatology Cons., Atlanta, 2002—. Co-author: Dermatology Textbook, 2003; contbr. articles to profl. jours. Fellow, U. Ala., Birmingham, 2000—01. Mem.: Am. Coll. Mohs Micrographic Surgery and Cutaneous Oncology, Phi Beta Kappa. Home: 1081 Woodruff Plantation Pkwy Marietta GA 30067 Office: 80 Lacy St Ste 100 Marietta GA 30060

CHASTAIN, MERRITT BANNING, JR., lawyer; b. Jan. 28, 1940; s. Merritt Banning and Lydia (Spock) Chastain; m. Virginia Anne Ferguson, July 21, 1962; children: Merritt Banning III, Grayson Anne Clark. BS, U. Okla., 1962; JD, La. State U., 1967. Bar: La. 1967, U.S. Dist. Ct. (we. dist.) La. 1968, U.S. Dist. Ct. (ea. dist.) La. 1972, U.S. Ct. Appeals (5th cir.) 1972, U.S. Supreme Ct. 1979. Law clk. La. Ct. Appeals (2d cir.), Shreveport, La., 1967—68; assoc. Smitherman, Lunn, Chastain & Hill, Shreveport, 1968—72, ptnr., 1972—. Mng. dir. Nat. Assn. of Pipe Coating Applicators, 1979—; spl. counsel La. Pub. Facilities Authority, 1985—87. Chmn. United Way of Shreveport/Bossier City, 1975, Ark.-La.-Tex. Ambs., Inc., 1989; pres. Vols. Am., 1976, Norwela Coun. Boy Scouts Am., 1977—78, Demoiselle Club, 1992, Cotillion Gov. Bd., 1989, Shreveport Opera, 1981—95, sec., 1981; trustee Loyola Coll. Prep. Sch., 1984—89, exec. com., 1985—89, pres. bd. trustees, 1986—87; chmn. bd. Loyola Found., Shreveport, La., 1987—88; corp. sponsor chmn. Arthritis Found. Telethon, 1990. Named Outstanding Young Man of La., La. Jaycees, 1975, Outstanding Young Man of Shreveport, Shreveport Jaycees, 1975; named to Hall of Fame, Nat. Assn. Pipe Coating Applicators, 2003. Mem.: ABA (La. mem. chmn. 1976—82), La. Law Inst., Shreveport Bar Assn. (exec. coun. 1971—75, sec.-treas. 1972, bd. govs. young lawyer's sect. 1967—74, pres. young lawyer's sect. 1974), La. State Bar Assn. (spl. com. 1974—75), So. Trace Country Club (Shreveport), Rotary, Shreveport Club. Democrat. Episcopalian. Home: 330 Corinne Cir Shreveport LA 71106-6004 Office: Smitherman Lunn Chastain & Hill 333 Texas St Ste 717 Shreveport LA 71101-3673

CHASTON, DEANNE WINTERTON, editor; b. Ogden, Utah; d. Kelly Bert and Ruth Ann Winterton; m. Ty Victor Chaston, Jan. 2, 1998. AA, Weber State U., 1998, BA, 2000. Online editor The Signpost, Ogden, Utah, 1998—99, asst. news editor, 1998—99; reporter The Morgan County News, Utah, 1998—99, editor, 1999—. Merit badge counselor Boy Scouts Am., Washington, Utah, 2000. Mem.: Soc. Profl. Journalists, Golden Key Honor Soc., Phi Kappa Phi. Mem. Lds Ch. Avocations: sewing, writing, crocheting. Home: 366 W 4775 S Washington Terrace UT 84405 Office: The Morgan County News PO Box 190 Morgan UT 84050

CHATARD, PETER RALPH NOEL, JR., aesthetic plastic surgeon; b. New Orleans, June 25, 1936; s. Peter Ralph Sr. and Alberta Chatard; m. Patricia Myrl White, Jan. 31, 1963; children: Andrea Michelle, Faedra Noelle, Tahra Deonne. BS in Biology, Morehouse Coll., 1956; MD, U. Rochester, 1960. Diplomate Am. Bd. Plastic Surgery, Am. Bd. Otolaryngology. Intern Colo. Gen. Hosp., 1960-61; asst. resident in gen. surgery Highland Gen. Hosp., Rochester, N.Y., 1963-64; resident in otolaryngology Strong Meml. Hosp., Rochester, 1964-67; resident in plastic and reconstructive surgery U. Fla., 1980-82; staff otolaryngologist Group Health Corp. of Puget Sound, Seattle, 1967-68; practice medicine specializing in otolaryngology Seattle, 1968-80; practice medicine specializing in plastic surgery, 1982—; clin. asst. prof. otolaryngology, head and neck surgery U. Wash., Seattle, 1975—. Plastic surgery cons. western sec. Maxillofacial Rev. Bd. State of Wash., 1982-90, cons. Conservation of Hearing Program, 1968-80; trustee Physicians and Dentist Credit Bur., 1974-80, 84-87, pres. 1976-77, 84-85; active staff mem. Northwest Hosp., Seattle; courtesy staff Swedish Hosp., Overlake Hosp., Bellevue, Stevens Meml. Hosp., Edmond, Wash., Seattle, others. Capt. USAF, 1961-63. Fellow ACS, Am. Rhinologic Soc., Seattle Surg. Soc., Am. Acad. Facial Plastic and Reconstructive Surgery, Am. Acad. Otolaryngology-Head and Neck Surgery, Northwest Acad. Otolaryngology and Head and Neck Surgery, Soc. for Ear, Nose and Throat Advances in Children, Pacific Oto-Ophthalmological Soc.; mem. Am. Soc. Plastic Surgery, Am. Soc. for Aesthetic Plastic Surgery, Inc., Lipoplasty Soc. N. Am., Wash. Soc. Plastic Surgeons, Nat. Med. Assn., King County Med. Soc., Wash. Med. Assn., N.W. Soc. of Plastic Surgeons. Avocations: photography, cynology, microcomputing, architecture and design. Home: 13211 Frazier Pl NW Seattle WA 98177-4132 Office: AEsteem Aesthetic Plastic Surgery Inc 1200 N Northgate Way Seattle WA 98133-8916 E-mail: chatard@aol.com.

CHATEAUNEUF, JOHN EDWARD, chemistry educator, researcher; b. Lynn, Mass., Apr. 19, 1957; s. Edward Andre Chateauneuf and Blanche Louise Foley-Chateauneuf. BS in Chemistry, Salem (Mass.) State Coll., 1981; PhD in Chemistry, Tufts U., 1986. Rsch. assoc. Nat. Rsch. Coun. of Can., Ottawa, Ont., 1986-88; rsch. assoc. radiation lab. U. Notre Dame, Ind., 1988-90, mem. faculty, staff scientist, 1990-96; asst. prof. Western Mich. U., Kalamazoo, 1996-2000, assoc. prof., 2000—. Contbr. articles to profl. jours. Mem. AIChE, Am. Chem. Soc., Inter-Am. Photochem. Soc. Office: Western Mich U Dept Chemistry Kalamazoo MI 49008 E-mail: chateauneuf@wmich.edu.

CHATELAIN, DALIA DE LA PAZ, elementary education educator, counselor; b. Manzanillo, Oriente, Cuba, Oct. 13, 1954; arrived in U.S., 1967; d. Ciro V. and Dalia de la Paz; divorced; children: Katie, Kerri. BS, U. New Orleans, 1977; MA in Counseling, Our Lady of Holy Cross Coll., 1997. Lic. profl. counselor, nat. cert. sch. counselor, lic. marriage and family therapist. Tchr. Health and Phys. Edn. Archdiocese of New Orleans, Gretna, La., 1977-82; tchr. pre-kindegarten, kindegarten, resource bilingual tchr. Jefferson Parish Schs., Gretna., 1986-97, counselor, 1997—, bilingual counselor, 1998—. Co-chair Safe and Drug Free program, Gretna, 1996—. Vol. ARC, Gretna, 1994—; vol. Cath. ch., Gretna. Mem. Am. Counseling Assn., Am. Sch. Counselor Assn., La. Sch. Counselor Assn., Chi Sigma Iota (Alpha Zeta chpt. rep.-at-large 1997-98, pres. 1999-2000, Outstanding Mem. award 1998, pres. 1999—).

CHATELAINE, KENNETH LEO, education educator, psychoanalyst; b. Mpls., Minn., Oct. 16, 1931; s. Frank Arthur Chatelaine and Rose L. Ney. BA, St. Thomas Universtiy, 1954—57; MLA, The Johns Hopkins U., 1967—69; PhD, The U. of Md., 1970—78; NcPsyA, The Wash. Sch. of Psychiatry, 1982—86. DABPS-Specialties, Child Psychology and Psychoanalysis Springfield, MO., 1992, lic. cert. profl. counselor State of Md., 1995, cert. instr. Nat. Air and Space Mus., Wash., DC, 1996, aerospace tech. specialist Nat. Air and Space Mus., Wash., DC, 1999. Prof. of psychology Anne Arundel C.C., Arnold, Md., 1970—; lectr. Shephard Pratt Sch. of Mental Health Studies, Towson, Md., 1981—82, Wash. Sch. of Psychiatry, 1982—83; psychoanalyst Pvt. Practice, Severna Park, Md., 1991—2002. Cons. Margaret Mahler Found., Philadelphia, 1995—; founder Anne Arundel County Mental Health Edn. Coalition, Annapolis, Md., 1982—90. Author: (book) Harry Stack Sullivan, The Formative Years, 1981, Good Me, Bad Me, Not Me, 1992, Harry Stack Sullivan, Founder of Interpersonal Psychiatry, (monogram) Harry Stack Sullivan, The Man and Clinican, 1991. Vice chmn. Md. State Mental Health Adv. Coun., 1980—85; mem. Anne Arundel Mental Health Adv. Com., Annapolis, Md., 1982—88. Recipient Centennial Spkr., APA, 1991. Mem.: Internat. Soc. for the Psychol. Treatment of Schizophrenia and Other Psychoses, Wash. Sch. of Psychiatry, APA (life). Achievements include research in scholor on the interpersonal theory of psychiatry. Avocations: skiing, tennis, sailing, flying. Home: 359 Gatewater Ct #402 Glen Burnie MD 21060 Office: Dr Kenneth L Chatelaine 124 Riggs Ave Severna Park MD 21146 Home Fax: 410-768-7924.

CHATELIER, PAUL RICHARD, aviation psychologist, training company officer; s. Paul and Mary Chatelier; m. Mary Lu Moss; children: Michael, Suzanne. BS in Biology, Chemistry, Psychology, U. Fla., 1960; MA in Psychology, U. Miss., 1962; postgrad., U. N.Mex., 1967-69. Commd. ensign USN, 1962, advanced through grades to capt., 1986; sr. v.p. strategic planning Perceptronics, Inc., Washington, 1986-93; with Office Sci. and Tech. Policy Exec. Office of President U.S., Washington, 1993-96; dir. for edn. tech. edn. activity Dept. Def., Washington, 1996—. U.S. rep. on human factors NATO, Brussels, 1978—86; mem. task force tng. and wargaming Def. Sci. Bd., 1986—88, task force edn. and tng., 1999; U.S. rep. on tng. Tech. Coop. Panel, Washington, 1986—87; mem. indsl. adv. com. U. Ctrl. Fla. Inst. for Simulation and Tng.; edn. and tng. cons. Office Sci. and Tech. White Ho., 1993—96; workshop dir. internat. tng. and human factors; del. at large human factors and medicine panel NATO, 1999; dep. dir. Advanced Distributed Learning Co-Lab., Alexandria, Va., 1999—2001; cons. Potomac Inst. for Policy Studies, 2002—. Co-author: (book) Psychology of Reality, 1985; editor: Manprint & System Integ, 1988, International Human Factors, 1991, Advanced Technology for Training Design, NATO, 1993, Opening the Classroom Doors...Distance Learning, 1995, Virtual Reality Trainings Future?, 1997. Career advisor Fairfax County Pub. Sch., 1982—88. Mem.: Nat. Security Indsl. Assn. (chmn. manpower pers. tng. 1986—89), Va. Human Factors Soc. (pres. 1982—83), Nat. Human Factors Soc. (mem. exec. coun. 1982—85). Avocations: tennis, community activities. Home: 8021 W Point Dr Springfield VA 22153-3023 E-mail: pchat@mindspring.com.

CHATFIELD, JUDITH SPENCER, garden historian; b. N.Y.C., Sept. 20, 1942; d. Sherwood Clarke and Helen Spencer Chatfield; m. Frederick Woodbury Schwerin, Jr., July 12, 1975. BA, Syracuse U., 1964, MA, 1969; MPhil, Courtauld Inst. Art, U. London, 1972. Art and garden tour dir., 1980—. Garden history lectr., 1988—; vis. Am. Acad. in Rome, 2003. Author: Boboli Gardens, 1972, A Tour of Italian Gardens, 1988, The Classic Italian Garden, 1991, Gardens of the Italian Lakes, 1992; contbr.: The Grove Dictionary of Art, 1996; photographer gardens Rizzoli Pub., 1988—. Dir. Hotchkiss Libr. Bd., Sharon, Conn., 1992—. Recipient Fulbright fellowship Fulbright Assn., 1967-68. Mem. City Gardens Club N.Y.C., Sharon Garden Club (pres. 1992), Mad Gardeners. Episcopalian. Avocations: travel, photography, languages, history, literature. Home: 44 Morey Rd Sharon CT 06069

CHATFIELD, MARY VAN ABSHOVEN, librarian; b. Bay Shore, N.Y. d. Cornelius and Elma Elizabeth (Sumner) van Abshoven; m. Robert W. Chatfield, June 22, 1963 (div. 1981); 1 child, Robert Warner Jr.; m. Alexander Watts, Jan. 6, 1996 (div. 2000). AB, Radcliffe Coll., 1958; SM, Columbia U., 1961; MBA, Harvard U., 1972. With library system Harvard U., Cambridge, Mass., 1961-92, librarian Bus. Sch., 1963-78, head libr., 1978-92; acting head libr. Countway Libr. Harvard Med. Sch., 1988-89; head libr. Angelo State U., San Angelo, Tex., 1992-95; collections care mgr. Fosterfields, Morristown, N.J., 1996-97; mgr. libr. svcs. Montclair (N.J.) Art Mus., 1997; exec. dir. Mendham (N.J.) Free Pub. Libr., 1997-99; coord. tech. svcs. Tom Green County Libr., San Angelo, Tex., 1999—. Mem. Daughters of Brit. Empire. Democrat. Episcopalian. Avocations: reading, embroidery, collecting, museum studies, public art. Home: 115 N Jackson St San Angelo TX 76901-3215 E-mail: marychat@wcc.net.

CHATFIELD, MICHAEL, accounting educator; b. Seattle, June 13, 1934; s. Chester and Thelma (McCormick) C. BA in Bus. Adminstrn., U. Wash., 1957, MBA, 1962; D in Bus. Adminstrn., U. Oreg., 1966. CPA, Wash. Jr. acct. Yergen and Meyer CPAs, Astoria, Oreg., 1957-58; acct. Mill Factors Corp., N.Y.C., 1959; staff acct. R.C. Mounsey and Co. CPAs, Seattle, 1959-61; tchg. asst. acctg. U. Oreg., Eugene, 1962-63, instr. acctg., 1963-65; asst. prof. acctg. UCLA, 1965-72; sr. lectr. acctg. U. Canterbury, New Zealand, 1972-73; prof. acctg. Calif. State U., Hayward, 1973-82, 84-90, Fresno, 1982-84, So. Oreg. U., Ashland, 1990—. Mem. numerous coms. So. Oreg. U., 1991-96; presenter confs. in field. Author: A History of Accounting Thought, 1974 (rev. edit. 1978, Japanese edit. 1979, Korean edit. 1985, Chinese edit. 1989); co-author: (with Denis Neilson) Cost Accounting, 1983, (with Richard Vangermeersch) The History of Accounting: An International Encyclopedia, 1996; editor: Contemporary Studies in the Evolution of Accounting Thought, 1968 (Spanish edit., 1970, 79), The English View of Accountants' Duties and Responsibilities, 1881-1902, 1978; mem. editl. bd. The Acctg. Rev., 1970-72, 74-75, The Accounting Historians Jour., 1976-95; contbr. articles to profl. jours. Mem. Am. Acctg. Assn., Acad. Acctg. Historians (Hourglass award 1974, 96), Beta Alpha Psi. Office: So Oreg Univ Bus Sch Ashland OR 97520

CHATFIELD-TAYLOR, ADELE, historic preservationist; b. Jan. 29, 1945; d. Hobart and Mary Owen (Lyon) C-T; m. John Guare, May 20, 1981. BA, Manhattanville Coll., 1966; MS in Hist. Preservation, Columbia U., 1974; postgrad., Harvard U., 1978-79; ArtsD (hon.), Lake Forest Coll., 1995. Archtl. historian Hist. Am. Bldg. Survey, Washington, 1967; co-founder, dir. Urban Deadline Archs., Inc., 1968-73; with N.Y.C. Landmarks Preservation Commn., 1973-80; founder, exec. dir. N.Y. Landmarks Preservation Found., 1980-84; dir. design arts program Nat. Endowment for Arts, 1984-88; pres. Am. Acad. in Rome, N.Y.C., 1988—. Adj. prof. hist. preservation program Grad. Sch. Arch. and Planning, Columbia U., 1976-84; guest lectr. Harvard U., MIT, Columbia U., NYU, U. Va. Contbr. articles to profl. jours. Mem. Thomas Jefferson Found. for Monticello, 2001—; bd. dirs. Preservation ACTION, 1976—84; trustee Ctr. for Bldg. Conservation, 1978—84; mem. U.S. del. to China Women in Arch., 1977, 1980, Hist. Preservationists, 1982; mem. exec. com. U.S./Internat.

Coun.on Monuments and Sites, 1979—84, vice chmn. design arts policy panel, 1978—82; trustee Tiber Island History Mus., 1983—; bd. dirs. Internat. Design Conf., Aspen, 1986—90, Nat. Bldg. Mus., 1989—95; mem. commn. Fine Arts, 1990—94; trustee Nat. Trust for Hist. Preservation, 1999—; mem. restoration com. South St. Seaport Mus., 1975—84; mem. adv. bd. Jeffersonian Restoration, 1989—; bd. dirs. Greenwich Village Trust for Hist. Preservation, 1983—84; mem. lawn adv. bd. U. Va., 1982—86. Recipient Rome prize Am. Acad. in Rome, 1983-84; Loeb gellow Harvard U, 1978-79; archtl. fellow Ednl. Facilities Lab. Acad. Ednl. Devel., 1982-83, fellow N.Y. Inst. Humanities, 1983-89. Fellow Am. Acad. Arts & Scis.; mem. Nat. Trust Hist. Preservation, Friends of Cast Iron Arch., Met. Mus. Art, Century Assn., Pug Dog Club of Greater N.Y. Office: Am Acad in Rome 7 E 60th St New York NY 10022-1001 E-mail: a.chatfield-taylor@aarome.org.

CHATHAM, LLOYD REEVE, lawyer; b. Jackson, Miss., Aug. 16, 1958; s. Archie Reeves Chatham and Anna C. Smith; m. Louise Lucas, July 2, 1983; 1 child, Christopher Lloyd. Student, Hinds Jr. Coll., Raymond, Miss., 1977-78; BS, Miss. State U., 1981; JD, Miss. Coll. Sch. Law, 1996. Bar: Miss. Supreme Ct. 1996, U.S. Dist. Ct. (no. and so. dist.) Miss. 1996, U.S. Ct. Appeals (5th cir.) 1996. Mgr. Miss. State U. Food Svcs., Starkville, 1981-83; gen. mgr. Dobbs Houses, Inc., Jackson, 1983-92; lawyer Waller & Waller, Jackson, 1996-99; pvt. practice Chatham Law Office, Brandon, Miss., 1999; gen. counsel Financial Technologies, Inc., Jackson, 1999—. Dir. Miss. Restaurant Assn., Jackson, 1989-92; v.p. Jackson Restaurant Assn., 1990, pres., 1991. Choir mem. St. Peters By-The-Lake, Brandon, Miss., 1997, Miss. Chorus, Brandon, 1998. Named Miss. Restaurant Mgr. of Yr., Miss. Restaurant Assn., Jackson, 1992. Mem. ATLA, ABA, Miss. Bar Assn., Hinds County Bar Assn., Rankin County Bar Assn., Jackson Young Lawyers, Christian Legal Soc., Federalist Soc., Phi Delta Phi, Alpha Phi Omega (v.p., pres.). Avocations: antique collecting, travel, antique collecting, traveling, music. Home: 1201 Martin Dr Brandon MS 39047-6448 Office: 200 Briarwood West Drive Jackson MS 39206 E-mail: chathaml@bellsouth.net.

CHATHAM, RICHARD DOUGLAS, mathematics educator; b. Statesville, NC, June 5, 1968; s. Ricky Morgan and Geraldine Lyn Chatham. BS, Wake Forest U., 1990; PhD, U. of Tenn., 2000. Vis. asst. prof. Wake Forest U., Winston-Salem, NC, 2000—01; asst. prof. Morehead (Ky.) State U., 2001—. Mem.: Math. Assn. of Am., Am. Math. Soc. Home: 253 Chestnut Ln Morehead KY 40351 Office: Morehead State U Dept Math Morehead KY 40351 Personal E-mail: d.chatham@moreheadstate.edu. E-mail: d.chatham@moreheadstate.edu.

CHATIGNY, ROBERT NEIL, judge; b. 1951; AB, Brown U., 1973; JD, Georgetown U., 1978. Atty. Williams & Connolly, Washington, 1981-83; ptnr. Chatigny and Palmer, Hartford, Conn., 1984-86, Chatigny & Cowdery, Hartford, 1991-94; pvt. practice Hartford, 1986-90; dist. judge U.S. Dist. Ct., Hartford, Conn., 1994—. Office: 450 Main St Hartford CT 06103-3022

CHATLEN, STANLEY LEE, logistics executive; b. Washington, Nov. 6, 1937; s. Louis and Hannah (Fisher) C.; m. Patricia Adams, May 9, 1965 (dec. Nov. 1988); m. Martha Cahill, June 9, 1990; children: Sarah and Emily (twins), John Louis. BS, U Md., 1964; MBA, Wayne State U., 1968. Supr. Ford Motor Co., Detroit, 1964-66; divsn. traffic mgr. Chrysler Corp., Centerline, Mich., 1966-70; regional mgr. Airborne Freight Corp., Detroit, 1970-75; v.p., regional mgr. Shulman Air Freight, Chgo., 1975-78; v.p. svc. Associated Air Freight, New Hyde Park, N.Y., 1978-81; dir .mktg. and sales Pilot Air Freight, Newark, 1981-83; v.p. Central Air Freight, Inc., Valley Stream, N.Y., 1983-87; exec. v.p. Apollo Express Inc., Norwich, NY, 1987-88; pres. Chatlen Transp. Enterprises, Inc., Huntington, N.Y., 1988-97, New Media, Inc., 1996-98; v.p. sales Americold Logistics, Atlanta, 1998—2002; sr. ptnr. Stanley L. Chatlen, LLC, 2002—03; sales and mktg. mgr. Atlas Cold Storage, McDonough, Ga., 2003—. Instr. Henry Ford C.C., Dearborn, Mich., 1973-75, adv. bd., 1975; adj. prof. sales and mktg. SUNY, Westbury, 1997. Served with U.S. Army, 1958-60. Recipient Alcoa Found. award, 1964. Mem. Am. Mgmt. Assn., Coun. Logistics Mgmt. (dir. Atlanta Roundtable), Assn. Transp. Practitioners, Am. Soc. Transp. and Logistics, Delta Nu Alpha (past local dir.). Home: 3300 Sundew Ct Alpharetta GA 30005-4200 E-mail: schatlen@hotmail.com.

CHATLOS, WILLIAM EDWARD, management consultant; b. Turtle Creek, Pa., Aug. 28, 1927; s. Rudolph and Elizabeth (Mraz) C.; m. Margaret Eileen Jackson. Student, U. Pitts., 1946-47, Ursinus Coll., 1948-49; BS magna cum laude, Boston U., 1951; postgrad., N.Y. Inst. Fin., 1955-56. With Georgeson & Co., N.Y.C., 1952-81, prin. in charge mgmt. cons. for investor rels., 1957-81; prin. Chatlos & Co. Inc., North Caldwell, N.J., 1981—. Bd. dirs. Kelso Inst.; cons. state govts.; lectr. in field. Editor Trends in Mgmt.-Investor Rels., 1957-81; contbr. articles to profl. publs. Mem. Soc. Profl. Mgmt. Cons., Pub. Rels. Soc. Am., Am. Mgmt. Assn., Assn. Corp. Growth, Investor Rels. Assn. (pres. 1966-67), Nat. Investor Rels. Inst. (co-founder, pres. 1974-75). Office: Chatlos & Co Inc 165 Grandview Ave Caldwell NJ 07006-4743

CHATMAN, ELEANOR LOUISE, secondary school educator; b. Nashville, Aug. 30, 1959; d. Donald Leveritt and Eleanor Scrutchions Chatman. BA, Oberlin Coll., 1982; MA, Ea. Mich. U., 1991. Substitute tchr. Chgo. Pub. Schs., 1984—87, Spanish/French tchr., 1991—; grad. asst. Ea. Mich. U., Ypsilanti, 1989—91; Spanish tchr. Diversified Ednl. Svcs., Detroit, 1990. Singer: (TV series) The Tonight Show, 1996. Singer Christ Universal Temple, 1994; mem. Christ Universal Temple Ensemble, 1994—99. Scholar, Nat. Bd. for Profl. Tchg. Stds., 2002. Avocations: singing, dancing, religious study.

CHATO, JOHN CLARK, mechanical and bioengineering educator; b. Budapest, Hungary, Dec. 28, 1929; s. Joseph Alexander and Elsie (Wasserman) C.; m. Elizabeth Janet Owens, Aug. 1954; children: Christine B., David J., Susan E. ME, U. Cin., 1954; MS, U. Ill., 1955; PhD, MIT, 1960. Co-op student, trainee Frigidaire div. GMC, Dayton, Ohio, 1950—54; grad. fellow U. Ill., Urbana, 1954—55; grad. fellow, inst. MIT, Cambridge, 1955—58, asst. prof., 1958—64; assoc. prof. U. Ill., Urbana, 1964—69, prof., 1969—96, prof. emeritus, 1996—, chmn. exec. com. bioengring. faculty, 1972—78, 1982—83, 1984—85, asst. dean of engring., 1997—98. Cons. Industry and Govt., 1958—; dir., founder Biomed. Engring. Systems Team, Urbana, Ill, 1974-78; assoc. editor Jour. Biomech. Engring., 1976-82. Patentee in field; contbr. articles to profl. jours., chpts. to books on heat transfer, bio-heat transfer, refrigeration, air conditioning, cryogenics, and thermal systems. Com. mem. troop 6 Boy Scouts Am., Urbana, 1984—86; com. mem. Urbana Plan Commn., 1973—78; mem. adv. com. Urbana Park Dist., 1981—84; 2nd v.p. Champaign County Izaak Walton League, 1986, 1st v.p., 1987, pres., 1988—92, bd. dirs., state dir., 1992—; mem. Urbana Postal Customer Adv. Coun., 2002—; trustee 1st Presbyn. Ch., Urbana, 1976—78, 1999—2001, elder, 1982—85; bd. dirs. Univ. YMCA, Champaign, Ill., 1976—78, 1987—90. Recipient Tobin award Champaign County Izaak Walton League, 1992, Cmty. Svc. award Urbana Park Dist., 1996, Russell Scott Meml. award, Cryogenic Engring. Conf., 1979; named Disting. Engring. Alumnus, U. Cin., 1972, NSF fellow 1961, Fogarty Sr. Internat. fellow 1978-79; Japan Soc. Promotion of Sci. fellow, 1997. Fellow: ASME (exec. com. bioengring. divsn. 1992—96, sec. 1993—94, chmn. 1994—95, Charles Russ Richards Meml. award 1978, N.R. Lissner award 1992, Dedicated Svc. award 2000), Am. Inst. Med. and Biol. Engrs.; mem.: ASHRAE (treas. East Ctrl. Ill. chpt. 1984, sec. 1985, 1987, 1st v.p. 1988, pres. 1989), IEEE (sr.), Am. Soc. Engring. Edn., Internat. Inst. Refrigeration (assoc.), Audubon Soc. Champaign County (bd. dirs. 1988—89, v.p. 1990, treas. 1991—93, v.p. 1995—96, treas. 1998—99, pres. 2000—02, bd. dirs. 2002), Exch. Club Urbana (bd. dirs. 1989—91, 1995—96, pres.-elect 1996—97, pres. 1997—98, dist. dir. 2001—). Achievements include research in fields of heat transfer, bio-heat transfer, refrigeration, air conditioning, cryogenics, and thermal systems. Office: U Ill Dept Mech Indsl Engring 1206 W Green St Urbana IL 61801-2906 E-mail: jbchato@staff.uiuc.edu.

CHATOFF, MICHAEL ALAN, lawyer; b. N.Y.C., Aug. 18, 1946; s. Alexander Zelig and Leona Rhoda (Weiss) C. BA, CUNY, 1967; JD, Bklyn. Law Sch., 1971; LLM, NYU, 1978. Bar: N.Y. 1971, U.S. Dist. Ct. (so. and ea. dists.) N.Y. 1978, U.S. Ct. Appeals (2d cir.) 1980, U.S. Supreme Ct. 1980. Reader Chgo. Title Ins. Co., N.Y.C., 1972; chief U.S. Code Congl. and Adminstrv. News West Pub. Co., Westbury, N.Y., 1972-97. Cons. N.Y. Sch. for Deaf, N.Y.C. Mayor's Office for Disabled, Westchester County Legis.; lectr. N.Y. State Dept. of Edn. Vocat. Ednl. Svcs. for Individuals with Disabilities, N.Y. Sch. Deaf, Lexington Sch. for Deaf, Parents for Deaf Awareness, Am. Profl. Soc. for Deaf, N.Y. Ctr. for Law and the Deaf, Coun. on Jewish Deaf Edn. and Rehab., Nat. Coun. on Deaf People and Deafness, NYU. Assoc. law editor Ency. on Deaf People and Deafness; contbr. articles to Nat. Law Jour., N.Y. Law Jour., Able Adv., Communication Outlook, Deaf Spectrum. Bd. dirs. Westchester Cmty. Svcs. for Hearing Impaired; counsel Conn. African-Am. Deaf Advocate; mem. Supreme Ct. Hist. Soc.; del. nominee Dem. Nat. Conv., 1992. Mem. ABA, Queens County Bar Assn., Assn. of Bar of City of N.Y., Nat. Assn. Deaf, Am. Contract Bridge League, Nassau Bar Assn. Avocations: bridge, jogging, weight-lifting. Home: 26909T Grand Central Pkwy Floral Park NY 11005-1010

CHATT, ALLEN BARRETT, psychologist, neuroscientist; b. Phoenix, July 17, 1949; s. Arthur Beecher Ellis and Helen (Scheidt) Chatt; m. Gail Nancy Anguish, Aug. 21, 1971. BS in Psychology with honors, SUNY, Buffalo, 1971; MS in Psychology, Fla. State U., 1974, PhD in Psychology and Neuroscience, 1978. Rsch. asst. Fla. State U., Tallahassee, 1971-76; predoctoral fellow U. Tex. Med. Br., Galveston, 1977; postdoctoral fellow sch. medicine Yale U., New Haven, 1978-80, rsch. asst. prof. neurology Sch. Medicine, 1981-87, rsch. assoc. prof., 1988—91, scholars chair, 1991; rsch. psychologist VA Med. Ctr., West Haven, Conn., 1978-84, sr. rsch. psychologist, 1985-90, sr. rsch. psychologist disability retirement pension, 1991—; founder, exec. dir., consulting psychologist Phoenix Fund for Neurologically Challenged, New Haven, Tallahassee, 1991—. Grant reviewer NSF, 1982—, NIH, 1982—, VA, 1982—; vis. prof. neuroscience Beijing Normal U., 1987, U. Glasgow, 1994—95; neuroscience reviewer Am. Psychol. Soc. Convs., 1991—; sci.-by-mail scientist Mus. Sci., Boston, 1991—; psychol. cons., case mgr. nuerologically impaired; pvt. funding nuerol. rsch.; courtesy prof. movement scis. Fla. State U., 1999—. Contbr. chapters to books, articles articles to profl. jours.; mem. editl. bd. Brain Rsch., 1983—86, Exptl. Neurology, 1982—86, Exptl. Brain Rsch., 1984—88, Quar. Jour. Exptl. Physiology, 1986. Sponsor Bobby Bowden Classic Fellowship Christian Athletes, 1992—, Bill Campbell Challenge Children's Miracle Network, 1996—99, Sandels Fund Excellence Coll. Human Scis., 2000; bd. dirs. Wal-Mart/Children's Miracle Network, No. Fla., 1996—99, Jennifer Harrison Fund, 1995—; judge Sam Walton Cmty. Leadership Scholarship Program, 1998—99, Phoenix Fund Collegiate Scholarship Human Scis., 1999—; sponsor Jennifer Harrison Meml. Golf Tournament, 1991—2000, Freedom Scholarship Batavia HS Class 1965, 1992—, Camp Sunshine, 1992—, Goodspeed Opera Ho., 1995—, Fla. State U. Seminole Classic, 1998—2000, Boy's Town Invitational N. Fla., 1998—2000, Fla. State U., 1999—, Scholarship Applied Biomedical Undergrad. Study, 1999—; mem. Rep. Senatorial Inner Cir., Washington, 1985, Eisenhower Commn., 1995; life mem. Rep. Nat. Com., 1993—; mem. adv. bd. Ellingsworth Press, 1998—. Recipient Most Sr. Benefactor award, Children's Miracle Network, 1996—99, Gold Miracle Maker award, 1998, Platinum Miracle Maker award, 1999; Regents scholar, N.Y. State, 1965—69, VoHab scholar, 1965—71, Rsch. grantee, NIH, 1982—87. Mem.: AAAS, Soc. Pain Practice Mgmt., Am. Epilepsy Soc., Soc. Neuroscience, Epilepsy Found. Am., Am. Psychol. Soc., Yale Neurology Alumni Assn. (charter), Pres.'s Club. Republican. Methodist. Achievements include development of neurosurgical procedure increasing the effectiveness of stellate ganglion blocks for the treatment of relfex sympathetic dystrophy in humans; discovery of differential neuronal circuits involved in focal and secondarily generalized seizure activity in neocortical model of epilepsy; brain cells that become abnormal initially in focal and secondarily generalized seizure activity; mid brain neuronal circuits modulating pain; thermal evoked potential in humans and the localization of cortical cells responsive to pain. Home: PO Box 1449 699 Goose Ln Guilford CT 06437-0549 also: 2949 Golden Eagle Dr E Tallahassee FL 32312-4008

CHATTERJEE, AMITAVA, finance educator, consultant; b. Calcutta, West Bengal, India, Jan. 10, 1961; came to U.S., 1986; s. Nepal and Shila Chatterjee; m. Rupa Bhattacharjya, Dec. 15, 1993; 1 child, Anirudha. BS, U. Calcutta 1983, MS, 1985; postgrad. diploma in operational rsch., Ops. Rsch. Soc. India, Calcutta, 1985; PhD, U. Miss., 1992. Cert. cash mgr. Assn. Fin. Profls., 2002. Jr. rsch. fellow U. Calcutta, India, 1985—86; tchg. and rsch. asst. U. Miss., University, 1987-90, 1990-92; coord. area econs. and fin., asst. prof. fin. Lemoyne Owen Coll., Memphis, 1992-96; asst. prof. fin. Fayetteville (N.C.) State U., 1996-99, assoc. prof. fin., 1999—2001; prof. fin. Tex. So. U., Houston, 2001—. Advisor Econs. and Fin. Club, Fayetteville, 1996—2001. Co-author: Principles of Finance, 2d edit., 1998—; contbr. articles to profl. jours. Named All India Nat. scholar of merit, Govt. Of India, 1977, All India Jr. Rsch. fellow, 1985, Grad. fellow, Internat. Fedn. Operational Rsch., 1985—, Tchr. of Yr., Fayetteville (N.C.) State U., 2000; recipient citation of excellence, Anbar Electronic Intelligence, 1998, Disting. Rsch. Award, Allied Academies, 2001; Classroom Tchg./Learning grantee, Carolina Colloquy for Univ. Tchg., Cullowhee, N.C., 1999, Rsch. grantee, Tex. So. U., 2001, 2002. Mem.: Acad. Econs. and Fin. (bd. dirs. Hattiesburg, Miss. 1996—, track chair 1999, 2000, 2001), Acad. Fin. Case Rsch. (founder, mem. editl. bd. jour. 1999—), Fin. Mgmt. Assn., Am. Fin. Assn. Hindu. Avocations: reading, cooking. Home: PO Box 16665 Sugar Land TX 77496 Office: Texas Southern U Sch of Bus 3100 Cleburn Ave Houston TX 77004 E-mail: chatteramit@hotmail.com.

CHATTERJEE, HEM CHANDRA, electrical engineer; b. Hirapur, W. Bengal, India, Jan. 3, 1940; came to U.S., 1969; s. Kishory Mohon and Katayani (Mukherjee) C.; m. Kamal Renu Mukherjee, Feb. 27, 1967; children: Madhumita, Biswajit. Diploma E.E., Indsl. Tng. Inst., India, 1960; diploma engring., Brit. Inst. Engring. Tech., 1965; MSEE, U. Pa., Phila., 1972; PhD in E.E., City U., L.A., 1979. Registered profl. engr., Pa., N.J., Md., Va., Ga., W.Va., Mass., Maine; cert. profl. mgr.; chartered engr., India; lic. nat. elec. supr. Govt. of West Bengal; cert. cogeneration profl. Elec. chargehand Rallis India Ltd., Calcutta, West Begal, 1961-62; elec. engr. Schindler Aufzuge G.m.b.H., Berlin, 1965-67; sr. elec. engr. Simco, Lessard, Thomson, Dixon Assocs., Windsor, Ont., Can., 1967-69; chief elec. engr. Vinokur-Pace Engring. Svcs., Inc., Jenkintown, Pa., 1969-80; mgr. elec. dept. Walter F. Spiegel, Inc., Jenkintown, 1980-82; sole proprietor, prin. Chatterjee Internatl Engrs., Jenkintown, 1982-85; dir. elec. engring. GSGSB Architects, Engrs. & Planners, Clarks Summit, Pa., 1986-87; chief elec. engr. Robert G. Werden & Assocs., cons. engrs., Jenkintown, 1987-88; v.p. engring. Marvin Waxman Cons. Engrs., P.C., Wyncote, Pa., 1988-90; dir. elec. engring. Mark Ulrick Engrs., Inc., Phila., 1993-95; sole propr., prin. Unique Engrs., Willow Grove, Pa., 1991—. Contbr. more than 20 engring. articles to profl. jours. Founder, mem. Pragati-Bengali Cultural Assn., Phila., 1970. Fellow India Soc. Engrs. (pres. U.S. chpt. 1970-82), Inst. Engrs. (India), Inst. Elec. & Telecom. Engrs. (New Delhi); mem. IEEE (sr.). Hindu. Achievements include interior and exterior power distbn. systems, interior and exterior lighting systems, interior and exterior comm. systems, generating plants, substas. and switchgears, motor controls and ctrs., remote monitoring and controls. Completion of several thousand projects with industrial, commercial, institutional, and residential applications. Home and Office: Unique Engrs 1703 Alba Rd Willow Grove PA 19090-3708

CHATTERJEE, JAYANTA, architecture and planning educator; b. Calcutta, India, Mar. 19, 1936; came to U.S., 1959; s. Hari Charan and Asha (Mukherjee) C.; m. Janet Ley Smith, Aug. 31, 1968; children: Eric, Brinda. BArch, Indian Inst. Tech., 1958; M in Regional Planning, U. N.C., 1962; MArch in Urban Design, Harvard U., 1965. Asst. prof. U. of Cin., 1967-72, assoc. prof., 1972-77, assoc. dean, 1975-77, prof., 1977—, dir. sch. planning, 1977-82, acting dean, 1982-83, dean, 1982-2001, prof. arch. and planning, 2001—. Regional designer Met. Area Planning Commn., Boston, 1965-67; urban scholar Cities Recovery Program, Cleve., 1981-82. Co-author: The Partnership Planning, 1982, Rebuilding American Cities, 1983, Breaking the Boundaries, 1989; co-editor/founder: Jour. Planning, Education and Research, 1981-84. Mem. Ohio Eminent Scholar Rev. Panel, 1985, Urban Design Rev. Bd., Cin., 1988—; bd. dirs. Arts Consortium, Cin., 1983—87, Contemporary Arts Ctr., Cin., 1983—, Hillside Trust, Cin., 1983—84, Bethesda Hosp., Inc., Cin., 1982—95, Total Living Concept, Inc., Cin., 1976—88, Ctr. Mediation of Disputes, Cin., 1989—92, The Emery Ctr., Cin., 1988—90, Better Housing League, Cin., 1989—92, Archtl. Found., Cin., 1990—, pres., 2004—; bd. dirs. Season Found. for Good Govt., 2003—, pres., 1997—. Recipient Apple award Archtl. Fedn. Cin., 1996, Disting. Alumnus award U. N.C., 1996, Disting. Svc. award Assn. Coll. Schs. of Planning, 1991. Fellow Am. Inst. Cert. Planners (editl. bd. AICP Casebook 1991-93, tech. adv. bd. 1993-96); mem. AIA (assoc.; Thomas Jefferson award pub. arch. 2000), Am. Planning Assn. (pres. Ohio chpt. 1970-72, editorial adv. bd. Jour. APA), Ptnrs. of Ams. (Ohio-Parana), Assn. Collegiate Schs. of Planning (pres. 1983-85, Jay Chatterjee Svc. award 1998--), Internat. Coun. Fine Arts Deans, Cin. Post/Corbett Found. (Lifetime achievement award in Arts 1999). Office: U Cin Coll of Design Architecture Art and Planning PO Box 210016 Cincinnati OH 45221-0016 Fax: 513.556.3288. E-mail: Jay.Chatterjee@uc.edu.

CHATTERJEE, MALAYA, immunologist; b. Cooch-Behar, W. Bengal, India, Jan. 16, 1946; came to US, 1969; d. Nalini Nath and Kanak Prova (Chakraborty) Bhattacharya; m. Sunil K. Chatterjee, Oct. 25, 1972; children: Indranil, Sumana. BS, Presidency Coll., Calcutta, India, 1963; MS, U. Calcutta, 1965, PhD, 1969. Cancer rsch. scientist III Roswell Park Cancer Inst., Buffalo, N.Y., 1972-78, cancer rsch. scientist IV, 1979-92; assoc. prof. U. Ky., Lexington, 1993-97, prof. dept. medicine, 1997-99, U. Cin., 1999—. Mem. The Barrett Cancer Ctr., Cin., 1999—; cons. study sect. Nat. Cancer Inst.-NIH, Bethesda, Md., 1992-96, 97—. Contbr. numerous peer-reviewed articles to profl. jours., 14 chpts. to books; holder 7 patents. Mem. Hindu Cultural Soc. We. N.Y., Buffalo, 1972-92. Grantee Nat. Cancer Inst. NIH, 1976-79, 89—, Am. Cancer Soc., 1979-82, Pharm. Corp., 1996-99, Dept. Def., 1995-98. Mem. Am. Assn. Immunologists, Am. Assn. Cancer Rsch., N.Y. Acad. Scis., Blue Grass Indo-Am. Assn. Democrat. Hindu. Avocations: travel, music, camping, gardening, international cooking. Office: U Cin Med Ctr 3125 Eden Ave Cincinnati OH 45267-0509

CHATTERJEE, SHARMILA, marketing educator; b. Cuttack, Orissa, India, Dec. 4, 1961; arrived in U.S., 1986; d. Sunil N. and Pronoti Chatterjee; m. Arup K. Chakraborty, July 8, 1992; 1 child, Meenakshi. PhD in Mktg., U. Pa., 1994. Asst. prof. Fairfield (Conn.) U., 1995—98, Golden Gate U., San Francisco, 1998—2000, assoc. prof., chair dept. mktg., 2000—. Contbr. articles to profl. jours. Mem.: Informs, Am. Mktg. Assn. (mgr. collegiate activities San Francisco chpt. 1998—). Avocations: reading, music. Office: Golden Gate U 536 Mission St San Francisco CA 94105 Office Fax: 415-442-6579.

CHATTERJEE, SUNIL KUMAR, cancer research scientist; b. Calcutta, Aug. 7, 1940; came to U.S., 1966; s. Bhupendra Nath and Parimal Bala (Banerjee) C.; m. Malaya Bhattacharya, Oct. 25, 1972; children: Indranil, Sumana. BS, Presidency Coll., Calcutta, 1959; MS, U. Calcutta, 1961, PhD, 1966. Postdoctoral fellow dept. microbiology U. Pa., Phila., 1966-68; rsch. assoc. Inst. Cancer Rsch., Fox Chase/Phila., 1968-69; rsch. officer U. Calcutta, 1969-71; rsch. fellow Max-Planck Inst., Goettingen, W. Germany, 1971-72; asst. cancer rsch. scientist dept. pathology Roswell Park Cancer Inst., 1972-73, cancer rsch. scientist I, 1973-76, cancer rsch. scientist III, 1976-86, 93-97; assoc. prof. dept. ob/gyn., internal medicine U. Ky., Lexington, 1993-99; prof. dept. internal medicine Vontz Ctr. Molecular Studies, U. Cin., 1999—. Vis. scientist divsn. oncology, Stanford (Calif.) U., 1993. Contbr. articles to profl. jours. Grantee Elsa U. Pardee Found., 1991-93, Am. Cancer Soc., 1992, Audrey Lippman Cancer Rsch. Fund, 1990-92, NIH, 1991—, Ephrain McDowell Cancer Found., 1993-94. Democrat. Hindu. Avocations: photography, music, drama. Home: 3512 Reeves Dr Fort Wright KY 41017-9436 Office: U Cin Vontz Ctr Molecular Study 3125 Eden Ave Cincinnati OH 45267-0001 Fax: 513-558-6703. E-mail: sunil.chatterjee@uc.edu.

CHATTERJI, ANGANA P. anthropologist; b. Calcutta, India, Nov. 17, 1966; d. Bhola and Anubha (Sengupta) C.; m. Richard Murray Shapiro, May 10, 1998. MA, U. Delhi, 1989; PhD, Calif. Inst. Integral Studies, San Francisco, 1999. Cons. Planning Com. India, New Delhi, 1990-92; dir. rsch. Asia forest network program Ctr. South Asia Studies U. Calif., Berkeley, 1992—. Asst. adj. prof. Calif. Inst. Integral Studies, 1997—; cons. Swed Forest Internat., Stockholm, 1997—; cons. in field Author: In Search of Reality, 1984. Ford Found. grantee, 1993. Mem. Am. Anthropol. Assn. Avocations: gliding, reading, computers, travel, symphony.

CHATTERJI, DEBAJYOTI, retired manufacturing company executive, educator; b. Puri, India, Aug. 4, 1944; came to U.S., 1967, naturalized, 1980; s. Kumud Chandra and Mrinmoyee (Mukherji) C.; m. Smee Banerjee, July 11, 1968; children: Ananya, Kooheli, Miabi. BS with honors, Utkal U., India, 1963; B in Metall. Engring., Indian Inst. Tech., Kharagpur, India, 1966; MS, Purdue U., 1968, PhD, 1971. Vis. scientist Wright-Patterson AFB, Ohio, 1971-73; with Research & Devel. Center, Gen. Electric Co., Schenectady, 1973-83, mgr. electrochemistry br., 1975-79; mgr. Chem. Systems and Tech. Lab., 1979-80, Inorganic Materials and Structures Lab., 1980-83; v.p. tech. affairs The BOC Group, Inc., Murray Hill, N.J., 1983-89, chef exec. tech. activities, 1990, mng. dir. tech., 1990-99. Bd. dirs. The BOC Group, plc., Indsl. Rsch. Inst.; vis. prof. Lehigh U., 1999-2000; pres. Far Hills Group Inc. Chmn. editl. bd. Rsch. and Tech. Mgmt.; mem. editl. bd. R&D Mgmt.; contbr. articles to profl. jours.; patentee in field. Bd. dirs. BOC Found. for Environment, Imperial Coll., London. Recipient Disting. Engring. Alumnus award Purdue U., 1987; Disting. fellow Indian Inst. Mgmt., Calcutta, Maurice Holland award Ind. Rsch. Inst. Mem. Internat. Assn. Mgmt. of Tech. (adv. bd.). Office: The BOC Group 100 Mountain Ave New Providence NJ 07974-2069

CHATTERLEY, JAMES PHILIP, retired automotive development engineer; b. Toronto, Ont., Can., July 21, 1923; came to U.S., 1956; s. Philip and Gertrude Louisa (Trickey) C.; m. Shirley Florence Esther Spicer, Mar. 23, 1946 (dec. 1970); children: Maureen, Jamie Philip, Cheryl. Student, No. Vocat. Sch., Toronto, 1938-40, Galt Aircraft Sch., St. Thomas, Ont., 1940-41, RCAF Aircraft Sch., 1941-42, Armed Services Rehab. Sch., Toronto, 1946-48. Supr. archtl. design A.B. Cairns & Sons, Toronto, 1948-50; with archtl. design and bldg. dept. S. Sugarman Architects, Toronto, 1950-52; ptnr. Neilson's Wood Products, Richmond Hill, Ont., 1952; research and devel. exptl. engr. A.V. Roe Aircraft Ltd., Malton, Ont., 1952-56; with GM, Warren, Mich., 1956—; leader engring. model shop Chevrolet div. GM, Warren, Mich., 1956-66, mem. chevä engring. R & D staff, 1966-70, devel. engr. engring. staff, 1970-85; prototype vehicle devel. and build engr. Cadillac div. GM, Warren, Mich., 1985-91; ret., 1991. Developer of patented "Quickbuild" system for devel. and fabrication of dimentionally accurate prototype vehicles; inventor, co-developer plastic die fabricating system for accurate forming of sheet metal; developer lazer non contract measuring and dimentional data transfer system for model makers work sta.; developer the body and chassis "Quickbuild" tooling system for various prototype vehicles (i.e., 1st 7 GM Saturn vehicles, 1st 3 GM electric E.V.-l vehicles, 1st 11 GM Cadillac 93 DeVille vehicles, 6 Cadillac presdl. armored security vehicles). Served with RCAF, 1941-45, ETO. Achievements include designing, building and flying first parawing tricycle aircraft, 1961. Home: 60701 Apache Ln Washington MI 48094-2010 E-mail: jchatt@michigan-net.com.

CHATTERTON, ROBERT TREAT, JR., reproductive endocrinology educator; b. Catskill, N.Y., Aug. 9, 1935; s. Robert Treat and Irene (Spoor) Chatterton; m. Patricia A. Holland, June 24, 1956 (div. 1965); children: Ruth Ellen, William Matthew, James Daniel; m. Astrida J. Vanags, June 4, 1966 (div. 1977); 1 child, Derek Scott; m. Carol J. Lewis, May 24, 1985. BS, Cornell U., 1958, PhD, 1963; MS, U. Conn., 1959. Postdoctoral fellow Med. Sch. Harvard U., 1963-65; rsch. assoc. div. oncology Inst. Steroid Rsch. Montefiore Hosp. and Med. Ctr., N.Y.C., 1965-70; asst. prof. Coll. Medicine U. Ill., 1970-72, assoc. prof. Coll. Medicine, 1972-79; prof. Med. Sch. Northwestern U., Chgo., 1979—. Mem. sci. adv. com. AID, chairperson Instnl. Rev. Bd. Northwestern U., 1982—83, mem. intellectual properties com., 1987—95, chairperson radiation safety com., 2000—02; dir. Immunoassay Facility, R. H. Lurie Cancer Ctr. Northwestern U. Med. Sch., 1997—; dir. clin. labs., dept. ob-gyn. Northwestern Med. Facutly Found., 1996—99, dir. shared clin. labs., 1999—. Contbr. articles to profl. jours. Grantee, NIH, 1972—90, 1995—, NSF, 1975, 1995—98, AID, 1971—86, Army Office Rsch., 1987—94. Mem.: AAAS, Chgo. Assn. Reproductive Endocrinologists (pres. 1987—88), Soc. Study Reproduction, Soc. Gynecologic Investigation, Endocrine Soc., Am. Chem. Soc., N.Y. Acad. Scis., Phi Kappa Phi, Sigma Xi. Presbyterian. Achievements include patents for method of totally suppressing ovarian follicular devel. and method of ovulation detection. Home: 6001 N Knox Ave Chicago IL 60646-5821 Office: Northwestern U Olson 8319-710 N Fairbanks Ct Chicago IL 60611-3015 E-mail: chat@northwestern.edu.

CHATTIN, GILBERT MARSHALL, financial analyst; b. Decherd, Tenn., Jan. 13, 1914; s. Murrell Emmett and Lena Katherine (Jones) C.; m. Hester Stroud, June 18, 1938; 1 child, Marsha Jane. BA, U South Sewanee, 1937; JD, Blackstone Sch. Law, 1965. Chief credit analyst, mgr. city dept. Dun and Bradstreet, Inc., Knoxville, Tenn., 1938-43; ptnr. A&A Service and Supply Co., Atlanta, 1946-70; chief auditor Ga. Dept. Health, 1963-72; chief auditor, audit

mgr. Ga. Dept. Human Resources, 1972-84; corp. auditor Ga. Dept. Revenue, 1955-63; pvt. practice fin. analyst, investor, cons., 1955—. Served with AUS, 1943-46, ETO. Mem. NRA, Am. Assn. Individual Investors, Nat. Assn. Investors, Am. Numismatic Assn., Am. Legion, Phi Gamma Delta. Mem. Ch. of Christ. Avocations: hunting, fishing.

CHATTMAN, RAYMOND CHRISTOPHER, foundation executive; b. San Rafael, Calif., Apr. 11, 1956; s. Raymond Rene Chattman and Virginia Mae (Kirkland) Robinson; m. Patti Lyn Barnard Garbers, Feb. 14, 1975 (div. 1977); m. Dawn Irene Russell Kilpatrick, Aug. 21, 1993 (div. 1998); children: Christian Paige, Bradley Charles Kilpatrick. BS, SUNY, Albany, 1988; MBA, Averett Coll., 1995. Dir. planning, ops. Comms. Media Group Inc., Alexandria, Va., 1981; comms. mgr. ANPA Found., Reston, Va., 1982-84; graphics editor Times-Herald Record, Middletown, N.Y., 1984-85; editor employee comms. Washington Gas Light Co., 1985-86; exec. dir., CEO Soc. Newspaper Design, Reston, 1986-96; dir. AIAA Found., Reston, 1996—. Asst. coach Herndon (Va.) Optimist Youth Football, 1994, Herndon Youth Soccer, 1992. Served in U.S. Army, 1974-81, Korea, Germany, Res., 1981-90. Recipient Thomas Jefferson award Dept. Def., 1979, Keith L. Ware award Dept. Army, 1978, 83, 86, 87. Mem. Am. Soc. Assn. Execs., Nat. Assn. Govt. Communicators (blue pencil award 1978), Am. Mgmt. Assn., Greater Washington Soc. Assn. Execs. Avocations: travel, reading, golf. Office: AIAA Found 1801 Alexander Bell Dr Ste 500 Reston VA 20191-4344

CHATTON, BARBARA ANN, education educator; b. San Francisco, Aug. 4, 1948; d. Milton John and Mildred (Vick) C.; m. Andrew M. Bryson, May 1, 1993. BA, U. Calif., Santa Cruz, 1970; MLS, UCLA, 1971; PhD, Ohio State U., 1982. Libr. John Steinbeck Pub. Libr., Salinas, Calif., 1971-79; prof. U. Wyo., Laramie, 1982—. Author: Using Poetry Across the Curriculum, 1993; co-author: Creating Connections, 1986, Blurring the Edges, 1999. Mem., past chair Friends of Libr.,, Albany County, Wyo., 1989—. Recipient Ellbogen award U. Wyo., 1990. Mem. ALA, Nat. Coun. Tchrs. English, Internat. Reading Assn., Phi Delta Kappa. Office: U Wyo Coll Edn PO Box 3374 Laramie WY 82071-3374 E-mail: bchat@uwyo.edu.

CHATTOPADHYAY, NAIBEDYA, physiologist, educator, researcher; b. Kharagpur, India, May 25, 1965; s. Nirmal Chandra and Minati Chattopadhyay. BSc with honors, Presidency Coll., Calcutta, 1985, MSc in Physiology, 1988; PhD in Endocrinology, S.G. PGIMS, Lucknow, India, 1994. Rsch. fellow Brigham & Women's Hosp., Boston, 1994-98, Harvard U. Sch. Medicine, Boston, 1994-98, instr. medicine, 1998—. Reviewer Am. Jour. Physiology, Endocrinology, European Jour. Neurosci; editor: Calcium-Sensing Receptor, 2001; contbr. numerous articles to sci. an dprofl. jours. Mem. Am. Physiol. Soc., Am. Soc. for Neurochemistry, N.Y. Acad. Scis., Endocrine Soc., Physiol. Soc. U.K., London Diplomatic Assn. (life). Office: Brigham and Women's Hosp 221 Longwood Ave Boston MA 02115 E-mail: nchattopadhyay@partners.org.

CHATURVEDI, PRAVIN R. pharmaceutical executive; B in Pharmacy, U. Bombay; PhD in Pharm. Scis., W.Va. U. With Alkermes Inc.; pres., CEO Scion Pharms., Inc., Medford, Mass. Office: Scion Pharms Inc 200 Boston Ave Ste 3600 Medford MA 02155

CHATZIDAKIS, LARRY, assemblyman; b. June 24, 1949; m. Randy Chatzidakis; 3 children. BA in Psychology, Villanova U., 1971. Coun. Mt. Laurel Twp., 1985—2000, mayor, 1988, 1992, 1996, 2000; freeholder Burlington County, 1995—97; assemblyman N.J. Gen. Assembly, 1997—. Republican. Office: 3000 Midlantic Dr Ste 103 Mount Laurel NJ 08054*

CHATZKY, HERBERT, music educator; b. Balt., Apr. 8, 1935; s. Samuel and Sonia (Greenspun) C.; m. Sally Anne Rush, Feb. 13, 1973; children: Christine, Lisa, David. BS, Juilliard Sch. of Music, 1957; MS, 1958, postgrad., 1959. Cert. tchr. music, Conn. Accompanying staff Juilliard Sch. Music, N.Y.C., 1952-57, tchr. class piano, 1958-60; instr. in piano Bowling Green (Ohio) State U., 1960-61; asst. prof. piano and accompanying Hart Coll. Music, Hartford, Conn., 1961-72; music staff South Windsor (Conn.) Sch., 1972-97; choirmaster Hartford (Conn.) Symphony Chorale, 1972-73, ofcl. pianist, 1962-73; dir. 2nd Congregational Ch., Manchester, Conn., 1967-86, North United Meth. Ch., Manchester, 1986—. Dir. Manchester Young Artist Competition, Conn., 1974—; music dir., sr. organist, Temple Beth Israel, Conn., 1986-98, dir. Jewish music competition; mem. Scehovic-Chatzky Piano Duo; dir. Newcomb Friends for Music Concerts, Newcomb Young Composer Contest. Composer: (symphonic composition) Night Music for Orchestra, 1952, Variations, 1952 (hon. mention N.Y. Philharmonic 1952), Music for Orchestra and Chorus: 29th Psalm, 1973; arranger for organ; Lincoln Portrait, 1978; performed concert series Lake Placid Synagogue. Performer holocaust music, Conn. Pub. Radio, Hartford, 1970, 2nd Congregational Ch., Manchester, 1978; dir. concert series, 2nd Congregational Ch., 1975-86; lectr. on sight-reading, New Eng. Piano Tchrs. Assn., 1967; trustee Newcomb United Meth. Ch.; v.p. Newcomb C. of C.. Sgt. USANG, 1960-70. Recipient full piano scholarship Juilliard Sch. Music, 1952-57, french-horn scholarship, 1952-57; award of Philo-Music Soc., N.Y.C., 1955; winner of concerto competition, Juilliard Sch. of Music, 1958; concerto soloist under Arthur Fiedler, Hartford Symphony Orchestra, 1972. Jewish. Avocations: mountain climbing, hiking, reading, travel in motorhome. Home: PO Box 214 Newcomb NY 12852-0214 also: 5461 Rte 28N Newcomb NY 12852 E-mail: hchatzky@capital.net.

CHAU, MAY YING, librarian, educator; b. Hong Kong, Feb. 16, 1952; d. Zea Wan Chau and Yok Mei Chen. BFA, BS, Brigham Young U., 1984, MS, 1987; MSLS, Wayne State U., 1990. Rsch. asst. Wayne State U., Detroit, 1987—89; rsch. technician Strohtech Inc., Detroit, 1989—90; plant sci. libr., asst. prof. Colo. State U., Ft. Collins, Colo., 1991—94; agrl. sci. libr., assoc. prof. Oreg. State U., Corvallis, Oreg., 1994, agrl. sci. libr., 1994—. Co-chmn. pres. commn. Oreg. State U., 2000—01. Contbr. articles to profl. jours. Mem.: ALA (racial & ethnic diversity com. 1997—98), Oreg. Libr. Assn. (honor, award & scholarship com. 1999—). Office: Oregon State University 121 The Valley Library Corvallis OR 97330-4551 Business E-Mail: may.chau@orst.edu.

CHAUDHARI, PRAVEEN, materials physicist; b. Ludhiana, Punjab, India, Nov. 30, 1937; came to U.S., 1961; s. Hans Raj and Ved (Kumari) C.; m. Karin Romhild, June 13, 1964; children: Ashok, Pia. BS with honors, Indian Inst. Tech., Kharagpur, 1961; MS in Phys. Metallurgy, MIT, 1963, ScD in Phys. Metallurgy, 1966. Rsch. assoc. MIT, Cambridge, Mass., 1966; rsch. staff mem. IBM T.J. Watson Rsch. Ctr., Yorktown Heights, N.Y., 1966-70, mgr., 1970-80, dir. phys. scis., 1981-82, v.p. sci., dir. phys. scis., 1982-91, v.p. sci., tech. com., 1988-91, rsch. staff, 1991—2003; dir. Brookhaven Nat. Lab., Upton, NY, 2003—. Exec. sec. Presdl. Wise Men Com. on Super Conductivity, 1988; mem. Presdl. Commn. on Super Conductivity, 1989; mem. vis. coms. various univs.; co-chmn. Materials Sci. and Engring. Study by NRC; chmn. U.S. Liaison Commn. to Internat. Union of Pure and Applied Physics; mem. com. on Physics for the Next Decade, sponsored by NRC/NAS, Nat. Critical Tech. panel; chmn. sci. coun. Internat. Ctr. for Theoretical Physics, Trieste, Italy; chmn. adv. coun. math. and phys. scis. NSF. Author of papers on mechanical properties and defects in crystalline solids, amorphous solids, quantum transport, superconductivity and magnetic monopoles and neutrino mass experiments. Recipient Nat. Medal of Technology, 1995. Fellow Am. Phys. Soc. (George Pake prize 1987); mem. NAS (bd. physics and astronomy, governing bd.), AIME (leadership award 1986), NAE, IEEE (Liebmann prize 1992), Am. Inst. Physics (mem.-at-large of governing bd.), N.Y. State Inst. of Superconductivity (mem.-at-large), Am. Acad. Arts and Scis., N.Y. Acad. Scis. (governing bd.). Office: Brookhaven Nat Lab PO Box 5000 Upton NY 11973

CHAUDHARY, BHARAT INDU, chemical engineer; b. Dehradun, India, July 29, 1964; s. Khairati Lal and Pushap Bala Chaudhary; m. Sunita Ranjhan, Aug. 25, 1990; 1 child, Abha. B in Chem. Engring., U. Benin, Benin City, Nigeria, 1985; MSc in Advanced Chem. Engring., Imperial Coll., London, 1986, PhD in Chem. Engring., 1990. R & D scientist Smith and Nephew Rsch., Gilston Park, England, 1989—90; sr. rsch. engr. Dow Deutschland Inc., Rheinmuenster, Germany, 1990—94; rsch. specialist The Dow Chem. Co., Granville, Ohio, 1994—97, sr. rsch. specialist Freeport, Tex., 1997—2002, Somerset, NJ, 2002—. Patentee (U.S. and European) in polymer rsch.; contbr. articles to profl. jours. and conf. procs. Recipient cert. of Appreciation, Soc. of Plastics Engineers, 1999, Overseas Rsch. Students award, Com. of Vice Chancellors and Prins., Univs. of the U.K., 1988 89, Indsl. Sponsorship, BXL Plastics, 1986—89. Office: The Dow Chemical Co 1 Riverview Dr Somerset NJ 08873 Office Fax: 732-271-7949. Business E-Mail: bichaudhary@dow.com.

CHAUDHARY, KAMRAN, internist; MD, U. Mo., Kansas City; BA, U. Mo. Physician internal medicine U. Ill., Chgo., 1999—2002. Home: 1522 N Campbell Ave # 1 Chicago IL 60622

CHAUDHARY, SATVEER, state senator; b. June 12, 1969; BA, St. Olaf Coll., 1991; JD, U. Minn., 1995. Mem. Minn. Ho. Reps., 1996-2000, Minn. State Senate, 2000—, vice chair transp. com., mem. crime prevention com., edn. com., E-12 edn. budget divsn. com., fin. com., transp. and pub. safety budget divsn. com.; owner Chaudhary Cons. Law clk., intern Hennepin County Atty.'s Office, Minn.; aide Minn. Atty. Gen. Hubert H. Humphrey III. Co-chair Anoka County Legis. Delegation; hon. adv. coun. Asian-Pacific Endowment for Cmty. Devel.; mem. Coalition of Labor Union Women, Minn. Outdoor Heritage Alliance; hon. chair Minn. Cricket Assn.; mem. Minn. Welcome Com. for The Dalai Lama, U. Minn. Indsl. Rels. Adv. Coun., Twin Cities Internat. Citizen Award Com.; Fridley Human Resources Commn.; vol. Mounds View Festival in the Park; mem. New Brighton Hist. Soc., New Brighton Sportsmen's Club, Minn. Pheasants Forever Soc.; state affirmative action officer Minn. DFL Party; co-founder, chair Minn. Asian-Indian Dem. Assn.; bd. dirs. World Trade Ctr., St. Paul, A Blanket of Hope. Named Legislator of the Yr., Coll. Dems. of Minn., 1999; recipient Cert. of Commendation, Legal Aid Soc. of Minn., Cert. of Appreciation, DFL Party, 1995, Achievement award, Indian Assn. Minn. Mem.: New Brighton Eagles, Bass Anglers Soc. Am., Columbia Hts. Lions. Dfl. Home: 1601 N Innsbruck Dr Fridley MN 55432 Office: 325 Capitol 75 Constitution Ave Saint Paul MN 55155-1206 E-mail: sen.satveer.chaudhary@senate.leg.state.mn.us.

CHAUDHRI, AMIN QAMAR, film company executive; b. Gujrat, Punjab, India, Apr. 18, 1942; came to U.S., 1959; s. C.D. and Sardar (Begum) C.; children: Asif Qamar, Asha Noor, Amina Yasmin. Grad., CUNY, 1965. Owner Filmasia Prodns., N.Y.C., 1961-87; pres. Gross Chaudhri Prodns., N.Y.C., 1961-64; film cameraman, editor Francis Thompson, Inc., N.Y.C., 1964-65; music and effect editor Musifex Inc., N.Y.C., 1965-66; pres. Artscope Ltd., N.Y.C., 1965-78; owner Filmart Internat., Bombay, 1974-2000; pres. Filmart Enterprises, Ltd., N.Y.C., 1980-2000, Continental Cinema Industries, Inc., Kenilworth, N.J., 1985-87; chmn., chief exec. officer Continental Film Group, Ltd., Sharon, Pa., 1987—; pres. Continental Entertainment Group, Ltd., 1991-97; chief exec. officer, pres. Heron Internat. Pictures, Ltd., 1993-2000; pres. Continental Actors/Models Agy., Ltd., 1997. Dir. dept. film Jazz Arts Soc., Inc., N.Y.C., 1961-68; pres. Livingston (N.J.) TV 36, 1985. Filmmaker (documentary) Khajuraho Eternal, 1965 (award); dir. photography (TV spl.) Medium is the Message, 1968 (Emmy award); photographer (slides) Pakistan Photography Salon, 1969 (Gold medal), cameraman, editor (film) Right On, 1970 (Cannes Film Festival award 1970); dir.. prodr.: (films) An Unremarkable Life, Tiger Warsaw, Once Again, Seventh Veil; prodr. (film) Diary of a Hitman, The Master Mechanic. Mem. Montclair (N.J.) Hist. Soc., 1972, Nat. Assn. for the Blind, Livingston, 1985. supervising producer, Scent of Harvest, 2001 Recipient Spl. award City of Sharon, Pa., 1987; Amin Qamar Chaudhri Day proclaimed by City of San Francisco, Amin Qamar Chaudhri Day proclaimed by City of Farell, Pa., 1987, City of Sharon, 1997. Fax: 818-907-0814. E-mail: acmoviemogul@earthlink.net.

CHAUDHRY, HUMAYUN JAVAID, physician, medical educator, flight surgeon, writer; b. Karachi, Pakistan, Nov. 17, 1965; came to U.S., 1971, naturalized, 1978; s. Hukam Dad and Riffat Sultana (Bhatti) C.; m. Nazli Tabasum Iqbal, June 7, 1992; children: Shaun Hatim, Haris Iqbal. BA, NYU, 1986, MS, 1989; DO, N.Y. Coll. Osteo. Medicine, 1991; SM, Harvard Sch. of Pub. Health, 2001. Diplomate Nat. Bd. Osteo. Med. Examiners, Am. Bd. Internal Medicine; lic. physician, surgeon, N.Y. Intern St. Barnabas Hosp., Bronx, NY, 1991-92; resident in internal medicine Winthrop-U. Hosp., Mineola, NY, 1992-95, chief med. resident, 1995-96; asst. prof. medicine N.Y. Coll. Osteo. Medicine, Old Westbury, 1997—2003, chmn. dept. medicine, 2001—, med. dir., 2003—, assoc. prof. medicine, 2003—; attending physician, dir. med. edn. Long Beach (N.Y.) Med. Ctr., 1996-2001; attending physician Island Park Med. Care, 1996-98, Family Care Ctr., Long Beach, N.Y., 1996-99, Academic Health Care Ctr., N.Y. Coll. Osteopathic Medicine, 2001—; mem. staff Winthrop U. Hosp., 2001—. Reporter, news editor, TV anchorman Third World Broadcasting Network, N.Y.C., 1986-95; asst. clin. instr. medicine SUNY Stony Brook Sch. Medicine, 1995-96. Mem. editl. bd. New Physician, Reston, Va., 1991-99; contbr. articles to profl. jours. Bd. mem. Multifaith Forum of LI. Capt. USAF Res., 1999—2002, maj. USAF Res., 2002—. Regents Coll. scholar State of N.Y., Albany, 1982; recipient Essay Competition award N.Y.C. Fire Dept., 1979. Fellow: ACP (Nassau West dist. pres. 2000—), Am. Coll. Osteo. Internists, Nassau Acad. of Medicine, Royal Soc. Medicine UK; mem.: AMA, Nassau County Med. Soc. (bd. dirs. 2002—03), So. Poverty Law Ctr., Am. Acad. Osteopathy, Med. Soc. State of NY, Islamic Soc. N.Am., Nassau Soc. Internal Medicine (bd. dirs. 1996—98, v.p. 1998—99, pres. 1999—2000), NY State Osteo. Med. Soc., Assn. Osteo. Dirs. Med. Educators (bd. dirs. 2001—03, treas. 2003—), Islamic Med. Assn. N.Am., Am. Coll. Osteo. Internists (founding pres. NY chpt. 1998—, bd. dirs. 1999—), NY State Soc. Internal Medicine (pres. resident physicians sect. 1995—96, bd. dirs. 1996—2000), Am. Osteo. Assn., World Wildlife Fund, Islamic Ctr. LI, NY Coll. Osteo. Medicine Alumni Assn. (sec. bd. dirs. 1995—98, pres. 1998—2000, bd. dirs. 2000—02), Amnesty Internat. Muslim. Avocations: reading, cinema, travel. Home: 53 Timber Ridge Dr Commack NY 11725-1739 Office: NY Coll Osteo Medicine Dept Medicine Hannah & Charles Serota Acad Ctr Rm 1225 Old Westbury NY 11568-8000 E-mail: hchaudhr@nyit.edu.

CHAUDHRY, NAUMAN AHMED, computer scientist; b. Lahore, Pakistan, Aug. 7, 1968; s. Nazir Chaudhry and Kishwar Nazir. BSc in Elec. Engring., U. Engring. and Tech., Lahore, 1991; MSE in Computer Sci., U. Mich., Ann Arbor, 1994, PhD in Computer Sci., 1998. Sr. mem. tech. staff Oracle Corp., Redwood Shores, Calif., 1998—2003; asst. prof. U. New Orleans, 2003—. Contbr. articles to profl. jours., chpts. to books. Office: Oracle Corp 500 Oracle Pky 50p534 Redwood Shores CA 94065 E-mail: chaudhry@umich.edu.

CHAUDOIR, JEAN HAMILTON (JEAN HAMILTON), educator; b. Lake Charles, La., July 31, 1945; d. John Gardiner and Nora (Alford) Hamilton; divorced; 1 child, Elizabeth Jean. BS, La. State U., 1967, MEd, 1986, postgrad., 2002. Tchr. 3d grade St. Pius X Sch., Baton Rouge, 1967-69; tchr. 2d grade St. Francis Cabrini Sch., Alexandria, La., 1969-75; tchr. 3d grade St. Theresa Sch., Shreveport, La., 1975-76; tchr. 4th grade Sacred Heart Sch., Baton Rouge, 1976-79, West Baton Rouge Parish, Brusly, La., 1979-80; tutor Ed-U-Care, Baton Rouge, 1987-88; with summer program East Baton Rouge Parish, Baton Rouge, 1990-91, tchr. Chpt. 1 summer sch., 1993, 94; part time tchr. Modern Curriculum Press, Baton Rouge, 1995—; tchr. for instrnl. support Lanier Elem. Sch., Baton Rouge, 1997—2002, chair improvement team. Chair Adopt-A-Sch. at Park Forest Elem., Baton Rouge, 1986-94; chair mktg. com. Park Forest Elem. Sch., Baton Rouge, La., 1986-94, mem. adv. coun., 1993-94, chair monitoring com., 1993-94; mem. Title 1 Sch. Wide Com., 1995. Sustaining mem. Jr. League Baton Rouge, 1985—2001. Mem.: Delta Kappa Gamma (pres.). E-mail: jchaudoir@ebrpss.k12.la.us.

CHAUHAN, VIJAY LAKSHMI, English educator, writer; b. Srinagar, Kashmere, India, Apr. 25, 1943; came to U.S., 1982; d. Dewan Chand and Subhadra Devi Sharma; m. Pradyumna S. Chauhan, Apr. 14, 1982; children: Prabodh, Nidhi. BA, U. Rajasthan, Jaipur, India, 1961, MA in English, 1963, PhD in English, 1976. Asst. prof. U. Rajasthan, Jaipur, 1969 82; adj. prof. C.C. Phila., 1989-91, asst. prof., 1991-95, assoc. prof., 1995—, curriculum facilitator, 1996-98. Author: Virginia Woolf, 1976, (under Vijay Lakshmi) Pomegranate Dreams and Other Stories, 2002; contbr. articles to profl. jours.; contbr. short stories to periodicals. Fulbright fellow Yale U., 1979; grantee NEH, 1994. Mem. Multi Ethnic Studies of Europe and the Ams. Democrat. Hindu. Avocations: gardening, music, reading, cooking. Office: CC Phila 1700 Spring Garden St Philadelphia PA 19130 E-mail: vchauhan@comcast.net.

CHAURASIA, VISHAL, physician, writer, computer programmer; b. Agra, India, Jan. 3, 1971; s. Raj and Renu Chaurasia; m. Shruti Chaurasia, Apr. 13, 1995. MBBS, All India Inst. Med. Scis., New Delhi, 1994. Diplomate Am. Bd. Internal Medicine. Intern Albert Einstein Coll. Medicine and Affiliated Hosps., Bronx, N.Y., 1994-95, resident, 1995-97; fellow SUNY, Buffalo, 1997-98; physician Med. Ctr. Eastern Ariz., Pima, 1998—2000; freelance emergency rm. physician Ariz., 1998—; pvt. practice, 1999—2000. Chmn. ICU, respiratory, cardiology Mt. Graham Cmty. Hosp., Safford, Ariz., 1998-2000. Served with Naval Nat. Cadet Corps, 1986. Nat. Talent scholar Govt. of India, 1986. Mem.: MENSA, AMA. Home: 9808 E Becker W Scottsdale AZ 85260 E-mail: chaurasia@email.com.

CHAUVETTE, CLAUDE R. building materials company administrator; b. Montreal, Que., Can., Mar. 19, 1939; s. Bruno and Germaine (Handfield) C. BA, U. Montreal, 1959; postgrad., Ecole Polytechnique, Montreal, 1959-60; LSc Comm., LSc Compt., Hautes Etudes Comm., Montreal, 1963; CA, Can. Inst. Chartered Accts., Montreal, 1964. Pub. acct. Riddell Stead & Co., Montreal, 1963-67; asst. to v.p. Marine Industries, Montreal, 1967-71; contr. Forano Ltd., Plessisville, Can., 1971-73; sec.-treas. Demix Ltd., Demix (Laval) Ltd., Montreal, 1973-76; mgr. adminstrn. Montreal area St. Lawrence Cement Inc., Montreal, 1977-79, mgr. adminstrn. Que. div., 1979-81, treas., asst. sec., 1981-87, sec.-treas., 1987-2000, corp. sec., 2000—, also bd. dirs. Bd. dirs. St. Lawrence Cement Group Inc. Mem. Can. Inst. Chartered Accts., Risk and Ins. Mgmt. Soc., Cash and Treasurer Mgmt. Inst. Office: St Lawrence Cement Inc 1945 Graham Blvd Mount Royal QC Canada H3R 1H1 E-mail: cchauvette@stlawrencecement.com.

CHAUVIN, LEONARD STANLEY, JR., lawyer; b. Franklin, Ky., Feb. 13, 1935; s. Leonard Stanley Sr. C.; m. Cecilia McKay; children: Leonard Stanley III, Jacqueline, McKay. Grad., Castle Heights Mil. Acad., 1953; AB in Polit. Sci., U. Ky., 1957; JD, U. Louisville, 1961, LLD (hon.), 1990, Ohio No. U., 1990. Bar: Ky. 1961, U.S. Dist. Ct. (we. dist.) Ky. 1962, U.S. Ct. Appeals (6th cir.) 1964, U.S. Ct. Mil. Appeals 1966, U.S. Ct. Claims 1966, U.S. Supreme Ct. 1966, N.Y. 1983, Ind. 1983, Tenn. 1983, D.C. 1983, U.S. Dist. Ct. (so. and na. dists.) Ind. 1983, U.S. Dist. Ct. D.C. 1983, U.S. Ct. Appeals (7th, D.C. and Fed. cirs.) 1983, U.S. Tax Ct. 1983, U.S. Ct. Internat. Trade 1983, Wis. 1984, U.S. Dist. Ct. (so.and ea. dist.) 1984, U.S. Ct. Appeals (2d cir.) 1984, Fla. 1985, Nebr. 1985, Minn. 1985, Mass. 1986, W.Va. 1986. Assoc. Daniel B. Boone, Louisville, 1962-63, Laurence E. Higgins, Louisville, 1963-68; ptnr. Brown & Chauvin, Louisville, 1968-78, Carroll, Chauvin, Miller & Conliffe, Louisville, 1978-82; sole practice Louisville, 1982-83; ptnr. Barnett & Alagia, Louisville, 1983-92, Chauvin & White, Louisville, 1992-93, Chauvin & Chauvin, 1993—. Asst. Commonwealth atty. Jefferson County Commonwealth Attys. Office, Louisville, 1962-63; asst. gen. counsel dept. hwys. Commonwealth of Ky., Louisville; judge pro tem Louisville Police Ct.; master commr. Jefferson Cir. Ct., Louisville, 1992—; asst. county atty. of Jefferson County, 1978-87. Chmn. Registry of Election Fin.; mem. Ky. jud. retirement form system, Frankfort, Ky. Fellow Am. Bar Found. (chmn.); mem. ABA (chmn. ho. of dels. 1982-84, pres. 1989-90), Am. Coll. Tax Counsel, Ky. Bar Assn. (Lawyer of Yr. award), Nat. Jud. Coll., Am. Judicature Soc. (pres. 1986-88, Harley award), Am. Coll. Trust and Estate Counsel. Office: 235 S 5th St Ste 300 Louisville KY 40202 Home: 1028 Cherokee Rd Louisville KY 40204-1226

CHAVAS, JEAN-PAUL, economist, educator; b. Pélussin, France, Jan. 4, 1951; arrived in U.S., 1974; s. Robert Chavas, Marie Chavas; m. Eloisa Divinagracia, June 18, 1977; children: Nicole, Daniel. PhD, U. Mo., Columbia, 1978; B, U. Lyon. Asst. prof. Tex. A&M U., College Station, 1978—82; prof. agrl. econs. U. Wis., Madison, Wis., 1982—2003, U. Md., College Park, 2003—. Home: 3218 Knollwood Way Madison WI 53713 Office: Univ of Maryland Dept Agrl and Resource Econs 2200 Symons Hall College Park MD 20742-5535 Personal E-mail: jchavas@facstaff.wisc.edu. Business E-Mail: chavas@aae.wisc.edu.

CHAVASSE, PHILIPPE, foreign languages educator; b. Mar. 31, 1968; BA, U. Lyon, France, 1989, MA, 1990; PhD, U. Oreg., 1997. Asst. prof. Marshall U., Huntington, W.Va., 1997-98, So. Ill. U., Carbondale, 1998—. Office: Fgn Langs & Lits So Ill U Carbondale IL 62901-4521 E-mail: chavasse@siu.edu.

CHAVE, CAROLYN MARGARET, arbitrator, retired lawyer; b. Chgo., Jan. 30, 1948; d. Grant Carruthers and Priscilla Morrison (Shaw) C.; m. Robert Edmund Hand; children: Joshua, Chloe, Robert, Grant. BA, U. Chgo., 1970; MAT, Oakland U., 1971; JD, Loyola U., Chgo., 1976. Bar: Ill. 1976, N.Y. 1980. Tchr. corps intern Pontiac (Mich.) Pub. Schs., 1970-71; sec., receptionist Grad. Sch. Bus., U. Chgo., 1971; counselor Sonia Shankman Orthogenic Sch., Chgo., 1972; pvt. practice Chgo., 1976-78; asst. v.p., assoc. counsel Bank of Tokyo, N.Y.C., 1978-85; substitute tchr. N.Y.C. Pub. Schs., 1986-88; with Breckenridge Law Offices, 1986-88; sr. v.p., counsel, mgr. human resources Tokai Bank, N.Y.C., 1988-97; dir., counsel Deutsche Bank, N.Y.C., 1997-99. Arbitrator Am. Arbitration Assn., N.Y.C., 1986—. Vol. lawyer Chgo. Vol. Legal Svcs., 1977-78; designer playground PS 41 Parent Assn., Greenwich Village, N.Y., 1987. Avocations: weaving, dancing, patchwork quilting.

CHAVERS, BLANCHE MARIE, pediatrician, educator, researcher; b. Clarksdale, Miss., Aug. 2, 1949; d. Andrew and Mildred Louise C.; m. Gubare Mpambara, May 21, 1982; 1 child, Kaita. BS in Zoology, U. Wash., 1971, MD, 1975. Diplomate Am. Bd. Pediats. Intern U. Wash., Seattle, 1975-76, resident in pediatrics, 1976-78; instr. U. Minn., Mpls., 1982, asst. prof. pediatrics, 1983-90, assoc. prof. pediatrics, 1990-99, prof. pediatrics, 1999—. Attending physician dept. pediatrics, U. Minn. Sch. Medicine, Mpls., 1982. Co-editor: Am. Jour. Kidney Diseases, 2001—; contbr. articles to profl. jours. Recipient Clin. Investigator award NIH, 1982; Pediatric Nephrology fellow U. Minn., 1978-81. Mem. Am. Soc. Nephrology, Am. Soc. Pediatric Nephrology, Internat. Soc. Nephrology, Internat. Soc. Pediatric Nephrology, Am. Soc. Transplantation. Democrat. Methodist. Avocations: tennis, reading, collecting african artifacts, art. Office: Univ Minn MMC 491 420 Delaware St SE Minneapolis MN 55455-0348

CHAVERS, DANE CARROLL, lawyer; b. Cleve., Mar. 20, 1956; s. Clarence Louis and Lee Myrtle (Simpson) C.; m. Christine Kumer, Sept. 21, 1991; stepchildren: Mary Elizabeth Curtin, Laura Louise Curtin. BA, Hiram Coll., 1978; JD, Ohio State U., 1981. Bar: U.S. Dist. Ct. (so. dist.) Ohio 1981. Staff atty. common pleas unit Franklin County Pub. Defender, Columbus, Ohio, 1980—. Lectr. Ohio Assn. Criminal Def. Attys., Columbus, 1997—. Bd. dirs. Friends of Homeless, Columbus, Summit United Meth. Ch., Columbus, West Ohio Conf. United Meth. Ch. Bd. Ministry. Democrat. Avocations: reading, tennis, church choir. Bus. Office: Franklin County Pub Defender 373 S High St Columbus OH 43215-4591 E-mail: dcchaver@co.franklin.oh.us., dchavers@allvantage.com.

CHAVES, JOSE MARIA, diplomat, foundation administrator, lawyer, educator; b. Bogotá, Colombia, Aug. 19, 1922; s. Carlos Chaves and María García de C.; m. Elena Gómez y Samperio; children: Cristina María, Tomás José. Bachiller, Bogotá, 1939, cert. in anthropology, 1942, JD, 1945; DSc (hon.), U. Antióquia, 1948; MA, Columbia U., 1951, PhD, 1953; LLD, U. Popayán, Colombia, 1957, Mercy Coll., 1991. Bar: Colombia 1944, InterAmerican 1953. Editor in chief Revista Colegio del Rosario (arts and letters mag.), Colombia, 1944; gen. legal duties specializing in public adminstrn. Bogotá, 1942-45; instr. Romance langs. Columbia U., N.Y.C., 1945-48, 50-51; founder, 1st dean faculty U. Andes, Bogotá, 1948-49; head area studies Queens Coll. NYU, 1951-53; counselor Colombian Embassy, Washington, 1953-55; prof. internat. law U. Colombia, 1955-58, U. Paris, 1957; guest prof. internat. law and relations Brit. Council, various univs. Eng., Scotland, 1957; dir., chief exec. Am. Found. for Cultural Popular Action, Inc. (pvt. internat. orgn. for mass edn. by radio), N.Y.C., 1958—; amb. of Kyrgyzstan to UN, 1992—. Dir. Center Latin Am. Studies, CUNY; chmn. Hispanic Am. editorial bd. Grolier, Inc., 1971—; ambassador extraordinary, permanent del. Iberoam. Bur. Edn. to UN; A.E. and P., permanent rep. Grenada to OAS; permanent rep. orgn. Iberoam. Countries to UN and OAS, 1986—; alt. gov. World Bank and Internat. Monetary Fund, 1974-77, 94; chmn. C.I.P., 1972—; organizer, dir. tech. assistance mission Unitarian Service Com. in Latin Am.; dir. gen. Nat. Univ. Fund, Colombia, 1955-58; amb. extraordinary Spl. Mission to Brazil, 1995. Editor-in-chief: Grolier Spanish Universal Ency; author: Chaves Plan for settlement religious conflict between Caths. and Protestants in Latin Am; Author: Francisco de Vitoria. Founder International Law, 1945, Intergroup relations in the Spain of Cervantes, 1953, University Reform in Colombia, 1957. Pres. Assn. Latin Am. Unity, 1984; chmn. Summit Coun. World Peace, 1985-92; ambassador extraordinary and plenipotentiary of Kyrgyztan to the UN, 1992-93. Decorated Legion

of Honor (France); gran cruz Order of St. Constantine the Great; comdr., knight comdr. Grand Order Isabel La Católica (Spain); knight comdr. Alfonso El Sabio; grand cross Vasco N'nez de Balboa Panama, 1970; grand cross Juan P. Duarte Sanchez y Mella Dominican Republic, 1970, Medal of Jerusalem Israel, 1972; grand cross Order of Malta, 1976; grand cross Order Justice Law and Peace of Mex., 1977, grand cross Order Latin Am. Unity 1986, grand cross Order of St. Michael (Portugal), 1990; grand cross Order of Holy Cross of Jerusalem, 1991, grand cross of Saint Dennis of Zanthe, 1991; recipient medaglia universitaria U. Po Deo, Rome, 1957, medalla de los Andes U., 1958, medaille de Versailles, France, 1990, medalla Universidad, Lima, 1990, Lord Perry World prize for Edn., 1993, Order of Manas of Kyrgyzstan 1995. Mem. Internat. Law Assn., Inter-Am. Bar. Assn., Acad. Polit. Sci., MLA, Academia Hispano Americana, Assn. for Latin Am. Unity (founder, pres. 1984), Summit Coun. for World Peace (dir. 1987), Met. Club, Columbia U. Club (N.Y.C.), Quill Club USA (pres.), Brook Club, Phi Delta Kappa (v.p. Univ. World). Clubs: Metropolitan, Brook, Columbia U. (N.Y.C.), Quill of U.S.A. (pres.). Home: 118 E 60th St New York NY 10022-1103 Office: 401 5th Ave New York NY 10016-3317 *Faith in God is also faith in man. Service of man is also service of God. As we enter a new period of peace in the world, our faith can sustain our peace building efforts and help create a better life for all mankind.*

CHAVES, MARK ALAN, sociologist, educator; b. Jersey City, Apr. 13, 1960; s. Alan Bertram and Joan Dorathea (Mezger) C. AB, Dartmouth Coll., 1982; MDiv, Harvard U., 1985, MA in Sociology, 1987, PhD in Sociology, 1991. Instr. sociology Harvard U., Cambridge, Mass., 1989-90; instr. sociology and anthropology Loyola U. Chgo., 1990-91, asst. prof., 1991-92; from asst. prof. to assoc. prof. U. Notre Dame, 1992—96; from assoc. prof. to prof. U. Ariz., Tucson, 1998—. Author: Ordaining Women: Culture and Conflict in Religious Organizations, 1997; contbr. articles to profl. jours. Office: U Ariz Dept Sociology Tucson AZ 85721 Home: 2034 E 7th St Tucson AZ 85719

CHAVES-CARBALLO, ENRIQUE, neuropediatrician; b. San Jose, Costa Rica, Dec. 2, 1936; arrived in U.S., 1955,arrived in Saudi Arabia, 1996; s. Enrique Chaves and Celina Carballo; m. Vilma Irene Peralta, Aug. 26, 1961; children: Antonio, Maria, Miguel, Karen. MD, U. Okla., 1963. Diplomate Am. Bd. Psychiatry and Neurology, Am. Bd. Pediatrics. Prof. pediatrics and neurology Ea. Va. Med. Sch., Norfolk, 1979-89, U. Kans., Kansas City, 1990-94; chief pediatric neurology King Faisal Specialist Hosp. and Rsch. Ctr., Riyadh, Saudi Arabia, 1996—2002; fellow pediatrics Mayo Clinic, 1964—67, fellow neurology, 1972—75; clin. prof. pediatrics U. of Kans., Kans. City, 2003. Contbr. articles to profl. jours, chpts. to books; reviewer numerous jours. Recipient award Am. Neurol. Assn.; fgn. scholar Wesleyan U., 1955; grantee Rockefeller Archives, 1979. Fellow Am. Acad. Neurology; mem. Costa Rica Assn. Neuroscis. (hon.), Child Neurology Soc., Internat. Child Neurology Soc., Iberoam. Acad. Pediat. Neurology, Profs. Child Neurology, Soc. for Study of Inborn Errors of Metabolism, Soc. for Inherited Metabolic Disorders. Achievements include research in Reye syndrome and inborn errors of metabolism. Office Fax: 913-451-4975. E-mail: echaves17@hotmail.com.

CHAVEY, WILLIAM E. physician; b. Amarillo, Tex., Oct. 21, 1961; s. William Edward and Dorothy Dean Chavey; m. Kara Ann McGrath, Sept. 28, 1990; children: Halley Elizabeth, William Edward, III, Sarah Marie, Joseph Anthony, Margaret Ann, Lucy Marie. MS in biomedical engring., U. of Tex., 1984—87; M.D., U. of Tex. Med. Br., 1987—92. Instr. U. of NC, 1995—97; clin. asst. prof. U. of Mich., 1997—. Office: University of Michigan 1500 E Medical Center Dr Ann Arbor MI 48109 E-mail: wchavey@umich.edu.

CHAVEZ, ALBERT BLAS, financial executive; b. L.A., Jan. 1, 1952; s. Albert Blas and Yolanda (Garcia) C.; m. Irma Laura Cavazos, Dec. 21, 1996. BA, U. Tex., El Paso, 1979; MBA, Stanford U., 1985. CPA, Calif. Mem. profl. staff Deloitte Haskins and Sells, L.A., 1980-83; planning analyst corp. fin. planning Boise (Idaho) Cascade Co., 1984; treasury analyst corp. treasury RCA Corp., N.Y.C., 1985; asst. contr. RCA/Ariola Records, Mexico City, 1986; fin. analyst corp. exec. office GE Co., Fairfield, Conn., 1987-90; corp. fin. cons. Entertainment Industry and Litigation Support Svcs., L.A., 1990-91; co-founder, sr. v.p., CFO El Dorado Comm., Inc., L.A., 1991-98; fin. cons. entertainment and tech. industries, 1999—. Bd. dirs., treas. L.A. Conservation Corps, 1990—; bd. dirs. Wave Cmty. Newspapers, 1999-2000. Mem. AICPA, Calif. Soc. CPAs. Democrat. Home: 18744 Strathern St Reseda CA 91335-1221 E-mail: albert.chavez@earthlink.net.

CHAVEZ, ANDREW, writer, poet; b. San Antonio, Tex., Oct. 9, 1950; s. Alfonso Jr. and Mary Chavez. BA in Sociology and Polit. Sci., Kans. Wesleyan U., Salina, 1975; MA in English, Kans. State U., Manhattan, 1997. Commd. lt. U.S. Army, 1979, advanced through grades to sgt., 1983. Contbr. poetry Sun Flower Anthology, Vol. I, 1996; author: A New Romanticism, 2000. With U.S. Marine Corps., Vietnam, 1969-71. Mem. Acad. Am. Poets, New Romantic Soc. (pres. 1995-2001). Home: 1000 Vattier Manhattan KS 66502 E-mail: Andrewchav@aol.com.

CHAVEZ, CESAR T. ophthalmologist, cosmetic surgeon; b. Mexicali, Mex., Mexico, Aug. 3, 1952; s. Felipe and Norbertha Chavez; m. Teresa Cardenas, June 1977; children: Elena, Esteban, Ela. BA, UCLA, 1973; MD, MPH, U. Wash., 1977. Diplomate Am. Board Ophthalmology (assoc. examiner), Nat. Bd. Med. Examiners. Intern Kaiser Permanente Hosp., Fontana, Calif., 1977-78; resident Jules Stein Eye Inst.-UCLA Med. Ctr., 1983-85; chief divsn. comprehensive ophthalmology UCLA, 1985-88, asst. prof. ophthalmology, med. dir. Jules Stein Eye Inst., 1985-88; med. dir. Univ. Ophthalmology Assocs., Los Angeles, 1986-88, Camino Coastline Eye Surgeons, Encinitas, Calif., 1988—; clin. dir. Aesthetically You, 1998—. Qualified med. evaluator State of Calif.; founder LASIK Internat., 1999—. Contbr. articles to profl. jours. Bd. dirs. Calif. State U., San Marcos Found. Lt. USPHS, 1978-81. Fellow Am. Acad. Ophthalmology, Am. Acad. Cosmetic Surgery; mem. Med. Group Mgmt. Assn., San Diego County Med. Soc., Calif. Med. Assn. Roman Catholic. Avocation: trout fishing. Office: Camino Coastline Eye Surgeons 477 N El Camino Real Ste C200 Encinitas CA 92024-1354

CHAVEZ, EDWARD, protective services official; b. Stockton, Calif., Mar. 22, 1943; m. Nancy Ruhr; children: Eric, Jill. AA, San Joaquin Delta Coll., 1971; BA, Calif. State U., 1972; MS, Calif. Polytechnic Pomona, 1990; grad., POST Command Coll., Delinquency Control Inst., Leadership Stockton Program, FBI Nat. Acad. With USAF, 1962-70; officer Stockton Police Dept., 1973, sgt., 1980, lt., 1986, capt., 1990, dep. chief of police, 1990, acting chief of police, 1993, chief of police, 1993—. Bd. dirs. St. Joseph's Med. Ctr., San Joaquin United Way, Lilliput Childrens Svcs., Greater Stockton C. of C.; active Hispanics for Polit. Action; adv. com. Leadership, Stockton. With USAF, 1962-70. Mem. Calif. Peace Officers Assn., Hispanic Am. Police Command Officer's Assn., Mexican Am. C. of C., Stockton E. Rotary, Coun. for Spanish Speaking (past bd. dirs.), Leadership Stockton Alumni Assn. Office: Stockton Police Dept 22 E Market St Stockton CA 95202-2802

CHAVEZ, GILBERT T. librarian; s. Severo J. and Stella I. Chavez. BA, Calif. State U., 1969—72, MLS, 1972—74; MEd, Heritage Coll., 1998—99; D Libr. and Info. Studies, U. of Wisc., 2002—. Libr. dir. Oreg. Trail Libr. Dist., Boardman, Oreg., 1996—2000; vol. Peace Corps, Wash., DC, 2000—02. Pres. Boardman C. of C., Oreg., 1997—98. Recipient Advanced Study Fellowship, U. of Wis. - Madison, 2002. Mem.: ALA. Home Fax: 866-369-1642. Personal E-mail: chxx@onebox.com.

CHAVEZ, JOHN ANTHONY, lawyer; b. Auburn, Calif., Oct. 5, 1955; s. Marco Antonio and Barbara Ann (Lawrence) Chavez-Rivas. BA, U. Calif., Santa Barbara, 1977; JD, Stanford U., 1981. Bar: Calif. 1981, Tex. 1982, U.S. Dist. Ct. (so. and no. dists.) Calif. 1982, (cen. dist.) Calif. 1983, U.S. Dist. Ct. (so. dist.) Tex. 1982, (we. dist.) Tex. 1983, (no. dist.) Tex. 1991, N.Y. 1986, U.S. Dist. Ct. (ea. and so. dists.) N.Y. 1986, U.S. Supreme Ct. 1986. With legal dept. Exxon Co. U.S.A., Houston, 1981-85, N.Y.C., 1985-86; assoc. gen. counsel Sybron Corp., Saddlebrook, N.J., 1986-88, Crown Equipment Corp., New Bremen, Ohio, 1989-90; trial atty. Exxon Co. U.S.A., Houston, 1990-92; counsel complex litigation Exxon Chem. Co., Houston, 1992-95; counsel internat. oil and gas exploration Exxon Exploration Co., Houston, 1995-96; counsel antitrust, mergers and acquisitions Exxon Chem. Co., Houston, 1996-2000; counsel intellectual property licensing ExxonMobil Chem. Co., Baytown, Tex., 2000—. Presenter numerous legal edn. seminars and programs. Contbr. articles to profl. jours. Mentor Ft. Bend Ind. Sch. Dist., 1998, Houston Bar Assn., 1998. Chancellor's scholar U. Calif., 1976; Univ. Svc. award for dist. svc. to campus cmty. U. Calif., Santa Barbara, 1977. Fellow Houston Bar Found.; mem. ABA (antitrust sect., vice chair corp. counseling com. 1998-2000, vice chair intellectual property com. 2000-03, vice chair Sherman Act sect. 2003—), Houston Bar Assn. (chair antitrust and trade regulation sect., 1997-98, vice-chair 1996-97, sec.-treas. 1995-96, coun. 1993-95), Wong Sun Soc. Republican. Avocations: hiking, theatre, travel. Home: 4908 Cedar St Bellaire TX 77401 Office: Exxon Chem Co 5200 Bayway Dr Baytown TX 77520-2100 Fax: 281-834-2911. E-mail: J.Anthony.Chavez@exxonmobil.com.

CHAVEZ, JULIO CESAR, professional boxer; b. Ciudad Obregon, Mex., July 12, 1962; s. Rodolfo and Isabelita Chavez; m. Amalia Carrasco; children: Julio Jr., Omar, Christian. Profl. boxer, 1980—; six time world champion; winner WBC super featherweight championship, 1984; winner WBA lightweight championship, 1987; winner WBC jr. welterweight championship, 1988; world title fight record 31-1-1. Office: World Boxing Coun Genova 33 Despacho #503 DF 06600 Mexico City Mexico

CHAVEZ, MARTIN JOSEPH, lawyer, mayor; b. Albuquerque, Mar. 2, 1952; s. Lorenzo Armijo and Sara (Baca) C.; m. Margaret Aragon de Chavez, July 29, 1988; children: Martinique, Ezequiel Lorenzo. BS, U. N.Mex., 1975; JD, Georgetown U., 1978. Staff asst. U.S. Senate, Washington, 1976-77; dep. dir. LULAC Nat. Scholarship Fund, Washington, 1977-78; law clk. N.Mex. Atty. Gen., 1978-79; pvt. practice, 1979-86, 87-93, 98—; first and founding dir. N.Mex. Workers Compensation Adminstrn., 1986-87; mem. N.Mex. Senate, 1988-93; mayor City of Albuquerque, 1993-97, 2001—. Mem. Med. Rev. Commn., 1990—; bd. dirs. Senior Arts Project, 1987—, Tree New Mex., 1991-92. Mem. Citizens Rev. Bd., 1988—; bd. dirs. N.Mex. First, Sr. Arts; founding mem., bd. dirs. Tree N.Mex.; mem. Citizens Adv. Bd., N.Mex. Med. Rev. Commn.; Dem. candidate for Gov., 1998. Recipient Outstanding Young Men of Am. award, 1984, Appreciation award Friends of Albuquerque Petroglyphs, 1989, Cert. Appreciation, Am. Merchant Marines, 1989, Disting. Svc. award N.Mex. Dietetic Assn., 1989, Appreciation award West Mesa Little League, 1989, Excellence in Edn. award Friend of Edn., 1990, Appreciation award FHP N.Mex., Inc., 1990, Devoted and Invaluable Svc. award Indian Pueblo Cultural Ctr., 1990, Recognition award Ind. Ins. Agts. N.Mex., 1991, Accomplishment, Dedication and Performance award West Mesa High Sch., 1991, N.Mex. State Meml. award, 1991, Exemplary Dedication and Svc. award Sec. of State, 1991, Cert. Spl. Appreciation, MADD, 1991, Disting. Svc. award Hispanic Bar Assn., 1992, Legis. Recognition award Dem. Party N.Mex., 1992, Commitment to Edn. award Alamosa Elem. Sch., 1992, Recognition and Appreciation award N.Mex. First, 1992, Dedication award Albuquerque Hispano C. of C., 1993, Pride of N.Mex. award Hispanic Round Table, 1993; named Outstanding Youth Advocate, Youth Devel., Inc., 1993. Mem. N.Mex. State Bar Assn. (Pub. Svc. Recognition award 1989). Avocation: fly fishing. Office: Office of the Mayor PO Box 1293 Albuquerque NM 87103

CHAVEZ, MARY ANN, osteopathic family physician; b. York, Pa., Dec. 6, 1942; d. Henry David Gross and Mary Ellen (Ness) Rhoads; m. Richard L. Ziegler, Dec. 24, 1965 (div. Jan. 1983); children: Richard L. Ziegler Jr., Mara L. Tammaro, Brian L. Ziegler. BS, Alvernia Coll., 1983; DO, Coll. Osteo. Medicine, Phila., 1992. Legal sec. Louis Sager, Esquire, Pottstown, Pa., 1962-67; homemaker, tailor in pvt. practice Pottstown, 1967-85; intern Riverside Hosp., Wilmington, Del., 1992-93, resident in family practice, 1993-95; pvt. practice Spring Grove, Pa., 1995-97, Lancaster, Pa., 1997-999, Chillicothe, Ohio, 1999-2000, Sullivan, Ind., 2001—. Pell grantee, Beog grantee Alvernia Coll., 1979-83. Mem. AMA, Am. Osteo. Assn., Am. Coll. Osteo. Family Physicians, Am. Acad. Osteopathy, Pa. Osteo. Med. Assn., York County Osteo. Med. Assn, Nat. Osteo. Women's Physicians Assn., Ohio Osteo. Medicine, Ohio State Med. Soc., Ind. State Med. Assn., Sullivan Rotary Club, Sullivan Bus. and Profl. Women's Club. Avocations: oil painting, piano, tailoring, gardening. Home: 204 W Giles St PO Box 450 Sullivan IN 47882-0450 Office: Sullivan Med Clinic 222 W Beech St Sullivan IN 47882 E-mail: maryann.chavez@verizon.net.

CHAVEZ, MARY LYNN, pharmacy educator; b. Detroit, May 8, 1950; d. Gilbert E. and Dorothea J. (Munro) Van Sickle; m. Pedro I. Chavez, May 12, 1973; children: Pedro C., Stephen J. BS in Pharmacy, U. Tex., 1973; PharmD, Purdue U., 1985. Instr. Coll. Pharmacy U. P.R., San Juan, 1983-84, 87-88, asst. prof. pharmacy practice, 1988-92, clin. pharmacy specialist Med. Sch.-Pediat. Oncology Group, 1990-93, assoc. prof. pharmacy, 1990-93; assoc. prof. dept. pharmacy practice Chgo. Coll. Pharmacy, Midwestern U., Downers Grove, Ill., 1993-98, acting asst. chmn. clin. edn., 1997-98; dir. didactic edn. Midwestern U. Coll. Pharmacy, Glendale, Ariz., 1998—; dir. complementary therapies Rsch. Ctr. Advancement Pharmacy Practice, Glendale, 1998—, prof. pharmacy practice, 1999—. Writer pharmacy exam. CAT-NAPLEX/NABPLEX Licensure, Park Ridge, Ill., 1996; reviewer posters and presentations Am. Assn. Health Sys. Pharmacies, Bethesda, Md., 1996—; reviewer manuscripts Annals of Pharmacotherapy, Cin. Therapeutics, Am. Jour. Pharm. Edn., Jour. Pharmacy Tech., Am. Jour. Health Sys. Pharmacy, 1995—. Mem. editl. bd. Jour. Am. Pharmacy Assn., Prima Pub., Jour. Herbal Pharmacotherapy; contbg. editor Hosp. Pharmacy. Asst. to cub pack leader area coun. Boy Scouts Am., Naperville, Ill., 1995, 96. Mem. Am. Pharm. Assn., Am. Assn. Colls. of Pharmacy, Am. Soc. Hosp. Pharmacists, Am. Coll. Clin. Pharmacists, Sigma Xi, Rho Chi. Office: Midwestern U Coll Pharmacy Glendale AZ 85308

CHAVEZ, VICTOR EDWIN, judge; b. L.A., Aug. 28, 1930; s. Raymond C. and Sarah (Baca) C.; children: Victoria, Catherine, Stephanie, Christopher, Robert, Elizabeth. BS, Loyola U., L.A., 1953, JD, 1959. Bar: Calif. 1960. Mem. firm Early, Maslach, Foran and Williams, L.A., 1960-69, Pomerantz and Chavez, L.A., 1969-90; judge L.A. Superior Ct., 1990—, mem. exec. com., 1991—92, asst. presiding judge, 1997, 98, presiding judge, 1999—2000, mem. exec. com., 1996, 2003. Mem. com. State Bar Examiners, 1972-76; del. to State Bar, 1971-75; bd. regents Loyola Marymount U., 1973-78. 1st lt. USAF, 1953-55. Mem. ABA (standing com. on fed. judiciary 1979-86), L.A. County Bar Assn., Mex.-Am. Bar Assn. of L.A.(pres. 1971), Am. Bd. Trial Advocates (pres. L.A. chpt. 1979), Law Soc., Internat. Acad. Trial Judges. Office: Dept 96 111 N Hill St Los Angeles CA 90012-3117

CHAVEZ-THOMPSON, LINDA, labor union administrator; b. Lubbock, Tex., Aug. 3, 1944; m. Robert Thompson (dec.); 2 children. Union sec. Am. Fedn. State, County & Mcpl. Employees, 1967-71, internat. rep., 1971-73, asst. bus. mgr., bus. mgr., exec. dir. local 2399, 1973-95, exec. dir. coun. 42, 1977-95, nat. v.p. labor coun. L.Am. Advancement, 1986-96, internat. v.p., 1988-96, exec. dir. Tex. Coun. 42, 1977-95; v.p. AFL-CIO, Washington, 1993-95, exec. v.p., 1995—. Office: AFL-CIO 815 16th St NW Washington DC 20006-4145

CHAVIN, WALTER, biological science educator and researcher; b. N.Y.C., Dec. 6, 1925; s. Isidor and Fanny (Kesch) C. BS, CCNY, 1946; MS, NYU, 1949, PhD, 1954. Rsch. asst. N.Y. Aquarium, N.Y.C., 1947-48; instr. dept. zoology U. Ariz., Tucson, 1949-51; rsch. specialist dept. fishes Am. Mus. Natural History, N.Y.C., 1951-53; prof. biol. scis. Wayne State U., Detroit, 1953-90, prof. emeritus, 1990—; prof. radiology Wayne State U. Med. Sch., Detroit, 1975-80; dir. Radiation Biology Inst. Wayne State U., Detroit, 1959-71. Research assoc. Argonne (Ill.) Nat. Lab., 1955-58. Contbr. 225 articles to profl. jours. NSF Sr. Postdoctoral fellow, 1960-61; Rsch. grantee NSF, AEC, NIH. Fellow AAAS (sec. 1978-85), N.Y. Acad. Scis.; mem. Am. Physiol. Soc., Am. Soc. Zoologists (treas., sec.), Soc. Exptl. Biology and Medicine (com. 1986-90), Endocrine Soc., Am. Orchid Soc., South Fla. Orchid Soc., Pan Am Orchid Soc., Am. Bonsai Soc., Gold Coast Bonsai Soc., Lighthouse Bonsai Soc., Palm Beach Bonsai Soc., Sigma Xi (chpt. pres. 1974). Independent. Home: 16484 Bridlewood Cir Delray Beach FL 33445-6678 E-mail: raja25@bellsouth.net.

CHAVOOSHIAN, MARGE, artist, educator; b. NYC, Jan. 8, 1925; d. Harry Mesrob and Anna (Tashjian) Kurkjian; m. Barkev Budd Chavooshian, Aug. 11, 1946; children: J. Dean, Nora Ann. Student, Art Students League, 1943, Reginald Marsh, N.Y.C., 1943, Mario Cooper, 1977. Designer Needlework Arts Co., N.Y.C., 1943-44; illustrator John David Men's Store, N.Y.C., 1944-45; illustrator, layout artist Fawcett Publs., N.Y.C., 1945-47; designer, illustrator Pa. State U., University Park, 1947-49; art tchr. Trenton Pub. Sch., N.J., 1958-68, art cons. Title One Program, 1968-74; painting instr. Princeton Art Assn., N.J., 1974-77, 96, Jewish Cmty. Ctr., Ewing, N.J., 1974-85, Comtemporary Club, Trenton, 1974-85, YMCA, YWCA, Trent Ctr., Trenton, 1974—, various watercolor workshops, N.J., 1990—. Artist-at-large Alliance For Arts Edn., NJ, 1979—80; adj. asst. prof. art instr. Mercer County Coll., West Windsor, NJ, 1985—93; tchr. watercolor workshops Chalfonte, 2001, Cape May, NJ, H. Leeche Studio, Sarasota, Fla., 1998, Sarasota, 99, Art Ctr., Sarasota, 2001, Sarasota, 02. One-woman shows include Rider U., 1974, 2000, Rider Coll., 2002, Jersey City Mus., 1980, N.J. State Mus., 1981, 2001, Trenton City Mus., 1984, 1987, Arts Club, Washington, 1991, Magnolia Rm., Cape May, 1993—2003, Coryell Gallery, Lambertville, N.J., 1993, Chalfonte Cape May, 1993—96, 2001—03, Louisa Melrose Gallery, 2002, exhibited in group shows at Douglas Coll., N.J., 1977, Bergen Mus., Paramus, NJ, 1980—82, Hunterdon Art Ctr., Clinton, N.J., 1982, 1995, Morris Mus., Morristown, N.J., 1984, Allied Artists of Am., 1984, 1986, 1989, 1991—99, Salmagundi Club, N.Y.C., 1988, 1991—92, 1994—99, German Mus., 1995—96, Barron Art Ctr., Woodbridge, NJ, Ridgewood (N.J.) Art Inst., Art Works of Princeton and Trenton, 1995, Hunterdon County Cultural and Heritage Commn. Show, Clinton, N.J., 1995, Trenton City Mus., 2001; actor: others; Represented in permanent collections Mercer County Cultural and Heritage Commn., Arts Club of Washington, N.J. State Mus., Jersey City Mus., Trenton City Mus., Morris Mus., Rider U., Art Mus. San Lazarre, Italy, Bristol Myers Squibb, Johnson and Johnson, Schering Plough Corp., Pub. Svc. Electric and Gas Co., U.S. Trust, N.J. Blue Cross and Blue Shield, Eden Inst., Princeton, N.J., others. Recipient numerous awards Union Coll., E. Jane Given Meml. award, 1996, Pres. award, 1996, Rockport Pubs. Mass. Pub. Inclusion: Best of Watercolor, 1995, Watercolor Places, 1996, Graphic-Sha Pub. Co., The Best of Watercolor, Tokyo, 1996, Landscape Inspirations, 1997, Best of Sketching & Painting, 1998, The Artistic Touch 3, Creative Art Press, 1999, Mercer County Cultural and Heritage Commn. purchase award, 1999, Phillips Mill, Walter E. Martin Meml. award 1992, Patrons award for watercolor 1994, Am. Watercolor Soc., Phila Watercolor Club, Ligorno and Solansky award Hunterdon County Cultural and Heritage Commn., 1991, Cynthia Goodgal Meml. award, Moshe Bahire award Ridgewood Art Inst., 1992, 99, Ruth Ratay award Cmty. Arts Assn. Mid Atlantic Show, 1994, Elliot Liskin Meml. award Salmagundi Open Show, 1995, Thomas Moran Meml. award Salmagundi Open Show, 1999, Mus. award Trenton City Mus., 2000, D. Rodney and DaVinci Paint award Garden State Watercolor Soc., 2000, Dale Meyers medal, Salmagundi Club, NY, 2002, Niece Lumber award, Coryell Gallery, Lambertville, 2003; named Woman of Month Woman's Newspaper of Princeton, 1984, NJ State Coun. Arts fellow, 1979. Fellow Am. Artists Profl. League (Am. Arts Clon award 1973, Winsor Newton award 1980, Gold medal, Barron Art Ctr. award 1991, 93, Merit award 1993, Am. Artists Profl. League award 1994, Best in Show award, Best in Watercolor award 1995, others, representational painting award 1995); mem. Nat. Assn. Women Artists (two yr. nat. travel award 1985, Jeffrey Childs Willis Meml. award, Natl. Assn. Women Artists award 1999), S. Winston Meml. award 1988, (two yr. travel award 1996—), Catherine Lorillard Wolfe Art Club (Bee Paper Co. award 1977, Anna Hyatt Huntington bronze medal, 2000, Cynthia Goodgall Meml. award 1995), Allied Artists Am. (elected mem., Henry Gasser Meml. award 1992), N.J. Watercolor Soc. (Newton Art Ctr. award 1972, Helen K. Bermel award 1984, Howard Savs. Bank award 1986-87, Forbes Mag. award 1997, Lambertville Hist. Soc. award Coryell Gallery, 1995, 2001), Painters and Sculptors Soc. (Medal of Honor, Digby Chandle medal, others), Garden State Watercolor Soc. (Triangle Art Ctr. award 1976, 89, 94, Grumbacher Silver medal 1981, Merit award 1982, Trust Co. award 1987, Triangle award 1994, Art Express award, 1995, Rider U. Gallery award 1995, Cranbury Sta. Art Gallery award 1997, Daler Rowney and Da Vinci paint award 2000), Midwest Watercolor Soc., Nat. Arts Club (John Elliott award 1988), Phila. Watercolor Club (Village Art award 1991), Nat. Watercolor Soc. (signature), Am. Watercolor Soc. (signature). Democrat. Mem. Apostolic Ch. Armenia. Home: 222 Morningside Dr Trenton NJ 08618-4914

CHAWLA, NIKHILESH, engineering educator; b. Rio de Janeiro, Jan. 8, 1972; arrived in U.S., 1984; s. Krishan Kumar and Nivedita Chawla; m. Anita Chawla. BS, N.Mex. Tech., 1993; MS, U. Tenn., 1994; PhD, U. Mich., 1997. Rsch. fellow U. Mich./Ford Motor Co., Ann Arbor, 1997-98; sr. devel. engr. Hoeganaes Corp., Cinnaminson, N.J., 1999; asst. prof. materials engring., grad. chair Ariz. State U., Tempe, 2000—03, assoc. prof. materials engring., 2003—. Contbr. articles to profl. jours.; patentee in field. Recipient R.L. Thakur Meml. award, Indian Ceramic Soc., 1998, Office Naval Rsch. Young Investigator award, 2001, Early Career award, NSF, 2001; grantee, U.S. Automotive Materials Partnership, 2000. Mem. ASM (composite materials com. 1999—, 1st pl. grad. student award 1996), Soc. for the Promotion of Indian Classical Music, The Minerals, Metals and Materials Soc. (chair young leaders com., vice-chair composite materials com.). Avocations: violin, basketball, flag football. Office: Ariz State U Dept Chem/Materials Engrg PO Box 876006 Tempe AZ 85287-6006

CHAWNER, LUCIA MARTHA, English educator; b. Ithaca, N.Y., Dec. 2, 1933; d. Lowell Jenkins and Lucia Mary (Soule) C.; m. Movses Guichen Andreassian, Mar. 18, 1967 (div. June 1971). Student, Earlham Coll., 1951-53; BA, U. Colo., 1956; MA, So. Meth. U., 1975. Provisional cert. elem., secondary and talented and gifted, Tex.; profl. cert. reading specialist, Tex. Tchr. grade 7 lang. arts and social studies Stonewall Jackson, Dallas Ind. Sch. Dist., 1959-63; reading clinician Reinhardt, Dallas Ind. Sch. Dist., 1963-66; Reading Resource Pilot Project Lakewood, Dallas Ind. Sch. Dist., 1972-74; devel. curriculum specialist El Centro Coll., Dallas County C.C. Dist., Dallas, 1977-78; English tchr. Health Magnet, Dallas Ind. Sch. Dist., 1979-95; univ. supervising tchr. U. Tex. Dallas, Richardson, 1996—. Part-time instr. El Centro & Richland Colls., Dallas, 1978-88, Brookhaven Coll., Farmers Branch, Tex., 1996-98; mem. English lit. textbook adoption com. Dallas Ind. Sch. Dist., 1988-89; chmn. English dept. Health Magnet, Dallas Ind. Sch. Dist., 1989-94, mgr. innovative grant, 1994-95. Co-leader child and youth study U. Md., Dallas, 1967-69; pres. English-Speaking Union-Dallas Br., 1992-96; mem. Leadership Arts, Dallas Bus. Com. Arts, 1994-95, World Affairs Coun. Greater Dallas; region 7 chmn., nat. bd. mem. English-Speaking Union of USA, 1996-2000. Recipient Instrnl. grant Richland Coll., 1980; Advanced Study grantee Dallas Ind. Sch. Dist., 1973; Named Tchr. of the Yr., Health Magnet, 1991, Rotary Tchr. of the Yr., Health Magnet, 1993, nat. Merit award, English-Speaking Union of USA, 2000. Mem. Dallas Mus. Art League (bd. dirs. 1997—), New Conservatory of Dallas (bd. mem. 1999—, sec. 2002-), Friends SMU Librs. (bd. dirs. 1995-98), Assemblage (pres. 1987-88), Brit. Am. Commerce Assn., Dau. Brit. Empire, Soc. Mayflower Descs., Dallas Knife and Fork Club, Inc. (Bd. Dirs. 2003—), Delta Delta Delta, Phi Delta Kappa, Pi Lambda Theta (Alpha Sigma chpt. pres. 2002-). Avocations: sculpture, needlepoint, fitness exercise, travel. Office: PO Box 141179 Dallas TX 75214-1179

CHAYES, JENNIFER TOUR, mathematical physicist, educator; b. N.Y.C., Sept. 20, 1956; d. Eli and Hedy Tour; m. Christian Borgs. BA summa cum laude, Wesleyan U., 1979; PhD, Princeton U., 1983. Postdoctoral fellow Harvard U., Cambridge, Mass., 1983-85, Cornell U., Ithaca, N.Y., 1985-87; prof. math. UCLA, 1987—; prof. math. and physics U. Wash., Seattle, 1997—; mgr. theory group Microsoft Rsch., Redmond, Wash., 1997—. Mem. bd. math. scis. NRC, Washington, 1997—; bd. govs. Inst. for Math. and its Applications, Mpls., 1998-2000; bd. mem. external adv. bd. Ctr. for Discrete Math. and Computer Sci., New Brunswick, N.J., 1997—; mem. adv. com. Office on the Pub. Understanding Sci., NAS, Washington, 2000—. Contbr. articles to profl. jours. Sloan Found. Rsch. fellow Alfred P. Sloan Found., 1989, NSF postdoctoral fellow, 1984. Mem. AAAS, Am. Math. Soc. (v.p. 1998-2001), Am. Phys. Soc., Internat. Assn. Math. Physics. Office: Microsoft Rsch 1 Microsoft Way Redmond WA 98052 Office Fax: 425-936-7429. E-mail: jchayes@microsoft.com.

CHAYKIN, ROBERT LEROY, manufacturing and marketing executive; b. Miami, Fla., May 2, 1944; s. Allan Leroy and Ruth (Levine) C.; m. Patty Jean Patton, Feb. 1971 (div. May 1975); m. Evalyn Marcy Slodzina, Sept. 3, 1989; children: Stephanie Lee, Michele Alee, Catrina Celia, Ally Sue. BA in Polit. Sci., U. Miami, Fla., 1965, LLB, 1969. Owner, operator Serrating Svcs. Miami, 1969-71, Serrating Svcs. Las Vegas, Nev., 1971-84; pres. Ser-Sharp Mfg., Inc., Las Vegas, 1984—; nat. mktg. dir. Coserco Corp., Las Vegas, 1987—. Patentee in mfg. field. With U.S. Army, 1962. Recipient 2d degree black belt Tae Kwon Do, Profl. Karate Assn., 1954-61. Avocations: travel, camping.

CHAZELLE, BERNARD, computer science educator; b. Clamart, France, Nov. 5, 1955; s. Jean and Marie-Claire (Blanc) C.; m. Celia Martin, June 26, 1982; children: Damien, Anna. Engring. diploma, Ecole Nat. Supérieure des Mines de Paris, 1977; PhD, Yale U., 1980. Rsch. assoc. Carnegie-Mellon U., Pitts., 1980-82; from. asst. prof. to assoc. prof. Brown U., Providence, R.I., 1982-86; assoc. prof. Ecole Normale Superieure, Paris, 1985-86, Princeton (N.J.) U., 1986-89, prof., 1989—. Cons. Xerox Parc, Palo Alto, Calif., 1984, DEC SRC, 1984-93. Editor Algorithmica, Siam Jour. Computing, Jour. Algorithms, Computer Geometry: Theory & Applications, Internat. Jour. Computations Geometry and Applications, Discrete and Computational Geometry, Jour. Assn. for Computing Machinery; contbr. articles to profl. jours. Fellow French Ministry Fgn. Affairs, 1977, J.S. Guggenheim Meml. Found., 1994, NEC, 1998—. Fellow: Assn. for Computing Machinery; mem.: European Acad. Sci. Avocation: blues guitar. Office: Princeton U Dept Computer Sci Princeton NJ 08544-0001

CHAZEN, HARTLEY JAMES, lawyer; b. N.Y.C., Feb. 14, 1932; s. Joseph and Helen (Jacobson) C.; m. Lois Audrey, Dec. 12, 1967; 1 child, Nicole Joanna. AB, CCNY, 1953; LLB, Harvard U., 1958; LLM, NYU, 1959. Bar: N.Y. 1959. Assoc. Hays, St. John, Abramson & Heilbron, N.Y.C., 1959-65, Shea & Gould, N.Y.C., 1965-68, Rosenman & Colin, N.Y.C., 1968-70; ptnr. Monasch Chazen & Stream, N.Y.C., 1970-82; pvt. practice N.Y.C., 1982-88; ptnr. Chazen & Fox, N.Y.C., 1988—; of counsel McLaughlin & Stern, N.Y.C., 1992-2000. Lectr. in field. Capt. USAR, 1958-68. Mem. Assn. Bar City N.Y., ABA (subcom. corp. taxation 1987—), Harvard Club. Home: 75 Perkins Rd Greenwich CT 06830-3510 Office: Chazen & Fox 767 Third Ave Fl 35 New York NY 10017 E-mail: hchazen@chazenfox.com.

CHAZEN, STEPHEN I. oil company executive; b. Buffalo, N.Y., Aug. 26, 1946; s. Michael M. and Marcia Chazen; m. Patricia L. Orr, Dec. 18, 1971. AB, Rutgers Coll., 1968; PhD, Mich. State U., 1973; MS, U. Houston, 1977. Lab. mgr. Northrop Svcs., Inc., Houston, 1973-77; dir. project evaluation Columbia Gas Devel. Corp., Houston, 1977-81; v.p. Merrill Lynch, Houston, 1982-86, mng. dir. N.Y.C., 1987-93; exec. v.p. Occidental Petroleum Corp., L.A., 1994—, CFO, exec. v.p. corp. devel. Dir. Lyondell Chem. Corp., Houston, Premcor Inc., Old Greenwich, Conn. Mem. L.A. C. of C. (dir. 1996—). Home: PO Box 427 Pacific Palisades CA 90272-0427 Office: Occidental Petroleum Corp 10889 Wilshire Blvd Los Angeles CA 90024-4201

CHAZHUR, BESS JOHN, health facility administrator; b. N.Y.C., Dec. 2, 1973; d. Thomas and Annamma John; m. Jaison Francis Chazhur, Oct. 21, 2000; 1 child, Christopher. BA, SUNY, Albany, 1995; MS, Iona Coll., New Rochelle, N.Y., 1999. Devel. asst. Archdiocese of N.Y., N.Y.C., 1995—98; devel. coord. Sound Shore Med. Ctr., New Rochelle, NY, 1998—2001; dir. devel., chair devel. com. Marian Woods Retirement Ctr., Hartsdale, NY, 2001—. Adj. prof. Westchester Bus. Inst., White Plaines, NY, 2002—. Vol. Westchester Christian Worship Ctr., White Plains, 2001—, Dem. Com., White Plains, 2002—. Mem.: Nat. Cath. Devel. Conf., Assn. of Fundraising Profls. Avocations: songwriting, singing.

CHEADLE, DON, actor; b. Kansas City, Mo., Nov. 29, 1964; Actor: (TV series) Fame, 1982, L.A. Law, 1986, Hill Street Blues, 1981, The Bronx Zoo, 1987, Hooperman, 1988, Night Court, 1984, Booker, 1989, China Beach, 1988, The Fresh Prince of Bel-Air, 1990, Hangin' with Mr. Cooper, 1992, The Simpsons, 1989, The Bernie Mac Show, 2001, ER, 1994; (films) Moving Violations, 1985, Punk, 1986, Hamburger Hill, 1987, Colors, 1988; (TV series) The Golden Palace, 1992; (films) Roadside Prophets, 1992, The Meteor Man, 1993; (TV films) Lush Life, 1993; (TV series) Picket Fences, 1992; (films) Things to Do in Denver When You're Dead, 1995, Devil in a Blue Dress, 1995; (TV films) Rebound: The Legend of Earl The Goat Manigault, 1996; (films) Rosewood, 1997, Volcano, 1997, Boogie Nights, 1997, Bulworth, 1998, Out of Sight, 1998; (TV films) The Rat Pack, 1998, A Lesson Before Dying, 1999; (films) Mission to Mars, 2000; (TV films) Fail Safe, 2000; (films) The Family Man, 2000, Traffic, 2000, Things Behind the Sun, 2000, Manic, 2001, Swordfish, 2001, Rush Hour 2, 2001, Ocean's Eleven, 2001, The Hire: Ticker, 2002. Office: William Morris Agy Attn Arnold Rifkin 151 El Camino Dr Beverly Hills CA 90212*

CHEADLE, LOUISE, concert pianist, educator; b. Donora, Pa., July 4, 1935; d. Max Raphael and Helen Louise Busto; m. William George Cheadle, Feb. 12, 1959 (dec. Dec. 1993); children: William Robert, Amy Louise Fleming. BMusic, The Juilliard Sch., 1959. Founder, dir. Westminster Conservatory of Music/Rider U., Princeton, NJ, 1972—82; head piano dept. Amherst Summer Music Ctr., Raymond, Maine, 1971—72; adj. instr. music Bucks County C.C., Newtown, Pa., 1982-85; nationwide concert tours and workshops, various mgmts. and agys., throughout U.S., 1980s; nat. adjudicator Nat. Guild Piano Tchrs., Austin, Tex., 1999—; freelance recitals, workshops and pvt. tchg. includes Lincoln Ctr., Carnegie Hall, N.Y.C., 1980—. Debut recital with Pitts. Concert Soc., 1954; contbg. author: Teaching Piano, 1981; CD release Virtuoso Piano Music by Cecile Chaminate and Fanny Mendelssohn-Hensel, 2002. Bd. dirs., chair Cmty. Outreach. Juilliard Sch. scholar, 1956-59. Mem. Music Tchrs. Nat. Assn., N.J. Music Educators Assn. (bd. dirs., v.p.), N.J. Music Tchrs. Assn. (chair Young Artist Competition 1999, 2000, chair Master Class Competition 1999, 2000), Rossmoor (N.J.) Music Assn. (bd. dirs.), Piano Tchrs. Congress N.Y., Music Club of Princeton. Avocations: writing, reading, cooking, cultural events. Office: PO Box 7792 Princeton NJ 08543-7792 E-mail: chealou@aol.com.

CHEAH, KEONG-CHYE, psychiatrist, educator; b. Georgetown, Penang, West Malaysia, Mar. 15, 1939; came to U.S., 1959; s. Thean Hoe and Hun Kin (Keong) C.; m. Sandra Massey, June 10, 1968; children: Chylynn, Maylynn. BA in Psychology, U. Ark., 1962; MD, U. Ark., Little Rock, 1967, MS in Microbiology, 1968. Diplomate Am. Bd. Psychiatry and Neurology (examiner 1982, 85); cert. Ark. State Sci. Bd., Ark. State Med. Bd. Intern U. Ark. Med. Ctr., 1967-68; resident VA Med. Ctr. and U. Ark. Med. Ctr., Little Rock, 1968-72; chief addiction sect. Little Rock VA Med. Ctr., 1972-73, staff psychiatrist, 1975-80; chief psychiatry American Lake VA Med. Ctr., Tacoma, 1981-86; chief consultation, liason Am. Lake divsn. Puget Sound Health Care Sys., Tacoma, 1986-94; asst. prof. medicine, psychiatry U. Ark., Little Rock, 1975-81; asst. prof. psychiatry and behavioral scis. U. Wash., Seattle, 1981-86, clin. assoc. prof., 1987—2002, clin. assoc. prof. emeritus, 2002—. Mem. dist. br. com. The CHAMPUS, 1977-91; surveyor Jt. Commn. for Accreditation of Healthcare Orgns., 1990-93; site visitor AMA Continuing Med. Edn., 1979-83; book reviewer Jour. Am. Geriatrics Soc., 1984-85; mem. task force alcohol abuse VA Med. Dist. 27, 1984, survey mem. Sytematic External Rev. Process, 1985; mem. mental health plan adv. com. State of Ark., 1976-81, chmn. 1979-81, chmn. steering com., 1979; mem. Vietnamese Resettlement Program, 1979; many coms. Am. Lake VA Med. Ctr. including chmn. mental health com. 1981-84, utilization rev. com., 1981-86. Contbr. articles and abstracts to profl. jours.; presenter to confs. and meetings of profl. socs. Mem. Parents Adv. Com., Lakes H.S., Wash., 1987-91; mem. Mayor's Budget and Fin. Foresight Com., 1992—, chmn. 1990-92; sch. cons. Child Study Ctr. U. Ark., 1972-74; bd. dirs. Crisis Ctr. Ark., 1974-79, chmn. pub. rels. com., 1975-79, mem. pers. com. 1974, vice chmn. bd. 1977; pres. Chinese Assn. Ctrl. Ark., 1977; mem. gifted edn. adv. coun. Clover Park Sch. Dist. 400, Wash., 1983-85, Parent Tchr. Student Orgn. Recipient U.S. Govt. scholarship 1959, cert. merit State of Ark., 1973, Leadership award, Mental Health Svcs. Divsn., State of Ark., 1980. Fellow Am. Psychiat. Assn. (sec. treas. Asian Am. caucus 1985-87, pres. 1987-94); mem. Assn. Mil. Surgeons U.S., Wash. State Psychiat. Assn. (mem. peer rev. com. 1982-92, chmn. pub. psychiatry com. 1985-93, exec. coun. 1985-93), N. Pacific Soc. Neurology and Psychiatry Assn. (sec.-treas. 1986-99, pres. 1993), S. Puget Sound Psychiat. Assn., Assn. Chinese-Am. Psychiatrists, Chapel of Four Chaplains, Ark. Caduceus Club, Alpha Epsilon Delta, Psi Chi, Phi Beta Kappa, Alpha Omega Alpha. Avocations: reading, target shooting.

CHEATHAM, BELZORA, writer; b. Lodi, Tex., Mar. 13, 1932; d. Calvin and Hattie Geneva Brown; m. Andy Cheatham, Sept. 9, 1950 (dec. Jan. 1979); children: Jacqueline, Russell E., David R. Divsn. head Sears Roebuck & Co., Chgo., 1970-93. Author: Whittaker Cemetery Index, 1995, The History of Whittaker Memorial Cemetery, 1996 (Tex. Hist. Marker award 1996), Slaves and Slave Owners of Bowie County, Tex., 1850, 1996. Mem. Afro-Am. Geneal. and Hist. Soc. Chgo. (treas. 1992-97, pres. 1999-2001). Methodist. Avocation: genealogy. E-mail: mscheats@aol.com.

CHEATHAM, JOHN BANE, JR., retired mechanical engineering educator; b. Houston, June 29, 1924; s. John Bane and Winnie (Carr) C.; m. Juanita Faye Burns, July 19, 1947; children— Preston, Curtis. BME, So. Methodist U., 1948, MS, 1953; ME, M.I.T., 1954; PhD, Rice U., 1960. Registered profl. engr. Design engr. Linkbelt Co., Dallas and Houston, 1949-50; rsch. engr. Atlantic Refining Co., Dallas, 1950-53; rsch. assoc., head drilling rschr. Shell Devel. Co., Houston, 1954-63; prof. mech. engring. Rice U., 1963-96; chmn. dept. mech. engring. and materials sci., 1994-96; pres. Cheatham Engring. Inc., Houston, 1977-94, Techaid Corp., Houston, 1978-88. Cons. in field. Contbr. to profl. jours.; tech. editor: Jour. Energy Resources Tech, 1979-81. Served to 2d lt. USAAF, 1943-45. Fellow ASME; mem. Am. Inst. Mining and Petroleum Engrs., Am. Soc. Engring. Edn., Sigma Xi. Address: 5671 Longmont Dr Houston TX 77056-2344 E-mail: john_cheatham@hotmail.com.

CHEATHAM, ROBERT WILLIAM, lawyer; b. St. Paul, June 4, 1938; s. Robert William and Hildegard Frances Cheatham; m. Kay C. Sarnecki, Mar. 20, 1964; children: Ann Marie, Lynn Marie, Paul William. BCE, U. Minn., 1961, JD, 1966. Bar: Calif. 1967, U.S. Dist. Ct. (no. dist.) Calif. 1967. Assoc. Brobeck, Phleger & Harrison, San Francisco, 1967-74, ptnr., 1974-88, Cheatham & Skovronski, San Francisco, 1988-96, Cheatham & Tomlinson, San Francisco, 1996-97, Cassidy, Cheatham, Shimko & Dawson, San Francisco, 1997-2000, Foley & Lardner, 2000—. Speaker on continuing legal edn., San Francisco. Co-author: Calif. Attorneys Guide to Real Estate Syndicates, 1970, Cheatham and Merritt California Real Estate Forms and Commentaries, 1984-90. Mem. ABA, Calif. Bar Assn. Office: Foley & Lardner 1 Maritime Plz Fl 6 San Francisco CA 94111-3416 E-mail: rcheatham@foleylaw.com.

CHEATHAM, WALLACE MCCLAIN, music educator; b. Cleveland, Tenn., Oct. 3, 1945; s. Martin Luther and Ollie Frances (Simpson) Cheatham; m. Willie Faye Watson, May 22, 1971; children: Tosca Carmé, Kimberly Ann. BS, Knoxville Coll., 1967; MS, U. Wis., Milw., 1972, DFA, 2002; PhD, Columbia Pacific U., 1982. Music tchr. Knoxville (Tenn.) City Sch. Sys., 1967—68, Unified Sch. Dist., Racine, Wis., 1968—71, Milw. Pub. Schs., 1971—2003. Organist St. Mark African Meth. Episcopal Ch., Milw.; pianist, condr. various singers, instrumentalists, choral groups and other performing arts orgns.; presenter in field. Editor: Dialogues on Opera and the African American Experience, 1997; recordings include: U. Maine Singers, Spiritual Fantasy, Beginnings; contbr. articles to profl. jours.; composer: My Soul is a Witness, Dese Bones Gonna Rise Again, I Belong To That Band, You Must Come In Through The Door, Sinner, Please Don't Let This Harvest Pass, When the Roll is Called Up Yonder, Glory Hallelujah, My Hope Is Built, On Our Knees, Kwanzaa Songs, Anthology of Art Songs, I Am A Soldier, Praise, Thanksgiving, Missa, Portraits, O Holy Yahweh, Hymn Suite, Ode To An Organism, Children Go Where I Send Thee, For Unto Us A Child is Born, Symphony No. 1, String Quartet No. 1, Over My Head, Passacaglia and Fugue, Drinking Of The Wine, Dies Irae, Theme and Variations on Austria, Charge From A Pauline Epistile, Statements From The Light, Do Not Press Me To Leave You, Yonder Comes Mary, He Shall Purify The Sons of Levi, The Glory of The Lord, Fanfare and Tocatta, Tone Poem, Three Preludes, The inaugural anthem for the investiture of Coppin State Coll. Pres. Stanley Battle, 2003; Choral Compositions and works for solo voice published by Shawnee, Marvel, Warner Brothers, and William Grant Still; unpublished compositions (symphonic, choral, and chamber scores) housed at Ctr. for Black Music Rsch., Columbia Coll., Chicago. Participant Operation Crossroads Africa, 1966. Recipient Sullivan-Spaights Prof. Leadership award, U. Wis., Milw., 1999, Lifetime Achievement award, Civic Music Assn. Milw., 2000, Morris D. Hayes award, Wis. Choral Dirs. Assn., 2003, Achievement award, Unity Grand chpt. Order of Ea. Star State of Wis., Prince Hall Affiliation, 2003. Mem.: Nat. Assn. Negro Musicians, Internat. Consortium for the Music of Africa and its Diaspora (bd. mem.), Wis. Alliance Composers, Am. Choral Dirs. Assn., Music Educators Nat. Conf., Am. Guild Organists (svc. playing cert.), Phi Beta Sigma. African Methodist Episcopal. Home: 2961 N Fifth St Milwaukee WI 53212

CHEATHEM, MARK R. historian, educator; b. Cleveland, Tenn., July 29, 1973; s. Danny and Brenda Cheathem; m. Amber Dawn Livingston, May 15, 1999; 1 child, Laney Marie. BA in History, Cumberland U., 1995; MA in History, Mid. Tenn. State U., 1998; PhD of History, Miss. State U., 2002. Lectr. Miss. State U., Starkville, 2002—. Lectr. Miss. U. for Women, Columbus, 1999—. Contbr. Fellow, White House Hist. Assn., 2001. Mem.: Tenn. Hist. Soc. (Wills Rsch. fellow 2000), So. Hist. Assn., Orgn. Am. Historians. Avocation: chess. Office: Miss State Univ 214 Allen Hall Starkville MS 39762

CHEATWOOD, ROY CLIFTON, lawyer; b. Rome, Ga., Aug. 27, 1946; s. Herman Arthur and Dorothy Mary (Griffin) C.; m. Cynthia Morrison, June 27, 1969; children: Clifton, Scott, Dancy. BA, U. South Fla., 1968; JD, Tulane U., 1974. Bar: La. 1974, U.S. Dist. Ct. (ea. dist.) La. 1974, U.S. Dist. Ct. (mid. dist.) La. 1975, U.S. Ct. Appeals (5th cir.) 1975, U.S. Dist. Ct. (we. dist.) La. 1977, U.S. Supreme Ct. 1977, U.S. Ct. Appeals (11th cir.) 1981, U.S. Dist. Ct. (no. dist.) Tex. 1990. Assoc. Jones, Walker, Waechter, Poitevent, Carrere & Denegre, New Orleans, 1974-78, ptnr., 1978-91, Phelps Dunbar, New Orleans, 1991—, practice coord., comml. litigation practice group, 1992—, mem. mgmt. com., 1995—2003. Adj. prof. La. State U., Baton Rouge, 1980, Loyola U., New Orleans, 1981, 84-86; faculty mem. Nat. Inst. Trial Advocacy, 1986—; master barrister Tulane Inn of Ct. Co-author: Louisiana Courtroom Evidence, 1993. Firm campaign rep. United Way, New Orleans, 1982, 98, recruiter, 1983-86, 88, acct. exec. area lawyers, 1989; bd. dirs. Children's Bur., New Orleans, 1988, 1st v.p., 1991, pres., 1993-95; mem. session St. Charles Presbyn. Ch., 1988-91, session New Covenant Presbyterian Church, 2000—, clk. of session, chair pastor-nominating com., 2000—02. 1st lt. U.S. Army, 1968-71, Vietnam. Mem. ABA (litigation sect./vice chmn. 5th cir. trial practice com. 1975-76, co-chmn. 1976-78, judge regional nat. appellate adv. com. 1978, co-chmn. ann. litigation meeting 1981, judge nat. appellate adv. competition 1978, membership chmn. litigation sect. 1983-86), La. State Bar Assn. (bd. legal specialization 1998—, chmn. 2000-02). Office: Phelps Dunbar 365 Canal St Ste 2000 New Orleans LA 70130-6534 E-mail: cheatwor@phelps.com.

CHECCHI, ALFRED A. airline company executive; b. 1948; m. BA, Amherst Coll., 1970; MBA, Harvard Univ., 1974. V.p. Marriott Corp., 1975-82; with Bass Bros., 1982-86; pres. Alfred Checchi Assocs., Inc., 1986—; co-chmn., bd. dirs. NWA Inc., 1997—, Northwest Airlines Inc., 1997—, Wings Holdings Inc., 1997—; bd. dirs. Northwest Airlines, Inc., St. Paul, 1997—. Office: NW Airlines Inc 5101 Northwest Dr Saint Paul MN 55111-3034

CHECCHI, VINCENT VICTOR, economist; b. Calais, Maine, Nov. 25, 1918; s. Arthur R. and Dina I. (Pisani) C.; m. Mary E. Pate, Aug. 2, 1941; children: Dina Ann, Mary Jane, Vincent Arthur. AB, U. Maine, 1940; postgrad., Harvard U., 1941; MA, George Washington U., 1942. Various posts in U.S. Government, Allied Military Government, UNRRA, The World Bank, 1941-50; founder, CEO, chmn. bd. dirs. Checchi and Co., Washington, 1951—. Co-author: Honduras, A Problem in Economic Development; author articles on econs. Home: 9206 Watson Rd Silver Spring MD 20910-4136 Office: Checchi and Co 1899 L St NW Ste 800 Washington DC 20036-3804 E-mail: checchi@checchiconsulting.com.

CHECK, MELVIN ANTHONY, lawyer; b. Milw., Nov. 12, 1951; s. Mathew N. and Lorraine L. (Michels) C.; m. LuAnn E. Mueller, July 10, 1976. BBA, U. Wis., Milw., 1976; JD, Marquette U., 1979. Assoc. atty. Miller Law Office, Jefferson, Wis., 1979-81; atty. Check Law Office, Port Washington, Wis., 1981-82, 85—; corp. counsel Mutual Savs. and Loan Assn., Milw., 1982-85; owner Coldwell Banker N. Suburban Realty, Port Washington, Wis., 1994—. Instr. Wis. Realtors Assn., Madison, 1991—, Milw. Area Tech. Coll., 1985-91. Bd. dirs. Econ. Devel. for Grafton Enhancement, Inc., Grafton, 1990-93. With U.S. Army, 1971-73. Recipient Outstanding Svc. by an Individual Atty. Milw. Young Lawyers Assn. Vol. Lawyers Project, 1987. Mem. Ozaukee Realtors Assn. (Affiliate of Yr. 1990, Realtor of Yr. 1995), Wis. Realtors Assn. (Instr. of Yr. 1995, 2001), Nat. Assn. of Realtors, Ozaukee County Bar Assn., State Bar of Wis., Beta Gamma Sigma. Avocations: softball, bowling, woodworking. Office: 429 W Grand Ave Port Washington WI 53074-2143 E-mail: melcheck@coldwellbanker.com.

CHEDID, ANTONIO, pathologist, educator, researcher; b. Barranquilla, Colombia, May 5, 1939; came to U.S., 1966; s. Aziz Antonio and Maria (Turbay) C.; m. Hoda Abi-Rached; children: Anthony John, Marie-Claude, Erica Houda. BS, Coll. of Barranquilla, 1954; MD, U. Madrid, 1962. Diplomate Am. Bd. Pathology. Intern Columbus Hosp., Chgo., 1967-68; resident in pathology Michael Reese Hosp., Chgo., 1968-72; instr. pathology Pritzker Sch. Medicine U. Chgo., 1972-73; asst. prof. pathology U. Cin. Coll. Medicine, 1973-76; assoc. prof. pathology Chgo. Med. Sch., North Chicago, Ill., 1976-84, prof. pathology, 1985—, prof. microbiology and immunology, 1995—, prof. medicine, 1997—. Current work: aging, immunology of alcoholic liver disease and hepatitis C; specialties include pathology, medicine, hepatology and immunology. Mem. Am. Assn. Pathology, Internat. Assn. for Study of the Liver, Am. Assn. for Study Liver Diseases, Am. Soc. for Cell Biology, Fedn. Am. Socs. Exptl. Biology, Internat. Acad. Pathology. Home: 650 Rockefeller Rd Lake Forest IL 60045-3142 Office: 3333 Green Bay Rd North Chicago IL 60064-3037

CHEDID, JOHN G. retired bishop; b. Eddid, Lebanon, July 4, 1923; Educated, Sems. in Lebanon and Pontifical Urban Coll., Rome. Ordained to ministry Cath. Ch., 1951. Ordained priest Faithful of the Oriental Rite, 1951—80; apptd. St. Maron of Bklyn., 1980—81, titular bishop of Callinico and aux bishop, 1981—94; apptd. Our Lady of Lebanon, LA, 1994—2000; ret., 2000. Office: Our Lady of Lebanon Ch 333 S San Vicente Blvd Los Angeles CA 90048-3313*

CHEE, ANN-PING, music educator; b. July 26; came to U.S., 1964; d. To-Khiem Thi and Thanh-Phuc Dong; m. Anthony N.C. Chee, Dec. 27, 1969; children: Andrew, Lawrence. BA in Music cum laude, Conn. Coll., 1970. Tchr. piano, music theory, Houston, 1972—. Mem. Associated Bd. Royal Schs. Music, London. Named to Piano Guild Hall of Fame, Austin, Tex., 1997. Mem. Nat. Guild Piano Tchrs. (cert.), Music Tchrs. Nat. Assn. (cert.), Tex. Music Tchrs. Assn., Houston Music Tchrs. Assn., Houston Fedn. Music Clubs, Forum Music Tchrs. Assn., Associated Bd. Royal Schs. Music London.

CHEE, CHENG-KHEE, artist, educator; b. Xienyou, Fujian, China, Jan. 14, 1934; came to the U.S., 1962, naturalized, 1980; s. Ya-Jie and Xien-chun (Zheng) C.; m. Sing-Bee Ong, Aug. 28, 1965; children: Yi-Hung, Yi-Min, Wan-Ying, Yen-Ying. BA, Nanyang U., Singapore, 1960; MA, U. Minn., 1964. Asst. libr. Nanyang U., 1961-62; tchg. asst. U. Minn., Mpls., 1963-64, libr. Duluth, 1965-68, instr., 1968-80, asst. prof., 1981-88, assoc. prof., 1988—. One-man shows include Zhejiang Acad. Fine Arts, 1984, 87, Tweed Mus. Art, U. Minn., 1982-83, 91-92, Shanghai U. Acad. Fine Arts, China, 1987, Tianjin Acad. Fine Arts, China, 1988, Phipps Ctr. for Arts, Wis., 1991, Cannon Rotunda U.S. Ho. Office Bldg., Washington, 1993, Singapore Nat. Art Mus., 1997, Minn. Mus. Am. Art, 1997, Bloomington Ctr. for Arts, Minn., 2003; exhibited in group shows Am. Watercolor Soc. Ann., Nat. Acad. and Salmagundi Club, N.Y.C., 1975, 78, 79, 81, 91, 94, 95, 98, 2001, 03, Rocky Mountain Nat. Watermedia Exhbn., Foothills Art Ctr., Golden, Colo., 1976, 78, 80, 84, 90, 92, 93, Allied Artists Am. Ann. Exhbn., Nat. Arts Club, N.Y.C., 1980, 82, 91-97, 99-2001, Adirondacks Nat. Exhbn. Am. Watercolors, Cmty. Arts Ctr., Old Forge, N.Y., 1982, 83, 86, 89, 91, 92, 95, 96, 97, 98, 2000, 02, Nat. Watercolor Soc. Ann. Exhbn., 1983, 84, 85, 92, 96, 2002, Knickerbocker Artists USA Ann. Exhbn., 1980-81, 89-93, Sumi-e Soc. Am. Ann. Exhbn., 1979-84, 86, Mitchell Mus., Ill., 1983, Mpls. Inst. Arts, 1978, Nat. Taiwan Art Edn. Inst. Watercolor Exhbn. Artist of Taiwan, U.S. and Australia, 1994; author portfolio Cheng-Khee Chee Watercolors, 1984, 87, 91, 94, 96, (book) The Watercolor World of Cheng-Khee Chee, 1997; author exhbn. catalog, 1973-82, Retrospective Exhbn., 1982, China Exhbn. Tour, 1987, Singapore Nat. Art Mus. Exhbn., 1997, Bloomington Art Ctr., Minn., 2003; contbr. to books: Watercolor Energies, 1983, Learn Watercolor, The Edgar Whitney Way, 1994, Splash 3: Ideas and Inspirations, 1994, The Best of Watercolor, 1995, Splash 4: The Splendor of Light, 1996; illustrator: (children's books) Old Turtle, 1992 (AABBY award, Internat.Reading Assn. award 1993), Splash 5: The Glory of Color, 1998, The Best of Watercolor, Vol. 3, 1999, Swing Around the Sun, 2003.. Recipient Gold medal of honor Allied Artists of Am. exhibit, 1980, Knickerbocker Artists Exhbn., 1989, Silver medal of honor Am. Watercolor Soc. Exhbn., 1991, High Winds medal Am. Watercolor Soc. Exhbn., 1994, Grand award Akron Soc. Artists Grant Nat. Exhbn., 1994, Colo. Centennial award Rocky Mountain Nat. Watermedia Exhbn., 1976, Grumbacher Gold medal Midwest Watercolor Soc. Exhbn., 1984, 85, 98, Gold award Ga. Watercolor Soc. Exhbn., 1985, 98, Gold medal and Purchase prize Knickerbocker Artists 43rd Ann. Grand Nat. Open Juried Exhbn., 1993, Chancellor's Disting. Svc. award U. Minn., 1994, Silver award Calif. Watercolor Assn., 1998; named Best in Show Sumi-e Soc. Am., 1984, 86, New Orleans Art Assn. 11th Nat. Art Exhbn., 1986, Western Colo. Watercolor Soc. Ann. Nat. Exhbn., 1993, Red River Watercolor Soc. 1st Nat. Art Exhbn., 1994, La. Watercolor Soc. 26th Ann. Internat. Exhbn., 1996, Duluth's Cultural Amb. to the World, Mayor Doty, 1994. Mem. Am. Watercolor Soc. (Dolphin fellow), Nat. Watercolor Soc., Rocky Mountain Nat. Watermedia Soc., Allied Artists Am., Knickerbocker Artists USA, Midwest Watercolor Soc. (Master Watercolorist), Watercolor USA Honor Soc., Sumi-e Soc. Am., others. Home: 1508 Vermilion Rd Duluth MN 55812-1526 Fax: 218-724-6153.

CHEE, PERCIVAL HON YIN, ophthalmologist; b. Honolulu, Aug. 29, 1936; s. Young Sing and Den Kyau (Ching) C.; m. Carolyn Tong, Jan 27, 1966; children: Lara Wai Lung, Shera Wai Sum. BA, U. Hawaii, 1958; MD, U. Rochester, 1962. Intern Travis AFB Hosp., Fairfield, Calif., 1962-63; resident Bascom Palmer Eye Inst., Miami, 1965-68, Jackson Meml. Hosp., Miami, 1965-68; ptnr. Straub Clinic, Inc., Honolulu, 1968-71; practice medicine specializing in ophthalmology Honolulu, 1972—; mem. staff Queen's Med. Ctr. St. Francis Hosp., Honolulu; assoc. prof. surgery U. Hawaii Sch. Medicine, 1971—. Cons. Tripler Army Med. Center; adv bd. Svcs. to the Blind; bd. dirs. Lions Eye Bank, Makana Found. (organ bank), Multiple Sclerosis Soc.; assoc. examiner Am. Bd. Ophthalmology. Contbr. articles to profl. jours. Capt. USAF, 1962-65. Fellow Am. Acad. Ophthalmology, ACS; mem. AMA, Pan Am. Med. Assn., Pan Pacific Surg. Assn., Am. Assn. Ophthalmology, Hawaii Ophthal. Soc. Pacific Coast Ophthal. Soc. Home: 3755 Poka Pl Honolulu HI 96816-4409 Office: Kukui Pla 50 S Beretania St Ste C116 Honolulu HI 96813-2225 E-mail: ophth@hawaii.rr.com.

CHEEK, ARTHUR LEE, administrative professional; b. Raleigh, N.C., Aug. 6, 1940; s. Arthur Lee Sr. and Margaret Louise (Bradburn) C.; m. Sandra Lee Tigges, July 21, 1958 (wid. Sept. 1971); children: Michael Sidney, Robert Bruce; m. Sheila Ann Waters, June 27, 1987. Comml. pilot. Capt. Air America, Inc., Far East, 1965-66; corp. pilot Am. Enka Corp., Asheville, N.C., 1966-68; capt. TWA/Saudi Arabian Airlines, Jidda, Saudia Arabia, 1968-71; owner Custom Homes, Inc., Asheville, 1971-80; corporate pilot SEU Constrn., Inc., Cape Coral, Fla., 1980-85, contract adminstr., 1985-89, v.p. contract adminstrn and constrn. litigation support svcs., 1989-96; v.p., gen. mgr. Coral Rock, Inc., Punta Gorda, Fla., 1994-96, West Coast Industries, Ft. Myers, Fla., 1990-96, Advantage Transp., Punta Gorda, Fla., 1994-96; ins. sales, 1998-99, Gen. Elec. Fin. Assurance, 1999-2000, cons. in constrn. claims and litigation, 2000—. Personal fin. adv. to srs. With USMC, 1957-60, U.S. Army, 1960-65, ETO. Mem. Masons. Republican. Avocations: golf, reading, fishing.

CHEEK, BARBARA LEE, college reading program director, educator; b. Springfield, Mo., Oct. 25, 1935; d. Curtis Earl and Gertrude Helen (Ahonen) Nelson; m. Lee Roy Clyde, June 16, 1961; children: Michael, Paul, Daniel. BA in Edn. cum laude, Pacific Luth. U., 1957; postgrad., U. Wash., Seattle, 1961-62; MA in Elem. Reading Edn., Boise (Idaho) State U., 1982; postgrad., Ea. Oreg. U., 1983, Seattle U., 1989. Cert. elem. and secondary edn. tchr., Wash. Sec. engring. dept. Boeing Aircraft Co., Seattle, 1957; instr. Edmonds (Wash.) Sch. Dist., 1957-61, Clover Pk. Sch. Dist., Tacoma, 1961-62, Payette (Idaho) Sch. Dist., 1970-74; bookkeeper Cheek Dairy Supply, Payette, 1970-71; instr. Ontario (Oreg.) Sch. Dist., 1975-79; prof. Treasure Valley C.C., Ontario, 1979-89, Pierce Coll., Tacoma, 1989-2001, dir. reading dept., 1989-96; dir. Alternative Learning Ctr. at Pierce Coll., Puyallup, Wash., 1996—2001; mem. faculty emeritus Pierce Coll., Puyallup, Wash., 2001—; instr. Profl. Excellence Program Tacoma (Wash.) Sch. Dist., 1994; pvt. reading tutor and cons., 2001—; Stephen min. Luth. Ch., 2003—. Sec. Malheur Reading Coun., Ont., 1986—87; faculty exec. bd. Treasure Valley C.C. Faculty, Ont., 1986—88; mem. Peer Evaluation Orgn. Devel. Edn., Ont., 1986; cons. Tacoma Sch. Dist. Profl. Excellence Program, 1993—; exec. Pharmanex/Nu-Skin Enterprises, 1994—; rep. Avon Cosmetics, 2003—. Moderator Ont. candidate's fair AAUW, 1985, state sec., Payette, 1972-74, sec. N.W. region, 1974, br. pres., 1970-72, 75-77; bd. dirs. Boy Scouts Am., Oregon, Idaho, 1971-84; deacon, v.p. Luth. Ch., 1986; mem. basic literacy steering com. Tacoma, 1992; mem. Pierce County

Literacy Coalition, Tacoma, Scandinavian Cultural Ctr., Pacific Luth. U.; asst. min. Luth. Ch., 1984—, Stephen Min. Leader, 2003-, Stephen Min., 2002-. Recipient Faculty Devel. award Higher Edn. State of Wash., 1990-91. Mem. AAUW (chpt. pres. 1970-72), ASCD, Western Coll. Reading Assn., Wash. State C.C., Faculty Devel. (state com.), Wash. Devel. Edn. Assn., Am. Assn. Women in Comty. and Jr. Colls., Wash. Fedn. of Tchrs. (faculty exec. bd.), Coll. Reading and Learning Assn. (pres-elect Washington, Idaho 1998-99, pres. N.W. region 1999-2001), Tchr. English to Spkrs. of Other Langs., Sweet Adelines (pres. Tacoma chpt. 2001-02), Internat., Alpha Delta Kappa (v.p. 1986), N.W. Coll. Reading and Learning Assn. (pres. 1999-2000). Republican. Avocations: handbell choir, soloist, reading, golf, skiing. E-mail: tracinda@worldnet.att.net.

CHEEK, JAMES HOWE, III, lawyer, educator; b. Nashville, Nov. 28, 1942; s. James H. and Anne H. C.; m. Sigourney Woods, June 1, 1968; children— James Howe, IV, Daniel W., Matthew H. AB, Duke U., 1964; JD, Vanderbilt U., 1967; LL.M., Harvard U., 1968. Bar: Tenn. 1967. Assoc. firm Shearman & Sterling, N.Y.C., 1967; asst. dean, asst. prof. law Vanderbilt U. Law Sch., 1968-70, adj. prof. law, 1970—; ptnr. Bass, Berry & Sims, PLC, Nashville, 1970—; chmn. legal adv. com. N.Y. Stock Exch., 1989-92. Vis. fellow Jesus Coll., Cambridge U., 1985—86; cons. Securities and Investments Bd. U.K., 1985—86; cons. comml. crime unit Commonwealth Secretariat, 1985—86; trustee Elliott E. Cheatham Fund; pres. dean's coun. Vanderbilt U. Law Sch., 1986—89, pres. law alumni bd., 1997—99; chair San Diego Securities Regulation Inst., 2000—; chmn. legal adv. bd. NASD Inc., 1996—98; lectr. CLE at seminars and insts. Contbr. articles to law jours. Trustee SEC Hist. Soc., 2000—02, Montgomery Bell Acad., Nashville, 2000—; chmn. Met. Nashville Airport Authority, 2000—. Recipient Disting. Alumnus award Vanderbilt Univ., 1994. Fellow Tenn. Bar Found. (trustee 1993-97); mem. ABA (chmn. subcom. on 1933 Act 1978-85, sec. com. on corp. law 1980-85, chmn. fed. regulation of securities com. 1987-91, chmn. sect. bus. law 1998-99, chmn. nat. task force on corp. responsibility 2002--), Nashville Bar Assn., Am. law Inst., Order of Coif, Belle Meade Country Club, Queen's Club. Home: 4404 Honeywood Ave Nashville TN 37205-3404 Office: Bass Berry & Sims PLC AmSouth Ctr Nashville TN 37238

CHEEK, JAMES RICHARD, ambassador; b. Decatur, Ga., Apr. 27, 1936; s. Woodrow Wilson and Dorothy (Webb) C.; m. Carol Ruth Rozzell, Sept. 1, 1957; children— Leesa Lynn, Forrest Craig, Surya Tamang BA, Ark. State Tchrs. Coll., 1959; M. Internat. Service, Am. U., 1961. Dep. chief mission Am. Embassy, Montevideo, Uruguay, 1977—79; dep. asst. sec. state U.S. Dept. State, Washington, 1979—81; dep. chief mission Am. Embassy, Kathmandu, Nepal, 1982—85, charge d'affaires, chief mission Addis Ababa, Ethiopia, 1985—88; diplomat-in-residence Howard U., Washington, 1988—89; U.S. amb. to Sudan Am. Embassy, Khartoum, 1989—92, U.S. amb. to Argentina Buenos Aires, 1993—96; global cons., amb. in residence U. Ark., Little Rock, 1997—; pres. Am. Internat. Airports, LLC, 2002—. Served to capt. U.S. Army, 1954-56 Recipient spl. commendation Women's Orgn., Dept. State, 1979, Disting. Alumnus award U. Ark., 1992, U. Ctrl. Ark., 1997. Mem. Am. Fgn. Service Assn. (William R. Rivkin award 1974) Avocations: antique clocks, fishing, trekking, playing squash. Home: 31 Saint Andrews Dr Little Rock AR 72212-2908 Office: U Ark 2801 S University Ave Little Rock AR 72204-1099

CHEEK, JIMMY GEARY, university administrator, agricultural education and communications educator; b. Gorman, Tex., Sept. 7, 1946; s. Geary B. and Mayme (Wright) C.; m. Ileen Griffin, Aug. 23, 1969; children: Jennifer Leigh, Jeffrey Stewart. BS with high honors, Tex. A&M U., 1969, PhD, 1975; MEd, Lamar U., 1972. Agrl. edn. instr. Beaumont (Tex.) High Sch., 1969-73; supr. manpower tng. Beaumont Ind. Sch. Dist., 1971-73; grad. fellow Tex. A&M U., College Station, 1973-74, instr., 1974-75; asst. prof. U. Fla., Gainesville, 1975-80, assoc. prof., 1980-85, prof., 1985—, asst. dean for acad. programs Coll. Agr., 1992-99, dean Coll. Agrl. and Life Scis., 1999—. Cons., seminar leader Pa. Coop. Extension Svc., 1985, Dept. Agrl. and Extension Edn., Pa. State U., 1985; cons. Gainesville (Fla.) Bd. Realty, Inc., 1988, 89, 90, 91, 92; review team mem. So. Assn. Colls. and Schs., 1977, 78; reviewer various books. Sr. author: (with others) Effective Oral Communication, 2d edit., 2000. Chair Rawlings Elem. Sch. Adv. Com., 1982-83, 85-86; pres. Rawlings Elem. Sch. PTA, 1985, v.p., 1984; mem. Ft. Clarke Sch. Adv. Com., 1987—; mem. Hidden Oak Elem. Sch. Adv. Com., 1988-90. Recipient Hon. Tex. State Future Farmers Am. degree, 1972, Hon. Fla. State Future Farmers Am. degree, 1978, Hon. Am. Future Farmers Am. degree, 1984, Outstanding Rsch. Paper award So. Agrl. Edn. Rsch. Conf., 1984, 88, 92; Merit award scholar Tex. A&M U., 1967-69; named of the 30 Notable Grads. Coll. Edn., Tex A&M U., 1999. Fellow Nat. Assn. Colls. and Tchrs. Agr. (Ensminger-Interstate Disting. Teaching award 1990); mem. Am. Vocat. Ednl. Rsch. Assn. (pres. 1986), Fla. Vocat. Assn. (pres. 1992), Am. Assn. Agrl. Edn. (v.p. 1991-92, Disting. Svc. award 1998), Am. Vocat. Assn., Nat. Vocat. Agr. Tchrs. Assn. (Outstanding Svc. award so. region 1987), Fla. Vocat. Agr. Tchrs. Assn., Fla. Assn. Vocat. and Adult Tchr. Educators, Nat. Future Farmers Am. Alumni Assn., Assn. Internat. Agrl. Edn., U. Fla. Agrl. Alumni and Friends, Sigma Xi, Phi Kappa Phi (pres. 2003—), Gamma Sigma Delta, Alpha Zeta, Phi Delta Kappa, Iota Lambda Sigma, Alpha Gamma Rho (hon.). Office: U Fla PO Box 110270 2001 McCarty Gainesville FL 32611 E-mail: jgcheek@ufl.edu.

CHEEK, MICHAEL CARROLL, lawyer; b. Fostoria, Ohio, Aug. 28, 1948; s. Carroll Wright and Mabel A. (Smith) C. BA, Hanover Coll., 1970; JD, U. Cin., 1974. Bar: Ohio 1974, Fla. 1974, U.S. Dist. Ct. (mid. dist.) Fla. 1975. Pub. defender, Clearwater, Fla., 1974-77; lawyer sole practice, 1977—. Vice chmn. bar grievance Clearwater, 1990-94; trustee Pinellas County Law Libr., Clearwater, 1977-92; chmn. Ct. Law Libr., 1982-89. Pres. 1st Step Corp., Clearwater, 1986-93; vice chmn. Long Ctr. Found., Clearwater, 1994-95; founder Head Start Learn-to-Swim Program, 1994. With Ohio NG, 1970—74, with Fla. NG, 1974—76. Mem. Nat. Assn. Criminal Def. Lawyers, Pinellas Criminal Def. Assn. (v.p. 1987).

CHEELY, DANIEL JOSEPH, lawyer; b. Melrose Park, Ill., Oct. 24, 1949; s. Walter Hubbard and Edith Arlene (Orlandino) C.; m. Patricia Elizabeth Dorsey, May 14, 1977; children: Mary Elizabeth, Daniel, Katherine, Laura. Anne-Marie, Thomas, Susan, Michael, William. AB, Princeton U., 1971; JD, Harvard U., 1974. Bar: Ill. 1974, U.S. Dist. Ct (no. dist.) Ill. 1975, U.S. Ct. Appeals (7th cir.) 1975. Ptnr. Baker & McKenzie, Chgo., 1974-81, ptnr. litigation, 1981-85, capital ptnr. litigation, 1985-94; ptnr. Mauck, Bellande & Cheely, Chgo., 1994-2000; ptnr. Bellande, Cheely & O'Flaherty, Chgo., 2000—. Liaison counsel Asbestos Claims Facility, Chgo., 1985-88, bus. devel. com., 1987-90, Chgo. assoc. train com., 1988-91, chmn. Chgo. assoc. evaluation; liaison coun. Com. for Claims Resolution, 1988-89; cons. Midwest Theol. Forum, 2003—. Advisor Midtown Sports and Cultural Ctr., Chgo., 1974—; mem. River Forest Regular Reps., Ill., 1980-88, Ill. Rep. Assembly, Chgo., 1984—; pres. Cath. Evidence Forum, 1984—; pres. Ch. History Forum, 1994—; dir. Cath. Citizens of Ill., 1997—; bd. dirs. Cath. Lawyers Guild, 2000—; cons. Midwest Theological Forum, 2003-. Mem. ABA (vice chmn. environ. law sect. 1989-97), Ill. Bar Assn., Appellate Lawyers Soc. Ill., Chgo. Bar Assn., Trial Lawyers Club. Chgo., Serra Club (v.p. Chgo. chpt. 1988-89, 92-94, 96—, treas. 1989-92), United Rep. Fund, Phi Beta Kappa. Roman Catholic. Avocations: history, parent effectiveness training, education, christian apologetics, travel consulting. Office: Bellande Cheely & O'Flaherty 19 S La Salle St Ste 1203 Chicago IL 60603-1406

CHEEMA, MOHAMMAD ASLAM, retired cardiothoracic surgeon, community leader; b. Faisalabad, Pakistan, Apr. 7, 1927; came to U.S., 1972; s. Barkat Ali and Rasul Bibi Cheema; m. Soraiya Jabeen Zafar, Mar. 14, 1953; 1 child, Tehmina. MBBS, King Edward Med. Coll., Lahore, Pakistan, 1951. Lic. physician, Wis., Ill. Rotating intern Provident Hosp., Chgo., 1956; resident in general surgery Presbyn.-St. Luke's Hosp., Chgo., 1957-60, fellow in cardiothoracic surgery, 1961-62; asst. prof. surgery K.E. Med. Coll., Lahore, 1966-72; attending surgeon St. Mary's Hosp., Milw., 1974-88, chair dept. surgery, 1986-88, advisor dept. quality assurance/utilization rev., 1988-92. Founder mem. Islamic Soc. of Milw., 1976—, pres., 1986-88; mem. Majis Shura, Islamic Soc. N.Am., Plainfield, Ind., 1984-86; chmn. bd. dirs. Am. Muslim Coun., Washington, 1993-96. Recipient plaque in recognition of outstanding svcs. Am. Muslim Coun., 1997; Disting. Surgery scholar Presbyn.-St. Luke's Hosp., Chgo., 1962. Avocations: reading, speaking, writing. Home: 10707 N Magnolia Dr Mequon WI 53092-1765 E-mail: Mcheema@aol.com.

CHEEMA, ZAFARULLAH K. management consultant; b. Gakkhar, Pakistan, Apr. 21, 1934; arrived in U.S., 1957; s. Nasrulla Khan Cheema and Aisha Bibi Varraich; m. Bilquees Cheema, Aug. 12; children: Yusufullah, Shahjehan. BS in Pharmacy, U. Punjab, 1954; PhD, U. Tübingen, 1957; MBA, U. Chgo., 1983. Prof., chmn., chemistry dept. Knoxville (Tenn.) Coll., 1960—64; tech. supr. Allied Chem. (Honeywell), Morristown, NJ, 1964—71; prof., chmn., chemistry dept. Fairleigh Dickinson U., Madison, NJ, 1967—68; rsch. mgr. Keuffel and Essex Co., Morristown, NJ, 1971—78; v.p. Richarson Co. (WITCO), Melrose Pk., Ill., 1978—84, Polaroid Graphic Imaging, Waltham, Mass., 1985—2001. Cons. Oak Ridge (Tenn.) Nat. Lab., 1961—64, AMOCO Ctrl. Rsch., Napervill, Ill., 1984. Author: (publs.) Jour. Am. Chem. Soc., 1963—64. Achievements include patents for commercially successful products. Avocations: tennis, golf, hiking, reading, travel. Home: 5 Joan Ave Sudbury MA 01776 Fax: 978-579-0966. E-mail: zcheema@gsb.uchicago.edu.

CHEESEBORO, MARGRIT, economics educator; b. Zurich, Switzerland; BA of Bus. Mgmt., U. Redlands, 1980; MSEd, U. So. Calif., 1981; MA in Ednl. Adminstrn., Calif. State U., L.A., 1982; postgrad, UCLA, 1990. Cert. tchr. and adminstr. Sch. office adminstr. Mid-City Alternative Sch., L.A., 1973-80; tchr. econ., govt., U.S. and world history Crenshaw H.S., L.A., 1982—; LEARN lead tchr., mentor tchr., chpt. chmn., co-chmn. governing bd., 1991-98. Mem. United Tchrs. L.A. (chpt. chmn. 1991-98), Kappa Delta Pi. Home: 3525 S Bronson Ave Los Angeles CA 90018-3636 Office: Crenshaw High Sch 5010 11th Ave Los Angeles CA 90043-4816

CHEESEMAN, DOUGLAS TAYLOR, JR., wildlife tour executive, photographer, educator; b. Honolulu, July 16, 1937; s. Douglas Taylor Cheeseman and Myra Bettencourt; m. Gail Macomber, Apr. 7, 1963; children: Rosie M., Ted F. BA, San Jose (Calif.) State U., 1959, MA, 1964. Cert. secondary tchr., Calif. Naturalist Crater Lake (Oreg.) Nat. Park, summers 1959-60; tchr. biology Woodside High Sch., Redwood City, Calif., 1961-65; teaching asst. U. Colo., Boulder, 1966-67; prof. biology De Anza Coll., Cupertino, Calif., 1967—, dir. environ. study area, 1970—, dir. Student Ecology Rsch. Lab., 1990—; pres. Cheeseman's Ecology Safaris, Saratoga, Calif., 1981-98; expedition leader Ioffe, Antarctic, 1998—. Instr. wildlife and natural history photography, Saratoga, 1984—; rsch. cooperator Fish and Wilflife Svc., 1972—, guest lectr. numerous conservation groups, No. Calif., 1978—; spkr. on rainforest destruction, zone depletion, global warming; participant, spkr. to save planet; spkr. Calif. Acad. Antarctic Ecology, Am. Acad. African Birds, 1996; expdn. leader Sengey Vavilov, Antarctic, 1994; active in saving flora and fauna in third world; expdn. leader, Antarctica, 1996, ship Alla Tarasova, 1996; expdn. leader in Antarctic, 1998, 2000, Polar Star Antartic, 2002, 2003. Photographs represented in books and on calendars. Recipient Outstanding Svc. and Tchr. award, Pres.'s award De Anza Coll., 1988, Nat. Leadership award U. Tex., Austin, 1989; NSF fellow, 1969, 71; NEDA Title III grantee, 1970. Mem. Ecol. Soc. Am., Am. Ornithologists Union, Am. Soc. Mammalogists, Brit. Trust Ornitology, Brit. Ornithologists Union, AfricanWildlife Soc., Marine Mammal Soc. (founding), Calif. Native Plants Soc., Bay Area Bird Photographers (co-founder), Santa Clara Valley Audubon Soc. (bd. dirs., v.p., program chmn. 1983—), Cooper Soc. Avocations: wildlife research and photography, rainforest conservation. Home: 20800 Kittridge Rd Saratoga CA 95070-6322 Office: De Anza Coll Dept Biology Cupertino CA 95014

CHEESMAN, KERRY LEE, education educator, researcher; b. Santa Barbara, Calif., Sept. 28, 1954; s. Theodore Richard and Barbara Jean (Wyckoff) C.; m. Sara Day Cheesman, June 17, 1978; children: Ian Walling, Nathan Elisha. BA, U. Calif., Santa Barbara, 1976; PhD, U. Ill., 1981; MS, Ind. U., 1987. Rsch. asst. U. Ill. Med. Ctr., Chgo., 1977-80; rsch. assoc. Med. Sch. Northwestern U., Chgo., 1981-82, asst. prof., 1983-86, St. Francis Coll., Ft. Wayne, Ind., 1987-90, assoc. prof., 1991-92, Capital U., Columbus, Ohio, 1993—96, prof., 1996—, chair biology dept., 1994—2001. Assoc. dir. endocrine labs. Northwestern U. Med. Sch., Chgo., 1983-86; dir. med. tech. program St. Francis Coll., 1989-92; health prof. dir. Capital U., 1993-. Bd. dirs. Habitat for Humanity, Ft. Wayne, 1985-92, Boy Scouts Am., Ft. Wayne, 1985-92, Columbus, Ohio, 1994—, Boy Scouts Am. Nat. Coun., 1999-, Native Am. Indian Ctr., Columbus, 1996-, Ohio Sci. & Ednl. Rsch. Assn., 1997-, Central Assn. Adv. in the Health Professions, 2002-. U. Calif. scholar, 1972. Mem. AAAS, Endocrine Soc., Soc. for Study Reprodn., Soc. for Health and Human Values, N.Am. Assn. Environ. Edn., N.Y. Acad. Scis., Ohio Acad. Scis., Nat. Sci. Tchrs. Assn., Nat. Assn. Biology Tchrs. Avocations: camping, backpacking, working with youth. Office: Capital U Biol Scis Dept 2199 E Main St Columbus OH 43209-2394

CHEETHAM, ALAN HERBERT, paleontologist; b. El Paso, Tex., Jan. 30, 1928; s. Herbert and Hildegard Marguerite (Moreton) C.; m. Marjorie Rogers, Apr. 20, 1951; children: Alan Christopher, Jan Alison, Susan Hilarie, Hilary Taber. BS, N.Mex. Inst. Mining & Tech., 1950; MS, La. State U., 1952; PhD, Columbia U., 1959. Instr. paleontology La. State U., Baton Rouge, 1954-60, asst. prof., 1960-63, assoc. prof., 1963-66, cons. prof., 1966-72; assoc. curator Smithsonian Instn., Washington, 1966-69, curator, 1969-87, sr. invertebrate paleontologist, 1987-2001, sr. scientist emeritus, 2001—. Guest prof. U. Stockholm, 1964—65; adj. prof. U. N.Mex., 1994—97. Author: Geological Society of America, Memoir 91, 1963; editor: Animal Colonies, 1973, Fossil Invertebrates, 1987; contbr. articles. Recipient Raymond C. Moore medal for paleontol., 1997, Disting. Achievement Alumni award, N.Mex. Inst. Mining and Tech., 1990; fellow Humble Oil Co., 1951, NSF, 1952, 1961. Fellow: AAAS; mem.: Paleontol. Rsch. Instn., Soc. Sedimentary Geology, Paleontol. Soc. (medal 2001), Internat. Bryozoology Assn. Home: 3101 Old Pecos Trail #647 Santa Fe NM 87505 Office: Smithsonian Instn Mrc Nhb 121 Washington DC 20560-0121 E-mail: cheetham.alan@nmnh.si.edu.

CHEEVER, GEORGE MARTIN, lawyer; b. Boston, Jan. 13, 1947; s. Francis Sargent and Julia Whitney (Martin) C.; m. Mary Margaret Duplain, Feb. 10, 1979; children: Charles Duplain, Frances Sargent, Mary Conner. AB, Harvard U., 1969; JD, U. Pa., 1973. Bar: Pa. 1973, U.S. Dist. Ct. (we dist.) Pa. 1973, U.S. Ct. Appeals (3d cir.) 1978, U.S. Ct. Appeals (4th cir.) 1985, U.S. Supreme Ct. 1992. Law clk. to assoc. justice Pa. Supreme Ct., Pitts., 1973-74; assoc. Kirkpatrick & Lockhart LLP, Pitts., 1974-82, ptnr., 1982—. Mem. ABA, Am. Bankruptcy Inst., Pa. Bar Assn., Allegheny County Bar Assn., Comml. Law League. Office: Kirkpatrick & Lockhart LLP Henry W Oliver Bldg 535 Smithfield St Pittsburgh PA 15222-2312 E-mail: gcheever@kl.com.

CHEEVER, MEG, non-profit organization administrator; b. Boston, Apr. 10, 1949; d. Charles J. and Mary A. (Malloy) Duplain; m. George M. Cheever, Feb. 10, 1979; children: Charles, Frances, Mary. AB, Wellesley Coll., 1970; JD, Boston U., 1975. Bar: Pa. Assoc. Thorp, Reed & Armstrong, Pitts., 1975-78; gen. counsel QED Comm., Pitts., 1979-89, dir. corp. planning, 1989-91; publisher Pitts. Mag., 1991-97; pres. Pitts. Parks Conservancy, 1997—. Pres. bd. Shenley Conservancy, 1996—; bd. mem. Regional Indsl. Devel. Corp., 1995—. Columnist Pitts. mag., 1992. Bd. mem. Pitts. History & Landmarks, 1997—, The Ellis Sch., Pitts., 1995-2003, Pitts. Ctr. for the Arts, 1994-96; adv. bd. The Pitts. Symphony, 1996-2002; bd. mem. Greater Pitts. C. of C., 1992-98. Named Person of Yr. in Comm., Vectors Pitts., 1996; recipient Leadership award in comm. Pitts. YWCA, 1995; recipient Gold medal City and Regional Mag. Assn., 1995. Mem. Internat. Women's Forum (we. Pa. chpt.), Pitts. Women's Forum. Roman Catholic. Office: Pitts Parks Conservancy 2000 Tech Dr Pittsburgh PA 15219

CHEFITZ, JOEL GERALD, lawyer; b. Boston, Aug. 27, 1951; s. Melvin L and Bernice L (Kahn) Chefitz; m. Sharon P Garfinkel, 1972; children: Sandra Beth, Meira Sarah, Michael Hanan. AB cum laude, Boston U., 1972, JD magna cum laude, 1976. Bar: Ill 1976, US Dist Ct (no Dist) Ill 1977, US Ct Appeals (3d cir) 1981, US Supreme Ct 1983, US Ct Appeals (7th cir) 1984, US Ct Appeals (9th cir) 1993, US Ct Appeals (2d cir) 1994, US Ct Appeals (5th cir) 1996, US Ct Appeals (4th cir) 1998, US Ct Appeals (fed cir) 2000, US Ct Appeals (DC cir) 2001. Law clk. to presiding justice U.S. Dist Ct., Boston, 1976-77; ptnr. Kirkland & Ellis, Chgo., 1977-82, 1982-86, Katten Muchin & Zavis, Chgo., 1986—2002; chgo., ptnr. Howrey Simon Arnold & White, 2002—. Editor: (jour) Boston Univ Law Rev, 1975—76; contbr. articles to profl. jours. Bd. dirs. Legal Assistance Found. Met. Chgo., Gastrointestinal Rsch. Found. Scholar Am Jurisprudence, Boston Univ, 1973—76, CJS, 1975, Bigelow, 1976. Mem.: ABA, 7th Cir Asn, Chicago Bar Asn, East Bank Club. Office: Howrey Simon Arnold & White LLP 321 N Clark St Ste 3400 Chicago IL 60610 E-mail: chefitzj@howrey.com.

CHEH, HUK YUK, electrochemist, battery company executive; b. Shanghai, Oct. 27, 1939; s. Tze Sang and Sue Lan (Che) C.; m. An-li, July 26, 1969; children: Emily, Evelyn. BASc in Chem. Engring., U. Ottawa, Can., 1962; PhD in Chem. Engring., U. Calif., Berkeley, 1967. Mem. tech. staff AT&T Bell Labs., N.J., 1967-70; asst. prof. chem. engring. Columbia U., N.Y.C., 1970-73, assoc. prof., 1973-79, prof., 1979-82, Ruben-Viele prof., 1982—2001, Ruben-Viele prof. emeritus, 2001—, chmn. dept., 1980-86; v.p. tech. Duracell, Inc., 1999—. Program dir. NSF, 1978-79; vis. rsch. prof. Nat. Tsinghua U., Taiwan, 1977 Mem. editorial adv. bd. Ency. of Phys. Sci. Tech.; mem. exec. adv. bd. Dictionary Sci. Tech.; contbr. articles to sci. jours.; patentee in biomaterials and in electrophoresis. Recipient Harold C. Urey award, 1980, sci. achievement award Am. Electroplaters and Surface Finishers Soc., 1989. Fellow Electrochem. Soc. (Electrodeposition Rsch. award 1988, Battery Tech. award 2000); mem. AIChE, Am. Electroplaters Soc., N.Y. Acad. Scis., Sigma Xi. Office: Duracell Berkshire Corp Park Bethel CT 06801 E-mail: Huk_Cheh@Gillette.com.

CHEIRIF, JORGE BERKSTEIN, cardiologist, consultant; b. Mexico City, June 21, 1956; came to U.S., 1981; m. Heidy Derzrvitch, June 14, 1981; children: Benjamin, Michelle, Mark. MD, Nat. U. Mexico, 1981; degree in internal medicine, Baylor U., 1984. Resident in cardiology Baylor U., 1987; dir. echocardiography VA Med. Ctr., Houston, 1987-92, Oschler Clin., New Orleans, 1992-97, Presbyn. Hosp. of Dallas, 1998—. Bd. dirs. Cardiopulmonary Rsch. Sci. and Tech. Inst., Dallas. Contbr. over 50 articles to med. jours. Fellow Am. Coll. Cardiology; mem. Am. Soc. Echocardiography, Am. Heart Assn. (clinician-scientist award 1992-97). Office: N Tex Heart Ctr 8440 Walnut Hill Ln Ste 700 Dallas TX 75231-3824 E-mail: jcheirif@nthc.com.

CHEIT, EARL FRANK, economist, educator; b. Mpls., Aug. 5, 1926; s. Morris and Etta (Warshausky) C.; m. June Doris Andrews, Aug. 28, 1950; children: Wendy, David, Ross, Julie. BS, U. Minn., 1947, LLB, 1949, PhD, 1954. Research economist, prof. Sch. Bus. Adminstrn. U. Calif., Berkeley, 1960—, exec. vice chancellor, 1965-69, dean Sch. Bus. Adminstrn., 1976-82, 90-91, dean emeritus Sch. Bus. Adminstrn., 1991—; dir. Inst. Indsl. Rels. Program officer in charge higher edn. and rsch. Ford Found., 1972-73; assoc. dir., sr. rsch. fellow Carnegie Coun. on Policy Studies in Higher Edn., 1973-75; sr. adv. con. Asian-Pacific econ. affairs Asia Found.; dir. CNF Transp., Inc., Shaklee Corp., 1976-2001, Simpson Mfg. Corp. Author: The Useful Arts and the Liberal Tradition, 1975, The New Depression in Higher Education, 1971, Foundations and Higher Education, 1979; Editor: The Business Establishment, 1964. Trustee Richmond (Calif.) Unified Sch. Dist., 1961-65, Russell Sage Found., N.Y.C., 1979-89; chmn. State of Calif. Wage Bd. for Agrl. Occupations, 1980-81. Office: U Calif Haas Sch Bus Berkeley CA 94720-1900

CHEITEN, MARVIN HAROLD, playwright, manufacturing executive; b. New Brunswick, N.J., Apr. 24, 1943; s. Samuel and Sarah (Peretzman) Cheiten. AB, Princeton U., 1965, MA, 1967, PhD, 1971. Ptnr. The Water Master Co., Highland Park, N.J., 1971-76, v.p., 1976-86, pres., 1986—. Author: (plays) Trial by Fire, 1972, Queen Jane, 1976, The Vault, 1978, The Golden Spy, 1996, Chowder, She Wrote, 1996, Le Coq d'Or, 2000, (novella) The Long Hello, 1995, (essays) The fate of Princeton Graduate School, 1991, Touching a Goddess, 1996, Two Voices in the Darkness, 1997, To the Millstone, 1997, Escape from Raritan Prep, 1998, Songs for My Love, 2000, (lyrics) The Inn Cabaret, 1978—80, Deborah, 1996, A Princess in Death, 1998, Dorothea, 2000, Terry Catherine, 2001, Ballade to 911, 2002, The Hunting of the Deer, 2002; contbr. short stories; mem. editl. bd.: Princeton Alumni Weekly, 1983—87. Trustee Princeton Symphony Orch., 1993—, Friends of Theatre Intime, 1996—; mem. coun. Princeton U. Libr., 2002—; bd. dirs. Princeton Rep. Assn., 1972—74. Mem.: Alliance L.A. Playwrights, Dramatists Guild, Assn. Princeton Grad. Alumni (gov. bd. 1973—88), Campus Club, Nassau Club. Jewish. Office: The Water Master Co Highland Park NJ 08904

CHELAPATI, CHUNDURI VENKATA, civil engineering educator; b. Eluru, India, Mar. 11, 1933; came to U.S., 1957, naturalized, 1971; s. Lakshminarayana and Anjamma (Kanumuri) Chunduri. B.E. with honors, Andhra U., India, 1954; MS, U. Ill., 1959, PhD, 1962. Jr. engr. Office of Chief Engr., State of Andhra, India, 1954-55; asst. prof. structural engring. Birla Coll. Engring., Pilani, India, 1956-57; research asst. dept. civil engring. U. Ill., 1957-62; asst. prof. engring. Calif. State U., Los Angeles, 1962-65, assoc. prof. Long Beach, 1965-70, prof. civil engring., 1970—96, vice chmn. dept., 1971-73, chmn. dept., 1973-79, coordinator profl. engring. rev. programs, 1972-81, dir. continuing engring. edn., 1982—96, dir. CADDS Research Ctr., 1986—96; pres. C.V. Chelapati & Assos., Inc., Huntington Beach, Calif., 1979—2001. Cons. USN Civil Engring. Lab., 1962—68, 1975—94, Holmes & Narver, Inc., Anaheim, Calif., 1968—73; pres. Profl. Engring. Devel. Publs., 1988—, Continuing Profl. Edn. Inst., 2000—, Irvine Inst. Tech., 2002—. Contbr. articles to profl. jours. Mem. ASCE, Am. Soc. Engring. Edn., Structural Engrs. Assn. So. Calif., Earthquake Engring. Research Inst., Seismol. Soc. Am., Am. Concrete Inst., Am. Inst. Steel Constrn., Sigma Xi, Chi Epsilon, Tau Beta Pi, Phi Kappa Phi. Home: 16292 Mandalay Cir Huntington Beach CA 92649-2107 Office: 8659 Research Dr Irvine CA 92618 *When a person is indeed fortunate enough to reach a position of responsibility, that person should even more zealously follow the path of truth and justice, keeping in mind the good of humanity. One should look for long range objectives and not be deterred by minor setbacks.*

CHELBERG, ROBERT DOUGLAS, army officer; b. Ironwood, Mich., Sept. 1, 1938; s. Raymond Rodahl and Marion Dora (Watson) C.; m. Patricia Tobey, Aug. 21, 1962; children: Robert, Kathryn. BS, U.S. Mil. Acad., West Point, N.Y., 1961; MBA, N.Mex. State U., 1973. Commd. 2d lt. U.S. Army, 1961, advanced through grades to lt. gen., 1991, ret., 1993; various assignments in U.S., Europe, 1961-78; student Nat. War Coll., Ft. McNair, Washington, 1978-79; asst. dir. pers. adminstrn. and svcs. Office Asst. Sec. Def. for Mil. Pers. Policy, Washington, 1979-80, staff dir., dep. to dep. asst. sec. def., 1980-81; comdr. 528th Arty. Group, U.S. Army So. Europe Task Force, 1981-83; chief of staff, dep. comdg. gen. Ft. Jackson, SC, 1983-86; asst. chief of staff, plans and policy Allied Forces So. Europe, 1986; exec. to supreme allied comdr. Europe, 1986-87; chief policy and programs br., policy div. Supreme Hdqrs., 1987-90; spl. asst. to supreme allied comdr. Europe for harmonization and verification Supreme Hdqrs., 1990; spl. advisor to sec.-gen. NATO, 1990-91; chief of staff U.S. European Command, Stuttgart, Germany, 1991-93; dep. dir. George C. Marshall European Ctr. for Security Studies, Garmisch, Germany, 1994-95; mng. dir. European region CUBIC Applications Inc., Stuttgart, Germany, 1995-98; sr. cons. European region Cubic Applications, Inc., 1998—2003; sr. advisor European affairs Econ. Devel. Partnership, Aiken, SC, 1999—; sr. fellow Joint Forces Staff Coll., 2001—; program mgr. Def. Threat Reduction Agy., European Field Office, 2003—. Dist. commr. Transatlantic coun. Boy Scouts Am., Brussels, Belgium, 1987-90. Decorated DSM, Def. Superior Svc. medal with oak leaf cluster, Army DSM. Legion of Merit, Bronze Star with four oak leaf clusters, 10 Air medals, Meritorious Svc. medal with oak leaf cluster; recipient Vet. of Yr. award VFW Post 3676, 1985, Outstanding Alumnus Svc. award Lake Superior State U., 1986, Army Exceptional Civilian Svc. award, 1995, Disting. Eagle Scout award, 1990; named to N.Mex. State U. Bus. Sch. Hall of Fame, 2001. Mem. Fedn. German-Am. Clubs (pres. 1994-96), S.C. Coun. Ret. Officers Assn. (v.p. 1999-2003), Rotary, Phi Eta Sigma, Phi Kappa Phi. Avocations: swimming, horses.

CHELEMER, HAROLD, engineering educator, consultant; b. Green Bay, Wis., Nov. 28, 1928; s. Benjamin and Jenny (Weiss) C.; m. Joan Sue Hirsh, June 30, 1957; children: Marc Jason, Scott Brian, Bruce Noah. AS, Jr. Coll. Kansas City, Mo., 1947; BSChemE, U. Mo., 1949, MSChemE, 1951; PhD in Chem. Engring., U. Tenn., 1955. Registered profl. engr., Pa. Asst. rsch. engr. dept. chem. engring. U. Tenn., Knoxville, 1951-54; sr. engr. atomic power div. Westinghouse, Monroeville, Pa., 1957-64, fellow engr. pressurized water reactor sys. div., 1964-70, adv. engr. nuclear fuel div., 1970-90; ret., 1990. Cons. nuclear fuel div. Westinghouse, Monroeville, 1992-96; instr. Duquesne U., Pitts., 1993-95; lectr. U. Pitts., 1992-01; tchr. Cmty. in Schs., 2000-03. Parent

rep. Pitts. Bd. Edn., 1970-71; vol. tutor Pitts. Pub. Schs., 1987-97. With U.S. Army Chem. Corps, 1955-57. Mem. Tau Beta Pi, Sigma Xi. Democrat. Jewish. Avocations: birding, billiards, bridge, basketball, guitar. Home: 5800 Wayne Rd Pittsburgh PA 15206-2110

CHELIOS, CHRISTOS K. hockey player; b. Chgo., Ill., Jan. 25, 1962; Student, U. Wis. With Montreal Canadiens, 1981—90; defenseman Chgo. Blackhawks, 1990—99, Detroit Red Wings, 1999—. Mem. NHL All-Rookie Team, 1984—85, NHL All-Star 1st Team, 1988—89, 1992—93, NHL All-Star 2d Team, 1990—91, WCHA All-Star 2d Team, 1982—83, Stanley Cup Champions Detroit Red Wings, 2002. Named All Star Tournament Team, NCAA, 1982—83, All-Star First Team, The Sporting News, 1988—89, All-Star 2d Team, 1990—91, 1991—92; recipient James Norris Meml. Trophy, 1988—89, 1992—93. Office: Detroit Red Wings 600 Civic Center Dr Detroit MI 48226-4419

CHELLAM, KRIS, data processing executive; Certificate in Edn., Cambridge U., 1968; Degree in Acctg., U. London, 1975. Chartered acct., Inst. Chartered Accts. Eng., 1975, Inst. Chartered Accts. Wales, 1975. Fin. mgr. Intel Corp., 1979—91; v.p. fin. & adminstrn., CFO Atmel Corp., 1991—98; sr. v.p. fin., CFO Xilinx, Inc., San Jose, Calif., 1998—. Office: Xilinx Inc 2100 Logic Drive San Jose CA 95124-3400

CHELLE, ROBERT FREDERICK, entrepreneurial leadership educator; b. New Brunswick, N.J., July 18, 1948; s. Robert and Frances (Brown) C.; m. Karen Ann Cederburg, Aug. 7, 1971; children: Robert, Pamela. BA, Bethany Coll., 1970; MBA, U. Dayton, 1972. Asst. contr. Tait Mfg. Co., Dayton, Ohio, 1972-73; pres. High Voltage Maintenance Corp., Dayton, 1973-99; dir. Crotty Ctr. for Entrepreneurial Leadership, U. Dayton, 1999—. Bd. dirs. The Siebenthaler Co., Dayton; adv. bd. U. Dayton Sch. Bus., 1994—. Contbr. articles to profl. jours. Chmn. Dayton C. of C., 1993, County Corp., Dayton, 1995. Recipient Cert. Appreciation Montgomery County Commn., Dayton, 1984-85, Up and Comer award for engring. City of Dayton, 1988. Mem. Nat. Elect. Testing Assn., Ohio Bar Assn. (mem. profl. ethics com. 2001—), Rotary (pres. 1984-85). Presbyterian. Avocations: yachting, fishing.

CHELLGREN, PAUL WILBUR, industrial company executive; b. Tullahoma, Tenn., Jan. 18, 1943; s. Wilbur E. Chellgren and Kathryn L. (Berquist) Chellgren; m. Sheila Mary McManus, Nov. 21, 1970; children: Sarah, Matthew, Jane. BS, U. Ky., 1964; MBA, Harvard U., 1966; diploma in devel. econ., Univ. Coll., Oxford, Eng., 1967. Assoc. McKinsey & Co., Washington and London, 1967—68; ops. analyst Office Sec. Def., Washington, 1968—70; adminstrv. asst. Boise Cascade Corp., Idaho, 1970—71, div. gen. mgr. L.A., 1971—72; pres. Universal Capital Corp., Kans. City, Mo., 1972—74; exec. asst. to chmn. Ashland (Ky.) Inc., 1974—77; adminstrv. v.p. Ashland Chem. Co., Columbus, Ohio, 1977—78, group v.p., 1978—80; sr. v.p., group operating officer Ashland Inc., Covington, Ky., 1980—88, sr. v.p., CFO, 1988—92, pres., COO, 1992—96, pres., CEO, 1996—97, chmn., CEO, 1997—2002, ret. chmn., CEO. Bd. dirs. PNC Bank Corp., U. Ky., Centre Coll., The Conf. Bd. Dir. Am. Friends of Univ. Coll. Oxford, Inc.; bd. dirs. Greater Cin. Found.; dir., trustee Taft Mus., Cin.; pres. Cin. Mus. Art. 1st lt. U.S. Army, 1968—70. Fellow: Univ. Coll. (Oxford, Eng.) (hon.); mem.: U. Ky. Fellows, Queen City Club (Cin.), Comml. Club, Met. Club. Home: 817 Squire Lake Dr Villa Hills KY 41017-1337 Office: 541 Buttermilk Pike #20 Crescent Springs KY 41017 E-mail: pwchellgren@ashland.com.

CHELLINE, WARREN HERMAN, English educator, clergy member; b. Jonesport, Maine, Sept. 26, 1923; s. Herman Albert and Olive Viola (Yarwood) C.; m. Bonnibelle Nelson, Jan. 1, 1950 (dec. June 1991); 1 child, Eric Warren; m. Frances Nadine Woodside, Aug. 7, 1993. Student, Brown U., 1941-43; DD, Am. Div. Sch., 1956; BA, MA, U. Mo., 1969, 70; MPhil, PhD, U. Kans., 1979, 82. Cert. secondary education tchr., Mo., Kans. Clergy member Remnant LDS Ch., Independence, Mo., 1942—; prof. English lang. and lit. Mo. We. State U., St. Joseph, 1971-97, prof. emeritus English lang. and lit., 1997—. Insp. U.S. Lighthouse Soc., 1997—. Author: John Milton and Roger Williams, 1982; contbg. editor Herald House Pubs., 1940-69; contbr. articles to profl. jours. Chmn. adv. bd. The Salvation Army, 1989—; bd. dirs. Boy Scouts Am., Can. and U.S.A., 1946— (Wood Badge award 1956, Silver Beaver award 1990), St. Joseph Pub. Libr., 1975—, St. Joseph Symphony, 1994—, Allied Arts Coun., 1995—. Chaplain USN, 1941-43. James E. West fellow, 1998. Mem. Am. Legion, Moila Shrine, Soc. Profl. Journalists, Milton Soc. Internat., Kiwanis Internat. (disting. lt. gov. 1982—), Am. Mason (32nd degree, chaplain 1988—). Avocations: clowning, lighthouses, circus lore, scottish bagpipe band. Home: Apt 1 421 N 25th St Saint Joseph MO 64501-2653 Office: 620 Francis St Saint Joseph MO 64501-2653 E-mail: chelline@magiccablepc.com.

CHELOHA, JOHN ANTHONY, city lobbyist, lawyer; b. Columbus, Nebr., Apr. 16, 1965; s. Carl C. and Julia J. Cheloha; m. Leigh Rademacher, May 5, 2000. BA, U. Nebr., 1987, JD, 1990. Assoc. Kennedy Holland Law Firm, Omaha, Nebr., 1990-94; city lobbyist City of Omaha, 1994—. Campaign mgr. Patrick Combs for Congress, 1994. Mem. Nebr. State Bar Assn. (legis. com. 1999—). Democrat. Roman Catholic. Office: 1819 Farnam St Omaha NE 68183-1000

CHELSTROM, MARILYN ANN, political education consultant; b. Mpls., Dec. 5; d. Arthur Rudolph and Signe (Johnson) C. BA, U. Minn., 1950; LHD, Oklahoma City U., 1981. Staff asst. Mpls. Citizens Com. Public Edn., 1950-57; coord. policies and procedures Lithium Corp. Am., Inc., Mpls., N.Y.C., 1957-62; exec. dir. The Robert A. Taft Inst. Govt., N.Y.C., 1962-77, exec. v.p., 1977-78, pres., 1978-89, pres. emeritus, 1990—; polit. edn. cons., 1990—; pres. Chelstrom Connection, 1992—. Home: 9600 Portland Ave Minneapolis MN 55420-4564 Office: 155 E 38th St New York NY 10016-2660

CHELTE, JUDITH SEGZDOWICZ, secondary education educator; b. Springfield, Mass., Aug. 23, 1951; d. Stanley (dec.) and Stella Margaret Segzdowicz; m. Raymond J. Chelte, Sr., July 31, 1982. BA in English/Secondary Edn., Westfield State Coll., 1973; MAT in English and Secondary Edn., Smith Coll., 1974; PhD in English, U. Mass., 1994. Cert. in adolescence young adulthood English and lang. arts Nat. Bd. for Profl. Tchg. Stds., 1999. Tchr. English Chicopee (Mass.) Pub. Schs., 1974—. Mentor Chicopee Comprehensive H.S., 2000—. Contbr. articles to profl. jours.; website creator New Eng. Adolescent Rsch. Inst., 2000. Sec. Friends of the Chicopee Pub. Libr., Inc., 1995-97, newsletter editor, 1997-99. Named Intel Master Tchr., 2001; grantee Mass. Dept. Edn., Malden, 1997, 98-99; finalist Mass. Tchr. of Yr., 2001. Mem. MLA, NEA, Mass. Tchrs. Assn., Chicopee Edn. Assn. Democrat. Roman Catholic. Avocations: reading, cross country skiing. Home: 63 Davenport St Chicopee MA 01013-2808 Office: Chicopee Comprehensive HS 617 Montgomery St Chicopee MA 01020-1634

CHEMA, SUSAN RUSSELL, lawyer; b. Dayton, Ohio, June 2, 1956; d. Thomas F. and Marjorie Bess (Wilson) Russell; m. J. Richard Chema, Aug. 7, 1982; children: Alexis K., Caroline K. BA, U. Dayton, 1977; JD, Ohio State U., 1982. Assoc. Smith & Schnacke, LLP, Dayton, 1982-83; lt. comdr. JAGC USN, various locations, 1983-91; lawyer Navy Gen. Counsel, Washington, 1991-95; chief litigation counsel NCR Corp., Dayton, 1995—. Office: NCR Corp 1700 S Patterson Blvd Dayton OH 45479-2260 Business E-Mail: susan.chema@ncr.com.

CHEMA, THOMAS V. government official, lawyer; b. East Liverpool, Ohio, Oct. 31, 1946; s. Stephen T. and Dorothy Grace (McCormack) C.; m. Barbara Burke Orr, Aug. 15, 1970; children: Christine, Stephen. A.B., U. Notre Dame, 1968; J.D., Harvard U., 1971. Bar: Ohio 1971, U.S. Supreme Ct. 1977. Assoc. Arter and Hadden, Cleve., 1971-79, ptnr. 1979-85, 1989—; pres. Gateway Cons. Group, Inc., 1995—; exec. dir. Ohio Lottery Commn., Cleve., 1983-85, Gateway Econ. Devel. Corp. Greater Cleve., 1990-95; chmn. Pub. Utilities Commn. Ohio, Columbus, 1985-89; chmn. Ohio Bldg. Authority, 1990-96. Candidate for Ohio Senate, 1980; campaign mgr., Senator Howard M. Metzenbaum, 1976; co-chmn. task force on violent crime, Cleve., 1981-83; trustee Hiram Coll., 1994—, Cleve. Works, Inc., 1995-98, Cleve. City Club, 1993-96, Sisters of Charity of St. Augustine Health Sys., 1994—, Historic Gateway Neighborhood, Inc., 1995—; dir. Transtechnology, Inc., Fairport Funds. Mem. ABA (adv. council), Nat. Assn. Regulatory Utility Commrs., Nat. Assn. State Lotteries (bd. dirs.), Greater Cleve. Bar Assn., Ohio State Bar Assn., Cleve. Legal Aid Soc., Ohio Legal Assistance Found. (chmn. 1996-99), Electric Power Research Inst., Sr. Citizens Resources Inc. (trustee), Hospice Council No. Ohio (sec., trustee, legal counsel), Citizens League, NAACP, League Women Voters, Am. Soc. Pub. Adminstrs. Trustee, St. Ignatius High Sch., Prospect Vision, Inc., Downtown Devel. Coordinators Cleve. Found. Arch.. Democrat. Roman Catholic. Club: City (Cleve., trustee 1993). Avocation: skiing. Home: 18580 Parkland Dr Cleveland OH 44122-3469 Office: Arter & Hadden 925 Euclid Ave 1100 Huntington Bldg Cleveland OH 44115-1475

CHEMERS, ROBERT MARC, lawyer; b. Chgo., July 24, 1951; s. Donald and Florence (Weinberg) C.; m. Lenore Ziemann, Aug. 16, 1975; children: Brandon J., Derek M. BA, U. So. Calif., 1973; JD, Ind. U.-Indpls., 1976. Bar: Ind. 1976, Ill. 1976, U.S. Dist. Ct. (so. dist.) Ind. 1976, U.S. Dist. Ct. (no. and so. dists.) Ill. 1977, U.S. Ct. Appeals 7th cir.) 1977, U.S. Ct. Appeals (5th cir.) 1985. Assoc. Pretzel & Stouffer, Chgo., 1976-79, officer, 1979-81, dir., 1981—. Author: IICLE - Civil Practice, 1978, rev. edit. 1982, 87; IICLE Settlements, 1984. Mem. ABA, Ill. State Bar Assn., Chgo. Bar Assn., Def. Rsch. Inst., Ill. Def. Counsel, Appellate Lawyers Assn. Office: Pretzel & Stouffer One S Wacker Dr Chicago IL 60606

CHEMLA, DANIEL S. physics educator; Grad., l'Ecole Nat. Super Telecomms., Paris; DSc, U. Paris, 1972. Mem. tech. staff, group leader, dept. head Ctr. Nat. d'Etudes des Telecomms., Berkeley; with AT&T Bell Labs., Holmdel, N.J., 1981-83, head of quantum physics and electonic rsch. dept., 1983-91; prof. physics, dir. materials scis. divsn. Lawrence Berkeley Nat. Lab., U. Calif., Berkeley, 1991—; dir. Advanced Light Source U. Calif., Berkeley, 1998—. Contbr. articles to profl. jours. Fellow IEEE (Quantum Electronics award 1995, Humboldt Rsch. award 1995), Optical Soc. Am. (R. W. Wood prize 1988), Am. Phys. Soc.; mem. NAS. Achievements include research in manybody interactions and quantum size effects in semiconductor nanostructures and detection and spectroscopy of single molecules and single molecular paris. Fax: 510-486-7769. E-mail: dschemla@lbl.gov.

CHEN, ADAM I. physician; b. Taipei, Taiwan, Sept. 9, 1956; came to U.S., 1961; s. Chwen-gu and Ai-Chi Chen; m. Pei-Jin Chen, June 19, 1981; children: Daniel, Patrick. BS, CCNY, 1981; MD, SUNY, Stony Brook, 1983. Diplomate in internal medicine and gastroenterology Am. Bd. Internal Medicine. Physician FHP/Talbert Med. Group, Fountain Valley, Calif., 1988-98, assoc. dept. chief gastroenterology, 1995-98; physician SCPMG, Riverside, Calif., 1998—. Contbr. articles to profl. jours. Fellow ACP, Am. Coll. Gastroenterology. Republican. Avocations: golf, travel. Office: SCPMG 10800 Magnolia Ave # 4H Riverside CA 92505-3043

CHEN, AN-BAN, physicist, educator; b. Chiayi, Taiwan, Taiwan, Oct. 10, 1942; s. Chei-Chung Chen and Weng Hou; m. Mayurase T Tuntirutanaront, Dec. 27, 1969; 1 child, William. PhD, Coll. William and Mary, 1971. Prof. Auburn (Ala.) U., Auburn, 1974—; Thomas and Jean Walter prof. Auburn U., Alumni prof. Cons. SRI Internat., Menlo Park, Calif., 1985—2001. Mem.: Am. Phys. Soc. Achievements include patents for in field. Office: Auburn University 305 Allison Lab Auburn University AL 36849-5311 Office Fax: 334-844-4613. E-mail: abchen@physics.auburn.edu.

CHEN, CARLSON S. mechanical engineer; b. Orange, N.J., Mar. 17, 1960; s. Kao and May Chen; m. Lynn Duong, Dec. 5, 1992; 1 child, Christopher D. BSME, Brown U., 1982; MBA, U. Pitts., 1987. Engr. Westinghouse Corp., Pitts., 1982-89; sr. engr. Gen. Dynamics, San Diego, 1989-91, GPS Techs., San Diego, 1991-93; sr. mech. engr. Nat. Steel & Shipbuilding (Gen. Dynamics divsn. since 1998), San Diego, 1993—. Contbg. author Standard Handbook of Powerplant Engineering, 1997. Active Brown Cmty. Outreach, 1979-80. Mem.: ASME, Soc. Naval Architects and Marine Engrs. (publicity, meetings, meeting chmn. San Diego chpt. 1998—99, sec. 2000—01, vice chmn. 2001—02, chmn. 2002—), Brown Club of San Diego. Office: Nat Steel & Shipbuilding Co Harbor Dr & 28th St San Diego CA 92186

CHEN, CATHLEEN, physician; b. Passaic, N.J., Mar. 30, 1963; d. Philip and Barbara Chen. BS in Pharmacy, Rutgers U., 1986; MD, UMDNJ-Robertwood Johnson, Camden, 1990. Diplomate in internal medicine, hematology and oncology Am. Bd. Internal Medicine. Intern Baystate Med. Ctr., Springfield, Mass., 1990-91, resident, 1991-93, fellow, 1995-96, Dartmouth Hitchcock Med. Ctr., Lebanon, N.H., 1993-95; physician, staff cons. Marquette Gen. Hosp., Mich., 1996—, chair instnl. rev. bd., 1997-2001, dir. outpatient outreach hematology/oncology clinic svcs., 1999—, chair cancer com., 2001—, chair cancer PI com., 2001—. Mem. ACP, Am. Soc. Hematology, Am. Soc. Clin. Oncology, Mass. Med. Soc. Office: UP Hematology Oncology Assocs 1414 W Fair Ave Ste 332 Marquette MI 49855-5493

CHEN, CHARLES, music educator, musician; s. Bingran Chen and Yan Xu; m. Xiao Wang, July 2, 1998. BA, Ctrl. Conservatory of Music, Beijing, 1982; MA, Boston U., 1990; MusM, Kent (Ohio) State U., 1992; ArtsD, Ball State U., 1994. Prin. clarinetist Ctrl. Opera Ho. Orch., Beijing, 1982—87; asst. condr. Muncie (Ind.) Symphony Orch., 1992—94; music dir./condr. East Ctrl. Ind. Youth Symphony Orch., Muncie, 1992—94; condr./gen. mgr. Am. Youth Symphony, L.A., 1995—98; music dir./condr. All Chinese Musician Symphony Orch., L.A., 1996—99; music prof. Lock Haven U. of Pa., 1999—. Chief cons. Global Cultural Exch. Ctr., Lock Haven, 2001—; vis. prof. Shanghai Tongji U., 2002—. Chmn. Chinese Student Assn., Muncie, 1992—94. Mem.: Coll. Music Soc. (assoc.). Home: 214 W Waterb St #2A Lock Haven PA 17745 Office: Lock Haven U of Pa 139 Sloan Fine Arts Ctr Lock Haven PA 17745 Fax: 570-893-2819. E-mail: cchen@lhup.edu.

CHEN, CHENGGANG, research scientist; b. Wenling, Zhejiang, China, Mar. 16, 1967; p. Rongquan Chen and Xiaohua Cao; m. Hong Zeng, Nov. 1, 1995. BS, Hangzhou (Zhejiang) U., 1987; MS, Zhejiang U., Hangzhou, 1989; PhD, Case Western Res. U., 1999. Rsch. asst. Zhejiang U., Hangzhou, 1987-89; asst. engr., lectr. Hangzhou U., 1990-93; rsch. asst. Case Western Res. U., Cleve., 1993-98; postdoctoral rsch. fellow Northwestern U., Evanston, Ill., 1998-99; postdoctoral rsch. assoc. Case Western Res. U., Cleve., 1999, The BFGoodrich Co., Cleve., 1999; assoc. rsch. scientist U. Dayton (Ohio) Rsch. Inst./Air Force Rsch. Lab., 2000—01, rsch. scientist, 2002—. Cons. The BFGoodrich Co., Cleve., 1999. Author: Polymer Preprints, 1998, Organic/Inorganic Hybrid Materials, 1998; contbr. over 30 articles to profl. publs. Alumni Grad. fellow Case Western Res. U., Cleve., 1995. Mem. Am. Chem. Soc., Materials Rsch. Soc. Achievements include 4 U.S. patents and 4 European patents. Office: U Dayton Rsch Inst Air Force Rsch Lab 300 College Park Dayton OH 45469-0168 Fax: 937-258-8075. E-mail: chenggang.chen@wpafb.af.mil.

CHEN, CHIA-EN JOHN, dentist; b. Taichung, Taiwan, Jan. 28, 1950; arrived in U.S., 1980; s. Kan-Kuo Paul Chen and Nie-Sen Ruth Tsai; m. Nightingale Li-Ing Chen, Dec. 30, 1989; children: Justina, Josephine, Joshiah. DDS, Coll. Medicine Taiwan, Taichung, 1980, NYU, 1987. Dental surgeon C. Chen Dental, N.Y.C., 1987—96, Bowen Dental & Assocs., Columbus, 1996—2002, C. Chen Dental LLC, Powell, Ohio, 2001—. Sunday sch. tchr., deacon Grace Chinese Christian Ch., S.I., NY, 1987—96, Columbus Chinese Christian Ch., 1996—. Republican. Avocations: gardening, tennis, ping pong, puzzles, music. Office: 84 S Liberty Powell OH 43065 Fax: 614-880-0576.

CHEN, CHIH-FAN, electrical engineer; b. Pa, Hopei, China, June 19, 1924; s. Shu-Chuang and Tung C. PhD, Cambridge U., 1971; LLD (hon.), Lewis Coll., 1963. Rsch. prof. Boston U., 1985—. Fellow Inst. Elec. Engrs. Office: Boston U Met Coll 808 Commonwealth Ave Boston MA 02215-1206

CHEN, CHIN-CHIN, music educator; b. Taipei, Taiwan, Jan. 29, 1964; came to the U.S., 1991. MMus in Piano Performance, U. Ill., 1993, MMus in Music Theory, 1995, DMA in Composition/Theory, 2000. Tchg. asst. U. Ill., Urbana, 1995-99; asst. prof. Grand Valley State U., Allendale, Mich., 1999—. Adj. asst. prof. Millikin U., Decatur, Ill., 1998-99. Author: (music for vibraphone and tape) Points of Departure, 1996, (music for 2-channel tape) Points of No Return, 1997 (1st prize, Internat. Luigi Russolo, 1997), (music for violin and tape) Points of Arrival, 1998, (music for orch.) The Marks of Life, 1999, (music for two mezzo-sopranos, baritone, horn and percussion) Next Door, 2000, (music for carillon) Prior to Landing, 2001, (music for wind ensemble) Like a Chinese Waterfall, 2002, (music for 2-channel electroacoustic sounds) Snow of Ages, 2003, (music for soprano, bivraphone and cello) Autumn Heart, 2003. Recipient electroacoustic music commn. U. Ill., Urbana-Champaign, 1995, 98, percussion commn. Kalamazoo Symphony. Mem. Can. Electroacoustic Cmty., Soc. Composers, Inc., Soc. for the Electro-Acoustic Music in the U.S., Broadcast Music, Inc., Coll. Music Soc. Office: Grand Valley State Univ Dept Music Allendale MI 49401 Fax: 616-331-3100. E-mail: chenc@gvsu.edu.

CHEN, CHING-CHIH, information science educator, consultant; b. Foochow, Fukien, China, Sept. 3, 1937; came to U.S, 1959; d. Han-chia and May-ying (Liu) Liu; m. Sow-Hsin Chen, Aug. 19, 1961; children: Anne, Catherine, John. BA, Nat. Taiwan U., Taipei, 1959; MLS, U. Mich., 1961; PhD, Case Western Res. U., 1974. Asst. Sch. Libr. Sci. U. Mich., Ann Arbor, 1960-61, svc. libr., 1961-62; sci. reference libr. McMaster U., Hamilton, Ont., Can., 1962-63, head sci. libr., 1963-64; sr. sci. libr. U. Waterloo, Ont., Can., 1964-65, head engring., math. and sci. libr., 1965-68; assoc. sci. libr. MIT, Cambridge, Mass., 1968-71; asst. prof. Grad. Sch. Libr. and Info. Sci. Simmons Coll., Boston, 1971-76, asst. dean for acad. affairs, 1977-79, assoc. dean, prof., 1979-96, prof., 1979—. Cons. Am. Soc. Info. Sci./Cath. U. Am., 1976-77, Chung-Shan Inst. Sci. Rsch., Taiwan, 1977-87, Abt Assocs., Inc., 1980 82, Sci. and Tech. Info. Ctr. Nat. Sci. Coun., Taiwan, 1973-77, S.E. Asia Region WHO, 1980, 81, Engring. Info. Inc., 1982, UNESCO, Paris, 1984, Nat. Geog. Soc., 1985, Norman Bethuen U. Med. Scis. Libr., 1986, Getty Trust, 1988, USIA, 1988, Ont. Coun. Gradual Studies, 1989, FID, 1989, World Bank, 1990, UNESCO, 1991, DataConsult, Mex., 1991, Soros Found., 1992-93, USIA, 1993-95, UN Devel. Program, 1997, Tsinghua U., Taiwan, 1997, Nat. Sci. Coun., Taiwan, 1998—2001; mem. US President's Info. Tech. Adv. Com., 1997—2001; guest prof. Tsinghua U., Beijing, 1999-2002. Author, editor 36 books including Biomedical, Scientific and Technical Book Reviewing, 1976, Sourcebook on Health Sciences Librarianship, 1977, Quantitative Measurement and Dynamic Library Service, 1978, Scientific & Technical Information Sources, 2nd edit., 1987, (with others) Numeric Databases, 1984, HyperSource on Hypermdia/Multimedia Technologies, 1989, HyperSource on Optical Technologies, 1989, Optical Technologies in Libraries; Use & Trends, 1991, Planning Global Information Infrastructure, 1995, Consortium of Electronic Resources, 1999, IT and Global Digital Library Development, 1999, Global Digital Library Development in the New Millennium, 2001; editor-in-chief: Microcomputers for Information Management, 1983-96; also editor numerous conf. procs.; contbr. over 150 articles to profl. jours. Barbour scholar U. Mich., 1959-61, Case Western Res. U. fellow, 1973-74, NATO fellow, 1975, AAAS fellow, 1985; Emily Hollowell Rsch. grantee, 1972—, Simmons Coll. Fund Rsch. grantee, 1972-81; recipient Disting. Svc. award Chinese-Am. Librs. Assn., 1982, Cert. of Appreciation, Asian-Pacific-Am. Librs. Assn., 1983, Disting. Alumni award U. Mich., 1983, Outstanding Svc. award Nat. Cen. Libr., 1986, Disting. Svc. award Asian-Am. Libr. Assn, 1992, Cindy award Assn. Visual Comm., 1992, Grazella Shepherd Meml. award for Excellence in Edn., Case Western Reserve U. Educator's Forum, 1999, NSF Internat. Digital Libr. Program award Chinese Memory Net: U.S.-Sino Collaborative Rsch., 1999-2003, Ernest A. Lynton award Am. Assn. Higher Edn., 2001. Fellow AAAS; mem. ALA (disting. svc. award 1989, Humphrey award 1996), AAUP, Am. Soc. Info. Sci. (best Info. Sci. Tchr. award 1983), Assn. Am. Libr. Schs., Assn. Coll. and Rsch. Librs., Libr. Info. Tech. Assn. (Gaylord Libr. and Info. Tech. Achievement award 1990, Outstanding Achievement Libr. Hi Tech. award 1994), New Eng. Libr. Assn. (Emerson Greenaway award 1994), Assn. Libr. and Info. Sci. Edn. (1st ALISE Pratt-Severn Nat. Faculty award 1997). Avocations: travel, stamp collecting. Home: 1400 Commonwealth Ave Newton MA 02465-2830 Office: Simmons Coll 300 Fenway Boston MA 02115-5820 E-mail: chen@simmons.edu.

CHEN, CHIN-JUNG, mechanical engineer; b. Kaohsiung, Taiwan, 1963; came to U.S., 1988; m. Yuh-Ying Chu; children: Abbie, Rebecca. BS, Chung Yuan Christian U., Chungli, Taiwan, 1985; MS, Nat. Chiao Tung U., Hsinchu, Taiwan, 1987; PhD, U. Iowa, 1994. Lectr. So. Asia Coll., Chungli, 1987-88; rsch. asst. U. Iowa, Iowa City, 1989-94; cons. Ford Motor Co., Dearborn, Mich., 1994-98; computer-aided engring. engr. Visteon Automotive Sys.-An Enterprise of Ford Motor Co., Dearborn, 1998—2000; tech. fellow Visteon Corp., Dearborn, Mich., 2000—. Contbr. over 20 papers and articles to profl. jours. and confs. Mem. Internat. Soc. for Structural and Multidisciplinary Optimization. Achievements include a continuum approach second-order shape design sensitivity for robust design, development and implementation of several structural optimization softwares, development of methodology for applying optimization techniques to improve automotive design involve manufacturing processing optimization development and implemenation.

CHEN, CHIN-TU, medical physics educator; b. Taipei, Republic of China, Nov. 21, 1951; came to U.S., 1976; s. Cheng-Li Chen and Tsai-Lan Chen-Wu. BS in Physics, Nat. Tsing-Hau U., Hsinchu, Republic of China, 1974; MS in Physics, Northwestern U., 1978; PhD in Med. Physics, U. Chgo., 1986. Physicist U. Chgo., 1982-87, asst. prof. med. physics, 1987—94, dir. Frank Ctr. for Image Analysis, 1986—, assoc. prof. med. physics, 1994—. Contbr. articles to sci. jours. Mem. Am. Physics Soc., IEEE, Soc. Nuclear Medicine. Office: U Chgo MC-2026 5841 S Maryland Ave Chicago IL 60637-1463

CHEN, CHONG, research scientist; s. Yiwei Chen and Yuan Guo; m. Ning Chen; 1 child, Yunxi. PhD, East China U. Sci.and Tech., Shanghai, 1997. Asst. rsch. engr. Luoyang Petro-Chem. Engring. Co., Luoyang, China, 1985—88; asst. prof. China U. Mining and Tech., Xuzhou, China, 1992—98; rsch. assoc. Tohoku U., Sendai, Japan, 1998—99; postdoctoral fellow W. Va. U., Morgantown, 2000—. Author (with others): The Chemistry of Coal Liquefaction, 2002; contbr. articles to profl. jours. Mem.: Am. Carbon Soc., Am. Chem. Soc. Achievements include research in coal chemistry and carbon material chemistry; discovery of the effect of the anion on the aggregation behavior of coal molecule in solution; development of coal-based carbon materials. Avocations: music, photography, swimming, travel, driving.

CHEN, CHUANSHENG, education educator; b. Yongkang, Zhejiang, China, Sept. 2, 1963; s. Lianbu and Xiangqin (Zhang) C.; m. Panfang Fu, May 24, 1990; children: Anthony, Brandon. BS, Hangzhou U., China, 1982; postgrad., Beijing Normal U., 1982-84; MA, U. Mich., 1987, PhD, 1992. Rsch. asst. U. Mich., Ann Arbor, 1985-88, rsch. assoc., 1989-92, teaching asst., 1989-90; asst. prof. U. Calif., Irvine, 1992—96, assoc. prof., 1996—, chmn. dept., 2001—. Contbr. articles to profl. jours. and chpts. to books. Recipient Rsch. award Johann Jacobs Found., 1992-94, Pacific Rim Rsch. Program, 1993-94, U. Calif.-Irvine, 1992 , Spencer fellowship Nat. Acad. Edn., 1993-95. Mem. APA, AAAS, Am. Psychol. Soc., Soc. for Rsch. in Child Devel., Am. Edl. Rsch. Assn. Avocation: hiking. Office: U Calif Sch Social Ecology Irvine CA 92697

CHEN, CHUNGTE WILLIAM, optical engineer; b. Taipei, Taiwan, June 24, 1950; came to U.S., 1974; s. Dwan-In and Atz Chen; m. Jenna Angela Chen, Jan. 18, 1975; children: Julia Shouann, Stacy Shouru. BS, Tunghai U., Taichung, Taiwan, 1972; MS, Creighton U., 1976; PhD, U. Ariz., 1980. Sr. engr. Perkin-Elmer Co., Norwalk, Conn., 1980-82; chief optical designer Hughes Optical Products Inc., Des Plaines, Ill., 1982-84; sr. optical designer Perkin-Elmer Co., Danbury, Conn., 1984-88, R&D mgr. Garden Grove, Calif., 1988-89; sr. scientist Hughes Aircraft Co., El Segunda, Calif., 1989-97; engring. fellow Raytheon Systems, El Segunda, Calif., 1997—. Over 30 patents in field. Mem. Zool. Soc. San Diego, 1989—. Recipient Optical Tech. award Electro-Optics Network, 1994, Electro-Optic Sensor and Tech. award Hughes Aircraft Co., 1996. Mem. Internat. Soc. Optical Engrs. (guest editor 1980), Optical Soc. Am., Soc. Info. Display. Avocations: tennis, tai-chi, camping, spending time with family. Home: 33 Allegheny Irvine CA 92620-2604 E-mail: cbchen@west.raytheon.com.

CHEN, CHUNGUANG, cardiologist; b. Fuging, Peoples Republic of China, Dec. 27, 1955; came to the U.S., 1989; s. Xiatong and Surong (Lin) C.; m. Kim Frances Cronin, Dec. 5, 1991; children: Sarah, Catherine, Laura. Student, Fujian Med. Coll., 1976-79; diploma, Chongqing Med. U., 1981; MD, U. Hamburg, 1984. Resident Hamburg (Germany) U. Hosp., 1983-84; staff physician Hamburg U. Hosp., 1990-92; fellow in cardiology Freiburg (Germany) Univ. Hosp., 1985-86; attending physician, chief Fujian Med. Coll., Fuzhou, Peoples Republic of China, 1987-88; rsch. fellow Mass. Gen. Hosp., Boston, 1989-90, clin. and rsch. fellow, 1992-93; attending cardiologist Hartford (Conn.) Hosp., 1993—; dir. cardiac non-invasive lab. Newark Beth

Israel Med. Ctr., 1999—. Dir. echocardiography Hamburg U. Hosp., 1990-92; assoc. dir. echocardiography Hartford Hosp., 1993—; asst. prof. medicine U. Conn., 1993—; assoc. prof. Fujian Med. Coll., 1988—; dir. echocardigraphy UMDNJ-N.J. Medicine Sch., 1998—; dir. Cardiac Non-Invasive Lab., Beth Isreal Med. Ctr., Newark, 1999—. Contbr. articles to profl. jours. Named Best Young Investigator Chinese Assn. Sci. and Tech., 1988; recipient Rsch. awards Ministry of Sci., Peoples Republic of China, 1986, 87; rsch. grantee Alexander-von-Humboldt Found., 1988. Mem. Coun. on Clin. Cardiology, Am. Heart Assn., Am. Soc. Echocardiography. Avocation: table tennis. Office: Newark Beth Israel Med Ctr Cardiac Non-Invasive Lab 201 Lyons Ave Newark NJ 07112-2027

CHEN, CHUN-HUNG, engineering educator; b. Kaohsiung, Taiwan, Oct. 27, 1964; came to U.S., 1991; s. Ping-Ho and Pao-Yu Chen; m. Mei-Mei Liu, June 15, 1991; 1 child, Valerie. PhD, Harvard U., 1994. Asst. prof. U. Pa., Phila., 1994-2000, acting grad. group chair, 1999-2000; assoc. prof. George Mason U., Fairfax, Va., 2000—. Cons. Computer Command and Control Co., Phila., 1997—. GAANN fellow U.S. Dept. Edn., 1998; recipient Motion Planning and Simulation award U.S. Army Rsch. Office, 1997, Engring. Design award NSF, 1998, Robust Design Optimization award Sandia Nat. Labs., N.Mex., 1998, Small Aircraft Sys. Transportation Devel. award NASA, 2002. Mem. IEEE (sr.), Inst. Ops. Rsch. and Mgmt. Scis. Achievements include development of simulation tool, 1992 (MasPar award); patents for optimal computing allocation, 1999 (Eliahu Jury award 1994). Avocations: trains, aircraft, weather forecasting. Office: George Mason U Dept Sys Engring & Ops Rsch 4400 University Dr MS 4A6 Fairfax VA 22030

CHEN, CONCORDIA CHAO, mathematician; b. Peiping, China; came to U.S., 1955, naturalized, 1969; d. Chun-fu and Kwie Hwa (Wong) Chao; BA in Bus. Adminstrn., Nat. Taiwan U., 1954; MS in Math., Marquette U., 1958; postgrad. Purdue U., 1958-60, M.I.T., 1961-62; m. Chin Chen, July 2, 1960; children: Marie Hui-mei, Albert Chao. Teaching asst. Purdue U., Lafayette, Ind., 1958-60; system analysis engr. electronic data processing div. Mpls.-Honeywell, Newton Highlands, Mass., 1960-63; mgmt. planning asst. Lederle Labs., Am. Cyanamid Co., Pearl River, N.Y., 1964, computer applications specialist, 1967, oper. analyst, 1967; staff programmer IBM, Sterling Forest, N.Y., 1968-73, adv. programmer Data Processing Mktg. Group, Poughkeepsie, 1973-80, mgr. systems programming and systems architecture, Princeton, N.J., 1980-82, sr. systems analyst, 1982-83, data processing mktg. cons., Beijing, 1983-88; sr. planner IBM DSD, Poughkeepsie, 1988-92; program mgr. Chiang Indsl. Charity Found Ltd., 1993-94; mgr. software engring. China Weal Bus. Machinery Co., Ltd., Hong Kong, 1995-99, exec. gen. mgr., 1999—. Chmn. ednl. council Hudson region MIT. Mem. Am. Math. Soc., Soc. Indsl. and Applied Maths., MIT Club Hudson Valley (pres.). Home: 12 Mountain Pass Rd Hopewell Junction NY 12533-5331 Office: Guangzhou World Trade Ctr Huan Shi East Rd 52709-13 Guangzhou 510095 China

CHEN, DEANFORD FREDERICK, software engineer; b. Taiwan, Jan. 2, 1965; came to U.S. 1975; BS in Computer Sci., San Jose State (Calif.) U., 1991. Software devel. Computer Sci. Corp., Sunnyvale, Calif., 1993-94; software specialist Litton, San Jose, 1995—. Mem. IEEE Computer Soc., ACM, Toastmasters (awards, 1997, 98, 99), San Jose State Alumni Assn., U.S. Jaycees. Avocations: chess, sport, reading, travel, computers. Home: 5312 Ayrshire Dr San Jose CA 95118-3001 Office: Litton Santa Clara CA 95050

CHEN, DI, electro-optic company executive, consultant; b. Chekiang, China, Mar. 15, 1929; came to U.S., 1954, naturalized, 1972; s. Hsun Yu and chien (Wang) C.; m. Lynn C. Wang, June 14, 1958; children: Andrew A.J., Daniel T.Y. BS, Nat. Taiwan U., 1953; MS, U. Minn., 1956; PhD, Stanford U., 1959. Asst. prof. U. Minn., Mpls., 1959-62; rsch. fellow Honeywell Co., Bloomington, Minn., 1962-80; tech. dir. Optical Peripherals Lab., Colorado Springs, Colo., 1980-84; co-founder, exec. v.p. tech. Optotech, Inc., 1984-89; pres. Chen and Assocs. Cons., 1989—. V.p. tech. and engring. Literal Corp., Colorado Springs, 1990-91; chmn., then co-chmn., advisor, sr. advisor Optical Data Storage, 1983-98. Topical editor Applied Optics Jour., 1991-97; contbr. articles to profl. jours, chpts. to ref. books; patentee in field. Recipient Honeywell Sweatt Scientists and Engrs. award, 1972. Fellow IEEE (life, chmn. IEEE-MAG Twin Cities chpt. 1974); mem. SPIE, Optical Soc. Am., Sigma Xi, Eta Kappa Nu. E-mail: dichen2127@cs.com.

CHEN, DONGQING, medical image processing researcher; b. Wuhan, Hubei, China, Jan. 4, 1964; came to U.S., 1998; m. Huayuan Qian, July 11, 1990; 1 child, Zizhuang. BA, Changsha Inst. Tech., Hunan, China, 1985; PhD, Beijing Normal U., 1990. Asst. prof. Tsinghua U., Beijing, 1990-93, assoc. prof., 1993-98; rsch. scientist SUNY, Stony Brook, 1998—2001; sr. rsch. scientist Viatronix Inc., 2001—. Contbr. articles to sci. jours., including IEEE Trans., Annals Probability; patentee in field. Named Outstanding Young Tchr., Gov. of Beijing, 1998; young scientist fellow Nat. Sci. Found. China, 1992. Mem. IEEE, Soc. Photo-Optical Instrumentatin Engrs. Avocations: swimming, basketball. Office: 25 E Loop Rd Stony Brook NY 17790 E-mail: dchen@clio.rad.sunysb.edu.

CHEN, EDEN HSIEN-CHANG, engineering consultant; b. Koachsiung, China, Mar. 1, 1954; came to U.S., 1976; s. Wen-Wu and Wen-Chian (Tien) C.; m. Marilyn L. Haugan, Jan. 18, 1982; children: Jessica, Joshua, Justin, Jerilyn. BS in Indsl. Engring., Chung Yuan U., 1976; MS in Indsl. Engring., N.D. State U., 1980. Sr. engr. Gen. Instruments, Kaohsiung, Taiwan, 1976-78, Litton Industries, Sioux Falls, S.D., 1980-86; engring. mgr. DICKEY-John Corp., Auburn, Ill., 1986-88, TRW, Marshall, Ill., 1988-90; prin. cons. CTI, Springfield, Ill., 1990—. Adj. instr. George Washington U., Washington, 1989—, U. Wis., Madison, 1989, U. Dayton, 1996—; instr. Soc. Automotive Engrs., Warrendale, Pa., 1986—, Soc. Mfg. Engrs., Dearborn, Mich., 1989—. Chmn. Springfield Commn. Internat. Visitors, 1995-96, commr., 1992-97; advisor Ill. Staet Treas. Pat Quinn, Chgo., 1992-94, Overseas Chinese Affairs Commn., Taipei, Taiwan, 1995—. Office: CTI PO Box 9302 Springfield IL 62791-9302

CHEN, ERIC YEN-PO, accountant, consultant; b. Kaohsiung City, Taiwan, Nov. 7, 1971; came to the U.S., 1994; s. Jeng-Quey and Hsiu-Chuan C.; m. Irene Hsiao-pu Jao, May 22, 1997. BS in Atmospheric Sci., Nat. Taiwan U., 1994; MBA in Accountancy, CUNY, 1996. CPA, N.Y., N.J. Account analyst Dean Witter Trust Co., Jersey City, 1994-95; contr. APWM, Inc. (Roven Dino), Pine Brook, N.J., 1995-96; assoc., tax specialist Kuan C. Tsai & Assocs., P.C., CPA's, Metuchen, N.J., 1996-98; assoc. Rothstein, Kass & Co., P.C., CPA's, Roseland, N.J., 1998-99; bus. analyst mgr. Formosa Plastics Corp., Livingston, N.J., 1999—. Cons. Keydata Internat., Inc., South Plainfield, N.J., 1996-98, Aaeon Electronics, Inc., Hazlet, N.J., 1997-98, New Bay Corp., N.Y.C., 1997-98, Pine Tech. USA, Edison, N.J., 1997-98. Supporter Nutley (N.J.) Fire Dept., 1994-98, Nutley Police Dept., 1994-98. Mem. AICPA, N.J. Soc. CPAs (mem. polit. action com., internat. taxation, young CPAs com.), Beta Gamma Sigma. E-mail: ecij_cpaotr@yahoo.com.

CHEN, ER-PING, engineering executive; b. Ping-Liang, Kansu, China, May 19, 1944; came to U.S., 1967; s. Sheng-Huang and Tze-Yu (Chou) C.; m. Regina C. Chen, Mar. 31, 1973; children: Candice S., Benjamin B. BS, Nat. Chung-Hsing U., Taiwan, 1966; MS, Lehigh U., 1969, PhD, 1972. Asst., assoc. prof. Lehigh U., Bethlehem, Pa., 1972-78; mem. tech. staff Sandia Nat. Labs., Albuquerque, 1978-93, disting. mem. tech. staff, 1993-97, mgr., 1997—. Co-author: Cracks in Composite Materials, 1981; contbr. more than 100 articles to profl. jours. V.p. Albuquerque Sister Cities Found., 1986; pres. N.Mex. Chinese Assn., 1985, Assn. Chinese Engrs. and Scientists of N.Mex., 1990. Fellow ASME (chair tech. com. 1984-86). Avocation: tennis. Home: 303 Bonaire Ct Danville CA 94506-1414 Office: Sandia Nat Labs PO Box 969 Livermore CA 94551-0969 E-mail: epchen@sandia.gov.

CHEN, FEN, mathematician, educator, researcher; b. Lutsao Village, Chia-Yi Shien, Taiwan, Nov. 28, 1939; arrived in U.S., 1979; s. Shin-Ting Chen and Susan Liaw; m. Ann-Hua Shieh, Aug. 10, 1966; children: Chu-Yi, Chu-Win. BS, Nat. Taiwan Normal U, Taipei, Taiwan, R.O.C., 1968; MEd, Tokyo U, 1977; A.G.S., U of Md., 1984. Math. tchr. Tailin Jr. HS, Tailin, Chia-Yi, Taiwan, 1961—63, Pekung Sr. HS, Pekung, Iling Shien, Taiwan, 1963—66, Taichung First Sr. HS, Taichung City, Taiwan, 1966—70; math. instr. Tainan Pharmacy U, Tainan Shien, Taiwan, 1970—74; fellowship stud. Tokyo U of Edn., Tokyo, 1975—78; vis. student The U Mich., Ann Arbor, Mich., 1978—79, The U Wis., Madison, 1979—80; tchg. asst. U Md., Coll. Park, 1981—83, vol. instr. Coll. Pk., 1982—86; sub. math. tchr. Prince George's and Montgomery County Pub. Schs., 1984—90; pt. instr. Montgomery Coll., Md., 1985; sub. math. tchr. Fairfax County (Md.) Pub. Sch., 1990—98, Arlington (Va.) Pub. Sch. Sys., 1999—2002. Rsch. in the Euclidean Geometry publ New Theory of Trisection. Author: Elem. Calculus, 1972, New Theory of Trisection, 1999, Regular Polygons Vol. I, 2001, Regular Polygons Vol. II. Grantee fellowship, Kyo-Dai-Ken Math. Study Group, 1975—78. Mem.: Math. Edn. Rsch. Group at Toyko of Japan, Nat. Council of Tchrs. of Math., Am. Math. Soc., Math. Assn. of Am. (assoc.). Christian. Achievements include discovery of The most remarkable achievement of the New Theory of Trisection over 2500 years in the history of mathematics is to solve the controversial trisection-problem, work was published in 1999; Another achievement is to construct a regular p-gon (p=3, p is a natural number) by applying the new theory of trisection from a regular triangle, tetragon, pentagon etc. See Regular Polygons Vol. I. Home: 4520 King St No 902 Alexandria VA 22302 Office: Internat School Math & Sciences Inst PO Box 16707 Alexandria VA 22302

CHEN, GENDA, engineering educator; b. Zhejiang, China, Jan. 23, 1962; came to U.S., 1989; m. Sharon Chen; 1 child, Wendy. BS, Dalian (China) U. Tech., 1982, MS, 1985; PhD, SUNY, Buffalo, 1992. Registered profl. engr., Calif. Rsch. asst. SUNY, Buffalo, 1989-92, rsch. assoc., 1992-93; sr. engr. Steinman Consulting Engrs., N.Y.C., 1993-96; asst. prof. U. MO., Rolla, 1996—. Sprk. seminars, 1999, 2000. Contbr. articles to profl. pubis. Recipient Career award NSF, 1998; grantee Mo. Dept. Transp., 1998, 99, 2000, 01, 02. Mem. ASCE, Earthquake Engring. Rsch. Inst. (faculty advisor 1997—). Avocations: table tennis, volleyball, basketball, swimming. Office: U Mo-Rolla Dept Civil Engring 1870 Miner Cir Rolla MO 65409-0001

CHEN, GEORGE CHI-MING, energy company executive; b. Shanghai, Sept. 21, 1923; s. Harvey Kun-Fan and Margaret Wen-Yao (Sang) C.; m. Nora Tzu-Ling Pan, Oct. 15, 1953; children: Priscilla Hsu-Lu, Peter Hsu-Ling. BS, Harvard U., 1946. Mgr. Kian Gwan Co., Shanghai, 1947-49, Hong Kong, 1949-50, mng. dir. Taipei, 1950-51; chmn. George Chen & Co., Taipei, 1951-87, Lien Chen Ltd., Taipei, 1951-87; mng. dir. Shing Nung Group, Tai Chung, 1961-87, chmn. Shell Pacific Devel., Singapore, 1970-87. Trustee Northfield Mt. Hermon Sch., Mass., 1988-98, Libr. Found. of San Francisco, 1996—; mem. bd. overseers Harvard U., 1998—. Lt. Col. Chinese Army. Mem. China Petroleum Soc. (life). Republican. Roman Catholic.

CHEN, GUI-QIANG, mathematician, educator, researcher; b. Cixi, Zhejiang, People's Republic of China, May 25, 1963; came to U.S., 1987; parents Zhi-Biao and Jin-Er (Hu) C. BS, Fudan U., Shanghai, People's Republic China, 1982; PhD, Acad. Sinica, Beijing, 1987. Asst. prof. Inst. Systems Sci., Acad. Sinica, 1987; vis. scientist Courant Inst. Math. Scis., N.Y.C., 1987-89; asst. prof. math. U. Chgo., 1989-94; assoc. prof. math. Northwestern U., 1994-96, prof., 1996—. Cons. Argonne Nat. Lab., Chgo., 1989-95. Editor: SIAM Jour. Math. Analysis, Jour. Applied Math. and Physics, Jour. Partial Differential Equations, Acta Math. Sci., Acta Math. Applications Sci., Chinese Annals Math., Comm. Pure and Applied Analysis. Recipient Young Investigator award NSF, Beijing, China, 1987, Nat. Medal of Sci., People's Republic of China, 1989; Alfred P. Sloan Rsch. fellow, 1991, Alexander von Humboldt rsch. fellow, 2003; named Excellent Young Scientist, Beijing Soc. for Sci. and Tech., 1988. Mem.: Soc. for Indsl. and Applied Math. (editor jour.), Am. Math. Soc. Office: Northwestern Univ Dept Math Evanston IL 60208-2730 E-mail: gqchen@math.northwestern.edu.

CHEN, GUODONG, scientist, enzymologist, biochemical engineer; b. Huaian, Jiangsu, China, July 23, 1963; s. Tingzhu Chen and Xiuying Shi; m. Dan Tao, Jan. 3, 1996; 1 child, Lydia Sijia. B in Engring., Nanjing Inst. Chem. Tech., Nanjing, China, 1985, M in Engring., 1988; MSChemE, Tenn. Technol. U., 1992; PhD in Bioengring., U. Toledo, 1996. Engr. Rsch. Inst. Petroleum Processing, Beijing, 1988-90; postdoctoral scientist Ohio U., Athens, 1997-99; sr. mfg. scientist Wyeth-Lederle Vaccines and Pediatrics, Pearl River, N.Y., 1999-2001, sr. mfg. specialist, 2001—. Presenter in field. Contbr. articles to Enzyme and Microbial Tech., Biotech. and Bioengring., Biochemistry, Biofunctional Membranes, Biophys. Jour., Inorganic Chemistry. Mem. AIChE, Am. Chem. Soc., Am. Soc. for Engring. Edn., Parenteral Drug Assn., Sigma Xi. Achievements include development of optimal pH control technique for the multienzyme reaction system; dual automatic pH control and dextrose feeding technique for vaccine production; research in Helicobacter pylori survival in the gastric acidity of the human stomach; enzymology of vitamin B12, Prevnar and Pnu-Immune vaccines. Office: Wyeth Vaccines 401 N Middletown Rd Pearl River NY 10965-1215 E-mail: chengl@wyeth.com.

CHEN, HO-HONG H. H. industrial engineering executive, educator; b. Taiwan, Apr. 11, 1933; s. Shui-Cheng and Mei (Lin) C.; m. Yuki-Lihua Jenny, Mar. 10, 1959; children: Benjamin Kuen-Tsai, Carl Joseph Chao-Kuang, Charles Chao-Yu, Eric Chao-Ying, Charmine Tsuey-Ling, Dolly Hsiao-Ying, Edith Yi-Wen, Yvonne Yi-Fang, Grace Yi-Sing, Julia Yi-Jiun. Owner Tai Chang Indsl. Supplies Co., Ltd., 1967—; pres. Pan Pacific Indsl. Supplies, Inc., Ont., Can., 1975—, Maker Group Inc., Md., 1986—, Wako Internat. Co., Ltd., Md., 1986—. Prof. First Econ. U., Japan; commr. Overseas Chinese Affairs Commn., Taiwan; chmn. supervisory bd. Global Alliance for Democracy and Peace, Taiwan. Author: 500 Creative Designs for Future Business, 1961; A Summary of Suggestions for the Economic Development in Central America Countries, 1979; Access and Utilize the Potential Fund in Asia, 1980. Mem. Univ. Club (Washington), Kenwood Golf & Country Club (Bethesda, Md.). Office: PO Box 5674 Washington DC 20016-1274

CHEN, HONG YU, pediatrician; b. Tainan, Taiwan, May 6, 1957; came to U.S., 1985; s. Chiong Ming and Shu Yin (Ko) C.; m. Pei Ling Tsai, June 25, 1985; chldren: Maximillian, Anastasia, Belinda. MD, Nat. Taiwan U., 1983. Diplomate Am. Bd. Pediatrics. Mem. attending staff Md. Gen. Hosp., Balt., 1989-90, St. Agnes Hosp., Balt., 1989-00, Howard County Gen. Hosp., Columbia, Md., 1989—; pvt. practice pediatrics Ellicott City, Md., 1990—. Fellow Am. Acad. Pediatrics; mem. AMA, Med-Chi of Md. Office: Ste 104 5084 Dorsey Hall Dr Ellicott City MD 21042-7795

CHEN, HUABIN, education educator; PhD, Ind. U., 1994. Tchr. Shanghai Tchrs. U., 1982—87; assoc. prof. St. Martin's Coll., Lacey, Wash. Office: St Martin's Coll 5300 Pacific Ave Lacey WA 98503

CHEN, I-YU, computer software executive; b. Chongqing, China, Feb. 7, 1946; came to U.S., 1967; d. Ching-Hsueh and Chi-Kang (Fu) Tung; m. Robert Chen, Mar. 6, 1971; children: Clara, David. BA, Tunghai U., Taichung, Taiwan, 1967; MSW, U. Pitts., 1970; MS, Monmouth Coll., 1981; postgrad. Sloan Sch., MIT, 1998. Social worker Three Rivers Youth, Pitts., 1970-71, Bapt. Children's House, Phila., 1974-76; software engr. Intermetrics, Inc., Cambridge, Mass., 1981-86; prin. software engr. Prime Computer, Inc., Framingham, Mass., 1986-89; sr. tech. cons. Encore Computer Corp., Marlborough, Mass., 1989-91; mem. tech. staff Digital Equipment Corp., Maynard, Mass., 1991-94; mgr. lang., libns. and tools Mercury Computer Systems, Inc., Chelmsford, Mass., 1994—98; mgr. Intel Corp., Hudson, Mass., 1998—2000, 2000—. Specialist in compilers, langs., parallel tools. Member Chinese Bible Ch., 1981—. Maurice Falk fellow U. Pitts., 1968-70. Mem. Assn. for Computing Machinery, Women's Initiative for Tech. Leadership, Greater Boston Chinese Cultural Assn. Baptist. Avocations: music, painting, traveling, cooking. Home: 2 Wyndcliff Dr Acton MA 01720-4818 Office: Intel Corp 77 Reed Rd Hudson MA 01749-2895

CHEN, JAMES PAI-FUN, biology educator, researcher; b. Fengyuan, Taichung, Taiwan, May 1, 1929; came to U.S., 1952; s. Chuan and Su-wuo (Lin) C.; m. Metis Hsiu-chun Lin, Dec. 19, 1964; children: Mark Hsin-tzu, Eunice Hsin-yi, Jeremy Hsin-tao. BS, Houghton (N.Y.) Coll., 1955; MS, St. Lawrence U., 1957; PhD, Pa. State U., 1961. From instr. to assoc. prof. Houghton Coll., 1960-64; rsch. assoc. Coll. of Medicine U. Vt., Burlington, 1964-65; rsch. assoc. Sch. of Medicine SUNY, Buffalo, 1965-68; asst. prof. U. Tex. Med. Br., Galveston, 1968-75; sr. rsch. assoc. NASA/Johnson Space Ctr., Houston, 1975-76; rsch. assoc. prof. U. Tenn. Meml. Rsch. Ctr., Knoxville, 1976-78; assoc. prof. Coll. of Medicine U. Tenn., Knoxville, 1978-84, prof. Grad. Sch. of Medicine, 1984—. Rsch. rev. com. Tex. affiliate Am. Heart Assn., Austin, 1974-76; co-investigator Spacelab I project, Johnson Space Ctr., Houston, 1976-83; vis. prof. Trnovo Hosp. Internal Medicine, Ljubljana, Yugoslavia, 1985. Contbr. over 50 articles to profl. jours. including Thrombosis and Haemostasis. Grantee Robert Welch Found., 1970-74, Ortho Rsch. Found., 1971-75, NIH, 1975-82, Am. Heart Assn. Tex. affiliate, 1969-72, 74-75, Am. Heart Assn. Tenn. affiliate, 1984-85, 89-90, U.S. Army Med. Rsch., 1988-91. Fellow Internat. Soc. Hematology; mem. Am. Assn. Immunologists, Am. Soc. Biochemistry and Molecular Biology, Internat. Soc. Thrombosis and Haemostasis, Internat. Fibrinogen Rsch. Soc., Internat. Soc. Fibrinolysis Proteolysis, Am. Bd. Bioanalysis (clin. lab. dir.). Achievements include research in thrombosis and hemostasis; discovery of additional proteolytic fragmentation in the high temperature trypsin cleavage of human IgM; development of a radioimmunoassay for fragment E-neoantigen and applied it to the clinical assay of hypercoagulable state; discovered evidence of the coagulopathy in Pichinde virus-infected guinea pigs; establishment of blood tests to monitor trauma patients for thromboembolism; recognized that hypercoagulability in preterm infants with intraventricular hemorrhage is associated with fibrinolytic shutdown; ascertained that complement and cytokines are responsible for antibody-mediated hypercoagulability in the anti-T-cell therapy of transplantation. Office: U Tenn Med Ctr Dept Med Genetics Box 2 1924 Alcoa Hwy Knoxville TN 37920-1511 E-mail: jchen@mc.utmck.edu, jpaifunchen@yahoo.com.

CHEN, JEN-CHI, polymer chemist; b. Taipei, Taiwan, Feb. 3, 1954; s. Chi-Hsien and Wen-Shiu C.; m. Audrey W. Wang, August 18, 1979; 1 child Ida H. BS, National Hsin-Hua U., Hsinchu, Taiwan, 1976; PhD, U. Fla., Gainesville, 1985. Postdoctoral assoc. U. Fla., Gainesville, 1985-87, asst. rsch. scientist, 1987-88; sr. chemist Rohm and Haas Company, Phila., 1988-90; sr. rsch. scientist BetzDearborn Inc., Trevose, PA, 1990-98; prin. scientist Delsys Pharmaceutical Corp., Monmouth Junction, NJ, 1998—2001; prin. sci. McNeil Consumer and Splty. Pharm., Ft. Wash., Pa., 2001—. Patentee in field. Mem. ACS, AAPS. Avocations: reading, listening to music, bike riding, playing chess. Office: McNeil Consumer and Specialty Pharms 7050 Camp Hill Rd Fort Washington PA 19034-2299

CHEN, JIAN, engineer; d. Fujun Chen and Qun Yan; m. Shuang Zhang; 1 child, Cheney Zhang. M in Engring., Harbin (China) Engring. U., 2000. Grad. asst. Rutgers U., Piscataway, NJ, 2000—, Harbin Engring. U., 1997—2000. Office: CAIP Ctr Rutgers Univ 96 Frelinghuysen Rd Piscataway NJ 08854

CHEN, JINLING, science administrator; b. Taiyuan, Shanxi, China, Sept. 10, 1963; arrived in U.S., 1991; d. Junhao Chen and Suijiang Zhao; m. Yunfeng Chang, Dec. 10, 1986; children: Lawrence Chang, Albert Chang. BSc, Nankai U., Tianjin, China, 1984; MSc, Acad. Sci., China, 1987; PhD, Monash U., Melbourne, Australia, 1990. Prin. scientist Zeneca Inc., Richmond, Calif., 1992—97; sr. scientist Purepac Pharm., Elizabeth, NJ, 1997—98; prin. scientist Schering-Plough Rsch., Keniworth, NJ, 1998—99; sr. rsch. investigator Bristol-Myers Squibb, New Brunswick, NJ, 2000—02; assoc. dir. Tex. Biotech. Corp., Houston, 2002—. 10 patents in field. Office: Tex Biotech Corp 7000 Fannin St Houston TX 77030 Office Fax: 713-578-6720. E-mail: JLChen@tbc.com.

CHEN, JINN-KUEN, mechanical engineer; b. Tainan, Taiwan, Oct. 12, 1949; arrived in U.S., 1980; s. Lau-Der and Wen Cao C.; m. Shwu-Meei Wang, Jan. 2, 1978; children: Mary, Peter, Tina. BS, Nat. Cheng-Kung U., 1973, MS, 1977; PhD, Purdue U., 1984. Rsch. assoc. Purdue U., West Lafayette, Ind., 1984-86; analytical methods engr. GM-Allison Gas Turbine Divsn., Indpls., 1986-87; vis. assoc. prof. Nat. Cheng-Kung U., Tainan, 1987-88; sr. engr. Advanced Composites Corp., West Lafayette, 1988-90; lead engr. GE Aircraft Engines, Cin., 1990-93; sr. rsch. mech. engr. USAF Rsch. Lab., Albuquerque, 1993—. Rsch. adviser NRC, Washington, 2000—. Contbr. articles to profl. jours. Mem.: AMSE. Avocations: tai-chi quan, jogging. Office: USAF Rsch Lab 3550 Aberdeen Ave SE Albuquerque NM 87117

CHEN, JIUHUA, physicist, geophysicist, educator; b. Shenyang, Liaoning, China, Dec. 2, 1962; arrived in U.S., 1994; s. Xixue Chen and Yukun Li; m. Hongyu Lu, Dec. 28, 1986; 1 child, Jeddy Chang. PhD, Nat. Lab. High Energy Physics, Tsukuba, Japan, 1994. Postdoctoral rsch. assoc. Ctr. High Pressure Rsch., Stony Brook, NY, 1994-96; rsch. asst. prof. geophysics SUNY, Stony Brook, 1996-2001, rsch. assoc. prof., 2001—, assoc. dir. Mineral Physics Inst., 2002—. Mem. dissertation com. SUNY, Stony Brook, 1996—97; organizer workshop high pressure tech., ann. user's meeting Nat. Synchrotoron Light Source, Upton, NY, 1998. *" Pioneered the two- dimensional high — pressure x-ray diffraction with a large volume press and synchrotron radiation. Invented double- film translating imaging plate x- ray camera for real- time diffraction measurements. Demonstrated the new pseudomartensitic phase transformation mechanism by time- resolved structural refinements. Explored high- pressure rheological behavior of minerals for understanding deep- focus earthquakes. Developed x-ray radiograph imaging method for melts density measurement under high pressures.* Author: (book) A Combined CCD/IP Detection System: Science and Technology of High Pressure, 2000. Fellow Rsch., Japan Soc. Promotion Sci., 1998; grantee, NSF, 1999—. Mem.: Japan Soc. High Pressure Sci. Tech., Am. Geophys. Union, Internat. Union Crystallography. Achievements include inventor in field. Office: SUNY Stony Brook ESS Bldg Stony Brook NY 11794-2100 Office Fax: (631) 632-8140. E-mail: jiuhua.chen@sunysb.edu.

CHEN, JOHN C. chemical engineering educator; b. Shanghai, Feb. 6, 1934; came to U.S., 1945. s. L.F. and Rena (Tsao) C.; m. Katherine Lee, Oct. 9, 1960; children: Christopher, Lisa, Peter. BS in Chem. Engring., The Cooper Union, N.Y.C., 1956; MS in Chem. Engring., Carnegie Inst. Tech., Pitt., 1959; PhD in Chem. Engring., U. Mich., 1961. Process engr. Lummus Co., 1956-58; rsch. chem. engr. Brookhaven Nat. Lab, Upton, N.Y., 1960-70; adj. prof. Poly. Inst. Bklyn., 1966-70, Stony Brook, N.Y.C., 1965-66; prof. mech. engr. Lehigh U., Bethlehem, Pa., 1970-81, Carl R. Anderson prof., 1981—. Nat. chmn. Fluidization and Fluid Particle, 1991-94; bd. dirs. Coun. for Chem. Rsch, 1985-88. Recipient Donald Q. Kern award AIChE, 1988, Alexander von Humbolt Sr. Rsch. award Humbolt Found., 1992, Max Planck Rsch. award Max Planck Soc., 1994, Heat Transfer and Energy Conversion Divsn. award AIChE, 1996, Fluidized Process Recognition award, Particle Tech. Form, 1999, Heat Transfer Divsn. Classic Paper award ASME Internat., 2001. Mem.: AIChE (exec. com. particle tech. forum 1993—94, bd. dirs. 1994—, sec. 2001—, Max Jakob award 2001). Achievements include seminal model for convective boiling, resulting in widely appied "Chen Correlation". Office: Lehigh U Dept of Chemical Engineering 316 Iacocca Hall Bldg 111 Bethlehem PA 18015 E-mail: jcc0@lehigh.edu.

CHEN, JOHN CALVIN, child and adolescent psychiatrist; b. Augusta, Ga. Apr. 30, 1949; s. Calvin H. Chen and Lora L. Liu. BA in History, Pacific Union Coll., 1971; MD, Loma Linda U., 1974; PhD in Philosophy, Claremont Grad. U., 1984; JD, UCLA, 1987. Bar: Calif. 1987, U.S. Dist. Ct. (ctrl. dist.) Calif. 1988; diplomate Am. Bd. Psychiatry and Neurology, Child and Adolescent Psychiatry. Resident in psychiatry Loma Linda U. Med. Ctr., 1975-77; fellow in child and family psychiatry Cedars-Sinai Med. Ctr., L.A., 1977-78; psychiatr cons. San Bernardino (Calif.) County Mental Health Dept., 1979-83; pvt practice Claremont, Calif., 1980-84; fellow in child and adolescent psychiatry U. So. Calif., L.A., 1983-84; law clk. to Hon. William P. Gray U.S. Dist. Ct. L.A., 1987-88; mental health psychiatrist LA County Dept. Mental Health, LA 1988-94, Alameda County Health Care Svcs. Agy., Fremont, Calif., 1994-97 physician specialist L.A. County Dept. Health Svcs., 1997—99; sr. physician 1999—2003; attending physician Martin Luther King Jr. Hosp., L.A., 1997—child and adolescent psychiatrist Augustus F. Hawkins Mental Health Ctr., L.A. 1997—, chief child/adolescent svc., 1998—2003; supr. psychiatrist L.A County Dept Mental Health, L.A., 2003—. Adj. instr. social scis., philosophy Fullerton (Calif.) Coll., 1989-90; adj. asst. prof. psychiatry Charles Drew U. 1998—; asst. clin. prof. psychiatry UCLA Sch. Medicine, 1998—. Vis. fellow Claremont Grad. Sch., 1980—81. Office: 745 E Valley Blvd PMB 120 San Gabriel CA 91776-3549

CHEN, JOHN J. biostatistician, educator; b. Peking, China, May 21, 1967; s Chuhui Chen, Ping Chao; m. Jenny Z. Xu, Oct. 29, 1967. BS, Peking U. Beijing, 1990; MA, MS, SUNY, Stony Brook, 1994; PhD, U. Calif., Berkeley 1999. Rsch. scientist Dept. Health Svcs., Berkeley, Calif., 1995—97; biostat

istician U. Calif., San Francisco, 1997—99; asst. prof. biostats. St. Louis U., 1999—2002; asst. prof. SUNY, Stony Brook, 2002—. Statis. cons. Genentech Inc., South San Francisco, 1995—95, Roche Molecular Sys., Emeriville, 1998—99, Washington U. Sch. Medicine, St. Louis, 2000—01. Contbr. chapters to books, articles to profl. jours. Tchg. expert panel mem. U. Calif., Berkeley, 1998—98. Fellow Sir R.R. Shaw Fellowship, SUNY-Stony Brook, 1991—93. Mem.: Am. Soc. Human Genetics, Am. Statis. Assn. Achievements include interpretation of statistical significant results; statistical analysis of the long-term effects of recombinanthuman deoxyribonuclease on pulmonary function in cystic fibrosis patients. Office: SUNY-Stony Brook Dept Prev Medicine HSC Level 3 Rm 086 Stony Brook NY 11794-8036

CHEN, JOSEPH TAO, historian, educator; b. Shanghai, Jan. 30, 1925; came to U.S., 1951, naturalized, 1964; s. Hung Chun and Wei Tseng (Sze) C.; m. Lucy Zhu; children: Barbara Joanne, Cynthia Anne. BA, Coll. Emporia, Kans., 1953; MA, U. Calif., Berkeley, 1958, PhD, 1964. Head librarian Center for Chinese Studies U. Calif., Berkeley, 1963-64; asst. prof. history Calif. State U., Northridge, 1964-68, assoc. prof., 1968-71, prof., 1971—2001; guest lectr. history U. Calif., Santa Barbara, 1970-73, Immaculate Heart Coll., Los Angeles, 1965-79. Author: The May Fourth Movement in Shanghai, 1971, (transl. into Chinese), 1981; contbr. articles to profl. jours. Served with Chinese Navy, 1944-45. Grantee Social Sci. Research Council; Grantee Am. Philos. Soc.; Grantee Calif. State U. Found., Northridge; asso. Danforth Found. Mem. Assn. Asian Studies. Office: Calif State U Dept History Northridge CA 91330-0001 *In this great land of America, with unfailing faith, perseverance and hard work, one has the ability and the power to influence and determine one's own destiny*

CHEN, JULIE, newscaster; b. N.Y.C., Jan. 6, 1970; B in Broadcast Journalism and English, U. of So. Calif., 1991. Prodn. asst. ABC News, LA, 1990—91; prodr. ABC News One, Dayton, 1991—95; reporter WDTN-TV, Dayton, 1995—97; reporter, anchor WCBS-TV, N.Y.C., 1997—99; news anchor, substitute anchor The Early Show, 1999—; anchor CBS Morning News, 1999. Substitute anchor CBS Morning News, 1999, This Morning, 1999; host Big Brother, 2000—. Office: CBS News 524 W 57th St New York NY 10019*

CHEN, KEVIN B. arts organization executive, artist; b. Princeton, N.J., Mar. 27, 1972; s. Chaur C. and Liang-Jyu Chen. BA, Columbia U., 1994. Adminstrv. asst. Kala Art Inst., Berkeley, Calif., 1994-97, programs mgr., 1997-98; program dir. Intersection for the Arts, San Francisco, 1998—. Bd. dirs. Youth Speaks, San Francisco, 2000—, SF Camerawork, San Francisco, 2000-02; youth vol. Harlem Restoration Project, N.Y.C., 1991-94; cmty. adv. bd. San Francisco Art Inst., 2001—; mem. program com. Headlanes Ctr. for Arts, 2001—. Mem. Nat. Assn. Arts Orgns., Phi Beta Kappa. Avocations: printmaking, sculpture. Home: 4250 Horton St # 2 Emeryville CA 94608 Office: Intersection for the Arts 446 Valencia St San Francisco CA 94103 E-mail: brainology@lycos.com.

CHEN, KEVIN S. corporate executive, consultant, educator; b. Dover, N.J., Aug. 17, 1960; s. Irving S. and Judy Chen; m. Peggy Eng, June 2, 1990. BS, Stevens Inst. Tech., Hoboken, N.J., 1984, MS, 1988. Purchase parts planning mgr. Rowe Internat. Inc., Whippany, N.J., 1984-86; materials mgr. KDI/Triangle Electronics, Whippany, 1986-90; prodn. control supr. Micron Powder Systems, Summit, N.J., 1990-93. Dir. Bus. Methods Cons., Cedar Knolls, NJ, 1989—, pres. bd. dirs., Randolph, NJ, 1995—; registered and cert. profl. cons. to mgmt. Nat. Bureau of Cert. Cons., 1993—, adv. coun., 1993—97, regional dir. (N.J.), 2001—, nat. com. for continuing edn. in consultancy, 1999—2001; edn. dir. Vols. Morris County, Morristown, NJ, 2000; Dovia focus group chmn., coord., adv. coun. chair Project Blueprint, 2000; dir. Logo In Motion, Randolph, NJ, 1999—; supr. Ctr. Assessment and Learning, County Coll. of Morris, 2000—. Mem. coll. coun. County Coll. of Morris, 2002—, mem. acad. std. com., 2002—; hon. chair State of N.J. bus. adv. coun. Nat. Rep. Com., 2002—; rsch. bd. advisors Am. Biog. Inst., 1992—; walk chair ADA, 1993—96, bd. dirs., 1995—97, mem. N.W. regional coun., 1993—97; mem. steering com. United Way's Mentoring Tng. and Cons. Ctr., 2001—02; vice chmn., chmn. spl. events., chmn. survey subcom. Randolph Township Environ. Com., 1985—89; dir. Custom Scholarship Search Program, 1991—94; instr. County Coll. of Morris, 1996—98, 2001—; racquetball events coord. Stevens Alumni Assn., 1994—2000; racquetball coord. Madison Area YMCA, 1999—2001; N.J. state dir. Cons. Inst., 1999—2001; regional dir. N.J. Nat. Bur. Cert. Cons., 2001—; bd. dirs. The Better Bus. Bur., NJ, 2001—02; mem. steering com. County Coll. of Morris' Ctr. for Teaching Excellence, 2001—. Recipient Nat. Leadership award, Nat. Rep. Congl. Com. Mem.: NJ Regional Cons. Assn. (founder, regional dir.). Avocations: racquetball, coaching, team sports. Home: PO Box 520 Mount Freedom NJ 07970-0520 Office: Business Methods Corp 503 State Route 10 Randolph NJ 07869-2152 E-mail: kchen@ccm.edu.

CHEN, KUEN HAI, physician; b. Tachia, Taiwan, May 23, 1937; came to U.S., 1966, naturalized, 1976; s. John Bei and Yeh (Liang) C.; m. Fu Mei Lai, Jan. 1, 1966; children: Richard, Humphrey, Christopher. BS, Nat. Taiwan U., Taipei, 1959, MD, 1964. Diplomate Am. Bd. Family Practice. Intern Ill. Central Hosp., Chgo., 1966-67; resident in gen. surgery Sisters Hosp., Buffalo, 1967-69, C & O Hosp., Huntington, W.Va., 1970-71; fellow spinal cord injury service VA Hosp., East Orange, N.J., 1971-72, chief, 1972-76; mem. staff First Ave. Med. Center, N.Y.C. Mem. adv. bds. Dupont, McNeil Health Network, 1999—; Shering/Key cons. Glaxo Wellcome Inc. Nat. Irritable Bowel Syndrome Awareness Registry, 2000—; mem. med. adv. bd. Agouron, Bristol Myers Roche, 2000—; physicians coun. Heritage Found., 1994—; dir. K.F.C. Corp; analyst Am. Bd. of Disability, 1999. Author: American Spoken English; founding prodr. GOP-TV, 1994—. Active Taiwan Union Presbyn. Ch. in N.Y., chmn. exec. com., 1983, pres. Parents' Assn., 1980-84; mem. Presdl. Adv. Commn., 1992, Presdl. Commn. Am. Agenda, 1992; del. Presdl. Trust, 1992; adv. mem. Rep. Nat. Commn. Am. Agenda, 1992—; hon. co-chmn. bus. adv. coun. Rep. Nat. Com., 1998; del. N.J. Rep. Presdl. Task Force, 1994-98; mem., chmn. adv. bd. Rep. Nat. Com., 1994—, hon. co-chmn. bus. adv. coun., 1998, hon. chmn. bus. adv. coun. 1999—; founding mem. Rep. Campaign Coun., 1994—, nat. campaign advisor, 1995—, Eisenhower Commn., 1995-96; mem. Rep. Senator Adv. Coun., 1997—, Rep. Senator Inner Circle, 1998 ; hon. co-chmn., 1999—, adv. coun. Rep. Nat. Com., 1998, chmn. adv. coun. 1999; hon. chmn. Physician's Adv. Bd.; co-chmn. Election Adv. Bd., 2000—; hon. co-chair inaugural com. 43d Pres. of U.S., 2001. Served with Taiwan Air Force, 1965. Recipient Physician Recognition award AMA, 1969, 72, 75, 78, 81, 84, 87, 90, 93; Disting. Service and Leadership award Nat. Taiwan U.; Patriotic award medal Pres. of U.S., Congl. Medal Distinction, 2001; Republican of the Yr. award, 2002; Republican Senatorial Medal of Freedom award, 2002; named Mem. of Yr. Rep. Presdl. Task Force, 1996, Physician of Yr., 2003; NRCC Physician of Year, 2002 Fellow Am. Acad. Family Physicians, Am. Geriatric Soc.; mem. Am. Bd. Disability Analysts, N.Y. Acad. Sci., Am. Coll. Emergency Physicians, AMA, N.Y. County Med. Soc. (com. health care agy.), Internat. Soc. Paraplegia, Heritage Found., Taita Jing-Fu Med. Found. (hon. dir.), Nat. Taiwan U. Med. Coll. Alumni Assn. (exec. dir. 1979-81, pres. 1981-83, permanent bd. dirs. 1984, chmn. edn. com. 1987-95, chmn. fund campaign com. 1988-94, N.Y. chpt. bd. dirs. 1994, bd. trustees 1985-88, chmn. by-law com. 1994—), Am Spinal Injury Assn., Nat. Bd. Addiction Examiners (dr. addiction counselor), W.Va. Med. Inst., N. Am. Taiwanese Med. Assn. (bd. dirs. greater N.Y. chpt. 1985—, pres. 1987-89, chmn. edn. com. 1989-95), Nat. Irritable Syndrome Awareness Registry, Nat. Taiwan U. Alumni Assn. (bd. dirs. 1981—, chmn. edn. com. 1984-94, chmn. by-law com. 1994-96, treas. 1991-94, pres. 1999-2001), Alpha Omega Alpha. Presbyterian. E-mail: kuenhchen@aol.com.

CHEN, KUN-MU, electrical engineering educator; b. Taiwan, China, Feb. 3, 1933; came to U.S., 1957, naturalized, 1969; s. Tsa-Mao and Che (Wu) C.; m. Shun-Shun Chen, Feb. 22, 1962; children: Margaret, Katherine, Kenneth, George. BS, Nat. Taiwan U., 1955; MS, Harvard, 1958, PhD, 1960. Research assoc. U. Mich., 1960-64; vis. prof. Chao-Tung U., Taiwan, 1962; asso. prof. elec. engring. Mich. State U., 1964-67, prof., 1967-95, Richard M. Hong Endowed prof. elec. engring., 1995—99, dir. elec. engring. grad. program, 1967-70, Richard M. Hong prof. emeritus, 1999—. Vis. prof. Tohoku U., Japan, 1989, Nat. Taiwan U., 1989. Author articles on electromagnetic radiation, plasma physics, electromagnetic bioeffects. Recipient Disting. Faculty award Mich. State U., 1976, Outstanding Achievement award in sci. and engring. Taiwanese Am. Found., 1984; Withrow Disting. scholar Coll. Engring., Mich. State U., 1993; C.T. Loo fellow, 1957; Gordon McKay fellow, 1958-60. Fellow IEEE, AAAS; mem. Internat. Union Radio Sci. (commn. A, B and C), AAUP, Sigma Xi, Phi Kappa Phi, Tau Beta Pi. Home: 4433 Comanche Dr Okemos MI 48864-2071 Office: Mich State U Dept Elec Engring East Lansing MI 48824 E-mail: chen@msu.edu.

CHEN, LI, computer scientist, software engineer; b. Lishui, Jian Su, China, Apr. 23, 1961; came to U.S., 1991; s. Zhengxi and Suqin (Wang) C.; m. Lan Zhang, Apr. 18, 1987; children: Boxi, Kyle. BS, Wahan (China) U., 1982; MS, Utah State U., 1995; PhD, U. Luton, U.K., 2001. Asst. engr. Rsch. Inst. of Geophys. Prospecting, Nanjing, China, 1982-85; lectr. Nanjing Inst. Tech., 1985-89, Wuhan U., 1989-91; sr. software engr. Spiricon, Inc., Logan, Utah, 1994-2000, Sorenson Media, Salt Lake City, 2000; prin. rsch. scientist Sci. and Practical Computing Lab., North Logan, 1997-2000; vis. asst. prof. U. N.D., Grand Forks, 2000—01; assoc. prof. U. D.C., Washington, 2002—. Adj. assoc. prof. Wuhan U., China, 1997-2000. Contbr. articles to profl. jours. Recipient Award Rsch. Fund of Chinese Acad. Sci. for Young Scientists, 1987, 2d Class award Chinese Min. Geology, 1991; named Outstanding Scientist of Wuhan U., 1991. Achievements include definition of gradually varied surfaces and interpolation algorithms; the definition of general discrete manifolds and the classification of digital surface points; optimal algorithm for optimal minimum odd-weigh-column SEC-DED code's check matrix; inventor fuzzy sub-fiber, possibility-based neural networks. Office: U DC EE & CS Dept Washington DC 20008 E-mail: lchen@udc.edu.

CH'EN, LI-LI, writer, Chinese language, literature and comparative literature educator; b. Beijing, Apr. 6, 1934; came to U.S., 1951, naturalized, 1963; d. Shujen and Yu-wu (Kuan) C. BA magna cum laude, Wilson Coll., 1957, Litt.D., 1980; MA, Radcliffe Coll., 1958; PhD (Harvard-Yenching Inst. fellow, Ford Found. fellow), Harvard U., 1969. Prof. Chinese lang., lit. and comparative lit., dir. Chinese program Tufts U., Medford, Mass., 1972—94, prof. emerita, 1994—. Translator: Master Tung's Western Chamber Romance, 1977 (Nat. Book Award for Transl.); Contbr. articles to profl. jours. Am. Council Learned Socs. grantee, 1976-77; MacDowell Colony fellow, 1980; Michael Karolyi Found. fellow, 1980; Recipient Nat. Mag. Award for Fiction, Criticism, and Belles Lettres for short story Peking! Peking!, 1977 Mem. Phi Beta Kappa. Home: 186 Upland Rd Cambridge MA 02140-3624 Office: Tufts U Olin Hall Medford MA 02155

CHEN, LILLY LIL-JING, neurologist, educator; b. Taipei, Taiwan, Feb. 5, 1963; came to U.S., 1965; d. En Chuan and Amy Huei Mei C.; m. Joseph Philip Hasapes, June 22, 1990; children: Nicholas, Christopher. BA, Wellesley Coll., 1985; MD, SUNY, Stony Brook, 1989. Diplomate Am. Bd. Neurology. Intern SUNY, Stony Brook, 1989-90; resident in neurology Washington U., St. Louis, 1990-93; fellow in neurorehab. U. Tex. Health Sci. Ctr., Houston, 1993-94; asst. prof. orthopedics and rehab. U. Tex. Med. Br., Galveston, 1994—97; asst. prof. U. Tex., Dallas, 1997-98; asst. prof. orthopedics and rehab. U. Tex. Med. Br., Galveston, 1999—. Mem. Am. Acad. Neurology. Avocations: traveling, music, theater, ballet. Office: U Tex 301 University Blvd Galveston TX 77555-5302 E-mail: llchen@utmb.edu.

CHEN, MEI-QIN, mathematics educator; b. Mar. 26, 1956; BS in Math., Ea. Ill. U., Charleston, 1983; MS in Math., U. Ill., 1985, PhD in Math., 1989. Prof. math. The Citadel, Charleston, S.C., 1989—. Office: The Citadel Dept Math 171 Moultrie St Charleston SC 29409-0002 E-mail: chenm@citadel.edu.

CHEN, OLIVER TSUNG-YU, chemical engineer, researcher; b. Taichung, Taiwan, Jan. 1, 1942; arrived in U.S., 1969, naturalized, 1977; s. I-Nan and Feng (Chien) Chen; m. Helen Hui-Wan Lin, Feb. 24, 1969; children: Andrew, Grace. PhD, U. Calif., Santa Barbara, 1976. Assoc. U. Calif., Santa Barbara, 1976-77; fellow Argonne (Ill.) Nat. Lab., 1977-78; vis. asst. prof. U. Ill., Chgo., 1978-79; sr. rsch. chem. engr. Thiokol Corp., Elkton, Md., 1979-82, rsch. scientist, 1982-96, sr. prin. scientist, 1996-2000, staff scientist, 2000—. Contbr. Grantee, Cheng Kung U. Taiwan, 1961—64. Mem.: Am. Inst. Aero. Astronautics, Am. Chem. Soc., Sigma Xi. Office: PO Box 241 Elkton MD 21922-0241 E-mail: oliver.chen@atk.com., oliverchen@comcast.net.

CHEN, PENG-HSIN, composer, music educator; b. Tokyo, Dec. 2, 1964; d. Tsung-Tsing Chen and Mitsuko Ota; m. Christopher B Durrenberger, Dec. 29, 1965; children: Isabelle Ai Durrenberger, Leon Xin Durrenberger. Advanced Studies in Composition for Motion Picture & TV, U. of So. Calif., 1993—94, MusM, 1990—93. Comml. & film music composer PH Music Prodn., Taipei, Taiwan, 1993—98; adj. instr. Wittenberg U., Springfield, Ohio, 2003—; comml. & Film music composer PH Music Prodn., LA, 1993—98. Composer: The Second Dream, Qing Xou Village, Dance Suite, Spring for Women Freshness. Office: Wittenberg University Ward St at North Wittenberg Avenue Springfield OH 45501-0720

CHEN, PETER PIN-SHAN, electrical engineering, computer science and internet/web educator, data processing executive; b. Taishan, Kwangtung, China, Jan. 3, 1947; came to U.S., 1969; s. Man-See and T.T. Chen; m. Li-Chuang Ho; children: Victoria, Angela, Gloria Lily. BSEE, Nat. Taiwan U., Republic of China, 1968; MS, Harvard U., 1970, PhD, 1973. Student assoc. IBM, Yorktown Heights, N.Y., 1970; teaching fellow Harvard U., Cambridge, Mass., 1970-71; prin. engr. Honeywell, Waltham, Mass., 1973-74; vis. researcher Digital Equipment Corp., Maynard, Mass., 1974; asst. prof. MIT, Cambridge, Mass., 1974-78; assoc. prof. UCLA, 1978-82; Sinclair vis. prof. MIT, 1986-87; Foster Disting. Chair prof. La. State U., Baton Rouge, 1983—. Vis. prof. Harvard U., Cambridge, 1990, MIT, Cambridge, 1990-92; chmn. Chen & Assocs. Inc., Baton Rouge, 1978—; pres. ER Inst., Baton Rouge, 1980—. Author: Entity-Relationship Approach to Logical DB Design, 1978, ER to Systems Analysis, 1980, ER to Information Modeling, 1983; patentee in field. Tech. officer with Republic of China mil. svcs., 1968-69. Named to Data Mgmt. Hall of Fame, 2000; recipient Faculty Career award, UCLA, 1979, Info. Tech. award, Data Adminstrn. Mgmt. Assn., 1990, Gt. Paper in Computer Sci. Achievement award, Data Adminstrn. Mgmt. Assn. Internat., 2000, Stevens award, 2001, Allen Newell award, ACM/AAAI, 2002; Rsch. grantee, NSF, NIST, NIH, Dept. Def., Air Force, Air Force Office Sci. Rsch., Navy, others, 1978—. Fellow: AAAS, IEEE (Harry Goode award 2003), Assn. Computing Machines. Office: La State Univ Computer Sci Dept Baton Rouge LA 70803-0001 E-mail: pchen@lsu.edu.

CHEN, PETER WEI-TEH, mental health services administrator; b. Fuchow, Fukien, China, July 20, 1942; came to U.S., 1966; s. Mao-Chuang and Sheu-Lin (Wang) C.; m. Lai-Wah Mui, Nov. 8, 1969; children: Ophelia Mei-Chuang, Audrey Mei-Hui. BA, Nat. Chung Hsing U., Taipei, Taiwan, Republic of China, 1964; MSW, Calif. State U., Fresno, 1968; D of Social Work, U. So. Calif., 1976. Case worker Cath. Welfare Bur., L.A., 1968-69; psychiat. social worker L.A. County Mental Health Svcs., 1969-78, mental health svcs. coordinator, 1978; sr. rsch. analyst Jud. and Legis. Bur. L.A. County Dept. Mental Health, 1978-79; Forensic In-Patient Program dir. L.A. County Dept. Mental Health, 1979-86, chief Jail Mental Health Svcs., 1986-89, asst. dep. dir. Adult Svc. Bur., 1989, dir. cmty. care programs, 1989—; clin. prof. dept. psychiatry Harbor/UCLA Med. Ctr., 1997—. Pres. Orient Social and Health Soc., Los Angeles, 1973-75; bd. dirs. Am. Correctional Health Assn., 1986-87. Author: Chinese-Americans View Their Mental Health, 1976. Bd. dirs. San Marino (Calif.) Cmty. Chest, 1986-87; trustee San Marino Schs. Found., 1987-90; advisor San Marino United Way, 1989-92, AIDS Commn. L.A. County, 1993; founder, past chmn., bd. dirs. Chinese Sch. of San Marino, 1981—. 2d lt. Chinese Marine Corps, Taiwan, Republic of China, 1964-65. Recipient several cmty. svc. awards, 3 spl. awards Nat. Assn. County Orgn. Mem. Nat. Assn. Social Workers (bd. dirs. Calif. chpt. 1979-80), Nat. Correctional Health Assn., Forensic Mental Health Assn. Calif., L.A. World Affairs Coun., Chinese Am. Profl. Soc. (pres. 1997-98, chmn. bd. dirs. 1998-2000), Chinese Am. Human Svcs. Assn. (chmn. bd. dirs. 1998-2000, pres. 2001-02). Clubs: Chinese of San Marino (pres. 1987-88), San Marino City. Avocations: sports, fishing, bridge. Home: 2161 E California Blvd San Marino CA 91108-1348 Office: LA County Dept Mental Health 1925 Daly St Los Angeles CA 90031-3309 E-mail: pchen@co.la.ca.us.

CHEN, PHILIP MINKANG, investment banker, corporate executive, lawyer, engineer; b. Chungking, Szechuan, China, Oct. 20, 1944; s. Yin Ching and Wansu (Wu) C.; m. Deborah Lynn Carlson, May 7, 1971; children: Martin, Emily. BME with distinction, U. Va., 1968; MS, Stanford U., 1969; JD, U. Minn., 1979. Bar: Minn. 1979, U.S. Dist. Ct. Minn. 1979, N.Y. 1982; registered profl. engr. Va., 1972, N.Y.; diplomate Am. Acad. Environ. Engrs., 1994. Copy boy Washington Star Newspaper, 1962-65; mech. engr. Pope, Evans & Robbins, Alex, Va., 1967-68; engr. Westinghouse Orec, Annapolis, Md., 1969-71; sr. environ. engr. Stone & Webster Engring. Corp., Boston, Denver, 1971-78; sr. engr. Dames & Moore, Denver, 1978; assoc. Dorsey & Whitney, Mpls., 1979-82, Mudge, Rose, Guthrie & Alexander, N.Y.C., 1982; mng. dir. Lehman Bros., N.Y.C., 1982-92; pres. Weston Internat., 1992-94; exec. v.p. Roy F. Weston, Inc., West Chester, Pa., 1992-94; investment banker The Chase Manhattan Bank, N.A., N.Y.C., 1995-96; mng. dir. South Africa Infrastructure Fund, Johannesburg, 1996-2000. Editl. adv. bd. American City and County Mag., 1986-87, Project Finance Monthly, 1989-92; mem. environ. technologies trade adv. com., Dept. Commerce, 1995-96, co-chmn. fin. subcom. Patentee for mooring system. Mem. Town Mtg. Winchester, Mass., 1973; past bd. dirs. U.S. Environ. Tech. Export Coun., Greater Phila. Internat. Network, Greater Phila. First Ptnrship. for Econ. Devel.; mem. The Union League of Phila., 1994-2001; participant Presdl. Bus. Devel. mission to Brazil, Argentina, and Chile, 1994. Mem. ABA (vice chmn. elec. power com. natural resources law sect. 1982-85, chmn. spl. com. on energy fin. 1988-89), ASME, Nat. Resource Recovery Assn. (adv. bd. U.S. conf. of mayors 1989), U. Va. Alumni Assn., Phi Sigma Kappa. Avocations: art, writing, fishing. E-mail: chenpm@aol.com.

CHEN, PHILIP S., JR., government official; b. St. Johns, Mich., July 3, 1932; s. Philip Stanley and Helen Y.C. (Feng) C.; m. Inger Lise Rasmussen, Apr. 2, 1955; children: Bodil Lynn Chen Morris, Iver Allan. BA, Clark U., 1950; PhD, U. Rochester, 1954. Sr. asst. scientist Nat. Heart Inst. NIH, Bethesda, Md., 1956-59; asst. prof. radiation biology, biophysics and pharmacology U. Rochester, N.Y., 1959-67; grants assoc. NIH, 1967-68, spl. asst., br. chief Office Program Planning and Evaluation, 1968-72, assoc. dir. program planning and evaluation Nat. Inst. Gen. Med. Scis., 1972-74, assoc. dir. intramural affairs, 1974-97, sr. advisor to the dep. dir. for intramural rsch., 1997—. Bd. dirs. NIH Fed. Credit Union, 1986-92; chmn. Patent Policy Bd., 1987-92; bd. dirs. Brooke Grove Found., Inc. Co-author: Biological Effects of Organic Fluorides, 1963; contbr. articles to profl. jours. Trustee Atlantic Union Coll., South Lancaster, Mass., 1986-92; bd. dirs. Found. for Advanced Edn. in Scis., Bethesda, 1982-91. Served to capt. USPHS, 1956-59. Recipient NIH Dirs. award, 1976, USPHS award, 1978, Disting. Svc. award DHHS, 1993; AEC predoctoral fellow, 1951-53, NSF postdoctoral fellow, 1954-55, Guggenheim Found. fellow, 1966-67. Mem. Am. Physiol. Soc., Am. Chem. Soc., Radiation Research Soc., Sigma Xi Avocations: music; auto mechanics; skiing; travel. Office: NIH Room 140 Bldg 1 9000 Rockville Pike Rm 140 Bethesda MD 20892-0003

CHEN, QIAN, cell biologist, developmental biologist; b. Shanghai, Feb. 20, 1964; s. Chao-Yu Chen and Ke-Ying Wei; m. Lii Fang Snen. BS in Biochemistry, FuDan U., Shanghai, 1985; PhD in Cell, Molecular and Devel. Biology, Tufts U., 1992. Vis. scientist Boston Biomed. Rsch. Inst., 1986-87; rsch. fellow Mass. Gen. Hosp., Harvard Med. Sch., Boston, 1992-94; asst. cellular biologist Mass. Gen. Hosp., Boston, 1994-95; instr. Harvard Med. Sch., Boston, 1994-95; asst. prof. Pa. State U. Med. Sch., Hershey, 1995-2001, assoc. prof., 2001—02; prof. Brown Med. Sch., Providence, 2002—, Michael G. Ehrlich endowed chair in ortho. rsch., 2002—. Author: (chpt.) Extracellular Matrix Assembly and Structure, 1994; contbr. articles to profl. jours. Arthritis Found. postdoctoral fellow, 1994-96, Arthritis Investigator awardee, 1997—; Nat. Eye Inst./NIH summer fellow, 1992; recipient First award NIH, 1997—, Ind. Scientist award, 1998—, Kappa Delta award Am. Acad. Orthop. Surgeons, 2000, award Hinkle Soc., 2001. Mem. AAAS, Am. Soc. for Cell Biology, N.Y. Acad. Scis. Achievements include research in endochondral bone formation and skeletal development. Office: Brown Med Sch Dept Orthped 1 Hoppin Street Ste 402 Providence RI 02903 E-mail: qian_chen@Brown.edu.

CHEN, ROGER (RONGXIN CHEN), management educator; b. Shanghai, China, Jan. 20, 1961; m. Hong (Emily) Xu, June 30, 1992; 1 child, Angela. MS, Shanghai Jiao Tong U., 1986; PhD, U. Tex., Dallas, 1995. Lectr. Sch. of Mgmt., Shanghai Jiao Tong U., China, 1986—89; assoc. prof. Sch. of Bus. and Mgmt., U. of San Francisco, San Francisco, 1995—. V.p. Silicon Valley Bus. Forum Inc., Palo Alto, Calif., 1999—. Recipient Silicaon Valley Roundtable Guru award, U.S. Nat. Bus. Econs. Assn. and Silicon Valley Roundtable, 1999, Abramson award for Outstanding Article, (jour.) Bus. Econs., 1998. Mem.: World Affairs Coun., Acad. of Mgmt. Assn. Office: Bus Sch U San Francisco 2130 Fulton St San Francisco CA 94117 Office Fax: 415-422-2502. Business E-Mail: chenr@usfca.edu.

CHEN, SHIYI, physicist, educator; b. Zhejiang Province, China, Oct. 1, 1956; s. Daji and Guimei (Ye) Chen; m. Fan Chen, Oct. 1, 1986; children: Cathy, Jenny. PhD, Peking U., Beijing, 1987. Rsch. staff mem. Phys. Sciences Dept., IBM Watson Rsch. Ctr., Yorktown Heights, NY, 1994—97; dep. dir. Ctr. for Nonlinear Studies, LANL, Los Alamos, N.Mex., 1997—99; prof. The Johns Hopkins U., Balt., 1999—. Chief advisor Exa Corp., Boston, 1999—2002. Named one of Rd100, RD100 Mag., 1994; fellow Los Alamos Nat. Lab., 1999. Fellow: Am. Phys. Soc. Office: The Johns Hopkins Univ Latrobe 105, 3400 N Charles St Baltimore MD 21218 Office Fax: (410)-516-7254. Personal E-mail: syc@taylor.me.jhu.edu. Business E-Mail: syc@titan.me.jhu.edu.

CHEN, SHOEI-SHENG, retired mechanical engineer; b. Taiwan, Jan. 26, 1940; s. Yung-cheng and A-shu (Fang) C.; m. Ruth C. Lee, June 28, 1969; children: Lyrice, Lisa, Steve. BS, Nat. Taiwan U., 1963; MS, Princeton U., 1966, MA, 1967, PhD, 1968. Research asst. Princeton U., 1965-68; asst. mech. engr. Argonne (Ill.) Nat. Lab., 1968-71, mech. engr., 1971-80, sr. mech. engr., 1980—2001; ret., 2001. Cons. to Internat. Atomic Energy Agy. to assist developing countries in R & D of nuclear reator systems components, 1977, 79, 80, 94; cons. NASA, NRC, Rockwell Internat., others. Author: Flow-Induced Vibration of Circular Cylinderical Structures, 1987; mem. internat. adv. editorial bd. Acta Mechanica Solida; adv. bd. JSME Internat. Jour.; assoc. editor Applied Mechs. Rev., Jour. of Pressure Vessels Tech.; contbr. articles to profl. jours. Recipient Disting. Performance award U. Chgo., 1986, ASME pressure vessel and piping medal, 2001. Fellow ASME (chmn. tech. subcom. on fluid and structure interactions pressure vessels and piping divsn. 1987-90, honors chmn. 1990-94, mem. exec. com. 1990-96, organizer symposia, tech. program chmn. 1994, conf. chair ASME/JSME pressure vessels and piping conf. 1995, pressure vessels and piping divsn., chmn. 1995-96, senate pres. 1997-98, honors and awards chair of materials and structures tech. group 1996-99), Instn. Diagnostic Engrs.; mem. Am. Acad. Mechanics, Acoustical Soc. Am., Sigma Xi. Home: 27721 Manor Hill Rd Laguna Niguel CA 92677 Home Fax: 949-360-7586. E-mail: sschen88@aol.com.

CHEN, SHUANG, computer science professional; b. China, Jan. 29, 1958; m. Hongwen Yan, Aug. 3, 1987; children: Jessica Y., Julia Y. BSEE, Nanjing Aeronautical U., 1982; MSEE, South China U. Sci. and Tech., Guangzhou, China, 1985; MPH in Computer Engring., Rutgers U., 1990, PhD in Computer Engring., 1991. Mem. faculty South China U. Sci. and Tech., Guangzhou, 1985-86; rsch. asst. Rutgers U., New Brunswick, 1986-91; sr. rsch. engr. Comm. Intelligence Corp., Redwood Shores, Calif., 1991-95; rsch. staff mem. IBM Thomas J. Watson Rsch. Ctr., Yorktown Heights, N.Y., 1995-98; pres., CEO, chmn. bd. Internat. Interactive Commerce, Ltd., Armonk, NY, 1999—2001; chmn. bd. Op40, Inc., White Plains, NY, 2002—. Author: (with others) Studies in Pattern Recognition, 1997; reviewer profl. jours. Grad. Rsch. Assistantship, Rutgers U., 1987-91. Mem. IEEE, Sigma Xi. Office: Op40 Inc 1311 Mamaroneck Ave White Plains NY 10605

CHEN, SHU-CHING, computer science educator; b. Taoyan, Taiwan, Oct. 16, 1963; m. Mei-Ling Shyu; children: Winnie, Tiffany, Jonathan. MS in Computer Sci., Purdue U., 1992, MSEE, 1995, MSCE, 1996, PhD, 1998. Sys. engr. United World Chinese Comml. Bank, Taipei, Taiwan, 1988—90; rsch. asst. Ctr. Environ. and Regulatory Info., West Lafayette, Ind., 1996—98; asst. prof. Fla. Internat. U., Sch. Computer Sci., Miami, 1999—. Author: Semantic Models for Multimedia Database Searching and Browsing, 2000. Grantee, Fla. Dept. Ins., 2000—, NSF, 2000—02. Mem.: ACM, IEEE. Office: Fla Internat Univ 11200 SW 8th St ECS 354 Miami FL 33199 Business E-Mail: chens@cs.fiu.edu.

CHEN, SHYH-KWEI, computer scientist, researcher; b. Kao-Hsiung, Taiwan, Aug. 9, 1961; s. Feng-Dou Chen, Chiou-Ying Lin Chen; m. Fei-Wen Chuang; children: Jasmine, Alison. BS, Nat. Taiwan U., 1983; MS, U. Minn., 1987; PhD,

U. Ill., 1994. Teaching asst. U. Minn., Mpls., 1986—87; rsch. asst. U. Ill., Urbana-Champaign, Ill., 1990—94; with IBM T.J. Watson Rsch. Ctr., Hawthorne, NY, 1994—97, rsch. staff mem., 1997—. Contbr. articles to profl. jours. Recipient Book Coupon award, Nat. Taiwan U., 1982. Mem.: IEEE. Office: IBM TJ Watson Rsch Ctr 19 Skyline Dr Hawthorne NY 10532 Office Fax: 914-784-7455. Business E-Mail: skchen@us.ibm.com.

CHEN, SOW-HSIN, nuclear engineering educator, researcher; b. Chia-Yi, Taiwan, Mar. 5, 1935; came to U.S., 1958, naturalized, 1974; s. Pi-Yu Chen and Liang Hsu; m. Ching-Chih Liu, Aug. 19, 1961; children: Anne, Catherine, John. BS in Physics, Nat. Taiwan U., 1956; MS in Physics, Nat. Tsinghua U., 1958; MS in Nuclear Engring., U. Mich., 1962; PhD in Physics, McMaster U., 1964. Postdoctoral fellow AERE Harwell, Berkshire, U.K., 1965; asst. prof. physics U. Waterloo, Ont., Can., 1964-67; rsch. fellow Harvard U., Cambridge, Mass., 1967; asst. prof., then assoc. prof. nuclear engring. MIT, Cambridge, 1968-74, prof. nuclear engring., 1974—. Vis. prof. Tsinghua U., Peking, China, 1982, Ecole Superieure de Physique et Chemie, Paris, 1981, Univ. Konstanz, Germany, 1988, Univ. Bayreuth, Germany, 1988, Univ. Brodeaux I, France, 1991, 93; chmn. Gordon Conf., 1986; co-organizer ACS Conf., Conf. Colloid and Interface Sci.: Trends and Applications, 1985; dir. NATO ASI on Scattering Techniques Applied to Supramolecular and Non-Equilibrium Systems, 1980, Structure and Dynamics of Supramolecular Aggregates and Strongly Interacting Colloids, 1991. Author: Spectroscopy in Biology, Chemistry and Physics-Neutron, X-Ray and Laser, 1975, Scattering Techniques Applied to Supramolecular and Non-Equilibrium Systems, 1981, Micellar Solutions and Microemulsions: Structure: Dynamics and Statistical Thermodynamics, 1990, Structure and Dynamics on Strongly Interacting Colliods and Supramolecular Aggregates in Solution, 1992, Interaction of Photons and Neutrons with Matter-An Introduction, 1997; contbr. 300 articles to sic. jours. Alexander von Humboldt U.S. sr. scientist award Govt. of Germany, 1987-88, 95. Fellow AAAS, Am. Phys. Soc., Japan Soc. for the Promotion of Sci. (Rsch. fellow 1995); mem. Sigma Xi. Home: 1400 Commonwealth Ave Newton MA 02465-2830 Office: MIT 24-209 77 Mass Ave Cambridge MA 02139-4307 E-mail: sowhsin@mit.edu.

CHEN, SOW-YEH, pathology educator; b. Chang-Hua, Taiwan, Aug. 28, 1939; came to U.S., 1966. s. Chung and Sue (Shieh) C.; m. Ming-Ming Hsu, Sept. 9, 1972; children: Howard K., Hubert M. BMD, Nat. Taiwan U., Taipei, 1965; MS, U. Ill., Chgo., 1970, PhD, 1972. Diplomate Am. Bd. of Oral and Maxillofac Pathology; cert. Dentist Dental Bd. of Commonwealth of Pa. Rsch. asst. U. Ill., Chgo., 1966-71, nat. inst. health fellow, 1971-73; from asst. prof. to prof. Temple U., Phila., 1973—. Cons. Hunan Med. U., Chengsha, Hunan, China, 1990, U. Campinas, Piracicaba, Brazil, 2002. Contbr. 2 book chpts., 47 articles to profl. jours. Mem. AAAS, Am. Acad. Oral and Maxillofac Pathology, Sigma Xi, Omicron Kappa Upsilon. Office: Temple Univ Hosp 3401 N Broad St Philadelphia PA 19140-5189

CHEN, STEPHEN S. F. retired diplomat; b. Nanking, China, Feb. 11, 1934; m. Rosa Te Chen; three children. BA, U. Santo Tomas, Philippines, 1957, MA, 1959; postgrad., U. Santo Tomas, 1959-60; DBA (hon.), Kensington U. Various positions in field to dir. gen. Coord. Coun. for N.Am. Affairs, L.A., 1988-89, dep. rep. Washington, 1989-93; vice-min. fgn. affairs Ministry Fgn. Affairs, China, 1993-96; dep. sec.-gen. Office of Pres., China, 1996-97; rep. TECRO, Washington, 1997-2000; ret., 2000. Avocations: fgn. langs. including Chinese, English, Spanish, Portuguese and six Chinese dialects.

CHEN, STEPHEN SHI-HUA, pathologist, biochemist; b. Taipei, Taiwan, Republic of China, Dec. 25, 1939; came to U.S., 1965; s. Ah-wen and Shun (Pan) C.; m. Hsin-Hsin Yii, July 5, 1969; children: Peter T., Margaret T. MD, Nat. Taiwan U., 1964; PhD, U. Pitts, 1972. Diplomate Am. Bd. of Pathology. Asst. prof. pathology U. Pitts., 1972-76; staff pathologist Presbyn. Hosp., Pitts., 1973-76; asst. prof. pathology dept. Stanford U., Palo Alto, Calif., 1976-80, clin. assoc. prof. pathology dept., 1980-96, clin. prof., 1996—; staff pathologist Veterans Affairs Med. Ctr., Palo Alto, 1976—. Contbr. articles to Jour. Cellular Physiology, Jour. Chromatography, Clinica Chimca Acta. Fellow Coll. Am. Pathologists; mem. Am. Soc. Investigative Pathology, U.S. and Can. Acad. Pathology Inc., Am. Soc. Clin. Pathologists, Am. Soc. Cytopathology. Achievements include chromatography of phospholipids. Office: Vets Affairs Med Ctr 113 3801 Miranda Ave Palo Alto CA 94304-1207

CHEN, TAK-MING, civil engineer, consultant; b. Changning, Hunan, China, July 29, 1936; came to U.S., 1970; s. Jenn-Chiu and Yin (Peng) C.; m. Taining Chou, July 1, 1973; children: Merry, Terry. BS in River/Harbor Engring., Taiwan Provincial Coll. of Marine Sci. and Tech., 1966; MSCE, U. Mo., 1971. Registered profl. engr., N.Y., Md., D.C. Project engr. Chinese Petroleum Corp., Taipei, Taiwan, 1973; structural designer Bellante, Clauss, Miller & Nolan, inc., Scranton, Pa., 1974-76; structural engr. Wayman C. Wings, Cons. Engrs., N.Y.C., 1978-80, Gibbs & Hills, Inc., N.Y.C., 1980-81; civil/structural engr. Bechtel Power Corp., Gaithersburg, Md., 1981-84; structural engr. Hazen & Sawyer, P.C., N.Y.C., 1984-85; civil/structural engr. N.Y.C. Dept. Sanitation, 1985-87; civil engr. N.Y.C. Dept. Bldgs., 1987-94, N.Y.C. Comptroller's Office, 1994—; pres. Chen's Cons. Engrs., Queens, N.Y., 1985-87. Bd. dirs. RFK Dem. Assn., Inc., Forest Hills, N.Y., 1994—. Recipient Cert. of Honor for leadership Dem. Nat. Com. Mem. NSPE, N.Y. State Soc. Profl. Engrs., Chinese Am. Assn. City of N.Y., MSM-UMR Alumni Assn., Comptr. Engrs. Assn. Home: 82-28 255th St Floral Park NY 11004 Office: New York City Comptrollers Office Bur of Engring 1 Centre St Rm 650 New York NY 10007 E-mail: takchen@aol.com.

CHEN, TAR TIMOTHY, biostatistician; b. Fuching, China, June 23, 1945; came to U.S., 1967, naturalized, 1979; s. Lin-Tsang and Ai-Ging (Chang) C.; m. Meei-Ming Li, Aug. 9, 1969; children: Stephen, Daniel. BS, Nat. Taiwan U., 1966; MS, U. Chgo., 1969, PhD, 1972; MDiv, Southwestern Bapt. Theol. Sem., 1989; postgrad., Southwestern Baptist Theol. Sem., 2002—. Statistician Ill. Bell Tel., Chgo., 1971-73; asst. prof. Calif. State U., Hayward, 1973-74; vis. assoc. prof. Chung-Hsing U., Taichung, Taiwan, 1974-75; biostatistician The Upjohn Co., Kalamazoo, 1975-79; asst. prof. biometrics M.D. Anderson Cancer Ctr. U. Tex., Houston, 1979-84; sr. biostatistician Alcon Labs., Fort Worth, 1984-89; math. statistician Nat. Cancer Inst., Bethesda, Md., 1989-98; prof., head biostats. sect. U. Md. Greenebaum Cancer Ctr., 1998—2001; pres. Timothy Statis. Cons., 2001—. Contbr. articles to profl. jours. Deacon, Houston Chinese Ch., 1981-83, McKinney Meml. Bible Ch., Ft. Worth, 1988-89. 2d lt. Republic of China Army, 1966-67. Fellow Am. Statis. Assn., Am. Scientific Affiliation; mem. Am. Assn. Chinese Studies, Internat. Chinese Statis. Assn., Evangelical Theol. Soc. E-mail: tar_timothy_chen@yahoo.com.

CHEN, TEH-HSUN BEAN, federal agency researcher; b. Ho-Long, Miau-Li, Taiwan, Mar. 15, 1951; s. Kai-Ee Chen and Yue-Mei Cheng; m. Wey-Tsyr Shaw, Mar. 26, 1983; 1 child: Stephanie. BS in Physics, Tunghai U., Taichung, Taiwan, 1974; MS in Biophysics, U. Rochester, 1979, PhD in Biophysics, 1982. Post doctoral fellow Inhalation Toxicology Rsch. Inst., Albuquerque, 1983-85, staff scientist, 1985-95; sr. risk assessment specialist GRAM Inc., Albuquerque, 1995-96; team leader Nat. Inst. for Occupl. Safeth and Health, Morgantown, W.Va., 1996—. Adj. prof. U. N.Mex., Albuquerque, 1990-95; cons. site-wide environ. impact statement GRAM Inc., Dept. Energy, Los Alamos Nat. Lab., N.Mex., 1995-96. Co-author: Encyclopedia of Environmental Control Technology, 1989, Aerosol Measurement: Principles, Techniques and Applications, 1993, 2000, Air Sampling Instruments, 1995, 2000; contbr. over 70 articles to profl. jours.; patentee virtual impactor. Cmty. adv. bd. KNME TV, Albuquerque. Grantee HUD, 2000—, Dept. Energy, 1984-95, NIH, 1993-95. Mem. Am. Conf. Govtl. Indsl. Hygientists (air sampling instruments com. 2001—), Am. Indsl. Hygiene Assn. (aerosol tech. com. 1988—, Best Poster award 1999), Am. Assn. Aerosol Rsch., European Aerosol Assn., Chinese Assn. Aerosol Rsch. (life, editl. adv. bd. 1993—). Avocations: reading, singing, playing tennis and volleyball. Office: NIOSH/HELD/EAB MS3030 1095 Willowdale Rd Morgantown WV 26505

CHEN, WAI-FAH, civil engineering educator; b. Chekiang, China, Dec. 23, 1936; m. Lily Chen; children: Eric, Arnold, Brian. BS, Cheng-Kung U., 1959; MS, Lehigh U., 1963; PhD, Brown U., 1966. From asst. prof. to prof. civil engring. Lehigh U., 1966-76; prof. civil engring. Purdue U., Lafayette, Ind., 1976-92, head structural engring., 1980-99, George E. Goodwin disting. prof., 1992-99; dean Coll. Engring. U. Hawaii, Honolulu, 1999—. Cons. Exxon Products, 1979—, Karagozian & Case Structural Engrs., 1985—, Ga. Tech., 1987—, Skidmore, Owings & Merrill, 1987, World Bank, 1988—. Editor-in-chief The Handbook of Structural Engineering, 1997, Bridge Engineering Handbook, 1999, Earthquake Engineering Handbook, 2002, The Civil Engring. Handbook, 2d edit., 2002. Mem.: ASCE (hon.), Academia Sinica, Nat. Acad. Engring., Am. Inst. Steel Constrn., Am. Concrete Inst., Am. Acad. Mech., Structural Stability Rsch. Coun., Internat. Assn. Bridge & Structural Engring. Office: U Hawaii Coll Engring 2540 Dole St Honolulu HI 96822-2303

CHEN, WAI-KAI, electrical engineering and computer science educator, consultant; b. Nanking, China, Dec. 23, 1936; came to U.S., 1959; s. You-Chao and Shui-Tan (Shen) C.; m. Shirley Shiao-Ling, Jan. 13, 1939; children—Jerome, Melissa BS in Elec. Engring., Ohio U., 1960, MS in Elec. Engring., 1961; PhD in Elec. Engring., U. Ill., Urbana, 1964. Asst. prof. Ohio U., 1964-67, assoc. prof., 1967-71, prof., 1971-78, disting. prof., 1978-81; prof., head dept. elec. engring. and computer sci. U. Ill., Chgo., 1981-2001; vis. assoc. prof. Purdue U., 1970-71; v.p. for acad. affairs Internat. Technol. U., 2000—. Hon. prof. Tianjing U., Peoples Republic of China, 1990, Beijing U. of Posts and Telecomms., Beijing U. of Aeronautics and Astronautics, 1992. Author: Applied Graph Theory, 1970, Theory and Design of Broadband Matching Networks, 1976, Applied Graph Theory: Graphs and Electrical Networks, 1976, Active Network and Feedback Amplifier Theory, 1980, Linear Networks and Systems, 1983, Passive and Active Filters: Theory and Implementations, 1986, The Collected Papers of Professor Wai-Kai Chen, 1987, Broadband Matching: Theory and Implementations, 1988, Theory of Nets, 1990, Linear Networks and Systems: Computer-Aided Solutions and Implementations, 1990, Active Network Analysis, 1991, Modern Network Analysis, 1992, Computer-Aided Design of Comm. Networks World Scientific, 2000; editor: Brooks/Cole Series in Electrical Engineering, 1982-84; editor in chief Advanced Series in Elec. and Computer Engring., World Sci. Pub. Co., Singapore, 1986—, Jour. Circuits, Systems and Computers, 1989—, The Circuits and Filters Handbook, 1995, 2d edit., 2002, The VLSI Handbook, 2000, Design Automation, Languages and Simulations, 2003, VLSI Technology, 2003, Memory, Microprocessor and ASIC, 2003, Analog Circuits and Devices, 2003, Logic Design, 2003; editor The Elec. Engring. Handbook, 1998—, Imperial Coll. Press, 1998—, others; editor The VLSI Series, 2000—; assoc. editor Jour. Circuits, Systems and Signal Processing, 1981—; editor in charge Advanced Series in Circuits and Systems, World Scientific Publ. Co., 1991—; sect. editor Encyclopedia of Physical Science & Technology, 1998-2001; editor-in chief Design Automation, Languages and Simulation, Memory, Microprocessor and ASIC, Analog Circuits and Devices, Logic Design, VLSI Tschmology, CRC Press, 2003. Recipient Lester R. Ford award Math. Assn. Am., 1967, Baker Fund award Ohio U., 1974, 78, Disting. Accomplishment award Chinese Acad. & Profl. Assn. in Mid-Am., 1985, Disting. Guest Prof. award Chuo U., Tokyo, 1987, Outstanding Svc. award Chinese Acad. & Profl. Assn. in Mid-Am., 1988, Outstanding Achievement award Mid-Am. Chinese Sci. & Tech. Assn, 1988, Disting. Alumnus award Elec. and Computer Engring. Dept. Alumni Assn. U. Ill. Urbana-Champaign, 1988, Alexander von Humboldt award Alexander von Humboldt Stiftung, Fed. Republic of Germany, 1985, Rsch. award U. Ill. Chgo. Coll. Engring., 2000, hon. prof. award Nanjing Inst. of Technology and Zhejing U., Peoples Republic of China, 1985, The Northeast U. Tech., East. China Inst. Tech., Nanjing Inst. of Posts & Telecommunications, AnHui U., Chengdu Inst. Radio Engring., Wuhan Univ.; Rsch. Inst. fellow Ohio U., 1972, Japan Soc. for Promotion of Sci., 1986, Sr. U. Scholar award U. Ill., 1986, Ohio U. Alumni Medal Merit for Disting. Achievement in Engring. Edn., 1987, Hon. Prof. award Hangzhan U. of Electronic Tech., China, 1990, Disting. Prof. award Internat. Technol. U., 1995, Hon. Prof. award Taichung U. Healthcare and Mgmt., Taiwan, 2002, Disting. Alumnus award Taiwan U. Sci. and Tech., Taiwan, 2002. Fellow IEEE (Circuits and Sys. Soc. Meritorious Svc. award 1997, Edn. award 1998, Golden Jubilee medal 2000, Third Millennium medal 2000), AAAS; mem. NSPE, IEEE Cirs. and Sys. Soc. (adminstrv. com. 1985-87, exec. v.p. 1987, assoc. editor Trans. on Cirs. and Sys. 1977-79, editor 1991-93, pres.-elect 1993, pres. 1994), Md.-Am. Chinese Sci. and Tech. Assn. (bd. dirs. 1984-86, 89-93, pres. 1991-92), Chinese Acad. and Profl. Assn. Mid-Am. (advisor to bd. dirs. 1984-89, pres. 1986-87), Soc. Indsl. and Applied Math., Assn. Computing Machinery, Tensor Soc. Gt. Britain, Sigma Xi (sec.-treas. Ohio U. chpt. 1981), Phi Kappa Phi, Eta Kappa Nu. Office: Internat Technol U 1650 Warburton Ave Santa Clara CA 95050-3714

CHEN, WEIGANG, applied mechanics scientist, research engineer; b. Changshu, Jiangsu, China, Nov. 3, 1970; arrived in U.S., 1997; s. Xiaodi Chen and Miaogen Lu; m. Zhenrong Shen. BS in Naval Architechture, Shangahi Jiao Tong University, Shanghai, China, 1988—92; MS in Structural Mechanics, Shanghai Jiao Tong U., China, 1995; MS in Mech. Engring., MIT, Cambridge, Mass., 1997—2000; PhD in Applied Mechanics, MIT, 2001. Asst. prof. Shanghai Jiao Tong U., China, 1995—97; rsch. asst. MIT, Cambridge, Mass., 1997—2001; rsch. engr. Ford Motor Co., Dearborn, Mich., 2001—. Guest editor Internat. Jour. Vehicle Design, 2002—; profl. reviewer Jour. Thin Walled Structures, 2001—, Jour. Structural Optimization, 2001, Internat. Jour. Crashworthiness, 2002—, Internat. Jour. Solids and Structures, 2002—. Contbr. articles to profl. jours. Recipient Tuition Scholarship Award, MIT, 1997-2000, Guang-hua First Class award, Shanghai Jiao Tong U., 1994. Mem.: ASME, US Assn. Computational Mechanics, Am. Acad. Mechanics, Soc. Automotive Engrs, Sigma Xi. Avocations: tennis, travel. Office: Ford Motor Co 5111 Auto Club Dr LM714 Dearborn MI 48126

CHEN, WEI-YIN, chemical engineering educator, researcher; b. Taipei, China, Apr. 5, 1950; came to U.S., 1973; s. Shao-Pong and Fong-Hwa (Tsai) C.; m. Tsuei-Ju Kao, May 18, 1987. BSChemE, Tunghai U., Taichung, Taiwan, 1973; MS in applied math., SUNY, 1975; MSChemE, Poly. Inst. N.Y., 1975; PhDChemE, CUNY, 1981. Sr. rsch. engr. Gulf South Rsch. Inst., New Orleans, La., 1981-85, mgr. fuel rsch., 1985-87; rsch. asst. prof. La. State U., Baton Rouge, 1987-90; asst. prof. U. Miss., 1990-93, assoc. prof., 1993-2000, prof., 2000—. Contbr. articles to profl. jours. Recipient numerous grants for rsch. in field. Mem. AIChE, Am. Chem. Soc., Combustion Inst., Sigma Xi. Office: U Miss Dept Chem Engr Anderson Hall University MS 38677 E-mail: cmchengs@olemiss.edu.

CHEN, WESLEY, lawyer; b. N.Y.C., Nov. 29, 1954; s. Tom Y.M. and Mary (Don) C.; m. Vivien Wong, Dec. 10, 1983; 2 children: Marissa, Jocelyn. BA, N.Y. U., 1976, JD, 1980. Bar: N.Y. 1981, U.S. Dist. Ct. (so. and ea. dists.) N.Y. 1981. Lawyer Meissner, Tisch & Kleinberg, N.Y.C., 1980-81; pvt. practice N.Y.C., 1982—85, 2003—, 1989—90; of counsel Serchuk, Wolfe & Zelermyer, White Plains, N.Y., 1985-88, ptnr. N.Y.C., 1995—2003, Cantwell & Chen, N.Y.C., 1988, Kimmelman, Sexter, Warmflash & Leitner, N.Y.C., 1990-91, Krasner & Chen, N.Y.C., 1992-94; pvt. practice, 2003—. Bd. dirs. United Orient Bank, N.Y.C., 1982-92, MFY Legal Svcs., Inc., 1993-96; mem. N.Y. State Banking Bd., 1992—. Pres. bd. trustees Union Ch. of Pocantico Hills, 2000—. Mem. ABA, N.Y. State Bar Assn. (mem. banking law com.), N.Y. County Lawyers Assn. (mem. banking law com.), Asian-Am. Bar Assn. of N.Y., Chinese C. of C. (legal adviser 1982—). Office: 641 Lexington Ave Fl 20 New York NY 10022-4503

CHEN, XIA, mathematician, educator; s. Dayong Chen and Yongjing Dling; m. Lin Wang, July 20, 1962; children: Amy Lynn, Roger. PhD, Case Western Res. U., 1997. Vis. asst. prof. Northwestern U., Evanston, Ill., 1998—99, U. of Utah, Salt Lake City, 1999—2000; asst. prof. U. of Tenn., Knoxville, Tenn., 2000—. Reviewer Am. Math. Soc., RI, 1995—. Contbr. articles to profl. jours. Grantee, NSF, 2001—. Mem.: Inst. of Math. Stats. Personal E-mail: xchen@math.utk.edu.

CHEN, YEN-CHU, physicist; arrived in US, 1990; s. Fai-Fan Chen and Ging-Ling Liao; m. Jennifer C. Chung, Mar. 21, 1962; 1 child, Rachel. M in physics, Nat. Cheng Kung U., 1984, D in physics, 1988; PhD, Nat. Cheng Kung U., Tainan, Taiwan, 1994. Postdoctoral staff Inst. Physics, Academia Sinica, Taipei, Taiwan, 1994—2001; vis. expert Nat. Sci. Coun., Taipei, 2001—; tching. asst. Nat. Cheng Kung U., 1987—88; rsch. asst. Inst. of Physics, Acad. Sinica, 1989—94. Co-leader CDF prodn. farm group The CDF Expt. at the Fermi Nat. Accelerator Lab., Batavia, Ill., 1998—. Vol., co-leader vol. tng. group Tzuchi Found., Midwest Region, USA, Chgo., 1998—2003. Buddhist. Achievements include development of The Data Acquisition System of the HyperCP experiment at the Fermilab; The CDF production farm computing system at the Fermilab.

CHEN, YENN-KUNN OLIVER, mathematician, educator; b. Taichung, Taiwan, Jan. 20, 1947; s. Gen-Shine and Lai Yuan Chen; m. Celia Shew-Fang Chen, Feb. 26, 1947; children: Ruth, Reuben, Raymond. PhD, U. of Wash., Seattle, Washington, 1983; MS, Tsing Hua U., Sinchu, Taiwan, 1973; BS, Taiwan Normal U., Taipei, Taiwan, 1969. Math. educator Mont. State U. at Billings, Billings, Mont., 1983—. U. of Wash., Seattle, Wash., 1983, Chung Yuan U., Chung Li, Taiwan, 1973—75, Taichung Normal Coll., Taichung, Taiwan, 1969—70. Author: (book) Advanced Console Application Oriented Java Programs with Cojava, Console Application Oriented Java Programs with Cojava. Second lt. Marine Corps, 1970—71, Pindon, Taiwan. Office: Montana State University at Billings 1500 University Drive Billings MT 59101 Office Fax: 406-657-2829. E-mail: oychen@msbillings.edu.

CHEN, YI-LENG, meteorologist, educator; b. Tien-Chung, Taiwan, Aug. 7, 1950; arrived in U.S., 1973, naturalized; s. Yi-Hui and Jin-Chun Chen; m. Jane-Shen Lee, Jan. 9, 1958; children: Theresa, Esther, Janice. PhD, U. of Ill., Champaign-Urbana, 1980. Scientist I Nat. Ctr. for Atmospheric Rsch., Boulder, Colo., 1980—83; asst. prof. U. Hawaii, Honolulu, 1984—90; assoc. prof. U. Hawaii, Honolulu, 1990—96, prof., 1996—. Vis. prof. Nat. Ctrl. U., Chungli, Taiwan, 2000. Contbr. articles over 40 to profl. sci. jours. Grantee numerous rsch. grants, 11 from NSF alone with seven other Grantors. Mem.: Am. Meteorol. Soc. Home: 1822 Hunnewell St Honolulu HI 96822 Office: Dept Meteorol Univ Hawaii 2525 Correa Road Honolulu HI 96822 Home Fax: 808-944-9521; Office Fax: 808-956-2877. Personal E-mail: cheny006@hawaii.rr.com. Business E-Mail: yileng@hawaii.edu.

CHEN, YU, acupuncturist, Chinese herbologist; b. Beijing, Sept. 10, 1942; arrived in U.S., 1985; d. Hai Chen and Xiu (Wang) C.; m. Paul L. Munson, Feb. 27, 1987; 1 child by previous marriage: Ming An. MD, Capital Med. Coll., Beijing, 1965; D Traditional Chinese Medicine, Chinese Traditional Med. Sch., Beijing, 1977; MS, Chinese Acad. Med. Sci., Beijing, 1981. Diplomate in acupuncture Nat. Commn. Cert. Acupuncture; cert. Chinese herbologist; lic. acupuncturist, Md. Physician Govt. China, Ching Yang, Gan Su, 1968-73; resident physician dept. ob-gyn. Worker's Hosp., Yen Shan Oil Factory, Beijing, 1974-78; attending physician dept. genetics Nat. Rsch. Inst. Family Planning, Beijing, 1982-83; WHO postdoctoral fellow Karolinska Inst., Stockholm, 1983-85; postdoctoral fellow dept. physiology U. Tex., Houston, 1985-87; postdoctoral fellow dept. pharmacology U. N.C., Chapel Hill, 1987-90; pvt. practice acupuncture and herbology Cmty. Wholistic Health Ctr., Carrboro, N.C., 1989-93; pvt. practice acupuncture, Chinese herbology, magnet therapy Pikesville and Parkville, Md., 1993—. Contbr. articles to profl. jours.; patentee in field; inventor of simple and effective way to treat panic attack by acupuncture and tiny hammer, ear magnet therapy to treat diabetes mellitus and control appetite, scalp magnet therapy to treat attention deficit disorder, herbal suppository for treatment of vaginal yeast infection, herbal treatment of AIDS meningitis. Recipient Best Essay award 1st Internat. Conf. Micro-Acupuncture Therapy, San Francisco, 1995. Democrat. Lutheran. Avocations: painting, photography, travel, classical music, gardening. Office: Beijing Acupuncture Chinese Herb & Magnetic Ctr 1401 Reisterstown Rd Baltimore MD 21208-6502

CHEN, YUDONG, engineer, researcher; b. Hangzhou, Zhejiang, People's Republic of China, Jan. 26, 1960; came to U.S., 1985; s. Weiniu and Zhiru (Wu) C.; m. Charlene X. Chen, Sept. 19, 1991; children: Edward J., Kevin J. BSME, Zhejiang Inst. Tech., Hangzhou, 1982; MSChemE, SUNY, Buffalo, 1987, PhDChemE, 1991. Postdoctoral fellow SUNY, Buffalo, 1991-92; rsch. scientist Arbor Rsch. Corp., Ann Arbor, Mich., 1992-95; engr. The BOC Group Tech. Ctr., Murray Hill, N.J., 1995—. Cons. PRAXAIR Co., Buffalo, 1987-89. Contbr. more than 20 articles to profl. jours.; patentee in field. Mem. AIChE (com. adsorption and ion exch. 1990—), Am. Chem. Soc. Home: 65 Shaffer Rd Bridgewater NJ 08807-5605 Office: The BOC Group Tech Ctr 100 Mountain Ave New Providence NJ 07974-2069 E-mail: yudong.chen@us.gtc.boc.com.

CHEN, ZHANGXIN JOHN, mathematics educator; b. Boying, Jiangxi, China, Oct. 15, 1962; arrived in U.S., 1986; s. Furong Chen and Hao-e Fang; m. Aijie Li, Jan. 5, 1986; children: Christina C., Paul Z., William L. BS, U. Jiangxi, Nanchang, 1983; MS, Xi'an (Shaanxi) Jiaotong U., 1985; PhD in Math., Purdue U., 1991. Asst. prof. Xi'an Jiaotong U., 1985-86; rsch. assoc. U. Minn., Mpls., 1991-93; vis. asst. prof. Tex. A&M U., College Station, 1993-95; asst. prof. So. Meth. U., Dallas, 1995-98, assoc. prof., 1999—2001, prof., 2001—. Cons. Rush Presbyn. St. Luke's Med. Ctr., Chgo., 1994-95; reviewer Math. Revs., Providence, 1994—. Contbr. articles to profl. jours. Recipient Sigma Xi Outstanding Rsch. award, 1999; grantee NSF, 1996—; univ. fellow Jiangxi U., 1981, 82; David Ross fellow Purdue U., West Lafayette, Ind., 1989, 90. Mem. Am. Math. Soc., Soc. for Indsl. and Applied Math., N.Y. Acad. Scis. Avocation: playing sports. Office: So Meth Univ Dept Math PO Box 750156 Dallas TX 75275-0156 E-mail: zchen@mail.smu.edu.

CHEN, ZHAOQING, electronics engineer; b. Nanchang, China, Jan. 18, 1956; s. Yuxiao and Yunkun (Ao) C.; m. Ying Hua; children: Xu, Wynter. BS, Jiangxi U., Nanchang, 1982; M in engring., Tsinghua U., Beijing, China, 1985; PhD, Tsinghua U., Beijing, 1989. Instr. Tsinghua Uv., 1989-91; assoc. prof. Tsinghua U., 1992-94; vis. scholar Univ Calif., Berkeley, 1991-92; assoc. prof. Tsinghua U., 1992-94; vis. scholar SUNY, Binghamton, 1994-97; sr. staff engr. Motorola, Austin, Tex., 1997-98; sr. engr. IBM, Poughkeepsie, N.Y., 1999—. Co-author: Cad of Microwave Circuits, 1988, Application Tech. for Microwave CAD, 1996; inventor in field. Recipient Outstanding Paper award, Chinese Inst. Electronics, 1986, Advanced Sci. and Tech. award Chinese State Coun., 1988. Mem. IEEE, Internat. Microelectronics and Packaging Soc. Office: IBM P371 2455 South Rd # P371 Poughkeepsie NY 12601-5463 E-mail: zhaoqing@us.ibm.com.

CHEN, ZHI, electrical engineering educator; b. Dazu, Chongqing, China; s. Jianguo Chen and Guoshu Huang; m. Chaoyuan Liu, Sept. 27, 1988; 1 child, Annie. BSEE, U. Electronic Sci. and Tech., Chengdu, Sichuan, China, 1984, MSEE, 1987; PhD in Elec. Engring., U. Ill., 1999. Lectr., asst. prof. U. Electronic Sci. and Tech., 1987-92; asst. prof. U. Ky., Lexington, 1999—. Mem. tech. staff Lucent Techs., Orlando, Fla., summer 1998. Contbr. numerous articles to profl. jours.; patentee in field. Recipient Nat. award for invention Ministry of Sci. and Tech., China, 1995, Career award NSF, 2001; NSF grantee, 2000—. Mem. IEEE (sr. mem., Com. Prize Paper award 1992). Home: 4604 Hobbs Way Lexington KY 40515 Office: U Ky 453 Anderson Hall Lexington KY 40506 Fax: (859) 257-3092. E-mail: zhichen@engr.uky.edu.

CHEN, ZHIKANG (KEN CHEN), remote sensing scientist; b. Tianjin, People's Republic of China, Apr. 14, 1960; came to U.S., 1989; s. Guowu and Yunjuan (Gao) C.; m. Lin Feng, Mar. 26, 1989; 1 child, Eileen. BS, Peking U., 1982, MS, 1985; PhD, U. Nev., 1995. Grad. rsch. asst. Peking U., 1982-85; lectr. Tianjin U., 1985-89; grad. rsch. asst. U. Calif., San Diego, 1989-90; temp. technician, grad. rsch. asst. Desert Rsch. Inst. U. Nev., Reno, 1991-94; sr. scientist Comml. Remote Sensing Program Lockheed Martin Stennis Ops., Stennis Space Ctr., Miss., 1994-98; sr. geographer South Fla. Water Mgmt. Dist., West Palm Beach, 1998—2001; sr. supr. profl. S. Fla. Water Mgmt. Dist., West Palm Beach, 2001—. Reviewer New Millenium program earth observing-1 Mission proposals NASA, 1999, SBIR proposals, 1996, 97, USDA proposals, 2001, 2002, 2003; reviewer articles Internat. Jour. Remote Sensing, PE&RS, Remote Sensing of Environ. Author: (with others) Remote Sensing Change Detection: Environmental Monitoring Methods and Applications, 1998; contbr. Dictionary of Remote Sensing, 1990; contbr. articles to profl. jours. Recipient numerous awards. Mem. Am. Geophys. Union, Am. Soc. Photogrammetry and Remote Sensing, IEEE Geosci. and Remote Sensing Soc. Avocations: tennis, swimming. Office: South Fla Water Mgmt Dist Eviron Monitoring and Assessment Dept 3301 Gun Club Rd West Palm Beach FL 33406-3007

CHENAL, THOMAS KEVIN, lawyer; b. Cin., Nov. 9, 1953; s. Robert C. and Marion K. Chenal; children: Robert, Cristina, Grace. Cert. d'honneur, U. Catholique de l'Ouest, Angers, France, 1974; BA cum laude, U. Notre Dame, 1976; JD, U. Ariz., 1979. Bar: Ariz. 1979, U.S. Dist. Ct. Ariz. 1979, U.S. Ct. Appeals (9th cir.) 1979. Ptnr. Mohr, Hackett, Pederson, Blakley & Randolph, P.C., Phoenix, 1979—; town atty. City of Carefree, Ariz., 2001—. Editor U. Ariz. Law Rev. Councilman Carefree (Ariz.) Town Coun., 1996-99. Mem. ABA (bus. law, trial practice internat. sect.), Ariz. State Bar Assn. (bankruptcy sect.,

chair internat. sect. 1999-2000), Ariz. Assn. Def. Counsel, Ariz. Trial Lawyers Assn. Avocations: private piloting, travel. Office: Mohr Hackett et al 2800 N Central Ave Ste 1100 Phoenix AZ 85004-1043 E-mail: tchenal@mhplaw.com.

CHENAULT, KENNETH IRVINE, financial services company executive; b. N.Y.C., June 2, 1951; s. Hortenius and Anne N. (Quick) Ch.; m. Kathryn Cassell, Aug. 20, 1977; children: Kenneth I. Jr., Kevin A. BA, Bowdoin Coll., 1973; JD, Harvard U., 1976; PhD (hon.), Morgan State U., 1990, Stony Brook U., 1996, Adelphi U., 1995, Bowdoin Coll., 1996, Xavier U., 1997, S.C. State U., 1997, Howard U., 1998, U. Notre Dame, 1998; LLD, Iona Coll., 1996. Bar: Mass. 1981. Assoc. Rogers & Wells, N.Y.C., 1977-79; cons. Bain & Co., Boston, 1979-81; dir. strategic planning Am. Express Co., N.Y.C., 1981-83; from v.p. to sr. v.p. Am. Express Travel Related Svcs. Co., Inc., N.Y.C., 1983-96, exec. v.p. platinum card/gold, 1986-88, exec. v.p. personal card divsn., 1988-89, pres. consumer card and fin. svcs. group, 1990-93, pres. U.S.A., 1993-95; vice-chmn. Am. Express Co., N.Y.C., 1995-97, pres., COO, 1997-2000, chmn., CEO, 2001—. Bd. dirs. IBM, Am. Express Co., NYU Hosp.'s Ctr./NYU Sch. Medicine. Dean's adv. bd. Harvard Law Sch.; mem. Coun. Fgn. Rels., N.Y.C., 1988. Mem. ABA. Congregationalist. Office: Am Express Co Am Express Tower World Fin Ctr 200 Vesey St New York NY 10285-5104

CHENEVERT, DONALD JAMES, JR., lawyer; b. New Orleans, June 8, 1967; s. Donald James Sr. and Elly Nae Chenevert; m. Elizabeth Boyd, June 1, 1991; children: Donald James III, Sarah Elizabeth. BA in History, Miss. Coll., 1989; JD, Emory U., 1993. Bar: Ga. 1993, Ill. 2000, U.S. Dist. Ct. (no. dist.) Ga. 1993, U.S. Dist. Ct. (so. dist.) Ga. 1996, U.S. Dist. Ct. (ctrl. dist.) Ill. 2001, U.S. Ct. Appeals (11th cir.) 1996. Sr. assoc. Lord, Bissell & Brook, Atlanta, 1993-2000; sr. litigation atty. Caterpillar Inc., Peoria, Ill., 2000—. Mem. Emory Law Alumni Coun., Atlanta; chair employers' duties and problems com. State Bar Ga., Atlanta, 1995-97. Coun. mem. Young Law Alumni Coun. Emory U., Atlanta, 1994-96; chair Commerce Soc. of the Commerce Club, Atlanta, 1995-97. Mem. Miss. Coll. Alumni Assn.-Ga. (pres. 1993-2000), Miss. Coll. Nat. Alumni Assn. (bd. dirs. 1995-2000). Avocations: backpacking, reading. Office: Caterpillar Inc 100 NE Adams St Peoria IL 61629-7310 Fax: 309-675-6620.

CHENEY, ANNA MARIE JANGULA, retired medical-surgical nurse; b. Wishek, N.D., Nov. 27, 1935; d. Jacob Jangula and Eva Wald; m. Edwin J. Cheney, Feb. 6, 1965; children: Alan, Deborah, Darrell. Diploma, Sisters of St. Joseph Sch. Nursing, Grand Forks, N.D., 1957; BSN, St. Louis U., 1960; MSN, UCLA, 1965. Oper. rm. instr. Sisters of St. Joseph, Grand Forks, 1957-58; staff nurse Cardinal Glennon Meml. Hosp., St. Louis, 1958-60, VA Med. Ctr., St. Louis and L.A., 1960-62, head nurse West L.A., 1963-64; staff nurse UCLA Med. Ctr., 1964-65; head nurse Meml. Hosp., Culver City and L.A., 1965-66; staff nurse West Pk. Hosp., Canoga Park, Calif., 1980-84, VA Med. Ctr., Sepulveda, Calif., 1984-89, clin. nurse specialist med./surg., 1989—94, clin. nurse specialist ambulatory care, 1994; charge nurse ambulatory care West L.A. Med. Ctr., Calif., 1996—97, ret., 1997. Instr. CPR Am. Heart Assn., L.A., 1991-94; facilitator stop smoking Am. Cancer Soc., L.A., 1991—, instr. breast self exams, 1991—. Contbr. articles to profl. jours. Vol. mem. spkr. bur. Am. Cancer Soc., 1997—. Named Outstanding Pub. Spkr., Am. Cancer Soc., 1993; recipient Outstanding Spkrs. award, 1998, Project Team Leadership award, 1999, 1st place age group, Am. Heart Assn. 5K Run, 1996, 1998; grantee, UCLA, 1963—64. Mem. Toastmaster Internat. (v.p. edn. 1991-92, pres. 1992-93, Cert. of Appreciation 1992, competent toastmaster, Toastmaster Leadership Excellence award 1995, Bronze award 1998). Democrat. Roman Catholic. Avocations: horticulture, singing, tennis, jogging. Home: 23741 Highlander Rd West Hills CA 91307-1825

CHENEY, BRIGHAM VERNON, physical chemist, consultant, retired physical chemist; b. Salt Lake City, June 11, 1936; s. Silas Lavell and Klara (Young) C.; m. Marsali McAllister, Aug. 20, 1964; children: Jill, Mark Vernon, Heather, Karin, Brigham McAllister, John David. BA, U. Utah, 1961, PhD, 1966. Rsch. asst. U. Utah, 1964-66; rsch. scientist Upjohn Co., Kalamazoo, 1966-71, scientist, 1971-75, sr. rsch. scientist, 1975-98; cons. Vis. scientist Oxford (Eng.) U., 1986-87. Contbr. articles to profl. jours. Missionary LDS Ch., Germany, 1956-59, high councilor, Lansing, Mich., 1969-75, Grand Rapids, Mich., 1975-78, bishop, Kalamazoo, 1978-84; leader Boy Scouts Am., 1972-98. With U.S. Army NG, 1959-67. Mem. Am. Chem. Soc., Sigma Xi, Phi Eta Sigma, Sigma Pi Sigma. Home: 1765 N 2000 W Provo UT 84604-1128 E-mail: bvcheney@juno.com.

CHENEY, DANIEL LAVERN, retired magazine publisher; b. Vernon, N.Y., May 26, 1928; s. Luke Lavern and Estella Mae (Clinch) C.; m. Eleanora Louise Stevenson, Aug. 8, 1959; stepchildren: Patricia Walter, Nancy Fulcher Shannon, Jon Dinsmore (dec.). AB, Colgate U., 1950. Cost acctg. clk. Gen. Electric Co., Auburn, N.Y., 1955-58; mng. editor, cons. Smith, Kline & French, Phila., 1958-70; founder, pres. Nursing mag.; co-owner Springhouse Corp., Jenkintown, Pa., 1970—; founder, pres. Skillbooks, 1977—; founder, pub. Photobooks.; retired, 1992. Bd. dirs. Meth. Hosp., Phila., 1992—, Robins' Nest, Woodbury, N.J., 1995—, Health Link, 2001--, Lamb Found., 2001--; founder, pres. Danellie Found., 1990; mem. adminstrv. coun. Haddonfield (N.J.) United Meth. Ch., 1993, 99—. Methodist. Home: 5 Snapdragon Ln Marlton NJ 08053-4421

CHENEY, DAVID WARREN, science and technology policy analyst, executive; b. La Jolla, Calif., Jan. 27, 1958; s. Elliott Ward C. and Elizabeth Jean (Helsley) Root; m. Alexandra S. Fairfield, Dec. 27, 1990; children: Alexander Ward, Austin Elizabeth. BS in Geology-Biology, Brown U., 1979; MS in Tech. and Policy, MIT, 1983. Engr. Core Labs. Internat., Inc., Dallas, 1979-81; analyst sci. and tech. Congl. Rsch. Svc. Libr. of Congress, Washington, 1983-89; sr. assoc. Coun. on Competitiveness, Washington, 1989-94; staff dir. tech. subcoun. Competitiveness Policy Coun., Washington, 1992-94; assoc. dep. undersec. U.S. DOE, Washington, 1994-97; assoc. dir. sci. and tech. policy program SRI Internat., Arlington, Va., 1998—; v.p. Internet Policy Inst., Washington, 1999-2000. Adj. lectr. George Mason U., Fairfax, Va., 1991; vis. rschr. Saitama U., Urawa, Japan, 1987, 88; exec. dir. Optoelectronics Industry Devel. Assn., 1993-94; cons. U.S. Dept. Commerce, other orgns., 1998—. Witness hearing Com. on Sci. U.S. Congress, Washington, 1989, 91. Mem. AAAS. Achievements include contributions to the Clinton administration's technology policy. Office: SRI Internat 1100 Wilson Blvd Ste 2800 Arlington VA 22209-3915 E-mail: Dcheney@compuserve.com.

CHENEY, ELEANORA LOUISE, retired secondary education educator; b. Seneca Falls, N.Y., June 3, 1923; d. Guy Darrell and Alice Augusta (McCoy) Stevenson; m. John C. Dinsmore, Jan. 13, 1941 (div. 1953); children: Patricia Walter, Nancy Shannon, Jon Dinsmore (dec.); m. Daniel Lavern Cheney, Aug. 8, 1959. BA, Rutgers U., 1966; MA, U. Glassboro, 1971. Account clk. GE, Auburn, N.Y., 1953-58; supr. accounts payable Sylvania Electric, Camillus, N.Y., 1958-60; cost acctg. clk. RCA, Cherry Hill, N.J., 1960-64; honors English tchr. Lenape Regional High Sch., Medford, N.J., 1966-74; guidance counselor Shawnee High Sch., 1974-82; owner Another World of Travel, Marlton, N.J., 1984-86; co-founder, trustee, sec. Danellie Found., 1991—. Part-time travel agt., 1986—; notary pub., 1983 . Counselor Contact Ministries, Moorestown, N.J., 1976—; mem. fin. com., nominating com. Haddonfield (N.J.) United Meth. Ch., 1987-92, supr. ch. sch., 1980-82; bd. dirs. Fellowship House, Camden, N.J., 1994—, Robins' Nest, Glassboro, N.J., 1995—; mem. adminstrv. coun. Haddonfield (N.J.) United Meth. Ch., 1996-99, 2003—, leader small group, 1990—, mem. adminstrv. coun., 2003—; established Jon W. Dinsmore Meml. Math. Scholarship Cherry Hill West, NJ, 1997—. Named to Nat. Woman's Hall of Fame, 1994. Mem. AAUW. Republican. Methodist. Avocations: reading, knitting, gardening. Home: 5 Snapdragon Ln Marlton NJ 08053-4421

CHENEY, GLENN ALAN, writer, educator; b. Melrose, Mass., Sept. 6, 1951; s. Theodore Albert and Dorothy (Bates) C.; m. Solange Aurora Cavalcante, Apr. 26, 1948; 1 child, Ian Alan. BA in Philosophy, Fairfield U., 1974, MA in Communication, grad. cert. in profl. writing, Fairfield U., 1982; MA in English, Universidade Federal de Minas Gerais, 1990; MFA, Vermont Coll., 1991. Writing cons. Fairfield (Conn.) U., 1980-82, adj. prof., 1988-94, Conn. Coll., 1994—; freelance corp. writer Conn. and N.Y., 1980-84; account exec. Grey Advt., Inc., N.Y.C., 1982-85; pres. English Communications Ltd., Belo Horizonte, Brazil, 1984-98; liaison Fedn. Industries of the State of Minas Gerais, Brazil, 1998—. Instr. Inst. for Children's Lit., Redding Ridge, Conn., 1988-91; mktg. cons. Strategies, Stratford, Conn., 1988—; ptnr. Cheney & Assocs.; adj. prof. Albertus Magnus Coll., 1991. Author: El Salvador: Country in Crisis, 1982, rev. edit., 1990, Television in American Society, 1983, Mohandas Ghandi, 1983, The Amazon, 1984, Mineral Resources, 1984, Revolution in Central America, 1985, Responsibility, 1985, Mariana Scouts in the Valley of Spirits, 1986, Drugs, Teens and Recovery, 1993, Chernobyl: The Ongoing Story of the World's Deadliest Nuclear Disaster, 1993, Teens with Physical Disabilities, 1995, Acts of Ineffable Love, Collected Stories, 1995, Journey to Chernobyl: Encounters in a Radioactive Zone, 1995, They Never Know the Victims of Nuclear Testing, 1996, Nuclear Proliferation: Problems and Possibilities, 1998; contbr. chpts. to books, short stories to lit. mags. and articles to profl. acctg. and bus. jours.; host Nuclear Safety Issues, 1995-96; host, prodr. Sprague Today!, 1997—; announcer Music of Brazil, WCNI-FM, 2002— Bd. dirs. Suzuki Music Sch., New Haven, 1988-94; chmn. Sprague Pub. Libr., 1995—; founder Citizen's Regulatory Commn., 1995—; activist Green Party Conn., 1996—; emergency med. technician, Baltimore Fire Dept., 2001—; founder Southeast Conn. Peace Network. Recipient honorable mention Writers Digest Short Story, Poetry and Articles Contests, 1991, 2d pl. winner arts and entertainment reporting New England Press Assn. Avocations: philosophy, gardening, travel, photography, beekeeping. Home: PO Box 284 Hanover CT 06350-0284 E-mail: cheney@99main.com.

CHENEY, JAMES ADDISON, civil engineering educator; b. Los Angeles, Feb. 2, 1927; s. Burton Howard and Esther Jesse (Dumaresq) C.; m. Frankyee Jane Jackson, June, 23, 1951 (dec. Oct. 1966); children: John Addison, Linanne Dando, Matthew Jackson, Sarah Allan, Sharla Ryan, Jennifer Dumaresq; m. Barbara Louise Chadwick, June 1967 (div. Feb. 1987); children: Michael Chadwick, David Grant; m. Elaine Disbrow Barratt, Apr. 1988. BS, UCLA, 1951, MS, 1953; PhD, Stanford U., 1963. Registered profl. civil engr., Calif. Assoc. engr. L.T. Evans, Foundation Engrs., Los Angeles, 1953-55; staff engr. Lockheed Missile and Space Co., Sunnyvale, Calif., 1955-65; prof. civil engring. U. Calif., Davis, 1962-91, prof. emeritus civil engring., 1991—. Contbr. over 50 articles to scientific jours. Served with USN, 1944-45. Recipient Silver Beaver award, Golden Empire coun. Boy Scouts Am., 2002. Fellow ASCE; mem. Alpha Sigma Phi. Republican. Episcopalian. Home: 418 Anza Ave Davis CA 95616-0404 Office: U Calif Dept Civil Engring Davis CA 95616 E-mail: jacheney@ucdavis.edu.

CHENEY, LYNNE V. humanities educator, writer; b. Casper, Wyo., Aug. 14, 1941; d. Wayne and Edna (Lybyer) Vincent; m. Richard Bruce Cheney, Aug. 29, 1964; children: Elizabeth, Mary. BA, Colo. Coll., 1963; MA, U. Colo., 1964; PhD, U. Wis., 1970. Freelance writer, 1970-83; lectr. George Washington U., Washington, 1972-77, U. Wyo., Casper, 1977-78; researcher, writer Md. Pub. Broadcasting, Owings Mills, 1982-83; sr. editor Washingtonian mag., Washington, 1983-86; chmn. NEH, Washington, 1986-93; W.J. Brady Jr. fellow Am. Enterprise Inst., Washington, 1993-95, sr. fellow, 1996—. Commr. U.S. Constitution Bicentennial Commn., Washington, 1985-87. Author: Executive Privilege, 1978, Sisters, 1981, Telling the Truth, 1995; (with others) Kings of the Hill, 1983, 96, The Body Politic, 1988; contbr. articles to profl. jours. Mem. Women's Forum Washington. Mem. Congl. Club, Phi Beta Kappa, Kappa Alpha Theta. Republican. Methodist. Office: Am Enterprise Inst 1150 17th St NW Ste 1100 Washington DC 20036-4603

CHENEY, RICHARD B. (DICK CHENEY), Vice President of the United States; b. Lincoln, Nebr., Jan. 30, 1941; s. Richard Hebert and Marjorie Lauraine (Dickey) C.; m. Lynne Anne Vincent, Aug. 29, 1964; children: Elizabeth, Mary Claire. BA, U. Wyo., 1965, MA, 1966. Deputy asst. to Pres. The White House, Washington, 1974—75, asst. to Pres., 1975-77; mem. 96th-100th Congresses from Wyo., Washington, 1977—89, chmn. republican house policy comm., 1981—88, house minority whip, 1988—89; sec. U.S Dept. Def., Washington, 1989-93; sr. fellow Am. Enterprise Inst., Washington, 1993-95; chmn., CEO, Halliburton Co., Dallas, 1995-2000; v.p. of U.S, The White House, Washington, 2001—. Recipient Presidential Medal of Freedom, The White House, 1991. Republican. Office: The White House 1600 Pennsylvania Ave NW Washington DC 20501*

CHENEY, RICHARD EUGENE, public relations executive, psychoanalyst; b. Pana, Ill., Aug. 30, 1921; s. Royal F. and Nelle E. (Henke) C.; m. Betty L. McCray, Oct. 17, 1943; children: R. Christopher, Elyn G. Cheney MacInnis; m. 2d, Virginia B. Burns, Jan. 23, 1966; children: Benjamin, Anne. AB, Knox Coll., Galesburg, Ill., 1943; MA, Columbia U., 1960; postgrad., Ctr. Modern Psychoa. Studies, 1995. Assoc. editor Tide Mag., 1953; dir. pub. relations Tri Continental Corp., 1953-55; asst. mgr. pub. relations dept. Mobil Corp., 1955-60; chmn. bd., emeritus chmn. Hill & Knowlton, Inc., N.Y.C., 1987-91, 91—, chmn. bd., 1987-91, chmn. emeritus, 1991-93. Bd. dirs. Chattem Inc., Chattanooga, Stoneridge, Inc., Warren, Ohio, Rowe Furniture, Salem, Va. Served to lt. (j.g.) USNR, 1943-47, PTO. Mem. Soc. for Modern Psychoanalysis (trustee), Edgewood Club (Tivoli, N.Y.), Century Assn. Home: 108 E 86th St New York NY 10028-1024 Office: 108 E 86th St, 14 N New York NY 10028 E-mail: dcheney212@juno.com.

CHENEY, THOMAS WARD, retired insurance company executive; b. Union, Nebr., Dec. 17, 1914; s. Gilbert Ward and Vernie (Barnum) C.; m. E. Margaret Phillippe, Oct. 15, 1938; children: Patricia Kay Cheney Keim, Thomas Charles. BS, U. Nebr., 1936; student, Life Ins. Mktg. Inst., U. Kans., 1950. With Modern Woodmen of Am., 1935-79, dir., asst. to pres., 1954-60, pres., 1960-79, also dir. Dir. 1st Nat. Bank of Quad Cities, mem. exec. com., 1974-87. Bd. dirs. Rock Island Community Chest, 1956-58, 65-66, YMCA, Rock Island, 1965-69; v.p. Blackhawk Indsl. Devel. Assn., Rock Island County, 1959; mem. bus. advisory com. Coll. Bus. U. Ill., 1969-81; bd. dirs. Augustana Coll., 1970-78, mem. exec. com., 1972-78, chmn. devel. com., 1972-78; bd. govs. Rock Island Found., 1967-76, Trinity Med. Found., 1994-99; trustee, mem. exec. com. Rock Island Franciscan Med. Center, 1971-78, chmn. bd. trustees, 1974-75; mem. lay advisory bd. St. Anthony's Hosp., Rock Island, 1965-72. Served to lt. col. USAAF, 1941-46, PTO. Decorated Legion of Merit.; Recipient Distinguished Service award U.S. Jaycees, 1940 Mem. Fraternal Ins. Counsellors Assn., Life Underwriters Assn., Gen. Agents and Mgrs. Conf., Nat. Fraternal Congress Am. (mem. exec. com. 1961-62, pres. 1967-68), Ill. Fraternal Congress, Ill. (dir. 1966-72), Ill. Fraternal Congress (vice chmn. 1971-72); Ill. C. of C. (bd. dirs. 1966-72, vice chmn. 1970-72), Rock Island C. of C. (pres. 1965), Delta Upsilon. Republican. Presbyterian (elder, trustee, deacon). Club: Rock Island Arsenal Golf (bd. govs. 1975-81, pres. 1979, exec. com.). Home: 3930 38th St Apt H Rock Island IL 61201-7091

CHENG, ALEXANDER HUNG-DARH, engineering educator, consultant; b. Taipei, Taiwan, May 25, 1952; came to U.S., 1976; s. Chia-hua and Yu-Chuen (Chwang) C.; m. Daisy T. Cheng, Nov. 23, 1979; children: Jacqueline, Julia. BS, Nat. Taiwan U., Taipei, 1974; MS, U. Mo., 1978; PhD, Cornell U., 1981. Asst. prof. Cornell U., Ithaca, 1981-82, Columbia U., N.Y.C., 1982-85; assoc. prof. U. Del., Newark, 1985-93, prof., 1993—2001; dept. chair, prof. U. Miss., Oxford, 2001—. Author: Multilayered Aquifer Systems, 2000; editor: Engineering Analysis with Boundary Elements, 1996, editor 9 books; editor-in-chief Progress in Water Resources Series, 1998—; assoc. editor Jour. Engring. Mech., 1998—; contbr. over 100 articles to profl. jours. Recipient Basic Rsch. award U.S. Nat. Com. Rock Mechanics NRC, 1994, 99, Eminent Scientist award WIT. Mem. ASCE (sec., exec. com. engring. mech. divsn., W.L. Huber Civil Engring. prize 1994), Am. Geophys. Union, Am. Inst. Hydrology (v.p. acad. affairs). Office: U Miss Dept Civil Engring University MS 38677 E-mail: acheng@olemiss.edu.

CHENG, ALEXANDER LIHDAR, information technology executive; b. Taichung, Taiwan, Aug. 1, 1956; came to US, 1980; s. Pei-Kao and Kuang-Kun (Shiong) C.; m. Wei-Hong Mao, Feb. 16, 1988; children: Alexander Raymond, Bernard King. BS, Nat. Taiwan U., 1978; MS, U. Ky., 1982; PhD, Poly. U., Bklyn., 1992. Rsch. asst. Taiwan Hydraulic Bur., Taichung, Taiwan, 1978; tchg. asst. U. Ky., Lexington, Ky., 1981-82; sci. programmer Megadata Corp., Bohemia, NY, 1982-83; sr. software engr. Siemens Data Switching, Inc., Hauppauge, NY, 1983-87; tech. staff NYNEX S&T, Inc., White Plains, NY, 1987-94; pres. C-cation, Inc., 1994—; pres., chmn. and CEO Zheng Std. Comm. Tech. Co., 1995—97; CEO Renaissance Tech. Co., 1999—2001; found. and pres. Natural Lighting Systems, Inc. Bd. dir. C&M 1st Svc.; adj. prof. dept. computer sci. Pace U., 1992—95; advisor to ministry of post and telecomm. devel program UN, China, 1993—95. V.p. Woodcrest Hts. Assn., White Plains, 1991—2000. Mem. IEEE, IEEE Computer Soc., Assn. Computing Machinery, Upsilon Pi Epsilon. Avocations: music, stereo, skiing, bicycling, travel.

CHENG, BAOLIAN, physicist; d. Tairan Cheng and Yuqing Wang; 3 children. PhD, U. Ill., 1993. Postdoctoral fellow U. Chgo.; physicist Los Alamos Nat. Lab., Los Alamos, N.Mex., 1994—. Invited spkr. in field. Contbr. articles to profl. jours. Mem.: N.Y. Acad. Scis., Am. Astron. Soc., The Am. Phys. Soc.

CHENG, CHE PING, cardiologist, researcher, educator; b. People's Republic of China, Jan. 24, 1950; came to U.S., 1982; d. Ji and Yu Zhi (Pan) C.; m. Ping Tan, Feb. 23, 1951; 1 child, Xiao Tan. MD, Nanjing (People's Republic of China) Railway Med. U., 1976; PhD, Wayne State U., 1986. Diplomate Am. Bd. Internal Medicine. Attending physician dept. cardiology First Hosp. of Harbin (People's Republic of China) Med. Sch., 1977-81; rsch. assoc. Harbin Cardiovascular Rsch. Inst., 1980-81; teaching asst. dept. pathology Wayne State U., Detroit, 1982-83, teaching asst. dept. physiology, 1983-86; postdoctoral fellow cardiology rsch. Bowman Gray Sch. Medicine, Winston-Salem, N.C., 1986-88, rsch. instr. medicine dept. internal medicine, 1989-91, asst. prof. medicine dept. internal medicine, 1991-95, assoc. prof. medicine dept. internal medicine, 1995—2001, assoc. physiology and pharmacology, 1991, mem. grad. faculty Ctr. Neurobiol. Investigation Drug Abuse, 1993—, prof. intermedicine dept. sect. on cardiology, 2001—. Lectr. in field. Author: Novel Pharmacological Interventions for Alcoholism, 1992, Diastolic Relaxation of the Heart: Modulation of Diastolic Dysfunction in the Intact Heart, 1994, Effect of Felodipine on Left Ventricular Performance in Conscious Dogs: Assessment by Left Ventricular Pressure-Volume Analysis, 1994, Left Ventricular Systolic and Diastolic Performance, 1995, Altered Ventricular and Myoyte Response to Antiotensic II in Pacing-induced Heart Failure, 1996, Response of Left Ventricular Filling to Exercise Before and After Heart Failure, 1996; contbr. articles to profl. jours. Established Investigator award Am. Heart Assn., 1997-2000. Travel grantee Internat. Soc. for Biomed. Rsch., Rsch. Soc. on Alcoholism, 1990, grantee Am. Heart Assn., 1988-94, 95-97, NIH, 1986-95, 2000—, Hassle Pharm., Sweden, 1991-94, travel grantee Nat. Inst. Alcohol Abuse and Alcoholism, 1994; recipient Exptl. Biology Losartan Travel award, 1996. Mem. Am. Heart Assn. (coun.), Am. Fedn. Clin. Rsch., Am. Physiol. Soc., Internat. Soc. Biomed. Rsch. on Alcoholism, Internat. Soc. for Heart Rsch. Avocations: swimming, music, reading, knitting, cooking. Home: 651 Dover Dr Winston Salem NC 27104-1529 Office: Wake Forest U Sch Medicine Cardiology Dept Medical Center Blvd Winston Salem NC 27157-0001 E-mail: ccheng@wfubmc.edu.

CHENG, CHU YUAN, economics educator; b. Kwangtung Province, China, Apr. 8, 1927; came to U.S., 1959, naturalized, 1964; s. Hung Shan and Shu Cheng (Yang) C.; m. Alice Hua Liang, Aug. 15, 1964; children: Anita tung I, Andrew Y.S. BA in Econs., Nat. Chengchi U., Nanking, China, 1947; MA, Georgetown U., 1962, PhD, 1964. Rsch. prof. Seton Hall U., 1960-64; vis. prof. George Washington U., Washington, 1963; sr. rsch. economist U. Mich., Ann Arbor, 1964-69; assoc. prof. Lawrence U., Appleton, Wis., 1970-71; assoc. prof. econs., chmn. Asian studies com. Ball State U., Muncie, Ind., 1971-73, prof. econs., 1974—. Cons. NSF, Washington, 1964—; rsch. mem. presdl. Coun. for Nat. Unification, Republic of China, 1992-98. Author: Scientific and Engineering Manpower in Communist China, 1966, The Machine-Building Industry in Communist China, 1971, China's Petroleum Industry: Output Growth and Export Potential, 1976, China's Economic Development: Growth and Structural Change, 1981, The Demand and Supply of Primary Energy in Mainland China, 1984, Taiwan as a Model for China's Modernization, 1986, Sun Yat-sen's Doctrine in Modern World, 1988, Taiwan Experience and China's Reconstruction, 1989, Behind the Tiananmen Massacre, Social, Political and Economic Ferment in China, 1990, Economic Development and Interaction between Two Sides of the Taiwan Straits, 1993, The Transformation of Social, Political and Economic Structure in China, 1994, China's Transition From A Planned to A Market Economy, 1994, Township-Village Enterprises: China's New Route to Industrialization, 1995, China's Economic Reform: Programs, Effects and Prospects, 1997, China's Economic Reform and Cross-Strait Economic Relations, 2000, Economies on the Two Sides of the Taiwan Straits: Reforms and Development, 1950-2000, 2002. Bd. dirs., pres. Dr. Sun Yat-sen Inst., Chgo., 1978—. Grantee NSF, 1960-64, Social Sci. Rsch. Coun., 1965-67, 74, Chiang ching-Kuo Found., 1996; recipient Outstanding Rsch. award Ball State U., 1976, Outstanding Educator in Econs., Ball State U., 1981-82. Mem. Am. Econ. Assn., Assn. Asian Studies, Assn. Comparative Econ. Studies, Am. Acad. Polit. and Social Sci., Assn. Chinese Social Scientists in N.Am. (bd. dirs., pres. 1994-96), Am. Assn. Chinese Studies (bd. dirs., pres. 1996-98), Chinese-Am. Soc. (pres. Washington 1989-92), Chinese Acad. and Profl. Assn. Mid-am. (pres. 1983-84), Ind. Acad. Social Sci., Omicron Delta Epsilon. Home: 1211 N Greenbriar Rd Muncie IN 47304-2934 Office: Ball State U Coll Bus Rm 123 Muncie IN 47306-0340 E-mail: ccheng@bsu.edu.

CHENG, CHUEN YAN, biochemist, educator; b. Hong Kong, June 18, 1954; came to the U.S., 1981, naturalized, 1993; s. C. Yin and Tak Ying (Ho) C.; m. Po Lee, Mar. 17, 1978; children; Yan Ho, Chin Ho. BS with honors, Chinese U., Hong Kong, 1978; PhD, U. Newcastle, Australia, 1982. Fellow Population Coun., N.Y.C., 1981-82, rsch. investigator, 1983-84, staff scientist, 1985-87, scientist, 1988-90, sr. scientist, 1991—; assoc. dir. Internat. Consortium on Male Contraception, N.Y.C., 1994-95, dir., 1996—. Asst. prof. Rockefeller U., N.Y.C., 1986-90; prof. U. Rome, 1990—; cons. Angelini Pharms., Inc., River Edge, N.J., 1985-91, Angelini Rsch. Inst., Rome, 1992-93, Fidia Pharms., Inc., Italy, 1997, Bioprogress Pharms., Rome, 2001—. Contbr. over 180 articles to profl. jours. Recipient Sea Horse award, Newcastle U., Australia, 1982. Mem. Am. Soc. Andrology (Best Sci. Paper award 1996), Endocrine Soc. (Richard E. Weitzman Meml. award 1988). Achievements include patents for abnormally glycosylated variants of alpha-2-macroglobulin and serum proteins used to detect autoimmune disease, monoclonal antibody specifically detects abnormal glycosylation site on alpha-1-antitrypsin used to detect autoimmune conditions, testicular protein that regulates androgen production for male fertility control; 3-substituted 1-benzyl-1H indazole derivatives as antifertility agents. Office: Population Coun 1230 York Ave New York NY 10021-6307 E-mail: ycheng@popcbr.rockefeller.edu. *Do what is right, not what is popular.*

CHENG, DAVID HONG, mechanical engineering educator; b. I-Shing, China, Apr. 19, 1920; came to U.S., 1945, naturalized, 1956; s. Tze Kuen (dec. Sept. 2002) and Tseng Sun (Sheng) C.; m. Lorraine Hui-Lan Yang, Sept. 4, 1949; children: Kenneth, Gloria. MS, U. Minn., 1947, PhD; William Richmond Peters, Jr. fellow, Columbia U., 1950; LHD (hon.), William Paterson U. N.J., 1997. Instr. Rutgers U., 1949-50; structural engr. Ammann & Whitney, N.Y.C., 1950-52; sr. engr. M.W. Kellogg Co., N.Y.C., 1952-55; lectr. CCNY, 1955, asst. prof. civil engring., 1955-58, assoc. prof., 1959-65, prof., 1966-86, dir. grad. studies and exec. officer Ph.D. programs in engring., 1977-78, dean engring., 1979-86. Cons. M.W. Kellogg Co., Inst. Def. Analyses, N.Y.C. Transp. Adminstrn., ASME; pres. Techtran Inc., 1986; dir., v.p. China-Am. Tech. Corp., 1995— Author: Nuclei of Strain in the Semi-infinite Solid, 1961, Analysis of Piping Flexibility and Components, 1973, On Lao Tzu, 2000, A New Interpretation of Lao Tzu's Thought (in Chinese), 2000. Trustee governing bd. William Paterson Coll. N.J., 1990-97, William Paterson U., 1997-99. Recipient 125th Anniversary medal Coll. City N.Y., 1973; Am. Soc. Engring. Edn.-NASA Faculty fellow, 1964-65; hon. rsch. fellow Harvard U., 1967; William Peterson Univ. Main Libr. renamed David and Lorraine Cheng Libr. Mem. ASCE, ASME, Chinese Inst. Engrs. (Achievement award 1984), Sigma Xi, Tau Beta Pi (Outstanding Tchr. award 1972), Chi Epsilon, Phi Tau Phi. Home: Fort Lee, NJ. Died Sept. 14, 2002.

CHENG, DAVID KEUN, engineering educator; b. Kiangsu, China, Jan. 10, 1918; came to U.S., 1943, naturalized, 1955; s. Han J. and Ying H.C.; m. Enid Kwok, Mar. 27, 1948; 1 child, Eugene. BS in Elec. Engring., Nat. Chiao Tung U., 1938; S.M., Harvard U., 1944, Sc.D., 1946; D.Engr. (hon.), Nat. Chiao Tung U., Taiwan, 1985; PhD (hon.), Xidian U., China, 1998. Electronics and project engr., rsch. labs. U.S. Air Force, Cambridge, Mass., 1946-48; asst. prof. elec. and computer engring. Syracuse U., N.Y., 1948-51, assoc. prof., 1951-55, prof., 1955—, Centennial prof., 1970—. Hon. prof. Beijing Univ. Posts and Telecomm., 1982—, N.W. Inst. Telecomm. Engring., 1982—, Shanghai Jiao Tong U., 1985—, China; exch. scientist NAS, Hungary, 1972, Yugoslavia, 1974, Poland and Romania, 1978; liaison scientist Office of Naval Rsch., London, 1975-76; disting. European lectr. IEEE, 1975-76; pres., chmn., bd. trustees Li Instn. Sci. & Tech., 1992-98; cons. IBM, GE, TRW. Author: Analysis of Linear

Systems, 1959, Field and Wave Electromagnetics, 1983, 2d edit., 1989, Fundamentals of Engineering Electromagnetics, 1993; cons. editor elec. sci. Addison-Wesley, 1961-78, elec. engring. monographs Intext Edn. Pubs., 1969-72; mem. editorial bd. Jour. Electromagnetic Waves and Applications, 1987—; mem. internat. adv. bd. book series on Progress in Electromagnetic Rsch., 1989—; contbr. numerous articles to profl. jours. Recipient Disting. Achievement award Chinese Inst. Engrs., 1962, Disting. Engr. award Li Inst. Sci. and Tech., 1979; Guggenheim fellow, 1960-61; Chancellor's citation, 1981. Fellow IEEE, AAAS, Inst. Elec. Engrs. (U.K.); mem. AAUP, Am. Soc. Engring. Edn., N.Y. Acad. Scis., Sigma Xi (7 Best Paper prizes), Eta Kappa Nu, Phi Tau Phi (Disting. Svc. award 1975). Home: 4620 N Park Ave Apt 104E Chevy Chase MD 20815-4550 E-mail: chengkeun@aol.com.

CHENG, DEPING, chemist, researcher; arrived in U.S., 2000; s. Zhengxin Cheng and Zhengjie Zhang; m. Jian Cheng, July 4, 1994; 1 child, Yucheng. BS, Hangzou U., 1985; PhD, Zhejiang U., Hangzhou, China, 1999. Assoc. prof. Zhejiang (China) U., Hangzhou, 1999—2000; rschr. fellow San Francisco (Calif.) State U., 2000; sr. rschr. U. of Okla., Norman, Okla., 2001—. Referee: Jour. Ion Exchange & Absorption, 1996—2000; contbr. articles to profl. jours. Recipient Second-Class Achievements award of Sci. and Tech. Improvement, Zhejiang Province Govt., 1992. Mem.: Am. Chem. Soc. (corr.; sr. rschr. 2001—). Achievements include research in synthesis of new coordination polymers. Office: University of Oklahoma 620 Parrington Oval Rm 208 Norman OK 73019 Office Fax: 405-325-6111.

CHENG, EDWARD HSIN-YI, gastroenterologist, researcher, educator; b. Tokyo, Feb. 28, 1955; came to U.S., 1959; s. Charles Kang and Shirley Sui-Lan (Lau) C.; m. Sue-Fong Leong, Sept. 19, 1981; 1 child, Wesley. BS, SUNY, Stony Brook, 1976; MD, NYU, 1980. Diplomate Am. Bd. Internal Medicine, Bd. Gastroenterology. Resident in medicine U. Calif., San Diego, 1980-83; gastroenterology fellow SUNY, Stony Brook, 1983-85; attending physician SUNY/VA Hosp. Northport, Stony Brook, 1985—; asst. prof. medicine SUNY, Stony Brook, 1989-99, assoc. prof. medicine, 1999—. Contbr. articles to profl. jours. Named Assoc. Investigator, VA Career Devel., 1983-85. Fellow ACP; mem. Am. Gastroent. Assn. Office: VA Med Ctr Northport 79 Middleville Rd Northport NY 11768-2200

CHENG, GRACE ZHENG-YING, music educator; arrived in U.S., 1982; d. Chang Cheng and Guan-Zhi Fang. B Music, Shanghai Conservatory Music, China, 1980; M Music, U. Nebr., 1985. Tchg. asst. Shanghai Conservatory Music, China, 1976—82, U. Nebr., Lincoln, 1983—85; piano tchr. Freehold (N.J.) Music Ctr., 1985—. Piano soloist Arts in the Aisles, Lincoln, Nebr., 1984, Cecilian Music Club, Monmouth County, NJ, 1986—92; pianist, NJ, 1985—. Recipient Laura R. Conover Pedagogy award Outstanding Tchg., Carnegie Hall, N.Y.C., 1998, 5th Yr. Tchr.'s award, Cecilian Music Club, 1997. Mem.: ASPCA, Nat. Guild Piano Tchrs. (piano adj. 1994—), N.J. Music Tchrs. Assn. (piano adj. 1998), Nat. Music Tchrs. Assn. (piano adj. 1993), Sierra Club. Avocations: internet, travel, photography, gardening. Home: 1 Swallow Ln Howell NJ 07731 Office: Freehold Music Ctr 3681 Unit 4 Rte 9 Freehold NJ 07728 Personal E-mail: gchennj@aol.com.

CHENG, HENG-JIE, physician scientist; b. Harbin, China, June 27, 1958; came to U.S., 1984; s. Ji Cheng and Yu-Zhi Pan; m. Tina Sun; 1 child, Daniel. MD, Harbin Med. U., 1983; PhD, Wayne State U., 1991. Rsch. assoc. Wayne State U. Sch. Medicine, Detroit, 1991-93, Wake Forest U. Sch. Medicine, Winston-Salem, N.C., 1997—. Recipient Nat. Rsch. award NIH, 1999-2000. Mem. Am. Heart Assn., Am. Physiol. Soc. Home: 101 Bradford Lake Count Lewisville NC 27023 Office: Wake Forest U Sch Medicine Medical Center Blvd Winston Salem NC 27157 E-mail: hcheng@wfubmc.edu.

CHENG, HERBERT SU-YUEN, mechanical engineering educator; b. Shanghai, Jan. 15, 1929; came to U.S., 1949; s. Chung-Mei and Jing-Ming (Xu) C.; m. Lily D. Hsiung, Apr. 11, 1953; children: Elaine, Elise, Edward, Earl. BSME, U. Mich., 1962; MSME, Ill. Inst. Tech., 1956; PhD, U. Pa., 1961. Jr. mech. engr. Internat. Harvester Co., Chgo., 1952-53; project engr. Machine Engring. co., Chgo., 1953-56; instr. Ill. Inst. Tech., Chgo., 1956-57, U. Pa., Phila., 1957-61; asst. prof. Syracuse (N.Y.) U., 1961-62; rsch. engr. Mech. Tech. Inc., Latham, N.Y., 1962-68; assoc. prof. Northwestern U., Evanston, Ill., 1968-74, prof., 1974—, Walter P. Murphy prof., 1987—, dir. Ctr. for Engring. Tribology, 1984-88, 92—. V.p. Gear Rsch. Inst., Naperville, Ill., 1985-90; cons. GM, Chrysler Corp., Deere Co., Nissan, E.T.C., 1970—. Contbr. articles to profl. jours. Deacon South Presbyn. Ch., Syracuse, 1961-62, 1st Presbyn. Ch. Schenectady, N.Y., 1962-68. Named a hon. prof. Nat. Zhejiang (People's Republic of China) U., 1985. Fellow ASME (hon., Mayo D. Hersey award 1990, D.F. Wilcock award 1999), Soc. Tribologists & Lubrication Engrs. (hon., Nat. award 1987, CAP Alfred Hunt award 1997); mem. NAE, Inst. Mech. Engrs. (U.K., Tribology gold medal 1992), Am. Gear Mfrs. Assn. (acad. mem.). Avocations: peking opera, tennis. Office: Northwestern U 219 Catalysis Bldg 2145 Sheridan Rd Evanston IL 60208-0834

CHENG, HSUEH CHING, physician; b. Taikang, Henan, Republic of China, Jan. 26, 1927; arrived in U.S., 1961; s. Chih-kuo and Noong (Hou) C.; m. Meio Chien, May 19, 1956; childen: Wen, Julie, Ken, Gene. MD, Nat. Def. Med. Ctr., Taipei, 1952. Diplomate Am. Bd. Internal Medicine, Am. Bd. Cardiovascular Diseases. Intern Buffalo (N.Y.) Gen. Hosp., 1961-62, St. Boniface (Can.) Gen. Hosp., 1962-63; resident physician in medicine Passavant Meml. Hosp., Chgo., 1963-65; fellow in cardiology Maine Med. Ctr., Portland, 1965-66; resident in physician in medicine Hamilton (Ont.) Civic Hosps., 1966-67; physician Mt. Sinai Hosp., Ste-Agathe-des-Monts, 1967-71; chief divsn. of medicine Augusta (Maine) State Hosp., 1971-72, chmn. dept. medicine, 1976-77; attending physician Kennebec Valley Med. Ctr., Augusta, 1972—. Maj. Chinese Nationalist Army, 1952-61. Fellow: ACP, Am. Coll. Cardiology, Royal Coll. Physicians and Surgeons Can.; mem.: AMA, Chinese Med. Assn. (Taiwan), Am. Soc. Internal Medicine, Maine Med. Assn. Office: 6 Middle St Augusta ME 04330-5211

CHENG, H(WEI) H(SIEN), soil scientist, agronomic and environmental science educator; b. Shanghai, Aug. 13, 1932; came to U.S., 1951, naturalized, 1961; s. Chi-Pao and Anna (Lan) C.; m. Jo Yuan, Dec. 15, 1962; children: Edwin, Antony. BA, Berea Coll., 1956; MS, U. Ill., 1958, PhD, 1961. Rsch. assoc. Iowa State U., Ames, 1962-64, asst. prof. agronomy, 1964-65; asst. prof. dept. agronomy and soils Wash. State U., Pullman, 1965-71, assoc. prof., 1971-77, prof., 1977-89, interim chmn., 1986-87, chmn. program environ. sci. and regional planning, 1977-79, 88-89, assoc. dean Grad. Sch., 1982-86; prof., head dept. soil, water, and climate U. Minn., St. Paul, 1989—2002, prof. emeritus, 2002—. Vis. scientist Juelich Nuclear Rsch. Ctr., Fed. Republic Germany, 1971-73, 79-80, Academia Sinica, Taipei, Republic of China, 1978, Fed. Agrl. Rsch. Ctr., Braunschweig, Fed. Republic Germany, 1980; mem. acad. adv. coun. Inst. Soil Sci., Academia Sinica, Nanjing, People's Republic China, 1987-2000; mem. adv. bd. Inst. Botany, Academia Sinica, Taipei, 1991-2000; mem. first sci. adv. bd. Dept. Ecology State of Wash., 1988-89; chief tech. advisor project on water-saving agr. for N.W. China, UNDP, 2001—; mem. Nat. Acad. Bd. Agr. and Natural Resources, 2003—. Editor: Pesticides in the Soil Environment: Processes, Impacts, and Modeling, 1990; assoc. editor Jour. Environ. Quality, 1983-89; mem. editorial bd. Bot. bull. Academia Sinica, 1988—, Jour. Environ. Sci. and Health, Part B-Pesticides, Food Contaminants, and Agrl. Wastes, 2000—; cons. editor: Pedosphere, 1991—; contbr. articles to profl. jours. Fulbright rsch. scholar State Agrl. U., Ghent, Belgium, 1963-64. Fellow AAAS, Am. Soc. Agronomy (bd. dirs. 1990-2000, exec. com. 1994-2000, pres. 1998-99), Soil Sci. Soc. Am. (divsn. chair 1985-86, bd. dirs. 1990-93, exec. com. 1994-97, pres. 1995-96, chmn. Smithsonian soils exhibit com. 2002—); mem. Am. Chem. Soc., Soc. Environ. Toxicology and Chemistry, Internat. Soc. Chem. Ecology, Internat. Humic Substances Soc., Coun. for Agrl. Sci. and Tech., Soil and Water Conservation Soc., Inst. Internat. Devel. in Edn. and Agrl. and Life Scis. (chair bd. dirs. 2000—), Sigma Xi (pres. U. Minn. chpt. 1995-96), Phi Kappa Phi, Gamma Sigma Delta (pres. Wash. State chpt. 1988-89, Award of Merit U. Minn. chpt. 2000). Methodist. Office: U Minn Dept Soil Water and Climate 1991 Upper Buford Cir Saint Paul MN 55108-0010 E-mail: hcheng@soils.umn.edu.

CHENG, JIAN-YU, mechanical engineer, researcher, application developer; b. Shanghai, Aug. 2, 1960; arrived in U.S., 1996; s. Dewu Cheng and Fan Shen; m. Xiaolin Lu; children: Jinliu, Bridget. BS, U. Sci. and Tech. of China, 1982; PhD, U. of Sci. and Tech. of China, 1989. Asst. prof. U. of Sci. and Tech. of China, Hefei, China, 1988—91; postdoctoral fellow Inst. de Mecanique de Grenoble, Grenoble, France, 1991; Alexander von Humboldt fellow U. of Saarlandes, Saarbruecken, Germany, 1991—93; rsch. staff U. of Leeds, Leeds, England, 1993; fellow St. Francis Xavier U., Antigonish, Canada, 1994—96; sr. mech. project engr. Smith Internat., Inc, Houston, 1996—97; fellow U. of Del., Newark, Del., 1997—99; sr. rsch. scientist Dynaflow, Inc, Jessup, Md., 1999—2002; software engr. onsite at NOAA/NESDIS/CLASS, Westover Cons., Inc., Silver Spring, Md., 2002—. Contbr. articles to profl. jours. (Natural Sci. prize of Academia Sinica, China, 1993). Fellow, Alexander von Humboldt Found., Germany, 1991—93, Natural Sci. & Engring. Rsch. Coun. of Can., 1994—96; grantee, NOAA, 2001. Mem.: ASME. Avocation: travel. Home: 7126 Natures Rd Columbia MD 21046 Office: NOAA/NESDIS/CLASS 5627 Allentown Rd Suitland MD 20746 Personal E-mail: cheng_jj@hotmail.com.

CHENG, JOSEPH YU-SHEK, political scientist, educator; b. Hong Kong, Nov. 11, 1949; s. Kan Yau and Suk Chun (Pang) C.; m. Grace Wong, Feb. 18, 1973; children: Felicia, Laurence. BSocial Sci., U. Hong Kong, 1972; BA, Victoria U., Wellington, New Zealand, 1973; PhD, Flinders U., South Australia, 1979. Office: City U Hong Kong Tat Chee Ave Kowloon Tong Kowloon Hong Kong Fax: 852-2788-7328. E-mail: rcccrc@cityu.edu.hk.

CHENG, KENNETH TAT-CHIU, pharmacy educator; b. Hong Kong, Feb. 24, 1954; came to U.S., 1972; s. Shiu Fun and Alice Shiu-Wing (Leung) C.; m. Ying Hsu, Aug. 11, 1984; children: Jonathan Yee-Hang, Hannah Yee-Shing. BS in Pharmacy, SUNY, Buffalo, 1977; PhD, Purdue U., 1985. Lic. pharmacist N.Y., Ind., Kans., N.Mex., S.C.; diplomate Am. Bd. Sci. in Nuclear Scis.; cert. expert nuclear medicine tng.; cert. nuclear pharmacist. Resident in hosp. pharmacy U. Kans. Med. Ctr., Kansas City, 1978-79; research/teaching asst. Purdue U., West Lafayette, Ind., 1980-84; research fellow Harvard U. Med. Sch., Boston, 1984-85; assoc. prof. U. N.Mex., Albuquerque, 1985-88; dir. nuclear pharmacy and radiology rsch., assoc. prof. Med. U. S.C., Charleston, 1988—, assoc. prof., 1992—, tenured assoc. prof., 1995—. Bd. dirs. Am. Bd. of Sci. in Nuclear Medicine, Nat. Assn. Nuclear Pharmacicies; chmn. APHA APPM, Nuclear Pharm. Practice, 1999-2000. Recipient Donald E. Francke award Drug Info. Assn., 1981, Glenn E. Jenkins Qualifying Research award Purdue U., 1984, Merit award APHA, 2003; named one of Outstanding Young Men of Am., 1986; David Ross fellow Purdue U., 1982-83, research fellow Am. Cancer Soc., 1984-85. Fellow Am. Pharm. Assn. (merit award 2003); mem. AAAS, Soc. Nuclear Medicine, Am. Soc. Hosp. Pharmacists, Am. Chem. Soc., Soc. Magnetic Resonance Imaging, Internat. Assn. Radiopharmacology, Health Physics Soc., Sigma Xi, Rho Chi, Eta Sigma Gamma. Avocations: music, fishing, swimming. Office: Med U SC Nuclear Pharmacy 171 Ashley Ave Charleston SC 29425-0001

CHENG, KUANG LU, chemist, educator; b. Yangchow, China, Sept. 14, 1915; came to U.S., 1947, naturalized, 1955; s. Fong Wu and Yi Ming (Chiang) C.; children: Meiling, Chiling, Hans Christian. PhD, U. Ill., 1951. Microchemist Comml. Solvents Corp., Terre Haute, Ind., 1952-53; instr. U. Conn., Storrs, 1953-55; engr. Westinghouse Electric Corp., Pitts., 1955-57; assoc. dir. research metals div. Kelsey Hayes Co., New Hartford, N.Y., 1957-59; mem. tech. staff RCA Labs., Princeton, N.J., 1959-66; prof. chemistry U. Mo., Kansas City, 1966-90, prof. emeritus, 1990—. Recipient Achievement award RCA, 1963, Benedetti-Pichler award Am. Microchem. Soc., 1989; N.T. Veatch award for Disting. rsch. and creative activity U. Mo., 1979; cert. of recognition U.S. Office of Naval Rsch., 1979, cert. of recognition Coll. Engring., Tex. A&M U., 1981; bd. trustees fellow U. Kansas City, 1984. Fellow AAAS, Chem. Soc. London; mem. Am. Chem. Soc., Electrochem. Soc., Soc. Applied Spectroscopy, Am. Inst. Physics. Home: 48 Steeplechase Dr Marlboro NJ 07746-1914 Office: U Mo Dept Chemistry Kansas City MO 64110 *Part of the art of research is to simplify complex phenomena and to elaborate the simple observations. Scientific research resembles gold prospecting — staying away from the spots crowded by people, exploring new territories.*

CHENG, LEO LING, biophysicist, researcher; b. Shanghai, Aug. 22, 1959; came to U.S., 1986; s. Jizhou Cheng and Yanzhuang Li; m. Emma Y. Wu, Dec. 15, 1985; 1 child, Andrew Y. MS in Chemistry, Nanjing (China) U., 1986; MA in Chemistry, Brandeis U., 1989, PhD in Chemistry, 1993. Postdoctoral fellow Harvard Med. Sch./Mass. Gen. Hosp., Boston, 1994-96, instr. pathology, 1997—2002, asst. prof. radiology and pathology, 2002—; postdoctoral fellow Harvard Med. Sch./Beth Israel Hosp., Boston, 1993-94. Vis. scientist MIT, Cambridge, 1993-95. Recipient 1st Ind. Rsch. Support and Transition award USPHS-NIH, 1999. Mem. Am. Assn. Cancer Rsch., Internat. Soc. Magnetic Resonance in Medicine. Home: 7 Village Way North Andover MA 01845 Office: Mass Gen Hosp/Harvard Med Sch Path Res CNY-7 149 13th St Charlestown MA 02129 E-mail: cheng@nmr.mgh.harvard.edu.

CHENG, LIANG, pathologist; b. Zhejiang, China, Nov. 9, 1965; came to U.S., 1988; MD, Beijing Med. U., 1987; MS, U. Ill., 1990. Diplomate Am. Bd. Pathology. Resident Case Western Res. U., Cleve., 1993-97, instr. pathology, 1994-97; fellow Mayo Clinic, Rochester, Minn., 1997-98; asst. prof. pathology Ind. U. Sch. Medicine, Indpls., 1998—, asst. prof. urology, 1999—. Spkr., cons. in field. Co-author: (chpts.) Therapeutics: Methods and Applications of Direct Gene Transfer, 1994, Immunotherapeutics Approaches for the Treatment of Cancer, 1995; editor: Essentials of Anatomic Pathology, 2002; contbr. articles to profl. jours. Recipient Resident Competition award Cleve. Soc. Pathologists, 1997, Young Investigator Travel award, 1998, Eminent Scientist of Yr. Gold award, Internat. Rsch. Promotino Coun., 2000; Am. Cancer Inst. grantee, Clarian Value Fund grantee, Biomed. Rsch. Fund grantee, Dept. Def. grantee; Molecular Biology Lab. fellow U. Ill., 1990. Mem. AAAS, Am. Assn. Cancer Rsch., Am. Urologic Assn., U.S. and Can. Acad. Pathology (Stowell-Orbison award 1996), Coll. Am. Pathologists (cert. recognition), Am. Soc. Clin. Pathologists (cert. recognition), Internat. Soc. Urologic Pathology, Assn. Molecular Pathology. Office: Ind U Sch Medicine UH3465 550 University Blvd Indianapolis IN 46202-5149

CHENG, LIANG, electrical engineer, researcher; BSEE with hons., Huazhong U. of Sci. and Tech., Wuhan, China, 1994; MSEE, Tsinghua U., Beijing, China, 1997; PhD, Rutgers U., New Brunswick, N.J., 2002. Grad. asst. Ctr. for Advanced Info. Processing, Rutgers U., Piscataway, NJ, 1998—2001; fellow Dept. of Elec. and Computer Engring., Rutgers U., Piscataway, NJ, 2001—02; founding scientist Signal Communication, Inc., Iselin, NJ, 2001—; dir. Lab. of Networking Group, Lehigh U., 2002—. Summer mem. of tech. staff Huawei Tech. Co., Ltd., Shenzhen, Guangdong, China, 1994; rschr. Dept. of Automation, Tsinghua U., Beijing, 1994—97; exec. peer-reviewer Ednl. Tech. & Soc. Jour., New York, NY, 1998—. Contbr. articles to profl. jours., papers to sci. confs., chpts. to books (One of the Best Papers, the 4th IEEE Internat. Conf. on ATM (ICATM2001), 2001); author: (poster) IEEE 2002 Sarnoff Symposium on Advances in Wired and Wireless Communications, 2002 (IEEE 2002 Sarnoff Symposium Poster Prize, 2002); contbr. articles to Computer Connections. Pres. Rutgers Yan Xin Qigong Assn., New Brunswick, NJ, 2000—01. Recipient Tsinghua U. & #8211; Hong Kong City U. Scholarship, Hong Kong City U. & Tsinghua U., 1995, Golden Spike Scholarship, Tsinghua U., 1996; fellow Elec. and Computer Engring Fellowship, Rutgers, U., N.J., 2001—2002; grantee Travel Grants, Internat. Workshop on Discrete Algorithms and Methods for Mobile Computing and Comm., 1999, 2000. Mem.: USENIX (Advanced Computing Systems Assn.), ASEE (Am. Soc. for Engring. Edn.), IEEE Comm. Soc., IEEE Computer Soc., ACM (Assn. for Computing Machinery), IEEE (The IEEE). Personal E-mail: liangcheng@ieee.org.

CHENG, LIANGSHENG, engineer, researcher, educator; b. Chaohu, Anhui, China, Sept. 14, 1962; came to U.S., 1991; s. Shaoda Cheng and Defang Li. BS, Hohai U., Nanjing, Jiangsu, China, 1983, MS, 1986; PhD, U. Minn., 1996. Engr.-in-tng. Asst. prof. Hohai U., 1986-91; rsch. asst. U. Minn., Mpls., 1991-96, rsch. specialist, 1996, rsch. fellow, 1996, rsch. assoc., 1997-99; software engr. Worldtrak Co., Mpls., 1999; sr. software engr. C.H. Robinson Worldwide, Mpls., 1999-2000, Firepond Inc., Mpls., 2000-01, sr. software engring. cons. St. Paul, 2001—. Mem. ASCE, MRS, Phi Kappa Phi. E-mail: liangshengc@yahoo.com.

CHENG, MARIETTA N. conductor, educator; b. Marietta, Ohio, June 25, 1952; d. Wen-Yu and Helen (Kuomei) Cheng; m. Paul D. Salmi. Prof. music Colgate U., 1976—. Music dir., condr. Syracuse (N.Y.) Vocal Ensemble, 1978—80, Orch. of the So. Finger Lakes, 1995—; guest condr. Chautauqua (N.Y.) Symphony Orch., Chautauqua Instn., 1998, Hudson Valley Philharm., Poughkeepsie, NY; condr. Young Peoples' Concerts, 2000—; lectr. in field; music dir. Syracuse Vocal Ensemble, 1980, Corning Philharm., 0786—1995; mem. choral conducting faculty Aspen Music Festival, 1981—83. Pianist: chamber music Manhattan String Quartet; performer: Corning Philharm.; contbr. articles to profl. jours. Avocations: corvettes, bichon frises, rock music professor. Office: Colgate Univ Dept Music 13 Oak Dr Hamilton NY 13346

CHENG, MEI-FANG, psychobiology educator, neuroethology researcher; b. Kee Lung, Taiwan, Republic of China, Nov. 24, 1938; came to U.S., 1959; d. Chao-Chin Hsieh and Ai Tsu; m. Wen-Kwei Cheng; m. June 7, 1963; children: Suzanne, Po-Yuan, Julie. BS summa cum laude, Nat. Taiwan U., Taipei, 1958; PhD, Bryn Mawr Coll., 1965. Postdoctoral fellow U. Pa., Phila., 1965-68; asst. rsch. prof. Inst. Animal Behavior Rutgers U., Newark, 1969-73, assoc. prof., 1973-79, prof., 1979, acting dir. Inst. Animal Behavior, 1989-94, dir., 1991-95. Cons. NIMH, mem. neurosci. study sect., 1991-95; cons., mem. behavioral neurobiology br. NSF; mem. NIH Reviewers Res., 1995—; cons. numerous granting agys. Author: Advance in the Study of Behavior, 1979; co-editor: Reproduction: A Behavorial and Neuroscientific Perspective, 1986; assoc. editor Hormones and Behavior, 1986-96; cons. Brain Rsch., Sci., others; contbr. articles to profl. jours. Fulbright scholar, 1959; recipient Rsch. Scientist Devel. award NIMH, 1974-79, 79-84, Johnson & Johnson Discovery award, 1989, Hoechst-Celanese Innovative award, 1993, award of excellence in rsch. Rutgers Bd. Trustees, 1998. Mem. Internat. Conf. Neuroethology, Neurosci. Achievements include discovery that a bird's own songs stimulate the endocrine changes; demonstration of the vocal-auditory-endocrine pathways involved in voice and sound mediation of endocrine change, and provide anatomical basis for emotion-sharing theory of vocal communication; discovery of cell loss can trigger neurogenesis in the adult brain and may be harnessed for brain repair and functional recovery. Office: Rutgers U Dept Psychology 101 Warren St Newark NJ 07102-1811

CHENG, PAUL HUNG-CHIAO, civil engineer; b. China, Dec. 1, 1930; arrived in U.S., 1958, naturalized, 1973; s. Yen-Teh and Shu-Yin (Tsou) Cheng; m. Lucial Jen Chen, Aug. 1, 1964; children: Maria, Elizabeth, Deborah, Samuel. BSCE, Nat. Taiwan U., 1951; MSCE, U. Va., 1961. Registered profl. engr., Ill., Calif. Structural engr. Swift & Co., Chgo., 1963—67; sr. structural designer P&W Engring., Inc., Chgo., 1967, A. Epstein & Son, Inc., Chgo., 1967—68; staff engr. Interlake, Inc., Chgo., 1968—71, supervising engr., 1971—73, chief structural engr., 1973—80, product engring. mgr., 1980—82, CAD/CAM devel. mgr., 1982—84; CAD/CAM sys. mgr. Continental Can Co., 1984—88, Continental Container sys. divsn. Figgie Internat., Inc., 1988—90; pres. Interactive Handbook, Inc., 1990. Mem.: ASCE, Am. Mgmt. Assn., Soc. Mfg. Engrs. (Computer and Automated Sys. Assn.). Home and Office: 5320 N Sheridan Rd Apt 1706 Chicago IL 60640-7345

CHENG, SHIDE, engineer, researcher; s. Cheng Mindun and Gao Guiyin; m. Xiufeng Huang, Apr. 3, 1996; 1 child, Cheng Wanli. BS, Lanzhou U., China, 1989; MS, Nanjing U., China, 1992; PhD, Nanyang Technol. U., Singapore, 2000—00. Cert. electronic engr., Shenzhen, 1994. Sr. R&D engr. Tianma Microelectronics Co, Shenzhen, Guangdong, China, 1992—97; mem. tech. staff Phosistor Technologies Inc., Pleasanton, Calif., 2001—. Contbr. articles to profl. jours. Mem.: OSA, IEEE. Achievements include invention of deposition of c-axis oriented sol-gel LiNbO3 on silicon; optical beam transformer module for light coupling between a fiber array and a photonic chip and the method of making the same; amorphous HTN-LCD with wide and uniform viewing angles; chirped acoustics superlattice and ultra-high-frequency wideband acoustic/optic device; two-dimensional propagation in a surface acoustic wave device. Home: 5635 Springhouse Dr #35 Pleasanton CA 94588 Office: Phosistor Technologies Inc 7079 Commerce Cir Pleasanton CA 94588 Office Fax: 925-846-1633. Personal E-mail: shide_cheng@yahoo.com. E-mail: shide_cheng@yahoo.com.

CHENG, TSEN-CHUNG, electrical engineering educator; b. Shanghai, Peoples Republic of China, Dec. 24, 1944; s. Yik Yu and Shun Lan (Tsui) C.; m. Doris Tin Gen Lee, Aug. 25, 1974; 1 child, Jason. BS, MIT, 1969, MSEE, 1970, ScD, 1974. Asst. prof. U. So. Calif., Los Angeles, 1974-80, assoc. prof., 1980-84, Lloyd F. Hunt prof., dir. electric power program, 1984—. Pres. T.C. Cheng ScD Inc., San Marino, Calif., 1981—; cons. Los Angeles Dept. Water and Power, 1984—, So. Calif. Edison Co., 1982—, Pacific Gas & Electric Co., San Francisco, 1982—, and numerous other pub. utilities and elec. and electronic mfrs. worldwide. Patentee in field; author over 120 pubs. Recipient Outstanding Elec. Engring. faculty award U. So. Calif., 1976, Engring. Service award U. So. Calif., 1981. Fellow IEEE (relay com. award 1986, Best Paper award 1988), Sigma Xi, Eta Kappa Nu, Tau Beta Pi. Office: Univ of So Calif Phe 634 Dept Ee Ep # 634 Los Angeles CA 90089-0001 E-mail: tccheng@socal.rr.com.

CHENG, TSUNG O, cardiologist, educator; b. Shanghai, Mar. 30, 1925; came to U.S., 1950, naturalized, 1960; s. Keith S. and Fanny (Wang) C.; m. Marie Ellen Roe, June 18, 1955; children: Mark Dudley, Yvonne Joyce. BS, St. John's U., China, 1945; MD, U. Pa., 1950, MS in Medicine, 1956. Diplomate Am. Bd. Internal Medicine (subsplty. cardiovasc. disease), Nat. Bd. Med. Examiners. Intern St. Barnabas Hosp., Newark, 1950-51; resident Cook County Hosp., Chgo., 1952-55; fellow in cardiovasc. disease George Washington U., D.C. Gen. Hosp., Washington, 1955-56; instr. cardiology Harvard Med. Sch. Mass. Gen. Hosp., Boston, 1956-57; fellow in cardiorespiratory physiology Johns Hopkins U. Sch. Medicine and Hosp., 1957-59; practice medicine specializing in cardiology Washington, 1970—; asst. prof. medicine SUNY Downstate, 1959-70; assoc. prof. medicine George Washington U., 1970-72; chief cardiology D.C. Gen. Hosp., 1971-72; prof. George Washington U., 1972—. Dir. cardiac catherization lab. George Washington U. Med. Ctr., 1972—78, assoc. dir. cardiology, 1972—75; asst. physician Cardiac Clinic Johns Hopkins Hosp., 1957—59; dir. cardiopulmonary lab. Bklyn. Hosp., 1959—66; co-chief Pediat. Cardiac Clinic, 1959—66; chief Adolescent Cardiac Clinic, 1961—66; attending physician Adult Cardiac Clinic, 1959—66; chief Pediat. Cardiac Clinic Cumberland Hosp., Bklyn., 1963—66; asst. chief cardiology VA Hosp., Bklyn., 1966—69; chief Cardiovascular Lab., 1966—70, chief cardiology, 1969—70; asst. vis. physician Kings County Hosp. Med. Ctr., Bklyn., 1964—70; attending physician Univ. Hosp., SUNY, Bklyn., 1967—70; cons. Beth Israel Med. Ctr., N.Y.C., 1970—82; guest lectr. Chinese Med. Assn., 1972, 73, 75, 77, 79, 83, 86, 89, 92, Chinese Ministry Health, 1990; prof. (hon.) Shanghai 2nd Med. Univ., 1986—, Qingdao Med. Coll., 1989—, Binzhou Med. Coll., 1992—, Taishan Med. Coll., 1992—, Tongji Med. U., Wuhan, China, 1994—, U. Cape Town (South Africa), 1995—; dir. (hon.) Quingdao Cardiovascular Rsch. Inst., 1990—; pres. (hon.) Dandong (China) 1st Hosp., Liaoning Province, 1988—, Shanghai St. Luke's Hosp., 1990—, Bizhou Med. Coll. Affil. Hosp., 1992—, Taishan Med. Coll. Affil. Hosp., 1992—, Jujiang (China) Med. Coll. Affil. Hosp., Jiangxi, 1994—, 2nd People's Hosp., Jin De Zhen, Jiangxi, 1994—; vis. prof. Peking Union Med. Coll., 1986—; cons. (hon.) Beijing Hosp., 1989—; vis. prof. Sun Yatsen Med. U., Canton, 1992—, Cairo U., Egypt, 1994—, U. Oxford, 1995—, U. Witwatersrand Med. Sch., Johannesburg, 1995—, U. Paris Hosp., Tenon, France, 1995—, U. Natal, Durban, South Africa, 1995—, Cath. U. Inst. Cardiology, Rome, 1996—; vis. prof. Inst. Clin. Physiology, Nat. Rsch. Coun. U. Pisa (Italy), 1996—, U. Milan; vis. prof. Inst. Pathol. Anatomy Med. Sch. U. Milan, 1996—; vis. prof. U. Dusseldorf (Germany), 1997—, U. Hamburg (Germany), 1997—, U. Hannover (Germany), 1997—, U. Melbourne (Australia), 1997—, U. NSW, Sydney, 1997—, U. Istanbul (Turkey), 1999—, U. Athens (Greece), 1999—, U. Cordoba (Spain), 2000—, U. Las Palmas (Spain), 2000—, U. Complutense, Madrid, 2000—; vis. prof. Med. Faculty Charite Humboldt U. Berlin, 2001—; vis. prof. Chinese U. Hong Kong, 2002—, Capital U. Med. Scis., Beijing, 2002—, U. Geneva, 2003—, U. Zurich, 2003—, U. Bern (Switzerland), 2003—; v.p. Am. Ctr. Chinese Med. Sci., 1982—91; pres. Friends of St. Luke's Hosp., Shanghai, 1991—, chmn. bd., 1992—; dir. (hon.) Inst. Invasive Therapy PLA 150th Ctrl. Hosp., Luoyang, China, 1994—; disting. sr. visitor Royal Brompton Hosp./Nat. Heart and Lung Inst. London, 1995—; advisor (hon.) Guangdong Soc. Interventional Cardiology, Guangzhou, China, 1996—; pres. (hon.) China Heart Failure Assn., 2001—. Sr. editor: Vascular Medicine, 1983—88, Angiology, 1986—97; editor: The International Textbook of Cardiology, 1986, 1987, Percutaneous Balloon Valvuloplasty, 1992; mem. editl. bd.: Catheterization and Cardiovasc. Diagnosis, 1991—99, Catheterization and Cardiovasc. Interventions, 1999—, Jour.

Noninvasive Cardiology, 1997—, Chinese Jour. Misdiagnostics, 1999—; co-editor: Congestive Heart Failure, 1991, Modern Cardiology, 1994, 2nd edit., 2002, Genetics of Cardiovasc. Diseases, 1995, Congestive Heart Failure, 2d edit., 1997, Textbook of Congestive Heart Failure, 2003; contbg. med. editor: Cortlandt Forum, 1997—98; contbr. articles to profl. jours. Fellow ACP, Am. Coll. Chest Physicians, Am. Coll. Cardiology (ofcl. rep. to stds. com. on catheters Assn. Advancement Med. Instrumentation 1971—), Am. Heart Assn., Coun. Clin. Cardiology, Soc. Cardiac Angiography and Interventions, Internat. Coll. Angiology, Am. Coll. Angiology, Soc. Geriat. Cardiology (founding), Royal Soc. Medicine; mem. AAAS, Am. Fedn. Clin. Rsch., Am. Heart Assn., Washington Heart Assn. Home: 7508 Cayuga Ave Bethesda MD 20817-4822 Office: George Washington U Med Ctr 2150 Pennsylvania Ave NW Washington DC 20037-3201 *My goal in life is to serve the people the best way that I know, that is, through medicine which knows no international boundary. Perseverance, patience, hard work and selflessness will always be rewarded by the satisfaction of a job well done.*

CHENG, WAN-LEE, mechanical engineer, industrial technology educator; b. Yi-Hsin, Chaing-Su, Republic of China, Dec. 28, 1945; came to U.S., 1971; s. Teh-Chih and Mei-Nung (Shih) C.; m. Viki Shu-Whei Lu, Dec. 16, 1972; children: Julio Wheichung, Paul Yichung, Lisa Yenchung. BS, Chung Yuan U., Taiwan, 1969; MEd, Sul Ross State U., 1972; PhD, Iowa State U., 1976. Mech. engr. Taiwan Power Co., Taipei, 1970-71; instr. Iowa State U., Ames, 1974-76; asst. prof., then prof. U. N.D., Grand Forks, 1976-85; prof., chmn. dept. design and industry San Francisco State U., 1985-2000, assoc. dean Coll. Creative Arts, 2000—. Cons. High-Tech Mobile Lab., N.D. Vocat. Edn. Dept., Bismarck, 1984-85; vis. prof. Nat. Sci. Coun. and Chung Yuan U., Taiwan, Republic of China, 1990-91; dean Coll. of Design, Chung Yuan Christian U., Taiwan, 1994-95. Author computer software; contbr. articles to profl. jours.; mem. rev. bd. Jour. Indsl. Tech., 1986— Session elder 1st Presbyn. Ch., Grand Forks, 1984-85; session elder Lakeside Presbyn. Ch., 1989-91. Recipient Indsl. Arts Profl. Devel. award N.D. Indsl. Arts Assn., Bismarck, 1985, Outstanding Teaching and Faculty Devel. award Burlington No. Found., Grand Forks, 1985, Outstanging Prof. Indsl. Tech. award Nat. Assn. Indsl. Tech., 1992; 10 grants U. N.D., 1979-85. Mem. Soc. Mfg. Engrs. (sr.), Chinese Inst. Engrs. (v.p. 1993), Chung Yuan Alumni Assn. No. Calif. (pres. San Francisco 1987-88), Chinese Am. Econ. and Tech. Devel. Assn. (pres. 1997-99), Joint Alumni Assn. Chinese Univs. and Colls. No. Calif. (pres. San Francisco, 1988-89), Phi Kappa Phi, Epsilon Pi Tau (trustee Gamma Gamma chpt. Grand Forks 1984-85, Laureate award Beta Beta chpt. San Francisco 1991, Disting. Svc. award 2000). Office: San Francisco State Univ Coll Creative Arts 1600 Holloway Ave San Francisco CA 94132-1722 E-mail: wlcheng@sfsu.edu.

CHENG, WU C. retired patent examiner; b. Shanghai, Aug. 11, 1922; came to U.S., 1948; s. Ting-yih and Wei-chi (Kiang) C.; married 1963; 1 child, Robert C. BS, St. John's U., Shanghai, 1944; MS, Kans. State Coll., 1949; PhD, Ga. Inst. Tech., Atlanta, 1954. Asst. prof. to prof., head chemistry dept. Union U., Jackson, Tenn., 1955-66; assoc. prof. chemistry George Peabody Coll., Nashville, 1966-72; tchr. with rank I Lyman H.S., Longwood, Fla., 1972-75; asst. prof. chemistry to assoc. prof. physics Paine Coll., Augusta, Ga., 1975-89; patent examiner U.S. Dept. Commerce, Washington, 1990-99. Vis. instr. chemistry Ga. Inst. Tech., Atlanta, summer 1956; chemist No. Regional Rsch. Ctr., Peoria, Ill., summer 1976, 88; faculty rsch. participant Savannah River Lab., Aiken, S.C., summer 1977, Argonne Nat. Lab., Chgo., summer 1982, Oak Ridge (Tenn.) Nat. Lab., summer 1984; mem. faculty Rockwell Hanford (Wash.) Ops., summer 1979; faculty rsch. fellow USAF Acad., Colorado Springs, Colo., summer 1986. Contbr. articles to prof. jours. Mem. Am. Chem. Soc., Armed Forces Comms. and Electronics Assn., Ga. Acad. Sci., N.Y. Acad. Scis., Sigma Xi. Achievements include patents in field. Address: PO Box 211336 Augusta GA 30917-1336

CHENG, YANG-TSE, research scientist, materials scientist, physicist; came to U.S., 1980; s. Che-Min (Zhemin) Cheng (Zheng) and Fengzai; m. Julie Yang; children: Laura, Eric. BS, Calif. Inst. Tech., 1982, MS, 1983, PhD, 1987. Sr. rsch. scientist GM Rsch. Labs., Warren, Mich., 1987-92; staff rsch. scientist GM R&D Ctr., Warren, 1992—2001, lab. group mgr., engineered surfaces and functional materials, 1999—, sr. staff rsch. scientist, 2001—. Contbr. over 90 articles to sci. jours., including Applied Physics Letters, Jour. Applied Physics, Jour. Alloys and Compounds, Phys. Rev. B. Rapid Comm., Sci; prin. editor Jour. Material Rsch., 2001-2003. Mem. Materials Rsch. Soc., Am. Phys. Soc. (forum on indsl. and applied physics 2001—), Am. Vacuum Soc. (chmn. Mich. chpt. 1990-92), Bohmische Phys. Soc. Achievements include patents for method of forming surface coatings and thin film sensors. Office: GM R&D Ctr MS: 480-106-224 30500 Mound Rd Warren MI 48092-2031 E-mail: yang.t.cheng@gm.com.

CHENG, YUNG SUNG, research scientist; b. Fong Shan, Taiwan, Apr. 23, 1947; arrived in U.S., 1971; s. Chang Jeng and Asai Yueh Cheng; m. Chui Fan Chen, June 22, 1974; children: Jennifer, Vincent. BS, Nat. Taiwan U., 1969; MS, Syracuse U., N.Y., 1973; PhD, Syracuse U., 1976. Aerosol engr. Inhalation Toxicology Rsch. Inst., Albuquerque, 1978—84, sect. supr., 1984—89, aerosol program mgr., 1990—96; program dir. Lovelace Respiratory Rsch. Inst., 1996—. Clin. prof. U. N.Mex., Albuquerque, 1992—; adj. prof. U. R.I., Kingston, 1998—. Assoc. editor Aerosol Sci. & Tech., 1999—2003. Pres. N.Mex. Chinese Sch., 1995. Mem.: Am. Conf. of Govtl. Indsl. Hygienists, Internat. Soc. for Aerosol in Medicine, N.Mex. Assn. of Asian Ams. (bd. dirs. 2000—), Assn. of Chinese-Am. Engrs. and Scientists (pres. 1996), Am. Assn. Aerosol Rsch. (bd. dirs. 2002—, conf. and com. chair 1982—). Avocations: calligraphy, yoga, hiking, skiing. Office: Lovelace Respiratory Rsch Inst 2425 Ridgecrest SE Albuquerque NM 87108

CHENGALVARAYAN, RATHINAVELU, engineering researcher; b. Chennai, India; s. Chengalvarayan Manickavasagan and Pushpavathi Chengalvarayan; m. Anandhi Ramakrishnan; children: Senthil Rathinavelu, Velvizhi Rathinavelu. B in Engring., Anna U., Guindy, India, 1985; M in Engring., Anna U., 1987; MA in Sci., U. Waterloo, Can., 1992; PhD, U. Waterloo, 1995. Dep. engr. Bharat Electronics Ltd., Bangalore, India, 1986—90; rsch. and tchg. asst. U. Waterloo, 1991—95, postdoctoral fellow, 1995—96; mem. tech. staff Lucent Techs. Inc., Naperville, Ill., 1996—. Patentee in field, 2001; contbr. articles to profl. jours. Recipient Best Paper award, Sys., Cybernetics and Informatics, Orlando, Fla., 2000; scholar, Can. Commonwealth, 1991. Mem.: IEEE (sr.), European Speech Comm. Assn. Home: 339 Millcreek Ln Naperville IL 60540 Office: Lucent Techs Inc 2000 N Naperville Rd Naperville IL 60566 Fax: 630-979-5915. Personal E-mail: rathic@att.net. Business E-Mail: rathi@lucent.com.

CHENGAPPA, ROY K. N. psychiatrist, educator; b. Bangalore, Karnataka, India, Sept. 26, 1955; m. Dara Ann Davis; children: Leela, Lara. MD, Kasturba Med. Coll., Manipal, Karnataka, India, 1980. Cert. Am. Bd. Psychiatry and Neurology. Asst. prof. psychiatry U. Pitts., 1990—97, assoc. prof. psychiatry, 1997—. Dir. Spl. Studies Ctr., Mayview State Hosp., Pitts., 1990—. Fellow: Royal Coll. Physicians and Surgeons Can.; mem.: Biol. Psychiatry, Royal Coll. Psychiatrists U.K. Achievements include research in clinical trials of newer agents being developed for patients with schizophrenia, schizoaffective disorder and bipolar disorder. Office: Western Psychiat Inst and Clinic 3811 O'Hara St Pittsburgh PA 15213-2593

CHENHALLS, ANNE MARIE, nurse, educator; b. Detroit, May 26, 1929; d. Peter and Beatrice Mary (Elliston) McLeod; m. Horacio Chenhalls, 1953 (dec.); children: Mark, Anne Marie Chenhalls Delamater. Student, Detroit Conservatory Music, 1946-47; grad., Grace Hosp. Sch. Nursing, 1951; B Vocat. Edn., Calif. State U., L.A., 1967; BS in Nursing, Calif. State U., 1968; MA, Calif. State U., Long Beach, 1985. RN, Calif. Nurse Grace Hosp., Detroit, 1951-52; pvt. duty nurse Mexico City, 1953-54; nurse St. Francis Hosp., Lynwood, Calif., 1957-63; assoc. prof. nursing Compton Coll., Calif., 1964-72; health educator, sch. nurse Santa Ana (Calif.) Unified Sch. Dist., 1972-76, 79—. Med. coord., internat. health cons. Agape Movement, San Bernardino, Calif., 1976-79; instr. community health, Uganda, 1982; med. evaluator Athletes in Action, 1979; pub. health nurse Orange County Health Dept., Calif., 1990-95. Assoc. staff mem. Campus Crusade for Christ; solo vocalist, Santa Ana, Orange, Seal Beach, Dinner Theater, Calif., Civic Light Opera, Buena park, Calif.; acting Master's Repertory Theater, 1990-94, Santa Ana. U.S. govt. grantee, 1968. Mem. Calif. Sch. Nurses Assn., Calif. Tchrs. Assn. Republican. Home: 2601 E Ocean Blvd 810 Long Beach CA 90803-2504 Office: Santa Ana Unified Sch Dist 1601 E Chestnut Ave Santa Ana CA 92701-6322 E-mail: AChenhalls@aol.com.

CHENICEK, LAURA, artist, educator; b. N.Y.C., Apr. 19, 1952; d. Albert George and Beth Mackey Chenicek; m. Donald Stephen Korn, June 14, 1980; children: Anna Chenicek Korn, Julia Chenicek Korn. BFA, U. Colo., 1974; MFA, Sch. Art Inst. Chgo., 1976. Adj. faculty Essex County Coll., West Caldwell, N.J., 1979-84; instr. Dist. Adult Sch., Maplewood, NJ, 1991—97; adj. faculty Kean U., Union, N.J., 1995. Grants selection com. N.J. State Coun. on Arts, Trenton, 1980; v.p., bd. mem. Artists Equity Assn. N.J., 1980-85; bd. mem., v.p., co-pres. Women's Caucus for Art N.J., 1980-85; bd. mem., founding mem. Gallery South Orange, N.J., 1994-2001. Exhbns. include Newark Mus., 1982, N.J. State Mus., Trenton, 1986, Bergen Mus., Paramus, N.J., 1996, Pierro Gallery of South Orange, N.J., 1996, Stamford (Conn.) Art Mus., 1997, Phoenix Gallery, N.Y.C., 1998, Monmouth Art Mus., Lincroft, N.J., 1998, Nabisco World Hdqrs., East Hanover, N.J., 1999, Johnson & Johnson World Hdqrs., New Brunswick, N.J., 1999, N.J. Ctr. for Visual Arts, Summit, 1999, Hunterdon Art Mus., Clinton, N.J., 1999, Cow Parade, West Orange, N.J., 2000, Vanderbilt U., Nashville, 2003; represented in permanent collections South Western Med. Ctr., Dallas, Johnson & Johnson, New Brunswick, Pub. Svc. Electric & Gas, Newark, Schering, Plough Pharms., Madison, N.J.; represented in pvt. collections. Recipient Whitney Mus. Ind. Study Program award Whitney Mus. Am. Art, N.Y.C., 1976; fellowship grantee N.J. State Coun. on the Arts, Trenton, 1983-84. Mem.: NOW. Studio: 1133 Clifton Ln Nashville TN 37204

CHENOWETH, KRISTIN, actress; b. Tulsa, Okla., July 24, 1968; MA in Opera, Oklahoma City U. Actress with roles on Broadway including: Steel Pier, 1999 (Theatre World award), You're a Good Man, Charlie Brown, 1999 (1999 Tony award for best featured actress, Drama Desk award, 1999, Clarence Derwent award, 1999, Outer Critics Circle award, 1999), Epic Proportions, 1999-2000; Off-Broadway plays include: A New Brain, Scapin, The Fantasticks, Dames at Sea, Strike Up the Band at City Ctr.'s Encores! series; performed leading roles at Goodspeed Opera House, Guthrie Theatre, Paper Mill Playhouse, North Shore Music Theatre; guest soloist West Side Story Suite of Dances, N.Y.C. Ballet; mem. AMC's Paramour TV series, Lateline (NBC), Blind Men (Pilot-NBC); TV appearances: Frasier, 1993, (TV movie) Annie, 1999, Kristin, 2001, The Music Man, 2003, Topa, Topa Bluffs, 2002, Baby Bob, 2002, (miniseries) Paramour, 2003; solo album (with Rob Fisher and the Coffee Club Orches.) Let Yourself Go, 2001. Metropolitan Opera award. Office: c/o SAG 1515 Broadway Fl 44 New York NY 10036-8901*

CHENOWETH-HAGE, HELEN P. former congresswoman; b. Topeka, Kans., Jan. 27, 1938; 2 children. Attended, Whitworth Coll., 1975-79; cert. in law office mgmt., U. Minn., 1974; student, Rep. Nat. Com. Mgmt. Coll., 1977. Bus. mgr. Northside Med. Ctr., 1964-75; state exec. dir. Idaho Rep. Party, 1975-77; chief of staff Congressman Steve Symms, 1977-78; campaign mgr. Symms for Congress Campaign, 1978, Leroy for Gov., 1985-86; v.p. Consulting Assocs., Inc., 1978—; mem. U.S. Congress from Idaho, Washington, 1995-2001. Mem. agriculture, resources, vets. affairs coms., chmn. forest subcom.; bd. dirs. Ctr. Study of Market Alternatives, Mountain States Legal Found.; chmn. bd. America 21. Deacon Capitol Christian Ctr., Boise. Republican.

CHEONG, JONATHAN CHEEYONG, medical researcher; b. Ipoh, Perak, Malaysia, Sept. 8, 1968; s. Sui-Fook Cheong and Kew-Lan Choong; m. Gwo-Jen Tong, Feb. 27, 1994; children: Ryan H, Kathryn. BA, U. Kans., 1993. Assoc. scientist Advanced Medicine, Inc., South San Francisco, Calif., 1997—2001, ZymoGenetics, Inc, Seattle, 2001—. Author: (journals) Pharmacokinetics. Mem.: Am. Biotech. Soc., Am. Assn. Pharm. Scientists, Internat. Soc. Study of Xenobiotics (life). Office: ZymoGenetics Inc 1201 Eastlake Ave E Seattle WA Personal E-mail: jonathan_cheong@yahoo.com.

CHER, (CHERILYN SARKISIAN), singer, actress; b. El Centro, Calif., May 20, 1946; d. Gilbert and Georgia LaPiere; m. Sonny Bono, Oct. 27, 1964 (div.); 1 child, Chastity; m. Gregg Allman, June 1975 (div.); 1 child, Elijah Blue. Student drama coach, Jeff Corey. Singer with husband as team, Sonny and Cher, 1964-74; star TV shows: Cher, 1975-76, The Sonny and Cher Show, 1976-77; concert appearances with husband, 1977, numerous recs., TV, concert and benefit appearances with Sonny Bono; TV appearances, ABC-TV, 1978, appearance with Sonny Bono in motion pictures, Good Times, 1966, Chastity, 1969; film appearances include Silkwood, 1983, Mask, 1985 (Best Actress, Cannes Internat. Film Festival), The Witches of Eastwick, 1987, Suspect, 1987, Moonstruck (Golden Globe award 1988, Acad. award for best actress 1988), 1987, Mermaids, 1990, The Player, 1992, Pret-a-Porter, 1994, Faithful, 1996, Tea With Mussolini, 1999; TV movies; If These Walls Could Talk, 1996, Happy Birthday Elizabeth: A Celebration of Life, 1997, AFI's 100 Years...100 Movies, 1998; helped form rock band, Black Rose, 1979; recorded albums include Black Rose, 1980, Cher, 1988, Heart of Stone, 1989 (Double Platinum and 3 Gold Singles), Love Hurts, 1991, It's A Man's World, 1996, The Casablanca Years, 1996, Believe, 1998 (Grammy award best dance recording 1999), Not Commercial, 2000, Living Proof, 2002; exec. prodr. Sonny & Me: Cher Remembers, 1998. Office: c/o ICM 8942 Wilshire Blvd Beverly Hills CA 90211-1934 also: Reprise Records 3000 Warner Blvd Burbank CA 19010-4694*

CHERAMIE, CARLTON JOSEPH, lawyer, business consultant; b. Raceland, La., Sept. 29, 1952; s. Antoine Joseph and Gladys Marie (Plaisance) C.; m. Myra Joan Diaz, July 15, 1973; 1 child, Andrea Ragan. B.A., Nicholls State U., Thibodaux, La., 1973; J.D., La. State U., 1976. Bar: La. 1976, U.S. Dist. Ct. (ea. dist.) La. 1977, U.S. Dist. Ct. (we. dist.) La. 1977, U.S. Ct. Appeals (5th cir.) 1982, U.S. Ct. Appeals (10th cir.) 1984, U.S. Supreme Ct. 1984. Law clk. Dist. Ct. 19th Jud. dist., Baton Rouge, 1975-76; assoc. Diaz & Herrin, Golden Meadow, La., 1976-77; assoc. Law Office of Ed Diaz, Golden Meadow, 1977-79; ptnr. Diaz & Cheramie, Golden Meadow, 1979-83, Cheramie & Smith, Cut Off, La., 1983— ; pres., dir. Tradewinds Marine, Cut Off, 1982— ; corp. cons. First Am. Investments, Dallas; atty. Town of Golden Meadow, 1980-83; dir. Westwind Capital, Cut Off. State advisor U.S. Congl. Adv. Bd., Cut Off, 1980. Mem. Fed. Bar Assn., Assn. Trial Lawyers Am., La. Trial Lawyers Assn., ABA, Phi Alpha Theta, Phi Delta Phi. Republican. Roman Catholic. Home: 134 W 47th St Cut Off LA 70345-3129 Office: Cheramie & Smith 2024 W Main St Cut Off LA 70345-9408

CHERCOVER, MURRAY, television executive; b. Montreal, Que., Can., Aug. 18, 1929; s. Max M. and Betty (Pomerance) (dec.) C.; m. Barbara Ann Holleran, Aug. 8, 1953; children: Hollis Denny, Sean Peter. Grad., Acad. Radio TV Arts, Toronto, Ont., Can., Neighborhood Playhouse Sch. Theatre, N.Y.C. With Radio Sta. CFPA, Port Arthur, Ont., 1944-46, New Play Soc. Jupiter Theater, Toronto, 1946-48; exec. dir. Equity Library Theatre, N.Y.C., 1948-52; producer, dir. network TV drama Louis G. Cowan Agy., N.Y.C., 1948-52; with Canadian Broadcasting Co., 1952-60; exec. producer all prodn. Sta. CFTO-TV, Toronto, 1960, dir. programming, 1961; exec. v.p., gen. mgr. CTV TV Network Ltd., Toronto, 1966, pres., chief operating officer, 1968, pres., mng. dir., 1969—, pres., chief exec. officer, 1987-90, 1990—; pres. Chercover Communications, 1990—. Pres., dir. Avanti Mgmt. Ltd., founding dir., fellow Internat. Coun. Nat. Acat. TV Arts and Scis.; past mem. adv. com. theatre arts George Brown Coll. Applied Arts and Tech.; past mem. adv. coun. film/TV prodn. program Humber Coll. Bd. dirs. Found. for Ocean Rsch. (founding), Can. Satellite Learning Svcs., Inc.; founding, past trustee Ruth Hancock Scholarship Found. Recipient Gold medal Can. Film and TV Assn., 1988, Rockie award for Lifetime Achievement Banff TV Festival, 1990, Excellence in Broadcasting Lifetime Achievement award Conestoga Coll., 1990, Achievement award for outstanding contbn. to broadcasting Broadcast Exec. Soc., 1991; named to Can. Broadcasting Hall of Fame, 1994. Fellow NATAS (internat. coun., spl. citation 1989); mem. Acad. Can. Cinema and TV, Internat. Press Inst., Can. Assn. Broadcasters (Disting. Svc. gold ribbon medal 1986), Ctrl. Can. Broadcasters Assn. (past bd. dirs., Broadcaster of Yr. award 1990), Toronto Radio Control Club, Model Aeros. Assn. Can., Giant Scale Club (Oshawa), 400 RC Club, Seaton Valley R/C Flying Club. E-mail: chercover@sympatico.ca.

CHERENZIA, BRADLEY JAMES, retired radiologist, consultant; b. Niagara Falls, N.Y., Aug. 22, 1931; s. Peter and Myrna (Bradley) C.; m. Paula Joyce, Mar. 9, 1978; children: Kevin, Lori, David, Robert, Lisa. BS in Pharmacy cum laude, U. Buffalo, 1953; MD, SUNY Upstate Med. Ctr., Syracuse, 1957. Cert. Am. Bd. Radiology, Am. Bd. Nuclear Medicine. Intern SUNY Upstate Med. Ctr. Hosps., Syracuse, 1957-58; resident in radiology Wayne State U. Sch. Medicine Hosps., Detroit, 1960-63; practice medicine specializing in radiology Diagnostic Radiology Cons., P.C., Warren, Mich., 1965-2000, also chmn. bd. dirs., ret., cons. Sr. attending radiologist St. John Macomb Hosp., med. dir. dept. diagnostic radiology. Served to capt. M.C., U.S. Army, 1958-60. Mem. AMA, Am. Soc. Nuc. Cardiology, Wayne County Med. Soc., Mich. State Med. Soc., Radiol. Soc. N.Am., Mich. Radiol. Soc., Am. Coll. Radiology, Soc. Nuclear Medicine, Am. Coll. Nuclear Medicine, Am. Coll. Physician Execs., Soc. Radiologists in Ultrasound, Am. Heart Assn., Am. Med. Tennis Assn. Republican. Roman Catholic. Avocations: photography, art, music, golfing, tennis. E-mail: drbradrad@aol.com.

CHEREWKA, MICHAEL, lawyer; b. Taylor, Pa., July 3, 1955; s. Michael Jr. and Anne (Regan) C.; m. Michele Mary Robinson, Aug. 2, 1980; children: Michael Colin, Matthew Bryan, Meaghan Kelly. Student, U. Bristol, Eng., 1976-77; BSBA cum laude, Bucknell U., 1978; JD cum laude, Dickinson Sch. Law, 1981. Bar: Pa. 1981, U.S. Dist. Ct. (mid. dist.) Pa. 1983, U.S. Tax Ct. 1983, U.S. Ct. Appeals (3d cir.) 1983, U.S. Supreme Ct. 1985. Sr. mem. tax staff Ernst & Whinney, Harrisburg, Pa., 1981-83; assoc. Ball, Skelly, Murren & Connell (formerly Ball & Skelly), Harrisburg, 1983-89; pvt. practice Harrisburg, 1989—96, Wormleysburg, Pa., 2002—; mng. ptnr. Cherewka & Radcliff, LLP, 1996—2002; pvt. practice, 2002—. Mem. Keystone Family Bus. Ctr., LLC, 2000—. Co-author: Pennsylvania Tax Service, 1987; contbg. editor (legal column) Cen. Penn Bus. Jour., 1985-88, Strictly Business, 2002; advisor Dauphin County Law Explorers Post, 1982-88. Mem. Country Club Park Civic Assn., 1983-98, pres., 1987-88; mem. Hist. Harrisburg Assn., 1982-84; active Tri-County United Way, 1985-90, cons. planning giving, mem. adv. com., 1988-90; bd. dirs. Capital divsn. Am. Heart Assn., chmn. 1989-91, bd. dirs. Pa. affiliate, 1989-98, exec. com., 1989-90, 93, treas., 1994-95, incoming chmn. bd., 1995-96, chmn. 1996-97; chmn., bd. dirs. Concertante Chamber Ensemble, 1996-97; bd. dirs. Pa. Assn. Nonprofit Orgns., 1996-; mem. planned giving com. Keystone Svc. Sys. Found., 1995-2000; mem. adv. bd. Found. Caths. United in Svc., Cath. Diocese of Harrisburg, 1991-97. Named Outstanding Young Man Am., U.S. Jaycees, 1983. Mem. Nat. Network Estate Planning Attys., Pa. Bar Assn. (tax sect. 1981—, real estate, probate and trust law sect. 1981—, com. state taxation 1984-99, chmn. subcom. on compromise tax 1986-97), Dauphin County Bar Assn. (interprofl. rels. com. 1984-89, estate planning sect. 1992—), Estate Planning Coun. Cen. Pa. (chmn. CPA subcom. 1982-83, bd. dirs. 1988-96, treas. 1989-90, v.p. 1990-91, pres. 1991-92), Polit. Info. Com. CPAs Pa. (treas. 1982-83), Greater Harrisburg C. of C. (bus. liaison com. 1984-87, econ. devel. com. 1988-89, 92-93, reaccreditation task force 1996), Nat. Assn. Estate Planners (charter 1988—), Pa. Chamber Bus. and Industry (bus. subcom. 1989), Greater West Shore Area C. of C. (comml.-indsl. devel. com. 1987-89), Alzheimer's Assn. of So. Ctrl. Pa. (bd. dirs. 1998-2001), Pa. Assn. Nonprofit Orgns. (bd. dirs. 2000—), Delta Mu Delta, Omicron Delta Kappa. Republican. Roman Catholic. Avocations: coin collecting, golf, basketball. Home: 125 Pelham Rd Camp Hill PA 17011-1353 Office: 624 N Front St Wormleysburg PA 17043-1022

CHERIN, STEPHEN J. computer programmer, management consultant; b. N.Y.C., Apr. 12, 1962; Student, Baruch Coll., 1982-84; AA, L.A. City Coll., 2001; postgrad., Calif State U., L.A., 2001—. Mgr. data processing Salesman's Guide, N.Y.C., 1982-84; v.p. N.Y. Jour., N.Y.C., 1984-86; pres. Genesis Software, L.A., 1986—. V.p. pub. rels. Road Angels, L.A., 1986-88; programmer acctg. program EOMIDS, 1983, Datalink, 1985, E.Z. Acctg., 1989. Sgt. U.S. Army, 1979-81. Avocations: reading, philosophy, psychology, history.

CHERKEN, HARRY SARKIS, JR., lawyer; b. Phila., Dec. 8, 1949; s. Harry Sarkis and Lorna G. (Demurjian) Cherken. BA, Lafayette Coll., 1971; JD, Villanova U., 1976. Bar: Pa. 1976, U.S. Dist. Ct. (ea. dist.) Pa. 1976, U.S. Supreme Ct. 1983. Assoc. counsel Albert M. Greenfield & Co., Inc., Phila., 1976-79; assoc. Drinker, Biddle & Reath, Phila., 1979-84, ptnr., 1984—, co-chmn. real estate group, 1991—, mng. ptnr., 1996-2000. Phila. adv. bd. Chgo. Title Ins. Co., 1986—; assoc. Wharton Real Estate Rsch. Ctr., U. Pa., 1996—; adv. bd. Advanced Comml. Leasing Inst., Georgetown U. Law Ctr.; bd. dirs. Urban Outfitters, Inc., Mikronite Techs. Group, Inc., Law Dept. Am. U. Armenia. Trustee Kulicke Fund, Phila., 1985—, Balch Inst., 1992—2000, Woodmere Art Mus., 2002—; fellow trustee Armenian Assembly Am., 1986—, bd. dirs., 1988—2000, vice-chmn. bd. dirs., 1988—91, 1994—95; bd. dirs. Howard Karagheusian Commemorative Corp., 2003—; sec., bd. dirs. Reading Terminal Market Preservation Fund, 1991—. Mem.: ABA, Am. Coll. Real Estate Lawyers, Pa. Land Title Assn. (affiliate), Phila. Bar Assn., Pa. Bar Assn., Internat. Coun. Shopping Ctrs. (assoc.). Armenian Apostolic. Home: 630 St Andrews Rd Philadelphia PA 19118 Office: Drinker Biddle & Reath LLP One Logan Sq 18th & Cherry Sts Philadelphia PA 19103-6996

CHERKIN, ADINA, interpreter, writer, poet, translator; b. Geneva, Nov. 22, 1921; came to U.S., 1940; d. Herz N. and Genia (Kodriansky) Mantchik; m. Arthur Cherkin, Mar. 14, 1943 (div. Sept. 1980); children: Della Peretti, Daniel Craig. BA in Premed. Studies, UCLA, 1942, MA in Russian Linguistics, 1977. Pvt. practice med. interpreter in 5 langs., L.A., 1942-80; translator UCLA Med. Sch., 1970-79. Pres. acad. forum Jewish studies Herz Mantchik Amity Cir., L.A., 1973-99. Author: Terse Verse and Oodles of Doodles, 2000; author numerous poems. Active L.A. Internat. Vis. Coun., 1991—; pub. rels. Judge Stanley Mosk's Campaign, L.A., 1960; vol. Senator Cranston's Campaign, 1960. Recipient Community Svc. award L.A. City Coun., 1992. Mem. Am. Soc. for Technion Israel Inst. Tech. (bd. regents). Avocations: dance improvisation, figure skating. Home and Office: 2369 N Vermont Ave Los Angeles CA 90027-1253

CHERKSEY, BRUCE DAVID, physiology educator; b. Phila., Oct. 3, 1946; s. Arthur C. and Jeanne (Braslaw) C. MS, NYU, 1973, PhD, 1980. NIH trainee ophthalmology NYU Med. Ctr., N.Y.C., 1980-81, asst. prof. physiology, 1985-90, assoc. prof. physiology, 1990—, assoc. prof. psychiatry, 1992—; founding scientist, cons. Theracell, Inc., 1993—; co-founder Aegeus, Inc., 1994—; founding scientist, cons. Phytotherapeutics, Inc., 1998—. Cons. Titan Pharm. Holdings, Inc., 1993—, Am. Found. AIDS Rsch. Contbr. articles to profl. jours. Mem. Soc. Neurosci., Assn. for Rsch. in Vision & Ophthalmology, Am. Chem. Soc., N.Y. Acad. Scis., Soc. Exptl. Biology and Medicine, NYU-Bellevue Psychiat. Soc. Achievements include patents in membrane channel protein and related therapeutic compounds, pyrones as potassium channel activators, use of pyrones to treat addiction; discovery of the regulation of transport proteins and therapeutic effects in Glaucoma, polyamine toxin in spider venoms; synthetic cacium channel blockers; technology for cell implantation into brain to treat Parkinson's and other diseases, therapeutics to increase lean body mass and to reduce cholestrol. Home: 59 Willow Ter Hoboken NJ 07030-2812 Office: NYU Med Ctr 550 1st Ave New York NY 10016-6402 E-mail: bruce@denbru.com., bruce.cherksey@med.nyu.edu.

CHERMAK, GAIL D. audiologist, educator; PhD, Ohio State U., 1975. Asst. prof. So. Ill. U., Edwardsville, Ill., 1975—77; prof. Wash. State U., Pullman, Wash., 1977—. Author: (book) Central Auditory Processing Disorders: New perspectives, Handbook of Audiological Rehabilitation; contbr. articles. Fellow, Kellogg Found., 1986—89; grantee, U.S. Fulbright Program, 1990. Fellow: Am. Speech-Lang.-Hearing Assn. (cert. 1976), Am. Acad. Audiology; mem.: Pan Am. Audiology Assn., Acoustical Soc. Am., Am. Auditory Soc. Avocations: gardening, boating. Office: Wash State Univ Dept peech & Hearing Sci Pullman WA 99164-2420

CHERMAYEFF, IVAN, graphic designer; b. London, Eng., June 6, 1932; s. Serge Ivan and Barbara Maitland (May) C.; m. Sara Anne Duffy, July 15, 1956; children: Catherine, Alexandra, Maro; m. Jane Clark, Sept. 24, 1978; 1 son, Sam. Grad., Phillips Acad., Andover, Mass., 1950; student, Harvard, 1950-52, Ill. Inst. Tech., 1952-54; BFA, Yale, 1955; LLD (hon.), Maine Sch. Art, 1981; BFA (hon.), Corcoran Sch. Art, 1991, U. of Arts, Phila., 1991. Asst. to Alvin Lustig (designer), 1955; asst. art dir. Columbia Records, 1956; prin. Brownjohn, Chermayeff & Geismar Assocs., 1956-59, Chermayeff & Geismar Inc., NYC, 1959—, Cambridge Seven Assoc., 1965-96. Bd. dir. Internat. Design Conf., Aspen, Colo., 1968-99; bd. dir. Mcpl. Art Soc. NY, 1972-76, Smithsonian Instn., 1988-96; trustee Mus. Modern Art, NYC, 1966-86, Archives of Am. Art, 1987-90, New Sch. Univ., 1988-2002; bd. overseers Parson's Sch. Design, 1988-2002; disting. vis. prof. UCLA, 1998; vis. prof. Kansas City Art Inst., Cooper Union; co-chmn. First Fed. Design Assembly, Nat. Endowment for the

Arts and Humanities, 1973. Author: Observations on American Architecture, 1972, Ellis Island, 1987. Mem. com. on art and arch. Yale U.; mem. bd. overseers com. on visual and environ. studies Harvard U. Recipient Awards Art Dir. Club, NY, awards Am. Inst. Graphic Arts, awards Type Dirs. Club, Indsl. Arts, medal AIA, 1967, Gold medal Phila. Coll. Art, 1971, Claude M. Fuess medal Phillips Acad., 1980, Pres.'s award RISD, 1981, Yale Arts medal 1985, Grand Prix Biennale Brno, 1992; named to NY Art Dir. Club Hall of Fame, 1981, Soc. of Illustrators, gold medal, 2002. Mem. SPEE, Am. Inst. Graphic Arts (pres. 1963-66, Gold medal 1979), Nat. Soc. Indsl. Designers, Alliance Graphique Internat., Royal Soc. Arts and Commerce (Benjamin Franklin fellow), Royal Designer for Industry (RDI hon.), Century Assn., Yale Arts Assn. (past v.p.). Home: 140 E 81st St New York NY 10028-1805 also: Sheep's Hill North Salem NY 10560 Office: 15 E 26th St New York NY 10010-1505 E-mail: ic@cgnyc.com.

CHERN, SHIING-SHEN, mathematics educator; b. Kashing, Chekiang, China, Oct. 26, 1911; s. Lien Ching Chern and Mei (Han); m. Shih-ning Chern, July 28, 1939; children: Paul, May. BS, Nankai U., Tientsin, China, 1930; D (hon.), Nankai U., 1985; MS, Tsing Hua U., Peiping, 1934; DSc, U. Hamburg, Germany, 1936, DSc (hon.), 1972, U. Chgo., 1969, SUNY-Stony Brook, 1985; LL.D. honoris causa (hon.), Chinese U., Hong Kong, 1969; DMath (hon.), Eidgenossische Technische Hochschule, Zurich, Switzerland, 1982; DSc (hon.), U. Notre Dame, 1994. Prof. math. Nat. Tsing Hua U., China, 1937—43; mem. Inst. Advanced Study, Princeton, NJ, 1943—45; acting dir. Inst. Mathematics, Academia Sinica, China, 1946—48; prof. math. U. Chgo., 1949—60, U. Calif., Berkeley, 1960—79, prof. emeritus, 1979—; dir. Math. Scis. Rsch. Inst., 1981—84, dir. emeritus, 1984—; dir. Inst. Math., Tianjin, China. Named hon. prof., various fgn. univs.; recipient Chauvenet prize, Math. Assn. Am., 1970, Nat. medal of Sci., 1975, Wolf prize, Israel, 1983—84. Fellow: Third World Acad. Sci. (founding mem. 1985); mem.: NAS, Russian Acad. Scis. (fgn.), Acad. der Lincei Rome (stranieri), Acad. des Scis. Paris (fgn.), Royal Soc. London (fgn.), Academia Peloritana (corr.), London Math. Soc. (hon.), N.Y. Acad. Scis. (hon. life), Indian Math. Soc. (hon.), Brazilian Acad. Scis. (corr.), Academia Sinica, Am. Philos. Soc., Am. Acad. Arts and Scis., Am. Math. Soc. (Steele prize 1983). Home: 8336 Kent Ct El Cerrito CA 94530-2548 Office: Univ Calif Berkeley Dept Of Mathematics Berkeley CA 94720-0001*

CHERNAK, JERALD LEE, television executive; b. Bklyn., Nov. 7, 1942; s. Jess and Alice Kay (Kosoff) C.; m. Gail Loraine Cooper, March 26, 1967; children: Hope Ann, David. BS in Radio-TV, Indiana State U., 1965. Freelance dir., assoc. dir., asst. dir., stage mgr., N.Y.C., 1965-67; producer, dir., assoc. dir., stage mgr. ABC-TV, N.Y.C., 1967-86; exec. producer, gen. mgr. TV Nat. Shopping Club, Orlando, Fla., 1987-89; v.p., exec. producer U.C. Mktg. Group, Orlando, 1989; v.p., gen. mgr. Channel 7, Orlando, 1989-90; broadcast cons. Orlando, 1990; corp. v.p. Vision Broadcasting, Inc., WHBS, Orlando, 1991-92; v.p., sta. mgr. Stas. WQBN, WHBS, Tampa, Fla., 1992-93; pres. HODA Svcs., Inc., Orlando, Fla., 1993-94; mgr. cellular comms. Radio Shack, Orlando, 1994-97; prodn. mgr. spl. events and entertainment Universal Studios Fla., Orlando, 1997-98; pres., exec. prodr. Am. Monogram Entertainment, Inc., 1999—. Instr. film direction and prodn. U. Ctrl. Fla. Film Sch., 1998—. Post prodn. (TV news spl.) America Held Hostage ABC-TV, N.Y.C. (Emmy award 1982), 20/20 The Ump ABC-TV, N.Y.C. (Emmy nomination 1980). Bd. dirs. Children Wish Found., Orlando, 1987-88; mem. Mid. Fla. Film Coun., 1988-90. Served with USAR, 1965-70. Recipient Bronze and Silver awards Internat. Film & TV Festival, 1968-71, 82, Nobel Peace prize nominee, 2001. Mem. NATAS (bd. govs. N.Y. chpt. 1976-80, 82-86), Dirs. Guils Am. (coun. rep. 1968-85, chmn. Fla. coord. com. 1988—), Soc. Profl. Journalists, Sigma Delta Chi. Avocation: amateur radio operator. Home: 136 Margate Mews Longwood FL 32779-5627

CHERNEV, ALEXANDER, marketing educator, researcher; arrived in U.S., 1992; s. Christo and Irina Chernev. BA, Sofia U., Bulgaria, 1986, PhD, 1990, Duke U., 1997. Asst. prof. mktg. Kellogg Sch. Mgmt., Evanston, Ill., 1998—2001, assoc. prof. mktg., 2001—. Author: (book) Strategic Marketing Analysis, 2002; mem. editl. bd.: Jour. Consumer Psychology, 2001—, Jour. Consumer Rsch., 2002—; contbr. articles to profl. jours. Soros fellow, Open Soc. Found., 1995. Fellow: Am. Mktg. Assn. Doctoral Consortium; mem.: Soc. for Judgment and Decision Making, Am. Mktg. Assn., Assn. for Consumer Rsch. Achievements include research in adaptive models of information processing. Avocations: tennis, chess, skiing. Office: Kellogg Sch Mgmt 2001 Sheridan Rd Evanston IL 60208

CHERNEV, MELVIN, retired beverage company executive; b. Bklyn., Nov. 29, 1928; s. Irving and Selma (Kulik) C.; m. Noemi Dohnert, May 29, 1955 (dec. July 1, 1985); 1 child, Celia Ann; m. Marlene G. Tonkin, Sept. 4, 1988. AB, Cornell U., 1950. Chief statistician Eversharp, Inc., N.Y.C., 1951-52, sales adminstr., 1952-55, asst. gen. sales mgr., 1955-58; sales promotion mgr. Internat. Latex Corp. (Playtex), N.Y.C., 1959-64, product mgr., 1964-66; pres. Snow White Corp., San Jose, Calif., 1966-67; dir. planning and research Fromm and Sichel, Inc., distbrs. Christian Bros. wines and brandy, San Francisco, 1967-70, dir. mktg. services, 1970-73, v.p. mktg. services, 1973-76, sr. v.p. mktg., 1976-77, exec. v.p., 1977-78, pres., chief operating officer, 1978-83, bd. dirs. Mem. Sacramento County Grand Jury, 2000—01; bd. dirs., trustee Cogswell Coll., San Francisco, 1976—86, chmn., 1983—85; bd. govs. City U., Seattle, 1985—99; bd. dirs., treas. The Lakes at Northridge Homeowners Assn.; pres. bd. dirs. Albert Einstein Residence Ctr., 1997—2000. Mem. Cornell Club No. Calif., Cornell Club (N.Y.C.), North Ridge Country Club (Fair Oaks, Calif.). Home: 7529 Pineridge Ln Fair Oaks CA 95628-4858 E-mail: mchernev@aol.com.

CHERNEY, JAMES ALAN, lawyer; b. Boston, Mar. 19, 1948; s. Alvin George and Janice (Elaine) Cherney; m. Linda Bienenfeld. BA, Tufts U., 1969; JD, Columbia U., 1973. Bar: Ill. 1973, U.S. Supreme Ct. 1977, U.S. Ct. Appeals (7th cir.) 1979, U.S. Ct. Appeals (3d cir.) 1982, U.S. Ct. Appeals (10th cir.) 1984, U.S. Ct. Appeals (8th and 9th cirs.) 1987. Assoc. Kirkland & Ellis, Chgo., 1973-76, Hedlund, Hunter & Lynch, Chgo., 1976-79, ptnr., 1979-82, Latham & Watkins, Chgo., 1982—. Mem. ABA, Chgo. Bar Assn. Office: Latham & Watkins Sears Tower Ste 5800 Chicago IL 60606-6306

CHERNIACK, NEIL STANLEY, physician, medical educator; b. Bklyn., May 28, 1931; s. Max and Rebecca (Roulnick) C.; m. Sandra Lebowitz, Dec. 31, 1954; children: Evan, Andrew, Emily. AB with honors, Columbia U., 1952; MD, SUNY, 1956; MA, U. Pa., 1972; hon. degree, Karolinska U., 1991. Intern U. Ill., Chgo., 1956-57, resident, 1957-58, 60-62; resident, fellow Columbia Presbyn. Hosp., N.Y.C., 1962-64; practice medicine specializing in pulmonary disease Chgo., 1964-69, Phila., 1969-77, Cleve., 1977—; asst. prof. medicine U. Ill., Chgo., 1964-68, assoc. prof., 1968-69, U. Pa., Phila., 1969-73, prof., 1973-77, Case Western Res. U., 1977—, chief pulmonary svc., 1977-89, prof. physiology, 1982—, assoc. dean, 1983-90, dean sch. medicine, v.p. med. affairs, 1990-95, vice chmn. div. gen. med. sci., 1986-90, vice chmn. dept. medicine, 1987-90; chief pulmonary svc., sr. attending physician Phila. Gen. Hosp., 1969-77; assoc. dir. pulmonary svc., attending physician U. Pa. Hosp., 1973-77, U. Hosps. of Cleve., Cleve. VA Med. Ctr.; vis. prof. Karolinska U., Stockholm, 1976-77; dir. of clin. svcs., acting chmn. dept. physiology & pharmacology U. Medicine & Dentistry N.J., Newark, 1995-97. Chmn. vis. com. neurosci. program Howard U., 1998—. Mem. editl. bd.: Circulation Rsch., Am. Rev. Respiratory Disease, Chest; editor: Jour. Applied Physiology, Handbook of Physiology; assoc. editor: Jour. Lab. Clin. Medicine, Respiration Handbooks of Physiology, Respiration. Capt. USAF, 1958-60. Mem.: N.Y. Clin. Soc., Neurosci. Soc., Ctrl. Soc. Clin. Rsch., Biomed. Engring. Soc. (bd. dirs. 1984—87), Biogengring. Soc., Am. Physiol. Soc., Am. Lung Assn., Am. Thoracic Soc., Am. Soc. Clin. Investigation, Am. Assn. Physicians, Soc. Columbia Grads., Beta Sigma Rho, Alpha Omega Alpha, Phi Beta Kappa. Home: 11 Wood Dr Morris Plains NJ 07950-1509 Office: Univ Med Dental NJ Newark NJ 07103-2714 E-mail: cherniac@umdnj.edu.

CHERNICHAW, MARK, television production, advertising and promotion executive, international media consultant; b. Newark, Mar. 31, 1946; s. Nathan H. and Irma (Walker) C.; m. Pauline Papernik, Nov. 22, 1967; children: Adam, Ian. BA, U. Miami, Fla., 1969; MS, Bklyn. Coll., 1972. Ind. TV prodr., dir., 1973-82; assoc. prof. NYU, 1972-82; exec. prodr. TV comms., video/film prodns., exec. in charge Avon Products, Inc., N.Y.C., 1982-92; pres. Entertainment Enterprises Inc., 1991-96; exec. v.p. creative svcs. and prodn. SLP & Co., N.Y. and L.A., 1995—97; v.p. advt., promotion and prodn. The Home Shopping Network, USA Network, 1997—99; v.p. global mktg. comm. Prudential Fin., 1999—. Commls.-writer/prodr. ABC-TV Sweeps; exec. prodr., prodr. and dir. shows featuring celebrities including Ricki Lake, Martin Sheen, Cindy Crawford, John Glenn,, George Burns, Henry Fonda, Crystal Gayle, Billy Dee Williams, Robert Mitchum, Frank Sinatra, Bob Hope, Carol Kane, Shari Lewis, Beverly Sills, Ben Vereen; exec. prodr. home video: Shape Up with Mary Hart (People Mag. citation as one of top 10 videos); cons. N.J. Coalition for Fair Broadcasting, Trenton; guest spkr. Directing for TV seminars Video Comms. Congress; lectr. Video Expo, N.Y.; judge for Emmy and Clio awards, N.Y. Dir. One Person Too Late, ABC-TV (Internat. Film and TV award), syndicated TV series The Road to the White House (represented in permanent collection Smithsonian Instn.), CBS Sports segment, Cable TV series The Home Shopping Show, various nat. and regional TV commls. (Clio award); mem. editl. adv. bd. Video Mgr. mag.; contbr. articles to profl. jours. Polit. media cons. Recipient Peabody Archives awards, 1 Grand, 2 Gold, 4 Silver and 3 Bronze awards Internat. Film and TV, Grand award, Gold award Internat. Assn. Bus. Communicators. Mem. NIMA Internat., NATAS, Am. Film Inst., Internat. TV Assn. Avocations: music, sports, travel.

CHERNICOFF, DAVID PAUL, osteopathic physician, educator; b. N.Y.C., Aug. 3, 1947; s. Harry and Lillian (Dobkin) C. AB, U. Rochester, 1969; DO, Phila. Coll. Osteo. Medicine, 1973. Diplomate Nat. Bd. Osteo. Examiners, Am. Osteo. Bd. Internal Medicine, also in Hematology/Oncology. Rotating intern Rocky Mtn. Hosp., Denver, 1973-74; resident in internal medicine Cmty. Gen. Osteo. Hosp., Harrisburg, Pa., 1974-76; fellow in hematology and med. oncology Cleve. Clinic, 1976-78; asst. prof. medicine sect. hematology/oncology Chgo. Coll. Osteo. Medicine, 1978-82, assoc. prof., 1982-89; co-chmn. tumor task force Chgo. Osteo. Med. Ctr., 1978-89, dir. clin. cancer edn., 1978-89; asst. clin. prof. medicine Pa. State U. Coll. Medicine, Harrisburg, 1993—; pvt. practice, 1979. Med. dir. Keystone Peer Rev. Orgn., 1997-2000; chmn. tumor task force Olympia Fields (Ill.) Osteo. Med. Ctr. Trustee, mem. clin. exec. com. Ill. Cancer Coun., 1982-89; bd. dir. Chgo. unit Am. Cancer Soc., 1981-86, chief sec. of Hematology-Oncology Hosp. of Chgo. Coll. Osteo Medicine, 1981-89; carrier adv. com. Xact Medicare Svcs., 1997-2000; med. dir. Keystone Peer Rev. Orgn., 1997-2000. Contbr. articles to med. jours. Fellow Am. Coll. Osteo. Internists, Pa. Osteo. Med. Soc. Ea. Coop. Oncology Group (sr. investigator 1981-89), Am. Soc. Clin. Oncology; mem. Am. Osteo. Assn. Office: 4830 Londonderry Rd Harrisburg PA 17109-5207 E-mail: BronJeffPA@aol.com.

CHERNIN, PETER, motion picture company executive; Pres. entertainment group Fox Broadcasting Co., L.A.; former chmn. Twentieth Century Fox Film Corp., Beverly Hills, Calif.; now chmn., CEO The Fox Group, Beverly Hills, Calif.; pres., COO News Corp., 1996—. Office: Fox Inc Rm 5080 10201 W Pico Blvd Bldg 100 Los Angeles CA 90064-2606

CHERNISH, LELIA MARGARET, fundraiser; b. Collins, Mo., Mar. 19, 1921; d. Aubra F. and Velta Lelia (Nance) Higgins; m. Stanley M. Chernish, June 19, 1949; 1 child, Dwight Landers. Student, U. Md., 1947-48. Tchr. kindergarten, Silver Springs Bethesda, Md., 1945-51; apptd. del. White House Conf. on Aging, 1971, Ind. Health Careers, 1974-84; mem. Ind. Impaired Physicians Com., 1976-79; appointee Ind. Mus. Art, 1976-84; apptd. bd. trustees Ind. Med. Distbn. Loan Fund, 1977-92, Ind. Med. & Nursing Distbn. Loan Fund, 1981-85; mem. Marion County Impaired Physicians Com., 1983-84. Liaison to med. student wives, rec. sec., program, publicity and fin. chmn., historian and by-laws chmn. Ind. State Med. Aux.; pres. Marion County Med. Aux., 1965-66, med. student liaison, historian, United Fund chmn., by-laws com., parliamentarian, chmn. cookbook prodn.; mem., fin. chmn., parliamentarian Boys Club Aux. Mem. Winona Meml. Hosp. Aux.; founder Vol. Observer Program, Ind., 1970-71; mem., yearbook chmn. Alliance of Indpls. Mus. of Art; active Women United Against Rape, 1975, Sch. Drop Out Program, Diabetes Detection Dr., drug and internat. health activities; regular ct. watcher Indpls. Anti-Crime Crusade; vol. Ronald McDonald House, 1982-2003, trustee, chmn. needle art project, facilities com., chmn. 10th anniversary calendar fund raising project, 1992, bd. dirs., 2003—, sec. to bd. dirs. 1992-99. Recipient Theta Sigma Phi award, 1969, Sagamores of the Wabash award for disting. pub. svc. Gov. Otis R. Bowen, 1977, by Gov. Robert D. Orr, 1981, Ind. Jefferson award, 1982, Lori Kleiman award for svcs. over and above call of duty Ronald McDonald House, 1992, Indpls. Mayors Vol. Partnership award, 1999; named Ind. Mother of Yr., 1981. Mem.: Crossroads Guild (pres. 1969, Heart of Gold award 2002), Women in Neighborhood Svc., Indpls. chpt. Embroiderers Guild Am. (chmn. nat. embroiderers guild exhibit 1989, dean of faculty seminar 1990, co-chmn. nat. seminar 1992, pres. 1997—98), Hillcrest Garden Club (treas., chmn. flower show), Faculty Women's Club of Ind. U. Sch. Medicine. Fax: 317-547-3563.

CHERNISS, CARY, psychologist, educator; b. L.A., Mar. 26, 1948; s. Jack and Shirley Cherniss; m. Deborah Spitz, Mar. 23, 1968; 1 child, Joshua. AB, U. Calif., Berkeley, 1969; PhD, Yale U., New Haven, Conn., 1972. Asst. prof. psychology U. Mich., Ann Arbor, 1972—80; sr. rsch. scientist Ill. Inst. for Developmentally Disabled, Chgo., 1980—83; assoc. prof. psychology Rutgers U., New Brunswick, NJ, 1983—87, prof. psychology, 1987—. Author: (Book) Professional Burnout, 1980, Beyond Burnout, 1995, Promoting Emotional Intelligence in Organizations, 2000. Pres. Friends of CARRI program, Piscataway, NJ, 1997—. Fellow Woodrow Wilson Fellowship Found., 1969; scholar Expert in Residence, Kellogg Found., 1997. Fellow: Soc. for Cmty. Rsch. and Action (pres. 2000—01); mem.: Consortium for Rsch. on Emotional Intelligence in Orgns. (co-chair 1996—), Acad. Mgmt., Phi Beta Kappa. Office: GSAPP Rutgers Univ 152 Frelinghuysen Rd Piscataway NJ 08854 Office Fax: 732-445-4888. E-mail: cherniss@rci.rutgers.edu.

CHERNO, MELVIN, humanities educator; b. El Paso, Feb. 24, 1929; s. Sol and Deborah (Andes) C.; m. Dolores Ellen Himelstein, Dec. 25, 1950; children— Steven Philip, Paige Elise, Julie Rosanne AB, Stanford U., 1950; AM, U. Chgo., 1952; PhD, Stanford U., 1955. Instr. Bakersfield Coll., Calif., 1955-60; successively asst. prof., assoc. prof., prof. Oakland U., Rochester, Mich., 1960-80; Vaughan prof. tech., culture and comm. U. Va., Charlottesville, 1980-2000, Vaughan prof. emeritus humanities, 2001—, prin. second residential coll., 1991-95, 2000-01, co-prin., 1995-96. Co-editor: (4-vol. anthology) Western Society ..., 1967; editor, translator: (essay) Feuerbach on Luther, 1968; contbr. articles on historical topics to profl. jours. Fellow Ford Found., 1953-55, Deutscher Akademische Austauschdienst, 1966, Inst. für Europäische Geschichte, 1966 Mem. Am. Hist. Assn., Am. Soc. Engring. Edn., So. Hist. Assn., Soc. for History of Tech., Soc. for Lit./Sci., Soc. for 19th Century Studies, Phi Beta Kappa. Office: U Va TCC Divsn A237 Thornton Hall PO Box 400744 351 McCormick Rd Charlottesville VA 22904

CHERNOFF, AMOZ IMMANUEL, hematologist, consultant; b. Malden, Mass., Mar. 17, 1923; s. Isaiah and Celia (Margolin) C.; m. Renate R. Fisher, Jan. 25, 1953; children: David F., Susan N., Judith A. BS in Chemistry with honors, Yale U., 1944, MD cum laude, 1947. Diplomate Am. Bd. Internal Medicine. Med. intern Mass. Gen. Hosp., Boston, 1947-48; asst. resident in medicine Barnes Hosp., St. Louis, 1948-49; fellow in hematology Michael Reese Hosp., Chgo., 1949-51, asst. dir. hematology research lab., 1950-51; A.C.P. fellow Washington U. Sch. Medicine, St. Louis, 1951-52; USPHS spl. research fellow, 1952-53; instr. in medicine, 1952-54; asst. prof., 1954-56; assoc. prof. medicine Duke U., 1956-58; chief sect. hematology VA Hosp., Durham, N.C., 1956-58. Rsch. prof. U. Tenn. Meml. Rsch. Ctr., Knoxville, 1958-79, dir., 1964-77; assoc. vice chancellor for acad. affairs Ctr. Health Scis., 1977-79; prof. medicine Coll. Medicine, Memphis, 1966-79; med. dir. Cystic Fibrosis Found., Atlanta, 1975-77; dir. div. blood diseases and resources Nat. Heart Lung and Blood Inst., NIH, Bethesda, Md., 1979-88; assoc. exec. dir. sci. affairs Am. Assn. Blood Banks, Arlington, Va., 1988-90; cons. transfusion medicine programs. Contbr. articles to profl. jours. Served with U.S. Army, 1943-45. Recipient Campbell award Yale U. Sch. Medicine, 1947, Research Career award USPHS, 1962-77 Fellow ACP; mem. Am. Soc. Clin. Investigation, Am. Soc. Hematology, Internat. Soc. Hematology, Cen. Soc. Clin. Rsch., So. Soc. Clin. Investigation, Soc. Exptl. Biology and Medicine, Am. Fedn. Clin. Rsch., Am. Assn. Blood Banks, Sigma Xi, Alpha Omega Alpha.

CHERNOFF, HERMAN, statistics educator; b. N.Y.C., July 1, 1923; s. Max and Pauline (Markowitz) C.; m. Judith Ullman, Sept. 7, 1947; children— Ellen Sue, Miriam Cheryl. BS, CCNY, 1943; Sc.M., Brown U., 1945, PhD, 1948; Sc.D. (hon.), Ohio State U., 1983, Technion, 1984; A.M. (hon.), Harvard U., 1985; laurea (hon.), U. Rome (Sapienza), 1996; PhD (hon.), U. Athens, 1999. Rsch. assoc. U. Chgo., 1948-49; asst. prof. U. Ill., Urbana, 1949-51, assoc. prof., 1951-52, Stanford (Calif.) U., 1952-56, prof. stats., 1956-74; prof. applied math. MIT, Cambridge, 1974-85, prof. emeritus, 1985—; prof. stats. Harvard U., Cambridge, 1985-97, prof. emeritus, 1997—. Researcher in large sample theory, optimal design of expts., sequential analysis, pattern recognition. Author: (with L.E. Moses) Elementary Decision Theory, 1959, Sequential Analysis and Optimal Design, 1972. Recipient Townsend Harris medal CCNY Alumni Soc., 1981. Mem. NAS, Internat. Statis. Inst., Am. Acad. Arts and Scis., Inst. Math. Stats. (pres. 1967-68), Am. Statis. Assn. (Wilks medal 1987, Statistician of Yr. award Boston chpt. 1991). Home: 75 Crowninshield Rd Brookline MA 02446-6777 Office: Harvard U Dept Statistics Cambridge MA 02138 E-mail: chernoff@stat.harvard.edu.

CHERNOFF, MARVIN, advertising executive; CEO Chernoff/Silver & Assocs., Columbia, S.C., 1974—. Named Amb. of Yr. Greater Columbia C. of C., 1999. Office: Chernoff/Silver & Assoc 801 Gervais St Columbia SC 29201

CHERNOFF, YURY OLEGOVICH, biologist, educator; b. St. Petersburg, Russia, June 23, 1960; s. Oleg Nikolaevich and Raisa Nikolaevna (Stolyarova) C.; m. Tatiana Alexandrovna Zhukova, Dec. 12, 1980; children: Irena, Kirill. BS in Biology, St. Petersburg State U., 1980, PhD in Biology, 1985. Sr. rsch. scientist in genetics USSR Supreme attestation. Rsch. tech., jr. rsch. fellow/assoc., to leading assoc. St. Petersburg State U., 1980-92; rsch. assoc. U. Ill., Chgo., 1992-95; asst. prof. Ga. Inst. Tech., Atlanta, 1995-2001, assoc. prof., 2001—. Vis. rsch. scholar Okayama U., Japan, 1989-90; mem. initial rev. bd. Alzheimer's Assn.; mem. adv. com. Biol. Sci. Curriculum Study, Colorado Springs, Colo.; mem of Peer Review Bd., Nat. Prion Rsch. Program, U"S Army Med. Rsch. and Mater. Command, 2002, spkr. in field. Mem. editl. bd.: Gene Expression jour.; contbg. author: (book) Prion Biology and Diseases, 1999; contbr. articles to profl. jour. Min. of Sci., Edn. and Welfare of Japan rsch. scholar, 1989; Internat. Human Frontier Sci. Program Orgn. long-term fellow, Strasbourg, France, 1993, Jr. Faculty Devel. Award, Ga. Tech., 2001; Sigma Xi Best Faculty Paper Award, Ga. Tech., 2002, rsch. grantee NIH, Bethesda, Md., 1997, 99, Amyotrophic Lateral Sclerosis Assn., 1999, US-Israel Binat. Sci. Found., 2000, US Civilian R&D Found., 2000, 2002, Huntingtons Disease Soc. of Am., 2002. Mem. AAAS, Genetics Soc. Am., Am. Soc. for Microbiology. Avocations: history, soccer. Office: Sch Biology/Inst Bioengring Ga Inst Tech 315 Ferst Dr Atlanta GA 30332-0363 E-mail: yc22@prism.gatech.edu.

CHERNOW, ANN LEVY, artist, art educator; b. NYC, Feb. 1, 1936; d. Edward P. and Mollie (Citrin) Levy; m. Philip Chenok, Aug. 11, 1957 (div. Jan. 1969); children: David Charles Chenok, Daniel Joshua Chenok; m. Burt Chernow, Dec. 11, 1970. MA, NYU, 1969. Instr. Mus. Modern Art, N.Y.C., 1966-71; prof., head art dept. Norwalk (Conn.) Cmty. Tech. Coll., 1974-96. Guest lectr., instr. studio and art history Silvermine Sch. Arts Silvermine Coll., 1968—80; vis. artist, lectr. Housatonic C.C., Conn., 1975—80; guest lectr. Am. Coll. in Paris, 1985, Salem State Coll., 1993, 94, Yale U., 1995, Westport Hist. Soc., 1994, Fairfield U., 1993; vis. artist CAP program Wesleyan U., 1979; coord. Bicentennial Exhbn. Norwalk C.C., 1976, Yale U. Art Gallery, 1996; master drawing class The Nat. Acad., N.Y.C., 2000—, N.Y.C., 2001; vis. artist & lectr. Bryn Mawr U., 2003, Ind. U., 2003. One-woman shows include Wesleyan U., Middleton, Conn., 1979, Beall/Lambremont Gallery, La., 1980—81, Gallery Suzanne Maag, Zurich, 1980, Douglass Gallery, Rutgers U., N.J., 1980, Queens Coll., N.Y.C., 1982, Alex Rosenberg Gallery, 1982, Mattatuck (Conn.) Mus., 1982, Munson Gallery, Conn., 1984, 1988—89, Snug Harbor Cultural Ctr., L.I., 1984, Stamford (Conn.) Mus., 1985, Conn. Fine Arts Mus., 1986, Katonah Gallery, N.Y., 1987, Fairfield U., Conn., 1988, U.F.O. Gallery, Princeton, N.J., 1988, Provincetown, Mass., 1990—91, 1994, Uptown Gallery, 1989, Uptown Galley, N.Y.C., 1995, Uptown Gallery, 1997, N.Y.C., 1999, 2002, Conn. Gallery, 1989, Lust Gallery, N.Y.C., 1992, Winfisky Gallery, Salem, 1993, Washington Art Assn., Conn., 1993, NCTC Gallery, Norwalk, Conn., 1994, New Rochelle Libr. Gallery, N.Y., 1995, Mcpl. Mus. of St. Paul de Vence, France, 1996, PMW Gallery, Stamford, Conn., 1997—98, Westchester C.C., 1997, Albert Merola, Provincetown, 1998, Stamford Mus., 1999, Queens Coll., N.Y.C., 2000, Erlich Gallery, Marblehead, Mass., 2002, Raclin Gallery Ind. U., 2003, Print Ctr., Phila., 2003, Dorothy Rogers Fine Art, Santa Fe, N.Mex., 2003, exhibited in group shows at Alex Rosenberg Gallery, 1980, Mus. Contemporary Art, Sao Paulo, Brazil, 1980, Aldrich Mus., Ridgefield, Conn., 1981, Silvermine Guild, 1982, Print Club, Phila., 1983, Artists Choice Mus., Marisa Del Re Gallery, N.Y.C., 1983, Morris Mus., Morristown, N.J., 1984, John Slade Ely House, New Haven, 1985, Munson Gallery, 1985, Stamford Mus., 1985—86, 1994—95, Katonah Gallery, 1986, Internat. Miniature Print Bienniale, New Canaan, 1987, Uptown Gallery, N.Y.C., 1994, Martin Sumers Gallery, 1994, Nat. Drawings Assn., 1994, SAGA Prints, 1994, Fairfield, Conn., 1994, Americas, 2000, S.D., 1994, Triton Mus., Santa Clara, Calif., 1994, Ctr. for Visual Arts, Oakland, Calif., 1994, Discovery Mus., Conn., 1995, Calif. Soc. Printmakers, San Francisco, 1995, Millennium Portfolio of Time and Place, 1999—2001, Bklyn. Mus., 2001, Nat. Acad., 2001, NY Soc. Etchers, 2002, Nat Arts Club, NYC, 2002, Mus. City of NY, 2002, Salle des Fetes, Paris, 2003, Trois Rivigres, Can., 2003, Represented in permanent collections Met. Mus. Art, Rose Art Mus., Brandeis U., Nat. Mus. Women in Arts, Washington, William Benton Mus. Art, Storrs, Conn., Mus. of City of N.Y., UN, Westport, Achenbach Found., San Francisco, New Britain Mus. Am. Art, Conn., Neuberger Mus., Purchase, N.Y., Housatonic Mus. Art Yale U., Mattatauk Mus., Lehigh U. Art Collection, Pa., Utah Mus. Fine Arts, U. Ariz. Art Collection, Lyman Allyn Mus., Conn., Bruce Mus., Butler Inst. Am. Art, Ohio, Rutgers U., Hofstra U., Elvejhem Mus., Wis., N.Y. Pub. Libr., Duxbury Mus. Mass., USO of Met. N.Y., Amity Art Found., Conn., Reading (Pa.) Pub. Mus., Portland (Oreg.) Art Mus., De Cordova Mus., Lincoln, Mass., Yale U. Art Gallery, Utah Mus. Fine Arts, Ohio Wesleyan U., Worcester Mus. Art, Mass., Oakland Mus., Calif., U.S.O. Greater Met. N.Y., Reading Pub. Mus., Pa.; author numerous poems; contbr. articles to profl. jours. Named Conn. Woman of Decade in Arts, UN Assn., 1987, U.S.A. rep., Agart World Print Festival, Ljubljana, Slovenia, 1999, UN Artist of Yr., 2002; recipient Purchase award, Delta Internat. Prints, 1996, Etching award, L.A. Printmaking Soc., 1997, Painting award, Manhattan Arts Internat., 1997, Etching award, Audubon artists, 1997, Print Biennial Silvermine Guild of Art, Conn., 1998, Four winners award, Stamford Mus. & Nature Ctr., Conn., 1998, Eisner Found. award, 1998, Richard Florsheim award, 1998, Exhbn. award/Boston Printamkers and Delta Internat. awards, Print Club, 2001, Purchase award, Delta Internat. Prints, 2001, Trustees Merit award, Housantonic C.C., 2003, Legion of Honor award, Achenbach Found., San Francisco; fellow Yale Mellon, 1993—94; grantee Yale/Mellon, 1995. Mem.: N.Y. Etchers Soc., Print Club Albany, Print Club Phila., L.A. Print Soc., Boston Printmakers, Calif. Soc. Printmakers, Nat. Acad. Art, Nat. Acad. Art (elected Academician Graphics), Soc. Am. Graphic Artists (coun.). Studio: 2 Gorham Ave Westport CT 06880-2531 E-mail: finearts@rcn.com.

CHERNOW, BART, critical care physician; b. N.Y.C., June 26, 1947; BA, Queens Coll., 1968; MD, SUNY, N.Y.C., 1976. Internal medicine intern Nat. Naval Med. Ctr., Bethesda, Md., 1976-77, internal medicine resident, 1977-79, endocrine fellow, 1979-81; dir. rsch. dept. critical care medicine Bethesda Naval Hosp., 1981-85, head acad. affairs, 1985-86; assoc. prof. anesthesia Harvard Med. Sch., Boston, 1986-90; assoc. dir. surg. ICU Mass. Gen. Hosp., Boston, 1986-90; prof. medicine, anesthesia and critical care Johns Hopkins U. Sch. Medicine, Balt., 1990-99; physician-in-chief Sinai Hosp., Balt., 1990-97; program dir. John Hopkins U./Sinai Hosp. Program in Internal Medicine, Balt., 1990-97; vice dean for rsch. and tech. Sch. Medicine Johns Hopkins U. Sch. Medicine, Balt., 1997-99; pres., CEO GMP Cos., Inc., Ft. Lauderdale, Fla., 1999—. Adj. prof. medicine Johns Hopkins U. Sch. Medicine, 1999—. Editor: Pharmacologic Approach to the Critically Ill Patient, 1983, 88, 94; editor-in-chief: Critical Care Medicine, 1990-97. Comdr. med. corps USNR, 1969-86. Recipient Achievement award Am. Coll. Nutrition, 1995. Fellow ACP (master), Am. Coll. Critical Care Medicine; mem. Soc. Critical Care Medicine (Presdl. citation 1997), Am. Coll. Chest Physicians (regent 1990-98, pres. 1996-97, master fellow, chair CHEST found.1996-2002). Home: 2100 N Ocean Blvd Ph 30 Fort Lauderdale FL 33305-1940 Office: GMP Cos Inc Ste 1701 One E Broward Blvd Fort Lauderdale FL 33301 Fax: 954-745-3511.

CHERNOW, RON, writer, columnist; b. Bklyn., Mar. 3, 1949; s. Israel and Ruth (Goldspinner) C.; m. Valerie Stearn, Oct. 22, 1979. BA in English summa cum laude, Yale U., 1970; MA in English, Cambridge (Eng.) U., 1972. Free-lance writer, N.Y.C., 1973-82; program officer for fin. policy studies The Twentieth Century Fund, N.Y.C., 1983-86; writer, essayist, lectr., book reviewer N.Y.C., 1988—; occasional columnist The Wall St. Jour., 1990-91; commentator Nat. Pub. Radio, 1994-97. Frum Meml. lectr., 1997; guest curator Mus. Am. Fin. History, 1998-99; hist. cons. WGBH Boston. Author: The House of Morgan, 1990, The Warburgs, 1993, The Death of the Banker, 1997, Titan, 1998; also 13 cover stories; contbr. articles to N.Y. Times, N.Y. Mag., Time mag., Bus. Week, Saturday Rev., Vanity Fair, Am. Heritage, Smithsonian and 30 other publs. Vice chmn. Cambridge U. Assn. of N.Y., 1986-87. Recipient Jack London award United Steelworkers, 1980, Nat. Book award Nat. Book Found., 1990, Books to Remember award N.Y. Pub. Libr., 1990, Ambassador Book award English Speaking Union, 1991, George S. Eccles prize Columbia Bus. Sch., 1993, Notable Book citation ALA, 1993, Annual Book award Colonial Dames Am., 1998, Scholar of Yr. award N.Y. Coun. Humanities, 1999, Ohiana Book award Ohiana Libr., 1999, Abraham Lincoln Literary award The Union League Club, 2000. Mem. PEN (chmn. readers and writers com. 1994-98, trustee 1997-2003, sec. 1999, v.p. 2000-03), Authors Guild, Modern Libr. Bd., Leo Baeck Inst., Wildlife Conservation Soc., The Nature Conservancy, N.Y. Hist. Soc., Rembrandt Club, Phi Beta Kappa. Democrat. Jewish. Address: 63 Joralemon St Brooklyn NY 11201-4003

CHERNY, ROBERT WALLACE, history educator; b. Marysville, Kans., Apr. 4, 1943; s. Clarence L. and Lena M. (Hobbs) C.; m. Rebecca Ellen Marshall, June 11, 1967; 1 child, Sarah Catherine. BA with distinction, U. Nebr., 1965; MA, Columbia U., 1967, PhD, 1972. Instr. history San Francisco State U., 1971-72, asst. prof., 1972-77, assoc. prof., 1977-81, prof., 1981—, assoc. dean behavioral and social scis., 1984, acting dean behavioral and social scis., 1985, chmn. history dept., 1987-92, mem. acad. senate, 1981—84, 1995—, chair acad. senate, 2002—03, 2003—. Disting. Fulbright lectr. Moscow State U., 1996; vis. rsch. scholar U. Melbourne, 1997; cons. in field. Author: A Righteous Cause: The Life of William Jennings Bryan, 1985, rev. edit., 1994, Populism, Progressivism and the Transformation of Nebraska Politics, 1981, American Politics in the Gilded Age, 1869-1868, 1997; co-author: (with William Issel) San Francisco, 1865-1932, 1986, San Francisco: Presidio, Port and Pacific Metropolis, 1981, (with Carol Berkin, Christopher L. Miller, James L. Gormly) Making America: A History of the United States, 1995, 3d edit., 2003. Woodrow Wilson fellow, 1965-66, Woodrow Wilson dissertation fellow, 1969, NEH fellow, 1992-93. Mem. Am. Hist. Assn., Orgn. Am. Historians (treas. 2003-), S.W. Labor Studies Assn. (pres. 1982-86), Calif. Hist. Soc., Soc. Historians of Gilded Age and Progressive Era (pres. 1995), Nebr. State Hist. Soc., HNet--Humanities and Social Studies Online (pres. 2003). Democrat. Office: San Francisco State U Dept of History 1600 Holloway Ave San Francisco CA 94132-4155

CHEROUTES, MICHAEL LOUIS, lawyer; b. Chgo., Apr. 27, 1940; s. Louis Samuel Cheroutes and Maria Jane (Zimmerman) Dodd; m. Trisha Flynn, Oct. 30, 1965; children: Michael Louis Jr., Trisha Francesca, Matthew Dodd. BA, Harvard U., 1962; LLB, Stanford U., 1965. Bar: Colo. 1965. Assoc., then ptnr. Sherman & Howard, Denver, 1965-85; chief of staff to Rep. Patricia A. Shroeder U.S. Ho. of Reps., Washington, 1972-74; ptnr. Davis, Graham & Stubbs, Denver, 1985-93, Hogan & Hartson LLP, various, Colo., 1993—. Contbr. articles to profl. jours. Mem. Colo. Commn. on Higher Edn., 1988-91, chmn., 1989-91; mem. state bd. Gt. Outdoors Colo. Trust Fund, 1996-97. Mem. ABA, Colo. Bar Assn., Nat. Assn. Bond Lawyers. Avocation: sailing. Home: 2625 E Cedar Ave Denver CO 80209-3205 Office: Hogan & Hartson 1200 17th St Ste 1500 Denver CO 80202-5840 also: One Angel Ct London EC2R 7HJ England

CHEROVSKY, ERWIN LOUIS, lawyer, writer; b. Dover, NJ, Dec. 31, 1933; s. Sam and Ida (Bluestein) C.; m. Edith Mayer, June 26, 1966; children: Kim, Karen; children by previous marriage: Debra, Jill. AB, U. Rochester, 1955; LLB, Harvard U., 1958. Bar: N.Y. 1958, U.S. Dist. Ct. (so. dist.) N.Y. 1964, U.S. Ct. Appeals (2d cir.) 1964. Assoc. Stamer & Haft, N.Y.C., 1958-63, Summit Rovins & Feldesman, N.Y.C., 1963-68, ptnr., 1968-88, Proskauer Rose LLC, 1988-89; chmn., legal cost containment cons. WIK Cons. Inc., N.Y.C., 1992-97; pres. Old Quarry Devel., Englewood, N.J., 1996—. Sec. Space & Leisure Time, Ltd., N.Y.C., 1972-80, Ghiordian Knot, Ltd., N.Y.C., 1978-88, ORS Automation, Inc., Princeton, N.J., 1983-86, Cook United, Inc., Cleve., 1986; lit. agt. for Random House Russian-English Dictionary of Idioms, Sophia Lubensky, 1995, From Central Park to Sinai, Roy S. Neuberger, 2000. Author: The Guide to New York Law Firms, 1991, Competent Counsel: The Business Guide to Selecting, Hiring Lawyers and Monitoring Their Work, 1992; contbr. articles to profl. jours. Fellow Phi Beta Kappa Soc.; mem. N.Y.State Bar Assn., Assn. Bar City of N.Y., Fed. Bar Coun. (chmn. winter meeting 1980, mem. alternative dispute resolution com. 1984), Can. Club (N.Y.C.) (bd. govs. 1988-89, editor Maple Leaf 1984-89), Met. Club (N.Y.C.).

CHERPAS, CHRISTOPHER THEODORE, lawyer; b. Toledo, Mar. 23, 1924; s. Theodore C. and Mary (Veronie) C.; m. Ortha N. Mollis, June 23, 1946; children— Maria, Patricia, Christopher T. B.S. in Polit. Sci., Akron U., 1949; postgrad. Akron Law Sch., 1949-50, Western Res. U., 1951; J.D., Cleveland Marshall U., 1951. Bar: Ohio 1952, U.S. Dist. Ct. (7th dist.) Ohio 1954, U.S. Ct. Appeals (6th cir.) 1966. Counsel United Rubber Workers, Akron, Ohio, 1954-57; ptnr. Cherpas, Manos & Syracopoulos, Akron, 1957-74, Cherpas and Manos, Akron, 1974-79, Teodosio, Cherpas and Manos, Akron, 1979— . Served to capt. U.S. Army, ETO, PTO, Korea, 1942-46, 51-53. Mem. ABA, Ohio Bar Assn., Akron County Bar Assn., VFW, Am. Legion, Disabled Am. Vets, 37th Div. Assn. Democrat. Greek Orthodox. Clubs: Pan Arcadian Fedn. (Chgo.) (supreme pres. 1957-58); Fairlawn Country, Am. Hellenic Edn. Progressive Assn. (chpt. pres. 1979-80). Lodges: Masons, Shriners, K.T. Home: 1594 Alton Dr Akron OH 44313-6458 Office: Teodosio Cherpas Manos and Ward 907 Landmark Bldg 7 W Bowery St Akron OH 44308-1138

CHERRICK, RUTH E. medical researcher, researcher; b. Jersey City, N.J., Oct. 14, 1958; d. Dolores F. Posse, George D. Cherrick; m. Tim P Wunz; children: Melissa Knouse, Kerrie Knouse. BSBA, U. Phoenix, 1995; MPH, U. Ariz., 1997. Rsch. scientist U. Ariz., Tucson, 1995—99; faculty rsch. assoc., adj. prof. Ariz. State U., Tempe, 1999—2001. Owner Cherrick Consulting, Tucson, 1999—2002; rschr. dept. family and cmty. medicine U. Ariz. Chair HIV/AIDS sect. Am. Pub. Health Assn., Washington, 2001—02. Recipient Svc. award, Ariz. Dept. Health Svcs. HIV/AIDS/STDS Divsn., 1998, award, Health Svcs. Adv. Group, Ariz. Health Care Cost Containment Sys.; grantee Barriers to Workforce Participation for HIV-Infected Persons grantee, Glaxo Wellcome, 1997, Rev. Health Care Purchasing Options for County Employer grantee, Pima County Supervisors, 1998, New Cost Pressures to Health Care System grantee, Ariz. State U., 1998—99, Grant - Quantitative and Qualitative Evaluation of Latina Leadership Project grantee, So. Ariz. AIDS Found., 1999—2001, Phoenix EMA Title I HIV Health Svcs. Planning Coun. grantee, Maricopa County Dept. Public Health, 2000, 2001. Mem.: Assn. Health Svcs. Rsch., Ariz. Dept. Health Svcs. (com. mem. AIDS drug assistance program advisory coun.), Ariz. Pub. Health Assn. (chair health administration, rsch. & planning sect. 1999), Am. Pub. Health Assn. (chair HIV/AIDS sect. 2001—, Section Svc. award 2000, 2001). Office: Cherrick Consulting 675 N Northern Vista Place Tucson AZ 85748 also: U Ariz Dept Family and Cmty Medicine Tucson AZ Home Fax: 520-296-3342; Office Fax: 520-296-3342. Personal E-mail: ruth@cherrickconsulting.com. Business E-Mail: ruth@cherrickconsulting.com.

CHERRY, ANDREW LAWRENCE, JR., social work educator, researcher; b. Dothan, Ala., Nov. 11, 1943; s. Andrew L. Cherry and Wyalene Cain; m. Mary Elizabeth Dillon, July 16, 1988. MSW, U. Ala., Tuscaloosa, 1974; D Social Work, Columbia U., 1986. Child welfare worker Escambia County Dept. Pensions and Securities, Brewton, Ala., 1968-72; psychiat. social worker Bryce State Hosp., Tuscaloosa, 1974-79; instr. Salisbury (Md.) State Coll., 1981-85; asst. prof. Marywood Coll. Sch. Social Work, Scranton, Pa., 1986-87; prof. Barry U. Sch. Social Work, Miami, Fla., 1987—2003; prof. mental health Sch. Social Work U. Okla., Tulsa, 2003—, endowed prof. mental health sch. social work, 2003—. Cons. Informed Families Dade County, Miami, 1990—98, Miami Coalition for Care to Homeless, 1991—93, NAACP Minority Media and Telecomm. Coun., 1992—2000; with drug abuse prevention program Cath. Charities, Miami, 1991—2000, Broward Children's Svc., Ft. Lauderdale, 1992—94, The Biscayne Inst., 1994—, St. Luke's Addiction Recovery Ctr., 1995—2000; interim dir. child welfare divsn. Cath. Charities, 1998—2000. Author: The Socializating Instinct: Individual, Family and Social Bonds, 1994, A Research Primer for the Helping Professions: Methods, Statistics, and Writing, 2000, Examining Global Social Welfare Issues Using MicroCase, 2002; co-author: Social Bonds and Teen Pregnancy, 1992; co-editor: Teenage Pregnancy: A Global View, 2001, Substance Abuse: A Global View, 2002; contbr. articles to profl. jours. Scholar, NIMH, 1979. Fellow: Am. Orthopsychiat. Assn.; mem.: NASW, N.Y. Acad. Scis., Conf. Social Work Edn. Achievements include research in and devel. of the social bond theory; extensive work and rsch. among the mentally disabled, homeless, at-risk children and the addicted. Office: Barry U Sch Social Work 11300 NE 2nd Ave Miami FL 33161-6628 E-mail: alcherry@bronline.com.

CHERRY, BARBARA WATERMAN, speech and language pathologist, physical therapist; b. Norfolk, Va., June 25, 1949; d. Robert Bullock and Dorothy Estelle (Walsh) Waterman; m. Albert Glen Cherry, Sept. 17, 1977; 1 child, Dorothy Louise. BS in Phys. Therapy, U. Fla., 1972, MA in Speech-Lang. Pathology, 1982. Lic. phys. therapist, speech and lang. pathologist, Fla.; cert. tchr., Fla. Staff phys. therapist Retreat for the Sick Hosp., Richmond, Va., 1973-75; clin. instr. in phys. therapy Sch. of Rehab. Scis., Tehran, Iran, 1975-76; staff phys. therapist Sulmaniya Hosp., Manama, Bahrain, 1976-77, Cathedral Rehab. Ctr., Jacksonville, Fla., 1978-80; staff speech-lang. pathologist S. Allen Smith Clinic, Jacksonville, 1982-87, Mt. Herman Exceptional Child Ctr., Jacksonville, 1987-91, Duval County Sch. System, Jacksonville, 1991-98, Mt. Herman Exceptional Student Ctr., Jacksonville, 1998—, Brooks Rehab. Hosp., Jacksonville, 2003—. Mem. Am. Speech, Lang., and Hearing Assn., Am. Phys. Therapy Assn., Phi Kappa Phi. Episcopalian. Avocation: Karate (black belt). Home: 8821 Ivey Rd Jacksonville FL 32216-3369 Office: Mt Herman Exceptional Student Ctr 1741 Francis St Jacksonville FL 32209 E-mail: cherryab@bellsouth.net.

CHERRY, DANIEL RONALD, lawyer; b. Mpls., Dec. 31, 1948; s. Clifford D. and Ruby E. (Norman) C.; m. Dianne Brown, Jan. 24, 1971 (dec.); children: Matthew A., Kathryn E.; m. Q. Rhea Walker, Oct. 25, 1998. SB, MIT, 1970; JD cum laude, Harvard U., 1976. Bar: Ohio 1976, U.S. Dist. Ct. (no. dist.) Ohio 1976, U.S. Patent and Trademark Office 1978, U.S. Ct. Appeals (6th and Fed. cirs.) 1982, Ill. 1987, U.S. Dist. Ct. (no. dist.) Ill. 1987. Assoc. Squire, Sanders & Dempsey, Cleve., 1976-85, ptnr., 1985-87; ptnr., prin. Welsh & Katz, Ltd., Chgo., 1987—. Co-author: Patent Practice, 1997. With USCG, 1970-73. Mem. ABA, Ohio State Bar Assn., Ill. State Bar Assn., Chgo. Bar Assn., Am. Intellectual Property Law Assn., Intellectual Property Law Assn. Chgo., Licensing Execs. Soc. Home: 1046 Vine St Winnetka IL 60093-1834 Office: Welsh & Katz Ltd 120 S Riverside Plz # 22 Chicago IL 60606-3913

CHERRY, DAVID EARL, lawyer; b. Ft. Worth, Sept. 10, 1944; s. Leonard Earl and Dorothy Hazel (Brown) C.; m. Katherine Ann Yarborough, Dec. 23, 1967; children: Lisa, Craig. BBA, Tex. Christian U., 1967; JD, Baylor U., 1968. Bar: Tex. 1968, U.S. Dist. Ct. (we. dist.) Tex. 1970, U.S. Dist. Ct. (so. dist.) Tex. 1977, U.S. Ct. Appeals (5th cir.) 1977, U.S. Supreme Ct. 1978, U.S. Ct. Appeals (11th cir.) 1981, U.S. Ct. Claims 1985, U.S. Dist. Ct. (no. dist.) Tex. 1988, U.S. Dist. Ct. (ea. dist.) Tex. 1988. Ptnr. Pakis, Cherry, Beard & Giotes, Inc., Waco, Tex., 1969—91, Cherry, Davis, Harrison, Montez, Williams & Baird P.C., Waco, 1992-99, Campbell, Cherry, Harrison, Davis & Dove, P.C., Waco, 1999—. Mem. Charter Commn., Woodway, Tex., 1973; chmn. Planning and Zoning Commn., Woodway, 1976-79; bd. dirs. Heart of Tex. coun. Boy Scouts Am., Waco, 1985; mem. Nat. Exploring Com. Boy Scouts Am., Waco, 1977-82. Fellow Tex. Bar Found. (life); mem. ABA, ATLA, State Bar Tex., Am. Bd. Trial Advocates, Tex. Trial Lawyers Assn., Tex. Bd. Legal Specialization (cert. civil trial law), Coll. of State Bar of Tex., Waco-McLennan County Bar Assn., Waco-McLennan County Legal Aid Soc. (dir. 1971-73), Waco-McLennan County Young Lawyers Assn. (pres. 1974-75, Outstanding Young Lawyer 1977). Avocations: running, camping, fishing, photography, hunting. Office: Campbell Cherry Harrison Davis & Dove PC 5 Ritchie Rd Waco TX 76712

CHERRY, HAROLD, insurance company executive; b. Bronx, N.Y., June 20, 1931; s. Isidor and Esther C.; m. Maida Welt, Aug. 12, 1961; children— Gina, Joshua. BS cum laude, CCNY, 1953. With N.Y. Life Ins. Co., N.Y.C., 1956-89, 2d v.p., actuary, 1972-78, v .p., actuary, 1978-89; pres. Actuarial Study Materials, Merrick, N.Y., 1983—. Cons. in field. Served with U.S. Army, 1954-56. Fellow Soc. Actuaries; mem. Am. Acad. Actuaries, Nat. Assn. Watch and Clock Collectors (past pres. L.I. chpt.) Jewish. Office: Actuarial Study Materials 3217 Wynsum Ave Merrick NY 11566-5549

CHERRY, JAMES DONALE, pediatrician; b. Summit, N.J., June 10, 1930; s. Robert Newton and Beatrice (Wheeler) C.; m. Jeanne M. Fischer, June 19, 1954; children— James S., Jeffrey D., Susan J., Kenneth C. BS, Springfield (Mass.) Coll., 1953; MD, U. Vt., 1957; MSc in Epidemiology, London Sch. Hygiene and Tropical Medicine, 1983. Diplomate Am. Bd. Pediat., Am. Bd. Pediat. Infectious Diseases. Intern, then resident in pediat. Boston City Hosp., 1957-59; resident in pediat. Kings County Hosp., Bklyn., 1959-60; rsch. fellow in medicine Harvard U. Med. Sch.-Thorndike Meml. Lab., Boston City Hosp., 1961-62; instr. pediatrics U. Vt. Coll. Medicine, also asst. attending physician Mary Fletcher DeGoesbriand Meml. hosps., Burlington, Vt., 1960-61; asst. prof., then assoc. prof. pediat. U. Wis. Med. Sch., Madison, 1963-66; assoc. attending physician Madison Gen., U. Wis. hosps., 1963-66; dir. John A. Hartford Rsch. Lab., Madison Gen. Hosp., 1963-66. Mem. faculty St. Louis U. Med. Sch., 1966-73, prof. pediatrics, 1969-73, vice chmn. dept., 1970-73; mem. staff Cardinal Glennon Meml. Hosp. Children, St. Louis U. Hosp., 1966-73; chief divsn. infectious diseases UCLA Med. Ctr. UCLA Sch. Medicine, 1973-2000, prof. pediat., 1973—; acting chmn. dept. pediatrics UCLA Med. Ctr., 1977-79; attending physician, chmn. infection control com. UCLA Med. Ctr., 1975-93; cons. Project Head Start; vis. worker dept. cmty. medicine Middlesex Hosp. and Med. Sch., London, 1982-83; vis. worker Common Cold Rsch. Unit, 1969-70; mem. immunization adv. com. Los Angeles County Dept. Health Svcs., 1978—; acad. visitor U. Cambridge, Eng., 2000-01. Co-editor Textbook of Pediatric Infectious Diseases, 1981, 2nd edit., 1987, 4th edit., 1998; assoc. editor: Clin. Infectious Diseases, 1990-99; Am. regional editor: Vaccine, 1991-2000; author numerous papers in field; editl. reviewer profl. jours. Bd. govs. Alexander Graham Bell Internat. Parents Orgn., 1967-69. With USAR, 1958-64. John and Mary R. Markle scholar acad. medicine, 1964 Mem. AAAS, APHA, Am. Acad. Pediat. (mem. exec. com. Calif. chpt. 2 1975-77, mem. com. infectious diseases 1977-83, assoc. editor 19th Red Book 1982), Am. Soc. Microbiology, Am. Fedn. Clin. Rsch., Soc. Pediat. Rsch., Infectious Diseases Soc. Am., Am. Epidemiol. Soc., Am. Pediat. Soc., L.A. Pediat. Soc., Internat. Orgn. Mycoplasmologists, Am. Soc. Virology, Soc. Hosp. Epidemiologists Am., Pediat. Infectious Diseases Soc. (pres. 1989-91), Alpha Omega Alpha. Office: UCLA David Gaffon Sch Medicine Dept Pediatrics Rm 22-442 10833 Le Conte Ave Los Angeles CA 90095-3075 E-mail: jcherry@mednet.ucla.edu.

CHERRY, JOHN D., JR., lieutenant governor; b. Sulphur Springs, Tex., May 5, 1951; s. John D. Sr. and Margaret L. (Roark) C.; m. Pamela M. Faris, 1979; children: Meghan M., John D. BA, U. Mich., 1973; MA, 1984. Chmn. 7th Cong. Dist. Dem. Com., Mich., 1973-75; adminstrv. asst. Mich. State Sen. Gary Corbin, 1975-81; Mich. polit. dir. Am. Fedn. State, County & Munic Employees AFL-CIO, 1981-82; mem. Mich. Ho. Reps. from 79th dist., Lansing, 1983-86, Mich. Senate from 29th dist., 1987-95, Mich. Senate from 28th dist., lansing, 1995—; senate minority leader, mem. legis. coun.; lt. gov., 2003—. Mem. Oakland county Dem. Exec. Bd., 1995—; mem. Mich. Jobs Commn. Bd., 1996—; del. Dem. Nat. Conv., 1996. Mailing: PO Box 30013 Lansing MI 48909*

CHERRY, KENNETH JEROME, JR., surgeon; b. Richmond, Va., Oct. 22, 1947; s. Kenneth Jerome and Alice (Cuttingham) Cherry; m. Robin Wheeler, Sept. 10, 1983; children: Katherine, Sarah, Kenneth III. Undergraduate, Duke Univ., Durham, N.C., 1970; MD, Univ. Va., Richmond, 1974. Diplomate Am. Bd. Surgery, Gen. Vascular Surgery. Intern, resident surgery U. Va., Charlottesville, 1974-80; resident vascular surgery U. Calif. San Francisco, 1980-81; instr. surgery Mayo Med. Sch., Rochester, Minn., 1981—84, asst. prof. of surgery, 1988—95, assoc. prof. of surgery, 1995—, prof. of surgery, 1995—. Surgeon Rochester Meth. Hosp., St. Mary's Hosps., Rochester. Contbr. articles to profl. jour. Mem. ACS, Internat. Soc. Cardiovascular Surgeons, Midwestern Vascular Surg. Soc., Peripheral Vascular Soc., Soc. for Vascular Surgeons. Avocations: reading, history, outdoor activites. Home: 3581 Wright Rd SW Rochester MN 55902-1416 Office: Mayo Clin 200 First St SW Rochester MN 55905-0001

CHERRY, MIKE E. state legislator; b. Princeton, Ky., Feb. 6, 1943; m. Gale Cherry; 1 child, Davis. BS, Murray State U., 1966; MS, U. Louisville, 1972, Nat. Def. U., 1992. Commd. ensign USN, 1967, advanced through grades to capt.; owner Capitol Cinemas, 1996—; mem. Ky. Ho. of Reps., Frankfort, 1999—; mem. agr. & small com.; vice chmn. appropriations & revenue com. Bd. dirs. Caldwell City (Ky.) Free Clinic; mem. based decision-making com. Caldwell City HS, mem. site-based coun.; chair Princeton Tourism Commn.; treas., pres. Ch. Men's Fellowship. Mem.: VFW, Kiwanis, Elks (Citizen of the Yr.), Am. Legion. Democrat. Presbyterian. Office: Capital Annex # 332 700 Capitol Ave Frankfort KY 40601 also: 803 S Jefferson St Princeton KY 42445 Business E-Mail: mike.cherry@irc.state.ky.us.*

CHERRY, PAUL STEPHEN, lawyer; b. Phila., Oct. 6, 1943; s. Herbert Isdor and Toby (Ring) C.; m. Hilary Kirwan, Apr. 8, 1972. BA, Temple U., 1966; JD, Widener U., 1982. Pa. 1983, U.S. Dist. Ct. (ea. dist.) Pa. 1983, U.S. Ct. Appeals (3d and fed. cirs.) 1983, U.S. Ct. Internat. Trade 1983, U.S. Ct. Claims 1983, U.S. Tax Ct. 1983, U.S. Supreme Ct. 1986, U.S. Ct. Vets. Appeals 1995, U.S. Ct. Appeals (11th cir.) 1996, Fla. 1997; registered sanitarian. Sci. tchr. Cen. High Sch., Phila., 1966-67; instr. physiology Regional Sch. Nursing, Owen Sound, Ont., Can., 1967-68; tchr. natural sci. Sir Sanford Fleming Coll., Peterborough, Ont., 1968-69; sanitarian Dept. Pub. Health, Phila., 1972-73, Chester County Health Dept., West Chester, Pa., 1974-79; pvt. practice law Wayne, Pa., 1983-95; asst. pub. defender 20th Jud. Cir., Fla., 1998—2001; sr. atty. child welfare svcs. Fla. DCF, 2001—03. Operating engr. Sound and Light Show at Independence Hall, Phila., 1961-82; bd. dirs. Hist. Soc. of U.S., Dist. Ct. (ea. dist.) Pa., Phila., 1985-95; mem. traffic com. Tredyffrin Twp., Berwyn, Pa., 1991. Recipient Annual recognition Women Against Abuse, Phila., 1986. Fellow Lawyers in Mensa (main line coord. 1985-95); mem. Pa. Bar Assn., B'nai B'rith (pres. Freedom Valley Lodge, Valley Forge, Pa. 1992-95). Democrat. Jewish. Avocations: classical music, acoustics, computers, pipe organ constrn. Home: 6625 Taeda Dr Sarasota FL 34241-9149 Office: 805 N Mills ave Arcadia FL 34266 E-mail: paul_s_cherry_esquire@msn.com.

CHERRY, PETER BALLARD, electrical products corporation executive; b. Evanston, Ill., May 25, 1947; s. Walter Lorain and Virginia Ames (Ballard) C.; m. Crissy Hazard, Sept. 6, 1969; children: Serena Ames, Spencer Ballard. BA, Yale U., 1969; MBA, Stanford U., 1972. Analyst Cherry Elec. Products Corp., Waukegan, Ill., 1972-74, data processing and systems mgr., 1974, treas., 1974-77; v.p. fin. and bus. devel. Cherry Elec. Products Corps., Waukegan, Ill., 1977-80; exec. v.p. Cherry Elec. Products Corp., Waukegan, Ill., 1980-82, pres., chief oper. officer, 1982-86; pres., chief exec. officer Cherry Corp., Waukegan, 1986-92, chmn., pres., 1992—. Trustee Lake Forest Coll., Ill., 1982-90; trustee Lake Forest Hosp., 1982—, chmn., 1989-92. Mem.Onwentsia Club. Office: Cherry Corp 3600 Sunset Ave Waukegan IL 60087-3214

CHERRY, ROBERT STEVEN, III, municipal administrator; b. Chgo., Aug. 13, 1951; s. Robert Lee and Jean Louise (Curry) C. BA, Kensington U., 1988. With Chgo. Pk. Dist., 1968—, aquatic supr., 1983—, supr. beaches and swimming pool lifeguards south side, 2003. Asst. capt. 37th precinct, 7th ward, City of Chgo., 1979-80, precinct capt., 1980-83, asst. precinct capt. 2d precinct, 42d ward, 1984-92, capt., 1992-2002. 1st lt. U.S. Army/Ill. Nat. Guard, 1970-82. Named one of Outstanding Young Men of Am., 1985. Mem. Am. Legion (Post 1976), Young Dems. Am. (Ill. del. 1985), Young Dems. Ill., Young Dems. Cook County, U.S. Water Polo, U.S. Lifesaving Assn., Res. Officers Assn. U.S., Pub. Svc. Employees Union, Lambda Alpha Epsilon. Roman Catholic. Avocations: reading, backgammon, table tennis, swimming. Office: Chgo Park Dist 541 N Fairbanks Chicago IL 60611

CHERRY, VIVIAN, photographer; b. N.Y.C., July 27, 1920; d. Samuel and Ida (Agranovitch) C.; m. Herb Tank; m. 2d Eric Schmidt; 1 child, Steven Schmidt; m. 3d Louis Finger; m. 4th Alex Redein. One-woman shows include 44th St. Gallery, N.Y.C., 1940, The Gallery, St. Mary's Coll. of Md., St. Mary's City, 1990, Ctrl. Fine Arts, Soho, N.Y.C., 1992, 1993, 1994, Donnell Libr. Ctr., 1996, 7th and 2d Photo Gallery, 1997, Bklyn. Mus. Art, 2000, Lee Gallery, Winchester, Mass., 2001, Soho Triad Fine Arts, N.Y.C., 2001, SK Josefsberg Studio, Portland, Oreg., 2003, exhibited in group shows at Art Dir.'s Exhibit, N.Y.C., 1950, Ctrl. Fine Arts, 1991, Mus. Modern Art, 1995, 2002, The Bklyn. Mus. Art, 1996, 1997, The N.Y. Pub. Libr., 1998, Stephen Daiter Gallery, Chgo., 2000, Represented in permanent collections Nat. Portrait Gallery, Smithsonian Instn., Washington, D.C., Internat. Mus. Fine Arts, Pretoria, South Africa, Bergen County Mus. Fine Arts Marquette U., Paramus, N.J., The N.Y. Pub. Libr., Bklyn. Mus. Art, Mus. Modern Art, N.Y.C., Columbus (Ohio) Mus. Art, Internat. Ctr. Photography, N.Y.C.; photographer Parents Guide to Child Problems, The Long Loneliness (Dorothy Day), Loaves and Fishes (Dorothy Day); prodr., photographer, photographer: (films) Hello Halloween, 1970; works featured in: Popular Photography, Salon Photography, Colliers, Jubilee, Amerika, Coronet, Scope mag., numerous others; contbr. photographs, photographs Cityscapes, 2001; photographer Cityscapes, The Lower East Side, This Was the Photo League; Exhibited in group shows at Monroe Gallery of Photography, Santa Fe, N.Mex., 2002, Represented in permanent collections Marquette Univ., Milw., Wis., Mus. Modern Art, N.Y.C., N.Y., Columbus Ohio Mus. Art, SK Josefsberg Studio, Portland, Oreg., Internat. Ctr. for Photography. Home: 343 E 30th St New York NY 10016-6417 E-mail: vivcherry@yahoo.com.

CHERRY, WILLIAM ASHLEY, surgeon, state health officer; b. Halls, Tenn., Oct. 25, 1924; s. and Bessie R. C.; m. Jacqueline Guidry, June 2, 1989; children by previous marriage: Neal, Darrell, Philip, Susan. BS, Tulane U., 1946, MD, 1949. Diplomate Am. Bd. Surgery. Rotating intern Phila. Gen. Hosp., 1949-51; resident gen. surgery La. State U. div. Charity Hosp., New Orleans, 1953-56, resident thoracic surgery, 1956-57, asst. chief fracture service, 1963-65; practice medicine specializing in gen. and thoracic surgery New Iberia, La., 1957-63; commd. med. officer USPHS, 1963; mem. surg. staff USPHS Hosp., New Orleans, 1963-66, dir., 1966-71, asst. chief surgery dept., 1963-65, dep. chief, 1965-66, dir., 1966-71; regional health dir. Health Services and Mental Health Adminstrn., HEW, USPHS, Region VI, Dallas, 1971-74; sec., state health officer La. Dept. Health and Human Resources, Baton Rouge, 1977-80; commd. ensign USN, 1946, advanced through grades to comdr., 1963; sr. surgeon, comdr. USPHS, 1963; advanced through grades to asst. surgeon gen., admiral; comdg. officer Naval Res. Med. Co. 8-32, 1953-55; ret., 1963; chief med. officer USCG, Washington, 1974-77; pres., CEO, S. La. Health Svcs., Inc., 1987; med. dir. Lallie Kemp Regional Med. Ctr., Independence, La., Div. Mental Retardation and Developmental Disabilities, State of La., Baton Rouge, 1992-93, La. Dept. Health and Hosps., 1992-93; CEO, La. Health Care Authority, 1993-96; staff Met. Health Group, 1996—. Asst. clin. dir. surgery Charity Hosp., 1956-57, vis. surgeon, 1963— ; chief of surgery Iberia Parish Hosp., 1959-61; chief of staff Dauterive Hosp., New Iberia, 1962-63; clin. asso. instr., surgery dept. La. State U. Sch. Medicine, 1953-57, clin. instr., 1963-66, clin. asst. prof. surgery, 1966-67; clin. asso. prof. surgery Tulane U. Sch. Medicine, 1967-70; adj. asso. prof. health services adminstrn. Tulane U. Sch. Medicine (Sch. Pub. Health and Tropical Medicine), 1969-70, adj. prof., 1970-73, clin. prof. surgery, 1970— Contbr. articles to med. jours. Chmn. ofcl. bd. First Methodist Ch., New Iberia, 1960-62; mem. ofcl. bd. Carrollton Meth. Ch., New Orleans, 1964-66; chmn. La. Inter-Agy. Council for Tb, 1966-70; mem. exec. com. New Orleans Poison Control Center, 1966-71; mem. Health Goals Task Force, State of La., 1969-70; mem. Fed. Exec. Bd., New Orleans, 1970-71, Dallas, 1972-73; med. adv. to sec. Dept. Transp., 1974-77; pres. So. Inst. Human Resources, Atlanta, 1979-80; mem. La. Gov.'s Adv. Com. on Edn. of Handicapped Children, 1977-80. Recipient Querens-Rives-Shore award Tulane U. Sch. Medicine, 1949; USPHS Commendation medal, 1969; USPHS Meritorious Service medal, 1974; USPHS Disting. Service award, 1980; USCG Meritorious Service award, 1977; cert. of merit State of La., 1980; Grace A. Goldsmith Disting. Alumnus lectr. Tulane U. Med. Alumni Assn., 1974 Fellow ACS; mem. USPHS Clin. Soc., Nat. Tb Assn., James D. Rives Surg. Soc., Commd. Officers Assn., Mil. Order World Wars, La. Heart Assn., La. Tb and Respiratory Disease Assn. (dir. 1964—), La. Thoracic Soc., La. Pub. Health Assn., Assn. Mil. Surgeons of U.S.,

Phi Beta Kappa, Alpha Omega Alpha, Delta Omega. Home: 12674 S Highmeadow Ct Baton Rouge LA 70816-2528 Office: 4550 North Blvd Ste 100 Baton Rouge LA 70806-4013 Fax: 225-926-3346. E-mail: quack_70817@yahoo.com.

CHERTOFF, MICHAEL, judge; b. Elizabeth, NJ, Nov. 28, 1953; BA, Harvard U., 1975, JD, 1978. Bar: D.C. 1980, N.Y. 1987, N.J. 1990. Summer assoc. Miller, Cassidy, Larroca & Lewin, 1978; law clk. to Hon. Murray Gurfein U.S. Ct. Appeals (2d cir.), N.Y.C., 1978-79; law clk. to Hon. William J. Brennan Jr. U.S. Supreme Ct., Washington, 1979-80; assoc. Latham & Watkins, Washington, 1980-83, ptnr., 1994—2001; asst. U.S. atty. U.S. Atty.'s Office, N.Y.C., 1983-87, 1st asst. U.S. atty. Newark, 1987-90, U.S. atty., 1990—94; spl. counsel for Whitewater com. U.S. Senate, 1994—96; asst. atty. gen. criminal div. U.S. Dept. Justice, Washington, 2001—03; circuit judge U.S. Ct. Appeals, 3rd cir., 2003—. Mem. lawyer's adv. com. U.S. Dist. Ct. N.J., Newark, 1990—, U.S. Atty. Gen.'s Adv. com. of U.S. Atty.'s, Washington, 1991—. Recipient John Marshall award U.S. Dept. Justice, Washington, 1987. Office: James A Byrne Cthse 601 Market St Philadelphia PA 19106*

CHERTOK, DANIEL LVOVICH, mathematician, researcher; b. St. Petersburg, Russia, Aug. 6, 1967; s. Lev Efimovich and Irina Alexandrovna Chertok; m. Bonnie Woo; children: Alexandra Natalie children: Matthew Daniel. MSc in Engring. Math., St. Petersburg Tech. U., St. Petersburg, Russia, 1990; PhD, Simon Fraser U., Burnaby, B.C., Can., 1998. Rschr. St. Petersburg Inst, for Problems of Mech. Engring., St. Petersburg, Russia, 1990—93; front office devel. analyst Bank of Nova Scotia, Toronto, Canada, 1998—2000; computer systems analyst/mathematician Deerfield Capital Mgmt., LLC., Chgo., 2000—. Contbr. articles. Mem.: Profl. Risk Mgrs. Internat. Assn., Global Assn. of Risk Profls. Avocation: tennis. Office: Deerfield Capital Mgmt LLC 8700 W Bryn Mawr Ave 12th Floor Chicago IL 60631 Office Fax: 773-380-1601. E-mail: daniel_chertok@hotmail.com.

CHERTOW, BRUCE S. endocrinologist; b. Chgo., July 19, 1941; MD, U. Ill. Coll. Medicine, 1965. Diplomate Am. Bd. Internal Medicine. Chief endocrinology clinic Madigan Army Hosp., Tacoma, Wash., 1970-72; from asst. prof. to assoc. prof. U. Ill. Coll. Medicine, Chgo., 1972-78; prof. medicine, chief endocrinology Marshall Univ. Sch. Medicine, Huntington, W.Va., 1978—. Fellow ACP, Am. Coll. Endocrinology, Am. Assn. Clin. Endocrinologists; mem. Am. Fedn. Med. Rsch., Am. Diabetes Assn., Endocrine Soc. Office: Marshall U Sch Medicine 1600 Medical Center Dr Ste G500 Huntington WV 25701-3659

CHERTOW, MARIAN RUTH, industrial ecologist, educator; b. Syracuse, N.Y., Apr. 14, 1955; d. Bernard and Doris (Saltzman) C.; m. Matthew L. Nemerson, Nov. 10, 1985; children: Elana, Joy. BA magna cum laude, Barnard Coll., Columbia U., 1977; MA in Pub. and Pvt. Mgmt., Yale U., 1981, PhD, 2000. Dir. mktg. devel. Resource Recovery Systems, Inc., Branford, Conn., 1978-79; fin. mgr. Solid Waste Mgmt. Program City and County of San Francisco, 1981-83; from asst. to town mgr. to asst. town mgr. Town of Windsor, Conn., 1983-86; pres. Conn. Resources Recovery Authority, 1986-88; sr. fellow, author The U.S. Conf. of Mayors, 1988-89; dir. indsl. environ. mgmt. program Yale U., 1991—. Bd. dirs. Tax Exempt Proceeds Fund, Eco-Indsl. Devel. Coun., 2002—; mem. adv. bd. Conn. Clean Energy Fund, Alliance for Environ. Innovation. Mem. editorial bd. Bio Cycle Magazine, Jou. Indsl. Ecology; contbr. articles to profl. jours. Mem. ASPA (past pres. Conn. Coun.). Home: 35 Huntington St New Haven CT 06511-1332 Office: Yale Sch of Forestry & Environ Studies 205 Prospect St New Haven CT 06511-2106

CHERWENKA, RICHARD WAYNE, anesthesiologist; b. Merrill, Wis., 1943; MD, Med. Coll. Wis., 1971. Diplomate Am. Bd. Anesthesiology. Intern Milw. County Gen. Hosp., 1971-72; resident Med. Coll. Wis., Milw., 1975-77; mem. staff Elmbrook Meml. Hosp., Brookfield, Wis., 1978—; pvt. practice Brookfield, 1978—. Mem.: AMA, Am. Soc. Anesthesiologists.

CHERY, REGINALD, minister; b. Bklyn., July 12, 1968; s. Pierre Charlot and Viviane Chery; m. Bernadette L. Armstrong, Sept. 16, 2001. BBA in Computer Info. Sys., Baruch Coll., 1993; MDiv, Andrews U., 1997. Ordained elder, lic. min. Seventh-day Adventist Ch. Sales person Superior Computer Svcs., NYC, 1988; sys. analyst Rsch. Found. Mental Hygiene, NYC, 1992—93; bible worker assoc. evangelist Grand Concourse Seventh Day Adventist Ch., Bronx, NY, 1998; min. Gen. Conf. Seventh Day Adventist Chs., Silver Springs, Md., 1999—. Computer cons. Northeastern Conf. Seventh Day Adventists, Queens, NY, 1997; sch. chaplain Oakview Prep. Sch., Yonkers, NY, 1999—2002. Author: (manual) Straight Talk Youth Ministry. Recipient Police Athletic Leagues award, 1984. Mem.: Black Ministers Assn. Greater NY (assoc.). Seventh-Day Adventist. Achievements include design of Hotel Software. Avocations: basketball, reading, football, travel, weightlifting. Office: Gen Conf Seventh-day Adventists 12501 Old Columbia Pike Silver Spring MD 20904 Personal E-mail: ministerchery@aol.com.

CHESBRO, WESLEY, state senator; b. 1952; m. Cindy Chesbro; children: Collin, Alan. Student, Humboldt State U.; BA in Orgnl. Behavior, U. San Francisco. Mem. Calif. State Senate, 1998—, chair standing com. on revenue and taxation, chair select com. on Calif.'s wine industry, chair select com. on devel. disabilities and mental health, mem. budget and fiscal rev. com., edn. com., mem. environ. quality com., govtl. orgn. com., VA com. Founding mem. Calif. INtegrated Waste Mgmt. Bd., 1990-98; mem. Humboldt County Bd. Suprs., 1980-90; mem. Arcata City Coun., 1974-80. Democrat. Office: 50 D St Ste 120A Santa Rosa CA 95404-6535 also: State Capitol Rm 3070 Sacramento CA 95814*

CHESEBRO, JAMES WILLIAM, communication educator; b. Mpls., June 24, 1944; s. Floyd Jerome and Jeanette Mary (Campbell) C. BA, U. Minn., 1966, PhD, 1972; MS, Ill. State U., 1967. Instr. Concordia Coll., Moorhead, Minn., 1967-69; tchg. assoc. U. Minn., Mpls., 1969-72; assoc. prof. Temple U., Phila., 1972-81; prof. Queens Coll. CUNY, Flushing, 1981-89; dir. ednl. svcs. Nat. Comm. Assn., Annandale, Va., 1989-92; prof. Ind. State U., Terre Haute, 1992—. Vis. prof. U. P.R., PR, 1980; adj. prof. George Mason U., Fairfax, Va., 1989—92; vis. prof. Ctr. for Media Design, Ball State U., 2002—. Author: Analyzing Media, 1996; Computer-Mediated Communication, 1989; contbr. over 100 articles to profl. jours. Recipient Disting. Svc. award Nat. Kenneth Burke Soc., 1993. Mem. Nat. Commn. Assn. (pres. 1995-96, Golden Ann. Monograph award 1985, Disting. Svc. award 1997), Ea. Comm. Assn. (pres. 1982-83, Disting. Svc. award 1989, Hunt Scholarship award 1989, 97). Avocations: antiques, geneology. Office: Ind State U Dept Comm Terre Haute IN 47809

CHESER, RAYMOND NORRIS, III, healthcare company executive; b. Louisville, Oct. 17, 1947; s. Raymond N. II and Martha June C.; m. Elena Tymoshkina; 1 child, Stephanie Cheser. BS, Tex. A&M U., 1970, MS, 1976; MBA, U. Conn., 1983; DBA, Nova Southeastern U., 1996. Rsch. chemist The Dow Chem. Co., Freeport, Tex., 1970-76; engring., mfg. mgr. Johnson and Johnson, Skillman, N.J., 1977-80, Southington, Conn., 1980-92, dir. quality assurance, 1995-96; engring. mgr. C.R. Bard, Billerica, Mass., 1992-95; dir. continous improvement U.S. Surg. Corp., North Haven, Conn., 1997—2000; dir. quality United Health Group, Uniprise, Hartford, Conn., 2001—. Adj. faculty Boston U., 1994-95; adj. assoc. prof. Albertus Magnus Coll., New Haven, 1996—, U. New Haven, 2000—; spkr. in field. Contbr. articles to profl. jours. Bd. dirs. New Britain Symphony, 1989-90. Recipient Shingo prize for mfg. rsch., 1999. Mem. Acad. of Mgmt., Assn. for Mfg. Excellence, Internat. Assn. of Facilitators. Avocations: music composition, clay sculpture, art collector. E-mail: rayc@ziplink.net.

CHESKIDOV, ALEXEY P. mathematics educator; b. Novosibirsk, Russia, Feb. 5, 1976; s. Petr A. Cheskidov and Svetlana I. Cheskidova. Assoc. instr. Ind. U., Bloomington, 1999—2002; lectr. Tex. A&M U., College Station, 2002—. Contbr. articles to profl. jours. Joseph & Frances Morgan Swain fellow, Dept. of Math., Ind. U., 2000. Mem.: Soc. Indsl. and Applied Math., Am. Math. Soc. Office: Dept Math Ind U Bloomington IN 47405 Office Fax: 812-855-0046. E-mail: acheskid@indiana.edu.

CHESLER, DORIS ADELLE, real estate professional; b. Lincoln, Ill., Sept. 23, 1924; d. Harry and Esther Pearl (Campbell) Schoth; m. Eugene Albert Aughenbaugh, May 23, 1943 (div. Sept. 1970); children: Judith C., Rodney E., Paula Sue; m. Arthur Bernard Chesler, Oct. 16, 1972 (dec. Oct. 1998). Lic. real estate broker Fla. Realtor, assoc. Kilgore Real Estate, Brandon, Fla., 1969-76; broker Doris A. Chesler, Brandon, 1976—. Den mother Cub Scouts Am., Tampa, 1961-62; leader 4-H Club, Decatur, Ill., 1956. Republican. Presbyterian. Avocations: interior decorating, sewing, gardening, music, painting.

CHESLER, GAIL, arts organization development executive; b. Phila., May 22; d. Leon William and Sylvia (Spiegel) C.; m. Richard Allen Lippe (div. May 1989); children; Wendy Ann, David Allen. BA in History, Beaver Coll.; MA in Performing Arts Adminstrn., NYU, 1988. Outreach coord. North Shore Cmty. Arts Ctr., Gt. Neck, N.Y., 1976-79; pub. rels. cons. Gt. Neck, 1979-85; dir. of devel. and mktg. ART/New York, N.Y.C., 1987-88; exec. dir. Jennifer Muller/The Works, N.Y.C., 1989; dir. of devel. Temple Beth-El, Gt. Neck, 1989-92; nat. dir. planned giving and endowments Women's Am. ORT, N.Y.C., 1993-96; planned giving officer N.Y. Presbyn. Hosp./Weill Med. Coll. of Cornell U., N.Y.C., 1996-2000; dir. planned and spl. gifts The Met. Opera, N.Y.C., 2000—. Co-founder, bd. dirs. Teen to Teen, Carle Place, N.Y., 1985-88. Mem. Planned Giving Group of Greater N.Y. (past pres. 1999—, pres. 1998-99, v.p. 1997-98, treas. 1996-97). Avocations: opera, travel, theater. Home: 128 Central Park S # 3B New York NY 10019-1565 Office: The Metropolitan Opera Lincoln Ctr New York NY 10023

CHESLEY, STANLEY MORRIS, lawyer; b. Cin., Mar. 26, 1936; s. Frankl and Rachel (Kinsburg) C.; children: Richard A., Lauren B. BA, U. Cin., 1958, LLB, 1960. Bar: Ohio 1960, Ky. 1978, W.Va. 1981, Tex. 1981, Nev. 1981. Ptnr. Waite, Schneider, Bayless & Chesley Co., Cin., 1960—. Contbr. articles to profl. jours. Bd. dirs., past chmn. bd. commrs. on grievances and discipline Supreme Ct. Ohio; past pres. Jewish Fedn. Cin.; nat. vice chair, bd. govs., trustee, joint distbn. com. United Jewish Coms.; exec. bd., nat. bd. govs. Am. Jewish Com.; nat. bd. govs. Hebrew Uninon Coll.; exec. com. U.S. Holocaust Meml. Mus. Mem. ABA, ATLA, FBA, Am. Judicature Soc., Melvin M. Belli Soc., Ohio Bar Assn., Ky. Bar Assn., W.Va. Bar Assn., Tex. Bar Assn., Nev. Bar Assn., Cin. Bar Assn. Office: Waite Schneider Bayless & Chesley 1513 Central Trust Towers Cincinnati OH 45202 E-mail: wsbclaw@aol.com.

CHESLIK, FRANCIS EDWARD, management consultant; b. Saginaw, Mich., July 26, 1942; s. Wallace Paul and Nellie Elizabeth (Spurbeck) C. BS, Ctrl. Mich. U., 1964; MA, Wayne State U., 1972, PhD, 1977. Cert. tchr. Mich. Gen. mgr. WSUP-FM, Platteville, Wis., 1983-85; comm. rsch. prof. Seton Hall U., South Orange, N.J., 1985-91; dir. Comm. Ctr. Lincoln Meml. U., Harrogate, Tenn., 1991-93; cons. Comm. Mgmt. Rsch. Assocs., Emerson, N.J., 1985—. Commr. Cable TV Commn., Dubuque, Iowa, 1983-85; regional dir. AERho Nat. Broadcasting Soc., Jonesboro, Ark., 1983; mem. bd. govs. WSOU-FM, South Orange, N.J., 1985-91; media application cons. St. Peters Coll., Jersey City, N.J., 1991. Contbr. articles to profl. jours. Charity contest judge Nabisco, Buffalo, 1995. Mem. Nat. Comm. Assn., Internat. Comm. Assn., Tau Kappa Epsilon, Tau Kappa Epsilon (Advisor Recognition 1985, 86, 91, Creation Dr. Cheslik award 1991), Alpha Epsilon Rho (Advisor Recognition 1983, 87). Avocations: computer network evaluation, reading, videography, golf, french cooking. Home: 134 E Ackerman Ave Emerson NJ 07630-1923

CHESNEY, LEE ROY, JR., artist; b. Washington, June 1, 1920; s. Lee Roy and Rena Ruth (Beach) C.; m. Betty J. Lamb, Jan. 28, 1943; children: Lee Roy III, Terril Ann Bauer. B.F.A., U. Colo., 1946; M.F.A., U. Iowa, 1948; postgrad., U. Michoacan, Mex., 1950-51. Instr. drawing U. Iowa, 1947-50; prof. art, dir. printmaking, head grad. printmaking and painting U. Ill., Urbana, 1950-67; assoc. dean fine arts U. So. Calif., Los Angeles, 1967-72; prof. art, chmn. grad. art programs U. Hawaii, Honolulu, 1972-84, prof. emeritus, 1984—; Louis D. Beaumont vis. disting. prof. Washington U. Vis. artist Otis Art Inst., L.A., U. Colo., U. Wash., Mich. State U., Honolulu Acad. Arts Sch., Visual Arts Center, Anchorage, Portland (Oreg.) State U., 1988, U. Fla., 1989, Lacoste Sch. Arts, France, 1989, UCLA, 1989-90 ; mem. com., nat. juror Sr. Fulbright Research Awards, 1968-71, com. chmn., 1969-71; mem. visual arts selection com., Calif. Arts Coun., 1990; juror Hawaii Print Exhbn., 1991, 10th Internat. Pacific Rim Exhbn. Hilo, Hawaii, 1994; mem. Pacific Rim Lectrs. and Workshops, 1992; artist-in-residence U. Tex., 1993, Pacific Rim Series, 1994. Symposium Amon Carter Mus., Ft. Worth, 1990, Archer M. Huntington Art Gallery, 1993; one-man shows include Newman Brown Gallery, Chgo., U. Fla., U. Louisville, U. Mich., U. Wis., Madison, Ohio State U., Ill. State U., Yoseido Gallery, Tokyo, Atrium Gallery, Seattle, Visual Arts Center, Anchorage, Washington U., St. Louis, U. Utah, U. Alaska, Am. Cultural Ctr., Paris, 1964, Fisher Galleries, U. So. Calif., 1968, Honolulu Acad. Arts, 1973, Comsky Gallery, Beverly Hills, Calif., 1970—76, Downtown Gallery, Honolulu, 1975, BIMC Galerie, Paris, 1979, 1981, 1983, Galerie Sandoz, 1979, Cité Internat. des Arts, 1979, Honolulu Acad. of Arts, Focus Gallery, 1985, Contemporary Arts Center, Honolulu, 1980, 25-yr. retrospective exhbn. of prints circulated by U. Fla., 1977—80, retrospective exhbn. Portland State U., 1988, U. Fla., 1989, Printmaking 1985, Tallahassee, So. Graphics Coun. Emeritus Printmaker Exhbn. Knoxville Mus. Art, 1992, Williams Lamb Gallery, Long Beach, Calif., 1990, 1992, West Tex. A&M U., 1993, Oracle (Ariz.) Art Ctr., 1995, Parsons Sch. Design, Paris, 1998, solo exhbn. of paintings, Davis Dominguez Gall., Tucson, Ariz., 1999—2000, exhibited in group shows at Am. Fedn. Arts traveling exhbn., Mus. Modern Art traveling exhbn., USIS traveling exhbn., Soc. Am. Graphic artists traveling exhbns., 1973—77, Nihon Sosaku Hanga Kyokai, 1957—84, Contemporary Am. Painting, Bucharest, 1977, Hawaii Nat. Biennial Print Exhbn., Honolulu Acad. Arts, 1971, 1973, 1975, 1977, 1978, 1980, 1983, BIMC Galerie, 1978, 1979, 1980, 1981, 1982, 1983, 70th Nat. Invitational Drawing Exhbn., Emporia, Kans., 1986, U. West Fla., 1986, Neville-Sargent Gallery, 1986, Northwest Printmakers, 1986, U. Calif., Davis, 1985, Calif. Artists exhbn. at Thomas Ctr. Gallery, Gainesville, Fla., 1987, 25th Anniversary Exhbn. State Found. for Culture and the Arts (reproduction), Honolulu, 1988, 50th Anniversary Exhbn. of Commd. Prints, Honolulu Printmakers, Honolulu Acad. of Arts, 1988, N.W. Print Coun. Exhbn., Australia, 1988, Overreact Gallery, Long Beach, 1989, U. Hawaii, Hilo, 1989, Williams Lamb Gallery, 1990, 1991, 1992, Worcester (Mass.) Art Mus., 1991, Amon Carter Mus., 1990, Ft. Worth, 1990, Artists Who Teach Exhbn., Champaign, Ill., 1990, Nelson Atkins Mus., Kansas City, 1990, Mona Bismark Found., Paris, 1991, Soc. Am. Graphic Artists (prize) Nat. Exhbn., N.Y.C., Internat. Exhbn. Artists of Lacoste, France, Paris, 1991, San Diego Art Inst. Invitational, 1991, Williams Lamb Gallery, Long Beach, Calif., 1991, 1992, 12th U. Dallas Nat. Print Exhbn., 1991, 1992, Nat. Exhbn. Copper Engraving, Portand, Oreg., 1992, Pacific States Biennial Exhbn., Hilo, 1992—94, Northwest Print Coun., Eugene, Oreg., 1993, Indpls. Mus. Art, 1993, Pacific Rim Internat., 1993, 1997 (award), Works on Paper, L.A., 1995, 1996, 1997, 1998, Southern Graphics Exhib. of Disting. Print Makers, Tampa, Fla., 1997, L.A. Print Soc. Exhbn., 1997, Portland Art Mus. Intern. Pr. Exhib., 1997, Davis Dominguez Gallery, Tucson, 1997, "Exclusively Etchings" Lankersheim Arts, Pacific Rim Internat. Monoprint Exhibition, Hilo, Hawaii, 1998, State Fedn. 30 yr. anniv. exhbn., Hofstra Univ. Mus. N.Y. Exhbn. "Abstract Expressionism: Then and Now", 2001, Represented in permanent collections Nat. Gallery Art, Washington, Biblioteque Nationale, Paris, Victoria and Albert Mus., London, Tokyo U. Fine Art, Tokyo Mus. Modern Art, Nat. Gallery Art, Stockholm, Tate Gallery, London, USIS, State Dept., Washington, Library of Congress, Bklyn. Mus., Mus. Modern Art, N.Y.C., Phila. Mus., Denver Mus., Dallas Mus., Pasadena Mus., Honolulu Acad. Arts, Hawaii Council for Arts, Art Inst. Chgo., Oakland Mus., L.A. County Mus., Seattle Mus., Worcester Art Mus., Am. Embassy, Bonn, Bank of Am., United Calif. Bank, U. Hawaii, IBM, Litton Industries Corp., Hartford Ins. Co., Fuji Bank Calif., Northrop Corp., 1st Hawaii Trust Bank, Mus. Contemporary Art, Honolulu, Portland (Oreg.) Mus. Art, 1993, Univ. Hawaii, Hilo, 1992, Indpls. Mus. Art, 1991-92, Elvehjem Mus. Art, Wis., West Tex. A&M U., 1993, Wycross Press, Auburn, Ala., 1994; contbr. Mem. Commn. for Founders' Portfolio for N.W. Printmakers, Portland, 1977. Served to capt. AUS, 1942-45. Recipient Francis G. Logan medal Art Inst. Chgo., 1962, Pauline Palmer award, 1966; Concora Found. prize, 1963; Vera List award Soc. Am. Graphic Artists, Am. Acad., Rome, 1964; appointee Cité Internat. des Arts, Paris, 1970, 78-83; Fondation Gardilanne-Moffat Studio award, 1978-80; purchase award Epinal (France) Biennial Invitational Exhbn., Pacific Rim Internat., 1993, 97; awards Hawaii State Found. for Culture and Arts, 1972, 74, 75, 78, 80; awards Honolulu Acad. Arts, 1973, 78; award San Diego Art Inst., 1991, Fulbright sr. rsch. award, 1956-57; U. Ill. rsch. grantee, 1963-64; Ford Found. faculty enrichment award, 1978, 82, Printmaker Emeritus award So. Graphics Coun., 1992. Mem. Coll. Art Assn. Am., Calif. Soc. Printmakers, N.W. Print Coun. (bd. dirs.), Japan Print Assn., Soc. Am. Graphic Artists, Color Print Soc., World Print Coun., L.A. Printmaking Soc. (hon. dir.), Honolulu Printmakers (past v.p., pres.), Painters and Sculptors League Hawaii, Hawaii Artists League, So. Graphics Coun., Fulbright Assn. Address: 14601 Whitfield Ave Pacific Palisades CA 90272-2645

CHESNEY, ROBERT HENRY, communications/computer/process executive, consultant; b. Rockville Centre, NY, Aug. 12, 1950; s. Robert Lewis and Maureen C. (Oates) C.; m. Donna Marie Mazian, May 1, 1976; 1 child, Alexis Mary. BA in Indsl. Psychology, Hofstra U., 1972, MBA in Qualitative & Quantitative Analysis, 1979. Internal auditor Grumman Aerospace, Bethpage, NY, 1974-77, sr. ops. specialist, 1978; sr. systems analyst Sta. WNET, N.Y.C., 1978-79, mgr. mgmt. info. systems and procedures, 1979-81, asst. dir. mgmt. info. systems and procedures, 1981-82; sr. tech. cons. N.Y. Telephone, Melville, 1982-83, AT&T Info. Systems, Melville, 1983-89; from sr. exec. data sales to mgr. territory AT&T Computer Systems, Melville, 1990-94; from sr. client cons. to mng. client cons. AT&T Ops. Cons. Group, Manhasset, NY, 1994-95; ptnr. AT&T Bus. Consulting, Manhasset, NY, 1995; dist. mgr. AT&T Bus. Cons., Atlanta, 1996-97; dist. mgr. CFO SAP Lucent Technologies Inc., Warren, NJ, 1997-99, dist. mgr. GSP IPS, 1999-2000, sr. mgr. SPN NNS CFO sys. and procedures, 2000—01; mgmt. cons. strategic planning and process reengring. UN Joint Staff Pension Fund Info. Mgmt. Sys., NYC, 2002—. Mem.: IEEE, Hostra U. Alumni Assn., N.Y. Acad. Scis., Assn. Computing Machinery, IEEE Computer Soc. Republican. Roman Catholic. Office: UN Joint Staff Pension Fund Secretariat Bldg, UN New York NY 10017 E-mail: chez01@aol.com., chesneyr@un.org.

CHESNEY, RUSSELL WALLACE, pediatrician; b. Knoxville, Tenn., Aug. 25, 1941; s. Jack and Helen Wallace (McColl) C.; m. Patricia Joan Cook, June 8, 1968; children: Karen, Christopher, Gillian. AB, Harvard U., 1963; MD, U. Rochester, 1968. Diplomate Am. Bd. Pediatrics. Intern then resident Johns Hopkins U. Hosp., Balt., 1968-70, 72-73; renal fellow NIH, Balt., 1970-72, Montreal Childrens Hosp., Montreal, Que., Can., 1973-75; asst. then prof. U. Wis., Madison, 1975-85; prof., vice chmn. U. Calif., Davis, 1985-88; prof., chmn. pediatrics U. Tenn., Memphis, 1988—. Mem. Rsch. Study Sect. NIH, Washington, 1983—88, mem. Nat. Kidney and Urology Diseases Adv. Bd., 1988—91; sec.-treas., pediat. dept. chmn. Am. Med. Schs., 1993—99, pres., 2001—; mem. coun. Am. Pediat. Soc., 1995—, v.p., 2001—02, pres., 2002—; chmn. Fed. Pediat. Orgn., 1995—96; vice chair Task Force on Pediat. Edn., 1996—99; chair Am. Bd. Pediats., 2000—02. Contbr. articles to profl. jours., chpts. to text and med. books. Lt. comdr. USPHS, 1970-72, Balt. Recipient Founders award in Pediatric Rsch., So. Soc. Pediatric Rsch., 1993; Jour. Pediatrics lectr. U. Rochester, 1985, Paul Gaffney lectr. U. Pitts., 1988. Mem. Am. Pediat. Soc. (mem. coun. 1995--, v.p. 2001-02, pres. 2002--), Am. Acad. Pediats. (pres. Tenn. state chpt. 1995-98, E. Meade Johnson award 1985, Nutrition award 1996, St. Geme award 2001), Soc. for Pediat. Rsch. (pres. 1986-87), Midwest Soc. for Pediat. Rsch. (pres. 1984-85), Am. Soc. for Pediat. Nephrology (pres. 1986-87), VA Merit Rev. Bd. (chmn. 1988-90). Office: U Tenn Dept Pediats 50 S Dunlap St Memphis TN 38103-4909

CHESNEY, SUSAN TALMADGE, writer, developer; b. N.Y.C., Aug. 12, 1943; d. Morton and Tillie (Talmadge) Chesney; m. Donald Lewis Freitas, Sept. 17, 1967 (div. May 1976); m. Robert Martin Rosenblatt, Apr. 9, 1980. AB, U. Calif., Berkeley, 1967. Placement interviewer U. Calif., Berkeley, 1972-74, program coord., 1974-79; pers. adminstr. Hewlett-Packard Co., Santa Rosa, Calif., 1982-84; pres. Mgmt. Resources, Santa Rosa, 1984-97; human resources mgr. BioBottoms Inc., Petaluma, Calif., 1990-91; human resources adminstr. Parker Compumotor, Rohnert Park, Calif., 1991-93; writer, developer The E-Myth Acad., Santa Rosa, 1997-98. Cons. Kensington Electronics Group, Healdsburg, Calif., 1984-85, Behavioral Medicine Assocs., Santa Rosa, 1985-86, M.C.A.I., Santa Rosa, 1986-87, Bowdon Designs, Santa Rosa, 1987-88, Bass & Ingram, Santa Rosa, 1988-96, Eason Tech., Inc., Healdsburg, 1995-96, Interim Svcs., Inc., Santa Rosa, 1995-98, Flex Products, Inc., Santa Rosa, 1996-97, Nev. Prodn. Co., 1998-99. Avocations: cooking, gardening, music.

CHESNUT, DONALD BLAIR, retired chemistry educator; b. Richmond, Ind., Dec. 27, 1932; s. James Lyons and Naomi Irene (Wright) C.; m. Deborah Berry, Dec. 21, 1954; children— Lauren, Blair, Lynn. BS, Duke U., 1954; PhD, Calif. Inst. Tech., 1958. Postdoctoral fellow, instr. physics Duke U., Durham, N.C., 1957-58, assoc. prof. chemistry, 1965-71, prof. chemistry, 1971-98; prof. emeritus, 1999—; research chemist E.I. duPont de Nemours, Inc., Wilmington, Del., 1958-65. Mem. Am. Chem. Soc., Am. Phys. Soc., Sigma Xi. Home: 4404 Malvern Rd Durham NC 27707-5646 Office: Duke U Dept Chemistry Durham NC 27706 E-mail: donald.chesnut@duke.edu.

CHESNUT, NONDIS LORINE, screenwriter, consultant, reading and language arts educator, instructor, counselor; b. South Daytona, Fla., June 29, 1941; d. Anthony Valentine and Myrtle Marie (Allen) Campbell; m. Raymond Otho Chesnut, Aug. 25, 1962; 1 child, Starlina Mintina Chesnut Kladler. BS in English and Speech, Concord Coll., 1962; postgrad., Frostburg U., 1967; MEd, Shippensburg U., 1972; postgrad., W.Va. U., 1973; Advanced Grad. Specialist Degree, U. Md., 1974; postgrad., Md. State Dept. Edn., 1976-95, Inst. Children's Lit., 1995-97, Screenwriters Unlimited, 1997; writing coursework, Charter Oak State Coll., 2000. Cert. adminstr., secondary prin., elem. prin., reading splist., tchr. English and speech, drama. Tchr. English and speech Harpers Ferry (W.Va.) H.S., 1962-64; with Sears Roebuck, summer 1965; libr. Great Mills (Md.) H.S., 1968-69; tchr. English and reading North Hagerstown H.S., Hagerstown, Md., 1964-73; tchr. South Hagerstown H.S., Hagerstown, 1974-77; reading resource tchr. Woodland Way Elem. Sch., Hagerstown, 1977-83; adj. instr. grad. sch. Hood Coll., Frederick, Md., 1982-83; reading specialist Fountain Rock Elem. Sch., Hagerstown, 1983-85; tchr. Williamsport (Md.) H.S., 1985-95. Reading and lang. arts cons., Md., 1973-95, Fla., 1996-2000; adj. reading instr. Daytona Comm. Coll., 1996-97, Galaxy Middle Sch., 1997-98, drama, lang. arts, reading tchr., 1997-98, key source, 1999; instr. English and writing Bethune-Cookman Coll., fall 2000, ajd. instr. reading, English, Daytona Beach C.C., 2001-02; spkr., presenter local, nat. and internat. workshops, 1973-2000; speech and debate coach. Writer for radio programs and advertisements for reading, 1986—, TV programs, 1974-78, 90-91; appeared on TV programs, 1974-78; co-editor column Beckley Post Herald, 1957-59; contbr. articles to newspapers and mags., 1964—; appeared in film Guarding Tess, 1993; screenwriter Heaven on Planet Earth, 2000, Love From Heaven, 2000. Mem. debating team Concord Coll., 1961-62, mem. newspaper staff, 1959-61; mem. Washington County Network of Orgns., 1984-88; co-dir. Billy Bud, 1962; v.p. Women's Ind. Club, 1962, treas., 1961; sec.-treas. Fgn. lang. Club, 1961, Debate Club, 1961-62; treas. Meth. Youth Fellowship, 1961; pres. Tri-Hi-Y, 1959; legis. chairperson State of Md. Reading Coun., 1977-78; active Life in Spirit Group, Emmanuel Meth. Ch., White Sul, 1953-84, St. Ann's Roman Cath. Ch., 1994-95, Grace United Meth. Ch., 1984-95, Lady of Hope Cath. Ch., 1996—; mem. Fla. State Reading Coun., 1996-99. Recipient Pres.'s award State of Md. Reading Coun., 1981, Pres.'s award Washington County Reading Coun., 1981, Guidance Helping award, 1987, Voice of Democracy award VFW/Ladies Aux., 1992, Am. Heritage Writing award Williamsport Lions Club, 1995, numerous others; W.Va. Legislature scholar, 1959-62. Mem. AAUW (ednl. chairperson 1983-85, legis. v.p. 1986-87, cmty. chairperson 1987-89), NEA (publicity and scholarship coms., bldg. rep. 1989-95, del.), ASCD, VFW (chairperson Voice of Democracy 1989-95, VFW award 1989-95), Md. Dist. Am. Heritage Lions (Region II Lions award, Williamsport Am. Heritage Lions award 1995), State of Md. Internat. Reading Assn. Coun. (sec. 1975-79, v.p. elect 1979-80, v.p. 1980-81, pres. 1981-82, nominating chairperson 1982-83), Washington County Tchrs. Assn. (rep., scholarship chair, publicity), Internat. Reading Assn. (sec.-treas. sex differences in reading group 1976-77, 83-85, mem. gender differences in reading group 1985-86, mem. readability interest group, mastery learning interest group, del. convs., internat. rsch. com. 1976-77, 84-85, disabled learners interest group 1975-82), Washington County Reading Assn. (pres. 1981-82), Am. Legion (chairperson oratorial contest 1989-95, speech coach), Fla. Devel. Edn. Assn. (mem. com. registration 1996). Democrat. Avocations: swimming, dancing, travel, psychology, writing. Home: 107 Old Sunbeam Dr Daytona Beach FL 32119

CHESNUTT, FLORENCE WALKER ANDREWS, artist; b. El Dorado, Ark., Nov. 17, 1925; d. Stanley and Florence Venita (Cox) Andrews; m. John Christy Chesnutt, Apr. 9, 1949 (dec. 1972); children: John Christy, Stanley Andrews, Alan Howard, Sarah Florence Walker Chesnutt; m. Carl C. Friedrichs,

Dec. 26, 1982. BA, U. N.C., 1947; postgrad., Goethe U., Frankfort, Germany, 1949, St. Martins Acad., London, 1950, Art Students League, 1961. Fashion illustrator Gus Blass Co., Little Rock, 1944-48; adult edn. art instr. Cherokee County, Iowa, 1960-68, St. Tammany Parish, La., 1970-82; art dir. City of Mandeville, La., 1976-80; owner, operator graphic arts studio Studio A, Covington, La., 1979-86, Pleasant Green Studio, Pilot Grove, Mo., 1986—. Set designer Cherokee County and St. Tammany Parish Community Theaters, 1960-72; organizer Cherokee County Arts Coun., 1962; design cons. Main St. Boonville Project, 1988-89. One-woman shows at St. Tammany Art Ctr., Covington, La., 1982, 86, Town Hall Gallery, Mandeville, La., 1983, 86, Mo. Festival of Arts, 1988, Boonslick Art Ann., Boonville, Mo., 1990; exhibited in group shows at Sanford Mus., Cherokee, Iowa, 1987, Columbia (Mo.) Art League, 1989, Witter Gallery, Storm Lake, Iowa, 1991, Rocheport Gallery, 2003; works commd. include murals, panels, posters for ch. and civic orgns.; illustrator for books, calendars. Co-organizer St. Tammany Parish Hist. Soc., 1973, Boone's Lick Tourism Commn., Mo., 1989; mem. extension coun. U. Mo. Mem. DAR, Cooper County Hist. Soc. (co-organizer, program dir. 1990-91), Am. Graphic Soc., Friends of Historic Boonville, Boonslick Hist. Soc., State Hist. Soc. Mo., United Daus. of Confederacy, Colonial Dames. Democrat. Episcopalian. Avocation: restoring historic and architecturally significant buildings. Home: RR 1 Box 81 Pilot Grove MO 65276-9735 Office: Pleasant Green Studio RR 1 Box 81 Pilot Grove MO 65276-9735

CHESNUTT, JANE, publishing executive; b. Kenedy, Tex., Oct. 10, 1950; m. W. Mallory Rintoul. BJ, U. Tex., 1973. Editorial asst. Am. Jour. Nursing, N.Y.C., 1975-78; asst. editor Woman's Day mag., N.Y.C., 1978-82, health editor, 1982-89, beauty, health, fashion editor, 1989-91, editor-in-chief, 1991—, sr. v.p., group editl. dir., 2002—. Sr. v.p. & group editl. dir. Transplant Am. Nat. Kidney Found. Mem. bus. adv. coun. Washington Irving H.S., N.Y.C. Named one of Editor of Yrl, Adweek, 1992, Top Players, Min Mag., 2000; recipient Editor of Yr., Adweek, 1992. Mem. Am. Soc. Mag. Editors, Women in Comms., Inc. (Clarion award 1985, Headliner award 1996), YWCA Acad. of Achievers. Office: Woman's Day Mag Hachette Filipacchi Mags Inc 1633 Broadway New York NY 10019-6708

CHESS, SONIA MARY, retired language educator; b. Ashton, Lancashire, Eng., Apr. 14, 1930; came to U.S., 1951, naturalized, 1963; d. Arthur and Sarah Ann (Hulme) Bradburn; m. Joseph Campbell Chess, Nov. 17, 1950; children: Denise Ann, Tanya Marie, Michele Elise, Luana Jo. BA in English Lit., U. Hawaii, Honolulu, 1970, MA, 1973, MA in Am. Studies, 1989, PhD in Am. Studies, 1996. Prof. English U. Hawaii/Honolulu Community Coll., 1971-93, chmn. English dept., 1980-84, div. chairperson lang. arts, 1989-91, ret. Tchr. cons. Hawaii Writing Project, Honolulu, 1983—; tchr. summer sch. Regent, Sandwich Isle chpt. Daus. of Brit. Empire, Honolulu, 1978-80. Recipient Excellence in Teaching medal, U. Hawaii Bd. Regents, 1983; Dickens fellow, Nat. Endowment for Humanities, 1985, Hawaii Writing Project fellow, U. Hawaii Found., 1983. Mem. Hawaii Council Tchrs. English, Assn. Women in Jr. Colls., Humanities Assn. Episcopalian. Avocations: writing, knitting, reading, swimming, travel, gardening.

CHESS, WILLIAM, public relations executive; BS in Mgmt. and Acctg., MBA in Fin., Fordham U. Air traffic controller USAF; with Lever Bros. Co., contr.; fin. v.p. Lever Foods; exec. v.p., CFO Ogilvy & Mather Pub. Rels.; sr. v.p. fin. Ogilvy & Mather; CFO Ogilvy & Mather Worldwide, 1993-95, CFO and COO, 1995, Ogilvy Pub. Rels. Worldwide, N.Y.C. Office: Ogilvy Worldwide 909 3rd Ave New York NY 10022-4731

CHESSER, AL H. union official; b. Pettis County, Mo., Feb. 26, 1914; s. James A. and Mary Pearl (Dirck) C.; m. Rose Burns. Grad. high sch. Brakeman-condr. Santa Fe Ry., Amarillo, Tex., 1941; sec.-treas., legis. rep. Brotherhood R.R. Trainmen, Local 608, 1945-56; sec. Tex. Legis. Bd., 1952-56, legis. dir., 1956-61; nat. legis. rep. Washington, 1961-71, United Transp. Union, 1969-71, pres., 1971-79, pres. emeritus, 1979—; v.p., mem. exec. council AFL-CIO; chmn. Congress of Ry. Unions, 1972—. Chmn. Amarillo Civil Svc. Commn., 1950-56, Amarillo Labor Polit. Council, 1954-56; mem. Gov.'s Indsl. Commn., 1957-61, Fed. Task Force on R.R. Safety, 1964-69, Pres.'s Consumers Adv. Council, 1964-68, Greater Cleve. Growth Bd. and Transp. Study Group of Domestic Affairs Task Force, 1973— ; mem. adv. panel U.S. Congress Office of Tech. Assessment, 1976; hon. co-chmn. Internat. Guiding Eyes, Inc., 1976 Author: Transportation and Energy, 1975, Economic Advantages of Transporting Coal by Rail, 1976. Bd. dirs. Dem. Nat. Com., 1973; mem. transp. adv. com. FEA, 1975; co-chmn. R.R. Safety Rsch. Bd., 1975; chmn. bd. CSC; bd. dirs. Amarillo Community Chest, Maverick Boys Club; hon. staff mem. U.S. Army Transp. Sch. Named to Smith-Cotton H.S. Hall of Fame, Sedalia, Mo.; United Transp. Union bldg. named Al H. Chesser Bldg. in his honor; recipient Eugene V. Debs award, 2001. Mem. Nat. Def. Execs. Res., Masons, Shriners. Office: United Transp Union Sundance Hills 10437 E Dorado Pl Greenwood Village CO 80111-3711

CHESSER, DAVID MICHAEL, lawyer; b. Pensacola, Fla., Aug. 12, 1947; s. Julian Edward and Arabelle (Martin) C.; m. Carolyn Anne Miller, Aug. 31, 1968; children: Patrick, Lanie, Anna, Matthew. BA in Psychology, U. Fla., 1969, JD, 1971. Bar: Fla. 1972, U.S. Dist. Ct. (no. dist.) Fla. 1972, U.S. Ct. Appeals (5th and 11th cirs.) 1972, U.S. Tax Ct. 1974, U.S. Supreme Ct. 1976. Ptnr. Chesser, Wingard, Barr, Ft. Walton Beach, Fla., 1971—. Founder, chmn. Bayou Book Co., Inc.; pres. Old South Land Title; bd. dirs. Vanguard Bank and Trust Co. Chmn. Zoning Revision Panel, Okaloosa County, Fla., 1982, chmn. 911 devel. com.; pres. Okaloosa Guidance Clinic, Ft. Walton Beach, 1978, Okaloosa Guidance Found., Ft. Walton Beach, 1978. Served to capt. U.S. Army, 1971-78. Mem. Fla. Bar Assn., Okaloosa-Walton Bar Assn. (pres. 1978), Niceville C. of C. (bd. dirs. 1980-82). Lodges: Kiwanis. Democrat. Methodist. Avocations: tennis, books, music, sports. Office: Chesser Wingard Barr et al 1201 Eglin Pky Shalimar FL 32579-1206

CHESSER, JUDY LEE, municipal official; b. Albany, N.Y., May 27, 1948; d. Owen Francis (deceased) and Sylvia Alice (Tefft) C. BA, Syracuse U., 1970; JD cum laude, Boston Coll., 1977. Bar: D.C. 1977. Legis. asst. Urban Environment Council, Washington, 1973-74, Project on Budget Priorities, Washington, 1974-77; atty. SEC Gen. Counsel's Office, Washington, 1977-78; congl. liaison officer HUD, Washington, 1978-79; spl. asst. to asst. sec. for legislation Health and Human Svcs., Washington, 1979-80; legis. rep. City of N.Y. Washington Office, 1980-83, dir., 1983-94; dep. commr. for legis. Social Security Adminstrn. Congressional and Legis. Affairs, Washington, 1994-2001; dir. pub. policy, acting exec. dir. United Cerebral Palsy Assn., Washington, 2001—; dir. City of N.Y., Washington Office, 2002—. Coordinator Goodell Senate Campaign, N.Y., 1970, McGovern Presdl. Campaign, Pa., 1972. Mem. D.C. Bar. Democrat. Home: 3901 Alton Pl NW Washington DC 20016-2209 Office: City NY WA Office 1301 Penn Ave NW 350 Washington DC 20004 E-mail: jchesser@cityhall.nyc.gov.

CHESSER, THELMA JO SYKES, early childhood educator, administrator; b. Hot Springs, Ark., Mar. 8, 1936; d. Harry Freeman and Dorothy Maldana (Bales) Sykes; m. Rev. Zane Leavell Chesser, July 2, 1954 (div. Nov. 1993); children: Michael Zane, Susan Diane C. Branch, Beverly Jo. Student, U. Ctrl. Ark., 1970-72; BS in Edn., Ouachita Bapt. U., 1973, MS in Edn., 1986; Ed.D., U. Ark., Little Rock, 2000. Cert. tchr. K-6, reading specialist K-12, ednl. leadership, Ark. Kindergarten tchr. Malvern (Ark.) Pub. Schs., 1973-83; kindergarten coord. and tchr. 1st Bapt. Children's Ctr., Malvern, 1983-91; 2d grade tchr. Terry Elem. Sch., Little Rock, 1992—; rsch. assoc. facilitating Ark.-Okla. Study Circles rsch. U. Ark., Little Rock, 1998—. Reading specialist cons., Little Rock, 1987—; adj. asst. prof. U. Ark., Little Rock, 2001—; qualitative rsch. cons., 2001—. Author (prayer guide) State Missions Program Material, 1995; contbr. articles to newsletters. Co-developer North Little Rock Day Care Ctr. for Pike Ave. Bapt. Ch., 1971; asst. and coord. cmty. outreach to needy and transients, various cities and states, 1958-92. Honored Zane and Jo Chesser Day proclamation, City of Malvern/First Bapt. Ch. of Malvern, 1987; Outstanding Tchr. nominee Channel 4, Little Rock, 1995; named Tchr of Yr. Malvern Sch. Dist., 1980, Terry Outstanding Educator, 1994; Edna McGuire Boye Internat. scholar, 1997. Mem. ASCD, NEA, Ark. Edn. Assn., The P.E.O. Sisterhood (chpt. pres. 1988-89), Ark. Bapt. Womens Missionary Union (state bd. mem. 1992-97, 5 yr. plaque 1997), Delta Kappa Gamma (Kappa state internat. forum liaison, 1995—, pres. Gamma chpt. 1993-95, mem. adv. bd. to Ark. Friends for Better Schs. 1997—, Dr. Rose Berry State scholar 1996). Baptist. Avocations: music, writing, swimming, travel. Home and Office: 401 Nix Rd Little Rock AR 72211-3278

CHESSLER, RICHARD KENNETH, gastroenterologist, endoscopist; b. N.Y.C., Apr. 6, 1944; BS, Fairleigh Dickinson U., Rutherford, N.J., 1965; MD, Chgo. Med. Sch., 1969. Diplomate Am. Bd. Internal Medicine and Gastroenterology. Asst. chief gastroenterology Englewood Hosp., N.J., 1982—, chief endoscopy, 1992-99; asst. prof. medicine Mt. Sinai Hosp., N.Y.C., 1994-97. Author: Chemical Technicians Ready Reference Book, 1996; mem. editl. bd. Practical Gastroenterology, 1977—. Fellow ACP, Am. Coll. Gastroenterology (bd. govs. 1989). Avocations: ski, racquetball, golf. Office: 1555 Center Ave Fort Lee NJ 07024-4612

CHESSMAN, REBECCA LEE, librarian; b. Balt., Nov. 8, 1945; d. Robert Lee and Hazel Rebecca (Pearce) Hildenbrand; m. Robert Blakley, Oct. 22, 1977. AB in Teaching, Colo. State Coll., 1967; MA, U. Denver, 1974. Tchr. English Astoria (Oreg.) High Sch., 1967-73; ref. and tech. svc. libr. Fresno (Calif.) County Office Edn., 1974-77; jr. high sch. libr. Fremont Jr. High Sch., Seaside, Calif., 1977-83; elem. sch. libr. Patton Sch. Mt. Penin Unified Sch.Dist., Marina, Calif., 1983-84; dist. libr. Belmont (Calif.) Sch. Dist., 1983-94; sch. libr. Buchser Mid. Sch., Santa Clara (Calif.) Unified Sch. Dist., 1994—. Editor: (newsletters) Lymphad, 1989-95, Coracle, 1989-91, BFA Update, 1992-94. Mem. com. English/Lang. Arts Task Force, Belmont, 1991-93. Mem. ALA, NEA, Calif. Assn. Sch. Librs. (treas. 1990-92), Calif. Tchrs. Assn. (sec. Golden Gate svc. ctr. coun. 1990-92), Belmont Faculty Assn. (pres. 1989-91), Clan Donald USA (editor regional newsletter 1989-95, editor, pub. An Ceargall Lan a Celtic Cultural Jour. 1995-98, Clan Donald, U.S.A., Cen. Pacific Regional Commr., 2000-. Democrat. Episcopalian. Home: 1720 Halford Ave Apt 322 Santa Clara CA 95051-2607 Office: Buchser Middle Sch Library 1111 Bellomy St Santa Clara CA 95050-5433

CHESSON, CALVIN WHITE, lawyer, educator; b. Williamston, N.C., July 23, 1936; s. Bruce Cecil Chesson and Debby Beatrice White; m. Ann Cooke; children: Courtney Ann Haas, Stephanie Lynn. BA in Bus. Adminstrn., East Carolina U., 1958; JD, U. N.C., 1962. Bar: N.C. 1962, U.S. Dist. Ct. (ea., we. and mid. dists.) N.C. 1995, U.S. Ct. Appeals (4th cir.) 1998. Assoc. Lassiter, Moore & Van Allen, Charlotte, N.C., 1962-65; dist. atty. for Mecklenburg County N.C. Superior Ct., Charlotte, 1965-68; sr. ptnr. Cole & Chesson, Charlotte, 1968-80, Curtis, Millsaps & Chesson, Charlotte, 1980-85; pvt. practice law Charlotte, 1985—. Dir., chmn. Voluntary Action Ctr. United Way, Charlotte, 1983-86; pres. Lions Club, Charlotte, 1984-85, 92-93; commr. Mecklenburg County Pk. and Recreation Commn., Charlotte, 1986-88; dir. Family Support Ctr., Charlotte, 1989-90, Hope Springs, Charlotte, 1991-93. Pvt. USAR, 1959-65. Mem. N.C. Bar Assn., N.C. State Bar, Mecklenburg County Bar Assn. Democrat. Methodist. Avocation: tennis. Office: 7804 Fairview Rd PMB 287 Charlotte NC 28226 E-mail: cchesson@mindspring.com.

CHESSON, EUGENE, civil engineering educator, consultant; b. São Paulo, Brazil, Dec. 1, 1928; s. Eugene and Mary Josie (Foy) C.; m. Marilyn Ryder Hershey, Aug. 21, 1954; children: Christopher Eugene, David Anson. BSC.E., Duke U., 1950; MS, U. Ill.-Urbana, 1956, PhD, 1959. Registered profl. engr., Ill., Del., Ariz. Refinery engr. Standard Oil Ind., Whiting, 1953; research asst., research assoc. civil engring. dept. U. Ill.-Urbana, 1953-59, asst. prof., 1959-62, assoc. prof., 1962-66; prof. civil engring. U. Del., Newark, 1966-86, dept. chmn., 1966-75; pres. Chesson Engring., Inc., Newark, 1981-85; treas., project mgr. HPR Investors, L.C., Prescott, Ariz., 1992—; treas. Sedona Pinon Woods Partnership, Prescott, 1992-2000, Hershey Partnership, Prescott, 1993—. Contbr. articles in field to profl. jours. Mem. Nat. Def. Exec. Res., U.S. Dept. Transp., 1973-84. Lt. (j.g.) Civil Engr. Corps, USN, 1950-53. Named Outstanding Young Faculty Mem., Dept. Civil Engring., U. Ill., 1962; Del. Outstanding Engr. Del. Soc. Profl. Engrs., 1981; recipient Teaching award AT&T Found., 1986 Fellow ASCE (pres. local sect. 1982-83); mem. Am. Soc. Engring. Edn. (W.E. Wickenden award 1981), No. Ariz. Geneal. Soc. (v.p., pres. 1989-91). Republican. Presbyterian. Home: 640 Cosmos Way Prescott AZ 86303-5049

CHESSON, MICHAEL BEDOUT, history educator; b. Richmond, Va., Sept. 5, 1947; s. Wesley Earle and Virginia Winborne (Ramsey) Chesson. AB with high honors in History, Coll. William and Mary, 1969; postgrad. (Gilman fellow), Johns Hopkins U., 1972-73; PhD in History (Grad. fellow), Harvard U., 1978. Clk. R.F. & P. R.R., Richmond, 1966-69; park ranger-historian Colonial Nat. Hist. Park, Nat. Park Svc., Yorktown and Jamestown, Va., 1969-70, 72, 73; tchg. fellow Harvard U., 1975-78; asst. prof. history U. Mass., Boston, 1978-82, assoc. prof. history, 1982-96, prof. history, 1996—. Author: Richmond After the War, 1865-1890, 1981, Exile in Richmond: The Confederate Journal of Henri Garidel, 2001. Served to capt. USNR, 1969—. Fellow Mass. Hist. Soc.; mem. Am. Hist. Assn., So. Hist. Assn., Va. Hist. Assn., Orgn. Am. Historians, Peabody Essex Mus., Cape Ann Hist. Assn., Mil. Hist. Soc. Mass., Naval Res. Assn., Res. Officer Assn., Fleet Res. Assn., Navy League. Clubs: Wardroom Club (Boston). Democrat. E-mail: omohundro@aol.com.

CHESTER, ALEXANDER CAMPBELL, III, physician; b. N.Y.C., Dec. 21, 1947; s. Alexander C. II and Gladys (Edelhauser) C.; m. Kimberly Robinson Chester, Dec. 20, 1970; children: Kristin Elizabeth, Alexander C. IV. BS cum laude, Georgetown U., 1969; MD, Columbia U., 1973. Diplomate Am. Bd. Internal Medicine, Nat. Bd. Med. Examiners; advanced achievement in internal medicine; voluntary recert., 1998. Intern Georgetown U., Washington, 1973-74, resident in medicine, 1974-76, clin. fellow in nephrology, 1976-77, research fellow in nephrology, 1977-78, clin. instr. medicine, 1978-80, clin. asst. prof. medicine, 1980-84, clin. assoc. prof. medicine, 1985-89, clin. prof. medicine, 1990—. Govs. com. for coll. affairs Am. Coll. Physicians, 1980-90; clin. prof. medicine Georgetown U. Med. Ctr.;reviewer Annals of Internal Medicine, Am. Family Physician. Contbr. articles to profl. jours. and publs. Named one of Top Doctors, Washingtonian Mag., 1999, 2002, Area Outstanding Specialists, Checkbook mag., 1998, Area Outstanding Specialists Checkbook mag., 2002; featured in Consumers' Guide to Top Doctors, editors of Checkbook Mag., 2002. Mem. AAAS, AMA, Am. Soc. Internal Medicine (alt. del. Nat. Meeting 1980), Am. Fedn. Clin. Rsch., Hippocrates-Galen Med. Soc. (sec., treas. 1991-2, pres. 1993-94), Osler Soc. (sec., treas. 1986-88, pres. 1989-90), Nat. Kidney Found. (coun. on clin. nephrology, dialysis and tranplantation, profl. adv. bd. 1983-86, program com. ann. kidney symposium 1983-86), N.Y. Acad. Sci., Am. Heart Assn. (coun. on kidney 1988-90), Clinico-Pathol. Soc. (pres. 2003—), Am. Rhinologic Soc., Soc. Gen. Internal Medicine, Am. Coll. of Physicians (mem. gov.'s nominating com.), N.Y. Acad. of Scis., Soc. for the Study of Human Behavior and Evolution, Clinico-Path. Soc., Pavlovian Soc. N.Am., Am. Assn. for the Advancement of Sci., Assn. Medicine and Psychiary, Am. Assn. Chronic Fatigue Syndrome, European Rhinologic Soc., Russian Rhinologic Soc., Cosmos Club, Phi Beta Kappa. Achievements include research in nasal reflexes, sick building syndrome and chronic fatigue syndrome. Home: 4618 Laverock Pl NW Washington DC 20007-2544 Office: 3301 New Mexico Ave NW Ste 348 Washington DC 20016-3622 E-mail: achester@foxhallinternists.com.

CHESTER, DANIEL LEON, computer scientist, educator, consultant; b. Albany, Calif., Feb. 26, 1943; s. Frederick Neil and Della Nettie (Zweifel) C. BA in Math., U. Calif., Berkeley, 1966, MA in Math., 1968, PhD in Math., 1973. Asst. prof. math. U. Tex., Austin, 1973-76, asst. prof. computer sci., 1973-80, U. Del., Newark, 1980-85, assoc. prof. computer sci., 1985—. Vis. scientist T. J. Watson Rsch. Ctr., IBM, Yorktown Heights, N.Y., 1978-79; cons. Quantum Leap Innovations, Inc., Newark, Del., 1985—. Mem. IEEE, Assn. for Computing Machinery, Assn. for Computational Linguistics, Am. Assn. for Artificial Intelligence, Cognitive Sci. Soc. Achievements include invention of. Office: Univ Del Computer and Info Sci Newark DE 19716 E-mail: chester@cis.udel.edu.

CHESTER, FRANCIS, political science educator, lawyer; b. Bklyn., Jan. 25, 1936; s. Frank and Mary (DeFrancesco) C.; m. Diane G. Charlson, Oct. 27, 1966; children: Francis Scott, Angelique, Jennifer, Sabrina. BA in Econs., Iona Coll., 1957; JD, St. John's U., Jamaica, N.Y., 1960, MA in Polit. Sci., cert. in internat. law & diplomacy, St. John's U., Jamaica, N.Y., 1988. Bar: N.Y. 1961, U.S. Dist. Ct. (ea. and so. dists.) N.Y. 1962, U.S. Ct. Claims 1964, U.S. Supreme Ct. 1964, Va. 1969, U.S. Dist. Ct. (we. dist.) Va. 1994, U.S. Bankruptcy Ct., 1994. Sole practice, Roslyn Heights, NY, 1961—68, East Norwich, NY, 1968—69, Gordonsville, Va., 1969—80, Raphine, Va., 1980—88; founder, owner Chester Farms, Churchville, Va., 1946—; pvt. practice Augusta County, Staunton and Front Royal, Va., 1980-92, 94-97, Churchville, Va., 1997—; asst. prof. polit. sci. So. Sem. Coll., Buena Vista, Va., 1989, faculty, asst. prof. polit. sci. and econs., 1989. Lectr. polit. sci. and econs. Piedmont Va. C.C., 1985-87; lectr. in sheep breeding; adj. asst. prof. govt. and econs. Blue Ridge C.C., Weyers Cave, Va., 1986-89; asst. prof. econs. and polit. sci. Christendom Coll., Front Royal, Va., 1989-98, 99—, dir. politics practica program, 1989-94. Mem. Va. Bar Assn., Augusta County Bar Assn., Nat. Columbia Sheep Breeders Assn., KC (4th deg.). Lodges: KC (charter grand knight, co-founder coun. 670). Republican. Roman Catholic. Home: 2490 Little Calf Pasture Hwy Swoope VA 24479-2401 Office: 3581 Churchville Ave Churchville VA 24421-2509

CHESTER, JAMES A. music educator; b. Bay, Ark. s. Harvey Ray and Anna Florence (Brown) Chester; m. Julia Ellen Williams, May 31, 1963; children: Autumn Elizabeth Chester Marshall, Tiffany Paige Chester Parkhurst. BA, Harding Coll., 1965; M in Music Edn., Memphis State U., 1968. Cert. music tchr. grades K-12 Tenn. Tchr., choral dir. Crowley's Ridge Acad., Paragould, Ark., 1965—66, Memphis City Schs.-Treadwell, 1967—69, Harding Acad. Memphis, 1969—. Guest clinician Harding U. Christian H.S. Choral Festival, Searcy, Ark., 1984, guest clinician Lipscomb U., Nashville, 2001. Music min., worship leader Highland St. Ch. Christ, Memphis, 1968—. With U.S. Army, 1959—67. Named Outstanding Alumnus, Crowley's Ridge Acad., Paragould, Ark., 1984, Outstanding Tchr., Tenn. Govs. Sch. for the Arts, Nashville, 1990, Harding Acad. Secondary Tchr. of Yr., 1992. Mem.: Tenn. Music Educator's Assn. (bd. mem. 1996—98, long-range planning com. 1999—2001), West Tenn. Vocal Music Educators Assn. (treas. 1990—94, pres. 1996—98, host jr. and sr. high honor choruses 1996—2002, past pres. 1998—2002), Am. Choral Dirs. Assn. (life). Mem. Ch. Of Christ. Avocations: carpentry, woodworking. Office: Harding Acad Memphis 1100 Cherry Rd Memphis TN 38117

CHESTER, JOHN JONAS, lawyer, educator; b. Columbus, Ohio, July 13, 1920; s. John J. and Harriet Bonnadine (Rice) C.; m. Cynthia Johnson, Apr. 18, 1959; children: John, James, Joel, Cecily. AB cum laude, Amherst Coll., 1942; JD, Yale U., 1948. Bar: Ohio 1948. Ptnr. Chester & Chester, Columbus, 1948-57, Chester & Rose, Columbus, 1958-70, Chester Willcox and Saxbe and predecessor firm, Columbus, 1971—. Spl. counsel Pres. of U.S.., 1974. adj. prof. Ohio State U. Coll. Law. Past bd. dirs. Grant Riverside Meth. Hosps.; past chmn. Doctor's Hosp.; chmn. bd. dirs. Ohio Health, 2001—; past trustee Doctor's Hosp., Columbus Sch. for Girls, Columbus Acad., Shepherd Hill Hosp., Ohio Hist. Found., Ohio Hist. Soc.; active Ohio Gen. Assembly, 1953-58. Lt. USNR, 1942-46. Mem. ABA, Ohio State Bar Assn., Columbus Bar Assn., Am. Coll. Trial Lawyers, Columbus Club (bd. dirs.), Columbus Athletic Club, Rocky Fork Hunt and Country Club. Republican. Episcopalian. Home: 4906 Riverside Dr Columbus OH 43220-2876 Office: Chester Willcox & Saxbe 65 E State St Ste 1000 Columbus OH 43215-3442

CHESTER, LINNES LEE, JR., healthcare association administrator; b. Hopkinsville, Ky., Dec. 15, 1958; s. Linnes Lee Chester, Sr. and Cozy Mae Chester. BS in health care admin., magna cum laude, SW Tex. State U., 1986; MS in logistics mgmt., Air Force Inst. of Tech., Wright-Patterson Air Force Base, OH, 1992; MS in sys. mgmt., U. Southen Calif., 1994. Cert. Health Care Management Am. Coll. of Healthcare Execs., 2001. Dir., patient affairs & med. readiness Peterson AFB Clinic, Peterson Air Force Base, Colo., 1986—89, dir., med. resource mgmt. & info. sys., 1989—90; dir., med. readiness 39rd Tactical Group Hosp., Incirlik, Turkey, 1990—91; grad. student Air Force Inst. of Tech., Wright-Patterson Air Force Base, Ohio, 1991—92; dir., med. logistics & pers. 42nd Med. Group, Loring Air Force Base, Maine, 1992—94; adminstr. 59th Med. Wing, Reid Health Clinic, Lackland Air Force Base, Tex., 1994—97; exec. officer to the comdr. Air Force Inspection Agy., Kirtland Air Force Base, N.Mex., 1999—2000; fellow, managed care, resource mgmt. Long Beach Meml. Med. Ctr., Long Beach, Calif., 2000—01; dir., dept. of def. uniform bus. office Office of Asst. Sec. of Def. for Health Affairs, Falls Ch., Va., 2001— Western regents adv. coun. Am. Coll. of Healthcare Execs., 2001—; adv. Presdl. Task Force Vets. Affairs-Dept. Def. Fin. Subcom. Mem. Pikes Peak Jaycees, Colo. Springs, Colo., 1988—90; instr. San Antonio Literacy Coun., San Antonio, 1996—97; co-chairman to chairman 59th Med. Wing Combined Fed. Campaign, Lackland Air Force Base, Tex., 1996—96. Lt. col. USAF. Decorated Meritorious Svc. medal Air Force, Mil. Outstanding Vol. Svc. medal; recipient Alpha Chi Honor Soc., Alpha Chi, 1985, Disting. Grad., Sch. of Healthcare Scis., Sheppard AFB, Tex., 1987, Air Force Med. Insp. of the Yr., Air Force Inspection Agy., 1998, Mil. Excellence in Healthcare Mgmt., Am. Coll. of Healthcare Execs., 2002; fellow Managed Care/Resource Mgmt. Fellow, Air Force Med. Svc., 2000. Fellow: Am. Coll. of Healthcare Execs.; mem.: Air Force Med. Svc. Corps Assn., Assn. of Mil. Surgeons of US, Air Force Assn. (life), Soc. of Logistics Engrs. Achievements include development of itemized medical billing at 127 military treatment facilites that aligned processes with industry standards; first automated appointment system in the continental United States; Persian Gulf medical evaluation operation ranked number one in 12 regions. Home: 5597 Seminary Rd Apt 1616-S Falls Church VA 22041-3525 Office: Oasd-Ha/Tma-Rm 5111 Leesburg Pike Ste 810 Falls Church VA 22041-3206 Personal E-mail: linnes.chester@verizon.net. E-mail: linnes.chester@tma.osd.mil.

CHESTER, LYNNE, foundation executive, artist; b. Fargo, N.D., May 29, 1942; BA in Music, Hillsdale Coll., 1964; MA in Guidance Counseling, Mich. State U., 1965; PhD in Psychology, U. Mich., 1971. Tchr. Warren (Mich.) Consol. Schs., 1965-70; curriculum advisor Royal Oak (Mich.) Pub. Schs., 1974-75; co-founder, exec. dir. Peace Rsch. Found., Carmel, Calif., 1993-98. Assoc. Hillsdale Coll., 1989—; guest lectr. ceramics James Milliken U., Decatur, Ill., 1991; guest lectr. creative covergence Carl Cherry Ctr. for Art, Carmel, 1991, Compton lectr., Monterey, Calif., 1996—; mem. Nat. Assn. Fund Raising Execs., 1991-96; co-founder, bd. dirs. Monterey Peninsula Coll. Art Gallery, 1991—; guest juror Monterey County Essay Contest, 1997; cons. Monterey Mus. of Art; guest lectr. Hillsdale (Mich.) Coll., 1997; juror Monterey County Poetry Contest, 1993—; juror photographic show Beauty at the Heart of Things, Carl Cherry Ctr. for Arts, Carmel, 1999. Artist of multiple commd. sculptures for pvt. collections; also ceramics, sculpture and photographs in pvt. and corp. collections; represented in permanent collection at Krammert Art Mus., Champaign, Ill., Fresno (Calif.) Mus. Art; juried show Ctr. for Photographic Art, Carmel, Calif., 1996; art represented at Who's Who in Art, Monterey, 1989-96, Christmas Miniatures/Invitational Ctr. for Photographic Art, Carmel, 1996, Holiday Print Show Ctr. for Photographic Art, Carmel, 1996 (Dir.'s Choice 1996); author of poetry; juror essay contest Personal Heroes Monterey County K-12, 1997; juror poetry contest Monterey County 9-12 grades, Carl Cherry Ctr. for the Arts, 1993-2001; exhibited in photography show at Asilomer Conf. Ctr., Monterey Peninsula Airport, Pacific Grove Art Ctr., Carl Chevry Ctr., Seaside City Hall, Pacific Grove Mus. Natural History, 1995-98, Hillsdale Coll., 1997, Monterey Peninsula Airport, 1998, Calif. State U., Monterey Bay, 1998, Pacific Grove (Calif.) Art Ctr., 1998, Carl Cherry Ctr. for Arts, Carmel, Calif., 1998, Pacific Grove Mus. Nat. History, 1998, Salinas (Calif.) Courthouse, 1998, Asilomar Conf. Ctr., Pacific Grove, 1998, Prints Charming Gallery, Carmel, 1998, Triton Mus. Art, 1998, Pre-auction show KTEH, 1998, 2000, Triton Mus., 1998; one-woman show Prints Charming Gallery, Carmel, Calif., 2000; represented by Prints Charming Gallery and Carmel Express Internat. Co-founder Southfield (Mich.) Symphony, 1972, World Rhythms Festival, Carmel, 1994; mem. citizens adv. bd. City of Royal Oak, 1978-83; co-founder, bd. dirs. Monterey Bay Artists Day, Sta. KAZU-FM, 1987-89; pres., bd. dirs. Carl Cherry Ctr. for Arts, Carmel, 1988-94, 95, 97; bd. dirs. Monterey Peninsula Mus. Art, 1991-94, Carmel Pub. Libr. Found., 1991-94, Monterey Inst. for Rsch. in Astronomy, 1985-95, Cultural Coun. for Monterey County, 1993-98; fundraiser Student Art Gallery, Monterey Peninsula Coll., 1990-97, mem. mentors program Women Helping Women, 1998—. Recipient Citizens Adv. Coun. award City of Royal Oak, 1983, Best of Show award for monoprint Monterey Peninsula Coll., 1990, Poetry prizes Carl Cherry Ctr. for Arts, 1990-94, Benefactor of Arts award Monterey County Cultural Coun., 1992, 93, 94, Soccer Mgr./Coach of Yr. 1976-81, 1st pl. award photography contest Monterey Regional Park Dist. Celebration of Open Space, 1998; artist-in-residence Naubinway, Mich., 1997. Mem. AAUW, Internat. Platform Assn., Internat. Sculpture Ctr., Nat. Soc. Fund Raising Execs., Nat.

Mus. Women in Art (charter mem.), Am. Crafts Coun., Sigma Alpha Iota (Ruby Sword of Honor 1963). Avocations: reading, playing piano, composing, hiking, photography. Home: 9645 Sandbur Pl Salinas CA 93907-1031

CHESTER, MARK VINCENT, lawyer; b. Chgo., Apr. 22, 1952; s. Alvin L. and Barbara (Segal) C.; m. Shelly L. Beeber, May 20, 1979; children: Jonathan Harry, Michael Steven, Susan Gayle. BA, MA, Emory U., 1974; JD, Northwestern U., 1977. Bar: Ill. 1977, U.S. Dist. Ct. (no. dist.) Ill 1977, Ga. 1979, U.S. Ct. Appeals (7th, 11th and 5th cirs.) 1981, U.S. Supreme Ct. 1981. Asst. states atty. Cook County, Ill., 1977-81, spl. asst. states atty., 1981-96, spl. asst. atty. gen., 1981-83; assoc. Butler, Rubin, Newcomer & Saltarelli, Chgo., 1981-83; ptnr. Johnson and Colmar, Chgo., 1983—. Bd. dirs. Project LEAP, 1976-94. Mem. Ill. Bar Assn., Ga. Bar Assn., Chgo. Bar Assn. Home: 1017 Prairie Ln Deerfield IL 60015-2814 Office: Johnson and Colmar 300 S Wacker Dr Ste 1000 Chicago IL 60606-6665 E-mail: mvchester@jocolaw.com.

CHESTER, NORMAN CHARLES, bank executive; b. Glen Ridge, N.J., Dec. 7, 1953; s. Norman Harding Chester and Barbara Wanda (Barber) Readie; m. Vivian Leslie Tarallo, Aug. 15, 1987; children: Alfred Eduardo, Caroline Carmen. BBA, Bucknell U., 1976; MBA, Rutgers U., 1981. Cert. mgmt. acct. Adj. instr. Bergen C.C., Paramus, N.J., 1983-85; rep. Equitable Life, E. Orange, N.J., 1976-77; mgmt. trainee U.S. Life Ins. Co., N.Y.C., 1977-79; from acct. to v.p. Chase Manhattan Bank, N.Y.C., 1979-97; v.p., contr. ABN AMRO Bank, Fin. Restructuring and Recovery, N.Y.C., 1997—. Guest speaker Exec. Enterprises, 1993-94. Trustee Westwood (N.J.) United Meth. Ch., 1988-92, fin. chair, 1989-94, sec. adminstrv. coun., 1986-89; publicity chair Hillsdale Vol. Ambulance Svc., 1986-99, fin. chair, 1993—, treas., 1994—; dir. Oradell Kids Found., 1996-97. Mem. Inst. of Mgmt. Accts. Methodist. Avocations: running, photography. Home: 782 Martin Ave Oradell NJ 07649-2338 Office: ABN AMRO Bank 350 Park Ave New York NY 10022

CHESTER, PRISCILLA (PERCI CHESTER), artist, educator; b. Mpls., Mar. 29, 1945; d. Alexander and Ella (Olin) C.; m. Mitchell Elliot Bender; 1 child, Alexander Bender. BFA, Washington U., St. Louis, 1967; MA in Tchg., R.I. Sch. Design, 1968, MFA, 1969. Instr. R.I. Sch. Design, Providence, 1968-69; art instr. N.Y. Pub. Sch., N.Y.C., 1969-70, Newton (Mass.) Pub. Sch., 1970-71; instr. 3-D design City Coll., San Francisco, 1974-76; artist-in-residence Alvarado Art Workshop, San Francisco, 1976-81; cultural arts coord. Intersection, San Francisco, 1978-81; dir. Artward Bound program St. Paul Acad., 1983-85; vis. artist, drawing instr. Mpls. Coll. Art and Design, 1993-94; vis. artist Macalester Coll., St. Paul, 1995-96. One person shows include Flanders Fine Arts, Mpls., 1998, Phipps Ctr. for Arts, Hudson, Wis., 1996, Carolyn Ruff Gallery, Mpls., 1990-91, Minn. Mus., St. Paul, 1985-86; exhibited in group shows in N.Y., Boston, Minn., and San Francisco. Invited to make sculpture Poriya Govt. Hosp., Tiberias, Israel, 2001; bd. dirs. TZ Ctr. Visual Arts, 2000—03. Grantee San Francisco Planning Dept., 1976; travel and study grantee Dayton Hudson, Gen. Mills & Jerome Found., 1993. Mem. Artist's Alliance (bd. dirs. 1990-93, treas. 1991-93). Avocations: photography, music, writing poetry and plays. Studio: 250 3d Ave N # 200 Minneapolis MN 55401 Home Fax: 612-204-9664. E-mail: perci@percichester.com.

CHESTER, ROBERT SIMON GEORGE, lawyer; b. Chelmsford, Essex, England, Feb. 11, 1949; arrived in Can., 1971. s. Robert John and Elizabeth Poyitt (Forteath) C.; m. Anna Tharyan, Sept. 18, 1975; 1 child, Rahael Elizabeth Anna. BA, Oxford U., England, 1971, MA, 1979; LLM, Osgoode Hall Law Sch., Toronto, 1972. Bar: Ontario 1982, England and Wales 1988. Vis. lectr. Osgoode Hall Law Sch., Toronto, 1972-74; rsch. staff Ontario Law Reform Commn., Toronto, 1974-77; exec. counsel Dep. Atty. Gen. Ontario, Toronto, 1977-82; counsel policy devel. Ministry Atty. Gen., Ontario, 1982-85; dir. rsch. McMillan Binch, Toronto, 1985—; ptnr. KNOWlaw Group, Toronto, 1988—. Counsel Study on Access to Legal Svcs. by Disabled, Ontario, 1982-83; cons. Royal Commn. on Employment Equity, 1983-84, Royal Commn. on Electoral Reform, 1990-91, Royal Commn. on Aboriginal Peoples, 1992. Author: (with others) Environmental Rights in Canada, 1981, The Quality Pursuit, 1988, ABA Guide to Legal Marketing, 1995, Barristers and Solicitors in Practice, 1998; co-editor: Winning with Computers, 1991, 2d vol., 1993; contbr. articles to profl. jours. Trustee Coll. Law Practice Mgmt. Can. Rhodes Found. scholar, 1972; fellow Coll. Law Practice Mgmt. Mem. ABA (chmn. New Media and Internet bd., chmn. edn. bd. law practice mgmt. sect. 1994-96, chmn. Techshow 1992-93), Can. Bar Assn. (com. legal opinions 1992—, Pres. tech. impact adv. group). Anglican. Home: 41 Walmsley Blvd Toronto ON Canada M4V 1X7 Office: McMillan Binch LLP Royal Bank Plz PO Box 38 Toronto ON Canada M5J 2J7 E-mail: simon.chester@mcmillanbinch.com.

CHESTER, RUSSELL GILBERT, JR., accountant, auditor; b. Lorain, Ohio, Aug. 6, 1947; s. Russell Gilbert and Elizabeth Jane (Eucker) C.; m. Martha Ann Mamula, Jan. 24, 1970 (div.); children: Sally Ann, Russell Theodore; m. Pamela Jean Huggins, Sept. 26, 1992. BS in Indsl. Mgmt., Purdue U., 1970; grad. with honors, USAF Comm. Analyst Sch., 1971; M Accountancy, Bowling Green State U., 1975; Exec. Mgmt. Program, U. Mich., 1985. CPA, Ohio; cert. systems profl. Staff and sr. acct. Arthur Andersen & Co., Cleve., 1975-77; chief internal auditor lighting fixture divsn. ITT, Vermilion, Ohio, 1977, comptr. Can. Lighting divsn. London, Ont., 1977-78, comptr. lighting fixture div. Vermillion, 1978-80; comptr., dir. pers., lighting fixtures div. Lithonia Lighting, Vermillion, 1980; supr. internal audit indsl. tech. group ITT, Chgo., 1980-81, mgr. internal audit engr. products group, 1981-83, dir. internal audit natural resources group Stamford, Conn., 1983-84; dir. audit svcs. Parker Hannifin Corp., Cleve., 1984-2001, v.p. audit, 2001—. Cons. Component Repair Tech. Mentor, Ohio, 1984-86, bd. dirs., 1986—; mem. acctg. student adv. bd. Cleve. State U., 1990-2000, Case Western Res. U., 1994-95. Asst. scoutleader Boy Scouts Am., Cleve., 1985; instr. Jr. Achievement, Cleve., 1986. Sgt. USAF, 1970-73. Mem. AICPA, Inst. Mgmt. Accts., Ohio Soc. CPAs, Inst. Internal Auditors (bd. dirs. Cleve.-Akron chpt. 1991-97, 99—, internat. conf. com. 1994-96, chmn. acad. rels. 1991-94, 1st v.p. 1994-95, pres. 1995-96, chmn. attendance and mem. 1996-98, dist. rep. 1997-2000), Assn. for Sys. Mgmt., Mfrs. Alliance for Productivity and Innovation (gen. auditors coun.), Am. Legion, VFW, Beta Alpha Psi. Republican. Avocations: philately, numismatics, books, yachting, computers. Office: Parker Hannifin Corp 6035 Parkland Blvd Cleveland OH 44124-4141 E-mail: rchester@parker.com.

CHESTER, SHARON ROSE, photographer, natural history educator, writer, illustrator; b. Chgo., July 12, 1942; d. Joseph Thomas and Lucia Barbara (Urban) C. BA, U. Wis., 1964; grad., Coll. San Mateo, 1974, U. Calif., Berkeley, 1977, San Francisco State U., 1989. Flight attendant Pan Am. World Airways Inc., San Francisco, 1965; free lance photographer San Mateo, Calif., 1983—; stock photographer Comstock, N.Y.C., 1987-98. Lectr. Soc. Expdns., Seattle, 1985-91, Abercrombie & Kent, Chgo., 1992-94, Seven Seas Cruise Line, San Francisco, 1994-95; owner Wandering Albatross, 1993. Author (checklist) Birds of the Antarctic and Sub-Antarctic, 1986, rev., 1994, Antarctic birds and Seals: A Pocket Guide, 1993, South to Antarctica, 1994, The Northwest Passage, 1994; author and illustrator, Birds of Chile, Aves de Chile, 1995; co-author: The Birds of Chile: A Field Guide, 1993, The Arctic Guide, 1996, The Marquesas Islands: Mave Mai, 1997, Ia Orana Tahiti, 1998, Guide to Maritime Britain and The European North Atlantic, 1999, Guide to Scottish Isles, Faroes and Iceland, 2000, Travel Guides to Namibia and Jordan, 2001, Travel Guides to Egypt and East Africa, 2002; photos featured in Mother Earth Through the Eyes of Women Photographers and Writers, 1992, 10th anniversary edit., 2002; photographer mag. cover Internat. Wildlife Mag., 1985, Sierra Club Calendar, 1986; exhibited photos at Royal Geographic Soc. London. Mem. Calif. Acad. Sci. Avocations: writing, ice dancing, birdwatching. Home: 724 Laurel Ave Apt 211 San Mateo CA 94401-4131

CHESTNUT, JOHN WILLIAM, lawyer; b. Berwyn, Ill., July 3, 1940; s. James Edward and Alice Mary (Cotter) C.; m. Margaret Barbara Angland, Aug. 8, 1964; children: Edward, Nancy. BS cum laude, U. Notre Dame, 1962; JD cum laude, Northwestern U., 1965. Bar: Ill. 1965, U.S. Dist. Ct. (no. dist.) Ill. 1965, U.S. Supreme Ct. 1978, U.S. Ct. Appeals (7th cir.) 1982. Assoc. Dawson, Tilton, Fallon & Lumgmus, Chgo., 1965-68; ptnr. Tilton, Fallon, Lumgmus & Chestnut, Chgo., 1968-94. Mem. editorial bd. The Trademark Reporter, N.Y.C., 1975—. Mem. ABA, Am. Intellectual Property Law Assn., Ill. State Bar Assn., Intellectual Property Law Assn. Chgo., Patent Law Assn. Chgo. (bd. govs. 1979-81). Office: Tilton Fallon Lungum & Chestnut 100 S Wacker Dr Ste 960 Chicago IL 60606-4002

CHESTNUTT, ELLEN JOANNE, state official; b. Milw., May 15, 1928; d. Arthur Herman and Lydia Boaz (Groff) Ziemann; m. William John Chestnutt, Sept. 3, 1954; children: David William C., Douglas John C., Gregory Mark C., Timothy Eric C. BS, U. Wis., 1950, JD, 1952. Bar: Wis. 1952, U.S. dist. Ct. Wis. 1952, Colo. 1964, U.S. Dist. Ct. Colo. 1964. Editor Shepards Citations, Colorado Springs, Colo., 1952-54; pvt. practice Colorado Springs, Colo., 1964-68; chief dep. dist. atty., 1966-85; appeal referee Colo. Dept. Labor, 1985-86; instr. law Pikes Peak C.C., Colorado Springs, 1978-96; ret., 1996. Instr. law Chapman Coll. Contbr. articles to profl. jours. Task force on child support HEW, 1974; adv. com. Fed. Child Support Law Regulations, 1975, citizens adv. com. Dept. Social Svcs., 1988-93; spkr. Secs. Nat. Conf. on Fraud, Abuse, and Error, 1978; judge regional sci. fair, 1978-88; v.p. Longfellow Sch. PTA, Colorado Springs; vol. swimming instr. YMCA; bd. dirs. Salvation Army; citizens adv. com., block capt. Colorado Springs Police Dept.; election judge Republican Party, 1988—. Recipient Disting. Faculty award Nat. Dist. Attys. Coll. Law, 1976, Dorothy Forney award United Coun. Welfare Fraud, 1988, Ted Cole Achievement award for lifetime excellence Colo. Welfare Fraud Coun., 1990, Portia award for outstanding female atty., 1999. Mem. Nat. Assn. Parliamentarians (pres. Henry Martyn Robert parliamentarian unit 1996-98, registered parliamentarian, 1996—, sec. Colorado Springs unit, 2001-03, sec. profl. parliamentary rsch. unit 2002—, pres. parliamentary unit 2003—, pres. Colo. Springs unit, 2003—), Wis. Bar Assn., Colo. Bar Assn., El Paso County Bar Assn. (past sec., trustee), Colo. Womens Bar Assn. (Silver honoree), Nat. Child Support Enforcement Assn. (hon. life), Nat. Dist. Attys. Assn., Colo. Family Support Coun. (past pres.), United Coun. on Welfare Fraud (past pres.), Colo. Welfare Fraud Coun. (past pres.), Nat. Reciprocal Family Support Enforcement Assn. (past pres.), Pikes Peak Geneal. Soc. (past v.p.), Alpha Gamma Delta (past v.p. alumni assn.). Republican. Methodist. Home: 718 Pioneer Ln Colorado Springs CO 80904-1745

CHESTON, GEORGE MORRIS, lawyer; b. Phila., Aug. 18, 1917; s. Radcliffe and Sydney (Ellis) C.; m. Winifred Dodge Seyburn, May 5, 1955; 1 dau., Sydney. AB, Harvard U., 1939, LL.B., 1947. Bar: Pa. 1947. Since practiced in, Phila.; atty. firm Ballard, Spahr. Andrews & Ingersoll, Phila., 1947-52; farmer Georgetown, S.C., 1968-94. Treas. Nat. Citizens for Eisenhower, 1955-56 Pres. Phila. Soc. for Svcs. to Children, 1959-69; trustee United Fund Phila., 1958-69; bd. dirs. Phila. Zool. Soc., 1977-86, Saratoga Performing Arts, Am. Fedn. Arts; trustee Phila. Mus. Art, 1962—, pres., 1968-76, Nat. Mus. of Racing. Served to comdr. USNR, 1941-46, PTO. Home: 229 Spruce St Philadelphia PA 19106-3906

CHESTON, SHEILA CAROL, lawyer; b. Washington, Nov. 5, 1958; d. Theodore C. and Gabrielle Joan (Hellings) C. BA, Dartmouth Coll., 1980; JD, Columbia U., 1984. Bar: N.Y. 1986, D.C. 1986, U.S. Dist. Ct. D.C. 1987, U.S. Ct. Appeals (D.C. cir.) 1987, U.S. Dist. Ct. (so. and ea. dists.) N.Y. 1989, U.S. Ct. Appeals (2d cir.), U.S. Supreme Ct. 1989. Law clk. to judge U.S. Ct. Appeals for 9th Cir., L.A., 1984-85; assoc. Wilmer, Cutler & Pickering, Washington, 1985-92, ptnr., 1992-93; gen. counsel Def. Base Closure and Realignment Commn., 1993; spl. assoc. counsel to Pres. of U.S., 1994; dep. gen. counsel Dept. Air Force, 1993-95, gen. counsel, 1995-98; ptnr. Wilmer, Cutler & Pickering, Washington, 1998—2002; sr. v.p., gen. counsel BAE Systems N.A., Rockville, Md., 2002—. Adj. prof. in internat. litigation Georgetown Law Sch., 1991—. Mem. ABA, D.C. Bar Assn., Women's Bar Assn., Am. Soc. Internat. Law. Democrat. Episcopalian. Office: BAE Systems NA 1601 Research Blvd Rockville MD 20850-3173 E-mail: sheila.cheston@baesystems.com.

CHESTON, THEODORE C. electrical engineer; b. Vienna, May 30, 1922; m. Gabrielle Joan Hellings, Oct. 8, 1956; children— Peter Charles, Sheila Carol B.Sc., U. Edinburgh, 1947. Engr. Marconi's W.T. Co. Research Lab., Great Baddow, Essex, Eng., 1947-52; sr. engr. Can. Westinghouse Co., Hamilton, Ont., 1952-56; prin. profl. staff Applied Physics Lab. Johns Hopkins U., Laurel, Md., 1956-76; group leader Office of Naval Research NATO, La Spezia, Italy, 1976-79; liaison scientist Office Naval Research, London, 1979-81; br. head Naval Research Lab., Washington, 1981-88; cons., 1988—. Contbr. articles to profl. jours; patentee in field Served as flying officer RAF, 1942-46 Fellow IEEE, Instn. Elec. Engrs. (Eng.)

CHET, GUY, historian, educator; b. Ramat-Gan, Israel, Sept. 5, 1968; arrived in U.S., 1994; s. Ilan and Ruth Chet; m. Carrie Lane, Dec. 14, 2001. BA, Haifa U., Israel, 1994; MA, Yale U., 1996, MPhil, 1998, PhD, 2001. Asst. prof. U. N. Tex., Denton, 2001—. Author: Conquering the American Wilderness, 2003. Jewish. Office: Univ North Tex Dept History PO Box 310650 Denton TX 76203-0650 E-mail: guychet@unt.edu.

CHEUNG, CHI PUI, internist; b. Canton, China, 1944; came to U.S., 1972; MD, Nat. Def. Med. Ctr., Taipei, 1969. Cert. in internal medicine, oncology, hematology. Intern Elmhurst City Hosp., N.Y.C., 1972-73; resident in pediatrics United Hosp., Newark, N.J., 1973-74; resident in medicine Arthur C. Logan Meml. Hosp., N.Y.C., 1974-75, Kingsbrook Jewish Med. Ctr., N.Y.C., 1975-76; fellow in hematology and oncology Brookdale Hosp. Med. Ctr., N.Y.C., 1976-79; pvt. practice Bklyn.; staff Kingsbrook Jewish Med. Ctr., Bklyn.; staff Kings Hwy. Divsn. N.Y. Cmty. Hosp., Bklyn., 1979—; clin. instr. SUNY Downstate Med. Ctr. Office: 3080 Nostrand Ave Brooklyn NY 11229-2601

CHEUNG, JOSEPH YAT-SING, biomedical scientist, nephrologist; b. Hong Kong, June 21, 1950; came to U.S., 1972; s. Wah Lun and Wai Ming (Ho) C.; m. Barbara Ann Miller, June 14, 1975. BSc with honors, McGill U., Mont., Can., 1972; MS, Pa. State U., 1974, PhD, 1976; MD, Duke U., 1978. Diplomate Nat. Bd. Med. Examiners, Am. Bd. Internal Medicine, Am. Bd. Internal Medicine and Nephrology. Resident Duke U. Med. Ctr., Durham, N.C., 1978-80; fellow Mass. Gen. Hosp., Boston, 1980-83; instr. in medicine Med. Sch. Harvard U., Boston, 1983-84, asst. prof. medicine, 1984-86; assoc. prof. medicine Pa. State U., Hershey, 1986-91, prof. medicine, 1991—2000; sr. scientist Weis Ctr. for Rsch., Geisinger Med. Ctr., Danville, Pa., 2000—. Mem. editorial bd. Am. Jour. Physiology, 1991-93; assoc. editor Exec. Sports Sci. Rev., 2002—; contbr. articles to Jour. Clin. Investigation, Jour. Biol. Chemistry, New Eng. Jour. Medicine. Grantee Whitaker Found., Juvenile Diabetes Found. Internat., NIH, Am. Heart Assn. Mem. Am. Physiol. Soc., Am. Soc. Nephrology, Am. Soc. Clin. Investigation, Am. Soc. Cell Biology, Biophys. Soc. Republican. Achievements include research in beneficial role of exercise training in postinfarction hearts, phospholemmen regulation of heart function, role of altered calcium regulation in congestive heart failure. Office: Weis Ctr for Rsch Geisinger Med Ctr Danville PA 17822

CHEUNG, JUDY HARDIN, retired special education educator; b. Santa Rosa, Calif., Feb. 3, 1945; d. Robert Stephens and Edna Rozella Hardin. BA, Calif. State U. at Sonoma, Rohnert Park, Calif., 1966; MA, U. San Francisco, 1981. Tchr. St. Thomas (V.I.) Dept. Edn., 1967—71; spl. edn. tchr., basic functional and Ednl. skills to disabled adults Sonoma Devel. Ctr., Eldridge, Calif., 1971—2001; co-adminstr. Redwood Empire Chinese Assn. Sch., 1996—. Co-chair Ednl. Svcs. Profl. Practice Group, Eldridge, Calif., 1989-90, 93-94; pres. Poets of the Vineyard, 1998—. Author, pub.: Acorn to Embers, 1987, Welcome to the Inside, 1984; author, photographer, pub. Captions, 1986. Recipient awards Silver Pegasus, 1983, Poets of the Vineyard, 1986, 87, 2000, 01, Ark. Writers Conf., 1988. Mem. Calif. Fedn. Chaparral Poets (pres. 1989-91, 93-95), Ina Coolbrith Cir. (pres. 1988-90), Calif. Writers Club (treas. Redwood writers br. 1985-86), Artists Embassy Internat. (v.p. 2003—, Amb. of Arts award 1992, 2001), World Congress of Cultures and Poetry (internat. bd. dirs. 1993-2000, Grand Cultures medal 1993, Cert. of merit 2000, medal for Poetic Achievement 2000), Redwood Empire Chinese Assn. (sec., co-adminstr. Chinese Lang. sch. 1996—, Appreciation award for col. svc. 2000). Avocations: photography, reading. Home and Office: 704 Brigham Ave Santa Rosa CA 95404-5245

CHEUNG, KAM-FONG MONIT, social worker, educator; b. Hong Kong; d. Man Cheung and Bick Ching Lam; m. Patrick Leung. MA, MSW, Ohio State U., 1982, PhD, 1986. Social svc. worker Hong Kong Christian Svc., 1975-79; program coord. UNHCR-AVS, Hong Kong, 1979-80; social worker, adminstr. Against Child Abuse, Hong Kong, 1982-83; planner Cen. Ohio Area Agy. Aging, Columbus, 1981-82, 84-86; asst. prof. U. Iowa, 1986-88, U. Denver, 1988-90, U. Hawaii, 1990-91; assoc. prof. U. Houston, 1991—2001, prof., 2001—. Cons. Am. Assn. for Protecting Children, 1988—; P.I. Child Welfare Edn. Project, 2001—; dir. clin. svcs. Asian Am. Family Counseling Ctr., 1999—. Mem. editl. bd. Social Devel. Issues, 1987—, Social Work, 2002—, Jour. Social Work Edn., 1995—, Jour. of Poverty, 1998; contbr. articles to Social Work, Social Work Rsch. and Abstracts, Child Welfare, Social Svc. Rev., Internat. Jour. Drug Addiction, Social Devel. Issues, Child Abuse and Neglect, Jour. Child Sexual Abuse, others. Office: U Houston Sch Social Work Houston TX 77204-4013 E-mail: mcheung@uh.edu.

CHEUNG-YUEH, MANDARIN GERMAINE, pianist; b. Hong Kong, Sept. 24, 1965; married; 2 children. BMus, U. Houston, 1986, MMus, 1988; DMA, Ariz. State U., 1999. Pvt. piano tchr., Scottsdale, Ariz. Founder, pres. Young Artist Com., Scottsdale, 1991-97. Mem. Music Tchrs. Nat. Assn., Ariz. State Music Tchrs. Assn., East Valley Music Tchrs. Assn. Roman Catholic. Avocations: reading, swimming, walking, architecture, book collecting.

CHEVALIER, PAUL EDWARD, retired retail executive, lawyer; b. N.Y.C., Jan. 30, 1939; s. Arthur and Grace (Eaton) C.; m. Maggie Helfer, Dec. 29, 1996; 1 child, Marc. BA, Columbia U., 1960, LLB, MBA, Columbia U., 1966; AMP, Harvard U., 1979. Bar: Ill. 1968, U.S. Supreme Ct. 1974. Dir. labor rels. Carter Hawley Hale Stores, Inc., L.A., 1972-74, v.p. employee rels., 1974-86, sr. v.p. employee rels., 1986-93; pres. Chevalier Cons. Group, 1993-98. Vice chmn. Western Fed. Credit Union, 1989-93; bd. dirs., exec. com. Sedona Cultural Park, 2000—. Past pres., bd. dirs. Calif. Employment Law Coun.; chmn. Art and Culture Commn., City of Sedona, 1999—; dir. Ariz. Humanities Coun. Lt. USN, 1960-66. Mem. Nat. Retail Fedn. (chmn. employee rels. com. 1979-82), Calif. Retail Assn., Harvard Bus. Sch. Assn. (bd. dirs. 1980-90, pres. 1984-85), Harvard Bus. Sch. Alumni Coun., Jonathan Art Found. (chmn. emeritus).

CHEVALIER, ROGER ALAN, astronomy educator, consultant; b. Rome, Sept. 26, 1949; came to U.S., 1962; s. Frank Charles and Marion Helen (Janhke) C.; m. Margaret Mary With, July 27, 1974.; children: Chase Arthur, Max Toussaint. BS in Astronomy, Calif. Inst. Tech., 1970; PhD in Astronomy (Woodrow Wilson and NSF fellow), Princeton U., 1973. Asst. astronomer Kitt Peak Nat. Obs., Tucson, 1973-76, assoc. astronomer, 1976-79; assoc. prof. astronomy U. Va., Charlottesville, 1979-85, prof. astronomy, chmn. dept., 1985-92, W.H. Vanderbilt prof. astronomy, 1990—; dir. Leander McCormick Obs., 1985-92. Cons. Lawrence Livermore Nat. Lab., Livermore, Calif., 1981-90; bd. trustees U. Space Rsch. Assn., 2000—. Contbr. numerous rsch. articles to Astrophys. Jour., other astronomy and physics jours. Recipient Heineman prize for astrophysics Am. Astron. Soc./Am. Inst. Physics, 1996; named Va. Outstanding Scientist, Sci. Mus. Va., 1991; Woodrow Wilson Found. fellow Princeton U., 1970-71, NSF fellow, 1970-73; elected to Nat. Acad. Scis., 1996. Mem. NAS, Am. Astron. Soc. (councilor 1988-91), Internat. Astron. Union, Ill. Sci. Lectr. Assn. (v.p. 1975-85), Univ. Space Rsch. Assn. (bd. trustees 2000—). Home: 1891 Westview Rd Charlottesville VA 22903-1632 Office: U Va Dept Astronomy PO Box 3818 Charlottesville VA 22903-0818

CHEVERS, WILDA ANITA YARDE, former state official and educator; b. N.Y.C. d. Wilsey Ivan and Herbert Lee (Perry) Yarde; m. Kenneth Chevers, May 14, 1950; 1 child, Pamela Anita. BA, CUNY, 1947; MSW, Columbia U., 1959, PhD, 1981. Probation officer, Office Probation for Cts., N.Y.C., 1947-55, supr. probation officer, 1955-65, br. chief, 1965-72, asst. dir. probation, 1972-77, dept. commr. dept. probation, 1978-86; prof. pub. adminstrn. John Jay Coll. Criminal Justice, CUNY, 1986-91. Conf. faculty mem. Nat. Council Juvenile and Family Ct. Judges; mem. faculty N.Y.C. Tech. Coll., Nat. Coll. Juvenile Justice; mem. adv. com. Family Ct., First Dept. Sec. Susan E. Wagner Adv. Bd., 1966—70; sec., bd. dirs. Allen Cmty. Day Care Ctr., 1971—75; mem. Las Vegas EMA Ryan White Title I Planning Coun., 1998—2000; chmn., bd. dirs. Allen Christian Sch., 1987—91; bd. dirs. Allen Sr. Citizens Housing, Queensboro Soc. for Prevention Cruelty to Children, Las Vegas LWV. Named to Hall of Fame, Hunter Coll., 1983. Mem. ABA (assoc.), ASPA (coun.), NASW, N.Y. Acad. Pub. Edn., Nat. Coun. on Crime and Delinquency, Acad. Cert. Soc. Workers, Mid. Atlantic States Conf. on Correction, Alumni Assn. Columbia U. Sch. Social Work, NYU Alumni Assn., NAACP, Counselors, Las Vegas LWV (bd. dirs.), SNCCW (pres. 2002-03), Hansel and Gretel Club (pres. Queens, N.Y. 1967-69), Delta Sigma Theta. Home: 9012 Covered Wagon Ave Las Vegas NV 89117-7010

CHEVINS, ANTHONY CHARLES, retired advertising agency executive; b. Frackville, Pa., Apr. 1, 1921; s. Charles A. and Mary (Swade) C.; m. Margaret Macy, Sept. 18, 1948; children: Cheryl L., Christopher M., Cynthia M. AB in Eng. and Advt. magna cum laude, Syracuse U., 1947; postgrad., Columbia U., 1948-49. Writer Batten, Barton, Durstine & Osborn (advt.), 1948-51; with Cunningham & Walsh, 1951-87, sr. v.p., 1959-61, creative dir., 1958-61, exec. v.p., 1961-68, pres., chief operating officer, 1968-84, chmn., chief exec. officer, 1984-87, The C&W Group Inc., 1985-87; vice chmn. N.W Ayer Inc., 1987-90, also bd. dirs. Contbr. articles to mags. Mem. Nat. Advt. Rev. Bd.; mem. dean's adv. coun. Newhouse Sch.; bd. dirs. Medic Alert Found. Internat. Served to lt. USNR, 1941-45. Mem. Phi Beta Kappa, Alpha Delta Sigma. Clubs: Sky, Union League (N.Y.C.); Woodway Country (Darien, Conn.); Nat. Golf Links Am. (Southampton, L.I.); Ocean Reef, Card Sound (Key Largo, Fla.). Home: 10 South Rd Key Largo FL 33037-3729

CHEVINSKY, AARON HARRY, surgeon; b. Bklyn., May 2, 1959; s. Irving and Laura (Kleinberg) C.; m. Dawn J. Chernoff, Aug. 28, 1982; children: Michael, Jennifer, Shayna, Jonathan. BS magna cum laude, CCNY, 1981; MD, SUNY, Stony Brook, 1983. Diplomate Nat. Bd. Med. examiners; cert. Am. Bd. Surgery; cert. BCLS, ACLS, Advanced Trauma Life Support, Surg. Critical Care. Intern Stony Brook (N.Y.) U. Hosp., 1983-84, resident, 1984-88; fellow Ohio State U. Hosp., Columbus, 1988-90; surg. oncologist Morris County Surg. Assocs., P.A., NJ, 1990—; dir. gastrointestinal oncology Carol G. Simon Cancer Ctr., 1998—; acting chmn. dept. surgery Morristown (NJ) Meml. Hosp., 2002—. Lectr. and presenter in field. Contbr. chpt. to book and articles to profl. jours. Named fellow Herbert J. Block Meml. Fund, 1989; recipient Am. Soc. Clin. Oncology Travel award, 1989. Fellow Acad. Medicine N.J., Am. Coll. Surgeons; mem. AMA, Am. Cancer Soc. (bd. mgrs., clin. fellowship grant 1989-90), N.J. State Med. Soc. (del.), Soc. Surg. Oncology, Am. Soc. of Colon & Rectal Surgeons, Am. Soc. of Breast Diseases, Am. Trauma Soc., Robert M. Zollinger/Ohio State U. Surg. Soc., Soc. Critical Care Medicine, Morris County Med. Soc., Oncology Soc. N.J. Office: Morris County Surg Assocs PA 182 South St Morristown NJ 07960-5350

CHEVLI, RENATE NAREN, obstetrician, gynecologist; b. Hannover, Germany, 1937; d. Johann and Martha (Bruns) Schmidt; m. Naren A. Chevli, Sept. 18, 1965. MD, SUNY, Syracuse, 1971. Diplomate Am. Bd. Ob-Gyn. Intern St. Joseph's Hosp., Syracuse, 1971-72; resident in ob-gyn. SUNY Upstate Med. Ctr., Syracuse, 1972-76; pvt. practice Syracuse, 1976—. Fellow: ACOG, Am. Coll. Ob-Gyn.; mem.: AAUW, AMA, Women's Med. Soc. NY State, N.Am. Menopause Soc., Med. Soc. NY State, Am. Med. Women's Assn. Office: The Womens Place 4117 Medical Center Drive Fayetteville NY 13066 Fax: 315-329-4969. E-mail: chevliMD@aol.com.

CHEVRAY, RENE, physics educator; b. Paris, Feb. 6, 1937; came to the U.S., 1962; naturalized U.S. citizen, 1989; s. Robert and Marie-Louise (Fracher) C.; m. Keiko Uesawa, Aug. 9, 1964; children: Pierre-Yves Masaki, Veronique Mie. BS, U. Toulouse, France, 1962; Dipl. Ing. (French Govt. Highest scholar), Ecole Nationale Supérieure d'Electronique, d'Electrotechnique et d'Hydraulique de Toulouse, 1962; MS (Alliance Française of N.Y. fellow), U. Iowa, 1963, PhD, 1967; D.Sc., U. Claude Bernard, Lyon, France, 1978. Product and mfg. engr. Centrifugal Pumps Worthington, Paris, 1963-64; research assoc. Iowa Inst. Hydraulic Research, Iowa City, 1964-67; postdoctoral fellow, lectr. aeronautics Johns Hopkins U., 1967-69; asst. prof. SUNY, Stony Brook, 1969-72, assoc. prof., 1972-79, prof., 1979-82; prof. dept. mech. engring. Columbia U., N.Y.C., 1982-87, chmn. dept. mech. engring., 1987-90. Cons. physics of fluids and instrumentation; vis. prof. Japan Soc. for Promotion Sci., 1975; vis. prof., von. Humboldt fellow U. Karlsruhe, 1975-76 Author: Topics in Fluid Mechanics, 1993; contbr. articles to profl. jours.; rschr. in transport processes in fluids. Recipient Great Tchr. award Soc. Columbia Grads., 1993; Fulbright scholar, 1962-63; grantee NSF, 1970-73, 73-91, Dept. Energy, 1979-89, Office Naval Rsch., 1985-90, Whitaker Found., 1995—; Rsch. Found. SUNY Faculty Rsch. fellow, 1970-71. Mem. Internat. Assn. Hydraulic Rsch., Am. Phys. Soc., N.Y. Acad. Scis., Sigma Xi Home: 300 Riverside Dr Apt 10A New York NY 10025-5239 Office: Columbia U Mech Enging New York NY 10027

CHEW, GEOFFREY FOUCAR, physicist; b. Washington, June 5, 1924; s. Arthur Percy and Pauline Lisette (Foucar) C.; m. Ruth Wright, June 10, 1945 (dec. Apr. 1971); children— Berkeley, Beverly; m. Denyse Odette Mettel, Dec. 30, 1971; children— Pierre-Yves, Jean-Francois, Pauline BS in Physics, George Washington U., 1944; PhD in Physics, U. Chgo., 1948. Research physicist Los Alamos Sci. Lab., N.Mex., 1944-46; research physicist Lawrence Berkeley Lab., Calif., 1948-49; asst. prof. physics U. Calif., Berkeley, 1949-50; asst. prof., assoc. prof. physics U. Ill., Urbana, 1950-56; prof. physics U. Calif., Berkeley, 1957—, chmn. dept. physics, 1974-78, Miller prof., 1981-82, dean physical scis., 1986-92. Group leader theoretical physics Lawrence Berkeley Lab., Calif., 1964-83; vis. prof. Princeton U., N.J., 1970-71; sci. assoc. CERN, Geneva, 1978-79; vis. prof. U. Paris, 1983. Author: S-Matrix Theory of Strong Interactions, 1961; Analytic S Matrix, 1966; contbr. articles to profl. jours. Chmn. passport com. Fedn. Am. Scientists, Washington, 1951-56 Recipient E.O. Lawrence award AEC, 1969, Disting. Alumni award George Washington U., 1974, Berkeley citation U. Calif., 1991; Churchill Coll. overseas fellow, 1962 Fellow Am. Phys. Soc. (Hughes prize 1962); mem. Nat. Acad. Scis., Am. Acad. Arts and Scis. Home: 10 Maybeck Twin Dr Berkeley CA 94708-2037 E-mail: gfchew@lbl.gov.

CHEW, KEITH ELVIN, healthcare services administrator; b. Webb City, Mo., Jan. 1, 1957, s. David Elvin and Melinda Lou (Barker) C. BS in Physiology with distinction, U. Ill., 1979, MS in Biol. Sci., 1981, postgrad., 1981-83; MA in Health Svc. Adminstrn., Sangamon State U., Springfield, Ill., 1986. Instr. Sangamon State U., 1985-86; program dir. So. Ill. U. Sch. Medicine, Springfield, 1984-86; dir. bus. and clin. affairs Tex. Tech Health Sci. Ctr., Lubbock, 1986-88; cons. Profl. Cons. Svcs., Long Grove, Ill., 1988-90; adminstr. Primary Care Family Ctr., Libertyville, Ill., 1988-90; instr. Coll. St. Francis, Joliet, Ill., 1991; adminstr. North Suburban Clinic, Skokie, Ill., 1990-91; cons. KEC Healthcare Mgmt. Cons., Forest Lake, Ill., 1991-92; dir. practice mgmt. Contemporary Mgmt. Assocs., Inc., Portsmouth, N.H., 1992-95; exec. dir. Network, Health Mgmt. Ltd. Partnership-Drs. Hosp., Springfield, 1995-96, v.p., 1996-97; CEO Imaging Radiologists, MSO, Inc., Springfield and Chgo, 1998-99, Imaging Radiologists, LLC, Springfield and Chgo., 2000—02; prin. Vinculum Cons., LLC, 2002—. Author reports and articles. Mem. Am. Coll. Med. Group Adminstrs. (cert. med. practice exec. 1994), Med. Group Mgmt. Assn., Healthcare Fin. Mgmt. Assn., Chgo. Health Exec. Forum. Avocations: music (aural and vocal), golf, fishing, aviation, gardening. Home: 18 Hawks Nest Chatham IL 62629-2016 E-mail: kechew@springnet1.com.

CHEW, LINDA LEE, fundraising management executive; b. Riverside, Calif., Mar. 3, 1941; d. LeRoy S. and Grace (Ham) Olson; m. Dennis W. Chew, July 23, 1965; children: Stephanie, Erica. B.Mus., U. Redlands, 1962. Cert. fund raising exec. Dir. pub. events U. Redlands, Calif., 1962-69; dir. fin. and comm. San Gorgonio Coun., Girl Scouts USA, Colton, Calif., 1969-71; exec. dir. United Cerebral Palsy Assn., Sacramento, 1972-73; fin. devel. dir. San Francisco Bay coun. Girl Scouts U.S.A., 1973-76; chief devel. and pub. info. East Bay Regional Park Dist., Oakland, Calif., 1976-86; cons. Chew & Assocs., Alamo, Calif., 1986-96; pres. Providence Hosp. Found., Oakland, Calif., 1991-92; assoc. dir. Alta Bates Summit Found., Berkeley, Calif., 1996—; exec. dir. United Cerebral Palsy Assn., Yolo counties, Calif., 1972—73. Bd. dir. San Ramon Valley Edn. Found., 1984-88; Calif. Conservation Corps Bay Area Ctr. Adv. Bd., 1988-89. Mem. AAUW (pres. Redlands br. 1968-69), Nat. Soc. Fund Raising Exec. (nat. bd. dir. 1981-90, nat. vice chmn. 1982-84, pres. Golden Gate chpt. 1979-80, bd. dir. 1987-90, Abel Hanson Meml. award 1977, Outstanding Fund Raising Exec. 1988), Assn. Healthcare Philanthropy (Region 11 cabinet mem. 1991-94), Am. Guild Organists (dean Riverside-San Bernardino chpt. 1969-71), Pub. Rels. Soc. Am., Alamo Rotary, mem., Oakland Rotary Endowment (pres. 2002-03), Oakland Rotary, Lamorinda Volleyball Club (pres. 1994-95). Office: 2450 Ashby Ave Berkeley CA 94705-2067

CHEWNING, MARTHA FRANCES MACMILLAN, lawyer; b. Orlando, Fla., Oct. 11, 1951; d. James Francis and Frances Sybil (Es'Dorn) MacMillan; m. John Quinton Chewning, June 3, 1978. BA in Social Work magna cum laude, LaGrange Coll., 1972; JD, Mercer U., 1979. Bar: Ga. 1979. Pvt. practice, Pine Mountain, Ga., 1979—85; judge probate ct., traffic ct., supt. of elections Harris County, Hamilton, Ga., 1985—98; pvt. practice Hamilton, Ga., 1985—. Bd. dirs. First Union Nat. Bank, Pine Mountain. Mem. State Bar Assn. Ga., Pine Mountain C. of C. (pres. 1985), Harris County C. of C. (pres. 1998). Methodist. Avocations: scuba diving, motorcycles. Office: PO Box 354 Hamilton GA 31811-0354

CHEWNING, RICHARD CARTER, retired religious business ethics educator; b. Charlottesville, Va., May 12, 1933; s. Carroll Wills and Vivienne Elizabeth (Akers) C.; m. Shirley Anne Clarke, Nov. 26, 1955; children: Karen Carter Chewning Barnard, John Jeffrey, David Clarke. BSBA, Va. Polytech. Inst., 1956; MBA, U. Va., 1958; PhD in Bus. Adminstrn., U. Wash., 1963. Instr. U. Richmond, Va., 1958-61, from asst. to full prof., 1963-85; part-time instr. U. Wash., Seattle, 1961-63; Chavanne prof. Christian Ethics in Bus. Baylor U., Waco, Tex., 1985-2000, prof. emeritus Christian ethics, 2000—; Disting. scholar in residence John Brown U., Siloam Springs, Ark., 2001—. Chmn. bd. trustees Covenant Coll., Lookout Mountain, Tenn., 1976-88; chmn. bd. dirs. Roger Clarke, Inc., Fredericksburg, Va., 1983-92; bd. dirs. chmn. Quarryville (Pa.) Presbyn. Home, 1977—; moderator Presbyn Ch. in Am., Atlanta, 1985. Author: Business Ethics In A Changing Culture, 1983, Biblical Principles and Business: The Foundations, 1989, Biblical Principles and Economics: The Foundations, 1989, Biblical Principles and Business: The Practice, 1990, Business Through the Eyes of Faith, 1990, Biblical Principles and Public Policy: The Practice, 1991; also articles. Bd. dirs. Ctr. for Pub. Justice, Washington, 1991-96; trustee LeTourneau U., Longview, Tex., 1993—. Named Disting. Educator, U. Richmond, 1980, Baylor U. Sch. Bus., 1993; The Ann. Richard C. Chewning Award funded by the Service Master Found. in his honor, 1998. Mem. Soc. Bus. Ethics, Assn. Christian Econs., Christian Bus. Faculty Assn. (life), Golden Key, Omicron Delta Kappa, Beta Gamma Sigma. Presbyterian. Avocations: traveling, music. E-mail: twochew@hotmail.com.

CHEY, WILLIAM YOON, physician; b. Ki Jang, Korea, Jan. 21, 1930; s. Kee Bok and Myungkwon (Lee) C.; m. Fan K. Tang, May 21, 1959; children: William D., Donna C., Richard D., Laura C. MD, Seoul (Korea) Nat. U., 1953; MSc, U. Pa., 1962, DSc, 1966. Intern N.Y.C. Hosp., 1954-55, resident, 1955-56; resident in pathology Mount Sinai Hosp., N.Y.C., 1956-57; fellow in hepatology Seton Hall Med Coll., Jersey City, 1957-58; practice medicine specializing in gastroenterology Phila., 1967-71; attending physician Temple U. Med Center, Phila., 1963—; rsch. fellow in gastroenterology Samuel S. Fels Rsch. Inst., 1959-60; rsch. assoc. Samuel S. Fells Rsch. Inst., 1961, instr. medicine, 1961, assoc., 1963, asst. prof., 1965-68, assoc. prof., 1968-71; prof. medicine U. Rochester, N.Y., 1971-77, clin. prof., 1977-88, prof. medicine, 1988—; sr. attending physician, founding dir. Isaac Gordon Ctr. for Digestive Diseases and Nutrition, The Genesee Hosp., 1971-91; dir. divsn. gastroenterology and hepatology U. Rochester Sch. Medicine and Dentistry, 1992-2000; physician Strong Meml. Hosp., Rochester, 1992-2000; founding dir. William B. and Sheila Konar Ctr. for Digestive Liver Disease, Rochester, 1995—. Dir. Rochester Inst. Digestive Diseases and Scis., NY, 2000—; cons. gastroenterologist Canadaigua VA Hosp., Canadagiua, 1977—; hon. prof. Cath. U. Med. Coll., Seoul, Republic of Korea, 1983—; clin. prof. medicine Yunsei U. Sch. Medicine, 1984—; vis. prof. Peking Union Med. Coll., Chinese Acad. Med. Scis., Beijing, 1985—, Hallym U. Coll. Medicine, Choonchun, Republic of Korea, 1986—, Shanghai Med. U., 1987, Korea U. Coll. Medicine, Seoul, 1991—; mem. surgery and bioengring. study sect. Nat. Inst. Diaetes, Digestive and Kidney Diseases, NIH, Bethesda, Md., 1982—86. Contbr. articles to profl. and sci. jours and textbooks; mem. editorial bd. The Pancreas, Am. Jour. Physiology. Fellow Am. Coll. Gastroent.; mem. AAAS, Am. Fedn. Clin. Rsch., Am. Gastroent. Assn., Am. Physiol. Soc., Am. Assn. Study Liver Disease, Am. Pancreatic Assn. (pres. 1999-2000), Internat. Assn. Pancreatology, Am. Motility Soc., Am. Soc. Gastrointestinal Endoscopy, Am. Soc. Acupuncture, Am. Coll. Acupuncture, Sigma Xi. Home: 133 Crescent Hill Rd Pittsford NY 14534-2406 Office: 222 Alexander St Ste 3100 Rochester NY 14607

CHHOEU, AUSTIN H. surgeon; b. Battambang, Cambodia, Feb. 15, 1967; arrived in U.S., 1981; s. Heng Un Chhoeu and Eang Seam Ung; m. Sokkun Kimpau, Jan. 11, 2003. AS, Long Beach City Coll., Calif., 1987; BS, U. Calif.-Irvine, 1991; DO, U. Osteo. Medicine and Health Sci., Des Moines, 1996; MPH and TM, Tulane U., New Orleans, 2001. Lic. osteo. physician Calif. Rsch. asst. Long Beach VA Med. Ctr., Calif., 1989—91; lab. asst. FHP Hosp., Fountain Valley, Calif., 1990—92; CPR instr. osteo. manipulation medicine TA, phys. diagnosis TA U. Osteo. Medicine and Surg., Des Moines, 1993—94; commd. U.S. Army, 1996, advanced through grades; transitional intern William Beaumont Army Med. Ctr., 1996—97; flight surgeon, gen. med. officer Wiesbaden Health Clinic, Germany, 1997—2000; task force 11 flight surgeon Comanche Base, Tulza, Bosnia-Herzegovina, 1998; task force Rijeka III flight surgeon Rijeka Port and Airport, Croatia, 1999; task force 1/1 flight surgeon Task Force Falcon, Camp Bondsteel, Kosovo, 2000; resident Tulane U. Med. Ctr., New Orleans, 2000—01; flight surgeon Naval Operational Medicine Inst./Naval Aerospace Med. Inst., Pensacola, Fla., 2001—. Army Health Profl. .scholar, 1996—97, Harvey Franklin scholar, 1987, Isabel Paterson scholar, 1986, Edward Eldridge Meml. scholar, 1985. Mem.: AMA, The Cranial Acad., Am. Acad. Osteopathy, Am. Coll. Osteo. Family Physicians, Assn. of Mil. Osteo. Physicians and Surgeons, Am. Osteo. Assn., Soc. of U.S. Army Flight Surgeons, Osteo. Physicians and Surgeons of Calif., Am. Soc. Tropical Medicine and Hygiene, Aerospace Med. Assn., Assn. Mil. Surgeons of U.S. Home: 8059 Baywind Cir Pensacola FL 32514 Office: Naval Operational Medicine Inst 360 Hulse Rd Code 33 Pensacola FL 32508

CHI, BENJAMIN E. computer network executive; b. Tianjian, China, June 18, 1933; came to U.S., 1940; s. Hilary Shou-Yu and Emily Exner Chi; m. Virginia, Feb. 17, 1967 (dec. July 2002). BS, Antioch Coll., 1955; PhD, Rensselaer Poly. Inst., Troy, N.Y., 1962. Postdoctoral fellow, instr. Case Western Res. U., Cleve., 1962-65; summer rsch. fellow U. Minn., Mpls., 1963; from asst. prof. to assoc. prof. physics, dir. computer ctr. SUNY, Albany, 1965-99; dir. network technologies NYSERNet, Troy, 1999—. Cons. in field. Mem. Assn. Computing Machinery, Sigma Xi. Home: 1424 River Rd Selkirk NY 12158-1603 Office: NYSERNet 385 Jordan Rd Troy NY 12180-7620 E-mail: bec@nysernet.org.

CHI, DENNIS S. oncologist, researcher; b. N.Y.C., May 4, 1964; s. Chul Young and Kyu Soo (Kim) C.; m. Hae-Young Lee, Mar. 14, 1992; children: Jessica, Stephanie, Andrew. BA magna cum laude, Columbia Coll., N.Y.C., 1986; MD, NYU, 1990. Diplomate Am. Bd. Ob-Gyn., Am. Bd. Gynecol. Oncology. Resident in ob-gyn. NYU Sch. Med., N.Y.C., 1990-94; fellow in gynecol. oncology Meml. Sloan Kettering Cancer Ctr., N.Y.C., 1994-97, clin. asst. surgeon gynecol. svc., 1997—, dir. med. student and resident edn., 1997—2002, dir. fellowship tng., 2002—. Lectr., presenter in field. Co-author: (with R.M. Lanciano and A. Kudelka) Cancer Management: A Multidisciplinary Approach, 3rd edit., 1999, 4th edit., 2000; (with W.J. Hoskins) Methods in Molecular Medicine: Ovarian Cancer, 2000; (with M. Hensley and K. Alektiar) The MD Anderson/Memorial Sloan-Kettering Handbook of Gynecologic Oncology, 2000; (with D.G. Gallup) Principles and Practice of Gynecologic Oncology, 3rd edit., 2000; contbr. articles to profl. jours. Recipient Trainee Investigator award Am. Fedn. for Clin. Rsch., 1994, Berlex Oncology Found. award, 1997, Stanley Zinberg Tchg. award NYU Downtown Med. Ctr., 2000. Fellow ACOG, Am. Cancer Soc.; mem. AMA, Soc. Surg. Oncology, Korean Am. Med. Assn., Soc. Gynecol. Oncologists, Am. Soc. Clin. Oncology, Assn. Profs. Gynecology and Obstet., Phi Beta Kappa. Office: Meml Sloan Kettering Cancer Ctr 1275 York Ave New York NY 10021

CHI, JACOB, music educator; b. Qingdao, China, Dec. 9, 1952; arrived in U.S., 1981; s. Frank Chi and Linda Li; m. Lin Chang, July 11, 1987; children: Julius, Juliet. BA in Violin, Siena Heights U., 1985; MusM in Violin, U. Mich., 1987; DMA in Conducting, Mich. State U., 1996. Concert master Qingdao (China) Beijing Opera, 1970—74, condr., 1974—81; artist-in-residence U. So. Colo., Pueblo, 1991—93, assoc. prof. music, 1997—; asst. prof. music Miami U., Oxford, Ohio, 1993—97. Music dir. Pueblo Symphony, 1991—93, 1997—, Miami U. Symphony, Oxford, 1993—97. Composer: (Operas) Apricots Field, 1975. Home: 811 W Golfwood Dr Pueblo CO 81007 Office: Univ So Colo 2200 Bonforte Blvd Pueblo CO 81001

CHI, KEON SOO, editor, educator, researcher; b. Taegu, Korea, Nov. 26, 1936; came to U.S., 1965; s. Chong-Yun Chi and Pun-Sun Kim; m. Insoon Chi; children: Ronald, John. BA, Yonsei U., 1959; MA, Claremont (Calif.) U., 1968, PhD, 1970. Prof. polit. sci. Georgetown (Ky.) Coll., 1970—; sr. fellow Coun. of State Govts., Lexington, 1981—, editor jour. of state govt., 2000—. Contbr. chpts. to books and articles to profl. jours. Recipient Ky. Prof. of Yr. Carnegie Found., 1999; recipient James E. Webb award Am. Soc. for Pub. Adminstrn., 1996. Democrat. Presbyterian. Avocations: reading, travel, painting. Home: 3641 Gloucester Dr Lexington KY 40510 Office: Georgetown Coll 400 E College St Georgetown KY 40324 E-mail: kchi@georgetowncollege.edu.

CHIA, DAVID THIEN-SHING, internist, gastroenterologist; b. Sandakan, Malaysia, Mar. 24, 1942; came to U.S., 1966; s. Kiam Vun Chia and Su Lan Lo; m. Gloria Chia; children: Timothy Than-Han, Catherine Loo Ling. MD, Nat. Def. Med. Ctr., Taipei, Taiwan, 1996. Diplomate Am. Bd. Internal Medicine, Am. Bd. Gastroenterology. Rotating intern Resurrection Hosp., Chgo., 1966-67; resident in internal medicine and gastroenterology Bklyn. VA Hosp. and Downstate Med. Ctr., 1967-71; chief divsn. gastroenterology Phelps Meml. Hosp., Sleepy Hollow, N.Y., 1989-99; pvt. practice Sleepy Hollow, N.Y. asst. prof. medicine N.Y. Med. Coll., N.Y.C., 1975. Fellow ACP, Am. Coll. Gastroenterology. Lutheran. Avocations: asian antiques, mountain bicycling. Office: 777 N Broadway Ste 305 Sleepy Hollow NY 10591-1040

CHIA, NING, history educator; b. Beijing, Dec. 14, 1955; d. Guangshi Jia and Fangying Sheng; m. Ko-Hsing Huang, June 18, 1983; children: Shenstone Chia Huang, Bellara Ann Sakda Huang. BA in World His., Beijing Normal U., 1981; grad. study, Ctrl. U. Nationalities, 1982—83; MA in U.S. His., Ill. State U., Normal, 1985; PhD in Chinese His., John Hopkins U., 1991. Asst. prof. Ctrl. Coll., Pella, Iowa, 1991—98, assoc. prof., 1998—. Bd. dirs. Chinese Hist., Inc., 1997—98. Contbr. articles to journ., chapters to books. Bd. dirs. Pella Pub. Libr., 2002—03. Fellow For Adv. Study in China, Com. Scholarly Comm. with China, 1994—95. Mem.: Assn. Asian Studies, Am. Hist. Soc., Asianetwork (bd. dirs. 2003—06, Freeman Student-Faculty Fellowship Grant 2002). Avocations: fishing, photography, history book collecting, Chinese and Manchu calligraphy, classical music. Home: 209 Hemlock Dr Pella IA 50219 Office: Ctrl Coll 812 Univ St Pella IA 50219 Office Fax: 641-628-5316. Business E-Mail: chian@central.edu.

CHIA, PEI-YUAN, banking executive; b. Hong Kong, Jan. 27, 1939; came to U.S., 1962, naturalized, 1970; s. Dewey T.H. and Kitty C.; m. Frances T.C. Yen, Feb. 20, 1965; children: Katherine, Douglas, Candice. BA, Tunghai U., Taiwan, 1961; MBA, U. Pa., 1965. Products group mgr. Gen. Foods Corp., White Plains, N.Y., 1965-73; mktg. dir. Citibank (N.A.), N.Y.C., 1974-77; mng. dir. Famibank, Belgium, 1978-80; pres., chief exec. officer Diner Club/Carte Blanche Corp., L.A., 1980, divsn. exec., 1982-84, group exec., mem. policy com., 1985-90; sector exec. global consumer banking Citibank, N.Y.C., 1991-92; sr. exec. v.p., mem. mgmt. com. Citicorp, 1992, vice chmn., 1994-96. Bd. dirs. Am. Internat. Group, Inc., Baxter Internat., Bank of China, Hong Kong. Trustee Mt. Sinai-NYU Med. Ctr. Health Sys.; sr. fellow SEI Ctr. for Advanced Studies in Mgmt., U. Pa. Wharton Sch., adv. coun. Rockefeller U. Office: 298 Bedford-banksville Rd Bedford NY 10506-1925

CHIACCHIERINI, RICHARD PHILIP, healthcare consultant; b. Elmira, N.Y., Mar. 21, 1943; s. Frank Andrew and Grace Rose (Spallone) C.; m. Kathleen Doris O'Grady, Aug. 14, 1965; children: Paul Thomas, Lisa Marie. BS, St. Bonaventure U., 1965; MES, N.C. State U., 1967; PhD, Va. Tech. Inst., 1973. Ir statistician bioeffects divsn. Nat. Ctr. Radiol. Health, Rockville, Md., 1967-72; chief stats. sect. Office Radiation Programs EPA, Washington, 1972-73; sr. statistician epidemiol. studies br. Bur. Radiol. Health-FDA, Rockville, Md., 1973-79, chief stats. sect., 1979-83; chief ionizing rad. and statis. br. FDA, Rockville, Md., 1982-84, chief stats. br. Ctr. Devices and Radiol. Health, 1984-85, dir. biometric sci. divsn., 1985-94; v.p. for statis. svcs. C.L. McIntosh and Assocs., Inc., 1994—2002; pres. R.P. Chiacchierini & Assocs., Rockville, 2002—. Chief scientist USPHS Commd. Corps, Rockville, 1987-91; chair UPSHS Epidemiol. Tng. Commn., Bethesda, Md., 1989-92. Mem. editl. bd. Statistics in Medicine, 1991-96. Chmn., bd. dirs. Bennington, Gaithersburg, Md., 1978. Capt. USPHS, 1967-94 Recipient Exemplary Svc. medal Surgeon Gen. USPHS, 1990, Citation, 1985, 87. Mem. Am Statis. Assn., Biometrics Soc., Commd. Officer Assn. (bd. dirs., chmn. 1991—), Food and Drug Law Inst., Regulatory Affairs Profl. Soc., Phi Kappa Phi. Roman Catholic. Avocations: jogging, golf, computers. Office: R P Chiacchierini & Assocs 15825 Shady Grove Rd Ste 30 Rockville MD 20855

CHIANDUSSE, RICHARD STEPHEN, music educator; b. Englewood, NJ, Apr. 9, 1953; s. Enso V. Chiandusse; m. Karen L. Mossay, Feb. 15, 1951; 1 child, Christopher. MusB, Manhattan Sch. Music, MusM, 1977. Dir. of bands and honors humanities Dumont (NJ) H.S., 1977—. Clinictian/adjudicator Classic Festival And Tours, Medford, 1985—2002. Composer arrangements for marching band and ensembles. Mem.: BCMEA, NJ Music Educators Assn., NY State Horse Coun. (publicity com. 2001—02). Office: Dumont HS 101 New Milford Ave Dumont NJ 06728

CHIANG, ALBERT CHINFA, polymer chemist; b. Pai-ho, Tainan, Taiwan, Jan. 3, 1946; came to U.S., 1973; s. Long and Ping (Su) C.; m. Geraldine Chin, June 4, 1978; 1 child, Scott Jinlong. BS, Nat. Chung-Hsing U., Taichung, Taiwan, 1970; MS, Georgetown U., 1977; PhD, Am. U., 1980. Teaching asst. Georgetown U., Washington, 1974-77, Am. U., Washington, 1977-80; assoc. chemist Pitney Bowes, Stamford, Conn., 1980-81, chemist, 1982-83, staff chemist, 1984-86, sr. chemist, 1987-89, tech. advisor, 1989-92; v.p. R&D Mearthane Products, Cranston, RI, 1992—. Mem. Chinese Oversea Scholar, Taipei, Taiwan, 1980—. Mem. adv. bd. Am. Security Coun., Washington, 1984. Dissertation fellow Am. U., 1979. Mem. Am. Chem. Soc. (rubber div. 1987—), Soc. Plastics Engring. (sr. mem.), Photography of Sci. and Engring. Achievements include 21 patents; development of processes for preparation of polyphenylacetylene and desulfurization of coal; invention of materials for electrophotographic toners, high solid content emulsion formation, flourescent thermal transfer ribbon formation, new dual-step thermal transfer printing; research in rubber, photopolymers, thermal printing, silicone casting, polyurethane manufacturing; conducting polymers including conductive urethane, conductive silicone, acrylate, highly conjugated rubber and plastics, and high temperature superconducting material formation; non-impact printing technology and printing materials for postage meter and other mailing system machines; development and production of laser printer rollers including charge roller, developer roller, toner pick-up roller, paper transport roller; development of in-line skate and hockey wheel and live action skate wheel having a breaking mechanism, multiple-layer skate wheel and various track hockey wheel; toner for office machine application and medical grade urethane and silicone for medical applications; thermostat urethanes for pneumatic nail bumper application. Home: 10 Fox Hollow Ledyard CT 06339

CHIANG, CHIA-CHU, computer scientist, educator; b. Nan-Tou, Taiwan, Apr. 11, 1959; s. Yi-Ting Chiang and Chin Nun Liao; m. Jung-Yung Wang; children: Robert, Michael, Jennifer. BBA, Soochow U., Taipei, Taiwan, 1981; MS, Ea. Mich. U., 1988; PhD, Ariz. State U., 1995. Software engr. ASG Co. (formerly Viasoft), Phoenix, 1996—2001; asst. prof. U. Ark., Little Rock, 2001—. Spkr. in field. Contbr. articles to profl. jours. 2d lt. Taiwanese Army, 1981—83, Taiwan. Recipient Outrageous Contbr., Viasoft Co., 1998. Mem.: ACM, IEEE, Upsilon Pi Epsilon, Tau Beta Pi, Phi Kappa Phi. Avocations: jogging, swimming, reading, travel. Office: University of Arkansas at Little Rock 2801 South University Ave Little Rock AR 72204-1099 Office Fax: 501-569-8144. E-mail: cxchiang@ualr.edu.

CHIANG, GEORGE DJIA-CHEE, retired engineer, educator; b. Shanghai, Sept. 29, 1938; came to U.S., 1963; s. Tai Yei and Wai Yui (Lai) C.; m. Betty Theresa Doue, June 11, 1965; children: Andrew H., Audrey H. BS, Harbin (China) Inst. Tech., 1961; MS, U. Calif., Berkeley, 1965; PhD, Ariz. State U., 1971. Registered profl. engr., Tex. Asst. engr. Harbin Steel Co., 1961-62; rsch. asst. U. Calif., 1964-66; sr. project engr. Sperry Rand Corp., Phoenix, 1966-70; faculty assoc. Ariz. State U., Tempe, 1970-71; head, prof. engring dept. U.S. Army Intern Tng. Ctr., Texarkana, Tex., 1971-77; litigation, tech. cons. Nat. Hwy. Traffic Safety Adminstn., Washington, 1977-94; chief trend and analysis divsn. Nat. Hwy. Traffic Safety Adminstrn., 1994-2001; ret., 2001. Adj. prof. engring. U. So. Calif., Washington, 1977-89; cons. Sperry Rand Corp., Phoenix, 1970-71, Edgewood (Md.) Arsenal, 1972-77. Contbr. articles to tech. jours. Active local PTA; bd. dirs. Potomac Chinese Sch., 1978-81, Chinese Culture and Cmty. Svc. Ctr., 1989-91, pres., 1991-92. Active local PTA; bd. dirs. Potomac Chinese Sch., 1978-81; bd. dirs. Chinese Culture and Community Svc. Ctr., 1989-91, pres., 1991-92. Mem. ASME (tech. adv. com. 1980—), Profl. Engring. Soc., Tau Beta Pi. Democrat. Avocations: reading, tennis, travel. Home: 113 Ivy Arbor Ct Lincoln CA 95648-8631 E-mail: gdchiang@hotmail.com.

CHIANG, HUAI CHANG, entomologist, educator; b. Sunkiang, China, Feb. 15, 1915; came to U.S., 1945, naturalized, 1953; s. Wentse Chiang and Hsiu Hsiu C.; m. Zoh Ing Shen, Sept. 8, 1946; children: Jeanne, Katherine, Robert. BS, Tsing Hua U., Peking, China, 1938; MS, U. Minn., 1946, PhD, 1948; D.Sc. (hon.), Bowling Green State U., 1979. Asst. instr. entomology Tsing Hua U., Peking, 1938-40, instr., 1940-44; asst. prof. U. Minn., St. Paul and Duluth, 1954-57, assoc. prof. St. Paul, 1957-60, prof., 1960-83, prof. emeritus, 1984—. Cons. UNDP FAO, 1970, 72, 75, 76, 80, 82, 85-88, USDA, 1975-83; mem. sci. del. Am. Entomol. Soc., 1974, NAS, 1975, USDA/EPA, 1978, 81, USDA, 1979, 81, FAO, 1980, 82; sci. panel Coun. Environ. Quality, 1977, U.S. Internat. Comm. Agy., 1979, Internat. Centre Insect Physiology and Ecology, Nairobi, Kenya, 1980, Taiwan Coun. Agr., 1979, 84, Chinese Ministry Agr., 1982. Editor 3 publs.; contbr. over 230 rsch. papers to profl. jours. Recipient Cert. Appreciation USDA, 1975, Disting. Svc. award Am. Inst. Biol. Scis., 1979, Regents Cert. Merit U. Minn., 1984, Disting. Svc. award Ministry Agr. and Coops., Thailand, 1988; named Tchr. of yr. Student Assn., U. Minn-Duluth Campus, 1961; Guggenheim fellow, 1955; Phi Kappa Phi nat. scholar, 1983. Mem. Can. Royal London Entomol. Socs., Am. Entomol. Soc. (hon. mem., sect. chmn., chpt. pres., C.V. Riley award, Master Entomologist award), Hungarian Entomol. Soc. (hon. mem.), Japanese Soc. Population Rsch., Internat. Assn. Ecologists, Internat. Orgn. Biol. Control (pres. Western hemisphere, pres., hon. pres. working group), AAAS, Minn. Acad. Scis., Sigma Xi, Gamma Sigma Delta (Merit award 1983), Phi Kappa Phi (scholar of Yr. award 1982, Minn. chpt.). Home: Sterling House # 307 103 Bundy Rd Ithaca NY 14850-9291

CHIANG, TZE I. economist, researcher, economist, consultant; b. Fuzhou, Fujian, China, Feb. 4, 1922; arrived in U.S., 1953; s. Swe-hwa and Wan-lun Chiang; m. Wei-chih Chou Chiang, Feb. 4, 1952 (dec. 1999); children: Chi, Ling, Ding. BA in Agrl. Econs., Fujian Christin U., Fuzhou, 1946; MS in Agrl. Econs., Okla. State U., 1955; PhD in Agrl. Econs., U. Fla., 1958. Tchr. Sin-Ding H.S., Fuzhou, 1946—47; asst. to gen. mgr. China Textile Industries, Inc., Shanghai, 1947—53; grad. asst. Okla. State U., Stillwater, 1954—55; rsch. asst. U. Fla., Gainesville, 1955—58; prin. rsch. scientist Ga. Inst. Tech., Atlanta, 1958—86. Advisor Qingdao (China) Spl. Econ. Zone, China, 1986; vis. scholar to scholar Ga. Inst. Tech., Atlanta, 1986; cons. tech. transfer China Tech., Atlanta, 1986—87. Contbr. articles to profl. jours. Mem.: Gamma Sigma Delta. Achievements include research in economic feasibility; market analysis; economic and industrial development; international trade. Avocations: reading, music, gardening. Home: 3165 Frontenac Ct NE Atlanta GA 30319

CHIANG, WEN-LI, hydrodynamicist; b. Choulan, Republic of China, Apr. 14, 1946; came to U.S., 1972; naturalized, 1985; s. Pen-Hsiu and Yanagi (Shizuko) C.; m. Hsiu-lan Wang, Dec. 26, 1974; children: Dean Tsung, Charles. BS, Nat. Taiwan U., Taipei, Republic of China, 1969; MS, Nat. Cen. U., Chungli, Republic of China, 1972, U. Kans., Lawrence, 1977; PhD, U. So. Calif., 1980. Registered civil engr., Calif. Prin. engr. Tetra Tech Inc., Pasadena, Calif., 1979-87; prin. systems engr. undersea systems div. Honeywell Inc., Pasadena, 1987-88; prin. engr. Engring. Methods & Applications, Arcadia, Calif., 1988-90; sr. engr. Flow Sci., Inc., Pasadena, Calif., 1991—. Cons. Environment and Ocean Tech., Arcadia, Calif., 1990-91. Contbr. numerous articles to profl. jours. Recipient Sea grant NOAAt, 1976-79; NSF grantee, 1982-83. Mem. ASCE, Nat. Cen. Univ. Alumni Assn. So. Calif. (pres. 1986, chmn. bd. dirs. 1990), Sigma Xi, Tau Beta Pi. Avocations: reading, dancing. Home: 1139 Calle Malaga Duarte CA 91010-2250 Office: Flow Sci Inc 723 E Green St Pasadena CA 91101-2118 E-mail: wchiang@flowscience.com., chiangwenli@yahoo.com.

CHIANG, YUNG FRANK, law educator; b. Taichung, Taiwan, Jan. 2, 1936; came to U.S., 1961; s. Ruey-ting and Yueh-yin (Ho) C.; m. Quay-yin Lin, Nov. 1, 1969; children: Amy P., David H. LLB, Nat. Taiwan U., 1958; LLM, Northwestern U., 1962; JD, U. Chgo., 1965. Bar: Taiwan 1960, N.Y. 1974.

Assoc. Yen & Lai Law Office, Taipei, Taiwan, 1960-61; editor The Lawyers Co-op Pub. Co., Rochester, N.Y., 1965; rsch. assoc. Harvard Law Sch., Cambridge, Mass., 1965-67; asst. prof. U. Ga. Sch. Law, Athens, 1967-72; assoc. prof. Fordham U. Sch. Law, N.Y.C., 1972-76, prof., 1976—. Bd. dirs. Taiwan Ctr., N.Y.C.; legal cons., vice-chmn. Asia Bank, N.A., Flushing, N.Y., 1983-88, also bd. dirs.; leader N.Y. judge and lawyers del. to China and Hong Kong, People to People Internat., 1994; organizer, moderator 5 Russian delegations to U.S., People to People Amb. Program, 1994-95; pres. Fordham U. Law Faculty Union, 2000—. Contbr. articles to profl. jours. Organizer, bd. dirs. The Taiwan Mcht. Assn. N.Y., Flushing, 1976-96, pres., 1980-84; pres. N.Y. chpt. Formosan Assn. for Pub. Affairs, Washington, 1991-92. Mem. N.Y. State Bar Assn., N.Am. Taiwanese Profs. Assn. (bd. dirs. 1994-2000, v.p. 1997-98, pres. 1998-99), Nat. Assn. of Securities Dealers (arbitrator 1976-98), Order of Coif. Avocations: reading, skiing, archery, swimming. Office: Fordham U Sch Law 140 W 62nd St New York NY 10023-7407 E-mail: fchiang@mail.lawnet.fordham.edu.

CHIAO, PAUL J. molecular biologist, educator; b. Muscatine, Iowa, Nov. 20, 1954; s. J.S. Chiao and Jean Q. Gwan; m. Jane Q. Shao; children: Lucia J., Christa J. PhD, U. Tex., 1991. Asst. prof. U. Tex. M.D. Anderson Cancer Ctr., Houston, 1995—. Mem. Am. Assn. Cancer Rsch., Am. Soc. Microbiology. Office: U Tex MD Anderson Cancer Ctr 1515 Holcombe Blvd Houston TX 77030-4009

CHIAPELLA, ANNE PAGE, epidemiologist; b. Oakland, Calif., Oct. 12, 1942; d. Karl Josef and Anne Elizabeth (Gorrill) C. BA in Polit. Sci., Stanford U., 1964, PhD in Neurosci., 1982, MS in Stats., 1985; MPH in Epidemiology, Johns Hopkins U., 1986. Med. rschr. Stanford (Calif.) U., 1966-75, postdoctoral fellow, 1983-85, Johns Hopkins U., Balt., 1986-88; program officer Inst. Medicine NAS, Washington, 1989-91; sr. analyst Nat. Inst. on Alcohol and Alcohol Abuse, Rockville, Md., 1991—. Statis. and intellectual property cons. various orgns., Washington, 1983—; internat. rsch. on alcohol-related problems, 1993—. Writer humorous, tech. and travel speeches, 1985—; reviewer grants and sci. jours., 1992—; contbr. articles to sci. jours. Pres. Nebr. Ave. Neighborhood Assn., Washington, 1987-91, 2000—; assoc. Smithsonian Instn., Washington, 1987—; active in Friends of Kennedy Ctr., Washington, 1987—, Friends of Nat. Zoo, Washington, 1987—, Textile Mus., Washington, 1986—, WETA, Pub. Broadcasting Svc., 1997—. Grantee and fellow NIH, 1975, 77, 83, 86; grantee Environ. Health Sci. Ctr., 1986. Mem. AAAS, APHA, Soc. Epidemiologic Rsch., Toastmasters Internat. (officer 1987-89), Am. Statis. Assn. Avocations: travel, writing, photography. Home: 5126 Nebraska Ave NW Washington DC 20008-2047

CHIAPPETTA, EUGENE LOUIS, science educator; b. Jamestown, NY, Apr. 17, 1940; s. Joseph and Joan C Chiappetta; m. Barbara Morianz, May 21, 1969; 1 child, Robert. BS biology, Allegheny Coll., Meadville, Pa., 1962; MS gen., Syracuse U, Syracuse, NY, 1968, PhD, 1972. Cert. ed. NY state. Tchr. Southwestern Sch. Dist., Lakewood, NY, 1964—67; prof. sci. edn. U of Houston, Houston, 1972—. Mem.: Nat. Sci. Tchr. Assoc. (assoc.), Nat. Assoc. for Rsch. in Sci. tchg. (assoc.). Home: 10010 Moorberry Houston TX 77080 Office: Univ of Houston Dept Curriculum Instrn Dept Houston TX 77204-5027

CHIAPPINELLI, VINCENT ALEXANDER, pharmacology educator; b. Pawtucket, R.I., Mar. 16, 1951; m. Suzanne Bakshian, 1983; 2 children. AB, Boston U., 1973; PhD in Neuropharm., U. Conn., 1977. Postdoctoral fellow Harvard Med. Sch., Boston, 1977-80; asst. prof. St. Louis U. Sch. Medicine, 1980-85, assoc. prof., 1985-89, prof., 1989-96; prof., chair pharmacology Sch. Medicine and Health Scis. George Washington U., Washington, 1997—, dir. neurosci. program Sch. Medicine and Health Scis., 1997—2002. Mem. neurological scis. study sect. NIH, Bethesda, Md., 1991-95. Contbr. articles to profl. jours. Fogarty sr. internat. fellowship NIH, 1986-87, recipient Health Svc. Rsch. award, 1981—; internat. rsch. grant NSF, 1986-89. Mem. AAAS (scientific cons. for literacy for health project 1995-97), Soc. for Neurosci., Am. Soc. for Pharmacology and Exptl. Therapeutics, Am. Physiol. soc., Internat. Soc. on Toxinology, Assn. for Rsch. in Vision and Ophthalmology. Office: George Washington U Sch Med and Health Scis 2300 Eye St NW Washington DC 20037-2336 E-mail: phmvac@gwumc.edu.

CHIARAMIDA, SALVATORE, cardiologist, educator, health facility administrator; b. Manhattan, N.Y., Sept. 15, 1948; s. Joseph and Dina (DiBlasi) C.; m. Susan Postula, June 14, 1970; children: Todd, Tory. BS in Chemistry, Fordham Coll., 1970; MD, N.Y. Med. Coll., 1974. Diplomate Am. Bd. Internal Medicine, Am. Bd. Cardiovasc. Diseases. Intern North Shore U. Meml. Hosp., 1974-75, asst. resident in internal medicine, 1975-76, sr. resident in internal medicine, 1976-77, fellow in cardiology, 1977-79; fellow in medicine Cornell U. Med. Coll., 1975-77; chief cardiology Raritan Bay Med. Ctr., 1979-89, Our Lady of Mercy Med. Ctr., Bronx, NY, 1989—2000, assoc. dir. medicine, 1992—2000; dir. coronary care unit Med. Univ. S.C., Charleston, 2000—, prof. medicine, 2000—. Instr. cardiology North Shore U. Hosp., 1977-79; clin. instr. medicine U. Medicine and Dentistry N.J., 1981-83, clin. asst. prof., 1983; clin. assoc. prof. N.Y. Med. Coll., 1990—, prof. clin. medicine, 1999-2002; cons. Woodbridge (N.J.) Devel. Ctr., 1989; v.p., trustee Mercy Care PHO, 1994-2000; bd. dirs. Cath. Health Care Network, Cath. Health Care Network Physicians Orgn., Servitas IPA, Cath. Healthcare Resources LLC, Benefice Health LLC, Cath. Health Care Sys. Contbr. articles to profl. jours. Fellow ACP, Am. Coll. Cardiology. Office: Med Univ SC Heart Ctr Divsn Cardiology 135 Rutledge Ave Ste 1201 PO Box 250592 Charleston SC 29464 E-mail: chiara@musc.edu.

CHIARAVALLOTI, NANCY DONOFRIO, neuropsychologist; b. Jersey City, Feb. 22, 1972; d. Victor A. and Micki Donofrio; m. Nicholas A. Chiaravalloti, Nov. 11, 2000. AB, Muhlenberg Coll., 1994; MA, Hahnemann U., 1996, PhD, 1999. Intern in neuropsychology Brown U., Providence, 1998—2001; rsch. fellow Kessler Med. Rehab. Rsch. and Edn. Corp./U. Medicine and Dentistry N.J./N.J. Med. Sch., West Orange, 1999—2002; instr. dept. phys. medicine and rehab. U. Medicine and Dentistry of NJ/NJ Med. Sch., Newark, 1999—2002, asst. prof., 2002—; clin. rsch. assoc. Kessler Med. Rehab. Rsch. and Edn. Corp., West Orange, 2001—02, clin. rsch. scientist, 2002—03; adj. faculty Fairleigh Dickinson U., Teaneck, NJ, 2002—; assoc. dir. Neuropsychology and Neuroscience, 2003—. Contbr. articles to profl. jours., chpts. to books; consulting reviewer: Scandinavian Jour. Rehab. Medicine, 2000—, Rehab. Psychology, 2000—. Trustee Bayonne Cmty. Mental Health Ctr., 2000—, Bayonne Econ. Opportunity Found., 2001—; mem. adult bd. Bayonne Search Simpson-Baber Found., 1999—; mem. Ireland's 32, Bayonne, 2001—. Fellow, Nat. Stroke Assn., 2000—02; grantee pilot rsch., Nat. Multiple Sclerosis Soc., 2000—01, 2003—04. Mem.: APA (divsn. 40 asst. editor newsletter 2001—), Internat. Neuropsychol. Soc. (consulting reviewer jour. 2000—), Nat. Acad. Neuropsychology (conf. com. 1997—99), Psi Chi. Home: 65 W 34th St Bayonne NJ 07002 Office: Kessler Med Rehab Rsch & Edn Corp 1199 Pleasant Valley Way West Orange NJ 07052 E-mail: n.chiaravalloti2@verizon.net.

CHIARCHIARO, FRANK JOHN, lawyer; b. Sept. 11, 1945; s. Joseph Russell and Mary Catherine (Salmieri) C.; m. Judith Ann Penna, July 5, 1970; 1 child, Peter. BEE, Manhattan Coll., 1967; MSEE, NYU, 1970; JD, Bklyn. Law Sch., 1976. Bar: N.Y. 1977, U.S. Dist. Ct. (ea. and so. dists.) N.Y. 1977, U.S. Ct. Appeals (11th cir.) 1985, U.S. Ct. Appeals (4th cir.) 1989, U.S. Ct. Appeals (5th cir.) 1991, U.S. Supreme Ct. 1987. Engr. USN, Bklyn., 1968-72, USCG, N.Y.C., 1972-77; ptnr. Mendes & Mount, LLP., N.Y.C., 1977—. Contbr. articles to profl. jours. Decorated knight commdr. of Holy Sepulchre. Mem. ATLA, N.Y. State Bar Assn., Def. Rsch. Inst. Roman Catholic. Office: Mendes & Mount 750 7th Ave New York NY 10019-6834 E-mail: frank.chiarchiaro@mendes.com .

CHIARELLA, DONALD JOSEPH GRAY, information systems specialist, educator; b. Kilmarnock, Scotland, June 21, 1956; came to the U.S., 1958; s. Donald Joseph and Margaret Gray Chiarella; m. Misae Fox, Dec. 24, 1979; children: Donald H., Mia M., David A., Michaela F. BA in Urban Planning/Info. Sys. Mgmt., U. Md., 1979; MS in Tech. Mgmt., Am. U., 1988; PhD in MIS, Kennedy-Western, 2001. Cert. pub. adminstr. Computer specialist Navy Med., Bethesda, Md., 1977-86; prof. in computer mgmt. info. sys. U. Md. U. Coll., College Park, 1986—99; project leader Orkand Corp., Silver Spring, Md., 1988-89, R.S. Carsons, Bethesda, Md., 1989-90; govt. wide computer regulations analyst Gen. Svcs. Adminstrn., Washington, 1990-97; supervisory database adminstr. Md. State Govt., Hanover, 1997—. V.p. Data Processing Mgmt. Assn., Am. U., Washington, 1987-88. Author: Programming is Natural, 1991, Life in God's Management Corps, 2002, One Plus One Equals Three: The Virtues and Value of Teamwork and Leadership, 2003, others; author of 20 software applications. Pres. United Meth. Men, Cheltenham, 1987-88, Savage, Md., 1990-91; arch. bd. Spring Breeze Assn., Columbia, Md., 1994; vol. McCain 2000, Alexandria, Va., 1999. With USAF, 1974-75. Mem. IEEE Computer Soc., Inst. Transp. Engrs. (assoc.), Assn. Computing Machinery, Profl. Mgrs. (treas. 1992-93), Naval Inst. (life), Scottish Am. Found., Am. U. Alumni (life). Republican. Avocations: finances, sports, home projects, writing, art. Home: 6335 Hanover Crossing Way Hanover MD 21076 Office: Md DOT 7491 Connelley Dr Hanover MD 21076 E-mail: dchiarella@sha.state.md.us.

CHIARELLA, PETER RALPH, vintner; b. Bklyn., Dec. 6, 1932; s. C. Ralph and Catherine (Zinzi) C.; m. Frances M. Crane, Oct. 10, 1953; children: Ralph, Thomas, John, Karen. BBA, St. John's U., 1957. C.P.A., N.Y. Sr. accountant Peat, Marwick, Mitchell & Co., N.Y.C., 1957—61; asst. controller Bonwit Teller, N.Y.C., 1961—62; accounting mgr. plastics div. Celanese Corp., Newark, 1963—67; v.p., controller Clairol, Inc., N.Y.C., 1967—72; pres., dir. Kleinert's, Inc., Kutztown, Pa., 1972—77; v.p., corp. controller United Brands Co., N.Y.C., 1977—79; sr. v.p., chief fin. officer Max Factor & Co., Hollywood, Calif., 1979—83; sr. v.p. fin. and adminstrn. Syncor Internat., Sylmar, Calif., 1983—85; exec. v.p. Doctors' Co., Napa, Calif., 1985—92; pres. Cakebread Cellars, Inc., Rutherford, Calif., 1992—97; pres., CEO Crane Family Vineyards, Napa, 1999—. Bd. dirs. Cakebread Cellars, Inc., Rutherford. Mem. budget com. United Fund, Stamford, Conn., 1970; bd. dirs. Vis. Nurse Assn., L.A., 1983-90, Napa Valley Opera House, 1991-96, Napa Valley Coll. Found., 1991-99, Napa Valley Fair Bd., 1994-2000, Napa Physicians IPA Bd., 1999-2001, Pacific Vision Found., 2001—. With USN, 1952-54. Mem. AICPA, Fin. Execs. Inst., Delta Mu Delta. Home: 1051 Borrette Ln Napa CA 94558-9702 E-mail: peter@cranefamilyvineyards.com.

CHIARELLI, ROBERT CHARLES, audio engineer; b. Mass., Jan. 13, 1963; s. Carmello Charles C.; m. Theresa Pauline; children: Robert Michael, Angela Maria. Student, U. Miami. CEO 3.6 Music, L.A. Mixer albums for Will Smith, Christina Aguilera, Madonna, Ricky Martin, Temptations, Michael Bolton, Janet Jackson. Bd. dirs. Great Leap, Santa Monica, Calif. Mem. Am. Fedn. Musicians, Nat. Acad. Arts & Scis. Office: Final Mix Inc 2219 W Olive Ave Ste 102 Burbank CA 91506-2625

CHIARENZA, CARL, art historian, critic, artist, educator; b. Rochester, NY, Sept. 5, 1935; s. Charles and Mary Rose (Russo) C.; m. Heidi Faith Katz, Aug. 13, 1978; children: Suzanne Mari, Jonah Katz, Gabriella Christine. B.F.A., Rochester Inst. Tech., 1957; MS, Boston U., 1959; MA, 1964; PhD, Harvard U., 1972. Lectr. Boston U., 1963-64, instr. dept. fine arts, 1964-68, asst. prof., 1968-72, univ. prof., 1972-73, assoc. prof., 1973-80, prof. dept. art history, 1980-86, acting chmn. dept. art history, 1973-74, chmn. dept. art history, 1976-81; Fanny Knapp Allen prof. U. Rochester, N.Y., 1986-98, acting chmn. dept. art history, 1986-87, prof. emeritus, artist-in-residence, 1998—. Adj. vis. prof. Visual Studies Workshop, SUNY, 1972-73; vis. prof. Cornell U., 1991; Harnish vis. artist Smith Coll., 1983-84; vis. artist/scholar, U. Ga., Athens, 2002; artists adv. panel Artists Found., Boston, 1977-81; guest curator Inst. Contemporary Art, Boston, 1980-81; cons. Nat. Endowment for Arts, 1978-80, mem. Artists' Fellowships panel, 1982; bd. dirs. Photographic Resource Ctr.; trustee Visual Studies Workshop; lectr. in field. One-man shows include George Eastman House, 1995, Southeast Mus. of Photography, 1995, Rochester (NY) Inst. Tech., 1996, The Witkin Gallery, NYC, 1996, Kennedy Ctr. Gallery, Hiram Coll., 1997, High Mus. Art, Atlanta, 1997, U. Iowa Mus. Art, 1997, Stephen Cohen Gallery, LA, 1999, Robert Klein Gallery, Boston, 1999, Spectrum Gallery, Rochester, 1999, 2002, Troyer Gallery, Washington, 1999, Alan Klotz/Photocollect, NYC, 2000, U. RI, 2003, U. Rochester, 2003, others, exhibited in group shows at Ansel Adams Gallery, 1996, Bibliotecheque Nat., Paris, 1997, Fitchburg Art Mus., 1998, 2001, Hugo de Pagano Gallery, NYC, 1998, The Hotchkiss Sch., Lakeville, Conn., 1998, Robert Klein Gallery, Boston, 1998, Mt. Holyoke Coll. Art Mus., 1998, Sun Valley Ctr. for the Arts., 1998, Princeton (NJ) Art Mus., 1999, Ctr. for Creative Photography, Tucson, 1999, 2001, Yale U. Art Gallery, 1999, The Fitchburg Art Mus., 2000, Harvard U. Art Mus., 2000, Mill Art Ctr. and Gallery, Honeoye Falls, NY, 2000, DeCordova Mus. and Sculpture Pk., Lincoln, Mass., 2001, Boise (Idaho) Art Mus., 2001, Kiyosato (Japan) Mus. Photographic Arts, 2001, Adirondack C.C., 2001, Amon Carter Mus., Ft. Worth, Tex., 2002, Visual Studies Workshop Gallery, 2002, others, Represented in permanent collections LA County Mus. Art, Nat. Mus. Am. Art, Washington, Phila. Mus. Art, Mus. Modern Art, NYC, J. Paul Getty Mus., LA, Art Inst. Chgo., Cleve. Mus. Art, Mpls. Inst. Arts, Mus. Fine Arts, Boston, Houston, San Francisco Mus. Modern Art, Amon Carter Mus., Ft. Worth, others; author: Aaron Siskind: Pleasures and Terrors, 1982, Landscapes of the Mind, 1988, Evocations, 2002; contbr. articles to over 180 profl. jours.. Served with U.S. Army, 1960-62. Mass. Art and Humanities Found. fellow, 1975-76; Nat. Endowment for Arts fellow, 1977-78, 90-91; recipient Artist award Arts and Cultural Coun. for Greater Rochester, 1996, Artist-in-Residence award Hiram Coll., 1997, Spl. Opportunity Stipend award N.Y. Found. for the Arts, 1997, Disting. Alumnus of Yr., Rochester Inst. Tech., 1997, Honored Educator award Soc. for Photographic Edn., 1999, Lillian Fairchild Artist award, 1999, Best of Show award Nazareth Coll., 2000, 02. Mem. Soc. Photographic Edn., Assn. Historians Am. Art. Office: U Rochester Morey # 424 Rochester NY 14627 E-mail: ccrz@mail.rochester.edu. *I am a switch-hitter. I have always made, written about, or lectured about pictures. Because I seem to do each best when working in a concentrated spurt, I am often torn between these modes of communication. I work intuitively and in a state of agitation until things find their rightful place on a page or in a picture. It is as if I am reaching for a place of equilibrium or understanding as I move through the world from a position of essential ignorance about the meaning of life.*

CHIARENZA, FRANK JOHN, English language educator; b. New Britain, Conn., Dec. 10, 1926; s. Sebastian X. and Josephine (Spoto) C. AB, Yale, 1949, PhD in Medieval Lit, 1956; MA in English, Rutgers U., 1950; certificate, Inst. for Ednl. Mgmt.; Sloan Found. grantee, Harvard, 1970. Lectr. English U. Conn., 1954-55; instr. English Hillyer Coll., Hartford, Conn., 1955-57; from asst. prof. to prof. Coll. Arts and Scis., U. Hartford, 1958-67, prof. English, 1978-89, emeritus, 1989, chmn. dept., 1958-67, acad. dean Coll. Arts and Scis., 1967-78. Cons., reader English Coll. Entrance Exam. Bd., 1959— ; reader advanced placement tests Ednl. Testing Service, Princeton, N.J., 1961— ; chmn. for Conn., Nat. Council Coll. Publs. Advisers, 1966-67; adv. council Career Opportunity Program, 1970— ; resource cons. Conn. Commn. for Higher Edn., 1972-73; chief reader Coll. Level Exam. Program, Ednl. Testing Service, N.J., 1978— Author: The Milk Glass Book, 1998; contbr. articles to profl. jours. Corporator Watkinson Sch., West Hartford, Conn.; bd. dirs. Nat. Milk Glass Collectors Soc., 1991—, pres., 1997-99; founder Frank Chiarenza Mus. of Glass, Meriden, Conn., Bd. Dirs., Rosa Pnselle Mus., Conn, Served with USNR, 1944-46. Fulbright grantee U. Rome, 1953-54. AAUP (pres. Hartford 1962-64), NEA, Am. Assn. Higher Edn., Am. Conf. Acad. Deans, Am. Coun. Edn., Conn. Acad. Arts and Scis., Nat. Milk Glass Collectors Soc. (bd. dirs. 1991—, v.p. 1994—, v.p., chmn. publs. com. 1994—, pres. 1997—), Yale Club. Home: 80 Crestview Dr Newington CT 06111-2405 Office: Dequaine Found 39 W Main Meriden CT 06451 E-mail: chiarenzaglassmuseum@snet.net., mgmfrank@aol.com.

CHIARIELLO, MARIO, surgeon; b. Salerno, Italy, May 3, 1951; came to U.S., 1978; MD, U. Bologna, Italy, 1978. Diplomate Am. Bd. Surgery. Intern, then resident in surgery Bklyn. Cumberland Hosp., 1979-84; pvt. practice Bklyn., 1984—; mem. staff Meth. Hosp., Bklyn.

CHIATE, KENNETH REED, lawyer; b. Phoenix, June 24, 1941; s. Mac Arthur and Lillian (Lavin) C.; m. Jeannette Jensen, Aug. 21, 1965; children: Gregory Jensen, Carley MkKay. BA with honors, Claremont Men's Coll., 1963; JD, Columbia U., 1966; postgrad., U. So. Calif. Law Sch., 1967. Bar: Calif. 1967, U.S. Dist. Ct. (cen. dist.) Calif. 1967, Ariz. 1971, U.S. Dist. Ct. Ariz. 1971, U.S. Dist. Ct. (no. Dist.) Calif. 1982. Law clk. presiding justice U.S. Dist. Ariz., 1971; ptnr. Lillick McHose & Charles, L.A., 1971-91, Pillsbury Winthrop, LLP (formerly Pillsbury Madison), L.A., 1991—. Arbitrator Los Angeles Superior Ct. Arbitration Panel, 1979-82; mcpl. ct. judge protem Los Angeles, 1979-81; vice chmn. Los Angeles Open Com., 1969-71. Named among Calif. Lawyers of Yr. 2000, Calif. Mag. Mem. ABA, L.A. County Bar Assn., Calif. State Bar Assn., Ariz. State Bar Assn., Maricopa County Bar Assn., Am. Trial Lawyers Assn., L.A. Bus. Trial Lawyers Assn. Office: Quinn Emanuel Urquhart Oliver & Hedges LLP 865 Figueroa St 10th Fl Los Angeles CA 90017 E-mail: kenchiate@quinnemanuel.com.

CHIAVERINI, JOHN EDWARD, construction company executive; b. Providence, Feb. 6, 1924; s. John and Sadie (Ginsberg) C.; m. Cecile Corey, Mar. 31, 1951; children: Caryl Marie, John Michael. Cert. advanced san. engring., U. Ill., 1945; BS in Civil Engring., U. R.I., 1947. Registered profl. engr., Mass., R.I. Project engr. Perini Corp., Hartford, Conn., 1950-51, project mgr., 1951-55, asst. project mgr. Pitts. and Que., 1955-61, v.p. Framingham, Mass., 1965-84, sr. v.p. San Francisco, 1984—; pres., dir. Compania Perini S.A., Colombia, 1961—; v.p., exec. mgr. Perini Yuba Assocs., Marysville, Calif., 1966-70, v.p. Western ops., 1970-78, 79-84, group v.p., 1978-79; sr. v.p. spl. projects Perini Corp., 1984-90, dir., asst. to chmn., 1991—. Mem. U.S. com. Internat. Commn. on Large Dams; bd.dirs. Building Futures Coun., 1990—, vice chmn., 1993, chmn., 1994—; active Civil Engring. Rsch. Found., 1990—, mem. corp. adv. bd., 1992—. Served to 2d lt. USAAF, 1944-46. Recipient Golden Beaver award Supervision, San Francisco Bay Area Coun. Boy Scouts Am., 1989, Good Scout award, 1989; named to R.I. Engring. Hall of Fame, 1997. Fellow ASCE (mem. exec. com. constrn. divsn., vice chmn. 1994-95, chmn. 1995—), Soc. Am. Mil. Engrs. (Acad. of Fellows 1997, pres. San Francisco post 1991-92, bd. dirs.); mem. NSPE (life), Am. Arbitration Assn., Calif. Soc. Profl. Engrs., Dispute Resolution Bd. Found., Beavers (bd. dirs.), Moles, Commonwealth Club of Calif., KC, Rotary (mem. dispute resolution bd. found.). Republican. Roman Catholic. Home: 37 Dutch Valley Ln San Anselmo CA 94960-1045 Office: Perini Corp 37 Dutch Valley Ln San Anselmo CA 94960 E-mail: CEEJAYIII3@comcast.net., ceejayIII@aol.com.

CHIAZZE, LEONARD, JR., biostatistician, epidemiologist, educator; b. Falconer, N.Y., June 19, 1934; s. Leonard and Jennie (Bondi) C.; m. Ellen Anne Bergman, June 12, 1954; children: Kathleen, Caroline, Michael, Ellen. AA, SUNY, Jamestown, 1953; BS, U. Buffalo, 1955, MBA, 1957; ScD, U. Pitts., 1964. Instr. stats. U. Buffalo, 1955-57; biostatistician Nat. Cancer Inst., Bethesda, Md., 1957-66, acting chief biometry br., 1975-76, dir. divsn. occupl. health studies, 1994—; dir. divsn. biostats. and epidemiology Georgetown U. Sch. Medicine, Washington, 1960-94, asst. prof., 1966-69, assoc. prof., 1969-77, prof., 1977—, founder, dir. grad. program in biostats., 1970-94, dir. divsn. occupational health studies, 1994—. Mem. com. on toxicology NAS/NRC; vice chair Georgetown U. Instl. Rev. Bd., Washington; mem. data and safety monitoring bd. Nat. Inst. on Drug Abuse. Contbr. articles to profl. jours. Served with USPHS, 1957-66. Fellow: APHA, Am. Coll. Epidemiology; mem.: Soc. Occupl. and Environ. Health (past pres. governing coun.), Internat. Epidemiol. Assn., Soc. Epidemiologic Rsch., Am. Statis. Assn., Sigma Xi, Beta Gamma Sigma. Home: 11237 Waycross Way Kensington MD 20895-1034 Office: Georgetown U 3750 Reservoir Rd NW Washington DC 20007-2111 E-mail: chiazzel@georgetown.edu.

CHICAGO, JUDY, artist; b. Chgo., July 20, 1939; d. Arthur M. and May (Levenson) Cohen. BA, UCLA, 1962, MA, 1964; doctorate (hon.), Russell Sage Coll., 1992, Lehigh U., 2000, Smith Coll., 2000, Duke U., 2003. Co-founder Feminist Studio Workshop, L.A., 1973, Through the Flower Corp., 1977; vis. artist Ind. U., fall 1999, Duke U. fall 2000, U. N.C., fall 2000, Cal Poly Pomona, fall 2003. Author: Through the Flower: My Struggle as a Woman Artist, 1975, The Dinner Party: A Symbol of Our Heritage, 1979, Embroidering Our Heritage: The Dinner Party Needlework, 1980, The Birth Project, 1985, Holocaust Project: From Darkness Into Light, 1993, Beyond the Flower: The Autobiography of a Feminist Artist, 1996, The Dinner Party, 1996, Women and Art: Contested Territory, 1999; one-woman shows include, Pasadena (Calif.) Mus. Art, 1969, Jack Glenn Gallery, Corona del Mar, Calif., 1972, JPL Fine Arts, London, 1975, Quay Ceramics, San Francisco, 1976, San Francisco Mus. Modern Art, 1979, Bklyn. Mus., 1980, 2002, Parco Galleries, Japan, 1980, Fine Arts Gallery, Irvine, Calif., 1981, Musee d'Art Contemporain, Montreal, 1982, ACA Galleries, N.Y.C., 1984, 85, 86, Nat. Mus. of Women in the Arts, 2002; group exhbns. include Jewish Mus., N.Y.C., 1966, 67, Whitney Mus., 1972, Winnipeg Art Gallery, 1975; represented in permanent collections Bklyn. Mus., San Francisco Mus. Modern Art, Oakland Mus. Art, Pa. Acad. Fine Arts, L.A. County Mus. Art, also numerous pvt. collections. Office: 101 N 2nd St Belen NM 87002 E-mail: throughtheflower@compuserve.com. *I am an artist, writer and committed to an enlarged role for art and a more humanized world.*

CHICHESTER, JOHN H. state senator; b. Fredericksburg, Va., Aug. 26, 1937; m. Sydney Collson. Grad. Va. Poly. Inst. Mem. Va. Senate, 1978—, pres. pro tempore, 2000- . Mem. Big Bros. Served with USAR, 1956-62. Mem. Fredericksburg Jaycees. Republican. Presbyterian. Lodges: Masons, Shriners, Rotary (past pres.). Office: Va Senate Gen Assembly Bldg 910 Capitol St, Rm 626 Richmond VA 23219*

CHICHETTO, JAMES WILLIAM, editor, educator; b. Boston, June 5, 1941; s. Francis Anthony and Christina McInnis C. B of Philosophy, Stonehill Coll., 1964; M of Theology, Holy Cross Coll., 1968; MA, Wesleyan U., 1978. Ordained to ministry, Cath. Ch. the Congregation of Holy Cross, 1968. Assoc. editor Gargoyle Mag., Cambridge, Mass., 1975-81, Conn. Poetry Rev., Stonington, 1981-84, 1984-88, asoc. editor, art editor, 1988-89, editor, 1989-91; prof. writing Stonehill Coll., North Easton, Mass., 1991—; art editor East & West Lit. Quar., San Francisco, 1995—. Author of poems, essays, revs. and plays. Mem. Easton Arts Coun., 1994-98. Recipient Sri Chinmoy award, 1986; NEA grantee, 1980, 83; NEH grantee, 1992. Fellow World Lit. Assn.; mem. Assn. Lit. Scholars. Democrat. Avocations: painting, sketching. Home: 474 Washington St North Easton MA 02357-0001 Office: Stonehill Coll 430 Washington St Easton MA 02357

CHICHILNISKY, GRACIELA, mathematician, economist, writer, educator, writer; b. Buenos Aires, Mar. 27, 1946; came to U.S., 1968, naturalized citizen, 1992; d. Salomon Chichilnisky and Raquel Gavensky; children: Eduardo Jose, Natasha Sable. Student, MIT, 1967-68; MA, U. Calif., Berkeley, 1970, PhD in Math., 1971, PhD in Econs., 1976. Postdoctoral fellow Harvard U., 1974, lectr. dept. econs., 1975-77, fellow Harvard inst. internat. devel., 1978; assoc. prof. Columbia U., N.Y.C., 1977-80, prof., 1981—, dir. Program on Info. and Resources, 1994—, prof. stats, 1996—, dir. Columbia Ctr. for Risk Mgmt., 1998—, UNESCO prof. math. and econs., 1995—99. CEO Cross Border Exch. Corp., 1999-2003, chmn. 2003-; mem. presdl. cabinet Banco Ctrl. Republica Argentina, 1971-74; co-prin. investigator Urban Inst., Washington, 1975-77; vis. scholar Internat. Inst. Applied Sys, Analysis Laxenburg, Austria, 1975-77; prin. investigator U.S. Dept. Labor, 1977-78, Rockefeller Found. Project Internat. Rels., 1981-83; project dir. UN Inst. Tng. and Rsch., N.Y., 1979-83; chaired prof. econs. U. Essex, 1980-81; vis. prof. inst. math and its applications U. Minn., 1983-84, U. Siena, Italy, summers, 1991-93, 2002; vis. prof. Stanford Inst. Theoretical Econs., Stanford U., summers, 1991-93, dept. econs., Inst. Internat. Studies, 1993—, vis. prof. depts. econ. and ops. rsch. Stanford U., 1993-94; prof. missionaire U. des Antilles et de la Guyane, spring 1984-85; NSF prof. dept. math. U. Calif., Berkeley, 1985-86; CEO, chmn. FITEL Ltd., 1985-89; exec. dir. Sci. Internat. Ltd., 1989-90; vis. prof. U. Cath. Buenos Aires, Aug. 1993; cons. in field; UNESCO chair in math. and econs., Columbia U., 1995—; Salinbemi chair U. Siena, Italy, 1994-95; CEO Cross Border Exchange, NY, 1999-, chmn. 2003-. Co-author: Catastrophe or New Society? A Latin American World Model, 1976; author: (with G. Heal) The Evolving International Economy, 1986, Oil in the International Economy, 1991, Sustainability: Dynamics and Uncertainty, 1998, Mathematical Economics, 1998, Topology and Markets, 1998, Markets, Information and Uncertainty, 1998, Environmental Markets: Equity and Efficiency, 1999; assoc. editor Jour. Devel. Econs., 1976-86, Advances in Mathematics, 1985, Risk Decision and Policy; mem. various editorial bds.; contbr. articles to profl. jours. Bd. trustees Nat. Resources Def. Coun., N.Y., 1994—. Recipient Internat. Rels. award Rockefeller Found., 1983-84; named Most Disting. Woman Economist, Newcombe Found. and Omega Delta Epsilon, 1991, Leif Johansen award U. Oslo, Norway, 1995; grantee NSF, 1974—; fellow Ford Found., 1967-69, Banco Ctrl. Republica Argentina, 1972-74, spl. fellow UN Inst. Tng. and Rsch., 1977-76. Mem. Coun. Social Choice and Welfare Soc. Office: Columbia U 629 Mathematics New York NY 10027 Mailing: 335 Riverside Dr New York NY 10025

CHICKERING, HOWARD ALLEN, insurance company executive, lawyer; b. San Francisco, Mar. 21, 1942; s. Allen Lawrence and Caroline Cranford (Rogers) C.; m. Elizabeth Douglas Dalton, June 29, 1968; children: Philip Dalton, Caroline Howe. BS in Econs., U. Pa., 1966; JD, Stanford U., 1971. Bar: Calif. 1972. Assoc. Chickering & Gregory, San Francisco, 1971-76; sr. counsel Itel Corp., San Francisco, 1976-79; v.p., gen. counsel, bd. dirs. Clarendon Ins. Co. (Bermuda) Ltd., N.Y.C., 1979-81; pres. Clarendon Group Svcs. Inc., N.Y.C., 1981-85; exec. v.p., bd. dirs. Clarendon Ins. Group, N.Y.C., 1985-88; founder, pres., chief underwriting officer R.V.I. Guaranty Co., Ltd., Hamilton, Bermuda, 1989—; founder, pres. R.V.I. Am. Ins. Co., Stamford, Conn., 1994—. Spkr. in field. Contbr. articles to profl. publs. Co-author, acting campaign chmn. San Francisco Proposition C (Open Space), 1974; campaign sec. Proposition J (Open Space and Park Renovation), 1974; mem. San Francisco Open Space Citizens Adv. Commn., 1976-78; deacon Stanwich Congregational Ch.; leader, adminstr. Alpha Course on Basic Christianity. Lt. (j.g.) USNR, 1966-68, Vietnam. Mem. State Bar Calif., Soc. Colonial Wars, Soc. Mayflower Descendents, Racquet and Tennis Club, N.Y. Yacht Club, Belle Haven Club (commodore 1996). Republican. Home: 80 Otter Rock Dr Greenwich CT 06830-7029 Office: RVI Am Ins Co 177 Broad St Ste 9 Stamford CT 06901-5003

CHICKY, JON EDWARD, JR., military officer; b. Lincoln, Nebr., Feb. 13, 1961; s. Jon Edward and Sharon Diane Chicky; m. Angela Marie LaRocco, Dec. 12, 1993; children: Michael, Edward, Rose. AA, Indian River C.C., La Placa, Fla., 1991; BA, Fla. State U., 1993; MA, U. Kans., Lawrence, 1993, U.S. Naval War Coll., Newport, R.I., 1998. Commd. U.S. Army, 1983; advanced through ranks to lt. col.; South Am. analyst U.S. Army South, Ft. Clayton, Panama, 1987—88; battalion intelligence officer 193d Inf. Brigade, Ft. Clayton, Panama, 1988—89; co. comdr. U.S. Army South, Ft. Davis, Panama, 1989—90; sr. fellow George C. Marshall Ctr., Garnisch, Germany, 1993—94; battalion ops. officer 1st Infantry Divsn., Tuzla, Bosnia and Wuerchung, Germany, 1995—97; chief, arms control inspection team European Divsn., Def. Threat Reduction Agy., Frankfurt, Germany, 1998—2001; ctrl. Asian polit.-mil. officer U.S. Ctrl. Command, Tampa, Fla., 2001—. Recipient Knowlton award, Mil. Intelligence Corps Assn., 1995. Mem.: Am. Hist. Soc. Germans from Russia (life), VFW, Am. Legion. Lutheran. E-mail: jon_chicky@hotmail.com.

CHICOINE, ROLAND ALVIN, farmer, former state legislator; b. Rural Elk Point, S.D., Dec. 10, 1922; s. Elmire Joseph and Louise Marie (Ryan) C.; m. Evelyn Marie Lyle, June 18, 1945; children: Jeffrey R., David L., Marcia M. Quinn, Daniel B., Timothy K., Brian Elmire, Ellen Little, Nicole Louise Klein. Owner, farmer, Elk Point, 1942-90; state rep. S.D. State Legislature, 1980—86, 1993—2000, state senator, 1987—92. Mem. Elk Point Local Dist. Sch. Bd., 1971-80; bd. dirs. Union County Farmers Home Adminstrn.; 4-H leader (40 yrs.) Sioux Livestock 4-H Club, state past pres.. Named Family of Yr., S.D. State U., 1989, Eminent Farmer of Yr., S.D. State U., 1998. Mem. County Crop Improvement Assn. (past chmn. bd. dirs.), County Livestock Improvement Assn. (past chmn. bd. dirs.), S.D. State Irrigators Assn. (past state chmn. and organizer), S.D. Water Congress (past bd. dirs.), Union County Livestock Assn. (resolutions com. 1980—), Fed. Land Bank Assn. (Sioux Falls area chmn., bd. dirs. 1970-84, Omaha 4 state adv. bd. 1976-80), S.C. State 4-H Leaders Assn. (state chmn.), Eminent Farmers Assn. (pres. 2001-02) Lions(pres. Elk Point chpt. 2002). Democrat. Roman Catholic. Avocation: golf. Address: 32648 480th Ave Elk Point SD 57025-6833

CHICOREL, MARIETTA EVA, publishing company executive, consultant; b. Vienna; came to U.S., 1939, naturalized, 1945; d. Paul and Margaret (Gross) Selby. AB, Wayne State U., 1951; MALS, U. Mich., 1961. Asst. chief libr. acquisitions divsn. U. Wash., Seattle, 1962-66; project dir. Macmillan Info. Scis., Inc., N.Y.C., 1968-69; pres. Chicorel Library Pub. Corp., N.Y.C., 1969-79, Am. Libr. Pub. Co., Inc., 1979—; pub. cons. Creative Solutions Co., 1986—. Asst. prof. dept. libr. sci. CUNY (Queens Coll.), 1986—; mem. edn. com. Gov.'s Commn. on Status of Women, Wash., 1963-65; instr. libr. scis. No. Ariz. U., Flagstaff, 1990; bd. dirs. Skills Devel. Tng. counseling; pub. cons. creative solutios. Chief editor: Ulrich's International Periodicals Directory, 1966-68; editor, pub.: Chicorel Indexes, 1969—; founding editor: Jour. Reading, Writing and Learning Disabilities International, 1985-90; contbr. chpt. on univs. to Library Statistics: A Handbook of Concepts, Definitions and Terminology, 1966. Mem. ALA (exec. bd. tech. svcs. divsn. 1965-68, chmn. libr. materials price index com. 1968-69, councillor 1969-73), Am. Assn. Profl. Cons., Am. Book Prodrs. Assn., Book League N.Y. (bd. govs. 1975-79), Am. Soc. for Info. Sci., Can. Libr. Assn., Pacific N.W. Libr. Assn., N.Y. Libr. Club, N.Y. Tech. Svcs. Librarians. Home and Office: PO Box 4272 Sedona AZ 86340-4272

CHICOREL, RALPH, composer, lyricist, playwright; b. Detroit, Dec. 4, 1930; s. Jacob and Judith (Louza) C.; m. Phyllis Philko, Feb. 3, 1957 (div. 1979); children: Steven Mitchell, Daniel Adam, Jacob; m. Debra Anne Lisch, Jan. 10, 1981; children: Matthew Aaron, Tyler William, Allison Anne. Grad., Am. Acad. Dramatic Arts, 1955. Performer various groups, Detroit, 1948-51; salesman Stein Ellbogen, Detroit, 1953-57; co-owner, entertainer Kenwood Restaurant and Lounge, Detroit, 1957-66; salesman Music Merchants, Detroit, 1966-67; co-owner Weight Watchers of Wis., Inc., Milw., 1968-92, also advt. spokesperson; pres. Chicorel Music Corp., Milw., 1970-92; co-owner Weight Watchers in Hawaii, Honolulu, 1989-91. Pres. Civic Music Assn., Milw., 1990-91. Producer, composer, lyricist 5 albums on Pleasure Records label, 1970-79; composer, lyricist (stage mus., album) Jean, 1973, 85, (CDs) C. Dickens' Great Expectations, 1995, Anna Karenina, 2002; composer: (songs) Milwaukee (premiere performance Milw. Symphony Orch. Feb. 1988); producer Lynn Redgrave and the World of Weight Watchers, The Milw. Auditorium, 1989; contbg. author: Milwaukee: The Best of All Worlds, 1991. Bd. dirs. Congregation Emanuel Bne Jeshurun Brotherhood, Milw., 1984-86, Comedy Sports Bd., Milw., 1992—. Served with USMC, 1951-53, Korea. Mem. Dramatists Guild, Song Writers Guild Am., ASCAP, Milw. Broadcasters Club. Sephardic. Avocation: collecting recordings of musical shows. Office: N64w14660 Poplar Dr Menomonee Falls WI 53051-5197

CHIDNESE, PATRICK N. retired lawyer; b. Neptune, N.J., May 26, 1940; s. Louis and Helen Chidnese; 1 child, Krista; m. Kathy J. Chidnese, Feb. 16, 1985; children: Patrick, Nicole. BA, U. Miami, 1964, JD, 1968. Assoc. Sinclair, Louis & Huttoe, Miami, 1968-69, Stephens, Demos, Magil & Thornton, Miami, 1969-70, Howell, Kirby, Montgomery, D'Aiuto, Dean & Hallowes, Ft. Lauderdale, Fla., 1970-71; sole practice Ft. Lauderdale, 1971-88; ret., 1988. County atty. Broward County Juvenile Ct., 1971—72. Mem. Fla. Bar Assn. (chmn. auto ins. com. 1977-78, chmn. 17th jud. circuit legis. com. 1977-80), Broward County Bar Assn., Acad. Fla. Trial Lawyers, Broward County Trial Lawyers Assn. (bd. dirs. 1974-80). Home: PO Box 18419 Asheville NC 28814-0419

CHIDSEY, RONALD GRANT, counseling; b. North Royalton, Ohio, July 30, 1948; s. Harold Jerome and Lee R. Chidsey; m. Barbara A., Aug. 5, 1972; children: Christopher S., Susan R. B. Baldwin-Wallace, Berea, Ohio, 1970; MA in Edn. Curriculum, Cleve. State U., 1975, MA in Edn. Counseling, 1986. Tchr. Strongsville (Ohio) City Schs., 1970—90, counselor, 1990—2002; cons. Chidsey seminars on parent tng. and tchr. insvc., 2002—. Recipient Martha Jennings Holden award Martha Jennings Holden Found., 1981, Excellent Sci. Tchrs. Workshop NSF, 1984, Baldwin-Wallace Coll. Outstanding Educator award, 2001. Mem. North Coast Elem. Counselor Assn. (pres. 1997-2001), Strongsville Edn. Assn. (treas. 1980-84). Avocations: golfing, singing, woodworking. Office: Strongsville City Sch-Kinsner 19091 Waterford Pkwy Strongsville OH 44149 E-mail: chidsey@strongnet.org.

CHIECHI, CAROLYN PHYLLIS, federal judge; b. Newark, Dec. 6, 1943; BS magna cum laude, Georgetown U., 1965, JD, 1969, LLM in Taxation, 1971, LLD honoris causa, 2000. Bar: DC 1969, U.S. Dist. Ct. DC, U.S. Ct. Fed. Claims, U.S. Tax Ct., U.S. Ct. Appeals (5th, 6th, 9th, DC, and fed. cirs.), U.S. Supreme Ct. Atty. advisor to Hon. Leo H. Irwin U.S. Tax Ct., Washington, 1969-71; assoc. Sutherland, Asbill & Brennan, Washington, 1971—76, ptnr., 1976—92; judge U.S. Tax Ct., 1992—. Mem. bd. regents Georgetown U., 1988—94, Washington, 1995—2001, mem. nat. law alumni bd., 1986—93; mem. bd. govs. Georgetown U. Alumni Assn., 1994—2000; bd. dirs. Stuart Stiller Meml. Found., 1986—99; prin. Coun. for Excellence in Govt., 1990—92. Dept. editor: Jour. Taxation, 1986—92; contbr. articles to profl. jours. Fellow: Am. Coll. Tax Counsel, Am. Bar Found.; mem.: FBA, ABA, Am. Judicature Soc., Women's Bar Assn., DC Bar Assn., Georgetown U. Law Alumni Assn. (Law Ctr. Alumnae Achievement award 1998, award 1994). Office: US Tax Ct 400 2nd St NW Washington DC 20217-0002

CHIEGER, KATHRYN JEAN, recreation company executive; b. Detroit, July 13, 1948; BA, Purdue U., 1970; MA, U. Mich., 1974; MBA, U. Denver, 1983. Libr. U. Mich., Ann Arbor, 1970-74; staff aide U.S. Sen. Gary Hart, Denver, 1974-79; dir. fin. rels. Petro-Lewis Corp., Denver, 1979-86; dir. investor rels. Kraft Inc., Glenview, Ill., 1987-89; v.p. corp. affairs Gaylor Container Corp., Deerfield, Ill., 1989-96; v.p. corp. and investor rels. Brunswick Corp., Lake Forest, Ill., 1996—. Mem. Nat. Investor Rels. Inst. (chpt. bd. dirs. 1979-84, v.p. mem. 1982-83, pres. 1983-84, nat. bd. dirs. 1984-88), Chgo. Execs. Club, Investor Rels. Assn., Sr. Investor Rels. Roundtable. Office: Brunswick Corp 1 N Field Ct Lake Forest IL 60045-4811 E-mail: kchieger@brunswick.com.

CHIEGO, WILLIAM J. museum director; b. Newark, Sept. 17, 1943; s. William Joseph and Rose Marie (Del Guercio) C.; m. Elizabeth Kimball Lee, July 3, 1971; children: Ruth Katharine, Rose Monica. BA in History with distinction, U. Va., 1965; MA in Art History, Case Western Reserve U., 1968, PhD in Art History, 1974. Asst. curator Toledo (Ohio) Mus. Art, 1973-74, assoc. curator European Paintings, 1974-76; curator Portland Art Mus., 1976-79, chief curator, 1979-82, N.C. Mus. Art, Raleigh, 1982-86; dir. Allen Meml. Art Mus. Oberlin (Ohio) Coll., 1986-91; dir. Marion Koogler McNay Art Mus., San Antonio, 1991—. Trustee Intermuseum Conservation Assn., Oberlin, 1986-91; mem., co-chmn. mus. liaison com. Midwest Art History Soc., 1987-91; mem. exhbn. adv. com. Am. Fedn. Arts, 1988-94; mem. conservation grant panel Inst. Mus. Svcs., 1991-93; chair membership com. Assn. Art Mus. Dirs., 1997-99, trustee, 2000-02; lectr. in field. Co-author, editor exhbn. catalog Sir David Wilkie of Scotland, 1987; co-organizer, author intro. to French Paintings from The Chrysler Museum, 1986; coord. rsch. The N.C. Mus. Art Intro. to the Collections, 1983; author: Master Prints from the Gilkey Collection, 1980, From Oregon Private Collections, 1977; organizer, author: (with others) Oberlin Alumni Collect Modern and Contemporary Art, 1989, Reginald Rowe: A Retrospective, 1996, Carl Rice Embrey: A Retrospective, 1997, O'Keeffe and Texas, 1998, César A. Martinez: A Retrospective, 1999; author/editor: Modern Art at The McNay, 2001; contbr. articles to profl. jours. Resident fellow Yale Ctr. for British Art, New Haven, Conn., 1982, Bingham Travel fellow Art History Case Western Reserve U., 1970-71, Univ. fellow Art History, 1969-70, Nat. Defense Edn. Act fellow Latin Am. History, 1965; Mus. Mgmt. Inst. scholar, 1981. Mem. Phi Beta Kappa. Office: Marion Koogler McNay Art Museum PO Box 6069 San Antonio TX 78209-0069 E-mail: william.chiego@mcnayart.org.

CHIEN, SUFAN, surgeon, educator; b. Zhejiang Province, China, July 20, 1938; came to U.S., 1982; s. Jiaxing and Julian (You) C.; m. Lorrain Wilson; children: Samson, Lynn. MD, Shanghai 1st Med. Coll., 1962. Resident dept. gen. surgery Zhongshan Hosp. Shanghai 1st Med. Coll., 1962-66, attending gen. surgeon, 1975-79; supr. cardiopulmonary bypass Shanghai Inst. Cardiovasc. Diseases, 1975-82, attending surgeon cardiovascular surgery, 1979-82; vis. scientist cardiovascular divsn. Mayo Clinic, Rochester, Minn., 1982-84; vis. scientist physiology and biophysics La. State U. Med. Ctr., Shreveport, 1984-85; vis. scientist surgery, physiology and biophysics U. Ky. Med. Ctr., Lexington, 1985-87, asst. prof. divsn. cardio-thoracic surgery, 1987-93, assoc. prof., 1993-96; assoc. prof. surgery U. Louisville, 1996—. Invited lectr., presenter in field; mem. sci. rev. com. study sect. NIH. Author: Hibernation Induction Trigger for Organ Preservation, 1993; mem. editl. bd. Internat. Medicine Rev., 1979-84; contbr. articles and abstracts to med. jours., chpts. to books. Grantee NIH, VA, U.S. Army, AHA, Univ. Fellow Am. Coll. Angiology; mem. AHA, N.Y. Acad. Scis., Chinese Med. Assn., Chinese Surg. Assn., Chinese Soc. Thoracic Surgeons, Shanghai Med. Soc., Internat. Soc. Heart and Lung Transplantation. Office: U Louisville Sch Medicine Rudd Heart-Lung Ctr 1200 201 Abraham Flexner Way Louisville KY 40202-3841 E-mail: sufanc@netscape.net.

CHIEN, YIE W. pharmaceutical science educator, university dean; b. Keelung, Taiwan, Oct. 20, 1938; came to U.S., 1967; s. Chou-lin and Ai-wen (Chen) C.; m. Margaret C. Chuang, Apr. 23, 1964; children: Steven, Linda. BSc in Pharmacy, Kaohsiung Med. Coll., Taiwan, 1963; PhD in Pharmaceutics, Ohio State U., 1972. Group leader, rsch. scientist Searle Lab., Skokie, Ill., 1972-78; sect. head Endo Lab. The Dupont Co., Garden City, N.Y., 1978-81; prof. pharmaceutics Coll. Pharmacy Rutgers U., Piscataway, N.J., 1981-86, prof. II, 1986-89, dept. chmn., 1982-88, Parke-Davis chair, 1989—; dir., founder Controlled Drug-Delivery Rsch. Ctr. Rutgers U., Piscataway, 1982-99; vis. prof. Nat. U. Singapore, 1999-2000; provost for univ. R & D Kaohsiung Med. U., 2000—. Cons. WHO, UN, 1988—; mem. editl. bd. several sci. jour., U.S., Spain, France, Taiwan, U.K., 1983—; com. of revision U.S. Pharmcopeial Conv., 1995—. Author: Novel Drug Delivery Systems, 1982, 2d rev. edit., 1992, Nasal Systemic Drug Delivery, 1989; editor: Transdermal Controlled Systemic Medications, 1987; contbr. more than 310 articles to profl. jours. Recipient Sci. and Tech. Achievement award, Bd. of Trustees award for rsch. excellence, Disting. Lecture Chair Parke-Davis Endowed chair. Fellow Acad. Pharm. Sci. Rsch./Am. Pharm. Assn., Am. Assn. Pharm. Scientists, Am. Inst. Chemists; mem. AAAS, Controlled Release Soc. (bd. dirs. 1984-87), Acad. Pharm. Rsch. and Sci., Parenteral Drug Assn., Fed. Internationale Pharmaceutique, Am. Chem. Soc. (polymeric materials scis. and engring. divsn.), Am. Assn. Coll. Pharmacy, Am. Found. for Pharm. Edn., N.Y. Acad. Scis., Sigma Xi, Rho Chi. Achievements include 24 patents for novel pharmaceutical delivery systems; for transdermal fertility control system and process; for transdermal absorption dosage unit for estradiol and other estrogenic steroids; for transdermal estrogen/progestin dosage unit, system and process; transdermal iontotherapeutic system, dosage unit and process. Office: Kaohsiung Med U R&D Office 100 Shih-Chuan 1st Rd Kaohsiung Taiwan E-mail: yiechien@aol.com.

CHIERCHIA, MADELINE CARMELLA, management consulting company executive; b. Bklyn., Jan. 30, 1943; d. Lawrence Cataldo Carrozzo and Victoria Angel (torchio) Carrozzo Petrisie; m. Jerry Chierchia, Oct. 3, 1959 (div. July 1975); children: Gertrude Chierchia Kraljic Teleisha, Geraldine Rosalie Gorga. Student parochial schs., Bklyn. Pres. mgr. Argyle Pers. Agy., N.Y.C., 1976-77; clk. typist Atlantic Mut. Ins. Co., N.Y.C., 1977-78; sec. ARC, N.Y.C., 1978-82; mgr. D.F. King & Co. Inc., N.Y.C., 1982-89, asst. v.p., 1989-90, v.p., 1990—. Mem. NAFE, Securities Industry Assn. (proxy div., exec. bd. 1990—), Southwest Securities Transfer Assn., Reorganization Securities Industry Assn., Am. Soc. for Profl. and Exec. Women. Corp. Transfer Agts. Assn. Democrat. Roman Catholic. Avocations: bowling, chess, reading, old movies. Office: DF King & Co 48 Wall St New York NY 10005

CHIGNOLI, C(ELSO) WILLIAM, health care center administrator; b. Santa Fe, Argentina, Apr. 19, 1938; MD, Universidad Nacional Cordoba, Argentina, 1961; MDiv, Eden Theol Sem., 1994. Telemedicine dir. Miami Children Hosp., 1985-89; pres. Global Outreach Network, Miami, 1989-93, Accion Social Comunitaria, St. Louis, 1993—; exec. dir. Am. Assn. of Family Counselors, 1999—. Founder, pres. Cross Cultural Studies Inst. Editor Family Counselor Jour., 1999. Sr. pastor Iglesia de la Nueva Comunidad/Sruggs U.M.C., 1995-2000; adv. mem. Nat. Coun. of the Chs. of Christ the USA, 1996-2000; conf. sr. min. The United Meth. Hispanic Ministry, 1995; bd. dirs. The Olive Br.-A Ctr. for Young Families, 1995-96; del. White House Conf. on Aging, Washington, 1995; mem. minority, elderly and disability com. State of Mo., 1994-95. Mem. NATAS, Am. Pub. Health Assn., Internat. Assn. for Cross-Cultural Psychology, Asociacion Para La Educacion Teologica Hispana, Internat. Teleconferencing Assn., Soc. of Satellite Profls. Internat., Nat. Religious Broadcasters, Am. Assn. of Christian Counselors, Health Scis. Comms. Assn., Assn. of Biomed. Communicators Dirs., Fla. Mortion Picture and TV Assn. Home: 9112 Desmond Dr Saint Louis MO 63126-2808 Office: Am Assn of Family Counselors 3646 Fairview Ave Saint Louis MO 63116-4747 E-mail: cchignoli@aol.com.

CHIHOREK, JOHN PAUL, electronics company executive; b. Wilkes-Barre, Pa., June 22, 1943; s. Stanley Joseph and Caroline Mary C.; m. Cristina Maria Marroquin, Dec. 28, 1968; children: Jonathan, David, Crista, Daniel. BSEE, Pa. State U., 1965; postgrad., Calif. State U., San Diego, 1970-71; MBA, Calif. State U., Sacramento, 1972. Program officer Hdqrs. Air Force Logistic Command, Dayton, Ohio, 1972-75; sr. engr. Hdqrs. Air Force Space Div., L.A., 1975-78; mgr. software systems dept. Logicon Inc., San Pedro, Calif., 1978; mgr. software product assurance dept. Loral Aeronutronics, Rancho Santa Margarita, Calif., 1978-85, mgr. software engring., 1985—. Pres. CMC Sys. Inc. Mem. Congl. Adv. Bd., 1980; active PTA, mem. Republican Nat. com. Served with USN, 1965-70, Vietnam. Decorated Bronze Star. Mem. IEEE (mgmt. bd. Computer Soc., exec. com. on standard), AAAS, Engring. Mgmt. Soc. (v.p. publs.), Air Force Assn., Internat. Platform Assn. Clubs: Lions, Odd Fellows. Roman Catholic. E-mail: johnp@cmail.com.

CHIKALLA, THOMAS DAVID, retired science facility administrator; b. Milw., Sept. 9, 1935; s. Paul Joseph and Margaret Ann (Dittrich) C.; m. Ruth Janet Laun, June 20, 1960; children: Paul, Mark, Karyn. BS in Metallurgy, U. Wis., 1957, PhD in Metallurgy, 1966; MS in Metallurgy, U. Idaho, 1960. Research scientist Gen. Electric Co., Richland, Wash., 1957-62; sr. research scientist Battelle Pacific N.W. Labs., Richland, 1964-72, sect. mgr., 1972-80, programs mgr., 1980-83, dept. mgr., 1983-86, assoc. dir., 1986-95; ret., 1995. Tchr. U. Wis., Madison, 1962-64. Contbr. articles to profl. jours. Fellow AEC. Fellow Am. Ceramic Soc. (counselor 1974-80); mem. AAAS, Am. Nuclear Soc., Sigma Xi. Clubs: Desert Ski (pres. 1958-59), Alpine. Republican. Roman Catholic. Avocations: skiing, golfing, woodworking, mountain climbing. Home: 2108 Harris Ave Richland WA 99352-2021 E-mail: healey1828@aol.com.

CHIKLIS, MICHAEL, actor; b. Lowell, Mass., Aug. 30, 1963; s. Charles Chiklis; m. Michelle Moran, 1992; 2 children. BFA in Acting, Boston U., 1986. Actor: (TV series) The Shield, 2002— (Emmy award, 2002, Golden Globe award, 2002, TV Critics Assn. award, 2002), Heavy Gear: The Animated Series (voice actor), 2001; (films) Sen to Chihiro no Kamikakushi (voice actor), 2001; (TV films) The Three Stooges, 2000; (TV series) Daddio, 2000; (films) Carlo's Wake, 1999, Last Request, 1999; (TV series) St. Michael's Crossing, 1999; (films) Do Not Disturb, 1999, The Taxman, 1999, Body and Soul, 1998, Soldier, 1998, Nixon, 1995; (TV films) Commish: In the Shadow of the Gallows, 1995; (TV series) The Commish, 1991—95; (films) The Rain Killer, 1990, Wired, 1989, (numerous TV guest appearances). Office: FX Networks LLC 1000 Santa Monica Blvd Los Angeles CA 90067*

CHIKWENDU, SUNDAY C. engineering educator, mathematician, educator; s. Joseph Chukwunwike and Cordelia Chikwendu; m. Eudora Ebitimi Kombo, May 25, 1968; children: Adaora Atonye Chikwendu-Henry, Zamafa Inodu, Meremu Ngozi, Azuka Biriye. BSE in Aerospace and Mech. Engring., Princeton U., N.J., 1966; MS, U. of Wash., 1969, PhD, 1971; postgrad., MIT, 1966—68. Vis. asst. prof. of math. UCLA, 1971—73; lectr., sr. lectr., assoc. prof. of mech. engring. U. of Nigeria, Nsukka, Nigeria, 1973—84; vis. asst. prof. U. of Wash., Seattle, 1977—78, vis. prof. of applied math., 1984—85; assoc. prof., prof. of math. SUNY, New Paltz, NY, 1985—, chair of math. dept., 2000—. Contbr. Fellow Tchrs. for Africa, Ghana fellow, Internat. Found. for Edn. and Self-Help, 1998—99, Du Pont fellow, MIT, 1966—67, Faculty Summer fellow, Smithsonian Instn., 1989; scholar African Scholarship Program of Am. Univs., Princeton U., African-Am. Inst., 1963—66. Mem.: ASME, AIAA, Math. Assn. of Am., Am. Math. Soc., Phi Beta Kappa, Sigma Xi. Achievements include first to A perturbation method for hyperbolic equations with small nonlinearities; research in Slow zone and N zone models for contaminant dispersion in shear flows; diffusion analogy for stresses in granular soils. Office: State University of New York-New Paltz 85 South Manheim Blvd New Paltz NY 12561

CHILA, ANTHONY GEORGE, osteopathic educator; b. Youngstown, Ohio, Dec. 14, 1937; s. Paul and Anne (Jurenko) C.; m. Helen Paulick, Oct. 9, 1965; 1 child, Anne Elizabeth. BA, Youngstown State U., 1960; DO, Kansas City Coll. Osteopathy and Surgery, 1965. Assoc. prof. family medicine Mich. State U. Coll. Medicine, East Lansing, 1977-78, Ohio U. Coll. Medicine, Athens, 1978-83, prof. family medicine, 1983, chief clin. research, 1982; chmn. instl. rev. bd. Ohio U., Athens, 1986-88. George C. Kozma Meml. lectr. Cleve. Acad. Osteo Medicine, 1979, Andrew Taylor Still Meml. lectr., Chgo., 1990, Sutherland Meml. Lectr., San Francisco, 1992. Contbr. numerous articles to profl. jours. Trustee Saint Vladimir's Orthodox Theol. Sem., Tuckahoe, N.Y., 1975-89; active Kootaga Area coun. Boy Scouts Am. Mem.: AAAS, Am. Assn. Orthopaedic Medicine, N.Y. Acad. Scis., Cranial Acad., Am. Acad. Osteopathy (pres. 1983—84, 1985—86, Scott Meml. lectr. Kirksville, Mo. 1984, Thomas L. Northup lectr. Las Vegas 1986, Gutensohn-Denslow award 1995, Andrew Taylor Still medallion of honor 1997), Am. Coll. Gen. Practitioners, Am. Osteo. Assn. (Louisa M. Burns lectr. Clearwater, Fla. 1987), Gen. Charles Grosvenor Civil War Round Table. Republican. Avocations: philately, coin collecting, chess, American Civil War history. Office: Ohio U Coll Osteo Medicine Grosvenor Hall Athens OH 45701

CHILCOAT, RICHARD ALLEN, army officer, university president; b. Wilmerding, Pa., Sept. 16, 1938; s. Floyd Donald and Edna Bailey (Moles0 C.; m. Dixie Lowers, June 6, 1964; children: Michael, Sharon A. BS, U.S. Mil. Acad., 1964; MBA, Harvard U., 1974. Commd. 2d lt. U.S. Army, 1964; speechwriter to Gen. John A. Wickham Jr., Office Chief of Staff, U.S. Army, Washington, 1984-87; comdr. Devil Troop Brigade, 5th Inf. Divsn. U.S. Army, Ft. Polk, La., 1987-89, chief of staff, 3d Inf. Divsn., 1989-90; exec. asst. to Gen. Colin L. Powell, Joint Chiefs of Staff, Washington, 1990-92; dep. comdg. gen. U.S. Army Tng. Ctr., Ft. Jackson, S.C., 1993-94; comdt. U.S. Army War Coll., Carlisle Barracks, Pa., 1994-97; pres. Nat. Def. U., Washington, 1997—. Decorated DSM, Legion of Merit, Bronze Star with oak leaf cluster, Air medals. Mem. Assn. of U.S. Army, U.S. Mil. Acad. Assn. of Grads. Avocations: tennis, golf. Office: Nat Def U Office of Pres 300 5th Ave Fort Mcnair DC 20319-5066

CHILCOTE, GARY M. museum director, reporter; b. St. Joseph, Mo., Nov. 2, 1934; s. Merrill and Mary Thelma C.; m. Mary Carolyn Abmeyer, April 2, 1958; children: Douglas A., Carolyn D. BA, Northwest Mo. State U., 1956. Newspress spl. corr. St. Joseph News-Press/Gazette, 1954—2002; mus. dir. Patee House Mus. and Jesse James Home Mus., St. Joseph, 1963—. Vocat. tchr. Hillyard Tech. Sch., St. Joseph, 1964-91. Author, editor Pony Express Mail, 1972—. Staff sgt. Mo. Air Guard, 1957-63. Mem. Nat. Pony Express Assn. (nat. dir., nat. v.p. 1990—), Pony Express Hist. Assn. (bd. dirs., co-founder 1963), James-Younger Gang (nat. pres. 1997—, 98-99). Republican. Home: 1910 N 32nd St Saint Joseph MO 64506-2313 Office: Patee Ho Mus/Jesse James Ho Mus 1202 Penn St Saint Joseph MO 64503-2560

CHILCOTE, SAMUEL DAY, JR., trade association administrator; b. Casper, Wyo., Aug. 24, 1937; s. Sam D. and Juanita C. (Cornelison) C.; m. Ellen Sheridan Spear, Nov. 11, 1966. BS, Idaho State U., 1959. Adminstrv. asst. Continental Oil Co., Glenrock, Wyo., 1960-63; asst. supt. public instrn., dir. Wyo. Surplus Property Agy., Wyo. Sch. Lunch Program, Cheyenne Wyo. Dept. Edn., Wyo., 1963-67; supr. North Ctrl. region Distilled Spirits Inst., Denver, 1967-71, exec. dir., COO North Ctrl. region Washington, 1971-73; exec. v.p., COO, Distilled Spirits Coun., Inc., Washington, 1973-77, pres., CEO, 1978-81; pres. Tobacco Inst., Washington, 1981-99; chmn. Chilcote Enterprises, Potomac, Md., 1999—; mng. ptnr. Tubac (Ariz.) Golf Resort and Spa, 2003. Adv. council consumer goods industry sect. Dept. Commerce. Pres. Sky Ranch Found. for Boys, 1975-81, pres. emeritus, 1981—; treas. Ford's Theatre, 1984-88, vice chmn., trustee, 1988—96, chmn., 1997—99; v.p. Santa Cruz County Citizens Assn., 2000—; bd. dirs., exec. com. Art Barn; chmn. Awards Dinner Com., 1989—2000, USO Met. Washington, past pres. Capt. U.S. Army, 1959-60. Recipient Profl. Achievement award Idaho State U. Coll. Bus., 1986, Man of Yr. award Anti-Defamation league, 1986, Humanitarian of the Yr. award Tobacco and Confectionery Div. Dinner for the UJA-Fedn. 1991 campaign, Good Scout award Greater N.Y. Coun. Boy Scouts Am., 1996. Mem. Santa Cruz Citizen Assn. (v.p. 1999—), Georgetown Club, Congl. Country Club (past pres., exec. com., bd. govs.), Burning Tree Club, Nat. Press Club, Capitol Hill Club, City Club, F St. Club, TPC Avenel (Washington), Jefferson Islands Club (bd. govs.), Masons, Elks, Shriners. Office: Chilcote Enterprises 5801 Nicholson Ln Ste 1701 North Bethesda MD 20852

CHILD, CARROLL CADELL, research nursing administrator; b. Vicksburg, Miss., Nov. 10, 1949; s. John Clifton and Marie Adelaide (Gerwig) C.; m. Nicole Louise Child, Feb. 11, 1984; children: Dylan Christopher, Brendan Thomas. BA in Philosophy, So. Ill. U., 1972; BSN with honors, U. Calif., San Francisco, 1980; MSc with honors, San Francisco State U., 1994. RN, Calif. Nurse supr. USDA/U. Calif., Berkeley; clin. rsch. supr. drug studies unit U. Calif., San Francisco; rsch. nurse educator Stanford (Calif.) U.; rsch. dir. Community Consortium U. Calif., San Francisco. Participant, co-presenter V

Internat. Conf. on AIDS, Montreal, Que., Can., 1989, VI Internat. Conf. on AIDS, San Francisco, 1990, VIII Internat. Conf. on AIDS, Amsterdam, 1992; co-presenter univ.-wide task force on AIDS conf. U. Calif., Berkeley, 1990; chair quality improvement com. Cmty. Programs for Clin. Rsch. on AIDS/NIH, 1993—. Contbr. to profl. jours. Mem. Internat. AIDS Soc., Soc. Clin. Trials, Assn. Nurses in AIDS Care, Assn. Rsch. Nurses.

CHILD, JUDITH, artist; b. Concord, Mass., June 22, 1948; d. Luther Moore and Virginia (Ellms) C.; m. Alan Leigh Schwartz, June 22, 1974; 1 child, Timothy Child Schwartz. BS, Colby Saywer Coll., 1971; postgrad., Auckland Soc. Arts, New Zealand, 1976; postgrad. program in artistry, Boston U., 1978-80. Artist, Boston, 1980-86, St. Louis, 1986—. Juror Art St. Louis, 1998. One woman shows include Colby Coll., New London, N.H., 1996; group shows include Art Chgo., 1994, Cedar Rapids Mus. Art, 1997-98; represented in permanent collection Anheuser-Busch Co., Emerson Electric Co. Painting fellow Nat. Endowment Arts, Washington, 1996.

CHILD, JULIA MCWILLIAMS (MRS. PAUL CHILD), cooking expert, television personality, author; b. Pasadena, Calif., Aug. 15, 1912; d. John and Julia Carolyn (Weston) McWilliams; m. Paul Child, Sept. 1, 1945 (dec.). BA, Smith Coll., 1934. With advt. dept. W.&J. Sloane, N.Y.C., 1939-40; with OSS, Washington, Ceylon, China, 1941-45. Co-founder Am. Inst. Wine & Food, 1982. Hostess (TV program) The French Chef, WGBH-TV, Boston, 1963—, Julia Child & Co., 1978—79, Julia Child & More Co., 1980, Dinner at Julia's, PBS, 1983, Cooking with Master Chefs series, PBS, Baking with Julia, Julia and Jacques Cooking at Home, PBS, (occasional cooking segment) Good Morning Am., ABC-TV, 1980—, (video cassettes) The Way to Cook, 1982;, 1982; author (with Simone Beck and Louisette Bertholle): Mastering the Art of French Cooking, 1961, Mastering the Art of French Cooking, Vol. II, 1970, rev. edit., 1983; author: The French Chef Cookbook, 1968; author: (with Simone Beck) From Julia Child's Kitchen, 1975; author: Julia Child & Company, 1978, Julia Child & More Company, 1979, The Way to Cook, 1989, Julia and Jacques Cooking at Home, 1999; columnist McCall's mag., 1975—82, Parade mag., 1982—86, Julia's Kitchen Wisdom, 2000. Recipient Peabody award, 1964, Emmy award, 1966, French Ordre de Merite Agricole, 1967, Ordre National de Merite, 1974, Ralph Lowell award, Corp. for Pub. Broadcasting, 1998, TV Cooking Show award James Beard Found., Emy for Oustanding Svc. Show host, 1995-96, Daytime Emmy for Oustanding Svc. Show Host, 2000-01; French Legion of Honor, 2000.

CHILDERS, ANDREW AISLE, educational association administrator; b. Washington, Sept. 3, 1957; s. Herman Malcolm and Mary Louis Childers. BA in Econs., George Washington U., 1981; MS in Acctg., George Mason U., 1992. Cer. Mgmt. Acct. Acctg. staff Nat. Collegiate Conf. Assn., Fairfax, Va., 1982-84; assoc. exec. dir. Nat. Coll. Conf. Assn., Fairfax, Va., 1984-86, exec. dir., 1986-89, bd. dirs., 1989—98, acting exec. dir., 1993; asst. contr. LGB of Am., 1999—2000, contr., 2002—. Mem. Inst. Mgmt. Accts., Beta Gamma Sigma. Republican.

CHILDERS, BOB EUGENE, educational association executive; b. Cleveland, Miss., Sept. 16, 1930; s. William Nick and Allie Jeanette (Doty) C.; m. Jo Ann Roberts, May 1, 1953; children: William Frank, Robert Clayton, John Murry, Julia Ann. BA, Union U., 1953; MA, Memphis State U., 1958; EdD, U. Tenn., 1964. Cert. tchr., adminstr., Tenn. Field engr. RCA, El Paso, Tex., 1955-57; instr. USN, Memphis, 1957-60; prin. Halls H.S., Knoxville, Tenn., 1960-61, McMinn County H.S., Athens, Tenn., 1961-64; asst. commr. Tenn. State Dept. Edn., Nashville, 1964-66; regional dir. USOE, Vocat.-Tech. and Adult Edn., Atlanta, 1966-69; exec. dir. Commn. Occupl. Edn., Atlanta, 1969-82, So. Assn. Colls. and Schs., Atlanta, 1982-92. Cons. U.S. Dept. Edn., Washington, 1963-79, Fla. State Legislature, Tallahassee, 1979, Md. Values Edn. Commn., Annapolis, 1979-80; founder, pres. Childers-Childress Family Assn., 1982-88, 90-96. Editor SACS Procs., 1982-92. Bd. dirs. Boy Scouts Am., Atlanta, 1990-97, Ctr. for Citizenship Edn., Washington, 1978-81; bd. trustees YMCA, Nashville, 1964-66; v.p. Religious Heritage of Am., St. Louis, 1979-86; active Rotary, Atlanta, 1981-92. With U.S. Army, 1953-55. Mem. Am. Vocat. Assn. (life 1966, cons.), Am. Tech. Edn. Assn. (life 1978, pres.1984, v.p. 1983), Am. Vocat. Rsch. Assn., Am. Soc. Assn. Execs., Phi Delta Kappa (past treas. 1960-61, sec. 1960-61), Iota Lambda Sigma, Sigma Alpha Epsilon (pres. 1952). Democrat. Baptist. Avocations: geneology, vitaculture, gardening. Home and Office: 960 River Rd Woodruff SC 29388-9110

CHILDERS, CHARLES, communications executive; Grad., Purdue U. Sr. sales exec. Pacific Bell; group v.p. Bell Can.; sr. v.p. sales and mktg. Bell Nexxia; chief mktg. officer Nortel Networks, pres. major accts.; pres. BCE Teleglobe, Reston, Va. Bd. dirs. Carter Group, PBS. Office: Teleglobe Comms Corp World Hdqrs 11480 Commerce Park Dr Herndon VA 20191

CHILDERS, JOHN R. education educator; b. El Centro, Calif., Oct. 8, 1954; s. Shirley Jean and Roy Juaquin Childers. PhD, Concordia Coll. and U., 2002. Cert. State Bd. of Dirs. for C.C. of Ariz., 2000. Chem. warfare specialist U.S. Army, 1974—95; assoc. instr. history Cochise Coll., Sierra Vista, Ariz., 1999—. Commr. Arts & Humanities Commn., Sierra Vista, Ariz., 1994—96. Staff sgt. U.S. Army, 1974—95. Mem.: Paralyzed Veterans Assn. (life). Avocations: wheel chair games, travel. Home: 101 N 7th St Apt 147 Sierra Vista AZ 85635 Office: Cochise Coll 901 N Columbo Ave Sierra Vista AZ 85635-2317 Personal E-mail: childersj@mail.com.

CHILDERS, L. DOYLE, state legislator; b. Ironton, Mo., Nov. 25, 1944; s. Lawrence Arlin and Jewel Nicks C. AS, Sch. Ozarks, 1964, BS, 1972; postgrad., Southwestern Mo. State U. Active U.S. Peace Corps., Cen. Am., 1965-69; sci. chmn. Reeds Spring RIV Sch. System, 1972-82; Mo. State rep. Dist. 29, 1983-96, Mo. state sen., 1996—. Active Reeds Spring Comm. Betterment Assn. Mem. Lions, Delta Kappa Phi. Home: PO Box 127 Reeds Spring MO 65737-0127

CHILDERS, LAWRENCE JEFFREY, superintendent of schools, personnel director; b. Newport News, Va., Oct. 24; m. Susan; 1 child. BS in Edn., Ohio U., 1972; MEd, Xavier U., Cinn., 1978. Cert. profl. secondary tchr., elem. prin., secondary tchr., local supt. and supt. Tchr. elem., jr. high sch., high sch. Tri-Valley LSD, Dresden, Ohio, 1967-80; head coach boys basketball Ohio U., Zanesville, 1977-80; prin., dir. in-sch. suspension, coach varsity boys basketball Maysville Local Sch. Dist., Zanesville, 1980-82; prin. South Zanesville (Ohio) Sch., 1982-85, Newton Elem. Sch., 1985-89, Millersburg (Ohio) Elem. Sch., West Holmes Local Sch. Dist., 1989-91, dir. spl. edn., prin., 1992-93; county supt. Holmes County Office of Edn., Millersburg, 1993-94; supt. Holmes County Ednl. Svc. Ctr., Millersburg, Ohio, 1995-96; dir. classified pers., site mgr. Tricounty Ednl. Svc. Ctr., Wooster, Ohio, 1997-98; ops. mgr. Tri-county Ednl. Svc. Ctr., Wooster, 1998-99; supt. Crooksville (Ohio) Exempted Village Schs., 1999—. Coach Ohio Regional Campus State Basketball Champions, 1978; developer Parent Vol. Network, 1990, in-sch. post office, 1990—; mem. strategic planning com. for bldg. and grounds improvement West Holmes Local Sch. Dist., 1992-93; spkr. Sch. Study Coun. Ohio, 1992; mem. Tchr. Expectation and Student Achievement; mem. sch. supt.'s adv. coun. Ashland U., 1993, adj. prof., 1995-96; supt.'s rep. Ohio East Regional Tchr. Devel. Ctr., 1994-97; adj. prof. Muskingum Coll., 2001. Mem. adv. bd. Holmes County 4-H, 1990-92; vol. Buckeye Book Fair, 1991, 92, 93; chair Holmes County Interagy. Cluster, 1994-95; mem. exec. bd. Ednl. TV of S.E. Ohio, 2002—; mem. governing bd., S.E. Ohio Spl. Edn. Reg. Resource Ctr., 2002—. Named Ohio Dist. 12 Coach of Yr., 1983, Muskingum Valley League Coach of Yr., 1983, Outstanding Adminstr., Ohio Sch. Bd. Assn. S.E. Region, 2002. Mem. ASCD, Ohio Assn. Elem. Sch. Adminstr., Ohio Sch. Bds. Assn., Buckeye Assn. Sch. Adminstrs., North Ctrl. Buckeye Assn. Sch. Adminstrs., Wayne-Holmes County Prins. Assn., Coun. for Exceptional Children, Sch. Study Coun. Ohio, Holmes County C. of C., Phi Delta Kappa. E-mail: ce_jchilders@seovec.org.

CHILDERS, NICOLE ANNELISE, journalist; b. San Diego, Calif., Oct. 4, 1977; B of Arts and Scis., U. of Pa, 1999. Assoc. prodr. ABC News, N.Y.C., 1999—.

CHILDERS, SUSAN LYNN BOHN, special education educator, administrator, human resources and transition specialist, consultant; b. Zanesville, Ohio, Mar. 01; m. Lawrence J. Childers; 1 child. AA, Ohio U., 1978, BS in Edn. cum laude, 1982; MEd in Supervision, Ashland U., 1991. Profl. cert. 1-8 elem. tchr., K-12 edn. handicapped, permanent cert., ; spl. edn. tchr., Ohio. Educator learning disabilities, developmentally handicapped Maysville Local Sch. Dist., South Zanesville, Ohio, 1982-89; work-study coord. Holmes County Office Edn., Millersburg, Ohio, 1990, editor spl. edn. newsletter, 1990-93, cons., supervisor work-study programming, 1991-93; spl. edn. supr. Wayne County Bd. Edn., Wooster, Ohio, 1993-94; adminstr. severe behavior handicapped program, supr. special edn. Ashland-Wayne County Bd. Edn., Wooster, 1994-95; cons. Tri-County Ednl. Svc. Ctr., Wooster, 1996-99; supr. spl. edn., supr. instrn. support Zanesville City Sch., Ohio, 1999-2000; dir. spl. edn. Licking County Ednl. Svc. Ctr., Newark, Ohio, 2000-01; supr. spl. edn. Lancaster City Sch., Ohio, 2001—; pres. Ohio Assoc. Supr. and Coord. of Exceptional Students, 2003. Mem. Holmes County Spl. Edn. Adv. Coun., 1990—93, E. Holmes Local Sch. Dist. Strategic Planning Action Team Job/Life Skills, 1993; rep. Ohio Devel. Handicapped Issues Forum; mem. steering com. Ohio Speaks, 1991—94; mem. strategic planning com. Ashland-Wayne County Bd. Edn., 1994—95; mem. Chippewa Local Sch. Dist. Child Care Bd., 1995—96; chmn. Direct Student Svcs. Strategic Planning Com., 1995—96; mem. safety com. Ashland-Wayne Ednl. Svc. Ctr., 1994—96; mem. svc. coordination com. Wayne County Children and Family First Initiative, 1995, 96, Edn. Rep. Safety Com., Tri-County Ednl. Svc. Ctr., Wooster, 1997—99; mem. exec. com. Licking County Children and Family First Initiative, 2000—01; mem. Licking County Mental Health and Recovery Bd., Newark, 2001, Licking County Behavioral Health Assessment Team, 2000—01, Newark Cmty. Corps Adv. Com., 2001, Fairfield County Children and Family First Clin. Cluster, 2001—02; pres.-elect Ohio Assn. Suprs. and Coords. of Exceptional Students, 2002; spkr. in field. Editor Spl. Edn. Newsletter Holmes County Office Edn., 1990-93. Mem. adv. bd. Holmes County Job Placement, Holmes County Litter Prevention Cmty. Action Plan Com., 1993; vol. Ohio Buckeye Book Fair, 1991—93, 1999, Holmes County Spl. Olympics, 1990—93, chairperson vols., 1993; mem. jr. assembly Bethesda Hosp., 1970—78; mem. Beaux Arts Zanesville Art Ctr., 1972—78; mem. spl. needs adv. bd. Ashland-West Holmes Career Ctr., 1990—93; mem. Transition and Comm. Consortium on Learning Disabilities, Ohio U. Alumni Career Resource Network, Holmes County Abuse Prevention Cmty. Action Plan Com., 1993, Ohio Staff Devel. Coun., Wayne County Family and Children First Coun. (Clin. Cluster), 1994—96; co-chairperson fundraising com. Creating Connections Symposium, Akron, Ohio, 1994; mem. Ashland-Wayne-Holmes Counties Adv. Com. for Tech. and Tng. Subcom., Ohio, 1996—97; adv. com. for tech. 3-county rep. Ashland, Wayne, Holmes, Ohio, 1996—98; A-site tech. tng. com., 1996—97; mem., regional rep. School/Net Communities of Practice, 1996; mem. Licking County Behavioral Health Assessment Team, 2000—01, Licking County Spl. Edn. Collaborative Com., 2000—01, Cmty. Corps Adv. Com., Newark, Ohio, 2001, Licking County Mental Health and Recovery Bd, Newark, 2001, Licking County Fostercare Collaborative Coun., Newark, 2000—01; mem. asst. tech. com., chair speech-lang. dept. Lancaster City Sch., Lancaster, Ohio, 2002—03. Recipient award Muskingum County Office Litter Prevention, 1988, Kids Care Project, 1989, Maysville Bd. Edn. commendation, 1989, Merit award Keep Ohio Beautiful program, 1991, Ohio Future Forum's Exemplary Transition from Sch.-to-Work Model award, 1993, Model Program designation Ohio's Employability Skills Project, 1987, Franklin B. Walter Outstanding Educator award, 1996, 98. Mem. ASCD, AAUW, Career Edn. Assn., Coun. Exceptional Children, Ohio Rural Edn. Assn., Ohio Sch. Supr. Assn., Ohio Assn. Vocat. Edn. Spl. Needs Pers., Ohio Assn. Supr. and Work-Study Coord. (award of Excellence 1992, reg. pres. 1993-94), Wayne-Holmes Elem. Adminstr. Assn., Ohio Pupil Pers. Assn., Ohio Assn. Supr. and Coord. for Exceptional Students (regional pres.-elect 2002, pres. 2003), Phi Delta Kappa. E-mail: s_childers@lancaster.k12.oh.us.

CHILD-OLMSTED, GISÈLE ALEXANDRA, language educator; b. Port-au-Prince, Haiti, Dec. 27, 1946; (parents Am. citizens); d. Daniel McGuire Child and Alice Dejean Child; m. Hans George Bickel, Sept. 1967 (div. Apr. 1984); children: Anna Kristina Villemez, Maia Selena Deubert; m. Jerauld Lockwood Olmsted, June 17, 1988. BA in French with honors, U. Md., 1970; MA in French, Johns Hopkins U., 1978, PhD in Romance Langs., 1981; cert. in translation, Georgetown U. Vis. instr. U. Md., College Park, 1980-81; instr. Johns Hopkins U., Balt., 1981-82; lang. instr. Holton-Arms Sch., Bethesda, Md., 1982-83; asst. prof. dept. modern langs. and lit. Loyola Coll., Balt., 1983-89, assoc. prof., 1989-98, chair dept. modern langs. and lit., 1989-94, prof., 1998—. V.p. faculty coun. Loyola Coll., 1998-2000, mem. steering com. Ctr. for Humanities, 1989-94; organizer, dir. Colloquia on Lang., Lit. and Soc., Balt., 1990, 95, 99, 2002. Author: Jean Genet: Criminalité et Transcendance, 1987; contbr. articles to profl. jours. Faculty rsch. grantee Loyola Coll., 1984, 89, study grantee French Embassy, 1986, 89; Gillman Fellow, 1970-73, 79-80; visitor's scholar U. Cape Town, South Africa, 1995. Mem. MLA (del. Mid-Atlantic region 1992-94, 96-98), Am. Assn. Tchrs. French, Soc. Prof. Français et Francophones d'Amérique, Les Amis de Stendhal, Phi Beta Kappa. Avocations: painting, golf, antiques, classical music, flamenco dancing. Home: 7735 Arrowood Ct Bethesda MD 20817-2821 Office: Loyola Coll 4501 N Charles St Baltimore MD 21210-2601 E-mail: gchildolmsted@loyola.edu.

CHILDRESS, DORI ELIZABETH, nursing consultant; b. Chgo., Jan. 25, 1945; d. John Fredrick and Doris Eleanor (Clark) Klafin; m. Larry Dunn, May 3, 1969 (div. Aug. 21, 1975); m. Terry Childress, May 17, 1986. BSN, Calif. State U., Chico, 1976, MSN, 1983. RN, Calif.; cert. profl. in healthcare quality. Critical care nurse Kaiser Permanente, Sacramento, 1977-82; dir. nursing edn. Rancho Arroyo Vocat. Tech., Sacramento, 1979-86; nurse cons., supr. med. managed care divsn. med. monitoring State of Calif. Dept. Health, Sacramento, 1986—. Chair Calif. State Dept. Health Svcs. Statewide Nurse Cons. Network, 1999-2000; spkr. in field. Author: Angel Wings, 1998. With U.S. Army N.G., 1980-84, flight nurse USAFR, 1984-88, 94. Recipient State Pub. Health award Dept. Health Svcs., State of Calif., Sacramento, 1994, Superior Sustained award for outstanding performance, 1997. Mem. ANA (nat. com. curriculum devel. managed care program 1994), Nat. Assn. Healthcare Quality Profls., Calif. Assn. Healthcare Quality Profls. (bylaws chair 1999-2000, sec. 2001—), Toastmasters Internat. (area gov. 1992-93, dist. sgt.-at-arms 1989-90, Outstanding Area Gov. award 1993), Sigma Theta Tau. Avocations: piano, horseback riding, swimming, walking, singing. Home: 2510 Auburn Rd Lincoln CA 95648-9451 Office: State of Calif Dept Health Medi-Cal Managed Care Divsn 714 P St Rm 692 Sacramento CA 95814-6401

CHILDRESS, DUDLEY STEPHEN, biomedical engineer, educator; b. Cass Co., Mo., Sept. 25, 1934; m., 1959; two children. BS, U. Mo., Columbia, 1957; MS, U. Mo., 1958; PhD in Elec. Engring., Northwestern U., 1967. From instr. to asst. prof. Elec. Engring. U. Mo., Columbia, 1959-63; rsch. asst. Physiology Control Sys. Lab. Northwestern U., Evanston, Ill., 1964-66, from asst. prof. to assoc. prof. Elec. Engring., Ortho. Sur., 1972-77, co-dir. Rehab. Engring. prog., 1972-85, prof. Elec. Engring., Tech. Inst., 1977-86, prof. biomed. engring., 1986—; prof. Orthopedic Surgery Northwestern Med. Sch., 1977-97, dir. Prosthetics Rsch. Lab., 1971—, dir. Rehab. Engring. prog., 1985—; prof. phys. medicine rehab. Northwestrn Med. Sch., 1997—. Elected to Inst. Med. Nat. Acad. Sci., 1995; mem. Com. Prosthetics Rsch. and Devel., Nat. Acad. Sci. Nat. Rsch. Coun., 1969-72. Recipient Nat. Inst. Gen. Med. Sci. rsch. career devel. award, 1970-75, Goldenson award, United Cerebral Palsy Found., Paul Magnuson award Va. RR&D Svc., 2002 Mem. AAAS, Applied Physiology and Bioengring. Study Sec., NIH, 1974-78, Biomed. Engring. Soc., Rehab. Engring. Soc. N. Am., Inst. Soc. Prosthetics and Orthotics, Sigma Xi.

CHILDRESS, JAMES FRANKLIN, theology and medical educator; b. Mt. Airy, N.C., Oct. 4, 1940; s. Roscoe Franklin and Zella Bessie (Wagoner) C.; m. Georgia Monroe Harrell, Dec. 21, 1958 (dec. Aug. 1994); children: (twins) Albert Franklin, James Frederic; m. Marcia Day Finney, May 10, 1997. BA, Guilford Coll., N.C., 1962; B.D. cum laude, Yale Div. Sch, New Haven, 1965; MA, Yale U., New Haven, 1967, PhD, 1968. Asst. prof. dept. religious studies U. Va.-Charlottesville, 1968-71, assoc. prof. dept. religious studies, 1971-75, chmn. dept. religious studies, 1972-75, 86-94, prof. religious studies and med. edn., 1979—, dir. Inst. Practical Ethics, 2000—; prof. Christian ethics Kennedy Inst. Ethics, Georgetown U., Washington, 1975-79. Vis. prof. U. Chgo. Divinity Sch., 1977, Princeton U., 1978, Coll. Physicians and Surgeons, Columbia U., 1978; cons. and lectr. in field. Author: Priorities in Biomedical Ethics, 1981, Moral Responsibility in Conflicts, 1982, Who Should Decide? Paternalism in Health Care, 1982, Practical Reasoning in Bioethics, 1997; co-author: Principles of Biomedical Ethics, 1979, 5th edit., 2001; co-editor: Westminster Dictionary of Christian Ethics, 1986; contbr. articles to profl. jours., chpts. to books. Trustee Guilford Coll., Greensboro, N.C., 1983-85; mem. subcom. on human gene therapy NIH, Bethesda, Md., 1984-92, mem. NIH recombinant DNA adv. com., 1988-90, 2002--; mem. Biomed. Ethics Adv. Com., 1988-89; mem. Nat. Bioethics Adv. Commn., 1996-2001; vice-chmn. Task Force on Organ Transplantation, HHS, 1985-86; bd. dirs. United Network for Organ Sharing, 1987-89. Recipient numerous awards and grants in field including Disting. Prof. award U. Va., 1984, Va. Prof. of Yr. award Coun. for Advancement and Support Edn., 1990; Am. Coun. Learned Socs. fellow, 1972-73, Wilson Ctr. fellow, 1984-85, Guggenheim fellow, 1984-85. Fellow Inst. Social Ethics and Life Scis., Am. Acad. Arts and Scis., Inst. Medicine; mem. Soc. Christian Ethics (bd. dirs. 1973-76), Am. Acad. Religion, Am. Theol. Soc., Am. Philos. Assn. Democrat. Mem. Soc. Of Friends. Avocations: tennis, reading, music. Office: U Va Dept Religious Studies Charlottesville VA 22903

CHILDRESS, RICHARD THOMAS, investment company executive; b. Huntington, W.Va., Nov. 22, 1942; s. Grover Burgess and Zenna Belle C.; m. Elli Lisbeth, June 13, 1962; 1 child, Tyrone Richard. BA in Psychology, U. Cin., 1964; MA in Asian Studies, U. Ariz., 1976. Commd. 2d lt. U.S. Army, 1964, advanced through grades to col., 1984; gen. staff officer Asian affairs, exec. officer Dept. of Army, 1978—81; dir. Asian and polit. mil. affairs White House, Nat. Security Coun., 1981—89; pres. Asian Investment Strategies, 1989—; pres., co-founder Asian Energy Corp., Tulsa, Okla., 1992—. Sr. adv. Sec. of State, 1982-88; US del. Assn. Southeast Asian Nations, 1982-88; leader, participant US Policy Del., Vietnam, Laos, 1982-89; designated White House Surrogate Spkr. for Pres. US; Rep. Nat. Comm., adv. bd. US-ASEAN Bus. Coun., Inc., US Global Strategy Coun.; policy adv. Nat. League Prisoners of War, Missing in Action families, mem. U.S.-Philippine Bus. Com.; exec. com. US-Thailand Bus. Coun.; co-chair adv. com. Nat. Ctr. S.E. Asian Studies, Georgetown U.; Indochina forum Aspen Inst.; spkr. in field. Contbr. articles to profl. jours. Decorated Def. Disting. Svc. medal, Legion of Merit with Oak Leaf, Bronze Star, Vietnamese Cross of Gallantry, others; recipient Humanitarian awards Fgn. Govts., Nat. League Prisoners of War/Missing in Action Families, Svc. to Mankind, Pace award Dept. Army. Mem. Asia Soc., Thai-Am. Assn. Mailing: PO Box 104 Flat Rock NC 28731

CHILDRESS, SCOTT JULIUS, medicinal chemist; b. Greenville, S.C., Apr. 6, 1926; s. Julius Dunford and Ola Irene (Scott) C.; m. Nelly Araxy Medzadour, Dec. 20, 1975 BS, Furman U., 1947; PhD, U. N.C., 1951. Research chemist Tenn. Eastman, Kingsport, 1951-52; research chemist Wallace & Tiernan, Belleville, N.J., 1952-58, Wyeth Labs., Radnor, Pa., 1959-62, mgr. medicinal chemistry, 1962-68, asst. to v.p. research and devel., 1968-73, asst. v.p. research and devel., 1973-85. Patentee in field; contbr. articles to profl. jours. Served with AUS, 1944-46 Fellow N.Y. Acad. Scis.; mem. Am. Chem. Soc. (treas. med. div. 1969-71, chmn. nat. med. chem. symposium 1968), Sigma Xi Home: 604 S Washington Sq Philadelphia PA 19106-4152

CHILDRESS, STEVEN ALAN, law educator; b. Mobile, Ala., Feb. 9, 1959; s. Roy and Mary Helen (Gillion) C.;children: Ani, Steven; m. Victoria Holstein, Oct. 19, 2002. BA, U. Ala., 1979; JD, Harvard U., 1982; PhD in Jurisprudence and Social Policy, U. Calif., Berkeley, 1995. Bar: Calif. 1983, U.S. Ct. Appeals (5th cir.) 1984, D.C. 1986, U.S. Ct. Appeals (9th cir.) 1986, U.S. Supreme Ct. 1987. Law clk. to judge U.S. Ct. Appeals (5th cir.), Shreveport, La., 1982-83; assoc. Morrison & Foerster, San Francisco, 1983-84; adj. lectr. law Golden Gate U. Sch. Law, San Francisco, 1984-86; grad. instr. U. Calif., Berkeley, 1985-86; assoc. Brobeck, Phleger & Harrison, San Francisco, 1987-88; assoc. prof. law Tulane U. Law Sch., New Orleans, 1988-96, prof. law, 1996—. Co-author: Federal Standards of Review, 1986, 3d edit., 1999; contbr. articles to profl. jours. Regents fellow U. Calif. at Berkeley, 1985. Mem. Law and Soc. Assn., Phi Beta Kappa. Office: Tulane U Sch Law School of Law New Orleans LA 70118 E-mail: achildress@law.tulane.edu.

CHILDRESS-BROWN, NAZARENE, small business owner, writer; divorced; 1 child. AA in Acctg. and Stenography, Detroit Inst. Commerce, 1964; AA in Guidance and Counseling, AA in Human Resource Devel., Oakland U., 1973; BA in Mass Comm., Wayne State U., 1984. With Superior Life Ins., 1961-62; claims examiner Mich. Employment Security Commn., 1962-76; bus. enterprise specialist Mich. State Dept. Commerce, 1976-79; real estate salesperson Braverman Reality, Southfield, Mich., 1979—. Tng. Re-employment Act rep. Mich. Employment Security Commn.; spl. instr. bus. edn. dept. Detroit Bd. Edn., 1979-81; mgr. metro Detroit sales Powers Travel Agy., Inc., 1984-86; bd. dirs. Consolidated Black Econ. Devel. Corp.; past owner recording studio, party store, laundromat; pres. Rio De World, Travel, Inc., 1984—, Lucayan Pub., 1998—, Lucayan Apts. Author: Smoking Barrel, 1998 (Literary award of Excellence, Nat. Assn. Urban Lit. Arts 1998). Founder Nazarism Advancement and Scholarship Soc.; class leader Bethel African Methodist Episcopal Ch.; vol. ARC; bd. mem. Wayne County Mental Health Bd.; mentor Breithaupt Technical Ctr.; mem., advisor Booker T. Washington Trade Assn.; mem. Detroit Urban League, Econ. Devel. Empowerment Zone Com., Eldicare Bd.; founder Bereavement Com.; foster mother Children's Aid Soc.; advisor, counselor to minority bus. entrepreneurs, 1977—. Recipient Spirit of Detroit award Detroit City Coun., 1997, 50 Yr. Membership award Bethel African Meth. Episcopal Ch., 1998, Cert. Recognition, New Ctr. Cmty. Mental Health Svcs., 2000, Resolution of Tribute, Gov. Mich. William G. Milliken. Mem. NAACP (life), LWV (2nd v.p.), Bus. and Profl. Women's Club (Detroit), Eastern Stars (Guiding Light chpt. # 50), Commanders Club (Bronze Leader award 1999), Delta Sigma Theta, Sigma Delta Chi. Office: Nazarism Advancement Scholarship Soc 453 Martin Luther King Blvd Detroit MI 48201 Fax: 313-567-8952.

CHILDRESS ORCHARD, NAN L. music educator; b. Prineville, Oreg., Oct. 30, 1956; d. Donald E. and Easie M. Childress; m. Joseph T. Orchard. BA, Portland State U., 1985; MMus, U. Cin., 1987; D of Mus. Arts, Rutgers U., New Brunswick, N.J., 1997. Prof. music Wagner Coll., S.I., NY, 1991—2001; prof. piano Caldwell Coll., NJ, 2001—; prof. music William Paterson U., Wayne, NJ, 2002—. Vis. docent The State Theatre, New Brunswick, NJ, 2001—. Musician: (performance) Solo piano and art song recitals; contbr. encyclopedia, music criticism. Ch. mem. and musician First Bapt. Ch., Metuchen, NJ, 1993—2002. Mem.: N.J. Music Tchrs. Assn., Music Tchrs. Nat. Assn., Music Educators Assn. (editor 1996—99). Protestant. Avocations: walking, cats. Office: Caldwell Coll 9 Ryerson Ave Caldwell NJ 07006

CHILDREY, JOHN A., JR., literacy educator; b. Richmond, Va., Mar. 21, 1943; s. John Albert and Frances Ashton Trice C.; m. Candace O'Hern Childrey, June 19, 1965; children: Amy Thomasson Childrey Nast, Sean O'Hern Childrey. BA in English, U. Va., 1965, MEd, 1968, EdD, 1973; MFA, Fla. Internat. U., 1994. Tchr. Lynchburg (Va.) Pub. Schs., 1965-69; instr. Randolph Macon Woman's Coll., Lynchburg, 1969-73; asst. prof. Purdue U., West Lafayette, Ind., 1973-77; from asst. to assoc. prof. Fla. Atlantic U., Boca Raton, 1977-88, from assoc. to prof. Davie, 1988—. Cons. Broward County Pub. Schs., Ft. Lauderdale, Fla., 1979-98. Author: (book) Shadow Words, 1986; editor: (book) Paradise, 1996. Chmn. Coral Springs Mid. Sch., 1982-86; editor: Fla. Reading Assn. Quarterly, 1991-94. Also, of Yr. Fla. Atlantic U., Boca Raton, 1991; recipient Svc. award Phi Delta Kappa, 1990. Mem. Nat. Coun. Tchrs. of English, Internat. Reading Assn., MLA, South Fla. Poetry Instr. (treas. 1984-86). Democrat. Home: 11055 NW 38th St Coral Springs FL 33065 Office: Fla Atlantic U 2912 College Ave Davie FL 33314

CHILDS, BARTON, retired physician, educator; b. Chgo., Feb. 29, 1916; s. Robert William and Katherine Sayles (Barton) Childs; m. Eloise L.B. MacKie, Mar. 29, 1950 (dec. 1980); children: Anne Lloyd, Lucy Barton; m. Ann E. Pulver, Dec. 1986. AB, Williams Coll., 1938; MD, Johns Hopkins, 1942. Successively intern, asst. resident, resident pediat. Johns Hopkins Hosp., 1942—43, 1946—48; research fellow Children's Hosp., Boston, 1948—49; Commonwealth Fund fellow Univ. Coll., London, 1952—53; mem. faculty Johns Hopkins Sch. Medicine, 1949—, prof. pediat., 1962—2000, prof. emeritus, 2000—. Mem. cons. coms. NIH, 1959—63, 1963—67, 1967—69, 1970—74, 1978—. Capt. Med. Corps U.S. Army, 1943—46. Recipient Rsch. Career award, NIH, 1962, Meade Johnson award pediat., 1959, Allen award human genetics, 1974, Howland award pediat., 1989; scholar John and Mary Markle, 1953—58, Grover F. Powers Disting., 1960—62. Mem.: Am. Acad. Arts and Scis., Inst. Medicine NAS, Genetics Soc. Am., Am. Soc. Human

Genetics, Am. Acad. Pediat., Soc. Pediatric Rsch., Am. Pediatric Soc. Home: 1019 Winding Way Baltimore MD 21210-1232 Address: John Hopkins Sch of Med 600 N Wolfe St Baltimore MD 21287-0005*

CHILDS, BREVARD SPRINGS, religious educator; b. Columbia, S.C., Sept. 2, 1923; s. Richard A. and Reaux (Jones) C.; m. Ann Taylor, Aug. 7, 1954; children— John, Catherine. BA, U. Mich., 1946, MA, 1948; BD, Princeton, 1950; ThD, U. Basel, Switzerland, 1955; DD (hon.), U. Aberdeen, Scotland, 1984, U. Glasgow, 1992. Ordained to ministry Presbyn. Ch., 1958. Prof. O.T., Mission House Sem., Plymouth, Wis., 1954-58; prof. religion Yale U., New Haven, 1958-99, Sterling prof. div., 1992-99, ret., 1999. Author: Myth and Reality in the Old Testament, 1960, Memory and Tradition in Israel, 1962, Isaiah and the Assyrian Crisis, 1967, Biblical Theology in Crisis, 1970, The Book of Exodus, 1974, Old Testament Books for Pastor and Teacher, 1977, Introduction to the Old Testament as Scripture, 1979, the New Testament as Canon: An Introduction, 1985, Old Testament Theology in a Canonical Context, 1986, Biblical Theology of the Old and New Testaments, 1992, Commentary on Isaiah, 2000. Served with AUS, 1943-45. Guggenheim fellow, 1963-64; Nat. Endowment for Humanities fellow, 1977-78; Fulbright-Hays fellow, 1981; Deutscher Akademischer Austauschdienst fellow, 1987. Fellow Am. Acad. Arts and Scis. Home and Office: 508 Amity Rd Bethany CT 06524-3015

CHILDS, CATHERINE OELAND See CATCHI

CHILDS, JOHN DAVID, computer hardware and services company executive; b. Washington, Apr. 26, 1939; s. Edwin Carlton and Catherine Dorothea (Angerman) C.; m. Margaret Rae Olsen, Mar. 4, 1966 (div.); 1 child, John-David. Student, Principia Coll., 1957-58, 59-60; BA, Am. U., 1963. Jr. adminstr. Page Comms., Washington, 1962-65; account rep. Friden Inc., Washington, 1965-67; Western sales dir. Data Inc., Arlington, Va., 1967-70; v.p. mktg. Rayda, Inc., LA, 1970-73, pres., 1973-76, chmn. bd., 1976-84; v.p. sales Exec. Bus. Systems, Encino, Calif., 1981—87, sr. v.p. sales and mktg., 1987—; sr. assoc. World Trade Assoc., Inc., 1976—2001; ret. Pres. Coll. Youth for Nixon-Lodge, 1959-60, dir. state fedn.; mem. OSHA policy formulation com. Dept. Labor, 1967; sec. supervisory com. SMW-FCU, Denver. Served with USAFR, 1960-66. Mem. Assn. Data Ctr. Owners and Mgr. (chmn. privacy com. 1975, sec. 1972-74, v.p. 1974, sec. supr. com.). Democrat. Christian Scientist. Home: PO Box 460904 Denver CO 80246-0904 E-mail: dchilds80246@yahoo.com.

CHILDS, JOHN FARNSWORTH, consultant, retired investment banker; b. N.Y.C., Nov. 24, 1909; s. Albert Ewing and Amelia (McGraw) C.; m. Mary Elizabeth Cardozo, Apr. 21, 1950; 1 dau., Susan Elizabeth. BS, Trinity Coll., Hartford, Conn., 1931, MS, 1932; MBA, Harvard, 1933; LLB, Fordham U., 1946. Bar: N.Y. 1946. Analyst Dick & Merle-Smith, N.Y.C., 1935-40; sr. v.p., head corporate services div. Irving Trust Co., N.Y.C., 1941-74; sr. v.p. Kidder-Peabody Inc., 1974-94, Paine Webber Inc., N.Y.C., 1994-97. Mem. tech. adv. com. on fin. Fed. Power Commn., 1973-74; adj. prof. Columbia Grad. Bus. Sch.; cons. in field. Author: Long-Term Financing, 1961, Profit Goals and Capital Management, 1968, Earnings Per Share and Management Decisions, 1971, Encyclopedia of Long Term Financing and Capital Management, 1976, Corporate Finance and Capital Management for the Chief Executive Officer and Directors, 1979; Contbr. articles to profl. publs. Past treas., trustee Lenox Sch.; bd. dirs. N.Y. Council on Econ. Edn.; past bd. dirs. Sch. Book Fair Inc., Fla. Power Corp. Served as lt. comdr. USNR, World War II. Mem. Am. Mgmt. Assn. (pres. coun., past dir.), Atomic-Indsl. Forum (past dir.), N.Y. Soc. Security Analysts, Pine Valley Golf Club (Clementin, N.J.). Home: 15 Washington Pl New York NY 10003-6641

CHILDS, LUCINDA, choreographer; b. New York, June 26, 1940; d. Edward Patterson and Lucinda Eustis (Corcoran) C. BA, Sarah Lawrence Coll., 1962. Choreographer, performer Judson Dance Theater, N.Y.C., 1963—73; owner, choreographer, performer Lucinda Childs Dance Co., N.Y.C., 1973—. Choreographer, dancer Judson Dance Theatre, N.Y.C., 1962-66, choreographer, dancer, artistic dir. Lucinda Childs Dance Co., N.Y.C., 1973—; choreographer, dancer: Einstein on the Beach, 1976 (Robert Wilson and Philip Glass) (Obie award 1978); actress I Was Sitting On My Patio This Guy Appeared I Thought I Was Hallucinating, 1977-78. Decorated officer Order Arts and Letters (France); Guggenheim Found. fellow, 1979, Nat. Endowment Arts fellow.

CHILDS, MARLETA MARIE, genealogist, library specialist; b. Center, Tex., Nov. 18, 1946; d. Melvin Auvy Childs and Birdie Virginia Weaver; m. John Raymond Ross, July 31, 1971 (div. 1986); m. Ronald Gene Monroe, Apr. 18, 1987. BA in History and Spanish, Stephen F. Austin State U., 1969, MA in History, 1971. Kinsearching various Tex. newspapers, Tex., 1976—; Rootsearching, West Tex. Times and Ft. Worth Como Monitor, Ft. Worth and Lubbock, 1977-78; Kinsearching in Tex. Vanishing Tex. mag., 1981—82; genealogical columnist Nat. Geneal. Inquirer, West Allis, Wis., 1980-82, Family Records Today, Kansas City, Mo., 1982-95. Author: (book) Those Tangled Vines, 1992; editor: (book series) North Louisiana Census Reports, 1975-99; author, complier: (2-vol. book) Rootsearching, 1978, 82; mem. editl. bd. The English Genealogist, 1976-90; editor, co-editor: Stirpes, 1979; tech. editor: Afro-Am. Hist. and Geneal. Soc. Jour., 1981. Recipient Cert. Appreciation, Am. Family Records Assn., 1990, Disting. Svc. as Geneal. Columnist award Tex. State Geneal. Soc., 1992, Cert. Appreciation, Shelby County Hist. Soc., 1993. Baptist. Avocations: travel, reading, playing and listening to music, swimming, movies.

CHILDS, RAND HAMPTON, data processing executive, consultant; b. Charlotte, N.C., Oct. 20, 1949; s. Wade Hampton and Francis Marion (Rand) C.; m. Anne Elizabeth Turner, Jan. 4, 1986; children: Ian Peter, Ryan Patrick. BS in Chemistry, Ga. Inst. Tech., 1971, MS in Chemistry, 1977; postgrad., Eidgenossische Technische Hochschule, Zurich, Switzerland, 1971-72. Sys. analyst computing svcs. dept. Ga. Inst. Tech., Atlanta, 1974-80, mgr. data processing computing svcs. dept., 1980-83, assoc. dir. office of computing svcs., 1983-87; v.p. software devel. Sirsi Corp., 1987-94, acting mgr. data conversion dept., 1995-97, v.p. R&D, 1994—2001, ind. software cons., 2002—. Cons. in field. Contbr. articles to profl. jours.; compiler: (with Naugle and Sherry) A Concordance to the Poems of Samuel Johnson. World Student Fund scholar Ga. Inst. Tech. and Swiss Govt., 1971-72. Mem. AAAS, Am. Chem. Soc., Assn. Computing Machinery, Info. Industry Assn., VIM (6000) (Control Data Corp. User Group), Sigma Xi, Alpha Iota Delta of Chi Psi (Atlanta). Home: 12451 N Shawdee Rd SE Huntsville AL 35803-3717 Office: SIRSI Corp 101 Washington St SE Huntsville AL 35801-4827

CHILDS, RHONDA LOUISE, motivational speaker; b. Albany, N.Y., Sept. 29, 1946; d. David Cornelius and Rhoda Louise (Rodeniser) Curley; m. Lindsay N. Childs, July 22, 1972; children: Ashley Louise, Nathan Shreeve David Curley, Justin David Curley. BA in Sociology and Anthropology, Cath. Convent Coll., Buffalo, 1966; cert. proficiency exam, McGill U., Montreal, Que., Can., 1968; student, Siena Coll., Loudonville, N.Y., Russell Sage Coll. Adminstrv. asst. Hypersonic Lab., McGill U., 1966-68; adminstrv. asst. dept. comparative religions Sir George Williams U., Montreal, 1966-68; with various cmty. svc. orgns., Europe, Can., Africa, 1968-71, tchr. N.Y. State Mental Hygiene Dept., Albany, 1971-72; non-teaching profl. SUNY, Albany, 1973-75; cmty. liaison Collins Bay Penitentiary, Kingston, Ont., Can., 1976-77; ct. monitor Family Ct., 1975-78; pres. Concerned Citizens Against Crossgates, Guilderland, N.Y., 1978-80; adminstrv. asst. St. Catherine's Ctr. for Children, Albany, 1980-85; dir. govt. and cmty. affairs Empire Blue Cross and Blue Shield, Albany, 1985-94; devel. counsel St. Peter's Hosp., Albany, 1994-96; prin. New Visions, A Childs Co., Slingerlands, N.Y. Cons. to numerous nonprofit orgns.; founder, coord. Family Agys. Committed to Svc., 1983-86; founder, pres. Corp. Vol. Coun.; lectr. numerous ednl. and exec. seminars; motivational spkr. in field. Author: My Own Telephone Book, 1988. Bd. dirs. Sr. Svc. Ctrs. Found.; grad. Capital Leadership, 1988-94; past pres. adv. bd. Ret. Sr. Vol. Programs; trustee, pres. St. Anne Inst. Recipient Outstanding Svc. award Family Agys. Committed to Svc., 1985, Community Svc. award Cystic Fibrosis Found., 1988, Tribute to Women award, YWCA, 1991, Franklin D. Roosevelt Vol. award March of Dimes, 1991, June A. Bonneau award Sr. Svc. Ctrs. Albany, Citizen of Yr. award Samaritans, 1994, Golden Rule award, 1994, Lifetime Achievement award Women of Excellence, 1994, Outstanding Svc. award St. Anne Inst., 1994. Mem. APHA, Nat. Soc. Fund Raising Execs., Albany-Colonie Regional C. of C. (numerous coms., guest lect.), Corp. Vol. Couns. Am., NAFE, SUNY Women's Club, Enterprising Women's Leadership Inst., Rotary (pres. Albany chpt., coms. Dist. 7190 Citizen of Yr. award 1990, Airport Citizen of Yr. award 1990, Paul Harris fellow 1990). Democrat. Roman Catholic. Office: New Visions A Childs Co 308 Quidor Ct Slingerlands NY 12159-9554 E-mail: lchilds1@nycap.rr.com., childs@global2000.net.

CHILDS, RICHARD FRANCIS, retired scientist, educator; b. Battle Creek, MI, Sept. 20, 1918; s. Francis Marion and Mary Florence (Crilly) C.; m. Marion R. Avmitage, 1943 (div., 1953), m. Virginia Helen (Ramsdell), Aug. 2, 1958; children: Allen, Bonnie, Kathleen. BA in chem., Olivet, Olivet, MI, 1937-41; BS, MS, U. Wisconsin, Madison, WI, 1954-55; PhD in pharm., U. Arizona, Tucson, AZ, 1962. Cert. Reg. Pharmacist. Indsl. chemist Cleaver Brooks, Milwaukee, WI, 1942-43; radio instr. US Army AF, Sioux Falls, SD, 1943-46; chemist ARMOUR, Chicago, IL, 1948-50; assoc. prof. Coll. Pharm., Tucson, 1955-75; ret., 1975. Dir., Southern AZ Sci. Fair, Tucson, 1957-58. Assoc. edit. (edit. Homer B. Titton), Lightworks, Pima Community Coll. East, Tucson, AZ, 1998. Served AAF, CPL, 1943-46. Recipient Sci. Faculty, Natl. Sci. Found., U. Arizona, Purdue, Tchg. Fellowship, Natl. SCi. Found., first PhD offered by Coll. of RX, 1962. Democrat. Home: Tucson, Ariz. Died Aug. 3, 2002.

CHILDS, STEVE DOUGLAS, artist, portrait painter; b. Atlanta, Jan. 20, 1956; s. Charles Henry and Miriam (Chatfield) C.; m. Nilla Dudley, June 10, 1978; children: Daniel Cooper, David Dudley. B Visual Arts, Ga. State U., 1980; MFA, Utah State U., 1993. Freelance artist, Winston-Salem, N.C., 1980—. Lectr. to art orgns; instr. art workshops including Acad. of Art Coll., San Francisco at the Am. Soc. Portrait Artists' Portrait Painting Workshop, 1999; juror, panelist at numerous art shows. Exhbns. in one and two-man shows since 1982; group shows include 1997 Ala. Faces of Destiny Collection of Am. Portraiture Exhbn.; commissions include Crosby Golf Tournament, AMC Entertainment, Book of the Month Club, Pinnacle Books, Ballantine Books, Neenah Paper, Country, G Magazine, Wake Forest U., Dance Magazine, RJ Reynolds and many others. Presented fund raising benefit exhbns. for Cin. Ballet, N.Carolina Dance Theater. Recipient Exceptional Merit award, Nat. Portrait Competition, 1996, Hon. Mention award & Jury's Top 50 award Salon Internat., Juror Internat. Portrait Competition, 2001, 2001, 2002; grantee Liquitex Excellence in Art Competition, 1993. Home and Office: 1833 Sussex Ln Winston Salem NC 27104-1125 E-mail: stevechilds@portraitartist.net.

CHILDS, WILLIAM PARKER, education educator; s. Jean Parker and William Striet Baker(Stepfather); m. Marcy Liane LaPlante, July 29, 1988; children: William Alexander, Amanda Elizabeth, Kathryn Olivia, Benjamin Parker. BA in History, U. of Richmond, 1971; MEd, U. of Va., 1975; EdD, Va. Tech, 1997. Social studies tchr. Culpeper County Pub. Schools, Va., 1971—80; asst. prin. Spotsylvania County Pub. Schs., Va., 1980—2001; asst. prof. edn. Frostburg State U., Md., 2001—. Pres. Spotsylvania County Crime Solvers, Va., 1985—86; congl. dist. com. chair 7th Dist. Dem. Com. of Va., 1987—89; chair Spotsylvania County Dem. Com., Va., 1990—91. Mem.: Edn. Law Assn. (assoc.), Assn. of Supervision and Curriculum and Devel. (assoc.), Phi Delta Kappa Internat. (assoc.), Kappa Delta Pi Edn. Honor Soc. (assoc.; pres. 1970—71). Liberal. Avocation: politics. Home: 246 East Main St Frostburg MD 21532 Office: Frostburg State U 101 Braddock Rd Frostburg MD 21532 Personal E-mail: wchilds@frostburg.edu.

CHILES, STEPHEN MICHAEL, lawyer; b. July 15, 1942; s. Daniel Duncan and Helen Virginia (Hayes) C.; m. Deborah E. Nash, June 13, 1964; children: Stephen, Abigail. BA, Davidson Coll., 1964; JD, Duke U., 1967. Bar: N.Y. 1970, Pa. 1978, Wis. 1981, Ill. 1986, U.S. Dist. Ct. (ea. dist.) Pa. 1978, U.S. Tax Ct. 1978, U.S. Supreme Ct. 1978. Officer trust dept. Irving Trust Co., N.Y.C., 1970-75, v.p., 1975-77; assoc. atty. Stassen Kostos & Mason, Phila., 1978-79, mem., shareholder, 1979-85; ptnr. McDermott, Will & Emery, Chgo., 1986—. Contbr. articles to profl. jours. Served to capt. U.S. Army, 1967-69. Decorated Bronze Star, Army Commendation medal. Mem. ABA, State Bar Wis., Exmoor Country Club (Highland Park, Ill.). Republican. Episcopalian. Office: McDermott Will & Emery 227 W Monroe St Ste 3100 Chicago IL 60606-5096 E-mail: schiles@mwe.com.

CHILGREN, D. DIANNE, concert pianist, piano teacher; b. New Ulm, Minn., Apr. 18, 1941; d. Hilding Samuel and Barbara Elaine Chilgren. BMus and Performer's Cert., Eastman Sch. Music, 1962; MMusic, Ind. U., 1963. Piano soloist N.Y.C. BAllet, 1971-77, Zurich Opera House, 1977-83, Pacific N.W. Ballet, Seattle, 1985—. Pres. bd. dirs. Evergreen City Ballet, Auburn, Wash., 1996-98, bd. officer, 1994—. Solo recitals at Alice Tully Hall, Carnegie Hall, Town Hall, N.Y.C., 1971-77; perfomances solo and with orch. at Zurich Tonhalle Orch., Geneva Symohony, London Royal Philharm., Seattle Symphony, San Francisco Symphony, Madrid Symphony, Monte Carlo Symphony, Rochester Philharm., others; musician silent film soundtracks George Banchine's Ballets, 1996-97; guest artist Northwest Chamber Orch., 1998—; pvt. tchr. piano, Seattle, 1985—. Recipient Notable Am. award, 1976. Mem. Musicians Union. Avocations: reading, hiking, films, cooking, computer games. Home: 2025 10th Ave E Seattle WA 98102-4105 Office: Pacific NW Ballet 301 Mercer St Seattle WA 98109-4600

CHILIVIS, NICKOLAS PETER, lawyer; b. Athens, Ga., Jan. 12, 1931; s. Peter Nickolas and Wessie Mae (Tanner) C.; m. Patricia Kay Tumlin, June 3, 1967; children— Taryn Tumlin, Nicole Tumlin, Nickolas Peter Tumlin. LL.B., U. Ga., Athens, 1953; LL.M., Atlanta Law Sch., Ga., 1955. Bar: Ga. 1952, U.S. Supreme Ct. 1965. Ptnr. Lester & Chilivis, Athens, Ga., 1953-58; ptnr. Erwin, Epting, Gibson & Chilivis, Athens, Ga., 1958-75; commr. of revenue State of Ga., Atlanta, 1975-77; ptnr. Powell, Goldstein, Frazer & Murphy, Atlanta, 1977-84, Chilivis & Grindler, Atlanta, 1984-95, Chilivis, Cochran, Larkins & Bever, Atlanta, 1995—. Adj. prof. U. Ga. Sch. Law, Athens, 1965-75. Author: Termination Settlement, 1955. Contbr. chpts. to books, articles to profl. jours. Bd. visitors U. Ga., Athens, 1983-85; trustee Skandalakis Found., Atlanta, 1984, Found. of the Holy Apostles; former trustee U. Ga. Found.; former mem. U. Ga. Rsch. Found. Bd.; pres. and sr. warden Ch. of Apostles. With USAFR, 1953-55. Recipient Archdiocesan medal Archbishop of North and South Am., 1980. Fellow Internat. Soc. Barristers, Am. Coll. Trial Lawyers, Am. Acad. Appellate Lawyers; mem. Am. Inns. of Ct. (emeritus, master), Old War Horse Lawyers Club, Lawyers Club Atlanta, Commerce Club, Heritage Club, (Atlanta), Pres.'s Club (U. Ga.), Elks. Avocations: handball, tennis, writing, lecturing. Home: 855 W Paces Ferry Rd NW Atlanta GA 30327-2655 Office: Chilivis Cochran Larkins & Bever Chilivis Bldg 3127 Maple Dr NE Atlanta GA 30305-2503

CHILL, MYRTLE N. advertising copywriter, promoter; b. Indpls., Apr. 5, 1906; d. Henry and Mathilda (Kuhn) Newman; m. George F. Chill, June 28, 1932. BSJ, Northwestern U., Medhill Sch. Journalism, 1927. Editor Armitage News, Chgo., 1927—28; mng. editor The Nor'wester, Chgo., 1928—29; asst. sales promotion editor Sears, Roebuck & Co., 1929—32; head copywriter Goldblatt Bros. Dept. Stores, Chgo., Ind., 1932—39; gen. mgr. Substantial Products Co., Chgo., 1939—65; part-time advt. work Edelstein-Nelson, Reich & Kahn; Chicago Bar and Restaurant Supply, Chgo., 1967—2001; promotion mgr. Barbara Newman Designs, Chgo., 2001—. Achievements include presently developing a fused glass pin that with a necklace or cord becomes a pendant; updating her exentsive 1992 Newman family med. history that now includes the fifth living generation; with med. rsch. and care so specialized it is important to know the allergies inherited from our genes.

CHILLIDA, EDUARDO, sculptor; b. Donostia, Basque Country, Jan. 10; s. Pedro Chillida and Carmen Juantegui Eguren; m. Pilar Belzunce, 1950. Student arch., U. Madrid, 1943-46; degree in arch. (hon.), High Coun. Arch.'s Assn., Spain, 1989, Dr. Honoris Causa, U. Alicante, Spain, 1996. Vis. prof. Harvard U., 1971. One-man shows include Clan Gallery, Madrid, 1954, Galerie Maeght, Paris, 1956, 64, McRoberts and Tunnard Gallery, London, 1965, Galeria Iolas Velasco, madrid, 1977, Carpenter Ctr. Visual Arts, Harvard U., Boston, 1977, Nat. Gallery, Washington, Mus. Art, Carnegie Inst., Pitts., 1979, Min. Culture Palacio Cristal, Parque Retiro, Madrid, 1980, Mus. Fine Art, Bilbao, Basque Country, 1981, Hayward Gallery, London, 1990, Tasende Gallery, L.A., 1997; group shows include Mus. Fine Arts, Houston, 1961, Galerie Art Moderne, Basel, Switzerland, 1974, Hastings Gallery Spanish Inst., N.Y.C., 1974, Solomon R. Guggenheim Mus., N.Y.C., 1980, Galerie Beyeler, Basel, 1982, Galerie Herbert MeyerEllinger, Frankfurt, Germany, 1983, Mary-Anne Martin/Fine Art, N.Y.C., 1984, Tasende Gallery, La Jolla, Calif., 1985; represented in permanent collections Kuntmuseaum, Basel, Nationalgalerie, Berlin, Museo Bellas Artes, Bilbao, Art Inst. Chgo., Museo Art, Cuenca, Spain, Mus. Fine Art, Houston, La Jolla Mus. Contemporary Art, Tate Gallery, London, Museo Espanol Arte Contemporaneo, Madrid, Museo Rufino Tamayo, Mexico City, Solomon R. Guggenheim Mus., N.Y.C., Mus. Art, Carnegie Inst., Pitts., Collezione Arte Contemporanea, Musei Vaticani, Rome, Galleria Nazionale Arte Moderna, Rome, Hirshorn Mus., Washington; illustrator Le Chernin des Devins, 1965, Meditation in Kastilien, 1968, Die Kunst und der Raum, 1969, Más Allá, 1973, Voz Acorde: Homenaje a Jorge Guillén, 1982, Ce Maudit Moi, 1983. Recipient Graham Found. prize, 1958, Kandinsky prize, 1960, Wilhelm-Lehmbruck prize, 1966, Nordrhein-Westfalen prize, 1966, Wellington prize, 1970, Critica Arte prize, 1971, Encomienda Ciudad, 1971, Engraving prize Internat. Exhbn. Rijeka, Yugoslavia, 1972, Internat. Biennale Ljubljana, Yugoslavia, 1973, La Taula award Josep Lluis Sert, 1973, Premio Internat. Diano Marino award, 1974, Rembrandt prize, Goethe Found., 1975, First prize Japanese Ministry Fgn. Affairs, 1976, Peace and Truce prize Victor Seix Inst. Polemics, 1978, Gold Merit medal Mus. Fine Art Madrid, 1981, European Fine Arts prize City of Strasbourg, 1983, Gold medal U. Basque Country, 1984, Grand Nat. prize Arts for Sculpture, French Govt., 1984, Internat. Wolf Found. prize, 1985, Imperial Ring, City of Goslar, 1985, Revista Euzkadi prize, 1986, Prince Asturias award, 1987, Lorenzo-il Magnifico prize, 1987, Order Sci. and Art, Fed. German Govt., 1988, Imperial prize Japan Art Assn., 1991, Fundacion Sabino Arana prize, 1992, Gold medal City of Donostia, 1992, Assn. Española Critica Arte, 1995, Cross, Portuguese Order Merit Mario Soares, 1995, Freedom prize, 1995; co-recipient Andrew W. Mellon prize, 1978, Ildefonso Cerda medal Engrs. Coll. Cataluna, 1990. Fellow Hispanic Soc. Am. (hon.), mem. AAAS, Royal Acad. Arts London, Hispanic Soc. N.Y. (hon.), REal Academia Bellas Arts (hon.). Office: Tasende Gallery 8808 Melrose Ave West Hollywood CA 90069-5604

CHILMAN, CATHERINE EARLES STREET, social welfare educator, author; b. Cleve., Sept. 20, 1914; d. Elwood Vickers and Augusta (Jewitt) Street; m. C. William Chilman, Sept. 27, 1936 (dec. 1977); children: Margaret Chilman Carpenter, Jeanne Chilman Klovdahl, Catherine Chilman Brown. AB, Oberlin Coll., 1935; MA, U. Chgo., 1938; PhD, U. Syracuse, 1958. Caseworker United Charities Chgo., 1937-39, Family Svcs., Roanoke, Va., 1939-40; psychiat. cons. ARC, Syracuse, N.Y., 1943-44; tchr. dept. child devel., family rels. Syracuse U., 1947-49, instr., 1949-57, asst. prof., 1957-61; sr. social worker N.Y. State Mental Health Rsch. Unit, Syracuse, 1955-57; parent edn. specialist Children's Bur. HEW, Washington, 1961-64; rsch. adminstr. U.S. Welfare Adminstrn., 1964-69; dean faculty Hood Coll., Frederick, Md., 1969-71; curriculum dir. Internat. Population Planning and Social Work Edn. Project, U. Mich., Ann Arbor, 1971-72; prof. Sch. Social Welfare, U. Wis., Milw., 1972-86, prof. emerita, 1986—; pres. Nat. Groves Conf. on the Family, 1975-78. Speaker, cons. on rsch., family life, pub. policy to univs., fed. govt. and profl. orgns. Author: Your Child: 6 to 12, 1966, Moving into Adolescence, 1966, Growing Up Poor, 1967, Adolescent Sexuality in a Changing American Society, 1983, Families in Trouble, 5 vols., 1988, (with others) Mental Health Crisis and the Nation's Children, 1972, Programs and Policies of National Family Organizations, 1997; mem. editl. bd. Jour. Marriage and Family, 1963-69; contb. articles to profl. jours., chpts. to books. U.S. Office Edn. grantee, 1960-62; Wis. State grantee, 1973-75; Nat. Inst. Child Devel. grantee, 1976-77; recipient Hon. Alumni award Sch. Social Svcs. Adminstrn., U. Chgo., 1978, Honored Scholar award Groves Conf. Marriage and the Family, 1989. Fellow APA; mem. Nat. Coun. on Family Rels. (bd. dirs. 1991-93, sec. 1992-93), Groves Conf. on Marriage and Family (hon. life, bd. dirs., nat. workshop dir. 1992). Home: Cluster 3110 10450 Lottsford Rd Mitchellville MD 20721-2734 *Although I have experienced many tragedies and hardships and have lived through tumultuous times, I am continuously surprised and grateful for the many blessings of my life: dear friends and family, the excitement of teaching and research, the marvels of aesthetic creations, and the beauty and wonder of our natural world and until recently, living and writing near our beleagured but stimulating national capital. I have now joined a wonderful retirement community near Washington.*

CHILOW, BARBARA GAIL, social worker; b. Grand Forks, ND, June 7, 1936; d. Alfred Thomas and Florence (Micken) Seeley; m. Steven Chilow, Aug. 15, 1987; children: John Mark Doss, Timothy Stephen Doss, Elizabeth De La Cruz, David Chilow. BS, UCLA, 1957; MSW, U. So. Calif., 1970; MPA, Calif. State U., Long Beach, 1985. Lic. social worker, Calif., Utah, marriage, family and child counselor, Calif. Social worker Dept. Pub. Welfare, San Diego, 1957, Dep. Pub. Assistance, Whitman, Mass., 1966-68; psychiat. social worker State of Calif., Pomona, 1971-73; clin. social worker Orange County Dept. Mental Health, Santa Ana, Calif., 1973-74, sr. clin. social worker, 1974-79; dep. dir. mental health Orange County Human Svcs. Agy., Santa Ana, 1979-80, dep. regional mgr., 1980-82, adminstrv. mgr. II, 1982-93; clin. coord. Brightway at St. George, Utah, 1993-2000; pvt. practice Newport Beach, Calif., 1977—93, Dessert Hills, Calif., 2002—. Chmn. So. Calif. Case Mgmt. Coun., 1987-89, Orange County Bd. and Care Quality Com., Santa Ana, 1984-89; owner, mgr. Desert Hills Therapeutic Svcs., Inc., St. George, 1998-2002. Pres. Winchester Hills Homeowners Assn., St. George, 1995-97; bd. advs. Southwestern Spl. Svc. Dist., 1997-, Leadership Dixie, 1998-99; trustee Music Hall Found.; mem. gala bd. Cancer Soc., 2003—. Mem. NASW, AAUW (v.p. 2002), DAR (Boston Tea Party chpt.), Alliance for Mentally Ill (pres. Orange County chpt. 1994-95), Phi Alpha Alpha, Gamma Phi Beta. Democrat. Presbyterian. Avocations: hiking, piano, reading, travel. Home: 1110 W 5830 N Saint George UT 84770-5944 Office: Desert Hills Therapeutic Svcs Troon Park Plz 1240 E 100 S Ste 18B Saint George UT 84790-3001

CHILSTROM, ROBERT MEADE, lawyer; b. San Diego, July 1, 1945; s. Arne Oswald and Margaret Myra (Kippax) C.; m. Buena Lelia Hamlin, Aug. 24, 1968; children: Per Benjamin, Mikaela Lynn. BA, Princeton U., 1967; MA, Columbia U., 1969; JD, Yale U., 1973. Bar: N.Y. State 1975, U.S. Dist. Ct. (so. dist., ea. dist.) N.Y. 1975, U.S. Ct. Appeals (2d cir.) 1975. Assoc. Cravath, Swaine & Moore, N.Y.C., Paris, London, 1973-85, Skadden, Arps, Slate, Meagher & Flom LLP, N.Y.C., 1985-87, ptnr., 1987—. Office: Skadden Arps Slate Meagher & Flom LLP Rm 31-100 4 Times Sq New York NY 10036-6595 E-mail: rchilstr@skadden.com.

CHILTON, BRADLEY STEWART, law educator, educator; b. Rockford, Ill., Oct. 28, 1955; s. Ermal Rural and Maybelle Rose (McNair) C.; m. Lisa Marie Hartmann, May 21, 1977. BA, Milton Coll., 1977; JD, U. Toledo, Ohio, 1980, MA, 1981, U. Wis., 1982; PhD, U. Ga., 1988; MLS, U. So. Miss., 1989. Instr. S.E. Mo. State U., Cape Girardeau, 1985-86; asst. prof. U. So. Miss., Hattiesburg, 1986-89, Wash. State U., Pullman, 1989-93; assoc. prof. U. Toledo, 1993-2000, U. North Tex., 2000—. Pre-law advisor U. Toledo, 1993—99; fellow Tex. Ctr. for Digital Knowledge, U. North Tex. Author: Prisons Under the Gavel, 1991. Recipient Ann. Dissertation award NASPAA, 1988. Mem. Acad. Criminal Justice Sci., Am. Polit. Sci. Assn., Am. Soc. Criminology, Am. Soc. Pub. Adminstrn. Avocations: music, home design and building, religion. Office: Criminal Justice Univ North Texas PO Box 305130 Denton TX 76203-5130

CHILTON, ELIZABETH EASLEY EARLY, newspaper executive; b. Williamson, W.Va., Dec. 9, 1928; d. Carl Brooks and Susie Mason (Easley) Early; m. William Edwin Chilton III, Apr. 5, 1952 (dec. Feb. 1987); 1 child, Susan Carroll Chilton Shumate. Student, Hollins Coll., Va., 1946-48; AA in Primary Edn., Marjorie Webster Coll., Washington, 1950. Pub. rels. staff The Charleston (W.Va.) Gazette, 1952-87; v.p., treas. Daily Gazette Co., Charleston, 1987-91, pres., 1991—, also dir., 1994—, chmn. bd. dirs. Mgmt. com. The Charleston Newspapers, 1991-99; adv. bd. Eberly Coll. Arts and Scis., 1996. Editl. bd. The Charleston Gazette, 1987—. Chmn. W.Va. Gov.'s Mansion Preservation Found., Charleston, 1989—; bd. trustees U. Charleston, 1989-98, Marshall U.-Yeager Scholars, Huntington, W.Va., 1990-96, W.Va. State Coll. Found., Inst., 1988-96, WSWP-TV Pub. Broadcasting, 1980-94, Faculty Merit Scholars, 1991—, W.Va. Humanities Coun., 1994-2000; bd. dirs. BIDCO, 1996-98, Advantage Valley, Charleston, 1996-98, Greater Kanawha Valley Found., 1980-86, adv. bd., 1986—; bd. dirs. Childrens Express, 1987—, Charleston Renaissance, 1995—, Washington, 1997—, Gunston Hall Plantation, 1977-92, pres., 1989-92; bd. dirs., exec. com. Worth Bingham Prize Found., 1987—; bd. dirs. Nat. Youth Sci. Found., 1998, trustee W.Va. U., 2000—, Sulgrave Manor Found., 2001; bd. dirs. Clay Ctr. for Arts and Scis., 1998—. Recipient John Marshall medal for civic responsibility, Marshall U., 1997, Pres. Disting. Svc. award, W.Va. U., 2000. Mem. So. Newspaper Pubs. (journalism edn. com.

1992-94, minority affairs com. 1994—), Nat. Soc. of Colonial Dames of W.Va. (pres.), Internat. Press Inst. (dir. Am. com. 1994—), Newspaper Assn. Am. (com. mem. 1987—), Nat. Trust for Historic Preservation, Garden Club of Am. (chmn. libr., bd. dirs. 1989-92), Jr. League of Charleston, Edgewood Country Club of Charleston, Yale Club of N.Y.C., Sulgrave Club of Washington, Briar Hills Garden Club, Kanawha Garden Club, Sea Pines Country Club of Hilton Head. Democrat. Presbyterian. Avocations: travel, reading, golf, gardening. Home: 806 Cedar Rd Charleston WV 25314-1206 Office: The Charleston Gazette 1001 Virginia St E Charleston WV 25301-2895

CHILTON, HORACE THOMAS, pipeline company executive; b. San Antonio, June 18, 1923; s. Horace Thomas and Lear Isabel (Word) C.; m. Betty Jane Gray, Oct. 18, 1947; children: Thomas G., William D. BS in Mech. Engring., BA in Bus. Adminstrn., U. Tex., 1947; grad., Advanced Mgmt. Program, Harvard U., 1958. Engr. Stanolind Pipe Line Co., Tulsa, 1947; div. chief engr. Service Pipe Line Co., Lubbock, 1950-52, supt. maintenance and constrn., 1956-60, asst. gen. mgr., 1960; mil. pipe line cons. U.S. Govt., Paris, 1955; mgr. products pipelines, lake tankers and barges Amoco Oil Co., Chgo., 1963-68; mgr. transp. ops., v.p. Amoco Pipeline, 1969-71, gen. mgr. transp., pres., chief exec. officer, 1971-74; pres., chief exec. officer Colonial Pipeline, Atlanta, 1974-88; retired, 1988. Mem. U. Tex. Engring. Advisory Found. Bd., 1977-85. Served with USN, 1944-46. Mem. Assn. Oil Pipe Lines (chmn. 1983-84), Am. Petroleum Inst. (bd. dirs. 1975-88), Nat. Petroleum Coun., Beta Theta Pi. Clubs: Cherokee Town and Country (Atlanta). Presbyterian. Home: 8920 River Landing Way Atlanta GA 30350-1620

CHILTON, WILLIAM DAVID, architect; b. Tulsa, Jan. 4, 1954; s. Horace Thomas Jr. and Betty Jane (Gray) C. BA in Architecture, Iowa State U., 1976; MArch, U. Minn., 1980. Registered arch., Mass.; Minn., Conn., Calif., Va., Tex., Okla., Wash., Oreg., D.C. Designer CDG, Tulsa, 1976; assoc. architect Olson-Coffey Architects, Tulsa, 1977-78, The Leonard Parker Assocs., Mpls., 1980-81; sr. architect Conoco, Inc., Ponca City, Okla., 1981-89; v.p., project mgr. Ellerbe Becket, Inc., Mpls., 1989, v.p., sr. project mgr., 1990, v.p., project dir., 1991-93, sr. v.p., project dir., 1994-98; dir. The Ellerbe Becket Co., Mpls., 1995-99, pres. arch., mng. prin., 1998-99, mem. mgmt. com., 1997-99; mng. prin. Pickard Chilton, New Haven, 1999—. Bd. dirs. Rainier Tech., Mpls., 1998-2001; mem. architecture adv. coun. Iowa State U., 1994-99, chair, 1997-98. Prin. works include as project designer Milne Point (Alaska) Ops. Complex (award Best of Engring. News Record, 1986, Excellence in Arch. award North Ctrl. Okla. chpt. AIA, 1987, Honorable Mention Builder mag., 1985), Conoco Corp. Offices, Wilmington, Del. (Excellence in Arch. award North Ctrl. Okla. chpt. AIA, 1987), Conoco Office/Housing Facilities, Luanda, Angola, 1985—88, prin. works include as mng. prin. Dow Chem. Corp. Hdqrs. Master Plan, Midland, Mich., 1991, Dow Chem. Global Data Ctr., 1992, Sci. Mus. Minn., St. Paul, 1991—99, Kingdom Centre, Riyadh, Saudi Arabia, 1996—2002, CalPERS Hdqrs., Sacramento, 1999—, AIM Corp. Hdqrs., Houston, 2000—, Colgate U. Case Libr. and Ctr. Info. Tech., Hamilton, N.Y., 2002—. Bd. dirs. Children's HeartLink, Mpls., 1997-99. Recipient Design Achievement award Iowa State U., 1995. Mem. Conn. Soc. AIA (sec. North Ctrl. Okla. chpt. 1986, v.p. 1987, pres. 1988, bd. dirs. 1986-88, bd. dirs. Okla. Coun. 1987-88), Leadership Mpls., Inst. Dirs. (London), Interlachen Country Club (Edina, Minn.), Mpls. Club. Lutheran. Avocations: fly fishing, golf, reading, music. Home: 452 E River Rd Guilford CT 06437-2289 Office: Pickard Chilton 980 Chapel St New Haven CT 06510-2045 E-mail: wchilton@pickardchilton.com.

CHILVERS, ROBERT MERRITT, lawyer; b. Long Beach, Calif., Oct. 23, 1942; s. James Merritt and Elizabeth Louise (Blackburn) C.; m. Sandra Lee Rigg, Sept. 5, 1969; children: Jeremy Merritt, Jessica Rigg. AB, U. Calif., Berkeley, 1972; JD, Harvard U., 1975. Bar: Calif. 1975, U.S. Dist. Ct. (no. dist.) Calif. 1975, U.S. Ct. Appeals (9th cir.) 1980, U.S. Supreme Ct. 1980, U.S. Dist. Ct. (ctrl. dist.) Calif. 1981, U.S. Ct. Fed. Claims, 1984, U.S. Dist. Ct. (ea. dist.) Calif. 1987, U.S. Ct. Appeals (fed. cir.) 1987, U.S. Dist. Ct. (no dist.) Calif. 2002. Assoc. Brobeck, Phleger & Harrison, San Francisco, 1975-82, ptnr., 1982-93; spl. master U.S. Dist. Ct. (no. dist.) Calif., 1994-99; pres. Chilvers & Taylor, PC, San Rafael, Calif., 1996—. Neutral evaluator and mediator in field, 2001—; faculty U. Calif. Hastings Sch. Law, San Francisco, 1983-89, Emory U., Atlanta, 1984-90, fed. practice program U.S. Dist. Ct. (no. dist.) Calif., 1984-86, Nat. Inst. for Trial Advocacy, 1986—, Cardozo Law Sch., Yeshiva U., N.Y.C., 1993-99, Stanford U. Law Sch., 1994—, Widener U. Sch. Law, Wilmington, 1994-96, U. San Francisco Sch. Law, 1994—. Mem. Calif. Sch. Bds. Assn., 1985—89; trustee Mill Valley Sch. Dist., Calif., 1985—89, chmn., 1987—89; bd. dirs. Marin County Sch. Bds. Assn., Calif., 1985—86, Artisans, Mill Valley, Calif., 1999—2001. With USMC, 1964—71. Mem. Calif. Bar Assn. (commendation for Outstanding Contbns. to the delivery of vol. legal svcs. 1984), Marin County Bar Assn., Tau Beta Pi, Sigma Tau. Office: Chilvers & Taylor PC 83 Vista Marin Dr San Rafael CA 94903-5228

CHIMA, FELIX O. social work educator; b. Aba, Imo, Nigeria, Oct. 10, 1953; came to U.S., 1976; s. Akposioha Okoye and Mkpokwo (Mercy) Onwubuariri; children: Christopher, Jerry Chike, Nena Jesica. BA in Bus. Adminstrn., Midland Luth. Coll., 1979; MBA, Atlanta U., 1981; MSW, Clark Atlanta U., 1988, PhD in Social Work Adminstrn., 1992. Sales mgr. Assoc. Industries, Aba, Imo, Nigeria, 1973-76; prodn. supr. Campbell Soup Co., Fremont, Nebr., 1976-79; account mgr. Greyhound Lines, Inc., Atlanta, 1979-84; rsch. asst. Atlanta U., 1984-87; prin. social worker City of Atlanta, 1987-90, dir. human svcs., 1990-93; prof. U. Ky., Lexington, 1993-99, Prairie View A&M U. Tex., 1999—. Ombudsman Tex. Dept. Aging. Contbr. articles to profl. jours. Bd. dirs. foster rev. Commonwealth of Ky., Lexington, 1995-99, cons. child welfare advocacy, 1994-99. Mem. NASW, Ky. Assn. Social Workers. Home: 13522 White Cliff Dr Houston TX 77065-3770

CHIMPLES, GEORGE, lawyer; b. Canton, Ohio, Oct. 8, 1924; s. Mark and Katherine (Hines) C.; m. Eileen Mary Grumm, July 14, 2003; children: Alicia Candace, Mark II, John Hines, Katherine Hines. AB, Princeton U., 1951; LLB, Harvard Coll., 1954. Bar: Pa. 1955, U.S. Dist. Ct. (ea. dist.) Pa. 1955, U.S. Ct. Appeals (3d cir.) 1955, U.S. Ct. Claims, 1965, U.S. Tax Ct., 1965. Assoc. Stradley, Ronon, Stevens & Young, Phila., 1954-61, gen. ptnr., 1961-92; pvt. practice Wayne, Pa., 1993—. Adj. prof. law U. Pa., Drexel U. Grad. Sch. Bus.; co-authored establishment of overseas infrastructure for securities mktg. in Europe and the Antilles. Trustee Christ Ch. Preservation Trust; permanent assoc. Phila. Mus. Art.; founding mem. Duxford (Eng.) Air Mus. Capt. USAAF, 1942-46, ETO. Decorated D.F.C., Air medal with four oak leaf clusters, Air Force Commendation medal, Victory medal, four Battle Stars; recipient Royal Air Force plaque, 1994. Mem. ABA (chmn. subcom. regulated investment cos.), Phila. Bar Assn. (tax sect.), Internat. Bar Assn., Internat. Fiscal Assn. (tax treaty sect.), Mid-Atlantic Coun., Newcomen Soc. U.S. (trustee emeritus, life mem.) Army and Navy Club (Washington chpt.), Penn Club (life, bd. dirs., historian) Athenaeum of Phila. (life), Libr. Co. of Phila. (life), Phila. Mus. Art (permanent assoc.), Phila. Club, Cannon Club (Princeton chpt.), Torresdale-Frankford Country Club. Home and Office: 1522 Overington St Philadelphia PA 19124-5808

CHIMSKY, MARK EVAN, publishing consultant; b. Cin., Jan. 24, 1955; s. Matthew and Jean (Berger) C.; life ptnr. Robert Ira Lustig. BA, Carnegie-Mellon U., 1976. Editor Anderson Pub. Co., Cin., 1977-79; copy editor Book-of-the-Month Club, Quality Paperback Book Club, N.Y.C., 1979-85; mng. editor Quality Paperback Book Club, N.Y.C., 1985-89, exec. editor, 1989-91; editor in chief Collier Books Macmillan Co., N.Y.C., 1991-94; dir. trade paperbacks Little, Brown and Co., N.Y.C., 1994-96; from exec. editor to editl. dir. Harper, San Francisco, 1996-98, exec. editor, 1998-99; editl. cons. Mark Chimsky Editl. Plus, Riverdale, N.Y., 1999—. Adj. instr. NYU, N.Y.C., 1999—; dir. NYU Summer Pub. Inst., N.Y.C., 2000, N.Y.C., 03. Contbr. essays and poetry to lit. jours. including Jour. AMA. Recipient New-Emerging Poet/Anna Davidson Rosenberg award, 1997. Office: Mark Chimsky Editorial Plus PO Box 630207 Riverdale NY 10463-0802

CHIN, ALLEN E., SR., athletic administrator, educator; b. Arlington, Va., Oct. 21, 1950; s. Tung Ock and Hai Ock (Moy) C.; children: Allen Jr., Denise Maria Michelle. BA, George Washington U., 1972, MA, 1974, EdD, 1980. Cert. secondary social studies educator, D.C. Tchr. D.C. Pub. Schs., Washington, 1972-87, 88-91, dir. athletics, 1987-88, 91—. Exec. cons. D.C. Coaches Assn., Inc., Washington, 1988—; exec. dir. AEC-10 Found., Inc., Washington, 1988—. Mem. Jefferson Club, Richmond, Va., 1990-91, Dem. Nat. Com., Washington, 1984—, Dem. Senatorial Campaign Com., Washington, 1984—. Named Athletic Dir. of Yr., NHSACA Region 2, 1995—98; recipient Coach of Yr. award, 1986, 1987, 1988, Disting. Svc. award, NHSACA, 1998. Mem.: Am. Soc. Notaries, Nat. Interscholastic Athletic Adminstrs. Assn., Nat. Coun. for Social Studies, D.C. Coun. for Social Studies, D.C. Coaches Assn. (Hall of Fame 2002), Nat. Geog. Soc., Met. Police Boys & Girls Clubs. Democrat. Avocations: stamp and coin collecting, golf. Home: 6150 Windward Dr Burke VA 22015-3832 Office: Hamilton Sch 1401 Brentwood Pky NE Washington DC 20002 E-mail: aecdciaa@hotmail.com.

CHIN, BARBARA, massage therapist; b. Watsonville, Calif., Aug. 17, 1948; d. Joseph Ock Ngon Chin and Poy Jean Wong; m. Kent Tanaka, Aug. 12, 1972 (div. 1979); m. Stanley Yorke, Aug. 1989 (div. 1994). AS, Cabrillo Coll., 1968. Lic. massage therapist, Hawaii. Owner Holistic Healing Hands, Fresno, Calif., Kihei, Hawaii, 1969—. Vacation rental agt. Chin Accommodations, 1989—. Mem.: Internat. Massage Assn. Avocations: swimming, weight lifting, yoga, tai chi, qi gong. Office: Holistic Healing Hands 2050 Kanoe Ste 104 Kihei HI 96753 E-mail: barbchin@maui.net.

CHIN, CECILIA HUI-HSIN, librarian; b. Tientsin, China; came to U.S., 1961; d. Yu-lin and Ti-yu (Fan) C. BA, Nat. Taiwan U., Taipei, 1961; MSL.S., U. Ill., 1963. Cataloger, reference librarian Roosevelt U., Chgo., 1963; reference librarian, indexer Ryerson & Burnham Libraries, Art Inst. Chgo., 1963-70, head reference dept. indexer, 1970-75; acting dir. libraries Art Inst. Chgo., 1976-77, assoc. librarian, head reference dept., 1975-82; chief librarian Smithsonian Am. Art Mus. and Nat. Portrait Gallery, Smithsonian Inst., Washington, 1982—. Compiler: The Art Institute of Chicago Index to Art Periodicals, 1975 Recipient awards, Nat. Portrait Gallery, Smithsonian Instn., 1984, 1989, Smithsonian Instn. Libr., 2001. Mem. Art Librs. Soc., D.C. Libr. Assn., Washington Rare Book Group. Office: 750 9th St # 2100 Washington DC 20560-0975 Fax: 202-275-1929. E-mail: chinc@si.edu.

CHIN, CHEN OOI, dean; b. Singapore; arrived in U.S., 1972; d. Sat-kai Chin and Piang-keow Lee; m. Charles Hsieh, Oct. 15, 1972; 1 child, Chih-Mao Hsieh. BA, Nat. Taiwan U., 1964, MA, 1966, Yale U., 1968; PhD, Ohio State U., 1976. Lectr. U. Singapore, 1968—72; asst. prof. U. Detroit, 1974—77; exec. dir. Chinese Am. Edn. and Cultural Ctr. of Mich., Ann Arbor, 1976—; adj. prof. Lawrence Technol. U., Southfield, Mich., 2000—; dean Ctr. for Cultural Diversity, Singapore, 2001—. Cons. Prudential, Chgo., 1999—, Internat. Oriental Resources, Chgo., 1999—, Berlitz Internat., Inc., NJ, 1999—, GMAC, Mich., 1999—. Prodr.(editor): (video) Twelve Years of Harvest, 1988. Asian Found. grantee, 1963—66, Fulbright-Hayes grantee, Malaysia, 1966, NEA grantee, 1977—94. Mem.: Acad. of Mgmt. Office: Chinese Am Ednl & Cultural Ctr 296 W Eisenhower Ann Arbor MI 48104 Home: 1826 Glenwood Ann Arbor MI 48104

CHIN, DAVIS, lawyer; b. Evansville, Ind., Dec. 13, 1947; s. Frank S. M. and Mamie (Shu) C.; m. Pauline C., Aug. 3, 1974; 1 child, Davis M. BS, Rose-Hulman Inst. Tech., Terre Haute, Ind., 1969; JD, U. Balt., 1974; LLM in Taxation, John Marshall Law Sch., 1981. Bar: Ill. 1974, U.S. Dist. Ct. (no. dist.) 1974, U.S. Ct. Appeals (7th cir.) 1974, U.S. Patent and Trademark Office 1974, U.S. Claims Ct. 1977, U. S. Tax Ct. 1977, U.S. Supreme Ct. 1977, U.S. Ct. Appeals (fed. cir.) 1982. Staff atty. CTS Corp., Elkhart, Ind., 1974; assoc. Petherbridge, Lindgren & Gilhooly, Chtd., Chgo., 1974-78; staff atty. Borg-Warner Corp., Chgo., 1978-80, Container Corp. Am., Chgo., 1980-84; pvt. practice Chgo., 1984—. Instr. Prairie State Coll., Chgo. Heights, 1987-90, 94, South Suburban Coll., South Holland, Ill., 1989-91, Research U., Olympia Fields, Ill., 1990-93. Elder United Presbyn. Ch., South Holland, 1986—; panel program atty. Chgo. Vol. Legal Svcs., 1988—. Mem. Am. Intellectual Property Law Assn., Chgo. Bar Assn., Intellectual Property Law Assn. Chgo., Patent Law Assn. Chgo. (bd. mgrs. 1985-87, 94-96). Avocations: tennis, golf, travel. Home: 11428 Plattner Dr Mokena IL 60448-9228 Office: 16061 S 94th Ave Tinley Park IL 60477-4623 E-mail: davischin@juno.com.

CHIN, DER-TAU, chemical engineer, educator; b. Zhejiang, China, Sept. 14, 1939; came to U.S., 1963, naturalized, 1977; s. Tsu-Kang and Shou-Chen (Chen) C.; m. Lorna Fe Gencianeo, July 17, 1971; children: Janet G., Lynn G. BSChemE, Chungyuan Coll. Sci. & Engring, 1962; MSChemE, Tufts U., 1965; PhD in Chem. Engring., U. Pa., 1969. Plant engr. Lungyen Sugar Factory, 1962-63; sci. programmer USAF Cambridge (Mass.) Rsch. Lab., Lexington, Mass., 1965; sr. rsch. engr. rsch. labs. GM Corp., Warren, Mich., 1969-75; prof. Clarkson U., Potsdam, N.Y., 1975—. Vis. scientist Brookhaven Nat. Lab., Upton, N.Y., summers 1977, 80, U.S. Army Belvoir Research Devel. Ctr., Ft. Belvoir, Va., summer 1985, U.S. Army Electronics Tech. and Devices Lab., Ft. Mammouth, N.J., summer, 1986, Armstrong Lab. Tyndall Air Force Base, Fla., summer 1995; vis. prof. U. Calif., Berkeley, 1981, Swiss Fed. Inst. Tech., Zurich, 1981, Nat. U. Singapore, 1982, 87, Nat. Tsing Hua UNI, 1989, King Fahd U. Petroleum and Minerals, Dhahran, Saudi Arabia, 2000-2001; cons. Centro de Pesquisas do Energia Electrica, Rio de Janiero, Brazil, summer 1979. Fellow Electrochem. Soc. (Young Authors award 1971); mem. AIChE, Am. Electroplaters Soc., Am. Chem. Soc. Office: Clarkson U PO Box 5705 Potsdam NY 13699-5705 E-mail: chin@clarkson.edu.

CHIN, JAMES YING, corporate executive; b. N.Y.C., Nov. 22, 1953; s. Bing Fon and Mung King (Chew) C.; m. Randy-Jo Gensler, June 28, 1981; children: Chelsea Ivy, Madeleine Rose. AAS, Queensborough Community Coll., Queens, N.Y, 1973; BS cum laude, U. Md., 1990. Customer engr. IBM, Bklyn., 1973—83, systems ctr. rep. Gaithersburg, Md., 1983—86, field mgr. Reston, Va., 1986—89, area tag mgr. McLean, Va., 1989—91, adv. info. systems analyst Bethesda, Md., 1991—92, mgr. billing and shipments devel., 1992—93, svc. billing contract mgr., 1993—94, systems assurance, 1994—95, project exec., 1995—96, mgr. Process, Techniques and Tools Initiative Ctr., 1996—97, mgr. quality assurance, program advisor, 1997—99, quality assurance program mgr. Gaithersburg, 1999—2000, sr. quality assurance mgr. pub. sector, 2000—03, risk mgmt. ptnr., 2003—. Mem. Montgomery Co. citizen acad. alumni assn. Mem. Phi Kappa Phi, Alpha Sigma Lambda. Democrat. Avocations: golf, tennis, literature, deep sea fishing, softball. Office: IBM 6710 Rockledge Dr Bethesda MD 20817 E-mail: jimchin@us.ibm.com.

CHIN, JANET SAU-YING, data processing executive, consultant; b. Hong Kong, July 27, 1949; came to U.S., 1959; d. Arthur Quock-Ming and Jenny (Loo) C. BS in Math, U. Ill., Chgo., 1970; MS in Computer Sci., U. Ill., Urbana, 1973. Sys. programmer Lawrence Livermore (Calif.) Lab., 1972-79; sect. mgr. Tymshare Inc., Cupertino, Calif., 1979-83, Fortune Systems, Redwood City, Calif., 1983-85; div. mgr. Impell Corp, Berkeley, Calif., 1985; pres. Chin Assocs., Oakland, Calif., 1985-88; bus. devel. mgr. Sun Microsystems, Mountain View, Calif., 1988-92; engring. dir. Cadence Design Systems, San Jose, Calif., 1992-94; quality dir. Cadence Design Sys., San Jose, Calif., 1994-95; asst. to CEO, Avant! Corp., Fremont, Calif., 1995-99; provost World Inst. Tech., Fremont, Calif., 1996-98; cons. Second Resource, Oakland, 2000—. Vice-chmn. Am. Nat. Standards Inst. X3H3, N.Y.C., 1979-82, internat. rep. X3H3, 1982-88. Co-author: The Computer Graphics Interface, 1991; contbr. tech. papers to profl. publs. Mem. Assn. Computing Machinery, Sigma Xi. Avocations: Karate, iaido, taiko, science fiction/fantasy, piano. E-mail: barronchin@earthlink.net.

CHIN, JENNIFER YOUNG, public health educator; b. Honolulu, June 22, 1946; d. Michael W.T. and Sylvia (Ching) Young; m. Benny Chin, Nov. 16, 1975; children: Kenneth Michael, Lauren Marie, Catherine Rose. BA, San Francisco State Coll., 1969; M.P.H., U. Calif., Berkeley, 1971. Edn. asst. Am. Cancer Soc., San Francisco, 1969-70; intern Luth. Med. Ctr., Bklyn., 1971; cmty. health educator Md. Dept. Healht and Mental Hygiene, Balt., 1971-74, N.E. Med. Svcs., San Francisco, 1975; pub. health educator Child Health and Disability Prevention San Francisco Pub. Health Dept., 1975-83; health educator maternal and child health, 1991-95; health educator Breast and Cervical Cancer Control Program, 1995—2000. Grantee USPHS, 1970-71. Mem. Am. Pub. Health Assn., Soc. No. Calif. Pub. Health Edn. (treas. 1976, 77).

CHIN, KATHERINE MOY, nutritionist, consultant; b. Washington, Apr. 13; d. David Chee Nie and Mary Ng Juie (Hie) Moy; m. Calvin Chin, Oct. 7, 1951; 1 child, Stephanie Anne Chung. BS, U. Md., College Park, 1951. Registered dietitian Md., lic. nutritionist Md. Clin. dietitian Johns Hopkins Hosp., Balt., 1954; instr. nutrition, dietetics Sch. Nursing Johns Hopkins Hosp., Balt., 1955—68; owner Chinese Gourmet Restaurant, Balt., 1980—83; nutrition edn. and tng. specialist Balt. County Pub. Sch., Md., 1983—98; partnership specialist Bur. Census Dept. Commerce, Balt., 1999—2000. Bi-lingual interpreter for Cantonese speaking students Balt. County Pub. Schs., 1983—; commr. Asian-Pacific Am. Adv. Coun., Md., 1997—; instr. chinese cooking sch. The Internat. Gourmet Ctr., 1969—79. Coord., fundraiser Asian Cmty., Balt., 1960; lay reader ch. Mem.: Towson U. Asian Arts/Culture Ctr., Balt. Asian Trade Coun. (chairperson 1968—), Am. Dietetic Assn., AAUW, Md. Sch. Food Svc. Assn. (pres. 1984—86), Md. Dietetic Assn. (pres. 1968—70). Democrat. Episcopalian. Avocations: travel, reading, music, volunteering. Home: Unit 208 4100 N Charles St Baltimore MD 21218 Office: Balt Asian Trade Coun 4100 N Charles St Unit 208 Baltimore MD 21218

CHIN, KHEW-VOON, medical educator; b. Perak, Malaysia, Dec. 2, 1958; s. Kwong-See Chin and Peng-Koon Teng; children: Andrew Jian-Bing, Jeffrey Jian-Wen. BA, Wittenberg U., 1983; PhD, Rutgers U., 1987. Fogarty postdoctoral fellow Nat. Cancer Inst., Bethesda, Md., 1988—91; asst. prof. U. Tex., Houston, 1991—93; asst. prof. Robert Wood Johnson Med. Sch., The Cancer Inst. N.J. UMDNJ, Piscataway, 1993—2002, dir. DNA microarray facility Robert Wood Johnson Med. Sch., The Cancer Inst. N.J., 1999—2002; assoc. rsch. prof. Rutgers U., Piscataway, 2002—. Cons. Bio Clues and Solutions, Inc., Seoul, Republic of Korea, 2001—02. Contbr. articles to profl. jours. Achievements include research in phospholipid transfer protein (PLTP) and cholesterol metabolism; nucleic acid and protein expressed thereby and their involvement in stress; first to study of drug resistance in cancer. Office: Rutgers University 164 Frelinghuysen Rd Piscataway NJ 08854

CHIN, LLEWELLYN PHILIP, lawyer; b. Saigon-Cholon, Vietnam, 1957; s. Thomas and Kim C. AA, Glendale (Calif.) Coll., 1980; BS, U. So. Calif., L.A., 1982; JD, Columbia U., 1986. Bar: Calif. 1988, U.S. Dist. Ct. (cen. dist.) Calif. 1988, U.S. Ct. Appeals (9th cir.) 1988. Sr. counsel Calif. Assn. of Realtors, L.A., 1989—. Polit. cons. Robert Kwan for Alhambra Sch. Bd., Monterey Park, Calif., 1990, bus. cons. Larry L. Berg, Inc., L.A., 1986-88; legal advisor L.A. chpt. Chinese Consol. Benevolent Assn., Elderly Indo-Chinese Assn.; adj. prof. Southwestern U. Sch. Law, summer 1995, Loyola Law Sch., 1996; speaker in field. Columnist L.A. County Bar Real Property Newsletter; contbr. articles to profl. jours. Bd. dirs. Chinese-Am. Polit. Action Com., Alhambra, 1986-93, Golden Tours, Alhambra, 1993; candidate Alhambra City Coun., 1992; pres. Chinese Am. Edn. Assn., Monterey Park, 1994-95; bd. dirs. San Gabriel Valley YMCA, 1995-97; planning commr. City of Alhambra, 1995-99; commr. L.A. County Local Govtl. Svcs., 1995-97; commr. State Bd. Dental Examiners, 1998—2001. Beren Found. scholar, 1983-86, Harlan Fisk Stone scholar, 1986. Mem. ABA (chair home improvements, constrn. and purchase and sale of residential real estate subcom. 1992-2001, vice chair real estate brokerage subcom. 1998-2001), L.A. County Bar Assn. (disaster relief com., corp. counsel, elderline, continuing edn. com., gen. real property subsect. steering com.), Calif. Trial Lawyers Assn., So. Calif. Chinese Lawyers Assn., Calif. State Bar (co-chair sales and brokerage subsect. real property sect., 1993-96, 98—2001, cons. real property sect. 1993-96, continuing edn. of the bar com. 1992-95), Chinese Am. Real Estate Profls. So. Calif. (bd. dirs.), Alhambra C. of C. (legis. com., chair anti-graffiti task force 1993-94). Avocations: reading, stamp and coin collecting, organizing political events, hiking. Office: Calif Assn Realtors 525 S Virgil Ave Los Angeles CA 90020-1403

CHIN, MING, state supreme court justice; b. Klamath Falls, Oreg., Aug. 31, 1942; m. Carol Lynn Joe, Dec. 19, 1971; children: Jennifer, Jason. BA in Polit. Sci., U. San Francisco, 1964, JD, 1967. Bar: Calif. 1970, U.S. Fed. Ct., U.S. Tax Ct. Assoc., head trial dept. Aiken, Kramer & Cummings, Oakland, Calif., 1973—76, prin., 1976—88; dep. dist. atty. Alameda County, Calif., 1970—72; judge Alameda County Superior Ct., 1988—90; assoc. justice divsn. 3 Ct. Appeal 1st Dist., 1990—94; presiding justice 1st Dist. Ct. Appeal Divsn. 3, San Francisco, 1994—96; state supreme ct. assoc. justice Calif. Supreme Ct., San Francisco, 1996—. Capt. U.S. Army, 1967—69, Vietnam, Capt. USAR, 1969—71. Mem.: ABA, Asian Am. Bar Assn., San Francisco Dist. Atty.'s Commn. Hate Crimes, Alameda County Bar Assn., State Bar Calif., Calif. Judges Assn., Commonwealth Club of Calif. (pres. 1998), Alpha Sigma Nu. Office: Supreme Court Calif 350 Mcallister St Fl 1 San Francisco CA 94102-4783

CHIN, NEE OO WONG, reproductive endocrinologist; b. Hong Kong, Nov. 27, 1955; came to U.S., 1958; s. Bing Leong and Din Sui (Gee) C.; m. Shelly Loraine Crumrine, June 25, 1977; children: Jason Lei, Taryn Mae. BA, U. Cin., 1977; MD, Ohio State U., 1981. Diplomate Am. Bd. Ob-Gyn. Resident Duke U. Med. Ctr., Durham, N.C., 1981-84, chief resident, 1984-85; fellow Ohio State U. Coll. Medicine, Columbus, Ohio, 1985-87; teaching staff Good Samaritan Hosp., Cin., 1987—; clin. asst. prof. U. Cin. Med. Ctr., 1987—; dir. assisted reproductive techs. The Christ Hosp., Cin., 1992—. Mem. High Sch. for the Health Profl. subcom., Cin., 1989—. Author: (with others) Current Therapy in Obstetrics, 1988; contbr. articles to profl. jours. Named to Honorable Order of Ky. Cols., Gov. Martha Collins of Ky., 1987. Fellow Am. Coll. Ob-Gyn.; mem. AAAS, Am. Fertility Soc., Soc. Assisted Reproductive Tech., Soc. for Immunology Repro., Cin. Ob-Gyn. Soc. (med. malpractice com. 1989—), Acad. Medicine Cin. Avocations: tennis, Karate. Office: Ste 220 11503 Spring Field Pike Cincinnati OH 45246-3550

CHIN, SUE SOONE MARIAN (SUCHIN CHIN), conceptual artist, portraitist, photographer, community affairs activist; b. San Francisco; d. William W. and Soo-Up (Swebe) C. Grad., Calif. Coll. Art, Mpls. Arts Inst.; scholar, Schaeffer Design Ctr.; student, Yasuo Kuniyoshi, Louis Hamon, Rico LeBrun. Photojournalist All Together Now Show, 1973, East-West News, Third World Newscasting, 1975-78, Sta. KNBC Sunday Show, L.A., 1975, 76, Live on 4, 1981, Bay Area Scene, 1981. Chmn. Full Moon Products; pres., bd. dirs. Aumni Oracle Inc. Graphics printer, exhbns. include: Kaiser Ctr., Zellerbach Pla., Chinese Culture Ctr. Galleries, Capricorn Asunder Art Commn. Gallery (all San Francisco), Newspace Galleries, New Coll. of Calif., L.A. County Mus. Art, Peace Pla. Japan Ctr., Congress Arts Comm., Washington, 1989; SFWA Galleries, Inner Focus Show, 1989—, Calif. Mus. Sci. and Industry, Lucien Labaudt Gallery, Salon de Medici, Madrid, Salon Renacimento, Madrid, 1995, Life is a Circus, SFWA Gallery, 1991, 94, UN/50 Exhibit, Bayfront Galleries, 1995, Somar Galleries, 1997, 2003 (Merit award 2003), Sacramento State Fair, 2000, Star Child, Women thru the Ages - Somarts Gallery, 2000, AFL-CIO Labor Studies Ctr., Washington, Asian Women Artists (1st prize for conceptual painting, 1st prize photography), 1978, Yerba Buena Arts Ctr. for the Arts Festival, 1994; represented in permanent collections L.A. County Fedn. Labor, Calif. Mus. Sci. and Industry, AFL-CIO Labor Studies Ctr., Australian Trades Coun., Hazeland and Co., also pvt. collections; author: (poetry) Yuri and Malcolm, The Desert Sun, 1994 (Editors Choice award 1993-94). Del. nat., state convs. Nat. Women's Polit. Caucus, 1977-83, San Francisco chpt. affirmative action chairperson, 1978-82, nat. conv. del., 1978-81, Calif. del., 1976-81. Recipient Honorarium AFL-CIO Labor Studies Ctr., Washington, 1975-76, Bicentennial award 1976; award Centro Studi Ricerche delle Nazioni, Italy, 1985; bd. advisors Psycho Neurology Found. Bicentennial award L.A. County Mus. Art, 1976, 77, 78. Mem. Asian Women Artists (founding v.p., award 1978-79, 1st award in photography of Orient 1978-79, Merit award 2003), Calif. Chinese Artists (sec.-treas. 1978-81), Japanese Am. Art Coun. (chairperson 1978-84, dir.), San Francisco Women Artists, San Francisco Graphics Guild, Pacific/Asian Women Coalition Bay Area, Chinatown Coun. Performing and Visual Arts. Address: PO Box 421415 San Francisco CA 94142-1415

CHIN, SYLVIA FUNG, lawyer; b. N.Y.C., June 27, 1949; d. Thomas and Constance (Yao) Fung; m. Edward G.H. Chin, July 10, 1971; children: Arthur F., Benjamin F. BA, NYU, 1971; JD, Fordham U., 1977. Bar: N.Y. 1978, U.S. Dist. Ct. (so. and ea. dists.) N.Y. 1979, U.S. Supreme Ct. 1990. Law clk. to dist. judge U.S. Dist. Ct. (so. dist.), N.Y.C., 1977-79; assoc. White & Case, N.Y.C., 1979-86, ptnr., 1986—. Adj. assoc. prof. law Fordham U., N.Y.C., 1979-81. Mem. editl. bd.: Bus. Law Today, 1996—2002; contbr. articles to profl. jours. Mem.: ABA, Am. Coll. Comml. Fin. Lawyers, Am. Coll. Investment Counsel

(bd. dirs. 1999—, pres. 2002—03), Nat. Asian Pacific ABA (treas. 1997—98), Women's World Banking (bd. dirs.), Asian Am. Bar Assn. N.Y. (bd. dirs. 1991—97, pres. 1994—96), N.Y. County Lawyers Assn., Assn. Bar City N.Y., AABANY Found. (treas.), Fordham Law Alumni Assn. (bd. dirs.). Office: White & Case LLP 1155 Ave of Americas New York NY 10036-2711

CHIN, WAYMAN, musician, educator; b. Boston, Mass., Dec. 15, 1958; s. Tim and Lorraine Chin. MusB cum laude, U. of Hartford, 1980; MusM, Yale U., 1983. Artist faculty Yellow Barn Music Sch. and Festival, Putney, Vt., 1987—98, chmn. chamber music program; mem. faculty piano, collaborative piano, modern Am. music depts. Longy Sch. of Music, Cambridge, Mass., 1994—. Peer reviewer merit aid funding Mass. Cultural Coun., 1988—92; vis. lectr. Coll. Visual and Performing Arts U. Mass., Dartmouth, 1988—; performer premieres of new works by composers Aaron Jay Kernis, Meyer Kupeferman and Paul Brust; solo pianist, chamber musician recitals as solo pianist and chamber musician throughout the U.S., Asia, and Italy; master class tours, concerts, Philippines, 1998. Contbr. articles to mags. Recipient Catherine S. Winchell Meml. scholarship, as outstanding maj. in pianoforte playing, Yale U. Sch. of Music, 1982, Dr. and Mrs. Maurice F. O'Connell scholarship, Hartt Sch., U. of Hartford, 1976—80, 1976—80, Ellen Battell Stoeckel fellowship for chamber music study, Yale Summer Sch. of Music and Art, 1983. Mem.: Alpha Chi, Pi Kappa Lambda. Office: Longy Sch Music One Follen St Cambridge MA 02138 Personal E-mail: wchin58@yahoo.com.

CHINA, NICK See DYBMAN, NICK NISON

CHINARD, FRANCIS PIERRE, physiologist, physician, consultant; b. Berkeley, Calif., June 30, 1918; s. Gilbert and Emma (Blanchard) C.; m. Josephine L. Wise, June 23, 1943; children: Suzanne F., Jeanne M., Marc F. AB, U. Calif., Berkeley, 1937; MD, Johns Hopkins U., 1941. Intern, jr. asst. resident in medicine Presbyn. Hosp., N.Y.C., 1941-42; asst. physician Hosp. Rockefeller Inst., N.Y.C., 1945-49; instr. to asso. prof. medicine and physiol. chemistry Johns Hopkins Sch. Med., Balt., 1949-54; asst. prof. medicine U. Md., 1954-62, asso. prof., 1962-63; physician Johns Hopkins Hosp., 1956-63; prof. exptl. medicine, dep. dir. med. clinic McGill U., Can., 1963-64; prof. medicine NYU, 1964-68, adj. prof., 1968-70; career scientist N.Y.C. Health Research Council, 1964-68; prof. medicine, chmn. dept. U. Medicine and Dentistry N.J., Newark, 1968-75, prof. exptl. medicine, 1975-77, prof. research medicine, 1977—, prof. physiology, 1978—, Disting. prof., 1989—, emeritus, 1996; physician-in-chief Balt. City Hosp., 1962-63; acting physician-in-chief Goldwater Meml. Hosp., N.Y.C., 1965-67; dir. med. service Martland Hosp., Newark, 1970-71; cons. physician VA Hosp., East Orange, N.J., 1971-79, 93-95. Mem. staff Balt. City Hosps., 1953-63; cons. in field; pres. Faculty Practice Svc. Corp., N.J. Med. Sch., 1986-88; vis. scientist Med. Rsch. Coun. Can., McGill U., Montreal, 1989-90. Author: (With J.W. Bauman Jr.) Renal Function, 1975; editorial com.: Jour. Clin. Investigation, 1954-59, Jour. Applied Physiology, 1959-65, Am. Jour. Physiology, 1959-65, Circulation Research, 1967-72, Microvascular Research, 1981-89, Revue française des Maladies respiratoires, 1979-93, clin. and investigative medicine, 1985-96; contbr. articles on indicator-dilution techniques, membrane permeability and transport, pulmonary, renal function, free radicals and history of medicine and physiology to med. jours. Mem. profl. adv. com. Martha's Vineyard Guidance Center, 1968-75; mem. pulmonary disease adv. com. Nat. Heart and Lung Inst., 1971-75, chmn., 1974-75, mem. bd. sci. counselors, 1976-80, chmn., 1978-80. Served to maj. M.C. USAAF, 1942-45. Decorated Legion of Merit; recipient Lucian award McGill U., 1989, Sir William Osler Humanitarian award N.J. Thoracic Soc., 1991, Laureate award N.J. chpt. Am. Coll. Physicians, 1993, Charles L. Brown award Alumni Assn. N.J. Med. Sch. Fellow ACP, N.Y. Acad. Scis., AAAS; mem. Am. Chem. Soc., Am. Soc. Biochemistry and Molecular Biology, Am., Canadian socs. clin. investigation, Harvey Soc., Interurban Clin. Club, Soc. Exptl. Biology and Medicine, Assn. Am. Physicians, Am. Physiol. Soc., Peripatetic Soc., Acad. Medicine N.J. (trustee 1972-78), Am. Heart Assn. (research com. N.J. affiliate 1975-81), Inst Français Washington (trustee 1994—), Microcirculatory Soc. (Landis award), Am. Thoracic Soc., Soc. Scholars (Johns Hopkins), N.Y. Clinical Soc., Med. History Soc. N.J. (pres. 1984-86), Am. Assn. History of Medicine (councilor), Century Assn. Club (N.Y.C.), Charaka Club, Paris-Am. Club (N.Y.C.), Sigma Xi, Alpha Omega Alpha. Democrat. Office: 40 Warren Pl Montclair NJ 07042-2534 E-mail: chinard@umdnj.edu.

CHIN-BING, STANLEY ARTHUR, physicist, educator; b. New Orleans, La., Nov. 3, 1942; s. Arthur Joseph Chin-Bing and Adele Viola Peavy; m. Hilda Faye Taylor, Aug. 12, 1995 (dec. Aug. 12, 1997). BS, Tulane U., 1964; MS, U. New Orleans, 1966, PhD, 1973. Spl. lectr. U. New Orleans, 1973, asst. prof. of engring., 1975—79, adj. prof. of physics, 1988—; sys. analyst Martin Marietta Corp., New Orleans, 1974—75; advanced systems sr. engr. space divsn. Chrysler Corp., New Orleans, 1976—77; rsch. physicist Naval Ocean R & D Activity, Bay St. Louis, Miss., 1978—88; supervisory rsch. physicist Naval Oceanog. and Atmospheric Rsch. Lab., Bay St. Louis, 1988—92; head, acoustic simulation, measurements and tactics br. Naval Rsch. Lab., Stennis Space Center, Miss., 1992—. Contbr. more than 40 articles to sci. jours.; author: Procs. of Parabolic Equation Workshop II. Fellow: Acoustical Soc. Am. (assoc. editor 1996—2003); mem.: AAAS, Soc. Indsl. and Applied Mathematicians, NY Acad. of Sciences, Math. Assn. of Am., IEEE Ocean Engring. Soc., Am. Assn. of Physics Teachers, Optical Soc. of Am., Am. Phys. Soc., Sigma Pi Sigma. Home: 3619 Bauvais St Metairie LA 70001-5005 Office: Naval Rsch Lab 1005 Balch Blvd Stennis Space Center MS 39529-5004 Office Fax: 228-688-5049. E-mail: chinbing@nrlssc.navy.mil.

CHINCHINIAN, HARRY, pathologist, educator; b. Troy, N.Y., Mar. 7, 1926; s. Ohaness and Armen (Der Arakelian) C.; m. Mary Corcoran, Aug. 22, 1952; children: Armen, Marjorie, Matthew. BA, U. Colo., 1952; MS, Marquette U., 1956, MD, 1959. Cert. anatomic and clin. pathologist. Co-dir. Pathologists Regional Labs., Lewiston, Idaho, 1964-96; chief of staff Tri-State Hosp., Clarkston, Wash., 1967, St. Joseph's Hosp., Lewiston, 1971; assoc. prof. pathology Wash. State U., Pullman, 1972—. Author: Antigens to Melanoma, 1957, Parasitism and Natural Resistance, 1958, Pathologist in Peril, 1996, Immigrant Son, 1996, Immigrant Son II, 1997, Murder in the Mountains, 1997, Princess and the Beggar, 1998, Holly and the Dragon Dingle, 1998, Beware of the Drifters, 1998, Pathologist on Call, 2002, Pathologist in Training, 2003; co-author: Malakoplakia, 1957, Pneumocystis, 1965. Pres. Am. Cancer Soc., Asotin County, Wash., 1968, Lewiston Roundup, 1972-73, N.W. Soc. Blood Banks, 1973-74. Sgt. U.S. Army, 1944-46. Fellow Am. Coll. Pathologists (cert., lab. inspector 1970-2000), Am. Soc. Clin. Pathologists; mem. Idaho Soc. Pathologists (pres. 1970). Avocations: writing, drawing, horses. Home: 531 Silcott Rd Clarkston WA 99403-9784

CHING, ANDY KWOK-YEE, minister; b. Shanghai, People's Republic of China, Apr. 12, 1956; arrived in Hong Kong, 1961; arrived in Can., 1973; came to U.S., 1989. s. Jan Wai and Hon Wah (Kwan) C.; m. Rosita Wai-Mui Tsoi, June 4, 1989; children: Abigail, Aaron. B of Applied Sci., U. Toronto, 1981; M of Theol. Studies, Ontario Theol. Sem., 1982; DD, Internat. Sem., 1988; D of Min., Fuller Theol. Sem., 1996. Ordained to ministry Christian and Missionary Alliance, 1989. Asst. pastor North York Chinese Bapt. Ch., Willowdale, Ont., Can., 1982-83; interim pastor Montreal Chinese Bapt. Ch., Quebec, Can., 1984; lit. coord. Christian Reformed Ch., Toronto, Ont., 1988; gen. sec. Harvester Evangelical Press, Willowdale, 1985-89; pastor Chinese Christian Alliance Ch., Northridge, Calif., 1989-95, The Lord's Grace Christian Ch., Mountain View, Calif., 1996—. Guest lectr., Christ Internat. Theol. Sem., Alhambra, Calif., 1990-95, Christ Wilness Theol. Sem., Concord, Calif., 2001-; interpreter, Toronto Bd. Edn., 1986-88, instr, 1986-87. Editor: Onward Christian Soldiers, Toronto, 1982, Three Episodes of Life, 1982; translator (books) Reasons to Believe, 1988, Called to Ministry, 1989; contbr. articles to profl. jours. Vol. Scot's Missions to Native People, Toronto, 1983-84; bd. dirs. China Grad. Sch. Theology San Jose Coun., 1997—; reporter Evangelical Press. Assn., Canoga Park, 1990-96; tchr. trainer Evangelical Tchr. Tng. Assn., Wheaton, Ill., 1989—. Mem. Cultural Regeneration Rsch. Soc., USA (bd. dirs. 1996—). Office: The Lord's Grace Christian Ch 1101 San Antonio Rd Mountain View CA 94043-1008 *The two Josephs in the Old and New Testament teach us one thing: there is a price to pay if we want to actualize the dreams given by God.*

CHING, ANTHONY BARTHOLOMEW, lawyer, educator, consultant; b. Shanghai, Nov. 18, 1935; came to U.S., 1956; s. William L.K. and Christina Ching; m. Nancy Ann Prigge, Apr. 10, 1961; children: Anthony, Alice, Alexander, Andrew, Ann, Audrey, Anastasia, Albert. Student, Cath. U. West, France, 1953-54, Cambridgeshire Tech. Coll., 1954-55; matriculated, Cambridge (Eng.) U., 1955, St. John's Coll., 1956; BS in Geology, U. Ariz., 1959, postgrad., 1959-60, LLB, 1965; LLM, Harvard U., 1971. Bar: Ariz. 1965, U.S. Dist. Ct. Ariz. 1965, U.S. Ct. Appeals (9th cir.) 1969, U.S. Supreme Ct. 1969, U.S. Ct. Appeals (5th cir.) 1972. Geologist Duval Sulphur and Potash, Kingman and Tucson, Ariz., 1959-60; part-time geologist Am. Smelting and Refining Co., Tucson, 1960-61; engr. Marum and Marum Cons. Engrs., Tucson, 1961-65; atty., sole practice Tucson, 1965-66; atty., chief trial counsel Pima County Legal Aid Soc., Tucson, 1966-70; fellow clin. legal edn. Harvard Law Sch., Cambridge, Mass., 1970-71; acting prof. law Loyola U. Law Sch., L.A., 1971-73, 74-75, adj. prof., 1982; dir. litigation, acting project dir. Hawaii Legal Aid Soc., Honolulu, 1973-74; chief counsel Econ. Protection divsn. Atty. Gen.'s Office, State of Ariz., Phoenix, 1975-79; solicitor gen. Ariz. Dept. Law, Phoenix, 1979-91, asst. atty. gen., 1991-97; pvt. practice Tempe, Ariz., 1997—. Chmn. We. Attys. Gen. Litigation Action Com., 1983-86; pres. Nat. Consumer Law Ctr., Boston, 1979—; judge pro tem Maricopa County Superior Ct., 1983-93, 94—, Ct. Appeals, 1994. Mem. Pima County Dem. Com., 1966-70, Tucson Cmty. Coun., 1968-70, Pio Decimo Ctr., 1968-70; bd. dirs., Ariz. Consumer Coun., 1968-70; pres. Young Dems. Greater Tucson, 1969-70. Mem.: ABA, Harvard Law Sch. Assn. Ariz. (pres. 1980—83), Nat. Legal Aid and Defender Assn. (treas. 1973—74, Reginald Heber Smith award 1969), State Bar Ariz. (100 Women and Minority Lawyers in Ariz. award 2000). Home: 2632 S Fairfield Dr Tempe AZ 85282-2924 Office: 2043 E Southern Ave Tempe AZ 85282 E-mail: abching@azbar.org.

CHING, BARON KWAI FONG, internist; b. Honolulu, May 10, 1952; s. Alvin K.F. and Ethel F.L. (Lau) C. MD, U. Hawaii, 1980. Diplomate Am. Bd. Internal Medicine. Resident in internal medicine John A. Burns Sch. Medicine U. Hawaii, Manoa, 1980-83, asst. clin. prof. medicine, 1983—; pvt. practice, Honolulu, 1984—. Mem. exec. com. Rehab Hosp. Pacific, 1998—; mem. exec. com. dept. medicine Queen's Med. Ctr., 2001—; team physician Huaka'i I Mauna ascent of Mauna Kea, 2002, Hukai ascent Mauna Key, Mauna Loa to Keauhou, 2003; coord. med. field stations Honolulu marathon, 2003. Pres. Sacred Times, Sacred Places, Honolulu, 1998, Hui Kipulani, 1998; co-chmn. 'Ahahui Malama 'o Kaniakapupu, 2000; vice-chair Organic Act Centennial Observance Com., 2000. Named hon. citizen Ka Lahui, Hawaii, 1988. Mem. ACP, Physicians for Social Responsibility, Hawaii Med. Assn., Honolulu County Med. Soc. Avocations: hula, olelo hawaii. Office: 321 N Kuakini St Ste 708 Honolulu HI 96817-2362

CHING, ERIC SAN HING, health care and insurance administrator; b. Honolulu, Aug. 13, 1951; s. Anthony D.K. and Amy K.C. (Chong) C. BS, Stanford U., 1973, MS, MBA, 1977. Fin. analyst Mid Peninsula Health Service, Palo Alto, Calif., 1977; acting dep. exec. dir. Santa Clara County Health Systems Agy., San Jose, Calif., 1977-78; program officer Henry J. Kaiser Family Found., Menlo Park, Calif., 1978-84; dir. strategic planning Lifeguard Health Maintenance Orgn., Milpitas, Calif., 1984-90; v.p. strategic planning and dir. ops. Found. Life Ins. Co., Milpitas, 1986-90; sr. planning analyst Kaiser Found. Health Plan, Oakland, Calif., 1990-94, coord. product and competition analysis, 1994-95, mgr. ins. ops. and competitive intelligence cons., 1995-97, nat. product leader, 1997—. Adj. faculty Am. Pistol Inst., 1991-94. Mem. vol. staff Los Angeles Olympic Organizing Com., 1984; mem. panel United Way of Santa Clara County, 1985, panel chmn., 1986-87, mem. com. priorities and community problem solving, 1987-90, Project Blueprint, 1988-90. Mem. NRA, Law Enforcement Alliance of Am., Am. Soc. Law Enforcement Trainers, Internat. Assn. Law Enforcement Firearms Instrs., Internat. Wound Ballistics Assn., Stanford Alumni Assn., Stanford Bus. Sch. Alumni Assn., Stanford Swordmasters (pres. 1980-89), Safari Club Internat., Am. Soc. of Criminology. Avocations: hunting, photography, travel, musical theater, reading. Office: Kaiser Found Health Plan Inc One Kaiser Pla 25th Fl Oakland CA 94612 E-mail: chingesh@ix.netcom.com.

CHING, JAMES MICHAEL, artistic director opera company, composer, conductor; b. Honolulu, Hawaii, Sept. 29, 1958; BA summa cum laude, Duke U., 1980. Pianist, composer Houston Opera Studio, 1980-81; music adminstr. Fla. Grand Opera, 1981-85; mus. dir. Triangle Opera Theatre, 1987-88; asst. to gen. dir. Va. Opera, 1989-91, assoc. artistic dir., 1991-92; artistic dir. Opera Memphis, Tenn., 1992—. Mem. Phi Beta Kappa. Office: PO Box 171413 Memphis TN 38187-1413 E-mail: Michael@operamemphis.org.

CHING, WAI YIM, physics educator, researcher; b. Shaoshing, China, Oct. 18, 1945; came to U.S., 1969; s. Di-Son and Hung-Wong (Sung) C.; m. Mon Yin Lung, Dec. 27, 1975; children: Tianyu, Kunyu. BSc, U. Hong Kong, 1969; MS, La. State U., 1971, PhD, 1974. Rsch. assoc., lectr. U. Wis., Madison, 1974-78; asst. prof. U. Mo., Kansas City, 1978-81, assoc. prof., 1981-84, prof. physics, 1984-88, curators' prof., 1988—, chmn. physics dept., 1990-98. Cons. Argonne (Ill.) Nat. Lab., 1978-82, vis. scientist, 1985-86; vis. prof. U. Sci. and Tech., Hefei, China, 1983; guest scientist Max-Planck Inst. für Metallforschung, Stuttgart, Germany, 1997. Contbr. articles to profl. jours. Recipient N.T. Veatch award for disting. rsch., 1985; Trustee fellow U. Mo., 1984, 90. Fellow: Am. Ceramic Soc.; mem.: AAAS, Materials Rsch. Soc., Am. Vacuum Soc., Am. Phys. Soc., Sigma Xi. Achievements include the study of theoretical dondensed matter physics and materials sciences; electronic, magnetic, optical, dynamical structural and superconducting properties of ordered and disordered solids. Home: 2809 W 119th St Leawood KS 66209-1104 Office: U Mo Dept Physics Robert H Flarsheim Hall 5100 Rockhill Rd Kansas City MO 64110-2481 E-mail: chingw@umkc.edu.

CHINN, MENZIE DAVID, economics educator; b. Richland, Wash., June 4, 1961; s. Gene S. and Susan F. (Louie) C. BA, Harvard U., 1984; MA in Econs., U. Calif., Berkeley, 1988, PhD in Econs., 1991. Lectr. econs. dept. U. Calif., Berkeley, 1988-90; asst. prof. econs. U. Calif., Santa Cruz, 1991—97, assoc. prof., 1997—2002, prof., 2002—; sr. economist Pres. Coun. Economic Advisors, 2000-01. Rsch. assoc. Nat. Bur. Econ. Rsch., Inc., 2002--. Co-editor-in-chief Harvard Internat. Rev., 1982-83; assoc. editor Jour. Internat. Econs., 1996-2002; contbr. articles to profl. jours. Recipient Young Economist prize Am. Express Bank Rev. Awards, London, 1988. Mem. Am. Econs. Assn., Econometric Soc., Internat. Econs. and Fin. Soc. Office: U Calif Dept of Econs Santa Cruz CA 95064

CHINN, REX ARLYN, chemist; b. Bosworth, Mo., Apr. 5, 1935; s. Loren Herbert and Lima (Stanton) C.; m. Wanda June Williams, May 31, 1959 (dec.); children: Timothy Michael, Sharon Rose Chinn-Heritch, Jonathan Daniel; m. Victoria Loraine Hunter. BS in Chemistry, S.W. Mo. State Coll., 1961; grad., Cleve. Inst. Electronics. Lic. Bapt. minister. Rsch. asst. U. Mo. Med. Ctr., Columbia, 1961-65, William S. Merrell Co., Cin., 1965-67; lab. supr. U.S. Indsl. Chem. Co., Rsch. div., Cin., 1967-72; mgr. quality assurance Cloudsley Co., Cin., 1972-74; dir. tech. affairs Woodson Tenent Labs., Memphis, 1974-77; quality engr. Nat. Ind. for the Blind, Earth City, Mo., 1977-96; owner/mgr. The Master's Image, Maryland Hts., Mo., 1987—. Freelance field prodns. KNLC, Channel 24, St. Louis, 1987—; freelance audo rec. for ACTS Inc., 1996-2000; dir. video ops. Mission Gate Prison Ministry, 2000-2001; video cons.; environ. control sys. cons. Contbr. articles to profl. jours; producer/dir.: More Than a Fighting Chance, 1989. Founder, dir. Christian Alliance of Video Ministries, 2002—. With U.S. Army, 1954—56. Mem. Media Comms. Assn. Republican. Avocations: art, photography, electronics, motorcycling, guitar. Home and Office: The Masters Image 12079 Ameling Rd Maryland Heights MO 63043-4148

CHINNI, PETER ANTHONY, artist, poet; b. Mt. Kisco, NY, Mar. 21, 1928; s. Antonio and Carmella Catherine (Lampo) C.; m. Elisabeth Angela Cott, Aug. 17, 1970 (div. 1986); children— Christine Elizabeth, Megan Margaret. Student, Art Students League N.Y., 1947-49, Accademia di Belle Arti, Rome, 1949-50. One-man shows include Albert Loeb Gallery, N.Y.C., 1966, Loeb-Krugier Gallery, N.Y.C., 1969, A. Monett Gallery, Brussels, 1976, Gallery Bouma, Amsterdam, 1976, Katonah Gallery, N.Y., 1983, Fairlawn Libr. Gallery, N.J., 1993, Galerie Lafitte, New Orleans, 2000; group exhbns. include Whitney Mus., N.Y.C., 1962-65, 75, Carnegie Internat., Pitts., 1964-65, Biennale di Roma, 1969, Audubon Artists Ann., 1995 (Gold medal for sculpture); commd. pub. works, N.Y.C., Columbia, Mo., Yorktown, N.Y.; represented in permanent collections at Whitney Mus., New Orleans Fine Arts Mus., Smithsonian Inst., Washington, City Art Mus., Colo., MIT, Beeckestijn (The Netherlands) Mus., Denver Art Mus., Rockefeller Collection, Boca Raton (Fla.) Mus. Served with U.S. Army, 1951-53. Mem. N.Y. Sculptors Guild, Artists Equity. E-mail: peter@peterchinni.com.

CHIOGIOJI, MELVIN HIROAKI, former government official, entrepreneur; b. Hiroshima, Japan, Aug. 21, 1939; came to U.S., 1939; s. Yutaka and Harumi (Yamasaki) C.; m. Pallas A. Chiogioji; children: Wendy A., Alan K. BS in Elec. Engring., Purdue U., 1961; MBA, U. Hawaii, 1968; D.Bus. Adminstrn., George Washington U., 1972. Registered profl. engr., Hawaii. Head weapons gen. component div. Quality Evaluation Lab., Oahu, Hawaii, 1965-69; dir. weapons evaluation and engring. div. Naval Ordinance Systems Command, Washington, 1969-73; dir. Office Indsl. Analysis Fed. Energy Adminstrn., Washington, 1973-75; asst. dir., div. bldg. and community systems Dept. Energy, Washington, 1975-79, dir. fed. program div., 1980—, dep. asst. sec. state and local assistance program, 1980-85, dir. office of transp. systems, 1985-90; constrn. mgr. Office of New Prodn. Reactors, Washington, 1990-92; pres. EFC, Inc., 1980-99, Precision Auto Care, Inc., 1989-97, Intemco, 1993-96, Mele Assocs., Inc., 1999—. Prof. mgmt. sci. George Washington U., 1972—. Author: Industrial Energy Conservation, 1979, Energy Conservation in Commercial and Residental Buildings, 1982; contbr. articles to profl. jours. Mem. Md. State Adv. Com. on Civil Rights, 1976—; mem. Nat. Naval Res. Policy Bd., 1977—; vestryman Grace Episcopal Ch., Silver Spring, Md., 1982—; bd. dirs. Japanese Am. Nat. Mus., 1996—; chmn. Nat. Japanese Am. Meml. Found., 1995—. With USN, 1961-65; rear adm. USNR. Decorated Navy Commendation medal, Meritorious Svc. medal, Legion Merit medal. Mem. IEEE (sr.), NSPE, Acad. Mgmt., Naval Res. Assn., Assn. for Sci., Tech. and Innovation (pres. 1979-81), Soc. Am. Mil. Engrs., Armed Forces Mgmt. Assn., Seabee Meml. Scholarship Assn. (bd. dirs. 1973—), Triangle Fraternity Edn. Found. (bd. dirs. 1995—), Purdue U. Alumni Assn., Nat. Japanese Am. Meml. Found. (chmn.), Japanese Am. Nat. Mus. (bd. dirs.). Address: 15702 Thistlebridge Dr Rockville MD 20853-3226 Office: 14660 Rothgeb Dr Rockville MD 20850-5309

CHIORAZZI, MARY LORRAINE, psychiatrist; b. New York; BS, Marymount Manhattan Coll., 1966; MD, Georgetown U., 1970. Diplomate Am. Bd. Psychiatry. Pvt. practice child, adolescent, adult psychiatry, Englewood, N.J., 1975—. Office: 163 Engle St Englewood NJ 07631-2530

CHIORAZZI, NICHOLAS, immunologist educator; b. Weehawken, N.J., Oct. 2, 1945; s. Joseph P. and Mary L. (Ippolito) C.; m. M. Lorraine Dziadowicz, June 19, 1971; children: Anne, Michael. BA, Holy Cross Coll., 1966; MD, Georgetown U., 1970. Intern Cornell Cooperating Hosps., Manhasset, N.Y., 1970-71, resident in medicine, 1971-74; post doctoral fellow in immunology Harvard U. Med. Sch., Boston, 1974-76; post doctoral fellow in clin. immunology Rockefeller U., N.Y.C., 1976-77; asst. prof. The Rockefeller U., 1977-82, assoc. prof., 1982-87, dep. head lab. immunology, 1984-87; prof. medicine Cornell U., N.Y.C., 1987-96; chief rheumatology and immunology North Shore U. Hosp., Manhasset, 1987—2000; prof. medicine and pathology NYU Sch. Medicine, N.Y.C., 1996—; dir., CEO North Shore -LIJ Rsch. Inst., 2000—. Contbr. articles to profl. jours. NIH grantee, 1980—. Fellow Am. Coll. Rheumatology, Am. Assn. Allergists and Immunologists, Am. Acad. Allergy Asthma and Immunology; mem. ACP, Am. Soc. for Clin. Investigation, Am. Assn. Immunologists, Assn. Am. Physicians. Office: North Shore LIJ Rsch Inst 350 Community Dr Manhasset NY 11030-3801

CHIOTELLIS, PHILIP NICOS, cardiologist; b. Kyrenia, Cyprus, May 31, 1942; s. Nicos Philip and Maria (Constantinides) C.; m. Lavinia Conroy; children: Nicos, Peter, Fiona. MD, Athens U., 1966. Resident in medicine N.J. Med. Sch., Newark, 1968-71; fellow in cardiology Mass. Gen. Hosp./Harvard Med. Sch., Boston, 1972-74; instr medicine Harvard Med. Sch., Boston, 1974-75; practice cardiology Boston/Cape Cod Area, 1974—; pres. Heart Ctr., Hyannis, Mass. Fellow Am. Coll. Cardiology, Paul Dudley Med. Soc., Algonquin Club (Boston), Everglades Club (Palm Beach, Fla.). Office: Heart Ctr 52 Park St Hyannis MA 02601-5206

CHIOU, ANDY C. surgeon; s. Wun San and Chung Yuh Chiou; m. Laurie Chiou, Aug. 0, 2001; 1 child, Alexander. BA, Boston U., 1988, MPH, MD, Boston U., 1992. Diplomate NBME, 1993. Vascular surgery fellow Northwestern U., Chgo., 1998—2000; staff vascular surgeon USAF, Lackland AFB, Tex., 2000—. Maj. USAF. Decorated Achievement medal USAF. Mem.: ACS. Achievements include research in work on etiology of abdominal aortic aneurysms. Office: Wilford Hall USAF Med Ctr Ste 1 2200 Bergquist Dr Lackland A F B TX 78236 Personal E-mail: andychiou@aol.com.

CHIOU, PAUL C.J. statistician, educator; b. Tainan, Taiwan, Nov. 18, 1950; s. T.S. and H.C. Chiou; m. Peen-Peen Ma, Mar. 9, 1990; 1 child, Jonathan. BS, Nat. Chung Hsing U., 1974; MA, U. Tex., Arlington, 1980, PhD, 1984. Instr. U. Tex., Arlington, 1982—83; asst. prof. East Tex. State U., Commerce, 1983—88; from asst. prof. to assoc. prof. Lamar U., Beaumont, Tex., 1988—97, prof., 1997—. Chief editor: Jour. Statis. Rsch., 2003—, Jour. Probability and Statis. Sci., 2002—; contbr. articles to profl. jours. Grantee Grad. Tchg. Assistantship grant, U. of Tex. at Arlington, 1978—83. Mem.: Inst. of Math. Stats., Am. Statis. Assn., Pi Mu Epsilon. Avocation: gardening. Office: Lamar University East Lavaca Beaumont TX 77710-0047 Office Fax: 409-880-8794. E-mail: chiou@math.lamar.edu.

CHIOU-TAN, FAYE, physician, educator; b. Hsin-Chu, Taiwan, Mar. 27, 1964; d. George and Tricia Chiou; m. Filemon Tan, Jr.; children: Filemon III, Michelle. AB, Princeton U., 1985; MD, Baylor U., 1990. Diplomate Am. Bd. Electrodiagnostic Medicine, Am. Bd. Phys. Med. Rehab. Asst. prof. Baylor Coll. Medicine, Houston, 1995—2003, assoc. prof., 2003—. Contbr. articles to profl. jours. Chief svc. phys. medicine and rehab. Harris County Hosp. Dist., Houston, 2000—, dir. electrodiagnosis, 1995—, dir. Ctr. for Trauma Rehab. Rsch., 2000—. Recipient Excellence in Rsch. Writing award Assn Acad. Physiatrists/Am. Jour. Phys. Medicine and Rehab., 1999, 2000; named one of Am's Top Physicians, Consumer's Rsch. Coun. Am., 2003. Mem. Am. Assn. Electrodiagnostic Medicine (rsch. com.), Assn. Acad. Physiatrists. Avocations: cooking, hiking, antiques. Office: Baylor Coll Medicine Dept PM&R 3601 N MacGregor Way Ste 240 Houston TX 77004

CHIPKIN, FREDERICK, textile designer, consultant; b. New York, New York, Mar. 11, 1963; s. Sidney and Pearl Chipkin; m. Rimma Zilman Chipkin, Feb. 28, 1985; children: Alexandra Elizabeth, Rebecca Tatiana. AS in culinary arts, Johnson and Wales Coll., 1983; BFA, Parsons Sch. of Design, 1989. Owner/designer Design Soc., Inc., NYC, 1987—90; textile designer Liz Claiborne, NYC, 1990—92, Bernard Chause, Inc., NYC; mgr., CAD dept. I. Appel, Inc., NYC, 1995—99; owner/designer Origin Inc., Textile Design Studio, 1999—. Author: (book/tutorial) ADOBE Photoshop for Textile Design, 2001—03. Home and Office: Origin Inc 117-14 Union Turnpike CD2 Kew Gardens NY 11415 Business E-Mail: design@origininc.com.

CHIPMAN, DANIEL MYRON, chemist, researcher, educator; b. Ames, Iowa, July 26, 1945; s. Myron Jesse and Maxine Ruth (Lewis) C.; m. Pamela Jo Pease, June 7, 1969; children: Shannon Eileen, Ian Daniel. BS, Iowa State U., 1967; PhD, U. Wis., 1972. Lectr., postdoc. scholar U. Calif., Santa Barbara, 1972-73; instr., vis. prof. U. Colo., Boulder, 1974-75; asst. prof. U. Iowa, Iowa City, 1975-76; scientist U. Notre Dame, Ind., 1976-87, 88—; program officer NSF, Washington, 1987-88. Assoc. dir. radiation lab. U. Notre Dame, 1996-98. Author: (chpt.) Understanding Chemical Reactivity, Vol. 13, 1995; contbr. articles to Jour. Am. Chem. Soc., Jour. Chem. Physics, Jour. Physical Chemistry. George W. Catt scholar Iowa State U., 1966-67; Tchg. Prize fellow U. Wis., 1967-69. Mem. Phi Kappa Phi, Alpha Chi Sigma, Phi Eta Sigma, Sigma Xi. Office: Radiation Lab U Notre Dame Notre Dame IN 46556

CHIPMAN, DEBRA DECKER, paralegal; b. Oneonta, N.Y., Sept. 21, 1959; d. Leon Hannibal and Patricia Elizabeth (Ainsworth) Decker; m. Michael A. Chipman, May 24, 1980 (div. Sept. 1990); 1 child, Amanda Michelle. Student, Robert Morris Coll., 1988-94. Sec., receptionist Power Engring. Corp., Binghamton, N.Y., 1977-78; accts. payable clk. Old Dominion U. Rsch. Found., Norfolk, Va., 1978-80; adminstrv. asst. U. Pitts., 1980-81; paralegal Papernick & Gefsky, Attys. at Law, Pitts., 1981-93; mgr. Preferred Settlement Svcs., Inc., Pitts., 1993-97; asst. v.p., agy. rep. First Am. Title Ins. Co., Pitts., 1997-2000,

Fidelity Nat. Title Ins. Co. of N.Y., 2000—. Recipient award Otsego County Bankers Assn., 1977. Mem.: Pa. Land Title Assn. (western Pa. chpt. sec., chair 2002), Pa. Assn. Notaries, Pitts. Paralegal Assn. (co-chair fundraising com. 1990). Methodist. Avocations: golf, skiing. Home: 2593 Hunters Point Ct S Wexford PA 15090-7986 Office: Fidelity Nat Title Ins Co Grant Building Ste 1412 Pittsburgh PA 15219-2203 E-mail: dchipman@fnf.com.

CHIPMAN, DENNIS CLARENCE, JR., psychiatrist; b. Seattle, Jan. 7, 1934; s. Dennis Clarence and Esther Ränghild Chipman; m. Karen Antoinette Ekern, Mar. 17, 1968 (div. Oct. 1982); children: Judith, Kimberly, Jason, Carolyn; m. Sandra Kay Woodell, Feb. 6, 1983. MD, U. Wash. Diplomate in psychiatry, adolescent psychiatry, forensic psychiatry Am. Bd. Psychiatry and Neurology. Intern U. Nebr. Hosp., Omaha, 1959-60; resident U. Wash. Hosp. Sys., Seattle, 1960-63; pvt. practice Seattle, 1963-66; dir. Mental Health Ctr., Kingsport, Tenn., 1969-84; pvt. practice Kingsport, 1969-84, Hickory, N.C., 1984-86; med. dir. Pinewood Hosp., Texarkana, Ark., 1986-89, Charter Hosp. of Mobile, Ala., 1989-94; chief psychiatrist Patrick B. Harris Hosp., Anderson, S.C., 1994—; cons. Forensic Psychiatry, Anderson, 1994—. Cons. Meth. Children's Home, Greenville, Tenn., 1969-75. Bd. dirs. Sheltered Workshop, Kingsport, 1973-80, Gateways Farm for Girls, New Boston, Tex., 1988-94, Home of Grace for Women, Mobile, 1990-94, New Haven Program, Mobile, 1990-94. Capt. U.S. Army, 1966-68. Mem. AMA, Am. Psychiat. Assn., Am. Mensa Ltd., U.S. Chess Fedn., Internat. Soc. for Philos. Enquiry, Civitan Club, Rotary Club, Kappa Sigma. Libertarian. Avocations: music, chess, reading, travel. Home: PO Box 5587 Anderson SC 29623-5587 E-mail: c1219d@aol.com.

CHIPMAN, JACK, artist; b. L.A., Oct. 31, 1943; s. George Geotz and June Naomi (Hanson) C. BFA, Calif. Inst. Arts, 1966. Dealer Calif. pottery Calif. Spectrum, Redondo Beach, 1980-90. Cons. Schroeder Pub., Paducah, Ky., 1982-99. Author: Complete Collectors Guide Bauer Pottery, 1982, Collector's Encyclopedia California Pottery, 1992, 2d edit., 1998, Collector's Encyclopedia Bauer Pottery, 1997, Barbara Willis: Classic California Modernism, 2003, (periodicals) Antique Trader Weekly, 1981—83, Am. Clay Exch., 1982—88; one-man shows include Oakland Mus., Calif., Long Beach (Calif.) Art Mus., U. Santa Clara Art Mus., Represented in permanent collections Oakland Art Mus., Long Beach Mus. Art, U. Santa Clara (Calif.) Art Mus. Bd. dirs. Angels Gate Cultural Ctr., San Pedro, Calif., jour. editor, 1990-93. Avocation: collecting Calif. pottery. Office: PO Box 1079 Venice CA 90294-1079

CHIPMAN, JOHN SOMERSET, economist, educator; b. Montreal, Que., Can., June 28, 1926; s. Warwick Fielding and Mary Somerset (Aikins) C.; m. Margaret Ann Ellefson, June 24, 1960; children: Thomas Noel, Timothy Warwick. Student, Universidad de Chile, Santiago, 1943-44; BA, McGill U., Montreal, 1947, MA, 1948; PhD, Johns Hopkins U., 1951; postdoctoral, U. Chgo., 1950-51; Doctor rerum politicarum honoris causa, U. Konstanz, Germany, 1991, U. Würzburg, 1998; Doctor social and econ. scis., U. Graz, Austria, 2001. Asst. prof. econs. Harvard U., Cambridge, Mass., 1951-55; assoc. prof. econs. U. Minn., Mpls., 1955-60, prof., 1961-81, Regents' prof., 1981—. Fellow Ctr. for Advanced Study in Behavioral Scis., Stanford, Calif., 1972-73; Guggenheim fellow, 1980-81; vis. prof. econs. various univs.; permanent guest prof. U. Konstanz, 1985-91; bd. dirs. Leuthold Funds, Inc., 1995—. Author: The Theory of Intersectoral Money Flows and Income Formation, 1951; editor: (with others) Preferences, Utility, and Demand, 1971, Preferences, Uncertainty and Optimality, 1990, (with C.P. Kindleberger) Flexible Exchange Rates and the Balance of Payments, 1980; co-editor Jour. Internat. Econs., 1971-76, editor, 1977-87; assoc. editor Econometrica, 1956-60, Can. Jour. Stats., 1980-82; mem. adv. bd. Jour. Multivariate Analysis, 1988-92. Recipient James Murray Luck award Nat. Acad. Scis., 1981, Humboldt Rsch. award for Sr. U.S. Scientists, 1992, 2003. Fellow AAAS, Econometric Soc. (coun. 1971-76, 81-83), Am. Statis. Assn., Am. Acad. Arts and Scis., Am. Econ. Assn. (disting.); mem. NAS (chair sect. econ. scis. 1997-2000), Internat. Statis. Inst., Am. Philosophical Soc., Inst. Math. Stats., Can Econ. Assn., Royal Econ. Soc., History of Econs. Soc. Home: 2121 W 49th St Minneapolis MN 55409-2229 Office: U Minn Dept Econs 1035 Heller Hall 217 19th Ave S Minneapolis MN 55455-0400 E-mail: jchipman@econ.umn.edu.

CHIPMAN, MARION WALTER, retired judge; b. Penokee, Kans., May 5, 1920; s. James Edwin and May Maude (Hatcher) C.; m. Thelma Nadine Clark, Nov. 1, 1941 (div. 1965); m. Nancy Jo Payne, May 28, 1983; children: Clark D., Jill Ellen. AB in Social Sci., Ft. Hays (Kans.) State U., 1942; JD, Washburn U., 1948. Bar: Kans. 1948, U.S. Dist. Ct. Kans. 1948, U.S. Ct. Appeals 1970, U.S. Supreme Ct. 1970. Supt. Prairieview (Kans.) Sch., 1942; dir. edn. Bous Indsl. Sch., Topeka, 1945—46; atty. County of Graham, Hill City, Kans., 1949-53; counselor County of Johnson, Olathe, Kans., 1967-68; judge 10th Jud. Dist. Kans. Dist. Ct., Olathe, 1980-91, sr. judge, 1996-2001. Sgt. USAAF, 1942-45. Mem. ABA (life), Johnson County Bar Assn. (life), Kans. Bar Assn. (life), Am. Judicature, Am. Judge's Assn., Am. Arbitration Assn., Am. Legion (life), Masons (life), Shriners (life), Elks (life). Methodist. Home: 6398 17th Pl N Saint Petersburg FL 33710-5520

CHIPMAN, MARTIN, neurologist, educator, retired army officer; b. Boston, June 16, 1930; AB in History cum laude, Harvard U., 1953, postgrad., 1956; MD, Baylor Coll. Medicine, 1960. Diplomate Am. Bd. Psychiatry and Neurology. Intern Walter Reed Army Med. Ctr., Washington, 1960-61, resident in neurology, 1961-64; assoc. in neurophysiology Walter Reed Army Inst. Rsch., Washington, 1964; neurologist Meml. and Univ. Hosps.; dir. stroke rsch. unit VA Hosp. and SUNY-Upstate Med. Ctr.; chief neurology svcs. VA Hosp.; resident tng. supr. SUNY-Upstate Med. Ctr., assoc. prof. neurology; asst. clin. prof. neurology U. Md., Balt.; chief neurology svc. Eisenhower Med. Ctr., 1980-81; attending neurologist Walter Reed Army Med. Ctr.; prof. neurology Uniformed Svcs. U. of the Health Scis., Bethesda, Md., 1984-86; chief neurology svcs. Womack Army Hosp., 1986-87; attending neurologist Cape Fear Valley Med. Ctr., Highsmith-Rainey Hosp.; dir. sleep disorders lab. Cape Fear Valley Med. Ctr. Rsch. neurologist tropical medicine SEATO Med. Rsch. Lab., 1964-67; cons. neurology Chulalongkorn U. and Prasad Neurol. Inst., Thailand; chief medicine Sioux Valley Hosp.; asst. clin. prof. neurology Sch. Medicine U. S.D.; mem. stroke com. Regional Program for S.D. and Nebr.; cons. neurology Southwestern Mental Health Ctr., VA Hosp., Geneva (N.Y.) Gen. Hosp., Eisenhower Med. Ctr. Svc. Region; neurol. cons. Marion Labs., Kansas City, Kans.; clin. prof. neurology Med. Coll. Ga.; chmn. quality assurance, dept. neurology Walter Reed Army Ctr., Bethesda; vis. prof. neurology Hebrew U., Hadassah Med. Ctr.; sci. exch. officer to Israel, U.S. Army liaison to Israeli Def. Forces; cons., attending neurologist Nat. Naval Med. Ctr., Bethesda; mem. ethics com. Cape Fear Valley Med. Ctr., 1987-88, chmn. therapeutics and pharmacy com., 1988-94, libr. com., 1988-89, ethics com. Southeastern Gen. Hosp.; cons. surveyor Joint Commn. for the Accreditation of Health Care Facilities, 1991-95; mem. exec. com., chmn. medicine Cape Fear Valley Med. Ctr.; vis. prof. neuroscis. Ross Med. Sch., Dominica, West Indies. Contbr. articles to profl. jours. Col. U.S. Army, ret., 1987. Fellow Am. Acad. Neurology; mem. N.C. Med. Soc., N.C. Neurol. Soc., Cumberland County Med. Soc. Office: 4140 Ferncreek Dr Ste 501 Fayetteville NC 28314-2568 E-mail: chipdudes@aol.com.

CHIPMAN, SUSAN ELIZABETH, psychologist, researcher; b. St. Paul, Feb. 12, 1946; d. Robert Louis and Margaret Alice Fitzgerald; m. Eric George Chipman, Aug. 27, 1966. AB in Math., Harvard U., 1966, MBA, 1967, AM in Psychol., 1969, PhD in Exptl. Psychol., 1973. Asst. prof. U. Mich., Ann Arbor, 1974-75; assoc. Nat. Inst. Edn., Washington, 1976-78, asst. dir., 1979-84; sci. officer U.S. Office Naval Rsch., Arlington, Va., 1984-85, cognitive sci. program mgr., 1985—. Mem. adv. bd. James S. McDonnell Found., St. Louis, 1987-98. Editor, author: Thinking and Learning Skills, 1985, Women and Mathematics, 1985, Foundations of Knowledge Acquisition, 1993, Cognitively Diagnostic Assessment, 1995, Cognitive Task Analysis, 2000; contbr. articles to profl. jours. Fellow APA, APS. Avocation: photography. Home: 2606 S Joyce St Arlington VA 22202-2214 Office: Office Naval Rsch 342 800 N Quincy St Arlington VA 22217-5660

CHIPPARONI, GUY, communications company executive; married; two children. BS in Journalism, Ill. State U., 1981. Sr. mng. dir. of pub. affairs Hill & Knowlton, Chgo., 1992-97; pres., pub. affairs KemperLesnik Comms., Chgo., 1997—. Apptd. to bd. Met. Pier and Exposition Authority to oversee Navy Pier and McCormick Place, Chgo., 1998. Office: KemperLesnik Comms Ste 1500 455 N Cityfront Plaza Dr Chicago IL 60611-5313 Fax: 312-755-0274.

CHIQUELIN, DAVID BRYAN, mechanical engineer; b. Warrington, Fla., Apr. 12, 1953; s. William Leonard and Margaret Celeste (Boudreaux) C.; m. Elena Mikhaltchuk. BSME, U.S. Naval Acad., 1976. Commd. ensign USN, 1976, advanced through grades to lt., divsn. officer, gunnery officer USS William H. Standley, 1977-78, legal officer, line divsn. officer patrol squadron 56, 1980-83; strategic computer models analyst Joint Strategic Target Planning Staff, Omaha, 1983-86; resigned USN, 1986; flight contrl. tng. guide editor Rockwell Space Ops. Co., Houston, 1988-95; crew on-orbit support sys. lead programmer United Space Alliance, Houston, 1996—. Programmer software in field. Mem. Nat. Mgmt. Assn. (sec. Rockwell-Houston chpt. 1992-93, pub. rels. dir. 1993-94, programs dir. 1994-95, pres. 1995-96). Avocations: golf, reading, computers. Home: 15302 Pleasant Valley Rd Houston TX 77062-3606 E-mail: david.chiquelin1@jsc.nasa.gov., dbchiq@swbell.net.

CHIRASEVEENUPRAPUND, PAT, internist, endocrinologist; b. Bangkok, Apr. 27, 1940; came to U.S., 1966; s. Ping and Keunghiang (Ngo) Cheung; m. Anuluck Nasrakeo, May 14, 1966; children: Dara, Pat Jr., Peter. MD, Chiengmai Med. Sch., Thailand, 1965. Diplomate Am. Bd. Internal Medicine with subspecialty in endocrinology and metabolism. Intern Carney Hosp., Dorchester, Mass., 1966-67; resident in medicine New Eng. Deaconess Hosp., Boston, 1967-69; clin. fellow in endocrinology Lahey Clinic, Boston, 1969-70; rsch. fellow in endocrinology Boston City Hosp./Boston U. Med. Svc., 1970-72; rsch. assoc. Boston U. Sch. Medicine, 1970-76; pvt. practice Ashland and Framingham, Mass., 1976—. Contbr. articles to profl. jours. Fellow Am. Coll. Endocrinology; mem. Am. Assn. Clin. Endocrinologists, Endocrine Soc., Mass. Med. Soc. Avocations: playing piano, classical music, reading. Office: 475 Franklin St Framingham MA 01702-6264

CHIRIAC, VICTOR ADRIAN, aerospace engineer, researcher; b. Bucharest, Romania, Feb. 22, 1969; arrived in U.S., 1994; s. Florea Nicolae and Michaela Cornelia Chiriac; m. Raluca Olga Butunoiu. BSc, Poly. U. Bucharest, 1992, MSc, 1993; PhD in Aero. and Mech. Engring., U. of Ariz., 1999. Registered Profl. Engr. Rsch. and tchg. asst. U. Ariz., Tucson, 1994—97; intern Motorola Inc., Tempe, Ariz., 1996—98, prin. staff engr., 1999—. Awareness sub.-com. Motorola Inc., 2001—02. Contbr. articles to profl. jours. (Prize Paper Award, 2001). Mem.: ASME (k-16 com. mem. thermal divsn. 2002—), Internat. Microelectronics & Packaging Soc. Orthodox. Achievements include patents for system and method for cooling using an oscillatory impinging jet; patents pending for airbag circuit driver optimization. Avocations: tennis, swimming, hiking. Home: 15016 S 28th St Phoenix AZ 85048 Office: Motorola Inc 2100 East Elliot Tempe AZ 85284 Personal E-mail: victor.chiriac@motorola.com. Business E-Mail: victor.chiriac@motorola.com.

CHIRIKOS, THOMAS N. healthcare economics educator; b. Chgo., Nov. 19, 1938; s. Thomas Nicholas and Wilma L. Chirikos; m. Linda Lou Waddell. BA cum laude, Coe Coll., 1960; PhD, Ohio State U., 1967. From asst. to full prof. Ohio State U., Columbus, 1967—85; prof. U. South Fla., Tampa, 1985—. Mem.-in-residence Moffitt Cancer Ctr., Tampa, 1997—. Contbr. numerous articles to profl. jours. Fellow, Orgn. for econ. Cooperation and Devel., 1963—64; grantee, OAS, Inter-American Statis. Inst., 1965, Nat. Sci. Found., 1975—77, U.S. Dept. Health and Human Svc., Office of Asst. Sec. for Planning and Evaluation, 1985—86, Social Security Adminstrn., 1987—88, Health Care Financing Adminstrn., 1994—97, Nat. Cancer Inst., 1999—2002.

CHIRINKO, ROBERT S. economics educator; b. Coatesville, Pa., July 10, 1953; s. John M. and Ann C.; m. Barbara G. Cohen, Sept. 10, 1988. BA, U. Pa., 1975; MA, Northwestern U., Evanston, Ill., 1979, PhD, 1982. Asst. prof. econs. Cornell U., Ithaca, N.Y., 1982-84; John Stauffer pub. policy fellow Stanford (Calif.) U., 1984-85; asst. prof. U. Chgo., 1985-92; vis. scholar Fed. Res. Bank, Kansas City, Mo., 1992-93; assoc. prof. U. Ill., Champaign, 1993-94; assoc. prof., prof., dir. grad. studies, co-chair Emory U., Atlanta, 1994—. Rsch. fellow CESifo, Munich, 1999—. Contbr. articles to profl. jours. Recipient James L. Barr award pub. econs. Assn. Pub. Policy Analysis and Mgmt., 1983. Mem. Royal Econ. Soc., Am. Fin. Assn., Am. Econ. Assn., Econometric Soc., Nat. Tax Assn. (co-recipient Outstanding Dissertation award 1982). E-mail: rchirin@emory.edu.

CHIRINOS, EDUARDO, writer, educator; b. Lima, Peru, Apr. 4, 1960; arrived in U.S., 1993; s. Eduardo Chirinos and Ana María Arrieta; m. Jannine Montauban, Aug. 16, 1993. B Humanities, U. Católica, Lima, 1985, MA, 1988; PhD, Rutgers U., 1997. Vis. asst. prof. U. de los Andes, Trujillo, Venezuela, 1998, SUNY, Binghamton, 1998-99, U. Pa., Phila., 1999-2000, U. Mont., Missoula, 2000—. Author: (Poetry) Cuadernos de Horacio Morell, 1981, Crónicas de un Ocioso, 1983 (Municipalidad de Lima prize), Archivo de Huellas Digitales, 1985 (Segunda Bienal de Poesía Copé award), Sermón Sobre la Muerte, 1986, Rituales del Conocimiento y del Sueño, 1987, El Libro de los Encuentros, 1988, Canciones del Herrero del Arca, 1989, Recuerda, Cuerpo, 1991, Raritan Blues, 1997, El Equilibrista de Bayard Street, 1998 (El Olivo de Oro prize), Chronicles of a Man of Leisure, 1998 (Concurso Carpeta luz Bilingue prize), Amores & Desamores: 35 Poemas, 1999, Naufragio de los Días (Anthology, 1978-1998), 1999, Abecedario del Agua, 2000, Breve Historia de la Música, 2001 (Casa de América Poetry prize), Escrito en Missoula, 2003, (essays) El Techo de la Ballena, 1991, La Morada del Silencio, 1998, Epístola a los Transeúntes, 2001; editor: (anthologies) Infame Turba, 1992, Infame Turba, 2d edit., 1997, Loco Amor, 1991, of books, articles, revs.; author: El Fingidor, 2003, Derrota del Otoño (Anthology 1978-02), 2003. Home: 3701 Stephens Ave # 2 Missoula MT 59801 Office: U Mont 32 Campus Dr Missoula MT 59812

CHIROT, DANIEL, sociology and international studies educator; b. Bélâbre, Indre, France, Nov. 27, 1942; came to U.S., 1949; s. Michel and Hélène C.; m. Cynthia Kenyon, July 19, 1974; children: Claire, Laura. BA in Social Studies, Harvard U., 1964; PhD in Sociology, Columbia U., 1973. Prof. internat. studies and sociology Henry M. Jackson sch. U. Wash., Seattle, 1975—, chair internat. studies program. Author: Social Change in a Peripheral Society, 1976, Social Change in the Twentieth Century, 1977, Social Change in the Modern Era, 1986, Modern Tyrants: The Power and Prevalence of Evil in Our Age, 1994, rev. edit., 1996, How Societies Change, 1994; translator: (with Holley Coulter Chirot) Traditional Romanian Villages (Henri H. Stahl), 1980; editor: The Origins of Backwardness in Eastern Europe, 1989, The Crisis of Leninism and the Decline of the Left, 1991, (with Anthony Reid) Essential Outsiders, 1997, (with Martin Seligman) Ethnopolitical Warfare, 2001. John Simon Guggenheim fellow 1991-92. Avocations: skiing, hiking. Office: U Washington Jackson Sch Intl Studies PO Box 353650 Seattle WA 98195-3650

CHISCANO, ALFONSO, surgeon; b. Tenerife, Spain, 1938; came to U.S., 1963; MD, U. Barcelona, 1963. Diplomate Am. Bd. Surgery, Am. Bd. Thoracic Surgery, Can. Bd. Gen. Surgery, Can. Bd. Thoracic Surgery. Intern Grace Hosp., Detroit, 1963-64; resident in gen. surgery Wayne State U. Affiliated Hosps., Dearborn, 1964-69, resident in cardiothoracic surgery, 1969-71; fellow in cardiothoracic surgery Tex. Heart Inst., Houston, 1971-72; hosp. appt. S.W. Tex. Meth. Hosp., San Antonio, 2002—, Bapt. Meml. Hosps., 2002—, Santa Rosa Hosp., 1999—; surgeon Cirujanos de Corazon Assocs PA, San Antonio, 2002—. Clin. prof. cardiothoracic surgery U. Tex., 1998; instnl. advisor Autonomous Govt. of Canary Islands, Spain, San Antonio, 1998—. Officer pilot Spanish Airforce, 1958-61, Spain. Recipient Gold medal Am. Heart Assn., 1999, medal of Gold, Canary Islands, 1999. Fellow ACS, Am. Coll. Cardiology, Royal Coll. Surgeons (Can.); mem. Tex. Med. Assn., Bexar County Med. Soc., San Antonio Surg. Soc., San Antonio Cardiology Soc., Soc. Thoracic Surgeons (com. on medico-legal affairs), So. Thoracic Surg. Assn., Internat. Cardiovasc. Surg. Assn., Internat. Soc. Minimally Invasive Cardiac Surgery, Denton A. Cooley Cardiovasc. Surgery Soc. Avocations: reading, travel, listening to music, learning computer. Home: 15243 Pebble Cove San Antonio TX 78232-4127 Office: Cirujanos de Corazon Assocs PA 4330 Medical Dr Ste 275 San Antonio TX 78229-3342 Fax: (210) 494-6629. E-mail: chicocor@texas.net.

CHISHOLM, ANDREA LYNNE, business association administrator, foundation administrator; b. Waterloo, Iowa, Mar. 11, 1961; d. Delbert Eugene Brix and Lynne Larsen; m. Colin Alexander Joseph Chisholm, Nov. 3, 2001. BA, Iowa Lakes U., 1982. Dir. human resources Lord & Taylor, New York, 1986—98; dir. membership Stamford (Conn.) C. of C., 1998—. Dir., vice chmn. ARC, Stamford, 2000—02. Bd. dirs. Women in Mgmt., Stamford, 1999—2002. Mem.: Landmark Club. Republican. Avocations: yachting, deep water diving, golf, animal rescue. Office: Stamford C of C 7 33 Summer St Ste 104 Stamford CT 06901 Home Fax: 203-363-5069; Office Fax: 203-363-5069. Personal E-mail: achisholm@stamfordchamber.com. E-mail: achisholm@tcnnetworks.com.

CHISHOLM, COLIN ALEXANDER JOSEPH, III, media professional; b. Salem, Mass., Nov. 23, 1951; s. Colin Alexander William XI and Mary Elizabeth (Brennan) Chisholm; m. Virginia Louise Nance, June 24, 1973 (div.); 1 child, Mary Kathryn; m. Andrea Lynne Brix, Nov. 3, 2001. MS, New England Inst., 1976. Dir. sales United Artists TV, 1979-80; v.p. Turner Program Svcs., 1981-85; pres. CST Entertainment, 1986-88; vice chmn., CEO Comship Corp., 1989; chmn., CEO Chisholm Bros. Inc. Founder, chmn. bd. The Caribbean Network, 1994, CaribTel Telephone Co., 1994. Contbr. articles to profl. jours. Bd. dirs. St. Andrew's Soc. of the State of N.Y., Maine Golf Hall of Fame; dinner com. The Bal Polonaise, 1988, 89; mem. English Speaking Union; patron Debutante Assembly; mem. Nat. Found. of Scottish Medieval and Mus. With USMC, 1969-74, Res., 1974-76. Mem. NATAS, N.Y. State Broadcasters Assn. (bd. dirs.), Internat. Radio and TV Soc., Nat. Assn. of TV Program Execs., Am. Film Inst., Am. Legion, Scottish-Am. Found., Clan Chisholm Soc., Scottish Heritage U.S.A., Nat. Trust for Scotland, Rotary (N.Y.), Squadron A Assn., OverSeas Press Club Am., Coffee House N.Y., China C. of C. (bd. dirs.). Office: 250 Harbor Dr Stamford CT 06902 E-mail: cajc@msn.com.

CHISHOLM, DEAN D. lawyer; b. Missoula, Mont., Feb. 15, 1967; s. Richard L. and Marilyn R.W. Chisholm; m. Penni L. Chisholm, Sept. 4, 1993; children: Henry R., Ava P. BA, Colo. State U., 1989; JD, U. Mont., 1992. Bar: Mont. 1992, U.S. Dist. Ct. Mont. 1992, U.S. Ct. Appeals (9th cir.) 1992, Colo. 2001. Dep. county atty. Cascade County, Great Falls, Mont., 1992—94, acting county atty., 1994; ptnr. Lynch & Chisholm, P.C., Great Falls, Mont., 1995—96, Kaplan & Chisholm, P.L.L.P., Columbia Falls, Mont., 1996—; dep. city atty. Columbia Falls, 1998—; apptd. spl. prosecutor Mont. Supreme Ct. Commn. on Practice, 2001—02. Bd. mem. Fed. Law Enforcement Grant Bd., Great Falls, 1994—96. Named one of Best Lawyers in Am., 2001—; recipient cert. of recognition for Nat. Mid. East Studies Symposium, Pa. State U., 1989, Am. Jurisprudence award for outstanding achievement in constl. law, 1991. Mem.: Colo. Bar Assn., N.W. Mont. Bar Assn., Mont. Trial Lawyers Assn., Mensa. Avocations: literature, golf. Office: Kaplan & Chisholm PLLP PO Box 2071 Columbia Falls MT 59912

CHISHOLM, LIONEL DONALD JOHN, ophthalmologist; b. Montreal, Que., Can., July 9, 1935; s. Donald Munro and Isabelle Anne (Frizzell) C.; m. Ann Violet Webster, Feb. 12, 1960; children: Sarah Ann, John Webster. MD, U. Toronto, 1959. Retina fellow Retina Found., Mass. Eye and Ear Infirmary, Boston, 1964-66; asst. to assoc. prof. opthalmology U. Toronto, 1966-79, prof., 1979-93; ophthalmologist in chief Toronto Western and Toronto Hosp., 1979-93; prof., dir. of retina vitreous unit dept. ophthalmologyy W.Va. U., 1993—. W.Va. state rep. diabetes 2000 Am. Acad. Ophthalmology, 1994—. Fellow: Assn. for Rsch. in Vision and Ophthalmology, Schepens Internal Soc., Am. Acad. Ophthalmology, Royal Coll. Surgeons (Can.); mem.: Can. Med. Assn., Retina Soc. (founding mem.). Avocation: equestrian. Office: WVa U Eye Inst PO Box 9193 Morgantown WV 26506-9193

CHISHOLM, MALCOLM HAROLD, chemistry educator; b. Bombay, Oct. 15, 1945; came to U.S., 1972; s. Angus MacPhail and Gweneth (Robey) C.; m. Cynthia Ann Truax, May 1, 1982; children: Calum R.I., Selby Scott, Derek Adrian. BS in Chemistry, Queen Mary Coll., London, 1966, PhD in Chemistry, 1969; DSc (hon.), London U., 1981. Postdoctoral fellow U. Western Ont., London, 1969-72; asst. prof. Princeton (N.J.) U., 1972-78; assoc. prof. chemistry Ind. U., Bloomington, 1978-80, prof., 1980-85, Disting. prof. chemistry, 1985-99; disting. prof. math., phys. scis. Ohio State U., 2000—. Cons. in field. Editor: Polyhedron, Chem. Comm., Dalton Transactions; mem. editl. bd. Inorganic Chemistry, Organometallics, Inorganic Chimica Acta, Inorganic Syn. Inc., Jour. Cluster Sci., Chem. European Jour., Can. Jour. Chemistry, Chem. Record; contbr. over 500 rsch. articles to profl. jours. Fellow AAAS, Ind. Acad. Scis., Royal Soc. (London, Davy medal), Royal Soc. for Chemistry (Corday Morgan medal 1981, award for Transition Metal Chemistry, Centenary Lectr. and medal, Mond Lectr. and medal), Am. Chem. Soc. (Akron sect. award 1982, Buck Whitney award 1987, Inorganic Chemistry award 1989, Disting. Svc. award 1999). Home: 100 Kenyon Brook Dr Worthington OH 43085-3629 also: 38 Norwich St Cambridge CB2 1NE England Office: Ohio State U Dept Chemistry 100 W 18th Ave Columbus OH 43210-1185 E-mail: chisholm@chemistry.ohio-state.edu.

CHISHOLM, MARGARET ELIZABETH, retired library education administrator; b. Grey Eagle, Minn., July 25, 1921; d. Henry D. and Alice (Thomas) Bergman; children: Nancy Diane, Janice Marie Lane. BA, U. Washington, 1957, MLS, 1958, PhD, 1966. Libr. Everett (Wash.) C.C., 1961-63; from asst. to assoc. prof. edn. U. Oreg., Eugene, 1963-67; assoc. prof. edn. U. N.Mex., Albuquerque, 1967-69; prof., dean U. Md. Coll. Libr. and Info. Svcs., College Park, 1969-75; v.p. univ. rels. and devel. U. Washington, Seattle, 1975-81; dir., prof. Grad. Sch. Libr. and Info. Sci., U. Wash., Seattle, 1981-92; ret., 1992. Adv. com. White House Conf. on Libr. and Info. Sci., 1989-91, Pub. Broadcasting Svc. Archive; commr. Western Interstate Commn. Higher Edn., Colo., 1981-85. Author: Information Technology: Design and Applications (with Nancy Lane), 1990. Mem. USIA del. to Mexican-Am. Commn. on Cultural Coop., 1990. Civilian aide U.S. Army, 1978-88. Recipient Ruth Worden award U. Wash., Seattle, 1957, Disting. Alumni award St. Cloud (Minn.) U., 1977, Disting. Alumni award U. Wash., 1979, John Brubaker award Cath. Libr. Assn., 1987, Pres.'s award Wash. Libr. Assn., 1991. Mem. ALA (exec. bd. 1989-90, pres. 1988-89, v.p. 1986-87), Assn. Pub. TV Stas. (trustee 1975-84, 87-93), White House Conf. on Libr. and Info. Svcs. (adv. com. 1989-91), U. Wash. Retirement Assn. (v.p. 1995-96, pres. 1996-98). Home: 20900 Big Basin Way Saratoga CA 95070-5750

CHISHOLM, MARTHA MARIA, dietitian; b. Havana, Cuba, Nov. 27, 1958; arrived in U.S., 1961; d. Robert Lester and Martha Clara (Latour) C. BS in Dietetics and Nutrition, Fla. Internat. U., 1983, MS Dietetics/Nutrition magna cum laude, 1995. Lic. dietitian, Fla. Pediat. clin. dietitian Miami (Fla.) Children's Hosp., 1983-86, 92-96, pediat. gastroenterology dietitian, 1986-92, dietitian Ketogenic Diet Ctr., 1994-96, pediat. clin. dietitian, staff relief, 1997; dietitian Pediatric Cystic Fibrosis Ctr., 1993-96, dietitian feeding and swallowing disorder team, 1994-96; clin. dietitian Oncology and Hospice Mercy Cath. Hosp., 1997—. Cons. United Cerebral Palsy Assn. Miami, 1989-94, Roche Labs., Miami, 1991-95, Children's Rehab. Network, Miami, 1990-95. Mem. Homeless Ministry, St. Louis Cath. Ch., Miami, 1991-94, Eucharistic min., 1993-96, young adult ministry co-leader, 1994-96; mem. fgn. mission ministry Amor En Accion, 1995—. Mem. Am. Dietetic Assn. (reg. dietician), Fla. Dietetic Assn. (Disting. Dietitian 1997), Miami Dietetic Assn. (sec. 1988-89, Recognized Young Dietitian award 1988, Hurricane Andrew Relief Fund chair 1992-93, mem. nominating com. 1993-94, Disting. Dietitian 1996), Sierra Club (Miami chpt. cert. outings leader 1998—), Phi Kappa Phi. Republican. Roman Catholic. Avocations: dog shows, backpacking, cycling, photography, canoeing, rowing. Home: 5935 Turin St Coral Gables FL 33146-3245 Office: Mercy Cath Hosp 3663 S Miami Ave Miami FL 33133-4253 E-mail: mmchisholm@cattbi.com.

CHISHOLM, TOMMY, lawyer, utility company executive; b. Baldwyn, Miss., Apr. 14, 1941; s. Thomas Vaniver and Rubel (Duncan) C.; m. Janice McClanahan, June 20, 1964; children: Mark Alan (dec.), Andrea, Stephen Thomas, Patrick Ervin. BSCE, Tenn. Tech. U., 1963; JD, Samford U., 1969; MBA, Ga. State U., 1984. Registered profl. engr., Ala., Del., Ga., Fla., Ky., La., N.H., Miss., N., Pa., Tenn., S.C., Va., W.Va. Civil engr. TVA, Knoxville, Tenn., 1963-64; design engr. So. Co. Svcs., Birmingham, Ala., 1964-69, coord. spl. projects Atlanta, 1969-73, sec., house counsel, 1977-82, v.p., sec., house counsel, 1982-98; v.p., assoc. gen. counsel, sec. So. Co., Atlanta, 1998—, asst. to pres., 1973-75, sec., asst. treas., 1977—; mgr. adminstrv. svcs. Gulf Power Co., Pensacola, Fla., 1975-77; sec. So. Energy, Inc., Atlanta, 1981-82; v.p., sec. So. Energy Resources Inc., Atlanta, 1982-2000. Mem. ABA, State Bar Ala., Am. Soc. Corp. Secs., Am. Corp. Counsel Assn., Nat. Assn. Corp. Dirs., Phi Alpha Delta, Beta Gamma Sigma. Office: The Southern Co 270 Peachtree St NW Ste 2200 Atlanta GA 30303-1247

CHISHOLM, WILLIAM DEWAYNE, retired contract manager; b. Everett, Wash., Mar. 1, 1924; s. James Adam and Evelyn May (Iles) C.; m. Esther Troehler, Mar. 10, 1956; children: James Scott, Larry Alan, Brian Duane. BSChemE, BS in Indsl. Engring., U. Wash., 1949; MBA, Harvard U., 1955. Cert. profl. contracts mgr. Chemist, unit leader, tech. rep. The Coca-Cola Co., Atlanta and L.A., 1949-59; contract administr. Honeywell Inc., L.A., 1959-61, mktg. administr., 1961-64, contracts work dir., 1964-66, contracts mgr. Clearwater, Fla., 1966-73, contracts supr., 1973-75, sr. contract mgmt. rep., 1975-80, prin. contract mgmt. rep., work dir., 1980-82, contracts mgr., 1982-89; ret. Chmn. bd. Creative Attitudes, Inc., 1987-96; adj. faculty Fla. Inst. Tech., 1976-96. Contbr. articles to profl. jours. Trustee John Calvin Found., 1974-82; mem. budget adv. com. City of Clearwater, 1983-85; commr. to 196th gen. assembly Presbyn. Ch. (USA), 1984; sec. bd. trustees, treas. Presbytery of Tampa Bay, 1990-96, 99-2003, sec. coun., 1996-98, mem. rev., evaluation and planning com., 1996-98, treas. 1999-2003, elder session mem., 1964-65, 73-76, 77-80, 81-84, 86-90, 97-2000, 2001—, treas., 1994-96; Clearwater rep. on Long Ctr. bd. dirs., 1991-97, mem. exec. com., 1992-97, treas., 1992-93, v.p., 1993-95. With USN, 1944-46. Recipient Award of Distinction Fla. Inst. Tech. Grad. Ctr., 1987. Fellow Nat. Contract Mgmt. Assn. (chmn. S.E. region fellows 1985-87, past nat. dir., pres., v.p. Suncoast chpt.). Home: 1364 S Hercules Ave Clearwater FL 33764-3748 *We can't be too generous in sharing understanding and words of comfort, encouragement, and support to those facing adversity and challenge at various times in their lives.*

CHISM, REBECCA LYNN, language educator; MA, Middlebury Coll., 1986—87; PhD, Fla. State U., 1996—2000; MAT, U. of Louisville, 1990—91. Asst. prof. of fgn. lang. pedagogy Kent State U., Kent, Ohio, 2000—. Office: Kent State University-MCLS 109 Satterfield Hall Kent OH 44242 Office Fax: 330-672-4009. E-mail: rlchism@kent.edu.

CHISU, IOAN, artist; b. Cluj-Napoca, Romania, Jan. 28, 1939; arrived in U.S., 88, naturalized, 96; s. Gheorghe and Hermina Chisu; m. Rodica Chisu, Mar. 24, 1961; children: Ioana, Daniel. M of Painting, Ion Andreescu Fine Arts Inst., Cluj-Napoca, 1963. Pres. Union Bd. Artists of Sibiu County, Romania, 1968-70, 80-89; mem. coun. Leadership Fine Arts Union Romania, 1980-89, mem., 1964-89. One-person shows include Sirius Gallery, Sibiu, 1965, 67, Apollo Gallery, 1970, Brukenthal Mus., Sibiu, 1973; exhibited in group shows Art Gallery, Brasov, 1964, 65-67, Art Movie Theater Show, Sibiu, 1965, Brukenthal Mus., Sibiu, 1964, 67, 68-70, 72, 88, Simu Mus., Bucharest, 1965, Dalles Gallery, Bucharest, 1965, 67-70, 73-88, Casa Armatei, Sibiu, 1966, 74, Sirius Gallery, Sibiu, 1967, 73-88, Mus. Art, Bucharest, 1968, Art Gallery Casa Artelor, Sibiu, 1971, 73-88, Culture's House, Medias, 1971, 74, Big Gallery, Cluj-Napoca, 1973, Ateneul Roman Gallery, Bucharest, 1976, Nat. Theater, Bucharest, 1977; exhibited in mus. Brukenthal Mus., Sibiu, Art Mus., Brasov, Art Mus., Tirgu Mures, Romania, Anchorage Mus. History and Art, 1997-98; monumental mosaic works: Tradition and Contemporary Times, 1973, Homage to Human Creativity, 1980, Archways, 1981. Recipient Nat. Order of Cultural Merit for spl. artistic merits, Bucharest, 1968, Nat. Prize for Romania at 3d Internat. Festival of Painting, Cagnes-sur-Mer, France, 1971, 1st prize for painting Nat. Festival Art, Bucharest, 1985, 87, Grant award Cmty. Arts Assistance Program from City of Chgo. Dept. Cultural Affairs and Ill. Arts Coun. Access Program, 1993, 95. Home: 2417 N Alton Rd McHenry IL 60050

CHISUM, EMMETT DEWAIN, historian, archeologist, researcher; b. Monroe, La., Mar. 19, 1922; BA in Social Sci., Northwestern State U., 1942; MA in Social Sci., La. State U., 1946; MA in History, U. Wyo., 1952, MA in Polit. Sci. an dAnthropology, 1961. Tchr. sci. Cameron (La.) Parish Sch. System, 1947-51; tchr. English Welsh (La.) High Sch., 1946-47; social sci. librarian U. Wyo., Laramie, 1954-77, prof. rsch. history, archeology, 1977—. Mem. faculty senate U. Wyo., 1986—. Author: (books) Guide to Library Research, 1969, Guide to Research in Political Science, 1970, Guide to Research in Education, 1974, Memories: University of Wyoming 1886-1986, 1987; contbr. articles to Ency. of Lir. and Info. Sci. (45 vols.), 1986—, profl. jours. Mem. AAAS, ALA, Am. Archeol. Soc., Western Pol. Sci. Assn., Am. Assn. for State and Local History for Wyo. Publs. (Agnes Milstead award for Outstanding Librarianship 1995). Home: 2032 Holliday Dr Laramie WY 82070-4803

CHISUM, MATTHEW EUAL, research scientist, laboratory administrator; b. Amarillo, Tex., Aug. 5, 1953; s. Donzell Eual and Ella Jean (Vincent) C.; m. Elizabeth Kay Neidhardt, Mar. 15, 1980; children: Brett Matthew, Kristen Marie. BS, West Tex. State U., 1975, MS, 1976. Instr. math. Frank Phillips Jr. Coll., Borger, 1976-77; from chem. tech. to sr. scientist Mason & Hanger Pantex Plant, Amarillo, 1977—90; owner Chisum Ranches, Ltd., Stinnett, 1987—, from project scientist to lab. mgr., 1990—97; project team leader for atomic spectroscopy Pantex Plant, Amarillo, 1994-97; lab. mgr. Engineered Carbons, Inc., Borger, Tex., 1997-2000, Sid Richardson Carbon Co., Borger, 2000—02, BWXT Pantex, Amarillo, 2002—. Mem. Comm. Task Force-Pantex, Amarillo, 1990-91, Emergency Spill Response-Pantex, Amarillo, 1987-92. Contbr. articles to profl. jours. Mem. Tax Appraisal Rev. Bd., Hutchinson County, 1996—97, Hutchinson Count Crisis Ctr., 1999—2000. Mem. Am. Chem. Soc., ASTM (sec. Sect. D 24, 51, 1997-2002), Ducks Unltd. (chmn. Canyon chpt. 1985-86), Lions Internat. (sec. Adobe Walls 1988-95), Hutchinson County Pioneers Assn. (pres. 1994-96), Sigma Phi Epsilon (alumni chmn. Tex. Xi chpt. 1976-81, Alumnus of Yr. award 1976, 78, Leadership Borger 1998-99). Avocations: hunting, ranching. Home: PO Box 3338 400 Lariat St Stinnett TX 79083-3338 Office: BWXT Pantex PO Box 30020 Amarillo TX 79120 E-mail: mchisum@pantex.com.

CHITESTER, ROBERT JOHN, television producer; b. Kane, Pa., Oct. 30, 1937; s. Palmer Rayburn and Ellen Louise (Huffman) C.; m. Carol Beth Lovell, Feb. 28, 1958; children: Cindee Lynn, Kimberly Jo, Mark Kevin, Amy Beth. BA in Radio/TV, U. Mich., 1959, MA in Radio/TV, 1962; D of Lit., Allegheny Coll., 1980. Dir. of TV prodn. Buena Vista H.S., Saginaw, Mich., 1959-61; dir. TV ops. Edinboro (Pa.) State Coll., 1962-66; pres. Public Broadcasting of N.W. Pa., Erie, 1966-82, Amagin Inc., McKean, Pa., 1980-85, Chitester Creative Assocs., McKean, 1984—, Palmer R. Chitester Fund, McKean, 1985—; mng. ptnr. Free to Choose Enterprise, McKean, 1988—; chmn. Share TV, Inc., 1992-98. Adv. bd. C. Northcote Parkinson Fund, N.Y.C., 1988—, ACES, Erie, Pa., 1984-94. Prodr., dir. writer many prodns. including Milton Friedman's Free to Choose. Pres. Planned Parenthood, Erie County, Pa., 1969-73; dir. Erie County Public Libr., 1976-78, Erie County Alcoholism Coun., 1975-78. Republican. Avocations: aquarist, physical fitness, gardening, wood sculpture. Home: 10539 Edinboro Rd Mc Kean PA 16426-1949 Office: Palmer R Chitester Fund 1502 Powell Ave Erie PA 16505

CHITRE, SHARADCHANDRA RAGHUNANDAN, physician; b. Apr. 11, 1936; came to U.S., 1968; s. Raghunandan Ballal and Sarojini Chitre; m. Rekha Balkrishna Chitnis, May 6, 1961; children: Nanda, Priya, Yash. MB, BChir, M.S. U., Baroda, India, 1961, MS, 1966. Resident in orthopaedic surgery Royal Sea Bathing Hosp., Margate, Eng., 1967-68; resident in surgery Beverly (Mass.) Hosp., 1968-70, emergency physician, 1971—2002, chief emergency and outpatient dept., 1975-85. Fellow in plastic surgery Meth. Hosp., Bklyn., 1970-71; instr. North Shore Community Coll., Beverly; former mem. state adv. bd. on emergency med. Services. Fellow Royal Soc. Health (London); mem. Mass. Med. Soc., Essex South Dist. Med. Soc., Indian Med. Assn. New Eng. (trustee), Am. Coll. Emergency Physicians, Barода Med. Coll. Alumni Assn. (pres. 1987-90, trustee 1997-00). Home: 901 Bay Rd Hamilton MA 01936-0327 Office: 75 Herrick St Beverly MA 01915-5900

CHITTICK, ELIZABETH LANCASTER, women's rights activist; b. Bangor, Pa., Nov. 11, 1908; d. George and Flora Mae (Mann) Lancaster. Student, Columbia U., 1944-45, N.Y. Inst. Fin., 1950-51, Hunter Coll., 1952-56, Upper Iowa U., Fayette, 1976. Adminstrv. asst., chief clk U.S. Naval Air Stas., Seattle and Banana River, Fla., 1941-45; v.p. treas. W.A. Chittick & Co., MAnila, 1945-52; 31062Smith; real estate salesperson, 1949; registered rep. Bache & Co., N.Y. Stock Exch., N.Y.C., 1950-62, Shearson & Hamil, 1962-63; investment adviser, 1962-65; revenue officer IRS, N.Y.C., 1965-72; pres. Nat. Woman's Party, Washington, 1971-89, Woman's Party Corp., 1978-91; commr. Washington Commn. on Status of Women, 1982-86; pres., adminstr. Sewall-Belmont House. Bd. dirs. Wexita Corp., N.Y.C., Pan Am. Liason Com. of Women's Orgns. Inc.; 1st v.p., bd. dirs. Nat. Coun. Women U.S. Lectr., TV and radio commentator on Equal Rights Amendment; author: Answers to Questions About the Equal Rights Amendment, 1973, 76. Mem. Coalition for Women in Internat. Devel., Internat. Women's Yr. Continuing Com., 1978-81, Women's Campaign Fund, Washington, 1975-80, Women's Nat. Rep. Club, N.Y.C., Women Govt. Rels., Washington; mem. U.S. com. of cooperation to Inter-Am. Commn. of Women, OAS, 1974-80; del. U.S. World Conf. of Internat. Women's Yr., Mexico City, 1975; mem. women's history ctr. task force Am. Revolution Bicentennial Adminstrn., 1973-76; mem. adv. com. U.S. Ctr. for Internat. Women's Yr., 1973-76; vice convenor com. on law and status of women Internat. Coun. of Women; chmn. UN Drive for war orphans and widows, Manila, 1949 Mem. Greater Washington Soc. Assn. Execs., Internat. Coun. Women (Paris), Nat. Fedn. Bus. and Profl. Women's Clubs, Gen. Fedn. Women's Clubs, Women's Press Club (N.Y.C.), Am. Newswomen's Club, Nat. Press Club, Order Eastern Star. Home and Office: 236 Orange Tree Dr Atlantis FL 33462-1130

CHITWOOD, DAVID JOSEPH, zoologist, researcher; b. Balt., Apr. 29, 1950; PhD, U. Md., 1980. Zoologist USDA, Beltsville, Md., 1981—. Editor-in-chief Jour. of Nematology, 1990-93; contbr. over 28 articles to profl. jours. Fellow Helminthological Soc. Wash. (pres. 1991-92); mem. Am. Soc. Parasitologists, Soc. Nematologists (editor-in-chief 1990-93), pres. 1995-96, N.Y. Acad. Scis. Achievements include research in nematode steroids and hormones and potentially exploitable biochemical differences between nematodes and their hosts. Office: USDA Nematology Lab Oiia Barc W Beltsville MD 20705 E-mail: chitwood@ba.ars.usda.gov.

CHITWOOD, JULIUS RICHARD, retired librarian; b. Magazine, Ark., June 1, 1921; s. Hoyt Mozart and Florence (Umfrid) C.; m. Aileen Newsom, Aug. 6, 1944. AB cum laude, Ouachita Bapt. Coll., Ark., 1942; M.Mus., Ind. U., 1948; MA, U. Chgo., 1954. Music supr. Edinburgh (Ind.) Pub. Schs., 1946-47; music and audiovisual librarian Roosevelt Coll., Chgo., 1948-51; humanities librarian Drake U., 1951-53; spl. cataloger Chgo. Tchrs. Coll., 1953; asst. circulation librarian Indpls. Pub. Library, 1954-57, coordinator adult services, 1957-61; dir. Rockford (Ill.) Pub. Library, 1961-79, No. Ill. Library System, Rockford, 1966-76; ret., 1979. Chmn. subcom. library system devel. Ill. Library Adv. Com., 1965— ; adv. com. U. Ill. Grad. Sch. Library Sci., 1964-68; cons. in field, participant workshops Pres. Rockford Regional Academic Center, 1974-76; Mem. history com. Ill. Sesquicentennial Commn.; mem. Mayor Rockford Com. for UN, 1962-70; sect. chmn. Rockford United Fund, 1966-70; exec. Rockford Civic Orch. Assn., 1962-70. Served to maj., inf. AUS. 1942-45, ETO. Recipient Ill. Librarian of Year award, 1974 Mem. ALA (chmn. subcom. revision standards of materials, pub. library div. 1965-66, pres. bldg. and equipment sect. library adminstrn. div. 1967-68, chmn. staff devel. com. personnel adminstrn. sect., library adminstrv. div. 1964-68, pres. library adminstrn. div. 1969-70), Ill. Library Assn. (v.p. 1964-65, pres. 1965-66). Unitarian Universalist. Home: 3662 E Covenanter Dr Bloomington IN 47401-4681

CHIU, BELLA CHAO, astrophysicist, writer; b. Beijing, May 24, 1931; came to U.S., 1938; d. Yuen Ren and Buwei (Yang) Chao; m. Hong-Yee Chiu, June 25, 1960 (div. 1966); 1 child, Lihu Mason Chiu. BA, U. Calif., Berkeley, 1953; MS, Cornell U., 1956. Rsch. staff MIT, Cambridge, 1971-81; tchr. ESL Ctrl. S. U. Tech., Changsha, China, 1982-83; fgn. expert Qinghua U., Beijing, 1986-87; writer Arlington, Mass., 1987-97; rschr., 1997—. English editor Nat. Assn. Chinese Ams., 1984-86. Grantee NSF, 1972, 75, 79. Mem. Am. Astron. Soc. (hist. divsn.), Archeol. Inst. Am., Women's Health Initiative.

CHIU, CHAO-LIN, civil engineer; b. Taiwan, Nov. 9, 1934; came to U.S., 1961, naturalized, 1972; s. Chien-Song and Pi-Yu (Chang) C.; B.S., Nat. Taiwan U., 1957; M.S.A., U. Toronto, 1961; Ph.D., Cornell U., 1964; m. Fuh-Mei Lee, Sept. 24, 1965; 1 son, Bruce. Asst. prof. civil engring. U. Pitts., 1964-67, assoc. prof., 1968-71; research hydrologist U.S. Geol. Survey, 1974; prof. civil engring. U. Pitts., 1972— ; vis. prof. U. Karlsruhe, W.Ger., 1980; vis. NSC chair prof. dept. civil engring. National Taiwan U., 1991-92; cons. World Bank for Chinese U. Devel. Project, 1986. Sr. Fulbright fellow, 1980; NSF grantee, 1965, 71, 74, 78, 81, 95; U.S. Office Water Resources grantee, 1967; recipient Faculty Fellowship award Oak Ridge Assoc. U., 1988. Mem. ASCE, Am. Geophys. Union, Internat. Assn. Hydraulic Research, Am. Inst. Hydrology. Democrat. Author: Stochastic Hydraulics, 1971; Applications of Kalman Filter to Hydrology, Hydraulics and Water Resources, 1978; mem. editorial bd. Civil Engring. Systems, 1983-87, Water Resources Monograph Series, 1982-86; contbr. articles to profl. jours. Home: 724 Field Club Rd Pittsburgh PA 15238-2431 Office: U Pitts Dept Civil Engring Pittsburgh PA 15261-0001

CHIU, CHICHIA, mathematician, educator; b. Beijing, May 1, 1959; married. PhD, Carnegie Mellon U., 1987. Assoc. prof. Mich. State U., E. Lansing, 1995—2002.

CHIU, CHRISTINA, writer, editor; b. N.Y.C., Feb. 13, 1969; d. Alice Yim and Paul Chiu; married. BA, Bates Coll., 1991; MFA, Columbia U., 1999. Editor Tin Ho. Mag., N.Y.C., 1998—2002. Author: Troublemaker and Other Saints, 2001, A Bit of Heart (on a Small Plate), 2004. Named winner, New Stone Cir. Fiction Contest, 2001; recipient 3d pl., Playboy Fiction Contest, 1999, Asian Am. Literary award, 2002; Van Lier fellow, Asian Am. Writers' Workshop, 1998, Claire Woolrich scholar, Columbia U., 1999, Robert Simpson fellow, Millay Colony, 2001. Personal E-mail: troublemsaints@aol.com.

CHIU, DAVID TAK WAI, surgeon; b. Kwangtung, China, Oct. 23, 1945; s. Bud Yick and Lai Kwai (Lum) C.; m. Lilian Wah-Ying Shen, June 19, 1973; children: Vincent, Edmund, Jerome, Miranda. BA, U. Mo., St. Louis, 1969; MD, Columbia U., 1973. Diplomate Am. Bd. Plastic Surgery. Intern Barnes Hosp., St. Louis, 1973-74, resident in gen. surgery, 1974-77; resident in plastic surgery Columbia-Presbyn. Med. Ctr., 1977-79; fellow NYU Med. Ctr., N.Y.C., 1980, instr. surgery, 1981, asst. prof., 1981-89; supervisory attending Bellevue Hosp. Hand Clinic, N.Y.C., 1981-89; assoc. dir. plastic surgery, chief hand/microsurgery and replantation surgery divsn. plastic surgery Columbia Presbyn. Med. Ctr., N.Y.C., 1989-94, dir. microsurgery ctr., 1993, chief plastic surgery divsn. dept. surgery, 1994-97, prof. clin. surgery, 1990—2001, Thomas S. Zimmer prof., 1994-2000, Calvin F. Barber prof., 2000—01, dir. ctr. restorative surgery, 2000—; prof. plastic surgery NYU Med. Ctr., 2001—, dir. nerve surgery ctr., 2003—. Adj. prof. Coll. Physicians and Surgeons Columbia U., N.Y.C., 2001—. Author: Introduction to Microsurgery: A Lab Manual, 1985; mem. editorial bd. Jour. Reconstructive Microsurgery, 1990—. Recipient Alumni Fedn. Columbia U. medal, 1995. Fellow: ACS; mem.: AMA, World Soc. Reconstructive Microsurgery (founding mem.), Tissue Engring. Soc., Sunderland Soc., Am. Acad. Pediatrics (splty. fellow 1992), Internat. Soc. of Reconstructive Microsurgery, Northeast Soc. Plastic Surgery, Royal Soc. Medicine, Am. Soc. Peripheral Nerve Surgery (pres. 1999—2001, founding mem.), Am. Assn. Hand Surgery, Am. Soc. Plastic and Reconstructive Surgeons, Am. Soc. Surgery of Hand, Am. Soc. Reconstructive Microsurgery (pres. 1998—99), N.Y. Regional Soc. Plastic and Reconstructive Plastic Surgery (pres. 1997—98), Coll. Physicians and Surgeons Alumni Assn. (dir. 1984, pres. 2001—02, Bronze medal 1973, Gold medal 1997), Plastic Surgery Rsch. Coun., N.Y. Soc. Surgery of Hand (pres. 1996—97), N.Y. State Med. Soc., N.Y. County Med. Soc., Am. Assn. Plastic Surgeons, Chinese Am. Med. Soc. (dir. 1983—, pres. 1985—87, Presdl. medal 1987, Disting. Svc. award 1988, Scientific award 2001), Fedn. Chinese Am. and Chinese Can. Med. Socs. (founding pres. 1994—96, chmn. bd. dirs. 1996—98, found. trustee 2002—, found. pres. 2002—, Outstanding Achievement award 1994). Office: 900 Park Ave New York NY 10021-0231 E-mail: dtwc@davidchiumd.com.

CHIU, DOROTHY, retired pediatrician; b. Hong Kong, Aug. 8, 1917; came to U.S., 1946; d. Yan Tse Chiu and Connie Kwai-Ching Wan; m. Kitman Au; children: Katherine, Margo, Doris, James, Richard. BS, Lingnan U., 1939; MD, Nat. Shanghai Med. Coll., 1945. Diplomate Am. Bd. Pediats. Sch. physician L.A. Sch. Dist., 1954-55; pvt. practice Burbank, Calif., 1954-55, San Fernando, Calif., 1955-2000. Staff pediatrician Holy Cross Med. Ctr., Mission Hills, Calif., 1961-2000. Bd. dirs. Burbank Cmty. Concert, 1970-80. Fellow Am. Acad. Pediats.; mem. Calif. Med. Assn., L.A. County Med. Assn. Republican. Avocations: handicrafts, music, travel, reading, photography.

CHIU, HUNGDAH, lawyer, legal educator; b. Shanghai, Mar. 23, 1936; came to U.S., 1960; s. Han-ping and Ming-non (Yang) C.; m. Yuan-yuan Hsieh, May 14, 1966; 1 son, Wei-hsueh. LLB, Nat. Taiwan U., 1958; MA with honors, L.I. U., 1962; LLM, Harvard U., 1962, SJD, 1965. Assoc. in rsch. East Asian Research Center, Harvard U., 1964-65; assoc. prof. internat. law Nat. Taiwan U., 1965-66; rsch. assoc. in law Harvard U., 1966-70, 72-74; vis. prof. law Nat. Chengchi U., Taipei, Taiwan, 1970-72; assoc. prof. law U. Md., Balt., 1974-77, prof., 1977—2002, prof. emeritus, 2002—. Chmn. bd. dirs. Modern China Studies, Ctr. for Modern China, Princeton, NJ, 2000—; min. of state Exec. Yuan (Cabinet), Republic of China, Taiwan, 1993-94; mem. Presdl. Com. on Nat. Unification, Taiwan, 1995-2000, amb.-at-large, 1998-2000. Author: The Capacity of International Organizations to Conclude Treaties, 1966, The People's Republic of China and the Law of Treaties, 1972, (with J.A. Cohen) People's China and International Law, 2 vols, 1974 (certificate of merit Am. Soc. Internat. Law 1976), Normalizing Relations with China: Problems, Analysis and Documents, 1978, China and the Taiwan Issue, 1979, Agreements of the People's Republic of China, 1966-80, A Calendar of Events, 1981; (with S.C. Leng) China: 70 years after the 1911 Hsin-Hai Revolution, 1984, Criminal Justice in Post-Mao China, 1985, (with Y.C. Jao and Y.L. Wu) The Future of Hong Kong, 1987, The Draft Basic Law of Hong Kong: Analysis and Documents, 1988, (with G. Knight) International Law of the Sea: Cases, Documents and Readings, 1991; Hsian-t'ai Kuo-chi-fa (Modern International Law), 1995, (with Chun-i Chen) Hsien-tai Kuo-chi-fa Ts'an-kao Wen-chien (Reference Documents of Modern International Law), 1996, 1996 Case and Documentary Supplement for Knight and Chiu's International Law of the Sea, 1997; contbr. numerous articles to profl. jours., chpts. to books; gen. editor: Contemporary Asian Studies, 1976—; editor in chief Chinese Yearbook of Internat. Law and Affairs, 1981—. Del. UN Conf. Law of the Sea, 1976—82; chmn. of the bd. Ctr. for Modern China, 2000—. Served to 2d lt. Chinese Army, 1958—60. Named One of 10 Outstanding Young Men, Jr. c. of C. of Republic of China, 1971; Social Sci. Rsch. Coun. fellow, 1968; recipient Cultural award Inst. Chinese Culture, 1980, Toulmin medal Soc. Am. Mil. Engrs., 1982, Nat. Reconstrn. award Chinese Profl. Assn. Mid-Am., 1980, Outstanding Achievement award Mid-Am. Chinese Sci. and Tech. Assn., 1991, 1st class Merit Svc. medal Exec. Yuan (Cabinet), Republic of China, 1994. Mem. Am. Soc. Internat. Law (panel on China and internat. order 1969-74, chmn. interest group on law Pacific region 1987-93), Assn. for Asian Studies (com. on Asian law 1976-89), Am. Assn. for Chinese Studies (v.p. 1982-84, pres. 1985-87), Assn. Am. Law Schs. (chair internat. legal exch. sect. 1986-88), Assn. Chinese Social Scientists, N.A. (pres. 1984-86), Chinese Soc. Internat. Law (pres. 1993-2000), Internat. Law Assn. (pres. 1998-2000, perm. v.p. 2000—). Home: 6168 Devon Dr Columbia MD 21044-3821 Office: U Md Law Sch 500 W Baltimore St Baltimore MD 21201-1786 E-mail: estasia@law.umaryland.edu.

CHIU, ING-MING, biochemistry educator; b. Taipei, Taiwan, July 19, 1952; came to U.S., 1976; naturalized, 1988; s. Shin and Chung Tse (Shih) C.; m. Mei-Ching Liu Chiu, Sept. 4, 1977; children: Cindy Nicole, Katherine Grace. BS, Nat. Taiwan U., 1974; PhD, Fla. State U., 1981. Postdoctoral fellow NIH, Bethesda, Md., 1981-85; sr. investigator Revlon Health Care, Springfield, Va., 1985-86; asst. prof. Ohio State U., Columbus, 1986-91, mem. cancer rsch. ctr., 1986—, assoc. prof., 1991-95, prof., 1995—, dir. brain tumor gene therapy prog., 1997—. Contbr. articles to profl. jours. Lt. missile corps Taiwanese Army, 1974-76. Recipient Fogarty Internat. fellowship NIH, 1981-85, Ohio Cancer Rsch. award, 1988-90, Rsch. Career Devel. award NCI, 1990-95. Mem. AAAS, Am. Soc. Biochemistry and Molecular Biology, Am. Assn. Cancer Rsch. Presbyterian. Achievements include isolation of the first human proto-oncogene which codes for a protein with known physiological function, identification of HIV as a lentiretrovirus, patented cell lines that overexpress an angiogenic factor, and a method to isolate and enrich neural stem cells. Home: 8664 Finlarig Dr Dublin OH 43017-9636 Office: Ohio State U 480 W 9th Ave Rm S-2052 Columbus OH 43210-1245 E-mail: chiu.1@osu.edu.

CHIU, MARGARET CHI YUAN LIU, retired real estate broker; b. Quangzhou, Quangdong, China, Nov. 3, 1926; d. Chien Shan and Wen Bing Liu; m. Wan-Cheng Chiu, Feb. 6, 1954; children: Linda, Ellen, Elaine Amy. BA, Nat. Taiwan U., 1950; MBA, N.Y.U., 1956. Clk. Taiwan Supply Bur., Taipei, Taiwan, 1950-53; realtor assoc. Tropic Shore Realty, Honolulu, 1973-79; realtor broker Urner & Assocs., Inc., Honolulu, 1979-93; realtor/broker Savio Realty, Ltd./Better Homes and Gardens, Honolulu, 1993—95; ret. Chinese paintings shown in various exhibitions, 1990— Joint U.S. and Republic of China fellow, 1951-52. Mem. Nat. Assn. Realtors, Hawaii Assn. Realtors, Honolulu Bd. Realtors, Chinese Women's Benevolent Assn. Hawaii (pres. 1987-91), Hawaii Chinese Assn. (v.p. 1984, hon. dir. 2003--), Lung Kong Kung Shaw Soc. (sec. 1990-92). Avocations: chinese painting, singing, dancing. Home: 216 Kalalau St Honolulu HI 96825-2012

CHIU, MING SUNG, physician; b. Taipei Hsien, Taiwan, July 24, 1944; came to U.S., 1973; s. Ting-Fang and Siu-Mei C.; m. Lois P. Lin, 1971; children: James, Grace. MD, Taipei Med. Coll., 1969. Diplomate Am. Bd. Internal Medicine, Am. Bd. Pulmonary Disease. Resident Vets. Gen. Hosp., Taipei, 1970-73, Allegheny Gen. Hosp., Pitts., 1973-76, intern, 1973-74; sr. resident Vets. Hosp., Hines, Ill., 1976-78; pvt. practice Hopewell, Va., 1978—; mem. staff South Regional Med. Ctr., Petersburg, Va. Fellow Am. Coll. Chest Physicians; mem. ACP, Am. Thoracic Soc. Office: Va Med Group 2905 Boulevard Colonial Heights VA 23834-2400

CHIU, PETER YEE-CHEW, physician; b. China, May 12, 1948; came to U.S., 1965; naturalized, 1973; s. Man Chee and Yiu Ying Chiu. BS, U. Calif., Berkeley, 1969, MPH, 1970, DrPH, 1975; MD, Stanford U., 1983. Diplomate Am. Bd. Family Practice, Am. Bd. Preventive Medicine; registered profl. engr., Calif.; registered environ. health specialist, Calif. Asst. civil engr. City of Oakland, Calif., 1970-72; assoc. water quality engr. Bay Area Sewage Services Agy., Berkeley, 1974-76; prin. environ. engr. Assn. Bay Area Govts., Berkeley, 1976-79; intern San Jose (Calif.) Hosp., 1983-84, resident physician, 1984-86; ptnr. Chiu and Crawford, San Jose, 1986-89, Good Samaritan Med. Group, San Jose, 1989-90, The Permanente Med. Group, 1991—. Adj. prof. U. San Francisco, 1979-83; clin. assoc. prof. Stanford U. Med. Sch., 1987—. Contbr. articles to profl. publs.; co-authored one of the first comprehensive regional environ. mgmt. plans in U.S.; composer, pub. various popular songs Southeast Asia, U.S. Mem. Chinese for Affirmative Action, San Francisco, 1975—; bd. dirs. Calif. Regional Water Quality Control Bd.,Oakland, 1979-84, Bay Area Comprehensive Health Planning Coun., San Francisco, 1972-76; mem. Santa Clara County Ctrl. Dem. Com., 1987—; mem. exec. bd. Calif. State Dem. Ctrl. Com.; commr. U.S. Presdl. Commn. on Risk Assessment and Risk Mgmt., Washington, 1993-97; mem. U.S. Presdl. Rank Rev. Bd., Washington, 2000; hearing bd. mem. alt. Bay Area Air Quality Mgmt. Dist., San Francisco, 2002—. Recipient Resident Tchr. award Soc. Tchrs. Family Medicine, 1986, Resolution of Appreciation award Calif. Regional Water Quality Control Bd., 1985. Fellow Am. Acad. Family Physicians; mem. Am. Pub. Health Assn., Chi Epsilon, Tau Beta Pi. Democrat. Avocations: songwriting, recording. Office: The Permanente Med Group 770 E Calaveras Blvd Milpitas CA 95035-5491

CHIU, WILLIAM CHIEN-CHEN, surgeon; b. Taipei, Taiwan, Jan. 25, 1963; s. Wu Shung and Hsiu Hui (Kuo) C.; m. Terri-Ann Anthony, May 25, 1991; children: Anthony Kohler, Katherine Anna, Victoria Louise. MD, U. Md. Sch. Medicine, 1988. Diplomate in gen. surgery and surg. critical care Am. Bd. Surgery. Intern in surgery R. W. Johnson Med. Sch. U. Medicine and Dentistry N.J., N.J., 1988-89, res. surgery R.W. Johnson Med. Sch., 1989-94; fellowship trauma surgery, surg. critical care U. Md. Med. Ctr.-R. Adams Cowley Shock Trauma Ctr., Balt., 1994-95; fellowship in surgery rsch. U. Md. Sch. Medicine, 1995-97; attending surgeon U. Md. Med. Ctr.-R. Adams Cowley Shock Trauma Ctr., Balt., 1997—; asst. prof. surgery U. Md. Sch. Medicine, 1999—. Fellow: ACS, Internat. Coll. Surgeons; mem.: Ea. Assn. for the Surgery of Trauma, Soc. Critical Care Medicine. Republican. Office: R Adams Cowley Shock Trauma Ctr U Md Med Sys 22 S Greene St Baltimore MD 21201-1544 E-mail: wchiu@umm.edu.

CHIULLI, E. ANTOINETTE, lawyer; b. Pescara, Italy, Oct. 30, 1950; arrived in U.S., 1955; d. Nino and Maria (Mezzanotte) C.; children: Christopher J., Jason A. BA, Marymount Coll., 1972; JD, Rutgers-Camden Sch. Law., 1976. Legal asst. Judge Manuel Greenberg, Atlantic City, N.J., 1976-77; pvt. practice Somerdale, N.J., 1978-86. Econ. analyst Nat. Econ. Research Assocs., N.Y.C., 1972-73; panelist Matrimonial Settlement Program, 1985—. Cons., Alternatives for Women Now, Camden, 1978-80, Women's Counseling Ctr., 1981-83, Glassboro (N.J.) Coll. Together Program, Jaycettes of Camden County; trustee,

Haddonfield Child Care, 1989—. Mem. N.J. State Bar Assn., Camden County Bar Assn. (family law com., scholarship com.), Burlington Co. Bar. Assn. Office: 100 Grove St Haddonfield NJ 08033 E-mail: echiulli@aol.com.

CHIVERS, C.J. journalist; b. Binghamton, N.Y., Dec. 5, 1964; s. James Leeds and Patricia (Dolan) C.; m. Suzanne Keating, Apr. 1999; children: John Peter, James Michael. BA cum laude, Cornell U., 1988; MS, Columbia U., 1995. Staff writer Providence Jour., 1995-99; correspondent The New York Times, N.Y.C., 1999—. Officer USMC, 1988-94. Recipient Livingston award for internat. journalism, Molly Parnis Livingston Found., 1996; Pulitzer fellow, 1995. Roman Catholic. Office: The New York Times 229 W 43d St New York NY 10036 E-mail: chivers@nytimes.com.

CHIVERS, JAMES LEEDS, lawyer; b. Pitts., Jan. 8, 1939; s. Joseph Hobart and Lorraine Anna (Silhol) C.; m. Patricia Ann Dolan, Sept. 3, 1960; children: Catherine Ann, Christopher John, Matthew Leeds. AB, Colgate U., 1960; LLB cum laude, Union U., Albany, N.Y., 1967. Bar: N.Y. 1967, U.S. Dist. Ct. (no. dist.) N.Y. 1967, U.S. Ct. Appeals (2d cir.) 1982, Fla. 1987, U.S. Dist. Ct. (so. and ea. dists.) N.Y. 1988, U.S. Supreme Ct. 1989, U.S. Dist. Ct. (we. dist.) N.Y. 1993. Assoc. Hinman, Howard & Kattell, Binghamton, N.Y., 1967-75, ptnr., 1975—, ptnr.-in-charge dept. litigation, 1981—. Bd. govs. N.Y. State Atty.-Client Fee Dispute Resplution Program, 2003—. Past pres. Vol. Am. Binghamton, bd. dirs., 1969-93; bd. govs. N.Y. State Atty.-Client Fee Dispute Resolution Program, 2003-. Lt. USNR, 1960-64, Vietnam. Mem. ABA (tort and ins. practice sect.), N.Y. State Trial Lawyers Assn., Internat. Def. Counsel, Am. Arbitration Assn. (arbitrator), Def. Rsch. Assn. (bd. govs. N.Y. State Disput Resolution Program, 2003—), N.Y. State Bar Assn. (torts, ins. and compensation, trial lawyers exec. com. 1996—, environ., comml. and fed. litigation sects., com. on profl. ethics 1994-98, spl. com. on unlawful practice of law 1998-2002), Broome County Bar Assn., Broome County C. of C., Broome County YMCA Found., Justinian Soc., Binghamton Club (pres. 1987-89), Harpur Forum, Am. Legion. Republican. Roman Catholic. Avocations: fishing, wine-making, gardening. Office: Hinman Howard & Kattell 700 Security Mutual Bldg Binghamton NY 13901 E-mail: chivers@HHK.com.

CHIVIAN, ERIC SETH, psychiatrist, environmental scientist, educator; b. Newark, June 10, 1942; children: Cybele, Dylan C., Judah B. AB, Harvard U., 1964, MD, 1968. Staff psychiatrist MIT, 1980—2000; asst. clin. prof. psychiatry Harvard Med. Sch., 1987—, dir. Ctr. for Health and the Global Environment, 1996—. Recipient Nobel Peace prize, 1985. Mem.: AAAS, Internat. Physicians Prevent Nuc. War (co-founder, treas. 1980—85), Physicians for Social Responsibility. Achievements include research in first large scale scientific survey of American and Soviet teenagers' attitudes about the future; US-USSR relations and nuclear war; health implications of species extinction and loss of biodiversity. Home: 136 Carter Pond Rd Petersham MA 01366-9728

CHIVUKULA, UPENDRA J. assemblyman, electrical engineer; b. Oct. 8, 1950; MEE, CCNY; BEE, Coll. of Engring., Madras, India. Councilman 5th Ward Franklin Twp., 1997—, dep. mayor, 1998, mayor, 2000; gen. assembly, 2002—. Vice chair commerce and econ. devel. Environ. and Solid Waste Telecoms. and Utilities. Democrat. Office: 888 Easton Ave Somerset NJ 08873 Fax: 732-247-4383.*

CHIZAUSKAS, CATHLEEN JO, manufacturing company executive; b. Little Rock, Dec. 26, 1954; m. Alan Michael Chizauskas, Nov. 11, 1978; children: Marc Alan, Danielle Kelley. Diploma in Mgmt., Simmons Coll., Boston, 1981. Clk. typist to direct materials buyer Gillette Safety Razor Co., Boston, 1972-79, buyer capital equipment, 1979, mgr. MRO and purchasing svcs., 1979-85, adminstrv. asst. to v.p. mktg., 1985-87, exec. asst. to pres., 1987-88, assoc. brand mgr. shave creams, 1988-89, bus. devel. mgr., 1989-91, product mgr., 1991-94, nat. trade mktg. mgr. grooming products, 1994-95; dir. ethnic mktg. Gillette Co., Boston, 1995-98, interactive mktg. mgr., 1998-2001, dir. civic affairs, 2001—. Bd. dirs. St. Edward Sch., Brockton, Mass. Coun. Econ. Edn.; mem. vis. com. Dana-Farber Women's Cancer Program. Mem. Simmons Coll. Grad. Sch. Alumnae Assn. Office: Gillette Co Prudential Bldg Boston MA 02199

CHLAMTAC, IMRICH, computer company executive, educator; b. Zlate Moravce, Czechoslovakia, Mar. 21, 1949; came to U.S., 1977; s. Zoltan and Klara (Csato) C.; children: Eddie, Noga. BS, Tel Aviv U., 1975, MS, 1977; PhD in Computer Sci., U. Minn., 1979. Prin. engr. Digital Equipment Co., Tewksbury, Mass., 1980-82; sr. lectr., assoc. prof. Technion, Haifa, Israel, 1987—93; Fulbright prof. U. Mass., Amherst, 1993-94; founder, CEO BCN, Inc., Boston, 1990—, pres.; prof. Boston U., 1995—; disting. chair in telecom. prof. U. Tex., Dallas. B. Kessler hon. prof. Trento U., Italy; Sackler hon. prof. Tel Aviv U., Israel; univ. hon. prof. BUTE, Budapest; lectr. and presenter in field. Co-author: Local Networks, 1980, Wireless and Mobile Network Architectures, 2000; editor-in-chief Wireless Networks Jour., 1995—, Jour. Spl. Topics on Mobile Networking and Applications, 1996—, Optical Networks Mag., 2000—. Recipient New Talents in Simulation award Soc. for Computer Simulation, 1982. Fellow IEEE (founder, chair MobiComm and Opticomm Conf. 1995—, Personal Comm. award 2002), ACM (Mobile Networking award 2001). Office: Univ Texas Dallas Engring EC-38 PO Box 830688 Richardson TX 75083-0688

CHLEBOWSKI, JOHN FRANCIS, JR., business executive; b. Wilmington, Del, Aug. 19, 1945; s. John Francis and Helen Ann (Cholewa) C.; m. Mary L. Ahern, Sept., 1997; children: J. Christopher, Lauren R. BS, U. Del., Newark, 1967; MBA, Pa. State U., State College, 1971. Fin. analyst Jones & Laughlin Steel, Pitts., 1971-74; mgr. fin. analysis W.R. Grace & Co., NYC, 1974-75, mgr. fin. planning Dallas, 1975-77; v.p. planning Polumbus Co., Denver, 1977-78; asst. treas. W.R. Grace & Co., NYC, 1978-83; v.p. fin. planning GATX Corp., Chgo., 1983-84, v.p. fin., 1984-86, v.p. fin., chief fin. officer, 1986-94; pres. GATX Terminals Corp., Chgo., 1994—97, pres., CEO, 1998, Lakeshore Op. Ptnr. LLC, Chgo. Bd. dir. Laidlaw, Inc. and PLP-GP, LLC, Heartland Alliance, pres. bd. dirs., 1992-93. Leadership Greater Chgo. fellow, 1984-85 Mem.: The Racquet Club, Anglers Club, Beta Gamma Sigma. Roman Catholic.

CHLOUBER, KEN, state legislator; b. Shawnee, Okla., Jan. 24, 1939; m. Pat Chlouber. BS, Okla. Bapt. U. Miner; auctioneer; shift boss Climax Molybdenum; former employee Liberty Mutual Ins. Co.; staff Okla. Dept. Wildlife; mem. Colo. Ho. Reps., 1987-96, Colo. Senate, Dist. 4, Denver, 1996—; vice-chair agr., natural resources and energy com.; mem. bus. affairs and labor com.; mem. joint legis. coun.; pres. pro tem. Colo. Senate, Dist. 4, Denver, 2001—. Active Colo. Tourism Bd., Western Legislators Conf. Water Policy Com., High Altitude Sports Fitness Coun., Lake County Civic Ctr. Assn.; organizer, pres. Leadville Improvement Group; founder, chair Leadville Trail 100; charter v.p. Colo. Pack Burro Racing Assn. With U.S. Army. Republican. Home: 220 W 8th St Leadville CO 80461-3530 Office: State Capitol 200 E Colfax Ave Ste 263 Denver CO 80203-1716*

CHLUDZINSKI, CHRISTOPHER JAMES, information systems professional, consultant; b. N.J. s. James J. and Joan Chludzinski; m. Cheryl L. DiBello, Oct., 1992. BS in Computer Sci., Marist Coll., 1987. Mgmt. adv. svcs. cons. Wiss & Co., Livingston, N.J., 1987-93; v.p. info. systems Mane USA, Wayne, N.J., 1993—. Cons. Chris Chludzinski Consulting, Boonton, N.J., 1991—. Office: Mane USA 60 Demarest Dr Wayne NJ 07470-6702

CHMELEV, VSEVOLOD, engineer, consultant; b. Czechoslovakia, Feb. 5, 1932; s. Vsevolod Ivanovich and Anna Maria Chmelev; m. Antaram Nina Nerses, June 17, 1956; children: Marianna, Alexander. BSME, Poly. Inst. Bklyn., 1957, MSME, 1958, PhD in Sys. Engring., 1978. Registered profl. engr., N.Y.; lic. pilot. Engr. Ford Instrument Co., Long Island City, N.Y., 1957-60; sr. engr. Fairchild Astrionics, Wyandanch, N.Y., 1960-61, UNISYS (merger Sperry with Boroughs), Great Neck, N.Y., 1961-93; cons. engr. Chmelev Cons. Engrs., Huntington, N.Y., 1964—. Pres. and founder Internat. Inst. for Info. Interchange, Huntington, 1982—; pres. Arbat Assocs., Ltd., 1993—; bus. and tech. cons.; engring contractor Loral Devel. Sys. East, Lockheed Martin. Home and Office: 4 Royal Oak Dr Huntington NY 11743-4428

CHMELIR, LYNN KAY, academic librarian; b. Berwyn, Ill., Jan. 11, 1946; d. John Joseph and Dolores Margaret (Svehla) C.; m. John Philip Webb, June 12, 1976; 1 child, Lauren Jane Webb. AB, U. Ill., 1967, AM, 1970, MS in Libr. Sci., 1976. Catalog libr. Lewis and Clark Coll., Portland, 1976-78; tech. svcs. libr. Linfield Coll., McMinnville, Oreg., 1978-81, coll. libr., 1981-99; asst. dir. pub. svcs. Wash. State U., Pullman, 1999—2002, asst. dir. collections, 2002—. Chair Portals Coun. of Librs., Portland, 1995-96, Orbis Consortium, Eugene, 1997-98. Mem. ALA, Assn. of Coll. and Rsch. Librs. (com. chair, pres. Oreg. chpt. 1983-84, pres. Wash. chpt. 2001-02), Oreg. Libr. Assn. (pres. 1988-89), Alpha Lambda Delta, Beta Phi Mu. Home: 1635 Nicole Ct E Pullman WA 99163-8881 E-mail: lchmelir@wsu.edu.

CHMELL, SAMUEL JAY, orthopedic surgeon; b. Chgo., Aug. 21, 1952; s. Samuel and Elsie (Wauterlek) C.; m. Nancy Jean Aumiller, June 22, 1974; children: Jessica, Carson, Alexis, Lesley, Samuel Jayson. BS, U. Notre Dame, 1974; MD, Loyola U., 1977. Diplomate Am. Bd. Orthop. Surgery. Intern Loyola U. Med. Ctr., Maywood, Ill., 1977-78, resident in orthop. surgery, 1980-84; emergency rm. physician USPHS Indian Health Svc., Chinle, Ariz., 1978-80; attending orthop. surgeon Hines (Ill.) VA Hosp., 1984-88, Shriners Hosp. for Crippled Children, Chgo., 1985-89, Gallup (N.Mex.) Indian Hosp., 1988-89, Humana-Michael Reese Hosp. and Health Plan, Chgo., 1989—99; chmn. sect. orthopaedic surgery Humana-Michael Reese Med. Ctr., Chgo., 1991—99; asst. prof. dept. orthopaedic surgery U. Ill., Chgo., 1991—. Clin. instr. in orthop. surgery Loyola U. Med. Ctr., Maywood, 1985-88; asst. prof. dept. orthop. surgery U. Ill., Chgo.; adv. coun. Coll. of Sci. U. Notre Dame. Contbr. articles to profl. jours. Active Olmsted Hist. Soc. Riverside, Ill. Sofield Travelling fellow Orthop. Rsch. Soc. Gt. Britain, 1985. Master: Alpha Omega Alpha; fellow: Am. Acad. Orthop. Surgeons, ACS; mem.: Founders' Cir. of Sorin Soc. U. Notre Dame, Notre Dame Orthop. Soc. Office: 23 Longcommon Rd Riverside IL 60546-2168

CHMIELARZ, SHARON LEE, writer, educator; b. Mobridge, S.D., Dec. 20, 1940; m. Tadeusz B. Chmielarz, June 27, 1964. BS, U. Minn., 1962, MA, 1976. Tchr. German and English Orono (Minn.) Sch. Dist., 1962-91. Editl. work New Rivers Press, Mpls., 1993, 96, Minn. State Arts Bd., St. Paul, 1992, 96. Author: Different Arrangements, 1982, But I Won't Go Out in a Boat, 1990, Pied Piper of Hamlin, 1990, End of Winter, 1992, Down at Angels, 1994, (chapbook) Stranger In Her House, 1995, The Other Mozart, 2001. Minn. State Arts Bd. fellow, 1991; Jerome Found. travel grantee, 1995. Mem.: Soc. Children's Book Writers and Illustrators, S.A.S.E./The Write Place, The Loft/A Place for Writing, Children's Lit. Network. Avocations: driving, swimming, reading. E-mail: schmielarz@aol.com.

CHMIELEWSKI, JERRY GEORGE, botanist, educator; b. Grimsby, Ont., Can. BS, U. Waterloo, Can., 1979; MS, U. Waterloo, 1981, PhD, 1985. Rsch. assoc. U. Waterloo, 1985-86, rsch. assoc., lectr., 1988-89; rsch. assoc. U. Calgary, Alberta, Can., 1986-89, rsch. assoc., lectr., 1989-90; asst. prof. Slippery Rock (Pa.) U., 1990-94, assoc. prof., 1994-98, prof., interim assoc. dean Coll. Arts and Scis., 1999-2001. Rsch. assoc. Carnegie Mus. Nat. History, Pitts., 1993—; curator Slippery Rock U. Herbarium, 1990—. Contbr. articles to profl. jours. Mem. Am. Bot. Assn., Can. Bot. Assn., Am. Soc. Plant Taxonomy, Internat. Assn. Plant Biologists, New Eng. Bot. Club, Commonwealth Pa. Biologists (pres. 1993-94), Sigma Xi (treas. chpt. 1993-97). Office: Slippery Rock U Dept Biology Slippery Rock PA 16057 E-mail: jerry.chmielewski@sru.edu.

CHMIELEWSKI, TERESE LYNN, physical therapist, educator; d. Steven John Chmielewski and Loree Clara Rudnitski. BS, Coll. St. Scholastica, Duluth, Minn., 1991, MA in Phys. Therapy, 1993; PhD, U. Del., 2002. Cert. sports clin. specialist Am. Bd. Phys. Therapy Spltys., 1999, group fitness instr. Am. Coun. on Exercise, 1993. Staff phys. therapist HealthSouth Sports Medicine and Rehab. Ctr., Birmingham, Ala., 1993—96, clin. coord., 1996—98; rsch. asst. U. Del., Newark, 1998—2002; asst. rsch. prof. U. Fla., Gainesville, 2002—. Clin. cons. U. of Del., Newark, 2000—02. Contbr. chapters to books, articles to peer-reviewed profl. jours. Mem.: Am. Phys. Therapy Assn. (sports sect., rsch. sect.), Am. Coll. of Sports Medicine. Roman Catholic. Avocations: cooking, travel, fitness, crafts, reading. Office: U Fla Box 100154 HSC Gainesville FL 32610

CHMIELINSKI, EDWARD ALEXANDER, retired electronics company executive; b. Waterbury, Conn., Mar. 25, 1925; s. Stanley and Helen Chmielinski; m. Elizabeth Carew, May 30, 1946; children: Nancy, Elizabeth, Susan Jean. BS, Tulane U., 1950; postgrad., Colo. U., 1965. V.p., gen. mgr. Clifton Products, Litton Industries, Colorado Springs, Colo., 1965-67; pres. Memory Products divsn. Litton Industries, Beverly Hills, Calif., 1967-69, Bowmar Instruments Can., Ottawa, Ont., 1969-73; gen. mgr. Leigh Instruments, Carleton Place, 1973—85; pres., CEO, dir. Lewis Engring. Co., Naugatuck, Conn., 1973—85, Liquidometer Corp., Tampa, Fla., 1975-85; pres. Lewis divsn. Colt Industries, 1985-90; ret., 1990. Pres. Acad. Water Bd., 1963-65; bd. dirs. United Way, Colorado Springs, 1965-67;fellow Tulane U. Served with USN, 1943-46. Mem. Air Force Assn., Navy League.

CHO, ALFRED YI, electrical engineer; b. Beijing, July 10, 1937; arrived in U.S., 1955, naturalized, 1962; s. Edward I-Lai and Mildred (Chen) Cho; m. Mona Lee Willoughby, June 16, 1968; children: Derek Ming, Deidre Lin, Brynna Ying, Wendy Li. BSEE, U. Ill., 1960, MS, 1961, PhD, 1968, D (hon.) Engring., 1999; DSc (hon.), City U. Hong Kong, 2000, Hong Kong Bapt. U., 2001. Rsch. physicist Ion Physics Corp., Burlington, Mass., 1961—62; mem. tech. staff TRW-Space Tech. Labs., Redondo Beach, Calif., 1962—65, Bell Labs., Murray Hill, NJ, 1968—84, dept. head, 1984—87; dir. Materials Processing Rsch. Lab. AT&T Bell Labs., Murray Hill, 1987—90; semicondr. rsch. lab. v.p. Bell Labs. Lucent Techs. (formerly AT&T Bell Labs.), Murray Hill, 1990—2002; fellow Bell Labs., Lucent Techs. (formerly AT&T Bell Labs.), 1992—; rsch. asst. U. Ill., Urbana, 1965—68. Vis. prof. dept. elec. engring., vic. rsch. prof. coordinated sci. lab. U. Ill., Urbana, 1977—78, adj. prof. dept. elec. engring., adj. rsch. prof. coordinated sci. lab., 1978—; bd. dirs. Riber, Edison, NJ; trustee Coll. of N.J., 1996—. Contbr. over 590 articles to profl. jours. Named to, N.J. Inventors Hall of Fame, 1997; recipient Elec. and Computer Engring. Disting. Alumnus award, U. Ill., 1985, Disting. Achievement award, Chinese Inst. Engrs., USA, 1985, Internat. Gallium Arsenide Symposium award, 1986, Heinrich Welker Gold medal, 1986, The Coll. Engring. Alumni Honor award, U. Ill., 1988, World Materials Congress award, ASM Internat., 1988, Achievement award, Indsl. Rsch. Inst., Inc., 1988, Thomas Alva Edison Sci. award, N.J. Gov., 1990, Internat. Crystal Growth award, Am. Assn. for Crystal Growth, 1990, Asian Am. Corp. Achievement award, 1992, Chinese Am. Engrs. and Scientists Assn. So. Achievement award, 1993, Nat. Medal of Sci., NSF, 1993, Elliott Cresson medal, The Franklin Inst., 1995, Computer and Comm. prize, Japan, 1995, W.E. Lamb medal for laser sci. and quantum optics, 2000. Fellow: IEEE (Morris N. Liebman award 1982, IEEE Medal of Honor 1994, Third Millennium medal 2000), Am. Phys. Soc. (Internat. prize for new materials 1982); mem.: Third World Acad. Scis., Nat. Acad. Engring., U.S. Nat. Acad. Scis., Am. Acad. Art and Scis., Am. Philos. Soc., Chinese Acad. Scis., Academia Sinica (Taiwan), Materials Rsch. Soc. (Von Hippel award 1994), Electrochem. Soc. (electronic divsn. award 1977, Solid State Sci. and Tech. medal 1987), Am. Vacuum Soc. (Gaede-Langmuir award 1988), Sigma Tau, Eta Kappa Nu, Tau Beta Pi, Sigma Xi. Achievements include development of molecular beam epitaxy; 75 patents related to crystal growth and electronic and photonic devices. Office: Bell Labs Lucent Tech PO Box 636 New Providence NJ 07974-0636 Fax: 908-582-2043. E-mail: ayc@lucent.com., alcho@aol.com. *I learned early in my life that hard work is a major ingredient for success. We can always do more than we think we are able to do. I drive myself to my utmost capacity so that I will not have regrets later that I did not try my best. My first love is art but I earn my living as an engineer. In my work as a research scientist, the secret for success is that I combine Oriental patience with Western technology. We should always try to enhance the best part of what we have and not be afraid to change.*

CHO, HYUN JU, retired veterinary research scientist; b. Chinju, Korea, June 12, 1939; s. Gil Rae and Sun Gae (Park) C.; m. Kim Bok Mee, June 13, 1967; children— Jae Shin, Elisa, Jane. D.V.M., Gyeongsang Nat. U., 1963; M.Sc., Seoul Nat. U., 1966; PhD, U. Guelph, 1973. Vet. rsch. scientist Inst. Vet. Rsch., Anyang, Republic of Korea, 1965—70; vis. scientist Wallaceville Animal Rsch. Ctr., New Zealand, 1968; rsch. scientist Animal Diseases Rsch. Inst. Can. Food Inspection Agy., Lethbridge, Canada, 1973—2000. Contbr. articles to profl. jours. Achievements include discovering virus of Aleutian disease of mink and developed practical diagnostic test for it. Home: 14 Coachwood Rd W Lethbridge AB Canada T1K 6B6 E-mail: chojdvm@shaw.ca. *A combination of persistent and repeated experimentation, original ideas and thinking and the ambition to succeed where others may have failed, tempered with loyalty and dedication to sound research principles, has been the key to my scientific achievements.*

CHO, JOHN YUNGDO NAGAMICHI, atmospheric research scientist; b. Tokyo, Nov. 24, 1963; s. Joseph Kisun and Lydia (Shoko) C.; m. Colleen Marie Kirby, Oct. 23, 1999; children: Linnea Kirby, Gavin. BS, Stanford U., 1985, MS, 1986; PhD, Cornell U., 1993. With U.S. Peace Corps, Freetown, Sierra Leone, 1986-88; rsch. asst. Cornell U., Ithaca, 1988-93; columnist The San Juan (P.R.) Star, 1996-97; rsch. assoc. Arecibo (P.R.) Obs., 1993-97; rsch. scientist MIT, Cambridge, 1997—2002, tech. staff Lincoln lab. Lexington, 2002—. Adj. rsch. assoc., U. Colo., 1996-98. Author: SPAM-ku: Tranquil Reflections on Luncheon Loaf, 1998; contbr. articles to profl. jours. Recipient CEDAR prize NSF, 1993. Mem. Am. Geophys. Union, Am. Meterol. Soc., Internat. Radio Sci. Union. (young scientist award 1996). Avocations: music, literature, cinema, travel. Office: MIT Lincoln Lab 244 Wood St Lexington MA 02420 Home: 16 Pamela Dr Arlington MA 02474 E-mail: jync@mit.edu.

CHO, KYUNG JAE, physician, radiologist, educator; b. Tokyo, Mar. 26, 1942; s. Bang Kap and Myo Soon (Chai) C.; m. Young Soon Jeung, Sept. 6, 1969; children: Catherine, David, James. MD, Cath. Med. Sch., Seoul, 1966. Instr. U. Mich., Ann Arbor, 1973-74, asst. prof., 1975-78, assoc. prof., 1978-82, prof., 1982—, dir. interventional radiology, 1976-96; courtesy prof. U. Fla., Gainesville, 1996-99, prof. radiology, 1999—, William Martel endowed prof., 1999—. Hon. disting. prof. radiology Cath. U., Seoul, 2000. Co-author: Gastrointestinal Angiography, 1986; contbr. chpt. to book, articles to profl. jours. Fellow Soc. Cardiovascular and Interventional Radiology, Am. Coll. Radiology; mem. AMA, Radiol. Soc. N.Am., Soc. Gastrointestinal Radiology. Home: 413 Dhu Varren Rd Ann Arbor MI 48105-9690 Office: U Mich 1500 E Medical Center Dr Ann Arbor MI 48109-0005 E-mail: kyungcho@umich.edu.

CHO, LEE-JAY, social scientist, demographer; b. Kyoto, July 5, 1936; came to U.S., 1969; s. Sam Soo and Kyung Doo (Park) C.; m. Eun Ja Chun, May 20, 1973; children: Kaia Nuy, Sang-Mun Ray, Han-Jae Jeremy. BA, Kookmin Coll., Seoul, Korea, 1959; MA in Govt., George Washington U., 1962; MA in Sociology (Population Council fellow), U. Chgo., 1964, PhD in Sociology, 1965; D in Econs. (hon.), Dong-A U., 1982; DSc in Demography, Tokyo U., 1983; D in Econs., Keio U., Tokyo, 1989; D in Econs. (hon.), Russian Acad. Scis., 2000. Statistician Korean Census Council, 1958-61; research assoc., asst. prof. sociology Population Research and Tng. Center, U. Chgo., 1965-66; asso. dir. Community and Family Study Center, 1969-70; sr. demographic adv. to Malaysian Govt., 1967-69; assoc. prof. U. Hawaii, 1969-73, prof., 1973-78; asst. dir. East-West Population Inst., East-West Center, Honolulu, 1971-74, dir., 1974-92; pres. pro tem East-West Center, 1980-81, v.p., 1987-98, sr. advisor, 1998—. Cons. in field; mem. Nat. Acad. Scis. Com. on Population and Demography; mem. U.S. 1980 Census Adv. Com., Dept. Commerce. Author: (with others) Differential Current Fertility in the United States, 1970; editor: (with others) Introduction to Censuses of Asia and the Pacific: 1970-74, 1976, (with Kazumasa Kobayashi) Fertility Transition in East Asian Populations, 1979, (with Suharto, McNicoll and Mamas) Population Growth of Indonesia, 1980, The OWN Children of Fertility Estimation, 1986, (with Y.H. Kim) Economic Development of Republic of Korea: A Policy Perspective, 1989, (with Kim) Korea's Political Economy: An Institutional Perspective, 1994, (with Yada) Tradition and Change in the Asian Family, 1994, (with Y.H. Kim) Hedging Bets on Growth in a Globalizing Industrial Order, 1997, (with Y.H. Kim) Korea's Choices in Emerging Global Competition and Cooperation, 1998, (with Kim) Ten Paradigms of Market Economies and Land Systems, 1998, (with Kim) The Multi-Lateral Trading System in a Globalizing World, 2000, Restructuring the National Economy, 2001, Restructuring the Korean Financial Market in a Global Economy, 2002; contbr. numerous articles on population and econ. devel. to profl. jours. Bd. dirs. Planned Parenthood Assn., Hawaii, 1976-77. Ford Found. grantee, 1977-79; Population Council grantee, 1973-75; Dept. Commerce grantee, 1974-78; recipient Award of Mugunghwa-Jang, govt. Republic of Korea, 1992, 4th N.E. Asia Niigata prize, 1996. Mem. Internat. Statis. Inst. (tech. adv. com. World Fertility Survey), Internat. Union Sci. Study Population, Population Assn. Am., Am. Statis. Assn., Am. Sociol. Assn., N.E. Asia Econ. Forum (founding chmn.). Home: 1718 Halekoa Dr Honolulu HI 96821-1027 Office: 1601 E West Rd Honolulu HI 96848-1601 *The survival and welfare of the future generations will depend largely upon what we do today to plan and manage human population growth and sustainable development.*

CHO, TAI YONG, lawyer; b. Seoul, Republic of Korea, May 27, 1943; came to U.S., 1966; s. Nam Suck and Sun Yeo (Yoon) C; m. Hea Sun Cho, July 14, 1973; children: Robert, Richard, Susan. BS, Seoul U., 1965; MS, Cooper Union, 1971; CE, Columbia U., 1971; JD, Fordham U., 1981. Bar: N.Y., 1982; registered profl. engr., N.Y., 1973. Engr. Ministry of Constrn., Seoul, 1965-66, Andrews & Clark, N.Y.C., 1967-68, Parsons, Brinckerhoff, Quade & Douglas, N.Y.C., 1969-71; v.p. John R. McCarthy Corp., N.Y.C., 1972-80. Mem. ASCE, ABA, N.Y. State Bar Assn., Am. Arbitration Assn. (panel of arbitrators), Am.-Korean Lawyers Assn. of N.Y. (pres. 1988), Korean TV Broadcasters Assn., Am. (pres. 1990), Internat. Korean Lawyers Assn. (v.p. 1991). Home: 56 Tuttle Rd Briarcliff Manor NY 10510-2233 Office: 445 5th Ave New York NY 10016-6509 E-mail: taicho7@aol.com.

CHO, YONG HYO, public administrator, educator; b. Sachon, Republic of Korea, Dec. 14, 1934; arrived in U.S., 60; s. Deuk Kyu Cho and Sue Nahm Park; m. Chung Soon Kim, May 6, 1960; children: Miyun Fellerhoff, Hearn Jay. PhD, Syracuse U., 1964. Prof. U. Nev., Las Vegas, 1964—67, U. Akron, 1967—89, San Francisco State U., 1989—97; dean Grad. Sch. Internat. Studies Sogang U., Seoul, 1997—2000; expert U.S. Dept. Edn., Washington, 2000—; sr. advisor Ctr. for Pub. Policy Edn., The Brookings Instn., Washington, 2002—. Author: The White House and the Blue House, 1997, Public Policy and Urban Crime, 1974, others. Nat. Conv. del. Dem. Party, Akron, Ohio, 1980. Recipient Diplomatic Svc. medal Govt. of Republic of Korea, 1998. Fellow Nat. Acad. Public Adminstrn. (life); mem. Am. Soc. for Pub. Adminstrn. (pres. 1996-97). Roman Catholic. Avocations: travel, golf. Home: 424 E Pine Lake Cir Vernon Hills IL 60061 Home Fax: (847) 362-7417. E-mail: yongcho@prodigy.net.

CHOATE, RAY, university librarian; b. Torrington, Wyo., July 16, 1941; s. Bill and Byrel Louise (Harden) C.; m. Rosia Pasteur, Apr. 24, 1965 (div. 1994); children: David, Julia. BA with honors, U. Wyo., 1963; postgrad., Free Univ., Berlin, 1963-65, U. Mass., Amherst, 1967-69; MLS, Columbia U., 1966. Reference libr. NYU, N.Y.C., 1966, U. Mass., Amherst, 1967-69; libr. Am. Sch., The Hague, The Netherlands, 1969-70; reference libr. La Trobe U., Melbourne, Australia, 1970-85, dep. libr., 1986-89; univ. libr. U. Adelaide, Australia, 1990—. Author: Guide to Sources of Information on the Arts in Australia, 1983; editor: Reference Services: The State of the Art, 1985, Reference Services: The Challenge of the Information Age, 1987, Illustration Index to Australian Art, 1990. Fulbright fellow Free Univ., Berlin, 1963-64, Tchg. fellow Deutsch Akademische Austausch Dienst, 1964-65. Fellow (hon.) Australian Acad. Humanities (Australian Govt. Centenary medal 2003); mem. Australian Libr. and Info. Assn., Australian Libr. Pubs. Soc., Art Librs. Soc./Australia and New Zealand (past pres.), Coun. Australia Univ. Librs. (mem. exec. com.). Episcopalian. Office: U Adelaide Barr Smith Libr Adelaide SA 5005 Australia

CHOBANIAN, ARAM, medical school dean, cardiologist; b. Pawtucket, R.I., Aug. 10, 1929; s. Van and Marina (Arsenian) C.; m. Jasmine Goorigian, June 5, 1955; children: Karin, Lisa, Aram. BA, Brown U., 1951; MD, Harvard U., 1955. Intern, resident Univ. Hosp., Boston, 1955-59, cardiovasc. rsch. fellow, 1959-62; asst. prof. Boston U. Sch. Medicine, 1964-67, assoc. prof., 1967-70, prof. medicine, 1970—, prof. pharmacology, 1975—, John Sandson disting. prof. health scis., 1992—, dir. U.A. Whitaker Labs. for Blood Vessel Rsch., 1973-88, dir. Hypertension Specialized Ctr. Rsch., 1975-95, dir. Cardiovasc. Inst., 1975-92, dean, 1988—, provost Med. Ctr., 1996—, Univ. prof., 1999—. Dir. Nat. Rsch. and Demonstration Ctr. in Hypertension, 1985-90; chmn. FDA Cardiovasc. and Renal Adv. Com., 1978-80, NIH Hypertension and Arteriosclerosis adv. com., 1977-78; chmn. Cardiovasc. Study Sect. B. NIH, 1982-84; chmn. Joint Nat. Com. on Hypertension, NIH, 1990-91, 2003; Sandoz lectr.

Royal Coll. Physicians and Surgeons Can., 1989; mem. NIH Nat. Heart, Lung and Blood Adv. Coun., 1993-96; mem. bd. extramural advisers NHLBI, 1999-2002. Author: Heart Risk Book, 1982; mem. editl. bd. New England Jour. Medicine, Hypertension, Jour. Hypertension, Jour. Vascular Biology, Hypertension Rsch., Cardiovasc. Pharmacology. Pres. Am. Heart Assn., Boston, 1974-75; mem. exec. com., trustee Boston Med. Ctr.; bd. dirs. Armenian Culture Soc.; trustee Roger Williams Med. Ctr., Wolfson Found., Quincy Med. Ctr., Mass. Tech. Collaborative, New Eng.Healthcare Inst.; fellow trustee Armenian Assembly of Am. Capt. USAF, 1956-57. Recipient Cmty. Edn. and Disting. Svc. award Am. Heart Assn., Boston, 1975, 78, Eastman Kodak award Nat. Acad. Clin. Biochemistry, 1987, Abbott award Am. Soc. Hypertension. Fellow ACP, Am. Heart Assn. (chmn. coun. high blood pressure rsch. 1984-86, Corcoran lectr. 1989, award of merit 1990, Modern Medicine award 1990, Lifetime Achievement award in hypertension Bristol-Myers Squibb), Nat. Heart, Lung and Blood Inst. (Freis award 1997), Am. Soc. Clin. Investigation, Assn. Am. Physicians, Am. Physiol. Soc., New England Cardiovasc. Soc. (pres. 1985-86), Mass. Med. Soc. (mem. publs. com.), Phi Beta Kappa, Sigma Xi, Alpha Omega Alpha. Home: 5 Rathburn Rd Natick MA 01760-1011 Office: Boston U Sch Medicine 715 Albany St Boston MA 02118-2307

CHOBOT, JOHN CHARLES, lawyer; b. N.Y.C., Feb. 14, 1948; s. Arthur E. and Eleanore L. (Lotito) Chobot; m. Catherine Anne Moran, Aug. 24, 1974; children: Christine, Keith. BA, Cornell U., 1969; MS in Edn., CCNY, 1971; JD, Fordham U., 1975. Bar: N.Y. 1976, U.S. Dist. Ct. (we. dist.) N.Y. 1976, N.J. 1985, U.S. Dist. Ct. N.J. 1985. Assoc. Phillips, Lytle, Hitchcock, Blaine & Huber, Buffalo, 1975-85; with The CIT Group/Sales Financing, Inc., Livingston, N.J., 1985-90; sr. v.p., chief counsel bus. fin. divsn. AT&T Capital Corp., 1990-98; v.p. law, asst. gen. counsel Newcourt Credit Group Inc., Parsippany, N.J., 1998-99, The CIT Group, Inc., 1999-2000; counsel Am. Express Co., 2000-01; corp. counsel Lucent Techs. Inc., Murray Hill, NJ, 2001—. Adj. prof. law Seton Hall Law Sch., 2000—. Contbr. articles to legal jours. Mem.: ABA, Comml. Law League, Am. Bankruptcy Inst., N.Y. State Bar Assn., Kappa Alpha Soc. Home: 27 Hilltop Rd Randolph NJ 07945-4632 Office: Lucent Techs Inc 600 Mountain Ave New Providence NJ 07974 Fax: 908-582-8048. Business E-Mail: chobot@lucent.com.

CHOBOTOV, VLADIMIR ALEXANDER, aerospace engineer, educator; b. Zagreb, Yugoslavia, Apr. 2, 1929; came to U.S., 1946; s. Alexander M. and Eugenia I. (Scherbak) C.; m. Lydia M. Kazanovich, June 22, 1957; children: Alexander, Michael. BSME, Pratt Inst., 1951; MSME, Bklyn. Poly. Inst., 1956; PhD, U. So. Calif., 1963. Dynamics engr. Sikorsky Aircraft, Bridgeport, Conn., 1951-53, Republic Aviation, Farmingdale, N.Y., 1953-57, Ramo-Wooldridge, Redondo Beach, Calif., 1957-62; mgr. The Aerospace Corp., El Segundo, Calif., 1962-93; adj. prof. Northrop U., L.A., 1982-91; instr. UCLA, 1984—. Cons. Univ. Space Rsch. Assn., Washington, 1984-85; ad hoc advisor USAF Sci. Adv. Bd., Washington, 1985-87; cons. NASA Space Sta. Adv. Com., Washington, 1990-91; course leader Space Debris, Washington, 1990-91. Author: Spacecraft Attitude Dynamics and Control, 1991; author, editor: Orbital Mechanics, 1991, 3d edit., 2002; contbg. author: Space Based Radar Handbook, 1989, Earth, Sea and Solar System, 1987; contbr. numerous articles and reports to profl. publs. Fellow AIAA (assoc., Achievement award 1993); mem. Internat. Acad. of Astronautics. Achievements include pioneering in the analysis and modeling of space debris. Office: The Aerospace Corp PO Box 92957 Los Angeles CA 90009-2957

CHOCK, ALVIN KEALI'I, retired botanist; b. Honolulu, June 18, 1931; s. Hon and Eleanor Kam Hoon (Au) C.; m. Yona Nahenahe Bielefeldt, June 18, 1962; children: T. Makana, D. 'Alana, D. Malama. BA, U. Hawaii, Manoa, 1951, MS in Botany, 1953; postgrad., U. Mich., 1953-55, U.S. Dept. Agr. Grad. Sch., 1959, Pacific Asian Mgmt. Inst., 1988, 90, U. Hawaii, 1988, 90. Tech. adminstrv. asst. European Exchange Svc., Katterbach bei Ansbach/Mfr., Germany, 1958-59; plant quarantine insp. Agrl. Rsch. Svc., U.S. Dept. Agr., N.Y.C., 1959-60, Honolulu, 1961-67, supervisory insp. Balt., 1967-70; program specialist Office of Pesticide Programs, EPA, Washington, 1970-71, supervisory program specialist, 1971-74, supervisory biologist, 1975; agrl. officer (plant quarantine) FAO, Rome, 1975-78; also tech. sec. Near East Plant and Caribbean Plant Protection Commn., 1976; supervisory biologist, registration div. Office of Pesticide Programs, EPA, Washington, 1978-81; acting coord. internat. programs Dept. Agr., Hyattsville, Md., 1981-82; dir. (Europe, Near East and Africa) Region II, 1981-82, dir. (European, Near East and Africe), 1982-88; dir. (Asia and Pacific) Region III, Hyattsville, 1988-92. Lectr. botany U. Hawaii, 1961-67, 69, 72, 79, 84, 86, 88, 90, 93, 95—, adj. instr. botany, 1993-95, adj. colleague, 1995—; asst. botanist B.P. Bishop Mus., Honolulu, 1961-65; botanist Kokee Natural History Mus., Hawaii, 1953-55; bot. cons. Nat. Park Svc., 1962-63; mem. work panels European and Mediterranean Plant Protection Orgn., Paris, 1976-78; plant quarantine cons. Coun. Agr. Rep. China, Taiwan, 1993; artist-in-residence Am. Folk Dance, Hawaii Dept. Edn. Founding editor Hawaii Bot. Soc. Newsletter, 1962-63, 66; editor Fed. Plant Quarantine Insps. Nat. Assn. newsletter, 1963-65, Ka Nupepa, 1968-71; chmn. editl. com. FAO Plant Protection Bull., 1976-78; contbg. author books; editor (with G.L. Addicott) Pavorite Songs of the Hawaii State Society, 1973; contbr. articles to profl. jours.; mem. Nā Kūpuna o Ko'olau Hawaiian Entertainment Group. Mem. governing bd. Nat. Conf. State Socs., Washington, 1972-75, dep. dir. gen., 1973-74, 2d v.p., 1974-75; governing bd. Asian Pacific Am. Heritage Coun., Inc., 1979-81, 88-92; sec. PTA, Overseas Sch. Rome, 1976-77l USDA rep., 1988, observer, 1990-91, governing bd. Am. Fgn. Svc. Assn., 1989-91; co-spokesperson Mayor's Ewa-Kapolei Vision Team, Honolulu, 1998-99. Served with inf. U.S. Army, 1955-57. Plant species Cyanea chockii named in his honor; recipient other awards in field. Mem. Hawaiian Acad. Sci. (dir. jr. acad. 1963-64), Lloyd Shaw Found., Assn. Tropical Biology (charter), Hawaiian Bot. Soc. (sec. 1962, dir. 1963, 65, 94-95, pres. 1964), Internat. Assn. Plant Taxonomists, Pacific Sci. Assn., Soc. Econ. Botany, FAO Assn. Profl. Staff (appeals and procedures com. 1976-77, standing com. career devel. 1976-78), Nat. Capital Area Square Dance Leaders Assn. (editor newsletter 1980-81), Mediterranean Area Callers and Tchrs. Assn. (founder, publicity dir. 1977-78), European Callers and Tchrs. Assn., Contralab, Hawaii State Soc. D.C. (dir. 1968-69, 89-91, 1st v.p. 1969-71, pres. 1971-72, adv. 1978-79, 2d. v.p. 1979-80, Hawaii rep. 1995—), Hawaii Fedn. Square & Round Dance Clubs (treas. 1996-98), Hawaii State Dance Coun. (bd. dirs. 1996—, sec. 1997-99), Consumers Union, Bishop Mus. Assn., Ramblin' Romans Sq. Dance Club (founder), Ewa Gentry Cmty. Assn. (v.p. 1993-95, pres. 1995-96, newsletter editor 1993-94), Arbors Assn. Apt. Owners (bd. dirs. 1994—, v.p. 1997—, newsletter editor 1994—), Roosevelt H.S. Alumni Assn. (bd. dirs. 1993—), Roosevelt Alumni Found. (v.p. 1994-96, pres. 1996-99, bd. dirs. 1994—), Pacific Sci. Assn., Benevolent and Protective Order of Elk (inner guard 2000—), Internat. Order Odd Fellows, Sigma Xi. Home: 91-1064 Laaulu St Apt E Ewa Beach HI 96706

CHOCK, CLIFFORD YET-CHONG, family practice physician; b. Chgo., Oct. 15, 1951; s. Wah Tim and Leatrice (Wong) C. BS in Biology, Purdue U., 1973; MD, U. Hawaii, 1978. Intern in internal medicine Loma Linda (Calif.) Med. Ctr., 1978-79, resident in internal medicine, 1979, U. So. Calif.-L.A. County Med. Ctr., L.A., 1980; physician Pettis VA Clinic, Loma Linda, Calif., 1980; pvt. practice Honolulu, 1981—. Chmn. dept. family practice, 1990-98, chmn. utilization rev. com. 1991, 95; physician reviewer St. Francis Med. Ctr., Liliha, Hawaii., 1985-2002, chmn. Quality Care for Family Practice, 1990-93, 95-98; chmn. credentials Family Practice, 1990-93, 95-96, acting chmn. credentials com., 1992; physician reviewer Peer Rev. Orgn. Hawaii, Honolulu, 1987-93. Fellow Am. Acad. Family Physicians, Internat. Platform Assn. Avocations: model building, toy collecting, bible study, Pacific Revival Ctr.. Office: 321 N Kuakini St Ste 513 Honolulu HI 96817-2361

CHOCOLA, CHRIS, congressman; b. Jackson, Mich., Feb. 24, 1962; m. Sarah Chocola; children: Caroline, Colin. Degree in Bus. Adminstrn. and Polit. Economy summa cum laude, Hillsdale Coll., 1984; JD magna cum laude, Thomas Cooley Law Sch., 1988. Mgmt. trainee Soc. Nat. Bank, Cleve., 1984, fgn. exch. trader; credit mgr. Chocola Cleaning Materials; corp. counsel CTB Internat. Corp., Milford, Ind., 1988—94, CEO, 1994, chmn. bd. dirs., 1999; mem. U.S. Ho. Reps. from 2nd Ind. dist., 2003—. Mem. coun. advisors South Bend Ctr. for the Homeless; bd. dirs. Oaklawn Psychiat. Ctr. Mem.: Rotary Club. Office: 510 Cannon House Office Bldg Washington DC 20515 also: Ste 330 100 E Wayne St South Bend IN 46601*

CHODES, JOHN JAY, photographer, writer; b. N.Y.C., Feb. 23, 1939; s. Ralph and Henrietta (Jonas) C. Comml. cert., Germain Sch. Photography, N.Y.C., 1963. Asst. editor Kauri, N.Y.C., 1966-67; sales promotion writer Business Week, N.Y.C., 1967-69, Fortune, N.Y.C., 1970, Forbes, N.Y.C., 1971, The N.Y. Times, N.Y.C., 1972-74; comms. dir. Libertarian Party of N.Y., 1980-93; photographer Long Distance Log, Phila., 1961-63. Photographer publicity Newsweek, N.Y.C., 1960-61, Athletics Weekly, London, 1963-64, Track & Field News, Los Altos, Calif., 1961-63, Brooklyn Eagle, 1997-99, Brooklyn Heights Press, 1998-00. Author: Corbitt, 1973, Bruce Jenner, 1976, (play) A Howling Wilderness, 2001, (concert) Dante's Cantos: From Hell to Paradise, 2002, numerous other theatrical prodns.; contbr. more than 110 articles to profl. jours. Recipient Journalistic Excellence award Road Runners Club of Am., 1974, Outstanding Svc. award Libertarian Party of N.Y., 1988. Mem. League of the South, Road Runners Club, Libertarian Party of N.Y. Jewish. Avocation: road racing. Home: 411 E 10th St Apt 22G New York NY 10009-4213

CHODOROW, NANCY JULIA, psychotherapist; b. N.Y.C., Jan. 20, 1944; d. Marvin and Leah (Turitz) C.; children: Rachel Esther Chodorow-Reich, Gabriel Issac Chodorow-Reich. BA, Radcliffe Coll., 1966; PhD, Brandeis U., 1975; grad., San Francisco Psychoanalytic, 1993, cert. in adult psychoanalysis, 2000. From lectr. to assoc. prof. U. Calif., Santa Cruz, 1974-86, from assoc. prof. sociology to prof. Berkeley, 1986—, clin. prof. dept. psychology, 1999—. Faculty San Francisco Psychoanalytic Inst., 1994—. Author: The Reproduction of Mothering, 1978 (Jessie Bernard award Sociologists for Women in Soc. 1979, named one of Ten Most Influential Books of Past 25 Years, Contemporary Sociology 1996), 2d edit., 1999, Feminism and Psychoanalytic Theory, 1989, Femininities, Masculinities, Sexualities, 1994, The Power of Feelings: Personal Meaning in Psychoanalysis, Gender, and Culture, 1999 (L. Bryce Boyer prize Soc. for Psychol. Anthropology 2000); contbr. articles to profl. jours. Fellow Russell Sage Found., NEH, Ctr. Advanced Study Behavioral Scis., ACLS, Guggenheim Found., Radcliffe Inst. for Advanced Study; recipient Contbn. to Women and Psychoanalysis award APA, L. Bryce Bryer prize Soc. for Psychol. Anthropology, 2000. Mem. Internat. Psychoanalytic Assn., Am. Psychoanalytic Assn., San Francisco Psychoanalytic Soc.

CHODOS, DALE DAVID JEROME, physician, consumer advocate; b. Mpls., June 5, 1928; s. John H. and Elvira Isabella (Lundberg) C.; m. Joyce Annette Smith, Sept. 9, 1951; children: John, Julie, David, Jennifer. AB, Carroll Coll., Helena, Mont., 1950; MD, St. Louis U., 1954. Diplomate Am. Bd. Pediatrics. Intern U. Utah, Salt Lake City, 1954-55, resident in pediatrics, 1955 57, chief resident in pediatrics, 1957, NIH fellow in endocrinology and metabolism, 1957-58; practice medicine specializing in pediatrics Idaho Falls, Idaho, 1958-62; staff physician Upjohn Co., Kalamazoo, Mich., 1962-64, head clin. pharmacology, 1964-65, research mgr. clin. pharmacology, 1965-68, research mgr. clin. services, 1968-73, group research mgr. med. therapeutics, 1973-81, med. dir. domestic med. affairs, 1981-85, exec. dir. domestic med. affairs, 1985-87; chief pediatrics Latter-day Saints Hosp., Sacred Heart Hosp., Idaho Falls, 1962; cons. to pharm. industry, 1988-91. Pres. Am. Health Advocacy, 1991—; chmn. med. rels. oper. com. Nat. Pharm. Coun., 1977-80; mem. med. sect. steering com. Pharm. Mfrs. Assn., 1977-87, chmn., 1984-86; sci. advisor Am. Coun. on Sci. and Health, 1991—. Contbr. articles to med. and pharm. jours. Bd. dirs. Family Service Ctr., Kalamazoo, 1965-71. Served with AUS, 1945-46. Recipient W.E. Upjohn award for excellence, 1969, Physician's Recognition award AMA, 1969, 73, 76, 79, 82, 85, 88. Fellow: Am. Acad. Pediat.; mem.: Advancement of Sound Sci. Coalition (mem. scientist). Republican. Home: 4567 Foxfire Trail Portage MI 49024 E-mail: dalekazoo@aol.com.

CHODOSH, ROBERT IVAN, retired middle school educator, coach; b. Elizabeth, N.J., May 29, 1946; s. Philip Richard and Jean (Landerman) C.; m. Norma Jean Ries, Feb. 14, 1999. BS in Edn., U. Tenn., Knoxville, 1968; MEd, U. Ctrl. Fla., Orlando, 1975. Cert. in phys. edn., health edn. Tchr. Old Dixie Elem. Sch., Titusville, Fla., 1968-78, Surfside Elem. Sch., Satellite Beach, Fla., 1978-79; tchr., basketball and track coach Andrew Jackson Middle Sch., Titusville, 1979-98; ret., 1998; substitute tchr. Corpus Christi Ind. Sch. Dist., 2002—, Gregory-Portland (Tex.) Ind. Sch. Dist., 2002—. Mem. comprehensive edn. com. Brevard County Schs., Melbourne, Fla., 1990-91. Com. mem. Brevard County Elementary and Secondary Physical Education Guide, 1977, 82, 85, 88. Gray leader, coach North Brevard YMCA, Titusville, 1968-78; recreation leader North Brevard Recreation Dept., 1968-78, summer program leader, 1970-75, 88; scorer, asst. coach, concession stand mgr. Indian River City Little Leauge, 1987, 89. Recipient Tchr. of Yr. award Old Dixie Elem. Sch., Titusville, 1974, Silver Svc. award Brevard County Sch. System. Mem. U. Tenn. Alumni Assn. Democrat. Jewish. Avocations: walking, watching sports, listening to music, swimming, reading. Home: 7721 Hartley Cir Corpus Christi TX 78413-6116 E-mail: bchod39788@aol.com.

CHODOSH, SANFORD, pulmonologist; b. Carteret, N.J., Jan. 14, 1928; s. m. Harriet Reznick; 3 children. BA in Biology and Chemistry, U. VA., 1948; MD, Johns Hopkins U., 1952. Intern Boston City Hosp., 1952-53, resident, 1956-58, fellow Lung Sta., 1958-59, physician-in-charge Sputum Lab., 1959-85, dir. dept. inhalation therapy, 1971-79, 80-81, dir. pulmonary outpatient dept., 1973-76; instr. in medicine Tufts U., Boston, 1960-61, asst. prof. medicine, 1962-70, assoc.. prof. medicine, 1970-74; assoc. prof. medicine Sch. Medicine Boston U., 1974—; chief pulmonary clinic VA Outpatient Clinic, Boston, 1979-2000, chief medicine, 1984-88, acting chief staff, 1986-87, chief staff, 1987-2000, assoc. chief medicine, 1988-91. Rsch. asst. dept. psychobiology Johns Hopkins U., 1949-51; asst. vis. physician I & III Tufts Med. Svc., Boston City Hosp., 1964-67, assoc. vis. physician, 1968-73; vis. physician Univ. Hosp., 1977-88; vis. physician VA Hosp., Boston, 1975-77; mem. utilization evaluation com. Dept. Health and Hosps., 1966-71, chmn. accreditation subcom., 1966-68, chmn. human studies com., 1972-84; mem. tuberculosis adv. com. Deans Com. Boston, 1967-68, tuberculosis implementation com., 1969-71; mem. pulmonary com. Tufts U. Sch. Medicine, 1969-71, sci. affairs com., 1972-74; chmn. pharmacy and therapeutics com. Dept. Health and Hosps., 1972-75, patient care com., 1972-74, human studies com., 1973-84; mem. Nat. Human Rsch. Protections adv. com. U.S. Dept. HHS, 2000-22; cons. in field. Contbr. numerous articles to profl. publs., chpts. to books. Active Am. Lung Assn. of Mass.; mem. Applied Rsch. Ethics Nat. Assn. Coun., 1986—. With U.S. Army and USAF Med. Corps, 1953-56. Fellow Nat. Tuberculosis Assn., 1958-60, 60-61, Edward Livingstone Trudeau fellow Nat. Tuberculosis Assn., 1961-62; recipient Rsch. Career Devel. award USPHS, 1963-67. Fellow Am. Coll. Chest Physicians; mem. Am. Thoracic Soc., Mass. Thoracic Soc. (v.p. 1968-70, pres. 1970-72, mem. coun. 1967-77, 79-82, mem. rsch. allocations com. 1982-84), Am. Coll. Chest Physicians, Mass. Med. Soc., Johns Hopkins Med. and Surg. Assn., Suffolk Dist. Med. Soc., Pub. Responsibility in Medicine and Rsch., Inc. (founding mem., bd. dirs. 1974—, pres. 1979-2001), Assn. Accreditation Human Rsch. Protection Programs, Inc. (founding mem., pres. 1999-2001), Sigma Xi, Phi Beta Kappa. Home: 35 Oak Hill Rd Wayland MA 01778-2917 E-mail: schodosh15@comcast.net.

CHOE, YUN HWANG, chemist, educator; d. Yang-Kyu Hwang and Jang-Sook Kim; m. Young Chul Choe, June 15, 1989; children: Benjamin, Gabrielle. PhD, Rutgers U., 1993. Registered pharmacist NJ. Postdoctoral rschr. Hoffmann-La Roche, Nurley, NJ, 1993—95; group leader /scientist Enzon, Inc., Piscataway, NJ, 1996—. Lectr. Rutgers U., New Brunswick, NJ, 1998—. Mem.: Am. Assn. for Cancer Rsch. Achievements include patents for in field. Avocations: singing, piano, organ. Office: Enzon Pharms Inc 20 Kingsbridge Rd Piscataway NJ 08812

CHOHAYEB, AIDA A. dentist, educator; DDS, Alexandria (Egypt) U., 1957; cert. in pediatric dentistry, Eastman Dental Hosp., London, 1958; cert. in orthodontics, Royal Dental Hosp., London, 1960; MS in Dentistry, U. Minn., 1968; cert. in clin. dentistry, NYU, 1978. Lic. dentist N.Y., Pa., D.C. Pvt. practice, Maadi, Egypt, 1961—66, 1968—74; chmn. dept. dentistry Geziera Hosp., Cairo, 1961—66, 1968—74; asst. dir. Gesundheightsamt, Pedodontic Clinic, Krefeld, Germany, 1974—76; pvt. practice Krefeld, Germany, 1974—76, N.Y.C., 1979—81; asst. dir. Inst. for Fgn. Trained Dentists NYU, N.Y.C., 1976—80, chief endodontic sect., 1976—80, asst. prof. dept. endodontics Coll. Dentistry, 1976—80, rsch. scientist dept. dental materials Coll. Dentistry, 1980—81; attending endodontist endodontics residency program Nassau County Med. Hosp., L.I., 1980—81; assoc. prof. Howard U. Coll. Dentistry, Washington, 1981—86, prof., 1986—. Guest scientist Am. Dental Assn. Health Found. Paffanburger Rsch. Ctr. NIST, Gaithersburg, Md., 1984—93; vis. prof. rsch. NYU Coll. Dentistry, N.Y.C., 2001—; guest scientist; cons. in field; presenter in field. Contbr. articles to profl. jours. Recipient Outstanding Svc. award, Am. Assn. Women Dentists, 1982, 1984, Lucy Hobbs Taylor award, 1987, Meritorious Svc. award to organized dentistry, 1989, D.C. Meritorious Pub. Svc. award, Mayor D.C., 1983, Outstanding and Valuable Contbn. to the Profession and to the Women in Dentistry award, Am. Assn. Women Dentists Md. State chpt., 1990, Dedicated Svcs. award, Am. Assn. for Dental Rsch.-Met. Washington sect., 1992. Fellow: Am. Coll. Dentists (numerous positions including chmn. Washington sect. 1992—94), Internat. Coll. Dentists, Acad. Dentistry Internat.; mem.: AAUP, ADA (reviewer Jour. ADA 1988—90), Am. Assn. Pub. Health Dentistry, Assn. Egyptian-Am. Scholars, Dist. Columbia Dental Soc., Fedn. Dentaire Internat., Am. Assn. for Dental Rsch. (numerous positions including 1998—99, mem. nat. affairs com. 1999—2002, mem. constn. and bylaws com. 1999—2002, ednl. rsch. group, sec.-treas. Met. Washington sect. 1982—83, v.p. Met. Washington sect. 1984, pres. Met. Washington sect. 1985, counselor Met. Washington sect. 1986—92), Internat. Assn. for Dental Rsch. (councilor Egyptian divsn. 1996—99, numerous positions including exec. com. ednl. rsch. group 1996—2001, mem. constn. and bylaws com. 1999—2002, chmn. various oral sessions), NYU Alumni Assn., Minn. Alumni Assn. Home: 15517 Grinnell Terr Rockville MD 20855

CHOHLIS, DANA MARIE, educator, theatre director; b. San Francisco, Dec. 8, 1957; d. Francis P. and Irene Marion (Edwards) Severn; children: Alyssa Katrina, Christina Alexis. BA, Calif. State U., Hayward, 1992, MA, 2000. Cert. English tchr. Tchr. San Leandro (Calif.) Unified Sch. Dist., 1992—; instr. pub. spkg. Peralta C.C., Oakland, Calif., 2000—. Dir. A Midsummer Night's Dream, 1999, Bridge to Terabithia, 1998, Circus in the Wind, 1997, A Case for Two Detectives, 1996, Electra, 2001; performer: Cypress, Taming of the Shrew, Edinburgh Fringe Festival, 2002. Tech. grantee San Leandro Bus. Assn., 1997, 98, 99, Long's Drugs Adopt-a-Class grantee, 2001. Mem. San Leandro Tchrs. Assn. (sec.), No. Calif. Edn. Theatre Assn. (rep.. mem. English/lang. arts stds. com., master tchr., retention program coord.). Avocations: sailing, yacht racing, acting, dancing, hiking. Home: 1448 Church Ave San Leandro CA 94579-1523 E-mail: danabegood@yahoo.com.

CHOI, BERNARD, laser scientist, researcher; s. Chang Ryul and Young Ja Choi; m. Erna Vanessa Trujillo. BS, Northwestern U., 1996; MS, The U. of Tex., Austin, TX, 1998, PhD, 2001. Postdoctoral fellow Beckman Laser Inst., Irvine, Calif., 2001—02, rsch. scientist, 2002—. Fellow Beckman Fellowship, Arnold and Mabel Beckman Found., 2002-present. Mem.: Am. Soc. for Laser Medicine and Surgery, Soc. for Photo-Optical Instrumentation Engrs. Office: Beckman Laser Institute 1002 Health Sciences Road East Irvine CA 92612 E-mail: bchoi@laser.bli.uci.edu.

CHOI, DENNIS W. pharmaceutical executive, neurologist, educator; b. Ann Arbor, Mich., Sept. 26, 1953; three children. AB, Harvard Coll., 1974; MD, Harvard Med. Sch., 1978; PhD, Harvard U., 1978. Diplomate Am. Bd. Psychiatry & Neurology, Am. Bd. Clin. Neurophysiology, Am. Bd. Electrodiagnostic Medicine. Clin. fellow in medicine Harvard U., Boston, 1978-79, fellow in neurology, 1979-83; from asst. prof. to assoc. prof. Stanford (Calif.) U., 1983-91; prof., head dept. Washington U. Med. Sch., St. Louis, 1991—2002, adj. prof., Neurology, 2002—; exec. v.p. Merck Research Laboratories, 2002—. Trustee Grass Found., Braintree, Mass., 1997—. Mem. Am. Neurol. Assn. (v.p. 1996-97), Inst. Medicine, Soc. Neurosci. (pres. 1999—), Korean-Am. Med. Assn. (advisor 1997—). Office: Washington U Med Sch 660 S Euclid Ave Saint Louis MO 63110-1010

CHOI, DOO-SUP, molecular biologist; b. Seoul, South Korea, Sept. 27, 1964; came to U.S., 1997; s. Byung-Man and Mi-Hong (Park) C.; m. Sun-Jung Lim, June 1, 1991; children: Ji-Won, Jung-Yeon, Jae-Hyun. BS, Yonsei U., Seoul, 1988, MS, 1990; PhD, Louis Pasteur U., Strasbourg, France, 1997. Rsch. assoc. Cheil Foods & Chems., Seoul, 1991-92; postdoctoral rschr. dept. biopharm. sci. U. Calif., San Francisco, 1997-98, sr. scientist Gallo Rsch. Ctr., 1998—. Contbr. articles to profl. jours. Grantee Ctr. Nat. Rsch. Sci., France, 1993-97, NIH, 1997-98, State of Calif., 1998—. Fellow: Ctr. Internat. des Etudiants et Stagiares; mem.: Internat. Behavioral & Neural Genetics Soc., Soc. Neurosci., Serotonin Club. Christian Ch. Avocations: reading, travel, mountain climbing, tennis. Office: Gallo Rsch Ctr Univ of Calif-San Francisco 5858 Horton St Emeryville CA 94608 E-mail: choids@itsa.ucsf.edu.

CHOI, KENT CHOUNG, surgeon, researcher; b. Canton, China, Oct. 14, 1960; arrived in U.S., 1984; s. Sidney S.N. and Feng E. (Wu) Tsoi; m. Minjun Wang Choi, Aug. 12, 1990; children: Allen B., Brian C., Derek M. Student, Jin-Nan U., Canton, 1981—84; BS, U. Fla., 1989; MD, Med. Coll. Ga., 1993. Bd. cert. gen. surgery. Surg. intern/resident U. Va., Charlottesville, 1993—95; surg. resident W.Va. U., Morgantown, 1995—99; critical care fellow Washington U., St. Louis, 1999—2001; asst. prof. surgery Iowa U., Iowa City, 2001—; tchr. med. students and residents dept. surgery U. Iowa, Iowa City, 2002—03. Master: AMA; fellow: ACS (assoc.; com. on trauma for Iowa state 2002—). Avocations: swimming, reading, movies, fishing. Home: 1713 Red Oak Dr Coralville IA 52241 Office: U Iowa Hosp and Clinics 1504 JCP 200 Hawkins Dr Iowa City IA 52242

CHOI, MICHAEL KAMWAH, aerospace engineer, mechanical engineer, researcher; b. Aug. 16, 1952; arrived in U.S., 1972, naturalized, 1987; s. Ying-Loi and Kan-Hau (Yuen) C.; m. Wendy Liang; 1 child, Natalie. BSc in Engring. magna cum laude, Brown U., 1976; MSME, MIT, 1978, Engr's. Degree in Mech. Engring., 1979. Registered profl. engr., Va. Rsch. asst. dept. mech. engring. MIT, Cambridge, Mass., 1977-79; sr. rsch. engr. Sci. Applications Internat. Corp., McLean, Va., 1979-87; sr. engr. spacecraft thermal control sys. Fairchild Space and Defense Corp., Germantown, Md., 1987-90; project leader, mgr. NASA Goddard Space Flight Ctr., Greenbelt, Md., 1990—. Intrument thermal mgr. WIND and POLAR spacecraft Global Geospace Sci. Mission, 1990-92; thermal sys. mgr. Far Ultraviolet Spectroscopic Explorer Project, 1992-94; lead thermal engr. High Energy Solar Imager project, 1994-96; thermal sys. mgr. LANDSAT-7 mission, 1994-2000; lead thermal engr. electron reflectometer and magnetometer instruments on Lunar Prospector spacecraft, 1995 97, Next Generation Space Telescope, 1996-97, low energy neutral atom instrument on MIDEX IMAGE spacecraft, 1996-2000, Solar Probe Study, 1996-2001, Triana PlasMag instrument, 1999—, Swift Burst Alert Telescope instrument, optical bench and instrument module, 1999—; thermal architect Space Solar Power Exploratory Rsch. and Tech., 1999-2000; cons. EO-1 Advanced Land Imager, 1997-2000; reviewer flight assurance office; organizer, chmn. spacecraft and instrument thermal control sessions 32d Intersoc. Energy Conversion Engring. Conf., 1997, chmn. spacecraft and aircraft thermal mgmt. sessions, 1998-2002, chmn. spacecraft and aircraft thermal mgmt. sessions, Internat. Energy Conversion Engring. Conf., 2003—; contbr. solar heating and cooling program U.S. Dept. Energy; spkr. nat. and internat. confs.; cons. MAP Star Tracker thermal design, 1999-2000, IRAC thermal cooldown, 2000, Balloon instrument thermal design, 2000. Contbr. articles to profl. jours.; reviewer Solar Energy Jour., ASME Solar Energy Divsn., 1983-87. Fellow AIAA (assoc., Cert. Merit Best Paper in Aerospace Power Sys. 1996); mem. ASME, Soc. Automotive Engring., Sigma Xi, Tau Beta Pi. Home: 2237 Halter Ln Reston VA 20191-5824 E-mail: michael.k.choi@nasa.gov.

CHOI, SOOK C. physiologist, educator; arrived in U.S., 1958; d. Dong-Sun Yoo and Kuan-Sum Kim; m. Paul W. Choi, Mar. 5, 1960; children: James Paul, William Augustine, Mary Anne. PhD, Rutgers U., 1973; BSN, Seton Hall U., 1964. Prof. of biology Upsala Coll., East Orange, NJ, 1973—95; the calman prof. of biology Caldwell (N.J.) Coll., 1995—. Recipient Women of the Yr. award, Soroptimist Internat. of the Am., 1984, The Christian R. and Mary Lindback Found. award, Upsala Coll., 1986. Mem.: Am. Physiol. Soc. (corr.). Roman Catholic. Home: 8 Medford Rd Morris Plains NJ 07950 Office: Caldwell College 9 Ryerson Ave Caldwell NJ Home Fax: 975-631-1059; Office Fax: 973 618-3477. Personal E-mail: schoi@caldwell.edu. E-mail: schoi@caldwell.edu.

CHOI, SOON CHAE, orthopaedic surgeon; b. Sept. 13, 1941; MD, Seoul Nat U., Korea, 1966. Diplomate Am. Bd. Orthopaedic Surgery. Intern Albert Einstein Med. Ctr., Phila., 1966-67; resident gen. surgery St. Peter's Med. Ctr., New Brunswick, N.J., 1967-69; resident orthop. surgery Columbia Presbyn.

Med. Ctr., Harlem Hosp. Ctr., N.Y.C., 1969-73; chief orthopaedic surgery Muhlenberg Regional Med. Ctr., Plainfield, N.J., 1992-96; clin. asst. prof. orthopedic surgery Robert Wood Johnson Med. Sch., U. Medicine and Dentistry N.J, 1975. Fellow Am. Acad. Orthopaedic Surgeons. Office: 1907 Park Ave South Plainfield NJ 07080-5530 E-mail: sooncchoi@aol.com.

CHOI, STEPHEN U.S. mechanical engineer; b. Sunsan, Korea, Feb. 15, 1942; s. Yong Soo and Boon Soon (Cho) C.; m. Sunja Kang, Oct. 20, 1969; children: Samuel, David, John, Paul. BS, Seoul Nat. U., 1964; MS, U. Tex., 1974; PhD, U. Calif., Berkeley, 1978; MDiv, No. Bapt. Theol. Sem., 1997. Asst. prodn. mgr. Moorim Paper Mfg. Co., Ltd., Taegu, Korea, 1964-69; assoc. investigator Korea Inst. Sci. and Tech., Seoul, 1969-73; nuclear staff Bechtel Power Corp., San Francisco, 1978-79; staff scientist Lawrence Berkeley Nat. Lab., Berkeley, Calif., 1980-83; mech. engr. Argonne (Ill.) Nat. Lab., 1983—. Vis. prof. Purdue U. Calumet, Hammond, Ind., 1990-93; chmn. Internat. Energy Agy. Advanced Fluids Expert Group, 1990-93. Contbr. articles to profl. jours. Mem. ASME, Korean-Am. Scientists and Engrs. Assn., Phi Kappa Phi. Mem. Bible Ch. Achievements include invention of nanofluids, an innovative new class of heat transfer fluids which can be engineered by suspending nanoparticles in conventional heat transfer fluids. Home: 6413 Pruthmore Ct Lisle IL 60532-3255 Office: Argonne Nat Lab 9700 S Cass Ave Argonne IL 60439-4803 E-mail: choi@anl.gov.

CHOI, SUNG RAK, mechanical engineer, researcher; b. Yechun, Kyung-buk, Korea, May 13, 1950; came to the U.S., 1980; s. Duk-Sung and Chul-Ja (Chung) C.; m. Jung-Hee Moon, Feb. 18, 1978; children: Dong-Hoon, Jinny U. B in Engring., Yonsei U., Seoul, Korea, 1975; MS, U. Wash., 1983, M in Engring., 1985; PhD, U. Mass., 1988. Rsch. engr. Korea Inst. Sci. and Tech., Seoul, 1975-80; postdoctoral fellow U. Mass., Amherst, 1988-89; sr. resident rsch. scientist NASA Glenn Rsch. Ctr., Cleve., 1989—. Adj. faculty Cleve. State U., 1996—. Contbr. articles to profl. jours. Mem. ASTM (Std. Authorship award 1998, 2000), ASME, Am. Ceramic Soc. (Best Paper award 1996, 99), Korean Scientists and Engrs. Assn. (chpt. pres. 1995-96). Avocations: tennis, travel, camping. Office: NASA Glenn Rsch Ctr MS24-1 21000 Brookpark Rd Cleveland OH 44135-3191 E-mail: sung.r.choi@grc.nasa.gov.

CHOI, YOUNG SOO, pharmacologist, toxicologist; b. Chonju, Rep. of Korea, Dec. 20, 1936; came to U.S., 1961; d. Sung Wook and Woo Bok Choi. BS, Chosun U., Kwangju, Rep. of Korea, 1959; MS in Pharmacology, U. R.I., 1963; PhD in Pharmacology, Hahnemann Med. Coll., Phila., 1968. Rsch. asst. U. R.I., 1961-63; rsch. fellow Hahnemann Med. Coll., 1963-65, grad. student instr., 1965-67; postdoctoral fellow Downstate Med. Ctr. SUNY, Bklyn., 1967-68; assoc. rsch. scientist NYU Med. Ctr., N.Y.C., 1969-74; asst. prof. Howard U. Med. Sch., Washington, 1974-76; cons. FDA, Rockville, Md., 1975-76, pharmacologist, 1976-90, expert pharmacologist, 1990-97. Guest worker NIH, Bethesda, Md., 1977-80 Mem. Soc. of Toxicology, Korean-Am. Scientists and Engrs. Assn. (mem. editl. bd. 1979), Phi Sigma, Rho Chi. Roman Catholic. Achievements include development of 3 sets of guidelines for preclinical toxicity studies required for FDA approval for new drug applications for surfactants, antiasthmatic and intralipid drugs; research in pulmonary surfactants, intralipids, leukotriene antagonists, and immunotoxic and pulmonary drugs. Avocations: gardening, sewing, singing, brush writing, painting. Home: 4200 Warner St Kensington MD 20895-4058

CHOICE, PRISCILLA KATHRYN MEANS (PENNY CHOICE), educational director, international consultant; b. Rockford, Ill., Nov. 8, 1939; d. John Z. and Margaret A. (Haines) Means; m. Jack R. Choice, Nov. 14, 1964; children: William Kenneth, Margaret Meta. BA, U. Wis., 1963; MEd, Nat.-Louis U., 1990; MA, N.E. Ill. U., 1995. Field rsch. dir. Tatham-Laird and Kudner Advt., Chgo., 1964-69; drama specialist Children's Theatre Western Springs (Ill.), 1969-81; gifted teaching asst. Sch. Dist. 181, Hinsdale, Ill., 1980-84; tchr. Sch. Dist. 99, Cicero, Ill., 1984-85; gifted edn. program coord. Cmty. Consolidated Sch. Dist. 93, Carol Stream, Ill., 1985-99; coord. gifted edn. and fine arts Ednl. Svcs. Divsn., Lake County Regional Office Edn., Grayslake, Ill., 1999—. Drama specialist, cons. Choice Dramatics, Hinsdale and Clarendon Hills, Ill., 1976—; producing dir. Mirror Image Youth Theatre, Hinsdale, 1986-88; adj. prof. Coll. DuPage, Glen Ellyn, Ill., 1990-92, Nat.-Louis U., Evanston, Ill., 1991—, Aurora (Ill.) U., 1995—, Govs. State U., University Park, Ill., 1992-93; internat. cons. in gifted edn. and drama-in-edn., 1989—; co-chair advocacy com. Ill. Assn. Gifted Children, 2002—; trustee Friends of the Lake Co. Discovery Mus., 2003—; chair arts divsn. Nat. Asson. for Gifted Children, 2003—. Contbg. author Gifted/Arts Resource Guide, 1990; contbg. editor Ill. Theatre Assn., Followspot News, 1992-95. 96-2002. Mem. gifted adv. com. Ednl. Svc. Ctr., Wheaton, Ill., 1987—90, 1992—95, Regional Office of Edn., Wheaton, 1995—99, Northeastern Ill. U.1993-95., Chgo., 1993—95; bd. dirs. Ill. Theatre Assn., Chgo., 1983—87; chair Arts Divsn. Nat. Assn. for Gifted Children, 2003—; co-chair advocacy Com. Ill. Assn. for Gifted Children, 2002—. Recipient Ill. State Bd. Edn. gifted edn. fellowship, 1988, AAUW continuing edn. scholarship, 1986, 90, Excellence award Ill. Theatre Assn., 1991, Excellence award Ill. Math. and Sci. Acad., 1990, 98, Recognition of Excellence, No. Ill. Planning Commn. Gifted Edn., 1990, Award of Excellence Ill. and Math. Sci. Acad., 1998. Mem. ASCD, World Coun. on Gifted Edn., Nat. Assn. Gifted Children, Ill. Assn. Gifted Children (membership chmn. 1992-94, advocacy com. 1995—, co-chair advocacy com. 2002—), Ill. Coun. Gifted, Am. Assn. Theatre in Edn., Ill. Theatre Assn. (bd. dirs. 1983-87, Outstanding Achievement award 1991), Inst. for Global Ethics, Ill. Alliance Arts Edn., Theatre Western Springs, Phi Delta Kappa. Avocations: swimming, walking, reading. Home: 113 S Prospect Ave Clarendon Hills IL 60514-1422 Office: Lake County Ednl Svcs 19525 W Washington St Grayslake IL 60030-1152

CHOI-YIM, HAEIN, research scientist; b. Seoul, Korea (South), Apr. 1, 1966; d. Sangjun Yim and Jungduk Lee; m. Jaisig Choi, Sept. 5, 1990; children: Boryoung Gloria Choi, David Choi, James Choi. B, Sookmyung U., 1989, M, 1991, Calif. Inst. of Tech., 1996, PhD, 1998. Postdoctoral scholar Calif. Inst. of Tech., 1999—2000, sr. rsch. fellow, 2000—. Cons. Liquid Metal Tech., Lake Forest, Calif., 2001—. Achievements include patents pending for ductile metal reinforced bulk metallic glass composites; Ni-based bulk metallic glass formation in the Ni-Nb-Sn alloy systems; research in metallic glass composites. Home: 848 W Huntington Dr Unit 36 Arcadia CA 91007 Office: California Institute of Technology MS 138-78 1201 E California Blv Pasadena CA 91125 Home Fax: 626-795-6132; Office Fax: 626-795-6132. Personal E-mail: hchoi@its.caltech.edu. E-mail: hchoi@its.caltech.edu.

CHOJNACKI, PAUL ERVIN, pharmacist, pharmaceutical company official; b. Chgo., Dec. 29, 1950; s. Ervin Edward and Monica (Jablonski) C.; m. Doris Warenberg, May 26, 1979; children: Brittany, James. BS in Bus., Chgo. State U., 1975; BS in Pharmacy, St. Louis Coll., 1977; MA in Mktg., Webster U., 1982. RPh, Mo., N.C., Ind. Clk. Filmanowicz Drug, Chgo., 1968-70; stock clk. Sears, Roebuck & Co., Chgo., 1974-75; sales rep. Chgo. Motor Club, 1975-76; pharmacist Family Pharmacy, St. Louis, 1977; sales assoc. Eli Lilly & Co., St. Louis, 1977-84; regional mgr. Hosp. Pharmacies Inc., St. Louis, 1984-85; hosp. rep. Glaxo Inc., St. Louis, 1985-91; assoc. product mgr. Oral Cephaloporins Glaxo, Inc., 1989; State of Ind. sr. dist. mgr. Allen & Hanburys/Glaxo Pharms., Fishers, 1991—, area mgr. Novartis; staff pharmacist Marsh Pharmacies, Indpls., 2002; neursci. specialist Eli Lilly & Co., 2002—03, clin. pharmacist Advance PCS, 2003—. Local campaign worker, St. Louis, 1985. Mem. Am. Pharm. Assn., Ind. Pharmacists Assn., Alpha Zeta Omega (treas. St. Louis 197-78, pres. 1978-79). Avocation: orchids. Home and Office: 10110 Bent Tree Ln Fishers IN 46038-9363 Business E-Mail: yockshei@aol.com.

CHOJNICKI, ERIC WALTER THEODORE, molecular geneticist; b. Pitts., Mar. 16, 1959; s. Walter Chojnicki and Eva Helen Simko; m. Estelle Helen Goldsmith, Aug. 27, 1994; children: Johanna Eva, Wolfgang Otto, Walter Samuel, Willem Arthur. BA, Washington and Jefferson Coll., 1981; MS, W.Va. U., 1984, PhD, 1988; MBA, Fairleigh Dickinson U., 2002. Rsch. investigator II Bristol-Myers Squibb, Co., Syracuse, NY, 1991—94; devel. scientist Athena Neuroscis., Inc., South San Francisco, Calif., 1994—95; rsch. scientist II Amgen, Inc., Thousand Oaks, Calif., 1995—98; sr. rsch. investigator I Bristol-Myers Squibb Co., Hopewell, NJ, 1998—2000; dir. bus. devel. Valigen, Inc., Newtown, Pa., 2000—01; postdoctoral assoc. Cornell U., Ithaca, NY, 1988—90, Vanderbilt U., Nashville, 1990—91; dir. product devel. Acorda Therapeutics, Inc., Hawthorne, NY, 2001—. Founder, bd. mem. PreGentis, Inc., Newtown, Pa., 2000—; sci. cons. Metacine, Inc., Princeton, NJ, 2000—. Grantee NIH, 2001—. Mem.: AAAS, Am. Assn. Pharm. Scientists, Parenteral Drug Assn., Am. Chem. Soc., Am. Soc. for Microbiology, Am. Soc. Mass Spectrometry, Soc. for Neurosci. Republican. Roman Catholic. Achievements include discovery of First Monolonal Antibodies to TGF-Beta. Avocations: padi divemaster, golf. Office: Acorda Therapeutics Inc 15 Skyline Dr Hawthorne NY 10532 Office Fax: 914-347-4560. E-mail: echojnicki@acorda.com.

CHOJNOWSKI, DONNA APPLEGATE, cardiac nursing administrator; m. John Chojnowski. BSN, Trenton (N.J.) State Coll., 1979; MSN, Drexel U., 2003. Cert. clin. transplant coord., provider ACLS; CCRN, CRNP, ACNP. Staff nurse ICU, asst. head nurse Albert Einstein Med. Ctr., Phila., 1981-84, 84-87, asst. head nurse, 1985-87; nurse mgr. cardiothoracic surg./trauma ICU Temple U. Hosp., Phila., 1987-90; cardiac transplant clin. nurse coord./adminstr. Allegheny U. Hahneman Hosp., Phila., 1990-98; clin. transplant nurse coord. Hosp. U. Pa., 1998—2003, clin. mgr. heart failure/heart transplant/HF ND, 2003—. Lectr., rschr. on cardiac transplantation and heart failure, 1990—. Mem.: AACN (S.E. Pa. chpt., cert., bd. dirs., coord. monthly edn. program, Mgr. of Yr. award 1989), Bux-mont Nurse Practitioners Assn., Am. Acad. Nurse Practitioners, Sigma Theta Tau.

CHOKSY, JAMSHEED KAIRSHASP, historian, religious scholar, language professional, humanities educator; b. Bombay, Jan. 8, 1962; arrived in Sri Lanka, 1962; permanent resident, U.S. 1995, naturalized, 1999. s. Kairshasp Nariman and Freny Kairshasp (Cooper) C.; m. Carol Emma Burnside, Sept. 12, 1993; 1 child, Darius Jamsheed. AB in Mid.-Ea. Langs. and Culture, Columbia U., 1985; PhD in History and Religions, Harvard U., 1991. Tchg. fellow dept. anthropology and archaeology Harvard U., 1988, jr. fellow, 1988-91; vis. asst. prof. depts. history and internat. rels. Stanford U., 1991-93; from asst. prof. to prof. Ind. U., Bloomington, 1993—2001, prof. ctrl. Eurasian studies and history, 2001—. Mem. Sch. Hist. Studies, Inst. for Advanced Study-Princeton, 1993—94; cons. PBS-TV, 1990, L.A. Times, 1998, Am. Mus. Natural History, 1998, Am. Hist. Rev., 1999—; presenter in field. Author: Purity and Pollution in Zoroastrianism, 1989, Conflict and Cooperation, 1997, Evil, Good and Gender, 2002, Archeological Surveys in Pakistan, 1988-90, 1999-2001; contbr. numerous articles to profl. publs. Rsch. fellow Govt. India, Bombay, 1998; John Simon Guggenheim Meml. Found. fellow, 1996-97; resident scholar Ind. U., 1996-97, grantee 1994—, grantee Am. Acad. Religion, 1995-96, Andrew W. Mellon fellow, 1991-93, 2001-02. Fellow: NEH, Royal Asiatic Soc. Great Britain, Ireland, Ctr. for Advanced Study in the Behavioral Scis.; mem.: Cosmos Club (Washington), Explorers Club (NY). Office: Ind U Dept Ctrl Eurasian Studies Goodbody Hall 157 1011 E 3rd St Bloomington IN 47405-7005 E-mail: jchoksy@indiana.edu.

CHOLAK, PETER, mathematics educator; PhD, U. of Wis., 1991. Assoc. prof Notre Dame, Ind., 1994—. Office: Univ of Notre Dame 255 Hurley Notre Dame IN 46530

CHOLDIN, MARIANNA TAX, librarian, educator; b. Chgo., Feb. 26, 1942; d. Sol and Gertrude (Katz) Tax; m. Harvey Myron Choldin, Aug. 28, 1962; children: Kate and Mary (twins). BA, U. Chgo., 1962, MA, 1967, PhD, 1979. Slavic bibliographer Mich. State U., East Lansing, 1967—69; Slavic bibliographer, instr. U. Ill., Urbana, 1969—73, Slavic bibliographer, asst. prof., 1973—76, Slavic bibliographer, assoc. prof., 1976—84, head Slavic and East European Libr., 1982—89, head, prof., 1984—2002, dir. Russian and East European Ctr., 1987—89, C. Walter and Gerda B. Mortenson Disting. prof., 1989—2002, dir. Mortenson Ctr. for Internat. Libr. Programs, 1991—2002, prof. emerita, 2003—. Author: Fence Around the Empire: Russian Censorship, 1985; editor: Red Pencil: Artists, Scholars and Censors in the USSR, 1989, Books, Libraries and Information in Slavic and East European Studies, 1986. Chair Soros Found. Network Libr. Program Bd., 1997—2000. Recipient Pushkin gold medal for contbns. to culture, Russian Presdl. Coun. on Culture, 2000. Mem. ALA, Am. Assn. for Advancement of Slavic Studies (pres. 1995), Internat. Fedn. Libr. Assns. and Instns., Phi Beta Kappa. Jewish. Home: 888 S Michigan Ave #403 Chicago IL 60605

CHOLE, RICHARD ARTHUR, otolaryngologist, educator; b. Madison, Wis., Oct. 12, 1944; s. Arthur Steven and Wendy Elveyn (Danielczyk) C.; m. Cynthia Beiseker, Dec. 27, 1969; children: Joseph Michael, Timothy Thomas, Katharine, Melinda. Student, U. Calif., Berkeley, 1962-65; MD, U. So. Calif., 1969; PhD in Otolaryngology, U. Minn., 1977. Diplomate Am. Bd. Otolaryngology (sr. bd. examiner). Rotating intern U. So. Calif. Med. Ctr., 1969-70; med. fellow dept. surgery Sch. Medicine U. Minn., 1972-73, med. fellow dept. otolaryngology Sch. Medicine, 1973-77; asst. prof. dept. otolaryngology-head and neck surgery Sch. Medicine U. Calif., Davis, 1977-81, assoc. prof., 1981-84, prof., 1984-98, acting chmn. dept., 1985, chmn., 1985-88; chmn. dept. otolaryngology Washington U., St. Louis, 1998—. Mem. sci. rev. com. Deafness Rsch. Found., 1986—; mem. communicative disorders rev. com. Nat. Inst. Deafness and Communication Disorders, 1989—94; staff cons. Dept. Air Force, David Grant USAF Med. Ctr., Travis AFB, Calif., 1981—98; keynote spkr. 92d Japan Oto-Rhino-Laryngol. Soc. Meeting, Fukuoka City, Japan, 1990—; faculty mem. 4th Internat. Cholesteatoma Conf., Niigata City, Japan, 1992; bd. dirs. Am. Bd. Otolaryngology, 2000—; adv. coun. Nat. Deafness and Other Communication Disorders, 2001—; lectr. in field. Mem. editorial bd. Laryngoscope, 1985-87; mem. exec. editorial bd. Otolaryngology-Head and Neck Surgery, 1990—; contbr. numerous articles to profl. jours., book chpts., revs.; patentee in field. Mem. profl. edn. com. Am. Cancer Soc., 1977-78, Sacramento Noise Control Hearing Bd., 1977—, Greater Sacramento Profl. Standards Rev. Orgn., 1978-79; deacon 1st Bapt. Ch., Davis, 1979-82, elder, 1983-88. Recipient 1st pl. award Am. Acad. Ophthalmology and Otolaryngology, 1977, care recognition awards U. Calif., Davis, 1988-91; rsch. grantee NIH, Nat. Inst. Aging, Nat. Inst. Neurol. and Communicative Disorders and Stroke, Nat. Inst. on Deafness and Other Communication Disorders, Deafness Rsch. Found., Am. Otol. Soc., U. Calif., 1978-91. Mem. Collegeum Otorhinolaryngologicum Amicitiae Sacrum (U.S. group), Am. Acad. Otolaryngology-Head and Neck Surgery (Honors award 1984, com. on rsch. 1987—, rsch. coordinating coun. 1987—, continuing edn. com. 1991—), Am. Otol. Soc. (trustee rsch. fund 1986—, sec.-treas. 1989—, pres. 2001—), Assn. for Rsch. in Otolaryngology (pres. 1999-2000, award of merit com. 1988—), Am. Laryngol., Rhinol. and Otol. Soc., Am. Soc. for Bone and Mineral Rsch., Assn. Acad. Depts. Otolaryngology-Head and Neck Surgery (coun. 1986—), Calif. Med. Assn. (sci. adv. panel, sect. on otolaryngology-head and neck surgery 1986-98), Sacramento Soc. Otolaryngology and Maxillofacial Surgery, Soc. Univ. Otolaryngologists-Head and Neck Surgeons. Achievements include research in in experimental cholesteatoma, experimental otosclerosis, the aging auditory system, osteoclast cell biology. Office: Washington U Sch Med CB8115 660 S Euclid Ave # 8115 Saint Louis MO 63110-1010 E-mail: choler@msnotes.wustl.edu.

CHOLEWKA, PATRICIA ANNE, health services administrator; b. Bronx, N.Y. m. Michael A. Cholewka; children: Maureen, Kathleen. Diploma, Bellevue Sch. Nursing, 1967; BSN magna cum laude, Castleton State Coll., 1979; MPA, NYU, 1987; EdD, Columbia U., 1999. RN; cert. nursing adminstrn. ANA; cert. Nat. Assn. Healthcare Quality. Mgr. med.-surg. clin. svcs. in acute and managed care orgns., 1967-95; educator, 1995—; rschr. healthcare policy and econ. mgmt., 1993—. Healthcare orgn. devel. cons. Razgrad Hosp., Bulgaria, 1993, Kaunas Med. Acad. Hosp., Lithuania, 1996-98, Lviv (Ukraine) Mcpl. Health Dept., 1998; lectr. in field. Author: Comparative Analysis of Two Post-Soviet Healthcare Organizations in Lithuania and Ukraine: Implications for Continuous Quality Improvement, 1999; editor Jour. Healthcare Quality; mem editl. bd Nursing Outlook, Jour. Nursing Scholarship, Jour. Transcultural Nursing. Recipient Disting. Rsch. award, Columbia U., Fed. Nurse Traineeship award, NYU, 2003. Mem. Phi Delta Kappa, Sigma Theta Tau. E-mail: pacholewka@aol.com.

CHOLLET, DEBORAH, economist, educator; b. St. Louis County, Mo., Sept. 3, 1950; d. Robert Xavier and Madalyn Marie (Crowe) C. BS, U. Mo., St. Louis, 1972; MA, Syracuse U., 1975, PhD, 1979. Asst. prof. econs. Temple U., Phila., 1977-79; sr. rsch. fellow Nat. Ctr. for Health Svcs. Rsch., Washington, 1979-81; sr. rsch. assoc. Employee Benefit Rsch. Inst., Washington, 1982-90; exec. dir. Adv. Counc. on Social Security, Washington, 1989-90; dir. Ctr. for Ins. Rsch. Ga. State U., Atlanta, 1990-94, assoc. prof. ins. and risk mgmt., 1990-94; v.p. Alpha Ctr., Washington, 1994—2000; sr. fellow Math. Policy Rsch., Washington, 2000—. Contbr. articles to profl. jours. Mem.: Acad. Health, Nat. Acad. Social Ins. Office: Mathematica Policy Rsch 600 Maryland Ave SW # 550 Washington DC 20024

CHOLST, SHELDON, psychiatrist, writer; b. N.Y.C., July 31, 1924; s. William and Celia (Reiss) C.; m. Betty Brody, June 20, 1950 (div. 1960); children Ina Naomi, David, Tony. AB, NYU; MD, Downstate Med. Ctr., Bklyn. Instr. dept. psychiatry NYU Sch. Medicine, N.Y.C., 1956-58; med. dir. Human Sci. Ctr. Catholic Charities, Queens, N.Y., 1973-76; psychiatrist Prison Health Service, Bklyn., 1976-78; dir. Inst. Genetic Psychiatry, N.Y.C., 1980—. Author: The Only Baby, 1958, Hydra, 1962, The Psychology of the Artist, 1978, Finding Love in a Cold World; producer (cable TV show) Hip Shrink TV Talk Show, 1984—. Served to capt. USAF, 1953-55. Mem. Am. Psychiatric Assn., N.Y. Council for Child Psychiatry. Democrat. Home and Office: 7 E 14th St New York NY 10003-3115

CHOMKO, STEPHEN ALEXANDER, archaeologist; b. Bklyn., Nov. 18, 1948; s. Paul and Lucy Isabella (Bisaccio) C.; m. Leslie M. Howard, Aug. 1972 (div. 1980); m. Sheila A. McCarthy, May, 2000; children: Anthony Daniel, Nicholas Alexander. BA in Anthropology cum laude, Beloit Coll., 1970; MA in Anthropology, U. Mo., 1976. Mem. rsch. staff Nassau County Mus. Natural History, Glen Cove, N.Y., 1969-71; grad. rsch. asst. U. Mo., Columbia, 1972-74, 75-78; rsch. asst. Ill. State Mus., Springfield, 1974-75; dist. archaeologist Bur. Land Mgmt., Rawlins, Wyo., 1978-80; archaeologist Office of Fed. Inspector, Denver, 1980-82; dir. Paleo Environ. Cons., Wheat Ridge, Colo., 1980-86; archaeologist Interagy. Archaeol. Svcs., Denver, 1982-92; chief rsch. and resource mgmt. Mesa Verde (Colo.) Nat. Park, 1992; chief tng. mgmt. Fort Carson, 1994-2000; cultural resources specialist Nat. Resources Conservation Svc., Indpls., 2001—03; cultural resources doord. Valles Caldera Nat. Preserve, Los Alamos, N.Mex., 2003—. Writer, dir. (video program) Our Past Our Future, 1992; contbr. articles to profl. jours. Grantee Cave Rsch. Found., Yellow Springs, Ohio, 1976; Anthropology scholar U. Mo., Columbia, 1978; recipient Quality Performance award Nat. Park Svc., Denver, 1992, 93, Environ. Quality award Dept. of Army, 1996, Environ. Stewardship award Dept. of Def., 1997, Achievement medal for civilian svc. Dept. of Army, 2000. Mem. Soc. Am. Archaeology, Am. Anthropol. Assn., Am. Quaternary Assn., Wyo. Assn. Profl. Archaeologists (exec. com. 1979-82), Mont. Archaeol. Soc., Plains Anthropol. Soc. (v.p. 1988-89, bd. dirs. 1986-89). Home: 904 Capulin Los Alamos NM 87544 Office: Valles Caldera Trust 2201 Trinity Dr Los Alamos NM 87544 E-mail: schomko@vallescaldera.gov.

CHOMSKY, (AVRAM) NOAM (AVRAM CHOMSKY), linguistics and philosophy educator; b. Phila., Dec. 7, 1928; s. William and Elsie (Simonofsky) C.; m. Carol Doris Schatz, Dec. 24, 1949; children: Aviva, Diane, Harry Alan. BA, U. Pa., 1949, MA, 1951, PhD, 1955, DHL (hon.), 1984, U. Chgo., 1967, Loyola U., Chgo., 1970, Swarthmore Coll., 1970, Bard Coll., 1971, U. Mass., 1973, U. Maine, 1992, Gettysburg Coll., 1992, Amherst Coll., 1995; LLD (hon.), U. Buenos Aires, 1996; DHL (hon.), U. Rovira i Virgili, Catalonia, 1998, McGill U., 1998, U. Guelph, Can., 1999, Columbia U., 1999, U. Conn., 1999, U. Toronto, 2000, U. Western Ont., 2000; LittD (hon.), U. London, 1967, Delhi (India) U., 1972, Visva-Bharati U., Santiniketan, West Bengal, 1980, Cambridge (Eng.) U., 1995; LittD (hon.), U. Calcutta, 2001; Doctorate (hon.), Scuola Normale Superiore, Pisa, Italy, 1999; LLD, Harvard U., 2000; DHL (hon.), McGill U., 1998, U. Nat. del Comahue, Argentina, 2001, U. Nat. Bogota, Colombia, 2002. Mem. faculty MIT, 1955—, prof. modern langs., 1961—, Ferrari P. Ward prof. modern lang. and linguistics, 1966—, Inst. prof., 1976—. Vis. prof. Columbia U., N.Y.C., 1957-58; mem. Inst. Advanced Study Princeton U., 1958-59; Linguistic Soc. Am. prof. UCLA, summer 1966; Beckman prof. U. Calif.-Berkeley, 1966-67; John Locke lectr. Oxford U., 1969; Bertrand Russell Meml. lectr., Cambridge, 1971; Nehru Meml. lectr., New Delhi, 1972; Huizinga lectr. U. Leiden, 1977; Woodbridge lectr. Columbia U., 1978; Kant lectr. Stanford U., 1979; Jeanette K. Watson disting. vis. prof. Syracuse U., 1982; Pauling Meml. lectr. Oreg. State U., 1995. Author: Syntactic Structures, 1957, Current Issues in Linguistic Theory, 1964, Aspects of the Theory of Syntax, 1965, Cartesian Linguistics, 1966, Topics in the Theory of Generative Grammar, 1966, (with Morris Halle) Sound Pattern of English, 1968, Language and Mind, 1968, American Power and the New Mandarins, 1969, At War with Asia, 1970, Problems of Knowledge and Freedom, 1971, Studies on Semantics in Generative Grammar, 1972, For Reasons of State, 1973, (with Edward Herman) Counterrevolutionary Violence, 1973, Peace in the Middle East, 1974, Logical Structure of Linguistic Theory, 1975, Reflections on Language, 1975, Essays on Form and Interpretation, 1977, Human Rights and American Foreign Policy, 1978, (with Edward Herman) The Political Economy of Human Rights, 2 vols., 1979, Language and Responsibility, 1979, Rules and Representations, 1980, Lectures on Government and Binding, 1981, Concepts and Consequences of the Theory of Government and Binding, 1982, Towards a New Cold War, 1982, Radical Priorities, 1982, Fateful Triangle, 1983, Turning the Tide, 1985, Barriers, 1986, Knowledge of Language, 1986, Pirates and Emperors, 1986, On Power and Ideology, 1987, Language and Problems of Knowledge, 1987, Language in a Psychological Setting, 1987, Generative Grammar, 1987, Culture of Terrorism, 1988, (with Edward Herman) Manufacturing Consent, 1988, Language and Politics, 1988, Necessary Illusions, 1989, Deterring Democracy, 1991, Chronicles of Dissent, 1992, What Uncle Sam Really Wants, 1992, Year 501, 1993, Rethinking Camelot, 1993, Letters from Lexington, 1993, The Prosperous Few and the Restless Many, 1993, Language and Thought, 1994, World Orders, Old and New, 1994, The Minimalist Program, 1995, Powers and Prospects, 1996, The Common Good, 1998, Profits Over People, 1998, The New Military Humanism, 1999, New Horizons in the Study of Language and Mind, 2000, Rogue States, 2000, A New Generation Draws the Line, 2000, Architecture of Language, 2000, 9-11, 2001, Propaganda and the Public Mind, 2001, Understanding Power, 2002, On Nature and Language, 2002, Middle East Illusions, 2003. Named Rsch. Fellow, Harvard Cognitive Studies Ctr., 1964—67; recipient Disting. Sci. Contbn. award, APA, 1984, Kyoto prize, Kyocera Found., 1988, 2001, Benjamin Franklin Inst. award, 1999, George Orwell award, Nat. Coun. Tchrs. English, 1987, 1989, James Kilian Faculty award, MIT, 1992, Lannan Lit. award for nonfiction, 1992, Joel Seldin Peace award, Psychologists for Social Responsibility, 1993, Homer Smith award, NYU Sch. of Medicine, 1994, Loyola Mellon Humanities award, Loyola U. Chgo., 1994, Helmhotz medal, Berlin-Brandenburische Akad. Wissenschaften, 1996, Benjamin Franklin Inst. award, 1999, Rabindranath Tagore Centenary award, Asiatic Soc. Calcutta, 2000, Rising Sun of Mehgarh award, Dawn Isalamabad, 2001, Adela Dwyer St. Thomas Villanova Peace award, Villanova U., Phila., 2002, Peace award, Turkish Publishers' Assn., Istanbul, 2002, award, Kurdish Human Rights Assn., Diyarbakir, 2002; fellow (Jr.) Soc. Fellows Harvard Univ, 1951—55. Fellow AAAS, Brit. Acad. (corr.), Brit. Psychol. Soc. (hon.), Royal Anthrop. Inst. Gt. Britain, Royal Anthrop. Inst. of Ireland, Utrecht Soc. Arts and Scis. (hon.), Gesellschaft für Sprachwissenschaft (hon.), Am. Acad. Philosophy; mem. APA (William James fellow 1990), NAS, Am. Acad. Arts and Scis., Linguistic Soc. Am., Deutsche Akademie der Naturforscher Leopoldina, Assn. for Edn. in Journalism and Mass Comm. (Profl. Excellence award 1991). Home: 15 Suzanne Rd Lexington MA 02420-1831 Office: 77 Massachusetts Ave Cambridge MA 02139-4301

CHONG, KEN PIN, editor, author, foundation administrator; b. Fung Shen, Kwangtung, China, Sept. 22, 1942; s. Sai-Chong Ho; m. Shuang-Ling Cheng, 1966; children: Frederic, Lillian. AM, MSE, PhD, Princeton U. Registered profl. engr., Wyo. Sr. R&D engr. Nat. Steel Corp., Houston, 1969-74; prof. U. Wyo., Laramie, 1974-89; Mechanics and Materials rsch. program dir. NSF, Arlington. Hon. prof. U. Hong Kong, Shanghai U. Author: 12 books; editor: Elsevier Jour. Thin Walled Structures; contbr. articles to profl. jours. Recipient Rsch. awards Dept. of Energy, others. Fellow ASCE (hon., co-editor control mem. divsn. exec. com. chair 1970—, chair exec. com. engring. materials divsn. 1995-96, Edmund Friedman Profl. Recognition award 1997), Am. Acad. Mechs.; mem. ASME, IEEE, SEM.

CHONG, PANG HYON, pharmacist, consultant; b. Rep. of Korea, Oct. 21, 1966; s. Chong K. and Haeng C. Chong. Postgrad., Creighton U., 1985—87, PharmD, 1991. Registered Pharmacist Am. Coll. Clinical Pharmacy, 1991. Clinical pharmacist in Lipid Clinic, med. cardiology, rsch. mem. of Inst. Rev. Bd. Cook County Hosp., Chgo., 1991—. Spkr. Pfizer, Inc., N.Y.C., 1999—, Wyeth-Ayerst, Chgo., 2002—, Merck & Co., West Point, 2001—; asst. prof. U. Ill., Chgo., 1992—; adj. instr. Midwestern U., Downers Grove, Ill., 2000—;

spkr. Key Pharmaceuticals, Inc., Kenilworth, NJ, 2002—. Contbr. and review articles to profl. jours. Mem.: Soc. Critical Care Medicine, Am. Coll. of Clinical Pharmacy. Presbyterian. Avocations: travel, sports. Office: Cook County Hospital 1900 W Polk St Ste 552 Chicago IL 60612 Business E-Mail: cpang@tigger.cc.uic.edu.

CHONG, RICHARD DAVID, architect; b. Los Angeles, June 1, 1946; s. George and Mabel Dorothy (Chan) C.; m. Roze Gutierrez, July 5, 1969; children: David Gregory, Michelle Elizabeth. BArch, U. So. Calif., 1969; MArch, UCLA, 1974. Registered architect, Utah, Calif., Wyo., Wash. Assoc. Pulliam, Matthews & Assocs., Los Angeles, 1969-76; dir. Asst. Community Design Ctr., Salt Lake City, 1976-77; prin. Richard D. Chong & Assocs., Salt Lake City, L.A., 1977—, Santa Ana, 1977—. Planning cons. Los Angeles Harbor Dept., 1974-76; asst. instr. So. Calif. Inst. Architecture, Santa Monica, 1973-74; vis. design critic Calif. State Poly. U., Pamona, 1975, U. Utah, Salt Lake City, 1976-78; design instr. Calif. State Poly. U., 1975-76; adj. asst. prof. urban design, U. Utah, 1980-84; bd. dirs. Utah Housing Coalition, Salt Lake City; Salt Lake City Housing Adv. and Appeals Bd., 1976-80; presenter Rail-Volution Conf., Washington, 1996. Author: Design of Flexible Housing, 1974; prin. works include Airmen's Dining Hall, 1985 (1st Pl. Mil. Facility Air Force Logistics Command, 1986), Oddfellows Hall, 1984 (Heritage Found. award, 1986), Light Rail Sys. for Salt Lake City. Mem. Task Force for the Aged Housing Com. Salt Lake County, Salt Lake City, 1976-77; Salt Lake City Mortgage Loan Instns. Rev. Com., 1978; bd. dirs. Neighborhood Housing Svcs. of Fed. Home Loan Bank Bd., Salt Lake City, 1979-81, devel. com.; vice-chmn. Water Quality Adv. Coun., Salt Lake City, 1981-83; vice-chmn. Salt Lake City Pub. Utilities Bd., 1985-87; mem. adv. bd. Pub. Utilities Commn., Salt Lake City, 1985—; bd. dirs. Kier Mgmt. Corp.; bd. mem. Camp Kostopulos, Altro Nat. Risk Mgmt. Adv. Bd., 1996—, Ft. Douglas Social Adv. Bd., 1996—, Altro Nat. Safety Bd., 1996-01. Mem. AIA (jury mem. Am. Soc. Interior Designs Ann. awards 1981-82, treas. Salt Lake chpt. 1988-89, treas. Utah Soc. 1991, sec. 1992, pres.-elect AIA Utah 1993, pres. 1994-95), Am. Inst. Planning (juror Ann. Planning award 1984-85), Am. Planning Assn., Am. Arbitration Assn., Nat. Panel Arbitrators, Cottonwood Country Club. Democrat. Avocations: tennis, sailing, fgn. travel. Office: Richard D Chong & Assocs 244 Edison St Salt Lake City UT 84111-2307 also: 714 W Olympic Blvd Ste 732 Los Angeles CA 90015-1439 also: 106 W 4th St Santa Ana CA 92701-4646

CHONG, STEPHEN CHU LING, lawyer; b. Lakewood, Ohio, Aug. 1, 1957; s. Richard Seng Hoon C. and Betty J. (Chong) Wamego; m. Sheryl Kay Horton, Nov. 23, 1984; children: Evan M. G., Erin M.L., Elena M.L., Eric M.K., Ethan M.L. BA, Calvin Coll., 1979; JD, Ohio State U., 1982. Bar: Fla. 1982, U.S. Dist. Ct. (mid. dist.) Fla. 1983, U.S. Ct. Appeals (11th cir.) 1982, U.S. Tax Ct. 1985; bd. cert. real estate lawyer Fla. Bar Bd. Legal Specialization and Edn. Assoc. Caudill, Drage, de Beaubien, Orlando, Fla., 1982-83; shareholder Caudill, Chong & Migliaccio, Winter Garden, Fla., 1983-84; assoc. Thomas R. Rogers & Assocs., Longwood, Fla., 1984-90; of counsel Litchford, Christopher, Orlando, 1990-92; pres., shareholder Marks & Chong, Orlando, 1992-2001; ptnr. Arnold Matheny & Eagan PA, Orlando, 2001—. Mem. nominating bd. City of Orlando, 1993-98, chmn. 1996-97; mem. area bus. com. Naval Tng. Ctr. Reuse Com., Orlando, 1994-95; bd. trustees Minority/Women Bus. Enterprise Alliance, Orlando, 1994-99; chair Realtor Rels. Com., Orlando, 1992-93; presenter in field. Contbr. articles to profl. jours. Mem. cultural diversity com. Orlando Sci. Ctr., 1993-2000; mem. cmty. adv. bd. WMFE-TV/FM, Orlando, 1994-95; mem. adv. bd. Ctrl. Fla. Family, Orlando, 1994-2000; mem. 9th Jud. Cir. Grievance Com., 2002—; pres. Asian Am. C. of C., Orlando, 1993-94; vol. Income Tax Assistance, 1996—; trustee Calvin Coll., Grand Rapids, Mich., 1999—; bd. dirs. Econ. Devel. Commn. of Mid-Fla., Inc., 2001—, Oalndo Citizen Corps Coun., 2002—. Recipient Vision award-Small Bus. Downtown Orlando Partnership, 1994. Mem. ABA, Fla. Bar Assn., Orange County Bar Assn., Christian Legal Soc. Ctr. Fla. (pres. 1999-2000). Presbyterian. Office: Arnold Matheny & Eagan PA 801 N Magnolia Ave Ste 201 Orlando FL 32803

CHONG, VERNON, surgeon, physician, air force officer; b. Fresno, Calif., Nov. 13, 1933; s. Seu Ling and Ruth (Lee) C.; m. Ann Sumiko Kawana, Sept. 7, 1957; children: Christopher Lee, Gerald Scott, Douglas James. BA, Stanford U., 1955, MD, 1958. Diplomate Am. Bd. Surgery. Intern Gen. Hosp. of Fresno (Calif.) County, 1958-59, resident in gen. surgery, 1959-63; commd. capt. USAF, l963, advanced through ranks to maj. gen., 1987; chief gen. surgery svc. USAF Hosp., Scott AFB, Ill., l963-65, staff surgeon, dir. edn. Tachikawa AFB, Japan, 1965-68; staff surgeon, instr. surgery David Grant USAF Med. Ctr., Travis AFB, Calif., 1968-70, dep. comdr., dir. hosp. svcs., comdr., 1976-81; surgeon, chief surgery, dir. hosp. svcs. USAF Acad. Hosp., Colorado Springs, Colo., 1970-74, dep. comdr. dir. svcs. March AFB, Calif., 1974-76; comdr. Malcolm Grow USAF MEd. Ctr., Andrews AFB, Md., 1981-85; command surgeon Hdqrs., Mil. Airlift Command, Scott AFB, 1985-87; comdr. Wilford Hall USAF Med. Ctr., Lackland AFB, Tex., 1987-90, Joint Mil. Med. Command, San Antonio; command surgeon Hdqrs. Air Tng. Command, Randolph AFB, Tex., 1990-91, Hdqrs. U.S. European Command, 1991-94; ret., 1994; network dir. Vets. Integrated Svc. Network, VA, Grand Prairie, Tex., 1995-2000; spl. asst. to network dir. Vets. Integrated Svc. Network-21, McClellan Clinic, Sacramento, Calif., 2000—. Bd. dirs. Alamo chpt. ARC, San Antonio, 1987-88; trustee Air Force Village Found., 1987-90; bd. dirs. San Antonio chpt. ARC, 1995—. Decorated D.S.M., Legion of Merit with bronze oak leaf cluster; recipient Order of Sword award USAF, 1989. Fellow ACS (gov. 1985-90); mem. Assn. Mil. Surgeons U.S., Soc. Air Force Clin. Surgeons (bd. govs. 1971-73), Am. Coll. Physician Execs. Methodist. Avocations: physical fitness, running. Home: 1820 Starview Ln Lincoln CA 95648 Office: Dept Vets Affairs VISN-21 5342 Dudley Blvd Mcclellan AFB CA 95652 E-mail: vernon.chong@med.va.gov.

CHONMAITREE, TASNEE, pediatrician, educator, infectious disease specialist; b. Bangkok, Dec. 9, 1949; came to U.S., 1975; d. Surajit and Arporn (Maitong) C.; m. Somkiat Laungthaleong Pong, June 27, 1981; children: Ann L. Pong, Dan L. Pong. BS, Mahidol U., Bangkok, 1971; MD, Siriraj Med. Sch., Bangkok, 1973. Diplomate Am. Bd. Pediatrics, Am. Bd. Pediatric Infectious Diseases. Rotating intern Siriraj Hosp., Bangkok, 1973-74, resident in pediatrics, 1974-75, Lloyd Noland Hosp., U. Ala., Birmingham, 1975-78; fellow infectious disease U. Rochester (N.Y.), 1978-81; asst. prof. pediatrics U. Tex. Med. Br., Galveston, 1981-87, asst. prof. pathology, 1985-87, assoc. prof. pediatrics and pathology, 1987-94; prof. pediatrics and pathology, 1994—. Assoc. dir. clin. virology lab. U. Tex. Med. Br., Galveston, 1985-92, dir. divsn. pediatric infectious disease, 1985-92. Contbr. 65 articles to profl. jours. Grantee NIH, 1993—. Fellow Am. Acad. Pediatrics, Pediatric Infectious Diseases Soc., Infectious Diseases Soc. Am.; mem. Soc. Pediatric Rsch., European Soc. for Pediatric Rsch., Tex. Infectious Disease Soc. Buddhist. Avocation: classical music. Home: 1906 Cherrytree Park Cir Houston TX 77062-2327 Office: U Tex Dept Pediatrics Med Br Ninth Street & Market Galveston TX 77555-0001

CHOO, KRISTIN E. journalist; b. Elgin, Ill., Oct. 10, 1950; d. Joseph B. and Patricia B. Egelhof. BA in Anthropology, SUNY, Albany, 1972; MA in Environ. Sci., Coll. S.I., 1982; MA in Sci. and Environ. Reporting, NYU, 1994. Freelance journalist, 1994—. Contbr. articles to profl. jours. and newspapers. Mem.: Newswomen's Club of NY (corr. sec. 2000—, Front Page award 1999). Home and Office: PO Box 60541 Staten Island NY 10306

CHOO, YEOW MING, lawyer; b. Aug. 1, 1953; s. Far Tong and Kim Fong (Wong) C. LLB with honors, U. Malaya, 1977; LLM, Harvard U., 1979; JD, Chgo.-Kent Coll., 1980. Bar: Malaysia 1977, Ill. 1980. Lectr. law U. Malaya Law Sch., Kuala Lumpur, 1977-78, Monash U. Law Sch., Melbourne, Australia, 1978; internat. lawyer Amoco Oil Co., Chgo., 1979-82; ptnr. Anderson, Liu and Choo, Chgo., 1982-84, Baer Marks and Upham, N.Y.C., 1984-85, Winston and Strawn, Chgo., 1985-87, Dorsey and Whitney, N.Y.C., 1987-92, Winthrop Stimson, Hong Kong, 1993-2001; exec. chmn. CSI, Hong Kong, 2001—. Chmn. tax subcom. Nat. Coun. for US-China Trade, 1980-84; legal adv. Shanghai Law Soc., China, 1989—. Mem. ABA, Am. Mining Congress (com. on law of sea alt. 1980-82), Ill. Bar Assn., Chgo. Bar Assn., Malayan Bar Council, U.S. Chess Fedn., Harvard Law Sch. Alumni Assn., Harvard Club. Office: 2505 Asia Pacific Finance Tower Citibank Plz 3 Garden Rd Cen Hong Kong Hong Kong

CHOOK, PAUL HOWARD, publishing executive; b. N.Y.C., Oct. 17, 1929; s. Abraham and Etta (Cohen) C. BBA, CCNY, 1949; MS, Columbia U., 1950. Cons. quality control Philip Morris, Inc., N.Y.C., 1951-55; pres. media studies div. Alfred Politz Rsch., Inc., N.Y.C., 1955-66; v.p. rsch. Young & Rubicam, Inc., N.Y.C., 1966-74; pres. W.R. Simmons Rsch. Assocs., N.Y.C., 1974-75; exec. v.p. mktg. and circulation Ziff Davis Pub. Co., N.Y.C., 1975-84, sr. v.p. mktg., 1986-93; mktg. cons., 1993-95; exec. v.p. CBS Mags., N.Y.C., 1985; ind. mktg. cons., 1995—. Instr. CCNY, 1951-63. Sgt. N.Y. NG., 1948-56. Mem. Advt. Rsch. Found. (bd. dirs. 1977-84), Am. Statis. Assn., Am. Mktg. Assn., Am. Assn. Pub. Opinion Rsch., Market Rsch. Coun. Jewish. Avocations: bridge, jogging. Home: 65-65 Wetherole St Flushing NY 11374-4764

CHOPER, JESSE HERBERT, law educator, university dean; b. Wilkes-Barre, Pa., Sept. 19, 1935; s. Edward and Dorothy (Resnick) C.; m. Mari Smith; children: Marc Steven, Edward Nathaniel. BS, Wilkes U., 1957, DHL, 1967; LLB, U. Pa., 1960. Bar: D.C. 1961. Instr. Wharton Sch. U. Pa., 1957-60; law clk. to Chief Justice Earl Warren U.S. Supreme Ct., 1960-61; asst. prof. U. Minn. Law Sch., 1961-62, assoc. prof., 1962-65; prof. Law Sch. U. Calif., Berkeley, 1965—, dean, 1982-92, Earl Warren prof. Pub. Law, 1991—. Vis. prof. Harvard U., 1970-71, Fordham U., 1999. Author: Constitutional Law: Cases-Comments-Questions, 9th edit., 2001, The American Constitution, Cases and Materials, 9th edit., 2001, Constitutional Rights and Liberties, Cases and Materials, 9th edit., 2001, Corporations, Cases and Materials, 5th edit., 2000, Judicial Review and the National Political Process, 1980, Securing Religious Liberty, 1995; contbr. articles to profl. jours. Mem. AAUP, Am. Law Inst., Am. Acad. Arts and Scis., Order of Coif. Jewish. Office: U Calif Sch Law Berkeley CA 94720-0001

CHOPEY, NICHOLAS P. editor; b. N.Y.C., Dec. 22, 1932; s. Nicholas W. and Alice I. (Keshelak) C.; m. Katherine J. Heaney, Sept. 12, 1959; children: Nicholas, Michael, John, James. BChE, U. Va., 1955; MA in Econs., NYU, 1972. Process engr. Esso Standard Oil Co., Linden, NJ, 1955-56, 58-59; asst. assoc. editor McGraw-Hill, Inc., N.Y.C., 1960-67, sr. assoc. editor, 1967-72, mng. editor, 1972-78, exec. editor, 1978-82, editor-in-chief, 1982-87, exec. editor, 1987-99, editor-in-chief, 2000—; exec. editor Chem. Week Assocs., 1999-2000, editor-in-chief, 2000—. Adv. com. Indsl. Energy Tech. Conf., Houston, 1992—. Editor: Handbook of Chemical Engineering Calculations, 1984, 2d edit., 1994; (reprint books) Environmental Engineering in the Process Plant, 1992, Fluid Movers, 1994. 1st lt. USAF, 1956-58. Mem. AIChE (past chair com.), Am. Soc. Engrng. Edn., Knights of Malta, Roselle Golf Club, Tau Beta Pi. Roman Catholic. Office: Chemical Week Assocs 110 William St New York NY 10038-3901

CHOPIN, L. FRANK, lawyer; b. New Orleans, Apr. 29, 1942; s. Alton Francis and Floretta (Thensted) C.; children: Philip, Alexandra, Christopher. BBA, Loyola U., New Orleans, 1964, JD, 1966; diploma in mil. law, Judge Adv. Gen.'s Sch., U. Va. Sch. Law, 1966; postgrad., Nat. Law Ctr., George Wash. U., 1967-68; LLM in Taxation, U. Miami, Fla., 1976; PhD in Law, Cambridge U., Eng., 1986. Bar: La. 1966, Fla. 1968, Iowa 1980, U.S. Dist. Ct. (so. dist.) Fla. 1968, U.S. Ct. Appeals (5th cir.) 1968. Ptnr. Chopin & Chopin, Miami, 1969-77; assoc. prof. law Drake U., Des Moines, 1979-80; ptnr. Cadwalader, Wickersham & Taft, Palm Beach, Fla., 1980-94, Chopin, Miller & Yudenfreund, Palm Beach, Fla., 1994-98, Chopin & Miller, Palm Beach, Fla., 1999—. Adj. prof. law U. Miami, 1982-96, U. Sherbrooke, Can., 1982-94. Author: The New Residency Rules for Canadian Tax Considerations, 1985; also numerous articles in legal jours. Mem. Housing Fin. Authority; trustee Preservation Found., Palm Beach Community Chest, Inc. Served to capt. U.S. Army, 1966-68. Mem. ABA, Internat. Bar Assn., Fed. Bar Assn., Fla. Bar (tax sect.), Loyola U. Alumni Assn., U. Miami Alumni Assn., St. Thomas More Law Soc., Phi Alpha Delta (charter). Republican. Roman Catholic. Office: Chopin & Miller 505 S Flagler Dr Ste 300 West Palm Beach FL 33401-5942

CHOPIN, SUSAN GARDINER, lawyer; b. Miami, Fla., Feb. 23, 1947; d. Maurice and Judith (Warden) Gardiner; children: Philip, Alexandra, Christopher. BBA, Loyola U., New Orleans, 1966; JD cum laude, U. Miami, 1972; MLitt (Law), Oxford U., Eng., 1983. Bar: Fla. 1972, Iowa 1979. Sr. law clk. to judge U.S. Dist. Ct. (so. dist.) Fla., Miami, 1972-73; ptnr. Chopin & Chopin, Miami, 1973-77; assoc. prof. law sch. Drake U., Des Moines, 1979-80; pvt. practice law Palm Beach, Fla., 1981—; ptnr. Chopin & Chopin, 1999—2003, Chopin, Chopin & Chopin, 2003—. Lectr. in family law. Editor (mem. editl. bd.): (jour.) Fla. Bar Jour., 1975; editor: (co-chair editl. bd.) Fla. Bar Family Law Commentator, 2000—01. Trustee Preservation Found. of Palm Beach, 1986-89. Mem.: Palm Beach County Bar Assn., Soc. Wig and Robe, Fla. Assn. Women Lawyers, Fed. Bar Assn., Iowa Bar Assn., Fla. Bar Assn., ABA, Phi Alpha Delta, Phi Kappa Phi. Office: Esperante Bldg 222 Lakeview Ave Ste 220 West Palm Beach FL 33401-6149

CHOPKO, MARK E. lawyer; b. Kingston, Pa., Nov. 4, 1953; s. Michael E. and Rose Ann C. (Gavlick) C.; m. Jane K. Chopko; children: Michael, Jessica, Laura, Sarah. BS summa cum laude, U. Scranton, 1974; JD cum laude, Cornell U., 1977. Bar: Pa. 1977, U.S. Supreme Ct. 1984, D.C. 1987. Gen. counsel Nat. Conf. Cath. Bishops, U.S. Cath. Conf., Washington, 1987—. Mem. religious liberty com. Nat. Coun. Chs., N.Y.C., 1987—. Mem. bd. editors Religious Freedom Reporter, N.C., 1987-2000; contbr. articles to profl. jours. Bd. advisors program on philanthropy and the law Sch. of Law, NYU, 1995-98; bd. dirs. Blessed Sacrament Sch., Alexandria, Va., 1986-88; legal advisor Ams. United for Life, Chgo., 1987-94; mem. legal scholars bd. DePaul Inst. for Ch.-State Studies, Chgo., 1988—; asst. coach basketball Cath. Youth Orgn., Alexandria, 1989-94. Recipient High Quality award U.S. Nuclear Regulatory Commn., 1982. Mem. ABA (vice chmn. religious, charitable and non-profit orgns. tort sect. 1990-92), Cath. Health Assn. (legal affairs com. 1988-96), Am. Corp. Counsel Assn. (com. on non-profit and profl. assn. law). Office: US Conf Cath Bishops 3211 4th St NE Washington DC 20017-1194

CHOPLIN, JOHN M., II, lawyer; b. Cedar Rapids, Iowa, Nov. 10, 1945; s. John M. and Joyce G. (Mickelson) C.; m. Linda H. Kutchen, Feb. 14, 1969; children: Julie, John, James. BA, Drake U., 1967; JD, U. Mich., 1974. Bar: Ind. 1974, U.S. Dist. Ct. (so. dist.) Ind. 1974, U.S. Ct. Appeals (7th cir.) 1976, U.S. Supreme Ct. 1977, U.S. Ct. Appeals (6th cir.) 1983, U.S. Dist. Ct. (no. dist.) Ind. 1991. Assoc. Wilson, Tabor & Holland, Indpls., 1974-80; ptnr. Norris, Choplin & Schroeder, Indpls., 1980—. Committeeman precinct Carmel Reps., Ind., 1982-84. Served to capt. USAF, 1969-73. Mem. ABA, Ind. Bar Assn., Indpls. Bar Assn., 7th Fed. Cir. Bar Assn., Lawyers-Pilots Bar Assn., Ind. Trial Lawyers Assn., Assn. Trial Lawyers Am., Christian Legal Soc., Phi Beta Kappa, Omicron Delta Kappa. Baptist. Avocations: water sports, tennis, flying. Home: 8553 Twin Pointe Cir Indianapolis IN 46236-8903 Office: Norris Choplin & Schroeder 101 W Ohio St Ste 900 Indianapolis IN 46204-4213

CHOPLIN, ROBERT HANLEY, physician, radiologist; s. Rodney David and Anne Virginia Choplin; m. Marjorie Ann Bowman, Oct. 12, 1991; children: Lane Hanley, Leslie Anne, Blake Riley, Bridget Williamson Foley, Skyler Weston. BA, Westminster Coll., 1962—66; MD, Northwestern U. Sch. of Medicine, 1966—70. Cert. Examination, Diagnostic Radiology Am. Bd. of Radiology, 1979, Cert. Examination Am. Bd. of Internal Medicine, 1975. Prof. of radiology Wake Forest U., Winston-Salem, NC, 1979—96, U. of Pa., 1996—2001; prof. of clin. radiology Ind. U. Sch. of Medicine, 2002—. Mem. editl. bd. Radiol. Soc. of N.Am., 1995 2003. Maj. USAF, 1972—74, Blytheville, AR. Fellow, Am. Coll. of Radiology, 2000. Fellow: Am. Coll. of Radiology; mem.: Soc. of Thoracic Radiology, Am. Roentgen Ray Soc., Radiol. Soc. of N.Am. Office: IU Radiology Associates 0279 550 N University Blvd Indianapolis IN 46202-5253 Office Fax: 317-274-1848. E-mail: rchoplin@iupui.edu.

CHOPP, FRANK, state official; m. Nancy Long; 2 children. BA magna cum laude, U. Wash., 1975. Exec. dir. Fremont Pub. Assn., 1983—; part-time lectr. U. Wash. Grad. Sch. Pub. Affairs, 1992-95; speaker of house State of Wash. 43d Dist., Olympia, 1999—. Dir. Cascade Cmty. Ctr., 1975-76; mgr. No. Cmty. Svc. Ctr. Seattle Dept. Human Resources, 1976-79, 81-83; administrv. dir. Pike Market Senior Ctr., 1980-81. Office: 3D Fl Legislative Bldg Olympia WA 98504-0001 also: 4209 Sunnyside Ave N Seattle WA 98103-7658*

CHOPP, REBECCA S. university president; Dir. grad. studies Inst. for Women's Studies Emory U., Atlanta, dean of faculty and acad. affairs Candler Sch. of Theology, 1993-97, Charles Howard Chandler prof. theology Emory's Grad. Divsn., provost, exec. v.p. for acad. affairs, 1998—2001; dean, Titus Street prof. theology and culture Yale U. Div. Sch., 2001—02; pres., prof. philosophy and religion Colgate U., 2002—. Chair Commn. on Tchg. Emory U., univ. bd. trustees acad. affairs com.; lectr. in field. Author: The Praxis of Suffering: An Interpretation of Liberation and Political Theologies, 1986, The Power to Speak: Feminism, Language, God, 1989, Reconstructing Christian Theology, 1994, Saving Work: Feminist Practices of Theological Education, 1995; theology editor Religious Studies Rev.; editor-at-large Christian Century; editl. bd. Emory Theol. Studies, Religion and Ideology, Jour. of Religion, Word and World, Internat. Jour. of Practical Theology; contbr. articles to profl. publs. Recipient Alumna Achievement award Kans. Wesleyan U., 1990, Disting. Alumna award St. Paul Sch. of Theology, 1991, Founder's Day award Baker U., 1995, Alumna of Yr. award U. Chgo. Divinity Sch., 1997. Mem. Am. Acad. of Religion (pres. southeastern divsn.), Am. Theol. Soc. (chair women in leadership project). Home: 13 Oak Drive Hamilton NY 13346

CHOPPIN, GREGORY ROBERT, chemistry educator; b. Eagle Lake, Tex., Nov. 9, 1927; s. Gilbert P. and Nellie M. (Guidroz) C.; m. Ann M. Warner; children: Denise, Suzanne, Paul, Nadine BS in Chemistry, Loyola U., New Orleans, 1949, DSc (hon.), 1969; PhD in Chemistry, U. Tex, 1953; DSc Tech. (hon.), Chalmers U., Göteborg, Sweden, 1985. Rsch. scientist Lawrence Radiation Lab., Berkeley, Calif., 1953-56; faculty Fla. State U., Tallahassee, 1956—, R.O. Lawton Disting. prof. chemistry, 1968—2001, prof. emeritus, 2001—. Vis. scientist Centre d'Etude Nucleaire Mol, Belgium, 1962-63; vis. prof. Sci. U. Tokyo, 1978; vis. scientist European Transuranium Inst., Karlsruhe, Germany, 1979-80, 95; cons. Argonne Nat. Lab., Los Alamos Nat. Lab., N.Mex., Lawrence Livermore Nat. Lab., Calif., Pacific N.W. Nat. Lab., Wash., Sandia Nat. Lab., N.Mex., Kaiser-Hill Co., Archimedes Tech. Co.; served on panels and coms. of NRC, including bds. chem. sci. and tech. and radioactive waste mgmt. Co-author: Nuclear Chemistry: Theory and Applications, 1980, 2d edit., 1995, 3d edit., 2001; editor: Plutonium Chemistry, 1983, Actinide-Lanthanide Separations, 1985, Lanthanide Probes in Life, Chemical and Earth Sciences, 1989, Principles and Practice of Solvent Extraction, 1992, 2d edit., 2003, Separations of f-Elements, 1995, Chemical Separation Technologies and Related Methods of Nuclear Waste Management, 1999; mem. editl. bd. sci. jours. including Handbook on Physics and Chemistry of Rare Earths; co-discoverer of chemical element 101 Mendelevium; contbr. over 450 articles to sci. jours. Served to cpl. U.S. Army, 1946-48. Recipient Alexander von Humboldt Stiftung award, 1979, Chem. Mfrs. Assn. Edn. award, 1979, Seaborg Actinide Separations Sci. award, 1989, Presdl. citation Am. Nuclear Soc., 1991, Scientist of Yr. award Fla. Acad. of Sci., 1992, Spedding award N.Am. Rare Earth Rsch. Conf., 1996, Chem. Pioneer award Am. Inst. Chemistry, 1997, The Becquerel medal Brit. Royal Soc. Chem., 2000. Fellow AAAS; mem. Am. Chem. Soc. (award Fla. sect. 1973, So. Chemist award 1971, award in Nuclear Chemistry 1985, OESPER award Cin. sect. 1995), Royal Soc. Arts and Sci. (hon. fgn. mem.) (Sweden), Rare Earth Rsch. Conf. (pres. bd. 1981-83, chmn. 16th conf. 1983), Sigma Xi, Phi Beta Kappa. Avocations: sailing, racquetball. Home: 3290 Longleaf Rd Tallahassee FL 32310-6406 Office: Fla State U Dept Chemistry and Biochemistry Dittmer Bldg Tallahassee FL 32306-4390

CHOPPIN, PURNELL WHITTINGTON, research administrator, virology researcher, educator; b. Baton Rouge, July 4, 1929; s. Arthur Richard and Eunice Dolores (Bolin) Choppin; m. Joan Harriet Macdonald, Oct. 17, 1959; 1 child, Kathleen Marie. MD, La. State U., 1953; DSc (hon.), Emory U., 1988, La. State U., 1988; MD, MD, D Medicine, U. Cologne, 1988; DSc (hon.), Tulane U., 1989, Washington U., 1991, Med. U. S.C., 1995, U. Md., Baltimore County, 1995; DHL (hon.), Mt. Sinai Sch. Medicine, 1996; DSc (hon.), U. Mass., 1999, Northwestern U., 1999; LLD (hon.), St. Francis Xavier U., 2000; DSc (hon.), Rockefeller U., 2000, Johns Hopkins U., 2002. Diplomate Am. Bd. Internal Medicine. Intern Barnes Hosp., St. Louis, 1953—54, asst. resident, 1956—57; fellow, rsch. assoc. Rockefeller U., N.Y.C., 1957—60, asst. prof., 1960—64, assoc. prof., 1964—70, prof., sr. physician, 1970—85, Leon Hess prof. virology, 1980—85, v.p. acad. programs, 1983—85, dean grad. studies, 1985; v.p., chief sci. officer Howard Hughes Med. Inst., Chevy Chase, Md., 1985—87, pres., 1987—99, pres. emeritus, 2000—; prin. Washington Adv. Group, 2000—. Chmn. sect. 43 microbiology and immunology NAS, 1989—92, chmn. class IV med. scis., 1983—86, mem. com. on reorganization structure, 1985—86, coun., 2000—, Inst. Medicine, 1987—92, exec. com., 1988—91; mem. virology study sect. NIH, 1968—72, chmn. virology study sect., 1975—78; bd. dirs. Royal Soc. Medicine Found. Inc., N.Y.C., 1978—93; mem. adv. com. fundamental rsch. Nat. Multiple Sclerosis Soc., 1979—84, chmn. adv. com. fundamental rsch., 1983—84; mem. adv. coun. Nat. Inst. Allergy and Infectious Diseases, 1980—83; mem. bd. scis., cons. Meml. Sloan-Kettering Cancer Ctr., N.Y.C., 1981—86, chmn. bd. scis., 1983—84; co-chair NRA Task Force Goals and Ops., 1999—2000; mem. commn. on life scis. NRC, Washington, 1982—87; mem. sci. rev. com. Scripps Clinic and Rsch. Found., La Jolla, Calif., 1983—85, chmn. sci. rev. com., 1984; mem. coun. for rsch. and clin. investigation Am. Cancer Soc., N.Y.C., 1983—85; mem. com. priorities for vaccine devel. Inst. Medicine, Washington; mem. governing bd. NRC, 1990—92. Contbr. articles to profl. pubs., chapters to books on virology, cell biology, infectious diseases; editor: Procs. Soc. Exptl. Biology and Medicine, 1966—69; assoc. editor: Virology, 1969—72; editor, 1973—86; assoc. editor: Jour. Immunology, 1968—72, Jour. Supramolecular Structure, 1972—75, mem. editl. bd.: Jour. Virology, 1972—85, Comprehensive Virology, 1972, mem. overseas adv. panel: Biochem. Jour., 1973—77. Capt. USAF, 1954—56, Japan. Named to alumni Hall of Distinction, La. State U., Baton Rouge, 1983; recipient Howard Taylor Ricketts award, U. Chgo., 1978, Waksman award for Excellence in Microbiology, NAS, 1984, Alumni Achievement award, Washington U. Sch. Medicine, 1990, Dean's medal, Harvard Med. Sch., 1992, Meml. Sloan-Kettering medal for outstanding contbns. to biomed. rsch., 1998, Spl. Recognition award, Assn. Am. Med. Colls., 1999, medal, U. Calif. San Francisco, 2000. Fellow: AAAS; mem.: NAS, Am. Soc. Virology (pres. 1985—86), Am. Clin. and Climatological Assn., Practitioners Soc. N.Y., Infectious Diseases Soc. Am., Soc. Cell Biology, Am. Assn. Immunologists, Harvey Soc., Am. Soc. Microbiology (chmn. virology divsn. 1977—79, divsn. group councilor 1983—85), Am. Soc. Clin. Investigation, Assn. Am. Physicians, Am. Philos. Soc. (coun. 1998—, v.p. 2000—), Am. Acad. Arts and Scis., Alpha Omega Alpha, Sigma Xi (chpt. pres. 1980—81). Office: Howard Hughes Med Inst 4000 Jones Bridge Rd Chevy Chase MD 20815-6789

CHOPRA, ANIL KUMAR, civil engineering educator; b. Peshawar, India, Feb. 18, 1941; came to U.S., 1961, naturalized, 1977; s. Kasturi Lal and Sushila (Malhotra) C.; m. Hamida Banu, Dec. 7, 1976. B.Sc. in Engring, Banaras Hindu U., Varanasi, India, 1960; MS, U. Calif., Berkeley, 1963, PhD, 1966. Design engr. Standard Vacuum Oil Co., New Delhi, India, 1960-61, Kaiser Engrs. Overseas Corps, India, 1961; asst. prof. civil engr. U. Minn., Mpls., 1966-67; mem. faculty U. Calif., Berkeley, 1967—, prof. civil engring., 1976-92, Johnson prof. engring., 1992— Dir. Applied Tech. Council, Palo Alto, 1972-74; mem. com. natural disasters NRC, 1980-85, chmn., 1982-83; cons. earthquake engring. to govt. and industry. Author: Dynamics of Structures, A Primer, 1981, Dynamics of Structures: Theory and Applications to Earthquake Engineering, 1995, 2001; mem. adv. bd.: MIT Press Series in Structural Mechanics.; contbr. articles to more than 250 profl. pubs. Recipient Gold medal Banaras Hindu U., 1960, Disting. Alumnus award, 1980, certificate of merit for paper Indian Soc. Earthquake Tech., 1974, honor award Assn. Indians in Am., 1985, AT&T Found. award Am. Soc. Engring. Edn., 1987, Disting. Tchg. award Berkeley Campus, 1999. Mem.: ASCE (EMD exec. com. 1981—87, chmn. 1985—86, mem. STD exec. com. 1988—92, chmn. 1990—91, Walter L. Huber prize 1975, Norman medal 1979, Reese rsch. prize 1989, Norman medal 1991, Newmark medal 1993, Howard award 1998, Norman medal 2001), U.S. Com. on Large Dams, Earthquake Engring. Rsch. Inst. (bd. dirs. 1990—93, George W. Housner medal 2002), Structural Engrs. Assn. No. Calif. (bd. dirs. 1987—89), Seismol. Soc. Am. (bd. dirs. 1982—83), Nat. Acad. Engring. Home: 635 Cross Ter Orinda CA 94563 Office: Univ Calif Dept Civil Engring Berkeley CA 94720-0001

CHOPRA, DEEPAK, preventive medicine physician, writer; Medical dir. of edn. prog., CEO, founder The Chopra Center, La Costa Resort and Spa, 1995—. Author: Return of the Rishi, 1989, Quantum Healing, 1990, Perfect Health, 1990, Unconditional Life, 1991, Creating Health, 1991, Creating Affluence,

1993, Ageless Body, Timeless Mind, 1993, Restful Sleep, 1994, Perfect Weight, 1994, Journey Into Healing, 1994, The Seven Spiritual Laws of Success, 1995, Return of Merlin, 1995, Como Crear Abundancia/How to Create Wealth, 1999, Everyday Immorality: A Concise Course in Spiritual Transformation, 1999, How to Know God: The Soul's Journey into the Mystery of Mysteries, 2000, The Daughters of Joy: An Adventure of the Heart, 2002, . Office: Chopra Ctr for Well Being 2100 Costa del Mar Rd Carlsbad CA 92009

CHOPRA, DHARAM VIR, statistician, educator; b. Oct. 15, 1930; s. Achhru and Vidya Wati (Sondhi) C.; m. Miran Devi Suri, Jan. 1969; 1 child, Sandeep K. MA, Panjab U., 1953; MS, U. Mich., 1961, MA in Psychology, 1963; PhD, U. Nebr., 1968. Lectr. math. M. Tech. Inst., Jalandhar, India, 1953—59; instr. math. U. Nebr., Lincoln, 1963—66; asst. prof. So. Colo. State U., Pueblo, 1966—67; asst. prof. stats. Wichita State U., Kans., 1967—71, assoc. prof., 1971—76, prof., 1976—, chmn. math. dept., 1985—. Contbr. articles to profl. jours. Mem.: Indian Statis. Assn., Indian Math. Soc., Internat. Assn. Survey Statisticians, Inst. Math. Stats., Am. Stats. Assn. Avocations: hiking, travel. Office: Wichita State U Dept Math and Stats Wichita KS 67260-0033

CHOPRA, INDER JIT, physician, endocrinologist; b. Gujranwala, India, Dec. 15, 1939; came to U.S., 1967; s. Kundan Lal and Labhwati (Bagga) C.; m. Usha Prakash, Oct. 16, 1966; children: Sangeeta, Rajesh, Madhu. B of Medicine and BS, All India Inst. Med. Scis., New Delhi, India, 1961, MD, 1965. Intern All India Inst. Med. Scis., New Delhi, 1961-62, clin. resident, 1962-65, registrar in medicine, 1966-67; resident Queens Med. Ctr., Honolulu, 1967-68; fellow in endocrinology Harbor Gen. Campus UCLA Sch. Medicine, 1968-71; asst. prof. of medicine UCLA, 1971-74, assoc. prof., 1974-78, prof., 1978—. Mem. VA Merit Review Bd in Endocrinology, 1988-91. Contbr. more than 250 rsch. articles, revs. and book chpts. to profl. lit. Recipient Rsch. Career Devel. award, NIH, 1972. Master Am. Coll. Physicians; mem. Endocrine Soc. (Ernst Oppenheimer award 1980), Am. Thyroid Assn. (Van Meter-Armour award 1977, Parke-Davis award 1988, Disting. Svc. award 1995), Am. Soc. Clin. Investigation, Assn. of Am. Physicians, Western Assn. Physicians, Am. Fed. for Clin. Rsch. Achievements include patent for radioimmunoassay for measurement of thyronine and triiodothyonine. Office: UCLA Sch Medicine Ctr for Health Scis 24-130 Warren Hall 900 Veteran Ave Los Angeles CA 90024-2703

CHOPRA, NAGESH, emergency physician, researcher; s. Priya Vrat and Sheel Prabha Chopra. MB and BChir, Med. Coll. Baroda of M.S.U., Baroda, Gujarat, India, 1990—96; MD, U. of Medicine and Dentistry of N.J., 1997—2000. Diplomate Am. Bd. of Internal Medicine, 2000, ECFMG Standard Certification Ednl. Commn. for Fgn. Med. Graduates, 1996. Asst. attending physician St. Clares Hosp., Denville, NJ, 2001, Dover Gen. Hosp., Dover, NJ, 2001, Morristown Meml. Hosp., NJ, 2001; attending/emergency rm. physician S.E. Colo. Hosp. & Long Term Care, Springfield, 2001—. Asst. chief of med. staff S.E. Colo. Hosp. & Long Term Care, 2002; physician adviser, emergency med. svc. of Baca County S.E. Colo. Hosp. Emergency Med. Services, Springfield, 2002—; physician adviser, continuous quality improvement bd. S.E. Colo. Hosp. & Long Term Care, 2002; physician adviser/mem. S.E. Colo. regional emergency med. services and trauma adv. coun., 2002—; med. dir. Hospice of S.E. Colo. Hosp. & Long term Care facility, 2002—; clin. instr., dept. of medicine U. of Colo. Sch. of Medicine, Denver, 2002—; chief of med. staff S.E. Colo. Hosp. & Long Term Care, 2003—. Author (presentor): (jour. abstract) Jour. of Am. Coll. of Cardiology & Am. Coll. of Cardiology Conv., 1999, Circulation/Am. Heart Assn. Conv., 1999, Pacing and Clin. Electrophysiology, North Am. Soc. of Pacing and Electrophysiology Conv., 1999; author: (jour. article) Annals of Allergy, Asthma, & Immunology; author: (presentor) (abstracts) Atlantic Health Sys. Rsch. Day, CHEST/ Am. Coll. of Chest Physician conv., 2001; author: Jour. of Gen. Internal Medicine & Soc. of Gen. Internal Medicine Conv., 2003, (jour. articles) Cardiovasc. Fellows Forum, (rsch. project article) Anemia in Pregnancy, (jour. articles) The Jour. of Urology, Jour. of Clin. Rheumatology, (articles) numerous newsletter and newspaper articles on common health problems. Mem.: ACP.

CHOPRA, PRADEEP, physician, educator; m. Shalini Chopra, Dec. 12, 1994. MD, Harvard U., 2001. Diplomate Am. Bd. Anesthesiology, 2002, sub speciality cert. in pain mgmt. Am. Bd. Anesthesiology, 2002. Asst. prof. Boston U. Med. Sch., 2001—; dir. Pain Mgmt. Ctr., So. New Eng. Anesthesia and Pain Assocs., Providence, 2002—. Contbr. chapters to books, articles to profl. jours. Recipient John Hedley-Whyte prize in Critical Care Medicine, Harvard Med. Sch., 2000, Nancy E. Oriol prize in Obstetric Anesthesia, 2000. Mem.: Am. Soc. for Interventional Pain Physicians (dir. R.I. divsn. 2002—). Achievements include design of medical simulation model for a stuck expiratory valve. Office: Southern New England Anesthesia and Pain 102 Smithfield Ave Pawtucket RI 02860 Home Fax: 815-425-1666; Office Fax: 401-729-6019. Personal E-mail: painri@yahoo.com. E-mail: painri@yahoo.com.

CHOPYK, DAN BOHDAN, language educator, poet; b. Beneva-Ternopol, Poland, Jan. 2, 1925; came to U.S., 1957; s. Gregory W. and Olga T. (Jankow) C.; m. Helen Nancy Sabin, June 28, 1956 (div. Nov. 1, 1977); children: Robin G., Mimi N., William B., Alexander R.; m. Alexandra A. Koudryasheva, Dec. 19, 1990. Degree in philosophy, Ukrainian Theol. Sem., Hirschberg, Germany, 1947; B in Commerce, U. Birmingham, Eng., 1953; MA, U. Colo., 1962; LLB, Ukrainian Free U., Munich, 1963; PhD in Philology, Ukrainian Free U. and U. Colo., 1970; PhD, Internat. Info. Acad., 1998. Tchr. Jefferson County (Colo.) Pub. Schs., 1958-65; instr. Regis Coll., Denver, 1965; tchg. fellow U. Colo., Boulder, 1966-67, asst. prof., prof. U. Utah, Salt Lake City, 1969-96; pres. World Cossack Acad., N.Y.C., 1998—. Author: Guide to teaching, 1963, Navchania Movy, 1976, Movonavchania, 1997, Metodologia, 1994, (poetry) Shlyakhy ta dumky, 1981, Zhyvy Zhyttya, 1983, 2000; poetry translations; co-editor: Nasha Mova Jour., 1975. Bd. dirs. Internat. Ctr. Nutrition and Health Rehab. Fellow Fulbright Found., 1986, NEH, 1983, 84. Mem. Internat. Franko Soc., Delta Tau Kappa. Democrat. Avocations: poetry, translating, cossackdom, travel. Home and Office: 106 Guadeloupe Dr Toms River NJ 08757

CHOQUETTE, PAUL JOSEPH, JR., construction company executive; b. Providence, July 24, 1938; s. Paul Joseph and Virginia Josephine (Gilbane) C.; m. Elizabeth Walsh, Aug. 18, 1962; children: Jeanne Marie, Denise Elizabeth, Suzanne, Christine Noell, Paul Joseph III. BA, Brown U., 1960; LL.B., Harvard U., 1963. Assoc. firm Edwards & Angell, Providence, 1963-65; gov.'s legal counsel State of R.I., Providence, 1965-67; assoc. Edwards & Angell, 1967-69; gen. counsel Gilbane Bldg. Co., Providence, 1969-71, v.p., 1971-75, exec. v.p., 1975-81, CEO, 1981-, dir., chmn., CEO, dir. Bd. dirs. Fleet Fin. Group, Ea. Utilities Assn., Carbide Corp.; chmn. bd. Gilbane Properties Inc. Nat. Football Found. scholar, 1959; recipient Silver Ann. award NCAA, 1985. Mem. Providence C. of C. (past pres., dir.) Clubs: Dunes, Hope, University. Roman Catholic. Office: Gilbane Bldg Co 7 Jackson Walkway Providence RI 02903*

CHORENGEL, BERND, international hotel corporation executive; Pres. Hyatt Internat. Corp., Chgo. Office: Hyatt Internat Hotels Corp Madison Plz 200 W Madison St Chicago IL 60606-3414

CHORIN, ALEXANDRE JOEL, mathematician, educator; b. Warsaw, June 25, 1938; came to U.S., 1962, naturalized, 1971; s. Joseph and Hannah (Judowicz) C.; m. Alice Louise Jones, Aug. 11, 1965; 1 son, Ethan Daniel. Diploma in engring., Swiss Fed. Inst. Tech., Lausanne, 1961; MSc, NYU, 1964, PhD, 1966; DSc (hon.), Israel Inst. Tech., 2003. Rsch. scientist NYU, 1966-69, asst. prof. math., 1969-71; assoc. prof. U. Calif., Berkeley, 1972-73, prof., 1973—, Miller rsch. prof., 1971-72, 82-83, dir. Ctr. Pure and Applied Math., 1980-82, 95—, Chancellor's prof., 1997-2000, Univ. prof., 2002—; sr. staff scientist Lawrence Berkeley Lab., 1980—. Disting. vis. prof. Inst. for Advanced Study, Princeton, N.J., 1991-92; faculty rsch. lectr. U. Calif., Berkeley, 1999-00; vis. prof. Coll. France, 1992. Author: (with J. Marsden) A Mathematical Introduction to Fluid Dynamics, 1979, Computational Fluid Mechanics, selected papers, 1989, Vorticity and Turbulence, 1994; contbr. articles to profl. jours. Recipient Nat. Acad. Scis. award in applied math. and numerical analysis, 1989, Norbert Wiener prize Am. Math. Soc. and Soc. for Indsl. and Applied Math., 2000; fellow Sloan Found., 1972-74, Guggenheim Found., 1987-88. Fellow Am. Acad. Arts and Scis.; mem. NAS. Home: 1800 Spruce St Apt 201 Berkeley CA 94709 Office: U Calif Dept Math Berkeley CA 94720-0001 E-mail: chorin@math.berkeley.edu.

CHOROSINSKI, EUGENE CONRAD, writer, poet, author; b. Sienno, Poland, Jan. 1, 1930; came to the U.S., 1954, naturalized, 1961; s. Jozef Chorosinski and Weronika Religa; m. Anni Homeier, Mar. 23, 1959; children: Heidi Marie, Ramona Angela, Veronica Ann. LLB, Blackstone Sch. of Law, 1968. Chief field classification AMS, Ehiopia-U.S. Mapping Mission, Addis Ababa, 1965-67; intelligence analyst Combined Intelligence Ctr. Vietnam, 1968-69; sr. intelligence advisor DCAT 70, Lai Khe, South Vietnam, 1970-71; intelligance analyst 1st Armored Divsn., Support Command, Nuremberg, Germany, 1971-73; pvt. investigator Alexandria, Va., Md., Va., Washington, 1973-74; chief zoning review Dept. of Consumer and Regulatory Affairs, Govt. D.C., 1974-85; chmn. disaster damage assessment ARC, Ctrl. Fla. chpt., Orlando, Fla., 1995-96; free-lance writer Eustis, Fla., 1996-99; ret., 1999. Author: (novels) Through the Years, 1995, Days Remembered, 1999, Eugene's Saga to Freedom, War and Poetry, 2001; co-author: (anthologies) The Nat. Libr. Poetry, Famous Poets Soc., Sparrowgrass Poetry Forum, Poetry Guild, Internat. Libr. Poetry; contbr. articles to profl. jours. Mem. Rep. Nat. com., 1994—; mem. Rep. Presdl. Trust; mem. City of Eustis Parks and Trees Commn., 1996—, chmn., 1998-99; vol. Orlando (Fla.) VA Healthcare Ctr., 2001—; literacy tutor, Lake County Libr. Sys., 2003—. Decorated Bronze star, Air medal, Joint Svc. Commendation medal, Army Commendation medal, Nat. DSM with bronze svc. star, Vietnam Svc. medal with silver star, others; recipient Editor's Choice award for Outstanding Achievement in Poetry Nat. Libr. of Poetry, Honor Award Spl. Citation for Exceptional Vol. Svc., ARC, 1994, Shakespeare Trophy of Excellence award, Eugene Conrad Chorosinski Poet of Yr. Medallion award, 2002; named Best Poet, 1995, 96; declared and selected as the Poet of the Millennium 2000, Internat. Poets Acad., Chennai-86, India, named to Famous Poets Soc.; Internat. Peace Prize award, United Cultural Convention U.S.A., 2002, Voluntary Svc. medal Dept. Vets. Affairs, U.S.A., 2003. Mem. VFW, DAV, Internat. Soc. of Poets (life, Poet of Merit award 2001), Nat. Assn. Ret. Fed. Employees. Roman Catholic. Avocations: chess, travel, table tennis. Home: 131 Madrona Dr Eustis FL 32726-2016

CHORPENNING, FRANK WINSLOW, immunology educator, researcher; b. Marietta, Ohio, Aug. 17, 1913; s. Roy Albert and Laura Leola (Klintworth) C.; m. Annie Laurie Kay; children: Anne Kay, Jonathan Edward, Kathleen, Jane Cecelia. AB, Marietta Coll., 1970; MSc, Ohio State U., 1950, PhD, 1963. Immunologist USAREUR Med. Lab./US Army, Germany, 1952-55; chief clin. pathology Brooke Gen. Hosp., Ft. Sam Houston, Tex., 1955-61; cons. Nationalist Chinese Army, Taiwan, 1960; from lectr. to prof. Ohio State U., Columbus, 1961-81, prof. emeritus, 1981—. Me. coop. study group WHO, 1953-55. Div. editor Ohio Jour. Sci., 1974-83; editor: Clinical Pathology Procedures, 1959; author: (chpt.) Regulation of Immune Response Dynamics, 1982, Immunology of Bacterial Cell Envelope, 1983; author: The Man from Somerset, 1993; contbr. articles to profl. jours. Mem. Epidemiol. Com., San Antonio, 1949; mem. Rep. Nat. Com., Delaware, Ohio, 1979-97, Rep. Presdl. Task Force, Delaware, 1983-97. Lt. col. US Army, 1941-61. Recipient Commendation, Chinese Surgeon Gen., 1960, C.G. Brooke Gen. Hosp., 1960. Fellow Am. Acad. Microbiology, Ohio Acad. Sci.; mem. Am. Assn. Immunologists, Ohio Acad. Sci., Assn. for Gnotobiotics, Ohio Hist. Soc., Shamrock Club Columbus, Sigma Xi, Beta Beta Beta, Alpha Sigma Phi. Roman Catholic.

CHORPENNING, H. R., III, minister; b. Arlington Heights, Ill., Aug. 28, 1960; s. Harry R. and Margaret E. Chorpenning; m. Jean M. Sanfacon, May 7, 1988; children: Cameron Hayes, Christopher Eddy. Student, U. St. Andrews, Scotland, 1981-82; BA magna cum laude, U. Calif., Santa Barbara, 1983; MDiv with distinction, Iliff Sch. Theology, Denver, 1999. Ordained minister United Ch. of Christ. Dir. devel. comms. U. Calif., Santa Barbara, 1985-87; sr. writer Stanford U., Calif., 1987-89; owner Hal Chorpenning Comm., Boulder, 1989-99; assoc. conf. minister Conn. Conf. United Ch. of Christ, Hartford, 1999—2002; sr. min. Plymouth Congl. Ch., Fort Collins, Colo., 2002—. Bd. dirs. Elderly Housing Mgmt., Hamden, Conn., 1999—, Cmty. Housing Mgmt., 1999—; bd. dirs. Peninsula Conservation Ctr. Found., Palo Alto, Calif., 1988-90. Mem. The Coalition, Interfaith Alliance, Westar Inst., Phi Beta Kappa. Avocations: sea kayaking, swimming, classical music. Office: Plymouth Congregational Church UCC 916 W Prospect Rd Fort Collins CO 80526

CHOU, CHUNG-KWANG, bio-engineer; b. Chung-King, China, May 11, 1947; came to the U.S., 1969, naturalized, 1979; s. Chin-Chi and Yu-Lien (Hsiao) C.; m. Grace Wong, June 9, 1973; children: Jeffrey, Angela. BSEE, Nat. Taiwan U., 1968; MSEE, Washington U., 1971; PhD, U. Wash., 1975. Postdoctoral fellow U. Wash., Seattle, 1976-77, asst. prof., 1977-81, rsch. assoc. prof., 1981-85; rsch. scientist, head biomed. engring. sect. City of Hope Nat. Med. Ctr., Duarte, Calif., 1985-98, dir. dept. radiation rsch. divsn. radiation oncology, 1985-98; dir. Corp. RF Dosimetry Lab. Motorola, Inc., Plantation, Fla., 1998-2000; chief EME scientist, dir. Corp. EME Rsch. Lab. Motorola Inc., 2000—. Sci. adv. Mobile Mfrs. Forum, 2001—. Mem. editl. bd. IEEE EMC, MTT, 1999—; assoc. editor Jour. Bioelectromagnetics, 1987-2003; contbr. over 170 articles to profl. jours. 2d lt. Army of Taiwan, 1968-69. Fellow: IEEE (subcoms. 1979—, com. on man and radiation 1990—2000, ad hoc task force on health care reform 1993—97, vice chmn. 1994—95, mem. med. tech. policy com. 1995—98, chmn. 1996—98, std. coordinating com.), Am. Inst. for Med. and Biol. Engring.; mem.: Internat. Radio Sci. Union, Electromagnetic Acad., Radiation Rsch. Soc., Bioelectromagnetics Soc. (bd. dirs. 1981—84, Curtis Carl Johnson Meml. award 1995), N.Am. Hyperthermia Soc., Internat. Microwave Power Inst. (1st Spl. Decade award 1981, Outstanding Paper award 1985), Nat. Coun. Radiation Protection and Measurements (subcom. vice chmn. 1995—2000, IEEE liaison 1997—99, coun. mem. 1998—), Commn. K., Tau Beta Pi, Sigma Xi. Office: Motorola Inc Fla Rsch Lab Plantation FL 33322 E-mail: ck.chou@motorola.com.

CHOU, CLIFFORD CHI FONG, research engineering executive; b. Taipei, Taiwan, Dec. 19, 1940; came to U.S., 1966, naturalized, 1978; s. Ching piao and Yueh li (Huang) C.; m. Chu hwei Lee, Mar. 23, 1968; children: Kelvin Lin yu, Renee Lincy. PhD, Mich. State U., 1972. Research asst. Mich. State U., East Lansing, 1967-70, Wayne State U., Detroit, 1970-72, research assoc., 1972-76; research engr. Ford Motor Co., Dearborn, 1976-81, sr. research engr., 1981-82, prin. research engr. assoc., 1982-89, prin. staff engr., 1989-93; sr. engring. specialist, 1993-95; staff tech. specialist, 1995—. Adj. prof. Mich. Technol. U., 1997-2002, 2003—; lectr. to China under UN Devel. Program, 1987, 93, 95, lectr. to Taiwan under Automotive Rsch. and Test Ctr., 1991, 97, 98; organizer Safety Test Methodology, SAE session chair, 1997-2003, IBEC session chair 1999, 2000, 02; coord. Detroit Automobile Tech. Conf., 1993, session chair, 1997; mem. safety and environ. systems planning com. IBEC '98, 1997-2000, 01-03; indsl. acad. adv. to PhD Coms., U. Mich., 1995-98, U. Va., 1997—, Mich. Tchrs. U., 1997-2000, Wayne State U., 1999—; tchr. in field; co-organizer 6th U.S. Nat. Conf. on Computational Mechs., crashworthiness session, Dearborn, 2001; mem. safety tech. com. China SAE, 2002-. Contbr. chpts. to books, articles to profl. jours.; holder 7 patents. Recipient Safety Engring. Excellence award Nat. Hwy. Traffic Safety Adminstrn., 1980, Best Paper award IBEC, 2002; grantee Soc. Automotive Engrs. Fellow: Soc. Automotive Engrs. (Forest R. McFarland award 2000); mem.: AIAA, ASME, Detroit Chinese Am. Assn., Mich. Chinese Acad. Profl. Assn. (bd. dirs. 1992—93, pres. 1993—94, advisor 1994—, seminar spkr. 2000), Ford Chinese Club (pres. 1991—92), Sigma Xi. Achievements include patents. Home: 28970 Forest Hill Dr Farmington MI 48331-2439 E-mail: cchou@ford.com.

CHOU, ERWIN C. economist; b. San Francisco, July 12, 1952; s. George H. and Suet F. Chou. BA, U. Calif., Berkeley, 1974; PhD, Stanford U., 1986. Economist World Bank, Washington, 1977-84; internat. economist U.S. Treasury/IRS, San Francisco, 1987-94; mng. dir., sr. economist Price Waterhouse LLP, 1994-99; sr. economist EC Cons., San Francisco, 2000—. Economic cons. Pacific Gas & Electric Co., San Francisco, 1986-87. Mem. Am. Econ. Assn. Democrat. Home: 2921 Privet Dr Hillsborough CA 94010-6247 Office: Econsultants 4150 17th St Ste 2 San Francisco CA 94114-1995

CHOU, KEVIN, mechanical engineer, educator; married. PhD in Indsl. Engring., Purdue U., 1994. Guest rschr. Nat. Inst. Stds. and Tech., Gaithersburg, Md., 1995—98; asst. prof. U. Mo., Kansas City, 1998—99, U. Ala., Tuscaloosa, 1999—. Recipient Faculty Rsch. award, U. Ala., 2001; David Ross fellow, Purdue U., 1991—92. Mem.: ASME (assoc.), Am. Soc. Engring. Edn. (assoc.), Am. Soc. Metals Internat. (assoc.), Soc. Mfg. Engrs. (sr.). Achievements include research in hard machining and superhard cutting tools. Office: U Ala 290 Hardaway Hall Box 870276 Tuscaloosa AL 35405 Office Fax: 205-348-6419. E-mail: kchou@coe.eng.ua.edu.

CHOU, KUO-CHEN, biophysical chemist; b. Guangdong, China, Aug. 14, 1938; came to U.S., 1980; s. Hsiu-Chi Chou and Bi-Kun Luo; m. Wei-Zhu Zhong, Apr. 12, 1968; 1 child, James Jeiwen Chou. BS, Nanking (Peoples Republic China) U., 1960, MS, 1962; PhD, Shanghai (Peoples Republic China) Inst. Biochemistry, 1976; DSc, Kyoto (Japan) U., 1983. Jr. scientist Shanghai Inst. Biochemistry, Chinese Acad. Sci., 1976-78, assoc. prof., 1978-79; vis. assoc., prof. Chem. Ctr. Lund (Sweden) U., 1979-80; vis. assoc. prof. Max-Planck Inst. Biophys. Chemistry, Göttingen, Fed. Republic Germany, 1979-80; vis. assoc. prof. chemistry Cornell U., Ithaca, N.Y., 1980-83, sr. scientist Baker Lab., 1984-85; prof. biophysics U. Rochester, 1985—86; sr. scientist Eastman Kodak Co., Rochester, 1986-87, Upjohn Labs., Kalamazoo, 1987—92, sr. prin. scientist, 1993—99, rsch. advisor, 1999—2002; sr. rsch. adviser Pharmacia & Upjohn, Kalamazoo, 1995—, Pfizer, 2002—; dir. and chief scientist Gordon Lab. of Life Sci., 2003—. Editor Jour. Molecular Sci., 1983-86, Progress in Physics, 1981-85; mem. editl. bd. Current Peptide and Protein Sci., 2000—; contbr. more than 200 rsch. articles and rev. papers to profl. jours. Recipient Sci. and Tech. award Shanghai Com. of Sci. and Tech., 1977, Nat. medal of Sci., Nat. Acad. of Sci., China, 1978, Disting. Leadership award Am. Biog. Inst., N.C., 1989, Commemorative medal of Honor, Am. Biog. Inst., 1991; named for Leadership and Achievement, Internat. Biog. Ctr., Cambridge, U.K., 1990. Fellow Am. Inst. Chemistry; mem. AAAS, N.Y. Acad. Scis., Biophysical Soc., Am. Chem. Soc., Sigma Xi. Achievements include rsch. in bioinformatics, protein conformation and folding; graph theory in chem. reaction systems; enzyme kinetics; DNA codon usage analysis; prediction of protein cellular location and structural class; structure and function of antifreeze protein; prediction of HIV protease cleavage site; low-frequency collective motions of biomacromolecules and their biol. functions; structures of growth hormone and membrane proteins, proton-pumping mechanism of membrane proteins, inhibition kinetics of HIV reverse transcriptase, structure and binding site of adhesion proteins, apoptosis, human GFAT, G-protein couple receptors; GABA and GPCR receptors, cyclin-dependent kinases, molecular mechanism of Alzheimer's Disease, prediction signal peptides and their cleavage sites. Home: 7088 Arbor Valley Ave Kalamazoo MI 49009-8540 Office: Pharmacia & Upjohn Labs Computer-Aided Drug Discov 301 Henrietta St Kalamazoo MI 49007-4940 E-mail: kuo-chen.chou@pharmacia.com.

CHOU, LAISHENG, education educator; b. Shanghai, Nov. 8, 1952; s. Licheng Chou and Lanying Yang; m. Jialing Zhang, May 20, 1983; children: Sophia, Tina. DMD, Shanghai No. 2 Med. U., China, 1977; PhD, The U. of Brit. Columbia, Can., 1994. Diplomate Oral Pathology U. of Calif., 1987, Oral Medicine U. of Calif., 1989. Assoc. prof. biomaterials, assoc. prof. diagnostic scis., dir. oral aids clinic Boston U., 1994—2000, prof. biomaterials, prof. oral medicine, dir. divsn. of oral medicine, dir. oral aids clinic, 2000—. Hon. prof. China Med. U., Shengyang, 1993—; guest prof. China No. 4 Med. U., Xian, 2001—; sr. cons. The Chinese HIV/AIDS Found., Beijing, 2001—; sci. cons. The Chinese Acad. of Scis., Beijing, 2002—. Author: Over 100 sci. articles, abstracts, and book chpts. publ.; sci. reviewer The Jour. of Biomedical Materials Rsch., The Jour. of Dental Rsch., The Jour. of Biomaterials. Chmn. clin. investigation com. Am. Acad. of Oral Medicine, 2001, mem. membershp com., 2001; mem. awards and nominations com. Am. Soc. of Biomaterials Surface Scis.; mem. Boston U. Goldman Sch. of Dental Medicine Appointments and Promotions Com. Recipient The First Ann. award, The AU Found., 1988; fellow, Med. Rsch. Coun. of Can., 1992; grantee Grant award, NIH, 1988, Rsch. Grant, Calcitek Co., 1996, USBiomaterials Co., 1997, 1999, 2002, AIDS Edn. and Tng. Ctr. Grant, Dept. of Pub. Health and Svcs., 1998, 1999, 2000, 2001, 2002; grant, NIH, 1997, Zoller Meml. Fellow award, The U. of Chgo., 1989, Fellowship, The U. of Brit. Columbia, 1991. Mem.: Am. Soc. of Biomatrials Surface Scis., Soc. for Biomaterials, Am. Acad. of Oral Medicine (chmn., clin. investigation com. 2001), Internat. Assn. of Dental Rsch., ADA, Am. Acad. of Oral Pathology. Achievements include invention of Gold chloride enhanced cellular and molecular labeling system; Osteogenic elements of implant materilas; Novel scaffolds for human bone tissue engineering; Bioactive coating/implant materials for enhancement of bone attachment and regeneration; New materials for skin wound healing; discovery of Real earth filters for intraoral radiography with exposure reduction; Reduction of Langerhans' cells in smokeless tobacco-associated oral mucosal lesions; Oral mucosal Langerhans' cells as target, effector, and vector in HIV infection; first to Molecular biocompatibility of implant and tissue engineering scaffold materials. Office: Boston Univ 801 Albany St S207 Boston MA 02118 Office Fax: 617-638-5689. Personal E-mail: lchou@bu.edu. E-mail: lchou@bu.edu.

CHOU, RICHARD CHUNWAH, neuroscientist, internist; b. Tsuen Wan, Hong Kong, Apr. 27, 1964; came to U.S., 1989; s. Sun Po and Hoy Tei (Chiu) C. BS (hon.), Chinese U. Hong Kong, 1987; PhD in Pathology, SUNY, Buffalo, 1995, MD, 2001. Instr. dept. pathology SUNY, Buffalo, 1994-95, postdoctoral fellow dept. neurology, 1995-97, instr. dept. neurology, 1995-2001, rsch. scientist neurology, 1997-2001; clin. instr., internal medicine Ohio State U. Med. Ctr., Columbus, 2001—03; fellow internal medicine Mass. Gen. Hosp., Harvard Med. Sch., Mass., 2003—. Contbr. articles to profl. jours. Lam Oi Tong fellow, 1987-88; Mark Diamond Rsch. grantee, 1993-94, Sigma Xi grantee, 1994-95. Mem. ACP, N.Y. Acad. Scis., Soc. for Neurosci., Sigma Xi. Achievements include research on relationship between neural function and the inflammatory response during experimental arthritis; cell cycle regulation in astrocytes and its implications in neurological disorders. Office: Dept Internal Medicine Ohio State U Med Ctr 206 E Means Hall 1654 Upham Dr Columbus OH 43210-1250 E-mail: chou-1@medctr.osu.edu.

CHOU, TING-CHAO, pharmacology educator; b. Taiwan, Sept. 9, 1938; arrived in U.S., 1965, naturalized, 1976; s. Chao-Yun and Sheng-Mei (Chen) C.; m. Dorothy Tsui-chin Tseng, June 26, 1965; children: Joseph Hsin-I, Julia Hsin-Ya. BS, Kaohsiung Med. Coll., Taiwan, 1961; MS, Nat. Taiwan U., 1965; PhD, Yale U., 1970. Tchg. asst. pharmacology Nat. Taiwan U., 1964-65; rsch. asst. pharmacology Yale U., 1969; postdoctoral fellow Johns Hopkins U., Balt., 1969-72; assoc. Sloan-Kettering Inst. Cancer Rsch., N.Y.C., 1972-78, assoc. mem., 1978-88, mem., 1988-95, head lab. biochmn. pharmacology, 1988-98, dir. preclin. pharmacology core facility, 1995—. Asst. prof. Grad. Sch. of Med. Sci. Cornell U., 1972—78, assoc. prof., 1978—88, prof. pharmacology, 1988—2000; cons. Biogen, 1989, Boehringer Ingelheim Pharm., Inc., 1990—96, Hoffman-La Roche, Inc., 1990—91, U. Tex., Houston, 1991—, Sphinx Pharms., 1992—94, Synaptic Pharms., 1993—95, Virologic, Inc., 1997—99, Tularik, Inc., 1999—, Mass. Gen. Hosp., Boston, 2000—, Novartis Pharms., 2001—, Kosan Biosci., 2001—; mem. adv. bd. div. biotech. and pharma. rsch. Nat. Health Rsch. Insts., Taiwan, 2000—02; vis. prof. Chinese Second Mil. Med. U., Shanghai, 1992—, Tonji Med. U., 1993—; hon. prof. Chinese Acad. Med. Scis., Beijing, 1993—, Nanjing Med. U., 1994—, Chinese Acad. Mil. Med. Scis., Beijing, 1995—. Author (with J. Chou): Dose Effect Analysis with Microcomputers, 1986; co-editor: Synergism and Antogonism in Chemotherapy, 1991; co-editor: (with M. Hayball) CalcuSyn for Windows, Biosoft, 1996; mem. editl. adv. bd. : Cancer Biochemistry Biophysics, 1984—, Jour. of the Nat. Cancer Inst., 1988—92, Kaohsiung Jour. Med. Scis., 1992—, chmn. pub. bd. : Bio/Pharma Quar., 1995—2002; contbr. Chmn. Lim-Wang Meml. Scholarship Fund, 1998—2003; mem. adv. bd. divsn. biotechnology and pharm. rsch. Nat. Health Rsch. Inst., Taiwan, 2001—02. Rsch. grantee Nat. Cancer Inst., Nat. Inst. of Allergy and Infectious Diseases, Elsa U. Pardee Found. and Am. Cancer Soc., 1975—. Mem. AAAS, Am. Assn. Cancer Rsch., Am. Soc. Pharmacology and Exptl. Therapeutics, Am. Soc. Preventive Oncology (founding mem.), Am. Soc. for Biochem. and Molecular Biol., Am. Bur. Med. Advancement in China (bd. dirs. 1991-2003, v.p. 1994-98), N.Y. Acad. Sci., Kaohsiung Med. Coll. Alumni Assn. Am. (bd. dir. 1968-91, pres. 1972), Harvey Soc., Sigma Xi. Achievements include 14 U.S. patents in anticancer agents including desoxyepothilones; creator median-effect equation, multiple drug effect equation, combination index, dose-reduction index and polygonogram. Office: 1275 York Ave New York NY 10021-6007

CHOU, WUSHOW, computer scientist, educator; b. Shanghai, Kiangsu, China, Feb. 12, 1939; m. Lena Sun, Apr. 17, 1965; children: Warren, Wesley. BEE, Cheng Kung U., Tainan, Taiwan, 1961; MEE, U. N.Mex., 1965; PhD in Elec. Engring. and Computer Sci., U. Calif., Berkeley, 1968. Acting asst. prof.

U. Calif., Berkeley, 1968-69; v.p. Network Analysis Corp., Glen Cove, N.Y., 1969-76; vis. prof. SUNY, Stony Brook, 1976; rsch. prof. George Washington U., Washington, 1975-76; prof. computer sci. dept. and elec. and computer engring. dept. N.C. State U., Raleigh, 1976—, dir. computer studies, 1976-88; dep. asst. sec. for info. systems U.S. Dept. Treasury, Washington, 1994-97, chief info. officer, 1996-97. Vis. prof. Poly. U., Bklyn., 1988-89; pres. ACK Computer Applications, Cary, N.C., 1978-93; cons. AT&T, IBM, U.S. Govt., Singapore Govt., French Govt, over 40 corp. and other internat. corps. and orgns. Author, editor: Computer Communication, Vol. 1, 1984, Vol. 2, 1985, Advances in Telecommunication, 1985-88; editor in chief Jour. of Telecom., 1982-85, IT Profl., 1998-2001, chmn. adv. bd., 2002-; contbr. over 70 articles to profl. jours. and confs. Recipient award GSA, Washington, 1988, Treasury Dept., 1997; rsch. grantee NSF, 1978, rsch. grantee Army Rsch. Office, Research Triangle Park, N.C., 1982, rsch grantee AT&T, 1987. Fellow IEEE (awards 2001, 02), Assn. Computing Machines. Office: NC State U Dept Computer Sci PO Box 8206 Raleigh NC 27695-0001

CHOUDHURY, ABDUL LATIF, physics educator; b. Dhaka, Bangladesh, Jan. 1, 1933; came to U.S., 1966; s. Abdur R. and Umme Arefa (Khatun) C.; children: Kadjol, Marcel. BSc with honors in Physics, Dhaka U., 1953, MSc in Physics, 1954; D Theoretical Physics, Free U, Berlin, 1961. Asst. to prof. physics Dhaka U., 1955; helping asst. to prof. theoretical physics Free U. Berlin, 1958-60; sr. lectr. physics Dhaka U., 1961-66, reader in physics, 1969; assoc. prof. math. and physics. Elizabeth City (N.C.) State Coll., 1966-68, assoc. prof., 1969-73, prof. physics, 1973—. Cons. Nat. Bur. Standards, Washington, 1964-66; gen. sec. Dhaka U. Tchrs. Assn., 1969. Contbr. numerous articles to sci. pubs. German exch. scholar DAAD, Berlin, 1955-58; rsch. fellow Fritz Haber Inst., Berlin, 1960; rsch. asst. Colombo Plan, Imperial Coll., London, 1960-61. Mem. AAUP (v.p. Elizabeth City unit 1986-87, pres. 1987-88), Am. Phys. Soc., Bangladesh Phys. Soc. (life), N.C. Acad. Sci. Avocations: tennis, swimming. Home: 605 Forest Park Rd Elizabeth City NC 27909-9095 Office: Elizabeth City State Univ PO Box 886 Elizabeth City NC 27909 E-mail: alchoudhury@mail.escu.edu.

CHOUDHURY, DEO CHAND, physicist, educator; b. Darbhanga, India, Feb. 1, 1926; came to U.S., 1955; s. Kapleshwar and Gutainya Choudhury; m. Annette Patricia DuBois, Aug. 3, 1963; 1 son, Raj. BSc, U. Calcutta, 1944, MS, 1946; PhD, UCLA, 1959. Rsch. fellow Niels Bohr Inst., Copenhagen, 1952-55; rsch. asst. physics U. Rochester, N.Y., 1955-56; rsch. and tchg. asst. physics UCLA, 1956-59; asst. prof. physics U. Conn., Storrs, 1959-62; assoc. prof. physics Poly Inst. of N.Y. (now Poly U.), Bklyn., 1962—67; prof. physics Poly Inst. of N.Y., Bklyn., 1967—97, prof. emeritus, 1997—. Vis. asst. physicist Brookhaven Nat. Lab., summer 1960; vis. physicist Oak Ridge Nat. Lab., summer 1962, Niels Bohr Inst., 1978-79. Govt. India Coun. Sci. and Indsl. Rsch. scholar U. Calcutta Coll. Sci., 1947-52. Contbr. chpt. to book, numerous articles on high energy nuclear scattering, nuclear models, structure, reaction, and theoretical astrophysics to profl. publs. Mem. AAAS, Am. Phys. Soc., N.Y. Acad. Scis., Indian Phys. Soc., Sigma Xi, Sigma Pi Sigma. Home: 90 Gold St # 25L New York NY 10038-1833 Office: Poly U Dept Physics 6 Metrotech Ctr Brooklyn NY 11201-3840 Fax: 718-260-3136. E-mail: dchoudhu@duke.poly.edu.

CHOUDHURY, DIPA, mathematician, educator; b. Dhaka, Bangladesh, Feb. 1, 1953; d. Sisir and Monorama Sarkar; m. Japobrata Choudhury, July 18, 1972; children: Progga-Paromita, Atish-Dipankar. PhD, Johns Hopkins U., 1986. Asst. prof. Loyola Coll., Balt., 1986—94, assoc. prof., 1994—. Contbr. articles to profl. jours. Pres. Sanskriti, Washington, 1998—99. Mem.: Math. Assn. Am. (program chmn. Md./D.C./Va. sect. 2002). Home: 13026 Broadmore Rd Silver Spring MD 20904 Office: Loyola Coll 4501 N Charles St Baltimore MD 21210 Office Fax: 410-617-2803. Personal E-mail: dsc@loyola.edu. Business E-Mail: dsc@loyola.edu.

CHOUDHURY, RAJ DEO, business development manager; b. N.Y.C., 1969; s. Deo Chand and Annette P. Choudhury; m. Margarete Haeusler, 2002. BA, Princeton U., 1990; MA, Stanford U., 1993. Evaluation analyst Arco Ak. Inc., Anchorage, 1993—96; sr. planning analyst Atlantic Richfield Co., LA, 1996—99; mgr. fuel infrastructure and bus. devel. fuel cell activities GM Corp., Mainz Kastel, Germany, 1999—2003, mgr. ops. /pub. policy, fuel cell activities Washington, 2003—. Author: On the Theory of Repeated Games, 1990; co-author: Well-to-Wheel Energy Use and Greenhouse Gas Emissions of Advanced Fuel-Vehicle Systems for North Am., 2001, Well-to-Wheel Energy Use and Greenhouse Gas Emissions of Advanced Fuel-Vehicle Systems for Europe, 2002. Mentor US Dept. Def. Dep. Sch., Wiesbaden, Germany, 1999—2003. Mem.: Nat. Hydrogen Assn., Soc. Automotive Engrs., Mountaineering Club Alaska, Sigma Xi. Avocations: photography, international travel, amateur radio, mountaineering. Office: GM 1660 L St NW Ste 400 Washington DC 20036

CHOUEIFATI, ANTOINE (TONY CHOUEIFATI), computer company executive; b. Sept. 14, 1946; s. Beatrice and Jim Choueifati; m. Sally Shar; children: Anthony, Angie. Bachelor in Computer Science, Sir George Williams, 1975. Western region ter. mgr. IBM Corp., Houston, 1983—; tech support mgr. Goldrus Drilling Co., Houston, 1980—83. Author: (book) Sealed, 2002 (Marketing Excellence award, 1997). Mem.: Data Processing Mgmt. Assn. (cert.). Roman Catholic. Avocation: golf. Personal E-mail: tony1c@swbell.net.

CHOUKAS-BRADLEY, JAMES RICHARD, lawyer; b. Hartford, Conn., Sept. 11, 1950; s. William Lee and Paula Ann (Elliott) Bradley; m. Melanie Rose Choukas, June 21, 1975; children: Sophia Crane, Jesse Elliott. BA cum laude, U. Vt., 1974; JD cum laude, Georgetown U., 1980. Bar: D.C. 1980, U.S. Ct. Appeals (D.C. cir.) 1981, U.S. Ct. Appeals (11th cir.) 1984, U.S. Ct. Appeals (10th cir.) 1985, U.S. Ct. Appeals (4th cir.) 1990, U.S. Ct. Appeals (6th cir.) 1993. Reporter, editor The Berlin (N.H.) Reporter, The Groveton (N.H.) News, The Northland News, 1973—74; editor, pub., creative dir. Ad Lib, Gorham, NH, 1974—75; asst. to city mgr. City of Berlin, 1975—77; contbg. reporter The Lewiston (Maine) Sun, 1976; legal intern Congl. Budget Office, Washington, 1978; rsch. assoc. Schlossberg-Cassidy & Assocs., Washington, 1978—80; assoc. Miller, Balis & O'Neil, P.C., Washington, 1980—84, mem., v.p., 1985—, exec. com., 1993—97. Legal advisor, first v.p. Sugarloaf Citizens Assn., Barnesville, Md., 1987-2000; counsel Mcpl. Gas Authority of Ga., Natural Gas Acquisition Corp. of City of Clarksville, Tenn., S.E. Ala. Gas Dist., Mcpl. Gas Authority of Miss.; gen. counsel Tenn. Energy Acquisition Corp., Lower Ala. Gas Dist.; spkr. in field; pioneer in joint action and pub. financing in deregulated natural gas industry. Author: The Early Days, 1975. Pres. D.C. Dukes Athletic Club, Washington, 1978-81, Montgomery Dukes, 1987-92; com. chmn. Berlin Bicentennial Commn., Berlin, 1975-76; youth soccer and flag football coach Seneca Sports Assn., 1999-. Regents scholar State of N.Y., 1968. Mem.: Hist. Medley Dist., Energy Bar Assn., For A Rural Montgomery, Nat. Youth Sports Coaches Assn., Sugarloaf Citizens Assn., Randolph Mountain Club, Phi Beta Kappa. Avocations: softball, guitar, songwriting, hiking, travel. E-mail: jchoukasbradley@mbolaw.com.

CHOUKAS-BRADLEY, MELANIE, writer, photographer; b. Jacksonville, N.C., Aug. 20, 1952; d. Michael Jr. and Juanita May (Crosby) Choukas; m. James Richard Bradley, June 21, 1975; children: Sophia Crane, Jesse Elliott. BA in English, U. Vt., 1974; student, Pierce Coll., Athens, 1971; postgrad., U.S. Dept. Agr. Grad. Sch., Chevy Chase, Md., 1995—. From reporter to news dir. Radio Sta. WBRL, Berlin, N.H., 1975-77; rsch. asst. subcom. on oversight and Investigations Commerce Com., U.S. Ho. of Reps., Washington, 1978; writer, 1978—. Earth Day chmn. Sugarloaf Citizens Assn., Barnesville, Md., 1990-92. Author: (Book) City of Trees, 1987, Sugarloaf: The Mountain's History, Geology and Natural Lore, 2003; contbr. articles to Washington Post, Audubon Naturalist News, others. Grantee Am. Forest Inst., Nat. Forest Products Assn., Time Inc., Bendix, Union Camp Corp., 1978-81; grantee Sugarloaf Regional Trails, 1995, 2001. Mem. Authors Guild. Democrat. Achievements include member Capitol Steps adult synchronized skating team, participant National Championships 2001 and 2002; member Capital Classics synchronized skating team, 2003. Avocations: hiking, cross country skiing, syncronized figure skating, running, naturalist activities including botany and birding. E-mail: choukas@erols.com.

CHOVANES, EUGENE, lawyer; b. Hazleton, Penn., Jan. 1, 1926; s. Michael and Anna (Watro) C.; m. Claire Amelia Puhak, Mar. 27, 1952; children: Michael, George, Nicholas, Joseph, John. BS in Engring., Lehigh U., 1950; JD, Villanova U., 1960. Bar: Pa. 1961. Assoc. William Steell Jackson & Sons, Phila., 1957-63; ptnr. Jackson & Chovanes, Phila. and Bala-Cynwyd, Pa., 1963—. Lectr. patent law Villanova U., 1957-80. Sgt. U.S. Army, 1943-46, to 1st lt. Ordnance Corps, 1951-52. Mem. ABA, Phila. Intellectual Property Law Assn., Phila. Bar Assn., Soc. Registered Profl. Engrs., Am. Intellectual Property Law Assn. Office: 1 Bala Plz Ste 319 Bala Cynwyd PA 19004-1405

CHOW, AMY, gymnast, Olympic athlete; b. San Jose, Calif., May 15, 1978; Mem. USA Team, Hamamatsu, Japan, 1993, World Championships Team, Dortmund, Germany, 1994, Pan Am. Games Team, Mar del Plata, Argentina, 1995, U.S. Olympic Team, Atlanta, 1996. Placed 1st vault U.S. Gymnastics Championships, Ohio, 1992, 1st all around, vault, uneven bars, balance beam, 2d floor exercise, Mex. Olympic Festival, 1992, 3rd all around, vault, 1st floor exercise, USA/Japan Competition, Hamamatsu, Japan, 1993, 3rd vault Coca-Cola Nat. Championships, Nashville, Tenn., 1994, 1st vault, 2d uneven bars, 3rd all around Pan Am. Games, Mar del Plata, Argentina, 1995; recipient Gold medal Women's Gymnastics Team competition and Silver medal uneven bars, Olympic Games, Atlanta, 1996. Mem., U.S. Olympic Team, Sydney, 2000. Address: c/o Octagon 50 Portland Pier Portland ME 04101

CHOW, BRIAN GEE-YIN, policy analyst, researcher; b. Macau, China, Aug. 10, 1941; came to U.S., 1964; s. Kai-chuen and Chi-shiu (Miao) C.; m. Pauline P. Chou, June 14, 1969; children: Kira, Albert. BS, Chinese U. Hong Kong, 1963; PhD, Case Western Res. U., 1969; MBA, U. Mich., 1977, PhD, 1980. Sr. rsch. specialist Pan Heuristics, Sci. Applications Internat. Corp., L.A., 1978-79, R&D Assocs., Marina del Rey, Calif., 1979-89; sr. phys. scientist Rand, Santa Monica, Calif., 1989—. Cons. Under Sec. Def. for Policy, Washington, 1987-88, Pres.'s Sci. Adv., Washington, 1988-89, Office Chief Naval Ops., Washington, 1989-90. Contbr. over 95 monographs and articles to govt. agencies and profl. publs. Mem. Am. Inst. Strategic Coop. (organizing com. 1989-2002). Avocations: reading, bridge, chess. Home: 926 Harvard St Santa Monica CA 90403-2208 Office: Rand 1700 Main St Santa Monica CA 90401-3297 E-mail: chow@rand.org.

CHOW, CHI-MING, retired mathematics educator; b. Tai-Yuan, Shansi, Republic of China, Nov. 15, 1931; arrived in U.S., 1959; s. Wei-Han Chow and Lu-Tsen Hsu. Cert. tech. officer, Chinese Air Force Tech. Inst., Republic of China, 1954; BS in Math., Ch. Coll. Hawaii, 1962; MS in Math., Oreg. State U., 1965. Tech. officer Chinese Air Force, Republic of China, 1954-59; prof. math. Oakland C.C., Mich., 1965-92, ret., 1992. Author (first author of the proof of the theorem): The sight area A of a moving body is inversely proportional to the square of the distance D between the body and observing point, i.e. A=C/(DxD), where C is a constant; contbr. articles to profl. jours. including The Math. Tchr. 1st Lt. Air Force of Republic of China, 1954-59. Mem.: Pi Mu Epsilon. Avocation: piloting aircraft. Home: PO Box 903 Novi MI 48376-0903

CHOW, EILEEN SIU-HA, computer retailing, investment company executive; b. Hong Kong, Jan. 18, 1951; came to U.S., 1969, naturalized, 1983. d. Hin To and Oi (Kuen) Choi; m. Chun Ping Chow, Aug. 25, 1973; children: Connie, Sandra, Eugene. BA cum laude, UCLA, 1972, MS, 1973. Sys. analyst GM Rsch. Lab., Warren, Mich., 1973-77; v.p. Cougar of Calif., Inc., South San Francisco, 1977-85, Choice Investment Co. N.V., Netherlands Antilles, 1978—2001, ComSelect, Inc., Milbrae, Calif., 1983—; pres. CSE Investments, Inc., 1993—. Mem. Soc. Women Engrs., ACM. Office: PO Box 1420 Millbrae CA 94030-5420

CHOW, FRANKLIN SZU-CHIEN, obstetrician, gynecologist; b. Hong Kong, Apr. 15, 1956; came to U.S., 1967; s. Walter Wen-Tsao and Jane Ju-Hsien (Tang) C. BS, CCNY, 1977; MD, U. Rochester, 1979. Diplomate Am. Bd. Ob-Gyn. Intern Wilmington (Del.) Med. Ctr., 1979-80, resident in ob-gyn, 1980-83; practice medicine specializing in ob-gyn Vail (Colo.) Valley Med. Ctr., 1983—, chmn. obstetrics com., 1984-85, 86-87, chmn. surg. com., 1987-88, vice chief of staff, 1989-91, chief of staff, 1991-92; tchr., dir. Derma Tart Internat., Aurora, Colo., 1997—; obstetrical cons. Aurora Nurse Midwives, Aurora, 2000—. Obstet. cons. Aurora Nurse, 2000 . Named to Athletic Hall of Fame, CCNY, 1983. Fellow Am. Coll. Ob-Gyn's; mem. AMA, Colo. Med. Soc., Intermountain Med. Soc. (pres. 1985-86), Internat. Fedn. Gynecol. Endoscopists, Am. Assn. Gynecol. Laparoscopists, Gynecologic Laser Soc., Am. Soc. Colposcopy and Cervical Pathology. Avocations: skiing, swimming, photography. Home: PO Box 5657 Vail CO 81658-5657 E-mail: dti@vail.net.

CHOW, GREGORY CHI-CHONG, economist, educator; b. Macau, South China, Dec. 25, 1929; came to U.S., 1948, naturalized, 1963; s. Tin-Pong and Pauline (Law) C.; m. Paula K. Chen, Aug. 27, 1955; children: John S., James S., Jeanne S. BA, Cornell U., 1951; MA, U. Chgo., 1952, PhD, 1955; hon. doctorate, Zhongshan U., 1986; LLD, Lingnan U., 1994. Asst. prof. MIT, 1955-59; assoc. prof. Cornell U., 1959-62, vis. prof., 1964-65; staff mem., mgr. econ. models IBM Research Center, Yorktown Heights, N.Y., 1962-70, prof., dir. econometric rsch. program, 1970-97; Class of 1913 prof. polit. economy Princeton U., 1979—. Adj. prof. Columbia U., 1965-70; vis. prof. Harvard U., 1967, Rutgers U., 1969; adviser Chinese Natural Sci. Found.; econ. adviser Shandong Provincial Govt. Author: Demand for Automobiles in the United States: A Study in Consumer Durables, 1957, Analysis and Control of Dynamic Economic Systems, 1975, Econometric Analysis by Control Methods, 1981, Econometrics, 1983, The Chinese Economy, 1985, Understanding China's Economy, 1994, Dynamic Economics: Optimization by the Lagrange Method, 1997; co-author: The Demand for Durable Goods, 1960; co-editor: Evaluating the Reliability of Macro-Economic Models, 1982, Asia in the 21st Century, 1997, Dynamic Economics, 1997, China's Economic Transformation, 2002, Sower of Modern Economics in China: Interview of Gregory C. Chow (in Chinese) by Professor Liu Sufen; contbr. articles to profl. jours. Named Hon. Prof., Fudan U., Hainan U., The People's U., Zhongshan U., Shandong U., Nankai U., City U. Hong Kong, hon. pres., Lingnan U., Coll. at Zhongshan U., Nankai U. Fellow Econometric Soc., Am. Statis Assn.; mem. Academia Sinica, Am. Philos. Soc., Am. Econ. Assn., Soc. for Econ. Dynamics and Control (pres. 1979-80). Home: 30 Hardy Dr Princeton NJ 08540-1211 E-mail: gchow@princeton.edu.

CHOW, HUMPHREY WAI, mechanical engineer; b. Hoi Ping, Guangzhou, China, Feb. 7, 1954; came to U.S., 1972; s. Lai and Ming-Kuen (Wong) C.; m. Joanna Qi Deng, Nov. 17, 1988; children: Genevieve Daisy, Daphne Jolie. BSME, U. Mass., Lowell, 1978; MS, Ga. Inst. Tech., 1984; PhD, Rensselaer Poly. Inst., 1993; MS in Engring. Mgmt., Tufts U., 2002. Product design engr. GE Medium Power Transformers, Rome, Ga., 1979-82; mech. design engr. GE Ordnance Sys., Pittsfield, Mass., 1984-85; rsch. asst. Rensselaer Poly. Inst., Troy, N.Y., 1985-87; sr. mech. design engr. GE Power Sys., Schenectady, NY, 1987—90; teaching asst. Rensselaer Poly. Inst., Troy, 1990-93; dynamic analysis engr. GE Naval & Drive Turbine Sys., Fitchburg, Mass., 1993-94; methods devel. engr. Knolls Atomic Power Lab., Schenectady, 1994-96; staff engr. GE Aircraft Engines, Lynn, Mass., 1996-98, 99—, GE Deutschland, Frankfurt, Germany, 1998-99. Contbr. articles to profl. jours. including European Jour. Mechanics. Mem.: AIAA, ASME, Am. Soc. for Engring. Mgmt. Achievements include patents for rotor coil connectors of turbine generators; design of propulsion turbine generator for the Navy integrated electric drive program; methods development for nuclear fuel and core design analysis in the Navy nuclear propulsion program; metal forming process modeling of compressor airfoils manufacturing for aircraft engines. Office: GE Aircraft Engines 1000 Western Ave Lynn MA 01910-0001

CHOW, I-SHANG JACKSON, mutual fund company executive; m. Yu-Fen Wang, Sept. 20, 1992; 1 child, Alina. PhD, U. of Calif., Riverside, 1992. Asst. v.p. Chase Manhattan Bank, N.Y.C., 1997—2000; v.p. J & W Seligman, N.Y.C., 2000—. Mem.: ASA.

CHOW, JIMMY TAI-NIN, chemist; b. Hong Kong, Aug. 8, 1967; s. Ka Ho Chow and Chung Yue Ng; m. Lorena Lee. BS in Chemistry, U. Costa Rica, San Jose, 1991; MS in Chemistry, U. Tex.-Dallas, Richardson, 1995, D in Chemistry, 1998; postgrad., Kans. State U. Rsch. asst. Ctr. Investigacion de Tecnologia del Cuero, Sabanilla, Costa Rica, 1990-91; student intern Refineria Costarricense del Petroleo, Limon, Costa Rica, 1991; rsch. and tchg. asst. U. Tex.-Dallas, Richardson, 1992-95; chemist Rohm and Haas Tex., Inc., Deer Park, Tex., 1995-96; rsch. asst. U. Tex. and Carrington Labs., Inc., Richardson, 1997-98; postdoctoral chemist Carrington Labs., Inc., Irving, Tex., 1999; sr. chemist Bayer Corp., Baytown, Tex., 1999—. Tex. Pub. Ednl. Grant scholar, 1993-95, 97-98. Mem. AIChE, Am. Chem. Soc., Am. Inst. Chemists Inc., Soc. Hispanic Profl. Engrs. (Texas Bay chpt.), Electrochem. Soc., Sigma Xi.

CHOW, JUDY, library science and information sciences educator; b. Taipei, Taiwan, Feb. 13, 1954; came to U.S., 1964; d. Charles and Lucy (Chu) C.; m. Steve Lee, July 3, 1982; children: Andrew Chow Lee, Mike Chow Lee. BA, UCLA, 1975, MLS, 1977. Libr. L.A. County Pub. Libr., 1979-84, L.A. Pub. Libr., 1984-90; faculty mem. L.A. C.C., 1990—, prof. internat rsch. methods, 1990—. Mem. Calif. Libr. Assn., Faculty Assn. of Calif. C.Cs Sgi Buddhist. Avocations: drawing, painting, travel, music, reading. Office: LA CC 4800 Freshman Dr Culver City CA 90230-3519

CHOW, POO, wood technologist, scientist; b. Shanghai, Apr. 27, 1934; arrived in U.S., 1960, naturalized, 1971; s. Kai and Yung-Kwan (Hsieh) C.; m. Ai-Yu Kuo, July 17, 1965; children— Eugenia, Andrew E. MS in Forest Products, La. State U., 1961, PhD in Wood Sci. and Tech., Forestry, Mich. State U., 1969. Lab. dir. Pope and Talbot, Inc., Oakridge, Oreg., 1962-67; asst. prof. wood sci. U. Ill., Urbana, 1969-74, assoc. prof., 1974-80, prof., 1980—. Sr. Fulbright scholar, Fed. Republic Germany; cons. to industry; external examiner U. Ibadan, Nigeria; expert witness. Contbr. numerous articles to profl. jours.; patentee in field. Mem. ASTM, Forest Products Soc., Am. Chem. Soc., Soc. Wood Sci. and Tech., Am. Railway Engrs. and Maintenance-of-Way Assn., Internat. Rsch. on Wood Preservation Group, German Wood Technology Soc., RR Tie Assn., Am. Wood Preservatives Assn., Sigma Xi, Gamma Sigma Delta, Xi Sigma Pi. Office: Univ Ill 1102 S Goodwin Ave Urbana IL 61801-4730 E-mail: P-Chow2@uiuc.edu.

CHOW, REY, literature educator; b. Hong Kong; D in Modern Thought and Lit., Stanford U. Former tchr. U. Minn.; prof. comparative lit. program U. Calif., 1992; prof. Eng. Emory U., Atlanta. Author: Women and Chinese Modernity: The Politics of Reading Between West and East, 1991, Writing Diaspora, 1993, Primitive Passions: Visuality, Sexuality, Ethnography, and Contemporary Chinese Cinema, 1995 (James Russell Lowell prize, 1996); co-editor: Asia Pacific: Culture, Politics, Society; contbr. articles. Office: Emory Univ N-302 Callaway Ctr 537 Kilgo Cir Atlanta GA 30322 Office Fax: 404-727-2605. E-mail: english@emory.edu.

CHOW, RITA KATHLEEN, nursing consultant; b. San Francisco, Aug. 19, 1926; d. Peter and May (Chan) Chow. BS, nursing diploma, Stanford U., 1950; MS, Case Western Res. U., 1955; profl. diploma in nursing edn. adminstrn, Columbia U., 1961, EdD, 1968; B of Individualized Studies, George Mason U., 1983. Asst. in teaching Stanford U., Calif., 1951—52; instr., dir. student health Fresno (Calif.) Gen. Hosp. Sch. Nursing, 1952—54; instr. Wayne State U. Coll. Nursing, Detroit, 1957—58; rsch. assoc., project dir. cardiovasc. nursing rsch. Ohio State U., Columbus, 1965—68; commd. officer USPHS, 1968, advanced through grades to nurse dir. (capt.), 1974; spl. asst. to dep. dir. Nat. Ctr. Health Svcs. Rsch., Health Svcs. and Mental Health Adminstrn., HEW, Rockville, Md., 1969—73, dep. dir. manpower utilization br., 1970—73; dep. dir. Office Long Term Care; dep. chief nurse officer USPHS, Rockville, 1973—77; chief quality assurance br. div. long-term care Office Stds. and Certification, Health Standards and Quality Bur., Health Care Fin. Adminstrn., HHS, 1977—82; supervisory clin. nurse and spl. asst. to health systems adminstr. USPHS Indian Hosp., HRSA, HHS, Rosebud, SD, 1982—83; dir. patient edn., asst. dir. nursing G. W. Long Hansen's Disease Ctr., USPHS, Carville, La., 1984—89; dir. nursing Fed. Med. Ctr., Ft. Worth, 1989—95; pvt. cons., 1995—98; dir. Nat. Interfaith Coalition on Aging, Natl. Coun. on Aging, Washington, 1998—. Author: (book) Identifying Nursing Action with the Care of Cardiovascular Patients, 1967, Cardiosurgical Nursing Care: Understandings, Concepts and Principles for Practice, 1975; mem. editl. bd. Nursing and Health Care, 1983—95; contbr. articles to profl. jours. Served with Nurse Corps U.S. Army, 1954—57 USAR, 1957—68. Recipient Nursing Svc. award, Assn. Mil. Surgeons U.S., 1969, Commendation medal, USPHS, 1972, Meritorious Svc. medal, 1977, Disting. Svc. medal, 1987, citation for outstanding contbn. to cardiovascular nursing, Am. Heart Assn., 1972—79, award for disting. achievement in nusring rsch., Nursing Edn. Alumni Assn., Columbia U. Tchrs. Coll., 1973, Disting. Alumnus award, Case Western Res. U. Sch. Nursing, 1979, Women's Honors in Pub. Svcs. award, ANA, 1988, Commendable Svc. medal, U.S. Dept. Justice, Bur. Prisons, 1995, Holistic Nurse of the Yr. award, Am. Holistic Nurses Assn., 2001, Artist of Life First prize, Internat. Womens Writing Guild, 1987, Chief Nurse Officer award, USPHS, 2003; fellow Nat. League Nursing fellow, 1959—61; grantee, Sigma Theta Tau, 1966; scholar, AAUW, 1955. Mem.: Am. Assn. of Integrative Medicine.

CHOW, TSU SEN, research scientist; b. China, Nov. 8, 1939; naturalized, 1973; s. Kong and Helen (Chen) Wang; m. Shang-Mei Tang, June 10, 1967; 1 child, Albert S. ME, Rensselaer Poly. Inst., 1966; PhD, Carnegie Mellon U., 1968. Rsch. assoc. U. N.C., Chapel Hill, 1968-72; scientist Xerox Corp. Rsch. Labs., Webster, N.Y., 1972-74, project mgr., 1974-81, sr. mem. rsch. staff, 1981-85, prin. scientist, 1985—. Lectr. CIE-Europe/Elsivier, Finspong, Sweden, 1988-92; spkr. various univs., profl. socs., internat. meetings, 1975—. Contbr. articles to profl. jours. NSF grantee, 1972. Mem. Am. Phys. Soc., Materials Rsch. Soc., Soc. Rheology. Achievements include one patent; major contbns. to glassy polymers, composites, colloidal dispersions and interfaces. Home: 6 Red Rose Cir Penfield NY 14526-9779 Office: Xerox Corp # 114-39D 800 Phillips Rd Webster NY 14580-9791

CHOW, WINSTON, engineering research executive; b. San Francisco, Dec. 21, 1946; s. Raymond and Pearl C.; m. Lilly Fah, Aug. 15, 1971; children: Stephen, Kathryn. BSChemE, U. Calif. Berkeley, 1968; MSChemE, Calif. State U., San Jose, 1972; MBA cum laude, Calif. State U., San Francisco, 1985. Registered profl. chem. and mech. engr.; instr.'s credential Calif. Community Coll. Chem. engr. Sondell Sci. Instruments, Inc., Mountain View, Calif., 1971; mem. R & D staff Raychem Corp., Menlo Park, Calif., 1971-72; supervising engr. Bechtel Power Corp., San Francisco, 1972-79; sr. project mgr. water quality and toxic substances control program Electric Power Rsch. Inst., Palo Alto, Calif., 1979-89, program mgr., 1990-97, product line mgr. environ. market sector, 1997-99, indsl. and agrl. energy techs. and svcs. bus. area mgr., 1999—2001, exec. dir. Energy Ctrs. Network, 1999—2001, dept. mgr. energy utilization rsch. and devel., 2001—02. Mem. steering com. Indsl. Energy Tech. Conf., 1999-2002. Editor: Hazardous Air Pollutants: State-of-the-Art, 1993; co-editor: Clean Water: Factors that Influence Its Availability, Quality and Its Use, 1996; co-author: Water Chlorination, vols. 4, 6; co-editor 1997 Internat. Clean Water Conf.-Today's Sci. for Tomorrows Policies, The Environ. Profl., 1997; contbr. articles to profl. jours. Pres., CEO Directions, Inc., San Francisco, 1985-86, bd. dirs., 1984-87, chmn. strategic planning com., 1984-85; mem. industry com. Am. Power Conf., 1988-2002; with strategic long-range planning and restructuring com. Sequoia Union H.S. Dist., 1990-93, chmn. dist. ctrl. com., 1992-94. Recipient Grad. Disting. Achievement award, 1985; Calif. Gov.'s Exec. fellow, 1982-83. Mem. ASME, AIChE (profl. devel. recognition award), NSPE, Calif. Soc. Profl. Engrs. (pres. Golden Gate chpt. 1983-84, v.p. 1982-83, state dir.), Water Environ. Fedn., Air and Waste Mgmt. Assn. (mem. electric utility com. 1990-2000), Calif. State U. Alumni Assn. (bd. dirs., treas. 1989-91), U. Calif. Alumni Assn., Beta Gamma Sigma. Democrat. Presbyterian.

CHOWDHURI, PRITINDRA, electrical engineer, educator; b. Calcutta, July 12, 1927; came to U.S., 1949, naturalized, 1962; s. Ahindra and Sudhira (Mitra) C.; m. Sharon Elsie Hackebeil, Dec. 28, 1962; children: Naomi, Leslie, Robindro, Rajendro. B.Sc. in Physics with honors, Calcutta U., 1945, M.Sc., 1948; MS, Ill. Inst. Tech., 1951; D.Eng., Rensselaer Poly. Inst., 1966. Jr. engr. lightning arresters sect. Westinghouse Electric Corp., East Pittsburgh, Pa., 1951-52; elec. engr. high voltage lab. Maschinenfabrik Oerlikon, Zurich, 1952-53; research engr. High Voltage Rsch. Commn., Daeniken, Switzerland, 1953-56; devel. engr. high voltage lab. GE, Pittsfield, Mass., 1956-59, elec. engr. research and devel. ctr. Schenectady, N.Y., 1959-62, engr. elec. investigations transp. systems div. Erie, Pa., 1962-75; staff mem. Los Alamos (N.Mex.) Nat. Lab., 1975-86; prof. elec. engring. Ctr. Elec. Power Tenn. Technol. U., Cookeville, 1986—. Lectr. Pa. State U. Behrend Grad. Ctr., Erie, 1969-75. Author: Electromagnetic Transients in Power Systems, 1996. Patentee

in field. Fellow AAAS, IEEE, Instn. Elec. Engrs. (U.K.), N.Y. Acad. Scis. Democrat. Unitarian Universalist. Home: 690 Valley Forge Rd Cookeville TN 38501-1574 Office: Tenn Technol U Ctr Elec Power PO Box 5032 Cookeville TN 38505-0001 E-mail: pchowdhuri@tntech.edu.

CHOWDHURY, ALI ASRAF, electrical engineer, researcher; b. Jaldi, Chittagong, Bangladesh, July 1, 1955; s. Hesamuddin Ahmed Chowdhury and Mahfuza Khatun Chowdhurani; m. Razia Khanam; 1 child, Fariha. MSEE with distinction, Belarus Poly. Inst., Minsk, 1980; MSEE, U. Sask., Saskatoon, Can., 1983, PhD in Elec. Engring., 1988; MBA, St. Ambrose U., 2002. Lic. profl. engr., Tex., registered Alta., Can., New Brunswick, Can., chartered engr., Gt. Britain. Design engr. GE Mfg. Co., Chittagong, Bangladesh, 1980—81; reliability engr. Atlantic Nuclear Svcs. Ltd., Fredericton, Canada, 1987—90; sr. engr. Alta. (Can.) Power Ltd., Edmonton, 1990—99; sr. engring. reliability planning specialist MidAm. Energy Co., Davenport, Iowa, 1999—. Chmn. composite sys. reliability working group Mid-Continent Area Power Pool, St. Paul, 1999—; chmn. MidAm. Engring. Conf. MidAmerican Energy Co., Davenport, 2002; mem. Coun. Energy Advisors, USA, Davenport, 2001—; tech. advisor Electric Power Rsch. Inst., CA, Davenport, 2001—; industry advisor Power Sys. Engring. Rsch. Ctr., Davenport, 2000—; chmn. reliability task force Alta. Electric Utility Planning Coun., Calgary, 1990—95; chmn. coord. of reliability info. group Grid Co. Alta., Calgary, 1996—99; mem. tech. program com. Internat. Assn. Sci. and Tech. Devel., Calgary, 1991—99; mem. exec. com. Quad City Expo-Tech Orgn., Davenport, 1999, Quad City Engring. and Sci. Coun., Davenport, 1999—2002; advisor Jr. Achievement of No. Alta., Edmonton, 1990; mem. fund raising com. United Way of City of Edmonton, 1995. Mem. scholarship award com. Quad City Engring. and Sci. Coun., Davenport, 1999—2002. Recipient Best Paper award, Power Sys. Value-Vased Reliability Planning, 1997, Sys. Rsch. Found. Germany, 1996; scholar Talent Scheme scholar (7), Govt. Bangladesh, U. Sask., Can., 1965—88. Fellow: Instn. Elec. Engrs. U.K. (membership examiner 1999); mem.: IEEE (sr.; mem. several working groups 1995, vice.chmn. Iowa-Ill. sect. 2002, Best Paper award 1996). Avocations: travel, music, reading, writing, gardening. Office: MidAmerican Energy Co 106 East Second St Davenport IA 52801 Office Fax: 563-333-8112. Business E-Mail: aachowdhury@midamerican.com.

CHOWDHURY, ANWARUL KARIM, international organization official; b. Dhaka, Bangladesh, 1943; MA in History and Internat. Rels., U. Dhaka; D (hon.), Soka U. Permanent rep. of Bangladesh to UN, N.Y.C., 1996—2001; high rep. for least developed countries, landlocked developing countries and small island developing states UN, N.Y.C., 2002—. Dir., Japan, Australia and New Zealand UNICEF, 1990—93; v.p., Econ. and Social Coun. UN, 1997—98, chmn. Fifth Com. Gen. Assembly, 1998—2000. Recipient U. Thant Peace Award, Gandhi Gold Medal for Culture and Peace, UNESCO .

CHOWDHURY, DHIMAN, physician, consultant; b. Chittagong, Bangladesh, Jan. 1, 1953; arrived in Can., 1996; s. Chitta Ranjan and Aruna Chowdhury; m. Smriti Chowdhury, Sept. 6, 1978; children: Muna, Chinmoy, Priyanka. MB, BS, Chittagong Med. Coll., 1975; Diploma in Child Health, U. Coll. Dublin, Ireland, 1983, Royal Coll. Surgeons, 1984. Intern Chittagong Med. Coll., 1975-76; med. officer Primary Health Care Ctrs., Chittagong, 1976-79; resident Arab Child Hosp., Baghdad, Iraq, 1979-80; gen. physician Suk Al-Shiukh Hosp., Thedar, Iraq, 1980-83; registrar Suleimania Children's Hosp., Riyadh, Saudi Arabia, 1984-90, cons. pediatrician, 1990-97, No. Regional Health Bd., Nova Scotia, Can., 1997; clin. assoc. IWK-Grace Health Ctr., Halifax, Novia Scotia, Can., 1997-99, cons. pediatrician, 1999—. Asst. prof. pediatrics Dalhousie U., 1999—; clin. asst. prof. King Saud U., Riyadh, 1993-97; program dir. Arab Bd. in Pediat. Residency Program, Riyadh, 1993-95, 96-97. Contbr. articles to profl. jours., chpt. to textbook. Fellow Royal Coll. Physicians (Edinburgh, U.K.); mem. Royal Coll. Physicians (Eng.), Saudi Pediat. Assn., N.Y. Acad. Sci., Bangladesh Med. Assn. Avocations: clinical photography, desert trips, travelling, reading journals, fishing. Home: 967 Winwick Rd Halifax NS Canada B3H 4L5 Office: IWK Grace Health Ctr Dept Pediatric Medi PO Box 3070 Halifax NS Canada B3J 3G9 E-mail: d.chowdhury@dal.ca., dchowdhury@ns.sympatico.ca.

CHOWDHURY, DIPAK K. pharmaceutical executive, researcher; b. Chittagong, Bangladesh, Bangladesh, Dec. 1, 1956; s. Bimal Kanti and Srimitikana Chowdhury; m. Debjani Majumder, Sept. 1, 1965; children: Sudipa, Urvi. PhD, U. Sagar, 1984. Rsch. assoc. sch. pharmacy U. Mo., Kansas City, 1996—99; assoc. mgr. Murty Pharmaceuticals, Lexington, Ky., 1999—. Dept. pharmacy, assoc. prof. U. Dhaka, Bangladesh, 1989—96. Contbr. articles to internat. pharm. jours. Fellow, Ministry Edn., Govt. India, 1980—84, U. Mo., Kansas City, 1996; grantee, Nat. Inst. of Drug Abuse, NIH, 1999—2003. Mem.: Am. Assn. Pharm. Scientist (assoc.). Hinduism. Achievements include patents for Trasdermal delivery of tetrahydrocannabinol; patents pending for Sublingual Delivery For Tetrahydrocannabinol; In situ gel delivery for clindamycin; Microemulsion Delivery Of Tetrahydrocannabinol. Avocations: swimming, travel, reading. Home: 4321 Sharon Dr Lexington KY 40515 Office: Murty Pharmaceuticals Inc 518 Codell Dr Lexington KY 40509 Office Fax: 859-266-6976. Personal E-mail: dipak56@hotmail.com. E-mail: dchowdhury@mpirx.com.

CHOWDHURY, KHALID, plastic surgeon, otolaryngologist, surgeon; b. Sept. 21, 1957; came to U.S. married; 3 children. BS in Econs., BS in Biology, U. Regina, 1975-77; MD, U. Saskatchewan, Saskatoon, Can., 1982; MBA, U. Colo., 2000. Diplomate Am. Bd. Otolargyngology, Am. Bd. Facial Plastic and Reconstructive Surgery. Intern St. Thomas Med. Ctr., Akron, OH, 1982-83; resident in gen. surgery U. Saskatchewan, Saskatoon, Can., 1984-85; resident in otolaryngology/head and neck surgery McGill U., Montreal, Montreal, Can., 1985-89; fellow in cranio-maxillofacial surgery U. Hosp., Bern, Switzerland, 1989-90; dir. med. student edn. Albert Einstein Coll. of Med., N.Y.C., 1991-92; asst. prof. otolaryngology head and neck surgery U. Ky., Lexington, 1992-96; with Ctr. for Craniofacial Surgery, Denver, 1997—, Centura Saint Anthony Central, Columbia Med. Ctr. of Aurora, North, Columbia Med. Ctr. of Aurora,South, Columbia Presbyterian/St. Luke's Med. Ctr., Columbia Rose Med. Ctr., Denver Health Med. Ctr., Exempla St. Joseph Med. Ctr., The Children's Hospital. Jr. faculty devel.-five year strategic plan U. Ky. Med. Ctr. Dept. Surg. Lexington; mem. Coll. Med. Rsch. Com., 1995-98, Monthly Multidisciplinary Maxillofacial Trauma Tchg. Conf.; coord. for Thursday Morning Weekly Tchg. rounds, Dept. Otolaryngology-Head and Neck Surgery Bronx Mcpl. Health Ctr. Hosp., N.Y.C. Editl. bd. dirs. Jour. of Otolaryngology, Toronto, 1993—; contbr. articles to profl. jours. Bd. dirs., founding mem. Cranio-Maxillofacial and Skull Base Soc. (course organizing com., 1996); mem. Total Quality Mgmt Com. Divsn. of Otolaryngology-Head and Neck Surgery, U. Ky. Med. Ctr., Lexington, Dept. Surgery trauma Morbidity Mortality/Quality Assurance Com, Dept. of Surgery, Us. Ky.,Coll. Med. Rsch Com., U. Ky., Ctr for Membrane Scis. Faculty Assoc., U. Ky., Am. Acad. of Otolaryngology-Head and Neck Surgery., Am. Acad. of Facial Pleastic and Reconstructive Surgery, Canadian Soc. of Otolaryngology-Head and Neck Surgery, Canadian Medical Assn., Royal Coll. of Surgeons of Can., Colo. Med. Soc., Denver Med. Soc. Rsch. Regenerating Cranial Bone Defects using Growth Factors, Internat. Optic Nerve Trauma Study, Guided Tissue Regeneration of Large Cranial bone Defects Using Membrane Techniques and Bone Growth Factors, Analysis and Biomechanical Testing of Miniplate Stability in Mandibular Fractures, Internal Fixation of Mandible Fractures: Analysis of Complications. Office: Center Crainofacial Surgery 1601 E 19th Ave Ste 3000 Denver CO 80218-1239

CHOWDHURY, SUBIR, business executive, author, researcher; b. Chittagong, Bangladesh, Jan. 12, 1967; came to U.S., 1991; s. Sushil Kumar and Krishna Keshi (Biswas) C.; m. Malini Guha, Feb. 26, 1997. BTech. in Aerospace Engring. with honors, Indian Inst. Tech., Kharagpur, India, 1989; MA in Indsl. Mgmt., Ctrl. Mich. U., 1993. Software and sys. mgr. Ciproco Computers Ltd., Dhaka, Bangladesh, 1989-91; quality mgmt. cons. Gen. Motors Corp., Saginaw, Mich., 1993-97; exec. v.p. ASI, Livonia, Mich., 1997—2002, chmn., CEO, 2002—. Author: QS-9000 Pioneers, 1996, Robust Engineering, 1999, Management 21C, 2000, The Power of Six Sigma, 2001, Design for Six Sigma, 2002, The Talent Era, 2002, The Power of Design for Six Sigma, 2002, Organization 21C, 2002; editor-in-chief Automotive Excellence, 1997-99; founding editor Silocon mag., 1990. Fellow Royal Statis. Soc. (U.K.), Quality Soc. Australia; mem. Am. Soc. for Quality (sr.; chair automotive divsn. 1999-2000, Philip Crosby medal 2003), Soc Mfg. Engrs. (sr.; Gold medal 2002), Inst. Indsl. Engrs. (sr.), Soc. Automotive Engrs. (sr.; Henry Ford II award of Excellence, 1996). Avocations: photography, music, writing, reading, surfing the internet. Office: ASI Cons Group LLC 38705 Seven Mile Rd Ste 345 Livonia MI 48152-3908

CHOWHAN, NAVEED MAHFOOZ, oncologist; b. Pakistan, Oct. 19, 1960; came to U.S., 1979; Student, Mao and Forman Christian Coll., Pakistan, 1979; MD cum laude, U Cetec, Dominican Republic, 1982. Bd. cert. internal medicine, 1986, hematology, 1992, oncology, 1993. Resident internal medicine Georgetown U. Svc., D.C. Gen. Hosp., Washington, 1983-86; fellowship oncology-hematology SUNY, Stony Brook, 1988-91, clin. asst. prof. dept. medicine divsn. oncology, 1992-94; pvt. practice New Albany, Ind., 1994—. Pvt. practice, South Bend, Ind., 1986—88; attending physician Meml. Hosp. and St. Joseph Med. Ctr., South Bend, 1987—88, Floyd Meml. Hosp., New Albany, 1994—, chair cancer conf., 1995—97, 2001, 03, dir. stem cell transplant unit, 1997—, chair cancer com., 1997—2000, sec. med. staff, 1998—2000, vice-chair staff, 2001, chair credentials com., 01, chmn. med. staff, 02; attending physician Clark Meml. Hosp., Jeffersonville, Ind., 1994—, mem. cancer com., 1995—, chair blood transfusion com., 1997, cancer liaison physician, 1999—2001; mem. Com. on Rsch. Involving Human Subjects, 1993—94; pioneer bone marrow transplant program SUNY, Stony Brook, 1994; investigator, rschr. and presenter in field. Contbr. articles to profl. jours. Named Physician of Yr., Nat. Rep. Congl. Com. Physician Adv. Bd., 2003; recipient Leadership award, 2002. Fellow ACP; mem. Am. Soc. Clin. Oncology, Am. Soc. Hematology, Am. Soc. Bone Marrow Transplantation. Office: 2210 Greenvalley Rd Ste 1 New Albany IN 47150-6809

CHOWNING, JOHN E. political scientist, educator, minister; s. Chattin D. and Elizabeth B. Chowning; m. Catherine Pence Chowning, Aug. 28, 1971; children: Kacey, Emily, Kaleb, Laura. AA, Lindsey Wilson Coll., 1971; BA, Transylvania U., 1973; MPA, Ea. Ky. U., 1977. Sch. tchr. Lincoln County Schs., Stanford, Ky., 1973—75; grad. asst. Ea. Ky. U., Richmond, 1975—76; dir. housing and cmty. devel. Lake Comb ADD, Russell Springs, Ky., 1977—80; dir. cmty. devel. City of Campbellsville, Ky., 1980—83; sr. cons., v.p. Pvt. Consulting, Lexington, Ky., 1983—95; dir. econ. devel. Congressman Ron Lewis, Elizabethtown, Ky., 1995—98; v.p., faculty polit. sci. Campbellsville U., 1998—. Pastor Saloma Bapt. Ch., Campbellsville; trustee, bd. chair Campbellsville U., 1999—08; chair Indsl. Devel. Authority Campbellsville, 1998—2003; parliamentarian Ky. Bapt. Conv., Louisville, 2001—03; founder Ctr. Bivocational Ministry Campbellsville U., founder, dir. Ky. Heartland Inst. on Pub. Policy; bd. of institute Religion and Public Policy, DC; chair Rural Telecom Inst.; mem. Ctr. for Study of the Presidency; pres. Hopewell Acres, Inc. Citizen mem. State Bd. Elections, Frankfort, 1991—2002; exec. bd. mem., former chair, vice chair Ctr. for Rural Devel., Somerset, Ky., 1996—2003; state exec. com. Rep. Party Ky., Frankfort, 1986—98. Named Citizen of Yr., Campbellsville C. of C., 1998, 2001, Man of Yr., BPW, Taylor County, 1999; recipient Econ. Devel. Leadership award, Gov. Ky., 1999. Mem.: C. of C., Ky. Indsl. Devel. Coun., Am. Soc. Pub. Adminstrn., Am. Polit. Sci. Assn. Avocations: reading, travel, politics, ministry. Home: 512 Fern Dr Campbellsville KY 42718 Office: Campbellsville Univ 1 University Dr UPO 1295 Campbellsville KY 42718

CHOWNING, ORR-LYDA BROWN, dietitian; b. Cottage Grove, Oreg., Nov. 30, 1920; d. Fred Harrison and Mary Ann (Bartels) Brown; m. Kenneth Bassett Williams, Oct. 23, 1944 (dec. Mar. 1945); m. Eldon Wayne Chowning, Dec. 31, 1959. BS, Oreg. State Coll., 1943; MA, Columbia U., 1950. Dietetic intern Scripps Metabolic Clinic, LaJolla, Calif., 1944; sr. asst. dietitian Providence Hosp., Portland, Oreg., 1945-49; contact dietitian St. Lukes Hosp., N.Y.C., summer 1949; cafeteria food svc. supr. Met. Life Ins. Co., N.Y.C., 1950-52; set up food svc. and head dietitian McKenzie-Willamette Meml. Hosp., Springfield, Oreg., 1955-59; foods dir. Erb Meml. Student Union, Eugene, Oreg., 1960-63; set up food svc. and head dietitian Cascade Manor Retirement Home, Eugene, 1967-68; owner, operator Veranda Kafe, Inc., Albany, Oreg., 1971-80; owner, operator, sec.-treas. Chownings Adult Foster Home, Albany, 1984-98. Contbr. articles to profl. jours. Lin County Women's chair Hatfield for Senator Spaghetti Rally, Albany H.S., 1966; food preparation chair Yi for You, Mae Yih for State Senate, Albany Lebanon, Sweet Home, 1982; Silver Clover Club sponsor Oreg. 4-H Found., Oreg. State U., Corvallis, 1994-96. Recipient coll. scholarship Nat. 4-H Food Preparation Contest, Chgo., 1939. Mem. Am. Dietetic Assn. (registered dietitian, gerontol. nutritionist dietetic practice group 1988—), Oreg. Dietetic Assn. (diet therapy chair, newsletter editor 1963-64), Willamette Dietetic Assn., Kappa Delta Pi (Kappa chpt.), Mu Beta Beta. Republican. Mem. Christian Ch. (Disciples Of Christ). Avocations: gardening, genealogy, swimming, travel, pet therapy. Home and Office: 4440 Woods Rd NE Albany OR 97321-7353

CHOY, CLEMENT KIN-MAN, research scientist; b. Fukien, China, Aug. 4, 1947; came to U.S., 1970. s. Yick-Chu and Hui-Keng (Sy) C.; m. Anna K. Chan, Oct. 4, 1975; 1 child, Jennifer. Diploma, Hong Kong Baptist Coll., 1970; MS, Cleve. State U., 1972; PhD, Case Western Reserve U., 1976. Technician Univ. Hosps., Cleve., 1974-76; asst. dir. Gen. Med.Labs, Warrensville, Ohio, 1974-76; tech. staff Procter and Gamble, Cin., 1976-80; scientist Clorox, Pleasanton, Calif., 1980-81, sr. scientist, 1981-82, project leader, 1982-89, sr. rsch. assoc., 1989-93; tech. mgr. Asia Pacific region Clorox Internat. Co., Hong Kong, 1993-94; rsch. assoc. Clorox Tech. Ctr., 1994-97, rsch. fellow, 1997—. Pres. Chinese Assn. of Greater Cleve., 1972-74. Mem. Am. Chem. Soc., Am. Soc. Oil Chemists (mem.-at-large, surfactant divsn., exec. bd. 2001-), Am. Assn. Clin. Chemists, Consumer Splty. Products Assn. (chair sci. com. 1998--, exec. bd. cleaning products divsn. 1999-). Home: 1345 Sugarloaf Dr Alamo CA 94507-1238 Office: Clorox Svcs Co 7200 Johnson Dr Pleasanton CA 94588-8004 E-mail: clement.choy@clorox.com.

CHOY, HERBERT YOUNG CHO, federal judge; b. Makaweli, Hawaii, Jan. 6, 1916; s. Doo Wook and Helen (Nahm) Choy; m. Dorothy Helen Shular, June 16, 1945. BA, U. Hawaii, 1938; JD, Harvard U., 1941. Bar: Hawaii 1941. Law clk. City and County of Honolulu, 1941; assoc. Fong & Miho, 1947—48; ptnr. Fong, Miho and Choy, 1948—57; atty. gen. Territory of Hawaii, 1957—58; ptnr. Fong, Miho, Choy & Robinson, Honolulu, 1958—71; sr. judge U.S. Ct. Appeals (9th cir.), Honolulu, 1971—. Adv. com. on constrn. judiciary bldgs. Chief Justice Hawaii, 1970—71; compilation commn. to compile Revised Laws of Hawaii, 1955, 1953—57; com. to draft Hawaii rules of criminal procedure Supreme Ct., 1958—59; com. on pacific ocean territories Jud. Conf. of U.S., 1976—79. Dir. Legal Aid Soc. Hawaii, 1959—61; trustee Hawaii Loa Coll., 1963—79. Capt. U.S. Army, 1941—46, lt. col. USAR. Recipient Order of Merit award, Republic of Korea, 1973. Fellow: Am. Bar Found.; mem.: ABA, Hawaii Bar Assn. (exec. com. 1953, 1957, 1961, legal ethics and unauthorized practices com. 1953, com. on legis. 1959). Office: US Ct Appeals 300 Ala Moana Blvd Rm C305 Honolulu HI 96850-0305

CHOYKE, PHYLLIS MAY FORD (MRS. ARTHUR DAVIS CHOYKE JR.), management executive, editor, poet; b. Buffalo, Oct. 25, 1921; d. Thomas Cecil and Vera (Buchanan) Ford; m. Arthur Davis Choyke Jr., Aug. 18, 1945; children: Christopher Ford, Tyler Van. BS summa cum laude, Northwestern U., 1942. Reporter City News Bur., Chgo., 1942-43, Met. sect. Chgo. Tribune, Chgo., 1943-44; feature writer OWI, N.Y.C., 1944-45; sec. corp. Artcrest Products Co., Inc., Chgo., 1958-88, v.p., 1964-88; pres. The Partford Corp., Chgo., 1988-90. Founder, dir. Harper Sq. Press div., 1966-90. Author: (under name Phyllis Ford) (with others) (poetry) Apertures to Anywhere, 1979; editor: Gallery Series One, Poets, 1967, Gallery Series Two, Poets—Poems of the Inner World, 1968, Gallery Series Three Poets: Levitations and Observations, 1970, Gallery Series Four, Poets, I am Talking About Revolution, 1973, Gallery Series Five/Poets—To An Aging Nation (with occult overtones), 1977; (manuscripts and papers in Brown U. Library). Bonbright scholar, 1942. Mem. DAR (corr. sec. Gen. Henry Dearborn chpt. 1991-92, treas. 1992—, regent. 2003-04), Soc. Midland Authors (bd. dirs. 1987—, treas. 1988-93, pres. 1993-95, membership dir. 1997-98, corr. sec. 1999—), Mystery Writers Am. (assoc.), Chgo. Press Vets. Assn., Arts Club Chgo., John Evans Club (Northwestern U.), Poetry Soc. Am. (N.Y.C.), Acad. Am. Poets (N.Y.C.). Home: 23 Windsor Dr Elmhurst IL 60126-3971

CHOYKE, WOLFGANG JUSTUS, physicist; b. Berlin, Ger., July 24, 1926; s. Frederick Samuel and Alice Sophia Amalia (Dessauer) C.; m. Helen Ruth Rubenfeld, June 19, 1949; children: Alice Mathea, Peter Lyle. BSc, Ohio State U., 1948, PhD, 1952. Rsch. physicist Westinghouse Rsch. Labs., Pitts., 1952-60, fellow physicist, 1960-63, adv. physicist, 1963-78, cons. physicst, 1978-88; adj. prof. physics U. Pitts., 1974-88, rsch. prof. physics, 1988—. Cons. Northrup-Grumman and Westinghouse Sci. & Tech. Ctr., Pitts., 1988-98; vis. prof. U. Erlangen-Nuremberg, 1990—. Contbr. some 355 rsch. articles to profl. jours. With U.S. Army Signal Corps, 1944-46. Recipient Westinghouse Order of Merit, 1983, Humboldt Rsch. prize, Bonn, 1990. Fellow: Am. Phys. Soc. (mem. com. applications physic 1977—86), AAAS; mem.: NRC (chmn. com. large band gap semiconductor devices 1993—95), Material Rsch. Soc. Achievements include fundamental studies and development of Silicon Carbide into what is presently the most promising high temperature semiconductor. Office: U Pitts Dept Of Physics Pittsburgh PA 15260 E-mail: choyke@imap.pitt.edu.

CHREBET, WAYNE, professional football player; b. Garfield, N.J., Aug. 14, 1973; Student, Hofstra U. Wide receiver N.Y. Jets, 1995—. Mem. AFC Ea. Championship team, 1998. Office: NY Jets 1000 Fulton Ave Hempstead NY 11550-1030

CHRENCIK, FRANK, chemical company executive; b. Osage, Iowa, Jan. 6, 1914; s. Tom and Agnes (Walashek) C.; m. Edith Jo Phelps, July 27, 1935; children: Charles Frank, James Phelps (dec.). BS in Chem. Engring, U. Iowa, 1937; grad., Advanced Mgmt. Program, Harvard, 1955. Plant engr., prodn. and constrn. supr. gen. chem. div. Allied Chem. & Dye Corp., 1937-40; mgr. various plants Diamond Shamrock Chem. Co., Cleve., 1946-56, gen. mgr. electrochems. div., 1956-60, co. v.p., sr. officer, 1960-72; dir., chmn. exec. com. Terra Chem. Internat., Inc., Sioux City, Iowa, 1969-72; exec. v.p. chems. and metals group Vulcan Materials Corp., Birmingham, Ala., 1972-77, also bd. dirs., mem. exec. com., vice chmn. bd., 1977-79, emeritus dir. and cons., 1979—. Bd. govs. Gulf Coast Devel. Co., Pasadena, Tex., 1955; past mem. adv. council Coll. Engring., U. Iowa.; bd. dirs. Chlorine Inst., 1968-72 Mem. internat. adv. bd.: Ency. of Chem. Processing and Design. Past trustee Nat. Hemophilia Found., N.Y. Served to lt. col. Chem. Corps AUS, 1940-46. Recipient Disting. Alumni Achievement award U. Iowa, 1977; inducted into Acad. of Disting. Engrs., U. Iowa, 1996. Mem. AICE (Outstanding Chem. Engr. award Ala. sect. 1983), U. Iowa Pres.'s Club. Clubs: The Club (Birmingham), Vestavia Country (Birmingham). Home: 104 University Park Dr Birmingham AL 35209-6766 Office: 11200 Urban Center Dr Birmingham AL 35238 5014 also: PO Box 385014 Birmingham AL 35238-5014

CHRÉTIEN, JEAN (JOSEPH JACQUES JEAN CHRÉTIEN), prime minister of Canada, lawyer; b. Shawinigan, Que., Can., Jan. 11, 1934; s. Wellie and Marie (Boisvert) C.; m. Aline Chaîné, Sept. 10, 1957; children: France, Hubert, Michel. Law degree, Laval (Que.) U., 1958; LLD (hon.), Wilfred Laurier U., 1981, Laurentian U., 1982, U. Western Ont., 1982, York U., 1986, U. Alta., 1987, Lakehead U., 1988, U. Ottawa, 1994, Meiji U., 1996; D (hon.), Warsaw Sch. Econs., Poland, 1999, Mich. State U., 1999, Hebrew U., Israel, 2000, Memorial U., 2000. Bar: Que. 1958. Former mem. firm Chrétien, Landry, Deschênes, Trudel & Normand; M.P. from St. Maurice Ho. of Commons, 1963-86; Parliamentary sec. to prime min., 1965; Parliamentary sec. to min. of fin., 1966; min. without portfolio, 1967; min. of nat. revenue, 1968; min. of Indian Affairs and No. devel., 1968-74; pres. Treasury Bd. Can., 1974-76; min. of industry, trade and commerce, 1976-77; min. of fin., 1977-79; min. of justice, atty. gen. of Can.; min. of state for social devel., min. responsible for Constln. negotiations, 1980-82; min. of energy, mines and resources, 1982-84; deputy prime min., sec. state for external affairs, 1984; external affairs critic for the official opposition, 1984-86; counsel Lang, Michener, Lawrence & Shaw, Toronto, Ottawa and Vancouver, 1986-90; leader Liberal Party of Can., 1990; M.P. from Riding of Beauséjour, 1990-93; M.P. from Riding of St. Maurice Que.; prime min., 1993—. Mem. Can. Bar Assn., Shawinigan Sr. C. of C. (dir. 1962) Liberal Party Of Can. Office: Parliament Bldgs 80 Wellington St Ottawa ON Canada K1A 0A2*

CHRETIEN, L. BIANCA, journalist; b. Lafayette, La., July 17, 1979; d. Tracy Thomas Sr. and Julie Ann Chretien. BA, U. La., Lafayette, 2000. Copy editor Daily Advertiser, Lafayette, 2000, reporter, 2000—. Mem.: Delta Sigma Theta. Avocation: reading.

CHRETIEN, MARGARET CECILIA, public administrator; b. Tupper Lake, N.Y., Jan. 19, 1953; d. William Lawrence and Catherine Eileen (Dowdle) LaGasse; m. Thomas J. Chretien, Oct. 1, 1977. BA, Siena Coll., 1975; MPA, SUNY, Albany, 1983, postgrad., 1992—. Program coordinator Saratoga County Office for Aging, Ballston Spa, N.Y., 1977-80; crime prevention specialist N.Y. State Div. Criminal Justice Svcs., Albany, 1980-84, pub. info. officer, 1984-86, criminal justice program rep., 1986—2000, S.T.O.P. Violence Against Women program adminstr., 2000—01, sr policy analyst, 2001—. Publicity chair Nat. Mus. Dance, Saratoga Springs, N.Y., 1987-90; peer review panelist U.S. Dept. Justice, Office of Justice Programs. Mng. editor NYS Crime Prevention Update, 1980-84; mem. editorial rev. bd. Mng. N.Y. State, 1987-89. Bd. dirs. Vol. Ctr. Albany, 1988—, sec., 1992, pres., 1994-2000; fundraising vol. St. Cecilia's Orch., 1992; life mem. Saratoga Performing Arts Ctr. Mem. Women's Press Club N.Y. State, Inc. (v.p. 1984-86). Roman Catholic. Avocations: biking, golf, mountain climbing. Home: 8 Wagner Rd Saratoga Springs NY 12866-3744 Office: NY Div Criminal Justice Svc Executive Pk Albany NY 12203

CHRETIEN, PAUL BERNARD, oncologist, medical researcher; b. San Angelo, May 13, 1931; s. Joseph Rodney and Celeste Regina Chretien; m. Jane Susan Henkel, Apr. 11, 1970; children: Jean Paul, Yves Rene. BS, St. Louis U., Coll. Arts and Sci., 1953; MD, St. Louis U., Sch. Medicine, 1957. Diplomate Am. Bd. Surgery, 1963, lic. State of Md. From intern to chief resident, dept. surgery N.Y. U. Bellevue Hosp. Ctr., NY, 1957—62; nat. cancer inst. fellow, oncology Mem. Sloan-Kettering Cancer Cent., 1962—66; sr. investigator, surgery br. Nat. Cancer Inst., 1966—72, chief, tumor immunology sect., surgery br., founding mem. immunotherapy contracts prog., 1972—80, coord., head, neck cancer contracts prog., div. cancer treatment, 1974—80; prof., dir. rsch., dept. surgery U. Md. Sch. of Medicine, 1983—93. Mem., sr. exec. svc. U.S. Civil Svc., 1976—80; co-originator, co-chmn. First Internat. Head and Neck Oncology Rsch. Conf., 1980—; cons., immunotherapy prog. Hoffmann-LaRoche Inc., 1980—82; v.p., med. affairs Alpha 1 Biomedicals Inc.; originator, chmn. First Internat. Conf. Head and Neck Cancer, 1984. Contbr. scientific papers over 200 abstracts, articles book chapters. Capt. Med. Corps. USAR, 1959—69. Mem.: Soc. Surg. Oncology, Clin. Immunology Soc., Am. Soc. Clin. Oncology, Am. Radium Soc., Am. Head Neck Soc., Am. Coll. Surgeons, Am. Fedn. Med. Rsch., Am. Assoc. Immunologists, Am. Assoc. Cancer Rsch., Am. Assoc. Advancement Sci. Achievements include assigned FDA IND 14,738 for first clin. trial of Thymosin alpa 1 (1978). Office: 10201 Grosvenor Pl Rockville MD 20852-4645

CHRÉTIEN, RAYMOND A.J. ambassador; b. Shawinigan, Que., Can., May 20, 1942; s. Maurice and Cécile (Marcotte) C.; m. Kay Rousseau; children: Caroline, Louis-François. BA, Sém. de Joliette, 1962; LLL, U. Laval, 1965. Bar: Que. 1966. Mem. legal affairs div. Dir. External Affairs Govt. of Can., 1966-67, policy dir. industry, investments and competition, asst. undersec. mfg., tech. and transp., insp. gen., assoc. undersec. state for external affairs, 1988-91, 3rd sec. permanent mission to UN, 1967-68, asst. sec. fed. and provincial rels. com. Privy Coun. Office, 1968-70, exec. asst. to sec., mem. treasury bd. Privy Coun. Office, 1970-71; exec. asst. to pres. Can. Internat. Devel. Agy., 1971-72; 1st sec. Can. Embassy, Beirut, 1972-75, 1st sec., counsellor Paris, 1975-78; Can. amb. to Zaïre, 1978-81; Can. amb. to Mexico, 1985-88; Can. amb. to Belgium and Luxembourg, 1991-94; Can. amb. to U.S. Washington, 1994—2000. Awarded Order of Aztec Eagle, Mex. Office: Canadian Embassy 501 Pennsylvania Ave NW Washington DC 20001-2111

CHRISANT, ROSEMARIE KATHRYN, law library administrator; b. Chgo., Oct. 9, 1946; d. Theodore and Angeline Frances (Pawlik) Layne; 1 child, Paula Ellen Marie. BS in Edn., No. Ill. U., 1967; MLS, Rosary Coll., 1971. High sch. English tchr. Chgo. Sch. System, 1967-70; asst. libr. Akron (Ohio) Law Libr. Assn., 1971-76, libr. dir., 1976—. Cons. law firms, Akron. Contbr. articles to profl. jours. Mem. ABA, Am. Assn. Law Librs., Ohio Regional Assn. Law Librs. (Outstanding Svc. award 1986), Spl. Libr. Assn., Ohio Libr. Assn. Office: Akron Law Libr Assn Summit County Courthouse 209 S High St Rm 4 Akron OH 44308-1625 E-mail: allarkc@akronlawlib.org.

CHRISANTHOPOULOS, PETER, advertising executive; b. N.Y.C. s. George and Marika Chrisanthopoulos. BBA, Baruch Coll., 1978; MBA, Fordham U., 1982. Media planner, broadcast account exec. Ogilvy & Mather, N.Y.C., 1978—82; broadcast supr. primetime Young & Rubicam, N.Y.C., 1983—84; sr. v.p., dir. broadcast Ohlmeyer Comms., N.Y.C., 1984—86; pres., COO RJR Nabisco Broadcast, N.Y.C., 1986—90; pres., CEO Network TV Assn., 1990—93; exec. v.p. rsch, mktg. and promotion ABC-TV Network Group, 1993—96; pres. broadcast and programming USA Ogilvy & Mather Advt., 1996—2000; pres., COO Sales and Mktg., Pappas Telecasting Cos., 2000—. Office: Pappas Telecasting 75 E 55th St New York NY 10022

CHRISMAN, BRUCE LOWELL, physicist, administrator; b. Stillwater, Okla., Mar. 16, 1943; s. Everett Lowell and Lavinia Evelyn (Roether) C.; m. Barbara JoAnn Karnuth, May 17, 1975; children: Brenden Lowell, Brady Kenneth. SB, MIT, 1964; MS, U. Ill., 1965, PhD, 1971; MBA, U. Chgo., 1975; MA (hon.), Yale U., 1983. With Fermi Nat. Accelerator Lab., Batavia, Ill., 1970-88, physicist, 1970-75, exec. asst., 1975-79, bus. mgr., 1979-83, assoc. dir. adminstrn., 1984-88, 91—; v.p. adminstrn. Yale U., New Haven, 1983-84; assoc. dir. adminstrn. Superconducting Super Collider, Dallas, 1988-89; dir. adminstrn. Wildman, Harrold, Allan & Dixon, Chgo., 1989-91. Bd. dirs. Sch. Dist. 41, Glen Ellyn, Ill., 1986-95; bd. overseers Ill. Inst. Tech. Rice Campus, 1997—. Mem. Sigma Xi (pres. 1981-83). Home: 701 Forest Ave Glen Ellyn IL 60137-3905 Office: Fermi Nat Accelerator Lab PO Box 500 Batavia IL 60510-0500 E-mail: chrisman@fnal.gov.

CHRISMAN, JAMES JOSEPH, management educator; b. Kansas City, Mo., Oct. 11, 1954; s. James John and Mildred Fay (Nelson) C.; m. Karen Waller, June 11, 1991. AA, Ill. Cen. Coll., 1977; BB, Western Ill. U., 1980; MBA, Bradley U., 1982; PhD, U. Ga., 1986. Machinst WABCO, Peoria, Ill., 1974-78; asst. prof. U. S.C., Columbia, 1986-91; assoc. prof. La. State U., 1991-93; prof. U. Calgary, Canada, 1993—2002, co-dir. venture devel. program, 1996, assoc. dean rsch. and PhD program, 1996-2001, endowed prof. family bus. entrepreneurship, 1999—2002, dir. Ctr. Family Bus. Mgmt. and Entrepreneurship, 1999—2002; prof. Miss. State U., Starkville, 2002—. Cons. UN Devel. Program, 1989-90, Internat. Civil Aviation Orgn., 1990, La. Lottery Corp., 1992, Assn. Small Bus. Devel. Ctrs., 1993—. Editor (assoc.): Case Rsch. Jour., 1984—87; mem. editl. bd.:, 1988—94; editor (case collection): McGraw Hill; editor: (assoc.) Strategic Planning Mgmt., 1987—88; editor: (advt. and circulation) Am. Jour. Small Bus., 1986—88; editor: (promotions) Entrpreneurship Theory and Practice, 1989; mem. editl. bd.:, 1990—94; editor, 1994—98, 2003; guest editor Jour. Bus. Venturing, 1993—, mem. editl. bd. Jour. Small Bus. Mgmt., 1986—87, Jour. Bus. Strategies, 1993—96, Acad. Mgmt. Jour., 1994—96, Jour. Mgmt., 1995—96, Family Bus. Rev., 1999—, ad hoc reviewer Jour. Mgmt. Studies, —, and many other jours., —; guest editor: Jour. Small Bus. Mgmt., 2003—; contbr. articles to profl. jours. Fellow, The Ctr. for Innovative Studies, 2002—. Fellow U.S. Assn. Small Bus. and Entrepreneurship (competitive papers chmn. 1988, v.p. corp. entrepreneurship 1989, bd. dirs. 1989-93, program chmn. 1991, v.p. rsch. 1992, pres. elect 1993, hon. pres. 1994); mem. N.Am. Case Rsch. Assn. (v.p. publs. 1987, proc. editor 1987, v.p. membership 1988-89, bd. dirs. 1987-89), Internat. Coun. Small Bus. (competitive papers chmn. 1988, v.p. programs 1989, dep. program chmn. 1990, bd. dirs. 1999-2001), Ea. Casewriters Assn. (bd. dirs. 1990), Acad. Mgmt. (exec. com. Entrepreneurship div. 1991-92). Republican. Roman Catholic. Avocations: collecting first edition books, chess, lacrosse, darts, bowling. Home: 1121 Edinburgh Dr Starkville MS 39759 Office: Miss State Univ Coll Bus and Industry Mississippi State MS 39762-9581 Business E-Mail: jchrisman@cobilan.msstate.edu.

CHRISMAN, WILLIAM HERRING, property tax consultant; b. Evanston, Ill., June 28, 1932; s. Roswell Herring and Virginia Ruth (Haynes) C.; m. Margaret Baker Craig, Apr. 17, 1989; children: Katherine Anne, Emily Louise. AB, Harvard U., 1955. Media buyer Leo Burnett Co., Chgo., 1958-60; account exec. Lennen & Newell Inc., N.Y.C., 1960-63; subsidiary pres. Clairol Inc., N.Y.C., 1963-72; exec. v.p. Metalware Corp., Chandler, Ariz., 1973-75; pres. Chrisman Farms, Inc., Scottsdale, Ariz., 1975-80, E. Allen Mgmt. Corp., Phoenix, 1980-85; gen. mgr. Oasis Family Water Park, Phoenix, 1985; asset mgr. Evans Withycombe Inc., Phoenix, 1985-87; prin. Real Estate Valuation Cons., Phoenix, 1987—2002; ret., 2002—. Advt. instr. Katherine Gibbs Sch., N.Y.C., 1963-65. 1st lt. U.S. Army, 1955-57. Mem. Christmas Cove Improvement Assn., Spa at Camelback Inn. Democrat. Methodist. Home: 6235 E Catesby Rd Paradise Valley AZ 85253-3583

CHRISMER, RONALD MICHAEL, federal agency administrator; b. Washington, May 4, 1954; s. Michael Joseph and Phyllis Ann (Long) C.; m. Dorothea May Shifflett, Sept. 20, 1986; 1 child, Jeffrey Ronald. BS magna cum laude, Towson State U., 1976; M in Gen. Adminstrn. and MIS, U. Md., 1987. Cert. purchasing mgr. Sr. proofreader Am. Assn. Life Ins., Washington, 1976-77; asst. supr. Coopers & Lybrand, CPAs, Washington, 1978-83, supr., 1983-85; purchasing mgr. APA, Washington, 1985-87; buyer U. Md., Balt., 1988; contract specialist IRS, Washington, 1988-98, contracting officer, 1994—, supr. contract adminstr., 1998—. Mem. telecom. adv. coun. Bell Atlantic, Washington, 1983-85. Block capt. Neighborhood Watch, Cardinal Forest Devel., 1987—; mem. World Affairs Coun., Washington, 1983-85, Nat. Trust for Hist. Preservation, Washington, 1983-85; asst. den leader Cub pack Boy Scouts Am., 1996-98, scoutmaster Boy Scouts troop, 1998—, Order of the Arrow, 2000—; mem. sch. bd. St. Mary's Sch., Laurel, Md., 1990-96, chmn., 1992-93, mem. parish coun., 1991-92; min. Children's Liturgy, St. Mary's, 1993-2000; coach Cath. Youth Orgn., 1994-2000; coach Laurel Boys and Girls Club, 2001. Mem. KC (mem. Patuxent coun. 1996—, bd. dirs. club #2203 1996-99, sec. 1997-99), Nat. Assn. Purchasing Mgmt., Purchasing Mgmt. Assn. Md. (chmn. edn. com. 1988), Purchasing Mgmt. Assn. Washington, Inst. for Supply Mgmt., Inc. (lifetime cert. 2003), Nat. Honor Soc., Psi Chi. Roman Catholic. Avocations: U.S. Civil War history, world history, music, art, literature. Home: 8810 Cardinal Ct Laurel MD 20723-1241

CHRISOHOIDES, ANTONIS, civil engineer, researcher; b. Thessaloniki, Greece, 1968; s. Michael and Alkmini C.. B, Aristotle U. Thessaloniki (Greece); M, postgraduate, Ga. Inst. Tech., Atlanta. Profl. engr., Ga., 2002, Greece, 1992. Hydrologist Moreland-Altobelli Assocs., Inc., Norcross, Ga. Contbr. articles. Scholar Erasmus scholar, European Union, 1990. Mem.: SIAM, ASME, APS, ASCE, Hellenic Acad. Soc. (sec.). Achievements include development of Developed a unique technique for the detection of Lagrangian Coherent Structures on the free surface of turbulent flows; research in Research on bridge scour.

CHRISS, TIMOTHY D.A. lawyer; b. Balt., Oct. 26, 1950; s. Evan Alevizatos and Ceres (Rogokos) C.; m. Karin Elizabeth Jones, Feb. 25, 1978; children: Alexander Wilhelm Alevizatos, Caroline Elizabeth. BA, Washington and Lee U., 1972; JD, Cath. U. Am., 1976. Bar: Md. 1976, U.S. Dist. Ct. Md. 1976. Assoc. Gordon, Feinblatt, Rothman, Hoffberger & Hollander, Balt., 1976-83, ptnr., 1983—. Com. on character Ct. Appeals Md., 1991—. Bd. dirs. Citizens Planning and Housing Assn., Balt., 1978—80, Devel. Credit Fund, Inc., 1996—, Union Meml. Hosp. Found., 1996—, chmn., 2002—; bd. dirs. Union Meml. Hosp., 2003—, Greater Homewood Cmty. Corp., 1997—99; trustee Gilman Sch., 1988—92, Maryvale Prep. Sch., 1997—. Fellow: Md. Bar Found.; mem.: ABA, Bar Assn. Balt. City (exec. coun. 1988—90), Md. Bar Assn. (coun. real property sect. 1988—2000, sec. 1992—94, chmn.-elect 1994—96, chmn. 1996—98, chmn. real property code revision com. 1988—92), Am. Coll. Real Estate Lawyers, Balt. City C. of C. (bd. dirs. 1993—2002), Md. Club, Ctr. Club, Balt. Country Club (bd. govs. 2001—). Republican. Greek Orthodox. Office: Gordon Feinblatt Rothman Hoffberger & Hollander 233 E Redwood St Baltimore MD 21202-3332 E-mail: tchriss@gfrlaw.com.

CHRISSOCHOIDIS, ILIAS, musicologist; Diploma in Piano Performance, Macedonian Conservatory, Greece, 1990, Diploma in Music Theory, 1992; MA in Musicology and Music Edn., Aristoteles U., Greece, 1992; MusM in Hist. Musicology, U. of London, 1995; MPhil, U. of Liverpool, Eng., 1996; postgrad., Stanford U., 2003. Lectr. Macedonian Conservatory, Thessaloniki, Greece, 1989—91; tchg. asst. Stanford U. Dept. of Music, Calif., 1997—. Co-founder, mem. editl. bd. Mousikotropies, Aristoteles U. Sch. of Music, Thessaloniki, Greece, 1989—91; co-dir. Grad. Musicology Forum, Stanford U. Dept. of Music, 1998—99; asst. Lully Archive, Stanford U. Dept. of Music, Calif., 1998—99; adminstrv. asst. Ron Alexander Memorial Lectures in Musicology, Stanford U. Dept. of Music, Calif., 1999—2000. Composer: (opera) The Great Decision of Pythagoras, 1992, piano concerto; author: (novel) In the Trails of the American Dream, 2002. Guest columnist The Stanford Daily, Calif., 1998—2002; organizer share internat. back cover photo exhbn. UN Assn. Film Festival, Stanford, Calif., 2001—02; organizer a spiritual perspective of the sept. 11 attacks Stanford Humanities Ctr., Calif., 2001. Recipient Excellence award, Rotary Club of Thessaloniki, Greece, 1990; fellow Undergraduate Fellowships, Greek State Scholarships Found., 1987—90, Doctoral Fellowship, Alexander S. Onassis Pub. Benefit Found., 1995—96, Vozou Fellowship, The Acad. of Athens, 1995—96, Doctoral Fellowship, Stanford U., 1996—2000, Panayotis and Effie Michelis Found., 2000—02, Geballe Fellowship, Stanford Humanities Ctr., 2001—02, Rsch. Fellowship, William Andrews Clark Meml. Libr. (UCLA), 2002—03, Lewis Walpole Libr., Yale U., 2002—03; scholar Scholarship, Greek Ministry of Edn., 1994—95. Mem.: Am. Musicological Soc., Am. Soc. of Composers, Authors and Pubs., Am. Soc. for Eighteenth-Century Studies, The Coll. Music Soc., Am. Handel Soc. Office: Dept of Music Braun Music Ctr 541 Lasuen Mall Stanford CA 94305-3076 Home: PO Box 12249 Stanford CA 94309

CHRIST, CARL FINLEY, economist, educator; b. Chgo., Sept. 19, 1923; s. Jay Finley and Maud (Trego) C.; m. Phyllis Tatsch, Mar. 16, 1951; children: Alice Trego, Joan Elizabeth, Lucy Martha. Student, Colo. Coll., 1940-42; BS in Physics, U. Chgo., 1943; PhD in Econs., 1950. Jr. physicist Manhattan Project, 1943-45; instr. physics Princeton, 1945-46; research assoc. Cowles Commn. Research Econs., 1949-50; asst. prof., assoc. prof. polit. economy Johns Hopkins, 1950-55; assoc. prof. econs. U. Chgo., 1955-61; prof. polit. economy Johns Hopkins U., 1961—, Abram G. Hutzler prof., 1977-89; chmn. dept., 1961-66, 69-70. Vis. prof. U. Tokyo, 1959; Keynes vis. prof. econs. U. Essex (Eng.), 1966-67; lectr. Kyoto (Japan) Am. Studies Summer Seminar, 1977, Brazilian Econometric Soc., 1981, Chinese U. Devel. Project, Fudan U., Shanghai, 1987; vis. scholar Bank of Japan, Tokyo, 1986; chmn. Univs.-Nat. Bur. Com. for Econs. Rsch., 1967-74; mem. Md. Gov.'s Coun. Econ. Advisers, 1969-77; bd. dirs. Nat. Bur. Econ. Rsch., 1975—, chmn., 1999-2002; mem. econ. adv. panel NSF, 1965-66, 67-68; cons. Fed. Res. Bd., 1979; mem. rsch. adv. bd. Com. Econ. Devel., 1989-91. Author: Econometrics, Macroeconomics and Economic Policy, 1996; editor: Simultaneous Equations Estimation, 1994; author: Econometrics, Macroeconomics and Economic Policy, 1996; bd. editors Am. Econ. Rev., 1969-73; adv. bd. Jour. Monetary Econs., 1983-91. Sr. Fulbright rsch. scholar U. Cambridge, Eng., 1954-55, Profl. Achievement award U. Chgo. Alumni Assn., 2001; fellow Ctr. Advanced Study Behavioral Scis., Palo Alto, Calif., 1960-61 Fellow Econometric Soc. (Council 1976-82), Am. Statis. Assn.; mem. Am. Econ. Assn. (v.p. 1980). Office: Johns Hopkins U Dept Econs Baltimore MD 21218

CHRIST, CAROL TECLA, academic administrator; b. NYC, May 21, 1944; d. John George and Tecla (Bobrick) Christ; m. Larry Sklute, Aug. 15, 1975 (div. Dec. 1983); children— Jonathan, Elizabeth BA, Douglas Coll., 1966; M.Ph., Yale U., 1969, PhD, 1970. Asst. prof. English U. Calif., Berkeley, 1970-76, assoc. prof. English, 1976-83, prof. English, 1983—, dean dept. English, 1985-88, dean dept. humanities, 1988, acting provost, dean, 1989-90, provost, dean Coll. Letters and Sci., 1990-94, vice chancellor, provost, 1994-2000; pres. Smith Coll., Northampton, Mass., 2002—. Former dir. summer seminars for secondary and coll. tchrs. NEH; former tchr. Bread Loaf Sch. of English; invited lectr. Am. Assn. Univs., Am. Coun. Edn. Author: The Finer Optic: The Aesthetic of Particularity in Victorian Poetry, 1975, Victorian and Modern Poetics, 1984; mem. editl. bd. Victorian Literature, The Victorian Visual Imagination, The Norton Anthology of English Literature; contbr. articles to profl. jours. Mem. MLA Office: Smith Coll College Hall 20 Northampton MA 01063*

CHRIST, CHRIS STEVE, lawyer; b. Canonsburg, Pa., Jan. 3, 1936; s. Michael C. and Katina (Hantzigorgis) C.; m. Lula Koutroulakis, Dec. 31, 1942; 1 child, Gina Reneè Caplan. BBA, U. Pitts., 1957; JD, Samford U., 1968. Bar: Ala., U.S. Dist. Ct. (no. dist.) Ala., U.S. Ct. Appeals (5th and 11th cirs.), U.S. Supreme Ct. Sales rep. Mennen Cos., Morris Plains, N.J., 1960-62, Boston, 1962-65, Beecham Cos., Atlanta, 1965-66; councilman City of Vestavia Hills, 1972-76; pvt. practice, Birmingham, Ala., 1968—. Pres., Jeff, Blount, St. Clair Mental Health/Mental Retardation Auth., 1981-83; bd. dirs. Kids-One-Transport, 199-2002. Served to 1st lt. USAF, 1958-60. Mem. ABA, Ala. State Bar Assn., Ala. Criminal Def. Lawyers Assn., Birmingham Bar Assn., Nat. Assn. Criminal Def. Lawyers, Ala. Trial Lawyers Assn., Comml. Law League of Am., Masons, Shriners, Scottish Rite, Summit Club, The Club, AHEPA, Phi Alpha Delta (pres. Alumni Club 1982-88). Greek Orthodox. Office: 205 20th St N Ste 923 Birmingham AL 35203-4708 E-mail: cscrst@aol.com.

CHRIST, DUANE MARLAND, computer systems engineer; b. Lakota, Iowa, Jan. 5, 1932; s. George Andrew and Esther Gertrude (Franke) C.; m. Lily Esther Shih, Sept. 14, 1963; 1 child, Wesley Anzo. BS, Iowa State U., 1953; MA, U. Minn., 1960; PhD, Rutgers U., 1998. Sci. programmer United Aircraft Corp., Hartford, Conn., 1960-63; computer sys. analyst IBM, N.Y.C., 1963-68, staff instr., 1968-76, adv. sys. engr., 1976-82, sr. sys. engr., 1982-87, prin., 1987—2003; ret., 2003. 1st lt. USAF, 1953-56. Recipient Ea. Regional Dir. award, 1983; named Area Specialist of Yr., 1986; IBM Resident Study fellow, 1966-68. Mem.: Am. Math. Soc., Soc. Indsl. and Applied Math., Assn. Computing Machinery. Home: 15 Tilton Dr Freehold NJ 07728-3359 E-mail: christdm3@aol.com.

CHRIST, EARLE L. lawyer; b. Racine, Wis., Aug. 8, 1915; s. Thomas Christ and Martha Peterson; m. Agnes Barbara Meurer, Dec. 4, 1943; children: Joellyn K. Keleske, Thomas E. LLB, JD, Marquette U., 1948. Pvt. practic, Racine. Maj. USAFR, 1942-64. Mem. Wis. State Bar Assn., Racine County Bar Assn. Republican. Roman Catholic. Avocations: camping, flying. Home (Winter): Apt 315 700 Starkey Rd Largo FL 33771-2326 Home (Summer): 1021 Prairie Dr # 204 Racine WI 53406

CHRIST, LILY ESTHER SHIH, mathematics educator; b. Korea, Sept. 19, 1936; came to U.S., 1955; d. Whan-Chang and Shin-Tze (Lin) Shih; m. Duane M. Christ, Sept. 14, 1963; 1 child, Wesley Anzo. BS, U. Minn., 1960; MA, Western Res. U., 1962; EdD, Columbia U., 1967. Tchr. Cleve. Pub. Schs., 1960-62; stats. lab. asst. Tchrs. Coll., Columbia U., N.Y.C., 1964-71; asst. prof. Coll. of Mt. St. Vincent, N.Y.C., 1966-68, John Jay Coll. Criminal Justice, CUNY, N.Y.C., 1969-73, assoc. prof., 1974—; HI-TECH PREP dir., 1993—. Fulbright-Hays Sr. scholar, 1972. Mem. Math. Assn. Am. (gov. 1990-93, Cert. of Merit Svc. 1987), Am. Statis. Assn. (dist. 2 gov. 1990-91), Nat. Coun. Tchrs. Mathematics. Office: CUNY John Jay Coll Criminal Justice 445 W 59th St New York NY 10019-1104 E-mail: christle@jjay.cuny.edu.

CHRIST, THOMAS WARREN, electronics research and development company executive, sociologist; b. New Haven, Dec. 16, 1944; s. David Lamar and Wilma Margaret (Zimmerman) C.; m. Patricia Player, Jan. 29, 1967; children: Michael Edward, Tyler Player. AB, Coll. William and Mary, 1966; MS, Cornell U., 1968, PhD, 1973. Asst. prof. sociology Coll. William and Mary, Williamsburg, Va., 1971-78; v.p. HDS, Inc., Reston, Va., 1979—95, chmn., 1985—. Contbr. articles to profl. jours. Mem. Am. Sociol. Assn. Lutheran. Office: Starkirke Tech Ptnrs 37265 Hunting Hill Ln Purcellville VA 20132-4331

CHRISTAKIS, MICHAEL N. academic administrator; b. Rochester, N.Y., Aug. 2, 1977; s. Nikolaos M. and Vasiliki Christakis. BA in Polit. Sci. & History, Alfred U., 1999; MA in Pub. Policy, PhD, SUNY, 2001—. Resident asst. Alfred U., Alfred, NY, 1996—99; asst. residence hall dir. SUNY, Albany, NY, 1999—2001, residence hall dir., 2001—02. Co-coord. first yr. programs SUNY, 2001—02, asst. dir. residential life, 2002—; intern N.Y. State Edn. Dept., Albany, 2000—01. Congl. intern N.Y. 28th Congl. Dist., Rochester, NY, 1997—98. Mem.: Internat. Ldrop. Assn., Am. Soc. of Pub. Adminstrn., Omicron Delta Kappa (v.p. cir. std. 2002—, nat. student v.p. 2000—02, Meritorious Svc. award 2000). Greek Orthodox. Office: Department of Residential Life 1400 Washington Avenue Albany NY 12222-0001 Office Fax: 518-956-6251.

CHRISTALDI, BRIAN, lawyer; b. Passaic, N.J., June 8, 1940; s. Peter Samuel and Helen (O'Brien) C.; m. Amy Edmonds, May 4, 1968; children: Kevin, Justin. BA, Amherst Coll., 1962; LLB, Harvard U., 1965. Bar: D.C. 1966, N.Y. 1967, Calif. 1988. Maxwell Pub. Svc. fellow, Papua, Guinea, 1965—66; with legal dept. Allied Chem. Corp., N.Y.C., 1967-69; assoc. then ptnr. Kelley Drye & Warren, N.Y.C., 1969-1995; counsel Kaye, Scholer, Fierman, Hays & Handler, LLP, N.Y.C., 1995-97; sr. comml. counsel, later asst. gen. counsel, then assoc. gen. counsel project fin. Overseas Pvt. Investment Corp., Washington, 1997—. Home: 4031 Oliver St Chevy Chase MD 20815-3432 Office: Overseas Pvt Investment Corp 1100 New York Ave NW Washington DC 20527-0001 E-mail: bchri@opic.gov.

CHRISTEN, ARDEN GALE, dental educator, researcher, consultant; b. Lemmon, S.D., Jan. 25, 1932; s. Harold John Christen and Dorothy Elizabeth (Taylor) Deering; m. Joan Ardell Akre, Sept. 10, 1955; children: Barbara, Penny, Rebecca, Sarah. BS, U. Minn., 1954, DDS, 1956; MSD, Ind. U., 1965; MA, Ball State U., 1973. Lic. dentist, Ind. Commd. 1st lt. USAF, 1956, advanced through grades to col., 1972; base dental surgeon Zaragoza Air Base, Spain, 1970-73; dental surgeon, cons. preventive dentistry RAF Bentwaters, Eng., 1973-75; air force preventive dentistry officer Sch. Aerospace Medicine, Brooks AFB, Tex., 1978-80; prof., chmn. dept. preventive dentistry Ind. U., Indpls., 1981-93, dir. preventive/cmty. dentistry, 1993-2000, co-dir. nicotine dependence program, 1997—, acting chair oral biology, 2000—. Sr. med. svc. cons. Surgeon Gen., U.S. Air Force, U.S. and Eng., 1974-80; spl. cons. to asst. surgeon gen. for dental svcs., Washington, 1975-80. Co-author: Primary Preventive Dentistry, 4th edit., 1995; contbr. over 250 articles to profl. jours. Bd. dirs. Bexar County chpt. Am. Cancer Soc., San Antonio, 1976-80, Marion County chpt., Indpls., 1980—; mem. Ind. divsn. Pub. Edn. Standing Com., Indpls., 1980. Decorated Service medal with 2 oak leaf clusters, Legion of Merit. Fellow Am. Coll. Dentists; mem. ADA, Am. Acad. Oral Pathology, Internat. Assn. Dental Rsch., Am. Acad. History of Dentistry (v.p. 1984-85, pres. 1986-87). Presbyterian. Avocations: photography, classical music, travel, writing. Home: 7112 Sylvan Ridge Rd Indianapolis IN 46240-3541 Office: Ind U Sch Dentistry 1121 W Michigan St Indianapolis IN 46202-5186 E-mail: achriste@iupui.edu.

CHRISTENBURY, LEILA, education educator; BA English, Hollins Coll., 1972; MA English, U. Va., 1973; EdD English Edn., Va. Tech., 1980. Tchr. English Roanoke Cath. High Sch., Va., 1973—75, William Fleming High Sch., 1975—78; asst. prof. dept. English lang. and lit. U. No. Iowa, Cedar Falls, 1979—80; asst. prof. English dept. James Madison U., Harrisonburg, Va., 1982—86; asst. prof., assoc. prof. Sch. Edn. Va. Commonwealth U., Richmond, 1968—95, prof. Sch. Edn., 1996—. Contbr. articles to profl. jours. Scholar, Va. Commonwealth U. Sch. Edn., 1993. Mem.: Va. Writers' Club, Va. Conf. English Educators, Va. Assn. Tchrs. English (treas., Frances Wimer award 2001), Assembly Women in Lit., Assembly Appalachian Lit., Assembly Lit. Adolescents, Nat. Conf. Rsch. Lang. and Lit., Nat. Coun. Tchrs. English (pres., Rewey Belle Inglis award Outstanding Women in English Edn. 1997), Omicron Delta Kappa, Phi Beta Kappa, Phi Kappa Phi, Phi Delta Kappa. Office: Va Commonwealth U Sch Edn PO Box 842020 Richmond VA 23284-2020

CHRISTENBURY, TIMOTHY LLOYD, music educator; b. Charlotte, NC, Nov. 8, 1963; MusM Edn., Furman U., 1993. Cert. tchr. Ga. Choral dir. Evans County Schs., Atlanta, 1990—. Edn. cons. Portmans Music Superstore, Savannah, Ga., 1991—99. Dir.: (stage musical ensembles), 1989 (Musical Dir. of the Yr., SC, 1988). Candidate asst. Rep. Conv., Savannah, 1993—2002. Recipient Tchr. of the Yr., Jasper County Sch. Dist., 1991. Mem.: Ga. Music Edn. Assn., Music Educators Nat. Conf. Republican. Avocation: marathon bicycling. Personal E-mail: videoservice@g-net.net.

CHRISTENSEN, A(LBERT) KENT, anatomy educator; b. Washington, Dec. 3, 1927; s. Albert Sherman and Lois (Bowen) C.; m. Elizabeth Anne Reynolds Sears, Aug. 26, 1952; children: Anne, Kathleen Martha, Albert David, Jennifer, John Sears. AB, Brigham Young U., 1953; PhD, Harvard U., 1958. Postdoctoral fellow Cornell Med. Coll., 1958-59, Harvard Med. Sch., Boston, 1959-60, instr. dept. anatomy, 1960-61; asst. prof. dept. anatomy Stanford Sch. Medicine, Palo Alto, Calif., 1961-68, assoc. prof., 1968-71; prof., chmn. dept. anatomy Temple U. Sch. Medicine, Phila., 1971-78; prof. anatomy and cell biology U. Mich. Med. Sch., Ann Arbor, 1978-99, chmn. dept. anatomy and cell biology, 1978-82, prof. emeritus, 1999—. Contbr. articles to profl. jours. With USMC, 1946-47. Mem. AAAS, Am. Soc. Cell Biology, Am. Assn. Anatomists (pres. 1984-85), Microscopy Soc. Am. Office: U Mich Med Sch Dept Cell & Devel Biology Med Sci II Bldg Ann Arbor MI 48109-0616 E-mail: akc@mich.edu.

CHRISTENSEN, ALLAN ROBERT, electrical engineer, enrolled agent; b. Newton, Kans., Jan. 5, 1953; s. John Clyde and Margaret Ann (Christensen) Simpson. BSEE cum laude, Wichita (Kans.) State U., 1976; MSEE, So. Meth. U., University Park, Tex., 1981. Registered profl. engr., Tex.; enrolled agt. lic. by U.S. Treasury; accredited tax preparer, accredited tax advisor, by Accreditation Coun. for Accountancy and Taxation, 1996—; notary public, Tex.; cert. emergency care attendant, 1995—; lic. Tex. Dept. Health; chartered mutual fund counselor, accredited asset mgmt. specialist Investment Co. Inst. and Nat. Endowment for Fin. Edn. Draftsman, civil engring. asst. Wichita State U. State Architect's Office, 1971-72; chem. lab. asst. Wichita State U., 1973; clk. U.S. Postal Svc., Wichita, 1976; electrical engr., magnetic modulator, defense systems and elec. group, spl. guidance program, harpoon and tomahawk antiship missile projects Tex. Instruments, Inc., Dallas, 1977-96, elec. engr. magnetic modulator, switchmode power supply, radar signal processing, automatic test equipment design, 1977-96, spl. program divsn., 1996-97, jr. engr., 1977-79, engr., 1979-87, lead engr., 1987—, with spl. projects dept., 1996-97; digital design engr. with spl. equipment/projects Raytheon Systems Company, 1997-99; digital design engr. spl. projects divsn. Raytheon TI Sys., Dallas, 1998-99, sr. design engr., level 1, digital and interconnect design, 1998-99; emergency care attendant, 1995—; lead engr. spl. projects divsn. Raytheon TI Sys., Dallas, 1997-98, digital design engr. spl. projects divsn., 1998-99; sr. test engr. divsn. Kone Elevators and Escalators Montgomery Kone, Inc., McKinney, Tex., 2000—. Co-facilitator semiconductor focus group Tex. Instruments Def. Systems Electronics Group, Dallas, 1993-94; ind. contbr. sr. des. engr. adv. Analog Components QIT, Dallas, 1993-94, core mem. Engring. Sys. Divsn. PWB Adv. Team, 1994-96; core mem. engring. sys. divsn. PWB Adv. Team, 1994-96; cons. engr. to the Nat. Coun. Examiners for Engring. and Surveying, 1996. Inventor in field; cons. engr. and published elec. engring. exam. problem author, 1997 Elec. Engring. Profl. Engrs. Exam, Nat. Coun. Examiners for Engring. and Surveying; pub. reports in field. Instr., cook Mormon Relief Soc., Rockwall, Tex., 1986; Christmas program com. Tex. Instruments for Hope Cottage, Dallas, 1988—89; vol. tax preparer IRS, Mesquite, Tex., 1990; fundraiser United Way, Dallas, 1990; ct. apptd. spl. advocate Dallas CASA, 305th Dist. Ct., 1995—97; bd. dirs. Cmty Restoration Svcs., Inc., Dallas, 1998—2000; sponsor, vol. Kans. State Math. Tchrs. Conf., 1970; vol., fundraiser March-of-Dimes, 1972; coord. Arnold Air Soc. Gift; active blood donor dr. Wichita State U., 1971—73; plant-a-tree coord. Arnold Air Soc., 1972; vol. Cook Dept. HHS, Tex., 1983. Grantee in field, 1992-94; Am. Citizenship scholar, 1970, State of Kans. Hon. scholar, Kans. Engring. Soc. Hungerford Meml. scholar, Martin K. Eby scholar, Western Electric scholar, Ahrens scholar, Nat. Elec. Contractors scholar, Walter H. Beech scholar, 1971; recipient Regional art Competition winner State of Kans., 1968, 1st place award Indsl. Arts Fair, Friends U., 1971, Outstanding Elec. Engring. Project award IEEE, 1976, Site Selection Blue Ribbon, Site Mgmt. and People's Choice award Tex. Instruments for Hope Cottage, 1989, Vol. and Edn. programs award IRS, 1990, Stretch award Tex. Instruments Def. Systems and Electronics Group, 1995, 96, continuing edn. cert. of achievement Tex. Bd. Registration for Profl. Engrs., 1996, 97, 98, 99, 2000, People Assets and Effectiveness award Systems Group, 1990, "Take-a-Shot" award Tex. Instruments, 1996, Group award, Dallas Ct. Appointed Spl. Advs., JC Penney Golden Rule award, 1996. Mem. NSPE, Nat. Assn. Tax Practitioners (Achievers Club 1992, 93, 94, 95, 96, 97, 99, Sunsetted Silver medal 1998, 99, Sunsetted Gold medal 2000), Tex. Soc. Profl. Engrs. (Cmty. Restoration Svcs. summer enrichment program award 1999), Internat. High IQ Soc., Mensa, Eta Kappa Nu, Tau Beta Pi. Republican. Achievements include rsch. in cross-talk characteristics of various laminates (FR-4 fiberglass, polyimides, tetraIld) in mixed analog/digital design; designed and executed Taguchi and statistical process control experiments with manufacturing and test processes. Home: 2629 Emberwood Dr Garland TX 75043-6047 *There are no extraordinary men, there are only ordinary men accomplishing extraordinary deeds.*

CHRISTENSEN, BRUCE LEROY, former academic administrator, commercial broadcasting executive; b. Ogden, Utah, Apr. 26, 1943; s. LeRoy and Wilma (Olsen) C.; m. Barbara Lucelle Decker, June 17, 1965; children— Jennifer, Heather, Holly, Jesse BA cum laude, U. Utah, 1968; MS, Northwestern U., 1969. Radio and TV news reporter KSL, Inc., Salt Lake City, 1965-68, state house corr., 1969-70; weekend sports writer WGN Radio and TV News, 1968-69; instr. U. Utah, 1969-70, adj. assoc. prof. broadcast regulation, 1980-81, gen. mgr. Sta. KUED-TV and KUER-FM, 1979-82, dir. media svcs., 1981-82; asst. to dir. univ. rels. Brigham Young U., 1970-72, asst. prof., 1971-79, dir. dept. broadcast svcs., 1972-79; pres. Nat. Assn. Pub. TV Stas., Washington, 1982-84; pres., chief exec. officer PBS, Washington, 1984-93; dean Coll. Fine Arts and Comm., prof. comm. Brigham Young Univ., Provo, 1993-2000; sr. v.p. New Media Bonneville Internat., Salt Lake City, 2000—. Bd. govs. Pacific Mt. Network, 1979-82, chmn., 1978-80; vice chmn. (USA) Internat. Coun. Nat. Acad. Arts and Scis., 1990-91, pres. Internat. Coun. NATAS, 1992-93; pres. Prix Italia, 1993; producer, writer Channel 5 Eye-Witness News, 1967-68; bd. dirs. Bonneville Internat. Corp., Fund for Ancient and Mormon Studies, Lance Armstrong Found. for Cancer Rsch. Exec. producer numerous TV documentaries including The Great Dinosaur Discovery, 1973, A Time to Dance, 1976, Navajo, 1976, Christmas Snows, Christmas Winds, 1978 (Emmy award 1978). Bd. dirs. Utah Lung Assn., 1976-82, pres., 1978-80 Recipient Disting. Alumnus award U. Utah, 1989; Allen-Heath fellow Medill Sch. Journalism Northwestern U., 1969; recipient Ralph Lowell medal Corp. for Pub. Broadcasting, 1994. Fellow Internat. Coun. NATAS; mem. Rocky Mountain Corp. for Pub. Broadcasting (bd. dirs.), Sigma Delta Chi (pres. U. Utah chpt. 1967-68), Kappa Tau, Phi Kappa Phi. Avocation: photography. Office: Bonnieville Internat PO Box 1160 Salt Lake City UT 84110-1160

CHRISTENSEN, C. LEWIS, real estate developer; b. Laramie, Wyo., June 3, 1936; s. Raymond H. and Elizabeth C. (Cady) C.; m. Sandra Stadheim, June 11, 1960; children: Kim, Brett. BS in Indsl. Engring., U. Wyo., 1959. Mgmt. trainee Gen. Mills, Chgo., 1959, Mountain Bell, Helena, Mont., 1962-63, data comms. mgr. Phoenix, 1964-66, dist. mktg. mgr., so. Colo., 1970-73; seminar leader AT&T Co., Chgo., 1966-68, mktg. supr. N.Y.C., 1968-70; land planner and developer Village Assocs., Colorado Springs, Colo., 1973, exec. v.p., 1975-77; v.p. Cimarron Corp., Colorado Springs, 1974-75; pres. Lew Christensen & Assocs., Inc. Ptnr., gen. mgr. Briargate Joint Venture, 1977-82; pres. Vintage Comtys., Inc., 1982-93. Bd. dirs. Pikes Peak coun. Boy Scouts Am., Citizens Goals, Colo. Coun. on Econ. Edn., Cheyenne Mountain Zoo, U. Wyo. Found., engring. adv. bd.; chmn. Colorado Springs Econ. Devel. Coun., 1978, 89; bd. dirs., chmn. bd. Penrose St. Francis Hosp., chmn. 1999-2001. Served with USAF, 1959-62. Mem. Colorado Springs Home Builders Assn. (bd. dirs.), Urban Land Inst., Colorado Springs C. of C. (bd. dirs., chmn. bd.), Colorado Springs Country Club (bd. dirs.), Garden of Gods Club. Republican. Presbyterian. Achievements include development of 1,000-acre Peregrine planned community, south of USAF Academy; the 7,000 acre planned community of Briargate, just east of the USAF Academy. Office: Lew Christensen & Assocs Inc 2520 Stagsleap Pt Colorado Springs CO 80904-1192

CHRISTENSEN, CAROLINE "CONNIE", vocational educator; b. Lehi, Utah, Oct. 5, 1936; d. Byam Heber and Ruth (Gardner) Curtis; m. Marvin Christensen, June 16, 1961; children: Ronald, Roger, Robert, Corlyn, Richard, Chad. BS, Brigham Young U., 1958, MS, 1964. Sec. student body orgn. Brigham Young U., Provo, Utah, 1956—58; instr. bus. Richfield (Utah) H.S., 1958—61, Sevier Valley Applied Tech. Ctr., Richfield, 1970-92, dept. chairperson, 1988-92. Historian, Sevier Sch. Dist. PTA, 1968, 69; chmn. Heart Fund Dist., 1983; chair Rep. Voting Dist., 1988-90; dist. chmn. Am. Cancer Drive, 1994-95, 98, regional chairperson, 2000; guide Hist. Cove Fort, Utah, 1996-98, election judge, Richfield City, 1998. Mem.: NEA, Profl. Bus. Leaders, Sevier Valley Tech. Tchrs. Assn. (sec. 1971—86, pres. 1986—87, adv. com. chair 1997—), We. Bus. Edn. Assn., Utah Bus. Edn. Assn. (sec. 1986—87), Nat.Bus. Edn., Utah Vocat. Assn., Am. Vocat. Assn., Utah Edn. Assn., Delta Kappa Gamma (treas. 1975—90, pres. 1990—92, state nominating com. 1993—97, chmn. 1995—97, historian 2002—, Chi chpt., chmn. state convention 1992, 1998, State Achievement award 2001), Delta Pi Epsilon (historian).

CHRISTENSEN, CHARLES BROPHY, lawyer; b. Altadena, Calif., July 3, 1948; s. Charles Warren and Barbara Louise C.; m. Susan Marie Stricklin, Aug. 22, 1970; children: Charles Brophy, Michelle K., Courtney Marie, Timothy Patrick. BA in Biology, Claremont Men's Coll., Calif., 1970; JD, U. San Diego, 1973. Bar: Calif. 1973, U.S. Dist. Ct. (so. dist.) Calif. 1973, U.S. Dist. Ct. (cen. dist.) Calif. 1994, U.S. Ct. Appeals (9th cir.) 1995, U.S. Supreme Ct. 1997. Assoc. Biafora & Weiner, Reseda, Calif., 1974-76; ptnr. Biafora, Weiner & Christensen, Reseda, 1977-78; gen. counsel Charles W. Christensen & Assocs., San Diego, 1978-90; ptnr. Detisch, Christensen & Wood, San Diego, 1983-95, Detisch & Christensen, San Diego, 1995—2002; mng. ptnr. Christensen Schwerdtfeger & Spath LLP, San Diego, 2002—. Mem. ABA, San Diego County Bar Assn. Republican. Roman Catholic. Avocations: golf, tennis. Home: 2684 Jonquil Dr San Diego CA 92106-1135 Office: Christensen Schwerdtfeger & Spath LLP 444 W C St Ste 200 San Diego CA 92101-3582 E-mail: cbc@csslawllp.com.

CHRISTENSEN, DAVID ALLEN, manufacturing company executive; b. 1935; BS, S.D. State U., 1957. With John Morrell & Co., 1960-62, Raven Industries Inc., Sioux Falls, S.D., 1962—, product mgr., 1964-71, pres., chief exec. officer, 1971-2000; ret., 2000. Served with AUS, 1957-60. Office: Raven Industries Inc PO Box 5107 Sioux Falls SD 57117-5107

CHRISTENSEN, DAVID WILLIAM, mathematician, engineer; b. San Francisco, Jan. 19, 1937; s. Christopher Drost and Wilma (Hallowell) C.; m. Felicity Ann Bush, Nov. 2, 1963; children: Karen Anne, Paul Thomas. Student, MIT, 1954-58; BA, BS in Math., U. Calif., Santa Barbara, 1960; MIM in Internat. Mgmt. with honors, Am. Grad. Sch., Glendale, Ariz., 1973. Registered profl. engr., Calif. Project engr. North Am. Rockwell, Anaheim, Calif., 1963-70, Litton Ingalls Ships, Pascagoula, Miss., 1970-73; coord. of fin. Sonatrach Oil Co., Algiers, Algeria, 1975-78; revenue cons. Saudi Arabian Bechtel, Jubail, Saudi Arabia, 1978-80; sr. planner Arabian Am. Oil Co., Dhahran, Saudi Arabia, 1980-86; strategic planning and project controls Bechtel Power Corp., San Francisco, 1987—. Mem. (from Jubail) Saudi Royal Commn. Com. on Indsl. Devel., Riyadh, Saudi Arabia, 1978-80; lectr. U. Calif., Santa Barbara, 1964, citizens adv. group, subcom. Savannah River Site, S.C.; cons. DOE, U.S. Congress on tritium and plutonium projects. Contbr. articles to profl. publs. Mem. Charcot-Marie-Toothe Assn., Balt., 1987—, Gertrude Herbert Art Inst., Augusta, Ga., 1990—, Jr. C. of C., Santa Barbara, Calif., 1960-64. Recipient Boit prize, 1957. Mem. NSPE (power group 1990), Soc. Am. Mil. Engrs. Republican. Episcopalian. Achievements include development with others of hydrocarbon and industrial resources in the Middle East (Algeria, Egypt, Saudi Arabia). Office: ETA-Z Inc 3408 Heather Dr Augusta GA 30909-2795

CHRISTENSEN, DAWN MICHELLE, family practice nurse practitioner, consultant; b. Coatesville, Pa., June 28, 1970; d. John Richard Lebid; m. Scott Evan Christensen, Jan. 6, 1996; 1 child, Nicholas Scott. BSN, Temple U., Phila., 1992; MS, Pa. State U., 1997. Family Nurse Practitioner, Am. Nurses Credentialing Ctr., 1998, Acute Care Nurse Practitioner, Ancc, Pa., 1999. Staff nurse Pa. State Milton S. Hershey Med. Ctr., 1992—97, nurse practitioner, 1997—99, circulatory support coord., nurse practitioner, 1997—; adj. faculty Pa. State U., Harrisburg, 2000—. Clin. cons. Thoratec Corp., Pleasanton, Calif., 1999—2002. Mem.: Pa. Nurses Soc. Dist. 15 (v.p. 1999), Am. Soc. Artificial Internal Organs, Internat. Soc. Heart and Lung Transplant, Am. Assn. of Critical Care Nurses. Home: 66 Cardinal Rd Pine Grove PA 17963 Office: Pa State Milton S Hershey Med Ctr 500 University Dr Hershey PA 17933

CHRISTENSEN, DENISE DANYEL, real estate broker; b. Portland, Oreg., Dec. 29, 1952; d. Robert Wayne and Patricia Ann C.; m. Joseph Patrick Cronin, Jan. 11, 1969 (div. 1983); 1 child, Bobbi Jo Cronin. Student, Ctrl. Oreg. C.C., Bend, 1978-79, Ea. Oreg. Coll., 1988, Treasure Valley Coll., 1988—. Notary, Oreg. Tchrs. aide Filmore Grade Sch., Burns, Oreg., 1976-77; bookkeeper Blackburn Real Estate, Burns, 1977-79; real estate sales Burns, 1979—; office mgr. Burns-Hines Cable, Burns, 1982-85; real estate broker Denise Christensen Real Estate, Burns, 1983—. Mayor City of Burns, 1979-80, city coun., 1977-79; chair fundraising Am. Cancer Soc., 1980-91; precinct com. mem. Rep. Ctrl. Com., Burns., 1996-2002.; mem. City of Burns planning commn., 1991-2001. Recipient Profl. Excellence award Ctrl. Oreg. Realtors, 1993, 94. Mem. Realtors, Harney County C. of C., Burns Rotary, Lions Club, Beta Sigma Phi (Order of Rose 1999). Republican. Lutheran. Avocations: write, paint, garden, raise livestock, travel. Home: 615 S Juntura Burns OR 97720 Office: Real Estate 615 S Juntura Burns OR 97720

CHRISTENSEN, DIETER, ethnomusicologist; b. Berlin, Apr. 17, 1932; PhD, Free U., Berlin, 1957. Curator, dir. Berlin Phonogramm Archiv, 1958-72; prof. Columbia U., N.Y.C., 1970—, dir. Ctr. for Ethnomusicology, 1971—2003; lectr. Free U., Berlin, 1962-70. Vis. prof. Hunter Coll.-CUNY, N.Y.C., NY, 1978—80, U. Hamburg, Germany, 1977; sec. gen. Internat. Coun. for Traditional Music, UNESCO, 1981—2001; dir. The Universe of Music-A History, UNESCO, 1985—93. Author: Die Musik der Kate, 1957, Die Musik der Ellice-Inseln, 1964; co-author: El Anillo del Tlalocan, 1975, 1990, Dictionary of Traditional Music in Oman, 1994; editor: Yearbook for Traditional Music, 1981—2001, (compact disc) UNESCO Collection of Traditional Music, 1995—2000. Office: Columbia U Music Dept MC 1815 New York NY 10027 E-mail: dc22@columbia.edu.

CHRISTENSEN, DONN WAYNE, insurance executive; b. Atlantic City, Apr. 9, 1941; s. Donald Frazier and Dorothy (Ewing) Christensen; m. Marshella Abraham, Jan. 26, 1963 (div.); children: Donn Wayne, Lisa Shawn; m. Mei Ling Fill, June 18, 1976 (div.); m. Susan Kim, Feb. 14, 1987 (div.); m. Christina Yee, Dec. 2, 2000. BS, U. Santa Clara, 1964. West coast divsn. mgr. Ford Motor Co., 1964-65; agt. Conn. Mut. Life Ins. Co., 1965-68; pres. Christensen & Jones Inc., L.A., 1968—99; v.p. Rsch. Devel. Systems. Inc. Pres. Northern B.C. Enterprises Ltd., Misty Meadows Ranch Ltd., B.C., Can.; registered investment advisor, SEC. Pres. Duarte Cmty. Drug Abuse Coun., 1972-75; pres. Woodlyn Property Owners Assn., 1972-73; mem. L'Ermitage Found., 1985-90, Instl. Rev. Bd. White meml. Hosp., L.A., 1975-2000, Friend's Med. Rsch., 1992-2000; bd. dirs. Moberly Lake Cmty. Assn., 2002--; pres. Bd. of Moberly Lake Fire Dept., 2002--. Recipient Man of Yr. award L.A. Gen. Agts. and Mgrs. Assn. Mem. Nat. Life Underwriters Assn., Calif. State Life Underwriters Assn., Investment Co. Inst. (assoc.), Soc. Pension Actuaries, Foothill Cmty. Concert Assn. (pres. 1970-73). Office: 23801 Calabasas Rd Calabasas CA 91302

CHRISTENSEN, DONNA RADOVICH, needlecraft designer, consultant, educator; b. Midvale, Utah, Sept. 16, 1925; d. Daniel and Clara Ellen (Turley) Radovich; B.A., U. Utah, 1947; M.A. Columbia U., 1951; m. John Whittaker Christensen, Feb. 2, 1952; children: Carlyn M. Christensen Szalanski, John Chipman, Craig Whittaker. Tchr. and guidance counselor Jordan High Sch., Sandy, Utah, 1947-50; sec. Placement Bur. of Columbia U. Tchr.'s Coll., N.Y.C., 1950-51; free-lance designer of needlecrafts, 1970—; tchr. of needlecraft, 1965—; tchr. 18th Century painted finishes Isabel O'Neil Found. for Art of Painted Finish, N.Y.C., 1975-77; cons. in crafts, 1965—. V.p. Silvermine Guild of Artists, 1965-68, hospitality chmn., 1958-65. Recipient Service award Silvermine Guild, 1963, Journeyman's medallion O'Neil Studio, 1974. Mem. Embroider's Guild of Am., Needle and Bobbin Club (v.p. 1977-82, pres. 1982-89, bd. dirs. 1989-91), New Canaan Sewing Group (exec. bd. 1977-81), Phi Kappa Phi, Pi Lambda Theta, Kappa Delta Pi. Mormon. Club: New Canaan Garden (exec. bd. 1972-77, v.p. 1987-89, pres. 1989-91), Federated Garden of Conn. Inc. (asst. civic devel. chmn. 1991-93). Home: 788 Ponus Rdg New Canaan CT 06840-3412

CHRISTENSEN, DORIS ANN, antique dealer, researcher, writer; b. Safford, Ariz., Dec. 31, 1938; d. Joseph Solomon Welson and Bernice Beatrice (Blasius) Van Order; m. Donald Edward Christensen, Apr. 22, 1967. Student, Eastern Ariz. Coll., 1961-66. Sec. to dean of admissions Eastern Ariz. Coll., Thatcher, 1963-67; sec. to pres. United Homes Corp., Federal Way, Wash., 1969-89; office mgr. Heller Co. Realtors, Federal Way, Wash., 1990-94; antique dealer All That & Everything, Buckley, Wash., 1995—. Author: (book) Violin Bottles, Banjos, Guitars and Other Novelty Glass, 1995. Recipient Good Citizen's cert., DAR, 1957, Oustanding Citizenship award, Am. Legion, Safford, 1957. Mem.: Violin Bottle Collectors Assn. (editor newsletter U.S. and Can. 1995—). Avocations: collectibles, writing, research. Office: All That & Everything 21815 106th St E Buckley WA 98321-9277

CHRISTENSEN, ERIK REGNAR, engineering educator, researcher; b. Copenhagen, Apr. 17, 1943; came to U.S., 1974; s. Regnar and Margrethe Cathrine (Lou) C.; m. Lone Normann Jensen, Aug. 10, 1968; children: Irene Normann, Eva Normann, Finn Normann. MSEE, Tech. U., Denmark, 1967; Phd in Environ. Engring., U. Calif., Irvine, 1977. Registered profl. engr., Wis. Asst. prof. engring. Tech. Univ. Denmark, Lyngby, 1969-73, assoc. prof., 1973-74; rsch. asst., teaching assoc. U. Calif., Irvine, 1974-77; asst. prof. U. Wis., Milw., 1977-82, assoc. prof., 1982-97, prof., 1997—. Cons. Dept. of Justice, Madison, 1986-87, Milw. Met. Sewer Dist., 1989-90; coun. mem. Wis. Coastal Mgmt. Coun., Madison, 1987—; organizer/convener First Internat. Specialized Conf. (IAWQ) on contaminated aquatic sediments, 1993; co-chair NSF workshop on coastal pollution in urban areas, 1997. Author: (with others) Hazard Assessment of Chemicals, 1989. NSF grantee, Washington, 1981-85, 87-89, 90—. Mem. ASCE, Am. Geophys. Union, Internat. Water Assn., Assn. Environ. Engring. and Sci. Profs., Soc. Environ. Toxicology and Chems. Achievements include development of multiple toxicity models and of models for sediment record deconvolution. Office: U Wis Dept Civil Engring and Mechanics 3200 N Cramer St Milwaukee WI 53211-3029

CHRISTENSEN, HAROLD GRAHAM, lawyer; b. Springville, Utah, June 25, 1926; s. Harold and Ruby (Graham) C.; m. Gayle Sutton, June 17, 1950; children: Steven H., David S., Susan; m. Jacquita W. Corry, Dec. 13, 1988. AB, U. Utah, 1949; JD, U. Mich., 1951. Bar: Utah 1952. Ptnr. firm Skeen, Worsley, Snow & Christensen (and successor firms), Salt Lake City; dep. atty. gen. of the U.S., 1988-89; of counsel Snow Christensen & Martineau, P.C., Salt Lake City, 1992—. Practitioner-in-residence, U. Utah, 1989; vis. prof. Coll. Law, U. Calif., San Francisco, 1990; disting. vis. prof. Bond U., Queensland, Australia, 1991. Served with USNR, 1944-46. Fellow Am. Coll. Trial Lawyers, Am. Bar Found.; mem. Utah State Bar (pres. 1975-76), Utah Bar Found. (trustee 1978), Salt Lake County Bar (pres. 1972-73), Am. Inns of Ct. Found. (trustee 1983-89). Home: 2269 Pheasant Way Salt Lake City UT 84121-1312 Office: 10 Exchange Pl 11th Floor Salt Lake City UT 84111 E-mail: hchristensen@scmlaw.com.

CHRISTENSEN, HAYDEN, actor; b. Vancouver, BC, Canada, Apr. 19, 1981; Actor, 1992—. Actor: (TV series) Family Passions, 1993; (films) Street Law, 1995, In the Mouth of Madness, 1995, Strike!, 1998, The Virgin Suicides, 1999, Life as a House, 2001, Star Wars: Episode II Attack of the Clones, 2002; (TV films) Love and Betrayal: The Mia Farrow Story, 1995, Harrison Bergeron, 1995, No Greater Love, 1996, Freefall, 1999, Trapped in a Purple Haze, 2000, Making of Life as a House, 2001, R2-D2: Beneath the Dome, 2001, numerous TV guest appearances. Office: c/o The Gersh Agy 232 N Canon Dr Beverly Hills CA 90210

CHRISTENSEN, HENRY, III, lawyer; b. Jersey City, Nov. 8, 1944; s. Henry Jr. and M. Louise (Brooke) C.; m. Constance L. Cumpton, July 1, 1967; children: Alexander, Gustavus, Elizabeth, Katherine. BA, Yale U., 1966; JD, Harvard U., 1969. Bar: N.Y. 1970, U.S. Tax Ct. 1973, U.S. Ct. Appeals (2d. cir.) 1973, U.S. Supreme Ct. 1975. Assoc. Sullivan & Cromwell, N.Y.C., 1969-77, ptnr., 1977—. Adj. assoc. prof. NYU, N.Y.C., 1985-88, U. of Miami Law Sch., 1997—. Author: International Estate Planning, 1999, ann. supplements, 1999—; contbr. articles to profl. jours. Chmn. Prospect Park Alliance, Bklyn., 1985—; trustee, 1st vice chmn. Peddie Sch., Hightstown, N.J., 1986—; trustee Am. Fund for the Tate Gallery, 1987—, Bklyn. Acad. Music, 1992—, Vincent Astor Found., 1993—, Alex Hillman Family Found., 2000—, Friends of the Prince's Trust, 2001—; dir., sec. Freedom Inst., N.Y.C., 1980—; dir., v.p. Am. Friends of Whitechapel Art Gallery Found., 1991—; trustee, mem. exec. com. Am. Ctr. Oriental Rsch. in Amman, 1993—. Fellow Am. Coll. Trust and Estate Counsel (chmn. internat. estate planning com. 2003-); mem. N.Y. State Bar Assn. (chmn. estate and gift tax com. 1983-84, chmn. exempt orgn. com. 1986, chmn. income taxation of trusts com. 1984-85, 87-89, exec. com. tax sect. 1983-89), Internat. Acad. Estate and Trust Law (academician). Home: 35 Prospect Park W Apt 8/9B Brooklyn NY 11215-2370 Office: Sullivan & Cromwell 125 Broad St Fl 29 New York NY 10004-2498

CHRISTENSEN, JUHA, information technology executive; Pres. licensing Psion; co-founder Symbian Ltd.; corp. v.p. Microsoft, Redmond, Wash. Office: One Microsoft Way Redmond WA 98052-6399

CHRISTENSEN, KAREN KAY, lawyer; b. Ann Arbor, Mich., Mar. 9, 1947; d. Jack Edward and Evangeline (Pitsch) C.; m. Kenneth Robert Kay, Sept. 2, 1977; children: Jeffrey Smithson, Braden, Bergen. BS, U. Mich., 1969; JD, U. Denver, 1975. Bar: Colo. 1975, D.C. 1976, U.S. Supreme Ct. 1979. Atty., advisor office of dep. atty. gen. U.S. Dept. of Justice, Washington, 1975-76, trial atty. civil rights div., 1976-79; legis. counsel ACLU, Washington, 1979-80; staff atty. D.C. Pub. Defender Service, Washington, 1980-85; asst. gen. counsel Nat. Pub. Radio, Washington, 1985-93; gen. counsel Nat. Endowment Arts, Washington, 1993-98, acting dep. chmn. for grants and partnership, 1997-98, dep. chmn. grants and awards, 1998—2001; arts cons., 2002—. Mem. D.C. Bd. Profl. Responsibility, 1990-98, chair, 1996-98; arts cons. Bd. dirs. Corcoran Art Mus., 2001—, Liz Lerman Dance Exchange, 2002—. Mem. D.C. Bar Assn., NCA/ACLU (exec. bd. 1986-93, chair 1993), Phi Beta Kappa.

CHRISTENSEN, KATHLEEN ELIZABETH, foundation administrator; b. Madson, Wis., May 25, 1951; d. Norbert Martin and Janet Cull C.; m. John Joseph Murray III, May 25, 1990; children: Clare, Grace. BS summa cum laude, U. Wis., Green Bay, 1973; MS, Pa. State U., 1979, PhD, 1981. Policy analyst Urban Inst., Washington, 1973-75; from asst. prof. to prof. psychology CUNY, N.Y.C., 1981-91, prof., 1991-99; program dir. Alfred P. Sloan Found., N.Y.C., 1994—. Cons. in field. Author: Women & Home-based Work, 1988, Contingent Work: Employment Relations and Transition, 1990; editor: Employment Relations in Transition: The New Era of Homebased Work, 1988, Contingent Work: American Employment Relations in Transition, 1998. Mem. adv. bd. Boston Ctr. Work & Family, 1990-94. Humanities fellow NEH, 1977-79, Danforth fellow Danforth Found., 1979-81, Mellon fellow Aspen Inst., 1982. Mem. AAAS, Am. Sociol. Assn., Am. Anthropol. Assn. Office: Alfred P Sloan Found 630 Fifth Ave New York NY 10111 E-mail: christensen@sloan.org.

CHRISTENSEN, KENNETH ASHLEY, composer, tenor, music educator; b. McHenry, Ill., Apr. 12, 1971; s. George Marshall Christensen and Carolyn Elizabeth Beardsley. AA, McHenry County Coll., 1992; BS, Elmhurst Coll., 1996. Violin and vocal instr. Piano Trends Music Co., Crystal Lake, Ill., 1993—96, Fox Hills (Ill.) Music Tchrs. Assn., 1997—. Tenor soloist, mem. Crystal Lake Cmty. Chorus, 1997—, St. John's Luth. Ch., Algonquin, Ill., 1997—2001, Shepherd of the Hills Luth. Ch., McHenry, Ill., 2002—. Mem.: Fox Hills Music Tchrs. Assn. Democrat. Lutheran. Avocations: creative writing, movies, audiophile, meteorology. Home: 771 Dover Ct Crystal Lake IL 60014

CHRISTENSEN, LAWRENCE O. historian, educator; b. Glasgow, Mont., Aug. 18, 1937; s. Andrew Lawrence and Orvella Sylvia (Oland) Christensen; m. Maxine Joyce Lahmann, Mar. 31, 1961. BS in Edn., Truman State U., 1960, MA in History, 1962; PhD in History, U. Mo., Columbia, 1972. Elem. sch. tchr., Columbia, Ill., 1957—58; tchr. William Chrisman HS, Independence, Mo., 1961—62, Westwood HS, 1963—64; secondary sch. tchr. Galesburg, Ill., 1960—61; instr. history Wis. U., Whitewater, 1968—69; instr. history to disting. tchg. prof. history U. Mo., Rolla, 1969—2000; program officer NEH, Washington, 1977—78; prof. U. Mo., Rolla, Mo., 1981—2000, prof. emeritus, 2000—. Co-author: Missouri: The Heart of the Nation, 3 edits., 1981—2002, UM-Rolla: A History of MSM-UMR, 1982, The History of Missouri, vol. 4, 1875-1919, 1998 (Best Book award, 1998); co-editor: Dictionary of Missouri Biography, 1999 (award of merit, spl. book award, State Hist. Soc. Mo., 1999). Bd. dirs. Mo. Humanities Coun., St. Louis, 1989—91. P.f.c. USAR, 1955—61. Grantee, NEH, 1979, 1998—2001. Mem.: State Hist. Soc. Mo. (pres. 1997—2001, trustee), So. Hist. Assn. (life), Orgn. Am. Historians (life). Democrat. Episcopalian. Avocations: reading, travel, fishing, wine. Home: 14190 State Rte Y Rolla MO 65401 Office: U Mo Rolla 131 Humanities Rolla MO 65401 E-mail: christen@umr.edu.

CHRISTENSEN, MADONNA DRIES, writer; b. Ashton, Iowa, Sept. 17, 1935; d. Frank Anton and Agnes Isabella (Guertin) Dries; m. Gary Lee Christensen, May 22, 1965; 1 child, Jill Christensen Buzby. Certs. in creative writing, U. Va., 1984, certs. in creative writing, 1988. Founder/facilitator Gulf Coast Writers, Sarasota, Fla., 1994—95; contbg editor Writer's Guidelines and News mag., Sarasota, Fla., 1998—2001, Jamaica, NY, 2001—02; contbg mem. Thema Lit. Soc., Metairie, La., 1992—. Contbr. chapters to books; co-editor: (anthology) Tapestry; author: Swinging Sisters; contbr. anthology. Ct. monitor Mothers Against Drunk Drivers, Arlington County, Va., 1978—79; mem. Arlington County Fair Bd., Va., 1985—93; contest coord., editor Doorways, Sarasota, 1997—. Mem.: Gulf Coast Writers, Thema Lit. Soc., Internat. Women's Writing Guild, Emerald Coast Writers, West Coast Writers. Avocations: genealogy, reading, doll collecting.

CHRISTENSEN, MARGARET ANNA, nurse, health management educator; b. Nov. 10, 1938; d. John Bernard and Catherine (Scott) Thielen; m. Robert Edwin Christensen, June 24, 1961; children: Marthe Elizabeth Christensen Groves, Katrina Marie Christensen Head, Andrea Susan Christensen Clark. BS, Wichita State U., 1978; EdM, U. Cen. Okla., 1984; EdD, Okla. State U., 1986. Staff devel. supr. St. Joseph Med. Ctr., Wichita, Kans., 1972-79; head nurse Bapt. Med. Ctr., Oklahoma City, 1979-80; clin. supr. Mercy Health Ctr., Oklahoma City, 1980-81, staff devel. coord., 1981-84; pres., sr. cons. Human Resource Cons., Inc., Edmond, Okla., 1982-90; dir. planning and devel. Allied Nursing Care, Inc., Oklahoma City, 1984-85; rehab. specialist LDH Cons., Oklahoma City, 1985-90; pres., CEO Christensen Mgmt. Co., Bella Vista, Ark., 1990—, sr. cons.; mktg. mgr. Holiday Retirement Corp., 2003—. Adj. faculty U. Cen. Okla., Edmond, 1986-90; assoc. prof. Ctrl. Mich. U., 2003—; asst. prof., coord. health scis. grad. programs Ohio U., 1990-94, coord. health sci. grad. program, 1994-96; coord. health care mgmt. program, assoc. prof. dept. bus. Shawnee State U., Portsmouth, 1996-2001; dir. Shawnee State Grad. Ctr., 1999-2001; author performance enhancement plans for long-term care employees, 1995, mgrs. and supr. Health Care, 1992; performance enhancement plans for profl., tech. workers in health care, 1992, performance enhancement plans for office/clerical svc. and maintenance workers Health Care, 1992. Author human resource devel. process, 1984, (booklet) Live-In Companion Guide, 1984, report on hosp. appraisal sys. impact, 1986. Bd. dirs. Ohio Presbyn. Retirement Svcs., Columbus. Mem. Am. Coll. Health Care Execs., Am. Coll. Health Care Adminstrs., Assn. Univ. Programs in Health Adminstrn., Alpha Chi, Kappa Delta Pi, Sigma Kappa, Phi Eta Sigma. Republican. Roman Catholic. Home: 33 Sherlock Dr Bella Vista AR 72715-4904 E-mail: rchris@cox-internet.com.

CHRISTENSEN, MARGUERITE ALICE, librarian; b. Trout Lake, Wis., Aug. 24, 1917; d. Peter Carl and Alice (Cady) Christensen; B.A., U. Wis., 1938, B.L.S., 1939. Librarian, high sch. and Pub. Library, Bloomer, Wis., 1939-41; asst. librarian Wis. State U., Superior, 1941-43, Carroll Coll., Waukesha, Wis., 1943-45; asst. reference librarian U. Wis.-Madison, 1945-66, head gen. reference dept., 1967-82. Mem. ALA, Assn. Coll. and Research Libraries. Home: 4469 Hillcrest Dr Madison WI 53705-5020

CHRISTENSEN, MARVIN NELSON, venture capitalist; b. W. Branch, Iowa, July 15, 1927; s. Peter Ancher and Martha Henrietta (Neilsen) C.; m. Mary Lou Miller, Dec. 17, 1949 (dec. June 1999); children: Stephen R., Barbara. BS, U. Iowa, 1950. Pvt. practice ins. and real estate, Iowa City, 1955-69; asst. to pres. Gen. Growth Cos., Des Moines, 1970-72; acquisitions dir. Life Investors of Iowa, Cedar Rapids, 1972-80; chmn. and chief exec. officer Bus. Comml. Realty, Denver, 1980—; chmn., CEO Colo. Internat. Devel., Colorado Springs, 1984—; chmn. Byers (Colo.) State Bank, 1987-89, Farmer's State Bank, Waubun, Minn., 1988-96. Founder, adminstr. Waubun Area Devel. Enterprises, 1988—. Columnist: View from My Window (monthly newspaper); contbr. many articles to nat. pubs. Lt. (j.g.) USNR, 1944-46. Mem. Am. Bankers Assn., Minn. Bankers Assn., Masons, Elks, Eagles, VFW. Avocations: writing, cabinet making, fishing. Home: RR 2 Waubun MN 56589-9802

CHRISTENSEN, NADIA MARGARET, writer, translator, editor, educator; b. Mpls., July 28, 1937; d. Bernhard Marinus and Lilly Gracia (Gundersen) C. BA, Augsburg Coll., Mpls., 1959; MA, U. Minn., 1964; PhD, U. Wash., 1972. Asst. prof. U. Minn., Mpls., 1972-73; asst. editor Scandinavian Rev., N.Y.C., 1976-78, editor in chief, 1978-82; dir. pub. Am.-Scandinavian Found., N.Y.C.,

1980-82; producer Adventure Film Prodns., Paris, 1982-84; exec. dir. Nordic Ctr., Mpls., 1991-96; sr. program devel. officer Augsburg Coll., Mpls., 1997-99, dir. internat. ptnrs., 2000—; freelance writer and translator, 1972—. Cons. U.S. & European Pubs., 1970—. Author: (coll. text) The Big Apple, 1985, (nonfiction) Action, Reflection, Celebration, 1988; co-author: The Magic Clock, 1979, Ecuador: Island of the Andes, 1988, Turkestan: Oasis de la Chine, 1991; translator: (poetry) Necropolis, 1977, Selected Poems, 1982; (drama) The Ice Goes Out, 1985; (fiction) Consider the Verdict, 1976, Baby, 1980, Sea-Swell, 1986, Dollar Road, 1989, Dina's Book, 1994, Dina's Son, 2001, Tales of Protection, 2002; contbr. articles to profl. jours. Decorated Knight's Cross of Royal Norwegian Order of Merit, King Harald V of Norway; recipient 2d Internat. Poetry Rev., 1979, Pegasus literary prize as translator, 1980, 89; winner Northwind Children's Story competition, 1984; Fulbright scholar US Govt., 1965; George Marshall fellow Am.-Scandinavian Found., 1968, Strong fellow, 1984. Mem.: PEN (finalist Translation award 2003), Am. Lit. Translators Assn., Am. Translators Assn., Fulbright Assn., Poets and Writers. Address: 6133 Chowen Ave S Edina MN 55410

CHRISTENSEN, NIKOLAS IVAN, geophysicist, educator; b. Madison, Wis., Apr. 11, 1937; s. Ivan Rudolph and Alice Evelyn (Ethen) C.; m. Karen Mary Luberg, June 18, 1960; children— Kirk Nathan, Signe Kay. BS, U. Wis., 1959, MS, 1961, PhD, 1963. Rsch. fellow in geophysics Harvard U., Cambridge, Mass., 1963-64; asst. prof. geol. scis. U. So. Calif., 1964-66; prof. U. Wash., Seattle, 1966-83, Purdue U., Lafayette, Ind., 1983-97; Weeks disting. prof. U. Wis., Madison, 1997—. Mem. Pacific adv. panel Joint Oceanographic Instns. for Deep Earth Sampling, Seattle, 1973-75, mem. igneous and metamorphic petrology panel, 1973-75, mem. ocean crust panel, 1974-77; mem. adv. panel on oceanography NSF, 1976-78, mem. adv. panel on earth scis. 1994-97; mem. adv. panel on continental lithosphere NRC, 1979-83; mem. adv. panel Internat. Assn. Geodesy, 1980-88. Contbg. author: Geodynamics of Iceland and the North Atlantic Area, 1974; Contbr. numerous articles to profl. jours. NSF grantee, 1968-2003. Fellow Geol. Soc. Am. (chmn. geophysics divsn. 1984-86, assoc. editor Geology 1985-89, George P. Woollard award 1996), Am. Geophys. Union (assoc. editor Jour. Geophys. Rsch. 1998-2001). Achievements include research on nature of Earth's interior. Home: 11310 Marine Ln Anacortes WA 98221 Office: Dept Geology and Geophys U Wisc Madison WI 53706

CHRISTENSEN, PATRICIA ANNE WATKINS, lawyer; b. Corpus Christi, Tex., June 24, 1947; d. Owen Milton Jr. and Margaret (McFarland) Watkins; m. Steven Ray Christensen, May 28, 1977 (dec. 1985); children: Geoffrey Holland, Jeremy Ladd. BS, U. North Tex., 1971; JD, U. Houston, 1977. Bar: Utah 1977, Tex. 1977, U.S. Dist. Ct. Utah 1977, U.S. Ct. Appeals (10th cir.) 1977, U.S. Supreme Ct. 1990. Assoc. Berman & Giauque, Salt Lake City, 1977-80; ptnr. Parr, Waddoups, Brown, Gee & Loveless, Salt Lake City, 1980—, pres., 1991-93, 2002—03. Adj. prof. law U. Utah Law Sch., Salt Lake City, 1979-81; judge pro tem Third Dist. Ct., 1995—. Legis. asst. U.S. Senate, 1970-74; bd. dirs. Comml. Law Affiliate, 1997-2001, co-chair litigation sect.; trustee Rowland Hall St. Mark's Sch., chair devel. com., 1987-90; mem. steering com., comprehensive capital campaign U. Utah Sch. Nursing; mem. steering com. Utah Electronic Law Project. Named Utah Woman Lawyer of Yr., 1992. Mem. ABA, Utah State Bar (Dorothy Merrill Brothers award 1996), State Bar of Tex., Salt Lake County Bar Assn. (exec. com. 1979-87, author editor Utah Lawyers Practice Manual 1986), Women Lawyers Utah (pres. 1988-89, bd. dirs. 1987-90), Phi Delta Phi, Delta Gamma, Alpha Lambda Delta. Office: Parr Waddoups Brown Gee & Loveless 185 S State St Ste 1300 Salt Lake City UT 84111-1537 E-mail: pwc@pwlaw.com.

CHRISTENSEN, PAUL NORMAN, English educator, writer; b. W. Reading, Pa., Mar. 18, 1943; s. Kenneth Serenus and Ann Theresa C.; m. Jane T. Flowers, Apr. 18, 1964 (div. Mar. 1968); 1 child, Sean Oliver; m. Catherine Anne Tensing, Aug. 30, 1969; children: Maxine Elizabeth, Signe Laura, Cedric Owen. BA in English, William and Mary Coll., 1967; MA in English, U. Cin., 1970; PhD in English, U. Pa., 1975. Assoc. editor Stock Car Racing Mag., Alexandria, Va., 1967-68; from asst. prof. to assoc. prof. English Tex. A&M U., College Station, Tex., 1974-83, prof. English, 1983—. Editor, pub. Cedarshouse Press, Bryan, Tex., 1977—; dir. Provence Writer's Workshop, Buoux, France, 1998—; Fulbright sr. lectr. Coun. Internat. Exch. of Scholars, Washington, 1989, 96. Author: Charles Olson: Call Him Ishmael, 1979, Minding the Underworld, 1990, In Love, In Sorrow, 1991, West of the American Dream: An Encounter with Texas, 2001, Blue Alleys: Prose Poems, 2001, The Mottled Air, 2003. Recipient Short Fiction award, Tex. Inst. Letters, 1996, Chautauqua 2000 award, Tulsa Arts Coun., 1999, Disting. Prose award, Antioch Rev., 1999, Creative Nonfiction award, Writers' League of Tex., 2001, Violet Crown Award for Lit., Writers League of Tex., 2002; fellow, U. Pa., 1970—72. Democrat. Roman Catholic. Avocations: cooking, wine collecting, photography. Office: Tex A&M U Dept English College Station TX 77843-4227 E-mail: p-christensen@neo.tamu.edu.

CHRISTENSEN, PAUL WALTER, JR., gear manufacturing company executive; b. Cin., Jan. 31, 1925; s. Paul Walter and Lucy (Sickler) C.; m. Sarah Ernst, Nov. 22, 1947; children: Delle (Mrs. Edmund W. Jones), Sarah (Mrs. William McC. Reynolds), Lucy (Mrs. Craig M. Davis). BS in Mech. Engring., Cornell U., 1945. With Cin. Gear Co., 1946-87, v.p., 1947-58, pres., 1958-78, chmn. bd., 1978-87, ret., 1987; chmn. bd. Cin. Steel Treating Co., 1961-68, 87, pres., 1968-87, ret., 1987. Commr. Hamilton County Park Dist., 1980-93. Mem. Am. Gear Mfrs. Assn. (past pres.), Ohio Mfrs. Assn. (past pres.), Ocean Reef Club, Queen City Club, Commonwealth Club, Camargo Club, Comml. Club, Key Largo Anglers Club, Card Sound Golf Club. Home: 4660 Drake Rd Cincinnati OH 45243-4118

CHRISTENSEN, RAY RICHARDS, lawyer; b. Salt Lake City, July 7, 1922; s. E.R. and Carrie (Richards) C.; m. Carolyn Crawford, July 9, 1954 (dec. 1986); children: Carlie, Paul Ray, Joan, Eric.; m. Jeanne F. Pyke, June 24, 1989. LL.B., U. Utah, 1944. Bar: Utah 1944. Enforcement atty. OPA, 1946; law clk. to Utah Supreme Ct. Justice Wolfe, 1947-48; practice in Salt Lake City, 1949—; ptnr. Christensen & Jensen, P.C. (and predecessors), 1949—. Mem. Utah Bar Commn., 1963-66. Bd. dirs. Salt Lake City Jr. C. of C., 1949-53, v.p., 1950-52. Served with AUS, 1943-46. Fellow Internat. Acad. Trial Lawyers (bd. dirs. 1982-88), Am. Coll. Trial Lawyers (state chmn. 1984-85); mem. ABA (mem. council jr. bar conf. 1952-56, ho. of dels. 1966-68, 73-79, mem. council bar activities sect. 1967-70), Utah State Bar (pres. 1965-66, Utah Lawyer of Yr. 1981, Utah Trial Lawyer of Yr. 1993), Salt Lake County Bar Assn., Western States Bar Conf. (pres. 1969-70), Internat. Assn. Def. Counsel, Fedn. Defense and Corp. Counsel, Phi Eta Sigma, Phi Kappa Phi. Home: 992 Oak Hills Way Salt Lake City UT 84108-2022 Office: Christensen & Jensen PC 50 S Main St Ste 1500 Salt Lake City UT 84144-2044 E-mail: ray.christensen@chrisjen.com.

CHRISTENSEN, ROBERT PAUL, lawyer; b. Mpls., June 26, 1949; s. Otto and Cora Alice C.; m. Cindy G. Christensen, July 15, 1972; children: Nicholas, Lindsey, Callie. BA, U. Minn., 1971, JD cum laude, 1974. Ptnr. Carlsen, Greiner & Law, Mpls., 1974-86, Dunkley, Bennett Christensen & Madigan, Mpls., 1986—. Mem. Minn. Trial Lawyers Assn. (bd. dirs. 1986-96), Creative Dispute Resolution Assn. (bd. dirs. 1995-97, pres. 1998—), Coll. of Master Advocates & Barristers, NBTA 1993-, Million Dollar Advocates Forum, 1997-. Office: Dunkley Bennett Christensen& Madigan PA 701 4th Ave S Ste 700 Minneapolis MN 55415-1812 E-mail: rpchristensen@visi.com.

CHRISTENSEN, ROBERT WAYNE, oral maxillofacial surgeon, minister; b. N.Y.C., Apr. 6, 1925; s. Charles Joseph Brophy and Eva Sutherland (Hart) Christensen; m. Ann Forsyth (div.); children: Robert, Joan, Elizabeth, Peter, Mary, Colleen, Patricia, Michelle; m. Lynne Blindbury; children: Andrew, Matthew. DDS, NYU, 1948. Oral surgery tng. L.A. County Gen. Hosp., 1950; oral maxillofacial surgeon, 1950-88; pres. TMJ Implants, Inc., Golden, Colo., 1988—. Minister, founder Covenant Marriages Ministry, Golden, 1988—; pres. Design Dynamics Internat., Golden, 1994—, Combined Med. Techs., 2000; R&D med. adv. bd. mem. Sch. Medicine, Loma Linda U.; pres.'s cabinet mem. Jerry Savelle Ministry, Ft. Worth, 1994—; adj. prof. bioengring. Sch. Engring., Clemson U., 1997; biomed. engring. program adv. bd. Colo. State U., 1999; mem. bd. advisors for BMES, Sch. Ceramic Engring., Alfred U., 2002. Inventor of 5 U.S. patents. Lt. USNR. Recipient Rep. of the Yr. award, Nat. Congl. Rep. Com., 2001; fellow Robert W. Christensen fellow, TM Joint Surgery, U. Tenn. Sch. Medicine, 1997. Fellow Am. Inst. Med. and Biol. Engring. (coll of fellows 2003); mem. Am. Coll. of Forensic Examiners, Sigma Xi. Republican. Avocations: skiing, gardening, photography. Office: TMJ Implants Inc 17301 W Colfax Ave Ste 135 Golden CO 80401-4880

CHRISTENSEN, RONALD, statistician, educator; b. Willmar, Minn., Dec. 11, 1951; s. George Emmanuel and Doris Marie Christensen; m. Sharon G. Christensen, Feb. 14, 1976 (div. Jan. 1999), 1 child, Fletcher. BA, U. Minn., 1974, MS, 1976, PhD, 1983. Asst. prof. Mont. State U., Bozeman, 1982-88; assoc. prof. U. N.Mex., Albuquerque, 1988-94, prof., 1994—, dir. stats. clinic, 1998—2001. Author: Plane Answers to Complex Questions, 1987, Log-Linear Models, 1990, Linear Models for Multivariate, Time Series, and Spatial Data, 1990, Analysis of Variance, Design, and Regression, 1996. Fellow Am. Statis. Assn., Inst. of Math. Stats.; mem. Internat. Biometric Soc., Am. Soc. for Quality, Phi Beta Kappa. Office: Univ N Mex Dept Math and Stats Albuquerque NM 87131

CHRISTENSEN, SYLVIA MIGNON (SIBBY CHRISTENSEN), editor; b. Dec. 19, 1934; d. Franklin Just and Bertha Catherine (Wamboldt) C. BS in Journalism, Tex. Woman's U., 1957. Cityside reporter Port Arthur (Tex.) News, 1956; publicity asst. Dallas Cmty Chest, 1957-58; publicity rep. William Blakley Senate Campaign, Dallas, 1958; proof reader, media asst. G.M. Basford Advt., N.Y.C., 1959-61; editl. asst. Bell Telephone Labs., N.Y.C., 1962-63; mng. editor Overseas Press Club Bull., N.Y.C., 1963-70; editor AP World mag., AP, 1970-84; spl. projects coord. corp. comms. AP, N.Y.C., 1984-88; editor Spl. Edition AP, N.Y.C., 1989—. Recipient Disting. Alumna award Tex. Woman's U., 1985. Mem. N.Y. Women in Comms. (pres. 1971-73), N.Y./Internat. Assn. Bus. Communicators (award of merit 1980, 83, award of excellence 1982, Gold award 1984), Overseas Press Club (awards judge). Home: 643 Pelham Rd Apt 6D New Rochelle NY 10805-1116 Office: AP 50 Rockefeller Plz New York NY 10020-1605

CHRISTENSON, CHARLES JOHN, retired business educator; b. Chgo., Sept. 25, 1930; s. John Edward and Ethel Dagmar (Osterberg) C. BS, Cornell U., 1952; MBA, Harvard, 1954, D.BA, 1961. Mem. faculty Harvard Grad. Sch. Bus., 1957-58, lectr., 1959-61, asst. prof., 1961-63, assoc. prof., 1963-68, prof., 1968-74, Jesse Isidor Straus prof., 1974-79, Royal Little prof., 1980-96, prof. emeritus, 1996—. Prin. Auerbach Christenson Tagiuri, Inc., 1983-92; bd. dirs. Profile Techs., Inc. Author: Strategic Aspects of Competitive Bidding for Corporate Securities, 1965, (with J.L. Bower) Public Management: Cases and Readings, 1978, (with W.L. Berry and J.S. Hammond III) Management Decision Sciences: Cases and Readings, 1979. Bd. dirs. Boston Baroque, 1980—; trustee, chmn. Deep Springs Coll., 1986-94. With AUS, 1955-57. Mem. AAAS. Home: 1 Chauncy Ln Cambridge MA 02138-2401 Office: Harvard Bus Sch Soldiers Fld Boston MA 02163-1317 E-mail: cchristenson@hbs.edu.

CHRISTENSON, GORDON A. law educator; b. Salt Lake City, June 22, 1932; s. Gordon B. and Ruth Arzella (Anderson) C.; m. Katherine Joy deMik, Nov. 2, 1951 (div. 1977); children: Gordon Scott, Marjorie Lynne, Ruth Ann, Nanette; m. Fabienne Fadeley, Sept. 16, 1979. BS in Law, U. Utah, 1955, JD, 1956; SJD, George Washington U., 1961. Bar: Utah 1956, U.S. Supreme Ct. 1971, D.C. 1978. Law clk. to chief justice Utah Supreme Ct., 1956-57; assoc. firm Christenson & Callister, Salt Lake City, 1956-58; atty. Dept. of Army, Nat. Guard Bur., Washington, 1957-58; atty., acting asst. legal adviser Office of Legal Adviser, U.S. Dept. State, Washington, 1958-62; asst. gen. counsel for sci. and tech. U.S. Dept. Commerce, 1962-67, spl. asst. to undersec. of commerce, 1967, counsel to commerce tech. adv. bd., 1962-67, chmn. task force on telecommunications missions and orgn., 1967, counsel to panel on engring. and commodity standards, tech. adv. bd., 1963-65; assoc. prof. law U. Okla., Norman, 1967-70, exec. asst. to pres., 1967-70; univ. dean for ednl. devel., central adminstrn. State U. N.Y., Albany, 1970-71; prof. law Am. U. Law Sch., Washington, 1971-79, dean, 1971-77; on leave, 1977-79; Charles H. Stockton prof. internat. law U.S. Naval War Coll., Newport, R.I., 1977-79; dean, Nippert prof. law U. Cin. Coll. Law, 1979-85, univ. prof. law, 1985-99, prof. emeritus, dean emeritus, 1999—. Assoc. professorial lectr. in internat. affairs George Washington U., 1961-67; vis. scholar Harvard U. Law Sch., 1977-78, Yale Law Sch., 1985-86, Law Sch. U. Maine, Portland, 1997; Wallace S. Fujiyama vis. disting. prof. law Univ. Hawaii Law Sch., 1997; participant summer confs. on internat. law Cornell Law Sch., Ithaca, N.Y., 1962, 64; cons. in internat. law U.S. Naval War Coll., Newport, R.I., 1969; faculty mem., reporter seminars for experienced fed. dist. judges Fed. Jud. Center, Washington, 1972-77. Author: (with Richard B. Lillich) International Claims: Their Preparation and Presentation, 1962, The Future of the University, 1969; Contbr. articles to legal jours. Cons. to Center for Policy Alternatives Mass. Inst. Tech., Cambridge, 1970-81; mem. intergovtl. com. on Internat. Policy on Weather Modification, 1967; Vice pres. Procedural Aspects of Internat. Law Inst., N.Y.C., 1962-2001, trustee, 1962—. Served with intelligence sect. USAF, 1951-52, Japan. Recipient Silver Medal award Dept. Commerce, 1967; fellow Grad. Sch. U. Cin. Mem. Am. Soc. Internat. Law (mem. panel on state responsibility), Utah Bar Assn., Cin. Bar Assn., Order of Coif, Phi Delta Phi, Kappa Sigma. Clubs: Literary (Cin.); Cosmos (Washington). Home and Office: 3465 Principio Ave Cincinnati OH 45208-4242 E-mail: christga@msn.com.

CHRISTENSON, GREGG ANDREW, bank executive; b. Kalamazoo, Mich., June 11, 1958; s. Elmer J. and Marie E. (Durrstein) C.; m. Karen Peterson. BA, Mich. State U., 1980. CPA. Auditor Price Waterhouse, N.Y.C., 1980-82; with Bankers Trust Co., N.Y.C., 1982-92, v.p., 1987-92; sr. v.p. Huntington Nat. Bank, Columbus, Ohio, 1992-2000, sr. v.p. retail market Troy, Mich., 2000—. Bd. trustees, v.p. Worthington Pub. Libr.; treas. Far North Columbus Communities Coalition. Mem. Jr. Achievement Alumni Assn. (charter), Mich. State Alumni Assn., Phi Kappa Phi, Beta Gamma Sigma. Republican. Roman Catholic. E-mail: gregg.christenson@huntington.com.

CHRISTENSON, LE ROY HOWARD, religious organization administrator, consultant; b. Rochester, N.Y., Oct. 28, 1948; s. Howard Le Roy and Sigrid (Anderson) Christenson; m. Pamala Jean Mattson, Jan. 26, 1974; children: Nathan Lee, David Wayne. BS, Valparaiso U., 1970; MS, Purdue U., 1972. CLU. Corp. actuary Western Life Ins. Co., St. Paul, 1972-84; v.p., reins. actuary Am. United Life Ins. Co., Indpls., 1984—99, exec. v.p., 1999—2000; pvt. practice cons. Fishers, Ind., 2001—02; Great Lakes assoc. dir. Advancing Chs. in Missions Commitment (ACMC), 2002—. Fin. cons. Mgmt. Assistance Program, Mpls., 1982. Mission conf. chmn. Faith Missionary Ch., Indpls., 1987—89, elder, 1991—93, 1999—2002, elder chmn., 1993, 2000—02, mission com. chmn., 1995—2000; bd. dirs. Lake Wapogasset Bible Camp, Mpls., 1982—83, Christian Businessman's Com., Indpls., 1985—88, Interserve, chmn. nominating com., 1999—, mem. exec. com., 1999—2001; age group leader Pioneer Club, Indpls., 1983, 1987. Fellow: Soc. Actuaries (chmn. audit working group reins. sect. 1985—88, vice chmn. reins. sect. 1988—89, 1995—96, chmn. 1989—90, 1996—97, sec.-treas. reins. sect. 1994—95); mem.: Indpls. Actuarial Club (pres. 1987—88), Tri-State Actuarial Club (Indpls. rep. 1984—90, chmn. 1989—90), Am. Acad. Actuaries. Avocation: Avocations: bible study, biking, motorcycling. Home and Office: 10955 Knightsbridge Lane Fishers IN 46038 E-mail: lhchristenson@iquest.net.

CHRISTENSON, MICHAEL D. federal agency administrator; BS, U. Wis. Fed. personnel intern NASA, Washington, 1967, mem. staff Kennedy Space Flight Ctr, mem. staff Johnson Space Ctr., mem. staff Goddard Space Flight Ctr. Greenbelt, Md., assoc. dep. adminstr. instns. Washington, 1995; dir. personnel, then assoc. dep. adminstr. mgmt. Agrl. Rsch. Svc., USDA. Office: NASA Hdqrs Mail Code A 300 E St SW Washington DC 20546

CHRISTENSON, SHEN, editor; b. Salt Lake City, Utah, Aug. 13, 1954; d. Nicholas G. and Isabelle Marion (Burrows) Smith; m. A. J. Martinez, Jan. 1, 1989; children: Chandra, Marissa, Karrilee, Nicholas, Jen, Claire, Jacob. BA, U. Utah, Salt Lake City, 1975, MA, 1987. Writer freelance, Salt Lake City, 1982—, editor, 1997—. Bd. dirs. Artvest, Salt Lake City, 1997—; cons. Three Orchids Press, Salt Lake City, 1999—. Contbr. short stories, articles in various literary jours. Recipient 1st Pl. award, Story Mag., 1996, Chgo. Mag., 1999, 2d Pl. award, Utah Fine Arts Coun., 1998. Mem.: Writers Guild. Achievements include raising children who had been abused, whose prognosis was poor to very poor; to make them feel secure and become loving adults who hold degrees from many universities.

CHRISTENSON, WILLIAM NEWCOME, retired occupational and internal medicine physician; b. Biltmore Forest, N.C., Dec. 2, 1925; s. William Lambert and Beth (Newcome) Christenson; m. Elizabeth Chandler White, Aug. 9, 1957; children: Lisa Ann, Laurie E., Susan. MD, Johns Hopkins U., 1948; BS, U. N.C., 1949. Intern, asst. resident Mass. Gen. Hosp., Boston, 1948-50; asst. resident N.Y. Hosp., N.Y.C., 1953-55, dir. personnel health svc., 1960-85, asst. attending physician, 1961-64, assoc. attending physician, 1964-85; attending physician Westchester County Med. Ctr., 1985-95, physician Employee Health Svc., 1985-95; ret., 1995. Postgrad. rsch. fellow USPHS; postgrad. Med. Sch. London, 1955—56; instr. medicine Cornell U. Med. Coll., N.Y.C., 1956—59, asst. prof., 1959—65, clin. assoc. prof., 1965—79, assoc. prof. clin. medicine, 1979—85; dir. Office Grad. Med. Advising N.Y. Med. Coll., 1985—88, 1988—95, prof., 1986—95, assoc. dean, 1988—95; cons. N.Y. Blood Ctr., 1976—90; practice medicine specializing in internal medicine and occupl. medicine, NY, 1960—85; co-chair com. med. ctr. Am. Occupl. Med. Assn., 1980—90. With USNR, 1950—52. Fellow: ACP, Am. Coll. Occupl. and Environ. Medicine; mem.: Am. Soc. Hematology, Am. Fedn. Clin. Rsch., Phi Beta Kappa, Delta Kappa Epsilon, Alpha Omega Alpha. Achievements include research in in hematology and human ecology.

CHRISTIAENS, CHRIS (BERNARD FRANCIS CHRISTIAENS), financial analyst, state legislator; b. Conrad, Mont., Mar. 7, 1940; s. Marcel Jules and Virgie Jeanette (Van Spyk) C. BA in Chemistry, Coll. Gt. Falls, 1962, M in human svcs., 1994. Fin. and ins. mgr. Rice Motors, Gt. Falls, Mont., 1978-84; mem. Mont. Senate, Dist. 23, Helena, 1983-87, 1991—; majority whip 49th legis., 1985-86; fin. planner Jack Stevens CPA, Gt. Falls, 1984-85; adminstr., fin. analyst Gt. Falls Pre-Release, 1986-92; mem. Reforming States Group Health Care Reform, 1994—. Owner Oak Oak Inn-Bed and Breakfast, 1989-95; faculty U. Gt. Falls, part-time 1995—; bd. dirs. World Wide Press Inc., svc. rep., 1994—; gen. mgr. Gt. Falls Transit Dist.; adj. faculty U. Great Falls, 1994—; steering com. Reforming States Group; lobbyist Mont. State Legislature, 2003—. Chmn. Balance of State Pvt. Industry Coun., Mont., 1984-2002; mem. Mont. Human Rights Commn., 1981-84; bd. dirs. St. Thomas Child and Family Ctr., Gt. Falls, 1983—, Coll. of Gt. Falls, 1984—, Cascade County Mental Health Assn., 1986—, Salvation Army, Habitat for Humanity, 1992-95; adv. bd. State Drug and Alcohol Coun., State Mental Health Coun., Cambridge Court Sr. Citizen Apt. Complex, 1986; bd. dirs. treas. Gt. Falls Cmty. Food Bank, 1984-86; Dem. committeeman Cascade County, 1976-82; Mont. del. to Nat. Rules Conv., 1980; pub. chmn. Cascade County chpt. ARC, 1986; treas. Cascade County Mental Health Ctr.; vice chmn. Gov.'s Task Force on Prison Overcrowding, regional jail com.; mem. Re-Leaf Gt. Falls Com., 1989—, steering com.; active Gt. Falls and Cascade County Housing Task Force, 1995—; sec. Montanan's for the Coal Trust, 2003—. Recipient Outstanding Young Alumni award Coll. of Gt. Falls, 1979, Hon. Alumni Achievement award, 1994; Disting. Svc. award Rocky Mountain Coun. Mental Health Ctrs., 1995. Mem. Gt. Falls Ski Club, Toastmasters, Optimists, Big Sky Cum Christo. Roman Catholic. Avocations: skiing, tennis, fishing, reading, hiking. Address: 600 36th St S Great Falls MT 59405-3508

CHRISTIAN, BETTY JO, lawyer; b. Temple, Tex., July 27, 1936; d. Joe and Mattie Manor (Brown) Wiest; m. Ernest S. Christian, Jr., Dec. 24, 1960. BA summa cum laude, U. Tex., 1957, LL.B. summa cum laude, 1960. Bar: Tex. 1961, U.S. Supreme Ct. 1964, D.C. 1980. Law clk. Supreme Ct. Tex., 1960-61; atty. ICC, 1961-68, asst. gen. counsel, 1970-72, assoc. gen. counsel, 1972-76, commr., 1976-79; ptnr. Steptoe & Johnson, Washington, 1980—. Atty. Labor Dept., Dallas, 1968-70 Fellow Am. Bar Found., Tex. Bar Found.; mem. ABA, FBA (Younger Fed. Lawyer award 1964), Tex. Bar Assn., Am. Law Inst., Am. Acad Appellate Lawyers, Adminstrv. Conf. U.S., City Tavern Club. Office: 1330 Connecticut Ave NW Washington DC 20036-1704 E-mail: bchristi@steptoe.com.

CHRISTIAN, DARRELL L. journalist; b. Henderson, Ky., Dec. 26, 1948; s. James Boyd and Thelma (Todd) C. BA, U. Ky., 1970. Sports writer Gleaner Jour., Henderson, Ky., 1964-65, sports editor, 1965-66; newsman AP, Charleston, W. Va., 1967-68, Indpls., 1972-75, news editor, 1975-80, supervising editor Washington, 1980-81, dep. sports editor N.Y.C., 1981-85, sports editor, 1985-92, mng. editor, 1992-98, dir. MegaSports, 1998-00, bus. editor, 2000—. Pulitzer prize juror, 1995-96. With USN, 1970-73. Avocation: golf. Office: AP 50 Rockefeller Plz New York NY 10020-1605

CHRISTIAN, DAVID MICHAEL, athletic director, parochial school educator; b. Niagara Falls, Oct. 8, 1969; s. Raymond John Christian and Jacqueline Margaret Harley; m. Meaghan Elizabeth Pickard, Oct. 30, 1993; children: Jacob, Zachary, Benjamin, Jack. BS in Phys. Edn., SUNY, Brockport, 1993. Lic. tchr. N.Y., 1993. Tchr. Holy Family Sch., Syracuse, NY, 1993—. Recreation supr. Merriday Sch., Syracuse, NY, 1993—95; football coach East Syracuse (N.Y.)-Minoa Ctrl. Sch., 1995—96; baseball coach Westhill Ctrl. Sch., Syracuse, 1996—99; camp counselor Syracuse U., 1995—2000. Democrat. Roman Catholic. Avocations: bowling, golf, softball, woodwork. Office: Holy Family Sch 130 Chapel Dr Syracuse NY 13219

CHRISTIAN, EDWARD KIEREN, broadcasting station executive; b. Detroit, June 26, 1944; s. William Edward and Dorothy Miriam (Kieren) C.; m. Judith Dallaire, Nov. 25, 1966; children: Eric, Dana. BA, Wayne State U., 1966, postgrad.; MA, Cen. Mich. U., 1980. Mgr. John C. Butler Co., Detroit, 1968-69; nat. sales mgr. WCAR Radio, Detroit, WSUN Radio, St. Petersburg, Fla., 1969-70; v.p., gen. mgr., ptnr. WCER Radio, Charlotte, Mich., 1970-74; pres. Josephson Internat. Broadcast, 1975-86; pres., CEO Saga Comm., Inc., Detroit, 1986—. Pres., CEO, bd. dirs. Stas. WSNY-FM, WODB-FM Columbus, Ohio, Sta. WNOR-FM, Norfolk, Va., Sta. WAFX, Norfolk, WJOI AM Norfolk, Stas. WKLH-FM, WLZR-FM, WJYI-AM, WFMR-FM, WJMR-FM Milw., Stas. KRNT, KSTZ-FM, KIOA-AM/FM, KAZR FM, KLTI FM, KPSR AM, Des Moines, Stas. WLRW-FM and WIXY-FM, WKIO-FM, Champaign, Ill., Stas. WYMG-FM, WQQL-FM, WDBR-FM, WMXH-FM, WTAX-AM, Springfield, Ill., Stas. WGAN-AM/WMGX, WZAN-AM/WYNZ-FM, WPOR/FM, WBAE-AM Portland, Maine, Sta. WFEA-AM/WZID-FM, WQLL-FM, Manchester, N.H., Sta. WAQY-FM, WHNP-AM, Springfield, Mass., WHMP-AM, WLZX-FM, Northampton, Mass., WHMQ-AM, WHAI-AM, Greenfield, Mass., KOAM TV, Joplin, Mo., WNAX-AM/FM, Yankton, S.D., KGMI, KISM-FM, Bellingham, Wash., KBAI-AM, KAFE FM, Bellingham, Wash., Victoria Tex., KUNU TV, KXTS TV, KAVU TV, KVCT TV, Victoria, WXVT TV, Greenville, Miss., KICD AM-FM, Spencer, Iowa, KLLT, Spencer, WXDN, WJMR-AM, WZZP-FM, WCVQ-FM, WVVR-FM, Clarkesville, Tenn., KDXY-FM, KDEZ-FM, KJBX-FM, Jonesboro A.K., WKNE-FM, WKBK-AM, WZBK-FM, WUQL-FM, WINQ-FM, Keene, N.H., WKVT-AM/FM, Brattleboro, V.T., Mich. Radio Network, Ill. Radio Network, others; Mich. Farm Radio Network; Bd. dirs., Nat. Assn. Broadcasters 2002-, bd. dirs., Broadcast Found. 2003-, chmn. Arbitron Radio Adv. Coun., 1978-79; bd. dirs. All Industry Music Licensing Com. Pres. United Way, Charlotte, 1973-74; del. Rep. State Conv., 1974; bd. dirs. Am. Auto Immune Related Disease Found., 1995—; consul Republic of Iceland for Mich., Ohio and Ind., 1996—. Mem. Alpha Epsilon Rho (nat. adv. coun. 1980—). Home: 21 Newberry Pl Grosse Pointe Farms MI 48236-3749 also: 3310 Sabal Cove Dr Longboat Key FL 34228-4154 Office: Saga Communications Inc 73 Kercheval Ave Grosse Pointe Farms MI 48236-3603 E-mail: echristian@sagacommunications.com.

CHRISTIAN, ELIOT JORDAN, federal agency administrator, computer specialist; b. Springfield, Mo., Aug. 17, 1952; s. Robert Aspel and Clara Mae (Hess) Smith; m. Marcia Bernadette FitzSimons Christian, July 4, 1976; children: Sikandra, Theresa, Sheila. BA in English, U. Wis., Milw., 1973. Dep. dir. field mgmt. svc. Office Data Mgmt. and Telecomm., VA, Washington, 1975-86; chief office mgmt. svcs. info. sys. divsn. U.S. Geol. Survey, Reston, Va., 1986—. Chmn. Spl. Interest Group on Wide Area Info. Servers, Washington, 1993—98; arch., leader Global Info. Locator Svc., 1995—. Author: fed. reports. Recipient Best Windows Application award, Windows World, 1993, Federal 100 award, Fed. Computer Week, 1995, 1996, Madison award for pub. right to know, ALA and AAAS, 1998. Democrat. Roman Catholic. Avocations: hiking, reading. Home: 2002 Lakebreeze Way Reston VA 20191-4006 Office: US Geol Survey 802 National Ctr Reston VA 22092-0001

CHRISTIAN, ERNEST SILSBEE, JR., lawyer; b. Gonzales, Tex., Jan. 15, 1937; s. Ernest Silsbee and Ruby Ruth (Hamon) Christian; m. Betty Jo Wiest, Dec. 24, 1960. LLB cum laude, U. Tex., 1961. Bar: Tex. 1961, D.C. 1961, U.S.

Supreme Ct. 1978. Atty. Treasury Dept., Washington, 1970-72, tax legis. counsel, 1973-74, dep. asst. sec. treasury (tax policy), 1974-75; ptnr. Patton, Boggs & Blow, Washington, 1975-94, E.S. Christian, 1995—. Mem.: ABA, Am. Law Inst. Republican. Home: Willows Farm PO Box 1140 Union Bridge MD 21791-0582 Office: 800 Connecticut Ave NW Washington DC 20006-2709

CHRISTIAN, FRANCIS JOSEPH, bishop; b. Peterborough, N.H., Oct. 12, 1942; s. Joseph Lucien and Dorothy May (Parent) C. BA, PhB, U. Ottawa, Can., 1964; MA in Theology, U. Louvain, Belgium, 1968, PhD in Religious Studies, 1975. Ordained priest Roman Cath. Ch., 1968. Asst. pastor Our Lady of Mercy Parish, Merrimack, N.H., 1968-71, St. Joseph Cathedral Parish, Manchester, N.H., 1971-72; asst. chancellor Diocese of Manchester, 1975-77, chancellor, sec. for administrn. canonical affairs Diocese Manchester, 1978—, vicar gen., 1996—, monsignor (prelate of honor), 1986—, aux. bishop of Manchester, 1996—. Roman Catholic. Office: Diocese of Manchester 153 Ash St Manchester NH 03104-4396

CHRISTIAN, GARY DALE, chemistry educator; b. Eugene, Oreg., Nov. 25, 1937; s. Roy C. and Edna Alberta (Trout) Gonier; m. Suanne Byrd Coulbourne, June 17, 1961; children: Dale Brian, Carol Jean, Tanya Danielle, Tabitha Star. BS, U. Oreg., 1959; MS, U. Md., 1962, PhD, 1964. Rsch. analytical chemist Walter Reed Army Inst. Rsch., Washington, 1961-67; asst. prof. U. Md., College Park, 1965-66, U. Ky., Lexington, 1967-70, assoc. prof., 1970-72; prof. chemistry U. Wash., Seattle, 1972—, acting chmn. dept., 1990, assoc. chmn., 1991-92, divisional dean Arts and Scis., 1993-2001. Vis. prof. Free U. Brussels, 1978-79; invited prof. U. Geneva, 1979; cons. Ames Co., 1968-72, Beckman Instruments, Inc., 1972-84, 88, Westinghouse Hanford Co., 1977-83, Tech. Dynamics, 1983-85, Porton Diagnostics, 1990-91, Bend Rsch., 1992-93, E.I. DuPont de Nemours, Inc., 1993; examiner Grad. Record Exam., 1985-90. Author: Analytical Chemistry, 6th edit., 2003, Instrumental Analysis, 1978, 2d edit., 1986, Atomic Absorption Spectroscopy, 1970, Trace Analysis, 1986, Problem Solving in Analytical Chemistry, 1988, Calculations in Pharmaceutical Sciences, 1993; editl. bd. Analytical Letters, 1971—, Can. Jour. Spectroscopy, 1974-96, Analytical Instrumentation, 1974-93, Talanta, 1980-88 (spl. editor USA honor issue, 1989), Analytical Chemistry, 1985-89, Critical Revs. in Analytical Chemistry, 1985—, The Analyst, 1986-90, Jour. Saudi Chem. Soc., 1995—, editor in chief Talanta, 1989—, Electroanalysis 1988—, Jour. Pharm. and Biochem. Analysis, 1990-97, Fresenius' Z. Analytical Chem., 1991-93, Laborator Automation, 1992—, Quimica Analitica, 1993—; contbr. articles to profl. jours. Named Fulbright Hays scholar, 1978—79; recipient Medal of Honor, Univ. Libre de Brussels, 1978, Talanta medal, Elsevier Sci., 1995, Commemorative medal, Charles U., 1999, Geoff Wilson medal, Deakin U., 2003. Mem. Am. Chem. Soc. (sect. chmn. 1982-83, chmn. elect divsn. Analytic chemistry 1988-89, chmn. 1989-90, divsn. Analytical Chemistry award for Excellence in Tchg. 1988, Fisher award in analytical chemistry 1996), Soc. Applied Spectroscopy (sect. chmn. 1982), Spectroscopy Soc. Can., Am. Inst. Chemists (cert.), Soc. Electroanalytical Chemistry (bd. dirs. 1993-98). Republican. Home: PO Box 26 Medina WA 98039-0026 Office: U Wash Dept Chemistry Box 351700 Seattle WA 98195-1700 E-mail: christian@chem.washington.edu.

CHRISTIAN, GARY IRVIN, lawyer; b. Albany, Ga., July 7, 1951; s. Rupert Irvin and Alice Amelia (Smith) C.; 1 child, Amy Margaret. BA in History, Polit. Sci., David Lipscomb Coll., 1973; MPA, U. Tenn., 1974; JD, Vanderbilt U., 1979. Bar: Fla. 1979, U.S. Dist. Ct. (no. and mid. dists.) Fla 1979. Rsch. dir. Ala. League of Mcpls., Montgomery, 1974-76; instr. in pub. adminstrn. David Lipscomb Coll., Nashville, 1977-79; assoc. Rogers, Towers, Bailey, Jones & Gay, Jacksonville, Fla., 1979-83, Foley & Lardner, Jacksonville, 1983-86; ptnr. Christian, Prom, Korn & Zehmer, Jacksonville, 1986-92, Rumph, Stoddard & Christian, Jacksonville, 1992—. Editor-in-chief Vanderbilt Jour. of Transnational Law, 1978-79. Bd. dirs. PACE Ctr. for Girls, Inc., Jacksonville, 1984-92, pres., 1984-86; mem. Leadership Jacksonville, 1986-87; chmn. site selection com. St. Johns County Sch. Bd., 1993-95; mem. site selection com., St. Johns County Sch. Bd., 1989-91. Mem. ABA (condominiums and planned devels. com.), Jacksonville Bar Assn. (coord. continuing edn. 1984-85, vice chmn. real property sect. 1986-87, chmn. 1987-88, chmn. corps., banking & bus. sect. 1991-92), Wavemasters Soc. (pres. 1986-87), Jacksonville C. of C. (com. 100 1986-94), Southpoint Bus. Assn. (bd. dirs. 1990-2001, pres. 1991-93), Oak Bridge Country Club, Seminole Club, Salt Creek Homeowners Assn. (bd. dirs. 1993-97, pres. 1994-96), Univ. Club, Deer Creek Country Club. Republican. Mem. Ch. of Christ. Avocations: golf, fishing, racquetball, hunting, stamp collecting. Home: 1719 Girvin Rd Jacksonville FL 32225-2620 Office: Rumph Stoddard & Christian 3100 University Blvd S Ste 101 Jacksonville FL 32216-2777

CHRISTIAN, JAMES WAYNE, economist; b. Ft. Worth, Oct. 7, 1934; s. Nap B. and Daphne (Wright) Christian; m. Jo June Maples, June 5, 1952; children: Amy Joella, Nicole Denise. BA, U. Tex., Austin, 1962, MA, 1964, PhD, 1965. Dir. internat. div. Fed. Home Loan Bank Bd., Washington, 1972—74; sr. v.p., chief economist Nat. Savs. and Loan League, Washington, 1974—80, U.S. League Savs. Inst., Chgo., 1980—91; pres. James Christian Assocs., Fair Oaks Ranch, Tex., 1991; dir. Real Estate Ctr. at Tex. A & M Univ., 1993—95. Prof. econs. Iowa State U., 1965—74; dir. Nat. Housing Conf., 1980—84; cons. 23 developing country govts., 1970. Contbr. articles to profl. jour. Served with USN, 1952—55, served with USAF, 1955—59. Recipient Am. Legion award, 1949; grantee Social Sci. Rsch. Coun. grantee, 1968—69; univ. fellow, 1964, NSF fellow, 1965. Mem.: So. Econ. Assn., Am. Fin. Assn., Am. Econ. Assn., Cosmos, Phi Kappa Phi, Pi Sigma Alpha, Omicron Delta Epsilon, Phi Beta Kappa.

CHRISTIAN, JOE CLARK, medical genetics researcher, educator; b. Marshall, Okla., Sept. 12, 1934; s. Roy John and Katherine Elizabeth (Beeby) C.; m. Shirley Ann Yancey, June 5, 1960; children: Roy Clark, Charles David. BS, Okla. State U., 1956; MS, U. Ky., 1959, PhD, 1960, MD, 1964. Cert. clin. geneticist, Am. Bd. Med. Genetics. Resident internal medicine Vanderbilt U., Nashville, 1964-66; asst. prof. med. genetics Ind. U., Indpls., 1966-69, assoc. prof., 1969-74, prof., 1974-99, assoc. dean basic scis. and regional ctrs., 1996-98, prof. emeritus, assoc. dean emeritus, 1999—. Served with USAR, 1953-60. Mem. AMA, Am. Soc. Human Genetics. Democrat. Methodist. Avocations: bicycling, farming. Office: Ind U Dept Med/Molecular Genetics 975 W Walnut St Dept Med Indianapolis IN 46202-5181 E-mail: jcristi@iupui.edu.

CHRISTIAN, JOHN CATLETT, JR., lawyer; b. Springfield, Mo., Sept. 12, 1929; s. John Catlett and Alice Odelle (Milling) C.; m. Peggy Jeanne Cain, Apr. 12, 1953; children: Cathleen Marie, John Catlett, Alice Cain. AB, Drury Coll., 1951; LLB, Tulane U., 1956. Bar: La. 1956, Mo. 1956, U.S. Supreme Ct. 1975. Assoc. Porter & Stewart, Lake Charles, La., 1956-58, Wilkinson, Lewis, Wilkinson & Madison, Shreveport, La., 1958-62, ptnr., 1962-64, Milling, Benson, Woodward, Hillyer, Pierson & Miller, New Orleans, 1964-92, of counsel, 1993-94. Pres. Sherburne Land Co., 1974-83, Pointe-Martin Mgmt., Inc., 1990-2000; dir. Emerald Land Corp. Pres. Kathleen Elizabeth O'Brien Found., 1963—. Served with USMCR, 1951-53. Fellow Am. Coll. Trial Lawyers; mem. ABA, Fed. Bar Assn., Mo. Bar Assn., La. Bar Assn., La. Landowners Assn. (bd. dirs. 1983-2001), Boston Club, Beau Chene Country Club, Highlands Falls Country Club, Kappa Alpha Order, Omicron Delta Kappa, Phi Delta Phi. Home: 807 Tete Lours Dr Mandeville LA 70471-1774 Office: PO Box 1317 Mandeville LA 70470-1317 E-mail: jcchristiansr@aol.com.

CHRISTIAN, JOHN EDWARD, health science educator; b. Indpls., July 12, 1917; s. George Edward and Okel Kandus (Waltz) C.; m. Catherine Ellen Spooner, July 23, 1948; 1 dau., Linda Kay. BS, Purdue U., 1939, PhD, 1944. Control chemist Upjohn Co., 1939-40; faculty Purdue U., Lafayette, Ind., 1940—, prof. pharm. chemistry, 1950-59, head dept. radiol. control, 1956-59, prof. bionucleonics, head dept., 1959-82; chmn. adminstrv. com. Trace Level Research Inst., 1960-88; dir. Inst. for Environmental Health, 1965-88; head Sch. Health Scis., 1979-82, Hovde Disting. prof., 1979-88, Hovde Disting. prof. bionucleonics and health scis. emeritus, 1988—. Vis. prof. radiation therapy Ind. U. Sch. Medicine, 1970-88; Harvey Washington Meml. lectr. Purdue U., 1955; Edward-Kremers Meml. lectr. U. Wis., 1956; vis. lectr. U. Tex., 1959, Taylor U. Ann. Sci. Lecture Series, Upton, Ind., 1960; Julius A. Koch Meml. lectr. U. Pitts., 1961 Assoc. editor Radiochem. Letters. Mem. revision com. U.S. Pharmacopeia, 1950-60, mem. adv. panel on radioactive drugs, 1960-70; adv. com. isotope distbn. AEC, 1952-58, mem. med. adv. com., 1967-75; mem. radiation and chem. def. sect. Ind. Dept. Civil Def., 1954— ; vice chmn. Radiation Control Adv. Commn., Ind., 1958— ; mem. exec. com. Ind. Comprehensive Health Planning Council, 1972-76; mem. adv. com. radiopharms. FDA, 1970-75; mem. Ind. Gov.'s Pesticide Council, 1970-73; Alumni research councilor Purdue Research Found., 1964-88; mem. Ind. Environmental Mgmt. Bd., 1972-87, Nat. Energy Policy Task Force, Dept. Energy, 1981-83; mem. Bd. Grants Am. Found. for Pharm. Edn., 1989—. Recipient award Chilean Iodine Ednl. Bur., 1956, Julius Sturmer award Phila. Coll. Pharmacy and Sci., 1958, Leather medal Purdue U., 1971, Hovde Faculty Purdue U. fellow, 1988. Fellow AAAS (past sec. and chmn. pharm. sci. sect., mem. council), Ind. Acad. Sci.; mem. AMA (spl. affiliate), AAUP, Am. Inst. Architecture (bd. dirs. 1998—, Gibson award 1999), Am. Assn. Colls. Pharmacy (past mem. exec. com., chmn. conf. tchrs., chmn. conf. grad. study and grad. tchrs., chmn. com. study grad. edn. in pharmacy), Am. Chem. Soc. (past chmn. Purdue sect.), Am. Pharm. Assn. (Ebert medal 1957, Justin L. Powers Research Achievement award 1963, past chmn. sci. sect.), Acad. Pharm. Sci. (past v.p.), Ind. Pharm. Assn., Am. Pub. Health Assn., Am. Nuclear Soc., Am. Soc. Bacteriology, Health Phys. Soc., Historic Landmarks Found. of Ind. (bd. dirs., exec. com. 1997—), Frank Lloyd Wright Bldg. Conservancy (Wright Spirit award 1997), Sigma Xi (past pres. Purdue chpt., research award Purdue chpt. 1950), Rho Chi, Phi Lambda Upsilon, Sigma Pi Sigma., Eta Sigma Gamma, Gamma Sigma Delta. Home: 1301 Woodland Ave West Lafayette IN 47906-2371 Office: Purdue U Sch Health Scis Civil Engring Bldg West Lafayette IN 47907

CHRISTIAN, JOHN KENTON, organization executive, publisher, writer, marketing consultant; b. Pana, Ill., Nov. 6, 1927; s. Ben Ross and Ruth (Stevenson) C.; m. Marjorie Adair Pollock, Nov. 28, 1958; children— Jefrey, Dwane, Kevin. Student, Westminster Coll., 1945, Colo. Coll., 1948, Emerson Coll., 1949; BS, Boston U., 1951; student, Am. U., 1954-55. Relief editor, rep., columnist St. Louis Daily Record, 1950-51; reporter Commerce Clearing House, Washington, 1952; with U.S. News and World Report, 1953-68, regional sales mgr., 1960-63, mktg. mgr. Washington, 1964-68; pub. Nation's Cities Mag., Washington, 1968-76; mem. U.S. Fed. Preparedness Agy. mission to Iran, 1975-76; pres. Internat. Center for Emergency Preparedness, Washington, 1977-80; also pub. Emergency Preparedness News, 1977-79; v.p. Nat. Radio Broadcasters Assn., 1979-84; pres. Communications Brokers, Inc., 1984-88; author, pub. and mktg. cons., 1988-92; mktg. dir. Marine Corps Assn., 1992-2000. Media and mktg. devel. cons., 2000—. Served with USAAF, 1945-48. Presbyterian. Home: 10867 Deborah Dr Potomac MD 20854-2716 E-mail: JKChristian@erols.com.

CHRISTIAN, JOHN ROBERT, music educator; b. Milw., Dec. 29, 1972; s. Charles Edward Christian and Carol Ann Christian (Wendorf). MusB, U. of Wis., Whitewater, WI, 1996; student, U. Wis., 1996—97; MusM, Ctrl. Mich. U., 1999; student, U. of Colo., 2002. Dir. bands Lake Highland Prep. Sch., Orlando, Fla., 2000—, Greensburg (Pa.) Ctrl. Cath. H.S., 1999—2000, De La Salle H.S., Concord, Calif., 2003—; prof. music Alma (Mich.) Coll., 1997—99; grad. tchg. asst. Ctrl. Mich. U., Mt. Pleasant, Mich., 1997—99; asst. condr. Milw. Youth Symphony Orch., Milwaukee, Wis., 1996—97; instr. of music U. of Wis., Milw., 1996—97. Cons. Festival of Orchestras; cons. Band Quest Program Am. Composers Forum. Conductor USS Arizona Memorial-Pearl Harbor, Hawaii. Mem.: Music Educators Nat. Conf., World Assn. of Symphonic Bands and Ensembles, Coll. Band Dir. Nat. Assn., Phi Mu Alpha Sinfonia (collegiate province rep. 1992—94). Home: 7464 Sugar Bend Dr Orlando FL 32819 Office: De LaSalle HS 1130 Winton Dr Concord CA 94523 Home Fax: 407-206-2854. Personal E-mail: dp7464@yahoo.com.

CHRISTIAN, JOHN THOMAS, civil engineer; b. N.Y.C., Nov. 2, 1936; s. Thomas Douglas and Evelyn Catherine (Maestri) C.; m. Lynda Ballou Gregorian, June 8, 1960; children: Douglas Arthur, Shirin Lynda. BSCE, MIT, 1958, MSCE, 1959, PhD in Civil Engring., 1966. Registered profl. engr., Mass., Maine. Asst. prof. civil engring. MIT, Cambridge, 1966-70, assoc. prof. civil engring., 1970-73; cons. geotech. div. Stone & Webster Engring. Corp., Boston, 1973-76, cons. engr., 1976-80, sr. cons. engr., 1980-89, v.p., 1989—; exec. v.p. Stone & Webster Advanced Systems Devel. Svcs., Boston, 1989-92. Mem. engring. accreditation com. Accreditation Bd. for Engring. & Tech., N.Y.C., 1984—, chmn. 1990-91; mem. adv. bd. seismic group Electric Power Rsch. Inst., Palo Alto, Calif., Nat. Ctr. for Earthquake Engring. Rsch., Buffalo, N.Y., Mass. Bd. Bldg. Regulations and Standards, Boston; mem. vis. com. for civil engring. U. N.H., Durham, Princeton U., N.J., U. Tex., Austin. Co-author, editor: Numerical Methods in Geotechnical Engineering, 1977, Productivity Tools For Geotechnical Engineers, 1997, Reliability and Statistics in Geotechnical Engineering, 2003; contbr. 100 articles to profl. jours. Vol. speaker Boston pub. schs., 1986—; reader Recordings for the Blind, Cambridge, 1990-1997. Lt. USAF, 1959-63. NSF fellow, 1963-66. Hon. mem. Am. Soc. Civil Engrs., 2001 (chmn. geotech. engring. div. 1985-86, various coms.); mem. Internat. Soc. Soil Mechanics and Found. Engring., Earthquake Engring. Rsch. Inst., Seismol. Soc. Am., Assn. for Computing Machinery, Boston Soc. Civil Engrs. (hon. mem., Desmond Fitzgerald medal 1973, chmn. computer group), NAE, 1999. Achievements include development of computer applications for geotechnical engineering, including finite element methods and scope stability; development of probabilistic methods for earthquake and geotechnical engineering. Home and Office: 23 Fredana Rd Waban MA 02468-1103

CHRISTIAN, JOSEPH RALPH, physician; b. Chgo., June 15, 1920; s. Ralph F. and Anna M. (Across) Co; m. Marcia Pomeroy, Sept. 25, 1944; children—Patricia Ann, Joseph Ralph. AA, U. Chgo., 1941; MD, Loyola U., Chgo., 1944. Diplomate: Am. Bd. Pediatrics. Intern Cook County Hosp., Chgo., 1944-45, resident, 1945-46, 48-49; faculty Stritch Sch. Medicine, Loyola U., Chgo., 1948-61; prof. Stritch Sch. Medicine, Loyola U. (pediatrics), 1957-61, chmn. dept., 1960-61; attending pediatrician Loyola Service at La Rabida Sanitarium, 1948-61; chmn. dept. pediatrics Mercy Hosp., 1960-61; chief pediatrics Lewis Meml. Maternity Hosp., 1951-61; chmn. dept. pediatrics Rush Presbyn.-St. Luke's Med. Center, Chgo., 1961-85; prof. pediatrics U. Ill. Coll. Medicine, Chgo., 1961-70; prof. Rush Med. Coll., Chgo., 1970-85, prof. emeritus, 1985—, chmn. dept. pediatrics, 1970-85. Sr. attending pediatrician children's div. Cook County Hosp., 1959-65 Editor: Pediatrics Digest, 1962-78; Mem. editorial bd.: Childcraft, 1963-87; Contbr. articles to med. jours. Chmn. poison control com. Chgo. Bd. Health, 1961-69; chmn. med. com. Infant Welfare Soc., Chgo., 1958-61; chmn. 9th Ill. Congress Maternal and Infant Health, 1962; chmn. bd. trustees Holy Cross Chgo., 1970-75. Served to capt. M.C. AUS, 1946-47. Recipient Clin. Faculty award Stritch Sch. Medicine, 1954, 57 Fellow Am. Coll. Chest Physicians, Am. Acad. Pediatrics (chmn. film rev. com. 1963-73, chmn. com. residency fellowships 1964-67), Am. Pub. Health Assn., A.C.P.; mem. A.M.A., Am. Fedn. Clin. Research, Am. Pediatric Soc., Am. Heart Assn., Ambulatory Pediatric Assn., Am. Assn. Poison Control Centers, Am. Assn. Maternal and Infant Health, Ill. Assn. Maternal and Infant Health (pres. 1964), Am. Pediatric Soc., Chgo. Pediatric Soc. (pres. 1964-65), Midwest Soc. Pediatric Research, Assn. Med. Sch. Pediatric Dept. Chairmen. Home: 3 Oakbrook Club Dr Apt E107 Oak Brook IL 60523-1330

CHRISTIAN, LORI COFFELT, marketing professional; b. Houston, Dec. 5, 1960; d. Donald Warren and Charlotte Hollopeter Coffelt; m. John Catlett Christian, III, June 25, 1988 (div. Mar. 5, 2002); children: Charlotte Elizabeth, Camille Corinne, Catherine Catlett. BS, So. Meth. U., 1983; postgrad., U. Tex., 1984—86. Media planner Bozell Jacobs Kenyon and Eckhardt, Dallas, 1986—88; account exec. Levenson and Hill, Dallas, 1988—90; account exec., supr. Rubin Postaer and Assocs., Santa Monica, Calif., 1990—96; dir. brand mgmt. MediaOne, L.A., 1996—98; mng. dir., brand strategy Reliant Energy, Houston, 1998—99; CEO, ptnr DotDash, Inc., Houston, 1999—2003; chief mktg. officer Remedy Corp., Mountain View, Calif., 2000—01; v.p., innovation Pennzoil-Quaker State, Houston, 2002. Vol. Dem. Party, Calif., 1995—98; Sunday sch. tchr. St. Paul's United Meth. Ch., Houston, 1999—2000, Redondo Beach (Calif.) United Meth. Ch., 1993—96; Sunday sch. tchr., mem. adminstrv. bd. Oak Lawn United Meth. Ch., Dallas, 1986—88; Sunday sch. tchr., choir mem. United Meth. Ch., Kingwood, 2003. Mem.: River Oaks Dem. Women. Democrat. Methodist. Avocations: cooking, travel, reading, writing, gearhead. Personal E-mail: mslorichristian@aol.com.

CHRISTIAN, MARY JO DINAN, educator; b. Denver, May 7, 1941; d. Joseph Timothy and Margaret Rose Dinan; m. Ralph Poinsett Christian, Aug. 27, 1966. BA, Loretto Heights Coll., Denver, 1964; MA, George Washington U., 1983. Cert. English educator, adminstrn. and supervision secondary edn. English tchr. Denver Pub. Schs., 1964-67, Prince George's County Pub. Sch., Md., 1967-81; vice-prin. Prince George's County High Sch., Md., 1981-97; program dir. Tchr. Equity Equals Achievement, 1997—99, tchr., mentor, 2002—. Presenter tchr. equity and student achievement Nat. Conf.; Generating Expectations for Student Achievement equity assurance coord. instrs. in-svc. and adminstrs., 1997—99; tchr. mentor, 2002; pres. Tchr. Equity Equals Student Achievement Inc.; owner Independence House Bed and Breakfast, Washington, 2000—. Columnist: WomenSpeak, 1981-91. Rep. Prince George's County Commn. Women UN Fourth World Conf. Women Forum, Beijing, 1995. Md. Ho. of Dels. recognition. Mem. NAFE, ASCD, NEA (chair adminstrs. caucus 1991-93, adminstr.-at-large resolutions com. 1986-92, polit. action com. 1984-86, coord.-at-large women's caucus 1981-91, Creative Leadership award 1989), Md. State Tchrs. Assn. (state coord. Sen. Sarbane campaign 1982, state voter registration coord. 1984, issue coord. Tom McMillen campaign 1986, Women's Rights award 1988), Phi Delta Kappa, Alpha Delta Kappa. Home: 504 Independence Ave SE Washington DC 20003-1143

CHRISTIAN, PEARL C, musician; b. New York, July 18, 1927; d. Joseph Obadiah and Clotilda Cecelia Clifton; m. Lloyd Micah Christian, Jan. 28, 1948; children: Peter Lloyd, Donna Laverne, Lawrence Micah. Piano instr. Queens Village Sch. of Music, N.Y., 1989—91, pvt. studio, N.Y., 1991—. Performer: (Concert) Bklyn. Queens Conservatory Music.

CHRISTIAN, RALPH GORDON, agricultural research and animal health consultant; b. Lethbridge, Alta., Can., Apr. 17, 1942; s. Wesley Peel and Mary (Patterson) C.; m. Brenda Esther Kheong, 1976. DVM, U. Guelph, Ont., Can., 1966; vet. pathology diploma, U. Sask., Saskatoon, 1970. Cert. in vet. pathology Am. Coll. Vet. Pathologists. Instr. Vet. Sch. U. Melbourne, Australia, 1977; dir. animal health divsn. Alta. Dept. Agr., Edmonton, 1982-87; acting asst. dep. min. Alta. Agrl. Prodn. Sector, Edmonton, 1987; exec. dir. Alta. Agrl. Rsch. Inst., Edmonton, 1987—2000; exec. dir. rsch. divsn. Alta. Dept. Agr., Food and Rural Devel., Edmonton, 1987-2000; pres. Ralph Christian Cons., Inc., 2001—. Br. head pathology br. Alta. Agr. Vet. Lab., Edmonton, 1972-79, 79-82; lab. head Vet. Lab., Fairview, Alta., 1970-72; instr., resident pathology dept. Western Coll. Vet. Medicine, Saskatoon, 1969-70. Mem. Am. Coll. Vet. Pathologists, Can. Vet. Med. Assn. (chmn. specialization com. 1986-88), Alta. Vet. Med. Assn. (pres. 1981-82). Avocations: skiing, equine driving. Home and Office: RR 1 Edmonton AB Canada T6H 5T6 E-mail: rbchristi@shaw.ca.

CHRISTIAN, RICHARD CARLTON, university dean, former advertising agency executive; b. Dayton, Ohio, Nov. 29, 1924; s. Raymond A. and Louise (Gamber) C.; m. Audrey Bongartz, Sept. 10, 1949; children: Ann Christian Carra, Richard Carlton Jr. BS in Bus. Adminstrn, Miami U., Oxford, Ohio, 1948; MBA, Northwestern U., 1949; LLD (hon.), Nat.-Louis U., 1986; postgrad., Denison U., The Citadel, Biarritz Am. U. Mktg. analyst Rockwell Mfg. Co., Pitts., 1949-50; exec. v.p. Marsteller Inc., Chgo., 1951-60, pres., 1960-75; bd. dirs., exec. com. Young and Rubicam, Inc., 1979-84; chmn. bd. Marsteller Inc., 1975-84, chmn. emeritus, 1984—; assoc. dean Kellogg Grad. Sch. Mgmt. Northwestern U., 1984-91, assoc. dean Medill Sch. Journalism, 1991-99. Dir., chmn. Bus. Publs. Audit Circulation, Inc., 1969-75; spkr. in field. Trustee Northwestern U., 1970-74, Nat.-Louis U., Evanston, Ill., 1970-92, James Webb Young Fund for Edn., U. Ill., 1962-95; pres. Nat. Advt. Rev. Coun., 1976-77; bd. adv. coun. mem. Miami U.; mem. adv. coun. J.L. Kellogg Grad. Sch. Mgmt., Northwestern U.; v.p., dir. Mus. Broadcast Comm.; dir. Can. U.S. Ednl. Exch. (Fulbright Found.), 1988-92. With inf. AUS, 1942-46, ETO. Recipient Ohio Gov.'s award 1977, Alumni medal, Alumni, Merit and Svc. awards Northwestern U.; named to the Advt. Hall of Fame, 1991. Mem. Am. Mktg. assn., Indsl. Mktg. Assn. (founder, chmn. 1951), Bus. Profl. Advt. Assn. (life mem. Chgo., pres. Chgo. 1954-55, nat. v.p. 1955-58, G. D. Crain award 1977), U. Ill. Found., Northwestern U. Bus. Sch. Alumni Assn. (founder, pres.), Am. Assn. Advt. Agys. (dir., chmn. 1976-77), Am. Acad. Advt. (1st disting. svc. award 1978), Northwestern U. Alumni Assn. (nat. pres. 1968-70), Mid-Am. Club, Comml. Club, Econ. Club Chgo., Kenilworth Club, Westmoreland Country Club, Alpha Delta Sigma, Beta Gamma Sigma, Delta Sigma Pi, Phi Gamma Delta. Baptist. Home: 2 Arbor Lane Apt 412 Evanston IL 60201

CHRISTIAN, ROLAND CARL (BUD CHRISTIAN), retired English language and speech communications educator; b. LaSalle, Colo., June 7, 1938; s. Roland Clyde and Ethel Mae (Lattimer) C.; m. Joyce Ann Kincel, Feb. 15, 1959; children: Kathleen Marie Christian, Kristine May Christian Sweet. BA in English and Speech, U. No. Colo., 1962, MA, 1966. Cert. tchr., N.Y., Colo. Tchr. Southside Jr. High Sch., Rockville Centre, N.Y., 1962-63, Plateau Valley High Sch., Collbran, Colo., 1963-67; prof. English Northeastern Jr. Coll., Sterling, Colo., 1967-93, prof. emeritus, 1993—. Presenter seminars, workshops, Sterling, 1967—; emcee/host Town Meeting of Am., Sterling, 1976, Sterling Cmty. Caring Hands Trivia Challenge, 2001, 02, 03. Author: Be Bright! Be Brief! Be Gone! A Speaker's Guide, 1983, Potpourrivia, A Digest of Curious Words, Phrases and Trivial Information, 1986, Nicknames in Sports: A Quiz Book, 1986; (poetry) Dusty Rivers, 2001; lit. adv. New Voices mag., 1983-93; contbr. Ways We Write, 1964, The Family Treasury of Great Poems, 1982, Our Twentieth Century's Greatest Poems, 1982, Anti-War Poems; vol. II, 1985, Impressions, 1986, World Poetry Anthology, 1986, American Poetry Anthology, 1986, Chasing Rainbows, 1988, The Poetry of Life, 1988, Hearts on Fire, 1988, Wide Open Magazine, 1986, 87, 88; columnist South Platte Sentinel, 1988—. Served with U.S. Army, 1956-59. Recipient Colo. Recognition of Merit scholarship, 1956, Merit cert. Poets Anonymous, 1983, Award of Merit (9), 1985, 86, Golden Poet of Yr. award World of Poetry Press, 1985, 86, 87, 88, Joel Mack Tchr. of Yr. award Northeastern Jr. Coll., 1986; Jr. Coll. Found. grantee, 1986, 87. Avocations: fishing, hunting, sports, trivia, music. Home: 603 Park St Apt 105 Sterling CO 80751-3855 E-mail: budnjoyce@plains.net.

CHRISTIAN, SANDRA SVEC, retired state official; b. Evanston, Ill., Dec. 11, 1947; d. Joseph Francis and Martha Marjorie (Randau) Svec; m. Terry L. Yonker, June 28, 1969 (div. 1990); m. Bernard L. Christian, Aug. 20, 2001. BS in Meteorology, U. Wis., Madison, 1969. Sec., sales asst. Moore Bus. Forms Inc., Lansing, Mich., 1970-72; rsch. asst. Mich. Dept. Social Svcs., Lansing, 1972-74; adminstrv. analyst Mich. Pub. Svc. Commn., Lansing, 1974-79, supr. orgn. devel., 1980-84; program mgr. Gov.'s Energy Awareness Adv. Com., Lansing, 1979-80; labor rels. rep. Mich. Dept. Agr., Lansing, 1984-87, acting personnel dir., 1987-89, asst. to chief dep. dir., 1989-93, dir. EEO/affirmative action office, 1991-97, program mgr. human resources, 1997—2000; benefit analyst Human Resource Mgmt. Network, 1998—2002, ret., 2002. Bd. dirs. Lansing Area Advocates for Choice, 1991-93, Downtown Neighborhood Assn., Lansing, 1990—, v.p., 1992-95, sec., 1998-2000; vol. Radio Talking Book, East Lansing, Mich., 1974-93, Am. Cancer Soc. Relay for Life, 2003—; active Stratford (Ont., Can.), Shakespearean Festival, 1974—; Marshal vol. co-chair Oldsmobile Classic Ladies PGA event, East Lansing, 1993-96, Marshal vol., 1997-98, mdse. vol. co-team leader, 1999-2000; mem. Covenant Assn. United Ch. of Christ, Church and Ministry Com., 1992-96, chair, 1996. Mem.: Am. Bus. Women's Assn. (treas. Virgo chpt. 1998—2000, Woman of the Yr. award 1977), Friday Frolics. Avocations: golf, walking, community theater, conservation. Home: 1512 Settlers Hill Dr Lansing MI 48917-1284 E-mail: kangaroo333@comcast.net.

CHRISTIAN, SONYA, college dean; b. Quilon, Kerala, India, July 28, 1966; d. Paul and Pamela Christian; m. Sriram Khe, Feb. 13, 1993; 1 child, Eisha Christian. BSc in Math., U. Kerala, India, 1987; MS, U. So. Calif., 1990, postgrad.; EdD, UCLA, 2002. Lectr. American River Coll., Sacramento, 1991; asst. prof. Bakersfield (Calif.) Coll., 1991-95, assoc. prof., 1995-2000, dean, 2000—. Me. Rotary (officer Bakersfield 1998). Home: 655 Goodpasture Rd Eugene OR 97401-1535 Office: Lane Cmty Coll 4000 E 30th Ave Eugene OR 97405 E-mail: christians@lanecc.edu.

CHRISTIAN, SUZANNE HALL, financial planner; b. Hollywood, Calif., Apr. 28, 1935; d. Peirson M. and Gertrude (Engel) Hall; children: Colleen, Carolyn, Claudia, Cynthia. BA, UCLA, 1956; MA, Redlands U., 1979. CFP. Instr. L.A. City Schs., 1958-59, Claremont (Calif.) Unified Schs., 1972-84, dept. chair, 1981-84; fin. planner Waddell & Reed, Upland, Calif., 1982-96, sr. acct. exec., 1986; br. mgr. Hornor, Townsend & Kent, Claremont, 1996—2002,

Linsco Pvt. Ledger Fin. Svcs., 2002—. Past corp. mem. Pilgrim Place Found., Claremont; lectr. in field. Author: Strands in Composition, 1979; TV cable host Money Talks with Suzanne Christian, 1993—. Legal and estate planning com. Am. Cancer Soc., 1988-95; profl. adv. com. YWCA-Inland Empire, 1987; treas. Fine Arts Scripps Coll., 1993-94; bd. dirs. Casa Colina Hosp., 1994-2003; past bd. dirs. Galelio Soc. Harvey Mudd Coll. Recipient Athena Internat. Businesswoman of Yr. award, 1997. Mem. Inst. CFPs, Fin. Planning Assn., Planned Giving Roundtable, Estate Planning Coun. Pomona Valley (pres. 2001-2002, bd. dirs.), Claremont C. of C. (pres., bd. dirs. 1994-95), Curtain Raisers Club Garrison (pres. 1972-75), Circle of Champions (pres.'s coun. 1994-95, Silver Crest award 1985-87, 94-95, HTK top ten leader 1996-2003), Harvey Mudd Coll. Galileo Soc. (bd. dirs. 1997-98), Kappa Kappa Gamma (pres. 1970-74). Avocations: tennis, gardening, archaeology. Home: PO Box 1237 Claremont CA 91711-1237 Office: Hornor Townsend & Kent 419 Yale Ave Claremont CA 91711-4340 Fax: 909-625-3661.

CHRISTIAN, TERRY CLIFTON, lawyer; b. Welch, W.Va., Aug. 4, 1952; s. Samuel Clifton and Mary Jane Christian; m. Wendy Lee McCoy, Feb. 14, 1991. BA, U. Del., 1984; JD, Ind. U., Indpls., 1987. Bar: Fla. 1988, U.S. Dist. Ct. (mid. dist.) Fla. 1989, U.S. Ct. Appeals (11th cir.) 1990, U.S. Dist. Ct. (no. and so. dists.) Fla. 1996, U.S. Supreme Ct. 1996; cert. Bd. Legal Edn. and Specialization, Fla.; cert. Nat. Bd. Trial Advocacy. Asst. state atty. Office of State Atty., Ft. Myers, Fla., 1988-89; mng. ptnr. Christian & Assocs., P.A., Tampa, Fla., 1989—2003; U.S. Immigration Judge Detroit, 2003—. Mem. criminal justice act panel U.S. Dist. Ct. for Mid. Dist. Fla., 1989—, for No. Dist., 1996—, for So. Dist., 1998—; spl. asst. pub defender Capitol and RICO cases only, Tampa, 1989-2003. Author immigration and criminal law seminars. Bd. dirs. Humane Soc. Tampa Bay, 2002-03. Capt. U.S. Army Res., 1986-90. Mem. FBA (exec. com. Tampa Bay chpt. 1996-2001, svc. award 1997-2001 Am. Immigration Lawyers Assn. (sec. Ctrl. Fla. chpt. 1992-94, treas. 1994-95, v.p. 1995-97, svc. award 1995-97), Fla. Bar, Hillsborough County Assn. Criminal Def. Lawyers (bd. dirs., sec. 1996-97, pres. 1997-98, svc. award 1998), Am. Inns of Ct. (exec. com. 2000-03, parliamentarian 2001—, sec. 2002-03). Democrat. Roman Catholic. Avocations: reading, sports, physical exercise and weight training. Office: US Immigration Ct 1155 Brewery Park Blvd Ste 450 Detroit MI 48207 Fax: 813 228-6223; Office Fax: 313-226-3053.

CHRISTIAN, THOMAS WILLIAM, lawyer; b. Tuscaloosa, Ala., Aug. 23, 1938; s. George William and Grace (Mandeville) C.; m. Dorothy Rosamond, Jan. 23, 1965; children: George, Ed, Delia. AB, U. Ala., 1960, LLB, 1965. Bar: Ala. 1965, U.S. Dist. Ct. (no. dist.) Ala. 1965, U.S. Ct. Appeals (5th and 11th cirs.) 1971, U.S. Supreme Ct. 1973. Ptnr. Balch & Bingham, Birmingham, Ala., 1965-81; firm Rives & Peterson, Birmingham, Ala., 1981-2000, Christian & Small, Birmingham, Ala., 2000—. Lt. U.S. Army, 1961-63. Fellow Internat. Acad. Trial Lawyers, Am. Bar Found., Am. Coll. Trial Lawyers; mem. ABA, Am. Bd. Trial Advocates, Ala. State Bar Assn., Birmingham Bar Assn. (pres. 1984), Ala. Def. Lawyers Assn. (pres. 1979), Internat. Assn. Ins. Counsel, Birmingham Country Club, Redstone Club. Presbyterian. Avocations: fishing, jogging, nautilis. Home: 4012 Old Leeds Ln Birmingham AL 35213-3235 Office: Christian & Small 1800 Financial Ctr Birmingham AL 35203-2696 E-mail: twchristian@csattorneys.com.

CHRISTIAN-CHRISTENSEN, DONNA MARIE, congresswoman; b. Teaneck, N.J., Sept. 19, 1945; d. Almeric L. Christian and Virginia Sterling; children: Rabiah Green, Karida Green; m. Chris Christensen; stepchildren: Lisa, Esther, Bryan, David. BS, St. Mary's Coll., Ind.; MD, George Washington U., 1970. Pvt. medical practice, 1973—74; cmty. health physician U.S. V.I. Dept. Health; med. dir. Gov. Juan F. Luis Hosp., St. Croix; vice chairperson U.S. V.I. Dem. Territorial Com., 1980; mem. U.S. V.I. Bd. Edn., 1984; committeewoman Nat. Dem., 1984; apptd. U.S. V.I. Status Commn., 1988-92; del. Dem. Nat. Conv.; at large repr. from V.I. U.S. Ho. of Reps., 1997—; chair Congl. Black Caucus Health Braintrust, 1999—; mem. resources com., small bus. com. Trustee, founding mem. Caribbean Youth Orgn. Mem. Nat. Med. Assn. (trustee), Caribbean Studies Assn., V.I. Med. Inst., V.I. Med. Soc. (pres., sec.), Women's Coalition St. Croix, St. Croix Environ. Assn. Democrat. Office: 1510 Longworth Ho Office Bldg Washington DC 20515-0001 E-mail: donna.christensen@mail.house.gov.*

CHRISTIANO, MELISSA, artist, educator; b. Jonesboro, Ark. d. Jimmy and Mary (Moore) Lincoln; m. Richard J. Christiano, June 30, 1990; 1 child, Wes. BFA, MA, Ark. State U.; MFA, Memphis State U. Art instr. Jones Sch. Art., Jonesboro, 1985-87; instr., owner Studio Art Gallery, Jonesboro, 1987-88; tchg. asst. printmaking Memphis State U., 1986-90; instr. art Mississippi Coll., Blytheville, Ark., 1988-93, Williams Coll., Walnut Ridge, Ark., 1993—. Asst. dir. SAI Gallery, N.Y.C., 1999. Exhbns. include The Forum Gallery, Jonesboro, 1986, Ark. Artist Registry, Little Rock, 1988, Meth. Hosp. Health Sys., Memphis, 1989, U. Memphis Gallery, 1990, U. Ark. Little Rock, 1990, 95, 97, Maddox Fine Art Gallery, Walnut Ridge, 1994, Ark. State U. Gallery, Jonesboro, 1995, 97, Enid Okla Homa Gallery, Chgo., 1995, Chroma Gallery, Little Rock, 1995, B Gallery, Memphis, 1996, Howell Gallery, Jonesboro, 1996, Gallery 479, N.Y.C., 1997, Madison Ave Gallery, Memphis, 1998, Budapest, 1999, Sai Gallery, N.Y.C., 1999, Ark. Artist Register, Little Rock, 1999, Kavehaz Gallery, N.Y.C., 1999, Delta Competition, Little Rock, 1999. Home: Apt 8 3753 46th Ave S Saint Petersburg FL 33711-4460

CHRISTIANS, CLIFFORD GLENN, communications educator; b. Hull, Iowa, Dec. 22, 1939; s. Arnold and Verbena Janette (Geerdes) C.; m. Priscilla Jean Kreun, June 13, 1961; children: Glenn Clifford, Ted Arnold, Paul Raymond. AB, Calvin Coll., 1961; ThM, Fuller Theol. Sem., 1965; MA, U. So. Calif., 1966; PhD, U. Ill., 1974. Dir. comms. Christian Ref. Home Ministries, Grand Rapids, Mich., 1966-70; rsch. asst. prof. comms. U. Ill., Urbana, 1974-80, rsch. assoc. prof. comms., 1980-87, rsch. prof. comms., 1987—. Rsch. fellow Calvin Ctr. for Christian Scholarship, Grand Rapids, 1983-84; vis. scholar in ethics Princeton (N.J.) U., spring, 1979; inst. fellow U. Chgo., 1986-87; Pew Evangel. scholar in ethics Oxford U., spring, 1995; dir. Inst. Rsch. Comms., Urbana, 1987—. Co-author: Jacques Ellul: Interpretive Essays, 1981, Good News: Social Ethics and The Press, 1993, Media Ethics: Cases and Moral Reasoning, 1998, Communication Ethics and Universal Values, 1997, Moral Engagement in Public Life: Theorists fro Contemporary Ethics, 2002; editor: Critical Studies in Mass Communication, 1992-95. Bd. dirs. Empty Tomb, Inc., Champaign, Ill., 1986—; elder Christian Ref. Ch., Champaign, 1974-82; bd. dirs. Univ. YMCA, Champaign, 1974-77, Judah Christian Sch., Champaign, 1984-90. Rsch. fellow Program for Cultural Values and Ethics, 1990. Mem. Soc. for Philosophy and Tech., Assn. for Edn. in Journalism and Mass Comm. (chair qualitative studies divsn. 1980-81), Internat. Assn. Mass Comm. Rsch. (program co-chair 1991-94), Ellul Studies Forum, Nat. Comm. Assn. Democrat. Avocations: fishing, travel, reading. Home: U Ill Inst Comm Rsch 1002 W William St Champaign IL 61821 Office: U Ill Comm Dept 810 S Wright St Urbana IL 61801

CHRISTIANSEN, BRYAN, marketing professional, consultant; b. Washington, June 2, 1960; s. Earle Grace and Catherine Wilma Gardner; m. Inna Berezhnaya, Feb. 14, 1998; m. Chun-Ting Liu, May 31, 1985 (div. Mar. 21, 1996); children: Stanislav, Tanya Ting Gardner, Nicole. AA, Tenri U., Tenri City, Japan, 1981; BS, SUNY, Albany, 1996; MBA, Capella U., 2003. Cert. profl. marketer Am. Mktg. Assn., 2001. Mktg. exec. Xionics, Inc., Orange, Calif., 1988—90; Asia region mgr. Babco-East, Ltd. (Hong Kong), Taipei, Taiwan, 1990—95; sales rep. IBM Corp., Dallas, 1995—97; pres. The Christiansen Corp., Atlanta, 1997—2002; mktg. assoc. PointClear, LLC, Norcross, Ga., 2002—. V.p. mktg., treas., bd. dirs. APICS, White Plains, NY, 1999—2000. Independent. Agnostic. Avocations: martial arts, swimming, writing, travel, foreign language study. Home: 4780 Ashford-Dunwoody Road Atlanta GA 30338 Office: Ste 120 670 Engineering Dr Atlanta GA 30092 Personal E-mail: bchristiansen@specialforces.us.

CHRISTIANSEN, DAVID K. healthcare administrator; b. Logan, Utah, Sept. 10, 1952; s. John R. and Lucele (Kartchner) C.; m. Cynthia Ann Kutsko, July 28, 1982. BS, Brigham Young U., 1977; M in Health Care Adminstrn., U. Ala., 1979. Purchasing asst. McDonald Health Clinic, Provo, Utah, 1975—77; adminstrv. resident Bapt.-Montclair Hosp., Birmingham, Ala., 1978—79, adminstrv. asst., 1979—80; asst. adminstr. Lakeview Cmty. Hosp., Bountiful, Utah, 1980—83; adminstr. Shasta Gen. Hosp., Redding, Calif., 1983—84; CEO Knoxville (Iowa) Cmty. Hosp., 1984—89; COO Med. Ctr. Independence, Kansas City, Mo., 1989—92; CEO Newman Regional Hosp., Emporia, Kans., 1992—96; exec. v.p. MED/MAX Health Mgmt., San Diego, 1996—99; exec. dir. Salt Lake Sr. Clinic, 1999—2001; area adminstr. CHD-Meridan Healthcare Mgmt., 2001—. Cons. Ctr. Health Studies, Nashville, 1981—83; mem. faculty Ctr. Health Studies/Hosp. Cor. Am., Nashville, 1981—83. Explorer advisor Boy Scouts Am., Birmingham, 1977-80; campaign coord. United Way, Bountiful, 1983; exec. bd. dirs. Boy Scouts Am., Topeka, Kans., 1994-96. Named Outstanding Young Man of Am., U.S. Jaycees, 1982. Fellow Am. Coll. Healthcare Execs.; mem. Knoxville C. of C. (chmn. commerce com. 1986-87), Emporia Kans. C. of C. (bd. dirs. 1994-96), Rotary (membership chmn. REdding 1984, Knoxville bd. dirs. 1987-89).

CHRISTIANSEN, DONALD DAVID, electrical engineer, editor, publishing consultant; b. Plainfield, NJ, June 23, 1927; s. David Carsten and Rita (Holmes) C.; m. Joyce Ifill, Jan. 1, 1951; children: Jacqueline, Jill. BEE, Cornell U., Ithaca, N.Y., 1950; postgrad., Mass. Inst. Tech., 1951, 54, U. Wis., Madison, 1966, 68, 71. Registered profl. engr., Mass. Engr. Philco Corp., Phila., 1948-50, CBS, Danvers, Lowell and Newburyport, Mass., 1950-62; solid-state editor Electronic Design, Hayden Pub. Co., N.Y.C., 1962-63; sr. editor EEE-Circuit Design Engring. Mactier Pub. Co., N.Y.C., 1963-66; sr. assoc. editor Electronics McGraw-Hill Pub. Co., N.Y.C., 1966, sr. editor, 1966-67, assoc. mng. editor, 1967-68, editor-in-chief, 1968-70, mgr. planning, devel. electronics publs., 1970-71; gen. mgr. Electronics in Medicine, 1971; editor and pub. Spectrum jour. of IEEE, N.Y.C., 1971-93, editor emeritus, 1993—, chmn. editorial bd., 1972-93; IEEE rep. to UN, 1974-87; pres. Informatica, Huntington, N.Y., 1993—. Lectr. Newark Coll. Engring., 1967, U. Mich., Ann Arbor, 1973, Walla Walla (Wash.) Coll., 1973, Ga. Inst. Tech., 1976, NASA Goddard Space Flight Ctr., 1981, Cornell U., 1982, Disting. lectr. Purdue U., 1986; cons. Bur. of Census, Dept. Commerce, NSF; mem. NRC Com. on Edn. and Utilization of the Engr.; elec. engring. adv. com. Worcester Poly. Inst.; mem. AIP mag. policy com., 1996-98; mem. AIP adv. com. on Indsl. Physicist, chmn., 2000-01; adv. bd. Encyclopedia Americana, 2000—; advisor Am. Inst. Physics Resources Ctr., 2000-01. Editor-in-chief: Electronics Engineers' Handbook, 4th edit., 1997; editor: Engineering Excellence, 1987; publ. com. Cornell Alumni News mag., 1986-91; contbr. articles to profl. jours. Bd. dirs. YMCA, Newburyport, Mass., 1962, Broadband Info. Svcs., N.Y.C., 1970-87, L.I. Mus. Sci. and Tech., 1993-96. With USN, WWII. Recipient medal and citation for advancement of culture Flanders Acad. Art, Sci. and Lit., 1980, citation Folio mag., 1991. Fellow IEEE (co-founder, charter exec. com. chpt. 1958, Centennial medal, Gruenwald award), World Acad. Art and Sci., Radio Club of Am., 1987; mem. Nat. Press Club, N.Y. Acad. Sci., Cornell Soc. Engrs., Coun. Engring. and Sci. Soc. Execs., Am. Soc. Assn. Execs., Am. Soc. Mag. Editors, Soc. Nat. Assn. Publs. (dir. 1976-79, chmn. editl. com. 1976-79, pres. 1981-83), NY Bus. Press Editors (dir. 1978-79), Cornell Engring. Alumni Coun., Delta Club, Union Internat. de la Presse Radiotechnique et Electronique, Deadline Club, Nat. Conf. Electronics in Medicine (chmn. 1971), Soc. for History Tech., Soc. for Indsl. Archeology, Jovians, Antique Wireless Assn., Franklin Inst., Royal Instn., Newcomen Soc., Eta Kappa Nu (eminent mem., chmn., Outstanding Elec. Engr. award 1976-78, dir. 1982-84, chmn. Vladimir Karapetoff award 1991—, chmn. eminent mem. com. 1998—, Disting. Svc. award 2001), Navy League of U.S. (life), USS San Jacinto Assn., Mu Sigma Tau, Sigma Delta Chi. Office: Informatica 434 W Main St Huntington NY 11743-3247

CHRISTIANSEN, JAMES EDWARD, agricultural educator; b. Douglas, Ariz., Sept. 1, 1930; s. Felix Lawrence and Ada Naomi (Squire) C.; m. Jean McInnes, Dec. 25, 1950; children: James Lawrence, Bruce John. BS, U. Ariz., 1951, M Agrl. Edn., 1957; PhD, Ohio State U., 1965. Tchr. vocat. agriculture Tolleson (Ariz.) Union High Sch., 1954-57, Snowflake (Ariz.) Union High Sch., 1957-58, Tempe (Ariz.) Union High Sch., 1958-61; project mgr. Near East Found., Resht, Iran, 1961-63; asst. instr. Ohio State U., Columbus, 1964; cons. ctr. for vocat.-tech. edn. Nat. Ctr. for Rsch. in Vocat.-Tech. Edn., Columbus, 1965; asst. prof. U. Fla., Gainesville, 1966-68; prof. Tex. A&M U., College Station, 1968—. Cons. agrl. edn. US AID, San Jose, Costa Rica, 1967, San Jose, 86, Asuncion, Paraguay, 83, Belize, 90, Malaysia, 92, El Salvador, 94, Mexico, 99, 2000, 02, Internat. Inst. Cooperation in Agrl., San Jose, 2001. Author: Exploring Agriculture, 6th ed., 1984, 5th ed., 1979; contbr. articles to profl. jours. Elder A&M Presbyn. Ch., College Station, 1969-72, 81-83, 90-92. Named Disting. Lectr. Am. Assn. Agrl. Edn., 2000. Mem. Am. Vocat. Assn. (resolutions com. 1988-91), Am. Assn. Tchr. Educators in Agr. (treas. 1977-80, chmn. editing-mng. bd. 1973-76, Disting. Svc. award 1985), Assn. for Internat. Agrl. and Extension Edn. (chmn. constn. and bylaws 1986-87, 96-99, scholarly activities 2000-03, Outstanding Svc. award 2000, Outstanding Leadership award 2003), Vocat. Agr. Tchrs. Assn. Tex. (Outstanding Tchr. Educator award 1979, Disting. Svc. award 1992, 2002), Kiwanis (sec. Snowflake chpt. 1957), Phi Beta Delta, Phi Delta Kappa, Phi Kappa Phi. Republican. Avocations: landscape and instructional photography, rifle target shooting, archaeology. Office: Tex A&M U Dept Agrl Edu College Station TX 77843-2116 E-mail: j-christiansen@tamu.edu.

CHRISTIANSEN, JAY DAVID, lawyer; b. Slayton, Minn., Mar. 22, 1952; s. Holger K. and Dagny (Fjelstad) C.; children: Tyler, Carrie, Jayne. BA, Luther Coll., 1974; JD, Vanderbilt U., 1977. Ptnr. Faegre & Benson, Mpls., 1977—. Mem. ABA (chair 1997-99, health law sect., mem. ho. dels. 1999-2002), Am. Health Lawyers Assn., Order of Coif. Office: Faegre & Benson 90 S 7th St Minneapolis MN 55402-3901 E-mail: jchristi@faegre.com.

CHRISTIANSEN, KEITH ALLAN, lawyer; b. Madison, Wis., Dec. 14, 1943; s. Herman Louis and Faith Louise (Haase) C.; m. Sheila Irene Stangel, Apr. 11, 1966; children: Douglas, Jeffrey. BS, U. Wis., 1965, JD, 1968. Bar: Wis. 1968, Fla. 1973, U.S. Dist. Ct. (ea. dist.) Wis. 1968. Assoc. Foley & Lardner, Milw., 1968-74, ptnr., 1975—. Co-author: Marital Property Law in Wisconsin, 1984, supplements. Active Potawatomi Coun. Boy Scouts Am. (past pres.), 1975—; v.p. Ctrl. Region Boy Scouts. Am., 1992—. Fellow Am. Coll. Trust & Estate Counselors; mem. Mid-winter Estate Planning Clinic, Estate Counselors Forum. Republican. Office: Foley & Lardner 777 E Wisconsin Ave Ste 3800 Milwaukee WI 53202-5367 E-mail: kchristiansen@foleylaw.com.

CHRISTIANSEN, LARRY K. college president; AA, North Iowa Area C.C.; BA in Bus. Edn., U. Northern Iowa; MS in Ednl. Adminstrn., Drake U.; DEd, U. N.D. Distributive edn. coord., chmn. bus. dept. Perry (Iowa) Cmty. H.S., 1967-74; assoc. prof., chmn. bus. divsn. U. Minn. Tech. Coll., Crookston, 1974-82; dean adminstrv. svc., acting dean of instrn., assoc. dean Glendale C.C.; pres. Mesa C.C. Chair acad. internat. exec. adv. bd. Nat. C.C.; mem. Megacorp Bd.; adv. bd. Nat. Campus Compact Cmty.; spkr. in field. Author: (with others) A Case Approach, 1980; co-author: To the Future and Counselor's Guide to the Future. Pres. East Valley Partnership Bd.; cabinet chair Mesa United Way, 1996; campaign chair Maricopa C.C. Dist. Mem. Mesa C. of C. (nat. campus compact cmty. adv. bd.), Mesa Baseline Rotary, Nat. Assn. of Distributive Edn. Tchrs. Office: 1833 W Southern Ave Mesa AZ 85202-4822*

CHRISTIANSEN, MARK D. lawyer; b. Olney, Tex., June 10, 1955; s. Leon H. and Doris J. (Jennings) C. BA, U. Okla., 1977, JD, 1980. Bar: U.S. Dist. Ct. (we. dist.) Okla. 1984, U.S. Dist. Ct. (ea. dist.) Okla. 1993, U.S. Ct. Appeals (10th cir.) 1987. Assoc. Crowe & Dunlevy, Oklahoma City, 1980-85, mem., 1986—. Editor: The Oil and Gas Reporter. Mem.: ABA (chmn. energy and natural resources litigation 2001—, chmn. oil and natural gas exploration and prodn. com. 1999—2001), Okla. Bar Assn., Oklahoma City Mineral Lawyers Soc. (pres. 1989—90). Home: 20 N Broadway Ave Ste 1800 Oklahoma City OK 73102-8296 Office: Crowe & Dunlevy Mid America Tower 20 N Broadway Ave Ste 1800 Oklahoma City OK 73102-8273

CHRISTIANSEN, NORMAN JUHL, retired newspaper publisher; b. Isle, Minn., Apr. 30, 1923; s. Arthur Theodore and Ingeborg Hansena (Clemensen) C.; m. Margaret Eleanor Whorton, June 13, 1948; children— Gregory Lowell, Susan Joy. BA in Journalism, Drake U., Des Moines, 1947. Reporter Bloomington (Ill.) Pantagraph, 1947; spl. agt. FBI, 1948-54; mem. labor relations staff Am. Newspaper Pubs. Assn., 1954-59; with Gannett Newspapers, 1959-67; asst. gen. mgr. Westchester-Rockland Newspaper Group, 1965-67; with Knight-Ridder Newspapers, Inc., 1967-80, group v.p. ops., 1975-80; pres., pub. Wichita (Kans.) Eagle and Beacon, 1980-87. Bd. dirs. William Allen White Found. Served with AUS, 1943-45. Home: 1136 Cobblestone Ct Fort Collins CO 80525-2832

CHRISTIANSEN, PATRICK T. lawyer; b. Mpls., 1947; BSEE summa cum laude, U. Notre Dame, 1969; JD, Harvard U., 1972. Bar: Fla. 1972, Minn. 1974, U.S. Tax Ct. 1977, U.S. Supreme Ct. 1980. Mem. Akerman, Senterfitt & Eidson P.A., Orlando, Fla. Chmn. bd. Orlando Mus. Art; mem., bd. dirs. The Greater Orlando C. of C., Jobs and Edn. Partnership; chmn. Orange County Transp. Roundtable, BusinessForce, 2002--; mem. Orange County Blue Ribbon Commn., steering com., chmn. transp. com.; bd. dirs. United Arts Cen. Fla., Orlando Downtown Devel. Bd.; trustee, chmn. Orlando Repertory Theatre, 2002--, U. Ctrl. Fla. Found., 2001--; bd. trustees U. Ctrl. Fla.; mem. Orange County Arts & Cultural Affairs Adv. Com., chmn. advancement com., 2001--. Mem. ABA (sects. on bus. law, taxation, real property), Fla. Bar (trial lawyers sect., co-chmn. land trust com. real property, probate and trust law sect. 1978-82, dir. real property divsn. 1982-84, vice chmn. 1984-85, chmn. 1985-86, vice-chmn. UCC subcom. corp., banking and bus. law sect. 1979-84, bd. govs. young lawyers sect. 1981-83), Am. Coll. Real Estate Lawyers, Minn. State Bar Assn., Orange County Bar Assn. Office: Akerman Senterfitt & Eidson PA Citrus Ctr 17th Fl PO Box 231 255 S Orange Ave Orlando FL 32801-3445

CHRISTIANSEN, RAYMOND STEPHAN, librarian, educator; b. Oak Park, Ill., Feb. 15, 1950; s. Raymond Julius and Anne Mary (Fusek) Christiansen; m. Phyllis Anne Dombowski, Nov. 25, 1972; 1 child, Mark David. BA, Elmhurst Coll., 1971; MEd, No. Ill. U., 1974. Dept. dir. Elmhurst (Ill.) Coll., 1971—73; asst. law libr. media svcs. Lewis U., Glen Ellyn, Ill., 1974—77; asst. prof. edn. Aurora (Ill.) U., 1977—90, assoc. prof., 1990—2003, emeritus prof., 2003—, media libr., 1977—82, instnl. developer, 1982—89, dir. univ. media svcs., 1985—2003, dir. ednl. facilities and tech. planning, 2003—; media cons., 1977—. Author: (video series) Rothblatt on Criminal Advocacy, 1975, (book) Index to SCOPE the UN Magazine, 1977. Lic. lay min. Episcopal Ch., 1990—. Mem.: ASCD, Assn. Tchr. Educators, Assn. Ednl. Comms. and Tech., Phi Eta Sigma, Alpha Psi Omega. Home: 424 S Gladstone Ave Aurora IL 60506-5370 Office: Aurora U Libr 347 S Gladstone Ave Aurora IL 60506-4877

CHRISTIANSEN, RICHARD DEAN, retired newspaper editor; b. Berwyn, Ill., Aug. 1, 1931; s. William Edward and Louise Christine (Dethlefs) C. BA, Carleton Coll., Northfield, Minn., 1953; postgrad., Harvard U., 1954; LHD (hon.), DePaul U., 1988. Reporter, critic, editor Chgo. Daily News, 1957-73, 74-78; editor Chicagoan mag., 1973-74; critic-at-large Chgo. Tribune, 1978-83, entertainment editor, 1983-91, chief critic, sr. writer, 1991—2002; ret., 2002. Served to cpl. U.S. Army, 1954-56. Recipient award Chgo. Newspaper Guild, 1969, 74, Joseph Jefferson award, 1996, Excellence in the Arts award DePaul U., 1998, Peter Lisagor award for criticism, 2002; named to Chgo. Journalism Hall of Fame, 1998. Mem. Am. Theatre Critics Assn., Chgo. Acad. TV Arts and Scis., Soc. Midland Authors, Headline Club Chgo. (Peter Lisagor award 2002), Arts Club Chgo. (dir.), Phi Beta Kappa, Sigma Delta Chi. Republican. Lutheran.

CHRISTIANSEN, RICHARD LOUIS, orthodontics educator, research director, former dean; b. Denison, Iowa, Apr. 1, 1935; s. John Cornelius and Rosa Katherine C.; m. Nancy Marie Norman, June 24, 1956; children— Mark Richard, David Norman, Laura Marie DDS, U. Iowa, 1959; MSD, Ind. U., Indpls., 1964; PhD, U. Minn., 1970; hon. doctorate, Nippon Dental U., Tokyo, 2000. Prin. investigator Nat. Inst. Dental Research NIH, Bethesda, Md., 1970-73, chief craniofacial anomalies program br., 1973-81, dir. extramural Nat. Inst. Dental Research, 1981-82; prof. dept. orthodontics U. Mich., Ann Arbor, 1982—, dean, Sch. Dentistry and dir. W.K. Kellogg Found. Inst., 1982—2001, prof., dean emeritus, 2001—. Organizer state-of-the -art workshops in field of craniofacial anomalies and other aspects of oral health; founder Internat. Union Schs. Oral Health, 1985; organizer oral health conf. in Poland, 1989, Jordan, 1995. Contbr. chpts. to books and articles to profl. jours. Chmn. Region III United Way, U. Mich., Ann Arbor, 1984; chmn., v.p. Trinity Luth. Ch., Rockville, Md., 1975; v.p. and chmn. planning task force Trinity Luth. Ch., Ann Arbor, chmn. bd. Sequois Sr. Housing; bd. dirs. Luth. Soc. Svcs. Mich., 1997—. With USPHS, 1959-82. Recipient Commendation medal USPHS, 1980; Cert. of Recognition NIH, 1982, numerous internat. awards. Fellow Internat. Coll. Dentists, Am. Coll. Dentists, Pierre Fauchard Acad.; mem. Am. Assn. Orthodontists, Am. Assn. Dental Sch., ADA (rsch. coun.), Mich. Dental Assn., Am. Assn. Dental Research (dir. craniofacial biology group 1975-79, v.p. 1979-80, pres. 1981-82), Omicron Kappa Upsilon (mem. numerous nat. and internat. coms. and bds.). Avocations: reading, jogging, tennis, sailing, econs. Home: 5612 N Dixboro Rd Ann Arbor MI 48105-9415 E-mail: vista@umich.edu.

CHRISTIANSEN, WALTER HENRY, aeronautics educator; b. McKees Rocks, Pa., Dec. 14, 1934; s. Walter Henry and Elizabeth (Miller) C.; m. Joan Marilyn Swisler, Aug. 5, 1960; children: Walter, Audrey. BS in Mech. Engring., Carnegie Inst. Tech., 1956; MS in Aero. Engring., Calif. Inst. Tech., 1957, PhD, 1961. Sr. scientist Jet Propulsion Lab., Pasadena, Calif., 1961-62, 1963-67; rsch. assoc. prof. aero. and aeronautics U. Wash., Seattle, 1967-70, assoc. prof., 1970-74, prof., 1974—, dept. chmn., 1992-98. Cons. Boeing Sci. Rsch. Lab., 1967-69, Math. Scis. N.W., 1970-85, Spectra Tech., 1985-88, 91. Contbr. articles to profl. jours.; patentee in field. Com. mem. Directions for 70's Bellevue (Wash.) Sch. Dist., 1970. Served to capt. U.S. Army, 1961-63. Dept. Def. grantee, 1970-91, NSF grantee, 1977, 80, NASA grantee, 1980-89; Mesa Machine fellow, 1952-56, Convair fellow, 1958, Boeing fellow, 1960. Fellow AIAA (Pacific N.W. chpt. Sect. award 1972); mem. Am. Phys. Soc., Sigma Xi, Tau Beta Pi, Pi Tau Sigma, Theta Xi. Home: 9633 NE 28th St Bellevue WA 98004-1846 Office: Dept Aero & Astro Box 352400 Univ Wash Seattle WA 98195-0001 E-mail: walt@aa.washington.edu.

CHRISTIANSON, GALE EDWARD, historian, educator; b. Charles City, IA, June 29, 1942; s. Donna Jean and John Edward Christianson; m. Rhonda Packer, June 2, 1992. ArtsD, Carnegie Mellon U, Pitts., PA, 1969—71. Disting. prof. of arts and sci. IN State U, Terre Haute, Ind., 1986—2003. Cons. John Simon Guggenheim Mem. Found., NYC, 2002—03. Author: (hist. books) In the Presence of the Creator: Isaac Newton and His Times, Greenhouse: The 200-Yr. Story of Global Warming, Edwin Hubble: Mariner of the Nebulae, Fox at the Wood's Edge: A Biography of Loren Eiseley (The Loren Eiseley Medal, 1992). Fundraising and Voter Canvassing Dem. Party, Terre Haute, Ind., 1980—98. Recipient Nat. Endowment For the Humanities, Am. Philos. Soc., Am. Inst. of Physics, Gov. and Pvt. Inst. Mem.: Am. Hist. Assoc., Hist. of Sci. Soc., Phi Alpha Theta. Democrat. Achievements include John Simon Guggenheim Memorial Foundation Fellow, Huntington Library Fellow. Avocation: horseback riding. Office: IN State U 621 Chestnut St Terre Haute IN 47809 Home: 2745 S Brown Ave Terre Haute IN 47802

CHRISTIANSON, GERYLD B. government relations consultant; b. Boyd, Minn., Dec. 31, 1934; m. Sue Singer, July 9, 1960; children: Stephen, Alexander. BA in Internat. Rels., U. Minn., 1957; postgrad., Johns Hopkins U., 1967-68. Fgn. svc. officer Dept. State, NATO Office, Bur. European Affaira, various fgn. locations, 1958-75; fgn. policy advisor Senator Claiborne Pell, Washington, 1975-81; minority staff dir. Senate Fgn. Rels. Com., Washington, 1981-87, staff dir., 1987-95; sr. counselor The Evans Group, Ltd., Washington, 1995, 97—; v.p. Jefferson Waterman Internat., Washington, 1995-97. With USAR, 1957—63. Mem. Coun. on Fgn. Rels., Internat. Inst. for Strategic Studies (London). Democrat. Episcopalian. Avocations: collecting political buttons, tennis. Home: 8716 Mary Lee Ln Annandale VA 22003-3659

CHRISTIANSON, JAMES D. real estate developer; b. Bismarck, N.D., Aug. 18, 1952; s. Adolph M. and Elizabeth M. (Barnes) C.; m. Deborah Jaeger, Oct. 10, 1987. Student, Bismarck Jr. Coll., 1970, 1971-72, U. N.D., 1971. Lic. pvt. pilot; lic. realtor. Gen. mgr. and supr. Nutrition Search, Bismarck, 1974-76; gen. mgr. Home Still, Inc., Bismarck, 1976-78; v.p. Good Heart Assocs., Bismarck, 1978-82; pres. N.W. Devel. Group, Bismarck, 1982—, First Realty Bismark Inc., 1990-93, N.W. Realty Group, Bismarck, 1994—. Chmn. bd. Basin State Bank, Stanford, Mont., 1986-94; mem., vice chair Ctr. City Partnership, 1994—; mng. prin. N.W. Lodging Group, LLC. Supr. editor: Nutrition Almanac, 1975. Mem. Bismarck Centennial Com., 1986-89, Bismarck Parking Authority, 1996—; bd. trustees Bismarck State Coll., 1999—. Recipient Outstanding Citizen award Mayor and City Commn., Bismarck, 1982. Mem. Downtown Bus. and Profl. Assn. (bd. dirs. 1989—, pres. 1991). Avocations: traveling, reading, computers, golf. Office: N W Devel Group Inc PO Box 1097 Bismarck ND 58502-1097

CHRISTIANSON, JOHN ROBERT, historian, educator; b. Mankato, Minn., Jan. 21, 1934; s. Kenneth Orvin Christianson and Marian Christine Peterson; m. Birgitte Povelsen, June 20, 1964; children: Erik-Kenneth Gyde, Paul Frederik Gyde. BA, Minn. State U., 1956; MA, U. Minn., 1959, PhD, 1964. Asst. prof. history U. SD, Vermillion, 1964—66; chair dept. Luther Coll., Decorah, Iowa, 1967—83, assoc. prof., 1967—72, prof. history, 1972—96, rsch. prof. history, 1996—. V.p., exec. bd. Norwegian-American Hist. Assn., Northfield, Minn., 1993—99; asst. dir., coll. liaison Vesterheim Norwegian-American Mus., Decorah, Iowa, 1969—96; commr. for Iowa Nordmanns-Forbundet, Oslo, 1991—96; vis. asst. prof. U. Minn., Mpls., 1966—67. Author: (history book) On Tycho's Island: Tycho Brahe and His Assistants, 1570-1601, 2000; editor: Scandinavians in America: Literary Life, 1985; co-editor (history book) Tycho Brahe and Prague: Crossroads of European Science, 2002. Chmn., mem. steering com. 5 Norwegian royal visits, Decorah, Iowa, 1968—99. Pvt. first class U.S. Army, 1958—60. Named Knight, Royal Norwegian Order of Merit, H. M. Harald V, King of Norway, 1995; fellow, Am. Coun. of Learned Societies, 1973—74. Mem.: Inst. Agrl. Biodiversity (bd. dirs. 1991—97), Danish Am. Heritage Soc. (bd. dirs. 1998—, editor jour. 1998—2002), Norwegian-Am. Hist. Assn. (exec. bd. 1971—), Symra Lit. Soc. (bd. dirs. 1968—, pres. 1969—70), Phi Beta Kappa. Democrat. Lutheran. Avocations: fly fishing, travel. Home: 110 Pleasant Hill Decorah IA 52101 Office: Luther College 700 College Drive Decorah IA 52101-1045 Home Fax: 563-387-1322; Office Fax: 563-387-1322. Personal E-mail: christjr@luther.edu. E-mail: christjr@luther.edu.

CHRISTIANSON, MARCIA LARAYE, middle school educator; b. Austin, Minn., June 14, 1947; d. Arnold Raymond and Rayma Arliene (Peterson) C. AA, Austin Community Coll., 1967; BA, Luther Coll., Decorah, Iowa, 1969; MEd in Ednl. Computing, Cardinal Stritch Coll., Milw., 1986. Cert. tchr., Wis. Tchr. Joint Sch. Dist. 1, West Bend, Wis., 1969—. Facilitator, instr. Profl. Improvement Inst., West Bend, 1985-90; co-chair tchr. incentive pilot program, West Bend and Madison, Wis., 1986-88, Dist. Staff Devel. Com., West Bend, 1990—. Bd. dirs. Waubun Girl Scout Coun., 1993-94. Mem. NEA, AAUW, Wis. Edn. Assn. Coun. (bd. dirs., alternate 1992-98), Cedar Lake United Educators (bd. dirs. 1990, vice chair bd. dirs. 1998-2003, pres. bd. dirs. 2003—), West Bend Edn. Assn. (exec. bd., chief negotiator 1982-99), Portside Weavers Guild (past pres.), Lutheran. Avocations: weaving, beading, spinning, tennis, swimming. Home: 125 N University Dr Apt 210 West Bend WI 53095-2948 Office: Badger Mid Sch 710 S Main St West Bend WI 53095-3940

CHRISTIANSON, PAUL ALAN, music educator; b. Jan. 21, 1964; s. Donald Alan and Faye Lorraine (Jensen) Christianson; m. Denise Ellen Barber, June 26, 1993; children: Hannah, David, Mark. BA, N.W. Nazarene Coll., 1986; MusM, U. Idaho, 1988; D Mus. Arts, U. Ga., 1997. Vis. prof. music N.W. Nazarene Coll., Nampa, Idaho, 1989; assoc. prof. music Trevecca Nazarene U., Nashville, 1993—, chmn. cultural arts com., 2001—. Dir. worship Trinity Presbyn. Ch., Murfreesboro, Tenn., 2000—. Composer: (musical recordings) Rain on the Lake, 1991, Timeless, 1994, Music for 5 Vanderbilt Med. Ctr. videos, 1998—2000. Recipient 1st place award Collegiate Artists Piano Competition, Idaho Music Tchrs. Assn., 1987, Tchg. Excellence award, Trevecca Nazarene U., 2000. Mem.: Music Tchrs. Nat. Assn., Nashville Music Tchrs. Assn., Tenn. Music Tchrs. Assn. Nazarene. Avocations: reading, outdoor activities.

CHRISTIANSON, PHILIP D. employee benefits executive; b. Mpls., July 31, 1955; s. William Philip and Mavis Irene Christianson; m. Francene Parco, Nov. 17, 1984; children: Leah, Jack. BA summa cum laude, Calif. Poly., 1977; JD, Loyola U., 1983; MBA, U. So. Calif., 1989. Mgr. group benefits Times Mirror, L.A., 1984-90; dir. employee benefits Phillips Van Heusen, N.Y.C., 1990-94; v.p. employee benefits Walt Disney Co., Burbank, Calif., 1994-96; pres. Christianson Cons., Pasadena, Calif., 1996-99; sr. v.p. bus. devel. iBenefits.com, El Segundo, Calif., 1999—2000; pres., CEO Corp. Benefit Svcs. Am., Mpls., 2001—. Bd. dirs. March of Dimes, So. Calif., 1994-99, chmn. bd. dirs., 1999. Avocations: hiking, surfing, travel, reading, children's issues. Home: 18441 Highpath Ln Minnetonka MN 55345

CHRISTIANSON, ROGER GORDON, biology educator; b. Santa Monica, Calif., Oct. 31, 1947; s. Kyle C. and Ruby K. (Parker) Christianson; m. Angela Diane Rey, Mar. 3, 1967; children: Lisa Marie, David Scott, Stephen Peter. BA in Cell and Organismal Biology, U. Calif., Santa Barbara, 1969, MA in Biology, 1971, PhD in Biology, 1976. Faculty assoc. U. Calif., Santa Barbara, 1973-79, staff rsch. assoc., 1979-80; asst. prof. So. Oreg. U., Ashland, 1980-85, assoc. prof., 1985-93, prof., 1993—, coord. gen. biology program, 1980—, chmn. biology dept., 1996, 1997—2003. Instr. U. Calif. Santa Barbara, 1976, 78, 80. Contbr. articles to sci. and ednl. jours. Active Oreg. Shakespeare Festival Assn., Ashland, 1983—87; mem. bikeway com. Ashland City Coun., 1986—88; organizer Bike Oreg., 1982—92, Frontline HS Staff, 1985—2003; short-term mission work Mex. Orphanage, 1986—; ofcl. photographer Ashland H.S. Booster Club, 1987—92; coord. youth program 1st Bapt. Ch., Ashland, 1981—85, mem. ch. life commn., 1982—88, bd. deacons, 1993—95, mem. outreach com., 1994, 1995; youth leader jr. and sr. H.S. students Grace Ch., Santa Barbara, 1973—80. Mem.: AAAS (chair Pacific divsn. edn. sect 1985—2001, coun. Pacific divsn. 1985—, exec. com. Pacific divsn. 1998—, chair local organizing com. Pacific divsn. ann. meeting 2000, chair Pacific divsn. student awards com. 2001, exec. dir. Pacific divsn. 2002—), Assn. for Biology Lab. Edn., Oreg. Sci. Tchrs. Assn., Am. Mus. Natural History, Beta Beta Beta, Sigma Xi (chpt. membership com. 1998—2000). Republican. Avocations: sports, photography, youth work, multimedia presentations, amateur radio operator. Home: 430 Reiten Dr Ashland OR 97520-8762 Office: Southern Oregon U Dept Biology 1250 Siskiyou Blvd Ashland OR 97520-5010 E-mail: rchristi@sou.edu.

CHRISTIANSON, STANLEY DAVID, corporate executive; b. Chgo., Dec. 8, 1931; s. Stanley Olai and Emma Josephine (Johnson) D.; m. Elin J. Ballantyne, July 25, 1959; children: Erica Joanna, David Ballantyne. BS, U. Ill., 1954; MBA, U. Chgo., 1960. Auditor Price Waterhouse & Co., Chgo., 1956-58; asst. to controller Miehle-Goss-Dexter, Inc., Chgo., 1960-67, v.p. adminstrn. Goss Div., 1967-69; dir. mgmt. systems MGD Graphics Systems-N.Am. Rockwell (formerly Miehle-Goss-Dexter), Chgo., 1969-70; v.p. fin. Duchossois/Thrall Group (formerly Thrall Car Mfg. Co.), Chicago Heights, Elmhurst, Ill., 1970-83; vice chmn., bd. dirs. Thrall Enterprises, Inc., Chgo., 1983—. Bd. dirs. Midwestern U., 1992—, chmn., 1997-98. Bd. govs. Internat. House, U. Chgo., 1988-2000, chmn. 1997-2000; trustee Cmty. Theatre Guild, Valparaiso, Ind., 2001-; mem. Hobart (Ind.) Plan Commn., 1986-92, pres., 1988-92. Capt. U.S. Army, 1954-56. Home: 141 Beverly Blvd Hobart IN 46342-4346 Office: Thrall Enterprises Inc 180 N Stetson Ste 3020 Chicago IL 60601-6223

CHRISTIE, GEORGE NICHOLAS, economist, consultant; b. Wilmington, N.C., Nov. 2, 1924; s. Nicholas and Helen (Lymbertis) C.; m. Mary Danatos, July 22, 1951; children: Sultana Helen, Stephanie Hope, Susan Adrianne, Sandra Alicia, Gregory Nicholas. BBA, U. Miami, 1948; MBA, NYU, 1956; PhD, 1963. With Dun and Bradstreet, Inc., N.Y.C., 1949-61; staff bus. writer, 1959-61; assoc. dir. Credit Rsch. Found.; asst. dir. edn. Nat. Assn. Credit Mgmt., N.Y.C., 1961-63; asst. sec. credit policy com., small bus. credit com., 1964-67; v.p., dir. rsch. Credit Rsch. Found., 1967-80; sr. v.p., 1980-82; exec. v.p., 1983-89; assoc. dir. Grad. Sch. Credit and Fin. Mgmt., 1967-86; exec. dir., 1986-87; dir. Nat. Inst. Credit, 1967-84; prin. Four Seas Cons. Group, Great Neck, N.Y., 1989—; instr. N.Y. Inst. Credit. Lectr. Dartmouth, Stanford U.; assoc. prof. L.I. U.; adminstr. 2d year banking course Stonier Grad. Sch. Banking, Rutgers U. Contbr. articles to profl. jours. Mem. Am. Econ. Assn., Am. Fin. Assn., Fin Mgmt. Assn., Shriner (recorder, past potentate), Masons (past master). Office: 65 Nassau Rd Great Neck NY 11021-4047 E-mail: gnchristie@aol.com.

CHRISTIE, GEORGE CUSTIS, lawyer, educator, author; b. N.Y.C., Mar. 3, 1934; s. Custis and Sophie (Velimahitis) C.; m. Susan D. Monserud, Apr. 20, 1965 (div. July 1974); 1 child, Constantine George; m. Deborah D. Carnes, Dec. 20, 1974; children: Rebecca Sophia, Nicholas George. AB, Columbia U., 1955, JD, 1957; diploma in internat. law (Fulbright scholar), Cambridge (Eng.) U., 1962; SJD, Harvard U., 1966. Bar: N.Y. 1957, D.C. 1958. Assoc. Covington & Burling, Washington, 1958-60; Ford Found. fellow in law teaching Harvard U., 1960-61; assoc. prof. law U. Minn., Mpls., 1962-65, prof. law, 1965-66; asst. gen. counsel for Near E. and S. Asia, AID, Dept. State, 1966-67; prof. law Duke U., 1967-79, James B. Duke prof. law, 1979—. Vis. lectr. U. Witwatersrand, South Africa, 1980, Fudan U., China, U. Otago, New Zealand, 1985; fellow Nat. Humanities Center, 1980-81; scholar-in-residence McGuire, Woods & Battle, Richmond, Va., 1983, vis. Freda Alverson prof. law George Washington U., spring 1988; vis. prof. law Northwestern U., 1991-92, U. Athens, Greece, 2000; vis. fellow Rsch. Sch. Social Scis., Australian Nat. U., 2002. Author: Jurisprudence: Text and Readings on the Philosophy of Law, 1973, 2d edit. (with P. Martin), 1995, The Sum and Substance of the Law of Torts, 1980, Law, Norms & Authority, 1982, Cases and Materials on the Law of Torts, 1983, 2d edit. (with J. Meeks), 1990, 3d edit. (with others), 1997, The Notion of an Ideal Audience in Legal Argument, 2000. Served with U.S. Army, 1957. Mem. ABA, Am. Law Inst., Am. Soc. Internat. Law, Phi Beta Kappa. Democrat. Greek Orthodox. Home: 17 Stoneridge Cir Durham NC 27705-5510 Office: Duke U Sch Law PO Box 90360 Durham NC 27708-0360 E-mail: gcc@law.duke.edu.

CHRISTIE, HANS FREDERICK, retired utility company subsidiaries executive, consultant; b. Alhambra, Calif., July 10, 1933; s. Andreas B. and Sigrid (Falk-Jorgensen) C.; m. Susan Earley, June 14, 1957; children: Brenda Lynn, Laura Jean BS in Fin., U. So. Calif., 1957, MBA, 1964. Treas. So. Calif. Edison Co., Rosemead, 1970-75, v.p., 1975-76, sr. v.p., 1976-80, exec. v.p., 1980-84, pres., dir., 1984-87; pres., chief exec. officer The Mission Group (non-utility subs. SCE Corp.)., Seal Beach, Calif., 1987-89, ret., 1989, cons., 1989—. Bd. dirs. L.A. Ducommun Inc., L.A., A.E. Com., L.A., Valero LP, Tex., Am. Mut. Fund, Inc., AMCAP, Am. Variable Ins., I.H.O.P. Corp., AECom Tech., L.A., Internat. House of Pancakes, Inc., Southwest Water Co., L.A., Smallcap World Fund, L.A., Bond Fund Am., Inc., L.A., Tax-Exempt Bond Fund Am., L.A., Ltd. Term Tax-Exempt Bond Fund Am., Am. High Income Mcpl. Bond Fund, Capital Income Builder, L.A., Capital World Bond Fund, L.A., Capital World Growth Fund, Capital World Growth and Income Fund, Intermediate Bond Fund Am., L.A., Intermediate Tax-Exempt Bond Fund Am., Capital World Growth 2d Income Fund, L.A.; trustee Cash Mgmt. Trust Am., New Economy Fund, L.A., Am. Funds Income Series, L.A., The Am. Funds Tax-Exempt Series II, Am. High Income Trust, L.A., Am. High-Inc Mun. Board Fund, Am. Variable Ins. Trust, U.S. Treasury Fund Am., L.A. Bd. councillor sch. policy, planning and devel. U. So. Calif., 1981—2001; trustee Occidental Coll., 1984—96, Idlwild Sch. Arts, Chadwick Sch., Nat. History Mus. L.A. County. With U.S. Army, 1953—55. Named Outstanding mem. Arthritis Found., L.A., 1975, Outstanding Trustee, Multiple Sclerosis Soc. So. Calif., 1979 Mem. Pacific Coast Elec. Assn. (bd. dirs. 1981-87, treas. 1975-87), L.A. C. of C. (bd. dirs. 1983-87), Calif. Club. Republican. Avocations: swimming, horseback riding, bicycling. Home: 548 Paseo Del Mar Palos Verdes Estates CA 90274-1260 Office: PO Box 144 Palos Verdes Peninsula CA 90274-0144

CHRISTIE, JOSEPH FRANCIS, city planner; b. Feb. 5, 1955; BA, Coll. of Charleston, S.C., 1977, MPA, 1981. Tech. assistance mgr. B-C-D Coun. of Govts., Charleston, 1977-82; cmty. svcs. dir. Berkeley County, Moncks Corner, S.C., 1982-84; planning dir. Town of Summerville, S.C., 1984—. Office: 104 Civic Ctr Summerville SC 29483-6000 E-mail: nospam@sc.rr.com.

CHRISTIE, LEONARD GEORGE, JR., cardiologist, public health service officer; b. N.Y.C., Sept. 20, 1939; s. Leonard George and Dorothea Anne Christie; m. Judith Ann Kohanski, Jan. 1, 1942; children: Zachary David, Tyler. BA, Va. Mil. Inst., 1961; MD, Temple U., 1965; MPH, Johns Hopkins Sch. Pub. Health, 2002. Cert. Am. Bd. of Internal Medicine, 1971. Intern, resident Hartford Hosp., Conn., 1965—68; sr. resident U. Calif., San Francisco, 1968—69; asst. prof. cardiology Dartmouth Hitchcock Med. Ctr., Hanover, NH, 1973—76; assoc. prof. cardiology U. Fla., Gainesville, 1976—82; interventional cardiology Cardiovasc Assocs., Eugene, Oreg., 1982—99; dir., cardiac catheterization and interventional cardiology Oreg. Health Scis. U., Portland, 1999—2001; cons. internat. health Oreg. Cardiovasc. Teachings, Ltd, Eugene, 2001—. Dir. Oreg. Heart Ctr., Eugene, 1986—96; chmn., coop. cardiovasc. project Oreg. Med. Peer Rev. Orgn., Portland, 1992—95; cons., proctor, interventional cardiology Scimed Corp., Mpls., 1992—99; vis. cardiologist U. Capetown, South Africa, 1999—99; cons. interventional cardiology Scimed Corp., Japan, 1996—96; dir. cardiovasc. database Sacred Heart Hosp., Eugene, 1990—97. Chair Boy Scouts Am., Eugene, 1992—94. Maj. U.S. Army, 1969—71. Fellow Cardiology, Johns Hopkins Sch. Medicine, 1971—73. Fellow: Am. Coll. of Cardiology (pres. Oreg. chpt. 1996—99). Avocation: sheep and llama farming. Home: South Ridge Farm 771 West 52nd Ave Eugene OR 97405 Office: Oregon Cardiovascular Teachings Ltd 1461 Hilyard St Eugene OR 97401 Home Fax: 541-683-1054. Personal E-mail: lenchristie@earthlink.net.

CHRISTIE, RICHARD WALLACE, retired structural engineer; b. Ridgewood, N.J., Jan. 21, 1928; s. William Donald and Dorothy Seberne (Bensen) C.; m. Jean Anne Grebenstein, Feb. 6, 1954; children: Susan, Douglas, Martha. BS in Engring., U. Mich., 1950; MEngring., Yale U., 1951. Registered profl. engr., N.J., Conn. Engr. Hardesty & Hanover, N.Y.C., 1951-56, assoc., 1956-71, ptnr., 1972-94, ptnr. emeritus, 1995—. Mem. steel structures com., 1974—, chmn. movable bridge subcom., 1993-2001 Am. Railway Engring. Assn.; mem. structural welding com., 1971-96 Am. Welding Soc.; mem. Can./CSA movable bridge design code com., 1992-2002. Co-author: 50-Yr. History of Movable Bridge Constrn., 1975. Mem. Ridgewood Planning Bd., 1976-81. Fellow ASCE (Roebling award 1989). Mem. Reformed Ch. of Am. (elder). Avocation: woodworking. Home: 87 Green Knolls Dr Wayne NJ 07470-6123 Office: Hardesty & Hanover 1501 Broadway Ste 310 New York NY 10036-5587

CHRISTIE, THOMAS PHILIP, federal agency administrator, research manager; b. Pensacola, Fla., May 28, 1934; s. Joseph Aloysius and Margaret Gabriel (Donaldson) C.; m. Kathleen Ann Lawson, June 27, 1964; children— Kevin Patrick, Stephanie Marie. BS, Spring Hill Coll., 1955; MS, NYU, 1962. Dir. analysis div. Air Force Armament Lab., Eglin AFB, Fla., 1970-73; dir. Tactical Air Div., Office of Sec. Def., Pentagon, 1973-77, dep. asst. sec. def. for operational test and evaluation, 1977-79, dep. asst. sec. def. for gen. purpose forces, 1979—85, dep. asst. sec. def. for programs and resources, 1985—87, dir. program integration, Under Sec. Def., acquisition, 1987—90; dir. Operational Evaluation Divsn. Inst. for Def. Analyses, Alexandria, Va., 1990-2001; dir. operational test and evaluation U.S. Dept. Defense, Washington, 2001—. Recipient Presdl. Merit Rank award, 1980, 88, Def. Disting. Svc. award, 1981, 83, 88, Presdl. Disting. Rank award, 1983. Roman Catholic. Office: US Dept Def Operational Test and Evaluation 1700 Defense Pentagon Rm 3A 1073 Washington DC 20301-1700 Office Fax: 703-693-5248.

CHRISTIE, WALTER SCOTT, retired state official; b. Indpls., 1922; s. Walter Scott and Nina Lillian (Warfel) C.; m. Betty W. Phelps, Dec. 14, 1991 (dec.); stepchildren: Thomas G. Phelps, Judith Phelps Cummings. BS in BA, Butler U., 1948. CPA, Ind.; cert. fin. examiner. With Roy J. Pile & Co., CPAs, Indpls., 1948-56, Howard E. Nyhart Co., Inc., actuarial cons., 1956-62, Ind. Dept. Ins., 1962-92, dep. commr., 1966-74, adminstrv. officer, 1974-79, sr. examiner, 1979-81, adminstrv. asst., 1981-82, chief auditor, 1982-91, ret., 1991. Bd. dirs., sec., treas. Sr. Enterprises. Treas. Delta Tau/Delta House Corp., 1967—, Butler U. With AUS, 1942-45. Named to Hon. Order Ky. Cols. Mem. Ind. Assn. CPAs, Soc. Fin. Examiners (state chmn.), Indpls. Actuarial Club, Nat. Assn. Ins. Commrs. (chmn. zone IV life and health com. 1970-75), Internat. Platform Assn. Episcopalian (assoc. vestryman 1948-60), Optimist Club Downtown Indpls. (bd. dirs., Outstanding Svc. award 1985-87, Optimist of Yr. 1990). Episcopalian (assoc. vestryman 1948-60).

CHRISTIE, WILLIAM GARY, finance educator, dean; b. Toronto, Sept. 22, 1955; s. Robert Louis and Margaret Elsa (Sparling) C.; m. Kelly Maureen McNamara, July 25, 1980. B in Commerce with honors, Queen's U., Kingston, Ont., Can., 1978; MBA in Fin., U. Chgo., 1980, PhD in Fin. and Econs., 1989. Fin. analyst Hewlett-Packard (Canada) Ltd., 1980-81, Ford Motor Co. of Canada Ltd., 1981-82; rsch. asst. in statistics and fin. U. Chgo., 1983-88; asst. prof. mgmt. Vanderbilt U., Nashville, 1989-96, assoc. prof. mgmt., 1996—; tchr. equities markets, managerial fin. MBA, exec. MBA programs; assoc. dean Grad. Sch. Mgmt., 2000—. Contbr. articles to profl. jours. Fellow U. Chgo., 1982-89, Social Scis. and Humanities Rsch. Coun. Can., 1982-86, Ctr. for Rsch. in Securities Prices, 1983-84; recipient Irwin Disting. Paper award, 1994—, Smith-Breeden award, 1995—. Mem. Am. Fin. Assn., Southwestern Fin. Assn., Western Fin. Assn., Am. Econs. Assn., European Fin. Assn. Avocations: jogging, tennis, travel. Office: Vanderbilt U Owen Grad Sch 401 21st Ave S Nashville TN 37240-1104

CHRISTINA, SONJA (ALISA MORRIS), writer, poetess; b. Dec. 21, 1925; m. Desmond Halton Morris, June 17, 1950; 1 child, Belinda. Owner La Esmeralda Club and Restaurant, London, 1947—50; owner art gallery Domani, N.Y.C., 1968. Model for painter Sir Augustus John, London, 1941-43; dancer Phillis Dixy Prodns., London, 1943-45. Author: (poetry) Emotions, 1973, If, 2002, The Secret to Her Heart, 2002, Ground Zero, 2002; prodr. (play) The Future Was Yesterday, 1952; poem displayed at Mus. of Tolerance. Recipient 10 Merit awards World of Poetry, Outstanding Poetry award Am. Poetry Assn., 1986, Golden Poet award World of Poetry, 1985, 86, 88, 90, 91, 1st prize in short story Globe Contest, 1984, Editors Choice award Internat. Libr. Poetry, 1999, Recognition award Famous Poets Soc., 1999, Poets Fantasy award, 2000, Outstanding Achivement award Drury's Publs., 2002; world record holder (for personal jours.-286) Guinness Book of World Records. Mem. Internat. Soc. Poets (hon. charter mem.). Home: PO Box 142 Lenox Hill New York NY 10021-0012

CHRISTISON, MURIEL BRANHAM, retired art museum director emeritus, fine arts educator; b. Mpls. d. Harold D. and Helen (Ferguson) Branham; children: Evelyn, Carolyn. BA, U. Minn., 1933, MA, 1940; diploma, U. Paris, 1936, U. Bruxelles, 1938. Grad. asst. Dept. Fine Arts U. Minn., Mpls., 1933-36; curatorial rsch. asst. Mpls. Inst. Arts, Mpls., 1936-42, head edn., 1944-47; assoc. dir. Va. Mus. Fine Arts, Richmond, 1948-61; oper. and assoc. dir. Krannert Art Mus. U. Ill., Champaign, 1962-74, dir. Krannert Art Mus., 1975-82; ret., 1982; interim dir. Muscarelle Mus., Coll. William and Mary, Williamsburg, Va., 1984-85, 94-96, mem. vis. com., 1982-96, vis. prof. fine arts, 1983-98. Head program mus. studies U. Ill., 1974—82; cons. U. Tex., Austin, Tex., Washington U. St. Louis, 1972—78; v.p. Midwest Mus. Conf. Am. Assn. Mus., regional rep., 1972—82. V.p. Midwest Mus. Conf.; mem. Va. Mus. Fine Arts, Coll. William and Mary Found., Colonial Williamsburg Fund. Carnegie scholar Inst. Internat. Edn., 1936; CRB fellow Beligan-Am. Edn. Found., 1953; recipient Disting. Svc. award Midwest Mus. Conf., 1982. Mem.: Soc. Preservation Va. Antiquities, S.C. Arts Coun. (examiner 1984, 1986), Ohio Arts Coun., Am. Assn. Museums (regional rep. 1972—82, coun. 1972—82, surveyor, examiner 1982—), Assn. Art Mus. Dirs. (hon.), Cosmopolitan Club (N.Y.C.). Home: 257 Littletown Quarter Williamsburg VA 23185-5555 E-mail: mbchri@aol.com.

CHRIST-JANER, ARLAND FREDERICK, college president; b. Garland, Nebr., Jan. 27, 1922; s. William Henry and Bertha Wilhelmina (Beckman) C.-J.; m. Sally Johnson Grice, Sept. 4, 1975 (dec.).; m. Uta Buehler, Dec. 31, 2002. BA, Carleton Coll., 1943; BD, Yale U., 1949; JD, U. Chgo., 1952; LLD (hon.), Coe Coll., 1961, Carleton Coll., 1967, Colo. Coll., 1971; LHD (hon.), Monmouth Coll., 1967, Curry Coll., 1972; LHD, Cornell Coll., 1999. Asst. to pres. Lake Erie Coll., Painesville, Ohio, 1952-53; asst. to pres. St. John's Coll., Annapolis, Md., 1953-54, tutor, treas., 1954-59, v.p., tutor, 1959-61; pres. Cornell Coll., Mt. Vernon, Iowa, 1961-67, Boston U., 1967-70, Coll. Entrance Exam. Bd., N.Y.C., 1970-73, New Coll., Sarasota, Fla., 1973-75, Stephens Coll., Columbia, Mo., 1975-83, Ringling Sch. Art and Design, Sarasota, Fla., 1984-96, interim pres., 1998-99, pres. emeritus, 1996—; dir. Ringling Ctr. for the Cultural Arts FSU, 2001—. Adv. bd. Sun Bank. Exhibiting artist. Trustee New Coll. Found., U. South Fla., Sarasota, 1973—, Marie Selby Bot. Gardens, 1984—, John and Mable Ringling Mus. Art, 1991-93; bd. dirs. Fla. Ind. Coll. Fund, 1984-96, Fla. Assn. Colls. and Univs., 1984-96. With USAAF, 1943-46. Mem. Am. Acad. Arts and Scis., Assn. Ind. Coll. Art and Design (trustee 1991-96), Nat. Assn. Schs. Art and Design (v.p. 1993-96), Ind. Colls. and Univs. Fla. (bd. dirs. 1984-96), Univ. Club Sarasota, Kiwanis, Phi Beta Kappa (hon.), Phi Delta Theta. Office: Ringling Sch Art and Design 2700 N Tamiami Trl Sarasota FL 34234-5895

CHRISTMAN, ALBERT BERNARD, historian; b. Colorado Springs, Colo., May 18, 1923; s. James S. and Olga Emelia (Nelson) C.; m. Kate Gresham, July 1945 (div. July 1952); 1 child, Lloyd James; m. Jean Stewart, Apr. 4, 1954 (dec. Sept. 1984); children: Neil Stewart, Laura Elizabeth. BA, U. Mo., 1949, BJ, 1950; MA, Calif. State U., Dominguez Hills, 1982. Reporter Comml. Leader, North Little Rock, 1950-51; tech. editor, writer Naval Ordnance Test Sta., China Lake, Calif., 1951-55, head presentation divsn., 1956-63; historian, info. specialist Naval Weapons Ctr., China Lake, Calif., 1963-72, head pubs., 1973-79; historian Navy Labs., San Diego, 1979-82; freelance historian, writer San Marcos, Calif., 1982—. Author: Sailors, Scientists and Rockets, 1971, Naval Innovators, 1776-1900, 1989, Target Hiroshima, Deak Parsons and the Creation of the Atomic Bomb, 1998; co-author: Grand Experiment at Inyokern, 1979; contbr. articles to profl. jours. Founding mem. Red Rock Canyon State Park Adv. Com., Tehachapi, Calif., 1969-74. Pvt. U.S. Army, 1942-45; maj. USAFR, ret. Recipient Robert H. Goddard Meml. award Nat. Space, 1972, Superior Civilian Svc. award Dept. of The Navy, 1982, Helen Hawkins Meml. Rsch. grants, 1994, 2000. Mem. Maturango Mus. (trustee-sec. 1973-76), USN Inst., OX-5 Aviation Pioneers, Libr. of Congress Assn. (founding mem.), San Diego Aerospace Mus., Authors Guild, Writers Studio. Democrat. Unitarian Universalist. Avocations: photography, golfing, tennis, hiking. Home and Office: 1711 Birchwood Dr San Marcos CA 92069-9609

CHRISTMAN, ARTHUR CASTNER, JR., scientific advisor; b. North Wales, Pa., May 11, 1922; s. Arthur Castner and Hazel Ivy (Schirmer) C.; m. Marina Ilia Diterichs, Apr. 17, 1945; children: Candace Lee Christman Canto, Tatiana Marina Christman Harvey, Deborah Ann Christman Clark, Arthur C. III, Keith Ilia, Cynthia Ellen Christman Buckwalter. BS in Physics, Pa. State U., 1944, MS, 1950. Teaching asst. dept. physics Pa. State U., State College, 1943-44, grad. asst., 1946-48; instr. dept. physics George Washington U., Washington, 1948-51; cons. U.S. Navy, 1950-51; physicist ops. research office Johns Hopkins U., Chevy Chase, Md., 1951-58; sr. physicist SRI Internat., Menlo Park, Calif., 1958-62, head ops. research group, 1962-64, dept. mgr., 1965-67, dir. dept., 1968-71, dir. tactical weapons systems, 1971-75; sci. advisor to comdg. gen. and dep. chief staff combat devel. U.S. Army tng. and doctrine command Ft. Monroe, Va., 1975-87; cons. in field, 1988—. Author numerous publs. Pres. Valle Verde Continuing Care Retirement Cmty. Coun., 1991-93, 94-95, Am. Bapt. Homes of West Assn. of CCRC Resident Presidents, 1991-92; mem. bd. mgrs. fin. com. Valle Verde, 1988—; mem. Valle Verde Adv. Bd., 1997—, mem. fin. com., 1988—, chair environ. svcs. com., 1999—, mem. exec. com., 2002—; bd. dirs. Am. Bapt. Homes of the West, 1997—, mem. fin. and investment com., 1998—, mem. audit com., 1999, 2001—, chair investment com., 2002—; bd. dirs. Ctrl. Coast Commn. for Sr. Citizens Area Agy. on Aging, 1993; mem. continuing care contract statutes rev. task force State of Calif., 1999-2000; umpire Palo Alto Little League, Calif., 1962-72. Lt. USNR, 1944-46, PTO. Decorated Meritorious Civilian Service award Dept. Army, 1983, Exceptional Civilian Service award Dept. Army, 1987; recipient Presdl. Rank, 1985. Fellow AAAS; mem. Am. Phys. Soc., Inst. for Ops. Rsch. and the Mgmt. Scis. (U.S. del. internat. confs. Operational Rsch., France 1960, Norway 1963, U.S. 1966, Ireland 1972), Santa Barbara Lawn Bowls Club (bd. dirs. 1990-93), MacKenzie Park Lawn Bowls Club, Sigma Xi, Sigma Pi Sigma, Delta Chi (chpt. pres.). Republican. Baptist (deacon, trustee). Avocations: golf, swimming, tennis, bowling, photography. Home and Office: 1028 B Senda Verde Santa Barbara CA 93105-4407 E-mail: achristman@abhow.com.

CHRISTMAN, BRUCE LEE, lawyer; b. Bethlehem, Pa., Apr. 1, 1955; s. Raymond J. Jr. and Irene May (Bowman) C.; m. Lynn Eloise Brodt, Oct. 11, 1980; children: Jennifer Lynn, Amy Nicole. BA, Coll. William and Mary, 1977; JD, U. Pa., 1980. Bar: Va. 1980, U.S. Ct. Appeals (4th cir.) 1980, U.S. Dist. Ct. (ea. dist.) Va. 1980. Assoc. Hunton & Williams, Richmond, Va., 1980-84; prin., ptnr. Reed Smith LLP, Fairfax, Va., 1984—. Adj. prof. George Mason Sch. Law. Mem. Leadership Fairfax Class of 1993, bd. dirs. 1997, 2000-02—. Mem. Va. State Bar Assn., Phi Beta Kappa, Omicron Delta Kappa, Kappa Sigma. Democrat. Avocations: tennis, basketball, swimming, bicycling, camping. Home: 13610 Flintwood Pl Herndon VA 20171-3331 Office: Reed Smith LLP 3110 Fairview Park Dr Falls Church VA 22042-4503

CHRISTMAN, EDWARD ARTHUR, physicist; b. Lakewood, Ohio, Aug. 3, 1943; s. John N.H. and Mary Elizabeth (Fuller) C.; m. Florence T. Cua, July 21, 1979. MS, Rutgers U., 1975, PhD, 1977. Cert. Am. Bd. Health Physics. Mech. engr. missile systems div. AVCO Corp., Wilmington, Mass., 1966-72; instr. Rutgers U., New Brunswick, N.J., 1975-77, radiol. physicist, 1977-89, assoc. dir., 1989-91; dir. environ. health and safety Columbia U., N.Y.C., 1991-99; cons. Princeton, N.J., 1999—. Cons. in field, 1977—; assoc. faculty Rutgers U.,

1978—; faculty Columbia U., 1991—. Mem.: NJ Tech. Coun., Health Physics Soc., Health Physics Soc. NJ (pres. 1989—90), Soc. for Risk Analysis, Am. Assn. Physicists in Medicine. Office: 443 Sayre Dr Princeton NJ 08540-5845 E-mail: eac8@comcast.net.

CHRISTMAN, LUTHER PARMALEE, retired dean, dean, consultant; b. Summit Hill, Pa., Feb. 26, 1915; s. Elmer and Elizabeth (Barnicoat) Christman; m. Dorothy Mary Black, Dec. 5, 1939; children: Gary, Judith, Lillian. Grad., Pa. Hosp. Sch. Nursing for Men, 1939; BS, Temple U., 1948, EdM, 1952; PhD, Mich. State U., 1965; LHD (hon.), Thomas Jefferson U., 1980; DSc (hon.), Grand Valley State U., 1998. Cons. Mich. Dept. Mental Health, Lansing, 1956—63; assoc. prof. psychiat. nursing U. Mich., 1963—67; rsch. assoc. Inst. Social Rsch., U. Mich., 1963—67; prof. nursing and sociology, dean nursing Vanderbilt U., 1967—72; DON Vanderbilt U. Med. Ctr. Hosp., 1967—72; prof. sociology Rush Coll. Health Scis., Chgo.; sr. scientist Rush-Presbyn.-St. Luke's Med. Ctr.; prof. nursing, v.p. nursing affairs Coll. Nursing Rush U., 1972—87; dean Rush U. Coll. Nursing, 1972—87, dean emeritus, 1987—; sr. advisor to pres. Ctr. of Nursing, Am. Hosp. Assn., 1989; pres. Christman-Cornesky & Assocs., 1990—94; adj. prof. Vanderbilt U., 1991—. Chmn. planning com. 1st Midwest Conf. Psychiat. Nursing, Mpls., 1956; cons. cmty. svcs. and rsch. br. NIMH, 1963—66, mem. team to survey mental health facilities of Colo., 1982, mem. team to survey mental health facilities of Ga., 84; psychiat. rsch. project So. Regional Edn. Bd., 1964—67; mem., workshop leader White House Conf. on Children, 1970; nursing panel Nat. Commn. for Study Nursing and Nursing Edn., 1968—70; regional med. programs rev. com. dept. health, edn. and welfare Health Svcs. and Mental Health Adminstrn., 1968—72; cons. dept. medicine and surgery VA Ctrl. Office, 1968—71, 1974—77; panel nurse cons. to com. on nursing AMA, 1968—71; health svcs. adv. com. Am. Assn. Med. Colls., 1968—71; acting com. pub. health Am. Health Found., 1970—72; membership com. Inst. Medicine-NAS, 1972—76, com. on edn. in health professions, 1973—75; mem. S.D. Bd. Nursing, Tenn. Bd. Nursing; cons. in field. Contbr. numerous articles to profl. jours. Named Elinor Frances Reed Disting. Vis. Prof., U. Tenn., Memphis, 2000, Luther Christman Endowed scholar in his honor, Rush Coll. Nursing, 2002; recipient Old Master, Purdue U., 1985, Coun. of Specialists in Psychiat. and Mental Health Nursing award, 1980, Hon. Recognition award, Ill. Nurses Assn., 1987, Edith Copeland Founders award for creativity, 1981, History Makers in Nursing award, Ctr. for Advancement of Nursing Practice, Beth Israel Hosp./Mass. Gen. Hosp., 1992, Lifetime Achievement award, Sigma Theta Tau, 1992, Tenn. Nurses Assn., 2002, Disting. Alumnus award, Temple U., 1992, Rush U., 1997, Coll. Social Scis. Outstanding Alumnus award, Mich. State U., 1999, Hon. Recognition award, Nat. Academicians of Practice, 1996, Cert. of Appreciation, Marshall County Adult Edn., 1997. Fellow: AAAS, Soc. Applied Anthropology, Inst. Medicine Chgo., Am. Acad. Nrusing (Living Legend award 1995); mem.: ANA (3d v.p., Jesse M. Scott award 1985), AACN (life Margurite Rodgers Kinney award 2002), Nat. Acad. Practice (chmn. acad. nursing 1985—92, sec. 1992—96, Disting. Practitioner award 1985, Cert. of Appreciation 1995), Biomed. Engring. Soc., N.Y. Acad. Scis., Inst. Medicine, Soc. Gen. Sys. Rsch., Am. Sociol. Assn., Mich. Nurses' Assn. (pres. 1961—65), Alpha Kappa Delta, Alpha Omega Alpha (hon.). Home and Office: 5535 Nashville Hwy Chapel Hill TN 37034-2074 E-mail: lchristman@united.net.

CHRISTMAN, VIRGINIA REECE, physician assistant; b. Virginia Beach, Va., May 11, 1970; d. William Carey Jr. and Judith Vail Reece; m. Brindon John Christman, June 26, 1999. BS in Sports Medicine, Guilford Coll., 1992; cert. physicians asst., Wake Forest U., 1998. Athletic trainer HealthSouth, Greensboro, N.C., 1992-96; physician asst. Cornerstone Surgery, High Point, N.C., 1998—. Mem. Am. Acad. Physician Assts., Nat. Athletic Trainers Assn. Mem. Soc. Of Friends. Avocations: reading, tennis, cross-stitch, pets.

CHRISTMAS, WILLIAM ANTHONY, internist, educator; b. Montreal, June 5, 1939; came to U.S., 1946; s. William Richard and Marcelle (Hudon) C.; m. Maribeth Hanson, July 14, 1962 (dec. Feb. 2001); children: William, Ann, Gillian, Ira; m. Margaret Raye, June 21, 2003. AB, Bowdoin Coll., 1961; MD, Boston U., 1965. Diplomate Am. Bd. Internal Medicine. Mixed medicine intern Sinai Hosp., Balt., 1965-66; resident in internal medicine Med. Ctrs. Hosps. Vt., Burlington, 1966-68; pvt. practice, Bennington, Vt., 1972-77; med. dir. univ. health svcs., asst. prof. medicine U. Rochester, N.Y., 1977-81; NIH fellow in infectious diseases U. Vt., Burlington, 1968-69, dir. Student Health Ctr., 1981-93, clin. asst. prof. medicine, 1983-89, clin. assoc. prof., 1989-93; assoc. clin. prof. cmty./family medicine/dir. student health Duke U., Durham, NC, 1994—2002, clin. prof. cmty./family medicine, 2002—. Sr. assoc. cons. The Spelman & Johnson Group. Cons. editor Jour. Am. Coll. Health, 1985—; contbr. articles to med. jours. Pres., bd. dirs. State Com. Vt. YMCA, Burlington, 1983-91; bd. dirs. Greater Burlington YMCA, 1990-93, Vt. Epilepsy Assn., Rutland, 1990-93; active Vt. Coalition for Disability Rights, 1991-93; chmn. Measles Mumps Rubella Varicella (MMRV) Action Group, Nat. Coalition for Adult Immunizations, 1995-98. Fellow ACP, Am. Coll. Health Assn. (pres. 1987-88, Ruth Boynton award 1989, Edward Hitchcock award 2001), Infectious Diseases Soc. Am. (emeritus); mem. Am. Coll. Health Found. Bd. (chmn. 1998-2003), New England Coll. Health Assn. (pres. 1985-86), Vt. Med. Soc., So. Coll. Health Assn. (pres. 1998-99). Avocations: bread baking, medical history. Office: Duke U Student Health Ctr PO Box 2899 Durham NC 27710-0001 E-mail: bill.christmas@duke.edu.

CHRISTOFFERSEN, RALPH EARL, chemist, researcher; b. Elgin, Ill., Dec. 4, 1937; s. Arthur Henry and Mary C.; m. Barbara Hibbard, June 10, 1961; children: Kirk Alan, Rachel Anne. BS, Cornell Coll., 1959, LLD (hon.), 1983; PhD, Ind. U., 1963. Asst. prof. chemistry U. Kans., Lawrence, 1966-69, assoc. prof., 1967-72, prof., 1972-81, asst. vice chancellor for acad. affairs, 1974-75, assoc. vice chancellor for acad. affairs, 1976-79, vice chancellor for acad. affairs, 1979-81; pres. Colo. State U., Ft. Collins, 1981-83; exec. dir. Upjohn Co., 1983-85, v.p. biotech. and basic research support, 1985-87, v.p. discovery research, 1987-89; v.p. rsch. SmithKline Beecham, King of Prussia, Pa., 1989-90, sr. v.p. rsch., 1990-92; CEO, pres. Ribozyme Pharms., Inc., Boulder, Colo., 1992-2001, chmn. bd., 2001—02; ptnr. Morgenthaler Ventures, 2002—. Bd. dirs. Serologicals Corp., Globe Immune Corp. Contbr. articles to profl. jours. NIH fellow, 1962-63, 64-66 Fellow Am. Inst. Chemists; mem. Am. Chem. Soc., Am. Phys. Soc. (v.p. theoretical div. 1981), Internat. Soc. Quantum Biology (pres. 1977-79), Pharm. Mfrs. Assn. (chmn. biotech. adv. com. 1983-86, chmn. R&D steering com. 1989-90), Sigma Xi, Phi Lambda Upsilon.

CHRISTOFIDES, PANAGIOTIS D. chemical engineer, educator; b. Athens, Greece, Jan. 3, 1970; arrived in U.S., 1992; s. Dimitrios and Euaggelia Christofides; m. Marina Foundi, Dec. 30, 1993; children: Dimitrios, Marios. BSChemE, U. Patras, Greece, 1992; MSEE, U. Minn., 1995, MS in Math., PhDChemE, U. Minn., 1996. Asst. prof. chem. engring. UCLA, 1996—2001, assoc. prof. chem. engring., 2001—. Author: Nonlinear and Robust Control of PDE Systems: Methods and Applications to Transport Reaction Processes, 2001. Recipient Career award, NSF, 1998, Young Investigator award, Office Naval Rsch., 2001, Hugo Schuck Best Paper award, Am. Automatic Control Coun. Mem.: AIChE, IEEE, Soc. Indsl. and Applied Math. E-mail: pdc@seas.ucla.edu.

CHRISTOFORIDIS, A. JOHN, radiologist, educator; b. Greece, Dec. 24, 1924; s. John P. and Ada A. C.; m. Ann Dimitriadis, Nov. 11, 1961; children: John, Gregory, Alex, Jimmy. MD summa cum laude, Nat. U. Athens, Greece, 1949; M.M.Sc., Ohio State U., 1957; PhD, Aristotelian U., Greece, 1969. Instr. to prof. Ohio State U., Columbus, 1956-74, clin. prof., 1974—; chmn. dept. radiology Aristotelian U., Salonika, Greece, 1971; prof., chmn. dept. radiology Med. Coll. Ohio, Toledo, until 1982; prof., chmn. dept. Ohio State U., Columbus, 1982—. Researcher in chest and gastrointestinal radiology; cons. Greek Ministry Health, Batelle Meml. Inst., Columbus. Contbr. to textbook Atlas of Axial Sagittal and Coronal Anatomy with Computed Tomography and Magnetic Resonance; author: Radiology for Medical Students, 4th edit., 1988, Diagnostic Radiology-Thorax, 1989; contbr. several chpts. to books, over 100 articles to med. jours. Served to lt. M.C. Greek Army, 1950-52. Recipient Silver award Ohio Med. Assn., 1969, awards Heart Assn., 1960, awards Batelle Meml. Inst., 1965, awards Astra Co., 1967, awards Lung Assn., 1970-71; named Hon. Citizen City of Thessalonike, 1973; Ohio Geriatrics Med. grantee, 1980; NSF grantee, 1980 Fellow Am. Coll. Chest Physicians, Am. Coll. Radiology; mem. AAA, AMA, AAUP, Ohio Radiol. Soc., Assn. Univ. Radiologists, Radiol. Soc. N. Am., Soc. Chmn. Acad. Radiology Depts., Fleishner Soc. (charter), Am. Hellenic Edn. Progressive Assn., Greek-Am. Progressive Assn., Acad. of Athens (corr. mem.). Greek Orthodox. Office: Ohio State U 410 W 10th Ave Columbus OH 43210-1240

CHRISTOL, CARL Q(UIMBY), lawyer, political science educator; b. Gallup, S.D., June 28, 1913; s. Carl and Winifred (Quimby) C.; m. Jeannette Stearns, Dec. 18, 1949 (dec.); children: Susan Quimby Christol-Deacon, Richard Stearns (dec.). AB, U. S.D., 1934, LLD (hon.), 1977; AM, Fletcher Sch. Law and Diplomacy, 1936; postgrad., Institut Universitaire des Hautes Etudes Internationales, Geneva, 1937-38, U. Geneva, 1937-38; PhD, U. Chgo., 1941; LLB, Yale U., 1947; postgrad., Acad. Internat. Law, The Hague, 1950. Bar: Calif. 1949, S.D. 1948. Assoc. firm Guthrie, Darling and Shattuck, Los Angeles, 1948-49; of counsel Fizzolio, Fizzolio & McLeod, Sherman Oaks, Calif., 1949-94; assoc. prof. polit. sci. U. So. Calif., 1949-59, prof., 1959-87, prof. emeritus, 1987—, chmn. dept. polit. sci., 1960-64, 75-77. Stockton chair internat. law U.S. Naval War Coll., 1962-63, cons., 1963-70 ; cons. World Law Fund; mem. L.A. Mayor's Adv. Com. Human Rels., Commn. to Study Orgn. of Peace; mem. adv. panel on internat. law Dept. State, 1970-76; v.p. Ct. of Man Found., 1971-77; scholar-in-residence Rockefeller Found. Bellagio Conf. and Study Ctr., Italy, 1980. Author: Transit by Air in International Law, 1941, Introduction to Political Science, 1957, 4th edit., 1982, Readings in International Law, 1959, The International Law of Outer Space, 1966, The International Legal and Institutional Aspects of the Stratosphere Ozone Problem, 1975, The Modern International Law of Outer Space, 1982, Space Law: Past, Present and Future, 1991; bd. editors: Western Polit. Quar, 1970-75, Internat. Lawyer, 1975-84, Space Policy, 1985—, Internat. Legal Materials, 1985—, Australian Internat. Law Jour., 1998—; contbr. articles on legal, polit. and mil. subjects to profl. jours. Bd. dirs. Los Angeles County Heart Assn., 1956-61. Served to lt. col. AUS, 1941-46; col. Res. ret. Decorated Bronze Star medal; recipient Dart award U. So. Calif., 1970, Assos. award for excellence in teaching, 1977, Raubenheimer award, 1982, Disting. Emeritus award, 1990, Rockefeller Found. fellow, 1958-59; Borchard Found. lectr., 2002. Mem. Am., Los Angeles bar assns., Am. Soc. Internat. Law (exec. council 1973-76), Internat. Studies Assn. (chmn. internat. law sect. 1977-78), Internat. Acad. Astronautics, State Bar Calif., UN Assn. Los Angeles (pres. 1961-63), Am. Polit. Sci. Assn., Internat. Inst. Space Law (pres. Am. br. 1973-75, Lifetime Achievement award 1998), Town Hall, AIAA, Internat. Law Assn., UN Assn. U.S. (dir. 1967-69), Masons, Blue Key, Skull and Dagger, Rotary, Phi Beta Kappa, Phi Kappa Phi (award 1987), Alpha Tau Omega. Republican. Presbyterian. Home: 1041 Anoka Pl Pacific Palisades CA 90272-2414 Office: U So Calif Polit Sci Dept Los Angeles CA 90089-0044

CHRISTOPH, FRANCES, painter; b. Bronxville, N.Y., Mar. 27, 1931; d. Charles DeGuire and Reba (Skipwith) Christoph; m. Charles Robert Salerno, Apr. 4, 1952; 1 stepchild, Franklin Robert Salerno; children: Lucia Salerno Lilien, Christoph Robert Salerno. Student, Art Students League, 1945-49, Adelphia Coll., 1948, Temple U., 1949-50, State U. Iowa, 1950-51, U. Paris Sorbonne, 1951-52, Acad. de la Grande Chaumiere, Paris, 1951-52. One-man show South Mainland Libr., Micco, Fla., 2003; exhibited in shows at Am. Students and Artists Ctr., Paris, Pietrantonio Galleries, N.Y.C., S.I. Mus., Richmond Art Gallery, S.I., Internat. Art Exhbn., Mojacar, Spain, others; writer, editor: Salerno Sculpture, 1965. Mem.: Royal Scottish Country Dance Soc., Nat. Mus. Women in the Arts (Fla. com.), Strawbridge Art League, Brevard Watercolor Soc., Archives Nat. Mus. Women in Arts, Art Students League (life). Democrat. Episcopalian. Avocation: gardening. Home: 5828 Lindsay Rd Micco FL 32976-2604 E-mail: fansale@aol.com.

CHRISTOPH, PETER RICHARD, historical editor, archivist; b. Albany, N.Y., Apr. 25, 1938; s. Hajo and Mathilda Bertha (Haage) Christoph; m. Florence Anna Weaver, June 6, 1959; children: Daniel William, Richard Peter, AnnaLise Hall. BA, Hartwick Coll., N.Y., 1960; MA, SUNY, 1964, MLS, 1968. Secondary tchg. English N.Y. State Edn. Dept., 1960, Profl. Libr. N.Y. State Edn. Dept., 1968, Archival Adminstrn. U. of Denver, 1969. Asst. libr. cataloging N.Y. State Libr., Albany, 1967—68, sr. libr. manuscripts and history, 1968—72, assoc. libr., 1972—91; editor N.Y. Hist. Manuscripts, Albany, 1974—, sr. editor Selkirk, NY, 1991. Dir. New Netherland Project, Albany, NY, 1974—84, N.Y. Hist. Manuscripts, Selkirk, NY, 1988—. Editor: (document collection) The Kingston Papers, 1661-1775, 1976, Diary of Henry Edgar Whittelsey, Catskill Mountain Storekeeper, 1835-1836, 1999, (document collection) The Leisler Papers, 1689-1691, 2002, Administrative Papers of Governors Richard Nicolls and Francis Lovelace, 1664-1673, 1980, Books of General Entries of the Colony of New York, 1664-1688, 1982, Records of the People of the Town of Bethlehem, 1690-1880, 1982, Records of the Court of Assizes for the Colony of New York, 1665-1682, 1983, The Andros Papers, 1674-1680, 1989—91, The Dongan Papers,1683-1688, 1993—96; author: (biography) Albert Andriessen Bradt, 2004, (book) A Norwegian Family in Colonial America. Pres. Town of Bethlehem Hist. Assn., Cedar Hill, NY, 1980—82, trustee, 1989—92; mem. Bethlehem Rural Cemetery Assn., Selkirk, NY, 1995—2000; archivist First Luth. Ch., Albany, NY, 1983—2003, lay preacher, 1985—99; rep. Bd. of the Luth. Archives Ctr., Phila., 1988—2003; mem. com. on minutes and protocol Upstate N.Y. Synod, Syracuse, 1988—2003; mem., congl. coun. First Luth. Ch., Albany, NY, 1986—89, 2000—03; archivist Upstate N.Y. Synod, Evang. Luth. Ch. in Am., Syracuse, 1993—2003; mem. Friends of Schuyler Mansion, Albany, NY, 1988—96. Grantee, Nat. Endowment for the Humanities, 1992—94. Fellow: Holland Soc. of N.Y.; mem.: Luth. Hist. Conf., Friends of Tombstone (Ariz.), Friends of New Netherland, N.Y. Geneal. and Biog. Soc. Lutheran. Avocation: travel. Home: 181 Maple Ave Selkirk NY 12158 Personal E-mail: pchrist1@nycap.rr.com.

CHRISTOPHER, ALEXANDER GEORGE, transportation company executive; b. Melrose Park, Ill., Apr. 17, 1941; s. George Alexander and Ann (Gianoulis) C.; m. Susan Bernice Breitweiser, May 12, 1979; children: Anna Bernice, Jason Woodrow. BA in Econs., BA in Philosphy, Elmhurst (Ill.) Coll., 1963; postgrad., DePaul U., 1963-64. Mgr. Dunn & Bradstreet, Chgo., 1965-67, various Chgo.-area currency exchs., 1967-71; v.p. Ill. Armored Car Corp., River Grove, 1971-82, dir.-in-exile, 1982-83, pres. Broadview, 1983-95, chmn., CEO, 1995—; CEO, United Armored Svcs, 1995—. Mem. adv. bd. fin. instns. sec. state Ill., 1983-97; mem. steering com. Security Cos. Organized for Legis. Action, 1988—, treas., 1993—. With USMCR, 1964-70. Mem. Ind. Armored Car Operators Assn. (pres. 1979-80, chmn. bd. 1980-81, chmn. legis. com. 1988—, bd. dirs. 1989-95), Nat. Armored Car Assn. (bd. dirs. 1999—). Greek Orthodox. Office: United Armored Svcs 2100 W 21st St Broadview IL 60155-4628

CHRISTOPHER, DORIS K. consumer products company executive; m. Jay Christopher, 1967; children: Julie, Kelley. BS in Home Econs., U. Ill., 1967. Cert. in family and consumer svcs. H.S. home econs. tchr.; with U. Ill. Coop. Extension Svc.; founder, chmn. The Pampered Chef Ltd., Addison, Ill., 1980—. Appeared on various TV programs including Oprah Winfrey Show, NBC Weekend Today, CNBC, CNN. Author: Come to the Table: A Celebration of Family Life, 1999. Mem.: Direct Selling Assn., Am. Assn. Family and Consumer Scis., America's Second Harvest, Com. of 200. Office: The Pampered Chef 1 Pampered Chef Lane Addison IL 60101-5630

CHRISTOPHER, IRENE, librarian, consultant; b. Greece, Nov. 17, 1922; came to U.S., 1923; d. George and Helen (Stephens) C. AB, Boston U., 1944; BLS, Simmons Coll., 1945. Gen. asst. Robbins Pub. Libr., Arlington, Mass., 1945-46, Boston U. Chenery Libr., 1946-47, head circulation dept., 1947-48, head reference dept., 1948-62; dir. libr. Emerson Coll., Boston, 1962-68; dir. Gordon McKay libr. Harvard U., Cambridge, Mass., 1968-70; chief libr. Boston U. Med. Ctr., 1970-92. Mem. AAUW, ALA (various coms. 1962-82, coun. 1970-74), Spl. Librs. Assn. (various coms. Boston chpt. 1952-75), Am. Soc. Info. Sci., Women's Nat. Book Assn., North Atlantic Health Scis. Librs., Med. Libr. Assn., New Eng. Online Users Group, Inc., Mass. Libr. Assn., Boston U. Women's Coun. Home: 790 Boylston St Apt 11C Boston MA 02199-7911

CHRISTOPHER, JAMES ROY, executive director; b. Fort Worth, Aug. 4, 1942; s. Roy Leslie and Mary Ruth (Hudson) C. Student, U. Tex., 1962-64, UCLA, 1978-79. Program dir. Priority One Outpatient Treatment Ctr., Beverly Hills, Calif., 1987-89; founder, exec. dir. SOS/Secular Orgns. for Sobriety, L.A., 1986—. Lectr. in field; originator events Funeral for the Unknown Smoker (annual), Unknown Smoker's Day, 2000, Memorial to the Unknown Smoker. Author: How to Stay Sober: Recovery Without Religion, 1988, Unhooked: Staying Sober and Drug Free, 1989, SOS Sobriety: The Proven Alternative to 12 Step Programs, 1992, Escape from Nicotine Country; How to Stop Smoking Painlessly, 1999; contbr. articles to profl. jours.; over 300 appearances in radio and TV. Mem. ACA, Am. Coun. on Alcoholism. Unitarian Universalist. Avocations: hiking, running, theatre, film. Office: Secular Orgns for Sobriety SOS Internat Clearinghouse 4773 Hollywood Blvd Los Angeles CA 90027 Office Fax: 323-666-4271. Business E-Mail: sos@cfiwest.org.

CHRISTOPHER, JAMES WALKER, architect, educator; b. Phila., Nov. 5, 1930; s. Arthur Bailey and Cornelia (Slater) C.; m. Carolyn Kennard, July 9, 1955; children: William W., Kathryn A., Kimberley, James S., Pamela W. BA, BS in Architecture, Rice U., 1953; M.Arch., MIT, 1956. Registered architect, Utah, Colo., Nev., Idaho, Wyo. Asst. prof. architecture U. Utah, Salt Lake City, 1956-60, adj. prof. architecture, 1983; archtl. designer various firms, Salt Lake City, 1960-63; founding prin. Brixen & Christopher Architects, Salt Lake City, 1963—. Architect, Phase I, Snowbird, Alta Canyon, Utah (AIA Western Mountain Region award 1971), Numemaker Place Chapel, Salt Lake City (AIA Western Mountain Region award 1977), Congregation Kol Ami, Salt Lake City (AIA Western Mountain Region award 1977), Block 53 Master Plan, Salt Lake City (Utah chpt. AIA award 1979). Mem. Utah Environ. Transp. Council, Salt Lake City, 1970-77, vice chmn., 1970-75; mem. Big Cottonwood Citizens Planning Com., Salt Lake County, Utah, 1975, Salt Lake City Downtown Planning Com., 1981, Utah Transit Authority Transplan, Salt Lake City, 1982. Served to lt. (j.g.) USNR, 1953-55. Fellow AIA (pres. Utah Soc. 1970 12 Utah Soc. Design awards, 12 Western Mountain Region Design awards 1968-83, 8 nat. Design awards 1975-83, Presdl. citation 1982, nat. design and planning com. 1976—, chmn. R/UDAT task group 1987-91, western mountain region Firm of the Yr. award 1987, Silver medal 1991, Utah Soc. Bronze medal 1999). Clubs: Alta. Episcopalian. Home: 2954 Millcreek Rd Salt Lake City UT 84109-3108 Office: Brixen & Christopher Architects 252 S 2nd E Salt Lake City UT 84111-2487

CHRISTOPHER, JOE RANDELL, English language educator; b. Bartlesville, Okla., June 27, 1935; s. Ernest Randell and Blanche (Woods) C.; m. Mary Lynn Hayes, June 9, 1958; children: Saralinda Michelle Evans, Vandy Maria, Randell Llewellyn-Hayes. BA, U. Okla., 1957, MA, 1959, PhD, 1969. Instr. Tarleton State U., Stephenville, Tex., 1963-67, asst. prof., 1967-68; vis. prof. Western N.Mex. U., Silver City, summer 1970; assoc. prof. Tarleton State U., Stephenville, Tex., 1968-87, prof., 1987-2001, prof. emeritus, 2001—. Invited lecturer Abilene Christian U. Ctr. for Christian Writing, 1990; keynote spkr. C.S. Lewis for 20th Century conf., Oklahoma City U., 1998. Author: (with Dean W. Dickinsheet, Robert E. Briney) A. Boucher Bibliography, 1969; (with Joan K. Ostling) C.S. Lewis: An Annotated Checklist of Writings about Him and His Works, 1974; author: (play) A Foretaste of Blood to Come, 1973, (books) C.S. Lewis, 1987, Musings Beneath a Tree of Amalion, 2d edit., 1993; editor: (chapbook) Chad Walsh Reviews C.S. Lewis, 1998, (Dark Fantasy issue) Niekas 45, 1998, (chapbook) Sayers on Holmes: Essays and Fiction on Sherlock Holmes by Dorothy L. Sayers, 2001; contbg. editor: The Lamp-Post of the Southern California C.S. Lewis Soc.; mem. editl. bd. Windhover: A Journal of Christian Literature, The Mythopoeic Press. Mythopoeic scholar for publ. books, 1976, 88; guest of honor Mythopoeic Conf., N.Y. C.S. Lewis Weekend, Tulsa C.S. Lewis Conf.; papers collected Western History Collections, U. Okla. Librs., Norman, Dick Smith Libr., Tarleton State U., Stephenville, Tex. Mem. MLA, South Ctrl. MLA, Conf. on Christianity and Literature, Mythopoeic Soc. (bd. advisors), various soc. devoted to authors: C.S. Lewis, Tolkien, Dorothy L. Sayers, Charles Williams, etc. Democrat. Episcopal. Office: Tarleton State U PO Box T-0300 Stephenville TX 76402-0001 E-mail: jchristopher@tarleton.edu.

CHRISTOPHER, LIN, artist; b. Talladega, Ala., Dec. 23, 1948; d. Newman and Mary Anna (Stewart) White; m. William Jackson Christopher, July 16, 1975. BS, Auburn U., 1971. Artist, Roswell, Ga., 1975—. Bd. dirs. Roswell Artists' Studio Tour. Represented in permanent collections at IBM, Sunkist, Bell South, Citicorp, Norcom, Hyatt Hotels, Ball Stalker, Royal Caribbean Cruise Lines, Ridgeview Inst., United Va. Bank, Price Waterhouse, John Harland Co., Taiyo Elec. Co., Equitable Life Ins. Co., Coopers & Lybrand, Allen & Co., Kinder Care, Hilton Hotels, Crestar Bank, Ala. Power, Ven Der Groen, Sharp Industries, World Carpets, King & Spalding, Workman & Co., Bluff Park Art Assn., Ctrl. Ill. Light Co., SAFE, A.R.T. Sta., Trammel Crowe, Shaw Industries, Perimeter Mall Atlanta, The Landmark Group, Eastman Pharm., James Madison U., Meadows Meml. Hosp., Gainesville Arts Coun., USAF, Bus. Coun. Ga., Albany Mus. Art, Merrill Lynch, Bank of the South, Arthur Anderson, Creative Arts Guild, South Trust Bank, The Marcus Group, Fuqua Industries, North Ga. Coll., So. Engring. Co., Walt Disney World, Springfield (Ill.) Civic Assn., Universal Studios, M G M, Royal Caribbean Cruise Lines. Recipient over 100 awards. Mem. Nat. Assn. Ind. Artists, Am. Crafts Coun. Avocation: gardening. Home: 1534 Jones Rd Roswell GA 30075-2726

CHRISTOPHER, MARY M. education educator, consultant; b. Post, Tex., Apr. 22, 1956; d. G. L. and Natalie C. Marable; m. Philip L. Christopher, Jan. 3, 1976; children: Jeremy Philip, Natalie Anne. BS in Edn., Tex. Tech. U., 1978, postgrad., 1999—2003; EdM, U. Louisville. Cert. elem. edn., English, gifted and talented Tex., Okla., Ky. Classroom tchr. Trinity Valley Sch., Ft. Worth, 1979—81; classroom tchr., gifted and talented facilitator Ardmore (Okla.) City Sch. Dist., 1981—87; classroom tchr., gifted and talented tchr., tech. specialist Jefferson County Pub. Schs., Louisville, 1987—95; asst. prof., cert. officer Hardin-Simmons U., Abilene, Tex., 1995—. Edn. cons. in field, Tex., 1996—; with Tech. Leadership Inst. U. Tex., Austin, 2002; presenter in field. Mem. editl. bd.: Gifted Child Today, 1997—; contbr. articles to profl. jours. Mem. grant com. Cmty. Found. Abilene, Tex., 2000—01; mem., grant com. Future Fund, Abilene, 2000—; mem. devel. coun. Baylor U., Waco, Tex., 2000—. Mem.: NAGC, Gifted and Talented Coords. Divsn., Tex. Assn. Gifted and Talented, Phi Kappa Phi. Baptist. Office: Hardin-Simmons U PO Box 16225 Abilene TX 79698

CHRISTOPHER, NICHOLAS, poet, novelist; b. N.Y.C., Feb. 28, 1951; m. Constance Barbara Davidson, Nov. 21, 1980. AB cum laude, Harvard Coll., 1973. Prof. Columbia U. Sch. Arts, Columbia U., 1988—. Author: On Tour with Rita, 1982, A Short History of the Island of Butterflies, 1986, The Soloist, 1986, Desperate Characters, 1988, In the Year of the Comet, 1992, 5 Degrees and Other Poems, 1995, Veronica, 1996, Somewhere in the Night: Film Noir and the American City, 1997, The Creation of the Night Sky, 1998, A Trip to the Stars, 2000, Atomic Field: Two Poems, 2000, Franklin Flyer, 2002; editor: Under 35: The New Generation of American Poets, 1989, Walk on the Wild Side: Urban American Poetry Since 1975, 1994. Recipient Lavan award Acad. Am. Poets, 1991, Melville Cane award Poetry Soc. Am., 1993; NEA fellow, 1987, Guggenheim fellow, 1993, Amy Lowell fellow. Mem. PEN, Poetry Soc. Am. Office: Janklow & Nesbit Assocs 445 Park Ave New York NY 10022-2606 E-mail: nc11@nyu.edu.

CHRISTOPHER, RAY LOUIS, pilot, journalist, author; b. Louisville, Ky., Jan. 11, 1943; s. Joseph Raymond and Margaret Edith (Nalley) C.; m. Karen Lynn Christopher, June 25, 1964; children: Richard, Traci, Amanda, Wendi. Student in Journalism, Fla. State U., 1965; grad. (hon.), U.S. Army Flight Sch., 1971; Med. Svc. Officer, Acad. Health Sci., San Antonio, 1979; Aviation Safety Officer, Army Aviation Safety Sch., Ft. Rucker, Ala., 1980; grad. in Aviation Safety Tech., Embry-Riddle Aero. U., 1980. Cert. aviation safety insp., USASC and FAA, accident investigator, USASC and FAA; lic. airline transport pilot, FAA, flight instr. airplane/helicopter single and multi engine. Sgt. U.S. Army, 1971, advanced through grades to chief warrant officer, 1991; capt. ICH Corp., Louisville, 1985-90; dir. aviation safety U.S. Army ARCENT HQ, Dhahrain, Saudi Arabia, 1990-92; chief pilot ISAIR, Ft. Lauderdale, Fla., 1992-94, Wings for Christ, Louisville, 1994—. Author: The Ten Commandments of Aviation Safety, 1980, Personal Enhancement Manual, 1994, Pillars of Success, 1997, 66 Routes to Corvette City, 1998, The Ragged Ol' Flag, 1991, Aviating Prayers, 1995. Chmn. Pilots Assn. Ky., Somerset, 1981; dir. Ky. Aviation Assn., Frankfort, 1983; flight safety counselor, FAA, Louisville, 1983-87; show car judge Corvette Club Am., Bowling Green, Ky., 1996-99. Decorated Bronze star, 1991; recipient Silver Plate of Honor, Ind. State Police, 1978, Ky. Merit medal Office of Gov., Frankfort, 1982, Million Mile Pilot Safety award Nat. Bus. Aviation, 1983, 12000 Hour Pilot Safety award Nat. Bus. Aviation, 1994. Mem. Aero Club Am., VFW (Chaplain 1989-90), Quiet Birdmen Assn. (life), NRA

(life, Disting. Life Mem. 1989), Disabled Am. Vets. (life). Republican. Roman Catholic. Avocations: corvette restoration, backpacking, sport shooting. Home: 8726 Running Fox Cir Fern Creek KY 40291 Office: Wings for Christ Bowman Field Louisville KY 40202 E-mail: chrisaire@aol.com.

CHRISTOPHER, RICHARD SCOTT, public relations and advertising executive, editor; b. Chgo., May 21, 1953; s. James J. and Geraldine A. (Kaulback) C.; m. Jacqueline D. Muter,Apr. 16, 1988; 1 child, Alyssa Lauren. B Journalism, U. Mo., Columbia, 1975. Gen. assignment reporter Salem (Mo.) News, 1975; news editor, tech. writer Am. Vet. Med. Assn., Schaumburg, Ill., 1975-77; sports reporter Daily Herald, Arlington Heights, Ill., 1977-78; assoc. editor, mktg. coord. Farm and Land Inst., Nat. Assn. Realtors, Chgo., 1978-80; mgr. project svcs. Kiwanis Internat., Chgo., 1980-82; account exec. Eckis Advt. & Design, Irvine, Calif., 1982-83; advt., pub. rels. exec. R.S. Christopher & Assocs., Newport Beach, Calif., 1983-86; pub. rels. account mgr., v.p. pub. rels. Basso & Assocs. Advt. Pub. Rels., 1986-92; mgr. internal comms. Nissan N. Am., Inc., 1992—2002, mgr. auto show events and news bur., 2002—. Editor, advt. mgr. Nat. Assn. Ind. Ins. Adjusters, Chgo., 1982—. Recipient Bronze award, Internat. Film and TV Festival N.Y., 1981, 1982, Helios award Excellence, 1992, Mercury award Gold winner, Internat. Film and TV Festival N.Y., 1992, Gold Quill, 1994, Advt. Design award Silver, 1997, CIPRA Intranet Devel. award, 1997. Mem. Internat. Assn. Bus. Communicators, Pub. Rels. Soc. Am., Kiwanis. Roman Catholic.

CHRISTOPHER, ROBERT PAUL, retired physician; b. Cleve., Apr. 27, 1932; s. Walter Matthews and Charity Marie (Roberts) C.; m. Doreen Mary O'Leary, Apr. 28, 1962; children: Robert Jr., Judith, Mark. BS, Northwestern U., 1954; MD, St. Louis U., 1959. Diplomate Am. Bd. Physical Medicine and Rehab. Chief rehab. medicine V.A. Hosp., Ann Arbor, Mich., 1963-67; asst. prof. rehab. medicine U. Mich., Ann Arbor, 1964-67; assoc. prof. rehab. medicine U. Tenn., Memphis, 1967-71, prof. rehab. medicine, 1971-2001; ret., 2001. Med. dirs. Les Passees Children's Rehab. Ctr., Memphis, 1976-98, Le Bonheur Hosp. Rehab. Svcs., Memphis, 1981-2001, Regional Med. Ctr. Rehab. Svcs., Memphis, 1967-2001, assoc. med. dir. St. Joseph Rehab. Ctr., Memphis, 1981-98. Contbg. author: Seating the Cerebral Palsey Child, 1983; author: sound/slide program Systems of Physical Therapy in Cerebral Palsy, 1971; contbr. articles to profl. jours. Pres. Mid-South Health Systems Agy., Memphis, 1980; mem. Mayor's Adv. Council for Disabled, Memphis, 1977-98. Recipient Disting. Svc. Commn. on Accredited Rehab. Facilities, 1982. Fellow Am. Acad. Phys. Medicine and Rehab. (sec. 1982-88, v.p. 1992—, pres. elect 1993, pres. 1994), Am. Acad. Cerebral Palsy (pres. 1987); mem. AMA, Am. Congress Rehab. Medicine, So. Soc. Phys. Medicine and Rsch. (sec. 1976-2000), Am. Bd. of Phys. Medicine and Rsch. (vice chmn. 1992-98), East Memphis Cath. Club (bd. dirs. 1969-80), K.C. (Grand Knight 1969-70). Avocations: travel, swimming. Home: 818 Island Club Sq Vero Beach FL 32963-5505 E-mail: drbobchris@aol.com.

CHRISTOPHER, RUSSELL LEWIS, baritone; b. Grand Rapids, Mich., Mar. 12, 1930; s. Russell Stewart and Violet (Jurewicz) C.; m. Gail B. Eldredge, Aug. 24, 1963 (div. 1985); 1 son, Russell Frederick. AA, Grand Rapids Jr. Coll., 1950; MusB, U. Mich., 1953, MusM, 1954. Music librarian NBC, N.Y.C., 1955-58. Elected U. Mich. Sch. Music Alumni Bd. Govs., 1997. Prin. artist, N.Y.C. Opera Co., 1958-60, San Francisco Opera Co., 1962, 63, Met. Opera Assn., N.Y.C., 1963-91, soloist, L.A., Montreal, Chgo., Richmond symphony orchs., 1963— ; sang role Maecenas in: world premiere Antony and Cleopatra at new, Met. Opera House, 1966; recs.: Carmen (Deutsche Grammophon), 1973, La Traviata (Electra Records), 1982, (CD) I'll Take Romance, 2002; numerous TV prodns. Live from the Met (Emmy award 1985); Miami Beach Symphony, Hollywood Bowl, Balt. Civic Opera, Central City Opera, Dayton Opera Assn., Phila. Lyric Opera Assn., Met. opera tour, Japan, 1975, 86; concert soloist, Spoleto (Italy) Festival, 1977. Mem. U. Mich. Sch. Music Alumni Bd., 1997. Recipient award Martha Baird Rockefeller Fund for Music, 1961; auditions winner Am. Opera, 1962; auditions winner Met. Opera, 1963; Mrs. Frederick K. Weyerhaeuser award, 1963; Disting. Alumni award Grand Rapids Jr. Coll., 1964, Alumnus of Yr. award U. Mich. Club of N.Y., 1978; recipient citation of merit award for outstanding contbns. to field of music, Alumni Bd., Sch. of Music, U. Mich., 1995. Mem. Am. Guild Musical Artists (nat. bd. govs. 1985-91, 94-99, exec. com. 1994-99).

CHRISTOPHER, STEVEN LEE, religious studies educator; b. Long Beach, Calif., May 29, 1956; s. Lehland James and Harriet Ann (Werner) C.; m. Doris Dianne Deterding, Aug. 19, 1978; children: LeAnna Helen, Brett Steven. BS in Edn., Concordia Coll., Seward, Nebr., 1979; MA, U. San Diego, 1989; PhD, Talbot Sch. Theology, 2001. Cert. tchr. and dir. Christian edn. Min. youth and edn. Bethany Luth. Ch., Long Beach, 1979-85; coord. youth ministries Christ Luth. Ch., La Mesa, Calif., 1985-88; prof., dir. Christian edn. program Concordia U, Calif., 1988-99; asst. to pres. CNH Dist., Luth. Ch. Mo. Synod, 1999—; dir. family ministry Our Savior Luth. Ch., Livermore, Calif., 1999—. Chmn. youth com. Pacific SW dist. Luth. Ch.-Mo. Synod, Irvine, 1983-88, mem. extended staff bd. for youth svcs., St. Louis, 1988-91, com. mem. nat. youth gathering, 1986, 89, 2001; chmn. 1991 Nat. Dirs. Christian Edn. Conf., River Forest, Ill., 1989-91; mem. youth bd. Abiding Savior Luth. Ch., El Toro, Calif., 1989-2002; spkr. various workshops and youth gatherings. Author young adult Bible study and youth Bible study, 1985, 3 devotions for children, 1988, chapel talks for children, 1989; contbr. articles to profl. jours. Mem. Theol. Educators in Assoc. Ministries (pres.-elect 1988-90, pres. 1990-92), Profl. Assn. Christian Educators, Religious Edn. Assn. Office: 1385 S Livermore Ave Livermore CA 94550-9532 E-mail: dceduo@aol.com.

CHRISTOPHER, WILLIAM GARTH, lawyer; b. Beaumont, Tex., Oct. 14, 1940; s. Garth Daugherty and Ollye Mittie (Harkness) C.; m. Kathleen S. Christopher; children: John William, David Noah, Michael O'Hara. BS in Engring., U.S. Mil. Acad., 1962; JD, U. Va., 1970. Bar: Va. 1970, D.C. 1970, U.S. Supreme Ct. 1975, Mich. 1977, Fla. 1988, Tex. 1989. Atty. Steptoe & Johnson, Washington, 1970-77; ptnr. Honigman MIller Schwartz & Cohn, Detroit, 1977-94, Holland & Knight, Tampa, Fla., 1994-95, Brown Clark Christopher & DeMay, P.A., Sarasota, Fla., 1995—. Contbr. articles to legal publ. Pres. Birmingham (Mich.) Hockey Assn., 1982-84; mem. Epsc. Diocese of Mich. Commn. on Ministry, 1983-88, co-chmn., 1987-88, standing com., 1988. Capt. C.E. U.S. Army, 1962-67. Mem.: Tex. Bar Assn., The Fla. Bar, Nat. Bd. Trial Advocacy, Sarasota County Bar Assn., Va. Bar, Order of Coif, Phi Delta Phi. Episcopalian. Office: Brown Clark Christopher & DeMay PA 1819 Main St Ste 1100 Sarasota FL 34236-5975 E-mail: wchristopher@sarasotafirm.com .

CHRISTOPHERSEN, BILL, editor, writer, educator; b. Bronx, N.Y., Oct. 8, 1949; s. George Wilhelm and Isabel (Thomson) C. BA in English, Columbia Coll., 1971; MA in Tchg. of English, Columbia U., 1976, PhD in Am. Lit., 1980. Bookstore staffer Tchrs. Coll. Bookstore, N.Y.C., 1974-79; adj. English instr. various colls., N.Y. and N.J., 1979-85; letters correspondent Newsweek, N.Y.C., 1985-90, mgr. letters dept., 1990-91, assoc. editor letters, 1991-95; freelance copy editor various mags., N.Y.C., 1996—. Adj. asst. prof. English Fordham U. Author: The Apparition in the Glass, 1994; contbr. revs., essays to profl. jours., newspapers, mags.; rec. artist with Fly By Night String Band, Lazy Aces String Band. Vol. literacy tutor Jewish Cmty. League, 1995-96; sponsor Save the Children, 1982-96. Nat. Merit scholar, 1967-71. Avocations: traditional musician, fiddle, guitar. Home: 414 W 121st St Apt 58 New York NY 10027-6008

CHRISTOPHERSON, ELIZABETH GOOD, broadcast executive; b. Cin. d. Walter R. and Jean S. Good; m. Paul C. Christopherson; 1 child, Katherine. BA, Wellesley Coll. Bd. dirs. N.J. State Coun. Arts, 1982—, chmn., CEO, 1989—91; exec. dir., CEO N.J. Pub. TV and Radio, Trenton, 1994—; pres., CEO NJN Found., 1994—. Bd. dirs. PNC Bank N.J., PBS, Liberty Sci. Ctr., Wellesley Coll. Bus. Leadership Coun. Pres., bd. dirs. Leadership Am. Assn., Alexandria, Va., 1991—92; bd. dirs. N.J. Tech. Coun. Mem.: Internat. Woman's Forum (pres. N.J. chpt.). Office: NJ Network PO Box 777 Trenton NJ 08625-0777

CHRISTOPHERSON, MYRVIN FREDERICK, college president; b. Milltown, Wis., July 21, 1939; s. Fred J. and Inger J. (Haug) C.; m. Anne Christine Marking, June 10, 1967; children: Kirsten, Berit, Bjorn, Nisse. BA, Dana Coll., 1961; MS, Purdue U., 1963, PhD, 1965; DD (hon.), Wartburg Theol. Sem., 1998. Teaching asst., instr. Purdue U., West Lafayette, Ind., 1961-65; asst. prof. speech U. Wis., Madison, 1965-69, assoc. prof. communication Stevens Point, 1969-76, prof. communication, 1976-86, assoc. dean. fine arts and communication, 1970-86; pres. Dana Coll., Blair, Nebr., 1986—. Cons. Wis. Telephone, Milw., 1968-78, AT&T, N.Y.C., 1969-71, 1st Fin. Corp., Stevens Point, 1980-86; commr. Nebr. Coordinating Commn. for Post Sec. Edn., 1989-91; mem. N.E. jud. nominating commn. Ct. Appeals No. 3 Steering Com.; bd. dirs. Found. for Ind. Higher Edn., 2003—; mem. adv. bd. Thrivent Fin. For Lutherans, 2002—. Author: Speaker's Trainer's Guide, 1970, The Company Speaker, 1979; editor: Jour. of the Wis. Communication Assn., 1978—80. Mem. adv. bd. The Lutheran, 1987—94, chmn., 1992—94; bd. dirs. Blair Cmty. Found., 1999—, Planned Giving Svcs., Nebr., chmn., 1992—94; ann. fund appeal chmn. Meml. Cmty. Hosp., 1994; trustee Palmer Chirpractic U., 1998—; mem. coun. pres. Evangel. Luth. Ch. in Am., 1999—, vice chmn., 1999—2000, chmn., 2000—, memls. com. churchwide assembly, 2001; mem. pastoral call com. First Luth. Ch., 1995, mem. ch. coun., 1999; mem. Nebr. Ednl. Fin. Authority, 1991—, chmn., 1992—99, 2001—, vice chmn., 2002—. Inducted into Wall of Honor, Unity High Sch., Polk County, Wis.; fellow Palmer Coll. Chiropractic, Palmer Coll. Chiropractic-West; named Knight of The Order of the Dannebrog, Queen Margrethe II of Denmark, 1997. Mem.: Found. for Independent Higher Edn. (bd. dirs. 2003—), Coun. of Pres., Luth. Edn. Conf. N.Am. (vice chmn. 1994—95, chmn. 1995—96), Nebr. Ind. Coll. Found. (exec. com. 1990—92, vice chmn. 1992—93, chmn. 1994—95), Nebr. Bus. Higher Edn. Forum, Nat. Assn. Intercoll. Athletics (couns. of pres. 1999—), North Ctrl. Assn. Colls. and Schs. (cons.-evaluator 1997—, accreditation rev. coun. 2001—, team chair 2002—), Nebr. Ednl. TV Coun. for higher Edn., Assn. Ind. Colls. Nebr. (chmn. 1992—93), Nat. Assn. Ind. Colls. and Univs. (bd. dirs. 1997—99, 2003—). Avocations: international travel, reading, writing, antique collecting and refinishing, study of theology. Office: Dana Coll Office of Pres Blair NE 68008

CHRISTOPHI, COSTAS A, statistician, accountant; b. Limassol, Cyprus, Aug. 16, 1971; BSBA, Boston U., 1990—94; MS, George Wash. U., Washington, D.C., 1997—99, PhD, 1999—. Chartered Accountant, Inst. of Chartered Accountants of Eng. and Wales, 1997. Sr. auditor KPMG Peat Marwick, Limassol, Cyprus, 1994—97; tchg. asst. George Wash. U., Washington, 1997—; sas programmer The Biostatistics Ctr. of GWU, Bethesda, Md., 2002—. Author: Statistics and Probability Letters. Vol. Nat. Cancer Inst., Bethesda, Md., 2001 . First rank pvt. with Cyprus armed forces, 1988—90. Recipient Minna Mirin Kullback Meml. Prize, George Wash. U., 2001—02; scholar Cyprus-America Scholarship Program, USAID - Fulbright Commn., 1990—94, 1997—99. Mem.: Am. Statis. Assn. Home: 6 Angelou Vlahou St Limassol 3083 Cyprus Personal E-mail: coschri@gwu.edu.

CHRISTOPHILLIS, CONSTANTINE S. lawyer; b. Greenville, S.C., Nov. 27, 1953; s. Gus and Fofo (Stamati) C.; m. Catherine Lynn Carr, May 14, 1978; children: Tina, Cory, Anna Kate. BA, Wofford Coll., 1975; JD, U. S.C., 1977. Bar: S.C. 1978, U.S. Dist. Ct. S.C. 1978, U.S. Ct. Appeals (4th cir.) 1981. Ptnr. Christophillis Law Offices, Greenville, 1978-88; shareholder Culbertson & Christophillis, Greenville, 1988—. Mem. ABA, S.C. Bar Assn., Greenville County Bar Assn., S.C. Trial Lawyers Assn., Nat. Orgn. Social Security Claimants Reps., Assn. S.C. Claimant Attys. for Workers Compensation, Rotary (bd. dirs. Greenville, Paul Harris fellow 1996). Office: Culbertson & Christophillis 707 E North St Greenville SC 29601-3010

CHRISTOV, CHRISTO IVANOV, mathematician, educator; b. Bulgaria; arrived in U.S., 97; MSc, U. Sofia, Bulgaria, 1973; PhD, Inst. Theoretical and Applice Math., Novosibirsk, Russia, 1980; DSc, Bulgarian Acad. Scis., Sofia, 1987. Vis. scholar U. Paris VI, 1991; vis. prof. Nat. Inst. Meteorology, Madrid, 1992, U. Complutense, Madrid, 1993—94, Free U. Brussels, 1994—95; asst. prof. Bulgarian Acad. Scis., 1978—84, assoc. prof., 1984—90, prof., 1986—87; vis. scholar Stanford (Calif.) U., 1997—98; prof. U. La., Lafayette, 1998—. Editor: (procs.) Fluid Physics, 1985, (collection of articles) Selected Topics in Nonlinear Wave Mechanics, 2001; author: (monograph) Random Point Functions, 1992. Recipient 1st place, Young People Soc. for Sci. Innovation, Bulgaria, 1985, state award for best young scientist, Bulgaria, 1986. Mem.: Am. Phys. Soc., Am. Math. Soc. Home: 112 Rue Fontaine Apt 1 Lafayette LA 70508 Office: U La Lafayette Dept Math Lafayette LA 70504-1010

CHRISTY, ARTHUR HILL, lawyer; b. Bklyn., July 25, 1923; s. Francis Taggart and Catherine Virginia (Damon) C.; m. Gloria Garvin Osborne, Feb. 14, 1980; children by previous marriage: Duncan Hill, Alexandra. AB, Yale U., 1945; LL.B., Columbia U., 1949. Bar: N.Y. 1950. Assoc. firm Baldwin, Todd & Lefferts, N.Y.C., 1950-52; spl. asst. atty. gen. Saratoga Investigation, N.Y., 1952-53; asst. U.S. atty. So. Dist. N.Y., 1953-54; chief prosecutor spl. asst. atty. gen. Saratoga and Columbia County Investigations, 1954-55; asst. atty. gen. N.Y., 1955; chief criminal div. U.S. atty.'s Office, So. Dist. N.Y., 1955-57; chief asst. U.S. atty., 1957-58; U.S. atty., 1958-59; partner firm Christy & Viener (and predecessors), N.Y.C., 1959—. Spl. asst. to Gov. Rockefeller, 1959-61; apptd. 1st spl. prosecutor Under Ethics in Govt. Act of 1978 to investigate charges against White House Chief of Staff, 1979-80. Artist in scrimshaw. Trustee, vice chmn. Bklyn. Hosp., Cmty. Svc. Soc.; v.p., gen. counsel, mem. coun. N.Y. Heart Assn. Lt. USNR, 1944-46. Mem. ABA, N.Y. State Bar Assn., Fed. Bar Assn., Assn. Bar City N.Y. (chmn. exec. com. 1966-67, v.p. 1968-69), Am. Coll. Trial Lawyers, Century Assn., Rockefeller Luncheon Club, Univ. Club (N.Y.C.), Mastigouche Fish and Game Club (Que., Can.). Republican. Episcopalian. Home: 430 E 57th St New York NY 10022-3061 Office: 620 5th Ave New York NY 10020-2402 E-mail: achristy@salans.com.

CHRISTY, AUDREY MEYER, public relations consultant; b. N.Y.C., Mar. 11, 1933; d. Mathias J. and Harriet Meyer; m. James R. Christy, Apr. 19, 1952; children: James R., III, Kathryn M. Smith, John T., Alysia A. Coleman, William J. BA, U. Buffalo, 1967. Pub. rels. officer Turgeon Bros., Buffalo, 1968-69; mem. pub. rels. staff Sch. Fine Arts, U. Nebr., Omaha, 1972; pub. rels. exec. Mathews & Clark Advt., Sarasota, Fla., 1974-75; profiles editor Tampa Bay mag., Tampa, Fla., 1972; pub. rels. cons. Bildex Corp., 1973-79; owner, operator Christy & Assocs., Venice, Fla., 1976-97; dir. mktg. comm. Northern Trust Bank, Naples, 1994-97. Trustee Big Bros./Big Sisters of Sarasota; vice chmn. Erie County March of Dimes, 1970; bd. dirs. Sarasota chpt. Am. Cancer Soc., Manasota (Pvt.) Industry Coun., 1987-89; mem. S.W. Fla. Ambulance Adv. Com., 1981; pres. Community Health Edn. Coun. Recipient various advt. awards. Mem. Pub. Rels. Soc. Am. (Outstanding Pub. Svc. award 1984), Fla. Hosp. Assn., Nat. Assn. Women Bus. Owners (charter mem. Sarasota chpt.), Sarasota County C. of C. (v.p., bd. dirs. 1990-91, vice chmn. mktg. 1984-85, 85-86, 86-87, 88-90, 90, vice chmn. 1989-90), Sarasota Manatee Press Club, LWV (editor Sarasota publ. 1978-79). Home: 5556 Bilbao Pl Sarasota FL 33578 Office: Christy & Assoc 216 Bayshore Cir Venice FL 34285-1407 E-mail: christy.pr@aol.com.

CHRISTY, CHARLES WESLEY, III, industrial engineering educator; b. Chester County, Pa., Apr. 29, 1942; s. Charles Wesley Jr. and Violet R. (Pierpont) C.; m. D. Jean Cullmann, Jan. 25, 1972; children: Richard Townsend, Charles Wesley IV, Michael Pierpont. BS, Widener U., 1973; MBA, Temple U., 1980. Chmn. indsl. engring. tech. Del. Tech. and C.C., Newark, 1970—. Pres. Pierpont Industries, Inc., Wilmington, Del., 1985—; adj. assoc. prof. U. Del., Newark, 1994; examiner Del. Quality Award, Wilmington, 1994. Bd. dirs., past pres. Opportunity Ctr., Inc., Wilmington, 1972—. Mem. Am. Inst. Indsl. Engrs. (bd. dirs. Del. chpt. 1970—, past pres.), Am. Soc. Quality Control. Home: 11 Harlech Dr Wilmington DE 19807-2507 Office: Del Tech & CC 400 Stanton Christiana Rd Newark DE 19713-2111 E-mail: cchristy@hopi.dtcc.edu.

CHRISTY, DAVID HARDACKER, music educator, consultant; b. El Reno, Okla., Sept. 4, 1955; s. Roy Myron and Mary Kathryn (Collins) C. B of Mus. Edn. summa cum laude, Southwestern Okla. State U., 1977, MEd summa cum laude, 1978. Cert. tchr., Okla., Tex. Dir. of bands Wichita County Pub. Schs., Leoti, Kans., 1978-80, Elk City (Okla.) Pub. Schs., 1980-93, Hale Ctr. Pub. Schs., 1993-95; prof. music Southeastern Okla. State U., 1995—. Mus. dir. Miss Elk City Pageant, 1981-93; dir. Elk City Concert Band Contest, 1981-93, Elk City Cmty. Band, 1981-85, 87-93, Southeastern Okla. State U. Music Festival, 1995—, Hale Ctr. Music Festival, 1993-95; bd. dirs. Elk City Coun. on the Arts, 1980-93, Elk City Pageant, 1986-93, Western Okla. Symphony Soc., 1980-93, Red River Arts Coun., 1997—, Red River Arts Acad., 1997—; site chmn. Southeast Okla. Dist. Band, 1995—; condr. SOSU Cmty. Band, 1995—. Recipient Music Dir.'s award Okla. Secondary Sch. Activities Assn., 1989, 90, 93, award Elk City C. of C., 1989, award of appreciation Denison H.S. Band, 1996, Broken Bow H.S., 1998, 2002, Durant H.S. Band, 2001, Faculty Senate award for tchg. excellence Southeastern Okla. State U., 1996-97, Ea. Okla. Band Dirs. Assn., 1998. Mem. Western Okla. Symphony soc. (bd. dirs. 1980-93), Okla. Bandmasters Assn. (parliamentarian 1982-83, recording sec. 1983-84, v.p. 1984-85, pres. 1986-87), Tex. Bandmasters Assn., Okla. Music Educators Assn. (v.p. 1987-89), Okla. Music Adjudicators Assn. (exec. sec. 1986-93),Tex. Music Adjudicators Assoc.(2003), Nat. Band Assn. (state chmn. 1985-86, rep nat. exec. bd. 1990-92, Citation of Excellence 1989, Dir. of Yr. 1989), Southwestern Okla. Band Dirs. Assn. (pres. 1983-84, Bandmaster of Yr. award 1982), Okla. Edn. Assn., Am. Sch. Band Dirs. Assn. (young band dir. of yr. 1986), Nat. Assn. Jazz Educators (Performance Cert. 1977, 78), Assn. Tex. Sml. Sch. Band Dirs. (assoc.), Southeastern State U. Tchg. Acad., Phi Beta Mu (internat. bd. dirs. 1992-94, state v.p. 1992-93), Phi Mu Alpha (Sinfonia Province Leadership award 1976), Kappa Kappa Psi (hon.). Democrat. Methodist. Avocations: golf, tennis, snow skiing, baseball card collecting. Home: 930 W Alabama Durant OK 74701 Office: Southeastern Okla State U Dept of Music Box 4047 Durant OK 74701 E-mail: dchristy@sosu.edu.

CHRISTY, GARY CHRISTOPHER, lawyer; b. L.A., July 23, 1948; s. Harry Voorhees and Theresa (Wolff) C.; m. Debra Deiter, June 29, 1984; 1 child, Casey. B.A., U. Tampa, 1971; J.D., Woodrow Wilson Coll. Law, Atlanta, 1976. Bar: Ga., U.S. Supreme Ct., U.S. Ct. Appeals (11th cir.), U.S. Dist. Ct. (no. and mid. dists.) Ga. Asst. dist. atty. Cordele Jud. Cir., Ga., 1976-79, dist. atty., 1979-85; ptnr. Davis, Pridgen, Jones & Christy, Vienna, Ga., 1985-86, Rainwater & Christy, Cordele, Ga., 1986-89, Davis, Gregory & Christy, 1990—; mem. faculty Ga. Inst. Trial Advocacy, Nat. Criminal Def. Coll. Mem. Organized Crime Prevention Coun. Ga., 1981-85; bd. dirs. Nat. Spinal Cord Injury Assn., Cordele, 1984. Recipient Disting. Svc. award Ga. Bur. Investigation, 1983. Fellow Ga. Bar Found.; mem. Nat. Dist. Attys. Assn., Assn. Trial Lawyers Am., Ga. Trial Lawyers Assn. (lectr. cross examination and closing argument 1986), Ga. Criminal Def Lawyers Assn. (lectr. 1990), State Bar Ga. (lectr.), Dist. Attys. Assn. Ga. (pres. 1984-85). Democrat. Roman Catholic. Home: Hwy 41 N PO Box 444 Vienna GA 31092-0444 Office: Davis Gregory Christy & Foxehand 708 16th Ave E PO Box 5230 Cordele GA 31010-5230

CHRISTY, JEFF, football player; b. Freeport, Pa., Feb. 3, 1969; m. Kristen; children: Nicolette, Krusty. Linebacker Tampa Bay Buccaneers. Active Children's Miracle Network, Leukemia Soc.; participant Moab Offroad Rally. Office: Tampa Bay Buccaneers 1 W Buccaneer Pl Tampa FL 33607-5797

CHRISTY, JOHN GILRAY, financial company executive; b. Silver Creek, N.Y., Aug. 27, 1932; s. John Van Vlack and Ruth (Gilray) C.; m. Helen Llewellyn, 1991; children: Andrew, Jennifer. BA, Dartmouth Coll., 1954; MA in Asian Studies, U. Calif., Berkeley, 1960. Loan officer U.S. Devel. Loan Fund, 1960-61; with AID, New Delhi and Washington, 1961-65, chief extended risk guaranty divsn., 1965; with ITT, N.Y.C., 1965-72, treasury dept., 1965-68, v.p. internat. comm., 1968-69, asst. group exec. internat. comm., 1969-70; pres. ITT World Directories, Inc., N.Y.C., 1970-72; group v.p. land transp. IU Internat., Inc., Phila., 1972-76, exec. v.p., 1976-78; pres., COO IU Internat. Corp., 1978-80, chmn., pres., CEO, 1982-85, chmn., CEO, 1985-88; chmn. Chestnut Capital Corp., Phila., 1988—, First Fidelity Bank, Phila., 1991. Bd. dirs. 1838 Bond Debenture Trading Fund, Phila. Contributorship. Chmn. emeritus Fgn. Policy Rsch. Inst.; former trustee Colby Coll.; trustee Phila. Orch., Eisenhower Exch. Fellowships Inc. Lt. USNR, 1958. Recipient Disting. Svc. award AID, 1965 Office: Chestnut Capital Corp PO Box 22 Flourtown PA 19031-0022 E-mail: christy@chapline.net.

CHRISTY, LARRY TODD, publisher; b. Tarentum, Pa., July 2, 1946; s. Todd Rowley and Eleanor Fern Christy; m. Kathleen Bernadette Braun, Nov. 26, 1976 (div. Feb. 1987); m. Lynn Elwell Sparrow, July 2, 1996. BA in Polit. Sci., Thiel Coll., 1968. Dir. Transact Corp., Geneva, 1972-76, pres. Pitts., 1976-96, Trendvest Corp., Virginia Beach, Va., 1978—, Thirders Found., Shelocta, Pa., 1989—; dir. Share Found., Inc., Pitts., 1994—; mgr. Trendvest Founders Ltd. Partnership Hedge Fund, 2000—, Trendvest Assocs. Ltd. Partnership, 2003—. Seminar speaker on Hedge Funds, Charles Schwab, Chgo., Phoenix, San Francisco, Pitts. and Columbus, 1989; publisher Internet World Wide Web Svc. for Investors, 1994—. Editor electronic investment svc./Trendvest Ratings, 1983—; author: Tax Trimmer Manual for Pennsylvania Corporations, 1980. Capt. mil. intelligence U.S. Army, Vietnam, Germany. Decorated Bronze Star. Mem. Thiel Coll. Alumni Assn. (pres. 1992-94, v.p. 1988-92, dir. 1983-95). Republican. Office: Trendvest Corp Ste 1805 923 First Colonial Rd Virginia Beach VA 23454 E-mail: larry@trendvest.com.

CHRISTY, NICHOLAS PIERSON, physician; b. Morristown, N.J., June 18, 1923; s. Leroy and Elizabeth (Baker) C.; m. Beverly Vairin Morris, June 21, 1947 (dec. Mar. 1997); children: Nicholas Pierson, Martha Vairin; m. Caroline P. Adams, June 26, 1999. AB, Yale, 1945; MD, Columbia, 1951. Diplomate: Am. Bd. Internal Medicine. Intern, asst. resident medicine, 1951—54; asst. vis. physician Delafield Hosp., N.Y.C., 1955-66, vis. physician, 1966-75; asst. vis. physician 1st med. div. Bellevue Hosp., N.Y.C., 1958-66; assoc. attending physician Presbyn. Hosp., N.Y.C., 1962-78, attending physician, 1978-93. Dir. med. svc. Roosevelt Hosp., N.Y.C., 1965-79; faculty Columbia Coll. Phys. and Surg., N.Y.C., 1956—, assoc. prof. medicine, 1962-65, assoc. clin. prof., 1965-67, clin. prof. medicine, 1967-71, prof. medicine, 1971-79, lectr. in medicine, 1979-88, sr. lectr. medicine, 1988-93, spl. lectr. in medicine, 1993—; mem. Columbia U. Health Scis. adv. coun., 1993—; prof. medicine, assoc. dean vets. affairs Health Sci. Ctr. at Bklyn., SUNY, 1979-88, prof. emeritus, 1988—; chief staff Bklyn. VA Med. Ctr., 1979-88; writer-in-residence, alumni writer Coll. Physicians and Surgeons, Columbia U., 1988—; assoc. Nat. Humanities Ctr., Research Triangle Park, N.C., 1979; cons. FDA, 1966, Bd. of Health, N.Y.C., 1965—, NIH Nat. Inst. Diabetes, Digestive and Kidney Diseases tng. grants divsn., 1969-72, endocrinology study sect., 1975-79; cons., bd. dirs. Royal Soc. Medicine Found., 1984-93. Editor, co-author: The Human Adrenal Cortex, 1971; editor-in-chief: Jour. Clin. Endocrinology and Metabolism, 1963-67; assoc. editor: Beeson-McDermott Textbook of Medicine, 1968-75; cons. editor, 1975-79; cons. Med. Dictionary (Dorland), 1988; adv. editor and contbr. Internat. Dictionary of Medicine and Biology (Endocrinology), 1986; mem. adv. bd.: Am. Jour. Medicine, 1971-88; contbr. numerous papers to profl. publs. Served to lt. (j.g.) USNR, 1943-46, PTO. Recipient Borden award, Joseph Mather Smith prize Columbia; John and Mary R. Markle scholar; NIH tng. grantee, 1959-65, endocrinology study sect. grantee, 1958-69; honoree St. Luke's Roosevelt Hosp. Alumni Assn., 2000. Fellow Am. Med. Writers Assn. (hon., Swanberg award 1989); mem. Harvey Soc., AAAS, Soc. Exptl. Biology and Medicine, Am. Soc. Clin. Investigation, Assn. Am. Physicians, Am. Fedn. Clin. Rsch., A.C.P., N.Y. Acad. Medicine, Laurentian Hormone Conf., Am. Physiol. Soc., N.Y. State Med. Soc., N.Y. County Med. Soc., Am. Clin. and Climatol. Assn. (recorder 1977-88, pres. 1990), Am. Assn. Study Liver Diseases, Endocrine Soc. (sec.-treas. 1978-89, Ayerst award 1986), N.Y. Clin. Soc., N.Y. Med. and Surg. Soc., Assn. Am. Physicians, Interurban Clin. Club, Hosp. Grads. Club, Peripatetic Soc., Practitioners Soc., Elizabethan (Yale), Colony (Yale), Century Assn. (pres. 1987-90, hon. 1995—). Home: 88 Rossini Rd Westerly RI 02891-4750 E-mail: calnick@earthlink.net.

CHRISTY, ROBERT ALLEN, investment advisor; b. Butler, Pa., Feb. 22, 1956; s. Allen B. and Jane (McMinn) C.; children: Kenneth Robert, Ashley Lynn. BA in Econs., Grove City (Pa.) Coll., 1978. Registered investment advisor. Investment broker Bache, Halsey, Stuart & Shields, Charlotte, N.C., 1982-87; v.p. investments Prudential-Bache Securities, Atlanta, 1987-90; v.p. Paine Webber, Inc., Atlanta, 1990-95, Oppenheimer & Co., Inc., 1995-96; chief fin. officer Profl. Karate Assocs.; pres., CEO Christy Investment Group, Roswell, Ga., 1996—. Pres. North-South Ventures, Atlanta. Pres. Roswell Jaycees, 1990-91; chmn. North Fulton Jr. C. of C., 1991-92; Served to capt. USMC, 1978-82. Mem. Am. Mgmt. Assn., Ga. Securities Dealers Assn., N.C. Securities Dealers Assn., Internat. Assn. Fin. Planning, Ofcls. Unltd. (assoc.), Atlanta Sports Coun., North Fulton Jr. C. of C. (chmn. 1991-92), North Fulton Found. chmn. 1992), Rotary (editor Charlotte chpt. 1984-85, Paul Harris fellow 1986). Republican. Presbyterian. Avocations: golf, baseball, umpiring. Office: Christy Investment Group 12600 Deerfield Pkwy Ste 100 Alpharetta GA 30004-

CHRISZT, DENNIS FRANCIS, priest; b. Cleve., Apr. 27, 1954; s. Francis Nicholas and Annette Marie (Frantz) Chriszt. BA, St. Joseph's Coll., Rensselaer, Ind., 1977; MDiv, Cath. Theol. Union, Chgo., 1982; DMin, Cath. Theol.

Union, 1998. Mem. Missionaries of the Precious Blood order Cin. province, 1978; ordained priest Roman Cath. Ch. Assoc. pastor St. John the Baptist Cath. Ch., Whiting, Ind., 1982—87, St. Andrew Cath. Ch., Orlando, Fla., 1987—93; dir. of formation Missionaries of the Precious Blood, Chgo., 1993—98, dir. vocation ministry Dayton, 1998—2002. Bd. trustees Calumet Coll. of St. Joseph, Whiting, Ind., 1995—; mem. Diocesan Liturgical Commn.i, Diocese of Orlando, 1988—93; founding mem. Diocesan Initiation Team, Diocese of Orlando, 1986—93; preacher of missions and retreats, 1993—; preacher Isaiah Ministries, 1993—. Author: (book) Creating an Effective Mystagogy: A Handbook for Catechumenate Leaders, 2001. Roman Catholic. Office: Missionaries of the Precious Blood Preaching Ministry 5326 S Cornell Ave Chicago IL 60615 Personal E-mail: dccpps@aol.com.

CHRITTON, GEORGE A. theater producer; b. Chgo. s. George A. and Dorothea G. Chritton; m. Martha Gilman, Aug. 26, 1956; children: Stewart, Andrew, Douglas, Laura, Neil, Lyle. BA, Occidental Coll., 1955; postgrad., Princeton U., 1955-57. With CIA & various U.S. govt. agys., 1960-89; gen. ptnr. Margeo Investment Co., L.A., 1963-76; pres. Wildacre Prodns., Inc., L.A., 1990—. Pres., CEO Fin. Svcs. Bancorp, Reno, 1990—; pres. Sycamore Prodns. Ltd., Nev. and Calif., 1994—. Prodr. theater prodns. Thornton Wilder's Youth, In Shakespeare and The Bible, A Ringing of Doorbells, The Rivers under the Earth, 1999. Mem. Am. Fgn. Svc. Assn., Washington, 1960—; chmn. bd. Neighborhood Learning Ctr., Capitol Hill, Washington, 1985-87; vol. Options House, Hollywood, Calif.; vol. coord. Rebuild L.A.; spl. advocate L.A. County Juvenile Ct., 2000—. Maj. USAF, 1957-60. Named Princeton Nat. Fellow, 1955-56, Vis. Fellow & Lectr. U. Calif., 1987-88. Mem. AFTRA, Am. Film Inst., Nat. Assn. Ind. Film & T.V. Prodrs., L.A. World Affairs Coun., Phi Beta Kappa, Phi Gamma Delta, Alpha Mu Gamma, Alpha Phi Gamma, Princeton Club (So. Calif.). Office: Wildacre Prodns Inc PO Box 719 Beverly Hills CA 90213-0719

CHROBOG, JUERGEN, ambassador; b. Berlin, Feb. 28, 1940; m. Magda Gohar; 3 children. Degree in law, U. Goettingen, Germany. Atty.; joined German Fgn. Svc., 1972; mem. German rep. UN, N.Y.C., 1972-73; responsible for European, Third World affairs and econs. Office of Fgn. Min., Bonn, 1973-77; dep. amb. Embassy of Germany, Singapore, 1977-80; spokesman German del. European Cmty., Brussels, 1980-83; dep. spokesman Fgn. Office, Bonn, 1983-84, spokesman, head press office, 1984, spokesman, head mgmt. staff, 1984-91, dir. polit. dept., 1991-94; amb. to U.S. Embassy of Germany, Washington, 1995-2001; state sec. German Fgn. Office, 2001—. Office: Embassy of Germany 4645 Reservoir Rd NW Washington DC 20007 1998

CHROMIZKY, WILLIAM RUDOLPH, accountant; b. Chgo., Jan. 21, 1955; s. Rudolph Joseph and Helen M. (Gniewek) C.; m. Laura Lee Lamoureux, Oct. 24, 1992. BS, No. Ill. U., 1977; M of Mgmt., Northwestern U., 1987. CPA, Ill. Sr. auditor Arthur Andersen & Co., Chgo., 1977-83; supr. internal audit AM Internat., Chgo., 1983-84, mgr. fin. reporting, 1984-85, dir. acctg., 1985; mgr. bus. analysis Premark Internat., Inc., Deerfield, Ill., 1985-87, dir. fin. reporting, 1987-2000; v.p., sec. and external reporting Aon Corp., Chgo., 2001—. Vol. CPAs for the Pub Interest, Chgo., 1990-92; mem. fin. com. Brother Rice H.S., 1995—, bd. dirs., 1999—. Mem.: AICPA, Fin. Execs. Inst. Avocations: skiing, tennis, bowling, competitive running. Office: Aon Corp 200 E Randolph St Chicago IL 60601 E-mail: william_chromizky@asc.aon.com.

CHROMOW, SHERI P. lawyer; b. N.Y.C., Aug. 27, 1946; d. Abe and Sara L. Pinsky. BA, Barnard Coll., N.Y.C., 1968; JD, NYU, 1971. Ptnr. Shearman & Sterling, N.Y.C., 1979—2001, Katten, Muchin, Zavis Rosenman, N.Y.C., 2001—. Lectr. Practising Law Inst., N.Y. County Bar Assn., Urban Land Inst.; mem. exec. com. N.Y. dist. coun. U. L.I.; mem. adv. bd. N.Y.U. Law Sch. Real Estate Inst.; mem. adv. bd. Ticor Title Ins. Co. Mem. Urban Land Inst. (gen. counsel), Assn. Fgn. Investors in Real Estate. Office: Katten Muchin Zavis Rosenman 575 Madison Ave New York NY 10022 E-mail: sheri.chromow@kmzr.com.

CHRONIS, HILDEGARD MARIA See TURKS, HILDEGARD

CHRONISTER, GREGORY MICHAEL, newspaper editor; b. York, Pa., Nov. 28, 1953; s. Francis Gilbert and Mary Jane (Hamberger) C. AB, Grove City (Pa.) Coll., 1975. Features editor The Ghent Press, Norfolk, Va., 1975, mng. editor, 1976; co-founder, editor Tidewater After Dark, Norfolk, 1977-79; asst. dir. New Va. Rev. Inc., Norfolk, 1979-80; editor univ. publs. Old Dominion U., Norfolk, 1980-85; assoc. editor Edn. Week, Washington, 1985-89, mng. editor, 1989—. Mem. Hist. Soc. Washington, Theodore Roosevelt Assn., Omicron Delta Kappa. Office: Edn Week 6935 Arlington Rd Ste 100 Bethesda MD 20814-5273

CHRONISTER, RICHARD DAVIS, physicist; b. Birmingham, Ala., Aug. 17, 1943; s. Richard D. and Mary Anne (Bealmear) C.; m. Vickie A. Bacon, Apr. 10, 1965; children: Susan K., Karen J. BS in Physics, U. Okla., 1965; MS in Nuclear Engring., Ohio State U., 1968. Cert. electromagnetic compatibility engr. Commd. 2d lt. USAF, 1965; advanced through grades to maj., 1977; Project mgr. USAF Aeropropulsion Lab., Dayton, Ohio, 1965-69; electronics survivability officer Field Command Def. Nuclear Agy., Livermore, Calif., 1969-72; grad. student U. Okla., Norman, 1972-75; mgr., transient radiation effects on electronics USAF Weapons Lab., Albuquerque, 1975-78; chief, radiation analysis lab. USAF Tech. Applications Ctr., Sacramento, 1979-83; chief aircraft and space sys. USAF Nuclear Criteria Group Secretariat, Albuquerque, 1983-86; prin. engr./physicist BDM Internat., Albuquerque, 1986-97; prin. engr./ops. rsch. TRW, Albuquerque, 1997—2002; prin. engr., physicist Northrop-Grumman, 2002—. Author, co-author tech. reports. Sr. mem. Am. Inst. Aeronautics and Astronautics; mem. AAAS, Am. Phys. Soc., Nat. Assn. Radio and Telecommunications Engrs. Methodist. Achievements include support of development of Army, Navy, Air Force, NASA and Department of Energy programs in the areas of environmental compliance, integrated electromagnetics, nuclear and natural environments, test and evaluation, distributed interactive simulation, verification, validation and accreditation. Home: 13005 Rebonito Rd NE Albuquerque NM 87112-4819 Office: Northrop-Grumman Inc 6001 Indian School Rd NE Albuquerque NM 87110-4182 E-mail: richardchronister@ngc.com.

CHRONISTER, VIRGINIA ANN, school nurse, educator; b. York, Pa, Sept. 25, 1940; d. Ernest B. and Mary L. (Anderson) Stokes; m. Burton F. Chronister, June 13, 1964; children: Scott E., Karen A. Student, York Jr. Coll., Millersville (Pa.) Coll.; diploma, Harrisburg (Pa.) Hosp., 1961; BS in Profl. Arts, St. Joseph's Coll., North Windham, Maine, 1985; M. (equivalency), Pa. State U., 1989; postgrad., St. Joseph's Coll., North windham, Maine. RN, Pa.; cert. sch. nurse (edn. specialist II), Pa. Charge nurse Harrisburg Hosp., 1961-64; instr., practical nurses York City Sch. Dist., 1964-68; instr., med. sec. Yorktowne Bus. Inst., York, 1985; sch. nurse West York Sch. Dist., York, 1985—. Substitute sch. nurse, 1972-85; health cons. for 2-day care ctr. ECELS. Recipient Cardiac Nursing award. Mem.: AAUW, NEA, West York Area Edn. Assn. (pres. 1990—2003, negotiator 1999—2001, pres. 2002, 2003), York County Coord Coun., United Ostomy Assn. (charter mem.), York County Sch. Nurse Assn. (pres. 1991—92, sec. 1998—), Harrisburg Hosp. Alumnae Assn., Nat. Assn. Sch. Nurses, Pa. Sch. Health Assn., Pa. State Edn. Assn. (sch. nurse sect.), Beta Sigma Phi (pres. Theta master chpt. 2000). Home: 2090 Loman Dr York PA 17404-4214

CHRONLEY, JAMES ANDREW, real estate executive; b. Springfield, Mass., July 31, 1930; s. Robert Emmett and Eleanor Agnes (Sullivan) C.; m. Monique Mary Delpech, July 29, 1955; children: Mary Elizabeth, James Michael, Jean Louise, Patricia, Joseph Patrick, John Peter, Robert Emmett. AB, Brown U., 1952; diploma in real estate, U. R.I., 1963; MBA, Peppderdine U., 1991. With Arco Co., 1954-74, Eastern area mgr., until 1972; nat. real estate dir. Atlantic Richfield Co., Los Angeles, 1972-74; v.p. restaurant real estate Marriott Corp., Washington, 1974-78; exec. v.p. Burger Chef Systems, Inc., Indpls., 1978-82, pres., 1982; sr. v.p. devel. Taco Bell, Irvine, Calif., 1983-94. Served with AUS, 1952-54. Mem. Nat. Assn. Corp. Real Estate Execs. (chpt. pres. 1979, chmn. bd. 1985-87, elected trustee 1987-92), Am. Arbitration Assn., Internat. Exec. Svc. Corps, Orange County Assn. Investment Mgrs. Roman Catholic. Office: Taco Bell 19800 Macarthur Blvd Ste 1450 Irvine CA 92612-2421

CHROPUFKA, MARK A. information management specialist, poet; b. West Islip, N.Y., Feb. 27, 1970; s. Edward and Regina (Abbatello) Seaman. BS in Mgmt., SUNY, Binghamton, 1992; MBA, St. John's U., 2001. Tech. and trade support Sanford Bernstein, N.Y.C., 1992-93; substitute prin., stenographer Wyandanch UFSD, N.Y., 1993-94; data analyst Pratt Inst., Bklyn., 1994-96, dir. info. mgmt., 1996-98; software analyst St. John's Univ., 1999—. Author of poems; Holly and OaK: A Crossroads in Life, 1996; prodr. TV spl. Crazy Dave's Magic Show, 1995; songwriter; creator, prodr. TV spl. Aggravated Cat!, 1999-2001. Guitarist, mem. music ministry Our Lady of Miraculous Medal Ch., Wyandanch, N.Y., 1999—; contbr. Friends of Karen Lavilla Fund, Purdys, N.Y., 1995, The Newman House, Binghamton, N.Y., 1992—; vol., participant Wyandanch Career Day, 1994; asst. coord. Wyandanch Book Fair, 1994; supporter, contbr. Manhattan Neighborhood Network, N.Y.C., 1995. Mem.: Beta Gamma Sigma. Avocations: writing, investing, biking, travel, independent tv production, guitar playing. Home: 11 Pearsall St Babylon NY 11702-2517 Office: St Johns University 8000 Utopia Pky Jamaica NY 11439-0002 E-mail: chropufm@stjohns.edu., mchropufka@aol.com.

CHRYSANTHIS, PANOS KYPROS, computer science educator, researcher; b. Nicosia, Cyprus, Feb. 1, 1958; came to U.S., 1983; s. Kypros and Loulla Chyrsanthis; m. Areti Papanastasiou, Jan. 7, 1989. BS in Physics and Math., U. Athens, Greece, 1982; MS in Computer and Info. Scis., U. Mass., 1986, PhD in Computer and Info. Scis., 1991. Rsch. scientist U. Athens, Greece, 1983; tchg. asst./assoc. U. Mass., Amherst, 1983-85, rsch. asst., 1984-91, rsch. vis. faculty mem., 1992-94; asst. prof. U. Pitts., 1991-97, assoc. prof. computer sci., 1997—. Vis. prof. U. Rome La Sapienza, 1994, Carnegie-Mellon U., 1999-2000; hon. rsch. fellow Alba Bus. Adminstrn., Athens, Greece, 1995—; co-chair 1998 NSF Info. and Data Mgmt. Workshop Rsch. Agenda for 21st Century; program co-chair ACM Mobide 1999, DEXA MDDS, 1999, 2000-01; mem. program com., referee, reviewer for numerous confs., orgns.; adj. assoc. prof. Carnegie-Mellon U., 2000—. Author: Advances in Concurrency Control and Transaction Processing, 1997; guest editor spl. issue Distributed Sys. Engring. Jour., 1996, ACM/Balzer Monet; contbr. articles to profl. publs., chpts. to books in field. Recipient award for understanding autonomy in multidatabase NSF, 1992-96, Career award for mobile data mgmt. NSF, 1995-2000, Reliable Mgmt. of Gigabit Networked Databases, NSF, 1998-2002, Intelligent Workflow Mgmt. Sys., DARPA, 1999-2001; grantee Rsch. Devel. Fund, U. Pitts., 1992-94, DEC Equipment Allowance, 1991, B-Right Trucking Co., 1994-95. Mem. IEEE, Assn. for Computing Machinery, Hellenic Soc. Computer and Info. Scientists, Sigma Xi. Office: U Pitts Computer Sci Dept Sennott Square Bldg Pittsburgh PA 15260

CHRYSLER, RICHARD R. former congressman; b. St. Paul, Apr. 29, 1942; m. Katie; children: Richard R., Phil, Christie Ann. With Chevrolet divsn. Gen. Motors Corp., 1960-64, Hurst Performance, Inc., Brighton, Mich., 1966-76; founder, chmn. Cars & Concepts, Inc., Brighton, 1976-86, RCI; U.S. congressman Mich. 8th Dist., 1995-96; pres. JPE, Inc., 1998-99; vice chmn. ASCET, Inc., 1999; pres. Ideal Steel, Hamburg, Mich., 1999—. Bd. dirs. Mich. Nat. Bank. Patentee skylite T-roof.

CHRYSSIS, GEORGE CHRISTOPHER, entrepreneur; b. Crete, Greece, May 21, 1947; came to U.S., 1966; naturalized U.S. citizen; s. Christopher and Ourania (Kamisakis) C.; m. Margo Sayegh, May 21, 1978; children: Rania, Lilian, Alexander. ASEE, Wentworth Inst., 1969; BEE, Northeastern U., 1972, MEE, 1977. Electronic engr. Orion Rsch., Boston, 1977-78; sr. engr. Datel, Inc., Mansfield, Mass., 1978-79; co-founder, v.p. ops. and engring. Power Gen. Corp., Canton, Mass., 1979-85; pres., founder, CFO Intelco Corp., Acton, Mass., 1985-90; pres., treas. G & M Enterprises, Inc., 1989-92; co-founder, chmn. Collegescape, Inc., 1997-98; pres. Arcadian Capital Mgmt., LLC, 1999—; founder, pub. The Hellenic Voice, 2001—02. Pvt. investor, 1992-97;mem. bd. trustees Hellenic Coll./Holy Cross, 1989-97, 99— vice chmn., 2001—; trustee U. Crete Endowment Fund, 1992-97, Wentworth Inst., 1996—, Anatolia Coll., 1999-2002; chmn. NU Nat. Coun., 2002—; bd. dirs. Nat. Coun. Northeastern U., 1986—, Nat. Coun. Wentworth Inst., 1987—; corporator Wentworth Inst., 1990-96, chmn. fund campaign, 1989, trustee, 1996—; mem. Capital Campaign Cabinet, 1992-97; mem. Wentworth Inst. investment com., 1996—, chair long range planning com., 1999—; bd. dirs. Delphi Comms., Inc., Continuum Control Corp., EliteView Corp.; corporator Northeastern U., 1990, bd. overseers, 1995-2002, trustee 2002—, mem. indsl. advisory bd., 1997—, mem. long-range planning com. 1995—, audit com. 2002—, devel. com. 2002—; founding dir. Gorbachev Found. of N.Am., 1999—; adv. bd. NU Sch. of Entrepreneurship, 2000. Author: High Frequency Switching Power Supplies, 1984, 89, Echoes and Re-Echoes (poetry), 1993, Heliotropia (poetry), 1996, Short Poems of Homecoming, 1999; contbr. articles to profl. jours. Bd. dirs. St. Demetrios Ch., Weston, Mass., 1987-99, parish coun. pres. 1998-99, chmn. ways and means com., 1992-93, ch. svcs. com., 1989-90, stewardship com., 1994-2002; fellow Orthodox Steward of Boston Diocese, 1986—, Greek Orthodox Archdiocese Leadership One Hundred, 2000—, Archon Ecumenical Patriarchate, 2000; active numerous cmty. and civic orgns.; friends Univs. of Crete, 1995, Greek Inst., 1989, bd. dirs., 1998; mem. Am. Hellenic Inst., 1985, Mass. High Tech. Coun., 1986-90. Recipient New Englander award Smaller Bus. Assn. New Eng. (SBANE), 1989, Golden Leopard award Wentworth Inst., 1991, Arete award Greek Inst., 1996, Hellenic Leadership award, 1997, Ellis Island medal of honor award, 2000; named finalist for Entrepreneur of Yr. Arthur Young Inc. and Inc. Mag., 1989; named parishioner of yr. 1993 Greek Orthodox Diocese Boston, recipient laity award, Minoan award 2002. Mem.: Hellenic Scientists Assn., Internat. Soc. Poets (disting.), PanCretan Assn. Am. (pres. Boston chpt. 1987—89, co-chmn. 30th nat. conv. 1988, bd. govs. dist. I 1990—92, nat. pres. 1995—97, Minoan award 2002), Huntington Soc., President's Club, 500 Club of Northeastern U., Alpha Omega (coun. 1990—, treas. 1994—97). Greek Orthodox. Avocations: writing, tennis, traveling.

CHRYSTAL, WILLIAM GEORGE, minister; b. Seattle, May 22, 1947; s. Francis Homer and Marjorie Isabell (Daubert) C.; m. Mary Frances King, Aug. 24, 1970; children: Shelley, Sarah, John, Philip. BA, U. Wash., 1969, MEd, 1970; MDiv, Eden Theol. Sem., 1978; MA, Johns Hopkins U., 1984. Ordained to ministry, United Ch. of Christ, 1977. Learning resources specialist Seattle C.C. Dist., 1970-71; dir. learning resources ctr. Whatcom C.C., Ferndale, Wash., 1971-73; minister St. Peter's United Ch. of Christ, Granite City, Ill., 1978-79; sr. minister 1st Congl. Ch., Stockton, Calif., 1979-83; minister Trinity United Ch. of Christ, Adamstown, Md., 1983-85; sr. minister Edwards Congl. Ch., Northampton, Mass., 1985-86, 1st Congl. Ch., Reno, Nev., 1991—. Hosp. chaplain Washoe Med. Ctr., Reno, 1993-99; host Thomas Jefferson Hour, on Nat. pub. radio stas. Author: Young Reinhold Niebuhr: His Early Writings, 1911-1931, 1977, 2d edit., 1982, A Father's Mantle: The Legacy of Gustav Niebuhr, 1982, The Fellowship of Prayer, 1987; author monographs; contbr. articles to profl. jours. V.p. Reno-Sparks Met. Ministry, Reno, 1994-97; Chautauqua scholar Great Basin Chautauqua, Reno, 1993, 94, 98, 99. Lt. comdr. USN, 1986-91, maj. Nev. Army N.G., 1992-96. Decorated (2) Meritorious Svc. medal. Mem. Am. Soc. Ch. History, Nev. Soc. Mayflower Descs. (past gov.), Am. Legion, Disabled Vets. (life), VFW (life), Rotary Club (Paul Harris fellow 1997). Home: 3820 Bluebird Cir Reno NV 89509-5601 Office: 1st Congl Ch 627 Sunnyside Dr Reno NV 89503-3515 E-mail: chrystal@intercomm.com.

CHRYSTIE, THOMAS LUDLOW, investor; b. N.Y.C., May 24, 1933; s. Thomas Witter and Helen (Duell) C.; m. Eliza S. Balis, June 9, 1955; children: Alice B., Helen S., Adden B., James McD. BA, Columbia U., 1955; MBA, NYU, 1960. With Merrill Lynch, Pierce, Fenner & Smith, Inc., N.Y.C., 1955-75, dir. investment banking divsn., 1970-75; sr. v.p. Merrill Lynch & Co., 1975-78, CFO, 1976-78; chmn. Merrill Lynch White Weld Capital Markets Group, 1978-81, Merrill Lynch Capital Resources, 1981-83; adv. on strategy Merrill Lynch & Co. Inc., 1983-88; pvt. investor Jackson, Wyo., 1988—. Bd. dirs. Jackson State Bank, Consumer Portfolio Svcs., Inc., Eeonyx Corp. Trustee emeritus Columbia U.; trustee Nat. Mus. Wildlife Art, Middleton Place Found. Capt. USAF, 1955-58. Mem. N.Y. Athletic Club, Teton Pines Tennis Club, Columbia Club. Home and Office: PO Box 640 Wilson WY 83014-0640 *Whatever you are involved in, see it as part of a larger picture.*

CHRZANOWSKA-JESKE, MALGORZATA EWA, electrical engineering educator, consultant; b. Warsaw, Nov. 26, 1948; came to U.S., 1985; d. Waclaw and Halina (Siedlanowska) Chrzanowska; m. Witold Norbert Jeske, July 21, 1978; children: Marcin, Olaf. MS in Electronics, Warsaw Tech. U., 1972; MS in Elec. Engring., Tuskegee (Ala.) Inst., 1976; PhD in Elec. Engring., Auburn (Ala.) U., 1988. Rsch. and tchg. instr. Warsaw Tech. U., 1972-75; rsch. and tchg. asst. Tuskegee Inst., 1975-76, Auburn U., 1976-77, rsch. asst., postdoctoral fellow, 1985-89; sr. rschr. Inst. Electron Tech., Warsaw, 1977-82, CAD project leader, 1983-85; asst. prof. Portland (Oreg.) State U., 1989-95, assoc. prof. elec. engring., 1995-2000, prof. elec. engring., 2000—. Cons. Inst. Electron Tech., Warsaw, 1985—; lectr. Tuskegee Inst., 1977; profl/lectr. Oreg. Ctr. for Advance tech., Beaverton, 1991-94. Contbr. articles to profl. jours. Troop leader Polish Scout Assn., Warsaw, 1958-66; sci. and activity com. chmn. Polish Student Assn., Warsaw, 1966-75; mem. Solidarity, Poland, 1980-85. Recipient First Level award Polish Dept. Sci., Higher Edn. and Tech., 1983; named to Women of Distinction in Engring. Columbia coun. Girl Scouts U.S., 1993. Mem. Assn. Computing Machinery, Internat. Conf. on Electronics, Circuits and Sys. (tech. program co-chair 2002), IEEE (sr., Oreg. sect. exec. com. 1994-96, sr. mem.), IEEE Electron Device Soc. (chair edn. com. Oreg. sect. 1989-96), IEEE Circuits and Sys. Soc., Eta Kappa Nu. Achievements include research in low temperature semiconductor device simulation; comprehensive logic and layout synthesis for VLSI and field programmable gate arrays. Office: Portland State Univ Dept Elec Engring 1800 SW 6th Ave Portland OR 97201-5204 E-mail: jeske@ee.pdx.edu.

CHRZANOWSKI, LEYE JEANNETTE, publisher; b. Aug. 28, 1946; Student, Ctrl. Tex. Coll., 1978-79, Enterprise State Jr. Coll., 1982-83. Pres., founder Excel Networking Group, Inc., Va., 1991-94; v.p., exec. editor EKA Comms., Md., 1993-97; pres. Disability News Svc., Chantilly, Va., 1997—. Mem. Soc. Profl. Journalists, Investigative Reporters and Editors, Soc. Disability Studies, Washington Ind. Writers. Office: 13703 Southernwood Ct Chantilly VA 20151-3345 E-mail: leyech@cox.net.

CHRZANOWSKI, ROSE-ANN CANNIZZO, art educator; b. Bklyn., Mar. 13, 1952; d. Francis Salvatore and Vincenza Pilaro Cannizzo; m. Raymond David Chrzanowski; 1 child, Karen Kuczenski. BA, CUNY, Bklyn., 1974; MS, Fordham U., 1977; postgrad., So. Conn. State U., 1990. Cert. in elem. edn. N.Y. Permanent Tchg. Cert., Conn. Profl. Tchg. Cert., in art Conn. Profl. Tchg. Cert., art EAYA. 3d grade tchr. St. Michael Sch., Bklyn., 1974—78; art tchr. Naugatuck Elem. Schs., Naugatuck, Conn., 1978—90; tchr. City Hill Mid. Sch., Naugatuck, 1990—2000, Naugatuck H.S., 2000—. Tchr., tutor supr. Naugatuck Youth Svcs., 1978—84; edn. program coord. Human Resources Devel. Agy., Naugatuck, 1985—87; adj. prof. Teikyo Post U., Waterbury, Conn., 1996; mem. adv. coun. Celebration Excellence, New Haven, 1998—. Contbg. author: Doing What's Right in the Middle, Promising Practices of Schools with Middle Grades, 1999. Chmn. Naugatuck Arts Commn., 1996—98; nat. tchr. forum rep. State Dept. Edn., 2001. Recipient Emeritus award, Celebration Excellence, 1999. Mem.: NEA, Conn. Art Edn. Assn., Nat. Art Edn. Assn., Phi Delta Kappa. Office: Naugatuck HS 543 Rubber Ave Naugatuck CT 06770 Personal E-mail: rayrochrz@earthlink.net.

CHU, ALLEN YUM-CHING, automation company executive, systems consultant; b. Hong Kong, June 19, 1951; arrived in Can., 1972; s. Luke King-Sang and Kim Kam (Lee) C.; m. Connie Ge Chen, June 29, 1999. BSc in Computer Sci., U. B.C., Vancouver, Can., 1977; BA in Econs., U. Alta., Edmonton, Can., 1986. Rsch. asst. dept. neuropsychology and rsch. Alta. Hosp., Edmonton, 1977-78; systems analyst dept. agr. Govt. of Alta., Edmonton, 1978-81; systems analyst for computing resources City of Edmonton, 1981-86; pres. ANO Automation Inc., Vancouver, 1986-92. V.p., bd. dirs. ANNOVA Bus. Group, Inc., Canada, 1993—98; dir. Capital Alliance Group, 1998—. Mem. IEEE Computer Soc., N.Y. Acad. Sci. Office: Capital Alliance Group 1200 777 W Broadway Vancouver BC Canada V5Z 4J7

CHU, BENJAMIN K. hospital administrator; BA, Yale U., 1974; MD, NYU, 1978; MPH, Columbia Mailman Sch. Pub. Health, 1985. Diplomate Am. Bd. Internal Medicine, 1982. Intern, resident Kings County Hosp., 1978; sr. assoc. dean Harlem Hosp. Affairs P&S; pres., CEO N.Y.C. Health and Hosp. Corp., 2002—. Office: 125 Worth St New York NY 10013

CHU, BENJAMIN THOMAS PENG-NIEN, chemistry educator; b. Shanghai, Mar. 3, 1932; came to U.S., 1953; s. Charles C. and Gladys (Chen) C.; m. Louisa King, Mar. 30, 1959; children: Peter, Joanne, Laurence. BS magna cum laude, St. Norbert Coll., 1955; PhD, Cornell U., 1959. Research assoc. Cornell U., Ithaca, N.Y., 1958-62; asst. prof. U. Kans., Lawrence, 1962-65, assoc. prof., 1965-68; prof. chemistry SUNY, Stony Brook, 1968-88, Leading prof. chemistry, 1988-92, Disting. prof., 1992—, chmn. chemistry dept., 1978-85, prof. materials sci. and engring., 1982—. Vis. prof. U. New South Wales, Australia, 1974, Australian Nat. U., 1974, Wayne State U., Hokkaido U., 1975, Japan Soc. Promotion Sci., 1975-76, 92-93; vis. scientist Inst. for Theoretical Physics, U. Calif., Santa Barbara, 1982; cons. Calgon, Pitts., 1978-80, E.I. DuPont de Nemours, Wilmington, Del., 1979—, W.L. Gore & Assocs., Inc., Elkton, Md., 1998-99, Dow Chem., Freeport, Tex., 1998-99, Brookhaven (N.Y.) Instruments, 1981, USRA, Microgravity Sci. and Applications divsn. NASA, 1988, Bristol-Myers Squibb Co., 1990-92; hon. prof. Academia Sinica, China, 1992—, Nankai U., China, 1996—, Xiamen U., China, 1998—. Author: Molecular Forces, 1967, Problems in Chemical Therodynamics, 1967, Laser Light Scattering, 1974; editor: NATO ASI series B: Physics, Vol. 73, 1981, SPIE Milestone series: Selected Papers on Quasielastic Light Scattering by Macromolecular, Supramolecular, and Fluid Systems, Vol. MS 12, 1990, Laser Light Scattering: Basic Principles and Practice, 2d edit., 1991; patentee prism light scattering cells, method and apparatus for determining viscosity, light scattering and spectroscopic detector, magnetic needle rheometer, electrophoretic mobility of fluorophore labeled particles in gels by fluorophore movement after photo bleaching, separation medium for capillary electrophoresis, effective surface treatment for a new separation medium in electrophoresis, compatibilizer for immiscible polymer blends. Sloan rsch. fellow, 1966-68, John Simon Guggenheim fellow, 1968-69; recipient Humboldt award 1976-77, 92-93, Disting. Achievement award St. Norbert Coll., 1981, Soc. Polymer Sci. Japan Disting. Svc. in Advancement Polymer Sci. award, 1997, Achievement award Chinese Inst. Engrs., U.S., 1998. Fellow Am. Phys. Soc. (High Polymer Physics prize 1993), Am. Inst. Chemists; mem. Am. Crystallographic Assn., Am. Chem. Soc. (Langmuir Disting. Lectr. award 1994). E-mail: bchu@notes.cc.sunysb.edu.

CHU, CHUNG KWANG, medicinal chemistry educator; b. Seoul, Republic of Korea, May 18, 1941; s. Jee Young Huh; children: Susan, Jackie. BS, Seoul Nat. U., 1964; MS, Idaho State U., 1970; PhD, SUNY, Buffalo, 1974. Rsch. assoc. Sloan-Kettering Cancer Inst., N.Y.C., 1974-80; asst. prof. Idaho State U., Pocatello, 1990-82; asst. prof. medicinal chemistry U. Ga., Athens, 1982-87, assoc. prof., 1987-89, prof., 1990-98, disting. rsch. prof., 1998—. Adv. bd. NIH, Pharmasset, Atlanta. Lt. (j.g.) Korean Navy. Mem. Am. Chem. Soc. (Rsch. grant 1988), Am. Assn. for Cancer Rsch., Am. Assn. Colls. Pharmacy, Internat. Soc. Antiviral Rsch. Achievements include patents for drug discovery field. Office: U Ga Coll Pharmacy Brooks Dr Athens GA 30602 Fax: 706-542-5381. E-mail: dchu@rx.uga.edu.

CHU, DAVID S.C. federal agency administrator, economist; b. N.Y.C., May 28, 1944; s. H. T. and Esther Chu; m. Laura L. Tosi. BA, Yale U., 1964, PhD, 1972. Asst. dir. nat. security and internat. affairs Congl. Budget Office, Washington, 1978—81; dir. then asst. sec. def. for program analysis and evaluation Dept. Def., 1981—93; economist RAND, Santa Monica, Calif., 1970—78, sr. fellow Washington, 1993—94, dir. Washington rsch. dept., 1994—96, dir. Washington office, assoc. chmn. of rsch. staff, 1996—98; v.p. army rsch. divsn., dir. Arroyo Ctr., 1998—2001; under sec. def. (pers. and readiness), 2001—. Capt. U.S. Army, 1968—70, Vietnam. Decorated Bronze Star, Army commendation medal. Fellow: Nat. Acad. Pub. Adminstrn. (chmn., bd. trustees 1999—2001); mem.: Phi Beta Kappa. Office: 4000 Defense Pentagon Washington DC 20301-4000

CHU, HSIEN-KUN, chemist, researcher; b. Shanghai, People's Republic of China, Oct. 14, 1947; came to U.S., 1971; s. Hwei-Teh and Yun-Hsiang (Chang) C.; m. Winnie K.S. Wong, Dec. 23, 1976; children: James C., Jason C. BS, Nat. Taiwan U., Taipei, Republic of China, 1970; PhD, Vanderbilt U., 1976. Vis. instr. U. Tex., Arlington, 1976-77; rsch. assoc. Tex. Christian U., Ft. Worth, 1977-80; rsch. specialist Dow Corning Corp., Midland, Mich., 1980-88; sr. scientist Loctite Corp., Rocky Hill, Conn., 1988—. Contbr. rsch. articles to sci. jours. Mem. Am. Chem. Soc., Sigma Xi. Achievements include patents on

silicone sealants; research into mechanistic studies of organic reactions, silicone research. Home: 6 Harvest Hl Wethersfield CT 06109-2422 Office: Loctite Corp 1001 Trout Brook Xing Rocky Hill CT 06067-3910 E-mail: hsien-kun.chu@loctite.com.

CHU, JACK J. (JACK ZHU), electrical engineer; b. Shanghai, Jan. 26, 1938; arrived in U.S., 1980; s. Baoling Zhu(Chu), Zhi Yin Mo; m. Shannon Chongshan Sun, Oct. 1, 1990; 1 child, Ling Zhu. BS in Automatic Control Engring., Tsinghua U., Beijing, 1960; MS in Automatic Control Engring., Tsinghua U., 1962; MSEE, U. Minn., 1990. Sr. control system engr. Spectra Engring., Inc., Roseville, Minn., 1991—92, Innovex Engring., Inc., Hopkins, Minn., 1992—95, Quickie Design Inc., Fresno, Calif., 1995—97, Sunrise Med. Inc., Longmont, Colo., 1997—98, Kriton Med., Inc., Citrus Heights, Calif., 1998, Avery Dennison Inc., Ft. Wayne, Ind., 1999; sr. control system and software engr. Balance Tech., Inc., Ann Arbor, Mich., 2000—01, Avionics Specialties Inc., Charlottesville, Va., 2001—. Recipient Nat. Merit Citation Class 2 in China, 1984. Achievements include development of microprocessor model reference adaptive control system; of adaptive thin-film sensor grinding system; of blood pump controller with indicator. Avocations: table tennis, swimming, cooking, travel, chess. E-mail: jackjchu@mybluelight.com.

CHU, JEFFREY CHUAN, business executive, consultant; b. Tianjen, China, July 14, 1919; came to US, 1940; s. Yao and Vanyi (Tang) C.; m. Loretta Y. Yung, Feb. 9, 1928; children: Lynnet Helbig, Bambi Rae, Dashie Kocica. BSEE, U. Minn., 1942; MSEE, U. Pa., 1945. Rsch. assoc. Moore Sch., U. Pa., Phila., 1944-48; sr. engr. Reeves Instrument Co., NYC, 1948-50; chief sr. scientist Argonne Nat. Lab., Lemont, Ill., 1950-56; dir engring. Sperry Univac, Phila., 1956-62; v.p. asst., gen. mgr. Honeywell Info. Systems Inc., Waltham, Mass., 1962-72; sr. v.p. Wang Labs., Lowell, Mass., 1972-74; prin. advisor Nat. Sci. Commn., ROC, Taipei, Taiwan, China, 1974-77; chmn., chief exec. officer Santec Corp., Amherst, NH, 1980-85; chmn. Columbia Internat. Corp., Weston, Mass., 1985—. Adj. prof. Nankai U., Tanjen, Xinjiang U., Uremaqi; adj. prof., mem. U. Coun., Jiao Tong U., Shanghai; vis. prof. and mem. of the Univ. Coun., Qingdao U., Peoples Republic of China; advisor Com. for Higher Learning, Shandong U., Jinan; advisor office of pres. SRI Internat., 1986—; bd. dir. Interproject Corp., BTU Eng. Internat.; econ. advisor to Gov. Shandong Province, Peoples Republic of China. Mem. adv. bd. Wharton Sch. in China, U. Pa., Babage Inst., U. Minn.; hon. chmn. Inst. for Soft Sci. Studies, Shandong U., Jinan; bd. dirs. Fairbank Inst. Harvard U. Fellow IEEE (computer pioneer award 1981), Chinese Inst. Engrs.; hon. mem. Chinese Nat. Acad. Social Scis., Chinese Assn. Sci. Studies, Acad. Mil. Med. Sci., Beijing; mem. Sigma Xi (life). Avocations: tennis, skiing. Home: 10 Baldwin Cir Weston MA 02493-1520 Office: BTU Internat 23 Esquire Rd North Billerica MA 01862 E-mail: chuanchu@attbi.com.

CHU, JOHNSON CHIN SHENG, retired physician; b. Peiping, China, Sept. 25, 1918; arrived in U.S., 1948, naturalized, 1957; s. Harry S.P. and Florence (Young) Chu; m. Sylvia Cheng, June 11, 1949; children: Stephen, Timothy. MD, St. John's U., 1945. Intern Univ. Hosp., Shanghai, 1944-45; resident, research fellow NYU Hosp., 1948-50; resident physician in charge State Hosp. and Med. Ctr., Weston, W.Va., 1951-56; chief services, clin. dir. State Hosp., Logansport, Ind., 1957-84, ret., 1998. Active mem. Meml. Hosp., Logansport, Ind., 1968—. Research in cardiology and pharmacology; contbr. articles to profl. jours. Fellow: Am. Coll. Chest Physicians, Am. Psychiat. Assn.; mem.: AAAS, AMA, Cass County Med. Soc., Ind. Med. Assn. Home: 36 E Lake Shafer Monticello IN 47960 Office: Southeastern Med Ctr Walton IN 46994

CHU, MARGARET S. Y. federal agency administrator; b. Jan. 10, 1946; BS in Chemistry, Purdue U., 1967; PhD in Phys. Chemistry, U. Minn., 1973. Mem. tech. staff Sandia Nat. Labs., Albuquerque, 1980-86, disting. mem. tech. staff, 1986-91, tech. mgr., 1991-97, sr. mgr. nuclear waste mgmt., 1997-99, dir. nuclear waste mgmt., 1999—2002; Dir Civilian Radioactive Waste Mgt Dept Energy, Washington, 2002—. Contbr. numerous articles to sci. and profl. jours. Founding faculty mem. Albuquerque Chinese Sch., 1980. Mem. Am. Chem. Soc., N.M. Chinese Assn., Chinese Inst. Engrs. (bd. dirs., officer N.Mex. chpt. 1997-98). Office: Dept Energy Cicilian Radioactive Waste Mgt 1000 Independence Ave SW Washington DC 20585-0001

CHU, MARY LYNN, pediatric neurologist; came to the U.S., 1984; BS cum laude, U. of The Philippines, Quezon City, 1974; MD, U. of The Philippines, Manila, 1978. Bd. cert. neurology with spl. qualification in child neurology, electrodiagnostic medicine, pediat. Intern and resident pediat. Albert Einstein Coll. Medicine Affiliated Hosps., Bronx, N.Y., 1984-86, fellow in pediat. neurology, 1986-89; fellow in neuromuscular disease and electrophysiology The Hosp. for Spl. Surgery-Cornell U. Med. Coll., N.Y.C., 1989-90; attending neurologist and electromyographer Hosp. for Spl. Surgery, N.Y.C., 1990-91; pediatric neurologist, co-dir. MDA Clinic The Hosp. for Joint Diseases-NYU Med. Ctr., N.Y.C., 1990—. Clin. asst. prof. neurology NYU Sch. Medicine, N.Y.C., 1993—; med. dir. Elly Hammerman Ctr,. Treatment of Neuromuscular Disorders, Hosp. for Joint Diseases, N.Y.C., 1996—, dir. pediat. neurology and neuromuscular diseases, 1999—; dir. Elly Hammerman Ctr. Spasticity Ctr. Children, Hosp. Joint Disorders, N.Y.C., 2003. Beerhausen scholar Filipino Chinese Med. Soc., Manila, 1984. Fellow Am. Acad. for Cerebral Plasy and Developmental Medicine, Am. Assn. Electrodiagnostic Medicine, Child Neurology Soc.; mem. Am. Acad. Neurology. Office: Hosp for Joint Diseases 301 E 17th St New York NY 10003-3804 E-mail: marylynn.chu@med.nyu.edu.

CHU, MORGAN, lawyer; b. N.Y.C., Dec. 27, 1950; m. Helen M. Wong, Dec. 29, 1970. BA, UCLA, 1971, MA, 1972, PhD, 1973; MSL, Yale U., 1974; JD magna cum laude, Harvard U., 1976. Bar: Calif. 1976, U.S. Dist. Ct. (ctrl. dist.) Calif. 1977, U.S. Dist. Ct. (no. dist.) Calif. 1980, U.S. Ct. Appeals (9th cir.) 1980, U.S. Dist. Ct. (so. dist.) Calif. 1984, U.S. Dist. Ct. (ea. dist.) Calif. 1986, U.S. Ct. Appeals (fed. cir.) 1989, U.S. Supreme Ct. 1991. Law clk. to judge U.S. Ct. Appeals (9th cir.), San Francisco, 1976-77; assoc. Irell & Manella, LLP, L.A., 1977-82; ptnr. Irell & Manella, L.A., 1982—, co-mng. ptnr., 1997—, exec. com., 1984—. Adj. prof. UCLA Sch. Law, 1979-82; judge pro tem L.A. Mcpl. Ct., 1980—. Mem. editl. bd. Litigation News, 1981-84. Named Best Intellectual Property Lawyer in Nation, 2001 Survey of Co. Dirs., Law Sch. Deans and Lawyers by Corp. Bd. Mem., one of 12 Superstars in all practice areas, one of 10 New Superstars of 1st ammendment law, Legal Times of Washington, 1986, one of 100 Most Influential Lawyers in Am., Nat. Law Jour., 1994, 1997, 2000, one of Top Ten Trial Lawyers in U.S., 1995, one of top 45 Lawyers in U.S. Under 45 Years Old, Am. Lawyer, 1995, Exec. of Yr. in Law, L.A. Bus. Jour., 1994, one of top 20 lawyers in L.A., Calif. Law and Bus., one of top 100 Most Influential Lawyers in Calif., Calif. Law Bus., 1998, 1999, 2000, 2001, one of top 100 Most Inluential Lawyers in Calif., 2002; recipient Significant Achievement award for excellence and innovation in alternative dispute resolution, Ctr. for Pub. Resources, 1987; fellow postdoctoral fellow, Yale U., 1974. Mem.: ABA (chmn. high tech. intellectual property and patent trials subcom. 1986—90, trial practice com., litigation sect.), L.A. Intellectual Property Law Assn. (bd. dirs. 1991—93, bd. dirs. pub. counsel 1993—, exec. com. bd. dirs. pub. counsel 1995—), L.A. County Bar Assn. (judiciary com. 1983—2001), Calif. Bar Assn. Office: Irell & Manella LLP Ste 900 1800 Avenue of the Stars Los Angeles CA 90067-4276 E-mail: mchu@irell.com.

CHU, PAUL CHING-WU, physicist, educator; b. Hunan, China, Dec. 2, 1941; arrived in U.S., 1963; m. May P. Chern; children: Claire, Albert. BS, Cheng-Kung U., Taiwan, 1962; MS, Fordham U., 1965; PhD, U. Calif., San Diego, 1968, Fordham U., 1988, Northwestern U., 1988, Chinese U. of Hong Kong, 1988, Fla. Internat. U., 1989, SUNY, 1989, Whittier Coll., 1991, Hong Kong Bapt. U., 1999. 2d lt. Nationalist Chinese Air Forces, 1962—63; tchg. asst. Fordham U., Bronx, NY, 1963—65; rsch. asst. U. Calif., San Diego, 1965—68; tech. staff Bell Labs., Murray Hill, NJ, 1968—70; asst. prof. physics Cleve. State U., 1970—73, assoc. prof., 1973—75, prof., 1975—79; prof. physics U. Houston, 1979—, dir. magnetic info. rsch. lab., 1984—88, dir. Space Vacuum Epitaxy Ctr., 1986—88, dir. Tex. Ctr. for Superconductivity, 1987—2001, dir. NSF/materials rsch. sci. and engring. ctr., 1996—97; prin. investigator, cons. Lawrence Berkeley Nat. Lab., 1999—; convenor Heads of Univs. Com., Hong Kong, 2003—; pres. Hong Kong U. Sci. and Tech., 2001—. Dir. Solid State Physics Program NSF, Washington, 1986—87; resident, rsch. assoc. Argonne (Ill.) Nat. Lab., 1972; vis. scientist Hansens Physics Lab., Stanford, 1973; vis. staff mem. Los Alamos (N.Mex.) Sci. Lab., 1975—80; cons. Bell Labs., 1973, 75, 78, NASA Marshall Space Flight Ctr., Huntsville, Ala., 1982—87, Dupont, 1987—88; chmn. organizing com. Internat. Conf. on High Pressure Low Temperature Physics, 1977; M.D. Anderson chair physics M.D. Anderson Found., 1987—89; T.L.L. Temple chair sci. T.L.L. Temple Found., 1987—; hon. prof. Zhongshan U., 1988, Chinese Acad. Scis. Physics Inst., 1979, Nankai U., 1991, Chinese U. Sci. and Tech., 1991, Nanjing U., 1996; mem. internat. adv. bd. Materials Chemistry and Physics, 1992—; bd. dirs. Coalition for the Commercial Application of Superconductors, 1989—, Indsl. Tech. Rsch. Inst., 1988—91; co-chmn. solid state physics symposium Vereschagin Internat. Conf. on High Pressure Physics and Tech., Moscow, 1979; mem. White House ad hoc rev. panel on long-range plan for R & D of superconductivity, 1989; mem. rsch. adv. com. Inst. for Tech. and Strateegic Rsch., 1989; adv. bd. Internat. Inst. Cond. Math., Physics U., Brasilia, 1993—; vis. Miller rsch. prof. U. Calif., Berkeley, 1991; mem. adv. com. to redesign the space sta. The White House, Washington, 1993; mem. sch. adv. bd. Ctr. Nanoscale Sci. and Tech., Rice U., 1995—; internat. adv. com. Hong Kong Bapt. U., 1995—; internat. adv. bd. China-Am. Tech. Corp., 1995—; mem. adv. com. on rsch. planning Higher Edn. Coordinating Bd., State of Tex., 1997—2000; invited contbr. Nat. Millenium Time Capsule, 2000; bd. dirs. S.S. Chem. Found. Mathematical Rsch., 2000—; pres. Applied Superconductivity Corp., 2000—02; bd. dirs. Applied Superconductivity Conference, 2000—; mem. Academia Sinica Inst. Physics Acad. Adv. Com., 2001—; adv. Hong Kong Area of Excellence Project on "Chinese Med. Rsch. and Further Development", 2001—; mem. Academia Sinica Central Adv. Com., 2002—, Academia Sinica Coun., 2002—; chmn. ad hoc Com. on Future Nat. Energy, 2002—; dir. search com. Academia Sinica Ctr. Applied Sci. Engineering Rsch., 2002—; mem. Condensed Matter Experiment Screening Com. Nat. Acad. Scis., 2003—; bd. dirs. Hong Kong Sci. & Tech. Park, 2003. Mem. editl. bd.: High Tech. Bus., 1988—, Modern Physics Letters B, 1988—, Applied Superconductivity, 1992—98, Indian Jour. Pure and Applied Physics, 1992—, News and Reviews of Physics in China Today, 1992—, Internat. Jour. Modern Physics, 1988—, Brazilian Jour. Physics, 1995—, Sci. in China, 1997—, Chinese Sci. Bull., 1997—, Applied Physics Rev. (Korea), 1998—2000; contbr. articles to profl. jours. Internat. adv. com. World Lab. Pan Am. Ctr. for Collaboration in Sci. and Tech., 1998—; bd. dirs. Houston Mus. Natural Sci., 1989—94, T.S. Chang Scholarship Found., 1999—. Named hon. citizen, State of Tex., 1987, City of Houston, 1987, Best Rschr. in U.S., U.S. News and World Report, 1990, one of 20th Century's 100 most intellectual people in gas and electric, Century of Power, Heat Energy, 2000, honoree, Alliance for Multicultural Cmty. Svcs., 2000; recipient Phys. and Math. Sci. award, N.Y. Acad. Sci., 1987, Leroy Randle Grumman medal, Grumman Corp., 1987, Achievement award, Chine Am. Acad. and Profl. Assn., 1987, Disting. Alumnus award, U. Calif., San Diego, 1987, Faculty Rsch. award, U. Houston, 1987, Sigma Xi Rsch. Excellence award, 1987, Achievement award, NASA, 1987, Nat. Medal Sci., Pres. of U.S., 1988, Disting. Alumnus award, Cheng-Kung U., 1988, Medal of Sci. Merit, World Cultural Coun., 1989, Founders' prize, Texas Instruments, 1990, St. Martin de Porres award, 1990, Superconductivity Excellence award in sci. accomplishments, World Congress on Superconductivity, 1994, Bernd Matthias prize, 4th Internat. Conf. on Materials and Mechanisms of Superconductivity, High Temperature Superconductors, 1994, Disting. Sci. Achievement award, Washington Met. Assn. Chinese Am. Profls., 1998, Houston Hall of Fame award, George Bush Internat. Airport, 1999, Sharif U., 1999, Esther Farfel award, U. Houston, 2000, Houston Hall of Fame award, Greater Houston Conv. and Vis. Bur., 1988, John Fritz medal, United Engring. Found., 2001. Fellow: Chinese Acad. Scis., Tex. Acad. Scis., Am. Phys. Soc. (teller divsn. Sol. St. Physics 1976, internat. prize com. 1988—89, Internat. prize for new materials 1988); mem.: NAS (mem. panel on High Temperature Superconductivity 1987, sect. co-chair 1992—95, Comstock award 1988), AAAS, State of Tex. Sci. and Tech. Coun., Electromagnetic Acad., Third World Acad. Scis., Academia Sinica (Taipei, mem. adv. com. Inst. Physics 1997—2000), Am. Acad. Arts and Scis., Royal Soc. Encouragement of Arts Mfrs. and Commerce. Office: U Houston Texas Ctr Superconductivity Houston TX 77204-0001 E-mail: cwchu@uh.edu.

CHU, STEVEN, physics educator; b. St. Louis, Feb. 28, 1948; s. Ju Chin and Ching Chen (Li) C.; children: Geoffrey, Michael. BS in Physics, AB in Math., U. Rochester, 1970; PhD in Physics, U. Calif., Berkeley, 1976. Post doctoral fellow U. Calif., Berkeley, 1976-78; mem. tech. staff Bell Labs., Murray Hill, N.J., 1978-83; head quantum electronics rsch. dept. AT&T Bell Labs., Holmdel, N.J., 1983-87; prof. physics and applied physics Stanford (Calif.) U., 1987—, Frances and Theodore Geballe prof. physics and applied physics, 1990—93, chmn. physics dept., 1999—2001. Morris Loeb lectr. Harvard U., Cambridge, Mass., 1987-88; vis. prof. Coll. de France, fall 1990; Richtmeyer Meml. lectr., 1990. Contbr. papers in laser spectroscopy and atomic physics, especially laser cooling and trapping, and precision spectroscopy of leptonic atoms, polymer and biophysics. Recipient Humboldt sr. scientist award, Sci. for Art prize, 1995; co-recipient King Faisal prize for sci., 1993, Nobel prize for physics, 1997; Woodrow Wilson fellow 1970, doctoral fellow NSF, 1970-74, postdoctoral fellow 1977-78, Guggenheim fellow, 1996. Fellow Am. Phys. Soc. (Herbert P. Broida prize for laser spectroscopy 1987, chair laser sci. topical group 1989, A.L. Schawlow prize 1994), Optical Soc. Am. (William F. Meggars award 1994), Am. Acad. Arts and Scis.; mem. NAS, Academica Sinica, Am. Philos. Soc., Chinese Acad. Sci. (fgn.), Korean Acad. Sci. and Tech. (fgn.).

CHU, SUNG NEE GEORGE, materials scientist; b. Shanghai, Sept. 11, 1947; came to U.S., 1971; m. Teresa T. Yang, Sept. 10, 1974; children: Karen, Eric. BS, Nat. Taiwan U., Taipei, 1970; MS, U. Rochester, 1974, PhD, 1978. Jr. physicist Microelectronic Ltd., Hong Kong, 1970-71; rsch. assoc. U. Rochester, N.Y., 1977-80; mem. tech. staff AT&T Bell Labs., Murray Hill, N.J., 1980-86, disting. mem. tech. staff, 1986-96, Bell Labs., Lucent Techs., Murray Hill, N.J., 1996-2000; cons. mem. tech. staff Agere Sys., Murray Hill, 2001—, Multiplex Inc., South Plainfield, NJ, 2003—. Fellow Electrochem. Soc. (chmn. compound semiconductor subcom. 1989—, Electronic Divsn. award 2000); mem. Am. Phys. Soc., Optical Soc. Am., The Minerals, Metals & Materials Soc. Home: 55 Murray Hill Blvd New Providence NJ 07974-2700 Office: Multiplex Inc 500 Hadley Dr South Plainfield NJ 07080

CHU, VALENTIN YUAN-LING, author; b. Shanghai, Republic of China, Feb. 14, 1919; came to U.S., 1956, naturalized, 1961; s. Thomas V.D. and Rowena S.N. (Zee) Tsu; m. Victoria Chao-yu Tsao, Sept. 25, 1954; 1 child, Douglas Chi-hua. BA, St. John's U, Shanghai, 1940. Asst. Shanghai Mcpl. Coun., 1940-42; asst. mgr., pub., printer Thomas Chu & Sons, Shanghai, 1943-45; chief reporter China Press, Shanghai, 1945-49; pub. rels. officer Cen. Air Transport Corp., Hong Kong, 1949; Hong Kong corr. Time & Life mags., Hong Kong, 1949-56; with Time, Inc., N.Y.C., 1956-76; writer, asst. editor Time-Life Books, N.Y.C., 1968-76; assoc. editor Reader's Digest Gen. Books, N.Y.C., 1978-83. Lectr. on China. Author: Ta Ta, Tan Tan---Fight Fight, Talk Talk, 1963, Thailand Today, 1968, (with others) U.S.A., A Visitor's Handbook, 1969, The Yin-Yang Butterfly---Ancient Chinese Sexual Secrets for Western Lovers, 1993; contbr. articles to popular mags. Recipient spl. award UN Internat. Essay Contest, 1948. Mem. Authors League Am., Authors Guild, China Inst. in Am., Inst. Noetic Scis. Presbyterian. Home: 2934 Saklan Indian Dr Walnut Creek CA 94595-3911

CHU, WEI-KAN, physicist, educator; b. Kunming, China, Apr. 1, 1940; came to the U.S., 1963; s. Din Yuan and Y.C. (Wong) C.; m. Agnes Kuen, May 28, 1966; 1 child, Lawrence D. BS in Physics, Cheng-Kung U., 1962; MS, Baylor U., 1965, PhD, 1969. Postdoctoral fellow Baylor U., Waco, Tex., 1969-72; rsch. fellow, sr. rsch. fellow Calif. Inst. Tech., Pasadena, 1972-75; staff advisor, sr. engr. IBM, Hopewell Junction, N.Y., 1975-81; rsch. prof. physics U. N.C., Chapel Hill, 1981-88; disting. prof. physics U. Houston, 1989—. Panel mem. NSF, Washington, 1992, U.S. Dept. Energy, Washington, 1992, 93, 94, 97. Co-author: Backscattering Spectrometry, 1978; co-editor: HTS Materials, Bulk Processing and Bulk Applications, 1992, Procs. of the 6th U.S.-Japan Workshop on High Tc Superconductors, 1994, Procs. of the 10th Anniversary High Temperature Superconductors Workshop on Physics, Materials and Applications, 1996, Procs. of 6th Internat. Conf. Materials and Mechanisms of Superconductivity and High Temperature Superconductors, VI, 2000; contbr. chpts. to books and numerous articles to profl. jours.; holder 20 U.S. patents in field. Recipient Disting. Achievement award Baylor U., Waco, 1991, Assn. Am.-Chinese Profls., 1994, Superconductivity award of excellence for outstanding individual accomplishment World Congress on Superconductivity, 1994, Outstanding Alumni of Yr. Nat. Cheng-Kung U., 1997, 98. Fellow Am. Phys. Soc.; mem. Materials Rsch. Soc. Office: U Houston Tex Ctr Superconductivity Houston TX 77204-5002 E-mail: wkchu@uh.edu.

CHUA, NAM-HAI, plant molecular biologist, educator; b. Singapore, Apr. 8, 1944; came to U.S., 1971; m. Suat-choo Pearl, 1970; children: Lu-leng Felicia, Lu-san Clarissa. BSc, U. Singapore, 1965; AM, Harvard U., 1967, PhD, 1969. Andrew W. Mellon prof., head lab. plant molecular biology Rockefeller U., N.Y.C., 1988—, head lab. plant molecular biology, 1988—. Bd. dirs. DNAP Holdings, Oakland, Calif.; cons., dir. Delta and Pine Land Co., Scott, Mich.; cons. Global Tech. Ctr. and Nutrition Monsanto Co., St. Louis, 1997; cons. Shanghai Rsch. Ctr. Life. Scis. Chinese Acad. Sci, 1996—98; dir. exec. com., bd. dirs. Singapore BioInnovators of Am., Redwood City, Calif., 1991—2000; advisor World Sci. Pub. Co. Ptd. Ltd., Singapore, 1996—2002; mem. Nat. Biotech. Com., Singapore, 1988—98; chmn. mgmt. bd. Inst. Molecular Agrobiology Nat. U. Singapore, Singapore, 1995—2001; hon. rsch. prof. biotech. Chinese Acad. Agrl. Sci., 1987—; Sir Edward youde vis. prof. U. Hong Kong, 1996; cons. in field. Contbr. articles to profl. jours. Gadsby Flying fellow Sainsbury Lab., John Innes Inst., 1992. Fellow Royal Soc. U.K.; mem. AAAS, Internat. Assn. for Plant Tissue Culture, Internat. Soc. Plant Molecular Biologists, Am. Soc. Biol. Chemists, Am Soc. Cell. Biologists, Am. Soc. Plant Physiologists, Am. Soc. for Microbiology, Soc. Chinese Bioscientists in Am., Japanese Biochem. Soc. (hon. mem.), N.Y. Acad. Scis. Office: The Rockefeller U 1230 York Ave New York NY 10021-6399

CHUANG, FRANK SHIUNN-JEA, engineering executive, consultant; b. Taiwan, China, Sept. 5, 1942; came to U.S., 1966, naturalized, 1974; s. Swiss S. and Chin-May C.; m. Lily L. Chuang, Aug. 14, 1971; 1 child, Eugene. BS, Nat. Taiwan U., 1964; MS, U. Mass., 1968, PhD, 1971. Instr. engring. U. Conn., 1971-72; dept. mgr. C.E. Maguire; cons. engrs. New Britain, Conn., 1972-78; v.p., cons. engrs. Hayden, Harding & Buchanan, Inc., East Hartford, Conn., 1978-82; pres., cons. engrs. L-C Assocs., Inc., Rocky Hills, Conn., 1982—. Bd. dirs. Equity Bank, Wethersfield Conn.; mem. Conn. State Bd. Examiners for Profl. Engrs. and Land Surveyors. Active Wethersfield Planning and Zoning Commn. U. Mass. Water Resource Rsch. Ctr. grantee, 1966-71. Mem. ASCE, Nat. Soc. Profl. Engrs., Water Pollution Control Fedn., Wethersfield Country Club. Home: 38 Stonegate Dr Wethersfield CT 06109-3652 Office: L-C Assocs Inc 1960 Silas Deane Hwy Rocky Hill CT 06067-1310 E-mail: lcct2@erols.com.

CHUANG, TSU-YI, dermatologist, epidemiologist, educator; b. Amoy, China, May 21, 1946; s. Hsi and Kia-Ling (Hwang) C.; m. Lydia Ling-Chuan Lee, Dec. 22, 1973; children: Chester, Nancy. B of Medicine, Nat. Taiwan U., Taipei, 1971; MPH, U. Wash., 1978. Diplomate Am. Bd. Dermatology, Am. Bd. Preventive Medicine. From asst. prof. to assoc. prof. dermatology U. Wis., Madison, 1984-92; chief dermatology svc. Middleton VA Med. Ctr., Madison, 1984-90; assoc. prof. dermatology Wright State U., Dayton, Ohio, 1990-95, dir. immunopathology lab., 1994-95; dir. dermatology clinic Frederick A. White Health Ctr., Dayton, 1995; prof. dermatology Ind. U., Indpls., 1995—, med. dir. melanoma program, 1996—, Arthur L. Norins prof., dir. dermatology clinic, 1999—2001. Vis. prof. Nat. Taiwan U., Taipei, 1991-97. Co-author: Conn's Current Therapy, 1992, The Challenge of Dermato-Epidemiology, 1997, Sleisenger & Fordtran's Gastrointestinal and Liver Disease, 2002; editl. cons. Arch Dermatol., Chgo., 1990-99; editor Dermatologica Sinica, Taipei, 1994-96; contbr. over 100 articles to profl. jours. Pres. Rochester (Minn.) Chinese Culture Assn., 1980-82; v.p. Orgn. of Chinese Ams., Madison, 1986-90; pres. Midwest Chinese Christian Assn., Dayton, 1993-94, Indpls., 1996-97. Rsch. grantee U. Wis., 1985-89, VA merit rev. bd. grantee Dept. Vets. Affairs, 1986-88, 90-94; recipient Burdette-Kunkel award Mary Margaret Walther Program for Cancer Care Rsch., 1996-97. Fellow Am. Acad. Dermatology (editl. cons. Am. Acad. Dermatology jour. 1986-2001), Am. Soc. for Dermatol. Surgery; mem. Soc. for Investigative Dermatology, Ind. Chinese Profls. Assn. (pres. 1998). Achievements include first historical cohort study of human papilloma virus infection in U.S. in a defined population, first historical cohort study of genital herpes virus infection in U.S. in a defined population, first incidence study of polymyalgia rheumatica in the U.S. in a defined population, first population-based incidence study of skin cancer in U.S. in two well-defined populations. Office: 1801 N Senate Blvd Ste 745 Indianapolis IN 46202 Home: 7618 Torbay Cir Indianapolis IN 46254-9659

CHUANG, YII-DER, diplomat; b. Chekiang, China, July 1, 1934; came to U.S., 1964; s. W.C. Chuang and Y.F. Chang; m. Chung-hwa Lee, Jan. 6, 1968; children: David, Michael, Nancy. BS in Automotive Engring., Chung-Cheng Inst., 1957; MS in Metall. Engring., Mich. State U., 1966; PhD in Materials Sci., NYU, 1971. Dir. hot lab. Inst. Nuclear Energy Rsch. Atomic Energy Coun., Exec. Yuan, Taoyuan, Taiwan, 1972-82; sr. scientist sci and tech. adv. group Exec. Yuan, Taipei, Taiwan, 1980-84; dep. dir. prep. office materials rsch. lab. Indsl. Tech. Rsch. Inst., Hsinchu, Taiwan, 1981-82; dep. dir. materials rsch. and devel. ctr. Chung Shan Inst. Sci. and Tech., Taoyuan, Taiwan, 1982-84; dir. sci. divsn. Coord. Coun. N.Am. Affairs, Houston, 1984-86, San Francisco, 1986-92, Taipei Econ. and Cultural Rep. Office, Washington, 1992—. Exec. sec. materials steering com. Exec. Yuan, 1981-84; dir. Rep. Office Hsin-Chu Sci.-based Indsl. Park Adminstrn., Taiwan, 1986-92; patent reviewer Nat. Bur. Standards, Taiwan, 1973-83; exec. sec. Commn. Third Asian-Pacific Corrosion Control Conf., 1981-83. Editor Nuclear Sci. Jour., 1978-79; contbr. over 35 articles to profl. jours. Scholar NYU, 1972. Mem. Nuclear Energy Soc. of Rep. of China, Chinese Soc. Materials Sci. (editor Materials Sci. Quarterly 1972-78), Chinese Inst. Mining and Metall. Engrs., Chinese Soc. Mech. Engrs., Monte Jade Sci. and Tech. Assn., Alpha Sigma Mu. Office: TECRO Sci Divsn 4201 Wis Ave NW MB-09 Washington DC 20016 E-mail: chuang@hotmail.com.

CHUBB, CHARLES RAY, physicist, researcher; b. Springfield, Mo., Apr. 18, 1931; s. Prosser Sylvester and Harriet Elizabeth Chubb; m. Jeanne R. C. (div. 1978); children: Alan C., Paula J. Mello, Thomas J., Lisa C. Rottler. *Son Alan is a Lieutenant Colonel, Hanscom Air Force Base, Massachusett. Daughter Paula's husband and two sons are descendants of Mayflower passenger John Howland. Son Thomas is a tire store service manager, Nashville Tennessee. Daughter Lisa is a medical technologist, BJC Hospital, St. Louis, Missouri. Both brothers served in World War II. Brother Robert S., retired, was a Marine fighter pilot, aeronautical engineer and marketing representative, Lockheed Aircraft. Brother James J., retired, was a Navy landing craft officer, attorney and Ferguson Missouri judge. Uncle Charles Broad, deceased, painted murals in the Kansas City Missouri train station.Grandfather Joseph W. Chubb, deceased, Illinois Infantry, was in many battles in the Civil War.* BS in Engring. Physics, U. Ill., 1953; MS in Physics, U. Mo., 1958, PhD in Physics, 1963. Rsch. engr. N.Am. Aviation, L.A., 1953-54; mem. scientific and profl. pers. U.S. Army, Ft. Lee, Va., 1955-56; cons. McDonnell Douglas, St. Louis, 1957-62, group engr. to sr. tech. specialist, 1962-90; cons. Storz Instruments, St. Louis, 1990-91; rschr. C. Chubb Assocs., Ferguson, Mo., 1991—. Patentee in field of skin light exposure control methods. Recipient Optical Fiber Innovation award NASA, Houston, 1983. Mem.: Mo. Acad. Sci. (past exec com., industry rep.), Am. Geophys. Union (charter mem.), St. Louis Met. (past pres.). Avocations: hiking, skiing. Home and Office: 438 Marie Ave Ferguson MO 63135-1904 E-mail: c.r.chubb@att.net.

CHUBB, JANET L. lawyer; b. Bremerton, Wash., Feb. 27, 1943; children: David, Aaron, Noah, Leah. BA, La Sierra Coll., 1964; JD, Loyola U., L.A., 1967. Bar: Calif. 1968; U.S. Dist. Ct. (cen. and no. dists.) Calif.; U.S. Dist. Ct. Nev. 1980, U.S. Ct. Appeals (9th cir.) 1975; cert. in consumer and bus. law Am. Bd. of Cert. Law clk. L.A. County Superior Ct., L.A., 1968-71; dep. atty. gen. State of Calif., 1971-74; city atty. Winnemucca, Nev., 1974-75; ptnr. Chubb & Silverman, Reno, 1975-82, Janet L. Chubb & Assocs., Reno, 1982-89, Jones Vargas (formerly Jones, Jones, Close & Brown), Reno, 1989—. Lawyer rep. 9th Cir. Conf., San Francisco, 1990-93, 2001--; expert witness various state cts.; settlement judge Nev. Supreme Ct., 1997—. Contbr. articles to profl. jours. Pres. Sparks (Nev.) YMCA, 1979-80; law adv. counsel Old Coll. Sch. of Law, 1981-86; bd. dirs. Boys and Girls Club of Truckee Meadows, 1993-98. Named one of Best Lawyers in Am., 1992. Fellow Am. Bar Found., Am. Coll. Bankruptcy; mem. ABA, No. Nev. Women Laywers (pres. 1990-91), Reno Bd. Realtors, State Bar of Nev. (bd. govs. 1979-91, chair bankruptcy sect. 1995-97), Nev. Law Fedn. (trustee 1982-90), Washoe County Bar Assn., Am. Bankruptcy Inst., No. Nev. Bankruptcy Bar Assn. (pres. 1995-99), others. Home: 2225 Thomas Jefferson Dr Reno NV 89509 Office: Jones Vargas PO Box 281 100 W Liberty St 12th Flr Reno NV 89504-0281 also: Jones Vargas Chartered 3773 Howard Hughes Pkwy Fl 3 Las Vegas NV 89109-0949

CHUBB, PERCY, III, insurance company executive; b. N.Y.C., Oct. 14, 1934; s. Percy, 2d and Corinne Roosevelt (Alsop) C.; m. Sally Gilady, Dec. 29, 1956; children— Percy Lee, Sarah Chubb-Sauvayre, Lucy Chubb-O'Connell. BA, Yale U., 1956. With Chubb & Son Inc., N.Y.C., 1957-97, dir., 1965-97; sr. v.p., dir. Chubb Corp., Warren, N.J., 1979-81, exec. v.p., dir., 1981-86, vice chmn., 1986-97, also bd. dirs. Bd. dirs. Fed. Ins. Co. Bd. dirs. N.J. Performing Arts Ctr.; trustee Mystic Seaport Mus., Woods Hole Oceanographic Inst.; pres., trustee Victoria Found. Inc. With U.S. Army, 1956-58. Office: Chubb Corp PO Box 1615 15 Mountain View Rd Warren NJ 07059-6795

CHUBB, STEPHEN DARROW, medical corporation executive; b. Newton, Mass., Mar. 16, 1944; s. Phillip Darrow and Clarissa Stoddard (Nye) C.; m. Kathleen Alice Zimmerman, 1973. BS, U.S. Naval Acad., 1965; MBA, Northwestern U., 1974. CPA, Ill. With Am. Can Co., 1970—73, Baxter Labs., Deerfield, Ill., 1974—81; pres. Hyland Diagnostics, 1978—81; pres., chief exec. officer, dir. Cytogen Corp., 1981—84, T Cell Scis., Inc., 1984—86, Matritech Inc., 1987—; dir. Charles River Labs., 1994—, Compucyte, Cambridge, Mass., 1992—2001, I-Stat, Princeton, NJ, 1999—2002. Alumni adv. bd. Northwestern U., 1998. Bd. dirs. Sherwood Cmty. Assn., 1978-79, v.p., 1979-80; trustee Huntington Theatre Co., Boston, 1991-95, treas., 1992-95; trustee Mt. Auburn Hosp., Cambridge, 1995—; mem. Literacy Vols. Mass. With USN, 1965-70; capt., USNR (ret.). Recipient Meritorious Svc. medal, Combat Action Ribbon, U.S. Navy. Mem. AICPA, John Evans Club Northwestern U., U.S. Naval Acad. Alumni Assn. Avocation: deep sea diving. Home: 1 Avery St #33B Boston MA 02111-1027 Office: Matritech Inc 330 Nevada St Newton MA 02460

CHUBB, TALBOT ALBERT, physicist; b. Pitts., Nov. 5, 1923; s. Charles F. and Mary Clare (Albert) C.; m. Martha Capps, Oct. 24, 1947 (dec. June 1990); children: Mary Carroll, Nancy Henderson, Talbot Spence, Constance Lamont. AB, Princeton U., 1944; PhD, U. N.C., 1950. Physicist, U.S. Naval Research Lab., 1950-58, head upper air physics br., 1958-82; pres. Research Systems, Inc., Oxon Hill, Md., 1982—. Recipient Elisha Mitchell Soc. award U. N.C., 1951, E.O. Hulbert award Naval Research Lab., 1963, Pure Sci. award Naval. Research Lab.-Research Soc. Am., 1970, Disting. Civilian Service award Dept. Navy, 1978 Fellow Am. Geophys. Union, Am. Phys. Soc.; mem. Am. Astron. Soc. Achievements include rsch. on solar flare x-rays, x-ray stars, UV aurora, cosmology, solar thermal power, cold fusion theory. Home and Office: 5023 38th St N Arlington VA 22207-2845 E-mail: tchubb@aol.com.

CHUDACOFF, BRUCE MICHAEL, lawyer; b. Appleton, Wis., Oct. 1, 1944, s. Lester H. and Mollie (Goldin) C.; m. Nancy Lynn Wilets, June 9, 1968; children: Tanya Elizabeth, Tamara Ann, Joshua Aaron. AB, U. Mich., 1966; JD, Harvard U., 1969. Bar: Wis. 1969, U.S. Dist. Ct. (ea. dist.) Wis. 1971, U.S. Supreme Ct. 1972. Ptnr. Chudacoff & Liebzeit, Appleton, 1969—2002; assoc. Block, Samson, Chudacoff, Seymour & Liebzgit SC, Appleton, 2002—. Dir. 1st Interstate Bank Wis.-Appleton, 1976-91. V.p. ops. Bay Lakes coun. Boy Scouts Am., 1983—85, legal counsel, 1985—; active Nat. Jewish Com. on Scouting, 1986—; state chmn. Israel Bond Orgn., Milw., 1984—85; comdr. Northeastern Wis. post Jewish War Vets, 1986—; chmn. NCCJ, Appleton, 1974—79, Outgamie County Rep. Party, 1998—2001. Served to capt. USAR, 1970—71, Vietnam. Recipient Disting. Merit citations, NCCJ, 1979, Gates of Jerusalem medal, Israel Bond Orgn., 1986; named Diting. Eagle Scout, 2002. Mem. Outgamie County Bar Assn., State Bar Wis., Wis. Acad. Trial Lawyers, NE Wis. U. Mich. Alumni (pres. 1980), B'nai B'rith, Fox River Lodge. Home: 43 N Crestway Ct Appleton WI 54913-9510 Office: Block Seymour Chudacoff Samson & Liebzgit SC 512 W College Ave Appleton WI 54911-5802

CHUDOBIAK, WALTER JAMES, electronics company executive, electronic engineer; b. Gliechen, Alta., Can., Apr. 2, 1942; s. John and Clara (Suchy) C.; m. Mary Annetta Budarick, Oct. 11, 1969; children: Michael, Anne. BSc in Elec. Engring., U. Alta., Edmonton, 1964; MEng in Electronic Engring., Carleton U., Ottawa, Ont., Can., 1965, PhD in Electronic Engring., 1969. Rsch. officer Def. Rsch. Bd., Ottawa, 1965-69; group leader, rsch. scientist Comm. Rsch. Ctr., Dept. Comm., Ottawa, 1969-75; assoc. prof. Carleton U., 1975-81; pres., founder, dir. Avtech Electrosystems Ltd., Ottawa, 1975—. Contbr. numerous articles to profl. jours.; patentee in field. Mem. IEEE, Assn. Profl. Engrs. (Ont.). Home: 12 Timbercrest Ridge Nepean ON Canada K2R 1B4 Office: 55 Grenfell Cres Ste 205 Nepean ON Canada K2G 0G3 E-mail: info@avtechpulse.com., walter@avtechpulse.com.

CHUE, RANDY SHEK-MING, aerospace scientist; b. Hong Kong, July 8, 1957; came to U.S., 1998; m. Patricia Yuk-Yee Leung, Aug. 20, 1989. BE with great distinction, U. Saskatchewan, Saskatoon, Can., 1980; SM, MIT, 1983; PhD, McGill U., Montreal, 1993. Design engr. Bristol Aerospace Ltd., Winnipeg, Man., Can., 1987-88; STA rsch. fellow Nat. Aerospace Lab., Kakuda, Japan, 1994-96; vis. scientist Deutsche Forschungsanstalt fur Luft-und Raumfahrt, Göttingen, Germany, 1996-97; chief engr. computational fluids GASL divsn. Allied Aerospace, Ronkonkoma, NY, 1998—. Cons. Adroit Sys., Inc., Bellevue, Wash., 1993-94; external examiner U. Queensland, Brisbane, Australia, 1999—. Contbr. articles to profl. jours. Sci. and Tech. Agy. Japan fellow, 1994-96; Fonds FCAR postgrad. scholar Fonds Pour La Formation De Chercheurs at L'Aide a La Rechereche, 1991, 92, U. Saskatchewan scholar, 1977-80; recipient Lawrence C. Sentence award Assn. of Profl. Engrs. of Ont., 1980. Mem. AIAA, Sigma Xi. Office: GASL Divsn Allied Aerospace 77 Raynor Ave Ronkonkoma NY 11779-6648 E-mail: randy_chue@yahoo.com.

CHUEH, CHUN FEI, import/export company executive; b. Chaozhou, China; s. Yung Hsing and Ruu Mei Chueh; m. Cecilia Shih-mei Hsing, Apr. 15, 1961; children: Angelina Mary Kitten, Daniel Francis. BSChE, Nat. Taiwan U., 1954; MSChE, Kans. State U., 1957; PhD in Chem. Engring., Ga. Inst. Tech., 1962. Chem. engr. Sci. Design Co., N.Y.C., 1962—78; dir. devel. Halcon Internat., Inc., N.Y.C., 1978—86; gen. mgr. Haarmann & Reimer Cosfra, Ltd., Shanghai, 1987—97; pres. Elan Trading (Shanghai) Co., 1998—, Elan (Shanghai) Flavors & Fragrances Co., 1998—. Patentee in field. Home: 187-16 Cambridge Rd Jamaica Estates NY 11432 2435 Office: Elan (Shanghai) Flavors & Fragrances Co #92 Ln 1129 Nanjing Rd W Shanghai 200041 China

CHUGH, ASHOK KUMAR, civil engineer; b. Amritsar, Punjab, India, Dec. 9, 1942; came to U.S., 1967; s. Malik Chand and Amrita Bai (Chawla) C.; m. Indu Kochar, Dec. 6, 1970; children: Anju, Ajay, Amita. BS, Punjab U., 1963; MS, U. Minn., 1968; PhD, U. Ky., 1973. Asst. engr. Pub. Works Dept., Chandigarh, India, 1963-67; civil engr. Meyer Mfg., Red Wing, Minn., 1968; structural engr. Cons. Engrs., Lexington, Ky., 1968-71; from rsch. asst. to adj. asst. prof. U. Ky., Lexington, 1971-76; structural engr. U.S. Bur. Mines, Denver, 1976-78; civil engr. U.S. Bur. Reclamation, Denver, 1978—. Adv. bd. Internat. Jour. for Numeric, London, Eng., 1988-2000, World Bank and Asian Devel., Washington, 1989—. Contbr. articles to profl. jours. Judge Sci. Fair, Golden, Colo., 1991. Fellow ASCE; mem. U.S. Com. Large Dams (com. chmn. 1991-94). Hindu. Achievements include research in embankment dam and structural engineering. Home: 13798 W Warren Dr Lakewood CO 80228-4531 Office: U S Bur Reclamation PO Box 25007 Denver CO 80225-0007

CHUI, HELENA CHANG, physician; b. Pitts., Apr. 1, 1953; d. Jerry C.L. and Ruth C. Chang; m. Robert T. K. Chui, June 22, 1974 (div. Aug. 28, 2002); 1 child, Benjamin. BA, Johns Hopkins U., 1974, MD, 1977. Prof. neurology U. So. Calif., 1994—, interim chair neurology, 1990—. Bd. dirs. Alzheimer Assn., LA, 2000—. Fellow: Am. Heart Assn.; mem.: Am. Neurol. Assn., Am. Acad. Neurology. Office: 410 Keith Adminstrn 1975 Zonal Ave Downey CA 90033

CHUKHMAN, NELLA, music educator; b. Bendery, Moldova, Sept. 30, 1976; d. Boris and Mila Chukhman. German, Russian (magna cum laude), U. of Vt., 1999, Piano Performance, 2003. Piano instr. Home-based Bus., Shelburne, Vt., 1995—2000, Studio at Hansen & Son's, Shelburne, Vt., 2000—. Musician at concerts, events, recitals, auditions. Archivist Burlington Br. of Vt. Music Tchr. Assn., 2001—02. Scholar Outstanding Young Women Leaders, Mary Kay Assn., 1995. Mem.: Music Tchrs. Assn. of Am. Home: 349 Farrell St #311 South Burlington VT 05403 Office: Hansen & Son's Pianos 86 Longmeadow Dr Shelburne VT 05482

CHUKWUMERIJE, NKEMDIRIM, medical educator; b. Okigwe, Imo, Nigeria, Dec. 30, 1967; arrived in U.S., 1994; s. Pius and Beatrice Chukwumerije; m. Eukay Chukwumerije, July 14, 2001. NIB, BS, U. Nigeria, Enugu, 1991. Cert. internal medicine. Resident physician Muhlenberg Regional Med. Ctr./ U. Medicine Dentistry N.J.-Robert Wood Johnson Med. Ctr., Plainfield, 1997—2000; physician scholar UCLA Sch. Medicine, 2000—01; acad. hospitalist Cleve. Clinic Found., 2001—. Mem.: ACP (poster presenter 2000), Nat. Assn. Inpatient Physicians (poster presenter 2000). Avocations: reading, travel, soccer. Office: Cleve Clinic Found 9500 Euclid Rd Cleveland OH 44195

CHUMACEIRO, ROLANDO JOSE MENDEZ, family practice physician; b. Orangestad, Aruba, Oct. 23, 1959; came to U.S., 1965; s. Rolando Jose and Regina Maria Chumaceiro; m. Cecilia Chumaceiro, Jan. 20, 1990; children: Jessica Marie, Emily Cristina. BS, Northeastern U., 1983; MD, U. Autonoma de Guadalajara, Mex., 1988. Bd. cert. family medicine. Attending physician (pvt. practice) So. Yonkers (N.Y.) Family Practice, 1993-95, Oxford Med. Group, Yonkers, 1996—; clin. faculty St. Joseph Med. Ctr., Yonkers, 1993—, med. dir. methadone maintenance program, 1994—. Med. bd. St. Josephs Med. Ctr., Yonkers, 1999—, Yonkers Gen. Hosp., 1999—; dir. 5th pathway program N.Y. Med. Coll. at St. Joseph Med. Ctr., Valhalla, N.Y., 1996—. Capt. med. team N.Y.C. Marathon, 1990—. Recipient Am. Heart Assn. award, 1992. Mem. AMA, Am. Acad. Family Practice, Spanish Am. Med. Soc. Republican. Roman Catholic. Avocations: tennis, golf, traveling, camping, reading. Home: 1506 Pondcrest Ln White Plains NY 10607-1356 Office: Oxford Med Group 970 N Broadway Ste 305B Yonkers NY 10701-1311 E-mail: chuma1023@aol.com.

CHUMAN, FRANK FUJIO, lawyer; b. Montecito, Calif., Apr. 29, 1917; s. Hitsuji Henry and Kiyo (Yamamoto) C.; m. Ruby Ryoko Dewa, June 22, 1948 (div. Oct. 1968); children: Daniel Christopher, Paul Randolph; m. Donna Daungvipar Karschamroon, Apr. 17, 1983; children Diana, Daniel, Paul. BA in Polit. Sci., UCLA, 1938; postgrad., U. So. Calif., 1940-42, U. Toledo, 1943-44; JD, U. Md., 1945. Bar: Md. 1945, Calif. 1947. Clk. with probation dept. County of Los Angeles, 1939-42; adminstr. Base Hosp., Manzanar, Calif., 1942-43; acct. Goodyear Tire and Rubber Co., Balt., 1945; sole practice Los Angeles, 1947—; ptnr. Chuman and McKibbin, L.A., 1950-68; judge pro tem L.A. Mcpl. Ct., 1968-83. Arbitrator Los Angeles County Superior Ct., 1968—83; gen. ptnr. Japanese Village Plz. Shopping Ctr., L.A., 1976—85; chmn. Founders Savs. and Loan; pres., CEO Chuman Internat. Author: "Bamboo People" Law and Japanese Americans, 1976. Mem. Japanese Am. Citizens League, nat. pres., 1960—62, bd. dirs. Recipient Bishop's Merit award Episc. Diocese of Los Angeles, 1963, Disting. Svc. award UCLA Alumni Assn., 1963, Eagle Scout award Boy Scouts Am. 1939, Silver Beavers award, 1974, Disting. Svc. award Govt. Japan, 1977, Disting. Eagle Scout award, 1979. Mem. ABA, Japanese Am. Bar Assn., Assn. Immigration Lawyers (chmn. Los Angeles chpt. 1958-59). Avocations: golf, music. Office: 400 S Skyline Dr Westlake Village CA 91361 Office Fax: 805-496-0672.

CHUMAS, LINDA GRACE, elementary school educator; b. Floral Park, NY, May 3, 1944; d. Vincent Armond and Alisandra (Simonelli) DeAngelis; m. Spero Nicholas Chumas; children: Spero Chris, Kara Alisandra. BS, Ea. Ky. U., 1967; MA, SUNY, New Paltz, 1983. Cert. health and phys. edn. Tchr. phys. edn. Valley Ctrl. H.S., Montgomery, N.Y., 1968-70, varsity girls tennis coach, 1968-70, jr. varsity girls sports coach, 1968-70, tchr. adult edn. and phys. edn., 1968-75; phys. edn. tchr. Leptondale Elem. Sch., Wallkill, N.Y., 1983—; aerobics, line dance tchr. Wallkill H.S. PTO, 1993-96, tchr. ballroom dancing, 1995-96; tchr. ballroom and line dancing Wallkill Reformed Church, Wallkill, 1996-98; tennis tchr. Town of Shawangunk Recreation, Wallkill, 1993-96; tchr. tennis and dance Wallkill Arts Cmty., 1996-98. Jump Rope for Heart coord. Am. Heart Assn., 1983—; mem. Wallkill Ctrl. Sch. Dist. Strategic Planning Com., 1991—; tchr. tennis Walkill Arts Cmty., summer, 1996-98; tchr. ballrm. dancing Mt. St. Mary's Coll., 1999—, Town of Newburgh Recreation program, 2001, Town of Hamptonburgh Sr. Citizens Ctr., 2001. Treas. Am. Field Svc., Wallkill, 1988-93; chair flower sales Am. Heart Assn., Leptondale Elem Sch., 1990-2001; co-dir. road race Shamrock Scramble, Wallkill, 1988-96; mem. Health and Safety Comm., Wallkill Central Sch. Dist., 1991-2001; solicitor Multiple Sclerosis Soc., Capital region, 1990-92, 97-2000, Am. Lung Assn., 1998; coord. Hoops for Heart program Am. Heart Assn., 1997—; mem Walkill Vol. Ambulance Corp., 1999. Recipient Outstanding Devel. award Am. Heart Assn., Kingston, N.Y., 1990, Straight from Heart flowers award 1992-96, Amazing Person award Elem. Physical Edn. Sect. N.Y. Assn. for Health, Physical Edn., Recreation and Dance, 1996. Mem. AAHPERD (mem. coun. svcs. for Ea. dist. assn. 1995-97), N.Y. State Assn. Health, Phys. Edn., Recreation and Dance (sec. 1993-95, Jump Rope for Heart Task Force 1992—, Jump Rope for Heart Catskill zone coord. 1992—, chairperson necrology 1996-98, Amazing Persons award 1996, Hoops for Heart AHA 1997—), N.Y. State United Tchrs. (health ins. rep. Ulster County 1991-2001), Nat. Dance Assn., Wallkill Woman's Club. Democrat. Greek Orthodox. Avocations: volleyball, tennis, gardening, home decorating, ballroom dancing. Home: PO Box 163 Wallkill NY 12589-0163 Office: Leptondale Elem Sch 48 Mill St Wallkill NY 12589-2803 Personal E-mail: LCNY44@aol.com.

CHUMBLEY, ROBERT EDWARD, performing arts association administrator; b. Miami, Fla., Oct. 22, 1954; s. Robert Edward and Nanette (Gibbons) C.; m. Shirley Irek, Dec. 31, 1978; 1 child, Vanessa Irene. MusB, Temple U., 1975; MusM, Juilliard Sch., 1977. Exec. dir. Chopin Found. of the U.S., Miami, 1981-84; dir. cultural affairs Appalachian State U. (U. N.C.), Boone, N.C., 1984-90; artistic dir. Lied Ctr. for Performing Arts, U. Nebr., Lincoln, 1990-97, Charles Bethea exec. dir., 1997—; exec. music dir., artistic dir. Atlanta Ballet Inc., 1997—; pres., CEO The Arts Coun. Winston-Salem, NC, 2002—. Composer-in-residence Entrecasteaux Festival, Nice, France, 1985, N.C. Symphony, Raleigh, 1987-91; concert tours U.S., 1980-90, Europe, 1980, 85, 86, Japan, 1986, Africa, 1982. Composer (opera) Ordinary People, 1990, (symphonies) Reflections on a Tropical Evening, 1989, Violin Concerto, 1988, Songs of Persuasion, 1989, (chamber music) Odyssey of Reminiscence, 1985 (N.C. Arts Coun. Composer fellow), Homage to Wordsworth, 1986, (solo) Homage to Keats, 1986 Vice-chair Tourism Devel. Authority, N.C., 1988-90; bd. dirs. Arts Coun., Lincoln, 1990—. Mem. Chamber Music Am., Broadcast Music, Inc., Am. Compoers Alliance, Internat. Soc. of Performing Arts Presenters, Assn. Performing Arts Presenters, Am. Music Ctr., N.C. Arts Coun. (Composer Fellowship award). Republican. Avocations: golf, gem collecting. Office: 305 W Fourth St Winston Salem NC 27101

CHUN, SHINAE, federal agency administrator; Dir. Labor Dept., Chgo., 1998; dir. women's bur. U.S. Dept. Labor, Washington, 2001—. Office: US Dept Labor Women's Bur 200 Constitution Ave NW Washington DC 20210 Office Fax: 202-693-6725.

CHUN FAT, GEORGE, writer; b. Guadalajara, Mexico, Nov. 9, 1964; arrived in U.S., 1966; s. Francis and Angelina Chun Fat. Programmer Quality Svcs., Santa Barbara, Calif., 1984—85, Budget Copy, San Diego, 1986—87, Microsteps, San Diego, 1990. Author: (Internet book) Intuitive Happiness, 2002, Conceptual Principles of Existential Parameters, 2002. Mem.: Mensa. Mem. Natural Law Party. Avocations: mathematics, physics, philosophy, psychology, logic. Home: 8560 Longwood St San Diego CA 92126 E-mail: george_chun_fat@hotmail.com.

CHUNG, BENJAMIN T. F. science educator; b. Lianing, China; arrived in US, 1960; s. Chung Chen-Yin and Lin Lian; m. Jane L. Chung, Aug. 22, 1984; children: Matthew S., Dean S. BSME, Nat. Cheng Kung U., Tainan, Taiwan, 1958; MSME, Kans. State U., Manhattan, 1962; MS in Math., U. Wis., Milw., 1965; PhD in Mech. Engring., Kans. State U., 1968. Rsch. engr. Allis Chalmers Mfg. Co., Milw., 1962—69; engring. analyst Babcock & Wilcox Co., Barberton, Ohio, 1977—78; from asst. prof. to assoc. prof. to prof. U. Akron, Ohio, 1969—84, dept. chair, Harrington prof., 1984—99, Harrington prof. emeritus, rsch. prof., 2000—. Author: (handbook) Heat Transfer of Mathematics, 1982, Encyclopedia of Environmental Control Technology, 1989; contbr. scientific papers to profl. jours. Recipient Outstanding Alumni award, Nat. Cheng Kung U., 1994, Norbert Wiener award, MCB U. Press, 1998. Fellow: ASME (assoc. editor Jour. Heat Transfer 1999—2003, Exemplary Svc. award for outstanding rev. 1998), Internat. ASME (life). Office: U Akron Akron OH 44325-3903

CHUNG, CAROLINE, foreign service officer; b. Washington, Apr. 27, 1970; d. Jae Wan and Soojun Chung. BS, U. Wis., 1992; MBA, Vanderbilt U., 1997. Cert. Mad Dogg Spinning, Aerobics and Fitness Assn. Am. Mgr. ops. rsch. and statis. analysis Continental Airlines, 1997—99; mgr. product devel. USAirways, 1999—2001; ops. rsch. cons. Warden Assocs., 2001—02; fgn. svc. officer U.S. Dept. of State, 2002—. Roman Catholic. Avocations: professional aerobics instructor, travel, reading, world maps, music.

CHUNG, CHIA MOU (CHARLES CHUNG), former Oriental art business owner; b. Chiao Ling Hsien, Guangdong, China, Feb. 21, 1918; came to U.S., 1946; s. Kiu-Sin and Yee-Mui (Lee) C.; m. Sylvia E.E. Tuck, Jan. 16, 1955 (div. Jan. 1970); children: Wilma, Cathie, Vivian, Calvin; m. Betty Lee Sung, July 22, 1972; stepchildren: Tina, Cynthia, Victor, Alan Sung. Grad., Ctrl. Police U., Chungking, Sichuan, China, 1940, Nat. Cheng-Chi U., Chungking, 1943; BS, MS, Wash. State U., Pullman, 1948; postgrad., NYU, 1948-51. Editor Ctrl. Police U., 1941-43; profl. officer Exec. Yuan, Chungking, 1943-45; calligrapher, transl., reviser Secretariat UN, N.Y.C., 1948-79; pres. Jade and Oriental Arts, Inc., N.Y.C., 1961-99. Author: The Road for ROC to be Readmitted to UN (in Chinese), 1994; co-editor China Anthology (in English), 1996, Chung's Selected Essays (in Chinese), 1998; contbr. articles to Chinese newspapers and profl. pubs. Sr. advisor Chinese Chee-Yue Cmty. Assn., NYC, 1996—; bd. mem. Chinese Consolidated Benevolent Assn., NY, 1996—. Recipient first prize Nat. Essay Contest on Police Sci. and Adminstrn. by Examination Yuan, 1941, Excellent Svc. award pres., Exec. Yuan, 1945, Chinese Rsch. Prof. award Tai-ti Found., 1951, Svc. award Sec. Gen. UN, 1985, Excellent Svc. award Ctrl. Police U. Alumni Assn., N.Am., 1993, Nat. Cheng-ta Alumni Assn. Ea. U.S., 1995, Svc. award Shanghai Tiffin Club, 1995. Mem. Ctrl. Police U. Alumni Assn. Eastern U.S. (chmn. 1991—, excellent svc. award 1996), Nat. Cheng-ta Alumni Assn. Eastern U.S. (exec. dir. 1991-94, hon. v.p. 1994-99, adviser 1999—), World Hakka Fedn. (pres. Ea. U.S. chpt. 1991-93, advisor 1993—), World Kwongtung Cmty. Assn. (advisor 1991—), ROC Nat. Devel. Assn. (mem. overseas com. 1991—), Taiwan Devel. Inst. (rsch. fellow 1993—), Chinese-Am. Jewelry Assn. (sr. adviser 1991—). Home: 165 Park Row Apt 20F New York NY 10038-1138

CHUNG, CONNIE (CONSTANCE YU-HWA CHUNG), broadcast journalist; b. Washington, Aug. 20, 1946; d. William Ling and Margaret Chung; m. Maurice Richard Povich. BS, U. Md., 1969; DJ (hon.) (hon.), Providence Coll., 1988; LHD (hon.), Brown U., 1987; LLD (hon.), Wheaton Coll., 1989. News copyperson, writer, reporter Sta. WTTG-TV, Metromedia, Washington, 1969—71; corr. CBS News, Washington, 1971—76; TV news anchor Sta. KNXT-TV, CBS, L.A., 1976—83; anchor NBC News, NBC News at Sunrise, NBC Nightly News (Saturday), NBC News Digests, NBC News Mag. 1986, NBC News Spls., N.Y.C., 1983—89, Saturday Night with Connie Chung, CBS-TV, 1989—90, CBS Evening News (Sunday edit.), 1989—93, Face to Face, 1990—91, Eye to Eye, 1993—95; co-anchor CBS Evening News, 1993—95; anchor, corres. 20/20 ABC, N.Y.C., 1997—2002; anchor CNN, New York, NY, 2002—03. Recipient Achievement Cert. for series of broadcasts, U.S. Humane Soc., 1969, Metro Area Mass Media award, AAUW, 1971, Outstanding Young Women of Am. award, 1971, Atlanta chpt. Nat. Assn. Media Women award, 1973, Outstanding Excellence in News Reporting and Pub. Svc. award, Chinese-Am. Citizens Alliance, 1973, Hon. award for news reporting, Chinese YMCA, Boston, 1974, Woman of Distinction award, Golden Slipper Club, Phila., 1975, Best TV Reporting award, Sta. KNXT-TV and L.A. Press Club, 1977, Outstanding TV Broadcasting award, Valley Press Club, 1977, Golden Mike award for best documentary, 1978, Emmy award for individual achievement, L.A. chpt. NATAS, 1978, 1980, Mark Twain trophy, Calif. AP TV and Radio Assn., 1979, Best News Broadcast 4:30 p.m., 1980, Women in Comm. award, Calif. State U. at L.A., 1979, George Foster Peabody award for programs on environ., Md. Ctr. Pub. Broadcasting, 1980, Portraits of Excellence award, Pacific S.W. region B'nai B'rith, 1980, Newscaster of Yr. award, Temple Emanuel Brotherhood, 1981, First Amendment award, Anti-Defamation League of B'nai B'rith, 1981, Best Newscast 6:00 p.m. award, AP, 1981, Calif. AP TV and Radio Assn. award, 1981, Golden Mike award for best news broadcast, 1981, Disting. Contbns. in area of Comm. Media award, L.A. Basin Equal Opportunity League, 1983, Women in Bus. award, 1983, L.A. Press Club award for 4:30 p.m. boradcast, 1983, L.A. Press Club award for 6:00 p.m. broadcast, 1983, Emmy award, 1986, Emmy award for outstanding interview, 1989, 1990, Silver Gavel award, ABA, 1991, Ohio State of Achievement of Merit award, 1991, Nat. Headliner award, NCCJ, 1991, Clarion award, Women in Comm., 1991, Commendation award for AIDS and rape stories, Am. Women in Radio and TV, Commendation award for best implant stories, 1991, Godl Apple award, Nat. Media Network Film and Video Competition, 1999, Edward R. Murrow award for best news documentary, Nat. Assn. Radio and TV News Dirs., 1999, Cine Golden Eagle award, 1999, East Seals EDI award, 1999, Comm. award, Crystal award of Excellence, 1999, plaque award, Nat. Network for Youth, 2000, Gold Camera award, U.S. Internat. Film and Video Festival, 2000, 1999 award, Chgo. Internat. TV Competition, 2000, Media Spotlight award, Amnesty Internat., 2000, Salute to Excellence award, Nat. Assn. Black Journalists, 2000.*

CHUNG, CYNTHIA NORTON, communications specialist; b. Milton, Mass., Apr. 14, 1955; d. Ralph Arnold and Mary Elizabeth (McDonald) N.; m. Chinsoo Chung; children: Sara Jane, Steven Joonmok. BFA in Archtl. and Graphic Design, U. Mass., 1977. Graphic designer Garber Travel, Inc., Brookline, Mass., 1977-78; graphic and exhibit designer Rust Craft, Inc., Dedham, Mass., 1978-80; corp. advt. artist Morse, Inc., Canton, Mass., 1980-83; pvt. practice designer Boston, 1983-84; asst. art dir. Cahners Pub. Co., Newton, Mass., 1984-86, art dir., 1986-87, Knapp, Inc., Brockton, Mass., 1987-89; customer svc. rep. TWA, Boston, 1990; communications specialist Boston Fin., Quincy, Mass., 1992—. Designer graphs and charts for Vols. I and II State Budget Commonwealth of Mass., 1982; art dir. Mini Micro Systems, 1984-87. Mem. Kappa Kappa Gamma (Pres. 1975-76). Avocations: photography, real estate, travel. Home: 134 Samoset Ave Quincy MA 02169-2452 Office: Boston Financial 2000 Crown Colony Dr Quincy MA 02169

CHUNG, ED B(AIK), pathologist, educator; b. Kilchoo, Korea, Mar. 16, 1928; came to U.S. 1954; s. Hi Sam and Ok Bong (Lee) C.; m. Ok Hyung Kang, Nov. 9, 1958; children: Sophia M., Jeanne M., Theodore D., Virginia M., Esther K. MD, Severance Union Med. Coll., Seoul, Korea, 1951; MS in Pathology, Georgetown U., 1956, PhD in Pathology, 1958. Diplomate Am. Bd. Pathology in Anatomic Pathology and Clin. Pathology. Resident in pathology Georgetown U. Med. Ctr., Washington, 1954-58; instr. in pathology Georgetown U., Washington, 1958-61, asst. prof. pathology, 1961-63; assoc. prof. pathology Howard U., Washington, 1964-70, prof. pathology, 1970-98; prof. emeritus pathology Howard U. Hosp., Washington, 1999—, attending pathologist, 1964-98, dir. surg. pathology, 1968-98. Cons. Glen Dale (Md.) Hosp., 1968-74, Coroner's Office, Washington, 1969-71; vis. prof. soft tissue pathology, Padua (Italy) U. Inst. Anatomic and Histologic Pathology, 1989. Contbr. numerous articles to profl. jours. Bd. dirs. Washington Korean Community Svc. Ctr., 1974 , vice chmn. 1974-81, chmn. 1981-86; trustee the Korean Sch., Washington, 1971-73; chmn. bd. deacons Washington Korean Bapt. Ch., 1959-69; elder Full Gospel (Assembly of God) First Ch., Washington, 1979—. Capt. Republic of Korea Army Med. Corps, 1952-54. Fellow Am. Soc. Clin. Pathologists, Coll. Am. Pathologists; mem. U.S. and Can. Acad. of Pathology (mem. emeritus), Washington Soc. Pathologists. E-mail: ebchung@juno.com.

CHUNG, FUNG-LUNG, cancer research scientist; b. Keelung, Taiwan, Republic of China, Nov. 10, 1949; came to U.S., 1973; s. Tse-Yung and Carol (Cheng) C.; m. Judy Chu, Aug. 2, 1975; children: Christine, Christopher, Clifford. BS in Chemistry, Chung-Yuan U., Chung-Li, Taiwan, 1971; PhD, U. Utah, 1978. Postdoctoral fellow Columbia U., N.Y.C., 1979-80; rsch. assoc. Am. Health Found., Valhalla, N.Y., 1980-85, sect. head, 1985-89, assoc. chief, 1990-95, chief, 1995—. Mem. study sect. Nat. Cancer Inst., Washington, 1990-94; assoc. mem. Sloan-Kettering Cancer Inst., 1993—; mem. sr. adv. com. Am. Health Found., 1991—; program leader Am. Health Found. Cancer Ctr. Core Grant; adj. prof. N.Y. Med. Coll., 1998—. Editl. bd.: Chem. Rsch. in Toxicology, Oncology Reports; contbr. over 100 articles to profl. jours. Recipient Young Investigator award Nat. Cancer Inst., 1982, grantee, 1982—; featured on cover of Cancer Rsch., 1999. Mem. Am. Assn. Cancer Rsch., Am. Chem. Soc., Am. Soc. Preventive Oncology, The Oxygen Soc. Office: Am Health Found 1 Dana Rd Valhalla NY 10595-1549

CHUNG, JENNIFER M. not-for-profit executive; d. Soo Kil and Soon Won Chung. BA, BS in Bible, Phila. Bibl. U., 2001. Payroll asst. Phila. Coll. of Bible, Langhorne, 1998; testing adminstrator asst. Law Sch. Admissions Coun., Newtown, Pa., 1999; ednl. outreach rschr. intern Rec. for the Blind and Dyslexic, Princeton, NJ, 2000; mgr. devel. comm. and rsch. Big Bros. Big Sisters of Am., Phila., 2001—. Mem.: Students in Free Enterprise. Office: Big Brothers Big Sisters of Am 230 N 13th St Philadelphia PA 19107 Office Fax: 215-567-0394. E-mail: jchung@bbbsa.org.

CHUNG, JIN SOO, ocean mining and ocean engineer; b. Seoul, Korea, Jan. 27, 1937; s. Hyun Mo and Soon Mo (Yoo) C.; m. Yang Ja Park, Aug. 11, 1967; children: Claude H., Christine M. BSE. in Naval Arch., Seoul Nat. U., 1961; MS, U. Calif., Berkeley, 1964; PhD in Engring. Mechanics, U. Mich., 1969. Sr. rsch. engr. Exxon Prodn. Rsch. Co., Houston, 1969—73; staff engr. Lockheed Missiles & Space Co., Sunnyvale, Calif., 1973—80; team leader advanced tech. Ocean Minerals Co., Mountain View, Calif., 1975—80; prof. Colo. Sch. Mines, Golden, 1980—2000; exec. dir. Internat. Soc. Offshore and Polar Engrs. (ISOPE), 1990—. Cons. hydrodynamics to Inter-Govtl. Maritime Consultative Orgn. UN, 1981; founder, editor, chmn. ISOPE Ocean Mining Symposium, 1995—. Sr. editor: Transactions Jour. Energy Resources Tech., 1980-85; editor: Internat. Jour. Offshore and Polar Engring., 1990—; assoc. editor: Applied Mechanics Rev., 1985-91; chmn., editor Proceedings 1st Offshore Mechanics/Arctic Engring. Symposium, New Orleans, 1981, 2nd Internat. Symposium, Houston, 1983, 3rd Internat. Symposium, New Orleans, 1984, 4th Internat. Symposium, Dallas, 1985, 5th Internat. Symposium and Exhibit, Tokyo, 1986, 7th Internat. Conf., Houston, 1988, 8th Internat. Conf., Hague, The Netherlands, 1989; contbr. articles to profl. jours. Rsch. grantee, Office Naval Rsch. Mem.: ASME (policy bd. comm. 1981—85, editor various publs. 1981—, chmn. offshore mechanics com. 1982—84, founding chmn. offshore mechanics and arctic engring. divsn. 1985—89, Eugene W. Jacobson award Energy Tech. Conf. Houston 1978, Ralph James award 1980, Outstanding Achievement award 1987), Soc. Naval Archs. Japan, Internat. Soc. Offshore and Polar Engring. (co-founder 1989, chmn. editor procs. ann. conf. 1991—, 1st elected pres. 1999—2000, Neptune award 1992), Internat. Coun. Offshore Mechanics and Arctic Engring. (chmn. 1986—95, founder), Tau Beta Pi, Sigma Xi. Achievements include pioneering in advanced tech. devel. and position control simulation of deep ocean mining system; development of laser Doppler anemometer for turbulence in non-Newtonian fluids flow. Home: 11149 Sutherland Ave Cupertino CA 95014-4730 Office: Internat Soc Offshore & Polar Engrs PO Box 189 Cupertino CA 95015-0189 Fax: 650-254-2038. E-mail: jschung@isope.org.

CHUNG, JONG-MOON, education educator; b. Lincoln, Nebr., June 30, 1969; s. Chin Wee and Young Cha Cho Chung; m. Seung-Won Han Chung, June 26, 1995; children: Yonhee, Yonju. BEE, Yonsei U., 1988—92, MEE, 1992—94; PhD electrical engring., Pa. State U., 1995—99. Rsch. asst. Info. and Telecom. Rsch. Inst., Yonsei U., Seoul, Korea (South), 1992—94, rschr., 1994—95; instr. Pa. State U., 1997—99, asst. prof. of elec. engring., 1997—99; asst. prof. Okla. State U., 2000—. Dir., ACSEL and OCLNB laboratories Okla. State U., 2000—. Mem.: IEEE (Conf. Outstanding Paper, First Pl. award 2000). Catholic. Achievements include research in sailors wireless communication badge (SWCB) systems; hybrid wireless and wired network systems; Navy wireless audio/video/data headset; development of direct sequence spread spectrum (DSSS) wireless modem module; telecommunications & virtual laboratory. Avocations: basketball, skiing. Office: Okla State U 202 Engineering South Stillwater OK 74078 Personal E-mail: jmc29@alumni.psu.edu. E-mail: jchung@okstate.edu.

CHUNG, JOSEPH SANG-HOON, economics educator; b. Unmun-myon, Chongdo-kun, Kyongbuk, Korea, Oct. 11, 1929; came to U.S., 1953; s. Anthony Doseng and Martha (Cho) C.; m. Louise Carol Guenther, Aug. 17, 1957; children: Vincent, Sara, Melissa. Student, Seoul Nat. U., Korea, 1949-51; BS in Econs., Marquette U., 1956, MA, 1958; PhD, Wayne State U., 1964. Lectr. in econs. Marquette U., Milw., 1958-60; from instr. to asst. prof. Kalamazoo Coll., 1962-63, 63-64; asst. prof. Ill. Inst. Tech., Chgo., 1964-68, chmn. dept. econs., 1975-82, assoc. prof., 1968-73, prof. econs., 1973-95, prof. emeritus, 1996—. Fulbright prof. Seoul Nat. U. Korea, 1966-68; cons. Hoover Instn., 1964-66, Def. Dept., 1969; assoc. Asia Sci. Rsch. Assocs., Menlo Park, Calif., 1968-85. Author: Evolution of the Japanese Electronics Industry, 1980, The North Korean Economy: Structure and Development, 1974; editor: Patterns of Economic Development: Korea, 1966. Social Sci. Rsch. Coun. fellow, 1962; Stanford U. Hoover Instn. grantee, 1964-65; Fulbright lectr. Dept. State, 1966-68; Gen. Electric Found. grantee, 1975 Mem. Am. Econs. Assn., Assn. Asian Studies, Midwest Econs. Assn. Roman Catholic. Home: 22 W County Line Rd Barrington IL 60010 E-mail: j1chung@aol.com.

CHUNG, KING-THOM, microbiologist, educator; b. Tou Fen, Taiwan, Apr. 25, 1943; came to U.S., 1966; s. Aa-Yuan and Yi-Ing (Buu) C.; m. Lan-Seng Fang, Oct. 27, 1973; children: Theodore, Serena. MA, U. Calif., Santa Cruz, 1967; PhD, U. Calif., Davis, 1972. Scientist Frederick (Md.) Cancer Rsch. Ctr., 1972-77; vis. asst. prof. Food Sci. Inst. Purdue U., West Lafayette, Ind., 1977-78; assoc. prof. Tunghai U., Taichung, Taiwan, 1978-80; prof., chmn. dept. Soochow U., Taipei, Taiwan, 1980-87, dean, 1983-87; vis. scientist U.S. Meat Animal Rsch. Ctr., Clay Center, Nebr., 1987-88; assoc. prof. biology U. Memphis, 1988-93, prof., 1993—. Mem. adv. bd. Dept. Agr. and Forestry, Taiwan Provincial Govt., Taichung, 1982-87; exec. sec. Internat. Symposium on Biogas, Microalgae and Livestock Wastes, Taipei, 1980. Author: (in Chinese) Environment and Pollution, 1987, Intellectuals and Academic Education, 1987, Stories of 25 World Leading Microbiologists, 1996; contbr. articles to profl. jours. Grantee Am. Inst. Cancer Rsch., 1992. Fellow Am. Acad. Microbiology; mem. Am. Soc. Microbiology, Am. Acad. Microbiology, Inst. Food Technologists, Sigma Xi. Achievements include the illustration of the significance of azo reduction in the azo dye mutagenesis and carcinogenesis, quantatitive structure activity relationships (QSAR) of aromatic amines, tannins and health, food safety, and history of microbiology. Office: U Memphis Dept Microbiol And Molecular Memphis TN 38152-0001 E-mail: kchung@memphis.edu.

CHUNG, KYUNG CHO, Korean specialist, educator, writer; b. Seoul, Korea, Nov. 13, 1921; s. Yang Sun and Kyung Ok (Peng) C.; m. Yosi S. Chung, Oct. 10, 1958; children: In Kyung, In Ja. Student, Waseda U., Tokyo, 1941-43; BA, Seoul Nat. U., 1947; postgrad., Columbia U., 1948-49; MA, N.Y. U., 1951; LL.D., Pusan Nat. U., 1965; Litt.D., Sungkyunkwan U., 1968; MA, Monterey Inst. Fgn. Studies, 1974. Mem. faculty U.S. Def. Lang. Inst., Monterey, Calif., 1951-92, Monterey Inst. Fgn. Studies, 1973-74, Hartnell Coll., Salinas, Calif., 1974-93. Pres. Korean Rsch. Coun.; adviser Korean Assn., Monterey, 1974—, Am.-Korean Found., Crossroads, Inc., 1992, Asia Devel. Inc.; treas. Korean Rsch. Bull.; hon. prof. Kunkuk U.; pres. South Carmel Hills Assn., 1962-99; hon. chmn. Inst. Far Eastern Studies Joint Rsch. Program U.S.-Russia-Korea-Japan-China, 1993—; chmn. Korea-Am. Assn. Author: Korea Tomorrow, 1957, New Korea, 1962, Seoul (Ency. Americana), 1965, Naeil Hankuk, 1965, Sae Hankuk, 1968, Korea: The Third Republic, 1972, Korean Unification, 1973, Korea Reunion and Reunification, 1974, Kankuk Gaido, 1988, The Korea Guidebook: North and South Korea, 6th edit., 2002, Korea edit., 2002, Hankuk-chongran, 1999, East and West 1000 Munsun, 1995, Japanese Kangoku Gaizobuk, 2002. Recipient Superior Performance award, U.S. Govt., 1964, Recognition award of 40 Yrs. Svc., 1991, Excellency medal, 1992, Korean Prime Min. citation, 1965, cert. of achievement, U.S. Def. Lang. Inst., 1976, Outstanding Performance award, 1980, Commendation award, 1991, Olympic-Svc. Gold medal, Korean Pres., 1989, Spl. Commendation award, 1990, Fifa World Cup Svc. award, 2002, Spl. award medal, Korean Govt., 2002, Excellency Svc. award medal, Overseas Korean Found., 2003. Mem. AAUP, Am. Assn. Asian Studies, Am. Assn. Modern Langs., Am.-Korean Polit. Assn., Carmel Found., Korean Rsch. Coun. (pres. 2002-03). Democrat. Mem. Korean Ch. Home and Office: 25845 S Carmel Hills Dr Carmel CA 93923-8310 *Dedicate and contribute toward better relations among the nations and the lasting peace in the world, teaching other languages to meet the other nations half way by speaking the same language.*

CHUNG, PAUL MYUNGHA, mechanical engineer, educator; b. Seoul, Dec. 1, 1929; came to U.S., 1947, naturalized, 1956; s. Robert N. and Kyungsook (Kim) C.; m. E. Jean Judy, Mar. 8, 1952; children: Maurice W., Tamara P. BSME, U. Ky., 1952, MS, 1954; PhD, U. Minn., 1957. Asst. prof. mech. engring. U. Minn., 1957-58; aero. research scientist Ames Research Center, NASA, Calif., 1958-61; head fluid physics dept. Aerospace Corp., San Bernardino, Calif., 1961-66; prof. mech. engring. U. Ill., Chgo., 1966-95, head dept. energy engring., 1974-79, dean engring., 1979-94, prof., dean emeritus, 1995—. Mem. tech. adv. com. Ill. Inst. Environ. Quality, 1975-77; corp. mem. Underwriters Lab., 1983-95; cons. to industry, 1966—. Author numerous papers in field; author: Electric Probes in Stationary and Flowing Plasmas, 1975, Russian edit., 1978; contbr. chpt. to Advances in Heat Transfer, 1965, to Dynamics of Ionized Gases, 1973. Bd. govs. Redlands (Calif.) YMCA, 1965-67. Fellow AIAA (nat. tech. com. on plasmadynamics 1972-74, com. on propellants and combustion 1976-80); mem. AIChE (nat. com. on internat. activities 1992-94), Am. Soc. Engring. Edn. (exec. bd. engring. dean's coun. 1983-84), Sigma Xi, Tau Beta Pi, Pi Tau Sigma, Phi Kappa Phi. Home: 2003 E Lillian Ln Arlington Heights IL 60004-4215 Office: Univ Ill Off of Dean Chicago IL 60680

CHUNG, PING TSAI, education educator; b. Taipei, Taiwan, Republic of China; s. Tai-Der and Kun-Sen Lin Chung; m. Hsin-Hwa Hsiao Chung, Jan. 18, 1987; children: Rebecca, Timothy. PhD Computer Sci., Polytechnic U., 1998; M.S. Computer Sci., Stevens Instit. of Tech., 1986. Mem. tech. staff. Lucent Tech. Bell Lab., Merrimack Valley, Mass., 1998—2000; software devel. AT&T Lab., Middle Town, NJ, 1997—98; asst. prof. dept. of computer sci. L.I. U., 2000—. Chmn. computer sci. pers. com. L.I. U., Bklyn., 2002—, computer sci. club adv., 2001—. Author: (journal) Congressus Numerantium, Vol. 157, 2002, (proceedings) Proceedings of SPIE Vol. 4527, 2001, Proceedings of CIC, 2003, Proceedings of IC, 2003. Mem.: IEEE, Assn. for Computing Machinery. Office: Dept of Computer Sci Long Island U 1 University Plz Brooklyn NY 11201

CHUNG, RICHARD S. health facility administrator; b. Jacksonville, Fla., Mar. 2, 1946; BA, Northeastern U., 1969; MD, Boston U., 1973. Bd. cert. Am. Bd. of Psychiatry and Neurology. Area dir., regional gen. mgr. Am. Biodyne, Inc., Honolulu, 1987-91, v.p. med. affairs San Francisco, 1991, v.p. clin. ops. and med. affairs, 1991-93; med. dir. Dept. Vet. Affairs, Honolulu, 1989-90; v.p. chief clin. officer Medco Behavioral Care, St. Louis, 1993-94; exec. v.p., chief clin. officer Merit Behavioral Care Corp., St. Louis, 1994-96; v.p., med. dir. Hawaii Med. Svc. Assn., Honolulu, 1996—. Rsch. asst. Sleep and Dream Lab E. Hartmann, Boston, 1970-73; unit chief E. Valley Mental Health, Sepulveda, Calif., 1979-80; chief psychiat. support team Dept. Vet. Affairs, Honolulu, 1980-87, chief psychiatry svcs. 1981-83; asst. clin. prof. dept. psychiatry U. Hawaii, 1981-84, assoc. clin. prof., 1984—. Author chpts. to books.; mem. edtl. review bd. Nat. Assn. Healthcare Quality, 1992-94. Co-founder United Self Help, Honolulu, 1984. Fellow Am. Coll. Med. Quality; mem. AMA. Office: Hawaii Med Svc Assn Rm 517 PO Box 860 Honolulu HI 96808-0860 E-mail: Richard_Chung@hmsa.com.

CHUNG, SOON MYOUNG, computer scientist, educator; m. Jongwha Chung; 1 child, Jaewon. PhD, Syracuse U., 1990. Prof. Wright State U., Dayton, Ohio, 1989—. Editor: Multimedia Information Storage and Management, 1996. Office: Wright State U Dept Computer Sci and Engring Dayton OH 45435

CHUNG, STEVEN KAMSEIN, lawyer; b. Honolulu, Oct. 13, 1947; s. Edward K.O. and Amy B.J. (Chun) C.; m. Evelyn Reiko, July 5, 1980; children: Chanelle Mari, Tiffany Rei. BA in Acctg., U. Hawaii, 1972; JD, U. Calif., San Francisco, 1976. Bar: Hawaii 1976, U.S. Dist. Ct. Hawaii 1976, U.S. Ct. Appeals (9th cir.) 1978, U.S. Supreme Ct. 1983. Assoc. Frank D. Padgett, Atty. at Law, Honolulu, 1976-80, ptnr. Chung, Lau, MacLaren & Lau, Honolulu, 1980-81, Walter G. Chuck & Assocs., Honolulu, 1981-86; pvt. practice, Honolulu, 1987-88; ptnr. Oshima, Chun, Fong & Chung, Honolulu, 1988—. Served to 1st lt. U.S. Army, 1966-69, Vietnam. Mem. Assn. Trial Lawyers Am., ABA, Hawaii Bar Assn. Roman Catholic. Home: 1826 Laukahi Pl Honolulu HI 96821-1337 Office: 841 Bishop St Ste 400 Honolulu HI 96813-3921

CHUNG, SUNG-SOOK (YOOJIN), music educator; b. Sungjin City, Hamkyung-puk-do, North Korea, Dec. 30, 1945; BA in Korean Music, Seoul Nat. U., 1970; MA in Ethnomusicology, U. Wash., Seattle, 1983; PhD in Ethnomusicology, U. Calif. Santa Barbara, 1998. Rsch. asst. Islamic Music in We. Africa, 1988—89; tchg. asst., vis. artist U. Wash., Seattle, 1972—74; lectr. Korean music and dance MIT, Cambridge, 1974; tchg. asst. Music Dept. U. Calif. Santa Barbara, 1984; performed worldwide with Zingaro of Paris, France, 1997—99. Singer: (songs) (multiple CDs) Hungbo-ga, 2002, Chokbyok-ga, 2002, (CD) P'ansori: The Art of Cosmic Voice, 1998. Grantee Spl. Rsch. grant, Pacific Cultural Found., 1988, Spl. Rsch. fellow, Harvard U., 1973—74. Mem.: AAUW, Ctr for Asian Arts Seattle, Korean Musicological Soc., Soc. Ethnomusicology U.S., Soc. Studies in P'ansoni, Korea, U. Wash. Alumni Assn. Home: 5015 21st Ave NE #7 Seattle WA 98105

CHUNG, YA-LI, music educator; b. Tadyan, Taiwan, June 4, 1962; arrived in U.S., 1999; d. Yung-Liang Chung and Yui-Chaio Lee; m. Tien-Un Yu, Aug. 12, 1990 (div. June 2001). B, Tung-Hai U, Taichung,Taiwan, 1986; M, Tex. Tech. U, 2001. Piano tchr. Yamaha Co., Chung-Lee, Taiwan, 1986—94; music tchr. Jr. HS, Chung-Lee, Taiwan, 1992, Tayan, Taiwan, 1993—94; piano tchr. pvt. practice, Taoyan, Taiwan, 1986—99; accompany tchg. asst. Tex. Tech. U, Lubbock, Tex., 1999—2002, piano tchr., 1999—2003. Composer (piano composition): Seasonal Songs, 2002. Recipient Excellent Tchr. Award, Govt. of Taoyan City, 1989, 1997, 1998, 1999. Mem.: MTNA - Music Tchr. Assn. (assoc.). Avocations: reading, composing, accompaniment, piano performance, travel. Home: 1612 Ave Y #210A Lubbock TX 79401 Office: School of Music in TTU MS 2033 18th St Boston Rd Lubbock TX 79409

CHUNG-WELCH, NANCY YUEN MING, biologist; b. N.Y.C., July 28, 1960; d. Thomas Richard and Jennie Kan Fee (Lew) Semler; m. James Michael Welch, June 29, 1985. BS, Northeastern U., Boston, 1982; PhD, Boston U., 1990. Rsch. technician dept. biology Boston U., 1983-85, tchg. fellow dept. biology, 1987-89; rsch. fellow surgery Mass. Gen. Hosp., Harvard Med. Sch., Boston, 1989-94; instr. in surgery Harvard Med. Sci., 1994-95; rsch. assoc. prof. Boston U., 1996-97; product mgr. Oncogene Rsch. Products, Cambridge, Mass., 1997-99, BD Bioscis., Bedford, Mass., 1999—2002; mktg. mgr. Fisher Sci., Hampton, NH, 2002—. Contbr. articles to profl. jours. including Jour. Cellular Physiology, Differentiation, Analytical Biochemistry, Surg. Forum, Microvascular Rsch., Biotechniques, Jour. Electrophoresis. Boston U. Grad. Sch. grad. rsch. award, 1987, Biology Dept. grad, travel award, 1988-89, Grega-Zacharkow Young Investigator award Microcirculatory Soc., 1988; named Outstanding Young Woman of Mass., 1988; Repligen Corp fellow, 1993-95. Achievements include devel. of tissue culture technique for the isolation and culture of pulmonary microvascular endothelial cells human omental microvascular endothelial cells and mesothelial cells in vitro; demonstrated presence of simple epithelial keratins in endothelial cells; rsch. on the phenotyptic properties between endothelial and mesothelial cells using histochemical and biochemical criteria and in vitro assays of angiogenic potential, vascular smooth muscle interactions with extracellular matrices as it relates to intimal hyperplasia. E-mail: nancy.chung-welch@nh.fishersci.com.

CHUN OAKLAND, SUZANNE NYUK JUN, state legislator; b. Honolulu, June 27, 1961; d. Philip Sing and Mei-Chih (Chung) Chun; m. Michael Sands Chun Oakland, June 11, 1994; children: Mailene Nohea Pua Oakland, Christopher Michael Sing Kamakaku Oakland, Lauren Suzanne LeRong Kemelenohea Oakland. BAs in Psychology and Comms., U. Hawaii, 1983. Adminstrv. asst. Au's Plumbing and Metal Works, Hawaii, 1979-90; community svc. specialist Senator Anthony Chang, Hawaii, 1984; adminstrv. asst. Smolenski and Woodell, Hawaii, 1984-86; rsch. asst., office mgr. City Coun. Mem. Gary Gill, Hawaii, 1987-90; mem. Hawaii Ho. of Reps., 1990-96, Hawaii Senate, Dist. 14, Honolulu, 1996—; chair com. health and human svcs. Hawaii Senate, 1999—, co-chair com. human resources, 1997—; mem. coms. health and environ., consumer protection; commerce and info. tech., 1997—. Past chair, mem. several coms. Hawaii State Senate; mem. Sterile Needle Exch. Oversight Com., 1992—; apptd. pres. Kalihi-Palama Svc. Area Bd. on Mental Health and Substance Abuse, gov. Hawaii, 1985-89. Mem. adv. bd. Lanakila Multi-Purpose Sr. Ctr., 1991—, Sex Abuse Treatment Ctr., 1993—, Teen Line, 1993, Hawaii Cmty. Found. Children's Trust Fund, 1995—, Habitat for Humanity, 1998—; mem. Grow For It Program, 1996—, Hawaii Early Childhood Alliance, 1995-96, Families Together Initiative Core Team, 1993-95; coun. mem. Hawaii Even Start Family Literact Program, 1993-94; mem. coord. coun. Hawaii Early Intervention, 1993—, Early Childhood Edn. and Care, 1992-96; mem. adv. coun. Children's Trust Fund, 1993—; mem. adv. com. West Honolulu Pub. Health Nursing Sect., 1992—, Honolulu divsn. Casey Family Program, 1994—, Early Childhood Svs. Cost/Implementation, 1992-94; chair Liliha/Kalapama Neighborhood Bd., 1984-90; mem. project steering com. Hawaii Summit 2011, 1996—; mem. Healthy Mothers, Healthy Babies Coalition, 1992; convenor Elder Abuse and Neglect Task Force, 1995—; mem. task force Blueprint for Change, Child Protective Svcs., 1994-96, Hawaii Assistive Tech. Tng. and Svcs. Project Cmty., 1995—; mem. coun. Hawaii Kids Count, 1994—; bd. dirs. Honolulu Neighborhood Housing Svcs., 1986-88, 89—, pres., 1987-88, 92-93, 93-94; bd. dirs. McKinley H.S. Found, 1989—; Catholic Immigration Ctr., 1991-97, Hawaii Dem. Movement, 1991-97, Hawaii Cmty. Svcs. Coun., 1993-97, Hawaii Cmty. Edn. Assn., 1984-98, Hawaii Lawyers Care, 1994—, Susannah Wesley Cmty. Ctr., 1994—, Hawaii Housing Devel. Corp., 1993—, YWCA, 1994—, ARC, 1998—, Breakthroughs for Youth at Risk, 1998—, Providing Awareness Referrals Edn. Nurturing Therapy Support, 1999—; precinct pres. Hawaii Dem. Party, 1990. Named Legis. of Yr. Hawaii Long Term Care Assn., 1993, 98, Healthcare Assn. Hawaii, 1993, 95, Hawaii Psychiat. Med. Assn., 1994, Autism Soc. Hawaii, 1994, Mental Health Assn. Hawaii, 1996, Aloha State Assn. of Deaf, 1999; recipient cert. of appreciation YMCA, 1985, Hawaii Assn. for Edn. of Young Children, 1992, Winners at Work, 1993, Am. Box Car Racing Internat., 1996, Congress of Visayan Orgn., 1996, Pack 201 Boys Scouts Am., 1997, Partners in Policymaking Hawaii, 1998, Excellence award Honolulu Neighborhood Housing Svcs. Inc., 1988, mini internship program cert. Honolulu County Med. Soc., 1993, Friend of Social Workers award NASW, 1995, Outstanding Govt. Svc. award Hawaii Pacific Gerontol. Soc., 1996, Outstanding Legislator award Hawaii Med. Assn., 1996, Na Lima Kokua Ma Waema O Makua award Pacific Gerontol. Soc., 1996, Friend of the Family award Hawaii Assn. for Marriage and Family Therapy, 1998. Mem. Liliha/Palama Bus. Assn. (bd. dirs. 1994—), Hawaii Women's Legal Found., Good Beginnings Alliance, Kalihi-Palama Culture and Arts Soc., Chung Wah Chung Kung Hui, Hawaii Chinese Civic Assn., Hawaii State Youth Vol. Bd. (past pres.), Ma'ema'e Sch. SCBM, Legis. Women's Caucus, Small Bus. Caucus, Keiki Caucus (co-chair 1991—), Chinese C. of C., McKinley Alumni Assn. (bd. dirs. 1989—). Democrat. Episcopalian. Avocations: raising animals, gardening, swimming. Office: State Senate 415 S Beretania St Rm 228 Honolulu HI 96813-2407*

CHUPITA, GREGORY FRANK, poet, security firm executive; b. Winona, Minn., Jan. 3, 1955; m. Maria Teresa Canete Chupita, June 8, 2000. BA, WSU, 1977. Certificate In International Business U. Of San Diego, Calif., 1993. Author (poet): (book of poetry) Macrossan Street, (book) Cat Of Nine Tails, (book of poetry) Nightshades, Vagabond Heart, (book) The Healing Art Of Poetic Qigong, (book of poetry) Little Buddha. Recipient President's Award For Lit. Excellence, The Nat. Authors Registry, 1997, 1998, 2001. Mem.: World Congress Poets (life).

CHUPKA, WILLIAM ANDREW, chemical physicist, educator; b. Pittston, Pa., Feb. 12, 1923; s. William and Antoinette C.; m. Olive Augusta Pirani, May 21, 1955; children: Jocelyn Terese, Marc William. BS, U. Scranton, 1943; MS, U. Chgo., 1949, PhD, 1951. Instr. Harvard U., 1951-54; asso. physicist Argonne (Ill.) Nat. Lab., 1954-67; sr. physicist, 1967-75; prof. chemistry Yale U., 1975-96, prof. emeritus, 1996—. Research, numerous publs. in chem. physics. Served with U.S. Army, 1943-46. Guggenheim fellow, 1961-62 Mem. Am. Chem. Soc. Office: PO Box 208107 New Haven CT 06520-8107 E-mail: chupka@ursula.chem.yale.edu.

CHUPP, RAYMOND EDWARD, mechanical engineer, researcher; b. Indianapolis, Ind., June 30, 1941; s. Nathan Dale Chupp, Jr. and Margaret Bell Chupp; m. Mary Lynn Harrison, Dec. 30, 1961; children: Michael Edward, Richard Lee, Brian Keith, Christopher Ryan, Andrew Wyatt, Priscilla Hope. BS, Kettering U., 1965; MS, Purdue U., 1965, PhD, 1973. Profl. Engr., Ind., 1975. Sr. project engr. Allison Gas Turbines (now Rolls Royce), Indpls., 1965—84; dept. head / project engr. Teledyne CAE, Toledo, 1984—92; fellow engr. Siemens Westinghouse Power Corp., Orlando, Fla., 1992—99; mech. engr. Gen. Electric Global Rsch., Niskayuna, NY, 1999—. Contbr. articles to profl. jours. Bd. mem. (past chair) Grace Missionary Ch., Mooresville, Ind., 1975—85; bd. mem. Sylvania Alliance Ch., Ohio, 1985—92; treas., bd. mem. Cmty. Alliance Ch., Winter Springs, Fla., 1995—98; chair of bd. Mooresville Christian Sch., Ind., 1975—82. Recipient Cert. of recognition, NASA, 1999. Fellow: ASME (heat transfer com. mem. 1988—2002); mem.: Inst. of Cert. Profl. Managers, Am. Inst. of Aeronautics and Astronautics, Tau Beta Pi. Conservative. Alliance/Baptist. Achievements include patents for turbine interdisk cavity cooling air compressor; a turbine interstage sealing arrangement; repositionable brush seal for turbomachinery; brush seal with positive adjustable clearance control; rotary machine having a seal assembly; patents pending for advanced sealing. Avocation: travel. Home: 119 Acorn Dr Glenville NY 12302 Office: General Electric Global Rsch Bld K1-4C5 One Research Circle Niskayuna NY 12309 Office Fax: 518-387-7292. Personal E-mail: rechupp@yahoo.com. E-mail: raymond.chupp@crd.ge.com.

CHURCH, AVERY GRENFELL, retired anthropology educator, poet; b. North Wilkesboro, N.C., Feb. 21, 1937; s. Avery Milton and Eulah May (Lowe) C.; m. Joyce Elaine Riggs, Jan. 29, 1965 (div. Oct. 1968); m. Dora Ann Creed, Oct. 5, 1991; 1 stepchild, Mark Donald Burney. Student, U. N.C., 1959-60, 61; BA cum laude, Baylor U., 1962; MA, U. Colo., Boulder, 1965. Tchg. asst. U. Colo., Denver, 1965; asst. prof. anthropology Memphis State U., 1965-66, 69-72; lectr. U. So. Ala., Mobile, 1972-83. Various positions with businesses, ednl. and humanitarian orgns., 1984-95; interviewer Navaho urban relocation project U. Colo., Boulder, 1964, rschr. Indian edn. project, 1966-69; mem. rsch. staff, bd. dirs. Sociol. and Anthrop. Svcs. Inst., Inc., Mobile, 1974-79. Author: (poetry) Rainbows of the Mind, 1982, Patterns of Thought, 1986, Waves of Life, 1995; contbr. over 200 articles, hist. sketches and poems to books, lit. mags., profl. and lit. jours., including Dan River Anthology, New Dawn Poetry, Yearbook Modern Poetry, Am. Bd., Bardic Echoes, Hoosier Challenger, Orphic Lute, Parnassus Lit. Jour., Pasque Petals, San Fernando Poetry Jour., Jour. Ala. Acad. Sci., So. Jour. Ednl. Rsch., Symposium on Drug Use for PTA Leaders, Am. at the Millennium, Poets' Paper, many others. Hon. trustee Am. Indian Relief Coun., 1997-2003; active Project Independence, campaign fin. reform Common Cause, Washington, 1997; freedom writer Amnesty Internat., N.Y.C., 1997-99; mem. Dem. Senatorial Campaign Com.; hon. mem. scholarship com. Am. Indian Edn. Found.; founding mem. Nat. Campaign for Tolerance, So. Poverty Law Ctr.; mem. Unitarian Universalist Svcs. com. Acton Alert Network for Internat. Human Rights; svc. coord. Unitarian Universalist Fellowship of Winston-Salem, N.C., 2001-2002. With USN, 1955-57. Woodrow Wilson fellow, 1962-63, Univ. fellow U. Colo., Boulder, 1964-65; recipient various lit. awards. Fellow Am. Anthrop. Assn., Internat. Acad. Poets; mem. Poetry Soc. Am., Ala. Acad. Sci. (vice chmn. anthropology 1975-76, exec. com. 1975-77, v.p. 1976-77), Nat. Com. to Preserve Social Security and Medicare (Leadership Circle), Nature Conservancy, USN Meml. Found., Pres.'s Club U. Colo. (Silver Circle 1994-95), World War II Meml. Soc. (charter), Ala. Ret. Tchrs. Assn., World Federalist Assn., Alpha Chi, Alpha Kappa Delta. Democrat. Unitarian Universalist. Avocations: hiking, golf. Home: 2749 Park Oak Dr Clemmons NC 27012-8619

CHURCH, BRYAN P. business owner, educator; b. Toledo, Oreg., Nov. 1, 1960; s. Harry P. and Nadine I. (Peace) Ch.; m. Rana B. Heller, Aug. 23, 1991; children: Schyler B., Matthew A. BS, Sacramento State U., 1982, MBA, 1983. Cert. cmty. coll. tchr., Calif.; lic. real estate broker, Calif. Terr. sales mgr. Coca-Cola USA, Atlanta, 1983-87; sales mgr. Macmillan/McGraw Hill Pub., Columbus, Ohio, 1987-93; western regional sales mgr. Dearborn Fin. Pub., Chgo., 1993-95; owner Accredited Real Estate Schs., Fair Oaks, Calif., 1995—; adj. assoc. prof. mktg. Sch. Mgmt. Golden Gate U., San Francisco, 1998—. Mem. bus. adv. bd. San Joaquin Delta Coll., Stockton, Calif., 1985, Hawaii Bus. Educators Assn., Honolulu, 1992, Sierra Coll., Rocklin, Calif., 1992, Saddleback Coll., Mission Viejo, Calif., 1994; guest speaker Inst. Mgmt. Accts., Sacramento, 1993, Svc. Corps of Ret. Execs., Sacramento, 1995; coord. tng. project Golden Gate U., San Francisco, 1994; nat. real estate cons. Hewlett Packard, 1999. Author: Playing the Corporate Game, 1994, Real Estate Principles, 1995, Real Estate Contracts, 1996, California Real Estate Practice, 1997. Vol. baseball coach Mills Jr. H.S., Sacramento, 1994. Recipient various awards. Mem. Hawaii Bus. Educators Assn., Calif. Assn. Realtors (affiliate). Avocations: bicycling, fly fishing, flying. Office: Accredited Real Estate Schs 6716 Madison Ave Ste 4 Fair Oaks CA 95628-3152

CHURCH, DALE WALKER, lawyer; b. Portland, Oreg., Dec. 17, 1939; s. Floyd Walker and Lydia Belle (Barnette) C.; m. Mollie Ann Harper, Apr. 11, 1964; 1 child, Forrest Gregory. BS, Oreg. State U., 1961; JD, George Washington U., 1967. Bar: D.C. 1968, Calif. 1971. Contracting officer, exec. sec. contract rev. bd. CIA, Langley, Va., 1963-69; corp. gen. counsel, asst. sec. directory of contracts ESL, Inc., Sunnyvale, Calif., 1969-77; dep. under sec. research and engring. U.S. Dept. Def., Washington, 1977-80; ptnr. Surrey and Morse, Washington, 1980-84, Seyfarth, Shaw, Fairweather & Geraldson, Washington, 1984-88, Pillsbury, Madison & Sutro, Washington, 1988-93, McDermott, Will & Emery, Washington, 1993-97; chmn., CEO, Ventures & Solutions, LLC, Williamsburg, Va., 1998—, Mechanical Tech., Inc., 2002—. Counsel def. mgmt. to pres.'s Blue Ribbon Commn.; cons. Def. Sci. Bd., Washington, 1980—; lectr. profl. orgns. and colls. Mem. task force on Industry-to-Industry Coop.; active Ctr. Strategic and Internat. Studies Def. Orgn. Project; trustee Oratorio Soc. Washington; co-founder, counsel, treas. Youth Engaged in Svc. Am. Mem. ABA, Am. Electronics Assn. (former gen. counsel, chmn. def. conversion com.), Nat. Security Indsl. Assn. (trustee, chmn. acquisition reform task force), Nat. Contracts Mgmt. Assn., Def. Sci. Bd. Acquisition Reform Task Force, Calif. Bar Assn., D.C. Bar Assn., Fed. Bar Assn., Soc. Logistics Engrs. (hon.), Delta Theta Phi, Sigma Phi Epsilon. Home: 9 Franklin St Alexandria VA 22314-3828 Office: Ventures & Solutions LLC 704 Fairfax Way Williamsburg VA 23185-8202

CHURCH, DAVID, music educator; s. George Frederick and Joy Eva Church; m. Lisa Michele Dupea, May 26, 1984; children: Philip, Evan. MusB, U. Colo., 1987; MA, Pacific Luth. U., 1996; MS in Edn./Adminstrn., U. So. Calif., L.A., 1998. Prin. First Luth. Sch., Glendale, Calif., 1996—98; prof. Calif. Bapt., Riverside, Calif., 1998—2000, George Fox U., Newberg, Oreg., 2000—. Adjudicator State Solo Competition, Oreg., 2002, Oreg., 03. Composer: (suite) Oreg. State U., 2003. Condr. The Chehalem Symphony, Newberg, Oreg., 2000—03, The Nutcracker, Newberg, Oreg., 2002. Mem.: Oreg. Band Dirs., Music Educators. Avocations: skiing, boating, running. Home: 242 NW Chardonnay St Dundee OR 97115 Office: George Fox Univ 414 N Meridien St Newberg OR 97132

CHURCH, EUGENE LENT, physicist, consulting scientist; b. Yonkers, N.Y., July 30, 1925; s. Wallace L. and Wilhelmina L. (Binger) C.; m. Anne Richardson Meirs, May 15, 1948; children— Rebecca Meirs, David Lent. AB, Princeton U., 1948; PhD, Harvard U., 1953. With U.S. Dept. Def., 1952-94; sr. phys. scientist Picatinny Arsenal, Dover, N.J., 1977-94; sr. physicist Frankford Arsenal, Phila., 1971-77. Guest physicist Argonne (Ill.) Nat. Lab., 1952-55, Brookhaven Nat. Lab., 1955-59, 61-71, 81—; vis. scientist Niels Bohr Inst., Copenhagen, 1959-61. Contbr. numerous articles to profl. jours. Served with USN, 1944-46 Recipient R&D-100 award, U.S. Army Achievement awards. Fellow Am. Phys. Soc., AAAS, Am. Optical Soc., Soc. Photo-Optical Instrumentation Engrs.; mem. IEEE (life sr.), St. Nicholas Soc. N.Y.C. Republican. Presbyterian. E-mail: echurch@ieee.org.

CHURCH, FRANK FORRESTER, minister, author, columnist; b. Boise, Idaho, Sept. 23, 1948; s. Frank Forrester and Bethine (Clark) C.; m. Amy Furth, May 30, 1970 (div. 1991); children: Frank Forrester, Nina Wynne; m. Carolyn Buck Luce, July 25, 1992. AB, Stanford U., 1970; MDiv, Harvard U., 1974, PhD, 1978. Sr. min. All Souls Unitarian Ch., N.Y.C., 1978—. Columnist The Chicago Tribune, 1987-88, The New York Post, 1989; vis. prof. Dartmouth Coll., Hanover, N.H., 1989. Author: Father and Son: A Personal Biography of Senator Frank Church of Idaho, 1985, The Devil and Dr. Church, 1985, Entertaining Angels, 1987, The Seven Deadly Virtues, 1988, Everyday Miracles, 1988, Our Chosen Faith: An Introduction to Unitarian Universalism, 1989, God and Other Famous Liberals, 1991, Life Lines, 1996, A Chosen Faith, 1998, Lifecraft, 2000, Bringing God Home, 2002, The American Creed, 2002; translator: Greek Word-Building (Matthias Stehle), 1976; editor: Continuity and Discontinuity in Church History, 1978, The Essential Tillich, 1987, 2d edit., 1999, The Macmillan Book of Earliest Christian Prayers, 1988, The Macmillan Book of Earliest Christian Hymns, 1988, The Macmillan Book of Earliest Christian Meditations, 1989, One Prayer at a Time: A 12 Step Anthology, 1989, The Jefferson Bible, 1989, Without Apology: The Liberal Faith of A. Powell Davies, 1998, Restoring Faith: America's Religious Leaders Answer Terror With Hope, 2001; contbr. (articles) Harvard Theol. Rev., (speeches) Rep. Am. Speeches, 1983—84, 1986—87, 1987—88, 1989—90, 1992—93, 1995—96, 1997—98; contbr. articles to profl. publs. Bd. dirs. Union Theol. Sem., N.Y.C., Coun. on Econ. Priorities, N.Y.C., 1984-91, Religion in Am. Life, Christianity in Crisis, 1991, Franklin and Eleanor Roosevelt Found., N.Y.C., 1990—, exec. com. 1999—, N.Y. Correctional Assn., Osborne Inst., 1991-94, Enterprise Found., N.Y.C. HIV Planning Coun.; chmn. Coun. on Environment N.Y.C., 1995—; mem. svc. com. Unitarian Universalist Ch., 1978—; founder Lifelines Ctr., 1999. Montgomery fellow Dartmouth Coll., 1989. Mem. Am. Acad. Religion, Unitarian Universalist Mins. Assn., Soc. Bibl. Lit., Citizens United for Separation of Church and State. Democrat. Home: 201 E 80th St New York NY 10021-0511 Office: All Souls Unitarian Church 1157 Lexington Ave New York NY 10021-0440

CHURCH, GAIL GRAHAM, television producer, consultant; b. Providence, May 10, 1924; d. Harry Jackson and Gertrude (Conners) Graham; m. William Rice Gerber, Jan. 20, 1951 (div. Jan. 1971); children: Cheryl Ann Gerber, Linda Lee Gerber; m. Herbert Church Jr., July 6, 1974. BS, R.I. State Coll., 1945; M of Nursing, Yale U., 1948. Nurse, instr. Mary Hitchcock Hosp., Hanover, N.H., 1948-49; head nurse rooming-in unit Grace New Haven Hosp., 1949-51; nurse, instr. Home Health Agy., Chicopee, Mass., 1951; educator, pub. health nurse N.H. Divsn. Pub. Health, Concord, N.H., 1972-74; ednl. advisor communicable diseases N.H. Dept. Edn., Concord, 1980; founder, prodr. pub. affairs TV series Life: Living It and Loving It, Concord, 1985-89, 2001—. Advisor Hospice Adv. Com., Concord, 1985; pres. Life: Living It and Loving It, Inc., Concord, 1985—. Founder, pres. Concord Area Drug Action Com., 1968; initiator first HELP-Line in N.H., Concord, 1969; organizer Reps. for Clinton/Gore, N.H. Dem. Party, Concord, 1992; mem. Task Force Against Racism, Concord, 1997—; mem. adv. bd. Internat. Health Found., 1999—. Recipient Leadership award YMCA, 1969, Dedicated Svc. to N.H. award Gov. Walter Peterson, 1970, Vol. Svc. award Gov.'s Coun. on Volunteerism, 1987. Mem. LWV, AAUW (membership chair Concord 1997, pres. Concord br. 1997—2000, co-pres. 1999—2000), Capital Area League Women Voters, UN Assn., N.H. Women's Lobby. Episcopalian. Avocations: painting, reading, walking, art, music, watercoloring, biking, reading, walking, art and music appreciation. Home: 1 Pleasant View Ave Concord NH 03301-2555

CHURCH, GEORGE MILLORD, retired real estate company executive; b. Philadelphia, Miss., Sept. 21, 1924; s. George W. and Maggie (Smith) C.; m. Ruth Green, Nov. 12, 1948; children: Ray, Gary. Diploma in acctg., So. Bus. Coll., 1947; AA with honors, Meridian (Miss.) Jr. Coll., 1954; BA in History and Polit. Sci., Coll. of Ozarks, 1957; disting. grad., U.S. Army Noncommd. Officer's Acad., 1961; grad., Realtor's Inst., 1971; postgrad., U. Miss., 1976. Boatswain's mate 1st class USN, South Pacific, Aleutian's, 1942-46; shipfitter Ala. Dry Dock and Ship Bldg., Mobile, 1946; acct. Milton Supply Co., Meridian, 1948 50; staff sgt. USMC, Camp Pendelton, Calif., 1950-51, Meridian, 1953-54; chief acct. Meridian Grain and Elevator Co., 1951-52; cost acct. Flintkote Co., Meridian, 1952-53; enlisted U.S. Army, 1954, advanced through grades to command sgt. maj., 1968, served in Vietnam, retired, 1969; pres. Church Realty Co., Meridian, 1969—; ret. Instr. real estate, real estate math Meridain Jr. Coll. Chmn. Toys for Tots, Meridian, 1954; active Lauderdale County Planning Commn., 1980-84, past chmn.; charter mem. Rep. Presdl. Task Force, Washington, 1982—. Decorated 3 Bronze Star medals, Air medal, Gallantry Cross with Palm (Republic of South Vietnam), Gallantry Cross with Silver Star. Mem. Miss. Assn. Realtors (bd. dirs. 1972-73, 91, past chmn. profl. stds. com., FHA and VA liason officer), Meridian Bd. Realtors (pres. 1972-73, 91, bd. dirs. 1972-73, 91, chmn. legis. and polit. action com., bd. congl. coord., Realtor of Yr. 1973, 89), Realtors Polit. Action Com. (life), Navy League U.S. (life commodore), VFW (life, Nat. Home for Children), Am. Legion (life), NRA (life), SCV (life; comdr. Camp 1221, 1992, 93, chief of staff Miss. divsn. 1993-95, comdr./founder Camp 1649, 1994, brigade comdr., Miss. divsn. 1995-96, gen. exec. coun. 1998, comdr. Army of Tenn. Svc. 2000—), The Jefferson Davis Soc. (life, co-founder, sec.-treas. 1994-96, dir. 1997—), Order of So. Cross (life). Baptist. Avocations: hunting, fishing, traveling, golf. Home: 4200 Pineview Dr Meridian MS 39305-3345 Office: Church Realty Co PO Box 224 Meridian MS 39302-0224

CHURCH, GLENN J. lawyer; b. Grand Island, Nebr., Aug. 20, 1932; s. Glenn Jennings and Rachel Frances (Cochran) C.; m. Mary L. Church; children: Susan Jo, Zackary William. AB, U. Ill., 1954, JD, 1959. Bar: Ill. 1959, U.S. Dist. Ct. (cen. dist.) Ill. 1960, U.S. Ct Appeals (7th cir.) 1967, U.S. Supreme Ct. 1971, Ohio 1983. Assoc. Kavanaugh, Bond, Scully, Sudow & White, Peoria, Ill., 1959-62; ptnr. Smith & Church, Peoria, 1962-64, Smith, Whitney & Church, Peoria, 1964-65; pvt. practice Peoria, 1965-88, Columbus, Ohio, 1988—. Spl. asst. atty. gen. water pollution div. State of Ill., 1960-61; hearing officer Am. Arbitration Assn., Chgo., 1966—; mem. Ill. Fair Employment Practice Commn., 1974-79. Liasion officer Air Force Acad., Colorado Springs, Colo., 1968-82; bd. dirs. W.D. Boyce council Boy Scouts Am., 1970-86, Heart of Ill. Fair and Exposition Gardens, Peoria, 1978-84; exec. bd. chmn. eagle rev. com. Boy Scouts Am., Peoria, 1977-86. Served to lt. col. USAF, 1954-82. Mem. Ill. Bar Assn., Ohio Bar Assn., Peoria Bar Assn., Assn. Trial Lawyers Am., Phi Alpha Delta. Lodges: Sertoma. Republican. Methodist. Home and Office: Apt 502 3740 Ocean Beach Blvd Cocoa Beach FL 32931-5405 Fax: 321-868-4343. E-mail: marychurch@bellsouth.net.

CHURCH, HERBERT STEPHEN, JR., retired construction company executive; b. Framingham, Mass., July 21, 1920; s. Herbert Stephen and Edith L. (Shaw) C.; m. Carol S. Orzech, Apr. 2, 1945; children: Carolyn, David, Kathryn, Patricia, Virginia. BS in Civil Engring, Northeastern U., Boston, 1943. Constrn. insp. N.Y., New Haven & Hartford R.R., 1940-43; with Turner Constrn. Co., 1943; from gen. supt. to v.p., gen. mgr. Chgo. terr., 1965-73; sr. v.p. Western region, 1974-80; sr. v.p. Central region, 1980-85. Dir., 1972-85 Trustee Nat. Commn. for Coop. Edn., 1981-90. Mem. Contractors Mut. Assn. (dir. 1974-84), Builders Assn. Chgo. (dir. 1969-74), Chgo. Club, Inverness Golf Club. Roman Catholic. Home: 811 W George St Arlington Heights IL 60005-1751

CHURCH, IRENE ZABOLY, personnel services company executive; b. Cleve., Feb. 18, 1947; d. Bela Paul and Irene (Chandas) Zaboly; children: Irene Elizabeth, Elizabeth Anne, Lauren Alexandria Gadd, John Dale Gadd II. Grad. HS. Pers. cons., recruiter, Cleve., 1965—70; CEO, pres. Oxford Pers., Pepper Pike, Ohio, 1973—89, Oxford Temporaries, Pepper Pike, Ohio, 1979—, Oxford Group Ltd., Inc., 1989—. Guest lectr. in field, 1974—; expert witness for ct. testimony, 1982—. Chpt. leader Nat. Coalition on TV Violence, 1983—; troop leader Lake Erie coun. Girl Scouts U.S., 1980—81; mem. Better Bus. Bur., 1973—82; mem. Christian action com. Federated Ch., United Ch. Christ, 1981—85, sub-com. to study violence in rels. to women, 1983, creator, presenter programs How Work Affects Family Life and Re-entering the Job Market, 1981, mem. Women's Fellowship Martha-Mary Circle, 1980—, program dir., 1982—84, 1987—; mem. The Federated Ch., United Ch. of Christ, Chagrin Falls, Ohio, program dir Mary-Martha Cir., 1982—, christian action com., 1981—85, mem. Mary-Martha Circle, Women's fellowship, 1980—. Mem.: Nat. Assn. Temp. Svcs., Internat. Platform Assn., Greater Cleve. Assn. Pers. Cons. (2nd then 1st v.p. 1974—76, chairperson bus. practices and ethics com. 1974—76, state trustee 1975—80, pres. 1976—77, bd. advisor 1977—78, chmn. nominating com. 1983—88, membership com. 1987, arbitration com. 1980, 1985—87, fundraising 1980—89, bd. dirs. 1980—89, trustee 1985—89, program chair 1987—89, Vi Pender Outstanding Svc. award 1977), Ohio Assn. Pers. Cons. (trustee 1975—80, sec. 1976—77, chairperson bus. practices and ethics com. 1976—77, 1981—82, 1st v.p., chairperson resolutions com. 1981—82, sec. 1985—87, chairperson membership com. 1985—89, trustee 1985—, 2d v.p. 1987—, pres. 1988—89, Outstanding Svc. award 1987), Nat. Assn. Pers. Cons. (mem. ethics com. 1976—77, co-chairperson ethics com. 1977—78, mem. bus. practices and ethics com. 1980—82, mem. cert. pers. cons. soc. 1980—82, regional leader for membership 1987—, cert., Pres.'s award 1988), Greater Cleve. Growth Assn. Coun. Small Enterprises, Chagrin Valley C. of C. (leader Chagrin Blvd./East chpt. 1987—, pres. bd. dirs 1990—, Pres.'s award for Outstanding Contbns. 1988), Am. Bus. Women's Assn., Euclid C. of C. (chair taskforce com. on funding in social security and vets. benefits 1981, small bus. com. 1981), Rotary (vocat. svc. chairperson, program com. 1987—, membership chairperson 1988—89). Home: 8 Ridgecrest Dr Chagrin Falls OH 44022-4218 E-mail: IreneZChurch@oxfordltd.com.

CHURCH, JANE EVELYN, executive director, counselor; b. Phila., May 5, 1930; d. Carl Roger Dillman and Elizabeth Jane Powell; m. Allen Clarke Church, June 28, 1952; children: Allen, Thomas, Kenneth, Steven. BA, U. Pa., 1952; M in Ednl. Guidance and Counseling, Xavier U., 1977. Intermediate head counselor, asst. tennis instr. Crystal Lake Camp, NY, 1948-51; social worker Hamilton County Sch. for Under Privileged Children, Scranton, Pa., 1953; founder elem. sch., Toronto, Canada, 1967; cert. coord. Carlson Learning Inst., various cities, 1978-98; founder, exec. dir. pres. One Earth One People (OEOP), Cin., 1990—2003. Lectr. in growth and personal devel. Contbr. articles to profl. jours. Founder Christmas Gift project for underprivileged children, 1968; mem. devel. com., program chair Cin./Kharkov Sister City project, 1989-91; pres. internat. study group Am. Women's Club, Brussels; drug chair Hamilton County PTA, Cin., 1974-76. Recipient Cert. of Appreciation, Cin. Pub. Schs., 1994, Excellence in Ecology award Movimento Ecologista Mexicano, Mexico City, 1995, recognition Pres. Clinton for outstanding achievement in environment protection svcs., 1997, 98, J.C. Penney Golden Rule award, 1999, 2000, Cin. Earth Coalition award, Outstanding Dedication to Caring for the Environment and its Finite Resources, Congressman Rob Portman, 2001. Mem. Delta Delta Delta. Office: One Earth One People PO Box 43144 Cincinnati OH 45243-0144 Fax: 513-561-8834.

CHURCH, JAY KAY, psychologist, educator; b. Wichita, Kans., Jan. 18, 1927; s. Kay Iverson and Gertrude (Parrish) C.; m. Dorothy Agnes Fellerhoff, May 21, 1976; children: Karen Patrice Turnbull, Caryn Annice Church Casey, Rex Warren, Max Roger. BA, Lipscomb U., 1948; MA, Ball State U., 1961; PhD, Purdue U., 1963. Chemist Auburn Rubber Corp., 1948-49; salesman Midwestern United Life Ins. Co., 1949-52; owner, operator Tour-Rest Motel, Waterloo, Ind., 1952-66; tchr., guidance dir. pub. schs., Hamilton, Ind., 1955-61; counselor Washington Twp. (Ind.) Schs., Indpls., 1961-62; asst. prof. psychology Ball State U., 1963-67, assoc. prof., 1967-71, prof., 1971-88, prof. emeritus, 1988—, chmn. dept. ednl. psychology, 1970-74, dir. advanced grad. programs in ednl. psychology, 1978-81; pvt. practice psychology, 1963—. Mem. APA. Home: 4025 W State Road 28 Ridgeville IN 47380-9068 E-mail: jkchurch@tmcsmail.com.

CHURCH, JO HALL, retired adult education educator; b. Bryan, Tex., Nov. 8, 1931; d. Dan and Inez (Etheridge) Hall; m. Donald Roussel Church, May 7, 1954; children: Lynn Church Jordan, Carol Church Wood, Donald Roussel Church Jr., John Hall Church, Joseph Cornay Church. BA, Sam Houston State U., 1953; MA, Tex. Woman's U., 1978, PhD, 1985. Tchr. Manvel (Tex.) Ind. Sch. Dist., 1953-55; substitute tchr. Mary Immaculate Sch., Dallas, 1965-70; staff and dir. writing lab. Tex. Woman's U., Denton, 1983-84, teaching fellow, 1980-84, teaching ESL Japanese, 1986, 87; asst. prof. Cameron U., Lawton, Okla., 1988; instr. North Ctrl. Tex. Coll., Corinth, 1989—2003; ret., 2003. Adj. prof. Tex. Woman's U., 1985-87, 88-89, coord. grad. student symposium in rhetoric, 1979. Organist, St. Thomas Ch., Pilot Point, Tex., 1976—. Mem. MLA, South Ctrl. MLA (sec. rhetoric sect. 1989, chmn. rhetoric sect. 1990), New Chaucer Soc., Rhetoric Soc. Am. (panel organizer 1988), Tex. Coun. Tchrs. of English, Phi Delta Gamma, Sigma Tau Delta. Roman Catholic. E-mail: jchurch@gte.net.

CHURCH, LILLIAN HAZEL See BROOKS, LILLIAN

CHURCH, MARTHA ELEANOR, retired academic administrator, scholar; b. Pitts., Nov. 17, 1930; d. Walter Seward and Eleanor (Boyer) Church. BA, Wellesley Coll., 1952; MA, U. Pitts., 1954; PhD, U. Chgo., 1960; DSc (hon.), Lake Erie Coll., 1975; LittD (hon.), Houghton Coll., 1980; LHD (hon.), Queens Coll., 1981, Ursinus Coll., 1981, St. Joseph Coll., 1982, Towson State U., 1983, Dickinson Coll., 1987, Coll. Notre Dame Md., 1995; LLD (hon.), Hood Coll., 1995; LHD (hon.), Ill. Coll., 2003. Instr. geography Mt. Holyoke Coll., South Hadley, Mass., 1953-57; lectr. geography Ind. U. Gary Ctr., 1958; instr., then asst. prof. geography Wellesley Coll., 1958—65; dean coll., prof. geography Wilson Coll., 1965-71; assoc. exec. sec. Commn. Higher Edn., Middle States Assn. Coll. and Secondary Sch., 1971-75; pres. Hood Coll., Frederick, Md., 1975-95, pres. emerita, 1995—; sr. scholar Carnegie Found. for Advancement of Tchg., Princeton, 1995—97; interim pres. Ill. Coll., 2002—03. Bd. dirs. Farmers and Mechanics Nat. Bank, 1982—2000, dir. emerita, 2000—; cons. Choice: Books for Coll. Librs.; co-chmn. nat. adv. panel Nat. Ctr. for Rsch. to Improve Postsecondary Tchg. and Learning, U. Mich., 1985—90; mem. bd. visitors Def. Intelligence Coll., 1988—91; mem. adv. bd. dirs. Automobile Club Md., 1991—2002; bd. dirs. AAA Mid-Atlantic, 1997—2002; mem. adv. bd. The Boyer Ctr. Messiah Coll., Grantham, Pa., 1997—. Author: The Spatial Organization of Electric Power Territories in Massachusetts, 1960; Co-editor: A Basic Geographical Library: A Selected and Annotated Book List for Am. Colls, 1966; cons. editor, Change mag., 1980-2001. Bd. dirs. Coun. for Internat. Exch. of Scholars, 1979-80, Japan Internat. Christian U. Found., 1977-91, Nat. Ctr. for Higher Edn. Mgmt. Sys., 1980-83; bd. dirs. Am. Coun. on Edn., 1976-79, vice chmn., 1978-79, mem. nat. identification panel, 1977-95, Nat. Rsch. Com., 1993-96; bd. advisors Fund for Improvement of Postsecondary Edn., HEW, 1976-79; mem. Sec. of Navy's Adv. Bd. on Edn. and Tng., 1976-80; chmn. Md. Commn. on Civil Rights, 1981-82; trustee Bradford Coll., Mass., 1982-87, Peddie Sch., N.J., 1982-98, chair acad. affairs com., 1987, 96-97, adv. trustee, 1998—, trustee; trustee Carnegie Found. for the Advancement of Tchg., 1986-96, vice chair, 1990-92, chair, 1992-94, immediate past chair, 1994-96; trustee Nat. Geog. Soc., 1989—, mem. com. for rsch. and exploration, 1998—, chair audit rev. com., 1993-98, chair mission, membership, medals and awards com., 2000—, mem. exec., audit and compensation coms.; trustee Nat. Geog. Soc. Edn. Found., 1989-96, 99—; chmn. bd. dirs. Medici Found., Princeton, N.J., 1985—; trustee United Bd. for Christian Higher Edn. in Asia, 1995—, sec. bd. trustees, 1998-2003, chmn. East and Intra-Asia program subcom., 1996-97, exec. com., 1998-2003; mem. Md. Humanities Coun., 1985-86, Md. Jud. Disabilities Commn., 1985-94; commr. Edn. Commn. States, Md., 1981-99; exec. com. Campus Compact: Project for Pub. and Cmty. Svc., 1986-89—; trustee Internat. Partnership for Svc. Learning, 1999-2002. Mem. AAUW, Am. Assn. Advancement of Humanities (bd. dirs. 1979-81), Am. Assn. Higher Edn. (chmn. 1980-81, bd. dirs. 1979-83), Assn. Am. Geographers, Nat. Assn. Ind. Colls. and Univs. (bd. dirs. 1983-86), Md. Ind. Colls. and Univs. Assn. (pres. 1979-81, mem. exec. com. 1988-92), Assn. Am. Colls. and Univs. (mem. adv. com. project on status and edn. of women 1980-85), Women's Coll. Coalition (mem. exec. com. 1976-80, 87-89), Am. Conf. Acad. Deans (sec., editor 1969-71), Coun. Protestant Colls. and Univs. (bd. dirs. 1969-71), Soc. Coll. and Univ. Planning (mem. editl. bd. 1979-95), Cosmos Club (mem. jour. editl. bd. 1990-94), Inst. Ednl. Leadership (bd. dirs. 1982-87), Sigma Delta Epsilon, Delta Kappa Gamma (hon.). Home: 3124 Chartwell Crescent Ln Adamstown MD 21710-9643 Fax: 301-644-1701. E-mail: marthachurch@edurostream.com.

CHURCH, RANDOLPH WARNER, JR., lawyer; b. Richmond, Va., Nov. 6, 1934; s. Randolph Warner and Elizabeth Lewis (Gochnauer) C.; m. Lucy Ann Canary, July 4, 1970; children: Leslie R. Pennell, L. Weeks Kerr. BA with honors, U. Va., 1957, LLB, 1960. Bar: Va. 1960, U.S. Dist. Ct. (ea. dist.) Va. 1962, U.S. Ct. Appeals (4th cir.) 1981, U.S. Supreme Ct. 1999. Assoc. McCandlish, Lillard & Marsh, Fairfax, Va., 1960-63; ptnr. McCandlish, Lillard & Church and successor partnerships., Fairfax, 1963-84; city atty. Fairfax, 1968-72; mng. ptnr. McCandlish, Lillard & Church and successor partnerships, Fairfax, 1975-83, Hunton & Williams, Fairfax, 1984-99, mem. exec. com., 1988-94, sr. counsel, 2000—. Bd. dirs. George Mason Bank, George Mason Bankshares, Inc., George Mason Mortgage Co., 1991-98, Va. Found. for Rsch. and Econ. Edn., Inc., 1994-2000. Author: Appellate Civil Litigation, 1984; panelist: Lawyer Professionalism: Is Change in Order? 1988, Marketing Legal Services: What's Hot and What's Not, 1990, (with others) Equity Practice and Tips on Brief Writing. Active Fairfax Com. of 100, 1988—, bd. dirs., 1989-92; bd. visitors George Mason U., Fairfax, 1982-90, rector, 1983-86, chmn. adv. bd. Coll. Arts and Scis., 1999—; bd. dirs. Fairfax Symphony, 1991-2002, gen. counsel, exec. com., 1996-2002; bd. dirs. Fairfax Symphony Orch. Found., Inc., 1999-, Va. Found. for Humanities and Pub. Policy, 1993-99, vice chmn., 1997-99; active Va. Mus. of Fine Arts Found., 2000—; pres. Fall for the Book, Inc., 2001—. Fellow Va. Law Found., Am. Bar Found.; mem. Va. Bar Assn. (v.p. 1975), Country Club Fairfax County, U. Va. Club, Phi Beta Kappa. Home: 5114 Forsgate Pl Fairfax VA 22030-4507 Office: Hunton & Williams 1751 Pinnacle Dr Ste 1700 Mc Lean VA 22102-3836

CHURCH, RICHARD DWIGHT, electrical engineer, scientist; b. Ogdensburg, N.Y., June 27, 1936; s. Dwight Perry and Carmeta Elizabeth (Walters) C.; m. Vernice Naomi Ives, Aug. 26, 1961; children: Joel, Benjamin. B of Elec. Engring., Clarkson Coll. Tech., 1963. Elec. design engr. IBM, Owego, N.Y., 1963-69; prin. engr., pres. ASL Systems, Inc., Afton, N.Y., 1969-94, chmn. bd. dirs.; sr. elec. design engr. Magnetic Labs., Inc., Apalachin, N.Y., 1980-82, power supply engring. cons., 1982—; scientist Two Forty-Eight Co., Afton, 1994—2002, Norwood, NY, 2002—. Guest lectr. Afton Sch., Clarkson U. Co-author: Career Oriented Problems for Secondary Mathematics, 1974; contbr. articles to profl. jours.; patentee in field. Treas., trustee Candor Congregational Ch., 1972-84; vice chmn. Town Planning Bd. Candor, 1975-82; rep., mem. Candor Fire Co., 1972-87; bd. dirs., treas. Candor Cmty. Club, 1970-72; initiator endowed fund for Clarkson Theatre Co., Clarkson U., 1999. With USAF, 1955-59. Recipient Dr. Carl Michel award Clarkson Coll. Tech., 1960. Mem. IEEE (sr. mem.), Assn. Energy Engrs. (sr.), Afton Bd. Fire Commrs. (fin. com. 1991-2002), Candor Coin Club (pres. 1978-81), Union of Concerned Scientists, The Cousteau Soc., N.Y. Forest Owners Assn. (dir. 2003--), Am. Soc. Dowsers, Nat. Warplane Mus. Avocations: maple syrup production, maple tree farm development, singing, pyramid geometry, bicycling. Home: 516 Obrian Rd Norwood NY 13668 Office: PO Box 248 Norwood NY 13668 E-mail: rchurch248@cs.com.

CHURCH, RUSSELL MILLER, psychology educator; b. N.Y.C., Dec. 24, 1930; s. Donald E. and Dee (Friedman) C.; m. Ruth Kutz, Apr. 4, 1954; children— Kenneth, Emily. BA, U. Mich., 1952; MA, Harvard U., 1954, PhD, 1956. Mem. faculty Brown U., 1955—, prof. psychology, 1965—, chmn. dept. psychology, 1980-83. Chair faculty exec. com. Brown U., 1995-96. Editor: (with E.E. Boe) Punishment: Issues and Experiments, 1968; editor (with B.A. Campbell) Punishment and Aversive Behavior, 1969. Fellow AAAS, Am. Psychol. Assn. (pres. div. exptl. psychology 1987-88, comparative and physiol. psychology 1991-92); mem. Ea. Psychol. Assn. (pres. 1991-92). Office: Brown U Dept of Psychology 89 Waterman St Providence RI 02912-9079 E-mail: Russell_Church@Brown.edu.

CHURCH-GAULTIER, LORENE KEMMERER, retired government official; b. Jordan, Mont., Oct. 18, 1929; d. Harry F. and Laura (Stoller) Kemmerer; m. Scott Johnston, Sept. 8, 1948 (div. 1953); children: Linda M., Theodore O.; m. Fred C. Church, May 9, 1956 (dec. 1967); children: Ned B., Nia J.; m. Charles F. Gaultier, Oct. 1996 (dec. Jan. 2000). Student, Portland Community Coll., 1973-76, Portland State U., 1978-79. Sec. intelligence div. IRS, Portland, Oreg., 1973-75; trade asst. Internat. Trade Adminstrn., U.S. Dept. Commerce, Portland, 1975-84, internat. trade specialist, 1984-94; ret., 1995. Mem. NAFE, World Affairs Coun., N.W. China Coun., Portland C. of C. (Europe 1992 com. 1988-89, internat. trade adv. bd. 1988-89, treas. dist. export coun. 1996—), Western Internat. Trade Coun. Democrat. Roman Catholic. Avocations: music, growing roses. Home: 19725 SW Pike St Beaverton OR 97007-1446 Office: US Dept Commerce US&FCS 121 SW Salmon St Portland OR 97204-2901

CHURCHILL, JAMES ALLEN, lawyer; b. Kingsport, Tenn., Sept. 13, 1935; s. Robert Lang and Jamie Louise (Hill) C.; m. Jackeen Kelleher, Aug. 9, 1958; children: James Allen Jr., Courtney Bartlett. AB, Princeton U., 1957; LLB, Harvard U., 1960; M in Civil Law, Tulane U., 1963. Bar: La. 1961, U.S. Dist. Ct. (ea. dist.) La. 1962, U.S. Ct. Appeals (5th cir.) 1965, Calif. 1989. Ptnr. Lemle, Kelleher, Kohlmeyer & Matthews, New Orleans, 1960-79; dir. Barham & Churchill, New Orleans, 1979-88; ptnr. Pillsbury Madison & Sutro, L.A. and Tokyo, 1988-95; sr. v.p., gen. counsel., corp. sec. Ventura Foods, LLC, City of Industry, Calif., 1995—. Mem. ABA, Am. Law Inst., Calif. Bar Assn., La. Bar Assn., Calif. Club (L.A.), Boston Club (New Orleans), Annandale Golf Club. Office: Ventura Foods LLC 14840 Don Julian Rd City Of Industry CA 91746-3109

CHURCHILL, JAMES GARTON, retired international finance consultant; b. Bklyn., July 16, 1930; s. S. Garton and Mary Ellen (Peck) C.; m. Nancy Barrett Wickers, July 31, 1954 (dec. Jan. 1997); children: Glenn Garton, Bruce Barrett, Ellen Wickers; m. Ruth Mathews Leiter, Mar. 24, 2001. BA, Dartmouth Coll., 1952; MBA, Harvard U., 1954. Fin. analyst Mobil Oil Corp., N.Y.C., 1958-62; treas. Mobil Inner Europe, Geneva, 1962-65, Mobil Europe, London, 1965-68; fin. dir. Mobil Sekiyu, Tokyo, 1968-70; treas. internat. ops. Kaiser Aluminum & Chem. Corp., Oakland, Calif., 1970-81, treas., 1981-87; pvt. practice fin. cons.

San Francisco, 1987-90. Served to lt. USNR, 1954-57. Avocations: history and french language study, reading. Home and Office: 2001 Grassy Ln Woodstock VT 05091-8053 Home (Winter): 6333 Kennett Pl Mission KS 66202

CHURCHILL, JOHN HUGH, college academic administrator; b. Hector, Ark., Apr. 1, 1949; s. Olen Raymond and Mary Josephine (Cheek) C.; m. Jean Ann Hill, Aug. 19, 1972; children: William Houston, Mary Katherine Salisbury, Hugh Olen Hill. BA, Rhodes Coll., 1971; BA, MA, Oxford (Eng.) U., 1973; MA, MPh, PhD, Yale U., 1978. Asst. prof. philosophy Hendrix Coll., Conway, Ark., 1977-82, assoc. prof., 1982-92, prof., 1992—, dean of students, 1983-84, v.p. for acad. affairs and dean of the coll., 1984—2001. Asst. Am. sec. The Rhodes Scholarship Trust, Middletown, Conn., 1974-77. Contbr. numerous articles to profl. jours. Mem. Rhodes Scholarship Com. Gulf Dist, 1977—, sec. Ark., 1980—. Recipient Rhodes scholarship Rhodes Trust, Oxford, Eng., 1971, NCAA Postgrad. scholarship, 1971. Mem. Soc. for Philosophy of Religion, Phi Beta Kappa (sec. 2001—), Omicron Delta Kappa. Democrat. Avocations: reading history, fiction, biography, and poetry, walking, cooking, canoeing. Office: 1606 New Hampshire Ave NW Washington DC 20009 Home: Apt 214 3133 Connecticut Ave NW Washington DC 20008-5104

CHURCHILL, JOSEPH LACY, lawyer; b. Roanoke, Va., Oct. 31, 1944; s. Robert Carr and Barbara (Key) c.; m. Phyllis Brennaman, Dec. 19, 1965; children: Lacy, Vance, Tyree, Nicole, Carr. BA, U. N.C., 1966; LLB, Washington and Lee U., 1969; LLM, Harvard U., 1970. Bar: Va. 1969, Ga. 1972. Ptnr. Morris & Churchill, Atlanta, 1977-82, Porter, Davis, Saunders & Churchill, Atlanta, 1982-83, Asbill, Porter, Churchill & Nellis, Atlanta, 1983-86, Churchill & Ferguson, Atlanta, 1986—; pvt. practice Atlanta, 1992—. Bd. dirs. Alo-Scherer Healthcare, Boca Raton, Fla., Behr Indsl. Equipment, Inc., Detroit and Stuttgart, Fed. Republic of Germany, Otto Wolff'sche Verwaltungs-GmbH, Germany. Author: (with others) Kapitalanlagen in den USA, 1987. Mem. Va. Bar Assn., Ga. Bar Assn., Richmond Bar Assn., Atlanta Bar Assn., Lawyers Club Atlanta, Ansley Golf Club, World Trade Club. Avocations: swimming, tennis, running. Home and Office: 205 N Chambord Dr NW Atlanta GA 30327-4588

CHURCHILL, LARRY RAYMOND, ethics educator; b. Russellville, Ark., June 24, 1945; s. Olen Raymond and Mary Josephine (Cheek) C.; m. Sandra Wade; children: Shelley, Blair Naylor. BA, Rhodes Coll., 1967; MDiv, Duke U., 1970, PhD, 1973. Asst. prof. U. N.C., Chapel Hill, 1976-82, assoc. prof., 1982-88, prof., 1988—, chmn. dept. social medicine, 1988-98; Ann Geddes Stahlman prof. med. ethics Vanderbilt U., Nashville, 2002. Cons. med. schs. and orgns. in bioethics, 1976—. Author: Rationing Health Care in America, 1987; co-author: Professional Ethics of Primary Care, 1986, The Physician As Captain of the Ship, 1988, Self-Interest and Universal Health Care, 1994, The Social Medicine Reader, 1997; co-editor: Ethical Dimensions of Health Policy, 2002. Charles E. Culpeper scholar in med. humanities, 1991-94. Fellow: The Hastings Ctr.; mem.: The Hume Soc., Inst. of Medicine, Soc. for Health and Human Values (pres. 1980—81). Office: Vanderbilt U 319 Oxford House Nashville TN 37232-4350

CHURCHILL, MALCOLM HUGHES, retired diplomat, financial analyst; b. Cedar Rapids, Iowa, Sept. 29, 1937; s. Irving Lester and Kathryn Margaret (Hughes) Churchill; m. Bernardita Abueg Reyes, Dec. 22, 1962; children: Paul Reyes, Cristina Reyes. Student, Silliman U., Dumaguete, The Philippines, 1955—56; BA in Internat. Rels. cum laude, Dartmouth Coll., 1960; postgrad., Cornell U., 1960—61; MA in Econs., George Washington U., 1972. Fgn. svc. officer U.S. Dept. State, Washington, 1961—87; editor, owner The Insiders' Way, Washington, 1986—; resource person on Australia, New Zealand and the Philippines Lloyd Thomas & Ball, Inc., Washington, 1987—; analyst on Australia and New Zealand BERI, Inc., Washington, 1992—99. Treas. Philippine-Am. Edn. Found., Manila, 1973—76. Author: A Family Odyssey, Churchills the Ct, 1999; contbr. articles to profl. jours. Pres. Dartmouth Coll. Club Philippines, Manila, 1974—76, Manila Boat Club, 1975—76; pres., treas., bd. mem. Philippines Arts, Letters & Media Coun., Washington, 1993—2000. Mem.: Am. Fgn. Svc. Assn., Assn. for Asian Studies, Nat. Economists Club, Phi Beta Kappa. Avocations: rowing, cycling, hiking, history, genealogy. Home: 4715 47th St NW Washington DC 20016 Office: The Insiders Way 4715 47th St NW Washington DC 20016

CHURCHILL, ROBERT WILSON, state legislator, lawyer; b. Waukegan, Ill., Apr. 10, 1947; s. George Oliver and Helga C. (Carlson) Churchill; children: Abigail Lee, Julia Aubrey, Christine Lizbeth. BA, Northwestern U., Evanston, Ill., 1969; JD, U. Iowa, 1972. Elected del. Rep. Nat. Conv., 1980, 92, 96, alt. del., 1984; trustee Lake Villa (Ill.) Township, 1981-83; mem. Ill. Ho. Reps., 1983-99, 2003—; minority whip Ill. Gen. Assembly, 1987-89, asst. minority leader, 1989-91, dep. minority leader, 1991-94, 97-99; majority leader, 1995-97; chmn. Rep. Ctrl. Com. for Lake County, Ill., 1990-94. Co-chmn. Ill. Econ. and Fiscal Commn., Springfield, 1991-95, Space Needs Commn., 1997-99; mem. Ill. Prisoner Review Bd., 1999-2001; chief counsel, dir. legis. Ill. Ho. Reps., 2001-02. Mem. ABA, Lake County Bar Assn., Ducks Unlimited, Lake Villa Lions. Republican.

CHURCHILL, STEVEN WAYNE, former state legislator, marketing professional; b. Akron, Ohio, May 8, 1963; s. Wayne Stevenson and Carol Sue (Gurney) C. BA, Iowa State U., 1985. Fin. asst. The Governor Branstad Com., Des Moines, 1986, fin. dir., 1988-90; mktg. mgr. Iowa Dept. Econ. Devel., Des Moines, 1987; devel. officer Simpson Coll., Indianola, Iowa, 1990-93; fund-raising cons. The Churchill Group, Johnston, Iowa, 1993-97; v.p. mktg. Mid-Am. Group, West Des Moines, Iowa, 1997—. State Rep., Johnston, Iowa, 1993-99; commr. Iowa Civil Rights Commn., Des Moines, 1991-92; deacon Plymouth Congl. Ch., 1988-91, 96-99; admissions amb. Iowa State U., 1990-92; mem. Greater Des Moines Leadership Inst., 1998-99; chmn. Chef's Auction Dinner, March of Dimes, 1999. Recipient Comdr.'s Award for Pub. Svc., Dept. of the Army, 1991; named one of 10 Outstanding Young Iowans, Iowa Jaycees, 1995, one of Forty under 40 Ctrl. Iowans for Profl. Accomplishments and Cmty. Involvement Des Moines Bus. Record, 2000. Mem. Bull Moose Club (pres. 1990-91), Rotary of Des Moines (pres. 1991-92, team leader group study exch. to The Netherlands 2000), Sigma Alpha Epsilon (pres. 1989-90, Order of the Lion 1990, 96, 99, Merit Key award 2000, chmn. Robert D. Ray scholarship golf benefit 2002), vol. mentor Big Brothers, Big Sisters. Avocations: history, travel, stand-up comedy. Home: 6140 Nottingham Johnston IA 50131-8713 Office: Mid-Am Group 4700 Westown Pkwy Ste 303 West Des Moines IA 50266-6718 E-mail: swc@midamericagroup.com.

CHURCHILL, STUART WINSTON, chemical engineering educator; b. Imlay City, Mich., June 13, 1920; s. Howard Heenan and Faye Erma (Shurte) C.; m. Donna Belle Lewis, Feb. 22, 1946 (div.); children: Stuart Lewis, Diana Gail, Cathy Marie, Emily Elizabeth; m. Renate Ursula Treibmann, Aug. 3, 1974. BS in Math, BSChemE, U. Mich., 1942, MS, 1948, PhD, 1952; MA (hon.), U. Pa., 1972. Technologist Shell Oil Co., 1942-46; tech. supr. Frontier Chem. Co., 1946-47; mem. faculty U. Mich., 1949-67, prof. chem. engring., 1957-67, chmn. dept. chem. and metall. engring., 1962-67; mem. faculty U. Pa., 1967—, Carl V.S. Patterson prof. chem. engring., 1967-90, Carl V.S. Patterson prof. emeritus, 1990—; chmn. region 2 edn. and accreditation com. Engrs. Council Profl. Devel., 1961-65, mem. nat. council. 1965-71, exec. com., 1968-71; mem. bd. trustees Chemical Heritage Found., 1983-99, mem. bd. dirs., 1999-2001, mem. fin. com., 1987-2001. Cons. heat transfer and combustion. Recipient S. Reid Warren, Jr. award for disting. tchg. U. Pa., 1976, Max Jakob Meml. award for heat transfer ASME/Am. Inst. Chem. Engrs., 1979, medal for disting. achievement U. Pa., 1993, Alumni Merit award U. MIch., 2002; Japan Soc. for Promotion of Sci. grantee, 1977. Fellow AIChE (nat. coun. 1962-64, pres. 1966, Profl. Progress award 1964, William H. Walker award 1969, Warren K. Lewis award 1978, Founders award 1980, eminent chmn. engr. Diamond Jubilee 1983, heat transfer and energy conversion divsn. award 1997, inst. lectr. 1998); mem. Nat. Acad. Engring. (Founders award 2002), Combustion Inst., Am. Chem. Soc., Am. Soc. for Engring. Edn. (Corcoran award for best paper 1993), Verein Deutscher Ingenieure (corr. mem.), Sigma Xi, Phi Kappa Phi, Phi Lambda Upsilon (award U. Mich. chpt. 1961), Tau Beta Pi. Unitarian Universalist. Home: 137 Pole Cat Rd Glen Mills PA 19342-1301

CHURCHILL, THOMAS JOHN, broadcast meteorologist; b. Dubuque, Iowa, Mar. 4, 1961; s. John Victor and Thoma Margaret (Grutz) C.; m. Rita Lucia Daniels, Apr. 25, 1987; 1 child, Georan Thomas Churchill. Meteorologist Sta. WDBQ, Dubuque, 1974-76, Teleprompter, Dubuque, 1976-79, Sta. KLXL-FM, Dubuque, 1979-81, Stas. WDBQ/KIWI-FM, Dubuque, 1981-82; meteorologist, pres. No. Data Group, Inc., Dubuque, 1982-87; chief meteorologist Athena Svcs. Group, Inc., Dubuque, 1987-91; pres. Weatheradio, Dubuque, 1992-2000; ret., 2000. Tech. cons. AccuWeather, State College, Pa., 1998-2000; guest meteorologist Sta. KRON-TV, San Francisco, July 1975, Tomorrow Show on NBC-TV, N.Y.C., Aug. 1976, Good Morning Am. on ABC-TV, N.Y.C., Sept. 1978; cons. in field. Inventor digital weatherman, weather automation system. Commr. Dubuque Cable Regulatory Commn., 1983; co-founder, spokesperson Citizens United for Respect Equality, Dubuque; voting mem. Dubuque County Rep. Ctrl. Com. Mem. Am. Meteorol. Soc. Republican. Roman Catholic. Avocations: electronics, politics. Office: Weatheradio Box 1400 Dubuque IA 52004-1400

CHURCHILL, WILLIAM DELEE, retired education educator, psychologist; b. Buffalo, Nov. 4, 1919; s. Glenn Luman and Ethel (Smith) C. AB, Colgate U., 1941; MEd, Alfred U., 1951; EdD, U. Rochester, 1969. m. Beulah Coleman, Apr. 5, 1943; children: Cherylee, Christie. Tchr. secondary sci., Canaseraga, N.Y., 1947-56; dir. guidance Alfred-Almond Sch., Almond, N.Y., 1956-63; grad. asst. U. Rochester, 1963-65; asst. prof. psychology Alfred (N.Y.) U., 1965-66; assoc. prof. edn. Ariz. State U., Tempe, 1966-86. Author: Career Survey of Graduates, 1973. Served with U.S. Army Air Corps 1942-46, USAF Res. 1946-79, ret. lt. col. Mem. Ariz. Psychol. Assn. Home: 11454 N 85th St Scottsdale AZ 85260-5727

CHURCHMAN, MICHAEL STEELE BRIGHT, educational consultant, educator; b. Indpls., Mar. 9, 1929; s. M. Steele and Luita Curtis Churchman; m. Jean Virginia Wood, Apr. 28, 1951; children: Jean Wood, Julia Churchman McCue, Diana Churchman Mason. BA, Wesleyan U, 1950; MA, U Mo., 1958; EdM, Harvard U, 1964. Tchr. The Barstow Sch., Kans. City, Mo., 1955—64; headmaster The Kent Sch., Denver, 1964—74, St. Catherine's, Richmond, Va., 1974—79; dir. external affairs The Nelson-Atkins Mus. of Art, Kans. City, Mo., 1985—96, cons., 1996—. Trustee The Barstow Sch., Kans. City, Mo., 1999—, St. Paul's Eiscopal Sch., Kans. City, Mo., 1994—2000, Episcopal Social Svcs., Kans. City, Mo., 2000—. Author: The Kent Sch. 1922-1972, 1972, High Ideals and Aspirations: The Nelson-Atkins Museum of Art, 1993. Capital campaign co-chair Mainstream Coalition, Shawnee Mission, Kans. 2001. Democrat. Episcopalian. Office: The Nelson Gallery Found 4525 Oak St Kansas City MO 64111

CHURCHVILLE, LIDA HOLLAND, librarian; b. Dallas, May 5, 1933; d. Norbert R. and Agnes J. (Buckley) Holland; m. Joseph J. Churchville, Oct. 6, 1952 (dec. 1974); children: Lisa, Zoe, Anthony (dec.), Stephen. BA in History, Russell Sage Coll., Troy, N.Y., 1965; MLS, SUNY, Albany, 1967. Libr. Office Legis. Rsch., N.Y. Senate, Albany, 1967-75; chief law libr. U.S. Army Libr., Washington, 1975-78; coord. fed. women's program Dept. Def., The Pentagon, 1976-78; chief libr. Nat. Archives and Records Svcs., 1978-81; reference and spl. project libr. Nat. Archives Libr., 1981-83; spl. project libr. publs. unit Nat. Archives Trust Fund, 1983—, info. specialist Patent & Trademark Office, 1989. With Archives Libr. Info. Ctr., Nat. Archives, 1989-93, chief libr., 1993-95, br. chief Archives Info. Ctr., 1999—. Mem. Women's Issues Task Force, 1981-83, Women's Nat. Dem. Club, 1981-92, Eleanor Roosevelt Dem. Club, Greenbelt, Md.; mem. Paint Branch Unitarian Ch., Adelphi, Md., sec. to bd. trustees, 1991-93; docent Greenbelt Mus., 1988-2000; active Bd. of Elections, Greenbelt, 1993-2000; vol. Arena Stage; active mem. FEDLINK Libr. of Congress, 1994-98; sec. Fed. Lib. Info. coun. com., 1994-96. Recipient Outstanding Performance award The Pentagon, 1977. Mem.: Nat. Archives Assembly, D.C. Libr. Assn. (program com. 1993). Office: Archives Libr Info Ctr Rm 2380 8601 Adelphi Rd College Park MD 20740-6002 Address: 907 6th St SW Apt 601 Washington DC 20024-3830 E-mail: lida.churchville@verizon.net.

CHURCHWELL, EDWARD BRUCE, astronomer, educator; b. Sylva, NC, July 9, 1940; s. Doris L. Churchwell; m. Dorothy S. Churchwell, June 24, 1964; children: Steven T., Beth M. BS, Earlham Coll., 1963; PhD, Ind. U., 1970. NASA fellow Ind. U., Bloomington, 1963; postdoctoral fellow Nat. Radio Astronomy Obs., Charlottesville, Va., 1970; Heinrich Hertz postdoctoral fellow Max Planck Inst. Radioastronomie, Bonn, Germany, 1970-72, staff scientist, 1972-77; asst. prof. U. Wis., Madison, 1977-79, assoc. prof., 1979-83, prof., 1983—, Alfred E. Whitford prof. astronomy, 2002—. Fellow NASA, 1985, Fulbright Rsch., 1988—89. Mem.: Union Concerned Scientists, Internat. Astron. Union, Am. Astron. Soc. Office: U Wis Washburn Observatory 475 N Charter St Madison WI 53706-1582

CHURGIN, AMY, publishing executive; Assoc. pub. Seventeen Mag., 1992—94; Pub. K III Mag. Corp. (now Primedia Corp.--N.Y. Mag.), N.Y.C., 1994—99; group pub., N.Y., Chgo. Automobile Mag., 1999; Pub. Archtl. Digest, Condé Nast, L.A., 1999—. Office: Architectural Digest Condé Nast 6300 Wilshire Blvd Ste 1100 Los Angeles CA 90048-9083

CHURGIN, MICHAEL JAY, law educator, educator; b. N.Y.C., Feb. 25, 1948; s. Raphael B. and Sylvia (Nussbaum) C. AB magna cum laude, Brown U., Providence, 1970; JD, Yale U., 1973. Bar: Conn. 1974, Tex. 1975. Supervising atty., teaching fellow Yale Law Sch., New Haven, 1973-75; asst. prof. U. Tex. Sch. Law, Austin, 1975-79, assoc. prof., 1979-81, prof., 1981-90, Raybourne Thompson prof., 1990—. Mem. adv. bd. Advocacy, Inc., Austin, 1985-90; vis. fellow Clare Hall, Cambridge, Eng., 1996; vis. fellow Wolfson Coll., Cambridge, Eng., 1992; Quatercentenary vis. fellow Emmanuel Coll., Cambridge, 2000. Co-author: Toward a Just and Effective Sentencing System, 1977; author: (monograph) Analysis of the Texas Mental Health Code, 1988, 2d edit., 1994; contbr. articles to profl. jours. Mem. pub. responsibility com. Austin Travis County MHMR, 1979-85; bd. dirs. Tex. Hillel, Austin. Fellow W.K. Kellogg Nat. Found., 1980-83. Mem. ABA (bar admissions com. 1998—), Am. Soc. for Legal History (chair com. 1987—), Phi Beta Kappa. Jewish. Home: 4006 N Hills Dr Austin TX 78731 Office: U Tex Sch Law 727 E Dean Keeton Austin TX 78705-3224

CHUTE, ALAN DALE, lawyer; b. International Falls, Minn. s. Lester Robert and Florence Adele (Jensen) C.; m. Sharon Marie McHenry, June 9, 1979; children: Andrew Alan, Anthony Lee, Alan Joseph. BS, U.S. Mil. Acad., 1977; JD, U. Minn., 1982; LLM, Judge Advocate Gen.'s Sch., Charlottesville, Va., 1987. Bar: Pa., Minn., U.S. Ct. Mil. Appeals, Army Ct. Mil. Rev., U.S. Ct. Appeals (3d, 9th cir.), U.S. Dist. Ct. (we. dist.) Pa. Commd. 2d lt. U.S. Army, 1977, advanced through grades to col., 2001, signal officer, 1977-79; claims judge adv. Office of Staff Judge Adv., Ft. Lewis, Wash., 1982-83, prosecutor, 1983-85; atty. U.S. Army Trial Def. Service, Ft. Lewis, Wash., 1985-86, sr. def. counsel 2d inf. div., 1987-88; staff and faculty Judge Advocate Gen.'s Sch., Charlottesville, 1988—; with Jones, Day, Reavis & Pogue, Pitts., 1990—. Editor-in-chief U. Minn. Law Rev., 1981-82. Col. USAR. Mem. ABA, Pa. Bar Assn., Allegheny County Bar Assn. Lodges: KC. Roman Catholic. Home: 2595 Rossmoor Dr Pittsburgh PA 15241-2581 Address: Jones Day Reavis & Pogue 500 Grant St Pittsburgh PA 15219-2502

CHUTE, CHRISTOPHER GREGORY, medical educator; b. Hartford, Conn., July 8, 1955; s. Christopher Edward and Dorothy Marie Chute; m. Jeanne L. Nevin, Feb. 4, 2001; m. Diana E. Chan, May 30, 1982 (div. Jan. 18, 2001); children: Jessica Alexandra, Ian David. AB, Brown U., 1977, MD, 1982; MPH, Harvard U., 1982, PhD, 1990. Diplomate Am. Bd. Internal Medicine, Nat. Bd. Med. Examiners. Dir. undergrad. computer consulting group Brown U., Providence, 1975—77; programmer-analyst divsn. labs. R.I. Dept. Health, Providence, 1975—81; H.S. tchr. Rongai (Kenya) Secondary Sch., 1977—78; resident internal medicine Dartmouth-Hitchcock Med. Ctr., Hanover, NH, 1982—85; physician Dartmouth Coll. Student Health Svcs., Hanover, 1983—85; clin. instr. Dartmouth Med. Sch., Hanover, 1985—87; physician Matthew Thornton Health Plan, Nashua, NH, 1985—88; project dir., health profls. follow-up study Harvard Sch. Pub. Health, Boston, 1985—88; adj. asst. prof. health scis. Boston U., Sargent Coll., 1986—87; asst. prof. epidemiology Mayo Med. Sch., Rochester, Minn., 1988—93; acting head sect. med. info. resources Mayo Clinic, Rochester, Minn., 1989—91, head sect. med. info. resources, 1991—2001; assoc. prof. epidemiology Mayo Med. Sch., Rochester, Minn., 1993—, prof. med. informatics, 1998—; prof., chair divsn. med. informatics Mayo Clinic, Rochester, Minn., 2002—. Vice-chair ANSI Health Informatics Standards Bd., New York, NY, 1999—2001, voting mem., 1995—, Helath Info. Systems Planning Panel, Am. Nat. Standards Inst. (ANSI), New York, NY, 1991—95; chair Internation Med. Informatics Assn., Working Group 6 on Med. Concept Representation, Geneva, 1994—; co-chair Computer-based Patient Records Inst., Working Group on Codes and Vocabulary, Washington, 1993—97; mem., pub. policy com. Am. Med. Informatics Assn., Bethesda, Md., 1995—, chair, by-laws com., 2002—, bd. mem., 1998—2001; program chair, nat. summit on clin. terminology Computer-based Patient Records Inst., Working Group on Codes and Vocabulary, Washington, 1997; program chair, ann. symposium Am. Med. Informatics Assn., Bethesda, Md., 1998, mem., program com., ann. symposium, 1994—98; bd. mem. Computer-based Med. Records Inst., Washington, 1997—99; exec. bd. mem. Computer-based Patient Records Inst., Working Group on Codes and Vocabulary, Washington, 1998—99; mem., long-range planning info. policy task force Nat. Cancer Inst., Bethesda, Md., 1998—2000; vice-chair ISO Tech. Com. 215, Working Group 3 on Health Concept Representation, Geneva, 1998—2000, chair, 2000—; program chair, nat. conf. on terminolgoy, part ii Computer-based Patient Records Inst., Working Group on Codes and Vocabulary, Washington, 1999; co-chair, terminology com. Health Level 7 (HL7), Ann Arbor, Mich., 2001—; program chair, trienial symposium Internation Med. Informatics Assn., Working Group 6 on Health Concept Representation, Ponte Vedra, Fla., 1997, Phoenix, 2000; mem., med. informatics study sect. NIH, Bethesda, Md., 1998—. Treas. Rochester (Minn.) Rowing Club, 1997. Recipient Nat. Rsch. Svc. award, NIH, 1985—88, Best Theoretical Paper award, Am. Med. Informatics Assn., 1993, 1994, Homar Warner award for most outstanding contbn., 1998; fellow Arnold Fellowship for Rsch. Travel Abroad, Brown U., 1980, Charles H. Smith fellow, Harvard U., 1981; scholar Nat. Health Svc. scholar, U.S. Dept HHS, 1978—82. Fellow: ACP, Am. Coll. Med. Informatics; mem.: Am. Coll. Epidemiology. Avocations: rowing, bicycling. Home: 710 9th Ave SW Rochester MN 55902 Office: Mayo Clinic 200 First St SW Rochester MN 55905 Office Fax: 507-284-0360. E-mail: chute@mayo.edu.

CHUTE, HAROLD LEROY, veterinary pathologist, former chemical company executive; b. Winnipeg, Man., Can., Sept. 4, 1921; came to U.S., 1949; naturalized, 1955; s. Kenneth Karl and Hilda Mae (Stoddart) C.; m. Marion B. Baker, Aug. 9, 1947; children: Pamela D., Hazel Lee., Cameron C. Student, N.S. Agrl. Coll., 1942-44, hon. assoc., 1976; DVM, Ont. Vet. Coll., U. Guelph, 1949; MS, Ohio State U., 1953; DVSc, U. Toronto, 1955; LLD (hon.), Dalhousie U., 1998. Poultry pathologist U. Maine, Orono, 1950-80, prof., 1949-76; treas., dir. MeBio Labs Inc., 1958-66; dir. pullorum typhoid testing U. Maine, Orono, 1958-68, dir. devel., 1967-76; pres. Chute Chem. Co., Bangor, Maine, 1977-95. Bd. dirs. Blue Cross Blue Shield, Maine, 1988-99, dir. Key Bank of Eastern Maine. Contbr. over 200 articles to profl. jours. Mem. cmty. rels. Coun. of Job Corps; mem. EMTEC, 1990—; dir. Machigonne Agy.,; pres., CEO Margaret Villa Inc.; bd. dirs. U. Maine Found.; trustee Grand Lodge Charity Fund, 1969—; mem. Orono Town Coun., 1963-72; pres. Pine Tree 4-H Found., 1986-93; mem., trustee, deacon Ch. Univ. Fellowship, U. Maine. Mem. Am. Assn. Avian Pathologists (past pres.), Am. Assn. Vet. Lab. Diagnosticians (past pres., Pope award 1990), AVMA (del. 1978-2000), Maine Vet. Med. Assn. (past pres.), Shriners (potentate Anah Shrine Temple, Bangor 1981), Order of DeMolay (exec. officer Maine 1971-80, grand master grand lodge of Maine 1968-70), Mason (33 degree). Republican. Home: 432 Main St Orono ME 04473-3435

CHU-ZHU, JANICE GAIL, social worker; b. NYC, Aug. 13, 1958; d. Lamtin Adam and Jane Yuk (Leung) C.; m. Xiang Zhu, May 29, 1994. BA, Binghamton State U., 1981; MSW, Fordham U., 1990. Cert. social worker, N.Y. Tchr. English Berlitz Sch. of Languages, Madrid, 1980-82, Leo Burnett, S.A., Madrid, 1982-84; caseworker-foster care Sheltering Arms Children's Svc., NYC, 1984-87; social worker-family ct.- PINS mediation & diversion Children's Aid Soc., NYC, 1987-89, social worker-foster care, 1989-91; pluralism strategy cons. Girl Scouts USA, NYC, 1991-95, quality recognition specialist, 1995-98, mgr., 1998-2001; tech. assistance specialist, cons. cmty. sch. Children's Aid Soc. Nat. Tech. Assistance Ctr., NYC, 2001—. Bd. dirs. Fordham U. Grad. Sch. Svc. Alumni Bd., N.Y.C., 1990-94. Mem. Nat. Assn. Social Workers. Democrat. Roman Catholic. Avocations: travel, reading, swimming, bowling. Home: 19 Liberty St Ossining NY 10562-5924 Office: Children's Aid Soc Nat Tech Assistance Ctr 4600 Broadway New York NY 10040- Fax: 212-544-7609. E-mail: janicec@childrensaidsociety.org.

CHWAST, SEYMOUR, graphic artist; b. N.Y.C., Aug. 18, 1931; Student, Cooper Union Sch., N.Y.C.; PhD (hon.), Parsons Sch. Design, 1992. Co-founder Push Pin Studios, 1954; dir., pres. The Pushpin Group Inc. Instr. Parsons Sch. of Design. One-man exhbns. include Royal Palm Gallery, Palm Beach, Fla., 1982, Galerie Delpire, Paris, 1974, Gutenburg Mus., Mainz, Germany, 1984, 35 yr. retrospective exhibition Cooper Union, 1986, Jack Gallery, N.Y., 1987, Mus. of Art, Sao Paulo, Brazil, 1989, Lustrare Gallery, N.Y., 1991, Ginza Graphic Gallery, Tokyo, 1992, Kunstschalter Gallery, N.Y.C., 1994, Sch. of Visual Arts Master Series, 1997, Warsaw Poster Mus., 2000; various group shows; work in permanent collections Mus. Modern Art, N.Y.C., Library of Congress, Washington, Met. Mus. Art, N.Y.C., Whitney Mus. Am. Art, N.Y. Recipient numerous awards including Saint-Gaudens medal, 1972; named to Art Dir.'s Hall of Fame, 1984. Mem. Am. Inst. Graphic Artists (former v.p., medal 1986), Art Dirs.' Club (v.p.), Alliance Graphique Internationale. Office: Pushpin Group 55 E 9th St New York NY 10003-3111 E-mail: seymour@pushpininc.com.

CHWATSKY, ANN, photographer, educator; b. Phila., Jan. 11, 1942; BS in Art Edn., Hofstra U., 1965, MS, 1971; postgrad., L.I. U., 1973-74. Cert. tchr. Photography editor L.I. Mag., 1976-80; instr. Internat. Ctr. Photography, N.Y.C., 1979-80, Parrish Art Mus., Southampton, N.Y., 1984—. Mem. art faculty NYU, 1991—. Author, photographer: The Man in the Street, 1989, photographer The Four Seasons of Shaker life; photographs featured in Time, Newsweek, Newsday, Manchete, N.Y. Times, MD Med. Times; one person shows include Lincoln Ctr., Buenos Aires, 1983, Photographers Gallery, London, 1985, shakers, Nassau County Mus. Fine Arts, 1987, Greater Lafayette (Ind.) Mus. Art, 1988, Bklyn. Coll., 1990, Kiev, USSR Exhbn. Hall, 1991, Bklyn. Coll., Carrie Haddad Gallery, Hudson, N.Y., 2001; group shows include The Other, Houston Ctr. Photography, 1988, L.I. Fine Arts Mus., 1984, Women's Interart Ctr., N.Y.C., 1976, 80, Parrish Art Mus., Southampton, 1979, Internat. Ctr. Photography, N.Y.C., 1980, 82, Nassau County Mus. Fine Arts, 1983, Soho 20 Gallery, N.Y.C., 1984, New Orleans World's Fair, 1984, Southampton Gallery, 1988, 89, Lizan Tops Gallery, L.I., 1994, Apex Art, N.Y.C., 1995, Am. Mus., Prague, 1997, First Seoul Internat. Tribunal, 1998; represented in permanent collections Forbes N.Y.C., Midtown YWCA, Nassau County Mus. Fine Arts, Susan Rothenberg, others. Recipient Estabrook Disting. Alumni award Hofstra U., 1984; Kodak Profl. Photographers award, 1984; Eastman Found. grantee, 1981-82, Poloroid grantee, 1980. Mem. Assn. Am. Mag. Profls., Picture Profls. Am., Profl. Women Photographers N.Y.C. Studio: 29 E 22nd St Apt 3N New York NY 10010-5305

CHYNOWETH, ALAN GERALD, retired telecommunications research executive, consultant; b. Harrow, Eng., Nov. 18, 1927; came to U.S. 1952; s. James Charles and Marjorie (Fairhurst) C.; m. Betty Freda Edith Boyce, Sept. 22, 1950; children: Trevor Alan, Kevin Ray. BS in physics, U. London Kings Coll., 1948, PhD, 1950. Demonstrator U. London Kings Coll., 1948-50; postdoctoral fellow NRC, Ottawa, 1950-52; mem. tech. staff Bell Labs., Murray Hill, N.J., 1953-60, dept. head, 1960-65, dir., 1965-76, exec. dir., 1976-83; v.p. applied rsch. Bellcore, Morristown, N.J., 1984-92; cons. R/D Strategy and Mgmt., 1993—. Mem. vis. com. Cornell U. Materials Sci. Ctr., 1973-76; cons. advanced study inst. and rsch. workshops com. NATO, Brussels, 1982-90; lectr. Electrochem. Soc., 1983; alt. dir. Microelectronics and Computer Tech. Corp., Austin, Tex., 1984-92; mem. The Conf. Bd. Internat. Coun. on Mgmt. of Innovation and Tech., 1990-97, mgr., 1995; dir. Optoelectronic Industry Devel. Assn., 1991-92; mem. adv. bd. dept. elec. engring. and computer sci. U. Calif., Berkeley, 1987-93; mem. natural sci. adv. bd. U. Pa., 1988-93; mem. adv. bd. dept. elec. engring. U. So. Calif., 1988-93; mem. Indsl. Rsch. Inst., 1980-92, dir., 1990-92, emeritus, 1993—; mem. indsl. and profl. adv. coun. elec. engring. dept. Pa. State U., 1993-98, chmn., 1995; mem. adv. task force on U.S. indsl. competitiveness U.S. Ho. of Reps., 1987; cons. European Commn. Telecom. Directorate, 1995; advisor to panel on high performance computing and comm. Office Sci. and Tech. Policy, The White House, 1991-92. Assoc. editor Solid State Communications, 1975-83; co-editor: Optical Fiber Telecommunications, 1979; contbr. articles to profl. jours.; patentee in field. Mem. Am. Mgmt. Assn., R & D Coun., 1989-93; chmn. tech. transfer merit program N.J. Commn. on Sci.

and Tech., 1992-98. Fellow IEEE (chmn. device rsch. conf. 1963, mem. com. on U.S. competitiveness 1988-89, bd. adv. task force on new initiatives 1989-90, chmn. Marconi award com. 1987, mem. Alexander Graham Bell prize com. 1990-94, chmn. 1992-94, mem. Frederik Philips award com. 1998-2002, W.R.G. Baker prize, 1967, Frederik Philips award 1992, engrng. leadership recognition 1996, mem. corp. achievement award com. 1999—, chmn. 2001-02, mem. awards policies and planning com. 2003), Am. Phys. Soc. (indsl. affiliates com. 1984-87, editl. bd. Physics Today 1985-88, George E. Pake prize 1992), Inst. Physics and Phys. Soc. (London), Internat. Engrng. Consortium; mem. NRC (survey dir. com. on survey of materials sci. and engrng. 1970-74, panel chmn. com. on mineral resources and environ. 1973-75, panel chmn. materials sci. engrng. study com. 1986-88, nat. materials adv. bd. 1976-80), Metall. Soc. of AIME (chmn. John Bardeen prize com. 1993-95), Materials Rsch. Soc., N.Y. Acad. Scis. Avocations: travel, boating. Home: 6 Londonderry Way Summit NJ 07901-2914 Office: Telcordia Techs Box 7040 331 Newman Springs Rd Red Bank NJ 07701-5657 also: 17 Mill Close Fishbourne Chichester West Sussex PO19 3JW England E-mail: algchy@aol.com.

CHYNOWETH, W. EDWARD, retired lawyer, farmer; b. Washington, Sept. 1, 1923; s. Bradford Grethen and Grace (Woodruff) C. BS in Mil. Sci. and Engrng., U.S. Mil. Acad., 1946; MS in Mech. Engrng., U. Calif., Berkeley, 1959; LLB, Stanford U., 1963. Bar: Calif. Pvt. practice law, Fresno, Calif., 1963—69; dep. dist. atty. Tulare County, Visalia, Calif., 1969—78; farmer Sanger, Calif., 1968—. Contbr. articles on social-constl. issues to cultural jours. of opinion and politics. With U.S. Army, 1946-57, maj. Res. Home: 403 S Indianola Ave Sanger CA 93657-9436

CHYTEN, EDWIN RICHARD, lawyer; b. Boston, May 15, 1925; s. William and Elizabeth (Carpenter) C.; m. Helen Siegal, Apr. 26, 1949 (div. Feb. 1981); children— Leslie, Kenneth, Neil; m. Rosalyn Levine, May 11, 1983. A.B., Harvard Coll., 1947; J.D., Boston Coll., 1971. Bar: Mass. 1971, U.S. Dist. Ct. Mass. 1971. Atty., legal counsel, v.p. Purity Supreme, Inc., North Billerica, Mass., 1974-79; ptnr. Meyers, Goldstein & Chyten, Chestnut Hill, Mass., 1979—. Served to lt. (j.g.) USN, 1943-46; PTO. Fellow Mass. Bar Assn., Mass. Acad. Trial Attys. Club: Newton Tennis (pres., 1978-80) (Mass.). Home: 250 Hammond Pond Pkwy Chestnut Hill MA 02467-1533 Office: Meyers Goldstein & Chyten 850 Boylston St Chestnut Hill MA 02467-2477

CHYTIL, FRANK, biochemist; b. Prague, Czechoslovakia, Aug. 28, 1924; came to U.S., 1965, naturalized, 1971; s. Frantisek and Ruzena (Vitouskova) C.; m. Lucie Scheinost, Nov. 26, 1949; children: Frank, Anna, Helena. MS, Sch. Chem. Tech., Prague, 1949, PhD, 1952; C.Sc., Czechoslovak Acad. Sci., Prague, 1956. Rsch. biochemist Charles U., Prague, 1949-51; rsch. fellow Inst. Human Rsch., Prague, 1952-63; sr. scientist Czechoslovak Acad. Sci., Prague, 1956-64; sr. rsch. fellow Brandeis U., Waltham, Mass., 1964, sr. rsch. assoc., 1965-66; head sect. enzymology S.W. Found. Rsch. and Edn., San Antonio, 1966-69; mem. faculty Vanderbilt U., 1969—2000, prof. biochemistry, 1975—2000, Gen. Foods Disting. prof. nutrition, 1984-89, Harvie Branscomb disting. prof., 1993-94, prof. emeritus, 2000—. Adj. assoc. prof. U. Tex., San Antonio, 1968—2000. Editor: Vitamins and Hormones, 1983; mem. editl. bd. Analytical Biochemistry, 1980-87, Jour. Biol. Chemistry, 1982-88, 96-99, Am. Jour. Clin. Nutrition, 1993-95; contbr. articles to profl. jours. Recipient Osborne-Mendel and Lederle awards; USPHS grantee, 1967-99. Fellow Am. Soc. Nutritional Scis.; mem. Am. Soc. Biochemistry and Molecular Biology, Endocrine Soc., Sigma Xi. Home: 914 Lynnwood Blvd Nashville TN 37205-4527 Office: Vanderbilt U Sch Medicine Dept Biochemistry Nashville TN 37232-0146 E-mail: frank.chytil@vanderbilt.edu.

CIALLELLA, EMIL ANTHONY, library director, consultant; b. Fall River, Mass., July 1, 1943; s. Emil Anthony Ciallella and Italia Carmela DiBiase; m. Carol Ann Cunniff, Nov. 30, 1974. BA, Providence Coll., 1965; MA, Assumption Coll., 1967; MLS, U. R.I., 1971. Cert. tchr., Ariz., county libr. Libr. dir. Ctrl. Falls (R.I.) Free Pub. Libr., 1974-84, Richard Salter Storrs Libr., Longmeadow, Mass., 1984-86, Gila County Libr. Dist., Miami, Ariz., 1989-93, Ector County Libr., Odessa, Tex., 1996-2000, Jefferson County Libr., 2000—. Pres., libr. cons. Cal-Em Assocs., Globe, Ariz., Odessa, 1976—. With U.S. Army, 1967-69. Mem. ALA (mem. numerous ALA assns. and programs), Tex. Libr. Assn., Am. Legion. Home: #506 3603 Jimmy Johnson Blvd Port Arthur TX 77642-8252 Office: Jefferson County Libr Ste 7 7933 Viterbo Rd Beaumont TX 77705 E-mail: onwheels@co.jefferson.tx.us., eciallella@co.jefferson.tx.us.

CIAMPA, ROY EMILIUS, religious studies educator; b. Medford, Mass., Oct. 9, 1958; s. Edwin Reynold and Joan Simpson Ciampa; m. Marcelle Marie Daigneault, June 27, 1981; children: Timothy David, Christina Marie. BA, Gordon Coll., 1982; MDiv, Denver Sem., 1986; PhD, U. Aberdeen, Scotland, 1996. Protestant chaplain Middlesex County She, Billerica, Mass., 1988; instr. Portuguese Bible Inst., Loures, Portugal, 1989—95; lectr., coord. grad. studies Portuguese Bible Inst. and Coll. of Evang. Theol. Edn., Loures, Portugal, 1995—2001; assoc. prof. New Testament Gordon-Conwell Theol. Sem., S Hamilton, Mass., 2001—. Translator Bible Soc. of Portugal, Lisbon. Author: (book) The Presence and Function of Scripture in Galatians 1 and 2, 1998. Fellow: Inst. Bibl. Rsch.; mem.: Tyndale Fellowship for Bibl. and Theol. Rsch., Soc. Bibl. Lit. Baptist. Home: 6 Stonehill Dr Ipswich MA 01982 Office: Gordon-Conwell Theol Sem 130 Essex St South Hamilton MA 01982

CIANCE, KARIN LORI (OHS), medical/surgical nurse; b. Worcester, Mass., Nov. 20, 1962; d. Lawrence William and Kerstin Martha (Carlson) Ohs; married May 2, 1992. Diploma, Worcester City Hosp. Sch., 1983; BSN, Worcester State Coll., 1988. RN, Mass. Charge nurse Worcester (Mass.) City Hosp., unit coord.; assoc. nurse mgr., night supr. Fairlawn Rehab. Hosp., Worcester, Mass., 1991-94; staff nurse urgent care Family Health and Social Svcs., Worcester, Mass., 1994—2001, nurse mgr. urgent care, 2001—. Mem. NAFE, Am. Nurses Assn., Mass. Nurses Assn., Worcester City Hosp. Sch. Nursing Alumni, Sigma Theta Tau. Home: 120 Mixter Rd Holden MA 01520-1048

CIANCIMINO, JOSEPH ANDREW, data processing executive; b. Austin, June 30, 1965; s. Joseph Ciancimino and Helen Kay Barbier; m. Melissa Kay McMahan, Mar. 7, 1989. Student aid North Harris Coll., Houston, 1985—86; mgr. Comics & Cards, 1988—96; self employed Spring, 1989—2001; with Altech Computers/Metals, Houston, 1996—97; telecomm. World Datacom, 1997—99; instr. North Harris Coll., 1999—2001; data comm. World Datacom, 2002—. Home: 22033 Jay Dr Spring TX 77373

CIANCIO, GAETANO, transplant surgeon, urologist; b. Roccapiemonte, Salerno, Italy, June 15, 1956; s. Luigi and Maria Ciancio; m. Vivian Ramos; children: Anthony, Joseph. MD, Sch. of Medicine "Luis Razetti", UCV, 1982; MBA, U. Miami, 2001. Diplomate Am. Bd. of Urology 1997. Intern in gen. surgery Jackson Meml. Med. Ctr., U. Miami, Fla., 1986—87, resident in gen. surgery, 1987—89, resident in urology, 1989—92, chief resident urology, 1992—93, fellow in multiorgan transplantation, 1993—95; asst. prof. surgery (multiorgan transplantation) and urology U. Miami, 1995—98, assoc. prof., 1998—, assoc. dir. divsn. of kidney and kidney-pancreas transplantation, 2000—, dir. transplant edn., 2000—, dir. transplant urologic surgery, 2000—. Prof. surgery multiorgan transplantation U. of Miami Sch. of Medicine, 2002—, prof. urology, oncology and gen. urology, 2002—. Contbr. (Miracle Maker award, 1997). Adv. bd. Nat. MOTTEP, Washington, 1997—98; vice chmn. adv. bd. Nat. MOTTEP Program, Washington, 1998—2001. Named The Person of the Mo., Italian Mag., 1998, Hon. Citizen, Comune di Roccapiemonte, Salerno, Italy, 2000, Atteding of the Yr., Award of Excellence for the outstanding dedication and commitment to patients, colleagues and residents, Dept. of Urologic Surgery, U. Miami, 1998—99; named to The Italians of Am., A tribute to America's most significant Italians, The Italians of Am., ed. Alfonso Panico, 1999; recipient Dean's Sr. Faculty Clin. Rsch. award, U. Miami Sch. Medicine, 1999—2000, Honoree, In recognition of extraordinary generosity and tireless dedication in support of organ donation and transplantation, Transplant Found., 2001, Dr. Martin Luther King Jr. Spirit award, 2002; fellow Surg. Rsch. fellow, VA Med. Ctr., Miami, 1984—86; scholar Exec. MBA Program scholar, University of Miami, 2000—01. Fellow: ACS; mem.: Soc. of Laparoendoscopic Surgeons, Soc. Univ. Surgeons, Am. Soc. of Transplant Surgeons, Urologic Soc. for Transplantation and Vascular Surgery, The Transplantation Soc., Am. Urol. Assn. Office: Univ of Miami Schl of Medicine 1801 NW 9th Ave Ste 517 Miami FL 33136 Office Fax: 305-355-5134. Business E-mail: gciancio@med.miami.edu.

CIANCIOLO-CARNEY, ROSSANA, investigative analyst; b. Knoxville, Tenn., July 4, 1964; d. Salvatore and Mariluz Cianciolo; m. Patrick Michael Carney, Jan. 8, 1961. BA in Polit. Sci./Fgn. Langs., Stephens Coll., 1986. Intelligence rsch. specialist Nat. Drug Intelligence Ctr., Johnstown, Pa., 1994-95; investigative analyst FBI, San Diego, Calif., 1995—. Informal resolution program counselor Nat. Drug Intelligence Ctr., Johnstown, 1995. Spkr. Cmty. Outreach, 1995—, participant/San Diego Elder Abuse Fraud Task Force, 1998—; wish grantor Make-a-Wish, San Diego, 1997—; bd. dirs. Women in Bus. Aiding the Cmty., 1996—. Republican. Roman Catholic. Avocations: running, swimming, reading, travel. Office: FBI 9797 Aero Dr San Diego CA 92123-1829 Home: 369 Park Street NE Vienna VA 22180

CIANGIO, SISTER DONNA LENORE, religious organization administrator; b. Newark, N.J., Feb. 2, 1949; d. Nicholas Gabriel and Elizabeth Helen (Cwikla) Ciangio. BA, Caldwell (N.J.) Coll., 1971; MA, NYU, 1980; DMin, Drew U., Madison, N.J., 2003. Joined Sisters of St. Dominic of Caldwell, N.J., Roman Cath. Ch., 1967. Tchr. Blessed Sacrament Sch., Bridgeport, Conn., 1971-73, St. Ann Sch., Newark, 1973; chairperson art dept. St. Dominic Acad., Jersey City, 1974-78; art instr., gallery dir. Caldwell Coll., 1978-80; art dept. chairperson St. Cecilia High Sch., Englewood, N.J., 1979-81; assoc. dir. internat. office RENEW, Plainfield, N.J., 1981-94, also coord. for internat. tng. and planning; project dir. and dir. small Christian cmty. svcs. Nat. Pastoral Life Ctr., N.Y.C., 1994—. Cons. in art for secondary schs. Archdiocese of Newark, 1976—79. Recipient Papal Proecclesia award and Medal for Svc., Diocese of Malolos, Philippines. Office: Nat Pastoral Life Ctr 18 Bleecker St New York NY 10012-2404

CIANI, ALFRED JOSEPH, language professional, associate dean; b. N.Y.C., June 29, 1946; s. Joseph Alfred and Aurora Smiles (VanOver) C.; m. Sharon Skolkey, Aug. 16, 1968 (div. 1979); children: Mieke Jo, Gabriel Wolf; m. Lesley Lockwood, Aug. 9, 1980; children: Joseph Alfred, Clinton Lockwood. BA, U. Albany, 1969; MA, Coll. of St. Rose, 1972; EdD, Ind. U., 1974. Tchr. Greater Amsterdam (N.Y.) Schs., 1969-72; rsch. asst. Ind. U., Bloomington, 1972-73, assoc. instr., 1973-74; vis. prof. U. Wis., Milw., 1980; asst. prof. U. Cin., 1974-79, assoc. prof., 1979—2002, assoc. dean, info. officer, 1988—2003, prof. emeritus, 2003—. Pres. Ohio Internat. Reading Assn., Columbus, 1981-82; outside cons. State of Miss., Jackson, 1982-84, State of Ky., 1996-99, State of W.Va., 1972-74, 97-98, City of N.Y. Pub. Schs.; cons., U. Oreg. Profl. Devel., Eugene, 1979-80, Nashville Schs., 1982-83, State of W.Va., N.Y.C. Pub. Schs.; mem. Dean's Cabinet; mem. Urban Schs. Task Force. Author: Motivating Reluctant Readers, 1981; editor: (book series) Reading in Content Areas, 1979-81; rev. editor: Rsch. in Mid. Level Edn., 1995—. Grantee Ford Found., 1990, IBM, 1990. Mem. AAUP, Internat. Reading Assn., Am. Ednl. Rsch. Assn. (nat. coms.), Assn. Tchr. Educators (nat. coms.), Nat. Coun. Tchrs. English (nat. coms.),, Nat. Mid. Sch. Assn. (nat. coms.), Nat. Reading Coun., Phi Delta Kappa, Kappa Delta Pi (counselor). Democrat. Roman Catholic. Avocations: reading, walking, family oriented activities. Office: U Cin Mail Location 02 Cincinnati OH 45221-0001 E-mail: alfred.ciani@uc.edu.

CIANI, JUDITH ELAINE, retired lawyer; b. Medford, Mass., July 24, 1943; d. A. Walter and Ruth Alice (Bowman) C.; m. Marion M. Smith, Sept. 29, 1982. Grad., Thayer Acad., Braintree, Mass., 1961; MA, Mt. Holyoke Coll., 1965; JD, Boston Coll., 1970. Bar: Calif. 1971, U.S. Dist. Ct. (no. dist.) Calif. 1971, U.S. Ct. Appeals (9th cir.) 1971. Aide/press sec. Rep. James A. Burke, Washington, 1965-67; atty. Pillsbury, Madison & Sutro, San Francisco, 1970-78, ptnr., 1978-90; ret., 1990. Del. Calif. Bar Conv., San Francisco, 1973-78, 83-85. Mem. San Francisco Police Commn., 1976-80, Juvenile Justice Task Force, San Francisco, 1981-83; bd. dirs. Bernard Osher Found., San Francisco, 1977—; pres. Common Fund for Legal Svcs., San Francisco, 1985—, Sinfonia San Francisco, 1985-86. Fellow Am. Bar Found.; mem. Bar Assn. San Francisco (bd. dirs., pres. Found. 1978—, bd. dirs. 1981-83, treas. 1987). Home: PO Box 960 Inverness CA 94937-0960 E-mail: jeciani@svn.net.

CIANNELLA, JOEEN MOORE, museum director; b. Warren, Ohio, Mar. 20, 1948; d. Joseph Alvie and Elizabeth Dorthea Moore; m. Christopher M. Ciannella, July 31, 1976 (div. Jan. 1987); children: Bryce C., Tara E. BA in French, Denison U., 1970. Profl. staff U.S. Senate Rep. Policy Com., Washington, 1971-75; owner Jo Moore-Sophisticated Country, Park Ridge, NJ, 1984—; dist. dir. Congresswoman Marge Roukema U.S. Ho. Reps., Ridgewood, NJ, 1985—2002; exec. dir. Hermitage Mus., Hohokus, NJ, 2003—. Mem. Nat. coun. Boy Scouts Am., 1995—98; trustee Greater Roles and Opportunities for Women N.J. GOP, 1997—; mem. Park Ridge Bd. Health, 1984—86; founding mem. Pioneer Women Bergen County, 1992—; mem. exec. bd. Bergen coun. Boy Scouts Am., 1991—98, co-chair Pascak Valley Dist. Luncheree, 1991—92, chair spl. events fin., 1993—94, mem. exec. com., 1993—98, vice chmn. fin., 1995—98, mem. exec. bd. No. N.J. coun., 1999—, vice chair fin., 2000—02; mem. exec. bd. Ramapo Coll. Found., 1991—, theme chairperson fundraiser, 1991—94, disting. citizen dinner com., 1991—, mem. bus. network com., 1994—97, chmn. pub. rels. and mktg. com., 1996—2000, mem. exec. com., 1996—, chmn. mktg./instl. rels., 2000—; com. mem. N.J. Network Found. Gala, 2000—02; bd. dirs. Helen Hayes Theater Co., Nyack, NY, 2001—, mem. devel. com. spl. events, 2002—, mem. devel. com. Christmas Day in the Garden, 2003; chairperson spl. effects West Bergen Mental Health 40th Anniversary Ruby Ball, 2003; active Bush for Pres. Campaign, 1988, 1992, Dole for Pres. Campaign, 1996; elected mem. Park Ridge County Com., 1983—, mcpl. chairperson, 1986—96; active Bergen County (N.J.) Rep. Com., 1983—, Park Ridge Rep. Orgn., 1983—, v.p., 1988—89; active N.E. Rep. Orgn. Dist. 39, NJ, 1984—, sec., 1990—91, treas., 1991—92, chairperson, 1992—93; ofcl. com. mem. N.J. GOP Conv., 1991; charter mem. Women Leadership Summit Rep. Network to Elect Women, 1996—97. Recipient Mission award, Ramapo Coll. Found., 1999, Silver Beaver award, Boy Scouts Am., 1999. Mem.: Jr. League Bergen County (com. mem. Festival of Trees 1988), Ridgewood Unit Rep. Women, Bergen County Women's Rep. Club, N.J. Fcdn. Rep. Women, Rep. Women of 90's State N.J., Rotary (mem. com. annual auction Park Ridge chpt. 1990—, chairperson holiday party 1991—). Avocations: gardening, antiques, sports, travel. Home: 34 Spring Valley Rd Park Ridge NJ 07656-1860 Office: The Hermitage Mus 335 N Franklin Turnpike Ho Ho Kus NJ 07423 E-mail: j.cianella@thehermitage.org.

CIAO, FREDERICK J. school system administrator, educator; b. Phila. married; 3 children. BA, LaSalle U., 1962; MEd, Temple U., 1965; MA, Villanova U., 1972; PhD, Southwest U., 1990. From tchr. to counselor to dept. chmn. N.E. Cath. High Sch., Phila., 1962-73; vice prin. Archbishop Wood High Sch., Warminster, Pa., 1973-85; prin. Bishop McDevitt H.S., Wyncote, Pa., 1985-93, pres., 1993—2003, Archbishop Wood H.S., Warminster, Pa., 2003—. Mem. adj. faculty St. Agnes Hosp. Nursing Sch., Phila., 1963-71, Spring Garden Coll., Phila., 1971-73, Gwynedd Mercy Coll., Gwynedd Valley, Pa., 1976-84, LaSalle U., 1980—; presentor Nat. Diffusion Network, 1992—. Mem. edn. advisor Phila. Orch., 1993—, Italian Lang. Preservation Found., 1999—. Named Man of the Yr., N.E. Cath. Alumni Assn., 1972, Educator of the Yr., Millay Club, 1986; named to Legion of Honor, Chapel of Four Chaplains, 1980; recipient John Neumann medal St. John Neumann High Sch., 1985. Mem. Nat. Assn. Secondary Sch. Prins., Nat. Cath. Edn. Assn., Nat. Coun. Tchrs. of Maths., Maths. Assn. Am., Nat. Assn. Curriculum Devel., Nat. Coun. for Self Esteem, Mid. States Assn. of Colls. (chair). Office: Archbishop Wood HS 655 York Rd Warminster PA 18974

CIARDULLO, ROBERT CARL, plastic surgeon; b. N.Y.C., Oct. 2, 1950; s. Sam and Amy (Bonicoro) C.; m. Kira A. Geraci, Oct. 25, 1980; children: Jean-Paul, Christina. BA, Vassar Coll., 1972; MD, Johns Hopkins U., 1976. Diplomate Am. Bd. Plastic Surgery. Intern in gen. surgery and resident Columbia Presbyn. Hosp., N.Y.C.; resident in plastic surgery N.Y. Hosp.-Cornell, N.Y.C.; intern Columbia-Presbyterian Hosp., resident in gen. surgery; resident in plastic surgery N.Y. Hosp.-Cornell; pvt. practice, White Plains, N.Y., 1981—. Plastic surgeon White Plains Hosp., 1981—. Contbr. articles to med. jours. Mem. AMA, Am. Soc. Plastic and Reconstructive Surgeons (govt. rels. com. 1995—), N.Y. State Med. Soc., Westchester County Med. Soc. (pub. rels. com. 1994—). Avocations: deep sea fishing, golf, landscaping. Office: 170 Maple Ave White Plains NY 10601-4710

CIARLILLO, MARJORIE ANN, musician, educator; b. Cleve., Nov. 1, 1940; d. Nicolo and Madelaine (DaMico) C. AB in Fine Arts, Lake Erie Coll., 1962; cert., U. London, 1962; MA in Musicology, Western Res. U., 1971; postgrad., Ind. U., 1965, 82, 83; cert. Chinese music, Shanghai Conservatory Music, 1983. Dir. lower sch. music dept. Univ. Sch., Shaker Heights, Ohio, 1963-70; br. cood. Cleve. Inst. Music/Beaumont Sch. for Girls, Cleveland Heights, 1971-75; mem. piano faculty Cleve. Inst. Music, 1971—; dir. China Music Project, Cleve., 1980—. Musicologist Glen Oak Sch., Gates Mills, Ohio, 1978-82; instr. piano Lake Erie Coll., Painesville, Ohio, 1975-82, other ednl. instns. and pvt. students, 1961—; dir. China Music Project, 1980—; spl. asst. to dean of coll. Case Western Res. U., Cleve., 1987-94; asst. head The Andrews Sch., Willoughby, Ohio, 1994—. Performer Chinese Cultural Arts Symposa, 1988, 92, 94, Cleve. Mus. Art., Cleve. Inst. Music, 1981, 82, 86; performer radio programs on Chinese music WCLV-FM, Cleve., 1981—, WRUW-FM, Cleve., 1987; pianist Cleve. Women's Orch., 1972-75; contbr. articles to arts and scholastic publs. Trustee Andrews Sch., Willoughby, Ohio, 1991—94, Lake Erie Coll., 1975—78; mem. Leadership Lake County, 1998. Recipient Disting. Alumna award Andrews Sch., 1978, Disting. Alumna award Lake Erie Coll., 1997; Ednl. Rsch. Coun. fellow, 1968. Mem. AAUW, Adult Edn. Assn. U.S., Am. Musicol. Soc., Assn. Chinese Music Rsch. (founding), Coun. Advancement and Support Edn., Soc. Asian Music, Soc. Ethnomusicology, Cleve. Chamber Music Soc. (trustee 2003—), Mu Phi Epsilon. Avocations: chinese art, literature and music, horseback riding, embroidery. Office: The China Music Project Inc 334 Claymore Blvd Cleveland OH 44143-1730

CIARROCCHI, MAYA, dancer; d. Raymond W. Ciarrocchi and Sandra Caplan; life ptnr. Rebecca A. Nichols, Dec. 22, 2001. MFA in Computer Art, Sch. of Visual Art, N.Y.C., 2000—01; BFA in Dance, SUNY Purchase, 1985—89. Dancer Dance By Fred Darsow, N.Y.C., 1989—98, Dance by Neil Greenberg, N.Y.C., 1990—91, Core Performance Co., Atlanta, 1995—97, Beacon Dance Co., Atlanta, 1995—97, Ondine and Co., Atlanta, 1996—97; media adminstr. Dance Theater Workshop, N.Y.C., 2003—. Tchr. of dance Core Performance Co., Atlanta, 1995—97, 3rd Internat. Contemporary Dance Conf. and Festival, Bytom, Kracow, Poland, 1996—96. Video designer (performance) I Can See You, The Color Project, (video installation) Maya In Plane Movement; performance, Shift Scene, Morph: Live Remix, AIR: The Elemental Project, video installation, Black On White. Artists residents coun. Westbeth Artist's Housing, N.Y.C., 1999—2000, dance admissions com., 1999—2003. Home: 55 Bethune St #H353 New York NY 10014 Home Fax: 212-645-7022. Personal E-mail: oh_my@earthlink.net. E-mail: maya@dtw.org.

CIARVELLA, DAVID R. music educator, plastics company executive; b. Rochester, N.Y., Aug. 29, 1970; s. Robert John Ciarvella and Donna Marie Dolan; m. Julie Mae Aarssen, July 28, 2001; stepchildren: Amber Lehman, Jessie Lehman, Marcie Lehman. BS Music Edn., Robert Wesleyan Coll., Rochester, N.Y., 2000. Prodn. mgr. Helvic Plastic Extrusions, Rochester, NY, 1991—2002; music tchr. Churchville-Chili H.S., Churchville, NY, 2000—02; adj. prof. Robert Wesleyan Coll., Rochester, 2002; music tchr. Chestnut Ridge Elem. Sch., Rochester, 2002—. Cpl. USMC, 1998—2001, Buffalo, N.Y. Republican. Free Methodist. Home: 5786 Buffalo Rd Churchville NY 14428-9785

CIBBARELLI, PAMELA RUTH, information executive; b. Odessa, Tex., Mar. 26, 1946; d. Everett M. and Geneva (Hill) Johnson; 1 child, Shawn Edward. AA, Orange Coast Coll., 1966; BA, Calif. State U., Long Beach, 1971; MSLS, Calif. State U., Fullerton, 1973. Libr. clk. Golden West Coll., Huntington Beach, Calif., 1967-70; pres., founder Cibbarelli & Assocs., Huntington Beach, 1973-82; dir. rsch. Korn-Ferry Internat., L.A., 1982; Western regional mgr. Battelle Software Products Ctr., Costa Mesa, Calif., 1983-85; v.p. mktg. INLEX, Inc., Monterey, Calif., 1985-86; pres. Cibbarelli's, Huntington Beach, 1986—. Libr. svcs. supr. City of Commerce (Calif.) Pub. Libr., 1995—; lectr., assoc. prof. UCLA Grad. Sch. Libr. Sci., Calif. State U., San Jose, Fullerton, San Bernardino; mem. organizing com. Integrated Online Libr. Sys. Meeting, 1994, 95, 96, 97, 98, 99, 2000, Computers in Libr. Meeting, 1996, 97, 98, 99, 2000, E-Librs., 2001, 02, 03, Internet Libr., 97, 98, 99, 2000, 01. Editor: Directory of Information Management Software, 1983, 85, 87, 89, 91, Procs. of the Integrated Online Library Systems Meeting, 1994, 95, 96, 97, 98, 99, 2000, Directory of Library Automation Software, Systems, and Services, 1994, 96, 98, 2000, 2002; contbr. numerous articles to profl. jours. Mem. adv. com. UCLA Grad. Sch. Libr. Info. Scis. Mem. ALA, Am. Soc. Info. Sci., Spl. Librs. Assn., Calif. Libr. Assn.

CIBES, WILLIAM JOSEPH, JR., chancellor, educator; b. Newton, Kans., Aug. 25, 1943; s. William Joseph and Dorothy Beulah Cibes; m. Margaret Ann Collins, Sept. 2, 1967; 1 child, Julia Katherine. BA, U. Kans., 1965; PhD, Princeton (N.J.) U., 1975. Instr. to prof. Conn. Coll., New London, 1969-91; sec. Office of Policy and Mgmt., State of Conn., Hartford, 1991-94; chancellor Conn. State U. System, Hartford, 1994—. State rep. Conn. Gen. Assembly, Hartford, 1979-91. Democrat. Roman Catholic. Office: Conn State Univ System 39 Woodland St Hartford CT 06105-2337 E-mail: cibesw@so.ct.edu.

CIBLEY, LAURENCE JAY, obstetrician, gynecologist; b. Boston, July 7, 1951; s. Leonard Jonathan and Shirley I. (Idelson) C.; m. Bonnie Lisa, June 2, 1974; children: Jared Maurice, Ariana Lynn. BA, Boston Coll., 1973; MD, U. Autonoma Guadalajara, Mex., 1978. Diplomate Am. Bd. Ob/Gyn. Intern in ob/gyn. Boston City Hosp., 1979-80, jr. resident in ob/gyn., 1980-81, sr. resident in ob/gyn., 1981-82, chief resident in ob/gyn., 1982-83, attending physician ob/gyn clinic, 1983, Cambridge (Mass.) Hosp., 1983-84; active staff, assoc. ob/gyn. Beth Israel Hosp., Newton, Mass., 1984-93; acting chief dept. ob/gyn. Waltham (Mass.) Weston Hosp. and Med. Ctr., 1986-87, acting staff mem., 1993—. Clin. instr. ob/gyn Boston U. Sch. Medicine, 1984-86, asst. clin. prof., 1986, co-dir. residency ob/gyn., 1992-93, co-dir. update on ob/gyn., 1991, 92, co-dir. controverside in contraception, 1995; assoc. prof. dept. ob-gyn Tex. Tech U. Health Scis. Ctr., Odessa, 1995, assoc. program dir.; co-dir. colposcopy dysplasia clinic Boston City Hosp., 1991-93, dir., 1991-93; lectr. in field; cons. maternity unit video Waltham Weston Hosp., 1991. Contbr. articles to profl. publs.; mem. editl. bd. Am. Jour. Ob/Gyn., 1991; asst. to prodr. film A Labor of Love, 1973; appeared on various TV programs. Maj. USAR, 1990, Desert Storm, 1991. Fellow Internat. Soc. for Study of Vulvar Diseases (editl. bd. 1989); mem. Mass. Med. Soc. Home: 26 Hialeah Cir Odessa TX 79761-3527

CIBOROWSKI, PAUL JOHN, counseling psychology educator; b. NYC, Jan. 15, 1943; s. Paul J. and Mary (Deptuch) C.; m. Doris E. Carlo, June 24, 1973; children: Philip Alan, Kevin Michael. BA, U. Dayton, 1965; MA, NYU, 1969; PhD, Fordham U., 1979. Cert. counselor. Counselor Christ the King H.S., Queens, N.Y., 1967-70; coord. drug edn. Sachem Sch. Dist., Holbrook, N.Y., 1971-73; sr. counselor, grant coord. Sachem Schs., Holbrook, N.Y., 1973-89; mental health counselor, 1980—; assoc. prof. counseling and psychology L.I. U., 1989—. Pres. Stratmar Ednl. Systems; pvt. practice marriage and family therapy; coord. Dept. Counseling and Devel., Brentwood, N.Y.; cons., trainer Family Life Bur., Diocese of Rockville Centre; adv. coun. WSHO radio; contact person for sexual harassment complaints C.W. Post Coll., 2003. Author: The Changing Family I, 1984, 2d edit., 1986, Survival Skills for Single Parents, 1987, Working with Tomorrow's Teens: A 21st Century Challenge, 2000; contbr. articles to profl. jours. Fellow Ctr. for Study of the Changing Family, Port Chester, NY; active Brookhaven Anti-Bias Coalition; co chair Suffolk County Interfaith Anti-Bias Task Force; chair N.Y. Youth Bd., Western Suffolk Coalition on Child Abuse and Neglect; project dir. Suffolk County Gang Prevention, 2000—, grant coord., 2000—; active Suffolk County Youth in Crisis Task Force, 2003—; chmn. fin. com. St. Mark's Roman Cath. Ch., parish coun.; bd. dirs. Soundview Civic Assn. Grantee in field. Mem.: ACA (com. on children, youth and families), Western Suffolk Counselors Assn. (past treas., past v.p.), Am. Mental Health Counselors Assn. (chmn. spl. interest network on children and adolescents, coord. Child Adv. Network, exec. bd., nat. com. for the rights of children 1992—96), N.Y. State Assn. for Counseling and Devel. (legis. chmn. 1989—92, v.p., state curriculum com. 1981—82), Phi Delta Kappa. Home: 38 Mary Pitkin Path PO Box 284 Shoreham NY 11786-0284

CICCARELLI, CHICK, marketing professional; b. Oakland, Calif., Apr. 30, 1956; s. Wanda Bridges, Bernard Ciccarelli; m. Julia Barinova. Student, Calif. State U., Long Beach, 1976—78. Sr. art dir. Reeds, Farris & Lewis, Studio City, Calif., 1989—93; co-founder, exec. v.p. Theafilm Distribn. Network, Inc., Hollywood, Calif., 1993—95; pres. System X Entertainment, Hollywood, 1995—97; v.p. comm. Moviola, Hollywood, 1997—99, L.A. Digital Post, West Toluca Lake, Calif., 1999—2000; pres. Chick, Inc., Valley Village, Calif., 2000—. Creator (Online Digital Video Delivery System) Editvu, 2001. Recipi-

ent Cert. of Achievement, Voyager Flight, Smithsonian Inst., 1987, Cert. of Achievement, Design, Printing Industries of Am. Awards, 1985, 1986, 1988, Art Dirs. Club of L.A., 1987. Democrat. Roman Catholic. Avocation: traveling abroad.

CICCARONE, RICHARD ANTHONY, financial executive; b. Akron, Ohio, June 15, 1952; s. Andrew and Marie Antoinette Ciccarone; m. Marilyn Douglas DeBorde, May 26, 1984. BA, Miami U., Oxford, Ohio, 1974; MA, U. Akron, 1978. Mcpl. bond analyst Harris Bank, Chgo., 1977-82, mcpl. rsch. mgr., 1982-83; v.p., dir. rsch., sr. analyst Van Kampen Merritt Investment Adv. Corp. (formerly Am. Portfolio), Lisle, Ill., 1983-89; sr. v.p., dir. fixed income rsch. Blunt Ellis & Loewi, Inc., Chgo., 1989-90; exec. v.p., dir. tax exempt fixed income rsch. Everen Securities Inc. (formerly Kemper Securities), Chgo., 1990-96; sr. v.p., co-dir. mcpl. investments, dir. mcpl. rsch., co-head fixed income dept. Van Kampen Inv. Adv. Corp. unit of Morgan Stanley, Oakbrook Terrace, Ill., 1996—2001; pres. Merritt Rsch. Svcs. LLC, Oakbrook Terrace, Ill., 2001—; mng. dir. McDonnell Investment Mgmt. LLC, Oakbrook Terrace, Ill., 2001—. Publisher MuniNet Guide Review, 1996—. Contbr. articles to profl. jours. and fin. pubs. Mem. exec. com., bd. dirs. Civic Fedn. Chgo.; mem. Village of Hinsdale Plan Commn., 1995-99; bd. trustees Village Hinsdale, 1999-2003, Hinsdale Theater Found., 2002—; co-chair Am. Heart Assn., DuPage County Walkathon, 2000; bd. dirs. Hinsdale Libr. Found. Named All-Am Mcpl. Analyst (2d team), Global Guaranty, 1990, 91, The Bond Buyer, 1993, All-Am. Mcpls. Analyst, Generalist (2d team), 1993, Institutional Investor Mag., 1992, 94, Mcpl. Analyst Generalist (1st team), Institutional Investor Mag., 1995, 1st Team All-Star Smith's Rsch. and Ratings as Mcpl. Generalist, 1995, 96, 97, 98, 99, 1st Team All-Star Buyside Mcpl. Rsch. Dir., 1997, 98, 99. Mem. Nat. Fedn. Mcpl. Analysts (nat. chmn. 1984-85, Disting. Svc. award 1988, Standards and Practices chair 1991-92, Long Term Planning Chair 1993-94, govt. acctg. standards adv. coun. 1996-99), Soc. Mcpl. Analysts, Chgo. Mcpl. Analysts Soc. (pres. 1984), So. Mcpl. Fin. Soc., Miami (Ohio) U. Alumni Assn. (pres. Chgo. chpt. 1988-89), Com. of One Hundred (Hinsdale, Ill., pres. 1998-99), Omicron Delta Kappa. Roman Catholic. Home: 733 S Bodin St Hinsdale IL 60521-4316 Office: McDonnell Investment Mgmt LLC 1515 W 22d St 11th Fl Hinsdale IL 60523 E-mail: ciccaroner@mcdmgmt.com.

CICCHELLI, JOSEPH VINCENT, principal; b. Jersey City, Sept. 14, 1953; s. Anthony Charles and Julia Marie (Libri) C.; m. Joanne Barrino, July 11, 1981; children: Jaime Michele, Jason Michael. AA, Bergen C.C., 1973; BA, William Paterson Coll. of N.J., 1975; MA, Seton Hall U., 1981. Tchr.'s aide Bergen County Spl. Svcs. Sch. Dist., Paramus, 1975-76; tchr. Hackensack High Sch., 1976-98; asst. prin. Fairmount Elem. Sch., Hackensack, 1998—2003, prin., 2003—; educator Hackensack Adult Edn. Ctr., Hackensack, N.J., 1978-92; supr. Hasbrouck Heights Adult Edn. Ctr., Hackensack, N.J., 1987-92, Hackensack Adult Edn. Ctr., 1992-94. Cons. Belville (N.J.) Pub. Sch. Dist., 1987. Active Fairmount Creative Playground Com., Hackensack. Mem. Prins. and Suprs. Assn., N.J. Prins. and Suprs. Assn., N.J. Social Studies Coun., Kappa Delta Pi. Roman Catholic. Avocations: photography, fishing, woodcrafting, automobile restoration and shows. Office: Fairmount Elementary Sch 105 Grand Ave Hackensack NJ 07601

CICCI, DAVID ALLEN, aerospace engineer, educator; b. Greensburg, Pa., May 29, 1951; s. Henry and Ann (Bischan) C.; m. Christine Maryanne Smith, July 16, 1977; children: Corey Dylan, Darby Austin. BSME, W.Va. U., 1973; MSME, Carnegie-Mellon U., 1976; PhD in Aerospace Engring., U. Tex., 1987. Registered profl. engr., Pa., Ala. Engr. power systems div. McGraw Edison Co., Canonsburg, Pa., 1973—74; engr. Bettis Atomic Power Lab. Westinghouse Electric Corp., West Mifflin, Pa., 1974—77; sr. engr. Swanson Engring. Assocs. Corp., McMurray, Pa., 1977—81; engring. specialist Bell Helicopter Textron, Ft. Worth, 1981—82; from asst. instr. to rsch. asst. U. Tex., Austin, 1982—87; prof. dept. aerospace engring. Auburn (Ala.) U., 1987—, dir. minority introduction to engring., 1996—2000. Cons. Sverdrup Tech., Inc., Stennis Space Ctr., Miss., 1989-90, Gen. Dynamics Corp., Ft. Worth, 1984, Swanson Engring. Assocs. Corp., McMurray, 1982-83; instr. NASA, Huntsville, Ala., 1989, 90, 92, NSWC, Dahlgren, Va., 2001, U.S. Army, Huntsville, Ala., 2001-02, NRL, Washington, 2002. Contbr. articles to profl. jours. Mem. City Coun., Auburn, Ala., 1998-2002. Mem. AIAA (astrodynamics tech. com. 1991-94, 96—, astrodynamics stds. com. 1991-94), ASME, Am. Astronautical Soc., Tau Beta Pi, Sigma Gamma Tau. Home: 1960 Canary Dr Auburn AL 36830-6902 Office: 211 Aerospace Engring Bldg Auburn U Auburn AL 36849-5338 E-mail: dcicci@eng.auburn.edu.

CICCIARELLI, JAMES CARL, immunology educator; b. Toluca, Ill., May 26, 1947; s. Maurice and Helen (Ippolito) Cicciarelli; m. Mary Jane Manning, June 2000; 1 child from previous marriage, Nicola. BS, Tulane U., 1969; PhD, So. Ill. U., 1977. Lic. clin. lab. dir., Calif. Fellow dept. surgery UCLA, 1977-79, asst. prof. immunology, 1980-87, assoc. prof., 1987-91; prof. urology, surgery and microbiology U. So. Calif., L.A., 1992—. Lab. dir. Metic Transplant Lab., Inc., L.A., 1984—; bd. dirs.. So. Calif. Organ Procurement Agy.; clin. lab. dir. Am. Bd. Bioanalysis, 1991—; mem. histocompatibility com. United Network Organ Sharing, 1991-94; mem. scientific adv. com. United Network for Organ Sharing, 1997—; lab. dir. Sharp Hosp. and Clinic, San Diego; mem. scientific adv. bd., BioArray Solutions, 2001—. Contbr. articles to profl. jours., chpts. to books. Rsch. grant NIH, 1985-88. Mem. Am. Soc. Histocompatibility and Immunogenetics, Internat. Transplant Soc., Am. Soc. Transplant Physicians, Internat. Soc. Heart Lung Transplantation. Libertarian. Roman Catholic. Avocations: boating, hiking, skiing, tennis, running. Home: 5 Ringbit Rd W Rolling Hills Estates CA 90274-5241 Office: USC Dept Urology Metic Transplant Lab 2100 W 3rd St Ste 280 Los Angeles CA 90057-1922

CICCONE, AMY NAVRATIL, art librarian; b. Detroit, Sept. 19, 1950; d. Gerald R. and Ruth C. (Kauer) Navratil. BA, Wayne State U., 1972; AM in Library Sci., U. Mich., 1973. Rsch. libr. Norton Simon Mus., Pasadena, Calif., 1974-81; chief libr. Chrysler Mus., Norfolk, Va., 1981-88; head libr. Architecture and Fine Arts Libr. U. So. Calif., L.A., 1988-97, acting asst. univ. libr. pub. svcs., 1993-95, ref. libr., 1997—. Contbr. articles to profl. jours.; cons. editor Art Reference Svcs., 1990-98. Mem. Art Libraries Soc. N.Am. (moderator Decorative Arts Roundtable, 1991-93, facilities standards com. 1986-91, chmn. strategic planning task force 1994-96, vice-chmn. So. Calif. chpt. 1989, chmn. 1990, chmn. 2001 conf.), Rsch. Librs. Group, Art & Architecture Group (steering com. 1992-94). Office: U So Calif Libr Los Angeles CA 90089-1823 Office Fax: 213-821-1776.

CICCONE, MADONNA LOUISE VERONICA See MADONNA

CICCONI, CHRISTOPHER M. lawyer; b. Anaheim, Calif., Aug. 19, 1949; s. Samuel A. and Ercilia (Silva) C.; m. Cynthia Anne June 20, 1981; children: Christina Michelle, Kelly Melissa. BA in Comm. Arts, U. Notre Dame, 1971; JD, Villanova U., 1974; LLM in Taxation, Temple U., 1978. Bar: Pa., U.S. Dist. Ct. (ea. and mid. dists.) Pa., U.S. Ct. Appeals (3d dist.), U.S. Tax Ct., U.S. Supreme Ct. Assoc. Rocap, Rocap & Guinta, Media, Pa., 1974-77; 1st asst. pub. defender Pub. Defender's Office of Delaware County, Media, 1977-78; ptnr. Hepford Zimmerman & Swartz, Harrisburg, Pa., 1978-90, mng. ptnr., 1985-90; atty., mem. Eckert Seamans Cherin & Mellott, Harrisburg, 1990—, chairperson corp. dept., 1999—. Bd. dirs. York Saw & Knife Co., Inc., dBi Labs., Inc., Harrisburg, Ollie's Bargain Outlets, Inc., Harrisburg, sellstufflocal.com., Inc.; instr. Coll. Med., Pa. State U., 1992-98. Author, editor: Buying and Selling a Business, 1998. Mem., chair Zoning Hearing Bd., Derry Twp., Pa., 1984-89; mem. Preservation of Hershey Com., Derry Twp., 1987-88. Recipient Cmty. Achievement award Derry Twp., 1989, award of yr. Notre Dame Alumni Assn., 1995. Mem. Pa. Bar Assn. (chair legal affairs of older persons com. 1986-88, arbitrator dispute resolution com. 1988—), Dauphin County Bar Assn., Estate Planning Coun. Ctrl. Pa., Sorin Soc. of U. Notre Dame. Avocations: playing piano, wine collecting, travel, golf. Home: 1045 Fairdell Dr Hummelstown PA 17036-8710 Office: Eckert Seamans et al 213 Market St Harrisburg PA 17101-2132 E-mail: cmc@escm.com.

CICCONI, JAMES WILLIAM, lawyer; b. Elmira, N.Y., June 8, 1952; s. Raymond Joseph and Doris Arlene (Strong) C.; m. Patricia Olivia Burgess, Aug. 10, 1974; children: Jill, Sara, Rachel. BA, U. Tex., 1974, JD, 1977. Bar: Tex. 1977, D.C. 1985. Issues dir. Jim Baker for Atty. Gen. campaign, Austin, Tex., 1977-78; adminstrv. asst. to the gov. State of Tex., Austin, 1979-80, gen. counsel to the sec. of state, 1980-81; spl. asst. to the pres., to the chief of staff The White House, Washington, 1981-85; sr. issues advisor Bush-Quayle '88 campaign, Washington, 1987-88; asst. to the pres., dep. to the chief of staff The White House, Washington, 1989-90; atty. Akin Gump Strauss Hauer & Feld, Washington, 1985-88, 91-98, ptnr., 1991—; gen. counsel, exec. v.p. law and govt. affairs AT&T, N.Y.C., 1998—. Issues dir. Bush-Quayle '92 Campaign; dep. dir. strategy Dole-Kemp '96 Campaign; dir. El Paso Electric Co., Am. Coun. Germany; cons. U.S. State Dept.; advisor Bush-Cheney transition. V.p. George Bush Presdl. Libr. Found., College Station, Tex., 1991—; del. Conf. Security Cooperation Europe (CSCE); mem. Adminstrv. Conf. U.S., U.S. Reform Observation Panel for UNESCO. Mem. D.C. Bar Assn., State Bar Tex. Republican. Roman Catholic. Avocations: baseball, tennis. Office: AT&T 1120 20th St NW Ste 1000 Washington DC 20036

CICERCHI, ELEANOR ANN TOMB, fundraising executive; b. Sayre, Pa., Dec. 11, 1944; d. William Horton and Brinton Elizabeth (Cauffiel) Tomb; m. Robert A. Weskerna, Nov. 19, 1966 (div. Feb. 1981); children: Amy Marie, Robert Campbell; m. Philip J. Cicerchi, July 1982. AB with great distinction, Mt. Holyoke Coll., 1966; MS, New Sch. Social Rsch., 1992. Cert. fundraising exec. Sr. mktg. rep. Group Health Plan, Guttenberg, N.J., 1976-79; dir. comty. rels. Burke Rehab. Ctr., White Plains, N.Y., 1979-84; exec. dir. Bergen comty. Coll. Fedn., Paramus, N.J., 1984-86; campaign counsel Brakeley John Price Jones, Inc., Stanford, Conn., 1986-88; v.p. instnl. advancement Marymount Coll., Tarrytown, N.Y., 1988-93; dir. maj. gifts Am. Found. for AIDS Rsch., N.Y.C., 1993-95, chief devel. officer, 1995-96; v.p. devel. and external affairs ORBIS Internat., Inc., N.Y.C., 1996-2000; assoc. v.p. devel. Save the Children, Westport, Conn., 2000—02; dir. devel. The Corning Mus. of Glass, 2002—. Faculty mem. Fundraising Sch., Ctr. Philanthropy, Ind. U., Indpls., 1989—; adj. grad. faculty mem. NYU, N.Y.C., 1990-97, New Sch. for Social Rsch., N.Y.C., 1995—, chmn. PR Group for Vision 2000: The Right to Sight, Geneva, 1998-99; bd. dirs. AMD Alliance, 1999—. Author: Raid!, 1978, Anonymous Giving, 1991; co-author: The Earth Shook and the Sky Was Red, 1976, The Flower of the Virginian, 1980; editor: The Architecture of Bergen County, 1991. Pres. Dem. Club, River Vale, N.J., 1978-81; bd. dirs., immediate past chmn. Philharmonia Virtuosi, Dobbs Ferry, N.Y., 1985-2002; v.p. Orch. of the Finger Lakes, 2003—; bd. dirs., sec. Am. Anorexia-Bulimia Assn., N.Y.C., 1984-1999. Woodrow Wilson fellow, 1966; Sarah Williston scholar, 1964, Mt. Holyoke scholar, 1963. Mem. Nat. Soc. Fundraising Execs. (Greater N.Y. chpt. v.p. 1993-95, Finger Lakes chpt. bd. dirs. 2002—), Assn. for Rsch. on Nonprofit Orgns. and Voluntary Action, Phi Beta Kappa. Office: The Corning Museum of Glass One Museum Way Corning NY 14830 E-mail: ecicerchi@att.net.

CICERO, FRANK, JR., lawyer; b. Nov. 30, 1935; s. Frnk and Mary (Balma) Cicero; m. Janice Pickett, July 11, 1959; children: Erica, Caroline. AB with hons., Wheaton Coll., 1957; M in Pub. Affairs, Woodrow Wilson Sch. of Pub. & Internat. Affairs, 1962; JD, U. Chgo., 1965. Bar: Ill., U.S. Supreme Ct. 1965, various U.S. Ct. of Appeals and Dist. Cts. Polit. sci. instr. Wheaton Coll., Ill., 1957—58; assoc. Kirkland & Ellis, Chgo., 1965—70, ptnr., 1970—. Mem. vis. com. U. Chgo. Law Sch., 1971—74, 1996—99, 2003—, lectr., 1989—90, 1991—92; del. 6th Ill. Constl. Conv., 1969—70. Bd. editors: law rev. U. Chgo. Law Rev.; contbr. articles to profl. jours. Recipient Joseph Henry Beale prize, U. Chgo., 1963, Outstanding Young Man award, Evanston Jaycees, 1970. Fellow: Am. Coll. Trial Lawyers; mem.: ABA, Bar Assn. 7th Fed. Cir., Ill. State Bar Assn., Internat. Bar Assn., Saddle and Cycle Club (bd. govs. 1984), Mid-Am. Club (gov. 1981—84), Ventana Canyon Golf Club, Glen View Club, Chgo. Club. Office: Kirkland & Ellis 200 E Randolph Dr Ste 6000 Chicago IL 60601-6636

CICERO, J. DEBORAH, management consultant; b. Pitts., Mar. 24, 1948; d. James Francis and Margaret V. (Wuillmier) H. Diploma, Columbia Sch. Nursing, Pitts., 1969; BSN, La Roche Coll., Pitts., 1987; M in Pub. Mgmt./Healthcare, Carnegie Mellon U., 1988. RN, Pa.; cert. med. staff coord.; cert. profl. in healthcare quality. Clin. asst. to exec. v.p. Forbes Health System, Pitts., 1983-88; dir. med. staff svcs. Monongahela Valley Hosp., Pitts., 1988-90; quality tracking mgr. Humana, Louisville, 1990-91, regional quality mgmt. dir., 1991-92; sr. cons. MetriCor, Inc., Louisville, 1992-94, mgr. accreditation svcs., 1994-95, HCIA-Sachs, Louisville, 1995-96, sr. quality mgmt. cons., JCAHO liaison, 1996-98; mgr. accreditation svcs. Performance Improvement, 1998-99; dir. accreditation svcs. and performance improvement Soluciant, LLC, 2000—. Author study guide and publ. newsletter. Mem. Nat. Assn. Med. Staff Svcs., Nat. Assn. for Health Care Quality (study guide task force 1996-99), Ky. Assn. for Healthcare Quality (treas. 1996-99, pres. 2000-02), Am. Hosp. Assn., Ky. Assn. for Risk Mgmt. Avocations: exercising, biking, reading, music. Office: Solucient, LLC 216 Rodilin Dr Pittsburgh PA 15235-3312 Business E-Mail: dcicero@solucient.com.

CICERONE, RALPH JOHN, academic administrator, geophysicist; b. New Castle, Pa., May 2, 1943; married; 1 child. SB, MIT, 1965; MS, U. Ill., 1967, PhD in Elec. Engring. and Physics, 1970. Physicist U.S. Dept. Commerce, 1967; rsch. asst. aeronomy U. Ill., 1967—70; assoc. rsch. scientist aeronomy space physics rsch. lab. U. Mich., Ann Arbor, 1970—78; assoc. rsch. chemist ocean rsch. divsn. U. Calif., San Diego, 1978—80, rsch. chemist Scripps inst. oceanography, 1980—81, Daniel G. Aldrich prof., chair geosci. dept. Irvine, 1989—94, dean Sch. Phys. Scis., 1994—98, chancellor, 1998—; sr. scientist, dir. atmospheric chemistry divsn. Nat. Ctr. Atmospheric Rsch., Boulder, Colo., 1980—89. Lectr., asst. prof. elec. engring. U. Mich., Ann Arbor, 1973—75. Assoc. editor: Jour. Geophysics Rsch., 1977—79; editor, 1979—83. Recipient Bower award for Achievement in Sci., Franklin Inst., 1999. Fellow: AAAS, Am. Geophys. Union (Macelwane award 1979, Revelle medal 2002), Am. Meteorol. Soc., Am. Chem. Soc.; mem.: NAS (elected 1990, mem. com., bd. sustainable devel. 1995—98, com. on women in sci. and engring. 2000—, chair com. on climate sci. 2001), Am. Philos. Soc., Am. Acad. Arts and Scis. Office: U Calif Irvine Chancellors Office 501 Administration Bldg Ofc Irvine CA 92697-1900

CICET, DONALD JAMES, lawyer; b. New Orleans, May 24, 1940; s. Arthur Alphonse and Myrtle (Ress) C.; m. Iona Perry. BA, Nicholls State U., 1963; JD, Loyola U., New Orleans, 1969. Bar: La. 1969, U.S. Dist. Ct. (ea. dist.) La. 1972, U.S. Dist. Ct. (mid. dist.) La. 1978, U.S. Dist. Ct. (we. dist.) La. 1979, U.S. Ct. Appeals (5th cir.) 1972, U.S. Supreme Ct. 1972. Pvt. practice, Reserve, La., 1969—88, LaPlace, La., 1988—; staff atty. La. Legis. Coun., 1972-73; legal counsel Nicholls State U. Alumni Fedn., 1974-76, 78-80; spl. counsel Pontchartrain Levee Dist., 1976—2001. Adminstrv. law judge La. Dept. Civil Svc., 1981—. Pres. Boys' State of La. Inc., 1990-92, bd. dirs., 1988—. With AUS, 1964, USNG, 1964-70. Recipient Am. Jurisprudence award Loyola U., 1968. Fellow La. Bar Found.; mem. ABA, La. Bar Assn. (ho. dels. 1973-77, 79-85), 40th Jud. Dist. Bar Assn. (pres. 1985-87). ATLA, La. Trial Lawyers Assn., Nicholls State U. Alumni Fedn. (exec. coun. 1972-76, 77-85, pres. 1982, James Lynn Powell award 1980), Am. Legion (post cmdr. 1976-77, dist. judge adv. 1975-95, judge adv. La. dept. 1990-92, 93-96, mem. La. dept. commn. on nat. security and govtl. affairs 1974-89, chmn. 1977-78, 79-81, 85-89, M.C. Gehr blue cap award 1983). Roman Catholic. Home: 263 Central Ave Reserve LA 70084-6003 Office: 197 Belle Terre Blvd La Place LA 70069-0461

CICIO, ANTHONY LEE, lawyer; b. Birmingham, Ala., July 8, 1926; s. Joseph and Rosa (Tombrello) C.; m. Yvonne Antonio, Nov. 4, 1959; children: Valerie, Anthony Jr., Mark. BS, Samford U., 1951; LLB, Birmingham Sch. Law, 1955. Bar: Ala. 1956, U.S. Dist. Ct. Ala. 1956, U.S. Supreme Ct. 1961, U.S. Ct. Appeals (11th cir.) 1968. Ptnr. Cicio & Cicio, Birmingham, 1976—, sr. ptnr., 1994—. Served as Spl. asst. Atty. Gen. State of Ala., 1980; served Brimingham-Jefferson County Transit Authority, 1962; appt. Birmingham-Jefferson County regional planning com., 1999—. Served with USAF, 1944-46, PTO. Mem. ABA, Ala. Bar Assn. (chmn. pub. relations com.), Birmingham Bar Assn. (ethics com., ch. com. on media and pub. relations), Trial Lawyers Assn. Am., Ala. Trial Lawyers Assn. (exec. com. 1983—), State Indsl. Revenue Bond (adv. coun.), The Club, Vestavia Country Club (Birmingham). Democrat. Roman Catholic. Home: 3128 N Woodridge Rd Birmingham AL 35223-2750 Office: Cicio & Cicio PC Cicio Profl Bldg 2153 14th Ave S Birmingham AL 35205-3921

CICIRELLI, VICTOR GEORGE, psychologist; b. Miami, Fla., Oct. 1, 1926; s. Felix and Rene (DeMaria) C.; m. Jean Alice Solveson, Aug. 9, 1953; children: Ann Victoria, Michael Felix, Gregory Sheldon. BS, Notre Dame U., 1947; MA, U. Ill., Urbana, 1950; M.Ed., U. Miami, 1956; PhD (Univ. fellow), U. Mich., 1964; PhD, Mich. State U., 1971. Asst. prof. ednl. psychology U. Mich., 1963-65; dir. student teaching for elem., secondary and M.A.T. programs U. Pa., 1965-67; assoc. prof. early childhood edn. Ohio U., 1967-68; dir. research Nat. Evaluation of Head Start Westinghouse Learning Corp. at Ohio U., 1968-69; Office Edn. postdoctoral fellow U. Wis. Inst. Cognitive Learning, 1969-70; prof. human devel. Purdue U., 1970-73, prof. devel./aging psychology, 1974—, dir. devel. psychology program, 1977-78, 80-81, 82-83, 92-93, 96, 99-2001. Vis. sci. fellow Max Planck Inst. for Human Devel. and Edn., Berlin, 1991; fellow Ctr. for Health Policy Rsch., J. Hillis Miller Health Sci. Ctr., Sch. Medicine, U. Fla., Gainesville, summer 1991; cons. in field; mem. research adv. bd. Calif. Commn. for Tchr. Preparation and Licensing, 1973-78; scholar NSF Inst., Ohio U., 1956, Am. U., 1958, U. Fla., 1960. Author: Helping Elderly Parents: Role of Adult Children, 1981, Family Caregiving: Autonomous and Paternalistic Decision Making, 1992, Sibling Relationships Across the Life Span, 1995, Older Adults' Views on Death, 2002; mem. editl. bd.: Jour. Marriage and the Family, 1990—; contbr. articles to profl. publs. Bd. dirs. Nat. Com. on Prevention of Elder Abuse, 1988-91; mem. adv. com. Ind. Geriatric Edn. Ctr., U. Ind., 1991. Grantee OEO, 1968-69, 71-73, U.S. Office Edn., 1971-73; Nat. Inst. Edn., 1973-74, NIH, 1973-74, Office Child Devel., 1973-74, Nat. Ret. Tchrs. Assn./Am. Assn. Ret. Persons Andrus Found., 1978-82, 90-91, 92, 95, Retirement Rsch. Found., 1984-85, 87-89; fellow Andrew Norman Inst. Advanced Study, Andrus Gerontology Ctr., U. So. Calif., 1984, Gerontology Soc., 1983, 84. Fellow APA, Gerontol. Soc.; mem. Internat. Soc. Study Behavioral Deve., Am. Psychol. Soc., Am. Assn. Aging, Nat. Coun. on Family Rels. Soc. for Chaos Theory, Phi Kappa Phi. Roman Catholic. Home: 1221 N Salisbury St West Lafayette IN 47906-2415 Office: Purdue U Dept Psychol Sci West Lafayette IN 47907 E-mail: victor@psych.purdue.edu.

CICOLANI, ANGELO GEORGE, research and development company executive, operating engineer; b. Norwood, Mass., Mar. 4, 1933; s. Luigi and Maria (Fossa) Cicolani; m. Marilyn Adell Griffith, June 4, 1955 (div. Jan. 1968); children: George, Susanne, Diana; m. Patricia Anne Kirsch, Nov. 1, 1979 (dec. July 1995); m. Christine Elizabeth Blair, Apr. 1, 2001. Student, Northeastern U., 1950; BS, U.S. Naval Acad., Annapolis, Md., 1955, Naval Postgrad. Sch., 1969. Commd. ensign U.S. Navy, 1955, advanced through grades to lt. comdr., 1975, chief reactor operator, 1958-62, exec. officer, 1963-67, sys. analyst for Strategic Sys. Project Office, 1969-75; cons. Arlington, 1975-77; sr. rschr. R&D Assocs., Arlington, 1977-82, program mgr., sr. scientist, 1982-87, chief staff, tech. dir. Springfield Rsch. Facility, 1988—2003. Underwriter music commns., 1997—. Author: The Role of Systems Analysis, 1974; contbr. . Pres. emeritus bd. dirs. Dumbarton Concerts, Washington, 1982—. Mem.: Mineral Soc. D.C. (pres. 1972—77), Ops. Rsch. Soc. Am., Nature Conservancy, Mil. Officers Assn., Naval Submarine League, Naval Inst. Achievements include development of installation and undeground facilities vulnerability assessment techniques and courses of instruction.

CICONTE, EDWARD THOMAS, lawyer; b. Wilmington, Del., Dec. 14, 1948; s. Joseph John and Josephine E. (Roda) Ciconte; m. Diane Marie Penza, Mar. 3, 1973; children: Andrea, Michele, Jacklyn. BS, St. Josephs U., Phila., 1970; JD, Villanova U., 1973. Bar: Del. 1973, US Dist. Ct. Del. 1973. Ptnr. Ciconte, Roseman & Wasserman, Wilmington, 1973—. Co-author: Delaware Collection Law, 1982. Capt. USAF, 1974. Mem.: ABA, Am. Bd. Trial Advocates (past pres. Del. chpt.), Comml. Law League Am., Del. Trial Lawyers Assn., Am. Trial Lawyers Assn., Del. Bar Assn. Democrat. Roman Catholic. Home: 4009 Springfield Ln Wilmington DE 19807-2251 Office: Ciconte Roseman and Wasserman 1300 N King St Wilmington DE 19801-3220 E-mail: crw@dol.net.

CIELINSKI-KESSLER, AUDREY ANN, technical writer, publisher, small business owner; b. Cleve., Sept. 10, 1957; d. Joseph and Dorothy Antoinette (Hanna) Cielinski. BJ with high honors, U. Tex., 1979. Reporter, writer Med. World News mag., N.Y.C., 1979, asst. copy chief Houston, 1983-84; free-lance writer, editor, 1984—; editorial asst. Jour Health and Social Behavior, Houston, 1980-81; sec. dept. psychiatry Baylor Coll. Medicine, Houston, 1980-81; procedures analyst, tech. writer, tech. librarian Harris County Data Processing Dept., Houston, 1981-83; communications specialist III, Wang systems adminstr. office of planning and rsch. Houston Police Dept.; tchr. tech. writing class, 1985-89; tech. writer Chevron Exploration and Prodn. Svcs. Co., Houston, 1990-92; freelance tech. writer, 1992—; owner The Write Hand of Ohio, Kent, 1992—. Contbr. stories and articles newspapers and mags.; editor newsletters At the Summit, Signals, CEPS Synergy, PCLIBtm Letter, Insights, Steps & Specs., The Voter, LPC Portage County Leader. Vol. writer, graphic designer, office religious edn. St. Ambrose Roman Cath. Ch., Houston, 1983-92; vol. editor newsletters Greater Houston area Am. Cancer Soc. and VGS, Inc., West Knoll News, At the Summit; mem. City of Kent Bd. of Zoning Appeals, 1996—, vice chair, 1998, chair, 1999-2002; mem. City of Kent Shade Tree Commn., 1996—, chair, 1999-2002; mem. City of Kent Assessment Equalization Bd., 1998—, City of Kent Fair Housing Bd., 1998—, City of Kent Environ. Commn. 1999, Akron Metropolitan Area Transportation Study Citizen Involvement Com., 1999—, vice chair, 2000, chair 2001-02; mem. Leadership Portage County, 1999; bd. mem. Keep Kent Beautiful, vice chair, 2002-03; trustee Cath. Charities of Portage County, v.p. 2002, pres. 2003. Recipient Commendation award Chief of Police, Houston, Chief's Command Employee of Month award June, 1989. Mem. NAFE, Women in Comm., Nat. Assn. Desktop Pubs., Am. Med. Writers Assn., Soc. for Tech. Comm. (mgr. policies and procedures spl. interest group), Soc. Children's Book Writers (assoc.), Women's Network, Kent Area C. of C. (newsletter staff 1999), Sigma Delta Chi, Phi Kappa Phi, Alpha Lambda Delta. Home and Office: 1638 S Lincoln St Kent OH 44240-4449

CIENFUEGOS, MAURICIO, professional soccer player; b. San Salvador, El Salvador, Feb. 12, 1968; Profl. soccer player El Salvador's First Divsn., 1988—91, 1993—95, Mex. Nat. Team, 1991—93; midfielder L.A. Galaxy, 1996—. Three time MLS All-Star; named Galaxy's Most Valuable Player, 1997; one of six Galaxy players selected to 1996 All-Star game. Office: Los Angeles Galaxy 1010 Rose Bowl Dr Pasadena CA 91103-2864

CIESLA, ANDREW R. state legislator; b. Point Pleasant, N.J., July 24, 1953; m. Debra Holmes; children: Alexander, Andrew, Adam. BA, Montclair State Coll., 1975; postgrad., Syracuse U., 1976. Councilman Brick (N.J.) Twp., 1987-91; mem. N.J. Senate, Dist. 10, Trenton, 1991—; v.p. L&H Plumbing & Heating Supply Inc., Lakewood, N.J. Republican. Address: 852 Highway 70 Brick NJ 08724-2951*

CIESLAK, WILLIAM, academic administrator; b. East Chgo., Sept. 12, 1946; s. Walter Bernard and Irene Joan (Koziol) C. BA in Philosopy, BA in Theology, St. Joseph Coll., Rennasalear, Ind., 1969; MDiv., Franciscan Sch. Theology, Berkeley, Calif., 1973; PhD, Grad. Theol. Union, Berkeley, Calif., 1979. Prof. Franciscan Sch. Theology, Berkeley, 1980—, pres., 1993—. Mem. Soc. Liturgica, N. Am. Acad. Liturgy, Cath. Theol. Soc. Am. Democrat. Office: Franciscan Sch Theology 1712 Euclid Ave Berkeley CA 94709-1294

CIESZEWSKI, SANDRA JOSEPHINE, artist, retired manufacturing company manager; b. Cleve., June 7, 1941; d. Chester L. and Cecilia (Laska) C. BA in Chemistry, Ursuline Coll., 1962; BA in Art History, Cleve. State U., 1981; Exec. MBA, Baldwin Wallace Coll., 1989. Chemist Harshaw Chem. Co., Cleve., 1962-65, Union Carbide Corp., Parma, Ohio, 1965-79; project mgr. Gould, Inc., Eastlake, Ohio, 1979-91; product engring. mgr.- lithium Duracell Global Bus. Mgmt. Group, Lexington, N.C., 1992-2001; ret. Interim exhbns. coord. Davidson County C.C., 2003—. Mem. Soc. of Women Engrs. (N.E. Ohio sect.) Cleve. Garden Ctr., Cleve. Mus. Art. Mem.: Electrochem. Soc. (treas. 1980), Soc. Applied Spectroscopy, Am. Chem. Soc., Winston-Salem Cinema Soc. (programming chmn. 1997—98, bd. dirs. 1997—, treas. 1998—2002), Assoc. Artists of Winston-Salem (bd. dirs. 1998—, sec. 1999—2002, interim exec. dir. 2002, pres. 2002—03), Women's Club (sec. Walton Hills chpt. 1985, treas. 1991). Avocations: gardening, skiing, cycling. Home: 1494 Hickory Tree Rd Winston Salem NC 27127-9142 E-mail: scies@aol.com.

CIFALDI, ROSALIE, private investigator; Lic. pvt. detective Wis. Pvt. detective, Brookfield, Wis. Office: Rapid Results Investigations LLC PO Box 143 Brookfield WI 53008

CIFARELLI, THOMAS ABITABILE, lawyer; b. Queens, N.Y., Feb. 7, 1967; s. Philip S. and Gina A. Cifarelli; m. Lilian G. Cifarelli, Sept. 20, 1997; children: Vincent Thomas, Michael Greco. BA magna cum laude, UCLA, 1989; JD, Loyola U., 1992. Bar: Calif. 1992, U.S. Dist. Ct. (cen. dist.) Calif. 1994, U.S. Supreme Ct. 2001. Assoc. atty. Mazursky Schwartz & Angelo, L.A., 1992-94; trial atty. Law Offices of Philip Michels, L.A., 1994-97; trial atty., ptnr. The Cifarelli Law Firm, Santa Ana, Calif., 1997—. Lead trial & appellate atty. M.G. vs. Time Warner, Inc., etal. privacy rights case; lectr. Consumer Attys. Assn. Calif. Contbr. articles to law pubs. Mem. Million Dollar Advocates Forum (life), L.A. World Affairs Coun., 1998. Named one of 10 Up and Coming Litigators in Calif., L.A. Daily Jour., 2001. Mem. ATLA, Consumer Attys. Assn. Calif. (seminar spkr., bd. govs. 2000—, diplomat's club), Orange County Trial Lawyers Assn. Avocations: fitness, writing, family, travel, reading. E-mail: tomc@cifarellilaw.com.

CIFELLI, JOHN LOUIS, lawyer; b. Chicago Heights, Ill., Aug. 19, 1923; s. Antonio and Domenica (Liberatore) C.; m. Irene Romandine, Jan. 4, 1948; children— Carla, David, John L., Bruce, Thomas, Carol. Student, Bowdoin Coll., 1943, Norwick Mil. Acad., 1943, Mt. Piliar Acad., 1943, U. Ill. Extension Ctr., 1946-47; LLB, DePaul U., 1950, JD (hon.), 1975. Bar: Ill. 1950, U.S. Supreme Ct. 1960. Ptnr. Piacenti, Cifelli & Sims, Chicago Heights, 1950-78; pres. John L. Cifelli & Assocs., Chicago Heights, 1978-85; sr. ptnr. Cifelli Baczynski & Scrementi Ltd. (now Cifelli & Scrementi), Chicago Heights, 1985—; spl. counsel City of Chicago Heights, 1961-72; village atty. Village of Richton Park, Ill., 1962-77, Village of Ford Heights, Ill., 1984-89. Counsel Maj. League Umpires Assn., 1973-78, Ill. High Sch. Baseball Coaches Assn., 1975-89. Sec. Bd. Fire and Police, Chicago Heights, 1959-65; co-founder Small Fry Internat. Basketball, 1969, pres., 1969— ; coach, baseball coordinator Chicago Heights Park Dist., 1970-75; coach Babe Ruth League Baseball, 1972, 74, 75, asst. Ill. dir., 1973; dir. Ill. tournament, 1973. Served to 2d lt. USAAF, 1942-45, ETO. Mem. ABA, Ill. Bar Assn., Ill. Trial Lawyers Assn., Assn. Trial Lawyers Am., Justinian Soc. Lawyers, Isaac Walton League, Italo Am. Vets. Group, VFW (judge adv. 1951-72), Cath. War Vets. (judge adv. 1951-70), Am. Legion. Clubs: Chicago Heights Country (bd. dirs. 1972-76), Mt. Carmel; Pike Lake Fishing (Wis.). Lodges: Moose, Amaseno. Republican. Avocations: hunting, fishing, golf. Home: 879 Amico Dr Chicago Heights IL 60411 Office: Cifelli & Scrementi 1700 S Halsted St Ste 201 Chicago Heights IL 60411-3555 E-mail: cifellilawfirm@msn.com.

CIKOVSKY, NICOLAI, JR., retired curator, art history educator; b. N.Y.C., Feb. 11, 1933; s. Nicolai and Hortense (Hilbert) C.; m. Sarah Eden Greenough, June 17, 1978; children— Emily Hilbert, Sophia Greenough. AB magna cum laude, Harvard Coll., 1955; A.M., Harvard U., 1958, PhD, 1965. Asst. prof. Skidmore Coll., Saratoga Springs, N.Y., 1961-63; chmn., assoc. prof. Pomona Coll., Claremont, Calif., 1964-68; vis. assoc. prof. U. Tex., Austin, 1969-70; dir. art gallery, assoc. prof. Vassar Coll., Poughkeepsie, N.Y., 1971-74; prof., chmn. dept. art U. N.Mex., Albuquerque, 1974-83; curator Am. & British painting Nat. Gallery Art, Washington, 1983—2003, sr. curator Am. and Brit. painting, 1998—2003; ret., 2003. Author: Sanford Robinson Gifford, exhbn. catalogue, 1970; editor: Lectures on the Affinity of Painting with the Other Fine Arts (Samuel F.B. Morse), 1983; George Inness, 1971, The Life and Work of George Inness, 1977, Winslow Homer, 1990, Winslow Homer Watercolors, 1991, George Inness, 1993; contbg. author: exhbn. catalogues George Inness, 1985, Ansel Adams: Classic Images, 1985, William Merritt Chase: Summers at Shinnecock, 1987, Raphaelle Peale Still Lifes, 1988, William M. Harnett, 1992, James McNeill Whistler, 1994, Winslow Homer, 1995; also articles on William Merritt Chase, George Inness, Winslow Homer, Thomas Eakins, Am. landscape painting, Am. impressionism. Am. Council Learned Socs.-Smithsonian Instn. postdoctoral research fellow, 1968-69; Guggenheim fellow, 1978-79; Kress sr. fellow Nat. Gallery Art, 1983 Mem. Phi Beta Kappa. Clubs: Harvard (N.Y.C.). E-mail: nicolai.cikovsky@verizon.net.

CILELLA, MARY WINIFRED, director; b. Oak Park, Ill., Aug. 24, 1943; d. Charles William Sr. and Theresa Mary (Gilligan) Broucek; m. Salvatore G. Cilella Jr., Aug. 29, 1970; children: Salvatore George III, Peter Dominic. BA, Dominican U., 1965; MAT, U. Notre Dame, 1966; grad. The Prin.'s Inst., Harvard U., 1993; postgrad., U. S.C., 1994-97. Tchr. Miner Jr. H.S., Arlington Heights, Ill., 1966-67; sec. White House, Washington, 1969-70; devel. officer Textile Mus., Washington, 1982-83; dir. meetings and continuing edn. Am. Assn. Mus., Washington, 1983-87; interim lower sch. head, lower sch. head Heathwood Hall Episc. Sch., Columbia, S.C., 1989-94, dir. acad. adminstrn., 1994-95, dir. fin. and adminstrn., 1995-96, asst. head, 1996-98, assoc. head fin. and ops., 1998—2001; cons. Park Tudor Sch., Indpls., 2001—02, dir. Russel and Mary Williams Learning Project, 2002—. Mem. profl. edn. unit adv. com. U. S.C., 1996-2001; mem. U.S. Dept. of Edn.'s Blue Ribbon Schs. Planning Group, 1996; examiner Malcolm Baldrige Nat. Quality award bd. U.S. Dept. Commerce and Nat. Inst. Stds. and Tech., 1999, 2000. Mem. ASCD, Phi Delta Kappa. Roman Catholic. Avocations: gardening, collecting antiques, music, aerobics. Home: 905 Tamarack Cir S Dr Indianapolis IN 46260 Office: Park Tudor Sch 7200 North College Ave Indianapolis IN 46240 E-mail: mcilella@parktudor.org.

CILELLA, SALVATORE GEORGE, JR., museum director; b. Chgo., Oct. 19, 1941; s. Salvatore G. and Mary Genevieve (LaRocque) C.; m. Mary Winifred Broucek, Aug. 29, 1970; children: Salvatore G. III, Peter Dominic. BA, U. Notre Dame, 1963, MA in Am. History, 1966; MA in museum adminstrn., Univ. N.Y., Oneonta, 1971. Community amb. Experiment in Internat. Living, Iran, 1965; exec. dir. No. Ind. Hist. Soc., South Bend, 1970-72; registrar, asst. dir. N.Y. State Hist. Assn., Cooperstown, 1973-76; exec. dir. Historic Bethlehem (Pa.) Inc., 1976-79; dir. devel. and membership Old Sturbridge (Mass.) Village, 1979-81; devel. officer Smithsonian Instn., Washington, 1981-87; exec. dir. Columbia (S.C.) Mus. Art, 1987-2001; pres., CEO Ind. Hist. Soc., Indpls., 2001—. Cons. various mus., 1979—; overseer Old Sturbridge Village, 1982-89; lectr. Seminar for Hist. Adminstrn., Williamsburg, Va., 1983—, Mus. Mgmt. Program, Boulder, Colo., 1993. Contbr. articles to profl. jours. Co-chmn. United Black Fund, 1999; chmn. search com. Hist. Columbia; vice chair Gov.'s Commn. on Heritage; bd. dirs. Indpls. Conv. and Visitors Assn. Decorated Army commendation medal, 1969. Mem.: Am. Assn. for State and Local History, Am. Hist. Print Collections Assn., Am. Assn. Mus. (chmn. devel. and membership com. 1984—89, bd. dirs. 1989—92), Univ. Club, Columbia Club. Roman Catholic. Avocations: collecting 18th and 19th century American prints and maps, antiques, Civil War artifacts and tribal rugs. Office: Ind Hist Soc 450 W Ohio St Indianapolis IN 46202-3269

CILZ, DOUGLAS ARTHUR, lawyer; b. Rugby, N.D., Feb. 22, 1949; s. Fred W. and Arliene (Nelson) C.; m. Kathy Ann Walker, June 10, 1972; children: Jennifer, Nicholas. BS, Dickinson State U., 1976; JD, U. N.D., Grand Forks, 1980. Bar: N.D. 1980, U.S. Dist. Ct. N.D. 1980, Minn. 1981, U.S. Tax Ct. 1981, U.S. Claims Ct. 1981. Atty. Qualley Larson & Jones, Fargo, N.D., 1980-81, Pearson & Christensen, Grand Forks, N.D., 1981-87; ptnr. Juntunen, Cilz & Hager, Grand Forks, 1987—98; atty. N.D. Dept. Transp., Grand Forks, 1998—. Instr. East Grand Forks (Minn.) Tech. Coll., 1989-92; apptd. spl. asst. atty. gen. Bank N.D., 1993—; apptd. temporary adminstrv. law judge N.D. Office Adminstrv. Hearings, 1995-2003. Sgt. USAF, 1968-71. Mem. ABA, Minn. Bar Assn., N.D. Bar Assn., Grand Forks C. of C. Lutheran. Avocations: golf, sailing, fishing. Office: ND Dept Transportation 1951 N Washington St Grand Forks ND 58203-1420

CIMA, CHERYL ANN, medical/surgical nurse; b. St. Charles, Mo., Jan. 29, 1965; d. Harry H. and Margaret Mary (Schuette) C. Diploma in nursing with honors, St. Luke's Sch. Nursing, St. Louis, 1986; BSN magna cum laude, U. Mo., St. Louis, 1988. RN, Mo. Staff nurse cardiothoracic stepdown unit Barnes Hosp., St. Louis, 1986-93, staff nurse interventional and vascular radiology, 1993-99; staff nurse, acute dialysis unit Barnes Jewish Hosp., 1999—2003; clin. rsch. nurse coord. Dept. Surgery Washington U., St. Louis, 2003—. John Sullivan Waggoner scholar, St. Luke's Merit scholar, Bridgeton Kiwanis scholar. Mem. U. Mo.-St. Louis Nursing Honor Soc., Sigma Theta Tau. Home: 12480 Larkwood Dr Saint Louis MO 63146-4634

CIMBALA, STEPHEN JOSEPH, political science educator; b. Pitts., Nov. 4, 1943; s. Helen Alice and Stephen Joseph Cimbala; m. Elizabeth Ann Harder, Aug. 19, 1967; children: David Craig, Christopher John. PhD, U. Wis., 1969. Asst. prof. SUNY, Stony Brook, 1969—73; assoc. prof. Penn State U., Media, 1973—86, prof., 1986—. Author numerous books on national security. Cmty. outreach, lectures, Delaware County, Pa., 1973—2002. Recipient Eisenhower award for Disting. Tchg., Pa, State U. Office: Pa State Delaware County Campus 118 Vairo Library Media PA 19063 E-mail: sjc2@psu.edu.

CIMINI, JOSEPH FEDELE, law educator, lawyer, former magistrate; b. Scranton, Pa., Sept. 8, 1948; s. Frank Anthony and Dorothy Theresa (Musso) C. AB in German and Polit. Sci., U. Scranton, 1970; JD Columbus Sch. Law, Cath. U. Am., 1973. Bar: Pa. 1973, U.S. Dist. Ct. (mid. dist.) Pa. 1973, D.C. 1976, U.S. Ct. Appeals (3d cir.) 1978, U.S. Supreme Ct. 1978. Law clk. to judge Ct. Common Pleas Lackawanna County (Pa.), 1973-75; asst. U.S. atty. Middle Dist. Pa., Pa. Dept. Justice, 1975-80; spl. asst. to U.S. Atty. Middle Dist. Pa., 1980-81; asst. prof. sociology/criminal justice U. Scranton, 1980-94, assoc. prof., 1994—, chmn. dept., 2001—. U.S. magistrate judge U.S. Dist. Ct. (mid. dist.) Pa., 1981-92; spl. trial master Lackawanna County Ct. Common Pleas, 1995—. Past pres., trustee Lackawanna Hist. Soc.; v.p. adv. bd. Holy Family Residence, Scranton, Pa., 1997-2001, pres., 2002—; v.p. pastoral coun. St. Francis Ch., 1994-96; mem. cmty. adv. bd. MINSEC-Scranton, 2003. Recipient Meritorious award Dept. Justice; German Acad. Exchange Service fgn. study travel grantee, W.Ger., 1981. Mem. ABA, Fed. Bar Assn. (past v.p. mid. dist. Pa. chpt.), Am. Judges Assn., Fed. Magistrate Judges Assn., Am. Justinian Soc. of Jurists, Acad. Criminal Justice Scis., Pa. Bar Assn., Northeastern Assn. Criminal Justice Scis. (pres. 1987-88), Lackawanna Bar Assn., Pa. Sociol. Soc. (treas.), U. Scranton Alumni (nat. sec. 1997-99), Cath. U. Law Alumni, Purple Club, Victor Alfieri Lit. Soc., UNICO Nat., Dante Lit. Soc. Republican. Roman Catholic. Address: Univ Scranton Dept Sociology/Criminal Justice Scranton PA 18510-4605 E-mail: ciminij1@scranton.edu.

CIMINO, JAMES JOSEPH, physician, researcher, educator; b. Buffalo, May 23, 1955; s. James Ernest Cimino and Dorothy Hillary Naperkoski; m. Andria Marie Brummitt; children: Sara, Rebecca, Rachel. BSc, Brown U., 1977; MD, N.Y. Med. Coll., 1981. Diplomate Am. Bd. Internal Medicine. Resident in internal medicine St. Vincent's Hosp., N.Y.C., 1981-84, attending physician, 1985; clin. rsch. fellow Harvard U., Boston, 1985-88; asst. prof. Columbia U., N.Y.C., 1988-95, assoc. prof., 1995—2002, prof., 2002—. Co-arch. hosp. info. sys. Columbia-Presbyn. Med. Ctr., 1988; bd. sci. counsellors Nat. Libr. Medicine, Bethesda, Md., 1991-95. Fellow ACP, Am. Coll. Med. Informatics; mem. Am. Med. Informatics Assn. (fellow 1992, bd. dirs. 1994-97, sci. program chair 1996, sec. 1998-99). Office: Columbia U 622 W 168th St New York NY 10032-3720 Fax: 212-305-3302.

CIMINO, JAY, automotive company executive; BA, U of Denver, Denver. CEO Phil Long Dealerships, Colorado Springs, Colo. Office: Phil Long Ford 1212 Motor City Dr Colorado Springs CO 80906-1392*

CIMINO, JOSEPH ANTHONY, physician, educator; b. N.Y.C., Jan. 1, 1934; m. Margaret Langan; children: Andrea, Laura, Lisa, Joseph, Linda, Margaret, John BA in Am. History, Harvard U., 1956, M.I.H., 1964, M.P.H., 1965; MS in Biology, Fordham U., 1958; MD, U. Buffalo, 1962. Diplomate: Am. Bd. Preventive Medicine. Intern Grasslands Hosp., Valhalla, N.Y., 1962-63; AEC fellow in environ. medicine Harvard U. Sch. Public Health, 1963-65; research asso., health officer N.Y.C. Dept. Health, 1965-66; dir. Bur. Community Safety and Occupational Health, 1968-71, dep. commr. health, 1971-72, commr. health, 1972-74; chief med. officer N.Y.C. Dept. Sanitation, 1966-69; med. dir. N.Y.C. Poison Control Center, 1966-72; dir. health and safety N.Y.C. Environ. Protection Adminstrn., 1968-71; commr. hosps. Westchester County, N.Y., 1974-78; pres., chief exec. officer N.Y. Med. Coll., 1978-81, prof. preventive medicine, 1976—, chmn. dept. preventive medicine, 1980—; pres. Occupational Medicine Assocs., 1978—. Assoc. prof. environ. medicine and pub. health NYU, 1971—76; prof. cmty. dynamics Pace U., 1977—78; adj. prof. pub. health and tropical medicine Tulane U., 1972—76; lectr. in pub. health Columbia U., 1973—76; vis. prof. cmty. health Albert Einstein Coll. Medicine, 1973—76, N.Y. State Pub. Health Coun.; pres. bd. Dominican Sisters Family Health Svcs., Inc. Author: Safety: Protection from Injury, 1969, Medical Service Manual, 1971, Drug Abuse Treatment Agencies in New York City, 1972; author numerous profl. monographs; contbr. articles to profl. publs. Chmn. Cath. Interracial Coun. of Westchester County; chief med. cons. N.Y.C. CSC, 1966-71. Civilian U.S. Army, 1964-65; mem. exec. com. Med.Bd. West Med. Ctr., chair greivance com., N.Y. med. Coll., mem. N.Y.S. Pub. Health Council. Fellow Am. Coll. Preventive Medicine, N.Y. Acad. Medicine, Am. Coll. Occupational Medicine, N.Y. Acad. Sci.; mem. Am. Pub. Health Assn., N.Y.C. Pub. Health Assn., Indsl. Med. Assn., Assn. Govtl. Hygienists, Aerospace Med. Assn., Westchester County Med. Soc., N.Y. State Med. Assn., AMA, Am. Soc. Clin. Nutrition. Home: 50 Willard Ave Tarrytown NY 10591-1210 Office: NY Med Coll Dept Preventive Med Valhalla NY 10595

CIMINO, LEWIS R., JR., surgeon; b. New London, Conn., 1945; Grad., U. Notre Dame, 1968; MD, Creighton U., 1972. Diplomate Am. Bd. Surgery. Intern San Francisco Gen. Hosp., 1972-73; resident gen. surgery U. Calif. Hosps., 1973-76, Highland Gen. Hosp., Oakland, Calif., 1976-77; fellow vascular surgery Scenic Gen. Hosp., Modesto, Calif., 1977-78; surgeon Drs. Med. Ctr., Modesto, Calif.; asst. clin. prof. U. Calif., Davis; pvt. practice. Fellow ACS; mem. AMA, Stanislaus Med. Soc. Office: Orangeburg Med Ctr 1448 Florida Ave Modesto CA 95350-4424

CIMINO, RICHARD DENNIS, lawyer; b. Omaha, June 6, 1947; s. Lewis Raymond and Louise (Monaco) C.; m. Mary Scott Reins, Feb. 12, 1977; children: John Damon, Mary Drusilla, Robert Andrew, Ann Marie. BBA, U. Notre Dame, 1969; JD, St. Louis U., 1974. Bar: Nebr. 1975, Kans. 1989, Fla. 1994, U.S. Dist. Ct. Nebr. 1975, U.S. Dist. Ct. Kans. 1989, U.S. Dist. Ct. Fla. 1995. Assoc. Kutak, Rock & Campbell, Omaha, 1975-78, ptnr., 1979; v.p., gen. counsel Silvey Refrigerated Carriers, Omaha, 1980-86, pres., 1987; ptnr. Dwyer, Pohren, Wood, Heavey & Grimm, Omaha, 1988-89; pvt. practice St. Marys, Kans., 1989-93; ptnr. Treadwell, Cimino & McElrath, Naples, Fla., 1993—. Editor St. Louis U. Law Jour., 1972-74. Bd. dirs. Bergan Mercy Hosp Found., Omaha, 1986-87. With U.S. Army, 1969-71, Vietnam. Mem. Fla. Bar Assn., Kans. Bar Assn., Nebr. Bar Assn., Collier County Bar Assn., Notre Dame Alumni Club (pres. Omaha chpt. 1980), Alpha Sigma Nu. Republican. Roman Catholic. Avocations: golf, family activities. Office: 3838 Tamiami Trl N Naples FL 34103-3590 E-mail: dome96@aol.com.

CINABRO, ROBERT HENRY, lawyer; b. Kalamazoo, June 10, 1948; s. Louis and Maria (Breviglieri) C.; m. Pamela Mae Eschenburg, Aug. 19, 1972; children: Jennifer Elise, Michael Thomas. BA cum laude, Kalamazoo Coll., 1970; JD, Cornell U., 1973. Bar: Mich. 1973, U.S. Dist. Ct. (we. dist.) Mich., 1975, U.S. Supreme Ct. 1979, U.S. Ct. Appeals (6th cir.) 1983, Fla. 1987. Law clk. to presiding judge 9th Judicial Ct., Kalamazoo, 1973-74; asst. city atty. City of Kalamazoo, 1974-77, dep. city atty., 1977-88, city atty., 1988—. Civil mediator 9th Jud. Cir. Ct., Kalamazoo, 1985—; civil arbitrator U.S. Dist. Ct. for We. Dist. Mich., Grand Rapids, 1986—; legal counsel Kalamazoo Met. Transit Authority, 1985-88. Mem. Kalamazoo Criminal Justice Commn., 1982-83, Kalamazoo Safety Coun., Drunk Driving Task Force, 1983—85 commr. Kalamazoo Hosp. Fin. Authority, 1988—; bd. dirs. Kalamazoo County Humane Soc., 1983-85. Mem. ABA, Kalamazoo County Bar Assn., Fed. Bar Assn., Fla. Bar Assn., Phi Beta Kappa. Roman Catholic. Avocations: civil war history, travel, animal welfare. Home: 2525 Frederick Ave Kalamazoo MI 49008-2149 Office: Office of City Atty 234 W Cedar St Kalamazoo MI 49007-5151 E-mail: cinabror@kalamazoocity.org.

CINAT, MARIANNE EVA, surgeon; b. Detroit, Mich., Oct. 1965; d. Larry Joseph and Gloria Mary Lucia Cinat. MD, U. of Mich., 1990. Lic. Calif. Asst. prof. of surgery Univ of Calif. - Irvine, Orange, 1996—. Dir. surg. critical care fellow U. Calif.-Irvine, Orange, dir. burn ICU, 1998—, dir. trauma/critical care rsch. Contbr. articles to rsch. jours. (Resident Tchg. award, 1998, Student Tchg. award, 1998). Recipient Plenary award, Am. Fedn. for Med. Rsch., 1999, Scholarship Essay Contest award, Plastic Surgery Edn. Found., 1999, grant, Internat. Assn. of Firefighters. Fellow: ACS (assoc.; asst. program chairperson 2002—03, So. Calif. chpt., Young Surgeon Rep. So. Calif. chpt. 2000, Resident Paper Competition winner 2000); mem.: Orange County Burn Assn. (bd. dirs. 2000), Shock Soc., Soc. of Critical Care Medicine, Am. Burn Assn., Orange County Surg. Soc. (treas. 2002—03, program chairperson 2002—03). Avocations: scuba diving, golf, travel. Office: U Calif-Irvine Med Ctr Bldg 53 Rte 81 101 The City Dr Orange CA 92868 Office Fax: 714-456-6048. E-mail: mecinat@uci.edu.

CINBERG, JAMES ZUBOW, otolaryngologist, educator; b. N.Y., June 19, 1945; BA, Dartmouth Coll.; MD, Columbia U., 1970. Intern Mt. Sinai Hosp., N.Y.C., 1970—71, resident in surgery, 1971—72; resident in otolaryngology Columbia-Presbyn. Med. Ctr., N.Y.C., 1972—75; fellow in otolaryngology Lenox Hill Hosp., N.Y.C., 1975; otolaryngologist St. Barnabas Hosp., NJ, Union Hosp., NJ, St. James Hosp., NJ. Clin. asst. prof. Seton Hall Postgrad. Med. Sch. Recipient Ira Tresley award, 1985, honor award Am. Acad. Otolaryngology, 1985. Mem.: ACS, Soc. Head and Neck Surgeons, Am. Acad. Otolaryngology-Head and Neck Surgery. Unitarian-Universalist. Office: 219 S Broad St Elizabeth NJ 07202-3453 E-mail: info@balancecontrol.com.

CINCA, SILVIA (ROBERTA KING), writer, producer; b. Bucharest, Romania; came to U.S., 1977; d. Stephan Niculescu and Alexandrina (Mosu) Niculescu; married, Feb. 19, 1968; children: Robert, Shelby. Grad., Inst. I.L. Caragiale, Inst. Dramatic Art & Cinema, 1960, Tex. U., 1978-79, No. Va. C.C., 1979-80, Amb. Bible Coll., 1992. Editor, film critic, TV sect. Romanian Nat. Broadcasting Sys., 1960-73, Radio Free Europe/Radio Liberty, Washington, 1982-99. Author in Romanian lang.; The Cat and The Words, 1966, Destroy the Mirrors, 1969, The Non-Stop Express, 1971, The Unseen Snow, 1973, Scream, 1989, X Ray for Love, (Romfest award Can. 1992), 1992, The Ocean, 1992, X Ray for Success, 1993 (Contact Internat. award 1993), Himera: Leaves on Route 7, 1993, Gabriel Speaks, 1996, Gabriel Comes Back, 1997, Fascination of Misteries, 1998, Texas Hit, 1998, Forest of Angels, 1998, Messenger of Hope, 1999, The Change, The Stroke, 2000; author in Eng. lang.: The Night of the Rising Dead, 1985, Comrade Dracula (ARA award 1988), Homo Spiritus (ARA award 1988), 1988, Scream, Romania Ceausescu's Era, 1990, Hoot of the Owl, Forest of Angels, 1999, Lumina, Magical Journey of Life, Dreams, Success, 2002; Texas H4, 2003; contbr. articles to Romanian periodicals; founder Moonfall Press. Mem. Am. Romanian Acad., Pen Am. Writers Club (founder), LiterArt-XXI Internat. Assn. Romanian Writers and Artists, Owner Editura. Home: 202 N George Mason Dr #3 Arlington VA 22203 E-mail: cincaSilvia@aol.com.

CINFICI, WILLIAM FRANK, historian; b. Little Rock AFB, Dec. 6, 1969; s. William and Rose Concetta (Floriani) C. BA in History cum laude, Gettysburg (Pa.) Coll., 1991; student, Widener U. Sch. of Law, 1991-92. Rsch. specialist Berks County Register of Wills Office, Reading, Pa., 1992-94; office support Berks County Employment and Tng. Office, Reading, 1994-95; supr. victim/witness assistance unit Berks Country Dist. Atty.'s Office, Reading, 1995; temp. adminstrv. asst. Chris Talarico Assocs., Inc., West Reading, Pa., 1995-97; mem. election staff Pennsylvanians for Effective Govt., Muhlenberg, 1996; exec. dir. Berks County Rep. Com., Reading, 1997; local registrar divsn. vital records Pa. Dept. Health, Reading, 1997—. Contbr. articles to Italian-Am. Perspective. Chmn. Berks County Young Reps., 2001—; elected mem. Berks County Rep. Com., 1992—, Rep. State Com. Pa., 1998—. Mem. Italian-Am. Cultural Ctr. (bd. dirs.), Order Sons of Italy, Phi Beta Kappa. Home and Office: 1238 Linden St Reading PA 19604-2017

CINO, MARIA, federal agency administrator; b. Buffalo, Apr. 19, 1957; d. Richard J. and Lucy M. (Tripi) C. BA in Polit. Sci., St. John Fisher Coll. Project supr. Rep. Nat. Com., 1981-82, dir. local programs, 1983-84, exec. asst. field dir., 1985-86; rsch. analyst Am. Viewpoint, Inc., 1986-88; adminstrv. asst. Rep. L. William Paxon, 1989-93; exec. dir. Nat. Rep. Congl. Com., 1993—97; asst. sec. and dir. general, U.S. comml. svc. U.S. Dept. Commerce, Washington, 2001—; sr. advisor Wiley, Rein & Fielding, 1997—99; nat. polit. dir. Bush for Pres., 1999—2000; dep. chmn. polit. and congl. rels. Rep. Nat. Com., 2000—01. Mem. Ho. Adminstrv. Assts. Assn. Republican. Avocations: antiques, travel, golf. Office: US Dept Commerce US & Foreign Comml Svc 14th & Constitution Ave NW Washington DC 20230 Office Fax: 202-482-5013.

CINQUEGRANA, AMERICO RALPH, lawyer; b. July 8, 1942; s. Americo and Caroline (Pettine) C.; m. Hope Frances Meader, Aug. 24, 1968; children: Faith, Amelia. Cert., U. Md. Overseas, 1964; BA, U. N.H., 1968; JD, U. Va., 1973. Bar: Conn. 1973, U.S. Dist. Ct. Conn. 1973, U.S. Dist. Ct. (ea. and so. dists.) N.Y. 1973, U.S. Ct. Appeals (2d cir.) 1973. Intelligence officer CIA, Washington, 1968-70; asst. gen. counsel, 1976-79; dep. insp. gen. investigations, 1991-98; chief investigative counsel House Select Com. on Tech. Transfer to China, 1998; spl. counsel to CIA inspector gen., 1999; chief counsel Nat. Commn. for Review of Nat. Reconnaissance Office, 2000; spl. counsel Policy and Security Intelligence Cmty. Mgmt. Staff, 2001. Assoc. Day, Berry, & Howard, Hartford, Conn., 1973-76; dep. counsel to Atty. Gen. for Intelligece Policy, U.S. Dept. Justice, Washington, 1979-91; lectr. UVa. Law Sch., Charlottesville, 1983-85, Cath. U. Law Sch., Washington, 1986—; guest lectr. Brookings Inst., Washington, 1983, 84, Ctr. Law and Nat. Security U. Va. Law Sch., 1990—. Co-author course manual internation Simulation, 1968; author law rev. articles. Served with USAF, 1961-65. Ctr. for Law and Nat. Security grantee, 1983; named to Italian-Am. hall of Fame. Mem. U. N.H. ALumni Assn. (pres. Washington chpt. 1982). Office: Ford House Office Bldg Wasington DC 22102

CIOBANU, NICULAE, oncologist, researcher; b. Bucharest, Romania, Feb. 7, 1947; came to U.S., 1978; s. Niculae and Maria (Dimitriu) C.; m. Ellen J. Ferranti, Sept. 7, 1985; children: Christian, Alexandra. Baccalaureat degree, Lyceum Balcescu, Bucharest, 1965; MD, Bucharest Sch. Medicine, 1971. Diplomate Am. Bd. Internal Medicine, Am. Bd. Med. Oncology, Am. Bd. Hematology. Asst. prof. medicine Albert Einstein Sch. Medicine, Bronx, N.Y., 1983-88, assoc. prof. medicine, 1988—; dir. bone marrow transplant program Montefiore Med. Ctr. Albert Einstein Cancer Ctr., Bronx, 1986-92; dir. bone marrow transplant program St. Vincent's Hosp. and Med. Ctr., N.Y.C., 1993-97; med. dir. stem cell transplant program L.I. Coll. Hosp., Bklyn., 1994-98; chief hematology/oncology St. Clare's Hosp. Health Ctr., 2000—. Dir. bone marrow transplant svc. Schneider Children's Hosp., L.I. Jewish Med. Ctr., 1997-98; dir. hematology/oncology sect. St. Clare's Hosp., N.Y.C., 2000—. Contbr. chpts. to books and numerous articles to profl. jours. in field of bone marrow transplantation, immunotherapy with interleukin-2/LAK, infection in immunocompromised host. Recipient Rep. scholarship of Romania Ministry Edn., 1966-71, nat. rsch. award U.S. Dept. Health, 1982-83, spl. fellowship Leukemia Soc. Am., 1983-85. Fellow ACP; mem. Internat. Soc. Exptl. Hematology, Am. Soc. Clin. Oncology, Am. Soc. Hematology, Am. Radium Soc., Am. Assn. Cancer Rsch. Internat. Soc. Hematotherapy and Graft Engring. (founding mem.). Achievements include initiation of bone marrow transplant programs for British Hosp., Montevideo, Uruguay, Instituto De Criopreservacion Y Transplante Medula Osea, Buenos Aires. Office: 10 E 38th St Fl 7 New York NY 10016-0004

CIOC, CHARLES GREGORY, b. Scottsbluff, Nebr., Apr. 16, 1951; s. Charles John and Beatrice Devona C.; children: Christopher, Connor. AA in Bus. Adminstrn., Casper (Wyo.) Coll., 1971; BA in Bus. Adminstrn., Wash. State U., 1973; M in Urban Planning, U. Wash., 1990. Indsl. engr. Boeing, Seattle, 1974-77, database adminstr., 1980-81; database analyst Transp. Sys. Ctr., Cambridge, Mass., 1978-80; systems officer Seafirst Bank, Seattle, 1981-83; airport planner TRA-Arch Engr., Seattle, 1986-90; sr. transp. planner King County Dept. Transp., Seattle, 1990-96, prin. planner Puget Sound Regional Coun., 1997—2001; trans. planning mgr. KITSAP Co. Pub. Works, 2001—. Avocations: choral music, archaeology. Home: 7534 NE Emerald Way Bainbridge Island WA 98110

CIOCIOLA, CECILIA MARY, development specialist; b. Chester, Pa., Feb. 9, 1946; d. Donato Francis Pasqual and Mary Theresa (Dugan) C. BA, Immaculata Coll., 1975; MA, West Chester U., 1984. Tchr. Archdiocese of Phila., 1964-72, Harrisburg Diocese, Pa., 1972-74, Camden Diocese, NJ, 1974-76; tchr., elem. sci. chairperson Archdiocese of Phila., 1976-86; ednl. cons. Macmillan Pub. Co., Delran, NJ, 1986-88; program officer PATHS/PRISM, Phila., 1988-90; mgr. spl. programs minority engring., math., sci. program Prime, Inc., Phila., 1988-99; dir. partnership and cmty. devel. FOUNDATIONS, Inc., 1999-2001; grants adminstr. Chester Cmty. Charter Sch., Pa., 2001—. Tchr. cert. adv. com. U. the Scis., Phila.; cons. Delaware County Intermediate Unit, Media, Pa.; chair elem. (grades 1-8), sci. com. Phila. Archdiocese, 1985-86; coord. Chester County Cath. Schs.: Computer Edn., Pa.,

1982-84, Fed. Nutrition Program, St. Agnes Sch., West Chester, Pa., 1982-84, Justice Edn. Teaching Strategies, St. Agnes Sch., West Chester, 1983-84; mem. Mayor's Telecom. Policy Adv. Com., Phila., 1998-2000, Phila. 4-H Program Devel. Com., 1998-2000. Author, editor: (curriculum) Elementary Life and Earth Science, 1984. Mem. adv. com. environ. edn. program Fairmount Pk. Commn., 1998. NSF grantee Operation Primary Phys. Sci., La. State U., 1997—, Project GLOBE, 1997-2000. Mem. ASCD, Nat. Sci. Tchrs. Assn., Pa. Biotech. Assn. (edn. coun.), U. of the Scis. in Phila. (sci. edn. adv. com.), Pa. Sci. Tchrs. Assn. Avocations: poetry, country music, reading, photography, fitness. Office: 214 E 5th St Chester PA 19013-4510

CIOCZEK, HENRYK ANTONI, medical oncologist, internist; b. Lublin, Poland, May 27, 1961; came to U.S., 1987; s. Jan and Marianna (Szyszkowska) C.; m. Anna Wlaz, June 11, 1988. MD, Med. Acad., Lublin, 1985. Surgical intern Teaching Hosp. nr 1, Lublin, 1985-86, resident in neurosurgery, 1986-87; rsch. worker NYU Med. Ctr., N.Y.C., 1987-89, intern in surgery, 1991-92; intern in medicine Flushing (N.Y.) Hosp. Med. Ctr., 1992-93, resident in medicine, 1993-95; fellow in oncology Albert Einstein Cancer Ctr./Montefiore Med. Ctr., 1995-97; physician pvt. practice, 1997—; rsch. coord. Montefiore Med. Ctr./Albert Einstein Cancer Ctr., 1996-97, attending physician, 1997—, Maimoninides Med. Ctr., 1997—, Flushing Hosp. Med. Ctr., 1997—. Rsch. coord. Flushing Hosp., 1993-94, del. com. interns and residents, 1993-94; rsch. coord. Harvard U., 1993-94. Author: (in Polish) Intern of Bellevue Hospital N.Y., 1994, Woman's Victory-Dr. Marie Zakrzewska (1829-1902) First Lady of American Medicine, 1995, Bishop in Stripes - The Life and Martyrdom of God's Servant Wladyslaw Goral 1898-1945, 1998; contbr. articles to profl. jours. Active Student Orgn. Solidarity, Lublin, 1980-85. Recipient Rectors award and Sci. scholar Med. Acad., Lublin, 1982, 84, 85. Mem. ACP, Polish Med. Soc. Club. Avocations: sports, travel, movies, music, history of medicine.

CIOFFI, EUGENE EDWARD, III, retired educational administrator; b. Somerville, N.J., July 26, 1948; s. Eugene E. and Carmela Agnus (Montenegro) C.; m. Ellen Gertrude Coolbaugh, Sept. 12, 1969; children: Christopher, Daniel. BS in Edn., Bloomsburg U., 1970; MEd, Coll. of N.J., 1973. Cert. sch. adminstr., prin., elem. and secondary tchr., N.J. Asst. adminstr., tchr. 6th-8th grades Salah Tawfik Elem. and Mid. Sch., Sunrise, Fla.; chief sch. adminstr., prin. Frelinghuysen (N.J.) Twp. Bd. Edn., 1994-2000; ret., 2000. Pres. Warren County Spl. Svcs. Sch. Dist. Bd. Edn. Mem. ASCD, Warren County Assn. Sch. Adminstrs., N.J. Assn. Sch. Adminstrs., Warren County Prins. and Suprs. Assn., N.J. Sch. Bds. Assn., Phi Delta Kappa.

CIOFFI, MICHAEL LAWRENCE, lawyer; b. Cin., Feb. 2, 1953; s. Patrick Anthony and Patricia (Schroeder) C.; children: Michael A., David P., Gina M. BA magna cum laude, U. Notre Dame, 1975; JD, U. Cin., 1979. Bar: Ohio 1979, U.S. Dist. Ct. (so. dist.) Ohio 1980, U.S. Dist. Ct. (no. dist.) Ohio 1983, U.S. Ct. Appeals (6th cir.) 1985. Asst. atty. gen. Ohio Atty. Gen., Columbus, 1979-81; from assoc. to ptnr. Frost & Jacobs, Cin., 1981-87; staff v.p., asst. gen. counsel Penn Cen. Corp., Cin., 1988-93; v.p., asst. gen. counsel Am. Fin. Group, Cin., 1993-2000; ptnr. Blank Rome LLP, Cin., 2001—. Adj. prof. law U. Cin. Coll. Law, 1983—. Author: Ohio Pretrial Litigation, 1991; co-author: Sixth Circuit Federal Practice Manual, 1993. Bd. dirs. Charter Com. of Greater Cin., 1985—88. Recipient Goldman Prize for Tchg. Excellence U. Cin. Coll. Law, 1995, Nicholas Longworth Disting. Alumni award, 1996. Mem. ABA, Fed. Bar Assn. (mem. exec. com., pres.1994), Ohio Bar Assn., Cin. Bar Assn. Avocations: tennis, travel. Office: Blank Rome LLP 201 E 5th St Cincinnati OH 45202

CIONGOLI, ALFRED KENNETH, neurologist; b. Phila., Jan. 11, 1943; s. Alfred Anthony and Antoinette Marie (Ragano) C.; m. Barbara, Nov. 22, 1966; children: Adam, Happy, Gregory, Alessandra, Antonio. AB, U. Pa., 1964; DO, Phila. Coll. Osteopathic Med., 1968. Diplomate Am. Bd. Psychiatry & Neurology. Resident in neurology, chief resident neurology unit U. Vt. Coll. Medicine, 1968-73; attending neurologist U. Pa. Med. Sch., Phila., 1974-75; rsch. fellow in neuroimmunology Danish Muscular Sclerosis Soc., Copenhagen, 1973-74, Hosp. U. Pa., Phila., 1975-77; pres. Neurol. Assocs. Vt., Burlington, 1977—. Attending neurologist Hosp. U. Pa. Med. Sch., 1975-77; clin. assoc. prof. neurology U. Vt. Coll. Medicine, Burlington, 1977-87, clin. assoc. prof., 1987—, dir. Multiple Sclerosis clinic, 1975; pres. Bd. Alumni Dirs. Phila. Coll. Osteopathic Med., 1994—, chmn. internat. fellowship com., 1990—; chmn. com. NIH, 1990—. Apptd. boxing commr. State of Vt., 1982; sr. med. officer U.S. Olympics team, 1986. Recipient Ellis Island Medal of Honor, 1998, Grand Officiale Order Merit Republic Italy, Italian Pres. Scalfero, 1998. Mem. AMA, Am. Assn. Neurology, Phila. Neurol. Soc., Ethan Allan Club (bd. govs.), Nat. Italian-Am. Found. (sr. v.p. 1992-95, pres. 1996—, vice chmn. 1999—). Office: Neurol Assn Vt 89 S Williams St Burlington VT 05401-3405

CIOROIU, MICHAEL GELU, surgeon; b. Brasov, Romania, July 27, 1947; came to U.S., 1978; s. Marin and Margareta (Juranescu) C.; m. Monica Moca, Aug. 4, 1978; 1 child, Monica Comana. BS, Nr 1 Liceum, Romania, 1965; MD, U. Medicine Cluj, Romania, 1971. Diplomate Am. Bd. Surgery. Instr. clin. surgery Inst. Medicine & Pharmacy, Cluj, Romania, 1971-77; resident in surgery Cabrini Med. Ctr., N.Y.C., 1980-85, attending physician, surgeon, 1985—; dir. surg. edn. Cabrini/Mt. Sinai Residency Tng. program, N.Y.C., 1994-2000; med. dir. Cabrini Wound Care Ctr., 1995; asst. clin. prof. surgery Mt. Sinai Sch. Medicine, 2000—. Assoc. prof. clin. surgery N.Y. Med. Coll., Valhalla, 1985—. Contbr. articles to profl. jours. Recipient cert. appreciation Bayley Seton Hosp., 1984; listed among Best Drs., N.Y. Mag., 2001, 02. Fellow ACS, Internat. Coll. Surgeons, Am. Soc. Abdominal Surgeons; mem. AMA (award 1987, 90), Soc. Am. Gastrointestinal Endoscopic Surgeons, Soc. Laparoendoscopic Surgeons, Surg. Soc. N.Y. Med. Coll., Romanian Laparoscopic Soc. (hon.), Am. Coll. Physicians Execs. Republican. Avocations: tennis, photography, travel. Office: 247 3rd Ave Rm L-3 New York NY 10010-7453 E-mail: gcioroiu@aol.com.

CIOVACCO, ROBERT JOHN, lawyer; b. Bklyn., June 23, 1941; s. Frank and Frances (Grieci) C.; m. Phyllis Marie Russo, Aug. 14, 1966; children— Jennifer Jude, Lauren Marie. B.A., Adelphi U., 1963; LL.B., St. John's U., Bklyn., 1967 Bar: N.Y. 1967, U.S. Dist. Ct. (so. and ea. dists.) N.Y. 1975. Assoc., Roth Carlson Kwit Spengler & Mallin, N.Y.C., 1966-68; asst. counsel Celanese Corp., N.Y.C., 1968-71; ptnr., officer Whiteman, Ciovacco & Gorray, P.C., Westbury, N.Y., 1971— ; bd. dirs., sec., mem. exec. com. L.I. Forum for Tech., Farmingdale, N.Y., 1980-84. Bd. dirs. Community Program Ctrs. of L.I., Inc., Deer Park, N.Y., 1983—. Mem. Nassau Club (Glen Cove, N.Y.). Republican. Roman Catholic. Office: Whiteman Ciovacco & Gorray PC 1600 Stewart Ave Westbury NY 11590-6696

CIPARICK, CARMEN BEAUCHAMP, judge; b. N.Y.C., 1942; Grad., Hunter Coll., 1963; JD, St. John's U., 1967. Staff atty. Legal Aid Soc., N.Y.C.; asst. counsel Office of Jud. Conf., 1969—72; chief law asst. N.Y.C. Criminal Ct., 1972—74, judge, 1978—82; counsel Office of N.Y.C. Adminstrv. Judge, 1974—78; judge N.Y. Supreme Ct, 1982—94; assoc. judge N.Y. State Ct. Appeals, N.Y.C., 1994—. Former mem. N.Y. State Commn. Jud. Conduct. Trustee Boricua Coll.; bd. dirs. St. John's U. Sch. of Law Alumni Assn. Named to Hunter Coll. Hall of Fame, 1991. Office: NY State Ct Appeals 122 E 42nd St New York NY 10168-0002

CIPLIJAUSKAITE, BIRUTE, humanities educator; b. Kaunas, Lithuania, Apr. 11, 1929; came to U.S., 1957; d. Juozas and Elena (Stelmokaite) C. BA, Lycee Lithuanien Tubingen, 1947; MA, U. Montreal, 1956; PhD, Bryn Mawr Coll., 1960. Permanent mem. Inst. Rsch. in Humanities U. Wis., Madison, 1974, asst. prof., 1961-65, assoc. prof., 1965-68, prof., 1968-73, John Bascom prof., 1973—. Author: La Soledad y la poesia española contemporánea, 1962, El poeta y la poesia, 1966, Baroja, un estilo, 1972, Deber de plenitud: La poesia de Jorge Guillén, 1973, Los noventayochistas y la historia, 1981, La mujer insatisfecha, 1984, La novela femenina contemporánea (1970-85), 1988, Literaturos eskizai, 1992, De signos y significaciones. I: Juegos con a vanguardia, 1999, Carmen Martin Gaite, 2000, Guilleniana, 2002; editor: Luis de Gongora, Sonetos completos, 1969, critical edit., 1981, Jorge Guillén, 1975, (with C. Maurer) La voluntad de humanismo: Homenaje a Juan Marichal, 1990, Novisimos, postnovisimos, clásicos: la poesia de los 80 en España, 1991; translator: Juan Ramón Jiménez, Sidabrinukas ir as, 1982, María Victoria Atencia, Svenciausios Karalienes Ekstazes, 1989, Voces en el silencio: Poesia lituana contemporánea, 1991, Birute Pukeleviciute, Planto, 1994, (with Nicole Laurent-Catrice) Vingt poètes lituaniens d'aujourd'hui, 1997, Vidmante Jasukaityte, La milagrosa hierba de la raiz amarga, 2002, Entre el sol y la desposesion, 2002, Moteris tarp balandziu, 2002, others. Guggenheim fellow, 1968 Mem. Assn. For Advancement Baltic Studies (v.p. 1981), Asociación Internacional de Hispanistas. Office: U Wis Inst Rsch in Humanities 1401 Observatory Dr Madison WI 53706-1209

CIPOLLONE, ANTHONY DOMINIC, judge, educator; b. N.Y.C., Mar. 15, 1939; s. Domenico and Caterina (Brancazio) C.; m. Eileen Mary Patricia Kelly, Sept. 14, 1963; children: Catherine Mary, Kelly Ann, Mary Rose. BA, CCNY, 1961, MA, 1968; JD, Seton Hall U., 1978. Bar: N.J. 1978, Pa. 1978, U.S. Patent Office 1978, Fla. 1980, N.Y. 1984, D.C. 1985, Mass. 1988; cert. civil trial atty. N.J., 1987. Chemist Am. Chicle Co., Long Island City, N.Y., 1961-65; research chemist Denver Chem. Mfg. Co., Stamford, Conn., 1965-66; chem. sales engr. GAF Corp., N.Y.C., 1966-68; nat. acct. rep. Stauffer Chem., N.Y.C., 1968-72; sales mgr. Rhone-Poulenc Inc., South Brunswick, N.J., 1972-78; prosecutor Town of Elmwood Park, N.J., 1981-85, Town of Paramus, N.J., 1982-85; mcpl. ct. judge Town of Paramus (N.J.), 1985-90, Town of Little Ferry (N.J.), 1986-89; atty. planning bd. Twp. Saddle Brook, 1986-87; mcpl. ct. judge Town of Elmwood Park (N.J.), 1991, Town of Saddle Brook (N.J.), 1991-94; atty. Twp. Saddle Brook, 1987-90. Adj. faculty MBA program for chmn. and pharm. mgrs. Fairleigh Dickinson U.; atty. Zoning Bd., City of Hackensack, N.J., 1989-90, atty. Planning Bd., 1991—. Served to sgt. USMC, 1961-66. Mem. ABA, Bergen Bar Assn., N.J. Bar Assn., Pa. Bar Assn., N.Y. Bar Assn., D.C. Bar Assn., Fla. Bar Assn., Mass. Bar Assn., Am. Chem. Soc., Am. Mensa. Roman Catholic. Home: 130 Overlook Ave Hackensack NJ 07601 Office: 15 Main St Ste 215 Hackensack NJ 07601 E-mail: cipollone@aol.com.

CIPPARONE, ROCCO C., JR., lawyer; b. Phila. BA, St. Joseph's U., Phila., 1984; JD, U. Pa., 1987. Bar: N.J. 1987, Pa. 1987, U.S. Dist. Ct. (ea. dist.) Pa., U.S. Dist. Ct. N.J. 1987, U.S. Dist. Ct. (ea. dist.) Mich.; cert. criminal trial atty., N.J. Law clk. to Hon. Anthony J. Scirica U.S. Ct. Appeals, 3d Cir., Phila., 1987-88; asst. U.S. atty., criminal divsn. U.S. Dept. Justice, Camden, N.J., 1988-92; atty. in pvt. practice, Phila., also Haddon Hts., N.J., 1992—. Adj. faculty Rutgers U. Law Sch., Camden, 1991—; lectr. N.J. Inst. for Continuing Legal Edn. Contbr. articles to profl. jours. Apptd. bd. trustees by Gov. NJ Ancora Psychiat. Hosp., 2000—. Recipient Spl. Achievement award U.S. Atty. Gen., 1992, others. Mem. Camden County Bar Assn. Office: 205 Black Horse Pike Haddon Heights NJ 08035-1009

CIPRIANO, MICHAEL ROCCO, information technology consultant; b. Newark, N.J., Nov. 17, 1953; s. Michael Robert and Catherine Kay Cipriano; m. Marie Louise Schissler; children: Michael Richard, Michelle Renee, Melissa Marie, Megan Lynn. M in Theoretical Engring., Pacific Western U., San Cristobal, Mex., 1982. MCSE CsGa, N.J., 1988. CEO Palm Rsch. Group Inc., Union, NJ, 1980—94; pres. & founder GCC Inc., Union, NJ, 1984—88. Squadron comdr. Civic Air Patrol, Morristown, NJ, 1991—97. Capt. U.S. Army. Libertarian. Roman Catholic. Achievements include invention of The use of optical compact disc to store digitized data for retrival by computers. Avocations: flying, movies, computers. Office: Cipricorp Inc PO Box 103 Liberty Corner NJ 07928 Personal E-mail: mikrcip@cipricorp.com.

CIRANDO, JOHN ANTHONY, lawyer; b. Syracuse, N.Y., June 25, 1942; s. Daniel John and Anne Marie (Farone) C.; m. Carolyn Joyce Lace, Sept. 17, 1966; children: Lisa Marie, Julie Lynn, Jennifer Mary. BA in History, St. Bonaventure (N.Y.) U., 1963; JD, SUNY, Buffalo, 1966. Bar: N.Y. 1966, U.S. Dist. Ct. (no. dist.) N.Y. 1966, U.S. Dist. Ct. (we. dist.) N.Y. 1994, U.S. Claims Ct. 1991, U.S. Ct. Mil. Appeals 1967, U.S. Ct. Appeals (2d cir.) 1985, U.S. Supreme Ct. 1974. Chief asst. dist. atty. Onondaga County Dist. Atty.'s Office, Syracuse, N.Y., 1971-87; atty. D.J. & J.A. Cirando, Syracuse, 1966—. Treas. N.Y. State Dist. Atty.'s Assn., 1977-87; chair Govs. Jud. Screening Com. 4th Jud. Dept., 1997—. Pres. bd. dirs. Vera House, Shelter for Women and Children in Crisis, Syracuse, 1988-90, gen. counsel, 1991—; bd. trustees Leukemia Soc. Am., 1995—, asst. sec., 1995-96, sec., 1996-2000, adv. bd., 2000—. Capt. JAG, U.S. Army, 1967-71. Mem. N.Y. State Bar Assn. (chair com. on county cts. 1975-78, chair com. on pub. rels. 1979-83), Onondaga County Bar Assn. (bd. dirs. 1974-77, sec. 1979). Office: DJ & JA Cirando 101 S Salina St Ste 1010 Syracuse NY 13202-4303

CIRASUNDA, ESTHER BOND, librarian; b. Richmond, Va., July 10, 1950; d. Hobart Genues and Beulah Ann (Neal) Bond; m. Gary Lee Musser, June 3, 1977 (div. 1989); children: Laura Beth Musser, Jessica Lynn Musser; m. Francis Peter Cirasunda, July 4, 1990. BS, Madison Coll., Harrisonburg, Va., 1972; MS, Radford U., 1983. Sch. libr. Botetourt County Pub. Schs., Fincastle, Va., 1972-74, Roanoke (Va.) City Pub. Schs., 1974—2003; ret., 2003. Del. Gov.'s Conf. on Libr. and Info. Svcs., Richmond, 1990; teaching homebound students and private tutoring, 2003-. Mem. NEA (del. conv. 1993, vice-chair libr. info. tech. caucus), Va. Edn. Assn., Roanoke Edn. Assn. (v.p. instrn. 1992-93, Polit. Action Com chair 1994-95, pres. 1996-98, dist. 5 pres. 1998-2000), Roanoke Valley Reading Coun., Va. Ednl. Media Assn. (workshop presenter 1986), Phi Kappa Phi. Avocation: to obtain doctoral degree and teach at the college or university level. Home and Office: 436 Arbutus Ave SE Roanoke VA 24014-1208 E-mail: ecirasun@yahoo.com.

CIRAULO, DOMENIC ANTHONY, psychiatrist, educator; s. Salvatore and Josephine Ciraulo; m. Ann Marie B. Ciraulo; children: Nicole Bosh, Danielle, Jon. BA, U. Hartford, 1971; MD, Georgetown U., 1975. Diplomate in psychiatry with added qualification in addiction psychiatry Am. Bd. Psychiatry and Neurology. Med. resident Inst. Living, Hartford, 1975—77; chief resident psychiatry Mass. Mental Health Ctr., Boston, 1977—78; clin. fellow psychiatry Harvard Med. Sch., Boston, 1977—78, clin. instr., 1978—79, lectr. psychiatry, 2002—; asst. prof. psychiatry U. Conn. Sch. Medicine, Farmington, 1979—84; prof. psychiatry Tufts U. Sch. Medicine, Boston, 1992—96, lectr. pharmacology, 1993—; chief psychiatry svc. VA Med. Ctr./Outpatient Clinics, Boston, 1995—2001; psychiatrist in chief Boston Med. Ctr., 1996—; prof., chmn. divsn. psychiatry Boston U. Sch. Medicine, 1996—. Chair R&D com. VA Outpatient Clinic, Boston, 1987—94; mem. exec. com. dept. psychiatry Tufts U. Sch. Medicine, Boston, 1989—93, mem. addiction medicine com., 1989—96; sr. cons. Norcap Addictions Program, Norfolk, Mass., 1990—96; mem. dean's com. VA Med. Ctr., Boston, 1996—; mem. exec. com. Boston U. Sch. Medicine, 1996—, com. mem., 2001—02; gen. clin. rsch. ctr. adv. com. Boston U. Med. Ctr., 1997—; sci. adv. com. Boston U. Cmty. Tech. Fund, 1997—. Author: (book) Drug Interactions In Psychiatry, Clinical Manual of Chemical Dependence; contbr. chapters to books. Psychiat. cons. Canton (Mass.) Pub. Sch. Sys., 1990—96. Grantee, Nat. Inst. On Drug Abuse, 1995—, Nat. Inst. On Alcoholism and Alcohol Abuse, 1997—, Nat. Inst. On Drug Abuse, 2002—, 2002—, 2002—. Fellow: Am. Psychiat. Assn. (disting. fellow); mem.: AMA (ad hoc com. on physicians health 1996), FDA Adv. Bd., Am. Bd. Psychiatry and Neurology (examiner), Mass. Med. Soc., Mass. Psychiatry Soc. (com. on alcohol and addiction 1984—). Office: Boston Univ Sch Medicine Ste 914 720 Harrison Ave Boston MA 02118 Home Fax: 617-414-1996; Office Fax: 617-414-1996.

CIRAULO, STEPHEN JOSEPH, nurse, anesthetist; b. Danville, Pa., Feb. 25, 1960; s. Leonard Joseph and Mary Louise (Purpuri) C. Diploma, Geisinger Med. Ctr. Sch. Nursing, Danville, 1980; cert., Sch of Anesthesia for Nurses Univ. Health Ctr. Pitts., 1983; BA Mgmt. Health Scis., Ottawa U., Kansas City, 1997. Nursing asst. Geisinger Med. Ctr., Danville, 1978-80; staff RN, part time charge RN cardiac care unit Williamsport (Pa.) Hosp., 1980-81; asst. gastroenterology research group Presbyn. Univ. Hosp., Pitts., 1982-83; staff nurse anesthetist dept. anesthesia Duke U. Med. Ctr., Durham, N.C., 1983-90; with Anesthesia Anytime, Winston-Salem, N.C., 1990, Nash Gen. Hosp., Rocky Mount, N.C., 1991-92, staff nurse anesthetist, mem. epidural analgesia svc., 1991-92; staff nurse anesthetist Wake Anesthesiology Assocs., Inc., Raleigh, NC, 1992—; asst. chief nurse anesthetist We. Wake Med., Cary, NC, 2003—. Mem. coun. for nurse anesthetists dept. anesthesia Duke U. Med. Ctr., Durham, 1985-89; Wake Anesthesiology Assocs., Inc., 1992—; mem. faculty devel. com. Raleigh Sch. Nurse Anesthesia, 1999—, staff clin. instr., 1992—. Charter mem. Outstanding Young Ams., 1988; mem. Duke U. Artists Series Adv. Bd., 1994-97, Friends of Duke artist series devel. com. 1997—; bd. dirs. Whitehall Homeowners Assn., Raleigh, N.C., 1995-2001, sec., 1996-2000. Mem. Am. Assn. Nurse Anesthetists, N.C. Assn. Nurse Anesthetists (bylaws com. 1984-86, chmn. fin. com. 1986-88, fin. com. 1988-95, fall program com. 1988, spring program spkr. 1990, treas. 1991-93, pres. 1994-95, chmn. history com. 1995-97, strategic planning com. 1995-97), Triangle Transplant Recipient Internat. Orgn. (charter), Triangle Bus. and Profl. Guild, Internat. Platform Assn. Republican. Avocations: music, art, weight lifting, traveling, gardening. Home and Office: 836 Valerie Dr Raleigh NC 27606

CIRCEO, LOUIS JOSEPH, JR., research scientist, civil engineer; b. Everett, Mass., Aug. 31, 1934; s. Louis Joseph and Matilda (Marotta) C.; m. Brigitta H. Rockstroh, Jan. 26, 1961 (dec. 1986); children: Renata B., Craig L. BS in Engring., U.S. Mil. Acad., West Point, 1957; MS in Soils Engring., 1961; PhD in Civil Engring., Iowa State U., 1963. Registered profl. civil engr., D.C. Commd. 2d lt. U.S. Army, 1957, advanced through grades to col., 1987; rsch. assoc. Lawrence Radiation Lab., Livermore, Calif., 1962-64; civil engr. Bangkok Bypass Road, Thailand, 1965—66; instr. dept. engring. and mil. sci. U.S. Army Engr. Sch., Ft. Belvoir, Va., 1966—68; civil engr. advisor Vietnamese Nat. Mil. Acad., Dalat, Vietnam, 1968-69; rsch. tech. mgr. Def. Atomic Support Agy., Washington, 1969-72; comdr. 20th Engr. Bn., Ft. Campbell, Ky., 1973-75; ops. rsch. analyst nuclear activities br. SHAPE, NATO, Mons, Belgium, 1975-79; dir. U.S. Army Constrn. Engring. Rsch. Lab., Champaign, Ill., 1979-83; dir. Nuclear Survivability, Security and Safety Directorate, Hdqrs. Def. Nuclear Agy., Washington, 1983-87; ret., 1987; dir. Constrn. Rsch. Ctr., Ga. Inst. Tech., Atlanta, 1987—98; prin. rsch. scientist Ga. Tech Rsch. Inst., Atlanta, 1998—. Mem. ASCE, Soc. Am. Mil. Engrs., Assn. U.S. Army, Sigma Xi. Roman Catholic. Achievements include patents for recovery of fuel products from carbonaceous matter using plasma arc; in-situ plasma soil stabilization method and apparatus; in-situ plasma remediation and vitrification of contaminated soils, deposits and buried materials. Avocations: reading, travel. Home: 4245 Navajo Trl NE Atlanta GA 30319-1532 Office: Ga Tech Rsch Inst Atlanta GA 30332-0837 E-mail: lou.circeo@gtri.gatech.edu. *It is important that an individual does the most with his God-given talents for the betterment of mankind.*

CIRELLO, JOHN, utility and engineering company executive; b. Bound Brook, N.J., Apr. 17, 1943; s. Fiore Avanti and Assunta Cirello; m. Sherron Anne Thomas, July 31, 1965; children: Sueann, Elizabeth Rose, Sherron Marie. BS, Rutgers U., 1965, MS, 1971, PhD, 1975. Registered profl. engr., N.J., Pa. Engr. Calif. Dept. Water, L.A., 1965-66, U.S. Army Corps of Engrs., Ft. Belvoir, Va., 1966-68, Balt. Gas and Elec., 1968-69; rschr. Rutgers Water Resources Inst., New Brunswick, N.J., 1969-71; asst. prof. Rutgers U., New Brunswick, 1971-80; pres. Princeton Aqua Sci., Edison, N.J., 1980-85; v.p. IT Corp., Edison, N.J., 1985-88; v.p. ea. region Chem. Waste Mgmt., Inc., Princeton, N.J., 1988-92; pres. Metcalf & Eddy Svcs., Inc., Branchburg, N.J., 1992-95; with Environ. Engring. Svcs. Inc., 1995-96; pres., CEO Fla. Water Svcs. Corp., 1995—2002; exec. v.p. Allete Corp., Duluth, Minn., 1995—2002; pres. Resource Ventures Inc., 2002—. Editor (tng. manuals) Land Application of Effluents & Sludges, 1976, Ultimate Disposal of Organic and Inorganic Sludges, 1976, Water and Wastewater Polishing and Rennovation Techniques, 1976; co-editor (tng. manual) Construction and Environmental Inspectors Training Manual, 1977; contbr. articles to profl. jours. Mem. Bd. Adjustment, Bound Brook, N.J., 1976-81; councilman, pres., Bound Brook Town Coun., 1981-87; chmn. Dem. com. Bound Brook, 1982-86; Grad. Leadership Fla. Class XVI. Capt. U.S. Army Engr. Corps, 1966-68. Recipient award N.J. Water Pollution Control Assn., 1990. Mem.: ASCE, Fla. Water Wks. Assn. (bd. dirs. 1997—2002), Am. Chem. Soc., Water Environ. Fedn., Fla. State C. of C. Roman Catholic. Avocations: antique and classic cars, golf. Home: 540 Winding Creek Pl Longwood FL 32779-6119

CIRESE, ROBERT CHARLES, economist, real estate investment counselor; b. Oak Park, Ill., Feb. 25, 1938; s. Ferd Louis and Ruth (Olson) C.; m. Sarah Jane Williams, Apr. 3, 1965 (div. 1973); children: Lesley Mesarchik, Jeffrey Robert. BS, DePaul U., 1961; MS, U. Ill., 1963; postgrad., U. Calif., Berkeley, 1964. Lic. real estate broker Calif.; cert. gen. real estate appraiser Calif.; cert. coll. tchr. Calif. Economist State of Calif. Employment Divsn., San Francisco, 1965—67; assoc. prof. Golden Gate U., San Francisco, 1967—72; v.p. Larry Smith & Co., San Francisco, 1972—77; dir. PricewaterhouseCoopers, San Francisco, 1977—79; v.p. Rubloff Inc., San Francisco, 1979—85; pres. Cirese Assocs., Sausalito, Calif., 1985—; concession mgr. bus. mgmt. divsn. Nat. Pk. Svc. Dept. of Interior, San Francisco, 1994—. Guest lectr., speaker in field; economic, fin. and real estate investment counselor to corps., govt. agys. and pvt. insts. Contbr. articles to profl. jours. Active Stanford U. Buck Fund, U. Calif. Berkeley Bear Backer, Berkeley Repertory Theater, Calif. Shakespeare Festival; bd. dirs. San Francisco Camp Fire Inc., 1988-92. With Ill. Nat. Guard, 1956-63. Recipient Spl. Achievement award U.S. Dept. Interior Nat. Park Svc., 1996. Mem. Am. Soc. Real Estate Counselors (past chmn. no. Calif. chpt. 1988-89, bd. dirs. no. Calif. chpt. 1986—), San Francisco Planning and Urban Rsch. Assn., Urban Land Inst., Stanford Alumni Assn., U. Calif. Berkeley Alumni Assn., San Francisco Commonwealth Club, San Francisco Ballet Assn., Am. Conservatory Theater, San Francisco Opera, Friends of Filoli, Sierra Club (San Francisco, Marin group), Sierra Singles. Avocations: hiking, theater, sports, humor writing. Home: 54 Buckelew St Sausalito CA 94965-1120 Office: Fort Mason Bldg 201 San Francisco CA 94123

CIRILLO, RICHARD ALLAN, lawyer; b. N.Y.C., Feb. 7, 1951; s. Paul F. and Edith A. (Flanagan) C.; m. Kathleen V. Rossi, Aug. 23, 1975; children: Benjamin F., Theodore T., Amanda K. BA, Yale U., 1972; JD cum laude, Fordham U., 1975. Bar: N.Y. 1976, U.S. Dist. Ct. (so. dist.) N.Y. 1977, U.S. Dist. Ct. (no. dist.) N.Y. 1990, U.S. Ct. Appeals (5th and 10th cirs.) 1978, U.S. Ct. Appeals (2d cir.) 1982, U.S. Ct. Appeals (9th cir.) 1984, U.S. Ct. Appeals (11th cir.) 1994, U.S. Tax Ct. 1984, U.S. Supreme Ct. 1983. Assoc. Rogers & Wells, N.Y.C., 1975-83, ptnr., 1983—99, King & Spalding, N.Y.C., 1999—. Bd. dirs. MIM Corp. Editor: Fordham Law Rev.; contbr. articles to profl. jours. Trustee Colony Found., New Haven, 1982-84. Republican. Presbyterian. Home: 246 E 33d St New York NY 10016 Office: King & Spalding LLP 1185 Ave of the Americas Ste 3400 New York NY 10036

CIRILLO, VINCENT J. medical historian, consultant; b. New Haven, Conn., Sept. 21, 1937; s. Joseph Oscar and Mary (Venezia) Cirillo; m. Annette Vellaccio, July 2, 1960; children: Vincent J. Cirillo Jr., Paul L. BA, U. Conn., 1959, MS, 1961; PhD, Rutgers U., 1999. Asst. dir. clinical rsch. Merck & Co., Inc., Rahway, NJ, 1962—93; assoc. Inst. for Health, Health Care Policy and Aging Rsch.-Rutgers U., New Brunswick, NJ, 1999—. Cons. Target Rsch., Scotch Plains, NJ, 1993, Transcend Therapeutics, Cambridge, Mass., 1995, N.J. Vets. Mus., East Orange, 1999—2001. Contbr. articles to profl. jours. Recipient Margaret Hastings and Margaret Judson fellowship, Rutgers U., 1994—95. Mem.: History of Sci. Soc., Am. Assn. for History of Medicine, Med. History Soc. N.J. (pres. 1986—88), Soc. Civil War Surgeons. Avocation: book collecting. Home: 1387 Joseph St North Brunswick NJ 08902-1509

CIRILO, AMELIA MEDINA, educational consultant, supervisor; b. Parks, Tex., May 23, 1925; d. Constancio and Guadalupe (Guerra) Cirilo; m. Arturo Medina, May 31, 1953 (div. June 1979); children: Dennis Glenn, Keith Allen, Sheryl Amelia, Jacqueline Kim. BS in Chemistry, U. North Tex., 1950; MEd, U. Houston, 1954; PhD in Edn. and Nuc. Engring., Tex. A&M U., 1975; cert. in radioisotope tech., Tex. Woman's U., Denton, 1962; cert. in pub. speaking, Dale Carnegie, 1993. Cert. in supervision, bilingual Spanish Tex., permanent profl. tchr. Tex. Tchr. sci. dept. Starr County Schs., Rio Grande City, Tex., 1950—53; elem. tchr. San Benito-Brownsville, Tex., 1953—54, Kingsville (Tex.) Schs., 1954—56; tchr. sci. dept. head chem. physics LaJoya (Tex.) Pub. Schs., 1956—70; tchg. asst. Tex. A&M U., College Station, 1970—74; instr. fire chemistry Del Mar Jr. Coll., Corpus Christi, Tex., 1974—75; exec. dir. Hispanic Ednl. Rsch. Mgmt. Analysis Nat. Assn., Inc., Corpus Christi, 1975—79; head dept. chem. physics San Isidro (Tex.) HS, 1979—82; tchr. chemistry W.H. Adamson HS, Dallas, 1982—84; ednl. cons. Skyline HS, 1992—, tchr. high intensity lang. sci., 1984—86, chmn. faculty adv. com., 1983—84, chemistry tchr., 1986—92. Mem. core faculty Union Grad. Coll., Cin., P.R., Ft. Lauderdale and San Diego, 1975—79; mathematician Well Instrument Devel. Co., Houston, 1950—85; panelist, program evaluator Dept. of Edn., Washington, 1977—79; program evaluator, Robstown, Tex., 1975—79; tchr., trainer Edn. 20 and 2 Region Ctrs., Corpus Christi and San Antonio, 1975—79; rschr., writer Coll. Edn. and Urban Studies Harvard U., Cambridge, Mass., 1978—80; vis. prof. bilingual dept. East Tex. State Coll., Commerce, 1978; ednl. cons. and supr. Adult Basic Edn. Dallas Pub. Schs., 1994—99, kindergarten tchr., 1999—2000, tchr. elem. sci. and math., 2000—02, newcomers ESL tchr., 2002—; conf. presenter program evaluation, 1977—79. Author, rschr. Com-

parative Evaluation of Bilingual Programs, 1978 (named one of best US books), (poetry) Reflections, 1983; contbr. chapters to books. Mem. Srs. Active in Life adv. com. Dallas City Parks and Recreation; Brazos County advisor Tex. Constl. Revision Commn., 1973—74; sec. Goals for Corpus Christi Com. of 100; Corpus Christi rep. Southwestern Ednl. Authority, Edinburg, Tex., 1977—79; pres. Elem. PTA, 1972—75; mem. Women's Polit. Caucus, Mex. Am. Dems.; exec. bd. Nat. Com. Domestic Violence, 1978—80; bd. trustees Sci. Cluster Skyline HS, 1994—; bd. dirs. Meth. Home for Elderly, Weslaco, Tex., 1968, Am. Cancer Soc. fund drive, College Station, 1971—74; co-founder, bd. dirs. Women's Shelter, Corpus Christi, 1977—78. Named Educator of Yr., Literary Couns. of Greater Dallas, 1997—98; recipient Sr. Salute award for achievements in edn., City of Dallas and NYL Care, 1996; grantee, NSF, The Women's U., 1963—65. Mem.: AAUW, NEA, Metroplex Educators Sci. Assn., Rocky Mountain Sociol. Assn., So. Sociol. Assn., Chem. Soc., Tex. Assn. Bilingual Educators, Tex. Tchrs. Assn., League United Latin Am. Citizens (pres. College Station 1973—74, past dist. dir. Corpus Christi), Pan Am. Round Table, Fiesta Bilingual Toastmasters. Avocations: ballroom dancing, comedy. Home and Office: 5005 Oak Trl Dallas TX 75232-1643

CIRINCIONE, ROSS JOSEPH, mathematician, educator; b. Cleve., Ohio, Apr. 8, 1948; s. Charles Ignatius and Mary Italia Cirincione. BA, Dartmouth Coll., Hanover, NH, 1970; MS, Harvard U., Cambridge, Mass., 1972; PhD, U. Calif., Berkeley, 1979. Radar systems analyst Hughes Aircraft Co., El Segundo, Calif., 1981—83, stats. quality control instr., 1983—86; instrnl. asst. El Camino CC, Torrance, Calif., 1996—98; math. lectr. Case Western Res. U., Cleve., 2000—. Author: (company manual) Concepts in Experimental Design, 1985. Mem.: Am. Math. Soc., Dartmouth Alumni Assn. Avocation: photography. Office: Case Western Res Univ 10900 Euclid Ave Cleveland OH 44106 E-mail: rjc13@po.cwru.edu.

CIRKER, BLANCHE, retired publishing executive; b. N.Y.C., Oct. 3, 1918; d. Frank and Tillie (Jager) Brodsky; m. Hayward Cirker, Aug. 11, 1939 (dec. Mar. 2000); children: Steven, Victoria. BA, Hunter Coll., 1939; MSW, U. Pa., 1941. Family social worker, intake office Jewish Child Care Assn., 1948-50; med. social worker Joint Disease Hosp., N.Y.C., 1950; book pub., 1950-2001; pres. Dover Publs., N.Y.C., 2000; ret., 2001. Author: Monograms and Alphabetic Devices, 1970 Dictionary of American Portraits, 1967, Golden Age of Poster, 1971, Book of Kells, 1982, Art Nouveau Postcards, 1983, Masterpieces of the Belle Epoch, 1983, Victorian House Designs, 1996. Mem. Otto Rank Assn. Home: 199 Woodside Dr Hewlett NY 11557-2417

CIRONA, JANE CALLAHAN, investment company executive; b. Detroit, Feb. 23, 1949; d. Earl J. and Madeline Katherine (Freihaut) Callahan; children from previous marriage: Christopher Randall, Elisabeth Anne; m. James M. Cirona, Aug. 29, 1992. BA, Albion Coll., 1970; postgrad., Aquinas Coll., 1989—. Asst. mgr. Nat. Bank of Detroit, 1971-75; program coord. Muskegon (Mich.) C.C., 1978-79; services coord. Muskegon (Mich.) County Cmty. Mental Health, 1979-81; supr. engring. services Teledyne Continental Motors, Muskegon; v.p. investment UBS PaineWebber Inc., Muskegon, 1982—. Dir. Muskegon Econ. Growth Alliance, 1987—, Every Woman's Place, Muskegon, 1979-86; mem. Albion Coll. Planned Giving Adv. Bd., 1989—; mem. Commn. on Growth and Devel. Episcopal Diocese of Western Mich., 1985-88, Consumers Power Citizen Adv. Panel, Muskegon, 1983-84; bd. dirs. Mercy Hosp., Muskegon. Mem.: Zonta Internat. Avocation: travel. Office: UBS PaineWebber Inc PO Box 959 Muskegon MI 49443-0959 E-mail: jane.cirona@ubspw.com.

CIRONE, WILLIAM JOSEPH, educational administrator; b. Bklyn., Dec. 27, 1937; s. Joseph Nicholas and Marie Ann (Basile) C.; m. Barbara Jane Skirkie, Dec. 22, 1962; 1 child, Peter Craig. BA, Providence Coll., 1959; MA, NYU, 1960; adminstrv. cert., U. Calif., Santa Barbara, 1977. Tchr. N.Y.C. Pub. Schs., 1960-68; dir. product devel. ednl. divsn. Mead Corp., Atlanta, 1968-70, dir. mktg., 1970-73; founder, dir. Ctr. Cmty. Edn. and Citizen Participation, Santa Barbara, Calif., 1973-82; supt. schs. Santa Barbara County, 1983—. Vis. fellow Chisholm Inst. Tech., Melbourne, Australia, 1986; vis. scholar Ctr. for excellence Tenn. State U., 1986. Host (cable talk shows) Education On-Line-A Line to Learning, Cirone on Schools. Bd. dirs., chair student aide com. Santa Barbara Cmty. Found.; bd. dirs., 1998-; bd. chmn., 2003-; bd. dirs. Cmty. Action Commn., 1973-81, Cmty. Resource Info. Svc., 1978-82, Fin. Crisis Mgmt. Assistance Team, 1993—, Nat. Partnership in Edn., 1998—, S.B. Fightnig Balk, 1994-, chmn.2002-, Calif. Alliance for Arts Edn., 1999—, Ctr. for Learning and Citizenship, Santa Barbara Anti-Defamation League, 2001--; bd. dirs., sec. Pvt. Industry Coun., Santa Barbara, 1999—; bd. dirs. Industry Edn. Coun. Santa Barbara, 1983—, pres., 1990, 99; bd. dirs. Coun. of Alcoholism and Drug Abuse, 1998—, Santa Barbara Lung Assn., 1983-87, Philip Francis Siff Edn. Found., 1986—; bd. dirs. Impact II, 1989—, pres., 1993-99; bd. dirs. Nat. Comm. Edn. Assn., 1989-92, pres., 1990; regional chair Calif. County Supt. Assn., 1990-96, bd. dirs. media and values, 1989-92; hon. bd. dirs. So. Coast Spl. Olympics; mem. Gov.'s Commn. on Earthquake Hazards, 1981; mem. state bd. Common Cause, 1974-77, organizer and 1st state chmn., Ga., 1970-73; mem. voter accessibility adv. bd. Santa Barbara County, 1986—; mem. adv. bd. CALM, Peace Resource Ctr., Marymount Sch., Women's Cmty. Bldg., Jodi House, Girl Scouts U.S.; comdrs. cmty. liaison com. Vandenberg AFB; mem. Access Theatre; mem. Hon. Commn. for Goleta Hosp.; mem. campaign cabinet Santa Barbara United Way, 1991, 98; adv. bd. Santa Barbara Brand Opera Assn., 1996—; co-chair State Supts. Statewide Arts Task Force, 1997. Recipient Smallheiser award United Fedn. Tchrs., 1968, Hon. Svc. award 15th Dist. PTA, 1979, 81, Intercongregation Orgn. Project Action award, 1995, Anti-Defamation League Santa Barbara Disting. Svc. award, 1996, Meritorious Svc. award Cmty. Action Com., Santa Barbara, 1981, Ind. Living Resource Ctr., 1985, Hon. Svc. award Calif. State PTA, 1995, 99 for '99 award, Santa Barbara C. of C., 1993-99, Profl. Publ. award Calif. County Supts. Assn., Comm. Achievement award Toastmasters Internat., 1999, Santa Barbara Wildlife Care Network award, 2000, Excellence in Svc. award South Coast Bus. and Tech., 2000, Vanguard award, 2002, Calif. Outstanding Art Educators' award Calif. Art's Commn., Emmanus Disting. Cmty. Svc. award, 2002-, Easy Lift Van Guard award, 2002; named Calif. Cmty. Educator of Yr., Calif. Cmty. Edn. Assn., 1984, Pub. Servant of Yr., Santa Barbara County, 1987. Mem. World Future Soc. (life), Am. Assn. Sch. Adminstrs., Assn. Calif. Sch. Adminstrs. (Region XIII Adminstr. of Yr. award 2002), So. Coast Coord. Coun. (past chmn., past exec. com.), Nat. Soc. Fundraising Execs., Automobile Assn. Am. (So. Calif. adv. bd.), Phi Delta Kappa. Democrat. Unitarian Universalist. Home: 953 Elk Grove Ln Solvang CA 93463-9608 Office: PO Box 6307 Santa Barbara CA 93160-6307

CISCO, BEDE DONALD, monk, priest; b. Indpls., Oct. 30, 1951; s. Donald David Cisco and Mary Catherine Masse. BA, Saint Meinrad Coll., St. Meinrad, Ind., 1973, MDiv, 1978; EdD, Columbia U., 1986. Mgr. The Scholar Shop Saint Meinrad Sem., Saint Meinrad, Ind., 1978—82; assoc. dean students Saint Meinrad Coll., Saint Meinrad, Ind., 1979—82, 1987—93, assoc. acad. dean, 1986—91, faculty mem., 1986—98, acad. dean, 1992—98; dir. Indpls. programs Saint Meinrad Sch. Theology, Indpls., 1999—. Bd. advisors Abbey Press, St. Meinrad, Ind., 1987—99; bd. trustees Saint Meinrad Coll. and Sch. Theology, St. Meinrad, Ind., 1993—; adv. coun. and devel. com. mem. Carmelite Monastery, Indpls., 2000—; mem. coun. of priests Archdiocese of Indpls., 2002—. Co-author: Lay Ministers and Their Spiritual Practices, 2003. Mem.: Nat. Assn. Lay Ministry, Acad. Mgmt., Assn. Study of Higher Edn. Roman Catholic. Office: Saint Meinrad Sch Theology 3200 Cold Spring Rd Indianapolis IN 46222 Office Fax: 317-955-6453. Business E-Mail: indyprogs@saintmeinrad.edu.

CISLER, THERESA ANN, osteopath, former nurse; b. Tucson, Dec. 20, 1951; d. William George and Lucille (Seeber) C.; 1 child, Daniel Luttrell. BSN, U. Ariz., 1974; DO, Kirksville Coll. Osteopathy, 1983. Diplomate Am. Bd. Osteo. Manipulative Medicine. Operating room technician St. Joseph's Hosp., Tucson, 1973-74, operating room nurse, 1974-78, operating room inservice coordinator, 1978-79; intern Tucson Gen. Hosp., 1983-84; family practice and manipulation Assoc. Jane J. Beregi, D.O., Tucson, 1984-87; practice medicine specializing in osteo. manipulation Tucson, 1987—. Active med. staff Tucson Gen. Hosp., 1984-91, med. records chmn., 1986-87; part-time med. staff Westcenter Drug & Rehab., Tucson, 1984-88; vol. med. staff St. Elizabeth Hugary Clinic, 1984-87; mem. substance abuse com. Westcenter-Tucson Gen. Hosp., 1986-88, osteo. concepts com., 1986-91, osteo. manipulative cons., 1986-91. Roadrunner Civitan, 2000—01; chair Ariz.-S. Nev. Jr. Civitan, 2001—; eucharistic min. St. Pius X Ch., Tucson, 1984—86, eucharistic min. coord., 1087—1990. Mem. Am. Osteo. Assn., Am. Acad. Osteopathy (chair med. econs. com. 1994-99, bd. govs. 1997—), Ariz. Osteo. Med. Assn. (at.-large ho. of dels. 1985-93), Kirksville Coll. Osteopathy-Century Club, Cranial Acad. (bd. dirs. 1997-2003, pres., 2003-2005). Roman Catholic. Avocations: sewing, country dancing. Home and Office: 2802 N Alvernon Way Ste 200 Tucson AZ 85712-1500

CISLO, AMY EISEN, language educator; b. Flint, Mich., May 3, 1971; d. Murray and Sharon Eisen; m. Geoffrey Scott Cislo; 1 child, Emily. BA, U. Mich.; MA, Mich. State U.; postgrad., Washington U., St. Louis. Tchg. asst. Wash. U., St. Louis, 1998—2003; lectr. So. Ill. U.; tchr. Ft. Zumwalt H.S.; tchg. asst. Mich. State U. Fellow Egon Schwarz Fellowship, Wash. U., 1997-1998, Fellowship, Andrew Mellon Found., 2002. Mem.: MLA, Schweizerische Paracelsus Gesellschaft, Sixteenth Century Studies, Am. Assn. Tchrs. .of German. Achievements include Dean's Award for Excellence in Teaching.

CISLOWSKI, JOSEPH A. association executive; b. L.A., Mar. 11, 1960; s. Al and Bela C.; m. Ruth Ellen Reaven, May 25, 1997; 1 child, Bailey Solomon. AB, U. Calif., L.A., 1981; M in Pub. Policy, Harvard U., 1984. Legis. aide Calif. Legislature, Sacramento, 1981-82; program analyst NIH, Bethesda, Md., 1983; analyst in social legis. Libr. of Congress, Washington, 1984-88; cons. Nat. Acad. Scis., Washington, 1989; policy analyst Nat. Commn. on Children, Washington, 1989-91; prin. The Generation Group, L.A., 1991-96; exec. dir. Ctr. for Health Care Rights, L.A., 1996-99, So. Calif. Leadership Network, L.A., 1999—. Faculty Ctr. Nonprofit Mgmt. So. Calif., L.A., 1994—. Commr. County of L.A. Pub. Libr., 1999—; trainer United Way Greater L.A., 1994-99; dir. Jewish Cmty. Rels. Com., L.A., 1994—, Jewish Pub. Affairs Com. Calif., 1999—; mem. Calif. State Democratic Ctrl. Com., 1979-81, 93—, L.A. chpt., 1994—; elector Calif. Electoral Coll., 2000. Recipient Spl. Achievement award Librarian of Congress, Washington, 1985, Marilyn Gilbert award UCLA Internship Program, L.A., 1990, Achievement award UCLA Dept. Pediats., 1993, Dem. of Yr. award L.A. County Dem. Party, 1998; fellow Calif. State Assemby, Sacramento, 1981. Mem. Calif. Assn. Libr. Trustees and Commrs., Calif. Libr. Assn., Calif. Assn. Leadership Programs (dir. 2000—), UCLA Alumni Assn. (life), Harvard-Radcliffe Club So. Calif., Phi Beta Kappa. Jewish. Avocation: photography. Office: 811 Wilshire Blvd Ste 1025 Los Angeles CA 90017 E-mail: JCislowski@aol.com.

CISNEROS, HENRY G. homebuilding executive, broadcast executive, former federal official; b. San Antonio, June 11, 1947; s. J. George and Elvira (Munguia) C.; m. Mary Alice Perez; children: Teresa Angelica, Mercedes Christina, John Paul. BA, Tex. A&M U., 1969, M. Urban and Regional Planning, 1970; MPA, Harvard U., 1973; D. Public Adminstrn., George Washington U., 1975. Adminstrv. asst. to city mgr., San Antonio, 1968, Bryan, Tex., 1969-70; asst. dir. dept. model cities San Antonio, 1969-70; asst. to exec. v.p. Nat. League Cities, Washington, 1970-71; White House fellow asst. Sec. of HEW, Washington, 1971-72; teaching asst. dept. urban studies and planning M.I.T., 1972; mem. City Coun., San Antonio, 1975-81, mayor City of San Antonio, 1981-89; chmn. Cisneros Asset Mgmt., 1989-93; sec. U.S. Dept. HUD, Washington, 1993-97; pres., COO, Univision Comm., Inc., L.A., 1997-2000; chmn., CEO Am. CityVista, San Antonio, 2000—. Chmn. Nat. Civic League; vice chair New Am. Alliance; bd. mem. KB Home, The Entprise Found. Recipient Thomas Jefferson award for pub. architecture AIA, 1995. Office: Am CityVista 454 Soledad St Ste 300 San Antonio TX 78205-1555 Fax: 210-228-9906.

CISNEROS, SANDRA, poet, short story writer, essayist; b. Chgo., Dec. 20, 1954; BA, Loyola U., 1976. Author: (books) The House On Mango Street, 1984 (Am. Book award Columbus Found. 1985), Woman Hollering Creek and Other Stories, 1991, (children's) Hairs=Pelitos, 1994, (poetry) Bad Boys, 1980, The Rodrigo Poems, 1985, My Wicked, Wicked Ways, 1987, Loose Women, 1994, La Casa en Mango Street, 1994, El Arroyo de la Llorona, 1996, Caramelo, 2002. Fellow NEA, 1982, 87, MacArthur fellow, 1995; recipient Lannan Found. Lit. award, 1991. Home and Office: Susan Bergholz Literary SvcsAgy 17 W 10th St # 5 New York NY 10011-8746

CISSELL, JAMES CHARLES, lawyer; b. Cleve., May 29, 1940; s. Robert Francis and Helen Cecelia (Freeman) C; children: Denise, Helene-Marie, Suzanne, James. Student, Sophia U., Tokyo, 1961; AB, Xavier U., 1962; JD, U. Cin., 1966; postgrad., Ohio State U., 1973-74; D. Tech. Letters, Cin. Tech. Coll., 1979. Bar: Ohio 1966, U.S. Dist. Ct. (so. dist.) Ohio 1967, U.S. Ct. Appeals (6th cir.) 1978, U.S. Supreme Ct. 1980, U.S. Dist. Ct. (ea. dist.) Ky. 1981. Pvt. practice law, 1966-78, 82—; asst. atty. gen. State of Ohio, 1971-74; first v.p. Cin. Bd. Park Commrs., 1973-74; vice mayor City of Cin., 1976-77; U.S. atty. So. Dist. Ohio, Cin., 1978-82. Adj. instr. law No. Ky. U., 1982-86; pres. Nat. Assn. Former U.S. attys., 2001—02. Author: Oil and Gas Law in Ohio, 1964, Federal Criminal Trials, 5th edit., 1999; editor; Proving Federal Crimes. Gen. chmn. amateur pub. links championship U.S. Golf Assn., 1987; mem. coun. City of Cin., 1974-78, 85-87, 89-92; clk of cts., Hamilton County, 1992-2003; judge Hamilton County Probate Ct., 2003-; commr. Recreation Bd. Cin., 1974, Planning Bd. Cin., 1977; pres. Ohio Clk. of Cts. Assn., 1998; mem. Ohio Bicentennial Commn., 1998-2003; mem. Ohio Cts. Futures Commn., 1998-2000; mem. Ohio Supreme Ct. Adv. Com. on Tech. and the Cts., 2000—, privacy of access subcom. of Supreme Ct. adv. com. on tech. of the Cts. Recipient Econ. Opportunity award, Dr. Martin Luther King Jr. Holiday Commn., 2002; fellow, Ford Found., 1973—74. Mem. Ohio Bar Assn., Cin. Bar Assn., Fed. Bar Assn. (pres. 2002-03), Former U.S. Attys. Assn. Avocations: golf, jogging. Home: 201B Belvedere 3900 Rose Hl Cincinnati OH 45229 Office: William Howard Taft Law Ctr 230 E 9th St 10th Fl Cincinnati OH 45202 E-mail: jcissell@cms.hamilton-co.org.

CISSELL, WILLIAM BERNARD, health studies educator; b. Fancy Farm, Ky., Apr. 21, 1941; s. James S. and Lucille Marie C.; m. Mary Ellen Siebe, Aug. 26, 1967; 1 child, Lisa Kyung Mi. BS, So. Ill. U., Carbondale, 1967; MS in Pub. Health, UCLA, 1970; PhD, So. Ill. U., 1977. Cert. health edn. specialist. Curriculum coord. Dept. Def. Schs., 1972-75; asst. prin. Teagu (Korea) Am. Sch., 1975-77; asst. prof. U. Tex., Austin, 1977-79, East Tenn. State U., Johnson City, 1979-84, assoc. prof., 1984-89; prof., chmn. health studies Tex. Woman's U., Denton, 1989-98, prof., 1997—; dir. Tex. Statewide Coordinated Statement of Need Project, 1997—2001; chmn. adv. bd. Prairie Area Health Edn. Ctr., 1997—2001. Vis. prof., acting coord. behavioral health promotion and edn. dept. pub. health Jackson State U., 2001-2002; project dir. AIDS Edn. & Tng. Ctr. Tex. and Okla.; mem. joint com. on grad. standards Am. Assn. for Health Edn. and Soc. for Pub. Health Edn., 1993-96; treas. Commn. Nat. Com. for Health Edn. Credentialing, 1989-91; mem. Nat. Task Force for Prep. and Practice of Health Educators, 1986-88; dep. coord. Coalition Nat. Health Edn. Orgns., 2002-; pres. Tenn./Amazonas Ptnrs. of the Ams., 1987-88, Tenn./Amazonas Venezuela Ptnrs. of the Ams., 1981-82. Co-editor: Community Orgn., 1990, (newsletter) SHESIGN, 1989-92, Tenn. So. Pub. Health Edn., 1985-88. Chmn. sch. health com. Am. Lung Assn., Dallas, 1990-92; mem. evaluation com. Smoke Free Class 2000, 1991-93; mem. school site task force Am. Heart Assn., 1985-90. Served with USMC, 1961-64. Mem. Tex. Assn. Health, Phys. Edn., Recreation and Dance (chair cmty. health sect. 1993), Soc. Pub. Health Edn. (historian 1990-92, chair nominating and leadership devel. com. 1991-92, trustee 1995-97, disting. fellow award 1996, co-chmn. history com. 2000-02), Soc. Pub. Health Edn. and Am. Assn. for Health Edn. (baccalaureate approval process com. 1993—), Tenn. Soc. Pub. Health Edn. (pres. 1987-88), Am. Pub. Health Assn. (chmn. SHE sect. 2001-, SHE sect. program com. 2000-02), Tex. Soc. Pub. Health Edn. (pres. 1995-96, Helen Hill Disting. Svc. award 1994, Past Pres. award 1995, Dorothy Huskey Disting. Career award 1997), Golden Key Honor Soc. (co-advisor 1992-97, 2002—), Phi Kappa Phi, Eta Sigma Gamma (co-advisor Alpha Phi chpt. 1992—, disting. svc. award 1997), Denton Breakfast Club (pres.-elect 1999, pres. 2000-01), Kiwanis Internat. (sponsor, U. North Tex. Cir. K 1995-98), Divsn. 39, Tex./Okla. Dist. Kiwanis Internat. (sec. 1993-94), TAMS Key Club (sponsor 1998-2001). Office: Tex Woman's U Dept of Health Studies PO Box 425499 Denton TX 76204-5499

CITRIN, YALE, light industry executive; BA, NYU, 1950; JD, Bklyn. Law Sch., 1954. Bar: NY 1954. CEO Millar Elevator, Inc., NYC, 1959-83; bus. cons. NYC, 1983—. Head rschr. neuropsychobiology pvt. found., NYC, 1975— Home: 54 Bradford Rd Scarsdale NY 10583-7650

CITROME, LESLIE LUCIEN, psychiatrist, educator; b. Montreal, Quebec, Canada; MD, CM, McGill U. Faculty of Medicine, 1983; MPH, Columbia U. Sch. of Pub. Health, 1996. Diplomate Am. B. Psychiatry and Neurology 1990. Dir., clin. rsch. and evaluation facility Nathan S Kline Inst. for Psychiat. Rsch., Orangeburg, NY, 1998—; clin. prof. of psychiatry NY U. Sch. of Medicine, New York City, NY, 2001—. Pres. West Hudson Psychiat. Soc., Rockland County, NY, 1999—2001. Editor: (bulletin) NY State Psychiatric Assn., 1998—2002. Recipient NAMI Families and Friends of NKI Yr. 2000 Award, NAMI, 2000. Fellow: Am. Psychiat. Assn. (dep. rep. to the assembly 1997—2003, Newsletter of the Yr. Award 2002). Achievements include research in Schizophrenia. Office: Nathan Kline Inst 140 Old Orangeburg Rd Orangeburg NY 10962

CITRON, BEATRICE SALLY, law librarian, lawyer, educator; b. Phila., May 19, 1929; d. Morris Meyer and Frances (Teplitsky) Levinson; m. Joel P. Citron, Aug. 7, 1955 (dec. Sept. 1977); children: Deborah Ann, Victor Ephraim. BA in Econs. with honors, U. Pa., 1950; MLS, Our Lady of the Lake U., 1978; JD, U. Tex., 1984. Bar: Tex. 1985; cert. all-level sch. libr., secondary level tchr. Tex. Claims examiner Social Security Adminstrn., Pa., Fla. and N.C., 1951-59; head libr. St. Mary's Hall, San Antonio, 1979-80; media, reference and rare book libr., asst. and assoc. prof. St. Mary's U. Law Libr., San Antonio, 1984-89; asst. dir. St. Thomas U. Law Libr., Miami, Fla., 1989-96, assoc. dir./head pub. svc., 1996-99, acting dir., 1997-98. Law libr. cons., 2000—. Mem.: ABA, South Fla. Assn. Law Librs. (treas. 1992—94, v.p. 1994—95, pres. 1995—96), S.E. Assn. Law Librs. (newsletter, program and edn. coms. 1991—98), S.W. Assn. Law Librs. (continuing edn. com. 1986—88, chmn. local arrangements 1987—88), Am. Assn. Law Librs. (publs. com. 1987—88, com. on rels. with info. vendors 1991—93, bylaws com. 1994—96).

CITRON, MARC LAURENCE, oncologist, researcher; b. Detroit, June 1, 1948; s. Arnold Brodie and Irene Gayle (Willis) C.; m. Christine Marie Schnetzer, May 14, 1976; children: Leah, Evan, Adam. BA, Brandeis U., 1970; MD, Wayne State U., 1974. Diplomate Am. Bd. Internal Medicine, Am. Bd. Med. Oncology. Intern Georgetown U. Med. Ctr., Washington, 1974-75, resident, 1975-77, chief med. resident, 1977-78, Daryl Rubenstein fellow in med. oncology, 1977—79; asst. attending physician Hutzel Hosp., Mt. Carmel Mercy Hosp., Detroit, 1979-80; pvt. practice Southfield, Mich., 1979-80; sr. staff physician dept. oncology Henry Ford Hosp., Detroit, 1980-81; asst. prof. medicine Georgetown U., Washington, 1981-84; head sect. med. oncology L.I. Jewish Med. Ctr., New Hyde Park, N.Y., 1984—; from asst. prof. medicine Albert Einstein coll. medicine to prof. Yeshiva U., N.Y.C., 1989—97, prof. medicine Albert Einstein coll. medicine, 1997—; chief dept. oncology Pro-Health Care Assocs, LLP, Lake Success, N.Y., 1997—; clin. prof. medicine Albert Einstein Coll. Med., 1997—. Asst. prof. Medicine SUNY, Stony Brook, 1984; attending physician L.I. Jewish Med. Ctr., 1993, mem. cancer com., 1984—. Contbr. articles to profl. jours. Mem. AMA, ACP, Med. Soc. County of Queens, Med. Soc. State of N.Y., Cancer & Leukemia Group B, Am. Soc. Clin. Oncology. Office: ProHealth Care Assocs LLP 2800 Marcus Ave New Hyde Park NY 11042-1052

CITRON, RICHARD IRA, management consultant; b. Chgo., Apr. 1, 1944; s. Irving I. and Ruth (Katz) C.; m. Phyllis Sarah Kalifey, Dec. 26, 1971; children: Brian Todd, Dana Ann. BS, Roosevelt U., Chgo., 1966; MS, Ill. Inst. Tech., 1968, PhD, 1972. Enrolled Actuary. Consulting prin. A.S. Hansen, Inc., Chgo., 1972-79, mng. prin. N.Y.C., 1979-82; exec. v.p. Frank B. Hall Consulting Co., N.Y.C., 1982-86; pres., CEO W F Corroon, Inc., Stamford, Conn., 1986-92; pres. Benefit Svcs. div., exec. v.p., dir. Hogg Robinson, Inc., N.Y.C., 1992-95; CEO Penn Gen. Svcs. Corp., Inc., N.Y.C., 1992-95; chmn. Hogg Robinson Consulting Group, Inc., N.Y.C., 1992-95, Group Plan Cons., Inc., N.Y.C., 1992-95; corp. dir. worldwide benefits Campbell Soup Co., Inc., Camden, NJ, 1996—2002; CEO Nortic Cons., LLC, 2002—. Chmn., CEO Citron & Assocs., Inc.; bd. dirs. Employee Benefit Rsch. Inst., Washington, HRI, Inc., N.A; adv. bd. mem. Am. Benefits Coun., 1998—. Author articles in profl. jours. Trustee Optometric Ctr. of N.Y., mem. Coll. Council of SUNY; cons. State of Ill. Pension Laws Commn. 1974-78 Recipient: Blum-Kolver Found. grant 1963-66, Nat. Sci. Found. grant 1968-70. Mem. Am. Acad. of Actuaries, Internat. Found. Employee Benefits (chmn actuaries com. 1981-82), Assn. of Private Pension and Welfare Plans, Am. Soc. for Advancement of Sci., Boardroom, Landmark, Elmwood Country Club. E-mail: mardino@aol.com.

CITTONE, HENRY ARON, hotel and restaurant management educator; s. Joseph and Devora C.; m. Liliane, Oct. 2, 1965; children: Henry Joseph, Marc Ely. Student, Trade and Tech. Coll., L.A., 1971; MS, U. Houston, 1990; postgrad. in edn., Fla. Atlantic U., Boca Raton, 1993-94. Food svc. mgr. U. So. Calif., L.A., 1971; mgr. food and beverage Sheraton Poste Inn, Cherry Hill, N.J., 1972-73; resident mgr. Aruba Caribbean Hotel, Netherlands Antilles, 1973-74, Lima (Peru) Sheraton Hotel, 1974-76; dir. food and beverage Bahia Mar Hotel, Ft. Lauderdale, Fla., 1978-79, Maison Dupuy, New Orleans, 1979-81, Virgin Isle Hotel, St. Thomas, 1981-84; asst. prof. hotel and restaurant mgmt. Galveston Coll. (Tex.), 1984-90; prof. Morehead (Ky.) State U., 1990-92; instr. Coll. V.I., 1983-84, Houston C.C., 1985-90; prof., assoc. dean Fairfax U., La.; dir. food and beverage Gov.'s Club of West Palm Beach, Fla., 2002—. Adj. faculty North Miami (Fla.) Johnson and Wales U., 1994. With Israeli Army, 1956-59. Recipient Cert. Hotal Adminstr. Designation award Ednl. Inst. AH & MA, 1986. Mem. Nat. Restaurant Assn., Am. Hotel and Motel Assn., Internat. Hotel Sales Mgmt. Assn., Internat. Soc. Food and Beverage Execs., Coun. on Hotel, Restaurant, and Instnl. Edn., CHRIE (internat. exch. com.), Conrad Hilton Coll. Alumni Assn. (Disting. Hospitality Educator of Yr. 1988), Global Hoteliers Club. E-mail: CittonHA@msn.com.

CIUBOTARU, ALEXANDRU AURELIAN, electronics engineer; b. Galati, Romania, Apr. 12, 1965; s. Constantin and Aurelia C.; m. Dana Mihaela Bedivan, Sept. 8, 1993. Diploma de inginer, Inst. Politehnic Iasi, Romania, 1989; PhD, Univ. Tex., 1996. Design engr. Tehnoton, Iasi, 1989-91; asst. instr. Inst. Politechnic, Iasi, Romania, 1991—92; grad. rsch., tchg. asst. Univ. Tex., Arlington, 1992-96; intermediate product/device engr. Nat. Semiconductor Corp., Arlington, Tex., 1996-98; lead design engr. Intersil Corp., Palm Bay, Fla., 1998-2000; sr. design engr. Maxim Integrated Products, Melbourne, Fla., 2000—. Contbr. articles to profl. jours. Home: 6900 Woodlake Dr NE Apt 101 Palm Bay FL 32905-6122 Office: Maxim Integrated Products 300 A-1 North Dr Melbourne FL 32934 Fax: 321 751-1491. E-mail: alex_ciubotaru@yahoo.com.

CIUFFO, ANTHONY FRANK, small business owner; b. Bklyn., May 26, 1938; s. Michael and Mary (Despirito) C.; m. Joan, Sept. 23, 1961. BS, SUNY, Westbury, 1982; MA, SUNY, Old Westbury, Saratoga Springs, 1994; postgrad., Union Inst., 1998—. Divsn. head Bankers Trust Co., N.Y.C., 1956-63; owner, ptnr. M & U Provision Co., Bklyn., 1963—. Owner Craft-A-Fair, 1994, Rent-A-Shelf. Patentee in field. Mem. Am. Mktg. Assn. Republican. Roman Catholic. Home: 561 Seminole Rd Franklin Square NY 11010-1820

CIULLA, JOANNE BRIDGETT, business ethics educator; b. Rochester, N.Y., June 16, 1952; d. Andrew Joseph and Corrine Margaret (Christiano) C.; m. René Petrus Franciscus Kanters, Dec. 15, 1990. BA in Philosophy, U. Md., 1973; MA in Philosophy, U. Del., 1975; PhD in Philosophy, Temple U., 1985. Adj. asst. prof. La Salle U., Phila., 1975-84; fellow in bus. and ethics Harvard U., Cambridge, Mass., 1984-86; sr. fellow Wharton Sch. U. Pa., Phila., 1986-71; Coston Family chair in leadership and ethics Jepson Sch. of Leadership Studies U. Richmond, Va., 1991—. Cons. bus. ethics and leadership, pvt. practice, Cambridge, Phila. Richmond, 1984—; UNESCO chair in leadership studies UN U., Amman, Jordan, 2000-2001. Author: The Working Life, 2000, The Ethics of Leadership, 2002; editor: Ethics, the Heart of Leadership, 1998; mem. editl. bd. Bus. Ethics Quar. Bd. dirs. Desmond Tutu Peace Found. Mem. Soc. for Bus. Ethics, Acad. Mgmt. Office: U Richmond Jepson Sch Richmond VA 23173

CIULLO, ROSEMARY, psychologist; b. Chgo. BA, U. Ill., Chgo., 1974; MA, Gov.'s State U., University Park, Ill., 1977; PsyD with high distinction, Forest Inst. Profl. Psychology, 1986. Pvt. practice, Ill. Mem. APA, Ill. Psychol. Assn., Orthopsychiatry.

CIUPARU, DRAGOS MIHAEL, research scientist, educator; b. Ploiesti, Prahova, Romania, July 6, 1967; s. Dumitru and Zinovia Ciuparu; m. Alina Madalina Vasile, Oct. 27, 1990; children: Andrei Catalin, Georgiana Eugenia. MSc, Petrol-Gaze U., Ploiesti, 1991; PhD, Denis Diderot U., Paris, France, 1999. Lectr. Petrol - Gaze U., Ploiesti, Romania, 1996—99; postdoctoral assoc. Yale U., 1999—2001, rsch. scientist, 2001—. Contbr. scientific papers. Grantee PhD fellowship, French Ministry of Superior Edn., 1996-1999, TEMPUS-PHARE, European Union, 1998, Tng. grant, USAID, 1995. Mem.: Am. Chem. Soc., North Am. Catalysis Soc., AIChE. Office: Yale University 9 Hillhouse Ave Mason Laboratory 310 New Haven CT 06520-8286 Office Fax: 203-432-4387. E-mail: dragos.ciuparu@yale.edu.

CIURCZAK, ALEXIS, librarian; b. Long Island, N.Y., Feb. 13, 1950; d. Alexander Daniel and Catherine Ann (Frangipane) C. BA Art History magna cum laude, U. Calif., L.A., 1971; MA Libr. Sci., San Jose State U., 1975; cert. tchr. ESL, U. Calif., Irvine, 1985. Intern IBM Rsch. Libr., San Jose, Calif., 1974-75; tech. asst. San Bernardino Valley Coll. Libr., Calif., 1975; tech. svcs. librarian Palomar Coll., San Marcos, Calif., 1975-78, pub. svcs. librarian, 1978-81, libr. dir., 1981-86, pub. svcs. librarian, 1987—, instr. Libr. Technology Cert. Program, 1975—; exchange librarian Fulham Pub. Libr., London, 1986-87; coord. San Diego C.C. Consortium Semester-in-London Am. Inst. Fgn. Study, 1988-89. Mem. ALA, San Diego Libr. Svcs. com., Calif. Libr. Media Educators Assn., Patronato por Niños, Kosciuszko Found., So. Calif. Tech. Processes Group, Pacific Coast Coun. Latin Am. Studies, Libros, Reforma, Libr. Assn. (British), Calif. Libr. Assn., Calif. Tchrs. Assn., Phi Beta Kappa, Beta Phi Mu. Office: Palomar CC 1140 W Mission Rd San Marcos CA 92069-1415 E-mail: aciurczak@palomar.edu.

CIVANTOS, FRANCISCO, pathologist, educator; b. June 25, 1935; m. Elsa Gonzalez, Dec. 20, 1959; children: Francisco, Marlene, Joseph, Gloria, John, Christine. BS, U. Havana, 1957; MD, Tulane U., 1961. Lic. physician, Fla. Intern Detroit Receiving Hosp., 1961-62; resident in pathology, then chief resident in pathology Mass. Gen. Hosp., Boston, 1962-66; pathologist Mt. Sinai Hosp., Miami Beach, Fla., 1968-73; dir. clin. lab. St. Francis Hosp., Miami Beach, 1973-78; anatomic and clin. pathologist Jackson Meml. Hosp., Miami, Fla., 1978—; prof. pathology Med. Sch., U. Miami, 1985-95, dir. J.B. Miale Coagulation Lab., 1985-95. Dir. urologic and hepatic pathology U. Miami at Cedars Med. Ctr., 1989—. Contbr. numerous articles to sci. publs. Chmn. adv. coun. on clin. labs. to gov. State of Fla., Tallahassee, 1989-92. Capt. M.C., USAF, 1966-68. Fellow Am. Soc. Clin. Pathology (dir./lectr. workshops on endocrine pathology, Coagulation, and urologic pathology), Coll. Pathology; mem. Internat. Acad. Pathology, Fla. Soc. Pathology (pres. 1990-92), Peruvian Soc. Pathology (hon.), Internat. Soc. Urologic Pathology, Randonneurs USA (Paris-Brest-Paris medal 1991, 95, 99, 2003), Everglades Bicycle Club. Democrat. Roman Catholic. Avocation: bicycling. Office: Cedars Med Ctr 4th Fl Pathology 1400 NW 12th Ave Miami FL 33136

CIVELEK, A. CAHID, nuclear medicine physician, medical researcher; b. Antakya, Turkiye, Turkey, Feb. 23, 1953; s. M. Cevri and Necdet Civelek; 1 child, A. Cevri. MD, Istanbul U Sch. of Medicine, Istanbul - Turkiye, 1970—76. Cert. Medical Diplomate Univ of Istanbul Sch. of Medicine, 1976, Fellow Johns Hopkins Sch. of Medicine, 1982, Board of Nuclear Medicine Am. Bd. of Nuc. Medicine 1986, 1984, Residency - Nuclear Medicine Hacettepe Med. Instn., 1981. Assoc. prof., radiology The Johns Hopkins Med. Inst., Balt., 1995—; med. dir., sch. of nuc. medicine technologists Johns Hopkins Hosp., Balt., 1995. Dir., sect. of nuc. cardiology The Johns Hopkins Med. Inst., Balt., 1992—. Recipient AMA Continuing Med. Ed. Physicians Recognition Award, 1990; fellow IAEA, 1982—84. Fellow: Am. Soc. Nuc. Cardiology (Founding Mem.), Am. Coll. Angiology, Am. Coll. Nuc. Physicians. Achievements include research in Nuclear Medicine - Clinical. Office: Johns Hopkins Med Inst 601 N Caroline St OPC Ste # 3235 Baltimore MD 21287-0817

CIVILETTI, BENJAMIN R. lawyer, former United States attorney general; b. Peekskill, N.Y., July 17, 1935; m. Gaile Lundgren. AB, Johns Hopkins U., 1957; LLB, Columbia U. and U. Md., 1961; LLD (hon.), U. Balt., 1978, N.Y. Law Sch., 1979, Tulane U., 1979, St. Johns U., 1979, U. Notre Dame, 1980, U. Md., 1983. Bar: Md. 1961. Law clk. to judge U.S. Dist. Ct. for Md., 1961-62; asst. U.S. atty., 1962-64; mem. firm Venable, Baetjer & Howard, 1964-77; asst. atty. gen., criminal div. U.S. Dept. Justice, Washington, 1977-78; dep. atty. gen. U.S., 1978-79, atty. gen., 1979-81; pvt. practice law Balt. and Washington, 1981—; chmn. bd., dir. Md. Healthcorp., Inc.; now with Venable, Baetjer and Howard, Balt. Dir. MNC Fin. Corp., Afro-Am. Pub. Co. Trustee Johns Hopkins U.; chmn. Md. Legal Services Corp.; chmn. bd. visitors Sch. Pub. Affairs U. Md.; chmn. Gov.'s Task Force for Funding of Pub. Edn.; bd. dirs. Inst. Against Violence and Prejudice Recipient Herbert H. Lehman ethics award Fellow Am. Coll. Trial Lawyers, Am. Law Inst., Am. Bar Found., Md. Bar Found.; mem. Am., Md., Balt. City, D.C. bar assns., Am. Judicature Soc. (dir.), Order of Coif, Phi Alpha Delta. Office: Venable Baetjer and Howard 1800 Merc Bank & Trust Bldg 2 Hopkins Plz Ste 2100 Baltimore MD 21201-2982 also: Ste 1200 1301 Pennsylvania Ave NW Washington DC 20004-1701

CIVITELLA, CORINE ANTOINETTE, retired health facility administrator; b. Ridley Park, Pa., Oct. 23, 1928; d. Charles Christopher and Antoinette Campiglia Suess; m. Domenic Civitella, May 20, 1950; children: Dennis, Corine. Diploma, Northeastern Hosp. Nursing Sch. Phila., 1949; BSEd, West Chester (Pa.) U., 1971. Various positions Bryn Mawr (Pa.) Hosp., 1949-64; mem. faculty Bryn Mawr Hosp. Sch. Nursing, 1964-70; adminstr. Rest Haven Nursing Ctr., Broomall, Pa., 1978-86; regional adminstr. Geriatrics and Med. Ctrs., Phila., 1986, Health Care and Retirement Corp., Toledo, 1986-89; dir. ops. IFIDA Health Care, Bryn Mawr, Pa., 1985-86; regional adminstr. Multi-Care, Hackensack, N.J., 1989-90; regional nurse adminstr. Central Park Lodge, Sarasota, Fla., 1991-93; health care cons. pvt. practice, Fort Myers, Fla., 1993-96. Various positions Bryn Mawr (Pa.) Hosp., 1949-71; faculty Bryn Mawr Sch. Nursing, 1971-77; dir. nurses Fair Acres Geriatric Ctr., Lima, Pa., 1970-77, Pocopson Geriatric Ctr., West Chester, Pa., 1977-78; sec. Bowling League, Pine Lakes Bowling Club, Ft. Myers, Fla., 1996. Bd. mem. Pine Lakes Home Owners Assn., Ft. Myers, Fla., 1997; sec. golf assn. Pine Lakes Nine Holers, Ft. Myers, Fla., 1997; elders affair bd. mem. Lee Meml. Health Sys., Ft. Myers, Fla., 1999; bd. mem. Shady Rest Care Pavilion, Ft. Myers, Fla., 1999-2000; vol. Medway Sr. Ctr., 2002—. Named Nat. Honor Soc. Marple-Newtown H.S., Newtown Sq., Pa., 1946. Mem. Am. Coll. Nursing Home Adminstrs., Harvard Med. Coll. Brigham and Womens Hosp. Avocations: golf, swimming, bowling, knitting, tole painting. E-mail address. Home: 37 Lovering Hts Medway MA 02053-1555 E-mail: cividom@ncounty.net.

CIZEK, JOHN GARY, safety and fire engineer; b. St. Louis, Sept. 16, 1948; s. John Ernst and Ann Margaret (Seith) C.; m. Carolyn Marie Haas, Dec. 4, 1971; children: Laura Suzanne, John David. BSChE, U. Mo., Rolla, 1971. Registered profl. engr.; cert. safety profl. Loss prevention engr. Factory Mutual Engring. Assn., St. Louis, 1971-76; safety engr. Diamond Shamrock Corp., Cleve., 1977-80, from corp. safety specialist to mgr. safety Dallas, 1980-87; cons. safety and fire protection, asst. v.p. M&M Protection Cons., Houston, 1987-90, v.p., 1990-99, sr. v.p., 1999—2002, energy and chem. industry practice leader, 1997-98; mem. Marsh Risk Consulting, Houston, 1997—2002; sr. cons. Baker Engring. and Risk Cons., Stafford, Tex., 2002—. Mem. AIChE, Am. Soc. Safety Engrs., Soc. Fire Protection Engr. Lutheran. Office: Baker Engring & Risk Cons 4100 Greenbriar Ste 130 Stafford TX 77477-3908 E-mail: GCizek@BakerRisk.com.

CIZIK, ROBERT, manufacturing company executive; b. Scranton, Pa., Apr. 4, 1931; s. John and Anna (Paraska) C.; m. Jane Morin, Oct. 3, 1953; children: Robert Morin, Jan Catherine, Paula Jane, Gregory Alan, Peter Nicholas. BS, U. Conn., 1953; MBA, Harvard U., 1958; LLD (hon.), Kenyon Coll., 1983. Acct. Price Waterhouse & Co. (CPAs), N.Y.C., 1953-54, 56; fin. analyst Exxon U.S.A., N.J., 1958-61; exec. asst. Cooper Industries, Inc., Houston, 1961-63, treas., 1963-64, contr., 1964-67, v.p. planning, 1967-69, exec. v.p., 1969-73, pres., 1973-92, COO, 1973-75, CEO, 1975-95, chmn., 1983-96; propr. Cizik Interests, Houston, 1996—; dir. Am. Indsl. Ptnrs., 1996-98; adv. dir. Wingate Ptnrs., 1994—; chmn. bd. dirs. Easco, Inc., 1997-98, Stanadyne Automotive, 1998-2000. Chmn. bd. dirs. Koppers Industries; mem. host com. Houston Econ. Summit Meeting, 1990. Bd. dirs. Assocs. Harvard Bus. Sch., Boston, 1984-96; mem. Tex. Bus. and Edn. Coalition, 1991-94; chmn. Heartstrings Benefit, Design Industries Found. for AIDS, 1991-92; mem. nat. adv. coun., trustee Tex. Heart Inst.; mem. devel. bd. U. Tex. Houston Health Sci. Ctr.; campaign co-chair Wortham Theater Ctr., 1981-83, United Way of Tex., Gulf Coast, 1994-95. 1st lt. USAF, 1954-56. Recipient Gen. Maurice Hirsch award Bus. Com. for Arts, 1984, CEO of Yr. bronze award Fin. World Mag., 1987, CEO of Decade bronze award in Indsl. Equipment Cos., 1988, Masterson award Houston Grand Opera, 1998, Maurice Hirsch award for philanthropy, 1999; named Best CEO in Machinery Industry, Wall St. Transcript, 1980, 81, 83, 86, 87, 88, 89, 90-91, Internat. Exec. of Yr., Greater Houston Partnership and Houston World Trade Assn., 1990. Mem. NAM (chmn. 1992-93), Elec. Mfrs. Club (bd. govs. 1984—, pres. 1990-92), River Oaks Country Club, Forum Club Houston (founding). Office: Cizik Interests 8839 Harness Creek Ln Houston TX 77024-7044 E-mail: bcizik@sbcglobal.net.

CLAAR, VICTOR VYRON, economics educator; s. Herbert Ellsworth and Marcille Elaine (Staton) C.; m. Elizabeth Greer Oswalt. BA in Bus. Adminstrn., Houghton Coll., 1987, postgrad. math., 1991; MA in Econs., W.Va. U., 1995, PhD in Econs., 2000. Grad. tchg. asst. W.Va. U., Morgantown, 1994-98, grad. rsch. asst., 1997-98, fellow dept. econs., 1999-2000; asst. prof. econs. Hope Coll., Holland, Mich., 2000—. Referee Jour. Pub. Econs., Jour. Money, Credit and Banking, Rev. Polit. Economy; pres. Thompson's Econs. Club, Morgantown, 1995-96; discussant Allied Social Sci. Assns., Chgo., 1998; vis. prof. econs. Houghton (N.Y.) Coll., 1999. Author: survey report for Regional Rsch. Inst., 1998; contbr. articles to profl. jours. Cantor, mem. choir Trinity Episcopal Ch., Morgantown, 1996-98; mem. evangelism com. Trinity Episcopal Ch., 1998; charter mem. Brotherhood St. Andrew, Trinity Episcopal Ch., 1998-2000. Presidential scholar Houghton Coll.; Swiger Supplemental fellow W.Va. U. Mem. Am. Econs. Assn., So. Econ. Assn. (presenter, discussant), Assn. Christian Economists, Omicron Delta Epsilon (grad.). Office: Hope Coll Dept Econs and Bus Adminstrn PO Box 9000 Holland MI 49422-9000

CLAASSEN, W(ALTER) MARSHALL, employment company executive; b. St. Paul, Jan. 16, 1943; s. Walter Marshall and Marie Christine (Petersen) C.; m. Nancy Rector Alcock, Mar. 2, 1974; children: Katherine, Walter. BA, BJ, U. Mo., 1966. Sr. adminstr. Honeywell, Inc., Chgo., 1968-74; pers. dir. Lyon-Healy, div. of CBS, Inc., Chgo., 1974-78; mgr., corp. placement CF Industries, Long Grove, Ill., 1978-82; mgr. of recruiting Newark Electronics, Chgo., 1983-84; dir. human resources Swift, div. of Reichold Chem., Downers Grove, Ill., 1984-86, ECM, Inc., Schaumburg, Ill., 1986-87; pres. GBX, Inc., dba Express Personnel Svcs. of Vernon Hills, Ill. and Express Pers. Svcs. of Arlington Heights, Ill., 1988—. Bd. dirs. Elk Grove-Schaumburg Mental Health Ctr., 1975-77, Pvt. Industry Coun. of Lake County, Waukegan, Ill., 1990-96, chmn., 1994-96; bd. dirs. Pvt. Industry Coun. Found., 1992—, Lake County Workforce Investment Bd., 2000—. Lt.(j.g.) USNR, 1966-68. Recipient Circle of Excellence award, 1992—. Mem. Libertyville-Vernon Hills C. of C., Lake County C. of C., Lincolnshire C. of C., Arlington Heights C. of C., Univ. Mo. Alumni Assn., Phi Delta Theta. Republican. Quaker. Avocations: fly fishing, scuba diving. Home: 25030 N Pawnee Rd Barrington IL 60010-1380 Office: Express Personnel Svcs 977 Lakeview Pkwy Ste 190 Vernon Hills IL 60061-1429 E-mail: marshall.claassen@expresspersonnel.com.

CLABAUGH, ELMER EUGENE, JR., retired lawyer; b. Anaheim, Calif., Sept. 18, 1927; s. Elmer Eugene and Eleanor Margaret (Heitshusen) C.; m. Donna Marie Organ, Dec. 19, 1960 (div.); children: Christopher C., Matthew M. BBA cum laude, Woodbury U.; BA summa cum laude, Claremont McKenna Coll., 1958; JD, Stanford U., 1961. Bar: Calif. 1961, U.S. Dist. Ct. (cen. dist.) Calif., U.S. Ct. Appeals (9th cir.) 1961, U.S. Supreme Ct. 1971. With fgn. svc. U.S. Dept. State, Jerusalem, Tel Aviv, 1951-53, Pub. Adminstrn. Svcs., El Salvador, Ethiopia, U.S., 1953-57; dep. dist. atty. Ventura County, Calif., 1961-62; pvt. practice, 1962-97; mem. Hathaway, Clabaugh, Perrett and Webster and predecessors, 1962-79, Clabaugh & Perloff, Ventura, 1979-97; state inheritance tax referee, 1968-78; ret. Bd. dirs. San Antonio Water Conservation Dist., Ventura Cmty. Meml. Hosp., 1964-80; trustee Ojai Unified Sch. Dist., 1974-79; bd. dirs. Ventura County Found. for Parks and Harbors, 1982-96, Ventura County Maritime Mus., 1982-94. With USCGR, 1944-46, USMCR, 1946-48. Mem. NRA, Calif. Bar Assn., Safari Club Internat., Mason, Shriners, Phi Alpha Delta. Republican.

CLABORN, DAVID MERRELL, entomologist; s. Benjamen Franklin and Jeanie (Jones) Claborn; m. Vicky Lynn Richardson, May 4, 1991; children: Lauren Meryl, Rebecca Asia. DPH, Uniformed Services U of Health Sci., Bethesda, Md., 1998—2001; MS, Tex. Tech U., Lubbock, Tex., 1983—85, BS, 1975—83. Officer in charge Navy Disease Vector Ecology and Control Ctr., Jacksonville, Fla., 2002—02; med. entomologist U. S. Navy, 1988—2002. Adj. faculty U of Md., U Coll., Naha, Okinawa, Japan, 1992—94, Union Inst., San Diego, 1996—97. Author: (jour. articles) 15 Peer-reviewed Articles On Control Of Vectors And Vector-borne Diseases. Comdr., med. svc. corps U. S. Navy, 1988—2002, Jacksonville, FL. Decorated Navy and Marine Corps Commendation Medal (5 awards) U. S. Navy, Navy Achievement Medal (3 awards), Combat Action Ribbon, Humanitarian Svc. Medal, Kuwait Liberation Medal. Mem.: Entomol. Soc. of Am. Presbyterian. Avocation: music. Home: 1486 Winston Ln Orange Park FL 32003 Office: Disease Vector Ecology and Control Ctr Naval Air Sta Box 43 Jacksonville FL 32212-0043 Personal E-mail: dmclaborn@dveccjax.med.navy.mil.

CLACK, JERRY, classics educator; b. N.Y.C., July 22, 1926; s. Christopher Thrower and Mildred Taylor (VanDyke) C. AB, Princeton U., 1946, MA, 1958; PhD, U. Pitts., 1962; MA, Duquesne U., Pitts., 1977. Documents officer U.S. Nat. Commn. for UNESCO, 1946-52; exec. dir. Allegheny County chpt. Nat. Found., Pitts., 1953-68; asst. prof. dept. classics Duquesne U., Pitts., 1968-71, assoc. prof., 1971-75, prof., 1975—, chmn. dept., 1973-75, 80-83, mem. preprofl. health com., 1970-76, mem. univ. library com., 1979-93, mem. univ. due process, core curriculum, arts and scis. curriculum coms., 1986-94, mem. univ. promotion and tenure com., 1988-90. Editor: The Classical World, 1977-93, Anthology of Hellenistic Poetry, 1982, Meleager: The Poems, 1992, Asclepiades of Samos and Leonidas of Tarentum: The Poems, 1999, Dioscorides and Antipater of Sidon: The Poems, 2001; mem. editl. bd. Duquesne Univ. Press, 1991-94; author books, articles, revs. in field. Pres. Western Pa. Pub. Health Conf., 1967; v.p. Western Pa. Coun. World Federalists, 1965—88, treas., 1987—, Pitts. Opera Theater, 2001—; U.S. del. to 3d UNESCO Gen. Conf., Florence, Italy, 4th UNESCO Gen. Conf., Paris; bd. dirs. Pitts. Opera Theater, 2001—. Mem. Classical Assn. Pitts. and Vicinity (treas. 1970-78, 85—, sec. 1988—), Pa. Classical Assn. (treas. 1977-99), Classical Assn. Atlantic States (pres. 1987, exec. com. 1974—, 2d v.p. 1975, 1st v.p. 1976, exec. dir. 1993-2001, archivist 2001—), Am. Philol. Assn. (chmn. working group editors classical jours. 1982-93, chmn. com. regional classical orgns. 1986-95), Vergilian Soc. Am. (trustee 1985-87), Phi Sigma Iota, Delta Phi Alpha, Alpha Epsilon Delta, Phi Alpha Theta. Home: Apt 512 5850 Centre Ave Pittsburgh PA 15206 Office: Duquesne U Department Of Classics Pittsburgh PA 15282-0001 E-mail: clack@duq.edu.

CLAES, DANIEL JOHN, physician; s. John Vernon and Claribel C.; m. Gayla Christine, Jan. 19, 1974. AB magna cum laude, Harvard U., 1953, MD cum laude, 1957. Intern UCLA, 1957-58; Bowyer Found. fellow for rsch. in medicine L.A., 1958-61; pvt. practice specializing in diabetes, 1962—. Biotech. cons. SIRA Techs., 1995—; v.p. Am. Eye Bank Found., 1978-83, pres., 1983—, dir. rsch., 1980—, chmn., CEO 1995—; pres. Heuristic Group, 1981—, Cavendish Assocs., 2002—. Contbr. papers on diabetes mellitus, computers in medicine to profl. lit. Mem. L.A. Mus. Art, 1960—. Mem.: AAAS, AMA, Cell Transplantation Soc., Diabetes Tech. Soc., Am. Math. Soc., Internat. Pancreas & Islet Transplant Assn., Internat. Diabetes Fedn, Am. Diabetes Assn. (profl. coun. on immunology, immunogenetics and transplantation), L.A. County Med. Assn., Calif. Med. Assn., Royal Commonwealth (London), Harvard and Harvard Med. Sch. of So. Calif. Club. Office: Am Eyebank Found 15237 W Sunset Blvd Ste 108 Pacific Palisades CA 90272-3690

CLAES, GAYLA CHRISTINE, writer, editorial consultant; b. L.A., Oct. 17, 1946; d. Henry George and Glorya Desiree (Curran) Blasdel; m. Daniel John Claes, Jan. 19, 1974. AB magna cum laude, Harvard U., 1968; postgrad., Oxford (Eng.) U., 1971; MA, McGill U., Montreal, 1975. Adminstrv. asst. U. So. Calif., L.A., 1968-70; teaching asst. English lit. McGill U., Montreal, 1970-71; editorial dir. Internat. Cons. Group, L.A., 1972-78; v.p. Gaylee Corp., L.A., 1978-81, CEO, 1981-88; writer, cons. L.A. and Paris, 1988—. Dir. pub. rels. Ctr. Internat. for the Performing Arts, Paris and L.A., 1991—2000. Author: (play) Berta of Hungary, 1972, (novel) Christopher Derring, 1990; contbr. articles to lit. and sci. jours. Co-founder White Swan Awards, ann. benefit for Crippled Children's Soc. dba AbilityFirst, 1999. Mem. Harvard-Radcliffe Club of So. Calif., Royal Commonwealth Soc. (London).

CLAFLIN, ARTHUR CARY, lawyer; b. Bowling Green, Ohio, July 7, 1950; s. Edward Scott and Mona Sophia (Cretney) C.; m. Gretchen Elaine Anders, May 31, 1975; children: Rachel Anders, Emily Anders. BA magna cum laude, Wesleyan U., 1972; JD, Yale U., 1975. Bar: Wash. 1975, U.S. Dist. Ct. (we. dist.) Wash. 1975, U.S. Dist. Ct. (ea. dist.) Wash. 1981, U.S. Ct. Appeals (9th cir.) 1979, U.S. Ct. Appeals (5th cir.) 1982. Assoc. Bogle & Gates, Seattle, 1975-81, ptnr., 1981-99, Claflin & Christensen, Seattle, 1999-2000; mem. Hall, Zanzig, Claflin, McEachern, Seattle, 2000—. Mem. Phi Beta Kappa. Presbyterian. Office: Hall Zanzig Zulauf Claflin McEachern 1200 5th Ave Ste 1414 Seattle WA 98101-3106

CLAFLIN, JAMES ROBERT, pediatrician, allergist; b. Apr. 30, 1946; m. Marcee Claflin; children: James Sean (dec.), Brian Scott (dec.), Susan Nicole, Timothy Lynn. Student, Northwestern State Coll.; MD, U. Okla., 1971. Diplomate Am. Bd. Pediatrics, Am. Bd. Allergy Immunology. Intern U. Tex. Med. Br., Galveston, 1971-72; advanced through grades to lt. col. USAF, 1969-84, chief pediatric svcs. Goodfellow AFB, 1972-73, 75-77, chief pediatric svcs. and hosp. svcs. RAF Upper Heyford, 1977-80, chief allergy and clin. immunology, 1982-84; fellow allergy/immunology Willford Hall USAF Med. Ctr., Lackland AFB, Tex., 1980-82; ret. USAF, 1984. Clin. asst. prof. pediatrics, Oklahoma U.; presenter in field. Contbr. articles to profl. jours. Advisor child welfare com. Tom Green County, 1976-77; mem. child welfare com. RAF, Upper Heyford, Eng., 1978-80; mem. sch. and pub. health com. Tarrant County Med. Soc., 1984-85, chmn., 1986-87, publs. com., 1988-89, religion and meml. com., 1989; mem. quality assurance and infectious disease coms. Cook-Ft. Worth Children's Hosp., 1986-89; v.p. Brenham State Sch. Parent Assn., 1987-88; pres. Parents Assn. for the Retarded of Tex., 1987-88; chmn. cmty. conscience com. Wedgwood Bapt. Ch. Recipient Svc. award Am. Diabetes Assn., 1976. Fellow Am. Acad. Pediatrics, Am. Coll. Allergy (mem. com. on allergic rhinitis, mem. com. on adverse reactions to food 1991-96), Am. Acad. Allergy; mem. AMA (alt. del.), Am. Coll. Allergy, Asthma and Immunology (spkr. ho. of dels. 2001—), Oklahoma County Med. Soc. (pres.-elect 2003—), Okla. State Med. Assn. (sec.-treas. 2003—), Okla. Allergy and Asthma Soc. (pres. 1998-2000). Home: 750 NE 13th St Oklahoma City OK 73104-5051

CLAGETT, BRICE MCADOO, lawyer, writer; b. Washington, July 6, 1933; s. Brice and Sarah Fleming (McAdoo) Clagett; m. Virginia Lawrence Parker, Sept. 18, 1965 (div.); children: John Brice, Ann Calvert Brooke; m. Diana Wharton Sinkler, July 26, 1987. AB summa cum laude, Princeton U., 1954; postgrad., U. Allahabad, India, 1954-55; JD magna cum laude, Harvard U., 1958. Bar: D.C. 1958, U.S. Supreme Ct. 1962. Assoc. Covington & Burling, Washington, 1958-67, ptnr., 1967-2000, sr. counsel, 2000—02. Jud. counsellor Cambodian del. Internat. Ct. Justice, 1960—62; legal advisor Transition Team U.S. Dept. State, 1980—81; mem. nat. steering com. U.S. Iran Claimants Com., 1982—99; adv. bd. Inst. Transt. Arbitration, 1989—2000; mem. lawyers com. Ctr. Individual Rights, 1992—. Co-author: (book) The Valuation of Property in International Law, vol. 4, 1987, An Illustrated History of St. Albans School, 1981; bd. editors: Harvard Law Rev., 1956—58; contbr. articles to legal, geneal. and hist. jours. Trustee Md. Hist. Trust, 1971—78, chmn., 1972—78; trustee Md. State Ho. Trust, 1972—76, Md. Environ. Trust, 1978—, vice chmn., 1981—85, chmn., 1985—89; bd. dirs. Chester-Sassafras Found., 1985—89; trustee New Eng. Hist. Geneal. Soc., 1989—92, 1995—98, Tudor Place Found., 1992—96, Found. Preservation hist. Georgetown, 2000—; bd. advisors Nat. Trust Hist. Preservation, 1978—81; Clagett family com. Chesapeake Bay Found., 1982—; mem. Human Rights Law Group del. to Romania, 1990; counselor to the Pres. Gen. Soc. Cin., 1988—89, solicitor, 1998—; mem. adv. coun. Accokeek Found., 1989—91, trustee, 1991—94; comdr. Royal Order Cambodia, 1962. Recipient Cert. Disting. Citizens, State of Md., 1978. Mem.: So. Md. Soc., Federalist Soc., Washington Inst. Fgn. Affairs, Internat. Law Assn., Am. Arbitration Assn., Am. Law Inst., Am. Soc. Internat. Law, Mil. Order Stars and Bars, City Tavern Club (D.C.), Radnor Hunt Club (Pa.), Soc. Cin. Md., Met. Club (D.C.), Marlborough Hunt Club (Upper Marlboro, Md.), Sons Confederate Vets., Phi Beta Kappa. Republican. Episcopalian. Home: Holly Hill PO Box 86 Friendship MD 20758-0086 also: 3331 O St NW Washington DC 20007-2814 Office: Covington & Burling PO Box 7566 1201 Pennsylvania Ave NW Washington DC 20044 E-mail: bclagett@cov.com.

CLAGETT, DIANA WHARTON SINKLER, museum docent; b. Phila., Aug. 24, 1943; d. James Mauran Rhodes and Sarah Brinton (Wentz) Sinkler; m. Peter John Knop, Nov. 23, 1966 (div.); children: Alexandra Brinton, Peter Rhodes Quast, William James Wharton; m. Brice McAdoo Clagett, July 26, 1987. BA, George Wash. U., 1966. Rsch. asst. Nat. Investigations Com. on Aerial Phenomena, Washington, 1966-69; docent Asia Hall Smithsonian Instn., Washington, 1982-83, docent Sackler Gallery, 1989—, docent Freer Gallery, 1993—; propr. Georgian Antiques and Decorative Arts, Washington, 1983—. Bd. dirs. Sinkler Corp., Wentz Corp.; mem. Smithsonian Ednl. Vol. Adv. Bd., 1990-93. Mem. bd. devel. Hosp. for Sick Children, Washington, 1980—, vice chmn. bd. devel., 1985-86, co-chmn. flower and garden festival, 1988-90; mem. bd. devel. Children's Hearing and Speech Ctr., Washington, 1988—; mem. women's com. Phila. Acad. Fine Arts, 1980—; mem. alumni bd. Foxcroft Sch., Middleburg, Va., 1983-86; trustee The McLean Sch., 1993-96; mem. The Founders Washington Com. for Historic Mt. Vernon, 2001—. Mem. City Tavern Club (bd. govs. 1990-98), Radnor Hunt Club (racing com.), Acorn Club, Evermay Club Georgetown, New Scotland Garden Club (pres. 1993-94), Sulgrave Club. Avocations: gardening, Asian art. Home: Holly Hill PO Box 86 Friendship MD 20758 also: 3331 O St NW Washington DC 20007-2814

CLAGG-CATHEY, SHEILA RENAE, music educator; b. McAlester, Okla., Dec. 7, 1969; d. John Wayne and Sharon Kay (Hance) Clagg; m. M. Todd Cathey, Aug. 15, 1992. BS in Ch. Music and Piano Performance cum laude, Free Will Bapt. Bible Coll., 1993; MM in Music Theory summa cum laude, Tex. Christian U., 2000; postgrad., Southwestern Bapt. Theol. Sem., 1994-95; postgrad. in D Arts program, U. Miss., 2002—. Nat. cert. tchr. music. Piano instr. Lake Arlington Acad. Music, Arlington, Tex., 1994—, Arlington Heights Music Acad., Fort Worth, 1994-99. Theory tchr. U. Tex. Piano Camp, Arlington, 1995, Arlington, 99; faculty accompanist Tex. Christian U. Suzuki Inst., Ft. Worth, 1995—96; staff accompanist Dallas Bapt. U., 1996; adjudicator Nat. Music and Arts Festival Free Will Bapts., Louisville, 1993, Nat. Guild Piano Tchrs., 2000—; adj. prof. music theory Dallas Bapt. U., 2000—, Tex. Christian U., 2000—. Recipient 1st place award Nat. Music and Arts Festival Free Will Bapts., 1991, 1st place award keyboard competition Okla. Music Tchrs. Assn., 1985-88, Okla. State U., 1987, Northeastern State U., 1986, Acad. award, Winesanker, T.C.U., 1999. Mem. Tex. Music Tchrs. Assn., Arlington Music Tchrs. Assn., Nat. Guild Piano Tchrs., Music Tchrs. Nat. Assn., Pi Kappa Lambda (cert. Kindermusik instr.). Avocations: boating, traveling.

CLAGUE, JOHN ROGERS, sculptor; b. Cleve., Mar. 14, 1928; s. John Rogers and Ernestine Marie (Honsberg) C.; m. Sarah Eddy Reynolds, Aug. 2, 1958; children: Jeannette R., Elizabeth H. BFA, Cleve. Inst. of Art, 1956. Instr. Western Res. U., Cleve., 1956; sculpture instr. Oberlin (Ohio) Coll., 1957-61; prof. sculpture Cleve. Inst. of Art, 1957-71. One man show at Waddell Gallery, N.Y.C., 1966; group exhbn. at Whitney Mus. Art, N.Y.C., 1965, sculpture in permanent collections: Flower of Erebus, Cleve. Mus. of Art, Syllogistic Construction, Art Gallery of Ont., Auriculum I, Ashland U., Astra, Trumbull Meml. Hosp. Cpl. U.S. Army, 1950-52. Recipient Cleve. Arts prize Women's City Club of Cleve., 1967; Ohio Arts Coun. Individual Artist grantee, 1977.

CLAIBORNE, LIZ (ELISABETH CLAIBORNE ORTENBERG), fashion designer; b. Brussels, Mar. 31, 1929; came to U.S., 1939; d. Omer Villere and Louise Carol (Fenner) C.; m. Arthur Ortenberg, July 5, 1954; 1 son by previous marriage, Alexander G. Schultz. Student, Art Sch., Brussels, 1948-49, Academie, Nice, France, 1950; DFA, R.I. Sch. Design, 1991. Asst. Tina Lesser, N.Y.C., 1951-52, Omar Khayam, Ben Reig, Inc., N.Y.C., 1953; designer Juniorite, N.Y.C., 1954-60, Dan Keller, N.Y.C., 1960-76, Youth Guild Inc., N.Y.C., 1976-89; designer, pres., chmn. Liz Claiborne Inc., N.Y.C., 1985-89, pres., 1976-89, chmn., chief oper. officer, until 1989; chmn. Liz Claiborne Cosmetics, 1985-89, cons. Guest lectr. Fashion Inst. Tech., Parsons Sch. Design; bd. dirs. Coun. of Am. Fashion Designers, Fire Island Lighthouse

Restoration Com. Recipient Designer of Yr. award Palciode Hierro, Mexico City, 1976, Designer of Yr. award Dayton Co., Mpls., 1978, Ann. Disting. in Design award Marshall Field's, 1985, One Co. Makes a Difference award Fashion Inst. Tech., 1985, award Coun. Fashion Designers, 1986, Gordon Grand Fellowship award Yale U., 1989, Jr. Achievement award Nat. Bus. Hall of Fame, 1990, Frederick A.P. Barnard award Barnard Coll., 1991, Hon. Doctorate, R.I. Sch. of Design, 1991; named to Nat. Sales Hall of Fame, 1991. Mem. Fashion Group. Roman Catholic.

CLAIBORNE, WILLIAM, journalist; b. N.Y.C., 1936; Diploma in English, Hobart Coll., 1959. Reporter Rochester Dem. & Chronicle, 1959—66; city editor L.I. Suffolk Sun, 1966—69; nat. corr. The Washington Post, Washington, 1969—74, N.Y.C. bur. chief, 1974—77, Jerusalem corr., 1978—82, New Delhi corr., 1982—85, Johannesburg corr., 1986—90, Toronto corr., 1990—92, nat. corr., 1992—94, L.A. corr., 1994—97, Chgo. bur. chief, 1997—, Midwest bur. chief. Office: The Washington Post 401 N Michigan Ave Chicago IL 60611-4255

CLAIR, THEODORE NAT, educational psychologist; b. Stockton, Calif., Apr. 19, 1929; s. Peter David and Sara Renee (Silverman) C.; m. Laura Gold, June 19, 1961; children: Shari, Judith. AA, U. Calif., Berkeley, 1949, AB, 1950; MS, U. So. Calif., 1953, MEd, 1963, EdD, 1969. Tchr., counselor L.A. City Schs., 1957-63; psychologist Alamitos Sch. Dist., Garden Grove, Calif., 1963-64, Arcadia (Calif.) Unified Sch. Dist., 1964-65; head psychologist Wiseburn Sch. Dist., Hawthorne, Calif., 1966-69; asst. prof. spl. edn., coord. sch. psychology program U. Iowa, Iowa City, 1969-72; dir. pupil pers. svcs. Orcutt (Calif.) Union Sch. Dist., 1972-73; adminstr. Mt. Diablo Unified Sch. Dist., 1973-77; program dir., psychologist San Mateo County Office Edn., Redwood City, 1977-91; assoc. prof. John F. Kennedy U. Sch. Mgmt., 1975-77; pvt. practice as ednl. psychologist specializing in Attention Defecit Disorders Menlo Park, 1978—; pvt. practice marriage and family counselor specializing in Attention Defecit Disorders, 1978—. Dir. Peninsula Vocat. Rehab. Inst., 1978—; psychologist Coll. Counseling Svc., Menlo Park, 1992-2001, Calif. Pacific Hosp., San Francisco, 1993—; mem. adv. bd. Kitty Petty ADD/LD Inst., Palo Alto. Author: Phenylketonuria and Some Other Inborn Errors of Amino Acid Metabolism, 1971; editor Jour. Calif. Ednl. Psychologists, 1992-94; contbr. articles to profl. jours. Served with USNR, 1952-54. Mem. Am. Assn. Marriage & Family Therapy (Calif. divsn.), Calif. Assn. Marriage and Family Therapists, Palo Alto B'nai B'rith Club (pres.), Stanford Club Palo Alto. Home and Office: 56 Willow Rd Menlo Park CA 94025-3654

CLAIRE, THOMAS ANDREW, consultant, financial executive, educator, writer; b. Cleve., Feb. 13, 1951; s. William Henry and Dorothy Helen (Taylor) C. BA, Kenyon Coll., 1973; MA, Brown U., 1977; MBA, Columbia U., 1978; diploma, Swedish Inst., N.Y.C., 1992. Account adminstr. Irving Trust Co., N.Y.C., 1978-80; dir. fin. planning and analysis W.R. Grace & Co., N.Y.C., 1980-83; asst. treasurer Harper & Row Publishers, Inc., N.Y.C., 1983-87; treas., asst. sec. Moët-Hennessy U.S. Corp., N.Y.C., 1987-92; pres., CEO Clairefontaine, Inc., N.Y.C., 1993—. Speaker in field. Author: numerous books in field; contbr. articles to various jours. Recipient Fulbright scholar Acad. Coms., Paris, 1974-75, Nat. Merit scholar, Ohio, 1969-73. Mem. Phi Beta Kappa, Beta Gamma Sigma. Home and Office: Grand Ctrl Sta PO Box 1040 New York NY 10163-1040

CLAIRMONT, WILLIAM EDWARD, real estate developer; b. Walhalla, N.D., Jan. 2, 1926; s. Emil O. and Mae E. (Bisenius) C.; m. Patricia Ann Filben, Oct. 7, 1950; children: Stephen, Julie, Cynthia, Nancy. Student, N.D. State U., 1948-49. Founder William Clairmont, Inc., Bismarck, N.D., 1949, owner, 1949—. Chmn. bd. First Southwest Bank, Mandan, N.D., 1975-89, Grant County State Bank, Carson, N.D., 1981-85; land developer, Bismarck; owner farm, N.D. Mem. City Council, Walhalla, 1955-56; owner ranch, irrigation farm, Costa Rica, 1975-83; owner, pres. Country West Real Estate, 1978—; trustee, mem. bd. regents U. Mary, Bismarck, chmn. bd., 1980-81; trustee Bismarck State Coll. Found.; bd. dirs. Theodore Roosevelt Medora Found., 2000—. Served with USMCR, 1944-46. Mem. N.D. Assn. Gen. Contractors (dir. 1964-72, pres. 1971). Home: 1938 Santa Gertrudis Dr Bismarck ND 58503-0865 Office: 1720 Burnt Boat Dr Bismarck ND 58503-0806

CLAMAR, APHRODITE J. psychologist; b. Hartford, Conn. d. James John and Georgia (Panas) Clamar; m. Richard Cohen, June 24, 1973. BA, CCNY, 1953; MA, Columbia U., 1955; PhD, NYU, 1978; student, S. Adler Conservatory Acting, 1987-91. Mgmt. cons., psychologist Milla Alihan Assocs., N.Y.C., 1957-62; rsch. psychologist coord. Inst. Devel. Studies N.Y. Med. Coll., N.Y.C., 1964; intern psychologist Bellevue Psychiat. Hosp., N.Y.C., 1964-66; assoc. prof. Fashion Inst. Tech., N.Y.C., 1966-69; supervising psychologist Lifeline Ctr. Child Devel., N.Y.C., 1966-67; chief psychologist I Spy Health Program Beth Israel Med. Ctr., N.Y.C., 1967-70; dir. community-sch. mental health programs Soundview Community Svcs., Albert Einstein Coll. Medicine Yeshiva U., N.Y.C., 1970-73; dir. treatment program court-related children, dept. child psychiatry Harlem Hosp.; mem. faculty dept. psychiatry Coll. Physicians and Surgeons Columbia U., N.Y.C., 1973-76; pvt. practice psychotherapy, N.Y.C., 1976—; co-founder, pres. Richard Cohen Assocs. Pub. Rels. Agy., N.Y.C., 1979—99; prof. John Jay Coll., CUNY, 2000—. Cons. to pub. health and mental health agys., N.Y.C., 1976-91; mem. faculty Lenox Hill Hosp. Psychoanalytic Psychotherapy Tng. Program, 1982-88; theater producer, artistic dir. Tom Cat Cohen Prodns., Inc., 1990—. Author: (with Budd Hopkins) Missing Time, 1981; contbr. articles to profl. jours. Fellow AAAS; mem. APA, Dramatists Guild, Authors Guild. Democrat. Greek Orthodox. Home: 155 W 68th St Apt 1618 New York NY 10023-5829

CLAMME, MARVIN LESLIE, recording engineer, electronic engineer; b. Hartford City, Ind., May 28, 1953; BSEET, Purdue U., 1976. Electronic technician engr. Holzer Audio Engring. Co., Van Nuys, Calif., 1976-77; electronic technician Audio Industries Corp., L.A., 1977-78; maintenance technician, rec. engr. Britannia Studios, Hollywood, Calif., 1978-85, The Way Internat., New Knoxville, Ohio, 1985-90; svc. mgr. Carlin Audio and Video, Dayton, Ohio, 1990-99; dir. rsch. The Guitammer Co., Columbus, Ohio, 1999—. Inventor in field. Office: The Guitammer Co PO Box 82 Westerville OH 43086 0082 E-mail: marvin@guitammer.com.

CLAMP, CHRISTINA A. sociology educator; b. Amityville, N.Y., Mar. 12, 1953; d. Theodore Edward and Margaret A. Clamp; m. Donald H. Gianniny, June 24, 1980; children: Caitlin, Megan. BA in Liberal Arts, Friends World Coll., Huntington,N.Y., 1976; MA in Sociology, Boston Coll., 1978, PhD in Sociology, 1986. Assoc. Ctr. for Internat. Affairs, Harvard U., Cambridge, Mass., 1984-88; prof. So. N.H. U., 1981—. Bd. dirs. The ICA Group, Boston, past pres. Contbr. chpts. to books; co-author rsch. report. Pres. bd. dirs. Allston Brighton Cmty. Devel. Corp., Boston, 2002—; mem. adv. bd. Jobs for Youth, Boston, 1999. Mem. Internat. Sociol. Assn., Am. Sociol. Assn. Avocation: swimming. Office: So NH Univ Sch Cmty Econ Devel 2500 N River Rd Hooksett NH 03106-1067

CLANCEY, WILLIAM JOHN, computer scientist, researcher; b. Newark, 1952; s. William Robert and Rosemary Lee Clancey; m. Danielle Lea Fafchamps. BA in Math. Scis., Rice U., 1974; PhD in Computer Sci., Stanford U., 1979. Sr. rsch. assoc. Stanford (Calif.) Knowledge Sys. Lab., 1979—87; sr. rsch. scientist Inst. for Rsch. on Learning, Menlo Park, Calif., 1988—97; chief scientist human-centered computing NASA/Ames Rsch. Ctr., Moffett Field, Calif., 1998—. Founder, dir., cons. Teknowledge, Inc., Palo Alto, 1981—89; founder, dir., pres. Modernsoft, Inc., San Mateo, 1989—. Author: (book) Situated Cognition, 1997, Conceptual Coordination, 1999; editor: Contemplating Minds, 1994, Readings in Medical Artificial Intelligence, 1984. Fellow, Am. Coll. Med. Informatics, 1986. Fellow: Am. Assn. Artificial Intelligence (councilor, editor-in-chief 1987—90). Roman Catholic. Achievements include invention of simulating work practice; creating and editing documents. Avocations: photography, writing, travel. Office: NASA/Ames Rsch Ctr MS269-3 Computational Scis Divsn Mountain View CA 94035

CLANCY, CAROLYN, science foundation director, researcher, educator; Grad., Boston Coll., U. Mass. Fellow Henry Kaiser Family Found. U. Pa.; clin. assoc. prof. dept. health care scis. George Washington U. Sch. Medicine; asst. prof. dept. internal medicine Va. Commonwealth U./Med. Coll. Va.; dir. Ctr. Primary Rsch. Agy. Healthcare Rsch. and Quality, HHS, internist Ctr. Outcomes and Effectiveness Rsch. (COER), 1997—, dir., 2002—. Rschr. in field. Sr. assoc. editor Health Svcs. Rsch. ; mem. editl. bd.: Am. Jour. Pub. Health ; Jour. Evaluation in Clin. Practice, Jour. Gen. Internal Medicine, Med. Care Rsch. and Rev. ; contbr. articles in peer-reviewed jours. Recipient award, APHA Women's Caucus . Mem.: Soc. Gen. Internal Medicine. Office: 2101 E EJefferson St Ste 501 Rockville MD 20852

CLANCY, JOHN PATRICK, real estate company executive; b. N.Y.C., Aug. 4, 1942; s. Joseph Edward and Rita Gertrude (Hass) C.; m. Carol Ann Furnari, May 26, 1962 (div. 1982); children: Laureen, Lisa, Janine; m. Maureen Kearney Rose, Oct. 1, 1988; 1 child, Kim. BBA, St. John's U., 1965. CPA, N.Y. Acct. McGrath, Doyle & Phair, N.Y.C., 1965-66; sr. mgr. Ernst & Young, N.Y.C., 1966—81; exec. v.p. CFO Douglas Elliman Gibbons & Ives, Inc., N.Y.C., 1981-97; CFO, exec. v.p. Julien J. Studley, Inc., N.Y.C., 1997—. Mem. AICPA, N.Y. State Soc. CPAs. Office: Julien J Studley Inc 300 Park Ave New York NY 10022-7402

CLANCY, LYNN ROGER, JR., retired educational administrator, educator; b. Niagara Falls, N.Y., June 7, 1929; s. Lynn Roger Clancy and Jennie Marie Anderson; m. Doris Elizabeth Mathews, May 14, 1951 (div. May 1980); m. Sandra Virginia Nichols, June 20, 1987; children: Stephen Lynn, Kathleen Elizabeth Clancy Ellis. AB magna cum laude, Niagara U., 1957; MA, San Fernando Valley State U., 1960; PhD, UCLA, 1971. Cert. adminstr., tchr. K-14, Calif. Acting dir. Simi Valley (Calif.) Sch. Dist., 1973, prin., 1968-79, tchr., 1979-94, ret., 1994. Lectr., ednl. adminstrn. Calif. Luth. Coll., Thousand Oaks, 1969-73; tchr. Simi Valley Sch. Dist., 1966-68, L.A. Sch. Dist., 1957-66. Author: History of the American Federation of Teachers in Los Angeles, 1919-1969, 1971. Pres. Simi Valley PTA Coun., 1978-79; officer Boy Scouts Am., 1961-65. With USN, 1948-52. Named hon. citizen Boy's Town, Nebr. Mem. AARP, Nat. Wildlife Fedn., Wolf Edn. and Rsch. Ctr., Nat. Geographic Soc., Mensa, Delta Epsilon Sigma, Phi Delta Kappa. Democrat. Baptist. Avocations: photography, hiking, travel, woodworking, reading. Home: 1975 Katahn Dr Prescott AZ 86305-3971

CLANCY, RICHARD FRANCIS, priest; b. Winchester, Mass., Apr. 18, 1960; BA in Philosophy, Merrimack Coll., 1982; MDiv, St. John's Sem., 1991; MEd, U. Mass., Boston, 2001. Parish priest Archdiocese of Boston, Hyde Park, Mass., 1991—96, archdiocesan dir. campus ministry, 2002—; campus min./chaplain Emmanuel Coll./U. Mass., Boston, 1996—2002. Archdiocesan director of campus ministry Archdiocese of Boston, Boston, 2002—. Roman Catholic. Avocations: jogging, reading, travel. Home: 841 East Broadway South Boston MA 02127

CLANCY, THOMAS L., JR., novelist; b. Balt., Mar. 12, 1947; m. Wanda Thomas, Aug. 1969; children: Michelle, Christine, Tom, Kathleen. Grad., Loyola Coll., 1969. Ins. agent, Balt., Hartford, until 1973, O. F. Bowen Agy., Owings, Md., 1973-80, owner, from 1980; writer; chmn. Red Storm Entertainment, Morrisville, N.C. Author: (novels) The Hunt for Red October, 1984, Red Storm Rising, 1986, Patriot Games, 1987, The Cardinal of the Kremlin, 1988, Clear and Present Danger, 1989, The Sum of All Fears, 1991, Without Remorse, 1993, Debt of Honor, 1994, Executive Orders, 1996, Balance of Power, 1998, Rainbow Six, 1998, The Beear and the Dragon, 2000, Red Rabbit, 2002, The Teeth of the Tiger, 2003; (non-fiction) Submarine, 1993, Armored Cav, 1994, Fighter Wing, 1995, Marine, 1996, Airborne, 1997, Into the Storm, 1997, Every Man a Tiger, 1999; creator: (with Steve Pieczenik) Tom Clancy's OP Center, 1995-97. Roman Cath. Office: Red Storm Entertainment 3200 Gateway Ctr Blvd Ste 100 Morrisville NC 27560-9294*

CLANIN, DOUGLAS EDWARD, editor, researcher; b. Anderson, Ind., May 5, 1940; s. Howard Paul and Sarah Elizabeth (Weatherford) C.; m. Rebecca Suzanne Flowers, Aug. 9, 1970 (div. Dec. 1974); children: Christopher Lee, David Matthew. BS, Purdue U., 1963; MA, Ind. U., 1964. Social studies tchr. Whitewater-Fountain City (Ind.) H.S., 1964-65; asst. editor history U. Wis., Madison, 1970-80; editor publs. divsn. Ind. Hist. Soc., Indpls., 1980—. Editor: Papers of William Henry Harrison 1800-1815, 1993, 1999, Lew and Susan Wallace Papers Project, 1999—; asst. editor: Documentary History First Federal Elections, 1976, Documentary History Ratification of Constitution, 1976—81. Staff sg. USAF, 1965-69. Mem. Assn. for Documentary Editing, Ind. Assn. Historians, Soc. for Historians Early Am. Rep., Am. Legion, Svc. Club Indpls. Methodist. Avocations: conducting oral history interviews, travel, classical music. Office: Ind Hist Soc 450 W Ohio St Indianapolis IN 46202-3269 E-mail: dclanin@indianahistory.org.

CLANTON, ORVAL GENE, historian, educator; b. Pitts., Kans., Sept. 14, 1934; s. Orval Elmer and Verl Anne Clanton; m. Jane Ann Buffington, Aug. 5, 1959; children: Spencer Miles, Kimberly Jean. BS in Edn., Kans. State Tchrs. Coll., 1959; MS in History, Kans. State Coll., 1961; PhD in History, U. Kans., 1967. Tchr. Lamar (Colo.) HS, 1960—62; asst. instr. U. Kans., Lawrence, 1962—64, instr., 1965—66; instr. history Tex. A&M U., College Station, 1966—67, asst. prof. history, 1967—68, Wash. State U., Pullman, 1968—77, prof. history, 1978—96, prof. emeritus, 1997—. Vis. prof. history Ga. State Coll., Atlanta, 1968. Author: Kansas Populism: Ideas and Men, 1969, Populism: The Humane Preference in America, 1890-1900, 1991, Congressional Populism and the Crisis of the 1890s, 1998. With U.S. Army, 1954—57. Mem.: ACLU, Soc. for Historians of Gilded Age and Progressive Era, So. Hist. Assn., Orgn. of Am. Historians. Avocations: pilot, golf. Home: 1755 Appaloosa Rd Moscow ID 83843

CLANTON, THOMAS OSCAR, orthopedic surgeon; b. Oklahoma City, May 21, 1950; s. Frances Clanton; m. Kay Beavers; children: Kelly Elizabeth, Laura Kathryn. BA, Rice U., 1973; MD, Baylor Coll. Medicine, 1976. Lic. Tex. State Bd. Med. Examiners, 1976, Bd. Medicine Wyo., diplomate Am. Bd. Orthop. Surgery. Pvt. practice, Houston, 1982—93; orthop. surgeon Baxter, Clanton and Winston, Houston, 1993—97; prof., chmn., dept. orthops. U. Tex. - Houston Med. Sch., 1997—. Orthopaedic cons., asst. team physician Rice U. Athletic Dept., Houston, 1982—85, team physician, 1985—; dir. Found. Orthop., Athletic and Reconstructive Rsch. Fellowship Program, Houston, 1991—; asst. team orthopedist Houston Texans, 2001—. Contbr. chapters to books, articles to profl. jours. Trustee Goodloe Found., Houston, 1988; deacon Second Bapt. Ch., Houston, 1982; bd. dirs. Houston chpt. Fellowship Christian Athletes, 1990; alumni rep. student health com. Rice U., Houston, 1988—90. Recipient Disting. R award, Rice U., 1999. Fellow: Am. Orthop. Foot and Ankle Soc. (v.p. 1997, pres. 1999, bd. dirs. 2000); mem.: AMA (Physician Recognition award for CME 1984—86, 1991—93, 2002—), Mann Fellows Soc., Tex. Soc. Sports Medicine (program chmn. 1986—87, v.p. 1986—87, pres. 1987—88), Am. Orthop. Soc. Sports Medicine, Am. Coll. Sports Medicine, Houston Acad. Medicine, Harris County Med. Soc., Alamo Orthop. Soc., Am. Orthop. Assn., Am. Diabetes Assn., Christian Med. and Dental Soc., S.W. Conf. Team Physicians Soc., Orthop. Foot Club (pres. 1995—96), Am. Acad. Orthop. Surgeons (chmn. foot and ankle com. 2000—01), Houston Orthop. Soc. (pres. 1997—98), Tex. Orthop. Assn., Tex. Med. Assn. Home: 430 Hunterwood Houston TX 77024 Office: U Tex Houston Med Sch 6431 Fannin MSB 6156 Houston TX 77030 Office Fax: 713-500-0688. E-mail: thomas.o.clanton@uth.tmc.edu.

CLAPMAN, PETER CARLYLE, lawyer, insurance company executive; b. N.Y.C., Mar. 11, 1936; s. Jack and Evelyn (Clapman); m. Barbara Posen, May 8, 1966; children: Leah, Alice. AB, Princeton U., 1957; JD, Harvard U., 1960. Bar: N.Y. 1961, Conn. 1972. Assoc. Sage, Gray, Todd & Sims, N.Y.C., 1961-63; asst. counsel Stichman Commn., N.Y.C., 1964; legal cons. OEO, Washington, 1965; assoc. counsel Equitable Life, N.Y.C., 1965-72; sr. v.p., chief counsel investments Tchrs. Ins. and Annuity of Am., Coll. Ret. Equities Fund, N.Y.C., 1972—. Chmn. Internat. Corp. Govt. Network; bd. dirs. Nat. Com. for Quality Assurance, Investor Responsibility Rsch. Ctr. Author: Fiduciary Responsibilities of Institutional Managers on Proxy Issues, Iowa Law Jour., 1994, SEC Market 2000 Report; co-author: Notre Dame U. Law Rev., 1981. Mem. ABA, Assn. Bar City N.Y. (com. on securities regulation spl. com. on mergers), Am. Law Inst. Home: 3 Valley Rd Scarsdale NY 10583-1123 Office: Tchrs Ins & Annuity Assn Am 730 3rd Ave New York NY 10017-3206

CLAPP, ALLEN LINVILLE, electric supply and communications utility consultant, mediator/arbitrator; b. Raleigh, N.C., Oct. 8, 1943; s. Byron Siler and Alene Linville (Hester) C.; m. Anne Stuart Calvert, Dec. 18, 1966. BS in Engring. Ops., N.C. State U., 1967, M in Econs., 1973. Lic. profl. engr., N.C., N.J. Asst. engr. Booth-Jones and Assocs., Raleigh, 1965-67, assoc., 1969-71; chief ops. analysis N.C. Utilities Commn., Raleigh, 1971-77, engring. and econs. advisor to commrs., hearing examiner, 1977-82; dir. tech. assessment N.C. Alterative Energy Corp., Rsch. Triangle Park, 1982-85; pres. Clapp Rsch. Assocs., P.C., Clapp Rch. Inc., Raleigh, N.C., 1985—, Utility Bookstore, 2000—. Pvt. practice elec. safety cons., Raleigh, 1971—; mem. nat. Elec. Safety Code Com., 1971—, chmn., 1984—93; lectr. in field. Author: National Electric Safety Code Handbook, 1984, 91, 92, 96, 2001, Assembly and Testing of Aerial Mines, 1968, Practical Utility Safety, 1999; editor, pub. Danesc Update Newsletter; contbr. to McGraw-Hill Std. Handbook for Elec. Engrs.; contbr. articles to profl. jours. Past co-chmn. Brookhaven/Deblyn Park Action Com., Raleigh. With U.S. Army, 1968-69. Recipient Cert. of Recognition and Appreciation Aerial Mine Lab., 1969. Mem. NSPE (past bd. dirs.), IEEE (stds. bd. 1989, 90), Profl. Engrs. N.C. (pres. 1980, Disting. Svc. award ctrl. Carolina chpt. 1978), N.C. Assn. Professions (pres. 1981), Power Engring. Soc., Nat. Safety Coun., Am. Soc. Safety Engrs., Soc. Cable TV Engrs., Indsl. Applications Soc., Am. Nat. Stds. Inst. (chair Z535.2 std. on environ. and facility safety signs). Republican. Baptist. Avocations: leather carving, golf, engraving, photography, raising orchids. Home: 3206 Queens Rd Raleigh NC 27612-6233 Office: Clapp Rsch Assocs 6112 Saint Giles St Raleigh NC 27612-7043

CLAPP, BEVERLY BOOKER, accountant; b. Savannah, Ga., Oct. 26, 1954; d. Herschel Ray and Ida Marie (Bove) Beville; m. William L. Clapp III; 1 child, Matthew Anthony. BS in Med. Tech., Med. Coll. Ga., 1976; MS in Clin. Lab. Sci., U. Ala., Birmingham, 1977, BS in Acctg., 1989. CPA, Ala. Blood bank technologist U. Ala. Hosp., Birmingham, 1976-77; asst. supr. physiology Bapt. Med. Ctr., Montclair, Birmingham, 1977-79; rsch. chemist Nephrology Rsch. and Tng. Ctr. U. Ala., Birmingham, 1979-91; med. technologist VA Med. Ctr., Gainesville, Fla., 1991-92; acct., mgr. J.J. Lucky & Co., Gainesville, 1992; sr. grants specialist U. Fla., Gainesville, 1992-93; acct. Beverly Booker Clapp Acctg. Svc., 1993—. Treas. U. Fla. Women's Med. Guild. Mem. AICPA, Ala. Soc. CPAs, Am. Soc. Clin. Pathology, Fla. Inst. CPAs, Fla. Soc. Med. Tech., U. Fla. Women's Med. Guild (treas.), Alpha Aeta, Phi Kappa Phi. Roman Catholic.

CLAPP, DAVID FOSTER, library administrator; b. Birmingham, Ala., July 17, 1952; s. Merwin Bailey and Katherine Lorraine (Aderholt) C.; m. Sara Louise Stephan, Sept. 18, 1982. BA in Classical Langs., Tulane U., 1975; MS in LS, U. Ill., 1980; cert. advanced study in info. mgmt., U. Chgo., 1987. Asst. mgr. Kroch's & Brentano's Bookstore, Chgo., 1976-79; libr. I acquisitions dept. Chgo. Pub. Libr., 1980-82, libr. II, 1st asst. Walker br., 1982-83, libr. II, head Clearing br., 1983-84, libr. III, head Rogers Park br., 1984-89; asst. dir. for ext. svcs. Chattanooga-Hamilton County Bicentennial Libr., 1989—2002, dir. libr. sys., 2002, dir., 2002—. Recipient Outstanding Pub. Svc. award Friends Chgo. Pub. Libr., 1987; Josie B. Houchens fellow U. Ill., 1979. Mem. ALA, Pub. Libr. Assn., Libr. Adminstrn. and Mgmt. Assn., Tenn. Libr. Assn. (exec. bd. 1991-92), Chattanooga Area Libr. Assn. (pres. 1991-92), Mensa, Beta Phi Mu. Avocations: genealogy, history, development and philosophy of religions, ancient history. Office: Chattanooga Pub Libr 1001 Broad St Chattanooga TN 37402-2620 E-mail: clapp_david@lib.chattanooga.gov.

CLAPP, JOSEPH MARK, federal agency administrator; b. Greensboro, N.C., July 29, 1936; s. Frederick Lawrence and Mary Beatrice (Flaherty) C.; m. Helen Grey Roberts, June 8, 1963; children: Kathryn Grey, Amy Elizabeth. BS in Bus. Adminstrn., U. N.C., 1958. Practitioner ICC. From mgmt. trainee to dir. safety, personnel Ryder Tank Line, Inc., Greensboro, N.C., 1959-66; asst. to pres. T.I. McCormack Trucking, Inc., Woodbridge, N.J., 1966-67; div. employee relations mgr. to sr. v.p. Roadway Express, Inc., Akron, Ohio, 1967-74; vice chmn. corp. services Roadway Services, Inc., Akron, 1985—86, pres., chief exec. officer, 1986—95, chmn., 1987—95, also dir.; adminr., fed. motor carrier safety admin. Dept. of Transp., Washington, 2001—. Past chmn. Transp. Research Bd. of NRC Mem. Nat. Motor Carrier Adv. Council, Washington, 1985; bd. trustees Akron City Hosp., 1985— ; bd. dirs. St. Edwards Home, Fairlawn, Ohio, 1985. Served to staff sgt. USAFR, 1959-65. Mem. Am. Trucking Assn. (v.p. at large), Transp. Practitioners Assn., Regular Commn. Carrier Conf. (chmn. 1984). Clubs: Congl. Country (Bethesda, Md.); Fairlawn Country (Akron). Roman Catholic. Office: Dept of Transp Fed Motor Carrier Safety Admin 400 7th St SW Washington DC 20590

CLAPP, NEAL KEITH, experimental pathologist; b. Waldron, Ind., Oct. 14, 1928; s. Worrill Groven and Dora M. (Hurst) C.; m. Dorothy Louise Stockwell, Dec. 19, 1953; children: Cheryl Lynne, Mark Allen, Stephen Neal. BS, Purdue U., 1950; DVM, Ohio State U., 1960; MS, Colo. State U., 1962, PhD, 1964. NIH postdoctoral fellow Colo. State Univ., Ft. Collins, 1961-64; experimental pathologist Oak Ridge (Tenn.) Nat. Lab., 1964-81; dir. Marmoset Rsch. Ctr. Oak Ridge (Tenn.) Assoc. U., 1981-92; dir. MARCOR U. Tenn. Med. Ctr., Oak Ridge, from 1992. Editor: A Model for Colon Diseases, 1993; contbr. over 150 articles to profl. jours. Min. Clinton (Tenn.) Christian Ch., 1972-94. With USAF, 1951-55. Mem. Am. Assn. Cancer Rsch., Am. Vet. Med. Assn., Inflammation Rsch. Assn., Am. Assn. Lab. Animal Sci., Am. Primatology Assn., Radiation Rsch. Soc., Optimist Club, Masons. Republican. Avocations: golfing, fishing, baseball, football. Home: Clinton, Tenn. Died July 4, 2003.

CLAPP, RICHARD ALLEN, lawyer; b. Cin., Mar. 20, 1948; s. Hubert Dickason and Eletha May (Armstrong) C.;m. Sonja Petkovic, Mar. 16, 1968 (div. Apr. 1982); children: Shawn, Christian; m. Lori Plaisted, Sept. 8, 1990 (div. 1998). Student, Hamline U., 1966-68, U. Minn., 1968; BA, U. N.D., 1972, JD with distinction, 1976. Bar: N.D. 1976, U.S. Dist. Ct. N.D. 1976, U.S. Ct. Appeals (8th cir.) 1976, Minn. 1982, U.S. Dist. Ct. Minn. 1989. Atty. Haughland & Heustis, Devils Lake, ND, 1976-79; ptnr. Letness Marshall Fiedler & Clapp Ltd., Grand Forks, ND, 1979-95, Pearson, Christensen, PLLP, Grand Forks, ND, 1995—. Instr. bus. law Lake Region Jr. Coll., Devils Lake, 1977-79; adj. prof. trial advocacy U. N.D. Sch. Law, Grand Forks, 1985-87. Mem. ABA, Am. Bd. Trial Advocates (advocate, sat. bd. dirs.), Def. Rsch. Inst., State Bar Assn. N.D. (inquiry com. cast 1977-80), Minn. State Bar Assn. (cert. civil trial specialist), Phi Delta Phi, Grand Forks Country Club. Republican. Presbyterian. Avocations: travel, golf, literature, fishing, theater. Home: 201 Plain Hills Dr Grand Forks ND 58201-7941 Office: Pearson Christensen Clapp Fiedler & Fisher PO Box 5758 Grand Forks ND 58206-5758 E-mail: rclapp@grandforkslaw.com.

CLAPP, ROGER HOWLAND, retired publishing executive; b. Scarsdale, N.Y., May 11, 1928; s. Kenneth John and Louise (Allen) Clapp; m. Patricia Anne Townshend, June 26, 1954 (dec. Nov. 18, 1998); children: Roger Howland Jr., Georgia Louise, Sarah Townshend. BA cum laude, Amherst Coll., 1954. V.p. Benton & Bowles, Inc., N.Y.C., 1954-67, Rumrill-Hoyt, Inc., N.Y.C., 1967-72; v.p., advt. dir. Richmond (Va.) Newspapers, Inc., 1972-93. Bd. dirs. Richmond chpt. Better Bus. Bur., 1986—88, ARC, 1987—93. With USN, 1948—52, Korea. Recipient Silver medal, Am. Advt. Fedn., 1980. Mem.: Internat. Newspaper Advt. and Mktg. Execs. (pres. 1988). Home: 15470 Cedarwood Ln # 103 Naples FL 34110-8638

CLAPP, STEPHEN CASWELL, journalist; b. Lawrence, Mass., Dec. 25, 1938; s. Edward Theodore and Ruth Elinor (Caswell) C.; m. Sara Victoria Sarfati, June 17, 1967 (div. Nov. 1995); children: Emilia, Melissa. BA, Harvard Coll., 1960; MS, Columbia U., 1966. H.s. tchr. U.S. Peace Corps, Yola, Nigeria, 1963-65; field program evaluator Office Econ. Opportunity, Washington, 1966-69; reporter Nat. Jour., Washington, 1969-70; investigative reporter Pub. Info. Ctr., Washington, 1970-71; pubs. dir. Cmty. Nutrition Inst., Washington, 1971-83; comms. dir. Interfaith Action for Econ. Justice, Washington, 1983-88; freelance journalist Washington, 1988-93, 95-00; European editor World Food Chem. News, Brussels, Belgium, 1993-95. Cons. Consultative Group on Internat. Agrl. Rsch., Washington, 1996; conf. organizer European Food Law Update Conf., Washington, 1996-98; columnist Meat & Poultry Mag., Kansas City, Mo., 1996-2000, Road Runners Club Am., Alexandria, Va., 1978-90. Internat. editor Food Chem. News, 2000—. Active Bread for the World, Peace Corps Nigeria Alumni Found., Reston Runners, New Dominion Chorale, Scouting for All. Mem. Washington Ind. Writers. Democrat. Unitarian Universalist. Avocations: running, choral singing, photography. Home: 17705-K Karbon Hill Ct Reston VA 20191 E-mail: sclapp@crcpress.com.

CLAPPER, GEORGE RAYMOND, retired accountant, computer consultant; b. New Palestine, Ind., June 29, 1931; s. Raymond Henry and Magdalene Barbara (Niedenthall) C.; m. Mary Vaneta Shine, June 29, 1957 (div. 1978); children: Christine M. Dux, Joseph W., Ann T. Wendling, Michael R. BS in Acctg., Ind. U., 1956. With The Upjohn Co., 1956-81, distbn. ctr. mgr., 1956-57, N.Y.C., 1957-62, Kalamazoo, 1962-66, 68-69, New Orleans, 1966-68, Mpls., 1969; mgr., controller Lab. Procedures, Inc. (name now SmithKline Clin. Labs), King of Prussia, Pa., 1969-72, v.p., gen. mgr., 1972-81, exec. v.p. Kalamazoo, 1981; v.p., gen. mgr. SmithKline Clin. Labs., St. Louis, 1981-82, MDS Labs., Inc., Buffalo, N.Y., 1982-84; COO Specialty Svcs. Group, Phila., 1985-86; pub. acct., computer cons. Indpls., 1987-96. With USMCR, 1947-60. Mem. Am. Legion, KC. Republican. Roman Catholic. Avocations: music, sports, crafts, cooking. Home and Office: 2041 Ticen Ct Beech Grove IN 46107-1474

CLAPPER, HENRY H. retired surgeon; b. Akron, Ohio, 1923; MD, Ohio State U., 1946. Diplomate Am. Bd. Surgery. Intern St. Francis Hosp., Columbus, Ohio, 1946-47; resident surgery Canton (Ohio) Mercy Hosp., 1949-52; chief of surgery MASH Hosp., Korea, 1953; resident surgery Highland Hosp., Rochester, N.Y., 1954-55; chief surgery Mash Hosp., 1953; ret., 1987. Capt. U.S. Army, 1947-49, Germany. Fellow: ACS; mem.: Stark County Med Assn. (past pres.).

CLAPPER, JAMES R., JR., government agency administrator; B. Govt. and Politics, U. Md.; M. Polit Sci., St. Mary's U., San Antonio; PhD in Strategic Intelligence (hon.), Joint Mil. Intelligence Coll. Advanced through grades to lt. gen. USAF; ret.; asst. chief of staff intelligence USAF, dir. intelligence Pacific Command, dir. intelligence Strategic Air Command, dir. intelligence U.S. Forces Korea; dir. Def. Intelligence Agy.; exec. v.p. Vrdenburg, Inc.; exec. dir. mil. intelligence programs Booz-Allen & Hamilton; v.p., dir. intelligence programs SRA Internat., Inc., 1998—2001; dir. Nat. Imagery and Mapping Agy., Bethesda, Md., 2001—. Vice chair Adv. Panel to Assess Domestic Response Capabilities for Terrorism Involving Weapons of Mass Destruction, 2000. Office: National Imagery and Mapping Agy 4600 Sangamore Rd Bethesda MD 20816-5003

CLAPPER, MARIE ANNE, magazine publisher; b. Chgo., Nov. 21, 1942; d. Chester William and Hazel Alice (Gilso) Reinke; m. William Neil Petersen, Aug. 17, 1963 (div. 1975); children: Elaine Myrtice Petersen, Edward William Petersen; m. Lyle N. Clapper, Jan. 1, 1980; children: Jeffrey Leland, Anne Reinkestepchildren: John Scott, Susan Louise Clapper Kashmier. Student, Augustana Coll., Rock Island, Ill., 1960-63; EdB, Northeastern U., 1964. Writer Pack-o-Fun mag., Park Ridge, Ill., 1976-77, editor Des Plaines, Ill., 1977-78, pub., 1990—; asst. to pub., circulation dir. Crafts 'n Things mag., Des Plaines, Ill., 1978-82, pub., 1982—, Decorative Arts Painting mag., Des Plaines, 1990—, The Cross Stitcher mag., Des Plaines, 1991—, 101 Bridal Ideas mag., Des Plaines, 1991—; pub., pres. Clapper pub. Host TV show The Crafts 'n Things Show, 1984-86, Crafting for the 90s, 1990-94; author: EveryDay Matters, 1996. Mem. TEC, Mag. Pubs. Am. (bd. dirs.), Hobby Industry Am. (bd. dirs., treas. 1998-99), Soc. Craft Designers. Office: Crafts 'n Things 2400 E Devon Ave Ste 375 Des Plaines IL 60018-4618

CLAPS, JUDITH BARNES, educational consultant; b. N.Y.C., Sept. 8, 1938; d. Milton and Marguerite (Goodkind) Tarlau; m. Wayne C. Barnes, July 17, 1957 (div. 1968); children: David, Dan; m. Francis S. Claps, June 25, 1978. BA, Antioch Coll., 1961; MEd, Lehigh U., 1964; AA, William Glasser Inst., Calif., 1984. Tchr. Cedarville (Ohio) Schs., 1960-61, Quakertown (Pa.) Schs., 1961-62, Bethlehem (Pa.) Schs., 1962-95, social worker, 1991-95. In-svc. cons. JB Claps & Assocs., Hellertown, Pa., 1982—; adj. prof. East Stroudsburg U., Pa., 1982-90, De Sales U., Pa., 2001—; pres. Lehigh Valley Coun. for Social Studies, 1990-92; judge Nat. History Day, U. Md., 1989—. Author: Making the Parent Connection, 2001, The Quality School: Tools to Use, 2001, Easy Writer: Learning to Write and Loving It, 2002; creator: pamphlet Rap It Up, 1984, Freemansburg-A Canal Town, 1984, Bethlehem, 1986. Ednl. creator, bd. dirs. Burnside Plantation, Bethlehem, 1982—; mem. adv. coun. Ret. and Sr. Vol. Program. Named History Tchr. of Yr., DAR, Bethlehem, 1984, Pa. Soc. Studies Tchr. of Yr., Pa. Coun. for Social Studies, 1989, nominated for Pa. Tchr. of Yr., 1990. Mem. NEA, William Glasser Inst., Pa. State Edn. Assn., Bethlehem Edn. Assn., Phi Delta Kappa. Avocations: cooking, theater, travel, books, walking. Home: 3430 Drifting Dr Hellertown PA 18055-9601

CLAPTON, ERIC, musician; b. Ripley, Surrey, Eng., Mar. 30, 1945; m. Patricia Anne Boyd, 1979 (div. 1988); 1 child, Conor (dec.). Student, Kingston Art Sch. Former mem. rock music groups Yardbirds, John Mayall's Bluesbreakers, Cream, Blind Faith, Delaney & Bonnie & Friends, Derek & the Dominos;, performer (now solo performer); : (films) A Concert for Bangladesh, 1972 (Grammy award Album of the Year), Tommy, 1975, Music Communion, 1989; composer: Badge, Let It Rain, Layla; musician: (albums) Eric Clapton, 1970, Rainbow Concert, 1973, 461 Ocean Boulevard, 1974, There's One in Every Crowd, 1974, EC Was Here, 1975, No Reason to Cry, 1976, Slowhand, 1977, Backless, 1978, Just One Night, 1980, Another Ticket, 1981, Money and Cigarettes, 1983, Behind the Sun, 1985, August, 1987, Crossroads (retrospective), 1988, Time Pieces/Best of Eric Clapton, 1988, Time Pieces II/Live in the Seventies, 1988, One Moment in Time, 1988, Journeyman, 1989, 24 Nights, 1991, Unplugged, 1992 (Winner of 6 Grammy awards including Album of the Year, Record of the Year), From the Cradle, 1994 (Grammy award Best Traditional Blues Album), Pilgrim, 1998, Chronicles, 1999, Riding With the King, 2000 (Grammy award Best Trad. Blues Album), Reptile, 2001 (Grammy award Best Pop Instrumental Perf.), One More Car, One More Rider, 2002; wrote songs: BBC miniseries Edge of Darkness, 1986; composer film score Homeboy, 1988, Lethal Weapon, 1986, Lethal Weapon 2, 1989, The Van, 1996, Nil by Mouth, 1997; co-composer film score: Lethal Weapon 3, 1992. Named into Rock and Roll Hall of Fame, 1993. Office: care Warner Bros Records 3300 Warner Blvd Burbank CA 91505-4632*

CLARE, FRANK BRIAN, neurosurgeon, neurologist; b. Southport, Eng., June 27, 1919; came to U.S., 1920; s. Joseph and Nellie Elam C.; m. Shirley Edmondson, June 28, 1950 (dec. Apr. 1992); children: Frank Brian Jr., Shelley Jo Williamson, Merry Lou Cales, William Thmas Clare. BS, MS, MD, U. Ill., Chgo. Diplomate Am. Bd. Neurosurgery. Chief neurosurgeon U.S. Naval Hosp., Stalbans, N.Y., 1946-48, Portsmouth, Va., 1950-60, San Diego, 1960-63; neurosurgeon Portsmouth Gen., 1963-98; staff neurosurgeon Maryview Hosp., Portsmouth, 1963-99, Norfolk (Va.) Gen., 1963-99. Pres. Neurosurg. Soc. Va., 1965-67. Contbr. articles to profl. jours. Commr. sister city City Gov., Portsmouth, 1990-96. Capt. USN, 1942-63. Mem. Portsmouth Acad. Med. Soc. (pres. 1968), Rotary Internat. (bd. dirs. 1964, Paul Harris fellow). Republican. Episcopalian. Avocations: sailing, airplane pilot. Home and Office: 3201 High Point Dr Portsmouth VA 23703-4407

CLARE, KENNETH GUILFORD, economist, consultant; b. Dallas, Wis., June 13, 1918; s. Hans and Josie Bertina (Jacobson) C.; m. Elizabeth Rae Padfield, Oct. 5, 1945 (div. 1959); children: Raymond, Loren; m. Anne Worth Liesmann, Aug. 27, 1961; children: Steven, Janice, Keith. PhB in Economics, U. Wis., 1941; MA in Economics, U. So. Calif., 1946, PhD in Economics, 1950. Asst. prof. U. So. Calif., L.A., 1947-50, 56-59, U. Utah, Salt Lake City, 1950-51; dist. economist Office Price Stabilization, Boise, Idaho, 1951-53; economist CIA, Washington, 1953-56; sr. economist Stanford Rsch. Inst., Menlo Park, Calif., 1959-65; v.p. Westwood Rsch., Inc., L.A., 1965-72; sr. economist World Bank, Washington, 1972-83, cons., 1983—2000; ret., 2000. Asst. prof. UCLA, 1960-62; cons. various govtl. bodies, several locations. Author: Southern California Regional Airport Study, 1962, Area Study of Korea, 1969, (with others) Persian Gulf States, 1985, (hist. novel) Promises, Promises, 2003, Restless Man, A Memoir, 2003. Mem. Transp. Rsch. Forum (Internat. chpt. pres. 1990—), Omicron Delta Epsilon. Presbyterian. Avocations: reading, art collecting, genealogy. Home: 1600 N Oak St Apt 320 Arlington VA 22209-2761 Office: Clare Assocs 1600 N Oak St Apt 320 Arlington VA 22209-2761

CLARENDON, JOHN MARSDEN, counselor, youth program director; b. Greenwich, Conn., Aug. 27, 1946; s. Jean Knight and Katherine Eleanor (Marsden) C.; m. Patricia Marie Vetrone, June 26, 1982; 1 child, Colin McHugh. BA in English, Bucknell U., 1968; MEd in Counseling Psychology, Cambridge Coll., 1992. Lic. mental health counselor; cert. deep tissue bodywork practitioner. Dir. youth programs Selectman's Com. on Youth and Human Resources, Westport, Conn., 1970-72; dir. Open Line (crisis ctr.), Westport, Conn., 1973-75; tng. dir. Hotline of Greenwich, Inc., Conn., 1976-78, exec. dir., 1978-88; youth program dir. Barnstable (Mass.) County Sheriff's Office, 1988—. Trainer Alternative to Violence project, Greenwich, 1976-84, Cmty. Mediation Svcs., Stamford, 1985-88; founder Pers. Devel. Workshops, 1990; Jin Shin Jyutsu practitioner, 1980—. Dep. sheriff Barnstable County, 1989; bd. dirs. Samaritans, 1990, Project Quest Mass Nat. Guard, 1992-93. Mem. Assn. for Humanistic Psychology, U.S. Assn. for Body Psychotherapy, Mass. Assn. Mental Health Counselors. Roman Catholic. Home: 31 Leonard Rd East Sandwich MA 02537-1995

CLAREY, DONALD ALEXANDER, government affairs consultant; b. Johnson City, N.Y., Feb. 8, 1950; s. James Roger and Dorothy (Wait) C. BA, Union Coll., Schenectady, 1972; M.P.A., Harvard U., Cambridge, Mass., 1977. Exec. asst. to dir. for Congl. affairs FEA, Washington, 1973-76; program assoc. to majority leader N.Y. State Senate, Albany, 1977-79, adminstrv. asst. to majority leader, 1979-82; cons. Dept. State, Washington, 1983; assoc. dir. cabinet affairs The White House, Washington, 1983-85, spl. asst. to Pres. of U.S., 1985-87; dep. adminstr. SBA, 1987-88; cons. govt. affairs, v.p. Strategic Mgmt. Assocs., Washington, 1989-96; pres. Minerva Group, 1996—. Republican candidate for N.Y. State Assembly, 1980, 82. Republican. Roman Catholic. Avocations: skiing; golf. Home: 234 Lenox Ave Albany NY 12208-1408 Office: PO Box 459 Albany NY 12201-0459

CLAREY, JOHN ROBERT, executive search consultant; b. Waterloo, Iowa, June 5, 1942; s. Robert J. and Norma (Knox) C.; m. Kathleen Ann Kingsley, June 5, 1965; children: Sharon Diane, Suzanne Marie. BSBA, Iowa State U., 1965; MBA, U. Pa., 1972. Fin. analyst Ford Motor Co., Dearborn, Mich., 1972-74; cons. Price Waterhouse, Chgo., 1974-75, mgr., 1975-76; assoc. Heidrick & Struggles, Chgo., 1976-81, v.p., ptnr., 1981-82; pres. Clarey, Andrews & Klein, Inc., Northbrook, Ill. Served to lt. USN, 1965-70, Vietnam. Mem. Stick and Rudder, Assn. Exec. Search Cons., Lifeline Pilots, Mid-Am. Club (Chgo.), Sunset Ridge Country Club (Northbrook). Republican. Roman Catholic. Avocations: flying, microcomputers, tennis. Home: 1347 Hillside Rd Northbrook IL 60062-4612 Office: Clarey Andrews & Klein Inc 1200 Shermer Rd Ste 108 Northbrook IL 60062-4563 E-mail: jackc@clarey-andrews.com.

CLARIDA, RICHARD H. federal agency administrator; married; 2 children. BS in Econs., U. Ill., 1979; MS, PhD, Harvard U., 1983. Asst. prof. econs. Yale U., New Haven, 1983—88; prof. econs. Columbia U., N.Y.C., 1988—, chmn. dept. econs.; sr. staff economist CEA, 1986—87; asst. sec. econ. policy U.S. Dept. Treasury, Washington, 2002—, sr. advisor to treasury sec. and dep. sec., 2002—. Vis. scholar Internat. Monetary Fund, 1992, 93, 95, 97, Fed. Res. Bd., 1992, 94, 97. Office: US Dept Treasury Office Sec 1500 Pennsylvania Ave Washington DC 20220

CLARIDGE, ELMOND LOWELL, retired engineering educator, consultant; b. Delaplaine, Ark, June 5, 1917; s. Elmond Lee and Irene Cynthia Gates (Compton) C.; m. Zola Ruth McDowell, Jan. 1, 1939 (dec. Oct. 9, 1990); children: David Elmond, Jonathan McDowell; m. Mary Lasley Moore, Feb. 11, 1995 (dec. Feb. 16, 1999). BS in Chem. Engring., U. Mo., Rolla, 1939, MS in Chem. Engring., 1941; PhD in Chem. Engring., U. Houston, 1979. Registered profl. engr., Tex. Rsch. chemist Shell Oil Co., Wood River, Ill., 1941-43, technologist, 1943-48, asst. chief rsch. Houston, 1948-55, 57-60, sr. technologist head office NYC, 1960-64; group leader Royal Dutch Shell, Amsterdam, 1955-57; sr. rsch. assoc. Shell Devel. Co., Houston, 1964-79; assoc. prof. chem. engring. dept. U. Houston, 1979-91, dir. petroleum engring. grad. program, 1979-87. Cons. Gulf Univs. Rsch. Consortium, Houston, 1979-85, TCA Reservoir Engring. Svcs., Houston, 1979—. Author: PE 506, Miscible Processes, 1992; contbr. articles to profl. jour. Recipient Disting. Life award St. Luke's United Meth. Ch., 1990. Mem. AIChE, AAAS, Am. Chem. Soc. (chmn. sub com. petroleum res. fund adv. com. 1985-88), Am. Petroleum Inst. (rsch. adv. bd. prodn. divsn. 1978-81), Petroleum Soc./Can. Inst. Mining, Metallurgy and Petroleum, Soc. Petroleum Engrs. (editor reprint book Surfactant/Polymer Chemical Flooding vols. I, II, 1982, Enhanced Oil Recovery Pioneer 1980), Sigma Xi, Alpha Chi Sigma. Achievements include ten patents. Home and Office: 3011 Flower Field Pearland TX 77584 E-mail: eclaridge@houston.rr.com.

CLARIDGE, RICHARD, structural engineer; b. Chgo., Feb. 22, 1932; s. Dalbert Otis and Lucille Alma (Lindquist) C.; m. Joan Elaine Powell, June 12, 1952; children: Cathy L. Jansen, Richard Allen Jr., Jaylynn P. Cook. BSBA, Fla. State U., Tallahassee, 1953; BCE, U. Fla., 1959; postgrad., U. Cen. Fla., 1972-75. Registered profl. engr. Fla., S.C. Structures engr. Douglas Aircraft Co., 1959-63, McDonnell Douglas Astro, 1963-89, ground supt. equipment, design engr., 1974-81, stress analyst Titusville, Fla., 1982-89; structural cons., analyst Atlantic CADD Assocs., Titusville, 1989—. Group engr. McDonnell Douglas Astro, Kennedy Space Ctr., 1963-74; sect. chief stress McDonnell Douglas Missile Sys., Titusville, 1983-89; structural analyst, designer Lockheed Martin Astronautics, Cape Canaveral, Fla., 1989-97; webmaster, First Bapt. Ch., New Smyrna Beach, Fla., 2000-. Mem. Titusville Shoreline Authority, 1965. Lt. (j.g.) USNR, 1953-57. Mem. NSPE, ASCE (computer practices reviewer), AIAA, Am. Welding Soc., Fla. Engring. Soc., U.S. Naval Inst. (life), Internat. Soc. Allied Weight Engrs, Nat. Assn. Tech. Mins.. Avocations: woodworking, photography, volleyball, surfing. Office: Atlantic CADD Assocs PO Box 386 New Smyrna Beach FL 32170-0386 E-mail: rclaridgesr@cfl.rr.com.

CLARIE, THOMAS CASHIN, II, librarian; b. Providence, Dec. 21, 1943; s. T. Emmet and Gertrude Clare (Reynolds) C.; m. Rosemary Dorr Hamilton, Nov. 16, 1985. *His father, District Court Judge T. Emmet Clarie (January 1, 1913-September 24, 1997), was a noted attorney and judge. He became Connecticut State Legislator at age twenty-four, and was a three-term Connecticut House minority leader beginning at age twenty-six. He was clerk of the Connecticut Senate, and appointed chairman of the State Liquor Control Commission, before being appointed to the federal judiciary by President Kennedy in 1961. He was a close friend of Connecticut political greats Thomas Dodd, Abraham Ribicoff, John Bailey, and Chester Bowles. His important cases include; Los Macheteros Puerto Rican terrorists' seven million dollar robbery, the United Aircraft strike, and the Cuban travel ban.* BS in History, Coll. of Holy Cross, 1965; MS in Libr. Sci., So. Conn. State U., 1972; MA in History, U. Conn., 1973. Reference libr. Hamden (Conn.) Libr., 1967-69; head libr. Avon (Conn.) Old Farms Sch., 1969-71; reference libr. U. Conn., Storrs, 1973; head reference libr. So. Conn. State U., New Haven, 1973-97. Author: Occult Bibliography, 1978, Occult/Paranormal Bibliography, 1984; creator various ednl. card games, 1991 (Parents' Choice mag. award 1992). Recipient Best Reference Book Idea award Carrollton Press, 1978. Mem. ALA, AAUP, UN Assn. of U.S.A. Roman Catholic. Avocations: golf, theatre, tennis. Home: 1 Huckleberry Ln Hampton NH 03842 Office: So Conn State U Buley Libr New Haven CT 06515 E-mail: TomClarie@aol.com.

CLARK, A. JAMES, real estate company executive; b. 1927; BCE, U. Md., 1950. CEO, chmn., founder Clark Enterprises, Bethesda, Md., 1951—. Laureate, Washington Bus. Hall of Fame. Office: Clark Enterprises Inc 7500 Old Georgetown Rd Bethesda MD 20814*

CLARK, ALAN MARTIN, band director; b. Chattanooga, Tenn., Sept. 1, 1955; s. Leroy B. and Ruth Olene (Martin) C.; m. Barbara Faye Brinkley Johnson, July 19, 1991); 1 child, Stephanie Nickole. BS in Music Edn. magna cum laude, Tenn. Tech. U., 1977; MA in Music Edn. summa cum laude, Western Ky. U., 1979. Cert. educator in instrumental music, Tenn. Grad. asst. Western Ky. U., Bowling Green, 1977-79; band dir., music tchr. Marion County Schs., Jasper, Tenn., 1979-81; performing musician, bus. mgr. Jack Daniels' Original Silver Cornet Band, Nashville, 1981-86; records analyst State of Tenn., Nashville, 1986-93; band dir. Sumner County Schs., Hendersonville, Tenn., 1993—. Performer Sumner County Symphony, 2001—; band dir. Hunters Lane Cmty. Band, Nashville, 1991-96; bd. dirs. Hunters Lane Cmty. Edn., Nashville, 1992-96; pvt. brass instrn. Sumner County Schs., Gallatin, Tenn., 1992—; band camp instr. Hillsboro/Harpeth/Beech High Sch., Nashville, Hendersonville, 1992—. Performer (music/band) Freelance Trombone/Bariton, 1992—, Nashville Wind Ensemble, 1993—, Sumner County Symphony, 2000—. Poll observer CNN/CBS/local affiliates, Nashville, 1991—; mem., treas. Madison Sertoma Club, Nashville, 1992-93. Nat. Soloist finalist Tubists Universal Brotherhood Assn., 1976. Mem. Music Educators Nat. Conf., Tenn. Edn. Assn., Tubists Universal Brotherhood Assn., Middle Tenn. Sch. Band and Orch. Assn., Phi Mu Alpha. Ch. of Christ. Avocations: golf, raquetball, reading, listening to music, radio controlled airplanes. Bus. Office: Merrol Hyde Magnet School 128 Township Drive Hendersonville TN 37075-3821 E-mail: clarka2@k12tn.net.

CLARK, ALICIA GARCIA, political party official; b. Vera Cruz, Mex. came to U.S., 1970; d. Rafael Garcia Aully and Maria Luisa (Cobos) Garcia; m. Edward E. Clark, Oct. 20, 1970; 1 child, Edward E. MS in Chem. Engring., Nat. U. Mex., Mexico City, 1951. Chemist Celanese Mexicana, Mexico City, 1951-53, lab. mgr., 1951-53, sales promotion mgr., 1958-65, sales promotion and advt. mgr., 1965-70; nat. chmn. Libertarian Party, Houston, 1981-83, coord. coun. state chairs, 1987-95. Pres. San Marino (Calif.) Guild of Huntington Hosps., 1981-82, chmn. Celebrity Series, 1989-90, 90-91. Pres. Multiple Sclerosis Soc., San Gabriel Valley, Calif., 1977-78, San Marino Woman's Club, 1989-90; bd. dirs. L.A. Opera League, 1990-96; founder, co-chair Hispanics for L.A. Opera, 1991-99; bd. dirs. L.A. Opera Assn., Guild Opera Co., 1994-96, L.A. Music and Art Sch., Pasadena Symphony; exec. brd. Club 100, 1996-99; mng. dir. L.A. Opera, 1995—; mem. opera panel Nat. Endowment for Arts, 1997. Recipient award La Mujer de Hoy mag., 1969, Heroes of L.A. award Hispanic Traditions and Heritage Coun., 1995, Star of Our Culture award Mex. Cultural Inst. L.A., 1998, Placido Domingo award, 2000. Mem. Fashion Group (treas. 1969-70, award 1970), San Marino Woman's Club (ways and means chmn. 1987-88). Fax: 626 796-3485.

CLARK, ANJA MARIA, lawyer; b. Vienna, Mar. 31, 1942; came to U.S., 1966, naturalized, 1982; BA in Sociology summa cum laude, Oglethorpe U., 1974; MA in Sociology cum laude, Ga. State U., 1977; JD, John Marshall Law Sch., 1977. Bar: Ga. 1978, D.C. 1984. Paralegal asst., Atlanta, 1976-78; sole practice, 1978-84; trial atty. oil, gas, and elec. litig. Fed. Energy Regulatory Commn., Washington, 1985—. Recipient Benjamin Parker Law award Oglethorpe U., 1974, Cross of the Holy Land award Vatican, 1987; named Dame of the Order of St. Stanislas, 2000. Republican. Roman Catholic.

CLARK, ARTHUR WATTS, insurance company executive; b. Seattle, Nov. 28, 1922; s. Irving Marshall and Nell (Watts) C.; m. Mary Dick Cannon, Nov. 21, 1942; children: Arthur Watts, Claiborne Marshall, Johnston Jewell. AB, U. N.C., 1943; MA, U. Calif., 1948. With Home Security Life Ins. Co., Durham, N.C., 1948-50, 52-85, pres., 1967-75, chmn., chief exec. officer, 1975-85, also dir.; chmn., chief exec. officer Peoples Life Ins. Co. of Washington, D.C., 1983-85; chmn., pres., chief exec. officer Peoples Security Life Ins. Co., 1985-86, chmn. bd., 1986-88. Mem. Res. Forces Policy Bd., Office Sec. Def., 1975-78. Treas. Research Triangle Regional Planning Commn., 1959-63; mem. N.C. Health Ins. Adv. Bd., 1966-70; chmn. bd. dirs. N.C. Ctrl. U. Found., Zool. Coun., 1994-96, chmn., 1996-2002; vice-chmn. bd. dirs. N.C. Med. Found.; chmn. Greater Triangle Cmty. Found., 1992-94, The Explorer's Club, 1999—. With USAAF, 1942-46, USAF, 1952, maj. gen. USAF, ret. Decorated D.S.M., Legion of Merit with oak leaf cluster, Bronze Star. Mem. Am. Life Conv. (dir. 1972), Am. Life Ins. Assn. (dir. 1973-75), Life Office Mgmt. Assn. (dir. 1973-76), Am. Council Life Ins. (dir. 1976), Life Insurers Conf. (exec. com. 1972-75, 1983-86), Assn. N.C. Life Ins. Cos. (chmn. 1986-87), Phi Beta Kappa, Sigma Xi. Home: 3540 Rugby Rd Durham NC 27707-5434 Office: 3100 Tower Blvd Ste 500 Durham NC 27707-2563

CLARK, BETH, minister; b. Bradford, N.H., Apr. 15, 1914; d. John Scott and Bessie (Murdock) Pendleton; m. John Guill Clark, June 20, 1940 (dec. June 1955); children: John Guill Jr. (dec. 1999), Beverly Estelle Clark Daggett. BA, Colby Coll., 1935; BD, Andover Newton Theol. Sch., 1938; MDiv, Ea. Bapt. Theol. Sem., 1967; D Ministry, Lancaster Theol. Sem., 1981; postgrad., U. Athens, 1970, Jungian Inst., Zurich, 1980, Mansfield Coll., Oxford, Eng., 1982, 85, Caribbean Inst., 1989. Ordained to ministry United Ch. of Christ, 1967. Exec. dir. YWCA, Bristol, Tenn., 1955-59, Asheville, N.C., 1959-60; dean of women Anderson (S.C.) Coll., 1960-61, Eastern Coll., St. Davids, Pa., 1961-65; vol. rsch. coord. Selinsgrove (Pa.) State Sch., 1965-78; interim min. various chs. Pa. Ctrl. Conf., United Ch. of Christ, Harrisburg, 1968-96. Author: Grief in the Loss of a Pastor, 1981; editor: Meditations on the Lord's Supper (John G. Clark), 1958. Bd. mgr. Bethany Children's Home, Womelsdorf, Pa., 1982-88; mem. adv. com. Sun Home Nursing Svcs., Northumberland, Pa., 1982-95, sec. bd. dirs., 1989-96; mem. stewardship coun. United Ch. of Christ, 1997—. Mem. Interim Network (steering com. 1978-80), Assn. Ret. State Employees, Alban Inst., Interagy. Club (pres. 1966-68), Triangle Club (v.p. 1970-74, pres. 1996-98), Phi Mu. Democrat. Home: PO Box 216 Manchester ME 04351-0216 E-mail: bpclark@mint.net. *Our world is crying out for honesty, for absolute truth. Communication is impossible without belief and trust in the sincerity of the other person. Better the bitter truth than favor catering deception.*

CLARK, BEVERLY ANN, lawyer; b. Davenport, Iowa, Dec. 9, 1944; d. F. Henry and Arlene F. (Meyer) C.; m. Richard Floss; children: Amy and Barry (twins); stepchildren: Heather, Gretchan. Student, Mich. State U., 1963-65; BA, Calif. State U., Fullerton, 1967; MSW, U. Iowa, 1975, JD, 1980; grad., Iowa Massage Inst., 1999. Bar: Iowa 1980; lic. social worker, Iowa; nat. cert. lic. massage therapist. Probation officer County of San Bernardino, San Bernardino, Calif., 1968, County of Riverside, Riverside, Calif., 1968-69; social worker Skiff Hosp., Newton, Iowa, 1971-73, State of Iowa, Mitchellville, 1973-74, planner Des Moines, 1976-77, law clk., 1980-81; corp. counsel Pioneer Hi-Bred Internat., Inc., Des Moines, 1981-2000; pvt. practice, 2000—; atty. Jasper County Legal Aid, 2002—. Instr. Des Moines Area C.C., Ankeny, Iowa, 1974—75, Ankeny, 2001—; adj. prof. Drake Law Sch., 1993—96, Buena Vista U., 2002—; pub. Sweet Annie Press; past owner Annie's Place, The B&B Connection Gift Catalog. Editor: Proceedings: Bicentennial Symposium on New Directions in Juvenile Justice, 1975; contbr. articles to prof. jours. Founder Mother of Twins Club, Newton, 1971; co-chmn. Juvenile Justice Symposium, Des Moines, 1974-75; mem. Juvenile Justice Com., Des Moines, 1974-75; mem. Nat. Offender Based State Corrections Info. System. Com., Iowa rep., 1976-78; incorporator, dir. Iowa Dance Theatre, Des Moines, 1981; mem. Pesticide User's Adv. Com., Fort Collins, Colo., 1981-88; co-developer Iowa Migrant Ombudsmen Project, Pioneer, Inc. and Proteus, Inc. Recipient Disting. Alumni award U. Iowa, 1990, Nat. award Ctr. for Pub. Resources. Mem.: ABA (termination-at-will subcom. 1982—2000, subcom. on devel. individual rights in work place, columnist), Am. Assn. Agrl. Lawyers, Jasper County Bar Assn., Iowa Bar Assn., Iowa Orgn. Women Attys. (bd. dirs., sec. 2001).

CLARK, BRADD EVANS, dean, mathematician, educator; b. Sioux Falls, S.D., Apr. 12, 1948; s. Oliver Wilcox and Alvina Anderson Clark; m. Carol Ann Bihler, May 19, 1979; children: Meredith Mae, Charlotte Ann. BA, Northwestern U., 1970; MA, U. Wis., 1974; PhD, U. Wyo., 1976. Asst. prof. U. La., Lafayette, 1976—81, assoc. prof., 1981—87, prof., 1987—, dean scis., 2001—. Office: U La Lafayette Dept Math Lafayette LA 70504

CLARK, BRIAN THOMAS, mathematical statistician, operations research analyst; b. Rockford, Ill., Apr. 7, 1951; s. Paul Herbert and Martha Lou (Schlensker) C.; m. Suzanne Drake, Nov. 21, 1992; 1 child, Branden Ward. BS cum laude, No. Ariz. U., 1973; postgrad., Ariz. State U., 1980-82; MBA, Heriot-Watt U., Edinburgh, Scotland, 1999. Math. aide Ctr. for Disease Control, Phoenix, 1973-74, math. statistician, 1979-83, Ctrs. for Disease Control, Atlanta, 1983-84; ops rsch. analyst U.S. Army Network Enterprise Technology Command (formerly U.S. Army Info. Systems Command), Ft. Huachuca, Ariz., 1984—. Math. statistician U.S. Navy Meteorology Engring. Ctr., Pomona, Calif., 1974-79; part-time instr. Western Internat. U., Fort Huachuca Campus, 2003—. Republican. Mem. Lds Ch. Office: US Army Signal Command Dep Chief Staff Resource Mgmt G8 Managerial Acctg Pricing Fort Huachuca AZ 85613

CLARK, BRUCE BUDGE, humanities educator, educator; b. Georgetown, Idaho, Apr. 9, 1918; s. Marvin E. and Alice (Budge) C.; m. Ouida Raphiel, Nov. 7, 1946; children— Lorraine, Bradley, Robert, Jeffrey, Shawn, Sandra. BA, U. Utah, 1943, PhD, 1951; MA, Brigham Young U., 1948. Teaching fellow Brigham Young U., 1946-47, U. Utah, 1947-50; asst. prof. Brigham Young U., 1950-55, assoc. prof., 1955-58, prof., 1959—, dir. humanities program, 1958-60, chmn. dept. English, 1960-65; dean Coll. Humanities, 1965-81. Author: The Spectrum of Faith in Victorian Literature, 1966, The Challenge of Teaching, 1966, Romanticism through Modern Eyes, 1968, Oscar Wilde, A Study in Genius and Tragedy, 1970, Brigham Young on Education, 1970, Idealists in

Revolt, 1975, History of the Brigham Young U. Coll. Humanities, 3 vols., 1984, Family History, 3 vols., 1998, Selected Essays and Other Writings, 1998; Editor: Richard Evans Quote Book, 1971; anthology (Out of the Best Books, vol. 1, 1964, vol. II, 1966, vol. III, 1967, vol. IV, 1968, vol. V, 1969, Great Short Stories for Discussion and Delight, 1979; Contbr. articles to profl. jours. Served with AUS, 1944-46. Recipient Karl G. Maeser Teaching Excellence award, 1972, David O. McKay Humanities award, 1983, Brigham Young U. Presdl. citation for disting. svc., 1994. Mem. MLA, Nat. Coun. Tchrs. English, Rocky Mountain Modern Lang. Assn., Coll. Conf. on Composition and Communication, Phi Kappa Phi. Mem. Lds Ch. Home: 365 E 1655 S Orem UT 84058-7903

CLARK, BRUCE ROBERT, geologist, consultant; b. Pitts., June 17, 1941; s. Harold Thomas and Florence (Miller) Clark; m. Karen Pelton Heath, Dec. 30, 1967; children: Adam, Andrea. BS, Yale U., 1963; PhD, Stanford U., 1967. Asst. prof. U. Mich., Ann Arbor, 1968-73, assoc. prof., 1973-77; v.p. Leighton and Assocs., Inc., Irvine, Calif., 1977-85, pres., 1986—2002, CEO, 1988—2002, sr. cons., 2002—. Contbr. articles to profl. jours. Commr. Calif. Seismic Safety Commn., 2000—, chmn., 2001—03; chmn. bd. dirs. YMCA Orange County, Calif., 1999—2002. Fellow: Geol. Soc. Am.; mem.: Seismol. Soc. Am., Assn. Engrng. Geologists, Am. Geophys. Union, Earthquake Engrng. Rsch. Inst. (bd. dirs. 2002—). Office: Leighton and Assocs Inc 17781 Cowan Irvine CA 92614-6009 E-mail: bclark@leightongeo.com.

CLARK, BURTON ROBERT, sociologist, educator; b. Pleasantville, N.J., Sept. 6, 1921; s. Burton H. and Cornelia (Amole) C.; m. Adele Halitsky, Aug. 31, 1949; children: Philip Neil (dec.), Adrienne. BA, UCLA, 1949, PhD, 1954; PhD (hon.), U. Strathclyde, 1998, U. Turku, Finland, 2000. Asst. prof. sociology Stanford U., 1953-56; research asso., asst. prof. edn. Harvard U., 1956-58; asso. prof., then prof. edn. and asso. research sociologist, then research sociologist U. Calif. at Berkeley, 1958-66; prof. sociology Yale U., 1966-80, chmn. dept., 1969-72, chmn. higher edn. rsch. group, 1973-80; Allan M. Cartter prof. higher edn. UCLA, 1980-91, prof. emeritus, 1991—. Author: Adult Education in Transition, 1956, The Open Door College, 1960, Educating the Expert Society, 1962, The Distinctive College, 1970, The Problems of American Education, 1975, Academic Power in Italy, 1977, The Higher Education System, 1983, The Academic Life, 1987, Places of Inquiry, 1995, Creating Entrepreneurial Universities, 1998; co-author: Students and Colleges, 1972, Youth: Transition to Adulthood, 1973, Academic Power in the United States, 1976, Academic Power: Patterns of Authority in Seven National Systems of Higher Education, 1978; editor: Perspectives on Higher Education, 1984, The School and The University, 1985, The Academic Profession, 1987, The Research Foundations of Graduate education, 1993; co-senior editor: Encyclopedia of Higher Education, 1992. Served with AUS, 1942-46. Recipient Comenius medal UNESCO, 1998. Fellow Brit. Soc. for Rsch. in Higher Edn.; mem. Am. Sociol. Assn., Am. Ednl. Rsch. Assn. (Am. Coll. Testing award 1979, Divsn. J. Disting. Rsch. award 1988, Outstanding Book award 1989), Assn. Study Higher Edn. (pres. 1979-80, Rsch. Achievement award 1985, Howard Bowen Distinguished Svc. award 1997), Am. Assn. Higher Edn., Nat. Acad. Edn. (v.p. 1989-93), Consortium Higher Edn. Rschrs., European Assn. for Instnl. Rsch. (disting. mem.) Home: 201 Ocean Ave 1710B Santa Monica CA 90402 Office: UCLA Dept Edn Los Angeles CA 90095-1521 E-mail: clark@qseis.ucla.edu.

CLARK, CALEB MORGAN, political scientist, educator; b. Washington, June 6, 1945; s. Tanner Morgan and Grace Amanda (Kautzman) C.; m. Janet Morrissey Sentz, Sept. 28, 1968; children: Emily Claire, Grace Ellen, Evelyn Adair. BA, Beloit Coll., 1966; PhD, U. Ill., 1973. Lectr. N.Mex. State U., Las Cruces, 1972-75, asst. prof., 1975-78, assoc. prof. govt., 1978-81; assoc. prof. polit. sci. U. Wyo., Laramie, 1981-84, prof., 1984-92, U. Auburn, 1992—, prof., head polit. sci. Co-author: Comparative Patterns of Foreign Policy and Trade, 1976, Development's Influence on Yugoslav Political Values, 1976, Taiwan's Development, 1989, Women in Taiwan Politics, 1990, Foresight, Flexibility and Fortuna in Taiwan's Devel., 1992; mng. editor IS Notes, 1984-92; co-editor: North/South Relations, 1983, State and Development, 1988, Polit. Stability and Economic Development, 1988, Polit. Stability and Economic Development, 1991, The Evolving Pacific Basin, 1992, Technological Change and Rurdal Development in Poor Countries, 1994, Beyond the Developmental State, 1998, The ROC on the Threshold of the 21st Century, 1999, Democracy and the Status of Women in East Asia; cons., assoc. editor Soviet Union, 1974-77, World Affairs, 1975-84, Social Sci. Jour., 1978-80; contbr. articles to profl. jours. NDEA fellow, 1966-69; Woodrow Wilson dissertation fellow, 1969-70; grantee N.Mex. Humanities Coun., 1975, Wyo. Coun. for Humanities, 1982, U.S. Dept. Edn., 1983-85, Pacific Cultural Found., 1984-86, Am. Coun. Learned Socs., 1976, Met. Life Edn., 1978-80, NEH, 1978, NSF, 1981, Chiang Ching-Kuo Found., 1993-95. Mem. Am. Polit. Sci. Assn., Am. Assn. Chinese Studies (exec. coun. 1995-97), Western Polit. Sci. Assn., Assn. Asian Studies, Southern Polit. Sci. Assn., Internat. Studies Assn. (exec. dir. West 1981-84), Ala. Polit. Sci. Assn. (v.p. 1993-94, pres. 1994-95), Phi Beta Kappa (treas. 1983-91), Pi Eta Sigma, Phi Kappa Phi, Phi Beta Delta.

CLARK, CANDY, actress; b. Norman, Okla. d. Thomas Prest and Ella Lee C. Student public schs., Ft. Worth. Appeared in movies Fat City, 1971, American Graffiti, 1973 (nominated for best supporting actress), The Man Who Fell to Earth, 1975, Citizens Band, 1976, The Big Sleep, 1977, When Ya' Coming Back Red Ryder, 1978, More American Graffiti, 1978, National Lampoon Goes to the Movies, 1981, Blue Thunder, 1981, Amityville 3-D, 1983, Stephen King's Cat's Eye, 1984, At Close Range, 1986, The Blob, 1988, Cool-As-Ice, 1991, Buffy the Vampire Slayer, 1992, Radioland Murders, 1994, Niagara, Niagara, 1996, Cherry Falls, 1999, The Month of August, 2000, appeared in TV movies Amateur Night at the Dixie Bar and Grill, 1978, Where The Ladies Go, 1980, Rodeo Girl, 1980, Popeye Doyle, 1986, Plan of attack, 1992; appeared in off-Broadway show A Coupla White Chicks Sitting Around Talking, 1981, (play) It's Raining on Hope Street, 1988, Loose Lips, 1995.

CLARK, CARLETON EARL, tax consultant; b. North Easton, Mass., Apr. 5, 1942; s. Carleton Earl and Amy Ella (Toner) C.; m. Judy Carol Johnson (div. 1983); children: Amy Laura, Carla Elaine; m. Janice E. Dutra, Apr. 30, 1989. BS in Acctg., Bentley Coll., 1980. Asst. v.p. BayBank Norfolk, Dedham, Mass., 1967-89; tax cons. E.W. Costa, Pub. Acct., Brockton, Mass., 1989-93; pres. Costa & Clark, Inc., Brockton, 1993-96; tax preparer H&R Block, 1997—. Pvt. practice tax cons., Brockton, Mass., 1985—. Mem.: Nat. Assn. Tax Preparers. Democrat. Congregationalist. Home: 670 Pearl St Brockton MA 02301-4527

CLARK, CAROL CANDA, art historian, educator; b. N.Y.C., July 21, 1947; d. Henry G. Canda and Dolores C. Adam; m. Jon D. Clark, May 24, 1969 (div. Apr. 1983); m. Charles Parkhurst, July 18, 1986. B.A. with distinction, U. Mich.-Ann Arbor, 1969, M.A., 1971; Ph.D., Case Western Res. U., Cleve., 1981. Registrar, U. Mich. Mus. Art, Ann Arbor, 1971-72; instr. Tex. Christian U., Ft. Worth, 1975-77; curator Amon Carter Mus. Ft. Worth, 1977-84; exec. prendergast fellow Williams Coll., Williamstown, Mass., 1984-87, lectr. art history, 1984-87; assoc. prof. fine arts Amherst (Mass.) Coll., 1987—, William R. Kenan, Jr. prof., 2001—; prof. fine arts and Am. studies; adj. prof. art history So. Methodist U., 1982-83; adj. curator of Am. Art, Clark Art Inst., Williamstown, Mass., 1984-87. Mem. adv. com. Hist. Deerfield, Whitney Adv. Bd., Buffalo Bill Hist. Ctr., Cody, Wyo., pub. trustee Williamstown Art Conservation Ctr. Author: Thomas Moran's Watercolors, 1980, Robert Lehman Collection VIII: American Drawings and Watercolors, 1992; (catalogue) American Impressionist and Realist Paintings, 1978; co-author Maurice and Charles Prendergast, 1990. Mem. art and architecture adv. panel Tex. Commn. on the Arts, 1981-83. Kress Found. fellow, 1972-75. Office: Amherst Coll Fayerweather Hall Amherst MA 01002-5000 E-mail: ccclark@amherst.edu.

CLARK, CAROLYN COCHRAN, lawyer; b. Kansas City, Mo., Oct. 30, 1941; d. John Rogers and Betty Charleton (Holmes) Cochran; m. L. David Clark, Jr., Dec. 29, 1967; children: Gregory David, Timothy Rogers. BA, U. Mo., 1963; LLB, Harvard U., 1968. Bar: N.Y. 1968, Fla. 1979. Assoc. Milbank, Tweed, Hadley & McCloy, N.Y.C., 1968-76, ptnr., 1977—2001, cons. ptnr., 2002—. Mem. deferred giving com., former regional chmn. major gifts com. Harvard Law Sch. Fund; mem. vis. com. Harvard Law Sch., 1982-88; mem. com. on trust and estate gift plans Rockefeller U.; trustee Madison Ave. Presbyn. Ch., 1984-86, N.Y. Bot. Garden, 1993-96, Vis. Nurse Assn. N.Y. and Vis. Nurse Health Care, 1991-96, Riverdale Country Sch., 1994-98, Milbank Meml. Fund, 1996—, The Woodlawn Cemetery, 1999—; del. John D. Rockefeller Conf. Philanthropy in the 21st Century, N.Y., 1989; bd. advisors NYU program Philanthropy and the Law; chmn. program taxation exempt orgns. NYU Tax Inst. Recipient Disting. Alumna award U. Mo., 1989. Fellow Am. Coll. Trust and Estate Counsel (ind. regent, chmn. com. on charitable giving and exempt orgns.), N.Y. Bar Found., Am. Bar Found.; mem. ABA (chmn. subcom. income taxation of charitable trusts 1976-78, chmn. com. charitable instns. 1989-94), Assn. Bar City of N.Y. (chmn. com. on non-profit orgns. 1986-89, sec. com. philanthropic orgns. 1976-82, mem. com. trusts, estates and surrogates cts. 1977-80, 85-86), N.Y. State Bar Assn. (com. estate planning, trusts and estates sect. 1978-89), Am. Law Inst., Practising Law Inst. (lectr.), Harvard U. Law Sch., Assn. Greater N.Y. (trustee 1978-80, v.p. 1980-81, pres. 1981-82), NYU Tax Inst. (chmn. conf. tax planning charitable orgns. 1993-95), Nat. Harvard Law Sch. Alumni Assn. (exec. com. 1978-80, v.p. 1986-90, pres. 1990-92), Soc. Colonial Dames Am. in Mo., Maidstone Club. Home: 161 E 79th St New York NY 10021-0480 Office: Milbank Tweed Hadley Et Al 46th Fl 1 Chase Manhattan Plz New York NY 10005-1401 E-mail: cclark@milbank.com.

CLARK, CELIA RUE, lawyer; b. N.Y.C., Aug. 16, 1951; d. Edward Frank and Rosemary (Reddick) Clark, Jr.; m. Edgar Crawford Gentry, Jr., Aug. 11, 1979; children: Diana Marron, Carl Edgar. BA with distinction, U. Wis., 1974; JD, U. Chgo., 1979; LLM, NYU, 1988. Bar: N.Y. 1980. Mng. editor Heldref Publs., Washington, 1974-78; assoc. Rogers & Wells, N.Y.C., 1979-84; adj. asst. prof. law Yeshiva U., 1985; assoc. Weitzner, Levine & Hamburg, N.Y.C., 1988-92; counsel Pirro, Collier, Cohen, Crystal & Block, White Plains, NY, 1992—96; ptnr. Smith, Buss & Jacobs, LLP, NYC, 1996—2002; pvt. practice N.Y.C., 2002—. Contbg. author: Asset-Based Financing, 1984; contbr. articles to profl. jours. Mem. planned giving coun. Am. Cancer Soc.; bd. govs. N.Y. chpt. Arthritis Found.; bd. dirs. Louis R. Cappelli Found. Mem. ABA, Westchester County Bar Assn. Democrat. Office: Law Offices of Celia R Clark 100 Park Ave 33d Fl New York NY 10017 E-mail: cclark@cclarklaw.com.

CLARK, CHAPIN DEWITT, law educator; b. Lawrence, Kans., Dec. 27, 1930; s. Carroll DeWitt and Pearl (Holl) C.; m. Dorothy L. Becker, May 25, 1952; children— Julia Kay, Jeffrey Becker. AB, U. Kans., 1952, LL.B., 1954; LL.M., Columbia U., 1959. Bar: Kans. 1954, Oreg. 1965. Asst. prof. law U. S.D., 1959-62; assoc. prof. law U. Oreg., 1962-67, prof., 1967-91, prof. emeritus, from 1991, dean Sch. Law, 1974-80. Vice chmn. Oreg. Water Policy Rev. Bd., 1975-77, chmn., 1977-79; vis. prof. U.S. Mil. Acad., West Point, N.Y., 1980-81, 86-87; pres. Pacific 10 Athletic Conf., 1984-85; vis. prof. Wash. U. Law Sch., 1992. Contbr. articles to profl. jours. Pres. Planned Parenthood Lane County, 1975-76; mem. Gov.'s Commn. on Oceanography, 1967-68. Served with JAGC U.S. Army, 1954-58; col. USAR. Mem. Am. Bar Assn., AAUP (pres. U. Oreg. chpt. 1970-71, pres. Oreg. State conf. 1985-86), Am. Alpine Club. Home: Eugene, Oreg. Died Oct. 8, 2002.

CLARK, CHARLES M., JR., medical school administrator; b. Greensburg, Ind., Mar. 12, 1938; s. Charles Malcolm and Mary Louise (Christian) C.; m. Julia Berg Freeman, Jan 27, 1963 (div. 1982); children: Margaret Louise, Brian Alexander; m. Eleanor DeArman Kinney, June 25, 1983; 1 child, Janet Marie Clark. BA, Ind. U., 1960, MD, 1963. From asst. prof. to prof. medicine Ind. U., Indpls., 1969—, from asst. prof. to prof. pharmacology, 1970—; assoc. chief staff rsch. and devel. VA Hosp., Indpls., 1988—2002; dir. Diabetes Rsch. and Tng. Ctr., Indpls., 1977—2002; co-dir. Regenstrief Inst., Indpls., 1993-97; assoc. dean Ind. U. Sch. Medicine, Indpls., 2002—. Chmn. Safety and Quality com. DCCT, 1982-93, Nat. Diabetes adv. bd., 1987-88; chair Nat. Diabetes Edn. Program, 1995-2002; vis. prof. Facultad de Ciencias Medicas, U. Nacional de la Plata, Argentina, 1999-2000. Editor Diabetes Care, 1996-2001; contbr. numerous articles to profl. jours. Lt comdr. USPHS, 1967-69. Mem. ACP, Am. Soc. Clin. Investigation, Internat. Diabetes Fedn., Am. Diabetes Assn. (Banting award 1989). Office: 714 N Senate Ave EF 200 Indianapolis IN 46202 E-mail: chclark@iupui.edu.

CLARK, CHARLES MICHAEL ANDRES, economics educator; b. West Islip, N.Y., May 16, 1960; s. John Edward and Carol Marilyn (Andres) Clark; m. Lisa Mary McCarthy, Sept. 20, 1980; children: Meghan, Kaitlin, Charles. BA, Fordham U., 1982; PhD, New Sch. for Social Rsch., 1990. Instr. econs. St. John's U., Jamaica, N.Y., 1984-89, asst. prof., 1989-91, assoc. prof., 1991-96, prof., 1996—. Vis. prof. econs. Univ. Coll., Cork, Ireland, 1994—95; sr. fellow Vincentian Ctr. for Ch. and Soc., 2000—. Author: (Books) Economic Theory and Natural Philosophy, 1992; author: (with John Healy) Pathways to a Basic Income, 1997; editor: History and Historians of Political Economy, 1994, Institutional Economics and the Theory of Social Value, 1995; editor: (with Catherine Kavanaugh) Unemployment in Ireland, 1998; editor: (with Janina Rosicka) Economic Transformation in Historical Perspective, 2001; contbr. articles to profl. jours and chpts. to books; author (with S. Lerner and W.R. Needham): Economic Security for all Canadians, 1999; author: The Basic Income Guarantee, 2002. Grantee, Bus. Rsch. Inst., 1990, 1991. Mem.: Assn. for Institutionalist Thought, Assn. for Evolutionary Econs., History Econs. Soc., Am. Econ. Assn. Roman Catholic. Avocations: collecting old and rare books, visiting cathedrals. Office: St John's U Dept Econs 8000 Utopia Pkwy Jamaica NY 11439-1343

CLARK, CHARLES STUART, editor; b. Washington, July 6, 1953; s. Keith Conrad Clark and Cynthia Hyde Landry; m. Ellen McCallister Clark; children: Elizabeth Land, Susannah McCallister. BA in History, McGill U., 1976. Sr. rschr. Time-Life Books, Alexandria, Va., 1976—82; mng. editor Nat. Jour., Washington, 1986—91; staff writer Congl. Quar., Washington, 1991—97; editl. writer Washington Post, 1997; sr. writer-editor Nat. Ctr. on Edn. and the Economy, Washington, 1997—99; sr. editor Assn. of Governing Bds., Washington, 1999—. Freelance writer, 1977—; columnist No. Va. Jour., Fairfax, 1999—2003. Author: Finish High School at Home: A Novel, 2000. Active PTA Arlington Schs., 1994—2000, parent vol. tchr. excellence com., 2000—03. Democrat. Avocations: humor writing, rock and roll, basketball.

CLARK, CHARLES SUTTER, interior designer; b. Venice, Calif., Dec. 21, 1927; s. William Sutter and Lodema Ersell (Fleeman) C. Student Chouinard Art Inst., Los Angeles, 1950-51. Interior designer LM.H. Co., Gt. Falls, Mont., 1956-62, Andreason's Interiors, Oakland, Calif., 1962-66, Western Contact Furnishers Internat., Oakland, 1966-70, Design Five Assocs., Lafayette, Calif., 1972-73; owner, interior designer Charles Sutter Clark Interiors, Greenbrae, Calif., 1973-91, San Rafael, Calif., 1991—. Served with USAF, 1951-55. Recipient prizes Mont. State Fair, 1953-55. Mem. Am. Soc. Interior Designers. Home: 429 El Faisan Dr San Rafael CA 94903-4517

CLARK, CHARLES T(ALIFERRO), retired business statistics educator; b. Danville, Ill., Mar. 18, 1917; s. Charles A. and Kathryn S. (Gentry) C.; m. Pearl W. DuBose, Oct. 6, 1943; children: Charles A., Mary D., Robert S. BBA, U. Tex., 1938, MBA, 1939, PhD, 1956. Asst. mgr. Austin C. of C., Tex., 1940-41; dir. personnel U. Tex., Austin, 1946-59, asst. prof. bus. stats., 1959-60, assoc. prof., 1961-79, prof., 1979-91, Mary Lee Harkins Sweeney Centennial prof. emeritus in bus., 1991—. Bd. dirs. Tex. Student Publs., Austin, 1964-69, Tex. Union, Austin, 1969-83, Univ. Fed. Credit Union, Austin, 1976-84, Univ. Coop. Soc., Austin, 1980-84. Author numerous text books; (with L.L. Schkade) textbooks Statistical Analysis for Adminstrative Decision, 1969, 4th edit., 1983, (with John R. Stockton) Introduction to Business and Economic Statistics, 1971, 3d edit., 1980; contbr. articles to profl. jours. Served to 2d lt. USAAC, 1941-46, PTO. Recipient 11 teaching awards U. Tex., 1960-80 Mem. Coll. and Univ. Personnel Assn. (pres. 1959), Austin Personnel Assn. (pres. 1950), Austin Stat. Assn. (pres. 1975) Home: 4106 Farhills Dr Austin TX 78731-2812 Office: U Tex Dept Mgmt Sci & Info Systems Austin TX 78712 E-mail: ctclark@orotech.net.

CLARK, CHRISTINE MAY, editor, author; b. Peoria, Ill., Apr. 25, 1957; d. Darrell Ronald and Alice Venita (Burkitt) French. BA, Judson Coll., 1978. Assoc. editor David C. Cook Pub., Elgin, Ill., 1978-80; editor Humpty Dumpty, 1980-94, Jack and Jill, 1983-86, Turtle mag., 1990—; editl. dir. Children's Better Health Inst., Indpls.; assoc. editor Highlights for Children, Honesdale, Pa., 1994-96, mng. editor, 1996—2001, v.p. editl., 1997—, editor, 2001—, also bd. dirs. Recipient Journalism award EDPRESS, 1986, 87, 88, 89, 90, 92, Outstanding Reporting award Soc. Profl. Journalists, 1990; Aurora Found. scholar, 1975. Mem. Am. Soc. Mag. Editors, Soc. Children's Book Writers and Illustrators, Ednl. Press Assn., Judson Coll. Alumni Assn. Reorganized Ch. of Jesus Christ of Latter-day Saints. Avocations: piano, travel. Office: Highlights for Children 803 Church St Honesdale PA 18431-1895

CLARK, CHRISTOPHER MICHAEL, neurologist, educator, clinic director; m. Anne Marshall, Sept. 17, 1978. BS, Pa. State U., 1967; student vet. medicine, U. Pa., 1967-69; MD, Jefferson Med. Coll., 1973. Diplomate Am. Bd. Psychiatry and Neurology. Intern Pa. Hosp., Phila., 1973-74, asst. neurologist, 1977-82, assoc. neurologist, 1982-85; resident in neurology Neurol. Inst. Columbia Presbyn. Med. Ctr., N.Y.C., 1974-77, Muscular Dystrophy rsch. fellow, 1976-77; asst. prof. neurology Duke U., Durham, N.C., 1986-89, U. Pa., Phila., 1990-99, dir. Memory Disorders Svc. The Grad. Hosp., 1989-95, dir. Memory Disorders Clinic, 1995—. Clin. asst. prof. neurology U. Pa., 1977-85, sr. rsch. fellow Inst. on Aging, 1994—; mem. neurology med. staff Daroff divsn. Einstein Med. Ctr., Phila., 1977-82; mem. cons. staff Hunterdon Med. Ctr., Flemington, N.J., 1977-84; dir. EMG-Evoked Potentials Lab. Pa. Hosp., 1981-85; sr. fellow Ctr. Study Aging and Human Devel. Duke U. Med. Ctr., Durham, 1987-89; clin. dir. Joseph and Kathleen Bryan Alzheimer's Disease Rsch. Ctr., assoc. dir., 1986-89; dir. memory Disorders Clinic Duke U. Med. Ctr., 1986-89; co-dir., clin. core leader Alzheimer's Disease Core Ctr. U. Pa., 1994—, dir. memory disorders clinic, 1995—, info. transfer core leader, 1995-99, assoc. prof. neurology, 1999. Author: Neurodegenerative Dementia, Clinical Features and Pathological Mechanisms, 1996; contbg. editor: Jour. Gerontology; contbr. chpts. to books, articles to profl. jours. Mem. World Fedn. Neurology (rsch. com. 1981-85), Am. Acad. Neurology, Am. Assn. Electromyography and Electrodiagnosis, Consortium to Establish Registry for Alzheimer's Disease (clin. task force 1987—), Alzheimer's Disease Coop. Studies (ethics com. 1994—), Phila. Neurol. Soc. (Myasthenia Gravis med. adv. bd. 1985), Alzheimer's Disease and Related Disorders Assn. Ea. N.C. (bd. dirs. 1987-88), Alzheimer's Assn. (med. and sci. adv. bd. Phila. chpt. 1990—), Alzheimers Assn. Southeastern Pa. (bd. dirs. 1998—), Phi Sigma Soc. Office: Dept Neurology U Pa 3400 Spruce St Philadelphia PA 19104-4206

CLARK, CLIFFORD DALE, university president; b. Moulton, Iowa, Feb. 26, 1925; s. Artie Seymour and Myrtle Ida (Severs) C.; m. Margery Blair Miller, June 19, 1949 (dec. Dec. 1987); children: Geoffrey, Kathryn. AB in Econs, U. Kans., 1948; MA, U. Chgo., 1950, PhD, 1953. Instr. stats. Loyola U., Chgo., 1950-51; fgn. affairs officer research div. CIA, 1951-55; asst. prof. econs. N.C. State U., Raleigh, 1955-57; assoc. prof. econs. Grad. Sch. Bus. Adminstrn. NYU, 1957-62, prof., 1962-68, head, research office, 1963-64, assoc. dean, 1964-65, vice dean, 1965-68; dean Sch. Bus., prof. econs. U. Kans., 1968-73; v.p. acad. affairs SUNY, Binghamton, 1973-74, acting pres., 1974-75, pres., 1975—, acting vice chancellor rsch. grad. studies-profl. programs, 1986-87. Bd.dirs. Chase Lincoln 1st Bank N.A., Security Mut. Life Ins. Co. N.Y. Contbr. articles to profl. jours. Bd. dirs. Broome County Urban League, 1979-81, 90, Wilson Hosp., 1980-81. With US Army, 1943-46. Decorated Bronze Star. Mem. Am. Council Edn., Am. Assn. Higher Edn., Nat. Assn. Land Grant Univs. and Colls., Broome County C. of C. (dir. 1978-83) Clubs: Live Wire (Binghamton). Office: SUNY Vestal Pkwy E Binghamton NY 13901

CLARK, CLIFFORD EDWARD, JR., history educator; b. BayShore, N.Y., July 13, 1941; s. Clifford Edward and Helen C.; m. Grace Williams, Aug. 20, 1966; children: Cynthia Williams, Christopher Allen, Susan McGrath. BA, Yale U., 1963; MA, Harvard U., 1964, PhD in Am. Civilization, 1968. History tutor Harvard U., Cambridge, Mass., 1966-67; instr. Amherst (Mass.) Coll., 1968-69, asst. prof., 1969-70; from asst. to assoc. prof. Carleton Coll., Northfield, Minn., 1970-80, prof. history, 1980—, M.A. & A.D. Hulings Prof. of Am. Studies, 1982—, dir. summer acad. programs, 1984—, chmn. history dept., 1986-89. Cons. Minn. Humanities Commn., Mpls., 1976—, Minn. Hist. Soc., Mpls., 1982—; Northfield Sch. Bd., 1978-87; editl. cons. Winterthur Portfolio, Del., 1983-92. Author: Henry Ward Beecher, Spokesman for a Middle-Class America, 1978, The American Family Home, 1800-1960, 1986, (with others) The Enduring Tradition, 5th edit. 2003; editor: Minnesota in a Century of Change: The State and Its People Since 1900, 1989. Mem. Northfield Heritage Preservation Commn., 1986—. Fellow Woodrow Wilson Found., 1964, 67; Demonstration grantee NEH, 1978, sr. fellow NEH, 1980; recipient Younger Humanist Summer Stipend, NEH, 1973. Mem. Am. Studies Assn., Am. Hist. Assn., Orgn. Am. Historians, Northfield Hist. Soc. Episcopalian. Avocations: tennis, squash. Home: 718 4th St E Northfield MN 55057-2316 Office: Carleton Coll Dept History One N College St Northfield MN 55057 E-mail: cclark@carleton.edu.

CLARK, CLIFTON BOB, physicist; b. nr. Fort Smith, Ark., July 8, 1927; s. Clifton Breckenridge and Coly (Stroud) C.; m. Sue Magruder, Sept. 1, 1950; children— Carol Jane, Charles Brian, Richard Thomas. BA, U. Ark., 1949, MA, 1950; PhD, U. Md., 1957. Asst. prof. sci. Florence State Tchrs. Coll., 1950-51; asst. prof. physics U.S. Naval Acad., 1951-55; asso. prof., 1956-57; physicist U.S. Naval Research Lab., 1955-56; asso. prof. physics So. Meth. U., Dallas, 1957-61, prof., 1961-65, head dept., 1962-65; physicist, head dept. U. N.C., Greensboro, 1965-75, prof., 1965-94, prof. emeritus, 1994—. Vis. prof. physics Fla. State U., 1975-76 Served with USNR, 1945-46. Mem. Am. Assn. Physics Tchrs. (pres. South Atlantic Coast sect. 1974-75, 77-78, pres. N.C. sect. 1996-97), Am. Phys. Soc. (treas. S.E. sect. 1973-91), N.C. Acad. Sci., Phi Beta Kappa, Sigma Xi, Sigma Pi Sigma, Pi Mu Epsilon, Kappa Mu Epsilon, Omicron Delta Kappa. Home: 800 Montrose Dr Greensboro NC 27410-5428 Office: U NC Dept Physics and Astronomy PO Box 26170 Greensboro NC 27402-6170 *I believe people who are happy are those who accept doing things they do not enjoy as the price they pay for getting to do the things they enjoy. The most pleasant of experiences is the completion of a task which demanded extremely hard work. The most unhappy people I have known are those who cheated themselves of this satisfaction, because they tired of hard work and quit before they completed an endeavor.*

CLARK, COLIN WHITCOMB, mathematics educator; b. Vancouver, B.C., Can., June 18, 1931; s. George Savage and Irene (Stewart) C.; m. Janet Arlene Davidson, Sept. 17, 1955; children: Jennifer Kathleen, Karen Elizabeth, Graeme David. BA, U. B.C., 1953; PhD, U. Wash., 1958; DSc (hon.), U. Victoria, 2000. Instr. math. U. Calif., Berkeley, 1958-60; asst. prof. math. U. B.C., 1960-65, assoc. prof., 1965-68, prof., 1968-94, acting dir. Inst. Applied Math., 1983-86, prof. emeritus, 1994—. Vis. prof. math. N.Mex. State U., 1970-71; vis. scientist Fisheries and Oceanography div. C.S.I.R.O., Cronulla, Australia, 1975-76, Ecology and Evolutionary Biology, U. Ariz., 1992; Regents lectr. U. Calif., Davis, 1986; vis. prof. Biol. Scis. Cornell U., 1987; vis. prof. Princeton U., 1997. Author: The Theoretical Side of Calculus, 1972, Mathematical Bioeconomics, 1976, 2d edit., 1990, Elementary Mathematical Analysis, 1982, Bioeconomic Modelling and Fisheries Management, 1985, (with J. Conrad) Resource Economics: Notes and Problems, 1987, (with M. Mangel) Dynamic Modeling in Behavorial Ecology, 1988, (with J. Yoshimura, eds.) Adaption in Stochastic Environments, 1993, (with M. Mangel) Dynamic State Variable Models in Ecology, 2000; contbr. articles to profl. jours. Fellow Royal Soc. Can., Royal Soc. (U.K.); mem. Can. Applied Math. Soc. (pres. 1981-83), Resource Modeling Assn. (pres. 1988-90). Office: Univ BC Dept Math Vancouver BC Canada V6T 1Z2

CLARK, CRAIG BOYD, cardiologist; b. Des Moines, Feb. 18, 1966; m. Jane Ellen Clark. DO, Des Moines U., 1995. Diplomate Am. Bd. Internal Medicine, Am. Bd. Cardiovasc. Disease. Resident in internal medicine U. Iowa, Des Moines, 1995—98; fellow in cardiovasc. diseases U. Iowa Hosps., Iowa City, 1998—2001; assoc. in medicine U. Iowa Coll. Medicine, Iowa City, 2001—02; attending cardiologist Iowa Heart Ctr., P.C., Des Moines, 2002—. Adv. bd. POxMD.com, 1999—2000. Contbr. articles to profl. jours. Fellow: Am. Coll. Cardiology (Bristol-Myers Squibb award 2001); mem.: Am. Coll. Osteo. Internists (govt. rels. com. 2001—), Am. Soc. Echocardiography, Heart Failure Soc. Am. Office: Iowa Heart Ctr 1250 E 9th St Des Moines IA 50316 E-mail: cclark@iowaheart.com.

CLARK, D. SCOTT, surgeon; b. St. Louis, Dec. 20, 1934; MD, Baylor U., 1961. Diplomate Am. Bd. Surgery. Intern Minn. Health Scis. Ctr., 1961-62, resident in surgery, 1962-69; resident in plastic surgery U. Ariz. Hosps., 1970; surgeon No. Inyo Hosp., Bishop, Calif., 1983—. Office: 152 Pioneer Ln Ste G Bishop CA 93514-2563

CLARK, DAVID ALBERT, pediatrician, consultant; b. Johnson City, N.Y., Nov. 20, 1947; s. David Richard Greene and Ruth Marie (Merritt) C.; m. Darlene Elizabeth Wombacher, Aug. 22, 1970; children: Jennifer, Kimberly, Melinda. BA in Biology, SUNY, Binghamton, 1969; MD, SUNY, Syracuse, 1973. Diplomate Am. Bd. Pediatrics. Asst. prof. pediatrics Health Sci. Ctr. SUNY, Syracuse, 1978-84; assoc. prof. pediatrics NY Med. Coll./Westchester County Med. Ctr., Valhalla, N.Y., 1984-88; prof. pediatrics La. State U., New Orleans, 1988-98, vice-chmn. pediatrics, 1990-98; prof., chmn. pediatrics dept. Albany (N.Y.) Med. Coll., 1998—. Mem. neo/peri medicine Am. Bd. Pediatrics, Chapel Hill, N.C., 1996—. Co-author: Infants at Risk, 2d edit., 1993, Atlas of Neonatology, 1999. Asst. scoutmaster Boy Scouts Am., New Orleans, 1996-98. Recipient Stewart Gurman award SUNY, 1976, Seale Harris award So. Med. Assn., 1996; named Physician of Yr. Parent Care Assn., 1993. Fellow Am. Acad. Pediat. (Pediat. Rsch. award 1983), Soc. Pediat. Rsch., Am. Pediat. Soc., Am. Coll. Nutrition, Alpha Omega Alpha; mem. AAP (chair N.Y. dist. II child advocacy com. 1998—). Avocations: viola, vocal ensembles, fishing, philately. Office: Children's Hosp Albany Med Ctr MC88 C614 43 New Scotland Ave Albany NY 12208-3412

CLARK, DAVID EUGENE, surgeon; b. New Orleans, Jan. 21, 1950; s. Frank Eugene and Lucille Sommer C.; m. Susan Mann, June 10, 1972; children: Emily, Sarah, Susannah. AB, Dartmouth Coll., 1971; MD, George Washington U., 1975; MS, U. So. Maine, 1995; MPH, Harvard U., 1995. Surg. intern Dartmouth Affiliated Hosps., 1975-76; resident in surgery Maine Med. Ctr., 1976-80; fellow in traumatology U. Md., 1981-82; attending surgeon Maine Med. Ctr., Portland, 1983—; clin. asst. prof. U. Vt., 1983—. Mem. faculty Harvard Injury Control Rsch. Ctr., 1998—. Contbr. articles to profl. jours. Fellow: ACS (trauma com. 2002—). Democrat. Office: Maine Med Ctr 22 Bramhall St Portland ME 04102-3134

CLARK, DAVID KEITH, lawyer, real estate developer; b. Lakewood, Ohio, July 28, 1952; s. Don Roger and Patricia Ann (Hunt) C.; m. Beth Moore Malone, June 14, 1980; children: Blaire Megan, Shannon Elizabeth. BArch, BSBA, U. Ariz., 1977; JD, U. Houston, 1980. Bar: Tex. 1980, U.S. Dist. Ct. (no., so. and ea. dists.) Tex. 1980, U.S. Ct. Appeals (5th cir.) 1980. Law libr., clk. Baker, Botts, Vinson & Elkins, Houston, 1977-78; assoc. Baker, Brown, et al, Houston, 1980-82; asst. gen. counsel, devel. officer Cadillac Fairview, Dallas, 1982-87; devel. officer Prentiss Properties Urban Devel., Dallas, 1987-90; v.p. Equity Group, Chgo., 1990-92; mng. dir. LaSalle Ptnrs., Chgo., 1992-97, Tishman Speyer Properties, Chgo., 1997—99, M-R Capital LLC, 1999—. Bd. dirs. Don R. Clark M.D., P.C., Roswell, N.Mex., 1972—. Chmn. Dallas Urban Design Task Force, Mich. Ave. dist. task force, 1995; bd. dirs. Chgo. Devel. Coun., 1997—; chmn. Zoning Com., Chgo., 1998. Mem. Tex. Bar Assn. (real estate, probate and trust sects.), Urban Land Inst., Univ. Club Chgo., Leadership Dallas, Phi Delta Phi. Republican. Methodist. Home: 1184 Cedar Ln Northbrook IL 60062-3544 Office: Box 98 Northbrook IL 60065-0098

CLARK, DAVID LEWIS, lawyer; b. Forest Grove, Oreg., Mar. 11, 1946; s. Virgil James and Lovina (Culbertson) C.; divorced; children: Emily Janis, Bradley David. BS in Sociology, U. Oreg., 1968, JD, 1975. Bar: Oreg. 1975, U.S. Dist. Ct. Oreg. 1976. Ptnr. Nicholson & Clark, Florence, 1978-86; sole practice Florence, 1986—. Atty. City of Florence, 1975-81, Port of Siuslaw, Florence, 1975-92. Bd. dirs. Western Ln. County Found., Florence, 1982-89; justice of peace, Florence, 1983-90. Served with USAF, 1968-72. Mem. U. Oreg. Law Sch. Alumni Assn. (bd. dirs. 1982-83). Lodges: Rotary (pres., bd. dirs. 1982-89), Elks (justice 1976—). Roman Catholic. Avocations: family activities, reading. Office: PO Box 146 Florence OR 97439-0005 E-mail: davec616@hotmail.com

CLARK, DAVID RANDOLPH, food distributor; b. Columbia, S.C., Mar. 25, 1943; s. Joseph Wilbur and Josephine (Timberlake) C.; m. Carole Jane Cooper, Aug. 21, 1965; 1 dau., Catherine. BA, Wofford Coll., 1965; MBA, U. S.C., 1966. V.p., gen. mgr. Thomas & Howard Co., Spartanburg, S.C., 1969-77, pres., CEO Columbia, S.C., 1977—. Chmn. T&H Ins. Agcy.; bd. dirs. Timberlake Grocery Co., Macon, Ga., Food Distributors Internat., 1999-2003; Columbia regional adv. bd. SCANA Corp.; sec. Flint Lake, Inc. 1993—; mng. ptnr. Timber Lands Co.; mng. gen. ptnr. Tanglewood Co., L.P., 1995-98; pres. WDM Co., Inc., 1998—. Mem. campaign cabinet United Way, 1975; Eagle Scout, Boy Scouts Am., 1958—, bd. dirs. Indian Waters coun.; trustee S.C. Found. Ind. Colls., S.C. Coll. Coun.; bd. dirs. Columbia YMCA. Lt. U.S. Army, Vietnam. Recipient Disting. Svc. award Wofford Coll., 1999; Paul Harris fellow. Mem. Nat. Am. Wholesale Grocers Assn., So. Food Dealers Assn. (sec.-treas. 1988-90, pres. 1998-2002, v.p. 2002—), S.C. Assn. Convenience Food Stores (bd. dirs.), Wofford Coll. Alumni Assn. (bd. dirs. 1984-87, 89-92, pres. 1990-91, v.p. 1991-92), Sapphire Valley Country Club, Wofford Club Greater Columbia (bd. dirs. 1979—), Forest Lake Club (mng. com. 1998-2001), Flamenco Club, Tarantella Club, Camellia Ball (treas. 1992-95, pres. 1995), Rotary (pres. Columbia 1989-90), Scabbard & Blade, Phi Beta Kappa, Pi Gamma Mu, Pi Kappa Alpha. Episcopalian. Office: Thomas & Howard Co PO Box 23659 Columbia SC 29224-3659

CLARK, DAVID WALTER, electronical engineer, author; b. Peru, Ill., May 27, 1945; s. Elver Vincent and Rena Elsie (Weise) C. B.E.E., Cleve. Inst. Electronics, 1971. 1st class radiotelephone lic. FCC, 1969. Quality control supr. Anixter Comm. Sys., Rock Falls, Ill., 1973-76; field svc. tech. Comm. Engring. Co., Hobbs, N.Mex., 1976-79; sales engr. Energy Instrument Sys., Corpus Christi, Tex., 1979-82; field svc. tech. Comm. Engring. Co., Victoria, Tex., 1982-87; flight simulator installer Simtec, Kingsville, Tex., 1988; comm., navigation, instrument mechanic United Nuclear Corp., Kingsville, 1989-94; prodn. tech. Electrosource, San Marcos, Tex., 1995; maint. engr. Nat. Linens, Austin, Tex., 1996; computer/instrumentation tech. Petron Industries, Alice, Tex., 1997—2001. Pressman Anchorage Daily Times, 1963, Sterling (Ill.) Daily Gazette, 1964-68; electronics analyst Lear Siegler, Grand Rapids, Mich., 1969; comm. tech. Motorola, Schaumburg, Ill., 1969-71; quality control inspector Borg Warner, Dixon, Ill., 1971-73. Mem. Rep. Nat. Com., Alice, 1994-95, Dem. Nat. Com., Alice, 1996; mem. ACLU. Eisenhower Commn. award Rep. Nat. Com., 1995. Avocations: reading, writing, photography, backpacking, body-building.

CLARK, DAVID WILLIAM, lawyer, councilman; b. Manchester, Eng., Jan. 27, 1954; s. Chandler Kinney and May Clark; m. Sally Catherine Clark, June 27, 1987; children: Hilary Alexandra, Gillian Noelle. AB in History, Princeton U., 1975; JD, Duke U., 1978. Bar: Calif. 1978, Colo. 1990, Fla. 1992. Assoc. Thelen, Marrin, Johnson & Bridges, L.A., 1978-84; counsel Ultrasys. Inc. (later Hadson Corp.), Irvine, Calif., 1984-89, Oxbow Corp., West Palm Beach, Fla., 1989—2003, FPL Energy, LLC, Juno Beach, Fla., 2003—. Councilman City of Palm Beach Gardens, Fla., 1993—, mayor, 1994-95; bd. dirs. Palm Beach County chpt. ARC, West Palm Beach, 1998-2001. Mem. State Bar Calif., Colo. Bar Assn., Fla. Bar Assn. Republican. Avocations: reading, history, ships and the sea. Home: 24 Thurston Dr Palm Beach Gardens FL 33418-7097 Office: FPL Energy LLC 700 Universe Blvd Juno Beach FL 33408 E-mail: David_W_Clark@fpl.com.

CLARK, DAVID WRIGHT, lawyer; b. West Point, Miss., May 19, 1948; s. Douglas Earl and Sarah Evelyn (Wright) C.; m. Victoria Baugher, Oct. 16, 1976; children: Alexander, Nicholas, Peter. BA with high honors, Millsaps Coll., 1970; MA, Harvard U., 1971; JD, U. Mich., 1974. Bar: Ill. 1974, Miss. 1978, U.S. Dist. Ct. (no. dist.) Ill. 1974, U.S. Ct. Appeals (7th cir.) 1974, U.S. Dist. Ct. (so. and no. dists.) Miss. 1978, U.S. Ct. Appeals (5th cir.) 1978. Adj. prof. Miss. Coll. Sch. Law, Jackson, 1978-82; assoc. Wildman, Harrold, Allen & Dixon, Chgo., Friedman & Koven, Chgo., 1974-78; shareholder Wise Carter Child & Caraway, P.A., Jackson, 1978-96; ptnr. Lake Tindall, LLP, Jackson, 1996-2001, Bradley Arant Rose & White LLP, Jackson, 2001—. Pres. Miss. Bar Rev., 1979—. Mem. Miss. Constitution Study Commn., Jackson, 1985-87; bd. dirs. Miss. First, Inc., Jackson, 1983-87; pres. U.S.A. Internat. Ballet Competition, Jackson, 1990-98; mem. Leadership Jackson, 1989-90. Mem. ABA (Miss. Bar del. to ho. dels. 1998—, sect. litigation, dir. divsn., com. chmn. and task force chmn. 1987-2000, chmn. gun violence coord. com. 1998-2002), Miss. Bar Assn. (chmn. litigation sect. 1994-95), Am. Law Inst., Charles Clark Am. Inn of Ct. Avocations: musicals, opera. Home: 110 Olympia Fields Jackson MS 39211-2509 Office: Bradley Arant Rose & White LLP One Jackson Pl Ste 450 Jackson MS 39201 E-mail: dclark@bradleyarant.com.

CLARK, DAYLE MERITT, civil engineer; b. Lubbock, Tex., Sept. 5, 1933; s. Frank Meritt and Mamie Jewel (Huff) C.; m. Betty Ann Maples, Apr. 11, 1968; 1 child, Alison. BS, Tex. Tech U., 1955; MS, So. Meth. U., 1967. Registered profl. engr.; registered profl. land surveyor. Field engr. Chgo. Bridge & Iron Co., 1955; mgr. L.K. Long Construction Co., 1958-64; prof. U. Tex. Arlington, 1964-99. Cons. AID, 1966, NSF, 1967-68; expert witness in court cases. Editor Tex. Civil Engr., 1967-71; contbr. articles to profl. jours. Served to capt. USAF, 1955-57. Fellow ASCE (pres. Dallas br. 1987, pres. Tex. sect. 1992-93, Profl. Svcs. award 1991, Award of Honor 1998), Tex. Soc. Profl. Engrs. (achievement award in civil engring. Dallas chpt. 1995), Rotary (pres. Arlington-West 1986, Paul Harris fellow, Rotarian of Yr. 1987). Office: PO Box 185 Arlington TX 76004-0185

CLARK, DEANNA DEE, civic leader and volunteer; b. Cedar Rapids, Iowa, June 1, 1944; d. Cyrus Dean and Isabelle Esther Thomas; m. Glen Edward Clark, July 16, 1966; children: Andrew Curtis, Carissa Jane. AA, Coll. of the Desert, 1964; BA, Coe Coll., 1966. Fund devel. chmn. Nat. Assistance League, 1992—94; resource devel. writer and trainer, 1992—2002; convenor U.S. Internat. Youth Exch. Initiative Cmty. Network, Utah, 1984—94; human svcs. subcom. child advocacy project, social justice and peacemaking min. unit Presbyn. Ch. U.S.A., 1992—93; pres. Provo-Jordan River Pkwy. Found., 1993—95; sustaining mem. Jr. League Salt Lake City, 1976—, Assistance League Salt Lake City, 1986—; bd. dirs. Friends of Libr., U. Utah, 1991—94; moderator, nominating com. Synod of the Rocky Mountains, 1999—2002; numerous civic coms. and found. Utah, 1992—; sec., vice-chmn. City of Holladay Interfaith Coun., 1999—; info practices com. Utah Legislature, 1990; exec. com. of Gen. Assembly Coun., Presbyn. Ch. (U.S.A.), 1993—97; elder Presbyn. Ch., 1983—; mem. coun. Presbytery of Utah, 1985—2001, moderator, 2000—01. Mem. LWV (Utah pres. 1981-83), P.E.O. (historian Utah chpt. 1992-95, chpt. H pres. 1995-97, Utah chmn. Gump & Agers Scholarship Com. 1998-99). Home: PO Box 711098 Salt Lake City UT 84171-1098

CLARK, DICK, former senator, ambassador, foreign affairs specialist; b. Central City, Iowa, Sept. 14, 1928; s. Clarence and Bernice C.; m. Jean Gross, 1954 (div. 1976); children— Thomas Richard, Julie Ann; m. Julie Kennett, 1977. Student, U. Md., Wiesbaden, Germany, 1950-52; BA, Upper Iowa U., Fayette, 1953, LL.D. (hon.), 1973; MA, U. Iowa, Iowa City, 1956; L.H.D. (hon.), Parsons Coll., 1973, Mt. Mercy Coll., Drake U., Cornell Coll., Haverford Coll., St. Ambrose Coll., Loras Coll.; LLD (hon.), Elizabethtown Coll., 1986. Instr. U. Iowa, Iowa City, 1956-59; asst. prof. history Upper Iowa U., 1959-64, pres. faculty; chmn. Office Emergency Planning, Iowa, 1963-64; adminstrv. asst. Congressman John C. Culver, 1965-72; nat. polit. organizer Presdl. campaign staff Robert F. Kennedy, 1968; mem. U.S. Senate from Iowa, 1973-79, chmn. African affairs sub-com. of fgn. relations Com., mem. rules com., fgn. relations com., agr. com., com. on aging, Democratic steering com.; dir. Congl. Program Aspen Inst., Washington, 1980—. Pres. Members of Congress for Peace through Law, 1975-76; ambassador-at-large U.S. Dept. of State in charge of Am. Refugee Program, 1979; dep. campaign mgr. for Presdl. campaign Edward M. Kennedy, 1980. Bd. dirs. Ctr. Responsive Politics. Recipient Congl. Common Cause award, 1978. Fellow Woodrow Wilson Fellowship Found. (sr.); Coun. Fgn. Rels. Democrat. Avocations: tennis, reading, music, theater. Address: Aspen Inst One Dupont Cir NW 7th Fl Washington DC 20036-1511

CLARK, DON EUGENE, music educator; b. Sulphur, Okla., Nov. 12, 1931; s. Dulie Elmos and Louise Clark; m. Wanda Fern Grant, 1954; children: David, Donna(dec.), Paul, Ken, Sharon. MusB, Okla. Bapt. U., 1958; MusM, George Peabody Coll., 1963; D of Musical Arts, U. Okla., 1986. Music tchr. Biggers/Pocahontas Schs., Ark., 1958—60; chmn. music dept. Free Will Bapt. Coll., Nashville, 1960—67; prof. music Okla. Bapt. U., Shawnee, 1967—. Clarinetist, vocalist 680th USAF Band Air R&D command, 1951—53. Major roles in La Boheme, Madame Butterfly, Gianni Schicchi, La Traviata, Rigoletto, Falstaff, The Consul, Amahl and the Night Visitors, The Telephone, L'Enfant Prodique, Elijah, others. Mem.: Okla. Music Adjudicators Assn., Okla. Music Tchrs. Assn., Music Tchrs. Nat. Assn., Nat. Assn. Tchrs. Singing (pres. Nashville chpt. 1962—65, performing artist, regional and nat. convs.). Presbyterian. Home: 1822 N Union Shawnee OK 74804-3753 E-mail: dwclarks@earthlink.net.

CLARK, DONALD H. lawyer; b. Washington, Jan. 29, 1937; BS, U.S. Naval Acad., 1959; JD, George Washington U., 1968. Bar: Va. 1968, U.S. Dist. Ct. (ea. dist.) Va. 1969, U.S. Ct. Appeals (4th cir.) 1974, U.S. Supreme Ct. 1974, U.S. Tax Ct. 1981, U.S. Ct. Fed. Claims 1998, U.S. Ct. Appeals (fed. cir.) 2002. Engr. Naval Elec. Sys., Washington, 1965—68; assoc. Kellam & Kellam, Norfolk, 1968—72; ptnr. Clark & Stant, Virginia Beach, Va., 1972—99; pres., COO Williams, Mullen, Virginia Beach, 1999—. Appointed to Va. State Bar disciplinary bd., 1982-86, med. malpractice rev. panel, 1978-85, 2d dist. ethics com. 1975-77, vice chmn. 1976, chmn. 1977; lecr. continuing legal edn. Co-author: Virginia Construction Law. Vice chmn., chmn. bd. dirs. Sentara Health Care, 1998—; chmn. bd. dirs., mem. exec. com. Tidewater Health Care Inc., 1993-98; chmn. bd. dirs. Virginia Beach Gen. Hosp., 1988-91; chmn. mayor's com. for reapportionment; mem. vestry Eastern Shore Chapel, 1971-74, sr. warden, 1974. Lt. USN, 1959-65. Fellow ACTL; mem. ABA (litigation and law practice mgmt. sects.), Va. State Bar Assn. (litigation and constrn. law sects., bd. govs. constrn. law sect. 1983-86), Virginia Beach Bar Assn. (pres. 1982), Am. Inns of Ct. James Kent Inn (master 1995—). Office: Williams Mullen 222 Central Park Ave Ste 1700 Virginia Beach VA 23462-3035 E-mail: dclark@williamsmullen.com.

CLARK, DONALD MALIN, professional association executive; b. Buffalo, Feb. 11, 1929; s. Jack Merritt Malin and Louise Mary C.; m. Joan Marie Coyle, Dec. 27, 1958; children— Kevin Malin, Michael John, Elizabeth Anne. BS magna cum laude, Canisius Coll., Buffalo, 1950, MA, 1952; Ed.D., SUNY, Buffalo, 1961; grad., U.S. Army Advanced Armor Sch., Ft. Knox, Ky., 1964, U.S. Army Command and Gen. Staff Coll., 1969, U.S. Army War Coll., 1975. Adminstrv. asst. Traveler's Ins. Co., Buffalo, N.Y., 1950-57; mem. faculty Orchard Park (N.Y.) Sr. High Sch., 1957-66; dir. Ctr. Econ. Edn. SUNY, Buffalo, 1966-70; exec. dir. Industry-Edn. Coun., Niagara Falls, N.Y., 1970-79; pres., CEO, Nat. Assn. Industry-Edn. Cooperation, Buffalo, 1979—. Radio and TV pub. info. news commentator, 1962-78; adj. prof. Canisius Coll. Grad. Sch., Buffalo, 1962-63, Lemoyne Coll. Sch. Mgmt., Syracuse, N.Y., 1973-79, Rochester Inst. Tech., 1983-84; adj. prof. Mt. Carmel Coll., Niagra Falls, Ont., Can., 1966; summer faculty Nat. War Coll., Washington, 1967-68; pres. Consumer Credit Counseling Svc., Buffalo, 1973, edn. chmn.; dir. Industry Edn. Coun. Calif., 1992-94; mem. Econ. Forum, Buffalo, 1994-2000; mem. editl. adv. bd. for Business Ethics, 1988-92; selected by People to People Internat.'s Citizen Amb. Program as del. leader for industry and edn. leaders in U.S. to visit Russia, Latvia, 1993, to China, 1995, South Africa, 1996, U.K., 1997, Australia/New Zealand, 1998, China, 1999; cons. (on site) to Ministry of Ed., Koror, Rep. of Palau, Micronesia, 1996; profl. pianist pvt. functions, spl. occasions for agencies and orgns., 1986—. Author: Meeting the Challenge of a Free Society, 1965; writer editls.: Buffalo News and Business First, also newsletters, handbooks, articles, guides for nat. publs.; prodr.: film on industry-edn. cooperation; contbr. articles over 100 articles to nat. and Can. publs. Apptd. by Pres. Reagan to Nat. Adv. Coun. on Ednl. Rsch. and Improvement, 1988-90; bd. dirs. N.Y. State Coun. Econ. Edn., 1980-84, Amherst (N.Y.) Symphony Orch., 1997-98; lectr. St. Michael's Roman Cath. Ch., Buffalo; mem. cmty. adv. coun. SUNY, Buffalo, 1981—; mem. adv. com. ERIc Clearinghouse adult, career, and vocat. edn. Ohio State U., 1982-84; mem. adv. bd. Erie C.C., Williamsville, N.Y., 1995-97. With U.S. ANG, col. USAR, 1948-83; held position of chief of the Western/East European Divsn., Directorate of Fgn. Intelligence, Dept. Army, 1980-83. Recipient Kazanjian Found. Coll. Econs. Tchg. award, 1968, Freedoms Found. medal, 1965, Presdl. Citation for Pvt. Sector Initiatives, 1985, Cert. of Recognition, U.S. Dept. Edn. for contbns. of time and talent toward adult literacy, 1984, Canisius Coll. Disting. Alumni award 1996; fellow NAM, 1965. Mem. Am. Soc. Tng. and Devel., Western N.Y. Export Coun. (assoc.), U.S. Dept. Commerce, Active Corps Execs., U.S. SBA, Ret. Officers Assn., Amherst Dance Club (pres. 1987-88), Phi Delta Kappa (rsch. award 1996). Republican. Roman Catholic. Avocations: piano, writing, ballroom dancing, reading, correspondence. Home: 235 Hendricks Blvd Amherst NY 14226-3304 E-mail: naiec@pcom.net. *Being in the vanguard of change has been the most exciting aspect of my professional career. To participate in effecting change, particularly in education and human resources, economic development requires risk taking and the determination to gain support for one's ideas.*

CLARK, DONALD OTIS, lawyer; b. Charlotte, N.C., May 30, 1934; s. Otis and Ruby Lee (Church) C.; m. Jo Ann Hager, June 15, 1957 (div. 1980); children: Deborah Elise, Stephen Merritt; m. Anja Maria Smith, Nov. 5, 1983. AB, U. S.C., 1956, JD cum laude, 1963; MA, U. Ill., 1957. Bar: S.C. 1963, Ga. 1964, D.C., 1999. Practice law, Atlanta, 1963-83; mem. Candler, Cox, McClain & Andrews, 1968-70, McClain, Mellen, Bowling & Hickman, 1970-75; ptnr. King & Spalding, 1975-78; sr. ptnr. Hurt, Richardson, Garner, Todd & Cadenhead, 1978-83; ptnr. Bishop, Liberman, Cook, Purcell & Reynolds, Washington, 1983-86, Kaplan Russin & Vecchi, Washington, 1986-92, Whitman & Ranson (merged with Breed Abbot & Morgan 1993), Washington, 1992-93; sr. ptnr. Whitman Breed Abbott & Morgan, Washington, 1993-95; ptnr. Keck, Mahin & Cate, Washington, 1995-97, Reed Smith LLP, Washington, 1997—. Mem. dist. export council U.S. Dept Commerce, 1974—; adj. prof. law Emory U., 1970—, U.S.C., 1974; lectr. Ga. State U., 1972; lectr. numerous internat. trade seminars and workshops Author: German govt. study on doing bus. in Southeastern U.S., 1974; editor-in-chief: S.C. Law Rev., 1963; contbr. articles to profl. jours. Served to capt. USAF, 1957-60. Decorated knight Order St. John of Jerusalem, Knights of Malta, knight Order St. Stanislas, knight and minister of justice Order of New Aragon, Sungrye medal Korea; recipient Nat. Leadership medal Air Force Assn., 1956, Coll. award Am. Legion, Outstanding Sr. award U. S.C., 1956, hon. consul Republic of Korea, 1972—. Mem. Atlanta Bar Assn., ABA, S.C. Bar Assn., Ga. Bar Assn., D.C. Bar Assn., Lawyers Club Atlanta, Am. Judicature Soc., Am. Soc. Internat. Law, Atlanta C. of C., Ga. C. of C. (exec. com. Internat. Councils), Inst. Internat. Edn. (chmn. Southeastern regional adv. bd. 1974—, nat. trustee), So. Consortium Internat. Edn. Inc. (dir.), Wig & Robe, Sigma Chi (pres. 1956 Province Balfour award), Omicron Delta Kappa, Kappa Sigma Kappa, Phi Delta Phi (pres. 1963 Province Grad. of Yr. award)

CLARK, DONALD ROBERT, retired insurance company executive; b. Chgo., Jan. 19, 1924; s. Sherman Fred and Frieda (Grossklags) C.; m. Lora Marie Steiner, Aug. 11, 1945; children: Gregory Wayne, Sharon Louise. Student, Northwestern U., 1941-43, U. Wis., 1943-44. With Kemper Nat. Ins. Cos., 1941-89; ret., 1989. Exec. v.p., dir. Am. Mfrs. Mut. Ins. Co., Am. Motorists Ins. Co., Kemper Corp., Lumbermen's Mut Casualty Co.; former v.p., dir. Am. Protection Ins. Co., Economy Fire & Casualty Co., Fed. Kemper Ins. Co., Fed. Kemper Life Assurance Co., Fidelity Life Assn., Kemper Internat. Corp., Kemper Europe Reassurances, Belgium, Kemper S.A., Belgium, Kemper Ins. Co., Australia, Kemper Reins. Co., Long Grove, Ill.; former dir. Kemper Reins. Co. London Ltd., Kemper Fin. Services, Inc., Kemper Fin. Cos., Inc., Kemper Investors Life Ins. Co. Chgo. Contbr. to: Insurance Accounting Fire and Casualty, 2d edit, 1965, Property-Liability Insurance Accounting, 1974. Mem. Ins. Acctg. and Systems Assn. (pres. 1968-69), Fin. Execs. Inst. Lutheran (past chmn. congregation and fin. com.). Home: 689 Glasgow Ln Prospect Heights IL 60070-2588

CLARK, DWIGHT EDWARD, sports team executive, former professional football player; b. Kinston, N.C., Jan. 8, 1957; BA, Clemson U., 1979. Wide receiver San Francisco 49ers, NFL, 1979—87, exec. v.p., dir. football ops., 1995—98, played in Super Bowl, 1981, 1984; v.p., dir of football ops. Cleve. Browns, 1998—. Mem. NFL All-Star Team, 1981, 82. Office: c/o Cleveland Browns 76 Lou Groza Blvd Berea OH 44017-1238

CLARK, DWIGHT WILLIAM, lawyer; b. Gothenburg, Nebr., Sept. 24, 1944; s. William Elwood Clark and Christina Antina Koster; m. Sharon Louise Anderson, Aug. 31, 1968; children: Andrea Christine, Nathan William. BS, U. Nebr., 1967; JD, Calif. Western Law Sch., 1974; MPA, U. So. Calif., 1976. Bar: Calif. 1975; cert. specialist in jud. adminstrn. Adminstrv. intern U.S. Probation Office, L.A., 1975-76; exec. asst. San Francisco Mcpl. Ct., 1976-84, clk.-adminstr., 1984-89; cons. justice systems IBM, 1989-95; chief dep. clk. U.S. Bankruptcy Ct., San Francisco, 1995-98; ct. exec. officer Humboldt County Superior Ct.; moot ct. judge U. San Francisco Sch. Anthropology, 1977; dir. Corp. Bus. Brokers No. Calif., Inc.; user rep. EDP priority com. City and County San Francisco, 1979, electronic info. steering com., 1983-86; assoc. faculty Nat. Judges Coll., Reno, 1985-88; lectr. in law and computer related fields. Mem. adv. bd. Coll. Bus. Adminstrn. U. Nebr., Lincoln, 1966, 67, chmn. placement bd. program, 1967; chmn. honor code revision com. Calif. Western Law Sch., San Diego, 1968, 69; trustee San Mateo Elem. Sch. Dist. (Calif.), 1983-91, San Mateo PTA; mem. adj. faculty Coll. Profl. Studies U. San Francisco, 1992-98. Recipient Am. Jurisprudence Scholastic award, 1969, Tech. Achievement award Fin. Pub. Tech., Inc., Washington, 1984, Hon. Svc. award PTA, 1986. Mem. ABA, Am. Judicature Soc., Calif. State Bar, Calif. Mcpl. Ct. Clks. Assn., San Mateo County Bar Assn., Nat. Assn. Ct. Mgrs., Nat. Conf. Bankruptcy Clerks, Fed. Ct. Clerks Assn., Western Internat. Law Soc. (founding mem.), Calif. Western Law Sch. Alumni Club, U. So. Calif. Alumni Club, Lawyers Club, Phi Delta Phi, Delta Sigma Pi (life), Trial Ct. Budget Commn., Calif. Ct. Exec. Com., Ct. Tech. Adv. Com., Calif. Trial Ct. Adminstrs. Assn., Calif. Ct. Clerks Assn., Humboldt County Bar Assn., Humboldt Law Enforcement Chief Assn. Contbg. author: (book) Handbook of Management Consulting Services, 1995. Democrat. Lutheran. Avocations: woodcrafts, music, reading. Home: 6000 Noe Ave Eureka CA 95503-6386 Office: Superior Ct Humboldt Cty Rm 226 825 5th St Eureka CA 95501-1153

CLARK, EARNEST HUBERT, JR., tool company executive; b. Birmingham, Ala., Sept. 8, 1926; s. Earnest Hubert and Grace May (Smith) C.; m. Patricia Margaret Hamilton, June 22, 1947; children: Stephen D., Kenneth A., Timothy R., Daniel S., Scott H., Rebecca G. BS in Mech. Engring, Calif. Inst. Tech., 1946, MS, 1947. Chmn., chief exec. officer Friendship Group, Baker Hughes, Inc. (formerly Baker Oil Tools, Inc.), L.A., 1947-89, v.p., asst. gen. mgr., 1958-62, pres., chief exec. officer, 1962-69, 75-79, chmn. bd., 1969-75, 79-87, 87-89, ret., 1989; chmn. The Friendship Group, Newport Beach, Calif., 1989—. Bd. dirs. Regenesis Inc. Past chmn., bd. dirs. YMCA of U.S.A.; past chmn. bd. YMCA for Met. L.A.; mem. nat. coun. YMCA; trustee Harvey Mudd Coll. With USNR, 1944-46, 51-52. Mem. AIME, Am. Petroleum Inst., Petroleum Equipment Suppliers Assn. (bd. dirs.), Tau Beta Pi. Office: Friendship Group 3822 Calle Ariana San Clemente CA 92672-4502 E-mail: ehclarkjr@cox.net.

CLARK, EDGAR SANDERFORD, insurance broker, consultant; b. Nov. 17, 1933; s. Edgar Edmund, Jr., and Katharine Lee (Jarman) C.; m. Nancy E. Hill, Sept. 13, 1975; 1 child, Schuyler; children by previous marriages: Colin, Alexandra, Pamela. Student, U. Pa., 1952-54; BS, Georgetown U., 1956; JD, 1958; postgrad., INSEAD, Fountainbleu, France, 1969, Golden Gate Coll., 1973, U. Calif. Berkeley, 1974. Staff asst. U.S. Senate, Washington, 1958-59; underwriter Ocean Marine Dept. Fireman's Fund Ins. Co., San Francisco, 1959-62; mgr. Am. Fgn. Ins. Assn., San Francisco, 1962-66; with Marsh & McLennan, 1966-72; mgr. for. Europe resident dir. Brussels Belgium, 1966-70; asst. v.p., mgr. captive and internat. div., 1970-72; v.p., dir. Risk Planning Group. Inc., San Francisco, 1972-75; v.p., dir. global constrn. group Alexander & Alexander Inc., San Francisco, 1975-94; exec. dir. The Surplus Line Assn. Calif., 1995-97; CEO Capital Risk Solutions Corp., 1997—. Lectr. in field.; guest lectr. U. Calif., Berkeley, 1973, Am. Grad. Sch. Internat. Mgmt., 1981-82, Golden Gate U., annually 1985-91; dir. Soc. Ins. Brokers, 1991-94; del. Calif. Agts. and Brokers Legis. Coun., 1992-95; pres. Ins. Forum of San Francisco. Mem. editl. bd. Risk Mgmt. Reports, 1973-76. With USAF, 1956-58. Mem. Am. Mgmt. Assn., Am. Risk and Ins. Assn., Internat. Insurance Soc., Chartered Ins. Inst., Am. Soc. Internat. Law, Soc. Calif. Pioneers San Francisco, Meadow Club, Fairfax, Calif., World Trade San Francisco. Republican. Episcopalian. E-mail: snarkclark@worldnet.att.net.

CLARK, ELIAS, law educator; b. New Haven, Aug. 19, 1921; BA, Yale U., 1943, LL.B., 1947, MA, 1957. Bar: N.Y. 1948, Conn. 1950. Assoc. Cleary, Gottlieb, Friendly & Cox, N.Y.C., 1947-49; mem. faculty Law Sch., Yale U., New Haven, 1949—, prof., 1958—, Lafayette S. Foster prof., 1968-92, Lafayette S. Foster prof. emeritus, 1992—, Myres S. McDougal professorial lectr. law, 1992—. Master Silliman Coll., 1962-81. Co-author: Gratuitous Transfers, 1996, Cases and Materials on Federal Estate and Gift Taxation, 2000; contbr. articles to legal jours. Bd. dirs. Mental Health Conn., 1957-67; bd. dirs.

New Haven Found., 1969-76. Mem. Conn. Bar Assn. (Disting. Pub. Service 1959) Home: 1179 Whitney Ave Apt B Hamden CT 06517-3434 Office: Yale U Sch Law SLB 336 127 Wall St New Haven CT 06511-6636

CLARK, ELOISE ELIZABETH, biologist, educator; b. Grundy, Va., Jan. 20, 1931; d. J. Francis Emmett and Ava Clayton (Harris) C. BA, Mary Washington Coll., 1951; PhD in Zoology, U. N.C., 1958; DSc, King Coll., 1976; postdoctoral rsch., Washington U., St. Louis, 1957-58, U. Calif. at Berkeley, 1958-59. Rsch. asst., then instr. U. N.C., 1952-55; instr. physiology Marine Biol. Lab., Woods Hole, Mass., 1958-62; from instr. to asst. prof. Columbia U., 1959—65, assoc. prof. biol. sci., 1966-69; with NSF, Washington, 1969-83, head molecular biology, 1971-73, div. dir. biol. and med. scis., 1973-75, dep. asst. dir. biol., behavioral and social scis., 1975-76, asst. dir. biol., behavioral and social scis., 1976-83; v.p. acad. affairs Bowling Green State U., Ohio, 1983—96, prof. biol. sci. to trustee prof. emeritus, 1983—2002, trustee prof. emeritus, 2002—. Contbr. articles to profl. jours. and congl. hearings. Mem. alumnae bd. Mary Washington Coll., U. Va., 1967—70; bd. regents Nat. Libr. of Medicine, 1973—83; mem. policy group competitive grants program U.S. Dept. Agr.; mem. White House Interdepartmental Task Force on Women, 1978—80, Task Force for Conf. on Families, 1980, Com. on Health and Medicine, 1976—80; vice chmn. Com. on Food and Renewable Resources, 1977—80; mem. selective excellence task force Ohio Bd. Regents, 1984—85; mem. Ohio Adv. Coun., Coll. Prep. Edn., 1983—84, Ohio Inter-Univ. Coun. for Provosts, 1983—96, chmn., 1984—85, 1995—96; nat. adv. rsch. resources coun. NIH, 1987—89; mem. informal sci. edn. panel NSF, 1986—88, adv. com., social, behavioral and econ. scis., 1997—2000; program adv. com. sci., tech. and pub. policy Harvard U., 1988—90, mem. editl. bd. Forum, 1997—2001; mem. governing bd. OhioLink, 1990—96, vice chair, 1992, chair, 1993—94. Named Disting. Alumnus Mary Washington Coll., 1975; Wilson scholar, 1956; E.C. Drew scholar, 1956; USPHS postdoctoral fellow, 1957-59; recipient Disting. Service award NSF, 1978 Mem. AAAS (coun. 1969-71, bd. dirs. 1978-82, pres.-elect, 1992, pres., 1993, chmn. bd. 1994), Soc. Gen. Physiology (sec. 1965-67, coun. 1969-71), Biophys. Soc. (coun. 1975-76), Am. Soc. Cell Biology (coun. 1972-75), Am. Inst. Biol. Scientists, Marine biol. Lab. (trustee 1993), NASULGC (higher edn. and tech. com. 1988-93, com. on info. tech. 1994-96), Consortium of Social Sci. Assn. (bd. dirs. 1993-96), Ohio Coun. rsch. and Econ. Devel., Assn. Women in Sci. (bd. dirs. 1998-2001), Phi Beta Kappa (com. on qualifications 1985—, chair 1998—, senate 1996—, exec. com. 1997--), Sigma Xi, Omicron Delta Kappa. Home: 1222 Brownwood Dr Bowling Green OH 43402-3503 Office: Bowling Green State U Dept Biol Scis Bowling Green OH 43403-0001

CLARK, EMORY EUGENE, financial planning executive; b. Opelika, Ala., Jan. 24, 1931; s. Bunk Henry and Dorothy (Bolt) C.; m. Jean F. Reed, Sept. 30, 1951; children: Steven E., Michael E. Grad. pubs. schs. CLU, CFP. With Mgrs. Life Ins. Co., 1956-74, agt. supr., 1956-60, mgr. Hawaii br., 1960-65, mgr. Pitts. br., 1965-68, mgr. Houston br., 1968-74; with Jefferson Std. Life Ins. Co., Fort Worth, 1974-82; fin. planner E.F. Hutton & Co., Inc., 1983-90; v.p. investments A.G. Edwards & Sons, Inc., Ft. Worth, 1990-99, sr. v.p. investments, 1999—. 1st lt. Inf. AUS, 1950-56. Mem. Fort Worth Life Underwriters Assn., Am. Soc. Life Underwriters, Fort Worth Soc. Life Underwriters, Ft. Worth Securities Dealers Assn., Inst. Cert. Fin. Planners (cert., registered practitioner). Home: 8109 Meadowbrook Dr Fort Worth TX 76120-5309 Office: AG Edwards & Sons Inc 420 Throckmorton Ste 1000 Fort Worth TX 76102 E-mail: emory.clark@agedwards.com.

CLARK, ERIC C. state official; b. Smith County, Miss. s. Mr. and Mrs. John S. C.; m. Karan C.; children: Charles, Catherine. BA, Millsaps Coll.; MA, U. Miss.; PhD in History, Miss. State U. Prof. history and govt. Miss. Coll., 1989-95; mgr. family tree farm Smith County; mem. Miss. Ho. of Reps., 1980-96; sec. of state State of Miss., 1996—. Democrat. Baptist. Address: PO Box 136 401 Mississippi St Jackson MS 39205-0136*

CLARK, ESTHER FRANCES, law educator; b. Phila., Aug. 29, 1929; d. John and Lucy (Scapula) Giaccio; m. John H. Clark, Jr., June 12, 1954; 1 child, Jacqueline. BA, Temple U., 1950; JD, Rutgers U., 1955. Bar: Pa. 1956. Pvt. practice law, Chester, 1976; prof. Widener U. Sch. Law, Wilmington, Del., 1976-98. Disting. vis. prof. law Roger Williams U., Bristol, R.I., 1994—. Assoc. editor: Rutgers U. Law Rev, 1954-55. Bd. dirs. Lindsay Law Libr. Fellow Am. Bar Found.; mem. ABA, Pa. Bar Assn., Delaware County Bar Assn. (pres. 1982), Delaware County Legal Assistance Assn. (dir. 1972-77, pres. bd. dirs. 1974-76) Roman Catholic. Home: Bristol, RI. Died Feb. 28, 2002.

CLARK, EUGENIE, zoologist, educator; b. N.Y.C., May 4, 1922; m. Hideo Umaki, 1942; m. Ilias Konstantinou, 1949; 4 children; m. Chandler Brossard, 1966; m. Igor Klatzo, 1969; m. Henry Yoshinobu Kon, 1997. BA, Hunter Coll., 1942; MA, NYU, 1946, PhD (Pacific Sci. Bd. fellow 1949), 1950; DSc (hon.), U. Mass., Dartmouth, 1990, U. Guelph, 1995, U. South Hampton, 1995. Rsch. asst. in ichthyology Scripps Instn. Oceanography, 1946-47; with N.Y. Zool. Soc., 1947-48; research asst. in animal behavior Am. Museum Nat. History, N.Y.C., 1948-49, research assoc., 1950-80; instr. Hunter Coll., 1954; exec. dir. Cape Haze Marine Lab., Sarasota, Fla., 1955-67; asso. prof. biology City U. N.Y., 1966-67; asso. prof. zoology U. Md., 1968-73, prof. zoology, 1973-92, prof. emerita, sr. rsch. scientist, 1992—. Vis. prof. Hebrew U., 1972; sr. rsch. scientist, dir. emerita Mote Marine Lab., Sarasota, Fla., 1999—. Author: Lady with a Spear, 1953, The Lady and the Sharks, 1969, Desert Beneath the Sea, 1991; subject of biographies Shark Lady (Ann McGovern), 1978, Adventures of the Shark Lady (Ann McGovern), 1998, Eugenie Clark, Adventures of a Shark Scientist (Ellen R. Butts, Joyce R. Schwartz), 2000, Fish Watching with Eugenie Clark (Michael E. Ross), 2000. Recipient Myrtle Wreath award in sci. Hadassah, 1964, Nogi award in art Underwater Soc. Am., 1965, Dugan award in aquatic sci. Am. Littoral Soc., 1969, Diver of Yr. award Boston Sea Rovers, 1978, David Stone medal, 1984, Stoneman Conservation award, 1982, Gov. of S. Sinai medal, 1985, Lowell Thomas award Explorers Club, 1986, Wildscreen Internat. Film Festival award, 1986, medal Gov. Red Sea, Egypt, 1988, Nogi award in Sci., 1988, Women's Hall of Fame award State of Md., 1989, Women Educators award, 1990, Alumnae award, Franklin Burr award Nat. Geographic Soc., 1993; named to Hunter Coll. Hall of Fame, 1990, DEMA Hall of Fame, 1993; Fellow AEC, 1950; Saxton Fellow, 1952; Breadloaf Writer's fellow, Fulbright scholar Egypt, 1951 . Fellow: AAAS; mem.: Am. Elasmobranch Soc. (disting. fellow 1999), Am. Littoral Soc. (v.p. 1970—89), Nat. Pks. and Conservation Assn. (vice chmn. 1976), Internat. Soc. Profl. Diving Scientists, Soc. Woman Geographers (Gold medal 1975, U. Md. Pres.'s medal 1993), Israeli Zool. Soc. (hon.), Am. Soc. Ichthyology and Herpetology (life). Achievements include special research in ecology and behavior of tropical sand fishes, morphology and taxonomy marine fishes, isolating mechanisms poecillid fishes and behavior deep sea sharks. Office: Mote Marine Lab 1600 Ken Thompson Pkwy Sarasota FL 34236 E-mail: yoppe@mote.org.

CLARK, FAYE LOUISE, drama and speech educator; b. La., Oct. 9, 1936; m. Warren James Clark, Aug. 8, 1969; children: Roy, Kay Natalie. Student, Centenary Coll., 1954-55; BA with honors, U. Southwestern La., 1962; MA, U. Ga., 1966; PhD, Ga. State U., 1992. Tchr. Nova Exptl. Schs., Ft. Lauderdale, Fla., 1963-65; faculty dept. drama and speech Ga. Perimeter Coll. (formerly DeKalb Coll.), Atlanta, 1967—; chmn. dept., 1977-81. Pres. Hawthorne Sch. PTA, 1983-84. Mem.: Ga. Comm. Assn., Ga. Psychol. Assn., Ga. Theatre Conf. (sec. 1968—69, rep. to Southeastern Theatre Conf. 1969), Nat. Comm. Assn., Atlanta Hist. Soc., Oglethorpe Mus., Thalian-Blackfriars, Atlanta Artists Club (sec. 1981—83, dir. 1983—89), Atlanta Press Club, Friends of Atlanta Opera, Kappa Delta Pi, Sigma Delta Pi, Pi Kappa Delta, Phi Kappa Phi. Home: 2521 Melinda Dr NE Atlanta GA 30345-1918 Office: Ga Perimeter Coll Humanities Dept Dunwoody Campus Dunwoody GA 30338

CLARK, FRED, legal writer, editor; b. Limón, Costa Rica, Dec. 12, 1930; came to U.S., 1968; s. Thomas and Irene (Penney) C.; m. Dorothy Hyacinth James, Aug. 4, 1956; children: Paul, Fred Jr., Lydia Ramona. Student, Ctrl. Am. Acad., 1944-49; BLitt, U. Costa Rica, 1951; postgrad., Stafford Coll., 1956-57; barrister-at-law, Inner Temple, London, 1960. Bar: Eng. 1960, Jamaica 1960; cert. in law Coun. Legal Edn. Master of langs. Merl Grove Sch., 1951-55; trust officer Govt. of Jamaica, 1960-61; pvt. law practice Kingston, Jamaica, 1961-67; legal editor Corp. Trust Co., N.Y.C., 1968-69; sr. legal editor Prentice-Hall, Inc., Englewood Cliffs, N.J., 1969-91. Cons. commonwealth law. Editor The Corp. Jour., 1968-69. Trustee United Ch. of Christ, 1970-78; spl. advisor U.S. Congl. Adv. Bd.; nat. adv. bd. Am. Security Coun. Recipient Disting. Leadership award, 1984, Presdl. medal of merit, 1986. Mem. Am. Mgmt. Assn., Internat. Platform Assn., Internat. Commn. Jurists, Am. Mus. Natural History, Nat. Geog. Soc., N.Y. Acad. Scis., Am. Ballet Theater, Met. Opera Guild, U.S. Naval Inst., Freeport Bus. Promotion (bd. dirs.), U.S. Power Squadron (asst. sec.), Inter-Am. Soc., Rosicrucians. Home: PO Box 291 Bergenfield NJ 07621-0291

CLARK, GARY CARL, lawyer; b. Flippin, Ark., Mar. 4, 1947; m. Jane W. Clark; children: Ross, Lauren. BS in Agrl. Edn., Okla. State U., 1969, MS, 1972; JD with honors, U. Tex., 1975. Bar: Okla. 1975, U.S. Dist. Ct. (no. dist.) Okla. 1975, U.S. Ct. Appeals (10th cir.) 1979. Tchr. Laverne H.S., Okla., 1969—70; assoc. Conner, Winters, Ballaine, Barry & McGowen, 1975—81, ptnr., 1981, Baker & Hoster, Tulsa, 1981—97; dir. Crowe & Dunlevy, PC, Tulsa, 1997—. Lawyer-staffed Panel of Ct. Appeals, 1991; speaker in field. Vol. Legal Svcs. Ea. Okla., 1993—; trustee Okla. State Univ., Tulsa, 1999-2001; mem. bd. regents Okla. State Univ. and A&M Colls., 1993-2001, chmn., 1997-98; past v.p. Jane Addams Elem. Sch. PTA, sch. vol.; chair site adv.; mem. Okla. Jud. Evaluation Com., 1999—. Recipient Silver Beaver award Boy Scouts Am., 1996. Fellow Am. Coll. Trust and Estate Coun., Am. Bar Found., Okla. Bar Found. (trustee); mem. Okla. Bar Assn. (pres. 2002, bd. govs. 1997-99, 2001-2003, John Shipp Ethics award 1999, chair estate planning and probate sect. 1988-89, vice chair probate code com. 1991, bd. dirs. young lawyers divsn., mem. real property sect.), Tulsa County Bar Assn. (pres. 1993-94, Golden Rule award 1993, Outstanding Sr. Lawyer 1996), Tulsa County Bar Found. (pres. 1994-95, treas. 1995-99, charter fellow), Tulsa Title and Probate Lawyers Assn. (pres. 1989-90), Okla. State U. Alumni Assn. (life), FFA Alumni Assn. (life), Order of Coif, Alpha Gamma Rho Alumni Assn. (Okla. chpt. dir., past pres.), Phi Delta Phi. Home: 5505 S 97th West Ave Sand Springs OK 74063-4726 Office: Crowe & Dunlevy 500 Kennedy Bldg Tulsa OK 74103 E-mail: clarkg@crowedunlevy.com.

CLARK, GARY R. newspaper editor; b. Cleve., June 27, 1946; s. Dale Francis and Mary Louise (Rozeski) C.; m. Caryn Elaine Helm, Dec. 18, 1976; children: Jessica Lynn, Brian Michael. BA, Ohio State U., 1973, MA, 1978. Reporter Chronicle-Telegram, Elyria, Ohio, 1973-77, The Plain Dealer, Cleve., 1978-88, state editor, 1988-89, nat. editor, 1989, city editor, 1989-90, mng. editor, 1990—. Tchg. assoc. Ohio State U., Columbus, 1977-78. Sgt. USMC, 1966-69, Vietnam. Mem. AP Mng. Editors, Am. Soc. Newspaper Editors, Investigative Reporters and Editors, Cleve. City Club. Office: The Plain Dealer 1801 Superior Ave E Cleveland OH 44114-2198

CLARK, GARY RAY, licensing board executive; b. Keokuk, Iowa, Jan. 18, 1944; s. G. Raymond and M. Lucille (Logsdon) C.; m. Marla S. Clark; children: Mary Ellen Shimmens, Kelley Barnard. BS, Quincy U., 1967. Pharmaceutical detail man Merck & Co., Jefferson City, Mo., 1968-71, Hoffmann La Roche, Jefferson City, 1971-75; lic. bd. adminstr. Mo. Bd. Healing Arts, Jefferson City, Mo., 1975-90; exec. dir. Okla. Bd. Osteo. Med. Examiners, Okla. City, 1990—. Cons. Nat. Bd. Osteo. Medicine, Des Plaines, Ill. Mem. Coun. Licensure Enforcement and Regulation (past pres.), Adminstrs. in Medicine (pres. 1996), Willow Creek Country Club (Okla. City, bd. dirs.). Avocations: golf, writing, cooking. Office: Okla Bd Osteopatic Exam 4848 N Lincoln Blvd Ste 100 Oklahoma City OK 73105-3321

CLARK, GEOFFREY, accountant; b. Blackpool, Eng., Feb. 2, 1946; came to U.S., 1946; s. Ernest and Lucy (Moss) C. AA, San Jacinto Coll., 1966; BBA, U. Houston, 1969. CPA, Tex. Pvt. practice acctg., Houston, 1970-74, 76-78, 80-82; acct. Weison & Kennedy, Houston, 1974-76, Alan D. Buck, Houston, 1978-80; assoc. Oscar Nipper & Co., Houston, 1982—, ind. assoc., 1991. Judge Precinct 191, Pasadena, Tex., 1983-95. Mem.: AICPA (Houston chpt.), The Forum, Clear Lake Area Tax Forum, Tex. Soc. CPA's, Plays and Players Club (Houston) (acting chmn. 1983—87, pres. 1992), Woodmen of World (Am. Hist. award 1960), Rotary (treas. Gulfway-Hobby Airport chpt. 1987—88, Paul Harris fellow 2000), Masons (32 degree), Shriners, U. Houston Alumni Assn. Avocations: reading, golf, archery, acting, fitness. Home: 421 Brown Dr Pasadena TX 77506-3109 Office: Oscar Nipper & Co 7654 Park Place Blvd Houston TX 77087-4526

CLARK, GEORGE WHIPPLE, physics educator; b. Evanston, Ill., Aug. 31, 1928; s. Robert Keep and Margaret (Whipple) C.; m. Elizabeth Kister, Dec. 1956 (div. 1972); children: Katherine, Jaqueline; m. Charlotte Huston Reischer, Jan. 1988. BA, Harvard U., 1949; PhD, MIT, 1952. Instr. MIT, Cambridge, 1952-54, asst. prof., 1954-60, assoc. prof., 1960-65, prof., 1965-98, Breene M. Kerr prof. physics, 1984-95, prof. emeritus, 1996—. Cons., dir. Am. Sci. and Engring., Inc., Cambridge, 1958-69; dir. Assn. Univs. for Rsch. in Astronomy, Washington, 1982-90. Contbr. numerous articles to profl. jours. Fellow Am. Phys. Soc., Am. Astronomy Soc.; mem. NAS, Am. Acad. Arts and Scis. Office: MIT 37-611 77 Massachusetts Ave Cambridge MA 02139-4301 E-mail: gwc@space.mit.edu.

CLARK, GLEN EDWARD, judge; b. Cedar Rapids, Iowa, Nov. 23, 1943; s. Robert M. and Georgia L. (Welch) C.; m. Deanna D. Thomas, July 16, 1966; children: Andrew Curtis, Carissa Jane. BA, U. Iowa, 1966; JD, U. Utah, 1971. Bar: Utah 1971, U.S. Dist. Ct. Utah 1971, U.S. Ct. Appeals (10th cir.) 1972. Assoc. Fabian & Clendenin, 1971-74, ptnr., 1975-81, dir., chmn. banking and comml. law sect., 1981-82; judge U.S. Bankruptcy Ct. Dist. Utah, Salt Lake City, 1982-86, chief judge, 1986—. Bd. govs. nat. Conf. Bankruptcy Judges, 1988-94; mem. com. on bankruptcy edn. Fed. Jud. Ctr., 1989-92; vis. prof. U. Utah, Salt Lake City, 1977-79, 83; pres. Nat. Conf. Bankruptcy Judges, 1992-93; chair bd. trustees Nat. Conf. Bankruptcy Judges Endowment for Edn., 1990-92; vis. assoc. prof. law Univ. Utah; instr. adv. bus. law Univ. Utah. Articles editor: Utah Law Review. With U.S. Army, 1966-68. Finkbine fellow U. Iowa. Fellow Am. Coll. Bankruptcy (charter, mem. bd. regents 1995-2000, dir. found. 2002—); mem. Jud. Conf. U.S. (mem. com. jud. br. 1992-99, 10th cir. bankruptcy appellate panel 1996—), Utah Bar Assn., Order of Coif. Presbyterian. Office: 365 US Courthouse 350 S Main St Salt Lake City UT 84101-2106

CLARK, GORDON HOSTETTER, JR., physician; b. New Haven, Aug. 5, 1947; s. Gordon Hostetter and Elizabeth Master (Mapes) C.; m. Gail Marie Theroux, July 23, 1988; children: Emily Blakeslee Clark Ehl, Christopher Robert, Heather Mays Richmond, Adam Arthur. BA, Yale U., 1970; MDiv, Pacific Sch. Religion, 1973; MD, George Washington U., 1977. Diplomate Am. Bd. Psychiatry and Neurology, Am. Bd. Med. Mgmt., Am. Coll. Physician Execs.; cert. in adminstrv. psychiatry, APA, 1992; cert. physician exec. Commn. in Med. Mgmt., 1998. Intern, then resident, then fellow Dartmouth-Hitchcock Med. Ctr., Hanover, N.H., 1977-81; staff psychiatrist Lakes Region Med. Health Ctr., Laconia, N.H., 1981-82, med. dir., 1982-86; dir. psychiat. unit Lakes Region Gen. Hosp., Laconia, 1986-89; med. dir. behavioral svcs. St. Vincent Health Ctr., Erie, Pa., 1990-93; dir. med./profl. adminstrn. Deerfield Mgmt. Group, Erie, Pa., 1991-94; pres. Deerfield Profl. Assocs., 1992-94; med. advisor Deerfield Behavioral Health Network, 1994-95; sr. psychiat. cons. Med. Groups Divsn. Maine Harvard Cmty. Health Plan, Portland, Maine, 1995-96; pres., med. dir. Integrated Behavioral Healthcare, Portland, Maine, 1995—; med. dir. Behavioral Health Network of Maine, 1995-99, Augusta (Maine) Mental Health Inst., 1995-96; assoc. med. dir. Maine Dept. Mental Health and Mental Retardation, Augusta, 1995-96; med. dir. med.-psychiat. program Westbrook (Maine) Comty. Hosp., 1996-97; sr. physician advisor CMG Healthsource Maine, Maine, 1996-97. Adj. asst. prof. clin. psychiatry Dartmouth Med. Sch., Hanover, 1983-90; clin. asst. prof. psychiatry U. Pitts. Sch. Medicine, 1990-96; clin. assoc. prof. psychiatry U. Vt. Med. Sch., 1996—; chmn. com. psychiatrists in N.H. Comty. Mental Health Ctrs., Concord, 1982-86; med. liaison to Pa. Office of Mental Health and Mental Retardation and Erie County Office Mental Health and Mental Retardation, 1991-94; bd. dirs. Med. Network, Inc. 1999—, mem. credentials com. 1995-98, mem. med. mgmt. com. 2002—, med. dir. depression mgmt. program, 2002—; mem. New Eng. region adv. com. Cigna Behavioral Health Care, 2000-2001; mem. New Eng. region pharmacy and therapeutics com. Cigna Health Care, 2000, mem. nat. pharmacy and therapeutics com., 2001; mem. depression work group MaineHealth, 2002—. Exec. v.p. Erie Phiharm., 1991-92. Recipient Exemplary Psychiatrist award Nat. Alliance for Mentally Ill, 1992; recipient Benjamin Manchester award George Washington U., 1977. Fellow: Am. Coll. Physician Execs., Am. Assn. Social Psychiatry (mem. coun. 1993—99), Am. Coll. Mental Health Adminstrn., Am. Psychiat. Assn. (disting., task force psychiat. practice in cmty. menatl health ctrs. devel., com. state and cmty. psychiatry sys., com. chronically mentally ill, examiner oral part of exams. cert. adminstrn. psychiatry 1993—96, com. on stds. and survey procedures 1998—2001, APA/Bristol-Myers Squibb fellowship selection com. 1999—2002, Falk fellow 1979—81); mem.: Maine Psychiat. Assn. (chiar program com. 1996—97), We. Pa. Psychiat. Soc. (pres. elect 1992—94), Psychiat. Physicians Pa. (coun., govt. rels. com., fed. legis. rep. pbu. psychiatry com. 1993—94, treas. 1994), Nat. Psychiatric Alliance (chmn. med. staff com. 1992—94, exec. com. 1992—95), Am. Coll. Psychiatrists, Am. Assn. Psychiat. Adminstrs. (coun. 1996—97, pres.-elect 1997—99, pres. 1999—2001, immediate past pres. 2001—), Am. Assn. Cmty. Psychiatrists (com. psychiat. practice in cmty. mental health ctrs. guideline devel., founding pres. 1984—90, bd. dirs. 1984—92, Disting. Svc. award 1990). Avocations: skiing, tennis, biking, hiking, camping. Home: 10 Park St Yarmouth ME 04096-7757 Office: Integrated Behavioral Healthcare 1 Forest Ave Portland ME 04101-2810 E-mail: gordon.clark@integratedbehavioralhealthcare.com.

CLARK, GRANT LAWRENCE, corporate lawyer; b. Syracuse, NY, Apr. 15, 1954; s. Robert William and Linda (Grant) C.; m. Diana Christine Baker, Aug. 5, 1983. BA, Framingham State Coll., 1979; JD, Suffolk U., 1983. Bar: Mass. 1983, Calif. 1992, U.S. Dist. Ct. Mass. 1983, U.S. Dist. Ct. (so. dist.) Calif. 1992, U.S. Ct. Appeals (D.C. cir.) 1995, U.S. Ct. Claims 1995, U.S. Ct. Mil. Appeals 1984. Judge advocate USAF, Washington, 1983-87; asst. gen. counsel GSA, Washington, 1987-88; assoc. Rivkin, Radler, Dunne & Bayh, Washington, 1988 91; assoc./ptnr. McKenna & Cuneo, Washington, 1991-94; asst. gen. counsel Sci. Applications Internat. Corp., San Diego, 1994-99; sr. v.p., gen. counsel Telcordia Tech., Inc., Morristown, NJ, 1999—. Instr. Fed. Publ., Inc., Washington, 1991—99. Capt., USAF, 1983-87. Mem.: ABA. Avocations: mountain biking, latin dance, medieval history. Home: 229 Mount Kemble Ave Morristown NJ 07960-6209 Office: Telcordia Tech Inc 445 South St Morristown NJ 07960-6454 E-mail: gclark@telcordia.com.

CLARK, H. WESTLEY, health facility administrator; BA, Wayne State U.; MD, MPH, U. Mich.; JD, Harvard U. Diplomate Am. Bd. Psychiatry and Neurology. Past chief assoc. substance abuse programs VA Med. Ctr., San Francisco; dir. Ctr. Substance Abuse Treatment, Rockville, Md., 1998—. Sr. program cons. Robert Wood Johnson Substance Abuse Policy Program; assoc. clin. prof. psychiatry U. Calif., San Francisco; adv. bd. Treatment-on-Demand Planning Coun., San Francisco. Contbr. articles to profl. jours., chpts. to books. Grantee Nat. Inst. Drug Abuse. Mem. Am. Soc. Addiction Medicine (cert., nat. bd. dirs.). Office: Ctr Substance Abuse Treatment 5600 Fishers Ln Rockwall II Ste 618 Rockville MD 20857-0001

CLARK, HARRY WARREN, public policy consultant; b. South Bend, Ind., Mar. 9, 1949; s. Harry Warren Jr. and Jacquelyn Milgram Clark; m. Katherine Knight, Apr. 30, 1987; children: Abigail, Taylor, Caitlin. Student, George Washington U., 1974-75; BS, Cornell U., 1992. Exec. asst. U.S. Congressman Jack N.Y., Washington, 1972-75; mng. dir. Young & Rubicam, N.Y.C., 1977-80; pres., prodr. One Eleven Com., N.Y.C., 1980-83; sr. v.p., sr. cons. Burson Marsteller, N.Y.C., 1983-85; sr. v.p., group dir. Bozell Inc., N.Y.C., 1985-87; pres., mng. ptnr. Clark & Weinstock Inc., N.Y.C., 1987—2000; counselor U.S. Trade Rep., Office of Pres., 2002—. Prodr. TV documentaries: Countdown to the White House: The Reagan Transition, 1981, Admiral William Crowe's the Future of Military Power, 1989. Trustee Greenwich (Conn.) Acad., 1987—93, Greenwich Pub. Lib., 1997—2001; trustee, mem. exec. com. U.S. Ski and Snowboard Team, Park City, Utah, 1994—2001. Republican. Avocations: skiing, tennis, squash. Office: Stanwich Group LLC 30 E Elm St Greenwich CT 06830 Office Fax: 203-861-6671. Business E-Mail: harry@stanwichgroupllc.com. E-mail: harrywclark@hotmail.com.

CLARK, HEATHER, speech pathology/audiology services professional, educator; PhD, U. of Iowa, 1996. Cert. clin. competence Am. Speech-Lang.-Hearing Assn. Assoc. prof. Appalachian State U., Boone, NC, 1996—. Office: Appalachian State U Dept of Lang Readingg Boone NC 28608

CLARK, HOWARD LONGSTRETH, JR., finance company executive, director; b. N.Y.C., Feb. 1, 1944; s. Howard Longstreth and Elsie (Dancaster) C.; m. Karen K. Burke, July 25, 1992; 1 child by previous marriage, Howard Longstreth III. BSBA, Boston U., 1967; MBA, Columbia U., 1968. Exec. v.p., chief fin. officer Am. Express Co., N.Y.C., 1981-90; vice chmn. Lehman Bros., Inc. Bd. dirs. The Maytag Co., White Mountains Ins. Group, Ltd., Walter Industries, Inc. Mem.: River, Racquet and Tennis, Round Hill, Blind Brook, Links, Seminole, Jupiter Island, Nantucket Golf. Episcopalian. Home: 404 Round Hill Rd Greenwich CT 06831-2637 Office: Lehman Bros Inc 745 7th Ave Fl 20 New York NY 10019 E-mail: hclark@lehman.com.

CLARK, I. E. publisher; b. Schulenburg, Tex., Dec. 9, 1919; s. Harvey Robert and Annie Ruby (Miekow) C.; m. Lila Rhea Norwood, Sept. 1, 1945; children: Candace Ann, Robin Rhea. BA, U. Tex., Austin, 1941, MA, 1945. Rancher, 1945-95; tchr., theatre dir., publs. dir., lang. arts coord. Schulenburg Pub. Schs., 1945-77; founder, owner I.E. Clark, Publs. pub. plays and books for theatre, 1959—. Tchr. Newspaper Fund seminars U. Tex. at Austin, summers, 1961-66; regional observer for Nat. Observer, 1961; mem. Tex. Edn. Agy. Commn. for Lang. Arts Curriculum Revision, 1958-59, State Com. Devel. of Speech-Drama Publ. of Tex. Edn. Agy., 1960-61. Author: (plays) Twelve Dancing Princesses, 1969, Hansel and Gretel, 1970, It's A Dungaree World, 1974, Once Upon a Texas, 1985; also several one-act plays including The Christmas Dream, transl. into Spanish, produced TV, Ecuador, 1973; (Tex. Sesquicentennial pageant) Fate of Fayette, 1986. Mem. Fayette County Hist. Survey Com., 1969—; founder, artistic dir., bd. dirs., officer Backstage, Inc., Fine Arts Coun. for South Cen. Tex., 1969—; adv. dir. 1st Nat. Bank of Schulenberg, 1974-80; Democratic precinct chmn. Fayette County Dem. Exec. Com., 1955-80; county campaign chmn. Lyndon B. Johnson, 1949, 55; area campaign chmn. Tex. Lt. Gov. Bill Hobby, 1972; bd. dirs. Schulenberg Hist. Soc. Recipient Finest Journalism Tchr. in Tex. award U. Tex. Interscholastic League, 1967, Outstanding Citizen award Colorado Valley Coun. on Drug and Alcohol Abuse, 1990; Order Golden Quill, 1977; named Hon. State Farmer, Future Farmers Am., 1956; Newspaper Fund fellow, 1959. Mem. Am. Theatre Assn. (nat. chmn. play publishers panel 1977, editor Secondary Sch. Theatre Jour. 1982-83), S.W. Theatre Assn. (hon., life), Dramatists Guild, Am. Alliance for Theatre and Edn., Tex. Secondary Theatre Conf. (dir., Newsletter editor 1966-69, mem. Interscholastic League adv. com.), Tex. Edn. Theatre Assn. (Founders award 1985), Modern Music Masters (hon. life), Masons, Phi Beta Kappa, Delta Tau Delta, Sigma Delta Chi, Phi Eta Sigma. Methodist. Home and Office: PO Box 246 Schulenburg TX 78956-0246

CLARK, IRA C. hospital association administrator, educator; BA Gen. Sci., U. Iowa, 1959, MA honors Health and Hosp. Adminstrn., 1966; grad. Bus. Adminstrn., Rider Coll., 1963. Adminstrv. asst. divsn. Hosps. Iowa State Dept. Health, Des Moines, 1964; spl. asst. dir. planning and devel. Montefiore Hosp. and Med. Ctr., Bronx, N.Y., 1970, asst. dir., 1965-70; assoc. dir. Jersey City Med. Ctr., 1970-71, exec. dir., 1971-75; CEO Woodhull Hosp. and Mental Health Ctr., 1982-84; exec. dir. Bellevue Hosp. Ctr., 1984-85; CEO, regional adminstr. Kings County Hosp. Ctr., Bklyn., 1976-87; pres. & ceo Pub. Health Trust Jackson Meml. Hosp., 1987—. Bd. dirs. Fla. Hosp. Assn., So. Fla. Hosp. Assn.; panelist Robert Wood Johnson Found. Symposium, Princeton, N.J., 1986; chmn. Coun. Exec. dirs. N.Y.C. Health and Hosps. Corp., 1978-82; chmn. com. strategic planning Coun. Exec. dirs. Counterpart com. bd. dirs.; spl. adv. panel Emergency Svcs. Act, Advanced Para-medic Tng. N.J.; adj. faculty, lectr. various Univs.; spkr. in field. Author: The History and Development of Continuing Physical Education, 1966. Recipient Disting. Svc. award Commr. Mental Health, N.Y., 1981. Mem. Am. Hosp. Assn. (house dels., charter mem. pub. gen. hosps. sect., com. nominations bd. trustees pub.-gen. hosp. sect.), Assn. Am. Med. Colls. (gen. assembly coun. teaching hosps.), N.J. Hosp. Assn. (vice chmn., chmn. coun. govt. ops. of bd. trustees, spl. com. polit. strategy). Office: Jackson Meml Hosp 1611 NW 12th Ave Miami FL 33136-1096

CLARK, JACK, retired hospital company executive, accountant; b. Munford, Ala., Feb. 23, 1932; s. Raymond E. and Ora (Camp) C.; m. Louise Omega Lackey, Jan. 30, 1951; 1 son, Terry Wayne. BS, Springhill Coll., Mobile, Ala., 1960. Staff acct. Max E. Miller, C.P.A., Mobile, 1960-62; comptr. Mobile Gen. Hosp., 1962-67; assoc. adminstr. fin. Univ. Med. Ctr., Mobile, 1967-74; regional mgr. Humana Inc., Mobile, 1974-75, v.p., 1975-80, sr. v.p., 1980-84, exec. v.p., 1984-93, Galen Health Care, Mobile, 1993-94; ret. Columbia-HCA Healthcare,

1994. Trustee Mid-South region Humana hosps., 1974-87, Southwestern region, 1987-89, region IV, 1989-91, region 2, 1991-93, Regional Hosps., Columbia/HCA, 1994—. Bd. dirs. Agape S. Ala., Mobile, 1983, Rainbow Omega, 2000—; trustee Faulkner U., Montgomery, Ala., 1993—. Served in USAF, 1952-56, Korea. Mem. Hosp. Fin. Mgmt. Assn. (assoc.), Am. Hosp. Assn., Ala. Hosp. Assn., Ala. Hosp. Assn. Accts. (pres. so. council, dir. 1967-68), Mobile C. of C. Democrat. Mem. Ch. of Christ. Home: 6449 Canebrake Rd Mobile AL 36695-3817

CLARK, JACK IVOR, civil engineer, researcher; BSc, Acadia U., 1955; B Engring., Tech. U. N.S., Can., 1957, DEng (hon.), 1970; MSc, U. Alta., Can., 1961; DSc (hon.), Laurentian U., 1998. With major civil engring. projects, 1957—; dir. Ctr. for Cold Ocean Resources Engring. Meml. U. Nfld., St. John's, Can, 1984-91, 1st pres., CEO, Ctr. for Cold Ocean Resources Engring., 1991-97, prin. cons. Ctr. for Cold Odean Resources Engring., 1997—. Past editor Can. Geotech. Jour. Decorated officer Order of Can.; recipient R.M. Hardy keynote address, 1996, Roger J.E. Brown award, 1996, Queen's Golden Jubilee Anniversary medal, 2002; Karl Terzaghi fellow Norwegian Tech. Inst., 1997, MMS Corp. Leadership award Minerals Mgmt. Svc., USDA, 1999, 25th Anniversary Achievement award Nfld. Ocean Industries Assn., 2002. Fellow Engring. Inst. Can. (Julian C. Smith medal 1987), Can. Soc. Civil Engrs.; mem. Can. Acad. Engring., Nat. Scis. and Engring. Coun. (v.p., exec. com. for coun. 1988-94), Can. Geotech. Rsch. Bd. (chmn. 1991-94), Founds. for Offshore Structures (chmn. Can. Stds. Assn. Com. S472), Can. Geotech. Soc. (G. Geoffrey Meyerhof award 1995). Office: C-CORE Saint John's NF Canada A1B 3X5 E-mail: Jack.Clark@c-core.ca.

CLARK, JAMES BENTON, railroad industry consultant, former executive; b. Sweetwater, Tenn., Jan. 3, 1914; s. John Edgar and Nancy Ella (Webster) C.; m. Maxine Jeanette Butcher, Oct. 14, 1939; children— Diana Clark Hudgens, Sylvia Clark Pulliam BS, U. Tenn., 1937; grad. transport course, Northwestern U., 1959. Registered profl. engr. Ky. Coop. student Bur. Pub. Rds., 1934-36; with Louisville & Nashville R.R., 1937-74, asst. dir. personnel, 1955-59, chief engr., 1959-69, asst. v.p. personnel and labor relations, 1969-73, v.p. personnel and labor relations, 1973-74; v.p. ops. Seaboard Coast Line R.R., Jacksonville, Fla., 1974-76, v.p. exec. dept., 1976; cons. Louisville, 1976-81, Franklin, Ky., 1982—. Pvt. industry council Barren River Area Devel. Dist., 1985-91; mem. Nat. Ry. Labor Conf., Southeastern Carriers Conf. Com., 1969-73. Chmn. bd. trustees Simpson County Libr. Dist., 1989-92; mem. Simpson County (Ky.) Solid Waste Mgmt. Bd., 1990-93, chmn., 1993. Mem. Am. Ry. Engring. Assn. (life, bd. dirs. 1965-68, v.p. 1969), Franklin-Simpson County C. of C. (pres. 1986), Chi Epsilon. Baptist. Home: 305 Hillcrest St Franklin KY 42134-2374 E-mail: jimclark@bowlinggreen.net.

CLARK, JAMES COVINGTON, journalist, historian; b. Washington, May 22, 1947; s. William Edward and Louise (Covington) C.; children: Randall Healy, Kevin Healy. BA, Lenoir-Rhyne Coll., 1975; MA, Stetson U., 1986; PhD, U. Fla., 1998. Reporter UPI, Washington, 1967, Columbia (S.C.) Record, 1968, AP, Charlotte, N.C., 1969-70, Phila., 1972-73, Hickory (N.C.) Daily Record, 1974-75; regional editor Tampa (Fla.) Tribune, 1976-77; asst. exec. editor The Orlando (Fla.) Sentinel, 1977-98; syndicated columnist UP Syndicate, 1997-99; editor Orlando mag., 2000—. Instr. U. Ctrl. Fla., Orlando, 1986—. Author: Last Train South, 1984, Faded Glory: Presidents Out of Power, 1985, The Murder of James Garfield, 1994, Trips Through Florida History, 2000. Recipient George Polk award L.I. U., 1983, Gerald Loeb award, L.A., 1983, Arthur Thompson prize Fla. Hist. Soc., Gainesville, 1989. Mem. Authors Guild, Orgn. Am. Historians, Am. Hist. Assn.

CLARK, JAMES E. lawyer; b. Strong, Ark., Feb. 10, 1929; s. Carey Eugene Clark and Mary (Braswell) Matthews; m. Susie Erskine (dec.); children: Christopher G., David D., Jeffrey F.; m. Linda Savoy. BBA, La. Tech U., 1952; JD, La. State U., 1957. Bar: La. 1957, U.S. Dist. Ct. (we. dist.) La. 1957, U.S. Ct. Appeals (5th cir.) 1957, U.S. Supreme Ct. 2001. Sr. ptnr. Cook, Clark, Egan, Yancey and King, Shreveport, La., 1957-72; dist. judge State of La. 1st Jud. Dist., Shreveport, La., 1972-90; pvt. practice arbitration and mediation Shreveport, La., 1991—. Pres. La. Dist. Judges Assn., 1982-83; mem. State-Fed. Jud. Coun., 1983-90. Active Caddo Parish Dem. Exec. Com., Shreveport, 1964-72, La. State Dem. Exec. Com., 1964-72; del. Dem. Nat. Conv., 1964, 68; chmn. bd. Live Oak Retirement Cmty., Shreveport. Capt. USAFR, 1952-64; corp. USMC, 1946-48. Recipient Communication award Shreveport Toastmaster Internat., 1987. Mem. ABA, La. State Bar Assn. (del. 1968-72), Shreveport Bar Assn., Mason, Scottish Rite, Shriner, Elks, Rotary (pres. 1990-91). Democrat. Episcopalian. Avocation: reading. Office: 400 Travis St Ste 211 Shreveport LA 71101

CLARK, JAMES KERMIT, JR., real estate executive; b. Atlanta, Nov. 17, 1942; s. George W. and Jean (Scutaro) K. BBA, U. Ga., 1965; grad., Realtor Inst, Ga., 1973. Lic. real estate broker, Ga. Chief appraiser First Fed. Savs. & Loan Assn., Atlanta, 1965-67; comml. appraiser Draper-Owens Co., Atlanta, 1967-69; pres. Tri-City Comml. Sales, Inc., College Park, Ga., 1969—2002; exec. v.p. Group VI Corp., Peachtree City, Ga., 1993—. Dir. Student Leadership Univ. Dir. Second Wind Ministries; advisor Bible Tng. Ctr. for Pastors; lead lay counselor First Bapt. Ch., Atlanta. Mem. Nat. Assn. Realtors, Ga. Assn. Realtors, Atlanta Bd. Realtors (comml. adv. coun., comml. dir. and ethics com., chmn. equal opportunity com. 1986-90), Million Dollar Club (active life; Phoenix award, Silver Phoenix award), Atlanta C. of C. (Southside devel. task force 1972), Phi Kappa Alpha, Rho Epsilon Real Estate Fraternity. Republican. Baptist. Office: 900 W Park Dr Ste 300 Peachtree City GA 30269-3521

CLARK, JAMES MILFORD, college president, retired; b. Mich., Apr. 11, 1930; s. Roy Wesley and Florence (Grice) C.; m. Patricia Ann Haynes, Mar. 11, 1960; children— Pamela, Matthew, Timothy. BA, U. Mich., 1952, PhD (Horace H. Rackham fellow), 1962; MA, U. Philippines, 1955; Doctor (hon.), U. North London, 1993; Dr. (hon.), Capital Normal U., Beijing, 1994. Fulbright travel grantee, France, 1955-56; teaching fellow U. Mich., 1957-59; asst. prof. polit. sci. U. Maine, Orono, 1960-64, asso. prof., 1964-79, asst. to pres., 1966-68, v.p. for acad. affairs, 1968-79; pres. SUNY Coll., Cortland, 1979-95; ret., 1995. Fulbright lectr. U. Toulouse (France), 1965-66; mem. Com. on Internat. Exchange Scholars, 1988-92. Author: Teachers and Politics in France, 1967. Chmn. Maine Health Planning Coun., 1970-72, mem. exec. com., 1972-76; bd. dirs. Penobscot Valley United Fund, 1972-77, Cortland County United Way, 1979-85, Eden Alternative, Inc., 2002--; bd. overseers Rockefeller Inst. Govt., 1988-91; mem. N.Y. State Citizens com. on Bicentennial of French Revolution, 1988-90; mem. Tioughnioga Waterfront Devel. Commn., 2000--, Cortland Rural Cemetary Found. (mem. bd. dirs 2002-); With U.S. Army, 1952-55. Mem. Nat. Assn. State Univs. and Land-Grant Colls. (exec. com. council for acad. affairs 1971-76, sec. council 1974-76), Am. Assn. State Colls. and Univs. (N.Y. rep. 1979-81), Phi Beta Kappa, Phi Kappa Phi, Phi Eta Sigma, Pi Sigma Alpha, Sigma Phi Epsilon.

CLARK, JAMES RICHARD, lawyer; b. Madison, Wis., Mar. 30, 1946; s. James F. and Gloria J. Clark; m. Martha C. Conrad, Mar. 18, 1950; children: Lindsey Kelley, Chad. BA, Ripon Coll., 1968; JD, U. Wis., 1971. Bar: Wis. 1971, U.S. Dist. Ct. (we. and ea. dists.) Wis. 1972, U.S. Ct. Appeals (7th cir.) 1973, U.S. Dist. Ct. (no. dist.) Ill. 1974, U.S. Supreme Ct. 1976. Assoc. Foley & Lardner, Milw., 1971-78, ptnr., 1978—. Editor-in-chief Wis. Law Rev., 1971. Trustee Ripon Coll., 1985—. 1st lt. U.S. Army, 1971. Mem. ABA, Am. Coll. Trial Lawyers, Am. Bd. Trial Advs., Def. Rsch. Inst., 7th Cir. Bar Assn., Wis. Bar Assn., Ripon Coll. Alumni Assn. (past pres.), Milw. Athletic Club, Tripoli Country Club, Order of Coif, Phi Beta Kappa. Home: 9719 N Dalewood Ln Mequon WI 53092-6210 Office: Foley & Lardner Firstar Ctr 777 E Wisc Ave Milwaukee WI 53202

CLARK, JANET EILEEN, political scientist, educator; b. Kansas City, Kans., June 5, 1940; d. Edward Francis and Mildred Lois (Mack) Morrissey; m. Caleb M. Clark, Sept. 28, 1968; children: Emily Claire, Grace Ellen, Evelyn Adair. AA, Kansas City Jr. Coll., 1960; AB, George Washington U., 1962, MA, 1964; PhD, U. Ill., 1973. Staff US Dept. Labor, Washington, 1962-64; instr. social sci. Kans. City Jr. Coll., Kans., 1964-67; instr. polit. sci. Parkland Coll., 1970-71; asst. prof. govt. N.Mex. State U., Las Cruces, 1971-77, assoc. prof., 1977-80; assoc. prof. polit. sci. U. Wyo., 1981-84, prof., 1984-94; prof. polit. sci., head dept. State U. West Ga., Carrollton, 1994—. Co-author: Women, Elections and Representation, 1987, The Equality State, 1988, Women in Taiwan Politics: Overcoming Barriers to Women's Participation in a Modernizing Society, 1990; editor Women and Politics, 1991-2000; contbr. articles to profl. jours. Wolcott fellow, 1963-64, NDEA Title IV fellow, 1967-69. Mem. Internat. Soc. Polit. Psychology (gov. coun., 1987-89), NEA (pres. chpt. 1978-79), Am. Polit. Sci. Assn., We. Polit. Sci. Assn. (exec. coun. 1984-87), Western Social Sci. Assn. (exec. coun. 1978-81, v.p. 1982, pres. 1985), Women's Caucus for Polit. Sci. (treas. 1982, pres. 1987), LWV (exec. bd. 1980-83, 2002-2003, treas. 1986-90, pres. 1991-93, 2004-06), Women's Polit. Caucus, Beta Sigma Phi (v.p. chpt. 1978-79, sec. 1987-88, treas. 1988-89, v.p. 1989-90, pres. 1990-91), Phi Beta Kappa Chi Omega (prize 1962), Phi Kappa Phi. Home: 2507 Waterford Rd Auburn AL 36832-4113 Office: State University of West Georgia Dept Polit Sci Carrollton GA 30118-0001

CLARK, JEFF RAY, economist; b. Waynesboro, Va., Nov. 6, 1947; s. Jefferson Davis and Mildred (Cameron) C.; m. Arlene Donowitz, Dec. 17, 1988. BS, Va. Commonwealth U., 1970; MA, Va. Tech. U., Blacksburg, 1972, PhD, 1974. Assoc. dir. Joint Coun. Econ. Edn., N.Y.C., 1974-78, dir., 1978-80; chmn. econ./fin. Fairleigh Dickinson U., Madison, N.J., 1980-87; rsch. fellow Princeton (N.J.) U., 1987; Hendrix chair econs. U. Tenn., Martin, 1987-92, Probasco chair econs. Chattanooga, 1992—. Cons. Pew Charitable Trusts, Phila., 1987—, IT&T, Nutley, N.J., 1985, Fed. Res. Bank N.Y., N.Y.C., 1980, The Johns Hopkins U., Balt., 1984-86; disting. teaching fellow NSF, Washington, 1977, 78. Author: The Science of Cost, Benefit and Choice, 1988, 93, 96, 00, Essentials of Economics, 1982, 86, Economics Cost and Choice, 1987, Macroeconomics for Managers, 1990, Survey of Economics, 1997. Bd. dirs. The William B. Cockroft Found., The Palmer Chitester Fund., The Freedom Found. Mem. Assn. for Pvt. Enterprise (v.p. 1991, pres. 1992, sec.-treas.), Am. Econ. Assn., Ea. Econ. Assn. (bd. dirs. 1980-85), Mont Pelerin Soc., Western Econ. Assn., So. Econ. Assn. Avocations: aviation, skiing, boating, scuba diving. Home: 1623 Ashley Mill Dr Chattanooga TN 37421-3259 Office: U Tenn 615 Mccallie Ave Chattanooga TN 37403-2504

CLARK, JEFFREY RAPHIEL, research and development company executive; b. Provo, Utah, Sept. 29, 1953; s. Bruce Budge and Ouida (Raphiel) C.; m. Anne Margaret Eberhardt, Mar. 15, 1985; children: Jeffrey Raphiel, Mary Anne Elizabeth, Edward William Eberhardt. BS, Brigham Young U., 1977, MBA, 1979. CPA, Tex. Fin. analyst Exxon Coal USA, Inc., Houston, 1979-83; constrn. mgr. Gen. Homes, Inc., Houston, 1983-84; controller Liberty Data Products, Houston, 1984-86; v.p. Tech. Rsch. Assocs., Inc., Salt Lake City, 1987—2001, also dir., 1987—2001; contr. Internat. Sports Broadcasting, LLC, 2001—, controller, 2001—. Scoutmaster Boy Scouts Am., Salt Lake City, 1989-91. Mem. AICPA, Utah Inst. CPAs, Salt Lake C. of C. (legis. action com.), Salt Lake Country Club. Republican. Mem. Lds Ch. Avocations: snow skiing, golf, mountain climbing. Home: 1428 Michigan Ave Salt Lake City UT 84105-1609 Office: PO Box 708039 Sandy UT 84070-8039

CLARK, JERE WALTON, economics educator, researcher; b. Rex, Ga., Jan. 31, 1922; s. Grover Cleveland and Jessie Beatrice (Butler) C.; m. Juanita Stone, June 13, 1947; children: Merrilyn, Melissa Clark Vickers. *Much of the credit for Jere Clark's professional recognition in economics and general systems education can be attributed to the artistic and poetic touch of the work of his wife, Juanita, who is a free-lance artist. In 1967, as a labor of love, they founded the center for interdisciplinary creativity at southern Connecticut State University- the world's first collegiate center for whole —mind creativity in general system education. For the next 24 years they directed the national and international programs of this center.* Student, Berry Coll., 1941-43; BBA, U. Ga., 1947, MA, 1949; PhD, U. Va., 1953. Asst. prof. W.Va. U., Morgantown, 1952-55; assoc. prof. U. Chattanooga, 1955-62; prof. econs. So. Conn. State U., New Haven, 1962-91, prof. emeritus econs., 1991—, chmn. econs. dept., 1962-71, 85-91. Dir. Ctr. for Interdisciplinary Creativity, 1966-91; pres. Quality Optimizer Assocs., 1991—; mem. Nat. Blue-Ribbon Expert Panel of Interdisciplinarians (Merit Commn. on Sci. Edn., New Mex.), 1992-93. Author: 10 book chpts., 1965-89; co-author: Full Circle...of United Science, 1974, (with Juanita S. Clark) The Joy Imperative, 2003; editor nat. yearbook Enterprising Teachers, 1963, 64, 65; mem. editorial bd. Jour. Creative Behavior, 1967-93, Gen. Systems Bull., 1968-72, Internat. Assns., 1970-72; contbr. articles to profl. jours. Moderator 12 TV panels on edn. Nat. League of Nursing, Chattanooga, 1961; author, narrator 60 radio econ-o-grams Nat./Joint Coun. Econ. Edn., New Haven, 1966; chmn. internat. task force on Gen. Systems Edn., SGSR, 1967-72. With U.S. Army, 1943-45, ETO. Recipient Best Coll. Course in Econs. for Tchrs. award Nat./Joint Coun. on Econ. Edn., 1965, 1st statewide Acad. Freedom Award in pub. higher edn. in Conn., 1992; grantee Kazanjian Found. (5), 1967-80, USOE/HEW, 1975-76. Mem. Am. Econs. Assn., New England Bus. Adminstrn. Assn. (bd. dirs. 1987—), World Future Soc. Conn. (pres. 1975-76), Creative Edn. Found. (colleague 1957—).

CLARK, JESSIE DONA, social worker; b. Rochester, N.Y., Feb. 28, 1922; m. James Governeau Banks, Jan. 23, 1943 (div. Nov. 1972); children: James Governeau Banks, Franklin Frazier Banks, David Robert Banks; m. Paul Andrews Clark, Jan. 21, 1973. BA, Howard U., 1947, MSW, 1960. Psychiat. social worker St. Elizabeths Hosp., Washington, 1960-65; family relocation officer D.C. Redey, Land Agy., 1965-73; supr. social worker Dept. Community Mental Health, St. Thomas, V.I., 1975; spl. asst. to comptroller V.I. Housing Auth., St. Thomas, 1975-85. Evaluator, vice chmn. Operation Sisters United, St. Thomas, 1975-83; cons. V.I. Labor Mgmt. Com., St. Thomas, 1984—; cons. human resources dept. U. V.I., 1992—. Bd. dirs. YWCA (Phyllis Wheatley Br.), Washington; commr. Youth Coun., Washington, Vis. Nurses Assn., Washington, Puns. for Health, St. Thomas (editor mo. newsletter 1988-89). Recipient Disting. Lady award Plymouth Congl. Ch., 1967, Outstanding Performance award D.C. Redevelopment Agy., 1971; NIMH fellow 1957-60. Mem. Internat. Assn. Pers. Mgrs. (v.p.), Nat. Assn. Housing and Renewal Ofcls., NASW (pres. V.I. chpt. 1985-87, Social Worker of Yr. award 1983, V.I. Pioneer award 1998), Eta Phi Beta (v.p. 1988-89). Home: PO Box 8485 Saint Thomas VI 00801-1485

CLARK, JIMMY HOWARD, nutrition educator; b. Sedalia, Ky., Feb. 22, 1941; s. Charlie Howard and Rosemary (Harris) C.; m. Karen Sue Knudson, Aug. 17, 1974; 1 child, Carol Ada. BS, Murray State U., 1963; PhD, U. Tenn., 1967. Rsch. assoc. Clemson (S.C.) U., 1967-68; asst. prof. nutrition U. Ill., Urbana, 1968-75, assoc. prof., 1975-80, prof., 1980—. Recipient Paul A. Funk Recognition award, 1983, Am. Feed Mfrs. award, 1980, H.H. Mitchell award for excellence in grad. tchg. and rsch., 1991, Am. Cyanamid Co. award for rsch. and edn. in the field of milk prodn., 1991, sr. faculty award Coll. Agr., 1993, Disting. Alumnus award Murray State U., 1997, award for outstanding rsch. in dairy prodn. Dean Foods, 1998, others. Mem. Am. Dairy Sci. Assn. (bd. dirs. 1985-88, coun. prodn. div. 1979-82, sec. 1983, vice chmn. prodn. div. 1984, chmn. 1985, v.p. 1992, pres. 1993, award of honor 2000, Disting. Svc. award 2002, fellow award, 2003), Am. Soc. for Nutritional Sci., Am. Soc. Animal Sci., AAAS, Nutrition Soc., Coun. Agrl. Sci. Tech., Gamma Sigma Delta, Sigma Xi. Home: 2106 Burlison Dr Urbana IL 61801-6606 Office: U Ill Dept Animal Sci 1207 W Gregory Dr Urbana IL 61801-4733

CLARK, JOAN HARDY, retired journalist; b. Toronto, Ont., Can., Apr. 17, 1934; came to the U.S., 1960; d. Henry Robert Hardy and Irene Elsie Stevens; children: Lisa Anne Hanson, Anthony David Stuart Hanson. BA, Carleton U., Ottawa, Can., 1954; postgrad., Sarah Lawrence Coll., 1973-75. Chmn. coun. conservators N.Y. Pub. Libr., N.Y.C., 1986—2001, bd. dirs., 1996—, hon. chmn., 2001—; mem. Nat. Com., 2002—; bd. dirs. Whitney Mus., N.Y.C., 1983—2003; chmn. Coun. Conservators, 2001—. Mem. Cosmopolitan Club. Home: 1 Gracie Sq New York NY 10028-8001 also: Deer Meadow Farm Andover VT 05143

CLARK, JOHN ARTHUR, lawyer; b. Glen Ridge, N.J., Dec. 22, 1920; s. Franklin Jones and Eleanor Newhall (Moss) C.; m. Dorothy Winton Bateson (dec.), Apr. 21, 1945; children: William F., Margaret W., John R. BA, Haverford Coll., 1942; JD, U. Pa., 1948. Bar: Pa. 1949, N.Y. 1954. Assoc. Moss, Rieser & Bingaman, Reading, Pa., 1948-51; special atty. IRS Regional Counsel, N.Y.C., 1951-53; assoc. Davies, Hardy, Ives & Lawther, N.Y.C., 1953-58, ptnr., 1958-70, Duane, Morris & Heckscher, Phila., 1970-88, of counsel, 1989—. Author: How To Save Time and Taxes Handling Estates, 1965; contbr. articles to profl. jours. Treas. Met. Christian Coun. Phila., 1980-93; trustee Upper Moreland Free Pub. Libr., 1995-97. 1st lt. AUS, 1942-46, PTO. Mem. ABA, Pa. Bar Assn., Phila. Bar Assn. (vice chmn. com. on income of estates and trusts, ABA tax sect. 1987-89, chair 1989-91), Order of Coif. Office: Duane Morris & Heckscher One Liberty Pl Philadelphia PA 19103

CLARK, JOHN F. aerospace research and engineering educator; b. Reading, Pa., Dec. 12, 1920; s. John F. Clark and Edith Dix (Long) Guenther; m. June Teubner Schweiger, July 14, 1974; children from previous marriage: Linda J. Marks, James C. BSEE with honors, Lehigh U., 1942, EE, 1947; MS in Math., George Washington U., 1946; PhD in Physics, U. Md., 1956. Registered profl. engr., N.J. Electronic engr. Naval Rsch. Lab., 1942-47, physicist, atmospheric electricity br. head, 1948-58; asst. prof. elec. engring. Lehigh U., 1947-48; dir. physics and astronomy programs NASA, 1958-63, dep. assoc. adminstr. space sci. and applications (scis.), 1963-65, chmn. space sci. steering com., 1963-65; dir. Goddard Space Flight Center, 1965-76; dir. space applications and tech. RCA Corp., Princeton, N.J., 1976-86; part-time cons. Gen. Electric Astro Space Div., 1987-88; NAVSPACE rsch. prof. U.S. Naval Acad. aerospace engring. dept., Annapolis, Md., 1988-90; dir. grad. studies, prof. space sytems Fla. Inst. Tech. Spaceport Grad. Ctr., 1990—. Part-time lectr. math. George Washington U., 1956-58; part-time cons. rsch. Grad. Coun., 1960-66; part-time lectr. physics U. Md., 1958; mem. indsl. and profl. adv. coun. Pa. State U., 1963-65; mem. vis. com. physics Lehigh U., 1966-74; mem. Com. on Fed. Labs., 1971-75, Md. Gov.'s Sci. Adv. Coun., 1972-76, N.J. Gov.'s Sci. Adv. Coun., 1980-86, Am. Geophys. Union-URSI Bd. Radio Sci., 1974-78; mem. study panel Office Telecommunications, Nat. Assembly Engring., 1976-77; chmn. adv. com. FCC, 1981-83; mem. U.S. del. to Internat. Telecommunication Union Conf., Regional Adminstrv. Radio Conf., 1983, World Adminstrv. Radio Conf., 1985; chmn. Direct Broadcast Satellite Assn., 1986; mem. spectrum planning adv. com. U.S. Dept. Commerce, 1986-92; bd. dirs. ECON Inc.; mem. Calif. Inst. Tech. Jet Propulsion Lab.'s Mars Observer Program Rev. Bd., 1986-93. Contbr. numerous articles to profl. jours.; cons. editor space tech. McGraw-Hill Ency. Sci. and Tech, 1977—. Recipient NASA medals for Disting. Service, Outstanding Leadership, Exceptional Service, Collier trophy Nat. Aero. Assn. Fellow Am. Astron. Soc., AIAA (gen. chmn. Communications Satellite System Conf. 1984, v.p. pub. policy 1986-90), IEEE, Explorers Club; mem. Am. Geophys. Union, Am. Meterol. Soc., Satellite Broadcasting and Communications Assn. (chmn. 1987, chmn.'s coun. 1989-90, 1st Pres.'s award 1993), Internat. Soc. Satellite Profls. (bd. dirs. 1985-89), Internat. Acad. Astronautics, Phi Beta Kappa, Sigma Xi, Pi Mu Epsilon, Tau Beta Pi, Sigma Phi Epsilon, Sigma Pi Sigma. Achievements include patents in electronic circuits and systems. Home: 947 Loggerhead Island Dr Satellite Beach FL 32937-3863

CLARK, JOHN H., JR., lawyer; b. Chester, Pa., June 6, 1928; s. John H. and Emma E. (Higler) C.; m. Esther F. Giaccio, June 12, 1954 (dec. Feb. 2002); 1 child, Jacqueline Ann. BA with honors, U. Pa., 1948, JD cum laude, 1951. Bar: Pa. 1951. Pvt. practice, Ridley Park, Pa., 1973—. Chmn. hearing com. Pa. Supreme Ct. Disciplinary Bd., 1980-86. Pres. Historic Delaware County, Inc., 1972; del. Democratic Nat. Conv., 1960; solicitor Tinicum Twp., 1960-64, Folcroft Borough Sch. Dist., 1959-63, Norwood Borough, 1972-76, Folcroft Borough, 1973-74. Served with USAF, 1952-53; to maj. Res. Mem. ABA, Pa. Bar Assn. (ho. of dels. 1972-82), Delaware County Bar Assn., Delaware County Hist. Soc. (pres. 1989-92), Rotary (pres. Chester Pike club 1973-74). Roman Catholic. Office: PO Box 152 204 E Chester Pike Ridley Park PA 19078-0152 Home: 207 Knoll Rd Wallingford PA 19086

CLARK, JOHN HALLETT, III, consulting engineering executive; b. Bristol, Va., Oct. 31, 1918; s. John Hallett, Jr. and Shirley (Winston) C.; m. Suzanne North Hazelet, Sept. 19, 1942; children: Craig Winston, John Hallett IV, Philip Winston. Student, Williams Coll., 1937-38, Colo. Coll., 1938-42; BS in Civil Engring, U. Ky., 1948. Registered profl. engr., Ky. Jr. engr. Austin Co., 1942; with Hazelet & Erdal, Louisville, 1942-43, 47—, partner, 1956—, mng. partner, 1973-82, pres., 1982-86, chmn., 1986-87, retired, 1987; co-designer major hwy. and bridge projects. Mem. Louisville and Jefferson County Planning and Zoning Commn., 1957-64, vice chmn., 1962-64; bd. dirs. Better Bus. Bur. Louisville, 1965-68; mem. town coun., Anchorage, Ky., 1969-71. With C.E., U.S. Army, 1943-46, PTO. Fellow ASCE (pres. Ky. 1954); mem. Am. Inst. Cons. Engrs. (councilor 1970-73), Nat., Ky. socs. profl. engrs., Cons. Engrs. Council U.S. (dir. Ky. 1968-70, pres. Ky. 1967), Tau Beta Pi, Delta Kappa Epsilon. Clubs: Red Lantern (Colo. Coll.). Episcopalian. Home: 520 Old Stone Ln Louisville KY 40207-2336

CLARK, JOHN J. economist, educator, finance educator; b. N.Y.C., June 21, 1924; s. John J. and Mary E. (Taylor) Clark; m. Margaret T. Norton, July 1, 1965; 1 child, Patricia Ann. BBA magna cum laude, St. John's U., 1948; MBA, CCNY, 1950; PhD, NYU, 1959. Prof. econs. Coll. Bus. Adminstrn., St. John's U., 1950-69, chmn. dept., 1959-62, dean, 1962-70; Royal H. Gibson Sr. prof. bus. adminstrn. Drexel U., Phila., 1971-90, prof. emeritus, 1990—, dir. doctoral studies LeBow Coll. Bus. Lectr. econs. Bklyn. Poly. Inst., 1954—58. Co-author: (book) The Impact of the Foundation Reports on Business Education, 1963, Business Fluctuations, Growth and Economic Stabilization, 1963, Professional Education for Business, 1964, The New Economics of National Defense, 1966, Financial Management: A Capital Market Approach, 1976, Management of Capital Expenditures, 1979, 3d rev. edit., 1989, Lease/Buy Decision, 1980, A Statistics Primer for Managers, 1980, Business Mergers and Acquisition Strategies, 1985, Restructuring Corporate America, 1996; contbr. articles to profl. jours.; editor: (book) Business and the Liberal Arts, 1962; contbg. editor: Fin. Mgmt. Jour., 1972—82. Mem. Borough Pres.'s Planning Com., Queens County, N.Y.C., 1964—69; economist joint legis. com. banking law N.Y. State Legislature, 1965—68 Recipient Mil. Rev. award, U.S. Army Command and Gen. Staff Coll., 1964. Mem.: Royal United Svc. Inst. Def. Studies, Ea. Fin. Assn. (exec. dir. 1974—77), Am. Econ. Assn., Phila. Maritime Mus. (advisor), U.S. Naval Inst. (medal 1969), Omicron Delta Epsilon, Delta Mu Delta, Beta Gamma Sigma. Home: White Horse Village 535 Gradyville Rd # V101 Newtown Square PA 19073-2815 Office: Coll Bus Adminstrn Drexel U Philadelphia PA 19104

CLARK, JOHN PETER, III, engineering consultant; b. Phila., May 6, 1942; s. John Peter Jr. and Victoria Mary (McQuaide) C.; m. Nancy Ann Lapin, June 22, 1968; children: Shannon John, Hannah Marie. BSChemE, Notre Dame U., 1964; PhD, U. Calif., Berkeley, 1968. Registered profl. engr., Va., Ill. Rsch. engr. Agrl. Rsch. Svc., USDA, Berkeley and Washington, 1968-72; from asst. to assoc. prof. Va. Poly. Inst. and State U., Blacksburg, 1972-78; dir. R & D, ITT Continental Baking, Rye, N.Y., 1978-81; pres. Epstein Process Engring. Inc., Chgo., 1981-94; pvt. practice, engring. cons., Oak Park, Ill., 1994-95; v.p. tech. Fluor Daniel, Inc., 1995-98. Co-author: Food Processing Operations and Scale-up, 1991; editor: Exercises in Process Simulation, 1977; contbg. editor Food Tech.; contbr. articles to profl. jours.; patentee (with C.J. King) in field for sys. for freeze drying. Fellow: AIChE (divns. chmn. 1982, award in chem engring. 1998); mem.: Inst. Food Technologists (divns. chmn. 1984). Roman Catholic. Avocations: reading, folk music, Indian art. Home and Office: 644 Linden Ave Oak Park IL 60302-1661 E-mail: JPC3@worldnet.att.net.

CLARK, JOHN RUSSELL, marine biologist; b. Seattle, Apr. 11, 1927; s. Donald Hathaway and Mildred (Taylor) C.; m. Catherine Lochner; children: John M., Jeffry R., George K., Linda J., Kerry S., Karen M. BS, U. Wash., Seattle, 1949. Research biologist Woods Hole (Mass.) Fishery Lab., Dept. Interior, 1950-59; asst. dir. Sandy Hook (N.J.) Marine Lab., Dept. Interior, 1960-70; dir. Narragansett (R.I.) Marine Lab., Dept. Interior, 1971; dir. water programs Conservation Found., Washington, 1972-81; mgr. coastal programs internat. affairs office Nat. Park Svc., Washington, 1982-87; sr. rsch. assoc. U. Miami Sch. Marine Sci., Fla., 1988—. Adj. scientist Mote Marine Lab., Sarasota, Fla., 1994—. Author: Through the Fish's Eye, 1973, Shark Watch, 1975, Coastal Ecosystems Management, 1977, The Sanibel Report, 1977, Wetland Functions and Values, 1979, Coastal Environment Management, 1980, Wetlands of Bottomland Hardwood Forests, 1981, Snorkeling: A Complete Guide, 1985, Integrated Management of Coastal Zones, 1992, Coastal Zone Management Handbook, 1996, Coastal Seas, 1998, Marine Protected Areas, 2000. Served with USNR, 1945-46. Named Conservationist of Year Am. Motors Corp., 1968; recipient Meritorious Publ. award U.S. Fish and Wildlife Service, 1969 Mem. Am. Littoral Soc. (founder, dir., past pres.) Office: Mote Marine Lab Field Office PO Box 420313 281 W Indies Dr Ramrod Key FL 33042-5462 E-mail: JohnRClarkX@cs.com.

CLARK, JOHN WALTER, JR., shipping company executive; b. Mobile, Ala., Oct. 21, 1919; s. John Walter and Mae (Kappner) C.; m. Evelyn Ruth Hamilton, Aug. 29, 1941 (dec.); children: Ann Clark (dec.), Ruth Clark Day, Susan Clark Wells; m. Sandra L. Sharp, June 21, 1977; stepchildren: Kirsten J. Acomb, Heidi J. Qualey. Grad., U.S. Mcht. Marine Acad., 1940; postgrad., Tulane U., 1950-55. Served as officer, master mariner U.S. Mcht. Marine, 1940-46; mgr. Argentina, Brazil, West Africa and Europe Delta Steamship Lines, Inc., 1946-50, asst. to pres., 1950-53, v.p., 1953-59, pres., 1959-79, chmn. bd., 1979-80; pres. Clark Maritime Assocs., Inc., 1979—. Bd. dirs. Panama Canal Commn., 1978-82; past pres., mem. exec. com., bd. dirs. World Trade Ctr. of New Orleans; maritime arbitrator New Orleans Bd. of Trade; commr., pres. Port of New Orleans, 1978-82; exec. dir. Miss. State Port Authority, 1982-85; nat. vice chmn. Coun.of Ams., 1974-80. Rear adm. U.S. Maritime Svc. Decorated Order of Crown of Belgium; Order of Star of Africa Liberia; Order of So. Cross Brazil; Comendador de la Orden de Mayo Argentina; Orden de Isabel La Catolica Spain; named Maritime Man of Year Port of New Orleans, 1965. Mem. U.S. Mcht. Marine Acad. Alumni Assn. (Alumnus of Yr. 1975, named to Hall of Fame 1998). Clubs: Plimsoll, So. Yacht, Pickwick, Pass Christian Yacht, Pass Christian Isles Golf. Methodist. Office: Clark Maritime Assocs Inc 23322 Woodland Way Pass Christian MS 39571-5711

CLARK, JONATHAN L. photographer, printer, publisher; b. Ottawa, Ill., Mar. 24, 1952; s. Keith S. and Harriet S. Clark. BA in Photography, U. Calif., Santa Cruz, 1974. Self employed artist, 1975—. Founder, propr. The Artichoke Press, Mountain View, Calif., 1975—. Editor The Hedgehog arts rev., San Francisco, 1997—, Frederick Sommer: Cut-Paper, 2000; exhibited 16 one man shows in U.S., Japan and Europe; exhibited in more than 60 group shows, including Photo Gallery Internat., Tokyo, 1987, U Calif., Santa Cruz, 1993, Am. Ctr., Warsaw, Poland, 1996, Triton Mus. Art, Santa Clara, Calif., 1997. Mem. visual arts com. City of Mountain View, Calif., 1989-95. Photography fellow Arts Coun. Santa Clara County, 1997, Book Club of Calif. grantee, 1997; USIS travel grantee, Poland, 1994; travel grantee, Barcelona, 1994. Avocation: bicycling. Home: 550 Mountain View Ave Mountain View CA 94041-1941

CLARK, JONATHAN MONTGOMERY, lawyer; b. Bklyn., Oct. 20, 1937; s. Russell Inslee and Lillian (Longmore) C.; m. Priscilla M. Jorgensen, Sept. 24, 1960; children: Jonathan M. Jr., Christopher D. BA, Yale U., 1959; LLB, U. Va., 1964. Bar: N.Y. 1965. Assoc. Davis Polk & Wardwell, N.Y.C., 1964-71, ptnr., 1971-93; gen. counsel, mng. dir. Morgan Stanley & Co., Inc., N.Y.C., 1993—98; sr. counsel Davis, Polk & Wardell, N.Y.C., 1999—. Advisor mission to Poland, Fin. Svcs. Vol. Corps, 1990, 92; cons. Warren Commn., Washington, 1965; bd. dirs. Greenwich Hosp. Assn., 1990-98, Prentice Cup Com. bd. dirs. Caramoor Ctr. Music & the Arts. 1st lt. USMC, 1959-61. Mem. ABA, N.Y. State Bar Assn., Assn. Bar City N.Y., Securities Industry Assn. (bd. dirs., 1995-96), N.Y. Stock Exchange Legal Adv. Com. Republican. Episcopalian. Avocations: golf, fly fishing, birding. Office: Davis, Polk & Wardell 450 Lexington Ave New York NY 10017 E-mail: jonathan.clark@dpw.com.

CLARK, JOSEPH FRANCIS, JR., lawyer; b. Tulsa, Okla., Jan. 20, 1949; s. Joseph F. and Betty Sue C.; m. Carol J. Coleman, Nov. 2, 1974 (div. 1981); m. Cathy A. Baker, Jan. 6, 1989; children: Joseph F. Clark III, Thomas S. Clark, Joshua B. Baker. BA, Villanova U., 1971; JD, Tulsa U., 1973. Bar: Okla. 1974. Atty. Gibbon, Gladd, Clark et al, Tulsa, 1974-78; pvt. practice Tulsa, 1979-80; atty. Williams, Clark et al, Tulsa, 1980-90; ptnr. Clark & Stainer, Tulsa, 1990-94, Layon, Cronin, Clark & Kaiser, P.L.L.C., Tulsa, 1994-99; pvt. practice Tulsa, 1999—. Mem.: Tulsa County Bar Assn. (fee dispute com. 1998—99, profl. responsibility com. 2001—), Am. Inns of Ct. (Council Oak chpt., term master 1996—98, master 1999—). Democrat. Roman Catholic. Home: 2922 E 39th St Tulsa OK 74105-3704 Office: 1622 S Denver Ave Tulsa OK 74119-4232 E-mail: jclarkatt@sbcglobal.net.

CLARK, JOYCE NAOMI JOHNSON, retired nurse, counselor; b. Corpus Christi, Tex., Oct. 4, 1936; d. Chester Fletcher and Ermal Olita (Bailey) Johnson; m. William Boyd Clark, Jan. 4, 1958; (div. 1967); 1 child, Sherene Joyce. Student, Corpus Christi State U., 1975-77. RN, CNOR, ACLS, TNCC; cert. instrument flight instr.; cert. core trauma nurse. Staff nurse Van Nuys (Calif.) Cmty. Hosp., 1963-64, U.S. Naval Hosp., Corpus Christi, 1964-68; patient care coord. Spohn Meml. Hosp. (formerly Meml. Med. Ctr.), Corpus Christi, 1968—2002; counselor Christus Spohn Wellness Program, 1999—2002; ret., 2002. Leader Paisano Coun. Girl Scouts U.S.A., Corpus Christi, 1968-74; vol. transporting those in need; past comdr. 3rd group USAF Aux., CAP Air Search and Rescue, wing chief pilot, ret. lt. col. 1993. Recipient Charles A. Mella award Meml. Med. ctr., 1981, Paul E. Garbert award CAP, 1986, cert. of appreciation in recognition of Support Child Guard Missing Children Edn. Program Nat. Assn. Chiefs of Police, Washington, 1987, Charles E. Yeager Aerospace Edn. Achievement award, 1985, Grover Loenig Aerospace award, 1986, Cert. of World Leadership Internat. Biographical Ctr., Cambridge, Eng., 1987, Gill Robb Wilson award #1021, 1988, Merit award Drug Free Am. Through Enforcement, Edn., Intelligence Nat. Assn. Chiefs of Police, Sr. Mem. of Yr. USAF Aux., CAP Air Search and Rescue, 1986. Mem. USAF Aux., CAP Air Search and Rescue (past comdr. 3rd group, wing chief pilot, ret. lt. col., Sr. Mem. of Yr. 1986), Aircraft Owners and Pilots Assn. Avocation: flying. Home: 2802 Cimmaron Blvd Apt 221 Corpus Christi TX 78414-3455 E-mail: jnccfi11@aol.com.

CLARK, KAREN HEATH, lawyer; b. Pasadena, Calif., Dec. 17, 1944; d. Wesley Pelton and Lois (Ellenberger) Heath; m. Bruce Robert Clark,Dec. 30, 1967; children: Adam Heath, Andrea Pelton. Student, Pomona Coll., Claremont, Calif., 1962-64; BA, Stanford U., 1964-66; MA in History, U. Wash., 1968; JD, U. Mich., 1977. Bar: Calif. 1978. Instr. Henry Ford Community Coll., Dearborn, Mich., 1968-72; assoc. Gibson, Dunn & Crutcher LLP, Irvine, Calif., 1977-86, ptnr., 1986—. Bd. dirs. Dem. Found. Orange County, 1989-91, 94—, Planned Parenthood Orange County, Santa Ana, Calif., 1979-82, New Directions for Women, Newport Beach, 1986-91, Human Options, 2001—; bd. dirs. Women in Leadership, chair, 1995-99; trustee Newport Beach Pub. Libr., 2001—; mem. deans adv. coun. Sch. Humanities, U. Calif., Irvine. Recipient 1996 Choice award Planned Parenthood of Orange & San Bernardino Counties. Mem. Women in Leadership (founder 1993), Comml. Real Estate Women, Bldg. Industries Assn. So. Calif., Internat. Coun. Shopping Ctrs., Calif. Mortgage Bankers Assn. Office: Gibson Dunn & Crutcher LLP 4 Park Plz Ste 1400 Irvine CA 92614-8557 E-mail: kclark@gibsondunn.com.

CLARK, KELLY, Olympic athlete; b. Newport, R.I., July 26, 1983; Grad., Brattleboro (Vt.) Union H.S., 2002. Former mem. U.S. Women's Snowboarding Team. Named World Jr. halfpipe champion, 2000, U.S. halfpipe and snowboardcross champion, 2001; recipient Gold medal, 2002 Olympic Games, Salt Lake City. Address: US Ski and Snowboarding Assn Box 100 1500 Kearns Blvd Park City UT 84060

CLARK, KENNETH COURTRIGHT, retired physics and geophysics educator; b. Austin, Tex., Sept. 30, 1919; s. Evert Mordecai and Grace (Courtright) C.; m. Eleanor Lorraine McKenna, June 10, 1947; children: David Templeton, Gracia Courtright. BA, U. Tex., 1940; A.M., Harvard U., 1941, PhD, 1947. Spl. research assoc. nat. def. research project Electro-Acoustic Lab., Harvard, 1942-45, instr. physics, 1947-48; mem. faculty U. Wash., Seattle, 1948—, asso. prof., 1955-60, prof., 1960-90, prof. emeritus, 1990—, chmn. geophysics, 1967-69; research asso. prof. Geophys. Inst., U. Alaska, Fairbanks, 1957-58, mem. sci. adv. bd., 1972-76. Vis. prof. div. theoretical and space physics LaTrobe U., Melbourne, Australia, 1979-80; cons. AID, State Dept. and Ministry Edn. India, Varanasi, 1964, Udaipur, 1966; dir. aeronomy program NSF, Washington, 1969-70. Fellow Am. Phys. Soc., Optical Soc. Am.; mem. Am. Geophys. Union, Am. Assn. Physics Tchrs., Phi Beta Kappa, Sigma Xi. Methodist. Home: 4739 University View Pl NE Seattle WA 98105-4035 E-mail: clark@phys.washington.edu.

CLARK, KEVIN ANTHONY, marketing executive, communications executive; b. Kansas City, Mo., Dec. 10, 1956; s. Harley Leon and Virginia Lee (Magee) C.; m. Heidi Jean Sawyer. BS, U. Tulsa, 1978. Producer, announcer Sta. KWGS-FM, Tulsa, 1976-78; assoc. communications specialist IBM Corp., Charlotte, N.C., 1979-80, communications specialist Tarrytown, N.Y., 1981-82, staff communications specialist White Plains, N.Y., 1983-84, corp. speak up adminstr., sr. communications specialist Armonk, N.Y., 1985-87, info. rep., program adminstr. White Plains, 1988-90, mgr. svcs. and mktg. media rels., 1991-93; mgr. U.S. pub. rels. IBM, 1993-94; mgr. Global Multimedia Comms., 1994-95; product mgr. global strategic mktg. mobile computing IBM PC Co., Research Triangle Park, N.C., 1995-96; program dir. strategic mktg. IBM Mobile Computing, 1997-98; program dir. brand stewardship IBM ThinkPad, 1997-98; program dir. brand mgmt. IBM Think and IBM Work Pad, 1999—; program dir. bus. strategy, brand mgmt., licensing and integrated mktg. IBM Pers. Device Brands: IBM ThinkPad, IBM Think Centre, IBM Think Vision, IBM Think Vantage Design & Techs.; mem. mktg. mgmt. exec. com. IBM Pers. Device Brands: IBM ThinkPad, IBM Net Vista; program dir., brand strategy, market intelligence and integrated mktg. IBM Pers. Computing Devices. Dir. corp. comms. Okla. Intercollegiate Legislature, Oklahoma City, 1977; mem. steering com. MIT Media Lab.; mem. adv. bd. Boston Coll. Mktg. Author: IBM Speak Up Manual, 1986; editor: (brochure) IBM in Real Estate and Construction, 1984 (Excellence award IBM 1984, cert. Merit Printing Industries Am. 1984); author: (with others) Strategic Public Relations and Integrated Communications, Wireless Rules: New Marketing Strategies for Customer Relationship Management Anytime, Anywhere. Named one of Outstanding Young Men of Am., 1985. Mem. Nat. Spkrs. Assn., Internat. Visitors Coun. Avocations: alpine skiing, reading, writing, public speaking. Home: 907 Linden Rd Chapel Hill NC 27517-8046 Office: IBM Corp 3039 Cornwallis Rd Research Triangle Park NC 27709

CLARK, LARRY DALTON, civil engineer; b. Sask., Can., May 12, 1942; s. Albert Ray and Christina Emily (Marum) C.; B.S. in Civil Engring., S.D. Sch. Mines, Rapid City, 1971; m. Janice Martina Kettleson, Aug. 16, 1969; children— Tamara Dayrie, Laura Janelle Clark Daycie, Jennifer Lynette, Daniel Jerod. Engr. in tng. Iowa Hwy. Commn., Ames, 1971-75; asst. resident engr. Iowa Dept. Transp., New Hampton, 1975-79, acting resident engr., 1977-78; county engr. Black Hawk County, 1979-91, Robinson Engring., 1992-93, Clark Engring. and Surveying, 1993-94; county engr. Cherokee County, 1995—. Active local United Way campaign, 1976-77; state del. People to People to Russia, 1989. Recipient award Nat. Assn. Counties Bridge Rehab., 4 awards Asphalt Paving Assn. Iowa. Registered profl. engr., Iowa; registered land surveyor. Mem. ASCE, NSPE, Iowa Soc. Profl. Engrs., Sigma Tau. Lutheran. Home: 338 Longview Dr Waterloo IA 50701-1638 Office: 5074 Highway 3 Cherokee IA 51012-7229

CLARK, LAUREL JAN, adult education educator, author, editor, minister, counselor; b. Denver, Jan. 29, 1957; d. C. Dale and Ethelyn (Goldberg) Fuller; m. John Gordon Clark, May 29, 1994 (dec. Sept. 2000). BA with honors, U. Mich., 1978; PsD, Sch. Metaphysics, 1987; DD, Coll. Metaphysics, 1992, DM, 1994. Cert. tchr., Mo.; ordained min. Interfaith Ch. Metaphysics. Tchr. adult edn. Sch. Metaphysics, 1979—, dir., teaching supr., 1979-82, bd govs., 1981—, v.p., 1988-98, sec., 1990—2002; cert. counselor Interfaith Ch. Metaphysics, Windyville, 1987—; author SOM Pub., Windyville, 1981—; mng. editor Thresholds Quar., Windyville, 1990—. Field dir. Sch. Metaphysics, 1984-94, 2002--; internat. adv. bd. Unity and Diversity World Coun., L.A., 1995—; bd. dirs. Sch. Metaphysics; spkr. U. Mo., St. Louis, U. Mo., Columbia, Am. Bus. Women's Assn., Boulder (Colo.) Sheriff's Dept., Penn Valley C.C., U. Colo., Ft. Collins, Mensa Regional Conf., others. Author: Shaping Your Life, 1994, Concentration, 1995, Vital Ingredient, 1998, Karmic Healing, 2000; co-author: Power of Structure, 1987, Total Recall, 1993; contbg. author: First Opinion, 1997; contbg. author, editor: Interpreting Dreams for Self Awareness, 2001; contbr. articles to profl. jours. Mem.: Unity and Diversity World Coun., Spiritual Frontiers Fellowship Internat., World Peace Prayer Soc., Inst. Noetic Scis., Interfaith Alliance, Am. Holistic Assn., Phi Beta Kappa. Avocations: writing, music, composing, broadcasting, children's books. Home and Office: Sch Metaphysics 163 Moon Valley Rd Windyville MO 65783-9703 E-mail: som@som.org.

CLARK, LAVERNE HARRELL, writer, photographer; b. Smithville, Tex., June 6, 1929; d. James Boyce and Belle Bunte Harrell; m. L.D. Clark, Sept. 15, 1951. BA, Tex. Woman's U., 1950; student, Columbia U., 1951-54; MA, U. Ariz., 1962, MFA, 1992. Reporter, libr., photographer Ft. Worth Press, 1950-51; with sales and advt. depts. Columbia U. Press, N.Y.C., 1951-53; asst. promotion-news Episcopal Diocese Bull., N.Y.C., 1958-59; founding dir. U. Ariz. Poetry Ctr., Tucson, 1962-66, photographer, 1966-99. Author, photographer: They Sang for Horses, 1966 (award U. Chgo. 1967), rev. edit., 2001, Revisiting the Plains Indian Country of Mari Sandoz, 1977, Focus 101, 1979, The Deadly Swarm and Other Stories, 1985, 87, Keepers of the Earth, 1997, 2d edit., 2002 (1st Novel award Western Writers of Am. 1998), Mari Sandoz's Native Nebraska, 2000; editor, photographer: The Face of Poetry, 1976, 2d edit., 1979. Recipient 19 awards Nat. League Am. Pen Women, 1985-96, Disting. Alumna award Tex. Woman's U., Denton, 1973; grantee Am. Philos. Soc., 1967, 69. Mem. PEN, Western Writers of Am., Westerners Internat., Women Writing the West, Sandoz Heritage Soc. (hon. mem. adv. bd. 1989—), Tex. Inst. Letters. Democrat. Episcopalian. Avocations: travel, bicycling, showing slides. Home: 604 Main St Smithville TX 78957 E-mail: lhldclark@aol.com.

CLARK, LAWRENCE D. state representative; b. Louisville, Ky, July 24, 1945; m. Violet Clark; children: Tim, Joy. HS Diploma, Flager HS. State Rep. House of Rep., Dist. #46, Ky., 1984—; Elec. Apprentice IBEW/NECA, 1966—70. Spkr. State House Pro Tempore, 1993—98; mem. Okolona Dem. Club, Spirit of 46 Dem. Club; Exec. Dem. Fin. Comm.; advisor Econ. Adv. Coun. to the Mayor of Louisville; mem. Appropriations and Revenue Comm., Licensing and Occupations, Rules, State Gov. Mem.: Pvt. Indus. Fund Coun., Nat. Elec. Code Comm., Ky. Young Advocates, Ky. State Labor/Mgmt. Adv. Coun., Heart of Parks Foundation, Task Force, Commission of Louisville & Jefferson county Cultural Complex, Bellarmine College, Bd. of Overseers, Am. Cancer Soc., IBEW - 369, State Solar Energy Task Force. Democrat. Catholic. Office: Capitol Capitol Annex, Rm 304 Frankfort KY 40601 also: District 5913 Whispering Hills Blvd Louisville KY 40219*

CLARK, LAWRENCE JAMES, minister; b. Greensboro, N.C., Feb. 1, 1957; s. Henry Walker and Katherine Margaret Clark; divorced; 1 child, Tyler James Little Eagle. AA, City Coll. Chgo., 1988; BBA, McKendree Coll., 2001; postgrad., Hood Theol. Sem., Salisbury, N.C. EMT. Tank comdr. U.S. Army, 1975—96; intern New Mt. Vernon United Meth. Ch., Winston-Salem, NC, 2001 ; min./student Bethany United Meth. Ch., Liberty, NC, Staley (N.C.) United Meth. Ch. Actor: (films) The Patriot, Shake Rattle and Roll, Juwana Man, Black Knight; (TV series) Dawson's Creek, 2 NASCAR commls. Soccer coach Optimist Club, Winston-Salem, 1997; county rep. Piedmont Fatherhood Initiative, Greensboro, NC, 2001; Rep. candidate for Pres., 1998—99; Libertarian candidate for gov. State of N.C., 1999; Libertarian candidate for senate, 2000. Named Ky. Col., Gov. John Y. Brown; recipient Order of St. George, US Armor Assn., 1995. Fellow: Am. Legion (local comdr. 1999—2000), Greensboro Lodge (jr. deacon 2001—02, sr. deacon 2003—); mem.: Optimist Club (v.p. 1985—86). Republican. Methodist. Avocations: boating, bowling, coaching sports, sports, walking. Home: PO Box 38132 Greensboro NC 27438-8132 Fax: 366-288-8982. E-mail: larryclark27408@yahoo.com.

CLARK, LEROY D. legal educator, lawyer; b. 1934; BA, CCNY, 1956; LLB, Columbia U., 1961. Bar: N.Y. 1961. Staff atty. Office of N.Y. Atty. Gen., 1961-62; asst. cousnel NAACP Legal Def. and Edn. Fund, Inc., N.Y.C., 1962-68; prof. law NYU Law Sch., N.Y.C., 1969-79, Cath. U., 1981—. Gen. counsel EEOC, 1979-81; arbitrator Am. Arbitration Assn., Fed. Mediation and Conciliation Svc.; mem. Pub. Employee Rels. Bd. Author: The Grand Jury: The Use and Abuse of Political Power, 1975, Employment Discrimination Law--Cases and Materials, 5th edit., 2000. Office: Law School Catholic Univ Am 3600 John Mccormack Rd NE Washington DC 20064-0001 E-mail: clarkl@law.cua.edu.

CLARK, LINDA WILSON, educational administrator; b. Milburn, Ky., Apr. 18, 1939; d. James Oscar and Bonnie Ophelia (Hayden) Wilson; m. Voris Wayne Clark, June 10, 1960; children: Angela Sharlet, John Wilson. BS, Murray State U., 1964, ME, 1970, rank I cert. in sch. adminstrn., 1972. Cert. tchr., sch. adminstr., Ky. Tchr. math. Hickman County High Sch., Clinton, Ky., 1964-68, Cen. Elem. Sch., Clinton, 1970-71, librarian, 1972-78, Hickman County High Sch., 1979-87; instrnl. supr., fed. program coord. Hickman County Bd. Edn., Clinton, 1987-94. Cons. Ky. Dept. Edn., Frankfort, 1975; speaker at profl. meetings. Costume designer, dir. local theater prodns., 1985—. Bd. dirs. Hickman County Pub. Libr., Clinton, 1981-93; mem. Hickman County Dem. Com., 1982; libr. First Bat. Ch., Fulton, 1997—. Named hon. Ky. Col., 1963, Woman of Woodcraft, 1969. Mem. ASCD, Ky. Coun. Adminstrs. Spl. Edn., West Ky. Assn. Adminstrs., West Ky. Assn. Sch. Suprs. (pres. 1991-92, sec.-treas. 1992-94), West Ky. Assn. Spl. Edn. Coords., Ky. Assn. Sch. Adminstrs., First Dist. Edn. Assn., Bykota Homemakers (pres. 1980-81, v.p. 1985-86, pres., 1995-99). Baptist. Avocations: gardening, reading, basket weaving, furniture refinishing, woodworking. Home: 7391 State Route 58 E Wingo KY 42088-8426 Office: Hickman County Bd Edn RR 3 Clinton KY 42031-9803

CLARK, LLOYD, historian, writer, educator; b. Belton, Tex., Aug. 4, 1923; s. Lloyd C. and Hattie May (Taylor) C.; m. Jean Reeves, June 17, 1950; children: Roger, Cynthia, Candyce. BSJ, So. Meth. U., 1948; B in Fgn. Trade, Am. Grad. Sch. Internat. Mgmt., 1949; MPA, Ariz. State U., 1972. String corr. AP, Dallas, 1941-42; reporter Dallas Morning News, 1947; editor, pub. Ex-Press, Arlington, Tex., 1945-48; publicity mgr. Advt. Counselors Ariz., Phoenix, 1949; reporter Phoenix Gazette, 1949-65; asst. pub. Ariz. Weekly Gazette, 1965-66; founder Coun. on Abandoned Mil. Posts-USA, 1966, Papago Trackers, 1985; project cons. City of Prescott, Ariz., 1971-72; dep. dir. adminstrv. svcs. No. Ariz. Coun. Govts., Flagstaff, 1972-73; regional adminstr. South Eastern Ariz. Govts. Orgn., Bisbee, 1973-75; local govt. assistance coord. Ariz. Dept. Transp., Phoenix, 1975-80, program adminstr., 1980-83; history instr. Rio Salado C.C., Phoenix, 1983-89, Ariz. State U.-West, Sun City, 1995-98; proprietor LC Enterprises, 1993—; columnist Daily News-Sun, Sun City, 1995—. Editor, pub. Clark Biog. Reference, 1956-62, mem. spkrs bur. Ariz. Humanities Coun., 1998-99, Author: Lloyd Clark's Scrapbook, Vol. 1, 1958, Vol. 2, 1960, Here's Looking at You, 1997, The Usual Suspects, 1998, You Must Remember This, 1999. Bd. dir. Friends of Channel 8, 1984-86; mem. transit planning com. Regional Pub. Transit Authority, 1988; bd. dir. Friends of Ariz. Hwys. Mag., 1989-92; mem. Ariz. State Geographic and Historic Names Bd., 1994—. Lt. AUS, 1942-46, maj., 1966-70, col. Res. Recipient Ariz. Press Club's exemplary gen. news coverage award, 1960, outstanding news reporting, 1961; Lloyd Clark Journalism scholarship named in honor U. Tex. at Arlington Alumni Assn., 1992. Mem. Soc. Profl. Journalists (pres. Valley of Sun chpt. 1964), Am. Grad. Sch. Internat. Mgmt. Alumni Assn. (pres. Phoenix chpt. 1965), Ariz. Hist. Soc. (bd. dir. cen. Ariz. chpt. 1992-93, state bd. dir. 1993-95), Sharlot Hall Hist. Soc. (life), Res. Officers Assn. (life), Ex-Students Assn. No. Tex. Agrl. Coll. Arlington (pres. 1946-48), U. Tex. Arlington Alumni Assn. (life, bd. dir. 1994—, Disting. Alumni Svc. award 1997, Mil. Sci. Dept. Hall of Honor 1998), The Westerners (sheriff Phoenix Corral 1986-88), University Club (Phoenix). Address: PO Box 1537 Surprise AZ 85378-1537

CLARK, LYNDA KAY, entrepreneur; b. Miami, Fla., Aug. 7, 1948; d. Conrad Todd and Clementene (Robinson) C. BFA, Fla. Atlantic U., 1969; MA with highest honors, Calif. State U., Long Beach, 1986. Asst. curator Long Beach Mus. of Art, 1984-86; curator I Ill. State Mus., Springfield, 1986-89; dir. No. Ill. U. Art Mus., Dekalb, 1989-93, S.D. Art Mus., Brookings, 1993-98; exec. dir. The Journey Mus., Rapid City, S.D., 1998-2000; ind. curator, fine art appraiser Rapid City, SD, 2000—; internat. sales Am. Indian Art, 2001—; mem. S.D. Arts Coun., 2003—. Grant reviewer Inst. Mus. and Libr. Svcs., Washington, 1999, S.D. Arts Coun., Pierre, 1999. Author, curator: The Ness Collection, 1995, Native Sons, 1997, Corporals, Cooks and Cowboys: African Americans in the Black Hills, 1999, Sacred Duty: Warriors and Weapons of the Northern Plains, 2000. Bd. dirs. City of Presidents, Rapid City, 1999. Fellow NEA, Kellogg Found., 1986. Mem. AAUW, Am. Assn. Museums, Upper Midwest Conservation Assn. (bd. dirs. 1995-2000), Am. Soc. Apprpaisers, Rotary Internat. Avocations: painting (acrylic on canvas), bicycling, gardening, travel. Home: 3011 Country Club Ct Rapid City SD 57702-5287 Office: Wild Horse Trading Co 605 Main St Ste 102 Rapid City SD 57701

CLARK, MARGARET ANN-CYNTHIA, television producer, writer; b. New Orleans, Aug. 20, 1964; d. Joseph Christian and Elizabeth Rose Muller; m. Samuel Varnell, Oct. 5, 1991 (div. Aug. 1997); m. Kenneth Clark, Sept. 12, 2000. Diploma, St. Mary's Dominican Coll., 1984; AS in Nursing, U. NY, 1990; BA in Journalism, 1999; postgrad., Harvard U., 2002. Pediatric, neonatal therapist Charity Hosp., New Orleans, 1984-86; therapist/nurse Touro Infirmary, New Orleans, 1986-91; therapist St. John's Mercy Hosp., St. Louis, 1991-92; nurse Grady Meml. Hosp., Atlanta, 1992-95; dir. pulmonary rehab. Touro Infirmary, 1995-98; writer prodr. WYES-TV, New Orleans, 1996-00; contbr. The Shakespeare Bulletin, Easton, Pa., 1996-01; corr. Advance News Mags., King of Prussia, Pa., 1990—; clin. coord. pulmonary medicine Boston U., 2001—; writer Ga. Med. Care Found., 2003. Author: Inspiration, 1998, Write for You, 2000, Dinner with Francis, 2001; editor: Medscape, 2001—; contbr. articles to profl. jours.; writer, producer (TV series) By Louisiana Hands, 1999, Steppin Out, 1996-99; 1st alto Jefferson Performing Arts Soc., 1996-98. Bd. dir. Shakespeare Festival, Tulane U., New Orleans, 1996—; pres. Officer's Wives Club, Ft. Gillen, Ga., 1993-95; mem. La. Cols., New Orleans, 1997—. Recipient Bird Lifetime Achievement award Am. Assn. Respiratory Care, 1996. Mem. Am. Assn. Respiratory Care, Am. Med. Writers Assn., Am. Coll. Chest Physicians, Nat. Acad. TV Arts & Sci. Roman Catholic. E-mail: maraisells@aol.com.

CLARK, MARK DAVID, public relations consultant; b. Pensacola, Fla., July 20, 1965; s. Kenneth Caro and Nancy Abbey C.; m. Noeline Rachel, June 27, 1998. AA, Pensacola Jr. Coll., 1985; BA in Pub. Rels., Auburn U., 1988; MA in Comms. Arts, U. West Fla., 1989. V.p. comms. United Way Northeast Fla., Jacksonville, 1990-98; pres. David Clark Pub. Rels., Jacksonville, 1999—. Vol. Big Brothers and Big Sisters, Jacksonville, 1997-98; bd. dirs. Arthritis Found., Jacksonville, 1999—, All Saints Early Learning & Cmty. Care Ctr., Jacksonville, 2000—. Mem. Pub. Rels. Soc. Am. (v.p. programs Jacksonville chpt. 1999-2000), Fla. Pub. Rels. Assn. (pres. 1996-97, North Fla. chpt., state v.p. fin. 2000-2001). Avocations: hiking, tennis. Office: 917 Dante Pl Jacksonville FL 32207 E-mail: dcpr@msn.com.

CLARK, MARK JEFFREY, paralegal, researcher; b. Alton, Ill., Nov. 2, 1953; s. William Alfred and Winifred May (Young) C.; m. Patricia Ann Newell, July 29, 1989; children: Jason William, Brandi Leigh. AS in Bus. Adminstrn., Lewis & Clark Coll., 1978; cert. paralegal, diploma in civil lit. and bus. law, Paralegal Inst., Atlanta, 1994, Commd. spl. officer Lake Ozark (Mo.) Police Dept., 1975-78; ind. paralegal J & B Enterprises, Woodriver, Ill., 1994—; criminal rschr. Pinkerton Svcs. Group, Charlotte, N.C., 1998—, MPC Legal Rsch. Consulting Svcs., Battle Creek, Mich., 1999—. Cons., rschr. Nationwide Corps., 1994—. With USN, 1972-75, Vietnam. Mem. Nat. Paralegal Assn., KC (4th degree), Am. Legion. Democrat. Roman Catholic. Avocations: scuba diving, golf, bowling. Home: 318 S Pence East Alton IL 62024 Personal E-mail: MJC3562002@yahoo.com. Business E-Mail: MJC356@netscape.net.

CLARK, MARK WILLIAM, dean, educator; b. Jacksonville, N.C., July 19, 1945; s. Herbert P. and Elsa M. Clark; m. Reiko Watanabe, Jan. 10, 1969; children: Midori, Saori. BA, U. Calif., Berkeley, 1973, MA, 1976; PhD, Stanford (Calif.) U., 1980. Asst. prof. Hofstra U., Hempstead, N.Y., 1977-81; assoc. prof. U. Mont., Missoula, 1981 86; asst. dean grad. sch., assoc. prof. U. Northern Colo., Greeley, 1986-92; asst. v.p. acad., dean grad. sch. affairs Adams State Coll., Alamosa, Colo., 1992-96; dean edn. Northeastern State U., Tahlequah, Okla., 1996—2001; dean profl. studies U. Wis., Eau Claire, 2001—. Author: (with others) Minorities in History Education, 1994, Cooperstown Symposium on Baseball and American culture, 1990, 91, Comparative Physical and Education and Sport, 1986, 88; contbr. articles to profl. jours. Bd. dirs. Great Expectations Found., Tahbquah, Okla., 1996-2001. Recipient Outstanding Adminstr. award Okla. Assn. of Health, Phys. Edn. Recreation and Dance, 1997. Mem. Am. Assn. of Colls. for Tchrs. Edn., Am. Edn. Rsch. Assn., Soc. for Am. Baseball Rsch., Kappa Delta Pi (Educators Who Make a Difference award 1998), Phi Delta Kappa. Avocations: blues music, japanese wood block prints. Office: Coll Profl Studies U Wis Eau Claire Eau Claire WI 54702 E-mail: clark@uwec.edu.

CLARK, MARY HIGGINS, writer, business executive; b. N.Y.C., Dec. 24, 1929; d. Luke J. and Nora C. (Durkin) Higgins; m. Warren Clark, Dec. 26, 1949 (dec. Sept. 1964); children: Marilyn, Warren, David, Carol, Patricia; m. John J. Coheeney, Nov. 3, 1996. BA, Fordham U., 1979; hon. doctorate, Villanova U., 1983, Rider Coll., 1986, Stonehill Coll., 1992, Marymount Manhattan Coll., 1992, Chestnut Hill, 1993, Manhattan Coll., 1993, St. Peter's Coll., 1993; 7 additional hon. doctorates. Advt. asst. Remington Rand, 1946; stewardess Pan Am., 1949-50; radio scriptwriter, prodr. Robert G. Jennings, 1965-70; v.p., ptnr.,

creative dir., prodr. radio programming Aerial Communications, N.Y.C., 1970-80; chmn. bd., creative dir. D. J. Clark Enterprises, N.Y.C., 1980—. Author: Silent Night, Aspire to the Heavens, A Biography of George Washington, 1969 (N.J. Author award 1969), Where Are the Children?, 1976 (N.J. Author award 1977), A Stranger Is Watching, 1978 (N.J. Author award 1978), The Cradle Will Fall, 1980, A Cry in the Night, 1982, Stillwatch, 1984, Weep No More, My Lady, 1987, While My Pretty One Sleeps, 1989, The Anastasia Syndrome and Other Stories, 1989, Loves Music, Loves to Dance, 1991, All Around the Town, 1992, I'll Be Seeing You, 1993, Remember Me, 1994, The Lottery Winner, 1994, Bad Behavior, 1995, Let Me Call You Sweetheart, 1995, Moonlight Becomes You, 1996, Pretend You Don't See Her, 1997, The Plot Thickens, 1997, You Belong to Me, 1998, All Through the Night, 1998, We'll Meet Again, 1999, Before I Say Good-Bye, 2000, Deck the Halls, 2000, Daddy's Little Girl, 2002, Silent Night/All Through the Night, 2002, On the Street Where You Live, 2002; (with Thomas Chastain and others) Murder in Manhattan, 1986; editor: Murder on the Aisle: The 1987 Mystery Writers Anthology, 1987. Recipient Grand Prix de Litterature Policiere, France, 1980, Horatio Alger Award, 1997, Gold Medal of Honor, Irish-American Historical Society, Spirit of Achievement Award, Albert Einstein Coll. of Med., Yoshiva University, Nat. Arts Club Gold Medal in Education. Mem. Mystery Writers Am. (pres. 1987, dir.), Authors League, Am. Soc. Journalists and Authors, Acad. Arts and Scis. Republican. Roman Catholic.*

CLARK, MATT, science writer; b. Chgo., Feb. 3, 1930; s. Matthew and Kathryn Clark; m. Ellen Ann Mitchell, Aug. 23, 1952 (dec. 1978); children: Thomasin, Geoffrey Beach, Douglas Mitchell; m. Phyllis Malamud, Nov. 9, 1986. Grad., Hill Sch., 1947; AB, Wesleyan U., Middletown, Conn., 1951. Reporter Boston Traveler, 1953-56, sci. editor, 1956-58; writer Med. News, N.Y.C., 1958- 61; medicine editor Newsweek mag., 1961-88; free-lance sci. writer, 1958—. Served with USNR, 1951-53. Recipient Albert Lasker Med. Journalism award, 1964, 67, Howard W. Blakeslee award Am. Heart Assn., 1965, 68, 73, 83, Penney-Mo. mag. award in health, 1967, 71, 75, med. journalism award AMA, 1969, Claude Bernard Sci. Journalism award Nat. Soc. Med. Rsch., 1971, Page One award Newspaper Guild N.Y., 1974, 83, Media award (mag.) Am. Cancer Soc., 1976, N.Y. Deadline Club award 1977, James T. Grady award Am. Chem. Soc., 1983, Am. Med. Writers Assn.-Searle Labs. journalism award, 1983. Fellow AAAS, mem. Nat. Assn. Sci. Writers, Century Assn., Coffee House Club (N.Y.C.).

CLARK, MATTHEW HARVEY, bishop; b. Troy, N.Y., July 15, 1937; s. M. Harvey and Grace (Bills) C.. Student, Coll. Holy Cross, Worcester, Mass.; BA, St. Bernard's Sem., Rochester, N.Y.; STL, N. Am. Coll., Rome; JCL, Gregorian U., Rome. Priest Roman Catholic Ch., 1962. Vice chancellor Diocese of Albany, NY; Cath. chaplain Albany Law Sch.; mem. faculty Vincentian Inst.; chmn. pers. bd. Diocese of Albany; spiritual dir. N. Am. Coll.; bishop Diocese of Rochester, Rochester, NY, 1979—. Office: Chancery Office 1150 Buffalo Rd Rochester NY 14624-1823*

CLARK, MAXINE, retail executive; b. Miami, Fla., Mar. 6, 1949; d. Kenneth and Anne (Lerch) Kasselman; m. Robert Fox, Sept. 1984. B.A. in Journalism, U. Ga., 1971. Exec. trainee Hecht Co., Washington, 1971, hosiery buyer, 1971-72, misses sportswear buyer, 1972-76; mgr. mdse. planning and research May Dept. Stores Co., St. Louis, 1976-78, dir. mdse. devel., 1978-80, v.p. mktg. and sales promotion Venture Stores div., 1980-81, sr. v.p. mktg. and sales promotion Venture Stores div., 1981-83, exec. v.p. mktg. and softlines, 1983-85; exec. v.p. apparel Famous-Barr, St. Louis, 1985-86; v.p. mdsing. Lerner Shops div. Limited Inc., N.Y.C., 1986-88; exec. v.p. Venture Stores, St. Louis, 1988-92; pres. Payless ShoeSource, Topeka, 1992-96; founder, CEO Smart Stuff, Inc. children's retail concept devel. firm and the Build-A-Bear Workshop, 1996—; bd. dirs. Earthgrains Co., Tandy Brands Accessories Co., Wave Techs., Inc., Dept. 56. Sec., Lafayette Sq. Restoration Com., 1978-79; mem. Com. 200 Nat. Coun. Coll. Arts and Scis. Washington U., St. Louis; trustee U. Ga. Found., 1995—; mem. nat. adv. coun. Girl Scouts U.S.A., 1995-97. Office: Build A Bear Workshop 1960 Innerbelt Business Center Overland MO 63114-5760

CLARK, MELVILLE, JR., physicist, electrical engineer; b. Syracuse, N.Y., Dec. 19, 1921; s. Melville and Dorothy Drew (Speich) C. BS, MIT, 1943, postgrad., 1943-44, U. N.Mex., 1945-46, Princeton U., 1946; MA, Harvard U., 1947, PhD, 1949. Registered profl. engr., Mass. Mem. staff Radiation Lab. MIT, Cambridge, Mass., 1942-45; mem. staff Manhattan dist. U. Calif., Los Alamos, N.Mex., 1945-46; physicist Brookhaven Nat. Lab., Upton, N.Y., 1949-53; dir. 416 South Salina St. Corp., Syracuse, NY, 1957—66, pres., 1965—66; mem. staff Radiation Lab. U. Calif., Livermore, 1953-55; dir. Clark Music Co., Syracuse, N.Y., 1948-60, v.p., 1957-60; pres. Meldor Corp., Cazenovia, N.Y., 1960-66; sr. engring. specialist Sylvannia Electric Products, Waltham, Mass., 1962-64, pres., 1965—66; sr. scientist AVCO, Wilmington, Mass., 1964-67; sr. scientist NASA, Cambridge, 1967-70; sr. devel. engr. Thermo Electron, Waltham, 1970-73; sr. cons. engr., sr. tech. strategist Combustion Engring., Windsor, Conn., 1973-83; pres. Melville Clark Assocs., Wayland, Mass., 1949—. Cons. Raytheon Mfg. Co., Waltham, 1955-58, United Shoe Machinery Co., Beverly, Mass., 1956, Arthur D. Little, Cambridge, 1957-58, Aerodyne Rsch., Inc., Billerica, Mass., 1983-84; tech. expert witness Pennie and Edmonds, N.Y.C., 1984—; trustee Inst. Sci. Rsch. in Music, Wayland, Mass., 1990—; assoc. prof. nuclear engring. MIT, Cambridge, 1955-62; adviser Congressman Robert Drinan. Author: (with Rose) Plasmas and Controlled Fusion, 1961, (with Hansen) Numerical Methods of Reactor Analysis, 1964; translator, editor: (with B. Daniel) Introduction to the Theory of Ionized Gases, 1960; contbr. articles to profl. jours.; patentee in field. MIT scholar, 1939-43; NRC predoctoral fellow Harvard U., 1946-49, NRC predoctoral and Hercules Powder Co. fellow Princeton U., 1946. Mem. AAAS, IEEE, Am. Phys. Soc., Am. Inst. Physics, Fusion Power Assocs., Acoustical Soc. Am., Assn. Computing Machinery (Greater Boston chpt.), Soc. Music Perception and Cognition, Sigma Xi. Home and Office: 8 Richard Rd Wayland MA 01778-4099 E-mail: mclarkjr@gis.net.

CLARK, MELVIN EUGENE, chemical company executive; b. Ord, Nebr., Oct. 2, 1916; s. Ansel B. and Ruth Joy (Bullock) C.; m. Virginia May Hiller, Sept. 16, 1938; children— John Robert, Walter Clayton, Dale Eugene, Merry Sue. BSChemE cum laude, U. Colo., 1937; grad. exec. program, Columbia U., 1952; grad. advanced mgmt. program, Harvard U., 1961. Asst. editor Chem. Engring., McGraw-Hill, N.Y.C., 1937-41; mktg. staff Wyandotte Chem. Corp., Mich., 1941-53; chief program br. War Prodn. Bd., Washington, 1942-44; v.p. mktg. Frontier Chem. Co., Wichita, 1953-69; exec. v.p. chems. div. Vulcan Materials Co., Birmingham, Ala., 1969-81, v.p. planning, chems. and metals group, 1981-82; cons., 1982—. Pres. Chlorine Inst., 1977-80 Contbr. numerous articles to profl. jours. Recipient U. Colo. Alumni Recognition award, 1972; named Chem. Market Rsch. Assn. Man of Year, 1963, Disting. Engring. Alumnus, U. Colo., 1985, Centennial medalist Coll. of Engring., U. Colo., 1994. Mem. AIChE, Comml. Devel. and Mktg. Assn., Am. Chem. Soc., Boulder Country Club, Tau Beta Pi, Pi Mu Epsilon. Republican. Mem. Christian Ch. Home and Office: 7145 Cedarwood Cir Boulder CO 80301-3716 E-mail: meclark1@aol.com.

CLARK, MERRELL EDWARD, JR., lawyer; b. Bklyn., Apr. 30, 1922; s. Merrell Edward and Eleanor Everest (Wild) C.; m. Hollis Logan, May 22, 1943; children: Julie Clark Goodyear, Kenyon Wild. BA, Yale U., 1943, LLB, 1948. Bar: N.Y. 1948, U.S. Dist. Ct. (so. dist.) 1949, U.S. Ct. Appeals (2d cir.) 1949, U.S. Tax Ct. 1951, Conn. 1952, U.S. Dist. Ct. (ea. dist.) N.Y. 1952, U.S. Dist. Ct. (ea. dist.) N.Y. 1952, U.S. Supreme Ct. 1956, U.S. Ct. Appeals (6th cir.) 1965, U.S. Ct. Appeals (8th cir.) 1973, U.S. Ct. Appeals (4th cir.) 1974, U.S. Dist. Ct. (no. dist.) N.Y. 1982, U.S. Dist. Ct. (we. dist.) N.Y. 1982. Assoc. Winthrop, Stimson, Putnam & Roberts, N.Y.C., 1948-55, ptnr., 1956-91. Editor Yale Law Sch. Jour., 1947-48. Mem. Town Meeting, Greenwich, Conn., 1953-56, com. on jud. appointments (Appelate Div. 1st Dept.), 1978-82, 2d cir. jud. conf. evaluation com., 1980-87; dir.; trustee Perrot Meml. Library, Old Greenwich, Conn., 1956-63, Pomfret (Conn.) Sch., 1966-74, Richard Found., N.Y.C., 1965-2002, William Nelson Cromwell Found., N.Y.C., 1979—, Steep Rock Assn., Washinton, Conn., 1993—, Internat. Coll. Hospitality Mgmt., 1994-2002; adviser women's rights project ACLU, 1976-90; mem. N.Y.C. Bd. Ethics, 1987-89; chair N.Y.C. Conflicts of Interest Bd., 1989-90, N.Y.C. Hardship Appeals Bd., 1993-2001; bd. dirs. N.Y. Legal Aid Soc., 1985-88. Served to capt. AUS, 1943-46. Decorated Bronze Star with two battle stars. Mem. ABA (ho. of dels. 1985-89), Assn. of Bar of City of N.Y. (pres. 1978-80), Am. Law Inst., Am. Coll. Trial Lawyers, River Club (N.Y.C.), India House Club (N.Y.C.), Washington Club (Conn.). Office: Pillsbury Winthrop LLP 1 Battery Park Plz New York NY 10004-1490 Personal E-mail: htgclark@aol.com. Business E-Mail: mclerk@pillsbury-winthrop.com.

CLARK, MERRELL MAYS, management consultant; b. Clifton Springs, N.Y., Feb. 8, 1935; s. Arthur Tillotson and Ruthanna Frame (Anderson) C.; m. Lynne Ruth Butcher, June 14, 1957; children: Elisabeth Lynne Clark Jenks, Aimee Ruthanna Clark Peterson, Catherine Merrell Clark Seda. BA, Yale U., 1957, MA in Religion, 1970. Asst. to advt. mgr. Armstrong Rubber Co., West Haven, Conn., 1959-60; mktg. analyst SSC & B, N.Y.C., 1960-62, account exec., 1962-64, v.p., account supr., 1964-68, v.p. mgmt. supr., 1968-70; prin. Knight, Gladieux & Smith, N.Y.C., 1970-72; v.p. Edna McConnell Clark Found., N.Y.C., 1972-77; exec. v.p. Acad. for Ednl. Devel., N.Y.C., 1977-81; prin. Clark Co., Scarsdale, N.Y., 1981—. Contbr. articles to profl. jours. Bd. dirs. Westchester Cmty. Svcs. Coun., White Plains, 1965-72, Elderhostel, Boston, 1977-98, pres. Elderworks, Scarsdale, 1978—, Nat. Sch. Vol. Program, Alexandria, Va., 1977-89, chmn. nat. adv. bd., Coun. for the Arts in Westchester, White Plains, 1978-83, Scarsdale Found., 1981-90; advisor Nat. Exec. Svc. Corps, N.Y.C., 1977-87, United Way Scarsdale-Edgemont, 1989-97; treas. Greenacres Assn. Scarsdale, Inc. 1993-97; treas. Yale Westchester Alumni Assn., 1995-97, pres., 1997—. Mem. Fox Meadow Tennis Club, Yale Club. Republican. Presbyterian. Avocations: piano, organ, painting, platform tennis. Office: PO Box 1385 Scarsdale NY 10583-9385

CLARK, MICHAEL EARL, psychologist; b. Berea, Ohio, July 20, 1951; s. William Gray and Marguerite Jane (Charles) C.; m. Laura Lynn Putt, June 19, 1976 (div. Nov. 1987); 1 child, Brian Gray. BA, Kent State U., 1974, PhD, 1978. Asst. dir. chem. dependency unit N.D. State Hosp., Jamestown, N.D., 1978-79; staff psychologist VA Med. Ctr., Chillicothe, Ohio, 1979-84, Bay Pines, Fla., 1984-89; clin. dir., pain program James A. Haley Vets. Hosp., Tampa, Fla., 1989—. Assoc. prof. dept. psychology U. South Fla., Tampa, 1986—, clin. asst. prof. dept. neurology Sch. Medicine, Tampa, 1991—; adj. psychologist, counseling ctr. U. South Fla.; cons. to the correctional med. authority, State of Fla., 1993—; adv. bd. Pain Program Accreditation and Nat. Pain Data Bank, nat. pain mgmt. coordinating com.; mem. nat. pain edn. com., chmn. nat. outcomes com. Dept. Vets. Affairs; cons. in field. Contbr. chpts. to Innovations in Clinical Practice, 1991, Social Psychology: A Sourcebook, 1983, Pain Management: A Practical Guide for Clinicians, 2001; contbr. articles to Biofeedback and Self-Regulation, Jour. Personality Assessment, Jour. Clin. Psychology, Brit. Jour. Clin. Psychology, Jour. Dental Rsch., The VA Practitioners, Psychol. Assessment, Pain Forum, Am. Jour. Pain Mgmt., Vets. Health Sys. Jour., Jour. Rehab. Rsch. & Devel., others; ad hoc reviewer Biofeedback and Self-Regulation, Psychol. Assessment, Clin. Jour. Pain, Jour. Personality Assessment, Clin. Jour. Pain, Jour. Rehab. R&D; editor Am. Pain Soc. website. Vice-chmn. Paint Valley Mental Health Bd., Chillicothe, 1980-84. Mem. Am. Pain Soc., Am. Acad. Pain Mgmt., N.Y. Acad. Scis., Internat. Assn. for Study of Pain, Soc. for Personality Assessment. Democrat. Home: 9645 Fox Hearst Rd Tampa FL 33647-1829 Office: Psychology Svc (116B) VAMC 13000 Bruce B Downs Blvd Tampa FL 33612-4745 E-mail: michaeleclark@highstream.net.

CLARK, MORTON HUTCHINSON, lawyer; b. Norfolk, Va., Apr. 21, 1933; s. David Henderson and Catharine Angelica (Hutchinson) C.; m. Lynn Harrison Adams, Aug. 12, 1961; children: Allison Adams, David Henderson, Susan West, Julia Dixon. BA in English, U. Va., 1954, LLB, 1960. Bar: Va. 1960, U.S. Dist. Ct. (ea. dist.) Va. 1960, U.S. Ct. Appeals (4th cir.) 1976, U.S. Ct. Appeals (1st cir.) 1993, U.S. Supreme Ct. 1993. Assoc. Vandeventer Black LLP, Norfolk, 1960-65, ptnr., 1965—. Co-editor: The Virginia Lawyer, 1991-93. Chmn. Va. Commn. for Children and Youth, Richmond. Fellow Am. Coll. Trial Lawyers, Va. Law Found.; mem. Maritime Law Assn. (exec. com. 1984-87), Hoffman I'Anson Am. Inns of Ct. (exec. com. 1993-95), The Harbor Club (pres.), Town Point Club, Princess Anne Country Club, Farmington Country Club. Episcopalian. Avocations: off shore racing, cruising. Home: 103 Rivers Edge Kingsmill Williamsburg VA 23185-8930 Office: Vandeventer Black LLP 500 World Trade Ctr Norfolk VA 23510-1679

CLARK, NANCI, elementary education educator; b. Reno, Apr. 11, 1957; d. Edwin Dail Baggett and Sharon Adair (Patterson) Marks; m. Rodney K. Clark, Oct. 25, 1986; children: Ashley Nichole, Sean Patrick. BS, Calif. State U., 1979, MS, 1983. Bilingual tchr. Moutain View Sch. Dist., 1979; resource specialist bilingual tchr. Orange (Calif.) Unified Sch. Dist., 1980-88; resource specialist Alvord Unified Sch. Dist., Riverside, Calif., 1988-90, Rialto (Calif.) Unified Sch. Dist., 1990-93, Corona (Calif.)-Norco Unified Sch. Dist., 1993—. Mem. ASCD, Assn. Calif. Sch. Adminstrs. Office: Corona-Norco Unified Sch Dist 1150 Paseo Grande Corona CA 92882-5608 E-mail: clark4@wwdb.org.

CLARK, NANCY ELLEN, podiatrist; b. Orange, N.J., Feb. 20, 1951; d. William Leonard and Rita (O'Boyle) Clark. BSN, Rutgers Univ., Newark, 1976; MD, N.Y. Coll. Podiatry, N.Y.C., 1992. Head nurse ICU Newark Beth Isreal Med. Ctr., Newark, 1976—85; clin. rsch. analyst Marian Pharm., NJ, 1985—89; dir. surgical svc. N.Y. Coll. Podiatry, N.Y.C., 1998—. Residency dir. N.Y. Coll. Podiatry, N.Y.C., 1999—, assoc. prof., 1995—; nat. rep. of edn. Enhancement Project, N.Y.C., 1994—99. Initiated, orgn., staffed Foot Care Ctr. at Ground Zero, N.Y.C., 2001. Recipient Podiatrist of the Yr., N.Y.C. Podiatrist Soc., 2002, Svc. Award, N.J. State Soc. (podiatry), 2002. Office: FCNY 55 E124th St New York NY 10035

CLARK, NANCY LUCINDA BROWN, retired music teacher; b. Akron, Ohio, Dec. 11, 1946; d. Gardner Lane Brown and Ruth Marie Thomas; m. Eugene Ernest Zielinski, Aug. 1968 (div. Mar. 1989); children: Ruth Karlotte Zielinski Hansen, Jennifer Jane Zielinski Webber; m. Douglas Napier Clark, Mar. 11, 1989. Student, Kent State U., 1964-66; BS in Mus. Edn., U. Ill., 1968; postgrad., Nazareth Coll., 1981-82. Music tchr. pre-kindergarten and kindergarten Diocese of Rochester, N.Y., 1970s; tchr., supr. Muzak Cranford (N.J.) Mid. Sch., 1982-87; asst. music dir. First Presbyn. Ch., Maplewood, N.J., 1984-89; music min. Salem Bapt. Ch., Lexington, Ga., 1990-96, ret., 1996. Author (book chpt.) Nantucket Postmarks to 1890, 1989, Philatelic Congress Book Maine Fancy Cancels, 2000; contbr. articles to profl. jours. Pres. Olymphilex 96, Atlanta, 1992—96; mem. Barnstable County Hist. Pres. Commn., 2001—; juror, team leader Juvalux 98, Luxembourg, 1998, 2000; chmn. 1st Nat. Youth in Philately Symposium, 2002; v.p. Barnstable County Hist. Pres. Commn., 2002—; dir. edn. Stamp Camp USA, 2003—; bd. dirs. Oglethorpe County Libr., Lexington, 1989—98, Athens-Clarke County Regional Libr., 1992—98. Recipient Internat. Gold award ROCPEX Taipei, China, 1981, Polska, 1997, Grand Stamporee award, Palm Beach, Fla., 1996. Mem. Am. Philatelic Soc. (bd. dirs. 1993-97, treas. 1999-2003), Collectors Club N.Y., Boston Philatelic Group, Am. Assn. Philatelic Exhibitors (sec. 1998-2000, bd. dirs. 2000—). Avocation: philately.

CLARK, NOREEN MORRISON, behavioral science educator, researcher; b. Glasgow, Scotland, Jan. 12, 1943; came to U.S., 1948; d. Angus Watt and Anne (Murphy) Morrison; m. George Robert Pitt, Dec. 3, 1982; 1 child, Alexander Robert. BS, U. Utah, 1965; MA, Columbia U., 1972, MPhil, 1975, PhD, 1976. Rsch. coord. World Edn. Inc., N.Y.C., 1972-73; asst. prof. Sch. Pub. Health Columbia U., N.Y.C., 1973-80, assoc. prof., 1980-81, Sch. Pub. Health U. Mich., Ann Arbor, 1981-85, prof., chmn. dept. health behavior and health edn., 1985-95, Marshall H. Becker prof. of pub. health, 1995—, dean, 1995—. Adj. prof. health adminstrn. Sch. Pub. Health Columbia U., 1988—; prin. investigator NIH, 1977—; mem. adv. com. pulmonary diseases Nat. Heart, Lung & Blood Inst., Rockville, Md., 1983-87, mem. adv. com. for prevention, edn. and control, 1987-91, coordinating com. Nat. Asthma Edn. Program, 1991—; assoc. Synergos Inst., N.Y.C., 1987-99; nat. adv. environ. health scis. coun. NIH, 1999—. Co-author: Evaluation of Health Promotion, 1984; editor Health Edn. and Behavior, 1985-97; mem. editorial bd. Women in Health, Advances in Health Edn. and Promotion, Home Health Care Services Quarterly; contbr. articles to profl. jours. Bd. dirs./advisors Aaron Diamond Found., 1990-97, Family Care Internat., N.Y.C., 1987—, Internat. Asthma Coun., Am. Lung Assn., N.Y.C., 1988—, World Edn., Inc., The Healthtrak Found. Prize. Fellow Soc. Pub. Health Edn. (pres. 1985-86, Disting. Fellow award 1987); mem. APHA (chair health edn. sect. 1982-83, Derryberry award in behavioral sci. 1985, Disting. Career award 1994), Am. Thoracic Soc. (Health Edn. Rsch. award Nat. Asthma Edn. Program 1992, Healthtrak Edn. prize 1997), Internat. Union Health Edn., Soc. Behavioral Medicine, Coun. Fgn. Rels., Nat. Acad. Sci. Inst. Medicine, Pi Sigma Alpha. Office: U Mich Sch Pub Health 109 Observatory St Ann Arbor MI 48109-2029

CLARK, PAT ENGLISH, lawyer; b. Austin, Tex., Feb. 26, 1940; s. Pat Wheeler and Jennie Bell (Lagrone) C.; m. Peggy Arnold Gray, March 16, 2002; 1 child, Susan Louise Beisert. BA, JD, U. Tex. Bar: Tex. 1963, U.S. Ct. Mil. Appeals 1964, U.S. Dist. Ct. (so. and no. dists.) Tex. Staff atty. Phillips Petroleum Co., Houston, 1967-69; atty. Amoco Production Co., Houston, 1969-75; ptnr. Vinson & Elkins, Houston, 1975-95, Borrego & Clark, 1996-99. Capt. JAGC, U.S. Army, 1964-67. Presbyterian. Office: 9809 Villa Maria Cove Austin TX 78759

CLARK, PATRICIA, molecular biologist; b. Lake Village, Ark., Mar. 21, 1928; d. Cleburn Clem and Helen Miller (Baker) C. BA, Washington U., St. Louis, 1950, MA, 1955; PhD, Purdue U., 1962. Microanalyst Washington U., St. Louis, 1950-51; rsch. chemist The Chemstrand Corp., Decatur, Ala., 1953-55; assoc. chemist So. Rsch. Inst., Birmingham, Ala., 1955-56; grad. asst. Purdue U., West Lafayette, Ind., 1956-61; biochemist Gerontology Rsch. Ctr. Child Health and Human Devel. NIH, Balt., 1961-78, Nat. Inst. on Aging NIH, Balt., 1978-96; ret. Vis. rschr. Gerontology Rsch. Ctr., NIA, NIH, 1997. Hon. mention Westinghouse Talent Search, 1946. Fellow Am. Inst. Chemists; mem. AAAS, Am. Chem. Soc., Gerontol. Soc., N.Y. Acad. Scis., Sigma Xi, Pi Mu Epsilon, Alpha Lambda Delta. Home: Dulaney Towers 1 Smeton Pl Apt 1206 Baltimore MD 21204-2737

CLARK, PATRICIA MAYE, oncology nurse; b. Mt. Pleasant, Mich., Oct. 8, 1957; d. Robert Eugene and Letha Elizabeth (Walling) C. BS in Nursing, Baylor U., 1980; MS in Nursing, U. Tex., Arlington, 1990. Advanced oncology cert. nurse. Staff nurse U. Tex. Med. Br., Galveston, 1980; clin. nurse III Baylor U. Med. Ctr., Dallas, 1981-83, asst. supr., 1983-84, oncology nurse educator, 1984-88, clin. rsch. nurse, 1988-90; nurse practitioner Dana-Farber Cancer Inst., Boston, 1991-96, 98; sr. assoc. Med. Affairs Genzyme Corp., Cambridge, Mass., 1997-98; founding ptnr. Newtonnet Prodns., LLC, Roscommon, Mich., 1998—2001; nurse practitioner U. Mich., 2001—03, fellow, 2003—. Mem. Oncology Nursing Soc. (assoc. editor Oncology Nursing Forum), Sigma Theta Tau.

CLARK, PETER BRUCE, newspaper executive; b. Detroit, Oct. 23, 1928; s. Rex Scripps and Marian (Peters) C.; m. Lianne Schroeder, Dec. 21, 1952 (dec. Jan. 1996); children: Ellen Clark Brown, James. BA, Pomona Coll., 1952, LL.D. (hon.), 1972; M.P.A., Syracuse U., 1953; PhD, U. Chgo., 1959; H.H.D., Mich. State U., 1973, Lawrence Inst. Tech., 1982; LL.D. (hon.), U. Mich., 1977. Research assoc., then instr. polit. sci. U. Chgo., 1957-59; asst. prof. polit. sci. Yale U., 1959-61; with Evening News Assn., Detroit, 1960-86, corp. sec., 1960-61, v.p., 1961-63, pres., 1963-86, chmn. bd., chief exec. officer, dir., 1969-86; pub. Detroit News, 1963-81, also dir.; dir. Gannett Co., Inc., 1986-99. Regent's prof. UCLA Grad. Sch. Mgmt., 1987; chmn. Fed. Res. Bank Chgo., 1975-77, former chmn. br. Fed. Res. Bank Detroit. Served with AUS, 1953-55. Mem.: Am. Soc. Newspaper Editors, Am. Newspaper Pub. Assn. (dir. 1966—74), Ironwood Country Club.

CLARK, PHILIP HART, retired urban and regional planner; b. Hartford, Conn., May 23, 1938; s. Raymond Gilbert and Phyllis Angeline (Hart) C. BArch, Cornell U., 1961, M in Regional Planning, 1968. Asst. project mgr. W.R. Grimshaw Co., Denver, 1964-65; project coord. U. Pa., 1968-69; sr. planner County of Fairfax, Va., 1969-72; urban planner Hellmuth, Obata & Kassabaum, Washington, 1972-73; chief air transp. planning Met. Washington Coun. Govts., 1973-77; urban planning cons. Reston, Va., 1977-78; with Gordian Assocs., Washington, 1978-79; program mgr. base comprehensive planning USAF Engring. and Svcs. Ctr., Tyndall AFB, Fla., 1979-81; program mgr. base comprehensive planning hdqrs. USAF Pentagon, Washington, 1981-92; environ. restoration program mgr. Sta. Hdqrs. USAF Pentagon, Washington, 1992-98; ret., 1998. Vis. lectr. George Washington U., 1975, Am. U. 1976-77, Air Force Inst. Tech., 1979-91, USAF Acad., 1989; speaker Soc. Am. Mil. Engrs. Mtgs., aviation assn. meetings. Mem. Paul Hill Chorale, 1970-76, Choral Arts Soc., 1977-79, 81-83, Reston Chorale, 1983-95, 99—, Kaleidoscope Theatre, Panama City, Fla., 1980-81, Washington Men's Camerata, 1995-97. Capt. USAF, 1961-64. Fellow Am. Inst. Cert. Planners; mem. Am. Planning Assn., Theta Chi. Democrat. Avocations: music, reading, swimming, travel, photography. E-mail: fpdphil@aol.com., phc3@cornell.edu.

CLARK, PRISCILLA ALDEN, retired elementary education educator; b. Ray, Ariz., June 4, 1940; d. Edmund A. and Rena F. White; m. Larry C. Clark, Sept. 5, 1959; children: Russell, Kenneth, Clifford, Thomas. BS, Tex. Woman's U., 1987. Cert. elem. tchr., ESL tchr. Tchr. kindergarten and pre-kindergarten, grade level chair Irving (Tex.) Ind. Sch. Dist.; kindergarten tchr. Shady Grove Day Care, Irving; tchr. Irving (Tex.) Sch. Dist.; ret., 2003. Active in ch. and boy scouts; dir. new beginnings Diocese of Dallas and Ft. Worth. Recipient Silver Beaver award. Mem. Sci. Tchrs. Assn. Tex. (dist. sci. trainer), Kindergarten Tchrs. Tex., Assn. Tex. Profl. Educators (state del.), Mortar Bd., Irving Theatre Guild, Pi Lambda Theta (chair nat. com., conf. chair region VII, nat. spkr., internat. v.p. 2001-, pres. Alpha Sigma chpt., pres. Region VII, Region 7 Outstanding award 1996, Internat. Thelma Jean Brown Outstanding Classroom Tchr. award 1997), Alpha Chi, Delta Delta Delta, Omega Rho Alpha, Delta Kappa Gamma (pres. Mu Omicron chpt., Internat. Woman of Yr. 1992-93). Home: 2717 Peach Tree Ln Irving TX 75062-3230

CLARK, RAYMOND OAKES, banker; b. Ft. Bragg, N.C., Nov. 9, 1944; s. Raymond Shelton and Nancy Lee (McCormick) C.; m. Patricia Taylor; children: Matthew Patrick, Geoffry Charles. BBA, U. Ariz., 1966; postgrad., U. Wash., 1984-86. Mgnt. trainee First Interstate Bank, Phoenix, 1966, credit analyst, 1968-69, asst. br. mgr. Scottsdale, Ariz., 1969-72, asst. v.p., br. mgr. Tempe, 1972-90, v.p. br. mgr. Scottsdale, 1990-92, v.p. mgr. main office Phoenix, 1992—.

CLARK, RICHARD EUGENE, music educator; b. Wenatchee, Wash., Apr. 16, 1930; s. Raymond Otto Clark and Maude Myrtle Bass. BA, Western Wash. U., 1952, MA, 1970; MDiv, Am. Bapt. Sem. of the West, 1955; MA, Calif. State U., Carson, 1989; postgrad., Wycliffe Coll., Toronto, 1960—61. Nat. cert. tchr. music. Sociology instr. Coll. of the Ozarks, Point Lookout, Mo., 1970—71, S.W. Mo. State U., Springfield, 1971—72, Whatcom C.C., Bellingham, Wash., 1972—73; cmty. planner Whatcom County Opportunity Coun., Bellingham, Wash., 1973—76; itinerant prof. sociology and religion Chapman U., Orange, Calif., 1977—83; journalist, former editor Record Jour. Newspaper, Ferndale, Wash., 1984—90; piano instr. Wash. State Music Tchrs. Assn.-Bellingham chpt., Blaine, Wash., 1990—. Editor The Clarion Wash. State Music Tchrs. Assn., 1994—97, pres. Bellingham chpt., 1997—99. Author: Point Roberts, USA: The History of a Canadian Enclave, 1980, Sam Hill's Peace Arch: Remembrance of Dreams Past, 2003. Founder Pacific Arts Found.; vicar Ch. Holy Nativity, Calgary, Canada, 1961—67; pastor First Bapt. Ch., Pincher Creek, Canada, 1955—59. Recipient Bob Robbins Performing Arts award, Close Up Found. & No. Light Newspaper, 1999, Dyson Hague Meml. Liturgics First prize, 1960. Mem.: Old Main Soc. E-mail: dclark30@peoplepc.com.

CLARK, RICHARD T. pharmaceutical executive; BA in Liberal Arts, Washington and Jefferson Coll., 1968; MBA, Am. Univ., 1970. Quality control insp., indsl. engr., quality control analyst, lead supr. pharm. prodn. MSD, 1972—78, sr. new products planner, 1978—81, prodn. mgr. Elkton Pharm. Labs., 1981—83, prodn. mgr. indsl. engring., 1983—84; sr. mgr. indsl. engring. MPMD, 1984—85, dir. ops. improvement, 1985—86; sr. dir. mgmt. engring. Merck Sharp & Dohme/MPMD, 1986—89; exec. dir. mgmt. engring. Merck Pharm. Mfg. Divsn., 1989—91; v.p. materials mgmt. and mgmt. engring. MMD, 1991—93, v.p. procurement and materials mgmt., 1993—94, v.p. N.Am. ops., 1994—96, sr. v.p. N.Am. ops., 1996—97; sr. v.p. quality comml. affairs Merck Mfg. Divsn., 1997; exec. v.p., COO Merck-Medco Managed Care, 1997—2000, pres., 2000—. Lt. U.S. Army, 1970—72. Office: Merck and Co Inc One Merck Dr Whitehouse Station NJ 08889-0100

CLARK, RICHARD WALTER, education consultant; b. Mt. Pleasant, Iowa, Apr. 14, 1936; s. Samuel Richard and Floreine Eunice (Walz) C.; m. Rosemary Helma Savage, June 10, 1958; children: Melissa O'Neal, Cameron Clark. BA,

U. Wash., 1957, MA, 1963, PhD, 1970. Cert. tchr., prin., supt., Wash. Lectr., grad. asst. U. Wash., Seattle, 1960-61; tchr. Bellevue (Wash.) Pub. Schs., 1961-65, adminstr., 1965-91, dep. supt., to 1991; sr. assoc. Ctr. for Ednl. Renewal, U. Wash., Seattle, 1987—, Inst. for Ednl. Inquiry, Seattle, 1992—; exec. dir. Nat. Network Ednl. Renewal, 2001—. Cons. Pew Charitable Trusts, Phila., 1988-2001, MacArthur Found., Chgo., 1991-92, Coalition of Essential Schs., Brown U., Providence, 1990-97, Ednl Commn. of the States, Denver, 1990-91, Calgary (Alta., Can.) Bd. Edn., 1990-91, others. Author: Effective Speech, 1982, 3d edit., 1994, (with others) Glencoe English 10, 11, 12, 1981, 2nd edit., 1985, (with others) Kids and School Reform, 1997, Effective Professional Development Schools, 1999; contbr. articles to profl. jours., chpts. to books. Pres. Youth Eastside Svcs., Bellevue, 1972. Capt. USMC, 1957-63. Recipient Outstanding Performance Pub. Svc. award Seattle King County Mcpl. League, 1987; named Educator of Yr., Lions Club, 1991. Mem.: Nat. Soc. Study of Edn., Wash. Assn. Sch. Adminstrs., Am. Edn. Rsch. Assn., Phi Delta Kappa. Methodist. Home and Office: 209 140th Ave Bellevue WA 98005 E-mail: clark@msn.com.

CLARK, RICHARD WARD, trust company executive, consultant; b. NYC, Oct. 23, 1938; s. Richard Leal and Dorothy Jane (Whittaker) C. BA with distinction, U. Rochester, N.Y., 1960; MBA in Fin., U. Pa., 1962. Corp. planning analyst Campbell Soup Co., Camden, N.J., 1965-67; asst. product mgr. Gen. Mills, Inc., Mpls., 1967-70; sr. fin. analyst McKesson Corp., San Francisco, 1970-71, asst. divsn. controller, 1971-72, divsn. controller, 1972-78, gen. mgr. grocery products devel., 1978-79; v.p., controller McKesson Foods Group/McKesson Corp., 1979—82, v.p. fin., 1982—85, dir. strategic planning, 1985-87; v.p. fin., CFO, Provigo Corp., San Rafael, Calif., 1987-90; cons. on hotel devel., Napa Valley Assocs., S.A., San Francisco, 1990-92, health care cons., 1993-97; mgmt. cons. securities and ins. litig., 1998—. Author: Some Factors Affecting Dividend Payout Ratios, 1962; musician (albums) Dick Clark at the Keyboard, I Love a Piano, 1990, I Play the Songs, 1993, On My Way to You, 1997, Christmas Piano with Violin, 1999. Mem. adv. bd. Salvation Army, San Francisco, 1984—, chmn., 1993-2000. Lt. (j.g.) USNR, 1962-64, PTO. Fellow, St. Andrew's Soc.; Sherman fellow, U. Rochester, 1960. Mem. Bohemian Club, Beta Gamma Sigma. Republican. Presbyterian. Avocations: piano, skiing, tennis, singing, jogging. Home: 2201 Sacramento St Apt 401 San Francisco CA 94115-2314

CLARK, ROBERT ARTHUR, mathematician, educator; b. Melrose, Mass., May 3, 1923; s. Arthur Henry and Persis (Kidder) C.; m. Jane Burr Crofut Kinder, June 25, 1966. Student, Colo. Coll., 1940-42; BA, Duke, 1944; MA, MIT, 1946, PhD, 1949. Instr., research asso. MIT, 1946-50, vis. asst. prof., 1956-57; faculty Case Inst. Tech. (now Case Western Res. U.), Cleve., 1950—, prof. math., 1964-85, prof. emeritus, 1985—, acting head dept. math., 1960-61, assoc. chmn. dept. math., 1974-79, 82-84, exec. officer, 1981-82. Vis. mem. U.S. Army Math. Research Center, Madison, Wis., 1961-62 Mem. AAAS, Am. Math. Soc., Math. Assn. Am., Soc. Indsl. and Applied Math., Phi Beta Kappa, Sigma Xi. Achievements include spl. research asymptotic integration theory of differential equations and theory thin elastic shells. Home: 7469 Sherman Rd Gates Mills OH 44040-9769 Office: Case Western Res Univ Dept Math Cleveland OH 44106

CLARK, ROBERT HENRY, JR., holding company executive; b. Manchester, N.H., Mar. 4, 1941; s. Robert Henry and Elva C. (Stearns) C.; m. Rosalie Foster Case, Dec. 21, 1963; children: Robert Henry III, Hilary Eagan, Hadley Case. BSBA, Boston U., 1964. Mcpl. bond underwriter Merrill Lynch, Pierce, Fenner & Smith, N.Y.C., 1964-70; v.p. Case, Pomeroy & Co., Inc., N.Y.C., 1971-75, exec. v.p., 1975-83, pres., 1983—, CEO, 1993—, chmn., 1999—; v.p. fin. Felmont Oil Corp., 1972-79, exec. v.p., 1979-84. Trustee Boston U., 1984-87. Mem. Sigma Alpha Epsilon Office: Case Pomeroy & Co Inc 529 5th Ave Fl 16 New York NY 10017-4684

CLARK, ROBERT KING, communications educator emeritus, lecturer, consultant, actor, model; b. Springfield, Mass., Apr. 12, 1934; s. Harry Robert and Alice (McClure) C.; m. Suzanne Chapin, Apr. 9, 1966; children— Jennifer, Jeffrey, Anne Elizabeth BA, U. Wyo., 1956; MA, U. Tenn., 1960; PhD, Ohio State U., 1971. Instr. journalism U. Tenn., Knoxville, 1958; instr. speech Westminster Coll., New Wilmington, Pa., 1959-61; faculty Bowling Green State U., Ohio, 1963—, prof. radio-TV film, 1980-84, prof. emeritus, 1985—; gen. mgr. Sta. WBGU-FM, 1976-85. Cons. in field; lectr. in field; seminar leader in field; yoga instr./therapist. Contbr. articles to profl. jours. Presbyterian. Office: 1064 Village Dr Bowling Green OH 43402-1231

CLARK, ROBERT LLOYD, JR., librarian; b. McAlester, Okla., Sept. 12, 1945; s. Robert Lloyd and Ruth Fairel (Nelson) C.; children: Roberta, Johnathan, Kathryn; m. Audrey Lynn Wolfe, 1987. BA, U. Okla., 1968, M.L.S., 1969. Dir. div. archives and records Okla. Dept. Librs., Oklahoma City, 1968-72, data processing coord., 1972-73, dir., 1976—. Asst. dir. pub. services Jackson (Miss.) Met. Library System, 1973-74; dir. Mid-Miss. Regional Library, Kosciusko, 1974-76; sec. Okla. Archives and Records Commn., 1976—; ex officio sec. Okla. Arts and Humanities Council, 1976-81; sec. adv. council Library Services and Constrn. Act., 1976—; adv. bd. Okla. Hist. Records, 1979—; adv. council U. Okla. Sch. Library and Info. Sci., 1985-88, 95—; adv. council State regents for Higher Edn. on Ednl. Outreach, 1985-88; cons. in field. Author: Archive-Library Relations, 1976; contbr. articles to library pubs. Mem. adv. com. State Regents for Higher Edn., 1984-88. Robert L. Clark, Jr. Day proclaimed by Gov. of Okla., Nov. 15, 1982 Mem. ALA (chmn. pub. library assn. interlibrary coop. com. 1974-77, mem. standards com. 1979-82), Okla. Library Assn., Southwestern Library Assn. (pres. 1980-82), Amigos Bibliog. Council (exec. bd. 1977-80), Assn. State Libraries (bd. dirs. 1977-80), Assn. Chief Officers of State Library Agys. (chmn. legis. com. 1979-81, chmn. 1982-84), Western Coun. State Librs. (pres. 2000). Office: Librs Dept 200 NE 18th St Oklahoma City OK 73105-3205

CLARK, ROBERT MUREL, JR., lawyer; b. Dallas, Mar. 7, 1948; s. Robert M. Sr. and Dorrace Helen (Schaerdel) C.; m. Kimberly Ann Kerss, Oct. 25, 1986; 1 child, Ashley Pendleton. BBA, U. Tex., 1972; MBA, So. Meth. U., 1978; JD, Oklahoma City U., 1982. Bar: Tex. 1982, U.S. Dist. Ct. (no. dist.) Tex. 1982, U.S. Ct. Appeals (5th cir.) 1982, U.S. Supreme Ct. 1988; cert. in civil trial law Tex. Bd. Legal Specialization; cert. trial specialist Nat. Bd. Trial Advocacy. Ptnr. Eddleman & Clark, Dallas, 1989—. Author: The Evangelical Knights of Saint John, 2003; contbr. articles to profl. jours. Del. state conv. Tex. Rep. Party, 1970, 72, 74, 82, 90; bd. dirs. Haile Selassie Fund for Ethiopian Children in Need; sec., bd. dirs. Dallas Goethe Ctr.; bd. dirs. Tex. Conf. of Chs. Decorated grand officer Order of Ethiopian Lion, 1998, hon. knight Order of Vitez (Hungary), 1997, knight Order of St. John (Brandenburg), 1996; recipient Grand Cross, Rwanden Order of the Lion, 2000. Fellow Tex. Bar Found. (life), Soc. Antiquaries (Scotland); mem. State Bar Tex., Am. Bd. Trial Advs. (Dallas chpt.), Oak Cliff Bar Assn. (pres. 1990), Am. Soc. Legal History, Soc. of the Cin., Aztec Club, Sons Republic of Tex., Founders and Patriots Am. (dep. atty. gen.), Nat. Huguenot Soc. (former coun. gen. and 3d v.p. gen.), St. Nicholas Soc., Johanniterorden-Bailiwick of Brandenburg, Johanniter Hilfsgemeinschaften (bd. dirs., Washington), Army and Navy Club (Washington), City Tavern Club (Washington), Phi Delta Phi, Phi Delta Theta. Episcopalian. Office: 4627 N Central Expy Dallas TX 75205-4022

CLARK, ROBERT NEWHALL, electrical and aeronautical engineering educator; b. Ann Arbor, Mich., Apr. 17, 1925; s. Ellef S. and Esther (Baker) C.; m. Mary Quiatt, Aug. 20, 1949; children: Charles W., John R., Timothy J., Franklin T. BSEE, U. Mich., 1950, MSEE, 1951; PhD, Stanford U., 1969. Registered profl. engr., Wash., Minn. Rsch. engr. Honeywell, Inc., Mpls., 1951-57; lectr. Stanford U., 1968; prof. elec. engring. U. Wash., Seattle, 1957—, prof. aeronautics and astronautics, 1986-94; prof. emeritus, 1994—. Vis. scientist Fraunhofer Gesellschaft, Karlsruhe, W.Ger., 1976-77; guest prof. U. Duisburg, W.Ger., 1983-84; cons. analyst Boeing Aerospace Co., Seattle, 1971-92. Author: Introduction to Automatic Control Systems, 1962, Fault Diagnosis in Dynamic Systems, 1989, Control System Dynamics, 1996, Issues of Fault Diagnosis for Dynamic Systems, 2000. With USMC, 1943-46. NSF fellow, 1966-68. Fellow IEEE (life), AIAA (assoc.). Home: 3900 50th Ave NE Seattle WA 98105-5238 Office: U Wash PO Box 352500 Seattle WA 98195-2500

CLARK, ROBERT PHILLIPS, newspaper editor, consultant; b. Randolph, Vt, Dec. 3, 1921; s. James S. and Gladys M. (Phillips) C.; m. Jeanne Orr Rice, Dec. 14, 1949; children: Patricia Orr Clark Roy, Elizabeth Phillips Clark Christiansen. AB, Tufts U., 1942; MA, U. Mo., 1948. Reporter Owensboro Messenger & Inquirer, Ky., 1948-49; reporter, sci. writer Courier-Jour., Louisville, 1949-62, Washington corr., 1958; mng. editor Louisville Times, 1962-71; exec. editor Courier-Jour. and Louisville Times, 1971-79; editor Fla. Times-Union and Jacksonville Jour., 1979-82; v.p news Harte-Hanks Newspapers, 1983-86; co-chmn. rsch. com. Newspaper Readership Project, 1982-83; news, editorial cons., 1987—. Disting. vis. prof. Baylor U., 1990-92, Slippery Rock U., 1990; mem. accrediting com. Accrediting Coun. on Edn. in Journalism and Mass Comm., 1986-89. Author: Success Stories: What 28 Newspapers Are Doing to Gain and Retain Readers, 1988, Keys to Success: Strategies for Newspaper Marketing in the '90s, 1989; also numerous articles. Bd. dir. Louisville Presbyn. Theol. Sem., 1968-73, past sec.; trustee S.W. Sch. of Art and Craft, 1993-96; bd. dir. San Antonio Bot. Soc., 1996—; Pulitzer Prize juror, 1968, 69, 88, 89. Served to capt. US Army, WWII, PTO. Decorated Bronze Star, Purple Heart; Nieman fellow Harvard U., 1960-61; named Editor of Yr., Nat. Press Photographers Assn., 1967. Mem. Am. Soc. Newspaper Editors (pres. 1985-86, v.p. Found. 1980-81, 85-86, contbr. Am. Editor), Soc. Profl. Journalists (contbr. Quill Jour.), AP Mng. Editors Assn. (pres. 1974-75, chmn. regents 1979-80), Internat. Press Inst. (bd. dir. Am. com. 1981-87), Soc. Mayflower Descendants (capt. San Antonio colony 1999-2003, elder 2003—), Club Giraud, Torch Club (San Antonio, pres. 1997-98, contbr. The Torch), Harvard Club, Delta Tau Delta. Democrat. Presbyterian. Home: 3506 Elm Knoll San Antonio TX 78230-2706

CLARK, ROBERT T. career officer; b. Aug. 28, 1948; Student, Tex. Tech. U., 1970. Commd. U.S. Army, advanced through grades to maj. gen., 1998, comdg. gen. 101st airborne div. air assault, 1998—. Office: 101st Airborne Div Air Assault Fort Campbell KY 42223

CLARK, ROBERT WESLEY, neurologist; b. Jamestown, N.Y., Apr. 16, 1946; s. Robert Wesley and Dorothy (Depue) C.; m. Linda Gray, June 15, 1968 (div. Jan. 1982); 1 child, Jennifer Marie; m. Marcia Ramm, June 10, 1983; 1 child, Robert Scott. BS in Biology, John Carroll U., 1968; MD, Ohio State U., 1972. Diplomate Am. Bd. Psychiatry and Neurology, Am. Bd. Med. Examiners, Am. Bd. Sleep Medicine. Intern Barnes Hosp., St. Louis, 1972-73, resident, 1973-74; resident in neurology Ohio State U. Coll. Medicine, Columbus, 1974-77, clin. instr. neurology and psychiatry, 1977-78, asst. prof., 1978-81; med. dir. clin. sleep lab. St. Anthony Med. Ctr., Columbus, 1981-85, dir. clin. sleep and electroencephalography labs., 1985-90; med. dir. Mt. Carmel East Sleep Disorders Ctr., Columbus, 1990-97, Columbus Cmty. Hosp. Regional Sleep Disorders Ctr., 1997—2001, Columbus Cmty. Health Regional Sleep Disorders Ctr., 2001—. Cons. neurology Columbus Children's Hosp., Columbus, 1982—, Doctor's Hosp., Columbus, 1984—; med. advisor Ohio Narcolepsy Assn., Akron, Ohio, 1983—; cons. Nat. Insts. Health Gen. Clin. Research Com., Bethesda, Md., 1979. Contbr. articles on neurology, other topics; also reviewer. Recipient Nu Sigma Nu award Ohio State U. Coll. Medicine, 1969, John Edwin Brown award Ohio State U. Coll. Medicine, 1972. Mem. Am. Acad. Neurology (Weir Mitchell award 1977), Am. Narcolepsy Assn. (bd. dirs. 1986-91), Sociedade Latinoamericano do Sono (mem.-at-large 1989-90), Ohio Narcolepsy Assn., Assn. Profl. Sleep Socs. (accredited clin. polysomnographer), Epilepsy Found. Ohio, Epilepsy Found. Franklin County, Jaleistas Club (San Diego chpt.). Roman Catholic. Avocations: flamenco guitar, photography. Office: 1430 S High St Columbus OH 43207-1093 E-mail: Flamenco@netexp.net.

CLARK, ROBIN ERVIN, public health educator; b. Elizabethtown, N.C., June 5, 1952; s. George Ellis and Martha (Campbell) C.; m. Judith Ann Freeman, May 12, 1984. BA, Appalachian State U., 1974; MA, U. Conn., 1979; PhD, Brandeis U., 1991. VISTA vol. ACTION, Jonesboro, Ark., 1974-75; counselor Alexander Children's Ctr., Charlotte, N.C., 1975-76; dir. youth svcs. City of Bristol, Conn., 1978-81; exec. dir. Agawam (Mass.) Counseling Ctr., 1981-86; rsch. assoc. Harvard U. Kennedy Sch. Govt., Cambridge, Mass., 1987-90; asst. prof. Dartmouth Med. Sch., Hanover, N.H., 1991-97, assoc. prof., 1997—; dir. Behavioral Health Policy Inst., 2000—. Author: (with Judith F. Clark) Encyclopedia of Child Abuse, 1989, (with R.E. Drake, C. Mercer et al) Readings in Dual Diagnosis, 1998, Substance Abuse Treatment for People with Severe Mental Disorders: A Program Manager's Guide, 1998, with Judith F. Clark and Christine Adamec) Encyclopedia of Chila Abuse, 2d edit., 2001; contbr. articles to profl. jours. Mem. Am. Pub. Health Assn., Internat. Health Econ. Assn., Acad. for Health Svcs. Rsch. and Health Policy, Assn. for Pub. Policy and Mgmt., Phi Kappa Phi. Office: Dartmouth Med Sch Dept Cmty & Family Medicine Strasenburgh 7250 Hanover NH 03755

CLARK, RODNEY GEORGE, retired obstetrician, gynecologist; b. Ortonville, Minn., July 1, 1924; BS in Medicine, U. N.D., 1946; MD, U. Ill., 1948. Diplomate Am. Bd. Ob-Gyn. Intern St. Lukes Hosp., Denver, 1948-49, resident in gen. surgery, 1949-50; resident in ob-gyn. Louisville Gen. Hosp., 1950-52, 54-55. Fellow AMA; mem. Am. Coll. Ob-Gyn.

CLARK, RON D(EAN), cosmetologist; b. Wagga Wagga, NSW, Australia, Nov. 4, 1947; came to U.S., 1976; s. J. D. and Lura A. (Bennington) C. M Internat. Cosmetology, U. Geneva, Switzerland; ed., Eng., France, Belgium, Fed. Republic Germany, The Netherlands. Registered cosmetologist, Tex. Free-lance cosmetologist, Houston and L.A. Cosmetologist N.Y.C. Make-up and hair stylist for feature films, TV, commls. and Broadway musicals, 1977—. Decorated Order of Svc. to the Empire (Eng.); Emmy nomination for spl. effects, 1989, 91. Home and Office: 1227 W Clay St Houston TX 77019-4153 E-mail: re-clark@swbell.net.

CLARK, RONALD DEAN, retired newspaper editor; b. Millersburg, Ohio, Aug. 29, 1943; s. Dean Eli and Lavaun Lurline (Glasgo) C.; m. Carole Ann Smith, Oct. 15, 1983; children from previous marriage— Kelly Jay, Carrie Anne, Courtney Erin BA, Kent State U., 1965; MS in Journalism, Northwestern U., 1966; MPA, Humphrey Inst. of Pub. Affairs, U. Minn., 1999; LLD, U. St. Thomas, St. Paul, Minn., 2003. Reporter Akron Beacon Jour., Ohio, 1966 67, asst. city editor, 1967-68, city editor, 1968-70, met. editor, 1970-71, statehouse bur. chief, 1971-76, chief editl. writer, 1976-81; editl. page editor St. Paul Pioneer Press, St. Paul, 1981—2003; ret., 2003. Past pres. Minn. Newspaper Found. Recipient Pulitzer Prize (shared) Columbia U., 1971. Mem. Soc. Profl. Journalists, Nat. Conf. Editorial Writers, World Press Inst. (bd. dirs.), Informal Club (St. Paul). Luth. Avocations: cycling, music. Home: 13823 Tomahawk Dr S Afton MN 55001-9706 Office: Saint Paul Pioneer Press 345 Cedar St Saint Paul MN 55101-1004 E-mail: clarkrd@attbi.com.

CLARK, ROSE SHARON, elementary school educator; b. Winslow, Ind., Oct. 31, 1942; d. William Noel Fettinger and Mary Emaline Jones; m. Charles Edgar Clark, June 2, 1968; children: Mary Elizabeth, Christopher Edgar. BS, Oakland City (Ind.) U., 1964; MS, Ind. U., 1968. Elem. edn. tchr. Hendricks Twp. Sch., Shelbyville, Ind., 1964—67, Thomas A. Hendricks, Shelbyville, Ind., 1967—74, 1984—. Mem. bd. First Ch. of the Nazarene, Shelbyville, 1994—, First Ch. of God, Shelbyville, 1969—90; bd. dirs. Bright Star Pre-Sch., Shelbyville, 2001—. Mem.: AAUW (v.p.-treas. 1972—2000), Alpha Delta Kappa. Home: 2466 N Richard Dr Shelbyville IN 46176 Office: Thomas A Hendricks Sch 1111 S Knightstown St Shelbyville IN 46176

CLARK, ROSS BERT, II, lawyer; b. Lafayette, Ind., Dec. 23, 1932; s. Ross Bert and Pauline Frances (Wilkinson) C.; m. Madge Logan, Dec. 27, 1959; 1 stepchild, George W. Johnson III. BA in History, U. of the South, 1954; JD, U. Tenn., 1960. Bar: Tenn. 1961, U.S. Dist. Ct. (we. dist.) Tenn. 1961, U.S. Dist. Ct. (no. dist.) Miss. 1981, U.S. Dist. Ct. (ea. dist.) Ark. 1996, U.S. Ct. Appeals (6th cir.) 1962. Law clk. to presiding judge U.S. Dist. Ct. (we. dist.) Tenn., Memphis, 1961-62; assoc. Rupert & Ewing, Memphis, 1962-64, Laughlin, Watson, Garthright & Halle, Memphis, 1964-68; ptnr. Laughlin, Halle, Clark, Gibson, McBride, Memphis, 1968-84, McKnight, Hudson, Lewis, Henderson & Clark, Memphis, 1985-91, Apperson, Crump, Duzane & Maxwell, Memphis, 1991-96, Armstrong Allen PLLC, Memphis, 1996—. Instr. med. and dental jurisprudence U. Tenn., Memphis, 1963-72; asst. city atty. City of Memphis, 1972-78. Tenn. commr. Nat. Conf. Commrs. on Uniform Laws, 1998—; chmn. bd. dirs. Memphis Heart Assn., 1971—72; mem. adv. coun. U. Tenn. Law Sch., 1983—90, chmn. adv. coun., 1986—88; trustee U. of the South, 1992—95, 1998—. Fellow: Tenn. Bar Found. (trustee 1989—98, chmn. 1996—97), Am. Bar Found.; mem.: Memphis Bar Assn. (treas. 1981, sec. 1982, v.p. 1983, pres. 1984), Tenn. Bar Assn. (ho. of dels. 1986—88, bd. govs. 1988—94), Tenn. Supreme Ct. Hist. Soc. (bd. dirs. 2002—), Rotary (sec. 1988, bd. dirs. 1988—90, 2002—, Paul Harris fellow 2002). Republican. Episcopalian. Office: Armstrong Allen PLLC Brinkley Plz Ste 700 80 Monroe Ave Memphis TN 38103-2481

CLARK, ROY THOMAS, JR., chemistry educator, administrator; b. Feb. 22, 1922; s. Roy Thomas and Ada Louise (Masur) C.; m. Lavanie Anne Busby, JAn. 3, 1948; 1 child, Thomas David. BS in Chemistry, S.W. Tex. State Coll., 1947, MA in Chemistry, 1950; student Air Force Inst. Tech., Aerojet Gen. Corp., Sacramento, 1964-65. Commd. 2d lt. USAAF, 1943; advanced through grades to lt. col. USAF, 1966; various assignments U.S., 1943-59; project officer propulsion br. Agena divsn. Directorate Space Sys., Air Force Ballistic Missile Divsn., L.A., 1959-60; chief propulsion sect., astrovehicle br. Agena divsn. Office Dep. Comdr. Satellite Sys., Space Sys. Divsn., L.A., 1960-61; asst. prof. chemistry USAF Acad., Colo., 1961-63, assoc. prof., 1963-64; project officer 6595th Aerospace Test Wing, Vandenberg AFB, Calif., 1965-66; chief Titan Launched Satellite Sys. Office, 1966 69; ret., 1969; adminstrv. officer dept. chemistry U. Tex., Austin, 1969-84. Investor, 1999—. Decorated Air medal. Mem. Am. Chem. Soc. Episcopalian. Home: 7711 Shadyrock Dr Austin TX 78731-1432 E-mail: tom.clark@mail.utexas.edu.

CLARK, R(UFUS) BRADBURY, lawyer, director; b. Des Moines, May 11, 1924; s. Rufus Bradbury and Gertrude Martha (Burns) C.; m. Polly Ann King, Sept. 6, 1949; children: Cynthia Clark Maxwell, Rufus Bradbury, John Atherton. BA, Harvard U., 1948, JD, 1951; diploma in law, Oxford U., Eng., 1952; D.H.L., Ch. Div. Sch. Pacific, San Francisco, 1983. Bar: Calif. 1952. Assoc. O'Melveny & Myers, L.A., 1952-62, sr. ptnr., 1961-93; mem. mgmt. com., 1983-90; of counsel O'Melveny & Myers LLP, L.A., 1993—. Bd. dirs. Econ. Resources Corp., Brown Internat. Corp., Brown Citrus Sys., Inc., Avoco Internat. Corp., John Tracy Clinic, also pres. 1982-88, Tracy Family Hearing Ctrs., Ch. Charitable Found. Episcopal Diocese L.A., 2000—. Editor: California Corporation Laws, 7 vols, 1976—. Chancellor Prot. Episcopal Ch. in the Diocese of L.A., 1967—, hon. canon, 1983—. Capt. U.S. Army, 1943-46. Decorated Bronze Star with oak leaf cluster, Purple Heart with oak leaf cluster; Fulbright grantee, 1952. Mem. ABA (com. law and acctg., task force on audit letters 1976-93, com. on opinions 1988-92), State Bar Calif. (chmn. drafting com. on gen. corp. law 1973-81, drafting com. on nonprofit corp. law 1980-84, mem. exec. com. bus. law sect. 1977-78, 84-87, sec. 1986-87, mem. com. nonprofit orgns. 1991—, mem. task force on opinions 1999—), L.A. County Bar Assn., Harvard Club, Chancery Club, Alamitos Bay Yacht Club (Long Beach, Calif.). Republican. Office: O'Melveny & Myers LLP 400 S Hope St Los Angeles CA 90071-2899

CLARK, SANDRA ANN, clinical social worker; b. Long Branch, N.J., Dec. 4, 1942; d. Richard Marshall and Margaret (Novak) C.; m. John Jacob Hoffman, May 4, 1969 (div. 1987); children: Rebecca L., Benjamin C., Rachael A.; m. William E. Wilbur, June 25, 1989. BA, Valparaiso U., 1966; MSW, SUNY, Albany, 1968. Lic. clin. social worker, Maine; cert. clin. hypnotist. Pvt. practice psychotherapy, Kittery, Maine, 1982—; asst. exec. dir., coord. children's program N.H. Parents Anonymous, Portsmouth, 1985-86; mental health cons. Strafford County Head Start, Somersworth, N.H., 1985-88; interim exec. dir. N.H. Parents Anonymous, Portsmouth, 1986-87; home sch. coord. Portsmouth Sch. System, 1986-87; clin. social worker Rackingham Counseling Ctr., Exeter, N.H., 1986-89, York County Counseling Svcs., Kittery, 1989-90; exec. dir. Growing Consciousness Assn., Saco, Maine, 1995-96. Mem. faculty U. Conn., Concord, N.H., 1987. Mem. NASW, Acad. Cert. Social Workers, Am. Hypnosis Tng. Acad., Hypnosis Info. Network, Eye Movement Desensitization Reprocessing Internat. Assn., N.H. Mediators Assn., No. N.E. Soc. Clin. Hypnosis, Hypnosis Info. Network, Portsmouth Group Psychotherapy Soc. Democrat. Home and Office: 25 Old Ferry Ln Kittery ME 03904-1305 E-mail: hausonhill@aol.com.

CLARK, SANDRA MARIE, school administrator; b. Hanover, Pa., Feb. 17, 1942; d. Charles Raymond Clark and Mary Josephine (Snyder) Clark Wierman. BS in Elem. Edn., Chestnut Hill Coll., 1980; MS in Child Care Adminstrn., Nova U., 1985; MS in Ednl. Adminstrn., Western Md. Coll., 1992. Cert. elem. tchr., elem. prin., Pa. Tchr. various elem. schs., Pa., 1962-75; asst. vocation directress Mt. St. Joseph Motherhouse, Chestnut Hill, Pa., 1975-76; tchr. St. Catharine's Sch., Spring Lake, N.J., 1976-77; asst. mgr. Jim's Truck Stop, New Oxford, Pa., 1977-81; adminstr. Little People Day Care Sch., Hanover, 1981-88, sec., treas. bd. dirs., 1985-86; coord. regional resource Magic Yrs. Child Care & Learning Ctrs., Inc., Hanover, 1987-88; prin. St. Vincent de Paul Sch., Hanover, Pa., 1988—. Presenter Hanover Area Seminar for Day Care Employees, 1983-86. Coord. sch. safety patrols St. Vincent's Sch., Hanover, 1969-75, vice-chmn. bd., 1982-84; multi-media instr. first aid ARC, Hanover, 1983-86, bd. dirs., 1984-88; exec. sec. of bd. of dirs. ARC, Hanover, 1988; 1st v.p. Hanover Area Coun. of Chs., 1988, pres., 1989; validator accredidation program Nat. Acad. Early Childhood Programs, Washington, 1987—; bd. dirs. Life Skills Unltd. Handicapped Adults, 1988—; facilitator Harrisburg Diocesan Synod, Hanover, 1985-88, parish del., 1988. Pa. Dept. Pub. Welfare tng. grantee, 1986. Mem. NAFE, Nat. Cath. Ednl. Assn. Clubs: Internat. Assn. Turtles (London). Democrat. Roman Catholic. Avocations: swimming, reading, writing children's stories. Home: 348 Barberry Dr Hanover PA 17331-1302 Office: St Vincent De Paul Sch Hanover PA 17331

CLARK, SARA M. artist, art educator; b. Richmond, Va., July 15, 1957; d. David Stafford and Janet (Bird) Miller; m. Scott Hughes Clark, May 13, 1989. Cert. in Studio Arts, Holden Sch. Art, Charlottesville, Va., 1976; BFA in Art History, Va. Commonwealth U., 1980, MFA in Painting, 1996. Adj. prof. of the arts Va. Commonwealth U., Richmond, 1996—. One-woman shows include Mabey Gallery, Richmond, 1996, Anderson Gallery, 1996, Artspace, 1997, Anton Gallery, Washington, 2001, Elizabeth Roberts Galery, 2003, NIH, Bethesda, Md., 2001, Starch, Richmond, Va., 2003, Elizabeth Roberts Gallery, Washington, D.C., 2003, exhibited in group shows at N.Am. Cultural Inst., Lima, Peru, 1997, Cudahy's Gallery, Richmond, 1998, 1999, Anton Gallery, Washington, 1999, Corcoran Gallery Art, 1998, 1999, Twentieth Century Gallery, Williamsburg, Va., 1999, Am. Ctr. for Physics, College Park, Md., 2000, Cath. U. Am., Washington, 2000, Frostburg (Md.) State U., 2002, Peninsula Fine Arts Ctr., Newport News, Va., 2002, Athenaeum, Alexandria, Va., 2002, Peninsula Fine Arts Ctr., 2002, Frostburg State U., 2002. Recipient award of merit, Twentieth Century Gallery, Williamsburg, 1999; Va. Mus. Fine Arts profl. fellow, 1999-2000. Mem.: 1708 Gallery (bd. dirs. 1999—). E-mail: sclark234@yahoo.com.

CLARK, SCOTT H. lawyer; b. Logan, Utah, Jan. 7, 1946; BA with honors, U. Utah, 1970; JD, U. Chgo., 1973. Bar: Utah 1973. Ptnr. Ray, Quinney & Nebeker P.C., Salt Lake City, 1980—. Mem. ABA, Utah State Bar, Salt Lake County Bar Assn., Phi Beta Kappa, Phi Kappa Phi, Pi Sigma Alpha. Office: Ray Quinney & Nebek PC PO Box 45385 Salt Lake City UT 84145-0385 E-mail: SClark@RQN.com.

CLARK, SHARON JACKSON, private school administrator; b. Istanbul, Turkey, Feb. 3, 1939; d. John Warren and Maxine Jett (Brient) Jackson; m. Ronald Eugene Clark, June 6, 1959; children: Kristen Anne, Kevin Brooks, Jeffrey Kimball. BFA, Calif. Coll. Arts and Crafts, 1968; MS in Edn., Wheelock Coll., 1978; student, Moore Coll. Art. Co-founder Jowanio, Syracuse, NY, The Thoreau Sch., Salt Lake City, Glen Urquhart Sch., Beverly, Mass.; head, founder Clark Sch. for Creative Learning, Danvers, Mass. Mem. Gifted/Talented Educators North Shore (bd. dir.), Danvers Hist. Soc. (bd. dir.). Home: 487 Locust St Danvers MA 01923-1252

CLARK, SHARON W. employee benefits company executive; b. Trenton, N.J., July 16, 1952; d. John J. and Virginia E. (Devey) Woods; m. Kevin A. Clark, Oct. 11, 1980; children: Matthew, Andrew. BA, Rosemont (Pa.) Coll., 1974; MBA, Pace U., 1976. Asst. sec. human rels. Mfrs. Hanover Trust, N.Y.C., 1975-77; human resources mgr. Exxon, N.Y., Conn., N.J., 1977-93; pres. Woods & Assocs., Summit, N.J., 1993-94; human rels. cons. Gemini Cons., Inc., Morristown, N.J., 1993-94; exec. v.p. Work and Family Benefits, Inc., Cedar Knolls, N.J., 1994—. Pres. bd. dirs. Youth Svcs., Summit, N.J., 1995—; mem. Parish Pastoral Coun., 2002--. Mem. Alliance of Work/Life Profls., Rosemont

Coll. Alumni Assn. (pres.-elect bd. dirs. 1997—). Democrat. Roman Catholic. Avocations: reading, golf, squash. Office: Work & Family Benefits Inc 100 E Hanover Ave Cedar Knolls NJ 07927-2020 E-mail: clark@wfbenefits.com.

CLARK, SHERYL DIANE, physician; b. Cleve., May 8, 1952; d. Crandall and Martha Jayne (McNeilly) C.; children: Milan, Gabriel. BA, Beloit Coll., 1974; postgrad., Hampstead Clinic Child Analysis and U. London, 1976-77; MD, Case Western Res. U., 1982. Diplomate Am. Bd. Dermatology. Intern Mt. Sinai Med. Ctr., Cleve., 1982-83; rsch. fellow Case Western Res. U., Kenya, Kenya, Africa, 1983-84, Washington U., St. Louis, 1984-88; resident in dermatology Barnes Hosp., St. Louis, 1985-88; vis. assoc. physician Rockefeller U. Hosp., N.Y.C., 1990-91; asst. attending physician N.Y. Presbyterian Hosp., N.Y.C., 1988—; asst. clin. prof. medicine Cornell Med. Ctr., N.Y.C., 1991—; pres. Sheryl Clark Enterprises, N.Y.C., 1991—. Cons. Rodale Press, N.Y.C., 1995—; speaker in field. Co-editor: Jour. of Biomed. Engring. and Technology, 1977-78; contbr. articles to profl. jours. Rep. rape task force N.Y. Hosp., 1988-90; crisis intervention vol. Crisis Intervention Hotline, Beloit, Wis., 1973-74. Fellow N.Y. Acad. Medicine, Am. Acad. Dermatology; mem. AMA (cons. scientific advisory coun. 1992), Am. Med. Women's Assn., Caribbean Med. & Edn. Found. (bd. dirs.), Soc. Investigative Dermatology, Internat. Soc. for Androgenic Disorders, Med. Soc. State of N.Y., N.Y. County Med. Soc., Phi Beta Kappa, Alpha Omega Alpha. Avocations: painting, scuba, skiing, sailing. Office: 109 E 61st St New York NY 10021-8101

CLARK, SONDRA, composer, musicologist, educator; b. Breckenridge, Minn., Jan. 20, 1941; d. Fritz William Scholder; m. Gordon L. Clark, June 24, 1960. PhD, Stanford U., Stanford, CA, 1971; MA Music, San Jose State U., San Jose, CA, 1966; BA Music, Juilliard Sch., New York, NY, 1965. Composer and educator self-employed, Los Altos, Calif., 1990—; educator San Jose State U., San Jose, Calif., 1966—81; annotator San Jose Symphony, San Jose, Calif., 1973—; music critic free-lance, San Francisco, Calif., 1967—. Lectr./clinician Music Teachers Assn., San Francisco, 1994—2001; adjudicator UNICEF concerts, San Jose, Calif., 1974—80. Composer: of various published classical music scores. Recipient Composing award, Music Tchrs. Assn. Calif., 1990—2003, Composition-Concert Music award, ASCAP, 2001—02. Mem.: Nat. Assn. of Composers, USA (selection com. 2000—02), Juilliard Sch. Alumni Assn., Stanford U. Alumni Assn., Sigma Alpha Iota Nat. Music Frat. (hon.). Avocation: walking. Office: Sondra Clark Music 430 Lassen Street #10 Los Altos CA 94022 E-mail: donson42@aol.com.

CLARK, STAN, association executive; b. Oakland, Calif., Aug. 27, 1927; s. Otto and Luella (Vestal) C.; m. Faye Juhls, Aug. 31, 1952 (div. May 1980); children: Valerie, Laury, Steven; m. Nancy Wood, June 1, 1980 (div. Aug. 1989); m. June Simmers, Dec. 26, 1990. AB, San Jose (Calif.) State Coll., 1954, MA, 1956; postgrad., Stanford U., 1959-60. Dir. aux. svcs. San Jose City Coll., 1956-62, Calif. State U., Hayward, 1963-68, SUNY, Cortland, 1968-70, New Paltz, 1970-72; exec. dir. Nat. Assn. Coll. Aux. Svcs., Staunton, Va., 1972-94; pres. Assn. Coll. Adminstrn. Profls., Staunton, Va., 1995—. Part-time tchr. acctg. San Jose City Coll., 1958-61, Foothill Coll., Los Altos, Calif., 1962-63, Chabot Coll., Hayward, 1964-67; cons.; pres. Calif. Assn. Coll. Stores, 1962. Served with USAAF, 1945-47. Mem. Eastern Assn. Coll. Aux. Svcs. (sec.-treas. 1969-94), Coll. Stores Assn. N.Y. State (sec.-treas. 1969-72), Tau Delta Phi. E-mail: acap@cfw.com.

CLARK, STAN W. state legislator; b. Oakley, Kans., Dec. 9, 1954; married; 1 child. Student, Colby C.C. Photographer; mem. Kans. Senate from 40th dist., Topeka, 1994—; chmn. arts and cultural resources com. Kans. Senate, Topeka, chair joint computer com., vice chmn. utilities com., mem. agr. com., mem. rules and regulations com., mem. fin. instns. com. Past pres. Oakley Industries, Inc.; pres. Oakley Planning Commn.; past vice chair Oakley Bd. Zoning Appeals; past vice chair Kans. Agrl. Value-Added Ctr.'s Leadership Coun. Mem. Nat. Fedn. Ind. Bus., Oakley C. of C. (past pres.). Republican. Office: 300 SW 10th Ave Rm 128-s Topeka KS 66612-1504*

CLARK, STANFORD E. accountant; b. Farmington, Utah, Sept. 21, 1917; m. Merrial Jane Knight Mackay, Nov. 16, 1942 (dec. July 1993); m. Evelyn Harrow, Nov. 3, 1995. Student, LDS Bus. Coll., Salt Lake City, 1935. With Utah Constrn. Co., Riverton, Wyo., 1955-57; rancher Riverton, 1948-55; office mgr. Superior Bit Svc., Riverton, 1958-68; v.p., sec., treas. Allied Nuclear Corp., Riverton, 1957-69, Western Std. Corp., Riverton, 1957-83, pres., treas., dir., 1989—; also bd. dirs. Treas., v.p., sec., bd. dirs. Snow King Resort Mgmt. Inc., Jackson, 1992-, Jackson Hole Springs Water Co., 1995—; treas. S.K. Land Ltd. Liability Co., 1992—; v.p., treas., bd. dirs. Snow King Resort Ctr., Inc., 1999—, Snow King Resort, Inc., 1999—; sec., treas., bd. dirs., 1991-99; pres. Western Recreation Corp., 1957—. With USCG, 1942-45. Republican. Office: Western Standard Corp 205 S Broadway Ave Riverton WY 82501-4331

CLARK, SUE JANET, business owner; b. Vancouver, Wash., Oct. 17, 1929; d. Day Walter and Dorothy Janet (White) Hilborn; children: Leslie Lora, Kyle Scott, Sidne Suzanne, Brian Casey. AA, Stephens Coll., 1949; student, Northwestern U., 1949-51; BA, U. Wash., 1952. Continuity dir. KING-TV, Seattle, 1952-54; traffic mgr. KTNT-TV, Tacoma, 1954; freelance pub. rels. cons., 1966-70; continuity dir. KTIM, San Rafael, Calif., 1966-68; coord. vol. svcs. Sunny Hills Residential Treatment Ctr. for Teenagers, San Anselmo, Calif., 1968-73; adminstr. asst. tech. publs. Bechtel Power Corp., San Francisco, 1973; dir. unv. rels. U. Calif., San Francisco, 1973-77; real estate agt. Home & Land Co., San Rafael, 1977-80; pres. Lindberg-Clark, Inc. and Innkeeper, Hotel Ledger, Mokelumne Hill, Calif., 1978-82; field trainer Pa. Life Ins. Co., 1983-84; owner, ptnr. Travel Cons., San Francisco, 1985-94; writer, 1966—; propr. SJ Clark Lit. Agy., 1982—; writing instr., 1993—; owner, ptnr. Light Age Pub. House. Guest spkr. numerous confs., workshops, seminars. Contbg. writer articles and poetry Terra Linda News, Pacific Sun, Ind. Jour., Lincoln Messenger, various anthologies, others; contbr. articles on fundraising and pub. rels. to profl. jours. Bd. dirs. Vol. Bur. Marin County, 1978-80, San Francisco Easter Seal Soc., 1974-77. Mem. Nat. Soc. Fund Raisers (charter; bd. dirs. 1969-77), Lions Internat. (pres. 1991-93, So. of Market club), Pub. Rels. Soc. of Am., Phi Beta, Alpha Delta Pi. Republican. Presbyterian.

CLARK, SUSAN (NORA GOULDING), actress; b. Sarnia, Ont., Can., Mar. 8, 1940; d. George Raymond and Eleanor Almond (McNaughton) Clark; m. Alex Karra; 1 child, Katie Karras. Student, Toronto (Ont.) Children's Players, 1956-59; student (Acad. scholar), Royal Acad. Dramatic Art, London. Ptnr. Georgian Bay Prodns. Actor: (stage prodn.) Appearances to the Contrary, 2000, Glass Menagerie, 2002, Sisters Rosensweig, 2002, BiCoastal Woman, 2003; (TV series) Webster, 1983, Emily of New Moon, 1998; (films) Nobody's Perfekt, 1981, Porky's, 1981, Butterbox Babies, 1995; (TV films) Babe, 1975 (Emmy for oustanding lead actress in a drama, 1975), Sherlock Holmes: The Strange Case of Alice Faulkner, 1981, The Choice, 1981, Maid in America, 1982, Tonya & Nancy: The Inside Story, 1994, Snowbound: The Jim and Jennifer Stolpa Story, 1994, (stage prodn.) Dancing at Lughnasa, 2003. Mem. ACLU, Am. Film Inst. Office: care Georgian Bay Prodns 13400 Riverside Dr Ste 308 Sherman Oaks CA 91423-2541

CLARK, SUSAN ATKINSON, clinical social worker, educator; b. Paterson, N.J., Jan. 28, 1942; d. Edward F. and Evelyn R. (Moore) Atkinson; m. Albert M. Clark III, Aug. 24, 1968; children: David M., A. Miles IV, Jonathan E. BA, Hope Coll., 1963; MSW, U. Conn., Hartford, 1965; MBA, U. New Haven, 1982. Cert. diplomate in clin. social worker, Conn. Program dir. West Haven (Conn.) Cmty. House, 1965-70; assoc. prof. So. Conn. State U., New Haven, 1970—97, prof. emeritus, 1997—; ptnr. Center Assocs., Orange, Conn., 1981—. Social work cons. Kennedy Ctr., Bridgeport, Conn., 1968-70; field coord. Fordham U., N.Y.C., 1984-86; clin. social worker Yale-New Haven Hosp., 1987—; profl. adv. com. South Central Regional VNA, New Haven, 1993-98; text reviewer Nelson-Hall Pubs. Chair Orange Human Svc. Commn., 1983-85; pres. Camp Hazen YMCA, 1986-88; elected mem. Bd. Edn., Dist. 5, Conn., 1991-96; trustee State of Conn. YMCA, 1992-95; mem. New Eng. Substance Abuse Task Force; mem. Orange host town com. World Spl. Olympics; fund distbn. com. United Way of Greater New Haven Cmty. Impact Coun.; vol. Am. Red Cross Nat. Disaster Mental Health, 1998—. Recipient Past Pres. award Camp Hazen YMCA, 1988; named Vol. of Yr., Town of Orange, 1983. Mem. AAUP (legis. chair 1985-87), Acad. Cert. Social Workers, Nat. Assn. Social Workers (bd. dirs. 1983-85, nominating com. 1993-95), PACE Nat. trustees, 1999—, treas., 2001-02); bd. trustees Congregational Ch., 2001—; Orange VNA (rec. rev. and profl. adv. com.). Republican. Mem. United Ch. of Christ. Avocations: skiing, golf. Office: Yale New Haven Hosp 20 York St New Haven CT 06504-1330

CLARK, SUSAN FRANCES, theater educator; b. Chgo., Mar. 25, 1953; d. Anthony and Frances Frigo. BA, Rockford Coll., 1973; MA, Emerson Coll., 1980; PhD, Tufts U., 1989. Dir. Young People's Theatre, Lincoln, Mass., 1977-80; stage dir. Boston Lyric Opera, 1979-80; designer Middlesex Sch., Concord, Mass., 1975-78, chair theatre dept., 1978-89; mem. faculty theatre dept. Emerson Coll., Boston, 1989-90; asst. prof. theatre U. So. Maine, Portland, 1990-92, Smith Coll., Northampton, Mass., 1992—99; dir. theatre Groton Sch., Mass., 2001—, Malcolm Straham chair English lit. and theatre, 2001—. Exec. dir. Co. of Women, Inc., Boston, 1992-99; artistic dir. Country Summer Theatre, Inc., Concord, 1978-83; adjudicator Am. Coll. Theatre Festival, New Eng., 1990-93, New Eng. Drama Festival, Boston, 1980-89, New Eng. Theater Conf., 1983-90; reader Bunting Inst., Radcliffe Coll., Cambridge, Mass., 1990-93; proposal reader NEH, Washington, 1986. Contbr. chpts. to books in field. Grantee Maine Coun. Arts and Humanities, 1991, U. So. Maine, 1991, Smith Coll., 1993; Nat. Endowment Arts and Humanities summer fellow, 1986, 98, NEH fellow, 1999-2000; Five Colls. Inc. rsch. assoc., 1999—. Mem. MLA, Am. Theater and Drama Soc., New Eng. Theatre Conf. (presenter), Assn. for Theatre in Higher Edn. (presenter), Am. Soc. Theatre Rsch., Theatre Comms. Group, Far West Popular Culture Inst. (referee). Office: Groton Sch Groton MA 01430 E-mail: sclark@groton.org.

CLARK, SUSAN GLASSON, economics educator; b. Flint, Mich., Mar. 11, 1948; d. Daniel Robert and Joyce Ann (Ambrose) Glasson; m. John David Clark, Jan. 26, 1968; children: J. Daniel, Crystal A. BS, U. Mich., 1974; MA, U. Okla., 1982. Cert. tchr., Mich. Tchr. programming Genesee County Skills Ctr., 1973—74; tchg. asst. U. Okla., Norman, 1980—82; comml. realtor Barbara Lee & Assocs., Ft. Smith, Ark., 1982—84; instr. part-time Westark Coll., Ft. Smith, 1986—89, asst. prof. econs., 1989—. Trustee, chmn. Ft. Smith Libr. Bd., 1982-92; sec. treas. Ft. Smith Symphony Guild, 1982-84; bd. trustees Immaculate Conception Sch., Ft. Smith, 1985-88. Office: U Ark-Ft Smith PO Box 3649 Fort Smith AR 72913-3649

CLARK, SUZANNE, accountant; b. San Bernadino, Calif., Sept. 10, 1948; d. Richard Grant and Dorothy Jean (C.; children: Chelsea A. Clark-James, Graeme W. Clark-James. BS in Mktg. and Acctg., U. Colo., 1970, M in Urban Affairs, 1978. CPA-Personal Fin. Specialist, CFP, Colo. Dir. adminstrv. svcs. Suburban Cmty. Tng. & Svc. Ctr., Englewood, 1973-78; staff adminstr Solar Energy Rsch. Inst., Golden, Colo., 1979-80; rschr. Cmty. Coll. Denver, 1980-81; staff acct. R.E. Weise & Co., CPAs, Denver, 1982-83; owner Suzanne Clark, CPA, P.C., Denver, 1983—. Author: Providing Personal Financial Planning Services in Your CPA Practice, 1987, Providing Fiduciary Accounting and Tax Services, 1990, The Personal Financial Planning Process An Introduction, 1993, Personal Financial Planning in Crisis Situations, 1993, Estates and Trusts: A Guide to Fiduciary Advisors, 1996, Individual Tax Update, 1999, 2000, 2001, 2002. Bd. dirs. Children's Ctr., Denver, 1982-84, Hospice of Peace, Denver, 1987-88. Mem. AICPA (personal fin. specialist edn. subcom. 1988-93), Colo. Soc. CPAs (specialization oversight bd. 1984-87, pers. fin. planning com. 1987-88, comms. com. 1994-97, bd. dirs. 1997-99). Office: Suzanne Clark CPA PC 50 S Steele St Ste 505 Denver CO 80209-2810 E-mail: sclark2240@aol.com.

CLARK, SUZANNE UNDERWOOD, writer; b. Nyack, New York, Oct. 4, 1950; d. Roger Leslie Underwood and Mary Lee Hester; m. Albert John Clark, June 17, 1978; children: Katy, Stephen, Emily. BS magna cum laude, James Madison U., 1972; MA, Johns Hopkins U., 1975. Adj. prof. English King Coll., Bristol, Tenn., 1991—. Copy editor Comml. Appeal, Memphis, 1975—76; presenter workshops, seminars on writing Va. Highlands C.C., Abingdon, 1996, Chalcedon Christian Sch., Roswell, Ga., 1997; adj. prof. English East Tenn. State U., Johnson City, 1999, Va. Intermont Coll., Bristol, 2000; weekly columnist Kingsport Times News, Kingsport, Tenn., 2001. Author: Blackboard Blackmail, 1988, Weather of the House, 1994, Sketches of Home, 1998, What a Light Thing, This Stone, 1999, The Roar on the Other Side, 2000. Bd. dirs. Steele Creek Nature Ctr., Bristol, Tenn.; mem. adv. bd. Abortion Alternative & Crisis Pregnancy Ctr., Bristol, Tenn., 1982—. Recipient 1st prize in poetry, Va. Highlands Creative Writing Contest, 1995, Honorable Mention in Poetry, Now & Then Mag., 1998, Sow's Ear Review, 1996; fellow, Va. Ctr. for Creative Arts, 1992. Mem.: Appalachian Writers Assn., Appalachian Ctr. for Poets and Writers. Presbyterian. Avocations: birdwatching, hiking, shelling. Office: Mercy Med Airlift 4620 Haygood Rd Virginia Beach VA 23455

CLARK, SYLVIA DOLORES, business educator; b. NYC, June 5, 1959; d. Barna and Eva Anna (Beniczky-Gabriel) Csuros. BBA, Bernard Baruch Coll. CUNY, 1979, MPhil, 1993, PhD, 1994; MBA, NYU, 1982. Rsch. analyst Kornhauser and Calene and predecessor firm, N.Y.C., 1979-80; project coord. Gen. Foods, Inc., White Plains, N.Y., 1980-82; rsch. assoc. Lord, Geller, Federico, Einstein, Inc., N.Y.C., 1982-83; instr. Coll. of S.I. CUNY, 1984-93, asst. prof., 1994-97; instr. Wagner Coll., S.I., 1993-94; asst. prof. Queensborough C.C. CUNY, 1997-98, St. John's U., Jamaica, N.Y., 1998—. Recipient Becker Family Fund scholar, 1978, Baruch Coll. Alumni Assn. scholar, 1979. Mem.: Am. Statis. Assn., Am. Mktg. Assn., Phi Beta Kappa, Beta Gamma Sigma (past exec. bd.). Home: 62 Renwick Ave Staten Island NY 10301-4216 Office: St John's U Spellman Hall TCB 300 Howard Ave Staten Island NY 10301-4496 E-mail: clark1094@aol.com.

CLARK, TERESA WATKINS, psychotherapist, clinical counselor; b. Hobart, Okla., Dec. 18, 1953; d. Aaron Jack Watkins and Patricia Ann (Flurry) Greer and Ralph Gordon Greer; m. Philip Winston Clark, Dec. 29, 1979; children: Philip Aaron, Alisa Lauren. BA in Psychology, U. N.Mex., 1979, MA in Counseling and Family Studies, 1989. Lic. profl. clin. counselor, N.Mex.; nat. cert. counselor. Child care worker social svcs. divsn. Family Resource Ctr., Albuquerque, 1978-79; head tchr., asst. dir. Kinder Care Learning Ctr., Albuquerque, 1979-80; psychiat. asst. Vista Sandia Psychiat. Hosp., Albuquerque, 1980-87; psychotherapist outpatient clinic Bernalillo County Mental Health Ctr.-Heights, 1989-91; therapist adult program Charter/Heights Behavioral Health Sys., Albuquerque, 1991-2000; therapist New Day Youth and Family Svcs., Albuquerque, 2001—. Vol. mental health svcs. disasters ARC. Mem. ACA, Am. Assn. Multicultural Counseling and Devel., Nat. Bd. Cert. Counselors, N.Mex. Health Counselors Assn. (former cen. regional rep., ethics chair, bd. dirs.), Mental Health Counselor's Assn., Billy The Kid Outlaw Gang Hist. Soc. Democrat. Avocations: music, camping, horseback riding, reading. Office: New Day Youth and Family Svcs 1330 San Pedro Ne Albuquerque NM 87110

CLARK, TERRY DEE, political scientist, educator; b. Washington, D.C., Dc, Nov. 6, 1951; s. DeLair Aubrey and Sally Ethel Clark; m. Bonnie M. Guy, July 31, 1954; 1 child, Jessica Renelle Barron. Ph.D., U. of Ill., Urbana-Champaign, Illinois, 1985—92; B.S., US Mil. Acad., West Point, NY, 1969—73. Prof. of polit. sci. Creighton U., Omaha, Nebr., 1993—. J. william fulbright sr. scholar peer rev. com. for ctrl. eurasia CIES, Washington, D.C., DC. Author: (books) 1) books: a) Unity or Separation: Center-Periphery Relations in the Former Soviet Union (Praeger, 2002), b) Going Beyond Post-Communist Studies (ME Sharpe, 2002), (journal articles) Slavic Review (two articles), (articles) Nationalities Papers (two articles), (journal article) European Politics and Society (EEPS), PS: Politics and Political Science, (journal articles (three articles) Journal of Baltic Studies, (journal article) Economic Development and Cultural Change (EDCC), Journal of Policy Studies. Capt. US Army, 1973—85, Goeppingen, Germany. Recipient Dean's Award for Excellence in Tchg., Creighton Coll. of Arts and Sciences, 1988; fellow Fulbright Scholar, Fulbright, 1999-2000; grantee IREX Advanced Individual Rsch. Grant, Internat. Rsch. Exch. Bd. (IREX), 1996, APSA Small Rsch. Grant, Am. Polit. Sci. Assn., 2003-2004. Mem.: Lithuanian Polit. Sci. Assn. (LPSA), Assn. for the Advancement of Slavic Studies (AAASS), Am. Polit. Sci. Assn. (APSA). R-Consevative. Charismatic Protestant. Avocations: hiking, international travel, writing. Office: Creighton University Department of Political Science Omaha NE 68178 Home Fax: 402-280-4731; Office Fax: 402-280-4731. Personal E-mail: tclark@creighton.edu. E-mail: tclark@creighton.edu.

CLARK, THOMAS ALONZO, retired federal judge; b. Atlanta, Dec. 20, 1920; s. Fred and Prudence (Sprayberry) Clark; m. Betty Medlock, July 16, 1978; children: Thomas Alonzo, Christopher S., Julia M.;stepchildren: Allen L. Carter, Rosalyn Lackey Howell. BS, Washington and Lee U., 1942; LLB, U. Ga., 1949. Pvt. practice law, Bainbridge, Ga., 1949—55; ptnr. Dykes, Marshall & Clark, Americus, Ga., 1955—57, Fowler, White et al, Tampa, Fla., 1957—61; sr. ptnr. Carlton, Fields, et al, Tampa, 1961—79; judge U.S. Ct. Appeals (5th cir.), 1979—81, U.S. Ct. of Appeals (11th cir.), Atlanta, 1981—91, sr. judge, 1991—99, ret., 1999. Pres. Fla. Assn. for Retarded Citizens, 1974—75; mem. Ga. Ho. of Reps., 1951—52. Lt. comdr. USN, 1942—46. Fellow: Am. Coll. Trial Lawyers; mem.: ABA, Fla. Bar Assn., Ga. Bar Assn.

CLARK, THOMAS ALLEN, planning and evaluation consultant; b. Terre Haute, Ind., Mar. 5, 1952; s. Elmer Junior and Charlotte (Rabbe) C.; stepmother, Grace Lingle Clark. BS, So. Ill. U., 1982, MSc, 1987, PhD, 1993. Rschr. So. Ill. U., Carbondale, 1985-91; distance learning adminstr. Iowa State U., Ames, 1993-95; planning and evaluation cons. TA Consulting, Springfield, Ill., 1995—. Fed. program evaluator U. North Tex., 2000—. Author: (with J.R. Verduin, Jr.) Distance Education: The Foundations of Effective Practice, 1991, also other works on virtual and distance learning, 1989—. Dissertation fellow So. Ill. U., 1992. Mem. Am. Evaluation Assn., Sierra Club, Phi Delta Kappa. Unitarian Universalist. Avocation: long-distance cycling. Office: TA Cons 920 S Spring St Ste 311 Springfield IL 62704 E-mail: taconsulting@yahoo.com.

CLARK, THOMAS ARTHUR, education educator, consultant; b. Cleve., Nov. 10, 1944; s. John Arthur and Sallie (Hanger) Clark; m. Diana Maiden, Feb. 3, 1969 (div. Feb. 1989); children: Anna E., Naomi S.; m. Patricia O'Leary, July 14, 2000. AB in Polit. Sci., Brown U., 1966; MA in Urban & Regional Planning, U. Iowa, 1969, PhD in Geography, 1975. Vis. asst. prof. McGill U., Montreal, Canada, 1972—73; asst. prof. Middlebury (Vt.) Coll., Middlebury, 1973—76, Rutgers U., New Brunswick, NJ, 1976—82; from asst. to assoc. prof. U. Colo., Denver, 1982—93, prof., 1993—. Dir. western lands resources and devel. U. Colo. Coll. Arch., Denver, 1999—; acting assoc. vice-chancellor U. Colo., Denver, 1987—89; cons. in field. Contbr. articles to profl. jours. Mem.: Assn. Collegiate Schs. Planning (treas. 2003—). Avocations: bicycling, hiking, skiing, music, travel. Office: Univ Colo Coll Arch and Planning 1250 14th St PO Box 173364 Denver CO 80217 Office Fax: 303-556-3687. Business E-Mail: tom.clark@cudenver.edu.

CLARK, THOMAS B., SR., real estate broker; b. Ann Arbor, Mich., Jan. 21, 1943; s. Thomas W. and Helen (Sheldon) C.; m. Dianne Stribley, Dec. 4, 1970; children: Thomas B. Jr., Andrea Lynn. BA, U. Mich., 1964. Dir. rec. U. Mich., Ann Arbor, 1965-70; sr. auditor Touche Ross (now Deloitte and Touche), Detroit, 1970-72; acctg. mgr. E.R.I.M., Ann Arbor, 1972-75; owner/developer Clark Apts., Ann Arbor, 1975—. Bd. dirs. Kenitis Corp. Mem. Ann Arbor Apt. Assn. (bd. dirs.). Avocation: golf. Address: PO Box 7822 Ann Arbor MI 48107-7822 Office: 621 S Forest Ave Ann Arbor MI 48104-3123 E-mail: tclark_1@msn.com.

CLARK, THOMAS CARLYLE, banker; b. Barbourville, Ky., Dec. 1, 1947; s. Buford Thomas and Eleanor Randolph (Owens) C. AB, Duke U., 1969; MBA, Harvard U., 1971; LLD, Cumberland Coll., 1991. Officer Chem. Bank, N.Y.C., 1975-78; divsn. pres., mng. dir., chief credit officer U.S. Trust Co. N.Y., N.Y.C., 1978—. Pres. emeritus bd. dirs. Lubovitch Dance Co.; chmn. emeritus bd. trustees Union Coll., Ky.; bd. dirs. Am. Composers Orch. Concert Artists Guild, past pres.; bd. dirs. EOS Orch., Svc. Mems. Legal Defense Network. With USN, 1971-75; comdr. USNR ret. Mem. Robert Morris Assn. (past chmn. pvt. lending com.), Lincoln's Inn Soc. (alumni coun.), Duke U. Met. Alumni Assn. (pres. 1984), Am. Banking Assn. (past chair exec. com. for pvt. banking, alumni coun.), Kentuckians N.Y. Club, Met. Opera Club (bd. dirs.); bd. dirs. Duke U. Alumni, Duke U. Cap. Campaign. Commn. Republican. Methodist. Office: US Trust Co NY One Pickwick Plz Greenwich CT 06830

CLARK, THREESE ANNE, occupational therapist, disability analyst; b. Bath, N.Y., Jan. 16, 1946; d. Frank George and Beulah Irene (Harris) Brown; m. Jacob Clark, Mar. 11, 1966 (div. Mar. 1977); 1 child, Jayson Todd. BS in Occupational Therapy, U. N.D., 1967, MS in Counseling and Guidance, 1977. Lic. occupl. therapist, Pa.; sr. diplomate Am. Bd. Disability Analysts (charter adv. bd. mem. 1995—). Occupational therapist U. N.D. Med. Ctr., 1968; chief occupational therapist, program developer Corning (N.Y.) Hosp., 1968-69, Arnot-Ogden Hosp., Elmira, N.Y., 1969-71; staff occupational therapist VA Ctr., Bath, N.Y., 1971-74; instr. occupational therapy U. N.D., Grand Forks, 1974-77; prin. investigator occupational therapy Ohio State U., 1977-79; occupational therapist Regional Ednl. Assessment and Cons. Team, Hillsboro, Ohio, 1979-81; occupational therapist, phys. medicine and rehab. Saint Mary's Hosp., West Palm Beach, Fla., 1981-82; chief occupational therapist Mercy Med. Ctr., Oshkosh, Wis., 1982-87; dir. occupational/recreational therapy HealthSouth Rehab. Hosp., Altoona, 1987-95, clin. dir. spinal injury program, 1987-95; pres., owner, sr. disability analyst Life Care Planning and Mgmt. Inc., Altoona, 1993—; sr. disability analyst, diplomate, 1998—; assoc. prof., program dir./curriculum coord. BS occupl. therapy program Mt. Aloysius Coll., Cresson, Pa., 1995—; co-owner, sec.-treas. Shears-a-GoGo, Inc., Altoona, 1996—2001. Cons. Founders Pavillion, Corning, 1969, Grafton (N.D.) State Sch. for the Retarded, 1975-76, Heart of Am. Rehab. Ctr., Rugby, N.D., 1976-77, Andrea Clifford program, 1978; guest lectr. support groups, cmty. groups, ednl. programs, 1987—; presenter in field. Contbr. articles to profl. jours. Charter mem. profl. adv. coun. Am. Bd. Disability Analysts; pres. adv. bd. Occupl. Therapy Asst. Program, Mt. Aloysius Jr. Coll., 1988-92, 94-96; mem. adv. profl. com. Home Nursing Agy., Altoona, 1988-93; mem. com. Health Care Adv. Com., 1994—; bd. dirs. Ctr. for Internat. Living of South Cen. Pa., 1992-95; mem. med. svc. com. Evergreen Manor, Oshkosh, 1985-87; chair home/family life and human rels. Northtowne Elem. Sch. PTA, Columbus, Ohio, 1978, others. Mem. Am. Occupl. Therapy Assn. (coun. edn. 1974-76, coun. affiliate pres. 1976), Nat. Rehab. Assn., Ohio Occupl. Therapy Assn., Columbus Dist. Occupl. Therapy Assn., Pa. Occupl. Therapy Assn., Am. Assn. Hand Therapists. Baptist. Avocations: needlecrafts, signing, reading, dog obedience/agility training, dog confirmation shows. Home and Office: Life Care Planning Mgmt Inc 5300 5th Ave Altoona PA 16602-1312 Office: Mt Aloysius Coll 7373 Adm Peary Hwy Cresson PA 16630 E-mail: tclark@mtaloy.edu., chcohosh@charter.net.

CLARK, TONY, state commissioner; Student, Mich. State U., 1990-91; BS in Polit. Sci., N.D. State U., 1994, BS in History Edn., 1996; MPA, U. N.D., 2002. Mem. Dist. 44 N.D. Ho. of Reps., 1994-97; adminstrv. officer N.D. Tax Dept., 1997-99; commr. N.D. Dept. Labor, 1999-2000, N.D. Pub. Svc., 2001—, 2001—. Adult leader Boy Scouts Am. Named Eagle Scout Boy Scouts Am. Mem. Phi Kappa Phi. Office: 600 E Boulevard Ave Bismarck ND 58505-0480

CLARK, VERNON E. chief of US Naval Operations; b. Sioux City, Iowa, Sept. 7, 1944; Commd. ensign USN, advanced through ranks to vice-adm.; various assignments to vice-adm., dir. for opers., J-3 Joint Staff/The Pentagon, Washington; comdr. Second Fleet/Striking Fleet Atlantic, Norfolk, Va., 1999—2000; chief of naval oper. US Navy, Washington, 2000—. Office: Office Chief Naval Oper Pentagon Washington DC 20350*

CLARK, VERONICA ANN WILDS (RONNI PATRIQUIN CLARK), journalist; b. St. Louis, May 22, 1943; d. Charles Ernest, Jr. and Marie Elizabeth (Perabo) Wilds; m. Guy Albert Luno, Jr., Aug. 10, 1961 (div. Nov. 1967); children: Judith Wilds Luno Adams, Guy Albert Luno III; m. Francis David Patriquin, Dec. 23, 1972 (dec. Apr. 1982); m. Farris Laray Clark, Jr., Nov. 25, 1995. Student, La. State U., 1961, N.E. La. U., 1964-1967. Soc. editor The Monroe (La.) News Star, 1964; news reporter The Monroe Morning World, 1967; news dir. Televisual News, Baton Rouge, 1972-73; capital corr. The Clarion Ledger, Jackson, Miss., 1974-76; capital bur. chief capital bur. The Shreveport Jour., Baton Rouge, 1976-91; polit. writer Gannett News Svc., Tallahassee, 1991-92; sr. reporter The Mobile (Ala.) Register, 1992-2000, asst. city editor, 2000—. Pres. Capital Corrs. Assn., Baton Rouge, 1979-80, Mobile Gridiron, 1993; judge Loyola U. Silver Scribe Competition, New Orleans, 1985-90. Pres. Hist. Spanish Town Civic Assn., Baton Rouge, 1982-85; mem. Hist. Dist. Commn., Baton Rouge, 1984-85. Recipient numerous 1st Pl. AP awards Miss., Ala., La., 1974-97, Best Coverage Gov. award La. Press Assn., 1986, 88, Media Environ. award Organized Fisherman Fla., 1992, Edward J. Meeman Nat. Journalism award Scripps Howard Found, 1993. Mem. Mobile

Press Club (News & Excellence award 1992, 98, Gen. Excellence/Cmty. Svc. award 1998), Soc. Profl. Journalists (pres. 1993-94). Roman Catholic. Avocations: canoeing, biking, gardening, reading, travelling. Office: The Mobile Register 304 Government St Mobile AL 36602-2600 E-mail: rpatriquin@mobileregister.com.

CLARK, WESLEY K. retired military officer; b. Little Rock, Ark., Dec. 23, 1944; m. Gertrude Kingston; 1 child, Wesley. Grad., U.S. Mil. Acad., West Point, 1966; M in philosophy, politics, and econs., Oxford U., 1966—68; grad., Nat. War Coll., Command and Gen. Staff Coll., Armor Officer Adv. and Basic Courses, Ranger and Airborne Sch. Fellow White House, 1975—76, special asst. to dir. office mgmt. and budget, 1975—76; instr. to asst. prof. social sci. U.S. Mil. Acad.; comdr. 1st Battalion, 77th Armor, 4th Infantry Divsn. US Army, 1980—82; chief plans integration divsn. Office Deputy Chief of Staff Oper. and Plans, US Army, Washington, D.C., 1983; chief army's study group Office Chief of Staff of Army, Washington, D.C., 1983—84; comdr. oper. group US Army, 1984—86, comdr. 3rd Brigade, 4th Infantry Divsn., 1986—88, comdr. Nat. Tng. Ctr., 1989—91; deputy chief staff for concepts, doctrine, and developments US Army Tng. and Doctrine Command, Fort Monroe, Va., 1991—92; comdr. 1st Cavalry Divsn. US Army, Fort Hood, Tex., 1992—94, dir, strategic plans and policy, JR, the Joint Staff, 1994—96, comdr.-in-chief - U.S. So. Command, 1996—97, comdr.-in-chief - U.S. European Command, supreme allied comdr.- Europe, 1997—2003, ret., 2003. Corp. cons. Stephens Group Inc., Little Rock, 2000—. Author: Waging Modern War: Bosnia, Kosovo and the Future of Combat, 2001, Winning Modern Wars: Iraq, Terrorism and the American Empire, 2003. Decorated Defense Disting. Svc. Medal (three awards), Disting. Svc. Medal, Silver Star, Legion Merit (four awards), Bronze Star Medal (two awards), Purple Heart, Meritorious Svc. Medal (two awards), Army Commendation Medal (two awards); Rhodes scholar, Oxford U., 1966—68. Achievements include led mil. negotiations for the Bosnian Peace Accords at Dayton; commanded three companies to combat in Vietnam.*

CLARK, WILDER CRAWFORD, medical psychologist; b. Timmins, Ont., Can., Oct. 15, 1926; came to U.S., 1953; s. Wilder Crawford and Vera Ellen (Nordenstierna) C.; m. Susanne Loewe, Oct. 18, 1965. BA, Queen's U., Kingston, Ont., 1952, MA, 1953; PhD, U. Mich., 1958. Analytical chemist Atomic Energy Commn., Port Hope, Ont., 1948-50; instr. U. Mich., Ann Arbor, 1957-59; sr. rsch. assoc. Courtney & Co., Phila., 1959-60; mem. tech. staff AT&T Bell Labs., Holmdel, N.J., 1967-68; hon. prof. CUNY, 1960—; prof. Coll. of Physicians and Surgeons Columbia U., N.Y.C., 1960—; rsch. scientist VI N.Y. State Psychiat. Inst., 1960—. Ad hoc cons. NIH, Washington, 1976—; cons. Cygnus Inc., Paterson, N.J., 1986—. Author: (with others) Marihuana: Biological Effects, 1979, Stress Induced Analgesia, 1987, Encyclopedia of Neuroscience, 1987, 98, Advances in Pain Research and Therapy, 22, 1995, Issues in Pain Measurement, 1989. Grantee NIH, 1970, 86, 92, 99. Fellow AAAS, N.Y. Acad. Scis., Am. Psychol. Assn.; mem. Eastern Pain Assn. (bd. dirs.), Am. Pain Soc. (exec.), Internat. Assn. for the Study of Pain (founder). Achievements include pioneering the application of mathematical models (signal detection theory and multidimensional scaling) to the measurement of memory, pain and sensory function in medicine. Office: Columbia U 1051 Riverside Dr Unit 50 New York NY 10032-2695 E-mail: clarkcr@pi.cpmc.columbia.edu.

CLARK, WILLIAM, JR., political advisor; b. Oakland, Calif., Oct. 12, 1930; s. William and Mary Edith (Coady) C.; m. Judith Lee Riley, Sept. 11, 1954; 1 child, Jared Riley. BA, San Jose State U., 1955; postgrad., Columbia U., 1967—68; diploma with distinction, Nat. War Coll., 1977; LittD (hon.), Calif. State U., 1992. Dir. liaison dept. U.S. Civil Adminstrn., Naha, Japan, 1970-72; U.S.-Japan Trade Officer Am. Embassy, Tokyo, 1972-74, minister, 1981-85, polit. counselor Seoul, Republic of Korea, 1977-80, minister Cairo, 1985-86, charge d'affaires, 1986; dir. spl. trade activities Dept. of State, Washington, 1974-76, dir. Japanese Affairs, 1980-81, dep. asst. sec. state, 1986-89; ambassador to India, 1989-92; asst. sec. of state East Asian and Pacific affairs Dept. of State, Washington, 1992-93; Japan chair, sr. advisor Ctr. for Strategic and Internat. Studies, Washington, 1993-95; pres. Japan Soc., N.Y.C., 1996—2003; sr. advisor Ctr. for Strategic and Internat. Studies, Washington, 1996—2003; pres. Japan Am. Student Conf., 2003—. Lt. (j.g.) USN, 1950-53. Recipient Superior Svc. award Dept. Army, 1971, Outstanding Svc. award Dept. Army, 1972, Disting. Svc. award Pres. U.S., 1985, Meritorious Svc. award Pres. U.S., 1987, 89, Disting. Honor award Dept. State, 1989, Charles E. Cobb award Dept. State, 1991, Disting. lectr. Fgn. Svc. Inst., 1995, Order of the Sacred Treasure, Gold and Silver Star, Emperor of Japan, 2000. Mem.: Coun. Fgn. Rels., Am. Japan Soc. (bd. dirs. 1981—85), Japan Am. Soc. (bd. dirs. 1994—2000), Asia Soc., Am. Fgn. Svc. Assn., Am. C. of C. (hon. mem. Tokyo 1981—85, Cairo 1985—86), Gizira Club (Cairo), Chevy Chase Club (Washington), Pres.'s Estate Polo Club (New Delhi), Tokyo Am. Club. Episcopalian. Avocations: tennis, riding, skiing, golf. E-mail: jlnwclark@aol.com., jascinc@jasc.org.

CLARK, WILLIAM ALFRED, federal judge; b. Dayton, Ohio, Aug. 27, 1928; s. Webb Rufus and Dora Lee (Weddle) C.; m. Catherine C. Clark, Apr. 5, 1952; children: Mary Clark Youra, Jennifer Clark Kinder, Cynthia S., Andrea G. AB, U. Mich., 1950, JD, 1952. Bar: Ohio 1952, Mich. 1953. Pvt. practice, Dayton, 1954-57; assoc. Frank J. Svoboda, Dayton, 1957-73; ptnr. Legler, Lang & Kuhns, Dayton, 1973-82, Pickrel, Schaeffer & Ebeling, Dayton, 1982-85; judge so. dist. Ohio U.S. Bankruptcy Ct., Dayton, 1985-99, chief judge, 1993-99; apptd. recalled bankruptcy judge, 1999—. Judge Montgomery County Ct., Dayton, 1958-62; trial counsel in eminent domain Asst. Atty. Gen. Ohio, Dayton, 1963-70; tchr. bus. law Dayton chpt. Cert. Property and Casualty Underwriters, 1963-83; arbitrator Montgomery County Common Pleas Ct., Am. Arbitration Assn., Better Bus. Bur. Contbr. to Ohio Practice and Procedure Handbook, 1962. Lt. USAF, 1952-54. Named Alumnus of Yr., U. Mich. Club, Dayton, 1965. Mem. ABA, Ohio State Bar Assn. (chmn. eminent domain 1979-82), Dayton Bar Assn. (treas. 1964-65), Nat. Conf. Bankruptcy Judges, Lawyers Club. Republican. Avocations: tennis, other sports, reading, travel. Office: US Bankruptcy Ct Federal Bldg 120 W 3rd St Dayton OH 45402-1872

CLARK, WILLIAM ANTHONY, religious studies educator; b. Waterville, Maine, Apr. 16, 1958; s. William Henry and Theresa Laflamme Clark. BA in history, Williams Coll., 1980; MA in philosophy, Loyola U., 1987; MDiv, Weston Jesuit Sch. of Theology, 1992, D Sacrae Theol., 2001. Cert. Priestly Ordination Soc. of Jesus (Jesuits), 1993. Instr. of religion Cheverus HS, Portland, Maine, 1980—82; instr. of history St. George's Coll., Kingston, Jamaica, 1986—87; pastoral assoc. St. Thomas Aquinas Ch., Kingston, Jamaica, 1987—89; instr. of history, philosophy St. Michael Sem., Kingston, Jamaica, 1987—89; dir. of music St. Matthew's Ch., Dorchester, Mass., 1989—93; pastor St. Thomas Aquinas Ch., 1994—97; asst. prof., religious studies Coll. of the Holy Cross, Worcester, Mass., 2001—. Bd. of dirs. St. George's Coll., 1995—97, Cheverus H.S., Portland, Maine, 2003—. Composer: Spirit Call, 2001; author: Philosophy & Theology, 2002. Mem.: Am. Acad. Religion, Coll. Theology Soc., Cath. Theol. Soc. Am., Karl Rahner Soc. Roman Catholic. Avocations: genealogy, folk guitar music. Home: Ciampi Hall 1 Coll St Worcester MA 01610 E-mail: wclark@holycross.edu.

CLARK, WILLIAM ARTHUR V. geographer, demographer; b. Christchurch, N.Z., Mar. 21, 1938; came to U.S., 1961; s. Edward Arthur and Gertrude Rita (MacDonald) C.; m. Valmai Ruth Kirkham, July 1, 1961 (div. Oct. 1971); m. Irene Stephanee Borah, Mar. 25, 1978; children: Elisa, Louisa, Clifton, Justin. BA, U. N.Z., 1960; MA, U. Canterbury, N.Z., 1961; PhD, U. Ill., 1964; Doctorem Honoris Causa, U. Utrecht, The Netherlands, 1992; DSc, U. Auckland, N.Z., 1994. Lectr. U. Canterbury, 1964-66; asst./assoc. prof. U. Wis., Madison, 1966-70; prof. geography UCLA, 1970—, chmn. dept. geography, 1987-92, 95-97, assoc. dir. Inst. Social Sci. Rsch., 1984-87. Vis. prof. U. Amsterdam, 1981; Belle Van Zuylen prof. U. Utrecht, 1989; cons. state atty. gens. Mo., Calif., Wis., Minn. Author: Human Migration, 1986, Households and Housing, 1996, The California Cauldron: Immigration and the Fortunes of Local Communities, 1998, Immigrants and the American Dream: Remaking the Middle Class, 2003; author/editor: Residential Mobility and Public Policy, 1980, Rediscovering Geography: New Relevance for Science and Society, 1997. Fellow-in-residence Netherlands Inst. Advanced Studies, The Hague, 1993, Guggenheim fellow, 1994-95. Fellow Royal Soc. New Zealand (elected hon. 1997), Am. Acad. Arts and Scis.; mem. Assn. Am. Geographers (Honors award 1986), Population Assn. Am. Anglican Ch. Achievements include research in district and appellate court rulings on demographic change and school desegregation. Office: UCLA Dept Geography 405 Hilgard Ave Los Angeles CA 90095-9000

CLARK, WILLIAM H., JR., lawyer; b. Phila., Apr. 10, 1951; s. William H. and Alice Kimes (Metts) C.; m. Cristine D. Merkel, Aug. 18, 1973; children: Matthew, Alison, Daniel. BA summa cum laude, Amherst Coll., 1973; MA in Religion, Westminster Sem., 1979; JD magna cum laude, Temple U., 1983. Bar: Pa. 1983. Assoc. Morgan, Lewis & Bockius, Phila., 1983-89; ptnr. Klett Lieber Rooney & Schorling, Pitts., 1989-98, Phila., 1998-99, Drinker Biddle & Reath LLP, Phila., 1999—. Chmn. corp. bur. advisory com. Pa. Dept of State, 1991—; cons. rules disciplinary bd. Supreme Ct. Pa., Harrisburg, 1983—. Fellow Am. Bar Found.; mem. ABA (com. on corp. laws, com. on bus. courts), Pa. Bar Assn. (draftsman, lobbyist, corp. law com. 1984—, coun. sect. corp. banking and bus. law 1989-93, officer 1993-2001), Allegheny County Bar Assn. (coun. sect. corp. banking and bus. law 1991-97, officer 1997-98), Phila. Bar Assn. (coun. bus. law sect. 1998—), Am. Law Inst., Phi Beta Kappa. Republican. Presbyterian. Office: Drinker Biddle & Reath LLP One Logan Sq Philadelphia PA 19103 E-mail: clarkwh@dbr.com

CLARK, WILLIAM HARTLEY, political science educator; b. Pitts., Apr. 29, 1930; s. Arthur Tillotson and Ruthanna Frame (Anderson) C.; m. Barbara Jean Rockne, June 27, 1953; children— Heather Anderson, Jill Eleanor, Robert Hartley, Edward Kirtland. BA, Carleton Coll., 1952; MA, N.Y. U., 1955, PhD, 1960. Researcher for Carnegie Endowment for Internat. Peace, Brookings Instn., N.Y. U., 1953-54; instr. polit. sci. Western Coll., Oxford, Ohio, 1954-55; instr. internat. relations Carleton Coll., 1955-60, asst. prof., 1960-66, assoc. prof., 1966-70, prof., 1970-92, prof. emeritus, 1992—, chmn. dept. polit. sci., 1972-76, Frank B. Kellogg prof. internat. rels., 1973-92. Lectr. U. Minn., 1970; dir. Geneva Seminar on Internat. Instns., 1975-91; pres. Clark Assocs., 1992—. Author: The Politics of the Common Market, 1967; contbr. articles and revs. to profl. publs. Fulbright research fellow, 1961-62; Ford Found. research fellow, 1967; NSF research fellow, 1970, 71, 79; von Humbolt-Stiftung fellow, 1961. Mem. Coun. Fgn. Rels. (St. Paul-Mpls. com. fgn. rels.), UN Assn. Home: 216 Nevada St Northfield MN 55057-2343 E-mail: clark@carleton.edu.

CLARK, WILLIAM JAMES, retired insurance company executive; b. Kansas City, Mo., Oct. 1, 1923; s. William LeRoy and Margaret (Theobald) C.; children: Holly Clark, Jane Clark, Nancy Clark Mundel, Patricia Clark Midura; m. Elizabeth A. Smith, May 1, 1984. Student, Kansas City Jr. Coll., 1941-42; BS, U. Mo., 1947. With Mass. Mut. Life Ins. Co., Springfield, 1947-96, v.p. sales, 1967-70, sr. v.p., 1971-74, pres., 1974-86, chief exec. officer, 1980-88, chmn., 1988-96; ret., 1996. Served to 1st lt. USAAF, 1943-45. Mem. Audubon Country Club, Longmeadow Country Club. Home: 577 Portsmouth Ct Naples FL 34110-8687

CLARKE, ALAN WILLIAM, lawyer; b. Arlington, Va., Aug. 19, 1949; s. William Garland and Josephine Sessions (Cornell) C.; 1 child, Benjamin Alan; m. Laurie Anne Whitt, Oct. 22, 1994. BA, William and Mary Coll., 1972, JD, 1975; LLM, Queen's U., Kingston, Ont., Can., 1994; postgrad., Western Mich. U., 1998—. Bar: Va. 1975, Mich. 1994, U.S. Dist. Ct. (ea. dist.) Va., U.S. Dist. Ct. (we. dist.) Mich., U.S. Ct. Appeals (4th and 6th cirs.), U.S. Bankruptcy Ct. (ea. dist.) Va., U.S. Supreme Ct. Assoc. Clarke & Johnston, P.C., Lively, Va., 1975-81; ptnr. Clarke & Clarke, Kilmarnock, Va., 1981-93; sole practitioner Chassell, Mich., 1994-97; asst. prof. criminal justice Ferris State U., 1997-2001, U. Wis.-Parkside, 2001—. Cons. in field; dir. Rappahanock Legal Svcs. Corp., Fredericksburg, Va.; adj. prof. bus. Rappahanock C.C., 1987-88; adj. prof. criminal justice Gogebic C.C., 1995-96; vis. scholar humanities dept. Mich. Technol. U., summers 1998, 2000; lectr. in field. Contbr. articles to legal jours. Fireman, Upper Lancaster Fire Dept.; bd. dirs. York chpt. Chesapeake Bay Found., 1974, No. Neck Audubon Soc., Kilmarnock, Va., 1982. Recipient Spl. Recognition award Lancaster County br. NAACP, 1993, Cert. of Recognition for pub. svc.. Coll. William and Mary, 1993, Cert. of Appreciation, Va. State Bar, 1993. Mem. ACLU, Am. Soc. Criminology, Can. Law and Soc. Assn., Nat. Assn. Criminal Def. Lawyers, Va. Bar Assn., Nat. Lawyers Guild, Upper Lancaster Ruritan (pres. 1982-83). Democrat. Episcopalian. Club: Upper Lancaster Ruritan (pres. 1982-83). Office: U Wis-Parkside Molinaw 380 900 Kenosha Rd Kenosha WI 53141-2000

CLARKE, SIR ARTHUR CHARLES, author; b. Minehead, Somerset, Eng., Dec. 16, 1917; s. Charles Wright and Norah (Willis) C.; m. Marilyn Mayfield, June 15, 1953 (div. 1964). B.Sc. in Physics and Math. with 1st class honors, King's Coll., London, 1948; D.Sc. (hon.), Beaver Coll., 1971, U. Moratuwa, 1979; D.Litt. (hon.), U. Bath, Eng., 1988, U. Liverpool, 1995, U. Hong Kong, Beijing, 1996. Auditor British Civil Service, His Majesty's Exchequer and Audit Dept., London, 1936-41; asst. editor Science Abstracts Inst. of Elec. Engineers, London, 1949-50; lectr., author, 1951—; chancellor U. Moratuwa, Sri Lanka, 1979—2002; Vikram Sarabhai prof. Phys. Rsch. Lab., Ahmedabad, India, 1980. Underwater explorer, photographer Great Barrier Reef of Australia and coast of Ceylon, 1954-64; commentator with Walter Cronkite Apollo missions, 1968-70; dir. Rocket Pub. Co., Underwater Safaris, Sri Lanka; founder Arthur C. Clarke Centre for Modern Technologies, Sri Lanka, 1984—; trustee Inst. Integral Edn.; fellow Franklin Inst., 1971, King's Coll., 1977, Inst. of Robotics, Carnegie-Mellon U., 1981; lectr. U.S. and Britain, 1957-74; bd. dirs. Nat. Space Soc., Space Generation Found., Internat. Astronomical Union, Planetary Soc., Rocket Pub. Co., Eng., Underwater Safaris, Sri Lanka; chmn. Second Internat. Astronautics Congress, London, 1951; moderator "Space Flight Report to the Nation", N.Y., 1961; fgn. assoc. Nat. Acad. Engring. (U.S.); mem. adv. coun. Internat. Sci. Policy Found., Fauna Internat., Sri Lanka, Earth Trust. Author: (non-fiction) Interplanetary Flight, 1950, The Exploration of Space, 1951 (Internat. Fantasy award 1952), The Young Traveller in Space, 1953 (pub. as Going Into Space, 1954), (with R.A. Smith) The Exploration of the Moon, 1955, The Coast of Coral, 1956, The Making of a Moon, 1957, The Reefs of Taprobane, 1957, The Scottie Book of Space Travel, 1957, (with Mike Wilson) Boy Beneath the Sea, 1958, Voice Across the Sea, 1958, The Challenge of the Spaceship, 1959, The Challenge of the Sea, 1960; (with Wilson) The First Five Fathoms, 1960, Indian Ocean Adventure, 1961, Profiles of the Future, 1962, The Treasure of the Great Reef, 1964, Indian Ocean Treasure, 1964; (with editors of Life mag.) Man and Space, 1964, Voices from the Sky, 1965, The Promise of Space, 1968; (with astronauts) First on the Moon, 1970, Report on Planet Three, 1972; (with Chesley Bonestell) Beyond Jupiter, 1972, The View from Serendip, 1977; (with Simon Welfare and John Fairley) Arthur C. Clarke's Mysterious World, 1980, Ascent to Orbit, 1984, 1984: Spring-A Choice of Futures, 1984, (with Welfare and Fairley) Arthur C. Clarke's World of Strange Powers, 1984, (with Peter Hyams) The Odyssey File, 1985, Arthur C. Clarke's July 20, 2019: Life in the 21st Century, 1986, Arthur C. Clarke's Chronicles of the Strange and Mysterious, 1987, Astounding Days, 1989, Opus 700, 1990, How the World Was One, 1992, (with Welfare and Fairley) Arthur C. Clarke's A-Z of Mysteries, 1993, By Space Possessed, 1993, The Snows of Olympus, 1994, Front Line of Discovery: Science on the Brink of Tomorrow, 1994, Greetings, Carbon-based Bipeds, 1999; (fiction) The Sands of Mars, 1951, Prelude to Space, 1951, Islands in the Sky, 1952, Against the Fall of Night, 1953, Childhood's End, 1953, Expedition to Earth, 1953, Earthlight, 1955, Reach For Tomorrow, 1956, The City and the Stars, 1956, Tales from the White Hart, 1957, The Deep Range, 1957, The Other Side of the Sky, 1958, Across the Sea of Stars, 1959, A Fall of Moondust, 1961, From the Oceans, from the Stars, 1962, Tales of Ten Worlds, 1962, Dolphin Island, 1963, Glide Path, 1963, Prelude to Mars, 1965, The Nine Billion Names of God, 1967, (with Stanley Kubrick) 2001: A Space Odyssey, 1968, The Final Odyssey, 1997, The Lion of Comarre and Against the Fall of Night, 1968, The Wind from the Sun, 1972, Of Time and Stars, 1972, The Lost Worlds of 2001, 1972, Rendezvous with Rama, 1973 (Nebula award Sci. Fiction Writers Am. 1973, Hugo award World Sci. Fiction Conv. 1974, John W. Campbell Meml. award Sci. Fiction Rsch. Assn. 1974, Jupiter award Instructors of Sci. Fiction in Higher Edn. 1974), The Best of Arthur C. Clarke, 1973, Imperial Earth, 1975, The Fountains of Paradise, 1979 (Nebula award Sci. Fiction Writers Am. 1980, Hugo award World Sci. Fiction Conv. 1980), 2010: Odyssey Two, 1982, The Sentinel, 1983, Selected Works, 1985, The Songs of Distant Earth, 1986, 2061: Odyssey Three, 1988, (with Gentry Lee) Cradle, 1988, A Meeting with Medusa, 1988, (with Lee) Rama II, 1989, Tales from Planet Earth, 1989, (with Gregory Benford) Beyond the Fall of Night, 1990, Ghost from the Grand Banks, 1990, (with Lee) Garden of Rama, 1991, More Than One Universe, 1991, The Hammer of God, 1993, (with Lee) Rama Revealed: The Ultimate Encounter, 1994, (with Mike McQuay) Richter 10, 1996, 3001: The Final Odyssey, 1997, (with Mike-Kube-McDowell) Trigger, 1999, (with Stephen Baxter) The Light of Other Days, 2000; screenwriter: (films) (with Stanley Kubrick) 2001: A Space Odyssey, 1968 (Academy award nomination best original screenplay 1968, Second Internat. Film Festival Spl. award 1969); writer, host: (TV series) Arthur C. Clarke's Mysterious World, 1980, Arthur C. Clarke's World of Strange Powers, 1984, Mysterious Universe, 1994; actor: (films) Beddagama, 1979; editor: Time Probe: The Science in Science Fiction, 1966, The Coming of the Space Age, 1967, Three for Tomorrow, 1972, The Science Fiction Hall of Fame Vol. III, 1982. With Lindbergh Award Noms. Com. Served to flight lt. RAF, 1941-46. Recipient Presdl. award U. Ill., 1997. Fellow Royal Astron. Soc., Royal Soc. Arts; mem. Brit. Interplanetary Soc. (chmn. 1947-50, 53), Internat. Council Integrative Studies, AIAA, Inst. Engrs. Sri Lanka (named hon. fellow 1983), Sri Lanka Astron. Soc., Royal Astron. Soc., Assn. Brit. Sci. Writers (life), Internat. Acad. Astronautics, World Acad. Art and Sci., Nat. Space Inst. (dir.), Brit. Sci. Fiction Assn. (pres.), Royal Soc. Arts, Brit. Sub-Aqua Club, Brit. Astron. Assn., H.G. Wells Soc. (hon. v.p.), Sci. Fiction Writers Am., Internat. Sci. Writers Assn., Sci. Fiction Found., Soc. Authors (mem. coun.), Am. Astronautical Assn., Am. Assn. for Advancement of Sci., Nat. Acad. Engring., Third World Acad. of Scis. (assoc. fellow), Sri Lanka Animal Welfare Assn., Sri Lanka Assn. Advancement Sci., Sri Lanka Nat. Inst. Paraplegics, Astron. Soc. Haringey, Soc. Satellite Profls. (hon. chmn., Hall of Fame 1987), Nat. Space Soc. (bd. dirs., R.A. Heinlein Meml. award 1990), Royal Asiatic Soc., Astron. Soc. Pacific, Nat. Acad. Engring. (fgn. assoc.), U.N. Assn. Sri Lanka (hon. life pres.).

CLARKE, CHARLES FENTON, lawyer; b. Hillsboro, Ohio, July 25, 1916; s. Charles F. and Margaret (Patton) C.; m. Virginia Schoppenhorst, Apr. 3, 1945 (dec. July 1989); children: Elizabeth, Margaret, Jane, Charles Fenton, IV; m. Lesley Wells, Nov. 13, 1998. AB summa cum laude, Washington and Lee U., Lexington, Va., 1938; LLB, U. Mich., 1940; LLD (hon.), Cleve. State U., 1971. Bar: Mich. 1940, Ohio 1946. Pvt. practice, Detroit, 1942, Cleve., 1946—; ptnr. firm Squire, Sanders & Dempsey, 1957—, adminstr. litigation dept., 1979-85. Trustee Cleve. Legal Aid Soc., 1959-67; pres. Nat. Assn. R.R. Trial Counsel, 1966-68; life mem. 6th Circuit Jud. Conf.; chmn. legis. com. Cleve. Welfare Fedn., 1961-68; master bencher Celebrezze Inn of Ct., 1991—; bd. dirs. Wheeling and Lake Erie R.R. Co. Pres. alumni bd. dirs. Washington and Lee U., 1970-72; pres. bd. dirs. Free Med. Clinic Greater Cleve., 1970-86; trustee Cleve. Citizens League, 1956-62, Cleve. chpt. ACLU, 1986-93, Cleve. Works Inc., 1995—; bd. dirs. citizens adv. bd. Cuyahoga County (Ohio) Juvenile Ct., 1970-73; bd. dirs. George Jr. Republic, Greenville, Pa., 1970-73, Bowman Tech. Sch., Cleve., 1970-91; vice chmn. Cleve. Crime Commn., 1973-75; exec. com. Cuyahoga County Rep. Orgn., 1950—; councilman Bay Village, Ohio, 1948-53; pres., trustee Cleve. Hearing and Speech Ctr., 1957-62, Laurel Sch., 1962-72, Fedn. Cmty. Progress, 1984-90; mem. planning commn. Cleveland Heights, 1994-2003. Fellow Am. Coll. Trial Lawyers; mem. Greater Cleve. Bar Assn. (trustee 1983-86), Cleve. Civil War Round Table (pres. 1968), Cleve. Zool. Soc. (dir. 1970), Phi Beta Kappa. Clubs: Skating, Union (Cleve.); Tavern, Rowfant. Presbyterian. Home: 2262 Tudor Dr Cleveland Heights OH 44106-3210 Office: Squire Sanders & Dempsey 4900 Key Tower 127 Public Sq Cleveland OH 44114-1304 E-mail: cclarke@ssd.com.

CLARKE, CORDELIA KAY KNIGHT MAZUY, management consultant, artist; b. Springfield, Mo., Nov. 22, 1938; d. William Horace and Charline (Bentley) Knight; m. Logan Clarke, Jr., July 22, 1978; children by previous marriage— Katharine Michelle Mazuy, Christopher Knight Mazuy. AB with honors in English, U. N.C., 1960; MS in Stats., N.C. State U., 1962; BFA, Lyme Acad. Coll., 1999. Statistician Research Triangle Inst., Durham, N.C., 1960-63; statis. cons. Arthur D. Little, Inc., Cambridge, Mass., 1963-67; dir. mktg. planning and analysis Polaroid Corp., Cambridge, 1967-70; dir. mktg. and bus. planning Transaction Tech. Inc., Cambridge, 1970-72; pres. Mazuy Assos., Boston, 1972-73; v.p. Nat. Shawmut Bank, Boston, 1973-74; sr. v.p., dir. mktg. Shawmut Corp., 1974-78; sr. v.p., dir. retail banking Shawmut Bank, 1976-78; v.p. corp. devel. Arthur D. Little, Inc., 1978-79; v.p. Conn. Gen. Life Ins. Co., 1979-85; pres. CIGNA Securities, 1983-85; chmn. Templeton, Inc., 1985-92, 95—; exec. v.p. McGraw-Hill Inc., 1988-90; pres. micromarketing divsn. ADVO, 1990-95. Faculty Williams Sch. Banking; adv. com. Bur. of Census, 1978-84; bd. dirs. Guardian Life Ins. Co., Berkshire Life Ins., Providence Jour. Co.; tchr. Amos Tuck Grad. Sch. Bus., Dartmouth Coll., 1964-65, exec.-in-residence, 1978, 80; bd. overseers, 1979-85; exec.-in-residence Wheaton Coll., 1978; vis. prof. Simmons Grad. Sch. Mgmt., 1978; mem. schs. adv. coun. Bank Mktg. Assn., 1976-78; mem. corp. adv. bd. Hartford Nat. Bank & Trust Co., 1980-87. Columnist Am. Banker, 1976-78. Mem. Mass. Gov.'s Commn. on Status of Women, 1977-79; bd. corporators Babson Coll., 1977-80; adv. bd. Boston Mayor's Office Cultural Affairs, 1977-79; bd. dirs. McGraw-Hill, Inc., 1976-88, Blue Shield of Mass., 1976-79, Greater Hartford Arts Coun., 1979-93, Cybex Internat. Inc., 1996-2000; trustee Children's Mus. Hartford, 1980-82; corporator Inst. of Living, 1981-92; regent U. Hartford, 1982—; bd. dirs. Hartford Art Sch., 1982-94, Hartford Stage Co., 1985-99, Manhattan Theatre Club, 1988-91, Inst. for Future, 1988-92, N.Y. Internat. Festival of Arts, 1988-91, Goodspeed Opera, 1990—, Inst. Design, 1990-98, Aeroflex Found., 1972—. Mem. Artists Assn. Nantucket (elected), Lyme Art Assn. (assoc.), Essex Art Assn. (assoc.), Internat. Womens Forum, Power 10, Phi Beta Kappa, Phi Kappa Phi, Kappa Alpha Theta. Home and Office: 89 River Rd East Haddam CT 06423-1462

CLARKE, EDWARD NIELSEN, engineering science educator; b. Providence, Apr. 25, 1925; s. Edward O.A. and Edith (Nielsen) C.; m. Vivian Constance Bergquist, July 23, 1949; children— Sandra J., David E., Allan R., Jeffrey B. BS, Brown U., 1945, PhD, 1951; MS, Harvard, 1947, M.Engring. Sci., 1948. Mem. tech. staff, sect. head for semiconductors, physics lab. Sylvania Electric Products Co., Bayside, N.Y., 1950-56; group head for research Sperry Semiconductor div. Sperry Rand Corp., Norwalk, Conn., 1956-59; v.p. ops. and dir. Nat. Semiconductor Corp., Danbury, Conn., 1959-65; assoc. dean faculty, assoc. dean grad. studies, dir. research Worcester Poly. Inst., 1965-86, prof. engring. scis., 1968-94, dir. Ctr. Solar Electrification, 1986-94, prof. emeritus, 1995—; tri-coll. coordinator research Clark U.-Holy Cross Coll.-Worcester Poly. Inst., 1974 85. Co-founder Nat. Semiconductor Corp., founder solar electrification ctr. Worcester Poly. Inst.; disting. vis. prof. Nichols Coll., 2002. Trustee Upsala Coll., East Orange, N.J., 1971-74. Served with USNR, 1943-46. Recipient Brown U. Engring. Alumni medal, 1998. Mem. IEEE, Am. Phys. Soc., Torch Club (Worcester), Sigma Xi (past chpt. pres.), Tau Beta Pi. Lutheran. Achievements include patents and inventions in semiconductor technology; pioneering development of solar powered racing car. Home: 85 Richards Ave Paxton MA 01612-1123 Office: Worcester Poly Inst Dept Interdisciplinary and Global Studies Worcester MA 01609 E-mail: encvcc@aol.com. *Helping others to achieve has been my own principal achievement. Retain mobility and be willing to use one's skills wherever they are needed. Do not become too comfortable and secure. Move on to find new challenges. Stay young with variety in one's life and a healthy use of the out-of-doors.*

CLARKE, EDWARD OWEN, JR., lawyer; b. Balt., Dec. 19, 1929; s. Edward Owen and Agnes Oakford C.; m. P. Rhea Parker, Dec. 18, 1954; children: Deborah Jeanne, Catherine Ann, Carolyn Agnes, Edward Owen III. AB magna cum laude, Loyola Coll., Balt., 1950; JD with honors, U. Md., 1956. Bar: Md. 1956, U.S. Dist. Ct. Md. 1956. Law clk. U.S. Dist. Ct. Md., 1956-57; assoc. Smith, Somerville & Case, Balt., 1957-62, ptnr., 1962-71, Piper & Marbury, Balt., 1971-94, mem. policy and mgmt. com., 1981-94, mng. ptnr., 1987-90, co-chmn. bus. div., 1991-94. Mem. Gov.'s Com. to Study Blue Sky Law, 1961; mem. Md. Commn. on Revision Corp. Law, 1965-66. Bd. dirs. Bon Secours Hosp., 1964-73, sec., 1968-73; bd. dirs. Hosp. Cost Analysis Svc., 1966-81; bd. pres. mem. exec. coun. Md. Hosp. Assn., 1968-74, chmn. com. on legislation, 1971-73, treas., 1973; trustee St. Mary's Coll. Md., 1983-94, chmn. bd., 1988-94; trustee St. Mary's Sem., U. Balt., 1986-89, Loyola H.S., Balt., 1984-90, Hannah More Ctr., 1980-83; bd. dirs. Helix Health Sys., Inc., 1995-98, Med Star Health, 1998—; mem. Md. Higher Edn. Commn., 1994—, chmn. 1995-2000. Lt. USNR, 1952-55. Recipient Alumni Laureate award Loyola Coll. in Md., 2001. Mem. ABA, Md. State Bar Assn. (mem. sect. coun. corp., banking and bus. law sect. 1968-71, chmn. 1970-71), Wednesday Law Club (sec., treas. 1984-88, v.p. 1988-89, pres. 1990), Center Club (Balt., bd. govs. 1988-94), Order of Coif, Order of the Ark and the Dove, Phi Beta Kappa, Alpha Sigma Nu, Tau Kappa Alpha.

CLARKE, FRANK HENDERSON, retired chemical company executive, scientist; b. Newcastle, N.B., Can., Dec. 6, 1927; came to U.S., 1950; s. Frank Henderson and Elsie Louisa (Scammell) C.; m. Virginia Nicholas, Sept. 4, 1954; children: Susan Virginia, Sarah Ann Clarke Ben-Shahar. BSc, U. N.B., Fredericton, 1949, MSc, 1950; PhD, Harvard U., 1954. Rsch. chemist Schering Corp., Bloomfield, N.J., 1955-59, sr. rsch. chemist, 1959-62; group leader Geigy Chem. Corp., Ardsley, N.Y., 1962-63, assoc. dir. medicinal chemistry, 1963-67, dir. medicinal chemistry, 1967-71; dep. dir. chemistry CIBA-GEIGY, Ardsley, 1971-83, disting. rsch. fellow Summit, N.J., 1983-93; pres. Chem-Clarke, Inc., Califon, N.J., 1993-2000; ret., 2000—. Participant 1st Internat. Conf. on Narcotic Antagonists, 1972. Author: Calculator Programming for Chemistry and Life Sciences, 1981; co-author: (computer disks) Molecular Graphics on the Apple IIe, 1985, Molecular Graphics on the IBM PC, 1985; editor: How Modern Medicines Are Discovered, 1973, How Modern Medicines Are Developed, 1977; editor-in-chief: Annual Reports in Medicinal Chemistry, 1976, 77, 78; mem. editl. bd. Jour. Medicinal Chemistry; contbr. articles to sci. jours., including Jour. Am. Chem. Soc. Lord Beaverbrook scholar U. N.B., 1945-49. Fellow AAAS, N.Y. Acad. Sci.; mem. Am. Chem. Soc. (chmn. N.Y. sect. 1972), Pharm. Mfrs. Assn. (chmn. com. on rsch. info.). Achievements include numerous patents in chemical field and for molecular models. Home: 41 Big Spring Rd Califon NJ 07830-3428

CLARKE, FRANK WILLIAM, communication executive; b. Quebec, Que., Can., Apr. 16, 1942; came to U.S., 1946; s. William Frank Clarke and Tolly (English) Wing; m. Barbara Jean Dreher, Mar. 1966 (div. Sept. 1975); children: Kathleen Julienne Clarke Smith, Lori Christine Clarke Genovese; m. Vera Gretel Thol, Nov. 14, 1977; stepchildren: Teo Capriles, Gretel Capriles Saade. Student, U. Va., 1958-61; BS in Commerce, NYU, 1964; MS in Journalism, Northwestern U., 1965. Staff asst., then asst. account exec. Grey Advt. Inc., N.Y.C., 1969-70, account exec., 1970-73, account dir. Caracas, Venezuela, 1973-75, v.p. account svcs., 1975-78, v.p., area dir., 1978-82, N.Y.C., 1982-88, sr. v.p., area dir., 1988-93, exec. v.p., area dir., 1993-99; sr. cons. Strategy XXI Group Ltd., N.Y.C., 1999-2000, ptnr., 2001—. Mem. product mktg. com. U.S. Fund for UNICEF, N.Y.C., 1989-93, nat. adv. coun., 1991-93, bd. dirs., 1994-2000, mem. exec. com., 1996-2000; bd. dirs. Street Law, Inc., Washington, 1999—, chmn., 2001—. Capt. U.S. Army, 1966-69. Mem. Racquet and Tennis Club N.Y. Republican. Avocations: gardening, cross country skiing. Office: Strategy XXI Group Ltd 515 Madison Ave New York NY 10022-5403

CLARKE, FRED W., III, architect, architectural firm executive; b. Houston, Feb. 24, 1947; Grad. with highest honors, U. Tex., 1970. Registered architect, Conn., Calif., Del., Fla., Iowa, Ill., La., N.J., N.Y., N.C., Ohio, Tex., Washington, Wyo.; 1st class registered architect, Japan. With Gruen Assocs., L.A., 1970-77; project prin., collaborating designer, co-founder, mgr. Cesar Pelli & Assocs., New Haven, Conn., 1977—. Instr. Sch. Architecture UCLA, 1972-76, Sch. Architecture Rice U., Houston, 1976; vis. critic arch. Yale U., 1977-82; keynote spkr. VIII Bienal de Arquitectura de Quito; guest lectr., spkr. Iberian-Am. Forum of Architecture and Urbanism of São Paulo, Profl. Design-Build Conf., Asia Soc.; guest critic Colegio Arquitecos de Chile, others; chmn. design juries, profl. panels Urban Land Inst. Prin. works include Mus. Modern Art expansion and renovation, U.S. Embassy in Toyko, Herring Hall Rice U., Carnegie Hall Tower in N.Y.C., World Financial Ctr. in N.Y.C., terminal at Wash. Nat. Airport, Petronas Towers in Kuala Lumpur, Goldman Sachs Hqrs., Performing Arts Ctr. of Greater Miami, Nat. Mus. Contemporary Art., Osaka, Japan, Mpls. (Minn.) Ctrl. Libr.; corp. hdqrs., hosps., rsch. labs., acad. bldgs., mus., performing arts ctrs., office towers, airports worldwide. MacDowell Colony fellow, 1998. Fellow AIA (chmn. design juries, profl. panels, Firm award 1989); mem. Philippine Inst. Architects. Office: Cesar Pelli & Assocs Inc care Public Relations 1056 Chapel St New Haven CT 06510-2402

CLARKE, GARRY EVANS, composer, educator, musician, administrator; b. Moline, Ill., Mar. 19, 1943; s. Clarence Henderson and Gladys Arlene (Hokinson) C.; m. Melissa Jane Naul, May 24, 1975; children: Catharine van Gelder, Margaret Elizabeth Jane. MusB summa cum laude, Cornell Coll., Mount Vernon, Iowa, 1965; MusM, Yale U., 1968; LittD (hon.), Washington Coll., 1988. Asst. prof. music Washington Coll., Chestertown, Md., 1968-73; assoc. prof., 1973-79; prof. Washington Coll., Chestertown, 1979—, dean coll., 1977-83, acting pres., 1981-82. Am. liaison Harrison & Harrison Ltd., Durham, Eng. Composer symphonic, chamber, vocal, piano and organ music and opera; lectr. and recitalist (U.S., Europe): Am. music; condr. piano workshops; opera coach; organist and choir master, St. Paul's Episcopal Parish, Centerville, Md., 1975-88; Chester Parish, Chestertown, Md., 1988—; author: Essays on American Music, 1977; contbr. articles, revs. to profl. jours.; co-editor: Varied Air and Variations (Ives), 1971; editor: Charles Ives. Soc. publs. Trustee Coun. Econ. Edn. Md.; bd. dirs. Talbot Chamber Orch. Ford Found. fellow, 1965, Woodrow Wilson fellow, 1965; Carnegie Found. rsch. grantee, 1964, NEH rsch. grantee, 1970; recipient Bronze medal Coun. for Advancement and Support of Edn., 1993. Mem. AAUP, Soc. Music Theory, Assn. Anglican Musicians, Sonneck Soc., Council Higher Edn. in Music, Am. Conf. Acad. Deans, Nat. Assn. Schs. Music, Am. Assn. Higher Edn., Yale Sch. Music Alumni Assn. (exec. com. 1975-80), Assn. Yale Alumni, Yale Club (N.Y.C.), Order of Omega, Pi Kappa Lambda, Omicron Delta Kappa, Phi Delta Theta. Episcopalian. Home: Fairways 7775 Waterview Ln Chestertown MD 21620-9507 Office: Washington Coll 300 Washington Ave Chestertown MD 21620-1197 E-mail: gclarke2@washcoll.edu.

CLARKE, GARVEY ELLIOTT, lawyer; b. Christ Church, Barbados, May 13, 1935; came to U.S., 1941; s. Elliott and Marion (Gibbs) C.; m. Yvonne E. Hayling, 1961; children: Wendy Y., Garvey H. AB, Dartmouth Coll., 1957; JD, N.Y. Law Sch., 1961. Bar: N.Y. 1963. Attorney legal dept. NBC, N.Y.C., 1963-65; v.p. A Better Chance, Inc., N.Y.C., 1965-75; pres. Nat. Fund for Minority Engring. Students, N.Y.C., 1975-82; v.p. Nat. Action Coun. for Minorities in Engring., N.Y.C., 1982-83; sr. assoc. Right Assocs., N.Y.C., 1983-85; dir. Morehouse Coll. Campaign The Oram Group, Inc., N.Y.C., 1985-86; dir. devel. Project Orbis, N.Y.C., 1986-87; dir. capital campaign United Negro Coll. Fund, N.Y.C., 1987-89; pres. Leadership Edn. and Devel. Progam in Bus., Inc., N.Y.C., 1989—2002; pvt. practice Sarasota, Fla., 2003—. Cons. Edn. Assoc., Washington, 1968-70, Frantzreb and Pray, N.Y.C., 1968-71. Pres. Stuyford Action Coun., Bklyn., 1963-70, Black Alumni of Dartmouth Assn., Hanover, N.H., 1976-78; mem. Dartmouth Alumni Coun., Hanover, 1977-79; bd. dirs. Boys Club of N.Y., N.Y.C., 1970-92; active Greater Centennial A.M.E. Zion Ch. Mem. New York County Lawyers Assn., Dartmouth Lawyers Assn. Home: Lake Ridge Falls 8086 Stirling Falls Cir Sarasota FL 34243 E-mail: bagner22@aol.com.

CLARKE, GEORGE ALTON, chemist, academic administrator, retired; b. N.Y.C., Apr. 4, 1933; s. Cecil and Linda Clarke; m. Janice E. Avery, July 16, 1966; children: Jill, Kristin. BS, CCNY, 1955; PhD, Penn. State U., 1960. Postdoctoral rschr. Columbia U., N.Y.C., 1960-62; asst. prof. SUNY, Buffalo, 1962-68; assoc. prof. Drexel U., Phila., 1968-71, U. Miami, 1971-84, assoc. dean, 1978-84; dean Sch. Arts and Scis., Ctrl. Conn. State U., New Britain, 1984-97, spl. asst. to pres., 1997-98, emeritus, 1998—. Contbr. articles to profl. jours. Bd. dirs., v.p. New Britain C. of C., 1985-92; bd. dirs., pres. Human Resources Agy., New Britain, 1991-96; bd. dirs. Am. Savs. Bank, New Britain, 1994-98; bd. dirs., v.p. Substance Abuse Action Coun., New Britain, 1992-97. Mem. Am. Phys. Soc., Am. Chem. Soc., Sigma Xi. Avocations: swimming, gardening, hiking, tinkering, computers.

CLARKE, HENRY LEE, foreign service officer, former ambassador; b. Ft. Benning, Ga., Nov. 15, 1941; s. Edwin Lee and Jane Iredell (Jones) C.; m. Kathleen Ann Smith, May 19, 1973 (div. 1996); children: Ann Marie, Edwin Lee; m. Elena Anatolyevna Fedyai, Jan. 8, 1997; children: Julia Chikerenda, Christopher Lee. AB, Dartmouth Coll., 1962; MPA, Harvard U., 1967. U.S. fgn. svc. officer Dept. State, 1967-99; econ. counselor Am. Embassy, Moscow, 1982-85, dep. chief Bucharest, Romania, 1985-89, econ. counselor Tel Aviv, 1989-92, amb. to Uzbekistan, Tashkent, 1992-95; internat. affairs advisor Nat. War Coll., Washington, 1995-98; sr. advisor for property restitution in Europe, Dept. State, Washington, 1998-2000; dep. high rep. for Bosnia and Brcko Supr., 2001—. Bd. dirs. Addex Inc., Boston. Chmn. bd. Am. Sch., Bucharest, 1985-89, Tashkent Internat. Sch., 1994-95.

CLARKE, J. CALVITT, JR., federal judge; b. Harrisburg, Pa., Aug. 9, 1920; s. Joseph Calvitt and Helen Caroline (Mattson) C.; m. Mary Jane Cromer, Feb. 1, 1943 (dec.1985); children: Joseph Calvitt III, Martha Tiffany; m. Betty Ann Holladay, May 29, 1986. BS in Commerce, JD, U. Va., 1945. Bar: Va. 1944. Practiced in, Richmond, Va., 1944-74; partner firm Bowles, Anderson, Boyd, Clarke & Herod, 1944-60; firm Sands Anderson, Marks and Clarke, 1960-74; judge U.S. Dist. Ct. (ea. dist.) Va., 1975-91, sr. judge, 1991—. Mem. 4th Circuit Judicial Conf., 1963; hon. consul for Republic of Bolivia, 1959-75 Chmn. Citizen's Advisory Com. on Joint Water System for Henrico and Hanover counties, Va., 1968-69; mem. Mayor's Freedom Train Com., 1948-50; del. Young Republican Nat. Conv., Salt Lake City, 1949, Boston, 1951; chmn. Richmond (Va.) Republican Com., 1952-54; candidate for Congress, 1954; chmn. Va. 3d Dist. Rep. Com., 1955-58, 74-75, Va. State Rep. Conv., 1958—; co-founder Young Rep. Fedn. of Va., 1950, nat. committeeman, 1950-54, chmn., 1955; chmn. 3d dist. Speakers Bur., Nixon-Lodge campaign, 1960, mem. fin. com., 1960-74; chmn. Henrico County Republican Com., 1956-58; fin. chmn. 1956; pres. Couples Sunday Sch. class Second Presbyn. Ch., Richmond, Va., 1948-50, mem. bd. deacons, 1948-61, elder, 1964-99, 1st Presbyn. Ch., Virginia Beach, 1999— ; bd. dirs. Family Service Children's Aid Soc., 1948-61, Gambles Hill Community Center, 1950-60, Christian Children's Fund, Inc., 1960-67, Children, Inc., 1967-75, Norfolk Forum, 1978-83; mem. bd. of chancellors Internat. Consular Acad., 1965-75; trustee Henrico County Pub. Library, chmn., 1971-73. Fellow Va. Law Found.; mem. Va. State Bar (mem. 3rd dist. com. 1967-70, chmn. 1969-70), Richmond Bar Assn., Norfolk-Portsmouth Bar Assn., Va. Bar Assn., Thomas Jefferson Soc. of Alumni U. Va. Lile Law Soc., McGuires U. Sch. Alumni (pres. 1995-96), Am. Judicature Soc., ABA, Va. Bar Assn. (vice chmn. com. on cooperation with fgn. bars 1960-61), Richmond Jr. C. of C. (dir. 1946-50), Windmill Point Yacht Club, Westwood Racquet Club (pres. 1961-62), Commonwealth Club, Delta Theta Phi. Office: US Dist Ct 600 Granby St Norfolk VA 23510-1915

CLARKE, JAMES WESTON, political science educator, writer; b. Elizabeth, Pa., Feb. 16, 1937; s. Alonzo Peterson and Beatrice (Weston) C.; m. Jeanne Nienaber; children— Julianne, Michael BA, Washington and Jefferson Coll., 1962; MA, Pa. State U., 1964, PhD, 1968. Asst. prof. Fla. State U., 1967-71; assoc. prof. U. Ariz., Tucson, 1971-76, prof. polit. sci., 1976—, chmn. dept., 1973-78, univ. disting. prof., 2000. Author: American Assassins: The Darker Side of Politics, 1982, Last Rampage: The Escape of Gary Tison, 1988, On Being Mad or Merely Angry: John W. Hinckley Jr. and Other Dangerous People, 1990, The Lineaments of Wrath: Race, Violent Crime, and American Culture, 1998. Served with USMC, 1955-58 Recipient James Gillespie Blaine prize Washington and Jefferson Coll., 1962, Matthew Brown Ringland prize, 1962, Burlington Northern Found. award for excellence in tchg., 1987, Golden Key Nat. Honor Soc. award for tchg., 1989, Social and Behavioral Scis. award for outstanding tchg., 1991, 96; Udall fellow, 1993; Fulbright scholar, Ireland, 1999. Mem. Am. Polit. Sci. Assn. (Outstanding Tchg. in Polit. Sci. 2000), Authors Guild Am. Home: 855 E Placita Leslie Tucson AZ 85718-1960 Office: U Ariz 315 Social Sci Bldg Tucson AZ 85721-0001 E-mail: jclarke@u.arizona.edu.

CLARKE, JAY A. art historian, curator; b. Lake Forest, Ill., May 16, 1966; BA, Coll. of Holy Cross, 1988; MA, Brown U., 1991, PhD, 1999. Nat. Endowment for Arts intern Art Inst. Chgo., 1991-92, rsch. asst., 1992-95, asst. curator, 1997-2001, assoc. curator, 2001—. Grantee Ferdinand Möller Found., Germany, 1996, Brown U. Rsch. & Travel grantee, 1996, Cmty. Assocs. of the Art Inst. of Chgo. Rsch. and Travel grantee, 1999, German Acad. Exch. grantee, 2000. Mem. Coll. Art Assn., Historians German and Ctrl. European Art, Historians 19th Century Art, NOW, Print Coun. Am., Am. Assn. Art Mus. Curators. Office: Art Inst Chgo Dept Prints & Drawings 111 S Michigan Ave Chicago IL 60603-6492

CLARKE, JOHN, physics educator; b. Cambridge, Eng., Feb. 10, 1942; came to U.S., 1968; s. Victor Patrick and Ethel May (Blowers) C.; m. Grethe Fog Pedersen, Sept. 15, 1979; 1 child, Elizabeth Jane. BA, Cambridge U., 1964, MA, PhD, Cambridge U., 1968. Postdoctoral scholar U. Calif.-Berkeley, 1968-69, asst. prof. physics, 1969-71, assoc. prof., 1971-73, prof., 1973—; chair exptl. physics Luis W. Alvarez Meml., 1994—. Contbr. numerous articles to profl. jours. Recipient Charles Vernon Boys prize Brit. Inst. Physics, 1977, award Soc. Exploration Geophysics, 1979, Outstanding Teaching award U. Calif., 1983, Fritz London award for low temperature physics, 1987, Fed. Lab. Consortium award for excellence in technology transfer, 1992, divsn. materials scis. award in solid state physics Dept. Energy, 1986, 92, IEEE U.S. Activities Bd. Electrotechnology Transfer award, 1995, Comstock prize Physics NAS, 1999, Coun. on Superconductivity award IEEE, 2002; fellow Sloan Found., 1970-72, Miller Inst. for Basic Rsch., 1975-76, 94-95; Guggenheim fellow, 1977-78; named Calif. Scientist of Yr., 1987, One of 50, Scientific Am., 2002. Fellow AAAS, Royal Soc. London, Am. Phys. Soc. (Joseph F. Keithley Advances in Measurement Sci. award 1998), Brit. Inst. Physics. Office: U Calif Dept Physics Berkeley CA 94720-7300

CLARKE, JOHN PATRICK, retired newspaper publisher; b. Mattoon, Ill., Oct. 29, 1930; s. Patrick Joseph Clarke and Lucille (Hennebry) Stoeckinger; m. Roberta June Steiner, July 25, 1959 (div. 1984); children: Shannon, Dana; m. Sheila Cordill, June 24, 1995. BS, Ind. U., 1958; MBA, Harvard U., 1962. With contr.'s staff Ethyl Corp., N.Y.C., 1958-60; bus. mgr. State Jour.-Register, Springfield, Ill., 1962-68, pub., 1968-96; ret., 1996. Sec., bd. dirs. Ill. Ambassadors, 1986—; mem. Atty. Registration and Disciplinary Commn., 1987—; chmn bd. dirs. State Farm Rail Classic (LPGA tour). With USN, 1949-50, 52-54. Mem. Am. Newspaper Pubs. Assn., Inland Daily Press Assn., Kensington Golf and Country Club, Sangamo Club (pres. 1978-79). Avocations: sailing, golf.

CLARKE, JOHN RODNEY, surgeon; b. Ft. Riley, Kans., Apr. 24, 1943; s. Alfred Nelson and Kathryn Helen (Brossard) C. BA, Wesleyan U., Middletown, Conn., 1965; MD, U. Pa., 1968. Diplomate Am. Bd. Surgery. Intern and resident Presbyn.-St. Luke's Hosp., Chgo., 1968-70; resident St. Joseph Mercy Hosp., Ann Arbor, Mich., 1972-75; trauma fellow Boston City Hosp., 1975-76; instr. in surgery Med. Coll. Pa. Drexel U., Phila., 1976—77, asst. prof. surgery Med. Coll. Pa., 1977-80, assoc. prof. Med. Coll. Pa., 1980-84, prof. Med. Coll. Pa., 1984—. Adj. prof. computer and info. sci. U. Pa., Phila., 1991—; mem. health care tech. study sect. U.S. Agy. Health Care Policy and Rsch., Washington, 1990—92; mem. com. patient safety data stds. Inst. Medicine, Washington, 2002—03. Author: Surgical Judgment Using Decision Sciences, 1984; assoc. editor Theoretical Surgery, 1991-94; mem. editl. bd. Med. Decision Making, 1988-91, Jour. Surg. Outcomes, 1998-2000; contbr. articles to profl. publs., chpt. to books. Maj. Med. Corps, U.S. Army, 1970-72. Recipient Resident Tour award Frederick A. Coller Surg. Soc., 1975, Samuel D. Gross prize for rsch. in surgery, 1983; Wellcome rsch. travel grantee Burroughs Wellcome Fund, 1984. Fellow ACS (gov. 2001—), Phila. Acad. Surgery (pres. 2000); mem. Am. Surg. Assn., Am. Assn. Surgery of Trauma, Am. Med. Informatics Assn., Assn. for Acad. Surgery, Soc. for Med. Decision Making (v.p. 1989-90), Soc. Univ. Surgeons, Am. Assn. Artificial Intelligence, Internat. Soc. Surgery, Am. Philos. Assn. Office: Drexel U 3300 Henry Ave Philadelphia PA 19129-1191

CLARKE, JOHN TERREL, astrophysicist; b. Chgo., Mar. 4, 1952; s. Terrel Edward and Catherine Evelyn (Carr) C.; m. Cleda Elisabeth Clarke, 1997. BS in Physics, Denison U., 1974; MA in Physics, Johns Hopkins U., 1978, PhD in Physics, 1980. Rsch. physicist U. Calif., Berkeley, 1980-84; assoc. project scientist, Hubble Space Telescope NASA Marshall Space Flight Ctr., Huntsville, Ala., 1984-85; advanced instruments, project scientist NASA Goddard Space Flight Ctr., Greenbelt, Md., 1985-87; rsch. scientist U. Mich., Ann Arbor, 1987—2000; prof. dept. astronomy Boston U., 2000—. Mem. Hubble Space Telescope user's com., NASA, 1996-99. Assoc. editor: Jour. of Geophys. Rsch., 1997-2002, Icarus, 1997—; contbr. articles to profl. jours. Mem. Internat. Astron. Union, Am. Geophysical Union, Am. Astron. Soc. (div. planetary sci. com. 1997-2000), Sigma Pi Sigma. Home: Jamaica Plain MA 02130 Office: Boston U Dept Astronomy and Ctr for Space Physics 725 Commonwealth Ave Boston MA 02215

CLARKE, KATHLEEN BURTON, federal agency administrator; b. Utah; Grad., Utah State U. From dir. constituent svcs. to exec. dir. Office of Congressman James V. Hansen, 1987—93; dep. dir. Utah Dept. Natural Resources, 1993—98, exec. dir., 1998—2001; dir. Bur. Land Mgmt. U.S. Dept. Interior, Washington, 2001—. Office: US Dept Interior Bur Land Mgmt 1849 C St NW Washington DC 20240

CLARKE, KENNETH KINGSLEY, electronics executive; b. Miami, Fla., June 7, 1924; s. Kenneth Kingsley and Mary (Coffin) Clarke; m. Nona Nelme, Sept. 15, 1945; 1 child, Kenneth Stephen. Student, Cornell U., 1941-43; MSEE, Stanford, 1948; DEE, Bklyn. Poly. Inst., 1959. Rsch. fellow Bklyn. Poly. Inst., 1949-50, faculty, 1955-69, prof. elec. engring., 1965-69, dir. grad. elec. engring. divsn., 1967-69; asst. prof. Madras (India) Inst. Tech., 1950-52; lectr. U. Ceylon, Colombo, 1952-54; asst. prof. Clarkson Coll. Tech., Potsdam, NY, 1954-55; pres. Clarke-Hess Comm. Rsch. Corp., N.Y.C., 1969-99. Cons. in field; vis. prof. Mid. E. Tech. U., Ankara, Turkey, 1961—62; dir. Julie Rsch. Labs., 1966—71. Author (with M. V. Joyce): (book) Transistor Circuit Analysis, 1961; author: (with D. T. Hess) Communication Circuit Analysis, 1971. 2d lt. AC U.S. Army, 1943—46. Recipient Svc. award, Parlar Found., 1992. Fellow: IEEE (life), Instrument and Measurement Soc. (mem. adminstrv. com. 1993—96, mem. visitor accreditation bd. 1983—88, bd. dirs. Instrumentation/Measurement Tech. Conf., tech. program chmn. 1995); mem.: AAAS, AAUP, Sigma Xi, Tau Beta Pi. Achievements include co-inventor frequency locked loop. Home: 300 Riverside Dr New York NY 10025-5279 E-mail: ken1924@ix.netcom.com.

CLARKE, LAMBUTH MCGEEHEE, retired academic administrator; b. Salisbury, Md., Oct. 4, 1923; s. Hawes Palmore and Jessie Lee (Ham) C.; m. Alice Royall Acree, July 16, 1955; children: Leighton Krips, Palmore, Jessica, Virginia Hitch. BA, Randolph-Macon Coll., 1944, LLD (hon.), 1969; MA, Johns Hopkins U., 1948; postgrad., U. Birmingham, 1948, Harvard U., 1982; LHD (hon.), Va. Wesleyen Coll., 2002. English instr. Randolph-Macon Coll., Ashland, Va., 1948-51, asst. to pres., 1951-58, v.p. devel., 1958-66; pres. Va. Wesleyan Coll., Norfolk, 1966-92, pres. emeritus, 1992—, also trustee; acting pres. Randolph-Macon Womans' Coll., 1993-94. Bd. dirs. Va. Symphony, Norfolk, 1970-88, trustee, 1990—; bd. dirs. Leigh Meml. Hosp., later Med. Ctr. Hosps., 1970-82, Norfolk Forum, 1970-80, World Affairs Coun., 1972-76, YMCA, Norfolk, 1972-78, Sta. WHRO-TV, 1972-76, Greater Norfolk Corp., 1978-92, Com. of 101-Future of Hampton Rds., Norfolk, 1983-92, Order of Cape Henry 1607, Norfolk, Va. Eye Found., Norfolk, 1973-92, Va. Coun. Chs., 1978-82; trustee Va. Found. Ind. Colls., Richmond, 1982-92, vice-chmn., 1990-92, assoc., 1992-97; trustee Randolph-Macon Womans Coll., 1992-97, hon. trustee, 1998—; univ. senate United Meth. Ch., Nashville, 1988-92, bd. dirs., gen. bd. higher edn., 1980-88, del. jurisdictional conf., 1976-96, gen. conf., 1980-92; adv. bd. DePaul Med. Ctr., Norfolk, 1988-96; bd. dirs. Lee's Friends, 1993-99, adv. bd., 1999—; bd. dirs. Tidewater Scholarship Found., 1994-2000, Westminster-Canterbury of Hampton Rds., 1995-2003, Norfolk Sr. Ctr., Portsmouth Mus. Found., Inc., 1997-2000, Norfolk Bot. Gardens Found.; chmn. adminstrv. bd. Larchmont United Meth. Ch., 1993. Lt. (j.g.) USNR, 1943-46. Recipient Brotherhood citation NCCJ, 1991, John Wesley Disting. Educator award, 1991, Francis Asbury Educator award, 1995, Jerry G. Bray Dist. Svc. medal Va. Wesleyan Coll., 1997, Lambuth M. Clarke Acad. Ctr. of Va. Wesleyan Coll., 1999. Mem. Soc. Alumni Randolph-Macon Coll. (bd. dirs. 1993-99), Soc. of the Cin., Rotary Club Norfolk, Phi Beta Kappa, Omicron Delta Kappa, Phi Kappa Phi, Lambda Chi Alpha. Methodist. Avocations: volunteerism, reading, music, art and church architecture, philately.

CLARKE, LAURENCE B. retired real estate broker, writer; b. Phila., Nov. 29, 1932; s. James David Clarke and Mary Wainwright Bowen/Steelman; m. Jean Lowman (div.); m. Joann Sloan (div.); m. Constance Bates (div.); children: Laura Grimmer, Janet Kennedy, Linne Haywood, Jennifer. BBA, U. Alaska, College, 1955. Assoc. real estate broker Banker Nat. Bank Alaska, Anchorage, 1959—68; sr. sales rep., exec. Xerox Corp., Anchorage, 1968—77; real estate broker Jack White Co., Anchorage, 1977—93, Re/Max Properties, Anchorage, 1993—2001, Across Alaska Real Estate Referral, Wrangell, Alaska, 2001—03; ret. Pres. Anchorage Multiple Listing Svc., 1987—94. Author: Ahnya, 2000, One Who Knows Something, 2001, Chitina Past, 2002. Alaska liaison N.W. Lions Found. for Sight and Hearing, 2000—03. 1st lt. U.S. Army, 1955—59. Mem.: Wrangell Golf Assn. (dir.), Elks (treas.), Lions (past dist. gov., Lion of Yr. 1997). Democrat. Methodist. Avocations: writing, sports, coaching softball, boating, golf. Home: PO Box 1379 Wrangell AK 99929

CLARKE, LEWIS JAMES, landscape architect; b. Eng., Mar. 10, 1927; s. Roland and May (Pringle) C.; children: Lewis Nigel, Jennifer Kay, Rachel May, Lisa Elaine. Dip. Arch., Sch. Architecture, Leicester, Eng., 1950; Dip. L.D., Kings Coll, U. Durham, 1951; M.L.A., Harvard U., 1952. Prof. Sch. Design N.C. State Univ., Raleigh, 1952-68; sr. partner Lewis Clarke Assos., Raleigh, 1952—. Served with Corps Royal Engrs., 1946-49. Smith Mundt fellow, Fulbright fellow, 1951-52. Fellow Inst. Landscape Architects, Am. Soc. Landscape Architects; mem. Royal Inst. Brit. Architects. Office: Lewis Clarke Assocs 1701 Glen Eden Dr Raleigh NC 27612-4335

CLARKE, LEWIS RYLAND, history educator; b. Balt., May 28, 1937; s. Lewis Ryland Clarke Jr. and Ida Helen Schubert; m. Jill Susan Bennett, Aug. 13, 1966; children: Jennifer Diane, Elizabeth Carole. BA, Duke U., 1959; Diplôme d'Études Universitaires Françaises, U. Clermont Ferrand, France, 1962; MA in Tchg., Johns Hopkins U., 1961; PhD, Emory U., 1976. English and history tchr. Lycée Blaise Pascal, Clermont Ferrand, 1961—62, U. de Clermont-Ferrand, 1962—63; history tchr. Balt. County Pub. Schs., Balt., 1963—64, 1969—70, Am. Sch. of Madrid, 1968—69; French and history tchr. Gilman Sch., Balt., 1964—68; head history dept. Collegiate Sch., N.Y.C., NY, 1975—. Participant summer seminar NEH, Spokane, Wash., 1995, Fargo, ND, 2000. Bd. dirs. Ludlow Pk. Homeowners' Assn., Yonkers, NY, 1987—92, 2003—; warden Christ Ch. Riverdale, Bronx, NY, 1991—97, mem. vestry, 2002—. With U.S. Army, 1959—60. Grantee, Coun. for Basic Edn., Washington, 1994. Mem.: Assn. Tchrs. in Ind. Schs., Nat. Coun. For History Edn. Democrat. Episcopalian. Avocations: reading, running, travel. Office: Collegiate Sch 260 W 78th St New York NY 10024

CLARKE, LOGAN, JR., management consultant; b. Atlanta, May 28, 1927; s. Leonard Warner Moore and Marion (Ray) C.; children: Logan III, Jeffrey Reed, Jonathan, Lisa Beth; m. Cordelia Kay Knight Mazuy. Student, U. Okla., 1944; La., State U., 1945; Stonier Grad., Sch. Banking, 1960; BA, U. Pa., 1949; MS, Hartford Grad. Center, 1981. Salesman Liberty Mut. Ins. Co., Boston, 1949-52; with Nat. Shawmut Bank Boston, 1952-70, asst. v.p., 1955-58, v.p., 1958-70; exec. v.p. County Bank NA, Cambridge, Mass., 1970-71, pres., dir., 1971-75; pres. Shawmut Bank of Boston, N.A.; pres., dir. Shawmut Corp., 1976-78; alt. dir. Atlantic Internat. Bank Ltd., London; alt. rep. Internat. Monetary Conf., 1976-78; lectr. Hartford (Conn.) Grad. Center, 1979-86, dean Sch. Mgmt., 1983-85; exec. v.p. Soc. for Savings, Hartford, 1986-90; acting pres. Hartford Coll. for Women, 1990-91; pres. Templeton Inc., 1991—. Trustee Lyme Acad. Fine Art, 1997—; cons. Arthur D. Little, Inc., 1979-85 ; dir. Scan-Optics, Inc., 1981— Mem. Town Meeting Lexington, Mass., 1961-70, appropriations com., 1960-66, sch. com., 1966-70; bd. overseers Children's Hosp. Med. Ctr., Boston, 1967-87; trustee Lesley Coll., Cambridge, 1971-86, Hartford Coll. for Women, 1985-92; chmn. bd. Govs. Higher Edn., Conn., 1992-97, chmn., 1994-97; corporator Northeastern U., Boston, 1976-85. Recipient Outstanding Young Man award Boston Jr. C. of C. Mem. Masons. Episcopalian. Home: 89 River Rd East Haddam CT 06423-1462

CLARKE, MARY ELIZABETH, retired career officer; b. Rochester, N.Y., Dec. 3, 1924; d. James M. and Lillian E. (Young) Kennedy. Student, U. Md., 1962; M.Mil.Sci., Norwich U., Northfield, Vt., 1978. Joined as pvt. U.S. Army, 1945, advanced through grades to maj. gen., 1978; exec. asst. to Chief of Plans and Policies Office of Econ. Opportunity, 1966-67; comdr. WAC Tng. Bn., 1967-68; office dep. chief of staff for pers., 1968—71; WAC staff adviser 6th Army, 1971-72; comdr., comdt. U.S. Women's Army Corps Ctr. and Sch., 1972-74; chief WAC Adv. Office U.S. Army Mil. Pers. Ctr., Washington, 1974-75, dir. Women's Army Corps., 1975-78; comdr. U.S. Army Mil. Police and Chem. Sch. Tng. Ctr., Ft. McClellan, Ala., 1978-80; dir. human resources devel. Office of Dep. Chief of Staff for Personnel, Washington, 1980-81; ret., 1981. Hon. prof. mil. sci. Jacksonville (Ala.) State U.; mem. Def. Adv. Com. on Women in the Svcs., 1984—, vice chmn., 1986—; mem. adv. com. Women

Veterans, 1989—, chmn., 1991; mem. The Presidential Com. on the Assignment of Women in the Armed Forces. Decorated D.S.M.; recipient Toastmasters Internat. award, 1984, Nat. Veteran's award, 1994. Mem. Assn. of U.S. Army (coun. trustees), United Svcs. Automobile Assn. (bd. dirs. 1978-88), WAC Assn., U.S. Army Women's Mus. Achievements include being 1st woman promoted to maj. gen. in U.S. Army. Address: 8406 Quebec Dr San Antonio TX 78239-3008

CLARKE, MERCER KAYE, lawyer; b. N.Y.C., Sept. 27, 1944; s. Fred Wylly and Helen Frances (Kaye) C.; m. Elizabeth Koebel (div. 1987); 1 child, James Wylly. BA in Econs., Washington and Lee U., 1966; JD, U. Fla., 1970. Bar: Fla. 1971, U.S. Dist. Ct. (so. dist.) Fla. 1971, U.S. Ct. Appeals (5th cir.) 1971, U.S. Supreme Ct. 1977, U.S. Dist. Ct. (mid. dist.) Fla. 1978, U.S. Ct. Appeals (11th cir.) 1981, U.S. Dist. Ct. (no. dist.) Fla. 1986. Assoc. Smathers & Thompson (now Kelley, Drye & Warren), Miami, Fla., 1970-75, ptnr., 1975-83, proprietary ptnr., 1983-93; ptnr. Clarke & Silverglate, 1993—. Bd. govs. Better Bus. Bur. S. Fla., Miami; trustee Beacon Council, Miami. Recipient Golden Key award City of North Miami Beach, 1988. Mem. ABA, Fla. Bar Assn., Dade County Bar Assn., Internat. Assn. Def. Counsel, Miami C. of C. (trustee), Miami City Club. Republican. Episcopalian. Home: 4880 Hammock Lake Dr Miami FL 33156-2218 Office: Clarke Silverglate & Campbell PA Ste 900 799 Brickell Plz Miami FL 33131 E-mail: bclarke@cswm.com.

CLARKE, MILTON CHARLES, lawyer; b. Chgo., Jan. 31, 1929; s. Gordon Robert and Senoria Josephine (Carlisa) C.; m. Dorothy Jane Brodie, Feb. 19, 1955; children: Laura, Virginia, Senoria K. BS, Northwestern U., 1950, JD, 1953. Bar: Ill. 1953, Mo. 1956, U.S. Dist. Ct. (we. dist.) Mo. 1961, U.S. Ct. Appeals (8th cir.) 1961. Assoc. Swanson, Midgley, Gangwere, Clarke & Kitchin, Kansas City, Mo., 1955-61, ptnr., 1961-91; of counsel Olsen & Talpers, P.C., Kansas City, 1994—. Served with U.S. Army, 1953-55. Mem. Rotary. Office: Olsen and Talpers PC 2100 City Center Square 1100 Main St Kansas City MO 64105-2125 E-mail: miltonclarke@hotmail.com.

CLARKE, PAULA KATHERINE, anthropology educator, sociology educator; b. Berkeley, Gloucestershire, Eng., July 27, 1946; d. Percy George and Grace Anne C.; m. Warren Ted Hamilton. Ba, U. Calif.-Berkeley, 1982; PhD, U. Calif., San Francisco, 1991. Prof. anthropology and sociology Columbia Coll., Sonora, Calif., 1997—. Contbr. articles (Nominated-Kathleen Gregory Klein Award by Women's Caucus/Popular and Am.Culture Assn. for best unpublished article on feminism and popular culture, 1999); contbr.: First International Encyclopedia Men and Masculinity, 2003. Creator Future Promise Award scholarship Columbia College, Sonora, 2001. Recipient Excellence in Tchg. award, Tuolumne County Bd. Edn., 2002. Office: Columbia Coll 11600 Columbia College Dr Sonora CA 95370 Personal E-mail: clarkep@yosemite.cc.ca.us. Business E-Mail: clarkep@yosemite.cc.ca.us.

CLARKE, PAULINE M. columnist; b. Great Barrington, Mass., Mar. 19, 1946; d. James Jordan Clarke and Germaine Anita Guertin; m. Michael T. Lynch (div. July 1980); children: Brendan, Kenneth, Jennifer, Catherine. Student, Norwich U., 2000—, Vt. Coll. Union Inst. and Univ., 2002—. Columnist Berkshire Record, Great Barrington, Mass., 1990—. Author: (column) Writing Down the Words, 1999. Avocations: hiking, gardening, sewing, writing, reading. Personal E-mail: Prophet122@excite.com.

CLARKE, PETER, communications and health educator; b. Evanston, Ill., Sept. 19, 1936; s. Clarence Leon and Dorothy (Whitcomb) C.; m. Karen Storey, June 4, 1962 (div. 1984); 1 child, Christopher Michael BA, U. Wash., 1959; MA, U. Minn., 1961, PhD, 1963. Dir., asst. prof. Comm. Rsch. Ctr. U. Wash., Seattle, 1965-68, assoc. prof. sch. comm., 1967-72, dir. sch. comm., 1971-72; prof. dept. journalism U. Mich., Ann Arbor, 1973-74, chmn., prof. dept. journalism, 1975-78, chmn., prof. dept. comm., 1979-80; dean, prof. Annenberg Sch. Comm., U. So. Calif., L.A., 1981-92, prof., 1993—; prof. preventive medicine U. So. Calif. Sch. Medicine, L.A., 1985—. Co-dir. From the Wholesaler to the Hungry, 1991—; dir. Ctr. for Health and Med. Comm., 1997—; cons. for various fed. and state govt. commns. on mass media and social problems Co-author: (with Susan H. Evans) Covering Campaigns: Journalism in Congressional Elections, 1983, Surviving Modern Medicine: How to Get the Best from Doctors, Family and Friends, 1998; editor: New Models for Communication Research, 1973; co-editor: (with Susan H. Evans) The Computer Culture, 1985; contbr. articles to profl. jours. Numerous Fed., corp., pvt. founds. grants. Office: U So Calif Annenberg Sch Comm 3502 Watt Way Los Angeles CA 90089-0054 E-mail: chmc@usc.edu.

CLARKE, PHILIP REAM, JR., retired investment banker; b. Chgo., Feb. 10, 1914; s. Philip Ream and Louise (Hildebr) C.; m. Valerie Mead, Oct. 20, 1939 (dec. Sept. 1965); children: Barbara Foster, Philip Ream III; m. Jan Finan, Dec. 2, 1967; m. Barbara Schroeder, Apr. 15, 1977. AB, U. Chgo., 1937. With Glore, Forgan & Co., Chgo., 1937-42, City Nat. Bank & Trust Co., Chgo., 1946-57, asst. v.p., 1947-51, v.p., 1951-57; with Lehman Bros., Chgo., 1957-65, mgr. indsl. dept., 1957-62, dir. new bus., 1962-65; v.p., treas., dir. Hinsdale Cemetery Co., 1946-66; from sr. v.p. to vice-chmn Chgo. Corp., 1965-86, vice-chmn. emeritus, 1986-96, vice chmn. emeritus, 1997-98, dir., 1965-86; pres., CEO Hollymatic Corp., 1978-79, chmn., CEO, 1979-81, dir., 1969-81. Mem. Midwest Stock Exchange, 1954-56; pres., treas., dir. Bronswood Cemetery, Inc., 1966-89, chmn., 1990—; vice-chmn. emeritus ABN Amro Inc., 1998-2001. Bd. dirs., exec. com. Cook County Sch. of Nursing, 1958-68, v.p., 1965-68; treas., dir. Chgo. Com. on Alcoholism, 1952-56, v.p., 1957, exec. v.p., 1958, pres., 1959, chmn., 1960-61; charter mem. bd. assocs., Chgo. Theol. Sem., 1980-84; vice chmn. Chgo. Non Partisan Com. to Bring Rep. Nat. Conv. to Chgo.; Mem. Rep. Nat. Conv., 1959-60; treas. Citizens Com. to Bring Rep. and Dem. convs. to Chgo., 1952, 56; bd. govs. Hinsdale Community House, 1968-70, vice chmn., 1969, chmn., 1970, life trustee 1993—; trustee, chmn. fin. com., 1951-55, Village of Clarendon Hills, Ill., 1956-60, pres., 1961-65; bd. govs. United Rep. Fund of Ill., 1948-74, treas., 1948-62, v.p., exec. com., 1955-69; bd. dirs. Ill. council Trout Unltd., 1972-75; trustee U. Chgo. Alumni Found., 1958-61, citizens bd., 1955-80; mem. exec. com. Citizens of Greater Chgo., 1960-61. Lt. comdr. USNR, 1942-46. Mem. Chgo. Assn. Commerce and Industry (dir., treas. 1952-53), Chgo. Zool. Soc. (governing mem. 1956-69, 79—), Nat. Council on Alcoholism (v.p. 1959-62), Alpha Delta Phi. Clubs: Chicago (Chgo.), Bond (Chgo.); Hinsdale Golf; Coleman Lake (dir. 1972-84, v.p. 1982) (Wis.); Plaza (Chgo.). Republican. Episcopalian. Home: 404 Burr Ridge Clb Burr Ridge IL 60527-5207

CLARKE, RICHARD STEWART, security company executive; b. Louisville, Aug. 23, 1934; s. Jesse Edward and Sarah Elizabeth (Pilkerton) C.; m. Constance Jean Koga, Sept. 29, 1956; children: Stewart Michael, Stephen James, Susan Michelle (dec.). BS in Biology/Sociology, Ill. State U., 1958; postgrad., Ill. Benedictine Coll., 1955-56, DePaul U., 1956-57, 80-81, N.E. Mo. State Coll., 1959, U. Chgo., 1960-61. With Autoquip Corp., Chgo., 1952-54, asst. gen. mgr., 1956-57, indsl. engr., 1958-62, prodn. mgr., v.p. mfg., 1962-73; with Ky. Trailer, Louisville, 1953, Shafer Bearing, Downers Grove, Ill., 1955-56; salesman Ency. Britannica, Chgo., 1956; sci. tchr., writer Wilmette (Ill.) Bd. Edn. and Children's Press, 1958-62; pres. Darci Assocs., 1973-82, Alert Security Cons., Inc., Chgo., 1982—. Cons. in field; sci. fair dir. Chgo. Area Tchrs. Sci. Assn. and Wilmette Bd. Edn., 1960-62; sci. lectr./writer; trainer indsl. mgmt.; dir. Parassistance Corp., Chgo., 1976-80. Co-designer 3-dimensional board game: Skew, 1958; developer various ednl./sci. rsch. methods; author poetry: The Chicago Spirit, 1988-91; editor: St. Margaret Mary Today, 1992. Com. chmn. South Hinsdale (Ill.) Improvement Assn., 1952-53; mem. Rodgers Park Community Coun., Chgo., 1967—; pres. Northtown Fair Housing Com., Chgo., 1966-67; campaign aide Ill. Constl. Conv., Chgo., 1970-71; leader, sect. pres. Christian Family Movement, Chgo., 1957-70; ch. leader, tchr. St. Margaret Mary Parish Orgn., Chgo., 1966—, coun. pres., 1986-88; bldg. fund chmn. St. Margaret Mary Gym & Social Ctr., Chgo., 1987-89, auxiliary minister, 1982—. Mem. Security Assocs., Nat. Fire & Burglary Alarm Assn., No. Ill. Indsl. Mgmt. Soc. (exec. officer), Kappa Delta Pi (hon. life), Pi Gamma Mu (hon. life). Republican. Roman Catholic. Avocations: violinist, singer, poet, gymnast, rockhound. Office: Alert Security Cons Inc 2453 W Morse Ave Chicago IL 60645-4611

CLARKE, ROBERT EARLE (BOBBY CLARKE), hockey executive; b. Flin Flon, Manitoba, Can., Aug. 13, 1949; m. Sandy Clarke; children: Wade, Lucas, Jody, Jakki. Player Phila. Flyers, NHL, 1969-84, gen. mgr., 1984-90; gen. mgr., v.p. Minn. North Stars, NHL, 1990-92; now pres., gen. mgr. Phila. Flyers, 1993—. Winner West Divsn. Rookie of Yr., 1970, Player of Yr. West Divsn. Sporting News, 1972-73, Bill Masterton Meml. trophy, 1972, Hart Meml. trophy, 1973, 75, 76, Player of Yr. Comp. Conf. Sporting News, 1974-75, Player of Yr. Sporting News, 1975-76, NHL Exec. of Yr. Sporting News, 1993-94, 94-95; co-winner Lester Patrick award, 1981; named to NHL Hall of Fame, 1987. Office: Phila Flyers First Union Ctr 3601 S Broad St Philadelphia PA 19148-5250

CLARKE, ROBERT LOGAN, lawyer; b. Tulsa, Okla., June 29, 1942; s. Ralph Logan and Faye Louise (Todd) C.; m. Jean (Puddin) Barrow Talbert, Sept. 23, 1967; 1 child, Robert Logan Jr. BA Econs., Rice U., 1963; LLB, Harvard U., 1966. Bar: N.Mex. 1966, Tex. 1967. Legis. asst. to U.S. Senator Edwin L. Mechem, Washington, 1964; assoc. Hinkle, Bondurant, Cox, Eaton & Hensley, Roswell, N.Mex., 1966, Bracewell & Patterson, Houston, 1968-73, ptnr., 1973-85, ptnr., head fin. svcs. sect., 1992—; comptr. of currency Washington, 1985-92; dir. FDIC, Washington, 1985-92, Resolution Trust Corp., Washington, 1989-92. Bd. dirs. Cmty. Bancorp. N.Mex., Inc., Cmty. Bank, Centex Constrn. Products, Inc., First Investors Fin. Svcs., Inc.; sr. advisor to pres. Nat. Bank Poland, 1992-2000; advisor to bank suprs. in Ea. Europe, Mexico, Argentina, Brazil and Kazakhstan. Precinct chmn. Harris County Reps., 1970-74, 76-85, legal counsel, 1984-85; trustee Mus. N.Mex. Found., 1992—, Southwestern Grad. Sch. Banking Found., 1993—, Internat. Folk Art Found., 1995-2002; dir. Santa Fe Chamber Music Festival, 2003—; founding dir. Houston Rep. Club, 1982-85; bd. dirs. Houston Polit. Action Com., 1983-85, Trout Unlimited, 1997—; mem. adv. com. Harris County Reagan-Bush campaign, 1984; asst. scoutmaster Boy Scouts Am., Houston, 1980-85, deacon 1st Presbyn. Ch. Houston. Capt. U.S. Army, 1966-68. Recipient Disting. Svc. medal U.S. Treasury Dept., 1992, Banking Leadership award Western States Sch. Banking, Albuquerque, 1993. Mem. Houston Bar Assn., Houston Bar Found., State Bar Tex., State Bar N.Mex., Rice U. Alumni Assn. (chmn. area club com. 1984-85, mem. exec. bd. dirs. 1987-89, Disting. Alumnus award 1992), River Oaks Country Club, Chevy Chase Club, Houston Club, Coronado Club, Houston City Club, Sangre de Cristo Racquet Club (Santa Fe), Rotary (trustee student's ednl. fund), Trout Unltd. (trustee 1997—). Avocations: tennis, fishing, hiking. Office: Bracewell & Patterson Pennzoil South Tower 711 Louisiana St Ste 2900 Houston TX 77002-2781

CLARKE, ROBERT RESIDE, biochemist, researcher; b. Londonderry, No. Ireland, Mar. 3, 1956; s. Thomas and Eileen (Mateer) C.; m. Leena Anikki Hilakivi, Sept. 24, 1989; children: Tomas, Johan, Robin. BSc, U. Ulster, No. Ireland, 1980; MSc, Queen's U., Belfast, No. Ireland, 1982, PhD, 1986, DSc, 1999. Guest rschr. NIH, Bethesda, Md., 1987-88; asst. prof. physiology and biophysics Georgetown U., Washington, 1989-95, assoc. prof. physiology and biophysics, 1995-99, prof. oncology, physiology and biophysics, 1999—, v.p. acad. outreach. Cons. Am. Inst. for Cancer Rsch., 1990—, Cancer Rsch. Found. of Am., 1995—, NIH, 1996—, U.S. Dept. Def., Frederick, Md., 1995—, State of Nebr., 1997—, State of Calif., 1999, 2001. Mem. editl. bd. Breast Cancer Rsch. and Treatment, 1992—, Oncology Reports, 1997—, Brit. Jour. of Cancer, 1997—, Cancer Rsch., 2001—, Jour. Steroid Biochemistry and Molecular Biology, 2002—, Cancer Genomics Proteomics, 2003—; guest editor: Jour. Mammary Gland Biology and Neoplasia, 2000; patentee in field; contbr. over 125 articles to profl. jours., chapters to books. Grantee NIH 1989—, Dept. Def. 1996—. Fellow: Inst. Biology, Royal Soc. Medicine, Royal Soc. Chemistry. Office: Georgetown Sch Medicine Rsch Bldg W405A VT Lombardi Comprehensive Cancer Ctr 3970 Reservoir Rd NW Washington DC 20057-2126 Fax: 202-687-7505. E-mail: clarker@georgetown.edu.

CLARKE, ROY, physicist, educator; b. Bury, Lancashire, England, May 9, 1947; BSc in Physics, U. London, PhD, 1973. Rsch. assoc. Cavendish Lab., Cambridge, U.K., 1973-78; James Franck fellow U. Chgo., 1978-79; prof. U. Mich., Ann Arbor, 1979-86; dir. applied physics program, 1986—2002. Co-founder k-Space Assocs. Inc. Editor: Synchrotron Radiation in Materials Research, 1989. Fellow Am. Phys. Soc. Achievements include development of novel methods for real-time x-ray and electron diffraction studies; patent for quasiperiodic optical coatings. Office: U Mich Randall Lab Ann Arbor MI 48109

CLARKE, SEAN PATRICK, nursing researcher, educator; b. Toronto, Ont., Can., Dec. 17, 1968; arrived in U.S., 1998; s. Stephen Alexander and Michele Annie Clarke; m. Beth Lynelle McNutt, May 8, 1993; children: Julianna, Cameron. BS, U. Ottawa, 1988; BA, Carleton U., 1989; MS, McGill U., 1992, PhD, 1998. Cert. Order of Nurses of Que., Coll. of Nurses of Ont., Pa. Bd. Nursing. Asst. prof., lectr. U. Ottawa, Can., 1996-98; postdoctoral fellow U. Pa., Phila., 1999-2001, asst. prof., 2001—, assoc. dir. Ctr. for Health Outcomes and Policy Rsch. Contbr. articles to profl. jours. Mem. ANA, APHA, Acad. for Health Svcs. Rsch. and Health Policy, Am. Assn. Critical Care Nurses, Sigma Theta Tau. Office: U Pa 420 Guardian Dr Philadelphia PA 19104-6096 Fax: 215-573-2062. E-mail: sclarke@nursing.upenn.edu.

CLARKE, STEPHAN PAUL, retired language educator, retired writer; b. Watertown, N.Y., Jan. 18, 1945; s. Albert John and Marjory Ruth (Grieb) Clarke; m. Mary Elizabeth Hawley, May 23, 1970; 1 child, Erin Elizabeth. BS in Edn., SUNY, Geneseo, 1966; MA, Bowling Green State U., 1968. Cert. secondary tchr. N.Y. Tchr. English E. J. Wilson HS, Spencerport, NY, 1970-99; ret., 1999. Spkr. N.Y. State Edn. Dept. Writer's Conf., Albany, 1982, Albany, 87. Author: (book) The Lord Peter Wimsey Companion, 1985 (Edgar Allen Poe Spl. award), The Lord Peter Wimsey Companion, rev. edit., 2002, Crimes and Clues, 1977. Chmn. supr. com. Spencerport Fed. Credit Union, 1985—2003, bd. dirs., sec. bd., 1999—; rec. sec. Ch. and Ministry Com. Genesee Valley Assn. United Ch. of Christ, Rochester, 1983—88. Lt. USNR, 1968—70. Recipient Excellence in Secondary Sch. Tchg. award, U. Rochester Grad. Sch. Edn. and Human Devel., 1991. Mem.: SAR (bd. mgrs. Rochester chpt. 1997—, chpt. historian 1999—, chpt. pres. 2001—, War Svc. medal 1996, Silver Good Citizenship medal 1997), Rochester Geneal. Soc., USN Meml. Found., Dorothy L. Sayers Soc. U.K. (spkr. 2002, 1985), Stratford Shakespearean Festival Found. Can., Sons Union Vets Civil War, U.S. Naval Inst. (life). Democrat. Avocations: reading, travel, photography, model railroads, genealogy. Home: 148 Greenway Blvd Churchville NY 14428-9210 E-mail: sclarke@rochester.rr.com. *Live with the realization that the greatest success is that in which the world partakes, the indestructable good you leave behind.*

CLARKE, TERENCE MICHAEL, public relations and advertising executive; b. Altoona, Pa., Apr. 9, 1937; s. Robert Ewing and Louise Mercedes (Eckley) C.; m. Judith Ann Lawson, Oct. 15, 1966; children: Lawson Robert, Penn Terence. Student, U. Pitts., 1955-57; cert., Inst. Far Ea. Langs., Yale U., 1958; BS, Boston U., 1963, MS, 1989. Pub. rels. mgr. Pepsi-Cola Co., N.Y.C., 1963, H.P. Hood & Sons, Boston, 1964-66; pres. The Taggart Co., Chgo., 1966-70; dir. pub. rels. Creamer, Trowbridge, Case & Basford, Boston, 1970; v.p., dir. Johnson, Raffin & Clarke Inc., Boston, 1971-76; assoc. prof. Boston U., 1976-77; chmn. Clarke Goward Advt. Inc., Boston, 1977—; chmn., CEO Clarke & Co. Inc., Boston, 1997—, Red 98 Interactive, 1999—. Bd. dirs. EPROPSHOP, Inc. Chmn. planning, site, constrn. com. Hingham (Mass.) Sch., 1971-86; exec. com. Coll. Comm., Boston U., 1987—; bd. dirs. Mass. Soc. for Prevention of Cruelty to Children, 1980-94; mem. Hingham Police Sta. Constrn. Com., 1987-90; trustee Belmont (Mass.) Hill Sch., 1988-2003, Boston U., 1995-97; bd. overseers Huntington Theatre Co., Boston, 1992—. With USAF, 1957-60. Recipient L.E. Sissman award Greater Boston Advt. Club, 1984. Mem. Greater Boston Advt. Club (bd. dirs. 1980-83), Soc. for Preservation of Barber Shop Quartet Singing in Am. (internat. quartet champions 1980), Boston U. Alumni (pres. 1995-97, Disting. Alumni award Coll. Comms.1984), Algonquin Club, Univ. Club. Republican. Presbyterian. Avocation: barber shop quartet singing. Office: Clarke & Company PR Clarke Goward Advt 535 Boylston St Boston MA 02116-3720

CLARKE, THOMAS HAL, lawyer; b. Atlanta, Aug. 10, 1914; s. James Caleb and Mary Cox (DeSaussure) C.; m. Mary Louise Hastings, July 12, 1951; children: Thomas Hal Jr., Katie Clarke Hamilton, Rebecca DeSaussure Morrison. LLB, Washington and Lee U., 1938. Bar: Ga. 1939, U.S. Dist. Ct. (no. dist.) Ga., U.S. Ct. Appeals (5th cir.), U.S. Supreme Ct., 1973. Ptnr. Clarke & Anderson, Atlanta, 1948-60, Mitchell, Clarke, Pate & Anderson, Atlanta, 1960-69, 73-85; of counsel Gambrell, Clarke, Anderson & Stolz, Atlanta, 1985-92. Copyright trustee Gone With the Wind and sequels, 1983—. Mem. Fed. Home Loan Bank Bd., Washington, 1969-73; past pres., bd. dirs. Atlanta Hist. Soc.; past bd. visitors Emory U.; trustee emeritus Washington and Lee U.; mem. Hibernian United Service Club, Dublin, Ireland. Served with USNR, 1942-46, ETO, PTO. Mem. Internat. Bar Assn. (past chmn. savs. and bldg. socs. com.), ABA (chmn. savs. and loan com. 1970-73, chmn. corp. banking and bus. law sect. 1973-74, mem. ho. of dels. 1974-80, editor The Business Lawyer 1972), Ga. Bar Assn., Atlanta Bar Assn., Am. Law Inst., Atlanta Lawyers Club (past pres.), Selden Soc., English Speaking Union (past pres., chmn. bd.), Metropolitan Club (Washington D.C.), Commerce Club, Piedmont Driving Club (Atlanta). Presbyterian. Home: 186 15th St NE Atlanta GA 30309-3511 Office: 600 W Peachtree St NW Ste 1580 Atlanta GA 30308-3631

CLARKE, VICTORIA, federal agency administrator; BA, George Washington U., 1982. Asst. sec. def. for pub. affairs Dept. Def., Washington, 2001—; editl asst., photographer, graphics editor Washington Star newspaper, 1979—82; press asst. to Vice-Pres. George Bush, 1982; press sec. to Congressman, then Sen. John McCain; asst. U.S. trade rep. under Amb. Carla Hills Pub. Affairs and Pvt. Sector Liaison, 1989—92; press sec. for reelection campaign Pres. George Bush, 1992; v.p. for pub. affairs and strategic counsel Nat. Cable TV Assn., 1993—98; pres. Bozell Eskew Advt., gen. mgr. Hill and Knowlton, Washington. Office: Dept Def Pub Affairs 1400 Defense Pentagon Washington DC 20301-1400

CLARKE, WM. A. LEE, III, lawyer; b. Balt., May 7, 1949; s. William Anthony Jr. and Eileen Sheila (Walsh) C.; m. Dara Ford, May 8, 1994. Student, John Carroll U., 1969-72; JD magna cum laude, U. Balt., 1975. Bar: Md. 1975, U.S. Dist. Ct. Md. 1975, U.S. Supreme Ct. 1979, U.S. Ct. Appeals (4th cir.) 1981. Trial atty. Tenn. Valley Authority, Knoxville, 1975-76; pvt. practice Salisbury, Md., 1977—. Vis. lectr. criminal law U. Md. Eastern Shore, Princess Anne, 1989. Pres. Wicomico County Dems., Salisbury, 1981-83; commr. Md. Human Rels. Commn., Balt., 1983-85. Served to cpl. USMC, 1967-69, Vietnam. Mem.: Nat. Bd. Trial Adv. (cert. criminal trial advocate 1987—2002), Md. Criminal Def. Attys. Assn. (bd. dirs. 1984—93), Salisbury Jaycees (legal counsel 1977—79). Office: 30644 Brandywine Ct Salisbury MD 21804-2558 E-mail: walc@clarkelaw.com.

CLARKIN, JOHN FRANCIS, health care management executive; b. Atlantic City, Dec. 30, 1936; s. John Francis and Agnes (Winterholer) C.; m. Dorothy Louise Piffath, 1 son, John F. BSBA, Rider Coll., 1959; postgrad., Temple U. Cert. mgmt. cons. Inst. Mgmt. Cons. Mktg. rep. Scott Paper Co., Indpls., 1960-62; systems and mktg. rep. Burroughs Corp., Phila., 1962-67; dir. Mid-Atlantic health care ops. mgmt. practice Coopers & Lybrand, Phila., 1967-92; v.p. corp. fin. svcs. Crozer-Keystone Health System, Upland, Pa., 1992-97; pres. The Clarkin Group, West Chester, Pa., 1997-98; v.p. bus. svcs. Thomas Jefferson U. Hosp., Phila., 1998—. Lead instr., speaker numerous profl. meetings and seminars. Author: Topics in Health Care Financing, 1982; (with others) Handbook of Health Care Accounting and Finance, 1982, 89, Billing Systems, 2 vols., 1982, 89, Managing Accounts Receivable, 1990; contbr. articles to profl. jours. Mem. Grand Oak Run Civic Assn., 1970—. With U.S. Army, 1959. Grantee Rotary Club, 1955—59. Mem. Inst. Mgmt. Cons., Hosp. Mgmt. Systems Soc., Hosp. Fin. Mgmt. Assn., Med. Group Mgmt. Assn., Am. Hosp. Assn., Vesper Club, Pickering Racquet Club. Republican. Roman Catholic. Home: 1421 Grand Oak Ln West Chester PA 19380-5951 Office: Thomas Jefferson U Hosp Bus Svcs 170 S Independence Sq W Philadelphia PA 19106

CLARK-JOHNSON, SUSAN, publishing executive; Pres., pub. Reno Gazette-Jour., 1985—2000; sr. group pres. Pacific Newspaper Group, Gannett, 1985—2000; chmn. & CEO Phoenix Newspapers, 2000—; publ. Arizona Republic, 2000—. Bd. dirs. Harrah's Entertainment, Inc.; bd. visitors John S. Knight Fellowships for Profl. Journalists, Stanford U. Office: Arizona Republic PO Box 1950 Phoenix AZ 85001*

CLARK-SIMPSON, CAROLYN A. aerospace technologist, life scientist; b. Leon County, Tex., Feb. 16, 1941; d. Ray Brooks and Dena Mae (Green) Archer; m. Frank Ray Clark, Nov. 20, 1960 (div. Oct. 1979); children: Frank Ray, Valerie Lynn, Bruce Layne; m. Jack G. Simpson, May 1993. BA, Sam Houston State U., 1961; MS, Tex. A&M U., 1973, PhD, 1977. Supr., bookkeeper Rep. Sewing Machine Distbrs., Dallas, 1961-65; door-to-door sales rep. Avon Products, Inc., Bryan, Tex., 1965-72; lectr. Tex. A&M U., College Station, 1977, rsch. assoc., 1977-79; sr. scientist Lockheed Emsco, Houston, 1979-82, prin. scientist, 1983-85, staff scientist, 1987-88; aerospace technologist, phys. scientist NASA Stennis Space Ctr., Miss., 1985-87; sr. project mgr., office mgr. Ctr. for Space and Advanced Tech., Houston, 1988-91; staff scientist Lockheed Engring. and Scis. Co., Houston, 1991-94. Adj. prof. Montgomery Coll., Conroe, Tex. Contbr. articles to profl. publs. Recipient Commendation for Outstanding Contbns. Lockheed, 1979-80, 91, Commendation for Excellence, 1984; Cert. of Merit U.S. Dept. Agr. 1980; Grad. Rsch. fellow Tex. A&M, 1975-76; NSF co-grantee Tex. A&M, 1976-77. Mem. Am. Soc. Plant Taxonomists, Bot. Soc. Am., Internat. Assn. Plant Taxonomy, Am. Inst. Biol. Scis., Sigma Xi, Phi Sigma, Alpha Chi, Kappa Delta Pi. Republican. Avocations: sailing, scuba diving, tennis, piano. E-mail: caclarksim@aol.com.

CLARKSON, ADRIENNE, Governor General of Canada; b. Hong Kong, 1939; m. John Ralston Saul. BA with honours, MA in English Lit., U. Toronto; postgrad., Sorbonne, Paris. Host, writer, prodr. CBC TV, 1965-82; first agt.-gen. for Ont. Paris, 1982-87; pres, pub. McClelland & Stewart, 1987-88; exec. prodr., host, writer Adrienne Clarkson's Summer Festival, Adrienne Clarkson Presents, 1988-98; gov. gen. Govt. of Can., 1999—. Chair, bd. trustees Can. Museum of Civilization, Hull, Que.; pres. exec. bd. IMZ, Vienna; active numerous arts and charitable orgns. Exec. prodr., host CBC TV program Something Special, others; writer, dir. several films, Can. Named to Order of Can., 1992; recipient numerous awards. Office: Rideau Hall 1 Sussex Dr Ottawa ON Canada K1A OA1

CLARKSON, CHARLES ANDREW, real estate investment executive; b. Grove City, Pa., Sept. 1, 1945; s. Harold William and Jean Henrietta (Jaxtheimer) C.; m. Patricia Holt, June 14, 1969; children: Thomas Byerly, Blair Elizabeth, John Holt. AB, Princeton U., 1967; JD, George Washington U., 1972. With N.Y. Urban League, 1967—68; real estate negotiator Safeway Stores, Washington, 1968-69; mortgage banker J.W. Rouse Co., Washington, 1970-73; pres. Alex Brown Realty, Balt., 1973-76; founder, pres. The Clarkson Co., Jacksonville, Fla., 1976—. Bd. dirs. Ramgow, Inc.; chmn. Intelligenxia, JCCI. Chmn. bd. dirs. Jacksonville Urban League, 1976; Cmtys. in Schs.; trustee UNF Found.; mem. Environ. Land Mgmt. Study Com III, Fla.; chmn. bd. trustees WJCT-TV; mem. Commn. on Future of the South, 1998; mem. Bd. Govs. FCCJ Found. Mem. River Club, Sawgrass Club, The Lodge at Ponte Vedra. Office: The Clarkson Co 3100 University Blvd S Ste 200 Jacksonville FL 32216-2727

CLARKSON, CHERYL LEE, healthcare executive; b. Chgo., Apr. 14, 1953; d. George Mendenhall and Carol Ann (Fertig) C.; m. Daniel J. Townsend; children: Drew Scott Clarkson-Townsend, Danielle Ann Clarkson-Townsend. BA in Sociology, Ariz. State U., 1975; MS in Mgmt., MIT, 1990. Sales rep. Am. Hosp. Supply, Inc., Phoenix, 1975-78, area sales mgr. Dallas, 1978-79, Edison, N.J., 1979-81, regional mgr. Boston, 1981-83, dir. sales Evanston, Ill., 1983-85; v.p. sales, mktg. Rudolph Beaver, Inc., Waltham, Mass., 1985-88; pres. Beaver Steriseal, Inc., Waltham, 1987-88, Clarkson and Assocs., 1988-90, Abiodent, Inc., Danvers, Mass., 1990-92; CEO, COO, bd. dirs. Peer Review Analysis, Inc., Boston, 1992-95; CEO, pres. SkinHealth, Inc., Newton, Mass., 1999—. Bd. overseers Boston U. Med. Ctr. Hosp., 1993—; bd. dirs. Visualization Tech., Inc., Andover, Mass., NMT Med. Inc., Boston. Trustee Kingsley Montessori Sch., Boston, 1996—; bd. mem. Northeastern U. Sch. of Bus., 1998—; bd. trustees Mass. Eye and Ear Infirmary, Boston, 1998—. Mem. Algonquin Club (Boston). Avocations: travel, golf, horseback riding. Office: SkinHealth Inc 233 Needham St Ste 300 Newton MA 02464-1502

CLARKSON, ELISABETH ANN HUDNUT, volunteer; b. Youngstown, Ohio, Apr. 20, 1925; d. Herbert Beecher and Edith (Schaaf) Hadnut; m. William M. E. Clarkson, Sept. 23, 1950; children: Alison H., David B., Andrew E. AB, Wilson Coll., 1947, LHD, 1985; MA, SUNY, 1973, postgrad. With J. L. Hudson Co., Detroit, 1947-50; writer Minute Parade daily Sta. WGR, Detroit, 1948-50. Author: (book) You Can Always Tell a Freshman, 1949, An Adirondack

Archive: The Trail to Windover, 1993; contbr. articles to profl. jours. Trustee Wilson Coll., Chambersburg, Pa., 1970—83, chmn. bd. trustees, 1979—82; collector, curator Graphic Controls Corp. art collection, 1976—83; active N.Y. State Mus., 1985—90; past chmn. jr. group Albright Knox Art Gallery; mem. Buffalo Art Commn., 1983—, chmn., 1990—96; sustainer Jr. League, 1983—; mem. exec. bd. arts adv. coun. SUNY, Buffalo, 1985—95; mem. cmty. adv. panel Niagara Frontier Transp. Authority, 1991—94; trustee Clarkson Ctr. Human Svcs., 1995—2000, Irish Classical Theatre Co., 1998—; mem. Trinity Episcopal Ch., 1950—, Trinity Vestry, 1996—99, mem. cultural leadership group, 1994—96, 1998—2000; mem. racism commn. Episcopal Diocese of Western N.Y., 1989—92; mem. Companion of the Holy Cross, 1971—, companion-in-charge soc., 1985—90; bd. dirs. Buffalo Mus. Sci., 1972—87, 1990—96, Bischoff Clarkson Hudnut Corp., North Creek, NY, 1973—83, Windover Corp., 1997—, pres., 1998—2001; bd. dirs. N.Y. State Mus. Assn., Albany, 1985—90; adv. bd. dirs. North Creek R.R. Mus., 2003—. Recipient Trustee award for disting. svc., Wilson Coll., 1983, award in the arts, NCCJ, 1998. Mem.: Sloane Club (London), Buffalo Tennis and Squash Club, Garret Club (bd. dirs. 2000—03, pres. 2001—02). Home: 156 Bryant St Buffalo NY 14222-2003

CLARKSON, JOHN G. academic administrator, ophthalmologist; m. Diana Teasdale; children: Paige, David. BS, Princeton U.; MD, Miami Sch. Medicine, 1968. Intern U. Hosp., Boston; resident ophthalmology U. Miami/Jackson Meml. Med. Ctr., Fla.; opthalmic pathology, retinal and vitreous surgery fellow Johns Hopkins U., Balt.; chmn. dept. ophthalmology, dir. Bascom Palmer Eye Inst., 1991—96; sr. v.p. med. affairs, dean Sch. Medicine U. Miami, 1995—. Mem.: Macula Soc., Retina Soc., Am. Ophthalmol. Soc., Am. Acad. Ophthalmology, Am. Bd. Ophthalmology (bd. dirs.), Club Jules Gonin. Office: U Miami Sch Medicine PO Box 016099 (R699) 1600 NW 10th Ave Miami FL 33136-1090*

CLARKSON, JULIAN DERIEUX, retired lawyer; b. Coral Gables, Fla., Mar. 12, 1929; s. Julian Livingston and Hazel (Lamar) C.; m. Joan Combs, Dec. 24, 1950, children— James L., Julian L., Joanna D., Melinda C.; m. 2d, Shirley Lazonby, Nov. 8, 1979; 1 child, Shirley Lamar. B.A., U. Fla., 1950, LL.B., 1955, J.D., 1967. Bar: Fla. 1955, U.S. Ct. Appeals (5th cir.) 1961, U.S. Supreme Ct. 1961, U.S. Ct. Appeals (11th cir.) 1981, D.C. 1983. Ptnr. Henderson Franklin, Starnes & Holt, Ft. Myers, Fla., 1955-76; sole practice, Ft. Myers, 1976-77; ptnr. Holland & Knight, Ft. Myers, 1977-79, Tampa, 1979-82, Tallahassee, 1982—; ret., 1993; lectr. in field. Chmn. Fla. Supreme Ct. Jud. Nominating Commn., 1976-78. Served to 1st lt. U.S. Army, 1950-53. Decorated Purple Heart, 1951; named Outstanding Grad. Province V Phi Delta Phi, 1955. Mem. Am. Coll. Trial Lawyers, Am. Acad. Appellate Lawyers, Fla. Blue Key, Order of Coif, Phi Beta Kappa. Democrat. Episcopalian. Author: Let No Man Put Asunder— Story of a Football Rivalry, 1968, Golden Era II, 1994. Home: Apt 220 12770 Waterford Cir Fort Myers FL 33919-8008

CLARKSON, LAWRENCE WILLIAM, air transportation executive; b. Grove City, Pa., Apr. 29, 1938; s. Harold William and Jean Henrietta (Jaxtheimer) Clarkson; m. Barbara Louise Stevenson, Aug. 20, 1960; children: Michael, Elizabeth, Jennifer. BA, DePauw U., 1960; JD, U. Fla., 1962. Counsel Pratt & Whitney, West Palm Beach, Fla., 1967-72, program dep. dir., 1972-75, program mgr., 1974-75, v.p., mng. dir. Brussels, 1975-78, v.p. mktg. West Palm Beach, 1978-80, v.p. contracts Hartford, Conn., 1980-82, pres. comml. products div., 1982-87; sr. v.p. Boeing Comml. Airplanes Group, Seattle, 1988-91; corp. v.p. planning and internat. devel. Boeing Co., Seattle, 1992-93, sr. v.p., 1994-99; pres. Boeing Enterprises, Seattle, 1997-99; sr. v.p. Project Internat., Seattle, 2000—. Chmn. Hitco Carbon, 2002—, Interturbine NV, 2000—02; bd. dirs. Partnership for Improved Air Travel, Washington, 1988—91, Atlas Air, Avnet Inc. Trustee DePauw U., Greencastle, Ind., 1987—, vice chmn., 1996—; trustee Embry Ridde Aero. U., Daytona Beach, Fla., Seattle Opera, 1990—, chmn., 1991—2002; overseer Tuck Sch. Dartmouth, Hanover, NH, 1993—99; corp. counsel Interlochen (Mich.) Ctr. Arts, 1987, trustee, 1988—, chmn., 1996—2001; pres. Japan-Am. Soc., Wash., 1993, Wash. State China Rels. Com., 1992—93; chmn. Nat. Bur. Asia Rsch., Coun. Fgn. Rels., U.S. Pacific Econ. Corp. Coun., 1993—2000. Mem.: Am. Inst. Contemporary German Studies (bd. dirs. 1997—99), Nat. Assn. Mfrs. (bd. dirs. 1993—99), Wings Club (bd. govs. 1987—91), Met. Club DC, N.Y. Yacht Club, Order St. John (bd. govs., comdr.). Episcopalian. Home: 10127 NE 66th Ln Kirkland WA 98033-6870 E-mail: lckarlsonpii@cs.com., larryclarkson@compuserve.com.

CLARKSON, PHYLLIS OWENS, early childhood educator; b. Spartanburg, S.C., Apr. 3, 1951; d. Thomas Dean and Mary Ann (Turner) Owens; m. Everett Clifford Clarkson Jr., June 6, 1970 (div. Oct. 1989); children: Stacey Daneè, Trey. BA in Edn. magna cum laude, U. S.C., 1993; MEd in Curriculum and Instrn., U. Va., 1999. Substitute tchr. Spartanburg Day Sch., 1984-88, libr. aide, 1988-94; kindergarten tchr. Cedar Road Christian Acad., Chesapeake, Va., 1994-96, office mgr., 1995-96; tchr. 2d and 3d grade Cedar Rd. Christian Acad., Chesapeake, Va., 1996-97, computer lab. asst., 1997-99; tchr. 3d grade Georgetown Primary Sch. Chesapeake Pub. Schs., 1999-2000, tchr. 4th grade Southwestern Elem. Sch., 2000—03, tchr. 5th grade, 2003—. Mem. Cowpens Garden Club, 1988-94. Mem. NEA. Avocations: reading, needlepoint, swimming. Home: 705 Cottage Pl Chesapeake VA 23322-4621 E-mail: poclarkson@aol.com.

CLARKSON, RICHARD CLAIR, publisher, editor, photographer; b. Aug. 11, 1932; s. Maurice Wolford and Mary Meta (Murphy) C. BS in Journalism, U. Kansas, 1956. Dir. photography Topeka (Kans.) Capital-Jour., 1958-79; asst. mng. editor/graphics The Denver Post, 1980-84; dir. photography, sr. asst. editor Nat. Geographic Soc., Washington, 1985-87; prin. Rich Clarkson and Assocs., LLC, Denver, 1987—. Organizer, producer ann. workshops in sports photography with U.S. Olympic Com., and editorial and wildlife photography in Jackson Hole, Wyo; past lectr. adj. faculty U. Kansas Sch. of Journalism; lectr. at Mo. and Maine photographic workshops and at the Internat. Ctr. of Photography, N.Y.C.; juror Pulitzer prize in photography, 1986-87; judge and advisor Sasakawa Sports Found. and Competition, Tokyo. Co-author: (books) (with Cordner Nelson) The Jim Ryun Story, 1967, (with Bill Bruns), Sooner, 1972, Montreal 76, 1976, (with Bob Hammel) Knight with the Hoosiers, 1975, Silver Knight, 1996, (with Billy Reed) The Final Four, 1988; compiling editor The Kansas Century: 100 Years of Jayhawk Basketball, 1997; dir. of photography (book) A Day in the Life of America, 1986; producer-coord. (Brian Lanker project) I Dream a World: Portraits of Black Women Who Changed America, 1989; compiling editor World Champion Broncos, 1998. Trustee William Allen White Found., U. Kans; mem. hon. adv. coun. Nat. Mus. Wildlife Art, Jackson, Wyo., exec. com. W. Eugene Smith Meml. Fund, chmn. grant jury, 1995; founding officer Nat. Press Photographers Found. Named 1 of 50 most influential individuals in Am. photography, Am. Photo Mag., 1988. Mem. Nat. Press Photographers' Assn. (pres. 1975-76, past chmn. edn. com., twice chmn. Picture of Yr. jury). Office: Rich Clarkson & Assocs Denver Place Plaza Tower 1099 18th St Ste 1840 Denver CO 80202-1918

CLARKSON, ROBERT NOEL, commercial photographer, magician; b. Clinton, Mo., Mar. 2, 1950; s. Arthur W. and Vivian (Noel) C. BA in Econs., Carroll Coll., 1973. Owner, founder Clarkson Studio, Helena, Mont., 1973—; owner Sleepy Senator B&B, Helena, 2003—. Press officer Mont. Army N.G., Helena, 1977-81; photographer Mont. Senate, Helena, 1981-85, Mont. Ho. of Reps., 1983-85; profl. magician, 1974—. Sec. Lewis and Clark County Emergency Services Council, 1982; pub. elected officer Helena Citizen's Coun., 1999—; moderator Disciples of Christ Ch., 1996. Recipient cert. of merit Profl. Photographers Am., 1979. Mem. Am. Soc. Mag. Photographers, Soc. Am. Magicians (life, pres. assembly 219 1988, nat. region v.p. N.W. chpt. 1989-92, master of ceremony conv. Magic Dealer Show, Mont Centennial Performer, Cert. of Appreciation 1991), World Clown Assn., Res. Officers Assn. U.S. (pres. Helena chpt. 1983, dept. judge adv. 1987-88), Mont. Exch. Club (sec. 1983-88, sec. Yellowstone dist. 1988, disting. club sec. award 1983-87, svc. award 1986, 87), Masons (32 deg., K.T., P.M., PHP, TPM, PEK), Shriners. Avocations: flying, scuba diving, skiing, computer programming, woodworking. Home: 916 8th Ave Helena MT 59601-4411 Office: 401 N Hoback St Helena MT 59601-3718

CLARKSON, STEPHEN BATCHELDER, lawyer; b. Hartford, Conn., July 1, 1937; s. Albert Batchelder and Elsie (Eden) C.; m. Nancy Lee Michelmore, Oct. 16, 1965; children: Janet, Leigh. BA, Yale U., 1959; LLB, U. Va., 1962. Bar: N.Y. 1963, D.C. 1969, U.S. Supreme Ct. 1967. Spl. asst. to gen. counsel and under-sec. U.S. Dept. Commerce, 1968-69; ptnr. Pierson, Ball & Dowd, Washington, 1982—. Adv. bd. Bur. Nat. Affairs Fed. Contracts Report, 1974-76; editorial cons., 1976—. Mem. ABA (antitrust litigation, corp. banking and bus. law, pub. contract law, ct. of claims com. sects.), Fed. Bar Assn., D.C. Bar Assn., Assn. Bar City N.Y. Office: Newport News Shipbldg & Dry Dock Co 4101 Washington Ave Bldg 86 Newport News VA 23607-9700 Home: PO Box 353 Rye Beach NH 03871-0353 E-mail: clarkson_sb@nns.com.

CLARKSON, THOMAS BOSTON, comparative medicine educator; b. Decatur, Ga., June 13, 1931; DVM, U. Ga., 1954; Diploma, Am. Coll. Lab. Animal Medicine, 1963. Rsch. assoc. pharmacology and exptl. therapeutics sect. S. E. Massengill Co., 1954—57; from asst. to assoc. prof. exptl. medicine, dir. vivarium Wake Forest U., Winston-Salem, NC, 1957—64, assoc. prof. lab. animal medicine, head dept., 1964—65, prof., chmn. dept. Bowman Gray sch. medicine, 1965—97, dir. arteriosclerosis rsch. ctr., 1971—91, dir. comparative medicine clin. rsch. ctr., 1989—97; prof. Wake Forest U. Sch. of Medicine, 1997—. Mem. sci. adv. com. regional primate rsch. ctr. U. Wash., 1971—; mem. adv. com. Cerbrovascular Rsch. Ctr., 1973—; mem. com. vet. med. sci. NAS-Nat. Rsch. Coun., 1975—; chmn. arteriosclerosis, hypertension and lipid metabolism adv. com. Nat. Heart Lung & Blood Inst., 1983—85. Recipient Grifin award, Am. Assn. Lab. Animal Sci., 1977, Albion O. Bernstein award, N.Y. State Med. Soc., 1992, Duphar lectr., British Menopause Soc., 1993, Joseph Price orator, Am. Ob-Gyn. Soc., 1993. Fellow: Soc. Behavioral Medicine, Acad. Behavioral Med. Rsch., Am. Soc. Primatology; mem.: Am. Vet. Medicine Assn. (Charles River prize 1978), Am. Soc. Exptl. Pathology, Am. Assn. Pathologists, Am. Assn. Advancement Lab. Animal Sci., Am. Heart Assn. (mem. com. coronary artery lesions and myocardial infarctions 1970—, chmn. task force rsch. animal use, vice-chmn. coun. arteriosclerosis 1979—81, chmn. 1981—83, G. Lyman Duff Meml. lectr. 1985, Award of Merit 1987, Lewis A. Conner Meml. lectr. 1991), NAS (task force animal models atherosclerosis 1975—, mem. clin. sci. panel study nat. needs biomedical and behavioral rsch. 1976—), Sigma Xi. Achievements include research in in comparative and experimental atherosclerosis, particularly factors affecting susceptibilty and resistance to the disease and the mechanisms by which risk factors affect the pathogenesis. Office: Wake Forest U Dept Pathology Medical Center Blvd Winston Salem NC 27157-0001

CLARKSON, THOMAS WILLIAM, toxicologist, educator; b. Eng., Aug. 1, 1932; came to U.S., 1957; s. William and Olive (Jackson) C.; m. Winifred Browne, Mar. 4, 1957; children: Ian, Jean, Ann. BSc, U. Manchester, 1953, PhD, 1956; Dr Medicine (hon.), U. Umea, Sweden, 1986. Sci. officer tox research unit Med. Research Council U.K., Carshalton, Surrey, 1962-64; sr. fellow polymer sci. Weizmann Inst. Sci., Rehovot, Israel, 1964-65; mem. faculty U. Rochester (N.Y.) Med. Sch., 1958—, prof. toxicology, 1971—, head div., 1980-86, J. Lowell Orbison Disting. Svc. Alumni prof., 1983—, dir. Environ. Health Scis. Ctr., 1986-98; chmn. Dept. Environ. Medicine, 1992-98. Dir. NASA Ctr. Rsch. and Tng. in Space Environ. Health, 1991-95. Mem. editorial bds. profl. jours.; author articles in field. Recipient Founders' award CIIT, 1997, Arthur Kornberg Rsch. award U. Rochester, 1999. Mem. Inst. Medicine of NAS, Permanent Commn. Internat. Assn. Occupational Health, Soc. Toxicology (Arnold J. Lehman award 1993, Merit award 1999), Brit. Pharm. Soc., Am. Soc. Pharmacology and Exptl. Therapeutics, Internat. Soc. for Trace Element Rsch. in Humans, Ramazzini Collegium, Polish Toxicology Soc. (hon.), La Academia Nacional de Medicina de Buenos Aires (hon. mem.). Office: Dept Environ Medicine U Rochester Med Sch Rochester NY 14642-0001

CLARKSON, WILLIAM MORRIS, children's pastor; b. Newport, R.I., Feb. 23, 1954; s. George and Lois Ruth (Terwilligar) C.; m. Janice Aiko Enoki, June 16, 1978; children: Kyle Hideo, Keith Hiroshi. BA, Muhlenberg Coll., Allentown, Pa., 1976; MPA, Ball State U., Muncie, Ind., 1977. Advanced cert. in Employee Relations Law, Mich., Ind.; cert. Rev., Assemblies of God, Springfield, Mo., 1997. Research asst. Ball State U. Bur. Govtl. Research, Muncie, Ind., 1977; field staff cons. Ind. U., Div. Pub. Service, Indpls., 1977-78; adminstrv. asst. City of Midland, Mich., 1978-81, pers. dir., 1981-91; asst. city mgr. for pers. and risk mgmt., 1991-96; children's pastor Christian Celebration Ctr., Midland, 1996—. Adj. instr. pub. adminstrn. Ctrl. Mich. U., Mt. Pleasant, 1982-91, mem. MPA program adv. bd., 1988-91; mem. planning and evaluation com. Mich. Inst. for Pub. Adminstrn., 1989-91; dir. apptd. com. on act 312/PERA Det., Mich. Employment Rels. Commn., 1987-91; chmn. edn. and tng. com. Mich. Mcpl. League, 1991-95; mem., govtl. sector chmn. Midland Area Chamber Quality Coun., 1992-96; mem. Dow Chem. Cmty. Adv. Panel, 1994-98; exec. dir. Mid-Mich. Royal Family Kids Camp, 1996—; mem. strategic leadership group Nat. Royal Family Kids' Camp, 2002—. Co-author: Manual Indiana Counties Model Personnel Policies, 1978. Bd. dirs. Salvation Army Adv. Bd., Midland Mich., 1978-81, trustee Meml. Presbyn. Ch., Midland Mich., 1984-87, Loaned Exec. United Way Midland Mich., 1985; vice-chair Midland County Drug Abuse Resistance Edn. Project, 1989-95; bd. dirs. Midland County Camping Coun., 1999—. Recipient Mcpl. Achievement award Mich. Mcpl. League 1984; named one of Outstanding Young Men of Am., 1981. Mem.: Rotary. Mem. Assembly of God. Avocations: guitar, soccer, bible study, religious retreat leadership, directing children's church camp. Home: 3806 Westbrier Ter Midland MI 48642-6658 Office: Christian Celebration Ctr 6100 Swede Ave Midland MI 48642-3199 E-mail: pastorbil@aol.com.

CLARREN, STERLING KEITH, pediatrician; b. Mpls., Mar. 12, 1947; s. David Bernard and Lila (Reifel) C.; m. Sandra Gayle Bernstein, June 8, 1970; children: Rebecca Pia, Jonathan Seth. BA, Yale U., 1969; MD, U. Minn., 1973. Pediatric intern U. Wash. Sch. Medicine, Seattle, 1973-74, resident in pediatrics, 1974-77, asst. prof. dept. pediatrics, 1979-83, assoc. prof., 1983-88, prof., 1988, Robert A. Aldrich chair in pediatrics, 1989—. Head divsn. congenital defects U. Wash. Sch. Medicine, 1987-95, head divsn. hosp. medicine, 2002—; dir. dept. congenital defects Children's Hosp. and Med. Ctr., Seattle, 1987-96, dir. fetal alcohol syndrome clinic Child Devel. and Mental Retardation Ctr. U. Wash., 1992-2001, dir. Fetal Alcohol Syndrome Network, 1995-2001; dir. inpatient svcs. Children's Hosp. and Med. Ctr., Seattle, 1996—. Contbr. articles to profl. jours.; patentee for orthosis to alter cranial shape. Cons. pediatrician Maxillofacial Rev. Bd., State of Wash., Seattle, 1984—, chmn. Health-Birth Defects Adv. Com., Olympia, 1980—; mem. gov.'s task force on FAS State of Wash., 1994-95; mem. fetal alcohol adv. com. Children's Trust Found., Seattle, 1988—; bd. dirs. Seattle Children's Home, 2003—; mem. adv. bd. Nat. Orgn. on Fetal Alcohol Syndrome; mem. fetal alcohol com. Inst. Medicine, NAS, 1994-95. Rsch. grantee Nat. Inst. Alcohol Abuse & Alcoholism, 1982—, Ctrs. for Disease Control, 1992—. Fellow AAAS; mem. Am. Acad. Pediatrics, Soc. for Pediatric Rsch., Teratology Soc., Rsch. Soc. on Alcoholism (pres. fetal alcohol study group 1993), Am. Cleft Palate Assn., N.Y. Acad. Scis. Avocations: cross-country skiing, fishing, hiking, sailing. Home: 8515 Paisley Dr NE Seattle WA 98115-3944 Office: Children's Hosp and Med Ctr Divsn Hosp Medicine PO Box C-5371 Seattle WA 98105

CLARY, ALEXIA BARBARA, management company executive; b. Waterbury, Conn., Sept. 17, 1954; d. John Joseph and Veza (Mandzik) Zurlis; 1 child, Jason Farrell. BBA, U. Miami, Coral Gables, Fla.; MBA, U. New Haven. Buyer Hewlett Packard, Cupeztino, Calif., 1981-83; purchase mgr. ICI, Redmond, Wash., 1983-84; commodity mgr. No. Telecom, St. Mountain, Ga., 1985-88; mfg. rep. Montgomery Mktg., Norcross, Ga., 1988-90; internat. purchasing agt. Sci. Atlanta, Norcross, Ga., 1990-91; sr. buyer Amphenol, Danbury, Conn., 1992-94; purchasing mgr. Danaher-Gulton Graphic, East Greenwhich, R.I., 1994-96; materials control mgr. Amphenol Corp., Danbury, Conn., 1996-2000; materials mgmt. The Siemon Co., Watertown, Conn., 2000—; purchasing agt. Boehinger-Ingelheim Pharms., Inc., 2001—. Prof. econs., internat. bus., logistics and mgmt. Teikyo Post U. Miami scholar, 1974-75. Mem. Women in Electronics (v.p. sponsors 1989-90, guest speaker 1989), NAFE, Nat. Assn. Purchasing Mgrs. Republican. Roman Catholic. Avocations: golf, tennis, swimming, reading, jogging. Home: 18 Cynthia St Waterbury CT 06708-2702 Office: Bochringher Ingelheim Purchasing Agt Ridgefield CT 06877

CLARY, BRADLEY G. lawyer, educator; b. Richmond, Va, Sept. 7, 1950; s. Sidney G. and Jean B. Clary; m. Mary-Louise Hunt, July 31, 1982; children: Benjamin, Samuel. BA magna cum laude, Carleton Coll., 1972; JD cum laude, U. Minn., 1975. Bar: Minn. 1975, US Dist. Ct. Minn. 1975, US Ct. Appeals (10th cir.) 1977, US Ct. Appeals (8th cir.) 1979, US Ct. Appeals (6th cir.) 1980, US Ct. Appeals (7th cir.) 1981, US Supreme Ct. 1986, US Ct. Appeals (4th cir.) 1989, US Ct. Appeals (9th cir.) 1991. Assoc. Oppenheimer Wolff & Donnelly, St. Paul, 1975-81, ptnr., 1982-2000; legal writing dir. Law Sch. U. Minn., 1999—, clin. prof. Law Sch., 2000—. Adj. prof. Law Sch. U. Minn., Mpls., 1985-99; adj. instr. William Mitchell Coll. Law, St. Paul, 1995-96, 98, adj. prof., 1997, 99. Author: Primer on the Analysis and Presentation of Legal Argument, 1992; co-author: Advocacy on Appeal, 2001, Successful First Depositions, 2001, Successful Legal Analysis and Writing: The Fundamentals, 2003. Vestryman St. John Evangelist Ch., St. Paul, 1978-81, 98-00, pledge drive co-chmn., 1989-90, sr. warden, 2000-2002; mem. alumni bd. Breck Sch., Mpls., 1981-85, 89-96, exec. com., 1991-96, dir. emeritus, 1996—; mem. adv. bd. Glass Theatre Co., West St. Paul, Minn., 1982-87; mem. antitrust adv. panel dept. health State of Minn., 1992-93. Mem. ABA (adv. group antitrust sect. 1987-89, corp. counseling com.), Minn. Bar Assn. (program chmn. antitrust sect. 1986-87, treas. 1987-88, vice-chmn. 1989-90, co-chmn. 1990-92, governing coun. appellate practice sect. 2001--), Phi Beta Kappa. Avocations: tennis, sailing. Office: U Minn Law Sch 229 19th Ave S Rm 444 Minneapolis MN 55455-0400

CLARY, KEITH UHL, retired employee relations executive; b. Logansport, Ind., Mar. 7, 1921; s. Glen Uhl and Lucile (Billman) C. BSBA, Ind. U., 1943, MBA, 1948. Asst. dir. personnel and placement bur. Ind. U., Bloomington, 1947-48; mgr. personnel RCA plant, Monticello, Ind., 1948-54, Indpls. RCA plants, 1954-57; mgr. orgn. devel., corp. hdqrs. RCA, Camden, N.J., 1957-59, mgr. personnel EDP div. Cherry Hill, N.J., 1959-64; v.p. employee rels. RCA Consumer Electronics World Hdqs., Indpls., 1964-86, ret., 1987. Asst. prof. Military Sci. and Tactics Howe Military Acad., Howe, Ind., 1945-46; adv. bd. Ind. Exec. program, Ind. U., 1970-71. Trustee, Indpls. Mus. Art, 1970—. Capt. inf., U.S. Army, 1943-46, ETO. Mem. Indpls. Urban League (founding mem., bd. dirs. 1972-76), Ind. State C. of C. (labor rels. com. 1964-74), Ind. Pers. Assn. (bd. dirs.), Ind. Hist. Soc. (libr. com. 1990), Oriental Art Soc., Indpls. Mus. Art (pres. 1991, human resources com. 1990—, donated numerous pieces of Chinese art and other objects to Indpls. Mus. of Art and Evansville Mus. of Art), Phi Eta Sigma, Beta Gamma Sigma. Republican. Methodist. Avocations: gardening, art collecting, travel. Home: 6407 Landborough South Dr Indianapolis IN 46220-4356

CLARY, REBECCA KRISTEN, social services administrator; b. Uniontown, Pa., Nov. 15, 1973; d. James Edward and Deborah Sue Enany; m. Ross Hampton Clary, Sept. 23, 2000. BS, Tex. A & M U., 1994—97. Spl. events mgr. The Family Pl., Dallas, 2001—02; dir. of devel. Mosaic Family Services Inc., Dallas, 2002—. Pr cons. Exclusive Access2, Dallas, 2002—. Corr. sec. The Family Pl. Partners Aux. Bd., Dallas, 2002—. Mem.: The Cotillion Club, Jr. League Of Dallas, Jonathan's Pl. (mem. of women's aux. 2003—). Avocations: yoga, cooking, reading, antiques. Office: Mosaic Family Services Inc 4144 N Central Expy Ste 530 Dallas TX 75204

CLARY, RICHARD WAYLAND, lawyer; b. Tarboro, N.C., Oct. 10, 1953; s. S. Grayson and Jean (Beazley) C.; m. Suzanne Clerkin, July 21, 1991; children: Grayson Edward, Taryn Fenner. BA magna cum laude, Amherst Coll., 1975; JD magna cum laude, Harvard U., 1978. Bar: N.Y. 1981, U.S. Dist. Ct. (so. and ea. dists.) N.Y. 1981, U.S. Dist. Ct. (no. dist.) N.Y. 1998, U.S. Dist. Ct. (no. dist.) Calif., 1982, U.S. Ct. Appeals (9th cir.) 1983, U.S. Supreme Ct. 1989, U.S. Ct. Appeals (3d cir.) 1990, U.S. Ct. Appeals (2d cir.) 1994, U.S. Ct. Appeals (fed. cir.) 1995, U.S. Ct. Appeals (11th cir.) 1999, U.S. Ct. Appeals (6th cir.) 2000, U.S. Ct. Appeals (5th cir.) 2003. Law clk. to judge U.S. Ct. Appeals (2d cir.), N.Y.C., 1978-79; law clk. to Justice Thurgood Marshall U.S. Supreme Ct., Washington, 1979-80; assoc. Cravath, Swaine & Moore LLP, N.Y.C., 1980-85; ptnr. Cravath, Swaine & Moore, N.Y.C., 1985—, mng. ptnr. litigation, 1997—. Bd. dirs. Legal Aid Soc., 1998—.(vice chair, 2003-) John Woodruff Simpson fellow Amherst Coll., 1975-76. Mem. ABA, Fed. Bar Found. (bd. dirs. 1998-2001), N.Y. State Bar Assn., Assn. Bar City N.Y., Fed. Bar Coun., Phi Beta Kappa. Roman Catholic. Office: Cravath Swaine & Moore LLP Worldwide Pla 825 8th Ave New York NY 10019-7475 E-mail: rclary@cravath.com.

CLARY, RONALD GORDON, insurance agency executive; b. Moultrie, Ga., May 2, 1940; s. Ronald Ward and Hazel (Collins) C.; m. Adrian Irene Baker; children: Lynn, Beth, Lindsay, Baker. Student, Young Harris Coll., 1958-60; BBA in Ins., U. Ga., 1963; LLB, Woodrow Wilson Coll. Law, 1966. Registered rep. fin. planner. Field rep. Comml. Union Ins. Cos., 1962-67; ind. ins. agt., 1967—; ins. agt., sec. of agy. Day, Reynolds & Parks, Gainesville, Ga., 1970-93, pres., 1993—. Fin. planner, registered rep. Am. Express Fin. Advisors, Inc. Mem. Profl. Ins. Agts. Am., Ga. Assn. Ind. Ins. Agts., Gainesville Assn. Ind. Ins. Agts. (past pres.), Young Agts. Com. Ga. (past chmn.), Am. Legion, Elks, Rotary. Republican. Baptist. Avocations: tennis, sailing. Home: 1184 Cumberland Valley Rd Gainesville GA 30501 Office: 454 Green St NE Gainesville GA 30501 Fax: 770-754-9690., 770-539-9832.

CLARY, ROY, hospital administration executive; b. Winnipeg, Man., Can., Aug. 20, 1939; s. Omar LeRoy and Lois Ruth (Corey) C.; m. Marlene Alice Kogan; children: Megan Jennifer, Ethan Samuel. BA, Ohio State U., 1961; BFA/MFA, Art Inst. Chgo., 1964. Actor Seattle Repertory Theatre, 1964-66, Barter Theatre, Abingdon, Va., 1969-70, Great Lakes Shakespeare Festival, Lakewood, Ohio, 1970-71; campaign dir. USO of Metro. N.Y.C., 1973-78; assoc. dir. devel. NYU, 1978-87; exec. v.p. Calvary Hosp. Fund, Bronx, 1987—. Mem. Rotary (pres. Bronx club 1996-97). Avocations: chess, golf, theatre. Office: Calvary Hosp Fund 1740 Eastchester Rd Bronx NY 10461-2322

CLASON, RICHARD LEWIS, retired protective services official, writer; b. Chinook, Mt., June 6, 1926; s. John Halifax and Nettie Westover Clason; m. Lillian Olga Schierer, Nov. 27, 1948; children: Kenneth Richard, Christopher Robert. AA, L.A. Valley Coll., L.A., Calif., 1982. Police officer Beverly Hills, Calif., 1956—90. Author: The Kid from Custer, 1996; complier The John Nettie Book, 2003. Newsletter editor Destroyer-Escort Sailors Assn., Calif., 2000—. First class signalman USN, 1943—49. Recipient Police Officer of the Yr., C.H.A. award, City if Beverly Hills, Calif., 1970, Felix Rothchild award, City of Beverly Hills, C.H.C.C. award for Profl. Excellence, Beverly Hills C. of C., 1981. Mem.: Western Writers of Am., Internat. Assn. for Indentifcation (worldwide), So. Calif. Assn. of Finger Paint Officers. Avocation: writing. Home: 10118 Gothic Ave North Hills CA 91343

CLASSEN, HENRY WARD, lawyer, educator; b. Balt., May 17, 1959; s. John Newell and Margaret Taylor (Speer) C.; m. Sibley Gillis, Aug. 19, 1989; children: Sibley Keena, Taylor Pierce. BA in Econs., Trinity Coll., 1982; JD, Cath. U. Am., 1985; MBA, U. Pa., 1990. Bar: Md. 1985, U.S. Dist. Ct. Md. 1986, D.C. 1987. Assoc. Weinberg and Green, Balt., 1985-87; assoc. gen. counsel, asst. sec. Internat. Mobile Machines Corp., Phila., 1987-90; gen. counsel, sec. CSC Intelicom, Inc., Hanover, Md., 1990—; asst. gen. counsel Computer Scis. Corp., 1996—. Bd. dirs. Dyn McDermott Petroleum Svcs. Corp.; adj. prof. U. Balt. Law Sch., 1991—; lectr. Inst. for Paralegal Tng., 1988-96. Editor-in-chief Jour. Contemporary Health and Law Policy, Washington, 1983-85, Cath. U. Law Rev., 1984-85; author: Classen's Commercial Forms, Classen's Merger and Acquisition Forms; mem. edit. bd. Bus. Law Today, 1999—; columnist health care The Daily Record, 1986-87, book rev. columnist, 1989-92; contbr. articles to profl. jours.; commentator series Sta. WMMR FM, 1987. Trustee Calvert Sch., Inc., 1996—, treas. bd. trustees, 2000—. Mem. ABA (corp. and bus. law sects.), Md. Bar Assn. (chmn. gen. counsel com.), Am. Corp. Counsel Assn., Computer Law Assn. Republican. Presbyterian. Home: 7822 Chelsea St Baltimore MD 21204-3641 Office: CSC Intelicom Inc 7459 A Candlewood Rd Hanover MD 21076 E-mail: hclassen@csc.com.

CLASSON, ROLF ALLAN, pharmaceutical company executive; b. Nassjo, Sweden, Aug. 20, 1945; s. Allan K.E. and May Britt (Lagerquist) C.; m. Birgitta Larsson, Feb. 3, 1968; children— Peter, Karin, Erik. M in Bus. Econs. Gothenburg U., 1969. Personnel mgr. Pharmacia, Uppsala, Sweden, 1969-74 mgmt. cons. Asbjorn Habberstad, Stockholm, 1974-77; mktg. mgr. Pharmacia Uppsala, 1977-80; div. gen. mgr. Tarkett, Ronneby, 1980; pres. Pharmacia Infusion, Uppsala, 1981-84, Pharmacia Devel. Co. Inc., Piscataway, N.J. 1984-90; pres., chief oper. officer Pharmacia Biosystems AB, 1990—91; exec v.p. Bayer Corp., 1995—2002, exec. v.p., worldwide mktg., sales & services group diagnostics, 1991—92, pres., group diagnostics, 1995—2002, sr. v.p.

sales & services, group diagnostics, 1992—95, chief exec., health care div., 2002—. Bd. dirs. Pharmacia Deltec, Inc., Pharmacia/LKB Biotech., Inc., Hillenbrand Indus. Office: Bayer Corp 100 Bayer Rd Pittsburgh PA 15205-9741

CLASTER, JILL NADELL, university administrator, history educator; d. Harry K. and Edith Lillian Nadell; m. Millard L. Midonick, May 24, 1979; 1 child from previous marriage, Elizabeth Claster (dec.). BA, NYU, 1952, MA, 1954; PhD, U. Pa., 1959. Instr. history U. Pa., 1956-58; instr. ancient and medieval history U. Ky., Lexington, 1959-61, asst. prof., 1961-64; adj. asst. prof. classics NYU, N.Y.C., 1964-65, asst. prof. history, 1965-68, assoc. prof., 1968-84, prof., 1984—, acting undergrad. chmn. history, 1972-73, dir. M.A. in liberal studies program, 1976-78; assoc. dean Washington Sq. and Univ. Coll., 1978, acting dean, 1978-79, dean, 1979-86; dir. Hagop Kevorkian Ctr. for Near Eastern Studies, NYU, 1991-96. Appointee N.Y.C. Commn. on Status of Women. Author: Athenian Democracy: Triumph or Travesty, 1967, The Medieval Experience, 1982; Contbr. articles to profl. jours. Danforth grantee, 1966-68; Fulbright grantee, 1958-59 Mem. Am. Hist. Assn., Medieval Acad. Am. Home: 161 W 15th St New York NY 10011-6720 Office: NYU Dept History 53 Washington Sq S Dept History New York NY 10012-1098 E-mail: jill.claster@nyu.edu.

CLATWORTHY, CATHERINE LYNN, educational trainer, graphics designer; b. Chatham, Ont., Can., June 10, 1963; d. John Ferguson Clatworthy and Patricia Anne (Maynard) Clatworthy. A.O.C.A., Ont. Coll. Art and Design, Toronto, 1985. Graphic designer Burton Kramer Assocs., Toronto, 1985—87; co-owner/mgr. The Allery, Toronto, 1987—98; tng. ctr. instr. Larson-Juhl Co., Atlanta, 1998—; v.p., mktg. mgr. Dakota Framing Specialties, Inc., Watertown, SD, 2000—02; propr., cons. LilyCrest, Huron, SD, 2002. Com./facilitator Color Mktg. Group, Alexandria, Va., 2000—; mem. Visual Arts Ont., Toronto, 1985—; educator/lectr. Profl. Picture Framers Assn., Jackson, Mich., 1996—; mem. Can. Conservation Inst., Ottawa, 1998—, Am. Inst. Conservation, Washington, 2002—. Author: The Art of Colour & Design for the Art and Framing Industry, 1999; contbr. mags., newspapers, and interviews in field. Mem.: Visual Arts Ont., Profl. Picture Framers Assn., Color Mktg. Group. Avocations: art, antiques, travel, photography, cooking. Office: LilyCrest PO Box 906 Huron SD 57350 E-mail: lilycrest@hur.midco.net.

CLAUDIO, MANUEL P.A. medical educator, health facility administrator; b. Manila, June 23, 1938; s. Eduardo L. and Gorgonia A. Claudio; m. Adelina C.B. Claudio, May 1, 1965; children: Basil, Kevin, Kenneth, Liesl. MD, U. E. Ramon Magsaysay Meml. Med. Ctr., Quezon City, The Philippines, 1962; MBA, Northwestern U., 1993. Cert. Am. Bd. Med. Mgmt., Am. Bd. Quality Assurance and Utilization Rev. Physicians. Chmn. dept. medicine Humana Hosp., Hoffman Estates, Ill., 1981—83; chief sect. pulmonary medicine Mercy Hosp. Med. Ctr., Chgo., 1981—2000, med. dir. respiratory care dept., 1988—2000, pres. med. and sci. staff faculty, 1989—91; clin. asst. prof. medicine U. Ill. Coll. Medicine, Chgo., 1983—98; program dir. pulmonary medicine Mercy Hosp. Med. Ctr., Chgo., 1979—98. Contbr. Pres. Philippine Med. Assn. Chgo., 1968; exec. dir. Assn. Philippine Practicing Physician Am., Chgo., 1972; bd. advisors Cath. charities, Chgo., 1986—; Bd. dir., pres. elect Am. Lung Assn., Metro Chgo., Ill., 1992—. Named to Chgo.'s Filipino-Am. Hall of Fame, 1997; recipient Leadership award, Philippine Med. Assn. Chgo., 1968, Disting. Physician award, Philippine Med. Assn., 1992. Fellow: ACP, Inst. Medicine Chgo.; mem.: Am. Thoracic Soc. Roman Catholic.

CLAUDIO, PIER PAOLO, surgeon, researcher; b. Naples, Italy, May 20, 1964; arrived in United States, 1992; s. Francesco Leandro Claudio and Paola Zappa; m. Candace Michelle Howard, July 5, 1995; children: Charlene, Daniela. MD, Universita degli Studi di Napoli "Federico II", 1983—89. Bd. cert. head & neck surgery Italy, 1994. Asst. prof. dept. of odontostomatologic and maxillo-facial scis. U. Naples, 1998—; asst. prof. dept. pathology, anatomy and cell biology Thomas Jefferson U., Phila., 1996—2002; assoc. prof. dept. biotechnology Temple U., Phila., 2002—. Asst. and contbg. editor: Women's Oncology Rev., 2001. Fellow, U. Naples Federico II, 1989-1994, Lega Nazionale Lotta contro i Tumori, 1994-1995, Am.-Italian Cancer Found., 1995-1997, Associazione Leonardo di Capua, 1999-2000. Achievements include invention of application of the PRINS technique to titer recombinant virus and evaluation of the efficiency of viral transduction; and methods of inhibiting smooth muscle cell proliferation and preventing restenosis with a vector expressing RB2/p130. Avocations: swimming, travel. Office: Temple U Biotechnology Dept 1900 N 12th St, BioLife Sci Bldg 333 Philadelphia PA 19122 Home Fax: 215-735-3083; Office Fax: 215-204-9522. Business E-Mail: claudio@temple.edu.

CLAUS, LAURENCE PAUL, law educator; b. Adelaide, Australia, Apr. 25, 1968; s. Raymond Paul and Gloria Joy Claus. B in Econs., U. Queensland, Australia, 1987, LLB, 1991; PhD, U. Oxford, 1998. Barrister: Supreme Ct. NSW, Australia 1993. Assoc. to chief justice Supreme Ct. Queensland, Brisbane, 1989; assoc. to justice Royal Commn. Comml. Activities of Govt., Perth, Australia, 1991—92; legal rsch. officer High Ct. Australia, Canberra, Australia, 1992—93; fgn. svc. nat. atty. office fgn. litig. U.S. Embassy, London, 1995—98; law clk. US Ct. of Appeals (7th cir.), Chgo., 1999—2000; asst. prof. law U. San Diego, San Diego, 2001—. Fellow vis. rsch. fellow, U. Melbourne, 1999, John M. Olin fellow, Northwestern U., 2000—01. Office: University of San Diego School of Law 5998 Alcala Park San Diego CA 92110

CLAUSE, STEVEN LEE, pharmacist, researcher; b. Fort Wayne, Ind., Jan. 13, 1953; s. Edmund M. and Hazel Clause; children: Brendan M., Ryan A., Travis A. BS in Pharmacy, Purdue U., 1983; PharmD, Albany Coll., 2001. Pharmacist Rite Aid Pharmacies, Charleston, W.Va., 1983—86, CVS Pharmacies, Albany, NY, 1986—90, Albany Med. Ctr. Hosp., 1989—2000; resident home health care Albany Coll. of Pharmacy, 2001—02, rsch. asst. prof., 2002—. With Am. Pharm. Care Pain Cons., Delmar, NY, 2001—02; cons. pharmacist NY State Medicaid, Albany. Contbr. articles. Sgt. U.S. Army, 1973—78. Langeloth Found. grant, Eddy Vis. Nurse Assn., Troy, N.Y., 2002—. Mem.: Internat. Soc. Pharmacoeconomics and Outcomes Rsch. (licentiate), Am. Colleges Clin. Pharmacy (licentiate), N.Y. Soc. Health-Sys. Pharmacists (licentiate), Am. Soc. Health-Sys. Pharmacists (licentiate). Achievements include Vietnam Era U.S. Army Veteran. Office: Eddy Visiting Nurse Assn 433 River St Ste 3000 Troy NY 12180 Home Fax: 518-274-2908; Office Fax: 518-274-2908. Personal E-mail: clauses@acp.edu. E-mail: clauses@nehealth.com.

CLAUSELL, DEBORAH DELORIS, artist, songwriter; b. Mobile, Ala., July 16, 1951; d. Stephen Joseph and Estell Abney Clausell. BA in Sociology, U. Mobile, 1976; cert., Barbizon Modeling Sch., 1984. Movie extra Century Casting, Santa Monica, Calif., 1984-85; libr. Mobile Pub. Libr., 1996-97. Exhibited in group shows Greater Gulf State Fair, Mobile, 1990, 96 (3d, 2d and 1st prize ribbons), 97 (3rd prize ribbon), 99, Mercy Med. Gallery, Daphne, Ala., 1993, Mus. of City of Mobile, 1993, Fine Art Mus. of the South, Mobile, 1993, Spring Hill Art, Mobile, 1993, Greater Gulf State Fair Exhibit Fine Arts, 1999, Monticello-Thomas Jefferson Meml., 1993; pvt. collection The White House, Heritage Hall, 2000 and Art Auction, Energen Corp. Artpark Exbhn., 2001. Mem. Smithsonian Inst., 2001, USS Constn. Mus., 2002, U.S. Border Control, 2003. 2d lt. USAF, res. Recipient Gold Eagles and Stars Letters from U.S. President Bush, 2001. Mem. VFW, Internat. Platform Assn., U.S. Naval Inst., Libr. Congress Assn., Nat. Trust for Hist. Preservation, Civil War Trust, Mt. Vernon Ladies Assn., Navel League, Preservation Alliance. Democrat. Roman Catholic. Avocations: classic guitarist, harmonica, swimming, vocal singing, reading. Home: 5859 Reams Dr N Mobile AL 36608-3652

CLAUSEN, BJØRN, materials scientist, researcher; s. Erik Bjørn and Inger Clausen; m. Lene Hessner, Mar. 7, 1997; 1 child, Anders Bjørn. BSc, Aarhus Teknikum, Denmark, 1998; MSc, Aalborg U., Denmark, 1993; PhD, Tech. U. of Denmark, Denmark, 1997. Postdoctoral rsch. assoc. Los Alamos Nat. Lab., N.Mex., 1997—99, tech. staff mem., 2002—; sr. postdoctoral scholar Calif. Inst. of Tech., Pasadena, 2000—02. Office: Los Alamos National Lab PO Box 1663 MS H805 Los Alamos NM 87545 E-mail: clausen@lanl.gov.

CLAUSEN, BRET MARK, industrial hygienist, safety professional; b. Hayward, Calif., Aug. 1, 1958; s. Norman E. and Barbara Ann (Wagner) C.; m. Cheryl Elaine Carlson, May 24, 1980; children: Kathrine, Eric, Emily. BS, Colo. State U., 1980, MS, 1983. Cert. indsl. hygienist, safety profl., hazard control mgr., hazardous materials mgr.; cert. in comprehensive practice Am. Bd. Inds. Hygiene; cert. in comprehensive practice and mgmt. aspects Bd. Cert. Safety Profls. Assoc. risk mgmt., indsl. hygienist, safety rep. Samsonite Corp., Denver, 1980-83, mgr. loss prevention, 1984-88; health, safety and environment rep. Storage Tech., Longmont, Colo., 1984; sr. project cons. Occusafe Inc., Denver, 1988; numerous indsl. hygiene and safety mgmt./tech. assignments Rocky Flats Environ. Tech. Site, Golden, Colo., 1988—2003; ind. cons. indsl. hygiene and safety, 2000—; sr. mgr., health, safety and environ. Ch2m Hill Constructors, Inc., 2003—. Mem. radiol. assistance program team U.S. Dept. Energy, Region VI, 1994—. Local emergency planning com. Weld County, Colo., 1996—. Mem. Am. Indsl. Hygiene Assn. (pres. Rocky Mountain sect. 1988-89), Am. Soc. Safety Engrs. (prof., acad. accreditation/site evaluator 1998—, profl. and ednl. stds. com. 1998-2000, alt. 2000—), Inst. Hazardous Materials Mgmt. (cert. sr. level), Ins. Inst. Am. (assoc. in risk mgmt.), Am. Nat. Stds. Inst. (com. on confined spaces 1993—),Acad. Indsl. Hygiene (diplomate, acad. accreditation com. site evaluator 1994—). Republican. Lutheran. Avocations: hunting, camping, hiking, farming. Home: 16794 Weld County Rd # 44 La Salle CO 80645

CLAUSEN, HUGH JOSEPH, retired army officer; b. Mobile, Ala., Dec. 25, 1926; s. Hugh Martin and Elizabeth Hazel (Orrell) C.; m. Betty Sue Richards, June 7, 1949; children: Melinda, Joseph. LL.B., U. Ala., 1950; grad., Advanced Mgmt. Program, Harvard U., 1970. Bar: Ala. 1950, U.S. Supreme Ct. 1959, U.S. Ct. Mil. Appeals 1959. Commd. 1st lt. U.S. Army, 1951, advanced through grades to maj. gen.; various assignments, 1951-62; asst. staff judge adv. (8th Army), Korea, 1962-64; judge adv. U.S. Disciplinary Barracks, Fort Leavenworth, Kans., 1964-66; instr. U.S. Army Command and Gen. Staff Coll., 1966-68; staff judge adv. 1st Inf. Div., Vietnam, 1968-69; assigned Office Legis. Liaison, Dept. Army, Washington, 1969-71; chief mil. justice div. Office JAG, 1971-72, exec. officer, 1972-73; staff judge adv. III Corps and Ft. Hood, Tex., 1973-76; chief judge U.S. Army Ct. Mil. Rev., Falls Church, Va., 1976-78; asst. judge adv. gen. for mil. law Dept. Army, 1978-79, asst. judge adv. gen., 1979-81, judge adv. gen., 1981-85. Vice pres. for adminstrn., sec. bd. trustees Clemson U., S.C., 1985-92, v.p. emeritus, 1992—. Decorated Disting. Service Medal, Bronze Star with 3 oak leaf clusters, Meritorious Service medal, Legion of Merit with oak leaf cluster, Air medal with oak leaf cluster, Army Commendation medal with oak leaf cluster; RVN Honor medal; RVN Gallantry Cross with palm; RVN Civic Action Honor medal with palm. Mem. Ala. Bar Assn., Phi Alpha Delta. Address: 107 Hermitage Mooring Dr Seneca SC 29672-9138 E-mail: hughclausen@nuvok.net.

CLAUSEN, JEANNE LORRAINE, musician; b. L.A., Calif., Oct. 16, 1944; d. Leslie Paul and Margaret Jack Clausen; life ptnr. John Wesley Cleveland, June 12, 1990; 1 child, Laura Alexandra Cleveland. BA, Sarah Lawrence Coll., 1967; MusM, Cleve. Inst. Music, 1972. Mem. Calif. New Music Ensemble, L.A., 1975—78; mem. trio in residence Claremont (Calif.) Grad. Sch., 1976—79; concert mistress Ensemble Concerto, dir. Roberto Gini, Milan, 1983—86; mem. Amsterdam Baroque Orch., dir. Ton Koopman, Netherlands, 1986—87; founder, 1st violin La Cetra, San Francisco, 1982—. Mem. Early Music Ensemble Calif. State U., 2002. Author: (video) The Rhapsodic Art Of The Ancients. Esoteric Christian. Achievements include Research on 16th century stringed instrument lira da braccia. Avocations: hiking, swimming, reading, good conversation, enjoying the mystical beauty of nature.

CLAUSEN, JERRY LEE, psychiatrist; b. Wausau, Wis., Nov. 5, 1939; s. Douglas William and Florence Jean (Amidon) C.; m. Nancy Eileen Longdon, Aug. 3, 1962; children: Keith Russell, Pamela Dawn. BA, Wesleyan U., Middletown, Conn., 1961; MD, Albany Med. Coll., N.Y., 1965. Diplomate in psychiatry and in addiction psychiatry Am. Bd. Psychiatry and Neurology; cert. Am. Soc. Addiction Medicine; cert. alcoholism and substance abuse counselor, N.Y. Psychiatry intern Upstate Med. Ctr., Syracuse, N.Y., 1965-66, psychiatric resident, 1966-67, 69-71, asst. attending, 1971-72, attending, 1972-80; staff psychiatrist Onondaga Mental Health Clinic, Syracuse, 1971-72; courtesy staff Benjamin Rush Psychiatric Ctr., Syracuse, 1971-84, active staff, 1984—; pvt. practice psychiatry Syracuse, 1971—; clin. asst. prof. SUNY, 1972—. Staff psychiatrist Onondaga Pastoral Counseling Ctr., Syracuse, 1971-73, 81-97, psychiatric dir., 1973-81; cons. psychiatrist Loretto Rest Geriatric Ctr., Syracuse, 1972-74. Tchr. First Universalist Ch., Syracuse, 1966—. Lt. comdr. USN, 1967-69. Fellow Am. Psychiat. Assn. (disting. life fellow; chmn. ins. mktg. com. 1979-88); mem. Onondaga County Med. Soc., N.Y. State Med. Soc. Universalist-Unitarian. Avocations: walking, tennis, cross-country skiing. Office: 300 Burnet Ave Syracuse NY 13203-2302

CLAUSEN, LARS, social scientist; b. Berlin, Apr. 8, 1935; s. Jürgen and Rosemarie (Kögel) C.; m. Bettina Feddersen, Feb. 28, 1964. Diploma, U. Hamburg, Germany, 1960; Dr. sc. pol., U. Münster, Germany, 1963, Habil. in Sociology, 1968. Rsch. asst. Sozialforschungsstelle, Dortmund, Germany, 1963-68; rsch. affiliate Rhodes-Livingstone Inst., Lusaka, Zambia, 1964-65; asst. prof. U. Münster, 1968-70; prof. sociology, dir. Inst. Sociology U. Kiel, Germany, 1970-2000, dir. Disaster Rsch. Ctr., 1987—2000, dean Faculty Econs. and Social Scis., 1991-92. Fellow Wissenschaftkolleg, Berlin, 1996-97. Author: Elemente einer Soziologie der Wirtschaftswerbung, 1964, Industrialisierung in Schwarzafrika, 1968, Jugendsoziologie, 1976, Tausch, 1978, Produktive Arbeit, destruktive Arbeit, 1988, Krasser sozialer Wandel, 1994; co-author: Assistenten in einer neuen Universität, 1968, Siedlungssoziologie, 1978, Einführung in die Soziologie der Katastrophen, 1983, Zu allem fähig, 1985, Zur Hilfe bereit, 1987, Zur Akzeptanz staatlicher Informationspolitik bei technischen Grossunfällen und Katastrophen, 1990, Deutsche Regelsysteme, 1994, Tönnies in Toronto, 1998, Entsetzliche soziale Prozesse, 2003; chief editor: Ferdinand Tönnies Gesamtausgabe, 1998—; editor publs. Mem. Gewerkschaft Erziehung und Wissenschaft, Ferdinand-Tönnies-Gesellschaft (pres. 1978—), Deutsche Gesellschaft für Soziologie (v.p. (1991-92, pres. 1993-94), Schutzkommission beim Bundesminister des Inneren (chmn. 2003—). Office: U Kiel Inst Sociology Olshausenstr 40 D-24098 Kiel Germany E-mail: lclausen@soziologie.uni-kiel.de.

CLAUSEN, WENDELL VERNON, classics educator; b. Coquille, Oreg., Apr. 2, 1923; s. George R. and Gertrude (Johnson) C.; m. Corinna Slice, Aug. 20, 1947; children: John, Raymond, Thomas; m. Margaret W. Woodman, June 19, 1970. AB, U. Wash., 1945; PhD, U. Chgo., 1948; A.M. (hon.), Harvard U., 1959. Mem. faculty Amherst Coll., 1948-59, assoc. prof. classics, 1955-59; prof. Greek and Latin Harvard U., 1959-82, Victor S. Thomas prof. Greek and Latin, 1982-88, Pope prof. Latin lang. and lit., 1988-93, prof. comparative lit., 1984-93, prof. emeritus, 1993—, chmn. dept. classics, 1966-71. Vis. prof. Univ. Coll., London, 1971; Sather prof. U. Calif., Berkeley, 1982; vis. prof. I Tatti, Florence, Italy, 1989. Author: Virgil's Aeneid and the Tradition of Hellenistic Poetry, 1987, A Commentary on Virgil's Eclogues, 1994, Virgil's Aeneid: Decorum Allusion and Ideology, 2002, articles in classical philology; editor: Persius, 1956, Persius and Juvenal, 1959, rev. edit., 1992, Appendix Vergiliana, 1966, Harvard Studies in Classical Philology, 1990—92; editor, contbr. The Cambridge History of Latin Literature, 1982, Premio Internazionale Virgilio, 1994, assoc. editor Am. Jour. Philology, 1976—81, Style and Tradition: Studies in Honor of Wendell Clausen, 1998. William Rainey Harper scholar U. Chgo., 1946-48; fellow Am. Acad. in Rome, 1952-53, Am. Council Learned Socs., 1962-63, fellow commoner Peterhouse, Cambridge. Fellow Am. Acad. Arts and Scis.; mem. Am. Philol. Assn., Cambridge Philol. Soc., Signet Soc., Phi Beta Kappa. Home: 8 Kenway St Cambridge MA 02138-4724 Office: Harvard U 201 Boylston Hall Cambridge MA 02138 E-mail: clausen@tas.harvard.edu.

CLAUSER, ANGELA FRANCES, medical surgical, pediatrics and geriatrics nurse; b. Leavenworth, Kans., June 25, 1955; d. Donald F. Sr. and Agnes Angela (Forge) C. AA, Kansas City (Kans.) Jr. Coll., 1984; BSN, Pitts. State U., 1986. RN, Kans.; cert. provider CPR, Am. Heart Assn. Sec. U.S. Army, Ft. Leavenworth, Kans., 1978, 79-80, USAF Acad., Colorado Springs, Colo., 1981-82, VA, Leavenworth, 1982-84; staff nurse St. John's Hosp., Leavenworth, 1989-96, unit edn. coord., 1995-96; oncology prn nurse U. Kans. Hosp., Kansas City, 1997-99; clin. nurse Gentry Clinic, Ft. Leavenworth, Kans., 1998—, instr. pediatric asthma class, 1998-99, mem. asthma PAT team, 1999—, instr. adult asthma class, 2000—, instr. pediatric/parent asthma class, 2000—. Substitute sch. nurse Ft. Leavenworth, Kans., 1997—. Mem. Nurses Svc. Orgn., Pitts. State U. Alumni Assn., Kans. City Jr. Coll. Alumni Assn.

CLAUSER, DONALD ROBERDEAU, musician; b. Fort Worth, Mar. 2, 1941; s. Donald Milton and Selina Almira (Sizer) C. B.F.A., U. N.M., 1962; Mus.M., Boston U., 1964; diploma, Curtis Inst. Music, 1967. Mem. viola sect., Phila. Orch., 1966— . Home: 1609 Chanticleer Cherry Hill NJ 08003-4820 *It is my conviction that music is a universal medium of communication— a factor which is surely of distinct value in these troubled times. Keeping this in mind has constantly been uppermost in the pursuit of my career, wherever this may have led me.*

CLAUSMAN, GILBERT JOSEPH, retired medical librarian; b. Los Angeles, Nov. 8, 1921; s. Pete John and Lila (Mason) C. AB, Willamette U., 1947; BS, Columbia U., 1948, MS, 1952. Med. librarian N.Y. Acad. Medicine, N.Y.C., 1948-55; med. librarian NYU Med. Ctr., N.Y.C., 1955-86, librarian emeritus, 1987—. Cons. Milton Helpern Library Legal Medicine, 1963-88. Served with USN, 1942-45 Mem. Med. Libr. Assn. (pres. 1977-78), Archons of Colophon, N.Y. Acad. Medicine, Acad. Health Info. Profls. (Disting. mem. emeritus). Home: 6 Cobble Hill Rd Westport CT 06880-2915

CLAUSON, F.L. STAN, JR., city planner, consultant; b. Chgo., Oct. 20, 1944; s. Frank Levin and Ethel (Emrich) C.; m. Judith Johnson, Aug. 3, 1968; children: Max, Elli, Fritz Per. BA, Denison U., 1966; MA, U. Wis., 1969; M in Landscape Arch., Harvard U., 1978. Asst. prof. Western Ill. U., Macomb, 1971-73; urban design planner City of Newton, Mass., 1978-81; dir. planning devel. City of Montpelier, 1988-91; cons. Stan Clauson Assocs., 1991-94, 1981-88, owner, prin. Aspen, Colo., 1998—; cmty. devel. dir. City of Aspen, 1994-98. France country contact Rotary Youth Exch., 2001—; dir., trustee Vt. Symphony Orch., Burlington, 1990—94; bd. dirs. Aspen Chamber Resort Assn., 1999—; dir. Sta. KAJX, Roaring Fork Pub. Radio, 2003—. Recipient Cert. Nat. Merit Dept. HUD, 1988, Outstanding Planning Project award Vt. Planners Assn., 1990, Archl. Preservation award Montpelier (Vt.) Heritage Group, 1992; winner Aspen Affordable Housing Design Competition, 2000. Mem.: Inst. Transp. Engrs., Urban Land Inst., Am. Soc. Landscape Archs., Am. Planning Assn. (bd. dirs. Colo. chpt. 2000—, v.p. 2001—), Am. Inst. Cert. Planners, Aspen Rotary Club. Avocations: skiing, hiking, classical music. Home: PO Box 6968 76 Meadow Ln Snowmass Village CO 81615 Office: Stan Clauson Assocs LLC 200 E Main St Aspen CO 81611-1956

CLAUSON, GARY LEWIS, chemist; b. Peoria, Ill., Feb. 25, 1952; s. Cecil Lewis and Virgie Grace (Shryock) C. AAS, Ill. Cen. Coll., East Peoria, 1974; BA in Chemistry, U. Calif., San Diego, 1977; MS in Chem., Bradley U., Peoria, 1981; PhD in Organic Chemistry, U. Ill., 1987. Engring. technician U.S. Naval Sta., San Diego, 1974-75; lab. analyst Lehn & Fink Products Co., Lincoln, Ill., 1978-79; part-time faculty Bradley U., Peoria, 1980-81; sci. asst. Ill. State Geol. Survey, Urbana, 1986-87; sr. chemist Ciba-Geigy Corp., McIntosh, Ala., 1987-92; rsch. scientist Gensia, Inc., San Diego, 1992-95, cons., 1995-96; prin. scientist Alliance Pharm. Corp., San Diego, 1996-99; rsch. scientist Yoh Scientific, San Diego, 1999-2000; sr. rsch. scientist Synthetic Blood Internat., Inc., Costa Mesa, Calif., 2001—. Mem. Am. Chem. Soc. Avocations: paleontology, tennis, basketball, softball, bicycling. Home: 1220 Bryan Ave Apt A Tustin CA 92780 E-mail: doctorwho@alumni.ucsd.edu., glc@sybd.com.

CLAUSON, SHARYN FERNE, consulting company executive, educator; b. Phila., Oct. 4, 1946; d. Eugene and Gertrud Jayn (Besser) C. BA in English, Temple U., 1968; MEd in Psychology, Arcadia U. (formerly Beaver Coll.), 1979; MBA in Marketing, Drexel U., 1982; postgrad. in law, Temple U., 1987. Market analyst Epstein Rsch., Bala, Pa., 1967-69; cons. Ednl. Testing Svc., Princeton, N.J., 1979-80; CEO CCX, Narberth, Pa., 1978-79; mem. faculty Cheltenham Twp. Sch. Dist., Elkins Park, Pa., 1969—2003; dir. Sharyn Clauson Bus. Comm., Narberth, Pa., 1975-85; pres. S. Clauson & Assocs., Inc., King of Prussia, Pa., 1985—; dir. Execuwriter, King of Prussia, 1985—. Mem. adj. faculty Drexel U., Phila., 1979-96, Phila. U., 1985-89, St. Joseph's U., Phila., 1986-92, Phila. Ctr. of Gt. lakes Coll. Assn., 1988; mem. adv. bd. Ergodyne, Inc., 1995-96; talk show host Sta. WDVT-AM, Phila., 1985; bd. dirs. Site Selex, Inc., Doylestown, Pa., dir. comm. and pub. rels., 1988-95. Editor: Curriculum for Optacon Music Reading, 1984; mem. editorial adv. bd. Bus. Communications and Concepts, 2d edit., 1985 Mem. com. Women's Polit. Caucus, Phila.; mem. Phila. Art Alliance; mem. exec. bd., arts and scis. alumni bd. Temple U. Women's Law Caucus; sec., v.p. bd. dirs. VFTW Coun., 2000-02. Golden Hearts honoree, 1999; recipient U.S. Congl. award, 1999. Mem. ASCD, AAUW, Am. Mktg. Assn., Nat. Spkrs. Assn. (chairperson 1985), Nat. Assn. Profl. Saleswomen (honoree 1982—), Nat. Coun. Tchrs. of English, Delaware Valley Writing Coun., Wallenberg Communicators, Phi Delta Kappa. Office: 21036 Valley Forge Circle King Of Prussia PA 19406 E-mail: sclaus@erols.com.

CLAUSS, JAMES JOSEPH, classics educator; b. Scranton, Pa., Sept. 1, 1953; s. James J. and Marion A. (Lynch) C.; m. Louise M. Betti, Aug. 12, 1978; children: Gerard, Michael, Elizabeth. BA, U. Scranton, 1974; MA, Fordham U., 1976; PhD, U. Calif., Berkeley, 1983; postgrad., Am. Sch. Classical Studies, Athens, 1982-83. Asst. prof. classics Creighton U., Omaha, 1983-84, U. Wash., Seattle, 1984-90, assoc. prof., 1990-97, prof., 1997—. Author: The Best of the Argonauts, 1993; co-editor: Medea: Essays on Medea in Myth, Literature, Philosophy and Art, 1997; author numerous articles and revs. Mem. Seattle Perugia Sister City Assn., 1991—. Thomas Day Seymour fellow Am. Sch. Classical Study, 1982-83. Mem. Am. Philol. Assn. (chmn. editorial bd. for textbooks, 1993-96), Classical Assn. Pacific N.W. (v.p. 1991-92, pres. 1992-93), Classical Assn. Middlewest and South, Am. Inst. Archaeology (v.p., pres. local chpt. 1990-92). Democrat. Roman Catholic. Avocations: music, sports. Office: U Wash Dept Classics PO Box 353110 Seattle WA 98195-3110

CLAUSS, WAYNE FRANCIS, court clerk; b. Rockaway Beach, N.Y., Jan. 5, 1947; s. Milton Leroy and Ruth Margaret (Van Seldan) C.; m. Linda Veronica Scavetti, Nov. 9, 1977. BA, CCNY, 1970. Cert. peace officer, N.Y. Ct. officer N.Y.C. Criminal Ct., 1974-79; sr. ct. officer N.Y. State Supreme Ct., Queens, 1979-81, sr. ct. clk., 1981-87, assoc. ct. clk., 1987—. Maj. USAR, 1970-96, ret. Mem. N.Y. State Supreme Ct. Officers Assn. (alt. del. 1978), DAV (judge advocate 1984—, chpt. comdr. 1980-83, life mem.), DAV Dept. of N.Y. State (legis. com.), N.Y. State Ct. Clks. Assn. (bd. dirs. 1993-95), Res. Officers Assn. (life), Ret. Officers Assn. (life), 77th RSC Officers Assn. Avocations: hiking, travel, photography, coin collecting. Office: NY State Supreme Ct Rm 140 A Trial Term 88-11 Sutphin Blvd Jamaica NY 11435

CLAUSSEN, DANE SHERMAN, newspaper consultant, journalism educator; b. Salem, Oreg., May 5, 1963; s. Jerrold Hugo and Earlene Ann (Conkey) C. BS, U. Oreg., 1984; MBA, U. Chgo., 1986; MS, Kans. State U., 1996; PhD, U. Ga., 1999. Chmn., pub. Oreg. Commentator Pub. Co., Inc., Eugene, 1983-84; mktg. intern The Times Leader, Wilkes-Barre, Pa., 1985; adv. dir. Chgo. Bus., 1985, prodn. dir., 1985-86; mktg. assoc. Chgo. Tribune, 1985-86; pub., pres. Chgo. Spectator Corp., 1984-86; pres., pub., editor The Press, Ltd., Tacoma, 1986-89; pres. Am. Newspaper Consultants, Ltd., Athens, Ga., 1987—; exec. editor Van Dahl Pub., Capital Cities/ABC, Albany, Oreg., 1989-90; pub., editor The Daily Reporter, Milw., 1991-92; mergers and acquisitions assoc. W.B. Grimes and Co., Kansas City, Mo., 1992-95; asst. prof. comm. and mass media S.W. Mo. State U., 1999—2001; assoc. prof. journalism and mass comm. and dir. grad. program Point Park Coll., 2001—. Author: Standing on the Promises: The Promise Keepers and the Revival of Manhood, 1999, The Promise Keepers: Essays on Masculinity and Christianity, 2000, Sex, Religion, Media, 2002, Anti-intellectualism in American Media: Magazines and Higher Education, 2003; editor: Industrial Marketing Practitioner newsletter, 1996-2003. Bd. dirs. Univ. Place C. of C., Tacoma, 1988-89; sec. Pierce County Centennial Commn., Tacoma, 1987-89; mem. State/Univ. of Oreg. Mus. of Art Ad. Com., Eugene, 1983-84. Named Future 1st Citizen, Corvallis (Oreg.) C. of C., 1981. Mem. Am. Philatelic Soc. Writers Unit (dir. 1991-95, v.p. west 1995-99, pres. 1999-2003), Am. Studies Assn., Nat. Communication Assn., Internat. Philatelic Press Club (pres. 1991-94), Soc. Profl. Journalists, Assn. Edn. Journalism Mass Communication, Royal Philatelic Soc. (London). Avocations: philately, reading, traveling, book collecting, newspaper collecting. Home: # 4 1211 Buena Vista St Pittsburgh PA 15212-4530

CLAUSSEN, EILEEN BARBARA, federal agency administrator; b. N.Y.C., June 9, 1945; d. Louis and Elsie (Young) Lerner; children: Hillary Anne, Geoffrey David. BA, George Washington U., 1966; MA, U. Va., 1967. Systems analyst USN, Washington, 1967-68; cons. Booz, Allen & Hamilton, Inc.,

Washington, 1968-69; asst. dir. ctr. for comml. devel. Boise Cascade Corp., Washington, 1969-72; various mgmt. positions Office of Solid Waste U.S. EPA, Washington, 1972-83, dir. characterization and assessment div., 1984-87, acting dep. asst. adminstr. air and radiation, 1988-89, dir. atmospheric and indoor air programs, 1987-93; spl. asst. to pres., sr. dir. global environ. affairs Nat. Security Coun., Washington, 1993—; asst. sec. Oceans, Intl. Enviromental & Sci. Affairs State Dept., Washington. Home: 4712 Chesapeake St NW Washington DC 20016-4466 Office: Dept of State Oceans Internat Environ Affairs 2201 C St NW Washington DC 20520-0001

CLAUTICE, EDWARD WELLMORE, retired industrial engineer; b. Balt., Oct. 13, 1916; s. George Joseph and Janet Harwood (Wellmore) C.; m. Mary Madelyn Spraker, Aug. 30, 1941; children: Elizabeth F., Stephen F., Christopher G., Michael J., Edward G. BS in Engring., Johns Hopkins U., 1938; MBA, Boston U., 1964. Registered profl. engr., Pa. Commd. 1st lt. U.S. Army, 1942-64, advanced through grades to lt. col., 1950, various tech. sci. teaching positions, 1947-52, ret., 1964; prodn. engr. Koppers Co., Balt., 1940-41; ptnr., co-owner Lane Clautice Engr. Co., Balt., 1945-47; coord. research and devel. Ballistics Research Labs., Aberdeen Proving Ground, Md., 1952-58; research and devel. liaison officer Can. Army Devel. Establishment, Ottawa, Ont., 1958-61; chief ops. Watertown (N.Y.) Arsenal, 1961-64; chief indsl. engr. Joy Mfg. Co., Franklin, Pa., 1964-66; mgr., indsl. engr. AMF, Inc., York, Pa., 1966-79; ret., 1979. Cons. in field, York, 1979—; tchr. Pa. State U., York, 1967-1973; lectr. Soc. Mfg. Engrs., Detroit, 1967, 69, Mgmt. Engring. Trng. Agy, Rock Island, Ill., 1965. Author: A Little Nonsense, 1987, A Lotta Nonsense, 1992, Madelyn, My Wife, Our Mother, 1995, A Potpourri of Poetry, 2002; author numerous poems (2 Golds, 1 Silver, 3 honorable mention awards World of Poetry 1986-89); contbr. articles to profl. jours. Counselor, Service Corps. Ret. Execs., York, 1982-87; active Township Sewer Authority. Recipient numerous athletic awards. Mem.: Tennis (York). Republican. Roman Catholic. Avocations: theatre, tennis, contract bridge, woodworking, cooking. Home and Office: 231 Lynbrook Dr N York PA 17402-3229

CLAVELLE, PETER, mayor; BA, St. Anselm Coll., 1971; MPA, Syracuse U., 1972. Town mgr., Castleton, Vt., 1972-76; city mgr. Winooski, Vt., 1976-79, exec. dir. Vt.'s State Atty.'s and Sheriff's Dept., 1979-80; project dir. Hamlin Cons. Engring., Inc., Essex Jct., Vt., 1980-82; pres. dir. Burlington, 1982-83; dir. cmty. and econ. devel. office City of Burlington, 1983-89, mayor, 1989-93, 95—; co-founder, prin. Burlington assocs. in Cmty. Devel., 1993-95. Office: City of Burlington Office of the Mayor City Hall 149 Church St Rm 34 Burlington VT 05401*

CLAVER, ROBERT EARL, television director, producer; b. Chgo., May 22, 1928; s. Louis E. and Sara M. (Sosna) C.; 1 child, Nancy Beth. BS in Journalism, U. Ill., 1950. Prodr.-writer: first 1000 Captain Kangaroo shows (Sylvania award, Peabody award); prodr., dir.: (TV shows) Here Comes the Brides, 1968-70, The Interns, 1970-71, Partridge Family, 1970-74, Gloria, CBS-TV, 1982-83, Small Wonder, 1985, New Love American Style, 1985, New Leave It to Beaver, 1986-87, Charles in Charge, 1987, Out of This World, 1987-91, numerous other series; dir.: (TV shows) Welcome Back Kotter, ABC-TV, 1977-78, All's Fair, CBS-TV, Housecalls, CBS-TV, 1979-80, Mork and Mindy, ABC-TV, 1981-82. With U.S. Army, 1951-53. Mem. Dirs. Guild Am.

CLAVERIE, PHILIP DEVILLIERS, lawyer; b. New Orleans, June 29, 1941; s. Louis Barbot and Viola Aimee (Schlegel) C.; m. Laura Lynn McCampbell, Apr. 27, 1974; children: Philip deVilliers Jr., Stephanie McCampbell. AB, Princeton U., 1963; JD, Tulane U., 1966. Bar: La. 1966. Assoc. Phelps Dunbar, New Orleans, 1966-70, ptnr., 1970—. Hon. consul of Finland, 2002—. Contbr. articles to profl. jours. Mem. bd. trustees Children's Hosp. New Orleans, 1978-, pres. 1985-87; mem. bd. govs. Isidore Newman Sch., 1982-2000, chmn. 1995-98; mem. exec. bd. New Orleans Police Found., 1998—, hon. counsel of Finland. Served to lt. comdr., JAGC, USNR, 1973-79. Fellow Am. Bar Found., La. Bar Found.; mem. ABA, La. State Bar Assn., New Orleans Bar Assn., Assn. Bar City N.Y., Am. Law Inst., Am. Judicature Soc., La. State Law Inst. Clubs: Pickwick, Stratford. Home: 14 Versailles Blvd New Orleans LA 70125-4114 Office: Phelps Dunbar LLP Ste 2000 365 Canal St New Orleans LA 70130-6534 E-mail: claverip@phelps.com.

CLAWSON, DAVID KAY, orthopedic surgeon; b. Salt Lake City, Aug. 8, 1927; s. David J. and Elva (Gundry) C.; m. Janet Dorothy Smith, June 1, 1952; children: Kim Debra, David Roger. Student, U. Utah, 1944-45, 47-48; MD, Harvard U., 1952. Diplomate: Am. Bd. Orthopedic Surgery. Intern Stanford U. Hosp., 1952-53, resident gen. surgery, 1953-54; resident orthopedic surgery Stanford U. Hosp., also San Francisco City and County Hosp., 1954-57; fellow in orthopedics Nat. Found. Infantile Paralysis, 1955-58; hon. sr. registrar Royal Nat. Orthopedic Hosp., London, Eng., 1957-58; asst. prof. UCLA Med. Sch., 1958; asst. prof. surgery, head div. orthopedic surgery U. Wash. Med. Sch., 1958-61, assoc. prof. surgery, head div. orthopedic surgery, 1961-65, prof., 1964-83, chmn. dept. orthopedics, 1964-75; dean Coll. Medicine, U. Ky., 1975-83, vice chancellor for clin. profl. services, 1982-83; exec. vice chancellor U. Kans. Med. Ctr., Kansas City, 1983-94, cons. to chancellor, 1994; prof. surgery/orthopaedics U. Ky., 1994—. Mem. Accreditation Coun. for Grad. Med. Edn., 1977-88; chmn. residency rev. com. on structure and functions, 1987-88; chmn. coun. of deans Assn. Am. Med. Coll., 1985-86, chmn. of the assembly, 1988-89, immediate past chmn., 1989-90, disting. svc. rep. to exec. coun., 1992-95; active Am. Orthopaedic Soc. for Sports Medicine, 1972-87, founder, 1972; active Assn. Orthopaedic Chmn., 1971-73, founder, 1971. Contbr. med. jours.; mem. editorial bd.: Clin. Orthopedics and Related Research, 1964—. Mem. Heart of Am. coun. Boy Scouts Am., 1989—, mem. adv. bd., 1989-92, Regional Task Force and Edn. Found., 1972—. With USNR, 1945-46. Exchange fellow Am. Orthopedic Assn., 1967 Mem. AMA (coun. for med. affairs 1988—), Am. Acad. Ortho. Surgeons (coun. on health policy 1990-95), Am. Orthopaedic Assn., Assn. Acad. Health Ctrs., Assn. Am. Univs., Assn. Bone and Joint Surgeons (pres. 1977), Ky. Med. Assn., Fayette County Med. Soc., Harvard Med. Sch. Alumni Assn. (pres. 1984-85). Home: 3785 Jamaica Ct Lexington KY 40509-9506 also: 10 E Roanoke St Seattle WA 98102-3257 E-mail: dkcjd@msn.com. *Look to the past only for the lessons we can learn, live today for the joy of being alive, plan to the future to insure that what should be, will be.*

CLAWSON, HARRY QUINTARD MOORE, retired business executive; b. N.Y.C., Aug. 8, 1924; s. Harry Marshall and Marguerite H. (Burgoyne) C.; m. Annemarie Korntner, Dec. 1967 (dec. 1988); m. Mary Louise Kirkland, July 1989. Student, NYU, 1951-52, New Sch. for Social Rsch., 1953. Supr. transp., liaison with U.S. Army ARC, 1945-46; asst. to dir. pers. UNESCO, Paris, 1947; resident rep. Tex. Co., Douala, French Cameroun, West Africa, 1948-50; asst. dir. overseas bus. svc. McGraw-Hill Pub. Co., 1951-58; dir. client svcs. Internat. Rsch. Assocs., N.Y.C., 1958-61; v.p., sec. Frasch Whiton Boats, Inc., 1961-63; gen. mgr. Sailboat Tng. Facility, 1961-63; pres. Harry Q.M. Clawson & Co., Inc., N.Y.C., 1961-76, Charleston, S.C., 1978-2000; dir. planning and adminstrn. splty. chems. div. Essex Chem. Corp., 1976-78; pres. Trident Seafarms Co., Charleston, 1980-85. Contbr. articles to profl. jours. With U.S. Army, 1943-45, ETO. Decorated Bronze Star. Mem. Soc. Colonial Wars, Ex-Mems. Assn. Squadron A., Carolina Yacht Club, Yeamans Hall Club, 112 Infantry Regiment Assn. Home: 2 1/2 Legare St Charleston SC 29401-2337 E-mail: harryqm@aol.com.

CLAWSON, JAMES F., JR., judge, mediator, arbitrator; b. Coryell County, Tex., Aug. 31, 1923; s. James F. and Julia Josephine (Doolittle) C.; m. Mary Louise Forester, May 4, 1945; children: Marylou Bowen, Cathy Jo Young. JD, Baylor U., 1948. Bar: Tex. 1948, U.S. Dist. Ct. (so. dist.) Tex. 1995. Atty. Clawson, Jennings & Clawson, Houston, 1948-59; banker, trust officer First Nat. Bank of Temple, Tex., 1959-67; county judge Bell County, Belton, Tex., 1967-69; presiding judge 3d Adminstrv. Jud. Region of Tex., Belton, 1985-90; dist. judge 169th Jud. Dist. of Tex., Belton, 1969-85, sr. judge, 1985—. Chmn. Bd. Regional Judges of Tex., 1985-90; chmn. Ctrl. Tex. Coun. Govts., belton, 1985-90. Served to capt. USAF, 1942-46, 51-53. Named Outstanding Citizen of Yr., Temple (Tex.) Jaycees, 1966. Fellow Tex Bar Found.; mem. State Bar Tex. (mem. exec. com. jud. sect. 1972-82, chmn. jud. sect. 1982-83). Home: 1211 N Pea Ridge Rd Temple TX 76502-4917 E-mail: clawson@stonemedia.com.

CLAWSON, JOHN ADDISON, financier, investor; b. Monaco, Pa., June 4, 1922; s. Ralph S. and Elsie (Winnett) C.; m. Patricia Harmon, July 5, 1947; children: Christine Brandwie, Hunter Winnett. BS, Miami U., 1943, LLD, 1979; postgrad., Harvard U., 1968. Vice pres., nat. mgr. bus. and labor reports div. Prentice-Hall, N.Y.C., 1948-55; with DuBois Chems. div. Chemed Corp., Cin., 1955-78, dist. mgr. N.Y.C., 1955-60, regional mgr. Ea. div., 1960-64, divisional mgrs. v.p., 1964-66, exec. v.p., dir. sales, 1966-70, gen. mgr., 1968-70, pres., chief exec. officer, 1970-79, group exec., 1975-79; v.p. Chemed Corp., 1971-77, exec. v.p., 1978-79, ret., 1979. Chmn. Whitehall Mgmt. Corp., Cin.; bd. dirs. Suburban Fed. Savs. & Loan Assn. Trustee Providence Hosp., 1974-76; dean's assoc. Miami U., 1973— . Lt. (j.g.) USNR, 1943-46. Mem. Cin. C. of C. (city and county planning com. 1971-74), Soap and Detergent Assn. (vice-chmn. bd. 1971-73, chmn. bd., chief exec. officer 1974-75, mem. exec. com., bd. dirs. 1976-79), Delta Sigma Phi, Sigma Alpha Epsilon. Clubs: Queen City (Cin.), Kenwood Country (Cin.); John's Island (Fla.), Cat Cay, Ltd., Commodore (Bahamas). Presbyterian. Home: Johns Island 301 Island Creek Dr Vero Beach FL 32963-3306

CLAWSON, JUDITH LOUISE, middle school educator; b. Cleve., Nov. 24, 1938; d. Frank Anthony and Bettie (Cerny) Lisy; m. Robert Wayne Clawson, June 25, 1961; children: Deborah Marie, Gregory Scott. BS in Edn. magna cum laude, Bowling Green State U., 1960; postgrad., UCLA, 1961-65, Kent State U., 1976-80. Cert. secondary sch. math. tchr. Elem. tchr. Long Beach (Calif.) Unified Sch. Dist., 1960-61, L.A. Unified Sch. Dist., 1961-65, Stow (Ohio) City Schs., 1969-78, middle sch. math. tchr., 1978—97; ret., 1997. Cons., presenter in field. Recipient Cert. of Recognition, Martha Holden Jennings Foundn., 1987. Mem. ASCD, AAUW, NEA, LWV, Nat. Coun. Tchrs. of Math., Stow Tchrs. Assn., Ohio Edn. Assn., Ohio Coun. Tchrs. of Math., Delta Gamma (fin. advisor Kent State U. chpt. 1978-90, pres. alumnae chpt. 1987-89, 91-93, Pres.'s award 1987, housing dir. at-large nat. coun. 1997-2001), Kappa Delta Pi. Republican. Methodist. Avocations: golf, tennis, skiing, scuba diving, reading. Home: 7336 Westview Rd Kent OH 44240-5912 Office: Kimpton Mid Sch 380 N River Rd Munroe Falls OH 44262-1331

CLAWSON, ROXANN ELOISE, college administrator, computer company executive; b. Dallas, Oct. 15, 1945; d. Robert Wellington Clawson and Jeannette Irene (Rodenhauser) Clawson Clayton. BFA, Mich. State U., 1968. Library asst. Cooper Union, N.Y.C., 1970-75, asst. librarian, 1976-82, assoc. to dean, 1985—; computer cons., 1986—. Acting appearance in The Dragon's Nest, La MaMa Theatre, 1989. Mem. NAFE, N.Y. Personal Computer Group. Democrat. Lutheran. Avocation: administration.

CLAXTON, HARRIETT MAROY JONES, retired language educator; b. Dublin, Ga., Aug. 27, 1930; d. Paul Jackson and Maroy Athalia (Chappell) Jones; m. Edward B. Claxton, Jr., May 27, 1953; children: E. B. III, Paula Jones. AA with honors, Bethel Woman's Coll., 1949; AB magna cum laude, Mercer U., 1951; MEd, Ga. Coll., 1965. Social worker Laurens County Welfare Bd., Dublin, 1951-56; HS tchr. Dublin, 1961-66; instr. Mid. Ga. Coll., Cochran, 1966-71, asst. prof. English, lit. and speech, 1971-85, assoc. prof., 1985-86, adj. prof., 1987; rsch. tchr. Trinity Christian Sch., 1986, 92, sr. English tchr., 1986-87; ret., 1987. Instr. Ga. Coll., 1987, E. Ga. Coll., 1988—99; weekly columnist Dublin Courier Herald, 1995—. Author: (book) History of Laurens Superior Court; editor: Laurens County History, II, 1987; contbr. articles to profl. jours. and newspapers. Pres., chmn. bd. Mensea/Laurens unit Am. Cancer Soc.; sec. Am. Assn. Ret. Persons, 1987—90; v.p. Dublin Cmty. Concert, 1991—98; mem. preservation com. Hardy Smith House, 1998—2000; bd. dirs. Laurens County Libr., 1960—68, Friends Vets., Heart Ga. Altamaha Regional Devel. Ctr., 1998, sec., 2002—; bd. dir. Laurens County Libr., Dublin-Laurens Arts Coun., 2001—. Named Woman of the Yr., St. Patrick's Festival, Dublin, 1979, Most Popular Tchr., Dublin Ctr., 1985, Olympic Torch Bearer, 1996; recipient Outstanding Svc. award, Cancer Soc., Dublin, 1985, 1993, 1998, Outstanding Alumni award for cmty. svc., Ga. Coll., 1996. Mem.: UDC (chaplain 1999—), DAR (regent, vice regent, historian, state, dist., nat. awards), Dublin Assn. Fine Arts (pres. bd. 1974—76, 1982—84, 1990—98, 2001—03), Dublin Hist. Soc. (pres. 1976—78, 1995—98), Erin Garden Club (pres.), Woman's Study Club (pres.), U.S. Daus. of 1812, Daus. Am. Colonists, Daus. Colonial Wars, Delta Kappa Gamma, Chi Delta Phi (sec.), Phi Theta Kappa (pres.), Alpha Delta Pi (Middle Ga. alumni chpt. 1999—, scholarship plaque 1950), Sigma Mu. Democrat. Baptist. Home: 101 Rosewood Dr Dublin GA 31021-4129

CLAY, CAROL ANN, family nurse practitioner; b. South Hill, Va., Sept. 21, 1967; d. Arthur Lee and Helen Irene Bottoms; m. Edward Alan Clay, Oct. 1, 1996. BSN, Radford U., 1990; MSN, Old Dominion U., 1995. RN Va., cert. clin. specialist, Am. Nurse's Credentialing Ctr., family nurse practitioner, Am. Acad. Nurse Practitioners. RN charge nurse Southside Regional Med. Ctr., Petersburg, Va., 1990; RN staff nurse Culpeper (Va.) Meml. Hosp., 1990-91; RN charge nurse W.S. Hundley Annex, South Hill, Va., 1991; charge nurse, house supr. Brian's Ctr., Lawrenceville, Va., 1991-92; PN, NA instr. Southside Va. C.C., Alberta, 1991-95, 97-98; RN PRN pool Cmty. Meml. Health Ctr., South Hill, 1993-97, family nurse practitioner urgent care, 1997-98, family nurse practitioner occupl. health svcs., 1998—. Mem.: APHA, Am. Acad. Nurse Practitioners. Avocations: reading, rescuing abandoned animals. Home: 19491 Highway One Brodnax VA 23920-2247 Office: Cmty Meml Health Ctr 412 Bracey Ln South Hill VA 23970-1431

CLAY, CASSIUS MARCELLUS See ALI, MUHAMMAD

CLAY, CHARLES COMMANDER (CHUCK CLAY), lawyer, state senator; m. Sara Murphree; 1 child, Erin. Degree, U. N.C.; JD, U. Ga. Asst. dist. atty. Cobb County, Ga.; ptnr. Brock & Clay, P.C.; senator 37th dist. Ga. State Legislature, 1988-99; ptnr. Brock Clay Calhoun Wilson & Rogers P.C., Marietta, Ga., 1999—. Senate minority leader, vice chmn. banking and fin. instns. com., mem. appropriations and rules coms., ethics and jud. coms., senate study com. on local edn. fin. rev., chmn. Gen. Assembly's World Congress Ctr. Overview Com. Ga. State Senate. Grad. Leadership Cobb, Ga.; mem. adv. bd. Cobb Justice Found., North Ctrl. Ga. Police Acad., Open Gate Child Abuse Ctr.; bd. dirs. Kennesaw Mountain Nat. Battlefield Pk., U. Ga. Law Sch. Assn.; mem. Cobb County Commn., 1986-88; tchr. Sunday sch. St. James Episcopal Ch., Marietta. Recipient Disting. Svc. award Ga. Mid. Sch. Assn., 1992-93, Outstanding Legislator award Ga. Coun. on Aging. Mem. Kiwanis (Marietta chpt.), Cobb Landmark Soc., Phi Beta Kappa. Republican. Office: Brock Clay Calhoun Wilson & Rogers PC 49 Atlanta St SE Marietta GA 30060-8611

CLAY, CLARENCE SAMUEL, acoustical oceanographer; b. Kansas City, Mo., Nov. 2, 1923; s. Clarence Samuel and Mary Else (Hall) C.; m. Andre Jane Edwards, Mar. 27, 1945; children: Arnold, Jo, David, Michael. BS, Kans. State U., 1947, MS, 1948; PhD in Physics, U. Wis., 1951. Asst. prof. U. Wyo., Laramie, 1950-51; physicist Carter Oil Co., Tulsa, 1951-55; rsch. scientist Columbia U., Dobbs Ferry, N.Y., 1955-67; prof. dept. geol. geophysics U. Wis., Madison, 1967-89, emeritus prof., 1989—. Author: Elementary Exploration Seismology, 1990, (with I. Tolstoy) Ocean Acoustics, 1966, (with H. Medwin) Acoustical Oceanography, 1977, Fundamentals of Acoustical Oceanography, 1997; (with I. Tolstoy) Ocean Acoustics, 1987. Fellow Acoustical Soc. Am. (Silver medal in Acoustical Oceanography, 1993); mem. Sigma Xi. Home: 5033 Saint Cyr Rd Middleton WI 53562-2424 Office: U Wis Weeks Hall 1215 W Dayton St Madison WI 53706-1600

CLAY, DISKIN, classical studies educator; b. Fresno, Calif., Nov. 2, 1938; s. Norman and Florence Patricia (Diskin) C.; m. Jenny Strauss, June 21, 1963 (div. 1977); 1 child, Andreia; m. Sara Christine Clark, Oct. 28, 1978 (div. 1999); children: Hilary, Christine; m. Andrea Purvis, 2000. BA, Reed Coll., 1960; MA, U. Wash., 1963, PhD, 1967. Asst. prof. Reed Coll., Portland, Oreg., 1966-70; from asst. prof. to assoc. prof. Haverford (Pa.) Coll., 1970-76; prof., Francis White prof. Greek Johns Hopkins U., Balt., 1976-88; Disting. prof. Grad. Ctr. CUNY, N.Y.C., 1988-90; RJR Nabisco prof. classical studies Duke U., Durham, N.C., 1990—. Elizabeth Whitehead prof. Am. Sch. Classical Studies in Athens, 1988-89; Blegen rsch. prof. Vassar Coll., Poughkeepsie, N.Y., 1985-86. Author: Oxychynchan Poems, 1973, Sophocles, Oedipus the King, 1978, Lucretius and Epicurus, 1983, John Locke: Questions Concerning the Law of Nature, 1990, Paradosis and Survival: Three Chapters in the History of Eipcurean Philosophy, 1997, Platonic Questions: Dialogues with the Silent Philosopher, 2000, Sophocles: Philoctetes, 2003. Fulbright fellow, Univs. Montpellier and Poitiers, France, 1960-61; Woodrow Wilson fellow, 1961-62; Am. Coun. Learned Socs., Turkey, 1975; NEH fellow, 1974-75. Mem. Am. Philol. Assn., Am. Inst. Archaeology, Dante Soc. Am., Soc. for Ancient Greek Philosophy (pres. 1991-92). Home: 2543 Sevier St Durham NC 27705 Office: Duke U Dept Classical Studies Durham NC 27708

CLAY, ERIC L. federal judge; b. Durham, N.C., Jan. 18, 1948; BA, U. N.C., 1969; JD, Yale U., 1972. Bar: Mich. 1972, U.S. Dist. Ct. (ea. dist.) Mich. 1972, U.S. Supreme Ct. 1977, U.S. Ct. Appeals (6th cir.) 1978, U.S. Dist. Ct. (we. dist.) Mich. 1987, U.S. Ct. Appeals (DC cir.) 1994. Law clk. to Judge Damon J. Keith U.S. Dist. Ct. (ea. dist.) Mich., 1972—73; private practice, 1973—97; shareholder, dir. Lewis, White & Clay, P.C., Detroit, 1997; now judge U.S. Ct. Appeals (6th cir.), Detroit, 1997—. Fellow John Hay Whitney, Yale U. Mem.: ABA, Wolverine Bar Assn., Detroit Bar Assn., Nat. Assn. Railroad Trial Counsel, Nat. Bar Assn., U.S. Sixth Jud. Conf. (life), Phi Beta Kappa. Office: Potter Stewart US Cthse 100 E 5th St Cincinnati OH 45202-3988*

CLAY, IRENE GIBSON, community activist, retired educational administrator, educator; b. Miami, Fla., Apr. 1, 1929; d. Samuel and Jane (Hanna) Gibson; m. Calvin Arthur Clay, Nov. 7, 1952; children: Sanjena, Calvina. BS, St. Augustine's Coll., Raleigh, N.C., 1950; BA, Bethune Cookman Coll., 1951; postgrad., Northwestern U., 1967; MA, Hampton U., 1969; postgrad., Fla. Atlantic U., 1970; cert. adminstrn. and supervision, 1989. Tchr. Rosenwald Elem. Sch., South Bay, Fla., 1951-59, asst. prin., 1959-87; dir. Luth. Ministries Head Start Program, Belle Glade, Fla., 1987-99, mem. adv. bd., 2003. Instr. Palm Beach Community Coll., Belle Glade, 1988-2000, Glades Cen. Community Sch. Adult Edn., 1989-2000; guardian ad litem, 1993-96; student mentor, 1993-2000. Apptd. to West County Mental Health Bd., 1995; mem. Foster Care Rev. Bd., 1996, apptd. Econ. Devel. Bd., City of Belle Glade, 1999; bd. dirs. Wee Care, Inc., 2001—; vol. Noah INc. Parenting, 2000-2003, Glades Diamond Retirement & Handicapped Cmty., 2000-2003. Mem. La Chic Mesdames, Cupidettes, Delta Sigma Theta. Democrat. Episcopalian. Home: 1216 SW Avenue C Pl Belle Glade FL 33430-3219

CLAY, LUCIUS DUBIGNON, III, surgeon, educator; b. Tampa, Fla., Oct. 11, 1948; s. Lucius Dubignon Jr. and Betty Rose (Commander) C.; m. Kathryn Ann Nay, Sept. 10, 1981; children: Lucius Dubignon IV, Geraldine Margaret. BA in History, Washington and Lee U., 1971; MD, U. Va., 1979. Surg. intern NYU/Bellevue Hosp., N.Y.C., 1979-80; surg. resident St. Luke's Hosp., N.Y.C., 1980-84; surg. fellow Ochsner Clinic, New Orleans, 1984-85; attending physician Princeton (N.J.) Med. Ctr., 1985—; clin. asst. prof. surgery Robert Wood Johnson Med. Sch., New Brunswick, N.J., 1985—; pvt. practice Princeton Surg. Assocs., 1985—; attending physician Twin County Regional Hosp., 2003—. Office: Princeton Surg Assocs 281 Witherspoon St Princeton NJ 08540-3210 also: Blve Ridge Surgical Assoc 225 Hospital Dr Galax VA 24333

CLAY, ORSON C. insurance company executive, director; b. Bountiful, Utah, July 26, 1930; s. George Phillips and Dorothy (Cliff) C.; m. Dianne Jones, June 13, 1961; children: Orson Cliff, Charles Kenneth, Elizabeth Temple. BS, Brigham Young U., 1955; MBA with distinction, Harvard U., 1959. With Continental Oil Co., various locations in, U.S.; mng. dir. Conoco A.G., Zug, Switzerland, 1962-63; dir. econs. divsn. Continental Oil Co. Ltd., London, Eng., 1964-65; gen. mgr. adminstrn. and ops. Continental Oil (U.K.) Ltd., London, 1965-66; asst. mgr. marine transp. Continental Oil, N.Y.C., 1966-68; exec. asst. fin. Pennzoil United, Inc., Houston, 1968-70; exec. v.p. fin., treas. Am. Nat. Ins. Co., Galveston, Tex., 1970-73, sr. exec. v.p., treas., 1973-76, pres., 1977-95, CEO, 1978-91, also bd. dirs., ret., 1995. Past mem. nat. adv. coun. mgmt. Brigham Young U. Past trustee United Way Galveston; past bd. dirs. Tex. Rsch. League; active LDS Ch., missionary in Can., 1951-53. 1st lt. USMCR, 1955-57. Donald Kirk David fellow Harvard U., 1959. Mem. Life Officers Mgmt. Assn. (bd. dirs. 1993-95). Home: 5682 169th Pl SE Bellevue WA 98006-5514

CLAY, PHILLIP L. academic administrator; AB with honor, U.N.C.; PhD with honor, Mass. Inst. Tech., 1975. Chancellor Mass. Inst. Tech., prof. of city planning. Chair Mass. Inst. Tech. Coun.; mem. bd. Media Lab Europe, Cambride-Mass. Inst. Tech.; assoc. provost Mass. Inst. Tech., 1994—2001, head dept. urban studies & planning, 1992—94, head assoc. depart., 1990—92, asst. dir. joint ctr. urban studies, 1980—84. Author: (books) Neighborhood Renewal: Middleclass Resettlement ; co-author (with Rob Hollister): Neighborhood Politics and Planning. Founding mem. Nat. Housing Trusts; vice pres. bd. Com. Builders; sr. adv. various numerous. Avocation: gardening. Office: Mass Inst Tech 77 Mass Ave Cambridge MA 02139-4307

CLAY, WILLIAM LACY, former congressman; b. St. Louis, Mo., Apr. 30, 1931; s. Irving C. and Luella (Hyatt) C.; m. Carol A. Johnson, Oct. 10, 1953; children: Vicki, Lacy, Michelle. BS in Polit. Sci, St. Louis U., 1953. Real estate broker, from 1964; mgr. life ins. co., 1959-61; alderman 26th Ward, St. Louis, 1959-64; bus. rep. state, county and municipal employees union, 1961-64; edn. coord. Steamfitters local 562, 1966-67; mem. U.S. Congress from 1st. Mo. dist., Washington, 1969-2001; former ranking minority mem. edn. and the workforce. Served with AUS, 1953-55. Mem. NAACP (past exec. bd. mem. St. Louis), CORE, St. Louis Jr. C. of C. Democrat.*

CLAY, WILLIAM LACY, JR., congressman; b. St. Louis, July 27, 1956; s. William L. and Carol Ann (Johnson) C.; m. Ivie Lewellen, Jan. 24, 1992. BS in Polit. Sci., U. Md., Coll. Park, 1983. Cert. paralegal; lic. real estate salesman, Mo. Mem. Mo. Gen. Assembly, Jefferson City, 1983—90, Mo. State Senate, 1991—98, U.S. Congress from 1st Mo. dist., 2001—; mem. fins svcs. com. and govt. reform com. Chmn. Mo. Jesse Jackson 1988 Presdl. Campaign; Jackson del. to 1988 Dem. Nat. Conv.; committeeman to Dem. Nat. Com.; bd. dirs. William L. Clay Scholarship and Rsch. Fund. Mem. Ams. Dem. Action (Outstanding Legis. Mo. chpt. 1985, 86). Roman Catholic. Office: US Ho of Reps 131 Cannon HOB Washington DC 20515*

CLAYBORNE, JAMES F., JR., state legislator; b. St. Louis, Mo., Dec. 29, 1963; Sen. from dist. 37 Ill. State Senate, 1995—. Office: First Ill Bank Bldg 327 Missouri Ave # 422 East Saint Louis IL 62201-3088*

CLAYCOMB, CECIL KEITH, biochemist, educator; b. Twin Falls, Idaho, Oct. 19, 1920; s. Cecil R. and Frilla E. (Reams) C.; m. Elizabeth Jane Gregg, Mar. 10, 1943; children: John K., Mary E. BS, U. Oreg., 1947, MS, 1948, PhD, 1951. Prof., head dept. biochemistry Dental Sch. U. Oreg., Portland, 1951-82, dir. minority recruitment, 1971-74, asst. to pres./dir. minority student affairs, 1974-84, coordinator basic sci. curriculum, 1951-77, chmn. admissions com., 1959-69, emeritus, 1985—; emeritus prof. biochemistry Oreg. Health and Sci. U., 1986—. Contbr. articles to sci. jours. Served to 1st lt. AUS, 1943-46. Scholar dental bd. New South Wales, Sydney, Australia, 1970 Mem. Am. Chem. Soc., Internat. Assn. Dental Research, AAAS, Res. Officers Assn., Sigma Xi. Home: 3326 SW 13th Ave Portland OR 97239-2922

CLAYCOMB, HUGH MURRAY, lawyer, author; b. Joplin, Mo., May 19, 1931; s. Hugh and Fern (Murray) C.; m. Jeanne Cavin, May 6, 1956; children: Stephen H., Scott C. BS in Bus., U. Mo., 1953, JD, 1955; LLM, U. Miss., 1969. Bar: Mo. 1955, Ark. 1957, U.S. Tax Ct. 1956, U.S. Dist. Ct. (ea. dist.) Ark. 1957, U.S. Supreme Ct. 1979. Asst. staff judge advocate USAF, 1955-57; law clerk Ark. Supreme Ct., Little Rock, 1957-58; ptnr. Gregory & Claycomb, Pine Bluff, Ark., 1958-69; partner Haley, Claycomb, Roper & Anderson, Warren, Ark., 1969—. Dir. The Strong Co., Inc., Pine Bluff, Ark., bd. dirs. Ark. Cmty. Found. Author: Arkansas Corporations, 1967, 82, 92. Pres. Jefferson County Bar Assn., Pine Bluff, 1969, Warren YMCA, 1973-75, S.E. Ark. Legal Inst., 1980-81, Ctrl. Ark. Estate Planning Coun., 1963-64; trustee Bradley County YMCA Found.; spl. assoc. justice Ark. Supreme Ct., 1978, 87. Lt. USAF, 1955-57. Recipient Pres.'s award Ark. Trial Lawyers Assn., 1985. Mem. Ark. Bar Found. (pres. 1990), Ark. Bar Assn. (sec.-treas. 1998-2000, C.E. Ransick award 1996, pres. 2002-03), Warren Rotary (pres. 1972, Paul Harris fellow). Episcopalian. Home: 619 E Cedar St Warren AR 71671-3001

CLAYMAN, GARY L. surgeon, educator; b. Cleve., Nov. 21, 1957; m. Judith K. Wolf. BS in Biology, Case Western Res. U., 1978, DDS, 1982; MD, Northeastern Ohio Univs., 1986; MS in Immunology, U. Minn., 1991. Diplomate Am. Bd. Otolaryngology/Head and Neck Surgery; lic. physician, Minn., Tex. Subintern dept. oral and maxillofacial surgery Case Western Res. U.,

Cleve., 1981—82; pvt. practice gen. dentistry, 1982—86; intern dept. gen. surgery Hennepin County Med. Ctr., Mpls., 1986—87; resident dept. otolaryngology U. Minn., Mpls., 1987—91; rsch. fellow dept. head and neck surgery M.D. Anderson Cancer Ctr., U. Tex., Houston, 1989—90, clin. fellow, 1991—92, jr. faculty assoc. dept. head and neck surgery, 1992—93, asst. prof. surgery, dir. rsch. dept. head and neck surgery, 1993—96; assoc. prof.assoc. prof. of surgery, assoc. surgeon, dir. rsch. dept. head and neck surgery M.D. Anderson Cancer Ctr., 1996—97, dep. chair, dir. rsch., assoc. prof. surgery and assoc. surgeon, 1997—2000, assoc. biologist, assoc. prof. cancer biology dept. cancer biology, 1997—2000, prof. surgery, surgeon, dir. rsch. and dept. chmn. dept. head and neck surgery, 2000—, prof. biology and biologist dept. cancer biology, 2000—. Jr. faculty assoc. dept. head and neck surgery M.D. Anderson Cancer Ctr., U. Tex., 1992-93, mem. assoc. faculty Grad. Sch. Biomed. Scis., 1993—. Ad hoc reviewer immunobiology sect. Am. Cancer Soc., 1991—; ad hoc reviewer Jour. Clin. Immunology, 1991—, New England Jour. Medicine, 1991—; reviewer Jour. Head and Neck Surgery, 1991—, Laryngoscope, 1991—, Archives of Otolaryngology/Head and Neck Surgery Tex. Medicine, 1993—; co-contbr. chpt. to: Current Therapy in Otolaryngology-Head and Neck Surgery, 5th edit.; contbr. articles to profl. jours., conf. procs. Recipient Scholastic award in Basic Sci. Rsch., Am. Soc. Head and Neck Surgery, 1992, Resident/Fellow Clin. award, 1990, Joseph A. Keller award, 1985, Career Devel. award Am. Cancer Soc., 1993—, Oncology Fellowship award Tex. divsn., 1991, Allergy and Immunology award Janssen Case History Contest, 1991; recipient Am. Cancer Soc. Career Devel. award, 1993-96, U. Tex.-M.D. Anderson Cancer Ctr. Faculty Scholar award, 1998, Am. Acad. Otolaryngology/Head and Neck Surgery Award of Honor, 2000; named Stubenbord Lectr., Cornell U. Coll. Medicine, 1997; DHHS-NIH-NCI grantee, 2002—, NCI-NIH grantee, 2001-03 Fellow Am. Acad. Otolaryngology-Head and Neck Surgery, Am. Coll. Surgeons (candidate, Med. Student fellow award 1985, Residents Rsch. award 1990); mem. AMA, Tex. MEd. Assn., Minn. Med. Assn., Harris County Med. Soc., Hennepin County Med. Soc., Ramsey County Med. Soc., Am. Acad. Facial Plastic and Reconstructive Surgery, Am. Assn. Cancer Rsch., Am. Soc. Clin. Oncology, Phi Beta Kappa, Alpha Omega. Office: U Tex MD Anderson Cancer Ct Box 69 1515 Holcombe Blvd Houston TX 77030-4009

CLAYPOOL, DAVID L. lawyer; b. Springfield, Ill., 1946; BA in History, Ill. Coll., 1968; JD with high distinction, U. Iowa, 1975. Bar: Iowa 1975. Ptnr. Dorsey & Whitney, LLP, Des Moines. Editor notes and comments Iowa Law Review, 1974-75. Capt. U.S. Army, 1968-72 Mem. Iowa State Bar Assn., Pol County Bar Assn., Nat. Assn. Bond Lawyers, Iowa Mcpl. Attys. Assn., Order of Coif. Office: Dorsey & Whitney LLP 801 Grand Ave Ste 3900 Des Moines IA 50309-2790 E-mail: claypool.david@dorseylaw.com.

CLAYSON, JANE, newscaster; b. Apr. 25, 1967; BA in Journalism, Brigham Young U., 1990. Reporter, anchor local sta., Salt Lake City, 1990—96; journalist World News Tonight ABC, L.A., 1996—99; co-host The Early Show CBS, N.Y.C., 1999—2002; corr. CBS News, 2002—. Recipient awards Soc. Profl. Journalists, Emmy, Edward R. Murrow award Radio and TV New Dirs. Am. Office: c/o CBS News 524 W 57th St New York NY 10019*

CLAYSON, SUSAN HOLLIS, art historian, educator; b. Dec. 26, 1946; BA, Wellesley Coll., 1968; MA, UCLA, 1975, PhD, 1984. Asst. prof. art history Northwestern U., Evanston, Ill., 1985-91, assoc. prof. art history, 1991-2000, assoc. dean Grad. Sch., 1995-98, prof. art history, 2001—. Asst. prof. art history U. Ill., Chgo., 1984-85. E-mail: shc@northwestern.edu.

CLAYTON, ANITA LOUISE, psychiatrist, physician; MD, U. of Va., 1982. Psychiatrist Nat. Bd. of Psychiatry, 1989. Prof. and vice chair, dept. of psychiat. medicine U. of Va. Health Sys., Charlottesville, Va., 1990—; asst. prof., dept. of psychiatry Uniformed Services U. of the Health Sciences, Bethesda, Md., 1988—2000. Vice chair, dept of psychiat. medicine U. of Va. Health Sys., Charlottesville, Va., 1992—. Editor (chapter author): (book) Women's Mental Health: A Comprehensive Textbook. Cdr USNR, 1978—94. Office: Univ of Virginia Health System 2955 Ivy Rd Ste 210 Charlottesville VA 22908 Office Fax: 434-243-4743.

CLAYTON, ANN ALLMAN, music educator, minister; b. Knoxville, Tenn., Jan. 6, 1951; d. Samuel Herbert and Sarah Aldridge Allman; m. Max I. Clayton, June 1, 1980; children: Sara, Lyle. B Music Edn., Oklahoma City U., 1973; postgrad., Southwestern Okla. State U., 1977, Cen. State U., Edmond, Okla., 1978, Okla. State U., 1983. Cert. secondary edn. Band/vocal music dir. Okarche (Okla.) Pub. Schs., 1974—78; band dir. Seiling (Okla.) Pub. Schs., 1978—80; band/vocal music dir. Pleasant View Sch., Stillwater, Okla., 1981—83; band dir., supr. music dept. Frederick (Okla.) Pub. Schs., 1984—. Condr. honor bands and clinics, Geary, Clinton, Hollis, Kingfisher, 1974—. Youth choir dir. United Meth. Ch., Frederick, 1993—2002. Mem.: Shortgrass Band Dirs. Assn. (pres. 1988—90), Southwestern Oklah. Band Dirs. Assn. (chair honor band 2002—), Music Educators Nat. Conf., Okla. Music Educators Assn. United Methodist. Avocations: snow skiing, water sports, camping. Office: Frederick Pub Schs 312 N 15th Frederick OK 73542

CLAYTON, APRIL DIANE, music educator, flutist; b. Salt Lake City, Dec. 13, 1974; d. Archer Robert and Julia Emily Bryson Clayton. Postgrad., Oberlin Coll., 1992—94; MusB, U. Cinn., 1994, MusM, 1996; D in Musical Arts, Juilliard Sch., 2001. Asst. prof. flute Brigham Young U., Provo, Utah, 2000—; flutist Orpheus Winds Quintet, Provo, Utah, 2000—. Flutist Sarasota (Fla.) Music Festival, 1998; prin. flute, concerto soloist Lyric Theatre Orch., Hoboken, NJ, 1998—2000; prin. flute Jupiter Symphony, N.Y.C., NY, 1999—2000; flutist Nat. Repertory Orch., Breckenridge, Colo., 2001. Musician: Carnegie Hall Solo Recital Debut (Artists' Internat. NY Debut award, 2002), N.Y. performances at Carnegie Hall, Alice Tully Hall, Summergarden Concert Series at Mus. Modern Art, Symphony Space, live broadcast on WQXR radio, performances in Incheon Cultural Arts Ctr., Seoul Cais Art Gallery, South Korea (Juilliard Outreach grant (with pianist Jihea Hong), BYU Profl. Devel. grant, 2002), Aspen Contemporary Ensemble (Fellow to Aspen Music Festival, 1999), Music Teachers' National Assn. Woodwind Competition, Jefferson Symphony Young Artist Competition (First pl. instrumental divsn., 1991), Cinn. Philharmonia Concerto Competition (1st place, 1995), Moscow Conservatory Residency with The New Juilliard Ensemble, Flutist in residence at the Holder's Season Festival in Barbados. Music chairperson Local Congregation, N.Y.C., 1997—99, Provo, Utah, 2002. Mem.: Am. Fedn. Musicians, Coll. Music Soc., Nat. Flute Assn., Utah Flute Assn. (bd. mem., publicity dir. 2000—02). Avocations: travel, hiking, running, investing, reading. Home: 2311 N 390 E Provo UT 84604 Office: Brigham Young Univ C550 Harris Fine Arts Ctr Provo UT 84602 Office Fax: 801-422-0533. E-mail: april_clayton@byu.edu.

CLAYTON, BRUCE DAVID, pharmacology educator; b. Grand Island, Nebr., Mar. 9, 1947; s. John David and Eloise Regnier (Camp) C.; m. Francine Evelyn Purdy, June 19, 1971; children: Sarah Elizabeth, Beth Anne. Student, Hastings Coll., 1965-67; BS, U. Nebr., 1970; D Pharmacy, U. Mich., 1973. Resident U. Mich., 1972-74; asst. prof. clin. pharmacy Creighton U., Omaha, 1974-77; assoc. prof. Coll. Pharmacy, U. Nebr. Med. Ctr., Omaha, 1978-85, vice chmn. dept. pharmacy practice, 1978-84, interim chmn., 1984-85; prof., chmn. dept. pharmacy practice U. Ark. for Med. Scis., Little Rock, 1985-87, prof. pharmacy practice, 1985-89; prof. Coll. Pharmacy, Butler U., Indpls., 1989—, assoc. dean, 1989-2000, acting dean, 1999-2000, chmn. dept. pharmacy practice, 2001. Unit coord. perinatal pharmacy svcs. Univ. Hosps., Omaha, 1978-80; clin. pharmacist pediatrics Ark. Children's Hosp., Little Rock, 1986-89; Ciba-Geigy vis. prof., Australia and N.Z., 1979; S.E. Wright traveling fellow Pharm. Soc. Australia, 1983; lectr. in field. Author: (with S.A. Ryan) Handbook of Practical Pharmacology, 1977, 2d edit., 1980; (with J.E. Squire) Basic Pharmacology for Nurses, 7th edit., 1981, Handbook of Pharmacology in Nursing, 1984, Handbook of Pharmacology, 1987; (with Yvonne Stock) Basic Pharmacology for Nurses, 11th edit., 1997, 12th edit., 2001; contbr. articles to profl. jours. Named Nebr. Hosp. Pharmacist of Yr., 1978; recipient Bristol award for Professionalism, 1970, Last Lecture award, Butler U., 2001, Bowl of Hygeia award, 2002. Mem. Nebr. Soc. Hosp. Pharmacists (dir. 1977-80, pres. 1978-79), Ind. Soc. Hosp. Pharmacists, Am. Soc. Hosp. Pharmacists (coun. on orgnl. affairs 1979-82, com. on nominations 1980-85, chmn. 1985, ho. of dels. 1980-88, coun. on ednl. affairs 1987-89, chmn. 1989), Am. Pharm. Assn. (APHA-PAC bd. govs. 1994-96), Ind. Pharm. Assn. (bd. dirs. 1991-97, 98-99, v.p. 1995-96, pres.-elect 1996-97, pres. 1997-98), Ind. Pharmacists Action Com. (bd. dirs. 1991—), Ind. Pharmacists Alliance (pres. 1998, past pres. 1999), Ctrl. Ind. Options in Edn. Inc. (pres. bd. dirs., 2002—), Am. Assn. Colls. Pharmacy, Rho Chi.

CLAYTON, CLAUDE F., JR., lawyer; b. Tupelo, Miss., June 15, 1948; s. Claude F. and Bronson (Munday) C.; children from a previous marriage: Frances, Claude III; m. Tacey Clark, July 25, 1997. Student, Stanton Mil. Acad., 1966; BA, Tulane U., 1971; JD, U. Miss., 1973. Bar: Miss. 1973. Mem. judiciary com. U.S. Senate, Washington, 1968; ptnr. Mitchell, Voge, Clayton and Beasley, Tupelo, 1973-85, Mitchell, McNutt & Sams, Tupelo, 1985—2001; pres. Mitchell, McNutt & Sams, Tupelo, 1995—97; ptnr. Clayton Law Firm, PLLC, 2001—03, Clayton O'Donnell Walsh, PLLC, 2003—. Mem. complaints tribunal Supreme Ct. Miss., 1990-93; speaker Miss. Jud. Coll., also various trial practice and ethics seminars; special justice Miss. Supreme Ct., 2000. Mem. ABA (young lawyers div., chmn. justice dept. liaison com. 1978-79), Miss. State Bar (pres. fellows of young lawyers 1990-91, vice chmn. specialization com. 1990-92, chmn., 1980-82, lawyer econs. com. 1988-89, ethics com. 1982-85, vice chmn. continuing legal edn. com. 1980-81, law jour.-law sch. liaison com. 1974-76, various coms. young lawyers sect. 1985-90, bd. dirs. 1975-80), Miss. Def. Lawyers Assn. (bd. dirs. 1992-95), Def. Rsch. Inst., Internat. Assn. Def. Counsel. Office: Clayton O'Donnell Walsh PLLC 115 N Broadway PO Box 755 Tupelo MS 38802-4869 E-mail: cclayton@northmslaw.com.

CLAYTON, DAVID A(LVIN), biology educator; b. Joliet, Ill., Feb. 5, 1944; m. Lauretta Swanson, 1965; children: Lindsay, Ryan, Megan. BS, No. Ill. U., 1965; PhD in Biophysics and Chemistry, Calif. Inst. Tech., 1970. Asst. prof. pathology Stanford U., 1970—76, assoc. prof., 1976—82, prof., 1982—89, prof. devel. biology, 1989—; sr. sci. officer Howard Hughes Med. Inst., 1996—99, v.p. sci. devel., 2000—02, v.p., chief scientific officer, 2002—. Mem. adv. com. nucleic acids and protein synthesis, Am. Cancer Soc., 1976-80; mem. molecular biology study sect., NIH, 1982-86, chmn., 1984-86; mem. sci. rev. bd. Howard Hughes Med. Inst., 1993-96; mem. nat. adv. bd. Gen. Med. Sci. Coun., 1996-99; Fisher lectr. So. Ill. U., 1989.. Recipient Warner-Lambert/Parke Davis award, 1982. Mem. Inst. Medicine Nat. Acad. Sci., Am. Soc. Biochemistry and Molecular Biology.

CLAYTON, DONALD DELBERT, astrophysicist, nuclear physicist, educator; b. Shenandoah, Iowa, Mar. 18, 1935; s. Delbert Homer and Avis (Kembery) C.; children: Donald, Devon, Alia, Andrew; m. Nancy McBride. BS, So. Meth. U., 1956; PhD, Calif. Inst. Tech., 1962. Rsch. fellow in physics Calif. Inst. Tech., 1961-63; faculty Rice U., Houston, 1963-65, assoc. prof. physics and space sci., 1965-69; prof. physics and space sci., faculty assoc. Wiess Coll., 1969-77, Andrew Hays Buchanan prof. astrophysics, 1975-89; prof. physics and astronomy Clemson (S.C.) U., S.C., 1989—, centennial prof., 1996—. Vis. assoc. physics Calif. Inst. Tech., 1966-67; vis. fellow Inst. Theoretical Astronomy, Cambridge, summers 1967-72. Author: Principles of Stellar Evolution and Nucleosynthesis, 1968, The Dark Night Sky, 1975, The Joshua Factor, 1986, Photo Archive for History of Nuclear Astrophysics, 2000, A Walking Tour of Residential Seneca, 2001, Handbook of Isotopes in the Cosmos, 2003; contbr. over 200 articles to profl. jours. Recipient Humboldt award Max Planck Inst., Heidelberg, 1977, 82, Exceptional Sci. Achievement medal NASA, 1992, Disting. Alumni award So. Meth. U., 1993, S.C. Gov.'s award for sci. excellence, 1994, Jesse Beams award, 1998; Sloan fellow, 1966-70, Fulbright fellow, Heidelberg, 1979-80. Fellow Am. Phys. Soc. (Jesse W. Beams medal 1998), Meteoritical Soc. (Leonard medal 1991), Am. Acad. Arts and Scis.; mem. AAAS, Am. Astron. Soc., Royal Astron. Soc. (G.H. Darwin lectr. 1981), Cosmos Club (Washington), Phi Beta Kappa, Sigma Xi. Office: Clemson U Dept Physics Astronomy Clemson SC 29634-0978 E-mail: cdonald@clemson.edu. *My life centers on love of nature. As a cosmologist studying the universe, I find the truth to be stranger than fiction, and the commonplace to be the spectacular. To share this joy with laymen, I wrote a personal memoir, The Dark Night Sky, and a scientific novel, The Joshua Factor.*

CLAYTON, EDDIE J. small business owner, writer; s. Robert Early and Florine Clayton; life ptnr. Sia'kendah Lillie Hobdy; children: Aljzana Pamri, Justice Uosa. Fin. and ins. advisor PRIMERICA, LA, Calif., 1991—93; founder and c.e.o C. P. Heritage, Inc, Las Vegas, 1998—; pub. C. P. Heritage, Inc., 1998—. Author: (non-fiction book) Please, Don't Use the 'N-Word' and Other Racial Slurs!. Avocations: lexicostatistics, physical fitness, and, traveling. E-mail: cph@cpheritage.com.

CLAYTON, ELLEN WRIGHT, medical educator, pediatrician; b. Houston, June 22, 1952; d. James Thomas and Maidel Wright; m. John Bunyan Clayton IV, 1982. BS, Duke U., 1974; JD, Yale U., 1979; MD, Harvard U., 1985. Diplomate Am. Bd. Pediat. Clk. to Hon. John C. Godbold U.S. Ct. Appeals (5th cir.), Montgomery, Ala., 1979-80; assoc. Vinson & Elkins, Houston, 1980-81; resident in pediat. U. Wis., Madison, 1985-88; asst. prof. Vanderbilt U., Nashville, 1988-96, assoc. prof., 1996-99, prof. pediat., law, genetics and health policy, 1999—, dir. Ctr. for Genetics and Health Policy. Mem. health svcs. policy bd. Inst. of Medicine, 2002—, mem. com. on the use of 3d party rsch. with human rsch. participants, 2002—03. Editor-in-chief: Jour. Law, Medicine and Ethics, 1997—2001. Mem. Nat. Adv. Coun. for Human Genome Rsch., Bethesda, Md., 1995-98. Fellow Am. Acad. Pediat.; mem. ABA (vice chair clin. ethics interest group health law sect. 1998-01), Am. Soc. Law, Medicine and Ethics (pres. 1996-97, Jay Healey award health law tchrs. sect. 1999), Phi Beta Kappa. Office: Ctr for Genetics and Health Policy 507A Light Hall Nashville TN 37232-0165

CLAYTON, EVA M. congresswoman, commissioner; b. Savannah, Ga., Sept. 16, 1934; m. Theaoseus T. Clayton; children: Theaoseus Jr., Martin, Reuben, Joanne. BS, Johnson C. Smith U., 1955; MS, NC Central U., 1965. Founder, pres. Tech. Resources Internat., NC, 1981—92; mem. U.S. Congress from 1st N.C. dist., Washington, 1993—; mem. agriculture com.; mem. com. on budget. Mem. Warren County NC Bd. Commrs., 1982—92, chair, 1982—90. Democrat. Presbyterian. Office: US Ho of Reps 2440 Rayburn Bldg Washington DC 20515-3301

CLAYTON, JAMES EDWIN, journalist; b. Johnston City, Ill., Nov. 14, 1929; s. John Herman and Vinnie Ethel (Black) C.; m. Elise Brookfield Heinz, June 3, 1961; children— Jonathan Brown, David Lake. BS, U. Ill., 1953; MPA, Princeton, 1956. Reporter So. Illinoisan, Carbondale, Ill., 1951-52; reporter Washington Post, 1956-64, asst. mng. editor, 1964-67, 72-74, editorial writer, 1967-72, assoc. editor, 1974-82; assoc. dir. Reporter's Com. for Freedom of Press, 1984; sr. fellow Airlie Found., 1984-94. Vis. lectr. Northwestern U., 1966-67, Johns Hopkins, 1970. Author: The Making of Justice, 1964; editor: The Rights of Free Men, 1984. Chmn. bd. trustees Sofia Am. Schs., Inc. Served to 1st lt. AUS, 1951-52. Recipient Interpretive Reporting awards Washington Newspaper Guild, 1959, 62, 63, Distinguished Washington Correspondence award Sigma Delta Chi, 1960, Worth Bingham prize, 1970, George Polk Meml. award for editorial writing, 1970 Mem.: Princeton (Washington, N.Y.C.). Baptist. Home: 2728 N Fillmore St Arlington VA 22207-4936

CLAYTON, JOHN, retired engineering executive and consultant; b. Marlboro, Mass., Aug. 16, 1930; s. John and Esther Elizabeth (Gray) C.; m. Carol Ann Kopp, Feb. 19, 1954; children: Susan A., Dianne G., Jacqueline. Various positions, 1948-52; with Tech. Instrument Corp., Acton, Mass., 1952-56; engring. mgr. R&D Waters Mfg. Inc., Wayland, Mass., 1956-94; ret., 1994. Cons. in field. Active Stow Bd. Selectmen; clk. Stow Zoning Bd. Appeals; pres. Stow Cmty. Housing Corp., Stow Elderly Housing Corp.; radio officer Mass. Emergency Mgmt. Agy., Stow, 1995-2001. Mem.: IEEE (life). Republican. Achievements include 9 patents in electro-mechanical transducers and conductive plastics. Home and Office: 15 Walnut Ridge Rd Stow MA 01775-1109 E-mail: jackclaytn@cs.com.

CLAYTON, JOHN CHARLES, scientist, researcher; b. Pittston, Pa., June 15, 1924; s. Charles Conrad and Madeline Eleanor (Hastings) Clayton; m. Mary Catherine Mulvaney, Aug. 9, 1968. BS, St. Joseph's U., 1949; MS, U. Pa., 1950, PhD, 1953. Postdoctoral fellow U. Pa., Phila., 1953—55; sr. scientist Westinghouse Electric Corp., Pitts., 1954—81, fellow, scientist, 1981—. Sec., dir. Mulvaney Corp., Pitts. Contbr. chapters to books; patentee in field. Cpl. U.S. Army, 1943—45, ETO. Fellow: AAAS, Am. Inst. Chemists; mem.: Am. Soc. Metals, Am. Nuc. Soc., Am. Ceramic Soc., Am. Chem. Soc., NY Acad. Scis., South Hills Cotillion Club (officer 1983—85), Pitts. Chemists Club (officer 1990—), Pitts. Ski Club (officer 1960—70), Am. Youth Hostels Club (officer Pitts. br. 1960—68), Toastmasters Internat. Club (area gov. Western Pa. br. 1981—83, officer Pitts. br. 1976—), Phi Lambda Upsilon, Alpha Chi Sigma. Roman Catholic. Avocations: skiing, ice skating, hiking, sailing, gardening. Home: 1663 Citation Dr Library PA 15129-8832 Office: Westinghouse Electric Corp Bettis Atomic Power Lab PO Box 79 West Mifflin PA 15122-0079

CLAYTON, JOHN MIDDLETON, JR., development officer; b. West Grove, Pa., May 4, 1941; s. John Middleton and Esther Marion (Myers) C.; m. Norma Louise Towne, Aug. 17, 1968; 1 child, Signe Louisa. BS, West Chester U., 1963; MS, Drexel U., 1966. Librarian Penn's Grove (N.J.) High Sch., 1963-66; tchr. Avon-Grove High Sch., West Grove, 1966-67; reader svcs. librarian U. Del., Newark, 1967-69, archivist, 1969-89, dir. records mgmt., 1975-89, asst. dir. univ. devel., 1989-97, asst. dir. planned giving, 1997—. Cons. Bloomsburg (Pa.) U., 1988-89. Mem. revenue sharing screening com. City of Newark, 1985-88; sec., bd. dirs. Oaklands Civic Assn., Newark, 1988-89; clk. of session 1st and Ctrl. Presbyn. Ch., Wilmington, Del., 1988, ruling elder, 1995-99; sec. Friends of Goodstay Gardens, 1995—; mem. adv. com. Sch. of Music West Chester U., 1996—; bd. dir. Presbyn. Hist. Soc., 1979-85. Mem. Lincoln Club Del. Republican. Home: 217 Walker Way Newark DE 19711-6121

CLAYTON, JONATHAN ALAN, banker; b. New Brunswick, N.J., Jan. 20, 1937; s. Llewellyn H. and Florence E. (Denton) C.; m. Carole Elaine Jolly, Sept. 23, 1961; children— David Alan, Susan Beth. BA in History, Lafayette Coll., 1959; postgrad., NYU Law Sch., 1959, N.Y. U. Grad. Sch. Bus. Adminstrn., 1961-64; grad., Robert Morris Loan Mgmt. Seminar, 1973. Trainee mgmt. program Mfrs. Hanover Trust Co., N.Y.C., 1961-64, asst. sec., 1966-69, asst. v.p., 1969-71, v.p., 1971-80, officer in charge credit and fin. group, 1972-74, officer in charge hdqrs. br., 1974-76, dep. officer in charge, 1976-78, dep. mgr. Bklyn. and S.I. brs., 1978-80, sr. v.p. Bklyn. and S.I. comml. and retail banking, 1980-83, sr. v.p. comml. and retail banking, 1983-85, sr. v.p. comml. ctrs. and brs., 1986-87, sr. v.p., mgr. Bus. Banking Group, 1987-90, mng. dir., gen. mgr. profl. credit unit, 1990-92; mng. dir., middle market banking group, asset mgmt. Chem. Bank, N.Y.C., 1992; ret., 1992; instr. comml. banking Stonier Grad. Sch. Banking Rutgers U., New Brunswick, N.J., 1973-84, N.Y. State Bankers Assn. Exec. Devel. Schs., West Point, 1973-81, Syracuse, 1979-81. Mem. bd. govs. N.Y. chpt. Robert Morris Associates, 1979-81 Vice pres. bd. trustees, treas., chmn. fin. com. Rutgers Preparatory Sch., Somerset, N.J., 1975-78; bd. regents St. Francis Coll., Bklyn., 1981— ; elder First Presbyn. Ch., Cranbury, N.J., 1981-83; v.p. Men's Fellowship, 1981-83; bd. dirs. Bklyn. Borough Hall Restoration Found. Served from 2d. lt. to capt. U.S. Army, 1959-66. Mem. N.Y. State Bankers Assn. (mem. edn. com. 1975-81), Downtown Bklyn. Devel. Assn. (vice chmn., dir. 1981-83), N.Y.C. C. of C., Bklyn. C. of C. (dir. 1980-82), Am. Arbitration Assn. (arbitrator 1971—) Clubs: Bklyn, Mcpl. of Bklyn, Marco Polo, Candy Execs. and Affiliated Industries. Lodges: Lions (Cranbury) (dir. 1981-82). Republican. Office: 270 Park Ave New York NY 10017-2014

CLAYTON, KATY, elementary education educator; b. Bellefonte, Pa., Feb. 21, 1956; d. Everette Lee and Donna June (Trowbridge) Swinney; m. Charles Edward Clayton Jr., July 15, 1977; children: Quinton, Meredith, Zachary. BS in Edn., Southwest Tex. State U., 1978, MEd in Reading, 1983. Tchr. kindergarten Lockhart (Tex.) Pub. Schs., 1978-80; owner pvt. day care San Marcos, Tex., 1980-84; tchr. 1st grade Crockett Elem. Sch., San Marcos, Tex., 1984-89, tchr. 2d grade, 1989-93, reading specialist, 1993—. Dept. leader Crockett Elem. Sch., 1995-2000;, 02— cons. S.W. Tex. Tchr. Ctr., San Marcos, 1991-92; trained Help One Student to Succeed, 1996—. Bd. dirs. Little League, San Marcos, 1987-89, Habitat for Humanity, 2002—; deacon 1st Christian Ch., San Marcos, 1988-92; presenter 23d Annual Tex. State Reading Assn. Conf., The Young Child and Literacy. Recipient Nat. Exemplary award HOSTS, 1997—. Mem.: Reading Recovery Tchrs., Internat. Reading Assn., Tex. Classroom Tchrs. Assn. (pres. 1990—91), San Marcos Bluebonnet Lions Club (sec. 1998—2001). Democrat. Mem. Christian Ch. (Disciples Of Christ). Avocations: reading, needle work, crafts, volksmarching. Home: 513 Willow Creek Cir San Marcos TX 78666-5025 Office: Crockett Elem Sch 1300 Girard St San Marcos TX 78666-2813 E-mail: katy.clayton@san-marcos.isd.tenet.edu.

CLAYTON, LAWRENCE OTTO, minister, writer, educator, alcohol and drug counselor; b. Fallon, Nev., Mar. 24, 1945; s. Lawrence Otto and Nathalie E. (Gow) C.; m. Janice Hodge, 1978 (div. 1988); children: Rebecca, Larry; m. Belinda Baker, 1996; stepchildren: Joy, Erin. BS summa cum laude, Tex. Wesleyan Coll., Ft. Worth, Tex., 1976; postgrad., Emory U., Atlanta, 1976-77; MDiv, Tex. Christian U., 1978; PhD, Tex. Woman's U., 1983; MA, U. Ctrl. Okla., 1997. Ordained minister United Christian Ministries Internat., 2001. Exec. dir. Johnson County Mental Health Clinic, Cleburne, Tex., 1981—83; adminstr. United Meth. Counseling Svcs., 1983—88; exec. dir. Okla. Family Inst., 1988—95; ret., 1996; assoc. pastor Gospel Celebration Fellowship, Oklahoma City, 1996—98; freelance author Oklahoma City, 1995—. Cons. Great Plains Correctional Facility, Hinton, Okla., 1993—96; prof. Mid-Am. Bible Coll., Oklahoma City, 1991—95, Bacone Coll., Muskogee, Okla., 1992—94. Author: Assessment and Management of the Suicidal Adolescent, 1990, Coping with Depression, 1990, Coping with a Drug Abusing Parent, 1991, Coping with Being Gifted, 1991, Coping with a Learning Disability, 1992, Careers in Psychology, 1992, Coping with Sports Injuries, 1992, Designer Drugs, 1993, Barbiturates and Other Depressants, 1994, Amphetamines and Other Stimulants, 1994, The Professional Alcohol and Drug Counselor Supervisor's Handbook, 1993, All You Need to Know About Sports Injuries, 1994, Steroids, 1995, Working Together Against Drug Addiction, 1996, Drugs and Drug Testing, 1997, Tranquilizers, 1997, Alcohol, 1999, Diet Pills, 1999, Drug Testing, 2001, Delayed Gratification, 2001, Careers in Behavioral Science, 2002, Managing Suicidal People, 2003, others; assoc. editor Family Perspective, 1987-95; columnist Woman's Weekly, 1991-93, Growthline, 1992-95. Vol. and trainer of ombudsman Rockland County Office of Aging, 2003—. With U.S. Army, 1962-68. Mem. Okla. Inst. Adult Children of Alcoholics (pres. 1987-91), Okla. Drug and Alcohol Profl. Counselors Cert. Bd. (vice chmn. 1988-90, pres. 1990-95, Counselor of Yr., 1994) Republican. Avocations: snorkeling, rock collecting, restoring classic cars. Home: PO Box 270605 Oklahoma City OK 73137

CLAYTON, M. COURTLAND, engineering, manufacturing sourcing and health wellness and internet technology consultant; b. Norwich, Conn., Feb. 19, 1938; s. Marvin C. and Peggy (Farmer) Clayton; children: Cheryll, Michelle, Deborah. BS in Indsl. Engring., Purdue U., 1963; MBA, U. Louisville, 1971; MPA, Penn. State U., 1986; grad., U.S. Army War Coll., 1986. Registered profl. engr., Calif., Ky., Mo., Pa.; cert. purchasing mgr., mfg. engr., mfg. mgr., profl. mgmt. cons., logistician, exec. in logistics. Mgr. shop ops. GE Appliances, Louisville, 1968-69, prog. mgr. mfg. engring., 1969-71, contracting agt. material handling and computer systems, 1973-76, program mgr., material resource systems, 1976-80, mgr., advance and indirect material purchasing, 1980-82, program mgr., purchasing programs, 1982-87, program mgr., sourcing integration, 1987-89, mgr. supplier productivity engring., 1989-93, purchasing mgr. range products bus., 1993; prin. The Clayton Group, Louisville, 1993-94; mgr. range bus. purchasing GE Appliances, Louisville, 1992-94; mgr. Strategic Sourcing, Louisville, 1994; mfg. mgr. engring. Emerson Electric Co., St. Louis, 1971-72; corp. engring. and mfg. cons. AMEDCO, Springfield, Mo., 1972-73; pres. Clayton Cons., Louisville, Ky., 1994—. Prin. The Clayton Group, Global Cons., sr. exec. dir. NuSkin, Pharmanex, Big Planet, 1990—. Patentee in field. Chmn. bd. deacons Bapt. Ch., Louisville, 1975; dir. ch. choir Bapt. Ch., Arkansas City, Kans., 1963. Col. U.S. Army, 1963—93. Named to Honorable Order of Ky. Cols. Mem. Res. Officers Assn. (exec. bd., pres. 1984, nat. councilman 1990-94), Ky. Res. Officers Assn., Inst. Indsl. Engrs., Assn. Internal Mgmt. Cons., Assn. of U.S. Army, Purdue Alumni Assn., U. Louisville Alumni Assn., Pa. State Alumni Assn., Army War Coll. Alumni Assn. Republican. Avocations: piano, gardening, sports. Home and Office: 8215 Camberley Dr Louisville KY 40222-5534

CLAYTON, NANCY YUVAL, music educator, writer; b. Castroville, Tex., July 19, 1949; d. Abner Ewing and Yuval Cleone (King) C. BS in Music Edn., S.W. Tex. State U., 1971; postgrad., Tex. Tech. U., 1993-94. Cert. instrumental music tchr., libr., Tex. Feature writer Citizen News newspaper, San Antonio, 1976-83; TV news anchor, reporter Sta. KENS-TV, San Antonio, 1976-79;

prodr., reporter U.S. Farm Report Sta. WGN-TV, Chgo., 1978-82; band and color guard dir. Burbank H.S., San Antonio, 1981-89; band dir. Lackland Ind. Sch. Dist., Lackland AFB, Tex., 1989-92; percussion instr. Northside Idn. Sch. Dist., San Antonio, 1992-93; writer Lowell House Juveniles, L.A., 1997—. Sch. assembly performer Civil War Drum and Story Programs, San Antonio, 1992—; children's lit. cons. US Civil War Ctr., Baton Rouge, 1996—. Author: Strange But True Civil War Stories, 1999, Draw History Civil War, 1999; composer: (percussion music) Drum Line on Parade, 1982, Melody Cadences, Vol. I and II, 1981. Citywide band festival prodr. Fiesta San Antonio Commn., 1981-93; mem. publicity com. Bexar county Jr. Livestock Show, San Antonio, 1978-80; charter mem. Order of the Cascaron Fiesta San Antonio; assoc. U.S. Civil War Ctr., La. State U. Named Pub. News Media Person of Yr., Alamo Soil and Water Conservation, 1979, S.W. Tex. Women-The First 100 Yrs. award S.W. Tex. State U., 2000. Mem. ASCAP, Nat. Assn. Rudimental Drummers. Baptist. Avocations: genealogy, mountain trout fishing, golf, civil war book collecting. E-mail: nyclay@rionet.cc.

CLAYTON, ORVILLE WOOLFORD, surgeon; b. Ft. Payne, Ala., May 30, 1921; s. Olney Walker Clayton and Flora Pauline Wheeler; m. Dorothy Nell Meadows, June 20, 1944; children: Stephen W., Kathy L. Stockham, Shelley E. BA, U. Ala., Tuscaloosa, 1943; B in Medicine, Northwestern U., 1945, MD, 1946. Post surgeon U.S. Army, Huntsville, Ala., 1946-48; chief resident surgery Univ. Hosp., Birmingham, Ala., 1948; chief surgery Bapt. Med. Montclair, Birmingham, 1969-74, pres. staff, 1982; clin. assoc. prof. surgery U. Ala., Birmingham, 1973-91. Bd. dirs. Am. Pulmonary Inst., Birmingham, 1996-99. Capt. U.S. Army, 1946-48. Fellow ACS, So. Thoracic Soc. Avocations: gardening, genealogy. Home: 3133 Ryecroft Rd Birmingham AL 35223-2715

CLAYTON, PAMELA SANDERS, special education educator; b. Sulphur Springs, Tex., Feb. 8, 1952; d. Carl Louis Sanders, Jr. and Beatrice Coletha Sanders; children: Chad, Cicely. BS, E. Tex. State U., 1974, MEd, 1991. Kindergarten cert., mental retardation cert. Tchr. Saltillo ISD, 1976—77, resource specialist, tchr., 1977—80, Lamar Elem. Sch., Sulphur Springs, 1980—98, Sulphur Springs H.S., 1998—. Dir. student coun., uil prose & poetry dir., taas tutorial coach Sulphur Springs H.S., 1999—2002. Actor: (plays) A Christmas Carol, 1997 (Best Supporting Actress, 1998); singer: (concert) N.E. Tex. Choral Soc., 1998. Mem. allocation com. Hopkins County United Way, Sulphur Springs, 2000—01; bd. dirs. Lakes Regional MHMR, Terrell, Tex., 1997—, Sulphur Springs Pub. Libr., 1994—96. Mem.: Tex. Classroom Tchrs., Delta Kappa Gamma. Methodist. Avocations: poetry, rollercoaster riding, reading, piano. Home: 404 Lamar St Sulphur Springs TX 75482 Office: Sulphur Springs ISD 1200 Connally St Sulphur Springs TX 75482 Office Fax: (903)439-6116. Personal E-mail: pclayton@ssisd.net.

CLAYTON, PAUL DOUGLAS, health care administrator; b. Salt Lake City, Mar. 9, 1943; PhD in Physics, U. Ariz. Dir. Ctr. for Advanced Tech., Columbia Presbyn. Med. Ctr., 1994-98, dir. clin. info. svc., 1992-98; chmn., prof. med. info. Columbia U., 1987-98; info. sys. dir., dir. clin. info. sys. Intermountain Health Care, 1998—; prof. med. info. U. Utah, 2001—. Mem. Inst. Medicine of Nat. Acad. Sci., Am. Med. Info. Assn. (pres. 1998-99).

CLAYTON, RAYMOND ARTHUR, purchasing executive; b. Newark, May 22, 1930; s. John Raymond and Marion Caroline (Haster) C.; m. Barbara Russell Langdon, Feb. 11, 1956; children: Matthew Arthur, Mark Thomas. BSBA, NYU, 1951, MBA in Indsl. Rels., 1962. Lifetime cert. purchasing mgr. Minor league baseball player Cin. Reds, Inc., Columbia, S.C., 1951, Detroit Tigers, Jamestown, N.Y., 1954; adminstrv. staff Western Elec. Co., Inc., N.Y.C., 1954-55, sect. chief, contract buyer, 1956-59; dept. chief, contract buyer Bell Telephone Labs., Inc., Whippany, N.J., 1960-63, exec. asst., 1964-67, head svc. ops. North Andover, Mass., 1968-74, head purchasing Whippany, N.J., 1975-76, Murray Hill, N.J., 1977-78, 81-83, head personnel systems Short Hills, N.J., 1979-80; mgr. purchasing, resident AT&T Bell Labs. North N.J. AT&T Techs. Inc., 1984-87; assoc. dir. materials mgmt. inst. Bloomfield (N.J.) Coll., 1989-95, dir., 1996-98; pvt. practice as cons. purchasing and materials mgmt. Stanton, N.J., 1989—. Contbr. articles to profl. jours. Dir. Prep Club Greater Lawrence (Mass.) C. of C., 1969-74, v.p. socio-econ. divsn., 1972; organizer, advisor Jr. Achievement, Lawrence, 1970-74; pres. Boxford (Mass.) Athletic Assn., 1973-74; treas., mem. exec. com. Union (N.J.) County Econ. Devel. Corp., 1979-83. Mil. svc., 1952-53, Korea. Mem. Nat. Assn. Purchasing Mgmt. (fin. com., 2000—, policy com., 2000—, orgn. and planning com. 1994-97, J. Shipman award com. 1996, 98, nat. bd. dirs. 1992-94, 2000—, asst. dir. 1990-91, N.J. chpt. program chair 1979-83, exec. v.p. 1983-84, pres. 1984-85, 89-90, dir. nat. affairs 1985-86, 90-91, 93-94, 96-97, trustee 1984-2000, dir. ednl. liaison 1999—, mktg. mgr. 2000, C.P.M. instr. 1989—, W.M. Moon award 1991, H.L. Erlicher award 1996, J. Shipman gold medal 2001), Luth. Ch. Mo. Synod (N.J. dist. fin. com. 1992-95, bd. dirs. 1995—, chair 2000—, chair ops. coun. 1995—). Republican. Lutheran. Avocations: hiking, tennis, coaching little league baseball. Home: PO Box 145 Stanton NJ 08885-0145 E-mail: rayclayton@mapm.org.

CLAYTON, RAYMOND EDWARD, government official; b. Saskatoon, Sask., Can., Nov. 6, 1942; m. Joan Ann Snodgrass, Sept. 21, 1963; children: Grant, Sheila, Matthew, Daniel. B. of Commerce, U. Sask., 1964; MA in Econs., 1965. Dir. rsch. Dept. Mcpl. Affars, Govt. Sask., Regina, 1965-67, Dept. Edn., Govt. Sask., Regina, 1967-69, dir. ednl. adminstrn., 1969-77, dep. minister, 1979-84; dir. taxation and fiscal policy Dept. Fin., Govt. Sask., Regina, 1977-78; dep. minister Dept. Urban Affairs, Govt. Sask., Regina, 1978-79; chmn. Govt. Fin. Commn., Regina, 1984-86; asst. dep. minister Dept. Energy & Mines, Govt. Sask., Regina, 1986-94, dep. minister, 1994—2002; pres. Sask. Property Mgmt. Corp., Regina, 2002—. Office: Sask Property Mgmt Corp 1840 Lorne St Regina SK Canada S4P 3V7 E-mail: ray.clayton@spmc.gov.sk.ca.

CLAYTON, REBECCA D. customer service administrator; b. Milw., Sept. 28, 1955; d. Willie B. and Bertha L Rodgers; m. Stanley J. Clayton, Feb. 12, 1983; children: Renita Rodgers, Stanley E.J. Rodgers II, Brandon I.P. Rodgers. Attended, Milw. Theoloical Inst., 1990; attending, Marquette U., 1999—; bible student, Grace Bible Coll., 2002—. Customer svc. specialist 1st WI Bank, Milw., 1978—80; investigator WI Gas Co., Milw, 1980—97; customer svc. specialist Legion Ins., Milw., 1999—2001; br. auditor YMCA, Northside, Milw., 2001—02. Author: Made in His Image, 2002. Named State Forensics Champion, State of WI Sch., 1973. Mem.: Alpha Sigma Lambda. Avocations: poetry, floral arranging, clothes design, inspiration. Home: 2011 N 37th St Milwaukee WI 53208-1804

CLAYTON, RICHARD REESE, retired holding company executive; b. St. Louis, Aug. 26, 1938; s. Lester Cox and Gladys Caroline (Reese) C.; m. Leigh Ila Smith, Feb. 25, 1961; children: Mark, Catherine, Christine. BS in Indsl. Econs., Purdue U., 1960. With Trane Co., 1960-73, mng. dir., 1970-73; pres. Hallowell div. Standard Pressed Steel Co., Hatfield, Pa., 1973-77; exec. v.p. domestic ops., dir. SPS Technologies Inc., Jenkintown, Pa., 1977-84; pres., CEO, dir. Vermont Castings, Inc., Randolph, Vt., 1984-87; exec. v.p., chief adminstrv. officer Ea. Enterprises (formerly Ea. Gas & Fuel Assocs.), Weston, Mass., 1987-89, exec. v.p., COO, 1990-91, pres., COO, 1991-98. Baptist.

CLAYTON, ROBERT NORMAN, chemist, educator; b. Hamilton, Ont., Can., Mar. 20, 1930; came to U.S., 1952, naturalized, 1995; s. Norman and Gwenda (Twist) C.; m. Cathleen Shelburne, Jan. 30, 1971; 1 dau., Elizabeth Jane. B.Sc., Queens U., 1951, M.Sc., 1952; PhD, Calif. Inst. Tech., 1955. Research fellow Calif. Inst. Tech., 1955-56; mem. faculty Pa. State U., 1956-58, U. Chgo., 1958—, prof. chemistry and geochemistry, 1966—. Fellow AAAS, NAS, Royal Soc. (London), Royal Soc. Can., Am. Acad. Arts Scis., Am. Geophys Union, Meteoritical Soc. Achievements include research distbn. stable isotopes of light elements in nature, application to problems in geology. Home: 5201 S Cornell Ave Chicago IL 60615-4207

CLAYTON, THOMAS SWOVERLAND, English educator; b. New Ulm, Minn., Dec. 15, 1932; s. Robert Schoonmaker and Vida Virginia (Swoverland) C.; m. Ruth Barbara Madson, Sept. 24, 1955 (dec. Dec. 1989); children; Pamela Alison, Katherine Anne, John Robert, David Montgomery. BA, U. Minn., 1954; DPhil, Oxford U., England, 1960. Instr. English Yale U., New Haven, Conn., 1960-62; asst. to assoc. prof. English UCLA, L.A., 1962-68; from prof. to Regents prof. English U. Minn., Mpls., 1968—. Editor: Shakespeare's Hand in the Booke of Sir Thomas Moore, 1969, The Non-Dramatic Works of Sir John Suckling, 1971, Cavalier Poets, 1977, The "Hamlet" First Published, 1992. Sp4 U.S. Army, 1955-57. Am. Coun. Learned Studies grantee, 1962, NEH grantee, 1988; Guggenheim fellow, 1978; Rhodes scholar, 1954. Mem.: MLA, Assn. Literary Scholars and Critics, Assn. Am. Rhodes Scholars, Internat. Shakespeare Assn., Shakespeare Assn. Am. Democrat. Home: 1866 Portland Ave Saint Paul MN 55104-5953 Office: U Minn Classical Civilization Prog 9 Pleasant St SE Minneapolis MN 55455-0125

CLAYTON, VERNA LEWIS, retired state legislator; b. Hamden, Ohio, Feb. 28, 1937; d. Matthews L. and Yail (Miller) Lewis; m. Frank R. Clayton, Feb. 4, 1956; children: children: Valerie S., Barry L. Office mgr. Village of Buffalo Grove, Ill., 1972-78, village clk., 1971-79, village pres., 1979-91; mem. Ill. Ho. of Reps., Springfield, 1993-99. Bd. dirs. Savannah Lakes Property Owners Assn., 2000, v.p., 2003. Mem. Lake County Solid Waste Planning Agy., chmn. tech. com., chmn. agy., Nat. League of Cities, chmn. transp. and comms. steering com. Recipient Disting. Svc. award Amvets, 1981; named Libr. Legislator of the Yr. 1997. Mem. N.W. Mcpl. Conf. (pres. 1983-84), Chgo. Area Transp. Study Coun. Mayors (vice chmn. 1981-83, chmn. 1985-91), Mcpl. Clks. Ill. (treas. 1978-79), Mcpl. Clks. Lake County (pres. 1977-78), Ill. Mcpl. League (bd. dirs., v.p. 1985-90, pres. 1989-90), Buffalo Grove Rotary Club (hon. mem.), Buffalo Grove C. of C. (bd. dirs.). Republican. Methodist. Home: 11 Overlook Pt Mc Cormick SC 29835-2850 E-mail: frclayton9@wctel.net.

CLAYTON, WILLIAM HOWARD, retired university president; b. Dallas, Aug. 16, 1927; s. William Howard and Blanche (Phillips) C.; children: Jill, Gregory. BS, Bucknell U., 1949; PhD, Tex. A & M U., 1956. Instr. Bucknell U., 1949; grad. asst. Ohio State U., 1949, U. N.Mex., 1949-50; research asst. oceanography and meteorology Tex. A&M U., College Station, 1950-51; asst. oceanography Tex. A. and M. U., 1951-54; assoc. oceanography, instr. math. Tex. A&M U., 1954-56, micrometeorologist U. Research Found., instr. math., 1956-58, faculty meteorology, 1958—, prof. oceanography, 1965—, prin. investigator Research Found., 1956-65; asso. dean Coll. Geoscis. Tex. A & M U., 1970-71; pres. Tex. A&M U., Galveston, 1977-87, pres. emeritus, 1987—; sec.-treas. Tex. Coastal Higher Edn. Authority, 1981-88; dean Moody Coll., Galveston, 1971-74, provost, 1974-77, pres. coll., 1977-79. Coastal coord. coun., State of Tex.; vis. prof. U. Hawaii, 1963-64; tech. dir. Project Themis, U.S. Army Electronics Command, 1967-74; chmn. field observing facility adv. panel Nat. Center for Atmospheric Research, 1973-74; bd. dirs. Bank of West. Contbr. articles to profl. lit., chpts. to books. Commr. Galveston Police and Fire Dept. CSC; mem. Galveston City Coun., 1990—, Galveston Marine Affairs Coun.; trustee Gulf Univs. Rsch. Consortium, 1971-84, chmn., 1977-79. Served with RCAF, 1940-44; Served with USAAF, 1944-45; rear admiral U.S. Maritime Service. Mem. Am. Geophys. Union, Am. Meteorol. Soc. (dir.), Galveston C. of C., Sigma Xi, Pi Mu Epsilon, Sigma Pi Sigma, Phi Kappa Phi, Sigma Phi Epsilon. Home: 5222 Denver Dr Galveston TX 77551-5943 Office: Tex A&M U PO Box 1675 Galveston TX 77553-1675 E-mail: wclay1@wt.net.

CLAYTON-TOWNSEND, JOANN, aerospace analyst; b. Ft. Smith, Ark., Dec. 8, 1935; d. James Wooley and Rachel (McLaughlin) C.; m. John David Clayton (dec.); children: Rachel Diana, David Edward; m. John W. Townsend, Sept. 17, 1996. BA, U. Tulsa, 1958; MA, George Washington U., 1990. Chief legis. asst. U.S. Ho. Reps., Washington, 1974-79; aerospace analyst Washington, 1979—. Dir. aeronautics and space engring. bd. NRC, 1990-98. Editor Procs. Internat. Inst. Space Law, 1998-2003. Pres. Turkish-Am. Cultural Soc., Ankara, Turkey, 1972-73. Recipient Disting. Profl. Staff award NRC, 1990; McClure scholar U. Tulsa, 1955. Fellow AIAA; mem. Internat. Inst. Space Law (editor procs. of the Inst. 1998—), Women in Aerospace (v.p. 1990, Outstanding Achievement award 1991, Svc. to Women in Aerospace award 1997), Internat. Acad. Astronautics, Kappa Alpha Theta. Avocation: oil painting. E-mail: joannct@starpower.net.

CLAYTOR, KATHARINE DRANEY, human resources executive; b. Ft. Monmouth, N.J., Nov. 2, 1959; d. Edward P. and Margaret (Heliker) Draney; m. Stephen M. Claytor, June 1, 1985; children: Emily G., William M. BA in Bus./Econ., Emory & Henry Coll., 1981; postgrad., Lynchburg Coll. Accredited profl. human resources. Pers. analyst County of Roanoke, Va., 1983-89, asst. dir. human resources, 1989—. Subcom. chair Am. Heart Assn., Roanoke; mem. alive and well bd. Coun. Community Svcs.; com. chair Christ Episcopal Ch. Mem. Soc. Human Resource Mgmt., Internat. Pers. Mgmt. Assn., Salem Jr. Women's Club (pres. 1991-92). Office: County of Roanoke PO Box 29800 Roanoke VA 24018-0798

CLAYTOR, KATHERINE W. MOSS, secondary education educator; b. Richlands, Va., Dec. 9, 1959; d. Robert Lincoln Moss and Katherine Kiser Gillespie Huffman. BEd, Radford (Va.) U., 1984. Phys. sci. tchr. Tazewell County Pub. Schs., Tazewell, Va., 1986—. Sci. fair coord. Richlands Tazewell (Va.) Middle Sch, 1989—. Mem. NEA, Va. Edn. Assn., Tazewell Edn. Assn., Nat. Middle Sch. Assn. Avocations: horseback riding, camping, horse showing. Office: Tazewell Middle Sch 100 Bulldog Ln Richlands VA 24651-9765

CLAYTOR, RICHARD ANDERSON, retired federal agency executive, consultant; b. Roanoke, Va., Sept. 4, 1927; s. William Graham and Gertrude (Boatwright) C.; m. Mary Lee Leary, June 18, 1949; children: Gale Catherine, Douglas Gordon, Richard Anderson Jr. BS, U.S. Naval Acad., 1949; BS in Marine Engring., MS in Naval Architecture, Webb Inst. Naval Architecture, 1956. Registered profl. engr., N.J., Calif. Commd. ensign USN, 1949, advanced through grades to capt., 1969; served in various ships, 1949-53; project mgr. nuclear power div. USN Bur. Ships, Washington, 1956-63; asst. mgr. Pitts. Naval Reactors Office, AEC, 1963-73; ret., 1973; v.p., asst. to pres. Burns and Roe, Inc., Oradell, N.J., 1973-79; pres. Burns and Roe-Humphreys & Glasgow Synthetic Fuels, Inc., Oradell, 1979-81, Burns and Roe Pacific Co., L.A., 1981-90; asst. sec. for def. programs U.S. Dept. Energy, Washington, 1990-93; ind. cons. Decorated Legion of Merit. Mem. ASME, Soc. Naval Engrs., Am. Nuclear Soc., Army-Navy Club. Republican. Episcopalian. Avocations: tennis, bridge, hiking, canoeing, oil painting.

CLEAR, ALBERT F., JR., retired hardware manufacturing company executive; b. N.Y.C., June 9, 1920; s. Albert F. and Edna (Coyle) C.; m. Jeanne Posselt, Aug. 7, 1947; children: Geoffrey Posselt, Gregory Stuart. BS, MIT, 1942; MBA, Harvard U., 1948. V.p., mgr. Mallory div. John B. Stetson Co., Danbury, Conn., 1948-57; mng. assoc. Booz-Allen & Hamilton, N.Y.C., 1957-65; v.p., gen. mgr. hardware div. Stanley Works, New Britain, Conn., 1965-69, v.p. consumer group, chmn. European ops., 1967-69, exec. v.p., 1969-76, pres., 1977-80, vice chmn., 1980-82. Chmn. Ansonia (Conn.) Copper & Brass, 1999-2001; bd. dirs. The Stanley Works, New Britain, Stanley Home Products, Westfield, Mass., Barden Corp., Danbury, Curtis Corp., Sandy Hook, Constructive Workshop, Inc., New Britain, D&L Corp., Danbury; adv. dir. Conn. Nat. Bank. Vice chmn. MIT Ctr. N.Y., 1965; bd. dirs. Danbury chpt. ARC, 1953; trustee Hartford Grad. Ctr., Hartford Coll. for Women, Housatonic Valley Assn., 1976-80. Capt. AUS, 1942-46. Mem. Builders Hardware Mfrs. Assn. (exec. com.), Danbury C. of C. (pres. 1954), New Britain C. of C. (dir. 1967-69, 72-80, pres. 1977). Home: 344 Westmont West Hartford CT 06117-2938

CLEAR, JOHN MICHAEL, lawyer; b. St. Louis, Dec. 16, 1948; s. Raymond H. and Marian (Clark) Clear; m. Isabel Marie Bone, May 10, 1980; 1 child, Thomas Henry. BA summa cum laude, Washington U., St. Louis, 1971; JD with honors, U. Chgo., 1974. Bar: Mo. 1974, D.C. 1975, U.S. Ct. Appeals (5th and D.C. cirs.) 1975, U.S. Supreme Ct. 1977, U.S. Ct. Appeals (3d cir.) 1978, U.S. Ct. Appeals (8th cir.) 1980, U.S. Ct. Appeals (9th cir.) 1990, U.S. Dist. Ct. (so. dist.) Ill. 1995, U.S. Ct. Appeals (7th cir.) 1997. Law clk. to judge U.S. Ct. Appeals (5th cir.), Atlanta, 1974-75; assoc. Covington & Burling, Washington, 1975-80; jr. ptnr. Bryan, Cave, McPheeters & McRoberts, St. Louis, 1980-81, ptnr., 1982—. Mem. ABA, Mo. Bar Assn., D.C. Bar Assn., St. Louis Met. Bar Assn., Am. Law Inst., Order of Coif., Racquet Club, Noonday Club, Fox Run Golf Club, Phi Beta Kappa. Office: Bryan Cave LLP One Metropolitan Sq Saint Louis MO 63102-2750 E-mail: jmclear@bryancave.com.

CLEAR, ROSEMARY ELAINE, translator, court interpreter, consultant; b. Ogden, Utah, Mar. 7, 1946; d. Deryl Thomas and Mary (Rukavina) C. Student, Watchtower Bible Sch. Gilead, Bklyn., 1967-68; AA with honors, Houston C.C., 2001. Missionary Watchtower Bible and Tract Soc., Santo Domingo, 1968-69; owner, operator Office Svcs. Consultants, Houston, 1977—. Jehovah'S Witness. Avocation: singing (dramatic soprano). E-mail: rclear@hotmail.com.

CLEARFIELD, HARRIS REYNOLD, physician; b. Phila., Aug. 8, 1933; s. Samuel and Rae (Lewis) C.; m. Louise Libby, June 30, 1957; children: Andrea, Jonathan. BS, Franklin and Marshall Coll., 1955; MD, Jefferson Med. Coll., 1959. Intern Grad. Hosp. U. Pa., Phila., 1959-60, resident in internal medicine, 1960-62, resident in gastroenterology, 1962-63, mem. staff, 1963-72, Episcopalian Hosp., Phila., 1967-72, head sect. gastroenterology, until 1972; sr. attending physician Phila. Gen Hosp., 1972-77; mem. faculty U. Pa. Med. Sch., Phila., 1963-72; clin. asst. prof. medicine Temple U. Med. Sch., Phila., 1967-72; dir. div. gastroenterology Hahnemann Hosp., Phila., 1972—, prof. medicine, 1972—. Lectr., cons. Naval Regional Med. Ctr., Phila., 1976-78; sr. cons. Phila. Gen. Hosp., 1972-74; mem. gov.'s adv. com. of ACP, 1980-88; dir. Krancer Ctr. for Inflamatory Bowel Disease Rsch., 1985—. Author: (with Dinoso) Gastrointestinal Emergencies, 1979, (with Borowsky) Case Studies in Gastroenterology, 1989; editorial cons. Am. Jour. Proctology, 1976-86; contbr. articles to profl. jours. Chmn. sci. adv. bd. Nat. Found. Ileitis and Colitis, 1976-80, trustee, 1990—. Recipient Lindback award Phila. chpt. Nat. Found. Ileitis and Colitis, 1979, named Physician of Yr., 1980, Janssen award, 1998. Fellow ACP (mem. bd. regents 1999-2003, chmn. coun. subspecialty socs. 1999-2003), Phila. Coll. Physicians; mem. Am. Gastroenterologic Assn., Bockus Internat. Soc. Gastroenterology (trustee, v.p., pres. 1993-95), Phila. Gastroenterology Group (pres. 1974-75), Am. Soc. Gastrointestinal Endoscopy, Am. Coll. Gastroenterology (Master; gov. Ea. Pa. 1990-92, trustee 1992-96), Pa. Soc. Gastroenterology (pres. 1993-95), Delaware Valley Soc. Gastrointestinal Rsch. Forum, Pa. Med. Soc. (commn. on accreditation 1986-92), Phila. Med. Soc. (bd. dirs. 1996—, sec. 1998—, v.p. 1999-, pres. 2001-02), Musical Fund Soc. Phila. (physician, 2003—). Home: 720 Oxford Rd Bala Cynwyd PA 19004-2112 Office: 230 N Broad St Philadelphia PA 19102-1121

CLEARWATER, JOHN MURRAY, political analyst; b. Winnipeg, Man., Can., Feb. 8, 1966; s. Thomas Murray Clearwater and Olga Pupeza; life ptnr. Pamela Jayne Wheat. BA with honors, U. Winnipeg (Can.), 1988; MA, Dalhousie U., Halifax, Can., 1990—; PhD, King's Coll. London, London, 1994. Sr. analyst Dept. Nat. Def., Ottawa, Canada, 1996—98; editor-in-chief Inst. Def. and Disarmament, Cambridge, Mass., 2000—01; pres. Clearwater Cons., Houston, 2002—; policy adv. Emirates Ctr. for Strategic Studies and Rsch., Abu Dhabi, United Arab Emirates, 2002. Advisor Diefenbunker: Can.'s Cold War Mus., Ottawa, 1998—. Author: Canadian Nuclear Weapons, 1998, Johnson, McNamara and the Birth of SALT and the ABM Treaty, 1999, U.S. Nuclear Weapons in Canada, 2000. Advisor Diefenbunker: Canada's Cold War Mus., Ottawa, Canada. Recipient William Barton Award, Canadian Inst. Internat. Peace and Security, 1993-1994. Mem.: Internat. Plastic Modellers Soc. Avocation: oil painting. Home: 2006 Shadybriar Houston TX 77077-5910 Office: Clearwater Consulting 2006 Shadybriar Dr Houston TX 77077-5910 Personal E-mail: da710@ncf.ca. Business E-Mail: da710@ncf.ca.

CLEARY, BEVERLY ATLEE (MRS. CLARENCE T. CLEARY), writer; b. McMinnville, Oreg., Apr. 12, 1916; d. Chester Lloyd and Mable (Atlee) Bunn; m. Clarence T. Cleary, Oct. 6, 1940; children: Marianne Elisabeth, Malcolm James. BA, U. Calif., 1938; BA in Librarianship, U. Wash., 1939; LHD (hon.), Cornell Coll., 1993. Children's librarian Pub. Libr., Yakima, Wash., 1939-40; post librarian U.S. Army Regional Hosp., Oakland, Calif., 1942-45. Author: Henry Huggins, 1950, Ellen Tebbits, 1951, Henry and Beezus, 1952, Otis Spofford, 1953, Henry and Ribsy, 1954, Beezus and Ramona, 1955, Fifteen, 1956, Henry and the Paper Route, 1957, The Luckiest Girl, 1958, Jean and Johnny, 1959, The Real Hole, 1960, Hullabaloo ABC, 1960, 98, Two Dog Biscuits, 1961, Emily's Runaway Imagination, 1961, Henry and the Clubhouse, 1962, Sister of the Bride, 1963, Ribsy, 1964, The Mouse and the Motorcycle, 1965, Mitch and Amy, 1967, Ramona the Pest, 1968, Runaway Ralph, 1970, Socks, 1973, (play) The Sausage at the End of the Nose, 1974, Ramona the Brave, 1975, Ramona and Her Father, 1977 (Newbery Honor Book award ALA 1978), Ramona and Her Mother, 1979, Ramona Quimby, Age 8, 1981 (Newbery Honor Book award ALA 1982), Ralph S. Mouse, 1982, Dear Mr. Henshaw, 1983 (ALA Notable Book citation 1984, John Newbery medal 1984), Ramona Forever, 1984, Lucky Chuck, 1984, The Ramona Quimby Diary, 1984, Beezus and Ramona Diary, 1986, Janet's Thingamajigs, 1987, The Growing Up Feet, 1987, A Girl from Yamhill: A Memoir, 1988, Muggie Maggie, 1990, Strider, 1991, Petey's Bedtime Story, 1993, My Own Two Feet: A Memoir, 1995, Ramona's World, 1999. Recipient Disting. Alumna award U. Wash., 1975, Laura Ingalls Wilder award ALA, 1975, Regina medal Cath. Libr. Assn., 1980, De Grummond award U. Miss., 1982, U. So. Miss. medallion, 1982, Hans Christian Andersen medal nominee, 1984. Mem. Authors Guild of Authors League Am. Office: c/o Harper Collins Children's Books 1350 Sixth Ave New York NY 10019-4702*

CLEARY, CATHLEEN ANN, psychiatrist; b. New Brunswick, N.J., Mar. 28, 1962; d. William Bernard and Mary Elizabeth (Grant) C.; m. Warren R. Lemoi, Mar. 25, 1995. BA, Rutgers U., 1985; MD, U. Medicine and Dentistry N.J., 1989. Diplomate Am. Bd. Psychiatry and Neurology. Intern St. Luke's Hosp., Bethlehem, Pa., 1989-90; resident in psychiatry Brown U., Providence, 1990-93; staff psychiatrist East Bay Mental Health Ctr., East Providence, R.I., 1993-94, Cmty. Counseling Ctr., Pawtucket, RI, 1993—2001; psychiatrist pvt. practice, Providence, 1993—2001; clin. asst. prof. Psychiatry and Human Behavior Brown U. Sch. of Medicine, Providence, 2000—; psychiatrist pvt. practice, Warner Robins, Ga., 2001—; attending staff Houston Med. Ctr., 2001—, chmn. dept. psychiatry, 2002—. Vol. Big Sister Big Sister Program, Providence, 1994-95. R.E. Salny Sci. fellow Rutgers U., 1985. Mem.: Med. assn. Ga., Ga. Psychiat. Physicians Assn., Am. Psychiat. Assn., Phi Beta Kappa. Avocations: bicycling, travel, art. Office: 310-B Margie Dr Warner Robins GA 31088

CLEARY, DAVID LAURENCE, lawyer; b. Rochester, N.Y., Mar. 5, 1941; s. James W. and Margaret (Neary) C.; m. Valerie Claire Smith, July 27, 1968; children: Sean Michael, Megan Lynne. BS, St. John Fisher Coll., 1963; JD, Cornell U., 1970. Bar: Vt. 1970, U.S. Dist. Ct. Vt. 1970, U.S. Ct. Appeals (2d cir.) 1971, U.S. Ct. Appeals (1st cir.) 1974, U.S. Dist. Ct. N.H. 1974, U.S. Dist. Ct. Mass. 1975. Dep. stats atty. Chittenden County, Burlington, Vt., 1970-72; assoc. Wilson, Curtis, Bryan & Quinn, Burlington, Vt., 1970-72; ptnr. R.E. Davis Assocs., Inc., Barre, Vt., 1972-78, Miller, Cleary & Faignant and predecessor firms, Rutland, Vt., 1978-91; pres. D.L. Cleary Assn. PC, Rutland, Vt., 1991-98, Cleary-Shahi Assoc. PC, Rutland, Vt., 1998—. Spl. counsel Nat. Ski Areas Assn., Wilmington, Del., 1977-2000, United Ski Industries Assn., Fairfax, Va., 1989-99; counsel Vt. Bd. Med. Practice, Montpelier, 1979-86. Capt. M.I., airborne inf. U.S. Army, 1964-68, Vietnam. Decorated Bronze Star. Mem. ABA, ATLA, Internat. Soc. Barristers, Internat. Acad. Trial Lawyers, Am. Coll. Trial Lawyers, Fedn. Ins. and Corp. Counsel, Am. Arbitration Assn., Am. Bd. Trial Advocates (pres. Vt. chpt. 1993-94), Def. Rsch. Inst. (chmn. spl. ins. problems com. 1981-86), Vt. Bar Assn. (del. bd. govs. 1977-78, bd. profl. conduct 1979-89, chmn. tort reform commn. 1988—), Vt. Def. Trial Lawyers (pres. 1992-93), Chittenden County Bar Assn., Washington County Bar Assn., Rutland County Bar Assn., Ethan Allen Club, Lake George Yacht Club (bd. dirs., officer), Rutland Country Club, Smith Basin Club, Gooley Club. Republican. Roman Catholic. Avocations: scuba diving, hunting, fishing, boating, woodworking. Office: Cleary-Shahi Assoc PC PO Box 6740 110 Merchants Row Rutland VT 05701-5928

CLEARY, DAVID MICHAEL, composer, critic, library assistant; b. Chelsea, Mass., Nov. 11, 1954; s. Robert Joseph and Sally Ann (Deuker) C.; m. Janice Tucker Rhoda, Jan. 21, 2001. MusB, New Eng. Conservatory Music, 1976; MusM, U. Hartford, 1978; MusD, U. Cin., 1982. Asst. to composition dept. New Eng. Conservatory Music, Boston, 1974-76; tchg. asst. in music theory U. Hartford, Conn., 1976-78, U. Cin., 1978-80, rotating instr. in music theory, 1980-81; libr. asst. Harvard U., Cambridge, Mass., 1984—. Assoc. prodr. The Composers Show, Sta. WGBH-FM, Boston, 1974-75; co-dir. Composers in Red Sneakers, 1994-2000, pres., 1997-2000. Compositions include Five Character Studies, 1979, A Gathering of Quokkas, 1985 (commd. Dinosaur Annex

Ensemble), Lake George Overture, 1988, String Quartet no. 1, 1988, Gryllus, 1988-89, Cruikshank Fantasy, 1989 (commd. Alea III), Woodwind Quintet no. 2, 1990 (commd. Arcadian Winds), String Quartet no. 2, 1991 (commd. Artaria Quartet Boston), Linsner Sextet, 1992 (commd. Northwestern U. Trombone Ensemble), Western Wind Fragments, 1993-94 (commd. Eos Ensemble), Fanfares for Teddy Roosevelt, 1994-95, The Deeper Magic, 1995-96 (commd. Duo Renard), Fourteen Movie Characters, 1996-97 (commd. Am. Composers Forum Boston Area chpt.), Postcards from Annaghmakerrig, 1998, One Chord Wonders, 1999 (commd. Quincy Symphony), composer piano accompaniments ABCs of Strings Method Series, 2001—, Crosscultural Variations, 2002 (commd. Continental Harmony/Am. Composers Forum), SICPP Fantasies, 2002 (commd. SICPP Festival); contbg. music writer (website) All-Music Guide, 1997—; (book) All Music Guide to Rock, 2d edit., 3rd edit., 4th edit.; contbg. music critic New Music Connoisseur, 1999—, The Enterprise, 1999—, 21st Century Music, 2000—, Living Music, 2003—, Boston Herald, 2003—; contbr. articles to profl. jours.; recordings on Centaur, Vienna Modern Masters, Musicians Showcase CD labels. Mem. fellows coun. Va. Ctr. for the Creative Arts, 1999-02; bd. advisors Kalvos and Damian's New Music Bazaar, 1999—. Recipient 1st pl. Rosenberger Meml. Comm. Competition, Cin., 1989, Harvey Gaul Composition Competition, 1990; ASCAP grantee U. Hartford, 1978, grantee Somerville Arts Coun., 1987, 90, Meet the Composer, 1990, ASTRAL grantee Nat. Found. for Advancement in Arts, 1994; rsch. fellow U. Cin., 1980, Douglas W. Bryant fellow, 1988, fellow Va. Ctr. for Creative Arts, 1988-89, Yaddo fellow, 1988, Cummington fellow, 1989, Millay fellow, 1990, fellow Ella Lyman Cabot Trust, 1990, Ragdale fellow, 1992, MacDowell fellow, 1995, Tyrone Guthrie Ctr. fellow, 1998, Djerassi fellow, 2002. Mem. BMI, Am. Music Ctr., Am. Composers Forum, Soc. Composers, Electronic Music Found. Home: 7 Arlington St Apt 34 Cambridge MA 02140-2736 Office: Harvard U Biolabs Libr 16 Divinity Ave Cambridge MA 02138-2020 E-mail: dcleary@fas.harvard.edu.

CLEARY, EDWARD WILLIAM, retired diversified forest products company executive; b. Sergeant Bluff, Iowa, May 21, 1919; s. Edward D. and Laura Helen (Rich) C.; m. Arita Louise Hefferan, June 12, 1946; children: John William, Kathryn Louise, Patricia Jane. BA, DePauw U., 1941; BSC, Ohio State U., 1947. Sr. acct. Price Waterhouse & Co., Portland, Oreg., 1947-53; treas., contr. Nat. Hosp. Assn., Portland, 1953-55, Valsetz Lumber Co., Portland, 1955-60; asst. compt. Boise Cascade (Idaho) Corp., 1960-63, compt., 1963-68, v.p., compt., 1968, v.p., treas., 1968-80, v.p., 1980-82, ret., 1982. Vice chmn. bd. dirs. Farmers & Merchants State Bank. Mem. Pacific N.W. Area coun. YMCA, 1967-70; mem. exec. com. Boise United Fund, 1966-69, chmn. budget com., 1966-69; pres., bd. dirs. YMCA, 1967-69; bd. dirs. Idaho Blue Cross Hosp. Assn., 1969-75, Discovery Ctr. of Idaho, 1990-99; past pres. Bogus Basin Recreation Assn., bd. dirs. 1973-91. With AUS, 1941-42, USNR, 1942-46. Mem. AICPA, Nat. Assn. Accts. (past pres. Boise chpt., past nat. dir.), Idaho Soc. C.P.A.'s, Hillcrest Country Club (past dir., past v.p.). Home: Apt 408 3110 Crescent Rim Dr Boise ID 83706 E-mail: ecleary1@mindspring.com.

CLEARY, JAMES C. audio-visual producer; b. N.Y.C., Mar. 15, 1921; s. James Charles and Elizabeth Adelaide (Anglin) C.; m. Adele Lillian Coe, Nov. 28, 1954. Grad., Scarsdale (N.Y.) H.S., 1940. Lithographer, camerman Advt. Lit. Inc., N.Y.C., 1940-41; advt. copy writer Grosset & Dunlap, book pubs., N.Y.C., 1942-44; advt. copy writer, editor Baker & Taylor, book wholesalers, N.Y.C., 1945-46; asst. mgr. sales Camera Craft Inc., retail photog. sales, White Plains, N.Y., 1946-50, Colortone Camera Inc., White Plains, 1950-57; prodr., lectr. Ansco divsn. Gen. Aniline & Film Corp., Binghamton, N.Y., 1959-61; lab. photographer Nevis Lab. Nuc. Rsch., Columbia U., 1959-75; audio-visual specialist Edgemont Sch. Dist., Scarsdale, 1975-83; owner-prodr. Cleary Sound-Slides, New Rochelle, N.Y., 1950—. Mem. AAAS, Scarsdale Camera Club (pres. 1948-49), Color Camera Club Westchester N.Y. (dir. 1958-59), Am. Security Coun. (advisory bd. 1970—), USAF Assn., Am. Def. Preparedness Assn., Westchester County Grand Jurors Assn., The Baker Street Irregulars, Three Garridebs, Sherlock Holmes Socs., Thomas Wolfe Soc. Achievements include patentee of complete sound-synchronized, dissolving slide projection control system, 1966; pioneer in use of dissolve projection and synchronized sound in presentation of color slide continuities. Address: Cleary Sound-Slides 28 Pengilly Dr New Rochelle NY 10804-3016

CLEARY, LYNDA WOODS, financial advisor, consultant; b. Birmingham, Ala., June 18, 1950; d. Eugene and Elizabeth (Wright) Woods; m. George Cassius Riley, Nov. 29, 1975 (div. 1979); m. Richard Charles Cleary, Dec. 12, 1987. Student, Dartmouth Coll., 1970-71; BA, Tougaloo (Miss.) Coll., 1972; postgrad., Rutgers U., 1981-83; MBA, N.Y. Inst. Tech., 1992. Comml. underwriter Continental Ins. Co., N.Y.C., 1973-74; lectr. John Ericson Sch., Ostersund, Sweden, 1974; asst. underwriting cons. Prudential Property and Casualty, Holmdel, N.J., 1975-80; market rsch. analyst Continental Ins. Co., Piscataway, N.J., 1981-86; bus. systems analyst Am. Internat. Group, N.Y.C., 1986-87; ins. agt. Equitable Fin. Cos., N.Y.C., 1988; spl. agt. Northwestern Mut. Life, Princeton, N.J., 1988-89; cons. Cleary Woods Cons., Princeton, 1989—; account exec. Dean Witter, N.Y.C., 1992-93; fin. cons. Fahnestock & Co., Inc., Red Bank, N.J., 1993-95, Securities Am., Inc., Princeton, N.J., 1995-99; fin. advisor Am. Express, Edison, N.J., 1999-2000; investment advisor USAllianz Securities Inc., Princeton, NJ, 2000—. Cons. Nat. Torque Tech. Labs., Piscataway, 1989—. Mem. fin. com. Princeton Walk Homeowners Assn., 1988-95; fundraiser Crossroads Theatre, New Brunswick, N.J., 1988-94; asst. troop leader Girl Scouts U.S., West Windsor; bd. dirs. Nat. Alumni Coun. United Negro Coll. Fund, 2002-. Recipient Cert. Appreciation, Concerned Cmty. Women of Jersey City, Inc., 1990, Pres.' Bridging-the-Gap award, United Negro Coll. Fund, 2002. Mem. Nat. Assn. Securities Profls., Coalition Black Investors, Princeton Scrabble Club (dir. 1998-). Republican. Baptist. Avocations: macramé, gardening, playing word games, birdwatching, golf. Office: 22 Springwood Ct Princeton NJ 08540-9403 E-mail: lwcleary@clearywoods.com.

CLEARY, MARTIN JOSEPH, real estate company executive; b. N.Y.C., July 27, 1935; s. Patrick Joseph and Kathleen Theresa (Costello) C.; m. Peggy Elizabeth McIntyre, June 22, 1957; children: Patrick Francis, Eileen Ann, Michael Thomas, Kathleen Marie, Maureen Elizabeth. BS, Fordham U., 1960; MBA, N.Y. U., 1963. With Tchrs. Ins. and Annuity Assn. and Coll. Retirement Equities Fund, N.Y.C., 1953-81; pres. Richard E. Jacobs Group, Westlake, Ohio, 1981—2001, ret., 2001. Bd. dirs. Guardian Life Ins. Co., Lamson & Sessions, CBL & Assocs. Mem. Internat. Coun. Shopping Ctrs. (trustee 1980—, pres. 1983-84). Office: 619 Ocean Ave Sea Girt NJ 08750

CLEARY, PAMELA ANN, symphony executive; b. Omaha, Jan. 24, 1947; d. Carson Poe Jr. and Helen D. (Nelson) Dole; m. David O. Gilson, June 18, 1965 (div. 1977); children: Kevin D., Kyle, Kreg; m. John P. Cleary, Sept. 13, 1980; children: Shawn, Robert, Kevin M., Daniel, Charles, Colleen. BSBA, U. Nebr., 1977. Acct., bus. mgr. Northwestern Steel & Supply, Omaha, 1977-84; sr. dir. fin. and adminstrn. Omaha Symphony Assn., Omaha, 1984-93, exec. dir., 1992—. Mem. DAR, Oak Hills Country Club. Republican. Roman Catholic. Home: 5706 Oak Hills Dr Omaha NE 68137-3316 Office: Omaha Symphony Assn 1605 Howard St Omaha NE 68102-2705

CLEARY, ROBERT EDWARD, government and public affairs educator; b. East Orange, N.J., Feb. 27, 1932; s. Charles A. and Mary J. (Solomon) C.; m. Marilyn F. Jacoby, Apr. 21, 1956; children— Barbara, Kevin, Charles. BA in Social Sci, Montclair (N.J.) State Coll., 1953; MA in Polit. Sci, Rutgers U., 1959, PhD, 1962; LL.D., Am. U., 1977. Asst. dir. secondary sch. project Eagleton Inst. Politics, Rutgers U., 1959-61; asst. prof. George Peabody Coll. for Tchrs., 1961-64; asst. dir. Am. Polit. Sci. Assn., 1966-67; assoc. prof., assoc. dean Sch. Govt. and Pub. Adminstrn., Am. U., Washington, 1965-70, prof. govt. and public adminstrn., 1970—2001, prof. emeritus, 2001—, dean acad. devel., 1970-72, provost, 1972-76, acting pres., 1975-76, dean Coll. Pub. and Internat. Affairs, 1980-87. Author: Political Education in the American Democracy, 1971; co-author: Managing Public Programs, 1989; contbr. articles to profl. jours. Exec. sec. Harry S. Truman Scholarship Found., 1976-78. Mem. Am. Polit. Sci. Assn. (Congl. fellow 1964-65), Am. Soc. for Pub. Adminstrn., Nat. Assn. Schs. of Pub. Affairs (pres. 1984-85). Clubs: Cosmos (Washington, pres. 1997-98). Home: 7503 Elmore Ln Bethesda MD 20817-5503

CLEARY, SEAN MICHAEL, executive; b. Somerset West, South Africa, Oct. 26, 1948; s. Thomas Stanislaus and Isobel Forsyth Cranston (Bell) C.; m. Sophia Natalie Smit, June 5, 1971; children: Sean Michael, Mary Siobhan. BA, U. South Africa, 1969; MBA, Brunel U., England, 1999. Vice consul, consul SA Consulate Gen., Tehran, Iran, 1971-75; deputy head econ. & fin. rels. divsn. Min. Fgn. Affairs, Pretoria, South Africa, 1976—77, head tng. divsn., 1978; polit. counsellor South African Embassy, Washington, 1978-82; consul gen. SA Consulate Gen., Beverly Hills, Calif., 1982-83; chief dir. Office of Adminstr. Gen., Windhoek, Nambia, 1983-85; mng. dir. Strategic Concepts Ltd., Johannesburg, 1985 . Guest lectr. Grad. Sch. of Bus., UNISA, Johannesburg, 1986—, Witwatersrand Bus. Sch., Johannesburg, 2002; faculty mem. Grad. Inst. Mgmt. and Tech., Johannesburg, 1996—, Internat. Ctr. for Mgmt. Devel., Johannesburg, Wits Bus. Sch., Gordon Inst. Bus. Sci.; forum fellow World Econ. Forum; vice chmn. Meridian Worldwide LLC, 1998—; mng. dir. Ctr. Advanced Governance; mgmt. bd. Think Tools AG, 1999—2003, supervisory bd., 2003—; mem. facilitating and prep. com. Nat. Peace Accord, 1992; chair Working Group on Code of Conduct for Polit. Parties/Orgn.; chmn. Erinys Internat., Ltd.; bd. dirs. Lead Internat. Contbr. articles to profl. jours. Mem. Africa Task Force, World Econ. Forum, South African Inst. Internat. Affairs, Africa Inst. South Africa, Soc. Advancement Socio-Econs. Avocations: fishing, riding, writing, music. Home: The Lodge Silverhurst Silverhurst Est Constantia Cape Town South Africa Office: Strategic Concepts Stratcon Ho Waterfall Park Halfway House 1685 South Africa E-mail: scleary@erinyinternational.com., sean.cleary@thinktools.com.

CLEARY, SHIRLEY JEAN, artist, illustrator; b. St. Louis, Nov. 14, 1942; d. Frank and Crystal (Maret) C.; m. (Leo) Frank Cooper, June 18, 1982; stepchildren: Clay Cooper, Alicia Cooper, Curt Cooper, Aaron Cooper. BFA, Wash. U., St. Louis, 1964; MFA, Temple U., Phila.. Rome, 1968; postgrad., The Corcoran, Washington, 1969-71. Stewardship dir. mem. adv. bd. Mont. Trout Unltd. Prin. works include illustrations in mags. Flyfishing Quar., Fly Fishers Mag., Flyfishing News, Mont. Outdoors, Flyfisherman, Flyfishing Heritage; contbr. articles to profl. jours.; exhibited in group shows at Mo. Hist. Soc., St. Louis, 1987, Wild Wings, Mpls., 1985-2002, Settlers West Galleries, Tucson, 1984, 96-2003, Tucson Mus. Art, 1995-96; one-woman shows include Am. Mus. Fly Fishing, Manchester, Vt., 1997; artist 1990 Oreg. Trout Stamp (Artist of Yr. award 1992, Assn. N.W. Steelheaders print winner 1992). Bd. dirs. Mont. State Arts Coun., Mont., 1973-81, Helena Civic Ctr., Mont., 1983-89; active leadership Helena, 1985; participant Mont. Gathering of Artists, Grant Kohrs Ranch Nat. Pk., 1999-2002. Apprenticeship grantee Western Starts Art Found., Artist in Residence, River Meadow, Jackson, Wyo., 1989-94, 97, Herning Hojskole, Herning, Denmark, 1981, Wyo. Artist in the Schools, Sheridan, Wyo., 1977; named Arts for Parks Top 100 Artist, 1989, 94, 97, 98, 2000, Jackson One Fly Artist of Yr., 1990-92, Artist of Yr., Trout Unltd., 2001; recipient Conservation Comm. award Nat. Trout Unltd., 1999. Mem. Coll. Art Assn. Democrat. Avocations: flyfishing, travel. Home: 1804 Beltview Dr Helena MT 59601-5801 Home (Winter): 15B Canning St Gore 9700 New Zealand E-mail: clearystudio@hotmail.com.

CLEARY, TIMOTHY FINBAR, professional society administrator; b. Cork, Ireland, Sept. 30, 1925; s. John Francis and Nora (Riordan) C.; m. Patricia Agnes Hanley, June 21, 1947; children: Timothy F. X., Maureen P., Therese A., Richard S., Gail P., Eileen P. BS, Fordham U., 1955, JD, 1959. Bar: N.Y. 1959, D.C. 1980. Atty. N.Y.C. Police Dept., 1959-67; asst. counsel Fair Labor Standards div. U.S. Dept. Labor, Washington, 1967-71, chief counsel, 1971-73, mem., 1973-85; cons. in occupational safety and health, 1985—; exec. dir. Nat. Trust for Tng., Edn. and Research in Constrn., 1987-1991; internal campaign contbn. administrator Internat. Brotherhood Elec. Workers. Chmn. U.S. Occupational Safety and Health Rev. Commn., Washington, 1977-81; mem. Adminstrv. Conf. U.S.; cert. arbitrator Nat. Mediation Bd.; lectr. labor law Practising Law Inst., U. Wis., Washington and Lee U., Cumberland Sch. Law, Ohio No. U., Brookings Instn., AFL-CIO Center for Labor Studies, Gompers-Murray Inst.Trade Assc., numerous others. Contbr. articles to profl. jours. Served with USN, 1943-45. Mem.: Friendly Sons St. Patrick, D.C. Home and Office: 5709 Cheshire Dr Bethesda MD 20814-2207

CLEARY, WILLIAM B. oil industry executive; b. Kansas City, Mo., Jan. 8, 1921; s. John Kearny and Helen (Boswell) C.; m. Helen Prentice Cleary, Mar. 30, 1948; children: Louise, Anne, Douglas. BA in English, Yale U., 1942. Co-owner Smith-Cleary Inc., Oklahoma City, 1950-52; CEO W.B. Cleary Inc./Cleary Petroleum Corp., Oklahoma City, 1952-73, merged with W.R. Grace, N.Y.C., 1973-76, Boswell Energy Corp., Oklahoma City, 1976-92; mgr. Cleary Exploration LLC, Oklahoma City, 1992—2001; CEO Cleary Petroleum Corp., Oklahoma City, 2001—. Pres. Oklahoma City Symphony Soc., Oklahoma City Philharm., Oklahoma City Art Mus. Mem. Soaring Soc. Am. (pres., Warren Eaton Trophy award), Oklahoma Ind. Petroleum Assn. (pres), Nat. Petroleum Coun., Ind. Petroleum Assn. (dir.), Econ. Club Okla. (pres.), Oklahoma City Golf and Country Club (bd. dirs.), Oklahoma City Petroleum Club (bd. dirs., v.p.), Com. of 100 (pres.). Avocations: building aircraft, restoring automobiles, golf, fly fishing, skiing. Office: Cleary Petroleum Corp 2601 NW Expressway Ste 801 W Oklahoma City OK 73112 E-mail: billcleary@clearypetroleum.us.

CLEARY, WILLIAM JOSEPH, JR., lawyer; b. Wilmington, N.C., Aug. 14, 1942; s. William Joseph and Eileen Ada (Gannon) C. AB in History, St. Joseph's U., 1964; JD, Villanova U., 1967. Bar: N.J., 1967, Calif. 1982, U.S. Ct. Appeals (3d cir.) 1969, U.S. Ct. Appeals (9th cir.) 1983, U.S. Dist. Ct. (ctrl. dist.) Calif. 1983, U.S. Supreme Ct. 1992. Law sec. to judge N.J. Superior Ct., Jersey City, 1967-68; assoc. Lamb, Blake, H&D, Jersey City, 1968-72; dep. pub. defender State of N.J., Newark, 1972-73; 1st asst. city corp. counsel Jersey City, N.J., 1973-76; assoc. Robert Wasserwald, Inc., Hollywood, Calif., 1984-86, Gould & Burke, Century City, Calif., 1986-87; pvt. practice Hollywood, 1989—. Mem. ABA, FBA, N.J. State Bar Assn., Calif. Bar Assn., L.A. County Bar Assn. (appellate cts. com.), Nat. Jesuit Hon. Soc., Alpha Sigma Nu. Democrat. Roman Catholic. Office: 1853 1/2 Canyon Dr Los Angeles CA 90028-5607 E-mail: wjclaw42@aol.com.

CLEASBY, JOHN LEROY, civil engineer, educator; b. Madison, Wis., Mar. 1, 1928; s. Clarence Allen and Othelia Amanda (Swanson) C.; m. Donna Jean Haugh, Sept. 2, 1950; children: Teresa, Richard, Lynne. BS, U. Wis., 1950, MS, 1951; PhD, Iowa State U., 1960. Diplomate: Am. Acad. Environ. Engrs.; registered profl. engr., Iowa. Inspection engr. Standard Oil Co. Ind., Whiting, 1951—52; project engr. Consoer Townsend & Assocs., Chgo., 1952—54; from instr. to prof. Iowa State U., Ames, 1954—83, disting. prof., 1983—94, disting. prof. emeritus, 1994—. Vis. prof. Univ. Coll. London, 1975-76; cons. World Bank, Washington, Pan Am. Health Orgn., WHO, U. Sao Paulo Co-author: Water Supply Engineering, 1962; contbr. articles to profl. jours. Served with USN, 1945-46. Recipient Outstanding Tchr. award, Iowa State U., 1977, David R. Boylan Eminent Faculty award for rsch., 1989. Mem. ASCE (sec. Environ. Engring. divsn. 1969-73, pres. Iowa sect. 1966, Hering medal 1968, 70, 83, Norman medal 1980), NAE (life.), Am. Water Works Assn. (trustee Water Quality divsn. 1981-87, chmn. 1985, chmn. Iowa sect. 1982, hon., Publs. awards 1962, 80, Divsn. Best Paper awards 1970, 92, 95, Rsch. award 1982, Abel Wolman award 1997), Kiwanis. Am. Baptist. Home: 4805 Dover Dr Ames IA 50014-4586 Office: Iowa State U 487 Town Engring Ames IA 50011-0001

CLEAVER, GERALD BRYAN, physicist, researcher; b. San Bernardino, Calif., Mar. 7, 1963; s. Gerald Charles and Arvona Kathryn (Malchow) C.; m. Lisa Rae Hauder, June 26, 1993; children: Bryan Alexander, Shawn Gregory, Karissa Nicole. BS in Physics and Math, Valparaiso (Ind.) U., 1985; MS in Physics, Calif. Inst. Tech., 1988, PhD in Physics, 1993. Postdoctoral rschr. Ohio State U., Columbus, 1993-96, U. Pa., 1996-98, Tex. A&M U., 1998-2000, vis. asst. prof., 2000-2001; asst. prof. dept. physics Baylor U., 2001—. Mem. Houston Advanced Rsch. Ctr. Contbr. articles to profl. jours. Presidential scholar Valparaiso U., 1981. Fellow Mensa Soc., Prometheus Soc.; mem. Internat. Soc. for Philophican Enquiry, Am. Phys. Soc., Math. Assn. Am., Am. Assn. Physics Tchrs., Am. Sci. Affiliation, Triple-9 Soc., Alpha Phi Omega, Sigma Pi Sigma. Avocations: skiing, Karate, radio-controlled model aviation. Home: 501 Angel Fire Dr Hewitt TX 76643 Office: Baylor Univ Dept Physics Waco TX 76798-7316 E-mail: Gerald_Cleaver@baylor.edu.

CLEAVER, WILLIAM LEHN, lawyer; b. Harrisburg, Pa., Dec. 7, 1949; s. Gene Franklin and Goldie Jean (Haldeman) C.; children: Benjamin Neville, Valerie Anne. BA, Augustana Coll., 1971; JD, U. Iowa, 1974. Bar: Iowa 1974, Ill. 1975, U.S. Dist. Ct. (so. dist.) Iowa 1975, U.S. Dist. Ct. (so. dist.) Ill. 1975. Ptnr. Bozeman, Neighbour, Patton & Noe, Moline, Ill., 1991—. Chmn. bd. govs. BBB Ctrl. Ea. Iowa. Mem. adv. coun. Luth. Social Svcs. of Ill. Adult Day Care Ctr., Rock Island; v.p., bd. dirs. United Way of Quad Cities, Rock Island; pres. adv. coun. Ret. Sr. Vol. Program, Moline; bd. govs. Rock Island Cmty. Found.; commr., chmn. Rock Island Preservation Commn.; mem. Citizen's Adv. Com.; bd. dirs. Quad Cities chpt. ARC; mem. Rock Island/Milan Dist. 41 Sch. Bd. Col. USAR. Mem. ABA, Ill. State Bar Assn (mem assembly), Iowa State Bar Assn., Rock Island County Bar Assn., Scott County Bar Assn. Lodges: Kiwanis (pres. 1983-84, bd. dirs. 1984-85). Lutheran. Avocations: fine arts, racquet sports. Home: 8806 Ridgewood Rd Rock Island IL 61201-7655 Office: Bozeman Neighbour Patton & Noe 1630 5th Ave Moline IL 61265-7910 E-mail: wcleaver@bnpn.com.

CLEAVES, PETER SHURTLEFF, foundation official; b. Washington, Dec. 4, 1943; s. Richard Delaplane and Margaret Grant (Shurtleff) C.; m. Dorothy Barcham, Aug. 31, 1968; children: Geoffrey, Rachel. AB, Dartmouth Coll., 1966; MA, Vanderbilt U., 1968; PhD, U. Calif., Berkeley, 1972. Escort interpreter U.S. Dept. State, Washington, 1966-68; assoc. rep. for Peru, Ecuador and Bolivia, Ford Found., Lima, Peru, 1972-76, rep. for Mex. and C.Am., Mexico City, 1977-82; vis. scholar Yale U., New Haven, 1976-77; v.p. 1st Nat. Bank Chgo., 1982-90; prof. U. Tex., Austin, 1990-99, dir. Inst. Latin Am. Studies, 1990-95, dir. Ctr. for Study Western Hemisphere Trade, 1995-97; exec. dir. Avina Found., Hurden, Switzerland, 1997—. Cons. UN U., Tokyo, 1977, various corp. and non-profit orgns. in Latin Am., 1990—. Author: Bureaucratic Politics and Administration in Chile, 1974, Agriculture, Bureaucracy and Military Government in Peru, 1980, Profession and the State, The Mexican Case, 1987, Latin America in the 21st Century, 2003; also numerous articles. Chmn., trustee Internat. Sch. Panama, Panama City, 1984-86; advisor on L.Am. policy position papers Nat. Dem. Com., Washington, 1988, 92, 96. William Hill Meml. fellow Dartmouth Coll., 1966, NDEA Title VI fellow U. Calif., 1968, Doherty rsch. fellow Doherty Found., 1970, Fulbright-Hays fellow, 1971. Mem. L.Am. Studies Assn., Barton Creek Country Club. Episcopalian. Avocations: tennis, languages. Office: AVINA 1015 Beecave Woods Rd Ste 203 Austin TX 78746-6752 Fax: 512-329-5016. E-mail: peter.cleaves@avina.net.

CLECAK, DVERA VIVIAN BOZMAN, psychotherapist; b. Denver, Jan. 15, 1944; d. Joseph Shalom and Annette Rose (Dveirin) Bozman; m. Pete Emmett Clecak, Feb. 26, 1966 (div. 1993); children: Aimée, Lisa; m. John Pricz, Sept. 12, 1998. BA, Stanford U., 1965; postgrad., U. Chgo., 1965; MSW, UCLA, 1969. Lic. clin. social worker, Calif.; lic. marriage, family and child counselor, Calif. Social work supr. Harbor City (Calif.) Parent Child Ctr., 1969-71; therapist Orange County Mental Health Dept., Laguna Beach, Calif., 1971-75, area coordinator, 1975-79; pvt. practice psychotherapy Mission Viejo, Calif., 1979—. Founder, exec. dir. Human Options, Laguna Beach, 1981—; mem, co-chmn. domestic violence com. Orange County Commn. on Status of Women, 1979-81; mem. mental health adv. com. extension U. Calif., Irvine, 1983, counseling psychologist, 1980, lectr., 1984-85; lectr. Saddleback Community Coll., Mission Viejo, 1981-82, Chapman Coll., Orange, 1979; field instr. UCLA, 1970-71, 77-78. Co-chair Nat. Philanthropy Day, Orange County, 1996. Recipient Women Helping Women award Saddleback C.C., 1987, Cert. for child abuse prevention Commendation State of Calif. Dept. Social Svcs., 1988, Comty. Svc. award Irvine Valley Coll. Found., 1989, Disting. Svc. award in field of domestic violence Nicole Brown Simpson Found., 1996, Amelia Earhart award for svc. to women Women's Opportunity Ctr., U. Calif.-Irvine, 1997, Lee Steelman award South Orange County Cmty. Svcs., 1998, Vision in Philanthropy awrd, 1999, Dove award Human Options, 2002, Orange County Bus. Jour. Women's Achievement award, 2003; named Orange County Non-profit Exec. of Yr., 1994, Humanitarian of Yr., Alexis de Tocqueville Soc., 1997, Woman of Distinction, Laguna Beach Soroptimists, 1998, Desert Dist. Soroptimists, 1998, Visionary award Freeman, Freeman & Smiley, 1999; Hesselbein fellow Peter Drucker Found. for Nonprofits, 1999. Mem. NASW, Calif. Marriage Family and Child Counselors' Assn., Phi Beta Kappa. E-mail: vclecak@hamanoptions.org.

CLECH, JEAN PAUL MARIE, mechanical engineer; b. Morlaix, France, Sept. 16, 1958; s. Edouard Marie and Marie Guillemette (Lozach) C. A in Econs., Sorbonne, Paris, 1980; diploma engr., Ecole Cen. of Paris, 1981; MSME, Northwestern U., 1982, PhD, 1985. Rsch. asst., lectr. Northwestern U., Evanston, Ill., 1982-85; tech. staff mem. AT&T Bell Labs., Whippany, N.J., 1985-90; mgr. Advanced Computer Rsch. Inst., Lyon, France, 1990-92; cons. Electronic Packaging, Bridgewater, N.J., 1992-93; sr. cons. electronic packaging & reliability The Kohl Group, Inc., Montclair, N.J., 1993-95; pres., CEO Electronics Packaging Solutions Internat. Inc., 1995—. Expert in design and reliability of electronic assemblies and solder interconnects; expert witness in electronic product litigation. Contbr. chpts. in book and articles to profl. jours. Mem. IEEE (tech. com. mem. and reviewer), ASME (tech. com. mem. and reviewer), Internat. Electronic Packaging Soc. Avocations: sailing, bicycling. Home: 101 Gates Ave Apt H10 Montclair NJ 07042-2520 Office: EPSI Inc PO Box 1522 Montclair NJ 07042-1522 E-mail: jpclech@aol.com.

CLECKLEY, FRANKLIN D. law educator; b. W.V. Prof. law W.Va. U. Coll. Law, Morgantown, 1969—; justice W.Va. Supreme Ct., Charleston, 1994—96. Office: WVa U Coll Law PO Box 6130 Morgantown WV 26506-6130

CLEESE, JOHN MARWOOD, writer, comedian; b. Weston-super-Mare, Eng., Oct. 27, 1939; s. Reginald and Muriel Cleese; m. Connie Booth, 1968 (div. 1978); 1 child, Cynthia; m. Barbara Trentham, 1981 (div. 1990); 1 child, Camilla; m. Alyce Faye Elchelberger, 1992. Student, Clifton Coll., Bristol, Eng.; MA, Cambridge (Eng.) U.; LLD (hon.), St. Andrews U. Andrew D. White prof.-at-large Cornell U., 1999—. Writer, performer (TV series) The Frost Report, 1966, At Last the 1948 Show, others; actor: (TV series) Monty Python's Flying Circus, Fawlty Towers, Cheers (Emmy award), Third Rock from the Sun, 1998 (Emmy nomination), The Human Face, 2001; (TV films) The Taming of the Shrew, 1981; (films) Interlude, 1968, The Magic Christian, 1970, The Rise and Rise of Michael Rimmer, 1970, And Now for Something Completely Different, 1972, Monty Python and the Holy Grail, 1975, Romance with a Double Bass, 1975, Life of Brian, 1979, The Secret Policeman's Ball, 1979, Time Bandits, 1981, Monty Python Live at the Hollywood Bowl, 1982, The Secret Policemen's Other Ball, 1982, Privates on Parade, Yellowbeard, 1983, The Meaning of Life, 1983, Silverado, 1984, Clockwise, 1986, Erik the Viking, 1988, Splitting Heirs, 1992, Mary Shelley's Frankenstein, 1994, Jungle Book, 1994, The Out-of-Towners, Isn't She Great, 1998, The World is Not Enough, 1999, Rat Race, 2000, Harry Potter and the Philosopher's Stone, 2001, Die Another Day, 2002, Harry Potter and the Chamber of Secrets, 2002; actor, writer : A Fish Called Wanda, 1988; actor(voice actor): Fierce Creatures, 1997; co-author: (book) The Strange Case of the End of Civilization as We Know It, 1977, Monty Python's Big Red Book, 1975, Families and How to Survive Them, 1983, Life and How to Survive It, 1993, The Human Face, 2001; founder, former dir. Video Arts Ltd., London, 1979—91 (Queen's award for Exports, 1982), creator TV and radio commls. Office: care David Wilkinson 115 Hazlebury Rd London SW6 2LX England

CLEETON, DAVID LAWRENCE, economist, educational administrator; b. Chillicothe, Mo., Aug. 10, 1952; s. Sam Jr. and Doris Maxine (Clark) C.; m. Betty Howell, July 19, 1986; children: Sarah Howell, Rebecca Lebo. AB, U. Mo., 1973, AM, 1975; PhD, Washington U., St. Louis, 1980. Asst. prof. econs. Oberlin (Ohio) Coll., 1980-85, chmn. dept. econs., 1986-92, 97-01, chmn. social sci. divsn., 1988-92, prof., 1991—, chmn. ctr. european studies, 1996-2000, chmn. internat. studies, 2000-2001; dir. Oberlin in Europe, 2000—. Vis. prof. Washington U., 1984, U. Wis., Madison, 1986-88, Econs. Inst., Boulder, Colo., 1990, 2000, U. Strasbourg, 1994-95, Mid. Ea. Tech. U., 2001; Fulbright prof. Coll. Europe, 2002; treas. bd. Allen Meml. Hosp., Oberlin, 1992-99. European Union corr. Tax Notes Internat., 1998-2000; contbr. articles to profl. jours. NIMH fellow, 1987-88, Sloan fellow, 1984-85, Earhart fellow, 1979-80. Mem. Am. Econ. Assn., Am. Fin. Assn., Am. Statis. Assn., Fin. Mgmt. Assn., Internat. Pub. Fin. Inst., Nat. Tax. Assn., European Econ. Assn., European Fin. Mgmt. Assn. Office: Oberlin Coll Rice Hall Oberlin OH 44074 E-mail: david.cleeton@oberlin.edu.

CLEGG, JAMES STANDISH, physiologist, biochemist, educator; b. Aspinwall, Pa., July 27, 1933; divorced; 3 children; m. Eileen Clegg; 1 stepchild. BS, Pa. State U., 1958; PhD in Biology, Johns Hopkins U., 1961. Rsch. assoc. biologist Johns Hopkins U., 1961-62; asst. prof. zoology U. Miami, 1962-64, from assoc. prof. biology to prof., 1964-70; prof. sect. molecular and cellular

biology U. Calif., Davis, 1986—, dir. Bodega Marine Lab., 1986-98. With CNRS Thias France, 1983; pres. Nat. Assn. Marine Labs., 1992-94. Recipient Fulbright Sr. Rsch. award U. London, 1978, U. Ghent, 1999; Wilson fellow, 1958-59. Fellow AAAS; mem. Am. Soc. Zoologists, Am. Soc. Cell Biology, Biophys. Soc., Soc. Cryobiology, Sigma Xi. Achievements include research in comparative biochemistry and biophysics; mechanisms of cryptobiosis; properties and role of water in cellular metabolism; cytoplasmic organization. Office: U Calif Bodega Marine Lab PO Box 247 Bodega Bay CA 94923-0247 E-mail: jsclegg@ucdavis.edu.

CLEGG, KAREN KOHLER, lawyer; b. Junction City, Kans., Jan. 7, 1949; d. John Emil and Delores Maxine (Letkeman) Kohler; m. Stephen J. Clegg Jr., Mar. 28, 1970. BS, Emporia State U., 1970; JD, U. Kans., 1975; MBA, Rockhurst Coll., 1989. Bar: Kans. 1975, U.S. Dist. Ct. Kans. 1975, Mo. 1977, U.S. Dist. Ct. (we. dist.) Mo. 1977. Asst. atty. gen. State of Kans., Topeka, 1975-77; atty. The Bendix Corp., Kansas City, Mo., 1977-81, sr. atty., 1981-84; counsel Allied Corp. (now Allied Signal, Inc.), Kansas City, 1984-90, v.p. adminstrn., 1990—; pres. Honeywell Fed. Mfg. and Technologies Honeywell Internat., 1999—. Mem. council human resources mgmt. adv. bd. Commerce Clearing House, Chgo., 1985-88. Sec. Assn. Greater Devel. Coll. Blvd., Shawnee Mission, Kans., 1986-87; bd. dirs. adv. council Avila Coll. Bus., Kansas City, 1984—, Dimension's Unltd., Kansas City, 1985-86. Mem. ABA, Mo. Bar Assn., Am. Soc. Personnel Adminstrn. (v.p., bd. dirs. EEO 1985, profl. services 1986-87), Greater Kansas City C. of C. (centurian leadership program). Avocations: music, theatre, art, reading, travel. Office: Honeywell 2000 E 95th St Kansas City MO 64131-3030 Home: 6909 Burnt Sienna Cir Naples FL 34109-7828

CLEGG, ROGER BURTON, lawyer; b. Odessa, Tex., Apr. 18, 1955; s. Joe Dunn and Margaret Elisabeth (Blau) C.; m. Joann Ruth Catalfamo, June 15, 1985; 1 child, Paul. BA magna cum laude, Rice U., 1977; JD, Yale U., 1981. Bar: D.C. 1981. Grad. fellow Office Gen. Counsel, CIA, Langley, Va.; mem. staff editorial and research div. Republican Nat. Com., Washington, 1980; law clk. to presiding judge U.S. Ct. Appeals, Washington, 1981-82; atty.- adviser office of legal policy U.S. Dept. Justice, Washington, 1982, spl. asst. to atty. gen., 1982-83, dep. asst. atty. gen., 1983-84, acting asst. atty. gen., office legal policy, 1984, assoc. dep. atty. gen., 1984-85, spl. litigation counsel civil div., 1985, asst. to solicitor gen., 1985-87, dep. asst. atty. gen. civil rights div., 1987-91, dep. asst. atty. gen. env. div., 1991-93; v.p., gen. counsel Nat. Legal Ctr. for Pub. Interest, Washington, 1993-97, Ctr. for Equal Opportunity, Washington, 1997—. Editor-in-chief Yale Studies in World Public Order, 1979-80. Mem.: D.C. Bar, Federalist Soc., Phi Beta Kappa. Republican. Methodist. Home: 9703 Flintridge Ct Fairfax VA 22032-1712 Office: Ste 500 14 Pidgeon Hill Dr Sterling VA 20165

CLEGHORN, JOHN EDWARD, business executive; b. Montreal, July 7, 1941; m. Pattie E. Hart; children: Charles, Ian, Andrea. B in Commerce, McGill U., Montreal, 1962; DCL (hon.), Bishop's U., 1989; LLD (hon.), Wilfrid Laurier U., 1991; DCL (hon.), Acadia U., 1996. Chartered acct. Articled with Clarkson Gordon, chartered accts., Montreal, 1962-64; sugar and futures trader St. Lawrence Sugar Ltd., Montreal, 1964-66; with Citibank, NY, Montreal, Winnipeg & Vancouver, 1966—74; with Royal Bank of Canada, Montreal, Toronto & Vancouver, 1974—86, pres., 1986-90; pres., COO RBC, 1990—94; CEO Royal Bank of Can., Montreal, 1994-95, chmn., CEO, 1995—2001; chmn., bd. dirs. SNC Lavalin Group, Inc., 2001—. Bd. dirs. Finning Internat. Inc., Nortel Networks, Can. Pacific Rlwy. Ltd., McGill U; chmn. internat. adv. bd. McGill Faculty Mgmt.; dir. Can. Spl. Olympics Found.; chancellor Wilfrid Laurier U. Chmn. Hist. Found. of Can. Fellow Order of Chartered Accts. Quebec, Inst. Chartered Accts. Ont.; mem. Can. Inst. Chartered Accts., Inst. Chartered Accts. Brit. Columbia. Office: Ste 3115 31st Flr S Tower 200 Bay St Royal Bank Plz Toronto ON Canada M5J 2J5 Office Fax: 416-974-4420. Business E-Mail: john.cleghorn@rbc.com.

CLEGHORN, JOHN MICHAEL, communications executive; b. Atlanta, Jan. 15, 1962; s. George Reese and Gwendolyn Michael C.; m. Ellison Kelly Johnston; children: Ellison, Sophie. BA, Washington and Lee U., 1984. Journalist Charlotte (N.C.) Observer, 1984-90; chief speech writer Bank of Am., Charlotte, 1990-97, issues mgmt. exec., 1995-2000, corp. affairs exec. consumer and comml. banking, 2001—. Dir. Issues Mgmt. Coun., Washington. Editor: Words That Mattered: The Speeches of Hugh L. McColl, Jr., 1990-2000, 2001. Dir. Washington and Lee U. Bd. Alumni, Lexington, Va., 2000; bd. advisors U. N.C. Sch. Social Work, Charlotte, 1998—; elder, past clk. session Covenant Presbyn. Ch., Charlotte; participant Leadership Charlotte; chair, bd. dirs. Family Ctr., Charlotte, 1994-95; vice chair Annual Fund Washington and Lee U., Lexington, Va.; dir. Seversville Ptnrs. Inc., Charlotte, 1987-92. Recipient Disting. Young Alumnus Washington and Lee U., 1989, Outstanding Grad. in Journalism Simga Delta Chi, 1984, Excellence in Consumer Edn. award Nat. Assn. Consumer Agy. Adminstrs., 1998, Sch. Bell award for excellence in edn. reporting N.C. Assn. Educators, 1986. Mem. Am. Bankers Assn. (mem. comms. coun.) Presbyterian. Office: Bank Am 101 S Tryon St Charlotte NC 28255

CLEHANE, DIANE CATHERINE, journalist, writer, communications executive; b. N.Y.C., Sept. 2, 1960; d. Charles and Rita (Morley) C. BA in Journalism and Sociology, U. Mass., 1982. Asst. buyer Macy's N.Y., N.Y.C., 1982-84; dir. pub. rels. Anne Klein II, N.Y.C., 1984-85; dir. publicity, pub. rels. Liz Claiborne, Inc., N.Y.C., 1985-87; dir. pub. rels. Esmark, N.Y.C., 1987-88; sr. promotion writer Vogue, N.Y.C., 1988; mktg. promotion mgr. Elle Mag., N.Y.C., 1989; pres., creative dir. Madeline Comms., N.Y.C., 1989—; contbg. editor TV Guide, 1996—; corr. People mag., 1999—. Author: Diana--The Secrets of Her Style, 1998; author: I Love You, Mom!, 2003; contbg. author: TV Guide Fifty Years of Television, 2002. Fundraiser, mktg. cons. Adopt-A-Dog, Greenwich, Conn., 1994-96; fundraiser, pub. rels. Montefiore Hosp., N.Y.C., 1994-96. Mem. Fashion Group Internat. (editor newsletter 1990-91, events com. 1994—), Women in Comm. (co-chmn. program com.) Cosmetic Exec. Women, Alpha Chi Omega. Office: Madeline Comms 700 Scarsdale Ave Apt 3H Scarsdale NY 10583-5129

CLELAND, CHARLES CARR, psychologist, educator; b. Murphysboro, Ill., May 15, 1924; s. Homer W. and Stella (Carr) C.; m. Betty Lou Woodburn, July 18, 1948 BS, So. Ill. U., 1950, MS, 1951; PhD, U. Tex., 1957. Lic. psychologist, Tex. Chief psychologist Lincoln State Sch., Ill., 1956-57; chief psychologist Austin State Sch., 1957-59; supt. Abilene State Sch. Tex., 1959-63; prof. spl. edn. and ednl. psychology U. Tex.-Austin, 1963—. Author: Mental Retardation, 1969, 2d edit., 1978, Handbook for Widowers, 1997, Profound Retardation, 1979, Exceptionalities, 1982; contbr. articles to profl. jours.; patentee in field Bd. dirs. Child Guidance Ctr., Austin, 1966-67. Served with USAAF, 1943-46, PTO Recipient Disting. Psychologist award Tex. Psychol. Assn., 1980, Edn. award Am. Assn. Mental Deficiency, 1978 Fellow AAAS, Am. Psychol. Assn., Am. Assn. for Mental Deficiency (v.p. psychology div. 1973); mem. Tex. Psychol. Assn. (pres. 1962-63) Republican. Presbyterian. Office: U Tex E Db408A Austin TX 78712

CLELAND, JOSEPH MAXWELL (MAX CLELAND), education educator, retired state official; b. Atlanta, Ga., Aug. 24, 1942; s. Joseph Hugh and Juanita (Kesler) C. BA, Stetson U., Deland, Fla., 1964, LLD (hon.), 1979; MA, Emory U., 1968, hon. degree. Mem. Ga. Senate, Atlanta, 1971-75; cons. Com. on Vets. Affairs, U.S. Senate, Washington, 1975, profl. staff mem., 1975-77; adminstr. VA, Washington, 1977-81; sec. of state State of Ga., Atlanta, 1982-95; U.S. senator; mem. armed svcs. com., govtl. affairs com., small bus. com.; disting. adj. prof. Am. Univs. Washington Semester Program, 2003—. Mem. commerce com. U.S. Senate, 1999-2003; strategic cons. The Carmen Group, 2003—. Author: Strong at the Broken Places, 2000, Going for the Max!: 12 Principles for Living Life to the Fullest, 2002. Candidate U.S. Senate, Ga., 1996. Capt. U.S. Army, 1965-68, Vietnam. Decorated Bronze Star, Silver Star; fellow Ctr. for Congrl. and Presdl. Studies, 2003—; recipient Disting. Alumnus award Stetson U., 1972, Gt. Georgian award WSB Radio, award for gallantry Easter Seal Soc., 1973, Outstanding Handicapped Citizen in Ga. award, 1973, Jefferson award for greatest pub. service by individual under 35 Am. Inst. Pub. Service, 1977, Inspiration award Assn. U.S. Army, Atlanta, 1978, AMP of Yr. award, 1978, Life Inspiration award Religious Heritage Am., 1978, Golden Key award Am. Assn. Sch. Adminstrs., 1978, Gold medallion Chapel of Four Chaplains, 1979, Am. Patriot's medal Valley Forge Freedom's Found., 1979, J.O. Wright award, 1979, Neal Pike award, 1979, Citizen of Yr. award Nat. Conf. Citizenship, 1986; named One of Five Outstanding Young Men in Ga. Ga. Jaycees, Outstanding Disabled Vet. DAV, one of 100 most influential people in Ga. by Ga. Trend mag. Democrat. Office: The Carmen Group Inc Ste 800W 1299 Pennsylvania Ave NW Washington DC 20004*

CLELAND, MAX, former senator; b. Atlanta, 1942; BA, doctorate (hon.), Stetson U.; MA in Am. History, doctorate (hon.), Emory U. Mem. Ga. State Senate, 1971-75, sec. of state, 1983-96; U.S. senator from Ga., 1996—2003. Head U.S. VA, 1977-81, mgr. GI Bill, VA Home Loan Guaranty program, VA Hosp. program; founder First Stop Bus. Info. Ctr.; mem. Senate Armed Svcs. com., 1997-2003, com. on commerce, sci. and transp., 1999-2003, com. on govtl. affairs, 1997-2003, com. in small bus., 1997-2003. Author: (autobiography) Strong at the Broken Places. Capt. U.S. Army, 1967, Vietnam. Decorated Bronze Star, Silver Star; named One of Rising Democrats, Time Mag.; recipient Victory award Nat. Rehab. Hosp., Washington, 1996, Nat. award U.S. Small Bus. Adminstrn. Democrat. Office: PO Box 1054 Snellville GA 30078-1054*

CLELAND, SHERRILL, college president; b. Galion, Ohio, Sept. 21, 1924; s. Fred Burr and Doris Louise (Gregg) C.; m. Betty Irene Chorpenning, July 6, 1946 (dec. June 1986); children: Ann Denise Cleland Feldmeier, Douglas Stewart, Sarah McDermott Cleland Allen, Scott Cameron; m. Diana Ashley Drake, Sept. 3, 1988; stepchildren: Cynthia Rush, Allison Abizaid, Linda Wiener, Carol Abizaid, Amanda Abizaid, Richard Abizaid. AB, Oberlin Coll., 1949; MA, Princeton U., 1951, PhD in Econs., 1957; LLD (hon.), Marietta Coll., 1989. Instr. econs. Princeton U., 1951-55; asst. prof. U. Richmond, 1955-56; mem. faculty Kalamazoo Coll., 1956-73, acad. v.p., 1964-67; prof. econs., pres. Marietta Coll., Ohio, from 1973, now prof. emeritus. Econs. adviser Hashemite Kingdom Jordan, 1963-64; Ford Found. vis. prof. econs. and devel. adminstrn. Am. U. Beirut, Lebanon, 1967-69, hon. prof. Southwestern U. Fin. and Econs., Chengdu Peoples Republic China, 1985; cons. examiner North Ctrl. Assn. Colls., 1960-90; dir. Cleve. Fed. Res. Bank, Cin. br., 1980-85. Co-editor, author: Continuity and Change in the World Oil Industry, 1970; contbg. author: Linear Programming and Theory of Firm, 1962; contbr. to profl. jours. Pres. Kalamazoo chpt. Human Rels. Coun., 1958-60; bd. dirs. Tuition Educ. Inc.; chmn. Student Loan Funding Corp., 1991-97; bd. dirs. AHEAD Corp., Coll. and Univ. Resource Inst., Amideast, Inc.; past pres. Ohio Coll. Assn.; chmn. East Ctrl. Coll. Consortium, Ind. Colls., Univs. Ohio; trustee Oberlin Coll., 1976-82, Mt. Vernon Coll., 1992-97; Trustee Knowledge Works Found., Cin., 1997—. With AUS, 1944-46. Decorated Bronze Star, Purple Heart.; recipient Kazanjian Found. teaching award econs., 1971; Leadership tng. fellow N. Central Assn. Colls., 1959 Fellow Middle East Studies Assn.; mem. Am. Econ. Assn., UN Assn. (past pres. Kalamazoo chpt.), Ohio Assn. for Freedom to Die. Presbyterian. Home: 4489 Highland Oaks Cir Sarasota FL 34235-5175 Home (Summer): 67 Birch Tree Ln Waitsfield VT 05673 E-mail: dadcleland@aol.com.

CLELAND, THOMAS EDWARD, JR., secondary school educator; b. Holyoke, Mass., Nov. 4, 1943; s. Thomas Edward and Hazel (Mitchell) C.; m. Patricia Helen Deitz, Apr. 10, 1965; children: David T., Donna J., Todd R. BA in Liberal Arts, U. Mass., 1965; MS in Guidance, Troy State U., 1976. Cert. tchr. Ark., Mass., USAF. Commd. 2d lt. USAF, 1965, advanced through grades to col., 1986, ret., 1991; dir. aerospace sci. Pine Bluff (Ark.) H.S., 1991-93; chmn. aerospace sci. dept. Ctrl. H.S., Springfield, Mass., 1993—. Author: (manual) Guide for Instructor Supervisors, 1978, AFJROTC Cadet Guide, 1992. Deacon, trustee United Congrl. Ch., Holyoke, 1994—; mem. Vets. Activities Com., Sprinfield, 1996, pastoral search com., Holyoke, 1994—. Recipient 13 Air medals, Letter of Appreciation Pres. Bush, 1991. Mem. Air Force Assn., Am. Legion, Ret. Officers Assn., Aircraft Owners & Pilots Assn., Red River Valley Fighter Pilots Assn., Springfield Tchrs. Assn., Order of Daedalians (flight capt.). Avocations: aviation history, running. Home: 36 Roosevelt Ave South Hadley MA 01075-2337 Office: Springfield Ctrl HS 1840 Roosevelt Ave Springfield MA 01109-2437 E-mail: flytec@aol.com.

CLELAND, W(ILLIAM) WALLACE, biochemistry educator; b. Balt., Jan. 6, 1930; s. Ralph E. and Elizabeth P. (Shoyer) C.; m. Joan K. Hookanson, June 18, 1967 (div. Mar. 1999); children: Elsa Eleanor, Erica Elizabeth. AB summa cum laude, Oberlin Coll., 1950; MS, U. Wis., 1953, PhD, 1955. Postdoctoral fellow U. Chgo., 1957-59; asst. prof. U. Wis., Madison, 1959-62, assoc. prof., 1962-66, prof., 1966—, M.J. Johnson prof. biochemistry, 1978—, Steenbock prof. chem. sci., 1982—2002. Contbr. articles to profl. biochem. and chem. jours. Served with U.S. Army, 1957-59. Grantee NIH, 1960—, NSF, 1960-94; recipient Stein and Moore award Protein Soc., 1999. Mem. NAS, Am. Acad. Arts and Scis., Am. Soc. Biochemistry and Molecular Biology (Merck award 1990), Am. Chem. Soc. (Alfred R. Bader Bioinorganic or Bioorganic Chem. award 1993, Repligen award 1995). Achievements include development of dithiothreitol (Cleland's Reagent) as reducing agent for thiol groups; development of application of kinetic methods for determining enzyme mechanism. Office: Enzyme Inst 1710 University Ave Madison WI 53726-4087 E-mail: cleland@biochem.wisc.edu.

CLELLAND, CARMEN C. pharmacist; b. Clinton, Okla., Dec. 27, 1963; s. Carmen E and Maudine E. Clelland; m. Laura A Scott; children: Kwsind, Ehoni, Nokomis children: Natasha. BS in Chemistry, Southeastern Okla. State U., 1986; BS in Pharmacy, U. Okla., 1989, PharmD, 2002. Registered pharmacist 1989. USPHS pharmacy resident Winslow Svc. Unit, Indian Health Svc., Winslow, Ariz., 1989—90; clin. pharmacist Yakima Svc. Unit, Indian Health Svc., Yakima, Wash., 1990—92; pharmacist Economy Pharmacy, Muskogee, Okla., 1992—99; clin. pharmacist, diabetes educator Columbia Diabetes Pharmacy, Tulsa, Okla., 1995—97; dir. pharmacy, diabetes educator Tulsa Indian Health Care, 1997—99; asst. chief pharmacist, clin. pharmacist, diabetes educator Winslow Svc. Unit, Indian Health Svc., 1999—. HIV/Aids counselor Yakima Svc. Unit, Indian Health Svc., 1991—92; cons. pharmacist, AIDS counselor New Hope Clinic, Yakima, 1991—92; EEO counselor Winslow Svc. Unit, Indian Health Svc., 2001—, cert. insulin pump trainer, 2000—; diabetes cons. Diabetsource, Okmulgee, Okla., 1997—99. Contbr. articles. Commdr. USPHS, 2003, Arizona. Recipient citation, USPHS, 2000, Achievement medal, USPHS, 2001, Area Dir.'s Award For Exceptional Performance, Navajo Nation, 2001, Area Dir.'s award for Health Promotion, 2001, Am. Indian/Alaska Native Commd. Officer's award, 2001. Mem.: Res. Officers Assn., Commd. Officers Assn., Am. Pharm. Assn., Phi Delta Chi. Presbyterian. Avocations: running, biking, tennis, travel. Home: 1900 Mountain Dr Winslow AZ 86047 Office: U S Public Health Service PO Drawer 40 / 500 N Indiana Winslow AZ 86047 Office Fax: 928-289-5668. Personal E-mail: lclelland@cybertrails.com. Business E-Mail: carmen.clelland@winslow.ihs.gov.

CLEM, ALAN LELAND, political scientist, educator; b. Lincoln, Nebr., Mar. 4, 1929; s. Remey Leland and Bernice (Thompson) C.; m. Mary Louise Burke, Oct. 24, 1953; children: Andrew, Christopher, Constance, John, Daniel. BA, U. Nebr., 1950; MA, Am. U., 1957, PhD, 1960. Copywriter, research dir. Ayres Advt. Agy., Lincoln, 1950-52; press sec. to Congressman Carl Curtis of Nebr., 1953-54, Congressman R. D. Harrison of Nebr., 1955-58; info. specialist Fgn. Agrl. Service, Dept. Agr., 1959-60; asst. prof. polit. sci. U. S.D., Vermillion, 1960-62, assoc. prof., 1962-64, prof., 1965—; assoc. dir. Govtl. Research Bur., 1962-76, chmn. dept. polit. sci., 1976-78; ptnr. Opinion Survey Assocs., 1964-88. State analyst Comparative State Elections Project, U. N.C., 1968-73; dir. Mt. Rushmore Presdl. Inst., 1970-71; mem. U.S. Census Bur. Adv. Com. on State and Local Govt. Stats., 1970-74 Author: several books, including Prairie State Politics: Popular Democracy in South Dakota, 1967, The Making of Congressmen: Seven Campaigns of 1974, 1976, American Electoral Politics: Strategies for Renewal, 1981, Law Enforcement: The South Dakota Experience, 1982, The Government We Deserve, 1985, 5th edit., 1995, Congress: Powers, Processes and Politics, 1989, Government by the People? South Dakota Politics in the Last Third of the 20th Century, 2001; contbr. articles to profl. jours.; editor: Contemporary Approaches to State Constitutional Revision, 1969. Mem. Vermillion City Coun., 1965-69; sr. warden St. Paul's Episcopal Ch., Vermillion, 1971-73, treas., 1996—. Named Outstanding Alumnus, U. Nebr. Coll. Arts and Scis., 1998; Nat. Conv. faculty fellow, 1964. Mem. Mensa, Midwest Polit. Sci. Assn. (exec. council 1970-72, editorial bd. Am. Jour. Polit. Sci. 1971-72), Am. Polit. Sci. Assn., Phi Beta Kappa, Phi Alpha Theta, Pi Sigma Alpha (nat. coun. 1986-89), Sigma Delta Chi. Clubs: Vermillion Golf Assn. (pres. 1986-87). Republican. Home: 608 Colonial Ct Vermillion SD 57069-3424 Office: U SD Dept Polit Sci Vermillion SD 57069 *Avoid haste, anxiety, contentiousness, and self-centeredness. Care, clarity, persistence, honesty, and grace will prevail in the long run.*

CLEM, HARRIET FRANCES, library director; b. Akron, Ohio, Nov. 8, 1940; d. Paul Milton and Mary Eva (Koppes) Miller; m. Ross Lynn Clem, June 23, 1979. BA cum laude, Kent State U., 1963, MLS, 1965. Teletype operator Babcock & Wilcox Co., Barberton, Ohio, 1958-59; bookmobile libr. Wadsworth (Ohio) Pub. Libr., 1963-64; head ext. dept. Rodman Pub. Libr., Alliance, Ohio, 1965-68, libr. dir., 1969—. Instr. children's lit. Mt. Union Coll., Alliance, 1970-71; instr. libr. sci. Kent (Ohio) State U., 1975-7 Trustee YMCA, Alliance, 1974-84; pres. ARC, Alliance, 1975-77; bd. dirs. Leadership Stark County, Canton, Ohio, 1997-2003. Named Boss of Yr., Assn. Secs., Alliance, 1982; honoree Stark County Bicentennial Wall of Fame, 2003. Mem. Ohio Libr. Coun. (founder acctg. divsn.), Alliance C. of C. (pres. 1983, 93, Athena award 1990), Greater Alliance Devel. Corp. (pres. 2000), Beatrix Potter Soc., C.S. Lewis Soc., Alliance Women's Club (pres. 1977), Aliiance Country Club, Coterie, Sorosis, Beta Phi Mu (nat. coun. 1978-80). Episcopalian. Avocations: travel, cooking. Home: 13484 Louisville St NE Paris OH 44669-9713 Office: Rodman Pub Libr 215 E Broadway St Alliance OH 44601-2650

CLEM, JOHN RICHARD, physicist, educator; b. Waukegan, Ill., Apr. 24, 1938; s. Gilbert D. and Bernelda May (Moyer) Clem; m. Judith Ann Paulsen, Aug. 27, 1960; children: Paul Gilbert, Jean Ann. BS, U. Ill., 1960, MS, 1962, PhD, 1965. Rsch. assoc. U. Md., College Park, 1965-66; vis. rsch. fellow Tech. U., Munich, 1966-67; from asst. prof. to assoc. prof. physics Iowa State U., Ames, 1967—75, prof., 1975—, disting. prof. in liberal arts and scis., 1989—, chmn. dept. physics, 1982-85. Vis. staff mem. Los Alamos Nat. Lab., 1971—83, cons., 1997—2001, Argonne Nat. Lab., Ill., 1971—76, Brookhaven Nat. Lab., Upton, NY, 1980—81, Oak Ridge (Tenn.) Nat. Lab., 1981, Allied-Signal, Torrance, Calif., 1990—92, Am. Superconductor Corp., Westborough, Mass., 1996—97, Pirelli Cable Corp., Lexington, SC, 1996—97; guest prof. U. Tuebingen, Germany, 1978; cons. IBM Watson Rsch. Ctr., Yorktown Heights, NY, 1982—85, vis. scientist, 1985—86, Electric Power Rsch. Inst., Palo Alto, Calif., 1992—93; vis. prof. applied physics Stanford U., 1992—93. Editor: Virtual Jour. Applications Superconductivity; sci. editor: newsletter High-To Update; contbr. articles to profl. jours. Recipient award for sustained outstanding rsch. in solid state physics, U.S. Dept. Energy; Fulbright Sr. Rsch. fellow, 1974—75, NATO grantee, 1979—82. Fellow: Am. Phys. Soc. (chair divsn. condensed matter physics 1994—95); mem.: AAUP, Iowa Acad. Sci., Sigma Xi, Phi Kappa Phi, Tau Beta Pi. Democrat. Presbyterian. Achievements include patents in field. Avocation: singing. Home: 2307 Timberland Rd Ames IA 50014-8251 Office: Iowa State Univ A517 Physics Ames IA 50011-3160 E-mail: clem@ameslab.gov.

CLEM, RALPH S. career officer; BA in Geography with honors, San Diego State Coll., 1965; MA in Geography and Soviet Studies, Columbia U., 1972, PhD in Geography and Soviet Studies with distinction, 1976; student, Air Command and Staff Coll., 1987, Air War Coll., 1989. Commd. 2d lt. USAF, 1965, advanced through grades to brig. gen., 1996; spl. agt. detachment 101 Office Spl. Investigations, Hartford, 1965-68, spl. agt. dist. 51 Bangkok, 1968-69, supervising case officer hdqs. Washington, 1969-70; chief intelligence 915th Airborne Early Warning and Control Group, Homestead AFB, Fla., 1976-78, 93rd Tactical Fighter Squadron, Homestead AFB, 1978-83, 482d Tactical Fighter Wing, Homestead AFB, 1983-90; intelligence staff officer, sr. strategic air ops. analyst Office Mil. Forces, Nat. Security Agy., Ft. George G. Meade, Md., 1990-93; mobilization asst. to asst. dep. dir. ops. Nat. Security Agy., Ft. George G. Meade, 1993-96; mobilization asst. to comdr. Hdqs. Air Intelligence Agy., Kelly AFB, Tex., 1996-98; dep. chief Air Force Res. Hdqs. USAF, Washington, 1998-2000; aide to chief of Air Force Res., 2000—. Contbr. articles to profl. jours. Decorated Rep. Vietnam Campaign medal. Office: HQ USAF/RE 1150 Air Force Pentagon Washington DC 20330-1150

CLEMA, JOE KOTOUC, computer scientist; b. Omaha, Sept. 23, 1938; s. Joseph Arthur and Sylva Marie (Kotouc) C.; m. Maria Estela Cobos, Apr. 1, 1960; children: Jennifer, Arta. Student, U.S. Mil. Acad., 1957-60; BS, U. Nebr., 1963; MS, U. Miami, 1969; PhD, Colo. State U., 1973. Systems analyst Gen. Electric, Louisville, 1969-70; head sci. applications Colo. State U., Ft. Collins, 1970-73; project engr. Gen. Dynamics, Ft. Worth, 1973-77; sr. mgr. Simulation Tech., Inc., Dayton, Ohio, 1977-79; program mgr. Pratt and Whitney, West Palm Beach, Fla., 1979-82; dept. mgr. CACI, Dayton, 1982-83; dir. spl. projects Systems and Applied Scis., Vienna, Va., 1983-85; chief software engr. IIT Rsch. Inst., Annapolis, Md., 1985-90; cons. to IBM with, pres. Neurosystems, Inc., Bethesda, Md., 1991-98; cons, on IRS tax system modernization TRW, Merrifield, Va., 1993-95, cons. simplified tax & wage sys., 1995-96; mgr. Sys. Resources Corp., 1997-98, Houston Assocs., Inc., Arlington, Va., 1998—2002; dir. Nat. Tech., Inc., McLean, Va., 2002—. Contbr. articles to profl. jours. Sustaining mem. Rep. Nat. Com., Washington, 1983—. Served to capt. U.S. Army, 1963-67. First Ann. Simulation Symposium Rsch. grantee, 1972; recipient Outstanding Svc. award Ann. Simulation Symposium Bd. Dirs., 1980. Mem.: ACM (nat. lectr. 1978—83), IEEE (sr.), Internat. Platform Assn., Ann. Simulation Symposium (chmn. bd. dirs. 1979), Spl. Interest Group on Simulation (chmn. 1979—81), Mid Atlantic Electronic Commerce Network (bd. dirs. 1995—98), Soc. Computer Simulation (bd. dirs., program chmn. 1988—96), Nat. Def. Indsl. Assn., Herndon C. of C., Toastmasters, No. Va. Tech. Coun., Armed Forces Comm. and Elec. Assn., Worldgate Athletic Club, Hidden Creek Country Club. Republican. Avocations: bridge, tennis. Home: 301 Missouri Ave Herndon VA 20170-5426 Office: Nat Tech Inc Ste 700 2010 Corporate Ridge Mc Lean VA 22102 E-mail: joe.clema@nt-i.com., joeclema2@cs.com.

CLEMEN, JOHN DOUGLAS, lawyer; b. Mineola, N.Y., Dec. 18, 1944; s. John Douglas and Amy Gertrude (Ackerson) C.; m. Judith Anne Davis, June 3, 1967; children: Elizabeth, Jennifer. BA, Hobart Coll., 1966; JD cum laude, Seton Hall U., 1974. Bar: N.J. 1974, U.S. Dist. Ct. N.J. 1974, U.S. Ct. Appeals (3d cir.) 1980, U.S. Supreme Ct. 1982, N.Y. 1984, U.S. Dist. Ct. (so. dist.) N.Y. 1985, U.S. Dist. Ct. (ea. dist.) N.Y. 1989, U.S. Ct. Appeals (2d cir.) 1989. Law sec. to assoc. justice N.J. Supreme Ct., Trenton, 1974-75; assoc. Shanley & Fisher, P.C., Newark, 1975-83, ptnr., 1983-99; founding ptnr. Hooker, Pucciarelli, Clemen & Tibbs (and predecessor firm), Woodcliff Lake, NJ, 1999—. Arbitrator U.S. Dist. Ct. N.J., 1985—, N.J. Superior Ct., Morristown, 1986—, N.J. Superior Ct., Hackensack, 2002—; guest lectr. Acad. Medicine N.J., 1980-82. Contbg. editor Seton Hall Law Rev., 1973-74. Bd. dirs. Acad. Decathalon of N.J., 1997—; mem. Mass Disaster Response Team, ARC, 1997—. Capt. USAF, 1966-71, Vietnam. Decorated Air medal. Mem. ABA, N.J. Bar Assn. (chmn. aviation sect. 1992-94), N.Y. State Bar Assn., Assn. Bar City N.Y. (mem. aeronautics com. 1992—), Trial Attys. N.J., Bergen County Bar Assn., Commerce and Industry Assn. N.J. (bd. dirs. 1986—, counsel 1988-92). Home: 574 Colonial Rd River Vale NJ 07675-6107 Office: Hooker Pucciarelli Clemen & Tibbs 172 Broadway Woodcliff Lake NJ 07677-8077 E-mail: jdclemen@aol.com.

CLEMENCE, ROGER DAVIDSON, landscape architect, educator; b. Worcester, Mass., Jan. 20, 1936; s. Luther Davidson and Dorothy (Kay) C.; m. Margaret Ann Weinandy, Aug. 19, 1961; children: Peter, Benjamin, Ellsabeth. AB, Amherst Coll., 1957; MArch, U. Pa., 1960, M in Landscape Architecture, 1962. Registered landscape architect, Minn. Instr., asst. prof. Coll. Architecture and Design U. Mich., Ann Arbor, 1962-66; assoc. prof. Sch. Architecture and Landscape Architecture U. Minn., Mpls., 1966-73, dir. Urban Edn. Ctr., Sch. Architecture and Landscape Architecture, 1970-77, interim head Sch. Architecture and Landscape Architecture, 1984, mem. urban studies faculty Coll. Liberal Arts, 1973—97, mem. am. studies faculty Coll. Liberal Arts, 1986—97, dir. grad. studies in architecture Sch. Architecture and Landscape Architecture, 1978-85, prof. dept. architecture, 1973, assoc. dean Coll. of Architecture and Landscape Architecture, 1989-95, acting dean, spring 1993, interim dean, 1995-96. Landscape arch., planner, Mpls., 1963; collegiate program leader Minn. Ext. Svc., 1993-97, prof. emeritus, summer 1997—. Co-creator 10-part TV series The Meanings of Place, 1986. Mem. Minn. Com. on Urban Environment, 1979-88, Designer Selection Bd., 1980-85, chmn., 1983-84; mem. Mpls. Fed. Cts. Master Plan Com., 1991-92. Recipient Morse-Alumni Disting. Tchg. award, 1974, Pub. Svc. award Minn. Soc. Landscape Architects, 1982, Lob Pine award, 1996, CALA Disting. Svc. award, 1995; T.P. Chandler fellow U. Pa. Grad. Sch. Fine Arts, 1960-62; HWS Cleveland Vis. scholar U.

Minn., 2000-03. Fellow Am. Soc. Landscape Architects; mem. AIA (prof. affiliate Minn. chapt. 1979), MASLA, Tau Sigma Delta. Democrat. Mem. Unitarian Universalist Assn. Avocations: photography, writing, golf, reading, gardening. Office: U Minn CALA 89 Church St SE Minneapolis MN 55455-0109

CLEMENDOR, ANTHONY ARNOLD, obstetrician, gynecologist, educator; b. Port-of-Spain, Trinidad, Trinidad, Nov. 8, 1933; came to US, 1954, naturalized, 1959; s. Anthony Arnold and Beatrice Helen (Stewart) C.; m. Elaine Browne, May 31, 1958 (dec. May, 1991); children: Anthony Arnold, David Alan; m. Janat Jenkins, Sept. 23, 1993. AB, NYU, 1959; MD, Howard U., 1963. Diplomate Am. Bd. Ob-Gyn. Intern USPHS, S.I., N.Y., 1963-64; resident Met. Hosp. Ctr., N.Y.C., 1964-68; chief outpatient dept. ob-gyn Metro. Hosp. Ctr., N.Y.C., 1969-73; med. dir. family planning Human Resources Adminstrn., N.Y.C., 1973-74; assoc. dean student affairs, dir. office minority affairs N.Y. Med. Coll., Valhalla, 1974-97, assoc. clin. prof. dept. ob-gyn, 1978-90, prof. clin. ob-gyn, 1990-98; clin. prof. ob-gyn., 1998—. Bd. dirs. Elmcore, Caribbean-Am. Ctr. N.Y.C., Nat. Assn. Minority Med. Educators, Inc., 1978-88, Empire State Med. Sci. and Ednl. Found., Inc., Caribbean Am. Ctr. N.Y., 1988-91; mem. Nat. Urban League, N.Y. Urban League; life mem. NAACP. Fellow ACOG, APHA; mem. AMA (mem. survey team liaison com. on med. edn. 1989—, del. N.Y. State 1998—), Am. Fertility Soc., Nat. Med. Assn., N.Y. State Med. Soc. (treas. PAC 1997, councilor 1999-2002, asst. sec. 2002), N.Y. County Med. Soc. (sec. 1989, v.p. 1990, pres. elect 1991, pres. 1992-93, bd. trustees, chmn. bd. trustees 1997-98), N.Y. Acad. Medicine, N.Y. Gynecol. Soc. (v.p. 1986, pres. 1988).

CLEMENS, CHARLES JOSEPH, insurance agent; b. Phila., Mar. 1, 1942; s. Charles Wesley and Jane Elizabeth (Nesselhauf) C.; m. Keiko Kobayashi, Aug. 12, 1965 (dec. 2002); 1 child, Charles S.; m. Pranomkorn Rungarunvasin, Apr. 7, 2000. BA, Calif. State U., Fullerton, 1970; MBA, U. So. Calif., 1972. CLU. Asst. mgr. ins. N.Y. Life Ins. Co., Anaheim, Calif., 1971-74; ins. agt. Santa Ana, Calif., 1974-77; brokerage mgr. Alliance Ins. Co., Santa Ana, 1977-79; regional mgr. CIGNA, Orange, Calif., 1979-87; ins. agt. Garden Grove, Calif., 1987-93; ins. agt., broker Anaheim, 1993-96, Morro Bay, 1996—2002; contract specialist U.S. Govt., 2002—. Lt. col. USAF, ret. Republican. Avocations: jogging, biking, auto restoration. Home: 1940 SW River Square Portland OR 97201 E-mail: cjclemens@yahoo.com.

CLEMENS, DAVID ALLEN, minister; b. Camden, N.J., Aug. 8, 1941; s. Arleigh and Mae C.; m. Janice, Feb. 13, 1965; children: Stephen David, Daniel Lee. BA magna cum laude, Houghton Coll., 1963; MA, Nat. Christian U., 1972; ThD, Clarksville Sch. Theology, 1980; PhD, Christian Bible Coll., 1990. Ordained to ministry Ind. Bapt. Ch., 1963. Missionary Pocket Testament League, Argentina, Paraguay, Chile, Peru, Bolivia, 1963-66; min. Richfield (Pa.) Mennonite Ch., 1966-67; itinerant Bible tchr. Bible Club Movement Inc., Upper Darby, Pa., 1968-2000, nat. rep., 1971-77, dir. Family Adult Ministries dept., 1977-80, min. at large, 1980-99, missionary, Bible tchr., 1999-2000; pres., Bible tchr. David Clemens Bible Tchg. Ministries, Inc., Marlton, 2000—. Preaching and teaching tours Eng., Scotland, The Netherlands, Belgium, Sweden, Spain, Ireland, Can., Middle East, The Philippines, Zimbabwe, Poland, Cuba, Italy, Germany, Switzerland. Author: Steps to Maturity, Vols. I-III, 1973-79, How to Get Along With Impossible People, 1978. Mem. Nat. Home Missions Fellowship. Home and Office: 72 Knox Blvd Marlton NJ 08053-2921 *To know, love, and serve God (as revealed in Jesus Christ) is the highest privilege of life.*

CLEMENS, DONALD FAULL, chemistry educator; b. Dover, Ohio, Aug. 14, 1929; s. John William and Ruth (Faull) C.; m. Martha Kay Lemmon, July 2, 1950; children: Richard, Nancy, Barbara, Rebecca, Margaret. BS, Fla. Southern, 1961; MS, U. Fla., 1963, PhD, 1965. Prof. chemistry East Carolina U., Greenville, N.C., 1965-95, prof. emeritus, 1995—. V.p. Whitehurst Assocs., New Bern, N.C., 1982—. Co-inventor, patentee processes for making chelating agents for metal ions from saccharides, wet process phosphoric acid brightening reagent for aluminum. Bd. dirs. Kiwanis Club, Greenville, 1986-89; chmn. bd. St. James Meth. Ch., Greenville, 1989-90. Mem. Am. Chem. Soc. (councilor ea. N.C. sect. 1985-94, nat. com. on chem. safety 1988-94), N.C. Acad. Sci., Masons, Sigma Xi. Avocations: woodworking, birdwatching, ham radio operator. Home: 405 Walnut Ridge Dr SE Floyd VA 24091-4709

CLEMENS, MICHAEL TERRENCE, furniture manufacturing representative; b. Dubuque, Iowa, Apr. 7, 1950; s. William Michael and Mary Ellen (Degear) C.; m. Christine Marie Busalacchi, May 17, 1975; children: James William, Anthony Michael, Jennifer Lee. BBA, Loyola U., New Orleans, 1972. Mfr. rep. Flexsteel Industries, Inc., Dubuque, Iowa, 1973-79, 1980—; asst. golf profl. Fort Dodge (Iowa) Country Club, 1972. Mem. Northville (Mich.) Jaycees, 1980, Flexsteel 1989 All-Star Sales Team. Mem. Mich. Home Furnishings Reps. Assn., Wis. Home Furnishings Reps. Assn. (pres. 1978), Internat. Home Furnishings Reps. Assn., Home Furnishing Reps. of Mich. (treas.), Flexsteel Seven Million Dollar Sales Club, Nat. of Evansville Million Dollar Club (charter), Walnut Creek Country Club, Beta Gamma Sigma, Alpha Sigma Nu. Avocations: golf, water skiing, photography. Office: Flexsteel Industries 42128 Crestview Cir Northville MI 48167-2205

CLEMENS, RICHARD GLENN, lawyer; b. Chgo., Oct. 8, 1940; s. James Ralston and Jeanette Louise (Moellering) C.; m. Judith B. Clemens, Aug. 19, 1967; 1 child, Kathleen. BA, U. Va., 1962, JD, 1965. Bar: Ill. 1965. Assoc. Sidley Austin Brown & Wood LLP, Chgo., 1965—66, Washington, 1968—71, Brussels, 1972—73, ptnr. Chgo., 1973—. Served to capt. U.S. Army, 1966-68. Mem. ABA, Chgo. Bar Assn., Lawyers Club, Mid-Day Club. Office: Sidley Austin Brown & Wood LLC 10 S Dearborn St Chicago IL 60603 E-mail: rclemens@sidley.com.

CLEMENS, ROGER, professional baseball player; b. Dayton, Ohio, Aug. 4, 1962; m. Debbie Lynn Godfrey, May 27, 1963; children: Koby Aaron, Kory Allen, Kacy Austin, Kody Alec. Student, San Jacinto North Jr. Coll., Houston, 1980—81, U. Tex., 1981—83. Baseball player Boston Red Sox, 1984—96, Toronto Blue Jays, 1997—98, N.Y. Yankees, 1998—. Named Major League Player of Yr., Sporting News, 1986, Pitcher of Yr., 1986, 1991, N.Y. Yankees World Champion Team, 1999; named to All-Star Game, Am. League, 1986, 1988, 1990—92; recipient Cy Young award, 1986, 1987, 1991, 1997, 1998, Most Valuable Player award, 1986, All-Star Game, 1986. Office: New York Yankees Yankee Stadium E 161 St & River Ave Bronx NY 10451

CLEMENS, T. PAT, manufacturing company executive; b. Hibbing, Minn., July 26, 1944; s. Jack LeRoy and Mildred (Coss) C.; m. 1966 (div. 1992); children: Patrick Michael, Heather Kristen. BS in Econs. and Mgmt., St. Cloud State U., 1968; student of theology, Coll. St. Thomas, 1985-87. Sales adminstr. Transistor Electronics Co., Eden Prairie, Minn., 1969; head instnl. sales Chiquita Brands, Edina, Minn., 1970; dist. sales mgr. Menley & James Labs., Phila., 1971-75; owner, pres. T.P. Clemens Labs., Eagan, Minn., 1975—. Instr community edn. Rosemount, Minn., 1977-78; bd. dirs. Rosemount Hockey, 1977-78, Relocation Assistance Assn. Am., 1984-85; v.p. Sch. Dist. #196 Booster Club, 1984-85; lectr. econs. to corps., high schs. and colls. in U.S., Scotland, Ireland, and Jamaica, 1979—. Author, editor: How Prejudice and Narcissism Control Economics of the United States and the World, 1979. Mem. Rosemont Cmty. Edn. Bd., 1985, chmn., 1986-87; chmn. speakers bur. Citizens Steering Com., 1984-85; coach Little League, 1970-82, 88-91; coach high sch. weight lifting team, 1975-95; vol. worker with comatose children, 1975-96, 97—. Recipient letter of recognition for stopping armed robbery Dakota County Atty.'s Dept., 1979, 93. Mem. Internat. Platform Assn., Kids-N-Kinship Program 1988-92. Home and Office: 1276 Vildmark Dr Eagan MN 55123-2801

CLEMENSON, DAVID LEE, philosopher, educator; b. Portland, Oreg., Feb. 18, 1957; s. Gale Lamont Clemenson and Carolyn Sue Gervasiio; m. Donna Carol Franklin, Sept. 4, 1999. BS in Math., Portland State U., 1980; MS in Physics, U. Wis., 1982, MA in History of Sci., 1984; PhD in History of Sci., Harvard U., 1991; PhD in Philosophy, Rice U., 2001. Instr. Harvard U., Cambridge, Mass., 1991—92; tutor St. John's Coll., Annapolis, Md., 1992—94; adj. U. Houston, 1997, Tex. A&M, Galveston, 1998; asst. prof. philosophy U. St. Thomas, St. Paul, 1999—. Grad. fellow, NSF, 1980—84, Harvard U., 1984—86, rsch. grantee, Aquinos Found., 2001. Mem.: Am. Philos. Assn. Achievements include research in new paradox of model logic that provides the resources for a formally rigorous derivation. Avocation: hiking. Office: Univ St Thomas 2115 Summit Ave Saint Paul MN 55105-1096

CLEMENT, BARBARA KOLTES SADTLER, academic administrator; b. Hutchinson, Kans., Mar. 1, 1940; d. Edwin Michael and Rose Marie (Meyers) Koltes; m. David R. Sadtler, Aug. 24, 1963 (div. June 1974); m. Charles F. Clement III, Mar. 7, 1987. BA, U. Minn., 1961. Analyst Nat. Security Agy., Ft. Meade, Md., 1963—66; journalist Newhouse Nat. News Svc., N.Y.C., 1966-71; v.p. advt., pub. rels. Leslie Fay, Inc., N.Y.C., 1971-79; v.p. internat. pub. rels. Estee Lauder Internat. Cos., N.Y.C., 1979-94; asst. v.p., dir. Office of Comm. and Pub. Affairs, Villanova (Pa.) U., 1994—. Author: Orbits of Venus, 1994; editor Villanova Mag., 1994—. Republican. Office: Villanova Univ 800 Lancaster Ave Villanova PA 19085-1478 E-mail: barbara.clement@villanov.edu.

CLEMENT, BOB, former congressman; b. Nashville, Sept. 23, 1943; m. Mary Carson; children: Greg, Jeff, Elizabeth, Rachel. BS, U. Tenn., 1967; MBA, Memphis State U., 1968. Founder, owner Bob Clement and Assocs., 1979—; with Clement Ctr. for Govt. Tng. U. Tenn., 1971-72; commr. Tenn. Pub. Svc., 1973-79; dir. TVA, 1979-81; ptnr., owner Charter Equities, 1981-83; pres. Cumberland U., 1983-87; mem. 100th-107th Congresses from 5th Tenn. dist., Washington, 1988—2002; mem. budget, transp. and infrastructure coms. With U.S. Army, 1969-71, with USNG, 1971-2000. Democrat. E-mail: bob.clement@mail.house.gov.

CLEMENT, CLAYTON EMERSON, lawyer; b. Oakland, Calif., Dec. 3, 1943; s. Robert Emerson and Dorothy Winslow (Deacon) C.; m. Barbara Jonas, Sept. 4, 1965 (div. Aug. 1984); children: Robert, Jason; m. Kimberly Anderson, Nov. 30, 1991. BA with honors, U. Pacific, 1965; JD, U. Calif., Berkeley, 1968. Bar: Calif. 1969, U.S. Dist. Ct. (no. dist.) Calif. 1969, U.S. Ct. Appeals (9th cir.) 1969, U.S. Supreme Ct. 1972. Assoc. Cox & Cummins, Martinez, Calif., 1968-71; ptnr. Arata, Misuraca & Clement, Santa Rosa, Calif., 1972-75; pvt. practice Santa Rosa, 1976-78; ptnr. Clement, Fitzpatrick & Kenworthy, Santa Rosa, 1978—. Instr. Santa Rosa Jr. Coll., 1977-85; assoc. prof. law Kennedy U., Martinez, Calif., 1969-72. Dir. Sonoma County Family YMCA, Santa Rosa, 1985-91; treas. BOSCO for Congress Com., Santa Rosa, 1982-90. Fellow Am. Coll. Trial Lawyers; mem. ABA, Assn. Bus. Trial Lawyers, Am. Bd. Trial Advocates. Democrat. Avocations: flying, fishing. Home: 4199 Pine Rock Pl Santa Rosa CA 95409-4014 Office: Clement Fitzpatrick & Kenworthy 3333 Mendocino Ave Ste 200 Santa Rosa CA 95403-2233 E-mail: cclement@cfk.com.

CLEMENT, DANIEL ROY, IV, accountant, assistant nurse, small business owner, tax preparation consultant; b. Kirtland, Ohio, Apr. 2, 1943; s. Roy A. Jr. and Evelyn Violet (Hale Chase) C.; m. Jennifer Ilean Handley, July 10, 1965 (div. 1975); children: Elizabeth Ann Clement Baitt, Catherine Lynn Clement Holder; m. Barbara Jane Griffiths, Dec. 10, 1985. Student, Fenn Coll., 1961-63, Alexander Hamilton Inst., 1963-67, Am. Inst. of Banking, 1963-65, Lakeland Coll., 1965-70, Case Western Res. U., 1970-73, Lake Erie Coll., 1973-85, Auburn Career Ctr., 1987—; PhD, Case Western Res. U., 1999. Shipping and cost acctg. Mentor (Ohio) Products, 1961; acctg. asst. N.Y. Cen. Transport, Cleve., 1963-65; acct. mgr. Am. Soc. of Metals, Novelty, Ohio, 1965-67; corp. fleet mgr. Addressograph Multigraph, Euclid, Ohio, 1967-72; treas. Debevec Salo & Assocs., Painesville, Ohio, 1972-74; with sales Pontiac Cadillac-Record Shack, Mentor, 1974-78; shipping coord. Ajax Mfg., Euclid, 1978-82. Notary pub. Active Jr. C. of C., Mentor, Willoughby, Brunswick, Novelty, Lake County, 1962-78; mem. Congl. Task Force Pres. Bush, 1981-94. Republican. Methodist. Avocations: gardening, dogs, cats, tropical fish, camping. Home: 5724C Lake Rd E Geneva OH 44041 Address: 5724C Lake Rd E 1 Geneva OH 44041

CLEMENT, EDITH BROWN, federal judge; b. Birmingham, Ala., Apr. 29, 1948; d. Erskine John and Edith (Burrus) Brown; m. Rutledge Carter Clement Jr., Sept. 3, 1972; children: Rutledge Carter III, Catherine Lanier. BA, U. Ala., 1969; JD, Tulane U., 1972. Bar: La. 1973. Law clk. to Hon. Herbert W. Christenberry U.S. Dist. Ct., New Orleans, 1973-75; ptnr. Jones, Walker, Waechter, Poitevent, Carrere & Denegre, New Orleans, 1975-91; judge U.S. Dist. Ct. (ea. dist.) La., New Orleans, 1991—2001, U.S. Ct Appeals (5th cir.), New Orleans, 2001—. Fellow La. Bar Found. (life); mem. Am. Law Inst., La. Bar Assn., Federalist Soc. Advisory Bd. Louisiana Chpt., Maritime Law Assn. U.S., Fed. Bar Assn., Am Inn Ct., Com. Admin. Office of the Judicial Conference of the U.S., 5th Cir. Judicial Coun. Office: US Ct Appeals 5th Cir 600 Camp Street Rm 200 New Orleans LA 70130-3313

CLEMENT, HENRY JOSEPH, JR., diversified building products executive; b. New Orleans, May 14, 1942; s. Henry Joseph Sr. and Margaret (Dowd) C.; m. Kathleen Erin Shean; children: Colleen and Collette (twins). BS, Loyola U., 1973. Sales rep. GE, New Orleans, 1972-77, mgr. product planning Louisville, Ky., 1977-79, mgr. internat. market Tyler, Tex., 1979-83; v.p. internat. sales Phillips Industries, Inc., Dayton, Ohio, 1983-84, pres. internat. div., 1984-88; pres. internat. group Tomkins Industries, Dayton, 1988-94; pres. Crescent Group, Inc., Dublin, Ohio, 1994—. Vice chmn., bd. dirs. Shaanxi-Hytec, Ltd., Xian, Chila, 1988-89. Loan exec. United Way, New Orleans, 1974, Tyler, 1979. Mem. Miami Valley (Ohio) Internat. Trade Assn. (trustee), Blue Key (Cross Key Svc. award 1973). Republican. Roman Catholic. Home: 4666 Chatham Ct Dublin OH 43017-8607 E-mail: cresgroup@cs.com.

CLEMENT, HOPE ELIZABETH ANNA, retired librarian; b. North Sydney, N.S., Can., Dec. 29, 1930; d. Harry Wells and Lana (Perkins) C. BA, U. of King's Coll., 1951; MA, Dalhousie U., 1953; BLS, U. Toronto, 1955; D of Civil Law (hon.), U. King's Coll., 1992. With Nat. Library of Can., Ottawa, Ont., 1955-92, chief nat. bibliography div., 1966-70, asst. dir. research and planning br., 1970-73, dir. research and planning br., 1973-77, assoc. nat. librarian, 1977-92. Editor: Canadiana, 1966-69. (Outstanding Svc. to Librarianship award 1992), Internat. Fedn. Libr. Assns. (medal 1991).

CLEMENT, JOHN EDWARD STRAUSZ, retired minister, retired religious organization administrator; b. Enid, Okla., Jan. 9, 1934; s. Joseph Alvis and Sarah Evelyn (Brown) C.; m. Judith A. Strausz-Clement; children: Stephen W., Paul E., Catherine K., Christopher S. Clark, Karen L. Clark. BA, Oberlin Coll., 1956; MDiv, Union Theol. Sem., 1960. Ordained to ministry Presbyn. Ch., 1960. Pastor, Williamsport, Pa., 1960-65, Wilmington, Del., 1965-69; project leader S. Cen. Ministry, Minn., 1969-74; mission enabler Los Ranchos Presbytery, Long Beach, Calif., 1974-78; exec. presbyter Cayuca-Syracuse Presbytery, Syracuse, N.Y., 1978-91, Pitts. Presbytery, 1991-95; interim exec. presbyter Carlisle Presbytery, Camp Hill, Pa., 1995-96; gen. presbyter Blackhawk Presbytery, Oregon, Ill., 1996—2001, ret., 2001. Mem. Ecumenical Execs. of No. Ill., 1996—2001, Campus Ministry Com. of Synod of Lincoln Trails, 1998-2000, Nat. Cooperative Com. on Partnership Funding, Presbyn. Ch. (USA), 1998—2001. Organizing mem. Habitat for Humanity, Syracuse, N.Y.; chmn. ecumenical exec. cabinet and v.p. Syracuse Interreligious Coun., 1985-87; ch.-wide adminstrv. coord. cabinet Presbyn. Ch. (USA), 1986-88, 91-92; chmn. pers. com. N.Y. State Coun. of Chs., 1989-91; chmn. Synod of N.E. Ecumenical Cabinet, 1987-91; mem. AIDS Task Force of Ctrl. N.Y.; mem. nat. com. Bicentennial Fund Campaign, Presbyn. Ch. (USA), 1988-92; organizing mem. Christian Leaders Fellowship, Pitts., 1991-95; exec. com. Coun. of Christian Assocs. of Western Pa., 1991-95; mem. coun. judicatory execs. Ill. Conf. Chs., 1996-200; mem. Downtown Chs. Ecumenical Com., Sante Fe, 2003—, N.Mex. Conf. Chs. Faith and Order Task Force, 2003—; chair Presbytery of Sante Fe Task Group on Korean Fellowship, 2003—. E-mail: 73523.1671@compuserve.com. *I believe God loves our world and has become one of us to redeem us and guide us toward a new humanity. I see our ministry standing on the side of the poor and oppressed as well as loving the oppressor.*

CLEMENT, KATHERINE ROBINSON, retired social worker; b. Balt., Dec. 19, 1918; d. Alphonso Pitts and Sue Seymour (Ashby) Robinson; m. Harry George Clement, 1941 (div. 1948). BA, Coll. Wooster, 1940; MSW, Smith Coll., 1953; post grad., Washington Sch. of Psychiatry, 1951. LCSW Calif. Social worker Family Svc., Cin., 1953-55, Hamilton, Ohio, 1955-57, Family Svc. Orange County, Calif., 1957-60; pvt. practice counselor Fullerton, Calif., 1959-63; social worker Family Svc., Long Beach, Calif., 1961-1963; child welfare worker San Mateo (Calif.) County Welfare Dept., 1963-1967; supr. child protection Yolo County Dept. Social Svcs., Woodland, Calif., 1967-79; pvt. practice Woodland, Calif., 1980-91; cons. psychiat. social svc. State Dept. Social Svcs., Sacramento, 1984—2001; ret., 2001. Pres., bd. dirs. Yolo Family Svc. Agy., 1977. Mem. Yolo County Health Coun.; active Yolo County Dem. Ctrl. Com.; founding bd. dirs. Yolo County Ct. Apptd. Spl. Advs. Mem.: AAUW, LWV, NOW, NASW, Mensa, Sorpotimists. Unitarian Universalist. Avocation: Rosarian. Home: 205 Modoc Pl Woodland CA 95695-6662

CLEMENT, LESLIE JOSEPH, JR., lawyer; b. Thibodaux, La., June 26, 1948; s. Leslie Joseph and Shirley Marie (Picou) C.; m. Sandra Ann Rome, June 18, 1971; children: Paul, Philip, Rebecca. BA, Nicholls State Coll., 1970; JD, La. State U., 1974. Assoc. Porteous, Toledano, Hainkel & Johnson, Thibodaux, 1974-76; ptnr. Boudreaux & Clement, Thibodaux, 1976-78; sole practice Thibodaux, 1978—. Served to 1st lt. La. N.G., 1970-76. Mem. ABA, La. Bar Assn., Lafourche Parish Bar Assn., La. Trial Lawyers Assn. Republican. Roman Catholic. Office: 409 Canal Blvd Thibodaux LA 70301-3413 E-mail: clement@triparish.net.

CLEMENT, MEREDITH OWEN, economist, educator; b. Colusa, Calif., June 7, 1926; s. Eldon Wilford and Lillian (Ohm) C.; m. Jacqueline Parker, Apr. 10, 1955; children— William, Christopher. Student, Yuba Coll., Marysville, Calif., 1946-48; BS, U. Calif. at Berkeley, 1950, PhD, 1958. Rsch. economist CIA, 1954-56; mem. faculty Dartmouth Coll., Hanover, N.H., 1956—, prof., 1967-96, prof. emeritus, 1996—. Vis. asst. prof. U. Calif. at Berkeley, 1961-62; Brookings research prof. Brookings Instn., 1964-65; Fulbright lectr. Robert Coll., Istanbul, Turkey, 1969-70; vis. scholar U. New S. Wales, 1988-89. Author: (with others) Theoretical Issues in International Economics, 1967, An Economic Evaluation of the Federal Grant-in-Aid Programs in New England, 1961, also articles. Served with USMCR, 1944-46. Mem. Am., So. econ. assns., Royal Econ. Soc., Econometric Soc. Unitarian Universalist. Home: PO Box 247 Etna NH 03750-0247 Office: Dartmouth Coll Dept Econs Hanover NH 03755

CLEMENT, PAUL PLATTS, JR., performance technologist, educator; b. Geneva, Ill., Aug. 30, 1935; s. Paul P. and Vera Elizabeth (Dahlquist) C.; m. Susan Alice Aikins, June 7, 1958; children: Paul P. IV, Kathleen Elizabeth. BA in Math., Coe Coll., 1957. Sales tech. rep. Burroughs Corp., Chgo., 1960-63; mgr. EDP, Harding-Williams Corp., Chgo., 1963-65; edn. coord. Standard Oil Co., Chgo., 1965-69; mgr. product planning Edutronics Systems Internat., Chgo., 1969-71; interactive video instrn. specialist Advanced Systems Inc., Chgo., 1971-88; ind. cons. in tng., media use, computers Downers Grove, Ill., 1988; prin. instr., developer UNISYS Corp., Lisle, Ill., 1988-89; mgr. employee devel. CNA Ins. Cos., Chgo., 1990-91; cons. media tng. Internet Systems Corp., Chgo., 1990-93; prin. Clement Consulting Group, Downers Grove, 1993—. Part-time data processing faculty Coll. of DuPage and Coll. extension, Harper Coll., Ill., DeVry Inst., Joliet Jr. Coll.; invited spkr. numerous computer and tng. confs., nat. and internat. assns.; developer, presenter workshops in field; mem. adv. bd. Northeastern Ill. U., Chgo. Developer and pub. 12 animated films with supplementary texts, 84 videotapes, 17 interactive videodiscs and over 7000 pages of expository texts; collaborator 100 other videotapes with supplementary texts; prin. developer micro-computer based People Compatability System, 1983; developer Decision Table Algorithms, 1986, 94th Inf. Div. Assn. Info. System, 1977, Basic Computer Programmer Tng. Curriculum for Eng. Govt., 1979, computerized Data Processing Curricula Devel. System, 1973, Early COBOL Lang. precompiler, 1967, AutoMagic Glossary, 1992; contbr. articles to Datamation Mag., Data Tng. Mag. Capt. USAF, 1958-60. Recipient Silver award WPC, 1996, Gold award, 1998. Home and Office: 4942 Linscott Ave Downers Grove IL 60515-3537 E-mail: PaulClementJr@worldnet.att.net.

CLEMENT, RICHARD WOLCOTT, librarian, educator; b. Phila., Aug. 28, 1951; s. Danforth and Patricia (Harshman) C.; m. Susanne Kofod, Aug. 24, 1974; children: Kristina Alexandra, Elizabeth Wolcott. BA, U. Nev., 1975, MA, 1977; AM, U. Chgo., 1984. Asst. prof. English Ill. State U., Normal, 1981-84; rare book cataloger U. Chgo. Libr., 1985-86; assoc. spl. collections libr. Spencer Libr., U. Kans., Lawrence, 1996-2000, spl. collections libr., head, 2000—. Author: The Book in America, 1996, Books in the Frontier: Print Culture in the American West 1763-1875, 2003; editor: Iberia and the Mediterranean, 1989, Greece and the Mediterranean, 1990, Spain and the Mediterranean, 1992, RBM: A Jour. of Rare Books, Manuscripts, and Cultural Heritage, 2003—. Summer fellowship NEH, 1983, fellowship Newberry Libr., Chgo., 1982, Andrew W. Mellon Found., St. Louis U., 1982. Mem. ALA, Mediterranean Studies Assn. (bd. dirs. 1994-, pres. 1994-98), Medieval Acad. of Am., Soc. for the History of Authorship, Reading and Publishing. Avocations: travel, reading, music, building houses. Home: 2205 Riviera Dr Lawrence KS 66047-1990 Office: Spencer Rsch Libr U Kans Lawrence KS 66045-7616 Fax: 785-864-5803. E-mail: rclement@ku.edu.

CLEMENT, RICHARD JOSEPH, obstetrician-gynecologist; b. Crowley, La., Apr. 10, 1937; BS in Biographical Scis., McNeese State U., 1959; MD, La. State U., 1963. Diplomate Am. Bd. Ob-Gyn. Intern Charity Hosp., New Orleans, 1963-64, resident in ob-gyn., 1964-67; pvt. practice, 1969—; chief of staff Lake Charles Meml. Hosp., 1993-94. Chmn. bd. Walter O. Moss Regional Hosp., 1994—; clin. asst. prof. La. State U. Sch. Medicine, New Orleans, 1974. Col. U.S. Army. Fellow ACOG, Am. Fertility and Sterility Soc., Soc. for Colposcopy and Colpomicroscopy, Internat. Coll. Surgery; mem. AMA, La. State Med. Soc., Calcasieu Parish Med. Soc., La. State U. Postgrad. Ob-Gyn. Soc. (pres.), Royal Soc. Medicine. Home: 517 S Ryan St Lake Charles LA 70601-5724

CLEMENT, ROBERT WILLIAM, retired air force officer; b. Columbus, Ohio, Aug. 8, 1927; s. Coleman Clay and Leola Marie (Barnett) C.; m. Leila Ann Cameron, Dec. 27, 1950 (dec. Nov. 1998); children: Susan Lee, Robert William, Sandra Gay, Randall Clay; m. Elizabeth deGaris Atherton, June 1999. Student, Yale U., 1945-46; BS, U.S. Mil. Acad., 1950; MS in Aero. Engring., U. Colo., 1957; postgrad., Army War Coll., 1966-67. Commd. 2d lt. USAF, 1950, advanced through grades to maj. gen., 1978; vice comdr. 12th Air Force, Tactical Air Command, Bergstrom AFB, Tex., 1976; dep. chief staff for ops. and intelligence USAF in Europe Ramstein Air Base, Federal Republic of Germany, 1978-80; comdr. 16th Air Force, Torrejon AB, Spain, 1980-84; ret., 1984; asst. prof. math U.S. Air Force Acad., 1956-59. Decorated Air Force DSM, Legion of Merit with 3 oak leaf clusters, DFC with one oak leaf cluster, Bronze Star, Air medal with 9 oak leaf clusters. Mem. Haines City Citrus Growers Assn. (pres. 1990-92). Home: PO Box 2207 Haines City FL 33845-2207

CLEMENT, THOMAS EARL, retired lawyer; b. Watertown, N.Y., Sept. 9, 1932; s. Andrew W. and Dorothy L. (Martin) C.; m. Marion Jeanne Flotow, May 7, 1955; children— Christopher M., Thomas M., Peter J., Martha E. BA, St. Lawrence U., Canton, N.Y., 1954; LL.B., Cornell Law Sch., 1959. Bar: N.Y., D.C., U.S. Supreme Ct. Assoc. Nixon Peabody LLP, Rochester, N.Y., 1959-64, ptnr., 1965—2000; ret., 2000—. Bd. dirs. The Genesee Corp., Rochester. Trustee Genesee Country Mus., Mumford, N.Y.; bd. dirs. St. Joseph's Villa. 1st lt. U.S. Army, 1955-57. Mem. ABA, N.Y. State Bar Assn., Monroe County Bar Assn., Cornell Law Assn., Country Club Rochester, Omicron Delta Kappa. Avocations: platform tennis, golf, bird-watching. Home: 421 Cobbs Hill Dr Rochester NY 14610-2825

CLEMENT, WALTER HOUGH, retired railroad executive; b. Council Bluffs, Iowa, Dec. 21, 1931; s. Daniel Shell and Helen Grace (Hough) C.; m. Shirley Ann Brown, May 1, 1953; children: Steven, Robert, Richard. AA, San Jose (Calif.) City Coll., 1958; PhD, World U., 1983. Lic. realtor, Utah. Designer J.K. Konerle & Assocs., Salt Lake City, 1959-62; with U.P. R.R. Co., 1962—; class B draftsman Salt Lake City, 1971-75; sr. right of way engr. real estate dept., 1975-80; asst. dist. real estate mgr., 1980-83; asst. engr. surveyor, 1983-87; owner, pres. Clement Sales and Svc. Co., Bountiful, Utah, 1987—. Mem. Rep. Nat. Com., Rep. Congl. Com. With USN, 1950-54, Korea. Mem. Am. Ry. Engring. Assn., Execs. Info. Guild (assoc.), Bur. Bus. Practice. Methodist. Home: 290 W 1200 N Bountiful UT 84010-6826 E-mail: wclem56157@aol.com.

CLEMENT, YVONNE MADELINE, librarian; b. Tacoma, June 17, 1924; d. Cecil Edward and Madeline Edith (Wink) DeGuire; m. Ralph Louis Clement, Jr., June 25, 1949 (dec. Dec. 1969); children: Lawrence E., Catherine E. Gilbert, Mary Susan Clement Zimmerman, Michele Y. Clement Cates, David L. BA

Holy Names Coll., Spokane, Wash., 1946; B.A.L.S., Rosary Coll., 1947. Asst. br. librarian Tacoma Pub. Library (Wash.), 1947-49; br. asst. Salt Lake County Library, Salt Lake City, 1967-69, br. librarian, 1969-71, assoc. dir., 1971-86. Author: (with B.M. Hepworth) Utah Libraries: Heritage and Horizons, 1976. Bd. dirs. Utah coun. Camp Fire, Salt Lake City, 1983-84.

CLEMENTE, CARMINE DOMENIC, anatomist, educator; b. Penns Grove, N.J., Apr. 29, 1928; s. Ermanno and Caroline (Friozzi) Clemente; m. Juliette Vance, Sept. 19, 1968. AB, U. Pa., 1948, MS, 1950, PhD, 1952; postdoctoral fellow, U. London, 1953—54. Asst. instr. anatomy U. Pa., 1950—52; mem. faculty UCLA, 1952—, prof., 1963—95, chmn. dept. anatomy, 1963—73, dir. brain rsch. inst., 1976—87; prof. surg. anatomy Charles R. Drew U. Medicine and Sci., LA, 1974—; prof. neurobiology and anatomy UCLA, 1995—. Hon. rsch. assoc. Univ. Coll., U. London, 1953—54; vis. scientist Nat. Inst. Med. Rsch., Mill Hill, London, 1988—89, London, 1991; cons. VA Hosp., Sepulveda, Calif., NIH; mem. med. adv. panel Bank Am.-Giannini Found.; chmn. sci. adv. com., bd. dirs. Nat. Paraplegia Found.; bd. dirs. Charles R. Drew U., 1985—94. Author: Aggression and Defense: Neurol Mechanisms and Social Patterns, 1967, Physiological Correlates of Dreaming, 1967, Sleep and the Maturing Nervous System, 1972, Anatomy: An Atlas of the Human Body, 1975, 4th edit., 1997, Clemente's Anatomy Dissector, 2001; editor: Gray's Anatomy, 1973, 30th Am. edit., 1985; editor-in-chief: Exptl. Neurology, 1973—86, assoc. editor: Neurol. Rsch., Jour. Clin. Anatomy; contbr. articles to sci. jours. Recipient award for merit in sci., Nat. Paraplegia Found., 1973, 23rd Ann. Rehfuss Lectr. and medal, Jefferson Coll., 1986, award for excellence in med. edn., UCLA, 1996, Award of Extraordinary medit, UCLA Med. Alumni Assn., 1997, Significant Early Contributor award, Sleep rsch. Soc., 2003; fellow John Simon Guggenheim Meml. Found., 1988—89. Mem.: NAS (mem. com. on neuropathology, mem. BEAR coms.), Soc. for Neurosci., Japan Soc. Promotion of Sci. (Rsch. award 1978), N.Y. Acad. Scis., Med. Rsch. Assn. Calif. (bd. dirs. 1976—87), AMA-Assn. Am. Med. Colls. (mem. liason com. on med. edn. 1981—87), Internat. Brain Rsch. Orgn., Biol. Stain Commn., Assn. Anatomy Chairmen (pres. 1972), Nat. Bd. Med. Examiners (bd. dirs. 1978—84, mem. anatomy test com. 1980—84), Coun. Acad. Socs. (mem. adminstrv. bd. 1973—81, chmn. 1979—80), Assn. Am. Med. Colls. (mem. exec. com. 1978—81, disting. svc. mem. 1982), Am. Neurol. Assn., Am. Assn. Clin. Anatomists (Honored Mem. of Yr. 1993), Am. Acad. Neurology, Am. Assn. Anatomists (v.p. 1972, pres. 1976—77, Henry Gray award 1993), Am. Physiol. Soc., Brain Rsch. Inst. (dir. 1976—87), Pavlovian Soc. N.Am. (pres. 1972, Ann. award 1968), Inst. Medicine of NAS (mem. sci. adv. bd.), Am. Acad. Cerebral Palsy (hon.), Penn Club (N.Y.C.), Sigma Xi, Alpha Omega Alpha (hon.). Democrat. Home: 11737 Bellagio Rd Los Angeles CA 90049-2158 Office: UCLA Sch Medicine Dept Neurobiology Los Angeles CA 90095-0001 E-mail: cdclem@ucla.edu.

CLEMENTE, CELESTINO, physician, surgeon; b. Penns Grove, N.J., June 11, 1922; s. Ermanno and Caroline (Friozzi) C.; m. Marie Ann Strangio, Nov. 16, 1946; children: Jeffrey, Roderick, Mark, Laurie Ann, Jonathan. BS, Rutgers U., 1942; MD, U. Pa., 1945. Diplomate Am. Bd. Surgery. Intern Jersey City Med. Ctr., 1945-46; resident in gen. surgery Martland Med. Ctr., 1950-53; practice medicine specializing in gen. surgery Newark, 1953—; dir. surgery Children's Hosp., Newark, 1962-70, St. Vincent's Hosp., Montclair, N.J., 1972-83; trustee United Hosps. Med. Ctr., Newark, 1972-88, v.p. med. affairs, 1975-88. Assoc. clinic prof. surgery N.J. Med. Sch., Newark, 1975—; dir. surgery Roseland (N.J) Surg. Ctr., 1983—, also chmn. bd. Rep. candidate for U.S. Ho. of Reps, N.J., 1968; active Nat. Ad Council/HEW, 1970-74. Served to lt. USNR, 1946-48. Fellow ACS, Internat. Coll. Surgeons; mem. AMA, AAAS. Clubs: Essex (Newark). Home and Office: 364 Ridgewood Ave Glen Ridge NJ 07028-1513 Office: 556 Eagle Rock Ave Roseland NJ 07068-1500 E-mail: ccmdnj@aol.com.

CLEMENTE, VINCE, journalist, retired English educator, historian; b. NYC, Apr. 28, 1932; s. Louis Ernest and Rose Ann Clemente; m. Ann J. Clemente, Jan. 30, 1960; children: Maryann, Gina. BA, St. Francis Coll., Bklyn., NY, 1953; MA, Columbia U., 1956, postgrad., 1959-60. Tchr. Farmingdale HS, NY, 1961-67; instr. Suffolk County C.C., Selden, NY, 1967-92, SUNY, Stony Brook, 1992-95; columnist Sag Harbor Express, NY, 1998—. Author, editor: (lit. criticism) John Ciardi: Measure of the Man, 1987, (lit. history) Paumanok Rising: Figures in a Landscape, 1981; poet: Watergaw Along the Thames, 1998; editor: Whitman Jours., West Hills, N.Y., 1970-95. Trustee Walt Whitman Birthplace, 1970-95. Cpl. U.S. Army, 1953-55. Grantee L.I. Anthology grantee, Am. the Beautiful Fund, 1976, grantee, N.Y. State Coun. on Arts, 1980, poetry grantee, Nat. Endowment for the Arts, 1982. Democrat. Roman Catholic. Avocations: archives at Univ. of Rochester, Rush Rhees Libr., flyfishing, clamming. Home: 25 Cornell Rd Sag Harbor NY 11963

CLEMENT-FOUTS, SHIRLEY GEORGE, educational services executive; b. El Paso, Tex., Feb. 14, 1926; d. Claude Samuel and Elizabeth Estelle (Mattice) Gillett; m. Paul Vincent Clement, Mar. 23, 1946 (dec. 1997); children: Brian Frank, Robert Vincent, Carol Elizabeth, Rosemary Adele; m. Robert Warren Fouts, Sept. 4, 1998. BA in English, Tex. Western Coll., 1963; postgrad., U. Tex., El Paso, N.Mex. State U., 1988; MEd in Reading, Sul Ross State U., 1987; postgrad. in art history, Paris Am. Acad., 1994-98. Tchr. lang. arts Ysleta Ind. Schs., El Paso, 1960-62; tchr. adult edn., 1962-64; tchr. reading/lang. arts, 1964-77; owner, dir. Crestline Learning Sys., Inc., El Paso, 1980-90; dir. Crestline Internat. Schs., 1987-90; instr. Park Coll., Ft. Bliss, Tex., 1992—, U. Phoenix, 1995—. Dir. tutorial for sports teams U. Tex., El Paso, 1984; bd. dirs. S.W. Inst., pres., 1993; dir. continuing edn. program El Paso Cmty. Coll., 1985; mem. curriculum com. Ysleta Ind. Schs., El Paso, 1974; mem. Right to Read Task Force, 1975-77; mem. Bi-Centennial Steering Com., El Paso, 1975-76; presenter Poetry in the Arts, Austin, Tex., 1992, 97; judge student poetry contest, Austin, Tex., 1995; Poetry Soc. Tex. program presenter Mesilla Valley Writers, 1993-96, El Paso Writers, 1994-2001, Poetry Soc. Tex., 1993-2001; instr. writing Paris Am. Acad., summer 1994, 98; cons. Ysleta Schs., 1995; poetry critic, judge Writers Workshop, Albuquerque, 1999, 2002; lectr. on reading in 4 states; poetry judge E.P. Writers League contest. Author: Writers Organizer, 2000; (poems) Echoes Through the Pass, 1998; co-author: Beginning the Search for God-The Edgar Cayce Approach, 1979; contbr. articles to profl. jours.; contbr. poems to Behold Tex., 1983. Treas. El Paso Rep. Women, 1956; facilitator Goals for El Paso, Rep. Women, 1956;mem. hospitality com. Sun Carnival, 1974, Cotton Festival, 1975. Recipient 1st prize Sky Blue Waters Poetry Contest, 2000, 1st prize EP Writer's League Hist. Memories Contest, 2001. Mem. Internat. Reading Assn. (pres. El Paso County coun. 1973-74, presentor 1978-87), Assn. Children with Learning Disabilities (tchr. 1980), Poetry Soc. Tex. (Panhandle Penwomen's first place award 1981, David Atamian Meml. award 1991, judge 1995), Nat. Fedn. State Poetry Soc. (1st place award ann. contest 1988, 1st prize El Paso Hist. Essay contest 1991, 2nd prize 1995, honorable mention Writer's Digest Contest 1996), Chi Omega Alumnae (pres. 1952-53). Home: 537 Spring Crest Dr El Paso TX 79912-4155 E-mail: clement@elp.rr.com.

CLEMENT MCKINLEY, SANDI, performing arts association administrator, not-for-profit fundraiser; b. Scranton, Pa., May 12, 1969; d. Brian James and Diane Edmunds Murray; m. Sean David McKinley, May 27, 2000. BA, Rosemont (Pa.) Coll., 1990; MA, U. Pa., Phila., 1992. Publicist Viking Penguin USA, NYC, 1992—94; dir. donor rels. Wharton Sch., U. Pa., Phila., 1994—98; dir. investor rels. edu.com, Boston, 1998—2001; assoc. dir. Am. Repertory Theatre, Cambridge, Mass., 2001—; bd. mem. Boston Fenway Civic Assn., 1998—. Bd. mem. Women's Coll. Coalition, Washington, 1990—92. Mem. Soc. Of Friends. Home: 103 Gainsborough St Boston MA 02115 Office: American Rep Theatre 64 Brattle St Cambridge MA 02138 E-mail: sandi_mckinley@yahoo.com.

CLEMENTS, ALLEN, JR., retired lawyer; b. Macon, Ga., Jan. 15, 1924; s. Allen C. and Mamie F. (Vinson) C.; children: Mary, Jill, Byng, Allen. BBA, U. Miami, 1948, JD cum laude, 1951. Bar: Fla. 1951, U.S. Tax Ct. 1951, U.S. Dist. Ct. (so. dist.) Fla. 1951, U.S. Ct. Appeals (5th cir.) 1952, U.S. Ct. Appeals (11th cir.) 1981. Sr. assoc. Claude Pepper Law Offices, Miami Beach, Fla., 1953-72; ptnr. Pepper, Clements, Hopkins & Weaver, Miami Beach, 1972-79; of counsel Tew, Critchlow, Sonberg, Traum & Friedbauer, Miami, Fla., 1979-82, Finley, Kumble, Wagner, Heinz, Underberg & Casey, Miami, 1982-87; pros. atty. City of West Miami, Fla., 1954-56, city atty., 1956-83; legal advisor Dade County Coun. Mayors, 1964-72; ret., 1987. Cons. atty. Dade County League of Cities, 1966-77; city atty. City of South Miami, 1969-72; atty. Miami Beach Tourist Devel. Authority, 1970-78, Village of Biscayne Park, 1972-75. Active West Miami Town Coun., 1952-53; bd. dirs. Claude Pepper Found., Tallahassee, 1992—, sec., 1994—. With U.S. Army, 1943-45. Decorated Bronze Star. Mem. ABA, Dade County Bar Assn. (bd. dirs. 1984-86, grievance com., ethics com.). Democrat. Methodist. Home and Office: 2205 7th Ave Dr E Bradenton FL 34208 Fax: 941-750-6784.

CLEMENTS, CATHY J. education educator; b. Spokane, Washington, Mar. 9, 1955; d. William Dale and JoAnne Sparkman Preston; m. Michael R. Clements, Aug. 9, 1986; children: Elizabeth Grace, Emily Rae Dooley, Lucas William. AA in English, State Fair CC, Sedalia, Mo., 1990; BS in English, Central Mo. State Coll., Warrensburg, Mo., 1990, MA in lit., 2000. Writing lab supr. State Fair CC, Sedalia, Mo., 1989—90, instr., intro. to writing, 1991—93; tutor Write Stuff; self employed, Quincy, Ill., 1993—98; tchg. asst. Ctrl. Mo. State U., Warrensburg, Mo., 1998—99; instr., composition State Fair C.C., Sedlia, Mo., 1999—2000, Ctrl. Mo. State, Warrensburg, Mo., 2000—03. Admin. Libr. Assn. for the Arts, Sedalia, Mo., 2000—; campaign organizer Max Mitchell for Cir. Judge, Sedalia, Mo., 1999—2000; scholarship com. Quincy Symphony Coun., Quincy, Ill., 1994—95. Recipient President's Scholar Award, Ctrl. Mo. State U., 1988, Regents Scholar, 1988—90, Outstanding Grad. English, 2000. Mem.: Mo. Assn. Teacher's English, Nat. Coun. teacher's of English, Phi Betta Kappa, 1989-91. Avocations: reading, essays, teaching.

CLEMENTS, HANA JOAN, physician; b. Olomouc, Czech Republic, May 17, 1966; came to U.S., 1991; d. Zdenek and Jana (Cechmankova) Pospisilova. MD, Med. Sch. Masaryk U., Brno, Czech Republic, 1990. Dipolomate Am. Bd. Internal Medicine, Am. Bd. Pediatrics. Resident physician Bridgeport (Conn.) Hosp., Yale U., Brigeport, 1994-98, emergency rm. physician, 1999—2002; physician dept. emergency medicine St. Vincent's Med. Ctr., Bridgeport, 2002—. Mem. AMA, ACP, Am. Acad. Pediatrics, Women's Med. Assn. Fairfield County. Home: 9 Ivy Terrace Westport CT 06880 Office: 2229 Black Rock Tpke Ste 211 Fairfield CT 06430

CLEMENTS, JAMIE HAGER, lawyer; b. Crockett, Tex., Dec. 9, 1930; s. Neal William and Alberta (Hager) C.; m. Ann Trigg, Apr. 28, 1962; children: Susan Clements Negley, Jamie Hager, Cynthia. BA with honors, U. Tex., 1952, JD, 1955. Bar: Tex. 1956. Gen. counsel Scott and White Med. Center, Temple, Tex., 1960—. Mem. Tex. Ho. of Reps., 1953-60; chmn. Tex. State Bd. Human Resources, 1977-78; chmn. Planning commn. City of Temple, 1969, mayor, 1970-74; pres. Temple United Fund, 1969; trustee Ralph Wilson Pub. Trust, Temple, 1980, 85; pres. Cultural Activities Ctr., Temple, 1981-82; mem. Tex. Bd. of Mental Health and Mental Retardation, 1986—; mem. State Commn. on Judicial Conduct, 1983-89, vice chmn. 1986-89. Served with USMC, 1956-58. Mem. ABA, Nat. Health Lawyers Assn. (pres. 1980-81), State Bar Tex. (chmn. com. on liaison with med. profession 1966-69), Bell-Lampasas-Mills Counties Bar Assn. (pres. 1966), Temple C. of C. (pres. 1975), East Tex. C. of C. (dir.). Democrat. Presbyterian. Home: 2644 Marlandwood Cir Temple TX 76502-2503 Office: Scott & White Med Ctr 2401 S 31st St Temple TX 76508-0001

CLEMENTS, JOHN ROBERT, real estate professional; b. Richmond, Ind., Nov. 2, 1950; s. George Howard and Mary Amanda (McKown) C. Grad. high sch., Phoenix. Sales assoc. Clements Realty, Inc., Phoenix, 1973-75, office mgr. Mesa, Ariz., 1975-78, v.p., co-owner Phoenix, 1978-80; broker, assoc. Ben Brooks & Assocs., Phoenix, 1980-88; pres. John R. Clements, P.C., 1984—; broker Keller Williams Realty, Phoenix and Mesa, Ariz., 1994-96; v.p. facilities/malls Viacom Outdoor, Phoenix, 1996—. Real estate dir. Circle K Corp., Western Region, 1989-92; bd. dirs., v.p. Big Sisters Ariz., Phoenix, 1974-80; trustee Ariz. Realtors Polit. Action Com., 1975-85, Realtors Polit. Action Com., Ill., 1985-88; appointee Govtl. Mall Co., Ariz., 1986—, commr. chair, 1991-95. Mem. Ariz. Assn. Realtors (bd. dirs., pres. 1981), Mesa-Chandler-Tempe Bd. Realtors (past bd. dirs., pres., 1978), Nat. Assn. Realtors (past bd. dirs., exec. com.), Coun. Residential Specialists (bd. govs. 19865, v.p. 1990, pres. 1991), Ariz. Country Club. Republican. Presbyterian. Home: 3618 N 60th St Phoenix AZ 85018-6708 Office: Viacom Outdoor 2502 N Black Canyon Hwy Phoenix AZ 85009-1800

CLEMENTS, LINDA L. materials engineer, educator, journalist; b. Phoenix, Oct. 6, 1945; d. Howard Abner Clements and Louella Tooley; m. John Laurence Crowley; children: Timothy Crowley, Colin Crowley. BS, Stanford U., 1967; MS Engring., U. Pa., 1971; PhD, Stanford U., 1974. Engr. Lawrence Livermore Lab., Livermore, 1974—78, program mgr., 1977—78; project dir. Advanced Rsch. and Applications Corp., Sunnyvale, Calif., 1978—81, NASA-Ames Rsch. Ctr., Moffett Field, Calif.; assoc. prof., materials engring. San Jose State U., 1981—85, full prof., materials engring., 1985—91; dir. of materials R& D TFI Inc., Pacifica, Calif., 1989—98; adj. prof. U. of Nev., Reno, 1995—99; nat. adj. faculty ASM Internat., Materials Park, Ohio, 1984—2002; instr. Soc. for the Advancement of Material and Process Engring., Covina, Calif., 1995—; adj. faculty Western Nev. C.C., Carson City, Nev., 1999—2002; dir. of materials r & d 2Phase Technologies, Inc., Dayton, Nev., 1998—; pres. C & C Technologies, Dayton, 1991—. Faculty advisor student chpt. Soc. of Women Engineers San Jose State U., 1980—86, San Jose State U. SAMPE, 1985—91; reviewer ASM Internat., Materials Park, Ohio, 1983—99, Technomic Pub. Co., Lancaster, PA., 1999—2000; peer rev. bd. Jour. of Advanced Materials, Covina, 1999—; steering com. Composites Fabrication mag., Arlington, 2000—. Mem. editl. bd.: SAMPE Jour., 2000—, correspondant: Advanced Composites Bull., 1999—2000, contbg. editor: High-Performance Composites Mag., 1998—2000, Composites Fabrication Mag., 2000—. Bd. dirs. Do-Mor for Dayton, 2002—; mem. engring. adv. bd. Western Nev. C.C., Carson City, 1998—, chair engring. adv. bd., 2001—03. Grantee Rsch. innovation grants (3), Northrop Corp., 1986—90. Mem.: ASTM (d-30 com. sec. 1976—78), Soc. of Plastics Engineers, Am. Chem. Soc., ASM Internat., Soc. for the Advancement of Materials and Process Engring. (internat. com. chmn. 1986—2003, chpt. dir. 1996—, bd. dirs., internat. sec. 2003—), Dayton (Nev.) Hist. Soc. (bd. dirs. 2002—), Dayton (Nev.) Mus. Hist. Soc. (bd. dirs. 2003—), Friends of the Dayton Valley Libr. (pres. 1995—2000, sec. 2000—02, Vol. of the Yr. 2002). Avocation: genealogy, historic preservation, science fiction, camping, sewing. Office: C & C Technologies PO Box 1089 Dayton NV 89403 Business E-Mail: llclements@composites-training.com.

CLEMENTS, LYNNE FLEMING, family therapist, programmer; b. Bklyn., Aug. 8, 1945; d. Daniel Gillies and Dorothy Frances (Zitzmann) Fleming; m. Louis Myrick Clements, Feb. 19, 1972; children: Ryan Louis, Glenn Fleming. BA in Sociology, Bradley U., 1967; MSW, Fordham U., 1973; postgrad. studies, Columbia U., 1970-71; cert. family therapy, Inst. for Mental Health Edn., 1990. LCSW NJ, cert. social work mgr. Computer programmer Employer's Comml. Union Group Ins. Cos., Boston, 1967-69, Harvard Bus. Sch., Cambridge, Mass., 1969-70, Volkswagon of Am., Englewood Cliffs, N.J., 1971; psychiat. social worker Associated Cath. Charities Family and Children's Svcs., Paramus, N.J., 1973-74, Christian Health Ctr., Wyckoff, N.J., 1976; owner, mgr. Wicker Wagon, Bergenfield, N.J., 1977-85; psychotherapist The Psychotherapy Counseling Ctr., Bergenfield, N.J., 1982-89; programmer analyst Atlas Computing Svcs., Secaucus, N.J., 1984-86; program coord., family therapist Divsn. Family Guidance, Hackensack, N.J., 1986-91; pres. Corp. Family Resources, Ridgewood, N.J., 1989—; family therapist cons. Family Recovery of Valley View, White Plains, N.Y., 1992-94, Furman Clinic, Fair Lawn, N.J., 1995-96, Van Ost Inst. for Family Living, Englewood, N.J., 1996; cert. social work mgr., 1997—. Part-time family therapist NJ Ctr Psychotherapy Inc, Ridgefield Park, 1990. Chmn entertainment Bergen County Children's Festival, 1993; app chmn, designer Bergenfield's Coun Arts, 1993—99, chmn author/poet program, 1996—2003; chmn curriculum enhancement comt Bergen County Acad Advancement Sci and Technology, 1992—96; mem. fundraising com., arts programming chmn. Bergenfield Cmty. Ctr., 2000—; appt. sec. Mayor's Beautify Bergenfield Com., 1991—95; Sunday sch teacher All Sts Ch, 1982—89, 1994—, chmn bd community play ctr, 1977—78; mem Twin-Boro Youth Ministry Coun, 1989—. Recipient 1st and 2d pl Awards, Bergenfield 1980 Art Contest, Best Practice award, N.J. State Edn., 2003; grantee NIMH, 1973. Mem.: NASW, AAUW, NJ Coalition Mental Health Profls., NJ Soc Clin Social Workers (bd. dirs., chmn. mktg. and vendor 1999—), NJ Commerce and Indust Asn (child care comt 1990—, mem human resources comt 1990—), Fordhan Univ Alumni Asn, Am Orthopsychiatric Asn, Acad Cert Social Workers, Gifted Child Soc (parent workshop coord 1989—, bd dirs 1991—), Women of Accomplishments (founder, pres 1990—, chmn women's coalition conf 1993—), Zonta (Amelia Earhart chmn 1987—88, chmn status women comt 1993—94, mem literacy comt 1995—). Episcopalian. Avocations: walking, art, music, crafts, boating. Home: 148 Harcourt Ave Bergenfield NJ 07621-1917 Office: Corp Family Resources 15 Godwin Ave Ste 1 Ridgewood NJ 07450-3739

CLEMENTS, MICHAEL CRAIG, health services consulting executive, retired renal dialysis technician; b. Cin., Sept. 17, 1945; s. Marvin Hubert and Mildred Helen (Rabe) C.; m. Minnie Faye Pospisil, Dec. 1, 1972; children: Melissa Ayn, Michael Aaron. Student, U. Cin., 1968-70; EMT/paramedic, Good Samaritan Health Ctr., 1980. Cert. renal dialysis technician. Hemodialysis technician Christ Hosp., Cin., 1968-79; tech. svcs. dir. Dialysis Clinic, Inc., Cin., 1980-91; pres. Critical Care Svcs., Inc., Mason, Ohio, 1987—. Firefighter/paramedic Mason Vol. Fire Co., 1978-85, EMS tng. officer, 1984, EMS capt., 1985; coop employers environ. and sci. lab. tech. programs Cin. State Coll. Contbr. articles to profl. jours. Mem. Mason Environ. Adv. Commn., 1990—, vice chmn., 1992-93, bus. and parent curriculum review com. Mason City Schs., 1992; employer advisor coop. program Cin. Tech. Coll. Biomed. Engring. Tech., 1986-91; with U.S. Naval Sea Cadet Corps, 2002—, exec. officer Cin. divsn., 2003—. With USN, 1964-70. Mem. Assn. for Advancement of Med. Instrumentation, Ohio Acad. Sci. Mem. Ch. of Christ. Office: Critical Care Svcs Inc PO Box 252 1091 A Reading Rd Mason OH 45040-1345 E-mail: ceo@critical-care-services.com.

CLEMENTS, MICHAEL TAYLOR, academic administrator, educator; b. Lynchburg, Va., Dec. 7, 1965; s. Shirby Jean Clements and James Ryland Clements, Jr.(Stepfather); m. Priscilla Anne Heyert. MBA, U. of Redlands, Redlands, CA; BS, Longwood Coll., Farmville, VA. Dir. of residential and commuter life Longwood U., Farmville, Va., 1999—.

CLEMENTS, ROBERT, insurance executive; b. Chgo., Sept. 7, 1932; s. John and Mildred L. (Chapman) C.; m. Marilyn Trexler, Dec. 27, 1955; children: Paula J., John, Jeffrey, Ben T. BA, Dartmouth Coll., 1954. Underwriter Royal Ins. Co., N.Y.C., 1956—59; sr. v.p. Marsh & McLennan, Ltd., Toronto, Canada, 1959—75; chmn. Marsh & McLennan Inc., N.Y.C., 1975—92; pres. Marsh & McLennan Cos., Inc., N.Y.C., 1992-94; chmn. Marsh & LcLennan Risk Capital Corp., 1994-96, Risk Capital Holdings, Inc., 1996—2000, Arch Capital Group Ltd., 2000—. Bd. dirs. EXEL Ltd.; chmn. bd. trustees Risk Found.; chmn. emeritus Conf. Ins. Bd. overseers Inst. for Civil Justice. With U.S. Army, 1954-56. Democrat. Office: Arch Capital Group 20 Horseneck Ln Greenwich CT 06830-6327

CLEMENTS, ROBERT DONALD, sculptor; b. Pitts., Dec. 24, 1937; s. Clyde Clifford and Rosa Theresa Clements; m. Claire Brown, June 24, 1961; children: David Cal, Megan Lynn Tyler. BFA in Painting and Design, Carnegie Mellon U., 1959; MA in Art, Pa. State U., 1962, PhD, 1964. Tchr. art Pitts. Pub. Schs., 1961-62; asst. prof. art Ball State U., Muncie, Ind., 1964-68; assoc. prof. art U. Ga., Athens, 1969-81, prof. art, 1981-94. Design cons. Corp. for Olympic Devel. in Atlanta, 1993-96. Initiator, designer outdoor sculpture park Folk Art Park, 1994-96 (award 1997); sculptor S.E. Natatorium, 1994 (award 1995), Indian Creek Marta Sta. Mural, 1993 (award 1994), Marietta Bollard, CODA, 1996; author: Emphasis Art, 5th edit. 1991, 6th edit. 1997, 7th edit. 2001. Recipient Indsl. Artists awards Ga. Coun. for the Arts, 1987, 91, Reg. Site Sculpture award Arts Festival of Atlanta, 1987, Recognition award Urban Design Commn., Atlanta, 1995, 97, Outstanding Rsch. and Tchg. awards U. Ga., 1991, 93. Mem. Internat. Sculpture Ctr. Unitarian Universalist. Home: 155 Bar H Ct Athens GA 30605-4702 E-mail: rclements1@charter.net.

CLEMENTS, THEODORE, lawyer, law educator, dean; b. 1940; BS, BA, Creighton U., 1962; JD, Georgetown U., 1965. Bar: Nebr. 1965. Assoc. Haney, Walsh & Wall, Omaha, 1965—67; asst. city atty. City of Omaha, 1967—68; dir. and staff atty. Omaha Legal Aid Soc., 1968—70; bd. dir., 1971—77; asst. prof. Creighton U., 1970—72; assoc. prof., 1972—75; prof., 1975—78; dean, prof. Gonzaga U. Sch. Law, 1978—; Bd. dir. Bergan Mercy Hosp., Omaha, 1975—80, Holy Family Hosp., Spokane, Wash., 1979—. Mem.: Georgetown Law Jour. (past mem. bd. editors), Phi Delta Phi. Office: Gonzaga U Sch Law Spokane WA 99258-0001

CLEMETSON, CHARLES ALAN BLAKE, physician; b. Canterbury, Eng., Oct. 31, 1923; came to U.S., 1961, naturalized, 1972; s. Charles Harold and Gwendoline Maude Winefred (Blake) C.; m. Helen Cowan Forster, Mar. 29, 1947 (dec. Nov. 2002); children: Claudia, Charles, David (dec.), Andrew. B.M.,B.Ch., Oxford (Eng.) U., 1948. Lic. physician, La., U.K. Research asst. Obstetric Hosp., Univ. Coll. Hosp., London, 1950-52; Nichols research fellow Royal Soc. Medicine, 1951-52; house surgeon obstetrics W. Middlesex Hosp., 1952-53; resident med. officer obstetrics Queen Charlotte's Hosp., 1953; house surgeon gynecology Hammersmith Hosp., 1953-54; obstetric and gynecol. registrar Lake Hosp., Ashton-under-Lyne, Lancashire, Eng., 1954-56; lectr. ob-gyn. Univ. Coll. Hosp., London, 1956-58; asst. prof. Univ. Hosp., Saskatoon, Sask., Can., 1958-61, U. Calif., San Francisco, 1961-67; dir. dept. ob-gyn. Meth. Hosp., Bklyn., 1967-81, Huey P. Long Meml. Hosp., Pineville, La., 1981-91; assoc. prof. SUNY, Bklyn., 1967-72; prof. Downstate Med. Ctr., SUNY, 1972-81, Tulane U., 1981-91, prof. emeritus, 1991. Mem. obstetric adv. com. N.Y.C. Dept. Health, 1968; cons. in field; mem. med. adv. com. Planned Parenthood N.Y.C., 1971; mem. physicians rev. com. Blue Cross-Blue Shield N.Y.C., 1975; lectr. maternal health U. Calif., Berkeley, 1964-65 Author: Vitamin C, 3 vols., 1989; contbr. articles to med. jours. Served in RAF, 1948-50. Recipient Rsch. Career Devel. award NIH, 1965-67. Fellow ACOG, Royal Coll. Obstetricians and Gynecologists, Royal Coll. Physicians and Surgeons Can.; mem. Bklyn. Gynecol. Soc. (pres. 1977-78). *Certainty of knowledge is the antithesis of progress.*

CLEMMER, DAN ORR, librarian; b. Etowah, Tenn., Dec. 28, 1938; s. Dan Orr and Nancy Elizabeth (Haney) C.; m. Elizabeth Louise Campbell, Aug. 25, 1962; children: Nancy Day, Helen, Stephen. BA, Davidson Coll., 1961; MA Teaching, Brown U., 1964; MS Libr. Svc., Columbia U., 1967. Intern Libr. of Congress, Washington, 1967-68, asst. head African-Asian exchange, 1968-70; asst. to librarian Smithsonian Inst. Libr., Washington, 1970-72, asst. chief access svc., 1972-73; chief, reader svcs. U.S. Dept. State Libr., Washington, 1973-92, chief librarian, 1992—2002; ret., 2002. Mem. Depository Libr. Coun., 1994-98. Contbr. articles to profl. jours. [e]m. ALA (pres. Fed. Librs. Roundtable 1993-94, exec. bd. of Fed. Libr. and Info. Ctr. com.); mem. D.C. Libr. Assn. (pres. 1995-96). Home: 5527 Trent St Chevy Chase MD 20815-5511

CLEMMONS, EVELYN YVONNE, administrative assistant; b. Toledo, Ohio, Oct. 14, 1939; d. Larry Rogers and Blondella Mims; m. Lucius Eugene Clemmons (dec.); children: Christa Dee, Christina Louise; m. James C. Kiner; children: Michelle A. Kiner, Stephen J Kiner, Carolyn L Kiner. *Father Larry Rogers was a musician and bandleader, a drummer. Daughter Michelle A. Kiner, oldest child is a professional singer of jazz and contemporary songs- has produced a cd titled Clear Days, currently for sale on Amazon.com. Evelyn Y. Clemmons poetry book- Lessons includes Poem Drummerman dedicated to father-Larry Rogers. Son Stephen J. Kiner —A veteran of the Dessert Storm War- A volunteer in Saudi Arabia for one year, after the end of the conflict.* Administrative Assistant Certification SUNY Buffalo EOC, 1995. Gs-5 sec. Soil Conservation Svc., Albany, NY, 1989—89; sr. corp. support clk. Computer Task Group, Buffalo, 1995—99; admin. asst. EPA, Atlanta. Contact person Computer Task Group, Buffalo, 1995—99. Author: (poetry book) Lessons. Officer VFW Aux. Post 2851, Fremont, Ohio, 1983—85; listing names Wall of Tolerance, Montgomery, Ala., 2002—02; pres. Bissel Ave. Block Club, Buffalo, 1981—81. Mem.: Internat. Soc. of Poets. Avocations: knitting, crocheting, sewing, dancing, cooking. Home Fax: 404-767-8367.

CLEMMONS, FRANCOIS SCARBOROUGH, vocalist; b. Birmingham, Ala., Apr. 23, 1945; s. Willie Clemmons and Inez Scarborough; m. Carole Etha Gregory, Sept. 12, 1968 (div. Jan. 1974). BM, Oberlin Coll., 1967; MFA, Carnegie-Mellon U., 1969; DA (hon.), Middlebury Coll., 1996. Vocalist Met. Opera Studio, Cleve., Pitts. Symphony Orch., Phila. Orch., Indpls. Symphony, Milw. Symphony; Officer Clemmons Mr. Rogers' Neighborhood; Sportin' Life Porgy & Bess. Singer (rec. Cleve. Orch.): Porgy & Bess, 1973; singer: (with Harlem Spiritual Ensemble) Live in Concert, 1991, Free At Last, 1992; singer: Mr. Rogers' Neighborhood & Friends, 1977. Mem.: Harlem Spiritual En-

semble, Inc. (founder, dir.), Ind. Black Opera Singers (founder, pres. emeritus), Am. Negro Spiritual Rsch. Found. Inc. (founder, dir.). Democrat. Unitarian. Home: 104 S Main St Middlebury VT 05753

CLEMMONS, JOHN B. bank executive, director, mathematician, educator; b. Rome, Ga., Apr. 11, 1916; s. Lewis Isaac Clemmons and Bessie Turner; m. Mozelle Dailey, children: John B. Jr., Sheila Mozelle. BS, Morehouse Coll.; MS, Atlanta U.; postgrad., U. So. Calif. Prin. Harlan (Ky.) H.S., 1941—43; asst. prin. Carver H.S., Cumberland, Md., 1943—47; dept. head Savannah (Ga.) State U., 1947—87; chmn. bd. dirs. Carver Bank, Savannah. Bd. dirs. Goodwill, 1975—2001. Recipient Silver Beaver award, Boy Scouts Am., 1963; fellow Mention, Boule Found., 1996—, Russell, 2000; grantee, Ford Found., 1951, NSF, 1960. Mem.: Am. Math. Assn., Masons (32d degree), Beta Kappa Chi, Alpha Kappa Mu. Home: 2201 E Victory Dr Savannah GA 31404 Office: Carver Bank PO Box 2769 Savannah GA 31498-1201 Fax: 912-232-8666.

CLEMMONS, NANCY WASHINGTON, library administrator, educator; b. Sept. 6, 1947; m. W. Ronald Clemmons. BS in Chemistry, Birmingham So. Coll., 1968; MLS, U. Ala., 1973. Grad. sci. libr. Samford U., Birmingham, Ala., 1973-76; sr. libr. govt. docs. La. State U., Baton Rouge, 1976-77, reference libr. Lister Hill Libr. U. Ala., Birmingham, 1977-81, vision sci. libr., 1981-82, head reference svcs., 1983-89, head info. and instrnl. svc., 1989-92, acting dir., assoc. prof., 1992-95, dep. dir., 1995—, prof., 1999—. Mem. regional adv. coun. Southeastern Atlantic Med. Library Svcs., Balt., 1994—96; mentor Acad. Health Info. Profls., 1995—; mem. adv. bd. HealthInfoNet, Jefferson County, Ala., 2000— Author: (with others) Reference and Information Services Quarterly, 1994; mem. edtl. bd. Med. Ref. Svcs. Quar., 1990—; various book reviews; contbr. articles to profl. jours. Mem. adopt a troop com. Boy Scouts Am., 1988-92; alt. rep. Faculty Senate U. Ala., 1996-98. Mem. Acad. Health Info. Profls. (distinguished mem., Med. Libr. Assn. (chair so. chpt. 1997-98, chpt. coun. rep. 1994-97, chair pub. svcs. sect. 1988-89, chair mem. com. 1988-89, chair awards com. 1993-94, chair Lucretia McClure Excellence in Edn. Award Jury 2000-2001, mem. nominating com. 2000, bd. dirs. 2003—), Ala. Health Librs. Assn. (pres. 1983-84), Beta Phi Mu. Office: U Ala at Birmingham Lister Hill Libr HealthScis 251C 1530 3d Ave S Birmingham AL 35294-0013 Office Fax: 205-934-3545. Business E-Mail: nclemmons@uab.edu.

CLEMMONS, ROGER MAYEDA, veterinarian, educator; b. Springfield, Mo., Aug. 10, 1949; s. James Neil and Eva Christine Clemmons; m. Janis Mayeda, Sept. 3, 1971. DVM, Wash. State U., 1973, PhD, 1979. Cert. vet. acupuncture 2001. Vet. small animal practice St. Frances Vet. Hosp., San Francisco, 1973—75; post-doctoral fellow Wash. State U., Pullman, 1975—79; asst. prof. U. Fla., Gainesville, 1979—85, assoc. prof., 1985—. Mem. sci. adv. bd. PawCare.com, Miami, Fla., 1999—; cons., lectr. Chi Inst., Reddick, Fla., 2000—. Author: (Book) Neurology for Small Animal Practitioners- -Made Easy Series, 2002. Active Team VetMed, Gainesville, 2000—02. Grantee, The Amerman Found., 1999—2002, Morris Animal Found., 2001—02. Mem.: Am. Physiologic Soc., Am. Vet. Med. Assn., Gainesville Cycling Club, Phi Kappa Phi. Avocations: running, bicycling, swimming, computer graphics, photography. Office: Univ Fla 2015 SW 16th Ave Gainesville FL 32610-0126 Home Fax: 352-392-6125; Office Fax: 352-392-6125. Personal E-mail: rmc@neuro.vetmed.ufl.edu. Business E-Mail: rmc@neuro.vetmed.ufl.edu.

CLEMONS, JOHN ROBERT, lawyer; b. Oak Park, Ill., June 9, 1948; BA, U. Iowa, 1970; JD, DePaul U., 1975. Asst. village mgr. Village of Riverside, Ill., 1970-72; co-dir. dist. 208 Youth Ctr., Riverside, 1970-73; area dir. S.W. area Cook County OEO, 1972-73; clk., legal researcher Klein, Thorpe & Jenkins, attys., Chgo., 1974-75; asst. state atty.'s Jackson County, Murphysboro, Ill., 1975-80, state's atty., 1980-88; asst. prof. So. Ill. U., Carbondale, 1977-79, lectr., 1987—; ptnr. Clemons & Hood, 1991—. Home: 375 Mount Joy Rd Murphysboro IL 62966-4464 Office: 813 W Main St Carbondale IL 62901-2537

CLEMONS, JULIE PAYNE, telephone company manager; b. Attleboro, Mass., June 13, 1948; d. John Gordon and Claire (Paquin) P.; m. W. Richard Johnson, Oct. 10, 1970 (div. Oct. 1980); m. E.L. Clemons, Apr. 23, 1988; adopted son, Jason Corey. BBA, U. R.I., 1970. Svc. rep. New England Telephone, East Greenwich, R.I., 1970-71, So. Bell, Jacksonville, Fla., 1971-73, bus. office supr., 1973-77, bus. office mgr., 1978-84, staff mgr. assessment, 1984-86, mgr. assessment ctr., 1987-89; dir. human resource assessment State of Fla., Jacksonville, Fla., 1987-89, Customer Svcs. Revenue Recovery Ctr., 1989-93, mgr. small bus. sales and svc., 1994-95, br. mgr. small bus. No. Fla., 1995-97; product support mgr. Small Bus. Mktg., 1997-98, sr. product support mgr., 1998-2000, project mgr. network and transport svcs., 2000-01, ISDN product mgr., 2001—02; ret., 2002. Subst. tchr. Gwinnett County Sch. Bd., 2003—. Vol. Learn to Read; bd. dirs. Duval Assn. Retarded Citizens, Jacksonville, 1981-86, treas., 1983-84; Boy Scouts den leader, Pack 569, 2002-2003; mem. Leadership Jacksonville, Class of '97; career network adminstr. St. Lawrence Ch., 2003—. Mem. NAFE, Am. Mgmt. Assn., Pioneers of Am., Jacksonville C. of C. Roman Catholic. Avocations: gardening, water and snow skiing. E-mail: jpc@bellsouth.net., julie.clemons@bellsouth.com.

CLEMONS, KAY K. librarian; b. Peru, Ind., Jan. 17, 1937; d. Ellis Allen and Ferne (Bowman) Metzger; widow; 1 child, Wayne Ellis Shafer. Diploma, Marion (Ind.) Bus. Coll., 1985. Mem. Grant County Genealogy Club (sec. 1994-99, rschr. 1994—, v.p. 2001—). Avocations: geneological and family history research, crosswords, jigsaw puzzles, collecting reader's digest condensed books, collecting unusual bookmarks. Home: 1200 S Hendricks Ave Trlr 27 Marion IN 46953-1283 E-mail: ckaykay4706@aol.com.

CLENDENEN, PATRICK THOMAS, lawyer; b. Washington, Apr. 5, 1966; s. William Herbert and Sandra (Allaire) C.; m. Patricia Marie Haffey, Aug. 13, 1988; children: Paul W., Andrew B., Claire M. AB magna cum laude, Colby Coll., 1988; JD, Catholic U. Am., 1991. Bar: Conn. 1991, Mass. 1993, D.C. 1994, U.S. Dist. Ct. Conn. 1992, U.S. Dist. Ct. Mass. 1995, U.S. Ct. Apeals (1st cir.) 1996. Law clerk U.S. Dept. Justice Civil Rights Div. Office Complaint Adj., Washington, 1989-90; assoc. Cleary, Gottlieb, Steen & Hamilton, Washington, 1990; law clerk Hon. Ellen B. Burns U.S. Dist. Ct. Conn., New Haven, Conn., 1991-93; assoc. Mintz, Levin, Cohn, Ferris, Glovsky and Popeo P.C., Boston, 1993-2000, ptnr., 2000—. Editor-in-chief, The Jour. of Contemporary Health Law and Policy, 1991. Contbr. articles to profl. jours. Bd. dirs. Wellesley Youth Hockey Assn., Inc., 1995-2001, pres., 1999-2001; bd. dirs. Mass. affiliate Am. Heart Assn. Recipient Harold Dubord prize Colby Coll., 1988, Nat. Collegiate Econs. award, 1988, Norman H. White award, 1988, Am. Jurisprudence award Property & Adminstry. Law, 1989, 90. Mem. Mass. Bar Assn. (budget and fin. com., lawyers referral svc. com., civil litigation sects. coun., co-chair pro bono subcom., del.-at-large), ABA (former chair Young Lawyers divsn. com. on litigation, dir., co-chair subcom. on membership, sect. of litigation com. on ethics and professionalism, bd. editors The Young Lawyer, bus. and corp. litigation com., co-chair bus. law sect. fellows program, co-chair subcom. pro bono), D.C. Bar Assn., Boston Bar Assn., Conn. Bar Assn., Pi Sigma Alpha, Phi Beta Kappa. Avocations: golf, tennis, hiking, running, ice hockey. Home: 16 Sturbridge Rd Wellesley MA 02481-1230 Office: Mintz Levin Cohn Ferris Glovsky and Popeo P C One Financial Ctr Boston MA 02111

CLENDENEN, WILLIAM HERBERT, JR., lawyer; s. William H. and Ethel L. (Clifford) C.; children: William, Patrick, Allison, Derek, Luke; m. Corinna P. Smith. BA, Providence Coll., 1964; JD, Cath. U. Am., 1967. Bar: Conn. 1967, U.S. Dist. Ct. Conn. 1971, U.S. Dist. Ct. (so. dist.) N.Y. 1977, U.S. Dist. Ct. R.I. 1977, U.S. Ct. Clms. 1977, U.S. Ct. Appeals. (2d cir.) 1971, U.S. Sup. Ct. 1976. Reginald Heber Smith Cmty. Lawyer fellow U. Pa. 1967-68; staff atty. New Haven Legal Assistance Assn., Inc., 1968-73; prin. William H. Clendenen Jr., PC, New Haven, 1973-2002; mng. mem. Clendenen & Shea LLC, New Haven, 2002—; supervising atty. Yale Law Sch., 1981; alt. pub. mem. Conn. State Bd. Mediation and Arbitration, 1976-78; co-chmn. U.S. Dist. Ct. Conn. Spcl. Masters Com., New Haven, 1985-89. Fellow Am. Coll. Trial Lawyers, Conn. Bar Found. (life, dir. 1991—, treas. 1992—); mem. ABA, ATLA, Conn. Bar Assn. (chmn. consumer law sect. 1974-78, chmn. lawyer referral com. 1987-89, jud. independence task force 1998—), New Haven County Bar Assn. (sec. 1986-87, treas. 1987-88, v.p. 1988-89, pres. 1989-90), Conn. Trial Lawyers Assn., New Haven County Bar Found. (dir. 1993—). Home: 102 River Edge Farms Rd Madison CT 06443-2756

CLENDENNING, WILLIAM EDMUND, dermatologist; b. Waynesburg, Pa., June 23, 1931; s. William Burdette and Anna Marie (Schellhase) C.; m. Elizabeth Woodbury Bennett, Sept. 6, 1958; children— William Alan, Joy Marie, Bruce Bennett, Sarah Elizabeth. BS, Allegheny Coll., Meadville, Pa., 1952; MD, Jefferson Med. Coll., Phila., 1956. Diplomate Am. Bd. Dermatology, Am. Bd. Dermatopathology. Intern St. Luke's Hosp., Cleve., 1956-57; resident in dermatology Univ. Hosps. of Cleve., 1957-60; sr. investigator dermatology br. Nat. Cancer Inst., USPHS, 1961-63; asst. prof. dermatology Western Res. U. Med. Sch., 1963-67; prof. medicine (dermatology) Dartmouth Coll. Med.; prof. emeritus, 1996—; also mem. staff Mary Hitchcock Meml. Hosp., Hitchcock Clinic, 1967-94. Mem. Nat. Mycosis Fungoides Coop. Group, N.Am. Contact Dermatitis Group; Prosser White Orator St. John's Hosp. Dermatol. Soc., London, 1985 Author articles in field, chpts. in books. Nat. Cancer Inst. grantee, 1963-67 Mem. Am. Acad. Dermatology, Soc. Investigative Dermatology, Am. Dermatol. Assn., Am. Soc. Dermatopathology, New Eng. Dermatol. Soc., Am. Fedn. Clin. Research, N.H. Med. Assn., AMA. Home: 7 Pleasant St Hanover NH 03755-2008 Office: 1 Medical Center Dr Lebanon NH 03756-0001 E-mail: william.e.clendenning@dartmouth.edu.

CLENDINEN, CYNTHIA A.A. healthcare professional, compliance specialist; b. St. Croix, U.S. V.I., July 29, 1970; d. Cletis Antonio Jr. and Dolores T. Clendinen. BA, Brown U., 1992; MPH, U. South Fla., 1997. Med. technician St. Thomas (V.I.) Hosp./V.I. Dept. Health, 1992-93; lab. asst. St. Joseph's Hosp., Tampa, Fla., 1995; program coord., trainer St. Joseph's-Bapt. Healthcare, Tampa, 1995—; investigator Healthcare Co-Third Party Adminstrn., Tampa, 1998—, quality svc. trainer, 1999—2000, quality auditor, 2000—01, corp. project mgr., 2001—03, privacy ofcl., 2003—. Youth coord./advisor Youth Experiencing Success, St. Thomas, 1991-93; prevention/intervention counselor Parents Resource Inst. Drug Edn., St. Thomas, 1993. Author original poetry. Contbg. mem. United Way, Tampa, 1995—; assoc. mem. Pembroke Ctr. for Tchg. and Rsch. on Women, Brown U., 1998—. U. South Fla. grad. scholar, 1994; Presdl. scholar, Washington, 1987. Mem. APHA, U. South Fla. Alumni Assn. Democrat. Christian. Avocations: fitness activities, logic puzzles, foreign languages, Biblical study, poetry. Office: HealthPlan Svcs Inc 3501 E Frontage Rd Tampa FL 33607-1742

CLERGUE, LUCIEN GEORGES, photographer; b. Arles, France, Aug. 14, 1934; s. Etienne and Jeanne (Grangeon) C.; m. Yolande Wartel, Jan. 10, 1963; children: Anne, Olivia. Dr. es Letters in Photography, U. Provence, 1979. Tchr. workshops New Sch., N.Y.C., Art Ctr., Pasadena, Osaka U., Japan, other U.S. univs. and colls. Freelance photographer, 1959—; artistic dir. Arles Festival, 1971-75, 86-88; founder, Rencontres Internat. de la Photographie, Arles, 1969, art dir. XXVth anniversary, 1994; one-man exhbns. include Kunstgewerbe Mus., Zurich, 1958, 63, Mus. Modern Art, N.Y.C., 1961—, Musée d'Arts Decoratifs, Paris, 1962—, Moderna Museet, Stockholm, 1969—, Art Inst. Chgo., 1970—, Kunsthalle, Düsseldorf, Fed. Republic Germany, 1970—, Gallery Witkin, N.Y.C., 1972-79, Bruxelles Musee d'Ixelles, 1974—, Israel Mus., Jerusalem, 1974—, Ctr. Pompidou, Paris, 1980—, Musée d'Art Moderne Paris, 1984, George Eastman House, Rochester, 1985, ICP, N.Y.,1986, Amos Anderson Mus., Helsinki, 1987, Real Maestranza Sevilla, 1991, Houston Photo Fest, 1992, Milw. Art Mus., 1993, Calif. Mus. Photography, Riverside, 1997, Centro de la Imagen, Mexico, 1997, Kunstmuseum Dortmund, 1999, John Stevenson Gallery, N.Y., 2000, 02, Gallery B. Lebon, Paris, 2000, Vitoria, Spain, 2002; works rep. books, movies; represented in permanent collection Fogg Mus., Harvard U., Cambridge, Mass.; films include Picasso War Love and Peace; books include Footprints of the Gods, 1988, Picasso my Friend, 1993, Grands Nus, 1999; author of 65 publs. Decorated chevalier Nat. Order Merit, 1980, Legion of Honor, 2003; recipient Louis Lumière prize, 1966, Grand Prix of Higashikawa Photo Fest, 1986, 3rd prize World Press Photo Internat., Amsterdam, 1997, Prix Polyedre, Aix, France, 1998. Mem. Nat. Photographers Createurs, Parc Regional Camargue, Ste. des Amis Jean Cocteau, Ste des Amis de La Fond, St. J. Perse, Aix en Pr., Rencontres Internat. de la Photographie Arles, Memoire, Union des Photographes Createurs. Roman Catholic. Home: 17 Rue Aristide Briand 13200 Arles France

CLERICI, PAUL CAMILIO, writer-photographer; b. Norwood, Mass., Dec. 8, 1965; s. Frank Anthony Clerici and Carol Elizabeth Hunt-Clerici. BA in Comms., Curry Coll., 1987. Radio personality, promotions dept. Sta. WZOU-FM, Boston, 1987; sports editor, photographer The Walpole (Mass.) Times, 1987-92, editor, photographer, writer, 1992-97; claim analyst, writer, photographer John Hancock Life Ins. Co., 1997—; freelance editor, photographer, writer, 1997—; road race dir. CAMY 5K Run and DAVID 5K Walk, 2001—. Author, editor: Newsreal, Walpole, Mass., 1982; editor, dir. (videos) Milton Cable TV, 1987, Walpole Girls Hoop State Champs, 1989, 94; writer, photographer North End Mag., State St. Jour., Marathon & Beyond mag. Grand prize fund raiser Ride-a-thon for Mentally Retarded, Walpole, 1978-79; bd. dirs. Walpole Cmty. TV, 1995—; vol., photographer, writer, mem. tournament com. Wrentham Devel. Ctr. for Mentally Retarded. Recipient 2nd pl. prize Walpole Mall Photo Contest, 1988; named to Walpole H.S. Hall of Fame, 2002. Mem. New Eng. Press Assn. (3d pl. feature story 1990, 3d pl. editl., 4th pl. sports photo, 1993, 3d pl. serious column 1994, 2d pl. spot news 1995), Mass. Press Assn. (1st pl. sports column 1990, 2d pl. sports feature 1991, 2d pl. editl., sports photo 1992, 1st pl. front page 1993), Italian-Am. Mut. Benefit Soc. Walpole (photographer, writer 1999—, v.p. 2003—). Avocations: running marathons, reading, collecting autographs, sports cards, comic books.

CLERMONT, YVES WILFRID, anatomy educator, researcher; b. Montreal, Que., Can., Aug. 14, 1926; s. Rodolphe and Fernande (Primeau) C.; m. Madeleine Bonneau, June 30, 1950; children— Suzanne, Martin, Stephane B.Sc., U. Montreal, 1949; PhD, McGill U., 1953. Lectr. anatomy McGill U., Montreal, 1953-56, asst. prof., 1956-60, assoc. prof., 1960-63, prof., 1963-97, prof. emeritus, 1997—, chmn. dept., 1975-85. Mem. Nat. Bd. Med. Examiners, Phila., 1979-82; mem. rsch. grant com. Med. Rsch. Coun., Ottawa, 1970-97; cons. WHO, NIH, Ford Found., Fonds pour la formation de chercheurs et l'aide à la recherche, Quebec; sec. Artur Lucian Award Com. for Rsch. in Circulatory Diseases, 1983-97, hon. mem., 1997-2000. Contbr. chpts. to books, numerous articles to profl. jours. Recipient Ortho prize Can. Soc. Study Fertility, 1958, Prix Scientifique Govt. of Que., 1963, S.L. Siegler award Am. Soc. Study Fertility, 1966, Van Campenhout award Can. Fertility and Andrology Soc., 1986, Osler Teaching award McGill U., 1990. Fellow Royal Soc. Can.; mem. Am. Assn. Anatomists (v.p. 1970-73), Soc. Study of Reprodn., Am. Assn. Andrology (Disting. Andrologist award 1988, Serono award lectureship 1992), Can. Assn. Anatomists (hon., J.C.B. Grant award 1986), Can. Assn. Microscopy (v.p. 1982-83). Home: 567 Townshend St Saint Lambert QC Canada J4R 1M4 Office: McGill U Dept Anatomy Cell Biol 3640 University St Montreal QC Canada H3A 2B2 E-mail: yvesclermont@mcgill.ca.

CLEVELAND, ASHLEY, musician; b. Knoxville, Tenn., Feb. 2, 1957; m. Kenny Greenberg. Rec. Big Town, 1991, Bus Named Desire, 1993, Lesson of Love, 1996 (Grammy award for Best Rock Gospel Album, 1996, Nashville Music award, 1996), You Are There, 1998 (Grammy award for Best Rock Gospel Album, 1999), Second Skin, 2002, singer on over 200 albums, appearances (TV series) Austin City Limits, Saturday Night Live, TNN Country News, American Music Shop, 1991, CCM-TV, 1993, Gospel Music Assn. Dove Awards, 1994, 1996, 1998, The Road, 1994, Prime Time Country, 1996, Peace In The Valley, CeCe's Place, Stone Country: A Tribute To The Rolling Stones, 1997, Profiles in Praise, 1999. Named Big Town one of 1991's Ten Most Overlooked Albums, Billboard; recipient Dove award for Praise and Worship Album of Yr., 1994. Office: PO Box 50181 Nashville TN 37205*

CLEVELAND, CEIL MARGARET, writer, journalist, education administrator, English language educator; b. Tex., Jan. 10, 1942; d. Joe Donaldson Cleveland and Margaret Ellen (Gowdy) Slack; m. Donald R. Waldrip; children: Wendy Gentile, James Hardy, Timothy Owen; m. Jerrold K. Footlick, Nov. 24, 1984; stepchildren: Robbyn Footlick, Jill Footlick. BA, Whitworth Coll., 1968; MA magna cum laude, Midwestern U., 1971; postgrad., NYU, Columbia U., 1978-82. Assoc. editor Univ. Press, U. Cin., 1975-77; sr. devel. officer, founding editor-in-chief Columbia mag. Columbia U., N.Y.C., 1976-85; founder, pres. Cleveland Comms., Centerport, N.Y., 1987-91; v.p. instnl. rels. Queens Coll., CUNY, Flushing, N.Y., 1991-95; prof. English, v.p. univ. affairs SUNY, Stony Brook, 1995-98; prof. English N.Y. U., 1998—. Dir. curriculum Cin. Arts and Humanities Consortium, 1972-74; adj. prof. English Xavier U., 1972-77, U. Cin., 1972-77, Queens Coll., 1990—; co-founder Syzygy, Women's Press; founder, pub. fiction and poetry The Mill Pond Press. Author: In the World of Literature, 1991, Whatever Happened to Jacy Farrow: A Memoir, 1997, The Bluebook Solution, a novel, 2002, Your Total Kit for Better Punctuation, 2002; editor: English Musical Culture 1776-1976, 1976; mem. editl. bd.: Liberal Edn., 1987—92. Trustee CNET, Cin., 1973-76, Cin. Symphony, 1973-76, Sch. for Creative and Performing Arts, Cin., 1973 76; founder Inner City Sch. Enrichment Project; mem. Coun. of Racial Equality, 1973-76; active Playhouse in the Park, 1973-76, Internat. Children's Village, Cin., 1973-76. Recipient Writer of Decade and Mag. Editor of Decade, Coun. for Advancement and Support of Edn., 1976—86, Edn. Comms. award, Ed Press, 1993, Internat. Bus. Comms. award, 1994; fellow Va. Ctr. for Creative Arts, 2002. Fellow Woodrow Wilson; mem. MLA, Coun. for Advancement and Support of Edn. (trustee 1981-83), Nat. Edn. Roundtable, N.Y.C. Women Leader's Roundtable, Am. Coun. Edn. (coord. 1994). Home: 11 Prospect Rd Centerport NY 11721-1129 Office: NYU 228 Shimkin Hall 50 W 4th St New York NY 10012-1156

CLEVELAND, EDWIN PITTMAN, music educator; b. Birmingham, Ala., July 25, 1962; s. Edwin Thomas Cleveland; m. Sharon Leigh Pate, Nov. 25, 1964; children: Lindsay Sue, Edwin Patrick. MusB Edn., Samford U., 1985; MusM Edn., U. Montevallo, 1992. Cert. Tchr. Ala., 1985. Choral music dir. Banks H.S., Birmingham, Ala., 1985—88, Pizitz Mid. Sch., Vestavia Hills, Ala., 1988—94; min. music South Avondale Bapt. Ch., Birmingham, Ala., 1989—92, Meadow Brook Bapt. Ch., Birmingham, Ala., 1992—; choral dir. Mountain Brook H.S., Mountain Brook, Ala., 1994—95, Vestavia Hills H.S., Vestavia Hills, Ala., 1995—99, Oak Mountain H.S., Birmingham, Ala., 1999—. Adj. faculty Samford U., Homewood, Ala., 1998—2001. Choral dir. Ala. Mid. Sch. Honor Choir, Montgomery, Ala., 2001—03. Mem.: So. Bapt. Music Conf. (assoc.), Music Educators Nat. Conf. (assoc.). Conservative. Baptist. Avocations: family, church activities, church activities, college basketball, fishing. Office: Oak Mountain High School 5476 Caldwell Mill Rd Birmingham AL 35242 Office Fax: 205-682-5205. Personal E-mail: eslpc@juno.com. E-mail: ecleveland@shelbyed.k12.al.us.

CLEVELAND, ELBIN L. theatre design and technology educator; b. Cedar Rapids, Iowa, Dec. 18, 1940; s. Loras L. and Helen Beatrice (Miller) C. BA, U. Northern Iowa, 1962; MA, U. Iowa, 1969, MFA, 1972. Cert. profl. tchr. Tchr. Belmond & Cedar Rapids (Iowa) Pub. Schs., 1962-67; instr. U. Iowa, Iowa City, 1969-72; asst. prof. U. Wis., LaCrosse, 1972-75; assoc. prof. theatre design and tech. U. S.C., Columbia, 1975-90, full prof., 1990—. Fulbright lectr. Traditional Opera Acad., Beijing, China, 1994; guest lectr. Shanghai Theatre Acad., 1994, Nat. Inst. for Arts, Taipei, Taiwan, 1994, Nat. Acad. Scenography, Seoul, 1993; mem. Fulbright Group Project Abroad, 2000. Scene designer of over 165 stage plays including Hamlet, Crucible, Coctail Hour, Peer Gynt; tech. dir. over 220 stage plays; lighting designer over 40 stage plays; theatre architecture cons. 18 bldgs.; author: SC Guidelines for Identification of Artistically Gifted and Talented Students, 1985, SC Curriculum Framework for Theatre/Drama Education, 1988, Bibliographic and Supplier Listing for Scenic Modelers, 1990, rev. edit., 1992, International Dictionary of Theatre and Related Terms, 1999; contbg. writer Stage Directions Mag., 1996-99; contbr. more than 100 articles to profl. jour.; assoc. editor for edn. Theatre Design and Tech. Mag., new products editor, 1988—; assoc. editor for scenography So. Theatre Mag., 1995-99, Sightlines, Tech. Resource Guide; new products editor Quar. Rev., 1997—; inventor Clevair Lift, 1997, Clevair Chair, 1997, Roller Rigging, 1999. Mem. Arts in Basic Curriculum Steering Com., SC, 1988—. Grantee S.C. Arts Commn., 1989, SC Humanities Coun., 1989, U. SC Venture Fund, 1989, Instrnl. Innovation, 1996, R&D, 1996, USITT, 1998. Mem. SC Theatre Assn. (past pres., Founders award 1988, 94), US Inst. Theatre Tech. (nat. chmn. publs. 1990-92, vice commr. edn. 1990-92, edn. editor 1990-96, ex-officio officer, bd. dir. 1988-1992), US Inst. Theatre Tech.-SE (life, commr. new products, commr. archives, Founder's award 1995), SC Alliance for Arts Edn. (chmn.-elect 1989-90), Southeastern Theatre Conf. (life; bd. dir. 1989-91, SC rep. 1990-92), Assn. Theatre in Higher Edn, Samsung Found. (MAMPIST, US dir. interns in theatre arts), Mortar Bd. Honor Soc. (Excellence in Tchg. award 2002). Avocations: films, sailing, travel. Office: U SC Dept Theatre Columbia SC 29250

CLEVELAND, HARLAN, political scientist, public affairs executive; b. NYC, Jan. 19, 1918; s. Stanley Matthews and Marian Phelps (Van Buren) Cleveland; m. Lois W. Burton, July 12, 1941; children: Zoë, Melantha, Alan Thorburn. Grad. cum laude, Phillips Acad., Andover, Mass., 1934; AB in Politics with high honors, Princeton U., 1938; recipient 22 hon. degrees. Intern Office of U.S. Senator Robert M. LaFollette, Jr., 1939-40; writer info. div. Farm Security Adminstrn., Washington, 1940-42; ovcl. Bd. Edn. Warfare and successor Fgn. Econ. Adminstrn., Washington, 1942—44; exec. dir. econ. sect. Allied Control Commn., Rome, 1944-45; mem. U.S. del. 3d session UNRRA Coun., London, 1945; acting v.p. in charge econ. sect. Allied Commn., Rome, 1945-46; dept. chief of mission UNRRA Italian Mission, Rome, 1946-47; dir. China office UNRRA, Shanghai, 1947-48; dir. China program ECA, Washington, 1948-49, dept. asst. adminstr., 1949-51; asst. dir. for Europe Mut. Security Agy., 1952-53; exec. editor The Reporter, N.Y.C., 1953-56, pub., 1955-56; prof. polit. sci., dean Maxwell grad. sch. citizenship and pub. affairs Syracuse U., 1956-61; chmn. Citizens for Kennedy, Central N.Y., 1960; asst. sec. for internat. orgn. affairs Dept. State, 1961-65; chmn. Cabinet Com. on Internat. Cooperation Yr., 1965; U.S. amb., rep. to NATO, 1965-69; prof. polit. sci., pres. U. Hawaii, Honolulu, 1969-74, pres. emeritus, 1974—; dir. program in internat. affairs Aspen Inst. Humanistic Studies, Princeton, N.J., 1974-80, disting. fellow, 1988—; chmn. U.S. Weather Modification Adv. Bd., 1977-78; disting. vis. Tom Slick prof. world peace LBJ Sch. Public Affairs, U. Tex., Austin, 1979; prof. pub. affairs and planning Hubert H. Humphrey Inst. Public Affairs, U. Minn., Mpls., 1980-88, prof. emeritus, 1988—, dean, 1980-87. Hon. chmn. The Am. Forum for Global Edn., Vols. in Tech. Assistance; bd. dirs. Vols. of Am., Mertz-Gilmore Found., Common Heritage Corp., Am. Refugee Com.; trustee Toynbee Found.; nat. adv. coun. World Learning; del. from N.Y. Dem. Nat. Conv., 1960; electronic faculty Western Behavioral Scis. Inst., 1983—91; faculty Connected Edn., 1987—96; hon. trustee The Atlantic Coun. Author: The Obligations of Power, 1966, NATO: The Transatlantic Bargain, 1970, The Future Executive, 1972 (Louis Brownlow award 1975), China Diary, 1976, The Third Try at World Order, 1977, The Knowledge Executive, 1985, The Age of Choice, 1990, The Global Commons, 1990, Birth of a New World, 1993, Leadership and the Information Revolution, 1997, Nobody in Charge, 2002; co-author: Next Step in Asia, 1948; The Overseas Americans, 1960, Humangrowth, 1978; editor: The Promise of World Tensions, 1961, The Management of Sustainable Growth, 1980, Energy Futures of Developing Countries, 1980; gen. editor: Readings for Leaders (series), 1988; co-editor: The Art of Overseasmanship, 1957, The Ethic of Power, 1962, Ethics and Bigness, 1962, Bioresources for Development, 1980, Prospects for Peacemaking, 1988. Decorated U.S. Medal of Freedom, gold star Order Brilliant Star (China), gran ufficiale Order of Merit (Italy); recipient Woodrow Wilson award, Princeton U., 1968, Prix de Talloires, 1981, Leader for Peace award, U.S. Peace Corps, 1985, Rhodes scholar, Oxford U., 1938—39. Fellow: Internat. Leadership Forum, World Bus. Acad., World Acad. of Art and Sci. (pres. 1991—2000); mem.: ASPA (pres. 1970—71, Dwight Waldo award 1988, Elmer Staats Lifetime Achievement award 2003), Coun. on Fgn. Rels., Am. Polit. Sci. Assn., Univ. Club (Washington), Century Club (N.Y.C.), Phi Beta Kapp. Home: 46891 Grissom St Sterling VA 20165-3593 E-mail: harlancleve@cs.com. *If you try too carefully to plan your life, the danger is that you will succeed—succeed in narrowing your options, closing off avenues of adventure that cannot now be imagined, perhaps because they are not yet technologically possible. When a student asks me for career advice, I can only suggest that he or she opt for the most exciting "next step" without worrying where it will lead, and then work hard on the job in hand, not pine for the one in the bush. When your job no longer demands of you more than you have, go and do something else. Always take by preference the job you don't know how to do. If you build into your life enough variety of experience, you will be training for leadership in the role I have called The Public Executive.*

CLEVELAND, HERSCHEL, state representative; b. 1946; BSBA, JD, U. Ark. Spkr. of ho. State of Ark., 2001—; mcpl. judge Ho. of Reps., 1999, 2001. Chmn. ALC/JBC Parks and Tourism Subcom., ALC/Performance-Based Budgeting Subcom., Legis. Facilities; mem. ALC-Adminstrv. Rules and Regulations, ALC-JBC Budget Hearings, ALC-Peer, others. Baptist. Office: Hixon and Cleveland Law Office 1727 East Walnut Paris AR 72855 Office Fax: 479-963-3011.*

CLEVELAND, PEGGY ROSE RICHEY, cytotechnologist; b. Cannelton, Ind., Dec. 9, 1929; d. "Pat" Clarence Francis and Alice Marie (Hall) Richey; m. Peter Leslie Cleveland, Nov. 25, 1948 (dec. 1973); children: Pamela Cleveland Litch, Paula Cleveland Bertloff, Peter L. Cert., U. Louisville, 1956, B in Health Sci., 1984. Cytotechnologist cancer survey project NIH, Louisville, 1956-59; chief cytotechnologist Parker Cytology Lab., Inc., Louisville, 1959-75; mgr. cytology dept. Am. Biomed. Corp., 1976-78, Nat. Health Labs., Inc., Louisville, 1978-89; with various hosps. and labs., 1990—. Leader cytotechnologist del. to China, 1986; clin. instr. cytology Sch. Allied Health, U. Louisville, 1989; ptnr. Sham Star Stable thoroughbred horse breeding and racing. Mem. Am. Soc. Clin. Pathologist (cert. cytotechnologist), Internat. Acad. Cytology (cert. cytotechnologist), Am. Soc. Cytology (del.-person to person cytology delegation, amb. USSR 1990), Kentuckiana Cytology Soc., Cytology Soc. Ind., Horseman's Benevolent and Protective Assn. Democrat. Roman Catholic. Home: 8774 Lieber Hausz Rd NE Lanesville IN 47136-8522

CLEVELAND, RAY LEROY, history educator; b. Scottsbluff, Nebr., Apr. 29, 1929; s. Harold and Florence Cleveland. BA, Westmont Coll., 1951; MA, Johns Hopkins U., 1956, PhD, 1958; DS (hon.), U. of the Pacific, 1970. Rsch. assoc. Johns Hopkins U., Balt., 1959-64; rsch. fellow Am. Found. for Study of Man, 1964-66; assoc. prof. U. Sask., Regina, Can., 1966-72, prof. history, 1972-74, U. Regina, 1974-94, prof. emeritus, 1994—. Assoc. editor Bull. of Am. Schs. of Oriental Rsch., 1960-64; editor publs. Am. Found. for Study of Man, 1959-75. Author: An Ancient South Arabian Necropolis, 1965, Middle East and South Asia, 20 edits., 1967-88; co-editor: Alexander The Great, 1992; contbr. numerous articles to profl. jours. Fellow Am. Sch. Oriental Rsch. in Jerusalem, 1955-56. Office: U Regina History Dept Regina SK Canada S4S 0A2 E-mail: ray.cleveland@uregina.ca.

CLEVELAND, SUSAN ELIZABETH, library administrator, researcher; b. Plainfield, N.J., Mar. 14, 1946; d. Robert Astbury and Grace Ann (Long) Williamson; m. Stuart Craig Cleveland, Aug. 21, 1971; children: Heather Elizabeth, Catherine Elisa. BA, Douglass Coll., Rutgers U., 1968; MLS, Rutgers U., 1969. Acquisitions libr. Jefferson U., Phila., 1970-71; biomed. libr. VA Hosp., Hines, Ill., 1972; med. cataloger U. Ariz., Tucson, 1973-74; dir. U. Pa. Hosp. Libr., Phila., 1974-87; exec. dir. Cleveland, Lamb, Urban Assocs., 1987-89; libr. dir. Mt. Sinai Hosp., Phila., 1989, West Jersey Health System (now Virtua Health Sys.), Voorhees, NJ, 1990—2002, Our Lady of Lourdes Med. Ctr., Camden, NJ, 2002—. Cons. in field, Phila. USPHS fellow, Detroit, 1969-70; recipient Chapel of 4 Chaplains Legion of Honor. Mem. Med. Libr. Assn. (Phila. chpt.), Spl. Libr. Assn., Basic Health Sci. Libr. Consortium, So. N.J. Consortium for Health Info. Svcs., Health Scis. Libr. Assn. N.J., Acad. Health Info. Profls., Caravan Club. Home: 9 Sylvan Ct Laurel Springs NJ 08021 E-mail: clevelands@lourdesnet.org.

CLEVEN, CAROL CHAPMAN, state legislator; b. Hanover, Ill., Nov. 2, 1928; d. Edward William and Vivian (Strasser) Chapman; m. Walter Arnold Cleven; children: Kern W., Jeffrey P. BS, U. Ill., 1950, postgrad., 1950-56. Elem. sch. tchr. Derinda Ctr., Ill., 1946-47; with rsch. staff U. Ill., Urbana, 1950-56; exec. dir. Crittenton Hasting House, Brighton, Mass., 1975-86; mem. Mass. Ho. of Reps., Boston, 1987—. Mem. edn. com., mem. human svcs. com., mem. election laws com. Mass. Ho. Reps.; mem. Rep. Task Force on Pediatric AIDS, Mass. Caucus of Women Legislators, Gov.'s Adolescent Health Adv. Coun., Spl. Commn. on Pub. Assiatance, Spl. Com. on Women and the Criminal Justice System; co-chair Legis. Caucus on Older Citizens' Concerns, Dept. Social Svcs. Working Group; mem. steering com. Mass. Legis. Children's Caucus. Mem. Chelmsford (Mass.) Sch. Com., 1969-87, mem. elem. needs com., 1969-71, mem. sch. bldg. com., 1971-76; bd. dirs. Camp Paul for Exceptional Children, 1987—; past pres. Lowell (Mass.) YWCA, Lowell Coll. Club; mem. Merrimack River Watershed Coun., Mass. Coalition for Pregnant and Parenting Teens, Alliance for Young Families; treas. Boston Ctr. Blind Children; bd. dirs. Chelmsford Ednl. Found.; bd. dirs. Greater Lowell Alzheimers Assn., Ea. Mass. Alzheimers Assn.; mem. spl. adv. bd. Cmty. Teamwork, Inc. Mem. Mass. Assn. Sch. Coms. (life), Friends of the Library, Chelmsford Hist. Soc., Chelmsford LWV, Florence Crittenton League of Lowell, Phi Sigma, Sigma Delta Epsilon. Congregationalist. Home: 4 Arbutus Ave Chelmsford MA 01824-1113 Office: State House Rm 167 State Capitol Boston MA 02133

CLEVENGER, MARK THOMAS, communications executive, writer; b. L.A., Aug. 21, 1928; s. John Thomas Clevenger and Alice Laura (Wilburn) Gable; m. Ann Marie Kelley, Oct. 27, 1957; children: Kelley Patricia, Maura Theresa, Sean Thomas, Kate Clevenger Westerlund. BS in Agronomy, U. Calif., Davis; MA in Journalism, U. So. Calif.; PhC in Higher Edn., U. Wash. USAF, 1951-55; pub. rels. rep. Lockheed Corp., Burbank, Calif., 1959-70; dir. pub. rels. Lockheed Shipbldg., Seattle, 1970-72, cons., 1974-82; dir. info. svcs. U. Wash., Seattle, 1972-73, instr. bus. comm., 1974-91; pres. Interface Comm., Grapeview, Wash., 1976-2001, Polychite Corp., Redmond, Wash., 1985-91. Editor various newspapers, Calif., 1955-59. Trustee Group Health Coop., Seattle, 1979-82. Various awards Calif. Newspaper Pubs. Assn. Mem. Soc. Naval Archs. Marine Engrs. Address: PO Box 390 Grapeview WA 98546-0390

CLEVENGER, PENELOPE, international business consultant; b. Denver, Dec. 6, 1940; d. Harold Friedland and Charlotte (Glatt) Friedland Beskin; m. Willie K. Clevenger, Oct. 15, 1961 (div.). AA, Stephens Coll., 1960. Pers. mgr. Rolm/Midwest, Chgo., 1979-82; office mgr. Malcolm S. Gerald, Chgo., 1977-79; office adminstr. Nutech Engrs., Chgo., 1982-83; office mgr. Am. Acad. Orthop. Surgeons, Chgo., 1983-85; dir. adminstrn. Telecomm. Industry Assn. (formerly U.S. Telecomm. Suppliers), Chgo., 1985-88; pres. InterWorld Svcs., Ltd., Chgo., 1988—2002, Vosges Haut-Chocolat, 2001—. Bd. dirs. Ctr. Tng. and Rehab. of Disabled, Chgo., 1981-84; vol. Northwestern Meml. Hosp., 1985-87, Christian Indsl. League, 1992-97. Mem. Meeting Profls. Internat., Chgo. Coun. on Fgn. Rels., U.S. China Friendship Assn. Democrat. Jewish. Home: 233 E Wacker Dr Apt 3910 Chicago IL 60601-5116 E-mail: clev104763@cs.com.

CLEVENGER, RAYMOND CHARLES, III, federal judge; b. Topeka, Kans., Aug. 27, 1937; s. Raymond and Mary Margaret (Ramsey) Clevenger; m. Celia Faulkner, Sept. 6, 1961 (div. Mar. 1987); children: Winthrop, Peter. BA, Yale U., 1959, LLB, 1966. Law clerk to Justice Byron S. White U.S. Supreme Court, Washington, 1966—67; ptnr. Wilmer Cutler & Pickering, Washington, 1967—71, 1972—90; special assist. to gen. counsel John W. Barnum US Dept. of Transp., Washington, 1971—72; judge U.S. Ct. Appeals (Fed. Cir.), Washington, 1990—. Mem. ABA, D.C. Bar Assn. Office: Howard T Markey Nat Ct Bldg 717 Madison Pl NW Washington DC 20439-0002*

CLEVENGER, ROY EDWARD, credit and collections manager; b. Kansas City, Kans., Nov. 24, 1953; s. Roy J. and Rosa E. (Johnson) C.; m. Judith Ann Elizabeth Kowalski, Aug. 25, 1976; 1 child, Judith Ann. BJ, U. Kans., 1975. Exec. dir., trustee Washington Crossing (Pa.) Found., 1973-76; with credit and collections dept. Milton Roy Co., Ivyland, Pa., 1979-82; asst. credit mgr. McGraw-Hill Publs., Hightstown, N.J., 1982-83, mgr. credit and collections, 1984-89, Wood Textures, Inc., Edison, N.J., 1989-91; mgr. collections div. HIAS Inc., N.Y.C., 1991—. Vol. Independence Nat. Hist. Park, Phila., 1983-92. Mem. Media Credit Assn., Nat. Assn. Credit Mgmt., Ea. Nat. Park and Monument Assn. Avocations: philately, geology, history. Home: PO Box 33 Washington Crossing PA 18977-0033

CLEVENGER, SARAH, botanist, computer consultant; b. Indpls., Dec. 19, 1926; d. Cyrus Raymond and Mary Beth (Stevens) C. AB, Miami U., 1947; PhD, Ind. U., 1957. Tchr sci. Radford Sch., El Paso, Tex., 1949-51, Hillsdale Sch., Cin., 1951-52; asst. prof. Berea (Ky.) Coll., 1957-59, 61-63, Wittenberg U., Springfield, Ohio, 1959-60, Eastern Ill. U., 1960-61, Ind. State U., Terre Haute, 1963-66, assoc. prof., 1966-78, prof., 1978-85, prof. emerita, 1985—. Mem. Am. Inst. Biol. Sci., Am. Soc. Plant Taxonomists, Bot. Soc. Am., Internat. Assn. Plant Taxonomy, Phytochem. Soc. N.Am. (past sec.). Home: 717 S Henderson St Bloomington IN 47401-4838

CLEVER, LINDA HAWES, physician; b. Seattle; d. Nathan Harrison and Evelyn Lorraine (Johnson) Hawes; m. James Alexander Clever, Aug. 20, 1960; 1 child, Sarah Lou. AB with distinction, Stanford U., 1962, MD, 1965. Diplomate Am. Bd. Internal Medicine, Am. Bd. Preventive Medicine in Occupl. Medicine. Intern Stanford U. Hosp., Palo Alto, Calif., 1965—66, resident, 1966—67, fellow in infectious disease, 1967—68; fellow in cmty. medicine U. Calif., San Francisco, 1968—69, resident, 1969—70; med. dir. Sister Mary Philippa Diagonostic and Treatment Ctr. St. Mary's Hosp., San Francisco, 1970—77; chmn. dept. occupl. health Calif. Pacific Med. Ctr., San Francisco, 1977—. Clin. prof. medicine U. Calif. Med. Sch., San Francisco; NIIH rsch. fellow Sch. Medicine, Stanford U., 1967—68; mem. nat. adv. panel Inst. Rsch. on Women and Gender, 1990—, chair panel, 1998—2000; mem. San Francisco Comprehensive Health Planning Coun., 1971—76; bd. dirs., mem. Calif.-OSHA Adv. Com. on Hazard Evaluation Sys. and Info. Svc., 1979—85, Calif. Statewide Profl. Stds. Rev. Coun., 1977—81, San Francisco Regional Commn. on White House Fellows, 1979—81, 1983—89, 1992, 95, chmn., 1977—81, 2001—02; bd. sci. counselors Nat. Inst. Occupl. Safety and Health, 1995—. Editor We. Jour. Medicine, 1990—98; contbr. articles to profl. jours. Trustee Stanford U., 1972—76, 1981—91, v.p., 1985—91; pres. RENEW, 2000—; bd. dirs. Sta. KQED, 1976—83, chmn., 1979—81; bd. dirs. Ind. Sector, 1980—86, vice chmn., 1985—86; bd. dirs. San Francisco U. H.S., 1983—90, chmn., 1987—88; active Womens Forum West, 1980—, bd. dirs., 1992—93; mem. Lucile Packard Children's Hosp. Bd., 1993—97, Lucile Packard Found. Children, 1997—99; mem. policy adv. com. U. Calif. Berkeley Sch. Pub. Health, 1995—, chair, 1995—2000; bd. dirs. The Redwoods Retirement Cmty., 1996—2001, Buck Inst. for Rsch. in Aging, 2000—; bd. govs. Stanford Med. Alumni Assn., 1997—2002; bd. dirs. No. Calif. Presbyn. Homes and Svcs., 2000—. Master: ACP (agov. No. Calif. region 1984—89, chmn. bd. govs. 1989—90, regent 1990—96, vice chair bd. regents 1994—95); fellow: Am. Coll. Occupl. and Environ. Medicine; mem.: APHA, We. Assn. Physicians (pres. 2003), We. Occupl. Medicine Assn., Calif. Acad. Medicine, Calif. Med. Assn., Inst. Medicine NAS, Stanford U. Women's Club (bd. dirs. 1971—80), Chi Omega. Office: 2340 Clay St Ste 106 San Francisco CA 94115-1931

CLEWELL, DON B. microbial geneticist, educator; b. Dallas, Sept. 5, 1941; AB, Johns Hopkins U., 1963; PhD, Ind. U., Indpls., 1967. Cert. molecular biologist, microbiologist. From asst. prof. to assoc. prof. schs. dentistry and medicine U. Mich., Ann Arbor, 1970-77, prof., 1977—. Burroughs Wellcome vis. prof. U. Rochester, N.Y., 1982; found. lectr. Am. Soc. for Microbiology, 1985-86; mem. recombinant DNA adv. com. NIH, Bethesda, Md., 1986-90. Mem. editl. bd.: Jour. Bacteriology, 1974—80, Plasmid, 1977—87, Infection and Immunity, 1985—96; contbr. over 200 articles to profl. jours., chapters to books. Recipient Rsch. Career Devel. award USPHS, 1975-80, Disting. Faculty Achievement award U. Mich., 2002, Disting. Faculty Lectureship award U. Mich. Med. Sch., 2003. Mem.: Am. Acad. Microbiology. Achievements include discovery and characterization of bacterial sex pheromone systems and conjugative transposons. Office: U Mich Sch Dentistry Biol and Materials Scis Ann Arbor MI 48109-1078 E-mail: dclewell@umich.edu.

CLEWETT, KENNETH VAUGHN, college official; b. Pomona, Calif., June 3, 1923; s. Heber Hovey and Thelma Lela (Sikes) C.; m. Margery Marie Haas, July 10, 1949; children: Richard A., Bruce D., Curtis L., Janet M. AA, Pomona Jr. Coll., 1943; student naval tng., U. Redlands, 1943-44, Columbia U., 1944; BA, Stanford U., 1947. Gen. clk. So. Counties Gas Co., Pomona, 1947; pers. examiner Calif. Pers. Bd., Sacramento, 1947-50; asst. pers. officer Calif. Dept. Mental Hygiene, Sacramento, 1950-52; pers. dir. Sonoma State Hosp., Eldridge, Calif., 1952-60, hosp. adminstr., 1960-72, Fairview State Hosp., Costa Mesa, Calif., 1972-75, 76; acting exec. dir. Patton (Calif.) State Hosp., 1975-76, exec. dir., 1976-78; bus. mgr. So. Calif. Coll., 1978-82, dir. planning and corp. rels., 1982-84; v.p. adminstrn., dir. external affairs Kona campus U. of the Nations (formerly Pacific and Asia Christian U.), 1985—. Preceptor George Washington U., Grad. Sch. Health Care Adminstrn., 1962-78, Northwestern U. Grad. Sch. Mgmt., 1975-78, U. Minn. Program Mental Health Adminstrn., 1976-78. Pres. Sonoma Valley C. of C., 1964; v.p. Sonoma-Mendocino coun. Boy Scouts Am., 1968—71, bd. dirs., 1965—72; v.p. Sonoma County United Crusade, 1969—70; chmn. Sonoma Valley Coun. Edn. Com., 1969—71; founding chmn. bd. dirs. Sonoma Valley United Crusade, 1969—70, bd. dirs., 1969—72; vice chmn. bd. dirs. Big Sisters Orange County, Calif., 1975—77; bd. dirs. Ctrl. Sonoma County ARC, 1956—60, So. Calif. Coll., 1977—78, Goodwill Industries Ctrl. Calif., 1951—52, Goodwill Industries Inland Counties, 1978, West Hawaii Housing Found., 1988—, vice chmn., 1994—, Cmty. Orgn.for Edn. Devel., 1995—, Bridge Ho. Rehab. Ctr., 1997—2000, Kona Pacific Condo Owners Assn., 1990—2001, pres., 1992—93, 1998—2001; mem. sch./cmty.-based mgmt. coun. Konawaena H.S., 1992—95, Kealakehe H.S., 1998—; mem. adv. bd. Orange County Rescue Ctr., 1980—84, Hawaii County Decisions, 1988—91, Salvation Army Kona, 1991—99, chmn., 1995—98; mem. adv. bd. West Hawaii Food Bank, 1994—, vice chair, 1998—99; mem. adv. bd. Kona Hosp., 1996—2001, 2003—; mem. adv. coun. West Hawaii ARC, 1988—; mem. West Hawaii adv. com. Hawaii Health Sys. Corp., 1997—, chair, 2001—03; trustee Sonoma Valley Unified Sch. Dist., 1971—72; pres. Redwood Empire Hosp. Conf., 1967, bd. dirs., 1966—68; founding co-chair West Hawaii Coalition on Homeless Concerns, 1991—92; founding chair Meet 'N Eat feeding program, 1992—, Kona Area Coun. of Svc. Clubs, 1993—; bd. dirs. Greater Kona Cmty. Coun., 1991—92, vice chmn., 1992; elder United Presbyn. Ch. in U.S.A., 1949—74; deacon Newport-Mesa Christian Ctr., Costa Mesa, Calif., 1975—76, 1979—84. Lt. (j.g.) USNR, 1943—46, PTO. Recipient Citizens award of Year Valley Moon Tchrs. Assn., 1970, Outstanding Svc. award Redwood Empire Hosp. Conf., 1972, Rotarian Club Mem. of Yr., 1996, Clara Barton vol. award ARC, 1999. Fellow: Assn. Mental Health Adminstrs. (pres. 1976, bd. dirs. 1967—72, 1974—77), Royal Soc. Health (bd. dirs. 1989—95); mem.: Kona-Kohala C. of C., Christian Mgmt. Assn., Am. Assn. Mental Retardation, Rotary (pres. Kona 1993—94, Club Mem. of Yr. 1996), Alpha Gamma Sigma (hon.; life). Home: 75-5787 Kakalina St Kailua Kona HI 96740-1909 *Each additional personal achievement further confirms the weakness of depending upon myself alone and that real success is dependent upon truly following the leading of God, our heavenly Father.*

CLEWETT, RAYMOND WINFRED, mechanical design engineer; b. Upland, Calif., Nov. 7, 1917; s. Howard Jasper and Pansy Gertrude (Macy) C.; m. Hazel Royer, June 11, 1938; children: Alan Eugene, Patricia Gail, Charles Raymond, Richard Howard, Beverly Lynn. Student, Chaffey Jr. Coll., 1937. Exptl. mechanic Douglas Aircraft Co., Santa Monica, Calif., 1937-51; shop foreman, exptl. designer Lear, Inc., Los Angeles, 1945-51; design engr., shop mgr. The RAND Corp., Santa Monica, Calif., 1951-83, also design cons.; owner, mgr. HY-TECH Engring. and Devel. Lab., Malibu, Calif., 1983—2001. Works include mech. design of JOHNNIAC early model electronic computer; designer various computer input/output devices, 1953-70; developer low vision reading aids for the blind, 1970-75; design and constrn. spl. equipment for sci. and research, 1983-99; stone sculptor, 1994-2001; exhbns. include Malibu Art Festival, 1998, Art Affair XIII, Pacific Palisades, Calif., 1998; patentee in field. Republican. E-mail: ray_clewett@juno.com.

CLEWS, WILLIAM VINCENT, writer; b. Richmond, Va., Sept. 5, 1943; s. Charles Gordon and Eleanora Maria (Marciano) C.; children: Christopher William, Ashleigh Elizabeth; m. Carol Ann Peterson, May 30, 1986; stepchild, Todd Clinton. BS, Frostburg State Coll., 1966; MS, Ind. State U., 1969. Tchr. pub. schs., Rivera Beach, Md., 1966-67; writer Md. Pub. TV, Balt., 1968-70, producer, 1970-78; pres. Vince Clews & Assocs., Balt., 1979—98; CEO VcAnet, Inc., 1995—99. Drama dir. Md. Pub. Schs., 1966-67; tchr. Am. U., Washington, 1977, Western Md. Coll., 1978; lectr. Internat. TV Assn., San Francisco, 1980-90, Internat. Quorum of Film and Video Producers, Rio de Janeiro. Writer (TV show) Inventory, 1971 (Golden Gate award 1971), (video prodn.) Medical 12 (N.Y. Film Festival award 1980); producer (TV shows) Consumer Survival Kit, 1973, 1974 (Emmy nominee 1974), Scepter of Violence, 1981 (Gold Cindy 1981), Fight for Freedom, 1988 (Telly 1988), (tng. video) Salesability, 1982 (Silver Screen 1982), (corp. image video) The Rouse Co., 1986 (N.Y. Film Festival 1986); producer, dir. (pub. rels. video) Safe and Sound, 1989 (Telly 1989). Mem. Balt. County Cable Commn., 1981-83. Named one of Oustanding Young Men in Am., U.S. C. of C., 1975, for Excellence in Consumer Reporting, Nat Press Club, 1974; recipient Gavel award ABA, 1977, 78. Mem. Internat. Quorum Film & Video Producers (v.p. North Am. 1988-90), Internat. TV Assn. Republican. Avocations: tennis, travel. Home: 1205 Nicodemus Rd Reisterstown MD 21136-5823

CLIBURN, VAN (HARVEY LAVAN CLIBURN JR.), concert pianist; b. Shreveport, La., July 12, 1934; s. Harvey Lavan and Rildia Bee (O'Bryan) C. Studied music with, mother, 1937-51; studied with, Mme. Rosina Lhevinne; grad. with highest honors; grad. (Frank Damrosch scholar), Juilliard Sch. Music, 1954; HHD (hon.), Baylor U., 1958; MFA, Moscow Conservatory, 1989; D (hon.), The Juilliard Sch. of Music, 1998. Pub. appearances, Shreveport, 1940, debut, Houston Symphony Orch., 1947; appeared with Dallas Symphony Orch., 1952, N.Y. Philharm. Orch., Carnegie Hall, 1954, 58; concert pianist on tour, U.S., 1955-56, Soviet Union, 1958, recs. RCA Victor; guest TV shows, concert with Symphony of the Air, Carnegie Hall, 1958, concert Brussels Fair, Belgium, 1958, other appearances: Phila., Chgo., Hollywood, Denver, London, Amsterdam, Paris, Athens, Monaco, The Hague, Copenhagen, Stockholm, Bucharest, Oslo, La Scala, Moscow, Leningrad, Kiev, Boston, Washington, Dallas, Rio de Janeiro, Mexico City, Tokyo, Berlin, Munich, Zurich, Geneva, Madrid, Barcelona, Lisbon, Vienna, Tel Aviv; nation-wide tour U.S., 1958—; extensive recs. of works by Rachmaninoff, Chopin, Beethoven, others; composer classical music; recordings include My Favorite Encores-Works by Chopin, et. al., A Romantic Collection, World's Favorite Piano Music. Recipient Tex. State prize, 1947; Nat. Music Festival award, 1948; G.B. Dealy award Dallas, 1952; Kosciuszko Found. Chopin award, 1952; grantee Olga Samaroff Found., 1953; 1st place Juilliard Concerto concert, 1953; Edgar M. Leventritt Found. award, 1954; Carl M. Roeder Meml. award Juilliard Sch. Music, 1954; 1st prize Internat. Tchaikovsky Piano Competition Moscow, 1958; citation Am. Assn. Sch. Adminstrs., 1959; U. Mich. Musical Soc. First Disting. Artist award, 1996; Arturo Toscanini award, Classical Music Broadcaster's Assn., 1998; named number one in classical field Top Artists on Campus Poll (album sales), 1968. Mem. Am. Guild Mus. Artists. Clubs: Thespian (Kilgore, Tex.) (pres.), Rotary (hon.), Lotos (life), Shreveport, Ft. Worth. Baptist. Office: care Ann Hilton PO Box 470217 Fort Worth TX 76147-0217 also: Van Cliburn /Foundation 2525 Ridgmar Blvd Ste 307 Fort Worth TX 76116-4583

CLIETT, CHARLES BUREN, aeronautical engineer, educator, academic administrator; b. Montpelier, Miss., July 10, 1924; s. James Thomas and Sallie Lou (Saul) C.; m. Grace Holland Campbell, Dec. 25, 1946; children— Susan Marie, Charles Buren. BS in Aero. Engring, Ga. Inst. Tech., 1945, MS in Aero. Engring, 1950; DSc (hon.), Miss. State U., 2003. Registered profl. engr., Miss. Faculty Miss. State U., 1947—, prof. aero. engring., 1957-91, prof. emeritus, 1991—, chmn. dept., 1960-91. Lt. j.g. USNR, 1943—46. Recipient Spl. Achievement award Miss. State U. Alumni Assn., 1987, Faculty award for Career Achievement Faculty of Coll. Engring., Miss. State U., 1988. Mem. Am. Soc. Engrng. Edn., AIAA, Am. Legion, Nat. Soc. Profl. Engrs., Miss. Engring. Soc., Aerospace Dept. Chairpersons Assn. (pres. 1979), Tau Beta Pi, Sigma Gamma Tau. Methodist. Home: 638 Commerce St West Point MS 39773-3016 Office: Engring Rsch Ctr Miss State PO Box 6176 Mississippi State MS 39762-6176

CLIFF, JOHNNIE MARIE, mathematics and chemistry educator; b. Lamkin, Miss., May 10, 1935; d. John and Modest Alma (Lewis) Walton; m. William Henry Cliff, Apr. 1, 1961 (dec. 1983); 1 child, Karen Marie. BA in Chemistry, Math., U. Indpls., 1956; postgrad., NSF Inst., Butler U., 1960; MA in Chemistry, Ind. U., 1964; MS in Math., U. Notre Dame, 1980; postgrad., Martin U., 2000. Cert. tchr., Ind. Rsch. chemist Ind. U. Med. Ctr., Indpls., 1956-59; tchr. sci. and math. Indpls. Pub. Schs., 1960-88; tchr. chemistry, math. Martin U., Indpls., 1989—, chmn. math. dept., 1990—, divsn. chmn. depts. sci. and math., 1993—. Adj. instr. math. U. Indpls., 1991, Ivy Tech State Coll., Indpls., 2002. Contbr. rsch. papers to sci. jours. Grantee NSF, 1961-64, 73-76, 78-79, Woodrow Wilson Found., 1987-88; scholarship U. Indpls., 1952-56, NSF Inst. Reed Coll., 1961, C. of C., 1963. Mem. AAUW, NAACP, NEA, Assn. Women in Sci., Urban League, N.Y. Acad. Scis., Am. Chem. Soc., Nat. Coun. Math. Tchrs., Am. Assn. Physics Tchrs., Nat. Sci. Tchrs. Assn., Am. Statis. Assn., Am. Assn. Ret. Persons, Neal-Marshall-Ind. U. Alumni Assn., U. Indpls. Alumni Assn., U. Notre Dame Alumni Assn., Ind. U. Chemist Assn., Notre Dame Club Indpls., Kappa Delta Pi, Delta Sigma Theta. Democrat. Baptist. Avocations: gardening, sewing. Home: 405 Golf Ln Indianapolis IN 46260-4108 Office: Martin U 2171 Avondale Pl Indianapolis IN 46218-3878

CLIFF, KARISSA, consumer researcher, recruiter; b. Lancaster, Calif., Dec. 15, 1965; d. John Oliver and Frances Kay (Spencer) Cliff; m. Kevin Kenneth Ross, Apr. 14, 1984 (div. June 1988); children: Kevin Kenneth Ross, II, Serenity Angeline Ross; m. Ira C. Baxter, 1998 (div. Feb. 2003); children: Madeline Elizabeth, Rosalyn Andrea Regina. BBA magna cum laude, Belmont U., 1995; MBA, Vanderbilt U., 1997. Mgr., liaison Mercantile Stores, Nashville, 1983-87; researcher Ericson Mktg. Comm., Nashville, 1994-95; marketer Armor All, Charleston, S.C., 1996; consumer rschr. Procter & Gamble, Nashville, 1997-2000; sr. analyst Clorox, Nashville, 2000—03. Cons. Am. Beauty Cosmetics, Gallatin, Tenn., 1995. Founder Homeless Day Labor, Nashville, 1996-97; chair 100% Owen Svc. Orgn., Nashville, 1996-97; vol. soup kitchen Union Rescue Mission, Nashville, 1995-97; vol. Refugee Relocation, Nashville, 1995-97. Wendell scholar for Mktg. Studies, Belmont U., 1994-95, Morris scholar Vanderbilt U., 1995-97. Fellow Ctr. for Transition and Orgnl. Design; mem. MENSA, Delta Gamma Beta. Democrat. Avocation: flute. E-mail: karissacliff@yahoo.com.

CLIFF, STEVEN BURRIS, engineering executive; b. Knoxville, Tenn., Mar. 30, 1952; s. Edgar Burris and Otella (Patterson) C.; m. Sharon Grace Davis, Sept. 11, 1971 ; children: Sarah Elizabeth, Susan Rebecca, Steven John. BS in Engring. Sci., U. Tenn., 1974, MS in Engring. Sci., 1976; postgrad., So. Sem., 1974-75. Rsch. asst. U. Tenn., Knoxville, 1972-75, asst. rsch. prof., 1975-76; program analyst Oak Ridge (Tenn.) Nat. Lab., 1976-77, rsch. engr., 1977-79; chief tech. officer Computer Concepts Corp., Knoxville, 1979-81; pres. Productive Programming Inc., Knoxville, 1981-82; v.p. R&D Control Tech. Inc., Knoxville, 1982 98, sr. v.p. R&D, 1998-2001, corp. sec., 1991-2001; sr. embedded systems software engr. Remotec/Northrop Grumman, 2001—. Ptnr. Middlebrook Indsl. Properties, 1985—, Cliff Bros. Investments, 1988-2000. Contbr. articles to profl. jours. Mem. exec. bd. Rocky Hill Parent-Tchr. Orgn., Knoxville, 1987, 91-97, pres. 1994-95; deacon West Knoxville Bapt. Ch., 1984-87, Loveland Bapt. Ch., Knoxville, 1976-82; tech. com. Bearden (Tenn.) Mid. Sch., 1996-97; bd. dirs. Rocky Hill Baseball League, 1995-2000; tchr. Bearden United Meth. Ch., 2001—. U. Tenn. scholar, 1970. Mem. Soc. Mfgs. Engrs. (sr.), Nat. Electronic Mfg. Assn. (chmn. com. 1987-94, seminar spkr. 1988-94), Am. Assn. for Artificial Intelligence, Instrument Soc. Am., Open DeviceNet Vendors Assn. (com. chair 1998-2001), ControlNet Internat. (com. chair 2000-2001), PT Cruiser Club (Tenn. dir. 2000—), Oak Ridge Sportsman Assn. Avocations: photography, gun sports, fishing, bluegrass guitar. Home: 8210 Northshore Dr SW Knoxville TN 37919-8711

CLIFF, WALTER CONWAY, lawyer; b. Detroit, Jan. 2, 1932; s. Frank V. and Virginia L. (Conway) C.; m. Ursula McHugh, Nov. 5, 1960; children: Walter C., Mary F., Catherine C. BS, LL.B., U. Detroit, 1955; LL.M., NYU, 1956. Bar: Mich. 1956, N.Y. 1958. Assoc. firm Cahill Gordon & Reindel, N.Y.C., 1958-66, ptnr., 1966-2000; sr. counsel, 2000—. Bd. dirs. Florence Gould Found., N.Y.C., 1983— ; bd. dirs. Austen Riggs Center, Stockbridge, Mass., 1983-89, Geoffrey Hughes Found., 1992—; mem. Collections com. Harvard U. Art Mus., 1992—. Served with U.S. Army, 1956-58. J.K. Lasser fellow NYU, 1955-56. Mem. ABA, Assn. of Bar of City of N.Y., N.Y. Bar Assn., Stockbridge Golf Club. Democrat. Roman Catholic. Office: Cahill Gordon & Reindel 80 Pine St Fl 17 New York NY 10005-1790 E-mail: wcliff@cahill.com.

CLIFFORD, CHRISTINE KAREN, speech professional, writer; b. Mar. 13, 1954; Student, U. Denver, 1972-75; student, U. Minn., 1975-76. Cert. Speaking Profl., 2002. Pres. The Cancer Club, Edina, Minn., 1995—. Author: Not Now..I'm Having a No Hair Day!, 1996, Our Family Has Cancer, Too!, 1998 (Benjamin Franklin award, 1998), Inspiring Breakthrough Secrets to Live Your Dreams, 2001, Cancer Has Its Privileges: Stories of Hope & Laughter, 2002. Hon. chair Christine Clifford Celebrity Golf Invitational, Mpls., 1998—2001. Office: The Cancer Club Enterprises 6533 Limerick Dr Edina MN 55439-122[illegible] E-mail: Christine@cancerclub.com.

CLIFFORD, DEBORAH PICKMAN, historian; b. Boston, Mar. 22, 1933; d. Edward Motley and Hester Marion (Chanler) Pickman; m. Nicholas Rowland Clifford, June 22, 1957; children: Mary Tittmann, Sarah Laughlin, Susannah Blachly, Rebecca. BA cum laude, Radcliffe Coll., Cambridge, Mass., 1957; MA in History, U. Vt., 1974. Assoc. editor Historic Roots: A Mag. of Vt. History Middlebury, 1995—2000. Author: (book) Mine Eyes Have Seen the Glory 1979, Crusader for Freedom, 1992, The Passion of Abby Hemenway, 2001

Pres. Vt. Hist. Soc., Barre, 1981—84, Henry Sheldon Mus. of Vt. History, Middlebury, 1981—84. Recipient Stephen Greene award, Vt. Hist. Soc., 1995, Ben Lane award, 1995. Home: 125 Sherman Ln New Haven VT 05472

CLIFFORD, EUGENE THOMAS, lawyer; b. Utica, N.Y., July 15, 1941; s. James Anthony and Mary Margaret (Ellard) C.; m. Joyce Victoria Siwinski, Sept. 4, 1965; children: Michael Sean, Elizabeth Joyce, Thomas More. BA, Boston Coll., 1963, LLB, 1966. Bar: N.Y. 1967, U.S. Dist. Ct. (we. dist.) N.Y. 1967. Assoc. Chamberlain, D'Amanda, Bauman, Chatman & Oppenheimer, Rochester, N.Y., 1967-72, Lamb, Webster, Walz, Telesca & Donovan, Rochester, 1972-76; ptnr. Webster, Sullivan, Santoro & Clifford, Rochester, 1976-86, Fulreader, Rosenthal, Sullivan, Clifford, Santoro & Kaul, Rochester, 1986-2001, Davidson, Fink, Cook, Kelly & Galbraith, 2001—. Bd. dirs. N.Y. state divsn. Am. Cancer Soc., Syracuse, 1972-78, 82-88, 90-97, chmn. bd. dirs., 1982-83, nat. bd. dirs., 1991-97; bd. dirs. Urban League of Rochester, 1988-91. Recipient Nat. Bronze award N.Y. state divsn. Am. Cancer Soc., 1984, Hope award Monroe County unit, 1983. Mem.: Monroe County Bar Assn. (pres. 2002—03). Office: 28 Main St E Ste 1700 Rochester NY 14614 E-mail: eclifford@dfckg.com.

CLIFFORD, JAY, artist; b. Worcester, Mass., Sept. 22, 1954; s. James L. and Lois (Brown) C. Student, Boston Mus. Sch., 1979, Worcester Art Mus. Sch., 1990; BA in English, Conn. Coll., 1998; MFA in Painting, Mass. Coll. Art, 2000. Case worker Devereaux Sch., Rutland, Mass., 1988-98; residential counselor CASCAP, Inc., Cambridge, Mass., 1998—2002; case worker Cerebral Palsy of Mass., 2002—03. One man shows include AS 220, Providence, R.I., 1995, Bromfield Gallery, Boston, 1995, Anna Maria Coll., Paxton, Mass., 1997, Copley Soc., Boston, 1997, San Francisco State U., 1998, Quansigamond C.C., Worcester, 1998, Tabor Acad., Marion, Mass., 1999, Fletcher/Priest Gallery, Worcester, 2001; exhibited in group shows at Artworks Gallery, Hartford, 1992, 96, Slater Meml. Mus., Norwich, Conn., 1992, 93, Arts Worcester, 1993, 95, Hera Gallery, Wakefield, R.I., 1993, Nat. Arts Club, N.Y.C., 1994, 95, Berkshire Mus., Pittsfield, Mass., 1994, Contemporary Artist Ctr., North Adams, Mass., 1994, Copely Soc., Boston, 1994, 95, 97-2001, 2003, N.E. Mo. State U., 1995, Springfield (Mass.) Art Mus., 1995, Brown U. Sarah Doyle Gallery, 1995, Providence Art Club, 1995, Fitchburg (Mass.) Art Mus., 1992-95, 99, Concord (Mass.) Art Assn., 1995, Pleides Gallery, N.Y.C., 1995, 98, Ward-Nasse Gallery, N.Y.C., 1995, Ctrl. Mo. State U., 1996, Ceres Gallery, N.Y.C., 1996, U. Hartford, 1996, Ea. Conn. State U., 1996, Faber Birren Nat. Color Show, Stamford, 1994, 96, 97, 2000, Chuck Levitan Gallery, N.Y.C., 1996, 97, Viridian Artists, N.Y.C., 1997, Gallery 84, N.Y.C., 1997, Judi Rotenberg Gallery, Boston, 1998, Truman State U., 1998, Nebr. Wesleyan U., 1998, 2000, Lamar U., Tex., 1998, 2000, 2001, No Bias Gallery, North Benington, Vt., 1998, Barrett House Galleries, Poughkeepsie, NY, 1998, Mass. Coll. Art, Boston, 1998, 99, 2000, 2001, 2002, 2003, Heywood Gallery, Worcester, Mass., 1998-2001, Worcester Cmty. Found., 1999, Art Ctr. No. N.J., 1999, Nexus Gallery, N.Y.C., 1999, 2000, Aljira Ctr. Contemporary Art, Newark, 1999, Meml. Hall Ctr. Arts, Wilmington, Vt., 1999, Artworks 2000, 2002, New Bedford, Mass., 1999, Nassau C.C., 1999, Rogue C.C., Grants Pass, Oreg., 1999, Cambridge Art Assn., 1999-2003, Harper Coll., Palatine, Ill., 2000, Rutgers Univ., 1999, Silvermine Guild Arts Ctr., New Canaan, Conn., 2000, Attleboro Mus., Mass., 2000, Fletcher/Priest Gallery, Worcester, 2000, 2001, Bromfield Gallery, Boston, 2000, Nat. Art League, N.Y., 2000, Boston City Hall, 2000, Fla. State Univ. Mus. Fine Arts, 2000, Ctr. Visual Arts, Wausau, Wis., 2001, Pittsburg State Univ., Kans., 2001, Palm Springs Desert Mus., 2001, Shippenburg Univ., Penn., 2001, Galesburg Civic Art Ctr., Ill., 2001, Masur Mus. Art, Monroe, La., 2001, Harrisburg Pa. Art Assn., 2001, Gallery on the Green, Canton, Conn., 2001, Proviencetown Art Assn. and Museum, Proviencetown, Mass., 2001, Nicolet Coll., 2001, Minot State U., 2001, Southern Exposure, San Francisco, 2001, 2002, Berkeley Art Assn., 2001, Clark U. Train & Arts Ctr., Worcester, Mass., 2003. Recipient Juror's award Cape Cod Art Assn., 1993, Copley Soc., 1995, Providence Art Club, 1995, Conn. Acad. Fine Arts, 1996, Outstanding Merit award Art Ctr. No. N.J., 1999, Nat. Art League Merit award, 2000, Purchase award, 2001, Ams. 2000 award Minot State U., N.D., 2001, Merit award 6A6X 35 Nat. Exhbn., 2001. Mem. Copley Soc., Conn. Acad. Fine Arts, Arts Worcester, Cambridge Art Assn. Home: 51 Hollywood St Worcester MA 01610-1346

CLIFFORD, MAURICE CECIL, physician, former college president, foundation executive; b. Washington, Aug. 9, 1920; s. Maurice C. and Rosa P. (Linberry) C.; m. Patricia Marie Johnson, June 15, 1945; children: Maurice Cecil III, Jay P.L., Rosemary Clifford McDaniel. AB, Hamilton Coll., 1941, ScD, 1982; AM, U. Chgo., 1942; MD, Meharry Med. Coll., 1947; LHD, LaSalle Coll., 1981, Hahnemann U., 1985, Meharry Med. Coll., 1992; LLD, Med. Coll. Pa., 1986. Diplomate Am. Bd. Ob-Gyn. Intern Phila. Gen. Hosp., 1947-48, resident in ob-gyn, 1948-51, asst. chief service ob-gyn, 1951-60; mem. faculty Med. Coll. Pa., Phila., 1955—, prof. ob-gyn., 1975-91, prof. emeritus, 1992—, v.p. for med. affairs, 1978-80, pres., 1980-86, trustee, 1980-96, pres. emeritus, 1992—; commr. pub. health City of Phila., 1986-92; chmn. HMA Found., Phila., 1991-93; exec. v.p. The Lomax Cos., Chalfont, Pa., 1993-96; pres. The Lomax Companies, Chalfont, Pa., 1996-98. Contbr. articles to profl. jours. Former trustee Phila. Award, Phila. Art Mus., 1982-93; hon. trustee Phila. Coll. Textiles and Sci., 1982-94; trustee emeritus Phila. Acad. Natural Scis.; life trustee Meharry Med. Coll.; trustee Allegheny U. Health Scis., 1996-98; former alumnus trustee Hamilton Coll.; mem. nat. med. com. Planned Parenthood, 1975-78; mem. adv. com. on arts John F. Kennedy Ctr. for Performing Arts, 1978-80. Capt. M.C., U.S. Army, 1952-54. Recipient Dr. Martin Luther King, Jr. award PUSH, 1981, Dr. William H. Gray, Jr. award Educators Roundtable Assn., 1981, Ann. award Phila. Tribune Charities, 1981, Disting. Am. award Edn. and Rsch. Fund Am. Found. for Negro Affairs, 1980; Outstanding Svc. award Phila. br. NAACP, 1965, others. Fellow Am. Coll. Obstetricians and Gynecologists (life); mem. Nat. Med. Assn., Pa. Med. Soc., Med. Soc. Eastern Pa., Philadelphia County Med. Soc., Phi Beta Kappa, Alpha Omega Alpha

CLIFFORD, RICHARD JOHN, religious studies educator; b. Lewiston, Maine, May 27, 1934; s. William Henry and Alice Emma (Sughrue) C. AB, Boston Coll, 1959; licentiate in Sacred Theology, Weston Jesuit Sch. Theology, 1967; PhD in Bibl. Langs., Harvard U., 1970. Ordained priest Roman Cath. Ch., 1966. From asst. prof. to assoc. prof. in Old Testament Weston Jesuit Sch. Theology, Cambridge, Mass., 1970-78, prof., 1978—, dean, 1984-87. Vis. lectr. Harvard Divinity Sch., 1970-80. Chief editor: Cath. Bibl. Quar., 1975-80; author: The Cosmic Mountain in Canaan and the Old Testament, 1972, Fair Spoken and Persuading, 1984, Creation Accounts in the Bible and in the Ancient Near East, 1994, Proverbs: A Commentary, 1999, Psalms, 2002. Trustee Coll. of Holy Cross, Worcester, Mass., 1970-79. Mem. Soc. Bibl. Lit., Cath. Bibl. Assn. (pres. 1992-93) Avocations: reading, opera, theater. Office: Weston (Jesuit) Sch Theology 3 Phillips Pl Cambridge MA 02138-3418

CLIFFORD, ROBERT A. lawyer; b. Evergreen Park, Ill., Mar. 24, 1951; s. George Leonard and Shirley Marie (Meyer) C.; m. Joan Elizabeth Makowski, July 29, 1973; children Erin Elizabeth, Tracy Ann. BS in Commerce, DePaul U., 1973, JD, 1976. Bar: Ill. 1976, U.S. Dist. Ct. (no. dist.) Ill. 1976, U.S. Supreme Ct. 1981. Assoc., Philip A. Corboy & Assocs., Chgo., 1974-82, Corboy & Demetrio, Chgo., 1982-84; ptnr. Clifford & Henely, Chgo., 1984-85, owner Robert A. Clifford and Assocs., 1985— ; cons. and lectr. in law; mediation panelist Endispute of Chgo., 1982— . Contbr. articles to profl. jours. Mem. exec. com., chmn. fin. aid com. DePaul U. Coll. Law, 1982— ; bd. dirs. exec. com. for U. Coll., Galway, Ireland, Chgo., 1983— ; bd. dirs. Access Living of Met. Chgo., 1982-84; trustee Deaul U., 1987—; mem. coll. of law vis. com. DePaul U., 1982-85, chmn. fin. aid subcom. coll. of law vis., 1982-85, mem. exec. com. coll. of law vis. com., 1982-85, mem. Soc. of Fellows Found., 1976-83; mem. City of Hope Fund Raising Com. Mike Royko and James Roberts Jr. Benefits, 1981-82, products liability ADR devel. Ctr. for Pub. Resources, 1985-86, 1985-86; mediation panelist Endispute of Chgo., 1982-84. Mem. ABA (coun., sect. of litigation, tort and ins. practice), Assn. Trial Lawyers Am., Fed. Bar Assn., Am. Soc. Law and Medicine, N.W. Suburban Bar Assn., Ill. State Bar Assn. (gen. assembly, spl. com. on reduction of ct. costs, delays and involvement), Ill. Trial Lawyers Assn. (membership com., polit. action com., chmn. med. malpractice com.), Trial Lawyers Club of Chgo., Chgo. Bar Assn. (tort litigation, civil practice and health and hosp. care coms., com. on coms.), DePaul U. Alumni Assn. (pres. 1983—), Soc. Fellows Found. Roman Catholic. Clubs: Butler Nat. Golf (Oak Brook, Ill.); Inverness Golf (Ill.); Dairymen's Country (Boulder Junction, Wis.). Office: Cifford Law Offices 33 N Dearborn St Fl 20 Chicago IL 60602-3102

CLIFFORD, ROBERT WILLIAM, state supreme court justice; b. Lewiston, Maine, May 2, 1937; s. William H. and Alice (Sughrue) C.; m. Clementina Radillo, Jan. 18, 1964; children: Laurence M., Matthew P. BA, Bowdoin Coll., 1959; LLB, Boston Coll., 1962; LLM, U. Va., 1998. Bar: Maine 1962, U.S. Dist. Ct. Maine 1965. Ptnr. Clifford & Clifford, Lewiston, 1964-79; justice Maine Superior Ct., Auburn, 1979-83, chief justice, 1984-86; assoc. justice Maine Supreme Jud. Ct., Auburn, 1986—. Mem. Lewiston City Coun., 1968-70, mayor, 1971-72; mem. Maine State Senate, 1973-76; chmn. Lewiston Charter Commn., 1978-79; mem. Maine Probate Law Revision Commn., 1973-79; bd. overseers St. Joseph's Coll. Maine, 2000—. Mem. Maine Bar Assn., Androscoggin County Bar Assn., Am. Judicature Soc. Roman Catholic. Home: 14 Nelke Pl Lewiston ME 04240-5318 Office: Maine Supreme Jud Ct PO Box 3488 Auburn ME 04212-3488

CLIFFORD, STEVEN FRANCIS, science research director; b. Boston, Jan. 4, 1943; s. Joseph Nelson and Margaret Dorothy (Savage) C.; children from previous marriage: Cheryl Ann, Michelle Lynn, David Arthur; m. Theresa Kavanagh, Aug. 1996. BSEE, Northeastern U., Boston, 1965; PhD, Dartmouth Coll., 1969. Postdoctoral fellow NRC, Boulder, Colo., 1969-70; physicist Wave Propagation Lab., NOAA, Boulder, 1970-82, program chief, 1982-87, dir. environ. tech. lab., 1987—2001; sr. rsch. scientist emeritus U. Colo., 2001—. Mem. electromagnetic propagation panel, NATO, 1989-93; vis. sci. closed acad. city Tomsk, Siberia, USSR; apptd. mem. NAS Bd. on Atmospheric Sci. and Climate, 1999—. Author: (with others) Remote Sensing of the Troposhpere, 1978; contbr. 130 articles to profl. jours.; patentee in acoustic scintillation liquid flow measurement, single-ended optical spatial filter, acoustic sensor of surface ocean current and waves, high resolution GPS scatteromoter. Recipient 5 Outstanding publs. awards Dept. Commerce, 1972, 75, 89, 96, Outstanding Career Performance, U.S. Presidental award, 1998; inducted NAE, 1997. Fellow: Acoustical Soc. Am., Optical Soc. Am. (editor atmospheric optics 1978—84, advisor atmospheric optics 1982—84); mem.: NRC (bd. atmospheric sci. and climate, chair panel on FAA weather forecasting accuracy, study team on homeland security), NAE, IEEE (sr.), Am. Geophys. Union, Internat. Radio Sci. Union. Avocations: running, cross country skiing. Office: CIRES/NOAA Environ Tech Lab 325 Broadway St Boulder CO 80305-3337

CLIFFORD, STEWART BURNETT, banker; b. Boston, Feb. 17, 1929; s. Stewart Hilton and Ellinor (Burnett) C.; m. Cornelia Park Woolley, Apr. 26, 1952; children: Cornelia Lee Wareham, Rebecca Lyn Mailer-Howat, Jennifer Leggett Danner, Stewart Burnett Jr. AB, Harvard U., 1951, MBA, 1956. Asst. cashier Citibank, N.A., N.Y.C., 1958-60, asst. v.p., 1960-63; exec. v.p., gen. mgr. Merc Bank, Montreal, Que., Can., 1963-67, v.p. planning Overseas div., 1967-68; v.p., adminstr. comml. banking group Citibank, N.Y.C., 1969-72, v.p. head world corp. dept. London, 1973-75, sr. v.p. domestic energy N.Y.C., 1975-80, sr. v.p., head pvt. banking and investment div., 1981-87, div. exec., head investment div., 1987-93; sr. banker Pvt. Bank U.S., 1993-94; cons. Munn Bernhard & Assocs., N.Y.C., 1995—. Elder Brick Ch.; trustee Presbyn. Ch. Found., 1996—2001, Princeton Theol. Sem.; mem. com. univ. resources Harvard Coll.; dir. Monumental Corp., Balt., 1974—89; pres. 120 East End Ave. Corp, Woolley Clifford Found.; vice chmn. Asphalt Green. 1st lt. U.S. Army, 1951—54. Mem.: Union Club (N.Y.C., pres.), Bath and Tennis Club (Palm Beach), Duxbury Yacht Club (Mass.), Pilgrims Club. Republican. Avocations: squash, tennis. Home: 120 E End Ave New York NY 10028-7552 Office: Munn Bernhard & Assocs 6 E 43rd St New York NY 10017-4609

CLIFT, ELEANOR, magazine correspondent; b. Bklyn., July 7, 1940; d. Erk and Inna Roeloffs; m. Brooks Clift, 1964-1981; children: Edward, Woodbury, Robert; m. Tom Brazaitis, 1989. Student, Hofstra U., Hunter Coll. Former White House corr. now contbg. editor Newsweek. Commentator The McLaughlin Group, also Fox News Channel. Co-author: War Without Bloodshed: The Art of Politics, 1996, Madam President: Shattering the Last Glass Ceiling, 2000, Founding Sisters and the Passage of the 19th Amendment, 2003. Office: Newsweek Washington Bur 1750 Pennsylvania Ave NW Washington DC 20006-4502 E-mail: eclift@newsweek.com., eclift@aol.com.

CLIFTON, ANNE RUTENBER, psychotherapist, educator; b. New Haven, Dec. 11, 1938; d. Ralph Dudley and Cleminette (Downing) Rutenber; 1 child, Dawn Anne. BA, Smith Coll., 1960, MSW, 1962. Lic. clin. social worker, Mass.; diplomate Clin. Social Work. Psychiat. case worker adult psychiatry unit Tufts-New Eng. Med. Ctr., Boston, 1962-68, supr. students, 1967-68; pvt. practice psychotherapy, Cambridge and Newton, Mass., 1966—. Supr. med. students, staff social workers out-patient psychiatry Tufts New Eng. Med. Ctr., 1973—, also mem. exec. bd. Women's Resource Ctr., interim co-dir., 1986-88; asst. clin. prof. psychiatry Tufts U. Med. Sch., 1974—, research dept. psychiatry, 1966-68, 73, 77—. Contbr. articles to profl. jours. Mem. NASW, Acad. Cert. Social Workers, Cambridge Tennis Club, Mt. Auburn Tennis Club, Phi Beta Kappa, Sigma Xi. Home: 126 Homer St Newton MA 02459-1518 Office: 59 Church St Ste 4 Cambridge MA 02138-3724 E-mail: annerclifton@aol.com.

CLIFTON, CHRISTOPHER W. researcher, educator; b. Upland, CA, Apr. 18, 1963; s. C W Bingham, Sharon F Bingham (Stepmother), Ronald S Clifton (Stepfather), Jeanette M Clifton; m. Patricia A. Stump, June 18, 1994; children: Eric Ellerbusch, Dennis Ellerbusch, Denise Wagner. PhD in Computer Science, MA, Princeton University, Princeton, New Jersey, 1986—91; MS in Electrical Engineering and Computer Science, BS in Computer Science and Engineering, Massachusetts Institute of Technology, Cambridge, Massachusetts, 1981—86. Assistant Professor Northwestern University, Evanston, IL, 1991—95; Principal Scientist The MITRE Corporation, Bedford, MA, 1995—2001; Associate Professor Purdue University, West Lafayette, IN, 2001—. Editor: (Journal) Knowledge and Information Systems, 2000; contbr. articles to profl. jours., chpt. to book. Mem.: Inst. of Electrical and Electronics Engrs. (sr.), Association for Computing Machinery. Home: 72 Limberlost Ln West Lafayette IN 47906-9400 Office: Purdue University Dept Computer Sci 250 N Univ St West Lafayette IN 47907-2066

CLIFTON, DAVID SAMUEL, JR., research executive, economist; b. Raleigh, N.C., Nov. 15, 1943; s. David Samuel and Ruth Centelle (Paker) C.; m. Karen Lisette Buhrer (div. June 1980); children: Derek Scott, Mark David; m. Eileen Lois Cooley, July 30, 1983; children: Dana Cooley, Michael Cooley. B in Indsl. Engring., Ga. Inst. Tech., 1966; MBA in Econs., Ga. State U., 1970, PhD in Econs., 1980. Customer facilities engr. Lockheed Ga. Co., Marietta, 1966-70; prin. rsch. scientist Ga. Tech. Rsch. Inst., Atlanta, 1970-93, dir. econ. devel. lab., 1979-90, dir. econ. devel. and tech. transfer, 1990-93, dir. Ctr. for Internat. Stds. and Quality, 1991-99; acting exec. assoc. dir. Ga. Tech. Econ. Devel. Inst., Atlanta, 1993-94, group dir. ctrs. Econ. Devel. Inst., 1998-99, group dir. bus. and industry, 1999—2001, prin. rsch. scientist emeriuts, 2001—. Bd. dirs. Sea Adventure Unltd., Inc., Atlanta; cons. UN Indsl. Devel. Orgn., Vienna, 1982, Inst. de Adminstn. Cientifica de los Empreos, Mexico City, 1978; apptd. by gov. So. Tech. Coun., Rsch. Triangle Park, N.C., 1992—. Co-author: Project Feasibility Analysis, 1977; contbr. articles to profl. jours. Mem. Am. Econs. Assn., Atlanta Power Squadron Club, Sigma Xi. Avocations: sailing, navigating. Home: 2486 Williamswood Ct Decatur GA 30033-2810 Office: Ga Tech Ctr Internat Stds & Quality Atlanta GA 30332-0001

CLIFTON, DOUGLAS C. newspaper editor; b. Bklyn., July 14, 1943; s. Norman Stanton and Anne Frances (Montesano) C.; m. Margaret E. Clifton, Dec. 18, 1965; children: Amy Elizabeth Clifton Gallup, Clay Norman. BA Polit. Sci., Dowling Coll., 1965. Reporter, editor Miami Herald, 1970-87; news editor Knight Ridder, Washington, 1987-89; mng. editor Charlotte (N.C.) Observer, 1989-91; sr. v.p., exec. editor Miami Herald, 1991-99; exec. editor Plain Dealer, Cleve., 1999—2001, editor, 2001—. Lt. U.S. Army, 1966-69, Vietnam. Named Second Most Influential Person of Top 50 in N.E. Ohio, Crain's Cleve. (Ohio) Bus., 2003. Mem.: Am. Soc. Newspaper Editors (freedom of info. com. 2003—). Home: 19 Shoreby Dr Bratenahl OH 44108-1161 Office: Plain Dealer 1801 Superior Ave E Cleveland OH 44114-2198 E-mail: dclifton@plaind.com.*

CLIFTON, GREGORY TODD, financial services company executive; b. Cin., Mar. 6, 1962; s. Eugene M. and Dolores J. (Coleman) C.; m. Marcia G. Gibson, Apr. 11, 1987; children: Morgan Elise, Natalie Briann. Grad. h.s., Mansfield, Tex., 1980. ChFC; CFP. Agt., reg. rep. Equitable Life, Equico Securities, Ft. Worth, 1983—90; pres. Clifton Capital Mgmt., Ft. Worth, 1990—99; dir. investment svcs. Higginbotham & Assocs., Inc., Ft. Worth, 1999—. Chmn., BBB, Ft. Worth, 1995-2000; bd. dirs. Casa Mañana Theatre, Ft. Worth, 1994-2002, pres.-elect, 1994-98, pres., 1998-2000; bd. dirs., Arts Coun. Ft. Worth, 2002—. Avocation: motor sports. Office: Higginbotham Capital Mgmt 500 W 13th St Fort Worth TX 76102

CLIFTON, GUY L. neurosurgeon, educator; b. Jacksonville, Tex., Apr. 29, 1949; BS, Tex. A&M U., 1971; MD with high honors, U. Tex., 1975. Intern in surgery U. Minn. Hosp., Mpls., 1975-76; resident in neurosurgery U. Tex. Med. Br., Galveston, 1976-80; dep. chief neurosurgical svc., dir. neurosurgical ICU Ben Taub Gen. Hosp., Houston, 1980-84; asst. prof. dept. neurosurgery Baylor Coll. Medicine, Houston, 1980-84; assoc. attending surgeon Hunter Holmes McGuire VA Med. Ctr., Richmond, Va., 1984-89, chief neurosurgery svc., 1987-90; assoc. prof. divsn. neurosurgery Med. Coll. Va., Richmond, 1984-89, interim chmn. dept. rehab. medicine, 1988-90, prof. divsn. neurosurgery, 1990; chief neurosurgery Hermann Hosp., Houston, 1990—; prof., dir. divsn. neurosurgery Health Sci. Ctr. U. Tex. Houston Med. Sch., 1990-92, prof., chmn. dept. neurosurgery Health Sci. Ctr., 1992—. Mem.-at-large med. bd. Harris County Hosp. Dist., 1983-84; dir. Vivian Smith Ctr. Neurologic Rsch., 2000—, Mission Connect, 2002—; mem. exec. com. joint sect. on trauma Am. Assn. Neurol. Surgery/Cong. Neurol. Surgeons, 1986—; cons., reviewer NIH/NINCDS, Nat. Inst. Disability and Rehab. Rsch., Ctrs. for Disease Control; invited lectr. in field. Mem. cons. bd. editors Orthopedics, 1983-90; mem. editl. bd. Jour. Neurotrauma, 1988—; contbr. 110 articles to sci. and profl. jours., 28 chpts. to books. Chmn. Save Our ERs, 2003—. Recipient Roche Neuroscis. award SAMA-UTMB Nat. Student Rsch. Forum, 1975, Nancy, Clive and Pierce Runnells Disting. Prof. in Neurosci., 1999; grantee Yale U., 1980-83, NIH, 1980-84, 94—, 93, 93—, Baylor Coll. Medicine, 1981-82, Mead Johnson, 1982-83, Moody Found., 1982-83, Ross Labs., 1983-84, Med. Coll. Va., 1986, Thomas F. and Kate Miller Jeffress Meml. Trust, 1986, VA, 1987-90, 90, Nat. Inst. on Disability and Rehab. Rsch., 1988-90, NIH/NINDS 1994-99, 2002—. Mem. AMA, ACS (Regional reidents Competition award com. on trauma, 1979), Am. Assn. Neurol. Surgeons (liason to Am. Acad. Phys. Medicine Rehab., Nat. Ctr. for Rehab. Rsch.), Am. Assn. Surgery for Trauma, Am. Spinal Injury Assn., Am. Trauma Soc., Soc. of Neurol. Surgeons, Nat. Head Injury Found. (profl. adv. bd. 1992—, Sheldon Berrol Clin. Svc. award 1993), Congress Neurol. Surgeons, Soc. Neurol. Anesthesia and Neurol. Supportive Care, Soc. Neurotrauma (founding officer, v.p. 1988, program chmn. 1991), Tex. Assn. Neurol. Surgeons (bd. dirs. 1991), Tex. med. Assn., Houston Neurol. Soc., Phi Kappa Phi, Alpha Omega Alpha. Office: U Tex Houston Med Sch 6431 Fannin Ste 7148 Houston TX 77030

CLIFTON, JAMES ALBERT, physician, educator; b. Fayetteville, N.C., Sept. 18, 1923; s. James Albert Jr. and Flora M. (McNair) Clifton; m. Katherine Rathe, June 25, 1949; children: Susan M.(dec.), Katherine Y., Caroline M. BA, Vanderbilt U., 1944, MD, 1947. Diplomate Am. Bd. Internal Medicine (mem. 1972-81, mem. subsplty. bd. gastroenterology 1968-75, chmn. 1972-75, mem. exec. com. 1978-81, chmn. 1980-81). Intern U. Hosps., Iowa City, 1947—48, resident dept. medicine, 1948—51; staff dept. medicine Thayer VA Hosp., Nashville, 1952—53; asst. clin. medicine Vanderbilt Hosp., Nashville, 1952—53; cons. physician VA Hosp., Iowa City, 1965—93; assoc. medicine dept. internal medicine Coll. Medicine, U. Iowa, 1953—54, chief divsn. gastroenterology, 1953—71, asst. prof. medicine, 1954-58, assoc. prof., 1958—63, prof., 1963—91, prof. emeritus, 1991—, traveling fellow, 1964, vis. prof. dept. physiology, 1964, vice chmn. dept. medicine, 1967—70, chmn. dept. medicine Coll. Medicine, 1970—76, Roy J. Carver prof. medicine, 1974—91, Roy J. Carver prof. emeritus, 1991—, dir. James A. Clifton Ctr. Digestive Diseases, 1985—90, interim dean, 1991—93. Investigator Mt. Desert Isle Biol. Lab., Salisbury Cove, Maine, 1964; vis. faculty mem. Mayo Found. and Mayo Clinic, 1966; vis. prof. dept. medicine U. N.C. Chapel Hill, 1970; cons. gastroenterology and nutrition tng. grants com. Nat. Inst. Arthritis and Metabolic Diseases, NIH, 1964—68, chmn., 1965—68; mem. Nat. Adv. Arthritis and Metabolic Diseases Coun., 1970—73; mem. gastroenterology tng. com. VA, Washington, 1967—71, chmn. tng. grants com., 1971—73; mem. med. adv. bd. Digestive Disease Found., 1969—73; vis. prof. gastroenterology U. London (St. Marks Hosp.), 1984—85; mem. sci. adv. com. Ludwig Inst. Cancer Rsch., Zurich, 1984—95. Internat. editl. bd. Italian Jour. Gastroenterology, 1970—90, Gastroenterology, 1964—68. Recipient Disting. Alumnus of Yr. award, Vanderbilt U. Sch. Medicine, 1984, Disting. Alumnus of Yr. Achievement award, U. Iowa Coll. Medicine, 2000, Disting. Mentoring award, 2002; fellow spl. rsch., NIH, USPHS, 1955—56, in medicine, Evans Meml. Hosp., Mass. Meml. Hosps., also Boston U. Sch. Medicine, 1955—56; scholar Phi Connell, Vanderbilt U., 1943—44. Fellow: ACP (bd. regents 1972—79, pres. 1977—78, Alfred Stengel award 1984, Laureate award 1989); mem.: AAUP, AAAS, AMA (liaison com. grad. med. edn. 1976—77), Internat. Soc. Internal Medicine (exec. com. 1978—80), Assn. Profs. Medicine (councillor 1972—73, sec.-treas. 1973—75), Assn. Am. Med. Colls., Am. Physiol. Soc., Soc. Exptl. Biology and Medicine, Assn. Am. Physicians, Am. Clin. and Climatol. Assn. (v.p. 1984), Am. Fedn. Clin. Rsch., Am. Soc. Internal Medicine (Internist of Yr. award Iowa chpt. 1986), Am. Assn. Study Liver Disease, Am. Heart Assn., Am. Gastroent. Assn. (pres. 1970—71), Inst. Medicine NAS, U. Iowa Assn. Emeritus Faculty (pres. 1999—2000), U. Iowa Retirees Assn. (pres. 1999—2000). Home: 39 Audubon Pl Iowa City IA 52245-3437 Office: U Iowa Hosp and Clinics 4 JCP Hawkins Dr Iowa City IA 52242 E-mail: jclifton@uiowa.edu., zylumjim@mchsi.com.

CLIFTON, LUCILLE THELMA, author; b. Depew, N.Y., June 27, 1936; d. Samuel Louis and Thelma (Moore) Sayles; m. Fred James Clifton, May 10, 1958 (dec. Nov. 1984); children— Sidney, Fredrica (dec. 2000), Channing, Gillian, Graham, Alexia. Student, Howard U., 1953-55, Fredonia (N.Y.) State Tchrs. Coll., 1955. Prof. literature and creative writing U. Calif., Santa Cruz, 1985-90; dist. prof. humanities St. Mary's Coll. Md., 1990 , Hilda C. Landers endowed chair in liberal arts, 2000—. Poet-in-residence, Coppin State Coll., Balt., 1972-76, Jenny Moore vis. writer, George Washington U., 1982-83. Author: Good Times, 1969, Good News About The Earth, 1972, An Ordinary Woman, 1974, Generations, 1976, Two-Headed Woman, 1980, Sonora Beautiful, 1981, Next, 1987, Good Woman, 1987, Quilting, 1991, The Book of Light, 1993, Blessing the Boats, 2000 (Nat. Book award); Everett Anderson books and other books for children; co-author: Free to Be You and Me, 1974 (Emmy award), Free To Be A Family. Named Poet Laureate, State of Md., 1979; recipient Discovery award Poetry Center, 1969, winner Nat. Book Award, 2000; YMHA grantee, 1969; Nat. Endowment Arts grantee, 1970, 72 Fellow Am. Acad. Arts and Scis.; mem. Authors League, Author Guild, P.E.N., Acad. Am. Poets (chancellor), Poetry Soc. Am. (bd. dirs., Lila Wallace/Reader's Digest award 1999). Office: St Marys Coll of Maryland Divsn Arts and Letters Montgomery Hall 126 Saint Marys City MD 20686

CLIFTON, NELIDA, social worker; b. Buenos Aires, Aug. 16, 1944; came to the U.S., 1968; d. Juan Antonio and Zaira Elizabeth (Vera) Tovar; m. Mark Earl Jolls, Nov. 8, 1968 (div. July 1984); children: Patricia Elizabeth, Michael Thomas, Diana Marie Kathleen; m. Anthony Gene Clifton, June 19, 1993. BA in Bus. Adminstrn., Nat. Sch. Commerce, Tucuman, Argentina; BA in Psychology magna cum laude, Fairleigh Dickinson U., 1986; postgrad., William Paterson Coll., 1988-89. Diplomate Am. Psychotherapy Assn.; lic. cert. social worker Bd. Social Work Examiners, N.J.; cert. bilingual. Social worker Bergen County Bd. Social Svcs., Rochelle Park, N.J., 1987—. Crisis intervention vol.; phone counselor; cmty. resources referral profl. Mem. APA, NASW, Am. Assn. Christian Counselors, Phi Zeta Kappa, Phi Omega Epsilon, Psi Chi Nat. Honor Socs. Republican. Avocations: reading, chess, tennis, gardening. Home and Office: PO Box 8581 Saddle Brook NJ 07663-8581

CLIFTON, RACHEL LETTER, music educator, performing arts educator; b. Barre, Vt, Oct. 12, 1955; d. Raymond Joseph and Louise Irene (Geake) Letter; m. Artie Dessie Clifton, July 3, 1976; children: Valerie Clifton Neal, Alison Marie Clifton. BME, Stetson U., 1978. Tchr. St. James Cathedral Sch., Orlando, Fla.; music instr. Muhlenberg Coll., Allentown, Pa., 1981-89; adj. prof. music Jacksonville U., Fla., 1989—; tchr. Resurrection Parish Sch., Jacksonville, Fla., 1989-96, The Bolles Sch., Jacksonville, Fla., 1996—. Adv. bd. mem. Camarata

Singers, Allentown, Pa., 1987-89; mem. Music Educators Nat. Conf. Composer: It's a Swing Thing, 2002; Withering Heights, the Musical, 2001. Named Girls Nation Del., Am. Legion, Washington, 1972; recipient Theodore Presser award Stetson U., Deland, Fla., 1976; Fla. tchrs. grantee Fla. Coun. on Humanities, Tampa, 1996 and 2002. Mem. Am. Fedn. of Musicians, Kappa Delta Pi, Pi Kappa Lambda, Am. Choral Dir. Assn. Roman Catholic. Avocations: travel, literature, history. Home: 3842 Musket Trl Jacksonville FL 32277-2244 Office: The Bolles Sch 7400 San Jose Blvd Jacksonville FL 32217-3499

CLIFTON, RICHARD RANDALL, judge; b. Framingham, Mass., Nov. 13, 1950; s. Arthur Calvin and Vivian Juanita (Himes) C.; m. Teresa Morano Aleshire, Oct. 15, 1988; children: David Madison, Katherine Kaleilani. AB, Princeton U., 1972; JD, Yale U., 1975. Bar: Ill. 1975, Hawaii 1976, U.S. Dist. Ct. Hawaii 1976, U.S. Ct. Appeals (9th cir.) 1976, U.S. Ct. Appeals (2d cir.) 1979, U.S. Supreme Ct. 1982. Law clk. to judge U.S. Ct. Appeals (9th cir.), Honolulu, 1975-76; from assoc. to ptnr. Cades, Schutte, Fleming & Wright, Honolulu, 1977—2002; judge U.S. Ct. of Appeals (9th cir.), 2002—. Adj. prof. law U. Hawaii, Honolulu, 1979-89. Co-author: The Shreveport Plan: An Experiment in the Delivery of Legal Services, 1974. Mem. dist. com. Nancy J. Stivers Meml. Fund, Honolulu, 1984—; bd. dirs. Hawaii Pub. Radio, Honolulu, 1991—, chmn., 1995-2000; mem. Hawaii State Jud. Conf., 1987-90; 1st vice chmn. Hawaii Rep. Party, 1989-93, chmn. rules com., 1987-90, gen. counsel, 1993-2001; bd. dirs. Hawaii Women's Legal Found., 1987—, Ninth Jud. Cir. Hist. Soc., 1996—; mem. Hawaii State Reapportionment Com., 1991-92. Mem. ABA, Hawaii Bar Assn. Office: US Ct of Appeals 1132 Bishop St Ste 601 Honolulu HI 96813

CLIFTON, RUSSELL B. banking and mortgage lending consultant, retired mortgage company executive; b. Maroa, Ill., Jan. 16, 1930; s. Russell Thomas and Clara Leoda (Luckenbill) C.; m. Mary Joyce Hartline, Oct. 10, 1948; 1 son, Steven Shawn. BA, Mich. State U., 1957. Bank auditor Arthur Andersen & Co., Detroit, 1957-59; v.p. Mich. Nat. Bank, Lansing, 1959-65; sr. v.p. Assoc. Mortgages Co., Kansas City, Mo., 1965-69; v.p. Fed. Nat. Mortgage Assn., Washington, 1969-85, ret., 1985; pres., chief exec. officer First Chesapeake Mortgage Inc., Beltsville, Md., 1985-86, also bd. dirs.; cons. banking and mortgage lending, 1986—. Mem. adv. com. Home Owner's Warranty Corp., Washington, 1978-81; bd. dirs., mem. exec. com., treas. Nat. Acad. Conciliators, Washington, 1979-91; bd. dirs. Lincoln Savs. & Loan (now Seasons Savs. Bank), Richmond, Va., 1987-89; bd. dirs., treas. Nat. Ctr. for Dispute Settlements, Washington, 1987-91. Served with U.S. Army, 1952-54. Named disting. fellow Nat. Assn. Cert. Mortgages Bankers, 1975 Mem. Phi Kappa Phi, Beta Alpha Psi, Beta Gamma Sigma, Tau Sigma. Methodist.

CLIFTON-SMITH, RHONDA DARLEEN, art educator, art center administrator; b. Dyersburg, Tenn., Mar. 19, 1954; d. Charles Burton Clifton and Mary Opal (Carter) Harris; m. Michael Frederick Smith, Feb. 14, 1980 (dec. Sept. 1981). BS in Art Edn., Columbus Coll., 1977; MA in Hist. Administrn., Eastern Ill. U., 1986. Asst. cataloging libr. Lawton (Okla.) Pub. Libr., 1978-79; registrar Mus. of the Great Plains, Lawton, 1979-82; curator Boot Hill Mus., Dodge City, Kans., 1982-94; exec. dir. Carnegie Ctr. for Arts, Dodge City, 1994—; drawing and painting instr. Dodge City H.S. Author: (booklet) Dodge City: The Early Years, 1985; co-author: (booklet) Cattle and Wheat: Agricultural Growth in 19th Century Dodge City, 1985. Mem. Am. Assn. Mus., Am. Assn. State & Local History (c-chair mem. com. 1990-92), Kan. Mus. Assn. (treas. 1989—, area rep. 1982-85), Mt. Plains Mus. Assn., Soroptimists Internat. Avocations: painting and drawing, theater. Office: Carnegie Ctr for Arts 701 2d Ave Dodge City KS 67801 E-mail: carnegie@dodgecity.net.

CLIMAN, RICHARD ELLIOT, lawyer; b. N.Y.C., July 19, 1953; s. David Arthur and Mary (Vitale) C. AB cum laude, Harvard U., 1974, JD cum laude, 1977. Bar: Calif. 1977. Assoc. Pettit & Martin, San Francisco, 1977-83, ptnr., 1984-94; ptnr., head mergers and acquisitions group Cooley Godward LLP, Palo Alto, San Francisco, Calif., 1994—. Mem. adv. bd. BNA Mergers & Acquisitions Law Report; lectr. and panelist in field; co-chair Doing Deals Practising Law Inst., 1997-02, Tech. Mergers and Acquisitions Inst. Glasser LegalWorks, 1999-2001; mem. adv. bd. Securities Reg. Inst., Corp. Counsel Ctr., Sch. Law Northwestern U. Contbr. articles to profl. jours. Mem. ABA (sect. bus. law, co-chair Nat. Inst. on Negotiating Bus. Acquisitions 2003). Home: 1 Tulip Ln San Carlos CA 94070-1551 Office: Cooley Godward LLP 5 Palo Alto Sq 3000 El Camino Real Palo Alto CA 94306-2120 E-mail: climanre@cooley.com.

CLIMER, JAMES ALAN, lawyer; b. Chillicothe, Ohio, Dec. 17, 1954; s. James Parker and Jane Louise (Halsey) C.; m. Mary Ellen Murray, Oct. 17, 1981. BA in Polit. Sci., Miami U., Ohio, 1977; JD, U. Toledo, 1980. Bar: Ohio 1980, U.S. Dist. Ct. (no. and so. dists.) Ohio 1981. Assoc. Jones, Schell & Schaefer Co., Toledo, 1980-81; sole practice W. Carrollton, Ohio, 1981-83; asst. law dir. City of Parma, Ohio, 1984-90; pvt. practice, Cleve., 1983-90; ptnr. Mazanec, Raskin & Ryder Co., LPA, Solon, Ohio, 1990—. Mem. Ohio State Bar Assn., Cuyahoga County Law Dirs. Assn. Presbyterian. Avocations: golf, skiing, reading. Office: Mazanec Raskin & Ryder Co 34305 Solon Rd 100 Franklin's Row Cleveland OH 44139 E-mail: jclimer@mrrlaw.com.

CLINARD, JOSEPH HIRAM, JR., securities company executive; b. N.Y.C., Jan. 29, 1938; s. Joseph Sr. and Bertha (Feins) C.; m. Marcia Blyer, Sept. 1, 1958; children: Susan Clinard Jacobs, Robert. Cert., N.Y. Inst. Fin., 1962, Am. Coll., 1976, Adelphi U., 1980. Cert. fin. planner. Account exec. Merrill Lynch, N.Y.C., 1964-68; v.p. Shearson Lehman, N.Y.C., 1968-73; nat. dir. fin. planning Herzfeld & Stern, N.Y.C., 1974-78; v.p. Chem. Bank, N.Y.C., 1978-83; pres. DESCAP Securities, Inc., Hauppauge, N.Y., 1983-90; CEO North Shore Capital Mgmt. Corp., Melville, N.Y., 1990—. Adj. prof. Adelphi U., Garden City, N.Y., 1980-90, asst. to dean, 1983-87; chief cons. Clinard Mgmt. Assocs., Huntington, N.Y., 1985-91; exec. dir. L.I. Ctr. Fin. Studies, Hauppauge, 1986-90; instr. C.W. Post U., 1991-98. Author: Increasing Your Worth Through Personal Financial Planning, 1987. Bd. dirs. L.I. div. Am. Cancer Soc., 1992—. With USAF, 1956-59. Mem. L.I. Internat. Assn. Fin. Planning (pres. 1980-83, chmn. bd. dirs. 1983-88) (Appreciation award 1988), Adelphi Soc. Fin. Planners (v.p. 1985-86), Kiwanis (bd. dirs. Huntington chpt. 1997-2000). Republican. Avocations: boating, skiing. Home: 3 Colyer Pl Greenlawn NY 11740-3004 Office: North Shore Capital Mgmt 1895 Walt Whitman Rd Melville NY 11747-3031

CLINARD, MARSHALL BARRON, sociologist, educator; b. Boston, Nov. 12, 1911; s. Andrew Marshall and Gladys (Barron) C.; m. Ruth Blackburn, Aug. 28, 1937 (dec. Jan. 19, 1999; children: Marsha Clinard, Stephen Andrew; m. Arlen Runzler Westbrook, Jan. 15, 2002. BA, Stanford U., 1932, MA, 1934; PhD, U. Chgo., 1941; LLD (hon.), U. Lausanne, Switzerland, 1985. Instr. U. Iowa, 1937-41; chief criminal stats. U.S. Bur. Census, 1941-43; chief analysis report, enforcement dept. OPA, 1943-45; assoc. prof. Vanderbilt U., 1945-46; mem. faculty U. Wis., 1946—, prof. sociology, 1951-79, prof. emeritus, 1979—. Fulbright rsch. prof. U. Stockholm, 1954-55; vis. prof. Makerere U. Coll., Kampala, Uganda, 1968-69; cons. urban cmty. devel. Ford Found., India, 1958-60, 62-63; UN expert Asian Seminar Urban Cmty. Devel., Singapore, 1962; rapporteur 3rd UN Congress Prevention Crime and Treatment Offenders, Stockholm, 1965; panel expert 4th UN Congress, Kyoto, 1970; cons. 5th UN Congress, Geneva, 1975, Dept. Labor, 1966-67. Author: The Black Market: A Study of White Collar Crime, 1952; (with Robert F. Meier) Sociology of Deviant Behavior, 1957, 10th edit., 1998, 11th edit., 2000; editor, contbr.: Anomie and Deviant Behavior: A Discussion and Critique, 1964, Slums and Community Development: Experiments in Self-Help, 1966; (with Richard Quinney and John Wildeman) Criminal Behavior Systems: A Typology, 1967, 3d edit., 1994; (with Daniel J. Abbott) Crime in Developing Countries: A Comparative Perspective, 1973, Cities with Little Crime: The Case of Switzerland, 1978, Illegal Corporate Behavior, 1979; (with Peter C. Yeager) Corporate Crime, 1980, Corporate Ethics and Crime: The Role of Middle Management, 1983, Corporate Corruption: The Abuse of Power, 1990. Recipient Sutherland award Am. Soc. Criminology, 1970, Cressey award Assn. Cert. Fraud Examiners, 1994; NSF rsch. grantee, Switzerland, 1973, U.S. Dept. Justice grantee, 1977, 81. Mem. Soc. Study Social Problems (exec. com. 1959-60, 62-63, 65-67, pres. 1961-62), Midwest Sociol. Soc. (pres. 1965-66), Am. Sociol. Assn. (coun. mem. at large 1966-68) Home: 250 E Alameda St Apt 802 Santa Fe NM 87501-6209

CLINARD, ROBERT NOEL, lawyer; b. Welch, W.Va., Nov. 1, 1946; s. Vernon Carlos and Mary Elizabeth (Noel) C.; m. Margaret Hawthorne Higgins, May 21, 1977; children: Elizabeth Kercheval, Edward Noel, Margaret Graham Robinson, Kathryn Moir. BA, Washington & Lee U., 1968, JD, 1976. Bar: N.Y. 1977, Va. 1978, U.S. Dist. Ct. (so. dist.) N.Y. 1977, U.S. Dist. Ct. (ea. dist.) Va. 1978, U.S. Ct. Appeals (4th cir.) 1986, U.S. Supreme Ct. 1990. Assoc. Winthrop, Stimson, Putnam & Roberts, N.Y.C., 1976-78, Hunton & Williams, Richmond, Va., 1978-86, ptnr., 1986—. Sec. Va. Cultural Laureate Soc., Richmond, 1981-86, bd. dirs., 1981-90. Served to lt. USNR, 1969-72. Mem. ABA (antitrust sect., franchising and healthcare coms.), Va. State Bar (vice chmn. antitrust com. health law sect. 1985-86, chmn. 1986-87, bd. govs. antitrust sect. 1989-95, vice chmn. antitrust sect. 1992, chmn. 1993), Nat. Health Lawyers Assn., Coun. of Franchise Suppliers, Internat. Franchise Assn., Order of Coif, Phi Beta Kappa, Omicron Delta Kappa. Republican. Episcopalian. Avocations: boating, saltwater fishing, house renovation. Home: 6010 York Rd Richmond VA 23226-2737 Office: Hunton & Williams Riverfront Plaza East Tower 951 E Byrd St Richmond VA 23219-4074

CLINCH, NICHOLAS, assistant principal; b. Tokyo, Dec. 20, 1950; arrived in U.S., 1969; s. Harold Kenneth and Galina (Voevodina) C.; m. Carol Ann Connell, May 27, 1978; children: Michael Alan Clinch, Stephen Alexsei Clinch. BA, Davidson Coll., 1972; MA, Appalachian State U., 1973; EdD, Nova Southeastern U., 2002. Cert. secondary tchr., S.C. Spanish tchr. Gaffney (S.C.) H.S., 1973-74, York (S.C.) Comprehensive H.S., 1974-94; asst. prin. York Jr. H.S., 1994—. Tennis coach York Comprehensive H.S., 1977-81, soccer coach, 1979-89; home-sch. coord. York County Migrant Program, 1975-81, dir., 1982. Office: York Junior High School 1280 Johnson Rd York SC 29745-2100

CLINCH, NICHOLAS BAYARD, III, business executive; b. Evanston, Ill., Nov. 9, 1930; s. Nicholas Bayard Jr. and Virginia Lee (Campbell) C.; m. Elizabeth Wallace Campbell, July 11, 1964; children: Virginia Lee, Alison Campbell. Student, N.Mex. Mil. Inst., Roswell, 1948-49; AB, Stanford U., 1952, LLB, 1955. Bar: Calif. 1959. Expedition leader First Ascent, Gasherbrum I (26,470 ft.), Pakistan, 1958, First Ascent, Masherbrum (25,660 ft.), Pakistan, 1959-60; assoc. Voegelin, Barton, Harris & Callister, L.A., 1961-68; pvt. practice Washington, 1968-70; v.p., counsel Lincoln Savs. & Loan Assn., L.A., 1970-74, exec. dir. Sierra Club Found., San Francisco, 1975-81; environ. cons. Fluor Corp., Grass Valley, Calif., 1981-84; v.p., sec. CCA, Inc., Denver, 1984—. Bd. dirs. Growth Stock Outlook Inc., Potomac, Md.; mem. adv. bd. Lowell Obs. Author: A Walk in the Sky, 1982. Leader Am. Antarctic Mountaineering Expdn., Sentinel Range, 1966-67; co-leader Chinese Am. Ulugh Muztagh Expdn., Kun Lun Range, Xinjiang, 1985, Am. Expdns. to Kang Karpo Range, Yunnan-Tibet border, 1988, 89, 92, 93; co-founder, trustee Calif. League Conservation Voters, San Francisco, 1972-97; bd. dirs. Environ. Law Inst., 1981-86, Recreational Equipment Inc., 1985-91, 93-2001. 1st lt. USAF, 1956-57. Recipient John Oliver La Gorce medal Nat. Geog. Soc., Washington, 1967. Fellow Royal Geog. Soc., Explorers Club; mem. ABA, Am. Alpine Club (hon., pres. 1967-70), Appalachian Mountain Club (hon.), State Bar Calif., Roxburghe Club of San Francisco, Alpine Club (hon. London), Chinese Assn. Sci. Expdns. (hon.). Republican. Episcopalian. Avocations: mountaineering, skiing, book collecting. Home: 2001 Bryant St Palo Alto CA 94301-3714 Office: CCA Inc 220 Josephine St 200 Denver CO 80206

CLINE, ANDREW HALEY, lawyer; b. Fountain Hill, Pa, Nov. 30, 1951; s. William Matthew and Eleanor Mary (Bosich) C.; children: Haley Andrea, Catherine Anne. BA, Guilford Coll., 1973; JD, U. Ala., 1978. Bar: Pa. 1978, U.S. Dist. Ct. (mid. dist.) Pa. 1982, U.S. Dist. Ct. (ea. dist.) 1989, U.S. Ct. Appeals (3rd cir.) 1988, U.S. Supreme Ct. 1990. Law clk. Commonwealth Ct. Pa., Harrisburg, 1978-80; asst. counsel Dept. Transport., Harrisburg, 1980-86; assoc. dep. gen. counsel Gov. Office, Harrisburg, 1986-87, dep. gen. counsel, 1987-89; assoc. Kirkpatrick & Lockhart, LLP, Harrisburg, 1989—91, ptnr., 1992—2001; dep. gen. counsel Gov. Office, Harrisburg, 2001—02; asst. counsel Pa. Dept. Transp., Harrisburg, 2003—; dep. chief counsel Dept. Transport., Harrisburg, Pa., 2003. Editor-in-chief Ala. Law Rev., 1978. Named one of Outstanding Young Men Am. Jaycees, 1978. Mem. Fed. Bar Assn. (pres. Ctrl. Pa. chpt. 1994-95, nat. del. 1995-97), Pa. Bar Assn., Dauphin County Bar Assn. (chmn. continuing legal edn. com. 1992-95, bd. dirs. 1993-95, chmn. govt. law sect. 1994, sec. 1996), Bench and Bar Soc., Am. Inns of Ct. (master emeritus J.S. Bowman chpt.), St. Thomas More Soc. (bd. dirs. 1997-98), Omicron Delta Kappa. Avocation: photography. Office: Office of Chief Counsel PO Box 8212 Harrisburg PA 17105-8212 E-mail: acline@state.pa.us.

CLINE, BOBBY JAMES, insurance company executive; b. Floydada, Tex., Mar. 12, 1932; s. Howard O. and Carrie (Tomlinson) C.; m. Martha Nolen, May 29, 1954; children: Carolyn, Pamela, Millie, Robert, Sean. BBA, U. Tex., Austin, 1954. Casualty underwriter Ins. Co. N.Am., Dallas, 1956-59; account exec./ptnr. Munger-Moore & Assocs., Dallas, 1959-68; ptnr. Harris-Moore & Assocs., Dallas, 1968-70; sr. v.p. Alexander & Alexander Inc., Dallas, 1970-72, exec. v.p., 1972-77, pres., 1977-96, vice chmn. bd.; exec. v.p. Aon Risk Svcs. Tex., Dallas, 1997-2000. Chmn. bd. Texas Banc Ptnrs. Inc., 2000—03; bd. dirs. Oaks Bank. Served with USN, 1954-56. Mem. Soc. CPCUs (dir.), U. Tex. Ex-Students Assn. (past pres.), Salesmanship Club, Preston Trail Golf Club, Dallas Club, Dallas Athletic Club, Garland Toastmasters, Riverhill Country Club. Baptist. Avocations: golfing, hunting. Home: 1944 Wynn Joyce Rd Garland TX 75043-2542 Office: Texas Banc Partners 9304 Forrest Ln Suite 245N Dallas TX 75243

CLINE, CAROLYN JOAN, plastic and reconstructive surgeon; b. Boston, May 15, 1941; d. Paul S. and Elizabeth (Flom) Cline. BA, Wellesley Coll., 1962; MA, U. Cin., 1966; PhD, Washington U., 1970; diploma, Washington Sch. Psychiatry, 1972; MD, U. Miami, 1975. Diplomate Am. Bd. Plastic and Reconstructive Surgery. Rsch. asst. Harvard U. Dental Sch., Boston, 1962-64; rsch. asst. physiology Laser Lab., Children's Hosp. Rsch. Found., Cin., 1964, psychology dept. U. Cin., 1964-65; intern in clin. psychology St. Elizabeth's Hosp., Washington, 1966-67; psychologist Alexandria (Va.) Cmty. Mental Health Ctr., 1967-68; rsch. fellow NIH, Washington, 1968-69; chief psychologist Kingsbury Ctr. for Children, Washington, 1969-73; sole practice clin. psychology Washington, 1970-73; intern internal medicine U. Wis. Hosp. Ctr. for Health Sci., Madison, 1975-76; resident in surgery Stanford U. Med. Ctr., 1976-78; fellow microvasc. surgery dept. surgery U. Calif., San Francisco, 1978-79; resident in plastic surgery St. Francis Hosp., San Francisco, 1979-82; practice medicine specializing in plastic and reconstructive surgery, San Francisco, 1982-95; free-lance writer profl. and popular publs., 1995—. Contbr. chpts. to plastic surgery textbooks, articles to profl. jours. Mem. Am. Soc. Plastic and Reconstructive Surgeons, Royal Soc. Medicine, Calif. Medicine Assn., Calif. Soc. Plastic and Reconstructive Surgeons, San Francisco Med. Soc.

CLINE, FRED ALBERT, JR., retired librarian, conservationist; b. Santa Barbara, Calif., Oct. 23, 1929; s. Fred Albert and Anna Cecilia (Haberl) C. AB in Asian Studies, U. Calif., Berkeley, 1952, MLS, 1962. Resident Internat. House, Berkeley, 1950-51; trainee, officer Bank of Am., San Francisco, Düsseldorf, Fed. Republic Germany, Kuala Lumpur, 1954-60; adminstrv. reference libr. Calif. State Libr., Sacramento, 1962-67; head libr. Asian Art Mus. San Francisco, 1967-93; ret., 1993. Contbg. author: Chinese, Korean and Japanese Sculpture in the Avery Brundage Collection, 1974; author, editor: Ruth Hill Cooke, 1985; contbr. articles and book revs. on AIDS to various publs. Bd. dirs. Tamalpais Conservation Club, 1990-94, 98-99; dissident AIDS activist. Sgt. M.C., U.S. Army, 1952-54. Mem. Metaphys. Alliance (sec., bd. dirs. San Francisco chpt. 1988-91), Sierra Club. Democrat. Avocations: hiking, music, reading. Home: 825 Lincoln Way San Francisco CA 94122-2369 E-mail: facpat@aol.com.

CLINE, JANICE CLAIRE, education educator; b. Wausau, Wis., Aug. 22, 1945; d. George Leroy and Irma Olga (Brummond) C.; m. Brent Buell, Jan. 28, 1979. BS, U. Wis., 1967; MA, NYU, 1972; student of Eli Siegel, 1978; student of Ellen Reiss, Aesthetic Realism Found., N.Y.C., 1977—2001; student of Aesthetic Realism Teaching Method, 1977—. Tchr. Hyde Park H.S., Chgo., 1967-69; instr. Chase Manhattan Bank JOB Tng. Program, N.Y.C., 1969-71; evaluator York Coll. Title I Evaluation Team, Jamaica, N.Y., 1972; adj. lectr. N.Y.C. C.C., CUNY, Bklyn., 1971-72, lectr. York Coll. Jamaica, 1972—. Lectr. Aesthetic Realism Assoc., N.Y.C., 1977-2001; guest spkr. WVON, Chgo., 1980. Contbr. articles to profl. jours. Coord. Conf. in Support of the Liberation of S. Africa and Namibia, York Coll., Jamaica, N.Y., 1985, Student/Faculty Consortium on Central Am., York Coll., 1986. Recipient Outstanding Contbn. award Afro-Am. Club, York Coll., 1985, Outstanding Contbn. award Conf. of African People, Jamaica, N.Y., 1986. Mem. AAUP, Profl. Staff Congress (sr. coll. officer, exec. com. 2002—, chpt. chmn.), Internat. Reading Assn., Am. Fedn. Tchrs. (del. 2000—), Nat. Coun. Tchrs. English, CUNY Women's Coalition, Nat. Action Network. Office: CUNY York Coll Dept English 94-20 Guy R Brewer Blvd Jamaica NY 11451-0001

CLINE, JOHN CARROLL, clinical psychologist; b. Staunton, Va., Sept. 6, 1955; s. Carroll Hubert and Naomi Edith (Hevener) C.; m. Diane Jeannette Goudreau, May 21, 1983; 1 child, Virginia Goudreau Cline. BA, U. Va., 1977; PhD, U. Toledo, 1984. Lic. psychologist, Conn.; cert. biofeedback; clin. assoc. Am. Bd. Med. Psychotherapists; diplomate Am. Acad. Pain Mgmt. Psychology intern U. Toledo, 1980-81; predoctoral intern VA Med. Ctr., West Haven, Conn., 1981-82, attending psychologist, 1984-85; clinician Alcohol Svcs. Orgn., New Haven, 1982-85; team leader, staff psychologist Elmcrest Hosp., Portland, Conn., 1985-86, asst. unit chief, 1986, dir. behavioral medicine svc., 1986-90; pvt. practice psychologist Hamden, Conn., 1986-94; dir. adult outpatient svcs. Inst. of Living, Hartford, Conn., 1990-93; psychol. svcs. cons. Hamden, Conn., 1994—; clin. dir. dept. counseling and psychiat. svcs. Grove Hill Med. Ctr., New Britain, Conn., 1994-2000, chair quality assurance & outcomes mgmt. dept. psychiat. svcs., 1995-2000; psychologist Gaylord Hosp., Wallingford, Conn., 2000—; cons. Conn. Edn. Svcs., Middletown, 2000—; pvt. practice Affiliated Clin. Therapists, Middletown, 1999—2002. Clin. affiliate Yale Psychol. Svcs. Clinic, Yale U., New Haven, 1985—; cons. psychologist VA Med. Ctr., West Haven, 1985—91; asst. prof. clin. psychiatry U. Conn. Med. Sch., Farmington, Conn., 1991—94; adj. asst. prof. phys. therapy, orthop. phys. therapy program Sch. Grad. and Continuing Edn. Quinnipiac U., Hamden, Conn., 1992—; sr. cons. network devel. Inst. of Living, Hartford, 1993—94; affiliate clin. faculty, Grad. Inst. Profl. Psychology U. Hartford, Conn., 1997—99, 2001—; asst. prof. clin. psychiatry, dept. psychiatry Yale U. Sch. Medicine, New Haven, 2002—. Mem. mission study com. 1st Presbyn. Ch., New Haven, 1990-91; mem. Conn. Coun. Mental Health Providers, 1993-96, chair, 1993-94. Mem. AAAS, APA (coun. rep. 1997-99), Conn. Psychol. Assn. (chair hosp. practice com. 1990-92, practice directorate coord. 1993, pres.-elect 1994, pres. 1995-96, past pres. 1997), Conn. Behavior Therapy Assn. (mem. exec. com. 1992-96), N.Y. Acad. Scis., Assn. Psychiat. Clinics of Conn. (mem. polit. com. 1993-94, mem. edn. com. 1993-94), Soc. Behavioral Medicine, Am. Pain Soc. Avocations: microcomputers, fitness walking, fatherhood. Home: 4 Lamkin St Hamden CT 06517-3309 Office: ACT 770 Saybrook Rd Bldg B Middletown CT 06457-4739 E-mail: jccclineusa@netscape.net.

CLINE, LANCE DOUGLAS, lawyer; b. Columbus, Ind., Oct. 8, 1951; s. Leon Dale and Jo Ann Alice (Fauser) C.; children: Rachel Ann, Natalie Brooke, Kathleen Nagle. BA, Ind. U., 1973, JD, 1980. Bar; Ind. 1980, U.S. Dist. Ct. (so. dist.) Ind. 1980. Ptnr. Cline, Farrell, Christie, Lee & Caress, Indpls., 1980—. Contbr. articles to profl. jours. Mem. ATLA, Am. Coll. Trial Lawyers, Am. Coll. Legal Medicine, Ind. Trial Lawyers Assn. (bd. dirs. 1984—), Ind. State Bar Assn., Indpls. Bar Assn., Trial Lawyers Pub. Justice, Phi Beta Kappa. Home: 8645 Bay Colony Dr Indianapolis IN 46234-2912 Office: Cline Farrell Christie Lee & Caress 951 N Delaware St Indianapolis IN 46202 E-mail: lance@cfclc-law.com.

CLINE, MICHAEL PATRICK, association executive; b. Washington, Oct. 31, 1945; s. William E. and Anna (Kraynik) C.; m. Diana Cline, Dec. 31, 1989; children: Tammy, Mike, Bill, John, Terri, Nikki. AA in Bus., Cuyahoga C.C., Cleve., 1988; BA in Bus. Mgmt., Malone Coll., North Canton, Ohio, 1989. Cert. tchr., Ohio; lic. real estate, Ohio. With Phoebus Trucking, Cleve., 1967-68, Allied Delivery Sys., Cleve., 1968-86; owner M&N Auto Truck Body, Cleve., 1968-90; exec. dir. Enlisted Assn. of the N.G., Alexandria, Va., 1990—. Notary pub., Va. Author: How to Improve Office Efficiency, 1989, How to Work with Congress, 1991. Pres. Homeowners Assn. Woodbridge, Va., 1993-98; trustee Nat. Guard Ins. Trust, Washington, 1993—; co-chmn. Mil. Coalition; mem. Sec. of Vets. Adv. Panel on Edn; mem. com. on edn. Vet. Affairs Com.; co-chmn. Mil. Coalition; hon. chief master sgt. Air N.G.; bd. dirs. N.G. Youth Challenge Fund. With U.S. Army, 1963-67, Ohio N.G., 1967-92. Recipient Cert. of Merit, Mil. Coalition, Washington, 1995, Dedication/Appreciation award Medal of Honor Soc., 1992, U.S. Army Disting. Svc. ribbon with cluster. Mem. Enlisted Assn. of N.G. (life, exec. coun.), Md. Enlisted Assn. N.G., NRA, ASAE. Methodist. Avocations: computers, camping, antiques, travel. Office: Enlisted Assn NG of US 3133 Mount Vernon Ave Alexandria VA 22305

CLINE, PAULINE M. educational administrator; b. Seattle, Aug. 25, 1947; d. Paul A. and Margaret R. Cline BA in Edn., Seattle U., 1969, MEd, 1975, EdD, 1983. Cert. tchr., prin., supt., Wash. Tchr. Marysville High Sch., Wash., 1969-70; tchr., adminstr. Blanchet High Sch., Seattle, 1970-78; asst. prin. Edmonds High Sch., Wash., 1978-84; prin. College Place Middle Sch., Edmonds, 1984-85, Mountlake Terrace High Sch., Wash., 1985-93; asst. supt. Mount Vernon Sch. Dist., 1993-2000, Bethel Sch. Dist., 2002—. Recipient Washington award for excellence in edn. Gov. and Supt. Pub. Instruction, 1992, IDEA Kettering fellow, 1984, 86-87, 90-95, 97. Mem. ASCD, Am. Assn. Sch. Adminstr., Rotary (charter mem., past pres. Alderwood club), Phi Delta Kappa. Roman Catholic. Avocations: skiing, kayaking, backpacking, golf.

CLINE, RICHARD RYAN, education educator; b. East Liverpool, Ohio, Mar. 14, 1970; s. Ronald Richard and Barbara Kay Cline; m. Heidi Lynn Kalista, July 23, 1994; 1 child, Ryan Francis. BS in pharmacy, Ohio State U., 1993, MS, 1998; PhD, U. of Wis.-Madison, 2001. Registered Pharmacist Ohio, 1993. Tchg. asst. U. of Wis.-Madison, 1998—2001; asst. prof. U. of Minn., 2001—. Contbr. articles to profl. jours. Rsch. grant, Am. Found. for Pharm. Edn., Am. Assn. of Colleges of Pharmacy, 2002. Mem.: Acad. Health, Am. Pharm. Assn. Presbyterian. Avocations: bicycling, reading, travel. Office: University of Minnesota 308 Harvard St SE Minneapolis MN 55455 Office Fax: 612-625-9931. E-mail: cline011@umn.edu.

CLINE, ROBERT STANLEY, retired air freight company executive; b. Urbana, Ill., July 17, 1937; s. Lyle Stanley and Mary Elizabeth (Prettyman) C.; m. Judith Lee Stucker, July 7, 1979; children: Lisa Andre, Nicole Lesley, Christina Elaine, Leslie Jane. BA, Dartmouth Coll., 1959. Asst. treas. Chase Manhattan Bank, N.Y.C., 1960-65; v.p. fin. Pacific Air Freight Co., Seattle, 1965-68; exec. v.p. fin. Airborne Express (formerly Airborne Freight Corp.), Seattle, 1968-78, vice chmn., CFO, dir., 1978-84, chmn., CEO, dir., 1984—2002. Bd. dirs. Safeco Corp., Esterline Techs. Corp. Trustee Seattle Repertory Theatre, 1974-90, chmn. bd., 1979-83; trustee Children's Hosp. Found., 1983-91, 96—, Corp. Coun. of Arts, 1983-2002; bd. dirs. Washington Roundtable, 1985-2002, chmn. 1995-96; chmn. bd. dirs. Children's Hosp. Found., 1987-89; trustee United Way of King County, 1991-93. With U.S. Army, 1959-60. Home: 1209 39th Ave E Seattle WA 98112-4403 Office: Airborne Express PO Box 662 Seattle WA 98111-0662

CLINE, ROBERT THOMAS, retired land developer; b. McClave, Colo., May 31, 1925; s. John Howard and Goldie Gladys (Hiltabidel) C.; m. Martha Carolyn Erwin, Mar. 6, 1946; children: Carolyn Cline Price, Roberta Cline Colquitt. Student, Pueblo (Colo.) Jr. Coll., 1943, Wofford Coll., 1944. Real estate salesperson George H. Williams Co., Arlington, Va., 1946; real estate broker Lyon Pk. Realty Co., Arlington, 1946-48; cartographic rep. Hearne Bros Map Co., Detroit, 1949-58; owner Aero Surveys Map Co., Marietta, Ga. 1958-65, Imperial Builders, Marietta, 1965-69; sec., treas. Personality Homes Landmark Realty, Smyrna, Ga., 1969-78, Landmark Bldg. & Devel. Inc./Landmark Realty Co., Smyrna, 1978-96; ret., 1996. State sec. Christian Men's Fellowship Christian Ch., Ga., 1962-64; bd. dirs. Campbellstone Apts for Elderly, Atlanta, 1980-86. With USAF, 1943-46. Republican. Avocation collecting and flying radio controlled aircraft. Home: 2665 Cold Springs Trl SW Marietta GA 30064-4461

CLINE, RUTH ELEANOR HARWOOD, translator, historian; b. Middletown, Conn., Oct. 31, 1946; d. Burton Henry and Eleanor May (Cash) Harwood. A.B., Smith Coll., 1968; M.A., Rutgers U., 1969; Ph.D., Georgetown U., 2000 cert. translation from French, Georgetown U., 1978; m. William R. Cline, June 10, 1967; children: Alison, Marian. Reviewer, U.S. Dept. State, Washington 1979-94. Former v.p. Smith Coll. Class of 1968; rsch. assoc. dept. history Georgetown U., 2002--. Mem. Am. Translators Assn. (cert. in French, Spanish

and Portuguese), MLA, Internat. Arthurian Soc. Episcopalian. Translator English verse: Yvain; or the Knight with the Lion (Chretien de Troyes), 1975; Perceval; or the Story of the Grail (Chretien de Troyes), 1983, Lancelot or the Knight of the Cart (Chretien de Troyes), 1990 (Lewis Galantiere Prize 1992), Erec and Enide (Chretien de Troyes), 2000, Cliges (Chretien de Troyes), 2000. Home: 5315 Oakland Rd Chevy Chase MD 20815-6638

CLINE, SANDRA WILLIAMSON, retired elementary school educator; b. San Francisco, Dec. 10, 1944; d. Wilburn Woodrow and Hazel Stewart (Cochrane) Williamson; 1 child, Jeffrey Charles. BA, Western Mich. U., 1970, MA, 1973, MA, 1986. Cert. tchr., Mich. 1st-3rd grade tchr. Portage Mich. Pub. Schs., 1971—2000, mem. sch. effectiveness team and report card rev. com., 1988-92, mem. sci. writing team, 1989-96; mentor coach Western Mich. U., 1993-97, ret., 2000; substitute tchr. Gwinnett County Schs., Ga., 2000—. Mus. co-dir. Lake Ctr. Elem. Sch., Portage, 1982-83, student tchr., mentor, safety patrol advisor, 1st grade chairperson, state com. for social studies, writing chairperson, 1988-94. Vol. parking enforcement Portage Police, 1992-2000; assoc. coord. city emergency sys., 1995-2000; vol. ch. office and ch. choir. Recipient Congress medallion for disting. participation, 1992-93, Dr. Ronald Selkow award for Disting. Vol. Svc., 1996. Mem. NEA, ASCD, NSTA, Am. Fedn. Police (Nat. Patriotism award 1994), Nat. Coun. Tchrs. English, Assn. for Study of Coop. in Edn., Mich. Edn. Assn., Portage Edn. Assn. (exec. bd., membership chairperson, elem. grievance chair, negotiating team), Mich. ASCD (conf. com.), Phi Delta Kappa. Avocations: reading, needlecraft, church work. Home: 1248 Renee Dr SW Lilburn GA 30047-4340

CLINE, THOMAS WILLIAM, real estate leasing company executive, management consultant; b. Flint, Mich., Oct. 17, 1932; s. Leo D. and Helen (Wolohan) C.; m. Joanne Greiner, July 18, 1959; children: Robert Arthur, Thomas John, Mary Elizabeth. BS, U. Detroit, 1954, JD, 1956. Bar: Mich. 1957. Gen. atty. Wickes Corp., Saginaw, Mich., 1958-61, sec., gen. counsel, 1961-69, sr. v.p., gen. counsel, 1969-71, sr. v.p., sec., 1971-80, dir., 1964-70, 74-80; sr. v.p., group officer, dir. Wickes Cos. Inc., Saginaw, 1980-83; pres. Cline Mgmt. Co., Saginaw, 1983—; pres., chief oper. officer Signature Corp., Chgo., 1984-85; exec. v.p., chief oper. officer Seitner Bros. Inc., Saginaw, 1986—. Bd. dirs. Mid-Am. Life Assurance Co., Mich. Nat. Bank, Saginaw, Can. West Fin. Svcs.(U.S.) Inc., Aristar Inc. Chmn. fin. com. Diocese of Saginaw, 1970-72; chmn. Saginaw Cath. Schs. Study Com., 1969, Nat. assn. Boys Clubs Am.; bd. dirs. San Diego Symphony Assn., 1975-78, Econ. devel. Corp. San Diego County, 1975-78, also vice-chmn., Saginaw Japanese Cultural Ctr. and Tea House; vice chmn. Boys Clubs San Diego, 1975-77; trustee Saginaw Gen. Hosp. Assn., 1971-72, 73-75; trustee, fin. chmn. Saginaw Coop. Hosp. Inc., 1972; trustee, v.p. United Way of Saginaw County; bd. fellows Saginaw Valley Coll., 1973-75, chmn. bus. fund dr., 1978; mem. adv. bd. Delta Coll., U. San Diego, 1975-78, San Diego State U. Bus. Sch., 1975-78, Saginaw Art Mus., 1986-94; mem. instnl. rev. bd. Saginaw Valley State U., 2002--; mem. fin. com. Diocese San Diego, 1975-78; bd. dirs. Mich. State C. of C., 1973-75, Saginaw Symphony Assn. 1984-88, also v.p.; chmn. Saginaw Met. Area Nat. Alliance of Bus., 1979-80; bd. dirs. San Diego C. of C., 1976-77; ann. programs fund stategic advisor Rotary Found., 2001-03; pres. Big Creek Fishing Lodge, 2000-03. With U.S. Army, 1956-58. Mem. Mich. Bar Assn., Mich. Mfrs. Assn. (bd. dirs. 1980-88), U.S. C. of C. (adv. com.), Saginaw Club (bd. dirs., v.p. 1991), Serra Club Saginaw County (pres., bd. dirs.), Rotary (pres. Saginaw 1990-91, dist. gov. 1994-95, chair dist. found.1996-2000, del. coun. on legis. 1998, nat. advisor to Rotary Found. 2001-03), Blue Key Soc., Delta Sigma Pi, Beta Alpha Psi, Delta Theta Pi. Home and Office: 4640 Ashland Dr Saginaw MI 48603-4605

CLINE, VIVIAN MELINDA, lawyer; b. Seneca, S.C., Oct. 6, 1953; d. Kenneth H. and Wanda F. (Simmons) Fuller; m. Terry S. Cline, June 15, 1974 (div. Oct. 1986); 1 child, Alicia C. BSBA, Calif. State U., Northridge, 1974; JD, Southwestern U., L.A., 1983. Bar: Calif. 1983, Tex., 1990. Paralegal Internat. House Pancakes, North Hollywood, Calif., 1976-78; assoc. Tuohey & Prasse, Santa Ana, Calif., 1983-85; paralegal Smith Internat., inc., Newport Beach, Calif., 1978-83, sr. corp. counsel Houston, 1985—. Bus. cons. Jr. Achievement, Houston, 1992—94, 1997—99. Mem. Exec. Women's Network (sec. 1993, pres. 1994, dir. programs 1995, sec. 1996, 2000, treas. 1998-2001), Am. Soc. Corp. Secs. Inc. (sec. Houston chpt. 1995-96, treas. 1996-97, v.p., program dir. 1997-98, pres. 1998-99). Republican. Presbyterian. Office: Smith Internat Inc 16740 Hardy Rd Houston TX 77032-1125 E-mail: vcline@smith.com.

CLINE, WILLIAM RICHARD, economist, educator; b. Denver, Oct. 30, 1941; s. John Russell and Marian Alice (Franklin) C.; m. Ruth Eleanor Harwood, June 10, 1967; children: Alison Margaret, Marian Harwood. AB Pub Affairs summa cum laude, Princeton U., Princeton U., 1963; MA in Econs., Yale U., 1964, PhD, 1969. Lectr. Princeton U., 1967-69, asst. prof., 1969-70; Ford Found. vis. prof. Brazilian Planning Ministry and U. Sao Paulo, 1970-71; dep. dir. trade and devel. research U.S. Treasury Dept., Washington, 1971-73; sr. fellow Brookings Instn., Washington, 1973-81, Inst. for Internat. Econs., Washington, 1982—; pres. Econs. Internat., Inc., Washington, 1981—; dep. mng. dir., chief economist Inst. Internat. Fin., Washington, 1996—2001; sr. fellow Ctr. for Global Devel., Washington, 2002—. Professorial lectr. Johns Hopkins Sch. Internat. Studies, 1981-82, 84; vis. lectr. Princeton U., 1983, 85; vis. prof. Aoyama Gakuin U., Tokyo, 1992-94; adv. bd. U.S. Export-Import Bank, 1986-87. Author: Economic Consequences of a Land Reform in Brazil, 1970, Potential Effects of Income Redistribution, 1972, Trade Negotiations in the Tokyo Round, 1978, World Inflation and the Developing Countries, 1981, International Debt: Systemic Risk and Policy Response, 1984, The U.S.-Japan Economic Problem, 1985, Exports of Manufactures From Developing Countries, 1984, The Future of World Trade in Textiles and Apparel, 1987, Informatics and Development, 1987, United States External Adjustment and the World Economy, 1989, The Economics of Global Warming, 1992, International Economic Policy in the 1990s, 1994, International Debt Reexamined, 1995, Trade and Income Distribution, 1997. Woodrow Wilson fellow, 1964, Ford Found. fellow, 1965; recipient Harold and Margaret Sprout award Internat. Studies Assn., 1993. Mem. Am. Econ. Assn., Council Fgn. Relations. Episcopalian. Home: 5315 Oakland Rd Chevy Chase MD 20815 Office: Inst Internat Econs 1750 Massachusetts Ave NW Washington DC 20036-1903

CLING, B. J. lawyer, psychologist; b. N.Y.C., Nov. 22, 1943; d. Isidore Irving and Josephine Jean (Friedman) Rosenbaum. BA, CUNY, 1966; PhD, NYU, 1980; postgrad. Inst. Psychiatry, Law and Behavioral Sci., U. So. Calif., 1982; JD, UCLA, 1985. Bar: Calif., N.Y.; lic. clin. psychologist, Calif. Instr. psychology Adelphi U., 1969-70; asst. prof. psychology La Guardia Coll., CUNY, 1970-71; editor Program Practices-Children CBS, Los Angeles, 1978; producer women's series Sta. KPFK, Los Angeles, 1980-81; pvt. practice clin. psychology, Los Angeles, 1980-86; instr. UCLA Extension, 1979-86; clin. instr. Inst. Psychiatry, Law and Behavioral Scis., U. So. Calif., 1982-85; clk., U.S. Ct. Appeals (9th cir.), 1985-86; assoc., Davis, Polk & Wardwell, N.Y.C., 1986-88, Debevoise and Plimpton, 1989—. Past bd. dirs. Women's Equal Rights Legal Def. and Edn. Fund. Mem. Screen Actor's Guild (past chmn. women's com.), Am. Psychol. Assn.

CLINGAN, CHARLES EDMUND, historian; b. N.Y.C., Oct. 12, 1962; s. Eldon Ray and JoAnn Kay (McNamara) C. BA, CUNY, Queens, 1985; MA, U. Wis., 1987, PhD, 1991. Vis. asst. prof. Montclair State Coll., Upper Montclair, N.J., 1991-92, CUNY, 1992-95, NYU, 1994-95; asst. prof. history U. N.D., Grand Forks, 1995-2000, assoc. prof., 2000—. Author: From the General Manager's Files, 1993, Finance from Kaiser to Führer: German Budget Politics, 1912-34, 2000. Vice pres. Broadway Dem. Club, N.Y.C., 1994-95. Fulbright scholar, 1988-89. Mem. Am. Hist. Assn., German Studies Assn., Austrian Studies Ctr., Conf. Group on Ctrl. European History, Soc. for French Hist. Studies, Fulbright Assn. (pres. No. Prairie chpt. 1995—), Phi Beta Kappa. Office: Univ ND PO Box 8096 Grand Forks ND 58202-8096 E-mail: edmund_clingan@und.nodak.edu.

CLINGER, WILLIAM FLOYD, JR., retired congressman; b. Warren, Pa., Apr. 4, 1929; s. William Floyd and Lelia May Clinger; m. Julia Whita, Aug. 2, 1952; children: Eleanore, William Floyd, James, Julia. BA, Johns Hopkins U., 1951; LLB, U. Va., 1965. Bar: Pa. 1965, U.S. Supreme Ct. 1975. Advt. exec. New Process Co., Warren, 1955-62; ptnr. Stone and Harper, and successor firm Harper, Clinger & Eberly, Warren, 1965-78; mem. 96th-104th Congresses from 5th (formerly 23d) Pa. dist., Washington, 1979-96; mem. govt. ops. com.; vice chmn. transp. and infrastructure com.; chmn. govt. reform and oversight com.; sr. fellow John Hopkins U., Balt., 1996—. Chief Counsel Econ. Devel. Adminstrn., 1975—77; del. Pa. Constl. Conv., 1968; chmn., bd. dirs. Ripon Ednl. Fund, Inc.; chmn. bd. dirs Chautaugua Inst., 2000—. Mem. editl. bd.: U. Va. Law Rev., 1964—65. Chmn. Kinzua Dam Dedication Com., 1966; pres. Warren Libr. Assn., 1957—62, 1967—70, Warren Hosp. Bd., 1971—75; del. Rep. Nat. Conv., 1972, 1988, 1996. Served to lt. USN, 1951—55. Decorated Spirit of Honor medal; named Man of the Yr., Pa. Jaycees, 1960. Mem.: ABA, Warren County Bar Assn., Pa. Bar Assn., Ho. Wednesday Group (former chmn.), Warren Jaycees (pres. 1959—60). Republican. Presbyterian.

CLINKENBEARD, JAMES HOWARD, principal; b. Alexandria, Va., Apr. 1, 1950; s. Howard Samuel and Ethel Jane (Schwager) C.; m. Janelle Darlene Turner, May 27, 1972; children: Adam James, Nathan Linton, Evan Joel. BS, Murray State U., 1977; MEd, Xavier U., 1985, postgrad., 1986-87, 89-92. Cert. tchr. and adminstr., Ky. Tchr. art Newport (Ky.) Ind. Schs., 1978-88, chief negotiator, 1985-88, asst. prin., 1988-91, 92-96, dir. Title V, 1991-92, acting prin., 1992, 94-95, prin., 1996—; freelance artist, designer Bellevue, Ky., 1977—. Juror various sch. and profl. art shows; speaker pub. sch. in-service programs. Featured in Kentucky Artist and Craftsman mag., 1977, Inside Kentucky Schools, Ky. Ednl. T.V., 2001; author various documents, ednl. reports. State advisor Ky. Imagination Celebration, 1984—85; advisor Ky. Task Force for Comprehensive Arts, 1984, Ky. Task Force on Acad. Competition, 1985; active Ft. Thomas and Newport PTAs, Bellevue Civic Assn.; chmn. Citizens for Bellevue Schs., 1980—81, Arts Subcom, Coun. on Higher Edn., 1985—86, Ky. Foster Care Rev. Bd., 1991—97; mem. select panel Ky. Disting. Educators Program; chmn. Sch. Based Decision Making Coun., 1996—; chair com. Troop 70 Boy Scouts Am., 1997—2001, Ky. Rewards Category Sch., 1996—98, 1998—2000; deacon First Christian Ch., Ft. Thomas, 1976—, chmn. bd., 1982—83, Sunday sch. tchr., 1976—97, 1999—2000; bd. dirs. Ky. Citizens for the Arts in Edn., 1983—85. Recipient commendation Ky. Supt. Pub. Instrn., 1984. Mem.: ASCD, NEA, Washington Evening Star Cartoonists Guild, Newport Adminstrs. Assn. (pres. 1994—97, 2001—), Newport Tchrs. Assn. (sec. 1982—83, vice chmn. polit. action com. 1984, treas. 1985—88, pres. 1988), Ky. Edn. Assn. (svcs. com. 1985—87, del. 1986—88, task force 1987—88), Ky. Art Edn. Assn. (various offices including pres. 1983—84, Project Art Tchr. award 1980), Nat. Art Edn. Assn. (Ky. del. 1976—77, 1981), Ft. Thomas Swim Club (bd. dirs. 1994—2000, pres. 1995—2000), Alpha Tau Omega (chpt. advisor 1987—91, chpt. housing corp. pres. 1993—, chpt. trustee 1995—). Republican. Mem. Christian Ch. (Disciples Of Christ). Avocations: reading, sports, working with children. Home: 30 Kathy Ln Fort Thomas KY 41075-1914 Office: Newport Ind Schs 101 E 4th St Newport KY 41071-1615 E-mail: jclink.nky@fuse.net.

CLINKSCALES, KEITH, media company executive; BS in Acctg. and Fin. magna cum laude, Fla. A&M U. Chmn., CEO Vanguard Media Inc., N.Y.C., 1999—; lectr. Stanford Profl. Pub. Course; pres., CEO VIBE Mag.; co-founder, pub., editor-in-chief Urban Profile mag. Treas. Apollo Theater Found. Office: 11th Fl 315 Park Ave New York NY 10010*

CLINTON, BILL See CLINTON, WILLIAM JEFFERSON

CLINTON, EDWARD XAVIER, lawyer; b. Chgo., July 13, 1930; s. Michael Xavier and Mary Agnes (Joyce) C.; m. Margaret Mary Clinton, May 1, 1965 (div. Oct. 1978); 1 child, Edward Xavier Jr. Student, DePaul U., 1949-50; JD, John Marshall U., 1953. Bar: Ill. 1953, U.S. Dist. Ct. (no. dist.) Ill. 1955, U.S. Ct. Appeals (7th cir.) 1955, U.S. Supreme Ct. 1995. Assoc. Schultz & Biro, Chgo., 1955-56; with securities dept. Ill. State Dept., Springfield, 1956-57; assoc. Hough, Young & Coale, Chgo., 1957-65, Keck, Mahin & Cate, Chgo., 1965-92; pvt. practice Chgo., 1992—; spl. counsel Bullwinkel Ptnrs., Ltd. Instr. John Marshall Law Sch., Chgo., 1965-74; arbitrator N.Y. Stock Exch. Contbr. articles to profl. jours.; speaker in field. Mem. adv. bd. Steppenwolf Theatre, Chgo., 1988—89; pastoral coun. Holy Name Cathedral, 1989—94; Chgo. Opera Theatre, 1983—88, Children's Care Found., v.p.; bd. dirs. Records Mgmt. Svcs., 1966—97. With U.S. Army, 1953—55. Postgrad. scholar John Marshall Law Sch., 1953, John Jewell scholar, 1953. Mem. ABA, Ill. Bar Assn., Chgo. Bar Assn., Bar. Assn. of 7th Cir., Lawyers Club of chgo., Rotary, Law Club, Union League Club, Execs. Club of Chgo. (bd. dirs. 1985-95), Evanston Golf Club, Am. Legion, KC. Roman Catholic. Avocations: golf, prisoner appeals (pro bono). Home: 990 N Lake Shore Dr Chicago IL 60611-1366 Office: 19 S La Salle St Ste 1300 Chicago IL 60603-1406 E-mail: EClinton@mac.com.

CLINTON, HILLARY RODHAM, senator, former First Lady of United States, lawyer; b. Chgo., Oct. 26, 1947; d. Hugh Ellsworth and Dorothy (Howell) Rodham; m. William J. Clinton, Oct. 11, 1975; 1 child. BA with high honors, Wellesley Coll., 1969; JD, Yale U., 1973; LLD (hon.), U. Ark., Little Rock, 1985, Ark. Coll., 1988, Hendrix Coll., 1992, U. Sunderland, 1993, U. Pa., 1993, U. Mich., 1993, U. Ill., 1994, U. Minn., 1995, San Francisco State U., 1995; D Pub. Svc. (hon.), George Washington U., 1994, U. Md., College Park, 1996; DHL (hon.), Drew U., 1996, Ohio U., 1997. Bar: Ark. 1973, U.S. Dist. Ct. (ea. and we. dists.) Ark. 1973, U.S. Ct. Appeals (8th cir.) 1973, U.S. Supreme Ct. 1975. Atty. Children's Def. Fund, Cambridge, Mass. and Washington, 1973-74; legal cons. Carnegie Coun. on Children, New Haven, 1973-74; counsel, impeachment inquiry staff Judiciary Com. U.S. Ho. of Reps., Washington, 1974; asst. prof. law, dir. Legal Aid Clinic U. Ark. Sch. Law, Fayetteville, 1974-77, asst. prof. law Little Rock, 1979-80; ptnr. Rose Law Firm, Little Rock, 1977-92; chair Presdl. Task Force on Nat. Health Care Reform, 1993; mem. U.S. Senate from N.Y., 2001—. Author: Handbook on Legal Rights for Arkansas Women, 1977, 87, It Takes a Village: And Other Lessons Children Teach Us, 1996, Living History, 2003; syndicated columnist Talking It Over, 1995—; contbr. articles to profl. jours. Bd. dirs. Childrens Def. Fund, Washington, 1976-92, chair, 1986-91, Legal Svcs. Corp., Washington, 1977-81, chair, 1978-80; founder, pres., bd. dirs. Ark. Advs. for Children and Families, 1977-84; bd. dirs. Child Care Action Campaign, 1986-92, Nat. Ctr. on Edn. and the Economy, 1987-92, Ark. Children's Hosp., 1988-92, Franklin and Eleanor Roosevelt Inst., 1988-92, Children's TV Workshop, 1989-92, Pub./Pvt. Ventures, 1990-92; chmn. Ark. Edn. Stds. Com., 1983-84; mem. commn. on quality edn. So. Regional Edn. Bd., 1984-92; chair ABA Commn. on Women in the Profession, 1987-91; former hon. pres. Girl Scouts of Am.; mem. adv. bd. HIPPY, 1988-92, bd. dirs.; former hon. chair Pres.' Com. on the Arts and Humanities, U.S. Del., UN Fourth World Conf. on Women, 1995; hon. mem. The Pen and Brush, 1996—. Named Outstanding Layman of Yr. Phi Delta Kappa, 1984, Health Educator of Yr., Ryan White Found., 1995; recipient Lewis Hine award Nat. Child Labor Law Com., 1993, Albert Schweitzer Leadership award Hugh O'Brian Youth Found., 1993, Iris Cantor Humanitarian award UCLA Med. Ctr., 1993, Friend of Family award Am. Home Econs. Assn., 1993, Charles Wilson Lee Citizen Svc. award Com. for Edn. Funding, 1993, Claude D. Pepper award Nat. Assn. for Home Care, 1993, Commitment to Life award AIDS Project L.A., 1994, Disting. Svc., Health Edn. and Prevention award Nat. Ctr. for Health Edn., 1994, First Ann. Eleanor Roosevelt Freedom Fighter award, 1994, Brandeis award U. Louisville Sch. of Law, 1994, Social Justice award United Auto Workers, 1994, Ernie Banks Positivism trophy Emil Verban Meml. Soc., 1994, Humanitarian award Alzheimer's Assn., 1994, Elie Wiesel Found., 1994, Internat. Broadcasting award Hollywood Radio and TV Soc., 1994, Ellen Browning Scripps medal Scripps Coll., 1994, Disting. Pro Bono Svc. award San Diego Vol. Lawyer Program, 1994, HIPPY U.S.A. award, 1994, C. Everett Koop medal Am. Diabetes Assn., 1994, Women's Legal Def. Fund award, 1994, Martin Luther King, Jr. award Progressive Nat. Bapt. Conv., 1994, 30th Anniversary Women at Work award in Pub. Policy, Nat. Commn. on Working Women, 1994, Greater Washington Urban League award, 1995, Servant of Justice award N.Y. Legal Aid Soc., 1995, Presdl. award Bklyn. Coll., 1995, Outstanding Mother award Nat. Mother's Day Com., 1995, Dedication, Annual Survey Am. Law, NYU, 1995, Nat. Breast Cancer Coalition Leadership award, 1995, Faith in Humanity award Nat. Coun. Jewish Women, 1996, NICHE Humanitarian award, 1996, Nat. Assn. Elem. Sch. Prins. Dist. Svc. award, 1996, Grammy award, 1997, Bully Pulpit award Nat. Coun. for Adoption, 1997, Nat. Family Advocate award Parents' Plus Newspaper, 1997, Disting. Svc. to Edn. award Coll. Bd., 1997, Disting. Svc. award Columbia U. Ctr. of Addiction and Substance Abuse, 1997, Commitment to Children award The Elizabeth Glaser Pediat. AIDS Found., 1997, Eleanor Roosevelt Living World award Peace Links, 1997; Paul Harris fellow Rotary Found., 1996. Fellow Am. Bar Found.; mem. Ark. Bar Assn., Ark. Trial Lawyers Assn., Ark. Women Lawyers Assn., Am. Trial Lawyers Assn., Pulaski County Bar Assn. Democrat. Office: 476 Russell Senate Office Bldg Washington DC 20510*

CLINTON, LAWRENCE PAUL, psychiatrist; b. Lubbock, Texas, Apr. 27, 1945; s. Lewis Paul Clinton and Dorothy E. (Higgins) Clinton-Billingslea; m. Bonnie Gail Orenstein, June 22, 1969; children: Kerry Elizabeth, Andrew James, Alexander Geoffrey, Kaylin Lee. BA with honors, So. Conn. State Coll., 1966; postgrad., Ohio State U., 1966-68; MD, Hahnemann U., 1972. Diplomate Am. Bd. Psychiatry and Neurology, Am. Bd. Forensic Examiners, Am. Acad. Experts in Traumatic Stress, Am. Bd. Psychotherapy, 2000, Am. Psychiat. Assn. Teaching asst. Ohio State U., Columbus, 1966-68, research fellow, 1966-68; clin. instr. psychiatry Hahnemann U., Phila., 1975-82, asst. clin. prof., 1982—. Chief exec. officer Bldg. Mgmt. Group, Vineland, NJ, 1986—; psychiat. dir. James Guiffre Med. Ctr., Phila., 1976-79; med. dir. PSI Group, 1990-2003; cons. Superior Ct. NJ, 1975—, Ranch Hope, Alloway, NJ, 1989-92. Contbr. articles to profl. jours. Mem. Am. Security Coun., 1975—, Rep. Senatorial Com., 1978—, Rep. Nat. Com., 1978, The Pres. Club, 1990—. Recipient awards Am. Security Coun., 1982, Buena Regional Sch. Dist., NJ, 1983, Vineland Parent Support and Adv. Group, 1990, Rep. Presdl. Legion of Merit medal, 1992; decorated Chevalier Comdr. Ordre Souverain et Militaire de la Milice du Saint Sepulcre, 1990—. Fellow Am. Bd. Forensic Examiners, Phila. Coll. Physicians and Surgeons, Am. Psychiat. Assn. (disting.); mem. AMA, Internat. Assn. Group Psychotherapy, NJ Psychiat. Soc., Med. Club Phila., World Fedn. Mental Health, InterAm. Coll. Physicians and Surgeons, Hahnemann Undergrad. Rsch. Soc. (treas. 1971-72), Confedn. of Chivalry, Am. Chem. Soc., Soc. d'Chemie (pres. 1965-66), South Jersey Psychiat. Soc. (sec.-treas. 1994—, pres. 2001-03), Internat. Churchill Soc., The Heritage Found., SPQR Club (pres. 1961-62) (Milford, Conn.), Union League Phila., Union League Phila. Yacht Club, Phi Lambda Kappa (v.p. 1972). Avocations: gardening, art collecting, book collecting, historical biography, golf, sailing. Office: 1138 E Chestnut Ave Bldg 6 Vineland NJ 08360-5053

CLINTON, LOTTIE DRY EDWARDS, retired state agency administrator; b. Wilmington, N.C., July 26, 1937; d. King Solomon Dry and Bessie Theresa Mouzon; m. Edmund Russell Edwards III, Aug. 30, 1954 (dec. Aug. 29, 1969); children: Desireé, Vickie, Edmonia, Cheryl, Michele, Kevin; m. Robert Clinton, June 24, 1993. AAS in Bus. Adminstrn., Cape Fear Cmty. Coll., 1972; student, U. N.C., Wilmington, 1974—75, Ctrl. Piedmont Coll., 1984. Cert. Notary Pub. N.C. From acctg. clk. to supr. shipping and receiving N.C. State Port Authority, Wilmington, 1976—80, supr. open dock, 1980, adminstrv. supr., 1980—83, 1985—98, adminstr. supr. Charlotte Intermodal Terminal, 1983—85; ret., 1998. Apptd. 1898 Wilmington Race Riot commn. State of N.C., 2002—. Chmn. Svc. to Disabled, Wilmington, 1970—80, Com. on African Am. History, Wilmington, 1980—90; bd. dirs. New Hanover Cmty. Health Ctr., Wilmington, 1997—. Named Woman of Yr. N.C. liberty light chpt., ABWA, 1979; named an Outstanding Citizen, Winston-Salem Alumni Assn., 1995. Democrat. African Methodist Episcopal Zionite. Achievements include appointed mem. of 1898 Wilmington Race Riot Commn. State of NC. Avocations: reading, sewing, gardening, music, beach. Home: 127 Blount Dr Wilmington NC 28411 Personal E-mail: loddec@aol.com.

CLINTON, MARIANN HANCOCK, educational association administrator; b. Dyersburg, Tenn., Dec. 7, 1933; d. John Bowen and Nell Maurine (Johnson) Hancock; m. Harry Everett Clinton, Aug. 25, 1956; children— Carol, John Everett. BMus, Cin. Conservatory Music, 1956; BS, U. Cin., 1956; MMus, Miami U., Oxford, Ohio, 1971. Tchr. music public schs., Hamilton County, Ohio, 1956-57; tchr. voice and piano Butler County, Ohio, 1964—; instr. music Miami U., 1972-75; exec. dir. Music Tchrs. Nat. Assn., Cin., 1977-86. Mng. dir. Am. Music Tchr., 1977-86. Mem. adminstrv. bd. Middletown (Ohio) 1st United Methodist Ch., 1968-72; bd. dirs. Friends of the Sorg Opera House; concert presenter Friends of Music of Charlotte County (Fla.). Mem. Music Educators Nat. Conf., Am. Ednl. Research Assn., Am. Soc. Assn. Execs., Nat. Fedn. Music Clubs, Pi Kappa Lambda, Kappa Delta Pi, Mu Phi Epsilon, Phi Mu. Republican. Home: 714 Macedonia Dr Punta Gorda FL 33950-8013 *I have found that a consideration for the interrelatedness of all parts so necessary in the presentation of music and a warm regard for the feelings of others which is implicit in the practice of good manners in daily observance create success in one's personal and professional lives.*

CLINTON, MARY ELLEN, neurologist; b. Evanston, Ill., Feb. 15, 1950; d. Merle P. and Corinne E. (Wolf) C.; m. William J. Wade Jr. BS, Loyola/Marymount U., 1972; MD, U. So. Calif., 1976. Intern internal medicine Vanderbilt U. Hosp., Nashville, 1976-77, resident in neurology, 1979-81, chief resident, 1981-82, fellow in neuromuscular disease and electrodiagnostics, 1982-83, asst. prof. neurology, 1983-91; staff physician emergency medicine Donelson Hosp., St. Thomas Hosp., Nashville, 1977-79; asst. clin. prof. Vanderbilt U., Nashville, 1991—. Dir. electrodiagnostic testing Neurosurg. Assocs., Nashville, 1991—; reviewing physician Mid South Found. for Med. Care, Inc., Memphis, 1991-94; med. expert Social Security and Disability Determination State of Tenn., 1987-95; dir. Vanderbilt Muscle Biopsy Lab., 1984-89; dir. neurodiagnostic labs. Nashville VA Hosp., 1989-91; mem. staff St. Thomas Hosp., Centennial Hosp., Nashville, cons. staff Bapt. Hosp., Nashville. Contbr. articles and abstracts to profl. jours. Co-dir. Nashville br. Muscular Dystrophy Assn., 1983-91. Recipient Marymount Coll. Pres's award, 1972, Sandoz award neurology, 1983, Disting. Alum award Loyola Marymount U., 1998. Mem. AMA, AAUW, Am. Soc. for Internal Medicine, Soc. for Neurosci., Am. Med. Women's Assn., Nashville Acad. Medicine, Tenn. Med. Assn., So. Clin. Neurol. Soc., Am. Acad. Clin. Neurophysiology, Am. Assn. for Electrodiagnostic Medicine, Am. Acad. Neurology, Kappa Gamma Pi. Office: Neurosurg Assocs 4230 Harding Pike Nashville TN 37205-2013

CLINTON, RICHARD LEE, international relations educator; b. Cookeville, Tenn., Sept. 20, 1938; s. Howard Cecil Clinton and Nelva Dee Webb; m. Susan Jeffries Clinton, Sept. 17, 1964 (div. Dec. 1985); children: Lara Franklin, Lisa Laurens; m. Rosalie Norwood, Nov. 1, 1986. BA, Vanderbilt U., 1960, MA, 1964; PhD, U. N.C., 1971. Asst. prof. U. N.C., Chapel Hill, 1971-76, Oreg. State U., Corvallis, 1976-78, assoc. dean Coll. Liberal Arts, 1978-82, assoc. prof. Coll. Liberal Arts, 1982-85, prof. Coll. Liberal Arts, 1985—. Cons. UN Fund for Population Activities, Bolivia and Guatemala, 1988, Internat. Planned Parenthood Fedn., Costa Rica and Honduras, 1984, Ford Found., Peru, 1977, U.S. Dept. State, Peru, 1974; Hanna Disting. Prof., Rollins Coll., Winter Park, Fla., 1990, 93, 94, 95; Fulbright sr. lectr. U.S. Govt., Peru, 1982, 97. Author: Problems of Population Policy Formation in Peru, 1971, Poblacion y desarrollo en el Peru, 1985, Environmental Politics and Policy: A Comparative Approach, 2002; editor: Political Science in Population Studies, 1972, Research in the Politics of Population, 1973, Population and Politics, 1973. Lance cpl., USMCR, 1958-64. Mem. Latin Am. Studies Assn. Office: Oreg State U Dept Polit Sci Corvallis OR 97331 E-mail: richard.clinton@orst.edu.

CLINTON, RICHARD M. lawyer; b. Milw., June 25, 1941; s. William J. and Idella (Loftis) C.; m. Barbara Lynch, June 14, 1969; children: Amanda, Camille, Rebecca. BS, U. Wis., 1963, JD, 1967; LLM, George Washington U., 1971. Bar: Wis. 1967, Wash. 1971, U.S. Dist. Ct. (ea. dist.) Wash. 1975, U.S. Ct. Appeals (9th cir.) 1972. Instr. legal writing U. Wis. Law Sch., Madison, 1966-67; trial atty. antitrust div. U.S. Dept. Justice, Washington, 1967-71; assoc. Bogle & Gates, Seattle, 1971-75, mem., 1975-99; ptnr. Dorsey & Whitney LLP, 1999—. Fellow Am. Coll. Trial Lawyers; mem. ABA, Wash. Bar Assn. (pres. antitrust sect. 1982-83), Fed. Bar Assn. (pres. 1986-87), Wash. Athletic Club, Columbia Tower Club. Roman Catholic. Avocations: sailing, skiing, fishing, hiking, travel. Home: 3863 50th Ave NE Seattle WA 98105-5235 Office: Dorsey & Whitney LLP US Bank Centre 1420 5th Ave Seattle WA 98101-4087

CLINTON, STEPHEN MICHAEL, academic administrator; b. Wichita, Kans., Aug. 21, 1944; s. Thomas Francis and Bettie Lee (Harrison) C.; m. Virginia Ann Schoonover, Aug. 30, 1964; children: Matthew, Michael, Shanna. MA in Philosophy, Trinity Evang. Div. Sch., Deerfield, Ill., 1969, MDiv, 1970; PhD in Theology, Calif. Grad. Sch. Theology, 1979; postgdoc. in philosophy, U. Calif., Riverside, 1985-87, PhD in Edn., 1997; MA in Counseling, Internat. Sch. Theology, San Bernardino, Calif., 1987; MA in Edn., Calif. State U., San Bernardino, 1988. Ordained to ministry Evang. Free Ch. Am., 1973; cert. gifted edn. tchr., Calif. Pastor Lake Zurich (Ill.) EFC, 1967-69, Faith Presbyn. Ch., Wichita, Kans., 1972-74, Highlander Evang. Free Ch., 1974—78, East Cmty.

Ch., Orlando, Fla., 1993-94, First Bapt. Ch., St. Cloud, Fla., 1999-2000; dir. extension degree programs Internat. Sch. Theology, 1974-86, assoc. prof., 1978-86; dir. Internat. Leadership Coun., 1986—; pres. Orlando (Fla.) Inst., 1991—, prof. edn. and religion, 1992—; dir. EdD program Iberia-Am. U. Leadership, 1998—. Pres. Ministry Devel., Inc., San Bernardino, 1978-86; chmn. bd. dirs. Masterlife Internat., 1999-2000; bd. dirs. Vision Orlando, 1992—; bd. reference Am. All Stars, 2000—; prof. Belhaven Coll., 2000-01; adj. prof. Moody Bible Inst., Valenia C.C., Asbury Theol. Sem. Author: The Doctrine of the Christian Life, 1981, Cultural Apologetics, 1983, Calvinism and Arminianism, 1985, The Everlasting God, 1989, Movements Which Changed History, 1993, Theistic Realism, 1998, The Role of the Holy Spirit in Spiritual Development, 2001; also 40 articles. Pres. Advs. for Gifted and Talented Edn., San Bernardino, 1979-85; chmn. state parent coun. Calif. Assn. for Gifted, 1978-83; pres. advocates for gifted and talented edn. San Bernardino Unified Sch. Dist., 1984-87; chmn. bd. dirs. Ctr. for Individuals with Disabilities, San Bernardino, 1984-88; Maitland C. of C., bd. dirs., 2002—. Mem. Evang. Philos. Soc. (editor 1979-81, 84-98, pres. 1983), Evang. Free Ch. Ministerial Assn., Evang. Theol. Soc. (chmn. 1982, 03), John Dewey Soc., Philosophy of Edn. Soc. Office: Orlando Inst 100 Lake Hart Dr Ste 3000 Orlando FL 32832 E-mail: sclinton@toi.edu.

CLINTON, WILLIAM JEFFERSON (BILL CLINTON), 42d President of the United States; b. Hope, Ark., Aug. 19, 1946; m. Hillary Rodham, Oct. 11, 1975; 1 child, Chelsea Victoria. BS in Internat. Affairs, Georgetown U., 1968; postgrad., Oxford U., 1968-70; JD, Yale U., 1973. Prof. U. Ark. Sch. Law, Fayetteville, 1973-76; pvt. practice law, 1973-76; atty. gen. State of Ark., Little Rock, 1977-79, gov., 1979-81, 83-92; of counsel Wright, Lindsey & Jennings, Little Rock, 1981-82; President of the United States, 1993-2001. Chmn. So. Growth Policies Bd., 1985-86. Chmn. Edn. Commn. of the States, 1986-87, mem. steering com.; mem. Task Force on Adolescent Edn., Carnegie Found.; chmn. Dem. Leadership Coun., 1990-91. Rhodes scholar Univ. Coll., Oxford U., 1968-70. Mem. ABA, Ark. Bar Assn., Nat. Govs. Assn. (vice chmn. 1986, chmn. 1986-87, exec. com., fin. com., com. on human resources, com. on internat. trade and fgn. rels., task force on rural devel., co-chmn. task force for edn. 1990-92). Democrat. Address: 55 W 125th St New York NY 10027*

CLIPPERT, CHARLES FREDERICK, lawyer; b. Detroit, May 21, 1931; s. Harrison Frank and Ethelyn (Reuss) C.; m. Lynne Davison, June 6, 1959; children: Martha G. Shannon, Charles Frederick III, Thomas Harrison. BA, U. Mich., 1953, LLB, 1959. Bar: Mich. 1959. Assoc. Dickinson, Wright, Moon, Van Dusen & Freeman, Bloomfield Hills, Mich., 1959-67, ptnr., 1967-97, mem. exec. com., 1986-89; mem. Dickinson Wright PLLC, Bloomfield Hills, Mich., 1998-2000, cons. mem., 2001—. Commr. City of Birmingham, Mich., 1964-70, mayor, 1969-70; gov. Cranbrook Schs., Bloomfield Hills, 1978-99; trustee Cranbrook Ednl. Community, Bloomfield Hills, 1980-98, sec., 1989-93. Lt. (j.g.) USNR, 1953-56; mem. endowment com. The Consortium of Endowed Episcopal Parishes, 1998—. Fellow Am. Bar Found., Mich. Bar Found.; mem. ABA, State Bar Mich. (real property law coun. 1980-85, mem. select com. on professionalism 1992-99, mem. alternate dispute resolution coun. 1999—), Oakland County Bar Assn. (bd. dirs. 1985-91, pres. 1990-91), Orchard Lake Country Club (gov. 1986-92, pres. 1991-92), Am. Arbitration Assn. (panel of neutral arbitrators 1997—), Pi Sigma Alpha. Office: Dickinson Wright PLLC Ste 2000 38525 N Woodward Ave Bloomfield Hills MI 48304-2971 Mailing: PO Box 509 Bloomfield Hills MI 48303-0509 E-mail: cclippert@dickinson-wright.com.

CLIPSHAM, JACQUELINE ANN, artist; b. Hertfordshire, Eng., July 27, 1936; (parents Am. citizens), July 27, 1936; d. George Frederick and Helene Lucille (Lees) C. BA, Carleton Coll., 1958; postgrad., Universita per Stranieri, Perugia, Italy, 1959; MA, Western Res. U., 1962. Mem. Clay Art Center, Port Chester, N.Y., 1963-66; dir. ceramics program and art workshop CORE Community Center, Sumter, S.C., 1965; mem. faculty Bklyn. Mus. Art Sch., 1968-79, Essex. County Coll., Newark, 1979-80. Mem. Atlantic Gallery, N.Y.C., 1974-83; mem. crafts task force Nat. Endowment for Arts, 1980; Culpeper Found. project coordinator, dept. community edn. Met. Mus. Art, N.Y.C., 1981-82; mem. grants panel for crafts N.J. State Council Arts, 1982; visiting artist, Dayton Hudson, 1987; instr. Carleton Coll., N. Field, Minn., 1987. One-woman show: Willoughby (Ohio) Fine Arts Ctr., 1982, Hunterdon Mus. Art, 2001; works exhibited: Mid-Atlantic States Arts Found., 1987, Schwab Rehabilitation Inst., Chgo., 1987, Cleve. Mus., Bklyn. Mus., Mus. Contemporary Crafts, N.Y.C., Butler Inst. Art, Youngstown, Ohio, Hunterdon Mus. Art, Clinton, N.J., Greenwich House Pottery, N.Y.C., Pratt Inst., Bklyn., Atlantic Gallery, N.Y.C., 1980, Webster Coll., St. Louis, 1981, Clay Art Ctr., Sound Shore Gallery, Port Chester, N.Y., 1983, Gemans Van Eck Gallery, N.Y.C., 1983, Thorpe Intermedia Gallery, Sparkill, N.Y., 1984, N.Y. Pub. Library, 1984; work loaned to Dept. Acad. Affairs, Met. Mus. Art, 1978; cons. dept. Am. art Met. Mus. Art, N.Y.C.; represented in permanent collections: Cleve. Mus. Art, Johnson & Johnson Corp. Collection, New Brunswick, N.J., Mus. Modern Art., N.Y.C., N.Y., Carnegie Mus., Pitts., Pa., N.J. State Mus., Trenton, N.J., Zimmerli Mus., Rutgers U., New Brunswick, N.J., Newark (N.J.) Pub. Libr., Hunterdon Mus., Clinton, N.J., Noyes Mus., Oceanville, N.J., Dance Libr. Rutgers U., Newark, N.J., Alexander Libr., Rutgers U., New Brunswick, N.J. Featured in Women Artists' Book, Women's Caucus for Art Exhbn., 1982, Artists' Books, From the Traditional to the Avant Garde, 1982, also govt. publ. on employment of disabled; reviewer NEA accessibility guidelines; artist in residence Balt. (Md.) Clayworks. Recipient awards for ceramics and sculpture Butler Inst. Am. Art, 1963, 64, 65, nat. merit award for ceramics Mus. Contemporary Crafts, 1966; N.Y. State Council Arts grantee, 1982-83. Mem. Coll. Art Assn., Am. Crafts Council, Women's Caucus for Art (chair panel Nat. Conf.), Images of Disabled People in Western Art), Alumni Assn. Cleve. Inst. Art. Home and Studio: PO Box 387 Califon NJ 07830-0387

CLITHEROE, ELEANOR, utilities executive; LLB, U. Western Ont., 1977, MBA, 1980; B Civil Law, McGill U., 1978. Dep. min. fin. Province of Ont., dep. min. treasury and econs.; v.p. corp. fin. Can. Imperial Bank of Commerce; pres., CEO HycroOne Inc., Toronto, Canada; dir. HydroOne Networks, Inc., Toronto, Canada; chancellor U. Western Ont., London, 2000—. Bd. dirs. Donafco Inc., TD Bank Fin. Group, Alcan Aluminum Ltd., INCO Ltd., Conf. Bd. Can. Trustee Wildlife Preservation Trust; mem. Richard Ivey Alumni Bd. U. Western Ont., mem. campaign cabinet; bd. dirs. Nature Conservancy Can., Canada, St. Joseph's Hosp. Found., Internat. Inst. Sustainable Devel. Named Can. Top Businesswoman, Nat. Post Power 50, 2002. Office: HydroOne Inc 483 Bay St 10th Fl Toronto ON Canada M5G 2P5

CLIVE, CRAIG N. compensation executive; b. Waltham, Mass., June 10, 1947; s. Craig Clive and Marie Hope (Smith) Hodge; m. Charlotte Cranford, Aug. 23, 1970; children: Sarah Putnam, Andrew Ross. BSBA with high honors, Northeastern U., 1974; MBA, Babson Coll., 1975. Cert. compensation profl., sr. profl. in human resources. Compensation staff analyst Mitre Corp., Bedford, Mass., 1971-74; pers. mgr. High Voltage Engring. Corp., Burlington, Mass., 1974-78; employment mgr. CompuGraphic Corp., Wilmington, Mass., 1978-80; compensation and benefits mgr. TRW Fasteners Divsn., Cambridge, Mass., 1981-84; corp. compensation mgr. TRW Inc., Cleve., 1984-87; v.p. U.S. compensation Alexander & Alexander Inc., Owings Mills, Md., 1987-96; mng. ptnr. Baylights Compensation Cons., LLC, Ellicott City, Md., 1996—, futures chair, 1996—2001. Lay leader Bethany United Meth. Ch., Elliott City, Md., 1992-95; bd. dirs. Grey Rock Homeowner's Assn., Elliott City, 1992; asst. den leader Cub Scouts Pack 944, Elliott City, 1992-95, asst. scoutmaster Troop 794 Boy Scouts Am., Ellicott City, 1995—, unit commr. Nat. Pike Dist., 1998-2001, advisor Venturing Crew 794, 1999—; cert. lay speaker Balt.-Washington Conf., 1993—. 1st lt. U.S. Army, 1967-69, Vietnam. Mem.: Balt.-Washington Corridor C. of C. (bd. dirs.), Christian Motorcyclists Assn., DAV (life), Mackenzie's Co. 71st Regiment of Highland Foot-Hist. Reenactment. Methodist. Avocations: hist. reenactment, computing, reading, travel. Home: 3748 Dorsey Search Cir Ellicott City MD 21042-3753 Office: Baylights Compensation Cons LLC 3748 Dorsey Search Cir Ellicott City MD 21042-3753 E-mail: craig@baylights.com.

CLIVER, DEAN OTIS, microbiologist, educator; b. Oak Park, Ill., Mar. 2, 1935; s. Milton Clarence and Ivy Ada (Erb) C.; m. Carolyn Elaine Parker, Aug. 13, 1960; children— Blanche Irena, Frederick Lajos, Carl Milan, Marguerite Estelle. BS, Purdue U., 1956, MS, 1957; PhD, Ohio State U., 1960. Postdoctoral rsch. assoc. Ohio State U., 1960; resident rsch. assoc. NAS-NRC, U.S. Army Biol. Labs., Ft. Detrick, Md., 1961-62; rsch. assoc., instr. Food Rsch. Inst., U. Chgo., 1962-66; asst. prof. dept. food microbiology and toxicology, dept. bacteriology Food Rsch. Inst., U. Wis., Madison, 1966—, assoc. prof., 1967-76; prof. Food Rsch. Inst. U. Wis., 1976-95, Dept. Animal Health and Biomed. Scis. U. Wis, 1992-95; prof. dept. population health and reprodn. Sch. Vet. Medicine, U. Calif., Davis, 1995—. Prin. investigator, head WHO Collaborating Centre for Food Virology, Davis. Contbr. articles to profl. jours. and chpts. to books; editor 4 books in field. Served as 2d lt. U.S. Army Res., 1957. Recipient Borden undergrad. award Purdue U., 1956; Ralston-Purina grad. fellow, 1956-57 Mem. Am. Soc. Microbiology, Inst. Food Technologists (food sci. communicator 1991—), Internat. Assn. Food Protection, Internat. Assn. Water Quality, Sigma Xi. Home: 920 Villanova Dr Davis CA 95616-1749 Office: U Calif Sch Vet Medicine Dept Population Health/Rep Davis CA 95616-8743 E-mail: docliver@ucdavis.edu.

CLIZBE, JOHN ANTHONY, psychologist, organization administrator; b. Council Bluffs, Iowa, June 28, 1942; s. Harold George and Margaret Jane (Fariday) C.; m. Rebecca Rose Maddox, Jan. 30, 1965; children: Mark Andrew, Diane Christine. BA, William Jewell Coll., Liberty, Mo., 1964; PhD, Washington U., St. Louis, 1967. Clin. psychology resident Norfolk (Nebr.) State Hosp. and Northeast Mental Health Clinic, 1967-68; cons. psychologist Nordli, Wilson Assocs., Worcester, Mass., 1968-97, gen. ptnr., 1975-97, resident mgr., 1978-83, mng. ptnr., 1983-93, sr. ptnr., 1993-97; v.p. disaster svcs. ARC, Falls Church, Va., 1997—2002; interim exec. dir. Triangle Area chpt. Am. Red Cross, 2003, interim CEO Price George's County chpt., 2003—. Pres. PCMS, Inc., 1984-97; dir., treas. PSI, Inc., 1983-97, Human Interface Group, Inc., 1986-97; dir., v.p., treas. Student Achievement Inst., Worcester, 1973-97. Columnist Bus. Times. Dir., treas., pres. Nat. Psychol. Cons. to Mgmt.; mem. bd. edn. Town of Madison, Conn., 1980-86; trustee Calvin K. Kazanjian Econ. Found., Inc., 1986—; dist. chmn. 101st Assembly Dist., 1992-97, Conn. Party, 1992—; chmn. Conn. Red Cross Disaster Mental Health Com., 1992-97, Nat. Bd. Emergencey Ford and Shelter Program, 1997—; facilitator Vision Project City of New Haven, 1994; coord. Mental Health Svcs., 1995, Spl. Olympics World Games; mem. exec. com. Nat. Hurrican Conf., 1997—; chmn. waterfront com. City of New Haven Vision Project; others; nat. chmn. disaster svcs. ARC, 1995-97; mem. exec. com. Internat. Conf. on Disaster Mgmt., 2000; mem. adv. com. Natural Hazards Rsch. and Applications Ctr., 1998--. NDEA fellow Washington U., 1967. Mem. APA (membership com. div. 14), Mass. Psychol. Assn., Am. Mgmt. Assn. (faculty President's Assn. 1987-97), New Haven C. of C. (bd. dirs. 1989-95), Sigma Xi, Pi Gamma Mu, Pi Kappa Delta. Home: 607 Queen St Alexandria VA 22314-2514 Office: ARC 8111 Gatehouse Rd Falls Church VA 22042-1203

CLODIUS, ALBERT HOWARD, history educator; b. Spokane, Wash., Mar. 26, 1911; s. William Sr. and Mary Hebner (Brown) C.; m. Wilma Charlene Candler, June 3, 1961; children: Helen Lou Namikas, John Charles Parker. BA in Edn., Ea. Wash. State U., 1937; postgrad., Stanford U.; MA in History, Claremont (Calif.) Grad. U., 1948, PhD in History, 1953. Cert. secondary edn. tchr., Calif. Editorial asst. Pacific N.W. Quarterly, U. Wash., Seattle, 1938-40; reader Stanford U., Palo Alto, Calif., 1940-42; instr. Claremont-McKenna Coll., 1946-50; asst. prof. Pepperdine U., L.A., 1952-53; instr. Ventura (Calif.) Community Coll., 1953-76; adj. prof. Northrop U., L.A., 1977-85; prof. Nat. U., San Diego, 1987-88; ret., 1988. English conversation tchr., vol. internat. student ctr. U. Calif., L.A., 1979—. John R. and Dora F. Haynes Found. fellow, 1950-52; Clarence D. Martin scholar Ea. Wash. State U., 1936-37. Mem. Plato Soc. U. Calif. Democrat. Unitarian Universalist. Avocations: classical music, swimming. Home: 4832 Salem Village Pl Culver City CA 90230-4324

CLODIUS, ROBERT LEROY, economist, educator; b. Walla Walla, Wash., Mar. 10, 1921; s. Hans Friedrich and Emma (Wellman) C.; m. Joan Elizabeth Coyle, Aug. 27, 1949; children: Catherine, Mark. Student, Whitman Coll., 1938-40, LLD, 1970; BS, U. Calif., Berkeley, 1942, PhD, 1950. Lectr. econs. U. Calif., 1949-50; mem. faculty U. Wis., 1950-90, prof. agrl. econs., 1958-90, chmn. dept., 1960-62, v.p. univ., 1962-71, acting pres., 1970, prof. agrl. econs. emeritus, 1990—, prof. econs., 1971-90, prof. econs. emeritus, 1990—, prof. ednl. adminstrn., 1971-90, prof. ednl. administr. emeritus, 1990—, prof. univ., 1971-90, prof. univ. emeritus, 1990—, v.p. univ. emeritus, 1990—; pres. Nat. Assn. State Univs. and Land Grant Colls., 1979-91; pres. emeritus, 1992—. Vis. assoc. Harvard Bus. Sch., 1954; lectr. Am. Coun. Edn., Inst. Coll. and Univ. Adminstrs.; State Dept. specialist in South Am., 1961; cons. Dept. Agr., 1961; mem. com. agr. scis. to Sec. Agr., 1961-69; cons. Rockefeller Found., 1963-67; adviser U. East Africa, 1963-67; chmn. Com. Instnl. Coop., 1968; cons. Ford Found., Philippines, 1970; chmn. exec. bd. commn. instns. higher edn. North Ctrl. Assn., 1972-74; v.p. Midwest Univs. Consortium Internat. Activities, Inc., 1964-70, chmn. bd., 1970-71; mem. Commn. on Higher Edn., Govt. Sierra Leone, 1969; adminstr. Indonesian Higher Agr. Edn. Project, 1971-77; adv. commr. Edn. Commn. of the States, 1980-91; mem. Nat. Commn. on Higher Edn. Issues, 1981-82, chmn. adv. com. Nat. Ctr. Food and Agrl. Policy, Resources for the Future, 1984-89; nat. adv. com. Adult Learning Svc. PBS, 1987-91, Debt for Devel. Coalition, Inc., 1988-92, chmn., 1988-91, chmn. adv. com., 1992-97; cons. U.S. Info. Agy., 1991-94; v.p. WM Acad. Search Consultants Internat. Inc., 1991-94. Author articles, monographs, chpts. in books; editor: Jour. Farm Econs, 1958-60. Bd. dirs. Univ. Corp. Atmospheric Rsch., 1962-67, Ctr. for Rsch. Librs., 1969-71, Argonne Univ. Assocs., 1978-84, USN Meml. Found., 1995-2000, sec., 1998-2000, trustee, 2001—; docent Navy Mus., Washington Navy Yard, 1997-2000. Lt. USNR, 1942-46. Decorated Commendation medal; recipient Kiekhofer Teaching award U. Wis., 1953 Mem.: AAUP (pres. U. Wis. 1957), Nat. Trust for Hist. Preservation, Am./Schleswig Holstein Heritage Soc. (adv. com. 1999—), U.S.-Indonesian Soc. Washington, Am. Agrl. Econs. Assn. (v.p. 1960), Navy Club of USA-Ship 1 (chaplain 2002—), Rotary Internat., Phi Beta Kappa, Phi Kappa Phi, Alpha Zeta. Home: 1909 Shaw Woods Dr Rockford IL 61107-1729

CLOGAN, PAUL MAURICE, English language and literature educator; b. Boston, July 9, 1934; s. Michael J. and Agnes J. (Murphy) C.; m. Julie Sydney Davis, July 27, 1972 (div. 1982); children: Michael Rodger, Patrick Terence, Margaret Murphy. BA, Boston Coll., 1956, MA, 1957; PhD, U. Ill., 1961; F.AAR., Am. Acad. in Rome, 1966; MDiv, Blessed John XXIII Sem., 1999. Asst. prof. Duke U., 1961-65; assoc. prof. Case Western Res. U., Cleve., 1965-72; prof. English U. North Tex., Denton, 1972—. Vis. prof. U. Keele, Eng., 1965, U. Pisa, Italy, 1966, U. Tours, France, 1978; vis. mem. Inst. Advanced Study, Princeton, N.J., 1970, 77; cons. Library of Congress, Ednl. Testing Service, NEH, Nat. Acad. Scis., NRC Commn. Human Resources, Nation Rsch. Council Comn. for the Study of Rsch.-Doctorate-Programs in the U.S., Am. Council Learned Socs., Nat. Enquiry into Scholarly Communication, Chilton Research Services; mem. Am. Arts Assn., Inst. Internat. Edn., nat. screening com. 1984-88. Author: The Medieval Achilleid of Statius, 1968, Social Dimensions in Medieval and Renaissance Studies, 1972, In Honor of S. Harrison Thomson, 1970, Medieval and Renaissance Studies in Review, 1971, Medieval and Renaissance Spirituality, 1973, Medieval Historiography, 1974, Medieval Hagiography and Romance, 1975, Medieval Poetics, 1976, Transformation and Continuity, 1977, Byzantine and Western Studies, 1984, Fourteenth and Fifteenth Centuries, 1986, The Early Renaissance, 1987, Literary Theory, 1988, Spectrum, 1992, Columbian Quincentenary, 1992, Renaissance and Discovery, 1993, Breaching the Boundaries, 1994, Convergences, 1994, Diversity, 1995, Historical Inquiries, 1997, Transitions, 1998, Civil Strife and National Identity in the Middle Ages, 1999, Literacy and the Lay Reader, 2000, Ethnicity and Self-Identity, 2002, Papal Letters, Manual for Confessors and Romance, 2003; editor: Medievalia et Humanistica, Studies in Medieval and Renaissance Culture, 1970—; contbr. articles to profl. jours. Grantee Duke Endowment l961-62, Am. Coun. Learned Socs., 1963-64, 70-71, 88, Am. Philos. Soc., 1964-69, U. North Tex., 1972-75, 80-81, 89; sr. Fulbright-Hays postdoctoral rsch. fellow, Italy, 1965-66, France, 1978, fellow Prix de Rome, 1966-67, Bollingen Found., 1966, NEH, l969-70, 86, 90-91. Mem. Internat. Assn. Univ. Profs. English, MLA (exec. com. 1980-86, del. assembly 1981-86), Internat. Comparative Lit. Assn., Internat. Arthurian Soc., Modern Humanities Research Assn., Medieval Acad. Am. (nominating com. 1975-76, John Nicholas Brown Prize com. 1981-83), Internat. Assn. for Neo-Latin Studies, The New Chaucer Soc., Fulbright Assn. Democrat. Roman Catholic.

CLOHESY, WILLIAM WARREN, philosopher, educator; b. Chgo., July 31, 1946; s. John Cecil and Mary Evelyn (Ahern) Clohesy; m. Stephanie June Jagucki, June 19, 1971. BS, Loyola U., Chgo., 1964-68; MA, So. Ill. U., 1968-71; PhD, New Sch. Social Rsch., N.Y.C., 1981. Instr. Loyola U., Chgo., 1967, asst. prof., 1982-83; tchg. asst. So. Ill. U., Carbondale, 1969; adj. prof. Montclair State Coll., Upper Montclair, NJ, 1981-82; asst. prof. Rochester (N.Y.) Inst. Tech., 1983-86, rsch. assoc., 1986-87; lectr. U. Belgrano, Buenos Aires, 1987; asst. prof. U. No. Iowa, Cedar Falls, 1987-93, assoc. prof., 1993—. BSN adv. com. Allen Coll., Waterloo, Iowa, 1991—2002; instnl. rev. bd. U. No. Iowa, 2002—. Editor: (book) Ethics at Work, 1992; contbr. articles to profl. jours. Recipient Kurt Riezler Meml. award, New Sch. for Social Rsch., 1982, Faculty Excellence award, Iowa Bd. Regents, 2001; fellow Fulbright fellowship to Argentina, 1987; grantee W.K. Kellogg Found., 1995—2001, Iowa Humanities Bd., 1991—92, NEH, 1991—92. Mem.: Soc. Advancement Am. Philosophy, N.Am. Kant Soc., N.Am. Soc. Social Philosophy, Hume Soc., Am. Philos. Assn., Internat. Soc. 3d Sector Rsch. Democrat. Roman Catholic. Avocation: Irish language, literature, and music. Office: U No Iowa Dept Philosophy & Religion Cedar Falls IA 50614-0501 E-mail: william.clohesy@uni.edu.

CLONINGER, CLAUDE ROBERT, psychiatric researcher, educator, genetic epidemiologist; b. Beaumont, Tex., Apr. 4, 1944; s. Morris Sheppard and Marie Concetta (Mazzagatti) C.; m. Sharon Lee Rogan, July 11, 1969; children: Bryan Joseph, Kevin Michael. BA U. Tex., 1966; MD, Washington U., St. Louis, 1970, (hon.) U. Umea, Sweden, 1983. Diplomate Am. Bd. Psychiatry and Neurology. Instr. psychiatry Washington U., St. Louis, 1973-74, asst. prof. 1974-78, assoc. prof., 1978-81, prof., 1981—, prof. genetics, 1978—, prof. psychology, 1989—, Wallace Renard prof. psychiatry, 1991—, head dept. psychiatry, 1989-94, dir. ctr. psychobiology personality, 1994—; psychiatrist-in-chief Barnes and Renard Hosps., St. Louis, 1989-94; vis. prof. U. Hawaii, Honolulu, 1978-79, U. Umea, Sweden, 1980; chmn. NIMH psychopathology Review Com., Washington, 1980-84; cons. WHO, Geneva, 1981—, Am. Psychiatric Assn., Washington, 1978—, Nat. Inst. on Alcohol Abuse and Alcoholism, 1984-99, Inst. Medicine, 1986; chmn. genetics initiative schizophrenia NIMH, 1989-97; mental health commr. State of Mo., 1990-95. Author 6 books; editor: Jour. Behavior Genetics, 1980-86, Am. Jour. Human Genetics, 1980-83; assoc. editor Genetic Epidemiology, 1983-92, Human Heredity, 1989—; mem. editl. bd. Arch. Gen. Psychiatry, Comprehensive Psychiatry, Neuropsychopharmacology, Jour. Comprehensive Psychiatry, Jour. Psychiat. Rsch., Jour. Med. Genetics; contbr. articles to profl. jours. Recipient Rsch. Scientist award NIMH, 1975, 80, 85, Strecker award Inst. Pa. Hosp., 1988, James B. Isaacson award, ISBRA, 1992, Lifetime Achievement award Am. Soc. of Addiction Medicine, 2000, Finnish Psychiatry Assn. Annual Medal, Fellow AAAS, Am. Psychiat. Assn. (Adolph Meyer award, 1993), Am. Psychopathol. Assn. (treas. 1984-89, v.p. 1990, pres. 1991-93, sec. 1994-96, Samuel Hamilton award 1993); mem. Am. Soc. Human Genetics (editl. bd. 1980-83), Behavior Genetics Assn. (editl. bd. 1980—), Inst. Medicine of NAS, Rsch. Soc. Alcoholism (bd. dirs. 1987-90). Avocations: gardening, reading, travel. Home: 7100 Delmar Blvd Saint Louis MO 63130-4303 Office: Washington U Dept of Psychiatry 4940 Childrens Pl Saint Louis MO 63110-1002

CLONINGER, KRISS, III, insurance company executive; b. Houston, Oct. 21, 1947; s. Kriss and Jewel JoAnn (Jones) C.; m. Lisa L. Welch; children: Laura Kay, Kriss Alan; stepchildren: J. Tanner Prewit, Presley N. Lanier. BBA, U. Tex, 1969, MBA, 1971. Actuary KPMG Peat Marwick, Dallas, 1973-74, Atlanta, 1977-92, Rudd & Wisdom, Austin, Tex., 1974-77; pres. and CFO AFLAC Inc., Columbus, Ga., 1992—, bd. dirs., 2001—. Bd. dirs. Tupperware Corp. Served to 1st lt. USAF, 1971-73 Fellow Soc. Actuaries; mem. Am. Acad. Actuaries Home: 612 Front Ave Columbus GA 31901-2924 Office: AFLAC Ctr 1932 Wynnton Rd Columbus GA 31999-0002 E-mail: kcloninger@aflac.com.

CLONTS, GEORGE GARY, packaging company executive; b. Alton, Ill., Mar. 22, 1940; s. George William and Fern Lorene (Miller) C.; m. Charlotte Joann Shelburn, Feb. 28, 1960; children: George Randall, Gary Deneal. Aero. engring. student, USAF, 1957-1961. Flight engr. USAF, Fairbanks, Alaska, 1957-61; prodn. worker Hoerner Boxes, Inc., Springfield, Mo., 1961-64, office mgr. Denver, 1964-69; sales rep. Hoerner Waldorf, Inc., Denver, 1969-72, South West Packaging, Oklahoma City, 1972-77, gen. mgr., 1977-87, Green Bay Packaging, Oklahoma City, 1987-88; pres., chief exec. officer Tech Pack, Inc., Oklahoma City, 1988—2001. Active Rep. Presdl. Task Force, Washington, 1982—. With USAF, 1957-61. Mem. Petroleum Club Okla., Gaillardia Golf and Country Club. Avocations: golf, antique automobiles, history. Home: 11729 Hackney Ln Yukon OK 73099-8130

CLOONAN, JAMES BRIAN, investment executive; b. Chgo., Jan. 28, 1931; s. Bernard V. and Lauretta D. (Maloney) C.; m. Edythe Adrianne Ratner, Mar. 26, 1970; children: Michele, Christine, Mia; stepchildren: Carrie Madorin, Harry Madorin. Prof. Sch. Bus. Loyola U., Chgo., 1966-71; pres. Quantitative Decision Sys., Inc., Chgo., 1972-73; chmn. bd. Heinold Securities, Inc., Chgo., 1974-77; prof. grad. sch. bus. DePaul U., Chgo., 1978-82; chmn. Investment Info. Svcs., 1981-86; pres. Mktg. Sys. Internat. Inc., 1985-87, Analytics Sys. Inc., 1987—. Bd. dirs., chmn. Mktg. Svcs. Internat., Inc. Author: Estimates of the Impact of Sign and Billboard Removal Under the Highway Beautification Act of 1965, 1966, Stock Options-The Application of Decision Theory to Basic and Advanced Strategies, 1973; An Introduction to Decision Making for the Individual Investor, 1980, Expanding Your Investment Horizons, 1983, A Lifetime Strategy for Investing in Common Stocks, 1988, Maximum Return Minimum Risk, 2003. Mem.: Am. Assn. Individual Investors (pres. 1979—92, chmn. 1992—), Am. Mktg. Assn. Home: 1242 N Lake Shore Dr Chicago IL 60610-2361 Office: Am Assn Individual Investors 625 N Michigan Ave Chicago IL 60611-3110 E-mail: jbcaaii@aol.com.

CLOONAN, PATRICK MICHAEL, radio producer, writer; b. Pitts., Oct. 13, 1954; s. Joseph Patrick and Margaret (Leister) C.; married. BA in Journalism, Pa. State U., 1976. Freelance journalist AP, 1975-82, 89—; news dir. WNCC-AM, Barnesboro, Pa., 1976-82; assignment editor WTAJ-TV, Altoona, Pa., 1982-83; editor, reporter News Publishing Co., Homestead, Pa., 1984-85; cashier's clk. Legg Mason Masten Inc., Pitts., 1986-87; columnist Expression, Pitts., 1986-97; freelance corr. Post-Gazette, Pitts., 1989-92; freelance journalist CBS Radio Network, N.Y.C., 1989-2000; prodr. KQV-AM, Pitts., 1989-2000; commentator WPLW-AM, Pitts., 1996-97; news writer WPXI-TV, Pitts., 1997-98; staff writer Daily News, McKeesport, Pa., 2000—. Editor The Keystone State Times Newsletter, Munhall, Pa., 1997-2001; contbr. articles to newspapers. Vol. Bush-Quayle '88, Pitts., 1988, Robertson for Pres., Pitts., 1987; Munhall, Pa., Mayor's adv. bd. rep. Salvation Army, Homestead, Pa., 1985-87. Mem.: South Hills Coin Club (newsletter writer 1988). Roman Catholic. Avocations: reading, travel, shortwave radio, dogs, lay ministry. E-mail: acloonan@highvision.net.

CLOONEY, GEORGE, actor; b. Lexington, Kentucky, May 6, 1961; s. Nick C.; m. Talia Blasam (div.). Actor: (TV series) E/R, 1984—85, The Facts of Life, 1985—86, Roseanne, 1988—89, Sunset Beat, 1990, Baby Talk, 1991, Sisters, 1992—94, ER, 1994—99; (films) Return of the Killer Tomatoes, 1988, Red Surf, 1990, Unbecoming Age, 1992, One Fine Day, 1996, Batman & Robin, 1997, From Dusk Till Dawn, 1996, The Peacemaker, 1997, The Thin Red Line, 1998, Out of Sight, 1998, Three Kings, 1999, (voice) South Park: Bigger, Longer and Uncut, 1999, O Brother, Where Art Thou, 2000, The Perfect Storm, 2000, Ocean's Eleven, 2001, Spy Kids, 2001, Solaris, 2002, Spy Kids 3-D: Game Over, 2003, Intolerable Cruelty, 2003; prodr., writer: (films) Kilroy, 1999; prodr., actor: (films) Fail Safe, 2000; actor, dir.: (films) Confessions of a Dangerous Mind, 2002. Recipient SAE awards, 1998, 99. Office: Creative Artist 9830 Wilshire Blvd Beverly Hills CA 90212-1804*

CLORE, LAWRENCE HUBERT, lawyer; b. Tulsa, July 31, 1944; s. Hubert Charles and Jessie Louada (Fowler) C.; m. Carol Jean Roegelein, June 3, 1967 (div. 1981); children: Robert William, James Lawrence; m. Martha Jo Lawyer; children: Kathryn Denise, Michael Hubert. BBA, Tex. Christian U., 1966; JD, U. Tex., 1969. Bar: Tex. 1969. Assoc. Fulbright & Jaworski, Houston, 1971-77, ptnr., 1977—. Capt. U.S. Army, 1969-71, Vietnam. Mem. ABA, Tex. Bar Assn. (labor and employment sect., coun. 1990-93, vice chair 1993-94, chair 1994-95), Indsl. Rels. Rsch. Assn., Houston Mgmt. Lawyers Forum (chmn. 1976-77). Republican. Methodist. Avocations: hunting, fishing, golf. Office: Fulbright & Jaworski 1301 Mckinney St Ste 5100 Houston TX 77010-3031 E-mail: lclore@fulbright.com.

CLOS, LYNNE MOBLEY, magazine publisher, paleontologist; b. Baton Rouge, Sept. 2, 1955; d. Ralph C. and Theodora A. Mobley; m. Christopher J. Clos, Sept. 14, 1979; children: Allison Lee, Mattie Michelle. BSME with dept.

honors, Oakland U., 1978; M Basic Sci. in Mus. Studies, U. Colo., 1991. Corrosion engr. GM Proving Ground, Milford, Mich., 1979-81; product engr. Rockwell Internat., Golden, Colo., 1981-87; paleontology demonstrator Denver Mus. Natural History, 1989; free-lance writer Boulder, 1990-97; editor, pub. Fossil News, Boulder, 1998—. Contbr. numerous articles on paleontology to sci. jour., including Jour. Vertebrate Paleontology, Fossil News; costume designer Kinetic Sculpture Challenge, 1984-89. Vol. paleontology dept. Denver Mus. Natural History, 1988-96; vol. Ross Perot Campaign, Boulder, 1992; guest spkr. on paleontology to local schs., Boulder, 1994—; paleontology mentor for jr. high and high sch. students over internet, 1999. Recipient award for ednl. excellnece in web site Field Study Web, 1999. Mem. Soc. Vertebrate Paleontology, Western Interior Paleontol. Soc. (bd. dirs. 1988-89, 98-00, newsletter editor 1994-00), Cycad Soc. (bd. dir. 1990-2001), Tau Beta Pi. Avocations: mac computers, horticulture (cycads), reading, travel. Office: Fossil News 1185 Claremont Dr Boulder CO 80305-6601 E-mail: lynne@fossilnews.com.

CLOSE, DAVID PALMER, lawyer; b. N.Y.C., Mar. 16, 1915; s. Walter Harvey and Louise De Arango (Palmer) C.; m. Margaret Howell Gordon, June 26, 1954 (dec. July 1992); children: Louise, Peter, Katharine, Barbara. BA, Williams Coll., 1938; JD, Columbia U., 1942; LHD, Mount Vernon Coll., 1998. Bar: N.Y. State bar 1942. Practice law, Washington, 1946—; ptnr. Dahlgren & Close. Mem. adv. council Nat. Capital area Boy Scouts Am., 1961— ; bd. dirs. Nat. Soc. Prevention Blindness, 1961-63, Internat. Eye Found., 1965—, chmn., 1985-89; bd. dirs. D.C. Soc. Prevention of Blindness, 1957-63, pres., 1961-63; bd. dirs. Internat. Humanities, Inc., 1960—, pres., 1989—; bd. dirs. Marjorie Merriweather Post Found., 1974—, sec.-treas., 1974-76, sec., 1991—; trustee Williams Coll., 1963-68; trustee Hill Sch., 1965-85, chmn., 1973-85 ; trustee Mount Vernon Coll., 1963-75, bd. pres., 1971-74; mem. am. coun. UN U., 1980—. Served with O.N.I., USN, 1942-46. Mem. ABA, Inter-Am. Bar Assn., D.C. Bar Assn., Assn. Bar City of N.Y., Pilgrims, Order of St. John, Chevy Chase (Md.) Club, Fauquier Springs Country Club (Warrenton, Va.), Univ. Club (Washington). Home: 40 Hungry Run Farm Ln Amissville VA 20106-4017 Office: Dahlgren & Close 1000 Connecticut Ave NW Ste 204 Washington DC 20036-5337 E-mail: dahlgrenclose@cs.com.

CLOSE, DONALD PEMBROKE, management consultant; b. Orange, N.J., July 11, 1920; s. Charles Mollison and Simah Close; m. L. Carolyn Reck, Apr. 22, 1950 (dec. Mar. 1983); children: Geoffrey Stuart, Cynthia Leigh, Sara Carolyn; m. Diane M. Wisdo Kendzor, Dec. 31, 1996. BS in Econs., U. Pa., 1942. Sales rep. IBM, Newark, 1946-47; asst. budget dir. L. Bamberger & Co., Newark, 1947-53; staff exec. Am. Express, N.Y.C., 1953; contr., sec. Ciba Co., Inc., N.Y.C., 1953-59; dir. fin. and control Avon Products Inc., N.Y.C., 1960-72; pres. Corp. Fin. Assocs., Inc., N.Y.C., 1973-76; v.p. Nelson Walker Assocs., N.Y.C., 1973-76, Internat. Mgmt. Advisors, Inc., N.Y.C., 1976-86; prin. Deven Assocs. Internat. Inc., N.Y.C., 1986-91, The Pembroke Close Mgmt. Group, N.Y.C., 1991—. Mem. Pvt. Sector Study on Cost Control in Fed. Govt., 1982. Trustee Morristown (N.J.) Beard Sch., 1974-77; pres. Jr. Essex Troop Calvary, 1964-68. With U.S. Army, 1942—45. Decorated Bronze Star with oak leaf cluster, Letter of Commendation, N.J. Disting. Svc. medal with oak leaf cluster. Mem. Fin. Execs. Inst., Am. Soc. Corp. Secs., Systems and Procedures Assn., Internat. Assn. Accts., Human Resources Planning Soc., Group for Strategic Organizational Effectiveness, St. Andrews Soc. N.Y., St. George's Soc. N.Y., Navy League U.S., 102d Inf. Divsn. Assn., U.S. Naval Inst., Campbell Soc., Internat. Assn. Corp. and Profl. Recruiters, Human Resources Exch. Assn., Univ. Club (N.Y.C.), Morristown Club, Wharton Club, Essex Hunt Club, Burnt Mills Polo Club, Phi Sigma Kappa (past sec.). Republican. Episcopalian. Home: 6 Ridge Rd Gladstone NJ 07934-2000 Office: The Pembroke Close Mgmt Group PO Box 226 Gladstone NJ 07934-0226

CLOSE, ELIZABETH SCHEU, retired architect; b. Vienna, June 4, 1912; came to U.S., 1932, naturalized, 1938; d. Gustav and Helene (Riesz) Scheu; m. Winston A. Close, 1938; children: Anne Miriam Close Ulmer, Roy Michel, Robert Arthur. Student, Technische Hochschule, Vienna, 1931-32; B.Arch., MIT, 1934, M.Arch., 1935; LHD (hon.), U Minn. Coll. of Arch., 2003. Draftsman Oscar Stonorov, Architect, Phila., 1935-36; designer Magney & Tusler, Mpls., 1936-38; ptnr., architect Elizabeth and Winston Close (changed to Close Assos., Inc., 1969), Mpls., 1938-92. Instr. Mpls. Sch. Art, 1936-37; instr. design U. Minn. Sch. Architecture, 1938-39 Prin. works include Garden City Devel, Brooklyn Center, Minn., 1957, Duff House, variety structures Met. Med. Center Complex, 1960-75, Golden Age Homes, 1960, Peavey Tech. Center, Chaska, Minn., 1970, Gray Freshwater Biol. Inst., Orono, Minn., 1974, U. Minn. Music Bldg., Mpls., 1985, Internat. Sch. Minn., Eden Prairie, 1988. Bd. dirs. Civic Orch. Mpls., 1951-68; bd. dirs. Minn. Opera Co.; past pres. New Friends Chamber Music; mem. Commn. on Minn.'s Future. Recipient Honor award Pub. Housing Adminstrn., 1964; hon. mention F.D. Roosevelt Meml. competition, 1960, 25 Yr. award MSAIA, 1988; named Outstanding Woman of Yr., YWCA, 1983, Gold Medal for Lifetime Achievement award Minn. chpt. Am. Inst. of Arch., 2002. Fellow AIA (dir. Mpls. chpt. 1964-69, jury of Fellows 1986-87, recipient Gold medal Minn. chpt., 2002); mem. Minn. Soc. Architects (pres., Honor award 1975), Minn. Hist. Soc. (jury bldg. competition 1986). Home: 1588 Fulham Ave Saint Paul MN 55108-1312

CLOSE, GLENN, actress; b. Greenwich, Conn., Mar. 19, 1947; d. William and Bettine Close; m. Cabot Wade (div.); m. James Marlas, 1984 (div.); 1 child, Annie Maude Starke BA, Coll. William and Mary, 1974. Profl. actress; also accomplished mus. performer (lyric soprano). Co-owner The Leaf and Bean Coffee House, Bozeman, Montana, 1991—. Joined New Phoenix Repertory Co., 1974; made Broadway debut in Love for Love; other Broadway appearences include The Rules of the Game, The Member of the Wedding, 1974-75, Rex, Barnum, 1980-81 (Tony award nominee), The Real Thing, 1984-85 (Tony award for Best Actress in Drama), Benefactors, 1986, Wine Untouched, Death and the Maiden, 1992 (Drama League N.Y. Distinguished Performance award, 1992, Tony award for Best Actress in Drama, 1992), Sunset Boulevard, 1994-95 (Tony award Lead Actress in a Musical, 1995); other theatre appearences include Uncommon Women and Others, The Singular Life of Albert Nobbs, 1982 (Obie award), Childhood, 1985, one performance oratorio Joan of Arc at the Stake, 1985, Sunset Boulevard (L.A.), 1993-94, The Vagina Monologues, 1998 and other repertory and regional theatres; films include The World According to Garp, 1982 (Acad. award nominee), The Big Chill, 1983 (Acad. award nominee), The Natural, 1984 (Acad. award nominee), Greystoke: The Legend of Tarzan, Lord of the Apes (voice), 1984, The Stone Boy, 1984, Maxie, 1985, Jagged Edge, 1985, Fatal Attraction, 1987, Light Years (voice), 1988, Dangerous Liaisons, 1988, Immediate Family, 1989, Reversal of Fortune, 1990, Hamlet, 1990, Hook (cameo), 1991, Meeting Venus, 1991, The House of the Spirits, 1994, The Paper, 1994, 101 Dalmations, Mars Attacks!, 1996, Air Force One, 1997, Paradise Road, 1997, Cookie's Fortune, 1999, Things You Can Tell Just by Looking at Her, 2000, 102 Dalmatians, 2000, The Safety of Objects, 2001; TV films include Too Far To Go, 1979, Orphan Train, 1979, The Elephant Man, 1982, Something about Amelia, 1984 (Emmy award nominee), The Elephant's Child (host), 1987, The Emperor's New Clothes (host), 1987, The Legend of Sleepy Hollow (narrator), 1988, Stones for Ibarra, 1988, (also exec. prodr.) Sarah, Plain and Tall, 1991, Skylark, 1993 (Emmy award nomine for Lead Actress in a Miniseries, 1993), Serving in Silence: The Margarethe Cammermeyer Story, 1995 (Emmy award), In the Gloaming, 1997, Sarah, Plain and Tall: Winter's End, 1999, The Ballad of Lucy Whipple, 2001, South Pacific, 2001, The Girl in Hyacinth Blue, 2002. Recipient Woman of Yr. award Hasty Pudding Theatricals, 1990, Dartmouth Film Soc. award, 1990. Mem. Phi Beta Kappa Office: Creative Artists Agy 9830 Wilshire Blvd Beverly Hills CA 90212-1804*

CLOSE, LANNY GARTH, otolaryngologist, educator; b. San Antonio, Aug. 13, 1946; s. James Garth and Nona Lee (Galbraith) C.; m. Sharron Maredith Smith, Nov. 22, 1980; children: Hunter, Maredith. BA summa cum laude, Tex. Tech. U., 1968; MD cum laude, Baylor Coll. Medicine, 1972. Diplomate Am. Bd. Otolaryngology. Resident in surgery Johns Hopkins Hosp., Balt., 1972-74; resident in otolaryngology Baylor Affiliated Hosps., Houston, 1974-77; asst/assoc. prof. otolaryngology U. Tex., Houston, 1977-82; asst. surgeon dept. head & neck surgery M.D. Anderson Hosp., Houston, 1978-79; from assoc. prof. to prof. otolaryngology U. Tex. Southwestern Med. Sch., Dallas, 1982-94; prof., chmn. dept. otolaryngology/head and neck surgery Columbia U., N.Y.C., 1994—. Guest examiner Am. Bd. Otolaryngology, 1993, 94, 96, 97; pres.-elect Columbia-Presbyn. Med. Bd. Contbr. numerous articles to profl. jours. Fellow ACS, Am. Laryngological Assn., The Triological Soc., Am. Rhinological Assn., Am. Broncho Esophageal Assn., Am. Soc. for Head & Neck Surgery, Soc. of Head and Neck Surgery; mem. Johns Hopkins Soc. Scholars, Alpha Omega Alpha. Office: Coll Physicians & Surgeons Columbia U 630 W 168th St New York NY 10032-3702

CLOSE, MICHAEL JOHN, lawyer; b. Sandusky, Ohio, Jan. 24, 1943; s. Robert J. and Mary Lee (Graefe) C.; m. Nancy L. Schelp, June 18, 1995; children: Christina C., Karen L. AB in History, Lafayette Coll., Easton, Pa., 1965; JD cum laude, U. Mich., 1968. Assoc. Dewey, Ballantine, Bushby, Palmer & Wood, N.Y.C., 1968-76; ptnr. Dewey Ballantine, N.Y.C., 1976-96. Chmn. Tax Rev., N.Y.C. Author: Tax Aspects of Oil and Gas Drilling Funds, 1972, Drilling Funds: The 1977 Perspective, 1977, Special Allocations in Oil and Gas Ventures, 1982, The Final Section 704 (b) Regulations: Special Allocations Reach New Heights of Complexity, 1986, Fringe Benefit Regulation and the New York Law Firm Culture: A New Era, 1989, Off Balance Sheet Financings, 1994; contbr. articles to profl. jours. Bd. dirs., adminstrv. vice-chmn. Conn. Swimming, Inc., 1992-99; chmn. ad-hoc com. on by-laws USA Swimming, Inc., 1995-96; bd. dirs. Sharks Swim Team, Inc., 1991-94, pres., 1992-94. Mem. ABA (mem. tax sect. com. on partnerships), Assn. of Bar of City of N.Y., N.Y. Law Inst. (life mem.), N.Y. State Bar Assn. (mem. tax sect. com. partnerships), Ohio State Bar Assn., India House (N.Y.C.), Burning Tree Country Club (Greenwich), Meadows Country Club (Sarasota, Fla.), Phi Delta Phi, Theta Chi. Republican. Home: 4951 Windsor Pk Sarasota FL 34235-2610 E-mail: thecloses@comcast.net.

CLOSE, THOMAS JAMES, school administrator; b. Adrian, Mich., Oct. 9, 1935; s. James Thomas and Katherin Bellenir Close; m. Beatrice L. Close, July 26, 1961 (div. Feb. 1990); m. Sandra Lee McAnaleen, Aug. 9, 1993; children: Thomas James, Jonathon D., Julia S. AB, St. Joseph Coll., 1958; MA, Cen. Mich. U., 1969, EdS, 1973; EdD, Calif. Coast U., 1999. LPC, Mich. Tchr. Kalkaska (Mich.) Pub. Sch., asst. prin., A.D., sch. counselor, sch./cmty. adminstr.

CLOSEN, MICHAEL LEE, law educator; b. Peoria, Ill., Jan. 25, 1949; s. Stanley Paul and Dorothy Mae (Kendall) Closen. BS, Bradley U., 1971, MS, 1971; JD, U. Ill., 1974. Bar: Ill. 1974; notary pub. Ill. Instr. U. Ill., Champaign, 1974; jud. clk. Ill. Appellate Ct., Springfield, 1974-76, 77-78; asst. states atty. Cook County, Chgo., 1978; prof. law John Marshall Law Sch., Chgo., 1976—2003. Reporter Ill. Jud. Conf., Chgo., 1981—; arbitrator Am. Arbitration Assn., Chgo., 1981—; lectr. Ill. Inst. Continuing Legal Edn., Chgo., 1981—; vis. prof. No. Ill. U., 1985—86, adj. prof., 1990, St. Thomas U., 1991, Loyola U., Chgo., 1999—2002; vis. prof. U. Ark., 1993, 96; arbitrator Cook County Cir. Ct. Mandatory Arbitration Program, 1990—2003, Will County Cir. Ct. Mandatory Arbitration Program, 1996—2003; dir. Ctr. for Legal Edn., Ltd., 1995—96. Author: (casebook) Agency and Partnership Law, 1984, Agency and Partnership Law, 3d edit., 2000; author: (with others) Contracts, 1984, Contracts, 3d edit., 1992, AIDS Cases and Materials, 1989, AIDS Cases and Materials, 3d edit., 2002, Notary Law and Practice, 1997, Contract Law and Practice, 1998; co-author: (book) The Shopping Bag: Portable Art, 1986, AIDS Law in a Nutshell, 1991, AIDS Law in a Nutshell, 2d edit., 1996, Legal Aspects of AIDS, 1991; contbr. articles to profl. jours. Named One of Outstanding Young Men in Am., 1981; recipient Svc. award, Am. Arbitration Assn., 1984—85, 5-Yr. Cmty. Achievement award, Ill. Politics Mag., 1998. Mem.: Notary Law Inst., Am. Soc. Notaries, Nat. Notary Assn. (Achievement award 1998). Home: 1243 Motorcoach Polk City FL 33868-9774 Office: John Marshall Law Sch 315 S Plymouth Ct Chicago IL 60604-3968

CLOSS, JAMES WILLIAM, retired non-commissioned officer, financial analyst, educator; b. Buffalo, Nov. 15, 1950; s. Charles Howard and Beatrice Florence Closs; children: Anne P. Childers, James W. Closs II, Lisa K. AAS in Lab. Tech., CC of the Air Force, Robins AFB, Ga, 1990, AAS in Instr. of Tech. and Mil. Scie, 1991, AAS in Pers. Adminstrn., 1992; AAS in Electronic Comm. Mgmt., Ga. Mil. Coll., Milledgeville, Ga, 1991—93; AA in Gen. Studies, Ga. Mil. Coll., Milledgeville, 1991—93; BS in Criminal Justice, Mercer U., Macon, Ga, 1995—96; MPA, Ga. Coll.and State U., Milledgeville, Ga, 1998. Automobile Claims Law Assoc.: Am. Ednl. Inst. 2003; cert. Aerospace Mgr. USAF, 1992. Adminstrv. specialist USAF Reserves, Niagara Falls, NY, 1969—72; automatic tracking radar technician USAF, Richmond, Ky., 1973—79, sci. analysis technician - depot mgmt. McClellan AFB, Calif., 1979—82, sci. analysis technician - hdqs. Patrick AFB, Fla., 1981—82; sci. analysis technician Linsdey Air Sta., Wiesbaden, Germany, 1982—85; systems repair technician USAF, Wheeler AFB, Hawaii, 1985—88, noncommissioned officer acad. instr. Robins AFB, Ga., 1988—91, 1st sgt., 1991—94; personal fin. analyst Primerica Fin. Svcs., Stockbridge, Ga., 2003—. Prof. Polit. Sci. Gordon Coll., Barnesville, Ga., 2000—; cert. continuing edn. instr. Ga. Dept. of Ins., Macon, Ga., 2001—; ind. mktg. exec. Melaleuca, The Wellness Co., Covington, Ga. Dist. commr. BSA, Macon, Ga., 1988, membership com. chmn. Covington. Named Non. Commissioned Acad. Instr. of Yr., USAF Logistics Command, 1991; recipient Silver Beaver, BSA, 1992, Disting. Commr., 1993, Dist. Award of Merit, 1991. Mem.: DAV, VFW (life; chpt. trustee 1993—95, post trustee 1993—95), Mil. Order of the Cootie (provost marshal 1994—96), United Armed Forces Assn., The Ret. Enlisted Assn., Non Commd. Officers Assn., Nat. Assn. for Uniformed Services, Air Force Sergeants Assn. (v.p. 1992, chpt. pres. 1992—93, trustee 1993—95, pres. award 1994—95). Avocation: travel. Home: 100 Pebble Brooke Pass Covington GA 30016-3905 Mailing: PO Box 81398 Conyers GA 30013 Personal E-mail: jwcloss@iglide.net.

CLOSSET, GERARD PAUL, forest products consultant; b. Longwy, France, Nov. 17, 1943; came to U.S., 1965, naturalized, 1976; s. Robert Joseph and Renee (Jacquemet) C.; m. Nicki Lynn Okin, June 29, 1968; children: Juliette, Jennifer. BS, U. Pitts., 1966, MS, 1968, PhD, 1973. Engr. Allied Chem. Corp., Morristown, N.J., 1968-69; rsch. engr. Westvaco Corp., Laurel, Md., 1973-77; mgr. coating St. Regis Paper Co., West Nyack, N.Y., 1977-83, dir. materials, 1983-85; dir. papermaking Champion Internat., 1985-87, v.p. tech., 1987-96, v.p. applied techs., 1996-2000; prin. Closset Cons., Pomona, N.Y., 2000—. Industry cons., 2000—. Contbr. articles to profl. jours. Pres. Rockland Suburban Symphony, 1984-89; bd. dirs. Rockland County Assn., 1987-92. Fellow TAPPI (past chmn., rsch. mgmt. com., trustee TAPPI found.); mem. AIChE, Am. Forest Products Assn. (past chmn. agenda 2020 com.). Avocations: photography, skiing, scuba diving.

CLOSSEY, DAVID F. lawyer; b. Cleve., Jan. 31, 1944; s. William M. and Josephine Clossey; m. Jeanne Marie Ives, June 15, 1967; 1 child, Sarah Woodson. A.B., Georgetown U., 1965; J.D., Cornell U., 1968. Bar: Ohio 1968, Tex. 1981. Assoc. Jones, Day, Reavis & Pogue, Cleve., 1968-74, ptnr., 1974-81, ptnr.-in-charge, Dallas, 1981-84, regional mng. ptnr., 1984— ; dir. TBS Internat., Inc., Dallas. Trustee Dallas Ballet, 1982— ; bd. govs. Dallas Symphony Assn., 1983— ; mem. corp. council Dallas Mus. Art, 1983— . Recipient Fraser award Cornell U., 1968. Mem. ABA, Dallas Bar Assn., Order of Coif. Home: 3727 Beverly Dr Dallas TX 75205-2805

CLOSSON, WALTER FRANKLIN, child support prosecutor; b. Phila., Dec. 24, 1944; s. David Mayard Jr. and Florence Louise (Anderson) C.; m. Irene Veronica Jones, Aug. 10, 1968; children: Forrest Troy, Carey-Walter Franklin. BS in Music Edn., West Chester U., 1967; JD, Potomac Sch. Law, Washington, 1981. Bar: Ga. 1983, Md. 1985. Tchr. music D.C. Pub. Schs., Washington, 1967-77; tchr. woodwinds D.C. Youth Orch. Program, Washington, 1969-71; dist. ct. commr. Dist. Ct. of Md., Ellicott City, 1978-89; supervising dist. ct. commr. Dist. Ct. of Howard County, Ellicott City, 1984-89; asst. state's atty. State's Atty.'s Office, Ellicott City, 1989-99, chief child support divsn., 1999-2000; supervising atty. Bur. of Supoort Enforcement, Howard County Dept. Social Svcs., Columbia, Md., 2000—. Mem.. Howard County Bar Assn., Waring-Mitchell Law Soc. (pres. 1992-94, Man of Yr. 1990), Masons (sr. deacon 1996-97, sr. warden 1997-98, worshipful master, 1998-99, Lodz treas. 2002-), Delta Theta Phi (v.p. 1979-80). Office: Howard County Dept Social Svcs 7121 Columbia Gateway Dr Columbia MD 21046 E-mail: walt024@earthlink.net.

CLOTHIER, JEFFREY LANE, neuropsychiatrist, educator; b. Plainview, Tex., Mar. 18, 1957; s. Gale Joseph and Mary Jo Clothier; m. Risa McSpadden, Dec. 29, 1956; children: Amy Nicole, Matthew Travis. MD, U. Tex., 1982. Diplomate Diplomate Am. Bd. Psychiatry and Neurology, 1989. Assoc. prof. U. Ark. for Med. Scis., Little Rock, 1990—; acting assoc. chief staff for mental health Ctrl. Ark. Veterans Healthcare Sys., 2001—. Mem. UAMS Founder's Soc., Little Rock, 1996—2002. Recipient Emil Eckart award, UAMS Dept. Psychiatry, 1992, Golden Apple Tchg. award, UAMS, 1996, 2000, Tchr. Yr. award- Region 7, Assn. for Academic Psychiatry, 1997, Robert Shannon, M.D. award, UAMS Dept. of Psychiatry, 2000, 2001. Mem.: Ark. Psychiat. Soc. (disaster com. chmn. 2002), Assn. Convulsive Therapy, Am. Psychiat. Assn. Avocations: golf, cooking, gardening. Office: Ctrl Ark Vets Adminstrn 2200 Fort Roots Dr North Little Rock AR Personal E-mail: clothier@swbell.net. E-mail: clothier.jeffreyl@med.va.gov.

CLOTWORTHY, JOHN HARRIS, oceanographic consultant; b. Balt., Mar. 23, 1924; s. Harris A. and Violet (Klein) C.; m. Martha D. Wilson, Mar. 22, 1947; 1 son, John S. B.E.E., U. Va., 1946; certificate, Harvard Bus. Sch., 1956. Registered profl. engr., Md. With Westinghouse Electric Corp., 1948-67, v.p. def. and space center, gen. mgr. underseas div., 1963-67; chmn. div. ocean engrng. U. Miami, Fla., 1967-68; cons. to oceanographic industry, 1967-68; founder, pres. Oceans Gen., Inc., Miami, 1968-71; dir. office congl. and legislative affairs NOAA, Washington, 1971-78; v.p., gen. mgr. Joint Oceanographic Instns. Inc., Washington, 1978-88, cons., 1988—. Sec., v.p. Oak Bldg. & Savs. Assn., 1946-56; Bd. govs. Va. Engrng. Found., 1965-68, 72-78 Trustee, co-chmn., bd. advisors Mare Nostrum Found., 1986-88. Fellow Marine Tech. Soc. (founding mem., bd. dirs. 1966-69, chmn. silver anniversary com. 1986-88, Lockheed award for ocean sci. and engrng. 1992); mem. AAAS, Am. Geophys. Union, Am. Guild Organists, Nat. Oceanography Assn. (pres. 1966-69), Internat. Club of Annapolis (pres. 1995-96), Annapolis Yacht Club, Atlantic City Convention Hall Organ Soc. (sec., treas. 1998), Alpha Tau Omega. Home: 2014 Gov Thomas Bladen Way Apt #201 Annapolis MD 21401

CLOUD, BRUCE BENJAMIN, SR., construction company executive; b. Thomas, Okla., Feb. 15, 1920; s. Dudley R. and Lillian (Sanders) C.; m. Virginia Dugan, June 5, 1944; children: Sheila Marie Cloud Kiselis, Karen Susan, Bruce Benjamin, Deborah Ann Cloud McKenzie, Virginia Ann Cloud Treadwell. BCE, Tex. A. and M. U., 1940. Registered profl. engr., Tex. With H.B. Zachry Co., San Antonio, 1940-42, 55-99, exec. v.p., 1963-87, pres., 1987-93, vice chmn., 1993-94, sr. corp. advisor, 1995-99, adv. dir., 1999—; ptnr., bd. dirs. Dudley R. Cloud & Son, Constrn., San Antonio, 1946-55; owner Cloud Enterprises, San Antonio. Mem. adv. bd. dirs. Capitol Cement Co./Aggregate Co., 1999—. Mem. adv. coun. Boysville Inc., 1978-79; bd. dirs. Tex. State Tech. Coll. Found., 1983-97, 98—, hon. life bd. mem.; mem. adv. bd. Tex. Engrng. Extension Svc., 1995— . Lt. col. C.E. AUS, 1942-46, ETO. Recipient Pro Deo Et Juventute award Nat. Council Catholic Youth, Soyr Svc. award, 2003. Mem. AIM, NSPE, KC (3d degree), Tex. Assn. Gen. Contractors (life, dir. hwy. and heavy br. 1947-48, 72-76, pres. 1974, chmn. corps engrs. joint com. 1989-90), Am. Concrete Paving Assn. (v.p. 1970-74, bd. dirs., 1st v.p. 1975, pres. 1976), Nat. Asphalt Paving Assn., Tex. Hotmix Paving Assn. (bd. dirs. 1972), Nat. Assn. Gen. Contractors (bd. dirs. 1976-88, life dir., exec. com. 1978-79, bur. reclamaton com. 1968-97, corps engrs. com. 1988-97, equipment mgmt. com. 1978-97, Nat. AGC Outstanding Com. chmn., 1997, chmn. heavy divsn. 1979, environ. com, 1971-76, energy and materials 1976-86, fin. com. 1979, engrng. documentation rev. com. 1985, ethics rules legis. com. 1979, water and power resource com. 1980-81, transp. policy com. 1980-95, quality in constrn. com. 1993-96), San Antonio Livestock Assn. (life), Tex. Soc. Profl. Engrs., Tex. Good Rds.-Transp. Assn. (dir. 1974-79, exec. com. 1975-81, 85-89), Am. Mgmt. Assn., San Antonio C. of C. (chmn. better rds. task force 1978-79, 85-93, bd. dirs. 1993-94), Tex. Transp. Inst. (adv. bd. 1993-97), Tex. Engrng. Ext. Svc. (adv. bd. 1995-97), Cons. Contractors Coun. Am. (chmn. 1989), Holy Name Soc. (v.p. 1962-63), Nocturnal Adoration Soc. Office: Cloud Enterprises 127 Cave Ln San Antonio TX 78209-2208 Fax: 210-826-6044. E-mail: bbcsat@swbell.net.

CLOUD, MARK F. video producer, director, writer, musician; b. Culver City, Calif., Sept. 17, 1955; s. Wade and Maxine Esther Cloud; m. Cheryl L. Sorensen, Jan. 22, 1977 (dec. Aug. 3, 1995); children: Rory S., Jaren S. AA, San Bernardino Valley Coll., 1975; BA, Calif. State Fullerton, 1978. Lic. fed. Comm. Commn., 1978. Mgr. corp. comm. Sav-On Drugs, Anaheim, Calif., 1983—85; owner Cloud Productions, Murrieta, Calif., 1985—. Instr. Santa Ana C.C., Calif., 1985—87. Musician (producer): (cd) Hard Choices, Wings of Silver, Live at the Emu Farm, From the Cobwebs of Our Minds, Joyous Songs of Sorrow; prodr.: (cd) Legacy by Cheryl Cloud, Songs of Christmas by Cheryl Cloud. Song leader Avaxat Elem. Sch., Murrieta, Calif., 1995—2000. Recipient Award of Excellence, Calif. Parks and Recreation Soc., 1990. Non-Partisan. Avocations: mountain biking, camping, snow skiing. Office: Cloud Prodns PO Box 1109 Murrieta CA 92564-1109 Personal E-mail: markcloud@uncommonlyround.com.

CLOUD, STANLEY WILLS, journalist, editor, writer; b. Los Angeles, Nov. 4, 1936; s. Wade and Esther Maxine (Sowers) C.; m. Nancy Jean Fuller, June 22, 1962 (div. 1979); children: Michael Sean, David Stanley, Matthew Wade; m. Christina Lynne Olson, Jan. 5, 1980; 1 child, Caroline Wills BA, Pepperdine Coll., Los Angeles, 1958; postgrad. in Russian lang., Def. Lang. Inst., Monterey, Calif., 1961-62. Editorial clk. Los Angeles Times Mirror Syndicate, 1954-58; reporter Monterey Peninsula Herald, Calif., 1964-66; editor The Advocate, Monterey, 1966-68; corr. Time Mag., San Francisco, 1968-69, Moscow, USSR, 1969-70, bur. chief Bangkok, Thailand, 1970-71, Saigon, Vietnam, 1971-72, Senate corr. Washington, 1972-74, polit. corr., 1974-76, White House corr., 1976-78, news services editor, 1978-79, dep. Washington bur. chief, 1987-89, Washington bur. chief, 1989-93, Washington contbg. editor, 1993-94; contbributor, 1994; asst. mng. editor Washington Star, 1979-80, mng. editor, 1980-81; exec. editor Los Angeles Herald Examiner, 1982-86; freelance journalist Alexandria, Va., 1986-87; writer, author, 1995—. Co-author: The Murrow Boys, 1996, A Question of Honor, 2003; playwright: The Murrow Boys. Exec. dir. The Citizens Election Project, 1995-96. Served to lt. USNR, 1958-64. Mem. Coun. on Fgn. Rels., The Cosmos Club. E-mail: stancloud@mac.com.

CLOUDSLEY, DONALD HUGH, library administrator; b. Buffalo, Jan. 11, 1925; s. James Rowland and Helen Margaret (Macgregor) C. BA, Bethany Coll., W.Va., 1948; MLS, Carnegie Inst. Tech., 1949. Jr. librarian Buffalo Pub. Library, 1949-52; sr. librarian I Erie County Pub. Library, Buffalo, 1952-58; sr. librarian II Buffalo and Erie County Pub. Library, 1958-59, dep. dir., 1974-83, dir., 1983-95; reference librarian Grosvenor Library, Buffalo, 1959-61; head Brighton br. Tonawanda Library, N.Y., 1961-65; dir. Tonawanda Library, 1965-73; trustee West N.Y. Libr. Resources Coun., Buffalo, 1983-93, treas., 1976-89. Mem. N.Y. State Regent's Adv. Coun. on Librs., 1988-93, chmn., 1990-91; mem. adv. com. on pub. librs. Online Computer Libr. Ctr., 1991-94. Mem. citizens adv. coun. SUNY-Buffalo, 1983-95. Named Boss of Yr., Am. Bus. Women's Assn., Buffalo, 1984; recipient Alumni Achievement award Bethany Coll., 1991, Buffalo (N.Y.) News Citizen of Yr. award, 1992. Mem. ALA, N.Y. Libr. Assn., N.Y. State Pub. Librs. Assn. (cert. com. 1971-75), Rotary (treas. Kenmore, N.Y. club 1975-76), Beta Theta Pi. Methodist. Home: 152 Hidden Ridge Cmn Williamsville NY 14221-5765

CLOUES, EDWARD BLANCHARD, II, lawyer; b. Concord, N.H., Dec. 28, 1947; s. Alfred Samuel and H. Jeannette (Callas) C.; m. Mary Anne Matthews, Aug. 21, 1971; children: E. Matthew, M. Elizabeth. BA, Harvard U., 1969; JD, NYU, 1972. Bar: Pa. 1972, U.S. Dist. Ct. (ea. dist.) Pa. 1973. Law clk. to hon. judge James Hunter III U.S. Ct. Appeals (3d cir.), Phila. and Camden, N.J., 1972-73; assoc. Morgan, Lewis & Bockius LLP, Phila., 1973-79, ptnr., 1979-98; chmn., CEO K-Tron Internat., Inc., Pitman, N.J., 1998—. Bd. dirs. K-Tron Internat., Pitman, N.J., vice chmn. bd., 1987-94; bd. dirs. Amrep Corp., chmn., 1995—; bd. dirs. Penn Va. Corp., Penn Va. Resource Ptnrs., L.P.. Republican. Lutheran. Avocations: travel, reading. Office: K-Tron Internat Inc PO Box 888 Rtes 55 & 553 Pitman NJ 08071

CLOUGH, GERALD WAYNE, academic administrator; b. Douglas, Ga., Sept. 24, 1941; married; 2 children. BSCE, MSCE, Ga. Inst. Tech., 1964; PhD, U. Calif., Berkeley, 1969. Registered profl. engr., Calif., Va. Assoc. prof. to prof. civil engring. Stanford U., Calif., 1974—82; prof. civil engring., coord. geotech. program Va. Polytechnic Inst. and State U., 1982—83, prof. civil engring., head dept. civil engring., 1983—90, dean Coll. Engring., 1990—93; provost, prof. civil engring. U. Wash., Seattle, 1993—94; pres. Ga. Inst. Tech., Atlanta,

1994—. Bd. dirs. Noro-Moseley Ptnrs.; appt. to Pres. Coun. Adv. on Sci. & Tech., 2001—. Trustee Ga. Rsch. Alliance. Mem.: NAE. Office: Ga Inst Tech Office of the Pres 225 N Avae NW Carnegie Bldg Atlanta GA 30332-0001*

CLOUGH, LAUREN C. retired special education educator; b. Canton, N.Y., Mar. 17, 1924; s. Hiram William and Lena May (Ladison) C.; m. Margaret Ellen Williamson, June 8, 1951; children: David Wayne, Carol Canty (dec.). BA, U. Ala., 1947; MA in Teaching, U. Jacksonville, 1969; cert. mental retardation, U. Fla.; cert. specific LDEH, U. North Fla. Tchr. Duval County Bd. Pub. Instrn., Jacksonville, Fla., 1964-70; tchr. history Nassau County Bd. Pub. Instrn., Fernandina Beach, Fla., 1970-71, tchr. mentally retarded, 1971-73, specific learning disabled and emotionally handicapped resource tchr., 1973-98; tchr. Hilliard (Fla.) Elem. Sch., 1973-98; ret., 1998; substitute tchr., 1998—. Improvement com. Hilliard Elem. Sch., 1991-98, chmn. sch. pub. rels. com., 1993-95, comm. com., 1994-98, Title I com., 1994-97; sch. accreditation com. SACS, 1995-96, student svcs. com., 1997-98. Alt. mem. adv. com. Fernandina HS, 2001—02, mem. adv. com., 2002—; mem. Cmty. Alliance, 2002. Mem. Nassau County Ret. Educators Assn. (chmn. legislation com. 1999—, pres.-elect 2001-02, pres. 2002-).

CLOUGH, RAY WILLIAM, JR., civil engineering educator; b. Seattle, July 23, 1920; s. Ray William and Mildred (Nelson) Clough; m. Shirley Claire Potter, Oct. 30, 1942; children: Douglas Potter, Allison Justine, Meredith Anne. BSCE, U. Wash., 1942; MS, Calif. Inst. Tech., 1943; SM, MIT, 1947, ScD, 1949; D.Tech. (hon.), Chalmers U., Goteborg, Sweden, 1979; D.Tech. (hon.), Norges Tekniske Høgskole, Trondheim, Norway, 1982. Registered engr., Wash. Faculty U. Calif.-Berkeley, 1949—, prof. civil engring., 1959—, chmn. div. structural engring. and structural mechanics, 1967—70, dir. Earthquake Engring. Rsch. Ctr., 1973—76, Nishkian prof. structural engring., 1983—87, prof. emeritus, 1987—. Cons. in field; adv. com. NAS-NAE Environ. Sci. Svcs. Adminstrn., 1967—70; mem. U.S. C.E. Structural Design Adv. Bd., 1967—79. Capt. USAF, 1942—46. Named Hon. Rschr., Lab. Nat. De Engenharia Civil Lisbon, 1972; recipient Sr. Rsch. award, Am. Soc. for Engring. Edn., 1986, Congress medal, Internat. Assn. Computer Mechanics, 1986, citation, U. Calif., 1987, A.C. Eringen medal, Soc. of Engring. Sci., 1992, U.S. Nat. Medal of Sci., presented by Pres. William J. Clinton, 1994, Prince Philip medal, Royal Acad. Engring., 1997, George W. Housner medal, Earthquake Engring. Rsch. Inst., 1996; fellow Fulbright, Rsch. Inst., 1956—57, Overseas fellow, Cambridge (Eng.) U. Fellow: ASCE (hon.; chmn. engring. mechanics divsn. 1964—65, Rsch. award 1960, Howard award 1970, Newmark medal 1979, Moissieff medal 1980, T. VonKarman medal 1980), Inst. Water Conservation and Hydroelectric Power Rsch. (hon.); mem.: NAE, NAS (dynamics panel adv. bd. on hardened electric power sys. 1964—70), Seismol. Soc. Am. (bd. dirs. 1970—73), Structural Engrs. Assn. No. Calif. (bd. dirs. 1967—70). Home: PO Box 4625 Sunriver OR 97707-1625

CLOUS, JAMES M. electrical equipment company executive, engineer; b. Traverse City, Mich., July 22, 1959; s. August J. and Beverly J. (Kroetsch) C.; m. Mimi M. O'Connell, June 28, 1979 (div. July 1983). AS, Northwetern Mich. Coll., 1979; BSME, Mich. Tech. U., 1981. Sales engr. Louis Allis-Litton, Houston, 1981-83; dist. mgr. Louis Allis-Magnetek, Baton Rouge, 1984-85, GEC Automation Projects, Houston, 1986-88; regional mgr. Ross Hill Controls, Houston, 1989-91; nat. sales mgr. ABB Indsl. Systems, New Berlin, Wis., 1991-94; v.p. sales and mktg. Ideal Electric, Mansfield, Ohio, 1994-96; pres. Clous Cons., Traverse City, Mich., 1996—; fin. advisor Waddell & Reed, Traverse City, 2001—. Pvt. practice mktg. cons., Houston, 1987-91. Mem. Nat. Rep. Com., Washington, 1988. Mem.: IEEE. Republican. Roman Catholic. Home: 887 Carver St Traverse City MI 49686 Office: Waddell & Reed 1760A Forest Ridge Dr Traverse City MI 49686

CLOUSE, JERRY ALLAN, architectural historian; b. Carlisle, Pa., Aug. 20, 1950; s. Elmer Ellsworth Clouse and Bessie Virginia Warner. BA, U. Ky., 1972; MA, Pa. State U., 1993. Archtl. rschr. Cumberland County Hist. Soc., Carlisle, 1987—88; preservation specialist Pa. Hist. & Mus. Commn., Harrisburg, 1988—95; archtl. historian McCormick, Taylor & Assocs., Inc., Harrisburg, 1995—. Mem. tours com. Vernacular Architecture Tours, 2000—. Author: The Whiskey Rebellion, 1994, Gayman Tavern: A Study of a Canal-Era Tavern in Dauphin Borough, 2003; co-author: Perry County: A Pictoral History, 1978, Briner Family History, 1984. Bd. dirs. The Perry Historians, pres., 1990—92, 1997—98, v.p., 1992—97. Republican. Lutheran. Avocations: genealogy, collecting stoneware, watercolors. Home: 118A S Railroad St Hummelstown PA 17036

CLOUSE, JOHN DANIEL, lawyer; b. Evansville, Ind., Sept. 4, 1925; s. Frank Paul and Anna Lucille (Frank) C.; m. Georgia L. Ross, Dec. 7, 1978; 1 child, George Chauncey. AB, U. Evansville, 1950; JD, Ind. U., 1952. Bar: Ind. 1952, U.S. Supreme Ct. 1962, U.S. Ct. Appeals (7th cir.) 1965. Assoc. Firm of James D. Lopp, Evansville, 1952-56; pvt. practice law, 1956—. Guest editorialist Viewpoint, Evansville Courier, 1978—86, Evansville Press, 1986—98, Focus, Radio Sta. WGBF, 1978—84; 2d asst. city atty. Evansville, 1954—55; mem. Com. for Implementation of Criminal Justice Act of 1964, 1965; mem. appellate rules sub-com. Ind. Supreme Ct. Com. on Rules of Practice and Procedure, 1980. Pres. Civil Svc. Commn. Evansville Police Dept., 1961-62, v.p., 1988; pres. Ind. War Memls. Com., 1963-69; mem. jud. nominating com. Vanderburgh County, Ind., 1976-80; dir. Ind. Fed. Cmty. Defender Project, Inc., 1993-98. With inf. U.S. Army, 1943-46. Decorated Bronze Star; named one of World's Most travelled Man Guinness Book of Records, 1993, Most Travelled Man, 1995-2001. Fellow Ind. Bar Found.; mem. Internat. Wood Collector's Soc., Evansville Bar Assn. (v.p. 1972, James Bethel Gresham Freedom award 1997), Ind. Bar Assn. (chmn. com. on civil rights 1991-92), 87th Inf. Divsn. Assn., Internat. Wood Collectors Soc., Club Internat. Des Grand Voyageurs, Travelers Century Club (L.A.), Pi Gamma Mu. Republican. Methodist. Office: 123 NW 4th St Ste 317 Evansville IN 47708-1712 E-mail: JDCMJS@aol.com.

CLOUSE, MELVIN E. radiologist; b. Vinita, Okla., June 6, 1934; s. Clifford Powell and Agnes Elizabeth (Betcher) C.; m. Marian Upton, Feb. 16, 1966; children: Graydon Melville, Thomas Philip. BS, Tex. Christian U., 1967; MD, U. Tex., 1960. Diplomate Am. Bd. Radiology; lic. physician, Mass., Tex. Intern Phila. Gen. Hosp., 1960-61; resident in radiology Mass. Gen. Hosp., Boston, 1962-64, fellow radiology, 1964-65, radiologist, 1966-69; fellow radiology Armed Forces Inst. Pathology, Washington, 1965; from asst. in radiology to prof. Harvard Med. Sch., 1966-87, Deaconess prof. radiology, 2000—; radiologist New Eng. Deaconess Hosp., Boston, 1969-96; chmn. dept. radiology Deaconess Hosp., Boston, 1975-96; vice chmn. dept radiology Beth Israel Deaconess Med. Ctr., Boston, 1996-98, chmn. dept. radiology, 1998-2000, vice chmn., 2000—. Vis. prof. radiology U. Conn. Med. Sch., 1980, U. Va. Med. Sch., 1980, Loyola U., Maywood, Ill., 1981; examiner Am. Bd. Radiology, various yrs., question devel. written exam., 1994; staff dept. radiology Dana Farber Cancer Inst., 1989—; mem. various coms. New Eng. Deaconess Hosp., 1975—, ex-officio mem. bd. dirs., 1979-81; clin. assoc. Cancer Rsch. Inst./New Eng. Deaconess Hosp., 1978-90; chief radiology svc. Quigley meml. Hosp./Soldiers Home, 1985-87; pres. Deaconess Profl. Practice Group/New Eng. Deaconess Hosp. Mem. reviewer Cardiovascular and Interventional Radiology, 1980—, Transplantation, 1981—, Radiology, 1982—, Radiographics, 1988—, Investigative Radiology, 1990—, assoc. editor Liver Transplantation and Surgery, 1994—, Gastroenterology, 1994—; contbr. articles to profl. jours. Trustee Beaver Country Day Sch., Chestnut Hill, Mass., 1988-91, v.p., trustee, 1991; mem. Town Meeting, Brookline, Mass. Grantee Nat. Inst. Arthritis, Diabetes, Digestive and Kidney Diseases, Nat. Inst. Neurol. Diseases and Blindness, Am. Cancer Soc., USPH; U. Tex. fellow, 1958; recipient 4th Pl. award Soc. Nuclear Medicine, 1983; named Hon. Prof. Xi'an Med. U., China, 1989. Fellow Am. Coll. Radiology (councillor 1971-75), Soc. Cardiovascular and Interventional Radiology; mem. AMA, Am. Roentgen Ray Soc., Radiol. Soc. N.Am. (councillor, program com. cardiovascular radiology 1983), Mass. Radiologic Soc. (exec. com. 1971-75, councillor 1973-76, tribunal com. 1980, com. on standards in radiol. practice 1984-85, standards on radiologistical practice com., others, 1992), Mass. Med. Soc., New Eng. Roentgen Ray Soc. (sec. 1974-77, pres. 1980-81, exec. com. 1981-82, chmn. exec. com. 1983-84, nominating com., profl. ethics com. 1984-85, chmn. nominating com. 1986-87), New Eng. Cardiovascular and Interventional Roentgen Soc. (pres. 1982-83), Soc. for Magnetic Resonance in Medicine, Assn. Univ. Radiologists (membership com. 1985-87), Am. Heart Assn. Office: Beth Israel Deaconess Med Ctr 1 Deaconess Rd Boston MA 02215-5321

CLOUSE, VICKIE RAE, biologist, paleontologist, educator; b. Havre, Mont., Mar. 28, 1956; d. Olaf Raymond and Betty Lou (Reed) Nelson; m. Gregory Scott Clouse, Mar. 22, 1980; 1 child, Kristopher Nelson. BS in Secondary Sci. Edn., Mont. State U. N., Havre, 1989, MEd in Sci., 2002; postgrad., Mont. State U., Bozeman, 1991—94. Tchg. asst. biology/paleontology, asst. prof. biology and earth scis. Mont. State U.-N., Havre, 1986-90; asst. prof. biology and earth scis. Mont. State U. Northern, Havre, 1990—; rsch. asst. dinosaur eggs and embryos Mus. the Rockies, Bozeman, 1992-95. Dir. Dinosaur Rsch. Expdns. Bd. Trustees H.E. Clack Mus., Havre, 1991—97, H.E. Clack Mus. Found., Havre, 1991—97; dir. Mont. Bd. Regents Higher Edn., Helena, 1989—90, Mont. Higher Edn. Student Fin. Assistance Corp., Helena, 1989—90; mem. Ea. Mont. Hist. Soc., 1993—; adj. prof. biology and paleontology Mont. State U. N., Havre. Named Young Career Woman of Yr., Bus. and Profl. Woman's Club, 1986. Mem.: AAAS, Mont. Geol. Soc., Soc. Vertebrate Paleontologists. Avocations: collecting vertebrate fossils, directing dinosaur excavations for laypersons, boating. Office: Mont State U-No Hagener Sci Ctr # 219 Havre MT 59501 E-mail: clousev@msun.edu.

CLOUSHER, FRED EUGENE (FREDDIE CEE CLOUSHER), entertainment producer, booking agent, musician; b. Hanover, Pa., May 6, 1941; s. Raymond Samuel and Helena Elizabeth (Geiman) C.; m. Vicky S. Sumile, Dec. 18, 1967 (dec. Mar. 2001); 1 child, Michelle Marie Clousher Lively. Student, USN Sch. Music, Little Creek, Va., 1964. Music instr. various music stores, Pa., 1958-63, 68-72; owner, pres. Clousher Prodns., Mechanicsburg, Pa., 1972—. Leader Freddie & The Hy-Lites, Hanover, Pa., 1959-63, Tremors rock band, Norfolk, Va., 1964-65, Hawaiian Revue Show Band, Harrisburg, Pa., 1974-90. Performer (recording ABS Records) Five Minutes More b/w Foolish Love, 1960; co-writer (with Slim Anderson, K-Ark Records), Navy Wings of Gold, 1966; guitarist, musician USO shows, Vietnam and far East, 1966, navy unit band, Europe, 1967. With USN, 1963-67, Vietnam. Mem. Nat. Assn. Orch. Leaders (dist. adminstr. 1981-91), Pa. State Assn. County Fairs, Md. Assn. Agrl. Fairs and Shows, Inc., Am. Legion, VFW. Avocations: fitness walking, football, concerts, music. Home and Office: Clousher Prodns PO Box 1191 Mechanicsburg PA 17055-1191 E-mail: clousher@webtv.net.

CLOUSTON, ROSS NEAL, retired food and related products company executive; b. Montreal, Que., Can., Sept. 13, 1922; came to U.S., 1963, naturalized, 1973; s. Alan Roy and Maude (Neal) C.; m. Brenda Kerson, Feb. 12, 1944; children: Robert, Brendan. B.Sc., McGill U., 1949; MBA, Harvard U., 1951. With fisheries plant, N.S., Can., from 1940; founder LaSalle Foods Ltd., 1953, Blue Water Sea Food Ltd., Montreal, 1959, Blue Water Sea Food Ltd. (merged into Gorton Corp., 1963, merged into Gen. Mills, Inc. 1968); pres. Gorton Group div. Gen. Mills, Inc., 1969-86, chmn., 1986-87, corp. v.p. parent co., 1970-87; v.p. Gen. Mills Can. Ltd. Pres. Nat. Fisheries Inst., 1975, Fisheries Council Can., 1962. Served with RCAF, 1941-45. Decorated Royal Norwegian Order of Merit; recipient Man of Yr. award Nat. Fisheries Inst., 1985. Mem. The Oaks.

CLOUTIER, MONIQUE LEGENDRE, lawyer; b. New Orleans, Sept. 29, 1965; d. Byron Peter Legendre and Barbara Ann Escoffier; m. Jude Anthony Cloutier, Aug. 6, 1993; children: Charles Pierre, Jacqueline Ann. Degree in computer info. processing, Loyola U., New Orleans, 1987; JD, So. U., 1992. Bar: La. 1992, U.S. Dist. Ct. (ea., we. and mid. dists.) La. 1992. Law clk. 15th Jud. Dist. Ct., Abbeville, La., 1992-95; atty. Pub. Defender Office, Lafayette, La., 1995—2001, 2002—. Mem. La. State Bar Assn., Lafayette Young Lawyers Assn. (ann. meeting chairperson 1997-2000), Lafayette C. of C. Democrat. Roman Catholic. Home: 319 Live Oak Dr Lafayette LA 70503-3903 E-mail: cloutier@cox.internet.com.

CLOUTMAN, EDWARD BRADBURY, III, lawyer; b. Lake Charles, La., Dec. 8, 1945; s. Edward Bradbury Jr. and Evelyn (Daniel) C.; m. Kathryn Sue Robinson, Aug., 1967 (div. 1974); children: Michael Edward, Chad Edward; m. Elizabeth Katherine Julian, June 11, 1976; 1 child, Edward Bradbury IV. JD, La. State U., 1969. Bar: La. 1969, U.S. Dist. Ct. (we. dist.) La., U.S. Ct. Appeals (5th cir.) 1970, Tex. 1971, U.S. Dist. Ct. (no., we., and ea. dists.) Tex., U.S. Supreme Ct. 1973, U.S. Ct. Appeals (10th cir.) 1974, U.S. Ct. Appeals (6th cir.) 1980, U.S. Ct. Appeals (11th cir.) 1982. Reginald Heber Smith fellow CENLA Legal Aid Soc., Alexandria, La., 1969-70, Dallas Legal Svcs. Found., 1970-71; ptnr. Johnston, Polk, Larson, Cloutman & Dixon, Dallas, 1971-73; assoc. Mullinax, Wells, Mauzy and Baab, Inc., Dallas, 1973-74; ptnr. Mullinax, Wells, Baab and Cloutman, P.C., Dallas, 1975-90; pvt. practice Dallas, 1990—. Adj. prof. So. Meth. U. Sch. Law, 1990-98. Mem. ABA, Inns of Ct. (master 1990—). Democrat. Office: 3301 Elm St Dallas TX 75226-2562

CLOVIS, SAMUEL HARVEY, academic administrator; b. Salina, Kans., Sept. 18, 1949; s. Samuel Harvey and Mildred Marie (Baize) C.; m. LaVeta Ross, Nov. 27, 1971 (div. Mar. 2000); children: Travis Justin, Matthew Allen; m. Charlotte Anne Chase, July 21, 2000; 1 stepson, Robert Khan Rosenberger. BS in Polit. Sci., USAF Acad., 1971; MBA, Golden Gate U., 1984; postgrad., U. Ala., Tuscaloosa, 1998—. Commd. 2d lt. USAF, 1971, advanced through grades to col., 1992, ret., 1996; mgr. tech. support Betac Corp., Colorado Springs, Colo., 1996-97; mgr. strategic solutions divsn. Logicon Inc., Herndon, Va., 1997-2000; assoc. dean, dir. of faculty Coll. Working Adults William Penn U., Oskaloosa, Iowa, 2000—02, founding dean Coll. of Bus. and Mgmt. Sci., 2002—. Mem. affiliate faculty Regis U., Denver, 1995—; cons. Rand Corp., Santa Monica, Calif., 1996—. Mem. ASPA, Am. Polit. Sci. Assn., Assn. of Grads. USAF Acad. Avocations: fishing, golf, weightlifting. Office: William Penn U 201 Trueblood Ave Oskaloosa IA 52577

CLOW, LEE, advertising agency executive; Formerly exec. v.p., creative dir. Chiat/Day, L.A., now pres., chief creative officer, chmn, cco, 1995, chief creative officer worldwide. Office: TBWA Chiat/Day 5353 Grosvenor Blvd Los Angeles CA 90066

CLOW, TIMOTHY JAMES, lawyer; b. San Antonio, Jan. 2, 1960; s. Don and Bonnie Mae (Zaloudek) C. BBA with distinction, U. Okla., 1982, JD, 1985. Bar: Okla. 1985, Tex. 1986. Pvt. practive landman, Norman, Okla., 1980-82; lawyer Lynch, Chappell, & Alsup, Dallas and Midland, Tex., 1985-92, Page & Addison, Dallas, 1992-96, Addison Law Firm, Dallas, 1996—. Active March of Dimes, Midland, 1986-87. Mem. ABA, Okla. Bar Assn., State Bar Tex., Tex. Young Lawyers Assn., Phi Eta Sigma, Alpha Lambda Delta, Phi Delta Phi, Beta Gamma Sigma, Sigma Chi (v.p.). Republican. Roman Catholic.

CLOWER, WILLIAM DEWEY, retired trade association executive; b. Salem, Va., Oct. 9, 1935; s. Alton Oliver and Addie Vane (Young) C.; m. Shirley Carol Tuttle, Sept. 1, 1956; children— Candice Denise, Michael DeWayne, Catherine Dione. BS, U. Va., 1958. Applications engr. ITT, Nutley, N.J., 1958-60; regional mktg. mgr. Litton Industries, Washington, 1960-61; propr. W.D. Clower Co., Gt. Falls, Va., 1961-70; spl. asst. to Pres. of U.S., 1970-75; exec. v.p. CISPI, Washington, 1975-76; pres. Food Processing Machinery and Supplies Assn., Washington, 1976-86; dir. Food Processors Inst., 1977-80; propr. Clower Assocs., Great Falls, Va., 1986-88; pres., CEO NATSO, Inc., Alexandria, Va., 1988—2003. Dir. Small Bus. Legis. Coun., 1991—92; chmn. Found. for Internat. Meetings, 1993; mem. Pres.'s adv. coun. Peace Corps, 1982—85; mem. Industry Policy Adv. Coun. for Export Policy, 1982—86; pres. The NATSO Found., 1991—2003; mem. campaign svcs. steering com. Rep. Nat. Com., 1977. With USAF, 1959—60. Va. Gen. Assembly scholar, 1954-58 Mem.: Am. Soc. Assn. Execs., Aircraft Owners and Pilots Assn., Fawn Lake County Club, Country Club at Two Rivers, Sertoma (pres. 1963—64), Capitol Hill Club, Gamma Delta Epsilon. Presbyterian. Home: Fawn Lake 11701 General Wadsworth Dr Spotsylvania VA 22553

CLOWES, ALEXANDER WHITEHILL, surgeon, educator; b. Boston, Oct. 9, 1946; s. George H.A. Jr. and Margaret Gracey (Jackson) Clowes; m. Monika Meyer (dec.); m. Susan E. Detweiler. AB, Harvard U., 1968, MD, 1972. Resident in surgery Case Western Reserve, Cleve., 1972-74, 76-79; rsch. fellow in pathology Harvard Med. Sch., Boston, 1974-76; fellow in vascular surgery Brigham and Womens Hosp. Harvard Med. Sch., 1979-80; asst. prof. surgery U. Wash., Seattle, 1980-85, assoc. prof., 1985-90, prof., 1990—, assoc. chmn. dept., 1989-91, acting chmn. dept., 1992-93, adj. prof. pathology, 1992, chief divsn. vascular surgery, 1995—, dept. vice chmn., 1995—. Contbr. ;, author (numerous sci. papers). Trustee Marine Biol. Labs, Woods Hole, Mass., 1989—2000, Seattle Symphony, 1994—, v.p., 1998—; bd. dirs. Seattle Chamber Music Festival, 1990. Recipient Rsch. Career Devel. award, NIH, 1982—87; fellow Tng. fellow, 1974—77; scholar Loyal Davis Traveling Surg. scholar, ACS, 1987. Mem.: N.Am. Vascular Biology Orgn. (pres. 2001-02), Soc. Vascular Surgery, Seattle Surg. Soc., Internat. Soc. Applied Cardiovasc. Biology, Am. Soc. Cell Biology, Am. Heart Assn. (coun. on arteriosclerosis), Am. Assn. Pathologists, Am. Surg. Assn., Quisset Yacht Club, Cruising Club Am., Sigma Xi. Episcopalian. Home: 3425 Perkins Ln W Seattle WA 98199-1858 Office: U Wash Dept Surgery PO Box 356410 Seattle WA 98195-6410

CLOWES, EDITH W. language educator, consultant, literature educator, consultant; b. Cleve., Dec. 23, 1951; BA, Oberlin U., 1973; MPhil, Yale U., 1977, PhD, 1981. Asst. prof. Knox Coll., Galesburg, Ill., 1981-82, U. Va., Charlottesville, 1983-84; from asst. prof. to assoc. prof. Purdue U., West Lafayette, Ind., 1984—94, prof., 1994—98, dir. program in comparative lit., 1992-94; prof. Russian lang. & lit. U. Kans., Lawrence, 1999—. Author: (book) Maksim Gorky, 1987, The Revolution of Moral Consciousness, 1988, Russian Experimental Fiction: Resisting Ideology after Utopia, 1993; editor: Between Tsar and People, 1991, Doctor Zhivago: A Critical Companion, 1995, Collaborator: Merchant Moscow, 1998; translator: Private Wealth-National Vision: The Memoirs of a New Russian Entrepreneur (Aleksandr Panikin), 2000. Fellow, NEH, 2001; grantee, ITT, Munich, 1973—74, IREX, Moscow, 1978—79, 1993, 1994, 1997, NEH, 1986—88, DAAD, 1998. Mem.: MLA, Am. Comparative Lit. Assn., N.Am. Nietzsche Soc., Am. Assn. Tchrs. Slavic and E. European Lang., Am. Assn. Advancement Slavic Studies, Phi Beta Kappa. Office: U Kans Dept Slavic Langs and Lits Lawrence KS 66045

CLOWES, GARTH ANTHONY, electronics executive, consultant; b. Didsbury, Eng., Aug. 30, 1936; came to U.S., 1957; s. Eric and Doris Gladys (Worthington) C.; m. Katharine Allman Crewdson, July 29, 1950 (dec. Jan. 1998); children: John Howard Brett, Peter Miles, Vicki Anne. BSc, Stockport Coll., Cheshire, Eng., 1953; postgrad., UCLA, 1965-66; higher nat. cert., Birmingham (Eng.) Coll. Tech., 1955-56. Gen. mgr., v.p., dir. Eldon Industries, Inc., El Segundo, Calif., 1962-69; CEO, founder Entex Industries, Inc., Compton, Calif., 1969-83; pres., founder Entex Electronics, Inc., Camano Island, Calif., 1982—. Pres., founder TTC, Inc., Carson, Calif., 1984-86; pres. Universal Telesis Electronics, Inc., Carson, 1986-87; gen. mgr. Matchbox Toys (U.S.A.) Ltd., Moonachie, N.J., 1987-88; dir. gen. Matchbox Spain, S.A., Valencia, 1988-89; cons. Matchbox Internat. Ltd., worldwide, 1986-89; spkr. in bus. field. Inventor electronic voice recognition devices, numerous others. Mem. pres.'s com. UNICEF, N.Y., 1972-74, Senate Adv. Bd., Washington, 1982-83; cons. Interracial Coun., L.A., 1967-69; mem. adv. bd. Santa Rosa Coll., 1993-99. Decorated Knight of Malta. Avocations: antiques, gardening, art, breeding scotch highland cattle. Home: 68 W Cross Island Rd Camano Island WA 98282-6667 E-mail: gaclowes@earthlink.com.

CLOYD, THOMAS EARL, broadcast designer, consultant; b. Washington, Sept. 1, 1944; s. Buford Thomas Cloyd and Florence Elizabeth (Green) Paterson; m. Linda Oblak, Apr. 17, 1968 (div. Mar. 1989); 1 child from previous marriage, Lisa; 1 child, Tobey. Broadcast designer Sta KYW-TV/CBS, Phila., 1965-90. Owner Barboza Assocs., Blackwood, N.J., 1970—; cons. emerging techs. Broadcast Designers Assn., San Francisco, 1981-89. Designer: (TV show) Mike Douglas Show, 1965-76, Sta. WWL-TV News Set, 1974, Shattered Dreams, 1985 (Emmy nomination 1985), (TV show logo) Steve Allen Show, 1971, and corp. trade exhibits. With U.S. Army, 1962-65, ETO. Home: 590 Lower Landing Rd Apt 183 Blackwood NJ 08012-4125 E-mail: tomcloyd@yahoo.com.

CLUBB, BRUCE EDWIN, retired lawyer; b. Blackduck, Minn., Feb. 6, 1931; s. Ernest and Abigail (Gordy) Clubb; m. Martha Lucia Trapp, Dec. 19, 1954 (dec. Nov. 2001); children: Bruce Allen, Christopher Wade. BBA, U. Minn., 1955, LL.B. cum laude, 1958. Bar: DC 1959. Atty. Covington & Burling, 1958-61, Devel. Loan Fund, 1961-62, Chapman, DiSalle and Friedman, 1962-67; commr. U.S. Tariff Commn., 1967-71; ptnr. firm Baker & McKenzie, Washington, 1971-96; disting. lawyer in residence U. Minn. Law Sch., 1981-82. Chmn. bd. dirs. Sunrise Properties, Inc., 1989—99. Author: (treatise) United States Foreign Trade Law (2 vols.), 1991; contbr. law revs. Served with U.S. Army, 1952—54. Mem. D.C. Bar Assn., Am. Arbitration Assn. (arbitrator 1994-2000), Order of Coif, Cosmos Club (pres. 1986), Met. Club, Army Navy Club. Republican. Home: 630 Tennis Club Dr Fort Lauderdale FL 33311-4055 E-mail: bclubb2@aol.com.

CLUFF, LEIGHTON EGGERTSEN, physician; b. Salt Lake City, June 10, 1923; s. Lehi Eggertsen and Lottie (Brain) Cluff; m. Beth Allen, Aug. 19, 1944; children: Claudia Beth, Patricia Leigh. BS, U. Utah, 1944, ScD (hon.), 1989; MD with distinction, George Washington U., 1949; ScD (hon.), Hahnemann Med. Sch., 1979, L.I. U., 1988, St. Louis U., George Washington U., 1990, U. Utah, 1990. Intern Johns Hopkins Hosp., Balt., 1949—50, asst. resident, 1951—52; asst. resident physician Duke Hosp., Durham, NC, 1950—51; vis. investigator, asst. physician Rockefeller Inst. Med. Research, 1952—54; fellow Nat. Found. Infantile Paralysis, 1952—54; mem. faculty Johns Hopkins Sch. Medicine, Balt.; staff Johns Hopkins Hosp., Balt., 1954—66, prof. medicine, 1964—66, physician, head divsn. clin. immunology, allergy and infectious diseases, 1958—66; prof., chmn. dept. medicine U. Fla., Gainesville, 1966—76, VA disting. physician, 1990—95, prof. emeritus dept. medicine, 1990—; exec. v.p. Robert Wood Johnson Found., Princeton, NJ, 1976—85, pres., 1985—90, trustee emeritus, 1990—. U.S. del. U.S.-Japan Coop. Med. Sci. Program, 1972—81; mem. coun. drugs AMA, 1965—67; mem. NRC-NAS Drug Rsch. Bd., 1965—71; mem. expert adv. panel bacterial diseases (coccal infection) WHO; mem. coun. Nat. Inst. Allergy and Infectious Diseases, 1968—72; cons. FDA; mem. tng. grant com. NIH, 1964—68. Author, editor books on internal medicine, infectious diseases, clin. pharmacology, long-term care and health-care policy; contbr. articles to profl. jours. Mem. U. Fla. Found., 2001—; bd. dirs. Hospice of Worth Ctrs., Fla., 1985—, Nat. Coun. on Aging, 1995—98. Recipient Ordronaux award for med. scholarship, 1949, Career Rsch. award, NIH, 1962, Edward Jill award, Acad. Medicine N.J., 1990, Disting. Alumnus award, Duke U. Sch. Medicine, 1978, Johns Hopkins Sch. Medicine, 1992, Theobald Smith award, Albany Med. Coll., 1988, Outstanding Contbn. to Health and Health Care award, Am. Acad. Nursing, 1996; Markle scholar, 1955—62, Mead-Johnson Postgrad. scholar, 1954—55. Mem.: ACP, Johns Hopkins U. Soc. Scholars, Bd. Inst. for Child Health Policy (bd. dirs. 1991—), Am. Social Health Assn. (bd. dirs. 1991—99, chair 1997—99, bd. dirs. 2002—), Am. Clin. and Climatol. Assn., So. Soc. Clin. Investigation, N.Y.Acad. Scis., Infectious Diseases Soc. Am. (pres. 1975—76), Harvey Soc., Am. Fedn.Clin. Rsch., Am. Assn. Immunolgists, Soc. Exptl. Biology and Medicine, Assn. Am. Physicians, Am. Soc. Clin. Investigation, Assembly Life Sics. of NAS, Inst. Medicine of NAS, Sigma Theta Tau (Archon award 1992), Alpha Omega Alpha. Home: 8851 SW 45th Blvd Gainesville FL 32608-4138 E-mail: leighcluff@aol.com.

CLUFF, LLOYD STERLING, earthquake geologist; b. Provo, Utah, Sept. 29, 1933; s. Colvin Sterling and Melba Cluff; m. Janet L. Peterson, Dec. 21, 1976; children: Tanya, Sasha, Branden. BS in Geology, U. Utah, 1960. Registered profl. geologist, Calif.; cert. engring. geologist, Calif. Jr. geologist El Paso Natural Gas Co., Salt Lake City, 1957-59; teaching asst. dept. geology U. Utah, Salt Lake City, 1958-60; geologist Lottridge Thomas & Assocs., Salt Lake City, 1960; v.p., prin. geologist Woodward-Clyde Cons., San Francisco, 1960-85; assoc. prof. geology and geophysics U. Nev., Reno, 1967-73; dir. dept. geoscis. Pacific Gas and Electric Co., San Francisco, 1985—. Cons. Trans-Alaska Pipeline Siting Study, 1972-74, Aswan High Dam seismic safety evaluation, Govt. of Egypt, 1982-86; mem. com. Nat. Earthquake Hazards Reduction Program, Washington, 1987, Decade for Natural Disaster Reduction, Washington, 1989; advisor Venezuela Pres.'s Earthquake Safety Com., 1967-72; advisor Joint Legis. Com. on Seismic Safety, State of Calif., 1970-74; chmn. seismic rev. panel Calif. Pub. Utilities Commn., San Francisco, 1980-81; mem. Calif. Seismic Safety Commn., 1985-99, chmn., 1988-90, 95-97; adv. bd. So. Calif. Earthquake Ctr., 1996-2001; chmn. Tech. Adv. Bd. on Earthquake Safety, Israel, 1996—; mem. adv. panel on earth scis. NSF, 1992-95, chmn. com. on practical lessons from the Loma Prieta Earthquake, 1994; mem. organizing com. for Pub. Policy Partnership 2000-White House Confs. on Natural Disaster Loss Reduction, 1997-98; com. on assessing costs of natural disasters NAS, 1998-99, bd. Natural Disasters NAS, 1997-2000, Natural Disaster Roundtable, 2000—; nat.

pre-disaster mitigation program adv. panel FEMA, 1998-99; external adv. panel for Pacific Earthquake Engring. Rsch. Ctr., 1998-99, implementation adv. bd., 1999—; natural disaster panel Heinz Ctr. Inst. for Natural Disasters, 2000-02; chmn. sci. earthquake studies adv. com. USGS Nat. Earthquake Hazards Reduction Program, 2002-. Recipient Hogentagler award ASTM, 1968, Alfred E. Alquist medal, Calif. Earthquake Safety Found., 1998, John Wesley Powell award, USGS, 2000; named Woodward lectr., San Francisco, 1979. Fellow Calif. Acad. Scis.; mem. NAE, Seismol. Soc. Am. (pres. 1982-83), Assn. Engring. Geologists (pres. 1968-69), Earthquake Engring. Rsch. Inst. (hon., pres. 1993-95, chmn. Internat. Conf. on Seismic Zonation, Nice, France 1995), Geol. Soc. Am., Structural Engrs. Assn. No. Calif. (H.J. Degenkolb award 1992), Nat. Acad. Delegation Islamic Rep. of Iran, 2000. Republican. Avocations: photography, skiing, mountain climbing, hiking, bicycling. Office: Pacific Gas & Elec Co 245 Market St San Francisco CA 94105-1797 E-mail: lsc2@pge.com.

CLULEE, NICHOLAS HARKINS, history educator; b. Oak Park, Ill., Feb. 13, 1945; s. Charles Rudge and Mary (Harkins) C.; m. Carol Ellen Kipp, June 16, 1973; children: Crystal Elaine, Nicole Marie. BA, Hobart Coll., 1966; MA, U. Chgo., 1968, PhD, 1973. History educator Frostburg (Md.) State U., 1971—, prof. history, 1985—, dir. Modern Humanities Inst., 1991—; chair history dept. Frostburg (Md.) State Univ., 1997—. Author: John Dee's Natural Philosophy, 1988. NEH fellow, 1984-85. Avocations: skiing, early music, building harpsichord. Office: Frostburg State U Dept History Frostburg MD 21532 E-mail: nclulee@frostburg.edu.

CLUMP, MICHAEL A. psychologist, educator; s. Aden H. and Dee Wagner Clump; m. Keli Braitman, Aug. 2, 2001. PhD, So. Ill. U., 2001. Asst. prof. psychology Boise (Idaho) State U., 2001—. Vis. asst. prof. psychology St. Mary's Coll., Notre Dame, Ind., 2001. Contbr. articles to profl. jours. Mem.: APA, Idaho Acad. Sci., Rocky Mountain Psychol. Assn., Midwestern Psychol. Assn., Psychologia Soc., Coun. Tchrs. Undergrad. Psychology, Am. Psychol. Soc., Phi Beta Kappa, Psi-Chi (pres. 1995—97). Avocations: travel, hiking, soccer, collecting native american artifacts, golf. Office: Boise State U 1910 Univeristy Dr Boise ID 83725-1715

CLURMAN, MICHAEL, newspaper publishing executive; b. N.Y.C., June 23, 1952; BA, U. Md.; PMD, Harvard Bus. Sch. Apprentice printer The Washington Post, 1971-76, mgmt. trainee prodn. staff, 1976-79, asst. v.p. ops., 1979-81, plant mgr., 1981-89, dir. prodn., 1989-90, v.p. prodn., 1990-99; v.p. ops., CIO, 2000—. Office: The Washington Post 1150 15th St NW Washington DC 20071-0002

CLUTE, ROBERT EUGENE, political and social science educator; b. Earlville, Iowa, July 12, 1924; s. Henry and Leta (Allen) C.; m. Doris Reams, 1947; children: Robert Eugene, Andrea Reams. BA, U. Ala., 1947; MA, George Washington U., 1948; PhD, Duke U., 1957. Selector U.S. Displaced Persons Commn., Frankfurt, Fed. Republic Germany, 1948-50; analyst USAF, Austria, 1950-54; rsch. assoc. Duke U., Durham, N.C., 1957-58; vis. asst. prof. Tulane U. La., New Orleans, 1958-59; asst. prof. U. Nev., 1959-62; assoc. prof. U. Ga., Athens, 1962-68, prof. polit. sci., 1968—, head dept. polit. sci., 1972-75, grad. coord., 1975-88, chmn. social scis. div., 1982-93, prof. emeritus, 1993—. Am. specialist to Anglophone Africa, Cultural Affairs div. U.S. Dept. State, 1977. Author: The International Legal Status of Austria, 1962; (with others) The International Law Standard and Commonwealth Developments, 1966, De lege pactorum, 1970, Law and Justice, 1970; contbr. articles to profl. jours. With U.S. Army, 1943-46. Fulbright scholar 1967-68; Danforth assoc. 1972. Mem. Am. Soc. Internat. Law, Am. Polit. Sci. Assn., Ga. Polit. Sci. Assn., So. Polit. Sci. Assn., Internat. Studies Assn., African Studies Assn., Phi Kappa Phi, Phi Alpha Theta, Pi Sigma Alpha, Phi Beta Delta. Democrat. Episcopalian. Home: Ste 214 Arbor Terr 3736 Atlanta Hwy Athens GA 30606-3159 Office: U Ga Dept Polit Sci Athens GA 30602 *It is important for me to have career opportunities which help people. The preservation, analysis and dissemination of the knowledge of the past is as essential as the creation of new knowledge. Practical application of knowledge is extremely important. One must be loyal to one's colleagues and the institutions in which one participates.*

CLUTZ, WILLIAM (HARTMAN CLUTZ), artist, educator; b. Gettysburg, Pa., Mar. 19, 1933; s. Paul Alexander and Catherine (Hartman) C. BA, U. Iowa, 1955. Instr. drawing, painting Parsons Sch. Design, N.Y.C., 1969-96. One-man shows include Condon Riley Gallery, N.Y.C., 1959, David Herbert Gallery, N.Y.C., 1962, Triangle Gallery, San Francisco, 1967, Bertha Schaefer Gallery, N.Y.C., 1963, 64, 66, 69, Bklyn. Coll., 1969, Graham Gallery, N.Y.C., 1972, Mercersburg (Pa.) Acad., 1972, Lamont Gallery, Phillips Exeter (N.H.) Acad., 1973, Addison Gallery Am. Art, Phillips Acad., Andover, Mass., 1973, Moravian Coll., Bethlehem, Pa., 1977, Brooke Alexander Gallery, N.Y.C., 1973, Alonzo Gallery, N.Y.C., 1977, 78, 79, Walther-Rathenau-Saal, Rathaus Kunstamt Wedding, Berlin, 1978, Mellon Art Center, Wallingford, Conn., 1979, Gallery 333, Dayton, Ohio, 1980, Tatistcheff & Co., N.Y.C., 1981, 82, 84, John C. Stoller & Co., Mpls., 1983, 87, Gallery van Voorst van Beest, The Hague, 1984, Tweed Mus., Duluth, 1986, Tatistcheff Gallery, L.A., 1988, Washington County Mus., Hagerstown, Md., 1991, Tatistcheff Gallery, L.A., 1992, Nicholas Davies Gallery, N.Y.C., 1997, Katharina Rich Perlow Gallery, N.Y.C., 1999, 2000, 01, 02; exhibited in group shows including Mus. Modern Art, N.Y.C., 1956, 62, Am. Fedn. Arts Traveling Exhbn., 1961-62, Contemporary Arts Mus., Houston, 1961, Am. Fedn. Fine Arts Traveling Exhbn., 1963-64, Pa. Acad. Fine Arts, Phila., 1964, 65, 66, U. Wis., 1967, Purdue U., 1968, Tweed Gallery, U. Minn., Duluth, 1968, Ringling Mus. Art, Sarasota, Fla., 1969, Columbus (Ohio) Gallery Fine Arts, 1970, Hall Gallery, Miami, Fla., 1972, Brooke Alexander Gallery, 1973, Smithsonian Traveling Exhbn., 1976-79, Westmoreland County Mus., Greensburg, Pa., 1979, Hirschl & Adler, N.Y.C. and L.A., 1980, Aaron Berman Gallery, N.Y.C., 1980, Stoller Gallery, 1980, 81, 83, 85, 88, Tatistcheff & Co., 1980, 81, 82, 84, 87, 89, 90, Corcoran Gallery Art, Washington, 1982, Bklyn. Mus., 1983, Mus. Modern Art, San Francisco, 1985, Chem. Bank, N.Y.C., 1987, Montclair (N.J.) Mus., 1989; represented in permanent collections, Addison Gallery Am. Art, Ball State U. Art Gallery, Muncie, Ind., Bklyn. Mus., Fogg Art Mus., Harvard U., Cambridge, Mass., Guggenheim Mus., N.Y.C., Hirshhorn Mus. and Sculpture Garden, Washington, Dayton Art Inst. (Ohio), Mercersburg Acad., Miles Coll., Atlanta, Milw. Art Center, Mus. Modern Art, N.Y.C.,, Mus. of City of N.Y., 2002, Met. Mus. Art, N.Y.C., N.Y. Sch. Interior Design, N.Y.C., N.Y. U. Art Collection, Newark Mus., Minn. Mus., St. Paul, Sheldon Meml. Art Gallery, Lincoln, Nebr., U. Mass., Amherst, Tweed Mus., Duluth, Washington County Mus. Fine Arts, Hagerstown, Md., also, AT&T, Ashland Oil, Inc., Chase Manhattan Bank, Schroder Bank, Topseal Corp., Wausaw Ins. Co., Lehman Bros., Milbank Tweed, Minn. Mut. Ins. Co., Simpson Thatcher & Bartlett, Solomon Bros., Third Nat. Bank, Dayton, Chem. Bank, McKinsey & Co., Mobil Corp., Mpls. Star Tribune, and many others. Address: Katharina Rich Perlow Gallery 41 E 57th St New York NY 10022-1908

CLYBURN, JAMES E. congressman; b. Sumter, S.C., July 21, 1940; m. Emily England; children: Mignon, Jennifer, Angela. Grad., S.C. State Coll., 1962; LHD (hon.), Winthrop Coll., 1987; DSc (hon.), Coll. of Charleston, 1992, Med. U. S.C., 1993; LHD (hon.), St. Augustine Coll., 1994; LLD (hon.), Claflin Coll., 1995; LHD (hon.), S.C. State U., 1995; LLD (hon.), Voorhees Coll., 1996. Teacher Charleston County Pub. Sch. System; counselor S.C. Employment Security Commn.; dir. Charleston County Neighborhood Youth Corps/New Careers Projects; exec. dir. S.C. Commn. Farmworkers Inc.; staffer for Gov. John C. West, Charleston, S.C., 1971-74; commr. S.C. Human Affairs Commn., Columbia, 1974-92; mem. 103rd Congress from 6th S.C. dist., D.C., 1993—; transp. & infrastructure com. Congressional Black Caucus 106th Congress. Pres. Nat. Assn. Human Rights Workers, 1980-81, Internat. Assn. Official Human Rights Agys., 1985-87. Active Southern Regional Coun., Atlanta; bd. dirs. Wofford Coll., Spartanburg, Allen U., Columbia, Brookgreen Gardens Murrell's inlet, James R. Clark Sickle Cell Anemia Found., Ctr. for Cancer Treatment and Rsch., S.C. Literacy Assn. Recipient ann. award for disting. svc. to state gov. Nat. Govs. Assn.; named Pub. Adminstr. of Yr. Am. Soc. Pub. Adminstrn. S.C. chpt. Mem. NAACP (life), Masons, Shriners, Omega Psi Phi. Democrat. Office: 319 Cannon House Office Bldg Washington DC 20515-4006 E-mail: jclyburn@mail.house.gov.*

CLYBURN, LUTHER LINN, real estate broker, appraiser, ship captain; b. Evansville, Ind., May 17, 1942; s. Luther and Robbie (Cobb) C.; children: Lisa Michelle, Luther Brent. Grad., Am. Savs. and Loan Inst., 1970; ABA, Pontiac (Mich.) Bus. Inst., 1972; BS, Detroit Coll. Bus., 1972; M of Bus. Mgmt., Ctrl. Mich. U., 1983. Lic. merchant marine; cert. scuba instr.; cert. Profl. Assn. Dive Instrs. Chief loan officer First Fed. Savs. and Loan Assn. Oakland, Pontiac, 1964-74; assoc. broker Bateman Real Estate Corp., Pontiac, 1975-77; regional rep. United Guaranty Residential Ins., Troy, Mich., 1977-83; sr. account mgr. Investors Mortgage Ins. Co., Boston, 1983-87; real estate broker, appraiser White Lake, Mich., 1977—, Clyburn Appraisal Svcs., White Lake, 1987—. Dir. sea ops. Mirek Standowicz shipwreck recovery expedition, Lake Mich., 2001, Drowned River project, Straits of Mackinac, 2001. Project dir., capt.: (documentary film) Angels of the Sea, 1982 (N.Y. Film Festival award 1983); photographer for Tundra Tours 25th anniversary of Alaska's Iditarod dog sled race, 1997, 2000. Capt., comdr. "Noble Odyssey" Tng. Ship, Mt. Clemens, Mich., 1977-89; dir., comdr. U.S. Naval Sea Cadet Corps Great Lakes div., Mt. Clemens, Mich., 1973—; nat. bd. dirs. U.S. Naval Sea Cadet Corps, 1988; project dir. Interseas Inc., Pontiac, 1982; ship capt. Great Lakes Botanical Island research project for Cranbrook Inst. Sci. (Thunder Bay Islands, Lake Huron, 1987, Islands of Green Bay, 1989, 90); dir. of Underwater Cinitofu, capt. Pride of Mich., 1989—; capt. Great Lakes Island Rsch. Project for Oakland U., Fox Islands, 1996; project dir. In Search of the Griffin, Great Lakes Rsch. Bd., Pride of Mich., 1998—; founder/pres. Inter-Seas Exploration Ltd., 1999—. Recipient Cert. Appreciation award Southfield Bicentennial Commn., 1976, Letter of Commendation award Sec. of Navy, 1983, Quality People award Meritorious Cmty. Svc., 1993, Oakland County Q2 award, 1993, Unsung Hero award Mich. Ho. of Reps., 1994. Mem. Internat. Ship Masters Assn., Navy League of U.S., Am. Soc. Appraisers, Mich. Assn. Real Estate Appraisers. Home and Office: 9000 Gale Rd White Lake MI 48386-1411 E-mail: lclyburn@aol.com.

CLYBURN, ROSE MARY REED, construction materials company executive; b. New London, Conn., July 31, 1954; d. Raymond Morgan and Bernice Joan (Zaugg) Reed; m. Collins G. Clyburn, Aug. 14, 1982. BS in Zoology, U. R.I., 1976; MBA in Fin., N.W. U., 1984. Market rsch. trainee PPG Industies Chems. Group, Pitts., 1976-77, field sales rep. Houston, 1977-78, sales rep. chems. divsn. Chgo., 1978-80, sales devel. rep. splty. products unit, 1980-83, market rsch. assoc. Chems. Group Pitts., 1983-86, product mgr. Chems. Group, 1986-91, mgr. customer svc. Chems. Group, 1991-94, dir. quality chems., 1994-96, dir. sales/mkt. silica products, 1996-97; sr. v.p. Cement Divsn. Cemex USA, 1998—. Home: 7 Highland Cir The Woodlands TX 77381-3847 Office: Two Allen Ctr 1200 Smith St Ste 2400 Houston TX 77002

CLYDE, CALVIN GEARY, civil engineer, educator; b. Springville, Utah, Sept. 5, 1924; s. Edward and Hannah (Mendenhall) C.; m. Brigitta Straumer, Nov. 24, 1948; children: Rixa, Eric S., DeAnn, Carla, Andrea, Loretta, Mark E., Tania. Student, Utah State U., 1942-43, No. State Tchrs. Coll., 1943-44, Brigham Young U., 1946; BS, U. Utah, 1951; degrees in civil engring., U. Calif., Berkeley, MS, 1952, PhD, 1961. Registered engr. and land surveyor, Utah; consecrated bishop Mormon Ch., 1976. Assoc. prof. civil engring. U. Utah, Salt Lake City, 1953-63; prof. Utah State U., Logan, 1963-89, prof. emeritus, 1989—, assoc. dir. Utah Water Research Lab., 1965-77, acting dir. Utah Water Research Lab., 1975-76. Cons. in ground water, fluid mechanics, hydraulics, hydropower, hydrology and water resources planning, 1953—. Contbr. articles to profl. jours. Served with U.S. Army, 1943-46, ETO. Science faculty fellow NSF, Berkeley, 1959-60. Fellow ASCE (pres. Utah sect. 1969-70, Utah Civil Engr. of Yr. 1979); mem. Am. Soc. Engring. Edn. (chmn. Rocky Mountain sect. 1962-63), AIAA, Nat. Water Well Assn., Internat. Assn. Hydraulic Research. Republican. Avocations: skiing, hiking, camping, fishing. Home: 839 N 1400 E Logan UT 84321-3629 Office: Utah State U Water Research Lab # 82 Logan UT 84322-0001

CLYDE, LARRY FORBES, banker; b. Heber, Utah, Nov. 19, 1941; s. Don and Kathryn (Forbes) C.; m. Barbara Eliason, Dec. 23, 1963 (div. Jan. 1985); children: Lynne, Karen Lee; m. Katharyn L. Decker, July 3, 1986. BA, Utah State U., 1963, MS, 1965. With Pitts. Nat. Bank, 1965-68; with Crocker Nat. Bank, San Francisco, 1968-86, mgr. investment banking, 1973-75, mgr. capital markets divsn., 1975-86, sr. v.p., 1976-78, exec. v.p., mem. policy com., 1978-86; mng. dir., chief exec. U.S. capital markets activities Midland Bank Group, N.Y.C., 1986-87; CEO Midland Montagu Govt. Securities, Midland Montagu Mcpl. Securities, and Midland Montagu Trust Co., 1986-87; exec. v.p., mgr. global fin. institutions mktg. Am. Express Bank, 1987-88; exec. v.p., mgr. global securities lending, mem. sr. mgmt. com. Mellon Bank N.A., Pitts., 1988-2000. Bd. dirs. Pub. Securities Assn., 1976-83, govt. borrowing com., 1981-87, vice chmn., 1981, chmn., 1982; treas., dir. No. Calif. chpt. Invest-In-Am., 1975-87; bd. dirs. ABA Securities Assn., 1995-97, Fed. Farm Credit Funding Corp., 2000—; mem. Farm Credit Sys. Audit Com., 2000—. Mem. Am. Bankers Assn. (vice chmn. bank investment and funds mgmt. divsn. exec. com. 1982, chmn. exec. com. 1983), Dealer Bank Assn. (bd. dirs. 1986-87), San Francisco Bond Club, Duquesne Club, Allegheny Country Club, The Club at Las Campanas. Office: 12 Mustang Mesa Santa Fe NM 87506-7702

CLYMER, ADAM, newspaper correspondent; b. N.Y.C., Apr. 27, 1937; s. Kinsey and Eleanor (Lowenton) Clymer; m. Ann Wood Fessenden, June 3, 1961; 1 child, Jane Emily (dec.). AB, Harvard U., 1958; postgrad., U. Cape Town, South Africa, 1959. Reporter Virginian-Pilot, Norfolk, Va., 1960—62, Balt. Sun, 1963—76, N.Y. Daily News, Washington, 1977; reporter, editor N.Y. Times, N.Y.C. and Washington, 1977—90, asst. Washington editor, 1991—97, Washington editor, 1997—99, Washington corr., 1999—. Author: (book) Edward M. Kennedy: A Biography, 1999; co-author: Reagan: The Man, The President, 1981; editor: N.Y. Times Yr. in Rev., 1986—87. Mem. Harvard Crimson Grad. Bd., Cambridge, Mass., 1958—; bd. dirs. Washington Press Club Found., 1995—, pres., 2000—. With U.S. Army, 1961—62. Recipient Everett Dirksen award, Dirksen Congl. Rsch. Ctr., 1994. Mem.: Nat. Press Club, Delhi Golf Club (India) (life). Avocation: fly fishing. Office: New York Times 1627 I St NW Ste 700 Washington DC 20006-4085 E-mail: adclym@nytimes.com.

CLYMER, BRIAN WILLIAM, diversified financial services company executive, former state official; b. Camden, N.J., May 16, 1947; s. Howard Young and Jean (Hatch) C.; children: Kathleen Norris, Richard Hatch; m. Valerie Clymer; children: Caitlin, Emily, Daniel Scott. AA in Bus., Mitchell Coll., 1968; BS in Bus. and Econs., Lehigh U., 1969; DSc in Commerce (hon.), Drexel U., 1999. CPA, Pa. Ptnr. Clymer, Merves & Amon, CPAs, 1982-89; adminstr. Fed. Transit Adminstrn., Dept. Transp., Washington, 1989-93; pres., CEO Railway Systems Designs Inc., 1993-94; treas. State of N.J., 1994-97; v.p. external affairs Prudential Ins. Co., 1997—. Vice chmn. Southeastern Pa. Transp. Authority, 1981—89; bd. dirs. exec. com. Am. Pub. Transit Assn., 1993—95; bd. dirs. N.J. Sports Exposition Authority, Casino Reinvestment Devel. Authority, N.J. Performing Arts Ctr., 1994—97. With Pa. N.G., 1970-76. Mem. AICPA, Pa. Inst. CPA, N.J. Soc. CPA. Republican. Presbyterian. Avocations: fishing, golf. Home: 62 Brookville Hollow Rd Stockton NJ 08559-2006 Office: Prudential Fin 751 Broad St Newark NJ 07102-3777

CLYMER, JAY PHAON, III, science educator; b. Lancaster, Pa., June 23, 1951; s. Jay Phaon Jr. and Jeannette (Armold) C.; m. Elizabeth Teresa Ruddy, June 4, 1988; children: Candace Rose, Colin Jay. BS in Zoology, U. R.I., 1973; MS in Biology, Lehigh U., 1975, PhD in Biology, 1978. Teaching asst. Lehigh U., Bethlehem, Pa., 1973-75, rsch. asst., 1975-78; asst. prof. Marywood U., Scranton, Pa., 1978-83, assoc. prof., 1983—, chmn. sci. dept., 1987-90, v.p. Faculty Senate. Tech. advisor Lackawanna River Corridor Assn., Scranton, 1985—; dir. Riverwatch program, Scranton, 1985—; chmn. edn. com. County Conservation Dist., Clarks-Summit, Pa., 1990—; cons. to environ. firms; rschr. fish survey Wetlands Inst., Stone Harbor, N.J. Author: (booklets) Perspectives on Matter Energy Technology - Study Guide, vol. I, 1987, vol. II, 1991, Ecology - The Science of Nature, vol. I, 1988, vol. II, 1993, Biology - The Study of Life, 1995, Life Science, 1995; contbr. articles to sci. jours. Bd. dirs., v.p. Lackawanna County Conservation Dist., Clarks-Summit, 1990—; coord. fundraising March of Dimes. Mem. Atlantic Estaurine Rsch. Soc. (Grad. award 1979), Internat. Ctr. Environ. Mgmt. Enclosed Coastal Seas, Register of Pa. Biologists, Register of Estaurine Scientists, Lackawanna Fedn. of Sportsmen (officer 1990—), Phi Kappa Phi, Sigma Xi. Avocations: fishing, hunting, woodworking, gardening. Home: 210 Melrose Ave Clarks Summit PA 18411-1440 Office: Marywood U 2300 Adams Ave Scranton PA 18509-1598 E-mail: Clymer@ac.marywood.edu.

CLYMER, JERRY ALAN, educational administrator; b. Easton, Pa., Nov. 3, 1946; s. Wilbur L. and Dorothy M. (Cutsler) C.; m. Theresa M. Merlo, July 26, 1969; children: Shane A., Marc A., Adam T. BA, Moravian Coll., Bethlehem, Pa., 1969; MA, Rider Coll., Lawrenceville, N.J., 1976; postgrad., Trenton (N.J.) State Coll., 1976-80, East Stroudsburg U., 1976-80. Cert. elem. tchr., prin., supr., sch. adminstr., student pers. svcs., N.J. Elem. tchr. Pohatcong Twp. Bd. Edn., Bloomsbury, NJ, 1969—77, asst. prin., 1977—89, chief sch. adminstr., 1989—99, dir. child study team, grants coord., testing coord., 1977—89, supr. summer sch., 1978—79, affirmative action officer, drug free liaison person, 1987—89; supt. schs. Andover Regional Bd. Edn., Newton, 1999—. Coord. N.J. instrnl. child study team dir. for mini grant dist. award FHA and N.J. Dept. Edn., 1989-90. Mem., coach Pohatcong Recreation Assn., 1969—; mem. Pohatcong Centennial Incorporation, 1980-81; chmn. Pohatcong Twp. Sch. Dist. Staff Scholarship Fund, 1971-77. Mem. Am. Soc. Sch. Admin. (N.J. chpt.), N.J. Prins. and Suprs. Assn., Warren Coun. Coun. Sch. Adminstrs., Warren County Elem. Sch. and Mid. Sch. Prins. (v.p. 1981-82, 85-86), Am. Assn. Sch. Adminstrs., N.J. Assn. Sch. Adminstrs. Avocations: camping, swimming, hiking, tennis, basketball. Home: 318 Ohio Ave Phillipsburg NJ 08865 Office: Andover Regional Bd Edn 707 Limecrest Rd Newton NJ 07860-8801 E-mail: jaclymer_08865@yahoo.com.

CLYMER, JOHN HOWARD, lawyer; b. Boston, Nov. 19, 1939; s. Russell Sturgis and Eileen Newell (Williams) C.; m. Diana Payne Walker, Aug. 22, 1964; children: Sarah Payne, Amy Newell. BA, Princeton U., 1962; JD, Harvard U., 1965. Bar: Mass. 1965. Assoc. Hutchins & Wheeler, Boston, 1965-71; ptnr. Hutchins Wheeler & Dittmar, Boston, 1972—2003, Nixon Peabody LLP, Boston, 2003—. Trustee Hyams Found. Contbr. articles to profl. jours. Mem. Concord Planning Bd., Mass., 1972-77, Concord Bd. Selectmen, 1988-94; trustee, treas. Walter E. Fernald State Sch., Waltham, Mass., 1975-82; bd. dirs., clk. Anatolia Coll., Boston, 1984—; trustee clk. Sofia Am. Schs., Boston, 1985—. Mem. Am. Bar Assn. (bus. law section, com. chmn. health law 1987, real propr., probate and trust law sect., com. chmn. exempt orgn. 1996-2000), Mass. Bar Assn., Boston Bar Assn., Am. Coll. Trust and Estate Coun., Union Club (Boston), Concord Country Club. Unitarian Universalist. Avocations: photography, travel. Office: Nixon Peabody LLP 100 Summer St Boston MA 02110

CLYMER, JOHN MARION, think-tank executive; b. Indpls., July 8, 1960; s. Richard Marion and Jean (Archibald) Clymer; m. Anne E. Weston. AB in Religion and Econs., Wabash Coll., 1982. Registered fin. planner; cert. fund raising exec. Mktg. rep. Springs Industries, 1982-85; fin. cons. Indpls. Fin. Group, 1986-89; mgmt. cons. Russell & Von Kannon, Geneva, Ill., 1989-90; dir. mktg. Devel. Dynamics Group, Fenton, Mo., 1990-91; v.p. Leadership Inst., Springfield, Va., 1991-93, Americans for Med. Progress, Alexandria, Va., 1993-96, Albert B. Sabin Vaccine Inst., Washington, 1996-2001; pres. Partnership for Prevention, 2001—. Ptnr. Strategic Comm., Alexandria, 1996—. Author: Escape!, 1981; contbr., articles to mags. and newspapers. Youth dir. Hudnut Mayoral Campaign, Indpls., 1975; mem. staff Ford Presdl. Campaign, 1976, Reagan Presdl. Campaign, 1980; precinct committeeman, Indpls., 1986-87; mem. Ch. Coun. on Ministries, 1988-89, mem. task force on cmty. preventive svcs., 2002—; mem. Nat. Immunization Coun., 2000—, mem. organizing com. ann. conf. on vaccine rsch., 1998-2001; mem. FDA/NIH Coun., 1998-2001; adv. bd. vaccine edn. ctr. The Children's Hosp., Phila., Pa., prevention rsch. initiative. Named Outstanding Young Men Am., 1986. Mem. Nat. Assn. Wabash Men (bd. dirs. 1984-88), Greater Washington Soc. of Assn. Execs. (mem. CEO adv. coun. 2002-2003), Phila. Soc., Nat. Eagle Scouts Assn. (Boy Scouts dist. com. 1987-88), Phi Kappa Psi (past pres. Alumni Assn.). Methodist. Avocations: writing, tennis. Office: 1015 18th Street NW Ste 200 Washington DC 20036

CLYMER, KENTON JAMES, history educator; b. Bklyn., Nov. 17, 1943; s. Wayne Kenton and Helen Elizabeth (Graves) C.; m. Marlee Joan Arrowsmith, Aug. 5, 1967; children: Aron Kenton, Megan Arrowsmith. AB in History with honors, Grinnell Coll., 1965; MA, U. Mich., 1966, PhD, 1970. Danforth lectr. U. Mich., 1969-70; from asst. to assoc. prof. of history U. Tex., El Paso, 1970-82, prof., 1982—2003, dir. grad. studies dept. history, 1975-80, 82-84; prof. history, dept. chair No. Ill. U., De Kalb, 2003—; asst. dean coll. liberal arts U. Tex., El Paso, 1980-84, interim dir. MA in interdisciplinary studies program, 1981-82, dir. religious studies program, 1983-85, 87-90, chair history dept., 1984-85, 93-96. Mem. exec. com. commn. archives and history United Meth. Ch., 1976-80; Fulbright lectr. Silliman U., Dumaguete City, Philippines and Taft Ave. Consortium Univs., Manila, 1977-78, U. Indonesia, Jakarta, 1990-91, Renmin U., Beijing, China, 2003-2004; assoc. provost Tex. Internat. Edn. Consortium Program Malaysia, 1986; cons. Indochina Project, Washington, summer 1989; George Bancroft vis. prof. history U. Göttingen, Germany, 1992-93; reviewer applications NEH, Fulbright Program, Indonesia; mem. Fulbright Com., 1994—. Author: John Hay: The Gentleman as Diplomat, 1975, Protestant Missionaries in the Philippines, 1898-1916: An Inquiry into the American Colonial Mentality, 1986,Quest for Freedom: The United States and India's Independence, 1995, (with others) Reapraising an Empire: New Perspectives in Philippine American History, 1984; reviewer Pacific Hist. Rev., The Historian, Pilipinas, Meth. History, Jour. Am. History; contbr. articles to profl. jours. Mem. health planning adv. com. West Tex. Coun. Govts., 1972-76; pres. bd. dirs. Houchen Community Ctr. and Newark Maternity Hosp., El Paso, 1974-76. Grantee Univ. Rsch. Inst., 1971, 72, 73-74, 74-75, 77, 80-81, 89, Am. Philos. Soc., 1972, 76, 81, U. Tex., 1982-83, 85, NEH, 1983, 85; Rackham fellow U. Mich., hon. rsch. fellow Inst. U.S. Studies, Univ. London, 1983; rsch. fellow Indo-U.S. Subcommission Edn. and Culture, New Delhi, 1986-87; residency Bellegio Study Ctr. Rockefeller Found., 2000; Grinnell Acad. scholar, Younker Honor scholar. Mem. Am. Hist. Assn., Orgn. Am. History, Soc. Historians Am. Fgn. Rels., Assn. Asian Studies (mem. Philippine studies group), Friars. Democrat. Presbyterian. Avocation: tennis. Home: 2837 Greenwood Acres Dr DeKalb IL 60115 2413 Office: History Dept No Ill Univ DeKalb IL 60115

CLYMER, WAYNE KENTON, bishop; b. Napoleon, Ohio, Sept. 24, 1917; s. George Arnold and Sallie Grace (Hulvey) C.; m. Helen Eloise Graves, Sept. 3, 1939; children: Kenton James, Richard George; m. Virginia R. Schoenbohm, Dec. 26, 2000. AB, Asbury Coll., 1939; MA, Columbia U., 1942; BD, Union Theol. Sem., 1944; PhD, NYU, 1950; LLD, Westmar Coll., 1969; DLitt, Hamline U., 1975; DD, Iowa Wesleyan Coll., Rust Coll., Garrett-Evang. Theol. Sem. Ordained to ministry Evang. Ch., 1942; pastor Emanuel Ch., Ozone Park, N.Y.C., 1939-41, St. Paul's Ch., Forest Hills, N.Y.C., 1941-46; prof. Evang. Theol. Sem., Naperville, Ill., 1946-57, dean, 1957-67, pres., 1967-72; bishop United Meth. Ch., Mpls., 1972-80, Des Moines, 1980-84. Lectr. St. Andrews Theol. Coll., Manila, 1966, Trinity Coll., Singapore, 1967, U. Dubuque, 1985, Ill. Coll., 1990, United Theol. Sem. in Twin Cities, 1990; pres. United Meth. Com. on Relief, 1976-84; mem. del. UN Conf. Refugee, 1979; liaison to theol. sems. Coun. of Bishops, 1984-87; chair Grannis-Martin Found., 1984-98. Author: Affirmation, 1971, Membership Means Discipleship, 1976; Contbr. to: Ency. Religious Edn. Pres. Naperville Sch. Bd., 1959-63; Mem. bd. Naperville Community Fund, 1966; pres. Chgo. Pastoral Counseling Center. Mem. Soc. Sci. Study Religion, Kiwanis, Kappa Delta Pi. E-mail: wclymer2000@yahoo.com.

CLYNCH, EDWARD JOHN, political science educator, researcher; b. South Bend, Ind., Nov. 30, 1942; s. James Harpster and June May (Roberts) C.; m. Barbara Meadow, Aug. 22, 1970; children: Barnaby Patrick, Jennifer Sarah. BA, Hillsdale (Mich.) Coll., 1965; MA, Ball State U., 1968; PhD, Purdue U., 1975. Tchr. Penn H.S., Mishawaka, Ind., 1967; instr. Elizabethtown (Ky.) C.C., 1968-70; asst. prof. polit. sci. U. New Orleans, 1974-78, Kans. State U., 1978-81; assoc. prof. Miss. State U., Mississippi State, 1981-87, prof., 1987—, head. dept. polit. sci., 1983-94, grad. coord., 1995—. Co-author: (with Tom Lauth) Governors, Legislators and Budgets: Diversity Across the American States, 1991; contbr. articles to profl. jours. Pres. Miss. Pub. Mgmt. Grad. Edn. Coun., 1985—; mem. Oktibbeha County Dem. Conv., 1984. Mem. Nat. Assn. Sch. Pub. Affairs and Adminstrn. (mem. exec. coun. 1984-86, chair polit. sci. based program of nation sect. 1987-89, mem. commn. on peer rev. and

accreditation 1988-91, 2003-2005), S.E. Conf. Pub. Adminstrn. (chair 1989 meeting), Am. Soc. Pub. Adminstrn. (pres. Miss. chpt. 1984-85, mem. pub. adminstrn. edn. nat. coun. sect. 1988—, pub. adminstrn. program evaluator 1990—, pres. pub. adminstrn. edn. sect. 1992-94), Am. Poli. Sci. Assn., So. Polit. Sci. Assn., Starkville C. of C. (mem. govtl. affairs com. 1987—), Rotary, Epsilon Delta Alpha, Omicron Delta Kappa, Pi Alpha Alpha, Pi Sigma Alpha, Phi Kappa Phi. Democrat. Presbyterian. Home: 401 Colonial Cir Starkville MS 39759-4213 Office: Miss State U Dept Polit Sci PO Drawer PC Mississippi State MS 39762 E-mail: eclynch@futuresouth.com.

CLYNE, ROSEMARIE BLACKSTONE, technical services librarian; b. Utica, N.Y., May 16, 1926; d. Arthur C. and Mary C. (Hofsass) Blackstone; m. Robert F. Clyne, Sr., Aug. 6, 1947; children: Robert Jr., Judi, James, Jeanne, Richard, Jeffrey, Cynthia, Debra, Lisa. AA, AS with honors, Polk Community Coll., 1970; BA magna cum laude, U. South Fla., 1972, MA magna cum laude, 1978. Cert. librarian. Ins. clk. Utica Mut. Ins. Co., 1943-46; clk. libr. Polk C.C., Winter Haven, Fla., 1971-73; libr. asst. Polk Community Coll., Winter Haven, Fla., 1973-78; libr. tech. svcs. Polk C.C., Winter Haven, Fla., 1978-91, libr. coord., 1989-91, prof. emeritus, 1991—. Sec. collection devel. com. U. South Fla. and related librs., 1990. Mem. Fla. Assn. Community Colls. (2nd v.p., chair learning resources com. 1990). Avocations: camping, needlework, miniatures, dolls. Office: Polk Community Coll 999 Avenue H NE Winter Haven FL 33881-4256

CLYNES, CAROLANN ELIZABETH, realtor; b. Hoboken, N.J., June 30, 1944; d. Merwin Cecil and Marie Dolores Beck; m. Patrick Robert Clynes, June 10, 1967 (div. Oct. 1986); m. Robert Bradford Bourne, Oct. 8, 1988; stepchildren: Jonathan Bourne, Christopher Bourne, Mark Bourne, Sarah Bourne, Susan Bourne, Molly Bourne. Student, Seton Hall U., 1964; BA in History and French, Georgian Ct. Coll., 1965; student, The Sorbonne, Paris, 1966; student in real estate courses, NYU Adult Edn., 1984; student, Inst. Residential Mktg., 1990. Cert. appraiser Nat. Realtors Appraisal Inst., 1987. Sales assoc. Helen Fisher Realty, 1970—72, Peter Farley Realtor, 1972—76; broker, sales assoc. Burgdorff Realtors, 1976—88; dir. sales Lois Schneider Realtor, 1988—94, Murray Hill Farm, 1988—94; broker Burgdorff Realtors, Summit, NJ, 1994—, broker, mgr., v.p. Summit office, 1994—96, v.p. corp. bus. develop., 1996—. Mem. Summit Hist. Preservation Commn., 1996—2000, mem. planning com. Summit Downtown, Inc., 1994—96; mem. capital cabinet Nat. Interfaith Hospitality Network, 1997—. Recipient award, Jr. League of Summit, N.J., 1997, appointment to N.J. Historic Trust, Gov. McGreevey, 2002. Mem.: Real Estate Brokerage Mgrs. Coun. (cert. 1995), N.J. Assn. Realtors Disting. Sales Club (Dist. Sales Club 1991). Democrat. Episcopalian. Avocations: antiques, reading, choral music and opera, French, historic preservation. Home: 130 Pine Grove Ave Summit NJ 07901 Office: Burgdorff Realtors 401 Springfield Ave Summit NJ 07901 E-mail: carolann-clynes@burgdorff.com.

CLYNES, MANFRED, musician, neuroscientist, inventor; b. Vienna, Aug. 14, 1925; came to U.s., 1946; s. Marcel William and Olga Clynes; m. Renate Clynes, Mar. 1951 (div. July 1972); children: Darius, Neville, Raphael. B Engring. Sci., U. Melbourne, Australia, 1946, DSc, 1964; MS in Piano, Juilliard Sch. Music, 1949; postgrad., Princeton U., 1952-54. Chief piano tchr. Cons. Music, U. Melbourne, 1950-52; concert pianist Europe and Australia, 1951-54; computer specialist Bogue Elec., Patterson, N.J., 1954-56; chief rsch. scientist Rockland State Hosp., Orangeburg, N.Y., 1956-73; vis. prof. U. Calif., San Diego, 1974-76; rsch. prof., dir. Music Rsch. Ctr. Cons. Music, Sydney (Australia) U., 1977-88; adj. prof. neuropsychology U. Melbourne, 1988-90; pres., CEO Microsound Internat., Ltd., Sonoma, Calif., 1991—. Adj. prof. Lombardi Cancer Ctr., Georgetown U., Washington, 2003—. Author: 6 books; contbr. articles to profl. jours.; piano recordings include, Goldberg Variations, Bach, Beethoven, Diabelli Vars. Op 120; composer: 5 songs; contbr. ; recordings, 6 Beethoven string quartets, 6 Brandenburg concertos. Recipient Baker award IEEE, 1960, Smith-Mundt award U.S. Govt., 1953-54, Fulbright award, U.S. Govt., 1953-54. Mem. AAAS, Soc. for Neurosci. (founder), Internat. soc. Rsch. on Emotion (charter), Am. Sci. Assn., Am. Sentic Assn. Achievements include development of field of sentics; patents for over 40 in field; invention of color ultrasound, CAT computer for neurophysiologic brain research; laws of lifelike, emotionally expressive musical microstructure, composer's pulse, SuperConductor advanced music interpretation program; expressive intonation tuning for all computers and synthesizers; discovery of of biologic law of unidirectional rate sensitivity. Home and Office: 19181 Mesquite Ct Sonoma CA 95476 Fax: 707-996-0997. E-mail: mclynes1@aol.com.

CMAR, JANICE BUTKO, home economics educator; b. Pitts., Nov. 10, 1954; d. Edward Michael and Ruth Lillian (Pickard) Butko; m. Dennis Paul Cmar, children: Michael, Nicole. BS, Mansfield U., 1976; MS, Duquesne U., 1990. Home econ. tchr. Duquesne (Pa.) Sch. Dist., 1978-83; special edn. tchr. Allegheny Intermediate Unit, Pitts., 1985-95; home econs. tchr. Peters Twp. Sch. Dist., McMurray, Pa., 1995—. Sponsor Duquesne High Sch., Y-Teens and Future Homemakers Am., 1979-83, Pathfinder Student Coun., Bethel Park, Pa., Mon-Valley Secondary Sch. Yearbook and Prom, Jefferson, Pa. Vol. Allegheny County Dept. Cmty. Svcs., Pitts., 1986—97; mem. com. Allegheny County Dem. Orgn.; elected Borough Jefferson Hills Coun., 1997, 2001—, coun. v.p., 2000, 2002; mem. cmty. adv. panel Hercules Corp., 2000; bd. dirs. South Hills Coun. Govts., 2000. Mem. Am. Fedn. Tchrs., Am. Assn. Family and Consumer Scis., State Assn. Family and Consumer Scis., Allegheny County Assn. Family and Consumer Scis. (pres. 1991-92), Phi Delta Kappa, Alpha Sigma Tau. Democrat. Home: 918 Old Hickory Ln Jefferson Hills PA 15025-3437 Office: 625 E Mcmurray Rd Mc Murray PA 15317-3497

COADY, JOSEPH WILLIAM, history educator, researcher; b. Bklyn. s. Nicholas Joseph and Adele Marie (Valaitis) C.; m. Mary Agnes Dress, Aug. 19, 1972; children: Loretta, Regina, Virginia, Andrew. BS, St. Peter's Coll., 1962; MA, St. John's U., Jamaica, N.Y., 1963; PhD, St. John's U., 1968. History tchr. St. Peters Boys H.S., Staten Island, N.Y., 1963-64, Nazareth H.S., Bklyn., 1964-66; prof. Coll. St. Rose, Albany, N.Y., 1966-68, Coll. Mt. St. Vincent, Bronx, N.Y., 1968—. Adj. history prof. numerous colls. in N.Y. area, 1970-98. Author: New York At Turn of Century, 1996. Scholar U. N.H., 1962. Mem. Am. Hist. Assn., Orgn. Am. Historians, Phi Alpha Theta (faculty advisor 1981—). Republican. Roman Catholic. Avocations: photography, film classics. Home: 6300 Riverdale Ave Bronx NY 10471-1034 Office: Coll Mt St Vincent 6301 Riverdale Ave Bronx NY 10471 E-mail: jwcoady@aol.com.

COADY, PHILIP JAMES, JR., retired naval officer; b. Boston, Aug. 25, 1941; s. Philip James and Helen (Mowles) C.; m. Judith Mary Greene, July 11, 1964; children: Meredith, Philip, Adrienne. AB, Tufts U., 1963; MS, Naval Postgrad. Sch., 1972. Commd. ensign USN, 1963, advanced through grades to rear adm., 1990; comdg. officer USS Conolly, 1981-83, dir. command and tactics dept., 1983-86, comdg. officer USS Antietam, 1986-89; dir. polit. and mil. policy and current plans div. Chief of Naval Ops. Washington, 1989-91; comdr. Cruiser-Destroyer Group Five, 1991-93; dir. surf warfare divsn. Chief of Naval Ops., 1994-95; pres. Navy Mutual Aid Assoc., Arlington, Va., 1995—2002. Author: (monograph) Shipbuilding: Perspective for the '80s, 1980. Nat. v.p. Surface Navy Assn., 1998—2002; treas. world bd. govs. USO, 2001—03. Decorated D.S.M., Legion of Merit with 5 gold stars. Mem.: Army and Navy Club. Roman Catholic. Office: Henderson Hall 29 Carpenter Rd Arlington VA 22204-4584

COADY, SEAN ARTHUR, statistician; b. Boise, Aug. 8, 1963; s. John Francis and Doris Dickinson Coady; m. Jane Dianne Wurtele, June 22, 1996; 1 child, Peyton Jon. BS, U. Tenn., 1985, MS, 1988; MA, U. Nebr., 1997. Rsch. asst. U. Tenn., Knoxville, 1988—90; rsch. technician U. Nebr., North Platte, Nebr., 1990—93, support technician Lincoln, Nebr., 1993—98; statistician Nat. Heart, Lung, Blood Inst., Bethesda, Md., 1998—. Contbr. articles to profl. jours. Recipient merit award, NIH, 2001. Avocations: kayaking, camping, woodworking. Office: NHLBI Rockledge II MSC 7934 Bethesda MD 20892

COADY, WILLIAM FRANCIS, information technology executive, consultant; b. Bklyn., June 16, 1940; s. Alexander Ignatius and Nora Monica (Dooley) C.; m. Kathleen Dolores McNerney, July 16, 1966; children: Noreen Theresa, Elizabeth Ann, Jennifer Patricia, Patricia Marie. AB in Classical Lang., St. Peters Coll., Jersey City, 1961. With IRS, 1961-88, exec. officer internal security divsn., 1973-76, regional dir. internal security divsn. Atlanta, 1976-88; pres. Info. Svcs. Internat., Inc., Dunwoody, Ga., 1989—. Cons. ethics and behavior IRS, Atlanta, 1982-88; adv. coun. Info. Am., Atlanta, 1990—. Contbr. articles to profl. jours. Fellow Fed. Computer Investigation Com. (Disting. Svc. award 1989). Roman Catholic. Home and Office: 5390 Seaton Dr Atlanta GA 30338-4537

COAKER, JAMES WHITFIELD, mechanical engineer; b. Boston, Nov. 12, 1946; s. George W. and Margaret N. Coaker; m. Ruth Johnson, May 17, 1969; children— James W., John A., Stephen D. BSME, Lafayette Coll., 1968; MSB, Va. Commonwealth U., 1976. Registered profl. engr., Va. Application engr. pump and condenser div. Ingersoll-Rand Co., Richmond, Va., 1972-76; project mgr. Reco Industries, Inc., Richmond, Va., 1976-77, asst. mgr. engring., 1977-79, mgr. engring., 1979-83; systems engr., program mgr. Advanced Tech., Inc., Arlington, Va., 1983-87; program mgr. Boiler and Elevator Safety U.S. Postal Svc., Washington, 1987—2002; prin. Coaker & Co. P.C., Fairfax, Va., 2002—. Lectr. and educator in field. With USN, 1969-72; capt. (ED) USNR, ret. Fellow ASME (sr. v.p. Codes & Stds., v.p. bd. on safey codes and stds., 1996-99, vice chmn. Elevator and Escalator Safety Code Com., mem. Bd. Profl. Devel. 1990-96, past national chmn. Plant Engring. & Maintenance Divsn.), Nat Coun. Examiners for Engring. and Surveying (affiliate), Naval Res. Assn. (life). Home: 11675 Captain Rhett Ln Fairfax Station VA 22039-1236 E-mail: coakerandco@aol.com.

COAKLEY, DEIRDRE, writer; b. Detroit, Aug. 10, 1927; d. Cecil Francis and Elizabeth Kearney Coakley. Grad., Hollywood (Calif.) H.S., 1944. Mem. editl. staff L.A. Examiner, 1943-46; mem. editl. staff various other newspapers L.A., to 1954; advt. exec., mag. editor Las Vegas (Nev.) Sun, 1954-66, Sunday mag. editor, 1977-85; freelance advt. and pub. rels. exec. Las Vegas, 1966-68; pub. rels. exec. Jimmy Snyder Info. Unltd. Tropicana Hotel, Las Vegas, 1968-74; pub. rels. dir. Desert Springs Hosp., Las Vegas, 1974-77; writer, columnist Gadsden (Ala.) Times, 1985—. Editor: The Way it Was: Diary of a Pioneer Woman, 1979-80; author: The MGM Grand Hotel Fire, 1982, Portrait of a City: An Informal History of Gadsden, Alabama 1846-1996, 1996; writer, curator Voices and Images of World War II. Publicist United Way of Etowah County, Gadsden, 1994—; bd. dirs. Metro. Arts Coun., 1988-95, Gadsden Symphony Orch., 1990-96; mem. Gadsden Ctr. Cultural Arts. Mem. Gadsden Art Assn., Etowah Hist. Soc. Democrat. Roman Catholic. Avocation: genealogy. Home: 739 Church Rd Gadsden AL 35904-3143

COAKLEY, DEXTER, football player; b. Mt. Pleasant, S.C. Degree in Comm. and Advt., Appalachian State U. Linebacker Dallas Cowboys, 1997—. Served as celebrity escort Children's Cancer Fund Fashion Show; guest football coach Let Us Play! Sports Camp for Girls, 2000. Named to Pro Bowl, 1999; recipient first-team All-Pro honors Sports Illustrated, second-team All Pro honors Coll. & Pro Football Newsweekly, Football Digest, 1999. Office: Dallas Cowboys 2401 Airport Fwy Irving TX 75062

COAKLEY, WILLIAM THOMAS, retired utilities executive; b. Dubuque, Iowa, Oct. 18, 1946; s. Harold Leo and Mary Margaret (Schwartz) C.; m. Deborah Dixon Leach, Nov. 25, 1971; children: Matthew David, Kenneth William. BA, Loras Coll., 1968; postgrad., Drake U., 1968-69, 71. Commd. U.S. Army, 1970, advanced through grades to capt., co. exec. officer, 1971-73, brigade staff officer Stuttgart, Fed. Republic of Germany, 1973-75; budget analyst U.S. Army Corps of Engrs., Frankfurt, Fed. Republic of Germany, 1975-77, budget officer Riyadh, Saudi Arabia, 1977-80, resigned, 1980; budget and fin. officer Western Area Power Adminstrn., Billings, Mont., 1980-85, fin. mgr., 1985-95, fin. sys. mgr. Golden, Colo., 1996-2000; co-project mgr. implementation of Oracle U.S. Fed. Fins., V10.7, Golden, Colo., 1997-99; ret., 2000. Tng. coord. for Oracle Fins. and PSDI Maximo software applications. Author, editor Fiscal Procedures and Control of Funds, 1975. Chmn. divsn. United Way Fundraiser of Yellowstone County, 1992, 93, mem. bd. dirs., 1994-96; mem. St. Patrick's Co-Cathedral Parish Coun., 1990-92, pres., 1991-92. Mem. Internat. Soc. Am. Mil. Engrs. (sec., treas. Frankfurt chpt. 1974-75), Yellowstone Country Club (bd. dirs. 1984-86, 95-96), Rotary, Pacific Northwest Golf Assn. (Mont. rep. 1995-96), Colo. Golf Assn. (rules ofcl. 1997—), Bear Creek Golf Club. Republican. Roman Catholic. Home: 2164 S Parfet Ct Lakewood CO 80227-1913 E-mail: wcoaks@hotmail.com.

COALE, KENNETH HAMILTON, biogeochemist, educator; b. N.Y.C., Jan. 24, 1955; s. Franklin Steele Coale and Mary Louise (Price) Moses; m. Susan Elizabeth Lange, June 23, 1979; children: Megan Elizabeth Coale, Tyler Hamilton Coale. BA in biology, U. Calif., 1977, PhD in biology, 1988. Marine tech. Moss Landing (Calif.) Marine Labs., 1976-77; asst. specialist U. Calif., Santa Cruz, 1978-83, assoc. specialist, 1983, rsch. asst., 1983-88; postdoctoral researcher Moss Landing (Calif.) Labs., 1988, sr. rsch. assoc., 1991-92, adj. prof., 1992—; acting dir. Moss Landing Marine Labs., 1998—2001, dir., 2001—. Vis. scientist KFA Juelich Germany, NIOZ, The Netherlands, 1982; guest editor Deep Sea Rsch., Oxford, Sidney, London, 1994—. Co-author: Dynamic Processing in the Chemistry of the Upper Oceans, 1986; contbr. articles to profl. jours. Sec., bd. dirs. Land Trust of Santa Cruz Co., 1991-2000; bd. dirs. Friends of MLML, 1998—. Recipient rsch. grants in field. Fellow Calif. Acad. Sci.; mem. AAAS, Am. Geophysical Union, Am. Soc. Limnology & Oceanography, Oceanography Soc., Am. Chemical Soc. Achievements include development of 234th; 238 U disequilibria as a tracer for chemical biological removal process; development of DPASV to determine copper complexation in the North Pacific Ocean, COPi and chief scientist of the Iron Ex and SOFex experiments. Office: Moss Landing Marine Labs 8272 Moss Landing Rd Moss Landing CA 95039-9647 E-mail: coale@mlml.calstate.edu.

COALTER, MILTON J., JR., library director, educator; b. Memphis, July 5, 1949; s. Milton J. and Jewel (Mitchel) C.; m. Linda M. Block, May 20, 1973; children: Martha Claire, Siram Jacob. BA, Davidson Coll., 1971; MDiv, Princeton Theol. Sem., 1975, ThM, 1977; PhD in Religion, Princeton U., 1982. Asst. prof. Am. Religion N.C. State U., Raleigh, 1981-82; pub. svcs. libr. The Iliff Sch. Theology, Denver, 1982-84, acting libr. dir., 1984-85; libr. dir., prof. bibliography and rsch. Louisville Presbyn. Theol. Sem., 1985—, acting pres., 2002—03. Acting pres. Louisville Presbyn. Theol. Sem., 2002-03, bd. dirs. Louisville Inst., Scholars Press; gen. assembly coun. task force on ch. membership growth Presbyn. Ch., Louisville, 1989-91, gen. assembly theol. task force for the peace, unity and purity of the ch., 2001-. Author: (with John M. Mulder) The Letters of David Avery, 1979, Gilbert Tennent, Son of Thunder, 1986; (with John M. Mulder and Louis B. Weeks) The Presbyterian Presence in the Twentieth Century, 7 vols., 1989-92, Vital Signs, 1996, Resources for American Christianity, 2002, website for religion divsn. Lilly Endowment, 2000--; editor: (with Virgil Cruz) How Shall We Witness?, 1995; contbr. articles to profl. jours. Mem. Gen. Assembly Task Force on Peace, Unity and Purity of the Ch., 2001—. Recipient Jonathan Edwards award Princeton U., 1977-80, Tchg. award Assn. Princeton Grad. Alumni, 1979-80, Francis Makemie award Presbyn. Ch. Dept. History; Lily Endowment grantee, 1987-90, 99—, N.J. Hist. Commn. grantee, 1979-80, Pew Charitable Trust grantee, 1990-93; Princeton U. Whiting fellow, 1980-81. Mem. Am. Theol. Libr. Assn. (bd. dirs. 1997-2003, pres. 1998-2000), Am. Soc. Ch. History, Am. Acad. Religion. Presbyterian. Office: Louisville Presbyn Theol Sem 1044 Alta Vista Rd Louisville KY 40205-1758

COAN, RICHARD MORTON, lawyer; b. N.Y.C., Sept. 17, 1948; s. Nelson W. and Phyllis (Tomashoff) C.; m. Kathleen M. Mitcheom, Sept. 5, 1983; children: Benjamin, Spencer, Eliza. AB, U. Rochester, 1969; JD, Yale U., 1974. Bar: Conn. 1974, U.S. Dist. Ct. Conn. 1981, U.S. Ct. Appeals (2d cir.) 1982. Ptnr. Belford, Belford & Coan, New Haven, Conn., 1977-81, Coan, Lewendon, Royston & Guliver, LLC, New Haven, 1981—. Mem. ABA (corp. banking and bus. law sects.), Conn. Bar Assn. (real estate and comml. law sects.). Home: 17 E Haycock Point Rd Branford CT 06405-5301 Office: Coan Lewendon Royston & Gulliver LLC 495 Orange St New Haven CT 06511-3809 E-mail: richcoan@aol.com.

COAR, RICHARD JOHN, mechanical engineer, aerospace consultant; b. Hanover, N.H., May 2, 1921; s. Herbert Greenleaf and Anne (Langille) C.; m. Cecilie Berle, 1942 (dec. 1971); children— Gregory, Candace, Andrea, Kenneth; m. Lucille Hicks, 1972. BS in Mech. Engring., Tufts U., 1942. Engr. Pratt & Whitney Aircraft, East Hartford, Conn., 1942-56; chief engr. Fla. Research and Devel. Ctr., 1956-70, asst. gen. mgr., 1970—2001; v.p. engring. Pratt & Whitney Aircraft, East Hartford, 1971—76, exec. v.p., 1976-83, pres., 1983-84; sr. v.p. United Techs., Hartford, 1983-84, exec. v.p., 1984-86. Patentee aircraft engines and controls Corporator Hartford Hosp., 1983; bd. dirs. Hartford Symphony, 1985-87. Recipient Franklin W. Koln Air Transp. Progress award Soc. Automotive Engrs., 1985, Daniel Guggenheim medal for contbns. to aeronautic and space propulsion sys., 1998, Franklin W. Kolk Air Transp. Progress award Soc. Automotive Engrs., 1998. Mem. ASME (George Westinghouse Gold medal 1986), NAE, Am. Soc. Metals (disting. life mem.), Tau Beta Pi, Water's Edge Country Club. Avocations: sailing, golf. Home and Office: 105 Blackwater Cir Penhook VA 24137-5260

COASE, RONALD HARRY, economist, educator; b. Willesden, Eng., Dec. 29, 1910; arrived in U.S., 1951; s. Henry Joseph and Rosalie (Giles) Coase; m. Marian Ruth Hartung, Aug. 7, 1937. B of Commerce, London Sch. Econs., 1932, DSc in Econs., 1951; Dr. Rer. Pol. honoris causa, Cologne U., Fed. Republic Germany, 1988; D of Social Sci. (hon.), Yale U., 1989; LLD (hon.), Washington U., St. Louis, 1991; LLD (hon.), U. Dundee, Scotland, 1992; DSc (hon.), U. Buckingham, Eng., 1995; DHL (hon.), Beloit Coll., 1996; docteur honoris causa, U. Paris, 1996. Sir Ernest Cassel Travelling scholar, 1931—32; asst. lectr. Dundee Sch. Econs., 1932—34, U. Liverpool, England, 1934—35; from asst. lectr. to lectr. to reader London Sch. Econs., 1935—51; prof. U. Buffalo, 1951—58, U. Va., Charlottesville, 1958—64, U. Chgo., 1964—, now Clifton R. Musser prof. emeritus, sr. fellow in law and econs. Law Sch. Statistician, then chief statistician Ctrl. Statis. Office, Offices War Cabinet, England, 1941—46. Author: British Broadcasting, A Study in Monopoly, 1950, The Firm, the Market and the Law, 1988, Essays on Economics and Economists, 1994; editor: Jour. Law and Econs., 1964—82. Mem. hon. com. Eurosci.; chmn. adv. bd. Contracting and Orgns. Rsch. Inst. U. Mo., Columbia. Named Rockefeller fellow, 1948; recipient Nobel prize in Econs., 1991; fellow Ctr. for Advanced Study Behavioral Scis., 1958—59, sr. rsch. fellow, Hoover Instn., Stanford U., 1977, hon. fellow, London Sch. Econs. Fellow: European Acad., Am. Econ. Assn. (disting.), Brit. Acad. (corr.), Am. Acad. Arts and Scis.; mem.: Internat. Soc. for New Instnl. Econs. (founding pres. 1997), Mont Pelerin Soc., Royal Econ. Soc. Office: U Chgo Laird Bell Law Quadrangle 1111 E 60th St Chicago IL 60637-2776 Home: The Hallmark 2960 N Lake Shore Dr Chicago IL 60637

COATE, DAVID EDWARD, acoustician, consultant; b. Kansas City, Mo., Sept. 10, 1955; s. Arthur Dale and Martha (Goodrich) C.; m. Sheryl Marie Luebbert, Aug. 8, 1981; children: Allison Marie, Brian Joseph, Michelle Grace. BA in Math./Chemistry/Physics cum laude, Westminster Coll., 1978; MS, MIT, 1980. Rsch. staff scientist MIT Energy Lab., Cambridge, 1980-81; energy auditor Volt Energy Systems, Boston, 1981-82; owner Turning Point Records, Boston, 1982-85; sr. scientist Bolt, Beranek, and Newman, Cambridge, 1986-89; dir. noise and vibration control Acentech Inc., Cambridge, 1989—. Albums include Time Keeps on Running, 1980, State of the Heart, 1985, Still Small Voice, 1990, Evidence, 1998, Face to Face, 2001. Mem. Acoustical Soc. Am., Inst. Noise Control Engring. (assoc.), Transp. Rsch. Bd. Avocations: stamp collecting, weight lifting, jogging, water skiing.

COATES, BEN TERRENCE, professional football player; b. Greenwood, S.C., Aug. 16, 1969; BS in Sports Mgmt., Livingstone Coll. Tight end New Eng. Patriots, Foxboro, Mass., 1991-99, Baltimore Ravens, Owings Mills, Md, 1999—. Named to Sporting News NFL All-Pro Team, 1994, 95, to NFl Pro Bowl Team, 1994-96. Office: Baltimore Ravens 11001 Owings Mills Blvd Owings Mills MD 21117-2857

COATES, BRADLEY ALLEN, lawyer; b. L.A., Mar. 27, 1951; s. Mark Edmund and Elizabeth (Allen) C.; m. Margaret Fife Bentley, Apr. 17, 1977 (div. Dec. 1980); m. Sachi Braden, Oct. 11, 1993. BA, U. So. Calif., 1973; JD, UCLA, 1976. Bar: Calif. 1977, Hawaii 1978, No. Marianas Islands 1978, Marshall Islands 1979, Federated States Micronesia 1981. Staff atty. Congress of Micronesia, Saipan, 1976-78; mng. ptnr. Rohlfing, Smith & Coates, Honolulu, 1978-85; prin. ptnr. Law Offices Bradley A. Coates, Honolulu, 1985-96; mng. ptnr. Coates and Frey, Honolulu, 1996—. Pres., exec. dir. Pacific Arbitration and Mediation, Honolulu, 1985—. Author: Divorce with Decency: The Complete How-To Handbook and Survivor's Guide to the Legal, Emotional, Economic and Social Issues. Chief counsel Hawaii State Rep. Party, Honolulu, 1981; founder, pres. Divorce with Decency Mediation Assn., Honolulu, 1985. Selected as Best Divorce Lawyer by Honolulu Weekly and Honolulu Mag. Mem. Hawaii Bar Assn. (family law sect.). Clubs: Outrigger Canoe, Honolulu. Avocations: all water sports, skiing, hiking. Office: 900 Fort Street Mall Honolulu HI 96813-3721 Home: Apt 3501 2600 Pualani Way Honolulu HI 96815-2702

COATES, DIANNE KAY, social worker; b. Adrian, Mich., Jan. 4, 1945; Student, Jackson Bus. U., 1962-63; AA with honors, Macomb C.C., Warren, Mich., 1977; BA with high distinction, Madonna Coll., 1979; MSW, Wayne State U., 1982; postgrad., Internat. Grad. Sch., 1984, Ea. Mich. U., 1989. Cert. social worker, Mich. Nat. svc. officer Mil. Order of the Purple Heart, Detroit, 1973-80; psychology technician VA Med. Ctr., Allen Park, Mich., 1980-84; clin. cons. HOMEBASE, Detroit, 1983-85; clin. social worker Cmty. Counseling Assocs., Adrian, 1983, Roseville, Mich., 1983-87, Ypsilanti (Mich.) Regional Psychiat. Hosp., 1987-90, Southgate (Mich.) Regional Ctr. for the Developmentally Disabled, 1990-92, 92-96, Lafayette Clinic, 1992; from intake/admissions/discharge coord. to dir. social work svcs. Southgate Ctr., 1996—2001; clin. social worker Northville Psychiat. Hosp., 2001—02, acting dir. social svcs., 2002—03; clin. social work mgr. Walter Reuther Psychiat. Hosp., 2003—. Group counselor Survivors of Homicide, Detroit, 1981-82; vol. HAVEN, Pontiac, Mich., 1986-87; internat. exch. counselor Edn. Found. Fgn. Study, 1987-92; field instr. Wayne State U., 1988—; ind. contract therapist Renaissance West Cmty. Mental Health Svcs. Clinic, Detroit, 1988-89, Caknipe-Kovach Assocs., 1988-92; area rep. Ednl. Resource Devel. Trust, 1991-94 Recipient Ann. Disting. Svc. award LA MOPH Dept. of Mich., 1992. Mem. NASW (bd. cert. diplomate), Acad. Cert. Social Workers, Assn. State Employed MSW's (v.p. 1991-93), Mich. Mental Health Assn., Mich. Assn. Mental Health Profls., Social Work Assn. Madonna Coll. (co-founder), Wayne State U. Alumni Assn., Bus. and Profl. Women, VietnamVets. Am. (hon. life assoc. mem.), Met. Svc. Officers Assn. (pres. 1990-92), Ladies Aux. Mil. Order of Purple Heart (region 2 v.p. 1985-86, nat. membership officer 1995-96), Ladies Aux. VFW, DAV Aux. Home: 1502 Elias St Westland MI 48186-4919 Office: Walter Reuther Psychiatric Hosp 30901 Palmer Westland MI 48186

COATES, DONALD ROBERT, geology educator, scientist; b. Grand Island, Neb., July 23, 1922; s. Frank Jefferson and Harriet (Ferris) C.; m. Jeanne Louise Grandison, Mar. 18, 1944 (dec. Jan. 1993); children: Cheryl D., Donald Eric, Lark J.; m. Marilyn Hilton Williams, Jan. 12, 1998. BA, Coll. Wooster, 1944; MA, Columbia U., 1948, PhD, 1956. Faculty Earlham Coll., Richmond, Ind., 1948-51; geologist, project chief U.S. Geol. Survey, Tucson, 1951-54; faculty Harpur Coll. (now Binghamton U./SUNY), Binghamton, N.Y., 1954-90, chmn. dept. geology, 1954-63, prof., 1963-90; prof. emeritus Binghamton U. SUNY, Binghamton, 1990—; research geologist U.S. Geol. Survey, Vestal, N.Y., 1958-61; vis. geoscientist Am. Geol. Inst., 1963-65; cons. C.E. U.S. Army, 1965-66. Cons. Empire State Electric Energy Research Corp., Consol. Edison N.Y., Niagara Mohawk Power Corp., Mohonk Preserve Corp., Protector Pine Oak Woods Inc., U.S. Army C.E., Town of Islip, N.Y. State Dept. Environ. Conservation, N.Y. State Electric & Gas Corp., N.Y. State Dept. Transp., N.Y. State Atty. Gen., N.Y. State Power Authority, N.Y. Low Level Nuclear Waste Siting Commn., Town of Vernon, N.Y., Broome County, Chemung County, Town of Vestal, N.Y., Town of Trenton, N.Y., Town of Deerfield, N.Y., Town of Norwich, Adastra West Pubs., 1999, Facts on File, Inc., 1987, 99, also pvt. cos.; assoc. program dir. NSF Found., 1963-64; vis. prof. Ind. U., 1955, U. Ill., 1963, Guangdong Seismol. Bur., China, 1987; vis. scholar Chinese Acad. Sci., 1995. Editor: Geology of South-Central New York, 1963, Environmental Geomorphology and Landscape Conservation, 3 vols., Coastal Geomorphology, Glacial Geomorphology, Geomorphology and Engineering, Landslides, (with John Vitek) Threshholds in Geomorphology, Urban Geomorphology, Environmental Geomorphology, 1971, Environmental Science Workbook, 1972, (with Charles Higgins) Ground Water Geomorphology, 1990; editor, author: Environmental Geology; author: Geology and Society; contbr. to Science - A Process Approach, 1965; also articles, reports. Lt. USN, 1943—46, lt. USNR, 1946—54. Recipient award for Sustained Superior Performance NSF, 1964; Rsch. grantee NSF, U.S. Dept. Commerce, U.S. Geol. Survey, N.Y. State Atomic and Space Devel. Authority, Rsch. Found. SUNY, 1958-61. Fellow

AAAS, Geol. Soc. Am. (Merit cert. engring. geology divsn. 1980, E.B. Burwell Jr. award 1995); mem. Assn. Engring. Geologists, Nat. Assn. Geology Tchrs. (pres. Eastern sect. 1962, Ralph Digman award 1972, Coll. Tchr. of Yr. award 1971), Am. Inst. Profl. Geologists, N.Y. State Geol. Assn. (pres. 1963, 81), Phi Beta Kappa. Home: 6608 17th Ave Court West Bradenton FL 34209 Office: Binghamton U SUNY Dept Geol Scis Binghamton NY 13902 E-mail: donormarilyncoates@earthlink.net.

COATES, ELEANOR SMITH, civic worker; b. Omaha, Aug. 1, 1924; d. Victor Bunnell and Esther (Devalon) Smith; m. Carl Wendell Coates, Oct. 23, 1947; children: Carl Victor, Richard Wendell. Student, Cen. Inst. for the Deaf, St. Louis, 1929-36, Brownell Hall, Omaha, 1936-42; BA in Chemistry, Grinnell Coll., 1946. Owner, operator Coates Mimeo Svc., 1962-82. Author autobiography: I Won't Stay Silent!, 1987. Treas. Lincoln Sch. PTA, Ponca City, Okla., 1957-59, Presbyn. Sixty-Niners, Ponca City, 1953-54, Band Parents, Ponca City, 1963-65, United Meth. Women, 1991-93, 98-99; cub scout den mother Boy Scouts Am., Ponca City, 1957-60; deacon First Presbyn. Ch., Ponca City, 1988; mem. mission coms. First United Meth. Ch., Ponca City, 1990-93, worship com., 1993-97; promoter of hearing ear dogs program Dogs for Deaf, Inc., Central Point, Oreg.; vol. Ret. Sr. Vol. Program., 1988-2000; assoc. mem. Quail Springs Meth. Ch., Oklahoma City, 2000—, Samuel King DAR chpt. Named Vol. of Yr., Ret. Sr. Vol. Program, 1989. Mem. AAUW (corr. sec. 1989-90), Ctrl. Inst. for Deaf Alumni Assn. (v.p. 1947-51), Red Rose Garden Club (treas. 1991-93, 99-2000), DAR (Sam King chpt., Ponca City chpt. treas. 1986-90, 92-94, 96-2000). Republican. Methodist. Avocations: reading, genealogy, sports, writing, bridge. Home: Apt 180 14901 N Pennsylvania Ave Oklahoma City OK 73134-5960 E-mail: escoates@poncacity.net.

COATES, GLENN RICHARD, lawyer; b. Thorp, Wis., June 8, 1923; s. Richard and Alma (Borck) C.; m. Dolores Milburn, June 24, 1944; children—Richard Ward, Cristie Joan Student, Milw. State Tchrs. Coll., 1940-42, NMA and MA, 1943-44; LLB, U. Wis., 1949, SJD, 1953. Bar: Wis. 1949. Atty. Mil. Sea Transp. Service, Dept. Navy, 1951-52; pvt. practice law Racine, Wis., 1952—; of counsel Dye, Foley, Krohn, Shannon, S.E. Sec., gen. counsel Racine Federated Inc.; lectr. U. Wis. Law Sch., 1955-56. Author: Chattel Secured Farm Credit, 1953; contbr. articles to profl. publs. Chmn. bd. St. Luke's Meml. Hosp., 1973-76, bd. dirs., 1990-91; pres. Racine Area United Way, 1979-81; bd. curators State Hist. Soc. Wis., 1986-2001, pres., 1995-97; bd. dirs. Racine County Area Found., 1983-89; bd. dirs. Wis. History Found., Inc., 1983-99, Hist. Sites Found., Inc., 1987-89, St. Luke's Hosp./St. Mary's Med. Ctr. Healthcare Found., 1992-96. With U.S. Army, 1943-46. Fellow Am. Bar Found. (life); mem. ABA, State Bar Wis. (bd. govs. 1969-74, chmn. bd. 1973-74), Wis. Jud. Coun. (chmn. 1969 72), Am. Law Inst. (life), Racine Country Club, Masons, Order of Coif. Methodist (chmn. fin. com. 1961-67). Home: 2830 Michigan Blvd Racine WI 53402-4254 Office: 1300 S Green Bay Rd Racine WI 53406-4469

COATES, JOHN PETER, technical executive; b. Coventry, Eng., Apr. 4, 1946; came to U.S., 1978; s. Harry and Barbara Joan (Snape) C.; m. Laura Frances Curran, July 28, 1979; children: Jonathan Edmund, Kristen Elizabeth, Ross James. BS/MS in Chemistry, Slough Coll. of Tech. now Thames Valley Univ., Eng., 1972; PhD in Chemistry, Brunel U., London, 1987. Analytical chemist Castrol Oil Co., Bracknell, Eng., 1964-73; sr. chromatographer Burmah Oil, Bromboro, Eng., 1973-74; sr., chief chemist Perkin-Elmer Ltd., Beaconsfield, Eng., 1974-78; sr. staff scientist Perkin-Elmer Corp., Norwalk, Conn., 1978-85; dir. mktg. Spectra-Tech Inc., Stamford, Conn., 1985-88; dir. analyzer div. Nicolet Instrument Corp., Madison, Wis., 1988-92; dir. mktg. real time systems divsn. (PAI) Perkin-Elmer, Norwalk, Conn., 1992-96; prin. cons. Coates Cons., Newtown, Conn., 1996—; dir. techs. Global Technovations, Inc., Atlanta, 1998—2002; interim dir. MCEC, U. Tenn., Knoxville, 1999—2001; ptnr. Personal Instruments, LLC, Sentelligence Corp. Co-author: (with L.C. Setti) Oils, Lubricants and Petroleum Products--Characterization by Infrared Spectra, 1985; patentee in field; contbr. chpts. to books and articles to profl. jours. Fellow Royal Soc. Chemistry; mem. Am. Chem. Soc., Instrument Soc. Am., Soc. Automotive Engrs., Soc. Applied Spectroscopy. Avocations: writing, photography, music, computers. Office: Coates Cons PO Box 3176 Newtown CT 06470-3176 E-mail: JohnC79051@aol.com.

COATES, KAREN JEANNE, journalist, educator; b. Racine, Wis., Aug. 7, 1971; BA in Journalism Anthropology, U. Mont., 1993; MS in Journalism, Anthropology, Internat. Studies, U. Oreg., 1997. Reporting intern Albuquerque Tribune, 1993; freelance writer Roseburg, Oreg., 1993—. Editl. asst., cons. Women of Vietnam Rev., Hanoi, 1996; copy editor, weekend edit. editor The Cambodia Daily, Phnom Penh, Cambodia, 1998-99; fellow, guest spkr. Poynter Inst. Media Studies, St. Petersburg, Fla., 1993-94; keynote spkr. U. Idaho Asian Conf., 2001; instr. Umpqua C.C., Roseburg, 2000-2001. Contbr. numerous articles to newspapers, mags. and literary jours. Fellow Oreg. Global Grads., 1996, Oreg. Literary fellow Oreg. Literary Arts, Icn., 2000; recipient 3rd place feature writing William Randolph Hearst Found., 1993, 1st Place non-fiction Willamette Writers Kay Snow Contest, 2000, 2d place nonfiction Quincy Writers Guild, 2001, 2d place nonfiction Willamette Writers, 2001, Short non-fiction award Coun. for Wis. Writers, 2002. Mem. U. Oreg. Alumni Assn., Willamette Writer, Soc. Profl. Journalists.

COATES, ROBERT JAY, retired electronic scientist, consultant; b. Lansing, Mich., May 8, 1922; s. Archie Louis and Ruth Agnes (Hutchings) C.; m. Gladys Buchhorn, Aug. 17, 1946; (dec.); 1 child, Bonnie; m. H. Regina Thorsen, Oct. 17, 1999. BSE.E., Mich. State U., 1943; MSE.E., U. Md., 1948; PhD in physics, Johns Hopkins U., 1957. Electronic scientist U.S. Naval Research Lab., Washington, 1943—49, electronic scientist, 1952—59; instr. physics Johns Hopkins U., Balt., 1949—52; assoc. chief tracking systems divsn., chief space data acquisition divsn., chief advanced devel. divsn., chief advanced data systems divsn.; mgr. crustal dynamics project Goddard Space Flight Ctr., Greenbelt, Md., 1959—88. Cons., 1989-93. Home constrn. vol. Habitat for Humanity, 1996-99. Served with USN, 1944-45. Recipient Outstanding Performance award NRL, 1959, Group Achievement award NASA, 1973, 1968, 1986, Apollo Achievement award, 1969, Exceptional Performance award Goddard Space Flight Center, 1971, Exceptional Service medal, 1986; Outstanding Leadership medal NASA, 1989. Fellow IEEE, mem. Am. Phys. Soc., Am. Geophys. Union, AAAS, Sigma Xi, Phi Kappa Phi, Tau Beta Pi. Home: 529 Whitingham Dr Silver Spring MD 20904-6330

COATES, SHIRLEY JEAN, finance educator, secondary school educator; b. Nashville, Tenn., Oct. 9, 1944; d. Jerry Baxter Springer and Cora Louise Green; m. Arthur Andrew Coates; children: Andrea, John. BS, Mid. Tenn. State U., 1968; MS, Brigham Young U., 1971. Lic. profl. tchr., cert. tchr. Tenn. career level III. Instr. Young Harris Coll., Young Harris, Ga., 1968—70, U. of Miss., Oxford, Miss., 1971—72; tchr. Dickson County Jr. H.S., Dickson, Tenn., 1972—73, Hickman County H.S., Centerville, Tenn., 1973—. Bus. dept. chmn. Hickman County H.S., Centerville, Tenn., 1994—. Sponsor, Hickman County - Tenn. type-a-thon Leukemia Soc. of Am., BPA Chpt., Nashville, 1989—99; sec. Hickman County H.S. Band Boosters, Centerville, Tenn., 1988—94, Hickman County H.S. Athletic Booster Club, Centerville, Tenn., 1995—96; pageant chmn. Hickman County 4-H Vol. Leaders, Centerville, Tenn., 1990—94; project dir. (head start book dr.) South Ctrl. Human Resources Agy., Centerville, Tenn., 1988—89. Named Tchr. of Yr., Hickman County HS Bd. of Edn., 1990, Bus. Dept. Tchr. of Yr., Hickman County H.S., 2000, Most Disting. H.S. Tchr., Hickman County Tenn. Edn. Assn., 2002; recipient, 2003. Mem.: Bus. Profls. Am. (honor adv. 1991, star advisor 1992), Assn. for Career and Tech. Edn., Daughters of Am. Revolution (asst. registrar, treas. 1998—2002).

COATES, WAYNE EVAN, agricultural engineer; b. Edmonton, Alta, Canada, Nov. 28, 1947; arrived in U.S., 1981; s. Orval Bruce Wright and Leora (Raesler) C.; m. Patricia Louise Williams, Aug. 28, 1970. BS in Agr., U. Alta., 1969, MS in Agrl. Engring., 1970; PhD in Agrl. Engring., Okla. State U., 1973. Registered profl. engr., Ariz., Sask. Forage systems engr. Agr. Can., Melfort, Canada, 1973-75; project engr., tech. advisor, asst. sta. mgr. Prairie Agrl. Machinery Inst., Humboldt, Canada, 1975-81; pvt. practice cattle, grain farmer Humboldt, 1975-81; assoc. prof. U. Ariz., Tucson, 1981-91, prof., 1991—; prof. titular ad honorem U. Nat. de Catamarca, Argentina, 1993—. Cons. Vols. in Coop. Assts. and Ptnr. of Am., 1991-98, Paraguayan Govt. UN Devel. Program, 1987-90, Argentine Govt., univ. and pvt. industry, 1991—, govt., univ. and agrl. orgn., Mid East agrl. projects, 1986-89, 98-99; spkr. at internat. conf., Australia, Paraguay, Argentina, Peru, Chile, US expert witness in field. Designer farm equipment primarily for alternative crops and tillage; patentee in field; contbr. articles to profl. jour. Pres. Sunrise Ter. Village Townhomes Homeowners Assn., Tucson, 1990-92, 98-2000. Grantee USDA, Washington, 1981—, Ariz. Dept. Environ. Quality, Phoenix, 1989-98, US Dept. of Energy, Washington, 1991-98, agrl. industries western US, 1982—. Fellow: Can. Soc. Agrl. Engring. (web master 2002—), mem.. NSPE, AAAS, Assn. Latinoamericana de Ingenieria Agricola, Asian Assn. for Agrl. Engring., Australian Soc. for Agrl. Engring., Coun. for Agrl. Sci. and Tech. (bd. mem. 2002—), Am. Kenaf Soc. (newsletter editor 2000—, webmaster 2001—, treas. 2002), Air and Waste Mgmt. Assn., Soc. Automotive Engr. (chmn. farm machinery com. 2000—), Assn. for Advancement of Indsl. Crops (pres. 1994—95, Outstanding Rschr. award 1997), Am. Soc. Agrl. Engr. (chmn. Ariz. sect. 1984—85, vice-chmn. Pacific region 1988—89, dir. dist. 4 1991—93, rep. to AAAS Consortium of Affiliates for Internat. Programs 1992—97, internat. dir. 1994—96, rep. to CAST 2002—), Sigma Xi. Avocations: running, hiking. Office: U Ariz Office Arid Lands Studies 250 E Valencia Rd Tucson AZ 85706-6800 E-mail: wcoates@u.arizona.edu.

COATES, WILLIAM ALEXANDER, lawyer; b. Newberry, S.C., Oct. 8, 1949; s. William Floyd and Clara Monette (Alexander). B.S. in Bus. Administrn., U. S.C., 1971, J.D., 1974. Bar: S.C. 1974, U.S. Dist. Ct. S.C. 1976, U.S. Ct. Appeals (4th cir.) 1977. Asst. legis. asst. to senator Strom Thurmond, Washington, 1974-75; counsel to minority subcom. adminstrv. practice and procedure Com. on Judiciary U.S. Senate, 1975-76; asst. U.S. atty. Dept. of Justice, Greenville, S.C., 1976-80; ptnr. Love, Thornton, Arnold & Thomason, Greenville, 1980—2001; instr. Atty. Gen. Adv. Inst. U.S. Dept. of Justice, Washington, 1979. Chmn. Citizens Adv. Council, Greenville Gen. Hosp., Greenville County Heart Fund, Easter Seal Soc. Greenville County; mem. S.C. State Ethics Commn., 1988-93, chmn. 1991-93. Served with Air N.G., 1970-76. Mem. ABA, S.C. Bar, S.C. Def. Trial Attys. Assn. (pres. 1994), Phi Delta Phi (magister 1973-74). Republican. Baptist. Clubs: Commerce, Heritage Sertoma Office: Roe Cassidy Coates & Price PO Box 10529 1000 East North Street Greenville SC 29603 E-mail: wac@roecassidy.com.

COATNEY, SHARON ANN, librarian, editor; b. Kansas City, Kans., June 12, 1946; d. William H. and Irene M. (Vallis) Smith; m. Jeffery Richard Coatney, Apr. 2, 1966; children: Mark Stephen, Rachel Ann. BS, U. Kans., 1973; MLS, Emporia State U., 1982, MS in Sch. Adminstrn., 1996. Tchr. lang. arts Linwood (Kans.) Jr. High, 1973-84; library media specialist Linwood Schs., 1984-87, Oak Hill Elem. Sch., Overland Park, Kans., 1987—2002; acquisition editor Libraries Unlimited Books, 2002—. Sec. KAW Valley Regional Inservice Coun., Lawrence, 1985-86, evaluator North Cen. Assn. Evaluation team, St. Mary's, Kans., 1987; coord. continuing edn. sch. libr. media Emporia State U., 2002—. Founder Citizens for Community Schs., Marquette, Kans., 1986-87; trustee Linwood Community Library, 1980-87, treas. 1986-87. Kans. Network Bd. grantee, 1986, 87. Mem.: ASCD, ALA (councilor at large), Kans. Reading Assn., Am. Assn. Sch. Libr. (pres. 1998—99, chair libr. media stds. com. 1998—2001, nat. bd. profl. tchg. stds. 2000—), Kans. Assn. Sch. Libr., Phi Delta Kappa. Republican. Baptist. Home: PO Box 38 Linwood KS 66052-0038 Office: Oak Hill Elem Sch Blue Valley District # 229 Overland Park KS 66204

COATS, ANDREW MONTGOMERY, lawyer, former mayor, dean; b. Oklahoma City, Okla., Jan. 19, 1935; s. Sanford Clarence and Mary Ola (Young) C.; m. Linda M. Zimmerman; children— Andrew, Michael, Jennifer, Sanford BA, U. Okla., 1957, JD, 1963. Assoc. Crowe and Dunlevy, Oklahoma City, Okla., 1963-67, ptnr., 1967-76, sr. trial ptnr., 1980—; dist. atty. Oklahoma County, Oklahoma City, Okla., 1976-80; mayor City of Oklahoma City, 1983-87; dean U. Okla. Coll. Law. Pres. Okla. Young Lawyers Conf., 1968-69; dir. Local Okla. Bank, Oklahoma City. Democratic nominee U.S. Senate, 1980; pres. Oklahoma County Legal Aid Soc., 1972-73. Served to lt. USN, 1960-63 Named Outstanding Lawyer in Okla., Oklahoma City U., 1977 Fellow Am. Coll. Trial Lawyers (pres. 1996-97, 10th Cir. regent 1992-96), Am. Bd. Trial Advocates (charter pres. Okla. 1986); mem. ABA, U.S. Supreme Ct. Hist. Soc. (trustee), Okla. Bar Assn. (pres. 1992-93), Oklahoma County Bar Assn. (pres. 1976-77), Order of Coif, Oklahoma City Golf and Country Club (bd. dirs. 1977-80, 93-96), Petroleum Club (pres. 1995), Phi Beta Kappa (pres. 1975), Pi Kappa Alpha (pres. 1956), Phi Delta Phi (pres. 1962). Clubs: Oklahoma City Golf and Country, Petroleum. Democrat. Episcopalian. Avocations: music, golf. Office: Crowe and Dunlevy Mid-Am Tower 20 N Broadway Ave Ste 1800 Oklahoma City OK 73102-8273 also: U Okla Coll Law 300 Timber Dell Rd Norman OK 73019-5081 E-mail: acoats@ou.edu.

COATS, DANIEL RAY, former senator; b. Jackson, Mich., May 16, 1943; s. Edward R. and Vera E. C.; m. Marcia Crawford, Sept. 4, 1965; children: Laura, Lisa, Andrew. BA, Wheaton (Ill.) Coll., 1965; JD cum laude, Ind. U., 1971. Bar: Ind. 1972. Mem. 97th-100th Congresses from 4th Dist. Ind., Washington, 1981-89; Dist. rep. U.S. Congressman Dan Quayle, 1976-80; U.S. senator from Ind., 1989-99; lobbyist Pharm. Rsch. and Mfrs. of Am.; spl. counsel Verner, Liipfert, Bernhard, McPherson and Hand, 1999—2001; amb. to Germany Bonn, 2001—. Mem. Armed Svcs. Com., Labor and Human Resources Com., Intelligence Com.; bd. dirs. IPALCO. Lear Siegler Svcs., Inc., Internat. Repub. Inst., The Empowerment Network. Pres., Big Bros./Big Sisters, Ft. Wayne, Ind. Served with U.S. Army, 1966-68. Office: US Embassy Deichmanns Aue 29 D-53179 Bonn Germany Fax: 202-371-6262.*

COATS, NATHAN B. state supreme court justice; m. Mary Ricketson; 1 child, Johanna. BA in Econs., U. Colo., 1971, JD, 1977. Assoc. Hough, Grant, McCarren and Bernard, 1977-78; asst. atty. gen. Appellate Sect., Colo., 1978-83, dep. atty. gen., 1983-86; adj. prof. U. Colo., Colo., 1990; chief appellate dep. dist. atty. 2d Jud. Dist., Denver, 1986-2000; justice Colo. Supreme Ct., 2000—. Chief reporter Erickson Commn. on Officer-Involved Shootings, 1996-97; lectr. Denver Police Acad., 1986-97; reporter Govs. Columbine Commn., 1999-2000; mem. Colo. Supreme Ct. Criminal Rules Com., 1983-2000, chmn., 1997-2000, Colo. Bd. Law Examiners, 1984-94, Colo. Supreme Ct. Appellate Rules Com., 1985-2000, Colo. Supreme Ct. Civil Rules Com., Colo. Supreme Ct. Criminal Pattern Jury Instructions Com., 1987-2000, Colo. Supreme Ct. Jury Reform Pilot Project Com., 1998-2000, Colo. Dist. Attys. Coun. Legis. Com., 1990-2000. Office: Colo State Supreme Ct Judicial Bldg 2 E 14th Ave Denver CO 80203-2115

COATS, WARREN L., JR., economist; b. Bakersfield, Calif., May 19, 1942; s. Warren L. and Sara Jane C.; m. Louise Wilkinson, Feb. 15, 1968 (div. June 1980); children: Brandon, Daylin. BA in Econs., U. Calif., Berkeley, 1965; MA in Econs., U. Chgo., 1967, PhD in Econs., 1972. Instr. econs. Ill. Inst. Tech., Chgo., 1966-67, 68-70; asst. prof. econs. U. Hawaii, Honolulu, 1968, U. Va., Charlottesville, 1970-76, asst. dep. chmn., 1972-74, dir. honors program, 1974-76; economist, sr. economist ctrl. banking dept. Internat. Monetary Fund, Washington, 1976-81, chief SDRs and divsn. treas. dept., 1982-88, advisor treas. dept., 1989-91, advisor monetary and exch. affairs dept., 1992-99, asst. dir. monetary and exch. affairs dept., 1999—2003; dir. Cayman Island Monetary Authority, 2003—. Tech. asst., advisor ctrl. banks fghanistan, Bangladesh, Bosnia, Bulgaria, Croatia, Czech Republic, Egypt, Hungary, Kazakhstan, Kosovo, Kyrgyz Republic, Malta, Moldova, Slovakia, Turkey, Yugoslavia and other countries; dir. Canyon Island Monetary Fund, 2003—; presenter in field. Co-author: The World Development Report, 1989, The Simple Analytics of Digital Money: Finance in Cyberspace, 1996; editor: Inflation Targetting in Transition Economics: The Case of the Czech Republic, 2000; co-editor: Money and Monetary Policy in Less Developed Countries: Survey of Issues and Evidence, 1980; contbr. articles to profl. jours. Mem. Am. Econ. Assn., We. Econ. Assn. Internat. (past mem. exec. com.), Order of the Golden Bear, Phil. Soc. (past bd. dirs.), Mt. Peleron Soc., Alpha Tau Omega (past pres.). Home: PH 7 1300 Crystal Dr Arlington VA 22202-3234

COBAU, JOHN REED, lawyer; b. New Castle, Pa., Aug. 28, 1934; s. William D. and Sarah M. (Weinschenk) C.; m. Arlene L. Gilbert, June 22, 1960; children: William, Joseph, Thomas, John. BA, Princeton U., 1956; LLB, Harvard U., 1960. Bar: D.C. 1960, Ohio 1961, Mich. 1966. Assoc. Kyte, Conlan, Wulsin & Vogeler, Cin., 1960-66, Freud, Markus, Slavin & Mountain, Detroit, 1966-73; pvt. practice Grosse Pointe Woods, Mich., 1974—. Mem. ABA, Mich. Bar Assn., Macomb County Bar Assn., Grosse Pointe Hunt Club (bd. dirs. 1976-78), Rotary (pres., bd. dirs. Grosse Pointe). Office: 20233 Mack Ave Grosse Pointe MI 48236-1769 E-mail: jrlawyer@cobau.net.

COBB, BRIAN ERIC, broadcasting executive; b. Berlin, N.H., Jan. 3, 1945; s. Everett Bryan and Eleanore (Bouchard) C.; m. Denise Leclair, Sept. 20, 1986; children: Jennifer, Heather. BS, U. Nev., 1967. Gen. sales mgr. Sta. WNGE-TV, Nashville, 1972, mktg. mgr., 1973-76, v.p., gen. mgr., 1977, Sta. WSIX AM/FM, Nashville, 1977, Gen. Electric Broadcasting of Colo., stas. KOA-AM, KOAQ, KOA-TV, Denver, 1978-81; v.p. TV Chapman Assocs., Washington, 1982-87; ptnr. Media Venture Ptnrs., Naples, Fla., 1987-2001; pres. Cobb Corp., N.Y.C., 2001—. Cons. Denver Broncos, 1982—2000; pres. Media Ventur Mgmt., Biltmore Broadcasting. Comml. chmn. Mile-Hi United Way, 1980; bd. dirs. Vanderbilt Children's Hosp., 1973-76; founder, chmn. Naples Children and Edn. Found.; trustee Fla. Gulf Coast U., 2001—. Named an Outstanding Young Man of Yr., Nashville Jaycees, 1978. Mem. Nat. Assn. Broadcasters, Nat. Assn. TV Program Execs., Tenn. Assn. Broadcasters (bd. dirs. 1975-77), Nat. Assn. Media Brokers (pres. 1993-95), Rotary. Republican. Roman Catholic. Avocations: golf, reading. Office: Cobb Corp LLC Ste 210 5811 Pelican Bay Blvd Naples FL 34108-7512 E-mail: cobbcorp@aol.com.

COBB, CALVIN HAYES, JR., lawyer; b. San Diego, Aug. 2, 1924; s. Calvin Hayes and Frances King (Halm) Cobb; m. Olive Latimer Watson, Mar. 19, 1955; children: Alice Cobb Parte, Joan Cobb Pettit, Calvin Hayes III, Robert Watson, Olive Latimer Waxter. BS with distinction, U.S. Naval Acad., 1944; LLB, Georgetown U., 1950. Bar: DC 1950, Md. 1950, U.S. Supreme Ct. 1953. Assoc. Law Offices Elisha Hanson, Washington, 1950-55; ptnr. Hanson, Cobb & O'Brien, Washington, 1955-69, Steptoe & Johnson, Washington, 1969—. Leading article editor: Georgetown Law Jour., 1949; contbr. articles to law revs. and profl. jours. Trustee Found. Mid. East Peace, 1969—, Naval Hist. Found., 1983—2003. Lt. (j.g.) USN, 1944—47. Recipient Disting. Pub. Svc. award, U.S. Sec. of Navy, 1979, 1991, Pub. Svc. award, USCG, 1991. Mem.: Soc. Cin., U.S. Naval Acad. Alumni Assn. (trustee 1955—58), Navy League U.S. (nat. judge adv. 1975—89, bd. dirs. 1975—, sr. v.p. 1988—89, pres. 1989—91, Nat. Pres.'s award 1976, 1983, 1986), Naples Athletic Club, Forum Club (bd. dirs. 2000—03), Barristers Club, Naples Bath and Tennis Club (pres. 1974), Royal Poinciana Golf Club (pres. 2003—), Gibson Island Club, Chevy Chase Club (pres. 1974—75), Lawyers Club. Republican. Roman Catholic. Avocations: tennis, golf, bridge. Home: 3571 Hamlet Pl Chevy Chase MD 20815-4822 Office: 1330 Connecticut Ave NW Washington DC 20036-1704 E-mail: chcobbjr@aol.com., ccobb@steptoe.com.

COBB, CHARLES KENCHE, lawyer, real estate broker; b. Canton, Ga., Aug. 23, 1934; s. Charlie Kench and Alice (Enloe) Cobb; m. Carolyn Webb, Aug. 31, 1963; children: Charlie Kenche III, Catherine Elizabeth Fryman. BS, Ga. Tech., 1956; MBA, Harvard U., 1962, postgrad., Emory U., 1963, Georgetown U., 1959; LLD, Woodrow Wilson, 1968. Bar: Ga. 1969. Pres. C. Cobb Properties, Atlanta, 1969—, Sterling Land Co., Atlanta, 1973—; dir. Canton Textile Mills, Inc., 1991—. Mem. exec. com. Ga. Tech. Wesley Found., Atlanta, 1983—2003; former treas., sec., trustee Reinhardt Coll., Waleska, Ga., 1974—; bd. dirs. Ga. Tech. YMCA, Atlanta, 1976—89; lay leader Northside United Meth. Ch., Atlanta, 1978. Served to 1st lt. USAF, 1956—59, ETO. Mem.: Ga. Assn. Exchangers (former pres., Ga. Exchangor of Yr. 1971, 1990), Atlanta Bd. Realtors (bd. dirs. 1983—90, Outstanding Transaction of Yr. award 1986), Ga. Bar Assn., Ga. Tech. Alumni Assn. (trustee 1976—79), Ga. Hist. Trust, Buckhead 50 Club (pres. 1997), Canton Golf Club, Shriners, Masons. Home: 2851 Howell Mill Rd NW Atlanta GA 30327-1333 Office: 1 Northside 75 NW Ste 102 Atlanta GA 30318-7715

COBB, DAVID KEITH, business executive; b. Calhoun City, Miss., Mar. 2, 1941; s. Bayne and Frances (Clements) C.; m. Dorothy Hill, June 15, 1963; children: Paul J., John D., Mark F. BS, U. So. Miss., 1963. Nat. mng. ptnr. fin. svcs. KPMG Peat Marwick, N.Y.C., 1963-95; CEO, vice chmn. Alamo Rent A Car, Inc., 1995-97. Bd. dir. RHR Internat., Inc., First Fleet Corp., Capitol Ins. Co., CRA Investment Fund, BankAtlantic Bancorp, Chateau Communities Inc. Bd. dirs. United Way of Broward County, Nova Southeastern U. Grad. Sch. Bus. Republican. Presbyterian. Home and Office: 2521 Del Lago Dr Fort Lauderdale FL 33316-2303 E-mail: kcobb@cobbcorner.com.

COBB, EDWARD RAY, actor; b. Reidsville, N.C., July 6, 1957; s. Robert Edward and Mary Elizabeth Cobb; life ptnr. David M. Glaser, Oct. 9, 1981. Student, Greensboro Coll., 1975—78. Actor: (plays) Picture Me, Picture You, 1985, Lady L, 1986, Untold Decades, 1988, On Tina Tuna Walk, 1989 (Robby award for best actor in a comedy Frontiers After Dark, 1989), Bud O'Connor's Coconut Angel Pies, 1990, Body and Soul, 1991. Bd. mem. The Espoir Found., N.Y.C., 1985—94. Mem.: SAG, Actors Equity Assn.

COBB, ELIZABETH H. lawyer; b. Birmingham, Ala., Nov. 11, 1947; d. John and Tay Cobb; m. Peter Maye. BS, La. State U., 1969, MLS, 1976, JD, 1981. Bar: La. 1981, N.Y. 1984, Minn. 1995. With U.S. Ct. Appeals 5th Cir., New Orleans, Skadden Arps, N.Y.C.; asst. gen. counsel N.Y. Life, N.Y.C.; with Mackall Crounse, Mpls.; asst. v.p. The St. Paul Cos., Inc., Mpls. Office: The St Paul Companies Mail Code 515A 385 Washington St Saint Paul MN 55102-1396 E-mail: elizabeth.cobb@stpaul.com.

COBB, G. ELLIOTT, JR., lawyer; b. Franklin, Va., July 11, 1939; s. Gardner E. and Thelma L. (Whitley) C.; m. Betty Minor, July 15, 1961; children: Polly, Susan, Gardner. BS, U. Va., 1960, LL.B., 1966. Bar: Va. 1966, Supreme Ct. U.S 1974. Asso. counsel Union Camp Corp., Wayne, N.J., 1967-74, counsel, mgr. adminstrn., 1974-76, gen. counsel, asst. sec., 1976, v.p., gen. counsel, sec., 1976-78; ptnr. Moyler, Rainey & Cobb, Franklin, 1978—. Mem. adv. bd. SunTrust Bank, Franklin. Mem. Franklin City Coun., 1980-88; vice mayor of Franklin, 1982-84, mayor, 1984-88; bd. dirs. SFranklin Southampton Charieies. Served with USMC, 1960-61. Mem. Va. Bar Assn., Southampton-Franklin Bar Assn. Clubs: Cypress Cove Country, Rotary. Episcopalian. Home: 913 Clay St Franklin VA 23851-1306 Office: Moyler Rainey & Cobb 506 N Main St Franklin VA 23851-1438

COBB, GEORGE EDWARD, surgeon; b. Oklahoma City, Aug. 10, 1930; MD, Harvard U., 1955. Diplomate Am. Bd. Surgery. Intern Johns Hopkins Hosp., Balt., 1955-56, resident in surgery, 1956-57, San Francisco USPHS Hosp., 1958-61; staff Providence Hosp., Calif., Merritt Hosp., John Muir Med. Ctr. Hosp., Calif., Mt. Diablo Hosp., Concord, Calif., Summit Hosp., Oakland, Calif., Walnut Creek Hosp. Mem. AMA, Am. Coll. Surgeons, Calif. Med. Assn., ACCMA. Office: 3501 School St Lafayette CA 94549-4505

COBB, HENRY NICHOLS, architect; b. Boston, Apr. 8, 1926; s. Charles Kane and Elsie Quincy (Nichols) C.; m. Joan Stewart Spaulding, June 5, 1953; children: Sara Quincy, Emma Trow, Pamela Codman. AB, Harvard, 1947, MArch, 1949; DFA (hon.), Bowdoin Coll., 1985; D Tech. Scis. (hon.), Swiss Fed. Inst. Tech., 1990. Designer in office Hugh Stubbins, 1949-50; mem. archtl. div. Webb & Knapp, Inc., 1950-60; ptnr. Pei Cobb Freed & Ptnrs. (formerly I.M. Pei & Ptnrs.), N.Y.C., 1960—. Vis. critic Yale U., 1963-66, Bishop vis. prof. architecture, 1973, 78, Davenport vis. prof., 1975; studio prof., chmn. dept. architecture Harvard U. Grad. Sch. Design, Cambridge, Mass., 1980-85. Prin. works include Pl. Ville Marie, Montreal, Can., 1962; acad. ctr. and residence halls State U. Coll., Fredonia, N.Y., 1967, John Hancock Tower, Boston, 1972, Collins Place, Melbourne, Australia, 1976, Wilson Commons, U. Rochester, 1976, World Trade Ctr., Balt., 1977, Dallas Ctr., 1979, Johnson & Johnson World Hdqrs., New Brunswick, N.J., 1981, 16th St. Mall, Denver, 1982, Mobil Rsch. Lab., Farmers Branch, Tex., 1983, Portland (Maine) Mus. Art, 1983, Arco Tower, Dallas, 1984, hdqrs. Pitney Bowes Corp., Stamford, Conn., 1985, Fountain Place, Dallas, 1986, Columbia Sq., Washington, 1986, Commerce Sq., Phila., 1987, First Interstate World Ctr., L.A., 1989, Anderson Grad. Sch. Mgmt. UCLA, 1994, AAAS Hdqrs., Washington, 1997, U.S. Courthouse, Boston, 1998, World Trade Ctr., Barcelona, 1999, Head Office ABN-AMRO Bank, Amsterdam, 1999, Coll.-Conservatory of Music, U. Cin., 1999, Tour EDF, Paris, 2001, 2099 Pennsylvania Ave., Washington, 2001, Friend Ctr. for Engring. Edn., Princeton U., 2001, U.S. Courthouse, Hammond, Ind., 2002, World Trade Ctr. and Grand Marina Hotel, Barcelona, 2002, Nat. Constn. Ctr., Phila., 2003. Trustee Am. Acad. in Rome, 1972-90, Brearley Sch., 1975-80. Served with USNR, 1944-46. Recipient Topaz medallion for excellence in archtl. edn. Assn. Collegiate Schs. of Architecture/AIA, 1995. Fellow AIA (medal of honor N.Y. chpt. 1982), Am. Acad. Arts and Scis.; mem. Am. Acad. Arts and Letters (Arnold W. Brunner Meml. prize in architecture 1977), Nat. Acad. Design. Office: Pei Cobb Freed & Ptnrs 88 Pine St New York NY 10005

COBB, HOWELL, federal judge; b. Atlanta, Dec. 7, 1922; s. Howell and Dorothy (Hart) C.; m. Torrance Chalmers (dec. 1963); children: Catherine Cobb Cook, Howell III, Mary Ann Cobb Walton; m. Amelie Suberbielle, July 3, 1965; children: Caroline Cobb Ervin, Thomas H., John L. Student, St. John's Coll., Annapolis, Md., 1940-42; LLB, U. Va., 1948. Assoc. Kelley & Ryan, Houston, 1949-51, Fountain, Cox & Gaines, Houston, 1951-54, Orgain, Bell & Tucker, Beaumont, 1954-57, ptnr., 1957-85; judge U.S. Dist. Ct. (ea. dist.) Tex., Beaumont, 1985—. Mem. jud. coun. U.S. Ct. Appeals (5th cir.), 1994-97; mem. adv. com. East Tex. Legal Svcs., Beaumont. Pres. Beaumont Art Mus., 1969, bd. dirs., 1967-68; mem. vestry St. Stephens Episcopal Ch., Beaumont, 1973; mem. bd. adjustment City of Beaumont, 1972-82; trustee All Saints Episcopal Sch., Beaumont, 1972-76. 1st lt. USMC, 1942-45, PTO. Mem.: ABA, Maritime Law Assn. U.S., Am. Bd. Trial Advs., Am. Judicature Soc., Jefferson County Bar Assn. (sec. 1960, bd. dirs. 1960—61, 1967—68), State Bar Tex. (grievance com. 1970—72, chmn. 1972, admissions com. 1974—, bd. dirs. 1993—94, adv. mem.). Office: US Dist Ct 118 US Courthouse PO Box 632 Beaumont TX 77704-0632 Business E-Mail: druann_wiley@txed.uscourts.gov.

COBB, HUBBARD HANFORD, magazine editor, writer; b. N.Y.C., Aug. 5, 1917; s. Frank I. and Margaret Hubbard (Ayer) C.; m. Elizabeth Youngblood Simon, Feb. 6, 1954. Grad., Avon Old Farms Sch., Conn., 1936. Bldg. editor Am. Home mag., 1952-61, editor, 1961-69; author syndicated column home problems, 1946-60; condr. radio program home bldg., 1947-54; contbg. editor Woman's Day mag., 1972-84. Author: How to Build Your Dream House, 1948, Home Handyman's Guide, 1949, Homeowners Guide to Remodeling, 1950, Complete Homeowner, 1965, The Dream House Encyclopedia, 1970, How to Buy and Remodel the Older House, 1972, How to Paint Anything, 1972; (with Betsy Cobb) Vacation Houses--All You Should Know Before You Buy or Build, 1973, City People's Guide to Country Living, 1973, Preventive Maintenance for Your House or Apartment, 1975, Improvements That Increase the Value of Your House, 1976, Woman's Day Homeowners Handbook, 1976, (with Betsy Cobb) Your Barn House, 1991, American Battlefields, 1995. With USAAF, World War II. Mem. Authors Guild. Home: 60 Main St Apt 203 Deep River CT 06417

COBB, JEANNE BECK, education educator, researcher, consultant; b. Thomasville, NC, Apr. 5, 1948; d. Howard Paul and Thelma Lorene (Clanton) Beck; m. James Paul Cobb, June 10, 1974; children: James Alexander, Rebecca Jeanne. BS in Elem. Edn., West Carolina U., 1970; MS in Elem. Edn. and Reading, U. Tenn., 1971, EdD in Reading and Lang. arts, 1992. Cert. tchr., Tex.; cert. reading specialist, Tex. Title one tchr. Decatur (Ga.) City Schs., 1976-80; grad. tchg. asst. U. Tenn., Knoxvlle, 1989-92, asst. dir. Reading Ctr., 1991-92; adj. prof. U. North Tex., Denton, 1992-93, lectr., site coord. Evers Park Profl. Devel. Sch., 1995-99, from lectr. to asst. prof., 1993—2002, TAMS selection com., 1995-96, dir. reading clinic, dir. Am. Reads, dir. reading svcs. child and family resource clinic; assoc. prof. reading Ea. N.Mex. U., Portales, 2002—. Adj. prof. Tex. Wesleyan U., Ft. Worth, 1992-93; cons. Greenhill Sch., Dallas, 1995; reviewer Multicultural Edn., 1995—. Contbr. articles to profl. jours. Dir. Sat. sch. scholars First Christian Ch., Ft. Worth, 1997-99; teams vol. L.D. Bell H.S., Hurst, Tex., 1996-97; active PTA Ga., Tenn., Tex., 1985-96; band boosters fundraiser HEB Parent Assn., Hurst, 1996—; asst. chair clinical divsn. nat. reading conf. Coll. Reading Assn. Mem. Internat. Reading, Assn. (corr. sect. 1971—), Nat. Coun. on Rsch. in Lang. and Literacy, Assn. Childhood Edn. Internat. (pres. 1975-80, v.p. 1993—), Internat. Listening Assn. (edn. task force 1994—), Phi Kappa Phi, Alpha Delta Kappa. Democrat. Avocations: reading, hiking, camping, collecting children's china and old basal readers. Mailing: 3001 Wolflin Ave Amarillo TX 79109 Office: U North Tex PO Box 31137 Denton TX 76203-1337 Home: 1401 W 17th St Portales NM 88130 Office: Eastern NMex Univ Sch Edn Station 25 Portales NM 88130

COBB, JOHN BOSWELL, JR., clergyman, educator; b. Kobe, Japan, Feb. 9, 1925; s. John Boswell and Theodora Cook (Atkinson) C.; m. Jean Olmstead Loftin, June 18, 1947; children: Theodore, Clifford, Andrew, Richard. MA, U. Chgo. Div. Sch., 1949, PhD, 1952. Ordained to ministry United Meth. Ch., 1950. Pastor Towns County Circuit, N.Ga. Conf., 1950-51; faculty Young Harris Coll., Ga., 1950-53, Candler Sch. Theology and Emory U., 1953-58, Sch. Theology, Claremont, Calif., 1958-90; Avery prof. Claremont Grad. Sch., 1973-90; ret., 1990; mem. commn. on doctrine and doctrinal standard United Meth. Ch., 1968-72; mem. commn. on mission, 1984-88. Author: A Christian Natural Theology, 1965, The Structure of Christian Existence, 1967, Christ in a Pluralistic Age, 1975, (with Herman Daly) For the Common Good, 1989. Dir. Center for Process Studies. Fulbright prof. U. Mainz, 1965-66; fellow Woodrow Wilson Internat. Ctr. for Scholars, 1976 Mem. Am. Acad. Religion, Am. Metaphys. Soc. E-mail: cobbj@cgu.edu.

COBB, JOHN CANDLER, medical educator; b. Boston, July 8, 1919; s. Stanley and Elizabeth Mason (Almy) C.; m. Helen Imlay-Franchot, July 27, 1946; children: Loren, Nathaniel, Bethany, Julianne. BS in Astronomy cum laude, Harvard U., 1941, MD, 1948; MPH, Johns Hopkins U., 1954. Diplomate Nat. Bd. Med. Examiners, Am. Bd. Preventive Medicine and Pub. Health; lic. physician, Conn., Md., N.Mex. Intern Yale New Haven Hosp., 1948-49, fellow in pediatrics, 1949-50; jr. asst. resident Yale Psychiatric Clinic, 1950-51; instr. pediatrics Johns Hopkins U., 1951-56, asst. prof. hygiene, 1954-56; cons. Indian Health divsn. USPHS, Albuquerque, 1956-60; prof. preventive medicine U. Colo., Denver, 1965-85, emeritus prof., 1985—, chmn. dept., 1966-73. Dir. med. social rsch. project on population Govt. of Pakistan, 1960-64; cons. Am. Friends Svc. Com., Algeria, 1964; short term cons. WHO, Indonesia and Western Pacific Region, 1969, 70-73, USAID, Togo and Niger, 1979; exch. prof. Guangxi Med. Coll., Nanning, China, 1985-86; coord. ethics seminars U. Health Scis. Ctr., 1980-85; pres. World Hand Assocs., 1985--; cons. in field. Contbr. numerous articles to profl. jours. Bd. dirs., pres. Am. Assn. Planned Parenthood Physicians, 1966-67; chmn. Task Force for Preparing 314(b) Agy. Grant Applicaiton, 1969; mem., chmn. health com. of Gov. Lamm and U.S. Congressman Wirth's Task Force on Rocky Flats Nuc. Weapons Plant, Denver, 1974-75; mem. Gov.'s Task Force on Health Effects of Air Pollution, 1978-79; commr. Air Pollution Control Commn. of Colo., 1976-79; mem. air quality policy com. Denver Regional Coun. of Govts., 1978-80, environ. council, U. Colo., 1970-75, Gov.'s Scientific adv. council, Colo., 1973-80, Gov.'s Blue Ribbon Task Force on Transportation, Colo., 1977; bd. dirs. ROMCOE Ctr. for Environ. Problem Solving, 1978-81, Colo. Coalition for Full Employment, 1978-80; mem. Am. Friends Svc. Com. Adv. Group on Rocky Flats/Nuclear Weapons Project, 1979-85. Recipient Florence Sabin award Colo. Pub. Health Assn., 1979, Jack Gore Meml. Peace award Am. Friends Svc. Com., 1980; U.S. EPA grantee, 1975-82. Mem. AAAS, WHO, Internat. Solar Energy Soc., Am. Solar Energy Soc., Internat. Physicians for Prevention of Nuclear War (del. to Congresses in Moscow and Montreal), Appropriate Rural Tech. Assn. (bd. dirs. 1987-2002, v.p. 1991-92), Nat. Resources Def. Coun. (bd. advisors 1991-92), N.Mex. Solar Energy Assn. (bd. dirs. 1995-98), Physicians for Human Rights, Physicians for Social Reponsibility. Home and Office: # 4320 10501 Lagrima De Oro NE Albuquerque NM 87111

COBB, JOHN CECIL, JR., (JACK COBB), communications specialist and executive; b. Walton, Ky., Apr. 10, 1927; s. John Cecil and Lucy (Dean) C. BA in Sociology, Antioch Coll., 1950; postgrad., U. Ams., Mex., 1950; MA in Communication, Mich. State U., 1964. Fgn. corr., pub. exec. Vision, Inc., Rio de Janeiro, N.Y.C., 1950-55; writer Mexico City, 1956-57; dir. Antioch Coll. Program, Guanajuato, Mex., 1958-62; communication research asst. Mich. State U., East Lansing, 1962-64, mem. research staff Computer Inst. Social Sci. Research, 1964-67; Fulbright prof. U. El Salvador, San Salvador, 1967-68; cons. Peace Corps, Lima, Peru, 1968-69, San Jose, Costa Rica, 1968-69; exec. dir. Latin Am. Studies Assn., Washington, 1969-71; cons. Washington, 1972-78; pres. Human Comm. Sys., Reston, Va., 1978-93, prin., 1994—. Cons. on new internat. curriculum Antioch Coll., 1990; prodn. mgr. Peace in Action mag., 1994-97; cons. World Wide Web, 1996. Author: (with Howard I. Blutstein) Area Handbook of El Salvador, 1971; also monographs on land reform in El Salvador, 1980-86, study of urban family income in Bolivia, 1986, 3 software manuals on linking of electronic mail networks, 1991-92. Mem. Common Cause No. Va., 1975-77, publicity chmn., 1975-77; mem. exec. com. Washington area UN Assn., 1977-79; mem. Fairfax County Democratic Com., 1975-78; mem. Cherrydale Tap Dancers, 1997-98, Gotta Dance troupe, 1998—, soloist, 2002. Served with USN, 1945-46 Mem. Social Sci. Computing Assn. (chair), Latin Am. Studies Assn., Inter-Am. Coun. (v.p. 1994-95, pres. 1995-96), Soc. Internat. Devel., Mid-Atlantic Conf. Latin Am. Studies (panelist 1997), Fulbright Assn., The Internet Soc. E-mail: jack678cobb@yahoo.com.

COBB, KENNETH ALAN, lawyer; b. Alliance, Nebr., Jan. 3, 1951; s. Chandler and Margaret Jane (Sargent) C.; m. Diane Lynn Brown, Sept. 2, 1978; 1 child, Elaine Allison. BS, U. Nebr., 1973; JD, U. Mich., 1976. Bar: Mo. 1976. Assoc. Swanson, Midgley et al, Kansas City, Mo., 1976-78, Brown, Koralchik et al, 1978—79, Burrell, Seigfried et al, 1980—82; sr. atty. IBP, Inc., Dakota City, Nebr., 1983—86; couns. comml. divsn. Payless Cashways, Inc, Kansas City, 1986—96; sr. counsel Blackwell Sanders Peper Martin, 1996—2000, ptnr., 2001—. Bd. dirs. Children's Mus. Kansas City, Kans., 1992-95, Kansas City (Mo.) Consensus, 1996-98. Mem. Kansas City Met. Bar Assn. (chmn. corp. counsel sect. 1990). Republican. Office: Ste 1100 2300 Main St Kansas City MO 64108-2416 E-mail: kcobb@bspmlaw.com.

COBB, LARRY RUSSELL, ethics educator; b. Clendenin, W.Va., Nov. 7, 1938; s. Ivan O. and Jessie E. Cobb; m. Naomi Faye Cobb, Jan. 19, 1939; children: Michael Kent, Cheryl Lynn. BA in Econs., W.Va. U., 1961; MA in Philosophy and Govt., So. Ill. U., 1963, PhD in Govt., 1967. Instr. Glenville (W.Va.) State Coll., 1963-64; assoc. prof., then prof. Slippery Rock (Pa.) U., 1967-97, prof. emeritus, 1997—. Exec. dir., founder. Ethicsworks Cons., Slippery Rock, 2000—; sec. bd. dirs. Inst. for Values Inquiry, Tulsa, 1990—; bd. dirs., exec. dir. Found. for Philosophy of Creativity, Denton, Tex., 1991—. Contbr. numerous articles to profl. jours., chpts. to books. Bd. dirs. Cmty. Svcs. and Learning Inst., Slippery Rock, 1999—. Mem. Nat. Assn. Housing and Devel. Ofcls. (sec. Mid-Atlantic coun., 1999-2001, Bd. Ethics and Credentialing Trustees, 2000-, v.p. Internat., 2001-, Bd of Govs., 2001-). Democrat. Unitarian Universalist. Avocation: skiing. Home: 250 Slippery Rock Rd Slippery Rock PA 16057 E-mail: ethicsworks@aol.com.

COBB, MILES ALAN, retired lawyer; b. Salt Lake City, May 8, 1930; s. Miles Cobb and June (Ray) Cobb Wilson; children: Jennifer, Melissa, Mary. BS, U. Calif.-Berkeley, 1953, LL.B., 1958. Bar: Calif. 1958. Assoc. Bronson, Bronson & McKinnon, San Francisco, 1958-65, ptnr., 1965-76, 78-84; gen. counsel FDIC, Washington, 1976-78; pres. Bell Savs & Loan Assn., San Mateo, Calif., 1984-85. Author: Federal Regulation of Depository Institutions, 1984. Served to 1st lt. U.S. Army, 1953-55; Korea Democrat. Avocations: photography, golf, gardening. E-mail: cobb7@earthlink.net.

COBB, ROBERT W. federal agency administrator; b. Washington, Apr. 29, 1960; Grad. cum laude, Vanderbuilt U., 1982; JD cum laude, George Washington U., 1986. Assoc. Ober, Kaler, Grimes & Shriver, 1986—92; with U.S. Office Govt. Ethics, 1992—2001; assoc. counsel to Pres. White House, Washington, 2001—02; inspector gen. NASA, Washington, 2002—. Office: NASA Hdqrs Mail Code W 300 E St SW Washington DC 20546

COBB, RONALD DAVID, pharmacist, educator; b. Louisville, May 10, 1945; s. Harry D. and Ruth (Roberts) C.; m. Patricia Lee Carroll, Sept. 4, 1964; children: Joy Ruth, Tracy Renee. BS in Pharmacy, U. Ky., 1968, PharmD, 1973. Staff pharmacist Kettering (Ohio) Meml. Hosp., 1968; pharmacist mgr. Lawrence Drugs, Inc., Lexington, Ky., 1969-70; asst. prof. Coll. Pharmacy U. Ky., Lexington, 1973-79, assoc. prof. Coll. Pharmacy, 1980—. Pharmacist cons. Blue Cross/Blue Shield of Ky., Louisville, 1976-90, Market Measures, Inc., West Orange, N.J., 1976-94. Contbr. numerous articles to profl. jours. Bd. dirs. Am. Found. for Pharm. Edn.; trustee Am. Pharm. Assn. Found., 1990-93. Fellow Am. Coll. Apothecaries (assoc.); mem. Blue Grass Pharmacists Assn. (treas. 1969, exec. com. 1969-76, pres.-elect 1970, pres. 1971), Ky. Pharmacists Assn. (bd. dirs. 1972-79, chmn. 1977-78, pres.-elect 1975-76, pres. 1976-77), Am. Inst. History Pharmacy (bd. dirs. 1994-96), Am. Pharm. Assn. (chmn. bd. 1989, pres. 1990, trustee 1985-91), Acad. Pharmacy Practice (pres.-elect 1982-83, pres. 1983-84, bd. dirs. 1980-86). Democrat. Baptist. Avocations: woodworking, photography, traveling, fishing, sports. Home: The Preserve 410 25th Ave SW Vero Beach FL 32962

COBB, ROWENA NOELANI BLAKE, real estate broker; b. Kauai, Hawaii, May 1, 1939; d. Bernard K. Blake and Hattie Kanui Yuen; m. James Jackson Cobb, Dec. 22, l962; children: Shelly Ranelle Noelani, Bret Kimo Jackson. BS in Edn., Bob Jones U., l961; broker's lic., Vitousek Sch. Real Estate, Honolulu, l981. Lic. real estate broker, Honolulu; cert. residential broker. Med. supr. Hawaii Med. Svc. Assn., 1964-65, 66-68; bus. mgr. Micronesian Occupl. Ctr., Koror Palau, 1968-70; prin. broker Cobb Realty, Lihue, Hawaii, 1983—; sec. Neighbor Island MLS Svc., Honolulu, 1985-87, vice chmn., 1987-88; chmn. MLS Hawaii, Inc., Honolulu, 1988-90. Assoc. editor Jour. Entymology, 1965-66. Sec. Koloa Cmty. Assn., 1981-98, pres., 1989, bd. dirs. 2002—; mem. Kauai Humane Soc., YWCA, Kauai Mus., Kauai Visitors Bur.; bd. dirs. Wong Care Home, Hoi'Ke Pub. TV, 1998—, treas., 1999, v.p., 2002, pres. 2000-01; vice chair Kauai Schs. Adv. Coun., 1995-98, pres., 2000; mem. adv. bd. KKCR Radio, 2000; bd. dirs. Kekahu Fund, 1999-2001, Kauai United Way, 2003. Mem. Nat. Assn. Realtors (grad. Realtors Inst., cert. residential specialist), Hawaii Assn. Realtors (cert. tchr., state bd. dirs. 1984, v.p. 1985, dir. 1995-96), Kauai Bd. Realtors (v.p. 1984, pres. 1985, bd. dirs. 1995-97, treas. 1999, Realtor Assoc. of Yr. award 1983, Realtor of Yr. award 1986), Kauai C. of C., Soroptomists (bd. dirs. Lihue chpt. 1986-89, treas. 1989). Avocations: reading, music, travel. Office: PO Box 157 Koloa HI 96756-0157 E-mail: ro@jrcobb.net.

COBB, ROY LAMPKIN, JR., retired computer sciences corporation executive; b. Oklahoma City, Sept. 23, 1934; s. Roy Lampkin and Alice Maxine Cobb; m. Shirley Ann Dodson, June 21, 1958; children: Kendra Leigh, Cary William, Paul Alan. BA, U. Okla., 1972; postgrad., U. Calif., Northridge, 1976-77. Naval aviation cadet USN, 1955, advanced through grades to comdr., 1970, ret., 1978; mktg./project staff engr. Gen. Dynamics, Pomona, Calif., 1978-80; mgr. dept. support svcs. Computer Scis. Corp., Point Mugu, Calif., 1980-97; ret. Decorated Navy Commendation medal, Air medal (13). Mem. Assn. Naval Aviators, Soc. Logistic Engrs. (editor Launchings 1990-98), Navy League, Las Posas Country Club, Spanish Hills Country Club. Republican. Home: 2481 Brookhill Dr Camarillo CA 93010-2112 E-mail: cobbweb@aol.com.

COBB, RUTH, artist; b. Boston, Feb. 20, 1914; d. Charles Edward and Bessie (Cohen) C.; m. Lawrence Kupferman, Apr. 29, 1937; children: Nancy Rose, David. Diploma, Mass. Coll. Art, 1935. One-woman shows include Shore Galery, Boston, 1958, 60, 63, 65, 70, DeCordova Mus., Lincoln, Mass., 1955, Art Unlimited Gallery, San Francisco, 1961, Cober Gallery, N.Y.C., 1962, 65, 67, McNay Mus., San Antonio, 1966, Phila. Art Alliance, 1962, Galerie Moos, Montreal, Que., Can., 1969, Witte Mus., San Antonio, 1967, Harold Ernst Gallery, Boston, 1974, 75, 76, Midtown Gallery, N.Y.C., 1981, 82, Foster Harmon Gallery, Sarasota, 1984, Francesca Anderson Gallery, Boston, 1984, 87, Cen. Pl. Galleries, Bangor, Maine, 1988, Thayer Acad., Braintree, Mass., 1994, Cataumet (Mass.) Art Ctr., 1997, A.R.A. Gallery, Hamilton, Mass., 1999, Women Studies Rsch. Ctr. Brandeis U.; featured in exhbn. Boston's Honored Artists, Danforth Mus., Framingham, Mass., 1995; represented in permanent collections Boston Mus. Fine Arts, Brandeis U., Butler Inst. Am. Art, Munson-Williams-Proctor Inst., Addison Gallery Am. Art, Va. Mus. Fine Arts, DeCordova Mus., Tufts U.; featured in TV program Artist At Work, 1981; work featured in Am. Artist mag., 1979. Recipient awards Pa. Acad. Fine Arts, 1967, awards Allied Artists N.Y.C., 1966 Mem. Am. Watercolor Soc. (award), New Eng. Watercolor Soc., Allied Artists Am. (award), NAD (award)

COBB, SHIRLEY ANN DODSON, public relations consultant, journalist; b. Oklahoma City, Jan. 1, 1936; d. William Ray and Irene Dodson; m. Roy Lampkin Cobb, Jr., June 21, 1958; children: Kendra Leigh, Cary William, Paul Alan. BA in Journalism with distinction, U. Okla., 1958, postgrad., 1972, Jacksonville U., 1962. Info. specialist Pacific Missile Test Ctr., Point Mugu, Calif., 1975-76; reporter, splty. editor Religion and Fashion News Chronicle, 1977-81; cons. pub. rels., cable tv, telecomm. Camarillo, Calif., 1977—; media mgr. pub. info. cable TV and telecom. City of Thousand Oaks, Calif., 1983-99. Contbr. articles to profl. jours. Pres. Point Mugu Officers' Wives Club, 1975-76; trustee Ocean View Sch. Bd., 1976-79; bd. dirs. Camarillo Hospice, 1983-85, Long Term Care of Ventura County, Inc., 2001-03; sec. Ednl. TV for Conejo, 1997-98, pres., 1998-2000, bd. dirs., 1997-2002; vice chair Greater Thousand Oaks Telecmty., 1999-2000; treas. Thousand Oaks Rep. Women Federated, 2001-03; v.p. pub. rels. Ventura County Leadership Acad., 2001-02; bd. dirs. LWV Ventura County, 1999-2003, comms. dir., 2002-03. Recipient Spot News award San Fernando Valley Press Club, 1979, First Pl. spl. program Calif. Assn. Pub. Info. Offcls., 1985, Helen Putnam award League of Calif. Cities, 1989, Telecomm. Proj. award, League of Calif. Cities Telecom., 1998, 1st place award Best Practice award Govt., Bus., Edn. Tech Expo '98. Mem. Pub. Rels. Soc. Am. (L.A. chpt. liaison 1991), Calif. Assn. Pub. Info. Ofcls. (pres. 1989-90, Paul Clark Lifetime Achievement award 1993), Conejo Valley Hist. Soc. (sec. 1993-96, co-chmn. oral history com., 2001-), Ventura County Leadership Acad., Las Posas Country Club, Spanish Hills Country Club, Town Hall of Calif. Club, Phi Beta Kappa. Republican. Home and Office: 2481 Brookhill Dr Camarillo CA 93010-2112 E-mail: cobbweb@aol.com.

COBB, STEPHEN A. lawyer; b. Moline, Ill., Jan. 27, 1944; s. Archibald William and Lucile Bates C.; m. Nancy L. Hendrix, Dec. 18, 1972. AB cum laude, Harvard U., 1966; MA in Sociology, Vanderbilt U., 1968, PhD in Sociology, 1971, JD, 1977. Bar: Tenn. 1978, U.S. Dist. Ct. (mid. dist.) Tenn. 1978. Asst. prof. Tenn. State U., Nashville, 1970-74, dept. head, 1972-74; mem., chair edn. oversight com. Tenn. Ho. Reps., Nashville, 1974-86; pvt. practice law Nashville, 1978-86; with Waller Lansden Dortch & Davis, Nashville, 1986-90, ptnr., 1990—. Fullbright Jr. lectr. U. Caen, France, 1977-78; lectr. dept. sociology Fisk U., 1981-86. Former pres. Sister Cities of Nashville, Inc.; mem, former vice chmn. commn. ednl. quality So. Regional Edn. Bd. Decorated officer Ordre des Palmes Academiques (France); recipient Paul Simon Internat. award, 1990, Edwin Cudeki Internat. Bus. award, 1992; NDEA fellow, NIMH fellow, 1966-70. Mem. ABA, Am. Immigration Lawyers Assn., So. Sociol. Soc., Tenn. Bar Assn., Tenn Fgn. Lang. Inst., Nashville Bar Assn., Fedn. Alliances Francaises (former pres.), Order of Coif. Home: 1929 Castleman Dr Nashville TN 37215-3901 Office: 511 Union St Ste 2100 Nashville TN 37219-1760

COBB, TERRI REAMER (CECI COBB), film and video producer; b. N.Y.C., Feb. 18, 1934; d. Leo Odell and Jean (Wister) Gruber; m. Ira Reamer, July 4, 1954 (div. May 1975); children: Jeff, David, Ellen; m. David G. Cobb, Aug. 2, 1975. Student U. Miami, 1953-54, Miami Dade C.C., 1970-72. Vocalist The Girlfriends, N.Y.C., 1952-53; dental asst. Miami, Fla., 1953-56; med. asst., 1956-58; prodr., host TV talk show People and Places, Tampa, Fla., 1981-95; freelance film and video prodr., prodn. coord. Encore Film & Video Prodn., Tampa, 1984—. Freelance model, actress, Fla.; seminar leader Tom Kirby Assocs., Fla., 1986—; cons. U. South Fla. Dept. Edn., Tampa, 1980—; location scout, coord. films and commls.; freelance TV prodr., tech. dir. Co-prodr., host: (TV show) Insights (Telly award 2003). Health educator, fund raiser, speaker Fla. March of Dimes, 1964—91; mem. planning com. Tampa/Hillsborough; bd. dirs. Fla. Healthy Mother-Healthy Baby Coalition; mem. Hillsborough River Tech. Adv. Coun. Recipient Jone Intercable Golden Cassette award, 1989, Crystal Reel award Fla. Motion Picture & TV Assn., 1990, award Alliance for Cmty. Media, 2001. Mem. Fla. Perinatal Assn. (bd. dirs.), Fla. Womens' Alliance, Fla. Motion Picture and TV Assn. (bd. dirs.), Fla. Soc. Assn. Execs. (bd. dirs.), LWV. Avocations: tennis, boating, walking. Home: 16612 Hutchinson Rd Odessa FL 33556-2327

COBB, WILLIAM DOWELL, JR., lawyer; b. Dallas, Oct. 3, 1958; s. William Dowell and Gail Palmer Cobb; m. Stacy Lee Brainin, May 4, 1985; children: Claire, Will. BA, U. Denver, 1981; JD, U. Tex., 1984. Bar: Tex. 1984, U.S. Dist. Ct. (no. dist.) Tex. 1985, U.S. Ct. Appeals (5th cir.) 1987, U.S. Dist. Ct. (we. dist.) Tex. 1989, U.S. Dist. Ct. (ea. dist.) Tex. 1992, U.S. Dist. Ct. (so. dist.) Tex. 1998. Shareholder Cowles & Thompson P.C., Dallas, 1984—. Co-author: Texas Torts Handbook, 1998. Mem. ABA (litigation sect., tort and ins. practice sect., comml. torts com., profls.', officers' and dirs. liability law com., ins. coverage com., profl. liability com.), Assn. Profl. Responsibility Lawyers, Def. Rsch. Inst., Tex. Assn. Def. Counsel, Dallas Bar Assn. (legal ethics com.), Dallas Assn. Def. Counsel. Office: Cowles & Thompson PC 901 Main St Ste 4000 Dallas TX 75202-3793

COBB, WILLIAM THOMPSON, environmental and agricultural consultant; b. Spokane, Wash., Nov. 10, 1942; s. Elmer Jean and Martha Ella (Napier) C.; m. Sandra L. Hodgson, Aug. 29, 1964 (div. 1988); children: Mike, Melanie, Megan, Bill II. BA, Ea. Wash. U., 1964; PhD, Oreg. State U., 1973. Cert. profl. agronomist, profl. plant pathologist, crop advisor, environ. inspector. Mgr., agronomist Sun Royal Co., Royal City, Wash., 1970-74; sr. scientist Lilly Rsch. Labs., Kennewick, Wash., 1974-87; environ. and agrl. cons. Cobb Cons. Svcs., Kennewick, Wash., 1988—. Bd. dirs. Bentech Labs., Portland, Oreg., 1989; dir. spl. projects Bioremediation, Inc., Lake Oswego, Oreg., 1990-92; adv. bd. Adv. Coun. Tri-Cities, Wash., 1991. Contbr. articles to profl. jours. 1st lt. U.S. Army, 1964-67. Mem. Am. Phytopath. Soc., Weed Sci. Soc. Am., We. Soc. Weed Sci., Am. Soc. Agronomy, N.W. Assn. Environ. Profls., Nat. Assn. Environ. Profls., N.Y. Acad. Scis., Environ. Assessment Assn., Sigma Xi. Republican. Home and Office: Cobb Cons Svcs 815 S Kellogg St Kennewick WA 99336-9369

COBBAN, WILLIAM AUBREY, paleontologist; b. Anaconda, Mont., Dec. 31, 1916; s. Ray Aubrey and Anastacia (McNulty) C.; m. Ruth Georgina Loucks, Apr. 15, 1942; children: Georgina, William, Robert. BA, U. Mont., 1940; PhD, Johns Hopkins U., 1949. Geologist Carter Oil Co., Tulsa, 1940-46; paleontologist U.S. Geol. Survey, Washington, 1948-92, emeritus scientist, 1992—. Contbr. numerous articles to profl. jours. Recipient Meritorious Svc. award Dept. Interior, 1974, Disting. Svc. award U.S. Dept. Interior, 1986. Fellow AAAS, Geol. Soc. Am.; mem. Soc. Econ. Paleontologists and Mineralogists (hon.; Disting. Pioneer Geologist award 1985, Raymond C. Moore Paleontology medal 1990), Rocky Mountain Assn. Geologists (hon.), Mont. Geol. Soc. (hon.), Wyo. Geol Assn. (hon.), Paleontol. Soc. Am. (Paleontol. medal 1985), Assn. Petroleum Geologists, Paleontol. Rsch. Inst. (Gilbert Harris award 1996), Rocky Mountain Assn. Geologists (Outstanding award 2001), Phi Beta Kappa, Sigma Xi. Republican. Mem. United Ch. of Christ. Office: US Geol Survey Federal Ctr PO Box 25046 # 980 Denver CO 80225

COBBE, JAMES HAMILTON, economics educator; b. July 24, 1946; arrived in U.S., 68, naturalized, 85; s. Clifford James and Beatrice Aileen (Blake) Cobbe; m. Louise Grant Barrett, June 14, 1969; 1 child, Andrew van Leer. BA, U. Cambridge, 1968; MPhil, Yale U., 1970, PhD, 1977. Fellow Yale U., New Haven, 1968—72; rsch. economist Carnegie Endowment for Internat. Peace, N.Y.C., 1971; lectr. in econs. London Sch. Econs. and Polit. Sci., 1972—73, U. Botswana, Lesotho and Swaziland, 1973—76; asst. prof. econs. Fla. State U., Tallahassee, 1976—81, assoc. prof., 1981—86, prof. econs., 1986—, assoc. dean Coll. Social Scis., 1985—91, dir. interdisciplinary program social sci., 1985—89, interim dean Coll. Social Scis., 1986—87, dir. grad. program in econs., 1992—97, chmn. dept. econs., 1997—, vice chmn. faculty sen. steering com., 2002—. Rsch. fellow Inst. So. African Studies Nat. U. Lesotho, 1981—82; cons. in field. Author: Governments and Mining Companies in Developing Countries, 1977, Lesotho: Dilemmas of Dependence in Southern Africa, 1985; contbr. articles to profl. jours., chpts. to books. Mem.: Soc. Internat. Devel., African Studies Assn., So. Econ. Assn., Am. Econ. Assn., Fla. Economic Club, Leander Club (Henley, Eng.), Hawks Club (Cambridge, Eng.). Democrat. Home: 2012 E Randolph Cir Tallahassee FL 32308-3354 Office: Fla State U Dept Econs Tallahassee FL 32306-2180 E-mail: jcobbe@mailer.fsu.edu.

COBBETT, STUART HANSON, lawyer; b. Montreal, June 3, 1948; s. Stuart Ashton and Adrienne Cobbett; m. Jill Rankin, Sept. 7, 1973; children: Alexander, William, Anne. BA, McGill U., 1969, BCL, 1972. Bar: Que. Ptnr. Heenan Blaikie, Montreal, 1974-85; sr. v.p., dir. Astral Comms., Montreal, 1985-92; sr. ptnr. Stikeman Elliott, Montreal, 1992, mng. prin. London, 1996-99, mng. ptnr. Montreal, 2000—. Bd. dirs. Aldeavision Inc., Montreal, Formula Growth Ltd., Montreal, McCord St. Sites, Montreal. Bd. dirs. Bishop's Coll. Sch., Lennoxville, Que., Can., 1982-95; chmn., bd. dirs. McGill News, Montreal, 1991-96; chmn. bd. visitors in arts McGill U., 1991-96; pres. McGill Alumni Assn., 2002—. Mem. Can. Bar Assn., Internat. Bar Assn., N.Y. State Bar Assn. Anglican. Avocations: skiing, tennis, golf, hiking. Office: Stikeman Elliott 1155 Rene Levesque Blvd Montreal QC Canada H3B 3V2 E-mail: scobbett@stikeman.com.

COBBLE, JAMES WIKLE, chemistry educator; b. Kansas City, Mo., Mar. 15, 1926; s. Ray and Crystal Edith (Wikle) C.; m. Margaret Ann Zumwalt, June 9, 1949 (dec.); children— Catherine Ann, Richard James. Student, San Diego State Coll., 1942-44; BA, No. Ariz. U., 1946; MS, U. So. Calif., 1949; PhD, U. Tenn., 1952. Chemist Oak Ridge Nat. Lab., 1949-52; postdoctoral research asso. U. Calif., Berkeley, 1952-55, instr. dept. chemistry, 1954; asst. prof. dept. chemistry Purdue U., Lafayette, Ind., 1955-58, asso. prof., 1958-61, prof., 1961-73; prof., dean Grad. div. San Diego State U., 1973—; v.p. rsch., dean Grad. divsn. San Diego State U., 1997—. Cons. in field. Contbr. articles to sci. publs. Mem. bd. visitors USAF Air Univ., 1984—92, chmn., 1988—90; vpres. San Diego State Univ. Found., 1975—; trustee Calif. Western Law Sch., 1987—93; mem. Joint Grad. Bd., 1973—78; Lt. (j.g.) USNR, 1945—46. Recipient E.O. Lawrence award U.S. AEC, 1970, Disting. Svc. award USAF, 1992; Guggenheim fellow, 1966; Robert A. Welch Found. lectr., 1971. Fellow Am. Inst. Chemists, Am. Phys. Soc.; mem. Am. Chem. Soc., Sigma Xi, Phi Kappa Phi, Alpha Chi Sigma, Phi Lambda Upsilon. Home: 1380 Park Row La Jolla CA 92037-3709 Office: San Diego State Univ Grad & Rsch Affairs San Diego CA 92182-8020

COBBLE, STEVEN BRUCE, political consultant, strategist; b. Perrysburg, Ohio, July 7, 1951; s. Milan H. and Nancy L. (Musselman) C.; m. Molly E. Smith, July 3, 1983; children: Elizabeth A., Julia S. BS in Math., BA in Govt., N.Mex. State U., 1974. Speechwriter, spl. asst. Office of Gov., Santa Fe, N.Mex., 1982-86; nat. del. selection dir. Jesse Jackson for Pres., Chgo. and Washington, 1987, 88; exec. dir. Keep Hope Alive Polit. Action Com., Washington, 1988-90; advisor Ron Brown for Dem. Nat. Com. Chair Campaign, Washington, 1988, 89; democracy reform cons. Ctr. for New Democracy, Grinnell, Iowa, 1991-93; polit. and fin. dir. Carol Moseley-Braun for U.S. Senate Campaign, Chgo., 1992; speechwriter, policy analyst Office of Mayor, Albuquerque, 1994, 95; speech writer, polit. dir. Nat. Rainbow Coalition, Washington, 1996, 97; exec. dir. Arca Found., 1998, 99. Dir. Campaign for a Progressive Future, 2000-02; strategist Ralph Nader for Pres., 2000, Dennis Kucinich for Pres., 2003; assoc. fellow Inst. for Policy Studies, 2001-02; sr. fellow Ctr. for Internat. Policy, 2002; pub. spkr. numerous groups, meetings, 1970-2001; panelist, presenter numerous polit. forums/panels, 1970-2001; adv. bd. Hotline Index, Campaign Hotline newsletter, Washington, 1995, 96. Editor Nat. Rainbow Coalition Jax Fax, 1996, 97; contbr. articles to profl. jours.; guest appearance CNN's Inside Politics TV show, Washington, 1995. Nat. conv. del. Dem. Nat. Conv., Miami, 1972; democracy trainer Nat. Dem. Inst./African Nat. Congress, South Africa, 1991; mem. nat. rules com. Nat. Dem. Party, Washington, 1992; polit. party trainer Nat. Dem. Inst., Panama, 1993. Fellow LBJ Sch. Pub. Affairs, Austin, Tex., 1974, Inst. Politics, Harvard U., Cambridge, Mass., 1990; named Young Polit. Leader Am. Coun. Young Polit. Leaders, Washington, 1986. Methodist. Avocations: travel, beatles music, reading. Home: 6909 Williamsburg Blvd Arlington VA 22213-1812 Office: 6909 Williamsburg Blvd Arlington VA 22213-1812

COBBS, ALFRED LEON, German language educator; b. Sept. 12, 1943; BA in German, Berea Coll., 1966; MA in German, U. Mo., 1968; PhD in German, U. Cin., 1974. Asst. prof. Germanic langs. and lits. U. Va., Charlottesville, 1973-79; asst., assoc. prof. Romance and Germanic langs. Wayne State U., Detroit, 1979-89, assoc. prof. German and Slavic studies, 1989—. Home: 14030 Faust Ave Detroit MI 48223-3540 Office: Wayne State U Dept German-Slavic Studies Wayne MI 48202 E-mail: aa2845@wayne.edu.

COBBS, JAMES HAROLD, engineer, consultant; b. Bristow, Okla., Aug. 25, 1928; s. Harold Martin and Ella A. (Rountree) C.; m. Charlotte Marie Fisher, Aug. 16, 1953 (dec. June 1990); m. Mary J. Armer, May 28, 1994; children: James Harold, David Charles, Gregory Lee, Matthew Louis. BS in Petroleum Engring., U. Okla., 1949, postgrad., 1949-51, U. Tulsa, 1955-68. Registered profl. engr. 8 states; cert. of qualification nat. Coun. Engring. Examiners. Assoc. engr. Tidewater Oil Co., Midland, Tex., 1951-52, reservoir engr. Houston, 1952-55, divsn. reservoir engr. Tulsa, Okla., 1955—59; pvt. practice cons. engr., 1959-63; sr. engr. Fenix & Scisson Inc., Tulsa, 1963-69; pres. Cobbs Engring., Inc., cons. engrs., Tulsa, 1969—. Faculty U. Wis. Extension. Contbr. articles to profl. jours.; patentee in field. Various positions including scoutmaster Indian Nations coun. Boy Scouts Am., 1962-81; instr. first aid ARC, 1969-81; active Vols. in Tech. Assistance, 1978—. Mem. NSPE, Am. Underground Constrn. Assn., Petroleum Engrs., Nat. Acad. Forensic Engrs., World Rock Boring Assn., Okla. Soc. Profl. Engrs. Republican. Mem. Christian Ch. (elder, chmn. bd. elders 1971, 79). Home and Office: 4620 E 55th Pl Tulsa OK 74135-4306 E-mail: james_cobbs@yahoo.com.

COBBS, NICHOLAS HAMMER, lawyer; b. N.Y.C., June 28, 1946; s. John Lewis and Phyllis Cobbs; children: Robert White, Rebecca Ann. AB cum laude, Amherst (Mass.) Coll., 1968; JD, U. Pa., 1974. Bar: N.Y. 1975, D.C. 1982, Md. 1984, Va. 1990, U.S. Dist. Ct. (so. dist.) N.Y. 1975, U.S. Dist. Ct. D.C. 1982, U.S. Dist. Ct. (ea. dist.) Va. 1990, U.S. Dist. Ct. (we. dist.) Va. 1990, U.S. Dist. Ct. Md. 1989, U.S. Supreme Ct. 1984. Assoc. Burlingham Underwood & Lord, N.Y.C., 1974-77, Haight, Gardner, Poor & Havens, N.Y.C., 1977-83; ptnr., of counsel Tigert & Roberts, Washington, 1984-89; ptnr. Law Offices of Nicholas H. Cobbs, Washington, 1989—. Of counsel Klimack, Kolodney & Casale, Washington, 1995-; mem. steering com. D.C. Bar Law Practice Mgmt., 2000-, litigation steering com., 2001-, co-chmn., 2002—. Contbr. articles to profl. jours. Arbitrator, mediator D.C. Superior Ct., Washington, 1990—; instr. D.C. Bar Continuing Legal Edn., 1993—. Lt. USNR, 1969-73. Recipient Spl. Merit award, D.C. Bar, 2003. Mem. ABA, Fed. Bar Assn., Lawyer-Pilot's Bar Assn., Maritime Law Assn. of the U.S. Episcopalian. Office: 1776 K St NW Ste 300 Washington DC 20006-2326 E-mail: ncobbs@erols.com.

COBBS, RUSSELL L(EWIS), English language educator; b. Beaumont, Tex., Jan. 10, 1937; s. Clyde Bryan and Lois Genevieve (Martin) C.; m. Doris Elizabeth Pelletier, Aug. 9, 1969; 1 child, Colleen Elizabeth. BS in English, S. F. Austin U., Nacogdoches, Tex., 1960; postgrad NDEA English Inst., U. Tex., 1966; MEd in Adminstrn. and Supervision, Inter-Am. U., San Juan, PR., 1971. Cert. tchr. English, Mass., Tex. Tchr. English, Justin F. Kimball H.S., Dallas, 1960-63; med. rsch. writer U. Tex., M.D. Anderson Rsch. Inst., Houston, 1963-64; chmn. English dept. Ernest Harmon Jr.-Sr. H.S., Stephenville, Nfld., Can., 1964-66, Kaiserslautern Am. H.S., Germany, 1966-68, 71-72; coor. English and lang. arts curriculum Ramey AFB (P.R.) Schs., 1968-71; chmn. English dept. Ramey Sr. H.S., 1968-71; tchr. English, Longmeadow (Mass.) H.S., 1972-83, chmn. English dept., 1983-97, dir. computer writing ctr. English dept., 1987-97; ret., 1997. Founder Computer Writing Ctr., Longmeadow High Sch., 1987; cons. Nat. Evaluation Sys., Inc., 1998—, editl. prodn. cons., 2002—; asst. chief reader Mass. Tchr. Licensure Exam., 1998—. Rsch. vol. Richard Salter Storrs Libr., Longmeadow, 1997-2002; sr. reader vol. for Longmeadow Elem. Schs., 1998-2002. Curriculum devel. grantee Longmeadow Educators Assistance Program, 1987, Writing Curriculum grantee Horace Mann, Longmeadow, 1989; LHS Class of 1987 Curriculum Devel. award 1993. Mem. NEA, Nat. Coun. Tchrs. English (bd. dirs. secondary English/lang. arts com.), Nat. Writing Ctrs. Assn., Assembly Computers in English, New Eng. Assn. Tchrs. English (coord. affiliate forum), New Eng. Writing Ctrs. Assn., Mass. Coun. Tchrs. English, New Eng. Assn. Tchrs. English (pres. 1991-92, profl. devel. and curriculum com. chair 1993-94, coord. cyber coaching program for tchrs., K-Coll., 1997—, website devel. com. 1997—), Phi Delta Theta (life, Tex. Eta chpt.). Roman Catholic. Avocations: gardening, physical fitness training, dog obedience training, hiking, reading. Home: 85 Cooley Dr Longmeadow MA 01106-1303

COBBS HOFFMAN, ELIZABETH ANNE, history educator; b. Gardena, Calif., July 28, 1956; d. Donald Cobbs and Joanne Shelby Davis; m. Daniel Hoffman, May 20, 1995; children: Gregory Theodore Shelby, Victoria Marie Shelby. BA, U Calif., 1983; MA, U. Calif., 1984, PhD, 1988. Dwight Stanford prof. Am. fgn. rels. San Diego State U., 1998—; assoc. prof. of history U. San Diego, 1989—98. Mem. hist. adv. com. Dept. of State, Washington, 1999—. Author: The Rich Neighbor Policy: Rockefeller and Kaiser in Brazil, 1992, All You Need is Love: The Peace Corps and the Spirit of the Sixties, 1998, Major Problems in American History: 1865 to the Present, 2001. Pres. Ctr. for Women's Studies and Svcs., San Diego. Recipient John D. Rockefeller III Youth award, Rockefeller Found., 1980, Allan Nevins prize, Soc. Am. Historians, 1989; fellow, OAS, 1986, Woodrow Wilson Ctr. /Wilson Internat. Ctr. for Scholars, 1993. Mem.: Soc. Historians of Am. Fgn. Rels. (coun. 1996—99, Stuart Bernath Book prize 1993). Office: Dept History San Diego State U 5500 Campanile Dr San Diego CA 92182

COBEY, JOHN GEOFFREY, lawyer, consultant; b. Cleve., Aug. 16, 1943; s. Herbert Todd and Phyllis Jean (Weston) C.; m. Jan M. Frankel, 1983; children: Max Todd, David William. BS, Cornell U., 1966; postgrad., U. de Deusto, Balbao, Spain, 1968, Exeter (Eng.) U., 1969; JD, U. Cin., 1969. Bar: Ohio 1969, U.S. Dist. Ct. (so. dist.) Ohio 1969, U.S. Ct. Appeals (6th cir.) 1970, Ky. 1978, U.S. Dist. Ct. (no. dist.) Ky. 1978. Mem. Cohen, Todd, Kite and Stanford LLC, 1969—. Bd. dirs. 1st Nat. Bank No. Ky., Armstel Corp., E.F. Food Systems, Inc., Armstrong Coffee Co.; sec. bd. dirs. Elegant Fare; bd. dirs., sec. Apt. Assn. Title Co.; bd. dirs. Real Time Sys., Inc.; counsel coop. housing City of Cin. Founder, pres. Young Men's Wing, Mercantile Libr., 1971, regional amb. Cornell U., 1998, 99; trustee Ohio chpt. Nature Conservancy, 1974-82, Hillel of Cin., 1980-86, Women's Def. Fund, 1977, Holmes House, 1978-80; sec. Arts Consortium, Cin., 1975-77, trustee, 1975-78; mem. exec. com. Cin. chpt. Am. Jewish Com., 1981—; trustee Hillel House, Better Housing League; chmn. bd. Friends Cin. Parks, 1982-84, pres. 1977-79; chmn. bd. dirs. Washington Park Housing Co., 1997—; bd. dirs. Cin. Law Libr., Greater Cin./No. Ky. Apt. Assn., 1975-94, Chinese Music Festival, 1996-00, Greater Cin. Oral Health Commn., 2000—, United Jewish Cemetary, 1999-2002, Friends of Spl. Treatment Ctr. for Juvenile Arthritis, Children's Hosp. Cin., 2000—, Opn. Smile, 1998. Mem. Ohio State Bar Assn., Ky. Bar Assn., Cin. Bar Assn., No. Ky. Bar Assn., Fed. Bar Assn., U. Coll. Life Scis. and Agr. Alumni Assn. (dist. dir. 1977-79), Ohio Apt. Assn. (bd. dirs. 1986-87), Cin. Apt. Assn. (bd. dirs. 1983-90, pres. 1986-87), U. Cin. Law Sch. Alumni Assn. (bd. dirs. 1973-76), Masons Scottish Rite. Home: 231 Oliver Rd Cincinnati OH 45215-2638 Office: Cohen Todd Kite and Stanford 250 E 5th St Ste 1200 Cincinnati OH 45202-3121 E-mail: JCOBEY@ctks.com.

COBEY, RALPH, industrialist; b. Sycamore, Ohio, Aug. 15, 1909; m. Hortense Kohn, Feb. 28, 1944; children: Minnie, Susanne. ME, Carnegie Inst. Tech., 1932; D.Sc. (hon.), Findlay Coll., 1958. Pres. Perfection Steel Body Co., Galion, Ohio, 1945-70, Perfection-Cobey, Co., Galion, Ohio, 1949-70, Eagle Crusher Co., 1954-90, chmn. bd., 1990—; pres. Philips-Davies Co., 1965-70, Cobey Co., 1946-70, Diamond Iron Works, 1972-90, Austin-Western Crusher Co., 1974-90, Scoopmobile Co., 1978-90, Madsen Co., 1979-90, World Wide Investment Co., 1950—. Aide in preparation of prodn. and design of Army tanks OPM, 1939-42. Mem. contbg. com. NCCJ, 1951-55, now area chmn. spl. gifts com.; founder, pres. Harry Cobey Found.; area chmn. U.S. Savs. Bonds; mem. pres.'s adv. coun. for devel. Ashland Coll., Ohio, mem. Ohio Gov.'s Citizens' Task Force on Environ. Protection, 1971-72, Pres.'s Tax Com., 1962-66; pioneer chaplain svcs. in indsl. plants; mem. Ohio Expns. Commn., 1964, Radio Free Europe Com.; chmn. Cmty. Heart Fund Campaign, 1971-72; pres., spl. gifts chmn. Crawford County Heart Fund, 1972-78; mem. Ohio fin. bd. Heart Fund, 1973—; mem. Ohio Rep. Fin. Com.; mounted dep. sheriff, Morrow County (Ohio), 1974-84; bd. dirs., chmn. long range planning com. Johnny Appleseed Area coun. Boy Scouts of Am.; hon. life mem. Galion Cmty. Ctr.; trustee Galion City Hosp. Found. Bd.; mem. pres.'s coun. Ohio State U.; chmn., founder Minnie Cobey Meml. Libr.; founder, chmn. bd. trustees Louis Bromfield Malabar Farm Found.; bd. dirs. Morrow County United Appeals; State of Ohio amb. of natural resources; numerous other civic activities. Capt. USAAF, 1942-46, 51, Korea. Baden-Powel World fellow King Carl Gustaf of Sweden, 1992; recipient Disting. Citizen of Yr. award Heart of Ohio Coun., Boy Scouts Am., 1995, Lifetime Commitment to Humanitarianism award from Rep. Joan Lawrence, Ohio Ho. Reps., 1996, award Louis Bromfield Soc., 2001, resolution from Ohio Dist. 5 Agy. on Aging, Cert. of Appreciation USDA, 2003; inductee Ohio State Fair Hall of Fame, 1992, Ohio Agrl. Hall of Fame, 1999, Ohio Natural Resources Hall of Fame, 2001, Ohio Sr. Citizens Hall of Fame, 2002, N. Ctrl. Ohio Entreprenureal Hall of Fame, 2003; Ralph Cobey Day in City of Galion, 1995, City of Bucyrus, 1999. Mem. NAM, Nat. Assn. 4-H Clubs, Future Farmers Am., U.S. C. of C. (mem. taxation, fgn. affairs, labor rels. coms.), Masons (32 degree), Shriners (sec.-treas.). Home: 4270 State Route 309 Galion OH 44833-9618 Office: Eagle Crusher Co Inc PO Box 537 Galion OH 44833-0537

COBEY, WILLIAM WILFRED, JR., political organization administrator; b. Washington, May 13, 1939; m. Nancy Sullivan, Feb. 20, 1965; children: Billy, Cathy. BS in Chemistry, Emory U., 1962; MBA in Mktg., U. Pa., 1964; M.Ed. in Health and Phys. Edn., U. Pitts., 1968. Dir. athletics U. N.C., Chapel Hill, 1976-80; prin. Cobey and Assocs., mgmt. cons., Chapel Hill, 1982-85; mem. 99th Congress from 4th Dist. N.C., 1984-86, mem. com. on sci. and tech., com. on small bus.; dep. sec. of transp. State of N.C.; sec. of the environment, health & natural resources State of N.C. Past. pres. Chapel Hill.-Carrboro YMCA; active Am. Field Service, Boy Scouts Am.; Republican candidate for lt. gov. N.C., 1980, for U.S. Congress, 1982; chmn. N.C. Rep. Party, 1999—, So. State Chmn.'s Assn., 1999-. Mem. Fellowship Christian Athletes. Office: NC Rep Party PO Box 12905, 1410 Hillsborough St Raleigh NC 27605-1829*

COBIANCHI, THOMAS THEODORE, engineering and marketing executive, educator; b. Paterson, N.J., July 7, 1941; s. Thomas and Violet Emily (Bazzar) C.; m. Phyllis Linda Asch, Feb. 6, 1964; 1 child, Michael. Student, Clemson U., 1963; BS, Monmouth Coll., 1968, MBA, 1972; postgrad., U. Pa., 1987; D Bus. Adminstrn., U.S. Internat. U., 1994. Sales mgr. Westinghouse Electric Corp., Balt., 1968-74, sr. internat. sales engr. Lima, Ohio, 1975-77, program mgr. Pitts., 1977-78, mgr. bus. devel., 1978-82, dir. mktg. Arlington, Va., 1982-86; acting dir., engring. mgr. General Dynamics Corp., San Diego, 1986-89; dir. bus. devel. RPV Programs Teledyne Ryan Aero., San Diego, 1989-90; pres. Cobianchi & Assocs., San Diego, 1990; v.p. strategic planning and program devel. S-Cubed div. Maxwell Labs., Inc., San Diego, 1991; v.p. corp. devel. Orincon Corp., San Diego, 1995-98; mgr. client bus. AT&T, Irvine, Calif., 1998-2001, tech. bus. mgr. Las Vegas, Nev., 2001—. Instr., lectr. various ednl. instns. Active various polit. and ednl. orgns.; mem. bus. adv. coun. U.S. Internat. U.; bd. dirs. Cath. Charities San Diego; vol. exec., sect. chmn. United Way San Diego. Mem. Armed Forces Communications and Electronics Assn. (acting chmn. 1988), Princeton Club of Washington, Nat. Aviation Club, General Dynamics Health Club, Delta Sigma Pi. Home: 412 Sonoma Aisle Irvine CA 92618-3949

COBLE, HOWARD, congressman, lawyer; b. Greensboro, N.C., Mar. 18, 1931; s. Joseph Howard and Johnnie (Holt) C. Student, Appalachian State U., 1949-50; AB in History, Guilford Coll., 1958; JD, U. N.C., 1962. Bar: N.C. 1966. Field claim rep., supt. State Farm Mut. Ins., 1961-67; asst. county atty. Guilford County, N.C., 1967-69; mem. N.C. Ho. of Reps., Raleigh, 1969, 1979—83; asst. U.S. atty. U.S. Dist. Ct. (mid. dist.) N.C., 1969-73; sec. N.C. Dept. Revenue, Raleigh, 1973-77; atty. Turner, Enochs & Sparrow, Greensboro, 1979-84; mem. U.S. Congress from 6th N.C. dist., Washington, 1985—; mem. judiciary com., transp. and infrastructure com. Served to capt. USCG, 1952-56, comdg. officer USCGR. Mem. N.C. State Bar Assn., Greensboro Bar Assn., Masons (32d degree master mason Guilford lodge # 656), Am. Legion, VFW, Lions, SAR Republican. Presbyterian.*

COBLE, WILLIAM CARROLL, computer engineer; b. Detroit, July 23, 1958; s. Haskin Frazier and Wilma Jolela (King) C.; m. Barbara Karen Smith, Aug. 22, 1987. BS in Physics, Morehouse Coll., 1981; BSEE, Ga. Inst. Tech., 1981, MSM Mgmt. of Tech., 1999; postgrad., U. Dayton, 1981-82. Electronics engr. Dept. of Def., Dayton, Ohio, 1981-82; jr. computer engr. Ga. Power Co., Norcross, 1983-85, engr. info. systems Atlanta, 1985-86, sr. engr., project leader, 1987-89, team leader, 1990; supr. Trans Info. Resources, Atlanta, 1991-94, ops. coord., 1994-97, tech. coord., 1997-2000, mgr. mktg. sys., 2000-2001; mgr. ebusiness, info. and applications mgmt. SCS Mktg. Svcs., Atlanta, 2001—. Gen. mgr. Masterplan Computer, Decatur, Ga., 1983-94; cons. Sprull Products, Inc., Atlanta, 1987-94; vice chmn. GEMS Internat. Users Group, 1992-93, chmn., 1993-94. Pres. Springwoods Community, Decatur, 1986-89; baseball coach Cen. DeKalb Baseball Assn., 1995—, Tucker Baseball Assn., 2002–; basketball coach St. Timothy UMC, 1999—. Avocation: antique automobiles. Home: 5620 Rutland Trce Lithonia GA 30058-3203 Office: 20th Fl Bin 10206 241 Ralph Mcgill Blvd NE Atlanta GA 30308-3374 E-mail: wccoble@southernco.com.

COBOS, PATRICIO, music educator; s. Henry A. and Maria V. Cobos; m. Andrea Marie Dean, Mar. 22, 1997. MusM in Performance, Violin, Fla. State U., 1969. Violinist Atlanta Symphony, Atlanta, 1961—62; concert master Chattanooga Symphony, Chattanooga, 1962—66; prof. violin Winthrop U., Rock Hill, SC, 1969—74; concert master Charlotte Symphony, Charlotte, NC, 1971—75; artist in residence U. N.C., Charlotte, NC, 1973—75, SUNY, Buffalo, 1975—79; first violinist with profl. string quartet Rowe Quartet, 1973—83; coll. prof. violin Akron U., Akron, Ohio, 1980—83; prof. violin Columbus State U., Columbus, Ga., 1983—. Assoc. music dir. Nat. Symphony of Chile, Santiago, Chile, 1991—95; artistic dir., condr. Lago Ranco Music Festival, Lago Ranco, Chile, 1996—98; music dir., condr. LaGrange Symphony Orch., LaGrange, Ga., 2001—; concert master Macon Symphony Orch., Macon, Ga., 1984—; assoc. concert master Columbus Symphony Orch., Columbus, Ga., 2001—. Toured as first violinist with a profl. string quartet U.S. State Dept. Recipient Peabody Award, George Foster Peabody, 1977, Silver Medal, N.Y. Film Festival, 1977, Award in Performing Arts, Nat. Assn. of TV Program Executives, 1977, Gabriel Award, 1977;, Rockefeller Found., 1961, Fellowship in Violin, Koussevitzky Found., 1968. Mem.: Phi Mu Alpha (life). Achievements include New York debut as first violinist of the Rowe Quartet in 1977 at the Lincoln Center, returned to perform at the Lincoln Center in 1978, Served on the Faculty of Switzerland's Sommer Musikowochen; Founded the University of North Carolina-Charlotte Orchestra; Toured Spain and Italy as a violinist with the Atlanta Virtuosi; Violin soloist in Japan and Germany 1996 - 1997; Performed with the Garth Newel Chamber Players in France in 1998. Home: 6901 Sandstone Ct Columbus GA 31907 Office: Columbus State University 4225 University Ave Columbus GA 31907

COBURN, D(ONALD) L(EE), playwright; b. Balt., Aug. 4, 1938; s. Guy Dabney and Ruth Margaret (Somers) C.; m. Nazlee Joyce French, Oct. 24, 1964 (div. Sept. 1971); children: Donn Christopher, Kimberly; m. Marsha Woodruff Maher, Feb. 22, 1975. Student pub. schs., Balt. Propr. Don Coburn & Assocs., Balt., 1966-70; with Stanford Agy., Dallas, 1970-73; propr. Donald L. Coburn Corp. Cons., Dallas, 1973-75; ind. playwright, 1975—. Playwright: The Gin Game, 1977 (Pulitzer prize in drama 1978, Tony award nomination 1978, Golden Apple 1978), Bluewater Cottage, 1979, The Corporation Man, 1981, Currents Turned Awry, 1982, Guy, 1983, Noble Adjustment, 1986, Anna-Weston, 1988, Return to Blue Fin, 1991; (screenplays) Flights of Angels, 1987, A Virgin Year, 1992; (teleplay) Hollywood Presents: The Gin Game, 2002. Served with USNR, 1958-60. Mem. Authors League Am., Writers Guild Am., Tex. Inst. Letters, Soc. des Auteurs et Compositeurs Dramatiques.

COBURN, ELIZABETH ANN, librarian; b. Hartford, Conn., Jan. 22, 1949; d. Arlington Richard and Ann Elizabeth (Hillen) Semmler; m. Richard Joseph Coburn, Jan. 2, 1993. BS, Ctrl. Conn. State U., 1971; MLS, So. Conn. State U., 1973. Ref. libr. Tunxis C.C., Farmington, Conn., 1973-74; children's libr. Plainville (Conn.) Pub. Libr., 1973-77, asst. dir., mus. curator, 1978-81, 82-84, acting dir., 1977-78, 80; libr. Avon (Conn.) Old Farms Sch., 1985—. Researcher for BBC project, 1988. Active Wolf Haven, Tenino, Wash., 1991—. Mem. ALA. Democrat. Roman Catholic. Avocations: writing poetry, film history, photography, interior decorating, native american art. Home: 15 Stratford Park Bloomfield CT 06002-2143 Office: Avon Old Farms Sch 500 Old Farms Rd Avon CT 06001-2799

COBURN, JAMES LEROY, educational administrator; b. Oak Park, Ill., Nov. 21, 1933; s. Forest Edward and Myrtle Emmaline (Clarke) C.; m. Julianne Whitty, Sept. 3, 1955; children: James, Gregory, Julie, Cheryl. BA, North Cen. Coll., Naperville, Ill., 1956; MS, No. Ill. U., 1965; EdD, Vanderbilt U., 1983. Cert. tchr., guidance counselor, supt., Ill. Tchr. Luther South High Sch., Chgo., 1956-58, Maine Township High Sch. East, Park Ridge, Ill., 1958-61, dean, counselor, 1961-64; dir. student pers. svcs. Maine Twp. High Sch. South, Park Ridge, 1964-67; asst. prin. for staff Maine Twp. High Sch. West, Des Plaines, Ill., 1967-73, prin., 1973-97; ret., 1997. Cons. Pitts. Pub. Schs., 1965; chmn. Ill. Blue Ribbon Com. on Edn., Bloomington, 1988; spkr. Internat. Ednl. Symposium, South Korea, 1996. Editor: Growth through Reading, 1960, 61. Pres. Inter-Suburban Assn.; chmn. judges 4th of July Parade, Des Plaines, 1980-86; mem. Des Plaines Beautification Com., 1987, Des Plaines Mayor's Adv. Com., 1989—; Ill. state commr. North Ctrl. Assn., 1992-95; pres. Des Plaines chpt. United Way, 1995—; pres. Twp. Sch. Bd. Caucus, 2002. Recipient Those Who Excel award Ill. Bd. Edn., 1977, Disting. Educator's award Idea Inst., 1984. Mem. Nat. Assn. Secondary Sch. Prins., Am. Assn. Sch. Adminstrs., Ill. Prins. Assn., Intersuburban Assn. Prins. (pres. 1986—), Des Plaines C. of C. (bd. dirs 1980-85, 92-95), Rotary (pres. Des Plaines 1976-77, Most Valuable Mem. award 1979, Paul Harris fellow 1989, John Vaughin excellence in edn. award 1997). Lutheran. Avocations: reading, travel, recreational sports, gardening. Home: 1843 Locust St Des Plaines IL 60018-2326 E-mail: jim0181@attbi.com.

COBURN, LEWIS ALAN, mathematics educator; b. Austin, Tex., Aug. 16, 1940; s. Nathaniel and Ann (Block) C.; m. Charlaine Elizabeth Ackerman, June 19, 1966; 1 child, Elinor Nadia. BS, U. Mich., 1961, MS, 1962, PhD, 1964. Asst. prof. NYU, N.Y.C., 1964-65, Purdue U., West Lafayette, Ind., 1965-66, Yeshiva U., N.Y.C., 1966-68, assoc. prof., 1968-72, prof. math., 1972-79; prof. SUNY, Buffalo, 1979—, chmn. dept. math., 1979-97. Mem. editorial bd. Jour. Integral Equations and Operator Theory, 1978—; contbr. over 40 articles to math. rsch. jours. NSF grantee, 1966—. Mem. Am. Math. Soc. Office: SUNY Dept Of Math Buffalo NY 14260-0001 E-mail: lcoburn@acsu.buffalo.edu.

COBURN, MARJORIE FOSTER, psychologist, educator; b. Salt Lake City, Feb. 28, 1939; d. Harlan A. and Alma (Ballinger) Polk; m. Robert Byron Coburn, July 2, 1977; children: Polly Klea Foster, Matthew Ryan Foster, Robert Scott Coburn, Kelly Anne Coburn. B.A. in Sociology, UCLA, 1960; Montessori Internat. Diploma honor grad. Washington Montessori Inst., 1968; M.A. in Psychology, U. No. Colo., 1979; Ph.D. in Counseling Psychology, U. Denver, 1983. Licensed clin. psychologist. Probation officer Alameda County (Calif.), Oakland, 1960-62, Contra Costa County (Calif.), El Cerrito, 1966, Fairfax County (Va.), Fairfax, 1967; dir. Friendship Club, Orlando, Fla., 1963-65; tchr. Va. Montessori Sch., Fairfax, 1968-70; spl. edn. tchr. Leary Sch., Falls Church, Va., 1970-72, sch. adminstr., 1973-76; tchr. Aseltine Sch., San Diego, 1976-77, Coburn Montessori Sch., Colorado Springs, Colo., 1977-79; pvt. practice psychotherapy, Colorado Springs, 1979-82, San Diego, 1982—; cons. spl. edn., agoraphobia, women in transition. Mem. Am. Psychol. Assn., Am. Orthopsychiat. Assn., Phobia Soc., Council Exceptional Children, Calif. Psychol. Assn., San Diego Psychological Assn., The Charter 100, Mensa. Episcopalian. Lodge: Rotary. Contbr. articles to profl. jours.; author: (with R.C. Orem) Montessori: Prescription for Children with Learning Disabilities, 1977. Office: 836 Prospect St Ste 101 La Jolla CA 92037-4206 E-mail: mcoburn@san.rr.com.

COBURN, RICHARD JOSEPH, company executive, electrical engineer; b. N.Y.C., Nov. 4, 1931; s. Elmer Roswell and Marie Veronica (Greenan) C.; m. Catherine Elizabeth Wilkinson (div. 1992); children: Jenifer, Catherine, Steven; m. Elizabeth A. Semmler, Jan. 1993. BSEE, Yale U., 1954. Devel. engr. Hamilton Standard, Windsor Locks, Conn., 1954-59; chief engr. Dynamic Controls Corp., South Windsor, Conn., 1959-66; mgr. digital logic Fairchild Industries, Germantown, Md., 1966-68; co-founder, pres. Scan Optics, East Hartford, Conn., 1968-72; pres. Coburn Tech., East Hartford, 1972-77, KCR Tech., East Hartford, Conn., 1977-91; co-founder, chmn. Accent Color Sciences, Inc., East Hartford, Conn., 1993—2001; mgr. SentryTec, LLC, Bloomfield, Conn., 2001—. Bd. dirs. Scan Optics, Manchester, Conn. Inventor electronic back pressure control, radio noise free switch, apparatus for image reproduction. Mem. Yale Club, Franklin & Eleanor Roosevelt Inst. Republican. Roman Catholic. Home: 15 Stratford Park Bloomfield CT 06002-2143 E-mail: dickacs@aol.com.

COBURN, ROBERT CRAIG, philosopher, educator; b. Mpls., Jan. 25, 1930; s. William Carl and Esther Therice C.; m. Martha Louise Means, July 12, 1974. BA, Yale U., 1951; B.D., U. Chgo., 1954; MA, PhD, Harvard U., 1958. Asst. prof. philosophy U. Chgo., 1960-65, assoc. prof., 1965-68, prof., 1968-71; prof. philosophy U. Wash., Seattle, 1971—. Vis. assoc. prof. philosophy Cornell U., 1966, U. Bergen, Norway, spring 1986; condr. NEH summer seminar, 1983; cons. ERDA. Author: The Strangeness of the Ordinary: Issues and Problems in Contemporary Metaphysics, 1989; contbr. articles to philos. jours., chpts. to books. Ordained elder Rocky Mountain Conf. United Methodist Ch. Andrew Mellon postdoctoral fellow in philosophy U. Pitts., 1961-62; NSF grantee,

1968-69 Mem. Am. Philos. Assn. (exec. com. Pacific div. 1973-74), AAUP, Soc. Values in Higher Edn., Phi Beta Kappa. Home: 6852 28th Ave NE Seattle WA 98115-7145 Office: Univ Wash Dept Philosophy Seattle WA 98195-3350

COBURN, RONALD MURRAY, ophthalmic surgeon, researcher; b. Detroit, Aug. 25, 1943; s. Sidney and Jean (Goldberg) C.; m. Barbara Joan Levy, Feb. 21, 1969; children: Nicholas Scott, Lauren Joy. BS, Wayne State U., 1965, MD, 1969; postgrad., Kresge Eye Inst., 1971—74. Diplomate Am. Bd. Ophthalmology, Am. Bd. Eye Surgery (surg. examiner). Dir. The Coburn Clinic, Dearborn, Mich., 1976—; chief ophthalmology Straith Hosp. for Spl. Surgery, Southfield, Mich., 1985—2000. Cons. CooperVision, Inc., Bellevue, Wash., 1985-88, Alcon Surg., Inc., Ft. Worth, 1988—. Co-author: Lens-Stat Intraocular Lens Modeling System; editorial advisor Phaco and Foldables, 1990. Trustee Straith Hosp. for Spl. Surgery, 1986—. Capt. Mich. N.G., 1969-76. Fellow ACS, Internat. Coll. Surgeons, Soc. Eye Surgeons, Royal Soc. Medicine (London), Leadership Soc. ACS, Soc. for Excellence in Eye Care; mem. AAAS, Am. Soc. Cataract and Refractive Surgery, Am. Diabetes Assn., Mich. Ophthal. Soc., Wayne County Med. Soc., Rsch. To Prevent Blindness, N.Y. Acad. Scis., Internat. Assn. Ocular Surgeons, Internat. Eye Found., Soc. Geriatric Ophthalmology, Internat. Glaucoma Congress, Phi Beta Kappa. Achievements include design of Am. Med. Optics PC19LB intraocular lens, CILCO CPLU CP20 intraocular lenses, CooperVision CP10BG posterior chamber intraocular lens, Alcon CZ20BD intraocular lens. Home: 1490 W Long Lake Rd Bloomfield Hills MI 48302-1340 Office: The Coburn Clinic 19855 Outer Dr Dearborn MI 48124-2022

COBURN, STEVEN D. musicologist, educator, musician; b. Albany, N.Y., Aug. 7, 1955; s. Richard and Nancy Coburn; m. Lynn K. Ostro, May 14, 1989; 1 child, Maxwell R. MusB, SUNY, Potsdam, 1978; MA, NYU, 1992, PhD, 2002. Adj. instr. New Sch. U., N.Y.C., 2001—. Accompanist The Pk. Slope Singers, Bklyn., 2000—, The Cmty. Chorus Bklyn., Bklyn., 2002—; choral asst. Vertical Players Repertory Opera, Bklyn., 2003. Author: (book) Mahler's Tenth Symphony: Form and Genesis; composer: (choral) Aspects of Prospect Park, Four Bird Songs, Alleluia, Jubilation, Motet, (chamber) String Quartet, Scherzo for Septet, Brass Quartet, Trumpet Sonata, Prelude and Allegro for Clarinet and Piano, (orchestral) Fantasy. Mem.: Soc. for Music Theory, Am. Musicol. Soc. Avocation: painting. Personal E-mail: stevendcoburn@aol.com.

COBURN, TOM A. former congressman; b. Casper, Wyo., Mar. 14, 1948; m. Carolyn Coburn; 3 children. BS in Acctg., Okla. State U., 1970; MD, U. Okla., 1983. Mfg. mgr. ophthalmic divsn. Coburn Optical Industries, 1970-78; resident surgery St. Anthony's Hosp., 1983-84; resident in family practice U. Ark. Area Health and Edn. Ctr., 1984-86; family practice physician, obstetrician, 1986—; mem. U.S. Congress from 2d Okla. dist., 1995-2001; commerce and sci. com.; co-chmn. Presidential Advisory Council on HIV and Aids, Wash., DC, 2002—. Mem. energy & power, health & environment, oversight & investigations coms. Republican. Office: 3330 W Okmulgee Muskogee OK 74401

COCANOUGHER, ARTHUR BENTON, business administration educator; b. Lubbock, Tex., July 6, 1938; s. Arthur Clifton and Bonnie Odell (Ford) C.; m. Dianne Esther Reisenauer, May 27, 1967; children: Carolyn, David. Mgr. Gen. Electric Co., N.Y.C., 1962-67; asst. prof. U. So. Calif., Los Angeles, 1970-72; assoc. prof. So. Meth. U., Dallas, 1972-73; prof. mktg. U. Houston, 1973-75, chmn. dept., 1975-76, dean Coll. Bus., 1976-85, sr. v.p., provost, 1985-87; dean Tex. A&M U. Coll. Bus., College Station, 1987-2001, emeritus, disting. prof. Trustee Investment Series Smith Barney, Citibank Mutual Funds; interim chancellor, Tex. A&M U. system, 2003— ;cons. in field. Contbr. articles to profl. jours. Bd. dirs. Better Bus. Bur., Houston, 1979-87, West Houston Assn., 1984-87. Served to 1st lt. U.S. Army, 1960-62. Recipient Nicholas Salgo award So. Meth. U., 1973, Outstanding Service award U. Houston Alumni Assn., 1982, Disting. Alumnus award Coll. Bus. U. Tex.-Austin, 1981. Mem. Am. Mktg. Assn., Acad. Mktg. Sci. Home: 4409 Nottingham Ln Bryan TX 77802-5904 Office: Tex A&M U Coll Bus Coll Bus 4112 Tamu College Station TX 77843-4112

COCCHIARELLA, ANTONIO, physician, educator; arrived in U.S., 1956, naturalized; s. Francesco Saverio Cocchiarella and Yolanda Padoan; m. Teresa Marie Arzonetti, Nov. 8, 1957; 1 child, Francesca Yolanda Militeau. MD, U. Padova & Bari, Italy, 1953. Diplomate Am. Bd. Phys. Medicine & Rehab. Resident in rehab. medicine NYU & Columbia U., 1960—63; attending physician Yonkers (NY) Gen. Hosp., 1964—80; med. dir. rehab. svcs. Phelps Meml. Hosp., Sleepy Hollow, NY, 1976—92, Cabrini Med. Ctr., N.Y.C., 1992—97; attending Presbyn. Hosp., NYC, 1999—; prof. clin. rehab. medicine Columbia U., NYC, 1999—. Flight lt. med. corp. Italian Airforce, 1953—56. Mem.: N.Am. Spine Assn. (hon.), NY Acad. Sci. (hon.), Easter Pain Soc. (assoc.), Acad. Phys. Medicine Rehab. (sr.), Am. Rheumatism Assn. (sr.), Westchester Med. Soc. (sr.), NY State Med. Soc. (sr.). Avocations: stamp collecting, cooking. Office: 200 S Broadway Tarrytown NY 10591 Home Fax: 914-478-5296; Office Fax: 914-478-5296. Personal E-mail: ninoter@aol.com.

COCCHIARELLA, JOHN PETER, pediatrician; b. Milford, Mass., Jan. 13, 1939; s. John Andrew and Jennie Marie (Ruscitti) C.; m. Joan Marie Carey, June 21, 1969; children: John C., Andrew J., Nancy J., Susan M. AB, Clark U., 1960; MD, Boston U., 1964. Diplomate Nat. Bd. Med. Examiners, Am. Bd. Pediatrics. Intern R.I. Hosp., Providence, 1964-65; resident Boston City Hosp., 1965-67; rsch. fellow Children's Hosp., Boston, 1967-68; staff pediatrician U.S. Naval Hosp., Newport, R.I., 1968-70; pvt. practice Milford (Mass.) Pediatrics, 1970—. Asst. clin. prof. of pediatrics Boston U. Lt. comdr. USN, 1968-70. Fellow Am. Acad. Pediatrics, Mass. Med. Soc.; mem. Worcester Dist. Med. Soc. Roman Catholic. Avocation: enology. Office: Milford Pediatrics 327 West St Milford MA 01757-1257

COCCHIARELLI, MARIA, artist, educator; b. Bklyn., Apr. 10, 1956; d. Joseph Paul and Mary Jannace Cocchiarelli. BA in Art History, Syracuse U., 1978; BA in Art, CUNY, N.Y.C., 1983, MS in Art Edn., 1985, postgrad., 2002—. Lic. art tchr. grades K-12, N.Y. Instr., curator Queens (N.Y.) Coll. Ctr. for Improvement of Edn., 1983-84, 88-89; instr. Museum's Collaborative and N.Y.C. Youth Bur., Queens, 1984-85; mus. educator The Queens Mus., 1985-87; journalist Cover Arts Jour., N.Y.C., 1986-88; curator Mission Graphics Support Gallery, N.Y.C., 1987-88; artist, tchr. Inst. for Contemporary Arts/P.S.1 Mus., L.I. City, N.Y., 1989-91; artist in residence Children's Mus. Manhattan, N.Y.C., 1989-93, N.Y. Found. for Arts, N.Y.C., 1989-93; edn. dir. Socrates Sculpture Park, L.I. City, N.Y., 1991-93; curator edn. U. Wyo. Art Mus., Laramie, 1993-96; dir. edn. Kemper Mus. Contemporary Art & Design, Kansas City, Mo., 1996-97; programs dir. Grand Arts, Kansas City, Mo., 1997-98; watercolor instr. summer H.S. residency program Kansas City Art Inst., 1999—2002; residence Mo. Arts Coun., 1999—2001; garden artist, project developer Gem Theater and Linwood YWCA Youth Arts Garden, Kansas City, 1999—2002; K-5 and H.S. art tchr. Kansas City (Mo.) Sch. Dist., 2000—, exhbn. planner, 2001; artist in residence P.S. #6 Manhattan, 2003—. Pub. arts commns. for N.Y.C. Pub. Sch. Commn./One Percent for the Arts, Science City/Union Sta., Kans. City. Nebr. Arts Coun., numerous others, Omaha, Assn. Queens Artists, 1994, one-woman shows include The Skyline, L.I. City, 1987, Nancy Bratton Gallery, N.Y.C., 1989, YWCA, Bklyn., 1993, Coal Creek, Laramie, Wyo., 1996, Prospero, Kansas City, 1999, Blue Bird, 1999, Commerce Bankshares, 1999, Muddy's, 1999, First Bank, Warrenton, Mo., 1999, State of the Art, 2000, Kansas City, Mo., 2000, exhibited in group shows at Clocktower Mus., N.Y.C., 1991, Gallery 72, Omaha, 1991—96, Tribeca 148 Gallery, N.Y.C., 1993, Wyo. Arts Coun. Traveling Exhibi, 1994—95, U. Wyo. Art Mus., Laramie, 1994, Urban Ctr. Mcpl. Art Soc., N.Y.C., 1994, Yale U. Art Gallery, New Haven, 1995, Bennington (Vt.) Ctr. for the Arts, 1995, Nicyolaysen Art Mus., Casper, Wyo., 1996, Late Show Gallery, Kansas City, 1998, Manelyst, Oslo, 1999, Leedy Volkos Art Ctr., Kansas City, 1999, State of the Arts, 1999—2000, Museo Internazionale dell'Immagine Postale, Comune di Belvedere Ostrense, Italy, 2001, Coll. of Art, Seoul, 2001, permanent collections, Hallmark Cards Inc., Kansas City, Wyo. State Mus., Cheyenne, Omaha Children's Mus. . Exhbn. planner UN World Habitat, N.Y.C., 1988; instr., organizer Environ. Arts, Laramie, Wyo., 1996; lectr., cons. J. Paul Getty Conf., Omaha, 1996; mem. steering com. Cmty. Anti-Violence Initiative, Kansas City, Mo., 1996-2001. Mem. NOW, Am. Assn. Mus., Nat. Orgn. Italian-Am. Women. Avocations: swimming, writing, singin. Studio: 184-36 Avon R Jamaica NY 11432

COCCIA, PETER F. physician, pediatric hematologist and oncologist; b. Rome, N.Y., May 27, 1941; s. Peter and Catherine M. Coccia; m. Phyllis I. Warkentin, Aug. 29, 1982; children: Kathryn Elizabeth, Jennifer Irene. BA, Hamilton Coll., 1963; MD, SUNY, Syracuse, 1968. Diplomate in pediatrics and pediatric hematology/oncology Am. Bd. Pediatrics, in clin. pathology and pathology-hematology Am. Bd. Pathology. Fellow in pediatric hematology/oncology U. Minn., Mpls., 1973-74, asst. prof. pediatrics, 1974-78, assoc. prof., 1978-80; assoc. prof. pediatrics Case Western Res. U., Cleve., 1980-87; prof. pediatrics U. Nebr. Med. Ctr., Omaha, 1987—, vice chair pediatrics, 1994—, Itner prof., 1988—. Contbr. articles to profl. jours. Lt. comdr. USPHS, 1970-72. Home: 16428 Jones Cir Omaha NE 68118-2712 Office: U Nebr Med Ctr Dept Pediats 982168 Nebr Med Ctr Omaha NE 68198-2168 Fax: (402) 559-6782. E-mail: pcoccia@unmc.edu.

COCCO, KAREN JEAN, school psychologist; b. Erie, Pa., Sept. 30, 1952; d. Donald Wilson and Cecelia Ida (Patchen) Clark; m. James Michael Cocco, Dec. 26, 1970 (div. Feb. 1984); 1 child, Carolyn Marie Cocco. BS, Gannon U., Erie, 1982; MEd, Edinboro (Pa.) U., 1986, postgrad., 1988. Cert. sch. psychologist; lic. psychologist. Substitute tchr. Gertrude A. Barber Ctr., Erie, 1982, Millcreek (Pa.) Sch. Dist., 1983-84; tchr. Iroquois Sch. Dist., Wesleyville, Pa., 1984-87; substitute tchr. N.W. Tri-County Intermediate Unit, Edinboro, 1987-88, Erie Sch. Dist., 1987-88; psychologist Harcourt Brace Jovanovich, Inc., Erie, 1987-89, Sarah A. Reed Children's Ctr., Erie, 1988-90, N.W Tri-County Intermediate Unit, Edinboro, 1990—, tchr. parenting class Erie, 1997—, cons. to Head Start staff and other preschool, 1997—2002; mem. Comprehensive Sys. of Pers. Devel. team N.W. Tri-County Intermediate Unit, Erie, 2002—03. Mem. scuba team Erie County Sheriff's Dept., Erie, 1977-87; vol. United Cerebral Palsy, Erie, 1965-68; vol., co-leader ARC, Girl Scouts, Erie, 1976-88; tchr., mem. coun. and numerous coms. Mt. Calvary Luth. Ch., Erie, 1968—. Recipient Letter of Commendation, Millcreek Police Dept., 1978. Mem. Nat. Assn. Sch. Psychologists, Assn. Sch. Psychologists of Pa., N.W. Pa. Psychologists Assn., Pa. State Edn. Assn., Phi Delta Kappa (sec.). Republican. Lutheran. Avocations: boating, skiing, whitewater rafting, birdwatching, travel. Office: NW Tri-County Intermed Unit 252 Waterford St Edinboro PA 16412

COCCO, MARIE ELIZABETH, journalist; b. Malden, Mass., Jan. 15, 1956, d. Morris Alfred and Dorothy Anne (Colameta) C.; m. Thomas Neal Burrows, Sept. 4, 1982; children: Matthew C. Burrows., Michael C. Burrows. BA, Tufts U., 1978; MS, Columbia U., 1979. Journalist Daily Register, Shrewsbury, N.J., 1979-80, Newsday, L.I., N.Y., 1980—. Nat. syndication through The Washington Post Writers Group, 2002. Recipient Nat. Reporting award Sigma Delta Chi, 1991, Excellence in Editorial Writing award N.Y. State Pubs. Assn., 1992, N.Y. State AP award, 1997, 99. Mem. White House Corrs. Assn. (Barnet Nover award 1991), Nat. Press Club (Washington Corr. award 1991). Office: Newsday Washington Bur 1730 Pennsylvania Ave NW Washington DC 20006-4706

COCHÉ, JUDITH, psychologist, educator; b. Phila., Sept. 2, 1942; d. Louis and Miriam (Nerenberg) Milner; m. Erich Coché, Oct. 16, 1966 (dec.); 1 child, Juliette Laura; m. John Anderson, Jan. 1, 1994. BA, Colby Coll., 1964; MA, Temple U., 1966; PhD, Bryn Mawr Coll., 1975. Diplomate Am. Bd. Profl. Psychology; lic. psychologist Pa., Md., N.J., Fla.; cert. in group psychotherapy Nat. Registry Group Psychotherapists. Rsch. asst. Jefferson Med. Coll., 1965-66; diagnostician Law Ct., Aachen, Germany, 1967-68; staff psychologist N.E. Community Mental Health Ctr., Phila., 1969-74; family clinician Inst. Pa. Hosp., 1974-76; instr. psychology Drexel U., 1976-77; lectr. Med. Coll. Pa., 1977-78; asst. clin. prof. Hahnemann Med. Coll., Phila., 1979—; pvt. practice Phila., 1974—, 1985—; assoc. prof. psychiatry U. Pa., 1985—, clin. coord. Psychology, 1999—; assoc. clin. prof. psychology in psychiatry U. Pa. Med. Coll., 1986—; mem. faculty Family Inst. of Phila., 1990—; sr. cons. Phila. Child Guidance Clinic, 1992-96; assoc. clin. prof. psychology in psychiatry U. Pa. Med. Coll., 1986—. Clin. cons. Hilltop Prep Sch., 1977-86; clin. supr. Am. Assn. Marriage and Family Therapy. Co-author: Couples Group Psychotherapy, A Clinical Practice Model, 1990, Co. author Powerful Wisdom: Voices of Distinguished Women Psychotherapists, (1993); contbr. chpts. to books, articles to profl. jours. Bd. dirs. Whitemarsh Art Ctr., 1977-78, Please Touch Museum, 1982-89; mem. prof. adv. bd. Parents Without Ptnrs., 1977-86; mem. adv. com. Pa. Ballet/Shirley Rock. Grantee Del. Children's Bur. Bryn Mawr Coll., 1974-75, Pa. Hosp., 1975-77. Fellow Am. Group Psychotherapy Assn.; mem. APA, Am. Assn. Marriage and Family Therapy (approved supr.), Am. Family Therapy Assn., Phila. Soc. Clin. Psychologists (pres. 1980-81), Family Inst. Phila., Pa. Psychol. Assn. (chmn. legis. com. 1982), Soc. Rsch. in Psychotherapy. Address: Acad House 1420 Locust St Ste 410 Philadelphia PA 19102-4202

COCHEO, JOHN FRANK, lawyer; b. Hartford, Conn., Jan. 28, 1944; s. Frank and Olga Freida (Zotter) C. B.A., Quinnipiac Coll., 1969; J.D., New Eng. Sch. Law, 1973. Bar: Mass. 1974, Conn. 1975, U.S. Dist. Ct. Conn. 1975, U.S. Ct. Appeals (2d cir.) 1983, U.S. Supreme Ct. 1979; cert. Nat. Bd. Trial Advocacy; cert. Criminal Trial Specialist Am. Bd. Trial Advocacy. With Lach & Barron Rsch., Hartford, 1973; assoc. Deloreto & Karanian Assocs., New Britain, Conn., 1973-76; dep. asst. state's atty. New Britain, 1976-82, asst. state's atty., New London, 1982— . Rep. Victim-Witness Orgn., 1984. Mem. New Britain Bar Assn., New London Bar Assn. Continuing Legal Edn. Acad. Democrat. Roman Catholic. Lodge: K.C. Home: 201 Judson Ave Mystic CT 06355-2159 Office: O'Brien Shafner Stuart Baratnik 475 Bridge St Groton CT 06340-3723

COCHETTI, ROGER JAMES, international communications and internet company executive; b. Albany, N.Y., Apr. 11, 1950; s. Roger Peter and Mary Ann Cochetti; m. Mary Remmers. BS in Fgn. Svc., Georgetown U., 1972; postgrad., Johns Hopkins U., 1975; cert., Cambridge U., 1976, U. Va., 1986. Dir. Washington office UN Assn. of U.S.A., 1972-77; asst. dir. for legis. and pub. affairs U.S. Internat. Devel. Coop. Agy., Washington, 1978-81; dir. pub. and investor rels. Communications Satellite Corp., Washington, 1981-85, dir. investor and internat. rels., 1985-87, v.p. maritime bus. planning and devel., 1987-88, v.p. mobile bus. planning and devel., 1989-93; author, cons., lectr., 1993—; program dir. Internet policy and bus. planning IBM Corp., 1994-2000; sr. v.p. policy Network Solutions, Inc., 2000; sr. v.p. Veri Sign, 2001—; cons. to Internet and technology industries, 2003. Cons. to John D. Rockefeller III, N.Y.C., 1975; bd. dirs. Truste, Inc., Internet Law and Policy Forum, Internet Edn. Found., Internet Content Rating ASsn. Author: Mobile Satellite Handbook, 1994. N.Y. State Regents scholar, 1968. Mem. Pacific Telecommn. Coun., Nat. Press Club (Washngton), Princeton Club (N.Y.C.). Democrat. Roman Catholic. E-mail: roger@cochetti.us.

COCHRAN, ADDIE MAE, small business owner, writer; b. Orrville, Ala., Sept. 25, 1930; d. John Henry Cochran and Bertha Mae Powell; children: Rosia Ellis, Nathanial, Emmia. Lic. cosmetologist N.Y.C. Pres. McNoveck of Alma Okeshia & Co. Author (as Alma Okeshia): (book of spiritual songs) Darker Than a Thousand Midnights, 1998; author: My Angel Child Faleshia; composer: (spiritual songs) When My Lord Looked Down On Me, I Am Going On Where Jesus Is. Mem.: AAUW. Democrat. Avocations: fishing, writing. Home and Office: 2410 Snyder Blvd Brooklyn NY 11226 Fax: 718-469-1807.

COCHRAN, CAROLYN, library director; b. Tyler, Tex., July 13, 1934; d. Sidney Allen and Eudelle (Frazier) C.; m. Guy Milford Eley, June 1, 1963 (div.). BA, Beaver Coll., 1956; MA, U. Tex., 1960; MLS, Tex. Woman's U., 1970. Libr. Canadian (Tex.) High Sch., 1970-71; rep. United Food Co., Amarillo, Tex., 1971-72; libr. Bishop Coll., Dallas, Tex., 1975-76, St. Mary's Dominican, New Orleans, 1976-77, DeVry Inst. Tech., Irving, Tex., 1978-98, libr. dir. emeritus, 1998—. With Database Searching Handicapped Individuals, Irving, 1983—; vol. bibliographer Assn. Individuals with Disabilities, Dallas, 1982-85. Mem. Am. Coalition of Citizens with Disabilities, 1982-85, Assn. Individuals with Disabilities, 1982-86, Vols. in Tech. Assistance, 1985—, Radio Amateur Satellite Corp., 1985-86; sponsor 500, Inc., 1988-95. Reviewer Libr. Jour., 1974, Dallas Morning News, 1972-74, Amarillo Globe-News, 1970-71. Mem. Dallas regional adv. com. Tex. Commn. for the Blind, 2001. HEW fellow, 1967; honored Black History Collection, Dallas Morning News, Bishop Coll., Dallas, 1973. Mem. ALA, Spl. Libr. Assn., Am. Coun. of Blind (sec. Dallas chpt. 1997-99), Toastmistress Club (pres. 1982-83) (Irving). E-mail: carolyn_cochran@sbcglobal.net.

COCHRAN, DAVID MACDUFFIE, management consultant; b. Greenwich, Conn., Aug. 6, 1942; s. James J. and Dorothy Goff (MacDuffie) C.; m. Maria A. Cochran; children: David M. Cochran Jr., Michele T. Cochran, Matthew Carluzzo, Philip Carluzzo. BA, Columbia U., 1968; MBA, NYU, 1971. Product mgr. Colgate Palmolive Co., Inc., N.Y.C., 1968-71; group product mgr. Colgate Palmolive Co.-Can., Toronto, 1971-72; v.p. mktg. and sales Colgate Palmolive Co.-Portugal, Lisbon, 1972-74, pres., gen. mgr., 1974-76; exec. v.p. Colgate Palmolive Co.-Brazil, Sao Paulo, 1976-77; pres. Latin Am. Joseph E. Seagram & Sons, Inc., N.Y.C., 1977-82; pres. internat. The Mennen Co., Morristown, N.J., 1982-85; ptnr. Barry Persky & Co., Westport, Conn., 1986-92; pres., owner Cochran & Co. Internat., Stamford, Conn., 1992—. Bd. dirs. New Canaan Inn, chmn. nominating com., 1998—. Pres. New Canaan (Conn.) Lacrosse Asn., 1987—; bd. dirs. Conn. Lacrosse Found., 1995—, Conn.-N.Y. Lacrosse Assn., New Haven, 1989—. With U.S. Army, 1962-65. Mem. Country Club New Canaan (bd. govs. 1990-93, 96—, chmn. nominating com. 1996—, chmn. tennis com. 1996—). Republican. Presbyterian. Avocations: tennis, scuba diving, reading, photography, biking. Home: 12 N Casey Key Rd Osprey FL 34229-9704

COCHRAN, EARL VERNON, retired manufacturing company executive; b. Poplar Bluff, Mo., May 14, 1922; s. Earl J. and Bertha M. (Merrit) C.; m. Eleanor J. Greene, July 20, 1950; 1 child, Tara Lang. BS, R.P.I., 1947. Registered profl. engr., Ohio. Test lab. engr. Stromberg-Carlson, Rochester, N.Y., 1947-48; dir. elec. engring. dept. Commonwealth Rsch. & Devel., Dayton, Ohio, 1948-52; sales mgr. Dayton Precision Mfg. Co., Dayton, Ohio, 1952-57, v.p. sales, 1957-60, Kirkwood Industries, Cleve., 1960-78, dir., exec. v.p., 1978—; ret., 1994. Dir. Aoyama Kirkwood, 1976-94; dir., pres. Kirkwood Can. Ltd., 1978-90. Bd. mem. Fairview Luth. Hosp. Found., Cleve., 1980-97. Ensign USN, 1941-46. Fellow IEEE; mem. Ohio Soc. Profl. Engrs. Avocations: tennis, computing, skiing, diving, golf. Home: 12550 Lake Ave Lakewood OH 44107-1575

COCHRAN, GEORGE CALLOWAY, III, retired bank executive, lawyer; b. Dallas, Aug. 29, 1932; s. George Calloway and Miriam (Welty) C.; m. Jerry Bywaters, Dec. 9, 1961; children: Mary, Robert BA, So. Meth. U., 1954; JD, Harvard U., 1957; cert., La. State U. Sch. Banking, 1969. Bar: Tex. 1957. Assoc. Leachman, Gardere, Akin and Porter, Dallas, 1960-62, with Fed. Res. Bank of Dallas, 1962-76, sr. v.p., 1976-92, ret., 1992. Adv. com. Bank Ops. Inst., Tex. A&M U., Commerce, 1982—2003; mem. task force on truth in lending regulation Bd. Govs. of Fed. Res. Sys., Washington, 1968—69; bd. dirs. Am. Inst. Banking, Dallas, 1986—90. Hist. landmark survey task force City of Dallas, 1974-78. Capt. USAF, 1958-60. Recipient Warner award for svc. to dance The Dance Coun., Dallas, 1999. Mem. State Bar Tex., Phi Beta Kappa (pres. North Tex. Assn. 1998-2000), Harvard Club. Methodist. Home: 3541 Villanova St Dallas TX 75225-5008 E-mail: ccjbc@earthlink.net.

COCHRAN, GEORGE MOFFETT, retired judge; b. Staunton, Va., Apr. 20, 1912; s. Peyton and Susie (Robertson) C.; m. Marion Lee Stuart, May 1, 1948; children— George Moffett, Harry Carter Stuart. BA, U. Va., 1934, LLB, 1936; LLD (hon.), James Madison U., 1991. Bar: Va. 1935, Md. 1936. Asso. law firm, Balt., 1936-38; partner firm Peyton Cochran and George M. Cochran, Staunton, 1938-64, Cochran, Lotz & Black, Staunton, 1964-69; justice Supreme Ct., Richmond, Va., 1969-87. Pres. Planters Bank & Trust Co., Staunton, 1963-69 Chmn. Woodrow Wilson Centennial Commn. Va., 1952-58, Va. Cultural Devel. Study Commn., 1966-68, Frontier Culture Mus. Va., 1986-98; mem. Va. Commn. Constl. Revisi on, 1968-69, Jud. Coun. Va., 1963-69, Va. Ho. Dels., 1948-66, Va. Senate, 1966-68; chmn. bd. dirs. Stuart Hall, 1971-86; mem. bd. visitors Va. Poly. Inst., 1960-68; trustee Mary Baldwin Coll., 1967-81, U. Va. Law Sch. Found., 1975-89, Woodrow Wilson Birthplace Found., 1955-93. Lt. comdr. USNR, 1942-46. Recipient Algernon Sydney Sullivan award Mary Baldwin Coll., 1981. Mem. ABA, Va. Bar Assn. (pres. 1965-66), Raven Soc., Soc. of Cin., Phi Beta Kappa, Phi Delta Phi, Beta Theta Pi. Episcopalian.

COCHRAN, GLORIA GRIMES, retired pediatrician; b. Washington, June 24, 1924; d. Paul DeWitt and Muriel Ann (Quackenbush) Grimes; m. Winston Earle Cochran, June 10, 1950; children: Edith Ann, Winston Earle, Jr., Donald Lee, Robert Edward. BS in Zoology, Duke U., 1945; MD, 1949; MPH, Johns Hopkins Sch. Hygiene, Balt., 1979. Diplomate Nat. Bd. Med. Examiners, 1950, Am. Bd. Pediatrics, 1958. Asst. resident Pathology Boston Children's Hosp., Boston, 1949—50, asst. resident Pediatrics, 1950—51; chief resident Pediatrics Charlotte Memorial Hosp., Charlotte, NC, 1952—53; clinic pediatrician, sch. med. advisor health dept. Montgomery County, 1955-65; fellow in pediat. habilitation St. Christopher Hosp. for Children, Phila., 1965-66; assoc. dir. Child Development Clinic Baylor Med. Sch., Tex. Children's Hosp., 1966-72; dir. Northern Va. Child Devel. Field Svcs. Bur. Child Health State Health Dept. Commonwealth Va., 1972-76; coord. Handicapped Svcs. Children's Hosp. Nat. Med. Ctr., Washington, 1976-78; acting chief Divsn. of Svcs. to Children with Spl. Needs Bur. Sch. Health Svcs., Washington, 1982-89; retired, 1989. Cons. Head Start Program, Md., Va., Tex., Pa., D.C., 1965-89; bd. mem. Ctrs. for Handicapped, Silver Spring, Md., 1982-89; Child Health com. Med. Soc. D.C., Washington, 1976-91. Producer, editor: (teaching film) Challenge for Habilitation: The Child with Congenital Rubella Syndrome, 1976. Steering com. Rock Days Inter-Church Camp, Washington, 1978-82; bd. mem. Open Door Cmty. Ctr., Columbus, Ga., 1993-94; co-chair curriculum com. Columbus Coll. Acad. of Life Long Learning, Columbus, 1994. Mem. Am. Assn. Mental Retardation, Am. Med. Women's Assn., Assn. for Retarded Citizens, Am. Acad. Cerebral Palsy, Am. Acad. Pediatrics, Phi Beta Kappa, Delta Omega. Democrat. Methodist. Avocations: travel, gardening. Home: 1605 Greenbriar Dr Norman OK 73072-6717

COCHRAN, JAMES ALAN, mathematics educator; b. San Francisco, May 12, 1936; s. Commodore Shelton and Gwendolyn Audrey (Rosenau) C.; m. Katherine Koehler Kern, Sept. 6, 1958; children: Cynthia Royal, Sarah Lynn. BS in Physics, Stanford U., 1956, MS in Physics, 1957; PhD in Math., Stanford U., 1962. Mem. tech. staff, supr. applied math. Bell Telephone Labs. Inc, Whippany, N.J., 1962-72; prof. math. Va. Poly. Inst. and State U., Blacksburg, 1972-78; prof., chmn. dept. math. Wash. State U., Pullman, 1978-84, prof., 1978-89, campus exec. officer and founding dean tri-cities Richland, Wash., 1989-98, prof. math., 1999—2003, prof. emeritus, 2003—; staff assoc. First Presbyn. Ch., Kennewick, Wash., 2001—. Vis. prof. math. Stanford U., 1968-69, Wash. State U., 1977, U. NSW, Sydney, Australia, 1985, Southeast U., Nanjing, China, 1994; fgn. scholar math. and mechanics Nanjing Inst. Tech., 1984; vis. fellow Deakin U., Victoria, Australia, 1985, 87. Author: Analysis of Linear Integral Equations, 1972, Applied Mathematics: Principles, Techniques, and Applications, 1982, Advanced Engineering Mathematics, 1987; also articles. Mem. nat. coun. Boy Scout Am., 1973-76, 99-2001, mem. local coun., 1974-77, 82-84, 93—, coun. pres., 1999-2001, mem. western region, 1996-02; chmn. bd. commrs. Morris County (N.J.) Area Libr. Sys., 1971-72; mem. bd. dirs. Tri-Cities Sci. and Tech. Park Assn., 1990-2003, chmn., 1990-93; bd. dirs. Wash. Environ. Industry Assn., 1990-95, TRIDEC, 1996-2001; dir. state bd. Math. Engring. Sci. Achievement, 1992-2001; mem. Am. Pub. TV Stas. Bd., 1992-96; exec. com. Tri-Cities Commercialization Partnership, 1993-97; mem. Hanford Adv. Bd., 1994—; sr. advisor Tri-Cities Corp. Coun. for the Arts, 1991-2000. Recipient Silver Beaver award Boy Scouts Am., 1997, disting. Eagle Scout award, 1997; Gordon vis. fellow, Deakin U., Victoria, Australia, 1985. Mem. Am. Math. Soc., Math. Assn. Am., Soc. Indsl. Applied Math., Nat. Eagle Scout Assn. (young man pres. 1957-58, adviser 1958-71, Disting. Service award 1976), Phi Beta Kappa, Sigma Xi, Golden Key, Alpha Phi Omega. Republican. Presbyterian. Home: 1927 Cypress Pl Richland WA 99352-2414 Office: Wash State U Tri-Cities 2710 University Dr Richland WA 99352-1671 E-mail: cochranj@tricity.wsu.edu.

COCHRAN, JAMES KIRK, dean, oceanographer, geochemist, educator; BS summa cum laude, Fla. State U., 1973; M in Philosophy, Yale U., 1975, PhD in Geochemistry, 1979. Rsch. staff geochemist Yale U. dept. geology and geophysics, New Haven, Conn., 1979-81; asst. scientist dept. chemistry Woods Hole (Mass.) Oceanographic Instn., 1981-83; asst. prof. marine scis. SUNY, Stony Brook, 1985-90, assoc. prof., 1985-90, prof., 1990—, assoc. dir. for rsch., 1990-92; assoc. dean for rsch. Marine Scis. Rsch. Ctr., SUNY, Stony Brook, 1992-94, dean, dir., 1994-98; rsch. assoc. dept. invertebrates and paleontology Am. Mus. Natural History, N.Y.C., 1986—. Invited lectr., UCLA, 1979, vis. scholar, Dept. Oceanography, U. Wash., Seattle, 1982, vis. scientist Ctr. des Faibles Radioactivités CNRS, Gif sur Yvette, France, 1989; vis. fellow Program

in Oceanic and Atmospheric Scis., Princeton (N.J.) U., 1990, vis. prof. Inst. di Geol. Marina, Bologna, Italy, 1992, 98; assoc. rschr. European Ctr. for Environ. Geoscis., Aix-en-Provence, France, 1998, 2000, vis. scientist Internat. Atomic Engr. Agency, Monaco, 1999; mem. Group of Experts on Sci. Aspects of Marine Pollution and Internat. Atomic Energy Agy. working group to formulate an oceanographic model for dispersion of wastes disposed in the deep sea, 1980-82; sci. rep. to Phys. Oceanography Task Group of the Internat. Seabed Working Group, 1983-87; mem. Alvin Rev. Com., 1984-87, Joint Global Ocean Flux Steering Com., 1990-93; dir. summer course Processes in the Coastal Ocean, Bologna, Italy, 2000. Contbr. more than 90 articles to profl. jours. Mem. Am. Geophys. Union, Geochem. Soc., Oceanography Soc., Sigma Xi. Office: SUNY at Stony Brook Marine Sciences Rsch Ctr Stony Brook NY 11794-0001

COCHRAN, JOHN EUELL, JR., aerospace engineer, educator, lawyer; b. Dawson, Ala., May 22, 1944; s. John Euell and Beatrice Ann (Raley) C.; m. Gladys Carol Holdbrooks, Dec. 26, 1965; children: Christopher, Jonathan. BAE., Auburn U., 1966, MS, 1967; PhD, U. Tex.-Austin, 1970; JD, Jones Law Inst., 1976. Bar: Ala. 1977; registered profl. engr., Ala. Asst. prof. aerospace engring. Auburn (Ala.) U., 1970-75, assoc. prof., 1975-78, alumni assoc. prof., 1978-80, alumni prof., 1980-81, prof., 1981—, assoc. athletic dir., 1981-84, interim head aerospace engring., 1992-93, head aerospace engring., 1993—. Cons. Northrup Svcs., Huntsville, Ala., 1970-71, U.S. Army Missile Command, Redstone Arsenal, Ala., 1975-82, numerous law firms, 1977—, SRS Tech., Huntsville, 1984-89, Dept. Justice, 1996-97, The Boeing Co., 1998; pres. Eaglemark, Inc., legal cons. Sigmatech, Inc. Contbr. articles to profl. jours.; assoc. editor Jour. Guidance Control and Dynamics, 1989-91. Tau Beta Pi fellow, 1965; Nat. Coll. Athletic Assn. fellow, 1965; NSF fellow, 1968 Fellow AIAA (assoc.), Am. Astronautical Soc.; mem. ABA, NSPE, Am. Helicopter Soc., Ala. Soc. Profl. Engrs. (Young Engr. of Yr. 1980, v.p. Auburn chpt. 1985, pres. 1986). Methodist. Achievements include (with others) analysis, simulation and reconstruction of aircraft accidents; rsch. in areas of dynamics and control, spacecraft attitude dynamics and control, dual-spin, tethered satellites; on the stability and control of aircraft (including towed vehicles); on missile launcher dynamics; and on the simulation of aerospace and transp. systems; short courses/seminars on engring. topics and engring. law and ethics. Home: 1887 Prim Dr Auburn AL 36830-7545 Office: Auburn U 211 Aerospace Engring Buil Auburn AL 36849 E-mail: jcochhran@eng.auburn.edu.

COCHRAN, JOHN P. economics educator; b. Ft. Collins, Colo., Dec. 22, 1949; s. Ira Williams and Elizabeth Ann C.; m. I. Ann Cochran, Aug. 23, 1977. BA in Econs., Met. State Coll. of Denver, 1978; MA in Econs., U. Colo., 1981, PhD in Econs., 1985. Intern as sr. economist Colo. Pub. Utility Commn., summer 1986; asst. prof. econs. Met. State Coll. of Denver, 1986-90, chair of econs., 1990-94, assoc. prof. econs., 1990-96, prof. econs., 1996-97, chair and prof. econs., 1997—. Vis. lectr. econs. Met. State Coll. of Denver, 1981-82, vis. asst. prof., 1982-86, dir. Ctr. for Econ. Edn., 1997—; adj. asst. prof. econs. Regis U., Denver, 1986-90; adj. scholar Ludwig von Mises Inst., 1997—; vis. prof. U. Colo., Boulder, 2001—; Mises Meml. lectr. at Austrian Scholars' Conf. 9, Ludwig Von Mises Inst., 2003; mem. faculty Young Am.'s Rd. to Freedom: The Friedrich Hayek Seminar at the Reagan Ranch Ctr., 2003; presenter in field. Co-author: (book) The Hayek-Keynes Debate: Lessons for Current Business Cycle Research, 1999; contbr. articles to profl. jours.; editor books/publs. in field. Mem.: Golden Key Honor Soc. (Outstanding Scholar/Rsch. award 2002). E-mail: cochranj@mscd.edu.

COCHRAN, JOHNNIE L., JR., lawyer; b. Shreveport, La., Oct. 2, 1937; BS, UCLA, 1959; JD, Loyola U., 1962; postgrad., U. So. Calif. Bar: Calif. 1963, U.S. Dist. Ct. (we. dist.) Tex. 1966, U.S. Supreme Ct. 1968. Dep. city atty. criminal divsn. City of L.A., 1963-65; asst. dist. atty. L.A. County, 1978-82; now pvt. practice atty. L.A. Former adj. prof. law UCLA Sch. Law, Loyola U. Sch. Law; lawyer rep. U.S. Dist .Ct. (ctrl. dist.) Calif., 1990, U.S. Ct. Appeals (9th cir.) Judicial Conf., 1990; bd. dirs. L.A. Family Housing Corp., Lawyers Mut. Ins. Co. Spl. counsel, chmn. rules com. Dem. Nat. Convention, 1984; spl. counsel com. on standard ofcl. conduct, ethics com. 99th congress U.S. Ho. Reps.; bd. dirs. L.A. Urban League, Oscar Joel Bryant Found., 28th St. YMCA, ACLU Found. So. Calif. Fellow Am. Bar Found.; mem. Am. Coll. Trial Lawyers, State Bar Calif. (co-chair bd. legal svc. corps 1993), L.A. African Am. C. of C. (bd. dirs.), Airport Commrs. City of L.A., Black Bus. Assn. L.A. (pres. 1989). Office: 4929 Wilshire Blvd Ste 1010 Los Angeles CA 90010-3825

COCHRAN, KATHY HOLCOMBE, music educator, conductor; d. Bobby Neal and Louise Bryant Holcombe; m. Alan Randolph Cochran, June 14, 1975. AA, North Greenville Coll., 1973; MusB, Furman U., 1975; M in Music Edn., U. S.C., 1978; postgrad., Clemson U., 1997—. Cert. tchr. pub. sch. choral music K-12 S.C., elem. sch. educator S.C. Gen. and choral music specialist grades 6-8 Lexington (S.C.) Intermediate Sch., 1975—76; elem. music specialist K-2 Pierce Ter. Elem. Sch., Ft. Jackson, SC, 1976—78; elem. music specialist grades 1-5 Greenville County Schs., 1978—90, lead tchr. for choral dirs., 1996—97; choral dir. Berea H.S., Greenville, 1991—97, fine arts dept. chair, 1995—97; tchg. intern, asst. Clemson (S.C.) U.; tchr. choral music edn. Furman U., Greenville, 2001—. Dir. Young Artists Piano Competition Greenville Symphony Orch., 1990—91; sec. choral divsn. S.C. Music Educators Assn., 1996—97, pres.-elect, 1997—98. Author, composer Music for All Ages, 1985. Mem. Greenville County Legal Aux., 1978—; trustee North Greenville Coll., Tigerville, SC, 1996—2001, bd. advisors, 1994—96. Named Outstanding Young Educator, Greenville Jaycees, 1987, Wade Hampton Jaycees, Taylors, S.C., 1980. Mem.: Am. Choral Dirs. Assn., Choristers Guild, Assn. for Supr. and Curriculum Devel., Nat. Reading Conf., Internat. Reading Assn., Music Educators Nat. Conf. (S.C. Music in Our Schs. coord. 1980), Pi Kappa Lambda, Kappa Delta Pi, Phi Delta Kappa. Avocations: reading, cooking, boating. Office: Furman U 3300 Poinsett Hwy Greenville SC 29613

COCHRAN, KENDALL PINNEY, economics educator; b. Newton, Kans., Oct. 12, 1924; s. William Walter and Enid (Pinney) C.; m. Mona S. Hersh, Dec. 19, 1975; stepchildren— Paula L. Hersh, Susan B. Hersh, Kenneth A. Hersh. BA cum laude, U. Tex., 1949, MA, 1950; PhD, Ohio State U., 1955. Instr. econs. Ohio State U., 1953-55, asst. prof., 1955-57; assoc. prof. North Tex. State U., 1957-59, prof., 1959-89, prof. emeritus, 1989—, chmn. dept. econs., 1969-81; vis. research scholar London Sch. Econs., 1981-82, U. York, Eng., 1981-82. Dir. NSF Econs. Inst., 1964-69; vis. prof. Bishop Coll., 1969; vis. prof. U. Auckland, N.Z., U. Newcastle, Australia, 1985; asso. editor Southwestern Social Sci. Quar., 1962-64; editorial bd. North Tex. Bus. Studies, 1961-67; asso. editor Southwestern Jour. Social Edn., 1970 Pres. Denton Credit Union, 1968-69, dir., 1961-69. Served with USAF, 1942-44. Mem. AAUP (nat. coun. 1967-70), ACLU, Am. Econ. Assn., Southwestern Econ. Assn. (pres. 1965), Assn. Evolutionary Econs. (exec. com. 1964), Assn. Social Econs. (exec. coun. 1973—, 1st v.p. 1977—, pres. 1978, Thomas Divine award 1993), Tex. Assn. Coll. Tchrs. (coord. rsch. 1960-64), Common Cause, Hemlock Soc., Sierra Club. Democrat. Address: 3765 Weeburn Dr Dallas TX 75229-2716

COCHRAN, KENNETH WILLIAM, toxicologist; b. Chgo., Nov. 2, 1923; m. Martha Louise Wells, May 10, 1945; children: Kenneth W. III, Kimberley W. Cochran Nelson (dec.). SB, U. Chgo., 1947, PhD, 1950. Rsch. asst. to instr., toxicity lab. and dept. pharmacology U. Chgo., 1946-52; from rsch. assoc., instr. to prof. emeritus U. Mich., Ann Arbor, from 1952. Contbr. articles to profl. jours. 1st lt. U.S. Army, 1943-46. Fellow AAAS; mem. Am. Soc. for Microbiology, Am. Soc. for Pharmacology and Exptl. Therapeutics, Mycol. Soc. of Am., N.Am. Mycol. Assn. (exec. sec. 1988-97). Home: Ann Arbor, Mich. Deceased.

COCHRAN, LINDA THORNTHWAITE, psychotherapist, social worker, consultant; b. Huntsville, Ala., Nov. 3, 1946; d. W.L. and Mildred (Bridges) Thornthwaite; m. Phillip O. Cochran, July 1, 1966; children: Jeremy, Amanda. BA in Psychology, U. N.C., Asheville, 1984; MSW, geriatric cert., U. S.C., 1986. LCSW. Dir. Coun. on Aging, Hendersonville, N.C., 1986; child protection svc. worker Transylvania County Dept. Social Svcs., Brevard, N.C., 1986-88; clin. social worker mental health unit Pardee Hosp., Hendersonville, 1988-93; wellness coord. for MOMS program Blue Ridge Health Ctr., Hendersonville, 1993-95; psychotherapist Hendersonville Psychol. Assocs., 1995-97, Alpha Ctr. for Solution Therapy, 1997—. Cons., Hendersonville, 1988—. Sec. Widowed Persons Svc., Hendersonville, 1989-97. Mem.: NASW, Assn. Cert. Social Workers. Democrat. Mem. Ch. of Christ. Avocations: reading, water color painting. Home: 239 Bradshaw Ave Hendersonville NC 28792-5423 Office: Alpha Ctr for Solution Therapy 223 Duncan Hill Rd Hendersonville NC 28792

COCHRAN, MONA SHEINFELD, economics educator, consultant; b. Phila., Dec. 3, 1934; d. Samuel and Sara (Baram) Sheinfeld; m. Kendall Pinney Cochran, Dec. 19, 1975; children: Paula, Susan, Kenneth, Hersh BA, Rutgers U., New Brunswick, N.J., 1956; MA, Temple U., Phila., 1968; PhD, So. Meth. U., Dallas, 1966. Systems analyst RemingtonRand UNIVAC, Phila., 1956-58; rsch. analyst Coopers & Lybrand, N.Y.C., 1958-60; tchg. asst. So. Meth. U., Dallas, 1961-65; vis. rsch. scholar London Sch. Econs., 1981-82; acad. visitor U. York, Eng., 1981-82; prof. econs. Tex. Woman's U., Denton, Tex., 1965-91, prof. emerita, 1991—. Avocations: travel, sewing, entertaining. Home: 3765 Weeburn Dr Dallas TX 75229-2716

COCHRAN, RAYMOND MARTIN, university auditor; b. Passaic, N.J., Aug. 10, 1943; s. Mark and Catherine (Brown) C.; m. Dorothy Parcells; children: Tamara Takoudes, Tania Secor. BS, Farleigh Dickinson U., 1966; MBA, NYU, 1968. CPA, N.Y., N.J. Mgr. audit KPMG, N.Y.C., 1968-79, Engelhard Minerals and Chems. Corp., N.Y.C., 1979-81; dir. internal audit Columbia U., N.Y.C., 1981—. Founder, coord. N.Y. Metro Region Coll. and Univ. Audit Dirs., 1993—. Bd. dirs., treas. Japan Internat. Christian U. Found., Inc., 1985—. 1st lt. U.S. Army, 1969-71. Mem. AICPA, Assn. Coll. and Univ. Auditors (pres. 1999-2000), N.J. Soc. CPAs, Inst. Internal Auditors (pres. N.Y. chpt. 2001-02, bd. govs. N.Y. chpt. 1992—). Home: 818 E Ridgewood Ave Ridgewood NJ 07450-3911 Office: Columbia U 475 Riverside Dr Ste 510 New York NY 10115-0510 E-mail: cochran@columbia.edu.

COCHRAN, ROBERT CARTER, surgical educator; b. Newton, Mass., Oct. 9, 1932; s. Williams and Mary Faith (Williams) C.; m. Norma Rae Creighton, Aug. 27, 1958 (div. Aug. 1986); children: Barbara, Gwen, Williams; m. Rebecca Anne Fain, Feb. 3, 1990. BA, Princeton (N.J.) U., 1955; MD, Boston U., 1960. Diplomate Am. Bd. Surgery. Intern Mass. Meml. Hosp., Boston, 1960-61; resident Bethesda (Md.) Naval Hosp., 1963-67; commd. ensign USN, 1956, advanced through grades to capt.; intern Mass. Gen. Hosp.; resident in surgery N.H. Bethesda Hosp.; mem. surg. staff USN, Bethesda, Md., 1961-80; chief of surgery USN Hosp., Bethesda, 1980-83; pvt. practice Hygeia Med. Specialist Group, Charleston, W.Va., 1983-86; prof. Med. Sch. W.Va. U., Charleston, 1986. Asst. prof. surgery Uniformed Svcs. Univ. of Health Scis. Decorated Cross of Gallantry (Vietnam), Meritorious Svc. medal USN. Episcopalian. Avocations: fishing, skiing. Office: U Health Assocs 3110 Maccorkle Ave SE Charleston WV 25304-1210

COCHRAN, ROBERT GLENN, nuclear engineering educator; b. Indpls., July 12, 1919; s. Lucian Glenn and Daisy P. (Wachstetter) C.; m. Mary Olive Worland, Mar. 1945; 1 son, Robert Glenn. BA, Ind. U., 1948, MS, 1950; PhD, Pa. State U., 1957. Registered profl. engr. Physicist Ohio State Health Dept., 1950; physicist, group leader Oak Ridge Nat. Lab., 1950-55; dir. research reactor, asso. prof. Pa. State U., 1955-59; prof., head dept. nuclear engring. Tex. A&M U., College Station, 1959-83, prof., 1983-96, emeritus prof. for life, 1996—. Vis. prof. nuclear engring. Tex. A&M U., 1985—; cons. USAF, U.S. AEC, NRC. Author: (textbook) The Nuclear Fuel Cycle: Analysis and Management, 1989, revised edit., 1999; contbr. articles to profl. jours. and textbooks. Served with USNR, 1942-45. Fellow Am. Nuclear Soc.; mem. Am. Phys. Soc., Am. Soc. Engring. Edn. (life), Sigma Xi, Phi Kappa Phi. Lodges: Mason. Home: 12305 Hopes Creek Rd College Station TX 77845-9241 Office: Tex A&M U Dept Nuclear Engring College Station TX 77843-0001

COCHRAN, SACHIKO TOMIE, radiologist, educator; b. Heart Mountain, Wyo., Feb. 17, 1945; d. Kay and Emiko Tomie. BA, UCLA, 1967; MD, U. Md. Sch. Medicine, 1971. Intern LAC/USC Med. Ctr., 1971-72; resident So. Calif. Permanente Med. Ctr., L.A., 1972-75; fellowship UCLA Med. Ctr., 1975-76; asst. prof. UCLA Sch. Medicine, 1976-84, assoc. prof., 1984-94, prof. radiol. scis., 1994—. Chmn. com. on rules and jurisdiction UCLA, univ. emeriti pre-retirement rels. com.; active Joint Commn. accreditation of Healthcare Orgns. Profl. and Tech. adv. Com., 1993-96, US Pharmacopeia; chair expert adv. com. Diagnostic Agts., 2000 ; oral bd. examiner Am. Bd. Radiology, 1994—. Cons. editor Investigative Radiology Jour., 1989-94, Acad. Radiology, 1994-2000; cons. reviewer Radiology Jour., 1979-82, 85—; mem. editl. bd. The Radiologist, 1992—; contbr. articles to profl. jours., chpts. to books. Grantee Mallinkrodt Inst., 1981, 91, Cancer Rsch. Coord. Com., 1984, E.R. Squibbs, 1985, 92, Jonsson Comprehensive Cancer Ctr., 1985, Cook Imaging, 1990-91, Upjohn Co., 1994. Fellow Soc. Uroradiology (exec. bd. 1998—), Am. Coll. Radiology, European Soc. Urogenital Radiology; mem. Radiol. Soc. N.Am., Assn. Univ. Radiologists, Am. Roentgen Ray Soc. (chair scientific program), Calif. Radiol. Soc., Am. Coll. Radiology (chmn. quality assurance com.), LA Radiol. Soc., Assn. Acad. Women (treas. 1989—). Office: Dept Radiology UCLA 10833 Le Conte Ave Los Angeles CA 90095-1721

COCHRAN, SUSAN MILLS, librarian; b. Grinnell, Iowa, Nov. 21, 1949; d. Lawrence Omen and Louise Jane (Morgan) Mills; m. Stephen E. Cochran, July 1, 1972; children: Bryan, Jeremy. Libr. Iowa Geneal. Soc., Des Moines, 1987-96; asst. to dir. Local History Ctr., Canon City (Colo.) Pub. Libr., 1997—. Editor: Mingo, Iowa 1884-1984, 1984; contbr. articles to profl. jours. Past bd. dirs. Jasper County Libr., Newton, Iowa; past mem. Jasper County Cemetery Commn., Newton; mem. Jasper County His. Soc. Mem. Iowa Geneal. Soc., Jasper County Geneal. Soc., State Assn. for the Preservation of Iowa Cemeteries (charter), Fremont County Geneal. Group (coord.), Colo. Coun. Geneal. Socs. Avocations: genealogy, history, birding. Office: Canon City Pub Libr 516 Macon Ave Canon City CO 81212-3310

COCHRAN, THAD, senator; b. Pontotoc, Miss., Dec. 7, 1937; s. William Holmes and Emma Grace (Berry) C.; m. Rose Clayton, June 6, 1964; children: Thaddeus Clayton, Katherine Holmes. BA, U. Miss., 1959, JD cum laude, 1965; postgrad. (Rotary Found. fellow), U. Dublin, Ireland, 1963-64. Bar: Miss. 1965. Practiced in Jackson, 1965-72; assoc. firm Watkins & Eager, 1965-72; mem. 93d-95th congresses from Miss., 1973-79; U.S. senator from Miss., 1979—; chmn. Rep. conf. 104th Congress, 1995. Mem. agr. nutrition and forestry com., appropriations com., govtl. affairs com., rules and adminstrn. com., senate Rep. conf. com. Mem. exec. bd. Andrew Jackson council Boy Scouts Am., from 1973. Served to lt. USNR, 1959-61. Named Outstanding Young Man of Jackson, 1971, One of Three Outstanding Young Men of Miss., 1971 Mem. ABA, Miss. Bar Assn. (pres. young lawyers sect. 1972-73), Omicron Delta Kappa, Phi Kappa Phi, Pi Kappa Alpha. Clubs: Rotarian. Republican. Baptist.*

COCHRAN, WILLIAM JOHN, physician, pediatrician, gastroenterologist, nutritionist, consultant; b. Binghamton, N.Y., Apr. 22, 1953; s. John Joseph and Natalie Jane (King) C.; m. Deborah Janaskie, May 26, 1979; children: Shawn Patrick, Shelby St. John. BA in Biology, Franklin and Marshall Coll., 1975; MD, Pa. State U., 1979. Diplomate Am. Bd. Pediats., Am. Bd. Nutrition, Am. Bd. Pediats. in Pediatric Gastroenterology. Intern U. Rochester, N.Y., 1979-80, resident pediats., 1979 82, fellow pediat. GI/Nutrition, 1982-83, fellow sects. gastroenterology and nutrition Dept. Pediats. Baylor Coll. Medicine, Houston, 1983-84, instr. sects. gastroenterology and nutrition dept. pediats., 1984-85, asst. prof. sects. gastroenterology and nutrition USDA/ARS Childrens Nutrition Rsch. Ctr., 1985-87; assoc. in pediat. gastroenterology and nutrition Geisinger Clinic, Danville, Pa., 1987—; clin. assoc. prof. dept. pediats. Jefferson Med. Coll., Phila., 1988-98, Pa. State U. Coll. Medicine, Hershey, 1998—, assoc. prof. clin. pediat., 1998—2001. Mem. infant formula expert panel FDA, 1997. Mem. editl. bd.: Healthy Kids mag., 1998—2002. Soccer coach Am. Youth Soccer Assn., Danville, Pa., 1988-89; vice-chmn. Geisinger Health Sys., 1999-2000; chmn. Geisinger Regional Med. Coun. Travel grantee IV Internat. Congress of Auxology, Montreal, 1985, XIII Internat. Congress of Nutrition, Brighton, Eng., 1985; recipient Jr. Investigator award Internat. Congress Auxology, Montreal, 1985. Mem. Am. Soc. Parenteral and Enteral Nutrition (mem. Ctrl. Pa. chpt.), Am. Acad. Pediats. (gastroenterology sect., nutrition com., exec. com. gastroenterology and nutrition sect., chmn. gastroenterology and nutrition sect. 2002, v.p. Pa. chpt.), Am. Gastroenterol. Assn., Am. Coll. Nutrition, Pa. Soc. Gastroenterology, Pa. Nutrition Coun., N.Am. Soc. Pediat. Gastroenterology, mem., Am. Acad. of Pediat. Task Force on Obesity, 2003-, Exec. Com. advocates for Nutrition and Physical Activity, Pa., 2001-, v.p. Pa. Chapt. Am. Acad. Pediat., 2002-, chmn., Am. Acad. of Reds, sect. of GI & Nutrition, 2001-. Roman Catholic. Avocations: scuba diving, tennis, cross country skiing. Office: Geisinger Clinic Dept Pediats GI and Nutrition 100 N Academy Ave Danville PA 17821-1203

COCHRAN, WILLIAM MICHAEL, librarian; b. Nevada, Iowa, May 6, 1952; s. Joseph Charles and Inez (Larson) Cochran; m. Diane Marie Ohm, July 24, 1971. BLS, U. Iowa, 1979, MA with distinction in Libr. Sci., 1983; MA in Pub. Adminstrn., Drake U., 1989. Dir. Red Oak (Iowa) Pub. Libr., 1984; patron svcs. libr. Pub. Libr. of Des Moines, 1984-87; LSCA program coord. State Libr. of Iowa, Des Moines, 1987-88, dir. libr. devel., 1988-89, asst. state libr., 1989-90; dir. Parmly Billings Libr., 1990—. Mem. White House Conf. on Libr. and Info. Svcs. Mem.: Libr. Adminstrn. and Mgmt. Assn., Pub. Libr. Assn., Mont. Gov.'s Blue Ribbon Telecommunications Task Force, Mont. Libr. Assn. (chair, pub. libr. divsn. 1991—92, legis. com. chair 1992—93, pres. 1998—99, named Libr. of Yr. 1998), ALA, Beta Phi Mu. Office: Parmly Billings Libr 510 N Broadway Billings MT 59101-1156

COCHRANE, BETSY LANE, state senator; b. Asheboro, N.C. d. William Jennings and Bobbie (Campbell) Lane; m. Joe Kenneth Cochrane, 1958; children: Lisa, Craig. BA cum laude, Meredith Coll., 1958. Tchr. for eleven yrs.; mem. N.C. Ho. of Reps., Raleigh, 1980-88, house minority leader, 1985-88; mem. N.C. Senate, Raleigh, 1988-2001, chmn. Commn. on Aging, 1989-99, vice chmn. higher edn. com., 1991-92, senate minority whip, 1993-94, senate minority leader, 1995-96, vice chmn. senate appropriations, 1995—2000, vice chmn. senate commerce comm., 1995—2000, ranking minority mem. senate agr., 1995—2000. Tchr. Winston-Salem Sch. System, Highland Presbyn. Ch. Sch; mem. Nat. Rep. Platform Com., Order of LongLeaf Pine, 1992, Joint Legis. Ethics Com., 1989—2000, So. Regional Edn. Bd., 1987—2001; chmn. Joint Legis. Ethics Com., 1989—90; mem. N.C. Parks Commn., 1989—96, Retail Merchants Adv. Bd., 1989—2000, Govtl. Ops., 1989—97, Select Com. on Redistricting, 1991, 92, Revenue Law, 1992—2000; vice chmn. Commerce Commn., 1992—2000; mem. Select Com. on Redistricting, 1994, Environ. Rev. Com., 1997—2001, Utility Rev. Com., 1997—2001, Gov.'s Advocacy Coun. on Children and Youth, 1990—2001. Trustee Davie County Hosp.; bd. advisors Z. Smith Reynolds Found., 1996—99, Meredith Coll., chmn. pres.'s adv. coun., 1999—2001, govs. adv. budget com., 1989—93, pub. sch. forum, 1985—99; mem. Davie County Schs. Task Force on Facilities, 2001—02, So. Regional Edn. Bd., 1987—2001; del. GOP Nat. Conv., 1976, 1988, 1992, 1996; mem. Bible Study Fellowship; bd. dirs. Forks of the Yadkin Mus., 2002—. Recipient Woman in Govt. award N.C. Jaycees, 1985; named One of 10 Outstanding Legislators in Nation, 1987, Disting. Citizen of Yr., N.C. Libr. Dirs., 1991, Legislator of Yr., N.C. Divsn. Aging, 1991, Legislator of Yr., N.C. Assn. for Home Care, 1992, Citizen of Yr., N.C. Health Facilities Assn., 1993, Legislator of Yr. award N.C. Wildlife Fedn., 1995, Legislator of Yr. award Autism Found., 1995, Myers-Honeycutt award for excellence in pub. svc., 1996, Disting. Alumnae of the Yr. Meredith Coll., 1996, Dr. Ewald W. Busse award Aging Advocates of N.C., 1997; named to N.C. GOP Hall of Fame, 2001, FWC N.C. Women Achievement award, 2002. Baptist. Home and Office: 122 Azalea Cir Advance NC 27006-9582 E-mail: betsyco@prodigy.net, betsyc@ncleg.net.

COCHRANE, JAMES LOUIS, economist; b. Nyack, N.Y., Aug. 31, 1942; s. Thomas and Anna (Yaroscak) C.; m. Katherine Prince Schirmer, Mar. 24, 1984; 1 child. BA, Wittenberg U., 1964; PhD, Tulane U., 1968. Instr. Tulane U., New Orleans, 1967-68; asst. prof. U. S.C., Columbia, 1968-70, assoc. prof., 1970-72, prof., 1972-77; sr. staff mem. NSC, Washington, 1978-79; directorate of intelligence CIA, Washington, 1980-83; sr. v.p., chief economist Tex. Commerce Bancshares Inc., Houston, 1984-88, N.Y. Stock Exch., 1988—. Assoc. staff Brookings Instn., Washington, 1972-76, 76-78; 1st v.p. So. Econ. Assn., U. N.C., 1976-77; vis. prof. U. Melbourne, Australia, 1972, U. Tex., Austin, 1973-74; mem. adv. bd. White Ctr. Fin. Rsch., U. Pa., Fin. Markets Rsch. Ctr., Vanderbilt U.; mem. bd. advisors N.Y. Assembly; bd. dirs. Catalyst Inst., Columbia U. Ctr. Law and Econ. Studies; mem. emerging econs. program bd. U. Pa. Wharton Sch.; mem. deans adv. bd. Hofstra U. Sch. Bus.; mem. study equities markets Pace U.; mem. internat. adv. com. Ctr. for Internat. Affairs, Harvard U., U.S. Nat. Com. for Pacific Econ. Cooperation. Author: Macroeconomics Before Keynes, 1970, Macroeconomics Analysis and Policy, 1974, Industrialism and Industrial Man in Retrospect, 1977; editor: Multiple Criteria Decision Making, 1975; mem. editl. bd. History Polit. Economy, Duke U., 1974-80, So. Econ. Jour., U. N.C., 1976-79. Mem. History of Econs. Soc. (treas. 1974-80), Asia Soc. (adv. dir. 1986), Am. Econ. Assn., Western Fin. Assn. Avocations: tennis, singing, writing. Office: NY Stock Exch 11 Wall St Fl 7 New York NY 10005-1974

COCHRANE, ROBERT LOWE, biologist; b. Morgantown, W.Va., Feb. 10, 1931; s. Thomas Joseph and Isabelle Durston (Lowe) C. BA, W.Va. U., 1953; MS, U. Wis., 1954, PhD, 1961. Rsch. asst. genetics U. Wis., Madison, 1953-55, rsch. asst. zoology, 1957-60; with Fur Animal Exptl. Sta., Petersburg, Alaska, 1955; agt. in animal husbandry U.S. Dept. Agr., Madison, Wis., 1955-61; biologist FDA, Washington, 1961-62; sr. research fellow dept. anatomy U. Birmingham (Eng.), 1962-65; project assoc. dept. physiology U. Pitts., 1965-66; sr. endocrinologist Eli Lilly & Co., Indpls., 1966-80; rsch. assoc. G.D. Searle & Co., Skokie, Ill., 1980-81; with Short's Fur Farm, Granton, Wis., 1981-83; rsch. assoc. Marshfield (Wis.) Med. Found., 1983-84; biologist Northwood Fur Farms, Inc., Cary, Ill., 1984. Cons. for FAO to Wildlife Inst. India, Dehra Dun, 1985; adj prof. div. animal and vet. sci., W.Va. U., Morgantown, 1987—. Ad hoc reviewer (various sci. jours.); ad hoc reviewer: grants U.S. Dept. of Agr. Competitive Rsch. Grants; participant Internat. Mink Show, Wis., 1976—2003, W. Va. State Fox Show, Morgantown, 1989. Rsch. bd. advisors The Am. Biog. Inst., 1988-98; mem. adv. coun. Internat. Biog. Centre, 1989-98; mem. Golden Horseshoe Reunion Com., W.Va. Homecoming '96. Recipient Knight of Golden Horse Shoe award W.Va. Pub. Sch. System, 1945, W.Va. Boy's State, 1948; U. Birmingham (Eng.) sr. rsch. fellow, 1962-65. Mem. AAAS, Am. Inst. Biol. Scis., Soc. Exptl. Biology and Medicine, Soc. for Reprodn. and Fertility, Soc. Study of Reprodn., Am. Soc. Animal Sci., Endocrine Soc., N.Y. Acad. Sci., Soc. Endocrinology, Coun. Agrl. Sci. and Tech., Internat. Platform Assn., NRA (life), Sigma Xi, Pi Kappa Alpha, Gamma Sigma Delta. Presbyterian. Achievements include major contributions to the establishment of the hormonal requirements for ova-implantation and embryonic diapause in the rat, the elucidation of the role played by prostaglandins in corpus luteum function, parturition and ductus arteriosus closure in the rat; the development of steroid synthesis inhibitors for controlling reproduction in mammals; the documentation of the timing, duration and pattern of reproductive cycles in martens; determining how to successfully raise ruffed grouse in captivity; the dissemination of scientific information on fur farming and raising ruffed grouse to the commercial trade and public. Home: 404 Junior Ave Morgantown WV 26505-2208

COCHRANE, SHIRLEY GRAVES, writer, educator; b. Chapel Hill, N.C., Mar. 5, 1925; d. Thornton Shirley and Margaret (White) Graves; m. William McWhorter Cochrane, June 3, 1945; children: William Daniel, Thomas McWhorter. AB with honors, Agnes Scott Coll., 1946; MA, Johns Hopkins U., 1970. Editor U. N.C. Press, 1946-50, 51-52; tchr. various univs. including Am. U., Georgetown U., Cath. U., Washington, 1974—. Instr., mem. Writer's Ctr., Bethesda, Md., 1978—. Author: Everything That's All, 1991, Letters to the Quick/Letters to the Dead, 1998; contbr. short stories and poems to lit. mags., anthologies, etc.; free-lance editor, Duke U. Press, Yale U. Press, Shakespeare Quar., others, 1951-73; work represented in Libr. of Congress Archive of Recorded Poetry and Lit. Recipient awards including PEN award for Syndicated Fiction, others. Mem. Writers Ctr. Bethesda, Phi Beta Kappa. Democrat. Presbyterian.

COCHRANE, WALTER E. academic administrator, music educator, conductor; b. Phila. s. Earl and Martha (Binder) C. BS, MS, U. Pa., Phila.; grad. study, Columbia U., 1959-60. Cert. sch. dist. adminstr., N.Y., Pa., N.J., Mass., Maine, Va.; cert. music supr., N.Y., Pa., Va.; supt. schs., N.Y., Mass.; sch. prin., N.Y., Pa., Mass. Clarinet soloist Phila. Brahms Cycle, 1950; dir. bands Upper Darby Pa. Schs., 1950-51; prof. clarinet and chamber music Phila. Musical Acad., 1950-52; solo clarinetist Phila. Symphonic Band, 1950-58; dir. music Alexandria Va. City Schs., 1951—58; clarinet soloist Alexandria String Quartet, 1952; dist. music dir. Sch. Dist. II, L.I., NY, 1958-60; supr. music N.Y. State Edn. Dept., Albany, 1960-67; conductor NY State Bands, 1960-67; v.p. Found. Am. Art Song, Albany, 1965-70; supr. music Hartford (Conn.) City Schs., 1967-69; instr. music edn. U. Hartford, 1967—69; asst. supt. Sch. Dist. 5, L.I., N.Y.,

1970-78; supt. schs. Maine Sch. Adm. Dist. 19, Lubec, Maine, 1978-80; v.p. and dean Inst. Security and Tech., Phila., 1980-87; corp. dir. edn. PTC Career Insts., Phila., 1987; pres. Career Guidance Corp., 1988-91, dir. GED home study program N.Y. State, 1992—. Founder, dir. Stony Brook Conservatory Music, L.I., 1958—61. Author: GED Home Study Program, Meet The Great Composers, The Gulf War, World Wars I and II, Mathematics Mastery Manual, Science Mastery Manual, Understand Music, Women Composers, Literature Mastery Manual, Who Was the Killer Composer?, Clarinet Curriculum, Flute Curriculum, Graded Music for Wind and String Chamber Music, Graded Music for Brass Instruments, Public Schools Can Help You, The AAA Method in American Education-Analysis, Action and Alleviation of Attrition, CATP: Cooperative Analysis of Teacher Performance, Non-Traditional Employment for Women, A Philosophy and Basic Procedures for Supervision, Understanding Students for the Improvement of Learning, Encyclopedia of Conductors. Recipient Humanitarian award Chgo. PTC. Mem. ASCD, NEA, MENC, SAR, NYSSMA (adjudicator, all-state conductor), NASSP, Am. Assn. Sch. Adminstrs., N.Y. Assn. Supr. and Curriculum Devel., Phila. Musical Soc.

COCHRANE, WILLIAM HENRY, former city official; b. Norfolk, Va., Apr. 3, 1912; s. William F. and Gretchen (Schneider) C.; m. Elizabeth J. Ballantine, Aug. 3, 1935 (dec. July 1977); children: William Henry, Susan B., Peter B.; m. Deborah E. Collyer, June 14, 1978; stepchildren, Nancy Havecotte, George Shepard, Elizabeth Shepard, Alexander Shepard. Student, Princeton, 1931-32. Successively chemist, salesman, dist. mgr., mgr. market and sales analysis, mgr. detergent project U.S. Indsl. Chems. Co., 1932-52; gen. mgr. indsl. div. Lever Bros. Co., 1952-57; exec. v.p. Neptune Internat. Corp., 1957-58, pres., 1958-69, chmn., 1966-72; also bd. dirs.; bd. dirs. Los Angeles Soap Co.; v.p. Mountain Lake Corp., 1975-77, pres., 1978-81, Indian River Lands Inc., 1987—, also bd. dirs. Mem. Vero Beach (Fla.) City Coun., 1980-87, vice mayor, 1980-82, mayor, 1982-87, chmn. fin. commn., 1987—; bd. dirs. Vero Beach Civic Assn., Humane Soc., Coun. of Aging; trustee Vero Beach Ctr. Arts, 1983-90, pres., 1984-89; mem. Fla. Arts Coun., 1990-91. Lt. USNR, 1944-46. Mem. Newcomen Soc., Princeton Club N.Y., Nassau Club, Riomar Bay Yacht Club, Mountain Lake Club, One Harbor Club, Grand Harbor Club. Home: 740 Saint Annes Ln Vero Beach FL 32967-7347 Office: Cardinal Dr Vero Beach FL 32963

COCHRUN, JOHN WESLEY, financial consultant; b. Spencerville, Ohio, May 4, 1918; s. Paul Wesley and Laura Edna (McClure) C.; m. Almut Boesel-Michaud, Aug. 26. 2000; children: Timothea Jourdan, David Wesley. BS, Purdue U., 1940; diploma, U.S. Army Command and Gen. Staff Coll., 1944; MS in Fin. Svcs., Am. Coll., 1985. CLU, chartered fin. cons. Spl. apprentice Bendix-Westinghouse A.A.B. Co., Pitts., 1940-41, asst. svc. mgr. Elyria, Ohio, 1945-50; mgr. customer svc. DeVilbiss Co., Toledo, 1950-58; exec. v.p. Elec. Products R & D Co., Toledo, 1958-60; spl. agt. Northwestern Mut. and other ins. cos., Toledo, 1961-81, St. Petersburg, Fla., 1981-87, Las Cruces, N.Mex., 1987-97. Registered investment adviser SEC, State of N.Mex., 1989-95; pres. Cochrun Inc., Sylvania, Ohio, 1976-81, Seminole, Fla., 1981-87. Author: Service of the Piece, 1945, Avoid Financial Shocks in Your Family's Future, 1976, Wills, Trusts, and Life Insurance Settlement Options, 1995. Pres. Community League Sylvania, 1954; lobbyist Ohio Pub. Expenditure Coun., Sylvania, 1955, Fed. Transp. Commn., Washington, 1947-50. Lt. col. U.S. Army, 1941-45. Mem. Am. Soc. CLU and ChFC, Million Dollar Round Table (life), Res. Officers Assn., Phi Kappa Psi. Republican. Avocations: gardening, canoeing. Home and Office: 1615 Thunderbird Las Cruces NM 88011-9123

COCKBURN, JOHN F. retired bank executive; b. Everett, Wash., Apr. 8, 1928; s. Charles G. and Florence S. Cockburn; m. Lynn F. Pierson, June 29, 1960; children: Steven, Matthew, Teresa, Patrick. BBA, U. Wash., Seattle, 1950. With Rainier Nat. Bank (now Bank of Am.), Seattle, 1948-88, exec. v.p., 1975-88; pres. Pacific Coast Banking Sch., 1977-79; fin. chmn. Wash. Coun. Econ. Edn., 1980-81, also bd. dirs.; ret., 1981. Trustee Forest Ridge Sch., Bellevue, Wash., 1983-89, chmn., 1988-89; trustee, fin. chmn. Horizon House, Seattle, 1988-91; exec. bd. Energy Northwest, 1989-93, apptd. by gov., 1995—, apptd. by bd., chmn. audit, legal, fin. com., 1995—, chmn. bd., 2001-03. Mem. Rainier Club (trustee 1987-90), Seattle Tennis Club, Broadmoor Golf Club (trustee, pres. 1994-95). Congregationalist. Home: 1524 Shenandoah Dr E Seattle WA 98112-3732

COCKE, WILLIAM MARVIN, JR., plastic surgeon, educator; b. Balt., Aug. 2, 1934; s. William M. and Clara E. (Bosley) C.; m. Sue Ann Harris, Apr. 25, 1981; children: Gregory William, Laura Marie, Julie Ann; children by previous marriage: William Marvin III, Catherine Lynn, Deborah Kay, Brian Thomas. BS with honors in Biology, Tex. A&M U., 1956; MD, Baylor U., 1960. Diplomate: Am. Bd. Plastic Surgery (guest examiner 1978). Intern surgery Vanderbilt U. Hosp., Nashville, 1960-61; fellow gen. surgery Ochsner Clinic and Found. Hosp., New Orleans, 1961-64; chief resident surgery Monroe (La.) Charity Hosp., 1963-64; resident reconstructive surgery Roswell Park Meml. Inst., Buffalo, 1965-66; chief resident plastic surgery VA Hosp., Bronx, N.Y., 1966; practice medicine specializing in plastic surgery Nashville, 1968-75, Sacramento, 1976-79; pvt. practice medicine specializing in plastic surgery Bryan, Tex., 1980-92; prof. surgery, head div. plastic/reconstructive surgery Marshall U. Sch. of Medicine, Huntington, W.Va., 1992—. Mem. staff St. Mary's Hosp., Cabell-Huntington Hosp., Huntington Vets. Med. Ctr.; asst. prof. plastic surgery Vanderbilt U. Sch. Medicine, Nashville, 1968-69, asst. clin. prof. plastic surgery, 1969-75; assoc. prof. plastic surgery Ind. U. Sch. Medicine, Indpls., 1975-76; chief plastic surgery service Wishard Meml. Hosp., Ind. U., 1975-76; assoc. prof. surgery U. Calif. Sch. Medicine, Davis, 1976-79, chmn. dept. plastic surgery, 1976-79; prof. surgery, chief div. plastic surgery Tex. Tech. U. Sch. Medicine, Lubbock, 1979-80, dir. Microsurg. Research Lab., 1979-80; clin. prof. surgery Tex. A&M U. Sch. Medicine, 1983-92; prof. plastic surgery, 1986-89; chief plastic surgery svc., dept. surgery, Olin Teague VA Med. Ctr., Temple, Tex., 1986-92; prof. head surgery divsn. plastic and reconstruction Marshall U. Sch. Medicine, 1992—. Author textbooks on plastic surgery; contbr. articles to profl. jours. Served with M.C. USAF, 1966-68. Recipient Dean Echols award Ochsner Hosp. Found., 1963 Mem. ACS, Am. Assn. Plastic Surgeons, Soc. Head and Neck Surgeons, Assn. for Acad. Surgery, Alton Ochsner Surg. Soc. Episcopalian. Home: 45 Olde Farm Rd Ona WV 25545-9747 Office: Marshall U Sch Medicine Dept Surgery 1600 Medical Center Dr Huntington WV 25701-3656

COCKERHAM, LORRIS G. radiation toxicologist; b. Denham Springs, La., Sept. 27, 1935; s. Warren Conrad and Leda Frances (Scivicque) C.; m. Patricia Ann Stagg, Aug. 16, 1957; children: Michael B., Richard L., Ann E., Joseph D. BA, La. Coll., 1957; MS, Colo. State U., 1973, PhD, 1979. Diplomate Am. Bd. Forensic Examiners. Commd. 2d lt. USAF, 1961, advanced through grades to lt. col., 1977, instr., 1963-66, squadron electronic warfare officer Fairchild AFB, Wash., 1966-71, asst. prof. dept. chemistry and biology USAF Acad., 1973-77, wing electronic warfare officer, 1977-78, comdr. 416 Munitions Maintenance Squadron, 1978-80; Armed Forces Radiobiology Rsch. Inst., Def. Nuc. Agy., Bethesda, Md., 1980-86; Air Force Office of Sci. Rsch., Bolling AFB, D.C., 1986-87; ret., 1987; exec. dir. NCTR-Associated Univs., Little Rock, 1988-89; pres. The Delta Agy., Little Rock, 1989-93, Phenix Cons. and Svcs. Ltd., Little Rock, 1993—. Dir. Product Safety Labs., East Brunswick, N.J., 1994-95; dir. Toxicol. SITEK Rsch. Labs., Rockville, Md., 1997-99; asst. prof. physiology Sch. Medicine, Uniformed Svcs. U. Health Scis., 1981-87; assoc. prof. U. Ark. for Med. Scis., 1988-89. Troop com. chmn. Iroquois coun. Boy Scouts Am., 1978-80. Decorated D.F.C. (2), Airman's medal, Air medal (12), Air Force Commendation medal, Joint Svc. Achievement medal; Air Force Systems Command Dioxin Rsch. grantee, 1974-79; recipient Order of Arrow, Boy Scouts Am.; named Disting. Alumnus La. Coll., 1989. Mem. Soc. Neurosci., Internat. Brain Rsch. Orgn., World Fedn. Neuroscientists, Soc. Toxicology, Am. Physiol. Soc., Am. Coll. Toxicology, Sigma Xi, Phi Kappa Phi. Republican. Baptist. E-mail: phenixLtd@aol.com.

COCKERHAM, SIDNEY JOE, professional society administrator; b. Waxahachie, Tex., Aug. 17, 1951; s. Sidney Julius and Joan (Barlow) C. BS in Biology, U. Tex., Arlington, 1973. Cert. tchr., Tex. Tchr. Tex. Pub. Schs., Waxahachie, 1973-77; dir., founder U.S. Nat. Tennis Acad., Waxahachie, 1982—. Lt. USN, 1977-82. Avocation: tennis. Home: 1010 Allen St Dallas TX 75204-5880 Office: PO Box 192704 Dallas TX 75219 E-mail: usnta@usnta.com.

COCKLIN, RUTH ELLEN, artist; b. Canton, Ohio, May 20, 1929; d. John Burton and Sarah Ann (Wood) Schoonover; m. Gerald D. Cocklin, Sept. 2, 1950 (div. Feb. 1974); children: Sally, Thomas, Elizabeth. BFA, Colo. State U., Ft. Collins, 1982. Exhibits at Colo. History Mus. 1970-2003,exhibited in group shows at Foothills Art Ctr., Golden, Colo., 1990, Sprigfield Art Mus., 1997, U. Colo., Colorado Springs, 1997, 98, 21st Internat. Watercolor Art Soc. show, Houston, 1998, Western Fedn. Watercolor Soc. Ann., San Diego, 1999, Colorado Springs Fine Arts Ctr., 1997-2003, Wyo. Nat. Natucolor Soc. exhibit 2003; represented in pvt. collections; contbr. to books and mags. Mem. Colo. Watercolor Soc. Home: 5923 S Willow Way Greenwood Village CO 80111-5105 E-mail: rellen10@juno.com.

COCKRELL, JAN MEYER, recreation therapist; b. Indpls., Nov. 12, 1953; d. Brud Richard and Betty Louise (Stine) Meyer and Barbara Ann Hamilton (stepmother). BS in Recreation, Ind. State U., 1975; MA in Recreation Edn. Adminstrn., U. Iowa, 1977. Cert. therapeutic recreation specialist. Asst. dir. Girls Club Terre Haute, Ind., 1973-74, exec. dir., 1974-75; youth dir. YWCA, Terre Haute, 1977-79; activity dir. Vermillion Convalescent Ctr., Clinton, Ind., 1979-80, adminstrv. asst., 1980-81; dir. leisure svcs. Westminster Village, Terre Haute, 1981—; instr. Ind. Vocat. Tech. Coll., Terre Haute, 1988—2000, Ind. State U., 2000—. Bd. mem. Wabash Valley Sr. Classics, Terre Haute, 1988-91, 93-95; mem. adv. bd., 1991-93, 96-98. Mem. Ind. Park and Recreation Assn., Ctrl. Ind. Dirs. Leisure Svcs. (chairperson 1988—), Area Activity Profls. (chairperson 1989—). Methodist. Home: 205 Bluebird Ln Terre Haute IN 47803-1451 Office: Westminster Village 1120 E Davis Dr Terre Haute IN 47802-4065

COCKRELL, JANICE LOUISE, pediatric physiatrist; b. Omaha, Nov. 27, 1946; d. Keith Lewis and Nelldeane (Smith) C.; m. Robert John Czerniejewski, Apr. 21, 1975; children: Andrea Vanessa, Marissa Louise, Erika May. BA, U. Nebr., 1968; MD, Northwestern U., 1972. Diplomate Am. Bd. Pediatrics, Phys. Medicine and Rehab., Electrodiagnostic Medicine, Nat. Bd. Med. Examiners; lic. MD, Oreg., Wash. Resident pediatrics Children's Meml. Hosp., Chgo., 1972-74, Milw. Children's Hosp., 1974-75; pediatrician Northpoint Med. Group, Milw., 1975-76; vis. pediatrician ad honorem Nat. Children's Hosp., San Jose, Costa Rica, 1977-78; instr. epidemiology U. Costa Rica, San Jose, 1978; asst. prof. pediat. Med. Coll. Va., Richmond, 1979-84, resident phys. medicine and rehab., 1984-87, chief resident pediat. rehab. Children's Hosp., 1985-87, instr., assoc. prof. phys. medicine and rehab. and pediats., 1986-91; pediat. physiatrist Rehab. Medicine Assoc., Portland, 1992-98. Clin. instr. Med. Coll. Wis., Milw. Children's Hosp., 1975-76; cons. regional burn unit St. Mary's Hosp., Milw., 1975-76; clin. assoc. pediat. Oreg. Health Scis. U., Portland, 1992—; med. dir. pediat. rehab. Pediat. Rehab. Svcs. Legacy Emanuel Children's Hosp., Portland, 1992—; vis. prof. pediat. rehab. Ea. Va. Med. Sch., Norfolk, 1991. Contbr. articles to profl. jours. Mem. Local Spiritual Assembly Baha'is of Lake Oswego, 1992—. Fellow Am. Acad. Pediatrics, Am. Acad. Phys. Medicine and Rehab., Am. Assn. Electrodiagnostic Medicine, Am. Acad. Cerebral Palsy and Devel. Medicine; mem. Health for Humanity, Northwest Soc. Phys. Medicine and Rehab., Northwest Soc. Devel. and Behavioral Pediatrics. Avocation: piano. Office: Legacy Emanuel Childrens Hosp 2801 N Gantenbein Ave Portland OR 97227-1623

COCKRELL, KENNETH D. astronaut; b. Austin, Tex., Apr. 9, 1950; s. Dale and Jewell Cockrell; 2 children. BSc in Mech. Engring., U. Tex., 1972; MSc in Aeronautical Sys., U. W. Fla., 1974. Commd. lt. USN, 1972, naval aviator, 1974—75; served on USS Midway, 1975—78; various assignments naval air test ctr. USN, 1979—82; comdr. USS Ranger Naval Sta., San Diego, 1982—85; aerospace engr., rsch. pilot Ellington Field, Houston, 1987—90; astronaut NASA, Houston, 1991—. Astronaut Discovery, 1993, Endeavour, 1995, Columbia, 1996, Atlantis, 2001. Decorated Meritorious Svc. medal USNR, Disting. Flying Cross, Commendation medal, Humanitarian Svc. medal; scholar, Alcoa Found. Mem.: Assn. Space Explorers, Soc. Exptl. Test Pilots. Avocations: sport flying, skiing, tennis, water skiing. Office: Astronaut Office CB NASA Johnson Space Center Houston TX 77058

COCKRELL, SANFORD ALONZA, III, accountant; b. Raleigh, N.C., Feb. 2, 1959; s. Sanford Alonza Jr. and Vivian Mercer Cockrell; m. Louise Heath, Dec. 5, 1960; children: L. Heath, Morgan. M. BSBA, U. N.C., 1982. CPA, N.Y. Staff acct. Rackley & Parker CPAs, Raleigh, N.C., 1982-84; mgr. Deloitte Haskins & Sells, Raleigh, 1984-89; sr. mgr. Deloitte & Touche, N.Y.C., 1989-93, ptnr., 1993—, bd. dirs., 2001—. Grad. Leadership Raleigh I, Greater Raleigh C. of C., 1985-86; pres., treas. N.C. Soc. N.Y., 1996—, chmn. fin. com.; chmn. Younger Mem.'s Activities Com.; mem. Coun. Nominating Com., The Univ. Club; adv. bd. U. N.C., Inst. for Arts and Humanities, Chapel Hill, N.C., 1999—; co-chair cons. adv. bd., Youth, Inc.; coun. mem. U. N.C. Chapel Hill Nat. Devel. Coun., 1995—; coach girls' basketball and T-ball Yorkville Youth Athletic Assn., N.Y.C., 2000—; elder, deacon Brick Presbyn. Ch., N.Y.C., 1994-2000; 2d v.p., N.Y. area dir. U. N.C., Chapel Hill Gen. Alumni Assn. Bd. Dirs., 1996-2000; mem. reunion gift com. U. N.C., Chapel Hill, 1991-92. Mem. N.C. Soc. CPAs (chmn. com. on taxation 1986-88), Coral Beach Club (Bermuda), Rockaway Hunting Club, Lawrence Beach Club. Presbyterian. Avocations: golf, running, sailing, travel, reading. Office: Deloitte & Touche 1633 Broadway New York NY 10019 Home: 1240 Park Ave Apt 2-B New York NY 10128-1755 Home Fax: 212-410-0208; Office Fax: 212-492-3881. E-mail: scockrell@deloitte.com.

COCKRELL, WILBURN ALLEN, archaeologist; b. Sikeston, Mo., Apr. 24, 1941; s. Wilburn Edward Cockrell and Martha Ann (Killian) Yancy; m. Rose Marie Roberson, Dec. 1961 (div. 1970); children: Padraic A., Timothy E.; m. Barbara O'Horo, 1984 (div. 1987). AB, U. Ala., Tuscaloosa, 1963; MA, Fla. State U., 1970; postgrad., Ariz. State U., 1970-72. Cert. scuba diver Profl. Assn. Diving Instrs.; cert. cave diver Nat. Assn. Cave Divers; cert. mix gas Fla. State U. Acad. Diving Program. Tchr. Mobile County Sch. Bd., Mobile, Ala., 1963-64, Okeechobee (Fla.) Sch. Bd., 1964-65, Yuma (Ariz.) Sch. Bd., 1968; state hwy. archaeologist State of Fla., Tallahassee, 1966-68, state underwater archaeologist, 1972-83; chief archaeologist, project dir. Warm Mineral Springs (Fla.) Archaeol. Rsch. Project, 1972-92; faculty Manatee C.C., 1984-87; chief archaeologist, project dir. Fla. State U., Tallahassee, 1987-92. Cons. archaeologist for various orgns., 1975—; lectr. for various orgns., 1965—. Editor: In the Realms of Gold, 1980; contbr. articles to profl. jours.; author poetry; photographer for many publs.; prodr. videos. Bd. dirs., 1st v.p. Friends of Libr., North Port, Fla., 1987-90; com. chmn. explorer post #157 Boy Scouts Am., North Port; mem. cultural execs. com. Sarasota County Arts Coun.; co-chmn. Sarasota French Film Festival, 1989. Recipient Disting. Svc. award Ctr. for Am. Archaeology, 1983; rsch. grantee Fla. State Legis., 1984-92; recipient Resolution, Fla. Senate for achievement in sci. and history, 1979, Sigma Xi, 1993. Mem. Register Profl. Archaeologists, Soc. for Am. Archaeology, Fla. Archaeol. Coun., Fla. Anthrop. Soc. (sec. 1973-74), Warm Mineral Springs Archaeol. Soc. (founder, pres. 1990-92), Am. Acad. Underwater Scis., Fla. Acad. Scis., Fla. Hist. Soc., Nat. Assn. Cave Divers, Soc. for Am. Archaeology, Sigma Xi. Republican. Avocations: photography, poetry, writing, underwater videography. Home: 4621 Autumn Woods Way Tallahassee FL 32303-6701 E-mail: cockrellw@yahoo.com.

COCKRILL, SHERNA, artist; b. Chgo., Dec. 19, 1936; d. Glenn Wesley and Ruby Jean Will; m. J. Mitchell Jr., Mar. 23, 1963; 1 child, Ashley. BA, U. Ark., 1958, MA, 1966. One-woman shows include KPMG Pete Marwick & Assocs. Collection, Little Rock, Ark., 1997, Arts Ctr. of Ozarks, 1997—98, Walton Art Ctr., Fayetteville, Ark., 1997, one-man shows include, 2000, one-woman shows include Sager Creek Art Ctr., Siloam Springs, Ark., 2000, exhibited in group shows at Philbrook Art Ctr., 1968—69, Tulsa Regional 5-State Exhbn., 1968, Okla. 8-State Painting and Sculpture Exhbn., 1968, Ark. Arts Festival, 1968—70, 1972—73, Okla. Mus. Art, 1970—71 (1st prize in oils, 1970), Artists N.W. Ark., 1969—72, Ft. Smith Art Ctr., 1972—74 (Grand prize, 1973), Greater New Orleans Nat. Exhbn., 1973, Ark. Arts Ctr., 1973—75, Little Rock Arts Fair, 1973 (1st prize in painting, 1973), Tex. Fine Arts Assn. Ann., 1973—74, S.E. Ark. Arts and Sci. Ctr., 1973, Ark. Festival Arts Invitational, 1974—76, Ark. Arts, Crafts and Design Fair, 1975—76, Gov.'s Disting. Artists Exhibit, 1976, U. Ark., 1979—86 (2d prize, 1981, 1984), Laguna Gloria Mus., Austin, Tex., 1984, 1986, Art Ctr. of Ozarks, 1999 (Pres. award, 2000), Walton Arts Ctr., Fayetteville, Ark., 2000—01, Represented in permanent collections Smithsonian Archives Am. Art, D.c., Mid Am. Mus., 1st Nat. Bank, Little Rock, Smithsonian Collection in Mid. Am. Mus., Hot Springs, Ark., WRMC, Butler Ctr., Little Rock, Ctrl. Ark. Libr. Sys., others, exhibitions include Arts Ctr. of the Ozarks, 2000, Walton Art Ctr., 2001, Butler Ctr. for Ark. Studies, Little Rock, Ctrl. Ark. Libr., 2000, Nat. Mus. of Women in the Arts Archives, Washington. Recipient 1st and 2d prizes Ozark Artist's Ann., 1972, Grand prize Ark. State Festival Art, 1973, 1st prize Ark. Arts, Crafts and Design Fair (8-State), 1974, 2d prize Greater New Orleans Nat., 1986, Gov.'s Collection, State of Ark., 1994, KPMG Collection 1995, Ark. Artists Registry Invitational, 1996, Sen. Pryor's Wash. Exhibit 1996, Arts Ctr. of the Ozark's one-woman exhibit, 1997, Walton Arts Ctr. one-woman exhibit, 1997, Arts Ctr. of the Ozark's Competitive Regional Pres.'s award for excellence in oils. Democrat. Episcopalian. Avocation: travel. Home: 1295 N Woodcreek Ln Fayetteville AR 72701-8881

COCKRILLE, STEPHEN, art director, business owner; b. Washington, Jan. 19, 1945; s. Donald Herbert and Dorothy Charolette (Hoover) C.; m. Éva Vágréti, May 17, 1987; children: Christopher Lewis, Micki Lee. BA, W.Va. State Coll., 1968; MA, U. N.D., 1972. Grad. tchg. asst. U. N.D., Grand Forks, 1971; design asst. Thomas Clayton Printing, N.Y.C., 1974-75; art dir. West Side Printing & Graphics, N.Y.C., 1975-76; studio mgr. Graphic Concern, Inc., N.Y.C., 1976-78; ind. art dir. N.Y.C., 1978-84; pres. Textart, Inc., N.Y.C., 1984-97; ret., 1997. Judge New Eng. Book Show, Boston, 1987; selected for presentation to the Jordanian Min. of Edn. and staff on the U.S. textbook industry, N.Y.C., 1995. Prodr. numerous basal ednl. programs for nat. distbn., 1984-97. With Ctrl. Intelligence Ctr., U.S. Army, 1968-70, Vietnam. Recipient hon. mention New Eng. Book Show, Boston, 1992, Pupil's Edit. and Theme Posters, Boston, 1992, bronze award Dimensional Illustrators Awards Show, N.Y.C., 1992, 1st place award Ednl. Sch. Divsn. N.Y. Book Show, N.Y.C., 1994. Republican. Avocations: painting, reading, skiing. Home: 1150 Kings Crown Rd Woodland Park CO 80863-7731

COCKRUM, WILLIAM MONROE, III, investment banker, consultant, educator; b. Indpls., July 18, 1937; s. William Monroe C. II and Katherine J. (Jaqua) Moore; m. Andrea Lee Deering, Mar. 8, 1975; children: Catherine Anne, William Monroe IV. AB with distinction, DePauw U., 1959; MBA with distinction, Harvard U., 1961. With A.G. Becker Paribas Inc., L.A., 1961-84, mgr. nat. corp. fin. div., 1968-71, mgr. pvt. investments, 1971-74, fin. and adminstrv. officer, 1974-80, sr. v.p., 1975-78, vice chmn., 1978-84, also bd. dirs.; prin. William M. Cockrum & Assocs., L.A., 1984—; mem. faculty Northwestern U., 1961-63. Vis. lectr. grad. sch. mgmt. UCLA, 1984-88, adj. prof., 1988—. Mem. Deke Club (N.Y.C.), UCLA Faculty Club, Alisal Golf Club (Solvang, Calif.), Bel-Air Country Club (L.A.), Delta Kappa Epsilon. E-mail: bcockrum@anderson.ucla.edu.

COCKS, FRANKLIN HADLEY, materials scientist; b. S.I., N.Y., Oct. 1, 1941; s. Charles Franklin and Ruth (Hadley) C.; m. Pamela Kay Pfaff, Aug. 6, 1966; children— Elijah Eugene, Josiah Charles. BS, MIT, 1963, MS, 1964, Sc.D., 1965; postgrad. (Fulbright fellow), Imperial Coll. Sci. and Tech., London, 1965-66. Registered patent agt. Staff scientist Tyco Labs., Waltham, Mass., 1966-67, sr. scientist, 1967-70, asst. head materials sci. dept., 1970-72; assoc. prof. Duke U., Durham, N.C., 1972-76, prof. dept. mech. engring. and materials sci., 1976—, chmn. dept. mech. engring. and materials sci., 1994—, dir. M of Engring. mgmt. program, 1997—. Cons. Los Alamos Sci. Lab., 1979— Author: (with M.L. Shepard, J.B. Chaddock, C.M. Harman) Introduction to Energy Technology, 1976, Manual of Industrial Corrosion Standards and Control; Editor ASTM spl. tech. publ., 1973; patentee in field. NSF fellow, 1964-65; recipient NASA award, 1974 Mem. Nat. Assn. Corrosion Engrs., AIME, Instn. Metallurgists (Brit.), Sigma Xi, Tau Beta Pi. Clubs: London House (life). Office: Duke U Dept Mech Engring & Materials Sci Durham NC 27708-0300 E-mail: hadley01@acpub.duke.edu.

COCKS, GEOFFREY CAMPBELL, history educator; b. New Bedford, Mass., Nov. 13, 1948; s. James Fraser and Lillias (Campbell) C.; m. Sarah Rogers, Aug. 28, 1971; 1 child, Emily Anne. AB, Occidental Coll., 1970; MA, UCLA, 1971, PhD, 1975. Instr. Occidental Coll., L.A., 1974-75; asst. prof. history Albion (Mich.) Coll., 1975-83, assoc. prof., 1983-87, prof., 1987-94, Royal G. Hall prof., 1994—2002, Juilian S. Rammelkamp prof., 2002—. Vis. asst. prof. UCLA, 1980. Author: Psychotherapy in the Third Reich, 1985, 2d edit., 1997, Treating Mind and Body, 1998, The Wolf at the Door, 2004; co-editor: German Professions, 1990, Medicine and Modernity, 1996, Depth of Field, 2004; editor: The Curve of Life, 1994. Fellow German Acad. Exch. Svc., 1973-74, 85, NEH, 1980, 87, 88-89, Fulbright fellow, 1989; Nat. Libr. Medicine grantee NIH, 1991-92. Mem. Am. Hist. Assn., German Studies Assn. Office: Albion Coll Dept History Albion MI 49224

COCKS, GEORGE GOSSON, retired chemical microscopy educator; b. Sioux City, Iowa, Mar. 22, 1919; s. George Green and Nellie Patricia (Gosson) C.; m. Marian L. Singer, May 11, 1942; children: Gary, Kathleen (Mrs. Thomas Sadlowski), Francis, Kenneth. BS in Chemistry, Iowa State U., 1941; PhD in Chem. Microscopy, Cornell, 1949. Researcher Battelle Meml. Inst., Columbus, Ohio, 1949-64; prof. chem. microscopy Cornell U., 1964-81, prof. emeritus, 1981—; cons. Los Alamos (N.Mex.) Nat. Lab., 1980-81, staff mem., 1981-90; ret., 1990. Patentee in field. Scoutmaster Central Ohio council Boy Scouts Am., 1956-64. Served to lt. comdr. USNR, 1942-45. NSF grantee to study crystallization inorganic materials in polymers, 1966-68, to study biomed. uses collagen, 1972—, DOE grantee in hot dry rock geothermal energy project, 1981-90. Fellow AAAS (coun. 1970-75); mem. Am. Optical Soc., Am. Chem. Soc., Microscopy Soc. Am. (exec. sec. 1964-76), Sigma Xi, Phi Kappa Phi. Home: 1719 Hyland St Bayside CA 95524-9302

COCKWELL, JACK LYNN, business executive; b. East London, South Africa, Jan. 12, 1941; s. William Henry and Daphne (Cound) C.; children: Linda, Lorie, Leslie, Tessa, Malcolm, Gareth. M.Com., U. Cape Town, 1964, postgrad. with distinction, 1966. Chartered Acct. Mgr. Touche Ross & Co., Cape Town and Montreal, 1959-67; exec. v.p., chief oper. officer Edper Enterprises Ltd., Toronto, Ont., Can., 1968-90, Brascan Corp., Toronto, 1979-91, pres. and CEO, 1991—2002, group chmn., 2002—. Bd. dirs. Falconbridge Inc., Noranda Inc., Nexfor Inc., Great Lakes Power, Inc., Brookfield Properties, Inc., Astral Media Inc. Chmn. bd. trustees Royal Ont. Mus.; bd. dirs. C.D. Howe Inst. Office: Brascan Corp Ste 300 181 Bay St PO Box 762 Toronto ON Canada M5J 2T3 E-mail: dhorton@brascancorp.com.

COCO, MARK STEVEN, lawyer; b. Alliance, Ohio, Nov. 1, 1952; s. John Robert and Mabel Ann C.; children: Steven, Matthew. BA cum laude, Ohio State U., 1974, JD summa cum laude, 1977. Bar: Ohio 1977, U.S. Dist. Ct. (no. and so. dists.) Ohio 1977. Assoc. Schwartz, Kelm, Warren & Rubenstein, Columbus, Ohio, 1977-80, Jones, Day, Reavis & Pogue, Columbus, Ohio, 1980-87; ptnr. Minton, Leslie & Coco, Columbus, Ohio, 1987-89, Jones, Troyan, Coco, Pappas & Perkins, Columbus, 1989-94, Harris, McClellan, Binau & Cox, Columbus, 1994—. Mem. ABA (litigation sect.), Ohio Bar Assn. (labor and litigation sect.), Columbus Bar Assn., Ohio State U. Alumni Assn., Order of Coif. Home: 8622 Gairloch Ct Dublin OH 43017-9754 E-mail: mcoco@hmbc.com.

COCO, SAMUEL BARBIN, venture consultant; b. Cottonport, La., Nov. 6, 1927; s. Samuel Barbin and Hattie (Smith) C.; m. Hannalou John, June 25, 1957; children: Harvey Samuel, Caroline Shannon BS in Mech. Engring., La. State U., 1950; postgrad., MIT, 1964. Engr. Cabot Corp., Ville Platte, La., 1950-52, mfg. dept. Pampa, Tex., 1952-56, sales rep. Akron, Ohio, 1956-60, exec. asst. Boston, 1960-64, asst. gen. mgr. carbon black div., 1964-70, v.p., gen. mgr. carbon black div., 1970-77, sr. v.p., 1977-85, exec. v.p., 1985-89, pres., 1989-91, also bd. dirs., 1992; pres. Barbin Corp., Wellesley Hills, Mass., 1992—. Co-chair Bd. of Overseers. Mem. Spaulding Rehab. Hosp., Boston, Corp. Ptnrs. Healthcare, Inc.; overseer Newton-Wellesley Hosp.; dir. Wellesley (Mass.) Cmty. Ctr. Avocations: running, cooking. Office: Barbin Corp 30 Sawyer Rd Wellesley Hills MA 02481-2936

COCOLIS, PETER KONSTANTINE, business development executive; b. Stamford, Conn., Sept. 22, 1942; s. Gus and Agnes (Vender) C.; m. Lorraine Patricia Marut, July 2, 1966; children: Peter Konstantine Jr., William Jonathan. BS in Engring., Boston U., 1964; MBA, Auburn U., 1976; cert., Def. Sys. Mgmt. Coll., 1973; cert. in nat. and internat. security mgmt., Harvard U., 1996. Commd. 2nd lt. USAF, 1964, advanced through grades to lt. col., 1980, ret., 1984; mktg. mgr. N.Am. Aircraft Rockwell Internat., Washington, 1984-87, dir.

mktg. and govt. affairs, 1987-89; dir. bus. devel. and govt. affairs Rocketdyne divsn. Rockwell Internat., Washington, 1989-95; sr. dir. bus. and govt. affairs N.Am. Aircraft divsn. Rockwell Internat., Washignton, 1995-96; sr. dir. bus. and govt. affairs The Boeing Co., Washignton, 1996-2000; v.p. Washington ops. ARES Corp., Alexandria, Va., 2001—02; sr. dir. domestic mktg. The Boeing Co., Arlington, Va., 2002—. Contbr. articles to profl. jours. Bd. dirs. Lakeforest Home Owners Assn., Springfield, Va., 1985-88; v.p. Morwood Estates Home Owners Assn.; swimming ofcl. U.S. Swimming Orgn., No. Va., 1981-91. Decorated DFC, Air medals. Mem. AIAA (sr., coun. mem., com. chmn., bd. dirs.), Am. Mgmt. Assn., Nat. Space Club, Air Force Assn., Navy League, Emeritus Found. (bd. dirs., com. chmn.), Clifton Lions. Avocations: racquetball sailing, reading, swimming. Office: The Boeing Co 1421 Jefferson Davis Hwy Arlington VA 22202 E-mail: peter.k.cocolis@boeing.com.

COCOVES, ANITA PETZOLD, psychotherapist; b. Princeton, N.J., June 2, 1957; d. Charles Bernard and Kathleen Marie (McDonald) Petzold; m. Nicholas John Cocoves, Oct. 11, 1997; 1 child, Nicholas Euthymius. AS in Bus., Indian River C.C., Ft. Pierce, Fla., 1986; BS in Liberal Studies, Barry U., 1988; MS in Human Svcs. Adminstrn., Nova U., 1989, postgrad., 1989-91; PhD in Human Svcs. Adminstrn., LaSalle U., 1994. Lic. mental health counselor, Fla.; cert. addictions profl.; internat. cert. alcohol and drug abuse counselor; nat. cert. counselor; cert. employee assistance counselor; nat. cert. clin. mental health counselor; nat. cert. addictions counselor; cert. DUI instr.; cert. family and county ct. mediator. Admissions coord. The Palm Beach Inst., West Palm Beach, Fla., 1985-86; dir. admissions Heritage Health Corp., Jensen Beach, Fla., 1986-89; drug abuse strategy coord. Martin County Bd. of County Commrs., Stuart, Fla., 1989—; health and human svcs. adminstr. Martin County Bd. of County Commr., Stuart, Fla., 2001—. Mem. Drug Resource Team for the 12th Congl. Dist., Fla., 1990—, Juvenile Justice Assn. of the 19th Jud. Ct., Fla., 1993—, vice chmn. 1999—; grant writer in field. Vol. Hist. Soc. Martin County, Stuart, 1986—; mem. United Way Martin County, Stuart, 1993; mem. bd. dirs. Cmty. AIDS Adv. Project, Stuart, 1993; chmn. treatment com. Martin County Task Force on Substance Abused Children, Stuart, 1993; chmn. Legis. Subcom. Martin County Juvenile Justice Com., 1998—. Recipient Outstanding Cmty. Svc. award United Way Martin County, Stuart, 1993. Mem. NASW, Am. Mental Health Counselors Assn., Nat. Criminal Justice Assn., Nat. Assn. Alcoholism and Drug Abuse Counselors, Nat. Consortium Treatment Alternatives to St. Crime Programs, Am. Coll. Addiction Treatment Adminstrs., Am. Labor-Mgmt. Adminstrs., Fla. Alcohol and Drug Abuse Assn. Republican. Roman Catholic. Avocations: walking, reading. Office: Martin County Bd County Commrs 400 SE Osceola St Stuart FL 34994-2504

COCOZZOLI, GARY RICHARD, library director; b. Detroit, Oct. 27, 1951; s. Berto and Yolanda Virginia Cocozzoli. BA in Geography, Wayne State U., Detroit, 1973, MLS, 1974. With serials and interloan dept. Lawrence Inst. Tech., Southfield, Mich., 1975-81; dir. libr. Lawrence Tech. U., Southfield, 1981—. Mem. exec. bd. Mich. Libr. Consortium, 1994-97. Author: (with others) German-American History and Life, 1980, Japan's Economic Challenge, 1988; reviewer: Am. Reference Books Annual, 1985—. Pres. Cambridge Village Assn., Southfield, 1987 . Recipient Disting. Alumnus award libr. sci. program Wayne State U., 1990, Marburger Exellence in Achievement award, Adminstr. of Yr. award, 1998. Mem. ALA, Mich. Libr. Assn. (acad. divsn. bd. 1986-88, continuing edn. com. 1992-94, bd. mgmt. and adminstrv. divsn. 1998-2000), Spl. Librs. Assn. (career devel. com. 1987-88), S.E. Mich. League Librs. (chair 1988-90, bd. dirs. 1996-98), Coun. on Resource Devel. (chmn. Oakland County, Mich. 1990-91, sec. coun. resource devel. 1996-97), Mich. Libr. Exch. (steering com. 2001—), Toastmasters. Office: Lawrence Tech U 21000 W Ten Mile Rd Southfield MI 48075-1058 E-mail: grc@ltu.edu.

CODD, RICHARD TRENT, JR., computer scientist, educator; b. June 1, 1945; s. Richard Trent and Mildred Joyce Codd; m. Celine Marie Morisset, Aug. 10, 1968; children: Richard Trent III, Patrick Timothy, Matthew Paul, Kevin Andrew. AA, Miami-Dade C.C., 1967; BS, U. Miami, 1970, MA, 1974; BS, Fla. Internat. U., 1985. Lic. tchr., ednl. adminstr., Fla. Audio technician U. Miami, Coral Gables, Fla., 1968-71; tchr. Archbishop Curley H.S., Miami, 1972-74, St. Brendan H.S., Miami, 1974-80, adminstr., 1980-87, asst. prin., dir. computer svcs., 1981-87; instr. St. Thomas U., Opa Locka, Fla., 1980-87, St. John Vianney Coll. Sem., Miami, 1985-87, A.C. Reynolds H.S., Asheville, N.C., 1988-90, U. N.C., Asheville, 1988—, Advanced Edn. Ctr., Asheville, 1990-92; instr. math. Asheville-Buncombe Tech. C.C., Asheville, 2000—. Math. instr., computer applications programmer Haywood C.C., Clyde, N.C., 1991-99; bus. ptnr. Raintree House, 1992—; software systems developer Archdiocese of Miami, 1984-87; bd. dirs. Archdiocese of Miami Credit Union, 1979-80; developer Master Acad. Record/Scheduling ADP System, Univ./C.C. Class Scheduling ADP System. Mem. Math. Assn. Am. Republican. Roman Catholic. Avocations: music, hiking, boating. Office: Asheville-Buncombe Tech C C 340 Victoria Rd Asheville NC 28801-4897

CODDINGTON, ANNE LILLIAN, retired English literature educator; b. Shearstown, Newfoundland, Can., Nov. 12, 1918; came to U.S., 1943; d. James and Emily (Beecham) Sparkes; m. Walter Goretski, Oct. 2, 1941 (div. 1950); m. David M. Archibald, Sept. 24, 1951 (dec. Sept. 1953); m. David L. Coddington, Mar. 16, 1958 (dec. June 1979); children: Patricia Anne Kilbourn, James Sparkes Goretski Coddington. BA, Rutgers U., 1972, MA, 1974, PhD, 1987. Part time English instr. Rutgers U., Newark, 1972-87, lectr., 1987-99; instr. N.J. Inst. Tech., Newark, 1993-2000; ret., 2000. V.p. Evang. Hour Inc., 1968-71. Republican. Presbyterian. Home: 90 Carteret St Glen Ridge NJ 07028-2004

CODDINGTON, CLINTON HAYS, lawyer; b. Honolulu, July 8, 1939; s. L. Clinton and Patricia Carolyn (Richer) C.; m. Martha Ann Stevens, June 20, 1970; children: Clinton Stevens, Catherine Hadley. BSCE, U.S. Mil. Acad., 1961; JD, U. Calif., Berkeley, 1968. Bar: Calif. 1969, U.S. Ct. Appeals (2nd, 5th, 7th, 8th and 9th cirs.), U.S. Supreme Ct. 1974. Assoc. Bronson, Bronson & McKinnon, San Francisco, 1969-70, Rogers Majeski Kohn Bentley Wagner & Kane, Redwood City, Calif., 1970-77, Tucker & Coddington, Palo Alto, Calif., 1977-78; ptnr., pres. Coddington, Hicks & Danforth, Redwood City, 1978—. Contbr. articles to profl. jours. Chmn. Easter Seals; vestryman, sr. warden, chancellor various Episcopal chs.; pres. Chinquapin Homeowners Assn., Lake Tahoe, Calif., 1991-92, Stanford Hills Homeowners Assn., Palo Alto, Calif. Capt. U.S. Army, 1961-64. Mem. ABA, Assn. Def. Counsel of No. Calif., Lawyer/Pilot Bar Assn., Internat. Assn. Def. Counsel, San Mateo County Bar Assn., Calif. Bar Assn., Def. Rsch. Inst., Am. Bd. Trial Advocates. Republican. Avocations: guitar, classical music, aviation, boating, reading. Office: Coddington Hicks & Danforth 555 Twin Dolphin Dr Ste 300 Redwood City CA 94065-2133 E-mail: codsqd@attbi.com., ccoddington@chdlawyers.com.

CODDINGTON, JONATHAN A. curator, research scientist; BS, Yale U., 1975; MA, PhD, Harvard U., 1984. Rsch. scientist, curator arachnida and myriapoda Nat. Mus. Natural History, Washington, 1983—. Contbr. articles to profl. jours. Office: Nat Mus Natural History Dept Entomology Smithsonian Instn NHB 105 Washington DC 20013-7012

CODE, ARTHUR DODD, astrophysics educator; b. Bklyn., Aug. 13, 1923; 4 children. MS, U. Chgo., 1947, PhD, 1950. Asst. Yerkes Obs. U. Chgo., 1946-49; instr. U. Va., Charlottesville, 1950; instr. then asst. prof. astronomy U. Wis., Madison, 1951-56, prof., 1969-92, prof. emeritus, 1992—; mem. staff Mt. Wilson and Palomar Obs. Calif. Inst. Tech., Pasadena, 1956-58, prof., 1958-69; adj. prof. U. Ariz., Tucson, 1992—. Hilldale prof., dir. Space Astronomy Lab. U. Wis. Recipient Disting. Pub. Svc. medal and Pub. Svc. award NASA, Profl. Achievement award U. Chgo. Mem. NAS, Am. Acad. Arts and Scis., Internat. Acad. Astronautics, Assn. of Univs. for Rsch. in Astronomy (chmn. bd. dirs. 1977-80.), Am. Astronomical Soc. (pres. 1982-84). Office: U Wis Madison WI 53714

CODELL, JULIE FRANCIA, academic administrator, educator; b. Chgo., Sept. 19, 1945; d. Seymour and Rosalie Codell; 1 child, Ethan Granger. AB in English, Vassar Coll., 1967; MA in English, U. Mich., 1968; MA in Art History, Ind. U., 1975, PhD in Comparative Lit., 1978. Instr. English Western Ill. U., Macomb, 1968-71; prof., dept. chair art dept. U. Mont., Missoula, 1979-90; dir. sch. of art Ariz. State U., Tempe, 1991—2001, prof. art history, English, 2001—. Author: The Victorian Artist, 2003; (with others) Reframing Pre-Raphaelites, 1995, Towards a Modern Art World, 1995, Collecting Pre-Raphaelites, 1997, Biographical Passages, 2000, John Everett Millais, 2001; editor: Imperial Co-Histories, 2003; co-editor, author: Orientalism Transposed, 1998; mem. editl. bd. Victorian Periodicals Rev., 1992—; contbr. articles to profl. jours. Fellowship Nat. Endowment for Humanities, 1992-93, travel grant, 1986, 90, fellowship Yale U., 1994, Sr. Scholar Travel fellowship Am. Inst. Indian Studies, 2002, Skaaren Film fellowship Ransom Humanities Ctr. U. Tex., Austin, 2002; recipient summer stipend NEH, 1988. Mem. MLA, Coll. Art Assn., Historians of Brit. Art (exec. bd. 1993-97), Rsch. Soc. for Victorian Periodicals (v.p. 1997-99, pres. 1999-2001), Assn. for Asian Studies, Assn. for Art Historians. Office: Sch of Art Ariz State U Tempe AZ 85287-1505 E-mail: julie.codell@asu.edu.

CODERE, HELEN FRANCES, anthropologist, educator, university dean; b. Winnipeg, Man., Can., Sept. 10, 1917; came to U.S., 1919, naturalized, 1924; d. Charles Francis and Mabelle (Prosser) C. BA summa cum laude, U. Minn., 1939; PhD, Columbia, 1950. Instr. Vassar Coll, 1946-50, asst. prof., 1951-53, asso. prof., 1955-57, prof., 1958-63; vis. lectr. anthropology U. B.C., 1954-55, Northwestern U., winter 1963; mem. faculty Bennington Coll., 1963-64; prof. anthropology Brandeis U., 1964-82; dean Brandeis U. (Grad. Sch. Arts and Scis.), 1975-77, retired, 1982; anthrop. fieldwork Kwakiutl Indians of, B.C., 1951-55, 1959-60. Mem. adv. panel on anthropology Nat. Sci. Found., 1968-71 Author: Fighting with Property: A Study of Kwakiutl Potlatching and Warfare, 1792-1930, 1950, The Biography of an African Society, Rwanda 1900-1960; also articles.; Editor: Kawkiutl Ethnography (Franz Boas), 1966. Faculty fellow Vassar Coll., 1956; Social Sci. Research Council fellow, 1956, 62-63; Guggenheim fellow, 1959-60 Fellow Am. Anthrop. Assn. (exec. council 1966-69), AAAS; mem. Am. Ethnol. Soc. (pres. 1972-73), Northeastern Anthrop. Assn. (pres. 1973), Phi Beta Kappa. Home: 100 Newbury Ct Ste 609 Concord MA 01742

CODERRE, DENIS, legislator; m. Chantale Renaud; children: Geneviève, Alexandre. BA in Polit. Sci., U. Montreal. Mem. Parliament, Canada, 1997—, sec. of state for Amateur Sport, 1999—2002, min., Citizenship and Immigration Can., 2002—. Former pres. Young Liberals of Can., organizer; chair Quebec Liberal Caucus, 1998. Liberal Party Can. Office: Honourable Denis Coderre Citizenship and Immigration Canada Ottawa ON Canada K1A 1L1

CODERRE, NANCY ADELE, financial analyst; b. Cleve., Aug. 21, 1962; d. Richard Alfred and Julia (Viedt) C. BA, U. Colo., 1984; MBA with high honors, Babson Coll., 1986. Cert. mgmt. acct. Sr. cost acct. M/A Com., Omni Spectra, Waltham, Mass., 1987-88; fin. analyst Analogic Corp., Peabody, Mass., 1988-93, Carrier Corp., Syracuse, N.Y., 1994 95; product specialist SAS Inst., Cary, NC, 1995—. Mem. Inst. Mgmt. Accts., Beta Gamma Sigma. Avocations: swimming, chess. Home: 205 Livingstone Drive Cary NC 27513 E-mail: nancy.coderre@SAS.com.

CODESPOTI, DANIEL JOSEPH, computer science educator; b. Charleston, S.C., Jan. 18, 1941; s. Peter J. Sr. and Eula Lee (Pellum) C.; m. Sandra Lynn Huey, Mar. 16, 1963; 1 child, Daniel J. Jr. BA, Auburn U., 1964; MS, U. Mo., Rolla, 1974; PhD, Kans. State U., 1977. Computer programmer Auburn (Ala.) U., 1964-66; computer programmer, instr. S.E. Mo. State U., Cape Girardeau, 1969-73; grad. tchg. asst. Kans. State U., Manhattan, 1974-77; asst. prof. U. S.C., Columbia, 1977-79, Spartanburg, 1980-82, assoc. prof., 1982-90, prof. computer sci., 1990—. Propr. So. Computer Svcs., Mayo, S.C., 1981—. Pres. Spartanburg PC Users Group, 1989-90; v.p. chpt. S.C. State Employees, Spartanburg, 1993-94, pres., 1994-95, 98-2001. Lt. USNR, 1966-69. Mem. IEEE, Assn. Computing Machinery, S.C. Acad. Sci. Avocation: fishing. Office: U SC Spartanburg 800 University Way Spartanburg SC 29303-4999 E-mail: dcodespoti@gw.uscs.edu.

CODEY, RICHARD J. state legislator; b. Orange, N.J., Nov. 27, 1946; m. Mary Jo Rolli; children: Kevin X, Christopher Y. BA, Fairleigh Dickinson U. Mem. N.J. Gen. Assembly, Trenton, N.J. Senate, Dist. 27, Trenton, 1982—. Pres. Olympic Agy.; former acting gov.; Dem. Senate pres. Recipient Svc. award N.J. Mental Health Assn., Svc. award N.J. Prosecutor's Assn.; named Citizen of Yr., N.J. Psychiat. Assn. Mem. Nat. Assn. Funeral Dirs., State Assn. Funeral Dirs. Office: NJ Senate PO Box 099 State Capitol Trenton NJ 08625 also: 449 Mount Pleasant Ave West Orange NJ 07052-2734*

CODISPOTI, ANDRE JOHN, allergist, immunologist; b. Bklyn., Apr. 27, 1938; s. Bruno Mario and Antoinette (Savarese) C.; m. Miranda Babini, June 14, 1967; children: Rita, Elisa, Andrew. BA, Coll. of Holy Cross, 1959; MD, U. Bologna, Italy, 1965. Diplomate Am. Bd. Pediatrics, Am. Bd. Allergy and Immunology. Rotating intern Long Island Coll. Hosp., Bklyn., 1966, resident in pediatrics, 1967-69, fellow in allergy and immunology, 1971-73; pvt. practice Suffern, N.Y., 1972—. Maj. M.C., U.S. Army, 1969-71. Fellow Am. Coll. Allergy, Asthma and Immunology, Am. Acad. Allergy, Asthma and Immunology. Republican. Roman Catholic. Avocations: reading, music, travel, tennis, skiing. Office: 7 Hemion Rd Suffern NY 10901-4903 also: 70 Gilbert St Monroe NY 10950-1538 E-mail: acodispotimd@aol.com.

CODRON, MICHAEL VICTOR, theatrical producer; b. June 8, 1930; s. I.A. and Lily (Morganstern) C. Ed., St. Paul's Sch.; BA, Worcester Coll., Oxford U. Dir. Hampstead Theatre; adminstr. Aldwych Theatre; Cameron Mackintosh prof. contemporary theatre Oxford U., Eng., 1993. Prodns. include: Breath of Spring, 1957; The Birthday Party, 1958; Pieces of Eight, 1959; The Caretaker, 1960; The Tenth Man, 1961; Rattle of a Simple Man, 1962; Next Time I'll Sing to You, Private Lives, The Lovers and the Dwarfs, Cockade, 1963; Poor Bitos, The Formation Dancers, Entertaining Mr. Sloane, 1964; Loot, The Killing of Sister George, Ride a Cock Horse, 1965; Little Malcolm and His Struggle Against the Eunuchs, The Anniversary, There's a Girl in My Soup, Big Bad Mouse, 1966; The Judge, The Flip Side, Wise Child, The Boy Friend, 1967; Not Now Darling, The Real Inspector Hound, 1968; The Contractor, Slag, The Two of Us, The Philanthropist, 1970; The Foursome, Butley, A Voyage Round My Father, The Changing Room, 1971; Veterans, Time and Time Again, Crown Matrimonial, My Fat Friend, 1972; Collaborators, Savages, Habeas Corpus, Absurd Person Singular, 1973; Knuckle, Flowers, Golden Pathway Annual, The Norman Conquests, John Paul George Ringo...and Bert, 1974; A Family and a Fortune, Alphabetical Order, A Far Better Husband, Ashes, Absent Friends, Otherwise Engaged, Stripwell, 1975; Funny Peculiar, Treats, Donkey's Years, Confusions, Teeth 'n' Smiles, Yahoo, 1976; Dusa Stas, Fish & Vi, Just Between Ourselves, Oh, Mr. Porter, Breezeblock Park, The Bells of Hell, The Old Country, 1977; The Rear Column, Ten Times Table, The Unvarnished Truth, The Homecoming, Alice's Boys, Night and Day, 1978; Joking Apart, Tishoo, Stage Struck, 1979; Dr. Faustus, Make and Break, The Dresser, Taking Steps, Enjoy, 1980; Hinge & Bracket, Rowan Atkinson in Revue, House Guest, Quartermaine's Terms, 1981; Season's Greetings, Noises Off, Funny Turns, 1982, The Real Thing, 1982; The Hard Shoulder, 1983; Look, No Hans!, Benefactors, 1984; Jumpers, Who Plays Wins, Clockwise (film), 1985, Made in Bangkok, 1986, Woman in Mind, 1986; Hapgood, Uncle Vanya, Re Joyce!, The Sneeze, Henceforward, 1988; The Cherry Orchard, 1989; Man of the Moment, Look, Look, Hidden Laughter, Private Lives, 1990, What the Butler Saw, 70 Girls 70, The Revengers Comedies, 1991, The Rise and Fall of Little Voice, 1992, Time of My Life, 1993, Jamais Vu, 1993, Dead Funny, 1994, Arcadia, 1994, The Sisters Rosensweig, 1994, Indian Ink, 1995, The Killing of Sister George, 1995, Dealer's Choice, 1995, The Shakespeare Revue, 1995, A Talent to Amuse, 1996, Tom and Clem, 1997, Silhouette Heritage, 1997, Things We Do For Love, 1998, Elton John's Glasses, 1998, Alarms and Excursions, 1998, The Invention of Love, 1998, Copenhagen, 1999 (Tony award, 2000), Quartet, 1999, Comic Potential, 1999, Peggy For You, 2000, Blue/Orange, 2001, Life After George, 2002, Bedroom Farce, 2002, Damsels in Distress, 2002, My Brilliant Divorce, 2003. Recipient Michael Victor Codron CBE; emeritus fellow ST. Catherin's Coll., Oxford. Mem.: Garrick Club. Office: Aldwych Theatre London WC2B 4DF England

CODY, ALAN MORROW, financial consultant; b. Huntington, WV, June 7, 1947; s. Peer John and Nancy (Speer) C.; m. Elisabeth Anne Allen, Nov. 29, 1969; 1 child, David Miles. AB, Cornell U., 1969; SM, MIT, 1974. Economist Data Resources Inc., Lexington, Mass., 1974-76, dir. indls. mktg., v.p., 1976-79; v.p. The Planning Economics Group, Woburn, Mass., 1979-81; sr. mgr. Mitchell and Co., Cambridge, Mass., 1982-84; sr. cons. Arthur D. Little, Inc., Cambridge, 1984-93; dir. valuation svcs., group Coopers & Lybrand, 1993-98; prin. Corp. Value Consulting Group Pricewaterhouse Coopers LLP, Boston, 1998—. Editor: Sloan Mgmt. Rev., Cambridge, 1973-74. Active Ripon Soc., Boston, 1982—; dir. bd. investment First Unitarian Soc. Newton (Mass.), 1984-92, chmn. bd. trustees, 1993-94; bd. dirs. Fgn. Film Soc. of Montgomery (Ala.), 1971-72, Newton Conservators, 1988-91, Newton Taxpayers Assn., 1988—, Newton Citizens Commn. on Energy, 1990-97. 1st lt. USAF, 1969-72. Mem. Inst. Chartered Fin. Analysts, Assn. Investment Mgmt. and Rsch., Boston Security Analysts Soc., Cornell Club (N.Y.). Republican. Unitarian Universalist. Office: PricewaterhouseCoopers LLP One Post Office Sq Boston MA 02109

CODY, ARLENE J. CLARK BRATTAIN, interior designer; b. Phila., July 27, 1938; d. Franklin Corning Clark and Nora May Robertson; children: Kathy, Kurt, Karen, David. Cert. in interior design, N.Y. Sch. Interior Design, 1975; BS, U. Minn., 1986. State cert. interior designer, Minn. Exec. United Way, Mpls., 1980; interior designer AB Interiors, Minnetonka, Minn., 1982—. Pvt. practice color analyst, Minnetonka, 1984—; cons. showroom Rollin B. Child Tile, Plymouth, Minn., 1985; interior designer Room & Bd. Stores, Minnetonka, 1985-86. Designer Window Fashions mag., 1988—, Am. Soc. Interior Designers Showcase Home, 1987, Showcase Home for March of Dimes, 1988, Showcase Vignette, 1989. Trainer dist. Camp Fire Girls, Minnetonka, 1967-78; trainer, leader Boy Scouts Am., Mpls., 1967-80; pres. PTA, Minnetonka, 1970; pres. Music Boosters, Minnetonka, 1976-84. Recipient Silver Fawn award Boy Scouts Am., 1973. Mem. Am. Soc. Interior Designers (profl.), Internat. Furnishings and Design Assn. (exec. 1988—), Nat. Trust for Hist. Preservation, Mensa.

CODY, FRANK JOSEPH, secondary school educator; b. Detroit, Sept. 13, 1940; s. Burns J. and Margaret (Dowley) C.; m. Shirley Black, May 16, 1992. AB, Loyola U., 1962, PhD, 1965, MA, 1966, MDiv, 1975; PhD, Ohio State U., 1980. Cert. tchr., prin., supr., Ohio, Mich. Headmaster St. Ignatius H.S., Cleve., 1977-81; dir. Chapel Sch., Sao Paulo, Brazil, 1981-83, U. Detroit Ctr. Econ. Edn., 1988-91; assoc. prof., tchr. adminstrv. edn. U. Detroit, 1983-91; adminstr. Grand Rapids Cath. Secondary Schs., 1991-95; headmaster Woodside Priory Sch., Portola Valley, Calif., 1995-97; tchr. Kalamazoo Ctrl. H.S., 1997—, asst. prin., 1998-99; dir. Small Learning Cmtys. Project, 2002—. Trustee Wheeling Coll., 1980-82, mem. Coun. Entrance Svcs. Coll. Bd., 1978-81; mem. Mich. Supt.'s Com. on Accreditation, 1984-88; commr. Nat. Assn. Secondary Sch. Prins./Carnegie Found. Commn. on Future of Am. H.S., 1994-96; dir. rsch. English lang. studies Unified Coll. Guarulhos, Sao Paulo, Brazil, 1998-2002. Co-author: Manual of Educational Risk Management, Escola e Communidade: Uma Parceria Necessaria, O Professor Do Terceiro Milenio; contbr. articles to profl. jours. Trustee Trinity Sch., Menlo Park, Calif., 1996-97; commr. planning commission City of Kalamazoo, 2003—. Mem.: Am. Classical League. Roman Catholic. Office: Kalamazoo Ctrl High Sch 2432 N Drake Rd Kalamazoo MI 49006-1361 E-mail: codyfj@kalamazoo.k12.mi.us.

CODY, HIRAM SEDGWICK, JR., retired telephone company executive; b. Nov. 1, 1915; s. Hiram Sedgwick and Harriett Mary (Collins) C.; m. Mary Vaughn Jacoby, Oct. 4, 1941; children: Margaret Vaughn, Harriett Mary, Hiram Sedgwick III, Henry Jacoby, William Collins. BS cum laude, Yale U., 1937, LLB, 1940. Bar: NC 1940. With Western Electric Co., Inc., 1946-71, regional mgr. engring. and installation, 1961-64, dir. orgn. planning N.Y.C., 1964-65, sec., treas., 1965-71; asst. treas. AT&T, N.Y.C., 1971-80; ret., 1980. V.p. Morris-Sussex coun. Boy Scouts of Am., 1970-80; vice-chmn. Zoning Bd. Adjustment Mountain Lakes, N.J., 1968-80; boro councilman, Mountain Lakes, 1960-61; trustee, treas. Asheville (N.C.) Sch., 1974-84; trustee Asheville Symphony Orch., 1981-91, Asheville Cmty. Concert Assn., 1981-91; bd. advisors Warren Wilson Coll., 1983—, chmn., 1987-90. With USN, 1941-45, MTO, comdr. USNR, 1946. Mem. N.C. State Bar, Tel. Pioneers Am. (v.p. 1969-71, treas. 1971-78), Tau Beta Pi. Home: 64 Wagon Trl Black Mountain NC 28711-2563

CODY, JUDITH, composer, writer; Student, U. Calif., Berkeley, 1977, Foothill Coll., Los Altos Hills, Calif., 1972—75; pvt. student in Japanese culture and music, 1966—68. Editor: Resource Guide on Women in Music, 1981; author: Vivian Fine: A Bio-Bibliography, 2001; (poems) Eight Frames Eight, 2002; contbr. poems to lit. jours.; composer: Trio for flute, classical guitar and poem, 1974, Firelights: Variations for classical guitar, 1976-77, City and Country Themes in G, 1976, Dances, opus 8, 1977, Nocturne, opus 9, 1977, classical guitar Seven Concert Etudes, opus 7, 10, 11, 13, 14, 15 & 18, 1977, classical guitar, Christmas Theme, opus 17, 1977, Opus 16, flute & guitar, 1977, Trio, opus 21, two flutes and guitar, 1978, Three Songs of Middle English, opus 26, voice and guitar, 1978, Sonata, opus 22, flute and guitar, 1978, Theme and Variations, opus 27, piano, 1978, Three Patterns, opus 29, piano, 1978, Two Patterns, opus 30, piano, 1978, Flute Poems, opus 19, 1978, Meditation for Four Hands, duet, steel string and classical guitars, 1983, Rain on the Face of Buddha at Kamakura, classical guitar, 1984, Three Haiku Love Songs, piano and soprano, 1986, Danger Dance, piano and soprano, 1986, Whales' Song, piano, 1986, Swan River, piano, 1986, Looking Under Footprints, voice and classical guitar, 1986, Two Songs, piano, 1999, Heart-Blood-Heart, piano, 1999, Death of a Small Animal, piano, 1999, Earth of Ukraine, piano, 1999, Song Cycle: Updated History of the Universe, classical guitr, flute ensemble, voice, 2003. Founder steering com., mem. 1st Bay Area Congress on Women in Music, San Francisco State U., 1980—81. Recipient 1st Prize poem Amelia Mag., 1993, music composition winner New Times Concerts, La. State U., 1979, winner Atlantic Monthly Poetry Contest, 1973, Hon. Mention Emily Dickinson Poetry award, 2003; poetry placed in permanent collection Smithsonian Instn., Washington, 1978. Mem. PEN, Am. Music Ctr., Poets and Writers, Inc., Bay Area Congress on Women in Music (founding Steering Com. mem.). Achievements include First to discover and document composer's creative explosions in youth and old age, 2001; first woman engineering drafter in city and county of San Francisco Power and Utilities Engineering Bureau, 1963. Avocations: soprano in opera chorus, classical guitar. E-mail: jcpoetnow@yahoo.com.

CODY, MARK EDWARD, small business owner, martial arts instructor; b. Winter Haven, Fla., Feb. 10, 1966; s. Edward Dewitt and Patricia Lynn Cody. 5th degree black belt, wado ryu karate, jujutsu kali instr. Owner Cody's Armory Inc., Winter Haven, Fla., 1986—99; owner, chief instr. Acad. of Self Def., Winter Haven, Fla., 1986—. Tactical firearms instr., 1986—; kobujutsu instr., 1986—. Author: (book) Bushido: A Modern Adaptation of the Ancient Code of the Samurai, 2000. Named Guro, Filipino Combat Systems Kali, 1999, Natas Lima, Remy Presas, Internat. Modern Arnis, 2000. Mem.: NRA (life; instr. 1986—2002). Avocation: philosophy. Home: 17 Oakwood Rd Winter Haven FL 33880-1055 Personal E-mail: bushido@tampabay.rr.com.

CODY, PETER MALCOLM, economist, development, management consultant; b. Paris, July 30, 1925; s. Edward Morrill C. and Frances (Ryan) Millington; m. Rosa Maria Alatorre, Jan. 28, 1957; children: Cornelia Francisca, Cecilia Leonor, Michael Peter, William Ryan, Peter Malcolm. BA in Internat. Rels., Yale U., 1947, MA in Econs., 1948, postgrad., 1949-50. Instr. econs. Yale U., 1948—50; economist Fed. Res. Bd., Washington, 1950—54; program economist U.S. Agy. Internat. Devel., Mexico, 1954—57, program officer, 1957—59, Laos desk officer, 1959—61, dep. dir., 1961—64; dir. Office Vets. Affairs, Washington, 1964—65; dep. dir. U.S. Agy. Internat. Devel., Laos, 1965—67, dir., 1967—71, 1971—75, dir. ops.appraisal staff, 1975—76, dir., 1976—79, 1979—80; freelance econ. and social devel. and mgmt. cons. Haiti, Mauritania, Liberia, Sudan, Zaire, Kenya, El Salvador, Guatemala, Bolivia and South Pacific, 1980—. Mem. sch. bd. Am. Sch. Laos, Vientiane, Laos, 1965-67, Am. Sch. Paraguay, Asunción, Paraguay, 1967-71, Paraguay Nat. Cultural Ctr., Asunción, 1964-71. Lt. USN, 1943—46. Recipient Orden Nacional del Merito Pres. of Paraguay, 1971, Meritorious Svc. award US AID, 1981. Mem. Am. Econ. Assn., 1947-85, Am. Fgn. Svc. Assn., 1960—, Cosmos Club, Washington, 1994—. Avocations: computers, reading, tennis, skiing, hiking. Home: 5600 Wisconsin Ave Apt 606 Chevy Chase MD 20815-4410

CODY, RICHARD A. army officer; b. Montpelier, Vt., Aug. 20, 1950; m. Vicki Lyn Cody; children: Clint, Tyler. BS, U.S. Mil. Acad., 1972. Master army aviator. Commd. 2d lt. U.S. Army, 1972, advanced through grades to brig. gen.; comdr. 1st bn., 101st aviation regt. 101stAairborne Divsn., Operation Desert Storm; bn. exec. officer, co. comdr. Attack Helicopter Bns.; asst. divsn. comdr. for maneuver 4th Inf. Divsn. (Mechanized), 1998—. Decorated Legion of Merit with 2 oak leaf clusters, DFC, Bronze Star medal, Air medals, others.

CODY, SARA ELIZABETH, librarian; b. St. Louis, Feb. 23, 1950; d. John Patrick and Martha Elizabeth (Brown) C. B Individualized Studies, George Mason U., 1983; MLS, N.C. Ctrl. U., 1991. Cert. libr., N.C., Ga. Libr. asst. Glencarlyn br. Arlington (Va.) Pub. Libr., 1981-84; reference dept. librarian Randolph County Pub. Libr., Asheboro, N.C., 1984-88; serials asst. Perkins Libr., Duke U., Durham, N.C., 1988-89; libr. tech. Durham Tech. C.C. Libr., 1989-91; extension librarian N.W. Ga. Regional Libr., Dalton, 1991—98; reference libr. Brunswick-Glynn Regional Libr., Brunswick, Ga., 1998—. Mem. ALA, Bus. and Profl. Women's Assn. (treas. 1994—). Avocations: walking, music. Office: Brunswick-Glynn Regional Libr 208 Gloucester St Brunswick GA 31525

CODY, THOMAS GERALD, management consultant, writer; b. Holyoke, Mass., Feb. 18, 1929; s. John Francis and Mary Gertrude (Scanlon) C.; m. Kathleen Mary Maguire, Nov. 17, 1956; children— Kathleen, Joseph. AB, Coll. of Holy Cross, 1950; postgrad., Boston Coll., 1950-52; MBA, Harvard U., 1957. Various corp. mgmt. positions, 1955—62; cons., prin., v.p. Fry Cons., Inc., Chgo., L.A., Washington, 1962—72; exec. dir. U.S. Equal Employment Opportunity Commn., Washington, 1972—74; asst. sec. for adminstrn. HUD, Washington, 1974—76; Washington v.p., mgr. L.B. Knight & Assoc., Inc., 1976—79; pres. Lester B. Knight Mgmt. Cons. Group, 1979—81, Thomas Cody & Assoc., Annapolis, Md., 1981—84; v.p. human resources Baxter Travenol Labs. Inc., Deerfield, Ill., 1984—86, corp. v.p., 1985—87; exec. v.p., Chgo. office Jannotta Bray & Assoc. Inc., 1987—, ptnr. Washington office, 1989—96; prin. The Washington Group, 1996—. Author: Management Consulting: A Game Without Chips, 1986, Strategy of a Megamerger, 1990, Innovating For Health, 1994. Mem. U.S. Arch. and Transp. Barriers Compliance Bd., 1974-76, Anne Arundel Commn. on Women, 1977-79, U.S. Comptr. Gen. Adv. Panel, 1983-88; bd. dirs. Found. for Jr. Blind, L.A., 1968-70, Baxter Am. Found., 1986-88, Suburban Cook County Area Agy. on Aging, 1988-89; trustee St. Mary of the Woods Coll., Terre Haute, Ind., 1987-90; mem. panel on employers and working families NAS. 1st lt. USMC, 1953-55. Mem. Harvard Club of N.Y.C. Home: 5450 Whitley Park Ter Apt 303 Bethesda MD 20814-2054 E-mail: thomas-cody@hotmail.com.

CODY, WILLIAM BERMOND, political science educator; b. Brunswick, Ga., Jan. 15, 1949; s. Bermond Hamp and Dorothy Jane (Satterfield) C.; m. Mildred Ann McInnis, Sept. 5, 1970; children: Margaret Jae, Elizabeth Joelle. AB, U. Ga., 1971, MA, 1973, JD, 1986; PhD, New Sch. Social Rsch., 1980. Bar: Ga. 1986. Student advisor New Sch. Social Rsch., N.Y.C., 1978-79; asst. to pres. Robeal Mgmt. Co., Charleston, S.C., 1983-85; assoc. Carr, Tabb & Pope, Atlanta, 1987; legal asst. Ga. Ct. Appeals, Atlanta, 1987-89; asst. prof. polit. sci. U. Ga., Athens, 1989-90; asst. prof. Oxford (Ga.) Coll. Emory U., 1990-93; assoc. prof. Oxford (Ga.) Coll. Emory U., 1993—. Adj. instr. Coll. New Rochelle, N.Y., 1978-79; vis. asst. prof. Clemson (S.C.) U., 1980-83; mem. Emory U. Senate, 1995-97, pres.-elect, 1996-97, pres., 1997-98. Vestryman St. Bede's Episcopal Ch., Atlanta, 1988-92, jr. warden, 1990, sr. warden, 1991; bd. dirs. Interfaith, Inc., Atlanta, 1989-90. Mem. ABA, Am. Polit. Sci. Assn., Ga. Polit. Sci. Assn., So. Polit. Sci. Assn., Am. Hist. Assn., Acad. Polit. Sci., Ga. Bar Assn. Democrat. Office: Polit Sci Dept Oxford Coll Emory U Oxford GA 30054 E-mail: bcodyW@emory.edu.

CODY, WILMER ST. CLAIR, retired educational administrator, educational policy consultant; b. Mobile, Ala., Jan. 1, 1937; s. Wilmer St. Clair and Madeline (Maygarden) C.; m. Caroline Marie Burns, Aug. 16, 1958; children: David Marshall, Alison Marie. AB, Harvard U., 1959, EdM, 1960, EdD, 1968. Tchr. Newton (Mass.) Schs., 1960, Mobile County Schs., 1960-62, prin., 1962-64; dir. tchr. edn. Atlanta Schs., 1966-67; supt. Chapel Hill (N.C.) Schs., 1967-71; sr. research assoc. Nat. Inst. Edn., 1971-73; supt. Birmingham (Ala.) City Schs., 1973-83, Montgomery County Schs., Rockville, Md., 1983-87; dir. nat. assessment project Council Chief State Sch. Officers, 1987-88; supt. edn. State of La., 1988-92; exec. dir. Nat. Edn. Goals Panel, Washington, 1992-93; dir. Nat. Faculty/So. Region, New Orleans, 1993-95; commr. edn. State of Ky., Frankfort, 1995-99. Cons. in field; mem. Nat. Assessment Governing Bd., 1998-2002. Contbr. articles to ednl. jours. Mem. Nat. Adv. Com. on Juvenile Justice and Delinquency Prevention, 1976-78; bd. dirs. Comty. Chest, Campfire Girls; trustee Nat. Coun. Econ. Edn., So. Assn. Colls. and Schs., 1990-92; chmn. Nat. Assessment Edn. Policy Com., 1983-87; dir. S.W. Edn. Devel. Lab., 1988-92; steering com. Edn. Commn. of the States, 1990-92, So. Region Edn. Bd., 1990-92, 96-99; exec. bd. Nat. Coun. for Accreditation of Tchr. Edn., 1990-92, 96-98, chair 1998; pres. Coun. Chief State Officers, 1997-98. Named Educator of Yr. ALA, 1977. Mem. Am. Assn. Sch. Adminstrs., Am. Edn. Research Assn., Phi Delta Kappa. Methodist. Home: 1535 Eleonore St New Orleans LA 70115-4242

COE, BENJAMIN PLAISTED, retired state official; b. Long Beach, Calif., Aug. 24, 1930; s. Benjamin and Mary Plaisted (Ricker) C.; m. Margaret Jane Butler, Sept. 5, 1953; children: Benjamin B., Elizabeth C., Mary Susan, Margaret Jane. AB, Bowdoin Coll., 1953; BS, Ch.E., MIT, 1953. Lic. profl. engr., N.Y. With silicone products dept. Gen. Electric Co., Waterford, N.Y., 1953-65, process econs. engr., 1963-65; exec. dir. Vols. for Internat. Tech. Assistance, Schenectady, 1965-68, exec. dir. U.S.A. div., 1969-73, v.p., 1971-73; exec. dir. Tug Hill Commn., N.Y. State, 1973-93; ret. Tug Hill Commn., 1993. Vestryman Trinity Episcopal Ch., 1978-81, warden, 1981-86, 93-96; bd. dirs. Schenectady Symphony, 1969; chmn. pub. svc. divsn. Jefferson County United Way, 1982-84, bd. dirs., 1985-88, 2d v.p., 1988-89, 1st v.p., 1990-91, pres., 1992-94; pres. Vol. Ctr. Jefferson County, 1994-96, 98—. Named Exec. of Yr. Watertown Profl. Secs. Internat., 1978-79; recipient Ageless Achievers award, N.Y. State. Mem. AIChE (chmn. N.E. N.Y. sect. 1965), ASPA, Rotary (pres. Watertown 1989-90, dist. gov. 1996-97, Citation for Meritorious Svc. 2002), Phi Beta Kappa, Sigma Xi, Tau Beta Pi. Home: 314 Paddock St Watertown NY 13601-3943 *I have come to think that success should be measured internally, between man and his maker, rather than by external signs. My goals are to involve myself with mankind in a worthwile way and at the same time keep my family fed, healthy, and in a position to work toward their own goals.*

COE, DONALD KIRK, retired university official; b. Tuscaloosa, Ala., Nov. 21, 1934; s. Glen Dale and Hazel Mae (Coley) C.; m. Frances Ellen Truman, May 31, 1958; children: Mark William, Sandra Elizabeth, Bonnie Lee. BA, U. Ala., 1957. Wire editor Xenia (Ohio) Daily Gazette, 1958-59; reporter, county editor Sharon (Pa.) Herald, 1959-61; asst. wire editor Pitts. Press, 1961-66; in public relations and fund raising Carnegie-Mellon U., Pitts., 1966-70; editorial writer St. Petersburg (Fla.) Times, 1970-75; chief editorial writer Chgo. Sun-Times, 1975-84; univ. dir. pub. affairs U. Ill., 1984-98, spl. asst. to pres., 1998-2000; ret., 2000. Pres. Nat. Conf. Editorial Writers Found., 1989-91. Capt. USAR, 1958-68. Recipient Ill. UPI award, 1977 Mem. Sigma Delta Chi (pres. coll. chpt. 1957) Presbyterian. Home: 723 Bonnie Brae Pl River Forest IL 60305-1930

COE, FREDRIC L. physician, educator, researcher; b. Chgo, Dec. 25, 1936; s. Lester J. and Lillian (Chaitlen) C.; m. Eleanor Joyce Brodny, May 5, 1965; children: Brian, Laura. AB, U. Chgo., 1955; MS, U. Chgo., 1957; MD, U. Chgo., 1961. Diplomate Am. Bd. Internal Medicine. Intern Michael Reese Hosp., Chgo., 1961-62, resident, 1962-65, U. Tex. S.W. Med. Sch., 1967-69; chmn. nephrology Michael Reese Hosp., 1972-82; prof. medicine U. Chgo., 1977—, prof. physiology, 1979—; chmn. nephrology A.M. Billings Hosp., Chgo., 1982—; founder, pres. Litholink Corp., 1995—. Author: Nephrolithiasis, 1978, 2d edit. (with J. Parks), 1987, (with B. Brenner and F.C. Rector) Renal Physiology, 1986, Clinical Nephrology; editor: Renal Therapeutics, 1978, Nephrolithiasis, 1980, Hypercalciuric States, 1983, (with M. Favus) Disorders of Bone and Mineral Metabolism, 1993, 2d edit., 2001; editor-in-chief Yearbook of Nephrology, 1991-96; editor: (with others) Kidney Stones: Medical and Surgical Management, 1996. Served to capt. USAF, 1961-67. Recipient Belding Scribner medal for lifetime achievement in clin. rsch. Am. Soc. Nephrology, 2000; Univ. of Chgo. Distinguished Svc. Award, 2001; grantee NIH, 1977— . Fellow ACP; mem. Am. Soc. Clin. Investigation, Am. Physiol. Soc., Assn. Am. Physicians Jewish. Achievements include first evidence for hyperuricosuria as cause of calcium renal stones; discovery of nephro calcin a protein inhibitor of crystal growth; first demonstration that human idiopathic hypercalciuris is hereditary. Home: 5490 S South Shore Dr Chicago IL 60615-5984 Office: U Chgo Med Ctr 5841 S Maryland Ave Chicago IL 60637-1463

COE, HENRY H. R. state legislator; b. Cody, Wyo., Apr. 29, 1946; married. Student, U. Wyo. Mem. Wyo. Senate, Dist. 18, Cheyenne, 1988—; mem. travel, recreation, wildlife, and cultural com. Wyo. Senate, Cheyenne, chair resources com., mem. rules and procedure com. Mem. Wyo. Heritage Soc., Yellowstone Regulatory Authority Bd.; commr. Park County, 1978-86; trustee Buffalo Bill Hist. Soc.; pres. Cody Med. Found.; mem. Cody Fire Dept. Republican. Home: PO Box 1088 Cody WY 82414-1088 Office: 1234 Sheridan Ave Cody WY 82414-3630 also: Wyo Senate State Capitol Cheyenne WY 82002-0001 Fax: 307-527-6853.*

COE, JUDITH ANNE, music educator, composer, performer; b. Denver, June 11, 1955; d. James Arnold and Sonya Diane (Regnier) Hall; m. Loren R. Coe, June 14, 1975 (div. Dec. 1993); children: Jared, Joshua, Jessica. BM, Colo. State U., 1981, MM, 1983; DMA, U. Colo., 1991. Rsch. intern Denver Ctr. for Performing Arts Voice Lab., 1984-91; vis. artist Denver Sch. of Arts, 1991-92; vocal coach, vis. artist Denver Ctr. Theatre Co., 1991-92; instr. Front Range C.C., Ft. Collins, Colo., 1988-91; designer Vestige Pub. Co., Ft. Collins, 1994-96; asst. prof. dept. music Miss. U. for Women, Columbus, 1996-2001; asst. prof. music & entertainment industry studies U. Colo., Denver, 2001—. Adj. prof. Colo. State U., Ft. Collins, 1990-94. Author: Report on the Status of Women in College Music, 2000; assoc. editor: (ency.) Women Musicians in America, 2000; author/compiler: (webliography) Cyberspace Music Resources, 1999. Performing arts roster Miss. Arts Coun., 1999—; cmty. outreach affiliate Columbus Arts Coun., 1999—. Miss. U. for Women Faculty Devel. grantee, 1996, 97, 98, 99, 2000; Nat. Inst. for Deafness and Other Comm. Disorders grantee, 1990, 91, Columbus Arts Coun. grantee, 1999, 2000, Blas Internat. Sch. Traditional Irish Music and Dance grantee, 1999. Mem. AAUW (Leadership award 1999), NOW, Internat. Alliance for Women in Music (coord. of pub. advocacy 1999—, bd. dirs. 1996—), Am. Soc. Composers, Authors and Pubs., Coll. Music Soc. (co-chair com. on music, women and gender 1999—, profl. devel. com./ann. planning com. 1999—), Acad. and Rec. Industry Alliances (team organizer 2000), Nat. Assn. Tchrs. Singing (v.p., adjudications chair 1983-85), Southeastern Composers League, Internat. Assn. for Study of Popular Music. Democrat. Avocations: web design and development, photography, architecture, popular culture, travel. Office: U Colo Arts Bldg 288H Campus Box 162 PO Box 173364 Denver CO E-mail: judith.coe@cudenver.edu.

COE, LAURIE LYNNE BARKER, photojournalist, artist; b. Miami, Fla., Nov. 26, 1954; d. George Felton Barker and Dorita Maria Comas; m. James Woodrift Coe, Sept. 29, 1980; children: Blake Alexander, Alexandra Noelle. Profl. photography, N.Y. Inst. Photography, 1994. Photographer Marie Selby Botanical Gardens, Sarasota, Fla., 1997—99; corr. North Port Rev., Englewood, Fla., 1997—99; pres. Artistic Endeavours, North Port, Fla., 1998—. Author: In The Beauty of the Morning, 2001; Sarasota, A Photographic Portrait, 2000. Photographer Sun Coast Humane Soc., Sarasota, 1998, North Port, 2000—01; bd. mem. Arts and Culture Alliance, Sarasota, 2002—. Recipient Muses award, Arts and Cultural Alliance, 2003. Mem.: N.Am. Nature Photographer Assn., North Port Area Art Guild (chairwoman all shows 1998—2001, chair ways and means 1998—2001, v.p. 1999—2001, photographic tchr. childrens summer workshop 2000—01). Avocations: mentor fo high schools, natural healing, gardening, music. Home and Office: Artistic Endeavours 4880 Wecoma Ave North Port FL 34287

COE, MICHAEL DOUGLAS, anthropologist, educator; b. N.Y.C., May 14, 1929; s. William Rogers and Clover (Simonton) C.; m. Sophie Dobzhansky, June 5, 1955; children: Nicholas, Andrew, Sarah, Peter, Natalie. AB, Harvard, 1950, PhD, 1959. Asst. prof. U. Tenn., 1958-60; mem. faculty Yale U., 1960—, prof. anthropology, 1968-90, Charles J. MacCurdy prof. anthropology, 1990-94, prof. emeritus, 1994—. Adviser Robert Woods Bliss Collection Pre-Columbian Art, Dumbarton Oaks, Harvard, 1963-80. Author: La Victoria, An Early Site on the Pacific Coast of Guatemala, 1961, Mexico, 1962, The Jaguar's Children: Pre-Classic Art of Central Mexico, 1965, The Maya, 1966, (with Kent V. Flannery) Early Cultures and Human Ecology in South Coastal Guatemala, 1967, America's First Civilization, 1968, The Maya Scribe and His World, 1973, Classic Maya Pottery at Dumbarton Oaks, 1975, Lords of the Underworld, 1978, (with Richard A. Diehl) In the Land of the Olmec, 1980, Young Lords and Old Gods, 1982, (with Dean R. Snow and Elizabeth P. Benson) Atlas of Ancient America, 1986, Breaking the Maya Code, 1992, (with Sophie D. Coe) The True History of Chocolate, 1996, (with Justin Kerr) The Art of the Maya Scribe, 1998, (with Mark Van Stone) Reading the Maya Glyphs, 2001, Angkor and the Khmer Civilization, 2003; contbr. articles to profl. jours. Chmn. bd. Planting Fields Found., 1985— ; pres. Heath Hist. Soc., Mass., 1984-90. Fellow Royal Anthrop. Soc.; mem. NAS, Am. Anthrop. Assn., Conn. Acad. Arts and Scis., Conn. Acad. Scis. and Engring., Limestone Trout Club, The Anglers Club of N.Y., Sigma Xi. Home: 376 St Ronan St New Haven CT 06511-2251 E-mail: olmecC@aol.com.

COE, NICHOLAS P.W. surgeon; b. Kingston, U.K., May 8, 1946; MB BS, U. London, 1969. Diplomate Am. Bd. Surgery. Intern St. Mary Abbots Hosp., 1969-70; resident in surgery Guys Hosp., London, 1970-75, Baystate Med. Ctr., 1976-79; fellow in surgery Harvard Med. Sch., Boston, 1975-76; mem. staff Baystate Med. Ctr., Springfield, Mass., 1979—; prof. surgery Tufts U. Sch. Medicine, Boston, 1990—. Fellow ACS, Royal Coll. Surgery Eng.; mem. Am. Assn. Endocrine Surgeons, Assn. Program Dirs. in Surgery, Assn. for Surg. Edn., New Eng. Sur. Soc., Am. Surg. Assn. Office: 3300 Main St Springfield MA 01199-0001 E-mail: nicholas.coe@bhs.org.

COE, ROBERT CAMPBELL, retired surgeon; b. Seattle, Nov. 14, 1918; s. Herbert Everett and Lucy Jane (Campbell) C.; m. Josephine Austin Weiner, Mar. 24, 1942; children: Bruce Everett, Virginia Austin, Matthew Daniel. BS, U. Wash., 1940; MD, Harvard U., 1950. Diplomate: Am. Bd. Thoracic Surgery, Am. Bd. Surgery. Intern Mass. Gen. Hosp., Boston, 1950-51, asst. resident, 1951-54, chief surg. resident, 1955, chief surg. clinics, 1956; instr. surgery Med. Sch. Harvard U., 1956; pvt. practice medicine specializing in thoracic and vascular surgery Seattle, 1957-84. Hon. mem. staff Children's Hosp.; attending surgeon Swedish Hosp.; cons. thoracic surgeon Firland Sanitarium, Seattle, 1957-68, Children's Hosp. Tumor Clinic, 1968-84; mng. ptnr. Invex & Inpark med. offices, Seattle, 1970-88; clin. prof. U. Wash., 1973-2000; mem. Wash. State Med. Disciplinary Bd., 1981-86; chmn. med. adv. bd. Physio-control. div. Eli Lilly, 1979-85; pres. 1st Mercer (Wash.) Corp., 1969-73, 80-91, treas., 1973-80; owner, operator Hidden Valley Guest Ranch Cle Elum, Wash., 1969-93; developer Kula Estate, Maui, Hawaii; treas. 13th Internat. Cancer Congress. Editor: King County Med. Soc. Bull, 1964-70; mem. adv. bd. Pacific N.W. Mag. 1968-85; contbr. articles to profl. jours. Mem. Mayor's Harbor Adv. Com., 1958-61; chmn. bd. N.W. Seaport, Inc., hist. mus. Seattle, 1974-75; mem. Mercer Island City Coun., 1988-92. With USNR, 1941-46. Decorated Bronze Star, Presdl. Unit citation. Fellow ACS; mem. North Pacific Surg. Assn. (sr. mem.), Pacific Coast Surg. Assn. (sr. mem.), King County Med. Soc. (jud. coun. 1972-78, chmn. 1976-78), Seattle Surg. Soc. (pres. 1969), Psi Upsilon, Seattle Yacht Club, Cruising of Am. Club (bd. govs. 1992-95). Episcopalian. Home and Office: 7260 N Mercer Way Mercer Island WA 98040-2132

COE, ROBERT STANFORD, retired management educator; b. Cin., July 9, 1919; s. Louis Herman and Alma Mary (Jenkins) C.; children: Carolyn Lee, William Ayres, Jon Bruce; m. Dorothy June Harris, Nov. 25, 1977 BS, Miami U., Oxford, Ohio, 1941; MS, U. Houston, 1948, PhD, 1957. Asst. to v.p. Dresser Industries, Dallas, 1956-58; personnel adminstr. Ling-Temco-Vought, Dallas, 1958-64; prof., grad. adviser Stephen F. Austin State U. (Tex.), 1964-69, chmn. dept. bus. adminstrn., 1969-74; mgmt. prof. Angelo State U., San Angelo, Tex., 1969-87; pres. Mgmt. Resources Assocs., San Angelo, 1970-87. Lectr. U. Tex.-Arlington, 1960-64. Contbr. articles to profl. jours. Mem. Gov.'s Com. on Goals for Tex., 1970; bd. dirs. YMCA, 1970-72, West Tex. Lighthouse for Blind, 1985-87. Served with USN, 1941-45. Mem. Am. Psychol. Assn., Acad. Mgmt., AAUP, Am. Inst. Decision Scis., Alpha Kappa Psi, Phi Kappa Phi, Pi Kappa Alpha Clubs: San Angelo Country, Rolling Hills Country. Lodges: Rotary. Presbyterian. Home: 3929 Millbrook Dr San Angelo TX 76904-5603 *Since my high school days, my life has been guided by the principle expressed by the Latin phrase, "Esse Quam Videre", which means, to be, rather than to appear to be.*

COE, RODNEY MICHAEL, medical educator; b. Marquette, Mich., Nov. 10, 1933; s. Roy Arthur and Renee Adelaide (Reeder) C.; m. Elaine Elwell, Sept. 6, 1954; children: Kevin Elwell, Curtis Daniel, Andrea, Douglas Arthur. BS, Iowa State Coll., 1955; MA, So. Ill. U., 1959; PhD, Wash. U., 1962. From asst. to assoc. prof. Wash. U., St. Louis, 1962-70; from assoc. prof. to prof. St. Louis U., 1970—, chmn. cmty. and family medicine, 1989—, prof. emeritus, 1999. Exec. dir. Med. Care Rsch. Ctr., St. Louis, 1963-73; vis. prof. L.Am. Faculty Social Scis., Santiago, Chile, 1969-70; cons. Chilton Rsch. Svcs., Radnor, Pa., 1970-79, NIH, Bethesda, Md., 1976—. Author: Sociology of Medicine, 1970, and eighteen others; contbr. articles to profl. jours. Mem. Health Care for the Homeless, St. Louis, 1985—; mem., past pres. SSM Rehab. Inst., St. Louis, 1968—. Capt. U.S. Army, 1956-58. Recipient Geriatric Leadership Acad. award NIH, 1986-92; grantee NIH, Dept. Vets. Affairs, pvt. founds. Avocations: swimming, golfing.

COELHO, SANDRA SIGNORELLI, secondary school educator, consultant; b. Torrington, Conn., Oct. 19, 1940; d. Ernest J. and Linda M. (Zanolli) Signorelli; m. Walter S. Coelho, July 11, 1964. BS, Cen. Conn. State U., 1962, MS, 1969, postgrad; Intermediate Administration Certification, Cen. Conn. State, 1980- 6th year certificate. Tchr. Torrington Bd. Edn., 1962-65; K-12 tech./math. coord. East Windsor (Conn.) Bd. Edn., 1965—2002; cons. Enfield Town Hall, 2002, Conn. Acad., 2003—, PIMMS, 2003—. Mem. assistive tech. task force State of Conn.; presenter C.A.B.E.;cons. Town of Enfield, Conn. Acad. Chmn. townwide curriculum com. East Windsor; mem. twp. com. Conn. Dept. Edn.; chmn. East Windsor Tech. Com. Recipient Golden Apple award; BEST Mentor-Assessor; Apple Computer scholar; PIMMS fellow. Mem. NEA, Conn. Edn. Assn., Conn. Educators Computing Assn. (adviser), East Windsor Edn. Assn. (past pres.), ATOMIC (sec. exec. bd., past chmn. ann. meeting), Pi Lambda Theta, Phi Delta Kappa (exec. bd.), Delta Kappa Gamma (past v.p. Rho chpt.) Home and Office: 50 Smalley Rd Windsor Locks CT 06096-1134 *Think about what you do before you decide to do it. People are most important. Try to do what you believe in and proceed in a respectful manner on your own merits and not at the expense of others.*

COELING, HARRIET VAN ESS, nursing educator, editor; b. Grand Rapids, Mich., Dec. 3, 1943; d. Louis and Helen Angeline (DeGraff) Van Ess; m. Kenneth J. Coeling, June 27, 1970; children: Valerie Coeling Nandor, Beverly Coeling Corder. BSN, U. Mich., 1966, MS, 1968; PhD, Bowling Green State U., 1987. RN, Ohio; clin. nurse specialist. Head nurse, clin. specialist Presbyn. Univ. Hosp., Pitts., 1968-70; instr. U. Pitts. Sch. Nursing, 1970-72; staff devel. instr. Braddock (Pa.) Hosp., 1976-78, Med. Coll. Ohio, Toledo, 1978-83; asst. prof. U. Mich. Sch. Nursing, Ann Arbor, 1987-88, Kent (Ohio) State U. Coll. Nursing, 1988-93, asoc. prof., 1994—. Editor, Online Jour. Issues in Nursing, ANA/Kent State U., 1998—; contbr. articles to profl. jours. Coord. St. Malachi Healthcare Clinic, Cleve., 1993-98. Tchr. and Nonsvc. fellow Bowling Green State U., 1983-87. Mem. Nat. Assn. Clin. Specialists, Ohio Assn. Advanced Practice Nurses, Ohio Nurses Assn. (chair human rights com. 1998—2002), Greater Cleve. Nurses Assn., Midwest Nursing Rsch. Assn., Christian Assn. Psychol. Studies, Sigma Theta Tau (Excellence in Use of Tehc. award 1997). Christian. Avocations: travel, swimming. Office: Kent State U 1743 Settlers Reserve Westlake OH 44145 E-mail: hcoeling@kent.edu.

COEN, ADRI STECKLING See ADRI

COEN, ETHAN, film director, writer; b. Saint Louis Park, Minn., Sept. 21, 1957; married. Student in Philosophy, Princeton U. Former statis. typist Macy's, N.Y.C. Screenwriter: (with Joel Coen) Crime Wave (formerly XYZ Murders); prodr., screenplay, editor as Roderick James) Blood Simple, 1984, Raising Arizona, 1987, Miller's Crossing, 1990, Barton Fink, 1991 (Palme D'Or and Best Dir. awards, Cannes Internat. Film Festival 1996), The Hudsucker Proxy, 1994, Fargo (Oscar award Best Writing 1997, CFCA award Best Screenplay 1997, Golden Satellite award Best Motion Picture 1997, Ind. Spirit award Best Feature 1997, Best Screenplay 1997, WGA Screen award Best Screenplay 1997), Big Lebowski, 1998, The Naked Man, 1998, writer, dir., prodr.: O Brother, Where Art Thou?, 2000, The Man Who Wasn't There, 2001, Intolerable Cruelty, 2003, exec. prodr. Down From the Mountain, 2000, writer A Fever in the Blood, 2002. Office: care UTA c/o Jim Berkus 9560 Wilshire Blvd Beverly Hills CA 90212-2427*

COEN, JOEL, film director, writer; b. Saint Louis Park, Minn., Nov. 29, 1954; s. Ed and Rena C.; divorced. Student, Simon's Rock Coll.; student in film, NYU. Writer, dir. The Man Who Wasn't There, 2001, Intolerable Cruelty, 2003; asst. editor Fear No Evil, Evil Dead,; worked with rock video crews; screenwriter: (with Ethan Coen) Crime Wave (formerly XYZ Murders); dir., screenwriter Blood Simple, 1984, Raising Arizona, 1987, Miller's Crossing, 1990, Barton Fink (Palme D'Or and Best Dir. awards, Cannes Internat. Film Festival), 1991, The Hudsucker Proxy, 1994, Fargo (Best Dir. award, Cannes Internat. Film Festival, 1996, Acad. award for best writing screenplay written for the screen 1997), The Big Lebowski, 1998, O Brother, Where Art Thou?, 2000; exec. prodr. Down From the Mountain, 2000. Office: United Talent Agy c/o Jim Berkus 9560 Wilshire Blvd Fl 5 Beverly Hills CA 90212-2400*

COEN, JOHN JOSEPH, physician, oncologist; s. Patrick Clement and Maureen Patricia Coen. MD, U of Mass., Worcester, MA, 1994—98. Resident in radiation oncology Mass. Gen. Hosp., Boston, Mass., 1999—. Grantee T32 Cancer Rsch. Tng. Grant, NIH, 2002-2003. Mem.: Am. Soc. of Therapeutic Radiology and Oncology. Roman Catholic. Avocations: sailing, skiing.

COENSON, BARBARA, marketing and sales professional; b. Phila., Dec. 20, 1956; d. Martin and Rita (Cassel) Coenson; m. Steve L. Crook, Mar. 6, 1994. BS, U. Fla., 1978; M in Mgmt., Fla. Inst. Tech., 1996. Mng. editor Heritage Fla. News, Fern Park, Fla., 1978-82; freelance photographer and writer Altamonte Springs, Fla., 1982-89; campaign mgr. Pearlman for Congress, Orlando, Fla., 1990; mktg. mgr. AAA Travel Pub., Orlando, 1991-96, AAA Ptnr. Sales, Orlando, 1996-97; mktg. cons. AAA Internat. Pub. Co., 1997, Pathfinder Mortgage and Investments, Inc., 1997; nat. sales mgr. AAA Partnership Programs and AAA Car and Travel mag., 1997-98, AAA Nat. Hdqrs., Heathrow, Fla.; v.p. mktg. HardwareStreet.com, Inc., Reno, Nev., 1999-2000; v.p. West Coast ops. Bus. and Trade Network, Reno, Nev., 2000—. Author: Tom and Jerry, 1989; contbr., editor articles to various pubs. Del. Fla. Rep. Conv., 1990; campaign mgr. Fla. State rep. Frank Stone, 1990; vol., advisor White House advance staff for Pres. Bush's visit to Fla., 1990. Recipient 7 Press awards Fla. Press Assn., 1980. Mem. Hadassah Club. Avocations: piano, tennis, travelling.

COERPER, MILO GEORGE, lawyer, priest; b. Milw., May 8, 1925; s. Milo Wilson and Rose (Schubert) C.; m. Lois Hicks, Apr. 11, 1953; children: Milo Wilson, Allison Lee, Lois Paddock. BS, U.S. Naval Acad., 1946; LLB, U. Mich., 1954; MA, Georgetown U., 1957, PhD, 1960. Bar: D.C. 1954, Md. 1960, N.Y. 1980. Since practiced in, Washington; asso. firm Wilmer & Broun, 1954-60; firm Coudert Bros., 1961-63, mem. firm, 1964-96, retired ptnr., 1996—; ordained deacon Episcopal Ch., 1978, priest, 1979. Cathedral chaplain Washington Nat. Cathedral, 1986—. Contbr. articles to profl. jours. Trustee, vice chmn. for U.S., Canterbury Cathedral Trust in Am., 1982-97, acting chmn., 1991, 97; mem. coun. The Friends of Canterbury Cathedral in U.S., 1999—. Ensign USN, 1946-49; to lt. 1951-53. Mem.: ABA, Internat. Assn. for Protection of Indsl. Property, Am. Soc. Internat. Law, Am. Law Inst., Md. State Bar Assn., Bar Assn. DC, Chevy Chase Club, Met. Club (pres. 1986), Army and Navy Club. Home: 7315 Brookville Rd Chevy Chase MD 20815-4057 Office: Coudert Bros 1627 I St NW Washington DC 20006-4007

COETZEE, JOHANNES CHRISTIAAN, orthopedic surgeon; b. Potgietersrus, Transvaal, South Africa, Aug. 23, 1960; arrived in U.S., 1995; s. Antoine Charles and Cecile Coetzee; m. Linda Anne Dames, Apr. 2, 1983; children: Antoine Charles, Peter Alphonso. MD, U. of Pretoria, South Africa, 1984; MMed Orthopaedic Surgery, U. of Stellenbosch, South Africa, 1993. Lic. orthopedic surgeon Med. and Dental Bd., Minn., med.dr. and orthopedic surgeon South African Med. Coun. Othopedic trauma fellow AO Trauma Soc., Davos, Switzerland, 1993; foot and ankle fellow U. of Wash., Seattle, 1995—96; asst. prof. U. of Minn. Med. Sch., Mpls., 1999—; orthopedic surgeon. Cons. DePuy, Warsaw, 1999—. Guest editor: Current Concepts in Ankle Replacement Surgery. Foot and Ankle Clinics, 2002, asst. editor: Foot and Ankle Internat. Jour., 2000—. Lt. M.C., 1995—97, South Africa. Decorated Highest Recommendation South African M.C. Fellow: Royal Coll. of Physicians and Surgeons of Can. (lic. med.dr. and orthopedic surgeon); mem.: AMA, Am. Orthopedic Foot and Ankle Soc., Am. Foot and Ankle Soc. United

Methodist. Achievements include first to ongoing design and development of ankle joint replacements; research in outcomes research on various foot and ankle issues including, bunion surgery, ankle replacement and tendon abnormalities. Avocations: marathon running, downhill and cross country skiing, travel, wine. Office: Dept of Orthopaedics Univ Minn 2450 Riverside Ave S Minneapolis MN 55454 Home Fax: 612-456-9329. E-mail: coetz001@tc.umn.edu.

COFER, BERDETTE HENRY, public management consulting company executive; b. Las Flores, Calif. s. William Walter and Violet Ellen (Elam) C.; m. Ann McGarva, June 27, 1954 (dec. Feb. 20, 1990); children: Sandra Lea Cofer-Oberle, Ronald William; m. Sally Ann Shepherd, June 12, 1993. AB, Calif. State U., Chico, 1950; MA, U. Calif., Berkeley, 1960. Tchr. Westwood (Calif.) Jr.-Sr. High Sch., 1953-54, Alhambra High Sch., Martinez, Calif., 1954-59; prin. adult and summer sch. Hanford (Calif.) High Sch., 1959-60, asst. supt. bus., 1960-67; dean bus. svcs. West Hills Coll., Coalinga, 1967-76; vice chancellor Yosemite Community Coll. Dist., Modesto, 1976-88; pres. BHC Assocs., Inc., Modesto, 1988—. Chmn. Valley Ins. Program Joint Powers Agy., Modesto, 1986-88. Contbr. articles to profl. publs. Pres. Coalinga Indsl. Devel. Corp., 1972-74, Assn. for Retarded Citizens, Modesto, 1985; mayor City of Coalinga, 1974-76; foreman Stanislaus County Grand Jury, Modesto, 1987-88. 1st lt. USAF, 1951-53. Recipient Outstanding Citizen award Coalinga C. of C., 1976, Walter Starr Robie Outstanding Bus. Officer award Assn. Chief Bus. Officers Calif. Community Colls., 1988, Humanitarian of Yr. award Stanislaus County Mayor's Com. for Employment of Persons with Disabilities, 1995, Man of Yr. award Am. Legion Post 74, 1999. Mem. Assn. Calif. C.C. Adminstrs. (life), Lions (dist. gov. 1965-66, pres. Lions Eye Found. of Calif.-Nev., Inc. 1999-2001, hon. life dir. Calif.-Nev. Student Spkrs. Found. 2000—), Phi Delta Kappa (pres. Kings-Tulare chpt. 1962-63), Am. Legion, 40 and 8 (comdr. 1997-98, chef de gare 1999-2000), Sons in Retirement (pres. 1996). Democrat. Avocation: bowling. Home and Office: 291 Leveland Ln # D Modesto CA 95350-6806

COFER, DEBORAH END, artist; b. Norfolk, Va., Feb. 27, 1954; d. Marion Albert End and Mary Virginia (Haga) Harbert; m. Richard Saunders Cofer III, May 26, 1973; children: Lee Victoria, Mark Thomas. BFA cum laude, East Carolina U., 1977; postgrad., N.Mex. State U., 1978. Ordained min. Kingsway Fellowship Internat. Asst. dir. Inst. of the Arts, El Paso, Tex., 1978-80. One-woman and group shows include Ghent Gallery, Norfolk, Va., R.J. Reynolds Industries, N.C. Artists Collection, Winston-Salem, Kate Lewis Gallery, Greenville, N.C., Mendenhall Gallery, East Carolina U., Greenville, Old House Gallery, Nags Head, N.C., Petersburg (Va.) Area Art Ctr., U. Tex., El Paso, N.Mex. State U., Las Cruces, Griffith Gallery, Miami, Fla., Chrysler Mus. Art, Norfolk, Nev. West Gallery, Reno, Aesthete Gallery, El Paso, N.C. Mus. Art, Raleigh, Va. Mus. Art, Richmond, El Paso Mus. Art, U. Nev., Reno, Sierra Nev. Mus. Art, Reno, Nat. Gallery Modern Art, Lisbon, Portugal, others; represented in permanent collections Chrysler Mus. Art, Norfolk, El Paso Mus. Art, R.J. Reynolds Industries World Hdqrs., Winston-Salem, East Carolina U., Greenville, Norfolk Pub. Libr., Appalachian State U., Boone, N.C., N.C. Mus. Art, Raleigh, Sierra Nev. Mus. Art, Reno, others. Spkr. Streams in the Desert Internat., Reno, 1995—. Mem. Aglow Internat. (area bd. 1985-96), Phi Kappa Phi, Delta Phi Delta (scholar). Republican. Avocations: writing, reading, raquetball, travel.

COFER, JONATHAN H. career officer; b. Pa., July 13, 1950; Commd. 2d lt. U.S. Army, 1972, advanced through grades to brig. gen., 1998; dir. joint rear area coord. U.S. Ctrl. Command, MacDill AFB, Fla., 1998—. Office: US Ctrl Command Macdill AFB FL 33602

COFER, JOSEPH BROADDUS, surgeon; b. Beckley, W.Va., Apr. 8, 1951; s. Joseph Pleasant and Ferne (Broaddus) C.; m. Juanita Wurtz, Nov. 25, 1978; children: Jessica Ann, Allison Jane. BIE, Ga. Inst. Tech., 1972; postgrad., U. Tenn., Chattanooga, 1973-75; MD, U. Tenn., Memphis, 1976-78. Diplomate Am. Bd. Surgery; lic. MD, Tenn., S.C., Va.; cert. surgery, 1990, recertified surgery, 1997, critical care, Am. Bd. Surgery, 1994. Intern in surgery Portsmouth (N.H.) Naval Hosp., 1979—80; flight surgeon, trainee Naval Aerospace Med. Inst., Pensacola, Fla., 1980-81; resident in surgery Erlanger Hosp., Chattanooga, 1983-88; transplant fellow Baylor U. Med. Ctr., Dallas, 1988-90; asst. prof. Med. U. of S.C., Charleston, 1990-95, dir. liver transplantation, 1990-95; assoc. prof. surgery, dir. residency program dept. surgery U. Tenn. Coll. Medicine, Chattanooga, 1995-2000, prof. surgery, dir. residency program, 2000—. Attending surgeon Med. U. S.C. Med. Ctr., Charleston, 1990-95, Charleston Meml. Hosp., 1990-95, Erlanger Med. Ctr., T.C. Thompson Children's Hosp., 1995—, Meml. Hosp. Chattanooga, 1995—, Parkridge Hosp., Chattanooga, 1995—. Contbr. articles to sci. and prof. jours. Fellow: ACS, So. Surg. Assn., Southeastern Surg. Congress; mem.: AMA, Chattanooga-Hamilton County Med. Soc. (pres 2002—03, bd. dirs. 1997), Tenn. Med. Assn. (interprofl. liaison com. 1998—), Assn. Acad. Surgery, Internat. Hepatobiliary Soc., Am. Soc. Transplant Surgeons, Assn. of Program Dirs. in Surgery. Avocations: hunting, gardening, farming. Office: u Tenn Dept Surgery 979 E 3d St Ste #401 Chattanooga TN 37403 E-mail: CoferJB@Erlanger.org.

COFFEE, GALE FURMAN, musician, educator; b. Oneonta, N.Y., Oct. 20, 1939; d. Delmar Robert and Charlotte Carolyn (Holloway) F.; m. Curtis Webb, June 13, 1961 (div. 1994); children: Nathan Robert, Ellen Jean Coffee Blickhan. MusB, Eastman Sch. of Music, 1961; MusM, Boston U., 1963. Flutist Am. Wind Symphony, Pitts., 1960, 62; piccolo player, 2d flute Spokane (Wash.) Symphony, 1970—; pers. mgr., 1989—; acting prin. flutist, 1990. Adj. instr. Whitworth Coll., Spokane, 1973-93, Gonzaga U., Spokane, 1984-90, Ea. Wash. U., Cheney, 1996—. Mem. Nat. Flute Assn. Home: 1616 E 19th Ave Spokane WA 99203-3716

COFFEE, JOSEPH DENIS, JR., retired college chancellor; b. Glens Falls, N.Y., Dec. 8, 1918; s. Joseph Denis and Kathryne Grace (Dwyer) C.; m. Margaret Mary Jennings, Oct. 7, 1941 (dec. Aug. 1998); children: John Allan (dec.), James Jennings, Mary Joyce Coffee Dies, Barbara Grace Coffee Wolf, Matthew Brian, Margaret Erin Coffee Giovannini, Ann Ellen Coffee Beach. AB, Columbia U., 1941. Asst. to gen. sec. Columbia U., N.Y.C., 1946-50, dir. devel., 1950-60, founder corp. matching gift program of alumni support, 1953, assoc. dean, 1959-60, asst. to pres. for alumni affairs, 1960-66; v.p. Eisenhower Coll., Seneca Falls, N.Y., 1966-69, exec. v.p., 1969-76, acting pres., 1975-76, pres., 1976-80, chancellor, 1980-81, chancellor emeritus, 1981—. Dir. scholarship program Joint Industry Bd., Elec. Industry of N.Y., 1947-81; exec. sec. Com. for Corporate Support Am. Univs., 1962-64 Chmn. March Dimes campaign, Closter, N.J., 1953; active Boy Scouts Am.; former treas., dir. Anglo-Am. Hellenic Bur. Edn.; pres. Seneca County United Way, 1973-75; Chmn. Teaneck Polit. Assembly, 1967-68; Trustee Teaneck Bd. Edn., 1961-64, 65-68, Columbia U., 1978-84; bd. dirs. Nat. Women's Hall of Fame. Served from ensign to lt. comdr. USNR, 1941-46. Mem.: Seneca Falls Hist. Soc. (past trustee), Rotary (past pres. Seneca Falls, Paul Harris fellow 1988, 2002). Roman Catholic.

COFFEE, MELVIN ARNOLD, retired lawyer; b. Chgo., July 8, 1934; s. Charles Hyman and Ida (Berson) C.; m. Beverly N. Segal, Aug. 26, 1956; children: Ronald M., Babette S. BS in Law, LLB, U. Denver, 1957; LLM, NYU, 1959. Bar: Colo. 1958. Ptnr. Drexler, Wald, Sobol & Coffee, Denver, 1959-63, Inman, Flynn & Coffee, Denver, 1963-78; sr. ptnr. Melvin Coffee & Assocs., Denver, 1978-2000; ret., 2000. Adj. prof. tax law U. Denver, 1974-83; chmn. IRS liaison com. Southwest Bar, 1989. Author: Taxation for Accountants, 1970, Protecting Client in Tax Fraud Investigation, 1972, New Directions in Guarding Client Records, 1973, Criminal Tax Investigations, 1983, The Colorado Lawyer, 1983. Prin. draftsman statute Colo. Income Tax Act 1964, pres. Denver and Tri-County Respiratory Disease Assn., 1962; active Citizen Budget Rev., 1963; Dem. rep. Colo. Ho. of Reps., 1967-69. With U.S. Army, 1958-64. Mem. Colo. State Bd. Accountancy (bd. dirs., pres. 1981), Colo. Soc. CPAs (hon.), Colo. Bar Assn. (bd. govs. 1980-82, chmn. taxation sect. 1970, chmn. continuing legal edn. 1981), Arapahoe County Bar Assn. (trustee 1980-82), Nat. Assn. State Bds. Accountancy (v.p. 1981-84), Greater Denver Tax Counsel (pres., sec. 1963-65), Masons, Columbine. Office: Melvin Coffee PC 4296 S Dahlia St Englewood CO 80113-5004

COFFEE, RICHARD JEROME, II, lawyer; b. Chgo., Nov. 12, 1954; s. James F. and Jean Marie (Hackman) C.; children: David Patrick Coffee, Brent William Coffee; m. Sue Heberlie, Dec. 12, 1997. BS, So. Ill. U., 1975; JD, U. Ill., 1978. Bar: Ill. 1978, U.S. Dist. Ct. (no. dist.) Ill. 1978, U.S. Dist. Ct. (ctrl. dist.) Ill. 1980, U.S. Dist. Ct. (so. dist.) Ill. 1998. Staff atty. Ill. Dept. Ins., Springfield, 1979-80; counsel Ill. State Employees Assn., Springfield, 1980-84; staff counsel Ill. Bd. Regents, Springfield, 1984-87, legal counsel Chancellor's Office, 1987-89; univ. legal counsel Sangamon State U., Springfield, 1989-90; chief legal advisor Ill. State Bd. Edn., Springfield, 1990-96; assoc. Rau & Rau Attys., Waterloo, Ill., 1997—. Mem.: Monroe County Bar Assn. (sec. 1998—99, treas. 1999—2000, v.p. 2000—01, pres. 2001—02), Chgo. Bar Assn. Avocations: licensed pilot, licensed amateur radio operator. Office: 119 E Mill St Waterloo IL 62298-1518 E-mail: coffee@ljextra.com., raulaw@htc.net.

COFFEE, VIRGINIA CLAIRE, civic worker, former mayor; b. Alliance, Nebr., Dec. 8, 1920; D. James Maddigan and Adelaide Mary (Forde) Kennedy; M. Bill Brown Coffee, June 21, 1942; children: Claire, Sara, Virginia Anne, Sue. BS, Chadron State Coll., 1942. H.s. prin. Whitman (Nebr.) High Sch., 1942; bookkeeper Coffee & Son, Inc., Harrison, Nebr., 1965—, officer, 1967, pres., 1987-97, v.p., 1998—; dir. Friends of Agate Fossil Beds, Inc., Harrison, 1988, v.p., 1988-2001. Chmn. compilation com. book Sioux County Memoirs of Its Pioneers, 1967; coordinator Harrison sec. book Nebraska Our Towns, 1988. Mayor City of Harrison, 1978-80; leader Girl Scouts U.S.A., 1953-63; mem. Harrison Elem. Sch. bd., 1958-64, liason com. Chadron State Coll., 1975, pub. rels. chmn Nebr. Cowbelles, 1968; hon gov. Nebr. Centennial, 1967; sec. NW Stock Growers, 1971-73; corp. officer Ft. Robinson Centennial, 1973-88; officer Gov's Ft. Robinson Centennial Commn., 1973-75; chmn. Sioux County Bicentennial, 1973-77; trustee Nebr. State Hist. Soc. Found., 1975—, Village of Harrison, 1973-80; bd. dirs. Chadron State Coll. Found., 1996—, sec., 2003—; bd. dirs. Harrison Cmty. Club, Inc., 1983-86, officer, 1984-86; apptd. Sioux County Vis. Com. 1989-2003, adm. Nebr. Navy, 1992; life mem. Nebr. State Hist., dir. 1979-85, 2d v.p. 1982-84, 1st v.p. 1984-85; mem. com. for marker to honor Harrison Centennial 1985-86; mem. Wyo. State Hist. Soc.; mem. Sioux County Hist. Soc., bd. dirs. 1975-81, 83-84, 87-90, 97—, pres. 1988-90, co-pres., 2d v.p.; mem. Sioux County History Book Com. 1985-86. Recipient Disting. Svc. award Chadron State Coll., 1994. Mem. Nebr. Cattle Women, Harrison Cmty. Inc., Cardinal Key. Roman Catholic. Address: PO Box 336 Harrison NE 69346-0336

COFFEN, RICHARD WAYNE, minister, editor; b. Stoneham, Mass., Nov. 19, 1941; s. George Albert and Dorothy Cowan (Hayward) C.; m. Rosalia Jane Clausen, June 9, 1963; children: Robert W., Ronald D. BA, Atlantic Union Coll., 1963; MA, Andrews U., 1964. Ordained to ministry Seventh-day Adventists, 1968. Pastor So. New Eng. Conf., Seventh-day Adventists, Mass., 1964-70; editor So. Pub. Assn., Nashville, 1970-81; editor, assoc. editor books div. Rev. & Herald Pub. Assn., Hagerstown, Md., 1981—85, v.p. editl. svcs., 1985—90, assoc. editor books div., 1990—95; v.p. editl. svc., 1995—2001; asst. to pres., 2001—03; v.p. period. divsn., 2003—. Author: Time of the Sign, 1975, Ten Steps to Successful Bible Study, 1976, When God Sheds Tears, 1993, When God's Heart Breaks, 1997. Mem. Soc. Bibl. Lit., Adventist Soc. for Religious Studies. Home: 25 Bittersweet Dr Hagerstown MD 21740-6713 Office: Rev & Herald Pub Assn 55 W Oak Ridge Dr Hagerstown MD 21740-7301 E-mail: Rcoffen@rhpa.org.

COFFEY, C(HARLES) EDWARD, physician; b. May 11, 1952; BS, Wofford Coll., 1974; MD, Duke U., 1979. Diplomate Am. Bd. Psychiatry and Neurology. Intern Duke U. Med. Ctr., Durham, N.C., 1980-81, resident in psychiatry, 1979-80, 83-84, resident in neurology, 1981-83, dir. neuropsychiatry, 1984-90; dir. Allegheny Neuropsychiat. Inst., Pitts., 1991-96; v.p. Henry Ford Behavioral Health, Detroit, 1996—. Office: Henry Ford Health Sys 1 Ford Pl Ste 1F Detroit MI 48202-3450 E-mail: ecoffey1@hfhs.org.

COFFEY, CHARLES MOORE, communication research professional, writer; b. Chgo., July 8, 1941; s. Charles Adams and Helen Marie (Moore) C. BA in Econs., Beloit Coll., 1963; postgrad., Purdue U., 1980. WDBJ radio and TV reporter Times-World Corp., Roanoke, Va., 1964-65; reporter, anchor, prodr. WHAS AM FM TV, Louisville, 1967-72; asst. to chancellor Ind. U. S.E., New Albany, 1972-77; dir. spl. events Ind. U., Bloomington, 1977-82; dir. alumni affairs Ind. U.-Purdue U., Indpls., 1982-88; comm. advisor Bayh-O'Bannon Campaign, Inpdls., 1988; comm. asst. Lt. Gov. of Ind., Indpls., 1989-97; dir. comm. rsch. Ind. Dept. Adminstrn., Indpls., 1997—. Lt. gov.'s rep. INTELENET Commn., Indpls., 1990-97, gov.'s rep., 1997—; gov.'s rep. Enhanced Data Access Rev. Com., Indpls., 1997—. Contbr. articles to profl. jours. Pres. Coun. for Retarded Children, Clark County, Ind., 1975-76, Bloomington Restorations, 1982; founding chmn. Clark-Floyd Conv. Bur., Jeffersonville, Ind., 1977; bd. dirs. YMCA Greater Indpls., 1989-95, 97-98, 2000-2003, sec. bd. 1998-2000, trustee 1999—. With USAF, 1963. Recipient AP award for comprehensive reporting Va. AP Broadcasters, 1964-65. Mem. Rotary Club Indpls. Democrat. Home: 3922 Alsace Pl Indianapolis IN 46226-5413 Office: Ind Dept Adminstrn 402 W Washington St Indianapolis IN 46204-2739 E-mail: ccoffey@idoa.state.in.us., coffeyc@iquest.net.

COFFEY, DENNIS JAMES, performance technology consultant; b. Detroit, Nov. 11, 1940; s. James Patrick Coffey and Gertrude Viola Rinne Coffey Schultz; m. Joyce Crim (div. 1967); children: Jordan Collard, Denise Van Patten, Dennis Michael; m. Kathryn Osborne (div. 1988); children: James Donald, Andrew Joseph. BA, Wayne State U., 1990, MEd, 1992. Artist, writer, producer Maverick/MGM Records, Detroit, 1964-68, Sussex/Buddah Records, L.A., 1970-74, West Bound/Atlantic Records, Detroit, 1974-78; studio guitarist Motown Records, Detroit, 1968-76; v.p., co-owner Theocoff Prodns., Detroit, 1978-80, Glen Ridge, N.J., 1980-82; free-lance guitarist Farmington Hills, Mich., 1982-85; instml. technologist GM, Warren, Mich., 1985-89, Detroit Art Svcs., Troy, Mich., 1989-92; tng. cons. Farmington Hills, Mich., 1993-94; tng. mgr. ISI Robotics Inc., Warren, 1994-95. Author: Guitars, Bars and Motown Superstars, 2002; artist, writer and prodr. record albums including Hair and Thangs, 1969, Evolution, 1971, Going For Myself, 1972, Electric Coffey, 1973, Instant Coffey, 1974, Finger Lickin Good, 1975, Back Home, 1976, A Sweet Taste of Sin, 1978, Motor City Magic, 1988, Under the Moonlight, 1990; contbr. articles to Discoveries Mag. and Tech. Skills and Tng. Mag.; cameo role in documentary film Standing in the Shadows of Motown, 2002; appeared in PBS TV spl. Rhythm, Love and Soul, 2003. With U.S. Army, 1959-61. Recipient 3 cert. gold singles Rec. Industry Assn. Am., cert. gold album, Australia, award for best instrumental record NATRA, 1972, Alumni Acad. Achievement award Wayne State U. Coll. Lifelong Learning, 1995; named top instrumentalist and outstanding prodr. Record World, 1978; featured on cover Cashbox mag., 1972. Mem. ASTD, Nat. Soc. Performance and Instrn., Am. Fedn. Musicians, Mich. Soc. Instructional Tech. (hon. Achievement award 1991, Recognition award 1992), Broadcast Music Inc. (Citation Achievement award), Soc. for Tech. Communication (award 1991). Lutheran. Achievements include first to guitar being featured in Motown exhibit, Henry Ford Museum, Greenfield Village, Dearborn, Mich., 1995; Scorpio sheet music, Wah Wha Pedal and fuzz tone in Motown exhibit, Rock and Roll Hall of Fame and Museum, Cleveland.

COFFEY, JOAN L. humanities educator; b. Chgo., Jan. 14, 1944; d. Elmer Rudolph Lueder and Leona Joan Patelczyk; m. Edward Charles Coffey, July 9, 1966. BA in History, Barat Coll. DePaul, 1965; MA in European History, U. Colo., 1986, PhD in Modern Europe, 1990. H.S. history tchr. Marywood Acad., Evanston, Ill., 1965—66, Elmhurst Acad., Portsmouth, RI, 1967—68, Convent of Sacred Heart, Halifax, Canada, 1969—70, Notre Dame H.S., Milw., 1973—74, Shorewood (Wis.) H.S., 1974—75, Woodlands Acad., Lake Forest, Ill., 1982—84; tchg. asst. U. Colo., Boulder, 1986—90; assoc. prof. Sam Houston State U., Huntsville, Tex., 1990—. Mem. adv. bd. dept. history U. Colo., Boulder, 2001—03. Léon Harmel Social Reformer as Catholic Entrepreneur, 2003. Gilbert Chinard scholar, Inst. Français de Washington, 1987. Mem.: Phi Delta Phi, Phi Alpha Theta. Avocation: painting. Home: 11 Box Turtle Ln The Woodlands TX 77380 Office: Sam Houston State Univ AB4 #457 Huntsville TX 77341

COFFEY, JOHN LOUIS, judge; b. Milw., Apr. 15, 1922; s. William Leo and Elizabeth Ann (Walsh) Coffey; m. Marion Kunzelmann, Feb. 3, 1951; children: Peter, Elizabeth Mary Coffey-Robbins. BA, Marquette U., 1943, JD, 1948; MBA (hon.), Spencerian Coll., 1964. Bar: Wis. 1948, U.S. Dist. Ct. 1948, U.S. Supreme Ct. 1980. Asst. city atty. City of Milw., 1949—54; judge Civil Ct., Milw. County, 1954—60, Milw. County Mcpl. Ct., 1960—62; judge criminal divsn. Cir. Ct., Milw. County, 1962—72, sr. judge criminal divsn., 1972—75, chief presiding judge criminal divsn., 1976, judge civil divsn., 1976—78; justice Wis. Supreme Ct., Madison, 1978—82; cir. judge U.S. Ct. Appeals (7th cir.), Chgo., 1982—; mem. Wis. Bd. Criminal Ct. Judges, 1960—78, Wis. Bd. Circuit Ct. Judges, 1962—78. Mem. adv. bd. St. Mary's Hosp., 1964—70; mem. Milw. County coun. Boy Scouts Am., 1970—78; chmn. vol. svcs. adv. com. Milw. County Dept. Pub. Welfare, 1970—72; chmn. St. Eugene's Sch. Bd., 1967—70; pres. St. Eugene's Ch. Coun., 1974; bd. dirs., mem. exec. bd. Milw.-Waukesha chpt. ARC; chmn. adv. bd. St. Joseph's Home for Children, 1958—65. With USNR, 1943—46. Named Outstanding Young Man of Yr., Milw. Jr. C. of C., 1951; recipient Marquette Univ. H.S. Alumni Merit award, 2001. Fellow: Am. Bar Found.; mem.: State Bar Assn. Wis., Ill. State Bar Assn., 7th Cir. Bar Assn., Marquette U. Law Alumni Assn. (Disting. Profl. Achievement Merit award 1985), Marquette U. M Club (former dir.), Nat. Lawyers Club, Am. Legion (Disting. Svc. award 1973), Alpha Sigma Nu, Phi Alpha Delta (hon.). Roman Catholic. *I have tried to the best of my ability to render justice to all and remember that "We are a country of laws, not of men" and while protecting the individual's rights I have not lost sight of the common good of all mankind and cautioned each and every one who appeared before me that with every right there is a corresponding obligation.*

COFFEY, JOSEPH IRVING, international affairs educator; b. St. Louis, Feb. 13, 1916; s. Joseph Aloysius and Catherine Elizabeth (Burns) C.; m. Marjorie Ann Strode, Nov. 15, 1939 (div. 1963); m. Rosemary Klineberg, June 28, 1963 (div. 1976); m. Maryann Bishop, May 13, 1978; children: John Patrick, Catherine Elizabeth, Judith Ann, Megan Forbes, Susan Fox, James Odell; 1 stepchild, Janet Lynn Bishop. BS, U.S. Mil. Acad., 1939; postgrad., Columbia U., 1943-45; PhD in Internat. Relations, Georgetown U., 1954. Asst. dir. programs, spl. studies project Rockefeller Bros. Fund, 1956-57; exec. asst. to spl. asst. to Pres. for security ops. coordination, Washington, 1958-60; mem. staff Pres.'s Com. on Info. Activities Abroad, White House, 1960; research analyst Inst. for Def. Analyses, Washington, 1960-63; chief office of nat. security studies Bendix Systems div., Ann Arbor, Mich., 1963-67; prof. public and internat. affairs U. Pitts., 1967-80, Disting. Service prof., 1980-82, prof. emeritus, 1982—, dir. Ctr. for Internat. Security Studies, 1975-81; sr. research fellow Univ. Ctr. Internat. Studies, 1981-90; vis. prof. internat. peace and security studies Carnegie-Mellon U., 1986-91. Adj. prof. Carnegie Mellon U., 1991—92; sr. vis. fellow Ctr. for Internat. Studies Princeton U., 1990—91, sr. rsch. assoc., 1993—95, vis. lectr. Woodrow Wilson Sch., 1992; cons. AID, ACDA, Dept. Def. Dept. State, Internat. Comm. Agy.; dir. program on religion and conflict resolution Tanenbaum Ctr. Interreligious Understanding, 1999—2001. Author/editor books in field including Strategic Power and National Security, 1971, Arms Control and European Security, 1977, Allied Perceptions of Threat, 1983, Deterrence and Arms Control: American and West German Perspectives on INF, 1985, The Atlantic Alliance and the Middle East, 1989, Defense and Détente: U.S. and West German Perspectives on Defense Policy, 1989, Germany, the EU and the Future of Europe, 1995, The Future Role of NATO, 1997, Religion, Law and the Role of Force, 2002. Served to col. U.S. Army, 1939-60. Internat. Inst. Strategic Studies rsch. assoc., 1972-73; Stockholm Internat. Peace Rsch. Inst. fellow, 1977, NATO rsch. fellow, 1981, 89 Mem. Coun. Fgn. Rels., Fgn. Policy Assn., Internat. Inst. Strategic Studies, Internat. Studies Assn., European Cmty. Studies Assn., Atlantic Coun. U.S., Istituto Affari Internat. Home: 89 Castle Howard Ct Princeton NJ 08540-4025

COFFEY, KENDALL BRINDLEY, lawyer; b. Merced, Calif., Dec. 5, 1952; s. John Brindley and Valerie Alethea (Kendall) C.; m. Joni Beth Armstrong, Jan. 28, 1984; 1 child, Meredith Armstrong. BS in Broadcasting, U. Fla., 1975, JD, 1978. Bar: Fla. 1978, U.S. Ct. Appeals (9th and 11th cirs.) 1982. Law clk. U.S. Ct. Appeals (5th cir.), Newnan, Ga., 1978; assoc., bd. dirs. Greenberg, Traurig, Askew, Hoffman, Lipoff, Rosen & Quentel, P.A., Miami, Fla., 1978-88; ptnr. Coffey, Aragon, Martin & Burlington, P.A., Miami, 1988-93, also bd. dirs.; U.S. atty. U.S. Dept. of Justice, Miami, Fla., 1993-96; ptnr. Coffey, Diaz & O'Naghten, Miami, 1996—. Lectr. in field. Contbr. articles to profl. jours. Named Outstanding Young Dem. in Fla., Fla. Dem. Women's Clubs, 1975. Mem. Dade County Bar Assn. (pres. 1990), U. Fla. Law Rev. Alumni Assn. (pres. 1986-88, Most Productive Young Lawyer in Fla.). Home: 1639 S Bayshore Dr Miami FL 33133-4213 Office: Coffey Diaz & O'Naghten LLP 2665 S Bayshore Dr Miami FL 33133-5448

COFFEY, MARILYN JUNE, writer, educator; b. Alma, Nebr., July 22, 1937; d. June Thomas and Zelma Theola Coffey; m. John Raymond Powell, III (div.); m. Tom Henshaw (div.); 1 child, Ian Michael Henshaw. BA in Journalism, U. Nebr., 1959; MFA in Creative Writing, Bklyn. Coll., 1981. Journalist Lincoln (Nebr.) Evening Jour., 1959—60, Good Housekeeping, N.Y.C., 1960—61, Home Furnishings Daily, N.Y.C., 1964—66; asst. prof. Boston U., 1969—71; tenured prof. Pratt Inst., Bklyn., 1966—69, 1973—90; comm. instr. St. Mary's Coll., Lincoln, 1990—92; prof. creative writing Ft. Hays State U., Hays, Kans., 1992—2000; ret., 2000. Literature artist Kans. Arts Commn., Topeka, 1990—92, Nebr. Arts Coun., Lincoln, 1990—91; creative writer-in-residence Lawrence (Kans.) Arts Ctr., 1991. Author: Marcella, 1973, 1976, Great Plains: Patchwork, 1989, (book-length poem) A Cretan Cycle: Fragments Unearthed from Knossos, 1991. Named Listed Writer, Poets and Writers, 1973—2002, Admiral Nebr. Navy, Nebr. gov., 1977, Marilyn Coffey collection, Love Libr. Archives, 1987—; recipient Pushcart prize, Pushcart Press, 1976; grantee rsch. grantee, Ludwig Vogelstein Found., 1985—87, Mellon Funds through Pratt Inst., 1987—88. Mem.: Charlotte Writers Club. Avocations: Hatha yoga, walking, music, confabulating. Home: 1646-6 Chippendale Rd Charlotte NC 28205 E-mail: mcoffey65@hotmail.com.

COFFEY, MARY MARGARET, pharmacist; b. Allentown, Pa., June 21, 1972; d. Stephen and Jenny Tar; m. Mark Douglas Coffey, Dec. 31, 1999. BS in Pharmacy, U. Scis. in Phila., 1995; DPharm, Shenandoah U., 2002. Registered pharmacist. Staff pharmacist Rite Aid Corp., Wilmington, Del., 1995—96, pharmacy mgr., 1996—97, clin. educator Camp Hill, Pa., 1997—2001, diabetes program mgr., 2001—02; mgr. drug info. Bristol-Myers Squibb Co., Plainsboro, NJ, 2002—. Mem. pharmacy work group Am. Lung Assn. Attack Asthma Program, Phila., 1998—; Flex PharmD preceptor U. Scis. in Phila., 1998—2002. Mem.: Am. Diabetes Assn., Am. Pharm. Assn., Kappa Epsilon.

COFFEY, MATTHEW B. trade association executive; b. Cumberland, Md., Jan. 20, 1941; s. Francis Wade and Mary Agnes (Stegmaier) C.; m. Sharon Harriet West, May 20, 1971; children— Julia Katherine West, Francis Matthew West AA, Potomac State Coll., 1960; BS, W.Va. U., 1962, MBA, 1969. Investigator U.S. CSC, Washington, 1964-65; staff asst. to Pres. Johnson The White House, Washington, 1965-69; dir. planning Corp. for Pub. Broadcasting, Washington, 1969-73; dir. recruiting Carter-Mondale Transition, Washington, 1976-77; pres. Assn. of Pub. Radio Stas., Washington, 1973-77; sr. v.p. Nat. Pub. Radio, Washington, 1977; exec. v.p. Nat. Alliance of Bus., Washington, 1977-78; dir. Washington Office Textron, Inc., Washington, 1978-79; v.p., chief fin. officer Bridgeport-Textron, Bridgeport, Conn., 1979-83; exec. dir. Nat. Assn. Counties, Washington, 1983-85; pres. Nat. Tooling and Machining Assn., 1985—. Bd. dirs. Coun. for Adult and Experiential Learning, 1996-97; co-chmn. Commn. on Workforce Skills in Indsl. Found. Firms, 1992-94; mem. Nat. Alliance Bus. Coun. on Work Force Excellence, 1992-97; mem. industry adv. bd. D.O.E. Labs., 1993-96. Author: Toward a Clinical Method of Executive Selection, 1969; pub. Precision Mag., 1992-96; contbr. articles to profl. jours. Chmn., bd. dirs. Pub. Interest Groups, Washington, 1985; bd. dirs. Bridgeport (Conn.) Econ. Devel. Corp., 1981-83, Naugatuck Valley Indsl. Devel. Com., 1980-83; chmn. Pvt. Industry Coun., Bridgeport, 1981-83; bd. govs. Nat. Cathedral Sch., 1988; mem. bldg. com. Washington Nat. Cathedral, 1989—, co-chair long range planning task group, 1994-98, chmn. bldg. com., 1998—; trustee Protestand Episcopal Cathedral Found., 1998—; prin. Ctr. for Excellence in Govt., 1988-98; bd. mem. Small Bus. Legis. Coun., 1990—, chmn., 1998-99. Fellow Nat. Acad. Pub. Adminstrn., Congl. Country Club, Univ. Club. Avocation: sailing. Home: 3602 Massachusetts Ave NW Washington DC 20007-1449 Office: Nat Tooling & Machining Assn 9300 Livingston Rd Fort Washington MD 20744-4998 E-mail: mattcoffey@earthlink.net., matt@ntma.org.

COFFEY, NANCY ANN, real estate broker; b. Palm Springs, Calif. d. Arthur Johnson and Joan (Hunter) Coffey. BA, MS in Engring., Stanford U. Indsl. real estate broker Coldwell Banker, Houston, 1977-79, comml. broker San Francisco, 1980-87, Cushman & Wakefield, N.Y.C., 1987-90; model Gilla Roos,

N.Y.C., 1991-96; real estate broker, 1990-96; comml. real estate broker The Rolfe Group, N.Y.C., 1997-98, Cushman & Wakefield, Inc., N.Y.C., 1998-2000, Halstead Property, NYC, 2001—. Active Jr. League, San Francisco, 1981—87, N.Y.C., 1987—2000, sustainer, 1999—2000, Palo Alto Jr. League, 2000—01, N.Y. Jr. League, 2001—; mem. exec. com. spl. projects bd. Meml. Sloan Kettering Cancer Ctr., N.Y.C.; vice chair membership com. Soc. Meml. Sloan Kettering, 1999—2000, adminstrv. bd. mem.; v.p. Class of 1967 Stanford U.; parish life com. mem. St. James Ch., 1997—2000. Mem.: River Club NY, Rockaway Hunting Club. Home: Smoke Tree Ranch Palm Springs CA 92264

COFFEY, ROBERT J. neurosurgeon; b. Hartford, Conn., Sept. 26, 1950; s. Harry E. and Mary E. Coffey; m. Cheryl A. Bakas, Sept. 1978 (div. Dec. 31, 1988); m. Lulu B. Longstocking, Apr. 9, 2001. BA, Columbia Coll., 1975; MD, N.Y. Med. Coll., 1980. Diplomate Am. Bd. Neurol. Surgery. Faculty U. Pitts., 1987—90, Mayo Clinic, Rochester, Minn., 1990—97, St. George's U., Grenada, West Indies, 1997—2001; med. dir. Medtronic Neurol., Mpls., 1997—. Physician/tchr. Tng. Exch., Managua, Nicaragua, 1989, Managua, 94. Author: A Neuroimaging Atlas for Surgery of the Brain, 1998. Recipient William L. Olendorf award, Am. Soc. Neuroimaging, 1985. Mem.: Alpha Omega Alpha. Address: PO Box 319 81 Pondfield Rd Bronxville NY 10708-3818

COFFEY, ROBERT JOHN, pediatrician; b. Tulsa, Okla., July 10, 1948; s. George Clinton and Blanche Nellie (Clewell) C. BA cum laude, Washington U., St. Louis, 1970; MD, U. Okla., 1974. Resident in pediatrics Bronx (N.Y.) Mcpl. Hosp., 1974-77, fellow in pediatrics, 1977-78, dir. pediatric emergency svcs., 1978-82; pvt. practice pediatrics Soho Pediatric Group, N.Y.C., 1982-98; dir. Childrens Urgent Care Ctr. St. Francis Med. Ctr., Tulsa, 2000-01; pvt. practice pediat. Warren Clinic, Tulsa, 2001—. Dir. Childrens Urgent Care Ctr. St. Francis Med. Ctr., Tulsa., 1999. Office: Ste 704 6565 So Yale Tulsa OK 74136

COFFEY, SUSANNA JEAN, artist, educator; b. New London, Conn. d. Edwin Raymond and Magel C. (Willingham) C. BFA magna cum laude, U. Conn., 1977; MFA, Yale U., 1982. Tchg. asst. Yale U., 1982; prof. painting Sch. of the Art Inst. of Chgo., 1982—, 1985—. Vis. artist various schs., 1983—; adj. assoc. prof. U. Ill, 1983; vis. critic Royal Coll. Art, London, 1995, Vt. Studio Ctr., 1994; panel mem. Harvard Ctr. for Religious Studies, 2001. Illustrator: The H Hymn to Demeter, 1989, Monovassia (Eleni Fourtouni), 1979; one-woman shows include The Cultural Ctr. of the Chgo. Pub. Libr., 1986, Weatherspoon Gallery, Greensboro, N.C., 1993, Alpha Gallery, 1995, Galeria Alejandro Sales, Barcelona, 1995, Tibor De Nagy Gallery, 1996-97, 2001, others; represented in permanent collections Northwestern U., Evanston, Ill., Art Inst. Chgo., Mpls. Mus. Art, Bryn Mawr (Pa.) Coll., Boston Mus. Fine Arts, Weatherspoon Gallery, and pvt. collections. Individual Artists grant Conn. Commn. on the Arts, 1980, Residency grant Ragdale Found., Lake Forest, Ill., 1984, Faculty Enrichment grant SAIC, 1987, 90-91, Chgo. Artists Abroad grant, 1990, Ill./Arts Coun. grant, 1985, 92, Studio Program grant Marie Walsh Sharpe Found., 1992, Nat. Endowment for the Arts grant, 1993; Guggenheim fellow, 1996; recipient Louis Comfort Tiffany Found. award, 1993, Acad. award in art Am. Acad. of Arts and Letters, 1995; named to Nat. Acad. Design, 2001. Office: Sch of the Art Inst of Chgo 37 S Wabash Ave Chicago IL 60603-3002

COFFEY, THOMAS FRANCIS, JR., writer; b. Walthourville, Ga., Feb. 14, 1923; s. Thomas Francis and Julian (Bacon) C.; m. Mary Corley, Apr. 6, 1946 (dec. July 1988); 1 child, Mary Cynthia Smith; m. Marjorie Kinsner Guice, Nov. 11, 1989. Student Am. Press Inst., Columbia U., 1964; student program for urban execs., MIT, 1970. Reporter Savannah (Ga.) Eve. Press, 1940-42, asst. city editor, sports editor, 1945-55, city editor, 1960-64, mng. editor, 1964-67; dir. civilian pub. relations U.S. Army, Camp Stewart, Ga., 1942; news dir. Sta. WSAV-TV, Savannah, 1955-57; sports editor Savannah Morning News, 1957-60, mng. editor, 1967-69, assoc. editor, 1974-87, editor, 1987-89, columnist, 1989-98. Commentator WJCL-TV, Savannah, 1990-99. Author: Working for God, 1992, Only in Savannah, 1995, Savannah Lore and More, 1997. Asst. city mgr., City of Savannah, 1969-74; Bd. dirs. United Way of Savannah. Served with AUS, 1943-45. Decorated Bronze Star, Purple Heart. Mem. Ga. A.P. News Coun., Greater Savannah Hall Fame Assn. (pres. 1969), Internat. City Mgmt. Assn., Nat. Conf. Edit. Writers, Nat. Soc. Newspaper Columnists, Midway Soc. Ga. (pres. 1985), SR (pres. Ga.), Am. Legion, Sigma Delta Chi. Republican. Episcopalian (lic. lay reader). Club: Am. Business (past pres. Savannah chpt.). Home: 6401 Habersham St Unit 1B Savannah GA 31405-5632 Office: Savannah News Bldg 111 W Bay St Savannah GA 31401-1108 *Dedication to the task at hand/Compassion and concern for others/Gratitude to those who have built this nation/Faith in God.*

COFFEY, TIMOTHY, physicist; b. Washington, June 27, 1941; s. Timothy and Helen (Stevens) C.; m. Paula Marie Smith, Aug. 24, 1963; children: Timothy, Donna, Marie. BS in Elec. Engring. (Cambridge scholar 1958), MIT, 1962; MS in Physics, U. Mich., 1963, Evening News Assn. fellow, 1964, PhD, 1967. Rsch. physicist Air Force Cambridge Rsch. Lab., 1964; theoretical physicist EGG, Inc., Boston, 1966-71; head plasma dynamics br., then supt. plasma physics div. Naval Rsch. Lab., Washington, 1971-80, assoc. dir. rsch. for gen. sci. and tech., 1980-83, dir. rsch., 1983—2001; sr. rsch. scientist U. Md., Coll. Pk., 2001—. Recipient award Naval Rsch. Lab., 1974, 75, Disting. Civilian award Dept. Defense, 1991, Robert Dexter Conrad medal Dept. of Navy, 2000. Fellow Am. Phys. Soc., Washington Acad. Scis.; mem. AAAS, Franklin Inst. (com. for sci. and arts, Delmar S. Fahrney medal 1991), Am. Phys. Soc. Office: Univ Md 2133 Lee Bldg College Park MD 20742

COFFIELD, CONRAD EUGENE, lawyer; b. Hot Springs, S.D., Nov. 26, 1930; s. Eugene M. and Alice (Hotvet) Coffield; m. Mona L. Enfield, May 2, 1992; children: Conrad Eugene, Michael, Megan, Edward, Philip. Student, S.D. Sch. Mines and Tech., 1948—49; BBA, Washington U., St. Louis, 1952; LLB, U. Tex., 1959. Bar: Tex. 1959, N.Mex. 1959. Mem. Hervey, Dow & Hinkle, Roswell, N.Mex., 1959—64; gen. ptnr. Hinkle, Cox, Eaton, Coffield & Hensley, Roswell, 1964—66, resident ptnr. Midland, 1966—94, Santa Fe, 1994—2002, of counsel, 2002—. Served with USCGR, 1952—56. Fellow: Tex. Bar Found.; mem.: ABA, N.Mex. Oil and Gas Assn., Santa Fe County Bar Assn., N.Mex. Bar Assn., Tex. Bar Assn. Episcopalian. Office: Hinkle Cox Eaton Coffield Hensley 218 Montezuma Ave Santa Fe NM 87501-2625

COFFIELD, SHIRLEY ANN, lawyer, educator; b. Portland, Oreg., Mar. 31, 1945; BA, Willamette U., 1967; MA, U. Wisc.-Madison, 1969; JD, George Washington U., 1974. Bar: D.C. 1975. Clk. Stitt, Hemmendinger and Kennedy, Washington, 1973-74; asst. gen. counsel Office U.S. Trade Rep., Washington, 1975-79; ptnr. Reaves & Coffield, Washington, 1979-82; sr. counsel to dep. asst. sect. textiles and apparel U.S. Dept. Commerce, Washington, 1982-85; spl. counsel Skadden, Arps, Slate, Meagher and Flom, Washington, 1985-87; ptnr. Piper & Marbury, Washington and Balt., 1987-90, Baker & Hostetler, Washington, 1990-94, Keller and Heckman, L.L.P., Washington, 1994-98, Duane, Morris & Heckscher, 1998-2000, Coffield Law, Washington, 2000—. Adj. prof. internat. econ. law Georgetown U. Law Sch., 1982—. Mem. Fed. Bar Assn., Am. Soc. Internat. Law, D.C. Bar, Pi Gamma Mu, Phi Delta Phi. Office: Coffield Law Ste 315 666 11th St NW Washington DC 20001-4530 E-mail: coffieldlaw@yahoo.com.

COFFILL, MARJORIE LOUISE, civic leader; b. Sonora, Calif., June 11, 1917; d. Eric J. and Pearl (Needham) Segerstrom; A.B. with distinction in Social Sci., Stanford U., 1938, M.A. in Edn., 1941; m. William Charles Coffill, Jan. 25, 1948, (dec.); children: William James, Eric John. Asst. mgr. Sonora Abstract & Title Co. (Calif.), 1938-39; mem. dean of women's staff Stanford, 1939-41; social dir. women's campus Pomona Coll., 1941-43, instr. psychology, 1941-43; asst. to field dir. ARC, Lee Moore AFB, Calif., 1944-46; partner Riverbank Water Co., Riverbank and Hughson, Calif., 1950-68. Mem. Tuolumne County Mental Health Adv. Com., 1963-70; mem. central advisory com. Supplementary Edn. Ctr., Stockton, Calif., 1966-70; mem. advisory com. Columbia Jr. Coll., 1972-89, pres., 1980—; pres. Columbia Found., 1972-74, bd. dirs., 1974-77; mem. Tuolumne County Bicentennial Com., 1974—; active PTA, ARC. Pres., Tuolumne County Rep. Women, 1952—, assoc. mem. Calif. Rep. Central Com., 1950. Trustee Sonora Union High Sch., 1969-73, Salvation Army Tuolumne County, 1973—; bd. dirs. Lung Assn. Valley Lode Counties, 1974—, life 1986—. Recipient Pi Lambda Theta award, 1940, Outstanding Citizen award C. of C., 1974, Citizen of Yr. award, 1987, Woman of Distinction award Soroptimist Internat., 1993; named to Columbia Coll. Hall of Fame, 1990; named Alumnus of Yr., Sonora Union High Sch., 1994. Mem. AAUW (charter mem. Tuolumne County br., pres. Sonora br. 1965-66). Episcopalian (mem. vestry 1968, 75). Home: 376 Summit Ave Sonora CA 95370-5728

COFFIN, ANNE GAGNEBIN, educational association editor, consultant; b. Neptune, N.J., Aug. 2, 1939; d. Albert Paul and Genevieve (Hope) G.; m. John Devereux Coffin, Apr. 7, 1962; children: Samuel Devereux, Thomas Huguenin. BA, Smith Coll., 1961. Asst. editor, feature writer Look mag., N.Y.C., 1961-71; N.Y. rep., newsletter editor Villa I Tatti, Harvard U. Ctr. for Italian Renaissance Studies, Florence, 1984-92; dir. Internat. Print Ctr., N.Y.C., 2000—. Curator, exhbn. organizer Am. Art: The Last 4 Decades, London, 1977. Bd. dirs N.Y. Landmarks Conservancy, N.Y.C., 1981—; bd. dirs. Chamber Music Soc. Lincoln Ctr., N.Y.C., 1984—, Leopold Schepp Found., 1991—, Brit.-Am. Arts Assn., 1985—; mem. Art Table; mem. Villa I Jatti Coun., 1992—. Mem.: Cosmopolitan Club. Office: 526 W 26th St Rm 824 New York NY 10001

COFFIN, BEATRIZ DE WINTHUYSEN, landscape architect; b. Madrid, July 20, 1930; came to U.S., 1952; d. Javier de Winthuysen and Maria Hector; m. Laurence E. Coffin Jr., Jan. 4, 1958; children: Thomas A., Alisa W. BS, Furman U., Greenville, S.C., 1954; M in Landscape Arch., Harvard U., 1957. Cert. landscape architect, Md., Va. Landscape architect A. Carl Stelling, N.Y.C., 1957-58, Vorhees-Walker-Smith-Haines Architects, N.Y.C., 1958-60; ptnr. Coffin & Coffin, Washington, 1963—. Landscape architect USN, Washington, 1968; instr. George Washington U., 1974, U. Md., 1985; pres. Internat. Inst. Site Planning, Washington, 1976—; lectr. U. Guanajuato, Mex., 1989, 92; lectr., cons. City of Quito, Ecuador (sponsored by USIA), 1990, 1994, 99, La Paz, Bolivia (sponsored by USIA), 1995. Co-author: A Maryland New Town Turns 50, Arquitectura Paisajista, Quito, Conceptos y diseños, 1991, Lexicon, 2001; contbr. numerous articles to profl. pubis. Mem. design adv. steering com. D.C. Commn. on the Arts and the Humanities, 1986-94; bd. dirs. The World Charter Pub. Sch., Washington, 1998-2001. Fellow Am. Soc. Landscape Archs.; mem. Latin Am. Mgmt. Assn. (treas. 1991, 92, 90-95), Grupo Cultural San Gil. Office: Internat Inst Site Planning 715 G St SE Washington DC 20003-2853

COFFIN, BERTHA LOUISE, telephone company executive; b. Atlanta, Aug. 19, 1919; d. William Wesley and Bertha Louise (Marsh) Mendenhall; m. J. Donald Coffin, Feb. 14, 1943 (dec. Sept. 1978). BA, U. Kans., 1940. Med. technologist Midwest Research Lab., Emporia, Kans., 1940-43; ins. agt. Comml Ins. Agy., Council Grove, Kans., 1943-99, sole owner, mgr., 1978-82; treas. Council Grove Telephone Co., 1947-50, sec.-treas., 1950-78, pres., chmn. bd., 1978-98, gen. mgr., 1978-99. Del. legis. confs. Nat. Tel. Coop. Assn., 1986, 88, 91-92, 94, 97, comem. comml. co. com., 1987-91, mem. govt. affairs com., 1991-98, exec. com., 1996-98; founder, pres., chmn. bd. Kans. Personal Comm. Svcs. Ltd., 1995—; officer Cities Unltd., Inc., 1999—. Copy preparation for book The Story of the Santa Fe Trail, 1982; author: History of Council Grove Telephone Company, 1991; ann. civic sects. tel. directory. Pres. various lit. clubs, Council Grove, 1945-72; speaker various civic, polit. and religious groups, 1962—; mem. adv. coun. Manhattan Christian Coll., 1983-86, trustee, 1986-92, 93-99, 2000—, chmn., 1991-92. Mem. Kans. Telecomm. Assn. (bd. dirs. 1992-95), Ind. Tel. Pioneers (dir. 1984-92). Democrat. Avocations: travel, church related activities, speaking.

COFFIN, DAVID ROBBINS, art historian, educator; b. N.Y.C., Mar. 20, 1918; s. H. Errol and Lois (Robbins) C.; m. Nancy Merritt Nesbit, June 10, 1947; children— Elizabeth, David Tristram, Lois, Peter. AB, Princeton, 1940, M.F.A., 1947, PhD, 1954; postgrad., Yale U., 1940-41. Instr. fine arts U. Mich., 1947-49; lectr. art and archaeology Princeton, 1949-54, asst. prof., 1954-56, assoc. prof., 1956-60, prof. art and archaeology, 1960-66, Marquand prof. art and archaeology, 1966-70, Howard Crosby Butler Meml. prof. history architecture, 1970-88, prof. emeritus, 1988—, chmn. dept. art and archaeology, 1964-70; editor-in-chief Art Bull., 1959-62. Kress prof. CASVA Nat. Gallery Art, 1995-96. Author: Villa d'Este at Tivoli, 1960, The Villa in the Life of Renaissance Rome, 1979, Gardens and Gardening in Papal Rome, 1991, The English Garden: Meditation and Memorial, 1994, Princeton University's Graduate College, 2000; editor: The Italian Garden, 1st Dumbarton Oaks Colloquium on History of Landscape Architecture, 1972. Recipient Howard R. Marraro book award Am. Cath. Hist. Assn., 1979; Fulbright research award to Italy, 1951-52; McCosh Faculty fellow, also Am. Council of Learned Socs. fellow, 1963-64; Guggenheim Meml. Found. fellow, 1972-73; recipient Alice Davis Hitchcock book award Soc. Archtl. Historians, 1960; Howard T. Behrman award for disting. achievement in humanities, 1982 Mem. Coll. Art Assn. Am. (dir. 1957-61), Soc. Archtl. Historians (dir. 1968-70, treas. 1970-71), Renaissance Soc., Phi Beta Kappa. Office: Princeton U Dept Art And Archaeology Princeton NJ 08544-0001

COFFIN, DWIGHT CLAY, retired grain company executive; b. Evansville, Ind., Aug. 21, 1938; s. Dwight DeWitt and Ruth Robertson (Clay) Coffin; m. Carol Ann Elsaesser, Dec. 27, 1986; 1 child from previous marriage, John Charles. Student, DePauw U., 1959-61; BA, U. Pitts., 1963; MBA, NYU, 1970; postgrad. in bus., Harvard U., 1976; cert. in counseling, Postgrad. Ctr. Mental Health, N.Y.C., 2001. With Chase Manhattan Bank, N.Y.C., 1964-72, employee rels. officer, 1968-70, mgmt. svcs. officer, 1970-72; dir. employment and tng. Continental Grain Co., N.Y.C., 1972-73, dir. internat. pers. Paris, 1973-75, v.p. pers. N.Y.C., 1975-85, v.p., sec., 1985-86, v.p. human resources, 1986-99; now ret., cons. Mem global adv coun Am Grad Sch Int Mgt, 1986—. Pres Bishop's Fund for Children; dir Greenwich Found; pres Greenwich chpt English Speaking Union; warden St Barnabas Episcopal Ch, 1992—; bd dirs St Luke's Life Works, Stamford, 1989—. Mem.: SAR (treas Capt Mead chpt), Human Resource Planning Soc, Nat Foreign Trade Coun (chmn mgt resources comt 1984), Innis Arden Golf Club. Republican. Home: 115 Oak Tree Pl Santa Barbara CA 93108 E-mail: dwightcc@sover.net.

COFFIN, FRANK MOREY, judge; b. Lewiston, Maine, July 11, 1919; s. Herbert Rice and Ruth (Morey) Coffin; m. Ruth Ulrich, Dec. 19, 1942; children: Nancy, Douglas, Meredith, Susan. AB, Bates Coll., 1940, LLD, 1959; postgrad. indsl. adminstrn., Harvard U., 1943, LLB, 1947; LLD, Bates Coll., 1959, U. Maine, 1967, Bowdoin Coll., 1969; degree (hon.), Colby Coll., 1975. Bar: Maine 1947. Law clk. to fed. judge Dist. of Maine, 1947—49; engaged in practice, 1947—52; with Verrill, Dana, Walker, Philbrick & Whitehouse, Portland, Maine, 1952—56; mem. 85th-86th Congresses from 2d Dist. Maine, House Com. Fgn. Affairs; mng. dir. joint econ. com. Devel. Loan Fund, Dept. State, Washington, 1961; dep. adminstr. AID, 1961—64; U.S. rep. devel. assistance com. Orgn. Econ. Coop. and Devel., 1964—65; judge 1st circuit U.S. Ct. Appeals, 1965—, chief judge, 1972—83, sr. judge, 1989—; chmn. com. jud. br. U.S. Jud. Conf., 1984—90. Adj. prof. U. Maine Sch. Law, 1986—89. Author: Witness for Aid, 1964, The Ways of a Judge-Reflections from the Federal Appellate Bench, 1980, A Lexicon or Oral Advocacy, 1984, On Appeal, 1994. Emeritus Bates Coll.; dir. The Governance Inst., 1987—; mem. emeritus The Examiner; chair Maine Justice Action Group, 1996—2001. Lt. USNR, 1943—46. Recipient Edward J. Devitt Disting. Svc. to Justice award, 2001. Mem.: ABA, ABA (co-chmn. com. on loan forgiveness and repayment 2001—02), Am. Acad. Arts and Sci., Am. Acad. Arts and Sci. Office: US Ct Appeals 156 Federal St Portland ME 04101-4152

COFFIN, GEORGE JARVIS, III, advertising executive; b. N.Y., Aug. 18, 1957; s. George Jarvis and Barbara Jerauld C.; m. Susanne Madeira, Apr. 24, 1982 (div. June 1989); children: Sarah Nielson, George Jarvis; m. Marcia Nichols, June 12, 1993; 1 child, Nathan Jerauld. BA in Political Sci., Hobart Coll., 1979. Account exec. Dancer, Fitzgerald, Sample, N.Y., 1979-81; sales rep. Advertising Age, N.Y., 1981-82; assoc. publisher World Press Review, N.Y., 1982-85; sales mgr. USA Today, Boston, 1985-90, dir. sales N.Y., 1990-91; v.p. sales Business Week, N.Y., 1991-93; dir. nat. sales L.A. Times, N.Y., 1993-95; founder, pres. Burst Media, Burlington, Mass., 1995—. Mem. Lantern Club; chair Newspaper Assn. of AMSUCA, 1994-95. Founder/editor: (mag.) Running Iron Mag., 1977. Mem. Princeton Club, Mass. Interactive Mktg. Assn. Avocation: cooking. Office: Burst Media LLC 8 New England Executive Park Burlington MA 01803-5007 E-mail: burst@burstmedia.com.

COFFIN, LAURENCE EDMONDSTON, JR., landscape architect, urban planner; b. Toronto, Ont., Can., May 28, 1928; came to U.S., 1930; s. Laurence Edmondston and Josephine (Hewitt) C.; m. Beatriz de Winthuysen, Jan. 4, 1958; children: Thomas Amory, Alisa Winthuysen. BS in Hort., Va. Poly. Inst. and State U., 1952; M.L.A., Harvard U., 1957. Ptnr. Coffin & Winthuysen, East Lansing, Mich., 1962-65; asst. prof. Mich. State U., East Lansing, 1960-65; adj. assoc. prof. Cath. U. Am., Washington, 1966-81; ptnr. Coffin & Coffin, Washington, 1966—; sr. landscape architect Nat. Capital Devel. Commn., Canberra, Australia, 1985-87. Mem. architect/engr. select bd. Pennsylvania Ave. Devel. Corp., Washington, 1978-90; mem. design adv. panel Dept. of Housing and Community Devel., Balt., 1978-87; sec. Internat. Inst. Site Planning, Washington, 1980—; lectr. city planning Georgetown U., 1968, George Washington U., 1973, U. Md., 1982; vis. evaluator Landscape Archtl. Accreditation Bd., 1979-85. Elder Presbyterian Ch., Washington, 1977— . Fellow Am. Soc. Landscape Architects; mem. Am. Inst. Cert. Planners, Cosmos Club Washington. Democrat. Home: 9600 Potomac Dr Fort Washington MD 20744 Office: 715 G St SE Washington DC 20003-2853

COFFIN, LOUIS FUSSELL, JR., mechanical engineer; b. Schenectady, Aug. 30, 1917; s. Louis Fussell and Laura C. (Glen) C.; m. Mary Elizabeth McCarthy, Apr. 24, 1943; children— John, Sarah (Mrs. Joseph Fitzgerald), Laura (Mrs. Thomas Koch), Robert, Patricia (Mrs. Jeffrey Mullen), Deborah (Mrs. Patrick Higgins), Louis Fussell III, Margaret (Mrs. Neil Sharkey). BS, Swarthmore (Pa.) Coll., 1939; Sc.D., Mass. Inst. Tech., 1949. From asst. to asst. prof. mech. engring. Mass. Inst. Tech., 1939-49; research asso., then supr. mech. metallurgy Knolls Atomic Power Lab., Gen. Electric Co., 1949-54; mech. engr. Corp. Research and Devel. Gen. Electric Co., Schenectady, 1954-86. Adj. prof. mech. engring. Rensselaer Poly. Inst., Troy, N.Y., 1955-60, disting. rsch. prof., 1986-96; adj. prof. Union Coll., Schenectady, 1965-86; vis. fellow Clare Hall, Cambridge (Eng.) U., 1976; cons. in field. Author; patentee in field. Recipient Alfred E. Hunt award Am. Soc. Lubrication Engrs., 1958; award excellence Carborundum Co., 1974; Francis Clamer medal Franklin Inst., 1984 Clayton lectr. Inst. Mech. Engrs., London, 1974; Coolidge fellow, 1974 Fellow ASME (Nadai award 1979), Am. Soc. Metals (Albert Sauveur Achievement award 1980), ASTM (chmn. E9 com. on fatigue 1974-78, Dudley award 1975, award of merit 1978, Kroll zirconium medal 1991); mem. Nat. Acad. Engring., Am. Inst. Metall. Engrs. (Disting. Career award 1978), Sigma Xi, Pi Tau Sigma, Sigma Tau. Home: 235 Walker St Apt 172 Lenox MA 01240-2747

COFFIN, MARY ANN, elementary school educator; b. Pasco, Wash., Feb. 28, 1950; d. Orville Bernard and Elizabeth Lucille Waddell; m. Jon William Coffin, Aug. 16, 1969; children: Jason, Rainey. BA in Edn., Ea. Wash. U., 1980. Tchr. Butte Sch. Dist., Arco, Idaho, 1981—83, Post Falls (Idaho) Sch. Dist., 1983—. Author: In Spite of It All, 1997. Negotiator Post Falls Edn. Assn. Named Tchr of Yr., Post Falls Edn. Assn., 1989, Tchr. of Month, 2002. Democrat. Avocations: reading, golf, interior decorating. Home: 5631 N Vista Grande Dr Otis Orchards WA 99027-9116

COFFIN, RICHARD KEITH, lawyer; b. St. Louis, Apr. 6, 1940; s. Kenneth and Agnes (Ryan) C.; m. June Springmeyer, Apr. 8, 1972; children: Jennifer, Joanna. BS, U. Notre Dame, 1962; MBA, St. Louis U., 1967, JD, 1971. Engr. Nooter Corp., St. Louis, 1962-72; spl. prosecutor U.S. Dept. Justice, St. Louis, 1972-74; ptnr. Coffin & Torrence, P.C., St. Louis. Gen. counsel Southwestern Linen & Indsl. Supply Assn., St. Louis; gen. counsel Mission Industries, Las Vegas, Nev., 1996. Mem. Citizens Adv. Com., Parkway Sch. Bd., Chesterfield, Mo., 1980-82; treas. PSO Com., Parkway Sch., 1982-83. Mem. ABA, Mo. Bar Assn., Met. Bar Assn. St. Louis, Assn. Trial Lawyers Am., Mo. Assn. Trial Attys., Optimist Club (sec. 1981), Phi Alpha Delta. Roman Catholic. Home and Office: 1748 Orchard Hill Dr Chesterfield MO 63017-5127

COFFIN, TRISTRAM POTTER, retired English educator, writer; b. San Marino, Calif., Feb. 13, 1922; s. Tristram Roberts Coffin and Elsie Potter Robinson; m. Ruth Anne Hendrickson, Feb. 15, 1944; children: Patricia, Mark, Priscilla, Jonathan. BS, Haverford Coll., 1943; MA, U. Pa., 1947, PhD, 1949. From instr. to assoc. prof. English and folklore Denison U., Granville, Ohio, 1949-58; from assoc. prof. to prof. U. Pa., Phila., 1958-84, emeritus prof., 1984—, vice dean grad. arts and scis., 1965-68. Vis. prof. UCLA, 1955, U.S. Mil. Acad., West Point, N.Y., 1962-63, U. R.I., Kingston, summers 1968-70, Providence Coll., 1985-93. Author: The British Traditional Ballad in North America, 1950, 63, 77, An Analytical Index to the Journal of American Folklore, 1958, Uncertain Glory: Folklore and the American Revolution, 1971, The Old Ball Game: Baseball in Folklore and Fiction, 1971, illustrated edit., 1972, The Book of Christmas Folklore, 1973, illustrated edit., 1974, The Female Hero, 1975, paperback edit., 1978, The Proper Book of Sexual Folklore, 1978, Great Game for a Girl, 1980, How to Play Tennis with What You Already Have, 1997, My Own Trumpet, 2001; co-editor: (with Helen Flanders and Bruno Nettl) Ancient Ballads Traditionally Sung in New England, 4 vols., 1960, (with MacEdward Leach) Critics and the Ballad, 1961, (with Hennig Cohen) Folklore in America, 1966, Folklore from the Working Folk, 1974, The Parade of Heroes, 1978, The Folklore of the American Holidays, 1987, 3d edit., 1998, America Celebrates, 1991; editor: Indian Tales of North America, 1961, Our Living Traditions, 1968, Born Again, 2002; contbr. over 100 articles and revs. to profl. pubs. Cond. Voice of Am. Forum, 1966-67; chmn. Athletic Coun. U. Pa., 1965-72; soccer ofcl. USSFA, Phila., 1959-74; chief cons. Time-Life Enchanted World series, 1982-87. Recipient Citation for Outstanding Reference Work ALA, 1988; Guggenheim fellow, 1953; ACLS grantee, 1963. Fellow Am. Folklore Soc. (sec.-treas. 1961-65, editor spl. series and supplements 1961-65); mem. Dunes Club, Point Judith Country Club (tennis pro 1954-76), Merion Cricket Club, Phi Beta Kappa. Episcopalian. Avocations: tennis, bowling. Home: PO Box 509 94 Edgewood Farm Rd Wakefield RI 02879-3903 E-mail: t.p.coffin@aol.com.

COFFINGER, MARALIN KATHARYNE, retired career officer, consultant; b. Ogden, Iowa, July 5, 1935; d. Cleo Russell and Katharyne Frances (McGovern) Morse. BA, Ariz. State U., 1957, MA, 1962; diploma, Armed Forces Staff Coll., 1972, Nat. War Coll., 1977; postgrad., Inst. for Higher Def. Studies, 1985. Commd. 2nd lt. USAF, 1963, advanced through grades to brig. gen., 1985; base comdr., dep. base comdr. Elmendorf AFB, Anchorage, Alaska, 1977-79; base comdr. Norton AFB, San Bernardino, Calif., 1979-82; chmn. spl. and incentive pays Office of Sec. Def., Pentagon, Washington, 1982-83; dep. dir. pers. programs USAF Hdqrs., Pentagon, Washington, 1983-85; command dir. NORAD, Combat Ops., Cheyenne Mountain Complex, Colo., 1985-86; dir. pers. plans USAF Hdqrs., Pentagon, Washington, 1986-89; ret. USAF, 1989; dir. software products ops. Walsh America, 1992-94. Mem. Phoenix Symphony Orch., 1954—63; prin. flutist Sonoran Wind Quartet, Scottsdale Cmty. Orch. Band, Scottsdale Concert Band, Ariz.; keynote spkr., mem. dedication ceremonies Vietnam Meml. Com., Phoenix, 1990. Decorated Air Force D.S.M., Def. Superior Svc. medal, Legion of Merit, Bronze Star.; recipient Nat. Medal of Merit. Mem. NAFE, Air Force Assn. (vet./retiree coun., pres. Sky Harbor chpt. 1990), Nat. Officers Assn., Ret. Officers Assn., Maricopa County Sheriff's Exec. Posse, Ariz. State U. Alumni Assn. (Profl. Excellence award 1981), Nat. Assn. Uniformed Svcs., Recording for the Blind and Dyslexic. Roman Catholic. Home: 8059 E Maria Dr Scottsdale AZ 85255-5418 E-mail: mcoffinger@att.net.

COFFMAN, BARBARA LEANN, environmentalist; b. Conrad, Mont., Nov. 21, 1968; d. Walter Lloyd and Loretta Louise (Tomsha) C. AS in Agrl. Tech., Mont. State U.-No., 1990, AS in Environ. Health, 1991, BS in Water Quality and Chemistry, 1993, MS in Gen. Sci. Edn., 2001. Cert. backflow assembly tester and proctor. Indsl. waste technician No. Mont. Coll., City of Havre (Mont.), Burlington No., 1990; rsch. technician No. Mont. Coll., Mont. Salinity Control Assn., 1990-93; EPA grant asst., tng. asst. No. Mont. Coll. (now Mont. State U.-No.), 1989-93, lab. technician, 1991-93, lab. tchg. asst., 1992; hydrotechnician, rsch. asst. Mont. Bur. Mines and Geology, Butte, 1993-94; tng. specialist Mont. Environ. Tng. Ctr., Gt. Falls, 1994-2000; Mont. class I wastewater treatment plant operator City of Havre, Mont., 2000—. Mem. continuing edn. credit rev. com. for Mont. water and wastewater cert., 1996-2000; adv. bd. Mont. State U. No. Sci., 1997-2000. Bd. dirs. Collins (Mont.) Cmty. Hall, 1994-2000. Recipient Earth Team Vol. award Soil Conservation Svc., Havre, 1989, cert. of achievement Dept. Energy, Richland, Wash., 1991. Mem. Am. Water Works Assn. (sec.-treas. Mont. sect. 1999-2003, exec. sec. Mont. sect. 2003—), Am. Backflow Prevention Assn. (cert. tester and proctor), Water Environment Fedn. Avocations: family farming, stamp and rock collecting, fly fishing, horseback riding, playing basketball. Office: City of Havre PO Box 231 Havre MT 59501

COFFMAN, CLAUDE T. law educator, lawyer; b. Robinsonville, Miss., Jan. 20, 1916; s. Tulus Jackson and Addie (Mick) C.; m. Ninna Carr Bailey, July 15, 1940; children: Mary, Margaret. AB, LLB, U. Miss., 1938; postgrad. Harvard

U., 1939. Bar: Miss. 1938. Atty., U.S. Dept. Agr., Washington, 1939-51, dep. gen counsel, 1968-74; asst. legal counsel Tech. Corp. Adminstrn., Washington, 1951-53; prof. law Memphis State U., 1974-86; prof. emeritus and interim dean, 1986-87. Contbr. articles to profl. jours. Mem. ABA. Episcopalian. Home: 1028 Cresthaven Rd Ste 206 Memphis TN 38119-3871

COFFMAN, DALLAS WHITNEY, financial consultant; b. Louisville, Sept. 18, 1957; s. Lawrence DuWaine and Jean (Smith) C.; m. Deborah Joan Schneider, May 18, 1980 (div. July 1987); 1 child, Robert Smith; m. Francine Ruth Chaput, Dec. 26, 1987 (div. Jan. 1995); m. Diana Elise Pivo, May 28, 1995 (div. Dec. 1999); m. Gayle Amanda Leinberry, Oct. 5, 2002. AS in Bus. Mgmt., No. Essex Community Coll., Haverhill, Mass., 1977; BS in Mktg. Mgmt., Bentley Coll., 1979. CLU, CFP; chartered fin. cons.; registered investment adviser; lic. ins. adviser, Mass. Mgr. McDonalds Corp., Westwood, Mass., 1975-79; fin. salesman Gold Assocs., Chestnut Hill, Mass., 1979-84; propr., fin. planner Whitman Fin. Svcs., Wakefield, Mass., 1984—; prin. gen. securities N.Y. Stock Exchange, 1987. Adj. faculty Am. Coll., Bryn Mawr, Pa., 1986—, Northeastern U., Boston, 1986—, Coll. for Fin. Planning, Denver, 1986—; enrolled agt. IRS, 1989; gen. securities prin. br. mgr. Office of Supervisory Jurisdiction for LINSCO/Pvt. Ledger, 1990—; former mem. Boston chpt. Am. Soc. CLUs and ChFCs, Mass. and Boston chpts. Nat. Assn. Life Underwriters. Pub. Who's Who in Life Ins., 1982-84; contbr. articles to profl. jours. Test participant Project PIPER IRS, 1990-92; sponsor Wakefield Little League. Mem. Orgn. Ams. for Legal Reform, Am. Arbitration Assn. (panel arbitrators), Nat. Assn. Securities Dealers (chairperson, mem. bd. arbitrators large and complex case pool 1990, chmn., 1997), Internat. Assn. for Fin. Planning, Registry Fin. Planning Practitioners, Boston Estate Planning Coun., Bentley Coll. Reps. for Admissions Vol. Orgn., Inst. of Cert. Fin. Planners (bd. stds. cert. exam, mem. intem writing com.), Fin. Planning Assn. Avocations: music, skiing, motorcycles, dancing, bicycling. Office: Whitman Fin Svcs 382 Lowell St Ste 203 Wakefield MA 01880-1985 E-mail: financial@compuserve.com.

COFFMAN, DANIEL RAY, JR., lawyer; b. Richmond, Va., Feb. 13, 1933; s. D. Ray and Clara (Noell) C.; m. Blanche Gray Coffman, Oct. 8, 1960; children— Elizabeth, Julia, Virginia, Emily. B.A., Vanderbilt U., 1954, J.D., 1960. Bar: Fla. 1960. Shareholder Coffman, Coleman, Andrews & Grogan, P.A., Jacksonville, Fla., 1971— ; labor counsel Fla. Jr. Coll., Jacksonville, 1975-88. Bd. dirs. Salvation Army; mem. adv. bd. Learn to Read, Jacksonville. Served to lt USNR, 1954-57. Mem. ABA, Jacksonville Bar Assn., Bar (chmn. labor and employment law com. 1969-70), Jacksonville Area C. of C. (gen. counsel 1985, v.p. 1987). Republican. Presbyterian Club: Exchange (past pres.). Home: 4061 Timuquana Rd Jacksonville FL 32210-8531 Office: Coffman Coleman Andrews & Grogan 2065 Herschel St Jacksonville FL 32204-3875

COFFMAN, EDWARD MCKENZIE, history educator; b. Hopkinsville, Ky., Jan. 27, 1929; s. Howard Beverly and Mada (Wright) C.; m. Anne Nelson Rouse, June 30, 1955; children: Anne Wright, Lucia Page, Edward McKenzie. AB, U. Ky., 1951, MA, 1955, PhD (So. Faculty fellow), 1959. Instr., asst. prof. Memphis State U., 1957-61; research asso. George C. Marshall Research Found., 1960 61; asst. prof., assoc. prof., prof. history U. Wis., Madison, 1961-92, prof. emeritus, 1992—. Dwight D. Eisenhower vis. prof. Kans. State U., 1969-70; vis. prof. mil. history U.S. Mil. Acad., 1977-78; disting. vis. prof. USAF Acad., 1982-83; Harold K. Johnson vis. prof. U.S. Army Mil. History Inst., 1986-87; mem. adv. com. Dept. Army Mil. History Program, 1971-76, 87-89, chair, 1989-93; mem. Nat. Hist. Publs. and Records Commn., 1972-76; John F. Morrison vis. prof. U.S. Army Command and Gen. Staff Coll., 1990-91. Author: The Hilt of the Sword: The Career of Peyton C. March, 1966, The War to End All Wars: The American Military Experience in World War I, 1968, The Old Army: A Portrait of the American Army in Peacetime, 1784-1898, 1986; mem. editorial bd. Mil. Affairs, 1974-77, Arno Press series The American Military Experience and The George C. Marshall Papers; chmn. editorial bd. Jour. Mil. History, 1995-99. Served with U.S. Army, 1951-53. Recipient Outstanding Civilian Svc. medal Dept. Army, 1978, Comdr.'s Pub. Svc. award, 1987, Disting. Civilian Svc. medal, 1991; Guggenheim fellow, 1973-74; Harmon Lectr. USAF Acad., 1976; Am. Philos. Soc. grantee, 1960; named U. Ky. Disting. Alumnus, 1995. Mem. Soc. for Mil. History (pres. 1983-85, Samuel Eliot Morison prize 1990, Moncado prize 1995), U.S. Commn. Mil. History, So. Hist. Soc., Phi Beta Kappa. Democrat. Home: 1089 Lakewood Dr Lexington KY 40502-2523

COFFMAN, HAROLD EMERSON, retired agricultural products supplier, retail merchant; b. Lafayette, Indiana, Sept. 5, 1927; s. Russell Ambrose and Irene Elizabeth (Wiggins) Coffman; m. Marrie Christine Nelson, Oct. 3, 1953. BS, Morningside Coll., Sioux City, Iowa, 1948—53; attended, U. Ill., Chgo., 1962—63. Asst. dir. mfg. budgets Oliver Corp., Chgo., 1955, sales analyst, Ter. mgr., market rsch. analyst; sales promotion mgr. Oliver Corp., White Farm Equip., Chgo., 1977; dir. dealer devel. White Farm Equip., Omaha; gen. sales mgr. White Outdoor Equip., Oak Brook, Ill.; shop owner Framing Loft, Sun City, Ariz., 1977—97, ret., 1997—. Pres. Prof. Picture Framing Assn., Ariz. Chpt., Phoenix, 1980—81. Author: (book) This is Our Forest, 2002. Quarter master 3 USN, 1946—47, Pacific, ensign USNR, 1956, retired LTJG USN, 1963. Recipient 1st Pl. Award, creative framing, needlework, Prof. Picture Frames Assn., 1989. Avocations: stained glass, golf, writing, reading. Home: 10128 Shasta Dr Sun City AZ 85351-1204 E-mail: COFF2@juno.com.

COFFMAN, JAMES RICHARD, academic administrator, veterinarian; b. Lyndon, Kans., July 19, 1938; s. Harry Thomas and Eleanor Louise (Lowe) C.; m. Sharon Sue Neill, June 10, 1960; children: David Neill, Michael James, Scott Thomas. BS, Kans. State U., 1960, DVM, 1962, MS, 1969. Pvt. practice equine vet., Wichita, Kans., 1962-65, Oklahoma City, 1969-71; inst. vet. medicine Kans. State U., Manhattan, 1965-69, prof., head dept. surgery and medicine, vet. medicine, 1981-84, prof. vet. medicine, dean, 1984-87, provost, 1987—; assoc. prof. vet. medicine and surgery U. Mo., Columbia, 1971-75, prof., 1975-81, dir. Equine Ctr., 1973-78; prof., head dept. surgery and medicine Sch. Vet. Medicine Kans. State U., Manhattan, 1981-84, prof., dean, 1984-87, provost, 1987—. Chair Nat. rsch. Coun., Bd. on Agr. subcom., 1999. Author: Equine Chemistry and Pathophysiology, 1991; equine editor Compendium on Continuing Edn. 1980-83, mem. editorial bd., 1980-85; editor in chief Equine Sportsmedicine, 1981-85; mem. editorial bd. Jour. Equine Medicine and Surgery, 1979-80; adv. bd. Equine Vet. Jour., 1980—; contbr. numerous articles to profl. jours. Bd. dirs. St. Mary Hosp., Manhattan, 1989—. Recipient Disting. Tchr. award Norden Labs., 1969. Mem. Am. Coll. Vet. Internal Medicine (diplomate, pres. 1978-79, chmn. bd. regents 1979-80), Am. Assn. Equine Practitioners (dir. at large 1982-83, v.p. 1984, pres. 1986-87), Am. Vet. Med. Assn. (trustee profl. liability ins. trust 1978-85, chmn. 1980-82), Nat. Acads. Practice Vet. Medicine (exec. bd. 1985-87, founding com. mem. 1985—), Kans. Vet. Med. Assn., Nat. Assn. State Univs. and Land Grant Colls. (coun. chief acad. officers 1987—, exec. coun. on acad. affairs), Rotary (bd. dirs. 1989-90), Phi Kappa Phi, Gamma Sigma Delta, Phi Zeta. Avocation: oil painting. Home: 200 Waterbridge Rd Manhattan KS 66503-2512

COFFMAN, JAY DENTON, physician, educator; b. Quincy, Mass., Nov. 17, 1928; s. Frank David and Etta (Kline) C.; m. Louise G. Peters, June 29, 1955; children: Geoffrey J., Joanne K., Linda J., Robert B. AB, Harvard U., 1950; MD, Boston U., 1954. Diplomate Am. Bd. Internal Medicine. Med. intern Univ. Hosp., Boston, 1954-55, asst. resident in medicine, 1955-56, chief resident in medicine, 1957-58, fellow in cardiovascular disease, 1956-57, sect. head peripheral vascular dept., 1960—; asso. in medicine Boston U. Med. Sch., 1960-65, mem. faculty, 1965—, prof. medicine, 1970—. Author: Raynaud's Phenomenon, 1989; co-author: Ischemic Limbs, 1973, Peripheral Arterial Disease, 2002. Trustee Solomon Carter Fuller Mental Health Center, Boston, 1975-81. Served to capt. M.C. USAR, 1958-60. Mem. ACP. Am. Soc. Clin. Investigation, Am. Fedn. Clin. Rsch., Am. Heart Assn., Begg's Soc., Phi Beta Kappa, Alpha Omega Alpha. Office: 88 E Newton St Boston MA 02118-2308

COFFMAN, JENNIFER BURCHAM, federal judge; b. 1948; BA, U. Ky., 1969, MA, 1971, JD, 1978. Ref. libr. Newport News (Va.) Pub. Libr., 1972-74, U. Ky. Libr., 1974-76; atty. Law Offices Arthur L. Brooks, Lexington, Ky., 1978-82; ptnr. Brooks, Coffman and Fitzpatrick, Lexington, 1982-92, Newberry, Hargrove & Rambicure, Lexington, 1992-93; judge U.S. Dist. Ct. (ea. dist. and we. dist.) Ky., 1993—. Adj. prof. Coll. Law, U. Ky., 1979-81. Elder Second Presbyn. Ch., 1993—96; bd. dirs. YWCA Lexington, 1986—92, Shepherd Ctr., 2000—. Mem. Ky. Bar Assn., Fayette County Bar Assn., U. Ky. Law Sch. Alumni Assn. Office: 306 US Courthouse 101 Barr St Lexington KY 40507-1313

COFFMAN, MATTHEW THOMAS, marketing executive, land use planner; b. Santa Monica, Calif., Apr. 16, 1962; s. Jerry Lee and Karen C.; m. Christine M. Didier, June 1, 1996; children: Michael Philip, Thomas Matthew. BS, Ind. U., 1985. Cert. planner Am. Inst. Cert. Planner. Prin. planner, mgr. City of Indpls., 1985-89; dir. real estate Eller Media, Indpls., 1989-94; account exec. Burkhart Advt., Fort Wayne, Ind., 1994-97, Viacom Outdoor, Fort Wayne, 1998—. Pres., bd. dirs. Theta Chi Realty Corp., Bloomington, 1990—, Greater Indpls. Rep. Fin. Com., 1993-94. Mem. Outdoor Advt. Assn. of Ind. (dir. 1991-94, bd. dirs. 2000—), Columbia Club Indpls., Theta Chi. Home: 10507 Oak Tree Rd Fort Wayne IN 46845

COFFMAN, MICHAEL S. international organization official; b. 1943; m. Susan Coffman; children: Jonathan, Tamera. BS in forestry, No. Ariz. U., 1966, MS in biology, 1967; PhD in forest sci., U. Idaho, Moscow, 1970. Pres. Environ. Perspectives, Inc.; dir. Sovereignty Internat. Pub. Discerning the Times Digest, 1999—. Author: Saviors of the Earth. Office: 1229 Broadway #313 Bangor ME 04401

COFFMAN, PENELOPE DALTON, judge; b. Pulaski, Va., Apr. 16, 1938; d. Gomez and Hazel (Davis) Dalton; m. Aldine J. Coffman, Mar. 27, 1965; children: D'Maris, Derek. AB, Randolph-Macon Women's Coll., 1958; JD, Coll. William and Mary, 1965. Bar: Va. 1966, Utah 1977, Colo. 1984. Law clk. Va. Supreme Ct., Richmond, 1966-68; asst. commonwealth atty. Commonwealth Atty.'s Office, Virginia Beach, va., 1970-73; ptnr. Coffman & Coffman, Virginia Beach, 1968-75, Moab, Utah, 1975-88, Dodd, Scott, Stockton & Coffman, Lakewood, Colo., 1990-94; substitute judge Cherry Hills Village and Greenwood Village, Colo., 1992—. Articles editor William and Mary Law Rev., 1964-66; book reviewer. Bd. dirs. Four County Travel Coun., Grand County, Utah, 1978-82, Health Coun., Grand County, 1978-82, Mental Health, Grand County, 1978-82, Va. Coun. Ednl. TV, 1970-72. Mem. Denver Women's Press Club (bd. dirs., treas.). Republican. Episcopalian. Avocation: competitive bridge. Home: 6 Cherry Lane Dr Englewood CO 80110-4210

COFFMAN, VANCE D. aerospace company executive; b. Kinross, Iowa, Apr. 3, 1944; BS in Aerospace Engring., Iowa State U.; MS in Aeronautics/Astronautics, PhD in Aeronautics and Astronautics, Stanford U. Guidance and control sys. analyst Space Sys. divsn. Lockheed, 1985—87, divsn. v.p., 1987—88, gen. mgr., 1988, pres. Space Sys. divsn., 1995, pres., COO Space & Strategic Missiles sector, 1995—97, CEO and vice chmn. bd. dirs., 1997-98, chmn., CEO, 1998—. Bd. dirs. Bristol-Myers Squibb, 3M, United Negro Coll. Fund Recipient Profl. Progress in Engring. award Iowa State U., 1989, Disting. Achievement award Iowa State U., 1999, Bob Hope Disting. Citizen award Nat. Def. Indsl. Assn. L.A. chpt., Exec. of Yr. Nat. Mgmt. Assn., 2002. Fellow AIAA, Am. Astron. Soc.; mem. Nat. Acad. Engring., Am. Def. Preparedness Assn., Nat. Security Indsl. Assn., Security Affairs Support Assn. Office: Lockheed Martin 6801 Rockledge Dr Bethesda MD 20817-1877

COFFMAN, WILMA MARTIN, women's health nurse, educator; b. Washington County, Tenn., Dec. 29, 1939; d. Oval Earnest and Buena (Light) Martin; m. Niles Lee Coffman, Aug. 26, 1961; children: Stephen Lee, Ruth Marie, Andrew William. BSN, East Tenn. State U., 1962; MS, U. Tenn., Knoxville, 1987. RN, Tenn. Staff nurse in maternal-child health Holston Valley Hosp. and Med. Ctr., Kingsport, Tenn.; instr. Kingsport City Schs., Johnson City Schs. Organist, pianist Beulah Bapt. Ch., Jonesborough, Tenn., Greenvale Bapt. Ch.; pianist First Bapt. Ch., Jonesborough, Tenn. Mem. Toonie Cash Evangelist Assn., Pi Lambda Theta. Home: 410 Lakeridge St Kingsport TN 37663-3770

COFIELD, ROBERT HAHN, orthopedic surgeon, educator; b. Cin., Oct. 24, 1943; s. Robert Hedrick and Virginia (Hahn) C.; m. Pamela Joyce Haarbauer, Aug. 12, 1967; children: Robert, Stacey, Virginia. BA, Washington and Lee U., 1965; MD, U. Ky., 1969; MS, Mayo Grad. Sch. Medicine, 1976. Diplomate Am. Bd. Orthopedic Surgery. Intern Charity Hosp./Tulane U., New Orleans, 1970; cons. Mayo Clinic, Rochester, Minn., 1975—; from instr. to assoc. prof. Mayo Med. Sch., Rochester, 1975-88, prof., 1988—; vice chmn. dept. orthopedics Mayo Clinic, Rochester, 1992-97, Frank R. and Shari Caywood prof. orthopedic surgery, 1993; assoc. dean Mayo Grad. Sch., Rochester, 1992-94, dean, 1994-98; chmn. dept. orthopedics Mayo Clinic, Rochester, 1997—; pres. Am. Bd. Orthopaedic Surgery, Chapel Hill, 1999-2000. Editor-in-chief Jour. Shoulder and Elbow Surgery, 1990-96; contbr. chpts. to books, more than 150 articles to profl. jours.; co-inventor humeral resect. guide; co-designer Cofield total shoulder sys. Lt. comdr. USNR. Mem. ACS, AMA, Am. Acad. Orthopedic Surgery, Am. Bd. Orthopedic Surgery (dir. 114—), Am. Orthopedic Assn., Am. Shoulder and Elbow Surgeons (founding sec.-treas. 1982-87, pres. 1988-89). Republican. Presbyterian. Office: Mayo Clinic 200 1st Ave NW Rochester MN 55901-3004

COFRAN, GEORGE LEE, telecommunication consultant; b. Buffalo, Sept. 30, 1945; s. Louis Lee and Virginia Carolyn Cofran; divorced; children: Jeffrey Todd, Jennifer Renee. BSEE, Purdue U., 1967; MBA, Dartmouth Coll., 1969. CPA, Tex. Sys. analyst Burlington Mgmt. Svcs., Greensboro, N.C., 1969-70; mgmt. cons. Arthur Young & Co., Houston, 1971-77; pres. Cofran & Assoc., Inc., Houston, 1977—. Comml. arbitrator Am. Arbitration Assn.; spkr., lectr. in field. Bd. dirs., pres. Huntwick Civic Assn., Houston; charter v.p. Active Corps of Execs., SBA, 1974, 75. 1st lt. AUS, 1970-71. Decorated Army Commendation medal. Mem. AICPA, IEEE, Assn. Sys. Mgmt. (past pres., dir. Houston chpt., Outstanding Svc. award 1978-79), Data Processing Mgmt. Assn. (cert.), Tau Beta Pi. Avocations: volunteer fireman and EMT paramedic, amateur radio. Home and Office: Cofran & Assoc Inc 1933 Lawrence Rd Kemah TX 77565-3122

COFRANCESCO, DONALD GEORGE, health facility administrator; b. New Haven, May 29, 1953; s. George William and Marie Teresa (Marra) C. BS with distinction in Chemistry and Life Scis., Worcester Poly. Inst., 1975; MA in Gerontology, U. New Haven, 1979; MPH, Yale U., 1992. Lic. nursing home adminstr., Conn. Dir. biostats. and health planning Dept. of Health, New Haven, 1980; adminstr. Golden Manor Convalescent Home, New Haven, 1980-81, West Haven (Conn.) Nursing Ctr., 1981-85, Independence Manor, Meriden, Conn., 1986-87, Hillside Manor, Hartford, Conn., 1987-88; asst. in rsch. Yale U. Sch. Medicine, New Haven, 1975-77; asst. adminstr., fin. analyst, lectr., clin. practice specialist Yale U. Sch. Medicine, New Haven, 1990—2001. Cons. Hospice: Project Care, Inc., Watertown, Conn., 1989—90; v.p., CFO Environ. Health Corp., Hamden, Conn., 1991—98; healthcare cons. Coe Cons. Co., Hamden, 2001—. Bd. dirs. Partnerships Ctr. for Adult Day Care, Inc., Hamden, 1991—, pres., 1997-98, treas., 1998-99, sec., 2001—; mem. Health Systems Agy. South Cen. Conn., Inc., Woodbridge, 1982-87; commr. human svcs. Town of Hamden, 1998—, vice chmn., 2002—. Named one of Outstanding Young Men of Am., 1983. Mem. APHA, Am. Chem. Soc., Assn. Yale Alumni Pub. Health, Am. Radio Relay League (tech. class amateur radio lic.) Roman Catholic. Avocation: amateur radio. Home: 104 Hillfield Rd Hamden CT 06518-1852 E-mail: DCofrancesco@msn.com.

COGAN, ARNOLD M. planning consultant; b. Bath, Maine, Dec. 3, 1932; s. David Solis and Anna (Arik) C.; m. Elaine Cogan, Dec. 21, 1952; children: Mark, Sue Van Brocklin, Leonard. BS, Oreg. State U., 1954. registered profl. engr. (ret.) Oreg. City planner City of Portland, Oreg., 1960-62; dir. planning Port of Portland, Oreg., 1962-67; coord. state planning Office of Gov., Portland, 1967-69, chief planner, 1969-72; dir. planning and econs. Daniel, Mann, Johnson & Mendenhall, L.A., 1972-74; dir. Oreg. Dept. Land Conservation & Devel., Salem, 1974-75; mng. ptnr. Cogan Owens Cogen LLC, Portland, 1975—. Contbr. articles to profl. jours., chpts. to books. Founder, pres. Portland Beautification Assn., 1965-67; vice chair Oreg. Environ. Quality Commn., 1970-74; bd. dires. Pioneer Courthouse Sq., Portland, 1993-99. Fellow Am. Inst. Cert. Planners (cert.); mem. Am. Planning Assn. (Oreg. chpt., ethics program 1987-90, Disting. Leadership award 1991, policy action com. 1992-94, intergovtl. affairs divsn. 1992-94), Soc. Profls. in Dispute Resolution, Oregon Mediation Assn. Avocations: sailing, writing. Office: Cogan Owens Cogen LLC 813 SW Alder St # 320 Portland OR 97205

COGAN, JOHN DENNIS, artist; b. Wichita Falls, Tex., Feb. 24, 1953; s. John Patrick and Thrasilla Barbara (Forster) C.; m. Karen Elizabeth Smith, May 15, 1976; children: Jennifer, Tiffany, Kimberly, Courtney. BS in Physics, Tex. A&M U., 1975; MA in Physics, Rice U., 1978, PhD in Physics, 1981. Geophysicist Shell Oil Co., Houston, 1980-82; artist pvt. practice, Houston, Farmington, N.Mex., 1982—. Artist: one man show San Juan Coll., Farmington, N. Mex., 1994. Recipient Landscape award of merit Nat. Park Acad. Arts, Jackson, Wyo., 1994, Collectors award, 1995. Mem. Grand Canyon's Trust Landscape Artists Invitational Expedition down the Colorado River, 1999. E-mail: jdcogan@infoway.lib.nm.us.

COGAN, JOHN FRANCIS, JR., lawyer; b. Boston, June 13, 1926; s. John Francis and Mary (Galligan) C.; m. Mary T. Hart, May 1, 1951 (div.); m. Mary L. Cornille, June 24, 1989; children: Peter G., Pamela E., Jonathan C., Gregory M. AB cum laude, Harvard U., 1949, JD, 1952. Bar: Mass. 1953. Ptnr. Hale and Dorr, Boston, 1957—2000, mng. ptnr., 1976—84, chmn., 1984—96, of counsel, 2000—; dep. chmn. Pioneer Global Asset Mgmt., SpA, Milan, 2000—; chmn. Pioneer Investment Mgmt., USA, Inc., Boston, 2000—. Trustee various Pioneer Funds, Inc., Boston, 1963—; bd. dirs. ICI Mutual Inst. Co.; chmn. exec. com. Western Res. Life Assurance Co., Ohio, 1968—79. Trustee Boston Symphony Orch., 1989—, overseer, 1984—92, chmn., 1989—92; overseer Mus. Fine Arts, 1989—90, trustee, 1990—, chmn., 1994—98; trustee Boston Ballet, 1986—89; mem. Mass. Dem. State Com.; trustee Univ. Hosp., Boston, 1965—95, chmn. bd., 1972—89; trustee Boston Med. Ctr., 1995—; bd. dirs. Wendell P. Clark Meml. Assn., Walker Home for Children, 1972—2000, Brigham Surg. Group, Inc., 1981—95, The Med. Found., 1986—90; trustee Boston U. Med. Ctr., 1973—90; bd. govs. Investment Co. Inst., 1971—74, 1975, 1981, 1982, chmn. bd. govs., 1978—80, 1982—85, 1986—89, 1991—. Served with USNR, 1944—46. Mem. ABA, Internat. Bar Assn., Mass. Bar Assn. (chmn. corp. banking and bus. law com. 1973-76), Boston Bar Assn. (past chmn. profl. svcs. sect., mem. bench-bar com.), Boston Estate and Bus. Planning Coun. (past pres.), Boston Probate and Estate Planning Forum (sec. 1958-73), Nat. Assn. Security Dealers (bd. dirs. 1983-86, legal adv. bd. 1988-94). Home: 975 Memorial Dr Apt 802 Cambridge MA 02138-5755 Office: Pioneer Investment Mgmt USA Inc 60 State St Boston MA 02109-1820

COGAN, KAREN ELIZABETH, author, educator; b. Houston, Sept. 24, 1954; d. Hugh and Kathryn (DeGaugh) Smith; m. John Cogan, May 15, 1976; children: Jennifer, Tiffany, Kimberly, Courtney. BS in Elem. Edn., U. Houston, 1976. Kindergarten tchr. Houston Ind. Sch. Dist., 1976-79; writer Farmington, N.Mex., 1981—. Author: My Little Brother Ben, 1999, When Animals Sleep, 1999, (novels) Prodigal Heart, 2001, The Secret of Castlegate Manor, 2002; contbr. to anthology; author articles and short stories. Mem. Nat. Writers Assn. (profl. mem.), Soc. Children's Book Writers and Illustrators. Avocations: reading, gardening. E-mail: kecogan@infoway.lib.nm.us.

COGAN, MARY JO GLEBER, lawyer; b. Wilmington, Del., Aug. 13, 1954; d. Jacob Adam and Marilyn Roberta (Fox) Gleber; m. Julian N. Cogan; children: Caitlin, Amanda. BA in Polit. Sci., U. Del., 1978; JD, U. San Diego, 1981. Bar: Calif. 1982. Assoc. Stebleton, Waters & May, El Cajon, Calif., 1982-83; ptnr. George & Allred, El Cajon, 1983-84; assoc. O'Dorisio, Wedell & Wade, San Diego, 1984-85; sole practice San Diego, 1985—. Lilliam Kratter Women's scholar U. San Diego, Law Sch., 1980-81. Mem. Calif. State Bar Assn., San Diego County Bar Assn., U. San Diego Law Sch. Alumni Assn. Democrat. Home: 11145 Calle Dario San Diego CA 92126-1714

COGAN, SARAH EDWARDS, lawyer; b. NYC, May 12, 1956; d. James R. and Arrial S. (Seelye) C.; m. Douglas H. Evans, May 28, 1983; children: Anne Morrill, Thomas Taylor Seelye, Elizabeth Hayward. BA, Yale U., 1978; JD, Georgetown U., 1981. Bar: N.Y. 1982. Assoc. Simpson Thacher & Bartlett LLP, N.Y.C., 1981-88, ptnr., 1989—. Mem. ABA, Assn. Bar City N.Y., Women's Investment Mgmt. Forum, Nat. Resources Def. Coun. (sec.). Office: Simpson Thacher & Bartlett LLP 425 Lexington Ave New York NY 10017-3954 E-mail: scogan@stblaw.com.

COGBURN, MAX OLIVER, lawyer; b. Canton, N.C., Mar. 21, 1927; s. Chester Amberg and Ruby Elizabeth (Davis) Cogburn; m. Mary Heidt, Oct. 15, 1949; children: Max O. Jr., Michael David, Steven Douglas, Cynthia Diane, Mary Christine. AB, U. N.C., 1948, LLB, 1950; LLM, Harvard U., 1951. Bar; N.C. 1950, U.S. Dist. Ct. (we. dist.) N.C. 1953, U.S. Ct. Appeals (4th cir.) 1984. Asst. dir. Inst. Govt., Chapel-Hill, N.C., 1951-52; staff mem. Atty. Gen. N.C., Raleigh, 1952-54; adminstr. asst. Chief Justice N.C., Raleigh, 1954-55; judge Gen. County Ct. Buncombe County, Asheville, N.C., 1968-70; sole practice Canton, Asheville, N.C., 1968, 1971—; ptnr. Roberts, Stevens & Cogburn, P.A., Asheville, 1986-95, Cogburn, Cogburn, Goosmann & Brazil, P.A., Ashville, 1995—. Chmn. Buncombe County Dem. Exec. Com., Asheville, 1974-76; mem. State Dem. Exec. Com., Raleigh, 1974-76. Mem. ABA, N.C. State Bar Assn., N.C. Bar Assn. (Gen. Practice Hall of Fame 1997), 28th Jud. Dist. Bar State of N.C., Buncombe County Bar Assn. (past pres.). Roman Catholic. Home: RR 1 Candler NC 28715-9801 Office: 77 Central Ave Ste H Asheville NC 28801-2451

COGDILL, DAVID, state representative; b. Long Beach, Calif., Dec. 31, 1950; m. Stephanie Cogdill; children: David Jr., Meghan. Real estate appraiser, 1971—79; founder Cogdill and Giomi, 1981—; mem. Calif. Assembly, 2000—. Capt. Vol. Fire Dept.; pres. Bridgeport Sch. PTA; mem. city coun. Modesto, Calif., 1991—97; bd. dirs. Bridgeport Fire Protection Dist., Mono County, 1975, Stanislaus County YMCA. Mem.: Modesto C. of C. (bd. dirs.). Republican. Office: PO Box 942849 Rm 4117 Sacramento CA 94249 Address: 1912 Standiford Ave Ste 4 Lathrop CA 95330*

COGDILL, KEITH W. librarian, educator; b. Huntsville, Ala., July 15, 1967; s. Thomas J. and Patricia Cogdill. BA, Univ.of then South, Sewanee, Tenn., 1989; MLS, Univ. Ala., Tuculossa, Ala., 1992; PhD, Univ. N.C., Chapel Hill, 1998. Libr. Univ. Ill., Chgo., 1992—95; asst. prof. Univ. Md., Coll. Pk., Md., 1999—2002; outreach libr. Nat. Libr. of Medicine, Bethesda, Md., 2002—. Contbr. articles to profl. jour. Recipient Phi Beta Kappa, 1989; inform. fellow, Nat. Libr. of Medicine, 1994—95, Goldsmith Scholarship, Hebrew Univ., Jerusalem, 1989—90. Mem.: Med. Libr. Assn (editl. bd. 1994—97, 1999—2002). Office: Nat Libr of Medicine 8600 Rockville pike Bethesda MD 20894

COGET, JEAN-FRANCOIS AXEL HUGUES, management researcher; b. Paris, Mar. 22, 1975; s. Gerald Coget and Yvette Maury. MBA, Hautes Etudes Commerciales, 1998; PhD, UCLA, 2003—. Fin. analyst Morgan Stanley, Paris, 1997—98; naval asst. of def. attaché French Embassy, Lisbon, Portugal, 1998—99; rsch. assoc. UCLA Ctr. Communication Policy, L.A., 2000—01; student rschr. The Anderson Sch. at UCLA, 1999—. Lt. French Mil., 1998—99. Decorated Nat. Def. medal French Def. Min.; scholar, UCLA, 1999—2003. Office: Anderson School at UCLA HR/OB dpt PO Box 951481 Los Angeles CA 90095-1481 Office Fax: 310-825-0218. E-mail: jcoget@anderson.ucla.edu.

COGGESHALL, BRUCE AMSDEN, lawyer; b. Brattleboro, Vt., Sept. 24, 1941; s. Theodore Ronna and Katharine (Emery) C.; m. Phyllis Conroy, June 22, 1963; children: Bruce Jr., John P. AB, Dartmouth Coll., 1963; LLB, Cornell U., 1967. Bar: Me. 1967, U.S. Dist. Ct. Me. 1967, U.S. Tax Ct. 1970, U.S. Ct. Appeals (1st cir.) 1972, U.S. Supreme Ct. 1972. Assoc. Pierce Atwood, Portland, Maine, 1967—72, ptnr., 1972—97, mng. ptnr., 1997—. Commr. Nat. Conf. Commn. Uniform State Laws, Chgo., 1987—; mem. Maine Small Enterprise Growth Bd., 1997—. Chmn. Cape Elizabeth (Maine) Charter Rev. Commn., 1986-87, Cape Elizabeth Harbor Commn., 1987-89, Cape Elizabeth Town Ctr. Com., 1994-96; mem. Dartmouth Coll. Alumni Coun., 1997-2000; mem. Maine Econ. Devel. Incentive Commn., 1998—. Fellow Am. Bar Found., Maine Bar Found.; mem. Am. Law Inst. (life), ABA, Nat. Assn. Bond Lawyers, Maine Bar Assn., Cumberland County Bar Assn. (pres. 1976-77). Avocation: skiing. Home: 336 Ocean House Rd Cape Elizabeth ME 04107-2419 Office: Pierce Atwood 1 Monument Sq Portland ME 04101-1110 E-mail: bcoggeshall@pierceatwood.com.

COGGIN, CHARLOTTE JOAN, cardiologist, educator; b. Takoma Park, Md., Aug. 6, 1928; d. Benjamin and Nanette (McDonald) C. BA, Columbia Union Coll., 1948; MD, Loma Linda U., 1952, MPH, 1987; DSc (hon.),

Andrews U., 1994. Diplomate Am. Bd. Pediatrics. Intern L.A. County Gen. Hosp., 1952-53, resident in medicine, 1953-55; fellow in cardiology Children's Hosp., L.A., 1955-56, White Meml. Hosp., L.A., 1955-56; rsch. assoc. in cardiology, house physician Hammersmith Hosp., London, 1956-57; resident in pediatrics and pediatric cardiology Hosp. for Sick Children, Toronto, Ont., Can., 1965-67; cardiologist, asst. prof. medicine, co-dir. heart surgery team Loma Linda (Calif.) U., 1961-73, assoc. prof., 1973-91, prof. medicine, 1991—. Asst. dean. Sch. Medicine Internat. Program, 1973—75; v.p. for global outreach Loma Linda U. Health Scis. Ctr., 1998—; assoc. .dean. Sch. Medicine Internat. Program, 1975—, spl. asst. to univ. pres. for interat. affairs, 1991; co-dir., cardiologist heart surgery team missions to, Pakistan and Asia, 63, Greece, 67, Greece, 69, Saigon, Vietnam, 1974—75, Saudi Arabia, 1976—87, China, 1984, China, 1989—91, Hong Kong, 1985, Zimbabwe, 88, Zimbabwe, 93, Kenya, 88, Nepal, 92, China, 92, Myanmar, 95, North Korea, 96. Author: Atrial Septal Defects, motion picture (Golden Eagle Cine award and 1st prize Venice Film Festival 1964); contbr. articles to med. jours. Recipient award for service to people of Pakistan City of Karachi, 1963, Medallion award Evangelismos Hosp., Athens, Greece, 1967, Gold medal of health South Vietnam Ministry of Health, 1974, Charles Elliott Weinger award for excellence, 1976, Wall Street Jour. Achievement award, 1987, Disting. Univ. Svc. award Loma Linda U., 1990; named Honored Alumnus Loma Linda U. Sch. Medicine, 1973, Outstanding Women in Gen. Conf. Seventh-day Adventists, 1975, Alumnus of Yr., Columbia Union Coll., 1984, Outstanding Achievement in Edn., Adventist Alumni Achievement award, 1999. Mem. AAUP, AAUW, Am. Coll. Cardiology, AMA (physicians adv. com. 1969—), Calif. Med. Assn. (com. on med. schs., com. on member svcs.), San Bernardino County Med. Soc. (chmn. comm. com. 1975-77, mem. comm. com, 1987-88, editor bull., 1975-76, William L. Cover, M.D. Outstanding Contbn. to Medicine award 1995), Am. Heart Assn., Med. Rsch. Assn. Calif., Calif. Heart Assn., Am. Acad. Pediatrics, World Affairs Coun., Internat. Platform Assn., Calif. Museum Sci. and Industry MUSES (Outstanding Woman of Yr. in Sci. 1969), Am. Med. Women's Assn., Loma Linda Sch. Medicine Alumni Assn. (pres. 1978), Alpha Omega Alpha, Delta Omega. Democrat. Home: 25052 Crestview Dr Loma Linda CA 92354-3415 Office: Loma Linda U 11060 Anderson St Rm 105 Loma Linda CA 92350-0001 E-mail: Jcoggin@Univ.LLU.edu.

COGGINS, PAUL EDWARD, JR., lawyer, b. Hugo, Okla., May 21, 1951; s. Paul E. and Rebecca (Cates) C.; m. Regina T. Montoya, June 12, 1976; 1 child, Jessica Chandler. BA in Polit. Sci. summa cum laude, Yale U., 1973; BA with honors, Oxford U., 1975; JD cum laude, Harvard U., 1978. Bar: Tex. 1978. Tchr. Project New Gate N.Mex. State Penitentiary, 1973; law clk. Mass. Ct. Appeals, 1978-79; fed. prosecutor U.S. Attys. Office, Dallas, 1980-83; assoc. Johnson & Swanson, Dallas, 1979-80, ptnr., 1983-86, Meadows, Owens, Collier, Reed & Coggins, Dallas, 1986-93; U.S. atty. U.S. Dept. of Justice, Dallas, 1993-2001. Mem. adv. com. Magnet Sch. in Dallas, 1984—. Author: The Lady is the Tiger, 1987; co-author: Out of Bounds, 1992. Pres. bd. dirs. Dem. Forum, Dallas, 1985—. Rhodes scholar, 1973-76. Mem. ABA, Dallas Bar Assn. (mem. pro bono panel), Harvard Club (v.p. 1987—), Yale Club. Office: Fish & Richardson PC 5000 Bank One Ctr 1717 Main St Dallas TX 75201 Fax: (214) 747-2091. Business E-Mail: coggins@fr.com. E-mail: Coggins@fr.com.

COGGIOLA, JILL ANGELA, musician, educator; b. Buffalo, Apr. 7, 1962; d. Nicholas Joseph and Ruth Marie (Hutten) Francescone; m. John Cimo Coggiola, Aug. 6; children: Nicholas Peter, Julie Angelise, John Joseph. Cert., BMus in Performance and Music Edn., SUNY, Fredonia, 1984; MMus in Performance, Fla. State U., 1987, DMus in Performance, 1994. Instrumental music tchr. Grand Island (N.Y.) Ctr. Sch. Dist., 1987-88; asst. prof. music Radford (Va.) U., 1992-95; gen. music tchr. Decatur County Ctrl. Sch. Dist., 1996-97; affiliate artist Syracuse (N.Y.) U., 1997—. Bass clarinetist Erie Philharm. Orch., Pa., 1983-86, Naples Philharm. Orch., 1989-90; substitute clarinetist Buffalo Philharm. Orch., Buffalo, 1987-88, 91-92, Tallahassee Symphony Orch., 1987-91, Roanoke Symphony Orch., 1992-95, Erie Philharm. Orch., 1997—, Syracuse Symphony Orchestra, 1998—, Fredonia Chamber Players, 1997—, Rochester Philarm. Orch., 2002—. Mem. Syracuse Musician Assn., Internat. Clarinet Soc., Sigma Alpha Iota, Pi Kappa Lambda, Kappa Delta Pi, Coll. Music Soc. Democrat. Roman Catholic. Home: 8235 Dampier Cir Liverpool NY 13090-4104 E-mail: jacoggio@syr.edu.

COGHILL, WILLIAM THOMAS, JR., retired lawyer; b. St. Louis, July 20, 1927; s. William Thomas and Mildred Mary (Crenshaw) C.; m. Patricia Lee Hughes, Aug. 7, 1948; children: James Prentiss, Victoria Lynn, Cathryn Anne. JD, U. Mo., 1950, undergrad., 1944-45, 46-47. Bar: Mo. 1950, Ill. 1958. Pvt. practice, Farmington, Mo., 1950-51; spl. agt. FBI, 1951-52; ptnr. Smith, Smith & Coghill, Farmington, 1952-57; assoc. Coburn & Croft, St. Louis, 1957-58; ptnr. Thompson Coburn (formerly Thompson & Mitchell and predecessor firm), Belleville, Ill., 1958—2001, ret., 2001. Co-author: Illinois Products Liability, 1991, Cavaliers, 1999. With USN, 1945-46. Fellow Am. Coll. Trial Lawyers; mem. ABA, Ill. State Bar Assn., Mo. State Bar Assn. Home: 715 W Moon Valley Dr Phoenix AZ 85023-6234 E-mail: tcoghill@rni.net.

COGHLAN, KELLY JACK, lawyer; b. Longview, Tex., Sept. 3, 1952; s. Howard and Peggy Coghlan. BBA with honors, So. Meth. U., 1975, JD cum laude, 1978. Bar: Tex. 1978, U.S. Dist. Ct. (so. dist.) Tex. 1979, U.S. Tax Ct. 1981, U.S. Ct. Appeals (5th cir.) 1981, U.S. Supreme Ct. 1984. Law clk. to presiding judge Finis E. Cowan U.S. Dist. Ct. (so. dist.) Tex., 1978-79; assoc. Vinson & Elkins, Houston, 1979-84; equity ptnr. Dotson, Babcock & Scofield, Houston, 1984-88, chmn. risk mgmt. com., head gen. litigation group, 1987-88; pvt. practice, Houston, 1988—. Bd. dirs. Sta. KSBJ, Houston, sec., 1990-93, chmn. long range planning com., 1989-93, mem. exec. com., 1990-97, v.p., 1994-97. Mem. So. Meth. U. Law Sch. Southwestern Law Jour. Mem. steering com. Palmer Drug Abuse Program, Houston, 1980-82; vol. jr. high and H.S. youth programs, 1990—, 2d Bapt. Ch., Houston, 1990—; mem. 1st Meth. Ch., Longview, Tex., 1962—; youth min., Wesley United Meth. Ch., Longview, 1972-77. Recipient So. Meth. U. M award, 1975, Russell Baker Moot Ct. 1st pl. award So. Meth. U. Law Sch., 1976; named Players of 1999, Tex. Lawyer. Fellow Houston Bar Found., Coll. State Bar Tex., Pro Bono Coll. State Bar Tex.; mem. ABA, Tex. Bar Assn., Houston Bar Assn., Houston Young Lawyers Assn. (chmn. com. on consumer rights 1981-82), Nat. Eagle Scout Assn. (life), So. Meth. U. Student Found. (hon.), Order of Coif (hon.), Am. Mensa, Gulf Coast Mensa, Blue Key Soc. (hon., pres. 1974-75), Beta Gamma Sigma (hon.), Phi Delta Phi (hon.), Lambda Chi Alpha. Avocations: drumming, singing, youth work. Office: 505 Lanecrest Ln Ste 1 Houston TX 77024-6716

COGLIANESE, CARY, lawyer, educator; b. Chgo., Ill., Sept. 30, 1964; s. Carmine Coglianese and Janice Vera.; m. Debra Elaine Branin; children: Patrick, John. PhD, MPP, JD, U. of Mich., Ann Arbor, MI. Bar: Mich. Chair, regulatory policy program & assoc. prof. of pub. policy Harvard U., John F. Kennedy Sch. of Govt., Cambridge, Mass., 1997—; affiliated scholar Harvard Law Sch., Cambridge, Mass., 1994—; asst. prof. of pub. policy Harvard U., John F. Kennedy Sch. of Govt., Cambridge, Mass., 1994—97, dir., politics rsch. group, 1995—. Co-chair, collaborative rsch. network on regulatory governance Law & Soc. Assn., Amherst, Mass., 2000—, mem., editl. bd. of law & soc. rev., 2000—; vice-chair, e-rulemaking com. ABA, Chicago, Ill., 2002—. Contbr. articles to profl. jours. Counsel, amicus brief submitted to us supreme ct. on behalf of twenty legal scholars and scientists. Recipient Teaching Asst. Book prize, 1992, Rackham Sch. Grad. Studies Rsch. Partnership award U. Mich., 1991-92; fellow U. Mich. Dept. Polit. Sci., 1992-93; grante Nat. Sci. Found. Dissertation, 1992-93. Mem. State Bar of Mich., Law and Soc. Assn., Am. Polit. Sci. Assn. Office: Harvard University 79 John F Kennedy Street Weil Hall Cambridge MA 02138 Office Fax: 617-495-1710. E-mail: cary_coglianese@harvard.edu.

COGLIANO, DAN, tax accountant; b. Bklyn., Aug. 20, 1952; s. Angelo and Adelaide Cogliano; m. Debra Hayden Barrett, Mar. 19, 1978 (div. Oct. 21, 1991); children: Daniel, David, Dustin. BBA in Acctg., Hofstra U., 1974. Tax acct., Ozone Park, NY, 1975—; jr. acct. ABC Radio Network, N.Y.C., 1978—80; v.p. internat. mktg. Merrill Lynch, N.Y.C., 1980—2003. Income maintenance screener Suffolk County Dept. Social Svcs., Amityville, NY, 1975—77. Author: (book) Thick Skinned, 2003. Actor West Side Repertory Theater, N.Y.C., 1977—93, treas., 1989—92; mem. Mens Sr. Baseball League, L.I., 1993—, mgr., player, 1999—2001; baseball player Legends of Baseball Tournament, Cooperstown, NY, 2000—. Avocations: baseball, writing, acting. Home: Apt 19H 340 E 80th St New York NY 10002 E-mail: coglida@aol.com.

COGSWELL, FREDERICK WILLIAM, English language educator, poet, editor, publisher; b. East Centreville, N.B., Can., Nov. 8, 1917; s. Walter Scott and Florence (White) C.; m. Margaret Hynes, July 3, 1944 (dec. May 1985); children: Carmen Patricia Cogswell Robinson (dec.), Kathleen Mary Cogswell Forsythe; m. Gail Fox, Nov. 6, 1985 (div. Aug. 1997); m. Adele Bartlett, Sept. 20, 1997 (dec. Jan. 2002). BA with honors, U. N.B., 1949, MA, 1950; PhD (Imperial Order Daus. Empire fellow), U. Edinburgh, Scotland, 1952; LLD (hon.), St. Francis Xavier U., 1982; DCL (hon.), King's Coll., 1985; LLD (hon.), Mt. Allison U., 1988. From asst. to assoc. prof. dept. English U. N.B., Fredericton, 1952-64, prof., 1964-83, prof. emeritus, 1983—. Exch. writer in residence Scottish Arts Coun., 1983—84. Editor: The Fiddlehead, 1952—66, Humanities Assn. Bull., 1967—72; pub.: Fiddlehead Poetry Books, 1956—82; author: Charles G.D. Roberts, 1983, Charles Mair, 1986, (poetry) The Stunted Strong, 1954, The Haloed Tree, 1957, Descent from Eden, 1959, Lost Dimension, 1960, Star People, 1968, Immortal Plowman, 1969, In Praise of Chastity, 1970, The Chains of Lilliput, 1971, The House Without a Door, 1973, Light Bird of Life, 1974, Against Perspectives, 1977, (collected poems) A Long Apprenticeship, 1980, Selected Poems, 1982, Pearls, 1983, Meditations: 50 Sestinas, 1986, An Edge to Life, 1987, The Best Notes Merge, 1988, Black and White Tapestry, 1989, Watching an Eagle, 1991, When the Right Light Shines, 1992, In Praise of Old Music, 1992, In My Own Growing, 1993, As I See It, 1994, The Trouble with Light, 1996, Folds, 1997, A Double Question, 1999, With Vision Added, 2000, Deeper Than Mind, 2001, Dry Flowers, 2002, Ghosts, 2002, Later in Chicago, 2003; translator: The Testament of Cresseid, 1958, One Hundred Poems of Modern Quebec, 1970, 1971, A Second Hundred Poems of Modern Quebec, 1971, The Poetry of Modern Quebec, 1976, Confrontation, 1973, The Complete Poems of Emile Nelligan, 1983; translator: (with Jo-Anne Elder) Unfinished Dreams: Contemporary Poetry of Acadie, 1991; editor: Five New Brunswick Poets, 1961; editor: (with W.S. MacNutt and Robert Tweedie) The Arts in New Brunswick, 1967; editor: (with Thelma Reid Lower) The Enchanted Land, 1968; translator: (anthologies) One Hundred Poems of Modern Quebec, A Second Hundred Poems of Modern Quebec, The Poetry of Modern Quebec, Atlantic Anthology, Vol. 1 (prose), 1983, Vol. 2 (poetry); translator: (with Jo-Anne Elder) Climates by Hermènègilde Chiasson, 1999; translator: Conversations, 2001; contbr. articles and poems to profl. jours. Mem. sr. arts fellowship awards com. Can. Council, 1972, mem. centennial poetry awards com., 1968; mem. Leave fellowship awards bd. humanities sect., 1973, 74; mem. poetry sect. Gov. Gen.'s award bd., 1973, chmn., 1974; bd. dirs. Can. Found., 1983— . Served with Canadian Army, 1940-45. Decorated mem. Order of Can., 1981; recipient Bliss Carman medal for poetry, 1945, 47, Douglas Gold medal, 1949, Gold medal for svc. to poetry as mag. editor Republic of Philippines, 1956, Gold medal as disting. poet, 1956, Coronation medal for 125 Can. anniversary, 1992, Alden Nowlan award for excellence in the arts N.B. Gov., 1995, Coronation medal, 1992; Nuffield fellow, 1959-60, Can. Coun. Sr. fellow, 1967-68. Mem. League Canadian Poets (regional exec. 1973-80, 1st v.p. 1985-86, hon. life mem.), Canadian Authors Assn., Assn. Can. Pubs. (hon. life, Honors for Contrbns. to Can. Lit. and Publs. 2000), Ind. Pubs. Assn., Atlantic Pubs. Assn. (pres. 1979-80), Assn. Can. and Que. Lits. (pres. 1978-80), N.B. Writers' Fedn. (hon. life.; pres. 1983-85) Home: 2118 Dublin St New Westminster BC Canada V3M 3A9 *Anything I have accomplished has come about because it has been very easy for me to work hard at anything in which I have been interested and I have been interested in a good many things.*

COGSWELL, JOHN HEYLAND, retired telecommunications executive, financial consultant; b. Southampton, N.Y., Oct. 18, 1933; s. John W. and Lucy A. (McCurdy) C.; m. Patricia A. Morrissey, June 18, 1955; children: Julie A., Catherine J. AB, Dartmouth Coll., 1955, MS, 1956. Registered profl. engr., Mass. Engr. New Eng. Telephone Co., Boston, 1956-61, planning engr., Pittsfield, Mass., 1961-63, staff acct., Boston, 1963-65, constrn. program engr., 1969-71, div. mgr. fin., 1971-83, sec.-treas., 1983-90; engr. Am. Telephone Co., N.Y.C., 1965-68, mgr. econs., 1968-69. Treas., bd. dirs. Neighborhood Health Plan, Boston, 1986-88, 90-98, pres. 1988-90. Pres., bd. dirs. Health Action Forum, Greater Boston, 1992-97, treas. 1983-92, 97-98; treas., bd. dirs. Muscular Dystrophy Assn., Greater Boston, 1978-91, Needham (Mass.) Hist. Soc., Inc., 1975-95, trustee, 1995—, Cmty. Health Ctr. Capital Fund, 1992-99; mem., chmn. Needham Planning Bd., 1977-87; mem. Needham Bd. Appeals, 1987-91; mem. Needham Bd. Selectmen, 1996—, chmn., 1998, 2001; bd. dirs. Pathway Health Networks, 1995-96, Care Group, 1996—, Health Agys. of Mass., 1996-99, Cmty Health Charities, 1999—, pres. 2001, Mass. Hosp. Assn., 2000—; bd. dirs. Bridgewater Goddard Park Med. Assocs., 2000-02, chmn. 2000-02; bd. dirs. Combined Health Appeal of Mass., 1991-96, pres. 1993-95; chmn. bd. dirs. Physician Svc. Network, 2003—; bd. dirs. Ctr. Cmty. Responsive Care, 1994-98, treas., 1994-95; trustee Deaconess-Glover Hosp., 1991-99, vice chmn. 1992-94, chmn. 1994-99; bd. dirs. Mass. Health Data Consortium, 1991-96, treas., 1994-96; bd. dirs. HealthPoint, 2001—, Deaconess-Waltham Hosp, 2002, New Eng. Health Care Found., 1992-96; mem. Needham Town Meeting, 1975—; bd. dirs., treas. Cogswell Family Assn., 1989—. Named Vol. of the Yr., Combined Health Appeal of Am., 1992. Mem. Fin. Mgmt. Assn. (bd. dirs. 1977-79), Fin. Exec. Inst. (bd. dirs. 1988-90), Treas.'s Club Greater Boston (pres. 1987-88), Republican Club (New Providence, N.J.; pres. 1966-68). Episcopalian. Avocations: gardening, golf. Home and Office: 1479 Great Plain Ave Needham MA 02492-1217 E-mail: j.cogswell@verizon.net.

COHAN, GEORGE SHELDON, advertising and public relations executive; b. Oak Park, Ill., May 30, 1924; s. Charles and Ann (Holt) C.; m. Natalie Holmes, Dec. 14, 1974; children— Barry, Gail, Charles, Victoria. Student, Colo. Sch. Mines, 1941-42, Ind. U., 1942-43; BS in Mech. Engring, U. Cin., 1948; postgrad., John Marshall Law Sch., 1954-56. Certified bus. communicator. Field engr. Indsl. Erectors, Inc., Chgo., 1948-50; sales engr. Fairbanks-Morse & Co., Chgo., 1950-56; v.p., account supr. Hoffman & York Advt. Agy., Milw., 1956-62, Tobias & Olendorf, Chgo., 1962-65; sr. v.p., gen. mgr. Bozell & Jacobs, Inc., Chgo., 1965-74; chmn. bd., pres. Cohan & Paul, Inc., Chgo., 1975-84; pres. Fletcher, Mayo & Assocs., Chgo., 1984-87, Doremus & Co., Chgo., 1987-89, George Cohan Co., Chgo., 1989—; chmn. Cohan Seafood Co., San Francisco, 1988—. Bd. dir. Forest Labs., N.Y.C., Universal Gift Cert., Inc. Author: (play) Black Mutiny, 1948; contbr. articles to profl. jours. Mem. Cen. Ind. coun. Boy Scouts Am., 1965-69; mem. exec. com. March of Dimes, 1965-69, ANTA, 1948-51. 1st lt. C.E. AUS, 1943-45, CBI. Recipient Outstanding Merit award 8th Pan Am. Ry. Congress, 1954, 1st pl. Nat. Lithographic Soc., 1955, 15th ann. G.D. Crain award, 1981, gold award Chgo. Assn. Direct Mktg., 1979, 80, Pres.'s Cup award, 1986; named to Advt. Hall of Fame, 1981. Mem. ASME, Bus. and Profl. Advertisers Assn. (internat. pres. 1976-77, Best Seller award 1954, Best of Show 1962, Best of Show Indpls. 1966-67, ABP award 1971, Addy Gold award 1979, Profl. Excellence award 1978, Gold medal 1979, 80, Pro-Com. Gold award, 1981, 83, 84, Career of Excellence Spl. award 1989, Lifetime Career of Excellence award 1989), Pub. Rels. Soc. Am., Screen Actors Guild. Unitarian Universalist. Avocations: flying, cooking, fishing, opera, acting. Home: 2048 Foxfire Ct Henderson NV 89012-2190 E-mail: geocoh@aol.com.

COHAN, LEON SUMNER, lawyer, retired electric company executive; b. Detroit, June 24, 1929; s. Maurice and Lillian (Rosenfeld) C.; m. Heidi Ruth Seelmann, Jan. 22, 1956; children: Nicole, Timothy David, Jonathan Daniel. BA, Wayne State U., 1949, JD, 1952. Bar: Mich. 1953. Pvt. practice, Detroit, 1954-58; asst. atty. gen. State of Mich., Lansing, 1958-61, dep. atty. gen., 1961-72; v.p. legal affairs Detroit Edison Co., 1973-75, v.p., 1975-79, sr. v.p., gen. counsel, 1979-93; counsel Barris, Sott, Denn & Driker, Detroit, 1993—. Bd. dirs. Oakland Commerce Bank. Trustee Mich. Cancer Found.; bd. dirs. Concerned Citizens for Arts in Mich., U. Mich. Musical Soc.; mem. arts commn. Detroit Inst. Arts; mem. Race Rels. Coun. Met. Detroit. With U.S. Army, 1952-54. Recipient Disting. Alumni award Wayne State U. Law Sch., 1972, Disting. Svc. award Bd. Govs., Wayne State U., 1973, Judge Ira W. Jayne award NAACP, 1987, Israel Histadrut Menorah award, 1987, Knights of Charity award Pontifical Inst. for Fgn. Missions, 1989, Fellowship award Am. Arabic and Jewish Friends of Met. Detroit, Judge Learned Hand Human Rels. award, 1991, Gov.'s Arts award for Civic Leadership in the Arts, Michiganian of Yr. award Detroit News, 1993. Mem. ABA, Detroit Bar Assn., State Bar Mich. (Champion of Justice award 1993), Mich. Gen. Counsel Assn., Detroit Club. Democrat. Jewish. Home: 17 Eastbury Ct Ann Arbor MI 48105-1402 Office: Barris Sott Denn & Driker 15th Fl 211 W Fort St Lbby 15 Detroit MI 48226-3244 E-mail: icohan@aol.com.

COHANE, HEATHER CHRISTINA, magazine publisher, editor; b. Camberley, Surrey, Eng. came to U.S., 1982; d. William Willoughby and Naomi Mary (Winder) Fausset; m. John Philip Cohane, May 13, 1961 (dec. Dec. 1981); children: Alexander, Candida, Ondine; m. Ossian Kare Berga, Nov. 2, 1985. (dec. Oct. 2000). Student pvt. schs., Isle of Wight, Eng. and Neuchatel, Switzerland. Founding editor, pub. Quest mag., N.Y.C., 1987—; exec. v.p. Gotham Mag., N.Y.C., 1999—2001; editor-at-large Avenue Mag., 2002—. Office: Avenue Mag 63 W 38th #206 New York NY 10018 Fax: 212-327-4280.

COHASSEY, JOHN FREDRICK, writer; b. Pontiac, Mich., Nov. 2, 1961; s. Theodore F. C. and Nancy (Aldrich) Chubb; m. Gretta Ann Abu-Isa, May 22, 1993. A of Psychology, Oakland C.C., 1985; B of History, Oakland U., 1990; MA in History, Wayne State U., 1993. Freelance writer, Detroit, 1993—. Author: Toast of the Town: The Life and Times of Sunnie Wilson, 1998 (Hist. Soc. Mich. award Merit 1998); contbr. articles to jours. Avocations: music, collecting antiques, reading. Home: 398 W Iroquois Rd Pontiac MI 48341-1539

COHEN, AARON, aerospace engineer; b. Tex., Jan. 31, 1931; s. Charles and Ida (Moloff) C.; m. Ruth Carolyn Goldberg, Feb. 7, 1953; children— Nancy Ann Santana, David Blair, Daniel Louis BS, Tex. A&M U., 1952; MS in Applied Math., Stevens Inst. Tech, 1958, D Engring. (hon.), 1982. Microwave tube design engr. RCA, Camden, N.J., 1954-58; sr. research engr. Gen. Dynamics, San Diego, 1958-62; mgr. Apollo command and service module lunar module guidance nav. and control NASA, Houston, 1962-70, mgr. command and service module project, 1970-72, mgr. shuttle orbiter project, 1972-82, dir. research and engring., 1982-86, dir. Johnson Space Ctr., 1986-93; prof. Tex. A&M U., College Station, 1993—. Editor Astronautics sect. Marks Mechanical Engineer's Handbook, 9th edit.; contbr. articles to profl. jours. Vice chmn. engring. task force Target 2000 Tex. A&M U., College Station, 1981-83. Served to lt. C.E., U.S. Army, 1952-54, Korea Recipient Exceptional Service medal NASA, Houston, 1969, Disting. Service medal, 1973, 81, 88, 93—, Goddard Meml. trophy, 1988; Presdl. Rank of Meritorious Exec., U.S. Govt., Washington, 1981, Presdl. Rank of Disting. Exec., 1982, 88; Named NASA Engr. of Yr., Washington, 1982, Engr. of Yr. Nat. Acad. Engring., 1988. Fellow Am. Astron. Soc. (W. Randolph Lovelace II award 1982), AIAA (Von Karman lectureship 1984, Von Braun award 1993, Hon. Fellow, 1995, Robert H. Goddard Astronautics award 1996); mem. NAE, ASME (medal 1984), AJAA, Tau Beta Pi. Jewish. Avocation: tennis. Office: Texas A&M U Dept Mech Engring Ms 3123 College Station TX 77843-0001

COHEN, ABRAHAM EZEKIEL, retired health care company executive; b. Calcutta, India; married. With Merck & Co. Inc., 1957-92, now sr. v.p.; mng. dir. Merck Sharp and Dohme Internat. Div., Patistan, 1962-64; retired, 1992; regional dir Merck Sharp and Dohme Internat. Div., S. Asia, 1964-67, No. Europe, 1967-69, v.p. Europe, 1969-74, exec. v.p., 1974-77, pres., 1977—. Office: Neurobiological Technologies Inc 3260 Blume Dr Ste 500 Richmond CA 94806

COHEN, ABRAHAM J. (AL COHEN), educational administrator; b. Chelsea, Mass., Mar. 19, 1932; s. Samuel and Sarah (Liskofsky) C.; m. Isabel M. Reardon, Aug. 23, 1959; children: David Joseph, Jonathan William, Jennifer Eve. BS, Salem State Coll., 1959; M.Edn., Boston U., 1960; postgrad., U. Calif. at Santa Barbara, 1968, Fordham U., 1965; Ed.D., Columbia U., 1974; grad., U.S. Army Command and Gen. Staff Coll., 1975, Indsl. Coll. Armed Forces, 1976, Air Force War Coll., 1977. Tchr. social studies Chelsea jr. high schs., 1959-61; coord. instructional materials and svc. North Reading (Mass.) Pub. Schs., 1961-64; supr. instructional materials and sch. libraries White Plains (N.Y.) Pub. Schs., 1964-92, coord. health edn., 1974-88. Pres. Ednl. Film Libr. Assn. and Am. Film Festival, N.Y.C., 1971-73; lectr. Sch. Continuing Edn., NYU, 1965-68, Sch. Libr. Svc., Columbia U., 1972-92; dir. audiovisual ctr. Salem (Mass.) State Coll., 1961-62; adj. prof. Westchester C.C., 1988-93; mem. adv. bd. Ednl. Products Info. Exch. Inst., N.Y.C., 1972-78; instr. U.S. Army Command Gen. Staff Coll.; comdt. 1150th USARF Sch., Ft. Hamilton, N.Y., 1983-87; dir. Sta. Cable 36-TV, White Plains, N.Y., 1982-92. Contbr. articles to profl. jours. Scoutmaster, instnl. rep. Muscoot-Westchester coun. Boy Scouts Am., 1971-72; pres. Westchester Libr. Assn., 1972-74; mem. expansion com. J.C. Hart Libr., Yorktown, NY., 1969-71; pres. Westchester County Ednl. Comm. Assn., 1968-69; chmn. bd. dirs., pres. Yorktown Jewish Ctr., 1969-70; bd. dirs. Westchester divsn. Am. Cancer Soc., chmn. pub. edn., 1981-83; mem. N.Y. State Employer Guard and Res. Com., 1987; exec. officer, duty officer, tng. officer, mem. Sheriff's Armed Posse Sun City West, Ariz., 1993—, bd. dirs., 1996-97, 2000-01, comdr., 2000; trustee Temple Beth Emeth. With U.S. Army, 1952-54; col. USAR ret. Decorated Legion of Merit; recipient Gen. John J. Pershing award U.S. Army Command and Gen. Staff Coll., 1975, Educator of Yr. award Am. Cancer Soc., 1983; named to U.S. Army Disting. Med. Rgt. Hall of Fame, 1987; Col. Cohen Day proclaimed by County of Westchester and Town of Yorktown, 1987. Mem.: Assn. Edn. Comm. and Tech., NY State Edn. Commn. Assn. (bd. dirs. 1968—69), Ednl. Media Coun. (bd. dirs. 1971—73, exec. com. 1972—73), Mass. Audio Visual Assn. (bd. dirs. 1962—64), Shriners, Masons (32 deg., master Yorktown 1992—93, sec. Sun City Lodge 2002—), Phi Delta Kappa. Home: 16014 W Sentinel Dr Sun City West AZ 85375-6681

COHEN, ADAM J. plastic surgeon; b. Bklyn., May 27, 1968; s. Abraham and Lori Cohen. BS in Acctg., Bklyn. Coll., 1991; MD, Albany Med. Coll., 1996. Internal medicine 1996intern, resident S.I. U. Hosp., 1996—98; resident in ophthalmology Nassau U. Med. Ctr., East Meadow, NY, 1998—2001; fellow in orbitofacial surgery and neuro-ophthalmology U. Vt. Fletcher/Allen Med. Ctr., Burlington, 2001—02; cons. surgeon Eye Care for N.Mex., Santa Fe, 2002—. Contbr. articles to profl. jours.; author: textbook in field. Office: Eye Care For NMex 510 N Guadalupe Ste C Santa Fe NM 87501 E-mail: ajcohenmd@prodigy.net.

COHEN, ALAN, investment banker; b. N.Y.C., N.Y., Jan. 1, 1945; s. Harold and Edith (Schneider) Cohen; m. Carolyn Zacks, Jan. 3, 1970; children: Davi Melissa, Michael Jarrett. BA in Econs., Bklyn. Coll., 1967; postgrad, N.Y.U. Commodity broker Reynolds Securities Inc., N.Y.C., 1977—78; v.p., regional commodity mgr. Loeb Rhoades Hornblower, N.Y.C., 1978—79; v.p., regional commodity dir. E.F. Hutton Co., N.Y.C., 1979—80; v.p., nat. commodities sales mgr., ltd. ptnr. and assoc. dir. Bear, Stearns & Co., N.Y.C., 1980—91; sr. mktg. dir. Stamford Co., N.Y.C., 1991—. Home: 7 Hemlock Ln Marlboro NJ 07746-1212 Office: Independence Cmty Bank Corp 182 Atlantic Ave Brooklyn NY 11201-5604

COHEN, ALAN BARRY, researcher, educator; b. Bklyn, Nov. 3, 1952; s. Max B. and Blanche (Katz) C.; m. Helaine Francine Hartman, Dec. 22, 1973; children: Jeremy Todd, Bradley Daniel, Melanie Ann, Brandon Adam. BA, U. Rochester, 1973; MS, Harvard U., 1975, ScD, 1983. Rsch. asst. Beth Israel Hosp. and Harvard Med. Sch., Boston, 1974-75; sr. analyst Urban Systems Rsch. & Engring. Inc., Cambridge, Mass., 1975-79; rsch. assoc. Harvard Sch. Pub. Health, Boston, 1979-81, Johns Hopkins Sch. Hygiene and Pub. Health, Balt., 1981-82, asst. prof., 1982-84; assoc. dir. John Hopkins Ctr. for Hosp. Fin. and Mgmt., Balt., 1983-84; program officer Robert Wood Johnson Found., Princeton, NJ, 1984-87, sr. program officer, 1987-88, v.p., 1988-92; rsch. prof. Heller Grad. Sch. Brandeis U., 1992-94; prof. health policy and mgmt. Boston U. Sch. Mgmt., 1994—, dir. health care mgmt. program, 1994—2003; exec. dir. Health Policy Inst. Boston U., 2003—. Nat. program dir. Robert Wood Johnson Found. Scholars in Health Policy Rsch. Program, 1992—; mem. nat. adv. com. Robert Wood Johnson Found. Info. for State Health Policy Program, 1994-98; cons. NJ Dept. Health, 1993; chmn. commr.'s cardiac svc. com. State of NJ, Trenton, 1990-92; mem. Inst. Medicine, Tech. Monitoring Panel on Access to Care, 1989-91; cons. DC State Health Planning and Devel. Agy., 1984, Nat. Ctr. Health Svc. Rsch., 1984. Mem. editl. bd. Inquiry, Health Affairs; contbr. articles to profl. jour. Recipient Charles F. Wilinsky award Harvard Sch. Pub. Health, 1979; Kaiser fellow in health policy and mgmt., 1973-74; Dissertation grantee Nat. Ctr. Health Svc. Rsch., 1979-80. Fellow Acad. Health; mem. APHA, Am. Econ. Assn., Am. Polit. Sci. Assn., Nat. Acad. Social Ins., Health Tech. Assessment Internat., Zeta Beta Tau (pres. Gamma Pi chpt. 1972-73, treas. 1970-72), Beta Gamma Sigma. Jewish. Avocations: reading, travel, cinema, basketball, gardening. Office: Boston U Health Policy Inst 53 Bay State Rd Boston MA 02215

COHEN, ALAN NORMAN, business executive; b. Clifton, N.J., Dec. 19, 1930; s. Samuel and Ida (Phillips) C.; m. Joan Meryl Fields, Nov. 25, 1953 (dec.); children: Laurie Elizabeth, Gordon Geoffrey; m. Carol F. Vasil, June 21, 1992; 1 child, Rebecca Samantha. Student, Dartmouth, 1948-49; AB, Columbia U., 1952, LLB, 1954. Bar: N.Y. 1954. Assoc. Cahill, Gordon, Reindel & Ohl, N.Y.C., 1954-55, Paul, Weiss, Goldberg, Rifkind, Wharton & Garrison, N.Y.C., 1957-63, ptnr., 1961-70, 78-80; pres. Andal Corp., N.Y.C., 1980—, also bd. dirs.; chmn. ANC Sports Enterprises, LLC, 1997—; co-chmn. Sportsco. Internat. Ltd. Partnership, Toronto, 1999—. Exec. v.p., dir., mem. exec. com. Warner Comms., Inc., N.Y.C., 1970-74; pres., CEO, dir., mem. exec. com. Madison Sq. Garden Corp., N.Y.C., 1974-77; chmn. N.J. Nets, 1978-83; vice chmn., treas., dir. Boston Celtics Ltd. Partnership, 1986-93; co-chmn., pres. dir. Boston Celtics Comms. Partnership, 1990-92; mem. bd. visitors Columbia Coll., 1988-94; mem. bd. visitors Columbia Law Sch., 1994-96, chmn. ann. fund, 1994-98. Mem. bd. govs. NBA, 1979—83, chmn., 1986—88; bd. overseers Grad. Sch. Mgmt. and Urban Professions; trustee Am. Friends of Tel Aviv U., 1999—; bd. advisors Pine Crest Prep. Sch., 2001; bd. dirs. Jewish Fedn. South Palm Beach County, 2000. With AUS, 1955—57. Named to Jewish Sports Hall of Fame, 1988; recipient John Jay award Columbia Coll., 1988. Office: 2500 Westchester Ave Purchase NY 10577-2540

COHEN, ALAN SEYMOUR, internist; b. Boston, Apr. 9, 1926; s. George I. and Jennie (Laskin) C.; m. Joan Elizabeth Prince, Sept. 12, 1954; children: Evan Bruce, Andrew Hollis, Robert Adam AB magna cum laude, Harvard Coll., 1947; MD magna cum laude, Boston U., 1952. Intern Harvard Med. Svc., Boston City Hosp., 1952-53, resident, 1953-55; exch. registrar in medicine Dundee Royal Infirmary and U. St. Andrews, Scotland, 1955-56. Rsch. and clin. fellow in rheumatology Mass. Gen. Hosp., Boston, 1956-58; instr. Med. Sch. Harvard Coll. and Mass. Gen. Hosp., 1958-60; head arthritis and connective tissue disease sect. Evans dept. clin. rsch. Mass. U. Hosp., Boston, 1960-72; Conrad Wesselhoeft prof. medicine Sch. Medicine Boston U., 1972-93, prof. pharmacology, 1974-92, disting. prof. medicine in rheumatology, 1993—; dir. Arthritis Ctr., 1977-94; dir. divsn. medicine Boston City Hosp., 1973-93; dir. Thorndike Meml. lab., 1973-93; bd. dirs. Hemagen Diagnostics Inc.; scientific bd. Neurochem. Inc., Can., 1997—. Editor: Laboratory Diagnostic Procedures in the Rheumatic Diseases, 1967, rev. edit., 1975, 3d edit., 1985, (with others) Symposium on Amyloidosis, 1968, (With R. Friedin and M. Samuels) Medical Emergencies: Diagnostic and Management Procedures from Boston City Hospital, 1977, (with J. Combes and H. Koh) 2d edit., 1983, Rheumatology and Immunology, 1979, (with J.C. Bennett) 2d edit., 1986, Progress in Clinical Rheumatology, 1984, (with D. Goldenberg) Drugs in the Rheumatic Diseases, 1986, Amyloidosis, 1986, Clinical Problems in Acute Care Medicine (J.J. Heffernan, R.A. Witzburg, A.S. Cohen), 1989; founder, editor-in-chief Amyloid Internat. Jour. of Exptl. and Clin. Investigation, 1994—; contbr. over 700 articles to profl. jours. Trustee Arthritis Found., Atlanta, 1976-82, trustee Mass. chpt., 1966-85, vice chmn., 1971-84, pres., 1981-94; vice sec. for N.Am., mem. exec. com. Pan Am. League Against Rheumatism, 1982-85; chmn. Boston City Hosp. Physician Alumni Reunion Com., 1992; pres. Boston City Hosp. Fund for Excellence, 1992. Served to surg. USPHS, 1953-55. Recipient Outstanding Alumnus award Boston U. Sch. Medicine, 1975, Purdue Frederic Arthritis award, 1979, James H. Fairclough Jr. award for disting. svc. to Mass. chpt. Arthritis Found., 1981, Alumni award for spl. distinction Boston U., 1981, Jan Van Bremeen Gold medal Dutch Rheumatism Soc., 1990, Commrs. Disting. Physician award Boston City Hosp., 1991, Gold medal Am. Coll. Rheumatology, 1994, Dr. Marian Ropes award Arthritis Found., 1995, Socius Honoris Causa, Hungarian Amyloid Soc., 2001, Hero award Arthritis Found., 2001. Master Am. Coll. Rheumatology (pres. 1978-79); fellow ACP, Am. Soc. Clin. Investigation, Assn. Am. Physicians, Am. Fedn. Clin. Rsch., Am. Soc. Exptl. Pathology, Interurban Clin. Club, Soc. Exptl. Biology and Medicine, Electron Microscopy Soc. Am., New Eng. Soc. for Electron Microscopy, Am. Soc. Cell Biology, N.Y. Acad. Sci., AMA, Mass. Med. Soc., New Eng. Rheumatism Assn. (past pres.), Italian Rheumatism Soc. (hon.), Spanish Rheumatism Soc. (hon.), Finnish Rheumatism Soc. (hon.), Brazilian Rheumatism Soc. (hon.), Irish Soc. Rheumatism and Rehab. (hon.), Italian Soc. Amyloidosis (hon.), Boston U. Sch. Medicine Alumni Assn. (past pres.), Harvard Club (Boston), Wightman Tennis Ctr. (Weston, Mass.), Boulders Club (Carefree, Ariz.), Phi Beta Kappa, Alpha Omega Alpha. Jewish. Office: Boston U Sch Medicine Amyloid Program 715 Albany St M-902 Boston MA 02118-2307

COHEN, ALBERT, musician, educator; b. N.Y.C., Nov. 16, 1929; s. Sol A. and Dora Cohen; m. Betty Joan (Berg), Aug. 28, 1952; children: Eva Denise, Stefan Berg. BS, Juilliard Sch. Music, 1951; MA, NYU, 1953, PhD (hon.), 1959; postgrad., U. Paris, 1956-57. Mem. faculty U. Mich., Ann Arbor, 1960-70, assoc. prof. music, 1964-67, prof., 1967-70; prof. music, chmn. dept. SUNY, Buffalo, 1970-73, Stanford U., 1973-87, William H. Bonsall prof. music, 1974—, prof. emeritus, 2000—. Editor: Broude Bros. Ltd., N.Y.C., Info. Coordinators, Detroit. Author: Treatise on the Composition of Music, 1962, Elements or Principles of Music, 1965; (with J.D. White) Anthology of Music for Analysis, 1965; (with L.E. Miller) Music in the Paris Academy of Sciences, 1666-1793, An Index, 1979, Music in the French Royal Academy of Sciences, 1981, Music in the Royal Society of London 1660-1806, 1987; editor: J.B. Lully, Ballet de Flore, 2001; contbr. articles to profl. jours. Guggenheim fellow, 1968-69; NEH fellow, 1975-76, 82-83, 85-89 Mem. Internat. Musical Soc., Am. Musical Soc., French Musical Soc., Music Libr. Assn. Office: Stanford U Dept Music Stanford CA 94305

COHEN, ALBERT DIAMOND, retail executive; b. Winnipeg, Man., Can., Jan. 20, 1914; s. Alexander and Rose (Diamond) C.; m. Irena Kankova, Nov. 6, 1953; children: Anthony Jan, James Eduard, Anna-Lisa. LLD (hon.), U. Man., 1987. Pres. Gendis Inc., Winnipeg, 1953-87; chmn., chief exec. officer Winnipeg, 1987-99; chmn., 1999—. Chmn. exec. com. Gendis Realty Inc., Winnipeg, 1961-88, also bd. dirs.; bd. dirs. SAAN Stores Ltd., Gendis Realty Inc. Author: The Entrepreneurs (Cert. of Merit Nat. Bus. Book award 1986), The Story of SAAN, 2002. Past pres. Winnipeg Clin. Rsch. Inst., 1975-80, Paul H.T. Thorlakson Rsch. Found., 1978-80, Man. Theatre Ctr., 1968-71, 76-81; past hon. chmn. St. John's Ravenscourt Sch., 1984-94; commr. Metric Bd. Ottawa, 1978. Named mem. Order of Can., 1983, promoted to officer, 1995; recipient Internat. Disting. Entrepreneur award U. Man., 1983, Man. of Yr. award Sales and Advt. Club, Winnipeg, 1974, Commemorative medal 125th Ann. Can. Fedn., 1992, Sony Lifetime Achievement award, 2000; inducted into Can. Bus. Hall of Fame, 1994. Office: Gendis Inc PO Box 9400 1370 Sony Pl Winnipeg MB Canada R3C 3C3 E-mail: finance@gendis.ca.

COHEN, ALLAN RICHARD, broadcasting executive; b. Bklyn., Dec. 27, 1947; s. Ike and Fae C.; m. Roberta Segal, July 12, 1970; children: Evan, Stacie. BS, Hofstra U., 1970; MM, Poly. Inst. Bklyn., 1976. Electronics engr. Sperry Systems Mgmt. Div., Great Neck, N.Y., 1970-74; with CBS/Viacom, 1974—; dir. planning and adminstrn. WCBS-TV, 1977-79; v.p. personnel CBS Broadcast Group, 1979-80; v.p., gen. mgr. Sta. KMOX-TV, St. Louis, 1980-86, Sta. KMOV-TV, St. Louis, 1986—. Lectr. in comm. and journalism Washington U., St. Louis; mem. affiliates adv. bd. CBS. Restaurant critic, travel editor St. Louis Bus. Jour. Vice chmn. bd. dirs. St. Louis Symphony; bd. dirs. Paraquad, Jewish Hosp., United Way, Variety Club; mem. adv. bd. Nat. Coun. Jewish Women, St. Louis. Recipient Flair awards, Emmy awards. Mem. NATAS (v.p. St. Louis chpt. 1987-88, pres. 1989-91), Mo. Broadcasters Assn. (bd. dirs.), Ill. Broadcasters Assn., Nat. Assn. Broadcasters, St. Louis Jr. League (adv. bd.), Westwood Club, St. Louis Variety Club (bd. dirs.).

COHEN, ALVIN P. language educator; b. L.A., Dec. 12, 1937; m. Dade Singapuri, 1984; children: Peter, James, Anil. BS, U. Calif., Berkeley, 1960, MA, 1966, PhD, 1971. Asst. prof. Chinese U. Mass., Amherst, 1971—77, assoc. prof. Chinese, 1977—83, prof. Chinese, 1983—, dept. chair, 1991—97. Author: Introduction to Research in Chinese Source Materials, 2000. Office: Univ Mass Amherst Dept Asian Lang & Lit Amherst MA 01003-9312

COHEN, ANNE CAROLYN CONSTANT, biologist; b. Durham, N.C., Mar. 1, 1935; d. Frank Woodbridge Constant and Carolyn Anne (Cook) Colwell; m. Daniel Morris Cohen, Nov. 4, 1955; children: Carolyn Annette Leech, Cynthia Sarah Cohen. BA, Stanford U., 1956; MS, U. Md., 1972; PhD, George Washington U., 1987. Waitress Stanford U., Palo Alto, Calif., 1953-56, rsch. asst., 1956; mus. technician Smithsonian Instn., Washington, 1963-66; tchg. asst. U. Md., College Pk., 1969-70; mus. technician Smithsonian Instn., Washington, 1973-76, mus. specialist, 1976-82; project dir. Natural History Mus. L.A., 1987; postdoctoral fellow UCLA, 1987-91, biol. rschr., 1991-97; rsch. assoc. Natural History Mus. L.A. County; fellow, rsch. assoc. Calif. Acad. Scis., San Francisco; non-U. Calif. rschr. Bodega Marine Lab. Active rschr. through affiliations with L.A. County Mus. Nat. History, Calif. Acad. of Scis., Bodega Marine Lab. Contbr. more than 25 rsch. articles to sci. jours. Grantee NSF, 1987-92, Mead Found., 1983-85, Learner-Gray Fund, 1981; recipient award for Exceptional Svcs., Smithsonian Instn., 1979, Antarctic Svc. medal NSF, 1967. Mem. Soc. Women Geographers, Crustacean Soc. Office: Bodega Marine Lab (UC Davis) PO Box 247 Bodega Bay CA 94923-0247 E-mail: acohen@monitor.net.

COHEN, ARMOND E. rabbi; b. Canton, Ohio, June 5, 1909; s. Samuel and Rebecca (Lipkowitz) C.; m. Anne Lederman; children: Rebecca Long, Deborah (dec.), Samuel. BA, NYU, 1931; rabbi, Jewish Theol Sem. Am., 1934, M Hebrew Lit., 1945, DD (hon.), 1966; LLD (hon.), Cleve. State U., 1969; LHD (hon.), Baldwin-Wallace Coll., 1989. Ordained rabbi, 1934. Rabbi Pk. Synagogue, Cleve., 1934—. Adj. prof. psychiatry Jewish Theol. Sem. Am., N.Y.C., 1970-75; bd. dirs. Inst. Religion and Health, N.Y.C. Author: All God's Children, Selected Readings on Zionism, Outline of Jewish History, Readings in Medieval Jewish Literature; mem. editorial bd. Jour. Religion and Health, 1943-67; contbr. articles to profl. jours. Bd. govs. Hebrew U., Jerusalem; trustee Am. Friends of Hebrew U., 1969—; bd. dirs. consumers League Ohio, Cleve., Jewish Community Fedn., Cleve., Coun. World Affairs, Cleve.; hon. v.p. Zionist Orgn. Am. Named Humanitarian of the Yr., Internat. Red Cross, 2002. Mem. Rabbinical Assembly Am., Cleve. Bd. Rabbis (founder), Lotos Club (N.Y.C.), Oakwood Club (Cleve.), Union Club (Cleve.). Home: 8 Sherwood Ct Cleveland OH 44122-7592 Office: The Park Synagogue 3300 Mayfield Rd Cleveland OH 44118-1899 *Anyone can struggle through life without faith but everyone needs faith if he would confront life's inevitable challenges and sorrows and stand erect. It is easier to go through this life with faith than without it.*

COHEN, ARNOLD NORMAN, gastroenterologist; b. N.Y.C., Nov. 5, 1949; s. Norman and Edna Clara (Arnold) C.; m. Colleen Ruth Carey; children: Eric Arnold, Leslie Carey. BA summa cum laude, Hobart Coll., 1971; MD, Harvard U., 1975. Diplomate Am. Bd. Internal Medicine, Am. Bd. Gastroenterology. Resident internal medicine U. Pa., Phila., 1975-78, asst. instr. medicine, 1977-78; fellow gastroenterology, instr. medicine Northwestern U., Chgo., 1978-80; asst. clin. prof. medicine U. Wash. Med. Sch., Seattle, 1980—; mem. faculty Spokane (Wash.) Family Medicine Residency, 1980—; pvt. practice gastroenterology Spokane, 1980—. Mem. various coms. St. Lukes-Deaconess Hosp., Spokane, 1980—; pres. med. staff St. Lukes Hosp., 1985-86. Contbr. articles to profl. jours. and textbooks. Fellow ACP, Am. Coll. Gastroenterology; mem. Am. Soc. Gastrointestinal Endoscopy, Am. Gastroent. Soc., Wash. Med. Soc., Spokane Internal Med. Soc., Phi Beta Kappa, Alpha Omega Alpha. Avocations: shooting sports, martial arts, swimming. Home: 3514 S Jefferson St Spokane WA 99203-1441 Office: Spokane Digestive Disease Ctr 801 W 5th Ave Spokane WA 99204-2823

COHEN, BERNARD CECIL, political scientist, educator; b. Northampton, Mass., Feb. 22, 1926; s. Louis Mark and Lena (Slotnick) C.; m. Laura Mae Propper, Sept. 1, 1947; children: Barbara Ellen, Janie Louise. BA, Yale U., 1948, MA, 1950, PhD, 1952. Rsch. asst. Yale U., New Haven, 1950-51; rsch. asst., then rsch. assoc. Princeton (N.J.) U., 1951-59, asst. prof., 1957-59; mem. faculty U. Wis., Madison, 1959—, prof. polit. sci., 1963-73, Quincy Wright prof. polit. sci., 1973-90, prof. emeritus, 1990—, chmn. dept., 1966-69, assoc. dean Grad. Sch., 1971-75, vice chancellor acad. affairs, 1984-86, 88-89, acting chancellor, 1987, vice chancellor emeritus, 1990—. Vis. rsch. scholar Carnegie Endowment Internat. Peace, 1965-66; mng. editor World Politics, 1956-59, mem. bd. editors, 1959-60, 72-78; mem. bd. editors Internat. Studies Quar., 1966-78; bd. dirs. Nat. Register Health Svcs. Providers in Psychology. Author: The Political Process and Foreign Policy, 1957, The Press and Foreign Policy, 1963, The Public's Impact on Foreign Policy, 1973, Democracies and Foreign Policy, 1995; editor: Foreign Policy in American Government, 1965. Served with AUS, 1944-46. Ford Found. Faculty Research fellow, 1969-70; fellow Center Advanced Study Behavioral Scis., 1961-62, 69-70; Fulbright-Hays research scholar Netherlands, 1975-76; Guggenheim fellow, 1981-82 Mem. Am. Polit. Sci. Assn. Home: 87 Oak Creek Trl Madison WI 53717-1509

COHEN, BERNARD LEONARD, physicist, educator; b. Pitts., June 14, 1924; s. Samuel and Mollie (Friedman) C.; m. Anna Foner, Mar. 30, 1950; children: Donald, Judith, Frederick, Ernest. BS, Case Inst. Tech., 1944; MS, U. Pitts., 1948; PhD., Carnegie Inst. Tech., 1950. With Oak Ridge Nat. Lab., 1950-58; prof. physics U. Pitts., 1958-94, prof. emeritus, 1994—, also adj. prof. chemistry, chem. engring., radiation health, environ. and occupl. health; dir. Sarah Mellon Scaife Nuclear Physics Lab., 1965-78. On leave with Gen. Atomic Lab., San Diego, 1959-60, Inst. for Def. Analysis, Washington, 1962, Brookhaven Nat. Lab., 1965, Los Alamos Sci. Lab., 1969, Inst. Energy Analysis, Oak Ridge, 1974-75, Electric Power Rsch. Inst., 1975, Argonne Nat. Lab., 1978-79; cons. numerous govtl. agys. and pvt. corps. Author: Heart of the Atom, 1967, Concepts of Nuclear Physics, 1971, Nuclear Science and Society, 1974, Before It's Too Late: A Scientist's Case for Nuclear Power, 1983, A Homeowner's Guide to Radon, 1987, The Nuclear Energy Option: Alternative For The Nineties, 1990; contbr. numerous articles to profl. jours. Fellow AAAS, Am. Phys. Soc. (chmn. divsn. nuclear physics 1974-75, Bonner prize for nuclear physics 1981); mem. Nat. Acad. Engring., Am. Assn. Physics Tchrs. (nat. coun. 1973-78), Am. Nuclear Soc. (chmn. divsn. environ. scis. 1980-81, Pub. Info. award 1984, Walter Zinn award 1996, Spl. award 1996), Soc. Risk Analysis, Health Physics Soc. (Disting. Sci. Achievement award 1992). Home: 307 S Dithridge St Apt 204 Pittsburgh PA 15213-3514 Fax: 412-624-9163. E-mail: blc@pitt.edu.

COHEN, BETH, art historian; BA, CUNY, 1968; MA, NYU, N.Y.C., 1970, PhD, 1977. Vis. asst. prof. U. Wis., Milw., 1978-79; asst. prof. Columbia U., N.Y.C., 1979-88; vis. asst. prof. Bard Coll., Annandale-on-Hudson, N.Y., 1991; assoc. prof. U. Rochester in Italy, Arezzo, 1994. Art historian studies abroad program U. Ga., Cortona, Italy, 1997, N.Y. Acad. Art, 1999-2001; Parker disting. lectr. Ctr. for Old World Archaeology and Art, Brown U., spring 1998; adj. assoc. prof. Columbia U., N.Y.C., 1999, Drew U., Madison, N.J., 1999; vis. assoc. prof. Bard Coll., Annandale-on-Hudson, N.Y., 2000; guest curator Edith C. Blum Art Inst., Bard Coll., Annandale-on-Hudson, 1989-92; contract lectr. Met. Mus. Art, N.Y.C., 1991—; chair, organizer art history session Coll. Art Assn. Ann. Conf., N.Y.C., 1994; vis. lectr. U. Canterbury, Christchurch, 1995; mem. Univ. Seminar in Classical Civilization, Columbia U., 1979—, co-chair, 1982-85; art historian N.Y. Acad. Art, N.Y.C., 1999-2001; vis. prof. SUNY, Stony Brook, 2002—03. Author: Attic Bilingual Vases and Their Painters, 1978; editor, contbg. author: The Distaff Side: Representing the Female in Homer's Odyssey, 1995; co-author: (art exhbn. catalog) The Odyssey and Ancient Art, 1992; co-editor: (art exhbn. catalog) Mother City and Colony: Classical Athenian and South Italian Vases in New Zealand and Australia, 1995; contbg. author, editor: Not the Classical Ideal: Athens and the Construction of the Other in Greek Art, 2000. J. Clawson Mills fellow Met. Mus. Art, 1983-84, 92, NEH fellow, 1990, Andrew W. Mellon fellow Met. Mus. Art, 1991-92; Paul Mellon vis. sr. fellow Ctr. for Advanced Study in Visual Arts, Nat. Gallery Art, 1996, Ailsa Mellon Bruce vis. sr. fellow Ctr. for Advanced Study in the Visual Arts, Nat. Gallery of Art, 1997; recipient stipend Am. Acad., Rome, 2001. Mem. Archaeol. Inst. Am. (exec. com. N.Y. Soc. 1984—2001, v.p. 1985-88, editor newsletter 1994-96), Classical Assn. Atlantic States, Coll. Art Assn., Women's Classical Caucus, Italian Art Soc., Renaissance Soc. Am. Home: 425 E 86th St Apt 4C New York NY 10028-6491

COHEN, BRADLEY, neurologist; b. N.Y.C., Aug. 16, 1968; m. Beth Cohen, Aug. 27, 1994; children: Sydney, Joshua. BS, SUNY, Stony Brook, 1989; DO, U. Iowa, 1994. Practice neurology, New Hyde Park, N.Y. Office: Mallin-Blau-Cohen 3003 New Hyde Park Rd New Hyde Park NY 11042-1214

COHEN, BRETT I. health products executive; b. Bronx, N.Y., Aug. 13, 1962; s. Gilbert Victor and Phyllis C. (Strassberg) C.; m. Elissa Bloom, Aug. 23, 1986; children: Harley Lennon, Jake Aaron. BS, SUNY, Albany, 1984, PhD in Chemistry, 1987. Postdoctoral fellow Rutgers U., New Brunswick, N.J., 1988; CEO, v.p. dental rsch. Essential Dental Systems, South Hackensack, N.J., 1989—. Mem. dental magnets subcom. Am. Dental Assn./ISO Specification No. 81 Magnets and Keepers, 1993—. Contbr. articles to profl. jours.; patentee in field. Mem. Am. Chem. Soc., Soc. for Dental Materials, Soc. for Lasers, Am. Soc. Quality Control. Avocations: reading, running, movies. Office: Essential Dental Systems 89 Leuning St South Hackensack NJ 07606-1326 E-mail: eds@pipeline.com.

COHEN, BRIAN S. public relations executive; CEO, chmn. The Global Comm. Group, N.Y.C. Office: Global Comm Group 136 Madison Ave Fl 14 New York NY 10016-6711

COHEN, BURTON DAVID, franchising executive, lawyer; b. Chgo., Feb. 12, 1940; s. Allan and Gussy (Katz) C.; m. LInda Rochelle Kaine, Jan. 19, 1969; children: David, Jordana. BS in Bus. and Econs., Ill. Inst. Tech., 1960; JD, Northwestern U., 1963. Staff atty. McDonald's Corp., Oak Brook, Ill., 1964-69, asst. sec., 1969-70, asst. gen. counsel, 1970-76, asst. v.p., 1976-78, dep. dir. legal dept., 1978-80, v.p. franchising, asst. gen. counsel, asst. sec., 1980-89, sr. v.p., chief franchising officer, 1989-98. Adv. dir., 1992-93, McDonald's Corp., 1992—; lectr. Practising Law Inst.; guest lectr. grad. sch. of bus. U. Chgo.; adv. bd. La. State U. Franchise U.; dir. Goodwill Enterprises Devel. Corp.; franchise mediator CPR Inst. for Dispute Resolution; cons. Exec. Svc. Corps Chgo.; adj. prof. Kellogg Grad Sch. of Mgmt., Northwestern U.; dir. The Dwyer Group. Author: Franchising: Second Generation Problems, 1969. With AUS, 1963-64. Mem. ABA, Ill. Bar Assn., Chgo. Bar Assn., Internat. Franchise Assn. (lectr.), Assn. Nat. Advertisers, Chgo. Coun. Fgn. Rels., Execs. Club (Chgo.), Tau Epsilon Phi, Phi Delta Phi. Office: 300 Cedar Ave Highland Park IL 60035

COHEN, CARL I. psychiatry educator, researcher; b. N.Y.C., Aug. 7, 1947; s. Louis and Louise Cohen; m. Katherine A. Henry, Sept. 12, 1987; children: Sara, Zachary. BA, CUNY, 1967; MD, SUNY, Buffalo, 1971; MA, NYU, 1974. Diplomate Am. Bd. Psychiatry and Neurology, Am. Bd. Psychiatry and Neurology with Added Qualifications in Geriatric Psychiatry. Intern Med. Coll. Pa., 1971-72; resident NYU Bellevue Med. Ctr., 1972-74; fellow NYU Med. Ctr., 1974-75, asst. prof., dir. social and cmty. psychiatry, 1976-81; prof. psychiatry, dir. divsn. geriatric psychiatry SUNY Health Sci. Ctr., Bklyn., 1981—. Dir. Downstate Mental Hygiene Assocs., Bklyn., 1983—, Bklyn. Alzheimer's Disease Assistance Ctr., 1988—; mem. adv. b.d L.I. Alzheimer's Found., N.Y., 1998—; spl. advisor White House Conf. on Aging, Washington, 1980; advisor to various coms. NIMH, 1985-99; presenter N.Y.C. Mayor's Conf. on Alzheimer's Disease, 1992-99. Author: Old Men of the Bowery, 1989, Schizophrenia Into Later Life, 2003; mem. editl. bd. Jour. Geriat. Psychiatry, London, 1983—99, Am. Jour. Geriat. Psychiatry, 1994—2000, spl. editor Cmty. Mental Health Jour., 1993; contbr. over 150 articles to med. jours., chapters to books. Bd. dirs. St. Francis Friends of Poor, N.Y.C., 1983—. Named one of Best Drs. in N.Y., N.Y. Mag., 1996, 1998, 2001; over 40 grants, including, NIMH, N.Y. State Dept. Health, pvt. founds. Fellow Am. Psychiat. Assn.; mem. Am. Assn. Geriatric Psychiatry, Am. Assn. Cmty. Psychiatrists (Psychiatrist of Yr. award 1991), Internat. Assn. Geriatric Psychiatry. Avocation: handball. Office: SUNY Health Sci Ctr Bklyn 450 Clarkson Ave # 1203 Brooklyn NY 11203-2056 E-mail: cohen_c@hscbklyn.edu.

COHEN, CAROL I. lawyer; b. Jersey City, Feb. 26, 1945; d. Harry and Sylvia Indursky; m. Burton David Cohen, June 18, 1967 (div.); children: Steven Corey, Richard Harris. BA, Douglass Coll., 1966; MA, NYU, 1967; JD, Seton Hall U., 1978. Bar: N.J. 1978; Calif. 1979, U.S. Ct. Appeals (3d cir.) 1978, U.S. Supreme Ct. 1999. Tchr. Jersey City Bd. Edn., 1966-67; social worker Monterey Welfare Dept., Salinas, Calif., 1967—69; adoption caseworker DYFS, New Brunswick, NJ, 1969-71; supr. adoptions Adoption Svc. Ctr., Highland Park, N.J., 1971-73; legis. aide Sen. Anthony Russo, Union, NJ, 1980—84; atty. Union County Bd. Social Svcs., Elizabeth, NJ, 1984—90; asst. county counsel County of Union, Elizabeth, 1988-94, freeholder, 1996-98, county counsel, 1998—2002; atty. in pvt. practice, Westfield, N.J., 1978-98; adminstrv. law judge Newark, 2002—. Vice chair Westfield Dem. Com., 1990—; mem. Union County Dem. Com., 1980—. Recipient award in govt. svc. N.J. Adv. Com. on Status of Women, 1998; NDEA fellow, 1966; NYU fellow, 1966. Mem. Women's Polit. Caucus (pres. 1999), N.J. County Counsel Assn., Union County Bar Assn. (trustee 1997—), N.J. Bar Assn., Phi Beta Kappa. Jewish. Home: 302 Roanoke Rd Westfield NJ 07090-2920 Office: 33 Washington St Newark NJ 07102- E-mail: ccohen@oal.state.nj.us.

COHEN, CAROLYN ALTA, health educator; b. Boston, Aug. 25, 1943; d. Haskell Mark and Sarah (Siegal) Cohen. BS, Boston U., 1965; postgrad., Boston State Coll., U. Mass., 1978, Boston Leadership Acad., 1989, Boston Leadership Inst., 1997. Health and phys. edn. tchr., coach, girls athletic coord. Roslindale H.S., Boston, 1965—76; health and phys. edn. tchr., coach, athletic coord. West Roxbury H.S., Boston, 1976—87; asst. dir. health phys. edn. athletics Madison Park Campus, Boston, 1979—87; health educator dept. phys. edn./athletics West Roxbury H.S., Boston, 1989—90, 1990—, lead tchr., 1995—2000; commr. girls' basketball Boston Pub. Schs., 1979—. Cheerleading judge various orgns., 1963, 64, 65, 70, 74, 80, 69-74; coach recreational programs N.E. Deaconess Hosp. Sch. Nursing, 1962-64, Beth Israel Hosp. Sch. Nursing, 1961-64; basketball ofcl. Bay State League, Pvt. Sch. League, Cath. H.S., 1961-80; coach phys. edn. dept. Boston U., 1962-65, 65-68; ofcl. Boston Park and Recreation Dept., 1962-75, summer playgrounds instr., 1961-65; instr. garening, athletic specialist agr. dept. Boston Schs., 1965-76. Trustee Adaptic Environ. Ctr., Boston, 1986—, treas., mem. exec. bd., 1990—; trustee Friends of Boston Harbor Islands, Inc.; instr. ARC, 1965—; rep. Office Children-Area IV, Roslindale, Boston, 1974—76; liaison West Roxbury H.S. and Cmty. Sch. New Move Unltd. Theatre, Boston, 1981—84; liaison spl. arts project West Roxbury H.S., 1993—94. Named to Boston U. Scarlet Key Soc., 1998; recipient Spl. Citation, Boston U. Sargent Coll. Alumni Assn., 1980, Cert. of Appreciation, ARC Mass. Bay, 1986, Disting. Svc. to Alma Mater award, Boston U., 1994, New Agenda award, Boston Salute to Women in Sport, 1993, Citation, Mass. Celebration Women in Sports Day, 2002, citation, Mil. Order of World Wars, 2002, Youth Patriotic & Leadership, 2002. Mem.: Sargent Coll. Alumni Assn. (class sec., editor class newsletter 1965—, Spl. Citation 1980, Black Gold award 1995), Boston U. Nat. Alumni Coun., Boston U. Alumni Assn. (v.p. 1980—82, 1987—89, v.p. cmty. 1995—97, sec. 1997—), Mass. Assn. Health, Phys. Edn., Recreation and Dance (state and exec. com. 1969—74, treas. 1981—94, coord. registration ann. state conv. 1975—94, Honor award recognition 1978, Presdl. Citation 1988, Joseph McKenney award 2002), AAHPERD (bud. mgr. nat. conv. 1988—89), Boston U. Women's Grad. Club (v.p. for scholarship 1981—83, 1985—). Home: 100 Corey St West Roxbury MA 02132-2330

COHEN, CHARLES LLOYD, history and religious studies educator; b. N.Y.C., N.Y., June 4, 1948; s. Robert Edward and Gladys Shandling Cohen; m. Christine Amber Schindler, Nov. 8, 1981; 1 child, Amber Shandling. PhD, U. of Calif, Berkeley, 1982. Asst. prof. of history U. of Wis., Madison, 1984—88, assoc. prof. of history, 1988—97, prof. of history and religious studies, 1997—. Dir. religious studies program U. of Wis., Madison, 1997—; vis. asst. prof. Vassar Coll., Poughkeepsie, NY, 1983—84. Author: (book) God's Caress. Recipient Allen Nevins prize, Soc. of Am. Historians, 1983. Mem.: Am. Soc. of Ch. History (coun. mem. 2000—03), Omohundro Inst. of Early Am. History and Culture (coun. mem. 2002—), Mass. Hist. Soc. (corr.), Colonial Soc. of Mass. (life), Madison Lit. Soc. (life). Office: U Wis Dept History 4115 Humanities Bldg 455 N Park St Madison WI 53706-1483 Office Fax: 608-263-5302. E-mail: clcohen@facstaff.wisc.edu.

COHEN, CHERYL DIANE DURDA, communications executive; b. Mpls., Jan. 26, 1947; d. Joseph and Dolores Catherine (Monahan) Durda; m. Miles Jon Cohen, June 24, 1967; children: Christopher, Michael, Brian, Katherine Kelly. BA, U. Minn., 1978; grad. Owner/Pres. Mgmt. program, Harvard Bus. Sch., 1992. Writer Aeration Industries Internat. Inc., Chaska, Minn., 1982-85, communications asst., 1985-86, communications mgr., 1986-88, v.p. pub. rels., 1988-93, v.p. mktg. and pub. rels., 1993-97, environ. mktg. cons., 1997—. Bd. dirs. Aeration Industries Internat., Inc. Editor AIRE-02 News, 1985—, AQUA-02 News, 1988—; contbr. articles on water restoration and aquaculture to U.S. and internat. profl. jours., also conf. proc.; film editor, producer, 1986—. Bd. dirs. Minn. Assn. Retarded Citizens, Mpls., 1984-85, The Joseph Durda Found., 1990—; St. David's Sch. for Exceptional Children, Minnetonka, 1980-85; mem. adv. bd. Minnetonka Schs. CARE, Minn., 1982-92; dir. communications Minnetonka Football Assn., 1986-92, founding mem., 1986; mem. adv. coun. U. Minn. Women's Intercollegiate Athletics; founding mem. Minnetonka Basketball Club, 1984; active legis. testimony, lobbying, pub.

speaking Adv. for Severely Disabled, 1981—; mem. U. Minn. Gopher Football Team's Parent Club, 1988-92; mem. USAF Acad. Parents Club, 1992-93, Harvard-Radcliffe Club Minn., 1992-96; co-facilitator Devel. Capable Young People series for Minnetonka community, 1983-84. Mem. Water Pollution Control Fedn., World Aquaculture Soc., Asian Fisheries Soc., Chesapeake Bay Found., Clean Water Found., U. Minn. Alumni Assn., U. Minn. Presidents Club (chartered), Minn. Press Club, Booster Club (producer cable TV sports show 1988-92, co-chair publicity 1988-92), Harvard Bus. Sch. Club Minn. (alumni mem.). Roman Catholic. Avocations: reading, sports, music. Office: Aeration Industries Internat Inc 4100 Peavey Rd Chaska MN 55318-2353 E-mail: cheric@aireo2.com.

COHEN, CLAIRE GORHAM, investors service company executive; b. St. Johnsbury, Vt., May 9, 1934; d. John David and Muriel (Somers) Gorham; m. Richard D. Cohen, Nov. 26, 1959; 1 son, James H. BA, Radcliffe Coll., 1956; student, U. Vt., 1953-54. Proofreader Dun & Bradstreet, Inc., 1956, mcpl. bond analyst, 1957-64, sr. state analyst, 1965-66, sr. analyst, 1970-71, Moody's Investors Svc. Inc., N.Y.C., 1971-75; v.p., assoc. dir. rsch. Mcpl. Bond Rsch. Divsn., N.Y.C., 1975-86, v.p. mng. dir. state ratings, 1986-89; exec. mng. dir. govtl. fin. Fitch Investors Svc., Inc., N.Y.C., 1989-91, exec. v.p., 1991-94, vice chmn., 1994-97, Fitch IBCA, 1997—. Mem. Govt. Acctg. Stds. Adv. Coun., 1999-2002; adv. bd. Fed. Acctg. Stds., 2002--. Mem. Task Force on N.Y. State Pub. Authorities, 1974-75. Mem. N.Y. Harvard-Radcliffe Schs. Com.; 1952 class agt. St. Johnsbury Acad., 1981-86; 1956 class agt. Radcliffe Coll., 1981-86. Recipient Disting. Svc. award State Debt Mgmt. Network, 1999. Mem. Mcpl. Forum N.Y. (Career Svc. award 2002), Mcpl. Analysts Group N.Y. (treas. 1983-84, chmn. 1984-85), Nat. Fedn. Mcpl. Analysts (bd. govs. 1984-86, chmn. awards com. 1984-85, Career Achievement award 1991), Soc. Mcpl. Analysts, India House Club (bd. govs. 2003—). Office: Fitch IBCA One State St Plz New York NY 10004-2614

COHEN, CLAUDIA, journalist, television personality; b. Englewood, N.J., Dec. 16, 1950; d. Robert B. and Harriet (Brandwein) C.; 1 child, Samantha. BA, U. Pa., 1972. Mng. editor The Daily Pennsylvanian; with More Mag., N.Y.C., 1973-76; mng. editor, 1976-77; reporter N.Y. Post, N.Y.C., 1977-78; editor, author Page Six column, 1978-80; daily columnist I, Claudia N.Y. Daily News, N.Y.C., 1980-81, tv entertainment reporter Live with Regis and Kathie Lee, 1983—; reporter Eyewitness News WABC, 1984—89. Bd. overseers Sch. Arts and Scis. U. Pa.; mem. adv. bd. N.Y. Hosp. Cornell Med. Ctr. Honoree Sarah Herzog Meml. Hosp. Centennial, 1995, Rita Hayworth Gala Benefit for Alzheimers, 2000. Office: Sta WABC 7 Lincoln Sq New York NY 10023-5900

COHEN, CORA, artist; b. N.Y.C., Oct. 19, 1943; d. George and Anne (Lenarsky) C. BA, Bennington Coll., 1964, MA, 1972. Vis. artist U. Pa., 1969-70, U. Chgo., 1983-95, Art Inst. Sch. Chgo., 1983-85, 97, Boston Mus. Sch. Fine Arts, 1994-95, U. Minn., 1996, Kunsthögskolan, Stockholm, 1996; vis. prof. Art Inst. Sch. Chgo., 1992-93; adj. faculty NYU, 1990-2000; assoc. prof. art, U. N.C., Greensboro, 1998-2003, Vt. Studio Ctr., 1999-2002; vis. artist Emory and Henry Coll., Emory, Va., 2003. One-person shows include Everson Mus. Art, Syracuse, N.Y., 1974, Max Hutchinson Gallery, N.Y.C., 1979-80, 84, Wolff Gallery, 1988, Holly Solomon Gallery, 1990, New Arts Program, Kutztown, Pa., 1993, Jason McCoy Gallery, N.Y.C., 1993-94, David Beitzel Gallery, N.Y.C., 1994, Sarah Moody Gallery Art, Tuscaloosa, Ala., 1996, Joslyn Art Mus., Omaha, 1996, Hering Raum, Bonn, Germany, 1997-98, Rena Bransten Gallery, San Francisco, 1997, Jason McCoy Gallery, N.Y.C., 1997, Belvedere Strasse, 1999, Bentley Gallery, Scottsdale, Ariz., 1999, 2002, Stefanie Hering, Berlin, 2000, McCoy Chelsea, 2001; exhibited in group shows at Baxter Art Gallery, Pasadena, Calif., 1985, Am. Acad. and Inst. Arts and Letters, N.Y.C., 1987, Barbara Krakow Gallery, Boston, 1987, Pamela Auchincloss Gallery, Contemporary Surfaces, N.Y.C., 1992, A/C Project Room, An Esemplastic Shift, N.Y.C., 1992, Sandra Gering Gallery, 1992, Piccolo Spoleto Festival, Charleston, S.C., 1992, The Fetish of Knowledge, A/C Project Room, N.Y.C., 1992, Daniel Weinberg Gallery, L.A., 1989, Wolff Gallery, N.Y.C., 1991, Feigen Gallery, 1991, Sytsema Galleries, Baarn, Holland, 1992, Jason McCoy Gallery, N.Y.C., 1993, The Painting Ctr., N.Y.C., 1993, White Columns, N.Y.C., 1993, Bill Maynes Contemporary Art, N.Y.C., 1994, Penine Hart Gallery, N.Y., 1994, Trans Hudson Gallery, Jersey City, Out of the Blue Gallery, Edinburgh, Scotland, 1994, Cepa Gallery, Buffalo, 1995, 2000, the Smart Fair, Stockholm, 1995, NYU, N.Y.C., 1995, Newhouse Ctr. Contemporary Art, S.I., N.Y., 1997, Galleri Mariann Ahnlund Umea, Sweden, 1996, Accrochage, Hering Raum, Bonn, 1996, Galerie Brigitte Schenk, Köln, Germany, Köln Art Fair, 1997, Cepa Gallery, Buffalo, Galleri Mariann Ahnlund, Stockholm, Stalke Out of Space, Copenhagen, Barbara Davis Gallery, Houston, 1998, Oppenhoff & Rädler, Leipzig, Stockholm Art Fair, Hunter Coll., Times Square Gallery, N.Y., The Art Fair, The 69th Regiment Armory, N.Y., 1999, McCoy, Kansas City, 2000, Open Studio to Benefit the Coalition for the Homeless, N.Y., 2000, U. Ariz. Mus. Art, Tucson, 2001, The Five and Dime Series, Jan Vande Donk, NY, 2001, Cynthia Broan Gallery, N.Y., 2002, Painting Painting N3 Project Space, Williamsburg, Brooklyn, N.Y.; photgrapher: Cohen, Cora: The Record, The Death, The Surprise, 1999. Recipient N.Y. Found. Arts Gottlieb Found. award, 1990, Pollock Krasner award, 1998, Kohler Fund award U. N.C., 1999; Painting fellow Nat. Endowment for the Arts, 1987; Yaddo Residence grantee, 1982, 95, New Faculty grantee U. N.C., 1999. Mem. Simon Wiesenthal Ctr., Coll. Art Assn. Jewish. Home: 287 Broadway New York NY 10007-2004 E-mail: ccohen287@earthlink.net.

COHEN, CYNTHIA MARYLYN, lawyer; b. Bklyn., Sept. 5, 1945; AB, Cornell U., 1967; JD cum laude, NYU, 1970. Bar: N.Y. 1971, U.S. Ct. Appeals (2nd cir.) 1972, U.S. Dist. Ct. (so. and ea. dists.) N.Y. 1972, U.S. Supreme Ct. 1975, U.S. Dist. Ct. (ctrl. and no. dists.) Calif. 1980, U.S. Ct. Appeals (9th cir.) 1980, U.S. Dist. Ct. (so. dist.) Calif. 1981, U.S. Dist. Ct. (ea. dist.) Calif. 1986. With Paul, Hastings, Janofsky & Walker, LLP, L.A., N.Y.C. Lawyer del. 9th Cir. Jud. Conf. Bd. dirs. N.Y. chpt. Am. Cancer Soc., 1977-80; active Pres.'s Coun. Cornell Women; lawyer del. Ninth Cir. Jud. Conf. Recipient Am. Jurisprudence award for evidence, torts and legal instns., 1968-69; John Norton Pomeroy scholar NYU, 1968-70, Founders Day Cert., 1969. Mem. ABA, Assn. Bar City N.Y. (trade regulation com. 1976-79), Assn. Bus. Trial Lawyers, Fin. Lawyers Conf., N.Y. State Bar Assn. (chmn. class-action com. 1979), State Bar Calif., Los Angeles County Bar Assn., Order of Coif, Delta Gamma. Avocations: tennis, bridge, rare books, wines. Home: 4531 Dundee Dr Los Angeles CA 90027-1213 Office: Paul Hastings Janofsky & Walker LLP 515 S Flower St 25th Fl Los Angeles CA 90071 E-mail: cynthiacohen@paulhastings.com.

COHEN, DANIEL, psychologist, educator; b. N.Y.C., Dec. 13, 1932; s. Harry and Mary Ida (Goldstein) C.; m. Nita Vilk, Feb. 9, 1957; children: Nancy Ellen Cohen Iankowitz, Steven Michael. BA, N.Y.U., 1955, MA, 1959, PhD, 1967. Secondary sch. tchr. sci. Bd. of Edn., N.Y.C., 1956-67; asst. prof. edn. psychology Pace U., N.Y.C., 1967-73; exec. dir. N.Y. Testing and Guidance Ctr., N.Y.C., 1964-90; dir. visual psychology Inst. Visual Psychology & Optics, N.Y.C., 1968-73; tchr., dean student Bd. of Edn., N.Y.C., 1973-90. Fellow Royal Soc. of Health, mem. Am. Psychol. Assoc. Office: 20983 18th Ave Bayside NY 11360-1444

COHEN, DANIEL EDWARD, writer; b. Chgo., Mar. 12, 1936; s. Milton M. and Sue Greenberg C.; m. Susan Lois Handler, Feb. 2, 1958; 1 child, Theodora (dec.). BA in Journalism, U. Ill., 1958. Mng. editor Sci. Digest mag., N.Y.C., 1959-68; writer, 1968—. Author: Myths of the Space Age, 1967, Secrets from Ancient Graves, 1968, Vaccination and You, 1968, The Age of Giant Mammals, 1969, Animals of the City, 1969, Mysterious Places, 1969, A Modern Look at Monsters, 1970, Night Animals, 1970, Conquerors on Horseback, 1970, Talking with Animals, 1971, Superstition, 1971, A Natural History of Unnatural Things, 1971, Ancient Monuments and How They Were Built, 1971, Masters of the Occult, 1971, Voodoo, Devils, and the New Invisible World, 1972, Watchers in the Wild, 1972, In Search of Ghosts, 1972, The Magic Art of Foreseeing the Future, 1973, How Did Life Get There?, 1973, Magicians, Wizards and Sorcerers, 1973, How the World Will End, 1973, reissued as Waiting for the Apocalypse, 1983, Shaka: King of the Zulus, 1973, ESP: The Search Beyond the Senses, 1973, The Black Death, 1974, The Magic of the Little People, 1974, Curses, Hexes, and Spells, 1974, Intelligence: What Is It?, 1974, Not of the World, 1974, Human Nature, Animal Nature, 1974, The Far Side of Consciousness, 1974, The Mysteries of Reincarnation, 1975, The Greatest Monsters in the World, 1975, The Body Snatchers, 1975, The Human Side of Computers, 1975, Monsters, Giants, and Little Men from Mars, 1975, The New Believers, 1975, The Spirit of Lord, 1975, Animal Territories, 1975, Mysterious Disappearances, 1976, The Ancient Visitors, 1976, Dreams, Visions, and Drugs, 1976, Gold, 1976, Biorhythms in Your Life, 1976, Supermonsters, 1977, Ghostly Animals, 1977, The Science of Spying, 1977, Real Ghosts, 1977, Meditation, 1977, What Really Happened to the Dinosaurs?, 1977, Creativity: What Is It?, 1977, Ceremonial Magic, 1978, The World of UFO's, 1978, The World's Most Famous Ghosts, 1978, Young Ghosts, 1978, rev. edit., 1994, Frauds, Hoaxes, and Swindles, 1979, Missing, 1979, Mysteries of the World, 1979, What's Happening to Our Weather, 1979, Dealing with the Devil, 1979, Famous Curses, 1979, Great Mistakes, 1979, Close Encounters with God, 1979, The Monsters of "Star Trek", 1980, Monsters You Never Heard Of, 1980, The Tomb Robbers, 1980, Bigfoot: America's Number One Monster, 1980, Everything You Need to Know about Monsters and Still Be Able to Sleep, 1981, Ghostly Terrors, 1981, The Headless Roommate and Other Tales of Terror, 1981, The Last Hundred Years' Medicine, 1981, The Great Airship Mystery, 1981, Re-Thinking, 1982, America's Very Own Monsters, 1982, How to Buy a Car, 1982, Horror in the Movies, 1982, How to Test Your ESP, 1982, Real Magic, 1982, The Last Hundred Years' Household Technology, 1982, Monster Hunting Today, 1983, The Encyclopedia of Monsters, 1983, The Simon and Schuster Question and Answer Book on Computers, 1983, Southern Fried Rat and Other Gruesome Tales, 1983, Monster Dinosaur, 1983, The Restless Dead, 1983, The Encyclopedia of Ghosts, 1984, Musicals, 1984, Horror Movies, 1984, Hiram Bingham and the Dream of Gold, 1984, Masters of Horror, 1984, America's Very Own Ghosts, 1985, Henry Stanley and the Quest for the Source of the Nile, 1985, The Encyclopedia of the Strange, 1985; (with Susan Cohen) The Kids' Guide to Home Computers, 1983, Teenage Stress, 1984, The Kids' Guide to Home Video, 1984, Screen Goddesses, 1984, Hollywood Hunks and Heroes, 1985, Rock Video Superstars, 1985, Wrestling Superstars, Vol. 1, 1985, Vol. 2, 1986, Heroes of the Challenger, 1986, A Six-Pack and a Fake ID, 1986, The Encyclopedia of Movie Stars, 1986, A History of the Oscars, 1986, ESP: The New Technology, 1986, Strange and Amazing Facts About Star Trek, 1986, (with Susan Cohen) Wrestling Superstars II, 1986, Teenage Competition, 1986, Hollywood's Newest Superstars, 1987, The Encyclopedia of Unsolved Crimes, 1988, UFO's: The Third Wave, 1988, (with Susan Cohen) What Kind of Dog is That, 1989, Zoo Superstars, 1989, When Someone You Know is Gay, 1989, Ancient Egypt, 1990, The Ghosts of War, 1990, Ancient Greece, 1990, The Magical World of Monsters, 1991, Beverly Hills 90210: Meet the Stars, 1991, (with Susan Cohen) Going for the Gold: Medal Hopefuls for Winter '92, 1991, Zoos, 1992, Where to Find Dinosaurs Today, 1992, Ancient Rome, 1992, Ghostly Tales of Love and Revenge, 1992, Prophets of Doom, 1992, Ghosts of the Deep, 1993, Ghost in the House, 1993, Animal Rights, 1993, Dinosaur Discovery, 1993, The Beheaded Freshman and Other Nasty Rumors, 1993, The Ghost of Elvis and other Celebrity Spirits, 1994, Cults, 1994, 101 of the World's Strangest Mysteries, 1994, Into The Darkness, 1994, Real Vampires, 1995, The Phantom Hitchhiker, 1995, Riddle of the Stones, 1995, Prohibition, 1995, The Modern Ark, 1995, Gus the Bear, The Flying Cat and the Lovesick Moose, 1995, Allosaurus and Other Jurassic Meat Eaters, 1995, Stegosaurus and Other Jurassic Plant Eaters, 1995, Tyrannosaurus Rex and Other Cretaceous Meat Eaters, 1995, Triceratops and Other Cretaceous Plant Eaters, 1995, Werewolves, 1996, The Alaska Purchase, 1996, Joseph McCarthy: The Misuse of Political Power, 1996, Ghostly Warnings, 1996, Dangerous Ghosts, 1996, Screaming Skulls: 101 of the World's Great Ghost Stories, 1996, (with Susan Cohen) Gold Medal Glory: The Story of America's 1996 Women's Gymnastics Team, 1996, Hollywood Dinosaur, 1997, Great Conspiracies and Elaborate Cover-ups., 1997, Raising the Dead, 1997, The Millennium, 1997, Watergate: Deception in the White House, 1998, Cloning, 1998, The Alien Files 1, 1998, Contact, 1998, The Alien Files 2, Conspiracy, 1998, Are You Ready, The Best and Worst Predictions for the Millennium, 1998, The Manhattan Project, 1999, Prophets of Doom, The Millennium Edition, 1999, Wrestling Renegades, Civil War Ghosts, 1999, The Impeachment of William Jefferson Clinton, 1999, Yellow Journalism, 2000, George W. Bush, 2000, Apatosaurus, 2000, Pteranodon, 2000, Velociraptor, 2000, Stegosaurus, 2000, Triceratops, 2000, Tyrannosaurus, 2000, (with Susan Cohen) PanAm 103, 2000, rev. edit., 2001, Jesse Ventura, 2001, Hauntings and Horrors, 2002, Ankylosaurus, 2002, Brachiosaurus, 2002, Diplodocus, 2002, Ichythosaurus, 2002, Iguanoden, 2002, Allosaurus, 2002, Spinosaurus, 2003, Miasaurus, 2003, Pachcephalosaurus, 2003, Parasauiolophus, 2003, Trodon, 2003, Sarcosuchus imperator, 2003. Mem. Authors Guild, Watson's Erroneous Deductions Club, The Wodehouse Soc., Chapter One, The Capers of Sherlock Holmes Club, Clumber Spaniel Club Am. Avocation: dogs. Home and Office: 877 W Hand Ave Cape May Court House NJ 08210-1865 E-mail: bladgscast@aol.com.

COHEN, DANIEL MORRIS, museum administrator, marine biology researcher; b. Chgo., July 6, 1930; s. Leonard U. and Myrtle (Gertz) C.; m. Anne Carolyn Constant, Nov. 4, 1955; children— Carolyn A. Leech, Cynthia S. BA, Stanford U., 1952, MA, 1953, PhD, 1958. Asst. prof., curator fishes U. Fla., Gainesville, 1957-58; systematic zoologist Bur. Comml. Fisheries, Washington, 1958-60; dir. systematics lab. Nat. Marine Fisheries Service, Washington, 1960-81, sr. scientist Seattle, 1981-82; chief curator life scis. Los Angeles County Mus. of Natural History, 1982-93, dep. dir. rsch. and collections, 1993-95; emeritus, 1995—. Adj. prof. biology U. So. Calif., 1982-98. Contbr. numerous articles to profl. jours. Bd. advisors All Species Found., 2000—. Fellow AAAS, Calif. Acad. Sci. (rsch. assoc.); mem. Am. Soc. Ichthyologists and Herpetologists (v.p. 1969, 70, pres. 1985, Gibbs award 1997), Biol. Soc. Washington (pres. 1971-72), Soc. Systematic Biology (mem. coun. 1976-78). Avocations: gardening, cooking, reading, hiking. Home: PO Box 192 Bodega Bay CA 94923-0192 E-mail: dmco@monitor.net.

COHEN, DAVID B. optical company executive; b. Bklyn., Apr. 22, 1943; s. Noah and Sylvia (Naimark) C.; 1 child, Ronald; m. Madeleine Goldman, Dec. 21, 1975; children: Lawrence, Louis, Linda. BA in Philosophy, SUNY, Buffalo, 1960-64; student, CUNY, Long Island U., Bklyn. Coll., St. John's U., Hofstra U., 1964-70; AS in Opticianry, Interboro Inst., 1972-74. Lic. ophthalmic dispenser, N.Y.; cert. optician. Educator N.Y.C. Bd. Edn., 1966—90, 2000—03; v.p. dir. ops. London Optical, L.I., 1990-96. Pres. Quick 'n Easy Convenience Stores, L.I., 1972-74, Eyesite, L.I., 1982-90; chmn. Optical Adv. Bd. Coun. to Interboro Inst., N.Y., 1993-96; mem. NYSSO Conv. Com., N.Y., 1993-97, dir. L.I. chpt., 1994-96, chpt. pres. 1996-00, state sec. 1995-96, 96-97, state treas., 1997-99, state v.p., 1999-00, state pres., 2000-02. Trustee, pres. Temple Beth El Men's Club, Cedarhurst, N.Y., 1992-94; trustee, L.I. regional Met. N.Y. Fedn. Jewish Men's Clubs, 1995-96, Nassau City liaison 1996-97; pres. Cedarhurst Bus. Assn., 1993-97; mem. Cmty. Chest Fair Com., Cedarhurst, 1992-98; Ann. CBA Mayoral Program Golf and Tennis Charity Tournament, 1993-95; chmn. revitalization com. Busn Investment Dist.; bd. govs. North Woodmere Civic Assn. and Park Found., cmty. liason; mem. 5 Towns Jewish Cmty. Coun., v.p., 1998-99. Mem. Kiwanis Internat., Rep. Club (committeeman, poll watcher). Republican. Jewish. Avocations: video photography, travel, reading. Home: 33 Captains Rd Valley Stream NY 11581-2806 Office: London Optical 494 Central Ave Cedarhurst NY 11516-2007

COHEN, DAVID HARRIS, neurobiology educator, university official; b. Springfield, Mass., Aug. 26, 1938; s. Nathan Edward and Sylvia (Golden) C.; m. Arline Wyler, June 17, 1960 (div. Aug. 1980); children: Bonnie, Daniel, Ian; m. Anne Helena Remmes, Jan. 17, 1981; 1 child, Kaitlin BA, Harvard U., 1960; PhD, U. Calif., Berkeley, 1963. Postdoctoral fellow UCLA, 1963-64; asst. prof. physiology Western Res. U., Cleve., 1964-68; assoc. prof. to prof. physiology U. Va. Med. Sch., Charlottesville, 1968-79; prof., chmn. neurobiology SUNY, Stony Brook, 1979-86; v.p. research, dean grad. sch. Northwestern U., Evanston, Ill., 1986-91, provost, 1992-95, prof. neurobiology and physiology, 1986-95; v.p. arts and scis., dean of faculty Columbia U., N.Y.C., 1995—, prof. biol. scis. and psychiatry, 1995—. Mem. adv. com. directorate biol., behavioral and social scis. NSF, 1982-89; mem. life scis. rsch. adv. bd. Air Force Office Sci. Rsch., 1985-91; mem. bd. govs. Argonne Nat. Lab., 1986-92; bd. dirs. Rsch. Librs. Group, 1993-97, 2001—, Zenith Electronics, Inc., 1990-95, Columbia U. Press, 1996—, Thuris Corp., 2000—, Trevor Day Sch., 2000—. Mem. various edit. bds. profl. jours.; contbr. articles to profl. jours. Bd. overseers Fermi Nat. Accelerator Lab., Batavia, Ill., 1987-94; exec. com. Ill. Gov.'s Sci. Adv. Com., 1989-95; mem. Liaison Com. Med Edn., 1987-89; bd. dirs. N.Y. Structural Biology Ctr., 1999—. Mem. Soc. Neurosci. (pres. 1981-82), Pavlovian Soc. (pres. 1978-79), Assn. Neurosci. Depts. and Programs (pres. 1981-82), Nat. Soc. Med. Rsch. (v.p. 1984-85), Nat. Assn. Biomed. Rsch. (bd. dirs. 1985-87), Coun. Acad. Socs. (adminstrv. bd. 1982-87, chmn. 1985-86), Assn. Am. Med. Colls. (exec. coun. 1984-91, chmn. 1989-90), Internat. Brain Rsch. Orgn. (cen. coun. 1978-82). Jewish. Home: 445 Riverside Dr Apt 72 New York NY 10027-6801 Office: Columbia Univ Low Meml Library 208 New York NY 10027

COHEN, DAVID JOHN, cardiothoracic surgeon; b. San Antonio, Jan. 13, 1947; s. Melvin David and Betty (Brown) C.; m. Deborah Milton, May 29, 1976; children: John, Christopher, Scott, Joshua, Benjamin. BA in Biochemistry, Rice U., 1968; MD, Washington U., 1972; BS in Mech. Engring. summa cum laude, U. Tex., San Antonio, 1999; grad., U.S. Army Command and Gen. Staff Coll., 2001; MPA, Harvard U., 2003. Intern Johns Hopkins Hosp., Balt., 1972-73, resident in gen. surgery, 1973-74, U. Wash. Affiliated Hosps., Seattle, 1976-79; resident in cardiothoracic surgery Hosp. of U. Pa., Phila., 1979-81; chief dept. cardiovasc. physiology Walter Reed Army Inst. of Rsch., Washington, 1981-83; staff Brooke Army Med. Ctr., Ft. Sam Houston, Tex., 1983-84, U. Wis. Hosp., Madison, 1984-87, William S. Middleton VA Hosp., Madison, 1984-87, chief thoracic surgery svc., 1986-87; staff Med. Ctr. Hosp., San Antonio, 1987-92, Audie L. Murphy VA Hosp., San Antonio, 1987-92, chief cardiothroacic surgery, 1991-92, dir. surg. ICU, 1988-92; asst. chief cardiothoracic surgery Brooke Army Med. Ctr., San Antonio, 1992-93, dir. heart transplant program, 1994—2001, chief cardiothroacic surgery, 1993—2002; sr. clin. cons. for combad doctrine and devel. U.S. Army Med. Ctr. and Sch., 2003—. Bd. dirs. Tex. Organ Sharing Alliance, San Antonio, 1994—2002; cardiac transplant fellow Tex. Heart Inst., Houston, 1993; cons. thoracic and cardiovasc. surgery U.S. Army Surgeon Gen., 1999—2002; sr. med. cons. Army Med. Ctr. and Sch., Ft. Sam Houston, Tex., 2003—. Asst. scoutmaster Boy Scouts Am., San Antonio, 1990—2002. Decorated Bronze Star, Meritorious Svc. medal (4), Army Commendation medal (4), Order of Mil. Med. Merit; recipient Nat. Collegiate Engring. award, U.S. Achievement Acad., 1998. Fellow ACS, Am. Coll. Cardiology, Am. Coll. Chest Physicians; mem. Am. Assn. Thoracic Surgeons, Soc. Thoracic Surgeons, Soc. Univ. Surgeons, San Antonio Cardiology Soc. (sec.-treas. 1997-98, pres. 1998-99), Golden Key, Tau Beta Pi. Jewish. Avocations: horseback riding, camping, skiing. E-mail: david_cohen@ksg03.harvard.edu.

COHEN, DAVID LEON, physician; b. St. Louis, Feb. 2, 1947; s. Benjamin David and Hannah (Finfer) C.; m. Sheila Zeisel, July 2, 1974; children: Robin, Lori, Jonathan, Jennifer. BS, Roosevelt U., 1967; MS, Chgo. Med. Sch., 1972; MD, Mt. Sinai Sch. Medicine, 1976. Diplomate Am. Bd. Dermatology. Intern in internal medicine Michael Reese Hosp., Chgo., 1976-77; resident Mt. Sinai Hosp., N.Y.C., 1977-80; pvt. practice Hewlett and Jamaica, N.Y., 1980—. Office: 1800 Rockaway Ave Ste 208 Hewlett NY 11557-1645 also: 86-75 Midland Pkwy Jamaica NY 11432

COHEN, DAVID MICHAEL, newspaper editor, journalist; b. Phila., Feb. 20, 1963; s. Albert Franklin and Lenore (Trainor) C.; m. Debbie Bodin. BA, Northwestern U., Evanston, Ill., 1985. Editor Virginian-Pilot, Norfolk, Va., 1985-86, Courier-Post, Cherry Hill, N.J., 1986-89; wire editor Bergen Record, Hackensack, N.J., 1989-97; mng. editor Nando Times, Raleigh, N.C., 1997-2000; copy editor Phila. Inquirer, 2000—. Author: Rugged and Enduring, 2001. Recipient 1st pl. award for sports writing Phila. Press Assn., 1989. Jewish. Home: 121 Ashford Rd Cherry Hill NJ 08003 Office: 400 N Broad St Philadelphia PA 19130-4015 E-mail: DaveNJNews@aol.com.

COHEN, DAVID WALTER, academic administrator, periodontist, educator; b. Phila., Dec. 15, 1926; s. Abram and Goldie (Schlein) C.; m. Betty Axelrod, Dec. 19, 1948 (dec. Mar. 1992); children: Jane Ellen, Amy Sue, Joanne Louise. DDS, U. Pa., 1950; DSc (hon.), Boston U., 1975; PhD (hon.), Hebrew U., Jerusalem, 1977, U. Athens, 1979; Dr Honoris Causa, U. Louis Pasteur, Strasbourg, France, 1986; DHL (hon.), U. Detroit, 1989. Diplomate: Am. Bd. Periodontology (chmn. 1972). Research fellow pathology and periodontia Beth Israel Hosp., Boston, 1950-51; mem. faculty U. Pa. Sch. Dentistry, Phila., 1951—, prof. periodontics, 1962-86, chmn. dept., 1962-73; dean Sch. Dental Medicine U. Pa., Phila., 1972-83; dean emeritus U. Pa. Sch. Dentistry, Phila., 1983—; pres. Med. Coll. Pa., 1986-93; chancellor Allegheny U. of Health Scis., 1993-98, chancellor emeritus, 1998—; mem. staff Albert Einstein Med. Center, Phila., Children's Hosp., Phila.; pres. Jewish Publ. Soc., 1993-96. Vis. prof. Boston U. Sch. Grad Dentistry, 1972—; nat. cons. periodontics USAF, 1965-70; bd. govs. Hebrew U., Jerusalem, Betty and Walter Cohen chair in periodontal rsch., 1986; D. Walter Cohen endowed chair in periodontics U. Pa., 1995. Author: (with H.M. Goldman) Periodontia, 1957, (with others) An Introduction to Periodontia, 1959, Periodontal Therapy, 1960, (with R. Genco and Goldman) Contemporary Periodontics, 1990, (with Genco, L. Rose and B. Mealey) Periodental Medicine, 1999; also numerous articles and chpts. V.p. Jewish Publ. Soc., 1985-89, pres., 1993-96; pres. Nat. Mus. Am. Jewish History, Phila., 1996—. Served with USN, 1944-45. Named to Ctrl. H.S. Hall of Fame, 1976; 1st Presdl. scholar U. Calif., San Francisco, 1985-86; named for him Hebrew U. Betty and D. Walter Cohen Chair in Periodontal Rsch., 1986, U. Pa. D. Walter Cohen Endowed Chair in Periodontics, 1995; D. Walter Cohen Mid. East Ctr. for Dental Edn. dedicated by Hebrew U. of Jerusalem, 1997. Fellow AAAS, Am. Acad. Oral Pathology, Am. Acad. Periodontology, Inst. of Medicine of Nat. Acad. Scis.; mem. Am. Soc. Periodontists (pres. 1967), Friends of Nat. Inst. Dental Rsch. (pres. 1998—). Office: Med Coll Pa 3300 Henry Ave Philadelphia PA 19129-1191

COHEN, DIANA LOUISE, psychology, educator, psychotherapist, consultant; b. Phila., Apr. 8, 1942; d. Nathan and Dorothy (Rubin) Blasberg; 1 child, Jennifer. BA, Temple U., 1964, MEd, 1969, PhD, 1996. Lic. psychologist, Pa., N.J.; lic. profl. counselor, N.J.; cert. mental health counselor. Caseworker Phila. Gen. Hosp., 1964-69, staff psychologist, 1969-70, Atlantic Mental Health Ctr., McKee City, N.J., 1970-80, unit dir., 1980-87, v.p. profl. svcs., 1987-91; pvt. practice Pa., N.J., 1991—. Adj. faculty Glassboro (N.J.) State Coll., 1988—; cmty. and family mediator Cmty. Justice Inst., Atlantic County, N.J., 1990—. Com. chmn. Atlantic County Commn. for Missing and Abused Children, 1984—89; co-project dir. Employee Assistance Program, 1994—. Grantee N.J. Dept. Edn., 1988-89, N.J. Job Tng. Partnership Act, 1990. Mem. APA (assoc.), N.J. Counseling Assn., N.J. Mental Health Counselors Assn. (pres.-elect 1996, pres. 1997), South Shore Region Mental Health Counselors Assn. (sec. 1994-97). Avocations: painting, tennis, cross-country skiing. Home: 2 Dee Dr Linwood NJ 08221-1910 Office: 2106 New Rd Ste El Linwood NJ 08221-1052

COHEN, DONALD JAY, pediatrics, psychiatry and psychology educator, administrator; b. Chgo., Sept. 5, 1940; m. Phyllis Cohen, 1964; children: Matthew, Rebecca, Rachel, Joseph. BA in Philosophy and Psychology summa cum laude, Brandeis U., 1961; Student in philosophy and psychology, U. Cambridge, 1961—62; MD, Yale U., 1966. Diplomate Am. Bd. Psychiatry and Neurology, Am. Bd. Child Psychiatry. Intern in pediatric medicine Children's Hosp. Med. Ctr., Boston, 1966—67; resident in psychiatry Mass. Mental Health Ctr., Boston, 1967—69; resident in child psychiatry Judge Baker Guidance Ctr., Children's Hosp. Med. Ctr., Boston, 1969—70; fellow in child psychiatry Hillcrest Children's Ctr. and Children's Hosp., Washington, 1970—72; asst. in medicine Children's Hosp., Boston, 1967—69; asst. to dir. child devel. Dept. Health, Washington, 1970—72; assoc. prof. pediat., psychiatry, and psychology Yale U., New Haven, 1972—79, prof. child psychiatry, pediat. and psychology, from 1979, Irving B. Harris prof. child psychiatry, pediat. and psychology, from 1987, dir. Child Study Ctr., from 1983. Clin. assoc. adult psychiatry bd. NIMH Sect. on Twin and Sibling Studies, 1970—72; vis. prof. Hebrew U. Hadassah Med. Ctr., 1982; mem. Nat. Commn. on Children, 1988; tng. and supervising analyst Western New Eng. Psychoanalytic Inst., from 1992; trustee Anna Freud Ctr., London, 1992; pres. publs. com. Yale U. Press, from 1995. Contbr. articles to profl. jours., chapters to books; author (monographs): Serving Sch. Age Children, 1972, Serving Preschool Children, 1974; editor: Schizophrenia Bull., Vol. 8, No. 2, Jour. Autism and Devel. Disorders, 1982; co-editor (monographs (with A. Donnellan): Handbook of Autism and Pervasive Developmental Disorders, 1985; co-editor: (monographs (with A.J. Solnit, J.E. Schowalter) Psychiatry, 1985, 1991, author (book revs.) ; mem. editl. bd.: Jour. Am. Acad. of Child Psychiatry, 1972—76, from 1980, Israel Jour. Psychiatry, from 1983, Am. Jour. Psychiatry, from 1996, mem. adv. bd.: Jour. Child Psychology and Psychiatry, 1977. Chmn. profl. adv. bd. Nat. Soc. for Autistic Children, from 1981; mem. med. adv. bd. Tourette Syndrome Assn., from 1980; served with USPHS, 1970—72; mem. profl. adv. bd. Benhaven, New Haven, from 1972; trustee Brandeis U., from 1982, Western New Eng. Inst. for Psychoanalysis, from 1984; bd. dirs. NIMH Treatment Devel. and Assessment Study Sect.,

1979—82, Psychoanalytic Rsch. and Devel. Fund, from 1982, Found.'s Fund for Rsch. in Psychiatry, 1977—81, Spl. Citizens, Futures Unlimited, Inc., from 1983, Ounce of Prevention Fund Nat. Adv. Com., from 1983, B'nai B'rith Hillel Found., Yale U., from 1984. Recipient Ann. Pub. Svc. award, Nat. Soc. for Autistic Children, 1972, Spl. Recognition, Hofheimer prize, Am. Psychiat. Assn., 1977, Ittleson award, Am. Pschiat. Assn., 1981, Strecker award, Inst. of Pa. Hosp., U. Pa., 1990; fellow Woodrow Wilson, 1961, Falk, Am. Psychiat. Assn., 1970—71; scholar Fulbright, Trinity Coll., 1961—62, U. Cambridge, 1961—62. Fellow: Am. Acad. Pediat., Am. Pediatric Soc., Am. Acad. Child Psychiatry (chmn. com. on rsch. 1975—81); mem.: Western New Eng. Psychoanalytic Soc., Am. Psychoanalytic Assn., Israel Psychoanalytic Soc. (corr.), Internat. Psychoanalytic Soc., Internat. Assn. Child and Adolescent Psychiatry and Allied Professions (pres. from 1992), Soc. for Rsch. in Child Devel., Inst. Medicine of NAS, Alpha Omega Alpha, Sigma Xi, Phi Beta Kappa. Home: Woodbridge, Conn. Died Oct. 2, 2001.

COHEN, EARL HARDING, lawyer; b. St. Paul, Mar. 24, 1948; s. Samuel W. and Sylvia S. (Peters) C.; m. Phyllis S. Bruzonsky; children: Melissa Anne, Amy Beth. BS with distinction, U. Minn., 1970, JD, 1973. Bar: Minn. 1973, D.C. 1980, U.S. Tax Ct. 1981. Trust officer Norwest Bank Mpls., 1973-76; atty. Halpern & Halpern, Mpls., 1976-77; prin. Halpern & Cohen, Mpls., 1977 80, Cohen & Bialick, Mpls., 1980-84, Cohen & Cohen, Mpls., 1984-90; pres. Kensington Properties, Inc., Mpls., 1978-90; of counsel Mansfield & Tanick, Mpls., 1990-92; CEO, dir. Mansfield, Tanick & Cohen, P.A., Mpls., 1992—. Counsel, bd. cons. No. Computer Sys., Inc., Mpls., 1987-92; dir. United Sys. Techn., Inc., 1995—. Bd. trustees Torah Acad. of Mpls., St. Louis Park, Minn., 1973-91, Talmud Torah of Mpls., 1988. Mem. ABA, Minn. State Bar Assn., Am. Bankruptcy Inst., St. Pauls Boys and Girls Club. Avocations: skiing, golf, travel. Home: 6700 Field Way Minneapolis MN 55436-1719 Office: Mansfield Tanick & Cohen PA 220 S 6th St Ste 1700 Minneapolis MN 55402-4502 E-mail: cohene@mainsfieldtanick.com.

COHEN, EDMUND STEPHEN, lawyer; b. Newark, June 25, 1946; s. Louis William and Edna (Medresch) C.; m. Lisa Beth Sonenthal, June 30, 1968; children: Ellen Paige, Paul Lawrence. BA cum laude, Dartmouth Coll., 1968; JD cum laude, Harvard U., 1971; LLM in Taxation, NYU, 1975. Bar: N.Y. 1972, U.S. Ct. Appeals (2d cir.) 1972, U.S. Ct. Claims, 1973, U.S. Tax Ct. 1973, U.S. Dist. Ct. (so. dist.) N.Y. 1975. Assoc. Davis Polk & Wardwell, N.Y.C., 1971-78; ptnr. Cole & Deitz, N.Y.C., 1978-81, Coudert Bros., 1981—. Adj. prof. law grad. tax program NYU Law Sch., 1977-86; chmn. seminars World Trade Inst., N.Y.C., 1977—, Practicing Law Inst., N.Y.C., 1977—, NYU Fed. Tax Inst. Mem. ABA, N.Y. State Bar Assn., Assn. Bar City N.Y., Internat. Fiscal Assn. Office: Coudert Bros LLP Fl 43 1114 Avenue Of The Americas New York NY 10036-7710

COHEN, EDWARD, civil engineer; b. Glastonbury, Conn., Jan. 6, 1921; s. Samuel and Ida (Tanewitz) C.; m. Elizabeth Belle Cohen, Dec. 19, 1948 (dec. June 1979); children: Samuel, Libby M. Wallace, James; m. Carol Simon Kalb, Jan. 11, 1981; stepchildren: Anne Kalb Bronner, Paul Kalb. BS in Engring., Columbia U., 1945, MS in Civil Engring., 1954. Registered profl. engr., N.Y., Conn., Fla., Ga., Md., N.J., La., Mass., Mich., Pa., D.C., Okla., Va., Wis., Del., Nat. Council Engring. Examiners; chartered civil engr., Gt. Britain; cert. Eur ING (FEANI Europe); lic. land surveyor, N.Y., Conn., Mass., N.J. Engring. aide Conn. Hwy. Dept., 1941-42; asst. engr. East Hartford Dept. Pub. Works, 1942-44; structural engr. Hardesty & Hanover, N.Y.C., 1945-47, Sanderson & Porter, N.Y.C., 1947-49; lectr. architecture Columbia U., 1948-51; with Ammann & Whitney, N.Y.C., 1949-96, assoc. engr., 1954-63, ptnr., 1963-74, sr. ptnr., 1974-77, mng. ptnr., 1977-95, dir. co. work as engrs. of record restoration of Statue of Liberty, West Face and Olmsted Ters. of U.S. Capitol Bldg. and Roebling Del. Canal Bridge; exec. v.p. Ammann & Whitney, Inc., 1974-77, in charge bldg., transp., communications, mil. and hist. preservation projects, chmn., CEO, 1977-96; v.p. Ammann & Whitney Internat. Ltd., 1963-73; pres. Safeguard Constrn. Mgmt. Corp., 1973-77, chmn., CEO, 1977-95; pvt. practice as civil engr. ECCE Internat., 1996—. Cons. RAND Corp., Santa Monica, Calif., 1958-72, Dept. Def., 1962-63, Hudson Inst., Croton-on-Hudson, N.Y., 1967-71, World Bank, 1984, TVA, 1987, Nat. Trust for Hist. Preservation, Drayton Hall Restoration, 1990; Stanton Walker lectr. U. Md., 1973, Henry M. Shaw lectr. N.C. State U., 1987; deptl. adv. com. Urban and Civil Engring. U. Pa., 1978-84, Rutgers U., 1982-90; mem. engring. coun. Columbia U., 1975—, vice chmn., 1985-86; chmn. Bldg. Rsch. Bd. Com. on Fed. Constrn. Stds. to control bldg. life-cycle costs, 1989-91; mem. Planning Group Nat. Consortium for infrastucture rsch. and tech. tranfer, 1987-90, NRC Com. for Infrastructure and Rsch. Agenda, 1992-94; commr. Bklyn. Bridge Centennial Commn., 1981-83; spl. adv. N.Y. State Centennial Commn. Statue of Liberty, 1985; chmn. engring. com. NEA first U.S. Presdl. awards for design excellence, 1985, mem., 1991, 95. Mem. adv. bd. Jour. Resource Mgmt. and Tech., 1981-91; co-editor: Handbook of Structural Concrete, 1983; contbr. more than 100 papers and articles to profl. jours. and govt. manuals on bridge, structural, siesmic, and hardened design, wind forces, dynamic analysis, ultimate strength and plastic design, restoration of bridges and aesthetics, guyed towers and shell structures. Bd. dirs. Cejwin Youth Camps, 1972-92; mem. com. of 100 Trailblazer Summer Camp for Underprivileged Children, 1985-89; trustee Hall of Sci., N.Y.C., 1976-99; mem. com. March of Dimes Transp. Award Luncheon, 1983-99; mem. exec. com. Architects/Engrs. divsn. United Jewish Appeal-Fedn., 1985-93; mentor in engring. N.Y. Alliance for Pub. Schs., 1986-91; N.Y. area chmn. engring. divsn. Orgn. for Rehab. Through Training, 1983-98, nat. dir., 1989-95. Recipient Illig medal in Applied Sci. Columbia U., 1946, Patriotic Civilian Svc. award Dept. of Army, 1973, Egleston medal Columbia U., 1981, Goethals medal for Engring. Achievement Soc. Am. Mil. Engrs., 1985, Mayor's Award of Honor for Sci. and Tech., N.Y., 1988, U.S. Presdl. Design Excellence award for Roebling Del. Aqueduct Bridge Restoration, NEA, 1988, Prize Bridge award Am. Inst. of Steel Contrn. for Engring. Trinity Ch. Pedestrian Bridge, 1989; Best of Program award for Achievement in Arc Welded Design Engring. and Fabrication for Trinity Ch. Pedestrian Bridge, Bronze award Roebling (Del.) Aqueduct Bridge James F. Lincoln Arc Welding Found., 1988, Nat. Historic Preservation award for engring. U.S. Capitol restoration U.S. Dept. Interior and Adv. Coun. Historic Preservation, 1988. Fellow Am. Cons. Engr. Coun. (life, Grand award for Engring. Excellence 1986), Inst. Civil Engrs. (Gt. Britain), N.Y. Acad. Scis. (hon. life fellow, Laskowitz Aerospace Rsch. Gold medal 1970, chmn. engring. sect. 1977-79, N.Y. Acad. Scis. award 1989, mem. bd. govs. 1991-97, v.p. 1991-95, Charles Darwin Assocs. inagural mem. 1992-98), ASCE (hon. fellow, chmn. com. design loads for bldgs. and other structures A7 (ANSI A58), 1968-88, chmn. reinforced concrete rsch. coun. 1980-89, Civil Engring. State of the Art award 1974, Outstanding Civil Engring. Achievement award 1987, Raymond Reese award 1976, Ernest Howard Gold Medal 1983, Svc. to People award 1987, met. sect. v.p. 1978-79, pres. 1980, Ridgeway award 1946, Met. Civil Engr. of Yr. 1986), Am. Concrete Inst. (hon. fellow, dir. 1966-76, v.p. 1970-72, pres. 1972-73, chmn. com. bldg. code requirements for reinforced concrete 1963-71, Wason medal 1956, Delmar Bloem award 1973), Am. Soc. Mil. Engrs.; mem. Nat. Acad. Engring., N.Y. Assn. Cons. Engrs. (bldg. code adv. com., bd. dirs. 1981-82, 85-89, emeritus mem. 1997—), N.Y. Concrete Industry Bd. (bd. dirs. 1976-98, pres. 1978-79, Leader of Industry award 1997, emeritus mem. 1998—), Columbia U. Sch. Engring. Alumni Assn. (bd. dirs. 1985-86), N.Y. Concrete Constrn. Design Inst. (pres. tall bldgs. coun. 1975-80), NSPE (Outstanding Engring. Achievement award 1987, N.Y. State/NSPE Engr. of Yr. 1986), Internat. Bridge and Turnpike Assn., Internat. Assn. Bridge and Structural Engrs., Am. Welding Soc. (life), Mcpl. Engrs. City of N.Y., Comite European de Beton (specialist), Moles (emeritus mem. 1996), Century Assn., Sigma Xi, Chi Epsilon, Tau Beta Pi. Clubs: Engrs. N.Y.C. (dir. 1974-75), Wings, Club at World Trade Ctr. Lodges: B'nai Brith. Avocation: golf. Home: 4702 Carlton Golf Dr Lake Worth FL 33467-8133 *Do not give up personal integrity for any apparent "practical" advantage . . . Strive for successful projects rather than personal credit. Make no adverse judgments of people unless it is an active consideration in a necessary decision. Judge people by their actions, not their words.*

COHEN, EDWARD, lawyer; b. Hamilton, Ohio, Dec. 20, 1954; s. Alfred Sylvan and Marilyn (Melnikoff) C.; m. Dee Anne Bryll; children: Daniel, Briana L. BA, U. Cin., 1976; MA, Ind. U., 1982; JD, U. Cin., 1982. Bar: Ohio 1982, U.S. Dist. Ct. (so. dist.) Ohio 1982, U.S. Ct. Appeals (6th cir.) 1982. Doctoral fellow U. Cin., 1978-79, instr. coll. law, 1982-83; assoc. Goodman & Goodman Co., Cin., 1982-84, Kondritzer, Gold & Frank Co., Cin., 1984-88; ptnr. Clements, Mahin & Cohen, LLP, Cin., 1988—. Mem. ABA, ASCAP, Ohio Acad. Trial Lawyers, Ohio Bar Assn., Cin. Bar Assn. (sec. workers compensation com. 1990-91, chmn. 1992—), Order of Barristers, Ohio Cmty. Theatre Assn. (bd. dirs. 1995-98). Office: Clements Mahin & Cohen LLP 708 Walnut St Ste 600 Cincinnati OH 45202-2022 Fax: 513-763-6415. E-mail: ecohen@cmclawyers.com.

COHEN, EDWARD BARTH, lawyer; b. Washington, Oct. 13, 1949; s. Stanley Edward and Marjorie Cohen; m. Charlene Barshefsky, Jan. 25, 1976; two children. BA with acad. honors, U. Wis., 1971; JD, Georgetown U., 1974. Bar: D.C. 1975, U.S. Ct. Appeals (D.C. and 9th cirs.) 1981, U.S. Supreme Ct. 1981, U.S. Ct. Internat. Trade 1982, U.S. Tax Ct. 1983. Mem. profl. staff, counsel commerce com. U.S. Senate, Washington, 1971-77; gen. counsel U.S. Office Consumer Affairs, Washington, 1977-79; dep. spl. asst. Pres. Jimmy Carter, Washington, 1979-81; assoc. Davis, Wright & Jones, Washington, 1981—93; ptnr. Davis Wright Tremaine (and predecessor firm Davis, Wright & Jones), Washington, 1983-94; counselor to Sec. of Interior U.S. Dept. Interior, Washington, 1994-95, dep. solicitor, 1995-2000; v.p. govt. & industry rels. Honda North Am. Inc., Washington, 2000—. Mem. Bar of D.C. Office: Honda N Am Inc 1001 G St NW Ste 950 Washington DC 20001

COHEN, EDWARD HERSCHEL, lawyer, b. Lewistown, Pa., Sept. 30, 1938; s. Saul Allen and Barbara (Getz) C.; m. Arlene Greenbaum, Aug. 12, 1962; children: Fredrick, James, Paul. AB, U. Mich., 1960; JD, Harvard U., 1963. Bar: N.Y. 1964. Assoc. Katten Muchin Zavis Rosenman, N.Y.C., 1963-72, ptnr., 1972—86, 1988—2002, counsel, 1987, 2003—; v.p., gen. counsel, sec. Phillips-Van Heusen Corp., N.Y.C., 1987. Mem. Fenway Golf Club (Scarsdale, N.Y.), Ventana Golf and Racquet Club (Tucson). Republican. Jewish. Avocations: golf, travel. Office: Katten Muchin Zavis Rosenman 575 Madison Ave New York NY 10022-2585 Home: 45 Club Pointe Dr White Plains NY 10605

COHEN, EDWIN LOUIS, lawyer; b. Louisville, May 7, 1930; s. Abe and Belle (Bass) C.; m. Helen Lois Kasdan, July 23, 1967; children: Deborah, Jennifer, Joseph. AB, U. Louisville, 1955, LLB, 1958. Bar: Ky. 1958, U.S. Dist. Ct. (we. dist.) Ky. 1960, U.S. Ct. Appeals (6th cir.) 1980, U.S. Supreme Ct. 1981. Ptnr. Cohen & Cohen, Louisville, 1958—. Served to staff sgt. USAF, 1951-55, Korea. Mem. Ky. Bar Assn. Democrat. Jewish. Office: Cohen & Cohen 3415 Bardstown Rd Ste 306 Louisville KY 40218-4605 E-mail: cohenattorneys@aol.com.

COHEN, EDWIN SAMUEL, lawyer, educator; b. Richmond, Va., Sept. 27, 1914; s. LeRoy S. and Miriam (Rosenheim) C.; m. Carlyn Labenberg, June 27, 1936 (dec. 1942); m. Helen Herz, Aug. 31, 1944; children: Edwin C., Roger, Wendy. BA, U. Richmond, 1933; JD, U. Va., 1936. Bar: Va. 1935, N.Y. 1937, D.C. 1973. Assoc. Sullivan & Cromwell, N.Y.C., 1936-49; ptnr. Root, Barrett, Cohen, Knapp & Smith (and predecessor firm), N.Y.C., 1949-65; counsel Root, Barrett, Cohen, Knapp & Smith, 1965-69; prof. law U. Va., Charlottesville, 1965-68, Joseph M. Hartfield prof., 1968-69, 73-85, prof. emeritus, 1985—, professorial lectr. law, 1994—; asst. sec. treasury for tax policy, 1969-72; under sec. treasury, 1972-73; of counsel Covington & Burling, Washington, 1973-77, ptnr., 1977-86, sr. counsel, 1986—. Vis. prof. Benjamin N. Cardozo Sch. Law, Yeshiva U., 1987-92, U. Miami Law Sch., 1993, 95-99, chmn. grad. program in taxation and estate planning, 1995-98; mem., counsel adv. group on corp. taxes ways and means com. U.S. Ho. of Reps., 1956-58; spl. cons. on corps. fed. income tax project Am. Law Inst., 1949-54; mem. adv. group Fed. Estate and Gift Tax Project, 1964-68; mem. Va. Income Tax Conformity Study Commn., 1970-71; cons. Va. Income Tax Conformity Study Commn., 1966-68; mem. adv. group to commr. IRS, 1967-68. Author: A Lawyer's Life Deep in the Heart of Taxes, 1994. Recipient Alexander Hamilton award Treasury Dept. Mem. Am. Judicature Soc., ABA (chmn. com. on corporate stockholder relationships 1956-58, mem. council 1958-61, chmn. spl. com. on substantive tax reform 1962-63, chmn. spl. com. on formation tax policy 1977-80, Disting. Svc. award taxation sect. 1997), Va. Bar Assn., D.C. Bar Assn., N.Y. State Bar Assn., Va. Tax Conf. (planning com. 1965-68, 85-95, trustee emeritus 1995—), C. of C. of U.S. (bd. dirs., chmn. taxation com. 1979-84), Assn. Bar City N.Y., N.Y. County Lawyers Assn., Am. Law Inst., Am. Coll. Tax Counsel, Order Coif, Raven Soc., Colonnade Club, Boar's Head Club, Farmington Club, City Club, Phi Beta Kappa, Omicron Delta Kappa, Pi Delta Epsilon, Phi Epsilon Pi (Nat. Achievement award) Home: 104 Stuart Pl Ednam Forest Charlottesville VA 22903 E-mail: ecohen@virginia.edu.

COHEN, ELAINE HELENA, pediatrician, pediatric cardiologist, educator; b. Boston, Oct. 14, 1941; d. Samuel Clive and Lillian (Stocklan) C.; m. Marvin Leon Gale, May 7, 1972; 1 child, Pamela Beth Gale. AB, Conn. Coll., 1963; postgrad., Tufts U., 1963-64; MD, Woman's Med. Coll. Pa., 1969. Diplomate Am. Bd. Pediats. Intern in pediats. Children's Hosp. of L.A., 1969-70, resident in pediats., 1970-71; fellow in pediat. cardiology UCLA Ctr. Health Scis., 1971-72, L.A. County/U. So. Calif. Med. Ctr., L.A., 1972-74; pediatrician Children's Med. Group of South Bay, Chula Vista, Calif., 1974—. Clin. instr. dept. pediats. UCLA Sch. Medicine, 1971-72, U. So. Calif., L.A., 1972-74; asst. clin. prof. dept. pediats. U. Calif., Calif. Sch. Medicine, San Diego, 1974-98, preceptor dept. pediats., 1992—, assoc. clin. prof. dept. pediats., 1998—. Fellow Am. Acad. Pediats.; mem. Calif. Med. Assn., San Diego County Med. Soc. Avocations: sketching, design. Office: Children's Med Group South Bay 280 E St Chula Vista CA 91910-2945

COHEN, ELIOT DORSEY, electrical engineer; b. Washington, Mar. 10, 1942; s. Walter and Clara (Goldberg) C.; m. Barbara Susan Linderman, June 22, 1968; children: Gregory, Bonnie. BEE, George Washington U., 1963, MS in Engring., 1966, postgrad., 1967-72. From electronics engr. to head high frequency devices sec. Naval Rsch. Lab., Washington, 1963-80; navy dir. very high speed integrated circuits program Space and Naval Warfare Sys. Com., Arlington, Va., 1980-86; dep. dir. microwave and millimeter wave programs Def. Tech. Analysis Office, Arlington, Va., 1986-88; from program mgr. to dep. dir. def. mfg. office Advanced Rsch. Project Agy., Arlington, Va., 1988-91, exec. dir. microwave and millimeter wave tech., 1991-95; exec. dir. tech. ops., v.p. Palisades Inst. for Rsch. Svcs., Inc., Arlington, Va., 1995—2002; pres. EBCO Tech. Advising, Inc., 1995—'. Mem. adv. group on electron devices Office Sec. Def., Arlington, 1971—95; mem. U.S. Govt. Sr. Exec. Svc., 1989—95, NASA Pioneer Revolutionary Tech. Subcom. of Aerospace Tech. Adv. Com., 2002—; disting. lectr. dept. elec. and computer engring. U. Mass., Amherst, 2000; presenter in field. Contbr. articles to profl. jours. Pres. Strathmore-Bel Pre Civic Assn., Silver Spring, Md., 1980-81; mem. bd. visitors dept. materials and nuc. engring. U. Md., College Park, 1995-98. Named to, Space Tech. Hall of Fame, 2003. Fellow: IEEE (3d Millennium medal); mem.: Microwave Theory and Techniques Soc. Adminstrv. Com. (v.p. 1994, pres. 1995). Achievements include research in microwave and millimeter wave circuits and management of the Department of Defense's Microwave and MM-Wave Monolithic Integrated Circuits (MIMIC) program.

COHEN, ELLIOT L. urologist, educator; b. Bklyn., Aug. 13, 1941; m. Eileen Cohen, Aug. 12, 1979; children: Seth, Dina. BA, NYU, 1963; MD, Chgo. Med. Sch., 1967. Diplomate Am. Bd. Urology. Chief dept. urology USPHS Hosp., S.I., N.Y., 1975-81; asst. prof. urology Mt. Sinai Sch. Med., N.Y.C., 1981—; attending urologist Mt. Sinai Hosp., N.Y.C., 1981—. Contbr. articles to med. jours. Maj. M.C., USAF, 1969-71. Fellow ACS; mem. Am. Urol. Assn., Soc. Univ. Urologists, N.Y. Sect. Am. Urol. Assn. Avocations: skiing, sailing, bicycling. Office: 103 E 80th St New York NY 10021-0305

COHEN, ERIC, optometrist; b. Balt., July 9, 1949; s. Isadore Rael and Frieda Rose Cohen; m. Lindalou Silverman Cohen, Aug. 19, 1971; children: Natalie Yve, Ira Charles. BA, U. Md., 1970; BS, Pa. Coll. Optometry, 1971, OD, 1974. Resident pediat. optometry Pa. Coll. Optometry, Phila.; pvt. practice Md. Optometric Assn., Balt., 1974—. Asst. prof. Howard C.C., Ellicott City, Md., 1980-83; pediat. optometrist Katzen Eye Group, Balt., 1988-98. Author: Renazicatative Techniques in Binocular Dysfunction, 1974. Mem. Am. Optometric Assn., Md. Optometric Assn. (treas., v.p., pres.-elect, pres., Optometrist of Yr. 1998). Democrat. Jewish. Avocations: tennis, golf. Home: 11006 Valley Heights Dr Owings Mills MD 21117 Office: 6660 Security Blvd Baltimore MD 21207-4012 E-mail: e.cohe@bcpl.org.

COHEN, EZECHIEL GODERT DAVID, physicist, educator; b. Amsterdam, Holland, Jan. 16, 1923; came to U.S., 1963; s. David Ezechiel and Sophia Louisa (de Sterke) C.; m. Marina Arnoldina Linnekamp, Apr. 19, 1950; children: Michael Benjamin, Andrea Margaret. BS in Math., Physics and Astronomy, U. Amsterdam, 1947, PhD, 1957. First asst. U. Amsterdam, 1950-61, assoc. prof., 1961-63; research assoc. U. Mich., 1957-58, Johns Hopkins, 1958-59; prof. Rockefeller U., 1963-93, prof. emeritus, 1993—. Vander Waals prof. U. Amsterdam, 1969; Lorentz prof. U. Leiden, 1979; vis. prof. Coll. de France, 1969, 72, 79, 83, 90, Inst. for Advanced Studies, Australian Nat. U., Canberra, 1982, 88, 92, 96, 99, U. Florence, Italy, 1999, 2000; Donders prof. U. Utrecht, 1988; Francqui prof. interuniversitaire U. Brussels and U. Leuven, 1997. Editor: Fundamental Problems in Statistical Mechanics, Vol. I, 1961, Vol. II, 1968, Vol. III, 1975, Vol. IV, 1978, Vol. V, 1980, Vol. VI, 1985, Statistical Mechanics at the Turn of the Decade, 1971, The Boltzmann Equation, Theory and Applications, 1973. Fellow Am. Phys. Soc.; mem. Royal Dutch Acad. Scis., Johns Hopkins Soc. of Scholars, Mexican Acad. Molecular Engring. (corr.). Home: 450 E 63rd St New York NY 10021-7957 Office: Rockefeller U 1230 York Ave New York NY 10021-6399

COHEN, EZRA HARRY, lawyer; b. Macon, Ga., Mar. 13, 1942; s. Harry M. and Rena C. Cohen; m. Bonnie E. Cohen, Feb. 1, 1969 (div. Mar. 1988); children: Aaron M., Eileen R.; m. Katherine C. Meyers, June 18, 1989. BA, Columbia U., 1964; JD, Emory U., 1969. Bar: Ga. 1969. Ptnr. Troutman, Sanders, Lockerman & Ashmore, Atlanta, 1969-76, 79—; judge U.S. Bankruptcy Ct., U.S. Dist. Ct. (no. dist.) Ga., Atlanta, 1976-79. Dir. S.E. Bankruptcy Law Inst., Atlanta. Contbg. author: Cowan's Bankruptcy Laws & Practices, 1979. Mem. Emory U. Law Sch. Coun., Atlanta, 1988—. With U.S. Army, 1964-66, ETO. Fellow Am. Coll. Bankruptcy; mem. Ga. Bar Assn. (chmn. bankruptcy law sect.), Assn. Former Bankruptcy Judges (bd. dirs.), Nat. Assn. Bank Judges (assoc.), Atlanta Bar Assn. (bd. dirs. 1988-90), Lawyers Club of Atlanta. Home: 546 W Wesley Rd Atlanta GA 30305-3534 Office: Troutman Sanders 600 Peachtree St NE Ste 5200 Atlanta GA 30308-2216 E-mail: ezra.cohen@troutmansanders.com.

COHEN, FELIX ASHER, lawyer; b. Pitts., Aug. 11, 1943; s. Alex Harry and Audrey Gwen (Williams) C.; m. Nancy Ann Wills, July 24, 1971; children: Timothy Asher, Blair Wills Lavey. AB, Princeton U., 1965; JD, U. Pitts., 1971. Bar: Pa. 1972, U.S. Dist. Ct. (we. dist.) Pa. 1972, U.S. Tax Ct. 1972. Systems engr. IBM Corp., Pitts., 1965-68; law clk. U.S. Dist. Ct., Pitts., 1971-72; assoc. Buchanan Ingersoll, Pitts., 1972-75; sr. v.p., sec., counsel, bd. dirs. Signal Fin. Corp., Pitts., 1975-92; counsel CoreStates Fin. Corp., Phila., 1994-98; ptnr. Wolf Block Schorr & Solis-Cohen, Phila., 1999—. Mem. ABA, Pa. Bar Assn., Allegheny County Bar Assn., Phila. Bar Assn., Del. State Bar Assn. Home: 3 Black Rock Rd Chadds Ford PA 19317-9271

COHEN, FLORENCE EMERY, retired financial services executive; b. Paterson, N.J., Mar. 6, 1944; d. Claude John and Esther (Belber) Emery; m. Harvey H. Cohen, Sept. 5, 1965; children: John Aaron, Jason Matthew. AB in History, Temple U., 1965; MA in Social Scis., U. Chgo., 1970. Product planning mgr. Penn. Mut. Ins. Co., Phila., 1970-77; dir. mktg. sys. Prudential Co., Newark, 1978-80, v.p. mktg. analysis, 1980-82, v.p. tax adminstrn., 1983-84, v.p. market devel., 1984-88, v.p. enterprise planning, 1988-90; sr. v.p. individual pensions Pruco Life Co., 1990-93, v.p., Prudential annuity svcs. exec., 1993—94; ret. Lectr. numerous industry assns.; mem. exec. coun. Jersey City (N.J.) State Coll., 1985; mem. bd. visitors St. Andrew's Presbyn. Coll., N.C. grad. study fellow U. Del., 1965, Temple U., 1965, U. Chgo. 1970. Rep. committeewoman West Windsor; elder First Presbyn. Ch. Dutch Neck, mission com., deacon; bd. dirs. Project Freedom; co-chmn. Affordable Housing Com., West Windsor; pres. Welcoming Svcs., L.L.C., 1999—. Recipient Prudential Cmty. Champions award, 2001, 02, Project Freedom Spirit award, 2000. Fellow Life Office Mgmt. Assn., Limra Life Inst.; mem. Am. Soc. CLUs, Soc. Advancement Mgmt. (N.J. chpt., exec. of yr. 1986), Rotary (Princeton Corridor), Friends of West Windsor Open Space, West Windsor Hist. Soc. Republican. Avocations: cooking, gardening, swimming. Home: 3 Stonelea Dr Princeton Junction NJ 08550 also: 1621 A Spoonbill Ln Naples FL 34105

COHEN, FRED HOWARD, lawyer, investment company executive; b. Pitts., Mar. 22, 1948; s. Morris and Sylvia (Kalickman) C.; m. Katherine Jane Litman, July 12, 1970; children: Julia Jackson, Joseph Litman. BA, Stanford U., 1970; MA, York U., Toronto, Ont., Can., 1971; postgrad., Princeton U., 1971-72; JD, Harvard U., 1976. Bar: Calif. 1976. Assoc. Latham & Watkins, L.A., 1976-82, ptnr., 1983-85; v.p. Salomon Bros. Inc., N.Y.C., 1985-86, dir., 1986-88; v.p. Goldman Sachs & Co., N.Y.C., 1988-89; ptnr. Shearman & Sterling, N.Y.C., 1989-94; mng. dir. Salomon Bros. Inc., N.Y.C., 1994-98; with Cohen Fin. Advisors, 1998-99; mng. dir., head global high yield and leveraged fin. Bank Am. Securities, 2000—. Mem. Phi Beta Kappa. Home: 86 Kellogg Hill Rd Weston CT 06883-2640

COHEN, GAIL EHRLICH, lawyer, banker; b. Jersey City, Mar. 7, 1956; d. Alex and Florence (Levine) Ehrlich; m. Ofer Cohen, Oct. 5, 1980; children: Daniel, Michelle, Michael; 1 stepchild, Jaime. BA, Mt. Holyoke Coll., 1978; JD summa cum laude, Bklyn. Law Sch., 1985. Bar: N.J. 1986, N.Y. 1986. Paralegal Law Office of E.S. Schlesinger, N.Y.C., 1978-85, assoc., 1985-88, Debevoise & Plimpton, N.Y.C., 1988-94; exec. v.p. gen. trust counsel Fiduciary Trust Internat., N.Y.C., 1994—. Mem. trust and estates com. UJA Fedn., N.Y.C., 1998—; mem. trusts and estates adv. bd. N.Y.C. Ballet, 1997—, Rockefeller U., N.Y.C., 2000—, planned giving com. Anti-Defamation League, N.Y.C., 1998-00. Martha Prince scholar Bklyn. Law Sch., 1984-85. Mem. Assn. Bar City N.Y. (chmn. com. on estate and gift tax 1998-01, com. on trusts, estates and surrogate cts. 1992-95), N.Y. State Bar Assn.

COHEN, GARY, lawyer; b. Bklyn, NY, June 26, 1948; s. Irving and Henrietta Elizabeth (Weinkofsky) C.; 1 child, Celeste. BS in Physics, Cooper Union, 1969; JD, Bklyn. Law Sch., 1977. Bar: N.Y. 1978, U.S. Patent Office 1979. Patent atty. Western Electric Corp., NYC, 1978; patent atty. Striker & Stenby, NYC, 1979-82; sole practitioner Bklyn., 1983—; pres. IDEA Mktg. Corp., 2002—. Mem. Bklyn. Bar Assn. (past chmn. com. on patents, trademark & copyright), Ind. Order Odd Fellows. Home: 141 Joralemon St Brooklyn NY 11201-4071 Office: PO Box 20618 Brooklyn NY 11202-0618 E-mail: gcohenlaw@aol.com.

COHEN, GEORGE LEON, lawyer; b. Covington, Ga., June 20, 1930; s. Leon and Callie (Harrison) C.; m. Jacqueline Lanier Edwards, Nov. 17, 1951 (dec. May 2001); children— George Leon, Gardner Edwards. AB, Va. Mil. Inst., 1951; LLB, U. Va., 1956. Bar: Ga. 1957, U.S. Ct. Appeals (11th cir.). Assoc. Sutherland, Asbill & Brennan, Atlanta, 1956-62, ptnr., 1962—. Editorial bd. Va. Law Rev., 1954-56 Mem.: ABA (various coms.), Am. Law Inst. (advisor to corp. governance project), Lawyers Club Atlanta, Atlanta Bar Assn., Ga. State Bar (chmn. corp. and banking law sect. 1968—69, chmn. Ga. bus. corp. code revision com. 1986—89, various coms.), Peachtree Club, Omicron Delta Kappa, Order of Coif. Office: Sutherland Asbill & Brennan 999 Peachtree St NE Ste 2300 Atlanta GA 30309-3996

COHEN, GLORIA ERNESTINE, elementary education educator; b. Bklyn., July 6, 1942; d. Victor George and Marion Theodosia (Roberts) C. BS in Edn., Wilberforce U., 1965; MA in Elem. Edn., Adelphi U., 1975; Profl. Diploma in Ednl. Adminstrn., L.I. U., 1984; MS in Edn., Bklyn. Coll., 1986. Tchr. Bd. Edn., Bklyn., 1965—; case worker Dept. Welfare, Bklyn., 1965—. Mem. comprehensive sch. improvement program Pub. Sch. 149, 1990—91, mem. open corridor planning com., 1990—91, mem. consultation com., 1990—; tchr. in charge of after sch. reading and math. tutorial program, 1995—96; dean grades 4-6, 1996—98; supr. Sat. Acad.; tchr. in charge of Read Extended Day program, 1997—98; cons. tchr. for 4th grade class, 1999; tchr. in charge of food and nutrition distbn. Maxwell H.S., Bklyn., 1999, P.S. 64 Dist. 27, Queens, 2000; tutorial tchr. Pub. Sch. 149, 2001—02; tchr. in charge of food and nutrition distbn. P.S. 174 Dist. 19, Bklyn., 2001—03. Mem.: U.S. Profl. Tennis Registry, U.S. Tennis Assn., Hempstead Lake Tennis Club, Rockville Racqhet Club, Kappa Delta Pi, Zeta Phi Beta. Democrat. Roman Catholic. Avocations: tennis, skiing, swimming. Office: Bd Edn PS 149 700 Sutter Ave Brooklyn NY 11207-4224

COHEN, GORDON S. health products executive; b. N.Y.C., May 18, 1937; s. Leon Lewis and Irene (Lipton) C.; m. Marjorie Rennick, June 12, 1960; children: Terri Susan, Lisa Michelle, Bonnie Lynne. AB, Brown U., 1959; MD, Yale U., 1963. Diplomate Am. Bd. Pathology, Anatomic Pathology and Clin.

Pathology. Instr. dept. pathology Yale U., New Haven, 1967-70, asst. prof. pathology, 1970-71, asst. clin. prof. pathology, 1971-76; pres. Jeneric Industries, Wallingford, Conn., 1975-86; chmn. Pentron Corp., Wallingford, 1977-87; pres. Jeneric/Pentron, Inc., Wallingford, 1987—; chmn. Pentron Corp., Wallingford, 1987—. Attending pathologist Yale-New Haven Hosp., 1970-71, Hosp. St. Raphael, New Haven, 1971-76; pathologist The Charlotte Hungerford Hosp., Torrington, Conn., 1967-70. Author numerous articles in field. Sr. edn. officer Milford (Conn.) U.S. Power Squadron, 1987; mem. Congressman DeNardis's Small Bus. Adv. Com., 1982. Capt. (M.C.) USAR, 1964-70. Mem. Internat. Acad. Pathology, N.Y. Acad. Scis., Phi Beta Kappa, Sigma Xi, Alpha Omega Alpha. Avocations: sailing, shooting, book collecting. Office: Pentron Corp 53 N Plains Industrial Rd Wallingford CT 06492-5841

COHEN, HARLEY, civil engineer, science educator; b. Winnipeg, Man., Can., May 12, 1933; s. Joseph and Ettie (Gilman) C.; m. Estelle Brodsky, Dec. 25, 1956; children: Brent, Murray, Carla. B.Sc. hons., U. Man., 1956; Sc.M., Brown U., 1958; PhD, U. Minn., 1964. Registered profl. engr., Man. Research engr. Boeing Co., Seattle, 1958-60; sr. research scientist Honeywell, Inc., Mpls., 1960-64; asst. prof. aero. and engring. mechanics U. Minn., Mpls., 1965-66; assoc. prof. civil engring. U. Man., Winnipeg, 1966—, prof., 1968-89, disting. prof., 1983—, head dept., 1984-89, prof. applied math., 1989-94, dean faculty of sci., 1989-94, prof. applied math. and civil engring., 1994-98, disting. prof. math. emeritus, 1998—. J.L. Record prof. U. Minn.; invited vis. prof. U. Pisa, Italian Rsch. Coun., 1987; bd. dirs. Man. Rsch. Coun., 1989-94, Tri-Univ.-Meson Facility, U. B.C., 1989-94, Premier's Econ. Innovation and Tech. Coun., 1989-94. Co-author: Theory of Psuedo-Rigid Bodies, 1988; contbr. over 100 articles to profl. jours. Killam scholar, 1982; Brit. sci. fellow, 1985 Fellow Am. Acad. Mechanics (bd. dirs. 1988-91); mem. Soc. Natural Philosophy, Soc. Engring. Sci. Home: 55 Tanoak Park Dr Winnipeg MB Canada R2V 2W6 Office: U Man Dept Applied Math Faculty of Sci Winnipeg MB R3T 2N2 Canada R3T 2N2 E-mail: hcohen@cc.umanitoba.ca.

COHEN, HARRIS L. diagnostic radiologist, consultant; b. Bklyn., Sept. 18, 1951; s. Samuel G. and Lola Estera (Altman) C.; m. Sandra Wilensky, Oct. 18, 1979; children: David Matthew, Lauren Elizabeth, Benjamin Adam. BA, CUNY Bklyn., 1973; MD, SUNY, Bklyn., 1976. Diplomate Am. Bd. Radiology, Nat. Bd. Med. Examiners; cert. added qualifications in pediatric radiology Am. Bd. Radiology. Asst. prof. radiology SUNY Health Sci. Ctr., Bklyn., 1981-88; asst. chief of imaging Brookdale Hosp. Med. Ctr., Bklyn., 1983-85; med. dir. diagnostic med. imaging program Coll. Health Related Professions, SUNY Health Sci. Ctr., Bklyn., 1985-88, 94-01; assoc. prof. radiology Cornell U. Med. Coll., NYC, 1988-93; chief pediatric CT and ultrasound North Shore U. Hosp.-Cornell, Manhasset, NY, 1988-93, assoc. dir. divsn. CT/ultrasound/magnetic resonance imaging, 1988-93; assoc. dir. radiology Kings County Hosp., Bklyn., 1993-2000; prof. radiology SUNY Health Sci. Ctr., Bklyn., 1993-2000, assoc. chmn. acad. affair and clin. rsch., 1998-2000; vis. prof. radiology, dir. divsn. pediat. imaging Johns Hopkins U., Balt., 2000—02; prof. radiology, vice chmn. dept. radiology, dir. divsn. CT/ultrasound/MR, chief pediatric body imaging SUNY, Stony Brook, 2002—, dir. div. US, CT, MR, 2003—. Dir. divsn. ultrasound U. and Kings County Hosps., Bklyn., 1985-88, 93-2000, dir. divsn. pediat. radiology, 1999-2000; cons. ultrasound and pediatric imaging Brookdale Hosp. Med. Ctr., Bklyn., 1988—; cons. diagnostic radiology Med. Mut. Liability, N.Y.C., 1992—. Article reviewer: Am. Jour. Roentgenology, 1988—, Radiographics, 1991— (Editor's Recognition award), Ultrasound in Ob-Gyn.; editor-in-chief: Am. Coll. Radiology Prof. Self Evaluation Syllabus Series;co-editor: (textbook) Ultrasonography of the Prenatal and Neonatal Brain, 1996, 2d edit., 2002, Obstetrics & Gynecology (Ultrasound), 1997, Fetal and Pediatric ULTRASOUND, 2001; mem. editl. bd. Jour. Diagnostic Med. Sonography, 1985—, Jour. Women's Imaging, 1999—, Jour. of ULTRASOUND in Medicine, 2000—; articles to profl. jours., chpts. to med. texts. Recipient Master Tchr. award in radiology SUNY Health Sci. Ctr. at Bklyn. Alumni Assn., 1996. Fellow Soc. Radiologists in Ultrasound (chmn. constitution com. 1996-98), Am. Coll. Radiology (stds. and accreditation com. 1992-98, commn. ultrasound edn. com. 1998-2000, mem. task force on disaster planning 2001—), Am. Acad. Pediatrics (chmn. radiology sect. 1992-94), Am. Inst. Ultrasound in Medicine (chmn. ctrl. program com. 1995-97, chmn. pediatrics sect. 1994-95, bd. dirs. 1999-2002, co-chair emergency ultrasound, 2001—, bd. govs. 1999-2002); mem. Soc. Pediatric Radiology (liaison to Am. Acad. Pediatrics 1993-94, liaison to Am. Inst. Ultrasound in Medicine 1995), Radiologic Soc. N.Am. (audiovisual com. 1992-96), SUNY-Downstate Alumni Assn. (councillor, bd. mgrs. 1998-2001), Alpha Omega Alpha. Avocations: computers and computer education, basketball, sports, american and jewish history. Home: 78 Grove Ave Cedarhurst NY 11516-2311 E-mail: hlcohen@erols.com.

COHEN, HARVEY, lawyer; b. Far Rockaway, N.Y., Sept. 20, 1918; s. Theodore Bernard and Gertrude (Gottlieb) C.; m. Norma Ruth Boiles, Nov. 2, 1947; children: Douglas Lee, Beth Cohen DeGrasse, Barry Scott. BA, Lafayette Coll., Easton, Pa., 1940; JD, Harvard U., 1947. Bar: N.Y. 1948. Atty. Bernhardt, Sahn, Shapiro & Epstein, N.Y.C., 1947-49; ptnr. Murtagh, Cohen & Byrne, N.Y.C., 1950-77, Garden City, N.Y., 1977—. Bd. dirs., officer L.K. Comstock Co., Inc., N.Y.C., 1965-88, Electrospace Corp., Glen Cove, N.Y., 1963-81, Radiation Dynamics, Inc., Westbury, N.Y., 1958-83, Med. Sterilization, Inc., Syosset, N.Y., 1983-97. Mem. housing bd. dirs. Unitarian Universalist Congregation at Shelter Rock, 1970-72, chmn. bd. govs., 1978, trustee, 1966-75, 95-98, pres., 1974-75; trustee Mental Health Assn. Nassau County, 1984—, pres., 1990-91; active Port Washington Youth Activities. Recipient Wittelsburger award Heros, Inc., 1984, Good Guy award Nassau County Lacrosse Ofcls. Assn., 1985, Man of Yr. award Nassau County Lacrosse Coaches Assn., 1988, Bernie Ullman award Nat. Collegiate Lacrosse Ofcls. Assn., 1996, others; named to L.I. Met. Lacrosse Hall of Fame, 1986, Nat. Lacrosse Hall of Fame, 1988, Pt. Washington Youth Activities Hall of Fame, 1991. Mem. Nasau County Bar Assn., Phi Beta Kappa. Democrat. Avocations: youth sports, lacrosse, charitable work. Home: 125 Woodhill Ln Manhasset NY 11030-1716 Office: Murtagh Cohen & Byrne 1100 Franklin Ave Ste 303 Garden City NY 11530-1601

COHEN, HARVEY JAY, physician, educator; b. Bklyn., Oct. 21, 1940; s. Joseph and Anne (Margolin) C.; m. Sandra Helen Levine, June 1964; children: Ian Mitchell, Pamela Robin. BS, Bklyn. Coll., 1961; MD, Downstate Med. Coll., Bklyn., 1965. Diplomate Am. Bd. Internal Medicine, Am. Bd. Hematology. Intern, then resident internal medicine Duke U. Med. Ctr., Durham, N.C., 1965-67, fellow hematology and oncology, 1969-71; chief hematology-oncology VA Med. Ctr., Durham, N.C., 1975-76, chief med. service, 1976-82, assoc. chief of staff-edn., 1982-84, now dir. geriatric research, edn. and clin. ctr.; assoc. prof. medicine Duke U. Med. Ctr., Durham, 1976-80, now prof. medicine, chief geriatric divsn., also dir. Ctr. for Study of Aging, interim chair dept. medicine, 2002—03. Chair bd. sci. counselors Nat. Inst. Aging, 1999. Author: Medical Immunology, 1977; co-author: (with H.G. Koenig) The Link Between Religion and Health: Psychoneuroimmunology and the Faith Factor, 2002, Taking Care After 50, 2000; editor: Cancer I and II, 1987, Jour. Gerontology: Med. Scis., 1988-92, Geriatric Medicine, 1997; contbr. numerous articles to profl. jours. Served as surgeon USPHS, 1967-69. Fellow ACP, Am. Geriatrics Soc. (bd. dirs. 1987-96, chair bd. dirs. 1995-96, sec. 1991-93, ethics com. 1992-96, pres. 1994-95), Gerontology Soc. Am. (clin. sec., rsch. com. 1987-92, chair publs. com. 1996-98, program chair 1994, pres. 2000); mem. Am. Soc. Clin. Oncology, Am. Soc. Hematology, Am. Assn. Cancer Rsch. (cancer and acute leukemia group B, chair cancer in the elderly com.), Assn. Am. Physicians, bd. dirs. Intl. Soc. Geri. Oncology Home: 2811 Friendship Cir Durham NC 27705-5521 Office: Duke U Med Ctr for Study Aging & Human Devel Box 3003 Durham NC 27710-0001

COHEN, HELEN HERZ, camp owner, director; b. N.Y.C., Oct. 29, 1912; d. Fred W. and Florence (Hirsch) H.; m. Albert F. Schliefer, Sept. 22, 1933 (dec. Nov. 1941); m. Edwin S. Cohen, Aug. 31, 1944: children: Edwin C., Roger, Wendy. PhB, Brown U., 1933; MA, Columbia U., 1934; postgrad., NYU, Columbia. Counselor Camp Walden, Denmark, Maine, 1930-38, owner, 1939—; tchr. social studies Alcuin Prep. Sch., 1935; office mgr. Lewis P. Weil Importer, 1935-40; pres. The Main Idea, 1968—. Founder, pres. Main Idea, Inc., 1969—. Author: Choosing a Camp for Your Child, Getting Ready for Camp; co-author: Fabulous Foods for Fifty, 1970; contbr. articles to instrnl. booklets, mags. Active alumni coun. Pembroke Coll., 1960; chmn. camp divns. Bridgton (Maine) Hosp. Fund, 1962—; trustee Fund for Advancement Camping, 1980-90. Recipient Gold Key award Columbia Scholastic Press, 1972, award Fund for Advancement of Camping Patron, 1982. Mem. Am. Camping Assn. (regional bd. dirs. 1947-50, 52-55, 56-59, 60-63, standards visitor 1957-93, chmn. pvt. camps 1961, bd. dirs. 1963—, v.p. N.Y. 1963-75, Va. sect. 1975), Pioneers of Camping, Maine Camp Dirs. Assn. (legis. com. 1960-63, bd. dirs. 1963—, Halsey Gulick award 1991), Pembroke Coll. Club (co-founder), Cosmopolitan Club, Cornell Club, Farmington Country Club, Boar's Head Sports Club. Home: Ednam Forest 104 Stuart Pl Charlottesville VA 22903-4740 Office: Camp Walden PO Box 3427 Charlottesville VA 22903-0427 E-mail: waldenherz@aol.com.

COHEN, HENRY, historian, retired educator; b. Bklyn. s. Sam and Lily Cohen. BA, Columbia Coll., 1955; PhD, Cornell U., 1965. Asst. prof. Calif. State Coll., Long Beach, 1964-69; from asst. prof. to prof. Loyola U., Chgo., 1969-94. Author: Business and Politics in America to the Civil War, 1971, Brutal Justice, 1981; founder, editor Criminal Justice History: An International Annual 1980-83; editor The Public Enemy, 1981. Mem. Civil Grand Jury, San Francisco, 2002—03. Social Sci. Rsch. Coun. fellow, 1960-62. Mem. Group for Use of Psychoanalysis in History, Internat. Soc. for Polit. Psychology. Avocations: the arts, travel, wine. Home: 491 Utah St San Francisco CA 94110-1434

COHEN, HENRY C. lawyer; b. Pitts., Mar. 12, 1945; BS, Miami U., 1967; JD, Cornell U., 1971. Bar: Maine 1972, Pa. 1973, Fla. 1999; CPA, Ohio (inactive), Pa. Ptnr. Cohen & Grigsby P.C., Pitts. Adj. prof. Duquesne U. Sch. Law, Pitts., 1976-88. Bd. Dirs. Estate Planning Coun. Pitts. 1984-87. Office: Cohen & Grigsby PC 11 Stanwix St Ste 15 Pittsburgh PA 15222-1312 also: Ste 309 27200 Riverview Center Blvd Bonita Springs FL 34134 E-mail: hcohen@cohenlaw.com.

COHEN, HENRY RODGIN, lawyer; b. Charleston, W.Va, May 7, 1944; s. Louis W. and Bertie (Rodgin) C.; m. Barbara Latz, Aug. 31, 1969; children: Sarah Abigail, Jonathan David. BA, Harvard U., 1965, LLB, 1968; LLB (hon.), U. Charleston, 1998. Bar: W.Va. 1968, N.Y. 1970. Assoc. Sullivan & Cromwell, N.Y.C., 1970-77, ptnr., 1977—, vice chmn., 1999-2000, chmn., 2000—. Contbg. editor Fin. Svcs. Regulation Newsletter, 1985; bd. advisors Banking Law Rev.; mem. editorial adv. bd. Banking Expansion Reporter; mem. nat. bd. contbrs. Am. Lawyers Newspaper Group. Trustee N.Y. Presbyn. Hosp., trustee Hampton Coll., Hackley Sch. With U.S. Army, 1968—70. Office: Sullivan & Cromwell 125 Broad St Fl 28 New York NY 10004-2489

COHEN, HERBERT JESSE, physician, educator; b. N.Y.C., Apr. 27, 1935; s. Barnet and Edith (Lepolstat) C.; m. Marion E. Finger, Aug. 29, 1960; children— Linda Elizabeth, Gerald Daniel, Seth Michael. BA (Ford Found. scholar), Columbia, 1955; MD, State U. N.Y., 1959. Intern Bellevue Hosp., N.Y.C., 1959-60; resident N.Y. Hosp., N.Y.C., 1960-62; asst. instr. Cornell Med. Sch., 1961-62; instr. Tulane Med. Sch., 1962-64; NIH fellow Albert Einstein Coll. Medicine, 1964-66, asst. prof. pediatrics and rehab. medicine, 1966-71, assoc. prof., 1971-76, prof., 1976—; dir. Children's Evaluation and Rehab. Ctr., Rose F. Kennedy Center for Mental Retardation and Human Devel., Bronx, N.Y., 1968-74, 78—, Bronx Developmental Services, N.Y. State Dept. Mental Hygiene, 1971-80, Rose F. Kennedy Univ Ctr. for Excellence in Devel. Disabilities Tng. Svcs. and Rsch., 1974—, dir. div. child devel. and devel. disabilities, dept. pediatrics, 1981—. Vice chmn. Pres.'s Com. on Mental Retardation, 1978-81; mem. study sect. human devel. NIH, 1978-82; mem. profl. adv. bd. various founds. and profl. orgns. Author 4 books; also contbr. over 80 articles to profl. pubs. Served with USPHS, 1962-64. Recipient Disting. Humanitarian Research and Devel. awards Mental Retardation Service Orgns.; United Cerebral Palsy Research and Edn. Found. fellow, 1966-68 Fellow Am. Acad. Pediatrics (chmn. child devel. sect., chmn. com. on children with disabilities); mem. AAAS, Am. Acad. Cerebral Palsy, Am. Assn. Univ. Affiliated Facilities (pres. 1980-81, dir. 1977-84), Am. Assn. Mental Retardation (Leadership award 1996). Office: R F Kennedy Center 1410 Pelham Pky S Bronx NY 10461-1101 E-mail: hcohen@aecom.yu.edu.

COHEN, HERMAN NATHAN, private investigator; b. Bklyn., June 3, 1949; s. Stanley and Hannah (Persky) C.; m. Carolyn P. Grillo, Jan. 8, 1989. BA, Bklyn. Coll., 1970; MS in Ednl. Adminstrn., Hofstra U., 1975. Investigator IRS, N.Y.C., 1970-72, adminstrv. intern Washington, 1972-73, employee devel. specialist Uniondale, N.Y., 1973-75, br. chief Bklyn., 1975-79; pers. officer Home Ins. Co., N.Y.C., 1979-81; asst. v.p. City Investing Co., N.Y.C., 1981-85; prin. H.N. Cohen Enterprises, Inc., N.Y.C., 1985-86; human resources dir. Empire Blue Cross Blue Shield, N.Y.C., 1986-89; v.p. adminstrn. ASPCA, N.Y.C., 1989-90, sr. v.p., 1990, exec. v.p., 1990-91, chief adminstrv. officer, 1991-92, chief law enforcement, 1992-94; CEO, pvt. investigator Due Diligence Plus, Amherst, N.Y., 1994—, pvt. investigator West Hartford, Conn., 1994—. Arbitrator Am. Arbitration Assn., 1986—; bd. dirs. Ashfield Corp.; adj. faculty Conn. Criminal Law Found. Bd. dirs. Owen Sch.; adjutant, dir. at large Centennial Legion of Hist. Mil. Commands; mem. amb.'s coun. Wadsworth Atheneum, Conn., 1st co. Gov. Foot Guard, Conn. Mem. Internat. Assn. Chiefs of Police (chmn. pvt. security com.), Conn. Police Chiefs Assn., Vet. Corps. Arty., Nat. Assn. Investigative Specialists, World Affairs Coun., Mensa, Ancient Free and Accepted Masons, Am. Soc. Indsl. Security. Democrat. Jewish. Office: Due Diligence Plus 3940 Harlem Rd Amherst NY 14226-4704 also: Due Diligence Plus 11140 Rockville Pike #213 Rockville MD 20852 E-mail: cyberpi@home.com., cyberpi@msn.com.

COHEN, HERRICK JAY, physician; b. N.Y.C., Aug. 17, 1937; s. Philip and Bess Helen (Leinward) C.; m. Ellyn Ruth Bustner, Dec. 21, 1961; children: Shari Lynn, Lorin Jill, Caryn Beth. BA, Yale U., 1959; MD, NYU, 1963. Diplomate Am. Bd. Pediatrics. Physician Great Neck (N.Y.) Pediatrics Assocs., P.C., 1968—. Asst. clin. prof. pediatrics Albert Einstein Coll. of Medicine, N.Y.C., 1989—. Capt. USAF, 1966-68. Fellow Am. Acad. Pediatrics. Office: Great Neck Pediatric Assocs PC 173 E Shore Rd Great Neck NY 11023-2415

COHEN, HOWARD MARVIN, lawyer; b. Bklyn., Mar. 22, 1926; s. A. Louis and Claire (Bisgier) C.; m. Judith Rothstein, July 6, 1952 (div. Apr. 1967); children: Jonathan David, Tamara Beth; m. Marjory Hexter, Oct. 12, 1969; children: Theresa Abrams, John Abrams. Student, Yale U., 1945; AB cum laude, Columbia U., 1947; JD magna cum laude, Harvard U., 1949. Bar: N.Y. 1949. Ptnr. Kaye Scholar Fierman, Hays & Handler, N.Y.C., 1963-65; v.p., gen. counsel Revlon Inc., N.Y.C., 1966-71; ptnr. Finley, Kumble, Underberg, Persky & Roth, N.Y.C., 1971—72, Poletti, Freidin, Prashker, Feldman & Gartner, N.Y.C., 1973-78, Warshaw, Burstein, Cohen, Schlesinger & Kuh, N.Y.C., 1978-2000, of counsel, 2001—. Past editor Harvard Law Rev. Trustee Assoc. YM-YWHA, N.Y.C., 1972-90. With U.S. Army, 1943-45. Mem. ABA, Bar of Assn. of City of N.Y., Phi Beta Kappa, Harvard Club, Euro-Am. Lawyers Group (mem. mgmt. com. 1997-2001), Internat. Inst. of Space Law. Jewish. Avocations: skiing, tennis, computers, reading, travel. Home: 16 Sutton Pl Apt 16A New York NY 10022-3057 Office: Warshaw Burstein Cohen 555 5th Ave Fl 12 New York NY 10017-2456 E-mail: hcohen@wbcsk.com.

COHEN, IDA BOGIN (MRS. SAVIN COHEN), import and export executive; b. Bklyn. d. Joseph and Yetta (Harris) Bogin; m. Barnet Gaster, June 26, 1941 (div. May 1955); m. 2d Savin Cohen, Aug. 30, 1964. Student, St. John's U.; BS, NYU. Sec.-treas. J. Gerber & Co., Inc., N.Y.C., 1942-54, v.p., dir., 1954-73. Pres., dir. Austracan U.S.A., Inc., N.Y.C., 1960-73; v.p. Parts Warehouse, Inc., Woodside, N.Y., 1970-72, sec.-treas., 1972-83; also engaged in pvt. investments. Contbr. articles to South African Outspan, newspapers. Home: 12 Shorewood Dr Sands Point NY 11050-1909

COHEN, IRA, legislative staff member; b. Chgo., Sept. 6, 1947; With Rep. Danny K. Davis, Washington, 1979—, issues and comm. dir., 1996—. Office: Office of Rep Danny K Davis 3333 W Arthington St Ste 130 Chicago IL 60624-4102

COHEN, IRA MYRON, aeronautical and mechanical engineering educator; b. Chgo., July 18, 1937; s. Harry Nathan and Esther (Lenchner) C.; m. Linda Barbara Einstein, June 12, 1960; children: Susan Ellen Bolstad, Nancy Beth Cavanaugh. B in Aero. Engring., Poly. Univ., Bklyn., 1958; MA, Princeton U., 1961, PhD in Aero. Engring., 1963; MA (hon.), U. Pa., 1971. Mem. tech. staff Sandia Labs., Albuquerque, summers 1971, 74, 77; asst. prof. engring. Brown U., Providence, 1963-66; asst. prof. mech. engring. U. Pa., Phila., 1966-67, assoc. prof., 1967-76, prof., 1976—, chmn. dept., 1992-97. Guest prof. Technische Hochschule Aachen, Germany, 1966; cons. fluid mechanics related problems to industry, 1966—, attys., 1966—; mem. bd. The Sch. in Rose Valley, Moylan, Pa., 1969-74 Author: (with P.K. Kundu) Fluid Mechanics, 2nd edit., 2002; contbr. articles to various publs. Travel grant, Fulbright, 1966. Fellow AIAA (sect. sec. 1977-80, 85—), ASME; mem. AAUP, Am. Phys. Soc., Internat. Microelectronics and Packaging Soc., Sigma Xi. Office: U Pa Dept Mech Engring & Applied Mechanics 297 Towne Bldg Philadelphia PA 19104-6315 E-mail: imcohen@seas.upenn.edu. *Persistant hard work and uncompromising high standards will eventually overcome greed, corruption, and evil. Never forget to treat every human being with dignity, respect, kindness, and compassion. A loving mate is a lifelong inspiration.*

COHEN, IRVING DAVID, science administrator; b. Bklyn., May 12, 1945; s. Harry and Fay (Minchenberg) C.; m. Dorothy Ann Joseph, Aug. 21, 1966; children: Miriam Susan, Esther Heidi, Daniel Marc, Aaron Michael. BSChemE, CCNY, 1967; MSChemE, NYU, 1970, postgrad. in environ. safety and health, 1970—. Cert. environ. profl.; cert. environ. insp.; cert. environ. specialist. Sr. process engr. Crawford & Russell, Inc., Stamford, Conn., 1967-71; assoc. chem. engr. Hoffmann-LaRoche, Nutley, N.J., 1971-72; sr. project mgr. Woodward-Envicon, Inc., Clifton, N.J., 1972-75; pres., CEO Enviro-Scis., Inc., Mt. Arlington, N.J., 1975—. Chmn. bd. Aero Instrumentation Resources, Inc., 1978—, Ecra Labs., Inc., 1986—, Art Internat. Inc., 1988—. Author environ. impact reports for energy related projects and environ. liability audits. Mem. Am. Inst. Chem. Engrs., Am. Indsl. Hygiene Assn., Internat. Assn. for Pollution Control, Scientists Com. for Pub. Info, Air Pollution Control Assn., Nat. Assn. Environ. Profls. (cert. environ. profl., cert. environ. inspector), N.Y. Acad. Scis. Jewish. Home: 19 Copeland Rd Denville NJ 07834-9603 Office: Enviro-Scis Inc 111 Howard Blvd Mount Arlington NJ 07856-1315

COHEN, IRVING ELIAS, real estate executive; b. Bklyn., Nov. 7, 1946; s. Daniel Arthur and Shirley B. (Kanner) C.; 1 child, Jonathan D. BA in Psychology, CCNY, 1968; MBA in Fin., NYU, 1973, 68. Mut. fund cashier Investors Funding Corp., Inc., 1968-69; syndication cashier Eastman Dillon, Union Securities, Inc., 1969-70; registered rep. Steiner, Rouse & Co., Inc., N.Y.C., 1970-72; instl. rep. Shearson Hayden Stone, Inc., N.Y.C., 1972-74; exec. v.p. Howard P. Hoffman Assos., Inc. subs. Lehman Bros. Kuhn Loeb, Inc., N.Y.C., 1974-81; sr. v.p. Security Pacific Realty Adv. Group, 1981-83; exec. v.p. E.F. Hutton Properties Inc., 1983-87; trustee, chmn. investment com. Mellon Participating Mortgage Trust, 1988-89; mng. dir. Real Estate Cons. Svcs. Group, Price Waterhouse, N.Y.C., 1989-90; mng. ptnr. Fuller Corp. Realty Ptnrs., 1990-94; pres. TimeMinder Ltd., N.Y.C., 1994-96; mng. dir., chief acquisition officer Dames & Moore/Brookhill LLC, N.Y.C., 1996-97; mng. dir. Cherokee Investment Ptnr. LLC, NYC, 1997—2003; CEO Greeneagle LLC, 2003—. Mem. Counselors of Real Estate, Turnaround Mgmt. Assn., Urban Land Inst. Jewish. Office: GreenEagle LLC 400 Chambers St Ste 5G New York NY 10282 E-mail: icohen@greeneagle.us.

COHEN, IRWIN, economist; b. Bronx, N.Y., Feb. 29, 1936; s. Samuel and Gertrude (Levy) C. BS in Accounting, N.Y. U., 1956, MBA in Finance, 1964, MA in Econs., 1969; BS in Math., CCNY, 1970. Financial analyst U.S. SEC, N.Y.C., 1965-67, Fed. Res. Bank N.Y., N.Y.C., 1967-72, Prudential Ins. Co. Am., 1973-74, SEC, 1974—. Life Fellow Internat. Biog. Assn., Am. Biog. Inst. Research Assn. (dep. gov.), World Acad. Scholars, World Literary Acad., World Inst. Achievement; mem. Internat. Biographical Ctr. (dep. dir. gen.), Internat. Platform Assn. (life), Math. Assn. Am., Am. Finance Assn., Econ. History Assn. Home: 372 Central Park Ave Apt #2K Scarsdale NY 10583-1308

COHEN, ISAAC LOUIS (IKE COHEN), small business owner; b. N.Y.C., Sept. 15, 1948; s. Louis and Dora (Dostis) C.; divorced; children: Janice, Matthew. AAS in Bus. Adminstrn., Kingsborough Community Coll., 1977. Asst. v.p. Mfrs. Hanover Trust Co., N.Y.C., 1966-87; data processing ops. mgr. First Boston Corp., Princeton, N.J., 1987—; owner ILC Liquidators Co., High Bridge, N.J., 1990—, ILC Vending Co., High Bridge, 1991—, ILC 900 Co., High Bridge, 1991—, ILC Fin. Mgmt. Co., High Bridge, 1991—; with M&I Interactive Svcs., 1995—; owner SkyBiz 2000, 1999—. Editor booklet: Annadale Memorial Day Parade, 1985, 86, 87. Asst. v.p. Annadale Community Assn., 1982-89; umpire S.I. High Sch. League & Semi-Pro Baseball, 1985—; assoc. scout Kansas City Royals Profl. Baseball Team, 1988—. With USNR, 1967-75. Mem. U.S. Submarine Vets., Am. Legion, Jewish War Vets., Vietnam Vets. Avocations: baseball, motorcycle riding, skiing, roller skating, stamp and coin collecting. Home: 137 Fairview Ave High Bridge NJ 08829-1214 Office: CS First Boston 700 College Rd E Princeton NJ 08540-6617

COHEN, JACOB MARC, physician; b. Dec. 24, 1921; MB BCh, Cairo U., Egypt, 1946. Diplomate Am. Bd. Geriatrics. Pvt. practice, N.Y.C., 1964—. Fellow ACP. Home: 2500 Johnson Ave Apt 7P Bronx NY 10463-4930

COHEN, JACQUELINE, university researcher, sociology educator; b. N.Y.C., Nov. 30, 1945; d. John William and Veronica Loretta McNulty; m. Stuart Louis Cohen, Aug. 27, 1965. BS in Math., U. Pitts., 1966, MA in Sociology, 1970; PhD in Urban and Pub. Affairs, Carnegie Mellon U., 1982. Rsch. asst. Learning Rsch. and Devel. Ctr., U. Pitts., 1967-68, Carnegie Mellon U., Pitts., 1971-79, rsch. assoc., 1979-82, assoc. dir. Urban Sys. Inst., 1982-89, sr. rsch. scientist, 1989-93, prin. rsch. scientist, 1993—. Cons. various panels NRC, Washington, 1975-76, 81-82, 83-85, 89-91. Contbr. articles to Law and Society, Criminology, Jour. Quantitative Criminology, Jour. Rsch. in Crime and Delinquency, Jour. Criminal Law and Criminology, others. Bd. dirs. Health Sys. Agy. Southwestern Pa. Nat. Inst. Justice grantee, 1979—; Alfred P. Sloan Found. rsch. grantee, 1995-98. Mem. Am. Soc. Criminology, Acad. Criminal Justice Scis., Law and Society Assn., Am. Sociol. Assn. Office: Carnegie Mellon U Heinz Sch 5000 Forbes Ave Pittsburgh PA 15213-3890 E-mail: jc63@andrew.cmu.edu.

COHEN, JAMES ROBERT, oncologist, hematologist; BA in English Lit., Cornell U., 1967, MD, 1971. Diplomate Am. Bd. Internal Medicine, Am. Bd. Oncology. Intern N.Y. Hosp./Meml. Sloan Kettering Cancer Ctr., N.Y.C., 1971-72, resident in medicine, 1972-73; sr. resident in medicine U. Calif., San Francisco, 1973-74; postdoctoral fellow in hematology, oncology Stanford (Calif.) U. Sch. Medicine, 1976-78, clin. instr., 1978-85, clin. asst. prof., then clin. assoc. prof., 1986-93; pvt. practice San Jose, Calif., 1978—. Clin. assoc. in medicine U. Nebr. Sch. Medicine, 1975-76; chmn. divsn. oncology Good Samaritan Hosp., 1981-83, dir. med. oncology, 1983—; bd. dirs. Hospice of the Valley, 1979-85, v.p. profl. svcs., 1981-83, pres. bd., 1983-85; clin. investigator No. Calif. Oncology Group, 1977-88; mem. regional steering com. Calif. Cancer Registry, 1987-92, chmn., 1990-92; prin. investigator S.W. Oncology Group, 1992-2000; mem. adv. bd. Saratoga Subacute Hosp., Los Gatos Health Care Ctr., 1994-96. Contbr. articles to profl. jours. Bd. dirs. Good Samaritan Hosp., 2001—. Maj. USAF, 1974-76. Fellow ACP; mem. ACS (liaison assoc. in cancer, bd. dirs. 2001—), AAAS, Santa Clara County Med. Soc., Calif. Med. Assn., Calif. Soc. Internal Medicine, Am. Soc. Internal Medicine, Am. Soc. Clin. Oncology, N.Y. Acad. Scis., Am. Acad. Med. Adminstrs., Am. Coll. Oncology Adminstrs., Alpha Omega Alpha. Office: 15400 National Ave Los Gatos CA 95032-2433 Home: 6605 Boulder Mountain Way San Jose CA 95120-1626 E-mail: jrcohenmd@aol.com.

COHEN, JAY, government agency administrator; Grad., U.S. Naval Acad., 1968; MS in Marine Engring. and Naval Arch., MIT. Commd. ensign USN, 1968, advanced through grades to rear adm., 1997; diver SEALAB Group, San Diego; supply and weapons officer USS Diodon, San Diego; with engring. dept. USS Nathanal Greene, New London; engr. officer USS Nathan Hale, Bremerton, Wash.; staff Comdr. Submarine Force, U.S. Atlantic Fleet; exec. officer USS George Washington Carver, New London; comdr. USS Hyman G. Rickover, New London; sr. mem. nuclear propulsion examining bd. Comdr. in Chief, U.S. Atlantic Fleet; dir. operational support Dir. Naval Intelligence, Pentagon, Washington; comdr. USS L.Y. Spear, 1991—93; dep. chief Navy Legis. Affairs SECNAV; dep. dir. ops. Joint Staff SECNAV, dir. Navy Y2K Project Office. Decorated Legion of Merit. Office: Office of Naval Rsch Ballston Ctr Tower One 800 N Quincy St Arlington VA 22217-5660

COHEN, JAY LORING, lawyer; b. Erie, Pa., Oct. 26, 1953; s. Harold H. and Adelle (Stein) C.; children: Natanel M., Katrielle Z. BA cum laude, U. Rochester, 1974; JD, Georgetown U., 1977. Bar: Pa. 1977, U.S. Claims Ct. 1978, U.S. Ct. Appeals (D.C. cir.) 1978, D.C. 1979, U.S. Supreme Ct. 1981, U.S. Ct. Appeals (fed. cir.) 1982, Md. 1986. Mem. firm Israel, Raley & Cohen, Chartered (formerly Israel & Raley), Washington, 1977-87; pvt. practice, Washington and Bethesda, Md., 1988—. Editor Am. Criminal Law Rev., 1977. Vice-chmn. Montgomery County Ethics Commn., 1986-90, chmn., 1990—; bd. dirs. Hebrew Day Inst., 1984—, v.p., 1987-88, 90-91, treas. 1988—. Mem. Assn. Trial Lawyers Am. (comml. litigation sect.), ABA (pub. contract law sect.), Fed. Bar Assn. (fed. litigation sect.), Fed. Cir. Bar Assn. (gov. contract appeals sect.). Office: 9007 Seneca Ln Bethesda MD 20817-3558

COHEN, JEFF, editor; b. Cheyenne, Wyo. m. Kathryn M. Kase. Degree in journalism, U. Tex., 1976; student jn Multicultural Mgmt. Program, U. Mo., 1987; student Newspaper Mgmt. Ctr., Northwestern U., 1990. Sports writer San Antonio (Tex.) Light, 1976—89, mng. editor, 1989—94; editor Times Union, Albany, NY, 1994—2002; editor, exec. v.p. Houston (Tex.) Chronicle, 2002—. Juror Pulitzer prize, 1999, 2000. Office: Houston Chronicle 801 Texas Ave Houston TX 77002 Office Fax: 713-220-6677.*

COHEN, JEFFREY, lawyer; b. Bklyn., Jan. 31, 1956; s. Fred and Ann (Piel) Cohen. AB in Politics and Philosophy with depart mental honors magna cum laude, Brandeis U., 1977; JD, Bklyn. Law Sch., 1980. Bar: N.Y. 1981, Colo. 1981. Assoc. Freedman & May, N.Y.C., 1980—81, Alter, Zall & Haligman, Denver, 1981—82; ptnr. Quiat & Dice, Denver, 1982—84, Koransky, Friedman & Cohen, P.C., Denver, 1984—89, Cohen & Kenney, 1989—. Recipient Am. Jurisprudence Award, 1977, Rose Meml. scholar, 1977. Mem.: ABA (bus. bankruptcy com.), Denver Bar Assn., Colo. Bar Assn., Colo. Mountain Club. Republican. Jewish. Office: 600 17th St Ste Denver CO 80202-

COHEN, JEFFREY MICHAEL, lawyer; b. Dayton, Ohio, Nov. 13, 1940; s. H. Mort and Evelyn (Friedlob) C.; m. Betsy Z. Zimmerman, July 3, 1966; children: Meredith Sue, Seth Alan. AB, Colgate U., 1962; JD, Columbia U., 1965. Bar: Fla. 1965, U.S. Supreme Ct. 1969; cert. civil trial lawyer Fla. Bar Bd. Cert.; diplomate Nat. bd. Trial Advocacy. Asst. pub. defender Dade County (Fla.), 1968-70, asst. state's atty., 1970-72, spl. asst. state's atty., 1973; ptnr. Fromberg Fromberg Gross Cohen Shore & Berke, P.A., 1972-84, Cohen, Berke, Bernstein, Brodie & Kondell, P.A., Miami, Fla., 1984-2000, Carlton Fields, 2000—. Adj. prof. litigation skills U. Miami Sch. Law, 1989—, adj. prof. trial skills Nova Southeastern U. Law Sch.; chair bd. of legal specialization and edn. Fla. Bar. Trustee Miami-Dade County Alliance for Ethical Govt. Mem. ABA, Dade County Bar Assn. (bd. dirs.), Acad. Fla. Trial Lawyers, Assn. Trial Lawyers Am., Am. Judicature Soc., Nat. Inst. Trial Advocacy (chair and faculty mem.), Fla. Criminal Def. Attys. Assn. Home: 3628 Saint Gaudens Rd Miami FL 33133-6533 Office: 4000 Internat Pl 100 SE 2d St Miami FL 33131 E-mail: jmcohen@carltonfields.com.

COHEN, JEROME, psychology educator, electrophysiologist; b. Pitts., May 27, 1925; s. Abraham Wolfe and Dorothy (Middleman) C.; m. Florence A. Chanock, Oct. 28, 1945; children— Marcus, Mara, Aaron. AA, Princeton U., 1943; BA, U. Pitts., 1947; MA, Cornell U., 1949; PhD, U. Pitts., 1951. Instr. U. Pitts., 1950-51; asst. prof., assoc. prof. Antioch Coll., Yellow Springs, Ohio, 1951-57; prof. psychiatry and behavioral sci. and neurology Northwestern U. Med. Sch., Chgo., 1957-93, prof. emeritus, 1993—. Dir. Electroencephalography Lab. Presbyn.-St. Lukes Hosp., Chgo., 1967-72, Cook County Hosp., Chgo., 1973-99; vis. scientist Neurol. Inst., U. London, 1963-64; vis. prof. Hebrew U., 1972-73, Stanford U., winter 1984. Lt. (j.g.) USNR, 1943-46. Commonwealth Fund fellow, 1963-64 Mem. Am. EEG Soc., Am. Psychol. Assn., Psychophysiol. Research Soc., Internat. Brain Research Soc., AAUP, AAAS, Am. Soc. for Applied Psychophysiology and Biofeedback, Sigma Xi.

COHEN, JOEL EPHRAIM, biologist, educator, demographer; b. Washington, Feb. 10, 1944; s. Hymen Ezra and Alice. C.; children: Zoe, Adam. BA, Harvard U., 1965, MA, 1967, MPH, PhD, Harvard U., 1970, DrPH, 1973; MA (hon.), Cambridge U., 1974. Jr. fellow in math. biology and sociology Soc. of Fellows Harvard U., 1967-71, asst. prof. biology, 1971-72, assoc. prof., 1972-75; prof. populations Rockefeller U., N.Y.C., 1975—, Abby Rockefeller Mauzé prof., 1996—; prof. populations Columbia U., N.Y.C., 1995—; dir.'s visitor Inst. for Advanced Study, Princeton, 1989-90. Chmn. bd. Societal Inst. Math. Scis., 1973—88; mem. ednl. adv. bd. John Simon Guggenheim Meml. Found., 1985—2001, mem. com. selection of fellows, 1990—99; mem. Mayor's Commn. for Sci. and Tech. City of N.Y., 1984—90; mem. sci. adv. bd. Inst. Sci. Interchange, Torino, Italy, 1991—; mem. bd. math. scis. NRC, 1991—92, mem. exec. com., panel on sci., tech. and law, 2000—, mem. governing bd., 2001—; mem. bd. govs. The Nature Conservancy, Arlington, Va., 2000—; trustee N.Y. Nature Conservancy, 2001—; mem. exec. com. Tyler Prize for Environ. Achievement, 2001—. Author: A Model of Simple Competition, 1967, Casual Groups of Monkeys and Men, 1971, Food Webs and Niche Space, 1978, Community Food Webs, 1990, Absolute Zero Gravity, 1992, How Many People Can the Earth Support?, 1995, Comparisons of Stochastic Matrices, 1998, Plants and Population: Is There Time?, 1999; mem. edit. bd.: American Scholar, 1994—99. Trustee Russell Sage Found., 1989-99, vice chmn. bd., 1996-99; trustee Black Rock Forest Preserve, 1989—. Recipient Mercer award Ecol. Soc. Am., 1972, disting. statis. ecologist award 6th Internat. Congress of Ecology, 1994, Olivia Nordberg award for excellence in writing on population scis. Population Coun., N.Y.C., 1997, Fred L. Soper award Pan Am. Health & Edn. Found., Washington, 1998, Tyler prize Environ. Achievement, 1999, N.Y.C. Mayor's award for excellence in sci. and tech., 2002; fellow Ctr. for Advanced Study in Behavioral Scis., Stanford, 1981-82, John Simon Guggenheim Meml. fellow, 1981-82, MacArthur Found. fellow, 1981-86. Fellow AAAS, Am. Acad. Arts and Scis. (mem. coun. 2000—), Am. Statis. Assn.; mem. Population Assn. Am. (Mindel Sheps award for math. demography 1992), Cambridge Philos. Soc., Am. Soc. Naturalists, Am. Philos. Soc., U.S. Nat. Acad. Scis. (mem. coun. 2001—, mem. exec. com. 2002—). Office: Rockefeller U 1230 York Ave Ste 20 New York NY 10021-6399

COHEN, JON STEPHAN, lawyer; b. Omaha, Nov. 9, 1943; s. Louis H. and Bertha N. (Goldstein) C.; children: Carolyn, Sherri, Barbara, Shayna, Jordan; m. Cheryl A. Jiroux, Oct. 7, 1994. Student, London Sch. Econs., 1963-64; BA, Claremont Men's Coll. (now Claremont McKenna Coll.), 1965; JD, Harvard U., 1968. Bar: Ariz. 1968. Assoc. Snell & Wilmer, Phoenix, 1968-73, ptnr., 1973—. Bd. dirs. Vika Corp., Phoenix, Enterprise Network, Phoenix, Ariz. Tech. Coun., Phoenix, Ariz. Sci. Ctr., Phoenix. Bd. dirs. Kronos Found., Phoenix, Aurora Found., Phoenix. Fellow Ariz. Bar Found.; mem. ABA, Ariz. Bar Assn., Maricopa County Bar Assn., Village Athletic Club, City Sq. Athletic Club. Avocations: record collecting, skiing, racquetball. Home: 6528 N 27th St Phoenix AZ 85016 Office: Snell & Wilmer One Arizona Ctr Phoenix AZ 85004-0001 E-mail: jcohen@swlaw.com.

COHEN, JONATHAN ALLAN, research psychoanalyst; b. Troy, N.Y., Dec. 4, 1939; s. Irwin Jeremiah and Gertrude Ann (Willig) C.; m. Erica Ducornet; children from a previous marriage: Joshua Cohen, Adrienne Cohen, Jean-Yves Ducornet. Student, Yale U., 1956-59; BS in Phys. Chemistry, UCLA, 1963, MD, 1967. Diplomate Am. Bd. Psychiatry and Neurology. Clin. instr. dept. psychiatry U. Colo. Med. Ctr., Denver, 1971—; pvt. practice psychoanalysis and psychiatry Denver, 1974—. Assoc. dept. psychiatry Med. U. S.C., Charleston, 1972-74; rsch. assoc. Program Psychoanalytic Rsch. Brunel U., Middlesex, Eng., 1982-99, rsch. fellow 1989-99; cons. video archives for holocaust testimonies Yale U., New Haven, 1981-99; cons. dept. psychiatry W. Va. U. Sch. Medicine, Charleston, 1985-90. Author: Apart From Freud: Notes for a Rational Psychoanalysis, 2001; contbr. numerous articles on psychoanalysis to profl. jours. Served to lt. comdr. USN, 1972-74. Mem. AAAS, Am. Psychiatric Assn., Fedn. Am. Scientists, ACLU. Democrat. Jewish. Avocations: skiing, sailing, travel. Home: 2240 S Cook St Denver CO 80210-4916 Office: 2005 Franklin St Ste 500 Denver CO 80205-5406 E-mail: jon.cohen@interfold.com.

COHEN, JONATHAN BREWER, molecular neurobiologist, biochemist; b. Akron, Ohio, Dec. 17, 1944; s. Saul G. and Doris E. (Brewer) C.; m. Victoria Ann Rhoden, July 20, 1981; children: Deborah Karen, Samuel Max. AB, Harvard U., 1966, MA, 1967, PhD, 1972. Postdoctoral fellow Pasteur Inst., Paris, 1971-74; asst. prof. pharmacology Harvard Med. Sch., Boston, 1975-80, assoc. prof., 1980-82; prof. neurobiology Washington U. Med. Sch., St. Louis, 1982-92, prof. biol. chemistry, 1982-92; prof. neurobiology Harvard Med. Sch., Boston, 1992—, interim chair neurobiology, 1998-2000. Head neuroscis. grad. program Washington U., 1987-92, Harvard Med. Sch., 1993—; mem. pharm. scis. rev. com. NIH, 1988-92. Mem. editorial bd. Jour. Biol. Chemistry, 1986-91, 94-98. Mem. Am. Chem. Soc., Soc. Neurosci., Am. Soc. Pharmacology and Exptl. Therapeutics, Am. Soc. Biochemistry and Molecular Biology, Phi Beta Kappa. Office: Harvard Med Sch Dept Neurobiology 220 Longwood Ave Boston MA 02115-5701 E-mail: jonathan_cohen@hms.harvard.edu.

COHEN, JONATHAN LITTLE, investment banker; b. N.Y.C., Feb. 18, 1939; s. Reuben and Marjorie (Little) C.; children: Gregory David, Suzanne Elizabeth; m. Allison B. Morrow, 1998. AB, Dartmouth Coll., 1960, MBA, 1961. Asst. v.p. Irving Trust Co., N.Y.C., 1963-68; assoc. Goldman, Sachs & Co., N.Y.C., 1969-73, v.p., 1973-84, gen. ptnr., 1984-96; ltd. ptnr. The Goldman Sachs Group, L.P., N.Y.C., 1996-99, adv. dir., 1999—. Former trustee 1st Presbyn. Ch., N.Y.C.; trustee Wildlife Conservation Soc., N.Y.C., 2000—; former trustee Oberlin Coll.; bd. overseers Amos Tuck Sch. Bus. Adminstrn., Dartmouth Coll., 1991—, chmn., 1995—2001; bd. overseers Hopkins Ctr. and Hood Mus. Art, Dartmouth Coll., 2001—; mem. pres.'s leadership coun. Dartmouth Coll., 1998—, former mem. coun. alumni, 1983—86; former mem. sch. com. Friends Sem., N.Y.C., 1985—91; trustee Pa. Acad. Fine Arts, 1998—. Lt. USN, 1961—63. Mem.: Coral Beach and Tennis Club (Bermuda), Downtown Athletic Club, Bond Club, Bellport Bay Yacht Club, India House. Office: Goldman Sachs & Co 22nd Fl 85 Broad St New York NY 10004 2456 E mail: jonathan.cohen@gs.com.

COHEN, JORDAN JAY, medical association executive; b. St. Louis, June 18, 1934; s. Bernard and Gladys (Brauer) C.; m. Carole Goldstein, Aug. 26, 1956; children: Deborah, Joel, David. BA, Yale U., 1956; MD, Harvard U., 1960; DSc, George Washington U. Sch. Med., and Health Scis., 1995, SUNY Health Sci. Ctr., Syracuse, 1996, Wake Forest U., 1997; LHD, Chgo. Med. Sch., 1998; DSc, U. Med. and Dental, N.J., 1998; DH Sci., Boston U., 1998; DSc, Thomas Jefferson U., 2001. Diplomate Am. Bd. Internal Medicine (mem. critical care medicine test and policy com. 1985-87, chmn. 1987-89, mem. subspecialty com. on nephrology 1981-86, chmn. 1986-88, chmn. com. on evaluation of clin. competency 1987-92, bd. dirs. 1986-94, mem. exec. com. 1990-94, chmn. 1993-94). Intern, asst. resident Boston City Hosp., 1960-62, sr. resident, 1964-65; rsch. fellow in renal medicine New Eng. Med. Ctr. Hosp., Boston, 1962-64; tchg. fellow Harvard U. Med. Sch., Boston, 1964-65, instr. in medicine, 1968-74, lectr. in medicine, 1974-82; asst. prof. med. scis. Brown U., Providence, 1965-68, assoc. prof. med. scis., 1968-71; assoc. prof. medicine Tufts U. Sch. Medicine, Boston, 1971-75, prof. medicine, 1976-82; prof., assoc. chmn. medicine Pritzker Sch. Medicine, U. Chgo., 1982-88; dean sch. medicine, prof. medicine SUNY, Stony Brook, 1988-94; dir. Univ. Med. Ctr., Stony Brook, 1993-94; pres. Assn. Am. Med. Colls., Washington, 1994—; clin. prof. dept. medicine Georgetown U. Sch. Medicine, 1995—. Dir. divsn. renal disease R.I. Hosp., Providence, 1965-71; chief renal svc. New Eng. Med. Ctr. Hosp., Boston, 1971-82, pres. med. staff, 1975-76, physician-in-chief and chmn., dept. medicine Michael Reese Hosp. and Med. Ctr., Chgo., 1982-88; pres. med. staff Univ. Hosp., Stony Brook, N.Y., 1988-94. Co-author: (textbooks) Acid-Base, 1982, Nephrology Forum, 1983, Repairing Bodily Fluids, 1989; author chpts. to books; editor Nephrology Forum, 1978—, Tufts Family Health Guides, 1979-82; manuscript reviewer Am. Jour. Physiology, Annals Internal Medicine, Jour. Clin. Investigation, Kidney Internat., New England Jour. Medicine; contbr. articles to profl. jours. Lt. col. M.C., U.S. Army, 1969-71. Recipient Scroll of Merit, Nat. Med. Assn., 1997. Master: ACP (mem. coun. on subsplty. socs. 1978—84, chmn. coun. 1981—82, nominating com. 1983—84, chmn. edn. policy com. 1983—89, bd. regents 1983—89, vice chmn. 1988—89, rep. to Coun. Med. Splty. Socs. 1991—94, chmn. search com. for assoc. exec. v.p. for edn., mem. nephrology com. med. knowledge self-assessment program, chmn.); fellow: Royal Soc. Medicine; mem.: Weill Cornell Med. Coll., Spl. Med. Adv. Group, Rsch. Am., Partnerships for Quality Edn., Edn. Commn. Fgn. Med. Grads., Coalition for Health Svc. Rsch., Carl J. Shapiro Inst. for Edn. and Rsch., Am. Bd. Internal Med. Found., Internat. Soc. Nephrology, Ctrl. Soc. Clin. Rsch., Nat. Med. Fellowships, China Med. Bd., Assn. Program Dirs. in Internal Medicine (mem. coun. 1984—90, pres. 1988—89), Assn. Am. Physicians, Soc. Med. Adminstrs., Nat. Kidney Found. (mem. task force on nephrology manpower 1987—89), Am. Soc. Nephrology (rep. to CSS 1978—82, chmn. manpower task force 1980), Am. Soc. Clin. Investigation, Am. Heart Assn., Am. Geriat. Soc. (mem. program com. 1985—88), Am. Fedn. Clin. Rsch. (chmn. Ea. sect. 1975), Am. Clin. and Climatol. Assn., Inst. Medicine of NAS, Dept. Vets. Affairs, Josiah Macy Found., Cosmos Club, Midwest Salt and Water Club, Sigma Xi, Phi Beta Kappa. Home: 1819 Kalorama Sq NW Washington DC 20008-4021 Office: Assn Am Med Colls 2450 N St NW Washington DC 20037-1127

COHEN, JUDITH W. academic administrator; b. N.Y.C., May 14, 1937; d. Meyer F. and Edith Beatrice (Elman) Wiles; BA, Bklyn. Coll., 1957, MA, 1960; cert. advanced studies Hofstra U., 1978; MA Columbia U., 1986, postgrad. 1986—. m. Joseph Cohen, Oct. 19, 1957; children: Amy Beth (dec.), Lisa Carrie, Adam Scott Frank, Elyssa Lily. Tchr. N.Y.C. Pub. Schs., Bklyn., 1957-60; tchr. Mid. Country Sch. Dist., Centereach, N.Y., 1970-93, retired 1993; prof. psychology 5 Towns Coll., Dix Hills, N.Y., 1994—. prof. edn. Dowling Coll., Oakdale, N.Y., Title IX compliance officer, 1980-86, team leader 1987-91; dir. Long Island U. Summer Adventure Program, 1994—. Bus. adv. Women's Equal Rights Congress, Suffolk County Human Rights; chmn. bd. edn., Temple Beth David, trustee, 1975-79; pres. CHUMS, 1979-82; Tchr. of Gifted Post-L.I. U. Saturday Program, 1985—; L.I. Writing Project fellow, Dowling Coll., 1979— ; cert. sch. dist. adminstr., supr., adminstr., N.Y. State; adj. prof. Five Towns Coll., 1994—; adj. prof. edn. Dowling Coll., Oakdale, N.Y., 1997—. Mem. Nassau Suffolk Coun. Adminstrv. Women in Edn. (prds. 1979-81), Assn. for Supervision and Curriculum Devel., Assn. Gifted/Talented Edn., Women's Equal Rights Congress Com. (exec. bd.), Suffolk County Coordinating Council Gifted and Talented, Phi Delta Kappa, Delta Kappa Pi. Author: Arts in Education Curriculum in Social Studies and Language Arts, 1981. Home: 35 Gaymor Ln Commack NY 11725-1305

COHEN, JULES, physician, educator, former academic dean; b. Bklyn., Aug. 26, 1931; s. Samuel S. and Dora (Goldstein) C.; m. Doris Eidlin, Mar. 25, 1956; children: Stephen E., David E., Sharon E. AB, U. Rochester, 1953, MD, 1957. Intern Beth Israel Hosp., Boston, 1957-58; resident, fellow in medicine U. Rochester (N.Y.) Strong Meml. Hosp., 1958-60, mem. faculty, 1963—, prof. medicine, 1973—; NIH research asso. Bethesda, Md., 1960-62; research fellow Postgrad. Med. Sch., London, 1962-63; physician in chief Rochester Gen. Hosp., 1976-82; sr. asso. dean med. edn. U. Rochester Sch. Medicine, 1982-97. USPHS research grantee, 1963-69; USPHS research grantee, 74-77; recipient USPHS Research Career Devel. award, 1970-75; Am. Heart Assn. grantee-in-aid, 1969-71 Fellow ACP, Am. Coll. Cardiology; mem. Am. Physiol. Soc., Am. Heart Assn. (fellow coun. on clin. cardiology), Monroe County Med. Soc., N.Y. State Med. Soc., Rochester Acad. Medicine. Jewish. Home: 152 Burkedale Cres Rochester NY 14625-1704 Office: U Rochester Sch Medicine and Dentistry 601 Elmwood Ave Rochester NY 14642-0001 E-mail: Jules_Cohen@urmc.rochester.edu.

COHEN, KARL PALEY, nuclear energy consultant; b. NYC, Feb. 5, 1913; s. Joseph M. and Ray (Paley) C.; m. Marthe H. Malartre, Sept. 20, 1938; children: Martine-Claude Lebouc, Elisabeth M. Brown, Beatrix Josephine Cashmore. AB, Columbia U., 1933, MA, 1934, PhD in Phys. Chemistry, 1937; postgrad., U. Paris, 1936-37. Research asst. to Prof. H. C. Urey Columbia U., 1937-40; dir. theoretical div., SAM Manhattan project, 1940-44; physicist Standard Oil Devel. Co., 1944-48; tech. dir. H.K. Ferguson Co., 1948-52; v.p. Walter Kidde Nuclear Lab., 1952-55; cons. AEC, sr. sci. Columbia U., 1955; mgr. advance engring. atomic power equipment dept. Gen. Electric Co., 1955-65, gen. mgr. breeder reactor devel. dept., 1965-71, mgr. strategic planning, nuclear energy div., 1971-73, chief scientist, nuclear energy group, 1973-78; cons. prof. Stanford U., 1978-81. Author: The Theory of Isotope Separation as Applied to Large Scale Production of U-235, 1951; contbr. articles to profl. jours. Recipient Energy Research prize Alfried Krupp Found., 1977 Fellow AAAS, Am. Nuclear Soc. (pres. 1968-69, bd. dirs.), Am. Inst. Chemists (Chem. Pioneer award 1979); mem. NAE, IEEE, Am. Phys. Soc., Phi Beta Kappa, Sigma Xi, Phi Lambda Upsilon. Home and Office: 928 N California Ave Palo Alto CA 94303-3405 E-mail: karlpc@earthlink.net.

COHEN, LARRY, film director, producer, screenwriter; b. Chgo., Apr. 20, 1947; TV writer: (series) Kraft Mystery Theatre, The Defenders, Arrest and Trial, NYPD Blue, 87th Precinct, Ice, Heatwave; (movies) Cool Million, 1972, Shootout in a One-Dog Town, 1974, Man on the Outside, 1975, Desperado: Avalanche at Devil's Ridge, 1988; creator: Branded, 1965-66, The Invaders, 1967-68; film writer: The Return of the Seven, 1966, Daddy's Gone A-Hunting, 1969, El Condor, 1970, I, The Jury, 1982, Best Seller, 1987, Deadly Illusion, 1987, Guilty as Sin, 1993; dir., prodr., writer: Bone, 1972, Black Caesar, 1973, Hell in Harlem, 1973, It's Alive, 1974, Demon, 1976, The Private Files of J. Edgar Hoover, 1978, It Lives Again, 1978, Full Moon High, 1982, Q, 1982, Perfect Strangers, 1984; story: Success, 1979, The Man Who Wasn't There, 1983, Scandalous, 1984, Body Snatchers, 1984; dir., writer: Special Effects, 1984, The Ambulance, 1990; exec. prodr., dir., writer: The Stuff, 1985, It's Alive III: Island of the Alive, 1987, Return to Salem's Lot, 1987, Wicked Stepmother, 1989; prodr., writer: Maniac Cop II, 1990.; writer, dir.: As Good As Dead, 1996; dir.: Original Gangstas, 1997, Phone Booth, 2001, Cellular, 2001.

COHEN, LAWRENCE BARUCH, neurobiologist, educator; b. Indpls., June 18, 1939; s. Gabriel Murel and Helen (Aronovitz) C.; children: Daniel, Avrum; m. Barbara Ellen Ehrlich; 1 child, Lily Rachel. BS, U. Chgo., 1961; PhD, Columbia U., 1965. Asst. prof. Yale U., New Haven, 1968-71, assoc. prof., 1971-79, prof. physiology, 1979—. Recipient Elizabeth R. Cole award, Biophys. Soc., 1987, McMaster Award, Columbia U., 1965; named Dist. Lectr., Am. Physiol. Soc., 1998. Office: Yale U Sch Medicine 333 Cedar St New Haven CT 06510-3289 E-mail: lawrence.cohen@yale.edu.

COHEN, LAWRENCE EDWARD, sociology educator, criminologist; b. L.A., July 20, 1945; s. Louis and Florence (White) C. BA, U. Calif., Berkeley, 1969; MA, Calif. State U., 1971; PhD, U. Wash., 1974; postdoctorate study, SUNY, Albany, 1973-75. Rsch. assoc. Sch. of Criminal Justice, SUNY, Albany, 1973-76; asst. prof. U. Ill., Urbana, 1976-80; assoc. prof. U. Tex., Austin, 1980-85; prof. Ind. U., Bloomington, 1985-88, U. Calif., Davis, 1988—. Cons. editor Social Forces, 1981-84, Jour. Criminal Law and Criminology, 1982-2000, Am. Sociol. Rev., 1982-84, Am. Jour. Sociology, 1990-98, Criminology, 1996-98; contbr. numerous articles to profl. jours. Sgt. USMC, 1963-66, Vietnam. Grantee NIMH, 1978-80, NSF, 1983-89. Mem. Am. Sociol. Assn., Am. Soc. Criminology, Acad. Criminal Justice Scis., Soc. for Study Social Problems. Office: U Calif Dept Sociology Davis CA 95616 E-mail: lecohen@ucdavis.edu.

COHEN, LAWRENCE SOREL, physician, educator; b. N.Y.C., Mar. 27, 1933; s. Max and Fannie (Cooper) C.; m. Jane Abramson, Aug. 5, 1961; children: Melanie, Wendy. AB, Harvard U., 1954; MD, N.Y. U., 1958; MA (hon.), Yale U., 1970. Diplomate: Am. Bd. Internal Medicine, Sub Bd. Cardiovascular Diseases. Intern, then resident in medicine Yale-New Haven Hosp., 1958-60, 64-65; asst. in medicine Harvard U. Med. Sch., 1962-64; sr. investigator Nat. Heart, Lung and Blood Inst., 1965-68, mem. task force on arteriosclerosis, 1978-80, chmn. clin. trials rev. com., 1984-85, 87-89; assoc. prof. medicine U. Tex. Med. Sch., Dallas, 1968-70; prof. medicine Yale U. Med. Sch., 1970-81, Ebenezer K. Hunt prof. medicine, 1981—, dep. dean, 1991-95, spl. advisor to dean, 1995—. Mem. editorial bd. Circulation, Am. Jour. Cardiology, Am. Heart Jour.; contbr. over 160 articles to med. jours. Active Am. Heart Assn., chpt. pres., 1980-81, affiliate pres. Conn. chpt., 1984-86. With USPHS, 1960-62. Recipient Francis Gilman Blake award for Teaching of Med. Scis., 1973 Fellow ACP, Am. Coll. Cardiology (trustee 1978-83, mem. editorial bd. jour.); mem. Assn. Univ. Cardiologists (pres.-elect 1990, pres. 1991), Interurban Clin. Club (pres. 1988), Alpha Omega Alpha. Home: 633 Whitney Ave New Haven CT 06511-2218 Office: Yale U Sch Medicine 333 Cedar St New Haven CT 06510-3289 E-mail: lawrence.s.cohen@yale.edu.

COHEN, LEWIS COBRAIN, security products firm executive; b. Boston, July 26, 1947; s. Maurice M. and Marilyn (Cobrain) C.; married; 2 children. BS in Bus., Babson Coll., 1969; M in Mgmt., Vanderbilt U., 1974. Dir. consumer affairs audit divsn. Better Bus. Bur. N.Y., N.Y.C., 1974-75; pres. Consumer Affairs Cons. Co., Newton, Mass., 1975-76, Apahouser Security Co., Needham, Mass., 1976—; mfrs. rep. Best Lock Corp., Indpls., 1987—; co-owner Eastview Enterprises, East Hardwick, Vt. Co owner Camp Samoset, Casco, Maine; cons. Bus. Advocacy Ctr., N.Y.C., 1976-78. Mem. U.S. Senator John F. Kerry Fin. Com., Boston, 1981—, Brookline (Mass.) Zoning Bd. Appeals, 1981—; trustee New Hampton (N.H.) Sch., 1984-89, Concord Acad., 1989-95; co-trustee Fund for Philanthropy and Edn., Chestnut Hill, Mass., 1984—; chmn. bd. trustees Sterling Coll., Vt., 1995—; trustee Inst. for Jewish Cmty. and Religion, Calif., 1995-99. Mem. CEO Orgn., WPO Orgn., Nat. Alliance Businessman (chmn. New Eng. 1975-78), Am. Soc. Indsl. Security. Democrat. Avocations: golf, sailing, internat. travel, collecting ancient mideastern oil lamps. Office: Apahouser Security 31 Thorpe Rd Needham MA 02494-1503

COHEN, LEWIS ISAAC, lawyer; b. N.Y.C., July 27, 1932; s. Benjamin and Jeannette (Klotzko) C.; m. Sheila Lipman, Sept. 8, 1957; children— Leslie, Bruce, Wendy. BA, U. Calif. at Los Angeles, 1953; LL.B., Columbia, 1958. Bar: N.Y. State bar 1959, D.C. bar 1964, U.S. Supreme Ct. bar 1966. Atty. FCC, Washington, 1959-64; 1995practiced in Washington, 1964—95; ptnr. Cohen & Berfield, 1964-95. Served with AUS, 1954-56. Mem. Fed., D.C. bar assns., FCC Bar Assn. Home: 45 Sunset Ct Edinburg VA 22824 E-mail: lihcohen@shentel.net.

COHEN, LORI, computer software developer; b. Bklyn., Feb. 25, 1958; d. Arnold and Rhoda (Gingold) Newman; children: Melanie Sue, Justin Marc, Tyler Philip. BA in Computer Sci., SUNY, Oswego, 1979. Jr. programmer Fedn. Employment and Guidance, N.Y.C., 1979-81; programmer/analyst Lehman Bros. Kuhn Loeb, N.Y.C., 1981-84; sr. programmer/analyst Merrill Lynch, N.Y.C., 1984-86; mgr. mortgage-backed securities devel. Shearson/Lehman, N.Y.C., 1986-88; mgr. workstation devel. Magna Software, N.Y.C., 1988-90; mgr. Instinet, N.Y.C., 1990-96; v.p. brokerage svcs. Conversion Svcs. Internat., East Hanover, 1996; SOROS fund mgmt. cons. Trading Floor Systems, 1997—, HP Fin. Svcs., 2000—, Compaq/HP Integration, 2000—. Avocations: photography, gardening, dressage. Office: Conversion Svcs Internat 100 Eagle Rock Ave East Hanover NJ 07936-3149 E-mail: lcohen@csiwhq.com.

COHEN, LOUIS RICHARD, lawyer; b. Washington, Nov. 28, 1940; s. Milton Howard and Rowna (Chaffetz) C.; m. Bonnie Rubenstein, Aug. 29, 1965; children: Amanda Carroll, Eli Augustus. AB, Harvard U., 1962, LLB, 1966; student, Wadham Coll., Oxford, Eng., 1962-63. Bar: DC. Law clk. to Hon. John M. Harlan U.S. Supreme Ct., Washington, 1967-68; assoc. Wilmer, Cutler & Pickering, Washington, 1968-74, ptnr., 1974-86, 88—; dep. solicitor gen. U.S. Dept. Justice, Washington, 1986-88; ptnr. Wilmer, Cutler & Pickering, Wash., DC, 1988—. Vis. prof. Stanford (Calif.) Law Sch., 1981; lectr. law Harvard Law Sch., Cambridge, Mass., 1986. Author: Book Review Michigan Law Review, 1993. Chair Harvard Law Sch. Fund 1993-96; mem. overseers com. to Visit Harvard Law Sch., 1986-92; bd. dirs. Woolly Mammoth Theatre Co., Washington, 1988-91, 96—; bd. of dir.; Ptnrs. for Sacred Places, 2002--. Mem.: Bd. of Dir., Telluride Soc. for Jazz (bd. dirs. 2001—), Am. Law Inst., Am. Acad. Appellate Lawyers, Supreme Ct. Hist. Soc. Jewish. Avocation: hiking. Office: Wilmer Cutler & Pickering 2445 M St NW Ste 500 Washington DC 20037-1420 E-mail: louis.cohen@wilmer.com.

COHEN, LYOR, recording industry executive; b. N.Y.C. married; 1 child. B in Mktg. and Fin., U. Miami. Co-pres. Island Def Jam. Office: Island Def Jam 825 8th Ave New York NY 10019-7416

COHEN, MALCOLM MARTIN, psychologist, researcher; b. New Brunswick, N.J., May 13, 1937; s. Nathan and Esther (Greenhaus) C.; m. Marilyn Jerrow, Jan. 2, 1959 (dec. 1967); m. Eleanor Johnson, June 30, 1969 (div. 1988); m. Suzana Gal, Feb. 14, 1988. BA, Brandeis U., 1959; MA, U. Pa., 1961, PhD, 1965. Lic. psychologist, Pa. Asst. instr. U. Pa., Phila., 1961-63; rsch. psychologist Naval Air Engring. Ctr., Phila., 1963-67; supervisory rsch. psychologist Naval Air Devel. Ctr., Warminster, Pa., 1967-82; asst. chief biomed. rsch. divsn. NASA-Ames Rsch Ctr., Moffett Field, Calif., 1982-85, chief neurosci. br., 1985-88, rsch. scientist, 1988—, chief human info. processing rsch., 2000—. Lectr. dept. aeros. and astronautics Stanford (Calif.) U., lectr. human biology program, 1994—95, consulting assoc. prof. human biology program, 1995—98, cons. prof. human biology program, 1998—; assoc. editor Aviation, Space and

Environ. Medicine, 2001—. Contbr. articles to profl. jours. Patentee light bar to monitor human acceleration tolerance. Founding mem. Common Cause of Phila., 1973. Recipient Exceptional Sci. Achievement medal NASA, 1994. Fellow Aerospace Med. Assn. (editorial bd. Aviation Space and Environ. Medicine 1985-93, Environ. Sci. award 1985, William F. Longacre award 1989), Aerospace Human Factors Assn. (pres. 1992); mem. AAAS, AIAA, N.Y. Acad. Scis., Psychonomics Soc., Sigma Xi. Jewish. Avocation: scuba diving. Office: NASA Ames Rsch Ctr Mail Stop 262-2 Moffett Field CA 94035 E-mail: mmcohen@mail.arc.nasa.gov.

COHEN, MALCOLM STUART, economist, business executive; b. Mpls., Jan. 17, 1942; s. Jack Alvin and Lorraine Ethel (Hill) C.; m. Judith Ann Arenson, Sept. 25, 1965; children: Laura, Randall, Ilona. BA in Econs. summa cum laude, U. Minn., 1963; PhD in Econs., MIT, 1967. Labor economist U.S. Bur. Labor Stats., Washington, 1967-68; lectr. U. Md., Coll. Pk., 1968; asst. to v.p. state rels. and planning U. Mich., Ann Arbor, Mich., 1968-70, various tchr. positions, 1968-85; co-rsch. dir. U. Mich. Inst. of Labor and Indsl. Rels., Ann Arbor, Mich., 1973-80, dir., 1980-93; cons. Corp. Pub. Broadcasting, 1994-97; lectr. indsl. rels. ctr. U. Minn., 1994-96; pres. Employment Rsch. Corp., Ann Arbor, Mich., 1997—. Cons. U.S. Dept. Labor, 1995-2001, EEOC, 1996—, Mich. Senate Fiscal Agy., Lansing, 1988; project dir. various projects Washington, 1968-92; expert witness discrimination and econs. various clients, 1982—. Co-author: A Micro Model of Labor Supply, 1970; contbr. articles to profl. jour.; author: Labor Shortages: As Am. Approaches the 21st Century, 1995; co-author: Global Skill Shortages, 2002. Mem. Nat. Assn. Forensic Economists, Indsl. Rels. Rsch. Assn., Internat. Indsl. Rels. Assn., N.Am. Econ. and Fin. Assn. Avocations: jogging, geneology. Office: Employment Rsch Corp Ste 250 3820 Packard Rd Ann Arbor MI 48108-3348 E-mail: malco@umich.edu.

COHEN, MARCY SHARON, lawyer; b. N.Y.C., Apr. 29, 1954; d. Morton Gilbert and Sue Cohen. AB, Lehman Coll., 1975; JD, N.Y. Law Sch., 1978. Bar: N.Y. 1979, U.S. Dist. Ct. (ea. and so. dists.) N.Y. 1979, U.S. Supreme Ct. 1982. Assoc. Marcus & Marcus, N.Y.C., 1978-80; v.p., assoc. gen. counsel Bank Leumi Trust Co. N.Y., N.Y.C., 1980-84; sr. v.p., gen. counsel Atlantic Bank N.Y., N.Y.C., 1984-93, 1st v.p., dep. gen. counsel Republic Nat. Bank N.Y., N.Y.C., 1993-99; counsel for N.Am., Westdeutsche Landesbank Girozentrale, 1999—. Mem. faculty Am. Inst. Banking, N.Y.C., 1984-88. Mem. ABA (mem. corp. bankig and bus. law com.), Assn. of Bar of City of N.Y. (mem. banking law com.), N.Y. State Bar Assn. (chair corp. counsel sect.), Assn. Comml. Fin. Attys. Avocations: photography, art history, english and french literature. Office: Westdeutsche Landesbank Girozentrale 1211 Ave of Americas New York NY 10036-8701

COHEN, MARK GEORGE, retired cardiologist; b. Phila., 1928; MD, Hahnemann U., 1952. Diplomate Am. Bd. Internal Medicine, Am. Bd. Cardiology. Intern Hahn Hosp., Phila., 1952-53; resident in medicine Phila. VA Hosp., 1955-57; mem. staff Christiana Med. Ctr., Wilmington, Del.; ret., 1994. Clin. assoc. prof. medicine Jefferson U. Hosp. Fellow ACP, Am. Coll. Cardiology; mem. AMA. Home: Apt 101 1820 Les Chateaux Blvd Naples FL 34109-0396

COHEN, MARK HERBERT, broadcasting company executive; b. Boston, Mar. 27, 1932; s. Henry I. and Francis C.; m. Mary Jane Pitman, July 30, 1961; children: Patricia Beth, H. Jonathan, Cathy Ann. BA in Bus. Adminstrn., U. Maine, 1954; MS in TV Prodn, Syracuse U., 1958. Announcer Sta. WGUY-AM-FM, Bangor, Maine, 1954, Sta. WGAN-AM-TV, Portland, Maine, 1954-55; various positions in sales, planning and station clearance ABC-TV network, N.Y.C., 1958-68, v.p. sales planning, 1967-70, v.p., assoc. dir. planning, bus. and fin. analysis, 1970-76, sr. v.p. fin. and planning, 1976-77, sr. v.p., 1977-85; v.p. Am. Broadcasting Cos. Inc., 1981-83, sr. v.p., 1983-85, exec. v.p. broadcast group, 1985-86; exec. v.p. ABC Network Div., 1986-88; v.p. Capital Cities/ABC, 1986-88; pres. distbn. and prodn. co. D.L. Taffner Ltd., N.Y.C., 1990-91; broadcasting cons., 1991—. Mem. exec. com. of alumni coun. U. Maine, 1980-86. Mem. adv. bd. Newhouse Sch., Syracuse U., 1985-88; mem. exec. com. of pres.'s coun. U. Maine, 1988, vice chmn. of pres.'s coun., 1992-93, chmn., 1993-95, vice chmn. Campaign for Maine, 1991-96. 1st lt. inf. U.S. Army, 1954—57. Fellow Nat. Acad. Arts and Scis. (pres. internat. coun. 1984-85, exec. com. 1986-92); mem. Internat. Radio and TV Soc. (gov. 1980-81, v.p. 1983-85), Whipporwill Club. E-mail: mhc001@aol.com.

COHEN, MARK STEVEN, dentist; b. N.Y.C., Dec. 10, 1948; s. Lawrence and Yetta (Grossman) C.; m. Arlene Debbie Deutsch, Aug. 23, 1970 (div. May 1984); 1 child, Aaron Philip; m. Donna Lynn Poissonnier, Nov. 27, 1985. BS, CCNY, 1971; DDS, Columbia U., 1975, cert. in Pedodontics, 1976. Practice dentistry, Yonkers, N.Y., 1975-76, Bristol, Conn., 1976-79, Brookfield, Conn., 1977—. Dir. dental service N.Y. Inst. for the Edn. Blind, Bronx, 1976-78; assoc. attending dentist Danbury (Conn.) Hosp., 1976-82, Blythdale Children's Hosp., Valhalla, N.Y., 1986-87; assoc. clin. prof. dentistry Columbia U., N.Y.C., 1976—, mem. quality assurance com., 1982-85. Patentee in field. Active Dental Guidance Council for Cerebral Palsy, N.Y.C., 1976-81. Chemistry fellow NSF, Washington, 1969-71, research fellow NIH, 1971, United Cerebral Palsy, 1975-76. Mem. ADA, Conn. State Dental Assn., Greater Danbury Dental Soc., Am. Dental Vols. for Israel, OKU Dental Honor Soc. Democrat. Jewish. Avocations: travel, photography, biking, collecting antiques. Office: Mark S Cohen 940 Federal Rd Brookfield CT 06804-1144 E-mail: mscddspc@aol.com., mscddspc@mindspring.com.

COHEN, MARVIN A. writer; b. N.Y.C., Feb. 3, 1932; s. Phillip and Minnie Cohen; m. Mary Catherine Quinn-Cohen, Feb. 17, 1982; children: Lauren Bufi, Dina. BA, Bklyn. Coll., 1958; MA, Columbia U., 1963. Cert. ednl. and vocat. counselor N.Y. Bd. Edn. English tchr., counselor N.Y.C. Bd. Edn., 1959—87; instr. psychology Mercy Coll., Dobbs Ferry, NY, 1982—89, Elmira (N.Y.) Coll., 1995—99; writer, presenter sales workshops Broome C.C., Binghamton, NY, 1997—99. Author: Dodgers-Giants Rivalry: 1900-1957, 1999, An Innocent Murderer, Doc Farrell's Odyssey. Mem.: Rotary Internat. (bd. dirs. 1992—). Home: 416 Main St Vestal NY 13850-1536

COHEN, MARY ANN, judge; b. Albuquerque, July 16, 1943; d. Gus R. and Mary Carolyn (Avriette) C. BS, UCLA, 1964; JD, U. So. Calif., 1967. Bar: Calif. 1967. Ptnr. Abbott & Cohen, P.C. and predecessors, L.A., 1967-82; judge U.S. Tax Ct., Washington, 1982—, chief judge, 1996-2000. Mem. ABA (sect. taxation), Legion Lex. Republican. Office: US Tax Ct 400 2nd St NW Washington DC 20217-0002

COHEN, MELANIE ROVNER, lawyer; b. Chgo., Aug. 9, 1944; d. Millard Jack and Sheila (Fox) Rovner; m. Arthur Wieber Cohen, Feb. 17, 1968; children: Mitchell Jay, Jennifer Sue. AB, Brandeis U., 1965; JD, DePaul U., 1977. Bar: Ill. 1977, U.S. Dist. Ct. (no. dist.) Ill., U.S. Ct. Appeals (7th cir.). Law clk. to Justice F.J. Hertz U.S. Bankruptcy Ct., 1976-77; ptnr. Antonow & Fink, Chgo., 1977-89, Altheimer & Gray, Chgo., 1989—2003, Quarles & Brady, Chgo., 2003—. Mem. Supreme Ct. of Ill. Atty. Registration and Disciplinary Commn. Inquiry Bd., 1982-86, hearing bd., 1986-94; instr. secured and consumer transactions creditor-debtor law DePaul U., Chgo., 1980-90; bd. dirs. Bankruptcy Arbitration and Mediation Svcs., 1994-96; instr. real estate and bankruptcy law John Marshall Law Sch., Chgo., 1996-98. Contbr. articles to profl. jours. Panelist, spkr., bd. dirs., v.p. Brandeis U. Nat. Alumni Assn., 1981—; life mem. Brandeis Nat. Women's Com., 1975—, pres. Chgo. chpt., 1975-82; mem. Glencoe (Ill.) Caucus, 1977-80; chair lawyers com. Ravinia Festival, 1990-91, chmn. sustaining com., 1991, mem. annual fund, 1991—. Brandeis U. fellow. Fellow: Am. Coll. Bankruptcy; mem.: ABA (co-chair com. on enforcement of creditors' rights and bankruptcy), Internat. Women's Insolvency and Restructuring Confederation, Internat. Fedn. Insolvency Profls., Internat. Insolvency Inst., Turnaround Mgmt. Assn. (pres. Chgo./midwest chpt. 1990—92, internat. bd. dirs. 1990—, mem. mgmt. com. 1995—, pres. internat. bd. dirs. 1999—2000, chmn. internat. bd. dirs. 2000—01), Comml. Fin. Assn. Edn. Found. (bd. govs.), Ill. Trial Lawyers Assn., Comml. Law League, Chgo. Bar Assn. (chmn. bankruptcy reorgn. com. 1983—85), Ill. State Bar Assn. Home: 167 Park Ave Glencoe IL 60022-1351 Office: Quarles & Brady 500 W Madison Ave Ste 3700 Chicago IL 60661 E-mail: cohenm@altheimer.com.

COHEN, MELVIN IRWIN, retired communications systems and technology executive; b. N.Y.C., June 25, 1936; s. Alexander and Fannie (Becker) C.; m. Elaine Chesin; children: Daniel Marc, Martha Rachel. SB, MIT, 1957, SM, 1958; PhD, Rensselaer Poly. Inst., 1965. Engr. Pratt & Whitney Aircraft, East Hartford, Conn., 1958-61; mem. tech. staff, supr. Bell Telephone Labs., Murray Hill, N.J., 1964-72; asst. dir. Western Elec. Co., Princeton, N.J., 1972-79; dept. head AT&T Bell Labs., Murray Hill, 1979-82, dir. Whippany, N.J., 1982-87, Murray Hill, 1987, v.p. mfg. R&D Princeton, 1987-88, exec. dir., 1988-90, exec. dir. electronics and photonics div. Breinigsville, Pa., 1990-93, v.p. rsch. effectiveness Murray Hill, N.J., 1993-96, Bell Labs/Lucent Techs., Murray Hill, 1996-2000; ret., 2001. Mem. panel on assessment of Nat. Inst. Standards and Tech. Programs, NRC, 1990-96; trustee AT&T Found., 1993-96; mem. sci. policy bd. Rutgers U., Newark, 1993-96. Patentee in laser tech. Trustee Temple Sinai Summit, N.J., 1977-79, N.J. Prison Complex, Trenton, 1975-83; bd. advisors Rahway Lifers Program, 1979-83; mem. deptl. adv. bd. Rensselaer Poly. Inst., 1988-92, mem. exec. bd. Anderson Ctr. for Innovation in Undergrad. Edn., 1992-98. Named Key Exec., Rensselaer Poly. Inst., 1986-99, chmn. Key Exec. Program, 1994-95; recipient Clarence E. Davies medal for engring. achievement, 1993, Fellow award Rensselaer Poly. Inst. Alumni Assn., 1993. Fellow IEEE (3d Millennium medal), Optical Soc. Am.; mem. AAAS, IEEE Lasers and Electrooptics Soc. (pres. 1989, Disting. Svc. award 2000). Home: 188 High Tor Dr Watchung NJ 07069-5412 E-mail: micohennj@aol.com.

COHEN, MELVIN LEE, pediatrician, psychiatrist, educator; b. San Antonio, Mar. 18, 1950; s. Melvin David and Elizabeth Catherine (Brown) C. BA summa cum laude, Rice U., 1972; MD, U. Va., 1977. Diplomate Am. Bd. Pediat., Am. Bd. Psychiatry and Neurology, Am. Bd. Child and Adolescent Psychiatry. Chief Pediat. Clin., 97th Gen. Hosp., U.S. Army, Frankfurt, Germany, 1980—83; fellow in devel. pediat. William Beaumont Army Med. Ctr., El Paso, Tex., 1983—85; regional coord. Army exceptional family mem. program Brooke Army Med. Ctr., San Antonio, 1985—87; pvt. practice pediat. San Antonio, 1987—89; chief dept. pediat. Bowling Green Hosp., San Antonio, 1988—89; resident in gen. and child psychiatry U. Tex. Health Sci. Ctr., San Antonio, 1989-93; pvt. practice child and adolescent psychiatry, San Antonio, 1993—; med. dir. child and adolescent partial hospitalization Laurel Ridge Hosp., San Antonio, 1992-95; clin. assoc. prof. pediat. U. Tex. Health Sci. Ctr., San Antonio, 1991—2002, clin. asst. prof. psychiatry, 1991—. Mem. exec. com. Laurel Ridge Hosp., San Antonio, 1987-88, 93-94; councilor Bexar City Psychiat. Soc., 2000-01. Bd. dirs. Jewish Family Svc., 1993-99, sec. bd. dirs., 1996-98, v.p. bd. dirs., 1998-99, v.p. bd. dirs., 2000-02; mem. sci. adv. bd. Winston Sch., 1993—, chmn. sci. adv. bd., 1998-2002. Rotary Found. scholar Rice U., 1972; recipient Cert. of Appreciation, Pres. Azcona of Honduras, 1986. Fellow Am. Acad. Pediatrics; mem. Tex. Med. Asn., Tex. Med. Found., Bexar County Med. Soc., Bexar County Psychiatric Soc. (pres. elect, 2003), Rice U. Alumni Assn., Phi Beta Kappa. Jewish. Avocations: travel, foreign language. Office: Ste 110 14800 San Pedro Ave San Antonio TX 78232-3733

COHEN, MELVIN R. physician, educator; b. Chgo., May 24, 1911; s. Louis M. and Anna S. (Friedman) C.; m. Miriam, May 19, 1946; children: Nancy, Alan BS, U. Ill., 1931, MS in Pathology, 1933, MD, 1934. Diplomate: Am. Bd. Ob-Gyn. Practice medicine specializing in infertility, Chgo.; sr. attending physician Michael Reese Med. Ctr., Chgo., Northwestern Meml. Hosp., Chgo.; founder, dir. Fertility Inst. Ltd., Chgo.; prof. Northwestern U. Med. Sch., Chgo., prof. emeritus; guest vis. prof. first Martin Clyman postgrad. course in infertility Mount Sinai Hosp., N.Y.C., 1982. Author: Laparoscopy, Culdoscopy and Gynecography: Technique and Atlas, 1970; contbr. numerous chpts. in med. books and articles to med. jours. on infertility, endometriosis and Spinnbarkeit. Dir., producer: 8 teaching films on infertility; video films during surgery; ektochrome slides established world-wide technique. Pioneer use of Pergonal for stimulating ovulation. Served with MC, AUS, 1942-45. Co-recipient Gold Medal for Infertility exhibit AMA, 1951; recipient award for film on endometriosis 10th World Congress of Fertility and Sterility, Madrid, Spain, 1980, Lifetime Achievement award for contbns. to gynecologic endoscopy and women's health care Internat. Congress of Gynecologic Endoscopy, 1994; named honoree Internat. Soc. Gynecologic Endoscopy for pioneering work in laparoscopy, 1996, named Father of Modern American Laparoscopy, 1974. Fellow Chgo. Gynecol. Soc. (life); mem. AMA, Am. Fertility Soc., Am. Coll. Ob-Gyn., Am. Assn. Gynecol. Laparoscopists (Lifetime Achievement award Internat. Congress 1994), Internat. Fertility Assn., Internat. Family Planning Research Assn., Ill. State Med. Soc., Chgo. Gynecol. Soc., Kansas City Gynecol. Soc. (hon.), Los Angeles Gynecol. Soc., Inst. Medicine Chgo., Midwest Bio-Laser Inst., Indian Assn. Gynecol. Endoscopists (hon.), Soc. Reproductive Surgeons, Chgo. Assn. Reproductive Endocrinologists (pres. 1984-85), Sigma Xi, Alpha Omega Alpha. Address: 990 N Lake Shore Dr # 26C Chicago IL 60611-1366

COHEN, MERRILL, chemist; b. Boston, Feb. 5, 1926; s. Alfred and Goldie (Baitler) C.; m. Eleanor Barbara Goldstein, Sept. 10, 1950; children: Mark Allen, Steven, Linda Lee Cohen Ben-Ezra. BA, Boston U., 1948; MS, U. Chgo., 1949, PhD, 1951. Devel. chemist Gen. Electric, Schenectady, Lynn, N.Y., Mass, 1951-56; mgr. Gen. Electric Lab., Lynn, Mass., 1956-87; owner, mgr. Chemco Consulting, Marblehead, Mass., 1987—. Contbr. articles to profl. jours.; patentee in field. Sgt. U.S. Army, 1944-46, with Res. 1946-49. Mem. Am. Chem. Soc., Geothermal Resources Coun., Soc. Plastics Engrs., Soc. for Advancement of Materials and Process Engring. Avocations: gardening, fishing. Office: Chemco Consulting Inc 8 May St Marblehead MA 01945-1708

COHEN, MICHAEL, psychologist; b. Yonkers, N.Y., Mar. 14, 1950; s. Joseph and Mary (Harris) C.; m. Amy Beth Siskind, Nov. 1, 1987; 1 child, Laura Reneé. BA, SUNY, Binghamton, 1972; MA, PhD, CUNY, N.Y.C., 1992. Pvt. practice psychotherapist, N.Y.C., 1973-89; rsch. cons. N.Y.C. Bd. Edn., 1986-87; sr. rsch. analyst Kennan Rsch. and Cons., N.Y.C., 1987-90; dir. qualitive rsch. KRC Rsch. and Cons., N.Y.C., 1990-91, pres., 1992-95; prin., founding ptnr. Applied Rsch. & Cons. LLC, N.Y.C., 1995—. Adv. bd. Handprints Prodns., N.Y.C., 1990—. Editor: The Einstein Connection, 1979. Avocation: poetry. Office: 149 Wooster St 3d Fl New York NY 10012

COHEN, MICHAEL E. physician; b. Buffalo, May 7, 1937; s. Herman Lawrence and Mamie (Woldman) Cohen Magil; m. Joan Ruth Neuman, June 21, 1959; children: Sharie, Pamela, Nancy. Student, Dartmouth Coll., 1954-57; MD, SUNY, Buffalo, 1961. Diplomate in neurology and in child neurology Am. Bd. Psychiatry and Neurology; diplomate Nat. Bd. Med. Examiners. Intern Univ. Hosps., Cleve., 1961-62, resident in internal medicine, 1962-63, resident in neurology, 1963-65; fellow, child neurology Children's Hosp. Boston, 1965-66; clin. fellow, child neurology Harvard Med. Sch., 1966; acting dir. pediatric neurology Children's Hosp. of Buffalo, 1968-78, dir. pediatric neurology, 1978—; from clin. asst. prof. neurology to prof. neurology SUNY, Buffalo, 1968—, from clin. asst. prof. to prof. pediatrics, 1968-83, chmn. dept. neurology, 1985-2000, chair faculty senate, 2001—03; clin. dir. neurology Kalidea Health Systems, Buffalo, 1999—. Vis. prof. and speaker in field. Contbr. articles to profl. jours. Capt. U.S. Army, 1966-68. Fellow Am. Acad. Neurology (pres. child neurology sect. 1999-2001); mem. AMA, Am. Neurologic Assn., Am. Acad. Cerebral Palsy, Am. Epilepsy Assn., Assn. Univ. Profs. Neurology, Child Neurology Soc. (pres. 1995-97), Profs. Child Neurology (pres. 1992-94), Buffalo Pediatric Soc., Internat. Soc. Pediatric Neurology, Pediatric Oncology Group, Am. Acad. Pediatrics, Alpha Omega Alpha. Avocations: swimming, tennis, golf, travel. Office: Children's Hosp Buffalo 219 Bryant St Buffalo NY 14222-2006

COHEN, MICHAEL PAUL, statistician; b. San Mateo, Calif., July 8, 1947; s. Herman Charles and Evadna Fern (Tull) C. BA, U. Calif. San Diego, La Jolla, 1969; MA, UCLA, 1971, PhD, 1978. Math. statistician Bur. Labor Stats., Washington, 1978-87; math. statistician, cons. Nat. Ctr. Edn. Stats., Washington, 1987-2000, Bur. Transp. Stats., Washington, 2000—, asst. dir. for survey programs, 2002—. Reviewer Inst. for Statis. Math., Tokyo, 1988-92, Jour. Bus. and Econ. Stats., Washington, 1988, Annals of Stats., Hayward, Calif., 1991, Survey Methodology, 1998-2003 Jour. Ofcl. Stats., 1998-2003; tech. adv. bd. Nat. Ctr. Edn. Stats., Washington, 1987-2000; invited spkr. Internat. Stats. Inst., Seoul, Republic of Korea, 2001. Contbr. articles to profl. jours. Recipient cash awards U.S. Dept. Edn., 1987, 89, 90, 92, 93, 97, 98, 99, Quality Step Increases, U.S. Dept. Edn., 1988, 91, 94, 96. Fellow Washington Acad. Scis. (bd. mgrs. 1996—, sec. 1997-2000, pres.-elect 2002-03, pres. 2003—); mem. Inst. Math. Stats., Am. Statis. Assn., Am. Math. Soc., Am. Assn. Pub. Opinion Rsch. (assoc. treas. D.C. chpt. 2003—), Soc. Indsl. and Applied Math., Washington Statis. Soc. (bd. dirs. 1990—, Pres. award 1999), Calif. State Soc., Capital PC Users Group, Philos. Soc. of Washington (bd. dirs. 1999—), Washington Acad. Scis. (bd. mgrs. 1996—), Am. Assn. Pub. Opinion Rsch. (assoc. treas. D.C. chpt. 2003). Achievements include significant statistical contributions to index aggregation and expenditure weights, consumer price index revision; proof of admissibility of empirical distribution function. Office: Bur Transp Stats 400 7th St SW # 4432 Washington DC 20590-0001 E-mail: mcohen@cpcug.org.

COHEN, MICHAEL VICTOR, cardiologist; b. N.Y.C., June 25, 1944; s. Jules and Florence Sue (Barengos) C.; m. Madelyn Sue Korman, Dec. 9, 1967; children: Ari Rishon, Andrew Joshua. AB, Harvard Coll., 1964; MD, Harvard U., 1968. Diplomate Am. Bd. Internal Medicine, Cardiovascular Disease Subspecialty Bd. Intern, resident Boston City Hosp., 1968-70; fellow cardiology Peter Bent Brigham Hosp., Boston, 1970-73; instr. Harvard Med. Sch., Boston, 1973; asst. prof., prof., attending physician Albert Einstein Coll., Montefiore Med. Ctr., Bronx, N.Y., 1974-91; disting. prof., attending physician U. South Ala. Sch. Medicine, U. South Ala. Med. Ctr., Mobile, 1991—. Author: Correlative Atlas of Adult Cardiac Disorders: Non-Invasive Diagnostic Techniques, 1980, Coronary Collaterals: Clinical and Experimental Observations, 1985; contbr. numerous articles to profl. jours. Col. USAR. Grantee NIH, 1978—, fellow 1986-87, Devel. award, 1977-82. Fellow Am. Soc. Clin. Investigation, Am. Coll. Cardiology; mem. Am. Fedn. Med. Rsch., Am. Heart Assn. Achievements include research on the importance of coronary collaterals to myocardial function and mechanism of ischemic preconditioning. Home: 6404 Tokeneak Trl Mobile AL 36695-2940 Office: Dept Physiology U South Ala Coll Medicine Mobile AL 36688-0001 E-mail: mcohen@usouthal.edu.

COHEN, MILDRED THALER, art gallery director; b. NYC, Oct. 30, 1921; d. William and Dora (Snow) Intner; m. Seymour R. Thaler, June 17, 1945 (dec. 1976); children: Frederic I., Joan Thaler Zimmer; m. Sidney Cohen, Mar. 20, 1982. BA, Hunter Coll., 1942; BLS, Pratt Inst., 1943. Libr. Queens Borough Pub. Libr., NYC, 1943-44, Mus. of French Art, French Inst., NYC, 1944-46; dir. Marbella Gallery, Inc., NYC, 1971—. Author: (catalogues) Women Students of William Merritt Chase, 1973, Robert Hallowell, 1983, Eliot Clark, 1990, Tonalism, America's Gift to Landscape Painting, 1993, (brochures) Ethel Paxson, 1976, Three Generations of Wiggins, 1981, Samuel Rothbart, 1989, Rachel V. Hartley, 1991, Frank Kleinholz, 1992, Anthony Springer, 1996, Joseph Margulies, 1997, Allen Blagden, 1998, Hildegarde Hamilton, 1999, Samuel Brecher, 1999, 2003, James Bowman Consor, 2000. Bd. dirs. Lenox Hill Settlement House, NYC, 1955—77. Mem. Appraisers Assn. Am., Hunter Coll. Alumni (pres. Queens chpt. 1951-54, past bd. dir., pres. scholarship and welfare fund 1958-60, mem. coll. art adv. com., named to Hall of Fame 1973). Democrat. Jewish. Home and Office: 28 E 72nd St New York NY 10021-4234 E-mail: marbella_gallery@aol.com.

COHEN, MILLARD STUART, diversified manufacturing company executive; b. Chgo., Jan. 17, 1939; s. Lawrence Irmas and Myra Paula (Littmann) C.; m. Judith E. Michel, Aug. 2, 1970 (dec. Dec. 1995); children: Amy Rose, Michele Lauren. BSEE, Purdue U., 1960. Design engr. GTE Automatic Electric Labs., Northlake, Ill., 1960-66; chief elec. engr. Nixdorff Krein Industries, St. Louis, 1966-68, dir. data processing, 1968-72, treas., 1970—, v.p., 1980-85, pres., 1985—, exec. v.p. Nixdorff Chain, 1972-76, pres. Grape Expectations, 1976, also bd. dirs. Mem. Mo. Wine Adv. Bd., 1980—, vice chmn., 1983, 93; mem. St. Louis County Restaurant Commn., 1979—, Augusta (Mo.) Wine Bd., 1981—. Dist. commr. Boy Scouts Am., 1968-72; judge Mo. State Fair; trustee Congl. Temple Israel. Recipient award of merit French Wine Commn., 1972. Mem. IEEE, Assn. for Computing Machinery, Internat. Wine and Food Soc. (gov. Ams. 1985—), Mensa, Les Amis du Vin, Chaine des Rotisseurs, Commanderie de Bordeaux, St. Louis Club. Home: 11233 Ladue Rd Saint Louis MO 63141-8318 Office: 555 N New Ballas Rd Ste 230 Saint Louis MO 63141-6886 E-mail: millardcohen@cs.com.

COHEN, MORREL HERMAN, physicist, biologist, educator; b. Boston, Sept. 10, 1927; s. David and Rose (Kemler) C.; m. Sylvia Zwein, June 18, 1950; children: Julie, Robert, Daniel, Lisa. BS in Physics, Worcester Poly. Inst., 1947, DSc (hon.), 1973; MA in Physics, Dartmouth Coll., 1948; PhD in Physics, U. Calif., Berkeley, 1952. Faculty U. Chgo., 1952-57, assoc. prof. physics, 1957-60, prof., 1960-72, prof. theoretical biology, 1968-72, Louis Block prof. physics and theoretical biology, 1972-81, com. developmental biology, 1973-74, publs. bd., 1969-70; acting dir. James Franck Inst., 1965-66, dir., 1968-71; dir. materials rsch. lab. NSF, 1977-81; sr. sci. advisor Corp. Rsch. Lab. Exxon Rsch. and Engring. Co., 1981-96. Cons. govt. and industry, 1953-81, 96—; vis. scientist NRC, Can., 1960, Xerox Corp., 1975, 78; disting. vis. scientist Rutgers U., 1998-99, dist. scientist 1999—; disting. scientist Princeton U., 2003—; vis. fellow Clare Hall U., Cambridge, 1972-73; Shrum lectr. Simon Fraser U., 1973; assoc. Clare Hall U. Cambridge, Eng., 1973-85; vis. prof. U. Va., 1976, Kyoto U., 1979; mem. adv. panel electrophysics NASA, 1962-66; mem. adv. com. Nat. Magnet Lab., 1963-66; mem. rev. com. solid state sci. and metallurgy div. Argonne Nat. Lab., 1964-67, chmn., 1966, bd. govs., 1982-89, sci. & tech. adv. com., 1983-91; chmn. Gordon Conf., 1968, 4th Internat. Conf. Armorphous and Liquid Semicondrs., 1971; mem. adv. com. Inst. Amorphous Studies, 1982—; mem. Army Basic Research Com., 1979-85, mem. steering com., 1980-85; adv. com. dept. physics U. Tex., Austin, 1982-91; chmn. vis. com. dept. Physics Colo. Sch. of Mines, 1987-94; vice chmn. IUPAP commn. on stats. mechanics, 1987-93; van der Waals prof. U. Amsterdam, 1991-92. Contbr. articles on physics of solids, liquids, gases, theoretical and developmental biology, geophysics, materials sci., chem. physics, and chem. engring.; assoc. editor Jour. Chem. Physics, 1960-63; mem. editorial bd. advanced physics monograph series McGraw-Hill Co., 1963-70; mem. editorial bd. The Physics of Condensed Matter, 1962-74, Advances in Chem. Physics, 1960-93; mem. publs. bd. U. Chgo., 1969-70; bd. editors Jour. Statis. Physics, 1970-75. AEC fellow, 1951-52, Guggenheim fellow, 1957-58, NSF sr. postdoctoral fellow Rome, 1964-65, Spl. fellow NIH, 1972-73. Fellow AAAS, Am. Phys. Soc. (divsn. coun. 1978-82, exec. com. solid state physics divsn. 1968-71, chmn. 1970, mem. panel on pub. affairs, 2002—); mem. AAUP, Am. Inst. Physics, Nat. Acad. Scis., N.Y. Acad. Scis. (class mem. com. 2003—), Sigma Xi (nat. lectr. 1966). Home: 1100 Crim Rd Bridgewater NJ 08807-1872 Office: Dept Physics and Astronomy Rutgers The State Univ NJ 136 Frelinghuysen Rd Piscataway NJ 08854-8019 E-mail: mhcohen@prodigy.net.

COHEN, MORRIS, engineering educator; b. Chelsea, Mass., Nov. 27, 1911; s. Julius Harry and Alice (Ovson) Cohen; m. Ruth Krentzman, Jan. 24, 1937 (dec.); children: Barbara Cohen Nordwind(dec.), Joel Alan. SB, MIT, 1933, ScD, 1936; DTekn (hon.), Royal Inst. Tech., Stockholm, 1977; DTech (hon.), Israel Inst. Tech., 1979; DEngring. (hon.), Colo. Sch. Mines, 1985; DSc (hon.), Northeastern U., Boston, 1989. Asst. prof. MIT, 1937-42, assoc. prof., 1942-46, prof., 1946-62, Ford prof. materials sci. and engring., 1962-74, Inst. prof., 1974-82, inst. prof. emeritus, 1982—. Hon. prof. Beijing U. Sci. and Tech., 1980—, Beijing U. Aeros. and Astronautics, 1980—. Recipient Mathewson Gold medal, AIME, 1953, Inst. Metals award, 1952, Robert F. Mehl award, 1953, Clamer medal, Franklin Inst., 1959, Gold medal, Japan Inst. Metals, 1970, Chevenard medal, French Metall. Soc., 1971, Killian Faculty Achievement award, MIT, 1974, Procter prize, Rsch. Soc. N.Am., 1976, Nat. Medal of Sci., 1977, Joseph R. Vilella award, ASTM, 1979, Gold medal, Acta Metallurgica, 1981, Hobart M. Kraner award, Am. Ceramic Soc., 1981, New Eng. award, Engring. Socs. of New Eng., 1987, Kyoto prize, 1987, Nat. Materials Achievement award, Fedn. Materials Socs., 1988, David Turnbull Lectr. award, Materials Rsch. Soc., 1993, J. Herbert Hollomon award, Acta Metallurgica, 1995. Fellow: Indian Nat. Sci. Acad., N.Y. Acad. Scis., Am. Acad. Arts and Scis., Metall. Soc. of AIME (Leadership award 1987), Am. Soc. Metals (hon.; past pres., trustee, Howe medal, 1945 1949, Gold medal 1968, Sauveur Achievement award 1977, Albert Easton White Disting. Tchr. award 1987, Charles S. Barrett award 1988); mem.: Inst. Metals London, Indian Inst. Metals (hon. Kamani Gold medal 1953), AIME (hon.), Korean Inst. Metals (hon.), Japan Inst. Metals, Iron and Steel Inst. Japan, Nat. Acad. Engring., Nat. Acad. Scis. Achievements include research in materials sci. and engring., materials policy, phys. metallurgy, phase transformations, strenthening mechanisms, mechanical behavior of alloy systems, materials policy. Home: 491 Puritan Rd Swampscott MA 01907-2819 Office: MIT 77 Massachusetts Ave Bldg 13 Cambridge MA 02139-4307

COHEN, MORRIS LEO, retired law librarian and educator; b. N.Y.C., Nov. 2, 1927; s. Emanuel and Anna (Frank) C.; m. Gloria Weitzner, Feb. 1, 1953; children— Havi, Daniel Asher. BA, U. Chgo., 1947; LLB, Columbia U., 1951; MLS, Pratt Inst., 1959. Bar: N.Y. bar 1951. Pvt. practice, N.Y.C., 1951-58; asst. law librarian Rutgers U. Law Sch., 1958-59, Columbia Law Sch., 1959-61; law librarian, assoc. prof. law State U. N.Y. at, Buffalo, 1961-63; Biddle law librarian, prof. law U. Pa. Law Sch., Phila., 1963-71; law librarian, prof. law Harvard U. Law Sch., 1971-81, Yale U. Law Sch., New Haven, 1981-91; prof. emeritus, 1991—. Lectr. Drexel Inst. Sch. Libr. Sci., 1964-70, Columbia Sch. Libr. Svc., 1965-70; vis. prof. Simmons Coll. Libr. Sch., 1977-80; mem. exec. bd. Phila. chpt. ACLU; bd. visitors Columbia U. Law Sch., 1977-95. Author: Legal Research in a Nutshell, 1968, 8th edit., 2003, How to Find the Law, 9th edit., 1989, Law and Science: A Selected Bibliography, 1980, Finding the Law, 2d edit., 1989, Law: The Art of Justice, 1992, A Guide to the Early Reports of the Supreme Court of the United States, 1995, The Bench and Bar: Great Legal Caricatures from Vanity Fair, 1997, Bibliography of Early American Law, 1998. Mem. Am. Antiquarian Soc. NEH grantee. Mem. ABA, ALA (chmn. law and polit. sci. sect. 1967-69), AAUP (pres. U. Pa. chpt. 1966-67), Am. Assn. Law Librs. (pres. 1970-71), Am. Soc. Legal History (hon. fellow), Jewish Publs. Soc. (v.p. 1975-80), Bibliog. Soc. Am., Internat. Assn. Law Librs., Grolier Club, Yale Club of N.Y.C. Jewish. Office: Yale U Sch Law PO Box 208215 New Haven CT 06520-8215 E-mail: morris.cohen@yale.edu.

COHEN, MORTON NORTON, English educator, writer; b. Calgary, Alberta, Can., Feb. 27, 1921; came to U.S., 1934; s. Samuel Cohen and Zelda Jenny Miller. AB, Tufts U., 1949; MA, Columbia U., 1950, PhD, 1958. Instr. English W.Va. U., 1950-51; lectr. English Rutgers U., N.J., 1952-53; vis. prof. Syracuse U., N.Y., 1965-66, 67-68; prof. CUNY, 1971-82, prof. emeritus, 1982—. Mem. faculty advisory coun. CUNY Rsch. Found., 1976-80; lectr. in field. Author: Lewis Carroll, Photographer of Children: Four Nude Studies, 1979, Lewis Carroll's Photographs of Nude Children, 1978, Lewis Carroll and Alice 1832-1982, 1982, Lewis Carroll: A Biography, 1995, 2d edit., 1996, Reflections in a Looking Glass, 1998; co-author: A Brief Guide to Better Writing, 1960, Rider Haggard: His Life and Works, 1960, 61, 2nd rev. edit., 1968, Essays in an Exhibition from the Jon A. Lindseth Collection of C. L. Dodgson and Lewis Carroll, 1998, The World of Interiors, 1998, numerous others; editor: Rudyard Kipling to Rider Haggard: The Record of a Friendship, 1965, 68, The Russian Jour.-II, 1979, Lewis Carroll and the Kitchins, 1980, The Selected Letters of Lewis Carroll, 1982, 2nd edit., 1990, 3rd edit., 1996, Lewis Carroll: Interviews and Recollections, 1989; editor: The Letters of Lewis Carroll, 1979; co-editor Lewis Carroll and the House of Macmillan, 1987, Lewis Carroll and His Illustrators, 2003; contbr. articles to profl. jours.; book reviewer; appeared in TV and radio programs, U.K., U.S.A.; guest curator Pierpont Morgan Libr., N.Y.C., 1982; reader, cons. maj. univ. and comml. presses; contbr. Cambridge Bibliography of English Literature, 3rd edit.; author children's books under pseudonym. Sgt. U.S. Army, 1943-45. Faculty fellow Ford Found., 1951-52; Fulbright fellow at U. Leeds, 1954-55; grantee Am. Philos. Soc., summers 1962, 64; grant-in-aid Am. Coun. Learned Socs., summer 1963; Guggenheim fellow, 1966-67; Sr. fellow NEH, 1970-71, 78-79; Fulbright Sr. Rsch. fellow at Christ Church, Oxford, Eng., 1974-75; Rsch. grantee NEH, 1974-75; Guggenheim Found. Publ. grantee, 1979. Fellow Royal Soc. Lit.; mem. Lewis Carroll Soc. N.Am., Lewis Carroll Soc. Japan, Lewis Carroll Soc., Am. Trust Brit. Libr. (mem. adv. coun. 1980), Century Assn. Democrat. Jewish. Avocations: travel, theater, antiques, watercolors. Home: 55 E 9th St Apt 10D New York NY 10003-6325 also: Condo Miramar Plz Apt 21-E 954 Ponce de León Ave San Juan PR 00907 also: 28 Pembridge Villas London W11 3EL England

COHEN, N. JEROLD, lawyer; b. Pine Bluff, Ark., June 13, 1935; s. Maurice and Gertrude L. Cohen; children: Pamela, Lindsey L., Giles T. BBA, Tulane U., 1957; LLB magna cum laude, Harvard U., 1961. Bar: N.Y. 1962, Ga. 1966, D.C. 1966. Assoc. Cleary, Gottlieb, Steen and Hamilton, N.Y.C., 1961-65, Sutherland, Asbill, and Brennan, Atlanta, Washington, 1965, ptnr., 1968-79, 81—; chief counsel IRS, 1979-81, adv. coun., 1999-2000, chmn. Former pres., former mem. nat. bd. dirs. ACLU Ga.; chmn. Atlanta Cmty. Rels. Commn., 1976-79. 1st lt. U.S. Army, 1958. Recipient Gen. Counsel's award U.S. Dept. Treasury, Commrs. award IRS. Fellow Am. Bar Found.; mem. ABA (past chair tax sect.), FBA, Am. Law Inst., Am. Coll. Tax Counsel (regent, chair). Office: Sutherland Asbill & Brennan 999 Peachtree St NE Ste 2300 Atlanta GA 30309-3996 E-mail: njcohen@sablaw.com.

COHEN, NANCY MAHONEY, lawyer; b. Boston, July 14, 1941; d. Gerald Murray and Margaret (Callahan) Mahoney; m. William Cohen, Aug. 8, 1976; 1 child, Margaret Emily. AB, Emmanuel Coll., 1963; JD, Stanford U., 1975. Bar: Calif. 1975. Asst. gen. counsel Bendix Forest Products Corp., San Francisco, 1976-81; assoc. Brown & Bain, Phoenix, 1981; counsel Syntex Corp., Palo Alto, Calif., 1982-86, sr. counsel, 1986-88, assoc. dir. comml. law, 1988-95; gen. counsel Dendreon Corp., Palo Alto, 1995-97; sr. v.p. and gen. counsel Roche Palo Alto LLC, Palo Alto, 1997—. Bd. dirs. Syntex Fed. Credit Union, Palo Alto. Chmn. Rental Housing Mediation Task Force, Palo Alto, 1972-74; mem. All Saints Vestry, Palo Alto, 1985-88, 93-95, 97-99, 2003. Mem. ABA, Calif. Bar Assn., Am. Corp. Counsel Assn. Office: Roche 3431 Hillview Ave Palo Alto CA 94304-1347 E-mail: Nancy.Cohen@Roche.com.

COHEN, NEIL M. state legislator; Grad., Howard U. Sch. Law. Freeholder County of Union, N.J.; state assemblyman dist. 21 N.J., 1989-92; state assemblyman dist. 20, 1994—. Ptnr. Gill & Cohen, P.C., Montclair, N.J.; atty. Hillside Bd. of Edn.; spl. counsel Hillside's Charter Study Commn., 1990—; former chmn. intergovtl. coop and legis. affairs coms., fiscal affairs com. N.J. State Assembly. Office: 315 Elmora Ave Ste 208 Elizabeth NJ 07208-1383*

COHEN, NELSON CRAIG, lawyer; b. Harrisburg, Pa., Nov. 8, 1947; s. Raymond and Rhea (Jaschik) C. BS in Acctg., Pa. State U., 1969; JD, George Washington U., 1973. Bar: Md. 1973, D.C. 1974. Assoc., ptnr. Levitan Ezrin West & Kerxton, Bethesda, Md., 1973-84; ptnr. Kerxton & Cohen Chartered, Bethesda, 1984-87, Zuckerman & Spaeder LLP, Washington, 1987—. Speaker on bankruptcy matters. Mem. ABA (bus. banking sec.), Bankruptcy Bar Assn. Md., Montgomery County Bar Assn., Md. State Bar Assn. Republican. Jewish. Avocation: golf. Office: Zuckerman Spaeder LLP 1201 Connecticut Ave NW Washington DC 20036-2605

COHEN, NICHOLAS, immunologist, educator; b. N.Y.C., Nov. 20, 1938; s. Saris and Frances (Pakett) C.; m. Jayne Sevin Rogal, July 1, 1962 (div. 1972); children: Jaime Anne, Jessica Sevin; m. Catharina Johanna van der Harst, Oct. 23, 1974; children: Misha Thomas, Mark Sebastian. AB, Princeton U., 1959; PhD, U. Rochester, 1965. Asst. prof. microbiology and immunology Sch. Medicine and Dentistry U. Rochester, N.Y., 1967-73, assoc. prof., 1973-80, prof. microbiology, immunology and psychiatry, 1980—, prof. oncology, 1997—, dir. divsn. immunology, 1980—; assoc. dir. Ctr. for Psychoneuroimmunology Rsch., Rochester. Vis. prof. Agrl. U., Wageningen, The Netherlands, 1982-83; mem. Basel Inst. for Immunology, Switzerland, 1975-76; mem. peer rev. bds. NIH, 1976-80; cons. NIH study sects., NIMH study sects., NSF. Co-author: Monograph; assoc. editor Brain, Behavior and Immunity Jour., Devel. Comparative Immunology; editor 5 books; contbr. articles to profl. jours. Postdoctoral scholar in immunology UCLA, 1965-67, Fulbright scholar, 1982-83; grantee NIH, NIMH, NSF, 1967—; recipient Rsch. Career Devel. award NIH, 1974-78, NIH Merit award, 1987-97. Mem. Am. Soc. Zoologists (chmn. divsn. comparative immunology 1977-79), Transplantation Soc., Am. Soc. Immunologists, Brit. Soc. Immunology, Internat. Soc. Devel. and Comparative Immunology (v.p. the Americas 1994-2000), Psychoneuroimmunology Rsch. Soc. (councilor 1993-97). Democrat. Avocations: music, travel. Home: 211 Highland Pkwy Rochester NY 14620-2544

COHEN, NICKI SANDRA, music educator, music therapist; b. Easton, Pa., Mar. 16, 1955; d. Merton Emil and Claire Sybil (Reichlin) C.; m. Bruce Cline Bond, June 16, 1984. BS in Mus. Edn., Duquesne U., 1977; MA in Voice, U. Denver, 1983; PhD in Music Edn., U. Kans., 1991. Bd. cert. music therapist. Clin. music therapist Colo. State Home, Wheat Ridge, 1980-81; pvt. practice Roundup, Bethpage, Ctr. Pines, Susqueview, Denver and Lock Haven, Pa., 1981-91, Cmty. MT Svcs., Waterloo, Ont., Can., 1991-92; instr. Lock Haven U., 1991; asst. prof. Wilfrid Laurier U., Waterloo, 1991-92; pvt. practice in guided imagry and music therapy Denton, Tex., 1992—; from asst. to assoc. prof. Tex. Woman's U., Denton, 1992—. Music therapy cons., Denton, 1992—. Co-author (chpt.): Case Studies in Music Therapy, 1991, Ethical Considerations for Therapists; contbr. articles to profl. jours. Mus. dir. Denton Cmty. Chorus, 1994—98, Congregation Kol Ami, 2000—; vol. AIDS Denton, 1996—97, Ann's Haven Hospice, Denton, 1998—99. Rsch. grantee Tex. Woman's U., 1992, 93, 95, 97, 99, 2000, 02, Wilfried Laurier U., 1991; student fellow/assistantships U. Denver and U. Kans., 1981-83, 87-90. Fellow: Assn. Music and Imagery (pres.-elect); mem.: Coll. Music Soc., Nat. Assn. Tchrs. Singing, Am. Music Therapy Assn. (coun. coord. for edn. and clin. tng., chair adv. bd. for edn. and tng., mem. exec. bd.), Sigma Alpha Iota (patroness), Phi Delta Kappa, Pi Kappa Lambda. Democrat. Jewish. Avocations: hiking, gardening, reading, book groups. Office: Tex Woman's U PO Box 425768 Denton TX 76204-5768 E-mail: ncohen@twu.edu.

COHEN, NOEL LEE, otolaryngologist, educator; b. N.Y.C., Sept. 20, 1930; s. Victor Max and Esther Lily (Schonfeld) C.; m. Baukje Philippina Boersma, June 1, 1957; 1 child, Mark Bennett. AB, NYU, 1951; MD, U. Utrecht, The Netherlands, 1957, NYU, 1999, U. Freiburg, Germany, 2002. Intern Stads-en Academi Ziekenhuis, Utrecht, 1955-57; resident in otolargyngology Bellevue Med. Ctr. NYU, N.Y.C., 1959-62, instr. Sch. Medicine, 1962-64, asst. prof., 1964-69, assoc. prof., 1969-73, clin. prof., 1973-80, prof. otolargyngology, 1980—, chmn. dept. otolaryngology, 1981—2003, interim dean, provost Sch. Medicine, 1997-98, vice dean for clin. affairs, 1998-99, sr. advisor to dean, 2000—, Mendik Found. prof., 1999—2003, prof. otolaryngology, 2003—; pres. NYU Hosp. Ctr., 1998. Bd. dirs. League for Hard of Hearing, Am. Auditory Soc.; mem. rsch. adv. bd. EAR Found., Nashville, 1987—; mem. adv. bd. Self Help for Hard of Hearing People, 1995, Alexander Graham Bell Assn., Acoustic Neuroma Assn.; sci. adv. bd. Sci. Deafness Rsch. Found., 2000—. Mem. editl. bd. Jour. of Otology & Neurotology, 1986—, Otolaryngology-Head and Neck Surgery, Internat. Cochlear Implant Jour., 1999—; reviewer articles and books for profl. jours.; contbr. numerous articles to profl. jours.; author chpts. in books. Lt. USNR, 1957—59. Fellow: ACS; mem.: N.Y. Acad. Scis., N.Y. Otol. Soc. (pres. 1998—99), Soc. Acad. Depts. Otolaryngology, Soc. Univ. Otolaryngologists, Am. Neuro-Otol. Soc., N.Am. Skull Base Soc., N.Y. Head and Neck Soc. (charter mem., pres. 1984), N.Y. State Soc. Otolaryngology-Head and Neck Surgery (pres. 1988—89), N.Y. Acad. Medicine, Am. Otol. Soc., Am. Bronchoesophagol. Assn., Am. Soc. Head and Neck Surgery, Rhinol. and Otol. Soc., Am. Laryngol., Am. Acad. Otolaryngology-Head-Neck Surgery (Honor award 1985, Disting. Svc. award 2001). Democrat. Jewish. Avocations: tennis, skiing, gardening, carpentry. Office: NYU Med Ctr 530 1st Ave New York NY 10016-6402 E-mail: noel.cohen@med.nyu.edu.

COHEN, NORM, chemist; b. N.Y.C., Dec. 13, 1936; s. Moshe and Yetta (Pickman) C.; m. Anne Elizabeth Billings, July 11, 1959 (div. 1987); children: Alexandra Elizabeth Rachel, Carson Benjamin; m. Verni Greenfield, Feb. 6, 1987; 1 child, Matthew Jonathan Greenfield. BA in Chemistry, Reed Coll., 1958; MA in Math., U. Calif., Berkeley, 1960, PhD in Chemistry, 1963. Mem. tech. staff Aerospace Corp., El Segundo, Calif., 1963-72, head dept. chem. kinetics, 1972-84, sr. scientist, 1984-94; adj. asst. prof. chemistry U. Portland, 1995-99, Portland C.C., 1995—. Exec. sec. John Edwards Mem. Forum, L.A., 1969-94; adj. faculty Lewis & Clark Coll., 1999—. Author: Long Steel Rail, 1981, 2d edit., 2000 (Chgo. Folklore prize 1982, Deems Taylor award ASCAP 1982, Botkin prize Am. Folklore Soc. 1983), Traditional Anglo-American Folk Music: An Annotated Disography of Published Recordings, 1994, A Finding List of American Secular Songsters Published 1860-99, 2002; editor: Ozark Folk Songs, 1982, John Edwards Meml. Forum Quar., 1966-83, 85-86; asst. editor Internat. Jour. Chem. Kinetics, 1977-83, editor, prodr. album Minstrels and Tunesmiths, 1982 (Grammy nomination 1982); contbr. articles and revs. to chemistry and folk, music jours. Grantee NEA, NEH, DOE, EPA, NIST. Mem. Am. Chem. Soc., Am. Folklore Soc., Sigma Xi. Democrat. Jewish. Achievements include research and publications in combustion chemistry, atmospheric chemistry, thermochemistry, chemistry of high energy chemical lasers. Home: 3001 Grant St Vancouver WA 98660-2053 E-mail: ncohen@teleport.com.

COHEN, NORMAN GIRARD, retired social worker; b. Rochester, N.Y., Nov. 5, 1940; s. Abraham Joseph and Ethel (Weinstein) C.; m. Mary Catherine Serafine, Dec. 26, 1964; children: Jonathan, Adrian, Jordan. BS, Syracuse U., 1962; student, Babson Coll., 1958-60; MSW., U. Tenn., 1964; postgrad., U. Mich., 1962-63. Diplomate Am. Bd. of Clin. Social Workers. Supervising psychiat. social worker Beeman Clinic, Niagara Falls, N.Y., 1966-73; psychotherapist, assoc. H.W. Goldfarb, M.D., Niagara Falls, 1973-76; pres., clin. dir. Quantum Bionomics, Inc., Niagara Falls, 1977-80; project dir., systems analyst Williams Group of Cos., Kenmore, N.Y., 1980-81; project analyst Office Mental Health, Albany, N.Y., 1981-83; pvt. practice psychotherapy Albany, 1983-86; assoc. and acting exec. sec. N.Y. State Bds. Social Work, Chiropractic, Albany, 1986-91, exec. sec., 1991—2003; ret., 2003—. Part-time faculty SUNY-Albany; part-time columnist The Spotlight, Delmar, N.Y., 1982-86; part time faculty Niagara County Community Coll., Sanborn, N.Y., 1974-75; project cons. sch. systems, govt. agys., profl. agys. Bd. dirs. Golden Agers; v.p. bd. dirs. Metanoia Drug Program, 1972-73; coach Little League, 1976. NIMH fellow, 1962-63. Mem. Acad. Cert. Social Workers, Nat. Assn. Social Workers, Am. Fedn. Musicians, Biofeedback Soc. Am.

COHEN, NORTON JACOB, lawyer; b. Detroit, Nov. 5, 1935; s. Norman and Molly Rose (Natinsky) C.; m. Lorelei Freda Schuman, June 16, 1957 (dec. Jan. 1998); children: Debrah Anne, Sander Ivan. Student, U. Mich., 1953-55, U. Detroit, 1955-56; JD, Wayne State U., 1959. Bar: Mich. 1959, Tex. 1962, U.S. Dist. Ct. (ea. dist.) Mich. 1963, U.S. Ct. Appeals (6th cir.) 1966, U.S. Supreme Ct. 1970. Law clk. to presiding justice Mich. Supreme Ct., Lansing, 1959; assoc. Zwerdling, Miller, Klimist & Maurer, Detroit, 1963—68; legal dir. ACLU of Mich., Detroit, 1968—69; sr. dir. Miller, Cohen, Martens, Ice & Geary, P.C., Southfield, Mich., 1971—97, Miller Cohen, P.L.C., Detroit, 1997—. Chmn. Southfield (Mich.) Dem. Party, 1965-67; co-chair Robert F. Kennedy for Pres., Oakland County, Mich., 1968; mem. exec. bd. Met. Detroit ACLU, 1969-93, chmn., 1972-74; vice chair Equal Justice Coun., Detroit, 1970-74; spl. counsel workers compensation Mich. AFL-CIO, 1983-86; mem. dir.'s adv. coun. Workers Compensation Bur., Mich. Dept. Labor, 1986-1999. Served to capt. U.S. Army, 1960-63. Recipient Spirit of Detroit award Detroit Common Coun., 1982; elected to Mich. Workers' Compensation Hall of Fame, 2000. Mem. ABA (labor co-chair workers compensation com. sect. labor and employment law 1989-96), Fed. Bar Assn., B'nai B'rith, Am. Jewish Com. Jewish. Office: Miller Cohen PLC 600 W Lafayette Blvd Fl 4 Detroit MI 48226-3125

COHEN, PETER GRAY, artist; b. NYC, Nov. 12, 1925; s. Lester and Eden Gray Cohen; m. Robin Phyllis Goodman, Sept. 15, 1981 (dec. July 4, 1994); children: Daniel H., Joshua A.stepchildren: Alexis Zohner-Nassi, Sarah Johnston Johns. Student, U. Chgo., 1942—43, Escuela Pintura y Escultura, Mexico City, 1950—51, The Art Students League, N.Y.C., 1946—48. Founder, ptnr. The Art Sch. in the Poconos, 1971—76. Exhibitions include Eggleston Galleries, NYC, 1948, Mural Commissions, Approximately a dozen murals for arch. and designers executed in alkyd, acrylic, colored cement and guaging plaster, 1951—76, exhibitions include Crown Galleries, NYC, 1957, Arch. League, 1956, 1st Ref. Ch., Somerville, NJ, 1965, Everhart Mus., Scranton, PA, 1966, Mountain Gallery, East Stroudsburg, PA, 1974, Earth & Fire Galleries, Allentown, PA, 1977, cover, Sci. mag., 1989, exhibitions include Am. Assoc. for the Advancement of Sci., Washington, DC, 1989, Open Space Gallery, Allentown, PA, 1990, cover, Lawrence-Berkeley Labs. Ann. Report, 1991. Ind. Peace cand. for U.S. Congress 15th congl. dist. Pa., 1968; exec. dir. New Dem. Coalition of Pa., 1969—70, founder and chair Lehigh-Pocono com., 1965—68. With Signal Corps U.S. Army, 1944—46. Recipient award, Nat. Cmty. Arts Competition, HUD, 1973; grantee, Pa. Coun. on the Arts, 1990. Mem.: Nat. Soc. Mural Painters. Home: 1116 N Milpas St Santa Barbara CA 93103

COHEN, PHILIP, retired hydrogeologist; b. N.Y.C., Dec. 13, 1931; s. Isadore and Anna (Katz) C.; m. Barbara Sandler, Dec. 26, 1954; 1 son, Jeffery. BS cum laude, CCNY, 1954; MS, U. Rochester, 1956. Cert. profl. geologist, Va. With U.S. Geol. Survey, 1956-94, chief Long Island program, 1968-72, assoc. chief land info. and analysis office, 1975-78, asst. chief hydrologist water resources div., 1978-79, chief hydrologist water resources div., 1979-94; ret., 1994. Contbr. numerous articles on geology and hydrology to profl. jours. Recipient Ward medal Coll. City, N.Y., 1954; Meritorious Ser. award Dept. Interior, 1975, Disting. Ser. award, 1979, Presdl. Meritorious Exec. Rank award, 1986, Presdl. Disting. Exec. Rank award, 1988. Fellow Geol. Soc. Am.; mem. Am. Inst. Hydrology (C.V. Theis award 1993), Sigma Xi. E-mail: kenaik1@aol.com.

COHEN, PHILIP GARY, English language educator, dean, academic administrator; b. Easton, Pa., July 18, 1954; s. Jacob and Gloria (Mardar) C. BA in English, Am. U., 1976; MA in English, U. So. Calif., 1978; PhD in English, U. Del., 1984. Asst. prof. English Columbia (S.C.) Coll., 1984-85, Marist Coll., Poughkeepsie, N.Y., 1985-86; asst. to full prof. English U. Tex., Arlington, 1986—, dean, vice provost for acad. affairs. Editor: Devils and Angels: Editing and Literary Theory, 1991, Texts and Textuality, 1997; contbr. numerous articles to profl. jours. Mem. MLA, CGS, Soc. Textual Studies, Faulkner Soc., Soc. Study of So. Lit. Office: U Tex at Arlington Grad Sch Box 19167 Arlington TX 76019

COHEN, PHILIP HERMAN, accountant; b. Bklyn., Dec. 4, 1936; s. David J. and Toby (Jaeger) C.; m. Susan Rudd; children: Davina Ellen, Tobias Samuel Dory. BS, NYU, 1957. From acct. to ptnr. Touche Ross & Co., N.Y.C., 1957-81; exec. v.p. fin., CFO Integrated Resources, Inc., N.Y.C., 1981-86, sr. exec. v.p. fin., CFO, 1986-90; fin. and real estate cons. Philip H. Cohen & Co., Cedarhurst, N.Y., 1990—. Chmn. bd. dirs., pres., CEO FRMT Ltd. (A Bermuda Mut. Ins. Co.), 1996—99; bd. dirs. FMRT Ltd. (A Bermuda Mut. Ins. Co.); chmn. exec. com. FRMT Ltd. (A Bermuda Mut. Ins. Co.), 1999—2001; bd. dirs. Diwal Corp., Mitcoi Corp., Odin Mgmt. Corp., Sy Sims Sch. Bus. Yeshiva U.; chmn. bd. dirs. Fraternity Risk Mgmt. Trust, 1994—99, chmn. exec. com., 1999—2000. Bd. dirs. Alpha Epsilon Pi Found., Inc., 1976—, Nat. Interfrat. Conf., 1975-86, Nat. Interfrat. Found., 1996—, State of Israel Bonds, N.Y.; bd. dirs. Sutton Pl. Synagogue, 1984-99, v.p., 1993-99; bd. dirs. joint purchasing com. Fedn. Jewish Philanthropies, 1977-78; mem. Cmty. Bd. Manhattan, N.Y., 1992—; internat. bd. dirs. Hillel Found. for Jewish Student Campus Life, 1999—. Recipient State of Israel Bond Peace award 1983, Accts. Bankers and Fin. award Am. Jewish Congress, 1984, Gold medal Nat. Interfraternity Conf., 1994, Disting. Svc. award Fraternity Exec. Assn., 1999. Mem. Found. Acctg. Edn., Am. Inst. CPA's (real estate com. 1987-90), N.Y. State Soc. CPA's (admissions com. 1968-69, chmn. fin. and leasing com. 1972-74, com. on rels. with the bar 1974-76, com. on real estate acctg. 1976-79, com. ins. 1980-81, fin. acctg. standards com. 1983-86, chmn. mem.-in-industry com. 1981-83, chief fin. officers com. 1984-86, furtherance com. 1986, annual conf. com. 1985-87, com. on ops. 1987-88, bd. dirs. 1983-86, v.p. 1985-86, Outstanding CPA in Industry award 1986), Fin. Execs. Inst., Am. Acctg. Assn., Nat. Assn. Accts., Soc. Ins. Accts., Alpha Epsilon Pi (supreme gov. 1966-73, nat. pres. 1974-76, mem. fiscal control bd. 1977-81, vice chmn. 1981-92, chmn. 1992—), Beta Alpha Psi, Areopagus Clubs: N.Y. Alumni of Alpha Epsilon Pi. Lodges: Masons. Jewish. Home: 30 Beekman Pl New York NY 10022-8060 Office: 123 Grove Ave Cedarhurst NY 11516-2302

COHEN, RACHEL RUTSTEIN, financial planner; b. Phila., June 10, 1968; d. Charles Lawrence and Ronna (Newman) Rutstein(Stepmother), Susan Ellen (Yokel) Sansweet; m. Kipp B. Cohen, Nov. 22, 1995; children: Brandon Erik, Ryan Cameron. BS in Bus. Adminstrn., Pa. State U., 1990; student, U. Tel Aviv, 1989; MBA in Fin., Temple U., 1997. CFP; cert. wealth mgmt. advisor. V.p. Merrill Lynch, Bala Cynwyd, Pa., 1990—. V.p. bd. dirs. Phila. chpt. Shaare Zedek Hosp.Charity, 1992-96, co-chair Phone-A-Thon, 1993. Mem.: Phila. Fin. Assn. (co-chair dinner com.), Pa. State U. Alumni Assn., Phila. C. of C. (diplomate 1991—95, mem. nursery sch. com. 2003), Green Valley Country Club. Republican. Avocations: golf, tennis, travel, language (spanish), reading. Office: Merrill Lynch 2 Bala Plz Bala Cynwyd PA 19004 E-mail: kicohen@comcast.net.

COHEN, RACHELLE SHARON, journalist; b. Phila., Oct. 21, 1946; d. Hyman and Diane Doris (Schultz) Goldberg; m. Stanley Martin Cohen, June 22, 1968; 1 dau., Avril Heather. BS, Temple U., 1968. Editor, Somerville Jour. (Mass.), 1968-70; reporter Lowell Sun (Mass.), 1970-72, AP, Boston, 1972-79; state house bur. chief Boston Herald Am., 1979-80, editorial page editor, 1980-82; editorial page editor, columnist Boston Herald, 1982— . Mem. Mass. Bar Assn. (bench, bar, press com.), Mass. Assn. Mental Health (bd. dirs. 1993—). Office: Boston Herald 1 Herald St Boston MA 02118-2200

COHEN, RAYMOND, mechanical engineer, educator; b. St. Louis, Nov. 30, 1923; s. Benjamin and Leah (Lewis) C.; m. Katherine Elise Silverman, Feb. 1, 1948 (dec. May 1985); children— Richard Samuel, Deborah, Barbara Beth; m. Lila Lakin Cagen, Nov. 30, 1986. BS, Purdue U., 1947, MS, 1950, PhD, 1955. Instr. mech. engring. Purdue U., 1948-55, asst. prof., 1955-58, assoc. prof., 1958-60, prof., 1960-98, asst. dir. Ray W. Herrick Labs., 1970-71, dir., 1971-93, acting head Sch. Mech. Engring., 1988-89, Herrick prof. engring., 1994-99, Herrick prof. emeritus engring., 1999—. Cons. to industry. Departmental editor: Ency. Brit., 1957-62; editorial bd. Jour. Sound and Vibration, 1971-87; editor Internat. Jour. of Heating, Ventilating, Air Conditioning and Refrigerating Rsch., 1994-98. Served as sgt. inf. AUS, 1943-46. Recipient Kamerlingh Onnes gold medal, 1995; NATO sr. fellow in sci., 1971 Fellow ASME, ASHRAE; mem. NSPE, Am. Soc. Engring. Edn., Soc. Exptl. Mechanics, Internat. Inst. Refrigeration (chmn. U.S. nat. com. 1992-95, U.S. del. 1992-99), Acoustical Soc. Am., Inst. Noise Control Engring. (pres. 1990), Sigma Xi, Pi Tau Sigma, Tau Beta Pi. Home: 2501 Spyglass Dr Valparaiso IN 46383 Office: Purdue U Ray W Herrick Labs 140 S Intramural Dr West Lafayette IN 47907-2031

COHEN, RICHARD EDWARD, journalist; b. Northampton, Mass., 1948; AB, Brown U., 1969; JD, Georgetown U., 1972. Corr. Nat. Jour., Washington, 1973—. Author: Washington at Work: Back Rooms and Clean Air, 1992. Office: Nat Jour 1501 M St NW Ste 300 Washington DC 20005-1700

COHEN, RICHARD B. grocery company executive; b. Worcester, Mass., July 25, 1952; s. Lester and Norma (Russem) Cohen. BA in Acctg., U. Pa., 1974. V.p. fin. C&S Wholesale, Worcester, Mass., 1977-81, gen. mgr. Brattleboro, Vt., 1981-83, pres., CEO, 1983—, chmn. bd., dir., CEO. Bd. dirs. The Food Distbn. Inst.; bd. trustees Deerfield Acad. Named Entrepreneur of the Yr., Ernst & Young, 2002. Jewish. Avocations: fishing, tennis, travel. Office: C & S Wholesale Grocers Inc 47 Old Ferry Rd Brattleboro VT 05302*

COHEN, RICHARD GERARD, lawyer; b. N.Y.C., June 11, 1931; m. Evelyn Streit, June 22, 1952; Children: Frances, Andrew Steven, Emilie, Sarah Jane Grossbard. BS in Econs, U. Pa., 1952; LL.B., Columbia U., 1955. Bar: N.Y. 1956. With Office Chief Counsel, IRS, Treasury Dept., 1957-64, tech. asst. to chief counsel, 1961-64; with Lord, Day & Lord, N.Y.C., 1964-86, ptnr., 1966-86, Pillsbury Winthrop LLP, N.Y.C., 1986—. Chmn. adv. bd. NYU Inst. Fed. Taxation, 1991; lectr. in field. Contbr. articles to profl. jours. Served with Audit Agy. U.S. Army, 1955-57. Mem. ABA, N.Y. State Bar Assn. (chmn. tax sect. 1986-87), Assn. Bar City N.Y. (chmn. coun. on taxation 1989-93), Am. Law Inst. (cons. fed. income tax project 1974-95, reporter ptnrship tax issues 1976-84). Jewish. Office: Pillsbury Winthrop LLP One Battery Park Plaza New York NY 10004 E-mail: rcohen@pillsburywinthrop.com.

COHEN, RICHARD MARTIN, journalist; b. N.Y.C., Feb. 6, 1941; s. Harry Louis and Pearl (Rosenberg) C.; m. Barbara Stubbs, May 3, 1969 (div.); m. Leslie Feely, July 17, 1992; 1 son, Alexander Prescott. BS, N.Y. U., 1967; MS in Journalism, Columbia U., 1968. With UPI, 1967-68; gen. assignment reporter Washington Post, 1968-76, syndicated columnist, 1976—. Author: A Heartbeat Away, 1973. Office: Washington Post Co 251 W 57th St New York NY 10019-1802 E-mail: cohenr@washpost.com.

COHEN, RICHARD NORMAN, insurance executive; b. N.Y.C., Oct. 28, 1923; s. Norman M. and Janet (Goldsmith) C.; m. Ann Robertson, Oct. 25, 1975; children: Daniel Hays, James Matthew; 1 stepchild, Mark Thompson. Grad., Phillips Exeter Acad., 1941; BA, Yale U., 1945. Salesman Cohen, Goldman & Co., N.Y.C., 1947-50; mens fashion editor Fawcett Publs., N.Y.C., 1951-52; life ins. broker Mass. Mut. Life Ins. Co., 1954—; account exec. John M. Riehle, Inc., N.Y.C., 1961-63, v.p., 1963-83, Leonard Newman Agy. Inc., White Plains, N.Y., 1984-94, Arthur Gallagher & Co., White Plains, 1994-2000. Served to 2d lt. USAAF, 1943-45. Mem. Country Club of New Canaan, Yale Club (N.Y.C.), Century Country Club (White Plains, N.Y.), Beta Theta Pi. Republican. Jewish. Home: 1062 Ponus Rdg New Canaan CT 06840-3420 E-mail: RNCI@optonline.net.

COHEN, ROBERT (ROBERT AVRAM COHEN), lawyer; b. Pitts., July 23, 1929; s. Max R. and Mollie (Segal) C.; m. Frances H. Steiner, Dec. 24, 1951 (div. Feb. 1974); children: Deborah E., David R.; m. Mary E. Connors, Mar. 11,

1974; children: Deborah A., Charles E., Chrisann (dec.). AB magna cum laude, Harvard U., 1951, JD, 1954. Bar: Pa. 1955, Fla. 1974, U.S. Dist. Ct. (we. dist.) Pa. 1955, U.S. Dist. Ct. (so. dist.) Fla. 1974, U.S. Tax Ct. 1983, U.S. Ct. Appeals (3d cir.) 1961, U.S. Supreme Ct. 1962. Assoc. Goldstock, Schwartz, Teitelbaum & Schwartz, Pitts., 1955-60; ptnr. Goldstock, Schwartz, Cohen & Schwartz, Pitts., 1960-67, Fine, Perlow, Stone & Cohen, Pitts., 1967-70, Cohen & Goldstock, Pitts., 1970-73; assoc. Herring, Evans & Fulton, West Palm Beach, Fla., 1974; from assoc. to ptnr. Rothman, Gordon, Foreman and Groudine, P.A., Pitts., 1974-86; sole practice Pitts., 1986-2000; atty. Behrend & Ernsberger, Pitts., 2000—. Trustee Western Allegheny Cmty. Libr., 1989-91, pres., 1991-98; pres. County Libr. Assn. Serving the People, 1993-94; mem. Zoning Bd. Borough of Oakdale, 1991—. Mem. ABA, Assn. Trial Lawyers Am. (pres. western Pa. chpt. 1972-73), Pa. Bar Assn. (com. on ethics and profl. responsibility 1988—, com. on professionalism 1990-94, civil rights com. 1995-97), Acad. Trial Lawyers Allegheny County, Pa. Trial Lawyers Assn., Allegheny County Bar Assn. (civil litigation coun. 1988-90, continuing legal edn. 1977—, profl. ethics com. 1996—), Golden Triangle Lodge (v.p. 1966-69), B'nai B'rith. Democrat. Jewish. Home: 205 Oak Heights Dr Oakdale PA 15071-1137 Office: Behrend & Ernsberger 306 4th Ave Pittsburgh PA 15222-2000

COHEN, ROBERT, medical device manufacturing and marketing executive; b. Glen Cove, N.Y., Sept. 23, 1957; s. Alan and Selma (Grossman) C.; m. Nancy A. Arey, Jan. 17, 1981. BA, Bates Coll., 1979; JD, U. Maine, 1982. Bar: N.Y. 1983, U.S. Dist. Ct. (so. and ea.) N.Y. 1983. Atty. Pfizer Inc., N.Y.C., 1982-86; asst. corp. counsel, asst. sec. Pfizer Hosp. Products Group, Inc., N.Y.C., 1986-88; v.p. bus. devel., dir. for med. device mfr. and marketer Deknatel Inc., Fall River, Mass., 1988-92; pres., CEO GCI Med., Braintree, Mass., 1992-93; v.p. bus. devel. Sulzermedica USA, Inc., Angleton, Tex., 1993-94, group v.p., 1994-98; v.p. bus. & tech. devel. St. Jude Med., Inc., St. Paul, 1998—2002; CEO, dir. of Advanced Circulatory Sys., Inc. Eden Prairie, Minn., 2003—; dir. Horizon Med. Products, Inc., Atlanta, 1998-2001, CardioFocus, Inc., Boston, 1999-2000; CEO Advanced Circulatory Sys., Inc., Eden Prairie, Minn., 2003—. Author: 19th Century Maine Authors, 1978. Mem. ABA, Am. Corp. Counsel Assn. Republican. Home: 18683 Bearpath Trl Eden Prairie MN 55347-3476 Office: Advanced Circulatory Systems Inc 7615 Golden Triangle Dr Ste A Eden Prairie MN 55344 E-mail: rcohenmeddev@aol.com.

COHEN, ROBERT ABRAHAM, retired physician; b. Chgo., Nov. 13, 1909; s. Ezra Harry and Catherine (Kurzon) C.; m. Mabel Jean Blake, Mar. 21, 1933 (dec. Oct. 1972); children— Donald Edward, Margery Jean; m. Alice L. Muth, Mar. 31, 1974. BS, U. Chgo., 1930, PhD, MD, 1935. Intern Michael Reese Hosp., Chgo., 1936-37; resident Henry Phipps Psychiat. Clinic Johns Hopkins U., 1937-38; resident Sheppard-Pratt Hosp., Towson, Md., 1938-39, 40-41; sr. fellow Inst. Juvenile Research, Chgo, 1939-40; pvt. practice psychiatry Washington, 1946-48; clin. dir. Chestnut Lodge, Rockville, Md., 1948-53, dir. psychotherapy, 1981-91; dir. clin. investigations NIMH, Bethesda, Md., 1953-69, dir. div. clin. and behavioral research, 1969-81, dep. dir. intramural research program, 1969-81. Pres. Washington Sch. Psychiatry, 1973-82; Bd. dirs. Founds. Fund for Research in Psychiatry, 1960-63, chmn. bd., 1962-63; trustee William Alanson White Psychiat. Found. Served from lt. (j.g.) to comdr. M.C. USNR, 1941-46. Recipient HEW Disting. Svc. award, 1970, Salmon medal N.Y. Acad. Scis., 1978, Fromm-Reichmann award Am. Acad. Psychoanylsis, 1979, Woodley House award, 1982. Fellow Am. Psychiat. Assn. (life); mem. Am. Psychoanalytical Assn., Am. Psychopathol. Assn., Assn. Research in Nervous and Mental Disease, Washington Psychoanalytic Soc. (pres. 1951-53), Washington Psychiat. Soc. (pres. 1958-59), Washington Psychoanalytic Inst. (chmn. edn. com. 1955-59), Washington Acad. Medicine, Cosmos Club. Home: 5216 Elsmere Ave Bethesda MD 20814-5734

COHEN, ROBERT EDWARD, chemical engineering educator, consultant; b. Oil City, Pa., Jan. 21, 1947; s. David M. and Minnie E. Cohen; m. D. Jane Woodman, Nov. 18, 1978; children: Genevieve Elizabeth, Eliot Lee. BS with distinction, Cornell U., 1968; MS, Calif. Inst. Tech., 1970, PhD, 1972. Postdoctoral rsch. fellow Calif. Inst. Tech., Pasadena, 1972; ICI rsch. fellow Oxford (Eng.) U., 1972-73; asst. prof. chem. engring. MIT, Cambridge, 1973-75, Harold and Esther Edgerton asst. prof., 1975-77, assoc. prof., 1977-82, prof., 1982—, founding dir. program in polymer sci. and tech., 1985-88, Bayer prof. chem. engring., 1988-95, St. Laurent prof. chem. engring., 1995—, assoc. chmn. of faculty, 1989-91, chem. engring. grad. officer, 1992-01; co-dir. DuPont-MIT Alliance, 2000—. Vis. appt. Sandia Nat. Labs., Albuquerque, summer 1979, Istituto Guido Donegani, Novara, Italy, 1981-82; vis. prof. dept. chemistry Harvard U., 1989; co-founder, bd. dirs., cons. MatTek Corp., Ashland, Mass., 1985—; bd. dirs. Kiser Rsch., Inc., Washington, 1992-94; chmn. sci. adv. bd. William and Mary Greve Found., N.Y.C., 1988—, bd. dirs., 1997—. Co-editor: Jour. Polymer Engring.; mem. editorial adv. bd. Jour. Applied Polymer Sci., 1989—, Chemistry of Materials, 1989-93; cons. editor AIP Series on Polymers and Complex Fluids, 1992-97; contbr. articles to profl. jours.; patentee in field. Bd. trustees The Advent Sch., Boston, 1996-99. Recipient Camille and Henry Dreyfus Tchr. Scholar award Dreyfus Found., 1977; Robert W. Vaughan Meml. lectr. Calif. Inst. Tech., 1984, Shell Disting. lectr. dept. materials sci. Northwestern U., 1996. Mem. AIChE (program chair materials divsn. polymer sect. 1993-97, dir. materials divsn. 1998-2001, Charles M.A. Stine award 2000), Am. Chem. Soc., Am. Phys. Soc., Materials Rsch. Soc., Soc. Rheology, N.Y. Acad. Scis. Jewish. Avocation: golf. Office: MIT Dept Chem Engring Bldg 66 Rm 554 Cambridge MA 02139

COHEN, ROBERT L. editor; s. Sol E. and Lorraine Sterling Cohen. BA, Empire State Coll., 1993. Pres. Sterling Media Prodns., N.Y.C. Bd. mem. Jewish Music Inst. Hebrew Coll., Newton, Mass. Prodr.: (CD) Open the Gates!: New American Jewish Music for Prayer, 2003. Recipient Simon Rockower award for excellence in arts and criticism, Am. Jewish Press Assn., 1994. Mem.: Am. Soc. for Jewish Music, Editl. Freelancers Assn. Office: Sterling Media Prodns 182-12 Horace Harding Expy 2M Fresh Meadows NY 11365

COHEN, ROBERT SONNÉ, physicist, philosopher, educator; b. N.Y.C., Feb. 18, 1923; m. Robin Gertrude Hirshhorn, June 18, 1944; children: Michael, Daniel, Deborah. BA, Wesleyan U., Middletown, Conn., 1943, LHD, 1986; MS, Yale U., 1943, PhD (NRC fellow), 1948. Instr. physics Yale U., 1943-44, instr. philosophy, 1949-51; sci. staff, war research div. Columbia U. and Communications Bd., U.S. Joint Chiefs Staff, 1944-46; asst. prof. physics and philosophy Wesleyan U., 1949-57; assoc. prof. physics Boston U., 1957-59, prof. physics and philosophy, 1959-93, chmn. dept. physics, 1959-73, chmn. dept. philosophy, 1986-88, prof. emeritus, 1993—; acting dean Coll. Liberal Arts, 1971-72. Chmn. Boston U. Center for Philosophy and History Sci., 1970-93, chmn. emeritus, 1993—; vis. lectr. humanities and philosophy of sci. Mass. Inst. Tech., 1958-59, 61-62; vis. prof. history of ideas Brandeis U., 1959-60; lectr. history and philosophy of sci. Am. U., Washington, summers 1958-68; vis. fellow Polish and Yugoslav Acad. Sci., 1963, Hungarian Acad. Sci., 1964; vis. prof. philosophy U. Calif., San Diego, 1969, Yale U., 1973; rsch. fellow history of sci. Harvard U., 1974; mem., chmn. U.S. Nat. Com. for Internat. Union History and Philosophy of Sci., 1969-75; trustee Wesleyan U., 1968-84, emeritus, 1984—; trustee Tufts U., 1984-93, emeritus, 1993—. Author, editor articles, books and jours. in field.; Editor: Boston Studies in Philosophy of Sci., Vienna Circle Collection, Sci. in Context. Trustee Bill of Rights Found. Am. Council Learned Soc. fellow philosophy and sci., 1948-49; Ford faculty fellow Cambridge, Eng., 1955-56; fellow Wissenschaftskolleg zu Berlin, 1983-84, Inst. fur Wissenschaften dem Menschen, Vienna, 1994. Fellow AAAS (chmn. sect. L history and philosophy of sci. 1978-79), Am. Phys. Soc.; mem. AAUP, Am. Assn. Physics Tchrs., Am. Philos. Assn. (exec. com. 1988-91), History Sci. Soc., Philosophy Sci. Assn. (v.p. 1972-75, pres. 1982-84), Nat. Emergency Civil Liberties Com. (mem. nat. coun.), Am. Inst. Marxist Studies (chmn. 1964-82), Fedn. Am. Scientists (nat. coun. 1967-70), Inst. for Unity of Sci. (exec. com. 1960-74). Home: 44 Adams Ave Watertown MA 02472-1391 Office: Boston U Dept Philosophy 745 Commonwealth Ave Boston MA 02215-1401

COHEN, ROBERT STEPHAN, lawyer; b. N.Y.C., Jan. 14, 1939; s. Abraham and Florence C.; children: Christopher, Ian, Nicholas; m. Stephanie J. Stiefel, Jan. 29, 1998. BA, Alfred U., 1959; LLB, Fordham U., 1962. Bar: N.Y. 1963, U.S. Dist. Ct. (so. and ea. dists.) N.Y. 1964, U.S. Ct. Appeals (2d cir.) 1965. Assoc. Saxe, Bacon & O'Shea, N.Y.C., 1963-68; mng. ptnr., chmn. Morrison, Cohen Singer and Weinstein and predecessor firms, N.Y.C., 1968—2003. Lectr. in field; mem. faculty Am Acad. Psychiatry and the Law, 1984—. Author: Reconcilable Differences, 2002; contbr. articles to legal jours. Bd. dirs. N.Y. Pops, 1983-02. 1st lt. JAG, USAR, 1965-67. Fellow Am. Coll. Family Trial Lawyers; mem. ABA, FBA, ATLA, N.Y. State Bar Assn., N.Y.C. Bar Assn., N.Y. Acad. Matrimonial Lawyers; Univ. Club (N.Y.C.). Office: Cohen Lans LLP 885 2d Ave New York NY 10017

COHEN, ROBERTA JANE, government executive; b. N.Y.C., Feb. 5, 1940; d. George H. and Ethel (Israel) Cohen; m. David A. Korn, Apr. 8, 1981; stepchildren: Marie Korn, David Korn, Philip Korn, Stephen Korn. BA, Barnard Coll., 1960; MA, Johns Hopkins U., 1963. Exec. dir. Internat. League for Human Rights, N.Y.C., 1971-78; sr. adviser to U.S. del. to UN and human rights officer Dept. of State, Washington, 1978-80, dep. asst. sec. state for human rights, 1980-81; head pub. affairs office U.S. Embassy, Addis Ababa, 1982-85; hon. sec. Parliamentary Human Rights Group, London, 1985-86; sr. adviser to refugee policy group Washington, 1989-96; sr. advisor NAS Com. on Human Rights, Washington, 1991-95; sr. advisor on internally displaced to rep. UN Sec.-Gen., 1994—; co-dir. project on internal. displacement Brookings Instn., Washington, 1994—, sr. fellow, 2001—. Cons. World Bank, various govt. and non-govt. orgns., 1991—94; chmn. task force on human rights UN Assn., Washington, 1993—94; chair task force on China Internat. Human Rights Law Group, Washington, 1997—99, vice chair, 1992—96; bd. dirs. Jacob Blaustein Inst. for Advancement Human Rights; mem. adv. com. Human Rights Watch/Africa, RFK Meml. on Human Rights, Internat. League Human Rights, Toda Inst., Trinity Coll. Human Rights Program; mem. Coun. Fgn. Rels., Women's Fgn. Policy Group, Fund for Peace, Human Rights Bus. Roundtable. Author: People's Republic of China: The Human Rights Exception, 1987; co-author: Masses in Flight: The Global Crisis of Internal Displacement, 1998; co-editor: The Forsaken People, 1998, Compliance of the Law of the South Caucusus with the Guiding Principles on Internal Displacment: Georgia, Armenia & Azerbaijan, 2003. Pub. mem. U.S. del. UN Commn. on Human Rights, 1998. Recipient Superior Honor award, U.S. Info. Agy., Addis Abada, 1985, Human Rights award, UN Assn., 1994, Fiftieth Ann. award for Exemplary Writing on Fgn. Affairs and Diplomacy, Diplomats and Consular Officers Ret., 2002.

COHEN, RONALD S. accountant; b. Lafayette, Ind., July 13, 1937; s. William and Stella (Fleischman) C.; m. Nancy Ann Plotkin, May 29, 1960; children: Philip, Douglas. BS in Acctg., Ind. U., 1958. CPA Ind. Staff acct. Crowe, Chizek & Co., South Bend, Ind., 1958—65, ptnr., 1965—2003, mng. ptnr., 1982—94, chmn. bd. dirs., 1994—2000. Chmn. Horwath Internat., 1999—; mem. dean's adv. coun. Ind. U. Sch. Bus., 1996—. Commr. Housing Authority of South Bend, 1976-85, also vice-chmn.; pres. Jewish Fedn., 1979-82; bd. dirs. United Way of South Bend, 1987-90. Served to lt. USAR, 1958-66. Mem. AICPA (bd. dirs. 1990-97, vice-chmn. 1994, chmn. 1995), Ind. Soc. CPAs, Ind. U. Sch. Bus. Alumni Assn. (bd. dirs. 1992-95). Democrat. Jewish. Office: Crowe Chizek & Co PO Box 7 330 E Jefferson Blvd South Bend IN 46601-2366 E-mail: rcohen@crowechizek.com.

COHEN, SAMUEL MONROE, physician, pathologist, researcher; b. Milw., Sept. 24, 1946; s. David A. and Harriett (Goldman) C.; m. Janet L. Olson, Jan. 27, 1968; children: Sheri Lyn, Benjamin A., Daniel E., Erica A. BS, U. Wis., 1967, MD, PhD, U. Wis., 1972. Diplomate Am. Bd. Anatomic and Clin. Pathology. Staff pathologist St. Vincent Hosp., Worcester, Mass., 1975-76, 77-81; assoc. prof. pathology U. Mass. Med. Sch., Worcester, 1977-81; vice chmn. dept. pathology U. Nebr. Med. Ctr., Omaha, 1981-92, chmn. dept. pathology and microbiology, 1992—. Vis. prof. 1st dept. pathology Nagoya (Japan) City U. Med. Sch.; mem. study sect. NIH, Bethesda, Md., 1982-86, 88, 89-91, chmn., 1991-93; mem. expert panel Flavor and Extracts Mfg. Assn., 2002—; mem. bd. sci. counselors Nat. Toxicology Program, 2002—; expert cons. to several cos. Editor: Pathology of Bladder Cancer, 1983; contbr. articles to profl. jours. Recipient Outstanding Rsch. and Creativity award U. Nebr., 1990. Mem. AMA, Am. Assn. for Cancer Rsch., Soc. Toxicology (Arnold J. Lehman award 2001), Am. Assn. Pathologists, Soc. Toxicologic Pathologists, Am. Soc. Clin. Pathologists. Avocations: reading, travel. Home: 2721 S 101st St Omaha NE 68124-2618 Office: 983135 Nebr Med Ctr Omaha NE 68198-3135

COHEN, SANDON LEE, lawyer; b. Balt., Mar. 12, 1960; s. Harold Shemer and Nancy Ann (Gershberg) C. BA, George Washington U., 1982; JD, U. Pa., 1985. Bar: Md. 1985, U.S. Ct. Appeals (4th cir.) 1987, U.S. Ct. Appeals (3d cir.) 1991. Assoc. Burke, Gerber, Wilen & Francomano, Balt., 1985-88, Cohan and Francomano, P.C., Balt., 1988-92; sr. assoc. David Rodman Cohan and Assocs., P.C., Balt., 1992-2001, Cohan and West, P.C., Balt., 2001—. Mem. ABA, Md. Bar Assn. Republican. Avocations: coin collecting, classical music.

COHEN, SANFORD IRWIN, physician, educator; b. N.Y.C., Sept. 5, 1928; s. George A. and Gertrude (Slater) C.; m. Jean Steinbruecker, Nov. 30, 1952; children— Jeffrey, Debra, John, Robert. AB magna cum laude, N.Y. U., 1948; M.B., MD, Chgo. Med. Sch., 1952. Intern Jackson Meml. Hosp., Miami, Fla., 1952-53; resident psychiatry U. Colo. Med. Center, 1953-54; resident Duke Med. Center, 1954-55, 57-58, mem. faculty, 1956-68, prof. psychiatry, 1964-68, head div. psychosomatic medicine and psychophysiol. research, 1964-68, lectr. psychology, 1960-68; instr. Washington Psychoanalytic Inst., 1964-68; cons. VA Hosp., Durham, N.C., 1957-65, NIMH, 1963-66; prof. psychiatry Boston U. Med. Sch., 1970-86, chmn. dept., 1970-86; vis. research scientist health and behavior br., div. basic scis. NIMH, 1986-88; prof. psychiatry U. Miami (Fla.) Sch. Medicine, 1988-2000, vice chmn. dept., 1990-2000, prof. emeritus, 2000—. Markle scholar med. sci., 1957-62; Commonwealth fellow, Czech Republic and USSR, 1966. Contbr. articles to profl. jours., chpts. to books. Recipient Robert Morse award excellence in sci. writing, 1965 Fellow Am. Psychiat. Assn. (life), Am. Coll. Clin. Pharmacology (life); mem. AAAS, Am. Psychosomatic Soc., Acad. Behavioral Medicine Rsch. Home: 15110 Rollinmead Dr Darnestown MD 20878-3906 E-mail: scohen@med.miami.edu.

COHEN, SANFORD NED, pediatrics educator, academic administrator; b. N.Y.C., June 12, 1935; s. George M. and Fannie Leah (Epstein) C.; m. Judith Luskind, June 22, 1958 (div. 1984); 1 child, Andrew B.; m. Elizabeth Prevot(div. 1991); m. Sandra Hoffmann, June 13, 1992. AB, The Johns Hopkins U., 1956, MD, 1960. Diplomate Am. Bd. Pediat. Intern in pediat. Johns Hopkins Hosp., 1960-61, resident, 1961-63; instr. to assoc. prof. NYU Sch. Medicine, N.Y.C., 1965-74; chmn., prof. pediat. Wayne State U. Sch. Medicine, Detroit, 1974-81, assoc. dean, 1981-86, sr. v.p. for acad. affairs, provost, 1986-91, prof. pediat., 1991-98, prof. emeritus, 1998—. Dir. Wayne State U. Devel. Disability Inst., 1983-86, Child Rsch. Ctr., Detroit, 1975-81; pediatrician-in-chief Children's Hosp. Mich., Detroit, 1974-81; adj. faculty U. Mich. Sch. Pub. Health, Ann Arbor, 1980-90; chair steering com. NIH Network of Pediat. Pharmacology Rsch. Units, 1994-98, mem. adv. com., 1999—; reviewer Inst. of Medicine Nat. Acad. Sci.; mem. profl. adv. coun. Children's Med. Rsch. Inst., Oklahoma City, 1999—; vol. cons. Lee Meml. Health Sys., Ft. Myers, Fla., 2000—. Editor: Progress in Drug Therapy in Children, 1981; contbr. articles to profl. jours. Mem. bd. health, Leonia, N.J., 1972-74; mem. Bd. Police Commrs., Detroit, 1995-99, chmn., 1997-98. John and Mary R. Markle scholar acad. medicine, 1968-74. Mem.: Soc. Pediat. Rsch. (v.p. 1980—81), Sr. & Ret. Physicians Assn. (pres. 2001—), Midwest Soc. Pediat. Rsch. (pres. 1979—80), Am. Pediat. Soc. Avocations: reading, golf. Office: Children's Hosp Mich 3901 Beaubien St Detroit MI 48201-2119 E-mail: scohen@med.wayne.edu.

COHEN, SARAH, reporter; BA, U. N.C.; M in Pub. Affairs Reporting, U. Md. Reporter Tampa Tribune, St. Petersburg Times, Investigative Reporters and Editors; database editor Washington Post, 1999—. Office: Washington Post 1150 15th St NW Washington DC 20071

COHEN, SAUL BERNARD, former college president, geographer; b. Malden, Mass., July 28, 1925; s. Barnett and Anna (Kaplinsky) C.; m. Miriam Friederman, June 11, 1950; children: Deborah Fae, Louise Esther. AB, Harvard U., 1947, AM, 1949, PhD, 1955; DSc (hon.), LLD (hon.), CUNY, 1986; DSc (hon.), Clark U., 1991. From instr. to prof. geography Boston U., 1952-65; vis. prof. U.S. Naval War Coll., 1957; prof. geography, dir. Grad. Sch. Geography, Clark U., Worcester, Mass., 1965-78; dean Grad. Sch. Geography, Clark U. (Grad. Sch.), 1967-70, chmn. faculty, 1973-76, 77-78; pres. Queens Coll., Flushing, N.Y., 1978-85; univ. prof. geography Hunter Coll., N.Y., 1986-96, univ. prof. emeritus, 1996—. Vis. prof. Hebrew U., Jerusalem, 1971, 74, 75; adj. prof. Haifa U., 1977; cons. social sci. div. NSF, 1966-74, U.S. Office Edn., 1966-77; mem. U.S. nat. delegation Internat. Geog. Union, 1966-69; chmn. com. geography Nat. Acad. of Scis.-NRC, 1966-69. Author: Geography and Politics in a World Divided, 1963, rev. edit., 1973, Problems and Trends in American Geography, 1967, Experiencing the Environment, 1976, Resources and Human Networks, 1977, Jerusalem-Bridging the Four Walls, 1977, Jerusalem Undivided, 1980, Israel's Defensible Borders: A Geopolitical Map, 1983, The Geopolitics of Israel's Border Question, 1987, Geopolitics of the World System, 2003; also articles; geog. editor The Oxford World Atlas, 1973; geog. advisor New Columbia Ency., 1991, 93; editor-in-chief Columbia Gazetteer of the World, 1998. Chmn. N.Y.C. Early Childhood Commn., 1985-86; co-chmn. N.Y. State Sch. and Bus. Alliance, 1986-94; mem. Temp. State Commn. on N.Y.C. Sch. Governance, 1989-91; at-large mem. N.Y. State Bd. Regents, 1993—, chmn. Regents Telecom. Policy Commn., 1994-97, Regents Elem., Secondary and Continuing Edn. Com., 1995-98, Regents Higher Edn. and Profession com., 1999—; mem. N.Y. State Archives Partnership Trust, 1994—; chmn. vis. com. N.Y. State Mus., 1997—. Mem. Consortium Profl. Assns. (chmn. 1965-71), Assn. Am. Geographers (exec. officer 1964-65, del. Am. Coun. Learned Socs. 1964-66, mem. coun. 1966-70, chmn. com. coll. geography 1965-67, v.p. 1988-89, pres. 1989-90, past pres. 1990-91, chmn. com. on geog. curriculum internat. exch. 1990-96), Am. Geog. Soc. (coun. 1970-79). Home: 82 Taymil Rd New Rochelle NY 10804-2802

COHEN, SELMA, reference librarian, researcher; b. N.Y.C., Mar. 14, 1930; d. George and Rose (Cohen) Unger; m. Irwin H. Cohen, Nov. 19, 1950; children: Barbara Katzeff, Joel. Grad. high sch., William Howard Taft High Sch., 1948. Asst. bookkeeper acctg. dept. Severud, Perrone et al, N.Y.C., 1970-75, Russell Reynolds Assocs., Inc., N.Y.C., 1976-77, rsch. asst., 1977—, reference libr., 1985—. Chairwoman Scott Tower Charity Com., Bronx, 1976-84, Scott Tower Property Improvement Com., Bronx, 1983-84. Home: 3400C Paul Ave # 10H Bronx NY 10468-1042 Office: Russell Reynolds Assocs 200 Park Ave New York NY 10166-0005

COHEN, SEYMOUR STANLEY, biochemist, educator; b. N.Y.C., Apr. 30, 1917; s. Herman and Lena (Tanz) Cohen; m. Elaine Pear, July 12, 1940; children: Michael, Sara. BS, CCNY, 1936; PhD in Biol. Chemistry, Columbia U., 1941; Dr.h.c., U. Louvain, Belgium, 1972, U. Kuopio, Finland, 1982. NRC fellow Rockefeller Inst., 1941—42; mem. faculty U. Pa., 1943—71, prof. biochemistry in pediatrics, 1954—71, Charles Hayden-Am. Cancer Soc. prof. biochemistry, 1957—71, Hartzell prof., chmn. dept. therapeutic research Sch. Medicine, 1963—71; Am. Cancer Soc. prof. microbiology U. Colo. Sch. Medicine, Denver, 1971—76; distinguished prof., Am. Cancer Soc. prof. pharm. scis. State U. N.Y., Stony Brook, 1976—85, prof. emeritus, 1985—. Chmn. council analysis and projection Am. Cancer Soc., 1972—74, adviser research, 1974—76; Guggenheim fellow Pasteur Inst., Paris, 1947—48; Jesup lectr. Columbia U., 1967; guest investigator Institut du Radium, Paris, 1967—68; vis. prof. Collège de France, Paris, 1970; vis. fellow Smithsonian Instn., 1973—74, 1986; vis. prof. U. Tokyo, 1974, Hadassah Med. Sch., 1974, Zuckerman lectr. tropical disease, 79; Guggenheim and Lady Davis fellow Faculty Agr., Israel, 1983; fellow Nat. Humanities Ctr., NC, 1982—83, NC, 1985; research assoc. history of sci. Smithsonian Instn., 1986; presdl. scholar U. Calif., San Francisco, 1988; lectr. Academia Sinica, Taiwan, 1989; trustee Marine Biol. Lab., Woods Hole, Mass.; bd. sci. cons. Sloan-Kettering Inst. Author: Virus-Induced Enzymes, 1968, Introduction to the Polyamines, 1971, Guide to the Polyamines, 1998, Biography of Thomas Cooper, 1999; editl. bd.: Virology, 1954—59, Jour. Biol. Chemistry, 1959—65, Jour. Cell Physiology, 1966—71, Bacteriol. Revs, 1969—73, Hist., Philos. Life Scis., 1985. Named Fogarty scholar, NIH, 1973—74; recipient cert. for war research, OSRD, 1945, War Manpower Commn., 1945, War Research medal, Columbia U., 1943, Eli Lilly award and medal, Am. Soc. Bacteriology, Immunology and Pathology, 1951, 1st Mead Johnson award, Am. Acad. Pediatrics, 1952, medal, Soc. de Chimie Biologique France, 1964, Borden award, Am. Assn. Med. Colls., 1967, Passano award, 1974, Townsend Harris medal, CCNY Alumni Assn., 1978, Forster award, German Acad. Sci. and Letters, Mainz, 1978. Master: Am. Acad. Arts and Scis.; fellow: AAAS (Newcomb Cleveland award 1955), Am. Acad. of Microbiology; mem.: NAS, Am. Assn. Cancer Rsch. (bd. dirs. 1974—77), French Soc. Microbiology (hon.), Inst. Medicine, Soc. Gen. Physiologists (councilor, pres. 1967—88), Phi Beta Kappa. Home: 10 Carrot Hill Rd Woods Hole MA 02543-1206

COHEN, SHARLEEN COOPER, interior designer, writer; b. L.A., June 11, 1940; d. Sam and Claretta (Ellis) White; m. R. Gary Cooper, Dec. 18, 1960 (dec. Feb., 1971); m. Martin L. Cohen, M.D., Aug. 27, 1972; children: Cami Gordon, Dalisa Cooper Cohen. Student, U. Calif., Berkeley, 1957-58, UCLA, 1958-60, L.A. Valley Film Sch., 1976-78. Owner, mgr. Designs on You, L.A., 1965-77; writer L.A., 1977—. Prodr. Jewish Repertory Theatre, N.Y.C., 1996. Author: The Day After Tomorrow, 1979, Regina's Song, 1980, The Ladies of Beverly Hills, 1983, Marital Affairs, 1985, Love, Sex and Money, 1988, Lives of Value, 1991, Innocent Gestures, 1994, (play) Solomon and Sheba, 1990, (musical) Sheba, 1996; assoc. prodr. : Broadway Street Corner Symphony; prodr.: Cookin' At The Cookery, The Best of Times; assoc. prodr. : Duet; writer: Stormy Weather, 1999, Blackout, 2000. Mem. exec. com. Women of Distinction United Jewish Appeal, 1990-95; chair L.A. chpt. Nat. Gaucher Found., 1991-95; bd. dirs., mem. com. chair Calif. Coun. for the Humanities, San Francisco, 1992-98; bd. dirs. Amas Mus. Theatre; mem. acquisitions com. Modern Contemporary Art Coun., L.A. County Mus. Art. Recipient Hon. Mention, Santa Barbara Writers Conf., 1978, Writer's Digest Writing Competition, 2000. Mem.: PEN, League of Profl. Theatre Women, The Drama League, Theatre Guild, Dramatists Guild, Writers Guild Am. E-mail: SccInc1@aol.com.

COHEN, SHELDON GILBERT, physician, historian, immunologist; b. Pittston, Pa., Sept. 21, 1918; s. Samuel H. and Dorthy (Goldberg) C. Grad., Wyo. Sem., 1936; student, Syracuse U., 1936-37; BA, Ohio State U., 1940; MD, NYU, 1943; DSc (hon.), Wilkes U., 1976. Diplomate Am. Bd. Allergy and Immunology. Intern Bellevue Hosp., N.Y.C., 1944; resident internal medicine Ft. Howard VA Hosp., Balt., 1947-48; resident in allergy VA Hosp., Aspinwall, Pa., 1948-49, U. Pitts. Med. Ctr., 1948-49; rsch. fellow U. Pitts. Sch. Medicine, 1949-50; rsch. assoc. U. Pitts., 1950-51; attending physician Allergy Clinic, Falk Clinics, 1950-51; chief of allergy Mercy Hosp., Wilkes-Barre, 1951-72; attending physician in allergy VA Hosp., Wilkes-Barre, 1951-60, cons. in internal medicine and rsch., 1960-72; assoc. prof. biol. rsch. Wilkes U., Wilkes-Barre, 1952-62, prof. biol. rsch., 1962-68, prof. exptl. biology, 1968-72, adj. prof. immunology, 1991—; cons. extramural programs Nat. Inst. Allergy and Infectious Diseases, 1972-73, chief allergy and immunology br., 1973-76, dir. immunology, allergic and immunologic diseases program, 1977-88, sci. advisor div. of intramural rsch. office of dir., 1988—; bd. sci. advisors Allergy and Immunology Inst. of Internat. Life Scis. Inst., 1989-97; sr. staff physician NIAID-NIH Clin. Ctr., 1974—. Adj. prof. medicine Northwestern U., 1988-98; scholar Nat. Libr. Medicine, 1988-99, vis. scholar history of medicine, 1999--; regional med. cons. Children's Asthma Research Inst. and Hosp., Denver, 1969-72; mem. medico adv. bd. CARE, 1977-89; cons. to Ministry Public Health, State of Kuwait, 1981-83; mem. expert adv. panel on immunology WHO, Geneva, Switzerland, 1979—, dir. WHO Collaborating Ctr. for Allergy, 1985-89; bd. dirs. Asthma and Allergy Found. Am., 1969-81, mem. com. public edn., 1976-81; bd. dirs. Lupus Found. Am., 1978-85, exec. v.p., 1981-85, mem. med. council, 1978-93; mem. aeroallergens com. NRC, 1976-80. Author: Excerpts from Classics in Allergy, 2d edit., 1992, Asthma Among the Famous, 1995-2002; mem. editl. bd. Jour. Devel. and Comparative Immunology, 1976-81, Allergy Proc., 1983-93; editor Hist. Notes, Allergy Proc., 1988-93, Allergy Archives, Jour. Allergy and Clin. Immunology, 2001--; cons. editor Am. Jour. Rhinology, 1986-93; contbr. articles to profl. jours., chpts. to books. Trustee Marywood Coll., Scranton, Pa., 1983-89; bd. govs. adv. coun. Wilkes U., Wilkes-Barre, 1991-92. Capt. M.C., USAF, 1944-46. Recipient Disting. Svc. award Wyo. Sem., 1978, Asthma and Allergy Found. Am., 1981, Clemens von Pirquet award Georgetown U., 1981, NIH Centennial award, Terri Gottheif Lupus Rsch. Inst., 1987, NYU Med. Alumni Achievement award in health sci., 1988, Achievement award Internat. Assn. Allergology and Clin. Immunology, 1988, Spl. Recognition award Am. Acad Allergy and Immunology, 1989, 2002, recognition citation ILSI Allergy and Immunology Inst., 1992. Fellow ACP, Am. Acad. Allergy (chmn. rsch. coun. 1963-66, historian 1963-69, v.p. 1979-80, Disting. Svc. award 1971), Am. Coll. Allergists, Coll. Physicians Phila.; mem. Am. Assn. Immunologists, Assn. Am. Physicians, Clin. Immunology Soc., Am. Thoracic Soc., Am. Coll. Rheumatology, Soc. for Exptl. Biology and Medicine, Collegium Internat. Allergologicum, Am. Fedn. Clin. Rsch., Am. Assn. for History of Medicine, Washington Soc. for History of Medicine (v.p. 1993-94,

pres. 1994-96), Cosmos Club, Sigma Xi, Alpha Omega Alpha (NYU alumni). Home: 5500 Friendship Blvd Apt 1927N Chevy Chase MD 20815-7272 Office: NIH NIAID MSC 6611 6610 Rockledge Dr Rm 2014 Bethesda MD 20892-7600 E-mail: scohen@niaid.nih.gov.

COHEN, SHELDON IRWIN, lawyer; b. Newark, July 25, 1937; BS in Ceramic Engring., AB in Humanities, Rutgers U., 1959; LLB, Georgetown U., 1964. Bar: Va. 1964, D.C. 1964, U.S. Ct. Appeals (D.C. and 4th cirs.) 1964, U.S. Supreme Ct. 1967. Assoc. Chapman, Disalle & Friedman, Washington, 1964-70; pvt. practice law Washington, Arlington, Va., 1970—. Author: Security Clearances and the Protection of National Security Information, Law and Procedure, 2000. Vice chmn. Arlington Dem. Com., 1968-70; mem. Va. Dem. Cen. Com., 1969-70. Capt. USAR, 1959-67. Mem. ABA (chmn. govt. pers. com. 1986-89, chmn. nat. security interests com. 1990-95), D.C. Bar Assn. (chmn. civil svc. law com. 1984-86). Democrat. Office: 2009 14th St N Ste 708 Arlington VA 22201-2514 E-mail: sicohen@sheldoncohen.com.

COHEN, SHELDON STANLEY, lawyer; b. Washington, June 28, 1927; s. Herman and Pearl (Jaffe) C.; m. Faye Fram, Feb. 21, 1951; children: Melinda Ann Cohen Goetzl, Laura Eve Cohen Apelbaum, Jonathan Adam, Sharon Ruevena Cohen Liebman. AB with spl. honors, George Washington U., 1950, JD with highest honors (Charles W. Dorsey scholar), 1952; DLit (hon.), Lincoln Coll.; LLD (hon.), George Washington U., 2003. Bar: D.C. 1952, U.S. Dist. Ct. D.C. 1952, U.S. Ct. Appeals (D.C. cir.) 1952, U.S. Claims Ct. 1956, U.S. Tax Ct., 1956, U.S. Supreme Ct. 1956, U.S. Ct. Appeals (fed. cir.) 1986; CPA, Md. Acct., 1950-52; legis. atty. Office Chief Counsel, IRS, Dept. Treasury, 1952-56, chief counsel, 1963-65, commr. internal revenue, 1965-69; assoc. Paul, Weiss, Rifkind, Wharton & Garrison, 1956-60; ptnr. Arnold, Fortas & Porter, Washington, 1960-63, Cohen & Uretz, Washington, 1969-85, Morgan, Lewis & Bockius, Washington, 1985—. Lectr. Howard U. Law sch., 1957-58; professorial lectr. George Washington U. Law Sch., 1958-81; adj. prof. U. Miami Law Sch., Fla., 1974-85; mem. adv. com. Inst. Estate Planning, U. Miami Law Ctr., 1969-86; chmn. exec. compensation com. U.S. Pay Bd., 1971-72; cons. Commn. for Revision of Tax Laws, 1969-71; cons. Filer Commn. on Pvt. Philanthropy and Pub. Needs, 1975-76; mem. Commn. on Founds. and Pvt. Philanthropy, 1969-70; mem. adv. group to commr. IRS, 1969-70; chmn. steering com. Adminstrv. Conf. U.S., 1974-84; mem. exec. com. Washington Lawyer's Com. for Civil Rights Under Law, 1975-, co-chmn., 1988-90; mem. Jimmy Carter Tax Task Force, 1976; advisor on tax and econs. Walter F. Mondale Campaign, 1984; mem. cons. panel to controller gen. U.S. Gen. Acctg. Office, 1982-2000, chmn. Audit Adv. Com, 1995-; pres. Am.-Israel Tax Found., 1969-80; mem. coun. Sch. Govt. and Bus. Adminstrn. George Washington U., 1969-79, mem. commn. on governance, 1970, trustee, 1980-2002, chmn. bd. of trustees, 2000-02, chmn. emeritus, 2003; pres. Law Assn., 1978-79; rapporteur CIAT Conf. in Can., 1987; adv. bd. The Lincoln Legals, 1988-; v.p. presdl. Inaugural Found., 1992-93; bd. dirs. Supreme Ct. Hist. Soc., treas. 1995-. Editorial and bus. sec.: George Washington U. Law Rev, 1952; case notes editor, 1951-52; bd. editors Nat. Law Jour., 1978—85; editorial bd. advisors Corporate Taxation. Mem. adv. com. to D.C. Ct. Appeals Admission Com.; past pres. Jewish Social Service Agy., Washington; bd. dirs. Adas Israel Congregation, Jewish Welfare Bd., United Synagogues Am., Common Cause, Nat. Council for a Responsible Firearms Policy, Inc., Nat. Found. for Jewish Culture, 1968-72, Am. Jewish Joint Distbn. Com., United Jewish Appeal Found. of D.C., 1969-2002, Supreme Ct. Hist. Soc., 1993-, treas. 1997-; past v.p. Jewish Community Ctr. Greater Washington; bd. dirs., past v.p. Jewish Community Found.; bd. regents Omar N. Bradley Found., U.S. Army Hist. Collection, 1970-73; bd. dirs., chmn. devel. com. Community Found. Greater Washington, 1982—; trustee B'nai B'rith Found. of U.S.; spl. tax counsel Democratic Nat. Com., 1969-72, gen. counsel, 1972-77; bd. overseers Jewish Theol. Sem. Am., 1972-; trustee United Jewish Endowment Fund, 1980-2002, trustee emeritus, 2003-; counsel Project Judaica Found., Inc., 1980—; v.p. Am. Jewish Hist. Soc., 1980-92, chmn., 1993-2000, honorary chair, 2001—; bd. dirs. Am. Assocs. Ben-Gurion U. of the Negev, Israel, v.p., 1988-90; sec., tax counsel Ctr. for Nat. Policy, 1981-2000; bd. dirs. Gomez Found. for Mill House, 1982-95, Ulysses S. Grant Assn., 1976-, v.p. 1994—, B'nai B'rith, 1979-85; treas. Nat. Jewish Dem. Coun., 1991-; chmn. endowment steering com. Coun. Jewish Fedns., 1991-2000, Am. Jewish Hist. Soc., 1993-; v.p. Presdl. Inaugural Found., 1992-93. With USNR, 1945-46, adv. com. Abraham Lincoln Bicentennial Commn., 2002-. Recipient Alumni Achievement award George Washington U., 1965, Arthur Flemming award, 1966, Alexander Hamilton award U.S. Treasury Dept., 1969, Joseph Ottenstein community service award Jewish Social Agy., 1976. Ourisman award for comm. svc. 1999. Mem. Nat. Acad. Pub. Adminstrn. (chmn. com. on energy 1978-79, trustee, sec. 1983-90, com. on ethics), ABA (chmn. spl. com. on retirement benefits legis. tax csect. 1972-73), Fed. Bar Assn. (coun. tax sect.), D.C. Bar Assn. (bd. dirs. 1969-72), D.C. Bar (Unified) (bd. govs. 1972-75, tax counsel 1972-, chair Iolta Study), Am. Coll. Tax Counsel, Am. Law Inst., J. Edgar Murdock Am. Inn of Ct. (counselor 1988—), D.C. Inst. CPAs (hon.), Inter-Am. Ctr. for Tax Adminstrs. (pres. 1967-68), Am.-Israel C. of C. (chmn. tax com.), Cosmos Club, Tournament Players Assn., Golf Avenel Club, Masons. Home: 5518 Trent St Bethesda MD 20815-5512 Office: Morgan Lewis & Bockius 1111 Penna Ave NW Washington DC 02004-5802

COHEN, STANLEY, pathologist, educator; b. N.Y.C., June 4, 1937; s. Herman Joseph and Eva (Lapidus) C.; m. Marion Doris Cantor, Aug. 30, 1959; children: Laurie Ellen, Ronald Nelson, Kenneth Stuart. AB, Columbia U., 1957, MD, 1961. Diplomate Am. Bd. Pathology (mem. immunopathology com.). Intern Albert Einstein Med. Ctr., Bronx, N.Y., 1961-62; resident Mass. Gen. Hosp., 1962-64; fellow NYU Med. Ctr., 1964-66; prof. pathology SUNY, Buffalo, 1968-74; acting dir. Ctr. for Immunology, Buffalo, 1973-74; prof. pathology U. Conn. Health Ctr., Farmington, 1974-87, assoc. chmn., 1976-80; prof., chmn. bd. Hahnemann U., Phila., 1987-94; prof., chmn. U. Medicine Dentistry-N.J. Med. Ctr., 1994—. Mem. study sect. allergy and immunology, 1981-85; chair study sect. tumor immunology ahd therapy TRDRP, 1992-94; co-chmn. 3d, 4th and 5th Internat. Lymphokine Workshops, 1982, 84, Congress on Cytokines, 1987, UCLA colloquium: molecular pathways of cytokines, 1990—, Keystone Symposium, 1992. Author: Mechanisms of Cell-Mediated Immunity, 1974, Mechanisms of Tumor Immunity, 1976, Mechanisms of Immunopathology, 1978, Biology of the Lymphokines, 1979, Interleukins, Lymphokines and Cytokines, 1983, Molecular Basis of Lymphokine Action, 1987, Role of Lymphokines in the Immune Response, 1989; assoc. editor-in-chief Clin. Immunology and Immunopathology; mem. editorial bds. 8 profl. jours.; contbr. more than 195 articles to profl. jours. Served to capt. U.S. Army, 1966-68. Recipient Kinne award, 1954, Borden award, 1961, Parke-Davis award in Exptl. Pathology, 1977, Outstanding Investigator award Nat. Cancer, Inst., 1986; Witobsky Meml. lectr., 1995. Mem.: Pluto Soc., Am. Soc. Exptl. Biology (fin. com. 2001—), Am. Soc. Investigative Pathology (sec.-treas. 2001—), Clin. Immunol. Soc. (councilor), Am. Assn. Immunologists, Am. Assn. Pathologists. Home: 79 Ettl Cir Princeton NJ 08540-2334 Office: UMDNJ Med Sch Newark NJ 07103

COHEN, STANLEY, biochemistry educator; b. Brooklyn, N.Y., Nov. 17, 1922; s. Louis and Fannie (Feitel) C.; m. Olivia Larson, 1951 (div.); children: Burt Bishop, Kenneth Larson, Cary; m. Jan Elizabeth Jordan, 1981. BA, Bklyn. Coll., 1943; MA, Oberlin Coll., 1945, PhD, 1989; PhD in Biochemistry, U. Mich., 1948; PhD, U. Chgo., 1985, Washington U., 1993. Instr. dept. biochemistry and pediatrics U. Colo., Denver, 1948-52; Am. Cancer Soc. fellow in radiology Washington U., St. Louis, 1952-53, assoc. prof. dept. zoology, 1953-59; asst. prof. biochemistry, sch. medicine Vanderbilt U., Nashville, 1959-62, assoc. prof., 1962-67, prof. biochemistry, 1967-86, disting. prof., 1986-2000, Am. Cancer Soc. rsch. prof. biochemistry, 1976, disting. prof. emeritus, 2000—. Charles B. Smith vis. rsch. prof. Sloan Kettering, 1984; Feodor Lynen lectr. U. Miami, 1986, Steenbock lectr. U. Wis., 1986. Mem. editorial bd. Abstracts of Human Developmental Biology, Jour. of Cellular Physiology. Cons. Minority Rsch. Ctr. for Excellence. Recipient Research Career Devel. award NIH, 1959-69, William Thomson Wakeman award Nat. Paraplegia Found., Earl Sutherland Research Prize Vanderbilt U., 1977, Albion O. Bernstein MD award Med. Soc. State N.Y., 1978, H.P. Robertson Meml. award Nat. Acad. Sci., 1981, Lewis S. Rosentiel award Brandeis U., 1982, Alfred P. Sloan award Gen. Motors Cancer Research Found., 1982, Louisa Gross Horwitz prize Columbia U., 1983, Disting. Achievement award UCLA Lab. Biomed. and Environ. Scis., 1983, Lila Gruber Meml. Cancer Research award Am. Acad. Dermatology, 1983, Bertner award MD Anderson Hosp. U. Tex., 1983, Gairdner Found. Internat. award, 1985, Fred Conrad Koch award Endocrine Soc., 1986, Nat. Medal Sci., 1986, 89, Albert and Mary Lasker Found. Basic Med. Research award, 1986, Nobel Prize in physiology or medicine, 1986, Tennessean of Yr. award Tenn. Sports Hall of Fame, 1987, Franklin Medal, 1987, Albert A. Michaelson award Mus. Sci. and Industry, 1987. Fellow Jewish Acad. Arts and Sci.; mem. Nat. Acad. Sci., Am. Soc. Biol. Chemists, Am. Chem. Soc., AAAS, Internat. Inst. Embryology, Internat. Acad. Sci. (hon. internat. coun. for sci. devel.).*

COHEN, STANLEY, commercial real estate developer; b. Cin., Jan. 4, 1929; s. Robert Lieb and Celia (Gordon) C.; m. Rae A. Cohen, Aug. 28, 1960; children: Gordon Alan, Gary Louis, Sharon Diann. BA, U. Cin., 1950. Promotion assoc. Ziv TV Programs, Inc., Cin., 1953-57; program dir. WDSU-TV, New Orleans, 1957-64; pres. Royal Street Devel. Co., Inc., Newport Beach, Calif., 1965-73, Mission Hills Ranch, Inc., Newport Beach, 1969-73; vice chair Greater Park City Co., Inc., Park City, Utah, 1971-74; sr. v.p. E.M. Warburg, Pincus & Co., Inc., Newport Beach, 1973-75; mng. ptnr. Stanley Cohen/Crocker/Pacific Assocs., Newport Beach, 1978-85, Shoreline Sq. Assocs., Newport Beach, 1985-94; owner Stanley Cohen & Assocs., Costa Mesa, Calif., 1975—. Bd. dirs. Flowline, Inc., Los Alamitos, Calif.; mem. exec. com. The Olson Co., Seal Beach, Calif., 1995—; guest lectr. UCLA Grad. Sch. Bus., U. So. Calif. Grad. Sch. Bus., U. Calif. San Diego Grad Sch. Bus. Contbr. articles to L.A. Times, Orange County Register. Bd. dirs. Calif. State U. Found., Long Beach, 1987-95; trustee St. Mary Med. Ctr., Long Beach, 1984-90; chmn. ednl. resources adv. com. Newport-Mesa Unified Sch. Dist., Newport Beach, 1982-83. Recipient Disting. Achievement award U. Cin., 1993, Disting. Bus. and the Arts award Pub. Corp. for the Arts, Long Beach, 1989, Outstanding Achievement award Long Beach Area C. of C., 1983, Outstanding Leadership award Newport Harbor Coun. PTA Pres., 1983, Outstanding Leadership award Newport-Mesa Unified Sch. Dist. Bd. Edn., 1983. Mem. Nat. Assn. TV Program Execs. (hon. life; founding pres. 1963-65), Lincoln Club of Orange County. Home: 1501 Antigua Way Newport Beach CA 92660-4917 Office: Stanley Cohen and Assocs 2183 Fairview Rd Ste 219 Costa Mesa CA 92627-5674

COHEN, STANLEY ALLEN, pediatric gastroenterologist; b. Columbus, Ohio, June 3, 1947; s. Norman Saul and Esther (Schlansky) C.; m. Judith Dee Adler, Mar. 22, 1970 (div. 1997). m. Jamie Ann Golsen, Nov. 10, 2002 ; children: David, Adam, Lauren. BS, Case Western Res., 1969; MD, Ohio State U., 1972. Diplomate Am. Bd. Pediat. and Pediatric GI/Nutrition. Intern Johns Hopkins Hosp., Balt., 1972-73, resident, 1973-75, intern, resident, 1972-75; pediatrician USAF, Langley AFB, Va., 1975-77; fellow Mass Gen. Hosp., Boston, 1977-80; pediatrician Roswell (Ga.) Pediatrics, 1980-87; physician, dir. Ctr. Pediatric Gastroenterology/Nutrition, Atlanta, 1987-99; physician Children's Ctr. Digestive Healthcare, 1999—; adj. clin. prof. pediatrics Emory U., Atlanta, 2001—. Med. dir. Healthfield/Hug Ctr., Altanta, 1989—. Author: Healthy Babies, Happy Kids, 1985, poem Two, 1990, Seeping Into/Out of the Well, 1991, Beyond Hell, 1992, Re-Re-, 1995, In Celebration, 2002; editor: Pediatric Emergency Mgmt., 1983; patentee in field. Chmn. 20th Century Art Acquisition Fund High Mus., Atlanta, 1985-86; pres. Scottish Rite Childrens Med. Ctr., Atlanta, 1986. Maj. USAF, 1975-79. Recipient Premiere Physicians award Crohn's and Colitis Found. Ga. chpt., 1995, Atlanta Alliance Devel. Disabilities award, 1999. Fellow Am. Acad. Pediatrics (chmn. com. on nutrition Ga. chpt., lay edn. award 1997, chmn. sect. subspecialists); mem. Greater Atlanta Pediatric Soc., N.Am. Soc. Pediatric Gastroenterology and Nutrition. Office: Children's Ctr Digestive Healthcare Ste 440 993-D Johnson Ferry Rd Atlanta GA 30342-4722

COHEN, STANLEY ALVIN, electrical engineer, consultant; b. Bklyn., Apr. 7, 1929; s. Moe and Bessie (Goldschmidt) C.; B.E.E., CCNY, 1951; M.E.E., Poly. Inst. Bklyn., 1954. Registered profl. engr., N.Y. Lectr. CCNY, 1958-65; group leader IIT Research Inst., Annapolis, Md., 1965-73; cons. Conic Research, Bethesda, Md., 1973-76, dir., 1973-78; staff engr. E-Systems Inc., Greenville, Tex., 1976-77; project leader, space div. Gen. Electric Co., Valley Forge, Pa., 1977-78; staff engr., applied physics lab. Johns Hopkins U., Laurel, Md., 1978-92. Contbr. articles to profl. jours. Inventor in fields of radar and electronics. Mem. IEEE (sr. mem.), Md. Soc. Profl. Engrs. (pres. Annapolis chpt. 1973-74), Sigma Xi (assoc.), Eta Kappa Nu. E-mail: ConicRes@consultant.com.

COHEN, STANLEY DALE, lawyer; b. Nassau County, N.Y., Mar. 14, 1952; s. Lester and Eleanor (Mait) C.; m. Janis Wendrow, Sept. 11, 1976; children: Adam Benjamin, Heather Jill. JD, Western New Eng. Coll., 1976. Bar: N.Y. 1977, D.C. 1980, Fla. 1981, U.S. Dist. Ct. (so. and ea. dists.) N.Y. 1977, D.C. 1980, Fla. 1981, U.S. Ct. Appeals (9th cir.) 1982. Mem. firm Ruben, Schwartz & Silverberg, N.Y.C., 1977-78; sole practice, N.Y.C., 1978-83; mem. firm Cohen & Jaeger, 1984—; sec., bd. dirs. Manhattan Mag. Found. Corp. Mem. steering com. Fed. Hall Bill of Rights Bicentennial. Mem. N.Y. County Lawyers Assn. Office: 250 Old Country Rd Mineola NY 11501-4299 Home: 3004 Shore Rd Bellmore NY 11710-4831

COHEN, STANLEY NORMAN, geneticist, educator; b. Perth Amboy, N.J., Feb. 17, 1935; s. Bernard and Ida (Stolz) Cohen; m. Joanna Lucy Wolter, June 27, 1961; children: Anne, Geoffrey. BA, Rutgers U., 1956; MD, U. Pa., 1960, ScD (hon.), 1995, Rutgers U., 1994. Intern Mt. Sinai Hosp., N.Y.C., 1960-61; resident Univ. Hosp., Ann Arbor, Mich., 1961-62; clin. assoc. arthritis and rheumatism br. Nat. Inst. Arthritis and Metabolic Diseases, Bethesda, Md., 1962-64; sr. resident in medicine Duke U. Hosp., Durham, N.C., 1964-65; Am. Cancer Soc. postdoctoral rsch. fellow Albert Einstein Coll. Medicine, Bronx, 1965-67, asst. prof. devel. biology and cancer, 1967-68; mem. faculty Stanford (Calif.) U., 1968—, prof. medicine, 1975—, prof. genetics, 1977—, chmn. dept. genetics, 1978-86, K.-T Li Prof., 1993—. Mem. com. recombinant DNA molecules NAS-NRC, 1974; mem. com. on genetic experimentation Internat. Coun. Sci. Unions, 1977—96. Trustee U. Pa., 1997—2002. With USPHS, 1962—64. Named to Nat. Inventors Hall of Fame, 2001; recipient Burroughs Wellcome Scholar award, 1970, Mattia award, Roche Inst. Molecular Biology, 1977, Albert Lasker basic med. rsch. award, 1980, Wolf prize, 1981, Marvin J. Johnson award, 1981, Disting. Grad. award, U. Pa. Sch. Medicine, 1986, Disting. Svc. award, Miami Winter Symposium, 1986, Nat. Biotech award, 1989, de la Vie prize, LVMH Inst., 1988, Nat. Medal Sci., 1988, City of Medicine award, 1988, Nat, Medal of Tech., 1989, Spl. award, Am. Chem. Soc., 1999, Lemelson MIT Prize, MIT, 1996; fellow Guggenheim fellow, 1973; scholar faculty scholar, Josiah Macy, Jr., 1975—76. Fellow: AAAS; mem.: NAS (chmn. genetics sect. 1988—91), Inst. Medicine, Assn. Am. Physicians, Am. Soc. Clin. Investigation, Am. Soc. Pharmacology and Exptl. Therapeutics, Am. Soc. Microbiology (Cetus award 1988), Genetics Soc. Am., Am. Soc. Biol. Chemists, Am. Acad. Microbiology, Phi Beta Kappa, Sigma Xi, Alpha Omega Alpha. Office: Stanford U Sch Med Dept Genetics Rm M-322 Stanford CA 94305

COHEN, STEPHEN BRUCE, lawyer; b. East Chicago, Ind., Mar. 14, 1939; s. Cecil Bernard and Ida Edith (Goldstein) Cohen; m. Lynn Sneider, Mar. 23, 1969; children: Debra Suzanne, Aaron Eliot, Sabrina Beth. AB, Harvard Coll., 1961; JD, Vanderbilt U., 1964; LLM in Internat. Law, Cambridge (Eng.) U., 1966, Diploma in Internat. Law, 1972. Bar: Ind. 1965, Ill. 1965, U.S. Dist. Ct. (no. dist.) Ill. 1967, U.S. Dist. Ct. (no. and so. dists.) Ind. 1965, U.S. Ct. Appeals (7th cir.) 1968, U.S. Tax Ct. 1981, U.S. Claims Ct. 1990, U.S. Supreme Ct. 1972. Ptnr. Cohen, Foss, Schuman & Drake and predecessor firms, East Chicago; assoc. Foss, Schuman, Drake & Barnard, Chgo., 1965-69, ptnr., 1969-86, Cohen, Starck & Burchett, Northbrook, Ill., East Chicago, 1986-87, Cohen, Starck & Weiner, Skokie, Ill., East Chicago, 1987-88; pvt. practice Law Offices of Stephen B. Cohen, P.C., Northbrook, 1988-94; ptnr. Cohen & Pinsel, Northbrook, 1995-99, Kelly, Olson, Michod & Siepker, 2000; mem. Kelly, Olson, Michod, DeHaan & Richter, L.L.C. Internat., 2000—, Cohen, Kelly, Olson, DeHaan & Richter, L.L.C. Internat., 2000—. Mediator Cohen Mediation Svcs., 1995—; arbitrator Cook County Mandatory Arbitration Program, 1993—; lectr. in field. Bd. dirs. U.S. Speedskating Charitable Found. Named to E. Chgo. (Ind.) Sports Hall of Fame, 2001; recipient Svc. award, Ill. Park Recreation Assn., 1986, Hall of Fame award, Northbrook Park Dist., 1992. Mem.: U.S. Internat. Speedskating Assn. (pres.'s adv. bd. 1988—2000, chmn. legal com. 1990—93, spl. counsel 1998—2001), East Chgo./Ind. Bar Assn. (pres. 1993—95), Lake County/Ind. Bar Assn. (grievance com. 1990—91), Chgo. Bar Assn. (chmn. condominium subcom. 1980—82, exec. com. real property law com. 1980—90), Ind. Bar Assn., Ill. Bar Assn. (ADR sect. coun. 1998—). Jewish. Avocations: weight lifting, racquetball, bicycling, masters track and field, fly fishing, reading. Office: Kelly Olson et al 30 South Wacker Drive Chicago IL 60606 also: Cohen Kelly et al 9337 Calumet Ave Ste A-1 Munster IN 46321 E-mail: scohen@komdr.com., lawcp@aol.com.

COHEN, STEPHEN FRAND, political scientist, historian, educator, author, broadcaster; b. Indpls., Nov. 25, 1938; s. Marvin Stafford and Ruth (Frand) C.; m. Katrina vanden Heuvel; children: Andrew, Alexandra, Nicola. BS, Ind. U., 1960, MA, 1962; PhD, Columbia U., 1969; cert., Russian Inst., 1969. Instr. Columbia U., N.Y.C., 1965-68; asst. prof. politics Princeton (N.J.) U., N.J., 1968-73; assoc. prof. Princeton U., N.J., 1973-80, prof., 1980-98, prof. emeritus, 1998—, dir. Russian studies, 1973-80, 88-94; prof. Russian studies and History NYU, 1998—. Cons. on Russia, CBS news TV commentator, 1989—; corr., chief cons. PBS WNET films on Russia, 1994-2001; adv. coun. U.S. Acad. Scis., Washington, 1979-82. Author: Bukharin and the Bolshevik Revolution, 1973 (Nat. Book Award nominee 1974, Bukharin prize 1989), Rethinking the Soviet Experience, 1985, Sovieticus: American Perceptions and Soviet Realities, 1985 (Page One award 1985), Failed Crusade: America and the Tragedy of Post-Communist Russia, 2000, 2d edit., 2001; editor: (with Robert C. Tucker) The Great Purge Trial, 1965, (with Rabinowitch and Sharlet) The Soviet Union Since Stalin, 1980, An End to Silence, 1982, (with Katrina vanden Heuvel) Voices of Glasnost: Interviews with Gorbachev's Reformers, 1989; mem. editl. bd. Slavic Rev., 1977-82, Post-Soviet Affairs, 1992-2002; assoc. editor World Politics, 1972-88; columnist The Nation Mag., 1982-87; contbg. editor, 1994—. Bd. dirs. NYU Ctr. for the Media. Recipient Page One award Column Writing, 1985, Ind. U. Disting. Alumn award, 1998, Columbia U. Harriman Inst. Alumnus of Yr. award, 2002; fellow Am. Council Learned Socs., 1971, 72-73; fellow John Simon Guggenheim Found., 1976-77, 88-89, Rockefeller Found., 1980-81; NEH fellow, 1985-86; Fulbright-Hays fellow, 1988-89. Mem. Council Fgn. Relations, Am. Polit. Sci. Assn., Am. Hist. Assn., Am. Assn. for Advancement Slavic Studies. Home: 340 Riverside Dr Apt 8B New York NY 10025-3436

COHEN, STEPHEN IRA, lawyer, state legislator; b. Memphis, May 24, 1949; s. Morris David and Genevieve (Goldsand) C. BA, Vanderbilt U., 1971; JD, U. Memphis, 1973. Bar: Tenn. 1974. Sole practice, 1974-75; legal advisor Memphis Police Dept., 1975-78; mem. Shelby County Commn., 1978-80; sole practice Memphis, 1978—; mem. Tenn. Senate, 1982—, deputy spkr., 2000—, chair, Senate State & Local Govt. Comm., 1991, mem., Senate Judiciary, Transp. & Fiscal Review Comm. Interim judge Gen. Sessions Ct., 1980; v.p. Tenn. Constnl. Conv., 1977; del. Democratic Nat. Conv., 1980, 92; chair lottery info. and recommendation com.; mem. coun. state govts. exec. com., 2002, exec. com. Nat. Conf. State Legislators. Trustee Memphis Coll. Art, 2000, bd. trustees, 1988-2002; mem. Redbirds Found., Memphis Shelby County Center City Commn, Memphis Zoological Soc., 1998-, (bd. dirs. 1988-). Recipient Public Leadership award, Tenn. Human Rights Campaign, 2002, Legislator of the Year, Boys & Girls Clubs of Tenn., 2003, Leadership Award, Gov.'s Awards in the Arts. Mem. Memphis Bar Assn., Shelby County Charter Commn. Democrat. Home: 349 Kenilworth Pl Memphis TN 38112-5405 Office: Legislative Plz Ste 8 Nashville TN 37243-0030*

COHEN, S(TEPHEN) MARSHALL, philosophy educator; b. N.Y.C., Sept. 27, 1929; s. Harry and Fanny (Marshall) C.; m. Margaret Dennes, Feb. 15, 1964; children: Matthew, Megan. BA, Dartmouth Coll., Hanover, N.H., 1951; postgrad., Harvard U., 1953; MA, Oxford U., 1977. Jr. fellow, Soc. of Fellows Harvard U., Cambridge, Mass., 1955-58, asst. prof. philosophy and gen. edn., 1958-62; asst. prof. U. Chgo., 1962-64, assoc. prof., 1964-67, acting chair Coll. Philosophy, 1965-66; assoc. prof. Rockefeller U., N.Y.C., 1967-70; prof. philosophy Richmond Coll. (now Coll. of S.I.), 1970-83; exec. officer program in philosophy Grad. Ctr. CUNY, 1975-83; prof. philosophy and law U. So. Calif., L.A., 1983-97, dean divsn. humanities, 1983-94, interim dean Coll. Letters, Arts and Sci., 1993-94, Univ. prof. philosophy and law emeritus, 1998—; dean emeritus Coll. Letters, Arts and Sci., U. So. Calif., LA, 1998—. Lectr. Lowell Inst., Boston, 1957-58; vis. fellow All Souls Coll., Oxford, Eng., 1976-77; mem. Inst. for Advanced Study, Princeton, N.J., 1981-82. Editor: The Philosophy of John Stuart Mill, 1961, Philosophy and Public Affairs, 1970-99, Philosophy and Society series, 1977-83, Ethical, Legal and Political Philosophy series, 1983-99; co-editor: Film Theory and Criticism, 1974, 79, 85, 92, 98, War and Moral Responsibility, 1974, The Rights and Wrongs of Abortion, 1974, Equality and Preferential Treatment, 1977, Marx, Justice and History, 1980, Medicine and Moral Philosophy, 1982, What Is Dance?, 1983, International Ethics, 1985, Punishment, 1995. Rockefeller Found. humanities fellow, 1977, Guggenheim fellow, 1976-77. Mem. Am. Philos. Assn., Am. Coun. Learned Socs. (bd. dirs. 1987-91, 93—), Coun. on Internat. Ednl. Exch. (bd. dirs. 1991-94). Democrat. Jewish. Office: U So Calif Law Sch Los Angeles CA 90089-0071 E-mail: mcohen@law.usc.edu.

COHEN, STEVEN ALAN, program director; b. Orange, N.J., Sept. 6, 1953; s. Marvin and Shirley Cohen; children: Gabriella Rose, Ariel Mariah. BA in Polit. Sci., Franklin Coll., 1974; MA in Polit. Sci., SUNY, Buffalo, 1977, PhD in Polit. Sci., 1979. Asst. prof. polit. sci. W.Va. U., Washington, 1979-80; environ. protection specialist EPA, Washington, 1980-81; asst. prof. polit. sci. Columbia U., N.Y.C., 1981-86, dir. grad. program, 1985-98, assoc. dean Sch. Internat. and Pub. Affairs, 1987-98, vice dean Sch. Internat. and Pub. Affairs, 1998-2001, dir. exec. MPA program pub. adminstrn., 2001—. Mgr. intergovernmental analysis unit Nat. Waste Terminal Storage Program, Washington, 1984; dir. hazardous waste mgmt. project Nat. Acad. Pub. Adminstrn., Washington, 1984-85; cons. N. Ward Ctr., Newark, 1999-00, Transitional Work Corp., Phila., 1999—; co-prin. investigator Earth Inst. Columbia U., N.Y.C., 1999—. Author: The Effective Public Manager, 1988 (Outstanding Author 1990); co-author: Environmental Regualtion Through Strategic Planning, 1991, total Quality Management in Government, 1993, Tools for Innovators: Creative Strategies for Managing Public Sector Organizations, 1998. Bd. dirs. Home for the Homeless, N.Y.C., 1999—. Fellow Ford Found., 1977-78, Rockefeller Found., 1978-79. Jewish. Home: 90 Morningside Dr Apt 5B New York NY 10027-7118 Office: Columbia U Sch Internat & Pub Affairs 420 W 118th St Rm 1314 New York NY 10027-7213

COHEN, STEVEN CHARLES, geophysicist; b. New Kensington, Pa., Aug. 27, 1947; s. Reuben and Rose Edith (Gordon) Cohen; m. Davria Eileen Millstone, Aug. 15, 1970; children: Amber, Phillip. BS, Drexel U., 1970; MS, U. Md., 1972, PhD, 1973. Physicist, Laser Tech. Br. Goddard Space Flight Ctr., Greenbelt, Md., 1970—76, geophysicist Lab. Terrestrial Physics, 1976—, sr. scientist, 1984—, asst. head geodynamics br., 1993—; U.S. del. geodynamics Working Group on U.S.-China Cooperation in Space Sci. and Tech., 1984—86; project scientist Geodynamics Laser Ranging System, 1986—90; vis. scholar U. Tex., 1991—92, Inst. of Geol. and Nuclear Sci., New Zealand, 1996—97, 2000; mem. Whitten medal award com. Am. Geophys. Union, 1998—2000. Del. Workshop on the interdisciplinary role of space geodynamics, 1988. Author (contbg.): Advances in Geophysics, Vol. 41; editor: AGU Geophysical Monograph: Slow Deformation and Transmission of Stress in the Earth, 1988—89; editor: (guest) Jour. Geophys. Rsch., 1985. Recipient Earth Sci. Spl. Achievement award, Goddard Space Flight Ctr., NASA, 1979, 1979. Mem.: Am. Geophys. Union, Sigma Xi, Pi Mu Epsilon, Sigma Pi Sigma, Phi Kappa Phi. Avocations: history, golf. Office: Goddard Space Flight Ctr Geodynamics Br Greenbelt MD 20771-0001

COHEN, STEVEN HOWARD, allergist, immunologist, educator; b. Akron, Ohio, May 15, 1946; s. Julius Abraham and Goldie Rebecca (Katzman) C.; m. Esta Rachel Ashrey, June 14, 1970 (dec. Aug. 1987); children: Hal, Beth; m. Deborah Mendeloff, Apr. 6, 1989. BS, Akron U., 1968; MD, Ohio State U., 1972. Intern Med. Coll. Wis.-Milwaukee County Hosp., 1972-73, resident internal medicine, 1973-75, fellow allergy and immunology, 1975-77; asst. prof. medicine Med. Coll. Wis., Milw., 1977-84, clin. assoc. prof. medicine, 1984—; physician Allergic Diseases S.C., Milw., 1984—, St. Lukes Hosp., Milw. Pres. Anshe Sfard Kehillat Torah, 1995-98. Mem. ACP, Am. Thoracic Soc., Am. Acad. Allergy Asthma and Immunology (ethics com. 1982-84), State Med. Soc. Wis. (ethics commn. 1994-2001). Office: 11121 W Oklahoma Ave Milwaukee WI 53227-4033 also: 721 American Ave Ste 205 Waukesha WI 53188-5071 E-mail: scgolf@allergiediseases.com.

COHEN, STEVEN PAUL, anesthesiologist, researcher; b. Philadelphia, Dec. 9, 1963; s. Allen Theodore Cohen and Harriet Ruth Hershfeld; m. Eun-Kyung Im, July 7, 2001; 1 child, Berklee Kordell. BA, SUNY, Stony Brook, 1985; MD,

Mt. Sinai U., 1989. Diplomate Am. Bd. Anesthesology. Intern Beth Israel Med. Ctr., N.Y.C., 1990—93; resident in anesthesia Presbyn. Hosp. Columbia U., N.Y.C., 1993; commd. 2d. lt. U. S. Army, 1993; asst. chief anesthesia & operavice svc. 121st Gen. Hosp., Seoul, Republic of Korea, 1993—95; chief anesthesia & operative svc. Wverzburg (Germany) MEDDAC, 1995—96, 121st Gen. Hosp., Seoul, Republic of Korea, 1996—99; fellow in pain mgmt. Mass. Gen. Hosp./Harvard Med. Sch., Boston, 1999—2000; dir. acute pain svc. Walter Reed Army Med. Ctr., Washington, 2000—; dir. inpatient pain svcs. NYU Med. Ctr., N.Y.C., 2002—. Contbr. articles. Lt. col. med. corps USAR. Recipient 1st pl., U.S. Army Photography Contest, 1998, 2d. pl., U.S. Army Forces Photography Contest, 1998, 2d ranked in black belt form N.Y./N.J. region, Karate Illustrated Mag., 1984. Mem.: N.Y. Acad. Scis., Am. Soc. Anesthesiologist, Am. Pain Soc. Avocations: martial arts, photography, writing, travel. Office: NYU Med Ctr Inpatient Pain Svc Dept 317 E 34th St 9th Fl New York NY 10016

COHEN, SUSAN LOIS, writer; b. Chgo., Mar. 27, 1938; d. Martin and Ida Handler; m. Daniel E. Cohen, Feb. 2, 1958; 1 child, Theodora (dec.). BA, New Sch. for Social Rsch., 1960; MA in Social Work, Adelphi U., 1962. Social worker, N.Y.C., 1962-67; various social work positions in N.Y.C., 1962-68. Author: The Liberated Couple, 1969, reassued under title Liberated Marriage, 1973; (under name Elizabeth St. Clair) Stonehaven, 1974, The Singing Harp, 1975, Secret of the Locket, 1975, Provenance House, 1976, Mansion in Miniature, 1977, Dewitt Manor, 1977, The Jeweled Secret, 1978, Murder in the Act, 1978, Sandcastle Murder, 1979, Trek or Treat, 1980, Sealed with a Kiss, 1981; (with Daniel Cohen) The Kids' Guide to Home Computers, 1983, The Kids' Guide to Home Video, 1984, Teenage Stress, 1984, Screen Goddesses, 1984, Rock Video Superstars, 1985, Wrestling Superstars, Vol. 1, 1985, Vol. 2, 1986, Hollywood Hunks and Heroes, 1985, Heroes of the Challenger, 1986, A Six-Pack and a Fake ID, 1986, The Encyclopedia of Movie Stars, 1986, A History of the Oscars, 1986, Teenage Competition: A Survival Guide, 1987, Young and Famous: Hollywood's Newest Superstars, 1987, Going for the Gold, 1987, What You Can Believe about Drugs, 1988, What Kind of Dog is That, 1989, When Someone You Know Is Gay, 1989, Zoo Superstars, 1989, Zoos, 1992, Where to Find Dinosaurs Today, 1992, Going for the Gold: Medal Hopefuls for Winter '92, 1992, Gold Medal Glow: The Story of America's Women's Gymnastic Team, 1996, Pop Am 103, 2000, rev. edit. 2001, Hauntings and Horrors, 2002. Mem. Wodehouse Soc. (pres.), Watson's Erroneous Deductions, Chapter One, The Capers of Sherlock Holmes, Clumber Spaniel Club of Am. Avocation: cats. Address: 877 W Hand Ave Cape May Court House NJ 08210-1865 E-mail: blindgscast@aol.com.

COHEN, TED, philosophy educator; b. Danville, Ill., Dec. 13, 1939; s. Sam and Shirley E. (Nimz) C.; m. Julie Simon, Apr. 18, 1940 (div. 1992); children: Shoshannah, Amos; m. Ann Rutherfurd Collier Austin, 1994. AB, U. Chgo., 1962; MA, Harvard U., 1965, PhD, 1972. Prof. philosophy U. Chgo., 1967—, chmn. dept. philosophy, 1974-79. Author: Jokes, 1999, Korean translation, 2002; editor: Essays in Kant's Aesthetics, 1982, Pursuits of Reason, 1993; contbr. articles to profl. jours. in German, Polish, Italian, French, Norwegian, Spanish, Finnish, Russian, Japenese, Serbo-Croatian and Dutch, 1972—. Bd. dirs. Ctr. for Rehab. and Tng. of Disabled, B'nai Brith Hillel Found. of U. Chgo., KAM Isaiah Israel Congregation, Chgo., 1980—, mem. faculty religious sch.; chmn. com. on gen. studies in humanities U. Chgo., 1991—. Named William R. Kenan Jr. Disting. Prof. Humanities Coll. of William and Mary, 1986-87; grantee Am. Council Learned Socs., 1980, 85. Mem. Am. Soc. Aesthetics (v.p., pres.-elect, pres. 1997—), Phi Beta Kappa (vis. scholar 2000-2001). Avocation: baseball theory and practice. Office: U Chgo Dept Philosophy 1050 E 59th St Chicago IL 60637-1559 Home: 5816 S Blackstone Ave Chicago IL 60637 E-mail: tedcohen@midway.uchicago.edu.

COHEN, WALTER STANLEY, accountant, financial consultant; b. Bklyn., Oct. 24, 1936; s. Harry and Ruth (Spitz) Cohen; m. Barbara Lee Cooper, June 18, 1960; children: Howard H, Andrea Sue. BS, U. Buffalo, 1958; postgrad., NYU, 1960-64. Jr. acct. Morris, Sherwood & May (CPAs), N.Y.C., 1958-59; semi-sr. acct. H. Merdinger & Co. (CPAs), 1960-61; sr. acct. Skillman & Michaels (CPAs), N.Y.C., 1961-62; with Blessings Corp., N.Y.C., 1962-84, sr. acct., 1962-66, asst. contr., 1966-69, asst. sec., 1969-70, sec., 1970-79, sec.-treas., 1979-84; v.p. fin. Sketchley Am., Inc., 1984-86; fin. cons. Thomson-McKinnon Securities, 1987-89; assoc. v.p. investments Prudential Securities, Bridgewater, N.J., 1989-94; assoc. v.p. Morgan Stanley Dean Witter, Somerville, N.J., 1994—. With AUS, 1959—60. Mem.: B'nai B'rith, Kappa Nu (treas 1995—96, vpres 1956—57). Republican. Jewish. Office: Morgan Stanley 166 W Main St Somerville NJ 08876-2204 Home: 9 Hazeltine Ln Jackson NJ 08527 E-mail: walter_cohen@msdn.com.

COHEN, WARREN I. history educator; b. Bklyn., June 20, 1934; s. Murray and Fay (Phillips) C.; m. Janice Prichard, June 22, 1957 (div. Mar. 1986); children: Geoffrey Scott, Anne Leslie; m. Nancy Bernkopf Tucker, June 12, 1988. AB, Columbia U., 1955; A.M., Fletcher Sch. Law and Diplomacy, Tufts U., 1956; PhD, U. Wash., 1962. Lectr. U. Calif.-Riverside, 1962-63, asst. prof., 1963-67, assoc. prof., 1967-71; prof. history Mich. State U., East Lansing, 1971-93, disting. univ. prof., 1990-93, dir. Asian Studies Ctr., 1979-89; disting. univ. prof. U. Md., Baltimore County, 1992—. Vis. prof. Nat. Taiwan U., Taipei, 1964-66, Columbia U., N.Y.C., 1971, Fgn. Affairs Coll., Beijing, 1986; mem. Com. on Am.-East Asian Rels., Balt., 1973—; mem. adv. com. on hist. diplomatic documentation Dept. State, 1986-90, chmn., 1988-90; scholar-in-residence Assn. for Diplomatic Studies and Tng., 1994-95; acting dir. Asia program Wilson Ctr., 1995-99. Author: The American Revisionists, 1967, America's Response to China, 1971, The Chinese Connection, 1978, Dean Rusk, 1980, Empire without Tears, 1987, East Asian Art and American Culture, 1992, America in the Age of Soviet Power, 1945-1991, 1993, East Asia the the Center, 2000, Asian American Century, 2002; editor Diplomatic History, 1979-82, New Frontiers in American-East Asian Relations, 1983, (with Akira Iriye) Japan and the United States in the Postwar World, 1988, Great Powers in East Asia, 1953-60, 1990, (with Nancy Bernkopf Tucker) Lyndon Johnson Confronts the World, 1994, Pacific Passage, 1996, (with Li Zhao) Hong Kong Under Chinese Rule, 1997. Bd. dirs. Mich. China Council, East Lansing, 1978-92; exec. sec. Gov's Mich. and China Com., Lansing, 1982-84; mem. Gov's Commn. on China, 1984-88; bd. dirs. Japan Council, 1979-92. Served to lt. (j.g.) USNR, 1956-59, PTO. Fulbright lectr. Tokyo, 1969-70; rsch. grantee Am. Coun. Learned Socs., 1968, Ford Found., 1976-77, Henry Luce Found., 1983-84; recipient Disting. Faculty award Mich. State U., 1988; Wilson Ctr. fellow, 1990-91, sr. scholar, 1999—; Presdl. rsch. scholar UMBC, 2001--. Mem. ACLU, Coun. on Fgn. Rels., Orgn. Am. Historians, Soc. for Historians of Am. Fgn. Rels. (v.p. 1983, pres. 1984). Democrat. Jewish. Office: U Md Balt County Dept History Baltimore MD 21250-0001 also: 11500 S Glen Rd Potomac MD 20854-1852 Business E-Mail: wcohen@umbc.edu.

COHEN, WILLARD, retired cardiologist, intensivist; b. Watertown, N.Y., Dec. 27, 1931; MD, SUNY, Syracuse, 1956. Diplomate Am. Bd. Internal Medicine, 1963, Cardiology, 1977, Critical Care Medicine, 1987; recert. in internal medicine, 1977. Intern Montefiore Hosp., N.Y.C., 1956-57; resident in internal medicine SUNY Upstate Med. Ctr., Syracuse, 1957-58, fellow in cardiovasc. disease, 1958-59, 62-63; clin. prof. emeritus internal medicine SUNY Upstate, Syracuse, prof. emeritus emergency and critical care medicine. Fellow Am. Coll. Cardiology, Coll. Critical Care Medicine, Coll. Chest Physicians; mem. Alpha Omega Alpha. Home: 119 Cherry Hl De Witt NY 13214-2303 E-mail: MDHEART@aol.com.

COHEN, WILLIAM, law educator; b. Scranton, Pa., June 1, 1933; s. Maurice M. and Nellie (Rubin) C.; m. Betty C. Stein, Sept. 13, 1952 (div. 1976, dec. 2000); children: Barbara Jean, David Alan (dec. 1995), Rebecca Anne; m. Nancy M. Mahoney, Aug. 8, 1976; 1 dau., Margaret Emily. BA, UCLA, 1953, LLB, 1956. Bar: Calif. 1961. Law clk. to U.S. Supreme Ct. Justice William O. Douglas, 1956-57; from asst. prof. to assoc. prof. U. Minn. Law Sch., 1957-60; vis. asso. prof. UCLA Law Sch., 1959-60, mem. faculty, 1960-70, prof., 1962-70, Stanford (Calif.) Law Sch., 1970—, C. Wendell and Edith M. Carlsmith prof. law, 1983-99, Carlsmith prof. emeritus, 1999—. Vis. prof. law European U. Inst., Florence, Italy, fall 1977; Merriam vis. prof. Ariz. State U. Law Sch., Spring 1981 Author: Constitutional Protection of Expression and Conscience: The First Amendment, 2003; co-author: The Bill of Rights, a Source Book, 1968, Comparative Constitutional Law, 1978, Constitutional Law Cases and Materials, 1981, 6th edit., 2001, Constitutional Law: The Structure of Government, 1981, Constitutional Law: Civil Liberty and Individual Rights, 1982, 4th edit., 2002. Home: 698 Maybell Ave Palo Alto CA 94306-3819 Office: Stanford Law Sch Nathan Abbott Way Stanford CA 94305

COHEN, WILLIAM ALAN, marketing educator, author, consultant; b. Balt., June 25, 1937; s. Sidney Oliver and Theresa (Bachman) C.; m. Janice Dawn Stults, Jan. 3, 1963 (div. Jan. 1966); 1 child, William Alan II; m. Nurit Kovnator, May 28, 1967; children— Barak, Nimrod. BS, U.S. Mil. Acad., 1959; MBA, U. Chgo., 1967; MA, Claremont Grad. Sch., 1978; PhD, Indsl. Coll. of the Armed Forces, 1989. Registered profl. engr., Israel. Project mgr. Israel Aircraft Industries, 1970-73; mgr. rsch. and devel. Sierra Engring. Co., Sierra Madre, Calif., 1973-76; pres. Global Assocs., 1973—2003; mgr. advanced tech. mktg. McDonnell-Douglas Co., Huntington Beach, Calif., 1976-78; prof. mktg. Calif. State U., L.A., 1979—2002, dir. bur. bus. and econ. rsch., 1979-83, chmn. mktg. dept., 1986—89; pres. Calif. Am. U., L.A., 2002—03, Inst. of Leader Arts, L.A., 2003—; prof. bus. adminstrn. Touro Univ. Internat., 2003—. Bd. dir. Inst. Bus. Devel.; cons. Fortune 500 cos. Author: The Executives Guide to Finding a Superior Job, 1978, 83, Principles of Technical Management, 1980, Successful Marketing for Small Business, 1981, How to Sell to Government, 1981, The Entrepreneur and Small Business Problem Solver, 1983, 89, Direct Response Marketing, 1984, Building a Mail Order Business, 1982, 85, 91, 96, Making It Big as a Consultant, 1985, 90, 2001, Winning on the Marketing Front, 1986, High Tech Management, 1986, Developing a Winning Marketing Plan, 1987, The Students Guide to Finding a Superior Job, 1987, 93, The Practice of Marketing Management, 1988, 91, The Entrepreneur and Small Business Financial Problem Solver, 1989, The Art of Leader, 1990, The Entrepreneur and Small Business Marketing Problem Solver, 1991, Get a Great Job Fast, 1993, The Paranoid Corporation and Eight Other Ways Your Company Can Be Crazy, 1993, The Marketing Plan, 1994, 98, 2001, Making It!, 1994, Model Business Plans for Service Businesses, 1995, Model Business Plans for Product Businesses, 1995, The Stuff of Heroes: The 8 Universal Laws of Leadership, 1998, The New Art of the Leader, 2000, Marketing Your Small Business Made E-Z, 2000, The Wisdom of the Generals, 2001, Break the Rules, 2001; contbr. numerous articles to profl. jours. Maj. USAF, 1959-70, maj.-gen. USAFR, ret. Decorated Disting. Svc. Medal, Legion of Merit, D.F.C. with 3 oak leaf clusters, Meritorious Svc. medal with 2 oak leaf clusters, Air medal with 11 oak leaf clusters, numerous other U.S. and fgn. awards; named Disting. Grad. Indsl. Coll. Armed Forces, 1989; recipient Ministry Def. award State of Israel, 1976, Outstanding Svc. award Nat. Mgmt. Assn., 1979, Pres.'s award West Point Soc., 1982, Outstanding Prof. award, 1983, Chgo. Tribune Gold medal, George Washington medal Freedoms Found. at Valley Forge, 1986, CSULA Statewide Outstanding Prof., 1996, Great Tchr. in Mktg. award Acad. of Mktg. Sci., 1999. Fellow Acad. Mktg. Sci.; mem. Direct Mktg. Assn. (fellow 1980, 83), World Mktg. Congress (del. N.S. 1983), Direct Mktg. Club So. Calif. (bd. dirs., grantee 1981), Am. Mktg. Assn. (award 1982), West Point Soc. (pres., bd. dirs. 1981-82), Beta Gamma Sigma, Phi Sigma Phi. Republican. Jewish.

COHEN, WILLIAM BENJAMIN, historian, educator; b. Jakobstad, Finland, May 2, 1941; came to U.S., 1957; s. Walter Israel and Rosi (Hirschberg) C.; m. Christine Matheu; children: Natalie, Leslie, Laurel. BA, Pomona Coll., 1962; MA, Stanford U., 1963, PhD, 1968. Vis. lectr. Northwestern U., Evanston, Ill., 1966-67; instr. history Ind. U., Bloomington, 1966-68, asst. prof., 1968-71, assoc. prof., 1971-80, prof., 1980—, chmn. West European studies, 1978-80, chmn. dept. history, 1980-87, acting chmn. dept. history, 2001—02. Author: Rulers of Empire, 1971, Robert Delavignette, 1977, French Encounter, 1980, European Empire Building, 1980, (with Thomas F. Noble et al) Western Civilization: The Continuing Experiment, 1994, 2d edit., 1998, Urban Government and the Rise of the French City, 1998, The Transformation of Modern France, 1997. NEH fellow, 1972, Fulbright fellow, 1983-84. Mem. Am. Hist. Assn. (mem. nominating com. 1987-90, George Louis prize com. 1997-00), Coun. for European Studies, Soc. French Hist. Studies (pres. 1980-81, exec. com. 1980-83) Democrat. Home: Bloomington, Ind. Deceased.

COHEN, WILLIAM NATHAN, radiologist; b. Balt., Dec. 10, 1935; s. Herbert and Lillian (Goldberg) C.; m. Sylvia Weinstein, Feb. 9, 1964; children: Elaine, Shirah, Jonathan. Student, Johns Hopkins U., 1952-55; MD, U. Md., 1959. Intern U. Mich. Hosp., Ann Arbor, 1959-60; resident in radiology Mallinckrodt Inst., Washington U., St. Louis, 1960-63; chief radiology sect. Gallup Indian Hosp., USPHS, 1963-65; asst. prof. radiology U. Iowa, Iowa City, 1965-69, asso. prof., 1969-73, prof., 1973-76; prof. radiology SUNY Health Sci. Ctr., Syracuse, 1976-83, clin. prof. radiology, 1983—. Attending radiologist Crouse-Irving Meml. Hosp., Syracuse; vis. prof. radiology Hebrew U., Jerusalem, 1971-72; examiner Am. Bd. Radiology, 1981-87. Contbr. articles in field to med. jours. Fellow Am. Coll. Radiology; mem. Radiol. Soc. N. Am., Am. Roentgen Ray Soc., Am. Inst. Ultrasound in Medicine (sr.), Alpha Omega Alpha. Office: Crouse Hosp 736 Irving Ave Syracuse NY 13210-1687

COHEN, WILLIAM SEBASTIAN, consultant, former federal official, former senator; b. Bangor, Maine, Aug. 28, 1940; s. Reuben and Clara (Hartley) C.; children: Kevin, Christopher. AB cum laude, Bowdoin Coll., 1962; LLB cum laude, Boston U., 1965; LLD, St. Joseph's Coll., Windham, Maine, 1974; LL.D., U. Maine, 1975, Western New Eng. Coll., 1975, Bowdoin Coll., 1975, Nasson Coll., 1975, Thomas Coll., 1988, Colby Coll., 1988. Bar: Maine, Mass., D.C. Ptnr. Paine, Cohen, Lynch, Weatherbee & Kobritz, Bangor, 1966-72; instr. U. Maine, 1968-72; asst. county atty. Penobscot County, Maine, 1968-70; U.S. Senator from Maine, 1979-96; U.S. sec. defense, 1997-2001; chmn., CEO The Cohen Group, Washington, 2001—. Mem. Bangor Sch. Com., 1970-71, Bangor City Council, 1969-72, mayor, Bangor, 1972; Trustee Unity Coll.; bd. overseers Bowdoin Coll., 1973-85; trustee and counselor Ctr. Strategic and Internat. Studies, Washington, 2001—; chmn. bd. advisors MIC Industries Author: Of Sons and Seasons, 1978, Roll Call, 1981, Getting the Most Out of Washington, 1982, A Baker's Nickel, 1986, One-Eyed Kings, 1991, (with Gary Hart) The Double Man, 1985, (with George Mitchell) Men of Zeal, 1988, (with Thomas B. Allen) Murder in the Senate, 1993. Recipient Alumni award for disting. pub. service Boston U., 1976; named to N.E. Hall of Fame Basketball Team, 1962, Silver Anniversary award Nat. Collegiate Athletic Assn., 1987; Outstanding Young Man of Yr. Nat. Jaycees, 1975; James Bowdoin scholar, 1961-62; Alumni Fund scholar, 1962, selected for Balfour Silver Anniversary All-Am. Team, Nat. Assn. Basketball Coaches U.S., 1987. Republican. Office: The Cohen Group 600 13th St NW Ste 640 Washington DC 20005-3096

COHEN-DEMARCO, GALE MAUREEN, pharmaceutical executive; b. Rochester, N.Y., June 4, 1947; d. Maurice Cohen and Florence Michaels; m. David Earl McCarty, June 16, 1975 (div. Nov. 1979); 1 child, Brock Adam; m. Peter Francis DeMarco, Aug. 3, 1984. BA, U. Rochester, 1969; MA, SUNY, Buffalo, 1971. Various pharm. cos.; hosp. rep., dirs. mgr., med. liason Glaxo Pharms., 1987—97; regional bus. mgr. Axcan Pharma, 1997—2003, sr. regional account mgr., 2003—. Grantee, NIH, 1969; scholar, N.Y. State Regents, 1964. Democrat. Jewish. Avocations: environmental activities, charity organizations. Home: 27621 W Lakeview Dr N Wauconda IL 60084-2362 Office: Axcan Pharma 22 Inverness Ctr Pkwy Ste 310 Birmingham AL 35242

COHEN-MANSFIELD, JISKA, psychologist, educator, researcher; b. Basel, Switzerland, Dec. 19, 1951; BA in Psychology and Statistics, Hebrew U., Jerusalem, 1974, MA in Statistics, 1976; MA in Clin. Psychology, SUNY, Stony Brook, 1978, PhD in Clin. Psychology, 1979; postgrad., NYU, 1980. Cert. Diplomate Behavioral Psychology, ABPP, 2001. Clin. psychologist Cmty. Psychiat. Clinic, Bethesda, Md., 1984-87; dir. Rsch. Inst. on Aging Hebrew Home of Greater Washington, 1984—; assoc. prof. Georgetown U., Washington, 1987-90, prof., 1990-98, dir. rsch. Ctr. on Aging, 1987-98; prof. Med. Ctr. George Washington U., Washington, 1998—. Contbr. articles to profl. jours. including Archives of Internal Medicine, Jour. of Am. Geriatrics Soc., The Gerontologist. Recipient Recognition award Md. Gerontol. Assn., 1994, Busse Rsch. award in social/behavioral scis. Internat. Assn. Gerontology, 1993; grantee Nat. Inst. Aging, 1989—, Nat. Inst. Nursing Rsch., 1997-99, Alzheimer's Assn., 1997—, Agy. Health Care Policy and Rsch., 1998-2000, Montgomery County Cmty. Devel., 1999-2002, among others. Office: Rsch Inst on Aging Hebrew Home Greater Washington 6121 Montrose Rd Rockville MD 20852-4856 Fax: 301-770-8455. E-mail: cohen-mansfield@hebrew-home.org.

COHEN-VADER, CHERYL DENISE, municipal official; b. Ft. Bragg, N.C., Mar. 23, 1955; BA, Princeton U., 1977; MBA, Columbia U., 1983. Treas. internat. divsn. commodity import-export financing Bank of N.Y., N.Y.C., 1977-81; v.p. Citicorp Securities Markets, Inc. Citicorp, N.Y.C., 1983-90; v.p. Weldon, Sullivan, Carmichael & Co., 1990-92; asst. v.p. Kirkpatrick Pattis, 1993-95; mgr. revenue dept. City of Denver, 1996—. Mem. Mcpl. Securities Rulemaking Bd., 1998-2001. Bd. dirs. Mile High chpt. ARC, Colo. Episcopal Found. Recipient Consortium of Grad. Mgmt. Edn. fellowship, 1981-83, Recognition of Achievement award Five Points Bus. Assn., Inc., 1995, Leadership Denver award Denver C. of C., 1994; honored in Living Portraits of African-Am. Women Nat. Coun. Negro Women, 1997. Mem. Govt. Finance Officers Assn. Office: City Denver Revenue Dept McNichols Bldg Rm 300 144 W Colfax Ave Denver CO 80202-5391

COHILL, MAURICE BLANCHARD, JR., federal judge; b. Pitts., Pa., Nov. 26, 1929; s. Maurice Blanchard and Florence (Clarke) C.; m. Suzanne Miller, June 27, 1952 (dec. May 1986); children: Cynthia Cohill Plattner, Jonathan, Jennifer Cohill O'Connor, Victoria. AB, Princeton U., 1951; LLB, U. Pitts., 1956. Bar: Pa. 1957. Judge family div. Common Pleas Ct., Allegheny County, Pitts., 1965-76; judge U.S. Dist. Ct. Pa. (we. dist.), 1976-94, chief judge, 1985-92, sr. judge, 1994—. Bd. dirs. Pa. George Jr. Republic, Grove City; chmn. bd. fellows Nat. Ctr. for Juvenile Justice. Served to capt. USMCR, 1951-53. Mem. ABA, Pa. Bar Assn. Allegheny County Bar Assns., Nat. Coun. Juvenile Ct. Judges (past v.p.), Pa. Coun. Juvenile Ct. Judges (past pres.), Phi Delta Phi. Republican. Presbyterian. Office: US Dist Ct US Courthouse 8th Fl Rm 803 7th and Grant Sts Pittsburgh PA 15219

COHLER, BERTRAM JOSEPH, social sciences educator, clinical psychologist; b. Chgo., Dec. 3, 1938; s. Jonas Robert and Betty (Cahn) C.; m. Anne Meyers, June 11, 1962 (dec. Dec. 1989); children: Jonathan Richard, James Joseph. BA, U. Chgo., 1961; PhD, Harvard U., 1967; cert. in adult analysis, Inst. Psychoanalysis, 1989. Diplomate Am. Bd. Psychoanalysis, Am. Bd. Examiners in Profl. Psychology. Lectr. social relations Harvard U., Cambridge, Mass., 1967-69; assoc. dir. Sonia Shankman Orthogenic Sch., 1969-72, 94-96; dir. Orthogenic Sch. U. Chgo., 1969-72, 94—; asst. prof. U. Chgo., 1969-75, assoc. prof., 1975-81, prof. depts. psychology, edn. and psychiatry, 1981—. Co-dir. Univ. Ctr. Health anf Aging Soc., 1987—; sci. and profl. staff dept. psychiatry Michael Reese Hosp., Chgo., 1980-90; cons. The Tresholds, Chgo., 1972-81, Inst. Psychoanalysis, Chgo., 1972—, Ill. State Psychiat. Inst., Chgo., 1977-82; pres. bd. Ctr. Religion and Psychotherapy, Chgo. Author (with H. Grunebaum et al.) Mentally Ill Mothers and Their Children, 1975, 1982, Mothers, Grandmothers and Daughters, 1981; author: (with others) Parenthood as an Adult Experience, 1983, The Invulnerable Child, 1987, Handbook of Clinical Research on Adolescence, 1993; author: (with R. Galatzer-Levy) The Essential Other, 1993; author: The Course of Gay and Lesbian Lives, 2000; author: (with R. Galatzer-Levy) The Psychoanalytic Study of Lives Over Time, 1999; author: (with others) Rethinking Psychoanalysis and the Homosexualities, 2002. Bd. dirs. Horizons Cmty. Svcs., Chgo.; mem. initial rev. group in aging NIMH, Washington, 1982—86, Mental Health Spl. Projects, 1988—2003. Recipient Quantrell prize U. Chgo., 1975, Lily Gondor award Postgrad. Ctr. for Mental Health, 2000; fellow Inst. Medicine, 1975; named William Rainey Harper chair U. Chgo., 1978. Fellow Gerontol. Soc., Soc. Projective Techniques Am. Orthopsychiat. Assn. (bd. dirs. 1981-84, pres. elect 1991, pres. 1992), Am. Psychol. Assn. (chmn. profl. affairs com. divsn. 39 1981-83, editor Psychoanalytic Psychology 1987-97, pres. sect. II 1992); mem. Am. Sociol. Assn., Am. Anthrop. Assn., Am. Assn. Psychiat. Svcs. to Children (Alexander Gralnick award), Soc. Rsch. in Child Devel., Chgo. Assn. Psychoanalytic Psychology (pres. 1983-84), Am. Psychoanalytic Assn. Home: 5408 S Blackstone Ave Chicago IL 60615-5407 Office: U Chgo 5730 S Woodlawn Ave Chicago IL 60637-1603 *Emphasis on community services has been an important tradition in my family for several generations. This concern includes making knowledge and skills available to others, providing leadership and giving of time where needed. Teaching, writing, and research and clin. svc. are all involved in making the world better for my having been a part of it. My own goal has been to improve the human condition and to inspire my students to carry on this concern for the welfare of others.*

COHLER, CHARLES B. lawyer. Ptnr. Lasky, Haas, Cohler & Munter, San Francisco. Office: Lasky Cohler & Munter 12th Floor 505 Sansome St San Francisco CA 94111-3106

COHN, AARON I. anesthesiologist, educator; b. L.A., Sept. 8, 1959; s. Alan Franklin and Louise Christine (Huff) C.; m. Nicola Ann Bernau, July 1984 (div. Aug. 1986). BS, U. Calif. Riverside, 1980; MA, Rice U., 1984; MD, U. Tex. Galveston, 1987. Diplomate Am. Bd. Anesthesiology. Med. intern Montefiore/Univ. Hosp., Pitts., 1987-88; postdoctoral fellow Ctr. for Med. Informatics, Yale U. Med. Sch., New Haven, 1988-90; resident in anesthesiology Yale-New Haven Hosp., New Haven, 1990-91, St. Elizabeth's Med. Ctr., Boston, 1991-93; asst. prof. dept. anesthesiology U. Tex. Med. Br., Galveston, 1993-96; anesthesiologist North Tex. Anesthesia, Dallas, 1996-97; asst. prof. dept. anesthesiology U. Okla., Oklahoma City, 1997-99, U. Colo., Denver, 1999—. Spl. study sect. mem. NIH, Rockville, Md., 1993—; reviewer Jour. Clin. Anesthesia, 1998-99. Contbr. articles to profl. jours. Mem. Internat. Anesthesia Rsch. Soc., Am. Soc. Anesthesiologists, N.Y. Acad. Scis. Republican. Jewish. Avocations: bicycling, pistol shooting, computers, scuba diving, underwater photography. Home: 939 Jersey St Denver CO 80220-4592 Office: U Colo Dept Anes CB B113 4200 E 9th Ave Denver CO 80262-0001 E-mail: aaron_cohn@cyberdude.com.

COHN, ANDREW HOWARD, lawyer; b. N.Y.C., Jan. 17, 1945; s. Maurice John and Margaret Ethel (Gordon) C.; m. Marcia Bliss Leavitt, July 10, 1977; children: Marisa Leavitt, David Herman. BA, U. Pa., 1966; AM, Harvard U., 1970, PhD, 1972; JD, Yale U., 1975. Bar: Mass. 1975, U.S. Dist. Ct. Mass. 1976, U.S. Ct. Appeals (1st cir.) 1976. Law clk. to presiding justice U.S. Ct. Appeals (1st cir.), Providence and Boston, 1975-76; assoc. Hill & Barlow, Boston, 1976-80; sr. ptnr. Hale and Dorr, Boston, 1980—. Chmn. exec. com. Hale and Dorr, 1990-91, real estate dept., 1991-97, energy group, 1992—; cons. for juvenile justice standards project ABA and Inst. for Judicial Adminstrn., N.Y.C., 1973-74; rsch. fellow MIT-Harvard U. Joint Ctr. for Urban Studies, Cambridge, Mass., 1969-71, Univ. Coll., Nairobi, Kenya, 1968. Contbr. articles to profl. jours.; note and project editor Yale Law Jour., New Haven, 1974-75. Advisor Newton (Mass.) Community SChs. Found., 1987-88. Named Law and Social Sci. fellow Russell Sage Found., 1972-74. Mem. ABA (environ.controls com., bus. law sect.), Am. Coll. Real Estate Lawyers, Boston Bar Assn. (chmn. real estate sect. 95-97), Yale Law Sch. Assn. Mass. (treas. 1985-87). Democrat. Jewish. Office: Hale and Dorr 60 State St Ste 25 Boston MA 02109-1816

COHN, ARNOLD KEITH, orthopedic surgeon; b. Chgo., Feb. 13, 1949; s. Irving Samuel and Violet S. (Kaplan) C.;children: Margo, Meredith, David; m. Darlene Ann Dudeck, Nov. 5, 1988; 1 child, Lauren. BA with high distinction, U. Ill., 1971; MD, Chgo. Med. Sch., 1975. Ptnr. Highland Park (Ill.) Orthopedic Clinic (now merged with Ill. Bone and Joint Inst., 1980—; resident in orthopedic surgery Loyola U. Med. Ctr., 1975-80; chmn. dept. orthopaedic surgery Highland Park Hosp., 1990-00; vice chmn. dept. orthopedic surgery ENH Hosps., 2002—. Assoc. prof. orthopedic surgery Loyola U. Med. Sch., Maywood, Ill., 1990—, instr., 1980-85, asst. prof., 1985-90. Patentee in field. Fellow Am. Acad. of Orthopedic Surgeons; mem. AMA. Avocations: saxaphone, sports, encouragement of innovation. Home: 1415 Meadow Ln Glenview IL 60025-2345 Office: Ill Bone and Joint Inst Ste 110 2101 Waukegan Rd Bannockburn IL 60015-1836 E-mail: acohn@yahoo.com.

COHN, AVERN LEVIN, district judge; b. Detroit, July 23, 1924; s. Irwin I. and Sadie (Levin) C.; m. Joyce Hochman, Dec. 30, 1954 (dec. Dec. 1989); m. Lois Pincus Cohn, June 1992; children: Sheldon, Leslie Cohn Magy, Thomas. Student, John Tarleton Agrl. Coll., 1943, Stanford U., 1944; JD, U. Mich., 1949. Bar: Mich. 1949. Practiced in, Detroit, 1949-79; mem. firm Honigman Miller Schwartz & Cohn, Detroit, 1961-79; sr. judge U.S. Dist. Ct., 1979—. Mem. Mich. Civil Rights Commn., 1972-75, chmn., 1974-75; Mem. Detroit Bd. Police Commrs., 1975-79, chmn., 1979; bd. govs. Jewish Welfare Fedn., Detroit, 1972—. Served with AUS, 1943-46. Mem. ABA, Mich. Bar Assn., Am. Law Inst. E-mail: avern_cohn@mied.uscourts.gov.

COHN, BERTRAM JOSIAH, investment banker; b. Newark, Sept. 12, 1925; s. Julius Henry and Bessie Ruth (Einson) C.; m. Barbara Biard, June 20, 1956; children: Daniel, Susan, Diana. AB cum laude, Harvard, 1949; MBA, NYU, 1957. Vice pres. Decatur Iron & Steel Co., Ala., 1951-67; chmn. bd. Schuylkill

Lead Corp., Baton Rouge, 1968-70, DPF, Inc., Hartsdale, N.Y., 1970—, Interstate Bakeries Corp., 1970-82. Mem. internat. adv. com. Cohn Inst. for History and Philosophy Sci., Tel Aviv U.. Trustee Washington Inst. for Near East Policy. With AUS, 1943-46. Mem. Wilderness Soc. (governing coun.). Home: 125 Woodbine Ave Larchmont NY 10538-3523 Office: First Manhattan Co 437 Madison Ave New York NY 10022-7001

COHN, BOB, public relations executive; b. N.Y.C., Oct. 12, 1934; Grad., U. Ala., 1961. Newspaper reporter, photojournalist, 1961—70; owner Cohn & Wolfe, N.Y.C., 1970—85, CEO, 1985—92, chmn. bd. dirs. Bd. dirs. Burson-Marsteller. Nominee Pulitzer prize, 1964; recipient 13 awards AP, UPI, Lifetime Achievement award, All-Star award, RP/Reputation Mgmt., 1999. Mem.: Arthur W. Page Soc. Office: Cohn & Wolfe 303 Peachtree St NE Ste 2600 Atlanta GA 30308-3267 Address: Cohn & Wolfe 225 Park Ave S Fl 17 New York NY 10003-1604

COHN, BRUCE, film and television company executive; b. San Francisco, Apr. 8, 1931; s. Theodore and Rosebud Enid (Schmulian) C.; 1 child, Mitchell Barry. M of Journalism, U. Calif., Berkeley, 1954. Writer, producer Clete Roberts News Sta. KTLA-TV, Hollywood, Calif., 1957-62, west coast producer Huntley-Brinkley and Today Show NBC, Burbank, Calif., 1962-63; news dir. Sta. KNBC-TV, Burbank, 1963-66; Washington producer ABC Evening News, 1966-68; west coast producer Los Angeles, 1968-71; exec. producer Nat. Pub. Affairs Ctr. for TV Pub. Broadcasting System, Washington, 1971-73; ind. producer, writer various film studios, Burbank, 1973-75, 1973—; pres. Bruce Cohn Prodns., Inc., Mill Valley, Calif., 1975—. Screenwriter ((film) Good Guys Wear Black, 1979; writer, producer (TV documentary) 1968-A Crack in Time, 1978, Secret Files of J. Edgar Hoover, 1990; producer (documentary series) Time Was, 1980; producer, dir. (documentary series) Rember When, 1981; writer, producer, dir. (documentary) Kisses with Lauren Bacall, 1991; writer, producer (documentary) Tom Clancy Presents John Ehrlichman In the Eye of the Storm, 1998, Couples, 2000. Recipient Cable Ace award, 1979, 81, 2 Gold medals N.Y. Internat. Film Festival, 1981, Gold plaque Chgo. Internat. Film Festival, 1982, Emmy award NATAS, 1984, 97. Mem. Writers Guild Am., Am. Film Inst. Home and Office: 1 Weatherly Dr Ste 101 Mill Valley CA 94941-3231 E-mail: bcp333@aol.com.

COHN, DANIEL ROSS, physicist; b. Berkeley, Calif., Nov. 28, 1943; s. Roy Wolfsohn and Betty (Black) C.; m. Helen Desfosses, Aug. 25, 1967 (div. 1974); 1 child, Adam Robsohn; m. Joanne Brecker, June 10, 1978. BA, U. Calif., Berkeley, 1966; PhD, MIT, 1971. Rsch. scientist, gp. leader Francis Bitter Nat. Magnet Lab., MIT, Cambridge, Mass., 1971-80; divsn. head Plasma Fusion Ctr., MIT, Cambridge, 1980—; sr. rsch. scientist Nuc. Engring. Dept., MIT, Cambridge, 1980—; acting asst. dir. plasma fusion ctr. MIT, Cambridge, 1992-96; pres., CEO Integrated Environ. Techs., 1996—2000. Cons. in field. Editor Jour. of Fusion Energy, 1984-92; contbr. more than 150 articles to profl. jours. Recipient Discover award for Technol. Innovation, Discover Mag., 1999. Fellow Am. Phys. Soc.; mem. Am. Nuc. Soc., Phi Beta Kappa. Achievements include holder of more that 20 U.S. patents on environmental, energy and monitoring technology; devel. of new energy and environmental technology. Home: 26 Walnut Hill Rd Chestnut Hill MA 02467-3125 Office: MIT Plasma Fusion Ctr 167 Albany St Cambridge MA 02139-4213 E-mail: cohn@psfc.mit.edu.

COHN, DAVID HERC, retired foreign service officer; b. Bklyn., July 29, 1923; s. Nathan and Blanche (Herc) C.; m. Verna Elizabeth Peterson, Jan. 29, 1949 (dec. Nov. 1992); m. Rosemarie M. Baiocchi, May 15, 1999. AB, Dickinson Coll., 1948; postgrad., NYU, 1948-49, U. Pa., 1963-64; MA, U. Miami, 1951. Instr. U. Miami, 1950-51; spl. asst. to div. dir. Dept. Commerce, 1951-56; joined U.S. Fgn. Service, 1956; consul, econ. officer Am. consulate gen., Istanbul, Turkey, 1956-60; 2d sec., economist U.S. Regional Orgn., Paris, 1960-63; economist Office Intelligence Rsch., Near East and South Asia; economist Bur. Near East and South Asian Affairs Dept. State, 1964-66, economist Pakistan-Afghanistan Country Directorate, 1966-68; dep. prin. officer Am. consulate gen., Karachi, Pakistan, 1968-70; econ. counselor Am. embassy, Kabul, Afghanistan, 1970-73, comml. counselor Jakarta, Indonesia, 1973-75, econ.-comml. counselor, 1975-76; econ. and social policy adviser Bur. Internat. Orgn. Affairs Dept. State, 1976-77, dir. Internat. Econ. Policy Office, Bur. Internat. Orgn. Affairs, 1977-78, dir. Office Econ. Research and Analysis, Bur. Intelligence and Research, 1978-80, ret., 1980; asst. v.p. U.S.-USSR Trade and Econ. Council, Inc., N.Y.C., 1981-85; program coord. for Chad Internat. Human Assistance Programs, Inc., N.Y.C., 1985-86; UN br. asst. adminstr. Chemical Bank, N.Y.C., 1987-88. Vol. assoc. City of N.Y. Office Bus. Devel. Not-for-Profit sector, 1988-91; vol. tutor N.Y. Pub. Libr. Ctr. for Reading and Writing Harlem Br., 1989-95; vestryman All Saints Episc. Ch., N.Y.C., 1985-90, warden, 1991-99, 2000—. With AUS, 1943-46. Mem. Nat. League of Nursing, Dacor Club, Dacor House Club (Washington), Omicron Delta Kappa. Clubs: Dacor, Dacor House (Washington). Home: 330 W 58th St Apt 7P New York NY 10019-1815 Office: All Saints Ch 230 E 60th St New York NY 10022-1402

COHN, DAVID STEPHEN, lawyer; b. Richmond, Va., June 19, 1945; s. Alfred Jerome and Jane Shaffer Cohn; m. Jane Boyle, Nov. 22, 1970; children: Elizabeth, Sarah. AB, U. Pa., 1967; JD, Harvard U., 1971. Bar: Pa. 1971, U.S. Dist. Ct. (ea. dist.) Pa. 1971, U.S. Ct. Appeals (3d cir.) 1971, Va. 1973. Assoc. Schnader, Harrison, Segal & Lewis, Phila., 1971-73; asst. prof. law T.C. Williams Sch. Law, U. Richmond, 1973-75; counsel Hunton & Williams, Richmond, 1975-84; mem., chmn., real estate dept. Browder, Russell, Morris & Butcher, P.C., Richmond, 1984-89; ptnr. Troutman Sanders LLP, Richmond, 1989—. Arbitrator Am. Arbitration Assn., 1972—; lectr. Marshall Wythe Sch. Law, Coll. William and Mary, Williamsburg, Va., 1977—81; mem. Va. Gov.'s Regulatory Reform Adv. Bd., 1983—85, Va. Gov.'s Com. on Efficiency in Govt., Richmond, 1985—87; chmn. Va. com. Harvard Law Sch. Fund, Cambridge, Mass., 1986—88, Cambridge, 2002—. Editor: (book) The Residential Real Estate Transaction, 1975. Bd. dirs., pres. Sci. Mus. Va. Found., 1987—2002; mem. Va. Hist. Landmarks Bd., 1988—89; chmn., pres. Richmond Goodwill Industries, Inc., 1988—2002; mem. Va. Vol. Formulary Bd., 1989—; mem. adv. coun. Va. Gov.'s Sch. Govt. and Internat. Studies for Gifted, 1991—93; mem. regulatory climate subcom. Va. Gov.'s Econ. Recovery Coun., 1991—92; mem. orgnl. structure team Gov.'s Commn. on Efficiency and Effectiveness, 2002; mem. state ctrl. com. Va. Dem. Party, Richmond, 1985—93; assoc. trustee U. Pa., Phila., 1984—94; bd. dirs. Better Housing Coalition, 1988—99; trustee, vice chair Sci. Mus. Va., 2002—. Mem.: ABA (chmn. govtl. assistance for real estate programs com. 1989—93), Va. State Bar (mem. bd. govs. real estate sect. 1984—87), Va. Bar Assn. (chmn. real estate com. 1985—87), Am. Coll. Real Estate Lawyers (chmn. affordable housing com. 1991—97). Jewish. Office: Troutman Sanders LLP Bank of Am Ctr PO Box 1122 Richmond VA 23218-1122 E-mail: david.cohn@troutmansanders.com.

COHN, DAVID V(ALOR), biochemist, educator; b. N.Y.C., Nov. 8, 1926; s. Ralph and Clara (Schenkman) C.; m. Evelyn Turner, 1947; children: Robert Warren, Emily. BS, CCNY, 1948; PhD, Duke U., 1952; postgrad., Western Res. U., 1953. Faculty U. Kans. Sch. Medicine, Kansas City, 1953-82, prof. biochemistry, assoc. dean rsch., 1974-82; assoc. chief staff for rsch. VA Med. Ctr., Kansas City, Mo., 1953-82; prof. biochemistry U. Mo., Kansas City, 1971-82; v.p. R&D Immuno Nuc. Corp., Stillwater, Minn., 1982; chmn. bd. sci. advisors Endotronics Corp., Mpls., 1983-85; rsch. prof. oral biology and biochemistry U. Louisville Sch. Medicine, Sch. Dentistry, 1984—2002, emeritus prof., 2002—, chmn. dept. oral health, 1989-91, chmn. dept. biol. and biophys. scis., 1992-97, univ. dir. tech. devel., 1996-99; asst. to v.p. rsch. U. Louisville, 1992-95, asst. v.p. econ. devel. and indsl. rels., 1999—2002; biomed. rsch. cons., 2002—. Pres. Internat. Conf. on Calcium Regulating Hormones, 1980-86, exec. sec., 1986-89; mem. bd. sci. counselors Nat. Inst. Dental Rsch., Bethesda, Md., 1980-84; bd. dirs. Cambridge Med. Tech., Inc., 1985-86; cons. VA, Washington, 2000—. Editor: Hormonal Control of Calcium Metabolism, 1981, Endocrine Control of Bone and Calcium Metabolism, 1984, Calcium Regulation and Bone Metabolism: Basic and Clinical Aspects, 1987, Calcium Regulating Hormones and Bone Metabolism: Basic and Clinical Aspects, vol. II, 1992; editor in chief Bone and Mineral, 1986-94; contbr. articles to profl. jours. With USN, 1945-46. Grantee USPHS, 1957—, Am. Cancer Soc., 1959-60, VA, 1975-82, Ky. Heart Assn., 1991-93. Mem. AAAS, AAUP (pres. Louisville chpt. 2000—), Am. Soc. Molecular Biology and Biochemistry, Am. Chem. Soc., Gordon Rsch. Conf. Chem. and Biol. of Bones and Teeth (chmn. 1974). Achievements include research on calcium metabolism, parathyroid gland parathormone/chromogranin biosynthesis and secretion, bone cell growth, differentiation and hormone responsivity, economic development, entrepreneurship, history of science and medicine. Home: 5709 Apache Rd Louisville KY 40207-1715 Office: U Louisville Health Scis Ctr Dept Bioland Biophys Scis Ctr Louisville KY 40292-0001 E-mail: dvcohn@attglobal.net., dvcohn@louisville.edu.

COHN, ELCHANAN, economics educator; b. Tel-Aviv, Israel; came to U.S. 1961; m. Sharon May, 1963. BA, U. Minn., 1963, MA, 1965; PhD, Iowa State U., 1968. Asst. prof. econs. Pa. State U., University Park, 1968-71, assoc. prof., 1971-74; prof. econs. U. S.C., Columbia, 1974—, fellow Bus. Partnerhip Found., 1990—. Cons. U.S. Dept. Edn., 1982-84, 86-88, World Bank, 1984, Orgn. for Econ. Coop. and Devel., Paris, 1995-97. Author: Public Expenditure Analysis, 1972, Economics of State Aid to Education, 1974, Input-Output Analysis in Public Education, 1975, Economics of Education, 1990, Recent Developments in Economics of Education, 1994, Market Approaches to Education: Vouchers and School Choice, 1997; editor Econs. of Edn. Rev., since 1980; contbr. articles to profl. jours. Grantee, Nat. Inst. Edn., U.S. Dept. Edn., 1985-87. Mem. Am. Edni. Fin. Assn., Am. Statis. Assn., Soc. Labor Economists, Omicron Delta Epsilon, Beta Gamma Sigma. Office: U SC Moore Sch Bus Columbia SC 29208-0001

COHN, GARY DENNIS, journalist; b. Bklyn., Mar. 9, 1952; s. Morton J. and Claire Cohn; m. Sally Denton, 1980 (div. 1983); 1 child, Jacob Max Cohn. BA in Psychology and Polit. Sci., SUNY, Buffalo, 1974; postgrad., U. Calif., Berkeley, 1974-75. Reporter Jack Anderson Column, Washington, 1975-80, Lexington (Ky.) Herald-Leader, 1980-84, Miami bur. Wall St. Jour., N.Y.C., 1984-86, Phila. Inquirer, 1986-93, Balt. Sun, 1993—. Atwood chair dept. journalism and pub. comm. U. Alaska, Anchorage, 2001—. Recipient Edward W. Scripps 1st Amendment award, 1980, Inter-Am. Press Assn. award, 1996, Overseas Press Club of Am. award, 1995, 97, Selden Ring award, 1996, 98, 1st Amendment award Soc. Profl. Journalists, 1997, 1st prize for investigative reporting Sigma Delta Chi, 1997, Investigative Reporters and Editors award, 1997, George Polk award, 1997, Pulitzer Prize for Investigative Reporting, 1998, finalist, Pulitzer Prize for Public Svc., 1996, finalist, Pulitzer Prize for Nat. Reporting, 2002. Office: U Alaska JPC Bldg K Rm 201 Anchorage AK 99508

COHN, HOWARD, retired magazine editor; b. N.Y.C., Nov. 1, 1922; s. Morris and Vivian (Siegel) C.; m. Regina Levy, Apr. 2, 1949; children— Steven B., Robert D. BA, Am. U., 1947. Assoc. editor Sportfolio mag., 1947-48; assoc. editor, then mng. editor Am. Lawn Tennis mag., 1948-50; assoc. editor Quick mag., 1950-51, Collier's mag., 1951-56; freelance writer, 1957-59; articles editor Pageant mag., 1959, exec. editor, 1959-63; mng. editor True mag., 1964-68, Med. World News mag., 1968, exec. editor, 1968-75, editor, 1975-77; exec. editor McGraw-Hill Newsletter Center, 1977-79; sr. staff editor McGraw-Hill Pub. Co., N.Y.C., 1979-81; editor-in-chief Graduating Engr. mag., 1981-88. Served with AUS, 1943-46. Home: 750A Heritage Hls Somers NY 10589-4009

COHN, IAN J. architect; b. Phila., Jan. 9, 1950; s. Isidore Jr. and Jacqueline (Heymann) C.; m. Vicki Hertzberg, June 23, 1973; children: Kevin Aton, Adrian Kirrin. Grad., The Gunnery, Washington, Conn.; BA, Washington U., St. Louis, 1971, MArch, 1974. Registered arch., N.Y. Staff arch. Howell, Killick, Partridge & Amis, London, 1974-76, George Nelson & Co., N.Y.C., 1977; assoc. Perkins & Will, N.Y.C., 1977-80; founding ptnr. Ian-Aaron Archs., N.Y.C., 1980-89, Ian-Aaron Architects Internat. (in assn. with Sheehan & Barry, Dublin, Ireland), Dublin, Ireland, 1985-89; prin. Diversity: Architecture & Design, N.Y.C., 1989—. 1st vis. young artist-in-residence The Gunnery Sch., 1989, vis. prof., 1992. Author: Structures: A Rule of Thumb Handbook, 1973; designs exhibited in mus. and mags. Bd. dirs. Kids of NYU Med. Ctr.; chair comm. com. Ctrl. Synagogue, N.Y., 1997-2000. Mem. The Gunnery Alumni Assn. Democrat. Jewish. Avocations: photography, tennis, traveling, wine, gourmet foods. Office: Diversity: Architecture & Design 250 E 87th St Apt 22A New York NY 10128-3101 E-mail: ddiversity@aol.com.

COHN, ISIDORE, JR., surgeon, educator; b. New Orleans, Sept. 25, 1921; s. Isidore and Elsie (Waldhorn) C.; m. Jacqueline Heymann, July 4, 1944 (div. Aug. 1971); children: Ian Jeffrey, Lauren Kerry; m. Marianne Winter Miller, Jan. 3, 1976. MD, U. Pa., 1945; M.Med. Sci. in Surgery, 1952, DMS in Surgery, 1955; LHD (hon.), U. S.C., 1995. Diplomate Am. Bd. Surgery (bd. dirs. 1969-75). Intern Grad. Hosp. U. Pa., 1945-46, resident in surgery, 1949-52; fellow dept. surg. rsch. U. Pa., 1947-48; vis. surgeon Charity Hosp., New Orleans, 1952-62, sr. vis. surgeon, 1962-2000, hon. sr. vis. surgeon, 2000—; surgeon in chief La. State U. Svc., Charity Hosp., New Orleans, 1962-89; prof. surgery La. State U. Sch. Medicine, New Orleans, 1959-2000, emeritus chmn., emeritus prof. surgery, 2000—. Cons. surgeon VA Hosp., New Orleans, Touro Infirmary, New Orleans; instr. surgery La. State U. Sch. Medicine, New Orleans, 1952-53, asst. prof., 1953-56, assoc. prof., 1956-59, prof., 1959-2000, chmn. dept. surgery, 1962-89; mem. surg. rsch. rev. com. VA, Washington, 1967-68; dir. Nat. Pancreatic Cancer Project, 1975-84; mem. Soc. Surg. Chairmen, 1962-89. Mem. editl. bd. Am. Surgeon, 1963-87, Current Surgery, 1964-90, Am. Jour. Surgery, 1968-96, emeritus, 1997—, Digestive Diseases and Scis., 1978-82, Surg. Gastroenterology, 1982—, Cancer, 1992—, Digestive Surgery, 1995—. Bd. dirs. New Orleans Met. Conv. and Visitors Bur., 1998-2000. Served to capt. M.C., AUS, 1946-47. Isidore Cohn, Jr. Professorship named in his honor at La. State U., 1987, Isidore Cohn, Jr., M.D. Student Learning Ctr. at La. State U. Health Sci. Ctr. Sch. Medicine dedicated in his honor, 2002, Spirit of Charity award Med. Ctr. La., 2003; named Outstanding Alumnus, Isidore Newman Sch., New Orleans, La., 2003. Fellow ACS (exec. com., bd. govs. 1987-91, vice-chmn. 1989-90, chmn. 1990-91, 1st v.p. 1993-94); mem. AMA, Am. Surg. Assn., So. Surg. Assn. (1st v.p. 1979-80, treas.-recorder 1981-82, pres. 1982-83), La. Surg. Assn. (pres. 1968), So. Med. Assn., La., Orleans Parish med. socs., Soc. Univ. Surgeons, Southeastern Surg. Congress (chmn. forum on progress in surgery 1967-69, councillor for La. 1967-73, pres. 1972), Surg. Biology Club II, Assn. Acad. Surgery, James D. Rives Surg. Soc., Internat. Surg. Soc., Am. Gastroenterol. Assn., Bockus Soc. Gastroenterology, Soc. Surgery Alimentary Tract (trustee 1969-80, president 1973-76, pres. 1976-77, chmn. bd. 1977-78), Am. Soc. Microbiologists, Soc. Surg. Oncology, N.Y. Acad. Scis., Am. Assn. Cancer Research, Southeastern Cancer Research Assn. (pres. 1975), Collegium Internationale Chirurgiae Digestivae, Am. Cancer Soc. (vice chmn. clin. investigation adv. com. 1969, chmn. clin. investigation adv. com. 1969-73), Tex. Surg. Soc. (hon.), Sigma Xi, Phi Beta Kappa, Alpha Omega Alpha, Omicron Delta Kappa. Office: La State U Med Sch New Orleans LA 70112 E-mail: icohn@lsuhsc.edu.

COHN, JAN KADETSKY, American literature and American studies educator; b. Cambridge, Mass., Aug. 9, 1933; d. Allan Robert and Beatrice (Goldberg) Kadetsky; m. Donald S. Solomon, Feb. 6, 1955 (div. 1968); children: Cathy Rebecca, David Seth; m. William Henry Cohn, Mar. 9, 1969. BA, Wellesley Coll., 1955; MA, U. Toledo, 1961; PhD, U. Mich., 1964. From instr. to asst. prof. U. Toledo, 1964-68; assoc. prof. U. Wis., Whitewater, 1968-70, Carnegie Mellon U., Pitts., 1970-79; prof., dept. chair George Mason U., Fairfax, Va., 1979-87; dean faculty Trinity Coll., Hartford, Conn., 1987-94, G. Keith Funston prof. Am. lit. and Am. studies, 1994—. Cons. in field. Author: The Palace or the Poorhouse, 1979, Improbable Fiction, 1980, Romance and the Erotics of Property, 1988, Creating America, 1989, The Saturday Evening Post (covers), 1995; editor: Henry James, The Portrait of a Lady, 2001. Bd. dirs. Nat. Bldg. Mus., Washington, 1987-91; trustee Norman Rockwell Mus., Sturbridge, Mass., 1997—; exec. bd. dirs. Conn. Pub. Broadcasting, Hartford, 1988-92. Fellow Am. Coun. Learned Socs., 1972, NEH, 1972-73. Mem. Modern Language Assn., Popular Culture Assn., Am. Culture Assn., Am. Studies Assn., Phi Kappa Phi. Democrat. Jewish. Office: Trinity Coll Dept English 300 Summit St Hartford CT 06106-3100

COHN, JAY N. cardiologist, educator; b. Schenectady, N.Y., July 6, 1930; s. Morris Mandel and Rose (Gold) C.; m. Syma Cheris, June 14, 1953; children: Cynthia, Lauren, Joshua. BS, Union Coll., 1952; MD, Cornell U. Med. Coll., 1956. Diplomate Am. Bd. Internal Medicine. Intern Beth Israel Hosp., Boston, 1956-57, asst. resident in medicine, 1957-58; rsch. fellow in medicine Georgetown U. Med. Ctr., Washington, 1960-61; chief resident in medicine VA Hosp., Washington, 1961-62, clin. investigator, 1962-65, chief hypertension and clin. hemodynamics divsn., chmn. rsch. and edn. com., 1965-74; asst. prof. medicine Georgetown U. Sch. of Medicine, Washington, 1965-68, assoc. prof. medicine, 1968-72, prof., 1972-74, co-dir. cardiovascular rsch. divsn., 1972-74, mem. exec. com. dept. medicine, 1972-74; prof. medicine, head cardiovascular divsn. U. Minn. Med. Sch., Mpls., 1974-96, prof. medicine, 1996—. Mem. cardiovascular studies merit rev. bd. VA Ctrl. Office, Dept. VA, 1970-75, chmn. VA Cooperative Study on Vasodilator Therapy of Acute Myocardial Infarction, 1974-81, VA Cooperative Studies-Vasodilator-Heart Failure Trials, 1980—; mem. cardiovascular and renal adv. com. FDA, 1977-81, chmn., 1979-81, mem. congrl. commn. fed. drug approval process, 1981-82; co-chair Coun. Hypertension and Atherosclerosis Edn., 1990-94; mem. subcom. Nat. Bur. Info. Coronary and Heart Disease Risk, 1996; mem. sci. adv. com. Victor Chang Cardiac Rsch. Inst., Sydney, Australia, 1997; mem. task force hypertension edn., steering com. WHO, 1994—, coun. geriatric cardiology, task force heart failure edn., 1994—, coun. geriatric cardiology, task force cardiac rehab. edn., 1995—; mem. numerous coms. NIH. Guest editor various jours.; contbr. over 600 articles to profl. jours., chpts. to textbooks. With USPHS, 1958-60. Scholar N.Y. State Coll., N.Y. State Med. Sch.; recipient Ann. award N.Y. State Arthritis and Rheumatism Found., 1955, Arthur S. Flemming award Fed. Govt. Svc., 1969; named one of 400 Best Drs. in Am., Good Housekeeping, 1992, 96, one of 250 Top Drs. In Twin City Area, Mpls.- St. Paul Mag., 1992, Arrigo Recordati Internat. prize for sci. rsch., 2003, others. Fellow AAAS, ACP, Am. Coll. Cardiology, Am. Heart Assn. (bd. dirs. 1979-85, coun. circulation, coun. high blood pressure rsch., coun. basic sci., Disting. Svc. award 1982, Sci. Coun. Disting. Achievement award 1998, Novartis Award in Hypertension Rsch. Coun. on High Blood Pressure Rsch. 2000, Hames B. Herrick award 2003); mem. Am. Fedn. Clin. Rsch. (chmn. eastern sect. 1969-70), Assn. Am. Physicians, Assn. Univ. Cardiologists, Assn. Profs. Cardiology (councilor 1992-94), Am. Soc. Hypertension (pres.- elect 1988-90, pres. 1990-92, chmn. intersocietal affairs com. 1995—, sci. awards com. 1996—, William S. Harvey award 1987), Am. Physiol. Soc., Am. Soc. Clin. Investigation, Am. Soc. Clin. Pharmacology and Therapeutics (chmn. program com. 1971-72, v.p. 1973-74, chmn. cardiopulmonary sect. 1976—), Am. Soc. Pharmacology and Exptl. Therapeutics, Internat. Soc. Hypertension (v.p. 1994-96, organizing com. 18th Sci. Meetings Year 2000, Chgo. chpt. 1994—, pres.- elect 1995-96, pres. 1996-98), Internat. Soc. Cardiovascular Pharmacotherapy (chmn. 5th Congress, Mpls. 1993), Heart Failure Soc. Am. (pres. 1995-98), Ctrl. Soc. Clin. Rsch. (chmn. cardiovascular subsect. 1980-81, mem. coun. 1987-89), Alpha Omega Alpha. Office: U Minn Med Sch Cardiovascular Divsn 420 Delaware St SE Minneapolis MN 55455-0374

COHN, JOHN L. merchant banker; s. Bernard G. and Charlotte Cohn; m. Eve K. Keller, June 28, 1970; children: Jessica C. Lutzker, Abby Keller. AB, Brown U., 1968. Gen. mdse. mgr. Ind. Retailers Syndicate, N.Y.C., 1980—85, pres., 1985—88; COO The Doneger Group, N.Y.C., 1988—90; chmn. Colt Merc. Corp, N.Y.C., 1991—2000; pres. Growth Resources Group, White Plains, NY, 2000—. Dir. Extebank, N.Y.C., 1984—91. Active United Hebrew Geriatric Ctr., New Rochelle, NY, 2001. Mem.: Quaker Ridge Golf Club. Office: Growth Resources Group Ltd 20 Allan Dr White Plains NY 10605-4433 E-mail: jlcohn@growthresourcesltd.com.

COHN, JOSEPH DAVID, surgeon; b. N.Y.C., Jan. 26, 1937; s. Samuel Theodor and Gertrude (Emsheimer) C.; m. Barbara Ester Forst, July 27, 1966; children: Michael, Russell. SB, MIT, 1957; MD, NYU, 1961; MBA, Rutgers U., 1993. Diplomate Am. Bd. Surgery, Am. Bd. Thoracic Surgery, Am. Bd. Critical Care Surgery. Intern Duke Hosp., Durham, N.C., 1961-62; surg. resident Bronx Mcpl. Hosp. Ctr., N.Y., 1962-67; thoracic surgery resident U. Calif., San Diego, 1969-71; from asst. dir. surgery to dir. St. Barnabas Med. Ctr., Livingston, N.J., 1971-83; thoracic surgeon Northfield Surg. Assn., Livingston, 1978-99; mem. staff Santa Rosa Meml. Hosp. Sutter Med. Ctr., Santa Rosa, Calif., 2001—. Clin. asst. prof. surgery UMDNJ, Newark, 1972—79, assoc. prof., 1979—90, prof., 1990—99. Editor sci. jours.; author software programs, 1988; contbr. articles to profl. jours. Capt. USAF, 1967-69. Fellow Am. Heart Assn. 1966-67, NIH 1964-66. Fellow ACS, Am. Coll. Critical Care Medicine; mem. Sigma Xi, Phi Lambda Upsilon, Alpha Omega Alpha. Avocations: skiing, scuba, flying. Office: 5773 Shiloh Ridge Road Santa Rosa CA 95403-7802 E-mail: jcohn@alum.mit.edu.

COHN, LAWRENCE STEVEN, physician, educator; b. Chgo., Dec. 21, 1945; s. Jerome M. an Francis Cohn; m. Harriett G. Rubin, Sept. 1, 1968; children: Allyson and Jennifer (twins). BS, U. Ill., 1967, MD, 1971. Diplomate Am. Bd. Internal Medicine. Intern Mt. Zion Hosp., San Francisco, 1971-72, resident, 1972-73, U. Chgo., 1973-74; practice medicine specializing in internal medicine Paramount, Calif.; pres. med. staff Charter Suburban Hosp., 1981-83. Mem. staff Long Beach Meml. Hosp., Harbor Gen. Hosp.; clin. prof. medicine UCLA. Maj. USAF, 1974-76. Recipient Disting. Tchg. award Harbor-UCLA Med. Ctr., 1980, 90. Fellow ACP; mem. AMA, Calif. Med. Assn., L.A. County Med. Assn., Am. Heart Assn., Soc. Air Force Physicians, Phi Beta Kappa, Phi Kappa Phi, Phi Lambda Upsilon, Phi Eta Sigma, Alpha Omega Alpha. Home: 6608 Via La Paloma Palos Verdes Peninsula CA 90275-6449 Office: 16415 Colorado Ave Ste 202 Paramount CA 90723-5054

COHN, LINDSAY PAMELA, political scientist, researcher; b. Phila., May 26, 1977; d. John and Judith Cohn. BA magna cum laude with distinction in Polit. Sci., Duke U., Durham, N.C., 1999. Asst. to mil. justice officer, staff judge adv. USMC, New Orleans, 1996; intern, humanitarian demining sect., office of internat. security and peacekeeping, bur. of politico-military affairs US Dept. of State, Washington, 1997; rsch. assoc. and author: project on gap between the mil. and civilian soc. Triangle Inst. for Security Studies, Durham, NC, 1999—2001; project assoc. (including transl. and editing) on project on comparative mil. law in German ptnr. states Inst. for Internat. Law, U. of Goettingen, Goettingen, Germany, 2001—02; tchg. asst.: internat. law and internat. politics Duke U., Durham, NC, 2001—01; rsch. assoc. Social Sciences Rsch. Inst. German Fed. Armed Forces, Strausberg, Germany, 2002—. Rsch. asst. to prof. of internat. rels. Duke U., Durham, NC, 1996—; del. Naval Acad. Fgn. Affairs Conf. Duke U., 1998; translator (german-english) Harald-Fischer Verlag, Erlangen, Bavaria, Germany, 2000—01; rsch. asst. to prof. of internat. rels. Duke U., Durham, NC, 2002—; panelist Inter-Univ. Seminar on Armed Forces and Soc. Contbr. chapters to books, articles to profl. jours.; singer: at various coll. concerts, 2001—02. Grantee Internat. Rsch. Grant, Ford Found., 1998, Grad. Rsch. Fellowship Hon. Mention, NSF, 2001, Grant in German Studies, German Academic Exch. Svc., 2001, Grad. Award for Rsch. and Tng., Ctr. for Internat. Studies, Duke U., 2001; German Federal Chancellor Fellowship, 2002—. Mem.: Am. Polit. Sci. Assn., Triangle Inst. for Security Studies, Women in Internat. Security. Avocations: Latin and ballroom dancing, miedieval, renaissance and Irish traditional music, horseback riding, Tae Kwon Do. Office: Duke University Box 90204 Durham NC 27708 Office Fax: 919-660-4330. E-mail: lindsay.cohn@duke.edu.

COHN, LINKIE SELTZER, professional speaker, author; b. Nov. 22, 1925; d. Nathan A. and Ann (Ravkind) Levine; m. Marcus Seltzer (dec. 1973); children: Adrienne Lithman, Cathy Brenda Negrel, Robert Michael. Student, So. Meth. U., 1943—44, U. Tex., 1944—45. Profl. dancer Starlight Operettas, Dallas, 1943—44; exec. dir. SW region Am. Friends of Hebrew U., Dallas, 1973; prin. Linkie Seltzer and The Exercise Co., Dallas, 1981; co-founder Anderson-Cohn Inc., DBA Winners for Life Found.; columnist Achievement Mag., 1985; profl. spkr. Love in Bus. Makes Dollars and Sense, 1981—84; pres. Spkrs. Source Internat. Spkrs. Bur., 1989—98; co-owner pubs. Winners for Life. Author (with Donny Anderson): Winners for Life: A Success Guide for Teenagers Using the Proven Power of Goal Setting, Dallas C.C., 1978—85; author: Spanish transl. Triunfadores de por Vida, 2002, How to Love and Be Loved, Communicate With Confidence, Winners for Life Parent's Instructor Guide, Spanish transl. Triunfadores de por Vida Parent and Instructor Guide; prodr.(TV series): Covenent, 1972—73; composer (lyrics and narration of song): The Star of David, 2001; appeared with husband : in Philanthrophy in Texas mag., 2001. Pres. women's divsn. Jewish Fedn. Dallas, 1972—73; chmn. human rels. commn. Dallas Ind. Sch. Dist., 1968; pub. rels. Greater Dallas Cmty. Rels. Commn., 1983—; judge Dallas Morning News ann. contest Teenage Citizen Tribute, 1984; trustee Callier Comm. Found., 2003; campaign chmn. women's divsn. Jewish Fedn. Dallas, 1970. Named Campaigner of Yr., Jewish Fedn. Dallas, 1969; recipient Individual Bridge-Builder award, Turtle Creek Chorale, 2002. Office: PO Box 1011 Addison TX 75001-1011

COHN, LUCILE, psychotherapist, nurse; b. Kokomo, Ind., Apr. 17, 1924; d. Jacob and Anna (Kaplan) Kohn; m. Norman Cohn; children: Richard Alan, Robert Irving. PhD, Marquette U. Diplomate Am. Psychotherapy Assn.; cert. med. hypnotherapist, registered clin. men. hypnotherapist, clin. hypnotherapist, cert. hosp. hospice grief counsel. Employee counselor Mt. Sinai Med. Ctr., Milw., 1965-70; adminstr. of patient care svcs. Milw., 1970-72; chmn. psychiat. nursing Milw. Region Med. Complex, 1972-82; cons. psychotherapist Cardinal Stritch Coll., Milw., 1982—; pvt. practice psychotherapy Milw., 1980—. Prof. nursing Columbia Coll. Nursing, Milw., 1976—, Carroll Coll. Nursing, Waukesha, Wis., 1976—; profl. vol. dying patients and grieving families nursing homes and hsops.; vol. counselor Alzheimer's and AIDS victims and their families, 1990—; spkr. in field. Contbr. Bereavement counselor St. Mary's Hosp. Hospice, Milw., 1996—; life mem. Women's Am. Orgn., Rehab. Through Tng., Mt. Sinai Med. Ctr. Aux., Jewish Home and Care Ctr., Hadassah; mem. Urban League, Pub. Libr. Lit. Soc., Milw. Heart Assn.; vol. docent Milw. Pub. Libr., 2001—; active The Women's Meml., Milw. Art Mus., Temple Shalom. 1st lt. Nurse Corps U.S. Army. Named 1 of 2000 Women of Achievement, London, 1972, Nurse of Yr., Wis. Nurses Assn., 1977. Fellow: Am. Med. Psychotherapists Assn. (diplomate); mem.: ANA, Am. Assn, Grief Counselors, U. Wis. Union (life), Women's Assn. Orgn. Rehab. Through Tng. (life; pres. Beal chpt., regional v.p., Women's Meml.), Women in Mil. Svc. Democrat. Jewish. Avocations: swimming, painting, gardening, travel, volunteering. Home: 929 N Astor St Unit 2406 Milwaukee WI 53202-3438

COHN, MARIANNE WINTER MILLER, civic activist; b. Denver, Jan. 15, 1928; d. Henry Abraham II and Esther (Sheflan) Winter; m. Benjamin K. Miller, Dec. 29, 1948 (dec. Dec. 1972); children: Judy Ellen, Philip Henry (dec. 1996); m. Isidore Cohn Jr., Jan. 3, 1976; stepchildren: Ian Jeffrey Cohn, Lauren Kerry Cohn Fouros. Student, Colo. U., 1946-47. Women's bd. dirs. Nat. Jewish Hosp. at Denver, 1951—80, pres. women's divsn., 1960—61, mem., sec. gov. bd., 1972—76; mem. nat. bd. Nat. Jewish Ctr., 1976—; mem. exec. bd. Greater New Orleans Tourist and Conv. Commn., 1985; chmn. spouse program arrangements Am. Coll. Surgons, La., 1985; mem. exec. bd. NCCJ, New Orleans, 1987—96, sec., 1991—92, treas., 1993—94, nat. bd. dirs., 1993; bd. dirs. Jewish Endowment Found., New Orleans, 1987—88, La. ArtWorks of Arts Coun. of New Orleans, 2000; mem. Arts Coun. of New Orleans, 1988—, v.p. devel., 1991—92, v.p. grants, exec. bd., 1993—96, pres., 1997—98, chmn. bd., 1999, v.p. grants, 2001; chmn. Exhibit Sunking, Louis XIV La. State Mus., 1984, pres. La. Mus. Found. of, 1989—90, bd. dirs., 1994—2001, mem. governing bd., 1992—; bd. dirs. New Orleans Symphony Aux., 1980; chmn. Odyssey Ball of New Orleans Mus. Art, 1992; bd. dirs. La. Coun. for Music and Performing Arts, 1991—92; regional vice chmn. Nat. Jewish Ctr., 1999—; mem. Sisterhood of Temple Emanuel Denver, pres., 1957—60. Recipient Edgar L. Feinberg Meml. award James D. Rives Surg. Soc., 1988, Woman of Fashion award Men of Fashion, 1989, Humanitarian award Nat. Jewish Ctr. Immunology and Respiratory Medicine, 1995, role model award Young Leadership Coun. New Orleans, 1998—, Nat. Jewish Ctr. Chmn.'s award, 1999. Republican. Avocations: travel, cooking.

COHN, MILDRED, biochemist, educator; b. N.Y.C., July 12, 1913; d. Isidore M. and Bertha (Klein) Cohn; m. Henry Primakoff, May 30, 1938; children: Nina, Paul, Laura. BA, Hunter Coll., 1931, DSc (hon.), 1984; MA, Columbia U., 1932, PhD, 1938; DSc (hon.), Women's Med. Coll., 1975, Radcliffe Coll., 1978, Washington U., St. Louis, 1981, Brandeis U., 1984, U. Pa., Phila., 1984, U. N.C., 1985; PhD (hon.), Weizmann Inst. Sci., 1988; DSc (hon.), U. Miami, 1990. Rsch. asst. biochemistry George Washington U. Sch. Medicine, 1937—38; rsch. assoc. Cornell Med. Coll., 1938—46, Washington U. Sch. Medicine, 1946—58; assoc. prof. biol. chemistry Washington U., 1958—60; assoc. prof. biophysics and phys. biochemistry U. Pa. Med. Sch., 1960—61, prof., 1961—71, prof. biochemistry and biophysics, 1971—82, Benjamin Rush prof. physiol. chemistry, 1978—82; emerita, 1982—; sr. mem. Inst. Cancer Research, Phila., 1982—85; chancellor's vis. prof. biophysics U. Calif., Berkeley, 1982; vis. prof. biol. chemistry Johns Hopkins U. Med. Sch., 1985—91. Research assoc. Harvard U. Med. Sch., 1950—51; established investigator Am. Heart Assn., 1953—59; career investigator, 1964—78; vis. prof. chemistry Yale U., 1973. Mem. editl. bd. Jour. Biol. Chemistry, 1958—63, 1967—72. Recipient Hall of Fame award, Hunter Coll., 1973, Disting. Alumni award, 1975, Cresson medal, Franklin Inst., award, Internat. Assn. Women Biochemists, 1979, Humboldt award, Germany, 1980, Nat. Medal Sci., 1982, award, Am. Acad. Achievement, 1984, Chandler medal, Columbia U., 1986, Women in Sci. award, N.Y. Acad. Sci., 1992, Gov.'s award for excellence in sci., Pa., 1993, Founders medal, Magnetic Resonance in Biology, 1994, Stein-Moore award, Protein Soc., 1997. Mem.: NAS, Inst. de Biologie Physico-Chimique, Coll. Physicians of Phila. (Disting. Svc. award 1987), Am. Biophys. Soc., Am. Soc. Biolchemistry and Molecular Biology (pres. 1978—79), Harvey Soc., Am. Chem. Soc. (chmn. divsn. biol. chemistry 1975—76, Garvan medal 1963, Remsen award Md. sect. 1988, Cinn. sect. Oesper award 2000), Am. Philos. Soc. (v.p. 1994—2000), Am. Acad. Arts and Scis., Iota Sigma Pi (hon. nat. mem. 1988), Sigma Xi, Phi Beta Kappa. Office: U Pa Med Sch 242 Anat Chem Bldg Dept Biochemistry & Biophys Philadelphia PA 19104-6059

COHN, NATHAN, lawyer; b. Charleston, S.C., Jan. 20, 1918; s. Samuel and Rose (Baron) C.; 1 child, Norman; m. Carolyn Venturini, May 18, 1970. JD, San Francisco Law Sch., 1947. BAr: Calif. 1947, U.S. Supreme Ct. 1957. Pvt. practice law, San Francisco, 1947—. Judge pro tem Mcpl. Ct., Superior Ct. Columnist, San Francisco Progress, 1982-86; contbr. and author seminars in field. Mem. Calif. State Recreation Commn., 1965-68; former mem. Dem. State Ctrl. Com. Served to 1st lt. USAF, 1950-55. Named to San Francisco Law Sch. Hall of Fame, 2000. Fellow Am. Bd. Criminal Lawyers (founder, past pres.), Am. Bd. Trial Advs. (diplomate; chpt. pres. 1984), Internat. Acad. Law and Sci., San Francisco Trial Lawyers (past pres., Lifetime Achievement award 2000), Criminal Trial Lawyers Assn. No. Calif., Irish-Israeli-Italian Soc. (co-founder, co-pres.), Internat. Footprinters Assn., Regular Vets. Assn. (national judge advocate), Calamari Club, Godfathers Club (past pres.), St. Vincent Sch. for Boys, Press Club (life), Masons (32 deg.), Shriners, South of Market Boys (past pres.), Ancient Order Hibernians Am. (hon. life). Jewish. Office: 2107 Van Ness Ave Ste 200 San Francisco CA 94109-2596

COHN, REBECCA, state representative; b. Vallejo, Calif., Mar. 30, 1954; m. Ron Cohn; 1 child, Andrew. BS, U. Tex., Galveston, 1975, degree in Physical Therapy, 1976. Physical therapist, 1976—91; sr. cons. Bus. Design Assocs., 1991—2000; mem. Calif. Assembly, 2000—. Mem. diversity task force, Joint Venture Silicon Valley, 1989—90, Santa Clara County Domestic Violence Coun., County Domestic Violence Coun., 1998—2000, Silicon Valley Dem. Forum, 1997—2000; bd. dirs. Support Network Battered Women, 1987—2000; bd. dirs., sec. Calif. Indsl. Med. Coun., 1991—96. Mem.: Emily's List, Century Club. Democrat. Jewish. Office: PO Box 942849 Rm 3173 Sacramento CA 94249 Address: 901 Campisi Way Ste 300 Campbell CA 95008

COHN, ROBIN JEAN, crisis management executive, author; b. Portsmith, Va., Oct. 18, 1952; d. Murry and Mildred (Schachtman) Cohn. BA magna cum laude (Pres.'s scholar), Temple U., 1974. Dir. David Gary Ltd., Ft. Lauderdale, Fla., 1974—75; advt. mgr. Tamarac Topic, Fla., 1975—76; dir. pub. rels. Biscayne Med. Ctr., Miami, Fla., 1976—78; staff v.p. Air Fla., Miami, 1978—84, Alamo Rent A Car, 1984—86; dir. pub. rels. NY Air, 1986—87, MacAndrews & Forbes, 1987—88; pres. Romann & Tannenholz Pub. Rels., N.Y.C., 1989—91, Robin Cohn and Co., 1991—. Spkr. UNLC Crisis Mgmt. Conf., 1992, Aviation Disaster Symposium, 1994, Am. Soc. Indsl. Security Conf., 1995, Surviving Crises Conf., 1996, IAEM Conv., 1996, Inst. Internat. Rsch. Conf., 1997; guest lectr. NY Women's Bar Assn., Yale U., 1991, U. Miami; expert witness, 1997—; adj. prof. MA program in corp. and orgnl. comms. Fairleigh Dickinson U., 1990—. Author: (bible) The PK Crisis Bible, PR Crisis Bible. Dir. Miami City Ballet, 1985—88; mem. NY Women's Agenda's Woman of the Future, 1997; guest expert CNN, 2001—; mem. pub. rels. com. Miami's For Me, 1982, 1983, host com., 1983; active Leadership Miami, 1982—85, Miami Forum, 1981—86, Fla. Tourism Adv. Coun., 1983—86; bd. dirs. Project Horizon, 1986; mem. exec. bd. Corp. Comm. Inst., Fairleigh Dickinson U., 2000—; mem. pub. rels. com. Broward Arts Coun., 1984—86; vol. N.Y.C. Sch. Vol. Program, 1992—; chmn. reentry employment com. YWCA, 1994—; mem. AEM Convention Crummer Grad. Sch. Bus., 2002. Mem.: NAFE (mem. com. 1994—), Crisis Mgmt. Symposium, Fin. Women's Assn., Fgn. Policy Assn.

COHN, SCOTT, television news correspondent; b. Chgo., Feb. 8, 1960; s. Daniel Harris and Lillian Liselotte (Klopstock) C.; m. Jessica Elizabeth Simonson, Nov. 23, 1985; children: Nathan George, Justin Reid. BA, U. Wis., 1981. Reporter WYEN Radio, Des Plaines, Ill., 1978; reporter, news anchor Wis. Pub. Radio, Madison, 1978-81; reporter, anchor WEAU-TV, WAXX Radio, Eau Claire, Wis., 1981-82, WZZM-TV, Grand Rapids, Mich., 1982-89; corr., anchor CNBC, N.Y.C., 1989-90, chief Medwest corr. Chgo., 1990-95, nat. corr., 1995-99, corr. anchor, analyst N.Y.C., 1999—. Recipient Best Broadcast Series award, Medill/Strong Fin. Writers and Editors award, Medill, Sch. of Journalism, 2000-01, N.Y. Festivals award, 2001, 02. Mem. Radio-TV News Dirs. Assn., Soc. Profl. Journalists, Deadline Club of NY (Citation of Merit 1994, 2001). Office: CNBC 2200 Fletcher Ave Fort Lee NJ 07024-5005

COHN, SHERMAN LOUIS, lawyer, educator; b. Erie, Pa., July 21, 1932; s. Jacob and Bella (Kaufman) C.; m. Lucy Diaz, July 5, 1998; children by previous marriage: Ronald Bruce, Jerald Seth, Joshua Biber, Steven David, Leah Sura Guihen. BS in Fgn. Svc. summa cum laude, Georgetown U., 1954, JD, 1957, LLM, 1960, M of Acupuncture (hon.), 1993. Bar: Va. 1957, D.C. 1957, Md. 1978. Law clk. to Judge Burton R. Laub Erie County Ct., Pa., 1955, Walton H. Hamilton, 1957, Judge Charles Fahy, U.S. Ct. of Appeals for D.C. Circuit, 1957-58; staff atty. Appellate sect. Civil divsn. Dept. Justice, Washington, 1958-62, asst. chief, 1962-65; prof. law Georgetown U. Law Ctr., Washington, 1965—, dir. continuing legal edn., 1977-84. Lectr. Cath. U. Law Sch., 1963-65; vis. prof. Am. U. Law Sch., 1969-78, 92-93, 94-95; adminstr. Preview of U.S. Supreme Ct. Cases, 1975-79; cons., litigation counsel Select Com. on Presdl. Campaign Activities U.S. Senate, 1973-74; mem. Jud. Conf. D.C. Circuit, 1965-70, 71-73, 75, 77-78, 86, Jud. Conf. D.C. Ct. Appeals, 1979-81; reporter Nat. Conf. on Appellate Justice, San Diego, 1976. Contbr. articles to profl. jours. Pres. H.M. and A.E. Himmelfarb Found., 2002—, Charles Fahy Am. Inn of Ct., 1985—86, Traditional Acupuncture Found., 1984—88; chmn. Nat. Accredited Commn. Schs. and Colls. Acupuncture and Oriental Medicine, 1983—93; trustee Am. Inns of Ct. Found., pres., 1985—96; trustee Tai Sophia; bd. dirs. Acupuncture and Oriental Medicine Alliance, 1999—; chmn. bd. dirs. Tai Hsuan Found., 1998—2001; trustee Rule of Law Found., 2002—. Recipient A. Sherman Christensen award Am. Inns of Ct., 1990, Younger Fed. Lawyer award for outstanding service to U.S., 1964, Civil Justice award Am. Bd. Trial Advocates, 1993. Mem. ABA, D.C. Bar Assn., Va. State Bar, Am. Law Inst., Internat. Assn. Jewish Lawyers and Jurists (pres. Am. sect. 1983-87, dep. pres. internat. 1985-91), Jewish Law Assn. (pres. 1998-2002), Soc. Am. Law Tchrs., Georgetown U. Alumni Assn. (chmn. alumni fund 1985-87, Presdl. citation 1978, 87, John Carroll award 1980) Lodges: B'nai B'rith. Office: Georgetown U Law Ctr 600 New Jersey Ave NW Washington DC 20001-2075 E-mail: cohn@law.georgetown.edu.

COHN, STEVEN FREDERICK, sociology educator, consultant; b. Chgo., Sept. 5, 1939; s. William Wolf and Sylvia Ann (Wechsler) C.; m. Kathleen Marie Cusick, May 8, 1968 (div. Jan. 1974); 1 child, Iain Cusick-Cohn. BA, Dartmouth Coll., 1961; PhD, Columbia U., 1975. Lectr. U. Strathclyde, Glasgow, Scotland, 1968-69, U. Glasgow, 1969-71; asst. prof. U. Maine, Orono, 1971-77; policy analyst NSF, Washington, 1978-79; assoc. prof. U. Maine, Orono, 1980-85, prof., 1986—. Cons. ACTION, Washington, 1970-72, The Royal Soc., London, 1984. Contbr. articles to profl. jours. Fulbright fellow Coun. for Internat. Exch. Scholars, 1984. Mem. Am. Sociol. Assn. (sect. program com. 1995-96), Ea. Soc. Assn. (publs. com. mem. 1990), Phi Beta Kappa. Jewish. Home: 99 N Main Ave Orono ME 04473-4430 Office: U Maine 201 Fernald Orono ME 04469-0001

COHN, STEVEN LAWRENCE, internist, medical educator; AB, Rutgers U., 1973, MS in Physiology, 1974; MD, U. Monterrey, Mex., 1978. Diplomate Am. Bd. Internal Medicine. Intern then resident Downstate Med. Ctr., 1979-82, Kings County Hosp., 1979-82, Bklyn. VA Hosp., 1979-82; dir. med. consultation svc. Kings County Hosp., Bklyn., 1986—; chief divsn. internal medicine SUNY Health Sci. Ctr. Univ. Hosp., Bklyn., 2000—, assoc. med. dir. quality assurance, 1993—, chief divsn. gen. internal medicine, 2001—, clin. prof. medicine, 2002—. Contbr.: Surgery '89, 1989; contbr. articles to profl. jours. Fellow ACP; mem. Soc. Gen. Internal Medicine, N.Y. Heart Assn. Office: SUNY Health Sci Ctr Box 68 470 Clarkson Ave Brooklyn NY 11203-2012

COHN, THEODORE ELLIOT, optometry educator, vision scientist, bioengineer; b. Highland Park, Ill., Sept. 5, 1941; s. Nathan and Marjorie (Kurtzon) C.; m. Barbara Adler, Nov. 29, 1975; children: Avery Simon, Adrienne Leah, Harris Samuel. SB in Elec. Engring., MIT, 1963; MS in Bioengring., U. Mich., 1965, MA in Math., 1966, PhD in Bioengring., 1969. Asst. prof. U. Calif., Berkeley, 1970-76, assoc. prof., 1976-84, prof., 1985—. Vis. fellow John Curtin Med. Sch., Australian Nat. U., Canberra, 1977; vis. scholar U. Calif., San Diego, 1981-90; chair grad. group in bioengring. U. Calif., Berkeley/U. Calif., San Francisco, 2000—; vice chair grad. affairs, dept. bioengring., U. Calif. Berkeley, 1999—. Author, editor: Visual Detection, 1993. Bd. dirs. Berkeley-Richmond Jewish Cmty. Ctr., 1995—. Fellow Optical Soc. Am. (chairvision tech. group 1984-86); mem. IEEE (sr. mem.), Assn. Rsch. Vision & Ophthalmology, Vision Scis. Soc., Human Factors and Ergonomics Soc., Sigma Xi. Office: U Calif Sch Optometry 360 Minor Hall Berkeley CA 94720-2020 E-mail: tecohn@spectacle.berkeley.edu.

COHN, WILLIAM ETTLINGER, cardiologist, thoracic surgeon, product designer; b. New York, Ny, Sept. 2, 1960; s. Hugh Karl and Judith Ettlinger Cohn; m. Mishaun Victoria Drever, May 30, 1961; children: Benjamen Mycroft, Elizabeth Emily, William Ettlinger, Robert Huntington, Christopher Michael. M.D., Baylor Coll. of Medicine, Houston, Tex., 1982—86. Diplomate Board of Thoracic Suregry Soc. of Thoracic Surgery, 1994. Assoc. prof. Harvard Med. Sch., Boston, Mass., 2002—; chief of minimally invasive cardiac surgery Beth Israel Deaconess Med. Ctr., Boston, Mass., 2001—. Author (investigator): (scientific publications) 1)use of ultrasonic welding in cardiac surgery, 2) myocardial revascularization with a pedicaled gastric submucosal flap 3)The Hgraft as a varient of minimally invasive coronary artery bypass. Achievements include invention of Coronary artery stabilizer to allow bypass surgery without stopping the heart; patents for Distinguished Inventor of the year, 2000, Intellectual Property owner's association; invention of Nextstitch suture chain for cardiac valve implantation; Catheters For Percutaniously Attaching One Blood Vessel To Another Without Requiring An Operation; patents for Multiple Patents For Cardiac Valve Procedures Withourt Stoppig The Heart. Office: Beth Israel Deaconess Med Ctr 110 Francic St Boston MA 02215 Home Fax: 617-632-7562; Office Fax: 617-632-7562. Personal E-mail: wcohn@caregroup.harvard.edu. E-mail: wcohn@caregroup.harvard.edu.

COHODES, ELI AARON, publisher; b. Iron Mountain, Mich., Sept. 12, 1927; s. Joseph Harry and Esther Ida (Albert) C.; m. Phyllis Hersh, Jan. 4, 1953; children: Stephen Eliot, David Bruce, Mitchell Joseph, Paul Andrew (dec.) BA, Harvard U., 1950. Assoc. editor Hosp. Mgmt. mag., 1953-54; mng. editor Trustee mag., 1957-59, Modern Hosp. mag., 1959-63; editor Nation's Schs. mag., Chgo., 1963-68, chmn. editorial adv. bd., columnist, 1968-75; v.p. Instructional Dynamics, Inc., Chgo., 1968-70; chmn. Teach'em, Chgo, 1970—2001; pres. Bonus Books, Inc., Chgo., 1985—2002. Lectr. profl. writing U. Chgo., 1959-63 Co-author: Planning Flexible Learning Places, 1977; mem. editorial bd. Coll. and Univ. Bus. mag, 1973-75. With AUS, 1945-46. Home: 37 Turnbull Woods Ct Highland Park IL 60035-5135

COHON, JARED L. academic administrator; m. Maureen Cohon; 1 child, Hallie. BA in Civil Engring., U. Pa., 1969; MA in Civil Engring., MIT, 1972, PhD in Civil Engring., 1973. Legis. asst. for energy and environment U.S. Senator Daniel P. Moynihan, 1997—98; from faculty to assoc. dean engring. to vice provost rsch. Johns Hopkins; prof. environ. systems analysis, dean Sch. Forestry and Environ. Studies Yale U., 1992—97; pres. Carnegie Mellon U., Pitts., 1997—; apptd. chmn. by Pres. Clinton Nuclear Waste Tech. Review Bd., 1997—2002. Recipient Joan Queneay Hodges award, Nat. Audubon Soc. and Am. Assn. Engring. Scis., Pareto-Edgeworth award, Multiple Criteria Decision Making Soc. Office: Carnegie Mellon Univ 5000 Forbes Ave Pittsburgh PA 15213-3890

COIFMAN, RONALD R. mathematician, educator; b. Tel Aviv; PhD, U. Geneva, 1965. Former prof. U. Chgo., Washington U.; prof. math. and computer sci. Yale U., New Haven, 1980—, chair math dept., 1986—89, Phillips prof. math., 1998—. Vis. prof. Tel Aviv U., Israel, U. Chgo. Co-author 3 books; contbr. articles and papers to profl. jours. Recipient State of Conn. medal of Sci., Gov. John G. Rowland, 1996, Nat. medal of Sci., 1999. Fellow: NAS. Office: Yale U Dept Math PO Box 208283 New Haven CT 06520-8283

COIL, CAROLYN CHANDLER, educational consultant; b. Washington, Aug. 22, 1943; d. William Chandler and Charlotte Eleanor (Lanhardt) Hendrix; m. Paul Douglas Coil; children: Paul William, Johnston Allan. BA, U. Md., 1965; MA, U. South Fla., 1985, MEd, 1990. Cert. gifted tchr., secondary tchr., ednl. leadership adminstr. Tchr. Prince Georges County Sch., Upper Marlboro, Md., 1965-71, Ledyard (Conn.) Pub. Schs., 1971-73; insvc. coord. Ednl. TV for S.E. Ohio, Athens, 1977-81; learning resources specialist Fla. Diagnostic and Learning Rsch., Bartow, 1981-92; ednl. cons. Creative Cons. and Tng., Lilburn, Ga., 1992—. Cons., author Pieces of Learning, Marion, Ill., 1991—. Author: Motivating Underachievers, 1992, Motivating Underachievers, rev. edit., 2000, Becoming An Achiever, 1994, Eye on Japan, 1995, Eye on Australia, 1995, Teaching Tools for the 21st Century, 1997, Teaching Tools for the 21st Century, rev. edit., 2000, Tools for Teaching & Learning in the Integrated Classroom, 1997, Hot Topics in Education, 1997, Celebrations, 1998, Encouraging Achievement, 1999, Teacher's Toolbox, 1999, Student Engagement: Raising Achievement for Student Success, 2000, Surviving the MiddleYears, 2001, Solving the Assessment Puzzle, 2001. Mem. exec. bd. New Beginnings for Youth, Orlando, Fla.; mem. cons. commn. Episcopal Diocese of Atlanta. Mem. Phi Delta Kappa, Phi Kappa Phi. Avocations: travel, reading. Home: 4141 Wash Lee Ct SW Lilburn GA 30047-7440 Office: Pieces of Learning 1990 Market Rd Marion IL 62959-8976 E-mail: carolyncoil@aol.com.

COILE, RUSSELL CLEVEN, electrical engineer, consultant; b. Washington, Mar. 11, 1917; s. Cecil Roy and Gunda Cristoffersen Coile; m. Ellen Miller Coile, Dec. 27, 1951; children: Jennifer Norah Miller, Jonathan Roy Miller, Andrew Cleven Miller. SB, MIT, 1938, SM, 1939, EE, 1950; PhD, City U., London, 1978; Grad., Naval War Coll., 1959, Air War Coll., 1964. Registered profl. engr., Pa., 1947, D.C., 1951, lifetime instr. credential in engring., Calif. Cmty. Colleges, 1989; cert. emergency mgr. Internat. Assn. of Emergency Managers, 1993. Rsch. asst. Elec. Engring. Rsch. Lab, M.I.T., Cambridge, Mass., 1938—39; magnetician Cargnegie Instn. Wash./Huancayo (Peru) Magnetic Obs., 1939—42; engr. Colton & Foss, Inc., Washington, 1946—47; ops. rsch. scientist Ops. Evaluation Group, M.I.T., Washington, 1947—62, dir. rsch. Ops. Rsch. Group, Office Naval Rsch., Washington, 1953—57; dir. marine corps ops. analysis group Ctr. For Naval Analyses, Franklin Inst., Washington, 1962—67; ops. rsch. analyst Ctr. for Naval Analyses, U. Rochester, Arlington, Va., 1967—78; sr. rsch. analyst Ketron, Arlington, 1978—81; dep. exec. dir./chief scientist Planning Rsch. Corp., Fort Ord, Calif., 1982—87; sr. analyst Evaluation Tech. Inc., Monterey, Calif., 1988—90; disaster coord./emergency program mgr. Pacific Grove Fire Dept., Pacific Grove, Calif., 1990—2000; adj. prof. Inst. for Joint Warfare Analysis, Naval Postgraduate Sch., Monterey, 1998—2000; dir. disaster svcs. Carmel Chpt., ARC, Carmel-by-the-Sea, Calif., 2000—01. Cons. Purdue U., Lafayette, Ind., 1978, NSF, Washington, 1997, Assn. Monterey Bay Area Govts., Marina, Calif., 2002—, Fed. Emergency Mgmt. Agy., Washington, 2000—02; lectr. on naval ops. rsch. Maritime Self-Defense Force, Tokyo, 1956; Am. del. Internat. Fedn. Operational Rsch. Socs., Oslo, 1963; mem. small arms adv. com. Advanced Rsch. Projects Agy., Dept. Def., Washington, 1968—70; instr. Neighborhood Emergency Response Teams, Pacific Grove, 1994—97; presenter in field. Asst. editor: Quality Control and Applied Statistics Abstracts, mem. editl. adv. bd.: Hungarian Acad. Scis. Internat. Jour. Scientometrics; contbr. articles to profl. jours. Chmn. cmtys. working group V.p. Gore's Global Disaster Info. Network Project. Capt. Army Signal Corps U.S. Army, 1942—46, col. ret. USAF. Recipient Exemplary Practices in Emergency Mgmt. award, Fed. Emergency Mgmt. Agy., 1998, 1999, 2000; Rschr. Exch. Travel fellow to visit Chinese Acad. of Sciences, NSF, 1997. Fellow: Inst. Civil Defence and Disaster Studies; mem.: IEEE (life; cons. 1955), Internat. Test and Evaluation Assn. (bd. dirs. 1985—88), Emergency Planning Soc., Inst. for Ops. Rsch. and the Mgmt. Scis., Am. Soc. for Info. Sci., Internat. Emergency Mgmt. Soc., Internat. Assn. Emergency Mgrs. (commr. of the cert. emergency mgr. commn. 1998—), Island Sailing Club, Marine Meml. Club. Avocations: sailing, amateur radio. Home: 970 Egan Ave Pacific Grove CA 93950-2406 Office: Sand City Police Dept 1 Sylven Pk Sand City CA 93955 Personal E-mail: russell@coile.com.

COIMBRA, CARLOS F.M. mechanical engineering educator, fluid dynamicist; s. Jose Antonio and Maria Luiza Coimbra; m. Kaori Y. Coimbra, Apr. 6, 1999; children: Miya Carina, Kaila Miki. PhD in Mech. and Aerospace Engring., U. of Calif., 1998. Asst. prof. mech. engring. and mechanics Drexel U., Phila., 1999—2000; asst. prof. mech. engring. U. of Hawaii-Manoa, Honolulu, 2000—. Dir. of multiphase flow lab. U. of Hawaii-Manoa, Honolulu, 2000—. Author: (jour. pubs.) Fundamental Dynamics of Particle Motion in Fluid Mechanics (AIAA Best Paper Award in Microgravity Sciences, 1999). Grantee Lift Effects on Motion of Suspended Particles in Rotating Vessel Grant, Am. Chem. Soc. - Petroleum Rsch. Fund, 2002—. Achievements include research in Introduced new fractional calculus methods for solving multiphase flow problems. Office: Univ of Hawaii-Manoa 2541 Dole St Holmes Hall #302 Honolulu HI 96822

COIN, SHEILA REGAN, organization and management development consultant; b. Columbus, Ohio, Feb. 17, 1942; d. James Daniel Regan and Jean (Hodgson) Cook; m. Tasso H. Colin, Sept. 17, 1967 (div.); children: Tasso, Alison Regan. BS, U. Iowa, 1964. RN staff nurse VA Hosp., Boston, 1964-66; field rep. ARC, Chgo., 1966-67, chief nurse, 1967; asst. divsn. dir. Am. Hosp. Assn., sec. Am. Soc. Hosp. Dirs. Nursing, Chgo., 1967-69; owner Coin & Assocs., Chgo., 1975-77; ptnr., orgn. devel. and performance mgmt. sr. cons. Coin, Newell & Assocs., Chgo., 1976-96, Buck Cons., Inc., Washington, 1996-2000; pres. Coin Alisso Group, 2000—03; sr. organizational effectiveness cons. Potomac Elec. Power Co., Washington, 2003—. Instr. dept. continuing edn. Loyola U., Chgo., 1975-77, Rock Valley Coll. Mgmt. Inst., Rockford, Ill., 1978-80, Ill. Ctrl. Coll. Inst. Personal and Profl. Devel., Peoria, 1979-85, Triton Coll. Continuing Edn., River Grove, Ill., 1983-86, No. Ill. U. Continuing Edn., DeKalb, 1983-86; mem. editl. bd. Tng. Today mag., 1992-94, assoc. editor, 1994-96. Vol. Art Inst., Chgo., 1968-69; mem. Chgo. Beautiful Com., 1968-73; chmn. Mayor Daley's Chgo. Beautiful Awards Project, 1972; mem. jr. bd. Girl Scouts Assn., Chgo., 1975-76; mem. jr. governing bd. Chgo. Symphony Orch., 1971-81, pres., 1977-78; governing mem. Orchestral Assn., Chgo., 1977-81; bd. dirs. Mid-Am. chpt. ARC, Chgo., 1979-81, 91-94, vice chmn., 1986-89, mem. planning and evaluation subcom., 1991-96, chmn. quality mgmt. steering com., 1992-94, bd. dirs. Chgo. dist., 1981-89, chmn. fin. devel. com., 1982-85, vice chmn. dist. bd., 1986-89; bd. dirs. Ill. chpt. Lupus Found. Am., 1991-93; bd. dirs., mem. Survive Alive House Found., 1989-96; dir. Com. for Thalossemia Chgo. Bd., 1981-82; mem. Women's bd. Nat. Com. Prevention Child Abuse, Chgo., 1981-82; mem. State of Ill. Disabled Persons Adv. Coun., 1988-97; acad. specialist in mgmt. devel. U.S. Info. Agy., 1994. Mem. ASTD (exec. com. of mgmt. devel. profl. practice area 1992-95), Christ Child Soc., Ill. State Soc., Soc. for Human Resources Mgmt.

COKE, FRANK VAN DEREN, museum director, photographer; b. Lexington, Ky., July 4, 1921; s. Sterling Dent and Elisabeth (Van Deren) C.; m. Eleanor Barton, 1943 (div. 1980); children: Sterling Van Deren, Eleanor Browning; m. Joan Gillberry Morgan, 1983 BA, U. Ky., 1956; MFA, Ind. U., 1958; postgrad., Harvard U.; LHD (hon.), San Francisco Acad. of Art, 1986. With Van Deren Hardware Co., Lexington, 1946-56, pres., 1953-56; asst. prof. art U. Fla., 1958-61; assoc. prof. art Ariz. State U., 1961-62; prof., dir. art mus. U. N.Mex., 1962-66, chmn. dept., 1963-70, dir. art mus., 1973-79; dep. dir., then dir. Internat. Mus. Photography, Rochester, N.Y., 1970-72; dir. dept. photography San Francisco Mus. Modern Art, 1979-87. Bd. dirs. Internat. Folk Art Found., U. N.Mex. Art Mus., Georgia O'Keeffe Mus., Santa Fe, Mus. Fine Arts, Santa Fe; chmn. Albuquerque Fine Arts Adv. Com.; cons. in field; Disting. vis. prof. art Ariz. State U., 1988-91. Author: books and catalogues, including Taos and Santa Fe; The Artist's Environment, 1882-1942, 1963, The Painter and the Photograph, 1972, One Hundred Years of Photographic History, 1975, Avant-Garde Photography in Germany, 1919-1939, 1981, Faces Photographed, 1984, Joel-Peter Witkin, 1985, Photography: A Facet of Modernism, 1986, Secular and Sacred: Photographs of Mexico by Van Deren Coke, 1992, Forecast: Shifts in Direction, 1994. Served as officer USNR, 1942-45. Recipient Photography Internat. award, 1955, 56 (2), Modern Photography Internat. award, 1956, U.S. Camera Internat. award, 1957, 58, 60, New Talent USA Art in Am. award, 1960, Gov.'s award State of N.Mex., 1986, Educator of Yr. Leica Medal of

Excellence, 1987, Joseph Sudek medal Ministry of Culture of the Czech Socialist Republic, 1989, Disting. Internat. Career in Photography award, 1992, Internat. Photometeing, Rep. San Marino, Peer award The Friends of Photography, San Francisco, 1992, Distinction in Art Adminstrn. award Nat. Coun. Art Adminstrs., 1997; Guggenheim fellow, 1975; Fulbright teaching fellow U. Auckland, N.Z., 1989 Mem. Coll. Art Assn. (bd. dirs. 1973-77, 88-92), Soc. Photog. Edn. (bd. dirs. 1965-70).

COKELET, GILES ROY, biomedical engineering educator; b. N.Y.C., Jan. 7, 1932; s. Roy S. and Anna M. (Trippel) C.; m. Sarah Drew, June 15, 1963; children— Becky, Bradford BS, Calif. Inst. Tech., 1957, MS, 1958; ScD, MIT, 1963. Rsch. engr. Dow Chem. Co., Williamsburg, Va., 1958-60; asst. prof. Calif. Inst. Tech., Pasadena, 1964-68; assoc. prof. Mont. State U., Bozeman, 1969-76, prof., 1976-78, U. Rochester, N.Y., 1978-98; rsch. prof. Mont. State U., Bozeman, 1998—. Contbr. articles to profl. jours. With U.S. Army, 1954-55, Japan. Recipient Sr. U.S. Scientist award Humboldt-Stiftung, Bonn, Fed. Republic Germany, 1981-82, 88. Fellow AAAS; mem. Biomed. Engrng. Soc., Microcirculatory Soc., Soc. Rheology, No. Am. Soc. Biorheology, Internat. Soc. Biorheology (past pres., Poiseuille medal 1999). Avocations: stamp collecting, hiking. Office: Mont State U Dept Chem Engrng Bozeman MT 59717-0001

COKER, CAROLINE TIFFANY, lawyer; b. Houston, June 7, 1974; d. Donald W. and Linda S. Coker. BA, BS, So. Meth. U., 1996; JD, Samford U., 1999. Bar: Ala. 1999, Ga. 2001, U.S. Patent Bar 2001. Patent examiner U.S. Patent and Trademark Office, Washington, 1999—2000; e-commerce, intellectual property and patent atty. Troutman Sanders, Atlanta, 2000—02; sr. patent strategist Cingular Wireless, Atlanta, 2002—03; intellectual property counsel Motorola, Inc., Phila., 2003—. Mem. Jr. League, Atlanta, 2000—. Mem. Ala. Trial Lawyers Assn., Cumberland Intellectual Property Assn. (founder, pres.). Episcopalian. Avocations: fashion, travel, writing, music. Office: 101 Tournament Dr Ste 1-3032 Horsham PA 19044 E-mail: ctcoker@aol.com., ccoker@motorola.com.

COKER, CHARLOTTE NOEL, political activist; b. New Orleans, Dec. 28, 1930; d. Cecil Eugene and Esta Reed (Williams) Mahaffey; m. Rainey Morris Coker, Nov. 17, 1950; children: Patricia A. Coker Ross, Carol J. Coker goebel, Teresa J., Robert M. Student X-ray technician tng., St. Mary's Hosp., Port Arthur, Tex., 1947-48; X-ray therapy, Emory U., 1949. Precinct committeewoman Spokane County Dem. Com., Spokane, Wash., 1970—, 6th legis. dist. leader, 1973-74, 77-78; Wash. State rep. to Dem. Nat. Com., Washington, 2000—. State committeewoman Spokane County Dem. Ctrl. Com., 1975-76, 79-80, 81-82, 95—; vice chmn. Wash. State Dem. Com., Seattle, 1981; region 6 dir. Wash. State Fedn. Dem. Women's Clubs, 1979-80, state dir., 1981-85; mem. Dem. Nat. Com., 1992—, mem. exec. com., 1995-97, pres. Nat. Fedn. Dem. Women, 1995-97; tour guide Wash. Ho. of Reps., Olympia, 1975; aide Office of Gov. Dixy Lee Ray, Spokane, 1978-80; presdl. elector for Wash. State, 2000—; chair Wash. State Electoral Coll., 2000. Mem. Spokane Quality of Life Coun., 1975-77, Spokane Task Force for Cmty. Devel. Funds, 1978, Human Rights Commn. Wash. State, 1998—, chair, 2003—. Mem.: Spokane Fedn. Women's Orgns. (pres. 1985—87), Nat. Fedn. Dem. Women (pres. 1995—97), Nat. Assn. Parliamentarians, Jane Jefferson Dem. Club (v.p. 1979). Avocations: plate collecting, bridge, public affairs. Home: 2215 E 45th Ave Spokane WA 99223-6466 Fax: 509 448-8091.

COKER, CHERYL ANN, kinesiologist; b. Schefferville, Can., Feb. 16, 1965; came to U.S., 1985; d. Roy Thomas and Ann Isabel Gertrude (Stark) C. BS, La. State U., 1988; MEd, U. Va., 1992, PhD, 1995. Assoc. prof. dept. phys. edn., recreation and dance N.M. State U., Las Cruces, 1995—. Author: Motor Learning and Control for Practitioners; co-author: Play for Power, 1996; contbr. articles to profl. jours. Fellow Rsch. Consortium; mem. NMAHPERD (Prof. Merit award 2001), Nat. Assn. for Sport & Phys. Edn. (project inspiration award 1999), Am. Alliance Health, Phys. Edn., Recreation & Dance, S.W. Assn. Health, Phys. Edn., Recreation & Dance (Honor award 2003), Nat. Assn. Girls & Women in Sport (Pathfinder award, 1998, Presdl. award 1998), Phi Epsilon Kappa. Avocation: outdoor activities. Office: NM State Univ Dept PERD Box 30001 Dept 3M Las Cruces NM 88003 E-mail: ccoker@nmsu.edu.

COKER, DONALD WILLIAM, economic, management, banking, evaluation, healthcare, international business and real estate consultant, stock trader; b. Mobile, Ala., Nov. 26, 1945; s. William Mack and Gloria Antoinette (Croker) C.; m. Linda Carol Sandlin, July 12, 1969; children: Caroline Tiffany, Brittany Blaire. BA, postgrad., U. Ala., 1968; postgrad, U. Houston, 1973, Spring Hill Coll., 1996. Approved comml. arbitrator Am. Arbitration Assn. Trust mortgage officer AmSouth Bank, Mobile, 1968-72; sr. loan officer Gibraltar Savs., Houston, 1972-73; mortgage officer, asst. treas. Citicorp Real Estate, Houston, 1973-74; comml. loan officer M Bank-Houston, 1974-77; regional mgr. Comml. Credit Co., Houston, 1977-83, Ford Motor Credit, Houston, 1983-84; sr. v.p., mgr. lending and mortgage banking First Fed. Savs., San Antonio, 1984-85; exec. v.p. Home Savs., Houston, 1985-86, also bd. dirs.; supr. banking Tex. Savs. & Loan Dept., Houston, 1986-88; mng. dir. Coker Consulting, Mobile, 1986—. Staff economist DC Corporacion Abogados Internationales, Mex., 2000—, Internat. Bus. Cons., Mex., 2000—; CEO Pangaea Banking Experts, 2000—, Coker Fin. Investment Banking Svcs., 2001—; cons. Prentice-Hall Pub., IRS, FDIC, Resolution Trust Corp., World Bank; cons. to fin. instns., attys., corps. and govt. agys.; legis. and govtl. cons.; nat. healthcare and profl. practice valuation cons.; expert witness on valuation, econ., fin., real estate and banking. Author: Complete Guide to Income Property Financing, 1984, Self-Management, 1985, The Complete Loan Officer's Handbook, 2003; editor: Complete Real Estate Computer Workbook, 1986; contbr. numerous articles to profl. jours. and Internet sites. Trustee Katy Ind. Sch. Dist., Houston, 1987; treas. Nottingham Country Civic Club, Houston; precinct leader, del. and dep. voters registrar Rep. party. Mem. Am. Bankruptcy Inst., Nat. Assn. of State Savs. and Loan Suprs., Am. Mortgage Bankers Assn., Tex. Mortgage Bankers' Assn., Am. Bankers Assn., U.S. Savs. & Loan League, Houston C. of C. (bus. devel. com.). Clubs: Sweetwater Country. Republican. Episcopalian. Home: 1600 Sugar Creek Dr E Mobile AL 36695-2728 Office: PO Box 91182 Mobile AL 36691-1182 E-mail: bankexpert@cs.com.

COKER, HOWARD COLEMAN, lawyer; b. Jacksonville, Fla., Apr. 30, 1947; B in Journalism, U. Fla., 1969, JD, 1971. Bar: Fla. 1972. Asst. state atty. Fourth Jud. Cir., 1972; assoc. Howell, Kirby, Montgomery, D'Aiuto & Dean, P.A., 1973-76; pres., dir. Coker, Myers, Schickel, Sorenson & Green, Jacksonville, Fla., 1976—. Guest lectr. more than 40 CLE seminars on litig. and trial matters throughout Fla., for Fla. Bar Assn., Acad. Fla. Trial Lawyers; advisor mock trial team U. Fla. Law Sch., 1991-98; adj. prof. U. North Fla. Chair edni. adv. coun. U. North Fla., 1992-94, chair adv. bd. for paralegals, 1990-92. Fellow Am. Bar Found., Internat. Soc. Barristers; mem. ABA (ho. of dels., jud. qualifications comm.), ATLA, Am. Arbitration Assn. (panel arbitrators 1983—), Fla. Bar Assn. (pres. 1998-99, bd. govs. 1994-99, exec. com. 1995-97, all bar fconf. del. 1990-92, 94, 96, 97, budget com. 1995-97, bd. rev. coml. on profl. ethics chair 1995-96, disciplinary rev. com. 1994-95, jud. qualification screen com. 1994-95, legis. com. 1994-95, profl. retreat chair 1996, program evaluation com. chair 1996-97, 4th jud. cir. grievance com. reviewer 1994-97, coun. sects. 1991 94, chair 1993-94, sect. leadership conf. chair 1995, trial lawyers sect. exec. coun. 1987-94, bd. govs. liaison 1996, chair 1992-93, exec. co. 1989-93, legis. com. 1988-93), Am. Bd. Trial Advocates (pres. Jacksonville chpt. 1988—, media rep. 1988, exec. com. 1988—, diplomate), Am. Judicature Soc., Chester Bedell Meml. Found. (trustee 1996-2001), First Coast Trial Lawyers Assn., Acad. Fla. Trial Lawyers (bd. dirs. 1995—, pres. 2002-2003, Eagle sponsor 1990—), Fla. Lawyers Assn. for Maintenance of Excellence (bd. dirs. 1995-97), So. Trial Lawyers, Nat. Conf. Bar Presidents, Fla. Supreme Ct. Hist. Soc., Jacksonville Bar Assn., Roscoe Pound Found., U.S. Supreme Ct. Hist. Soc., Internat. Acad. Trial Lawyers, Fla. Conservation Assn. (pres. 1993-94), Fla. Ducks Unltd. (Sportsman of Yr. 1994), Fla. Wildlife Fedn., Seminole Club (bd. dirs. 1988, pres., 1989), U. Fla. Nat. Alumni Assn. (pres.'s coun. 1992-2001), Sigma Alpha Epsilon, Phi Delta Phi. Office: PO Box 1860 136 E Bay St Jacksonville FL 32201 Home: 4931 River Point Rd Jacksonville FL 32207 E-mail: hcoker@cokerlaw.com.

COKER, JOHN MICHAEL, quality assurance professional; b. Kansas City, Mo., Aug. 18, 1949; s. Louis Michael and Hallie Elaine (Earnshaw) Coker; m. Vickie Jean Bolden, Sept. 9, 1992. BA, U. Kans., 1971. Quality control technician Wellcome Animal Health, Kansas City, Kans., 1972—95; quality assurance compliance specialist animal health divsn. Bayer Corp., Kansas City, 1996—. Shawnee, Kans., 1996—. Mem.: Am. Soc. for Quality, Am. Statis. Assn., Math. Assn. Am. Avocations: music, modern philosophy. Office: Bayer Corp Animal Health Divsn 5101 Speaker Rd Kansas City KS

COKER, SYBIL JANE THOMAS, counseling administrator; b. Elizabeth, La., Aug. 16; d. Andrew J. and Lillye M. Thomas; m. Charles Mitchell Dolo Coker (dec. Apr. 13, 1983). AA, L.A. City Coll., 1952; BA, Calif. State U., L.A., 1955, Pepperdine U., 1957; MS, Mt. St. Mary's Coll., 1980. Tchr. Barton Hill Sch., 1957—58, 96th St. Sch., 1958—63; tng. tchr., reading specialist Hooper Ave. Sch., 1963—65; reading specialist dept. chair Vermont Ave. Sch., 1965—68; head start tchr. L.A. Urban League, 1966—68; tng. tchr. Hooper Ave. Sch., 1980—87; tng. tchr., tchr. of gifted clusters, grades 4,5,6 Angeles Mesa Sch., 1970—87; Eng. tchr., speech coach Horace Mann Jr. High Middle Sch., 1987—88, speech coach, 1988—90, bilingual coord./ESL, career, college and chap. 1 counselor, 1988—92, 8th grade counselor, career counselor, 1992—94, counselor 8th grade sr., 1994; counselor David Starr Jordan H.S., L.A., 1995—. Pres., founder The Charles Dolo Coker Jazz Scholarship Found., Inc., L.A., 1983—; freelance wedding coord., cons., 1960—; freelance writer, 1983—; sponsor Motivating Our Students Through Experience, Horace Mann Jr. High Middle Sch., Young Black Profls., Horace Mann Jr. High Middle Sch., USC Med Core, UCLA Partnership, Horace Mann Hr. High Middle Sch. Contbr. columns in newspapers including. Founder, dir. Second Baptist Ch. Drama Guild, 1957—67. Named Media Woman of Yr., 1977; recipient Unsung Heroine in Edn. award, Top Ladies of Distinction, 1992, Dist. Svc. award, 2nd Baptist Ch., 1991, Trailblazer award for outstanding contbns. in field of music, Delta Mothers and Sponsors Club, 2002. Mem.: NEA, PTA (life), NAACP (life; subscribing Golden Heritage mem., past bd. mem. L.A. br.), The Soc., Inc., Internat. Assn. Jazz Educators, Counselor's Assn., Black Women's Forum, L.A. Press Club, Soc. Profl. Journalists, Top Ladies of Distinction (L.A. chap., area VI, pub. rels. chair), Nat. Assn. Media Women (nat. recording sec., charter mem. Beverly Hills/Hollywood chap., past pres.), Pol. Action Com. of Educators, United Tchrs. of L.A., Nat. Coun. Negro Women (life), Santa Barbara Jazz Soc., L.A. Jazz Soc., Internat. Assn. Jazz Appreciation, Emanon Birthday and Social Club (charter mem., past pres.), New Frontier Dem. Club, Order of the Ea. Star, Phi Delta Kappa, Delta Sigma Theta (life; Century City alumnae chap., L.A. alumnae chap., Delta Choraliers). Democrat. Baptist. Avocations: creative writing, knitting, singing with the Delta Choraliers, studying piano. Home: 5336 Highlight Pl Los Angeles CA 90016 Office: Charles Dolo Coker Jazz Scholarship Fund 5336 Highlight Pl Los Angeles CA 90016

COKUSLU, LYNDA ELIZABETH MCCORD, medical assistant; b. Atlanta, June 11, 1956; d. Joseph Adair and Yvonne (Champagne) McCord; m. Fethi Cokuslu, Aug. 24, 1985; children: Sasha, Sedef, Samantha. Cert. med. asst., Bryman Sch., 1975. Casuality/liability claims processor Continental Ins./UAC, Atlanta, 1978—82; nutrition asst. Fayette County Edn., Peachtree City, Ga., 2001. Host benefit Hapeville (Ga.) Hist. Soc., 1988; officer PTA, Hapeville, 1997; catechist Youth/Adult Sch. Religion, Hapeville, 1996—2002. Mem.: Am. Sch. Food Svc. Assn., Am. Med. Asst. Assn., Travelers Protective Assn., Learning Disorder Assn., Midtown Bus. Assn., Internat. Poet Soc. Roman Catholic. Avocations: travel, collector, gardening, guitar, archaeology. Home: 105 Buckeye Ln Fayetteville GA 30214 Office: Huddleston Fayette County Nutrition McIntosh Trail Fayetteville GA 30215

COLA, PHILIP ANDREW, research administrator; b. Cleve., Nov. 14, 1965; s. Augustine Daniel and Elaine Theresa C.; m. Diane Marie Piskos, Oct. 12, 1991; children: Adam Denton, Samantha Marie. BA in Psychology, Cleve. State U., 1987, MA in Exptl. Psychology, 1994. Adminstrv. dir., lab. of biol. psychiatry Case Western Res. U., Cleve., 1989-96; dir. grants and contracts office U. Hosps. of Cleve., 1996—, dir. divsn. clin. rsch., 2002—. Reviewer, UHC grant rev. com. U. Hosps. of Cleve., 1998—, IRB adminstv. office head, 1999—. Contbr. articles to profl. jours. Religious edn. instr. Saint Bartholomew Parish, Middleburg Heights, 1996—; vol. instr. Juvenile Detention Ctr. Sch., Cleve., 1996; vol. Am. Suicide Found., N.E. Ohio chpt., 1992-96. Mem. Soc. for Am. Baseball Rsch., Soc. of Rsch. Adminstrs., Applied Rsch. Ethics Nat. Assn. Democrat. Roman Catholic. Avocations: baseball history and research, psychology/psychiatry history, reading, sports publications. Office: U Hosps of Cleve 11100 Euclid Ave Cleveland OH 44106-7061 E-mail: Philip.Cola@UHHS.com.

COLABELLA, GEORGE MICHAEL, management, fund raising consultant; b. Yonkers, N.Y., Sept. 27, 1948; s. Vincent and Concetta (Onorato) C.; m. Linn Margaret Stanton, Nov. 4, 1995. BA in Psychology, Canisius Coll., 1970; MA in Psychology, Hunter C.U.N.Y., 1975. Mgmt./devel. cons. Grace Ch. Cmty. Ctr., White Plains, 1995-97; devel. cons. Westchester Ctr. Arts, Mt. Kisco, NY, 1997—2001; mgmt. cons. Family Svc. Soc. Yonkers, N.Y., 1998—; mgmt./fund raising cons. Westchester/Putnam Legal Svcs., White Plains, NY, 1997—, Project Children, N.Y.C., 2002—, Victims Assistance Svcs., Elmsford, NY, 1999—; devel. cons. UGC Found., New Rochelle, NY, 2001—. Adj. prof. Pace U., White Plains, NY, 1993—; columnist Mental Health News, New Rochelle, 1999—; devel. cons. Victims Asst. Svcs., 2000—; devel., mgmt. cons. Batoto Yetu Dance Co., 2000—, Project Kids Worldwide, 2002—; lectr. in field. Bd. dirs. Westchester Vol. Ctr., 1993—. Mem. Nat. Soc. Fund Raising Execs. Home: 30 Priscilla Ave Yonkers NY 10710-3606 Office: Colabella Assocs 30 Priscilla Ave Yonkers NY 10710-3606 E-mail: galluppe@aol.com.

COLACOT, THOMAS J. chemicals executive, researcher; b. Kerala State, India, India, May 9, 1961; s. John Koruthu Colacot, Achamma John Colacot; m. Reena Colacot; children: Manu, Rebekah. PhD, Indian Inst. Tech., Madras, 1989. Sr. devel. assoc. Johnson Matthey, West Deptford, NJ, 1995—; grad. adj. prof. Rutgers U., Camden, 2001—. Sr. rsch. assoc. So. Meth. U., Dallas, 1993—95. Recipient award, Indian Chem. Soc., 1986. Mem.: Am. Chem. Soc. (chmn. 2002), Royal Soc., Ala. Acad. Scis. (life). Office: Johnson Matthey 2001 Nolte Dr Paulsboro NJ 08066

COLAGE, BEATRICE ELVIRA, education educator; b. Cleveland, Ohio, Aug. 13, 1958; BSEdn., Bowling Green State U., 1980; M of Curriculum, Cleveland State U., 1985. Spanish tchr. Cleveland (Ohio) City Schs., 1980—84, Mayfield (Ohio) City Schs., 1984—85, Solon (Ohio) City Schs., 1985—86, Orange (Ohio) City Schs., 1986—; adult edn. tchr. Mayfield (Ohio) City Schs. Lectr. Italian, Spanish and English. Author: book of 101 poems, 2003. Humanitarian and supporter of arts, civic, social and cultural instns. Mem.: NEA, Il Cenacolo Cleve., Ohio Fgn. Lang. Assoc., Ohio Edn. Assn., Am. Assn. Tchrs. of Spanish and Portuguese.

COLAIANNI, JOSEPH VINCENT, judge; b. Detroit, Mar. 19, 1935; s. Pasquale and Marie D. (Mastrantonio) C.; m. Rita Milena Roll, Oct. 13, 1962; children: Marie Elena, Joseph Vincent, Michael Philip, Vincent Gerard. BEE, U. Detroit, 1956; postgrad., Wayne State U., 1956-58; JD with honors, George Washington U., 1961. Bar: Mich. 1962, Ohio 1963, Washington 1964. Assoc. firm Fay and Fay, Cleve., until 1965; trial atty. civil div. Dept. Justice, Washington, 1965-70; commr. U.S. Ct. Claims, Washington, 1970-73, trial judge, 1973-77; judge U.S. Ct. Claims D.C., 1977-84; mng. ptnr. Pennie & Edmonds, Washington, 1984-98; chair intellectual property Patton Boggs LLP, Washington, 1998—. Sci. liaison com. Sci. Ct., 1976-84; prof. grad. sch. Patent Resources Inst.; adj. prof. Am. U., 1984-87, Cath. U. Sch. Law, 1997—; adv. com. patents and trademarks U.S. Dept. Commerce, 1987-89; sr. adviser U.S. Claims Ct. Adv. Coun., 1984—; adv. com. U.S. Patent and Trademark Office. Adv. bd. Patent, Trademark and Copyright Jour., 1984-91. District Heights (Md.) Recreation Coun., 1969-70; bd. dirs. Henson Valley Montessori Sch.; pres. Tilden PTA, 1979-81; pres. Lido Civic Club, 1981, bd. dirs., 1982-90, 90—; trustee Western Coll. Medicine, 1982-85; co-pres. U. Md. at College Park Parents Assn., 1991-97; mem. pres. cabinet U. Detroit Mercy, 1982—, commn. on future Coll. Engring., 1995-96. Mem. Am., Fed. bar assns., Patent Office Soc., Mich., Ohio, Washington bars, Phi Delta Phi, Eta Kappa Nu., Omicron Delta Kappa, Phi Delta Kappa, George Washington U. Law Rev. (1960-61) E-mail: jcolaianni@pattonboggs.com.

COLAIANNI, LOUIS EDWARD, voice educator; b. Paterson, N.J., Apr. 29, 1959; s. James Francis and Patricia Kelly C. Student, Boston Conservatory, 1977-79. Instr. Ohio U., Athens, 1987-88; instr., master tchr. New Actors Workshop, N.Y.C., 1988-89; master tchr. Trinity Repertory Theatre and Conservatory, Providence, 1989-90; asst. prof. U. Mo., Kansas City, 1990—, assoc. prof., 2000—. Adj. prof. Atlantic C.C., Mays Landing, N.J., 1985-87; adj. lectr. Hunter Coll., N.Y.C., 1988-89; voice dialect coach Mo. Repertory Theatre, Kansas City, 1990—. Author: The Joy of Phonetics and Accents, 1994, Shakespeare's Names: A New Pronouncing Dictionary, 2000, How to Speak Shakespeare, 2001; assoc. editor The Voice and Speech Rev.; inventor phonetic pillows. Curator Quentin Crisp Mus. Mem. Actors Equity Assn., The Players. Democrat. Unitarian Universalist. Avocation: collecting books. Office: Univ Mo Kansas City Theatre 4949 Cherry St PAC 404 Kansas City MO 64110 E-mail: colaiannil@umkc.edu.

COLAIZZI, JOHN LOUIS, college dean; b. Pitts., May 10, 1938; s. Peter Richard and Lena M. (Sebastian) C.; m. Maria Rose Santoro, Aug. 12, 1967; children— James J., Patricia R., John Louis. BS, U. Pitts., 1960; MS, Purdue U., 1962, PhD, 1965. Asst. prof. Sch. Pharmacy, W.Va. U., Morgantown, 1964—65; asst. prof., asso. prof. Sch. Pharmacy, U. Pitts., 1965—76, prof., chmn., asso. dean, 1976—78; prof., dean Sch. Pharmacy Rutgers U., Piscataway, NJ, 1978—, acting v.p. acad. affairs, 2003. Chmn. Robert Wood Johnson Univ. Hosp., New Brunswick, N.J., 1997-2000, also bd. dirs.; mem. Medicaid Drug Utilization Rev. Bd. N.J., 1996-97; bioavailability cons. Drug Utilization Rev. Coun. N.J., 1997-2000. Mem. Am. Pharm. Assn., Am. Assn. Pharm. Scis., Am. Soc. Health-system Pharmacists, Am. Assn. Coll. Pharmacy, Pharm. Care Mgmt. Assn. (deans adv. coun. 1998—), Am. Inst. History of Pharmacy, Rho Chi, Alpha Zeta Omega, Sigma Xi. Democrat. Roman Catholic. Home: 21 Jason Dr East Brunswick NJ 08816-3342 Office: Rutgers U Sch Pharmacy 160 Frelinghuysen Rd Piscataway NJ 08854-8020 E-mail: jlcolaiz@rci.rutgers.edu.

COLANDER-RICHARDSON, LATASHA, Olympic athlete; b. Portsmouth, Va., Aug. 23, 1976; Degree in comms., U. N.C., 1998. Winner Gold Medal 4x400 meter relay U.S.A. Track and Field Team, Sydney, 2000. Office: USA Track and Field Team One RCA Dome Ste 140 Indianapolis IN 46225

COLANGELO, JAMES JOSEPH, psychotherapist; b. Jamaica, N.Y., Jan. 8, 1950; s. Joseph and Amalia (Bove) C.; m. Kathy DeGuardi, Nov. 12, 1983; children: Nicole, Steven, Christina. BA, Manhattan Coll., 1971; MSEd, St. John's U., 1974; PD, cert. in marriage, family therapy, L.I. U., 1987; Psy.D., So. Calif. U., 2001. Diplomate Am. Bd. Sexology; cert. clin. mental health counselor; diplomate AASECT. Ind. community mental health counselor, Queens, N.Y.; caseworker N.Y.C. Dept. Social Svcs., Queens; clin. cons. Ea. Met. Counseling and Consulting Svcs., Queens; supr. Dept. Health & Human Svcs., Adminstrn. Children & Families, N.Y.C. Specialist Children and Families Program (DHHS/ACF); adj. faculty C.W. Post Ctr., L.I. U.; EEO counselor; mem. Region II AIDS com., DHHS. Recipient C. Eugene Morris award in mental health counseling L.I. U., 1992, Disting. Svc. award Dept. Counseling & Devel. L.I. U., 2001, Disting. Svc. award, L.I. U., 2001; named to Nat. Disting. Svc. Registry in Counseling, 1990. Mem. ACA, Am. Assn. Marriage and Family Therapists (clin., approved supr.), Am. Assn. Profl. Hypnotherapists, Am. Assn. Sex Educators, Counselors and Therapists (cert.), Am. Psychotherapy Assn. (diplomate), Internat. Assn. Marriage and Family Counselors, N.Y. Assn. Marriage and Family Counselors, N.Y. Mental Health Counselors Assn. E-mail: JColangelo@ACF.hhs.gov.

COLANGELO, JERRY JOHN, professional sports team executive; b. Chicago Heights, Ill., Nov. 20, 1939; s. Larry and Sue (Drancek) C.; m. Joan E. Helmich, Jan. 20, 1961; children: Kathy, Kristen, Bryan. BA, U. Ill., 1962. Ptnr. House of Charles, Inc., 1962—63; assoc. D.O. Klein & Assocs., 1964—65; dir. merchandising Chgo. Bulls, 1966—68; gen. mgr. Phoenix Suns, 1968—87, now also exec. v.p., 1987, pres., chief exec. officer, 1987—; mng. gen. ptnr. Arizona Diamondbacks, Phoenix, 1998—. Mem. Basketball Congress Am. (exec. v.p., dir.), Phi Kappa Psi. Clubs: University, Phoenix Execs. Republican. Baptist. Office: Phoenix Suns 201 E Jefferson St Phoenix AZ 85004-2412 also: Arizona Diamondbacks 401 E Jefferson St Phoenix AZ 85004-2438

COLASURD, RICHARD MICHAEL, lawyer; b. Navarre, Ohio, Apr. 1, 1928; s. Michael and Adeline (Manack) C.; m. Jane Cooley, Dec. 20, 1986; children: Steven Michael, David Gerard, Cathie Marie. AB, U. Notre Dame, 1950; JD, Harvard U., 1953. Bar: Ohio 1953. Practice in, Toledo, 1960-99; spl. agt. FBI, 1953-56; asst. U.S. atty. charge Northwestern Ohio, 1956-60; mem. firm Shumaker, Loop & Kendrick, 1960-64; asst. city law dir. Toledo, 1964; mem. firm Mulholland, Hickey & Lyman, 1964-73; U.S. commr., 1963-67. Mem. Ohio Bar Assn., Toledo Bar Assn., Soc. Former Spl. Agts. FBI, Lexington C.C., Rotary. Roman Catholic. Home: 16133 Edgemont Dr Fort Myers FL 33908-3651

COLAVITA, PAUL GERARD, cardiologist, medical educator; b. Newark, May 14, 1953; s. Dominick Paul and Frances DiMartino Colavita; m. Anna Oberc Colavita, Nov. 26, 1977; children: Paul, Jessica, James, Laura. BA, Rutgers U., 1975; MD, Wake Forest U., 1979. Diplomate Am. Bd. Internal Medicine. Clin. cardiologist Sanger Clinic, Charlotte, N.C., 1988—, chief cardiology, 1995-98, pres., 1998—; clin. asst. prof. medicine U. N.C. Sch. Medicine, Chapel Hill, N.C., 1991-95, clin. assoc. prof. medicine, 1995—. Mem. arrhythmia bd. Procter & Gamble, Cin., 1998—. Contbr. chpts. to books. Mem. alumni bd. Wake Forest U. Med. Sch., 1996—99; trustee Providence Day Sch., Charlotte, 1998—2002; mem. Am. Heart Assn. Coun. on Clin. Cardiology, 1985—. Fellow Am. Coll. Cardiology (treas. 1992-94, counselor 1994-96); mem. Am. Coll. Physician Execs., Cardiac Electrophysiology Soc., Am. Heart Assn. (grantee 1987, coun. on clin. cardiology 1985—, bd. dirs. 1995-96), N.Am. Soc. Pacing and Electrophysiology. Avocations: hunting, dogs, sports, family activities. Office: Sanger Clinic 1001 Blythe Blvd Ste 300 Charlotte NC 28203-5860

COLBATH, BRIAN (BRIAN COLBATH WATSON), actor, script and live performance writer; b. Port Washington, N.Y., July 14; s. H. Desmond Watson and Mary (Colbath) Watson Haynes. BS in Speech and Drama, Ithaca Coll., 1965. Cert. tchr., N.Y. Tchr. speech Canandaigua (N.Y.) Acad., 1965-67; speech pathologist West Seneca (N.Y.) Ctrl. Schs., 1967-70; v.p. Projects Plus, Inc., N.Y.C., 1994—. Mem. Blue Ribbon panel Daytime Emmy Awards, N.Y.C., 1985-91. Appearances include daytime TV programs, Tony Awards show, N.Y.C., 1989-2000, various prodns. Studio Arena Theatre, Buffalo; scripwriter indsl. films; writer night club acts. Named one of Outstanding Young Men of Am., 1970. Mem. AFTRA, SAG, Actors' Equity. Home: 15 W 67th St New York NY 10023-6226 Office: Projects Plus Inc 145 W 45th St Ste 300 New York NY 10036-4008

COLBERG-OCHS, SHERI RENEE, physiologist, educator; b. Shawnee Mission, Kans., Nov. 2, 1963; d. Donald A. and Karen Stubbs Colberg, Nancy Colberg (Stepmother); m. Raymond A. Ochs, Aug. 8, 1998; children: Alex R. Ochs, Anton S. Ochs, Ray-J Ochs. BA, Stanford U., 1985; MA, U. of Calif., Davis, CA, 1987; PhD, U. of Calif., Berkeley, CA, 1992. Cert. exercise test technologist Am. Coll. of Sports Medicine, 1986. Diabetes exercise specialist Diabetes Treatment Ctrs. Am., San Francisco, 1988; post-doctoral fellow Sch. Medicine U. of Pitts., 1993—94; lectr., rsch. Calif. State U., Hayward, Calif., 1994—97; prof. Old Dominion U., Norfolk, Va., 1997—. Cons. Animas Corp., Frazier, Pa., 2001—02; mem. adv. bd. Diabetes Interview, San Francisco, 1999—2002; dir. human performance lab. Old Dominion U., 1998—; reviewer for medicine & sci. in sports & exercise Am. Coll. of Sports Medicine, Indpls., 2002—; lectr. in field. Author: The Diabetic Athlete, 2001; contbg. editor: Diabetes Today, 2002—; contbr. articles to profl. jours. Fellow: Am. Coll. of Sports Medicine (Fellowship in orgn. 1996); mem.: Diabetes Sports & Exercise Assn., Am. Diabetes Assn. (grantee 2001—03). Avocations: swimming, tennis, reading, writing. Office: Old Dominion University ESPER Department H&PE Bldg Rm 140 Norfolk VA 23529 Office Fax: 757-683-4270. Personal E-mail: scolberg@odu.edu. E-mail: scolberg@odu.edu.

COLBERT, DIA TERESA, legal assistant; b. N.Y.C., July 10, 1963; d. Mack and Sarah (St. John) C. BS in Gen. Mgmt., Boston Coll., 1985; paralegal cert., Katharine Gibbs, 1988; MBA in Mgmt., Barry U., 1995; JD, Nova Southea. U., 2003. Legal asst. Legal Assistants Corp., N.Y.C., 1988-89; litigation asst. Sullivan and Cromwell, N.Y.C., 1989-91; legal asst. Mandler & Silver, Miami, 1991-92, Jenner & Block, Miami, 1992-95, Gallway Gillman et al, Miami,

1995-96, Stearns Weaver et al, Miami, 1996—2001; freelance paralegal Davie, Fla., 2001—. Alumni admission vol., county chairperson Boston Coll., 1993-98, Broward County, Fla., 1991—. Democrat. Roman Catholic. Avocations: tennis, travel, daily fitness program.

COLBERT, DOUGLAS MARC, lawyer; b. N.Y.C., Feb. 8, 1948; s. Leonard M. and Estelle (Ginsberg) C.; m. Amy Jo Guryan, May 1, 1976 (div. 1977); m. Angel Mendez, Dec. 28, 1986. Student, Hunter Coll., N.Y.C., 1964-67; BBA cum laude, Bernard Baruch Coll., N.Y.C., 1969; JD, Bklyn. Law Sch., 1972. Bar: N.Y. 1974. Honor law intern N.Y. County Dist. Atty., N.Y.C., 1971; law asst. N.Y.C. Corp. Counsel, 1972-74; campaign staff writer, media coord. Gov. Hugh. L. Carey, 1974; arbitrator N.Y.C. Civil Ct., 1979—; atty. Hauser & Rosenbaum Esq., N.Y.C., 1974-76; pvt. practice law N.Y.C., 1974—. Vol. atty. Vol. Lawyers for the Arts, N.Y.C., 1979-85; spl. investigator N.Y. State Bd. Elections, N.Y.C., 1981-84. Mem. N.Y. State Trial Lawyers Assn., N.Y. County Lawyers Assn., USCG Aux., Moot Ct., Sigma Alpha Mu (founder). Avocations: scuba, health & fitness, travel, boating. Office: 350 5th Ave Ste 7220 New York NY 10118-7299

COLBERT, JAMES W., III, lawyer; b. N.Y.C., Sept. 1, 1945; AB magna cum laude, Yale U., 1967; JD magna cum laude, Harvard U., 1970. Bar: Calif. 1971. Law clk. to Hon. Shirley M. Hufstedler U.S. Ct. Appeals (9th cir.), 1970-71; mem. O'Melveny & Myers, L.A. Mem. L.A. County Bar Assn. Office: O'Melveny & Myers 400 S Hope St Los Angeles CA 90071-2899

COLBERT, KATHRYN HENDON, lawyer; b. Englewood, N.J., Aug. 26, 1947; d. Charles R. and Rosemary F. (Schrafft) C. AB, Vassar Coll., 1969; JD, Tulane U., 1972. Bar: La. 1972, D.C. 1975, U.S. Supreme Ct. 1977, Miss. 1989, Tex. 1994. Atty. SBA, Harrisburg, Pa., 1972-73; staff mem. for rep. Leonor K. Sullivan Ho. of Reps., Washington, 1973-74; sole practice New Orleans, 1975; atty. office of hearings and appeals Social Security Adminstrn., HHS, New Orleans, 1976-87; sr. trial atty. EEOC, New Orleans, 1987-92; pvt. practice New Orleans and Dallas, 1993-94; sr. regional atty. Advocacy, Inc., Dallas, 1994-98; atty. Legas Svcs. of North Tex., Dallas, 1999—2003, N.Mex. Legal Aid, Albuquerque, 2003—. Mem.: Chickasaw Nation. Democrat. Presbyterian. Home: 4517 Inspiration Dr SE Albuquerque NM 87108 E-mail: kathrync@isht.org.

COLBERT, MARGARET MATTHEW, artist; b. N.Y.C., Apr. 18, 1911; d. William Diller and Kate (Lee) Matthew; m. Edwin Harris Colbert, July 8, 1933 (dec. Nov. 15, 2001); children: George, David, Philip, Daniel, Charles. BFA, Calif. Coll. Arts and Crafts, 1931. Sci. illustrator Am. Mus. Natural History, N.Y.C., 1931-33. Contbr. numerous illustrations to books; executed murals of extinct life for Mus. No. Ariz., Big Bend Nat. Pk., Petrified Forest Nat. Pk., Albuquerque Natural History Mus.; one-person show Mus. No. Ariz., 1984; exhibited in group shows in N.Y., N.J., Calif. and Ariz. Recipient engraved crystal award Soc. Vertebrate Paleontology, plaque Dinosaur Soc. Avocations: watercolor and oil portraits, ceramics, various crafts.

COLBERT, MARVIN JAY, retired internist, educator; b. Spokane, Wash., Nov. 6, 1923; s. John B. and Elizabeth (Peters) C.; m. Eleanor Ruth Rott, June 2, 1951 (dec. July 2000); children: Janet Lynn, James Lee, Lawrence Jay. Student, U. Utah, 1940-43; BS, Yale U., 1946; MD, Boston U., 1949. Diplomate: Am. Bd. Internal Medicine. Intern, resident in internal medicine Presbyn. Hosp., Chgo., 1949-50, VA Hosp., Boston, 1953-54, U. Ill. Rsch. and Ednl. Hosp., 1954-55; pvt. practice internal medicine Belmond, Iowa, 1955-56; mem. faculty U. Ill., Chgo., 1956-58; dir. health svc. Med. Ctr., 1959-78, prof. medicine, 1969-78; dir. employee health svcs. Evang. Hosp. Assn., Oak Brook, Ill., 1978-86. Cons. internal medicine radiol. and environ. rsch. div. Argonne (Ill.) Nat. Lab., 1978-79. Pres. Hillcrest PTA, Downers Grove, Ill., 1960-62; Parent-Tchrs. Group Chiengmai Co-Ednl. Ctr., Thailand, 1965-66. Capt. M.C. AUS, 1943-46, 50-52. Fellow ACP; mem. Assn. for Advancement of Automotive Medicine (dir. 1969-76). Home: 1700 Robin Ln #544 Lemont IL 60532 E-mail: ERColbert@aol.com. *While on leave from The University of Illinois, Marvin Jay Colbert was a Visiting Professor of Internal Medicine. Between the years of 1965-66 he taught at The Chiengmai Medical School and Hospital in Chiengmai, Thailand.*

COLBERT, ROBERT IVAN, education association administrator; b. Lake Charles, La., Sept. 25, 1950; s. Robert Ivan Sr. and Lou Anna (Duplechin) C.; m. Annick Marie Saint Hubert, July 2, 1977; children: Benjamin David, Catherine Annick, Martin Charles, Sarah Jessica. BA Psychology, U. Dallas, 1972; BA Theology, U. Cath. de Louvain, Belgium, 1973, STB Theology, MA Theology, U. Cath. de Louvain, Belgium, 1975. Asst. dean student personnel U. Southwestern La., Lafayette, 1976-78; dir. religious edn. Sts. Peter and Paul Ch., Scott, 1978-81; asst. supt. schs. Diocese of Lafayette, La., 1981-86, diocesan dir. religious edn., 1986-88; asst. prof./coord. field edn. dept. theology St. Mary's U., San Antonio, Tex., 1988-89; dir. pastoral instr., asst. prof. Incarnate Word Coll., San Antonio, 1989-92; assoc. exec. dir. dept. religious edn. Nat. Cath. Edn. Assn., Washington, 1992-94, exec. dir., 1994—. Mem. com. on catechesis United States Cath. Conf., Washington, 1994—; adv. bd. The Living Light, 1994—. Mem. Assn. Grad. Programs in Ministry, Religious Edn. Assn. Roman Catholic. Office: Nat Cath Ednl Assn 1077 30th St NW Ste 100 Washington DC 20007-3816 E-mail: colbert@ncea.org.

COLBERT, VIRGIS W. food products executive; m. Angela Colbert; three children. BS in Indsl. Mgmt., Ctrl. Mich. U. Mfg. gen. supt. Chrysler Corp.; asst. to plant mgr. Miller Brewing Co., Reidsville, N.C., 1979-80, prodn. mgr. Ft. Worth, 1980-81, profn. mgr. Milw., 1981, plant mgr., 1981-87, asst. dir. can mfg., 1987-88, dir. can. mfg., 1988, dir. container and support mfg., 1988-89, v.p. materials mfg., 1989-90, v.p. plant ops., 1990-93, sr. v.p. ops., 1993-95, sr. v.p. worldwide ops., 1995 97, exec. v.p., 1997—, also bd. dirs. and exec. com. Bd. dirs. Weyco, Inc., Delphi Automotive Sys., Inc., The Manitowoc Co. Chmn. bd. Thurgood Marshall Scholarship Fund; chmn. bd. trustees Fisk U., Nashville; bd. mem. Bradley Sports and Entertainment Corp. Ctr., Greater Milw. Open; exec. adv. com. Nat. Urban League's Black Exec. Exch. Program. Recipient various awards Jarvis Christian Coll., Tyler, Tex., So. U., New Orleans, N.C. AT&T, Greensboro, Clark Coll., Atlanta, Grambling (La.) State Coll., Fla. Meml. Coll., Miami, U. N.C., Greensboro, Young Program of Nat. Alliance Bus., Svc. award Nat. Urban Leage, Trumpet award Turner Broadcasting Sys., 1996, Exec. Leadership Coun. Achievement award, 1998; named Harlem YMCA Black Achiever, Milw. YMCA Black Achiever, Phi Beta Sigma Fraternity Black Achiever, one of 50 Top Black Execs. in Corp. Am., Ebony Mag., 1992, one of 24 To Watch in '94, Ebony Mag., 1994, one of 12 Most Powerful Blacks in Corp. Am., Ebony Mag., 1998, one of Am.'s 40 Most Powerful Black Execs., Black Enterprise Mag., 1993, One of 50 Top Black Execs. in Corp. Am., Black Enterprise Mag., 2000, Beverage Exec. of Yr., Beverage Industry Mag., 2001, One of 50 Most Powerful Balck Execs. in Am., Fortune Mag., 2002; inductee Scott H.S. Hall of Fame, Toledo, 1987. Mem. NAACP (life, Svc. award), 100 Black Men of Am. (hon.), Omega Psi Phi. Office: Miller Brewing Co 3939 W Highland Blvd Milwaukee WI 53201

COLBERT, VIRGIS WILLIAM, brewery company executive; b. Jackson, Miss., Oct. 13, 1939; s. Quillie and Eddi Colbert. BS, Ctrl. Mich. U. With Toledo Machining Plant Chrysler Corp., 1966—79, foreman, 1968—70, gen. foreman, 1970—73, mfg. supt., 1973—77, gen. mfg. supt., 1977—79; asst. to plant mgr. Miller Brewing Co., Reidsville, NC, 1979—80, prodn. mgr. Ft. Worth, 1980—81, plant mgr. Milw. Container Plant, 1981—87, asst. dir. can mfg., 1987—88, dir. container and support mfg., 1988—90, v.p. materials mfg. and plant ops., 1990—91, v.p. plant ops., 1991—93, sr. v.p. ops., 1993—95, sr. v.p. worldwide ops., 1995—97, exec. v.p., 1997—. Bd. dirs. Delphi Automotive Sys., Inc., Manitowoc Co., Inc., Weyco Group, Inc., Miller Brewing Co., Milw., Fisk Univ., Thurgood Marshall Scholarship Fund, Bradley Ctr., Sports and Entertainment Corp., Greater Milw. Open. Mem.: NAAPC, Nat. Urban League Black Exec. Exchange Program, Frontiers Internat. Club, Shriners, Masons, Sigma Pi Phi, Omega Psi Phi. Office: Miller Brewing Co 3939 W Highland Blvd Milwaukee WI 53208-2866

COLBORN, GENE LOUIS, anatomy educator, researcher; b. Springfield, Ill., Nov. 23, 1935; s. Adin Levi and Grace Downey (Tucker) C.; divorced; children: Robert Mark, Adrian Thomas, Lara Lee Colborn Russell; m. Sarah Ellen Crockett, Aug. 14, 1976; children: Jason Matthew, Nathan Tucker. BA with honors, Ky. Christian Coll., 1957; BS with honors, Milligan Coll., 1962; MS in Anatomy, Wake Forest U., 1964, PhD in Anatomy, 1967. Postdoctoral fellow U. N.Mex. Sch. Medicine, Albuquerque, 1967-68; asst. prof. U. Tex. Health Sci. Ctr., San Antonio, 1968-72, assoc. prof., 1972-75; assoc. prof. anatomy Med. Coll. Ga., Augusta, 1975-88, prof. anatomy, 1988-2000, prof. surgery, 1993-2000, dir. Ctr. for Clin. Anatomy, 1987-2000, dir. med. gross anatomy, 1975—, cons. dept. surgery, 1977-2000, prof. surgery, 1993-2000, emeritus prof. anatomy and surgery, 2000—; clin. prof. surgery Emory U. Sch. Medicine, Atlanta, 1996—; chmn. divsn. anatomical scis. Ross U. Sch. Medicine, Dominica, 2000—01; prof. Am. U. Caribbean Sch. Medicine, St. Maarten, Netherlands Antilles, 2002—, chmn. anatomy, 2002—. Pres. Ga. State Anatomical Bd., 1983-93; cons. Eisenhower Army Med. Ctr., 1990-96. Author: Practical Gross Anatomy, 1982, Surgical Anatomy, 1987, Hernias, 1988, Musculoskeletal Anatomy, 1989, Workbook of Surgical Anatomy, 1990, Clinical Gross Anatomy, 1993, Modern Hernia Repair, 1996, The Embryological and Anatomical Basis of Surgery, 2002; mem. editl. bd.: Clin. Anatomy Jour.; contbr. numerous articles on cardiac conduction, nervous sys., primate anatomy, cell culture and clin. and surg. anatomy to profl. jours. Active San Antonio Symphony Mastersingers, 1970-75, Augusta Opera, 1975—, Augusta Choral Soc., 1975-95; judge Regional Sci. Fairs, Augusta, 1978-90. Recipient Golden Apple award, U. Tex. Health Sci. Ctr., 1975, Outstanding Med. Educator award, Med. Coll. Ga., 1976, 1977, 1978, 1982, 1987, 1988, 1990, 1991, 1997, Disting. Faculty award, 1978, 2000, Excellence in Tchg. award, 1997, 1999, Regents' award in tchg., 1998, others. Mem. AAUP, Am. Assn. Clin. Anatomists (membership chmn. 1982-86, mem. editl. bd. Jour. Clin. Anatomy 1994—), Am. Assn. Anatomists, Columbia County Choral Soc. (founding mem.), KC (4th degree). Republican. Avocations: opera, chorales, chess, tennis, camping. Address: 4115 Columbia Rd Ste 5 Martinez GA 30907-0410 E-mail: glcolb@yahoo.com.

COLBORN, JACK P. engineering company executive; b. Bangor, Maine, Oct. 12, 1967; s. Jerry Phillip and Shunko Colborn; m. Dana Renee Rierson, Apr. 8, 1995; children: Caitlin Taylor, Nathaniel Robert. BSME, Tex. A&M U., 1989. Sr. mech. engr. Sperry-Sun Drilling, Houston, 1991—95; sales/mktg. mgr. Japan Aviation Electronics, Houston, 1998—. Mem. Klein United Meth. Ch., Spring, Tex., 2000—. Mem.: ASME. Avocations: golf, reading. Office: JAE Electronics Inc 2500 Citywest Blvd Ste 300 Houston TX 77042

COLBORN, NANCY WOOTTON, school librarian; b. Emporia, Kans., Aug. 29, 1959; d. Calvin Richard and Linda Jean Wootton; m. James Randall Colborn; children: Elizabeth Milhander, Tyler. BS, Kans. State U., 1981; MLIS, Ind. U., 1993. Asst. libr. ref. Franklin D. Schurz Libr., Ind. U. South Bend, Ind., 1994—98, assoc. libr. ref., coord. pub. rels. and staff develop., 1998—2002, assoc. libr., coord. libr. instr. and staff devel., 2002—. Contbr. articles. Mem.: ALA (mem. machine-assisted ref. sect. of user access svc. com. 1998—2002, chair machine-assisted ref. sect. of user access svc. com. 1999—2000, occasional papers subcom. 2002—), Assn. Coll. Rsch. Librs., Ind. Acad. Libr. Assn. (exec. bd. mem. 1997—, sec./treas. 2001—, vice chmn. 2002—03, chmn. 2003—), Ind. Libr. Fedn., Beta Phi Mu (Chi chpt. exec. bd. 1999—2000). Office: Franklin D Schurz Library IUSB 1700 Mishawaka Ave PO Box 7111 South Bend IN 46634 Business E-Mail: ncolborn@iusb.edu.

COLBOURN, FRANK EDWIN, communications educator; b. New Haven, Conn., July 5, 1928; s. Ira and Justine (O'Connell) C.; m. Andrea M. Pilato, May 29, 1981; children: Daniel, David, Bruce, Ann Sally. BSBA, Boston U., 1948, JD, 1950; SJD magna cum laude, Bklyn. Law Sch., 1956. Bar: Mass. 1950, Ill. 1952, N.Y. 1956. With mgmt. staff Household Fin., Boston, N.Y.C., Chgo., 1950-52; real estate exec. F.W. Woolworth Co., N.Y.C., 1952-64; assoc. prof. communication Pace U., N.Y.C., 1964-72, prof., 1972—. Pres. Colbourn Communication Cons., Inc., N.Y.C., 1976—; cons. Citizens Campaign Environ., Massapequa, N.Y., 1990. Author: (text and record) The Art of Debate, 1971, How to Judge a Debate, 1973. Head debate coach Pace U., 1980—90, U.S. Merchant Marine Acad., 1968—71. With USN, 1944—46. Mem. AAUP (pres. Pace, N.Y. chpt. 1994-97), Am. Forensic Assn., Internat. Soc. Gen. Semantics, Speech Comm. Assn., Delta Sigma Rho, Phi Alpha Alpha. Avocations: critical thinking instruction, coaching debate and communication, tutoring. Home and Office: 145 Cedar Shore Dr Old Harbor Green Estates Massapequa NY 11758-8133

COLBOURN, TREVOR, retired university president, historian; b. Armidale, New South Wales, Australia, Feb. 24, 1927; came to U.S., 1948; s. Harold Arthur and Ella Mary (Henderson) C.; m. Beryl Richards Evans, Jan. 10, 1949; children: Katherine Elizabeth, Lisa Sian Elinor. BA with honors, U. London, 1948; MA, Coll. William and Mary, 1949, Johns Hopkins, 1951, PhD, 1953. From instr. to asst. prof. Pa. State U., 1952-59; from asst. prof. to prof. Am. history Ind. U., 1959-67; dean Grad. Sch., prof. history U. N.H., 1967-73; v.p. for acad. affairs San Diego State U., 1973-77, acting pres., 1977-78; pres. U. Central Fla., Orlando, 1978-89. Author: The Lamp of Experience, 1965, 2d edit., 1998, The Colonial Experience, 1966, (with others) The Americans: A Brief History, 1972, 4th edit., 1985; co-editor: (with others) The American Past in Perspective, 1970; editor: (with others) Fame and the Founding Fathers, 1974, 2d edit., 1998. Mem. Orgn. Am. Historians, Am. Assn. State Colls. and Univs. Office: U Cen Fla Office Pres Emeritus Orlando FL 32816-1110

COLBURN, DAVID DUNTON, investment manager; b. San Mateo, Calif., Aug. 18, 1958; s. Richard Dunton and Joan Francis (Garber) C.; m. Carolyn Louise Hadley, Sept. 30, 1989; children: Margaret Hadley, Ethan Dunton. BA, Harvard U., 1980; MBA, U. Pa., 1989. V.p. Bank of Am., L.A., 1981-87; investment mgr. CED Mgmt. Svcs. Inc., Northbrook, Ill., 1989-91; mng. ptnr. Lincolnshire Assocs., Ltd., 1991—. Dunton Foundries, LLC, 2000—. Bd. dirs. Haskel Internat., Inc., Alamac Am. Knits, LLC. Mem. Young Pres. Orgn., Harvard Club Chgo., Wharton Club Chgo. Office: 555 Skokie Blvd Ste 555 Northbrook IL 60062-2854 E-mail: davidcolburn@mac.com.

COLBURN, DONALD EUGENE, protective services official; b. Atlanta, Oct. 22, 1954; s. Dillard Eugene and Juanita Kuykendall C.; divorced; children: Allison, Lindsey, Kyle, Madelyn. Student, Clayton State Coll., Valencia State Coll. Ordained to ministry Bapt. Ch., 1988. Maintenance Eggo Frozen Foods, Atlanta, 1972-75; police officer City of Palmetto, Ga., 1975—76; detective Clayton County Police SWAT Dept., Jonesboro, Ga., 1976-81; police officer, advanced situation team Dekalb County Police Dept., Decatur, Ga., 1981—83; lt. comdr. narcotics Clayton County Dist. Attys. Office, 1983—95, capt., 1995—98; asst. comdr. narcotics Clayton County Drug Enforcement Task Force, 1998-99; mem. spl. enforcement team Clayton County Sheriff Office, 1983—99; investigator III Clayton County Dist. Attys. Office, Jonesboro, Ga., 1999—2002; capt. spl. ops., comdr. vice unit, gang unit, K-9 unit, sheet narcotics unit, intell unit, homeland def. terrorist task force Clayton Police Dept., 2002—. Firearms instr.; std. tng. instr. Ga. State Police; sr. instr. Clayton County Police Acad., Clayton County Dist. Atty. Office. Former asst. pastor, pastor and youth min. First Freewill Bapt. Ch. Mem. Ga State Power Engrs., Internat. Narcotics Officers Assn., Police Benevolent Assn., Ga. Assn. Law Enforcement Firearm Instrs. Office: Spl Ops Unit Clayton County Police Dept 7930 N McDonough St Jonesboro GA 30236 E-mail: dec5602@hotmail.com.

COLBURN, GENE LEWIS, insurance and industrial consultant; b. Bismarck, N.D., July 12, 1932; s. Lewis William and Olga Alma (Feland) C.; PhD, City U. L.A., 1983. Pres., gen. mgr. Multiple Lines Ins. Agy., Auburn, Wash., 1953-79; ins. and risk mgmt. cons., Auburn, Wash., 1980—; pres. Feland Safe Deposit Corp.; bd. dirs. Century Svc. Corp. subs. Capital Savs. Bank, Olympia, Wash.; mem. exec. com. Great Repub. Life Ins. Co., Portland, Oreg., 1971-75; mem. Wash. State Ins. Commrs. Test Devel. Com., 1986-87. cons. indsl. risk mgmt. Councilperson Auburn City, 1982-85; mayor-pro tem, City of Auburn, 1984; co-incorporator, chmn. bd. SE Community Alcohol Ctr., 1971-75; mem. Wash. State Disaster Assistance Coun., 1981-82, founding mem.; pres. Valley Cities Mental Health Ctr., 1980; mem. instn. rev. com. Auburn Gen. Hosp., 1978—; prin. trustee Dr. R. B. Bramble Med. Rsch. Found., 1980-90; bd. dirs. Wash. Assn. Chs. (Luth. Ch. in Am.), Asian Refugee Resettlement Mgmt. div., 1981-83, Columbia Luth. Home, Seattle, 1985-87. Wash. Law Enforcement Officers and Fire Fighter's Pension Disability Bd., Auburn, 1980-84. Cert. ins. counselor, 1978. Recipient Disting. Alumni award Green River Community Coll., 1982. Fellow Acad. Producer Ins. Studies (charter); mem. Internat. Platform Assn. Lodge: Auburn Lions (past pres.). Office: 720 L St SE Auburn WA 98002-6219

COLBURN, KEITH W. electronics executive; Chmn. bd., CEO Consolidated Electrical Distrs, Thousand Oaks, Calif., 1999—. Office: Consolidated Electrical Distributors Inc 31356 Via Colinas Ste 107 Westlake Village CA 91362*

COLBURN, KENNETH HERSEY, financial executive; b. Melrose, Mass., Jan. 8, 1952; s. Warren Edward and Maybelle (Hersey) C.; married. AB, Brown U., 1975; MPPM, Yale U., 1978. Assoc. Credit Suisse 1st Boston Corp./(formerly First Boston Corp.), N.Y.C., 1978-83, v.p., 1983-88, mng. dir., 1988—94; v.p. project and internat. fin. Raytheon Co., Lexington, Mass., 1995-98; chief operating officer Highfields Capital Mgmt. L.P., Boston, 1998—. Trustee Huntington Theatre Co., Boston, Bentley Coll., Waltham, Mass. Mem. Yale Club, Watch Hill Yacht Club, Boothbay Harbor Yacht Club, Dedham Polo and Country Club, Southport Yacht Club. Office: Highfields Capital Mgmt 200 Clarendon St Boston MA 02116-5021 E-mail: kcolburn@highfieldscapital.com.

COLBURN, NANCY DOUGLAS, social worker, educator; d. Cleaveland Fisher Colburn and Virginia Colburn Bahrs. BA, Rutgers U., 1963; MSW, U. Ill., Chgo., 1971; MDiv, McCormick Theol. Sem., 1971; MPA, San Diego State U., 1997. LCSW Calif.; Ordained to ministry Vineyard Christian Fellowship 1990, cert. tchr./adminstr. child devel. programs Calif. Social worker Dept. Social Svcs. County of San Diego, 1979—92; social worker Family Advocacy, USN, San Diego, 1992—97. Scholar, State of N.J., 1959. Mem.: ASPA, NASW.

COLBURN, RICHARD DUNTON, business executive; b. Carpentersville, Ill., June 24, 1911; s. Cary R. and Daisy (Dunton) C.; children: Richard Whiting, Carol Dunton, Keith Whiting, Christine Isabel, David Dunton, McKee Dunton, Daisy Dunton, Franklin Anthony. Student, Antioch Coll., 1929-33. Pres. Consol. Foundries Mfg. Corp. (and predecessors), 1944-64. Underwriting mem. Lloyds of London. Home and Office: 1120 La Collina Dr Beverly Hills CA 90210-2616 also: 30 Chester Sq London SW1W 9HT England

COLBY, GEORGE VINCENT, JR., electrical engineer, consultant; b. Montpelier, Vt., Sept. 4, 1931; s. George Vincent and Clara Pauline (Tebbetts) Colby; m. Barbara Ann Gardner, Sept. 5, 1955; children: George V. III, Ann G. Colby Cummings, Catherine M. Colby Sanders. BEE, MEE, MIT, 1954. Tech. staff engr. Gen. Electric Co., West Lynn, Mass., 1954-55; mgr. radar lab. L.F.E. Corp., Waltham, Mass., 1957-70; staff mem. MIT Lincoln Lab., Lexington, Mass., 1970-80; product team leader Textron Def. Systems, Wilmington, Mass., 1980-94; pres. Colby Studios, Lexington, Mass., 1994—. Treas. troop 159 Boy Scouts Am., Lexington, 1970-76; dir. teen mass St. Brigid's Ch., Lexington, 1974-81. 1st lt. U.S. Army, 1955-57. Mem. IEEE (life). Roman Catholic. Achievements include patents for Doppler radar system, phase shifter, radar altimeter, Doppler radar altimeter, data acquisition and analysis system. Home and Office: 7 Hawthorne Rd Lexington MA 02420-1731 E-mail: bgcolby@earthlink.net.

COLBY, GEORGE VINCENT, III, logistics executive; b. Ft. Huachuca, Ariz., May 24, 1957; s. George Vincent Jr. and Barbara Colby; m. Celina Paratore, Sept. 27, 1986; children: George Nicholas, Celina Marie. BSBA, Suffolk U., Boston, 1982; MBA, Bentley Coll., 1985. Materials mgr. Craig Sys., Inc., Amesbury, Mass., 1985-88, Summit Technology, Inc., Waltham, Mass., 1988-93, Madison Cable Corp., Worcester, Mass., 1994; v.p. logistics Elec. Americas, FCI USA Inc., Manchester, N.H., 1994—. Com. mem. Holy Cross Ch., Derry, N.H., 1999. Mem. Nat. Assn. Purchasing Mgrs., Am. Prodn. and Inventroy Control Soc. (past pres. Granite State chpt.). Avocations: kayaking, cross-country skiing. Home: 4 Cyril Rd Derry NH 03038 Office: FCI USA Inc 47 E Industrial Park Dr Manchester NH 03019

COLBY, JOY HAKANSON, critic; b. Detroit; d. Alva Hilliard and Eleanor (Radtke) Hakanson; m. Raymond L. Colby, Apr. 11, 1953; children: Sarah, Katherine, Lisa. Student, Detroit Soc. Arts and Crafts, 1945; BFA, Wayne State U., 1946; DFA (hon.), Coll. Art & Design, 1998, Ctr. for Creative Studies, 1998. Art critic Detroit News, 1947—; originator exhibit Arts and Crafts in Detroit, 1906-1976; with Detroit Inst. Arts, 1976. Author: (book) Art and A City, 1956; contbr. articles to art periodicals. Mem. visual arts adv. panel Mich. Coun. Arts, 1974—79; mayor's appointment Detroit Inst. Arts, 1974; mem. Bloomfield Hills Arts Coun., 1974. Recipient Alumni award, Wayne State U., 1967, Art Achievement award, 1983, Headliner award, 1984, award arts reporting, Detroit Press Club, 1984, Art Leadership award, Ctr. Creative Studies, 1989. Office: 615 W Lafayette Blvd Detroit MI 48226-3124

COLBY, KAREN LYNN See WEINER, KAREN

COLBY, MARVELLE SEITMAN, business management educator, administrator; b. N.Y.C., Oct. 31, 1932; d. Charles Edward and Lily (Zimmerman) Seitman; m. Robert S. Colby, Apr. 11, 1954 (div. Apr. 1979); children: Lisa, Eric; m. Selig J. Alkon, Dec. 6, 1986. BA, Hunter Coll., 1954; MA, U. N.Colo., 1973; PhD in Pub. Adminstrn., Nova U., 1977; cert., Harvard Grad. Sch. Bus., 1979. V.p. SE Region URC Mgmt. Services Corp., Washington, 1972-77; dir. devel. Hunter Coll. Woman's Ctr. Community Leadership, N.Y.C., 1977-78; dir. tng. and career devel. Girl Scouts U.S., N.Y.C., 1978-79; dir. Overseas Tour Ops. Am. Jewish Congress, N.Y.C., 1979-81; chief exec. officer Girl Scout Council Greater N.Y.C., 1981-82; prof. bus. mgmt. Marymount Manhattan Coll., N.Y.C., 1982—, chmn. bus. mgmt. and acctg. div., 1982-89, 93-99. Adj. prof. NYU, 1986-92; mem. exec. com. Assn. Recreation Mgmt., N.Y.C., 1982; cons. Rockport Mgmt., Washington, 1974-78. Author: Test Your Management IQ, 1984; co-author: Lovejoy's Four Year College Guide for the Learning Disabled, 1985, Introduction to Business, 1991; contbr. articles to profl. jours. Chmn. Met. Dade County Commn. Status Women, Miami, 1975-77; chief planner Met. Dade County U.S. SBA 1st annual conf. Future Women Bus., 1977. Named to Hunter Coll. Hall of Fame, 1986. Mem. Acad. Mgmt., Hunter Coll. Alumni Assn. (bd. dirs. 1978-79), Phi Delta Kappa. Clubs: Lotos (mem. literary com. 1983-89). Home: 242 E 72nd St New York NY 10021-4574 Office: Marymount Manhattan Coll 221 E 71st St New York NY 10021-4532 E-mail: mcolby@mmm.edu.

COLBY, ROBERT ALAN, retired library science educator; b. Chgo., Apr. 15, 1920; s. Meyer and Ida (Lewis) C.; m. Vineta Blumoff, May 8, 1947. BA, U. Chgo., 1941, MA, 1942, PhD, 1949; MS in L.S, Columbia U., 1953. Instr. English DePaul U., Chgo., 1946-47; asst. prof. English Lake Forest (Ill.) Coll., 1949-51; lectr. English Hunter Coll., N.Y.C., 1951-53; lang., lit. and arts librarian Queens Coll., Flushing, N.Y., 1953-64; assoc. prof. libr. sci. So. Conn. State Coll., 1964-66; assoc. prof. libr. sci. Queens Coll., 1967-69, prof., 1969-86, prof. emeritus, 1986—. Docent N.Y. Pub. Libr., 1986—; asst. editor Wellesley Index to Victorian Periodicals, 1978-89. Author: (with Vineta Colby) The Equivocal Virtue: Mrs. Oliphant and the Victorian Literary Marketplace, 1966, Fiction With a Purpose: Major and Minor Nineteenth-Century Novels, 1967, Thackeray's Canvass of Humanity: An Author and His Public, 1979; editor: spl. issue William Makepeace Thackeray, Studies in the Novel, 1981; contbr. Introduction to Vanity Fair, 1989, Victorian Periodicals and Victorian Society, 1994, Storia Della Civilta Letteraria Inglese, 1996, Dickens Studies Annual, 2002; mem. editl. bd. Dickens Studies Ann., Victorian Periodicals Rev., 1999—. Served with AUS, 1943-46. Penfield fellow N.Y. U., 1942-43; Guggenheim fellow, 1978-79; Newberry Library fellow, summer 1982 Mem. MLA, Typophiles Soc., Victorian Soc. Am., Rsch. Soc. for Victorian Periodicals (bd. dirs. 1969-95, sr. adv. coun. 1995—), Midwest Victorian Studies Assn. Home: 320 Central Park W Apt 9N New York NY 10025-7659

COLBY, VIRGINIA LITTLE, retired elementary school educator; b. Saugus, Mass., May 1, 1917; d. Guy L. and Alberta M. (Chadwick) Little; m. Robert G. Colby, Dec. 25, 1951. AB, U. Mass., 1940. Svc. rep. N.E.T. and T. Co. Bus. Office, Lynn, Mass., 1940-63, N.E.T. and T. Co., Concord, N.H., 1963-67; tchr. Shaker Regional Sch. Dist., Belmont, NH, 1967—77, ret., 1977. Author: (book) St. Paul's Episcopal Church Concord New Hampshire: A Guide and Story of its Heritage, Memorabilia for Posterity: The Rev. Dr. Samuel Wood; co-author: Concord Eastside: A History of East Concord, New Hampshire, The Past and Present Here with Blend Highlights from 236 Years of Education in Boscawen, 1761-1997; contbr. articles to profl. jours. Mem.: AAUW (past pres. Concord br.), Boscawen Hist. Soc., Inc. (sec. libr.), Concord Ch. Women United (past pres., v.p.), Lakes Region Ret. Tchrs. Assn. (past pres.), No. N.H. Tel. Pioneers Am. (past pres.), Delta Kappa Gamma (hon.). Home: 134 Mountain Rd Concord NH 03301-6931

COLBY, WILLIAM MICHAEL, lawyer; b. Pontiac, Mich., Jan. 24, 1942; s. Orville Edgar and Jeannette (Nadon) C.; m. Brenda Schneckenburger, Nov. 28, 1964; children: Kathleen C. Scott, Thomas Brownell. AB, U. Mich., 1963, JD, 1966. Bar: N.Y. 1966, U.S. Tax Ct. 1969, U.S. Supreme Ct. 1972, Fla. 1982. Assoc. Harter, Secrest & Emery, Rochester, N.Y., 1966-74, ptnr., 1975-99, counsel, 2000—. Cons. various tax pubs. Contbr. articles to profl. jours.; editor various tax publs. Bd. dirs., hon. mem. Rochester Mus. and Sci. Ctr., chmn. bd. dirs. Genesee Cmty. Charter Sch. Fellow Am. Bar Found.; mem. Monroe County Bar Found. (pres. 1980-81), Oak Hill Country Club. Avocations: golf, wine tasting, collecting ancient greek coins, travel. Home: 39 Granite Dr Penfield NY 14526-2851 Office: Harter Secrest & Emery LLP 1600 Bausch & Lomb Pl Rochester NY 14604-2711 E-mail: colbyw@hselaw.com.

COLBY-HALL, ALICE MARY, Romance studies educator; b. Portland, Maine, Feb. 25, 1932; d. Frederick Eugene and Angie Fraser (Drown) C.; m. Robert A. Hall, Jr., May 8, 1976 (dec. 1997); stepchildren: Philip, Diana Hall Goodall, Carol Hall Erickson. BA, Colby Coll., 1953; MA, Middlebury Coll., 1954; PhD, Columbia U., 1962. Tchr. French, Latin Orono (Maine) H.S., 1954-55; tchr. French Gould Acad., Bethel, Maine, 1955-57; lectr. French Columbia U., 1959-60; instr. Romance lit. Cornell U., Ithaca, N.Y., 1962-63, asst. prof., 1963-66, assoc. prof., 1966-75, prof. Romance studies, 1975-97, prof. emerita, 1997—, chmn. Romance studies, 1990-96. Author: The Portrait in Twelfth Century French Literature: An Example of the Stylistic Originality of Chrétien de Troyes, 1965; mem. editl. bd. Speculum, 1976-79, Olifant, 1974—. Fulbright grantee, 1953-54; NEH fellow, 1984-85; recipient Médaille des Amis d'Orange, 1985; decorated chevalier de l'Ordre des Arts et Lettres, 1997. Mem. Modern Lang. Assn., Medieval Acad. Am. (councillor 1983-86), Internat. Arthurian Soc., Société Rencesvals, Académie de Vaucluse, Phi Beta Kappa. Republican. Congregationalist. Home: 308 Cayuga Heights Rd Ithaca NY 14850-2107 Office: Cornell U Dept Romance Studies Ithaca NY 14853 E-mail: amc12@cornell.edu.

COLCHER, ROBERT ELY, surgeon; b. Phila., July 9, 1927; MD, Jefferson Med. Coll., 1950. Diplomate Am. Bd. Surgery. Intern Jefferson Med. Coll. Hosp., 1950-51, resident in gen. surgery, 1951-55; surgeon Valley Forge Med. Ctr. and Hosp., Norristown, Pa. Fellow Am. Coll. Angiology, Internat. Coll. Surgeons; mem. AMA, Am. Soc. Addiction Medicine. Office: 1033 W Germantown Pike Norristown PA 19403-3905

COLCORD, HERBERT NATHANIEL, III, (SKIP COLCORD), corporate communications executive; b. Quincy, Mass., Mar. 21, 1951; s. Herbert Nathaniel Jr. and Audrey Louise (Gunn) C.; m. Deborah Sue O'Brien, Nov. 8, 1975; children: Heather Michele, Jared Scott, Devon Elizabeth. BA in Journalism cum laude, Northeastern U., 1973; MA in Journalism, U. Mo., 1975. Accredited bus. communicator. Staff reporter The Patriot Ledger, Quincy, Mass., 1970-73, Columbia (Mo.) Daily Tribune, 1974-75; pub. affairs asst. Nat. Fire Protection Assn., Boston, 1975-77, mgr. editorial programs, 1977-79; mgr. pub. affairs Ocean Spray Cranberries, Inc., Plymouth, Mass., 1979-82, mgr. consumer affairs, 1982-89, mgr. mktg. comms. Lakeville, Mass., 1990-97, mgr. corp. comm. and pub. affairs, 1998-99; sr. mgr. corp. comm. Polaroid Corp., Cambridge, Mass., 1999—2001, dir. corp. comm., 2002—. Bd. dirs. Plymouth County Devel. Coun., Pembroke, Mass., 1989-92; bd. dirs. Nat. Guest Rels. Assn., 1984-86, pres., 1984-85. Contbr. articles to profl. jours. Recipient Gold Quill award for Excellence Internat. Assn. Bus. Communicators, 1983, Writing Excellence award Coop. Communicators Assn., 1980-81, Writing Excellence award Nat. Coun. Farmer Coop., 1981-82, 1st pl. Spl. Project Awards, Coop. Communicators Assn., 1992; named Pub. Rels. Allstar, Food and Beverage Mag., 1995, one of Top 10 Food Industry Pub. Rels. Profls., Food Bus. Mag., 1992. Mem. Internat. Assn. Bus. Communicators, Kappa Tau Alpha. Avocations: basketball, golf, genealogy. Home: 322 Nichols Dr Taunton MA 02780-4373 Office: Polaroid Corp 1265 Main St Waltham MA 02451 E-mail: Colcors@Polaroid.com.

COLDEWEY, JOHN CHRISTOPHER, English literature educator; b. Beloit, Wis., June 13, 1944; s. George Henry and Frances Mary (McLoughlin) C.; m. Carolyn Culver (div.); children: Christopher, Devin; m. Christine May Rose, Sept. 9, 1989. BA, Lewis U., 1966; student, U. London, Eng., 1966; MA, No. Ill. U., 1967; PhD, U. Colo., 1972. Acting asst. prof. English U. Wash., Seattle, 1972-73, asst. prof. English, 1973-79, assoc. prof. English, 1979-91, prof. English, 1991—, dir. grad. studies, 1995-99; postdoctoral rsch. fellow Nottingham (Eng.) U., 1979-80; Fulbright exchange prof. U. East Anglia, Norwich, Eng., 1986-87. Lectr., speaker and reader in field. Author: Pseudomagia: A 17th Century Neo-Latin Tragicomedy by William Mewe, 1979, Renaissance Latin Drama in England, Vol. IV, 1987, Vol. 14, 1991, Contexts for Early English Drama, 1989, Early English Drama: An Anthology, 1993, Drama: Classical Through Contemporary, 1998, rev., 2001; editor: Modern Lang. Quar., 1983-93; contbr. chpts. to books, articles to profl. jours. Bd. dirs. Friends U. Wash. Libr., 1991-99 (pres. 1995-97); hon. advisor Brit. Univs. Summers Schs. Program, 1977-94. Fellow Medieval Acad. Am., 1974-75; grantee Am. Coun. Learned Socs., 1974-75, 1976-77, 86-87, 89-90, grantee NEH, 1979-80, 82-83, 92-93, fellow, 1999-2000. Mem. Coun. Editors Learned Jours. (pres. 1992-94, v.p. 1990-92, sec.-treas. 1989-90), Medieval and Renaissance Drama Soc. (exec. coun. 1997-98, v.p. 1998-00), Medieval European Drama Coun. (Am. rep. 1997-99). Avocations: skiing, mountain travel, running, biking. Home: 333 35th Ave E Seattle WA 98112-4923 Office: U Wash Dept English Box 354330 Seattle WA 98195-0001 E-mail: jcjc@u.washington.edu.

COLDREN, IRA BURDETTE, JR., lawyer; b. Uniontown, Pa., June 15, 1924; s. Ira Burdette and Eleanor Clarke (Lincoln) C.; m. Phyllis Miles, Sept. 7 (div. Oct. 1970); children: Kathy, Lee Ellen, Janice, David; m. Frances Thomas, Aug. 27, 1971. BS, U.S. Mil. Acad., 1945; LLB, U. Pa., 1952; LLM in Estate Planning, U. Miami, 1982. Bar: Pa. 1952, U.S. Dist. Ct. (we. dist.) Pa. 1953, U.S. Ct. Appeals (3d cir.) 1983. Commd. 2d lt. U.S. Army, 1945, advanced through grades to lt. col., 1952, ret., 1956; assoc. Ray, Coldren & Buck, Uniontown, Pa., 1956-59; ptnr. Coldren & Coldren, Uniontown, 1959-62, Coldren & Adams, Uniontown, 1962—83, Coldren, Adams, DeHaas & Radcliffe, Uniontown, 1983-92, Coldren Adams, Uniontown, 1992—. Pres. Greater Uniontown United Fund, 1962, Fayette County Devel. Council, 1971-75. Fellow Am. Bar Found., Am. Coll. Trust and Estate Counsel; mem. Pa. Bar Assn. (ho. of dels. 1976-79, bd. govs. 1979-82, v.p. 1985-86, pres. 1986-87), Pa. Bar Inst. (pres. 1982-83), Fayette County Bar Assn. (pres. 1983), Am. Law Inst., Am. Judicature Soc., Internat. Assn. Ins. Counsel, Pa. Jaycees (pres. 1959), Club: Uniontown Country (pres. 1969-71). Lodges: Rotary (pres. Uniontown club 1964), Masons (master 1964, 69, mem. Scottish Rite Supreme Coun. 1991—). Democrat. Presbyterian. Home: 117 Belmont Cir Uniontown PA 15401-4759 Office: Coldren Adams 2 W Main St Ste 700 Uniontown PA 15401 E-mail: CALawFirm@aol.com.

COLDREN, LARRY ALLEN, engineering educator, consultant; b. Lewistown, Pa., Jan. 1, 1946; s. Roscoe Calvin and Mary (Hutchinson) C.; m. Donna Kauffman, Sept. 4, 1966; children: Christopher William, Bret Allen. BS and AB, Bucknell U., 1968; MS, Stanford U., 1969, PhD, 1972. Registered profl. engr., N.J. Mem. tech. staff Bell Labs., N.J., 1968-84, supr., 1984; prof. U. Calif., Santa Barbara, 1984—; chmn., CTO Agility Commns., 1998—. Contbr. 500 papers to tech. jours.; patentee in field. Fellow IEEE (mem. ad com. 1988—), Optical Soc. Am., IEE; mem. Phi Beta Kappa, Tau Beta Pi, Pi Mu Epsilon, Sigma Pi Sigma. Presbyterian. Avocation: flying. Home: 4665 Via Vistosa Santa Barbara CA 93110-2333

COLDWELL, PHILIP EDWARD, financial consultant; b. Champaign, Ill., July 20, 1922; s. Montgomery Ian and Donna Clare (Rose) C.; m. Norma Elaine Abels, June 1, 1947; children: Douglas Michael, Cameron Iliff. BA, U. Ill., 1946, MS, 1947; PhD, U. Wis., 1952. Teaching asst. U. Ill., at Urbana, 1947; instr. Southwestern La. Inst., Lafayette, 1947-48, asst. prof., 1950-51; instr. Mont. State U., 1949-50; research economist Fed. Res. Bank, Kansas City, 1951-52, economist, officer Dallas, 1952-62, 1st v.p., 1962-68, pres., 1968-74; mem. bd. govs. Fed. Res. System, Washington, 1974-80; fin. cons., 1980—. Lectr. Southwestern Sch. Banking, Dallas, 1962-74; dir. Maxus Energy Corp., 1987-93. Trustee Austin Coll., 1977-89; dir. Temp Fund, Fed Fund, Muni Fund, 1980-99. Pilot USNR, 1942-46. Mem. Am. Econ. Assn., So. Finance Assn., Phi Delta Theta. Presbyn. (elder). Club: Economists (Dallas) (founder, 1st pres.). Home: 3330 Southwestern Blvd Dallas TX 75225-7653

COLE, ANN HARRIET, psychologist, communications consultant; b. Phila., Feb. 27, 1949; d. Albert and Deborah (Mann) Brawerman; m. Stephen Cole, June 4, 1969 (div. June 18, 1987); children: Richard David, Robert Walter; m. Allan J. Besbris, Aug. 4, 1998. BA, SUNY, Stony Brook, 1971, MA, 1975. Dir. field rsch. Opinion Rsch. Assocs., 1974-76; v.p. Social Data Analysts, Inc., 1976-86; rsch. assoc. Jay Schulman, Inc., N.Y.C., 1986-87; cons. Litigation Scis., Inc., N.Y.C., 1988-90, Stanley S. Arkin, P.C., N.Y.C., 1990; cons. Chadbourne & Parke, N.Y.C., 1990-91; pres. Ann Cole Opinion Rsch. and Analysis, N.Y.C., 1991—. CBS news cons., 1994-95. Mem. Am. Soc. Trial Cons. (bd. dirs. 1994-99, v.p. 1996-97, pres. 1997-99), Nat. Coalition to Abolish the Death Penalty, Qualitative Rsch. Cons. Am. Office: Ann Cole Opinion Rsch and Analysis 1560 Broadway Ste 813 New York NY 10036-1518 E-mail: ahcole@acoraweb.com.

COLE, BASIL B. priest, religious studies educator; b. San Francisco, Mar. 14, 1937; s. Burr R. and Lucy M. Cole. BS, U. San Francisco, 1959; lic. in sacred theology, Le Saulchoir, Etiolle, Soisy-sur-Seine, France, 1968; STD in Sacred Theology, U. San Tommaso, Rome, 1991. Prior St. Dominic's Priory, San Francisco, 1970—75, Daniel Murphy H.S., L.A., Calif., 1975—79; mem. Western Dominican Preaching, 1979—98; assoc. prof. moral and spiritual theology Dominican House of Studies, Washington, 1998—. Invited prof. Pontifical U. St. Thomas Aquinas, Rome, 1985—97; adj. prof. St. Charles Seminary, Overbrook, Pa., 2001—. Author: Music and Morals, 1993; co-author: Christian Totality, 1997. Home: 487 Michigan Ave NE Washington DC 20017 Office: Dominican House of Studies 487 Michigan Ave NE Washington DC 20017

COLE, BRAD, mayor; b. Decatur, Ill., Nov. 27, 1971; s. Neal and M. Sue Cole. BA, So. Ill. U., Carbondale, 1994. Commr. Ill. Student Assistance Commn., Springfield, 1993-95; asst. dir. So. Ill. U. Alumni Assn., Carbondale, 1995-99; city councilman City of Carbondale, 1999—2003; asst. dep. chief of staff Office of Gov., Stat of Ill., Springfield, 1999—2001; dep. chief of staff Office of the Gov., State of Ill., Springfield, 2002—03; mayor City of Carbondale, 2003—. Dir. Lower Miss. Delta Devel. Ctr., Memphis, Tenn., 2000—. Precinct committeeman Ill. Rep. Party, Carbondale, 1990; trustee Carbondale Pub. Libr., 1997-99; commr. Carbondale Pk. Dist., 1997-99. Named one of Outstanding Young Men of Am., 1996, 98. Mem. So. Ill. U. Alumni Assn., Rotary (Club Rotarian of Yr. 1998), Masons (sec. lodge 2000—), Delta Chi (ritual com. 1997-). Home: PO Box 1071 Carbondale IL 62903 Office: City of Carbondale 200 S Illinois Ave Carbondale IL 62901 Office Fax: 618-351-5766.

COLE, BRUCE MILAN, Federal Agency Administrator, Art Historian; b. Cleve., Aug. 2, 1938; s. Jerome I. and Selma (Kaufman) C.; m. Doreen Luff, July 15, 1962; children: Stephaine Wren, Ryan Lawrence. BA, Western Res. U., 1962; MA, Oberlin Coll., 1964; PhD, Bryn Mawr Coll., 1969. Asst. prof. U. Rochester, 1969-73; assoc. prof. Ind. U., Bloomington, 1973-77, prof., 1973-88, disting. prof. fine arts, 1988—; mem. Nat. Found. on the Arts and the Humanities, Washington, 2001—. Author: Giott and Florentine Painting 1280-1575, 1976, paperback edit., 1977, Agnolo Gaddi, 1977, Italian Majolica from Midwestern Collections, 1977, Masaccio and the Art of Early Renaissance Florence, 1980, Sienese Painting from Its Origins to the Fifteenth Century, 1969, The Renaissance Artist at Work, 1983, London, John Murray, 1983, Sienese Painting in the Age of Renaissance, 1985, Italian Art 1250-1550: The Relation of Renaissance Art to Life and Soc., 1987, Art of the Western World, Piero della Francesca, 1991, Giotto: The Scrovegni Chapel, Padua, 1993, Studies in Italian Art 1250-1550, 1996, Titian and Venetian Painting, 1450-1590, 1998, The Informed Eye, 1999. Recipient Pres.' award Am. Assn. Italian Studies, 1987; NEH fellow, 1972, Guggenheim Found. fellow, 1975, Am. Coun. Learned Socs. fellow, 1981. Fellow Accademia Senese degli Intronati; mem. Nat. Coun. on the Humanities. Avocation: walking. Office: Nat Found on the Arts and Humanities NEH 1100 Pennsylvania Ave NW Washington DC 20506 Office Fax: 202-682-5603.

COLE, C. SUZANNE, librarian; b. Bryn Mawr, Pa., Oct. 2, 1967; d. Taylor Whitney and Mary Ann Cole; m. Daniel Conroy Bigelow, Aug. 15, 1992; children: Warren Andrew Bigelow, Margaret Frances Bigelow. BA, Bowdoin Coll., 1989; MA in Sociology, U. Pa., 1992; MS in Libr. and Info. Sci., Drexel U., 1995. Ref. intern Van Pelt Libr., U. Pa., Phila., 1994-95; info. svcs. libr. Lehigh U., Bethlehem, Pa., 1995-96, team leader, 1996-97; pres. Emerac Info. Svcs., Doylestown, Pa., 1997; libr. The Pew Charitable Trusts, Phila., 1997-99, chief libr., 2000—. Bd. dirs. Words in Time, Inc., Takoma Park, Md. Contbr. articles to profl. jours. Ruling elder Collenbrook United Ch., Drexel Hill, Pa., 1994-95. Mem. Spl. Librs. Assn., Consortium of Found. Librs. (chair 2000-02), Phi Beta Kappa, Beta Phi Mu. Democrat. Office: The Pew Charitable Trusts 2005 Market St Ste 1700 Philadelphia PA 19103 E-mail: scole@pewtrusts.com.

COLE, CAROLYN JO, brokerage company executive; b. Carmel, Calif. d. Joseph Michael Jr. and Dorothea Wagner (James) C. AB, Vassar Coll., 1965. Sr. v.p. UBS Painewebber, Inc., N.Y.C., 1975—95; exec. v.p. Tucker Anthony, Inc., Boston, 1995—97; chmn. Inst. Econ. & Fin., Inc., N.Y.C., 1997—98; mng. dir. Citigroup Pvt. Bank, N.Y.C., 1998—. Guest lectr. Harvard U. Bus. Sch.; lectr. Securities Industry Inst., Wharton Sch. U. Pa.; past chmn. bd. dirs. N.Y. Women's Bldg.; bd. dirs. Women's Venture Fund. Named to YWCA Acad. Women Achievers. Mem. NOW, DAR, N.Y. Soc. Security Analysts (past bd. dirs.), Assn. Investment Mgmt. and Rsch., Soc. Fgn. Analysts, Aspen Inst. Humanistic Studies, Fin. Women's Assn., Women's Econ. Roundtable, Econ. Club N.Y., Women in Need (past bd. dirs.), Vassar Club. Democrat. Office: Citigroup Alternative Investments 388 Greenwich St New York NY 10013-2339 E-mail: cali.cole@citigroup.com.

COLE, CHARLES DEWEY, JR., lawyer; b. Lower Merion Twp., Pa., Aug. 12, 1952; s. Charles Dewey and Margaret Ann (Leach) C. AB, Columbia U., 1974; JD, St. John's U., Jamaica, N.Y., 1979; ML Info. Sci., U. Tex., 1982; LLM, NYU, 1988; LLM in Environ. Law, Pace U., 1993; LLM in Trial Advocacy, Temple U., 1999; LLM in Advanced Litigation, Nottingham Trent U., 2003. Bar: N.Y. 1980, Tex. 1980, N.J. 1986, D.C. 1988, U.S. Dist. Ct. (we. and ea. dists.) Tex. 1980, U.S. Dist. Ct. (so. and ea. dists.) N.Y. 1980, U.S. Dist. Ct. (no. dist.) Tex. 1982, U.S. Dist. Ct. (no. dist.) N.Y. 1983, U.S. Dist. Ct. (we. dist.) N.Y. 1984, U.S. Dist. Ct. N.J. 1986, U.S. Dist. Ct. D.C. 1994, U.S. Ct. Internat. Trade 1980, U.S. Tax Ct. 1984, U.S. Ct. Appeals (5th and 11th cirs.) 1981, U.S. Ct. Appeals (Fed. cir.) 1982, U.S. Ct. Appeals (2d cir.) 1984, U.S. Ct. Appeals (D.C. cir.) 1987, U.S. Ct. Appeals (3d cir.) 1993, U.S. Supreme Ct. 1984; solicitor, Eng. and Wales, 1995; Higher Rights of Audience (civil procs.) Qualification, 2002. Law clk. to chief judge U.S. Dist. Ct. (ea. dist.), Beaumont, Tex., 1979-80, U.S. Ct. Appeals (5th cir.), Austin, Tex., 1981-82; assoc. Moore, Berson, Lifflander & Mewhinney, Garden City and N.Y.C., N.Y., 1982-85; assoc. and ptnr. Newman Schlau Fitch & Burns P.C., N.Y.C. and Mineola, N.Y., 1985-88; assoc. Meyer, Suozzi, English & Klein, P.C., Mineola and N.Y.C., 1988-95; of counsel, ptnr. Newman Fitch Altheim Myers, P.C., N.Y.C. and Newark, 1995—. Instr. trial techniques program Hofstra Law Sch., 1994-2000; instr. intensive trial advocacy program Widener Law Sch., 1999—. Author: Law Books as a Charitable Contribution, 1975, The EPA Lender Liability Regulations: EPA's Questionable Authority to Promulgate the Regulations as Part of the National Contingency Plan, 1993; contbr. book revs. to profl. publs. Mem.: Solicitors Assn. of Higher Ct. Advs., The Coll. of State Bar Tex., State Bar Tex., Selden Soc., Supreme Ct. Hist. Soc., Soc. Advanced Legal Studies, Am. Soc. for Legal History, Osgoode Soc. for Can. Legal History, Brit. and Irish Assn. Law Librs., Law Libr. Assn. Greater N.Y., Am. Assn. Law Librs., Fed. Bar Coun., Bar Assn. 5th Fed. Cir., Maritime Law Assn. U.S. (proctor), N.Y. County Lawyers Assn. (com. on fed. cts.), D.C. Bar, N.Y. State Bar Assn. (co-chair exec. and appellate practice coms., comml. and fed. litigation sect.), The Law Soc. (reference group on multi-party actions), Clarity, Scribes (dir., chair brief-writing competition com.). Republican. Home: 16 94th St Apt 3B Brooklyn NY 11209-6643 Office: Newman Fitch Altheim Myers PC 14 Wall St New York NY 10005-2101 E-mail: dcole@nfam.com., cdc27@columbia.edu.

COLE, CHARLES DUBOSE, II, law educator; b. Monroeville, Ala., May 14, 1938; BSBA, Auburn U., 1960; JD cum laude, Samford U., 1966; LLM, NYU, 1971; D (hon.), Faculdade Marcelo Tupinamba, Sao Paulo, Brazil, 1991. Bar: Ala. 1966, U.S. Supreme Ct., 1971, U.S. Ct. Appeals (fed. cir.) 1997, U.S. Ct. Internat. Trade, 1997. Law clk., assoc. atty. Porterfield & Sch., Birmingham, Ala., 1965-66; prof. law Cumberland Sch. Law Samford U., Birmingham, 1966-75, 81—; Lucille S. Beeson prof. law and dir. internat. programs, master comparative law degree program Cumberland Sch. Law, Birmingham, Ala., 1993—; dir. permanent study commn. Ala. Jud. System, 1972-74; dir. Ala. Jud. Conf. Criminal Justice Survey, 1973; dir. adv. com. Ala. jud. article implementation Ala. Dept. Ct. Mgmt., 1974-75; dir. so. regional office Nat. Ctr. for State Cts., Atlanta, 1975-79; adminstrv. dir. cts. Commonwealth of Ky., Frankfort, 1979-81. Lectr. Cumberland Inst. for Continuing Legal Edn., Ala. Continuing Legal Edn., Josephson/Kluwer Bar Rev. Ctr. Am., Inc., 1967-87; law and social sci. adv. coun. Coll. Liberal Arts/Auburn U., 1991-96, dean's coun., 1996—; chmn. profl. adv. com. Office Advancement Auburn U., 1992-93; reporter civil justice adv. group Middle Dist. Ala., 1991-93; del. Moscow Conf. on Law and Econ. Coop., The Kremlin Palace, 1990; legal specialist (pro bono) Parliament of Ukriane, 1993; v.p. faculty Samford U., 1989-90; policy com. mem. Cumberland Sch. Law, 1989-92, 2000-02; mem. faculty exec. com. Samford U., 1988-89; del. U.S./Japan Bilateral Session, 1988; presenter USIA, Internat. Meeting Brazil/U.S., 1988; participant seminar Claremont McKenna Coll./NEH, 1986; presenter in field. Author: (with Brewer) Alabama Constitutional Law, 1992, 2d edit., 1997; contbr. articles to profl. jours.; mem. editl. bd. Ala. Lawyer, 2000—. Bd. dirs. Auburn U. Bar Assn., 1991—. Named Outstanding Prof. Student Bar Assn./Cumberland Sch. Law, 1972-73, 83-84, Outstanding Alumnus, Phi Alpha Delta, 1973, Samford U. Cumberland Sch. Law, 1998. Mem. ABA (lectr. appellate judges seminar 1977-78), Am. Judicature Soc. (bd. dirs. 2000—, exec. com. 2000—), Supreme Ct. Hist. Soc., Am. Trial Lawyers Assn. (faculty mem.), Ala. Bar Assn. (action group mem. 1984-85, chmn. 1985-88, reporter task force on jud. selection 1988-89, com. on the future of the profession 1990-91, task force on legal edn. 1992-93, com. on judicial and legal reform 1994-95, chmn. 1995-96), Ukrainian Legal Found. (bd. fgn. advisors 1993-98), Birmingham Bar Assn. (mem. civil ct. rules com. 1998-99), Auburn U. Bar Assn. (adv. bd. 1992—), Phi Alpha Delta. Home: 1824 Mountain Laurel Ln Birmingham AL 35244 E-mail: cdcole@samford.edu., colecdII@aol.com.

COLE, CLARENCE RUSSELL, college dean; b. Crestline, Ohio, Nov. 20, 1918; s. Arthur Leroy and Anita Emma (Stephan) C.; m. Mary Piper, Mar. 15, 1945; children: Carole Ann, Larry Lee, Pamela Sue. Student pre-med., Otterbein Coll., Westerville, Ohio, 1937-39; DVM, Ohio State U., 1943, MS, 1944, PhD, 1947. Instr. dept. vet. pathology Coll. Vet. Medicine Ohio State U., Columbus, asst. prof., 1947-49, chmn. dept., 1947-67, assoc. prof., 1949-54, prof., 1954-67, asst. dean Coll. Vet. Medicine, 1960-67, dean Coll. Vet. Medicine, 1967—, prof. pathology Coll. Medicine, 1952—, prof. comparative pathology Grad. Sch., 1954—, now prof. emeritus. Regents prof. Ohio Bd. Regents, 1966 ; chmn. Mershon Ctr. Nat. Security, Ohio State U., 1965-67; mem. U. Coun. Rsch., 1960-67; adminstr. cons. Vet. Rsch., Archtl. Engring. Planning, Animal Med. Ctr., N.Y.C.; cons. nat. adv. rsch. resources coun. NIH, 1972—, NIH Health Manpower Grants Br; mem. nat. adv. com. Nat. Ctr. for Primate Biology, 1967-70; mem. com. on comparative pathology NRC, NAS, 1971—; mem. fellowship com. NATO. Recipient Hetzfeld lectr. award Auburn U.; 1st award sci. exhibit Ohio State Med. Assn., 1956; 2nd award AMA. Mem. Men and Women of Sci., Internat. Acad. Pathology (mem. exec. coun.), Internat. Toxoplasmosis Com. (vice-chmn. 1959—), AVMA (Gold award, chmn. adv. bd. vet. med. spltys. 1960-75), Am. Coll. Vet. Pathologists (Disting. citation 1967, pres. 1957, Disting. Mem. 1989), Assn. Am. Vet. Med. Colls. (sec.-treas. 1969—), Sigma Xi, Phi Zeta, Omega Tau Sigma. Clubs: Torch Internat. Address: 1925 Coffey Rd Columbus OH 43210-1005

COLE, CLIFFORD ADAIR, clergyman; b. Lamoni, Iowa, Nov. 16, 1915; s. Fayette V. and Mable F. (Adair) C.; m. Harriet Lucile Hartshorn, June 28, 1936; children: Alethea Rae (Mrs. Justus S. Allen), Beverly Sue (Mrs. Lloyd G. Hilburn, Jr.), Lawrence Dean. Student, Graceland Coll., Lamoni, 1934-35, 41-42, U. Wyo., 1938; BS in Edn, Central Mo. State Coll., 1943; postgrad., U. Iowa, 1946, U. Chgo., 1952; MA in Edn, U. Mo. at Kansas City, 1957. Ordained to ministry Reorganized Ch. of Jesus Christ of Latter Day Saints, 1939. High sch. tchr., Lamoni, 1943-46, Bellevue, Ia., 1946- 47; min. Iowa, 1947-51; dean students Graceland Coll., 1951-53. Dir. dept. religious edn. Reorganized Ch. of Jesus Christ of Latter Day Saints, 1955-58, apostle in council twelve, 1958-80, pres. council, 1964-80, cons. to 1st presidency, 1980-82; ret., 1982 Author: The Prophets Speak, 1954, Working Together in our Families, 1955, Celebrating Together in our Families, 1955, Faith for New Frontier, 1956, The Revelation in Christ, 1963, Modern Women in a Modern World, 1965, The Mighty Act of God, 1984 Mem. Phi Sigma Pi, Zeta Kappa Epsilon, Kappa Delta Pi. Reorganized Ch. Of Jesus Christ Of Latter-Day Saints. *Everyone who thinks deeply must answer the question: "What is the Ultimate Reality undergirding our universe?" The answer is not found in proof but rather in faith. The struggle has led me to a profound and abiding faith in God.*

COLE, DANIEL GERARD, geographer, information scientist, cartographer; b. Utica, N.Y., Dec. 8, 1954; s. William John and Mary Margaret Cole; m. Wanda Elaine Jones, June 23, 1984; 1 child, Robyn Alexander. BA in Geography, SUNY, Albany, 1977; MS in Geography, Mich. State U., 1979; postgrad., Oreg. State U., 1979—81. Dir. cartographic svcs. lab. U. Md., College Park, 1982—82; cartographer NOAA, Silver Spring, Md., 1983—83, Woods Hole (Mass.) Oceanog. Instn., 1983—84; lectr. Montgomery Coll., Rockville, Md., 1985—86; rsch. cartographer Smithsonian Instn., Washington, 1986—90, geog. info. systems coord., 1990—. Presenter in field. Co-curator (museum exhbn.) Global Positioning Systems: A New Constellation; contbr. articles to profl. jours. Nat. coun. mem. Fellowship of Reconciliation, Nyack, NY, 1985—90; bd. mem. Fund for Edn. and Tng., Washington, 1988—2003. Named Tchg. asst., Mich. State U., 1977—79, Oreg. State U., 1979—81; Regents scholar, N.Y. State, 1973—77. Mem.: Can. Cartographic Assn., Am. Congress on Surveying and Mapping, Am. Soc. Photogrammetry and Remote Sensing, Assn. Am. Geographers. Democrat. Quaker. Avocations: human rights, peace and justice work, jogging, travel. Office: Smithsonian Instn 10th & Constitution NW Washington DC 20013-7012 Office Fax: 202-357-4122. Personal E-mail: cole.w@worldnet.att.net. E-mail: cole.dan@nmnh.si.edu.

COLE, DANIEL JOHN, anesthesiologist, educator; b. Washington, July 8, 1956; s. Wendell John and Marjorie Eileen (Danielson) Cole. BS, Andrews U., 1978; MD, Loma Linda U., 1982. Resident in anesthesiology Loma Linda U. Med. Ctr., Calif., 1982-85, chief resident, 1985; neuroanesthesia rsch. fellow U. Calif., San Diego, 1985-86; clin. instr. anesthesiology Loma Linda U., 1986, asst. prof., 1986-92, assoc. prof., 1992-96, prof., 1996-97; prof. anesthesiology Mayo Med. Sch.; cons. anesthesiology Mayo Clinic Scottscale. Chmn. dept. anesthesiology Mayo Clinic Ariz.; attending anesthesiologist Loma Linda U. Med. Ctr., 1986—; cons. Baxter Healthcare Corp., Round Lake, Ill., 1992—. Editor: Manual of Post Anesthesia Care, 1992; contbr. articles to profl. jours. Grantee Baxter Healthcare Corp., 1993, 94, Am. Soc. Anesthesiologists, 1988; recipient Faculty Rsch. award Walter E. MacPherson Soc., 1990, 94. Mem. AMA, Internat. Soc. Cerebral Blood Flow and Metabolism, Soc. for Neurosci., Internat. Anesthesia Rsch. Soc., Soc. Neurosurg. Anesthesia and Critical Care (sec.-treas.), Alpha Omega Alpha. Avocations: Karate, travel, roller hockey. Office: Mayo Clinic Hosp Dept Anesthesiology 5777 E Mayo Blvd Phoenix AZ 85054 E-mail: cole.daniel@mayo.edu.

COLE, DAVID, information technology executive; V.p. Internat Client and Collaboration Divsn., Microsoft, Redmond, Wash., v.p. Web Client and Consumer Experience Divsn., v.p. Consumer Windows Divsn., sr. v.p. Svcs. Platform Divsn., sr. v.p. Consumer Svcs. Divsn., sr. v.p. MSN and Personal Svcs. Group. Mem. Bus. Leadership Team, Microsoft. Office: Microsoft One Microsoft Way Redmond WA 98052-6399

COLE, DAVID AKINOLA, educational administrator, educator; b. Jan. 8, 1954; s. Nathaniel Jonathan and Betsy (George) C.; m. Claudia Marcella Campbell, Oct. 4, 1980; children: Bryan, Claudette, Lynnette. Student, Milton Margai Tchrs. Coll., 1976-79; BS in Edn. cum laude, Lincoln U., 1985, MEd, 1986; cert. in teaching, U. Ga., 1990, postgrad., 1992, EdD in Ednl. Leadership, 1999. Cert. English tchr., edn. of the gifted, Ga. Asst. tchr. Holy Trinity Boys Sch., Freetown, 1973-76; tchr., asst. libr. S.L. Grammar Sch., Freetown, 1979-82, Lincoln U. Mo., 1983-86; educator Rutland and Clarke County Sch. Dist., Athens, Ga., 1987-89; ednl. therapist Rutland Psychoednl. Svcs./Ga. Psychoednl. Network, Athens, 1989-92; spl. edn. tchr. Burney-Harris-Lyons Sch., Athens, 1992-94; asst. prin. Carver Mid. Sch., Monroe, Ga., 1994-98; asst. prin., Ga. h.s. grad. test coord. Clarke Ctrl. H.S., Athens, Ga., 1998—. Cons. U. Ga., Athens, 1988-90, rsch. asst. nat. rsch. ctr. on the gifted and talented project, 1992-96; mem. adj. faculty Piedmont Coll., Athens; client counselor N.E. Ga.

Residential Svcs./Dept. Human Resources, Athens, 1988-95; h.s. instr. Clarke County H.S. Evening Program, 1996—. UNESCO scholar Milton Margai Tchrs. Coll., 1976-79; David A. Cole Outstanding Faculty award established by Clarke Ctrl. H.S., 1998-99. Mem. ASCD, Nat. Coun. Tchrs. English, Coun. for Exceptional Children, Assn. for the Gifted, Coun. for Children with Behavior Disorders, Profl. Assn. Ga. Educators, Ga. Ednl. Rsch. Assn., Psi Chi, Sigma Tau Delta (tchrs. adv. bd. 1992—), Kappa Delta Epsilon (Perfect Scholar award 1992), Pi Lambda Theta. Avocations: reading, travel, music, athletics, tennis. Home: PO Box 5932 Athens GA 30604-5932

COLE, DAVID EDWARD, university administrator; b. Detroit, July 20, 1937; s. Edward Nicholas and Esther Helen (Engman) C.; m. Carol Hutchins, July 9, 1965; children: Scott David, Christopher Carl. BS in Mech. Engring. and Math., U. Mich., 1960, MS in Mech. Engring., 1961, PhD, 1966. Engr. GM, Detroit, 1960—65; prof. U. Mich., Ann Arbor, 1967—, dir. Office for Study of Automotive Transp., 1978—2000; entrepreneur 6 cos., 1975—95; chmn. Ctr. Auto Rsch. and Mgmt., ptnr. The Altarum Inst. Mich, 2000—03; chmn. Ctr. for Automotve Rsch. (ind. not for profit), 2003—. Bd. dirs. MSX Internat., Detroit, Saturn Electronics, Aurburn Hills, Mich., Plastech, Dearborn, R.L. Polk, Southfield, Mich., Campfire Interactive, Ann Arbor, Mich., Mich. Econ. Devel. Corp., Lansing, Cunningham Motors, Livonia, Mich.; mem. energy engring. bd. NRC, 1989-94; select panel U.S.-Can. Free trade Pact, 1988-91. Author: Elementary Vehicle Dynamics, 1972; contbr. articles to profl. jours. Bd. trustees Hope Coll., 1994-98; mem. exec. com., Mich. Economic Devel. Corp.; bd. dirs. Automotive Hall of Fame, Dearborn. Fellow Soc. Automotive Engrs. (dir. 1980-83, 85-88, Teetor award 1969), Engring. Soc. Detroit (Horace H. Rackham medal 2000); mem. Chevalier of the Nat. Order of Merit from France, 1999, Soc. Mktg. Execs. (Mktg. Educator of Yr. 1998, Rene Dubos Environ. award 1998), Nat. Auto Dealers Assn. Found. (Freedom of Mobility award 1993), Swedens Royal Order of the Polar Star. Republican. Presbyterian. Avocations: hunting, fishing, boating, running, golf. Office: Ctr Auto Rsch 3025 Boardwalk Ann Arbor MI 48108-4004 E-mail: dcole@cargrop.org.

COLE, DONALD BARNARD, education educator; b. Lawrence, Mass., USA, Mar. 31, 1922; s. Arthur Whittier and Marion Barnard Cole; m. Susan Appleton Wilson; children: Douglas B., Robert W., Daniel Whittier, Susan H. AB, Harvard U., Cambridge, Mass., 1943, AM, 1947, PhD, 1957. Instr. Phillips Exeter Acad., Exeter, NH, 1947—71, prof., 1971—88, Dean of Faculty, 1975—80, Prof. Emeritus, 1988—. Cons. US Office of Edn., Washington D.C.; com. on tchg. Am. Hist. Assn., Washington D.C., 1968—73; visting com. Harvard U., Cambridge, Mass., 1968—73. Author: (history) Immigrant City: Lawrence Mass., 1963, Jacksonian Democracy in New Hampshire, 1970, Martin Van Buren And the Am. Polit. Sys., 1984; co-editor: Witness to the Young Republic, 1989, The Presidency of Andrew Jackson, 1993. Lt. USN, 1943—46. Mem.: Soc. For Hist. of the Early Am. Republic, Organization of Am. Hist., Am. Hist. Assn. Democrat. Congregational. Home: 25 Elliot St Exeter NH 03833

COLE, ELSA KIRCHER, lawyer; b. Dec. 5, 1949; d. Paul and Hester Marie (Pellegrom) Kircher; m. Roland J. Cole, Aug. 16, 1975; children: Isabel Ashley, Madeline Aldis. AB in History with distinction, Stanford U., 1971; JD, Boston U., 1974. Bar: Wash. 1974, U.S. Supreme Ct. 1980, Mich. 1989, Kans. 1997, Ind. 1999. Asst. atty gen., rep. dept. motor vehicles State of Wash., Seattle, 1974-75, asst. atty. gen., rep. dept. social and health svcs., 1975-76, asst. atty. gen., rep. U. Wash., 1976-89; gen. counsel U. Mich., Ann Arbor, 1989-97, NCAA, Indpls., 1997—. Presenter ednl. issues various confs. and workshops. Contbr. articles to profl. jours. Fellow: Nat. Assn. Coll. and Univs. Attys. (mem. nominations com., mem. site selection com. 1987—88, co-chair student affairs sect. 1987—88, program 1988—89, mem. fin. com., articles com., by-laws com. 1988—89, co-chair student affairs sect. 1988—89, bd. dirs. 1988—91, program 1989—90, chair profl. devel. com. 1990—91, program 1991—92, honors and awards ethics com. 1991—92, program 1992—93, bd. ops. 1992—93, mem. nominations com., mem. site selection com. 1995—96, CLE com. 1995—96, program 1995—96, CLE com. 1996—97, pub. com. 1996—97, CLE com. 2000—02, honors and awards ethics com. 2002—, 2002—03, named NACUA fellow 1998); mem.: Nat. Sports Law Inst. (bd. advisors 2001—), Sports Lawyers Assn. (bd. dirs. 2001—), Indpls. Bar Assn. (bd. dirs. 2001—), Seattle-King County Bar Assn., Wash. Women Lawyers (pres. Seattle-King County chpt. 1986, state chair candidate endorsement com. 1987, v.p. membership, state bd. dirs. 1987—88, state chair candidate endorsement com. 1988), Wash. State Bar Assn. (chair law sch. liaison com. 1988—89). Office: NCAA PO 6222 Indianapolis IN 46206-6222 E-mail: ecole@ncaa.org.

COLE, EVELYN MARIE, day care administrator; b. Alvon, W.Va., Sept. 14, 1928; d. Melvin Arthur and Lillie Mae (Fifer) C.; m. Delford Lee Cole, Jan. 31, 1950; children: Karen Lee, Phillip Quinton, Jonathon Avery. Owner, adminstr. Evelyn's Home Away from Home Day Care, Roanoke, Va., 1974—. Owner, adminstr. Foster Home and Shelter Home for State Va., Roanoke, 1969-72. Active Christ's Ch. at Northside. Home: 1719 Grandin Rd SW PO Box 4656 Roanoke VA 24015-0656 Office: 1731 Grandin Rd SW Roanoke VA 24015-2815

COLE, FIRST DANA, computer scientist, educator; b. Norwalk, Conn., Mar. 25, 1957; s. George Walter Cole and Elaine Delphine Illions. PhD, Columbia U., 1992. Cert. Unix NADPP, 1998. Prin. Info. Sys. Group, New Haven, 1989—; prof. N.Y. Inst. of Tech., New York, Conn., 1990—2003. Author: New Technologies for Learning. Exec. dir. Oxford Ho. Placement Svcs., New Haven, 1992—2003. Officer Coast Guard, 1992—93. Decorated Exemplary Svc. award U.S. Coast Guard. Fellow: Assn. for Computing Machinery (life; sec. 1981—84). Achievements include discovery of a plan-based metric for program complexity. Home and Office: Information Systems Group POB 200936 Yale Station New Haven CT 06520-0936 E-mail: jdc@jeraldcole.com.

COLE, GEORGE ARTHUR, marketing professional; b. Spokane, Wash., July 12, 1943; s. Russell W. and Ruth J. (Connick) C.; m. Susan Merie Bickell, July 3, 1965; children: Francine Tageant, Spencer Cole. BA, U. Mont., 1965; Grad. Cert. in Internat. Bus., U. San Diego, 1996. Cert. mediator. Pres. Media West, Inc., Spokane and Ferndale, Wash., 1978—, San Diego, 1978—; internat. bus. advisor USAID/Global Tech. Network, Washington and San Diego, 1996-99; econ. devel. dir. City of Imperial Beach, Calif., 1993-96; asst. dir. comms. San Diego State U., 1989-92. Cons. Pacific Southwest Airlines, San Diego, 1980-86. Author: (oral history) Chet Huntley: Reflections, 1972; screenwriter/dir.: (films and videos) Smokin', 1982 (Chgo. Internat. Film Festival award 1983), Community Colleges of Spokane, 1983 (CASE Regional Video awards/Spokane Advt. Fedn. award 1984); anchor/prodr.: (radio series) On the Move, 1972-72 (Sigma Delta Chi award 1971-72). Commr., chair Spokane Housing Authority, 1978-87; bd. dirs. Wash. State ACLU Seattle and Spokane, 1978-79, Spokane Pub. Broadcasting Assn., 1971-74, 78-87. Recipient U.S. Presdl. commendation Pres. Richard Nixon, 1973, Wash. State Gov.'s Cmty. Svc. award, Spokane, 1973. Mem. Internat. Exec. Svc. Corps. (internat. bus. advisor), U. Mont. Alumni Assn. (del. 1990-91). Democrat. Unitarian Universalist. Avocations: running, hiking, travel, writing. Office: LFG&E Internat 663 Greenfield Dr El Cajon CA 92021-2983

COLE, GEORGE THOMAS, lawyer; b. Orlando, Fla., Mar. 14, 1946; s. Robert Bates and Frances (Arnold) C.; m. Peggy Ellen Stimson, May 23, 1981; children: Leslie Elizabeth, Ashley Ellen, Robert Warren. AB, Yale U., 1968; JD, U. Mich., 1975. Bar: Ariz. 1975, U.S. Dist. Ct. Ariz. 1975, U.S. Ct. Appeals (9th cir.) 1978; cert. real estate specialist Ariz. Bar. With Fennemore, Craig, von Ammon, Udall & Powers, Phoenix, 1975-81; ptnr. Fennemore Craig, P.C., Phoenix, 1981—. Mem. Ariz. State U. Coun. for Design Excellence. Served to lt. (j.g.) USN, 1968-71. Fellow: Ariz. Bar Found. (founding); mem.: Maricopa Bar Assn., Ariz. Bar Assn. (coun.real property sect. 1985—88, chmn. 1987—88), Cmty. Assns. Inst., Nat. Golf Found. (assoc.), ULI (cmty. devel. coun. 1995—2001), Ariz. Assn. Home Bldrs., Nat. Assn. Home Bldrs., White Mountain Country Club (Pinetop, Ariz.), Paradise Valley Country Club (Phoenix), Yale Club (pres. 1984). Republican. Methodist. Home: 5102 E Desert Park Ln Paradise Valley AZ 85253-3054 Office: Fennemore Craig 3003 N Central Ave Ste 2600 Phoenix AZ 85012-2913 E-mail: gcole@fclaw.com.

COLE, GLEN DAVID, minister; b. Tacoma, Dec. 21, 1933; s. Ray Milton and Ruth Evelyn (Ranton) C.; m. Mary Ann Von Moos, June 6, 1953; children: Randall Ray, Ricky Jay. BA in Theology, Cen. Bible Coll., 1956; DD, Pacific Coast Bible Coll., 1983. Assoc. pastor Bethel Temple, Dayton, Ohio, 1956—57; pastor Assembly of God, Marion, Ohio, 1957-60, Maple Valley, Wash., 1960-65; assoc. pastor Calvary Temple, Seattle, 1965-67; sr. pastor Evergreen Christian Ctr., Olympia, Wash., 1967-78, Capital Christian Ctr., Sacramento, 1978-95, pastor emeritus, 1995—; dist. supr. Assemblies of God, Sacramento, 1997—. Exec. presbyter Assemblies of God, Springfield, 1985-95; bd. mem., ch. extension plan, Salem, Oreg., 1997-; bd. mem. fin. svcs. group, Assemblies of God, Springfield, Mo., 1998-; trustee Bethany Bible Coll., Santa Cruz, Calif., 1979—; bd. dirs. Cen. Bible Coll., Springfield, Mo., 1988-99; bd. dirs. Calif. Theol. Sem., Fresno, 1985-90. Mem. Rotary (pres. Olympia chpt. 1977-78). Republican. Mem. Assemblies Of God Ch. Office: Assemblies of God 6051 S Watt Ave Sacramento CA 95829-1304 *It seems that the people God uses most are not those with greater ability, or more education, or superior talent but those who become totally dependent on him.*

COLE, HEATHER ELLEN, librarian; b. Rochester, N.Y., Nov. 7, 1942; d. Donald M. and Muriel Agnes (Kimball) C.; m. Stratis Haviaras; 1 child, Elektra Maria Muriel BA, Cornell U., 1964; MS, Simmons Coll., 1973. Mgr. Brentano's, Boston, 1968-70; intern Harvard Coll. Libr., Cambridge, Mass., 1970-73, reference libr., 1973-77, libr., 1977—, Hilles and Lamont Librs., 1977—. Mem. AAUW, ALA, Am. Soc. Info. Sci. (New England chpt.), Assn. Coll. Rsch. Librs. Democrat. Episcopalian. Avocation: gardening. Home: 19 Clinton St Cambridge MA 02139-2303 Office: Harvard Coll Lamont Library Cambridge MA 02138

COLE, HENRY PHILIP, educational psychology educator; b. Buffalo, Jan. 5, 1937; s. Raymond James and Hannah Christina (Shapleigh) C.; m. Marion Margaret Montgomery, Aug. 19, 1961; children: Mark Douglas, David Arthur, Debra Lynn. BS in Chemistry, Nasson Coll., 1958; MEd, SUNY, Buffalo, 1966, EdD, 1968. Chemistry technician WASCO Chem. Co., Sanford, Maine, 1957-58; tchr. physics and sci. Holland (N.Y.) Ctrl. Sch., 1958-59; med. rsch. technician Buffalo Gen. Hosp., 1959-61; tchr. sci. Griffith Inst. and Ctrl. Sch., Springville, N.Y., 1961-65; instr. ednl. psychology SUNY, Buffalo, 1966-68; ednl. psychologist Ea. Regional Inst. for Edn., Syracuse, N.Y., 1968-71; prof. ednl. psychology U. Ky., Lexington, 1971—, prof. preventive medicine, 1990—, head behavioral rsch. aspects safety-health group (BRASH), 1984-97, Vis. prof. Syracuse U., 1968-70; rsch. psychologist U.S. Bur. Mines, Pitts., 1988-89; U.S. del. MINESAFE Internat. Conf., Western Australia, 1993; behavioral safety expert ILO, China, 1993. Author: Measuring Learning in Continuing Education for Engineers and Scientists, 1984; contbr. more than 200 tech. reports, articles to profl. jours., chpts. to books. Cubmaster Boy Scouts Am., Lexington, 1975-77, round table commr., 1976-78; v.p., team. rep. Little League Baseball, Lexington, 1975-78. With U.S. Army, 1959-61. Recipient Disting. Author award Jour. Allied Health, 1981, Best Paper award Am. Soc. Engring. Edn., 1985, Pub. of Yr. award Bur. of Mines-Pitts. Rsch. Ctr., 1987, Tech. Transfer award, 1989, Unsung Hero's award for outstanding rsch. contbns. U. Ky., Exceptional Achievement award for Rsch., Tchg., and Svc. Coll. of Edn., U. Ky., 2000. Mem. APA, APHA, Am. Ednl. Rsch. Assn., Am. Soc. Agrl. Engrs. Republican. Presbyterian. Avocations: jogging, bicycling, reading natural science, farming. Office: University Kentucky Dept Preventive Medicine 1141 Red Mile Rd Ste 102 Lexington KY 40504-9842 Business E-Mail: hcole@uky.edu.

COLE, JACK ELI, physician; b. Matamoras, Pa., Jan. 7, 1915; s. Eli Martin and Louise (Henneberg) C. m. Evelyn Gaston Darragh, Apr. 26, 1941; children: Jack Eli, Thomas, Beverly, Martin, Robert, Leslie, Christopher, Candace, Champa. BS, Pa. State U., 1937; MD, U. Pa., 1941. Diplomate Am. Bd. Family Practice. Intern Wilkes-Barre (Pa.) Gen. Hosp., 1941-42; practice medicine, specializing in family practice Matamoras, Pa., 1946-47; staff St. Luke's Hosp., Bethlehem, Pa., 1948—; practice medicine, specializing in family practice Bethlehem, 1952-68, 1973-89; sec. dept. family practice St. Luke's Hosp., Bethlehem, 1973-88; incorporator, mem. med. staff Muhlenberg Hosp., Bethlehem, 1960—, pres. med. staff, 1961-62; student health physician Lehigh U., Bethlehem, 1948-52; physician Peace Corps, Afghanistan, Swaziland, India, 1968-73; leader mission med. team United Ch. Christ, Honduras, 1987; preceptor Temple U. Med. Sch., Phila., 1978-86. Author: Wandering Voices, 1999, Richard and Sabina, 2001; contbr. poetry to anthologies, children's stories and articles to profl. publs. Charter mem. mission partnership com. N.E. Pa. conf. United Ch. of Christ, 1984. With U.S. Army, 1942-45 Decorated Purple Heart, Combat Medic badge; recipient Recognition award Temple U. Med. Sch., 1979; Boss of Yr. award Allentown Bus. Womens Assn., 1975. Fellow Am. Acad. Family Physicians; mem. AMA, Northampton County Med. Soc., Pa. Med. Soc., Lehigh Valley Acad. Family Physicians (v.p. 1979-81, pres. 1981-83), Pa. Acad. Family Physicians, Am. Acad. Family Physicians. Republican. Avocation: opera. Home: 782 Barrymore Ln Bethlehem PA 18017-2522

COLE, JAMES OTIS, lawyer; b. Florence, Ala., Feb. 6, 1941; s. Calloway and Eula (Reynolds) C.; m. Ada Dolores Cole, Dec. 16, 1961; children: James Otis Jr., Lerone Barrington. BA, Talladega Coll., 1963; JD, Harvard U., 1971. Bar: Ill. 1971, U.S. Dist. Ct. (no. dist.) Ill. 1971, Calif. 1977, U.S. Supreme Ct. 1981. Assoc. Kirkland & Ellis, Chgo., 1971-73; div. counsel The Clorox Co., Oakland, Calif.; sr. v.p., gen. counsel, sec. AutoNation, Inc, Ft. Lauderdale; of counsel Ruden, McClosky, Smith, Schuster & Russell, 2002—. Arbitrator Contra Costa County Superior Ct., Martinez, Calif., 1980—. Counsel East Oakland Youth Devel. Ctr.; bd. dirs. Oakland Ballet, Bay Area Urban League, Oakland; bd. dirs. Black Filmmakers Hall of Fame, Oakland, pres. 1980-83. Mem. ABA, Nat. Bar Assn. (bd. govs. 1981—), Calif. Assn. Black Lawyers (pres.-elect 1986—), Charles Houston Bar Assn. (pres. 1985—), Calif. Bar Jud. Nominees Evaluation Commn. (commr. 1985—). Clubs: Oakland Athletic, Lakeview (Oakland). Home: 10 Nurmi Dr Fort Lauderdale FL 33301-1403 Office: Ruden McClosky Smith Schuster & Russell 200 E Broward Blvd Fort Lauderdale FL 33302*

COLE, JAMES S. academic administrator; b. Mpls., Minn. BS, Stephen F. Austin State U., 1967; DDS, Baylor Coll. Dentistry, 1975. Instr., restorative scis. Baylor Coll. Dentistry, 1977—81, dir. computer svcs., 1981—92, prof., restorative scis., 1992—, interim pres. and dean, 1990, held positions of exec. v.p., assoc. dean, CFO, COO, and vice dean; pres. and treas. Baylor Oral Health Found., 1997—99; interim dean Baylor Coll. Dentistry, 1999—2000; interim pres. Tex. A&M U. Sys. Health Sci. Ctr., 2000—01; dean Baylor Coll. Dentistry, 2000—. Lt. USN, 1967—71. Recipient Dentist of Yr., Dallas County Dental Soc., 2000. Fellow: Internat. Coll. Dentists, Am. Coll. Dentists. Office: 3302 Gaston Ave Dallas TX 75246

COLE, JAMES W. academic administrator; BS, Northeast Mo. State U., Kirksville, 1963; DO, Kans. City Coll. Osteo. Medicine, Mo., 1967. Intern Tucson Gen. Hosp., 1967—68; resident in pathology and lab. medicine Cherry Hill Med. Ctr., NJ, 1976—79; fellow in fed. health care policy Ohio U. Coll. Osteo. Medicine, Athens, 1994—95; dean Midwestern U. Ariz. Coll. Osteo. Medicine, Glendale, 1996—. Office: Ariz Coll Osteo Medicine 19555 N 59th Ave Glendale AZ 85308

COLE, JAMES YEAGER, foundation administrator; b. Cleve., Sept. 20, 1957; s. Charles and Nancy Cole. JD, Blackstone Sch. Law, Dallas, 1980, U. N.C., 1989; MA, M.C.I., London, 1981; PhD, N.W. London U., 1981. CEO Cole Corp., Tallahassee, 1979-81; judge Inst. Advanced Law Study, Las Vegas, 1981-84; cons., sentencing adv. Cullowhee, NC, 1984-2001. Decorated Knight Comdr. Royal Knights Justice, London, Venerable Order of Knigths of Michael the Archangel Knight Chevalier; recipient Presdl. medal of Merit, U.S. Pres. Ronald Reagan, Washington, 1980, Disting. Leadership award, ABA jud. divsn., 1997. Mem.: N.C. Fraternal Order Police, N.C. Sheriff's Assn., Nat. Sherriff's Assn., Am. Fedn. Police, Internat. Bar Assn., Nat. Judges Assn., World Judges Assn., Am. Judges Assn., Maggic Valley C. of C., Island Found., Human Rights Inst., Haywood County C. of C., Heirs, Inc. Avocations: swimming, skiing, volleyball, tennis, movies. Home and Office: 389 Chestnut Walk Dr Waynesville NC 28786 E-mail: jim@forlegalhelp.com.

COLE, JANICE MCKENZIE, former prosecutor; b. Feb. 16, 1947; m. James Carlton Cole. BA summa cum laude, John Jay Coll Criminal Justice, 1975, MPA, 1978; JD, Fordham U., 1979. Bar: N.Y. 1980, N.C. 1983. Asst. U.S. atty. Eastern Dist. N.Y., 1979-83; sole practitioner, 1983-89; with firm Cole & Cole, 1989-90; dist. ct. judge First Jud. Dist. N.C., 1990-94; U.S. atty. N.C. Eastern Dist., 1994—2001; sole practitioner, 2001—. Office: Ste 106 1072 Harvey Point Rd Hertford NC 27944-1461

COLE, JEFFREY CLARK, public relations professional; b. Toledo, Jan. 20, 1966; s. Frank Herbert, Jr. and Mary Therese ((Clark)) Cole. BA, U. Toledo, 1989, MEd, 1996. Cert. fund raising exec., Nat. Soc. Fund Raising Execs. Admissions counselor U. Toledo, 1989-92, devel. officer, 1992-97; comm. specialist Dana Corp., Toledo, 1997-99, mgr., pub. rels., 1999-2000, mgr. mktg. com., 2000—. Instr. comm. U. Toledo, 1992-97, adj. prof. comm., 1997—. Editor-in-chief The Collegian, U. Toledo, 1988-89. Pres. student govt. U. Toledo, 1987-88; alumni bd. dirs. St. Francis deSales High Sch., Toledo, 1989-92; bd. mgrs. Univ. YMCA, 1991-95; mem. alumni affiliate steering com. U. Toledo Coll. Arts and Scis., 1992-97; mem. profl. staff coun. U. Toledo, 1993-96, chair, 1995-96; Lucas County Rep. Ctrl. Com., 1996—; exec. com. Lucas County Rep., 1998—; devel. adv. com. St. Francis de Sales H.S., Toledo, 2000—; bd. dirs. Mobile Meals of Greater Toledo, 1999—, vice chair, 1999—; trustee Collegian Media Found., 2001—; bd. trustees U. Toledo Student Affairs Com., 2002—, chair, 2003—. Recipient Crystal award for pub. rels. Women in Comm., Inc., 1996; named Outstanding Young Alumnus, U. Toledo, 1999. Mem. Blue Key Nat. Honor Soc. (hon.), Toledo Press Club (award 1989, Excellence in Media award 1995), Internat. Assn. Bus. Communicators, Soc. Profl. Journalists, Toledo Club, Pub. Rels. Soc. Am. (accredited pub. rels.), Omicron Delta Kappa Soc. (adv.). Republican. Avocations: travel, genealogy, writing. Home: 3843 Woodmont Rd Toledo OH 43613-4323 Office: Dana Corp PO Box 1000 Toledo OH 43697-1000 E-mail: jeff.cole@dana.com.

COLE, JEROME FOSTER, research company executive; b. Cin., Aug. 8, 1940; s. George F. and Arlene M. (McCoy) C.; m. Virginia E. Vaughn, July 6, 1963; children: Cheryl, Robert. BS in Pharmacy, U. Cin., 1962, MS, 1965, ScD in Environ. Health, 1968. Registered pharmacist, Ohio. Indsl. hygienist Procter and Gamble Co., Cin., 1968-69; mgr. environ. health Internat. Lead Zinc Rsch. Orgn., N.Y.C., 1969-73, dep. dir., 1973-75, v.p., 1975-83, pres. Research Triangle Park, N.C., 1983—. Served to sgt. USAFR, 1967-68. Mem. Soc. Toxicology, Am. Indsl. Hygiene Assn., N.Y. Acad. Scis., Governors Club. Avocations: sailing, tennis, golf.

COLE, JESSIE MAE, nursing assistant, writer; b. McGehee, Ark., Nov. 19, 1925; d. Alonso Smith and Estelle Hursey; m. Amos Burns, May 15, 1942; children: Bobbie D., Joyce R.; m. Mose Eddie Cole (div. Nov. 1972). AA, Fresno City Coll, 1985; BA, Charter Oak State Coll., 1999. Cert. tchr. Calif., 1979. Beautician Beauty Culture, Chgo., 1956—76; nursing asst. Hope Manor Facility, Fresno, Calif., 1983—. Pvt. piano tchr., Fresno, 1981—. Author: (website) How to Read Sheet Music, 1997. Mem. Wall of Tolerance Nat. Campaign for Tolerance, 2002—03; bible study instr. Coll. Ch. of Christ, Fresno, 1975—. Mem.: Nat. Assn. Black Journalists. Home: 3749 N Fruit Apt C Fresno CA 93705

COLE, JOAN HAYS, social worker, clinical psychologist; b. Pitts., Sept. 4, 1929; d. Frank L. Wertheimer and Edith H. Einstein; m. Robert M. Wendlinger, June, 1984; children: Geoffrey F., Douglas R., Peter Hays. BA, Western Res. U., 1951; MSSA in Social Work, Case Western Res. U., 1962; PhD, Wright Inst., 1975. Cert. clin. social worker; diplomate Am. Bd. Orthopsychiat. Social group worker Alta House Settlement House, Cleve., 1958-59; housing dir. Cleve. Urban League, 1961-62; dir. Citizens for Safe Housing, Cleve., 1963; housing dir. United Planning Orgn., Washington, 1963-68; asst. prof. cmty. orgn. U. Md. Sch. Social Work and Cmty. Planning, Balt., 1968—72; assoc. prof. Lone Mountain Coll., San Francisco, 1975-78; psychotherapist, supr., orgnl. cons., Berkeley, Calif., 1977—. Cons. various pub. and vol. social welfare, health and housing agys., 1969—; mem. adj. faculty Union Grad. Sch. and Antioch West Coll., 1978-80; lectr. U. Calif. Sch. Social Welfare, Berkeley, 1980-84; mem. faculty Berkeley Psychotherapy Inst., 1981—, pres., 1983-85. Grantee NIMH, 1971-72, Sr. Social Work Career Devel. grantee, 1973-75. Fellow Soc. Clin. Social Work (diplomate), Am. Orthopsychiat. Assn.; mem. NASW, ACLU, Soc. for Study Social Issues, Acad. Cert. Social Workers, Nat. Conf. on Social Welfare and Psychotherapists for Social Responsibility. Office: 6239 College Ave Oakland CA 94618-1384

COLE, JOHN ADAM, insurance executive; b. Odessa, Tex., May 6, 1951; s. Alling and Millicent (McWilliam) C.; m. Karen Elisabeth Jones, June 28, 1974 (dec. May 2002); children: J. Adam Jr., Robert H., Kathryn E. A in Occupational Studies in Acctg., Bus.i, Utica (N.Y.) Sch. Commerce, 1973; postgrad., New Sch. Social Rsch., 1984, Am. Coll., Bryn Mawr, Pa. ChFC, CLU. Sales mgr. Mohawk Frozen Foods, Marcy, N.Y., 1973-77; sole propr. From the C's, Inc., Rome, N.Y., 1975-77; agt., dist. asst. Equitable Fin. Svcs., Rome, 1978-83; advanced mktg. specialist Farm Family Ins. Cos., Albany, N.Y., 1984, dir. agt. and mgr. devel., 1985-87, dir. devel. and advanced life sales, 1987-96, dir. advanced markets, 1996-97, dir. life sales, 1997—2003, dir. life and fin. svcs., 2003—; mem. mktg. com. Farm Bur. Bank, 1998—. Adj. instr. various profl. tng. orgns., Rome, Utica and Albany, 1981—. Pres. Rome Cmty. Concerts Assn., 1978-80, Voorheesville (N.Y.) Ctrl. Sch. Bd., 1990—; cubmaster Boy Scouts Am.; mem. Holland Patent (N.Y.) Ctrl. Sch. Bd., 1982-85; mem. parents adv. bd. Pine Bush Little League, New Scotland Pop Warner, Guilderland Babe Ruth League; coach Ea. N.Y. State Champions team Babe Ruth Allstars, 1995; found. dir. Voorheesville Cmty. Schs. Found., 1999—. Mem. Ea. N.Y. Soc. CLUs & ChFCs (bd. dirs. 1986-91), Albany Assn. Life Underwriters (bd. dirs. 1987-92), Mohawk Valley Life Underwriters (pres., chmn. 1980-84), Kiwanis, N.Y. State Newsletter award 1992), Masons. Republican. Methodist. Office: Farm Family Ins Co PO Box 656 Albany NY 12201-0656

COLE, JOHN DEWEY, management consultant; b. Ironton, Mo., Apr. 1, 1942; s. Dewey John and Ola Jeanetta Cole; m. Barbara Jean Egan; 1 child, Shane. MBA, Trinity Coll. U., 1999. Mgr. Nat. Steel, Granite City, Ill., 1970—90; ptnr. Third Kingdom Concepts, Milw., 1990—97; cons., inventor Michal David Group Quantum Sys. Cons., Port Washington, Wis., 1997—. Author: Mysticism of Commerce. Trustee City Govt. Police Dept., Pontoon Beach, 1968—72; ptnr. Boy Scouts, Ozakee County. Named Best Shortline RR USA, Terminal RR Assn., 1988. Fellow: Masonic Lodge (32d degree); mem.: Am. Assn. Iron and Steel Engrs., Jr. Achievement. Achievements include invention of railroad remote brake system. Avocation: exploration of theories and physical fact. Home: 8501 West Melvina Milwaukee WI 53222 Personal E-mail: jcole5@wi.rr.com.

COLE, JOHN POPE, JR., lawyer; b. Washington, Jan. 12, 1930; s. John Pope and Helen (Gorman) C.; m. Patsy Nan Moss, Mar. 20, 1960; children— John Moss, Nina Gorman. BS, Auburn U., 1953; LL.B., George Washington U., 1956. Bar: D.C. 1956, Md. 1956, Ga. 1961. Atty. FCC, Washington, 1956-57; ptnr. Smith & Pepper, Washington, 1957-66, Cole, Raywid & Braverman, Washington, 1966—; staff U.S. Ho. Reps., Washington, 1961-62. Served with USAF, 1948-49. Home: 5309 Portsmouth Rd Bethesda MD 20816-2930 Office: Cole Raywid & Braverman 1919 Pennsylvania Ave NW Washington DC 20006-3458 E-mail: jcole@crblaw.com.

COLE, JOHN PRINCE, lawyer, university official; b. Carrollton, Ga., Mar. 18, 1963; m. Mary Stewart Donovan. AB, Harvard U., 1985; JD magna cum laude, Mercer Law Sch., 1991. Bar: Ga. 1991, U.S. Dist. Ct. (no., mid. dist.) Ga. 1991, U.S. Ct. Appeals (11th cir.) 1991. Law clerk Mitchell, Coppedge, Wester, Bisson & Miller, Dalton, Ga., 1989, Ga. Atty. Gen., Atlanta, 1990; assoc. Anderson, Walker & Reichert, Macon, Ga., 1991-94; gen. asst. to pres. Mercer U., Macon, Ga., 1994—2000, v.p. univ. admissions, 2001—. Trustee First Bapt. Ch., Macon, 1993-97, Ga. Children's Home, 1996-2000, bd. chair, 1999-2000; funds allocation com. United Way Ctrl. Ga., 1992-94. Maj. USAR, Bosnia, 2001. Mem. ABA, Nat. Assn. Coll. and Univ. Attys., Macon Bar Assn. (treas. 1997-98, sec. 1998-99, pres. elect 1999-2001, pres. 2001-02), Lawyers Found. Ga., Leadership GA, Phi Kappa Phi. Democrat. Avocations: hiking, music, golf. Office: Mercer U 1400 Coleman Ave Macon GA 31207-0003

COLE, JOHN WALLACE, retired anthropologist, researcher, educator, consultant; b. Oshkosh, Wis., July 7, 1934; s. Wallace Allen and Helan Audry Cole; m. Ellan Irene Leonard, Mar. 24, 1956; children: Sheryl Ann, Judith Lynn Tazelaar. AB in Anthropology, U. of Mich., 1952—57, MA in Anthropology,

1961—65, PhD, 1965—69; D Polit. Economy (hon.), U. Trento, Italy, 2002. Asst. prof. Wayne State U., 1967—71; vis. prof. U. of Bucharest, Romania, 1974—75; vis. scholar Columbia U., 1977—78, City Univerity of NY Grad. Ctr., New York, NY, 1977—78; vis. lectr. Yale U., 1980—80; hon. vis. fellow U. of Amsterdam, Netherlands, 1984—84; prof. U. of Mass., 1971—2000, prof. emeritus, 2001—. Cons. Internat. Rsch. and Exchanges Bd. (IREX), N.Y.C., 1975—78; editl. bd. jour. Ethnologia Europaea, Berlin, 1990—; cons. Internat. Rsch. and Exchanges Bd. (IREX), United States, 1991—94. Author: The Hidden Frontier, 1974, new edit., 1999, (ethnographic monograph) Estate Inheritance in the Italian Alps; editor: (cultural anthropology book) Ethnicity and Nationalism in Southeastern Europe, (research report monograph) Economy, Soc. and Culture in Contemporary Romania; contbr. article, numerous articles and book chapters. First lt. Army Signal Corps, 1957—61, Germany. Recipient Award for Rsch. in Romania, Ford Found., 1975 - 1978, Michelangelo Mariani Internat. Prize, Ethnographic Mus. of the Trentino, 1996; fellow Sr. Fellowship, Fulbright-Hays Found., 1974; grantee Rsch. Grant, NSF, 1965 - 1967, Support Grant for Conf. on Romania, Internat. Rsch. and Exchanges Bd., 1978, Rsch. in Tyrol, Wenner-Gren Found. for Anthrop. Rsch., 1988, Rsch. on Romanian Pronatalism, Internat. Rsch. and Exchanges Bd., 1992, Grant to Study Romanian Lang., Am. Coun. of Learned Societies. Fellow: Soc. for the Anthropology of Europe (pres. 1988—90), Northeastern Anthropology Assn. (pres. 1998—2000), Am. Anthrop. Assn.; mem.: Mass. Soc. of Professors (pres. 1987—91), Mass. Teachers Assn. (dir. 1989—94). Achievements include research in Political economy of property inheritance; contributions to debates in critical anthropology; contributions to debates in political economy; contributions to anthropology of Europe. Home: 642 West St Brookfield VT 05036 Office: Department of Anthropology Machmer Hall University of Massachusett Amherst MA 01003 Home Fax: none. Personal E-mail: jwcole@anthro.umass.edu. E-mail: jwcole@anthro.umass.edu.

COLE, JOHNNETTA BETSCH, university president, educator; b. Jacksonville, Fla., Oct. 19, 1936; d. John Thomas and Mary Frances (Lewis) Betsch; m. Robert Eugene Cole (div. 1982); children: David, Aaron, Ethan; m. Arthur J. Robinson, Jr. (div.). Student, Fisk U., 1953; BA in Sociology, Oberlin Coll., 1957; MA in Anthropology, Northwestern U., Evanston, Ill., 1959, PhD, 1967. Instr. UCLA, 1964; dir. black studies Wash. State U., Pullman, 1969-70; prof. anthropology U. Mass., Amherst, 1970-83, assoc. provost undergrad. edn., 1981-83; vis. prof. Hunter Coll., N.Y.C., 1983-84, prof. anthropology, 1983-87, dir. Inter-Am. Affairs Program, 1984-87; pres. Spelman Coll., Atlanta, 1987-97, pres. emeritus, 1997—; pres. Bennett Coll. for Women, Greensboro, NC, 2003—. Corp. bd. dirs. Merck & Co., Inc., Atlanta Falcons; presdl. disting. prof. anthropology, women's studies and Afro-Am. studies Emory U., 1998-2001. Author, editor: Anthropology for the Eighties, 1982, All American Women, 1986, Anthropology for the Nineties, 1988, Conversations: Straight Talk with America's Sister President, 1993, Dream the Boldest Dreams, 1998; author: (with Beverly Guy-Sheftall) Gender Talk: The Struggle for Women's Equality in African American Communicies, 2003; mem. editl. bd. The Black Scholar. Recipient numerous hon. degrees. Fellow Am. Anthrop. Assn.; mem. Am. Acad. Arts and Scis., Assn. Black Anthropologists (past pres.). Congregationalist. Office: Bennett Coll for Women 900 E Washignton St Greensboro NC 27401 E-mail: jcole@bennett.edu.

COLE, JONATHAN JAY, aquatic scientist, researcher; b. N.Y.C., Jan. 14, 1953; s. Leonard and Selma Ruth (Greenblatt) C.; m. Nina F. Caraco, Nov. 25, 1980; children: Aaska H. Puccoon, Zak LeH Puccoon, Champ Elijah, Ganesh Caraco. BA, Amherst Coll., 1976; PhD, Cornell U., 1982. Post-doctoral fellow Woods Hole (Mass.) Oceanographic Inst., 1981-82, Marine Biol. Lab., Woods Hole, 1982-83; asst. scientist Inst. Ecosystems Studies, Millbrook, N.Y., 1983-89, assoc. scientist, 1989-95; scientist, 1995—. Editor: Comparative Analysis of Ecosystems, 1991; co-editor: Handbook of Methods in Aquatic Microbial Ecology, 1995; contbr. articles to profl. jours. Mem. Am. Soc. Microbiology, Am. Soc. Limnology and Oceanography (editl. bd. 1987-90, mem.-at-large 1994—, pres-elect. 2003—), Internat. Soc. Limnology. Achievements include elucidation of the role of microorganisms in aquatic ecosystems. Office: Inst Ecosystem Studies 65 Sharon Tpke Millbrook NY 12543

COLE, JONATHAN RICHARD, sociologist, academic administrator; b. N.Y.C., Aug. 27, 1942; s. Richard and Sylvia (Dym) C.; m. Joanna Miller Lewis, June 5, 1968; children: Daniel Lewis, Susanna Dora. BA, Columbia U., 1964, PhD, 1969. Asst. prof. sociology Columbia U., N.Y.C., 1969-73, assoc. prof., 1973-76, prof., 1976—, Quetelet prof. social sci., 1989—2001, dir. Ctr. for Social Scis., 1979-87, v.p. Arts and Scis., 1987-89, provost, 1989-94, provost dean of faculties, 1994—2003, John Mitchell Mason prof., 2002—. Adj. prof. Rockefeller U., 1983-85; pres. Reid Hall Inc.; cons. Ford Found., NSF, Nat. Acad. Scis., Russell Sage Found., AT&T. Author: Social Stratification in Science, 1973, Fair Science: Women in the Scientific Community, 1979, Peer Review in the National Science foundation, Vol. 1, 1978, Vol. 2, 1981, The Wages of Writing: Per Word, Per Price, or Perhaps, 1986, The Outer Circle, 1990, The Research Library in a Time of Discontent, 1994; editor Am. Jour. Sociology; contbr. articles to profl. jours. Recipient Cavaliere Ufficiale Republic Italy, 1996, Commendatore of Gidine al Merito della Republilica Italiana, 2003; Guggenheim fellow, 1975-76, Ctr. for Advanced Study in Behavioral Scis. fellow, 1975-76. Fellow AAAS, Am. Acad. Arts and Scis.; mem. Am. Sociol. Assn., Internat. Sociol. Assn., Ea. Sociol. Assn., Soc. Rsch. Assn. (hon.), Coun. Fgn. Rels. Home: 404 Riverside Dr New York NY 10025-1861 Office: Columbia U 205 Low Libr 116th & Broadway New York NY 10027

COLE, KATHLEEN ANN, advertising agency executive, retired social worker; b. Nov. 22, 1946; d. James Scott and Kathryn Gertrude (Borisch) Cole; m. Brian Brandt, Mar. 21, 1970. BA, Miami U., 1968; MSW, U. Mich., 1972; MM, Northwestern U., 1978. Social worker Hamilton County Welfare Dept., Cin., 1969—70, Lucas County Children Svcs. Bd., Toledo, 1970—74, East Maine Sch. Dist., Niles, Ill., 1974—77; account supr. Leo Burnett Advt. Agy., Chgo., 1978—93; primary therapist Lifeline, Chgo., 1994—95; acct. dir. GreenHouse Comm., 1995—2001. Field instr. Loyola U., Chgo., 1976—77. Mem. North Shore United Meth. Congregation. Mem.: NASW, Kellogg Alumni Assn., Northwestern U. Prof. Women's Assn., Miami U. Alumni Assn. (dir. 1976—), Acad. Cert. Social Workers (chair pub. rels. task force). Home: 414 Kelling Ln Glencoe IL 60022-1113 E-mail: colemarketing@attbi.com.

COLE, KENNETH DUANE, architect; b. Ft. Wayne, Ind., Jan. 23, 1932; s. Wolford J. and Helen Francis (McDowell) Cole; m. Carolyn Lou Meyer, Apr. 25, 1953; children: David Brent, Denelle Hope, Diana Faith, Dawn Love. Student, Ft. Wayne Art Inst., 1950-51; BS in Architecture, U. Cin., 1957. Draftsman/intern Humbrecht Assocs., Ft. Wayne, 1957-58; ptnr., arch. Cole-Matott, Archs./Planners, Ft. Wayne, 1959-94, Cole & Cole Archs., Ft. Wayne, 1995—. Mem. adv. bd. Gen. Svcs. Adminstrn., Region 5, 1976, 78. Prin. works include Weisser Pk. Jr. HS, 1963, Brandt Hall, 1965, Bonsib Bldg., 1967, Lindley Elem. Sch., 1969, Young Elem. Sch., 1972, Study Elem. Sch., 1975, Old City Hall Renovation, 1978, Peoples Trust Bank Adminstrv. Svcs. Ctr., 1979, Cole Residence (Design award, 1988), Ossian Office Old 1st Nat. Bank, 1988, Perimeter Security Wall, Ind. State Prison. Bd. dirs. Ft. Wayne Art Inst., 1969—74, Izaak Walton League Am., Ft. Wayne, 1970—76, Arch. Inc., Ft. Wayne, 1975—77, Downtown Ft. Wayne Assn., 1977—82, Hist. Soc. Ft. Wayne and Allen County, 1982—88. Mem.: AIA (bd. dirs. No. INd. 1971—74, pres. 1974), Am. Arbitration Assn. (panel arbitrators 1980—96), Ft. Wayne Soc. Archs. (pres. 1970—71), Ind. Soc. Archs. (bd. dirs. 1973—76, sec. 1976, citation for remodeling Bonsib Bldg. 1978), Ft. Wayne C. of C. Lutheran. Home: 11602 Stellhorn Rd New Haven IN 46774-9775 Office: Cole and Cole Archs 903 W Berry St Fort Wayne IN 46802-3917 E-mail: kennethcole@grinsfelderarchitects.com.

COLE, LEWIS GEORGE, lawyer; b. N.Y.C., Mar. 9, 1931; s. Ralph David and Emma (Balterman) C.; m. Sara Livingston, June 22, 1952; children: Elizabeth, Peter. BS in Econ., U. Pa., 1951; LLB, Yale U., 1954. Bar: N.Y. 1954. Ptnr. Stroock & Stroock & Lavan, LLP, N.Y.C., 1958—. Bd. dirs. Ametek, Inc. Served as 1st lt. U.S. Army, 1954-57. Mem. ABA, Assn. Bar City N.Y., N.Y. State Bar Assn. Office: Stroock & Stroock & Lavan LLP 180 Maiden Ln New York NY 10038-4925

COLE, LINDA SUE, grant program planner, computer software professional; b. Orange Park, Fla., Jan. 14, 1951; d. Harold Earl and Alma (Griffis) Cole; m. Stuart Curtis Madsen, June 22, 1974 (div. July 1978). AA, St. John's River C.C., 1971; BS in Journalism, U. Fla., 1973. Cert. tchr. Fla. Public info. specialist Alachua County Bd. of County Commrs., Gainesville, Fla., 1974-76; comms. specialist Jacksonville C. of C., 1976-77; juvenile ct. liason, sr. counselor City of Jacksonville, 1977-78; news reporter Palm Beach (Fla.) Daily News, 1978-80; mgr. Terminus Media, Atlanta, 1980-83; cons. Jr. Achievement of Jacksonville, 1982-83; profl. cons. City of Jacksonville, 1983-84; planning and devel. dir. N.E. Fla. Cmty. Action Agy., Jacksonville, 1984-86, dept. head, 1986-87; grant adminstr. Putnam County Bd. of County Commrs., Palatka, Fla., 1988-91; grant adminstrn. cons. Sims Design Cons., Inc., Jacksonville, 1992-95; tech. support rep. AT&T Solutions/Customer Care, Jacksonville, 1996-98; grants human svcs. planner, program Sterling TQM Bd. Cmty. Svcs. Dept., City of Jacksonville, 1998—. Author: A Smile Goes Wild, 1994, and You Can Be Like This, 2001; contbr. articles. Cons., spkrs. bur. Jr. Achievement of Jacksonville, 1983-84; annual jail and bail vol. Am. Cancer Soc. of Jacksonville, 1984, 89; mem. Fla. beautification recycling com., Putnam, Fla., 1990-91; bd. dirs. Putnam County Friends of the Libr., Putnam County, 1989-93; staff dir. Citizen's Adv. Task Force for Cmty. Devel., 1989-91. Recipient Fla. Gov. Sterling award, 2001, Svc. award, U.S. Dept. Justice, 2000. Mem. Am. Assn. Planners, U. Fla. Alumni Assn., Woodmen of World. Democrat. Lutheran. Avocations: reading, writing, sports, computers, sewing. Home: 3145 Belden St Apt 1 Jacksonville FL 32207-3751

COLE, LOIS LORRAINE, retired elementary school educator; b. Rock Lick, Ky., Oct. 18, 1932; d. Charles Lorraine and Gwendolyn Pearl (Johnson) Blanchard; m. John Hamilton Cole, Jr., July 10, 1953; children: Stephen Wesley, Pamela Cole Winningham, Paula Cole Bruner. BS in Elem. Edn. cum laude, Ind. Wesleyan U., Marion, 1954; postgrad., Miami U., Oxford, Ohio, 1974, 82. Cert. kindergarten and elem. tchr., Ohio. Tutor of handicapped Marengo (Ohio) Elem. Sch., 1955-56; tchr. 6th and 7th grade lang. arts Harmony Elem. Sch., Mingo Junction, Ohio, 1957-59; instr. English God's Bible Sch., Cin., 1963-64; tchr. Parents Coop. Kindergarten, Cin., 1964-68, Mt. Healthy City Schs., Cin., 1968-94, ret., 1994. Tutor PALS, Mt. Healthy, Ohio, 1991, Easley (S.C.) Pub. Schs., 1995-96. Tchr., primary supt. Galbraith Rd. Ch. of God Sunday Sch., Cin., 1970-72, Fairfield Ch. of Nazarene Sunday Sch., Fairfield, Ohio, 1973-77; former local ch. dir. Wesleyan Women Internat., Easley, 1996-99; former 1st v.p. Newcomers' Club, Easley, 1997. Mem. Mt. Health Edn. Assn. (bldg. rep. 1986-87), Ohio Congress Parents and Tchrs. (life). Republican. Wesleyan. Avocations: reading, photography, travel, flower gardening, music. Home: 245 Andover Turn Easley SC 29642-8803 E-mail: jonlo2002@aol.com.

COLE, LUTHER FRANCIS, former state supreme court associate justice; b. Alexandria, La., Oct. 25, 1925; s. Clem and Catherine (Wiley) C.; m. Juanita Barton, Mar. 9, 1945; children: Frances Jeannette, Jeffrey Martin, Christopher Warren. Student, La. Tech. U., 1943-44; JD, La. State U., 1950. Ptnr. Cole, Mengis & Durant, Baton Rouge, 1950-66; judge 19th Jud. Dist., Baton Rouge, 1966-75, chief judge, 1975-79; judge Ct. Appeals, Baton Rouge, 1979-86; assoc. justice Supreme Ct. La., New Orleans, 1986-92. Chmn. Jud. Budgetary Control Bd., 1990-92; mem. La. Bd. Ethics for Elected Ofcls., 1994-95, La. Commn. on Law Enforcement and Adminstrn. of Criminal Justice, 1996—. Rep. La. Legis., Baton Rouge, 1964-66; v.p. Merchants Assn., Baton Rouge, 1954; chmn. awards Boy Scouts Am., Baton Rouge, 1956; mem. Civic Ctr. com., Baton Rouge, 1971-74; bd. dirs. Blundon Home, Baton Rouge, 1984-86. Served to lt. (j.g.) USN, 1943-46. Mem. ABA (ann. meeting 1991, Jury Standards award 1991), La. Bar Assn., Baton Rouge Bar Assn. (pres. 1966), La. Dist. Judges Assn. (pres. 1972-73). Clubs: Exchange (Baton Rouge) (pres. 1954). Democrat. Baptist. Avocations: hunting, cooking. Home: 9213 Hilltrace Ave Baton Rouge LA 70809-2614

COLE, MAX, artist; b. Hodgeman County, Kans., Feb. 14, 1937; d. Jack Delmont C. and Bertha (Law) Fakes; m. Richard Cole, Sept. 4, 1955 (dec. April 1958); children: Douglas, Janet, Cindy. BA, Fort Hays State U., 1961; MFA, U. Ariz., 1964. One-man shows include Louver Gallery, L.A., 1978, 80, Sidney Janis Gallery, N.Y.C., 1977, 80, Zabriskie Gallery, N.Y., 1987, Haines Gallery, San Francisco, 1988, 93, 96, 98, Galerie Schlegl, Zurich, 1990, 96, 99, 2000, Mus. Folkwang, Essen, Germany, 1993, Kunstraum Kassel (Germany), 1992, Roswell (N.Mex.) Mus. and Art Ctr., 1996, Stark Gallery, N.Y., Galerie Michael Strum, Stuttgart, 1997, 99, Mus. Modern Art, Otterndorf, Germany, 1998, Haus Konstructive und Konkrete Junst, Zurich, 2001Walter Storms Gallery, Munich, 2002, Kunstverein, Aschaffenberg, Germany, 2002; exhibited in group shows including L.A. County Mus. Art, 1976, Corcoran Gallery Art, Washington, 1977, La Jolla Mus., 1980, Santa Barbara Mus., 1980, Mus. Fine Arts of N.Mex., 1984, Neuberger Mus., Purchase, N.Y., 1984, Marilyn Pearl Gallery, N.Y.C., 1985, Pratt Manhattan Ctr. Gallery, 1985, UCLA, 1988, Nat. Gallery Modern Art, New Delhi, 1988, Panza Found., Verese, Italy, 1995, Aagauer Kunsthaus, Aarau, Switzerland, 1995, Trento (Italy) Mus., 1996, Galerie Schlegl, Zurich, 1996, Manif, 1997, Internat. Art Forum, Seoul, 1997, Mus. Modern Art, Otterndorf, Germany, 1998, Haines Gallery, San Francisco, 1998; represented in permanent collections L.A. County Mus. Art, Newport Harbor Mus. Art, La Jolla Mus. Contemporary Art, Mus. N.Mex., Dallas Mus. Art, Santa Barbara Mus., Everson Mus., Tel Aviv Mus., La. Mus., Van Der Heyt Mus., Wuppertal, Germany, Denmark, Panza Collection, Italy, Diozesan Mus., Cologne, Chiat Found., N.Y., Panza Collection, Italy, Lembach Haus, Munich, Ingolstaadt Mus., Germany. Address: PO Box 56 Ruby NY 12475

COLE, MERRILL GRANT, language educator; b. Chapel Hill, N.C., Apr. 16, 1966; s. Merrill Grant Cole and Carole Petit Lapensohn; life ptnr. Jeffrey Stackey, Jan. 3, 2003. BA, New Coll. Fla., 1990; MFA, Cornell U., 1993; PhD, U. Wash., 1999. Tchg. asst. U. Wash., Seattle, 1995—99, instr. English, 1999—2001; asst. prof. English U. Minn., Morris, Minn., 2001—02; adj. faculty Gulf Coast C.C., Panama City, Fla., 2002. Contbr. articles to profl. jours. Observer World Trade Orgn. meeting Health Global Access Project, Seattle, 1999. Mem.: Modern Lang. Assn.

COLE, MONROE, neurologist, educator; b. N.Y.C., Mar. 21, 1933; s. Harry and Sylvia (Firman) C.; m. Merritt Ellen Frindel, June 15, 1958; children: Elizabeth Anne, Victoria, Scott Frindel, Pamela Catherine. AB cum laude, Amherst Coll., 1953; MD magna cum laude, Georgetown U., 1957. Diplomate Am. Bd. Psychiatry and Neurology. Intern in medicine Seton Hall Coll. Medicine, Jersey City, 1957-58, asst. resident in medicine, 1958-59; asst. resident in neurology Mass. Gen. Hosp., Boston, 1959-60, rsch. fellow in neuropathology, 1960-61, rsch. fellow in neurology, 1961-62; teaching fellow in neurology Harvard U., Cambridge, Mass., 1959-60, 61-62, teaching fellow in neuropathology, 1960-61; clin. instr. in neurology Georgetown U., Washington, 1962-65; asst. prof. neurology, assoc. in anatomy Bowman Gray Sch. Medicine, Wake Forest U., Winston-Salem, N.C., 1965-69, assoc. prof., assoc. in anatomy, 1969-70; assoc. prof. neurology Case Western Res. U., Cleve., 1970, clin. assoc. prof., 1972—, assoc. prof., 1989-93, prof., 1993—2000; chief neurology Highland View Hosp., Cleve., 1970-72; neurologist U. Hosps. Cleve.; prof. emeritus Case Western Res. U., Cleve., 2000—. Contbr. chpts. and articles to med. publs. Served to capt. U.S. Army, 1962-65 Fellow ACP, Am. Acad. Neurology, AHA Stroke Coun.; mem. N.Y. Acad. Scis., Acad. of Aphasia, Assn. for Rsch. in Nervous and Mental Disease, Am. Assn. Neuropathologists (assoc.), Am. Neurol. Assn., Alpha Omega Alpha Office: Univ Hosps Cleve Dept Neurology 11100 Euclid Ave Cleveland OH 44106-1736 E-mail: mcole@nacs.net.

COLE, NANCY STOOKSBERRY, educational research executive; b. Brenham, Tex., Nov. 29, 1942; d. Joe Brady and Grace Darling (Pyburn) S.; m. James W.L. Cole, June 4, 1966; 1 child, David Leverett. BA, Rice U., 1964; MA, U. N.C., 1967, PhD, 1968. Rsch. psychologist Am. Coll. Testing Program, Iowa City, 1968-71, dir. test devel., 1971-73, asst. v.p., 1973-74; from assoc. prof. to prof. U. Pitts., 1975-85; prof., dean edn. U. Ill., Champaign, 1985-89; exec. v.p. Ednl. Testing Svc., Princeton, N.J., 1989-93; pres., 1994-2000; sr. advisor, 2000—. Contbr. articles on ednl. testing to profl. jours. Fellow Am. Psychol. Assn.; mem. Nat. Acad. Edn., Nat. Coun. on Measurement in Edn. (pres. 1983-84), Am. Ednl. Rsch. Assn. (pres. 1988-89).

COLE, NATALIE MARIA, singer; b. L.A., Feb. 6, 1950; d. Nathaniel Adam and Maria (Hawkins) C.; m. Marvin J. Yancy, July 30, 1976 (div.); m. Andre Fisher (div.). BA in Psychology, U. Mass., 1972. Rec. singles and albums, 1975—; albums include Dangerous, 1985, Everlasting, 1987, The Natalie Cole Collection, 1987, Inseparable, Thankful, Good To Be Back, 1989, Unforgettable, 1991 (4 grammys, 3 grammys 1992), Too Much Weekend, 1992, I'm Ready, 1992, I've Got Love On My Mind, 1992, Take A Look, 1993 (Grammy award nominee best jazz vocal 1994), Holly and Ivy, 1994, Stardust (2 Grammy awards), Magic of Christmas, 1999; television appearances include Lily in Winter, USA, 1994. Recipient Grammy award for best new artist, best Rhythm and Blues female vocalist 1975, 76; recipient 1 gold single, 3 gold albums; recipient 2 Image awards NAACP 1976, 77; Am. Music award 1978, other awards. Mem. AFTRA, Nat. Assn. Rec. Arts and Scis., Delta Sigma Delta. Baptist. Office: care Jennifer Allen 8500 Wilshire Blvd Ste 700 Beverly Hills CA 90211

COLE, PATRICIA EISENBISE, educational organzation executive; b. Kansas City, Kans. d. Robert Lee and Martha Jeanne Eisebise; m. James Howard Cole, Dec. 4, 1987. BA, U. South Fla., 1979. CPA. Staff asst. Arthur Andersen & Co. CPAs, Tampa, 1979-81, sr. auditor, 1981-84, audit mgr., 1984-86; bus. mgr. Yellowstone Assn., Yellowstone National Park, Wyo., 1987-89, exec. dir., 1989—. Contbr. articles to profl. jours. Bd. dirs. Nat. Assn. Accountants, St. Petersburg, Fla., 1985-86, Conf. Nat. Park Cooperating Assns., Charles Town, W.Va., 1993-2000; treas. Assn. Ptnrs. Pub. Lands, Millersville, Md., 1994-98, v.p., 1998-2000; founding bd. dirs., treas. Yellowstone Park Found., Bozeman, Mont., 1995-96. Office: Yellowstone Assn PO Box 117 Yellowstone National Park WY 82190

COLE, PHILLIP ALLEN, lawyer; b. Washington, Mar. 3, 1940; s. Gordon Harding and Dorothy Barbara (Jugel) C.; m. Mary Jo Ruff, July 2, 1994; children: Jennifer Leigh, Christopher Harding, Catherine Anne. BA, U. Md., 1961; JD, Georgetown U., 1964. Bar: Md. 1964, Minn. 1968, U.S. Supreme Ct. 1967, U.S. Ct. Appeals (8th cir.) 1968, U.S. Dist. Ct. Minn. 1965, U.S. Ct. Mil. Appeals 1965; cert. civil trial specialist. Assoc. Beatty & McNamee, Hyattville, Md., 1968; founder, sr. mem. Lommen, Nelson, Cole & Stageberg, Mpls., 1969—. Spl. counsel Md. Ho. of Dels., 1968. Contbr. articles to profl. jours. Capt. USMC, 1965-67. Mem. ATLA, Am. Bd. Profl. Liability Attys., Internat. Assn. Def. Counsel. Avocations: golf, reading. Office: Lommen Nelson Cole & Stageberg 1800 IDS Ctr Minneapolis MN 55402 E-mail: phil@lommen.com.

COLE, PHYLLIS BLUM, literature educator; b. St. Charles, Ill., Nov. 22, 1944; d. George Walter and Ruth Pennington Blum; m. Robert Franklin Cole, May 20, 1972; children: Sarah Hammond, Rachel Louise. BA, Oberlin Coll., 1966; MA, Harvard U., 1967, PhD, 1973. Asst. prof. English Wellesley (Mass.) Coll., 1973—83; vis. rsch. scholar Wellesley Coll. Ctr. for Rsch. on Women, 1983—89; rsch. assoc. and vis. lectr. in women's studies Harvard Div. Sch., Cambridge, Mass., 1984—85; lectr. Harvard U. Ext., Cambridge, 1987—88; assoc. prof. English and women's studies Penn State Del. County, Media, Pa., 1989—2000, prof. English, women's studies, and Am. studies. Book rev. editor Resources for Am. Lit. Study, University Park, Pa., 1999—. Author: (book) The American Writer and the Condition of England, 1815-1860, Mary Moody Emerson and the Origins of Transcendentalism: A Family History (Finalist for James Russell Lowell prize, MLA, 1999); contbr. articles to profl. jours. Recipient award for Excellence in Academic Integration, Penn State Commonwealth Coll., 2001; fellow, Woodrow Wilson Found., 1966—67, Rsch. Assocs. fellow in women's studies, Ellis Phillips Found., 1985; grantee, Penn State Rsch. and Grad. Studies Office, 1996, Penn State Inst. for the Arts and Humanistic Study, 1991, 1998; Harvard Grad. Prize fellow, Ford Found., 1967—71, Charles Warren Ctr. fellow in Am. History, Harvard U., 1980—81, fellow for Coll. Teachers, NEH, 1980—81, Rsch. Fellowship in Women's Studies, Rockefeller Found., 1984—85, Summer Stipend fellow, NEH, 1993. Mem.: MLA, Chester County Hist. Soc., Del. County Hist. Soc., Mid-Atlantic Am. Studies Assn. (exec. bd. 2000—03), Margaret Fuller Soc. (adv. bd. 2001—03), Soc. for the Study Am. Women Writers (adv. bd. 2002—), Ralph Waldo Emerson Soc. (program chair 1998—2001, pres.-elect 2002—03), Am. Lit. Assn., Royal Scottish Country Dance Soc., Phi Beta Kappa. Avocations: scottish country dancing, travel, hiking. Home: 74 East Greenwood Ave Lansdowne PA 19050 Office: Penn State Delaware County 25 Yearsley Mill Rd Media PA 19063 Personal E-mail: pbc2@psu.edu. E-mail: pbc2@psu.edu.

COLE, RANSEY GUY, JR., federal judge; b. Birmingham, Ala., May 23, 1951; s. Ransey Guy and Sarah Nell (Coker) Cole; m. Kathleine Kelley, Nov. 26, 1983; children: Justin Robert Jefferson, Jordan Paul, Alexandra Sarah. BA, Tufts U., 1972; JD, Yale U., 1975. Bar: Ohio 1975, D.C. 1982. Assoc. Vorys, Sater, Seymour and Pease, Columbus, Ohio, 1975—78, ptnr., 1980—86, 1993—95; trial atty. U.S. Dept. Justice, Washington, 1978—80; judge U.S. Bankruptcy Ct., Columbus, 1987—93; circuit judge U.S. Ct. Appeals (6th cir.), Cinn., 1995—. Mem.: ABA, Columbus Bar Assn., Nat. Bar Assn. Office: US Courthouse 85 Marconi Blvd Rm 127 Columbus OH 43215-2823 also: US Court of Appeals 6th Circuit 532 Potter Stewart US Courthouse 100 E Fifth St Cincinnati OH 45202*

COLE, REGINALD DAVID, water treatment executive; b. Indpls., July 26, 1945; s. Reginald H.E. and Dorothy Lois (Glassburn) C.; m. Roxie Lee Large, Oct. 14, 1966; children: Thomas David, Timothy Dwayne. Cert., DeVry Inst. Tech., 1976; student, U. Ctrl. Tex., 1982-84; MBA, Concordia U., 2002. Dist. sales mgr. Purcell's Goodyear Tire & Rubber Co., Killeen, Tex., 1984-87, asst. plant mgr., 1987-89; bookkeeper Citizen Nat. Bank, Killeen, 1989-90; acct. Sheraton Hotel, Killeen, 1990-91, comptr., 1993, auditor, 1991-93; comptr. Hilton Hotel, Killeen, 1993, Holiday Inn, Killeen, 1993; gen. mgr. 440 Plz. Shopping Ctr., Killeen, 1994, Ramada Inn, Killeen, 1993-94, Park Inn Internat. Hotel, Killeen, 1993-94; operator Ctrl. Tex. Water Supply Corp., Harker Heights, Tex., 1995-97, gen. mgr., 1997—. Mem. City of Killeen Bd. Fire Code Adjustments and Appeals, 1994—; bd. dirs. Greater Ft. Hood Area United Way, 1993-96. Mem. U.S. Army, 1964-84. Recipient Leadership award Greater Killeen C. of C., 1992. Mem. Am. Inst. Profl. Bookkeepers. Republican. Baptist. Avocations: amateur radio, volleyball, chess, reading, gardening.

COLE, RICHARD CARGILL, English language educator; b. Kansas City, Kans., Apr. 16, 1926; s. Horace Richard and Iris Verner (Cargill) C.; m. Florence Adaline Mason, June 27, 1956; children: Celia Elizabeth Cole Shaw, Paul Richard. BA, Hamilton Coll., 1950; MA, Yale U., 1951, PhD in English, 1955. English tchr. Manlius (N.Y.) Sch., 1951-52; asst. to dean of freshmen Yale U., New Haven, 1953-54; instr. English U. Tex., Austin, 1954-57; assoc. prof. Radford Va. Coll. (now Univ.), 1957-59, prof. English, 1959-61, Davidson (N.C.) Coll., 1961-93, prof. emeritus, 1993—. Author: Irish Booksellers and English Writers, 1740-1800, 1986; author, editor: Robert Colvill's Atalanta and Savannah, 1987, John Singleton's Grand Tour, 1815-1817, 1988, The General Correspondence of James Boswell, 1766-1767, 1993, Thomas Mante, Writer, Soldier, Adventurer, 1993, The General Correspondence of James Boswell, 1768-1769, 1997; contbr. articles to profl. jours. Sgt. USAAF, 1944-46, ETO. Robert Warnock rsch. fellow Yale U., 1975-76, rsch. fellow Yale U. Div. Sch., 1978; rsch. grantee Bd. Higher Edn., Presbyn. Ch., 1968, Piedmont U. Ctr. N.C., 1968; grantee Am. Coun. Learned Socs., 1976, Nat. Endowment for the Humanities grantee, 1985, 89. Mem. Phi Beta Kappa. Republican. Presbyterian. Home: 400 Avinger Ln Apt 101 Davidson NC 28036-9700

COLE, RICHARD A. retired lawyer; b. Syracuse, N.Y., Feb. 21, 1951; s. Victor and Marie (Pogacar) C.; m. Lois Hallonquist, Sept. 27, 1975. AB, Brown U., 1973; JD, Cornell U., 1976. Bar: Ill. 1976, U.S. Dist. Ct. (no. dist.) Ill. 1976. Assoc. Mayer, Brown, Rowe & Maw, Chgo., 1976—82, ptnr., 1983—2002. Trustee U. Notre Dame, London, 1981-2002. Avocation: travel. Home: 29 Beverley Rd London SW 13 England E-mail: randlcole@dial.pipex.com.

COLE, RICHARD CHARLES, lawyer; b. Albany, N.Y., Apr. 23, 1950; s. Charles Stanley and Doris Jean (Hatch) C.; m. Margaret O'Leary; children: Jack Patrick, Charles Michael. BA magna cum laude, Cornell U., 1972; JD, Harvard U., 1975. Bar: N.Y. 1976, U.S. Dist. Ct. (so. and ea. dits.) N.Y. 1977, U.S. Ct. Apeals (D.C. cir.) 1980, U.S. Ct. Appeals (2d and 5th cirs.) 1981, U.S. Dist. Ct. (no, ea., so. and ctrl. dists.) 1989, U.S. Supreme Ct. 1995. Assoc. LeBoeuf, Lamb, Leiby & MacRae, N.Y.C., 1975-83, ptnr., 1984-89, LeBoeuf, Lamb, Greene & MacRae, San Francisco, 1989-95; pvt. practice Mill Valley, 1996—. Mem. ABA. Avocations: woodwind instruments, sch. vol. Office: 41 Buena Vista Ave Mill Valley CA 94941-1231

COLE, RICHARD GEORGE, public administrator; b. Irvington, N.J., Mar. 11, 1948; s. Warner W. and Laurel M. (Wilson) C. AS in Computer Sci., Control Data Inst., Anaheim, Calif., 1972; BA in Sociology with high honor, Calif. State

U., Los Angeles, 1974; MA in Social Ecology, U. Calif., Irvine, 1976; postgrad., So. Oreg. State Coll., 1979. Computer operator Zee Internat., Gardena, Calif., 1971; teaching asst. U. Calif., Irvine, 1974-75; planner Herman Kimmel & Assocs., Newport Beach, Calif., 1976-78; program analyst The Job Coun., Medford, Oreg., 1980-81, compliance officer, 1981-82, bus. mgr., 1982—2002, exec. dir., 2002—. Instr. credential Calif. C.C.; chmn. bd. trustees Job Coun. Pension Trust, Medford, 1982-97; mem. curriculum adv. com. Rogue C.C., Grants Pass, Oreg., 1986; mgr. computer project State of Oreg., Salem, 1983-84; mem. Oreg. Occupational Info. Coordinating Com., Salem, 1982-84. Pres. bd. trustees Vector Control Dist., Jackson County, Oreg., 1985, treas., 1986, bd. dirs., 1984-87, mem. budget com., 1988-99, sec., 1988-89; cand. bd. dirs. Area Edn. Dist., Jackson County, 1981; treas. Job Svc. Employer Com., Jackson County, 1987-99 (Spl. Svc. award 1991), Oreg. Employers Coun., 1997-99; Rogue Valley Workforce Devel. coun. dir. fin. joint pub. venture System Devel. Project, Salem, Oreg., 1986-89; mem. adv. bd. New Jobs Planning, Medford, Oreg., 1987-88, Fin. Audit and Risk Mgmt. Task Force, 1987-91, chm., 1989-90. Fellow LaVerne Noyes, U. Calif., Irvine, 1974; Dr. Paul Doehring Found. scholar, Glendale, Calif., 1973; Computer Demonstration grantee State of Oreg., Salem, 1983; recipient Award of Fin. Reporting Achievement Govt. Fin. Officers Assn. of U.S. and Can., 1989-90, Fin. Ops. recognition Vector Control Dist., Jackson County, Oreg., 1990, Nat. 2d Pl. Chpt. award Jackson County Job Svc. Employer Com., 1989, Oreg. Job Svc. Employer Com. Stat award, 1991, Oreg. Individual Citation award Internat. Assn. Profls. in Employment Security, 1993. Mem. Soc. for Human Resources Mgmt., Assn. So. Oreg. Pub. Adminstrs., Oreg. Employment and Tng. Assn., Pacific N.W. Personnel Mgmt. Assn. (chpt. treas. 1985-87, orgnl. liaison dir. 1988-89, Appreciation award 1985), Govt. Fin. Officers Assn., Oreg. Mcpl. Fin. Officers assn., The Nature Conservancy. Home: 575 Morey Rd Talent OR 97540-9725 Office: The Job Council 673 Market St Medford OR 97504-6125

COLE, RICHARD JOHN, marketing executive; b. N.Y.C., Oct. 18, 1926; s. Arthur and Anna C.; m. Birgitta Ofling, Aug. 26, 1961; children— Catherine Ann, Richard Arthur, John Eric, Christopher Arne. BA, Yale U., 1946. Pres. Richard J. Cole, Inc., N.Y.C., 1954-61; gen. mgr. Dynasty of Hong Kong, N.Y.C., 1961-67; CEO, M.I. Group div. Manhattan Industries, Inc., 1967-83; mng. dir. B. Barclay Internat., Inc., 1983-87; prin. Sources Unltd., 1991—, R.&R. Internat., Inc., N.Y.C., 1995—. Served with USNR, 1943-46, 52-53. Congregationalist. Home and Office: 72 Main St Newtown CT 06470

COLE, RICHARD LOUIS, political scientist, educator; b. Dallas, Jan. 25, 1946; s. Louis Ray and Mary (Steely) C.; m. Pamela June Jacobs, Nov. 22, 1968; children: Jonathan, Ashley. BA, North Tex. State U., Denton, 1967, MA, 1968; PhD, Purdue U., 1973. Asst. prof. George Washington U., 1973-78, assoc. prof., 1978-79; research scholar Yale U., New Haven, Conn., 1979-80; prof. polit. sci., dean Sch. Urban and Pub. Affairs U. Tex., Arlington, 1980—; acting dean Coll. Liberal Arts, 2001—. Cons. Office Revenue Sharing Rand Corp. Author: Citizen Participation, 1974, Revenue Sharing, 1976, Introduction to Political Inquiry, 1980, Urban Life in Texas, 1986, Texas Politics and Public Policy, 1987, The Politics of American Government, 1994, Introduction to Political and Policy Research, 1996; mem. editl. bd. Am. Politics Quar., 1977-88, Jour. Cmty. Action, 1981—, Pub. Adminstrn. Rev., 1986-89, Jour. Urban Affairs, 1988—; contbr. articles to profl. jours. Mem. Leadership Arlington. Mem. Am. Soc. Pub. Adminstrn. (pres. N. Tex. chpt. 1989-90), S.W. Polit. Sci. Assn. (v.p. 1983-84, pres.-elect 1990, pres. 1991-92), Am. Polit. Sci. Assn. Democrat. Methodist. Home: 614 Portofino Dr Arlington TX 76012-2759 Office: Inst Urban Studies U Tex PO Box 19588 Arlington TX 76019-0001

COLE, RICHARD RAY, university dean; b. Forney, Tex., Apr. 20, 1942; s. Richard W. and G. Gladys C.; m. Lynda F. Painter, May 31, 1968. BJ, U. Tex., 1964, MA, 1966; PhD, U. Minn., 1971. Asst. city editor The News, Mexico City, 1966-67; freelance writer, 1966-67; reporter Harrow Observer, Harrow-on-the-Hill, Eng., 1968; asst. prof. W.Va. U., 1967-68; instr. U. Minn., 1968-71; mem. faculty U. N.C., Chapel Hill, 1971—, prof. journalism, 1979—, John T. Kerr Jr. disting. prof., 2002—, dean Sch. Journalism and Mass Comm., 1979—. Nat. scholarship com. Freedom Forum, 1980-86, chmn., 1987-93; chief judge H.L. Mencken Nat. Writing Award Competition, 1983-90; mem. journalism awards program steering com. William Randolph Hearst Found., 1981—, chmn., 1991—; chmn. accrediting teams U.S. journalism schs.; mem. faculty adv. com. World Press Inst.; mem. Nat. Accrediting Coun. on Edn. in Journalism and Mass Comm., 1987-96, v.p., 1989-95; cons. in field; creator cooperative programs with univs. in Mexico City, Santiago, Chile, Brazil, State of Parana, Havana, Cuba, United Arab Emirates; apptd. adh., coun. facultad comunicaciones Pontificial Cath. U. Chile, 1999—. Co-author: Gathering and Writing The News: Selected Readings, 1975; editor: Communication in Latin America: Journalism, Mass Communication, and Society, 1996; asst. editor Journalism Quar., 1973-85; contbr. articles to profl. jours. Chmn. U. N.C. Bicentennial Observance Planning Com., 1986-87; mem. Bicentennial Policy Com., 1988-94. Recipient Excellence award in undergrad. tchg. Amoco Found., 1978, Freedom Forum medal for lifetime accomplishments in journalism-mass comm. adminstrn., 1992; grantee U. Minn., U. N.C. Dept. State, Internat. Comm. Agy., Internat. Media Fund, U.S. AID, others; Fulbright fellow, Brazil, 2001. Mem. Assn. Edn. Journalism and Mass Communication (exec. com. 1977-79, 81-84, chmn. coms. 1974-75, 77-79, pres. 1982-83, nat. task force on future mass communication of edn. 1983-84), Internat. Assn. Mass Communication Rsch. (coun. 1980-88, v.p. 1984-88), Assn. Schs. Journalism and Mass Communication (exec. com. 1983-88, 1992-93, pres. 1986-87, mem. nat. steering com. to select 1st journalist in space NASA 1985-86), Inter Am. Press Assn., Sigma Delta Chi, Kappa Tau Alpha. Office: U NC Sch Journalism & Mass Communication PO Box 3365 Chapel Hill NC 27599-0001 E-mail: richard_cole@unc.edu.

COLE, RICKY, political organization worker; b. Ovett, Miss., 1966; Chmn. Miss. Dem. Party, 2001—. Former chmn. Miss. Young Dems. Office: PO Box 1583 832 N Congress St Jackson MS 39202

COLE, ROBERT CARLTON, English and journalism educator; b. Beaver, W.Va., June 2, 1937; s. Carlton Enfield and Naomi Ruth (Bowman) C.; children: Cathryn Alisa, Alan Robert; m. Nancy Elaine Knight, Mar. 14, 1973; children: Robin Matthew, Timothy Carlton. AB, Marshall U., 1959; MA, Wake Forest U., 1964; PhD, Lehigh U., 1971. Reporter Herald-Dispatch, Huntington, W.Va., 1957-59; reporter, columnist Jour. and Sentinel, Winston-Salem, N.C., 1959-64; from asst. to assoc. dir. of pubs. Lehigh U., Bethlehem, Pa., 1964-72, asst. prof. English, 1972-73, Coll. of N.J. (formerly Trenton State Coll.), 1973-83, assoc. prof. English and journalism, 1983-91, prof. English, 1991—. Cons. Edison State Coll., Trenton, 1985; dir. Dow Jones Newspaper fund N.J. Copyediting Intern Prog., Trenton, 1989; spkr. N.J. Press Assn., AP Mng. Editors, Am. Soc. Newspaper Editors, 1980—. Contbr. articles to profl. jours.; included in Best Sports Stories and Best American Sports Writing Anthologies, 1961-98. Mem. Planning Commn., Yardley, Pa., 1974-76; dir. social concerns Wesley United Meth. Ch., Bethlehem, Pa., 1969-71; boys' recreation baseball and basketball coach, 1988—. Recipient nat. tchg. award in journalism Am. Soc. Newspaper Editors and Poynter Inst. for Media Studies, 1984, 86; John Ben Snow fellow Am. Press Inst., 1983, 90; named N.J. Prof. of Yr., Coun. for Advancement and Support Edn., 1992. Mem. Am. Fedn. Tchrs., N.J. Press Assn. (Career Achievement award 1994), Sigma Delta Chi. Democrat. Home: 198 S Canal St Morrisville PA 19067-1702 Office: Coll of NJ Dept English Ewing NJ 08628-0718 E-mail: colerobt@tcnj.edu.

COLE, ROBERT E. sociologist, educator; b. N.Y.C., Oct. 14, 1937; s. Bernard M. and Elizabeth Cole; m. Ingrid L. Cole, Apr. 17, 1960; children: Anders Johan, Rebecca Leah. BA in Econs., Hobart Coll., 1959; MA in Indsl. and Labor Rels., PhD in Sociology, U. Ill., 1962. Asst. prof. sociology U. Mich., Ann Arbor, 1968—71, assoc. prof. sociology, 1972—78, prof. sociology, 1979—90, prof. sociology and bus. adminstrn., 1986—90; prof. bus. adminstrn. and sociology U. Calif., Berkeley, 1990—. Lectr., cons. various Fortune 500 cos., 1980—; bd. dirs. Am. Productivity and Quality Ctr., Houston, 1983—; dir. mgmt. of tech. program Haas Sch. Bus., Berkeley, 1996—. Author: Japanese Blue Collar, 1971, Strategies for Learning, 1989, Managing Quality Fads, 1999. Named Fulbright Rsch. Scholar, Fulbright program, 1977—78; recipient Disting. Alumni award, Inst. of Labor and Indsl. Rels., U. Ill., Champaign, 1999; fellow, Woodrow Wilson Internat. Ctr. for Scholars, 1984—85, Ctr. for Advanced Studies in Behavioral Scis., Stanford, Calif., 1995—96. Mem.: Sociol. Rsch. Assn., Acad. Mgmt., Am. Sociol. Assn. Achievements include research in documenting status and determinants of Japanese blue collar behavior; evolution of American and Japanese quality movements; discriminatory behavior of Japanese auto plants in U.S; clarifying sources of innovation and reliability in open source computing. Office: U Calif Berkeley Haas Sch Bus Berkeley CA 94720-1900 Office Fax: 510-642-2826. E-mail: cole@haas.berkeley.edu.

COLE, ROBERT THEODORE, lawyer; b. Bklyn., Mar. 16, 1932; s. Harold I. and Bella (Weissman) C.; m. C. Margaret Hall, Oct. 25, 1959; children: Elizabeth, Tanya, Judith Amy. BS, U. Pa., 1953; LLB magna cum laude, Harvard U. Law Sch., 1956; diploma in law, London Sch. Econs., 1958. Bar: N.Y. 1956, D.C. 1972. Assoc. Law Office Frank Boas, Brussels, 1960-62, Nixon Mudge Rose et al, N.Y.C., 1962-67; atty. U.S. Treasury Dept., Washington, 1967-73, internat. tax counsel, 1971-73; ptnr. Cole Corette & Abrutyn, Washington, 1973-96; ptnr., sr. counsel Alston & Bird LLP, Washington, 1997—; co-owner The Little Gym, No. Va. Lectr. on internat. tax. Editor, prin. author Practical Guide U.S. Transfer Princing; contbr. articles on internat. taxes to legal jours. Capt. USAF, 1957-59. Recipient exceptional svc. award U.S. Treasury Dept., 1973. Fellow Am. Coll. Tax Counsel; mem. Assn. Bar City N.Y., Nat. Fgn. Trade Coun. (vice-chair tax com. 1989-95), Harvard Club (N.Y.C.). Avocations: hiking, theatre. Home: 4000 Chancery Ct NW Washington DC 20007-2140 Office: Alston & Bird LLP 601 Pennsylvania Ave NW No Bldg 10th Fl Washington DC 20004-2601

COLE, ROLAND JAY, lawyer; b. Seattle, Dec. 15, 1948; s. Robert J. and Josephine F. C.; m. Elsa Kircher, Aug. 16, 1975; children: Isabel Ashley, Madeline Aldis. AB in Econs. magna cum laude, Harvard U., 1970, M in Pub. Policy, 1972, PhD in Pub. Policy, JD, 1975. Bar: Wash. 1975, U.S. Supreme Ct. 1980, U.S. Dist. Ct. (we. dist.) Wash. 1984, Mich. 1989. Rsch. scientist Battelle Human Affairs Rsch. Ctrs., Seattle, 1975-83; assoc. Appel and Glueck, P.C., Seattle, 1984-89; gen. counsel Indsl. Tech. Inst., Ann Arbor, Mich., 1990-94; founder, exec. dir. Software Patent Inst., Indpls., 1994—; of counsel Shughart Thomson & Kilroy PC, Overland Park, Kans., 1997-2000, Barnes & Thornburg, Indpls., 2000—. Co-author: Government Requirements of Small Business, 1980, The Containment of Organized Crime, 1984; co-programmer Quadrant I software program, 1983. HUD fellow, 1970-71. Mem. Assn. Personal Computer User Groups (dir., founding pres. 1986), Wash. Athletic Club, Indpls. Athletic Club. Congregationalist. Avocations: squash, racquetball, volleyball, music. Office: Barnes & Thornburg 11 S Meridian St Indianapolis IN 46204-3535 E-mail: rcole@btlaw.com.

COLE, SOLON ROBERT, pathologist, educator; b. McComb, Miss., Sept. 18, 1937; s. Robert Walter and Thelma Rebecca (Price) C. BS, Tulane U., 1959, MD, 1962. Diplomate Am. Bd. Pathology. Intern St. Vincent's Hosp., N.Y.C., 1962-64; resident in pathology Boston City Hosp., 1964-67; rsch. fellow Harvard Med. Sch., Boston, 1967-69; pathologist pulmonary sect. Armed Forces Inst. Pathology, Washington, 1970-72; sr. pathologist Hartford Hosp., 1972—2002, dir. electron microscopy, 1972—. Assoc. prof. pathology U. Conn. Health Ctr., Farmington, 1974—; with Hartford Pathology Assocs., 1992—; com. on nomenclature of lung disease WHO, Geneva, Switzerland, 1978—; lung pathology cons. Regional Hosps., Hartford, 1972—. Contbr. chpts. to books. Bd. dirs. Hartford Symphony Orch., 1985. Royal Hort. Soc. fellow, London, 1985; grantee HEW, 1976, Nat. Heart and Lung Assn., 1978, Combined Hosp. Fund, 1983; named one of the Top Doc. in Am., 2001, 02. Fellow: Coll. Am. Pathologists; mem.: Soc. Pulmonary Pathologists, New Eng. Cancer Soc., Electron Microscopy Soc. Am., Internat. Acad. Pathology, Sigma Xi. Democrat. Avocation: landscaping. Home: 1 Gold St Apt 23E Hartford CT 06103-2932 Office: Dept Pathology Hartford Hosp 80 Seymour St Hartford CT 06115-2701 E-mail: solonc@snet.net.

COLE, STEPHEN E. magistrate judge; b. Powell, Wyo., Apr. 18, 1947; BA, U. Wyo., 1969, JD, 1974. Pvt. law practice, Worland, Wyo.; judge Worland Mcpl. Ct., 1975-81, Ten Sleep Mcpl. Ct., 1977-81; justice of the peace Washakie County Justice Ct., 1977-81; magistrate judge U.S. Dist. Ct. Wyo., 1975—. Office: PO Box 387 Yellowstone National Park WY 82190-0387 E-mail: stephen_cole@wyd.uscourts.gov.

COLE, SUSAN A. university president, English language educator; m. David Cole, two children. BA in English and Am. Lit., Columbia U., 1962; MA in English and Am. Lit., Brandeis U., 1964, PhD in English and Am. Lit., 1972. Tchg. asst. Clark U., 1964-65; assoc. prof. CCUNY-N.Y.C. Tech. Coll., 1968-77; assoc. dean for acad. affairs Antioch U., 1977-80; v.p. for univ. adminstrn. and pers. Rutgers U., New Brunswick, N.J., 1980-92; pres., prof. English Met. State U., Mpls. and St. Paul, 1993-98; pres. Montclair State U., Upper Montclair, N.J., 1998—. Guest adj. assoc. prof. Pace U., fall 1977; vis. sr. fellow in acad. adminstrn. Office Acad. Affairs, CUNY, 1991-93; bd. dirs. Western State Bank; presenter in field. Contbr. articles to profl. jours. Chmn. edn. resolutions sessions, coord. edn. panels N.Y. State meeting Internat. Women's Year, Albany, 1977; agy. mem. N.J. Gov.'s Mgmt. Improvement Program, 1982; v.p., bd. dirs. Bklyn. Ecumenical Coops., 1988-90; mem. cmty. health care policy task force Robert Wood Johnson Univ. Hosp., New Brunswick, 1991; mem. blue ribon task force Mpls. Pub. Libr., 1994-95; mem. steering com. Greater St. Paul Tomorrow, 1994—; trustee Twin Cities Pub. TV, 1994—, Sci. Mus. Minn., 1994; bd. dirs., mem. exec. com. St. Paul Riverfront Corp., 1994—; v.p., founding bd. dirs. St. Paul Pub. Schs. Found., 1995—; bd. dirs. St. Paul Found., 1995—. Mem. Am. Assn. State Colls. and Univs. (urban and met. steering com. 1993—), Am. Coun. on Edn. (Commn. on Women in Higher Edn. 1993—), Greater Mpls. C. of C. (enterprise devel. task force 1994—). Office: Montclair State U Ofc of Pres 1 Normal Ave Montclair NJ 07043-1624

COLE, SUSAN STOCKBRIDGE, theatre educator; b. San Francisco, Jan. 26, 1939; d. Elmer Leroy Stockbridge and Martha Louise Rosenauer; m. John Michael Day, June 28, 1965 (div. May 1968); m. Willie Robert Cole, June 12, 1976. AB, Stanford (Calif.) U., 1960, MA, 1961; PhD, U. Oreg., 1972. Asst. prof. theatre Bakersfield (Calif.) Coll., 1962-69; grad. tchg. fellow U. Oreg., Eugene, 1969-72; asst. prof. theatre Keuka Coll., Keuka Park, N.Y., 1972-75; prof. Appalachian State U., Boone, N.C., 1975—, dept. chair theatre and dance, 1989—. Cons. Dept. Pub. Instrn., Raleigh, N.C., 1980—, N.C. Arts Coun., Raleigh, 1989-93. Author: American National Biography, 1999, Notable Women in American Theatre, 1990; designer more than 100 play prodns., 1962—; dir. more than 60 play prodns. Mem.: Nat. Assn. of Schs. of Theatre, Am. Soc. for Theatre Rsch., Assn. for Theatre in Higher Edn., N.C. Theatre Conf. (pres. 1991—92, Svc. award 1997), Southeastern Theatre Conf. (pres. 1998—99, Suzanne Davis award 2002), Lions Club Internat. (past pres., treas. 1999—, dist. officer 1997—), Alpha Psi Omega (pres. 1997—2002). Democrat. Episcopalian. Avocation: reading. Home: PO Box 220 Todd NC 28684-0220 Office: Dept of Theatre and Dance Appalachian State U Boone NC 28608-2123

COLE, SYLVAN, JR., art dealer; b. N.Y.C., Jan. 10, 1918; s. Sylvan and Dorothy (Stein) C.; m. Vivian Vanderpool, May 1944 (div. 1952); children: Nancy, Robert, James; m. Lillyan Wood, Aug. 20, 1953 (dec. Oct. 1987), m. Mary Rowena Myers Dec. 12, 1998. BA, Cornell U., 1939. Exec. trainee Sears, Roebuck & Co., 1939-41; with Asso. Am. Artists, Inc., N.Y.C., 1946-83, pres., dir., 1958-83, Sylvan Cole Gallery, 1983—. Editor: Raphael Soyer: Fifty Years of Printmaking, 1967, Graphic Work of Joseph Hirsch, 1969, Will Barnet Graphics, 1932-1972, 1972, The Lithographs of John Steuart Curry, 1976; co-editor: Stuart Davis a Catalogue Raisonne of the Prints, 1986. Former pres. N.Y. chpt. Friends of Herbert F. Johnson Mus.; mem. exec. com. Cornell U. Maj. AUS, 1941-46. Recipient Gari Melchers Meml. medal Artists Fellowship, 1989. Mem. Art Dealers Assn. Am. (former dir.), Internat. Fine Print Dealers Assn. (past pres., past v.p.), Appraisers Assn. Am., Nat. Arts Club. Home: 25 Sutton Pl S New York NY 10022-2441 Office: 101 W 57th St New York NY 10019-2215

COLE, TERRENCE M. historian, educator; b. Quakertown, Pa., Sept. 23, 1953; s. William P. and Anne E. Cole; m. Marjorie K. Cole, Dec. 20, 1977 (div. Oct. 1997); children: Henry L., Desmond E.; m. Eugenia F. Salisbury, Aug. 9, 2003. BA in Geography, U. Alaska, 1976, MA in History, 1978; PhD in History, U. Wash., 1983. Editor Alaska N.W. Pub. Co., Edmonds, Wash., 1980—88; prof. history U. Alaska, Fairbanks, 1988—. Author: (book) Nome: City of Golden Beaches, 1984, The Cornerstone on College Hill: History of the University of Alaska, 1992, Crooked Past, 1991, Banking on Alaska, 2000; contbr. Chair Fairbanks North Star Borough Libr. Commn., 1991—. Recipient Bullock Award for Svc., U. Alaska Found., 1998. Mem.: Alaska Hist. Soc. (v.p. 1986—88, Alaska Historian of the Yr. 1986). Office: Univ of Alaska-Fairbanks Dept History Fairbanks AK 99775

COLE, THEODORE JOHN, osteopathic and naturopathic physician; b. Covington, Ky., May 30, 1953; s. John N. and Florence R. (Bruener) C.; m. Ellen Cole; children: Joren, Emily, Kevin, Aidan, Ronan. BA, Centre Coll., Danville, Ky., 1975; MA, Western Ky. U., 1978; DO, Ohio U., 1986. Diplomate Am. Osteo. Bd. Gen. Practice, Nat. Bd. Osteo. Examiners, Am. Naturopathic Med. Assn. Psychologist Comprehensive Mental Health Svcs., St. Petersburg, Fla., 1978-82; intern Detroit Osteo. Hosp., 1986-87; resident Doctors Hosp., Columbus, Ohio, 1987-88; pvt. practice, West Chester, Ohio, 1989—. Preceptor Ohio U. Coll. Osteo. Medicine, Athens, 1990—, U. Cin. Med. Sch., 1990—; dir. So. Ohio Coll. Nursing. Coach, Soccer Assn. for Youth, West Chester, 1989, 90, Liberty Sports Orgn., West Chester, 1990. Mem. Am. Osteo. Assn., Am. Assn. Osteopathy, Am. Coll. Gen. Practitioners, Am. Acad. Environ. Medicine, Am. Acad. Advancement of Medicine, Occidental Inst. Rsch. Found. Avocations: collecting art, hunting, camping, farming, tai chi. Office: The Cole Ctr for Healing/Cin Hyperbarics Ste 228 11974 Lebanon Rd Cincinnati OH 45241-1700

COLE, THOMAS WINSTON, JR., chancellor, college president, chemist; b. Vernon, Tex., Jan. 11, 1941; s. Thomas Winston and Eva Mae (Sharp) C.; m. Brenda S. Hill, June 14, 1964; children: Kelley S., Thomas III. BS, Wiley Coll., Marshall, Tex., 1961; PhD, U. Chgo., 1966. Mem. faculty Atlanta U., 1966-82, prof. chemistry, chmn. dept., 1971-82, Fuller E. Callaway prof., 1969-80, project dir. Resource Ctr. Sci. and Engring., 1978-82, univ. provost, v.p. acad. affairs, 1979-82; pres. Clark Atlanta U., 1988—, W.Va. State Coll., Institute, 1982-86; chancellor W.Va. Bd. of Regents, 1986-88. Vis. prof. U. Ill., summer 1972, MIT, 1973-74; summer chemist Miami Valley Lab. Procter and Gamble co., 1967; Celanese Corp., Charlotte, N.C., 1974, UNCF lectr., 1975-84; bd. dirs. C&P Telephone Co., Nat. Pub. TV Stas., United Nat. Bank, Thomas Meml. Hosp. Mem. Leadership Atlanta. So. Regional fellow, summer 1961; Woodrow Wilson fellow, 1961-62; Allied Chem. fellow, 1963; Danforth scholar, 1971-82. Mem. Am. Chem. Soc., AAAS, Nat. Inst. Sci., Nat. Orgn. Profl. Advancement Black Chemists and Chem. Engrs., Sigma Xi, Sigma Pi Phi, Alpha Phi Alpha. Lodges: Rotary. Home: 691 Beckwith St SW Atlanta GA 30314-4112 Office: Clark Atlanta U 223 James P Brawley Dr SW Atlanta GA 30314-4358 also: Sta WCLK-FM 111 James P Brawley Dr SW Atlanta GA 30314-4207

COLE, TODD GODWIN, management consultant transportation; b. Coushatta, La., Mar. 5, 1921; s. Ira and Lucie (Triche) C.; m. Inez Hamilton, Feb. 9, 1953 (div. 1974); children: Michael H., Diane Cole Janusz (dec. 1994); m. Josephine Giovanetti, Oct. 1974 (dec. 1985); m. Pamela Wilds, Mar., 1987. Student, La. State U., 1935-37; LLB, Woodrow Wilson Coll., 1947. CPA, Ga. With Delta Airlines, 1940-63, dir., exec. v.p. adminstrn., 1955-63; sr. v.p. finance and adminstrn., dir. Ea. Airlines, 1963-67, vice chmn., chmn. finance com., dir., 1967-69; v.p., asst. to pres., dir. C.I.T. Fin. Corp., N.Y.C., 1969, v.p. fin., 1969-71, mem. exec. com., 1970-86, exec. v.p., 1971-73, pres., chief adminstrv. officer, 1973-80, pres., COO, 1980-83, pres., CEO, 1984-86; CEO, bd. dirs. Frontier Air Lines D.I.P., 1987-89; vice chmn., dir. Ea. Air Lines D.I.P., 1989-91; mng. dir. Simat, Hellesen & Eichrer, Inc., 1992-96; pres. Cole & Wilds Assocs., Miami, 1996—. Chmn. Arrow Air, Inc., 1997-98; bd. dirs. Kaiser Ventures, LLC. Mem. Ga. Bar Assn. Office: 6355 NW 36th St Ste 601 Miami FL 33166 E-mail: coletg@bellsouth.net.

COLE, TOM, congressman; b. Shreveport, La., Apr. 28, 1949; s. John D. and Helen Gale Cole; m. Ellen Decker; 1 child, Mason. BA, Grinnell Coll., 1971; MA, Yale U., 1974; PhD, U. Okla., 1984. Fellow Yale U., 1974; instr. U. Okla., 1975-78, Okla. Bapt. U., 1981; exec. dir. Okla. Rep. Com., 1980-81; dir. dist. svcs. congressman Mickey Edwards U.S. Congress, 1982-84; exec. dir. Reagan-Bush Campaign, Okla., 1984; chmn. Okla. State Rep. Party, 1985-89; mem. Okla. State Senate, 1988—91; pres. Cole, Hargrave, Snodgrass & Assocs., 1989—; sec. of state State of Okla., 1995-99; chief of staff Republican Nat. Com., Wash., 1999—; mem. U.S. Ho. of Reps. from 4th Okla. dist., 2003—. Lectr. Grinnell Coll., 1977, 79; mem. Cleve. County Rep. Exec. Com., 1979-85, Okla. County Rep. Exec. Com., 1983-85; campaign mgr. Helen Cole for State Rep., 1978, 80, 82, Helen Cole for State Senate, 1984, Ken Wilson for County Commr., 1981, Evelyn Orth for County Commr., 1981; dep. campaign mgr. Daxon for Gov., 1981-82. Fullbright fellow U. London; Watson felow Inst. Hist. Rsch., London; recipient Robert A. Taft award Okla. Rep. Party, Guardian Small Bus. award Nat. Fedn. Ind. Bus. Mem. Am. Hist. Assn., Inst. Hist. Rsch., Soc. Study Labor History, Ea. London Hist. Soc., Okla. C. of C., Phi Alpha Theta. Methodist. Office: 501 Cannon Ho Office Bldg Washington DC 20515-3604*

COLE, WAYNE STANLEY, historian, educator; b. Manning, Iowa, Nov. 11, 1922; s. Roy Eldon and Gladys Evelyn (Granseth) Cole; m. Virginia Rae Miller, Dec. 24, 1950; 1 child, Thomas Roy. BA with high honors, Iowa State Tchrs. Coll., 1946; MS, U. Wis., 1948, PhD, 1951. From instr. to asst. prof. history U. Ark., 1950-54; from asst. prof. to prof. Iowa State U., 1954-65; prof. U. Md., College Park, 1965-92, Disting. scholar tchr., 1989-90, prof. history emeritus, 1992—; Fulbright lectr. U. Keele, England, 1962-63. Author: (book) America First, 1953, Senator Gerald P. Nye and American Foreign Relations, 1962, An Interpretive History of American Foreign Relations, 1968, An Interpretive History of American Foreign Relations, 2d edit., 1974, Charles A. Lindbergh and the Battle Against American Intervention in World War II, 1974, Roosevelt and the Isolationists 1932-1945, 1983, Norway and the United States, 1905-55, 1989, Determinism and American Foreign Relations During the Franklin D. Roosevelt Era, 1995, A Life in Twentieth Century America, 2002. Served to 1st lt. USAF, 1943—45. Fellow Woodrow Wilson Internat. Ctr. for Scholars, 1973, NEH, 1978—79. Mem.: Soc. Historians Am. Fgn. Rels. (pres. 1973, Graebner award 1994). Lutheran. Home: 10203 Mcgovern Dr Silver Spring MD 20903-1612 E-mail: wc14@umail.umd.edu. *Work hard. Give your best. Never give up. Have compassion for those who are different. Remember you stand on shoulders of those who came before. Leave the world a better place than it was. Never forget that you could be wrong.*

COLE, WILLIAM EDWARD, economics educator, consultant; b. Mineola, Tex., Feb. 5, 1931; s. Isaac Harry and Anna Belle (Davis) C.; m. Evelyn Mallory Taylor, June 9, 1967 (div. 1977); 1 child, Mary Kathleen; m. Mary Elizabeth Riddle, Nov. 21, 1978. BA, U. Tex., 1952, PhD, 1965. Auditor Procter and Gamble, Cin., 1955-61; from asst. to assoc. prof. econs. U. Tenn., Knoxville, 1965-70, prof., 1972—; gen. ptnr. Tenn.-Tex. Assocs.; head dept. U. Tenn., Knoxville, 1983-86; indsl. devel. specialist UN Indsl. Devel. Orgn., Vienna, 1970-72. Cons. World Bank, Internat. Labor Orgn., TVA, People's Republic of China, 1989, Fgn. Ministry of Japan, 1990; adminstr. UN Productivity Quality Project in Brazil, 1990. Author: Steel and Economic Growth in Mexico, 1967, The Economics of Total Quality Management, 1995; editor: Economic Policy in Mexico, 1987; contbr. articles to profl. jours. Served to 1st lt. U.S. Army, 1952-55, Korea. NDEA fellow Dept. HEW, Washington, 1962-65, Fulbright fellow Dept. HEW, Washington, 1964; grantee Tinker Found., N.Y.C., 1987. Mem. Am. Econ. Assn., N.Am. Econs. and Fin. Assn. (bd. dirs. 1984—), Assn. Evolutionary Econs., Latin Am. Studies Assn. Democrat. Avocation: travel. Home: 9912 Mccormick Pl Knoxville TN 37923-1959 Office: Univ of Tenn Dept Economics Knoxville TN 37916

COLE, WILLIE, artist; b. Somerville, N.J., 1955; Student, Boston U., 1974—75; BFA, Sch. Visual Arts, N.Y., 1976; student, Art Students League, N.Y., 1976—79. Artist-in-residence Studio Mus., Harlem, NY, 1989, The Contemporary, Balt., 1994, Pilchuck Glass Sch., Seattle, 1994, Capp St. Project, San Francisco, 1995. One-man shows include Ednl. Testing Svc. Corp., Princeton, N.J., 1986, Inst. Contemporary Arts, L.I., 1990, Peter Miller Gallery, Chgo., 1991, 1993, Newark Mus., 1992, St. Louis Art Mus., 1992, Brooke Alexander, N.Y., 1992, 1994, Balt. Mus. Industry, 1994, Capp St. Project, San Francisco, 1995, U. Arts, Phila., 1995, Fabric Workshop Mus., 1995, Alerie Almine Rech, Paris, 1997, Alexander and Bonin, N.Y., 1997, John Berggruen Gallery, San Francisco, 1998, Mus. Modern Art, N.Y.C., 1998, Birmingham (Ala.) Mus. Art, 1998, Morris Mus., Morristown, N.J., 1999, exhibited in group shows at Littlejohn-Smith Gallery, N.Y., 1986, Robeson Ctr. Gallery, Rutgers U., 1987, Palais Exposition, Nice, France, 1988, Artworks, Princeton, 1989, Art in General, N.Y., 1990, Brooke Alexander, 1991; author: Brooke Alexander, 1993; Exhibited in group shows at Weatherspoon Art Gallery, Greensboro,

N.C., 1992, Tokushima Modern Art Mus., Japan, 1992—94, Newark Mus., 1993, 1997, N.J. Ctr. Visual Arts, Summit, 1994, 1996, Josh Baer Gallery, N.Y., 1994, Neuberger Mus. Art, Purchase, N.Y., 1994, 1997, Mus. Modern Art, N.Y.C., 1995, 1996, K&E Gallery, N.Y., 1995, Whitney Mus. Am. Art, Champion, 1995, City Gallery Chastain, Atlanta, 1996, Rhona Hoffman Gallery, Chgo., exhibited in group shows, N.Y., 1998, exhibited in group shows, Paine Webber Art Gallery, N.Y., 1998, Alexander and Bonin, 1998—99, Represented in permanent collections Bronx Mus. Art, Mus. Contemporary Art, Chgo., Dallas Mus. Art, Milw. Art Mus., Newark Mus. Art, N.J. Mus. Modern Art, N.Y.C., Whitney Mus. Am. Art, N.Y., St. Louis Art Mus., State Mus., Trenton, N.J., Nat. Gallery Art, Washington, FRAC Lorraine, Metz. Recipient Joan Mitchell Found. award, 1996; fellow Rutgers Ctr. Innovative Printmaking fellow, Rutgers U., 1991; Penny McCall Found. grantee, 1991, Wheeler Found. grantee, 1994, Louis Comfort Tiffany Found. grantee, 1995. Office: c/o Alexander & Bonin 132 10th Ave New York NY 10011-4727

COLEMAN, ARLENE FLORENCE, retired nurse practitioner; b. Braham, Minn., Apr. 8, 1926; d. William and Christine (Judin) C.; m. John Dunkerken, May 30, 1987. Diploma in nursing, U. Minn., 1947, BS, 1953; MPH, Loma Linda U., 1974. RN, Calif. Operating room scrub nurse Calif. Luth. Hosp., L.A., 1947-48; indsl. staff nurse Good Samaritan Hosp., L.A., 1948-49; staff nurse Passavant Hosp., Chgo., 1950-51; student health nurse Moody Bible Inst., Chgo., 1950-51; staff nurse St. Andrews Hosp., Mpls., 1951-53; pub. health nurse Bapt. Gen. Conf. Bd. of World Missions, Ethiopia, Africa, 1954-66; staff pub. health nurse County of San Bernadino, Calif., 1966-68, sr. pub. health nurse, 1968-73, pediatric nurse practitioner, 1973—. Contbr. articles to profl. jours. Mem. bd. dist. missions Bapt. Gen. Conf., Calif., 1978-84; mem. adv. coun. Kaiser Hosp., Fontana, Calif., 1969-85, Bethel Sem. West, San Diego, 1987—; bd. dirs. Casa Verdugo Retirement Home, Hemet, Calif., 1985—; active Calvary Bapt. Ch., Redlands, Calif., 1974—; mem. S.W. Bapt. Conf. Social Ministries, 1993—. With Cadet Nurse Corps USPHS, 1944-47. Calif. State Dept. Health grantee, 1973. Fellow Nat. Assn. Pediatric Nurse Assocs. and Practitioners; mem. Calif. Nurses Assn. (state nursing coun. 1974-76). Democrat. Avocations: gardening, travel, reading. Home: 622 Esther Way Redlands CA 92373-5822

COLEMAN, ARTHUR ROBERT, retired accountant; b. East Brady, Pa., July 16, 1916; s. William Robert and Bertha Etta (Erbe) C.; m. Avanell B. Crawford, Apr. 1, 1938 (dec.); 1 child, Arthur Clyde; m. Catherine Elizabeth Tiedt, Nov. 16, 1985. Student, Internal Corres. Sch., 1932-38, Franklin Comml. Coll., 1938-39, Pa. State U., 1952. Salesman Colonial Life Ins. Co., Butler, Pa., 1939-40; salesman, unit mgr. Comml. Credit Corp., Butler, 1940-42, 45-49; magnetic insp. Curtiss Wright Corp., Beaver, Pa., 1942-45; sales rep. Associates Discount Corp., Butler, 1949-52, 53-59; regional mgr., auditor Borg-Warner Acceptance Corp., Chgo., 1959-61; regional mgr. Westinghouse Credit Corp., Pitts., 1961-62; contr. McGowan Lumber Co., Slippery Rock, Pa., 1962-64, 65-75; sec. and treas. Morgans Restaurants, Butler, 1964-65. Owner A. R. Coleman Ins. Agy., Butler, Pa., 1949-52; co-founder Slippery Rock (Pa.) Plaza, Diamond Investments, Plaza Estates, 1966-75. Founder, chmn. bd. dirs. Tanglewood Sr. Ctr., Lyndora, Pa., 1979-91. Named Coleman Hall senior center in his honor. Mem. Masons, Am. Assn. Ret. Persons (v.p. local chpt. 1982-85), Acaccia Club (pres. 1966-67), YWCA Mr. & Mrs. Club (pres. 1966-68). Republican. Avocations: wood working, camping, reading. Home: 129 Jarrett Ave Butler PA 16001-1949

COLEMAN, BARBARA MCREYNOLDS, artist; b. Omaha, Neb., May 5, 1956; d. Zachariah Aycock and Mary Barbara (McCulloh) McR.; m. Stephen Dale Dent, Mar. 12, 1983 (div. Dec. 20, 1992); children: Madeleine Victoria, Matthew Stephen; m. Ross Coleman, Oct. 16, 1993; 1 child, Mia Jeanne Coleman. Student, U. N.Mex., 1979, MA in Cmty. and Regional Planning, 1984. Lectr. U. N.Mex. Sch. Arch., Albuquerque, 1979-82, 91—; assoc. planner, urban designer planning divsn. City of Albuquerque, 1982-84, city planner, urban designer N.Mex. redevel. divsn., 1984-88; v.p. Hydra Aquatic, Inc., Albuquerque, 1997—. Cons. City of Albuquerque Redevel. Dept., 1987-88; urban design cons. Southwest Land Rsch., Albuquerque, 1991, instr. at Ctr. for Action and Contemplation, Albuquerque, NM, 1999-present. Columnist for Kids and Art, 1990-92; author: Coors Corridor Plan (The Albuquerque Conservation Assn. Urban Design award 1984), Electric Facilities Plan, Downtown Core Revitalization Strategy and Sector Development Plan, contbg. author: Anasazi Architecture and American Design, 1994; contbr. articles to profl. jour.; exhibited in shows and solo exhibitions at Dartmouth St. Gallery, Albuquerque, 2000, Chimayo (N.Mex.) Trade and Mercantile, JoAnne Chappel Gallery, San Francisco, Southwest Arts Festival, Albuquerque, Act I Gallery, Taos, N.Mex., Nat. Arts Club, NYC, Hermitage Mus., Norfolk, Va., Schimmel Ctr. for the Arts, Pace U., NYC, Musée Granet, Aix-en-Provence, France, Fine Arts Gallery, Albuquerque, 1999 (1st pl.). Vol. art tchr. Chaparral Elem. Sch., Roosevelt Mid. Sch., Albuquerque, 1989-97. Recipient First Pl. for pastels N.Mex. Art League, 1991, Merit award Pastel Soc. of S.W., 1989, 1st pl. award N.Mex. State Fair Fine Arts Gallery, Albuquerque, 1999; finalist Nat. Cath. Reporter Jesus 2000 contest. Mem. Pastel Soc. of Am. (signature mem.), Pastel Soc. N.Mex. (pres. 1991-92, Best of Show 1990 award, 4th pl. Am. Artist Mag. award 1999). Democrat. Episcopalian. Avocations: hiking, skiing, running. Office: U NMex Sch Architecture Albuquerque NM 87131-0001

COLEMAN, BERNELL, physiologist, educator; b. Jefferson County, Miss., Apr. 26, 1929; s. Percy and Julia (Nailor) C.; m. Annie C. Richardson, Jan. 30, 1962; children— Rochelle, Ronald. BS, Alcorn A&M Coll., 1952; PhD (Univ. fellow), Loyola U. Stritch Sch. Medicine, Chgo., 1964. Research asst. in biochemistry U. Chgo., 1956-57; research in cancer Hines (Ill.) VA Hosp., 1957-59; instr. St. Louis U. Sch. Medicine, 1963-65, asst. prof. physiology, 1965-67; asst. prof. Chgo. Med. Sch., 1967-69, asso. prof., 1969-76, prof., 1976, Howard U. Coll. Medicine, Washington, 1976—, chmn. dept. physiology and biophysics, 1979—. Lectr. Cook County Grad. Sch. Medicine, U. Ill. Med. Sch.; vis. prof. Rush Med. Coll.; external examiner Godfrey Huggins Sch. Medicine, U. Zimbabwe, Salisbury, 1981; mem. cardiovascular and pulmonary study sect. Nat. Heart, Lung and Blood Inst./NIH, 1982-83, rsch. tng. rev. com., 1990-94. Peer rev. com. Am. Heart Assn., 1988-93, 95—, rsch. com., 1993—. With U.S. Army, 1953-56, Korea. Recipient research award Chgo. Med. Sch. Bd. Trustees, 1975; NIH research fellow, 1960-61; NIH grantee, 1966-68, 69-74, 74-76, 79— ; USPHS fellow, 1961-63; Dept. Def. grantee, 1965-67 Mem.: AAAS, AAUP, Am. Soc. Hypertension (charter), N.Y. Acad. Scis., Internat. Soc. of Hypertension in Blacks, Assn. Black Cardiologists, Fedn. Am. Socs. Exptl. Biology (vis. scientist for minority instns. programs 1982—83, 1989—90), Am. Heart Assn. (basic sci. coun.), Am. Physiol. Soc. (cardiovascular fellow 1985), Phi Rho Sigma, Sigma Xi. Democrat. Achievements include research numerous publs. in cardiovascular physiology. Home: 14200 Myer Ter Rockville MD 20853-2350 Office: 520 W St NW Washington DC 20001-2337 E-mail: bcoleman@howard.edu.

COLEMAN, BETH ANN See GLEBA, BETH

COLEMAN, BONNIE WATSON, assemblywoman; m. William E. Coleman; 1 child, William stepchildren: Troy, Jared. BA, Thomas Edison State Coll.; PhD (hon.), Richard Stockton State Coll. Cert. pub. mgr. Asst. commr. N.J. Dept. of Cmty. Affairs, 1980; assemblywoman N.J. Gen. Assembly, 1998—, chair appropriations com., 2002—, mem. assembly budget com. Bd. trustees Richard Stockton Coll., 1981—98, chair, 1990—91; mem. N.J. Governing Bds. Assn. of State Colls., 1987—98, pres., 1991—93; chair N.J. State Coll. of Governing Bds., 1991; mem. Ewing Twp. Planning Bd., 1996—97; chair Dem. State Com., 2002—. Field rep. N.J. Divsn. on Civil Rights; chief Bur. of Housing and Pub. Accommodations; establisher, dir. State Dept. of Transp. first office of Civil Rights, Contract Compliance and Affirmative Action, 1974—80; mem. exec. com. Assn. of State Dem. Chairs, 2002; mem., deaconess Shiloh Bapt. Ch., Trenton, NJ. Mem.: Nat. Polit. Congress of Black Women, Nat. Assn. for Advancement of Colored People to Met. Trenton (life), Alpha Kappa Alpha Sorority, Inc. Democrat. Office: 226 W State St Trenton NJ 08608 E-mail: AswWatsonColeman@njleg.org.*

COLEMAN, BRITTIN TURNER, lawyer; b. Tuscaloosa, Ala., Dec. 12, 1942; s. Jefferson Jackson and Rose Wallace (Turner) C.; m. Johanna M. Nicol, June 1963 (div. 1967); 1 child, Anna M. Shields; m. Jane M. Kirkman, June 27, 1970; children: Mary Elizabeth, Emily Jane. BA in Am. Studies, U. Ala., 1964, LLB, 1967. Bar: Ala. 1967, U.S. Dist. Ct. (no. dist.) Ala. 1972, U.S. Ct. Appeals (5th cir.) 1975, U.S. Ct. Appeals (11th cir.) 1981, U.S. Dist. Ct. (mid. and so. dists.) Ala. 1986. With Bradley, Arant, Rose & White, Birmingham, Ala., 1971—, ptnr., 1976—. Adj. prof. law, coach Nat. Mock Trial teams Cumberland Sch. Law, 1979-84 (2 Nat. Championships); former mem. faculty Ala. Def. Lawyers Assn. Trial Acad., 1992; former mem. Ala. Pattern Jury Instructions Com.; mem. ct.'s adv. group No. Dist. Ala., 1997. Bd. dirs. Downtown YMCA, 1993-99; active Canterbury United Meth. Ch. Capt. JAGC, U.S. Army, 1967-71. Decorated Bronze Star with first oak leaf cluster, Army Commendation medal with first oak leaf cluster, Vietnam Svc. medal. Fellow Am. Bar Found., Ala. Law Found.; mem. ABA, Am. Judicature Soc., Birmingham Bar Assn. (past chmn. civil cts. com., mem. exec. com. 1992-94, chmn. grievance com. 1989, past chmn. CLE com., past chmn. ins. com., past Liberty Bell award com., past chmn. election com., past exec. com. young lawyers sect., past chmn. long range planning com., pres. elect 1998, pres. 1999), Birmingham Bar Found. (bd. dirs.), Birmingham Inn of Am. Inns of Ct. (master), Ala. Law Inst., Am. Bd. Trial Advocates, Ala. Def. Lawyers Assn., Def. Rsch. Inst., Farrah Law Soc., Ala. Law Sch. Found. (pres. 1994-96), Ala. Alumni of Order of Coif (pres. 1992-94), The Club, Inverness Country Club, The Summit Club. Office: Bradley Arant Rose & White One Federal Pl 18195th Ave N Birmingham AL 35203

COLEMAN, C. NORMAN, radiation and medical oncologist, researcher, educator; b. N.Y.C., Jan. 24, 1945; s. Samuel A. and Minna (Kramer) C.; m. Karolynn Forsburg, May 25, 1970; children: Gabrielle, Keith. BA, U. Vt., 1966; MD, Yale U., 1970. Diplomate Am. Bd. Internal Medicine, Am. Bd. Radiology, Am. Bd. Med. Oncology. Intern in internal medicine U. Calif., San Francisco, 1970-71, resident in internal medicine, 1971-72; clin. assoc. Nat. Cancer Inst., NIH, Bethesda, Md., 1972-74; clin. fellow therapeutic radiology Stanford (Calif.) U. Med. Sch., 1975-78, asst. prof. dept. radiology and medicine, 1979-84, assoc. prof., 1984-85; prof., chmn. Joint Ctr. for Radiation Therapy, Harvard U. Med. Sch., Boston, 1985-99; dir. radiation oncology sci. program Nat. Cancer Inst., NIH, 1999—, dep. dir. Ctr. for Cancer Rsch., 2001—. Prin. investigator radiation therapy oncology group, chem. modifiers of cancer treatment NIH, 1983-99; chmn. sensitizer protector working group DCT, NIH, Bethesda, 1985-99; mem. radiation study sect. NIH, Bethesda, 1988-92; mem. Nat. Cancer adv. bd. subcom. Nat. Cancer Program, 1993-94; mem. Nat. Cancer Inst. Divsn. of Treatment Bd. of Sci. Councilors, 1995-99. Author: (monograph) Chemical Modifiers of Radiotherapy and Chemotherapy, 1989, Understanding Cancer: Patient's Guide to Diagnosis, Prognosis and Treatment, 1998; editor: (monograph) Interaction of Radiation and Chemotherapy, 1986. Lt. col. USPHS, 1972-74. Fellow ACP, Am. Coll. Radiology, Soc. Chmn. Acad. Radiology Oncology Programs, (pres.), Am. Soc. Therapeutic Radiology and Oncology (bd. dirs. 1996-99), Am. Soc. Clin. Oncology (bd. dirs.), Radiation Rsch. Soc. (counselor 1992-94, pres. 1997); mem. Phi Beta Kappa, Alpha Omega Alpha. Democrat. Avocations: triathlon, family activities. Office: ROSP ROB NIH Bldg 10 B3B69 Bethesda MD 20892 E-mail: ccoleman@mail.nih.gov.

COLEMAN, CHARLES CLYDE, physicist, educator; b. York, Eng., July 31, 1937; came to U.S., 1941; s. Jesse C. and Geraldine (Doherty) C.; m. Sharon R. Slutsky, Aug. 12, 1976; children: Jeffrey Andrew, Matthew Casey. BA, UCLA, 1959, MA, 1961, PhD, 1968. Asst. prof. physics Calif. State U., Los Angeles, 1968-71, assoc. prof, 1971-76, prof., 1976—2002, prof. emeritus, 2002—. Cons. Gen. Dynamics Corp., 1975-77, China Lake Naval Rsch. Labs., 1981; dir. Csula Accelerator Facility; exec. dir. Csula Applied Physics Inst., 1978-83; sr. rsch. fellow Darwin Coll., Cambridge (Eng.) U., 1975-76; project specialist Chinese Provincial Univs. Devel. Project of World Bank, 1987-90; vis. prof. physics U. Istanbul, Turkey, 1969, 72, U. Sydney, Australia, 1977, Arya Mar U., Iran, 1976, U. Natal, South Africa, 1977, UCLA, 1990-91, U. Leicester, U.K., 1995-2001, Huber U., Wuhan, China, 2002; mem. NASA review panel, 1992. Contbr. articles to sci. publs.; referee Solid State Electronics, Phys. Rev., Phys. Rev. Letters, Jour. Phys. Chem. Solids, Jour. Solid State Chem., Jour. Optical Materials. Trustee Calif. State U. L.A. Found., 1981-85. Grantee NSF, 1976—, Rsch. Corp., 1987-91; NATO Collaborative Rsch. grantee, 1991—; NATO Sr. Rsch. fellow Cavendish Lab. (U.K.), 1983-84, Am. Chem. Soc. Rsch. Faculty fellow, 1990. Fellow Brit. Interplanetary Soc., Royal Philatelic Soc. (London); mem. Am. Phys. Soc., Am. Radio Relay League, Sigma Xi, Phi Kappa Phi, Phi Beta Delta, Sigma Pi Sigma. Office: Calif State U Dept Physics Los Angeles CA 90032 E-mail: ccolema@calstatela.edu.

COLEMAN, CHARLES DAVID, statistician, demographer; BS in Econs., George Mason U., 1985, PhD in Econs., 1996; MS in Social Sci., Calif. Inst. Tech., 1987. Math. statistician U.S. Census Bur., Washington, 1998—99, statistician (demography), 1999—. Presenter in field. Contbr. articles to profl. jours. Former mem. Oakleigh Homeowners Assn., Oakton, Va. Mem.: Pub. Choice Soc., So. Demographic Assn., Population Assn. Am., Am. Statis. Assn., Econometric Soc., Am. Econ. Assn., Omicron Delta Epsilon. Achievements include research in Measures of Estimates and Forecasts Quality; development of Official U.S. County Housing Unit Estimates; Official U.S. Subcounty Population Estimates; research in expert on names from U.S. Census. Avocations: travel, music, languages, reading. Office: US Census Bureau 4700 Silver Hill Rd Stop 8800 Washington DC 20233-8800 Personal E-mail: chuckcoleman@yahoo.com. E-mail: ccoleman@census.gov.

COLEMAN, CLAIRE KOHN, public relations executive; b. New Castle, Pa., Nov. 19, 1924; d. Louis and Florence (Frank) K.; m. Frederick H. Coleman, Mar. 10, 1957; children: Franklin, Elliot. BA, Pa. State U., 1945. Market editor Fairchild Publs., N.Y.C., 1945-48; asst. home editor N.Y. Times, 1949-50; pub. rels. dir. United Wallpaper, Chgo., 1950-53, Assoc. Am. Artists, N.Y.C., 1953-54; dir. Wallpaper Info. Bur., N.Y.C., 1954; dept. head Roy Bernard, Inc., N.Y.C., 1955-58; pub. rels. dir. The Siesel Co., N.Y.C., 1972—, sr. v.p., 1988; pres. Tisch Trask Comm. Resources Pub. Rels. Group, 1988-89; sr. v.p. Anthony M. Franco, N.Y.C., 1989-90; pres. Coleman Comm., N.Y.C., 1990—. Ctrl. steering com. Sch. Dist. Critical Assessments, New Rochelle, NY, 1969—71; active Mayor's Adv. Coun. on Aging, 1966, Mayor's Adv. Coun. on Bd. Edn. Appts., 1969; v.p. Coun. of PTAs, 1969—70; chmn. women's divsn. United Jewish Appeal, New Rochelle, 1971; v.p. Found. of WEPR, 1992—93, pres., 1993—94, bd. dirs., 1998—; bd. dirs., v.p. Beechmont Assn., 1969—74, adv. bd., 1990—2003. Fellow: Internat. Furnishings and Design Assn. (founder 1947, nat. treas. 1977—78, nat. pres. 1980—81, N.Y. chpt. v.p. 1994, nat. v.p. mktg. 1998—2000, formerly Nat. Home Fashions League, exec. chmn. 1947, Cir. of Excellence award 1994, Internat. Hon. Recognition award 1998); mem.: Women Execs. Pub. Rels. (bd. dirs. 1983—84, sec. 1986—87, pres.-elect 1994—95, pres. 1996—97). Fax: 914-576-6885. E-mail: ckcpr@aol.com.

COLEMAN, COURTNEY STAFFORD, mathematician, educator; b. Ventura, Calif., July 19, 1930; s. Courtney Clemon and Una (Stafford) C.; m. Julia Wellnitz, June 26, 1954; children: David, Margaret, Diane. BA, U. Calif., Berkeley, 1951; PhD, Princeton U., 1955. Asst. prof. Wesleyan U., Middletown, Conn., 1955-58; from asst. prof. to full prof. Harvey Mudd Coll., Claremont, Calif., 1959-98. Lectr. Princeton (N.J.) U., 1954-55; rsch. in field. Author, editor: Differential Equations Models, 1983; editor, translator: Local Methods in Nonlinear Differential Equations, 1988; author: (with others) Differential Equations, 1987, Differential Equations Laboratory Workbook, 1992 (EDUCOM award for best math./computer course materials), Ordinary Differential Equations: A Modeling Perspective, 1998, ODE Architect, 1999 (award of excellence and Gold medal for best CD-ROM in edn.); mem. editl. bd. Jour. of Differential Equations, 1964—, UMAP Jour., 1980—. Mem. Am. Math. Soc., Math. Assn. Am., Soc. Indsl. Applied Math. Office: Harvey Mudd Coll Math Dept 1250 N Dartmouth Ave Claremont CA 91711 E-mail: coleman@hmc.edu.

COLEMAN, CY, pianist, composer, producer; b. N.Y.C. s. Max and Ida (Prizent) Kaufman. Classically trained pianist; grad. h.s., High Sch. of Music and Art; diploma, N.Y. Coll. Music, 1948; studied with, Rudolph Gruen, Adele Marcus, Bernard Wagenaar, Hall Overton.; MusD (hon.), L.I. U., 1994; LHD (hon.), Hofstra U., 2000. Pres. Notable Music Co., Notable Records Co. Began performing publicly at age six in N.Y.C.; pianist night clubs throughout U.S., 1948—; TV appearances on Dumont, 1947-48, Date in Manhattan, 1948-51, Kate Smith Show, 1951-52, Art Ford Greenwich Village Party, 1957-58; contbr. John Murray Anderson's Almanac, 1953; provided background music to Compulsion, 1957; appearances with Milw. Symphony Orch., Syracuse (N.Y.) Symphony Pops Orch., Detroit Symphony Orch., Indpls. Symphony Orch., San Antonio Symphony Orch., Ft. Worth, Edmonton (Can.), New Orleans, Toledo, Tulsa, Hartford Pops, Grand Rapids, Honolulu, Middletown and Spokane symphony orchs.; composer music for Broadway shows Wildcat, 1960, Little Me, 1962, Sweet Charity, 1963, also revival, 1986, See-Saw, 1973, I Love My Wife, 1977, On the Twentieth Century, 1978 (Tony award Best Original Score 1978), Barnum, 1980, City of Angels, 1989 (Tony award for Best Original Musical Score, 1990), Welcome to the Club 1989, The Will Rogers Follies, 1991 (Tony award for Best Score, 1991, Grammy award for Best Mus. Show Album, 1992, Grammy award for Record Producer and Composer, 1992), The Life (Best Musical), 1997, revival of Little Me, 1998, off Broadway Exactly Like You, Grace, Amsterdam, The Netherlands; also music for motion pictures Heartbreak Kid, Sweet Charity, 1969, Power, 1986, Garbo Talks, Family Business; rec. artist for Westminster, Capitol, Columbia, M.G.M., London records, (recipient Interborough awards Music Edn. League 1934, 35, 36, LaGuardia Meml. award 1961, 2 Emmy awards for TV spl. If They Could See Me Now 1974, Emmy award for Gypsy in My Soul 1975, Drama Desk award for best score I Love My Wife 1977, Cue mag. Golden Apple award for best score I Love My Wife 1977, Tony award Best Score for On the Twentieth Century 1977-78, for City of Angels, 1990); composer popular songs Why Try to Change Me Now, 1952, I'm Gonna Laugh You Out of My Life, 1955, Witchcraft, 1957, Firefly, 1958, It Amazes Me, 1958, You Fascinate Me So, 1958, The Best is Yet to Come, 1959, The Riviera, 1959, Play Boy Theme, 1960, Rules of the Road, 1961, Pass Me By, Pussy Cat, Hey Look Me Over, Big Spender, If My Friends Could See Me Now, Nobody Does It Like Me, I Love My Wife, Hey There Good Times. Recipient Johnny Mercer Songwriters Hall of Fame award, 1995, Elaine Kaufman Cultural Ctr. Honors Creative Arts award, 1999, Lifetime Achievement award Nat. Operatic Dramatic Assn. Eng., 1999, Achievement in the Arts award Northwood Univ., 2000. Mem. ASCAP (v.p., Richard Rogers award 2000), Acad. Motion Picture Arts and Scis. Office: 441 E 57th St New York NY 10022-3003

COLEMAN, D. CHRISTIAN, journalist; b. Cleve, Nov. 6, 1973; s. David T. and Toni (Raia) C.; m. Pamela Reinhard, Sept. 25, 1999. BA, Kent (Ohio) State U., 1996. Prodn. asst. Sta. WKYC-TV, Cleve., 1997; prodr., on-air talent Sta. WMIH-AM, Cleve., 1997; announcer, morning drive Sta. WTTF-FM, Tiffin, Ohio, 1997-98; reporter sports and news Sta. WEOL-AM, Elyria, Ohio, 1998—. Mem.: Kent State U. Alumni Assn. Roman Catholic. Avocations: golf, travel, internet. Office: Sta WEOL-AM PO Box 4006 Elyria OH 44036-2006 E-mail: DCsquared29@aol.com.

COLEMAN, D. JACKSON, ophthalmologist, educator; b. Waverly, N.Y., Dec. 1, 1934; s. Max Elliot and Frances Agnes (Henton) C.; m. Jane Marie Holmes, July 6, 1963; children: Jeffrey, Jonathan, Jeremy. BS, Union Coll., 1956; MD, U. Buffalo, 1960. Intern Columbia Med. Div., Bellevue Hosp., N.Y.C., 1960-61; lt. comdr. USPHS Bur. State Services Heart Disease Control Program, Washington, 1961-64; resident in ophthalmology Edward S. Harkness Eye Inst., Columbia Presbyn. Med. Center, N.Y.C., 1964-67, mem. faculty, staff, 1967-79; John Milton McLean prof. Cornell U. Med. Coll., N.Y.C., 1979—; chmn. dept. ophthalmology N.Y. Hosp.-Cornell Med. Ctr., 1979—, ophthalmologist-in-chief, 1979—. Sr. author: Ultrasonography of Eye and Orbit, 1977; contbr. articles to med. jours. Recipient Wacker award of Club Jules Gonin Internat. Retina Soc., 1976, Lucien Howe medal, 1988; NIH grantee. Fellow ACS, Am. Acad. Ophthalmology; mem. Am. Inst. Ultrasound Medicine (bd. govs. 1970-73), Am. Ophthamolgy Soc., Am. Retina Soc. (v.p. 1989-91, pres. 1991-93), Assn. Rsch. Ophthamology (Weisenfeld award 1996), Societas Interationalis de Diagnostic Ultrasonica in Ophthalmology (exec. bd. 1971-81), World Fedn. Ultrasound Medicine and Biology (exec. bd. 1973-82, sec.treas. 1973-77, treas. 1977-82), Am. Intraocular Lens Soc. (sci. advisor 1976-79), Am. Soc. Ophthalmic Ultrasound (bd. govs. 1976—), AMA, N.Y. County Med. Soc., Am. Eye Study Club, Jules Gonin Club (exec. com. 1992—, v.p. 1993-98, pres. 1998—). Republican. Methodist. Office: NY Presbyterian Hosp-Cornell Med Ctr 525 E 68th St New York NY 10021-4870 E-mail: djceye@aol.com.

COLEMAN, DAN, composer, arranger, recording engineer, educator; b. N.Y.C., Jan. 12, 1972; s. Peter and Jane Coleman. BA, U. Pa., 1993; MM, The Juilliard Sch., 1995. Composer-in-assn. Metamorphosen Chamber Orch., Boston, 1993—; composer-in-residence Young Concert Artists, N.Y.C., 1994-96; adj. faculty The Juilliard Sch., 1995-99; composer Crowded Air Music, Tucson, 1999—; resident composer Tucson Symphony, 2002—. Adj. asst. prof. U. Ariz., 2001-02; mem. fellows exec. com. The Macdowell Colony, Peterborough, N.H., 1998-99. Composer: (orchestral work) Whitaker Commission, 1998. Recipient ASCAP/Victor Herbert prize, 1997, Aaron Copland prize, 1999, Beyer award for chamber music, 2002; Charles Ives scholar Am. Acad. Arts and Letters, 1995; Macdowell Colony fellow, 1997, 99, Corp. of Yaddo fellow, 1998; Ariz. Commn. on the Arts fellow, 2000. Home: PO Box 609 Tucson AZ 85702-0609 E-mail: dan@dancoleman.com.

COLEMAN, DANIEL EUGENE, physician; b. Boston, Sept. 12, 1951; s. Bernard John and Lorraine Marie (Walsh) C.; m. Marguerite Marie Horrigan, Aug. 24, 1974; children: Patrick Michael, Daniel Christopher, Erin Kathleen. BA, Boston U., 1973; MD, Georgetown U., 1977. Diplomate Am. Bd. Internal Medicine, cert. pulmonary diseases, crit. care medicine. Resident St. Elizabeth's Hosp., Boston, 1977-80, intern, resident, 1977-80; fellowship Georgetown U. Hosp., Washington, 1980-82; med. dir. ICU Andrews AFB Hosp., Washington, 1983-86; flight surgeon Otis AFB, Cape Cod, Mass., 1986-90; asst. prof. medicine Uniformed Svcs. Hosp., Bethesda, Md., 1983-86; staff pulmonologist Holy Family Hosp., Methuen, Mass., 1986-94, chief of medicine, 1989-93, pres. med. staff, 1996-2001; assoc. clin. prof. medicine Tufts U., Boston, 1990—; med. dir. respiratory tng. No. Essex C.C., Haverhill, Mass., 1984-94; instr. in trauma care Mass. Gen. Hosp., Boston, 1989-94; Col. Mass. Air NG, 1993—, Mass. State Air Surgeon, 1993—. Dir. pulmonary rehab. Whittier Rehab. Hosp., Haverhill, 1987-94; dir. cardiac life support tng. Merrimack Valley, Mass., 1987-94. Mem. St. Luke's Guild, Boston, 1989—. Maj. USAF, 1982-86. Fellow: Am. Coll. Chest Physicians; mem.: AMA, Soc. State Air Surgeons (pres. 1998—2001), Aerospace Med. Assn., Mass. Thoracic Soc. (councillor 1993—96), Mass. Med. Soc. Roman Catholic. Avocations: skiing, birding, nature, family. Office: 565 Turnpike St North Andover MA 01845-5922

COLEMAN, DAVID CECIL, financial executive; b. Topeka, Sept. 7, 1937; s. Merrill Orda and Cecil Jennie (Warders) C. BS in Fin., Kans. U., 1959; PhD in Bus. Adminstrn., Calif. Western U., 1979. Registered investment advisor. Cost acct. Am. Electronics, Inc., Orange, Calif., 1963-65; fin. mgr. Univ. Calif. San Diego, La Jolla, 1965-67; v.p. fin. Aero Titanium Products, San Diego, 1967-69; contr. Gen. Tire, Tustin, Calif., 1969-70; fin. mgr., satellite telecom. analyst Hughes Aircraft, El Segundo, Calif., 1970-76; proprietor Concept Pub., York, N.Y., 1976—. Realtor assoc. Mitchell Pierson Jr., Realtor, Mendon, N.Y., 1980-92; instr. MBA prog. Rochester (N.Y.) Inst., 1982-86. Author: Management of the Firm, 1977, For the Long Term Investor, 1979, Consistency in Market Forecasting, 1982, How to Collect Bad Checks, 1989, Tax Tricks for the Proprietor, 1990, Starting a Business for the Proprietor, 1992, How to Avoid Audit for the Proprietor, 1992, Asset Protection for the Small Firm, 1995. Fin. mgr. York (N.Y.) Hist. Soc., 1988. 1st Lt. USMC, 1959-63. Home: PO Box 500 York NY 14592-0500 Office: Concept Pub 2682 Main St York NY 14592 E-mail: conceptpublishing@hotmail.com.

COLEMAN, DAVID MICHAEL, religious organization executive; b. Cedar Hill, Tenn., Oct. 24, 1942; s. Julian Turner and Dorothy (Cobb) C.; m. Linda Ruth Gholdston, Dec. 21, 1963; children: Melissa Jeanette, Michael Carl. BS, Belmont U., 1965; postgrad., Midwestern Bapt. Theol. Sem., 1965-67, So. Bapt. Theol. Sem., 1979. Cert. fund raising exec. Pastor Maple Grove Bapt. Ch., Dickson, Tenn., 1963-65, Kingsville (Mo.) Bapt. Ch., 1965-67; office mgr. Bapt. Sunday Sch. Bd., Nashville, 1967-69; missionary Zimbabwe So. Bapt. Internat. Mission Bd., Richmond, Va., 1968-86; assoc. dir. vols. in missions dept So. Bapt. Fgn. Mission Bd., Richmond, Va., 1986-87, assoc. to v.p. for devel., 1987-89, dir. for devel., 1989-97; chmn./pres./CEO Atlanta Union Mission, Atlanta, 1999—. Chmn. Bapt. Internat. Mission Services Bd., Johannesburg, South Africa, 1982-83, 84-85. Co-author: (book) Baptist Beliefs, 1972. Pres. Frank Johnson Sch. PTA, Harare, Zimbabwe, 1975-77; chmn. Planning and Devel. Coun., Harare, 1983-85; chmn. bd. trustees Bapt. Theol. Sem., Gweru, Zimbabwe; mem. Ga. Planned Giving Study Group. Mem. Assn. of Fundraising

Profls., Kiwanis (pres. 1963-64, treas. 1965), Rotary. Republican. Avocations: golf, tennis. Home: 1237 Kenway Cir Smyrna GA 30082-6418 Office: Atlanta Union Mission PO Box 1807 Atlanta GA 30301-1807 Fax: 404-588-4016. E-mail: david.coleman@myaum.org.

COLEMAN, DEBRA LYNN, electrical engineer; b. Mobile, Ala., Apr. 7, 1966; d. Fred and Mattie Lois (Carter) C. BSEE, Boston U., 1988; MSEE, U. Wash., Seattle, 2002. Test engr. Raytheon Corp., Andover, Mass., 1987-88; liaison design engr. Boeing Co., Everett, Wash., 1988-89, software engr. Seattle, 1989-90, sr. sys. engr. Renton, Wash., 1990-95, specialist engr. Everett, Wash., 1995—98, acct. mgr., 1998—2001, sr. elec. engr., 2001—. Avocations: writing, history, art, travel, aerospace. Home: 3020 21st Ave S Seattle WA 98144-5906 Office: Boeing Co PO Box 3707 #MS 4A-11 Seattle WA 98124-2207

COLEMAN, DONALD GENE, education educator; b. Ft. Wayne, Ind., June 20, 1934; s. Clarence R. and Ruth F. (Wise) C.; m. Eileen E. Hoffman, Apr. 25, 1959; children: Suzanne Eileen, Jessica Ruth. BS, Ind. U., 1965; MA, St. Francis Coll., 1967; EdD, Ball State U., 1973. Tchr. Ft. Wayne (Ind.) Schs., 1965-67; asst. prof. Ind. U., Ft. Wayne, 1967-74; prof. N.E. Mo. State U., Kirksville, 1974-86, San Diego State U., 1986-88, Calif. State U., Fresno, 1988—. Cons. in field. Author: Slams, 1985. With U.S. Army, 1954-56. Danforth Found. grantee, St. Louis, 1990, 91, 92. Mem. Am. Assn. Sch. Adminstrs., Nat. Coun. Profl. Edn. Adminstrs., Nat. Assn. Elem. Sch. Prins., Calif. Profl. Edn. Adminstrn., Assn. Calif. Sch. Adminstrs., Phi Delta Kappa. Office: Calif State U Sch Edn Fresno CA 93740-0001 E-mail: donc@csufresno.edu.

COLEMAN, DOROTHY ZIPPER, retired educational administrator; b. Louisville, Apr. 18, 1937; d. William Buckner and Florence Marie (Gardner) Zipper; m. Elton B. Coleman, Aug. 16, 1958; children: Sanda Marie Staples, David William Coleman. BABA, Centre Coll. Ky., 1958; MAT, The Citadel, 1974; EdD in Vocat. Edn., U. Ga., 1985. Tchr. Charleston (S.C.) County Pub. Schs., 1968-82; grad. asst. U. Ga., Athens, 1982-85; program coord. So. Ill. U., Carbondale, 1986-97, asst. prof. emeritus, 1997—. Adj. prof. Webster U., 1997—. Mem. ASTD (bd. dirs., instnl. tech. excellence in leadership award 1994), Carolina Soc. for Tng. and Devel. (bd. dirs. 1990-92), Alpha Delta Kappa (past pres. Mu chpt.), Phi Delta Kappa. Avocations: travel, grandchildren. Home: 677 Highwood Cir Charleston SC 29412-9032

COLEMAN, EARL MAXWELL, publishing company executive; b. N.Y.C., Jan. 9, 1916; s. Samuel Sidney and Rose (Ensleman) C.; m. Frances Louise Allan, Mar. 23, 1942 (div. Mar. 15, 1965); children: Allan Douglass, Dennis Scott; m. Ellen Schneid, Aug. 19, 1973. Student, NYU, 1933-34, CCNY, 1934-35, Columbia U., 1946. Founder, pres. Plenum Pub. Corp. (and predecessors), N.Y.C., 1946-77, chmn. bd. dirs., 1960-77, cons., 1977—. Founder Earl M. Coleman Enterprises, Inc. (Pubs.), 1977—; pres. Nat. Pubs. The Black Hills Inc., 1984-89; cons. Prentice Hall Coll. div., 1989-90. Contbr. poems, short stories to mags. Served with USAAF, 1941-45. Mem. Info. Industry Assn. (dir. 1971—), Assn. Am. Publishers (exec. com. tech.-sci.-med. div. 1970—), Sci. Tech. Med. Publishers (Holland). Home: 131 Ridge Dr Montville NJ 07045-9473 *Do whatever you do passionately. Never be astonished at the fact that literally all the worldly affairs with which humans busy themselves and into which they pour so much energy, are games, sometimes bloody games, but games. Not only does the passionate player have a greater chance to get ahead in the game, he also enjoys it more than the passive player. Only the person who is willing to be stark naked before his own eyes, which can be the cruelest of mirrors, gets to savor his life to the fullest. Here too, passion serves, for ruthless honesty with self is key to an honest appraisal of anything else.*

COLEMAN, EMMETT See REED, ISHMAEL SCOTT

COLEMAN, ERNEST ALBERT, plastics and materials consultant; b. N.Y.C., Nov. 21, 1929; s. Del Rey and Rozelle (Weed) C.; m. Sonia Dimon, Aug. 22, 1953 (div. 1967); children: Donna Leslie, David Winslow; m. Ann G. Royer, Jan. 20, 1968. BS in Chemistry, Rensselaer Poly. Inst., 1951; MS in Phys. Organic Chemistry, U. Pa., 1955, PhD in Phys. Organic Chemistry, 1959. Sr. rsch. chemist DuPont, Wilmington, Del., 1957-71; phys. scientist Libr. of Congress, Washington, 1971-73; mgr. tech. svc. GAF, Wayne, N.J., 1973-79; mgr. thermoplastics R & D Dart & Kraft Corp., Paramus, N.J., 1979-82; rsch. mgr. Union Carbide, Tarrytown, N.J., 1982-86, Norton Performance Plastics, Wayne, N.J., 1986-88; key technologist Norton Co., Worcester, Mass., 1986-88. Cons., 1986—; adj. prof. U. Conn., Stamford, 1982-86, Naugatuck State Tech. Coll., 1992-2002; CEO CP Tech., Inc. Inventor over 50 patents (U.S. and fgn.) engring. thermoplastics composites, fast crystallizing PET, improvement of mech., chem. and thermal properties of thermoplastic resins and abrasives; assoc. editor Jour. Vinyl & Additive Tech., 1994-96. V.P. consistory Reformed Ch., Kinnelon, N.J., 1982; elected elder, Turn of River Presbyn. Ch., Stamford, 2000. Fellow Soc. Plastics Engrs. (edn. chmn. 1985-86, 91-92, chmn. tech. program 1987-89, 93-95, seminar chmn. 1990-92, nat. publs. com. 1991-96, nat. edn. com. 1991-96, polymer modifiers and additives divsn. coun. 2001—, nat. intellectual property com. 2002-2003, chair tech. vols. com., 2003—, sec. mktg. & mgmt. divsn. 2000—, adv. com. Stamford, Conn., 2003—); mem. AAAS, Am. Chem. Soc. (chair southwestern Conn. sect. 2002), Assn. Cons. Chemists & Chem. Engrs. (pres. 1996-98), Inventors Assn. Conn., Sigma Xi, Phi Lambda Upsilon. Avocations: rehabilitation of injured/orphaned animals, numismatics, woodworking. Home and Office: 293 Janes Ln Stamford CT 06903-4822

COLEMAN, FRANCES MCLEAN, secondary school educator; b. Jackson, Miss., Feb. 17, 1940; d. Robert Beatty and Dorothy Trotter (Witty) McLean.; m. Thomas Allen Coleman, Aug. 29, 1964; children: James Plemon, Robert McLean, Dorothy Witty McLean, Josiah Dennis, Leonidas McLean. BA, U. Miss., Oxford, 1962; MS, U. Miss., Jackson, 1964, PhD, 1970. Cert. tchr., Miss.; cert. in young adult/adolescent sci., Nat. Bd. Prof. Tchg. Stds. Adolescent/Young Adult Scis. Coord. Title I ESEA Choctaw County, Ackerman, Miss., 1970-73; instr. anatomy and physiology Wood Jr. Coll., Mathiston, Miss., 1977-78; instr. math. Miss. State U., Starkville, 1978-81; tchr. Choctaw City Sch. Dist., Ackerman, 1982—2003, dist. tech. coord., 1995—2003. Adj. faculty Lesley U., Cambridge, Mass., 2002—. Contbr. articles to profl. jours. including Surgery, T.H.E. Jour., Learning and Leading with Tech. Active Miss. State Bd. of Health, Jackson, 1980-94. Recipient Presdl. award for excellence in sci. teaching NSF, 1990, Sci. Tchr. awards Disney, 1993; named to Women Hall of Master Tchrs. Miss. U., 1994; named Educator of Yr. Milken Family Founds., 1991; Tandy scholar, 1991; Tapestry grantee, 1995; Coun. for Basic Edn. Sci.-Math. fellow, 1994, Access Excellence fellow Genentech, 1995, Am. Physiol. Soc. fellow, 1995, Einstein Disting. Educator fellow Dept. of Energy, 2000. Mem. Nat. Sci. Tchrs. Assn., Am. Assn. German Tchrs., Am. Assn. French Tchrs., Am. Assn. Physics Tchrs., Nat. Assn. Biology Tchrs., Miss. Edn. Computer Assn. (Miss. Computer Educator of Yr. 1990, pres.-elect 1995, pres. 1996), Miss. Fgn. Lang. Assn. (pres. secondary sect. 1992-94). Episcopalian. Avocations: reading, travel. Home: PO Box 268 Ackerman MS 39735-0268 Office: Choctaw County Sch Dist PO Box 398 Ackerman MS 39735-0398 E-mail: fcoleman@telepak.net. *We advise students to do what they like in life. Perhaps we should advise them that with imagination and hard work they can transform almost any job so that they like what they do.*

COLEMAN, FRANCIS J., JR., lawyer; b. McCook, Nebr., Jan. 28, 1945; BA, Rice U., 1966; JD (with hons.), U. Tex., 1972. Bar: Tex. 1972. City atty. City of Houston, Tex., 1982-84; ptnr. Vinson & Elkins L.L.P., Houston. Office: Vinson & Elkins 2300 1st City Tower 1001 Fannin St Houston TX 77002-6760

COLEMAN, GARY WILLIAM, retired elementary school educator; b. Davenport, Iowa, Dec. 16, 1945; s. Robert Earl and Mildred Margaret (Mast) C.; m. Janice Marie Coleman, Dec. 29, 1973; children: Heidi Marie, Sean Robert. BS in Elem. Edn., U. S.D., 1987; BSBA, Ariz. State U., 1969. Cert. elem. tchr., EMT, S.D. Tchr. Marty (S.D.) Indian Sch., 1987-91, Parkston (S.D.) Elem. Sch., 1991-2000, ret., 2000; acct./bookkeeper Ulland Bros Constrn., Austin, Minn.; realtor assoc. Myre-Sorenson Real Estate, Albert Lea, Minn.; bldg. constrn. contractor, landscaper, Alcester, S.D.; site mgr. Heritage Ct. Apts., Oak Leaf Real Estate Mgmt. Ltd., 2001—03; preschool tutor South Ctrl. Edn. Coop., 2002—03; tutor Avon Elem. Sch., SD, 2003—; human resources coord. Boys and Girls Club, Wagner, SD, 2003—. E.M.T., 1982—2003. Sgt. USAF, 1969-73. Mem. NEA, Parkston Edn. Assn. (v.p. 1995-96, pres. 1996-97, founder scholarship fund 1997), Am. Legion (vice-comdr. S.D. 7th Dist. 2003-2005).

COLEMAN, GEORGE EDWARD, tenor, alto and soprano saxophonist; b. Memphis, Mar. 8, 1935; s. George Edward and Indiana (Lyle) C.; m. Gloria Bell, Aug. 3, 1959; children: George, Gloria; m. Carol Ann Hollister, Sept. 7, 1985. Grad. high sch., Memphis. Ind. saxophonist with numerous jazz combos, 1952-74; leader George Coleman Quartet/Quintet/Octet, 1974—. Cons. Lenox (Mass.) Jazz Sch. Music, 1958, L.I. U., 1984—, NYU, 1987—, New Sch. Social Rsch., 1987—, Thelonious Monk Inst., 1996, New Eng. Conservatory, 1998; judge Thelonious Monk Inst. Internat. Jazz Competition, Washington, 2002; pvt. instr. Saxophonist B.B. King Band, 1952-53, 55, Max Roach Quintet, 1958-59, MIles Davis quintet, 1963-64, Lionel Hampton Orch., 1965-66, Lee Morgan quintet, 1969, Elvin Jones Quartet, 1970; composer, arranger mus. shows, films: Sweet Love Bitter, 1970, Comedie (French), 1985, Freejack, 1991, The Preacher's Wife, 1996. Grantee NEA, 1975, 81, 85; recipient award for contbns. to music Beale St. Assn., 1977, Tip of the Derby awards, 1978, 79, N.Y. Jazz Audience award, 1979, Gold Note Jazz award, 1985, Key to the City of Memphis, 1991, Lifetime Achievement award Jazz Found. Am., 1997, Concertgebow Jazz award, 2002; selected by Internat. Jazz Critics Poll, 1958; named Artist of Yr., Record World mag., 1969. Address: 63 E 9th St New York NY 10003-6302 E-mail: biggeorgecoleman@aol.com.

COLEMAN, GEORGE JOSEPH, III, (JAY COLEMAN), lawyer; b. Plainfield, N.J., Aug. 25, 1958; s. George Joseph and Alice Burke (McHugh) C. BA in Philosophy, U. Notre Dame, 1980, JD, 1983. Bar: Conn. 1984, Ariz. 1984, U.S. Dist. Ct. Ariz. 1984, U.S. Ct. Appeals (9th cir.) 1985, N.Y. 1993. Law clk. Hon. William E. Eubank, Ariz. Ct. Appeals, Phoenix, 1983-84; assoc. Snell & Wilmer, Phoenix, 1984-90, ptnr., 1991—. Mem. Men's Arts Coun. of Phoenix Art Mus., 1991—. Mem. ABA (sect. of litigation). Democrat. Roman Catholic. Home: 111 E Alvarado Rd Phoenix AZ 85004-1413 Office: Snell & Wilmer One Arizona Ctr Phoenix AZ 85004 E-mail: jcoleman@swlaw.com.

COLEMAN, GLORIA JEAN, chemical manufacturing company professional; b. Hannibal, Mo., May 9, 1952; d. Gene Hughes and Joan (Wiley) Carroll; m. Larry Dean Coleman, Nov. 25, 1971. BBA, Culver-Stockton Coll., Canton, Mo., 1992. Cert. profl. sec. Sec., bookkeeper, cashier Western-So. Life Ins., Hannibal, Mo., 1970-77; exec. sec. Marion County Mut. Savs. and Loan, Hannibal, 1977; acctg./info. svcs. dept. sec. Am. Cyanamid, Hannibal, 1977-85, users svcs. coordinator, 1985-88, analyst office systems, 1988-90, analyst computer edn. and tng., 1990-94; supr. computer edn. and tng., 1995-2000; owner, CEO G.J. Coleman Cons., 2000—; sr. J.D. Edwards implementation assoc. PSS World Med., 2002—. Mem. adv. bd. Hannibal area Vocat. Tech. Sch. Bus. Edn. Com., 1985-91; pub. speaker area schs. and svc. orgns., Quincy, Ill., Hannibal, Springfield, Mo., 1986—. Bd. dirs. ARC, Hannibal; mentor Bus. and Profl. Women's Club, Hannibal, 1985-86,also coord. individual devel. program for pub. speaking; fundraiser Convocom Pub. Broadcasting Sta., Quincy, 1986, Hannibal, 1988. Mem. Cert. Profl. Sec. Acad., Profl. Secs. Internat. (sec. Quinsippi chpt. 1984-85, v.p. Heartland chpt. 1988-89, pres. 1989-91, parliamentarian 1991-93, pres. Mo. div. 1993-94, Sec. of Yr. 1985), Kiwanis (Early Bird 1990-94). Mem. Assembly of God Ch. Avocations: walking, traveling, golf, music, sports. Home: 106 Butternut St Hannibal MO 63401-6517 Office: GJ Coleman Cons 106 Butternut St Hannibal MO 63401-6517

COLEMAN, GREGORY G. former magazine publisher; V.p., gen. mgr. Readers Digest, 1995—97; pub. Reader's Digest mag., Pleasantville, N.Y., Readers Digest, U.S. edit., 1991—97; sr. v.p., worldwide pub. Reader's Digest mag., 1997—2001; xec. v.p. North Am. Ops. Yahoo! Inc., 2001—. Office: Yahoo! Inc. 701 1st Ave Sunnyvale CA 94089

COLEMAN, HENRY EDWIN, art educator, artist; b. Charlottesville, Va., Oct. 26, 1938; s. Albin Clayton and Mary Louise (Nay) C.; m. Charlotte Heyne, Dec. 29, 1962 (dec. 1984); children: Edwin Randolph, Mary Clayton; m. Leslie W. Rose, Jan. 4, 1993; 1 stepson, John A. Rose. AB in Fine Arts, Coll. William and Mary, 1961; MA, U. Iowa, 1963. Instr. art Lawrence Coll., Appleton, Wis., 1963-64; mem. faculty Coll. William & Mary, Williamsburg, Va., 1964-99, prof. fine arts, 1989—91, chair dept. fine arts, 1987—91. Cons. for purchasing CSX Corp. Art Collection, Richmond, Va., 1985. Illustrator: Oscar Wilde's Remarkable Rocket, 1974; one-man shows include Radford Coll., Va., 1975, Gallery II West, St. George, Utah, 1984, U. Maine, Presque Isle, 1989, Andrew & Laura McLain Mus., Florenceville, N.B., Can., 1989, Muscarelle Mus. of Art, William & Mary Coll., Williamsburg, Va., 1999, exhibited in group shows at Patio Show, Iowa City, 1962, 1963, Des Moines Art Ctr., 1963, Lawrence Coll., Appleton, 1964, 20th Century Gallery, Williamsburg, 1964, 1965, 1966, Chrysler Mus., Norfolk, Va., 1972, So. Ill. U. at Carbondale, 1975, Peninsula Art Ctr., Newport News, Va., 1980, Nat. Small Image Exhbn., Spokane, Wash., 1984, Am. Drawing Biennial Muscarelle Mus. of Art, Coll. William and Mary, Williamsburg, 1988, 1990 (Honorable Mention award), 1992, Internat. Cultural Exch. Art Exhibit, Neyagawa, Japan, 1988, Bowery Gallery, N.Y.C., 1988, Invitational D'Art Ctr., Norfolk, 1991, Peninsula Fine Arts Mus., Newport News, 1995, 1996, 2001. Commr. Williamsburg Arts Commn., 1985-91; bd. dirs. Yorktown (Va.) Arts Found., 1989-93; juror Occasion for the Arts, Williamsburg, 1988, 27th Regional Art Exhbn., W.C. Rawls Libr. & Mus., Courtland, Va., 1990; commr. archtl. rev. bd., City Williamsburg, 1994-2000. Summer Rsch. grantee Coll. William & Mary, 1976, Semester Faculty grantee, 1985, Faculty Rsch. grantee, 1991-92. Office: Coll William and Mary Andrews Hall Williamsburg VA 23185

COLEMAN, HENRY JAMES, JR., management educator, consultant; b. Cleve., Nov. 28, 1947; s. Henry James and Kathryn Adele (Ketchum) C.; m. Sharon Ann Boothe, Sept. 12, 1971 (div. Jan. 1975). AB, Dartmouth Coll., 1969, MBA, 1970; PhD, U. Calif., Berkeley, 1978. Employment mgr. Lima (Ohio) Meml. Hosp., 1977-78; strategic planner NCR Corp., Dayton, Ohio, 1980-81; vis. asst. prof. Calif. Poly. State U., San Luis Obispo, 1983-85; dean Sch. Mgmt., Columbia Pacific U., San Rafael, Calif., 1985-92; assoc. prof. mgmt. St. Mary's Coll. Calif., Moraga, 1992-2000; mgmt. cons. Lafayette, Calif., 2000—. Adj. prof. Holy Names Coll., Oakland, Calif., 1987, 90-92; mgmt. cons. Orgn. Dynamics, Berkeley, 1970, Comm. Workers Am., San Francisco, 1971, Exide Corp., Reading, Pa., 1988-89, Retirement Fin. Ctrs. Am., Las Vegas, Nev., 1996. Contbr. articles to profl. jours. Nat. Def. Grad. fellow, 1971. Mem. Western Acad. Mgmt., Phi Beta Kappa. Episcopalian. Avocations: color photography, music appreciation. E-mail: hcoleman@silcon.com.

COLEMAN, JACK ANDREW, JR., otolaryngologist; b. Mpls., Oct. 17, 1951; s. Jack Andrew and Patricia Marie Coleman; m. Margaret Overton, June 14, 1987; children: Kelley Anne, Jennifer Allison, Jack Andrew Christian. Ba, U. Va., 1973; postgrad., U. Autonoma Guadalajara, Mex., 1973-77; MD, U. Cin., 1979. Diplomate Am. Bd. Gen. Otolaryngology, Nat. Bd. Med. Examiners. Resident in surgery Cin. Gen. Hosp., 1979-81; resident in otolaryngology Eye and Ear Hosp. Pitts., 1981-84; staff physician Southside Cmty. Hosp., Farmville, Va., 1984-85, Univ. Med. Ctr., Lebanon, 1985-88; instr. Vanderbilt U. Med. Ctr., Nashville, 1988-93, asst. prof., 1993-96; chief otolaryngology Nashville Gen. Hosp., 1988-93; staff physician Centennial Med. Ctr., St. Thomas Hosp., Nashville, 1996-2000, Chesapeake Gen. Hosp., 2000-01, Sentera Bayside Hosp., 2000—; asst. clin. prof. otolaryngology Eastern Va. Med. Sch., 2000-01. Chmn., mem. com. sleep disorders Am. Acad. Otolaryngology, 1990-99; mem. edn. com. Laser Inst. Am., Cin., 1991-96; cons. In-Fluent, San Francisco, 1998-99; mem. med. adv. bd. Pi Med., 2001; physician Police S.W.A.T. Team, Chesapeake, Va.; cons. Ethicon EndoSurg., 2001. Editor: Management of Lower Airway Stenosis, 1995, Sleep Apnea Vols. 1 and 2, 1998-99. Cub scout leader Boy Scouts Am., 1998-99; hon. chmn. physician adv. bd. Nat. Rep. Congl. Com., 2001. Comdr. USNR. Grantee Laserscope Co., 1988, Karl Storz Instruments, 1989, Vanderbilt U. Rsch. Coun., 1994. Fellow ACS, Am. Acad. Otolaryngology and Head and Neck Surgery, Am. Acad. Facial Plastic and Reconstructive Surgery; mem. Amateur Athletic Union (coach, ofcl. Tae Kwon Do program 1998-2001), Rotary Club. Avocations: military history, military awards, military miniatures, sky diving. Office: Middle Tenn ENT 1255 N Highland Ave Murfreesboro TN 37130

COLEMAN, JAMES J. electrical engineer, educator; b. Chgo., Il, May 15, 1950; s. Harry A. and Lorita Marie (Kelly) C.; m. Teresa Ann Stoerger, Mar. 10, 1984; children: Amelia, Harry T., Lucy. BSEE, U. Ill., 1972, MSEE, 1973, PhD, 1975. Fellow U. Ill., Urbana, 1975-76; tech. staff Bell Labs., Murray Hill, N.J., 1976-78, Rockwell Internat., Anaheim, Calif., 1978-82; from assoc. prof. to prof. elec. and computer engring. U. Ill., 1982—, Franklin W. Woeltge Prof. Electrical and Computer Engineering, 2002—. Pres. Bd. Edn. Monticello (Ill.) Bd. Edn., 1997—. Fellow IEEE, AAAS, Optical Soc. Am., Am. Phys. Soc. Achievements include patents in field. Office: U Ill Dept Elec & Computer Engring 208 N Wright St Urbana IL 61801-2355

COLEMAN, JAMES H., JR., former state supreme court justice; b. Lawrenceville, VA, May 4, 1933; s. James H. Sr. and Neda Coleman; m. Sophia Coleman, May 12, 1962; 2 children. BA cum laude, Va. State U., 1956, LLD (hon.), 1995; JD, Howard U., 1959. Bar: N.J. 1960, U.S. Dist. Ct. N.J. 1960, U.S. Supreme Ct. 1963. Asst. and/or cons. various N.J. commns. and divs., 1960-64; pvt. practice law Elizabeth and Roselle, N.J., 1960-70; judge N.J. Workers' Compensation Ct., 1964-73, Union County Ct., 1973-78, Law div. N.J. Superior Ct., 1978-81; mem. spl. three-judge resentencing panel N.J. Superior Ct., 1979-81; judge Appellate div. N.J. Superior Ct., 1981-87, presiding judge, 1987-94; assoc. justice Supreme Ct. of N.J., Springfield, 1994—. Mem. various Supreme Ct. coms.; lectr. in field. Chmn. Elizabeth Good Neighbor Coun.; mem. Elizabeth Adv. Bd. on Urban Renewal; incorporator, bd. dirs. Union County Legal Svcs., Elizabeth Anti-Poverty Program; v.p., bd. dirs., counsel to Urban League of Union County; counsel to Elizabeth NAACP; v.p. Scotch Plains-Fanwood Human Rights Coun.; Mem. N.J. Com. on Hiring the Handicapped; mem. Union County Coordinating and Adv. Com. on Higher Edn.;mem. Essex County Coll. Equal Edn. Opportunity Fund Bd., others. Fellow ABA; mem. Nat. Bar Assn. (judicial coun.), N.J. Bar Assn., Union County Bar Assn., Am. Law Inst., Am. Judicature Soc., Garden State Bar Assn., Omega Psi Phi. Baptist. Avocations: tennis, gardening. Office: Supreme Ct of NJ 99 Mount Bethel Rd Warren NJ 07059-5126*

COLEMAN, JAMES JULIAN, lawyer; b. New Orleans, May 5, 1915; s. William Ballin and Millie (Davis) C.; m. Dorothy Louise Jurisich, July 30, 1940; children: James Julian, Thomas Blaise, Peter Dee, Dian Judith. BA, Tulane U., 1934, JD, 1937; LL.D. (hon.), Hampden-Sydney Coll., 1982. Bar: La. 1937. Sr. ptnr. Coleman, Johnson, Artigues & Jurisich, New Orleans. Past pres. Internat. Trade Mart, New Orleans Philharmonic Symphony; hon. consul gen. Republic of Korea; chmn. La. Jud. Compensation Commn. Past pres. New Orleans C. of C., Jr. Achievement New Orleans, Adult Edn. Ctr.; past bd. dirs. U.S. C. of C., Internat. House, Fed. Rels. Assn.; past chmn. New Orleans coordinating com. NASA; founder Peoples League; trustee emeritus Principia Coll.; past chmn. Tulane U. Bus. Sch. Coun.; chmn. bd. trustees Crimestoppers. Decorated Order of Oranje-Nassau Diplomatic Service Merit Republic Korea; recipient Nat. Achievement award Jr. Achievement, Loving Cup award New Orleans Times-Picayune, 1980, Joseph W. Simon, Jr. award, 1981, Disting. Alumnus award Tulane U., 1982, New Orleans Activist award, 1984, C. Alvin Bertel award, 1985; named to Bus. Hall of Fame, 1984; named Pres. Emeritus, World Trade Ctr., N.Y.C., Chmn. Emeritus, The City Energy Club, Humanitarian of Yr. ARC, 2000; recipient Benementi Papal Honor, 1989. Mem. ABA, Internat. Bar Assn., La. Bar Assn., New Orleans Bar Assn., Am. Judicature Soc. (past dir.), Beta Gamma Sigma (hon.) Christian Scientist (1st reader 1953-56). Home: 10 Audubon Pl New Orleans LA 70118-5526 Office: 321 Saint Charles Ave New Orleans LA 70130-3145 *Success in Family Enterprises depends on an inbred family loyalty supported by love, compassion and understanding for and between family members and their spouses from generation to generation.*

COLEMAN, JAMES JULIAN, JR., lawyer, industrialist, real estate executive; b. New Orleans, May 7, 1941; s. James Julian Sr. and Dorothy Louise (Jurisich) C.; m. Carol Campbell Owen, Dec. 19, 1970 (dec. Sept. 1979); 1 child, James Owen; m. Mary Olivia Cochrane Cushing, Oct. 12, 1985. BA, Princeton U., 1963; postgrad. in law, Oxford (Eng.) U., 1963-65; JD, Tulane U., 1968. Bar: La. 1969, U.S. Supreme Ct. 1969. Chmn. Internat.-Matex Tank Terminals, New Orleans, 1969—; pres. Coleman Devel. Co., New Orleans, 1969—, IMTT, Quebec, 1993—, Nfld. Transhipment Terminal Inc.; ptnr. Coleman, Johnson & Artigues, New Orleans, 1972—; chmn. DownTown Parking Service, New Orleans, 1978—; pres. City Ctr. Properties, New Orleans, 1980—. Mng. ptnr. Windsor Court Hotel, New Orleans Hilton Hotel, Exxon Bldg., Chevron Bldg., Freeport Cooper Gold Bldg., Internat. River Ctr.; chmn. East Jersey R.R. and Terminal Co., 1993; trustee Loving Found., New Orleans, R.L. Blaffer Found., Houston; dir., v.p. U.S. Coast Guard Found., pres. Natl. Coast Guard Museum Assn. 2001—. Author: Gilbert Antoine de St. Maxent: The Spanish Frenchman of New Orleans, 1975. Mem. history coun. Princeton U., 1982—; mem. N.J. Commn. on Sci. and Tech., 1992—; bd. dirs. Hampden Sydney Coll., 1982-92, Liberty Sci. Ctr., Liberty State Park, N.J., 1999—; bd. overseers N.J. Inst. Tech., 1999—; mem. N.J. Commn. on Jobs and Econ. Growth, 2003—. Named H.M. Hon. Brit. Consul for La., Brit. Consulate, New Orleans, 1975—, to Order of Brit. Empire, Queen Elizabeth II, London, 1986. Mem. ABA, La. Bar Assn., N.Y. Yacht Club, N.Y. Racquet Club, Newport Reading Room, So. Yacht Club, New Orleans Lawn Tennis Club, USN League (bd. dirs. New Orleans), Union League Club. Office: Coleman Johnson & Artigues 321 St Charles Ave 10th Fl New Orleans LA 70130-3145 E-mail: jimmyjr504@aol.com.

COLEMAN, JAMES SCOTT, environmental research executive; b. Pitts., Dec. 30, 1960; s. Morton and Greta Bernice Coleman; m. Adele Ruth Johnson, June 25, 1999. BS, U. Maine, 1982; MS, MPhil, PhD, Yale U., 1987. Postdoctoral scholar Stanford (Calif.) U., 1987-88; postdoctoral fellow Harvard U., Cambridge, Mass., 1988-90; prof. biology Syracuse (N.Y.) U., 1990-97; program dir. NSF, Arlington, Va., 1995-96; exec. dir. bio. scis. ctr. Desert Rsch. Inst., Reno, 1997-99; dir. State of Nev. NSF EPSCoR program U. and C.C. Sys. Nev., Reno, 1998—; v.p. rsch. and bus. devel. Desert Rsch. Inst., Reno, 1999—. Mem. bd. dirs. Nev. Tech. Coun., Reno, Nat. EPSCoR Coalition, Washington, Internat. Arid Lands Consortium, Tucson; councilor Oak Ridge (Tenn.) Associated Univs., 2000-01. Mem. editl. bd. Ecology and Ecol. Monographs, 1996-99, Internat. Jour. Plant Sci., 1998—; contbr. numerous articles to profl. jours. Recipient grant NSF, 1992-96, 98—, Young Investigator award NSF, 1993-99, grant Andrew W. Mellon Found., 1993—, grant USEPA, 1999—, grant U.S. Dept. Energy, 2000—. Mem. AAAS, Ecol. Soc. Am. (pres. physiol. ecology sec. 1997-2000), Bot. Soc. Am., Western Indsl. Nev., Nev. Tech. Coun. (chair tech. adv. bd. 2000). Avocations: guitar, hiking, dogs, basketball. Office: Desert Rsch Inst 2215 Raggio Pky Reno NV 89512 Fax: 775-673-7421. E-mail: jcoleman@dri.edu.

COLEMAN, JEAN BLACK, nurse, physician assistant; b. Sharon, Pa., Jan. 11, 1925; d. Charles B. and Sue E. (Dougherty) Black; m. Donald A. Coleman, July 3, 1946; children: Sue Ann Lopez, Donald Ashley. Grad., Spencer Hosp. Sch. Nursing, Meadville, Pa., 1945; student, Vanderbilt U., 1952-54. RN, Ga. Nurse, dir. nursing Bulloch Meml. Hosp., Statesboro, Ga. 1948-51, nurse supr. surgery, 1954-67, dir. nursing, 1967-71; physician's asst., nurse anesthetist Office Dr. Robert H. Swint, Statesboro, 1971-96; physician asst. Office Dr. Earl L. Alderman, Statesboro, 1996-98, Dr. Swaroop Reddy, Statesboro, 1998—. Mem. physician's asst. adv. com. Ga. Med. Bd., 1989-97; mem. physician assts. adv. com. Ga. Bd. Med. Examiners, 1987-97, ex-officio mem., 1994-95. Recipient Dean Day Smith Svc. to Mankind award, 1995; named Woman of Yr. in med. field Bus. and Profl. Women, 1980; Paul Harris fellow Rotary Club. Mem. ANA, Am. Acad. Physician Assts., Ga. Nurses Assn., Ga. Assn. Physician Assts. (bd. dirs. 1975-79, v.p. 1979-80, pres. 1980-81). Democrat. Roman Catholic.

COLEMAN, JEFFREY PETERS, lawyer; b. Providence, Nov. 21, 1959; s. Gerard Giles and Molly Claire (Armbrecht) C.; m. Vonnie Lynn Hendrickson, July 11, 1981; children: Chelsea Adelle, Rebecca Rose, Martin Daniel, Angelyn Marie. BA in Psychology, Davidson (N.C.) Coll., 1981; postgrad., Exeter (Eng.) U., 1984; JD, Coll. of William and Mary, 1985. Bar: Fla. 1985, U.S. Dist. Ct. (mid. dist.) Fla. 1986. Assoc. Harris, Barrett, Mann & Dew, St. Petersburg, Fla., 1985-86; ptnr. Bonner, Hogan & Coleman, P.A., Clearwater, Fla., 1986-97; pres. Coleman Law Firm, 1997—. Author: Spotting Those Bad Apples: Investment Fraud in the New Millenium, 1999. Counsel Pinellas County (Fla.) Habitat for Humanity, 1989, Boy Scouts Am. Pinellas County; advisor Phiomont Expdn., 2002; worship leader Heritage United Meth. Ch. Mem. Fla. Bar Assn., Clearwater Bar Assn. (pres. young lawyers divn., coord. pub. rels.

com. 1989-90), Publ. Investors Arbitration Bar Assn. (chmn. 1999 Fla. mid-year conf.), Nat. Assn. Securities Dealers (arbitrator 2000), Am. Trial Lawyers Assn. (nat. chmn. securities litigation sect.). Republican. Avocations: scuba diving, camping, boating. Office: Coleman Law Firm 581 S Duncan Ave Clearwater FL 33756 Fax: 727-461-7476. E-mail: jeff@colemanlaw.com.

COLEMAN, JOEL CLIFFORD, lawyer; b. Reading, Pa., Nov. 6, 1930; s. Thomas and Lee (Jason) Iscovitz; m. Lois M. Schulman, Feb. 4, 1960; children: Teri, Thomas. BS in Econs., U. Pa., 1952, LLB cum laude, 1955. Bar: N.Y. 1956. Assoc. Kaye, Scholer, Fierman, Hays & Handler, N.Y.C., 1955-67; atty. Twentieth-Century Fox Film Corp., N.Y.C., 1967-69; gen. counsel Internat. Playtex, Inc., N.Y.C. and Stamford, Conn., 1969-86, sec., 1975-86, v.p., 1980-86, also dir.; v.p., gen. counsel, sec. Playtex Inc., 1986-88, Playtex Family Products Corp., 1989-94, Playtex Products, Inc., 1994, assoc. gen. counsel, asst. sec., 1994-95. Editor U. Pa. Law Rev., 1953-55, case editor, 1954-55. Trustee Larchmont (N.Y.) Temple, 1973-75; bd. dirs. Jewish Home for the Elderly of Fairfield County, 1996—; bd. dirs. Bruce Mus., Greenwich, Conn., 1997—. Mem. Order of Coif. Home and Office: 61 Ridgeview Ave Greenwich CT 06830-4755

COLEMAN, JOHN JAMES, III, lawyer, educator; b. Birmingham, Ala., Apr. 10, 1956; s. John James Jr. and Yonceil Oden (Foster) C.; m. Lizabeth Gaines, Aug. 24, 1985; 1 child, John J. IV. AB in History and Econs. magna cum laude, Duke U., 1978, JD, 1981. Bar: Ala. 1981, U.S. Dist. Ct. (no. and mid. dists.) Ala., U.S. Ct. Appeals (4th and 11th cirs.) 1982, U.S. Supreme Ct. 1987, Ga. 2000, Tex. 2001. Law clerk Judge Donald Russell, U.S. Ct. Appeals 4th cir., Richmond, Va., 1981-82; assoc. Balch & Bingham, Birmingham, 1982-88, ptnr., 1989-2000, Burr & Forman LLP, Birmingham, 2000—. Adj. instr. Cumberland Sch. Law, Birmingham, 1990—, Birmingham Sch. Law, 1994—; v.p. Indsl. Rels. Rsch. Assn., Birmingham, 1990-91; bd. dirs. Indsl. Health Coun. of Ala., Inc., Birmingham, 1991—. Author: Employment Discrimination in Alabama, Supplement to Employment Discrimination in Alabama, 1991, Disability Discrimination in Employment, 2001; co-author: (guide publ.) Workers Compensation Practice, 1994; contbr. articles to profl. jours. Ballot security atty. Rep. Party, Ala., 1988, 92, 94; co-chmn. Kidschance Scholarship, Birmingham, 1992. Mem. ABA (labor and employment law sect. OSHA com.), Am. Arbitration Assn. (mem. panel arbitrators), Ala. State Bar (exec. com. labor and employment sect. treas. 1995-96, vice chmn. 1996-97, chmn. 1997-98), Shades Mountain Sunrise Rotary Club (treas. 1994-96), Redstone Club. Republican. Roman Catholic. Avocations: tennis, cycling, riding, writing. Home: 10 Peachtree St Birmingham AL 35213-3018 Office: Burr & Forman LLP 3100 SouthTrust Tower 420 N 20th St Birmingham AL 35203 Fax: (205) 458-5100. E-mail: jcoleman@burr.com.

COLEMAN, JOHN JOSEPH, telephone company executive; b. Boston, Aug. 2, 1937; s. Martin Joseph and Anna Veronica (Leonard) C.; m. Carol Ann Holmes, May 6, 1961; children: Mark Christopher, Cara Romaine. BA cum laude, Boston Coll., 1964; postgrad., Harvard U., 1970. With New Eng. Telephone Co., 1955—, various supervisory positions plant, acctg., sales, mktg., now v.p.; prin. The Coleman Group, Walpole, Mass. Bd. dirs. Mchts. Nat. Bank, Manchester. Bd. dirs. United Way of Greater Manchester, chmn., 1980; chmn. Gov.'s Mgmt. Rev., 1981; chmn. fundraising campaign Manchester Crimeline, Inc., 1982; bd. dirs. Boston Mcpl. Rsch. Bur., 1984-86, Mass. Taxpayers Found. Inc., 1984-86; mem. New Spirit in Boston Com., 1984-85. With USN, 1956-58. Mem. Bus. and Industry Assn. of N.H. (dir.), N.H. Safety Coun. (adv. bd.), Am. Automobile Assn. Mass. (mem. adv. bd.), Greater Boston C. of C. (chmn. pub. safety com. 1985-86). Office: The Coleman Group 1240 Old North St Walpole MA 02081-2325

COLEMAN, JOHN JOSEPH, III, surgery educator; b. Boston, Nov. 15, 1947; MD, Harvard U., 1973. Intern Emory U. Affiliated Hosp., Atlanta, 1973-74, resident in gen. surgery, 1974-78, residentin plastic surgery, 1978-80; fellow in surg. oncology U. Md., Balt., 1980; prof. surgery Ind. U., Indpls., 1980—; chief plastic surgery Ind. U. Med. Ctr., Indpls., 1980—; chmn. American Board of Plastic Surgery, 2002—. Office: U Plastic Surg Assocs 235 Emerson Hall 565 Barnhill Dr Indianapolis IN 46202-5112

COLEMAN, JOHN ROYSTON, writer; b. Copper Cliff, Ont., Can., June 24, 1921; came to U.S., 1946, naturalized, 1954; s. Richard Mowbray and Mary Irene (Lawson) C.; m. Mary N. Irwin, Oct. 1, 1943 (div. 1966); children: John M., Nancy J., Patty A., Stephen W. BA, U. Toronto, 1943; MA, U. Chgo., 1949, PhD, 1950; LLD (hon.), Beaver Coll., 1963, U. Pa., 1968, Gannon Coll., 1975; L.H.D. (hon.), Manhattanville Coll., 1975, Emory and Henry Coll., 1977, Green Mountain Coll., 1984; DLitt (hon.), Haverford Coll., 1980, Elizabethtown Coll., 1987; D.Litt. (hon.), Marlboro Coll., 1991; DSL (hon.), U. Toronto Victoria Coll., 1994. Rsch. assoc. U. Chgo., 1947-49; instr. econs. Mass. Inst. Tech., 1949-51, asst. prof., 1951-55; asso. prof., asst. head dept. econs. Carnegie Inst. Tech., 1955-60, prof., head dept. econs., 1960-63, dean div. humanities and social sci., 1963-65; assoc. dir. econ. devel. and adminstrn. Ford Found., 1965-66, program officer in charge social devel., 1966-67; pres. Haverford Coll., Pa., 1967-77, Edna McConnell Clark Found., N.Y.C., 1977-86; chmn. Coleman Assocs. Inc., 1985-97; pres. Home Town Press, Inc., 1995-2001. Chmn. bd. dirs. Fed. Res. Bank Phila., 1973-76; labor arbitrator, cons., 1953-85; cons. indsl. rels. rsch. Ford Found. in India, 1960-61; tchr. Am. Economy CBS-TV, 1962-63 Author: Goals and Strategy in Collective Bargaining, 1951, Readings in Economics, 1952, 55, 58, 64, 67, Labor Problems, 1953, 59, Working Harmony, 1955, The Changing American Economy, 1967, Comparative Economic Systems, 1968, Blue Collar Journal, 1974, The Ballad of Clarence Adams, 1992, Pieces from the Quilt, 1993, The Play of the Three Kings, 1995, Takeoff at the North Pole, 2002; contbr. numerous articles to mags. Justice of peace, chmn. bd. civil authority Town of Chester, Vt., 1991—; prodr., dir. Chester Players Guild, 1991—; dir. Green Mountain Union H.S. Bd., 1998—; v.p. So. Windsor United Way, 1997-2003; chmn. Reparative Parole Bd., Springfield, Vt., 1997—. Lt. Royal Can. Navy, Vol. Res., 1943-46. Mem. Religious Soc. of Friends. Home: PO Box 995 Chester VT 05143-0995

COLEMAN, JOHN WESLEY, fluid mechanics engineer, heat transfer engineer; b. Dearborn, Mich., July 13, 1966; s. John Wesley and Terry May Coleman. BSME, U. Mich., 1989; MS in Engring., Western Mich. U., 1995; PhD, Iowa State U., 2000. Engr. Westinghouse Electric Corp., Chgo., 1990-92; instr. Western Mich. U., Kalamazoo, 1995-98, doctoral assoc., 1997-98; rsch. engr. Iowa State U., Ames, 1998-2000. Contbr. articles to sci. jours., including Internat. Jour. Heat and Mass Transfer, ASHRAE Trans., Jour. Enhanced Heat Transfer. Scholar Western Mich. U., 1996-97. Mem. ASHRAE (grantee 1999), Epeians (v.p. 1989-90), Phi Kappa Phi. Democrat. Avocations: music, travel, art history. Home: 41485 Savage Rd Belleville MI 48111-3058 Office: Brazeway 2711 E Maumee Adrian MI 49221 E-mail: jcoleman@brazeway.com.

COLEMAN, JOHN WILLIAM, urologist; b. Jersey City, Jan. 26, 1939; s. John William and Marion Cecille (McAuliffe) C.; m. Rosemary Elizabeth Romano, July 13, 1963 (div. 1984). AB, Georgetown U., 1960, MD, 1964. Diplomate Am. Bd. Urology. Intern, resident in surgery N.Y. Hosp., 1964-66, resident in urology, chief resident in urology, 1968-72, asst. attending surgeon urology, 1972-75; assoc. attending urologist N.Y. Hosp./Cornell Med. Ctr., 1975—. Assoc. prof. urology Cornell Med. Coll., 1975—; cons. Rockefeller U. Hosp., N.Y.C., 1985—; Vets. Gen. Hosp., Taipei, Taiwan, 1987; bd. dirs. Am. Bur. for Med. Advancement in China. Chief med. officer USMC/USN, 1966—68, Vietnam. Recipient John K. Lattimer award, 1997, N.Y., N.J. sect. Nat. Kidney Found. award, 1997. Fellow ACS, Am. Acad. Pediatrics; mem. Asian Surg. Soc., Chinese Am. Med. Soc., Soc. Pediat. Urology, Soc. Urologie Internat, Kidney and Urology Found Am. (bd. dirs.). Roman Catholic. Avocations: golf, study of southeast asia. Office: 53 E 70th St New York NY 10021-4941 also: 254 Canal St Rm 3001 New York NY 10013-3501

COLEMAN, JONATHAN MARK, writer, English language educator; b. Allentown, Pa., Sept. 26, 1951; s. Frederic Edward Coleman and Sylvia (Berkowitz) Coleman Harris; m. Kathryn Diana Court, July 8, 1978 (div. Feb. 1989); m. Eileen S. Dinan, May 30, 1992 (div. 1997). BA, U. Va., 1973. Editorial asst. The New Rev., London, 1974; publicity writer Alfred A Knopf, N.Y.C., 1975-77; assoc. editor Simon & Schuster, N.Y.C., 1977-78, sr. editor, 1978-81, mem. editorial bd., 1980-81; assoc. producer CBS News, N.Y.C., 1981-83; lectr. English U. Va., Charlottesville, 1986-93. Advisor Pres. Clinton Race Initiative, 1997. Author: At Mother's Request, 1985, Exit the Rainmaker, 1989, Long Way to Go, 1997. Fellow Va. Ctr. for Creative Arts; mem. Am. PEN. Avocations: reading, sports (watching and participating). Home: 801 Park St Charlottesville VA 22902-4317 E-mail: jonacoles@aol.com.

COLEMAN, JOSEPH DALE, architect; b. Sarasota, Fla., Apr. 1, 1939; s. Joseph Paul and Frances Corinne (Stockstill) How; m. Rosemary Peduzzi, Nov. 24, 1965 (div. Feb. 1978); children: Lisa Anne, Laura Frances, Anna Elizabeth; m. Feay Shellman, Dec. 27, 1986; 1 child, Weslie Selena. BA, U. Miss., 1961; postgrad., Claremont Grad. Sch., 1961-62, U. Calif., Berkeley, 1968-69; BArch, Tulane U., 1974; MA in History, U. South Fla., 1992; PhD, U. Fla., 1998. Registered architect, Ga., NCARB. Archtl. draftsman Leo S. Wou and Assocs., Honolulu, 1969-69, Ray Bergeron and Assocs., New Orleans, 1974-76; planner Wolf/Kirkman Assocs., Albany, N.Y., 1970-72; architect N. Grant Nicklas and Assocs., Altoona, Pa., 1976-77, Maddox and Assocs., Savannah, Ga., 1977-80; pvt. practice architecture Savannah, 1980-88, Tampa, Fla., 1998—2000. Instr. drafting and design Pasco-Hernando C.C., New Port Richey, Fla., 1998-2000; asst. prof. Coll. Applied Sci., U. Cin., 2000—; judge Nat. Coun. Archtl. Registration Bds., Archtl. Record Exam., Ft. Lauderdale, Fla., 1985. Prin. works include pvt. residences. Mem. adv. bd. Hillsborough County Libr., 1989-92. With USN, 1962 67, Vietnam. U. Miss. scholar, 1958-61, Claremont Coll. fellow, 1961-62. Mem. AIA, Assn. for Preservation Tech., Icomos, Phi Eta Sigma, Phi Kappa Phi. Democrat. Roman Catholic. Avocation: sailing.

COLEMAN, JOSEPH MICHAEL, truck lease and logistics consultant; b. Washington, Mar. 6, 1945; s. Francis Thomas and Helen (Hile) C.; m. Dorothy Burke, Feb. 14, 1976; children: Caroline Dalton, Joseph Michael Jr., Elizabeth O'Keefe. BSBA, Georgetown U., 1971. Asst. to pres. Leaseway Transp. Corp., Cleve., 1971-73; pres. Leaseway Transp. Mktg. Corp., N.Y.C., 1973-77; v.p. Colorlab Corp., Rockville, Md., 1977-78; area dir. Hertz Corp., N.Y.C., 1978-82; nat. account exec. Hertz Penske Truck Leasing, Reading, Pa., 1982-86; v.p. Indsl. Fleet Mgmt., Towson, Md., 1986-88; pres. Friedman, Fuller & Coleman, Inc., Rockville, Md., 1988-93, Joseph M. Coleman & Assocs. Ltd., Bethesda, Md., 1992—. Mem. Am. Truck Hist. Soc., Washington Hist. Soc., Md. Motor Truck Assn., Soc. of Friendly Sons of St. Patrick, Gentleman Afield Sporting Club, Traffic Club (Balt.), Kenwood Country Club, Assn. of the Oldest Inhabitants of Washington. Republican. Roman Catholic. Office: Coleman & Assocs 7315 Wisconsin Ave Ste 450N Bethesda MD 20814 E-mail: jmc45@georgetown.edu.

COLEMAN, JOYCE KIT, English literature educator, literary historian; b. Bklyn., Nov. 12, 1949; d. Alexander and Harriet (Yanover) C. BA, Barnard Coll., 1971; MA, U. Tex., 1979; PhD, U. Edinburgh, Scotland, 1993. Proofreader Svc. Typesetters, Austin, Tex., 1976-77; proofreader, prodn. asst. U. Tex. Press, Austin, 1977-79; freelance copy editor, Austin and Berkeley, Calif., 1979-83; copy editor Boston Mag., 1983-84; staff editor Boston Bus. Jour., 1984-85; mng. editor Am. Soc. Law and Medicine, Boston, 1985-88; assoc. prof. English lit. U. N.D., Grand Forks, 1994—. Author: Public Reading and the Reading Public in Late Medieval England and France, 1996. Mem. MLA, Early Book Soc., Internat. Courtly Lit. Soc., Medieval Acad. Am., New Chaucer Soc. Avocation: photography. Office: Univ ND PO Box 7209 Grand Forks ND 58202-7209 E-mail: joyce_coleman@und.nodak.edu.

COLEMAN, K(ATHERINE) ANN, behavioral psychology educator; b. Plattsburg, N.Y. d. John and Anna C. BS, Elms Coll., 1963; MS, Springfield Coll., 1964; PhD, Boston Coll., 1971; MPH, Harvard U., 1978. Psychologist Exec. Office of the Pres., Washington, 1964-66; rsch. assoc. Harvard U., Cambridge, Mass., 1970-71; asst. prof. SUNY, Stony Brook, 1971-75, assoc. prof., 1975-78, Boston U., 1978—. Owner, pres. La Di Da Properties, Cambridge, 1986—. Co-author: Behavioral Statistics: The Core, 1994, Fundamentals of Behavioral Statistics, 9th edit., 2000; contbr. articles to profl. jours. Fellow APA, Am. Psychol. Soc.; mem. New Eng. Ednl. Rsch. Orgn. (bd. dirs. 1974-86, v.p. 1985-86, pres. 1986-87), Ea. Ednl. Rsch. Orgn. (div. chmn. 1979-91, bd. dirs. 1985-91). Home: 44 Concord Ave Cambridge MA 02138-2380 Office: Boston U Dept Psychology 64 Cummington St Boston MA 02215-2407 E-mail: kaycole@bu.edu.

COLEMAN, KIMBERLEE MICHELE, critical care nurse; b. North Tonawanda, N.Y., July 11, 1962; d. Samuel and Joan (Newhart) C.; married; children: Joshua, Kaylee; m. Ronald L. Coleman, May 23, 1997 (dec. July 1999). AS, Niagara County C.C., Sanborn, N.Y., 1982; student, U. Buffalo, 1984. Staff and relief charge nurse, preceptor Erie County Med. Ctr., Buffalo, 1983—86; staff and relief charge nurse Lawnwood Regional Hosp., Ft. Pierce, Fla., 1986—88, Sebastian Humana Hosp., Roseland, Fla., 1988—89; staff nurse surg. ICU Buffalo Gen. Hosp., 1989—91; staff nurse Sisters of Charity, Buffalo, 1991—93; ICU nurse DeGraff Meml. Hosp., North Tonawanda, 1993—98; case mgr. Staffbuilders Home Care, Niagara Falls, 1997—2002; case mgr., inpatient rev. Ind. Health, Amherst, NY, 2002—. Adult leader Girl Scouts U.S. Mem.: AACN. Home: 2714 Stenzil Ave North Tonawanda NY 14120-1008

COLEMAN, LAWRENCE GERALD, II, music educator; b. Norfolk, Va., Sept. 8, 1972; s. Lawrence Gerald Coleman and Priscilla Elaine Holman; m. Denise Armstrong, June 29, 1996; 1 child, Ryan Patrick. MusB Edn., Lander U., 1994; MS, Radford U., 1997. Cert. K-12 instrumental music tchr. Va. Claims assoc. Walmart Stores, Inc., Christiansburg, Va., 1989—97; band dir. Patrick County H.S., Stuart, Va., 1997—, fine arts chmn., 2000—, dept. chmn., 2001—. Percussion instr. Radford (Va.) H.S., 1997—2000. Entertainment coord. Am. Cancer Soc. - Relay for Life, Stuart, 2002. Recipient Louis Armstrong Jazz award, Instrumentalist Mag./Nat. Band Assn., 1994. Mem.: NEA, Music Educator's Nat. Conf., Amateur Radio Relay League (Technician Lic. 1999, Gen. Lic. 2000), Handyman Club of Am., Phi Mu Alpha Sinfonia (Cert. of Membership 1997). Republican. Methodist. Avocations: amateur radio, arranging, golf, travel. Home: 15 Honeymoon Dr Stuart VA 24171 Office: Patrick County HS 215 Cougar Ln Stuart VA 24171 Home Fax: 276-694-0183; Office Fax: 276-694-6997. Personal E-mail: lgcolema@sitestar.net.

COLEMAN, LOUIS KRESS, prosecutor; b. Balt., Mar. 8, 1947; s. Edward Lee and Bernice Edith (Kress) C.; m. Laura Lee Vulgaris, May 14, 1980, 1 child, John M. K. BA, Washington & Lee, 1969; JD, U. Md., 1973; LLM in Taxation, U. Balt., 1996. Bar: U.S. Ct. Appeals Md. 1973, U.S. Dist. Ct. Md. 1974. Assoc. Lichter, Coleman, Pezzula & Rogers, Balt., 1973-75; asst. state's atty. Baltimore City, 1975—. Bd. dirs. Beth Am Synagogue, Balt., 1993-95; pres. parents assn. Norbel Sch., Balt., 1992-94; hon. mem. N.W. Citizens Patrol, Balt., 1992. Home: 2508 Guilford Ave Baltimore MD 21218-4618 Office: Office of State's Atty 110 N Calvert St Baltimore MD 21202-1705

COLEMAN, MARSHALL DONALD, psychiatrist, psychoanalyst; b. Utica, N.Y., Dec. 27, 1925; s. Jacob and Lucille (Smith) C.; m. Beverly Sitrin, June 28, 1949; children: Charles Theodore, Jacqueline Sue. BA, Harvard Coll., 1947; MD, Harvard Med. Sch., 1952. Diplomate Am. Bd. Psychiatry and Neurology. Intern Mass. Meml. Hosps., Boston, 1952-53; resident Boston Psychopathic Hosp., Boston, 1953-56; tchg. fellow Med. Sch. Harvard U., Boston, 1953-56; instr. Albert Einstein Sch. Medicine, Bronx, N.Y., 1956-57, asst. prof., 1957-63, asst. clin. prof., 1963—; sr. vis. staff Jacobi Hosp., Bronx, N.Y., 1962—; pvt. practice Mamaroneck, N.Y., 1968—. Dir. walk-in psychiat. clinic Albert Einstein Sch. Medicine, 1956; pres. N.Y. State Psychoanalytic Coordinating Com., 1988—. Author: Winston S. Churchill: Overcoming Childhood Adversities Help Form the Heroic Character of the Statesman, 1994; contbg. editor: Generations of Holocaust, 1982; editor articles on psychiat. walk-in clinics, brief psychotherapy and agoraphobia. Co-chairperson mental health profls. N.Y. area United Jewish Appeal, 1990—. With U.S. Army, 1943-46, ETO. Recipient M. Jucovy Lifetime Achievement award, 2000. Fellow Am. Psychiat. Assn. (life); mem. N.Y. Psychoanalytic Soc., Internat. Psychoanalytic Soc., Westchester Psychoanalytic Soc. (pres. 1978-79), Internaat. Psychoanalytic Soc. Office: 1030 Greacen Point Rd Mamaroneck NY 10543-4609

COLEMAN, MARY SUE, academic administrator; b. Richmond, Ky, Oct. 2, 1943; m. Kenneth Coleman; 1 child, Jonathan. BA, Grinnell Coll., 1965; PhD, U. N.C., 1969. NIH postdoctoral fellow U. N.C., Chapel Hill, 1969—70, U. Ky., 1971—72, instr., rsch. assoc. depts. biochemistry and medicine, 1972—75, asst. prof. dept. biochemistry, 1975—80, assoc. prof. dept. biochemistry, 1980—85, prof. dept. biochemistry, 1985—90; prof. dept. biochemistry and biophysics U. N.C., Chapel Hill, 1990—93; provost, v.p. for academic affairs, prof. biochemistry U. N.Mex., 1993—95; pres., prof. biochemistry, prof. biol. scis. U. Iowa, Iowa City, 1995—2002; pres. U. Mich., 2002—. Pres. Iowa Health Sys., 1995—2002; vice chancellor grad students and rsch. U. N.C., 1992—93, assoc. provost, dean rsch., 1990—92; trustee U. Ky., 1987—90, assoc. dir. rsch. L.P. Markey Cancer Ctr., 1983—90, dir. grad. studies biochem., 1984—87; acting dir. basir rsch. U. Ky. Cancer Ctr., 1980—83; NSF summer trainee Grinnell Coll., 1962; scientific cons. Abbott Labs., 1981—85, Collaborative Rsch., 1983—88, Life Techs., Inc., 1992; bd. trustees Univs. Rsch. Assn., 1998—; mem. rsch. accountability task force Am. Assn. Univs., 2000—, chair undergrad. edn. com., 1997—, mem. exec. com., 2001—; mem. task force on tchrs. edn. Am. Coun. Edn., 1998—; bd. dirs. Meredith Corp., Am. Coun. Edn.; mem. Big Ten Coun. Pres.'s, 1995—2002; mem. stds. success adv. bd. Am. Assn. Univs. and he Pew Charitable Trusts, 2000—; co-chair Inst. Medicine Com. on Consequences of Uninsurance, 2000—; mem. Gov.'s Strategic Planning Coun., 1998—2000, Imagining Am. Pres.'s Coun., 1999—, Bus.-Higher Edn. Froum, 1999—, Knight Commn., 2000—01; presenter in field. Mem. editl. bd.: Jour. Biol. Chemistry, 1989—93; contbr. articles to profl. jours. Trustee Crinnell Coll., 1996—; mem. bd. govs. Warren G. Magnuson Clin. Ctr., NIH, 1996—2000, State of Iowa Gov.'s ACCESS Edn. Commn., 1997; bd. dirs. United Way, Albuquerque, 1995. Fellow postdoctoral fellow, Clayton Found. Biochem. Inst., U. Tex., 1970—71. Fellow: AAAS, Am. Acad. Arts and Scis.; mem.: Nat. Coll. Athletic Assn. (bd. dirs. 2002—), Nat. Assn. State Univs. ans Land Grant Colls. Coun. Cchief Acad. Officers (exec. com. 1993—95), Am. Soc. Biochem. and Molecular Biology, Am. Assn. Cancer Rsch.

COLEMAN, MICHAEL B. mayor; s. John and Joan Coleman. Student, U. Cin.; JD, U. Dayton, 1980. Pvt. practice; mem. City Coun. Columbus, Ohio, 1992—99; mayor Columbus, Ohio, 2000—. Pres. Columbus (Ohio) City Coun., 1997—99. Office: Mayors Office 90 W Broad St Rm 247 Columbus OH 43215-9014*

COLEMAN, MICHAEL DORTCH, nephrologist; b. Jackson, Tenn., June 19, 1944; s. Ivery R. and Kathleen (Campell) C; children from a previous marriage: Michael Dortch, Christopher Matthew, Cassandra Sherean; m. Jennifer Lynn Baxter. BA in Chemistry, U. Ark., 1966; MD, Duke U., 1970. Diplomate Am. Bd. Internat. Medicine. Intern Duke U. Med. Sch., Durham, N.C., 1970-71, resident internal medicine, 1971-72; practice medicine specializing in nephrology Durham, 1972-74, Kannapolis, N.C., 1973-74, Dr. Smith, Ark., 1974—. Nephrology cons. Cabarras County Hosp., Kannapolis, 1973; chief dept. nephrology Holt Krock Clinic, Ft. Smith, 1974-99, Cooper Clinic, 1999—; dir. dialysis Holt Krock Dialysis Ctr., 1974-99; dir. dialysis Sparks Regional Med. Ctr., Ft. Smith, 2000—, chief medicine, 1994-96; dir. dialysis St. Edward's Mercy Med. Ctr., Ft. Smith, 1980—, Ft. Smith Regional Dialysis Ctr.; assoc. prof. medicine U. Ark., Ft. Smith, 1976—; mem. med. rev. bd. Ark. Kidney Disease Commn., 1974—; mem. exec. com. and med. rev. bd. Ark.-Okla. Endstage Renal Disease Coun., 1977—. Contbr. articles to profl. jours. Bd. dirs. Ark Tennis Assn., Jr. Tennis Coun., Holt Krock Clinic, Ft. Smith; bd. dirs., mem. fin. com. Holt Krock Clinic, Cooper Clinic, 1999—. Nephrology fellow Duke U. Med. Sch., 1972-74. Mem. AMA, Ark. Med. Assn., Sebastian County Med. Assn., Intenat. Soc. Nephrology, Renal Physician Assn., Am. Soc. Nephrology, Am. Heart Assn., St. Smith Racquet Club (bd. dirs., pres.), Town Club Ft. Smith, Hardscrabble Country Club, Alpha Ometa Alpha. Office: 1500 Dodson Ave Fort Smith AR 72901-5128

COLEMAN, MICHAEL MURRAY, polymer science educator; b. Herne Bay, Eng., Jan. 24, 1938; s. Ronald and Winifred L. (Legg) C.; m. Mary Jane Ogorek, June 25, 1977; 1 child, David Spencer. BSc in Polymer Sci., Borough Poly., London, 1968; MS in Macromolecular Sci., Case Western Res. U., 1971, PhD in Macromolecular Sci., 1973. Analytical chemist Rhokana Corp. Ltd., Nkana, Zambia, 1955-61, Johnson-Mathey Ltd., Wembley, Eng., 1963-64; rsch. chemist Revertex Ltd., Harlow, Eng., 1968-69, E.I. du Pont de Nemours & Co., Wilmington, Del., 1973-75; asst. prof. polymer sci. Pa. State U., 1975-78, program chmn. polymer sci., 1976-84, assoc. prof., 1978-82, prof., 1982—2002, head, dept. materials sci. and engring., 1983-91, prof. emeritus, 2002—. Author: (with others) The Theory of Vibrational Spectroscopy and its Application to Polymeric Materials, 1982, Specific Interactions and the Miscibility of Polymer Blends, 1991, Fundamentals of Polymer Science, 1994, 2d edit., 1997; contbr. over 200 tech. articles to profl. jours. Fellow Am. Phys. Soc. (high polymer physics divsn.); mem. Am. Chem. Soc. (polymer and polymeric materials sci. and engring. divsns.), Soc. Plastics Engrs. Office: Pa State Univ 330 Steidle Bldg University Park PA 16802-5007 Fax: (814) 865-2917. E-mail: MMC4@psu.edu.

COLEMAN, MORTON, oncologist, hematologist; b. Norfolk, Va., Sept. 15, 1939; s. Isadore and Bessie (Levin) C.; m. Joyce Goodman, May 26, 1968; children: Ingrid Alexandra, Benjamin Lee, Abigail Rachael. AA, Coll. William and Mary, 1958; BA, Johns Hopkins U., 1959; MD, Med. Coll. Va., 1963. Diplomate Nat. Bd. Med. Examiners, Am. Bd. Internal Medicine, Am. Bd. Hematology, Am. Bd. Clin. Oncology. Intern Grady Meml. Hosp.-Emory U. Med. Ctr., Atlanta, 1963-64, resident, 1964-65, N.Y. Hosp.-Cornell U. Med. Ctr., N.Y.C., 1967-68; NIH fellow in hematology Cornell U. Med. Coll., 1968-70, asst. prof. medicine, 1970-74, assoc. prof., 1974-86, clin. prof., 1986—; asst. attending N.Y. Hosp., N.Y.C., 1970-74, assoc. attending, 1974-86, attending, 1986—99, assoc. dir. oncology svc., 1974-86; assoc. program dir. Nat. Cancer Inst. Clin. Chemotherapy Program Cancer Control, 1974-80; attending N.Y. Presbyterian Hosp., 1999—. Dir. Ctr. for Lymphoma and Myeloma, divsn. hematology-oncology, 1997—; attending staff Manhattan Eye and Ear Hosp., 1972—82, Doctors Hosp., 1973—90, Beth Israel NorthMed. Ctr., 1990—94, New Rochelle Med. Ctr., 1980—91; chmn. new agts. com. Cancer and Leukemia Group B, 1975—82; chmn. bd. dirs. Fund for Blood and Cancer Rsch., 1975—; sci. advisor United Leukemia Fund, 1976—82; program chmn. N.Y. Cancer Soc., 1993—94, sec., 1994—95, treas., 1995—96, v.p., 1996—97, pres.-elect, 1997—98, pres., 1998—99, coun. of advisors, 2002—, 2002—; bd. dirs. Cure for Lymphoma Found., 1997—2001, chmn. med. affiliates bd., 2000—01; chmn. lymphoma/Hodgkins' diseases symposium com. Internat. Union Against Cancer Congress, 1993—94; co-chmn. clin. rsch. rev. com. Israel Cancer Rsch. Fund, 1988—93, chmn. bd. dirs. Affiliated Physicians Network, Inc., 1996—2001; Internat. Adv. Cancer Care Trust and Rsch. Found., India, 1995—; mem. sci. adv. com. Lymphoma Rsch. Found., 1998—, bd. dirs., 2001—, chmn. med. affiliates bd., 2001—; dirs. Immunomedics, Inc., 1999—; bd. dirs. BML Pharms., 2000—02; mem. Pub.Com, 2001—; chmn. Policy and Procedures Subcom., 2002—. Assoc. editor: Cancer Investigation, 1987—; mem. editl. adv. bd. Hem/Onc Today, 1999—, internat. adv. bd. Indian Jour. Med. and Pediatric Oncology, 1994—; contbr. articles to rsch. publications on blood and cancer. V.p. alumni coun. Cornell U. Med. Ctr., 1992-94, pres., 1994-96. Lt. comdr. USN, 1965-67. Recipient Disting. Alumni award, Old Dominion U., 1994, Together award, Cure for Lymphoma Found., 2000, 2001. Fellow: ACP; mem.: AMA, AAAS, N.Y. County Med. Soc., N.Y. State Med. Soc., Soc. Study of Blood, N.Y. State Soc. Med. Oncology and Hematology (mem. exec. com. 1991—99), N.Y. Acad. Sci., Internat. Soc. Hematology, Harvey Soc., Cornell U. Med. Ctr. Alumni Assn., Am. Soc. Hematology, Am. Soc. Clin. Oncology (mem. clin. practice com. 1997—2001, pub. com., chmn. policy and procedures subcom., 2002— 2001), program com., chmn. hematologic malignancy sub com., 2002— 2001—), Am. Radium Soc., Am. Fedn. Clin. Rsch., Am. Assn. Cancer Rsch., Explorers Club, Sigma Zeta, Alpha Omega Alpha. Office: 407 E 70th St 3rd fl New York NY 10021-5302 also: NY Presbyn Hosp-Weill Cornell U Med Ctr Div Hematology-Oncology 525 E 68th St New York NY 10021-4870 E-mail: mortoncolemanmd@aol.com.

COLEMAN, NICHOLAS VASS, microbiologist; b. Goulburn, Australia, May 4, 1973; s. Frances Mildred and Michael John Coleman; m. Belinda Judith Norman, Feb. 12, 2000. BS, U. of Sydney, 1990—94, PhD in microbiology, 1996—2000. Cons. Total Environment Ctr., Sydney, 1995—98; postdoctoral fellow (microbiologist) Air Force Rsch. Lab., Tyndall AFB, Fla., 2000—. Composer: (electronic music) Sykmuzak - Cytokromatix; contbr. articles to profl. jours. Postdoctoral fellowship, Oak Ridge Inst. for Sci. and Edn. (U.S. Dept. of Energy), 2000—03. Mem.: Am. Soc. for Microbiology. Green Party. Buddhist. Achievements include discovery of a bacterium that can grow on the toxic pollutant dichloroethene as a carbon source; research in ten different bacteria that biodegrade the carcinogenic pollutant vinyl chloride, and vinyl chloride-degrading bacteria were widespread in the environment; discovery of a cytochrome p-450 enzyme was involved in the bacterial biodegradation of the

explosive compound RDX; the genes encoding vinyl chloride biodegradation in Mycobacterium strain JS60; first to demonstrate Coenzyme M is required for epoxide metabolism in vinyl chloride-degrading bacteria. Avocations: hiking, music, muscle cars, computer games.

COLEMAN, NORM, senator, former mayor; b. Brooklyn, NY, Aug. 17, 1949; m. Laurie Coleman; 2 children. BA, Hofstra U.; JD, U. Iowa. Bar: Minn. Asst. atty. gen., solicitor gen., dir. crim. justice policy Minn. Atty. Gen.'s Office, 17 yrs.; mayor City of St. Paul, 1994—2002; U.S. senator Minn., 2003—. Active in creation of Minn. Drug Abuse Resistance Edn. program, also The Partnership for a Drug Free Minn. Humphrey fellow U. Minn. Republican. Office: SD-B40 Ste 3 Dirksen Senate Off Bldg Washington DC 20510*

COLEMAN, PAUL DARE, electrical engineering educator; b. Stoystown, Pa., June 4, 1918; s. Clyde R. and Catharine (Livengood) C.; m. Betty L. Carter, June 20, 1942; children— Susan Dare, Peter Carter. AB, Susquehanna U., 1940; MS, Pa. State U., 1942; PhD, Mass. Inst. Tech., 1951, D.Sc. (hon.), 1978. Asst. physics Susquehanna U., 1938-40, Pa. State U., 1940-42; physicist USAF-WADC, Wright Field, Ohio, 1942-46, Cambridge Air Research Center, also; grad. research assoc. Mass. Inst. Tech., 1946-51; prof. elec. engring., dir. electro-physics lab. U. Ill. at Urbana, 1951—. Recipient meritorious civilian award USAAF, 1946 Fellow AAAS, IEEE, MTT (Disting. Educator award 1994, Centennial medal 1984), Optical Soc. Am., Am. Phys. Soc.; mem. Sigma Xi, Pi Mu Delta, Pi Mu Epsilon, Eta Kappa Nu. Achievements include research on millimeter waves, submillimeter waves, relativistic electronics, far infrared molecular lasers, beam wave guides and detectors, chem. lasers, nonlinear optics, solid state electronics. Home: 710 Park Lane Dr Champaign IL 61820-7633 Office: Univ Ill 133 Everitt Lab 1406 W Green St Urbana IL 61801-2918

COLEMAN, PAUL DAVID, neurobiology researcher, educator; b. N.Y.C., Dec. 2, 1927; s. A. Barnett and Martha L. (Michaels) C.; m. Zinia J. Cereska, Mar. 13, 1955 (div. Sept. 1978); children: Laura A., Paul David; m. 2d Dorothy G. Flood, Feb. 26, 1983. AB, Tufts U., 1948; PhD, U. Rochester, 1953. Asst. prof., research assoc. Tufts U., Medford, Mass., 1956-59; assoc. Computer Ctr. MIT, Cambridge, 1957-60; spl. fellow Johns Hopkins Sch. Medicine, Balt., 1959-62; assoc. prof. Sch. Medicine U. Md., Balt., 1962-67; prof. neurobiology and anatomy Sch. Medicine, U. Rochester, N.Y., 1967—. Editor in chief Neurobiology of Aging, 1988—; contbr. articles to profl. jours. 1st lt. U.S. Army, 1953—56. Recipient award for leadership and excellence in Alzheimer's disease Nat. Inst. Aging, NIH, 1990, Pioneer award Alzheimers Assn., 2000; Rsch. grantee NSF, 1958-67, NIH, 1963—; NIH spl. fellow Johns Hopkins U. Sch. Medicine, 1959-62. Mem. Soc. for Neurosci., Am. Assn. Anatomists, AAAS, Gerontol. Soc., Am. Psychol. Assn., Sigma Xi. Clubs: Yacht (Rochester, N.Y.) (bd. dirs. 1971-72). Home: 7 Durham Way Pittsford NY 14534

COLEMAN, PAUL JEROME, JR., physicist, educator; b. Evanston, Ill., Mar. 7, 1932; s. Paul Jerome and Eunice Cecile (Weissenberg) C.; m. Doris Ann Fields, Oct. 3, 1964; children: Derrick, Craig. BS in Engring. Math., BS in Engring. Physics, U. Mich., 1954, MS in Physics, 1958; PhD in Space Physics, UCLA, 1966. Rsch. scientist Ramo-Wooldridge Corp. (name now TRW Systems), El Segundo, Calif., 1958-61; instr. math. U. So. Calif., L.A., 1958-61; mgr. interplanetary scis. program NASA, Washington, 1961-62; rsch. scientist UCLA, 1962-66, prof. geophysics, space physics, 1966—; asst. lab. dir., mgr. Earth and Space Scis. divsn., chmn. Inst. Geophysics and Planetary Physics Nat. Lab., Los Alamos, N.Mex., 1981-86; dir. Inst. Geophysics and Planetary Physics UCLA, 1989-92; dir. Nat. Inst. for Global Environ. Change, 1994-96; pres. Univs. Space Rsch. Assn., Columbia, Md., 1981-2000, Girvan Inst. Tech., 2002—. Bd. dirs. Axcess Inc., Dallas, Biocentric Solutions, Inc., Madison, Wis., others; mem. adv. bd. San Diego Supercomputer Ctr., 1986-90, chmn., 1987-88, others; trustee Univs. Space Rsch. Assn., Columbia, Md., 1981-2000, Am. Tech. Alliances, 1990-2002, Internat. Small Satellite Orgn., 1992-96; vis. scholar U. Paris, 1975-76; vis. scientist Lab. for Aeronomy Ctr. Nat. Rsch. Sci., Verrieres le Buisson, France, 1975-76; com. mem. numerous sci. and ednl. orgns., cons. numerous fin. and indsl. cos. Co-editor: Solar Wind, 1972; co-author: Pioneering the Space Frontier, 1986; mem. editorial bd. Geophysics and Astrophysics Monographs, 1970—; assoc. editor Cosmic Electrodynamics, 1968-72; contbr. revs. to numerous profl. jours. Apptd. to Nat. Commn. on Space, Pres. of U.S., 1985, apptd. to Space Policy Adv. Bd., Nat. Space Coun., v.p. of U.S., 1991; bd. dirs. St. Matthew's Sch., Pacific Palisades, Calif., 1979-82, v.p., 1981-82. 1st lt. USAF, 1954-56, Korea. Recipient Exceptional Sci. Achievement Medal NASA, 1970, 1972, spl. recognition for contributions to the Apollo Program, 1979; Guggenheim fellow 1975-76, Fulbright scholar, 1975-76, Rsch. grantee NASA, NSF, Office Naval Research, Calif. Space Inst., Air Force Office Sci. Research, U.S. Geol. Survey. Mem. AIAA, Am. Geophys. Union, Internat. Acad. Astronautics, Bel Air Bay Club (L.A.), Birnam Wood Golf Club (Montecito, Calif.), Cosmos Club (Washington), Valley Club (Montecito, Calif.), Eldorado Country Club (Indian Wells, Calif.), Tau Beta Pi, Phi Eta Sigma. Avocations: flying, skiing, racquetball, tennis, golf. Home: 1323 Monaco Dr Pacific Palisades CA 90272-4007 Office: UCLA Inst Geophysics & Planetary Physics 405 Hilgard Ave Los Angeles CA 90095-9000

COLEMAN, RALPH EDWARD, nuclear medicine physician, educator; b. Otwell, Ind., Jan. 2, 1943; s. Ralph H. and Roxie Ellen (Arnold) C.; children: Kathryn Kinsley, Emily Elizabeth, Matthew Edward. BA, U. Evansville, 1965; MD, Washington U., 1968; DSc (hon.), U. Evansville, 2000. Diplomate Am. Bd. Nuclear Medicine, Am. Bd. Internal Medicine. Intern Barnes Hosp., St. Louis, 1968-69; med. resident Royal Victoria Hosp., Montreal, Que., Can., 1969-70; resident Mallinckrodt Inst. Radiology, St. Louis, 1972-74, asst. prof., 1974-76; assoc. prof. U. Utah Med. Ctr., Salt Lake City, 1976-78; prof. Duke U. Med. Ctr., Durham, 1978—. Author: ACR Nuclear Radiology Syllabus, 1983, 2d edit., 1990, Diagnostic Nuclear Medicine, 3d edit., 1995; assoc. editor Jour. Nuclear Medicine, 1989—; sr. editor Clin. Positron Imaging, 1997—. Capt. U.S. Army, 1970-72. Fellow Am. Coll. Radiology, Am. Coll. Chest Physicians; mem. Soc. Nuclear Medicine (trustee 1985-88, 89-93, bd. dirs. 1997—, pres. Southeastern chpt. 1987-88), Am. Coll. Nuclear Physicians, Radiol. Soc. N.Am., Inst. for Clin. Positron Emission Tomography (pres. 1990). Office: Duke U Med Ctr PO Box 3949 Durham NC 27710-0001 E-mail: colem010@mc.duke.edu.

COLEMAN, REXFORD LEE, lawyer, educator; b. Hollywood, Calif., June 2, 1930; s. Henry Eugene and Antoinette Christine (Dobry) C.; m. Aiko Takahashi, Aug. 28, 1953 (dec.); children: Christine Eugenie, Douglass Craig; m. Sucha Park, June 15, 1978. Student, Claremont McKenna Coll., 1947-49; AB, Stanford U., 1951, JD, 1955; M. in Jurisprudence, Tokyo U., 1960. Bar: Calif. 1955, Mass. 1969. Mem. faculty Harvard U., 1959-69; mem. firm Baker & McKenzie, 1969-83, income ptnr., 1971-73, capital ptnr., 1973-83, mng. ptnr. Tokyo office, 1971-78; sr. ptnr. The Pacific Law Group, L.A., 1983—. Adj. prof. McGeorge Sch. Law, U. Pacific, 1989—; lectr. Gray's Inn, The Inns of Ct. Sch. Law, London, 1989; cons. U.S. Treasury Dept., 1961-70; counselor Japanese-Am. Soc. for Legal Studies, 1964—; guest lectr. Ford Seminar on Comparative History, MIT, 1968; lectr. Legal Tng. and Research Inst., Supreme Ct., Japan, 1970-73; guest lectr. Colloguium Scholars, Calif. Luth. U., 1989; chmn. fgn. bus. customs consultative com. Bur. Customs, Ministry of Fin., Govt. of Japan, 1971-72; chmn. fgn. bus. consulatative commn. Japanese Ministry of Internat. Trade and Industry, 1973-76; mem. U.S. Del., U.S.-Japan Income Tax Treaty Negotiations, 1961, internat. bd. advisors, McGeorge Sch. Law, U. Pacific, 1989—. Author: Am. Index to Japanese Law, 1961, Standard Citation of Japanese Legal Materials, 1963, The Legal Aspects Under Japanese Law of an Accident Involving a Nuclear Installation in Japan, 1963, An Index to Japanese Law, 1975; editor: Taxation in Japan, World Tax Series, 1959-70; founding chmn. bd. editors: Law in Japan: An Ann., 1964-67; mem. bd. editors Stanford Law Rev., 1954-55, Japan Ann. Internat. Law, 1970-92; mem. Internat. Adv. Bd., The Transnational Lawyer, 1988—; contbr. articles to profl. jours. Participant in Japanese-Am. Program for Cooperation in Legal Studies, 1956-60; co-chmn. Conf. on Internat. Legal Protection Computer Software, Stanford Law Sch., 1986, Tokyo, Japan, 1987. Served to 1st lt., Inf. AUS, 1951-53; lt. col. Ret. Ford Found. grantee, 1956-60. Mem. ABA, State Bar Calif., Mass. Bar Assn., Japanese-Am. Soc. for Legal Studies, Internat. Fiscal Assn. Japan, Res. Officers Assn. (v.p. army dept. Far East 1974-75), Ret. Officers Assn., Internat. House Japan (Tokyo), Stanford U. Alumni Assn., Gakushi Kai (grads. of former Japanese Imperial Univs. Assn.), Internat. Law Assn. Japan, Japan-Western Assn., Pacific Basin Econ. Council, (U.S. exec. com. 1985-87), Nihon Shiho Gakkai, Nihon Kokusai Ho Gakkai, Nihon Kokusai Shiho Gakkai, Sozei Ho Gakkai, Phi Alpha Delta Episcopalian (vestryman 1966-69, del. Conv. Episcopal Diocese Mass. 1968, Conv. Episcopal Diocese L.A., 1989-91, Bishop's com. 1983-87, 91-93). Clubs: Tokyo Am; Harvard (N.Y.C.), North Ranch Country. Home: 32314 Blue Rock Rdg Westlake Vlg CA 91361-3912 Office: The Pacific Law Group 12121 Wilshire Blvd Ste 205 Los Angeles CA 90025-1164

COLEMAN, RICHARD WILLIAM, retired lawyer; b. Brookline, Mass., Dec. 9, 1935; s. Michael John and Mary Ellen (Motherway) C.; m. Mary M. Kilcommins, June 3, 1961; children: Lauren, Christopher. BS, Boston Coll., Newton, Mass., 1957; JD, Boston Coll., Brighton, Mass., 1960. Bar: Mass. 1960, U.S. Dist. Ct. Mass. 1961, U.S. Ct. Appeals (1st cir.) 1981. Field atty. NLRB, Newark, 1960-61; assoc. Segal & Flamm, Boston, 1961-69; labor rels. advisor Scott Paper Co., Phila., 1969-70; labor rels. mgr. Harvard U., Cambridge, Mass., 1970-72; ptnr. Segal, Roitman & Coleman, Boston, 1972-93; pres. Richard W. Coleman, P.C., Needham, 1994—2002; ret. Contbg. editor Development of Law Under National Labor Relations Act, 1988. Bd. dirs. Little Bros. of St. Francis, 1998-2001. Recipient Cushing award Cath. Labor Guild Boston, 1976. Mem. ABA, Am. Prepaid Legal Svcs. Inst. (bd. dirs. 1997—), Indsl. Rels. Rsch. Assn., Mass. Bar Assn., Boston Bar Assn., AFL-CIO Lawyers Coord. Com. Democrat. Roman Catholic. Avocations: golf, reading, choir singing. E-mail: rcolegolf@aol.com.

COLEMAN, RITA KAY, writer, literature educator; b. Dayton, Ohio, Apr. 23, 1948; d. Robert Glenn and Suzie Modina Coleman; m. Robert Eugene Speer, June 20, 1970 (div. Feb. 1975); 1 child, Samantha Perrin Speer; m. Frank Orion Baxley, July 8, 1990. BA in English, Wright State U., 1995, MA in English, 1997. Founding mem., actress Dayton Women's Theatre Workshop, 1978—80; journalist Dayton Daily News, 1978—80; freelance writer, 1981—90, 1998—; educator Wright State U., Dayton, 1995—2002, 2001, tutor writing and French, 1993—95; educator U. Dayton, 2001—02. Author in residence St. Brigid Middle Sch., Xenia, Ohio, 1994—95; writing mentor Imagine, Xenia, 1998—; co-founder, writer Mudrock Writers, Dayton, 1998—2002. Author poetry. Initiator City of Moraine (Ohio) Hideaway Neighborhood Watch, 1980; vol. Dem. Candidate Coroner, Dayton. Mem.: NOW, AAUW. Democrat. Unity. Avocations: hiking, theology, reading, gardening, movies. Home: 1216 Nash Rd Xenia OH 45385

COLEMAN, ROBERT GRIFFIN, geology educator; b. Twin Falls, Idaho, Jan. 5, 1923; s. Lloyd Wilbur and Frances (Brown) C.; m. Cathryn J. Hirschberger, Aug. 7, 1948; children: Robert Griffin Jr., Derrick Job, Mark Dana. BS, Oreg. State U., 1948, MS, 1950; PhD, Stanford U., 1957. Mineralogist AEC, N.Y.C., 1952-54; geologist U.S. Geol. Survey, Washington, 1954-57, Menlo Park, Calif., 1958-80; prof. geology Stanford U., Calif., 1981-93, prof. emeritus, 1993—. Vis. petrographer New Zealand Geol. Survey, 1962-63; br. chief isotope geology U.S. Geol. Survey, Menlo Park, 1964-68, regional geologist, Saudi Arabia, 1970-71, br. chief field geochemistry and petrology, Menlo Park, 1977-79; vis. scholar Woods Hole Oceanographic Inst., Mass., 1975; vis. prof. geology Sultan Qaboos U., Oman, 1987, 89; cons. geologist, 1993—; instr. geobotany field sch. Siskiyou Inst., Oreg., 1998-99. Author: Ophiolites, 1977, Geologic Evolution of the Red Sea, 1993, Ultrahigh Pressure Metamorphism, 1995; contbr. articles to profl. jours. Named Outstanding Scientist, Oreg. Acad. Sci., 1977; Fairchild scholar Calif. Inst. Tech., Pasadena, 1980; recipient Meritorious award U.S. Dept. Interior, 1981 Fellow AAAS, Geol. Soc. Am. (coun.), Am. Mineral Soc. (coun., editor), Am. Geophys. Union; mem. Nat. Acad. Scis., Russian Acad. Sci. (fgn. assoc.). Republican. Avocations: wood carving, art. Home: 2025 Camino Al Lago Atherton CA 94027-5938 E-mail: coleman@pangea.stanford.edu.

COLEMAN, ROBERT J. lawyer; b. Phila., Dec. 24, 1936; s. Francis Eugene and Mary Veronica (McCullough) C.; m. Mary Patricia Coleman, June 26, 1955; children: Debra, Robert P., Linda, Martin S. AB, Villanova U., 1959; JD, Temple U., 1964. Bar: Pa., U.S. Dist. Ct. (ea. dist.) Pa., U.S. Ct. Appeals (3d cir.), U.S. Supreme Ct. With First Pa. Bank, Phila., 1955-57; underwriter Employer's Mut. Co., Phila., 1957-59; claim adjuster Safeco Ins. Co., Phila., 1959-62; claim supr. Gen. Accident Ins., Phila., 1962-64; assoc. Rappaport & Lagakos, Phila., 1964; trial atty. Allstate Ins. Co., Phila., 1964-67; chmn., CEO Marshall, Dennehey, Warner, Coleman & Goggin, Phila., 1967—. Chmn. hearing com. Pa. Disciplinary Bd., Phila., 1986-94; mem. Pa. Bd. Law Examiners, 1997-2003; bd. dirs. Republic First Bancorp, 2003. Assoc. editor Phila. County Reporter, 1984-96; contbr. articles to legal publs. Bd. dirs. Ins. Soc. Phila., HERO Scholarship Fund Delaware County; bd. vis. Temple U. Law Sch. With USAR, 1954-62. Mem. ABA, Pa. Bar Assn., Phila. Bar Assn., Phila. Bar Found. (trustee), Pa. Def. Inst., Internat. Assn. Def. Lawyers, Def. Rsch. Inst. Republican. Roman Catholic. Avocations: tennis, boating, travel. Home: 908 Penn Valley Rd Media PA 19063-1652 Office: Marshall Dennehey Warner Coleman & Goggin 1845 Walnut St Philadelphia PA 19103-4797

COLEMAN, ROBERT LEE, retired lawyer; b. Kansas City, June 14, 1929; s. William Houston and Edna Fay (Smith) C. BMus Edn., Drake U., 1951; LLB, U. Mo., 1959. Bar: Mo. 1959, Fla. 1973. Law clk. to judge U.S. Dist. Ct. (we. dist.) Mo., Kansas City, 1959-60; assoc. Watson, Ess, Marshall & Engas, Kansas City, 1960-66; asst. gen. counsel Gas Svc. Co., Kansas City, 1966-74; v.p., corp. counsel H & R Block, Inc., Kansas City, 1974-94; retired, 1994. With U.S. Army, 1955-57. Mem. ABA.

COLEMAN, ROBERT MARSHALL, biology educator; b. Bridgton, Maine, Sept. 27, 1925; s. Louis Elmer and Helen (Marr) C.; m. Patricia Ann Stocum, Dec. 29, 1947; children: Mary Deborah, Kevin Robert. BS, Bates Coll., 1950; MS, U. N.H., 1951; PhD, U. Notre Dame, 1954. Faculty Russell Sage Coll., Troy, N.Y., 1954-62, asst. prof. biology, 1956-58, asso. prof., 1958-62, Boston Coll., 1962-68; prof. biol. scis. U. Mass., Lowell, 1968-97, prof. emeritus, 1997—. Cons. AID NSF, India, 1965, 68, Lowell Tech. Inst., 1964-67, Smithsonian Instn., 1976, WHO, Egypt, 1977, NSF Internat. Programs, 1980—, Biotech at Tufts U., 1984, Cath. U., 1985, 86, 87, Harvard U., 1986, Marine Biol. Lab, Woods Hole, Mass., 1988, NSF Young Scholars Program, 1991; ednl. dir. Mass. Bioprocess Ctr., Lowell, 1993; dir. Ctr. for Tropical Diseases, U. Mass., Lowell, 1997. Author: (with others) Fundamental Immunology, 1989, 2d edit., 1992; contbr. articles profl. jours. Served with AUS, 1943-46. Mem. AAAS, Assn. Med. Lab. Immunology, Am. Soc. Parasitology, Am. Soc. Tropical Medicine and Hygiene, Am. Soc. Microbiology, N.Y. Acad. Scis., Sigma Xi, Phi Sigma. Home: 48 Blanchard St PO Box 640 Moody ME 04054-0640 Office: U Mass Lowell Biol Scis Dept Lowell MA 01854

COLEMAN, ROBERT WINSTON, lawyer; b. Oklahoma City, Mar. 1, 1942; s. Clint Sheridan and Genevieve (Ross) C.; m. Judith Moore, Sept. 7, 1963; children: Robert Winston, Jr., Claire Elizabeth. BA, Abilene Christian Coll., 1964; JD with hons., U. Tex., 1968. Bar: Tex. 1968, Ga. 1970. Law clk. to presiding justice U.S. Ct. Appeals (5th cir.), Montgomery, Ala., 1968-69; assoc. Kilpatrick, Cody, Rogers, McClatchey & Regenstein, Atlanta, 1969-75; ptnr. Meyers, Miller, Middleton, Weiner & Warren and predecessor, Dallas, 1975-80, Jones, Day, Reavis & Pogue, Dallas, 1981-85; dir. Baker, Glast and Middleton, P.C., Dallas, 1985-92; ptnr. Vial, Hamilton, Koch & Knox, LLP, Dallas, 1992-2000, Brown McCarroll LLP, Dallas, 2000—. Mem. exec. com. Dallas County Dem. Com., 1980-87. Mem. ABA, Dallas Bar Found., Dallas Bar Assn., Tex. Bar Assn., Ga. Bar Assn., Am. Judicature Soc. Office: Brown McCarroll LLP 2000 Trammell Crow Ctr 2001 Ross Ave Dallas TX 75201 E-mail: RColeman@mailbmc.com.

COLEMAN, RODNEY ALBERT, government affairs consultant; b. Newburgh, N.Y., Oct. 12, 1938; s. Samuel and Rebecca (Belden) Coleman; children: Terri Lynn, Stephen Anthony. BArch, Howard U., 1963; grad. exec. devel. program, U. Mich., 1988. Commd. 2nd lt. USAF, 1963, advanced through grades to capt., separated, 1973; White House fellow Washington, 1970-71; exec. asst. to chmn. D.C. City Coun., Washington, 1973-78; archtl. design cons. Pennsylvania Ave. Devel. Corp., Washington, 1978-80; dir. govt. rels. Gen. Motors, Detroit, 1980-85, dir. mcpl. govt. affairs, 1985-90, exec. dir. urban and mcpl. affairs, 1990-94; asst. sec. of Air Force for manpower, Res. affairs, installations, and environ. Dept. of Air Force, Washington, 1994-98; exec. v.p. ICF Kaiser Internat., Fairfax, Va., 1998-99; ptnr. Alcalde & Fay, Arlington, Va., 1999—. Chmn. bd. adv. Mus. Aviation of Ga., 1998—; trustee Air Force Aid Soc., 1998—; bd. dirs. Washington Hosp. Ctr., 2002—. Decorated Bronze Star medal, Air Force Commendation medal Republic of Vietnam, Honor medal First Class, Air Force Meritorious Svc. medal; recipient Disting. Alumni award for postgrad. achievement in corp. and govt. svc. Howard U., 1996, Disting. Alumnus award Newburgh Free Acad., 1994, Black Engr. of Yr. dean's award, 1996, Lt. Gen. Benjamin O. Davis Jr. Disting. Achievement award of The Tuskegee Airmen, 1996, decoration for exceptional civilian svc. Dept. of Air Force, 1997, Eagle award Nat. Guard Bur., 1998. Mem. White House Fellows Assn., Exec. Leadership Coun, Air Force Assn., Tuskegee Airmen. Methodist. Avocation: golf. Home: 1200 Crystal Dr Arlington VA 22202-4320 E-mail: honrc@aol.com., coleman@alcalde-fay.com.

COLEMAN, ROGER DIXON, bacteriologist; b. Rockwell, Iowa, Jan. 18, 1915; s. Major C. and Hazel Ruth Coleman; m. Lee Aden Skov, Jan. 1, 1978. AB, UCLA, 1937; postgrad., Balliol Coll., Oxford, Eng., 1944; MS, U. So. Calif., 1952, PhD, 1957. Diplomate Am. Bd. Bioanalysts. Sr. laboratorian Napa (Calif.) State Hosp., 1937-42; dir. Long Beach (Calif) Clin. Lab., 1946-86, pres., 1980-86. Mem. Calif. State Clin. Lab. Commn., 1953-57. Author papers to profl. publs. Officer AUS, 1942-46. Mem. Am. Assn. Bioanalysts, Am. Assn. Clin. Chemists, Am. Soc. Microbiologists, Am. Chem. Soc., Am. Venereal Disease Assn., Calif. Assn. Bioanalysts (past officer), Med. Rsch. Assn. Calif., Bacteriology Club So. Calif., Sigma Xi, Phi Sigma (past chpt. pres.). Office: PO Box 7073 Laguna Niguel CA 92607-7073

COLEMAN, RONALD LEE, insurance claims executive; b. Danville, Va., June 10, 1941; s. Raymond Lee and Mildred Sue (Floyd) C.; m. Stephanie Walther Barton Ewalt; children: Ronald Lee, Christopher Brent. BSBA summa cum laude, Va. Poly. Inst. and State U., 1964; BS in Pub. Adminstrn. summa cum laude, U. Richmond, 1964, postgrad., 1971; postgrad. law sch., U. Va., 1980. Pres. Johnson & Coleman, Ltd., Richmond, 1974-79, Ron Coleman & Assocs., Ltd., Richmond, 1981—; v.p. Schnell, Johnson & Coleman, Ltd., Richmond, Va., 1979-81. Adj. prof. U. Tex., Austin, Pa. State U., State College; adv. coun. Pamplin Bus. Sch., Va. Tech. Author: Investigation and Handling of Aviation Claims, 1981, Presentation of Evidence in Accident Reconstruction Cases, 1989, others; editor-in-chief Claimsman mag., 1971-76; contbr. articles to profl. jours. Mem. U.S. Senatorial Bus. Adv. Bd., 1988; mem. adv. coun. Paplin Coll. Bus., Va. Tech.; mem. Rep. Presdl. Task Force, 1988; mem. Va. Rep. Com., Chesterfield County, 1984; mem. The Pres.'s Coun., 1990, Pres. Club Rep. Party; bd. dirs. Va. Tech. Found., Va. Tech. Athletic Fund., Va. Tech. Athletic Bd. Mem. ABA (torts and ins. practice sect.), Richmond Claims Assn. (pres. 1971-72, Man of Yr. award 1971), Va. Claims Assn. (Bob Anderson Humanitarian award), Def. Law Inst., Atlanta Claims Assn., Profl. Claims Assn. Richmond, Truck Ins. Def. Assn., 1872 Soc. at Va. Poly. Inst. and State U., Assn. Lloyds Mems. (London), Pilon Soc. at Va. Poly. Inst. and State U., Ut Prosim Soc. at Va. Poly. Inst. and State U., Va. Tech. Found., 1789 Soc. at Hampden-Sydney Coll., Soc. of Founders Hampden-Sydney Coll., Va. Hist. Soc., Rotunda Soc. U. Va., Reform Club (London), St. James Club (London), Salisbury Country Club, Hurlingham Club (London), Sloane Club (London), Quinnipiack Club (New Haven), Yale Club N.Y.C., Pilon Soc., Va. Tech. Methodist. Avocations: jazz, golf.

COLEMAN, ROY EVERETT, secondary education educator, computer programmer; b. Chgo., Oct. 16, 1942; m. Dianna Joy Uchida, Nov. 12, 1988. BS in Physics, Ill. Inst. of Tech., 1964; MS in Physics, DePaul U., 1974; Sci. Edn., Ill. Inst. of Tech., Chgo., 1990; Computer Sci., Chgo. State U., Chgo., 1984. Physics tchr. Morgan Park H.S., Chgo., 1965—, St. Xavier Coll., Chgo., 1977-80; S.M.I.L.E. staff specialist Ill. Inst. of Tech., Chgo., 1982—, computer edn. staff, 1988—. Dir. comp. lit. Chgo. Pub Schs., 1983—84; exec. chair Chgo. Sci. Fair, 2002—. Author: Equipment Evaluation, 1982; co-author: Physics Text Evaluations, 1984. Mem. Pursuit of Excellence Com., Chgo., 1982-88, Scholarship Com., 1985-89; chmn. student sci. fair Chgo. Pub. Schs., 2002—. Recipient Phoebe Aperton Hurst award Nat. PTA, Washington, 1985, Tchr. of Yr. award Chgo. PTA, 1978-80, Presdl. award of Excellence, U.S. Dept. Edn., 1987, Supt. award Chgo. Pub. Schs., 1979, 80, H.S. Tchr. of Astronaut Dr. Mae C. Jemison award, Kohl Internat. Tchg. award, 1994, First pl. Chgo. Rd. Rally Series, 1997, 99; Tandy Tech. scholar, 1995; finalist Golden Apple awards, 1995. Mem.: Am. Assn. Physics Tchrs. (treas., pres. Chgo. chpt.), Sports Car Club Am. (Ind. N.W. region). Avocations: road rallies (rallyemaster, driver scca road rallye), computer games, auto mechanics. Home: 5436 S Kimbark Ave Chicago IL 60615-5284

COLEMAN, SIDNEY RICHARD, physicist, educator; b. Chgo., Mar. 7, 1937; s. Harold Albert and Sadie (Shanas) C. BS, Ill. Inst. Tech., 1957; PhD, Calif. Inst. Tech., 1962. Research fellow dept. physics Harvard U., 1961-63, asst. prof., 1963-66, assoc. prof., 1966-69, prof., 1969—, Donner prof. of sci. Vis. prof. U. Rome, Italy, 1968, Princeton U., 1973, Stanford U., 1979-80, U. Calif., Berkeley, 1989, 95. Author: Aspects of Symmetry, 1985. Trustee Aspen Ctr. Physics. Recipient prize for physics lectures Ettore Majorana Centre Sci. Culture, Boris Pregel award N.Y. Acad. Sci., Disting. Alumnus award Calif. Inst. Tech., Dirac medal Internat. Centre for Theoretical Physics 1990. Fellow NAS (J. Murray Lack award for sci. revs.), Am. Acad. Arts and Sci., Am. Phys. Soc. (Dannie Heineman prize); mem. Lilapa. Home: 1 Richdale Ave Unit 12 Cambridge MA 02140-2610 Office: Harvard U Physics Dept Cambridge MA 02138 E-mail: coleman@physics.harvard.edu.

COLEMAN, TERRY LEWIS, state legislator; m. Carol Cofield; 2 children. AA, Reinhardt Coll.; BS, Brenau Coll.; JD, Woodrow Wilson Coll. Law, 1981. Estate planner Assoc. of Wealth Planning Cos.; rep. 118th dist. Ga. Ho. of Reps., 1973—, spkr., 2003—. Chmn. house appropriations com., 1991-2002, house natural resources and environment com., 1987-88, house pub. safety com., 1978-86, house ways and means com., 1989-90, mem. budget conf. com., 1991-2002, chmn. joint com. of budget responsibility, 1991-2002, oversight com., 1991-2002. Mem. Eastman Vol. Fire Dept.; bd. govs. Mercer Med. Sch., 1990-2003. With Ga. N.G. Mem.: Million Dollar round Table, C. of C. (pres. 1985—87), Pacific Mutual Nat. Leaders Club. Democrat. Home: PO Box 157 Eastman GA 31023-0157 Office: State Capitol Rm 338 Atlanta GA 30334*

COLEMAN, THOMAS YOUNG, lawyer; b. Richmond, Va., Jan. 6, 1949; s. Emmet Macadium and Mary Katherine (Gay) C.; m. Janet Clare Norris, Aug. 30, 1980; children: Dana Alicia (dec.), Amanda Gay, Blair Norris. BA, U. Va., 1971, JD, 1975. Bar: Va. 1975, U.S. Dist. Ct. (we. dist.) Va. 1975, U.S. Ct. Appeals (4th cir.) 1976, Calif. 1977, U.S. Dist Ct. (no. dist.) Calif. 1977. Law clk. chief judge U.S. Dist. Ct. (we. dist.) Va., Charlottesville, 1975-76; assoc. Morrison & Foerster, San Francisco, 1976-79; v.p., counsel Calif. 1st Bank (now Union Bank of Calif.), San Francisco, 1979-85; of counsel Orrick, Herrington & Sutcliffe, San Francisco, 1985-86, ptnr., 1987—. Speaker in field; vis. atty. Clifford-Turner Solicitors (now Clifford Chance), London, 1984. Mem. bus. gifts com. San Francisco Symphony. Mem. Internat. Bankers Assn. in Calif. (co-counsel). Office: Orrick Herrington & Sutcliffe 400 Sansome St San Francisco CA 94111-3143

COLEMAN, TRAVIS BRENT, music educator; b. West Palm Beach, Fla., Aug. 11, 1971; s. Travis and Arllinda Coleman; m. Andrea Michelle Williams, July 27, 1996; 1 child, Sophia Michelle. B in Mus. Edn., Auburn U., 1994. Cert. tchr. Ala., 1994. Choral dir. Pizitz Mid. Sch., Vestavia Hills, Ala., 1994—. Mem.: Tex. Music Educators Assn., Ala. Vocal Assn., Ala. Music Educators Assn., Music Educators Nat. Conf., Am. Choral Directors Assn. Home: 342 Old Cahaba Tr Helena AL 35080 Office: Pizitz Mid Sch 2020 Pizitz Dr Vestavia Hills AL 35216 Office Fax: 205-402-5354. E-mail: bcoleman@vestavia.k12.al.us.

COLEMAN, WADE HAMPTON, III, management consultant, mechanical engineer, former banker; b. Tuscaloosa, Ala., June 24, 1932; s. Wade Hampton, Jr. and Margaret Pauline (James) C.; m. Kate Shannon Stabler, June 2, 1958 (div. 1966); children— Shannon Hunter, Wade Hampton IV; m. Eileen Marie Lincoln, Dec. 23, 1967; 1 child, Lydie Elizabeth BA, U. N.C., 1954; BS and BSM.E., U. Ala., 1960; MSI.E., Lehigh U., 1965. Registered profl. engr., Pa. Rsch. engr. Western Electric Co., Princeton, N.J., 1960-65; tech. staff mem. MITRE Corp., Arlington, Va., 1965-66; mgmt. cons. Booz, Allen & Hamilton, Washington, 1967-70; prin. Auerback Corp., Phila., 1970-72; spl. asst. to sec. HEW, Washington, 1972-73; sr. v.p. Citibank, NA, N.Y.C., 1973-85; chmn., chief exec. officer Asbestos Claims Facility Inc, Princeton, N.J., 1985-87; pres. ELW Devel. Group, Lawrenceville, N.J., 1987-89, Coleman & Evans Inc., Princeton, 1989—. Mem. Civic Assn., Lawrenceville, N.J., 1973—, bd. dirs.

Lower Eastside Services Ctr., N.Y.C., 1978—, pres. 1986-90; bd. dirs. Capstone Found., Tuscaloosa, 1980— . Served with USN, 1954-57, lt. comdr. res. ret. Mem. Nat. Soc. Profl. Engrs., Am. Bankers Assn., Sigma Pi Sigma, Tau Beta Pi, Delta Kappa Epsilon Republican. Episcopalian. Home: 4 Monroe Ave Lawrenceville NJ 08648-1606

COLEMAN, WILLIAM THADDEUS, JR., lawyer; b. Germantown, Pa., July 7, 1920; s. William Thaddeus and Laura Beatrice (Mason) Coleman; m. Lovida Hardin, Feb. 10, 1945; children: William Thaddeus III, Lovida Hardin Jr., Hardin L. AB summa cum laude, U. Pa., 1941; LLB magna cum laude, Harvard U., 1943. Bar: Pa. 1947, DC 1977. Law sec. Judge Herbert F. Goodrich, U.S. Ct. of Appeals, 3d Cir., 1947—48, Justice Felix Frankfurter (assoc. justice Supreme Ct. U.S.), 1948—49; assoc. Paul, Weiss, Rifkind, Wharton & Garrison, N.Y.C., 1949—52, Dilworth, Paxson, Kalish, Levy & Green, Phila., 1952—56; ptnr. Dilworth, Paxson, Kalish, Levy & Coleman, 1956—75; sec. Dept. Transp., Washington, 1975—77; sr. counsellor, sr. ptnr. O'Melveny & Myers, Washington, L.A., San Francisco, N.Y.C., Tokyo, London, Hong Kong, Shanghai, Beijing, China, 1977—. Spl. counsel for transit matters City of Phila., 1952—63; rep. atty. gen. Pa. and Commonwealth of Pa. in litig. to remove racial restrictions at Girard Coll., 1965; mem. Pres.'s Com. on Govt. Employment Policy, 1959—61, cons. ACDA, 1963—74, sr. cons., asst. counsel Pres.'s Commn. on Assassination of Pres. Kennedy, 1964; co-chmn. planning sessions White House Conf. to Fulfill These Rights, 1965—66; mem. U.S. del. 24th Session UN Gen. Assembly, 1969; mem. legal adv. com. Coun. on Environ. Quality, 1970; pub. mem. Pres.'s Nat. Commn. on Productivity, 1970; commr. Price Commn., 1971—72, Phila. Fairmount Pk. Commn., 1967—75, White House Commn. Aviations Safety and Security, 1996—97; mem. Gov.'s Commn. on Constl. Revision, 1963—65. Contbr. articles to profl. jours. Former chmn. bd. NAACP Legal Def. and Ednl. Fund; v.p., trustee, mem. exec. com. Phila. Art Mus.; trustee Brookings Instn., Nat. Gallery Art, 1999; mem. Trilateral Commn.; mem. exec. com. Lawyers Com. for Civil Rights Under Law; bd. overseers Harvard U., 1975—81; bd. dirs., adv. dir. NY City Ballet. Decorated officer French Legion of Honor; recipient Joseph E. Beale prize, 1946, Presdl. Freedom medal, Pres. Clinton, 1995, NAACP Legal Def. Fund Thurgood Marshall Lifetime Achievement award, 1997, Marshall Wythe medallion, 2003; fellow Langdell, 1946—47. Fellow: Am. Coll. Trial Lawyers; mem.: Coun. Fgn. Rels., Am. Arbitration Assn. (gov.), Am. Acad. Arts and Scis., Am. Philos. Soc., Phila. Bar Assn. (past chmn. jud. com.), Am. Law Inst. (coun., Henry J. Friendly medal 2000), Am. Acad. Appellate Lawyers, Met. Club (Washington), Jr. Legal Club (Phila.), Alfalfa Club, Cosmos Club, Order of Coif, Harvard Law Sch. Club, Pi Gamma Nu (Wickersham award 1997, The Fordham Stein prize 2000), Phi Beta Kappa. Office: O'Melveny & Myers 555 13th St NW Ste 500W Washington DC 20004-1159

COLEMAN, WINIFRED ELLEN, academic administrator; b. Syracuse, N.Y., Oct. 3, 1932; d. Peter Andrew and Josephine (Fahey) C. BA, Le Moyne Coll., Syracuse, N.Y., 1954; MA, Marquette U., 1956; DHL (hon.), Le Moyne Coll., 1993. Dean of students Cazenovia (N.Y.) Coll., 1957-70, Trinity Coll., Washington, 1970-80; exec. dir. Nat. Coun. Catholic Women, Washington, 1980-85; pres. Cashel House, Ltd., Syracuse, NY, 1985—, St. Joseph Coll., West Hartford, Conn., 1991—. Trustee LeMoyne Coll., Syracuse, 1995—, The Mark Twain House, Hartford; trustee emerita Loretto Geriatric Ctr., Syracuse, N.Y.; pres. Assn. Mercy Coll. Presidents, 1993-97, Hartford Consortium for Higher Edn., 1993-97; bd. dirs. Conn. Higher Edn. Student Loan Adminstrn., Hartford Mutual Funds. Bd. dirs. St. Francis Hosp. and Med. Ctr. Hon. membership Trinity Coll. Alumnae, Washington, 1978, Cazenovia (N.Y.) Coll. Alumnae, 1961, Naming of Winifred E. Coleman Student Union, Cazenovia Coll., 1963; recipient Chantal Award, Catholic Woman of the Yr., 1965. Mem.: Nat. Jesuit Honor Soc. for Women, Gamma Pi Epsilon. Roman Catholic. Avocations: reading, composing lyrics. Home: 27 Buckingham Ln West Hartford CT 06117-2758 Office: St Joseph Coll 1678 Asylum Ave West Hartford CT 06117-2764

COLE-MCCREA, CANDACE, social sciences educator; b. Glens Falls, N.Y., May 25, 1948; d. Arthur Eugene and Jane Evelyn (McCrea) Cole; m. William Martin Paris, Mar. 1976 (div. 1985); children: Daric, Kestrel. BA in Sociology and Ethnic Studies, Calif. State U., Fullerton, 1980; MA in Sociology, U. N.H., 1983; PhD in Psychology, Kennedy-Western U., 2001. Cert. family support counselor; cert. HIV/AIDS counselor; cert. yoga instr.; cert. in music therapy, art therapy, logotherapy; cert. hospice ministry. Mem. faculty, chair dept. social scis., human svcs., edn. N.H. Cmty. Tech. Coll., Stratham, 1990—. Spkr., cons. and jazz poet. Contbr. articles and poetry to profl. pubIs. Min., counselor Native Am. Ch.; specialized foster parent, 1993—; mentor 4-H Club; mem. Milton Town Sch.-to-Work Com. Mem. N.H. Native Am. Assn., N.H. Poetry Soc. Mem. Soc. Of Friends. Avocations: native american poetry, jazz band, textile arts. Home: PO Box 1033 Milton NH 03851-1033 Office: NH Cmty Tech Coll Dept Human Svc Social Sci 67 New Hampshire Ave Portsmouth NH 03801-2864 E-mail: snowyowl@metrocast.net.

COLEN, FREDERICK HAAS, lawyer; b. Pitts., May 16, 1947; married, 1972. BSChemE, Tufts U., 1969; JD, Emory U., 1975. Bar: Pa. 1975, Ga. 1975, U.S. Patent Office 1976, U.S. Dist. Ct. (we. dist.) Pa. 1975, U.S. Dist. Ct. (no. dist.) Ga. 1975, U.S. Ct. Appeals (fed. and 3d cirs.) 1975, U.S. Supreme Ct. 1980. Chem. engr. Shell Oil Co., New Orleans, 1969-71; san. engr. USPHS, Morgantown, W.Va., 1971-73; patent atty. Mobay Chem. Corp., Pitts., 1975-79; assoc. Reed Smith, LLP, Pitts., 1979-86, ptnr., 1986—. Contbr. articles to profl. jours. Mem. ABA, Allegheny County Bar Assn., Pa. Bar Assn., Ga. Bar Assn., Am. Intellectual Property Law Assn. Home: 4940 Ellsworth Ave Pittsburgh PA 15213-2807 Office: Reed Smith LLP 435 6th Ave Ste 2 Pittsburgh PA 15219-1886 E-mail: fcolen@reedsmith.com.

COLEN, HELEN SASS, plastic surgeon; b. Bytom, Poland, Jan. 9, 1947; came to the U.S., 1963; d. Karl Julius and Sabina (Orgel) Sass; m. Stephen Robert Colen, Mar. 25, 1972; children: Kari, Michael. BA, NYU, 1968, MD, 1972. Diplomate Am. Bd. Plastic Surgery. Intern Jefferson U. Hosp., 1972-74; gen. surgeon U. Colo., Denver, 1974-79; plastic surgeon U. Columbia-St. Lukes, N.Y.C., 1979-81; microsurgeon Bellevue Hosp., N.Y.C., 1981-82; practice medicine specializing in plastic surgery N.Y.C., 1982—. Fellow ACS; mem. Am. soc. Plastic Surgeons, Phi Beta Kappa. Office: 784 Park Ave New York NY 10021-3553

COLENDA, III, CHRISTOPHER COLUMBUS, psychiatrist; b. Baltimore, Md., Feb. 14, 1952; s. Christopher Columbus Colenda, Jr. and Janet A. Colenda; m. Kathyryn Winclkhofer Colenda, July 24, 1976; children: Meredith Lee Colenda, Stephanie Adair Colenda. BA, Wittenberg U., 1970—73; MD, Med. Coll. of Va., 1973—77; MPH, Johns Hopkins U., 1981—82. Certified Psychiatry Am. Bd. of Psychiatry and Neurology, 1991, Psychiatry Am. Bd. of Psychiatry and Neurology, 1986. Dir. of geriatric psychiatry Med. Coll. of Va., Commonwealth U., Richmond, Va., 1985—90; vice chmn. and sect. head, geriatric psychiatry Wake Forest U. Sch. of Medicine, 1990—96; chmn., dept. of psychiatry Mich. State U., 1997—2002; acting dean Mich. State U., Coll. of Human Medicine, 2000—01; dean Coll. of Medicine, Tex. A&M U. Health Sci. Ctr., 2003—. Vice-chairman, geriatric psychiatry test writing com. Am. Bd. of Psychiatry and Neurology, Deerfield, Ill., 2000—; faculty fellow Liason Com. for Med. Edn., Washington, 2001—02. Author: (health services and policy research) American Journal of Geriatric Psychiatry. Mem.: AMA, Am. Assn. for Geriatric Psychiatry (treas. elect and treas. 2002—, bd. dirs. 2000—01), Am. Psychiat. Assn. (chair, coun. of aging 1997—2000). Office: Coll of Medicine Tex A&M U Health Sci Ctr College Station TX 77843-1114 E-mail: colenda@medicine.tamu.edu.

COLER, MYRON A(BRAHAM), chemical engineer, educator; b. N.Y.C., Mar. 30, 1913; s. Marcus and Bertha (Bebarfald) C.; m. Viola Ethel Buchbinder, Nov. 15, 1942 (dec. Jan. 1993); children: Mark D., Sandra Coler Carson; m. Lena Amark, Feb. 16, 1996 (div. Mar. 1998). AB, Columbia U., 1933, BS, 1934, ChE, 1935, PhD, 1937; postgrad., NYU, Bklyn. Poly. Inst. With NYU, N.Y.C., 1941-75, prof., dir. surface tech. program dir. creative sci. program. Supr., rsch. scientist Manhattan Project, 1943-45; founder, pres., dir. chmn. bd. Markite Co., Markite Corp., Markite Engring. Co., 1948-67, Coler Engring. Co., 1967—, The Vulcan Press Divsn., Valmath, 1988—; sponsor-in-residence Franklin Inst. Rsch. Labs., 1975-81; cons. numerous cos. and govt. agys. Author: Aircraft Engine Finishes, 1941; editor, contbg. author: Essays on Creativity in the Sciences, 1963, Essays on Invention and Education, 1977; numerous articles to profl. jours.; patentee in field. Bd. dirs. Marcus and Bertha Coler Found.; mem. adv. com. dept. phys. and engring. metallurgy Polytechnic Inst. N.Y.; mem. pres.'s com. for Sch. Continuing Edn., NYU; appointee Nat. Inventors Coun., 1966-74; mem. state tech. svc. com. Dept. Commerce; with divsn. cultural studies UNESCO-Dept. State, 1982. Named hon. prof. Polytechnic Inst. N.Y.; Weston fellow Electrochem. Mem. AAAS, Am. Math. Soc., Materials Rsch. Soc., Am. Nuclear Soc., N.Y. Acad. Sci., Electrochem. Soc., Am. Ceramic Soc., Am. Chem. Soc., Am. Soc. for Metals, Am. Def. Preparedness Assn., Internat. Precious Metals Inst., Sigma Xi, Phi Beta Kappa, Phi Lambda Upsilon, Tau Beta Pi, Epsilon Chi. Address: Empress Hotel 7766 Fay Ave La Jolla CA 92037-4309

COLES, ANNA LOUISE BAILEY, retired university official, nurse; b. Kansas City, Kans., Jan. 16, 1925; d. Gordon Alonzo and Lillie Mai (Buchanan) Bailey; children: Margot, Michelle, Gina. Diploma, Freedmen's Hosp. Sch. Nursing, 1948; BSN, Avila Coll., Kansas City, Mo., 1958; MSN, Cath. U. Am., 1960, PhD in Higher Edn., 1967. Instr. VA Hosp., Topeka, 1950—52, supr. Kansas City, Mo., 1952—58; asst. dir. in-service edn. Freedmen's Hosp., Washington, 1960—61, adminstrv. asst. to dir. nursing, 1961—66, assoc. dir. nursing services, 1966—67, dir. nursing, 1967—69; dean Howard U. Coll. Nursing, Washington, 1968—86, dean emeritus, 1986—; cons. pvt. practice, Kansas City, Kans.; dir. minority devel. U. Kans., 1991—95. Pres. Nurses Examining Bd., 1967—68; cons. Gen. Rsch. Support Program, NIH, 1972—76; mem. Inst. Medicine, NAS, 1974—; cons. VA Ctl. Office continuing edn. com., 1976—; mem. D.C. Health Planning Adv. Com., 1967—68, Tri-State Regional Planning Com. for Nursing Edn., 1969, Health Adv. Coun., Nat. Urban Coalition, 1971—73; bd. dirs. Hilton Grand Vacation CLub Seaworkd Internat. Ctr. Contbr. articles to profl. jours. Trustee Cmty. Group Health Found., 1976—77, cons., 1977—; bd. regents State Univ. Sys. Fla., 1977; adv. bd. Am. Assn. Med. Vols., 1970—72; bd. dirs. Iona Whipper Home for Unwed Mothers, 1970—72, Nursing Edn. Opportunities, 1970—72. Recipient Sustained Superior Performance award, HEW, 1962, Meritorious Pub. Svc. award, Govt. of D.C., 1968, medal of honor, Avila Coll., 1969, Disting. Alumni award, Howard U. Nat. Assn. for Equal Opportunity in Higher Edn., 1990, Cmty. Svc. award, Black Profl. Nurses Kansas City, 1991, Lifetime Achievement award, Assn. Black Nursing Faculty in Higher Edn., 1993, Svc. award, Midwest Regional Conf. on Black Families and Children, 1994. Mem.: ANA, Am. Assn. Colls. Nursing (sec. 1975—76), Am. Congress Rehab. Medicine, Nat. League Nursing, Societas Docta (charter, pres. 1996—99), Freedmen's Hosp. Nursing Alumni Assn., Alpha Kappa Alpha, Sigma Theta Tau. Home: 15107 Interlachen Dr Apt 205 Silver Spring MD 20906-5627

COLES, BERTHA SHARON GILES, visual information specialist; b. Paris, Tenn., Aug. 13, 1949; d. Charles Ray and Etter Bell (Lightfoot) Giles. Student, Profl. Edn. Divsn. Dallas, 1979, Dynamic Graphics Ednl. Found., 1980, No. Va. C.C., 1981. Typesetter, illustrator Def. Printing, Washington, 1979-83; editl. asst. Exec. Office of Pres., Washington, 1983; visual info. specialist Naval Media Support Ctr., Washington, 1983—. Design, layout, paste-up specialist for various publs., including USN Medicine, 1981, 83, Bull., 1983, Playbook, 1995; cover design July 1996 issue All Hands Mag.; design, layout Posture Statement Mag., 1997; cover design USN-(Joint Civilian Orientation Conf.)-Dept. Def.; cover design and layout of Dept. Navy Posture Statement, 1998. Bd. dirs. London Woods Cmty. Assn., Capitol Heights, Md., 1995. Democrat. Avocations: painting, gardening, interior decorating, collector. Home: 5634 Onslow Way Capitol Heights MD 20743-3059 Office: Navy Media Support Ctr 2713 Mitscher Rd SW Washington DC 20373-5819

COLES, DONALD EARL, retired aeronautics educator; b. St. Paul, Feb. 8, 1924; s. Courtney J. and Lorna (Addison) C.; m. Ellen Searight, Sept. 11, 1947; children: Christopher Lee, Elizabeth Anne, Kenneth Spencer, Janet Jacqueline. B.Aero. Engring., U. Minn., 1947; MS, Calif. Inst. Tech., 1948, PhD, 1953. Research engr. Jet Propulsion Lab., Pasadena, Calif., 1950-53; research fellow Calif. Inst. Tech., Pasadena, 1953-56, mem. faculty, 1953-96, prof. aeros., 1964-96; ret., 1996. Cons. to industry, 1954—; mem. Nat. Com. Fluid Mechs. Films, 1960 Producer ednl. film Channel Flow of a Compressible Fluid, 1966. Served with AUS, 1943-46. Fellow AIAA (Lawrence Sperry award 1953, Dryden medal 1985), Am. Phys. Soc. (Otto Laporte award 1996); mem. Nat. Acad. Engring., Sigma Xi. Home: 1033 Alta Pine Dr Altadena CA 91001-1409

COLES, GRAHAM, conductor, composer; b. London, May 7, 1948; arrived in Canada, 1951; s. Walter Harold and Phyllis Irene Gwendoline (Conn) C. MusB, U. Toronto, 1972, MusM, 1974, EdB, 1991. Music dir. Kitchener-Waterloo (Ont.) Chamber Orch., 1985—. Mem. coll. of examiners Royal Conservatory of Music, Toronto. Composer numerous instrumental and vocal compositions. Mem. Can. League Composers, Can. Music Ctr. (assoc. composer), Assn. Can. Orchs. Home: 86 Weber St E Kitchener ON Canada N2H 1C7 E-mail: kwchamberorchestra@on.aibn.com.

COLES, H. BRENT, former mayor; m. Julie Allred; 5 children. B in Polit. Sci., Brigham Young U., 1977; MPA, Calif. State U., Long Beach, 1980. Asst. city mgr. City of Boise, city planner, mem. city coun., mayor, 1993—2003. Mem. adv. bd. U.S. Conf. Mayors. Bd. dirs. Assn. Idaho Cities, Boise Future Found., Ada Planning Assn.; co-chair Drug Control Task Force.

COLES, ROBERT, child psychiatrist, educator, author; b. Boston, Mass., Oct. 12, 1929; s. Philip and Sandra (Young) C.; m. Jane Hallowell; children—Robert, Daniel, Michael. AB, Harvard U., 1950; MD, Columbia U., 1954; MD (hon.), Temple U., Notre Dame U., Bates Coll., 1972, Wayne State U., 1973, Western Mich. U., Holy Cross Coll., 1974, Hofstra U., 1975, Coll. William and Mary, Bard Coll., U. Lowell, U. Cin., 1976, Stonehill Coll., Lesley Coll., Rutgers U., 1977, Wesleyan U., Columbia Coll., Knox Coll., Cleve. State U., Wooster Coll., 1978, U. N.C., Manhattan Coll., St. Peter's Coll., Coll. New Rochelle, Pratt Inst. and Sch. Design, 1979, Berea Coll., Bklyn. Coll., Emmanuel Coll., 1980, Colby Coll., 1981, Sienna Heights Coll., Salem State Coll., Williams Coll., 1983, Beloit Coll., 1984, Emory U., Fairfield U., Macalaster Coll., Colgate U., 1986, Dartmouth Coll., 1987. Intern U. Chgo. Clinics, 1954-55; resident in psychiatry Mass. Gen. Hosp., Boston, 1955-56, McLean Hosp., Belmont, Mass., 1956-57, Judge Baker Guidance Center-Children's Hosp., 1957-58; mem. staff children's Unit Met. State Hosp., Waltham, Mass., 1957-58; mem. staff alcoholic clinic Mass. Gen. Hosp.; teaching fellow in psychiatry, mem. psychiat. staff and clin. asst. in psychiatry Harvard Med. Sch., 1955-58; research psychiatrist Harvard U. Health Services, 1963—; lectr. gen. edn. Harvard U., 1966—, prof. psychiatry and med. humanities, 1977—; founder and editor DoubleTake Magazine, 1995—. Child psychiat. fellow Judge Baker Guidance Center, Children's Hosp., Boston, 1960-61; mem. Nat. Adv. Com. on Farm Labor, 1965— ; cons. Appalachian Vols., 1965—, Rockefeller Found., 1969—, Ford Found., 1969— ; mem. Inst. of Medicine, Nat. Acad. Scis., 1973-78; vis. prof. public policy Duke U., 1973— ; cons. supr. dept. psychiatry Cambridge (Mass.) Hosp., 1976— ; cons. Center for Study of So. Culture, U. Miss., 1979— ; bd. dirs. Ctr. for Documentary Studies, Duke U.; vis. prof. psychiatry, Dartmouth Coll., 1989. Author: Children of Crisis: A Study of Courage and Fear, 1967, Dead End School, 1968, Still Hungry in America, 1969, The Grass Pipe, 1969, The Image is Yours, 1969; Wages of Neglect, 1969, Uprooted Children: The Early Lives of Migrant Farmers, 1970, Teachers and the Children of Poverty, 1970, Erik H. Erikson: The Growth of His Work, 1970, The Middle Americans, 1970, Migrants, Sharecroppers and Mountaineers, 1972, The South Goes North, 1972, Saving Face, 1972, Farewell to the South, 1972, A Spectacle Unto the World, 1973, Riding Free, 1973, The Darkness and the Light, 1974, The Buses Roll, 1974, Irony in the Mind's Life: Essays on Novels by James Agee, Elizabeth Bowen and George Eliot, 1974, Headsparks, 1975, The Mind's Fate, 1975, Eskimos, Chicanos and Indians, 1978, Privileged Ones, Vol. V of Children in Crisis book series, 1978, (with Jane Hallowell Coles) Women of Crisis Lives of Struggle and Hope, 1978, Walker Percy: An American Search, 1978, Flannery O'Connor's South, 1980, Women of Crisis; Lives of Work and Dreams, 1980, Dorothea Lange: Photographs of a Lifetime, 1982, (with Ross Spears) Agee, 1985, The Political Life of Children, 1986, Dorothy Day: A Radical Devotion, 1987, Simone Weil: A Modern Pilgrimage, 1987, Times of Surrender: Selected Essays, 1988, Harvard Diary, 1988, That Red Wheelbarrow, 1988, The Call of Stories: Teaching and the Moral Imagination, 1989, Rumors of Separate Worlds, 1989, The Spiritual Life of Children, 1990; contbg. editor: The New Republic, 1966—, Am. Poetry Rev, 1972—, Aperture, 1974—, Lit. and Medicine, 1981—, New Oxford Rev, 1981— ; mem. editorial bd.: Integrated Edn., 1967—, Child Psychiatry and Human Devel., 1969—, Rev. of Books and Religion, 1976—, Internat. Jour. Family Therapy, 1977—, Grants mag., 1977—, Learning mag., 1978—, Jour. Am. Culture, 1977—, Jour. Edn., 1979— ; bd. editors: Parents' Choice, 1978— ; editor: Children and Youth Services Rev., 1978— . Bd. dirs. Field Found., 1968— ; trustee Robert F. Kennedy Meml., 1968—, Robert F. Kennedy Action Corps, State of Mass., 1968—, Miss. Inst. Early Childhood Edn., 1968—, Twentieth Century Fund, 1971— ; bd. dirs. Reading is Fundamental, Smithsonian Inst., 1968—, Am. Freedom from Hunger Found., 1968—, Am. Parents Com., 1971— ; mem. corp. Boston Children's Service, 1970; mem. adv. council Inst. for Nonviolent Social Change of Martin Luther King, Jr. Meml. Center, 1971—, Ams. for Children's Relief, 1972— ; mem. nat. com. for Edn. of Young Children, 1972— ; mem. nat. adv. council Rural Am., 1976— ; trustee Austen Riggs Found., Stockbridge, Mass., 1976— ; mem. nat. adv. com. Ala. Citizens for Responsive Public Television, 1976— ; mem. adv. com. Nat. Indian Edn. Assn., 1976— ; visitor's com. mem. Boston Mus. Fine Arts, 1977; bd. dirs. Boys Club Boston, 1977; vis. com. Boston Coll. Law Sch., 1977; adv. Center for So. Folklore, 1978— ; mem. children's com. Edna McConnell Clark Found., 1978— ; bd. dirs. Lyndhurst Found., 1978— ; mem. nat. adv. bd. Foxfire Fund, Inc., 1979— . Recipient Ralph Waldo Emerson prize Phi Beta Kappa, 1967; Anisfield-Wolf award in race relations Saturday Rev., 1968; Hofheimer award Am. Psychiat. Assn., 1968; Sidney Hillman prize, 1971; Weatherford prize Berea Coll. and Council So. Mountains, 1973; Lilliam Smith Award So. Regional Council, 1973; McAlpin medal Nat. Assn. Mental Health, 1972; Pulitzer prize, 1973 (all received for Children of Crisis, Vols. II, III); disting. scholar medal Hofstra U., 1974; William A. Shonfeld award Am. Soc. Adolescent Psychiatry, 1977; MacArthur Found. award, 1981; Josepha Hale award, 1986; fellow Davenport Coll., Yale U., 1976— Fellow Am. Acad. Arts and Scis., Inst. Soc., Ethics and the Life Scis.; mem. Am. Psychiat. Assn., Am. Orthopsychiat. Assn. (past dir.), Acad. Psychoanalysis, Nat. Orgn. Migrant Children. Office: Harvard U Univ Health Svcs 75 Mount Auburn St Cambridge MA 02138-4960

COLES, ROBERT NELSON, SR., religious organization administrator; b. Aug. 1, 1929; married; 6 children. Grad., Salvation Army Officers Coll., 1956; postgrad., DePaul U., 1968. Field officer Salvation Army, 1960-68; with Vols. Am., 1946-55, 60-80; editor-in-chief Rescue Herald Orgn. Am. Rescue Workers, Phila., 1981-92, ordination com. chmn., dir. spl. svcs., 1988-96; nat. comm. sec. Am. Rescue Workers, 1980—, also nat. bd. mgrs., 1956-2001; Ordained. Chmn. ordination com., aid-de-camp to gen. Am. Rescue Workers, 1985-96. Editor Rescue Herald. Active Comty. Svc. Coun.; organizer numerous youth baseball and basketball teams, and semi-profl. football team Vols. Am., Elmira, N.Y.; established 3 group homes for children from broken homes, Hagerstown, Md., 1969-81; dir. food program Am. Rescue Workers, Phila., 1981-92. Named to Elmira Sports Hall of Fame, 1990. Mem. Am. Correctional Chaplains Assn., Am. Correction Assn., Md. State Sheriff's Assn., Washington County Ministerial (treas. 1993-94), Scottish Rite Bodies, Masons (32 degree), Hagerstown Exch. Club. Office: Am Rescue Workers Nat Field Office 1209 Hamilton Blvd Hagerstown MD 21742-3340 E-mail: chiefcoles@aol.com.

COLES, ROBERT TRAYNHAM, architect; b. Buffalo, Aug. 24, 1929; s. George Edward and Helena Vesta (Traynham) C.; m. Sylvia Rose Meyn, Mar. 28, 1953; children: Marion Brigette, Darcy Eliot. Student, Hampton Inst., 1947-49; BA, U. Minn., 1951, B. Arch., 1953; M.Arch., M.I.T., 1955; Litt.D. (hon.), Medaille Coll., 1977. Designer, Perry, Shaw, Hepburn and Dean (Architects), Boston, 1956-57, Shepley, Bulfinch, Richardson and Abbott (Architects), Boston, 1957-58, Carl Koch and Asso., Cambridge, Mass., 1958-59; architect, custom design mgr. Techbuilt, Inc. (housing prefabricators), Cambridge, 1959-60; coordinating architect Deleuw, Cather and Brill, Engrs., Buffalo, 1960-63; prin. Robert Traynham Coles, Architect, P.C., Buffalo, 1963—; Langston Hughes Disting. prof. architecture and urban design U. Kans., 1989. V.p. Buffalo Archtl. Guidebook Corp., 1979-82; cons. housing rsch. Union Carbide Corp., 1963; vis. prof. SUNY, Buffalo, summer 1967, U. Kans., 1969; v.p. Eastside Cmty. Orgn. Inc., 1965-68, pres., 1968-77; chmn. Com. for an Urban U., 1966-67, Goals for Met. Buffalo, 1967-68; pres. Cmty. Planning Assistance Ctr. Western N.Y., Inc., 1972-74, Archtl. Mus. and Resource Ctr., 1980-84; mem. N.Y. State Bd. for Architecture, 1984-94, vice chmn., 1990, chmn., 1991; assoc. prof. architecture Carnegie Mellon U., Pitts., 1990-95; mem. jury U.S. Post Office Nat. Design Competition, Wash., D.C., 1994, City Plaza Nat. Design Competition, Lexington, Ky., 2001; chair jury, N.Y. State Assn. Architects Design Awards, N.Y.C., 1995. Treas., v.p., editor (newsletter) Nat. Orgn. Minority Architects, 1972—80, contbr. The Urban Ecosystem: A Holistic Approach, 1974, exhibitor Design Diaspora, Black Architects and International Architecture, 1970-1990, Chgo. Athenaeum, 1993, Robert Traynham Coles: Architect, Buffalo, N.Y., 1996, Between Tradition and Memory: Constructed Shleters, Black Architects, Inst. Rsch. African Diaspora in Americas and Caribbean, N.Y.C., 1999, Robert Traynham Coles: Inner City Architect, Buffalo and Erie County Hist. Soc., Buffalo, N.Y., 2002. Mem. coun. Burchfield Art Ctr., Buffalo, 1989-92, nat. adv. com. Arts in Am., 1989, Erie County Horizons Waterfront Commn., 1988-91; bd. dirs. Build a New City, Inc., 1973-75; trustee Preservation League N.Y. State, sec., 1978; trustee Western N.Y. PBS, 1981-87, hon. trustee, 1987—. Recipient Centennial award Medaille Coll., 1975, Alumni Achievement award U. Minn. Coll. Architecture and Landscape Architecture, 1997; Edward H. Moeller scholar, 1949-53, Rotch Travelling Scholar Boston Soc. Architects, 1955; named Citizen of Distinction Mayor of Buffalo, N.Y., 1997. Fellow AIA (mem. nat. housing com. 1969-71, nat. urban design and planning com. 1971-73, chmn. social responsibility com. Buffalo-Western N.Y. chpt. 1970-71, dir. 1978-81, nat. dep. v.p. minority affairs 1974-75, Whitney E. Young award 1981, sec. Coll. of Fellows 1991-93, vice-chancellor 1993-94, chancellor 1995); mem. Nat. Orgn. Minority Architects (treas. 1976-78, dir. 1978, v.p. 1978), Alpha Kappa Mu. Home: 321 Humboldt Pkwy Buffalo NY 14208-1023 Office: 730 Ellicott St Buffalo NY 14203-1102 *Because they have the ability to see things as they can be, today's architects have a special task which goes beyond simply designing the physical environment. They must be activists involved in the social and political life of the community. They must address their efforts to change in these areas as well, so that people can make the needed adjustments to an increasingly challenging and rich urban world. They must, in their works, build the demonstrative alternative to the way we live today. They must be initiators as well as implementors—leaders more than followers. They must truly be revolutionaries who see their architecture as a broad movement to enchance the quality of life of urban people.*

COLES, WILLIAM HENRY, ophthalmologist, educator; b. Rochester, N.Y. BA, Ohio Wesleyan U., 1958; MD, Emory U., 1962; MS, La. State U., 1970. Diplomate Am. Bd. Ophthalmology. Intern Grady Hosp., Atlanta, 1962-63; resident Charity-La. State U., New Orleans, 1966-70; prof. ophthalmology Emory U., Atlanta, 1980-86, dir. postgrad. edn., 1981-86; prof. ophthalmology SUNY, Buffalo, 1986—, chmn. dept., 1986—. Clin. assoc. prof. Med. Univ. S.C., Charleston, 1980-86; chief of svc. Grady Meml. Hosp., Atlanta, 1981-84; chief ophthalmology svc. VA Hosp., Atlanta, 1984-86; chmn. adv. coun. Ophthalmic Surgery, 1998. Author: Ophthalmology: A Diagnostic Text, 1989; sect. editor: Medicine for the Practicing Physician, 1984 (Med. Textbook of Yr. award). Dir. Inst. Health Assessment, 1997—. Nat. Eye Inst. grantee, 1975-78. Mem. AMA, ACS (chair adv. coun. 1997—, regent 1998-), AAUP, Am. Acad. Ophthalmology (Disting. Svc. award 1989, sr. honor award 1998), Med. Soc. State of N.Y., Assn. Rsch. and Vision in Ophthalmology, Assn. Univ. Profs. in Ophthalmology (trustee, pres. 1996-97). Home: 120 Donegal Dr Chapel Hill NC 27517

COLE SCHIRALDI, MARILYN BUSH, occupational therapy educator; b. N.Y.C., Jan. 29, 1945; d. George Lyman and Theis (Maurer) Bush; m. Carl E. Cole, Aug. 31, 1968 (div. June 1981); children: Charlot E. Sleeper, Bradley Eric Cole; m. Martin M. Schiraldi Sr., July 3, 1982. BA, U. Conn., 1966; grad. cert., U. Pa., 1969; MS, U. Bridgeport, 1982. Registered occupational therapist, Conn. Staff occupational therapy Ea. Pa. Psychiat. Inst., Phila., 1968-69; dir. occupational therapy Middlesex Meml. Hosp., Middletown, Conn., 1973-76; supervising occupational therapist Lawrence & Meml. Hosps. Day Treatment Ctr., New London, Conn., 1976-79; staff occupational therapist Newington Children's Hosp., Newington, Conn., 1980-82; asst. prof. occupational therapy Quinnipiac Coll., Hamden, Conn., 1982-95, assoc. prof., tenured, 1995—. Vis. faculty fellow Yale U., 1999-2001; cons. psychiat. svcs. VA Med. Ctr., West Haven, Conn., 1983-91; cons. Fairfield Hills Hosp., Newtown, Conn., 1989-91. Author: (textbook) Group Dynamics in Occupational Therapy, 1993, 3d edit.,

2003; co-author Structured Group Experiences, 1982; contbr. chpts. to books, articles to profl. jours. Grantee Quinnipiac Coll. 1986; recipient Best Seller award Slack, Inc., 1999. Fellow: Am. Occupl. Therapy Assn. (Comms. award 1976, Svc. awards 1998, cert.); mem.: AAUW (cultural chair 1972, publicity chair 1973—76, edn. chair 1989—91, nominations 1993—96, membership treas. 1998—2001), Ctr. Study Sensory Integrative Dysfunction (cert. 1979), World Fedn. Occupl. Therapists, Conn. Occupl. Therapy Assn. (sec. 1978, nominations chair 1982—89, state mental health chair spl. interest sect. 1999—), U.S. Sailing Assn., U.S. Power Squadron, Sigma Xi. Republican. Episcopalian. Office: Quinnipiac U Dept Occupl Therapy 275 Mount Carmel Ave Hamden CT 06518-1961 E-mail: marilyn.cole@quinnipiac.edu.

COLESCOTT, WARRINGTON WICKHAM, artist, printmaker, educator; b. Oakland, Calif., Mar. 7, 1921; s. Warrington W. and Lydia (Hutton) C.; m. Frances Myers, Mar. 15, 1971; children by previous marriage: Louis Moore, Julian Hutton, Lydia Alice. AB, U. Calif. at Berkeley, 1942, MA, 1947; postgrad., Acad. de la Grand Chaumiere, Paris, France, 1950, 53, Slade Sch. Art, U. London (Eng.), 1957. Mem. faculty U. Wis., Madison, 1949-86, prof. art, 1957-86, Leo Steppat chair, prof., 1979-85, Leo Steppat chair (emeritus prof.), 1986—. Printmaker emeritus So. Graphics Coun., 1991; academician Nat. Acad. Design. One-man shows include Perimeter Gallery, Chgo., 1985, 87, 88, 91, 93, 95, 99, 2002, Milw. Mus. Art, 1996, Rockford (Ill.) Art Mus., Bradley U., Peoria, Ill.; print retrospective Elvehjem Mus., Madison, Wis., 1989, Nelson-Atkins Mus., Kansas City, 1990, SUNY, Albany, N.Y., 1995, New Orleans Mus. Art, 2003; represented in permanent collections Mus. Modern Art, Victoria and Albert Mus., London, Bibliotechque Nat., Paris, Met. Mus., Chgo. Art Inst., Bklyn. Mus., Phila. Mus. Art, Milw. Art Mus., Elvehjem Art Mus.; co-author (with Arthur Hove) Progressive Printmakers, 1999; etchings commd. Milw. Art Mus., N.Y. Print Club, 2002. Recipient Print award NAD, 1991, 92, 95, 97, NSAL Award of Excellence, 1993, 99, award Internat. Triennial of Print, Cracow, Poland, 1997, award Boston Printmakers, 2003; Fulbright fellow, 1957, Guggenheim fellow, 1965, Nat. Endowment Arts Printmaking fellow, 1975, Artist fellow, 1979, 83-84, 93-94. Fellow Wis. Acad. Sci. Arts and Letters. Office: 8788 County Hwy A Hollandale WI 53544-9801

COLESON, RICHARD EUGENE, lawyer, minister; b. Bulsar, India, Feb. 6, 1951; came to U.S., 1952; s. Ralph James and Olive Leone Coleson; m. Linda Sue McCrory, Aug. 19, 1972; children: Nathan Edward, Heather Anne, Jason Andrew. BA, Ind. Wesleyan U., 1973; MA in Religion, Asbury Theol. Sem., Wilmore, Ky., 1975; JD, Ind. U., 1987. Bar: Ind. 1987, U.S. Dist. Ct. (so. and no. dists.) Ind. 1987, U.S. Ct. Appeals (7th cir.) 1994, U.S. Ct. Appeals (5th cir.), 1991, U.S. Ct. Appeals (4th cir.) 1995, U.S. Supreme Ct. 1990. Pastor Wyoming (Mich.) Wesleyan Ch., 1975-78; prof. Bartlesville (Okla.) Wesleyan Coll., 1978-82; pastor Blue River Wesleyan Ch., Arlington, Ind., 1983-87, Oak Hill & Riley (Ind.) United Meth. Chs., 1990—; assoc. Brames, Bopp, Abel & Oldham, Terre Haute, Ind., 1987-92; staff counsel Nat. Legal Ctr. for the Medically Dependent and Disabled, Terre Haute, Ind., 1992-99; sr. assoc. Bopp, Coleson & Bostrom, Terre Haute, Ind., 1992—. Contbr. articles to profl. jours. Mem. Vigo County Election Bd., Terre Haute, 1993-97. Recipient Outstanding Achievement award Ind. Wesleyan U. Alumni Assn., 1997. Office: Bopp Coleson & Bostrom 1 South 6th St Terre Haute IN 47807-3510

COLESSIDES, NICK JOHN, lawyer; b. Kavala, Greece, Jan. 14, 1938; came to U.S., 1958; s. John T. and Maroula C.; m. Sophia Simons Symeonidis, Oct. 5, 1970. BS in Polit. Sci., U. Utah, 1963, MS Polit. Sci., 1967, JD, 1970. Bar: Utah 1970, U.S. Dist. Ct. Utah 1970, U.S. Ct. Appeals (10th cir.) 1970, U.S. Dist. Ct. (so. dist.) Ohio 1975, U.S. Ct. Appeals (9th cir.) 1976. Chief deputy county atty. Salt Lake County (Utah) Atty.'s Office, 1970-74; city atty. West Jordan (Utah) City Atty.'s Office, 1971-78, Park City (Utah) Atty.'s Office, 1976-80; atty. pvt. practice, Salt Lake City, 1970—. Bd. dirs. Merrill Lynch Bank, U.S.A., Salt Lake City City. Trustee Greek Orthodox Ch., SaltLake City, 1976, 77, 87, 88, 98, 99, Utah Cmty. Reinvestment Corp. Mem. Assn. Trial Lawyers Am., Utah Trial Lawyers Assn., U. Utah Coll. of Law Alumni Assn. (trustee 1995-98), Utah State Bar Assn., Salt Lake County Bar Assn., Am. Inn of Ct. VII (master of the bench, pres. 1997, 98). Greek Orthodox. Avocations: gardening, cooking, reading. Office: 466 S 400 E Ste 100 Salt Lake City UT 84111-3301 Home: Apt 410 150 S 300 E Salt Lake City UT 84111-2087

COLETTA, GERARD CHARLES, management consultant; b. Cambridge, Mass., Dec. 9, 1944; s. Gerard Charles and Eileen Gertrude (Barrett) C.; m. Pamela S. Wight, June 30, 1984; children: Nadine, Sean. BSChemE, Tufts U., 1966; MSChemE, MIT, 1968; postgrad., U. Calif., Berkeley, 1969-71. Design engr. Standard Oil of Calif., San Francisco, 1968-71; staff cons. Arthur D. Little, Inc., Cambridge, 1971-78; corp. dir. of safety and health Nat. Semiconductor Corp., Santa Clara, Calif., 1978-81; sr. cons. Risk Planning Group, Darien, Conn., 1981-83; pres. Risk Control Services, Tiburon, Calif., 1983-86; prin. and practice mgr. Tillinghast div. Towers Perrin Co., San Francisco, 1986-91; sr. v.p., nat. practice mgr., bus. continuity cons. Marsh USA (formerly Sedgwick of Calif.), San Francisco, 1991-2000; v.p., nat. practice leader, bus. continuity cons. Palmer & Cay, Boston, 2000—. Spkr. in field. Contbr. articles to profl. jours. Mem. ASTM (chmn. com. 1980-85, bd. dirs. sub-com. 1987-91, Spl. Service award 1985, Achievement award 1986), Am. Soc. Safety Engrs., Nat. Safety Mgmt. Soc., Tufts U. Chem. Engring. Alumni Council, Tau Beta Pi. Republican. Avocations: tennis, skiing, jogging. Office: Palmer & Cay 189 State St Boston MA 02109-2647 E-mail: jerry_coletta@palmercay.com., jcoletta@attglobal.net.

COLETTA, RALPH JOHN, retired lawyer; b. Chillicothe, Ill., Dec. 13, 1921; s. Joseph and Assunta Maria (Aromatario) C.; m. Ethel Mary Meyers, Nov. 19, 1949; children: Jean, Marianne, Suzanne, Joseph, Robert, Michele, Renee. BS, Bradley U., 1943; JD, U. Chgo., 1949. Bar: Ill. 1949. Practice law, Peoria, Ill., 1949-99; gen. ptnr. Ralet Ltd. Partnership, Peoria, Ill.; ret., 1999. Pres. White Star Corp., Mark Tidd, Inc.; asst. state's atty. Peoria County. Chmn. United Fund. Served to 1st lt. AUS, 1943-46. Mem. ABA, Ill. State Bar Assn., Peoria County Bar Assn., Chgo. Bar Assn., Creve Coeur Club, Mt. Hawley Country Club, K.C., Union League Club. Republican. Roman Catholic. Home: 301 W Crestwood Dr Peoria IL 61614-7328

COLETTE, LOIS MARIE, artist; b. L.A., Mar. 31, 1950; d. Conrad Valenzona and Irene Iacona; children: Jason Collette, Hunter Fine. BA, Antioch Coll., Yellow Springs, Ohio, 1980. Painting fellow Nat. Endowments for the Arts, 1987-88. Home: 9 Fillmore Pl Brooklyn NY 11211-4001

COLETTI, JOHN ANTHONY, lawyer, furniture and realty company executive; b. Cherry Point, N.C., Sept. 22, 1952; s. Joseph Nicholas and Gloria Lucy (Fusco) C.; m. Barbara Nancy Carlotti, July 20, 1975; children: Lisa M., Kristen B. Student, Biscayne Coll., 1970-72; BA summa cum laude, Boston Coll., 1974, JD, 1977. Bar; R.I. 1977, U.S. Dist. Ct. R.I. 1977. Assoc. Resmini, Fornaro, Colagiovanni & Angell, Providence, 1979-81; ptnr. Coletti & Tente, Cranston, R.I., 1981—. Pres. Coletti's Furniture, Inc., Johnston R.I., 1983-95, Coletti's Realty, Inc., Johnston, 1983-96. Legal counsel Cranston Housing Authority, 1988—; interviewer alumni admissions coun. Boston Coll., 1980—. Mem. ABA, R.I. Bar Assn., R.I. Conveyancers Assn., Nat. Assn. Retail Collection Attys., Phi Beta Kappa. Roman Catholic. Avocations: horseback riding, golf, figure skating. Office: Coletti & Tente 311 Doric Ave Cranston RI 02910-2903

COLEY, BRENDA ANN, elementary education educator; b. Indpls., Sept. 17, 1958; d. Jack Louis Mullis and Margaret Ann (Crites) Farris; m. Keith Alan Coley, Feb. 17, 1978; children: Amy Michelle, Jared Wesley, Adam Jacob. B Music Edn., Ind. U., 1981; MS in Music Edn., Ind. State U., 1987. Tchr. music Clay Community Sch. Corp., Staunton, Ind., 1981-84; choral dir. Spencer (Ind.)-Owen Community Sch. Corp., 1984-90, tchr. music, 1990—2000; asst. prin. McCormick's Creek Elem. Sch., Spencer, Ind., 2000—. Composer children's musical: Up! Up to the Moon!!, 1992; composer gospel music., founder "Jubilation in Christ", gospel singing group, 1997-. Choir dir. 1st Christian Ch., Spencer. Mem. NEA, Music Educators Nat. Conf., Ind. Music Educators Assn., Spencer-Owen Edn. Assn., Order Ea. Star, Kappa Kappa Kappa, Pi Lambda Theta, Delta Theta Tau. Democrat. Avocations: singing, sports, bowling. Home: 40 Mozart Ln Spencer IN 47460-9344 Office: McCormick's Creek Elem Sch 1601 Flatwoods Rd Spencer IN 47460-1499

COLEY, F(RANKLIN) LUKE, JR., lawyer; b. Monroeville, Ala., Apr. 17, 1958; s. Franklin Luke and Margaret Boyce (Green) C. BA in History, U. Ala., 1980, JD, 1983. Bar: Ala. 1985, U.S. Dist. Ct. (so. dist.) Ala. 1987, U.S. Ct. Appeals (11th cir.) 1990. Law clk. Robert S. Edington, Mobile, Ala., 1983-85; pvt. practice Mobile, 1985—. Active Mobile County Dem. Exec. Com., 1986-98; bd. dirs. United Methodist Children's Home, 1999—. Mem. ABA, Mobile Bar Assn., Kiwanis (sec. local chpt. 1987-89, v.p. 1989-91, pres. 1991-92). Methodist. Home: 5906 Reams Dr N Mobile AL 36608-3658 Office: 273 Azalea Rd Ste 2-512 Mobile AL 36609-1957 E-mail: flcoley@bellsouth.net.

COLEY, JOAN DEVELIN, education educator; b. Phila., Nov. 12, 1944; d. Paul Kennedy Develin and Lillian Marian Stiles; 1 child, David Kennedy. AB, Albright Coll., Reading, Pa., 1966; MEd, U. Md., 1970, PhD, 1973. Reading specialist Prince George's County (Md.), 1966-70, dir. secondary sch. vol. program, 1970-71; adj. prof. Univ. Coll., U. Md., College Park, 1971-73; prof., chair edn. dept., dean grad. programs, provost McDaniel Coll. (formerly Western Md. Coll.), Westminster, 1973—, pres. Reading cons. Simon & Schuster Pub., 1986—. Editor: Reading: Issues and Practices, 1984-88; editorial adv. bd. Reading Rsch. and Instrn., 1977-81; author programmed reading vocabulary for tchrs. Mem. Internat. Reading Assn. (pres. Carroll County 1979-81, Tchr. Educator of Yr. 1989, Outstanding Educator in Reading 1982), Coll. Reading Assn. (bd. dirs. 1980-83), Nat. Reading Conf., Md. Higher Edn. Reading Assn. (pres. 1975-76). Home: 1 College Hill Westminster MD 21157-4450

COLEY, LINDA MARIE, retired secondary school educator; b. Albany, Ga., Apr. 19, 1945; d. Leonard Earl and Hazel (Brady) C. BS in Math., Piedmont Coll., 1966; MS in Math., U. Ga., 1972, postgrad. Cert. tchr., Ga.; certed gifted tchr. Tchr. Toccoa (Ga.) Pub. Schs., 1966-67, Hall County Sch. Dist., Gainesville, Ga., 1967-68, Clarke County Sch. Dist., Athens, Ga., 1968—2001. Sec., 1st v.p. Clarke County Dem. Com., Athens, 1981—, Gov.'s Club. Mem. NEA, Ga. Edn. Assn., Clarke County Assn. Educators (treas., sec.), Alpha Delta Kappa (treas., sec., pres., dist. treas.), Phi Delta Kappa. Democrat. Baptist. Home: 135 Ravenwood Pl Athens GA 30605-3344

COLFER, CAROL JEAN PIERCE, anthropologist, researcher; b. Melrose Park, Ill., Aug. 27, 1945; d. Joe Eugene Pierce and Gwendolyn Marie Harris Pierce; m. Richard George Dudley, Feb. 2, 1985. MA, U. Wash., 1969, PhD, 1974; MPH, U. Hawaii, 1979. Field rschr. Abt Assocs., Quilcene, Wash., 1972—77; exec. dir. PACT: Social Analysts, Seattle, 1976—77; field rschr. Man and Biosphere Program, Long Segar, Indonesia, 1979—80; women in devel. asst. specialist U. Hawaii, Honolulu, 1980—82, farming systems assoc. rschr. Sitiung, Indonesia, 1992—96; assoc. prof. Sultan Qaboos U., Al Khodh, Oman, 1988—90; cmty. specialist Asian Wetlands Bur., Danau Sentarum Wildlife Res., Indonesia, 1992—93; prin. scientist Ctr. Internat. Forestry Rsch., Bogor, Indonesia, 1996—98, program leader, 1998—2002; vis. fellow Cornell U., Ithaca, NY, 2002—03. Cons. Ctr. Internat. Forestry Rsch., Bogor, Indonesia, 1994—, FAO, Portland, Oreg., 1990—91. Author: (book) Toward Sustainable Agriculture in the Humid Tropics, 1991, Shifting Cultivators of Indonesia, 1993, Beyond Slash and Burn, 1997; editor: People Managing Forests, 2001, Which Way Forward?, 2002; contbr. articles to profl. jours. Named William S. Main Disting. Visitor, U. Calif. Berkeley, 1991, Profl. Affiliate Award, East-West Ctr., 1979; recipient Invitation to give Plenary Address, Internat. Union Forestry Rsch. Orgns., 2000, Appointment to Adv. Group, Ctr. Social Forestry, Mulawarman U., E. Kalimantan, Indonesia, 1999, Participant award for productivity, stability, sustainability and the small-mcalesFarmef, East-West Ctr., 1985, Profl. Affiliate award, 1977, Cert. of Outstanding Contbn./Rural Edn., Rural/Regional Ednl. Assn., 1976; fellow Fellow on population info., edn. and comm., East-West Ctr., 1975, Fulbright-Hayes Predoctoral fellow/Iran, Fulbright Hayes/U.S. Govt., 1972, fellow to study langs., NDEA, 1964—67; grantee to study interactions between people and forests in E. Kalimantan, U.S. Man and Biosphere program, 1979—80. Fellow: Internat. Union Forestry Rsch. Orgns. (vice chair 2001), Soc. Applied Anthropology, Med. Anthropology Soc., Am. Anthrop. Assn.; mem.: Soc. Study of Common Property. Liberal. Avocations: reading, beading, swimming, canoeing, travel. Home: 14845 SW Murray Scholls Dr Ste 110 Beaverton OR 97007-9237 Office: Ctr Internat Forestry Rsch PO Box 6596 JKPWB Jakarta 10065 Indonesia Office Fax: 62-21-622100. E-mail: c.colfer@cgiar.org.

COLFIN, BRUCE ELLIOTT, lawyer, video producer; b. Bklyn., June 9, 1951; s. Abraham and Sylvia (Laykin) C.; m. Virginia Mary Faszczewski, Sept. 27, 1981. BA, CUNY, 1977; JD, N.Y. Law Sch., 1980. Bar: N.Y. 1982, U.S. Dist. Ct. (so., ea. dists.) N.Y., 1987, U.S. Ct. Internat. Trade, 1990. Audio engr. Snowball Sound Systems, N. Bergen, N.J., 1974-77; producer, dir. cable TV program What's On, N.Y.C., 1976-84; stage mgr. Peter Tosh U.S. tour Rolling Stones Records, 1978; v.p., producer Upswing Artists Mgmt., N.Y.C., 1979-86; pres., producer, dir. LegalVision, Inc., N.Y.C., 1982-87; ptnr. Jacobson & Colfin, N.Y.C. and Washington, 1985-90; mem. Jacobson & Colfin, P.C., N.Y.C. and Washington, 1990—; pres. Fifth Ave. Media, Ltd., N.Y.C., 1996—. Assoc. prof. music bus. and tech. Five Towns Coll., 1999—; spkr. Discovery Ctr., N.Y., 1st Ann. Musicians Seminar, L.I., N.Y. Law Sch. Media Law Soc., 1986; vis. lectr. SUNY, Oneonta, 1988—; panelist New Eng. Music Orgn. Conf., 1998, Emerging Artists and Talent in Music, 1999, 2002. Assoc. producer music video Blues Alive, 1982; exec. prodr., dir. video series Entertainment Law Video Primer, 1984; exec. prodr. (CD) Zen Tricksters, 1999; monthly columnist Ind. Music Producers Soc. Jour., NARAS N.Y. chpt. newsletter; contbr. articles to profl. jours.; columnist: Replication News, 1998, Medialine, 2000. Mem. ABA (com. on entertainment sports law, subcom. chmn. patent, trademark and copyright com. 1989, subcom. chmn. internat. law and practice, internat. intellectual property rights com., spl. subcom. on multimedia 1994—, editl. advisor pubs. com. internat. law sect. 1990-92, exec. com. entertainment law cir. 1989-91, com. on authors of intellectual property law sect. 2001--), Nat. TV Acad. (N.Y. chpt., mem. new media com., internet sub-com.), N.Y. State Bar Assn. (entertainment, arts and sports law sect., com. on talent agys. and talent mgmt., com. on rights of publicity 1994—), Nassau County Bar Assn. (vice chmn. entertainment, sports and media law com.), Spkrs. Bur. Entertainment and Sports Law Comm., Copyright Soc. U.S.A. (editl. bd. 1986-88), Nat. Acad. of Recording Arts and Scis. (N.Y. chpt.). Jewish. Avocations: traveling, writing, stamp collecting, hockey. Office: Jacobson & Colfin PC 19 W 21st St Rm 603A New York NY 10010 E-mail: BRUCE@Thefirm.com.

COLFLESH, GERTRUDE PATTERSON (TRUDY P. COLFLESH), counselor; b. Steubenville, Ohio, June 6, 1939; d. Robert Meade and Gertrude (Lippincott) Patterson; m. George William Colflesh, Aug. 5, 1961; children: Michael, Christopher, Karen (dec.). BA in Religious Studies, Coll. Wooster, 1961; postgrad., Oberlin Sch. Theology, 1962; MA in Counseling and Human Devel., Montclair State U., 1990. Nat. cert. counselor; lic. profl. counselor. Dir. Christian Edn. Calvary Presbyn. Ch., Canton, Ohio, 1961-63; counselor Christian Counseling Ctr., Clifton, NJ, 1990—2001; pvt. practice lic. profl. counselor, 2001—. Founder women's support groups St. Andrew's Presbyn. Ch., Berea, Ohio, 1966-72, elder, 1972; founding v.p. Women's Aglow Fellowship Internat., Miami, Fla., 1973-75, area v.p. Outreach and Retreats, No. N.J., 1980-86; founder Neighborhood Women's Bible Study, 2000. Author: Too Precious to Die, 1984, Soulcry, 2002. Named Adult Sunday Sch. Tchr. of Yr., Bethany Assemblies of God Ch., Wyckoff, N.J., 2001. Mem. Am. Assn. Christian Counselors, N.J. Counseling Assn., Nat. Assn. for Christian Recovery, Phi Kappa Phi. Home and Office: 33 Northwood Dr West Milford NJ 07480-3724 E-mail: trudy@encouraginghope.com. *While the accomplishments of my years of service and achievements are presented in this book with pride and delight, my greatest joy is in the accomplishment of Jesus Christ who saved and redeemed me and entered my name in His Book of Life.*

COLGAN, STEPHEN THOMSON, analytical chemist; b. Rochester, N.Y., June 11, 1957; s. Frank John and Margaret Ann (Thomson) C.; m. Karen Elita Koudal, June 30, 1983; children: Christopher, Patrick, Kimberly. BS in Chemistry, SUNY, Cortland, 1980; MS in Forensic Chemistry, Northeastern U., 1982, PhD in Analytical Chemistry, 1986. Rsch. scientist Pfizer Inc., Groton, Conn., 1987-90, sr. rsch. scientist, 1990-94, sr. rsch. investigator, 1994-99, prin. rsch. investigator, 1999—. Presenter in field. Contbr. articles to profl. jours. Active Boy Scouts Am., North Stonington, Conn., 1994—. ACS Summer fellow, 1983; recipient Gustel Giessen Advanced Rsch. award, Northeastern U., 1985, Dr. Y. Tapuhi Meml. award, Northeastern U., 1983; named Outstanding Student in Chemistry, SUNY Cortland, 1980. Mem. ACS (analytical chemistry divsn.). Avocations: basketball, volleyball, mountain biking, fishing, science fiction. Home: RR 2 Box 95 North Stonington CT 06359-9801 Office: Pfizer Inc Central Research Eastern Point Rd Groton CT 06340

COLGAN, SUMNER, manufacturing engineer, chemical engineer; b. Framingham, Mass., Sept. 11, 1934; s. Joseph and Leora C.; student Boston Coll., 1957-61, Boston U., 1961, Banff Climbing Sch.; married; 1 son, Scott Paul. Chem. engr. Beam Tube Corp., Western, Mass., 1962-63; reliability engr. Gen. Motors Corp., Framingham, 1963-86, mfg. engr., 1986-91; chemist Envirotech Operating Systems, North Haven, Conn., 1991-92; lab. mgr. New England Fertilizer, 1992—. Served in USAF, 1953-57. Mem. Hunting Ravine Avalanche Patrol, 1970-78. Mem. Matterhorn Climbers Assn. Zermatt, Pvt. Pilot Assn., Mt. Rainier Summit Climbers Assn. Clubs: Appalachian Mountain, Sea Urchins. Office: 97 E Howard St Quincy MA 02169-8711 Home: PO Box 6501 Laconia NH 03247-6501

COLGATE, DORIS ELEANOR, sailing school owner and administrator; b. Washington, May 12, 1941; d. Bernard Leonard and Frances Lillian (Goldstein) Horecker; m. Richard G. Buchanan, Sept. 6, 1959 (div. Aug. 1967); m. Stephen Colgate, Dec. 17, 1969. Student, Antioch Coll., 1958-60, NYU, 1960-62. Rsch. supr. Geyer Moyer Ballard, N.Y.C., 1962-64; administrv. asst. Yachting Mag., N.Y.C., 1964-68; v.p. Offshore Sailing Sch. Ltd., Inc., N.Y.C., 1968-78; pres. Offshore Sailing Sch. ltd., Inc., Ft. Myers, Fla., 1978—2001; pres., CEO On and Offshore, Inc., Ft. Myers, 1984-2001; v.p. Offshore Travel, Inc., City Island, 1978-88; CEO Offshore Sailing Sch. Ltd., Inc., Ft. Myers, Fla., 2001—. Pres. bd. dirs. Women's Sailing Found., 1998-2000, chmn. 2000-02, adv. coun., 2002—. Author: The Bareboat Gourmet, 1983, Sailing: A Woman's Guide, 1999; contbr. articles to profl. jours. Recipient Betty Cook Meml. Lifetime Achievement award, 1994, Sail Industry Leadership award, 1996, Southam award, 2000. Mem. Royal Ocean Racing Club (London chpt.), Nat. Women's Sailing Assn. (founder, chair nat. women's adv. bd. 1990-94, pres. 1994-2000, chair 2000-02), Am. Women's Econ. Devel. Corp. (adv. bd. 1980-86), Boat U.S. (nat. adv. coun. 1995—), Sail Am. (bd. dirs. 2000—). Avocations: piano, sailing, photography, writing, cooking. Home: 15400 Catalpa Cove Ln Fort Myers FL 33908 Office: Offshore Inc 16731 McGregor Blvd Fort Myers FL 33908-3810 E-mail: doris@offshore-sailing.com

COLGATE, STEPHEN, small business owner; b. N.Y.C., June 25, 1935; s. Gilbert Colgate and Nina (King) Heiner; m. Doris Eleanor Horecker, Dec. 17, 1969. BA, Yale U., 1957. CEO, owner Offshore Sailing Sch., Ltd., Ft. Myers, Fla., 1964—, Offshore Travel, Inc., N.Y.C., 1978-88, On and Offshore, Inc., Captiva Island, Fla., 1975—, Cafe Offshore Inc., City Island, Fla., 1981-84. Author: (book) Colgate's Basic Sailing Theory, 1973, Fundamentals of Sailing, Cruising and Racing, 1978, The Yachtsman's Guide to Racing Tactics, 1981, Steve Colgate on Sailing, 1991, Steve Colgate on Cruising, 1991, Steve Colgate on Racing Rules, 1991. Served to capt. USAF, 1958—60. Mem.: Nat. Marine Mfrs. Assn., U.S. Olympians (Fla. chpt.), Internat. Sailing Schs. Assn. (pres.), Internat. Sailing Fedn., U.S. Sailing Assn., Cruising Club Am., Royal Bermuda Yacht Club, Royal Ocean Racing Club (London), N.Y. Yacht Club (N.Y.C.). Republican. Episcopalian. Avocations: bicycling, sailing.

COLGATE-LINDBERG, CATHARINE PAMELLA, educator; b. Cedar Rapids, Iowa, Dec. 17, 1939; d. Fred Joseph and Emma H. Petrick; m. Gary N. Lindberg; children: Shannon Colgate, Stephen Colgate, Stewart Colgate, Stanley Colgate, Travis Lindberg, Heidi Lindberg Roberts. BS, Ariz. State U., 1973, MA, 1977. Cert. tchr., jr. coll. educator, Ariz. Tchr. English Mesa (Ariz.) Pub. Schs., 1975—99; instr. English Mesa C.C., 1982—, prof. English. Writing specialist Associacao Escola Graduada, Sao Paulo, Brazil; vis. prof. edn. U. Sao Paulo. Patentee sch. lecterns. Mem. NEA, AAUP, Nat. Sch. Bds. Assn., Nat. Coun. Tchrs. English, Mesa Edn. Assn., Ariz. Sch. Bd. Assn., U.S. Air Force Acad. Alumni Parents' Orgn. and Assn., U.S. Mil. Acad. Alumni Parents Orgn., Phi Delta Kappa, Phi Lambda Theta.

COLGLAZIER, E. WILLIAM, science academy administrator, physicist; BS in Theoretical Physics, Calif. Inst. Tech., 1966, PhD in Theoretical Physics, 1971. Rschr. theoretical physics various instns.; congl. sci. fellow U.S. Rep. George Brown, 1976-77; rsch. fellow Ctr. Sci. and Internat. Affairs, Kennedy Sch. Govt. Harvard U.; prof. physics U. Tenn., Knoxville, 1983—91, dir. numerous sci. and tech. policy ctrs.; internat. affairs exec. dir. NRC, 1991—94, exec. dir. Office of Internat. Affairs, 1994; acting exec. officer NAS, NRC, 1994, exec. officer, 1994—. Bd. dirs. Fermilab High-Energy Physics Accelerator. Author numerous publs. in field. Bd. dirs. Oak Ridge Associated Univs. Recipient Lifetime Contbn. award, sect. environ. and nat. resources adminstrn. ASPA, Commendation, State Planning Coun. on Radioactive Waste Mgmt. Office: NAS & NRC 2101 Constitution Ave NW Washington DC 20418-0007

COLGRASS, MICHAEL CHARLES, composer; b. Chgo., Apr. 22, 1932; s. Michael Clement and Ann (H) C.; m. Ulla Damgaard, Nov. 25, 1966; 1 child, Neal. MusB, U. Ill., 1956; studied with Paul Price, studied with Eugene Weigle, studied with Darius Milhand, studied with Lukas Foss, studied with Wallingford Riegger, studied with Ben Weber. Author: Tuning the Human Instrument, 1993-94, My Lessons with Kumi-How I Learned to Perform with Confidence in Life and Work, 2000; freelance solo percussionist maj. N.Y. mus. orgns., 1956—, Narrator, Boston Symphony, 1969, Phila. Orch, 1970; dir. : Virgil's Dream, Brighton Festival; Soloist, Danish Radio Orch., 1965; dir. opera Nightingale Inc, U. Ill. Contemporary Music Festival, 1975; author, poet own theatre works, 1966—; composer: Divertimento, 1961, Fantasy Variations, 1961, Wind Quintet, 1962, Light Spirit, 1963, Rhapsody, 1963, Rhapsodic Fantasy, 1965, Sea Shadow, 1966, As Quiet As, 1966, Virgil's Dream, 1967, Three Brothers, 1951, Percussion Music, 1953, Chamber Music for Four Drums and String Quintet, 1954, Chamber Music for Percussion Quintet, 1955, Variations for Four Drums and Viola, 1957, The Earth's a Baked Apple, 1968-69, New People for mezzosoprano, viola, piano, 1969, Nightingale, Inc, Auras for Harp and Orch, 1973, Image of Man, 1974, Concertmasters for 3 violins and orch, 1975, Best Wishes U.S.A. for black and white choruses, folk instruments, jazz band and orch, 1976, Theatre of the Universe for soloists, chorus and orch, 1976, Wolf for solo cello, 1976, Letter from Mozart for orch, 1976, Dèjà Vu, 1977 (Pulitzer prize 1978), Mystery Flowers of Spring for soprano and piano, 1978, Something's Gonna Happen, children's musical theatre, 1978; Flashbacks, musical play for 5 brass, 1979; Night of the Raccoon, 5 songs for soprano and 4 players, 1979, Ghosts of Pangea-A Fantasy of Cultures Meeting for full orchestra, 2000; Delta, for violin, clarinet, percussion and orch, 1979; Tales of Power, a mus. drama for solo piano on the writings of Carlos Castaneda 1980; Metamusic for solo piano, 1981; Memento for 2 pianos and orch., 1982; Demon for amplified piano, tape, radios and orch., 1983; Chaconne for viola and orch., 1984, Winds of Nagual, for wind ensemble, 1985; Strangers: Irreconcilable Variations for clarinet, viola and piano, 1986, (Jules Legèr Chamber Music Prize 1988), Dèjà Vu for percusssion quartet and wind ensemble, 1987; Folklines: A Counterpoint of Musics for string quartet and wind ensemble, 1988, The Schubert Birds, 1989, Snow Walker for organ and orch., 1990, arctic Dreams for symphonic band, 1991, Wild Riot of the Shaman's Dreams for solo flute, 1991, Arias for clarinet and orchestra, 1992, Te Tuma Te Papa for solo percussionist, 1994, a Flute in the Kingdom of Drums and Bells, 1994, Urban Requiem for four saxophones and wind ensemble, 1995, "Hammer & Bow" for violin and marimba, 1997, 98, Dream State for solo piano, 1998, Baroque Blues for solo piano, 1998, Drummers for solo piano, 1998, "Chameleon" for solo saxophone, 1999, Memento Trio for flute, cello and piano, 1999, "Old Churches" for young band, 1999, Crosswords for flute, piano and orch., 2002 "The Beethoven Machine" for young band, 2003, "Apache Lullaby" for young band, 2003, "Bach-Goldberg Variations" for chamber orchestra, 2003; works commd. N.Y. Philharm., CBC, U. Ill. Symphonic and Concert Bands, Boston Symphony, Toronto Symphony Orch., Lincoln Center Chamber Mus. Soc., New Eng. Conservatory Wind Ensemble, Fromm Found., Corp. for Pub. Broadcasting, Ford Found., Spokane, Detroit, Springfield, Minn. symphony orchs., Musica Aeterna Orch. N.Y., Young Concert Artists N.Y., Nat. Arts Centsre Orch. of Can., Calgary Internat. Organ Festival, New World Festival Arts, Delos, Manhattan and Muir string quartets, U. Miami, Nexus percussion ensemble: works recorded various cos.: contbr. articles to publs.; columnist Music Mag.; author: My Lessons with Kumi- How I Learned to Perform with Confidence in Life and Work, 2000, Ghosts of Pangea (for orchestra), 2000, Dream Dancer (for saxophone and wind ensemble), 2001. With AUS, 1954-56. Scholar Tanglewood, Mass., 1952, 54, Aspen, Colo., 1953;

Guggenheim fellow, 1964-65, 68-69; recipient Fromm award, 1966, Chem. Bank award, 1971, Emmy award for Sta. WGBH-TV film Soundings: The Music of Michael Colgrass for best documentary Nat. Acad. TV Arts and Scis., 1982; Rockefeller grantee, 1967-69; Ford Found. grantee, 1972; recipient Pulitzer prize, 1978; Winds of Nagual winner Louis B. Sudler Internat. Wind Band Composition Competition, 1985, De Moulin prize Nat. Band Assn., 1985, Barlow Internat. prize, 1986. Office: 583 Palmerston Ave Toronto ON Canada M6G 2P6 E-mail: colgrass@interlog.com. *I see the composer as a person not separate from life and community but indigenous to it. How to bridge the gap that has developed between the artist and people is the biggest challenge I know, but I find the more I reach out to people the less indifferent they are to the artistic experience.*

COLI, GUIDO JOHN, chemical company executive; b. Richmond, Va., Sept. 12, 1921; s. Guido and Rena (Pacini) C.; m. Vonda L. Coli; children: Pamela, Patricia, Deborah, Rebecca Smith. BS, Va. Poly. Inst., 1941, MS, 1942, PhD, 1949. Registered profl. engr., N.Y., Va. Asst. engr. Va. Health Dept. bur. indsl. hygiene, 1941; assoc. chemist Naval Research Lab., 1942-43; instr. chem. engring. Va. Poly. Inst., 1947-48; chem. engr. Mobil Oil Co., Paulsboro, N.J., 1949-50; with Allied Chem. Corp., N.Y.C., 1950-72, group v.p. corp., 1968-72, dir., 1970-72; pres. Am. Enka Co., Enka, N.C., 1979-82; dir. Akzo Am. Inc., 1979-86, pres., chief exec. officer, 1982-86; chmn., chief exec. officer Armira, Inc., Asheville, N.C., 1986—; pres., CEO Sisters of Mercy Svcs. Corp., Asheville, 1999—. Mem. Gov. Va. Commn. to Establish Urban Univ. in Richmond Area, 1966-67, mem. adv. council Coll. of Engring., Va. Poly. Inst. Lt. USN, 1943-46. Fellow Am. Inst. Chemists; mem. Am. Chem. Soc. (chmn. Va. 1957), Am. Inst. Chem. Engrs., Sigma Xi, Phi Lambda Upsilon, Tau Beta Pi, Phi Kappa Phi, Alpha Kappa Psi. Clubs: University (N.Y.C.); Country of Asheville. Home: 314 Town Mountain Rd Asheville NC 28804-3821 Office: Sisters of Mercy Svcs Corp 445 Biltmore Ave Asheville NC 28801-4119 E-mail: v.coli@home.com.

COLIJN, GEERT JAN, academic administrator, political scientist; b. Naarden, The Netherlands, Sept. 23, 1946; came to US, 1969; s. Izak and Aaltje Cornelia (Rozeboom) C.; m. Sarah Ellen Griffith, Jan. 4, 1986; 1 child, Cornelia Alice. Kandidaat, U. van Amsterdam, 1969; MA, Temple U., 1971, PhD, 1977. From asst. prof. to assoc. prof. polit. sci. Richard Stockton Coll. NJ, Pomona, NJ, 1978-91, prof., 1991—, chmn. social and behavioral sci., 1982-85, dean of gen. studies, 1988—. Trustee Internat. House, Phila., 1990-2002; steering com. Visions of Higher Edn. Conf., Zurich, Switzerland, 1988-94; vis. fellow U. Warwick, 1987-88 Co-editor: Confronting the Holocaust, 1997, From Prejudice to Destruction, 1995, Hearing the Voices, 1999; mem. editl. bd. Jour. Genocide Studies; contbr. articles to profl. jour. Mem. exec. com. Holocaust Resource Ctr., Pomona, 1988—; trustee Community Justice Inst., Atlantic City, NJ, 1982-85; mem. nat. adv. coun. Anne Frank Ctr., 1992-94. Avocations: classical music, speedskating, travel. Home: 135 Old New York Rd Port Republic NJ 08241-9739 Office: Richard Stockton Coll NJ Jimmie Leeds Rd Pomona NJ 08240 E-mail: jan.colijn@stockton.edu.

COLINA, RAMON ENRIQUE, gastroenterologist; b. Las Villas, Cuba, Dec. 12, 1963; came to the U.S., 1972; s. Ramon Colina and Noemi Gutierrez; m. Cristina M. Simas, July 3, 1998. B in Biology, U. P.R., San Juan, 1986; MD, U. P.R., 1990. Diplomate Nat. Bd. Med. Examiners, Am. Bd. Internal Medicine, Am. Bd. Internal Medicine-Gastroenterology. Resident internal medicine VA Hosp., San Juan, 1990-93; chief internal medicine USAF 14th Med. Group, Columbus AFB, Miss., 1993-95; fellow gastroenterology Walter Reed Army Med. Ctr., Washington, 1995-97; staff gastroenterologist Malcolm Grow Air Force Med. Ctr., Andrews AFB, Md., 1997-99; gastroenterologist Ctr. for Digestive Diseases, St. Petersburg, Fla., 1999—. Asst. prof. medicine Uniformed Svcs. U. Health Scis., Bethesda, Md., 1997-99. Contbr. articles to profl. jours. Maj. USAF, 1992-99. Mem. ACP, Am. Gastroenterol. Assn., Am. Coll. Gastroenterology, Alpha Omega Alpha. Avocations: sports, bicycling, running, theater. Office: 7126 Beneva Rd Sarasota FL 34238 E-mail: rcolina38@yahoo.com.

COLINO, RICHARD RALPH, communications consultant; b. N.Y.C., Feb. 10, 1936; s. Victor and Caroline (Pauline) C.; m. Wilma Jane Rubinstein, June 10, 1962 (div. Oct. 1991); children: Stacey Anne, Geoffrey William; m. Charmaine Mallory Kelly, 1997. BA, Amherst Coll., 1957; JD, Columbia U., 1960. Assoc. Sargoy & Stein, N.Y.C., 1960-61; atty. FCC, Washington, 1962-64, U.S. Info. Agy., Washington, 1964-65; dir. internat. affairs Comm. Satellite Corp., Washington, 1965-68, dir. Europe/Middle East Geneva, 1968-69, asst. v.p. Washington, 1969-75, v.p. and gen. mgr. internat. ops., 1975-79; pres., CEO Continental Home Theatre, Burlingame, Calif., 1979-80, DynaCom Enterprises Ltd., Chevy Chase, Md., 1980-83; dir. gen., CEO Internat. Telecomm. Satellite Orgn., Washington, 1983-86; v.p. W. L. Pritchard & Co., Inc., Cons. Engrs., Bethesda, Md., 1990-92, Jackson-Richards Cons. Ltd. Telecom. Cons., Irvine, Calif., 1992-97; artist Oro Valley, Ariz., 1997-2000; ind. bus. cons., 1997—. Contbr. to more than 30 books and articles; group shows include Ariz. Art Gallery, Arte-Spazio, Tucson, 2000. Bd. dirs. Washington Opera, 1986-87, Overseas Devel. Coun., 1986-87, Internat. Inst. Communication, London, 1985-86, Big Bros., Washington, 1975-77; co-chmn., chmn. various fundraisers, Washington, 1983-89, AFCEA, Washington, 1975-79; docent The Irvine Mus., 1994-98. With U.S. Army, 1961-62. Named one of top 15 people in U.S. comms. Comms. Week, 1986; recipient Adam Thompson award Amherst Coll., 1982. Avocations: tennis, skiing. Home: 2 Pheasant Ln South Hadley MA 01075 E-mail: rccolino@aol.com.

COLINVAUX, PAUL A. research scientist, writer; b. St. Albans, Eng., Sept. 22, 1930; arrived in U.S., 1963; s. Henri Jean and Flora Rosalind (Kingsman) Colinvaux; m. Llewellya Hillis, June 17, 1961; children: Catherine, Roger. BA, Cambridge (Eng.) U., 1956; PhD, Duke U., 1962. Rsch. biologist Yale U., New Haven, 1963—64; prof. Ohio State U., Columbus, 1964—89; sr. rsch. scientist Smithsonian Intn., Washington, 1990—98; adj. scientist Marine Biol. Lab., Woods Hole, Mass., 1999—. Chmn. The Inst. Ecology, 1975; adj. prof. U. Wash., Seattle, U. Ga., Athens, U. Mich., Ann Arbor. Author: Why Big Fierce Animals are Rare, 1978 (Ohioana award, 1982), The Fates of Nations, 1982; contbr. articles to profl. jours. Pres. Gansett Woods Assn., Woods Hole, 2001—; counselor Charles Darwin Found. for Galapagos Islands, 1968—88; treas. Ecol. Soc. Am., 1984—87. Lt. Royal Arty., 1949—51, Germany. Fellow Guggenheim Found. Fellow: AAAS, Artic Inst. N.Am., Explorers Club. Avocations: rowing, woodworking, reading. Home: 20 Brooks Rd Woods Hole MA 02543 Office: Marine Biol Lab 7 Mbl St Woods Hole MA 02543 Fax: 508-540-6902. E-mail: pcolinva@mbl.edu.

COLISH, MARCIA LILLIAN, history educator; b. Bklyn., July 27, 1937; d. Samuel and Daisy (Kartch) C. BA magna cum laude, Smith Coll., 1958; MA, Yale U., 1959, PhD, 1965; DHL (hon.), Grinnell Coll., 1999. Instr. history Skidmore Coll., Saratoga Springs, N.Y., 1962-63; instr. Oberlin Coll., Ohio, 1963-65, asst. prof., 1965-69; assoc. prof. Oberlin Coll, Ohio, 1969-75; prof. history Oberlin Coll., Ohio, 1975-2001, Frederick B. Artz prof. history, 1985-2001, chmn. dept. history, 1973-74, 78-81, 85-86; vis. fellow Yale U., 2001—. Vis. prof. history and religious studies Yale U., 2002-03, vis. scholar Am. Acad. Rome, 1968-69; lectr. history Case Western Res. U., Cleve., 1966-67; editl. cons. W.W. Norton & Co., 1973, John Wiley & Sons, Inc., 1981, SUNY Press, 1983, 85, U. Chgo. Press, 1988, U. Calif. Press, 1988, Princeton U. Press, 1988, 96, 98, U. Notre Dame Press, 1991, 92, 94, U. Ill. Press, 1995, U. Pa. Press, 1995, 97, 99, Yale U. Press, 1997, 98, Oxford U. Press, 1998, 2001, Blackwell's, 1998, Liturgical Press, 1999, Cambridge U. Press, 2002; cons. dept. history Grinnell Coll., 1974, Knox Coll., 1981, St. John's U., 1981, Whitman Coll., 1982, Hope Coll., 1995, Kenyon Coll., 1996; mem. exec. bd. Ohio Program Humanities, 1976-81, exec. bd., 1978-81, vice chmn., 1979-81; writing residency, Villa Serbelloni, Bellagio, 1995; mem. Sch. Hist. Studies, Inst. for Advanced Study, Princeton, 1986-87 Author: The Mirror of Language: A Study in the Medieval Theory of Knowledge, 2d rev. edit., 1983, The Stoic Tradition from Antiquity to the Early Middle Ages, 1985, enlarged paperback edit., 1990, Peter Lombard, 1994, Medieval Foundations of the Western Intellectual Tradition, 400-1400, 1997, 2d printing, 1998, paperback edit., 1999, (Italian transl.) La Cultura del Medioevo, 2001. Mem. exec. bd. Oberlin ACLU, 1970-74, chmn., 1972-74, rec. sec., 1976-77, vice chmn., 1979-80; mem. exec. bd. Oberlin YWCA, 1966-70. Recipient Wilbur Cross medal Yale Grad. Sch. Alumni Assn., 1993, Marianist award U. Dayton, 2000; Etienne Gilson lectr. Pontifical Inst. of Mediaeval Studies, Toronto, 2000; Samuel S. Fels fellow Yale U., 1961-62, Younger Scholar fellow Inst. for Rsch. in Humanities, U. Wis., 1974-75, Nat. Humanities Ctr. fellow, 1981-82, Guggenheim fellow, 1989-90, Woodrow Wilson Ctr. fellow, 1994-95, NEH fellow, 1968-69, 81-82; NEH summer grantee U. Calif., 1993. Fellow Medieval Acad. Am. (coun. 1987-89, 2d v.p. 1989-90, 1st v.p. 1990-91, pres. 1991-92, Haskins medal 1998); mem. Am. Hist. Assn., Medieval Assn. Midwest (coun. 1978-81), Midwest Medieval Conf. (pres. 1978-79), Renaissance Soc. Am., Cen. Renaissance Conf., Soc. Internat. pour Etude Philosophie Medievale, Internat. Soc. for Classical Tradition, Internat. Soc. Intellecutal History, Phi Beta Kappa. Home: 80 Seaview Terr #29 Guilford CT 06437 E-mail: marcia.colish@yale.edu.

COLIZZA, WAYNE ANTHONY, orthopaedic surgeon; b. Hamilton, Ont., Can., Sept. 12, 1958; came to the U.S., 1992; s. Vincent Patrick and Velma Louise C.; m. Marlene Catherine Morin, Aug. 13, 1983; children: Wayne Jr., Christina, Michael. BSc in Biochemistry with honors, McGill U., Montreal, 1982, MD, 1987. Diplomate Am. Bd. Orthopaedic Surgery. Fellow Insall Scott Kelly Inst. for Orthopedics and Sports Medicine, N.Y., 1992-93; attending surgeon St. Clares Med. Ctr., Denville, N.J., 1993—, Beth Israel Med. Ctr., N.Y., 1995-99, Morristown (N.J.) Meml. Hosp., 1996—; pvt. practice Newton, Cedar Knolls, N.J., 1996—. Contbr. articles to profl. jours. Pres. Canadian Orthopaedic Residents Assn., 1992. Recipient Zimmer Travelling Fellows award Am. Orthopaedic Assn., 1994. Fellow ACS, Internat. Coll. Surgeons, Royal Coll. Surgeons Can. (cert.), Am. Acad. Orthopaedic Surgeons; mem. Can. Orthopaedic Assn., Can. Med. Assn., N.J. Med. Soc., N.J. Orthopedic Soc. Office: 63 Newton Sparta Rd Newton NJ 07860 2715 also: 218 Ridgedale Ave Ste 104 Cedar Knolls NJ 07927-2109

COLKER, DAVID, trade association administrator; JD, U.Va., 1982. Gen. counsel Cin. Stock Exch., 1984—90, exec. v.p., 1991—95, COO, 1995—98, pres., COO, 1998—2001, pres., CEO, 2001—. Office: Cincinnati Stock Exch 440 S LaSalle St 26th fl Chicago IL 60605*

COLKER, EDWARD, artist, educator; b. Phila., Jan. 5, 1927; Grad., Phila. Coll. Art, 1949; BS, NYU, 1965, MA, 1985. Instr., critic Phila. Coll. Art, Cooper Union, N.Y.C., 1949-66; assoc. prof. Grad. Sch. Fine Arts, U. Pa., 1968-70; dir. Sch. Art and Design, U. Ill., Chgo., 1972-78, research prof. art, 1977-80; dean of visual arts SUNY, Purchase, 1980-85; chmn. dept. art Cornell U., 1985-86; provost Univ. of the Arts, 1986-91, Cooper Union for the Advancement of Sci. and Art, N.Y.C., 1991—95, Pratt Inst., Bklyn., 1995—98, 2003. Cons. Nat. Endowment Arts, USIA; cons. in field One-person shows, Print Club, Phila., 1961, 89, Amel Gallery, N.Y.C., 1965, East Hampton Gallery, N.Y.C., 1969, Douglas Kenyon Gallery, Chgo., 1975, Ctr. Book Arts, N.Y.C., Neuberger Mus., Purchase, U. Ill., Chgo., 1985, 86, SUNY, Albany, 1990, Cooper Union, 1993, U. of Ariz. Mus. of Art, Bates Coll. Mus. of Art, 1998, Neuberger Mus. of Art, 1999, Poets House, 2002-03, others; represented in permanent collections, Mus. Art, Phila., Library of Congress, Washington, Mus. Modern Art, N.Y.C., Nat. Mus., Stockholm, Rosenwald Collection, NYU, U. Ariz., others. Guggenheim Found. fellow, 1961-62; Ill. Arts Council grantee, 1973, 80; Graham Found. grantee, 1977, R. Florsheim Art Fund grantee, 1997. Mem. Coll. Art Assn. Am., Caxton Club, Grolier Club.

COLL, EDWARD GIRARD, JR., university president; b. Pitts., Aug. 9, 1934; s. Edward G. and Alive V. (Ebeling) C.; m. Carole Hulse, Feb. 3, 1958; children— Thomas, Jean Coll Mendenhall, Peter, Karen, Kelly. BA, Duquesne U., 1960, LHD (hon.), 1983, Alfred U., 2000. Div. dir. United Fund Allegheny County, Pitts., 1959-61; asst. to exec. v.p. United Fund Dade County, 1961-63; asst. to v.p. for devel. affairs U. Miami, Fla., 1963-66, dir. corp. and found. relations, 1966-67, dir. devel., 1967-72, sec. univ. corp., 1972-73, v.p. for devel. affairs, 1973-82; pres. Alfred U., N.Y., 1982-2000; ret., 2000. Bd. dirs. Steuben Trust Co.; lectr. in field. Contbr. articles to profl. jours. Chmn. zoning bd. appeals Dade County, 1973-82; bd. dirs. Nat. Ctr. Child Abuse and Neglect, 1985-90; pres. com. NCAA, 1988-92, coun. mem. 1993-97, vice-chair divsn. III, 1990, v.p., 1994-96; trustee Coun. for Support and Advancement Edn., Washington, 1981-82, 87-89, chair, 1991-92. With U.S. Army, 1953-56. Univ. Adminstr. Fulbright fellow U. Warwick, Coventry, Eng., 1985. Mem. Ind. Colls. and Univs. N.Y. (bd. dirs. 1982-86), Duquesne Univ. Alumni Assn., Am. Mktg. Assn. (hon.), Miami Club, University Club, Genesee Valley Club, Wellsville Country Club, Delta Mu Delta, Phi Kappa Phi, Beta Gamma Sigma. Roman Catholic. Office: PO Box 121 Alfred Sta Alfred NY 14803 E-mail: coll@alfred.edu.

COLL, JOHN PETER, JR., lawyer; b. Pitts., Oct. 5, 1943; s. John Peter and Lelia (Nicolussi) C.; m. Nancy Kaye Swan; children: John Peter, Alexis S. AB in Polit. Sci., Duke U., 1965; JD, Georgetown U., 1968. Bar: N.Y. 1969, U.S. Dist. Ct. (so. dist.) N.Y. 1970, U.S. Dist. Ct. (ea. dist.) N.Y. 1974, U.S. Ct. Appeals (2d cir.) 1972, U.S. Supreme Ct. 1974, U.S. Ct. Appeals (5th cir.) 1981, U.S. Ct. Appeals (11th cir.) 1981, U.S. Ct. Appeals (8th cir.) 1980, U.S. Ct. Appeals (6th cir.) 1991, U.S. Ct. Appeals (1st cir.) 1993, U.S. Ct. Appeals (3d cir.) 1994, U.S. Ct. Appeals (9th cir.) 1994, U.S. Dist. Ct. (no. dist.) Calif. 1983, U.S. Dist. Ct. (no. dist.) N.Y. 1984, U.S. Dist. Ct. (we. dist.) N.Y. 1988, U.S. Tax Ct. 1990, U.S. Ct. Appeals (fed. cir.) 1999. Assoc. Donovan Leisure Newton & Irvine LLP, N.Y.C., 1968-76, ptnr., 1976-98, chmn. exec. com., 1989-98; ptnr. Orrick, Herington & Sutcliffe, LLP, N.Y.C., 1998—, mem. exec. com., 2000—. Bd. advisors product safety and liability rep. BNA, 1991—; mem. litigation steering com. Def. Rsch. Inst., 1991—97. Contbg. author: Preparing for and Trying the Civil Law Suit, 1987, Supplement, 2003, Commercial Litigation in New York State Courts, 1995, Supplement, 2003, Products Liability in New York, Strategy and Practice, 1997. Mem. ABA (litigation sect. 1983—), Fed. Bar Coun., N.Y. State Bar Assn., Assn. of Bar of City of N.Y., N.Y. Coun. Law Assocs. (mem. steering com. 1971-72), Lawrence Beach Club (bd. govs. 1991-2000), Cherry Valley Club, Univ. Club. Democrat. Roman Catholic. Home: 385 Stewart Ave Garden City NY 11530-4615 Office: Orrick Herrington and Sutcliffe LLP 666 5th Ave New York NY 10103-1798

COLL, STEPHEN WILSON, editor; b. Washington, Oct. 8, 1958; s. Robert Wilson and Shirley Lee (Baldwin) Coll; m. Susan Keselenko, May 17, 1984; children: Alexandra, Emma, Maxwell. BA cum laude, Occidental Coll., 1980. Contbg. editor Calif. mag., L.A., 1983—85, staff writer The Washington Post, 1985—87, Wall St. corr., 1987—89, New Delhi bur. chief, 1989—93, investigative journalist, London bur., 1993—95; editor and pub. The Washington Post Mag., 1995—98; mng. editor Washington Post Newspaper, 1998—. Author: (book) The Deal of the Century, 1986, The Taking of Getty Oil, 1987; co-author (with David A. Vise): Eagle on the Street, 1990; author: On the Grand Trunk Road, 1994. Recipient Pulitzer Prize for explanatory journalism, 1990, Gerald Loeb award, UCLA, 1990, Livingston award, Molly Parnell Livingston Found., 1992, Ed Cunningham award, Overseas Press, 2000, Robert F. Kennedy Internat. Print award, 2001. Mem.: Phi Beta Kappa. Office: Washington Post 1150 15th St NW Washington DC 20071-0002

COLLADAY, ROBERT S. trust company executive, consultant; b. Flint, Mich., Sept. 24, 1940; s. Robert Harold and Mary Elizabeth (Strong) C.; m. Joan M. Hartsock; children: David, Jill, James, Christopher. BA, Alma Coll., 1962; postgrad., Nat. Trust Sch., Northwestern U., 1967. Asst. trust officer Comerica Bank-Detroit, 1968-71, trust officer, 1971-74, v.p., 1974-80, 1st v.p., 1980-83, sr. v.p., 1983-91, Comerica Inc., 1984-91; pres., prin. cons. Trust Consulting Svcs., Inc., Bloomfield Hills, Mich., 1991—. Cons. to bd. dirs. Found. Southeast Mich. Trustee, chmn. investment com. Alma Coll., Mich. Republican. Presbyterian. Avocations: photography; fishing. Home: 22241 Village Pines Dr Franklin MI 48025-3568 Office: Trust Consulting Svcs Inc PO Box 1131 Bloomfield Hills MI 48303-1131

COLLAMER, SONJA MAE SOREIDE, retired veterinary facility administrator; b. Rapid City, S.D., Sept. 3, 1937; d. Louis Severin and Mae Marie (Barber) Soreide; m. John Harry Collamer, Dec. 30, 1959; children: Debra, Michael, Kenneth, Kerry. BS in Bacteriology, Colo. State U., 1959. Practice mgr. Saratoga (Wyo.) Vet. Clinic, 1966-94, ret., 1994. Sec., v.p., pres. Wyo. Bd. Medicine, 1995-2003. Pres., mem. Wyo. Jaycettes, 1962-70; mem. deacon, elder, treas., clk. session 1st Presbyn. Ch., Saratoga, 1966—, chair pastor nominating com., 1998, 2001-02; neighborhood chmn., leader Girl Scouts Am., Saratoga, 1967-77; sec., mem. Snowy Range Cattlewomen, Carbon County, Wyo., 1967—; active bd. of edn. Sch. Dist. #9, Saratoga, 1968-72; chmn., treas. bd. edn. Sch. Dist. #2, Carbon County, 1972-81; mem. Platte Vallley Rep. Women, 1972—, Carbon County Rep. Ctrl. Com., 1980—, Wyo. state com. woman, 1982-86, 2001-03; vice chair, mem. Saratoga Sr. Ctr. Bd., 1982-86; pres., mem. Snowy Range Ambs., Saratoga, 1984-97; chair Region VIII Child Devel. Program, Carbon County, 1985-90; mem., fundraiser Saratoga Cmty. Choir, 1988—; mediator Wyo. Agrl. Mediation Bd., 1988-97; co-chair Thomas for Congress Com., Carbon County, 1990; chair Saratoga Hist. and Cultural Assn. Bd., 1988-97; active Planning & Devel. Commn., Carbon County, 1994—; steering com. Town Saratoga Assessment Team, 2001-02. Mem. AVMA Aux., Wyo. Vet. Med. Assn. Aux. (pres.), Kappa Delta. Republican. Presbyterian. Home: PO Box 485-806 Rangeview Saratoga WY 82331

COLLAMORE, THOMAS JONES, corporate executive; b. Hartford, Conn., Jan. 29, 1959; s. H. Bacon Jr. and Elizabeth Caldwell (Jones) C.; m. Jacqueline Ann Kelly, Nov. 21, 1992; children: Thomas Jones Jr., Pauline Elizabeth, Sallie Ann, Katherine Muse. BA magna cum laude, Drew U., 1981. Personal aide Rome for Gov., Bloomfield, Conn., 1978, dep. dir., 1982; staff asst. George Bush for Pres., Hartford, 1979-80; confidential asst. to sec. commerce Malcolm Baldrige Washington, 1981-82; spl. asst. to sec. commerce, 1982-85; dep. asst. to V.p. of U.S. The White House, Washington, 1985-87, asst. to V.p. of U.S., 1987-89; dir. secretariat Office of Pres.-elect of U.S., Washington, 1988-89; asst. sec. for adminstrn. U.S. Dept. Commerce, Washington, 1989-91, chief of staff, asst. sec. commerce, 1991-92; v.p. corp. affairs policy and adminstrn. Philip Morris Cos. Inc., N.Y.C., 1992-95, v.p. corp. pub. affairs, 1995—. Chmn. govt. ops. com. Pres.'s Coun. on Mgmt. Improvement, Washington, 1989-91; mem. bd. advisors George Bush Presdl. Libr., 1996—. Bd. dirs. Malcolm Baldrige Scholarship Fund, Hartford, 1988—, City Meals-on-Wheels of N.Y.; trustee Kingswood-Oxford Sch., West Hartford, 1991—, Drew U., Madison, N.J., 1992—; alt. del. Rep. Nat. Conv., Detroit, 1980, del., Houston, 1992. Mem. Pi Sigma Alpha. Episcopalian. Home: 5206 Norway Dr Chevy Chase MD 20815-6672 Office: Philip Morris Cos Inc 120 Park Ave New York NY 10017-5592

COLLARD, ROBERTA R. emeritus educator, researcher; b. Lamesa, Tex., Oct. 7, 1917; d. Clarence Benjamin and Nannie (Van Cleave) C. BS, U. Tex., 1940; cert., Inst. for Psychoanalysis, Chgo., 1951; PhD, U. Chgo., 1962. Libr., editor Inst. for Psychoanalysis, Chgo., 1943-52; tchr. U. Chgo. Nursery Sch., 1946-47; play therapist St. Lukes Hosp., Chgo., 1952-54; rsch. asst. Yale Child Study Ctr., New Haven, Conn., 1954-55; asst. prof. U. Calif., Davis, 1962-67; from assoc. prof. to prof. U. Mass., Amherst, 1968-86, prof. emeritus, 1986—; rsch. assoc. Smith Coll., Northampton, Mass., 1985—. Founder, cons. U. Mass. Infant Ctr., Amherst, 1977-91, Smith Coll. Infant Ctr., Northampton, 1983-92. Editor: Dynamic Psychiatry, 1952; contbr. rsch. papers to profl. jours., including Child Devel., Developmental Psychology, Infancy Grantee NIH, 1958-59. Mem. AAAS, APA, Soc. for Rsch. in Child Devel., Nat. Assn. for Edn. Young Children, Internat. Soc. Infant Studies, Sigma Xi (grantee 1972). Avocations: piano, gardening, travel, writing poetry. Home: 581 Pfersick Rd Shelburne Falls MA 01370-9590

COLLAROS, PANDEL LEE, music educator; b. Steubenville, Ohio, Mar. 3, 1954; s. Jack Peter and Frankie Zanetos Collaros; 1 child, Zachariah Tobias. BA cum laude with honors, Ohio State U., 1989, MA, 1993. Gen. mgr. John Lotas Productions, Inc., NYC, 1984—86; lectr. in music theory U. of Kans., 1996—98; lectr. in fine arts Bethany Coll., W.Va., 1999—. Composer: Three Short Pieces for Oboe, Kyrie, Fantasy for Flute and Piano; author: (short stories) Mannequin Man (winner of lit. contest for short fiction sponsored by Mosaic, the Ohio State U. undergraduate arts and lit. mag., 1989). Judge for Ohio state sci. day Ohio Wesleyan U., 1989; faculty sponsor Kans. Composers Project at the U. of Kans., 1997—98; mem. of the Anthony B. Cius composition award com. U. of Kans. Recipient Cert. of appreciation, Ohio State U. Office for Disability Services, 1989; scholar Grad. Tchg. Assoc., Ohio State U., 1990—96; scholarship, Pan Icarian Found., 1989. Mem.: Soc. for Music Theory, Coll. Music Soc., The Biol. Sciences Honor Soc., Golden Key Nat. Honor Soc., Internat. Premedical Honor Soc., Pi Kappa Lambda Musical Honor Soc., Sigma Tau Epsilon, Bethany Coll. Music Honor Soc. (hon.), Phi Kappa Phi (Ohio State U. chpt. initiation, and mem. com. 1994—95). Home: 623 Lovers Lane A1 Steubenville OH 43953 Office: Bethany College 210 Steinman Hall Bethany WV 26032 Personal E-mail: collaros@1st.net. E-mail: collaros@1st.net.

COLLAZO, SERGIO I. computer company executive; b. Havana, Cuba, Sept. 9, 1967; came to U.S., 1969; s. Carlos and Madeline Collazo; m. Assunta Collazo, May 20, 1981. AS in Engring., Computer Processing Inst., Paramus, N.J., 1986. Application engr. Custom Video Sys., Rockaway, N.J., 1986-93; project mgr. Integrated Access Sys., Rockaway, 1992-93; mgr. security products group Toshiba Am Info. Sys., Irvine, Calif., 1993—. Adv. bd. Stevens Pub., Dallas, 1999—. Office: 2 Allaire Way Aliso Viejo CA 92656

COLLE, HERBERT A. psychologist, educator; b. Milw., Aug. 27, 1943; s. J. Edgar and Martha Colle; m. Claudine Colle, June 19, 1965; children: Brian, Gregory. BS, U. Wis., 1965; PhD, U. Wash., 1969. NDEA title IV fellow U. Wash., Seattle, 1967-69; rsch. assoc. NASA Ames Rsch. Ctr., Mountain View, Calif., 1969-70; asst. prof. U. Chgo., 1969-73; faculty rsch. assoc. Human Resources Lab., Williams AFB, Ariz., 1977; assoc. prof. psychology Wright State U., Dayton, Ohio, 1973—, chair dept. psychology, 1985-95; vis. scientist Air Force Rsch. Lab., Wright-Patterson AFB, Ohio, 1995—. Liaison Armstrong Lab., 1989-2000; mem. accreditation guidelines com. Internat. Ergonomic Assoc., 1998-2000. Author: Labs and Demos in Introductory Psychology, 1998; mem. editl. bd. Human Factors Jour., 1997—; contbr. articles to profl. jours. including Human Factors, Jour. Exptl. Psychology, among others. Rsch. fellow NASA, 1969. Fellow Human Factors and Ergonomics Soc. (chair accreditation 1998—, pres. So. chpt. 1988-89, Paul M. Fitts Ednl. award 1999); mem. APA (chair edn. and tng. divsn. 21 1983-87), Soc. for Computers in Psychology, Midwestern Psychol. Assn., Coun. on Undergrad. Rsch. Office: Wright State U Dept Psychology Dayton OH 45435

COLLE, RONALD, research chemist; b. Milw., Feb. 11, 1946; s. J. Edgar and Martha (Kopaczewski) C.; m. K.A. Maroufi-Colle, Oct. 11, 1990; children: Arthur, Sophie. BS in Chemistry, Ga. Inst. Tech., 1969; PhD, Rensselaer Poly. Inst., 1972; MS in Adminstrn., George Washington U., 1978. Rsch. assoc. Yale U., New Haven, 1972, SUNY, Albany, 1971-73, Brookhaven Nat. Lab., Upton, N.Y., 1972-74, U. Md., College Park, 1974-76, Atomic Indsl. Forum, Washington, 1974-76; rsch. chemist Nat. Inst. Stds. Tech., Gaithersburg, Md., 1976—. Contbr. over 90 articles to profl. jours. Recipient Bronze medal U.S. Dept. Commerce, 1981. Office: Nat Inst Stds Tech Radiation Physics C114 Gaithersburg MD 20899-8462 E-mail: rcolle@nist.gov.

COLLEA, JOSEPH VINCENT, perinatologist, educator; b. Utica, N.Y., Sept. 10, 1940; s. Anthony and Jennie Collea; m. Margaret Elizabeth Collea, Mar. 4, 1974; children: Amy Elizabeth, Lisa Anne, Jennie Louise. AB, Hamilton Coll., 1962; MD, SUNY, Syracuse, 1966. Bd. cert. in maternal-fetal medicine Am. Bd. Ob-Gyn. Instr., resident Johns Hopkins Hosp., Balt., 1966-72; asst. prof. L.A. County-U. So. Calif. Med. Ctr., 1974-79; assoc. prof. Georgetown U., Washington, 1979-91, prof., 1991—. Cons. Matria, Inc., Atlanta, 1998—, Am. Jour. Ob-Gyn., 1978—. Contbr. articles to jours. and textbooks. Maj. U.S. Army, 1972-74. Named Outstanding Citizen of Yr., Health Babies Project, Inc., 1999, one of Best Drs. in Washington, Washington Mag., 1998; N.Y. State Regents scholar, 1958-62. Fellow ACOG; mem. Maternal-Fetal Medicine Soc., Washington Ob-Gyn. Soc., Bethesda Country Club. Office: Georgetown U Dept Ob-Gyn 3800 Reservoir Rd NW Washington DC 20007-2196

COLLEN, JOHN, lawyer; b. Chgo., Dec. 26, 1954; s. Sheldon and Ann Collen; m. Lauren Kay Smulyan, Sept. 20, 1986; children: Joshua, Benjamin, Sarah, Joel. AB summa cum laude, Dartmouth Coll., 1977; JD, Georgetown U., 1980. Bar: Ill. 1980, U.S. Dist. Ct. (no. dist.) Ill. 1980, Trial 1982, U.S. Ct. Appeals (7th cir.) 1984, U.S. Supreme Ct. 1990. Ptnr. Duane Morris, LLC, Chgo. Mem. editl. adv. bd. Journal of Bankruptcy Law & Practice. Author: Buying and Selling Real Estate in Bankruptcy, 1997; contbr. articles to profl. jours.; lectr. in field. Mem. ABA, Chgo. Bar Assn., Am. Bankruptcy Inst. (co-chmn. com. real estate bankruptcy), Phi Beta Kappa. Avocations: water sports, magic, biographies. Office: Duane Morris LLC 227 W Monroe St Chicago IL 60606-5016 Fax: 312-499-6701. E-mail: jcollen@duanemorris.com.

COLLEN, MORRIS FRANK, medical association administrator, physician, medical researcher; b. St. Paul, Nov. 12, 1913; s. Frank Morris and Rose (Finkelstein) Collen; m. Frances B. Diner, Sept. 24, 1937; children: Arnold Roy, Barry Joel, Roberta Joy, Randal Harry. BEE, U. Minn., 1934, MB with distinction, 1938, MD, 1939. Diplomate Am. Bd. Internal Medicine. Intern Michael Reese Hosp., Chgo., 1939—40; resident L.A. County Hosp., 1940—42; chief med. service Kaiser Found. Hosp., Oakland, Calif., 1942—52, chief of staff, 1952—53; med. dir. West Bay divsn. Permanente Med. Group, Oakland, 1953—79, dir. med. methods rsch., 1962—79, dir. tech. assessment, 1979—83, cons. divsn. rsch., 1983—. Chmn. exec. com. Permanente Med. Group, Oakland, 1953—73; dir. Permanente Svcs., Inc., Oakland, 1958—73; lectr. Sch. Pub. Health, U. Calif., Berkeley, 1966—78; lectr. info. scis. U. Calif., San Francisco, 1970—85; lectr. U. London, 1972, Stanford U. Med. Ctr., 1973, 75, 1984—86, Johns Hopkins U., 1976, others; adj. asst. prof. biomed. informatics Uniformed Svcs. U. Health Scis., 2000—; cons. Bur. Health Svcs. USPHS, 1965—68, chn. health care sys. study sect., 1968—72, mem. adv. com. demonstration grants, 1967, advisor VA, 68; cons. European region WHO, 1968—72; cons. med. fitness program USAF, 1968; cons. Pres.'s Biomed. Rsch. Panel, 1975; mem. adv. com. Automated Multiphasic Health Testing, 1971; discussant Nat. Conf. Preventive Medicine, Bethesda, Md., 1975; mem. com. on tech. in health care NAS, 1976; mem. adv. group Nat. Commn. on Digestive Diseases, U.S. Congress, 1978; mem. adv. panel to U.S. Congress Office of Tech. Assessment, 1980—85; mem. peer rev. adv. group TRIMIS program Dept. Def., 1978—90; program chmn. 3rd Internat. Conf. Med. Informatics, Tokyo, 1980; chmn. bd. sci. counselors Nat. Libr. Medicine, 1985—87, cons., 1985—88, mem. lit. selection tech. rev. com., 1997—2002, chmn., 2000—02; chmn. tech. evaluation group Application of Advanced Network Infrastructure in Health and Disaster Mgmt., 2002, chmn. tech. group, 02. Author: Treatment of Pneumococcic Pneumonia, 1948, Hospital Computer Systems, 1974, Multiphasic Health Testing Services, 1978, History of Medical Informatics, 1995; editor: Permanente Med. Bull., 1943—53; mem. edit. bd.: Preventive Medicine, 1970—80, Jour. Med. Sys., Methods Info. Medicine, 1980—97, Diagnostic Medicine, 1980—84, Computers in Biomed. Rsch., 1987—94; contbr. articles to profl. jours., chpts. to books. Fellow Ctr. Advanced Studies in Behavioral Scis., Stanford U., 1985—86; scholar Johns Hopkins Centennial scholar, 1976, scholar-in-residence, Nat. Libr. Medicine, 1987—2002. Fellow: Am. Inst. Med. and Biol. Engring., Am. Coll. Chest Physicians, Am. Coll. Cardiology, ACP; mem.: AMA, Salutis Unitas (v.p. 1972), Internat. Health Evaluation Assn. (pres. 1995—96, Morris F. Collen Permanente Rsch. award named in his honor 2003, Lifetime Achievement award 1992, Computers in Health Care Pioneer award 1992, David E. Morgan award for achievement in health care info. 1998, Japan Shigeaki Hinohara award for preventive medicine 2001, Cummings Psyche award for behavioral medical rsch. 2001), Am. Med. Informatics Assn. (bd. dirs. 1985—96), Nat. Acad. Practice in Medicine (chmn. 1982—88, co-chmn. 1989—91), Soc. Adv. Med. Sys. (pres. 1973), Am. Coll. Med. Informatics (pres. 1987—88, Morris F. Collen medal named in his honor 1993), Am. Fedn. Clin. Rsch., Inst. Medicine of NAS (chmn. tech. subcom. for improving patient records 1990, chmn. workshop on informatics in clin. preventive medicine 1991), Internat. Med. Informatics Assn. Sr. Officers Club, Tau Beta Pi, Alpha Omega Alpha. Home: 4155 Walnut Blvd Walnut Creek CA 94596-5834 Office: 2000 Broadway Oakland CA 94612-2304 E-mail: mfcollen@aol.com.

COLLEN, SHELDON ORRIN, lawyer; b. Chgo., Ill., Feb. 7, 1922; s. Jacob Allen and Ann (Andalman) C.; m. Ann Blager, Apr. 8, 1946; 1 child, John O. BA magna cum laude, Carleton Coll., 1944; JD, U. Chgo., 1948. Bar: Ill. 1949, Minn. 1976, U.S. Dist. Ct. (no. dist.) Ill. 1949, U.S. Supreme Ct. 1965. Assoc. Adcock, Fink & Day, Chgo., 1948-51; mem. Simon & Collen, Chgo., 1951-59, Friedman & Koven, Chgo., 1959-86, Epton, Mullin & Druth, Ltd., Chgo., 1986-89; of counsel Lawrence Walner and Assocs., Ltd., 1989-90; prin. Sheldon O. Collen P.C., 1990—. Specialist fed. antitrust litigation; sec. Jupiter Industries, Inc. and subs., Chgo., 1961-86. Mem. adv. bd. Antitrust Bull. and Jour. Reprints for Antitrust Law and Econs. Curator Prince Art Gallery, Chgo.; mem. bd. edn. U. Chgo. Law Rev., 1948-49; bd. dirs. J.G. Inds. Inc., Lower Northcenter, Chgo. Youth Ctrs., Union League Found. for Boys and Girls, Contemporary Art Workshop, Edward P. Martin Soc., Ctr. for Study of Multiple Births; sec., bd. dirs. 3750 Lake Shore Dr., Inc., 1982-87; pres. Union League Civic and Arts Found., 1984-86, life trustee. With AUS, 1943-46. Fellow Norwegian Am. Mus., Decorah, Iowa. Mem. ABA, Am. Judicature Soc., Chgo. Bar Assn. (coun. corp. and securities law coms., chmn. antitrust 1976-77), Bar Assn. 7th Cir., Am. Arbitration Assn. (arbitrator), Art Inst. Chgo., Mus. Contemporary Art, Lawyers for Creative Arts, Chgo. Hist. Soc. Home: 3750 N Lake Shore Dr Apt 16C Chicago IL 60613-4234

COLLENETTE, DAVID MICHAEL, Canadian government official; b. London, 1946; m. Penny Hossack, Oct. 11, 1975; 1 child, Christopher. BA, York U., 1969; postgrad., Carleton U. Former exec. v.p. leading exec. search co., Toronto and Ottawa; adminstrv. officer Int. Life Ins. Co., London, 1970-72; coord. 41st Ann. Couchiching Conf., 1972; exec. dir. Liberal Party of Ont., 1972-74; M.P. from Don Valley East dist. Ho. of Commons, Ottawa, Ont., Can., 1974-79, 80-84; min. state multiculturalism, 1983-84; sec. gen. Liberal Party Canada, 1985-87; min. nat. def., min. vets. affairs Govt. of Can., Ottawa, 1993-97, min. transport, 1997—; min. responsible for Can. Mortage and Housing Corp., Can. Post Corp., Royal Can. Mint, Can. Lands Coun., Queens Quay West Lands Corp., 2002—. Del. NATO, Brussels, UN, N.Y.C., EEC, Strasbourg, S.Am.; party sec. to Postmaster Gen., Dep. Govt. House Leader; chmn. Standing Com. Energy Legis.; vice chmn. External Affairs and Nat. Def., Subcom. on Van. Rels. with L.Am. and Caribbean, 1982-83. Vol. overseas dem. devel. work; monitor elections in Haiti, Chile, Romania, Czech Republic; mem. internat. adv. com. Inst. Internat. Affairs, Stanford (Calif.) U. Mem. Univ. Club (Toronto), Nat. Liberal Club (London). Liberal Party Can. Anglican. Avocations: squash, swimming, classical music, theatre. Office: Transport Can 330 Sparks St Ottawa ON Canada K1A ON5 E-mail: colled@parl.gc.ca.

COLLENS, LEWIS MORTON, university president, legal educator; b. Chgo., Feb. 10, 1938; BS, U. Ill., Urbana, 1960, MA, 1963; JD, U. Chgo., 1966. Bar: Ill. 1966. Assoc. Ross, Hardies, Chgo., 1966-67; spl. asst. to gen. counsel EEOC, Washington, 1967-68; asst. prof. Ill. Inst. Tech., Chgo. Kent Coll. Law, 1970-72, assoc. prof., 1972-74, prof., 1975—90; dean Coll. Law, Ill. Inst. Tech., 1974-90, pres., 1990—. Bd. dirs. Amsted Industries, Inc., Dean Foods Co., Inc. Chmn. Ill. Gov.'s Commn. on Y2K; mem. Chgo. Mayor's Coun. Tech. Advisors; bd. dirs. Latin Sch., Chgo.; dir. Ill. Coalition. Mem. ABA, Ill. Bar Assn., Chgo. Bar Assn., Am. Law Inst., Econ. Club of Chgo. (dir.), Order of Coif. Office: Ill Inst Tech 10 W 33rd St Rm 223 Chicago IL 60616-3730

COLLER, BARRY SPENCER, medicine and pathology educator, hematologist; b. N.Y.C., Nov. 21, 1945; s. Arthur L. and Ruth (Degenshein) Coller; m. Barbara Nan Gelfand; children: Hilary Ann, Alyssa Brook. BA magna cum laude, Columbia U., 1966; MD, NYU, 1970. Diplomate Am. Bd. Internal Medicine, 1973, Hematology Subspecialty Am. Bd. Internal Medicine, 1974, Am. Bd. Pathology, 1975. Intern, resident Bellevue Hosp., N.Y.C., 1970-72; clin. assoc., hematology svc., clin. pathology dept. NIH, Bethesda, Md., 1972—74, staff physician, hematology svc., clin. pathology dept., 1974—76; asst. prof. medicine SUNY Health Scis. Ctr., Stony Brook, 1976-78, clin. chief hematology lab., 1976-93, assoc. prof., 1978-82, clin. dir. hematology div. dept. medicine, 1978-83, prof. medicine and pathology, 1982-93, head hematology div., 1984-93, Disting. Svc. prof., 1993; assoc. dir. biomed. rsch. Advanced Ctr. Biotech. SUNY, Stony Brook, 1992-93; Murray M. Rosenberg prof. medicine Mt. Sinai Sch. Medicine, N.Y.C., 1993—2001, chmn. dept. medicine, 1993—2001, clin. prof. medicine, 2001—; dir., chief medicine Mt. Sinai Hosp., N.Y.C., 1993—2001; David Rockefeller prof. medicine, head lab. blood and vascular biology, v.p. med. affairs Rockefeller U., N.Y.C., 2001—; physician-in-chief Rockefeller U. Hosp., N.Y.C., 2001—. Surgeon USPHS, NIH, Bethesda, Md., 1972—76; clin. instr. Georgetown U. Sch. Medicine, Washington, 1972—76; Anna and Leo Roon lectr. Scripps Clinic and Rsch. Found., La Jolla, Calif., 1986; Martin Rosenthal lectr. Mt. Sinai Hosp., N.Y.C., 1991; vis. prof. Cornell U., Ithaca, NY, 1992, Ithaca, 96, U. Nebr., Omaha, 1994, SUNY, Bklyn., 1994, U. Wash., 1999, U. Utah, 2002, U. Calif., San Francisco, 2002; Hymie Nossel Meml. lectr. Columbia U., N.Y.C., 1994; Herion-Walker lectr. U. N.C., Chapel Hill, 1997; Oscar D. Ratnoff lectr. Case Western Reserve U., 1997; vis. lectr. U. Okla., 1997; Teichman lectr. Tel Aviv U., 2002; dir. Stony Brook Found., 1991—93, 2001—, L.I. High Tech. Incubator Facility, Stony Brook, 1991—93; scientific advisor Ariad Pharm., Cambridge, Mass., 1991—; cons. Centocor Inc., Malvern, Pa., 1986—95, Northport VA Med. Ctr., NY, 1986—94, Genentech, South San Francisco, 1994—95; scientific adv. bd. mem. Otsuka Pharm. Co., Rockville, Md., 1985—93, N.Y. Blood Ctr., N.Y.C., 1994—, N.Y. Biotech. Assn., 1995—99, Oxford Found., 1996—98, Accumetrics, San Diego, 1996—2001; bd. govs. NIH Clin. Ctr., 2002—; bd. extamural advisors Nat. Heart, Lung and Blood Inst., 2000—. Editor: Progress in Hemostatis and Thrombosis, Vol. 8, 1986, Vol. 9, 1988, Vol. 10, 1990, Williams' Hematology, 5th and 6th edits.; mem. editorial bd. Blood, 1981-85, Current Opinion in Hematology, 1991-, Blood Cells, Molecules & Diseases, 1999-, Circulation, 1993-, Mt. Sinai Jour. Medicine, 1994-, Haemostasis, 1996-2002, Thrombosis and Haemostasis, 1999-, Pathophysiology of Haemostasis and Thrombosis, 2003-; reviewing editor Jour. Lab. and Clin. Medicine, 1991-; cons. editor Jour. Clin. Investigation, 1992-97; contbr. over 100 articles, revs. and abstracts to sci. jours., chpts. to books. Recipient citation Fight for Sight, 1977, Jane Nugent Cochems prize, 1977, Internat. Investigator recognition award, 1987, Solomon A. Berson Med. Alumni Achievement award NYU Med. Ctr., 1991, Inventor of Yr., N.Y. Intellectual Property Law Assn., 1997, Disting. Career award Internat. Soc. on Thrombosis and Haemostasis, Nat. Rsch. Achievement award Am. Heart Assn., 1998, Warren Alpert Found. award, 2001, Jacobi medallion Mt. Sinai Sch. Medicine, 1997; grantee NIH, 1976—, Am. Heart Assn., 1983-86, SUNY, 1987-89; Guggenheim fellow Weizmann Inst. Sci., Rehovot, Israel, 1982. Mem.: NAS, Am. Heart Assn., Assn. Profs. Medicine (bd. dirs. 2000—01), World Fedn. Hemophilia, Internat. Soc. on Thrombosis and Haemostasis (councilor 1986—92, publs. com. 1986—92, chmn., fin. com. 1990—92), Harvey Soc., Am. Soc. Hematology (treas. 1983—87, fin. com. 1983—90, exec. com. 1984—87, corp. adv. com. 1986—87, adv. com. 1987—92, com. on pub. info. and govtl. affairs 1988—98, chmn., com. on pub. info. and govtl. affairs 1992—94, fin. com. 1993—, v.p. 1995—96, pres.-elect 1996—97, exec. com. 1996—98, edn. com. 1996—98, com. on practice 1996—98, pres. 1997—98, adv. com. 1998, chair, adv. com. 1999—2000), Am. Fedn. Med. Rsch. (councilor, ea. sect. 1981—86), Assn. Am. Physicians, Am. Soc. Clin. Investigation, Alpha Omega Alpha (sec.-treas., MU chpt. 1985—86, councilor, MU chpt. 1985—90), Phi Beta Kappa (v.p., Alpha Beta N.Y. 1990—91, pres., Alpha Beta N.Y. 1991—92). Achievements include discovery of a monoclonal antibody that was modified to produce the drug abciximab which was approved by the FDA in 1994. Office: Rockefeller U Lab of Blood/Vasc Bio 1230 York Ave New York NY 10021

COLLER, ROBERT BURTON, music educator, musician; b. Greenfield, Mass., July 1, 1924; s. Alton Barnald and Dorothy Shumway Coller; m. Virginia Marjorie Ware, Sept. 3, 1946; children: Diane Coller Wilson, Brian Thomas Wilson, Marsha Coller Wilson. MusB in Edn., Boston U., 1949; MS in Music Edn., SUNY, Potsdam, N.Y., 1959. Cert. permanent tchg. cert. N.Y., sailing master. Tchr. jr. high Schenectady (N.Y.) Pub. Schs., 1949—59; tchr. high sch. and jr. high Huntington (N.Y.) Pub. Schs., 1959—74; tchr. Lincoln Acad. High Sch., Newcastle, Maine, 1970—82. Condr., adjudicator N.Y. State Sch. Music Assn., Maine Music Educators Assn.; innkeeper Chance Along Inn, Belfast, Maine, 1970—82, sailing instr., 1970—82; church choir dir. various churches, 1949—2002; cons. in music edn. Co-author: (educational publ.) 5 Steps to a Song, 1970. Quartermaster 3/C USN, 1943—46, ATO. Named Man of Yr., Lions Club, Schenectady, Belfast. Mem.: Music Edn. Nat. Conf., N.Y. State Sch. Music Assn., Maine Music Educators Assn. (Ret. Tchr. of Yr. award). Avocation: reading, singing, acting, computing, boatbuilding. Home: 101 Waldo Ave #2-4 Belfast ME 04915

COLLERAN, KEVIN, lawyer; b. Spalding, Nebr., July 16, 1941; s. James Edward and Helen Marcella (Vybiral) C.; m. Karen Ann Rooney, Aug. 1, 1964; children: Mary Jane, Patrick. BS, U. Nebr., 1964, JD with distinction, 1968. Bar: Nebr. 1968, U.S. Dist. Ct. Nebr. 1968, U.S. Dist. Ct. (we. dist.) La. 1975, U.S. Dist. Ct. (no. dist.) Tex. 1978, U.S. Supreme Ct. 1980, U.S. Ct. Appeals (8th cir.) 1981. Law. clk. U.S. Dist. Ct. Nebr., 1968-69; assoc. Cline, Williams, Wright, Johnson & Oldfather, LLP, Lincoln, Nebr., 1969-74, ptnr., 1975—, mng. ptnr., 1985-89, 96—. Bd. dirs. Lancaster County unit Am. Cancer Soc., 1972-83, pres., 1979. Fellow Am. Coll. Trial Lawyers; mem. ABA, Am. Bd. Trial Advocates, Nebr. Bar Assn. (chmn. worker's compensation com. 1980-82, chmn. civil practice and procedure com. 2001-02), Internat. Assn. Def. Counsel, Nat. Assn. Trial Attys., Order of Coif. Democrat. Office: Cline Williams Wright Johnson & Oldfather LLP US Bank Bldg Ste 1900 233 S 13th St Lincoln NE 68508 E-mail: kcolleran@cline-law.com.

COLLETT, CAMILLE, family physician; b. Denver, May 31, 1957; BA, Westminster Coll., 1979; MD, U. Utah, 1983. Intern and resident U. Utah, Salt Lake City, 1983-86, family practice fellow, 1986-87; clin. instr. U. Utah Family Practice Residency, Salt Lake City, 1986-88, asst. prof., 1988—2001; assoc. prof. UUMC, DFPM, Salt Lake City, 2001—; assoc. residency dir. St. Mark's Family Practice Residency, 1997-2000; family physician Oquirrh View Cmty. Health Ctr., Salt Lake City, 2000—. Proctor for no scalpel vasectomy, 1992—. Bd. dirs. Am. Cancer Soc., Salt Lake City, 1986-95. Mem. Am. Acad. Family Practice, Physicians for Social Responsibility, Utah Acad. of Family Practice, Utah Med. Assn., Women and Math., Sigma Xi. Office: Oquirrh View Cmty Health Ctr 4745 South 3200 West Salt Lake City UT 84118 E-mail: ccollett@chc-ut.org.

COLLETT, ROBERT LEE, financial company executive; b. Ardmore, Okla., July 1, 1940; s. Pat (Dowell) Conway; m. Sue Walker Healy; 1 child, Catherine April. BA in Math., Rice U., 1962; MA in Econs., Duke U., 1963. Actuary Milliman & Robertson, Inc., Phila., 1966-70, prin. Houston, 1970-89, pres., 1990, pres., CEO Houston and Seattle, 1991-92, Seattle, 1992—2002. Bd. dirs. Seattle Symphony, 1992—2002; chmn. Millenium Global, 2000—. Fellow Soc. Actuaries (chmn. internat. sect. 1992—); mem. Rainier Club. Episcopalian. Avocations: travel, music. Office: Milliman & USA Inc 1301 5th Ave Ste 3800 Seattle WA 98101-2646

COLLETT, WALTER LEE, electrical engineer; b. Morristown, Tenn., Oct. 11, 1968; s. William and Bonnie June (Lefevers) C.; m. Candi Renea Henry, July 11, 1992; children: Aaron Shaw, Ian Christopher. BS, Tenn. Tech. U., Cookeville, 1990, MS, 1992, PhD, 1999. Instrumentation engr. Quaker Oats Co., Newport, Tenn., 1992-94; grad. rsch. asst. Ctr. for Electric Power, Cookeville, 1994-99; sr. elec. engr. Square D Co., Nashville, 1999-2000, supr. engring., 2000—03, mgr. engring., 2003—. Adj. faculty Nashville State Tech. Inst., 1995-99, Volunteer State C.C., 2002—; tchg. assoc., dept. elec. and computer engring., Tenn. Tech. U., spring 1997; presenter conf. papers. Contbr. articles to profl. jours. Mem. IEEE (student chpt. treas. 1989-91), Am. Phys. Soc., Sigma Xi, Eta Kappa Nu (student chpt. treas. 1990-91). Home: 802 Partridge Cir Mount Juliet TN 37122 Office: 1010 Airpark Center Dr Nashville TN 37217-5200

COLLETTE, BRUCE BADEN, ichthyologist; b. N.Y.C., Mar. 14, 1934; s. Raymond Hill and Agnes Helen (Larson) C.; m. Sara Elizabeth Foster, June 14, 1956; children: Karen Cali Collette, Sheila Helen Collette Bell, Claire Elizabeth Shaw. BS, Cornell U., 1956, PhD, 1960. Rsch. asst. Cornell U., Ithaca, N.Y., 1956-57, teaching asst., 1957-60; systematic zoologist Systematics Lab. Nat. Marine Fisheries Svc., Washington, 1960-82, sci. editor Fishery Bull, 1974-77, dir. Systematics Lab., 1982-98, sr. scientist, 1999—. Professorial lectr. George Washington U., Washington, 1978-79; vis. prof. Northeastern U., Nahant, Mass., summers 1967-85, adj. prof. biology, 1980—; instr. Bermuda Biol. Sta., summers 1984—; rsch. assoc. Smithsonian Instn., Washington, 1967—, Mus. Comparative Zoology, Harvard U., Boston, 1977—; adj. prof. biology Va. Inst. Marine Sci., 1992—. Co-author: (text book) Diversity of Fishes, 1997, Fishes of Bermuda, 1999; editor: Ecology of Coral Reef Fishes, 1972, Bigelow and Schroeder's Fishes of the Gulf of Maine, 2002; contbr. over 210 articles to sci. jours. Mem. exec. bd. Little Hunting Creek Citizens Assn., Mt. Vernon, Va., 1971-77; Mt. Vernon rep. Fairfax County Environ. Quality Adv. Coun., Fairfax County, Va., 1974-77; mem. natural resources com. No. Va. Planning Dist. Coun., 1974-77. Team recipient Hammer award U.S. V.p. Gore, 1998; recipient Conservation award Internat. Wildlife Found., 1981, awards Fishery Bull., 1969, 75, 84, 96. Fellow AAAS, Am. Inst. Fishery Rsch. Biologists; mem. Am. Soc. Ichthyologists and Herpetologists (ichthyology editor 1964-68, sec. 1974-78, pres. 1981, Frederick H. Stoye award 1956, 58, 59, Robert A. Gibbs Meml. award 1989), Biol. Soc. Washington (pres. 1976-77), Am. Assn. Zool. Nomenclature (pres. 1987), Soc. Systematic Zoologists (councilor 1986-88), Willi Hennig Soc. (councilor 1988-90). Avocations: collecting beer bottles and cans, raising thoroughbred horses. Home: Pageland Farm Casanova VA 20139-0108 Office: Nat Marine Fisheries Svc Systematics Lab Nat Mus Natural History Washington DC 20560-0153 E-mail: collette.bruce@nmnh.si.edu.

COLLETTE, FRANCES MADELYN, retired tax consultant, lawyer; b. Yonkers, N.Y., Aug. 5, 1947; d. Morris Aaron and Esther (Gang) Volbert; m. Roger Warren Collette, Dec. 25, 1971; children: Darren Roger, Bonnie Frances. BEd summa cum laude, SUNY, Buffalo, 1969; JD cum laude, U. Miami, 1980. Bar: Fla. 1980. Employment counselor Fla. Bur. Employment Security, Miami, Fla., 1969-73; unemployment claims adjudicator Fla. Bur. Unemployment, Miami, 1973-77; owner Unemployment Svcs. Fla., Inc., Miami, 1977-93. Cons. Fla. unemployment tax and personnel; lectr. in field. Ad hoc comm. students with Asperger's Syndrome Dade County Pub. Schs., 1998-2000; vol. child advocate Exceptional Student Edn., 1996—; 1st v.p. BBB South Fla., 1980-81, bd. govs., 2d vice chair, 1990-91; mem. Supt.'s Dist. Adv. Panel for Exceptional Student Edn., Miami-Dade County Pub. Schs., 2003—. Jewish.

COLLETTE, MARIA D. librarian; b. Villamagna, Chieti, Italy, Aug. 25, 1951; d. Alfio and Isolina (Iezzi) D'Onofrio; m. Gene L. Collette, May 26, 1973; 1 child, Jacqueline A. BS in Edn., Kutztown State Coll., 1973; MLS, Kutztown U., 1980. Serials clk. Kutztown State Coll., 1973; libr. Sch. Nursing St. Luke's Hosp., Bethlehem, Pa., 1974, med. libr., 1975-92, dir. libr. svcs., 1992—; mus. curator St. Luke's Hosp. Fowler Family Mus., Bethlehem, Pa., 2001—. Mem. Cooperating Hosp. Librs. of the Lehigh Valley (sec. 1984-85, pres. 1986-87, treas. 1988-91), Med. Libr. Assn. Avocations: reading, gardening. Office: St Luke's Hosp 801 Ostrum St Bethlehem PA 18015-1004

COLLETTE, TONI, actress; b. Sydney, Australia, Nov. 1, 1972; Appeared in films: Efficiency Expert, 1991, Spotswood, 1992, This Marching Girl Thing, 1994, Muriel's Wedding, 1994, Lilian's Story, 1995, Arabian Knight, 1995 (as voice of nurse/good witch), Cosi, 1996, The Pallbearer, 1996, Emma, 1996, The Boys, 1997, Clockwatchers, 1997, The James Gang, 1997, Diana & Me, 1997, Velvet Goldmine, 1998, Hotel Sordide, 1999, Dead by Monday, 1999, 8 1/2 Women, 1999, The Sixth Sense, 1999, Shaft Returns, 2000, Changing Lanes, 2002, About a Boy, 2002, Hotel Splendide, 2000, Dirty Deeds, 2002, The Hours, 2002, Japanese Story, 2003; TV appearances include The panel, 1998, Frontline, 1994, Dinner With Friends, 2001. Office: United Talent Agy care Adam Isaacs 9560 Wilshire Blvd Ste 500 Beverly Hills CA 90212-2427

COLLEY, CAREN R. language educator; b. Medford, Oreg., Oct. 12, 1972; d. Stephen Paul and Corinne Lucille Colley. BA in Art History, BA in French, Portland State U., 1998, M of French Lit., 2001. Instr. English Min. L'educ. Nat., Amieus, France, 1998—99, Portland State U., 1999—2002; instr. English, French Call Internatl., Brussels, 2002—. Avocations: reading, jogging, travel, music.

COLLEY, JOHN LEONARD, JR., educator, author, management consultant; b. Wilmington, N.C., Feb. 17, 1930; s. John L. and Icie (Hall) C.; m. Tommie Lancaster, Dec. 14, 1950; children: John Lawrence, Claire Ellen, Thomas Michael. BS, N.C. State U., 1957; MS, Yale U., 1959; D.BA, U. So. Calif., 1964. Planning engr. ops. and systems analysis Western Electric Co., 1959-62; chief ops. analysis Hughes Aircraft Co., 1962-65; group leader Research Triangle Inst., Durham, N.C., 1965-67; also lectr. U. So. Calif., 1963-65; adj. prof. indsl. engring. N.C. State U., 1965-67; prof. bus. adminstrn. Darden Grad. Sch. Bus., U. Va., 1967—, Almand R. Coleman prof. bus. adminstrn., 1979—, dir. div. research, 1973-74; Sesquicentennial asso. of Center for Advanced Studies, 1974-75; pres. Southeastern Cons. Group, Ltd., 1969-92. Bd. dirs. Blue Cross/Blue Shield of Va., 1981-97, chmn. bd., 1985-86, Worldwide Cryogenics Ltd., Hillcrest Group, Dominion Holdings, LLC, Avid Med. Co-author: Operations Planning and Control-Text and Cases, 1977, Operations Planning and Control, 1978, Corporate Strategy, 2002; author: Corporate and Divisional Planning, 1984, Case Studies in Service Operations, 1996. Served with USAF, 1952-56. Recipient Disting. Prof. award U. Va. Alumni Assn., 1987, Disting. Faculty award The Z Soc., 1996, Raven award Raven Soc., 1998, IMP Faculty award, 1999, Frederick S. Morton Leadership award Darden Sch./U. Va., 2000. Mem. Ops. Research Soc. Am., Inst. Mgmt. Sci., Am. Inst. Decision Scis., Raven Soc., Sigma Xi, Tau Kappa Epsilon, Tau Beta Pi, Alpha Pi Mu, Beta Gamma Sigma, Phi Kappa Phi, Omicron Delta Kappa. Clubs: Farmington (Charlottesville); Yale (N.Y.C.). Home: 1423 Foxbrook Ln Charlottesville VA 22901-3119 Home (Summer): 8 Pelican Dr Charlottesville VA 28480-3119 E-mail: colley@virginia.edu.

COLLEY, KAREN J. medical educator, medical researcher; b. Nov. 3, 1958; BS in Chemistry, Duke U., 1981; PhD in Molecular Biology, Washington U., St. Louis, 1987. Postdoctoral fellow dept. biol. chemistry UCLA, 1987—91; postdoctoral fellow NIH, 1990; asst. prof. dept. biochemistry U. Ill., Chgo., 1991—97, assoc. prof., 1997—. Mem. med. adv. bd. Leukemia Rsch. Found., 1994—, reviewer study sect., 1994—; outside reviewer NSF Grants, 1995—, VA Rsch. Grants, 1995—; mem. pathiobiochemistry study sect. NIH, 1998—. Reviewer: Jour. Biol. Chemistry, Jour. Cell Biology, Molecular and Chem. Neuropathology, Jour. Cell Sci., Devel. Biology; contbr. articles to profl. jours.; patentee in field. Recipient Established Investigator award, Am. Heart Assn., 1996; fellow (sr.), Am. Cancer Soc., 1991; grantee, 1992, U. Ill., 1992, 1996, Leukemia Rsch. Found., Inc., 1993. Mem.: AAAS, Soc. Glycobiology, Am. Soc. Biochemistry and Molecular Biology, Am. Soc. Cell Biology, Sigma Xi. Office: U Ill Dept Biochemistry and Molecular Biology 1819 W Polk St Chicago IL 60612-7331

COLLI, BART JOSEPH, lawyer; b. Englewood, N.J., Feb. 13, 1948; s. Bart Joseph and Marie (Burns) C.; m. Mary Ellen Diemer, May 20, 1972; 1 son, Michael John. BA summa cum laude, Fordham Coll., 1968; JD cum laude, Harvard U., 1971. Bar: N.Y. 1972, Tex. 1975, N.J., 1988, Pa. 2002. Assoc. White & Case, N.Y.C., 1971-75; ptnr. Hughes & Luce, Dallas, 1976-85, McCarter & English, L.L.P., Newark, 1985—2000; exec. v.p., gen. counsel, sec. ARAMARK Corp., Phila. Judge Entrepreneur of the Yr. awards program, 1993, 95, 96, North Jersey Venture Fairs, 1993, 94, N.J. Family Bus. of Yr. awards program, 1997, 99; lectr. in field; mem. resources com. Edison Partnership Tech.; chmn. 1st annual Mergers and Acquisitions Conf., 1999, spkr. 2d annual Conf.; lectr. in field. Contbr. numerous articles to legal publs. Trustee Tri-County Scholarship Fund, No. N.J. chpt. Leukemia Soc. Am., Inc.; coun. Lincoln Ctr. Bus. Coun. of the Consol. Fund. Capt. M.I., USAR, 1968-76. Mem. ABA (fed. regulation of securities com., sect. on corp.), N.J. State Bar Assn. (securities law com., bus. orgn. com. of the corp. and bus. law sect.), Phi Beta Kappa. Address: ARAMARK Corp ARAMARK Tower 1101 Market St Philadelphia PA 19107-2934 E-mail: colli-bart@aramark.com.

COLLIAS, NICHOLAS ELIAS, zoology educator, ornithologist; b. Chicago Heights, Ill., July 19, 1914; s. Elias and Marina (Giatras) C.; m. Elsie Cole, Dec. 21, 1948; 1 child, Karen. BS, U. Chgo., 1937, PhD, 1942. Instr. biology Amherst (Mass.) Coll., 1946-47; instr. zoology U. Wis., Madison, 1947-51; wildlife biologist Wis. Conservation Dept., Madison, 1952-53; postdoctoral fellow Cornell U., Ithaca, N.Y., 1953-54; prof. zoology Ill. Coll., Jacksonville, 1954-58; from asst. prof. to prof. zoology UCLA, 1958—. Author: Evolution of Nest-building in the Weaverbirds, 1964, Nest Building and Bird Behavior, 1984; editor: External Construction by Animals, 1976. 1st lt. USAAC, 1943-46. Guggenheim fellow, 1962-63; NSF grantee, 1960-80. Fellow AAAS, Am. Ornithologists Union (Elliott Coues award 1980), Animal Behavior Soc. (Disting. Animal Behaviorist 2000); mem. Cooper Ornithol. Soc. (hon.), Wilson Ornithol. Soc. (Margaret Morse Nice medal 1997). Avocations: natural history, birding. Office: U Calif Dept Org Biology/Ecology Los Angeles CA 90095-1606

COLLIE, JOHN, JR., insurance agent; b. Gary, Ind., Apr. 23, 1934; s. John and Christina Dempster (Wardrop) Collie; m. Jessie Fearn Shaw, Aug. 1, 1964; children: Cynthia Elizabeth Lunsford, Douglas A. H., Jennifer F. Weaver. Student, Purdue U., 1953; AB in Econs., Ind. U., 1957. Assoc. risk mgmt. (A.R.M.). Operator Collie Optical Lab., Gary, 1957-62; owner, operator Collie Ins. Agy., Gary, 1962—. Pres. Collie Realty and Investment, Ins. and Fin. Adv., Lake Michigan Global Industries; lectr. High Frontier, dist. chmn. 1st dist. com. secure; mem. employer support Guard & Res., Dept. Def.; affiliated broker Agy. One INs., INc., Valparaiso, Ind.; instr. Command and Gen. Staff Coll., 1973—77. Lt. col. USAR, 1957—86. Mem.: Nat. Fedn. Ind. Bus. (guardian,

state adv. bd., N.W. Ind. adv. bd.), Leadership Coun. Am., Res. Officers Assn. (sec., pres. N.W. Ind. chpt., v.p. Ind. chpt.), Ret. Officers Assn., Mil. Order World Wars, Shriners, Masons (32 degree), Phi Kappa Psi. Republican. Methodist. Home: 871 Camelot Mnr Portage IN 46368-6632 Office: 4004 N Campbell Valparaiso IN 46383

COLLIE, PAULA RENEA, secondary school educator; b. Gonzales, Tex., Dec. 23, 1971; d. Paul Jr. and Kathy (Maulding) C. BA in Geography and Polit. Sci., SW Tex. State U., 1994. Clk. City of Gonzales, 1989-90; salesperson Laurel Ridge Antiques, Gonzales, 1990; subs. tchr. Gonzales Ind. Sch. Dist., 1990—94; with Gonzales County Archives, Gonzales Hist. Commn., 1993-94; geography tchr. Luling (Tex.) H.S., 1994—, social studies dept. head, 1995—, student coun. sponsor, 1996—, summer sch. tchr., 2000—. Participant All State Tex. Alliance Conf., Clear Lake, 1994, Nat. Conf. for Geographic Edn., Lexington, Ky., 1994. Mem. Nat. Geographic Soc., Nat. Coun. for Geographic Edn., Tex. Alliance for Geographic Edn., NEA, Tex. Student Edn. Assn. Avocations: genealogy, fishing. Home: 1611 Gardien St Gonzales TX 78629-4318 Office: Luling Ind Sch Dist 218 E Travis Luling TX 78648

COLLIER, ALBERT M. pediatric educator, child development center director; b. Elba, Ala., May 3, 1937; s. Milford William and Ida Ruth C.; m. Mary Gaynell Wehler, July 17, 1960; children: Albert Mark, Dennis Murray, Jonathan Lee. BS, U. Miami, 1959, MD, 1963. Pediatric resident U. Miami, Coral Gables, Fla., 1963-66; infectious diseases fellow U. N.C., Chapel Hill, 1968-70, from asst. prof. to assoc. prof., 1971-80, prof., 1980—, divsn. chief infectious disease, 1980—, assoc. dir. ctr. environ. med. lung bio, 1980—, acting dir. Frank Porter Graham Child Devel. Ctr., 1990-92, assoc. chmn. of pediatrics for rsch., 1997—, med. sch. sci. integrity officer, 2000—. Contbr. over 100 articles to profl. jours. Recipient Louis Dienes award Internat. Orgn. Mycoplasmology, Vienna, Austria, 1988. Mem. Gideons (zone leader 1990-93). Baptist. Office: U NC Chapel Hill Dept Pediatrics 5135 Bioinformatics Cb 7220 Chapel Hill NC 27599-0001 E-mail: uncacl@med.unc.edu.

COLLIER, ALICE ELIZABETH, retired community organization executive; b. Akron, Ohio, June 9, 1927; d. Christian and Virginia (Schulmeister) Becker; m. John Robert Fenwick, Aug. 28, 1954 (dec. 1980); 1 child, Beth Alice; m. Thomas Collier, Mar. 8, 1980. BA in Edn., Heidelberg Coll., Tiffin, Ohio, 1949; MA in Ednl. Adminstrn., U. Akron, 1968. Cert. tchr., ednl. adminstr., Ohio. Tchr. Air Force Dependent Schs., Fed. Republic Germany and Eng., 1960-64, Akron Pub. Schs., 1964-68, adminstr., 1968-80; dep. mayor City of Akron, 1980-84; pres. Collier Pub. Rels./Mktg., Akron, 1984-86; gen. mgr., broker Coldwell Banker Real Estate, Akron, 1986-90; dir. comms. Area Agy. on Aging, Akron, 1990-94; v.p. Mktg. and Creative Solutions, 1994-97; ret., 1997. Author, editor: (Manual) Visual-Motor Training for the Developmentally Disabled Child, 1972, Different Strokes for Little Folks, 1974. Chmn. adv. coun. U. Akron, 1977-88; mem. Akron Health Commn., 1978-80, Akron Sr. Citizens Commn., 1980—, Nat. Adv. Coun. on Aging, Bethesda, Md., 1982-84; pres. Tri-County Employee Assistance Program, Summit, Medina and Portage, 1985-97; charter rev. commn. Summit County, 1991; mem. women's adv. coun. Summa Health Sys., 1994—; v.p. Women's Network, Akron, 1987-88; trustee Comty. Health Rsch. Group, Inc., 1980—, Cuyahoga Falls Gen. Hosp. Found., 1992—; pub. rels. chmn. State of Ohio Atty. Gen. Health Info. Com.; bd. trustees No. Ohio Golf Charities Found., Firestone Country Club, 1999—, World Series of Golf, Firestone Country Club, 1983—; vol. World Golf Championships, 2001—. Recipient Svc. to Elderly award Am. Gerontol. Soc., 1982, Excellence in Comm. award Nat. Assn. Area Agys. on Aging, 1991. Mem.: AAUW, Akron Bd. Realtors (Salesperson of Yr. award 1988, Hall of Fame award 1988), Ohio Assn. Realtors (trustee 1988—90), Am. Mktg. Assn. (pres. Akron-Canton chpt. 1988—89, Spl. Merit award 1990), Mission Valley Country Club (Venice, Fla.), Heidelberg Coll. Alumni Assn., Akron Women's City Club, Medina Country Club, Phi Lambda Theta (founding, charter). Republican. Avocations: church organist, golf, tennis, collecting hummel figurines. Home: Beechwood # 11 333 N Portage Path Akron OH 44303-1218 also: 255 The Esplanade N Apt 204 Venice FL 34285-1518

COLLIER, BOYD DEAN, finance educator, management consultant; b. Waco, Tex., Jan. 16, 1938; s. Denis Lee and Anne Alice (Berry) C.; m. Barbara Nell Joseph, June 20, 1966; children: Diedra Michelle, Christopher Boyd. BBA, Baylor U., 1963, MS, 1965; PhD, U. Tex., 1970. Diplomate Am. Bd. Forensic Acctg.; CPA, Tex. Asst. prof. Univ. of NC, Greensboro, NC, 1969-72, asst. dean, 1970-72; assoc. prof. U. Houston, Tex., 1972-73; chief ops. auditor Glastron Boat Co., Austin, Tex., 1973; prof. bus. econs., dean Ctr. for Bus. Adminstrn. St. Edward's U., Austin, Tex., 1974-83; prof. fin., head dept. acctg. and fin. Tarleton State U., Stephenville, Tex., 1983-96, exec. dir. office planning, evaluation and instrnl. rsch., accreditation liaison officer, 1996—. Co-owner Vranich, Collier Co., CPA's, Austin, Tex., 1974-83; v.p. fin. Execucom Sys., Austin, 1979; sr. lectr. U. Tex., Austin, 1980-83; compliance officer Tex. A&M U.; bd. dirs. Acctg. Info. Sys., Houston, 1974-78; advisor Office of Atty. Gen., State of Tex., Austin, 1986, Office of Comptr., State of Tex., Austin, 1986. Author: Measurement and Environmental Deterioration, 1971; editl. advisor Jour. Accountancy, NYC, 1982—; contbr. articles to profl. jours. Faculty advisor Coll. Reps. of Tex., Stephenville, 1984-1988. With USN, 1955-59. Fellow Earhart Found., Ann Arbor, Mich., 1963, 68, NSF, Washington, 1966. Mem. AICPA, Nat. Acctg. Assn. (v.p. 1978-83, Outstanding Svc. award 1983, Sargent Americanism award 1989), Am. Acctg. Assn., Tex. Soc. CP's, Southwestern Fin. Assn., U. Tex. Austin Ex-Students Assn. (life), Sigma Xi. Libertarian. Avocations: tennis, hiking, collecting coins and walking canes. Home: 930 N Charlotte Ave Stephenville TX 76401-2004 Office: Tarleton State U 1603 W Washington PO Box 505T Stephenville TX 76401-0505 E-mail: collier@tarleton.edu.

COLLIER, CHARLES ARTHUR, JR., lawyer; b. Columbus, Ohio, Apr. 18, 1930; s. Charles Arthur and Gertrude Clara (Roe) C.; m. Linda Louise Biggs, Aug. 5, 1961; children: Sheila Collier Rogers, Laura Collier Prescott. AB magna cum laude, Harvard U., 1952, LLB, 1955. Law clk. U.S. Dist. Ct. (cen. dist.) Calif., L.A., 1959-60; assoc. Freston & Files, L.A., 1960-66; assoc., ptnr. Mitchell, Silberberg & Knupp, L.A., 1967 82; ptnr. Irell & Manella, L.A., 1982-95, of counsel, 1995—2003. Lectr. Calif. Continuing Edn. of Bar, 1976-89; advisor Restatement of Property, Donative Transfers, 1990—; speaker numerous local bar assns. Contbr. articles to profl. jours. Recipient Arthur K. Marshall award Probate and Trust sect. L.A. County Bar Assn. Fellow Am. Coll. Trust and Estate Counsel (chmn. state laws com. 1986-89, regent 1989-98, joint editl. bd. uniform trust and estate acts, 1988—, chmn. expanded practice com. 1989-92, chmn. nominating com. 1998-99, spkr. 1988, exec. com. 1989-98, treas. 1992-93, sec. 1993-94, v.p. 1994-95, pres.-elect 1995-96, pres. 1996-97, immediate past pres. 1997-98), ABA Found.; mem. ABA (mem. real property, trust and probate law sect. spkr. 1985, 89, moderator teleconf. 1998, coun. 1989-93, chmn. com. trust adminstrn. 1982-85, chmn. task force on fiduciary litigation 1986-89, sr. lawyers divsn., vice chair wills, probate and trusts com. 1999-2000, chair 2000-2001, vice chair book pub. com. 2000-2002, chair editl. bd. 2001--, others), Estate Planning, Trust and Probate Law Sect. of State Bar Calif. (chmn. 1980-81, vice chmn. 1979-80, mem. exec. com. 1977-82, advisor 1982-85, chmn. probate com. 1977-78, mem. legislation com. 1977-80, sect. liaison to Calif. Law Revision Commn. 1982-88), Internat. Acad. Estate and Trust Law, Harvard Alumni Assn. (dir. 1975-77, v.p. 1979-82), Harvard Club So. Calif. (pres. 1970-72). Republican. Methodist. Office: Irell & Manella LLP 1800 Ave Of Stars Ste 900 Los Angeles CA 90067-4276 E-mail: ccollier@irell.com.

COLLIER, CHRISTOPHER, history educator, writer; b. N.Y.C., Jan. 29, 1930; s. Edmund and Katherine Brown C.; m. Virginia W. Collier, Aug. 21, 1954 (div. Sept. 1969); children: Edmund Q., Sally Collier Lovegrove; m. Bonnie B. Collier, Dec. 6, 1969; 1 child, Christopher Z. AB, Clark U., 1951; MA, Columbia U., 1955, PhD, 1964. Pub. sch. tchr. Greenwich (Conn.) Pub. Schs., 1955-59, New Canaan (Conn.) Pub. Schs., 1960-61; from instr. to prof. U. Bridgeport, Conn., 1961-84; prof. U. Conn., Storrs, 1984-2000, prof. emeritus, 2000—. Conn. state historian, 1984—. Author: Roger Sherman's Connecticut, 1971; co-author: My Brother Sam is Dead, 1974, Decision in Philadelphia, 1986, others; editor: Pub. Records of State of Conn., 1965-69, 84—. With U.S. Army, 1952-54. Mem. Conn. Hist. Soc., Am. Hist. Assn., Orgn. Am. Historians, Acorn Club. Avocations: ice dancing, ice hockey, trumpet playing, swimming, tennis. Home: 344 W River Rd Orange CT 06477-2742

COLLIER, DIANA GORDON, publishing executive; b. Ottawa, Ont., Can., June 15, 1945; came to U.S., 1984; d. Edward Cecil and Vera (Lowrie) C.; m. Y. Naim, Apr. 17, 1982; 1 child, Sundiata. BA, U. B.C., 1963; MA, U. Montreal, 1975. Writer, 1972-83; editor Black Rose Books, Montreal, Que., Can., 1973-75; bus. mgr. Studies Polit. Economy, Ottawa, Ont., Can., 1980-82; pub. Clarity Press, Inc., Atlanta, 1984—. Dir. comms. Internat. Human Rights Assn. of Am. Minorities, Chgo., 1988—; program dir. First Internat. Conf. on the Right to Sefl-Determination and the UN, GEneva, 2000. Author: Invisible Women of Washington, 1989 (Best of U.S. Small Press 1989), Minnesota Review, 1988; editor: Restructuring of America, 1991, Israeli Peace-Palestinean Justice, 1994, A Popular Guide to Minority Rights, 1995, American Indians: Stereotypes and Realities, 1996, Societal Development and Minority Rights, 1997, A Land to Die For, 1998, The Legacy of Ibo Landing: Gullah Roots of African American Culture, 1998, The Piracy of America: Profiteering in the Public Domain, 1999, Discovering America As It Is, 1999, In Pursuit of the Right to Self Determination: Collected Papers & Proceedings of the First International Conference on the Right to Self Determination and the United Nations, 2001, The Criminality of Nuclear Deterrence, 2002, Child Rights and Remedies, 2002, Palestine, Palestineans and International Law, 2003. Pub. grantee European Human Rights Found., Brussels, 1992; Can. Coun. grantee, Ottawa, 1975, 77; Bell Can. fellow, Montreal, 1973, 74. Mem. NAACP, ACLU, Soc. Scholarly Pub., Pub. Mktg. Assn. Office: Clarity Press Inc 3277 Roswell Rd NE Ste 469 Atlanta GA 30305-1854 E-mail: claritypress@usa.net.

COLLIER, DUAINE ALDEN, manufacturing and distribution company executive; b. Chambersburg, Pa., Aug. 19, 1950; s. Clyde Alden and Etta Jean (Browell) C.; m. Trudy Jean Shoap, Aug. 22, 1970; children: Patrick, Crystal. BS in Math., Shippensburg U., 1972. Product specialist ITT Domestic Pump, Shippensburg, 1972-77; pres., CEO College Town, Inc., Shippensburg, 1971—; gen. mgr. Shippensburg Pump Co., Inc., 1985—. Bd. dirs., sec.-treas. Beidel Printing House, Inc., Shippensburg, 1975—, White Mane Pub. Co., Inc., Shippensburg, 1987—. Committeeman Franklin County Rep. Party, 1989-92; pres. Shippensburg Area Devel. Corp., 1983-84, bd. dirs., 1982-84; bd. dirs. Shippensburg Midget Football Assn., Inc., coach, 1984-94, head coach, 1991-94; pres. Maroon & Grey Football Club, 1991-94; bd. dirs. Shippensburg U. Found., 1995—; bd. dirs., pres. Shippen Place, Inc., 1996-99; mem. adv. bd. Orrstown Bank, 1998—; v.p. Main St. Nonprofit Redevel. Corp. Mem. Harrisburg Regional C. of C. (bd. dirs. 2000—), The Wednesday Club, Masons (master Orrstown lodge 1979), Shippensburg Lions Club (pres. 1989-90), Sons of the Am. Legion. Methodist. Avocations: hunting, fishing, skiing, photography, painting. Office: College Town Inc PO Box 337 17 W Burd St Shippensburg PA 17257-1223

COLLIER, HERMAN EDWARD, JR., retired college president; b. St. Louis, Aug. 8, 1927; s. Herman E. and Evelyn (Saville) C.; m. Jerline L. Weston, Mar. 25, 1948; children: Herman Edward III, Michael F., Thomas W. BS, Randolph-Macon Coll., 1950, Sc.D., 1977; MS, Lehigh U., 1952, PhD, 1955, LL.D., 1971; Litt.D., Coll. of Charleston, 1976; LHD, Muhlenberg Coll., 1986, Moravian Coll., 1987. Chmn. dept. chemistry Moravian Coll., 1955-57; research chemist E. I. duPont de Nemours Co., Wilmington, Del., 1957-63; prof. chemistry, chmn. div. natural scis. Moravian Coll., 1963-69, pres., 1969-86; pres., dir. I&I Planning Assocs., 1987—89; interim pres. Salem Acad. and Coll., 1991, N.C., Wesleyan Coll., 1994-95, Chowan Coll., 1995-96, Lees-McRae Coll., 1997-98. Sr. cons. Acad. Search Consultation Svc., 1998—; bd. dirs. Horizon Health Sys. Inc., First Health Found., 2003-; cons. sci. adv. bd. EPA, 1979-85; chmn. Commn. Ind. Colls. and Univs. Pa.; bd. dirs. Bethlehem Steel Corp., 1987-95. Patentee mfg. tech. and product quality organo-lead compounds; sodium tetraphenyl boron for potassium detection; periodic table for lecture room, 1953; flame spectra Metallic ions from the H-F Flame, 1957. Mem. Com. to Employ the Handicapped, 1970-75; mem. Northampton County Citizens for Regional Progress; bd. dirs. United Fund Bethlehem, Hist. Bethlhem, Inc., Moravian Music Found., 1992-94, Roanoke Island Hist. Assn., Inc., 1996—98; trustee St. Luke's Hosp., R.K. Laros Found., Moravian Acad., Salem Acad. & Coll., 1995—. With USN, 1945-46. Mem. Lehigh Valley Assn. Ind. Colls. (dir.), Am. Chem. Soc., AAUP, Lehigh Valley Automobile Assn. (dir. 1981-86), Bethlehem C. of C. (dir.), The Club at Longleaf, Phi Beta Kappa, Sigma Xi, Omicron Delta Kappa, Kappa Alpha. Clubs: Saucon Valley Country (dir.), Duckwoods Country Club, Longlea Country Club. E-mail: hcollier2@earthlink.net.

COLLIER, JAMES BRUCE, lawyer; b. Ironton, Ohio, Sept. 25, 1920; s. James W. and Faye L. (Clark) C.; m. Bette E. Fawcett, Mar. 24, 1943; children: James B. Jr., Gretchen J. Randall. Student, Miami U., Oxford, Ohio, 1938-41; LLB, State U. Iowa, 1949. Bar: Iowa 1949, Ohio 1949, U.S. Dist. Ct. (so. dist.) Ohio 1950, U.S. Ct. Appeals (6th cir.) 1961, U.S. Supreme Ct. 1960. Pvt. practice, Ironton, 1949—. Chmn. Lawrence County Rep. Ctrl. Com., Ironton, 1955-85; mem., pres. Ironton City Sch. Bd., 1962-66. Capt. USAAF, 1941-46. Mem. Ohio Bar Assn., Lawrence County Bar Assn. Episcopalian. Avocations: fishing, boating, competitive pistol shooting. Home: 1111 Mastin Ave Ironton OH 45638-2223 Office: Collier & Collier 411 Center St Ironton OH 45638-1506

COLLIER, JAMES WARREN, lawyer; b. Dallas, July 31, 1940; s. J.W. and Mary Gertrude (Roberts) C.; m. Judith Lane, Dec. 27, 1964; children: Anne Elizabeth, Jennifer Susan. BA, U. Mich., 1962, JD, 1965. Bar: N.Y. 1966, Mich. 1968. Assoc. Simpson Thacher & Bartlett, N.Y.C., 1965-66; tax atty. office gen. counsel Ford Motor Co., 1966-67; assoc. Dykema Gossett, Detroit, 1967-73, ptnr., 1973—. Mem. Dykema Gossett. Mem. ABA, Mich. Bar Assn., Econ. Club Detroit, Lochmoor Club. Office: Dykema Gossett 400 Renaissance Ctr # 3500 Detroit MI 48243-1603 E-mail: jcollier@dykema.com.

COLLIER, JUDITH BRANDES, elementary education educator; b. Chgo., June 11, 1941; d. Rico G. and Frances (Miller) Bosca; m. Stanley H. Brandes, June 14, 1964 (div. May 1, 1987); children: Nina Stonebarger, Naomi; m. Neil Adrian Collier, June 11, 1987. BA, U. Calif., Berkeley, 1965. Bilingual tchr., resource tchr., reading recovery tchr. West Contra Costa Unified Sch. Dist., Richmond, Calif., 1978-97, project asst. Title VII, curriculum guide, 1997—. Mem.: Phi Beta Kappa, Phi Delta Kappa. Avocations: gardening, walking, traveling, birding. Home: 1335 Peralta Ave Berkeley CA 94702-1127 Office: Bayview Sch 3001 16th St San Pablo CA 94806 E-mail: jbcnajc@pacbell.net.

COLLIER, NATHAN MORRIS, musician, music educator; b. Clinton, Okla., July 23, 1924; s. Lotan Morris and Annie Carlletta (Willsey) C.; m. Frances Aleta Snell, June 24, 1955; children: Susan Aleta Kowalski, Ray Morris. MusB, U. Okla., 1949; MusM, U. Rochester, 1951. String music cons. Lincoln (Nebr.) Pub. Schs., 1951-68; asst. concertmaster Lincoln Symphony Orch., 1953-2001; 1st violinist Lincoln String Quartet, Nebr., 1955—; first violin Omaha (Nebr.) Symphony, The Nebr. Sinfonia, 1956-79; asst. prof. violin, theory Nebr. Wesleyan U., Lincoln, 1968-84; asst. concertmaster Nebr. Chamber Orch., 1973-91; assoc. concertmaster Omaha (Nebr.) Symphony, The Nebr. Sinfonia, 1977-78; concertmaster Lincoln Symphony, Lincoln Little Symphony, 1977-78; acting concertmaster Omaha (Nebr.) Symphony, The Nebr. Sinfonia, 1978; prin. second violinist Des Moines Symphony, 1979—; asst prof. music, condr. symphony orch. Kans. State U., Manhattan, 1980-81, pvt. tchr., 1st violinist Resident String Quartet, 1980-81; string tchr. St. John Luth. Sch., Seward, Nebr., 1983-89; acting concertmaster on occasion Nebr. Chamber Orch.; concertmaster Omaha Pops Orch., 1988-90; 1st violinist Avanti String Quartet, 1990; sect. I violinist Nebr. Symphony Chamber Orch., 1995—. Vis. instr. music Concordia U., Seward, 1985, 90; 1st violinist Lincoln String Quartet, 1951—; guest prin. violinist Des Moines Symphony, 1979, 87; guest violinist, violist Myron Cohen Met. and the Midlands String Quartets, Omaha, 1988—, Hastings (Nebr.) Symphony, 1990—; concertmaster and solo violinist with Collegium Musicum Concordia, 1999—; viola instr. chamber music coach summer course U. Nebr., Lincoln, 1991; concertmaster, soloist Nebr. Camerata-Orch. Berlin tour, 1992; mem. adv. bd. Rocky Ridge Music Ctr., 1972; cons., lectr. in field. Composer various mus. pieces; arranger numerous compositions for string quartet, 1980. Tchr., co-organizer Brownville (Nebr.) Summer Music Festival, 1972-77. With USN, 1943-46. Grantee U.S. Govt., 1966; inducted into Nebr. Music Educators Hall of Fame, 2002. Mem. Am. String Tchrs. assn. (nebr. Pvt. Studio Tchr. of Yr. 1994), Music Tchrs. Nat. Assn. (nationally cert. 1994—), Music Educators Nat. Conf., Violin Soc. Am.(inducted into NMEA Hall of Fame, 2002), Chamber Music Am., Lincoln Music Tchrs. Assn., Nat. Sch. Orch. Assn., NEA, Nebr. State Edn. Assn., Lincoln Musicians Assn., Omaha Musicians Assn., Lincoln Arts Coun. (co-recipient Lincoln Mayor's Arts award 1995), Pi Kappa Lambda. Democrat. Methodist. Home: 4544 Mohawk St Lincoln NE 68510-4838 E-mail: acorelli@aol.com.

COLLIER, SAMUEL MELVIN, aerospace engineer; b. Atlanta, Aug. 19, 1941; s. Samuel Roland Collier and Dixie Pauline (Sorrells) Terry; m. Gail Lee Grenfel Simmons, Sept. 22, 1962 (div. 1982); children: Phyliss, Sheri, Suzan, Samuel, Donica, Michele; m. Betty Lou Morris, Feb. 22, 1985. Grad., Officer's Candidate Sch., 1964; BS, U. Tex., 1973; MS in Bus. Adminstrn., U. No. Colo., 1977. Enlisted U.S. Army, 1959, advanced through grades to maj., ret., 1979; sr. staff engr. LTV Missiles & Electronics, Grand Prairie, Tex., 1979-85; engring. project mgr. LTV Aircraft, Dallas, 1985-93, ret., 1993; technology transfer mgr. La. State U., Shreveport, 1996-97; sr. staff engr. Lockheed-Martin, Dallas, 1999-2000; cons. sys. engr. joint strike fighter devel. Lockheed Martin Aeronautics Corp., Ft. Worth, 2002—. Grants cons. Town of Vivian, 1993-95. Author, pub. Terrapin Neck, Frog Level, Horseshoe, 2000. Pres. Hist. Soc. North Caddo, Vivian, 1995-99; grants review panelist Shreveport Regional Arts Coun., 1996, 97; mem. Vivian Preservation Commn., 1995-96. Mem. Ret. Officers Assn., Inst. Ops. Rsch. and Mgmt. Sci. Avocations: bass fishing, archery, genealogy, achievements include leading the operations research engineering team in a highly competitive tactical missile system production program won by the company, managing research and development programs that defined future military aircraft designs based upon the application of stealth technologies, authoring winning grant applications for small, local non-profit corporations. Home: 1701 N Pine St Vivian LA 71082-9515

COLLIER, STEPHEN N, educational consultant; b. Atlanta, Ga., June 29, 1942; s. William E and Dora G Collier; m. Judy Ann Gordon, Aug. 17, 1968; children: Stephen Christopher, David Gordon, Katherine Marie. BA, Emory U., 1960—64; MA, Ga. State U., Atlanta, Georgia, 1965—71; PhD in Polit. Sci., Ga. State U., 1973—80. Respiratory therapist Emory U. Hosp., Atlanta, 1962—67; instr. and grad. counselor Grad. Sch. of Bus. Adminstrn., Ga. State U., Atlanta, 1967—71; chmn. and assoc. prof. Dept. of Cardiopulmonary Care Sci., Ga. State U., Atlanta, 1971—76; assoc. dir. for health programs So. Regional Edn. Bd., Atlanta, 1976—80; prof. and assoc. dean U. of Ala., Birmingham, Ala., 1980—85; pres. MGH Inst. of Health Professions, Boston, 1985—87, john hilton knowles prof. of health policy, 1985—88; dean, coll. of health professions Towson U., Towson, Md., 1989—98, dir. and prof., ctr. for health policy and workforce rsch., 1998—; prof. and dir., office of health professions edn. and workforce devel. U. of Ala., Birmingham, Ala., 2002—. Fellow Inst. for Ednl. Leadership, Washington, 1985—86; health policy fellow W.K. Kellogg Found. and Assn. of Schools of Allied Health Professions, Washington, 1985—86; mem. Commn. on Academic Health Centers and the Economy of New Eng., Boston, 1986—87; chmn., state policy task force Pew Health Professions Commn., Durham, NC, 1990—93; chmn., commn. on health and human services So. Regional Edn. Bd., Atlanta, 1993—95. Mem. bd. dirs. Assn. of Sch. of Allied Health Professions, Washington, 1993—95; mem. Am. Lung Assn., Atlanta, 1973—80. Comdr. USNR, 1966—90. Fellow: Assn. of Schools of Allied Health Professions (life); mem.: Acad. of Polit. Sci. (life). Home: 13811 Cuba Road Hunt Valley MD 21030-1206

COLLIER, VIRGINIA UPCHURCH, internist; b. Birmingham, Ala., June 26, 1950; d. Samuel Earl and Ann Samford Upchurch; m. Thomas Austin Collier, Dec. 27, 1975; children: Ann Upchurch, Katherine Margaret, Louisa Samford. BA, Sweet Briar Coll., Va., 1972; MD, Johns Hopkins U. Sch. of Medicine, Balt., 1976. Diplomate Nat. Bd. of Med. Examiners, 1976, Am. Bd. of Internal Medicine, 1980, in Nephrology Am. Bd. of Internal Medicine, 1982. Pvt. practice in internal medicine and nephrology Kent And Queen Anne' s Hosp., Chestertown, Md., 1980—89; dir., fourth yr. student program, dept. of medicine Med. Ctr. of Del., Newark, 1989—91; residency program dir. internal medicine Med. Ctr. Del., Newark, 1991—94; vice chair, residency program dir., dept. medicine Christiana Care Health Sys., Newark, Del., 1994—. Author: (jour. articles) Jour. of the Am. Med. Assn., Annals of Internal Medicine, Jour. of Gen. Internal Medicine. Gov. Am. Coll. of Physicians and Am. Soc. of Internal Medicine, Phila., 1999—2003; bd. mem. Sweet Briar Coll., Va., 2002; coun. mem. Assn. of Program Dirs. in Internal Medicine, Washington. Recipient Parker Palmer award, Accrediation Coun. for Grad. Med. Edn., 2002. Fellow: ACP (gov., Del. chpt. 1999—2003). Avocations: travel, sailing, tennis, opera, reading. Office: Christiana Care Health Svcs 4755 Ogletown Stanton Rd Newark DE 19718 E-mail: vcollier@christianacare.org.

COLLIER, WILLIAM GAYLE, psychology educator, researcher; b. Albuquerque, July 31, 1970; s. William Robert and Judith Church Collier. BS in Psychology, Okla. Christian U., 1992; MA in Exptl. Psychology, U. Ctrl. Okla., 1994; MS in Exptl. Psychology, Tex. Christian U., 1997, PhD in Gen. Exptl. Psychology, 1998. Grad. asst. Multimedia Ctr., Coll. Edn., U. Ctrl. Okla., Edmond, 1994; dep. asst. dept. psychology Tex. Christian U., Ft. Worth, 1995-96, acad. tutor athletic dept., 1997-98, dep. asst. dept. psychology, 1998; lectr. psychology U. Tex., Tyler, 1998-99, vis. asst. prof., 1999—, undergrad. student advisor dept. psychology, 1999—. Undergrad. student advisor dept. psychology U. Tex., 1999—. Author poetry; contbr. articles to profl. jours. Mem. APA, Am. Psychol. Soc., Internat. Soc. Poets (disting. mem.), Psi Chi, Alpha Chi. Avocations: science fiction, history, poetry, music, theatre. Office: 504 East 14th Street Lumberton NC 28358 Fax: 903-565-5656. E-mail: captcrohn@aol.com.

COLLIN, THOMAS JAMES, lawyer; b. Windom, Minn., Jan. 6, 1949; s. Everett Earl and Genevieve May (Wilson) C.; m. Victoria Gatov, Oct. 11, 1985; children: Arielle, Elise, Sarah. BA, U. Minn., 1970; AM, Harvard U., 1972; JD, Georgetown U., 1974. Bar: Ohio 1975, U.S. Dist. Ct. (no. dist.) Ohio 1975, U.S. Ct. Appeals (10th cir.) 1977, U.S. Supreme Ct. 1980, U.S. Ct. Appeals (6th cir.) 1981, U.S. Ct. Appeals (8th cir.) 1982, U.S. Ct. Appeals (7th cir.) 1997, U.S. Ct. Appeals (11th cir.) 1999. Law clk. to Judge Myron Bright U.S. Ct. Appeals, 8th Cir., St. Louis, 1974-75; assoc. Thompson, Hine LLP, Cleve., 1975-82, ptnr., 1982--. Author: Ohio Business Competition Law, 1994, (with others) Criminal Antitrust Litigation Manual, 1983; editor: Punitive Damages and Business Torts: A Practitioner's Handbook, 1998; contbr. articles to profl. jours. Active Citizens League, Cleve., bd. trustees, 1994-99, v.p. 1995-97, pres. 1997-99; bd. trustees Citizens League Rsch. Inst., Cleve., 1999-2002. Mem. ABA (chair bus. torts and unfair competition com. antitrust sect. 1995-98, chair annual mtg. com. 2001-02, chmn. franchise and dealership com. 2002-), Ohio State Bar Assn. (bd. govs. antitrust sect. 1988-98). Republican. Avocations: book collecting, music. Home: 7879 Oakhurst Dr Cleveland OH 44141-1123 Office: Thompson Hine LLP 127 Public Sq Cleveland OH 44114-1216

COLLINE, MARGUERITE RICHNAVSKY, maternal, women's health and pediatrics nurse; b. Bayonne, N.J., Nov. 30, 1953; d. John P. and Margaret M. (Conaghan) Richnavsky; m. Richard L. Colline, Oct. 8, 1977; children: Jennifer, Nicole, Danielle, James Michael. Diploma in practical nurse, Union County Tech. Inst., Scotch Plains, N.J., 1973; BSN, Seton Hall U., 1978. RN, N.J., Md. Practical nurse oncology unit John E. Runnell's Hosp., Berkley Heights, N.J.; staff nurse infant unit Johns Hopkins Hosp., Balt.; staff nurse neonatal unit Overlook Hosp., Summit, N.J. Mem. Nat. Assn. Neonatal Nurses, Sigma Theta Tau.

COLLINGS, KAY P. legal office administrator; b. Swansea, S.C., Dec. 18, 1944; d. Elvin Hampton and Sue D. Poole; m. Benny Lewis Collings, Apr. 25, 1992. AS, U. S.C., 1978, BS, 1987. Sec. Eastman Chem., Columbia, S.C., 1967-76, buyer, 1976-77, engring. records coord., 1978-87, staff asst., engring., 1987-89, purchasing rep., 1989-92, legal staff asst. Kingsport, Tenn., 1992-93, legal office adminstr., 1993-95, sr. office adminstr., 1995-98, prin. office adminstr., 1998—. Mem. family life ministries Mountain View United Meth. Ch., Kingsport, 1995—. Avocations: painting (oil and acrylic), eggery, stained glass, crafts, travel. Office: Eastman Chem Co 100 N Eastman Rd # B-75 Kingsport TN 37660-5299

COLLINGS, ROBERT BIDDLECOMBE, judge; b. Aug. 31, 1942; s. Harry Biddlecombe and Juanita Beatrice (Huber) C.; m. Mary Clare Flintoft, Sept. 14, 1968; children: John Richard Biddlecombe, Christopher James More, Clare Yung Hee. AB, Hamilton Coll., 1964; JD, Harvard U., 1967. Bar: Mass. 1968, N.H. 1970, U.S. Ct. Mil. Appeals 1970, U.S. Dist. Ct. Mass. 1971, U.S. Ct. Appeals (1st cir.) 1971, U.S. Ct. Appeals (5th cir.) 1979, Temporary Emergency Ct. Appeals 1980. Asst. U.S. atty. Dept. Justice, Boston, 1971-82, chief criminal

divsn., 1976-82, 1st asst. U.S. atty., 1978-81; U.S. magistrate judge U.S. Dist. Ct., Boston, 1982—, chief magistrate judge, 1999—2001. Lectr. law Harvard Law Sch., 1988—92, Northeastern U. Sch. Law, 1989—90; guest lectr. Stanford Law Sch., 2000—03; mem. Magistrate Judge Ednl. Com. of Fed. Jud. Ctr., 1990—96, Def. Svcs. Com. Jud. Conf. U.S., 1991—97; mem. joint adv. group Adminstrv. Office of U.S. Cts., 1998—2000; mem. Fed. Jud. Ctr. Bd., 2001—. Co-editor: Federal Court Civil Litigation in the First Circuit, 1994. Lt. USNR, 1967-71. Mem. ABA (chair magistrate judges' com. nat. conf. fed. trial judges 1999-2000, exec. com. 2000-02, sec. 2002-03, vice-chmn. 2003-04), Nat. Coun. U.S. Magistrates (treas. 1990-91), Fed. Magistrate Judges Assn. (2d v.p. 1991-92, 1st v.p. 1992-93, pres.-elect 1993-94, pres. 1994-95, past pres. 1995-96, legis. chmn. 1995—, Founders award 1998), Mass. Bar Assn., Boston Bar Assn. Office: US Courthouse 1 Courthouse Way Boston MA 02210-3002

COLLINGS, ROBERT L. lawyer; b. May 22, 1950; AB, Harvard U., 1972; JD, Boston Coll., 1977. Bar: Pa. 1977, U.S. Ct. Appeals (D.C. cir.) 1981, U.S. Dist. Ct. (ea. dist.) Pa. 1985, U.S. Ct. Appeals (3d cir.) 1984, U.S. Dist. Ct. (mid. dist.) 1992. Atty. U.S. EPA, 1977-84, sect. chief, 1979-81, br. chief, 1981-84; ptnr. Morgan, Lewis & Bockrus LLP, 1984—98; ptnr., chair litig. dept. Schnader, Harrison, Segal & Lewis LLP, Phila., 1998—. Editor: Environmental Spill Reporting Handbook; contbr. Municipal Solicitors Handbook, 1994, 1999, 2003, Brownfields: A Comprehensive Guide, 1997, 2d edit., 2002. Mem. Phila. Bar Assn. (chair environ. law com. 1986), Water Resources Assn. (sec. exec. com. 1990—). Office: Schnader Harrison Segal & Lewis LLP 1600 Market St Ste 3600 Philadelphia PA 19103-7287

COLLINGWOOD, TRACY LYNN, career counselor; b. Jamestown, N.Y., Aug. 9, 1964; d. Edward William and Kay Collingwood. AA Social Scis., Jamestown C.C., 1992; BA in Psychology, SUNY, Fredonia, 1994; EdM in Coll. Student Svcs. and Devel., SUNY, Buffalo, 1997. Commuter svcs. coord. SUNY, Buffalo, 1995-96, peer edn. supr., 1996-97, acad. affairs advisor Fredonia, 1997; mem. faculty, counselor Jamestown (N.Y.) C.C., 1997-99; univ. website coord. media rels. office SUNY, Fredonia, 1998—. Internet steering com. SUNY, Buffalo, 1995-96, career counselor, 1996; tchg. asst. SUNY, Fredonia, 1994; mem. SUNY Career Devel. Orgn. Vol. Rosa Parks Scholarship Program, Fredonia, 1997, The Resource Cu., 1994-97. Seager Presdl. scholar SUNY, Fredonia, 1992-94, Crecraft Olsen scholar, 1993-94. Mem. Nat. Assn. Student Pers. Adminstrs., Am. Coll. Pers. Assn., Coll. Student Pers. Assn., Niagara Frontier Coll. Placement Assn., Psi Chi, Phi Theta Kappa. Avocations: singing, songwriting, guitar. Office: SUNY at Fredonia Central Ave Fredonia NY 14063

COLLINS, ADRIANA DELIA, banker; b. Port Jefferson, N.Y., Nov. 25, 1953; d. Domenic and Mary Delia; m. David Collins, Apr. 28, 1950 (dec. Feb. 2001); 1 child, Domenique Mara. BA in Social Sci., Fordham U., 1974; MPA in Internat. Devel., NYU, 1980. Mgmt. cons. FR Schwab & Assoc., N.Y.C., 1980-82; dir. econ. and rsch. N.Y. State Bankers Assn., N.Y.C., 1982-86; fin. acctg. officer Chem. Bank, N.Y.C., 1986-88; v.p. structured and corp. fin. Bank Austria, N.Y.C., 1988-92; sr. asst. mgr. loans/bus. devel. PT Bank Bumi Daya Indonesia, N.Y.C., 1992-95; 1st v.p. HSBC Bank USA, N.Y.C., 1995—. Mem. NYU Mentor Program, 1993; cons. Jr. Achievement. Contbr. articles to profl. jours. Cadette troop leader Girl Scouts U.S.; mentor NYU Wagner Sch. Alumni. Mem. Fordham Alumni Student Team. Avocations: running, skiing, internat. travel. Office: 452 5th Ave Fl 4 New York NY 10018-2333 E-mail: tanahlot96@aol.com.

COLLINS, ALLAN MEAKIN, cognitive scientist, psychologist, educator; b. Orange, N.J., Aug. 7, 1937; s. Clinton and Sarah Amy (Meakin) C.; m. Anne Marjorie Linstead, Aug. 24, 1963; children: Antony, Elizabeth. MA in Communication Scis., U. Michigan, 1962, PhD in Psychology, 1970. Sr. scientist Bolt, Beranek & Newman Inc., Cambridge, 1967-82, prin. scientist, 1982-2000; prof edn. and social policy Northwestern U., Evanston, Ill., 1989—; co-dir. Ctr. for Tech. in Edn., Bank St. Coll. of Edn., N.Y.C., 1991-94; rsch. prof. of edn. Boston Coll., 1998—2002. Lectr. various colls. and univs. Editor: Representation and Understanding, 1975, Cognitive Science, 1976-80, Readings in Cognitive Science, 1988; author: The Cognitive Structure of Emotions, 1988. Guggenheim fellow, 1974, Sloan fellow, 1980. Fellow AAAS; mem. Nat. Acad. Edn., Cognitive Sci. Soc. (chmn. 1979-80, goving. bd. 1979-87), Am. Assn. for Artificial Intelligence (fellow 1990), Am. Ednl. Rsch. Assn. Achievements include launched research on human semantic memory (with R. Quillian); development of first intelligent tutoring system (with J.R. Carbonell); development of cognitive apprenticeship (with J.S. Brown). Home: 135 Cedar St Lexington MA 02421-6516 E-mail: a-collins@northwestern.edu.

COLLINS, ALLEN HOWARD, psychiatrist; b. Washington, Sept. 6, 1942; s. Murray and Bertha (Baccalman) C.; m. Stephanie Evelyn Awn, May 22, 1976; children: Sasha Marie, Matthew Allen, Alyssa Beth. AB, Columbia Coll., 1964; MD, Tufts U., 1968; MPH, Columbia U., 1974. Diplomate Am. Bd. of Psychiatry and Neurology; Nat. Bd. of Med. Examiners; cert. psychoanalysis. Mental health career develop. fellow NIMH, Rockville, Md., 1968—74, staff psychiatrist Region II NYC, 1972—74, psychiat. cons., 1974—90; chief psychiat. consultation liaison svcs. Lenox Hill Hosp., NYC, 1974—76, chief psychiat. inpatient svc., 1976—78, chief of psychiatry svc., 1978—86, chmn. dept. of psychiatry, 1986—, pres. med. bd., 1994—96, 2000—02. Examiner in psychiatry Am. Bd. of Psychiatry and Neurology, Evanston, Ill., 1979—, chief proctor, 1991—; clin. prof. of psychiatry N.Y. Med. Coll., Valhalla, 1988-90; tng. and supervisory psychoanalyst divsn. of psychoanalytic tng., 1986-90; assoc. clin. prof. psychiatry Cornell U. Med. Coll., 1990-93; clin. prof. psychiatry NYU Med. Ctr., 1993—; vis. prof. psychiatry SUNY/Downstate Health Sci. Ctr., 1998—. Author: (with others) Provider's Guide To Hospital-Based Services, 1986; contbr. articles to profl. jours. bd. trustees Lenox Hill Hosp., 1994—. With USPHS, 1968-74. Fellow Am. Psychiatr. Assn., Am. Acad. of Psychoanalysis, N.Y. Acad. Medicine. Avocations: tennis, golf, reading biographies, history. E-mail: ahcolmd@aol.com.

COLLINS, ALMA JONES, English educator, writer; d. Walter Melville Jones and Anne Teresa Harrington; m. Daniel Francis Collins, Apr. 9, 1994. BA, Conn. Coll., 1943; MA, Trinity Coll., 1952, U. Conn., 1962. Tchr., counselor W. Hartford (Conn.) Bd. Edn., 1947-72; pres. Arts Universal Rsch. Assocs., 1978—. Interviewed Salvador Dali (CD located in archives Wadsworth Atheneum Mus. Art), 1978, 79; cons. for corp. product devel.; rep. for artists. *Since 1978 Arts Universal Research Associates has focused on concept development and publications by Alma Jones Collins with research associate Audrey Jones Burton. Art-related articles for national and international publications include Japanese woodblock prints, Oriental rugs, third world embassies, commemorative art objects, art collections and interior design. Concept development for corporations includes articles and monographs for Royal Doulton, Hallmark International and U.S. Historical Society. Presentations include Salvador Dali, Chaim Gross, Kamil Kubik, Dominic Mingolla, Eric Sloane, John Stobart, Carlos Paez-Vilaro and Bjorn Wiinblad. Book in process is titled DANIELLE AT THE WADSWORTH.* Contbr. articles and monographs in nat. and internat. publs. Mem. Phi Beta Kappa, Delta Kappa Gamma Internat. Avocation: writing poetry and fiction. Home and Office: 275 Steele Rd A318 West Hartford CT 06117-2763

COLLINS, ANGELO, science educator, educator; b. Chgo., June 15, 1944; d. James Joseph and Mary (Burke) C. BS, Marian Coll., 1966; MS, Mich. State U., 1973; PhD, U. Wis., 1986; hon. degree, Edgewood Coll. High sch. biology tchr. various schs., Wis., 1966-81; rsch. asst. U. Wis., Madison, 1981-86; asst. prof. Kans. State U., Manhattan, 1986-87, Stanford (Calif.) U., 1988-90, Rutgers U., New Brunswick, N.J., 1990-91; assoc. prof. Fla. State U., Tallahassee, 1991-95; prof. Vanderbilt U., 1995—2000; exec. dir. Knowles Sci. Tchg. Found., 2000—. Mem. Working Group on Sci. Stds., Washington, 1992, dir. 1993—; sci. com. Nat. Bd. Profl. Tchg. Stds., Washington, 1991—; chmn. adv. bd. BioQuest, Beloit, Wis., 1988—; bd. dirs. Jour. for Rsch. in Sci. Tchg. Editor Tchr. Edn. Quarterly, 1991; reviewer several books; contbr. articles to profl. jours. Henry Rutgers fellow Rutgers U., 1990; recipient Devel. Scholar award Fla. State U., 1993-94. Fellow AAAS; mem. Nat. Assn. Biology Tchrs. (Outstandng Biology Tchr. Wis. 1977), Nat. Assn. Rsch. Sci. Tchg., Assn. Edn. Tchrs. Sci., Am. Edn. Rsch. Assn., Sch. Sci. and Math., Assn. Tchr. Educators, Sigma Xi, Phi Delta Kappa. E-mail: angelo.collins@kstf.org.

COLLINS, ANNAZETTE R. state representative; b. Chgo., Apr. 28, 1962; m. Keith Langston; 1 child, Angelique. BS in Sociology, No. Ill. U.; MS in Criminal Justice, Chgo. State U., 1983. Social worker Ada S. McKinley Interventions, 1982—83; correctional officer Fed. Bur. Prisons, 1983—86; social worker Cook County Social Svcs., 1986—90; adminstr. Dept. Children Family Svcs., 1990—2000, Chgo. Pub. Schs., 2000; mem. Ill. Ho. of Reps., 2000—. Mem. St. Joseph Sch. Bd., 1992—95; v.p. pres.'s club Cosmopolitan Cmty. Ch., 2001. Democrat. Baptist. Office: 252-W Stratton Office Bldg Springfield IL 62706 Address: 110 N Pulaski Rd Chicago IL 60624*

COLLINS, ARLENE, secondary education educator; b. Mandan, N.D., Sept. 7, 1940; d. John Marcellus and Cecelia Magdalena (Schaaf) Weber; m. Abdul Rahman Rana (dec.); children: Fazale Rahman, Habeeb Rahman; m. Freddie L. Collins. BS in math., N.D. State U., 1962; postgrad., W.Va. Inst. Tech., 1974; M in Edn. Adminstrn., WVCOGS, 1988. Cert. mid. sch. tchr., W.Va. Tchr. physics, math. Montgomery (W.Va.) H.S., 1970; tchr. math., sci. Spencer (W.Va.) Jr. H.S., 1974-80; sci. tchr. Poca (W.Va.) Mid. Sch., 1980—, team leader, 1983-96. W.Va. textbook adoption com., W.Va. Bd. Edn., 1984-90. Leader Girl Scouts U.S.A., Montgomery, 1966-70, 99—, Boy Scouts Am., Montgomery, 1966; bd. dirs. Violet Twp. Womens League, 2002-. Mem.: NOW (bd. dirs. 1986), Am. Fedn. Tchrs., Laurel Soc., Am. Legion Aux. (sec. 2002—), Buckeye Sertoma, Soroptimists Internat. Home: 7292 Fox Den Ct Pickerington OH 43147-9019 E-mail: ac0907@aol.com.

COLLINS, ARTHUR D., JR., medical products executive; b. Lakewood, Ohio, Dec. 10, 1947; BS, Miami U., Oxford, Ohio, 1969; MBA, U. Pa., 1973. Pres. Medtronics Internat., 1992; exec. v.p. Medtronic Inc., Mpls., 1992, COO, pres., COO, 1994—96, pres., 1996—2001, CEO, 2001—, chmn., 2002—. Office: Medtronics 7000 Central Ave NE Minneapolis MN 55432-3576

COLLINS, AUDREY B. judge; b. 1945; BA, Howard U., 1967; MA, Am. U., 1969; JD, UCLA, 1977. Asst. atty. Legal Aid Found. L.A., 1977-78; with Office L.A. County Dist. Atty., 1978-94, dept. dist. atty., 1978-94, asst. dir. burs. ctrl. ops. and spl. ops., 1988-92, asst. dir. atty., 1992-94; judge. U.S. Dist. Ct. (Ctrl. Dist.) Calif., 1994—. Dep. gen. counsel Office Spl. Acad. scholar Howard U.; named Lawyer of Yr., Langston Bar Assn., 1988; honoree Howard U. Alumni Club So. Calif., 1989; recipient Profl. Achievement award UCLA Alumni Assn., 1997, Ernestine Stahlhut award, Women Lawyers Assn., 1999. Mem. FBA, Nat. Assn. Women Judges, Nat. Bar Assn. (life), State Bar Calif. (com. bar examiners, chmn. subcom. on moral character 1992-93, co-chmn. 1993-94), Los Angeles County Bar Assn. (task force on criminal justice sys. 2002-03), Assn. Los Angeles County Dist. Attys. (pres. 1983), Black Women Lawyers Los Angeles County, Women Lawyers L.A. (life, Ernestine Stahlhut award 1999), Calif. Women Lawyers (life), Order of Coif, Phi Beta Kappa. Office: US Dist Ct Edward R Roybal Fed Bldg 255 E Temple St Ste 670 Los Angeles CA 90012-3334

COLLINS, CARDISS, former congresswoman; b. St. Louis, Sept. 24, 1931; m. George W. Collins (dec.); 1 child, Kevin. Ed., Northwestern U.; hon. degree, Winston-Salem State U., Spelman Coll., John Marshall Law Sch., Rosary Coll., Forest Inst. Profl. Psychology. Barber Scotia Coll.; mem. 93d-104th Congresses from 7th Ill. Dist., 1973-97; ret., 1997. Ranking minority mem. govt. reform & oversight com.; former chair. govt. activity and transp. subcom.; former chair commerce, consumer protection and competition subcom.; former majority whip-at-large; former asst. regional whip; former chair Congl. Black Caucus, sec.; dir. emeritus, former chair Congl. Black Caucus Found.; former chair Mems. Congress for Peace through Law. Recipient award Roosevelt U., Loyola U. Mem. NAACP, Nat. Coun. Negro Women (past v.p.), Chgo. Urban League, Black Women's Agenda, The Chgo. Network, The Links, Dem. Nat. Com., Alpha Kappa Alpha. Democrat. Baptist. Home: 1110 Roundhouse Ln Alexandria VA 22314-5934

COLLINS, CARL RUSSELL, JR., industrial engineer; b. Williamsport, Pa., Dec. 29, 1926; s. Carl Russell, Sr. and Annis (Kilmer) C.; m. Rita Thomas, Oct. 3, 1959; children— James, Michael, Nancy BS in Indsl. Engring., Pa. State U., 1953. Div. sales mgr. Fla. Power Corp., St. Petersburg, 1961-64, asst. div. mgr., 1964-65, dist. mgr., 1965-67, div. mgr., 1967-79, v.p., 1979-85, George F. Young Inc., Architects and Engrs., St. Petersburg, 1986-91. Bd. dirs. Abilities, Inc. Bd. dirs. United Way, St. Petersburg, 1978, Com. of 100, 1981; v.p. Suncoasters, Inc., St. Petersburg, 1982; mem. adv. bd. Salvation Army, 1964—; active Meth. Ch., pres. Meth. Men, chmn. adminstrv. bd., lay leader, chmn. fin. com. With USN, 1944-46, as lt., 1953-56. Mem. Pa. State U. Alumni Club (life), Tau Beta Pi. Lodges: Kiwanis (pres. 1984). Republican. Avocations: photography, fishing, boating. Home: 5937 Tangerine Ave S Saint Petersburg FL 33707-4059

COLLINS, CAROLYN HERMAN, school media specialist, legislative aide; b. Lenoir, N.C., May 25, 1944; d. William Richard and Madeline Edith (Harris) Herman; m. Walter William Collins, Dec. 30, 1989. BA in English, Old Dominion U., 1968, cert. advanced study in ednl. adminstrn., 1992; MS in LS, Fla. State U., 1977. Cert. secondary prin. and libr., tchr. English, French, profl. librarian. Librarian Southampton County (Va.) Schs., 1973-79, TRADOC Army Library, Fort Monroe, Va., 1980-81; media specialist Portsmouth (Va.) Pub. Schs., 1981—; legis. aide Va. House of Dels., Richmond, 1984-97. Moderator White House Conf. on Libraries, Washington, 1991; state del. Gov.'s Conf. on Libraries, Richmond, Va., 1990; York regional dir. Va. Ednl. Media Assn. (VEMA), 1992-94. Del. Virginia Beach City Rep. Conv., 1985-87; mem. Red, White and Blue Club, Virginia Beach, 1987-88; elected rep. Rep. City Com., Virginia Beach, 1987-89; category 2 rehabilitator Va. Dept. Game and Inland Fisheries. Named Sch. Tchr. of Yr., Portsmouth Pub. Schs., 2003. Mem. Va. Ednl. Media Assn. (regional dir. 1992-94), Va. Reading Assn., Va. Assn. Tchrs. of English, Va. Square Dancing Assn., Libr. of Congress Assocs., Nat. Hist. Soc., Old Dominion Alumni Assn. (v.p. English chpt. 1987-89, House Dels. 1993-97), Fla. State U. Alumni Assn., Virginia Beach Shag Club, Alpha Delta Kappa (chpt. pres. 1978-80, dist. sec. 1980-82), Beta Phi Mu, Phi Kappa Phi. Republican. United Methodist. Avocations: square, ballroom and shag dancing, oil painting, traveling, reading, skiing. Home: 4026 B Tanglewood Trl Chesapeake VA 23325-2252

COLLINS, CHRISTOPHER CARL, manufacturing executive; b. Schenectady, N.Y., May 20, 1950; s. Gerald Edward and Constance (Messier) C.; m. Margaret Elizabeth Busby Cox, May 20, 1972 (div. Apr. 1978); 1 child, Carly Elizabeth; m. Mary Sue Kuhn, Jan. 9, 1988; children: Caitlin Christine, Cameron Christopher. BSME, N.C. State U., 1972; MBA, U. Ala., 1975. Sales engr. Westinghouse Elec. Corp., Birmingham, Ala., 1972-76, market rsch. analyst Buffalo, 1976-77, mgr. market planning, 1978-79, mgr. gearing divsn., 1980-82; pres., chmn., CEO Nuttall Gear Corp., Niagara Falls, N.Y., 1983-97; pres. Nuttall Gear, LLC, Niagara Falls, 1997-98; v.p. corp. devel. Wilson Greatbatch Ltd., Clarence, N.Y., 1999; chmn. bd., CEO, Bloch Industries LLC, Rochester, N.Y., 1999—; chmn. bd. Zepto Metrix Corp., Buffalo, 1999—; treas. Oakwood Classic & Custom Woodworks, Ltd., Rochester, 2000—, Volland Electric Equipment Corp., Buffalo, 2001—; v.p. Easom Automation Sys., Detroit, 2003—. Treas. Frontier Indsl. Supply, Buffalo, 2001—, Mead Supply, Buffalo, 2002—; chmn. Niagara Machinery Corp., Wilson, NY; mem. small bus. adv. coun. Fed. Res. Bank, NY, 1992—95. Bd. dirs. Kenmore Mercy Hosp., 1986-93; mem. ho. of dels. United Way, Buffalo, 1986-2003; mem. Buffalo Fin. Planning Com., 1994; exec. bd. dirs. Greater Niagara Frontier coun. Boy Scouts Am., 1998—; Rep. and Conservative candidate for U.S. Congress, 1998; mentor Ctr. for Entrepreneurial Leadership, SUNY, 1999—. Mem. Chief Execs. Orgn., World Pres.'s Orgn., Young Pres. Orgn. (chmn. edn. com. 1988-89, chpt. chmn. 1989-90, chmn. membership 1990-91, chmn. exec. com. 1991-96), Brookfield Country Club, Holimont Ski Club. Republican. Roman Catholic. Avocations: golf, skiing, aviation. Home: 9660 Cobblestone Dr Clarence NY 14031-1576 Office: Bloch Industries LLC 140 Commerce Dr Rochester NY 14623-3592 E-mail: ccc9660@prodigy.net.

COLLINS, CHRISTOPHER MICHAEL, engineering educator; b. Park Ridge, Ill., Oct. 1, 1971; s. William Gerard and Beverly Marie Collins; m. Belinda Gail Enders, July 1, 1994. BS in Engring. Sci., Pa. State U., 1993; PhD in Bioengineering, U. Pa., Phila., 1999. Contbr. articles to profl. jours. Choir dir. Washingtonboro (Pa.) United Meth. Ch., 2000—02. Mem.: IEEE, Internat. Soc. for Magnetic Resonance in Medicine. Office: Penn State Center for NMR Research H066 500 University Dr Hershey PA 17033

COLLINS, CURTIS ALLAN, oceanographer; b. Sept. 16, 1940; s. Ralph Charlie and Noma Lovella (Buckley) C.; m. Judith Ann Petersen, Dec. 22, 1962; children: Nathaniel Christopher and Hillary Victoria. BS, U.S. Mcht. Marine Acad., 1962; MS, Oreg. State U., 1964, PhD, 1967. Instr. Chapman Coll. (Calif.) in Barcelona, Spain, 1964; 3d mate on ship Reynolds Metals, Corpus Christi, Tex., 1967-68; rsch. scientist Govt. of Can., Nanaimo, B.C., 1968-70; ocean engr. Cities Svc. Oil, Tulsa, 1970-72; program dir. NSF, Washington, 1972-87; prof. dept. oceanography Naval Postgrad. Sch., Monterey, 1987—, chmn., 1987-94, faculty chmn., 2002. Guest investigator Woods Hole Oceanographic Instn. (Mass.), 1983; commr. Moss Landing Harbor Dist., 1993-94, pres. 1994. vis. prof. U. Calif., Santa Cruz, 1998. Oceanography editor Geophys. Rsch. Letters, 1996-98. Capt. USNR, ret. Decorated Armed Forces Res. Def. medal; recipient Admiral E.S. Land award Dept. Commerce, 1962, Meritorious Svc. award NSF, 1987, grad. fellow NSF, 1963-64, Fulbright fellow Instituto Investigaciones Oceanológicas U. Autonomia de Baja, Calif., 1994-95. Mem. Am. Geophys. Union (Oceans Scis. award 1985, pres. ocean scis. sect. 1993-94, chair editl. bd. 2002--), Ocean Soc. Japan. Home: 24010 Ranchito Del Rio Ct Salinas CA 93908-9652 Office: Naval Postgrad Sch Code Occo-833 Dyer Rd Rm 331 Monterey CA 93943 E-mail: collins@nps.navy.mil.

COLLINS, DANIEL FRANCIS, lawyer; b. N.Y.C., Mar. 5, 1942; s. Daniel Joseph and Madeline Elizabeth (Berger) C.; m. Margaret Mary Heyden, Jan. 15, 1966; children: Matthew C., Elizabeth C. BA in History and Polit. Sci., Hofstra U., 1964; JD, Am. U., 1967. Bar: D.C. 1968. Law clk. to Hon. E. Barrett Prettyman U.S. Ct. Appeals, Washington, 1967-68; assoc. Ross, Marsh & Foster, Washington, 1970-74, mem., 1974-78; ptnr. Brackett & Collins, P.C., Washington, 1978-87; v.p. regulatory law The Coastal Corp., Washington, 1987-2001; sr. v.p., dep. gen. counsel El Paso Corp., Washington, 2001—. Office: El Paso Corp Ste 750 555 11th St NW Washington DC 20004 E-mail: daniel.collins@elpaso.com.

COLLINS, DANIEL W. accountant, educator; b. Marshalltown, Iowa, Sept. 1, 1946; s. Donald E. and Lorine R. (Metge) C.; m. Mary L. Packer, June 27, 1970; children— Melissa, Theresa BBA with honors, U. Iowa, 1968, PhD, 1973. Asst. prof. acctg. Mich. State U., East Lansing, 1973-76, assoc. prof., 1976-77; vis. assoc. prof. U. Iowa, Iowa City, 1977-78, assoc. prof., 1978-81, prof., 1981-83, Murray chaired prof. acctg., 1983-88, Henry B. Tippie prof. of acctg., 1989—; vis. IBM prof. bus. Fuqua Sch. Bus., Duke U., 1988-89, chmn. dept. acctg., 1995—. Mem. Fin. Acctg. Stds. Adv. Coun., acad. adv. bd. Deloitte & Touche; mem. Arthur Andersen doctoral dissertation awards com., 1996—; bd. dirs. Ira B. McGladrey Inst., U.S. Bank, Iowa City, Christian Ret. Svcs., Iowa City. Assoc. editor Acctg. Rev., 1980-86; mem. editl. bd. Jour. Acctg. and Econs., 1978—, Jour. Acctg. Rsch., 2001—; contbr. articles to profl. jours. 2d lt. U.S. Army, 1972 Recipient All Univ. Tchr. scholar award Mich. State U., 1976, Gilbert Maynard Excellence in Tchg. award U. Iowa, 1985, Collegiate Tchg. award, 1998; Univ. Faculty scholar U. Iowa, 1980-82, Faculty Excellence award Iowa Bd. Regents, 2000, Outstanding Acctg. Alumnus award, U. Iowa, 2003. Mem. Am. Acctg. Assn. (disting. vis. faculty mem. Doctoral Consortium 1980, 89, dir. Doctoral Consortium 1987, program dir. ann. conv. 1988, dir. publs. 1989-91, exec. com. 1989-91, Outstanding Acctg. Educator award 2001), Acctg. Rschrs. Internat. Avocations: jogging, gardening. Home: 11 Wildberry Ct NE Iowa City IA 52240-9173 Office: U Iowa Coll Bus W252 PBAB Iowa City IA 52242-1000

COLLINS, DAVID BROWNING, religious institution administrator; b. Hot Springs, Ark., Dec. 18, 1922; s. Charles Frederick and Agnes Elizabeth (George) C.; m. Maryon Virginia Moise, Oct. 14, 1945; children: Melissa, Christopher, Matthew, Geoffrey. BA, U. of the South, 1943, BD, 1948, STM, 1962, DD, 1974. Ordained to ministry Episcopal Ch. as deacon, 1948, as priest, 1949. Rector St. Andrew's Episc. Ch., Marianna, Ark., 1948-53; priest-in-charge Holy Cross Episc. Ch., West Memphis, Ark., 1949-53; chaplain and assoc. prof. of religion U. of the South, Sewanee, Tenn., 1953-66; dean Cathedral of St. Philip, Atlanta, 1966-84; exec. dir. Windsong Ministries, Inc., 1984—; pres. House of Deps. Episcopal Ch., 1985-91. Trustee Ch. Pension Fund, N.Y.C., 1976-88; mem. Bd. of Clergy Deployment, N.Y.C., 1971-76. Contbr. articles to profl. jours. Pres. Christian Council of Met. Atlanta, 1977-78; chaplain Atlanta Braves Booster Club, 1966-84. Served to lt. (j.g.) USNR, 1943-46. Episcopalian. Avocation: baseball. Home and Office: 132 Hearthstone Dr Woodstock GA 30189-5298

COLLINS, DELORIS WILLIAMS, secondary school educator; b. Jackson, Miss., Oct. 24, 1959; d. Eddie (Stepfather) and Mary Louise Lewis; m. Bobby Collins, July 18, 1981; children: Garrian V., Bryan L. AA, Hinds Jr. Coll., Jackson, Miss., 1987; BBA in Office Adminstrn., Jackson State U., 2000. Circulation clk. Eudora Welty Libr., Jackson, Miss., 1989—91; tech. specialist/libr. circulation clk. H.T. Sampson Libr. Jackson State U., 1991—93; libr. media tech. specialist Canton Pub. Schs. Dist., 1993—96; with U.S. Postal Svc., Jackson, 1999—2000; substitute tchr. Jackson Pub. Schs. Dist., Jackson, 2000—. Cert. facilitator Family Connections, Jackson, 1999; seminar and workshop condr. Author: They Are Throwing Rocks, 1997, Chasing After the Wind, 1998, Anointed Hyms-Poems, 1999, Treasured Recipes, 1999, Marriage in Yesterday and Today Society: There is Hope, Its All in the Lord, 2000. Nominee Poet of the Yr., 2003; named to Wall of Tolerance, Civil Rights Meml. Ctr., 2003. Mem.: Internat. Soc. of Poets (hon.). Avocations: reading, cooking. Home: 403 Stillwood Dr Jackson MS 39206

COLLINS, DENNIS ARTHUR, foundation executive; b. Yakima, Wash., June 9, 1940; s. Martin Douglas and Louise Constance (Caccia) C.; m. Mary Veronica Paul, June 11, 1966; children: Jenifer Ann, Lindsey Kathleen. BA, Stanford U., 1962, MA, 1963; LHD, Mills Coll., 1994, Univ. San Diego. Assoc. dean admissions Occidental Coll., Los Angeles, 1964-66, dean admissions, 1966-68, dean of students, 1968-70; headmaster Emma Willard Sch., Troy, N.Y., 1970-74; founding headmaster San Francisco U. High Sch., 1974-86; pres. James Irvine Found., San Francisco, 1986—2002; ret. Trustee Coll. Bd., N.Y.C., 1981-85, Ind. Ednl. Svcs., Princeton, N.J., 1981-85, Calif. Assn. Ind. Schs., L.A., 1982-86, Branson Sch., 1987-89, Aspen Inst. Nonprofit Sector rsch. Fund, 1992—; chmn. bd. So. Calif. Assn. Philanthropy, L.A., 1989-91, No. Calif. Grantmakers, 1987-90; dir. Rebuild L.A., 1992-93. Trustee Cathedral Sch. for Boys, San Francisco, 1976-82, Marin County Day Sch., Corte Madera, Calif., 1978-84, San Francisco Exploratorium, 1984-86, Ind. Sector, Washington, 1987-95, Am. Farmland Trust, Washington, 1992—; bd. dirs., vice chmn. Children's Hosp. Found., San Francisco, 1984-86; chmn. bd. dirs. Coun. for Cmty. Based Devel., Washington, 1989-92. Mem. Council on Founds. Clubs: World Trade, University; California (L.A.). Democrat. Episcopalian. Home: 432 Golden Gate Ave Belvedere Tiburon CA 94920-2447

COLLINS, DENNIS GLENN, mathematics educator; b. Gary, Ind., June 26, 1944; s. Glenn and Irene Martha (Richman) C.; m. Barbara Jean Hamilton, July 14, 1979; 1 child, Glenn H. BA, Valparaiso U., 1966; MS, Ill. Inst. Tech., 1970, PhD, 1975. Temp. instr. Mich. State U., East Lansing, 1975-76; instr. U. New Orleans, 1976-79; asst. prof. Valparaiso (Ind.) U., 1979-82; from asst. prof. to prof. math. U. P.R., Mayaguez, 1982—, chmn. math. dept. pers. com., 1994-95. Vis. scholar, U. P.R., Mayaguez, 2003—; vis. assoc. prof. dept. math. Mich. State U., 1988-89; judge computer sci. 38th Internat. Sci. and Engring. Fair, San Juan, P.R., 1987; presenter optical echo theory of quasars Internat. Sem. Math. Investigation, Rio Piedras, P.R., 1995, organizer 15th conf., 2000, presenter 16th conf., 2001, 17th conf., 2002, 18th conf., 2003; Am. Math. Soc., Orlando, Fla., 1996; presenter 8th Quadrennial Internat. Conf. on Graph Theory, Kalamazoo, 1996, 9th, 2000, 1st Biennial Energy Analysis Conf., U. Fla., Gainesville, 1999, 2d conf., 2001. Created copyrighted set postcards of 120 mathematicians and physicists, 1983-2001; composed short Columbus Cantata and short Spaceship Cantata, Short Cosmic Cantata, 2001; contbr. articles to conf. proceedings. NSF fellow, 1966-67; vis. scholar Mich. State U., 1988-89, 96-97. Mem.: N.Y. Acad. Scis., U.S. Patents, 2003, Soc. Indsl. and Applied Mathematicians (presenter 50th anniversary, ann. meeting 2002), Am. Math. Soc. (presenter ann. meetings 1985—87, informatics and cybernetics 1990, presenter Internat. Symposium on Econ. Modelling, World Bank 1994, Detroit meeting 1997, dialog com. to rector 1997—2003, poster session 10th internat. math. conf. Chgo. 1998, invited address 5th internat. Conf. on info. rsch.), Internat. Soc. for Optical Engring., Soc. Photo-optical Instrumentation Engrs.,

Internat. Soc. for Sys. Sci. (presenter 1998, 2000), Sigma Xi (treas. local chpt. 2000—03, del. annual mtg. 2001, pres. 2003). Lutheran. Home: 7108 Grand Blvd Hobart IN 46342-6628 Office: U PR Dept Math Mayaguez PR 00681

COLLINS, DIANA JOSEPHINE, psychologist; b. Potsdam, N.Y., Apr. 27, 1944; d. Philip Joseph and Janet Dorothy (Lynke) C.; m. Philip J. Audett, June 12, 1999. Grad. with high honors, SUNY; PsyD, Mass. Sch. Profl. Psychology, 1981. Psychologist N.H. Hosp., Concord, 1974-79, asst. dir. forensic unit, 1979-80; founder, dir. Victim/Witness Svc. Country of Hillsborough, Manchester, N.H., 1980-84; pvt. practice Bedford, N.H. Adj. assoc. prof. U. N.H., 1974; adj. assoc. prof. Antioch Coll. of New Eng. Mem. APA, Assn. Applied Psycholphysiology and Biofeedback, Biofeedback Soc. Am. (cert.), N.H. Psychol. Assn. (bd. dirs.), Mass. Psychol. Assn., Ea. Psychol. Assn., Internat. Assn. Psychotherapists and Counselors, Am. Assn. Female Execs. Roman Catholic. Home: 17 Pine Ln Warner NH 03278-4630 Office: 40 S River Rd Unit 63 Bedford NH 03110-6724 E-mail: audco17@aol.com.

COLLINS, DONNELL JAWAN, lawyer; b. Nov. 13, 1970; s. Artis Lee and Ruby Collins; m. Tonia Yvette Holloway, Nov. 28, 1998; 1 child, Demi Arnell. BA summa cum laude, Morehouse Coll., 1993; JD, Emory U., 1996. Bar: Ga. 1996, Supreme Ct. Ga. 1998, U.S. Dist. Ct. (no. dist.) Ga. 1998, U.S. Ct. Appeals (11th cir.) 1998. Atty. King & Spalding, Atlanta, 1996-97; assoc. Zirkle and Hoffman, LLP, Atlanta, 1997—2001, ptnr., 2001—. Mem.: ABA, ATLA, Ga. State Bar Assn., Atlanta Bar Assn., Phi Delta Phi, Phi Beta Kappa Soc. Avocations: geography, travel, philosophy. Office: Zirkle and Hoffman LLP 5 Concourse Pkwy NE Ste 2900 Atlanta GA 30328-6104

COLLINS, DOUG See COLLINS, PAUL DOUGLAS

COLLINS, DUANE E. manufacturing executive; BSME, U. Wis.; postgrad., Harvard U. Sales engr. Parker Hannifin Corp., Cleve., 1961, gen. sales mgr., ops. mgr. hose products divsn., gen. mgr., 1973-76, v.p. ops. fluid connectors group, 1976-80, pres. fluid connectors group, 1980-83, corp. v.p., 1983-87, pres. internat., 1987-88, corp. exec. v.p., pres. internat., 1988-92, vice chmn., 1992-93, CEO, 1993—2001, chmn., 2001—. Bd. dirs. Nat. City Bank, Sherwin-Williams Co., MeadWestvaco, MTD Holdings. Office: Parker Hannifin Corp 6035 Parkland Blvd Cleveland OH 44124-4141

COLLINS, E. DORLEE (E. DORLEE WOODYARD), business counselor; b. Crown City, Ohio, July 10, 1954; d. Walter Woodyard and Ruth Evelyn Simmons; m. Gary Lee Collins, Nov. 27, 1971 (div. 1978); children: Angela Nycole, Tiara Dorlee Elizabeth Collins. AA, We. Wyo. Coll., 1986; BS in Women's Studies, U. Utah, 1991, BS in Psychology, 1994. Cert. hypnotherapist, child protection svcs./youth and family, adult protection; cert. bus. counselor. Rsch. asst. U. Utah, Salt Lake City, 1988-91; sales mgr. Life and Safety, Sandy, Utah, 1992-94; edn. specialist ITT Tech. Inst., 1994-95; br. mgr. SOS Staff Svcs., Inc., Jackson Hole, Wyo. br., Salt Lake City, 1995-96; social worker Wyo. Dept. Family Svcs., Rock Springs, 1997-99; bus. counselor Small Bus. Devel. Ctr., U. Wyo., Rock Springs, 2000—02; faculty Inst. for Social Rsch. U. Mich., Ann Arbor, 2002—; social worker Lincare, Inc., Rock Springs, Wyo. Mem. Nat. Inst. Survey Rsch. U. Mich., Ann Arbor, 2002. Named Miss Regal USA, Amarillo, Tex., 1981, Ms. Wyo. USA, 1997. Mem. AAUW, LWV, Psi Chi. Mem. Lds Ch. Avocations: reading, skiing.

COLLINS, EILEEN LOUISE, economist; b. Dec. 15, 1942; d. Theodore Milton and Louise Alma (Sweet) C. BA (regional scholar), Bryn Mawr Coll., 1964; MA, U. Wis., 1967, PhD, 1975. Lectr. dept. econs. U. Waterloo, Ont., Can., 1971-73; asst. prof. dept. econs. Barnard Coll., N.Y.C., 1975-76, Fordham U., N.Y.C., 1976-78; economist NSF, Washington, 1978-86, sr. economist, 1986-91, program dir., 1991-94, sr. coord., mgr. assessment studies, 1995—2003; dir., analyst Sci. and Tech. Studies, Washington, 2003—. Acting asst. dir. Social and Bevavioral Scis. Office of Sci. and Tech. Policy, Exec. Office of President of the United States, 1994. Editor: American Jobs and the Changing Industrial Base, 1984, The Economics of American Universities: Management, Operations, and Fiscal Environment, 1990; contbr. papers and reports in field. Recipient NSF Outstanding Performance award, 1979, 81, 83, 84, 91, 93, 95, 96, 97, 98, Office of Sci. and Tech. Policy award for extraordinary svc. to the USA, 1994, NIMH fellow, 1969-71; Nat. Inst. Public Affairs fellow, 1966-67. Mem. AAAS, Am. Econ. Assn., Nat. Economists Club (v.p. seminars 1986). Office: Sci and Tech Studies 1301 20th St NW #502 Washington DC 20036-6002 E-mail: drel.collins@verizon.net.

COLLINS, EILEEN MARIE, astronaut; b. Elmira, N.Y., Nov. 19, 1956; d. James Edward and Rose Marie (O'Hara) C.; m. James Patrick Youngs, Aug. 1, 1987. AS in Math., Sci., Corning C.C., 1976; BA in Math., Econs., Syracuse U., 1978; grad., USAF Undergrad. Pilot Tng., Vance AFB, Okla., 1979, USAF Test Pilot Sch., Edwards AFB, Calif., 1990; MS in Ops. Rsch., Stanford U., 1986; MA in Space Systems Mgmt., Webster U., 1989. Commd. 2d lt. USAF, 1978, advanced through grades to col., 1993, instr. pilot 71st flight tng. wing, 1979-82, aircraft comdr. 86th mil. airlift squadron Travis AFB, Calif., 1983-85; asst. prof. math. USAF Acad., Colorado Springs, Colo., 1986-89; astronaut Johnson Space Ctr. NASA, Houston, 1990—. Second in command, space shuttle Discovery, 1995, space shuttle Atlantis, 1997; comdr. space shuttle, Columbia, 1999. Decorated Air Force Commendation medal with one oak leaf cluster, Meritorious svc. medal with one oak leaf cluster, Air Force Expeditionary medal, Def. Meritorious Svc. medal, French Legion Honor Disting. Flying Cross; 1st woman pilot of the Space Shuttle; 1st woman comdr.

COLLINS, FLEDA MAE, librarian; b. Bolton, Miss., July 29, 1935; d. Norman Wingate and Sadie Lee (Dawson) McElvoy; m. James Felix Collins, May 31, 1968; 1 child, Rebecca Louise Collins Teatro. BA, Miss. Coll., Clinton, 1957, MEd, 1971; MLS, North Texas State U., 1975. Cert. Media Spl. and Libr. Sec. 1st Bapt. Ch., Clinton, 1957; sec. & youth dir. Ruleville (Miss.) Bapt. Ch., 1957-58; sec. Bapt. Sem. Ext. Dept., Jackson, Miss., 1958-62; clk. State Dept. Edn., Jackson, 1962-64; order libr. Miss. Coll. Libr., Clinton, 1964-68, head libr. Hardy Jr. High, Jackson, 1968-71; elem. libr. Jackson Pub. Schs., 1971-93, ret., 1993. Mem. Profl. Educators of Jackson (bd. mem. 1987), Kappa Delta Pi, Alpha Delta Kappa (v.p. 1986-88, pres. 1988-90). Southern Baptist. Avocations: traveling, crafts, baking. Home: 7750 Melanie Cir Talbott TN 37877-8951

COLLINS, FRANCIS S. medical research scientist; BS, U. Va., 1970; PhD, Yale U., 1974; MD, U. N.C., Chapel Hill, 1977. Former staff mem. Howard Hughes Med. Inst., U. Mich. Med. Ctr., Ann Arbor; now dir. Nat. Human Genome Rsch. Inst. NIH, Bethesda, Md. Co-recipient Gairdner Found. Internat. award for work on cystic fibrosis, 1990. Mem. NAS. Office: Nat Human Genome Rsch Inst 31 Center Dr Msc2152 Rm 4b09 Bethesda MD 20892-0001

COLLINS, FRANCIS WINFIELD, chemicals executive; b. NYC, Jan. 5, 1927; s. Francis W. and Lillian A. (Schaeffler) C.; m. Rhoda Henry Collins, May 30, 1952; children: Sharon, Russell, Margaret, Cynthia, Wayne. BA cum laude, Amherst Coll., 1948; MA, Columbia U., 1949. From control chemist to asst. dept. head Merck and Co., Rahway, N.J., 1949-60; tech. rep. E.I. DuPont de Nemours, Wilmington, Del., 1960-65, from supt. to sr. market rschr. Gibbstown, N.J., 1965-85; ret., 1985. Pres. Brandywine Cons., Inc., Wilmington, Del., 1985—; tchg. and tutoring, 1985—. Chair Hanby Civic Assn., Wilmington, 1978-80, West Milford (N.J.) Adv. Commn., 1969; chpt. chair Svc. Corps Ret. Execs., 1991-93, regional mktg. coord., 1994-95, regional computer coord., 1994-96 (spl. award 1996, Platinum award 1997); counselor Internat. Exec. Svc. Corps, 1993—; asst. chmn. bd. trustees Minikin Opera, Wilmington, 1985-94. Recipient Platinum award, Svc. Corp. Ret. Execs., 1998. Avocations: world travel, sailing, camping, gardening. Home and Office: Apt 312 3025 Chesbrough Blvd Rock Hill SC 29732

COLLINS, FRANK, JR., dentist, educator; b. Jackson, Miss., Mar. 1, 1965; s. Frank Collins, Sr. and Emma H. Collins. BS in Biology, U. So. Miss., 1988; DDS, Howard U., 1996; cert. advanced edn. in gen. dentistry, Luth. Med. Ctr., Bklyn., 2002. Instr. Hinds C.C., Raymond, Miss., 1997—2000; gen. practice resident St. Mary's Hosp., Waterbury, Conn., 2001. Mem.: ADA (Am. Dental Assn.), Acad. Gen. Dentistry. Avocations: music, jogging.

COLLINS, FRANK CHARLES, JR., industrial and service quality specialist; b. El Paso, Tex., Oct. 29, 1927; s. Frank Charles Sr. and Lucile Ellen (Reynolds) C.; m. Esther Frances Shiell, Aug. 16, 1948; children: Lucile Frances Collins Silveira, Sue Ellen Collins Hekman, Francene C. Collins Newman, Virginia Ann Collins Friesen, Melissa Esther Collins Fry, Laura Beth Collins Leach, Frank Charles III. BA in Sociology, La. State U., 1949; grad., Naval War Coll., 1966; postgrad., UCLA, 1976-77; PhD, Kennedy Western U., 1995. Enlisted USNR, 1945-46; commd. ensign USN, 1951, advanced through grades to rear adm. (upper half), 1951; comdr. U.S.S. LSS(L) 65, 1953-54, U.S.S. Saline CTY LST 1101, San Diego, 1957-59, U.S.S. John A. Bole DD 755, 1967-69; ops. officer Naval Support Activity, Danang, Vietnam, 1966-67; comdr. COMDESRON Nine, San Diego, 1974-76, Devel. and Tng. Center/Fleet Maintenance Assistance Group, Pacific, San Diego, 1976-78; chief Navy Sect., Army Mission, Mil. Assistance Adv. Group, Iran, 1978-79; dir. logistics plans Office Chief of Naval Ops., Washington, 1979-81; exec. dir. quality assurance Def. Logistics Agy., 1981-83, ret., 1983; v.p. quality ops. Avco Corp. and Textron, Inc., Providence, 1983-86; pres. Frank Collins Assocs. Survival Twenty-One, Alexandria, Va., 1987—. Chmn. bd. dirs. The Collins Group Internat., Inc., Washington. Author: Sixteen Steps in Establishing a Quality Improvement Process, 1986, Quality—The Ball in Your Court, 1987, Twenty Steps in Establishing a Quality Culture, 1991, Chiko and the Guv, 1992; contbg. author: Energy and Sea Power, 1981, Vietnam: The Naval Story, 1986; contbr. articles to profl. jours. Mem. exec. bd. Iran Am. Friendship Found., Washington, 1985—; bd. dirs. Malcolm Baldridge Nat. Quality Award Consortium, Milw., 1988-92, Nat. Found. Inc., Washington, 1988-93; mem. pastor's cabinet, lay preacher Alexandria Free Meth. Ch., 1990-93. Decorated Legion of Merit (2), Bronze Star, Navy Commendation medal (all with Combat V), Def. Superior Service medal, Def. Meritorious Service medal., Def. Disting. Service medal. Mem. Am. Soc. for Quality Control (chmn. aerospace and def. div. 1987-88, vice chmn. energy div. 1989-91), Assn. for Quality and Participation, Ret. Officers Assn., U.S. Naval Inst., Navy League, Nat. Security Indsl. Assn., Navy Surface Warfare Assn. Republican. Avocations: writing poetry, quality management doctrine, history of iranian revolution and the overthrow of the shah. *In an era now characterized by humanism and relativism, I thank God for having grown up in a period which recognized absolutes—absolutes of morality, self-discipline, individual effort, and national leadership and purpose. I pray we can set an example of concern for others, and as a nation set goals which can bring about a revival of justice, peace, morality and belief in a sovereign God and risen Christ.*

COLLINS, GALEN ROBERT, technology educator; b. Elkhart, Ind., Oct. 2, 1957; s. Galen Franklin and Ann Elizabeth C.; m. Melissa Ferguson, June 22, 1991; 1 child, Robert Jay. BBA, Fla. Internat. U., 1978, MS in Hotel Food Svc. Mgmt., 1980; PhD in Ednl. Tech., Nova Southeastern U., 2002, EdS in Ednl. Tech., 2000. Summer mgmt. trainee Walt Disney World, Orlando, Fla., 1979; asst. restaurant mgr. Tony Roma's, Miami, Fla., 1980-81; controller Indian Trail Country Club, Royal Palm Beach, Fla., 1981-82; asst. exec. mgr. Palm Beach (Fla.) Hilton, 1982-83; product tng. specialist Auditel Lodging Mgmt. Sys., Vienna, Va., 1983-84; program mgr. Robert Barrie & Ptnrs., Washington, 1984-85; asst. prof. Johnson & Wales U., Providence, 1985-87; from asst. prof. to prof. No. Ariz. U., Flagstaff, 1987—2003, assoc. dean, 1999—, prof., 2003—. Chairperson Abacus Internet Svcs., Phoenix, 1996—. Author: Hospitality Information Technology, 1992, 5th edit., 2003, Overcoming the Customer Service Syndrome, 2003; founding pub. Internat. Jour. Hospitality Info. Technology, 1998-2003; contbr. articles to profl. jours. Bd. dirs. Epiphany Episcopal Ch., Flagstaff, 1993-96; invited mem. Ariz. Town Hall, Phoenix, 1997—. Recipient Most Prolific Author award Hospitality Rsch. Jour., 1992. Mem. Hospitality Internat. Tech. Assn. (founding, pres. 1992-97), Assn. Computing Machinery, Hospitality Fin. Tech. Profls., Coun. Hotel Restaurant Instl. Edn., Lions (charter, pres. 1996, Lion of Yr. 1999), Continental Country Club (bd. dirs. 1995-99), Phi Theta Kappa, Phi Kappa Phi. Avocations: golfing, racquetball. Home: 2631 N Elk Run Flagstaff AZ 86004 Office: No Ariz U Nau Box 5638 Flagstaff AZ 86011 E-mail: galen.collins@nau.edu.

COLLINS, GEORGE WILLIAM, II, astrophysics educator, writer; b. Waukegan, Ill., July 18, 1937; s. William George and Louise Van Horsen (Jack) C.; m. Barbara A. Bartels, Dec. 28, 1961; children: Carol Louise, Deirdre Ann. AB in Physics, Princeton U., 1959; PhD in Astronomy, U. Wis., 1962. Asst. prof. U. Wis., Madison, 1962, 63; from asst. prof. to assoc. prof. Ohio State U., Columbus, 1963-71, prof. astrophysics, 1971-91, prof. emeritus, 1991—. Vis. prof. U. Wis., 1987; adj. prof. Case Western Res. U., 1991—; exec. editor Packart Pub. House, 1980—. Author: The Virial Theorem in Stellar Astrophysics, 1978, Foundations of Celestial Mechanics, 1989, The Fundamentals of Stellar Astrophysics, 1989; also numerous articles. Instr., trainer ARC, Columbus, 1980-90; canoeing coord. Ctrl. Ohio coun. Boy Scouts Am., 1978-91; canoeing instr. Am. Youth Hostels, Columbus, 1978-91. Recipient Silver Beaver award Boy Scouts Am., vigil honor, James E. West Fell.; sr. rsch. fellow (vis.) U. Sussex, 1982, 89, (hon.) U. Glasgow, 1989 Fellow AAAS, Royal Astron. Soc.; mem. Am. Astron. Soc., Internat. Astron. Union, N.Y. Acad. Sci. (life), Ohio Acad. Sci. Avocations: wilderness, canoeing.

COLLINS, GORDON DENT, recording company executive; b. Berkeley, Calif., Mar. 27, 1924; s. Edward Everett and Dorothy Janet C.; m. Louise Norma Krivicich, July 23, 1960; children: Daniel Edward, Patrick Doyle, Christine Anne, Gordon Jr. Student, U. Maine, 1943-44; BSEE magna cum laude, U. Wash., 1948; postgrad., Stanford U., 1960-63. Registered profl. engr., N.Y. Founder, chief executive officer Collins Rec. Co., Los Altos, Calif., 1962—. Assigned to Comissariat à l'energie Atomique, Ctr. Nuclear Studies, France. Served to lt. U.S. Army Signal Corps, 1943-52. Named Sr. of Yr. Elfun Soc., San Jose, Calif., 1980. Mem Soc. Engrs. and Scientists of France, Phi Beta Kappa, Tau Beta Pi, Phi Kappa Psi, Sigma Xi. Clubs: No. Calif. Golf Assn. (Pebble Beach). Achievements include patents in field of nuclear power, solution technology, fast breeder reactors; development of atomic power. Avocations: golf, travel, photography, genealogy. Office: PO Box 934 Los Altos CA 94023-0934

COLLINS, GWENDOLYN BETH, health administrator; b. Akron, Ohio; d. Emmett Samuel and Lillice Elizabeth (Matthews) Shaffer; 1 child, Holly Marie. BA, Case Western Res. U. Exec. dir. Canton Area Regional Health Edn. Network, 1981-88; project dir. Region VII Cancer Registry, Canton, Ohio, 1984-88; program dir. Diabetes Mgmt. Ctr., St. Petersburg, Fla., 1988-89, 92-94, Pasadena Sr. Health Ctr., St. Petersburg, 1995-96; health mgmt. and mktg. cons. Largo, Fla., 1986-88, 95—; practice adminstr. Santiago Morales, MD, P.A., Largo, Fla., 2000—02. Mem. continuing med. edn. com. Aultman Hosp., 1983-88; planner and evaluator Directions for Mental Health, Inc., Clearwater, Fla., 1990-92. Mem. adv. com. Camp Y-Noah, 1985-86. HHS grantee, Canton, 1986-88. Mem. Cancer Control Consortium Ohio (mem. cancer incidence mgmt. com. 1986-87). Republican. Avocations: reading, music, walking. Home and Office: 9508 Cavendish Dr Tampa FL 33626

COLLINS, HARKER, economist, manufacturing executive, publisher, marketing, financial, business and legal consultant; b. Denver, Nov. 24, 1924; s. Clem Wetzel and Marie (Harker) C.; m. Emily Harvey, Aug. 23, 1957; children: Catherine Emily, Cynthia Lee, Constance Marie. BS, U.S. Naval Acad., 1945. Asst. buyer Montgomery Ward & Co., N.Y.C., 1947-51; prodn. mgr. Diamond Hosiery Mills, High Point, N.C., 1953-55; v.p. Vanette Hosiery Mills, Dallas, 1955-59; v.p., dir. Grote Mfg. Co., Madison, Ind., 1959-71; group v.p., gen. mgr. Bendix Corp., South Bend, Ind., 1971-73; pres., dir. Bandag, Inc., Muscatine, Iowa, 1973-78, chief exec. officer, 1974-78; pres., chief exec. officer, bd. dirs. Harker Collins & Co., Lubbock, Tex., 1978-98; pub. newsletters The Economy and You, Update, 1978-96; econ. counsel Automotive Svc. Industry Assn., 1978-91; exec. v.p., bd. dirs. Indsl. Molding Corp., Lubbock, 1993-97; pres., bd. dirs. Indl. Molding Corp., Lubbock, 1997. Instr. U. Denver, 1948; Bd. dirs. Hwy. Users Fedn., 1970-86; chmn. automotive industry liaison com. with Dept. Transp., 1968-86, automotive industry excise tax com., 1964-70, automotive industry tariff com., 1964-70, joint operating com. for automotive trade shows, 1969-77 Mem. Pres.'s Com. Hwy. Safety, 1966-68; Bd. dirs. Iowa Ind. Coll. Found., 1976-86; bd. fellows Northwood Inst., 1974— ; alderman City of Rancho Viejo, Tex., 1980-87. Served to ensign USN, 1945-47; to lt. USNR, 1951-53. Recipient Automotive Industry Leadership award, 1965, 74; Fin. World award as chief exec. of yr., 1975, 77 Mem. Automotive Svc. Industry Assn. (vice chmn. 1966-67, chmn. 1968-69, chmn. heavy duty exec. com. 1969-71, chmn. safety and environ. protection com. 1962-67, 70-78), Automotive Sales Coun. (bd. dirs. 1966-67, sec. 1971-72, v.p. 1972-73, pres. 1973-74), Am. Nat. Standards Inst. (chmn. task force on used vehicle standards 1966-74), Home Products Safety Coun. (pres. 1960-63), Medicine Cabinet Mfg. Coun. (pres. 1960-63, bd. dirs. 1960-68), Truck Safety Equipment Inst. (pres. 1960-63, dir. 1960-68).

COLLINS, HARRIS EDWIN, real estate appraiser; b. Milton, Mass., June 14, 1969; s. Webster Alanson and Anne Katherine (O'Sullivan) C.; m. Melinda Anne Weinkam, Aug. 10, 1991; children: Lily Elizabeth, Everett Fuller. BS, Lehigh U., 1991. Cert. gen. real estate appraiser, Mass., N.H. Summer intern Whittier Ptnrs., Boston, 1988, 90; from sr. real estate appraiser to ptnr. CB Comml./Whittier, Boston, 1991—2003, ptnr., 2003—. Alt. mem. Valuation Internat., Ltd., Atlanta, 1995. Corp. vol. City Yr., Boston, 1994—96. Mem. Real Estate Fin. Assn. (Greater Boston Real Estate Bd.), Appraisal Inst., Nat. Coun. Real Estate Investment Fiduciaries. Republican. Episcopalian. Avocations: skiing, running, hiking. Office: CB Richard Ellis/Whittier Cons & Valuation Group 10 High St Fl 11 Boston MA 02110-1605 E-mail: hcollins@cbre-ne.com.

COLLINS, HARRY DAVID, forensic specialist, mechanical engineer, nuclear engineer, claims consultant; b. Brownsville, Pa, Nov. 18, 1931; s. Harry Alonzo and Cecilia Victoria (Morris) Collins; m. Suzanne DyLong, May 11, 1956; children: Cynthia L., Gerard P. BSME, Carnegie Mellon U., 1954; MS in Physics, U.S. Naval Postgrad. Sch., 1961; postgrad., U.S. Army Command and Gen. Staff Coll., 1970, George Washington U., 1971-72. Registered profl. engr., Miss., La. Commd. 2nd lt. C.E. US Army, 1954, advanced through grades to lt. col., 1969; comdr. 802d Heavy Engr. Constrn. Bn., Republic of Korea, 1972-73; dep. dist. engr. and acting dist. engr. Army Engr. Dist., New Orleans, 1973-75; v.p. deLaureal Engrs., Inc., New Orleans, 1975-78; v.p. Near East mktg. and project mgmt. Kidde Cons., Inc., 1978-82; dir. new bus. devel. and project mgmt. North Africa, Mid. East Am. Mid. East Co., Inc., 1982-84; sr. cons. Wagner, Hohns, Inglis, Inc., 1984-91; chief engr. bd. commrs. Orleans Levee Dist. State of La., 1991-92; pres. Harry D. Collins and Assoc., New Orleans, 1992—. Pres. La. Security Products & QuTech, 1994—97. Contbr. articles to profl. jours. Decorated Legion of Merit, Bronze Star with oak leaf cluster, Vietnam Nat. Commendation medal, Vietnam Tng. Svc. medal. Mem.: NSPE, ASME, Assn. Profl. Genealogists, Nat. Acad. Forensic Engrs. (diplomate, cert.), Am. Arbitration Assn. (mem. panel arbitrators), Am. Nuc. Soc., La. Engring. Soc., Am. Soc. Mil. Engrs., Sigma Xi. Home: 2024 Audubon St New Orleans LA 70118-5518 E-mail: hdc1@cox.net.

COLLINS, HARVEY ARNOLD, art educator, retired; b. High Springs, Fla., Aug. 22, 1927; s. Harvey Arnold and Pansy Henrietta (Bugg) C.; m. Thelma L. Haufler, Apr. 22, 1951; children: Cheryl, Patty, Marc. BFA, U. Fla., 1951, MFA, 1952; LLD (hon.), Olivet Nazarene Coll., Kankakee, Ill., 1982. Assoc. prof. Olivet Nazarene Coll., Kankakee, 1953-58; instr. art Largo (Fla.) Jr. High Sch., 1958-60, Oak Grove Jr. High Sch., Clearwater, Fla., 1960-71; assoc. prof., chair dept. art Olivet Nazarene U., Kankakee, 1971-91, ret., 1991. Adj. instr. art history Sante Fe C.C., Gainesville, Fla., 1994—. Painter murals various univs., hosps., librs. Cpl. Signal Corps, U.S. Army, 1946-47, Korea. Recipient George Washington Tchr. medal Freedoms Found., Valley Forge, Pa., 1962, Disting. Svc. award Coll. Ch., Bourbonnais, Ill., 1986. Mem. Coll. Art Assn., Kappa Delta Pi. Democrat. Avocations: travel, tropical plants, model bldg. Home: 4128 NW 133rd Street Gainesville FL 32606-4719 E-mail: harco5@cs.com.

COLLINS, HENRY JAMES, III, insurance company executive; b. Washington, July 9, 1927; s. Henry James and Genevieve (Downey) C.; m. Josephine Ann McDonald, July 13, 1946; children: Jonathan Alexander, Thomas James, Patricia Ann. B.C.S., Strayers Coll., 1951. With Govt. Employees Ins. Co., Washington, 1945, 46-80, treas., 1965-77, comptroller, 1972-80, v.p., 1977-80, Govt. Employees Life Ins. Co., 1980-83; with Collins Contracting, 1983—. Treas. Govt. Employees Corp., Washington, 1966-74, Govt. Employees Fin. Corp., Washington, 1966-74; asst. treas. Criterion Ins. Co., 1961-70, treas., 1970-72; dir. Md. Ins. Guaranty Fund.; Mem. auditors and comptrollers adv. com. Nat. Assn. Ins. Commrs. Treas. Oakview Citizens Assn., 1952-53. Served with AUS, 1945-46. Mem. Soc. Ins. Accountants, Ins. Accounting and Statis. Assn., Nat. Assn. Ind. Insurers (com. blanks and uniform accounting 1964—, fed. taxes com. 1969-74), Fin. Execs. Inst. (pres. D.C. chpt. 1979-80), Izaak Walton League Am., Am. Legion. Clubs: Bassmasters. Home: 13878 Foggy Bottom Ct Mount Airy MD 21771-4608 Office: 13812 Penn Shop Rd Mount Airy MD 21771-4626

COLLINS, HERBERT, JR., retired elementary education educator; b. Washington, Oct. 27, 1931; s. Herbert Sr. and Marie Eleanor (Paris) C. BS, U. D.C., 1955; MA, George Washington U., 1962; postgrad., Cath. U. Am., 1974; diploma paralegal, Barclay Career Sch., 1991. Tchr. kindergarten-6th grade D.C. Pub. Schs., 1955-80; legal asst. Legal Aid Soc. D.C., 1991; libr. asst. D.C. Pub. Libr. System, 1992—; paralegal, 1991—. Instr. Career Blazers Learning Ctr., 1999-2000. Active Columbia Sr. Ctr., Washington, 1992—; active share program Cath. Charities, Washington, 1992—. With U.S. Army, 1956-58, D.C. N.G. 1958-63. Mem.: Francis L. Cardozo Sr. H.S. Alumni Assn., Inc. (v.p. 1975, pres. 1977—79, 1986—, chmn. scholarship com.). Democrat. Unitarian Universalist. Avocations: organ, piano, museums, voice concerts, drama. Home: 1319 Allison St NW Washington DC 20011-4440

COLLINS, H(ERSCHEL) DOUGLAS, retired physician; b. Caribou, Maine, Jan. 19, 1928; married, 1950, 87; 3 children. BA, U. Maine, 1949; MD, Harvard U., 1952. Diplomate Am. Bd. Internal Medicine. Intern Mass. Gen. Hosp., 1952-53, asst. resident in medicine, 1953-54, 72-73, resident, 1954-55; sr. asst. surgeon USPHS, 1955-57; pvt. practice Caribou, 1957-72, 73-75, 1980-84; group practice, 1984-87. Dir. Ctrl. Maine Family Practice Residency, 1975-79, Maine-Dartmouth Family Practice Residency, 1979-80; gov. Am. Bd. Internal Medicine, 1988-91. Mem. Inst. Med.-Nat. Acad. Sci., AMA, ACP (master). Home: RFD Box 2179 Kingfield ME 04947

COLLINS, J. BARCLAY, II, lawyer, oil company executive; b. Gettysburg, Pa., Oct. 21, 1944; s. Jennings Barclay and Golda Olevia (Hook) C.; m. Janna Claire Fall, June 25, 1966; children: J. Barclay III, L. Christian. AB magna cum laude, Harvard U., 1966; JD magna cum laude, Columbia U., 1969. Bar: N.Y. 1969. Law clk. to presiding judge U.S. Ct. Appeals (2d cir.), N.Y.C., 1969-70; assoc. Cravath, Swaine and Moore, N.Y.C., 1970-78; v.p., asst. gen. counsel City Investing Co., N.Y.C., 1978-84; exec. v.p., gen. counsel Amerada Hess Corp., N.Y.C., 1984—, also bd. dirs. Bd. dirs. Premier Oil plc, Nuvera Fuel Cells Inc. Trustee Bklyn. Hosp., Bklyn.; bd. dirs. United Hosp. Fund N.Y., past gov. Bklyn. Heights Assn. Mem. ABA, N.Y. Bar Assn., N.Y.C. Yacht Club. Clubs: Heights Casino (Bklyn.); Harvard N.Y.C. Office: Amerada Hess Corp Ste 810 1185 Avenue Of The Americas Fl 800 New York NY 10036-2601

COLLINS, J. MICHAEL, retired public broadcasting executive; b. Buffalo, Feb. 17, 1935; s. John Lloyd and Celestine (Buhrle) C.; m. Marilyn Anne Mercer, Aug. 5, 1961; children: Kevin Michael, Timothy David, Sheila Anne, Jeanne Mary, Julie Lynn. BS in Social Scis., Canisius Coll., 1957, LHD (hon.), 1978; postgrad., Mich. State U., 1957-58. Promotion mgr. Western N.Y. Pub. Broadcasting Assn. (Stas. WNED-TV-AM-FM, WNEQ-TV, WNJA-FM), Buffalo, 1959-60, dir. devel., 1961-62, asst. sta. mgr., 1963-65, gen. mgr., 1966-69, pres., 1970-98; sr. cons., 1998-99; ret., 1999. Co-author: ETV: The Farther Vision, 1967. Mem. ho. of dels. United Way of Buffalo and Erie County, 1967-98; trustee Ea. Ednl. Network, 1965-95, treas., 1967-70, exec. com., 1967-74, 78-81, 84-85, 88-90, 92-94, chmn. budget and fin. com., 1967-70, pres., 1971-72, chmn., 1973-74, v.p., 1980-81, 88-90, 92-93, adv. bd. interregional progam svc., 1984-90; trustee Am. Program Svc., 1993-96, exec. com., 1993-96, fin. com., 1994-96; mem. CATV com., devel. adv. com. NAEB; exec. bd. Niagara Frontier coun. Boy Scouts Am., 1971-76; exec. com. Cantalician Ctr., 1978-85; trustee St. Joseph's Collegiate Inst., 1978-85 (mem. steering com. capital campaign, 1998-2000); chmn. PBS Border Sta.Consortium, 1986-88; bd. dirs. PBS, 1972-78, 80-86, vice-chmn., 1975, nat. program policy com., 1990-95; mem. Governance Task Force, 1996; bd. dirs. PBS Enterprises, 1985-90, Nat. Data Cast, Inc., 1989-90; trustee Assn. Am. Pub. TV Stas., 1987-93, exec. com., 1989-93, chmn. nominating com., 1989; mem. Kenmore-Tonawanda Pub. Schs. Bd. Edn., 1974-81, v.p., 1977, pres., 1978; trustee Chautauqua Instn., 1988-96, devel. com., 1989, program com., 1988-95, exec. com., 1989-95, personnel com., 1990-95, mktg. com., 1994-95, fin. com., 1995-96, bldg. and grounds com., 1995-96, edn./youth/recreation com., 1989-

93, 96-97, chmn., 1989-93, mission policy com., 1997-98; bd. dirs. Buffalo Coun. World Affairs, 1994-95, Blue Shield West N.Y., 1990-92; mem. fin. com. St. Amelia Ch., 1990—, mem. stewardship com., 1993—, chmn., 1993-2001, trustee, 2001—; chmn. bd. dirs. John Lodge McHugh Endowment, 2000—. Recipient Focus award Buffalo Courier Express, 1978, Signum Fidei award St. Joseph's Collegiate Inst., 1984, Man of Yr. award Nat. Columbus Day Com., 1985, 92, Matrix award Women in Comm., 1985; named one of 100 Most Influential People in Western N.Y., Bus. First, 1996; inducted into Buffalo Broadcast Pioneers Hall of Fame, 1999. Mem. N.Y. State Ednl. Radio and TV Assn. (trustee, pres. 1964-65, treas. 1963, editor newsletter 1962), Pub. Rels. Assn. Western N.Y. (pres. 1966), Nat. Assn. Ednl. Broadcasters, Canisius Coll. Alumni Assn. (bd. govs. 1960-62, 70-73). Avocations: reading, collecting and tasting wine, photography.

COLLINS, J. ROBERT, trade association administrator; BA, Tex. A&M U. With Dallas Fed. Res. Bank and Pioneer Futures; sr. v.p. El Paso (Tex.) Mcht. Energy, 1997—2001; pres. N.Y. Mercantile Exch., 2001—, mem., 1995—. Office: NY Merchantile Exch One North End Ave New York NY 10282*

COLLINS, JACK, retired state legislator; b. Atlantic City, June 25, 1943; m. Betsy Leeds, 1960; children: Joellen, Dawn, Rebecca, Sean. BA, Glassboro State Coll., 1964, MA, 1967; JD, Rutgers U., 1982. Exec. asst. to pres. Glassboro (N.J.) State Coll., faculty; operator livestock farm; spkr. N.J. Gen. Assembly, Dist. 3, 1986—2001; with Princeton Public Affairs Grp., Inc., 2002—. Asst. majority whip N.J. Gen. Assembly, 1986-87, dep. minority leader, 1990-91, majority leader, 1992-93, chmn. econ. growth agrl. and tourism com., 1988—. Republican. Office: Princeton Public Affairs Grp Princeton Ho 160 W State St Trenton NJ 08608-1102

COLLINS, JACQUELINE Y, state senator; b. McComb, Miss., Dec. 10; Grad. journalism, Northwestern Univ.; MA, Harvard's John F. Kennedy Sch. of Gov.; MA Human Svc. Admin., Spertus Coll.; MA Theol. Studies, Harvard Divinity Sch., 2003. State Senator US Senate, Dist. 16, 2003—; min. of Comm. St. Sabina Cath. Ch., Chgo.; journalist in print, radio and TV; press sec. Congressman Gus Savage. Mem. Appropriations I, Environ. and Energy, Revenue (VC), Revenue Subcommittee on Spl. Issues. Recipient Emmy Award - nominated news editor, CBS-TV/ Chgo.; fellow Legislative Fellow with US Senator Hillary Rodham Clinton. Democrat. Catholic. Office: Capitol Bldg M-108 Springfield IL 62706 Home: 1419 W 76th St Chgo. IL 60620*

COLLINS, JAMES DUFFIELD, marine engineer, editor; b. Logansport, Ind., Dec. 20, 1919; s. Louis Duffield and Gaynelle May (Mobley) C.; m. Barbara Cook, Mar. 12, 1949; children: Barbara Cook Jr., James Duffield II. BS in Marine Engring., U.S. Mcht. Marine Acad., 1946. Process engr. Gen. Motors Corp., Indpls., 1940-44; marine engr. Moore McCormack Lines, N.Y.C., 1946; sr. project engr. rsch. and devel. Gen. Motors Corp., Indpls., 1946-82; editor-at-large Marcel Dekker, Inc., N.Y.C., 1986—. Contbr. author: Materials and Processes, 1985; author: Bowline Knot, 1972; contbr. articles to profl. jours; patentee in field. Lt. (j.g.) USNR, 1946-57, ret. Mem. Soc. Naval Architects and Marine Engrs., Masons. Avocations: music, concert master, orchestra and symphony member. Home and Office: 5228 Bevedere Dr Indianapolis IN 46228-2137 E-mail: jcollin9@ix.netcom.com.

COLLINS, JAMES FRANCIS, toxicologist; b. Balt., Jan. 26, 1942; s. James Murphy and Mary M. (Dolan) C.; m. Barbara Joan Betka, June 21, 1969; children: Chris, Cavan. BS, Loyola Coll., Balt., 1963; PhD, U.N.C., 1968. Diplomate Am. Bd. Toxicology. Fellow NIH, Bethesda, Md., 1968-75; faculty mem., rsch. chemist U. Tex. Health Sci. Ctr. and VA Med. Ctr., San Antonio, 1975-86; staff toxicologist Calif. EPA and Dept. Health Svcs., Oakland, Calif., 1986—. Instr. U. Calif. Berkeley/Extension, 1987-95; instr. U. San Francisco, 1995—. Contbr. numerous articles to profl. jours., publs. Mem. Am. Soc. Biochemistry and Molecular Biology. Democrat. Roman Catholic. Avocation: reading. Home: 822 Rogers Way Pinole CA 94564-2409 Office: Calif EPA 1515 Clay St Fl 16 Oakland CA 94612-1499 E-mail: jcollins@oehha.ca.gov., collins113@juno.com.

COLLINS, JAMES FRANCIS, wildlife artist; b. Haverhill, Mass., Aug. 9, 1952; s. Francis Stanley and Elinor Marie (Clohecy) C.; m. Susan Elaine Woodburn, Sept. 24, 1977. Plumber Stark & Cronk, Groveland, Mass., 1975-84; truck driver various cos., Mass., 1984-89; wildlife artist self employed, Plaistow, N.H., 1989—. Designer State of N.H. Conservation Edition number plate yr. 2000. Recipient award for N.J. Trout Stamp Design, 1995, Ind. Trout Stamp Design, Dept. Fish and Wildlife, 1997, Vt. Waterfowl Stamp Design, 1997, N.H. Migratory Waterfowl Stamp Design, 1998, N.J. Pheasant Stamp Design, 1999, N.H. Migratory Waterfowl Stamp Design, 2002. Mem. Haverhill Artist Assn., Ducks Unltd., NRA (life). Republican. Roman Catholic. Avocations: hunting, fishing, woodworking, hiking, photography. Home: 37 Harriman Rd Plaistow NH 03865-2520

COLLINS, JAMES FRANKLIN, retired ambassador; b. Aurora, Ill., June 4, 1939; AB cum laude, Harvard Coll., 1961; MA, Ind. U., 1964, postgrad., 1964-67, Moscow State U., 1965-66. Asst. prof. history U.S. Naval Acad., 1967-69; vice consul Am. Consulate Gen., Izmir, Turkey, 1969-71; polit. officer European Affairs Bur., U.S. Dept. State, Washington, 1971-73; polit. officer Am. Embassy, Moscow, 1973-75; polit. analyst Bur Intelligence and Rsch. U.S. Dept. State, 1975-78, staff asst., polit. officer Near East Affairs Bur., 1978-82; polit. counselor Am. Embassy, Amman, Jordan, 1982-84; dir. ops. ctr. Dept. State, 1984-87; dir. for intelligence policy Nat. Security Coun., Washington, 1987-88; dep. exec. sec. for Europe and L.Am. U.S. Dept. State, 1988-90; dep. chief of mission Am. Embassy, Moscow, 1990-93; coord. for regional affairs for New Ind. States U.S. Dept. State, 1993-94, sr. coord. Office Amb.-at-Large for New Ind. State, 1994-95, amb.-at-large, spl. advisor to sec. state New Ind. States, 1995-97; U.S. amb. to Russian Fedn., Am. Embassy, Moscow, 1997-2001, ret., 2001; sr. internat. advisor Akin, Gump, Strauss, Hauer & Feld LLP, 2001—. Writer cons., 2001— Address: 1333 New Hampshire Ave NW Washington DC 20036 Business E-Mail: jcollins@akingump.com. E-mail: jfcollins@aol.com.

COLLINS, JEFFREY HAMILTON, research facility administrator, electrical engineering educator; b. Luton, Bedfordshire, Eng., Apr. 22, 1930; came to U.S., 1966; s. Ernest Frederick and Dora Gladys (Bromley) C.; m. Sally Parfitt, Mar. 31, 1956; children: Adrian Vincent, Kevin Allan. BS, London U., 1950, 51, MS, 1954, DSc, 1987; D of Engring. (hon.), Napier, 1997. Chartered engr., chartered physicist, Eng. Sci. staff mem. GEC Hirst Rsch. Ctr., London, 1951-56; sr. staff mem. Ferranti Ltd., Edinburgh, Scotland, 1956-57; sr. lectr. U. Glasgow, Scotland, 1947-66; rsch. engr. Stanford (Calif.) U., 1966-68; dir. phys. sci. Rockwell Internat., Anaheim, Calif., 1968-70; prof. elec. engring., then head dept. U. Edinburgh, 1977-84, emeritus prof., 1984; dir. Automation and Robotics Rsch. Inst., Ft. Worth, 1987-90; sr. tech. specialist Lothian Regional Coun., Edinburgh, Scotland, 1990—93. Specialist adviser to prin. Napier U., Edinburgh, 1994-97, prof., 1995-97; prof. elec. engring. U. Tex., Arlington, 1976-77, 87-90; bd. dirs. advent tech., Edinburgh, 1981-86, chmn. tech. adv. com., 1985-88; mem. Computer Bd. Univs. and Rsch. Couns., Eng., 1985-86, Info. Sys. com. U.K. Univs. Coun., 1992-94; chmn. Edinburgh Parallel Computing Centre, 1990-94; chmn. Scottish Electronics Mfg. Ctr., 1994-96. Editor: Computer-Aided Design of SAW Devices, 1976; editor Conf. Proc. Tech. and Edn., 1988-89; contbr. numerous articles to profl. jours. Recipient Hewlett Packard Europhysics prize European Phys. Soc., Paris, 1979, Bulgin Premiums, Marconi Premium Inst. Electronics and Radio Engr., London, 1974, 77, 78. Fellow Instn. Elec. Engrs. (Eng., chmn. electronics div. 1985-86, counc. mem. 1984-87), IEEE, Royal Soc. Edinburgh, Royal Acad. Engring. (Eng., coun. mem. 1984-87), Inst. Physics (Eng.). Address: 28 Muirfield Park Gullane EH31 2DY Scotland

COLLINS, JO ANNE DILWORTH, secondary school educator; b. Dayton, Ohio, Aug. 20, 1948; d. James Oliver and Madaline Madonna Dilworth; m. David Jerome Collins, Feb. 14, 1981; children: Kathleen Jo, Matthew Charles. BS in Edn., Wright State U., 1970, MEd, 1975. Cert. 7-12 libr. sci. and social studies tchr., K-12 ednl. media tchr., Ohio. Libr. tchr. Hardin-Houston (Ohio) local schs., 1970-71, Cumberland County Schs., Fayetteville, N.C., 1971-74; grad. asst. ednl. media Wright State U., Fairborn, Ohio, 1974-76; libr. tchr. Kettering (Ohio) City Schs., 1976—, dist. media coord., 1998—2002, girls track coach, 1977-81, girls volleyball asst. coach, 1978. Adj. prof. Wright State U., 1993; presenter in field. Contbr. articles to profl. jours. Leader Girl Scouts U.S., Fairborn, 1991-94. Recipient Golden Apple Achiever award Ashland Oil Co., 1993. Mem. ALA, Ohio Edn. Assn., Ohio Ednl. Libr. Media Assn. (chmn. mid. sch. sect.), Greater Miami Valley Ednl. Tech. Coun., Kettering Edn. Assn. (comm. sec., newsletter editor, bldg. rep.). Avocations: gardening, reading, cross-stitch, tennis. Office: Van Buren Mid Sch 3775 Shroyer Rd Kettering OH 45429 E-mail: joanne.collins@kettering.k12.oh.us.

COLLINS, JOAN HENRIETTA, actress; b. London, May 23, 1933; came to U.S., 1938; d. Joseph William and Elsa (Bessant) C.; m. Maxwell Reed (div.); m. Anthony Newley (div.); children: Tara, Sacha; m. Ronald S. Kass, Mar., 1972 (div.); 1 child, Katy; m. Peter Holm (div.); m. Percy Gibson, 2002. Ed., Francis Holland Sch., London; student, Royal Acad. of Dramatic Art. Actor: (films) Cosh Boy, Our Girl Friday, I Believe in You, Girl in the Red Velvet Swing, Sea Wife, Rally Round the Flag Boys, Island in the Sun, Seven Thieves, Road to Hong Kong, Sunburn, The Stud, Game for Vultures, The Bitch, The Big Sleep, The Good Die Young, Land of the Pharoahs, The Bravados, Esther and the King, Warning Shot, The Executioner, Subterfuge, Revenge, Quest for Love, Tales From the Crypt, The Bawdy Adventures of Tom Jones, The Opposite Sex, The Virgin Queen, Quest for Love, Decadence, 1994, In the Bleak Mid-Winter, 1995, The Clandestine Marriage, 1998, The Flintstones-Viva Rock Vegas, 1999, Joseph and His Technicolor Dreamcoat, 1999, Ozzie, 2001, (theater appearances) Jassey, Claudia, The Skin of Our Teeth, The Praying Mantis, The Last of Mrs. Cheyney, The 7th Veil, A Doll's House, Private Lives, 1990, Love Letters, 2000, Over the Moon, 2001; (TV films) Drive Hard, Drive Fast, 1973, The Man Who Came to Dinner, Paper Dolls, 1982, The Wild Women of Chastity Gulch, 1982, The Cartier Affair, The Making of a Male Model, 1983, Her Life as a Man, 1984; (TV miniseries) The Moneychangers, 1976, Sins, 1986, Monte Carlo, 1986, Tonight at 8:30, 1991, Dynasty: The Reunion, 1992; star (TV series) Dynasty, 1981—89; actor: (TV appearance) Faerie Tale Theater (Showtime TV), 1982, Roseanne (ABC), 1993, Mama's Back spl., 1993, Will and Grace, 2000, (TV movie) Annie: A Royal Adventure, 1995, Hart to Hart spl., 1995, Sweet Deception, 1998, These Old Broads, 2000; (TV series) Pacific Palisades, 1997, Guiding Light, 2002, (video spl.) Secrets of Fitness and Beauty, 1994; author: (autobiography) Past Imperfect, 1978, Katy, A Fight for Life, Joan Collins Beauty Book, 1980, (autobiography) Second Act, 1996, (novels) Prime Time, 1988, Love and Desire and Hate, 1991, My Secrets, 1994, Too Damn Famous, 1995, My Friends Secrets, 1999, Star Quality, 2002, Joan's Way, 2002. Decorated Order of Brit. Empire; recipient Emmy nomination, Golden Globe award, Ace award, People's Choice award; named to Order Brit. Empire. Avocations: travel, 18th century art. E-mail: pkeylock@aol.com.

COLLINS, JODA LEE, minister; b. Modesto, Calif., May 3, 1949; s. Joda William and Retha Mae Collins; DD, Universal Bible Inst., 1976; BA, Golden State U., 1980, PhD, 1982; B in Psychology, Calif. State U., 1988. So. Baptist pastor various chs., Calif., Fla., Tenn., 1974—. Author: (book) Dynamic Discipline, 1996, The Biblical Role of Woman in the Church, 1998, How to Successfully Pastor a Difficult Church, 1998, The Fun Presentation of the Book of Revelation, 1999, Every Word Spoken by Jesus on How to do Church, 2000, Thy Kingdom Come, 2002, Introduction to New Testament, 2003. With USAF, 1968—72, Vietnam. Republican. Baptist. Avocations: Karate, water-skiing, bowling, fishing. Fax: 423-629-1399. E-mail: kingwoodbaptist@aol.com.

COLLINS, JOE LENA, retired educator; b. Mt. Pleasant, Tenn., Nov. 18, 1922; d. Morton Daniel and Rosetta Francis C. BS in English, Tenn. Tech., 1949; MA in English, George Peabody, 1968, EdS in English, 1975. Cert. profl. tchr. Sec. to Dr. G.C. English and Dr. C.D. Walton, Mt. Pleasant, Tenn., 1942-46; tchr. Maury Co. Schs., Mt. Pleasant, Tenn., 1949-51, Tenn. Tech., Cookeville, Tenn., 1951; acct. Cookeville Prodn. Credit, Tenn., 1951-52; tchr. Metro Nashville Schs., 1952-88. Lectr. Ret. Learning Vanderbilt U., 2000—. Mem. Shepherd's Ctr. West End Book Club, 1989—2002, Metro Retired Tchrs. Assn., 1988—; chmn. Shepherd's Ctr. West Book Club; com. work Dem. Party, 1980—2003. Mem. AAUW (pres.), Tenn. Art League, Tenn. Writers Alliance, Tenn. Hist. Soc., Women in the Arts, United Meth. Women (Woman of Purpose award). Avocations: reading, writing, painting, sports. Home: 6212 Henry Ford Dr Nashville TN 37209-1738

COLLINS, JOHN ALFRED, retired obstetrician-gynecologist, educator; b. Kitchener, Ont., Can., Oct. 2, 1936; s. John Bandel and Vera Collins; m. Carole Joanne Sedwick West; children: John Bruce, Blayne Linda, Anne Catherine. MD, U. West Ont., 1960. Intern Victoria Hosp., London; resident ob-gyn. U. West Ont., 1961-65; McLaughlin Found. fellow Univ. Coll. Hosp., London; with clin. endocrinology rsch. unit U. Edinburgh, U.K., Middlesex Hosp., London, 1965-67; clin. rsch. fellow Ont. Cancer Found. London Clinic, 1967-76; with dept. ob-gyn. U. West Ont., 1967-77, asst. dean undergrad. edn. faculty medicine, 1975-77; prof., head dept. ob-gyn. Dalhousie U., 1977-83; prof., chmn. dept. ob-gyn. McMaster U., Hamilton, Ont., 1983-93; vis. chair internat. Francqui Found. Brussels Free U., 2000-01. Mem. editl. bd. New Eng. Jour. Medicine, 1991-96, Fertility and Sterility, 1991-96; assoc. editor Human Reprodn., 2003—; contbr. articles to profl. jours. Mem. Royal Coll. Physicians and Surgeons Can., Royal Coll. Obstetricians and Gynecologists U.K., Am. Coll. Obstetricians and Gynecologists, Am. Soc. Reproductive Medicine, Can. Fertility Soc., Soc. Obstetricians and Gynecologists Can. Home: RR#1 Mahone Bay Nova Scotia NS Canada B0J 2EO

COLLINS, JOHN CLEMENTS, physicist, educator; b. Colchester, Eng., Dec. 8, 1949; s. Hugh C. and Florence E. (Seymour) C.; m. Mary A. Brown, Oct. 24, 1991. BA, U. Cambridge, Eng., 1971, PhD, 1975. Postdoctoral fellow Princeton (N.J.) U., 1975-76, asst. prof., 1976-80; from asst. prof. to prof. Ill. Inst. Tech., Chgo., 1980-90; prof. Pa. State U., State College, 1990—. Author: Renormalization, 1984; contbr. articles to profl. jours. Guggenheim fellow, 1986; recipient Humboldt award, 2000. Mem. Am. Phys. Soc. Avocations: music, scottish country dancing, hiking. Office: Pa State U 104 Davey Lab University Park PA 16802-6300 E-mail: collins@phys.psu.edu.

COLLINS, JOHN F. lawyer; b. N.Y.C., Dec. 15, 1948; AB, Fordham U., 1970; JD, U. Chgo., 1973. Bar: N.Y. 1974. Ptnr. Dewey Ballantine, N.Y.C. Mem. ABA, N.Y. State Bar Assn., Assn. Bar of City of N.Y., Phi Beta Kappa. Office: Dewey Ballantine 1301 Avenue Of The Americas New York NY 10019-6022

COLLINS, JOHN TIMOTHY, lawyer; b. Springfield, Mass., Sept. 27; s. Edward T. and Elizabeth Collins; m. Kathleen M. Collins, Nov. 25, 1972. BA history, Holy Cross Coll., 1968; JD, Georgetown U., 1971; LLM taxation, 1976. Bar: Mass 1972, DC 1977. Atty. SEC, Washington, 1972—75; sr. atty. Fed. Res. Bd., Washington, 1975—77; gen. counsel US Senate Banking Com., Washington, 1977—85; mem. covenants and code com. Woodacres Citizens Assn., Bethesda, Md., 1982—83; ptnr. Steptoe & Johnson, Washington, 1985—. 2d. lt. U.S. Army, 1981—82, capt. USAR. Fellow John J. Cummings fellow, Stonier Grad. Sch. Banking, Rutgers U., 1983. Mem.: Fed. Bar Assn. (mem. banking law com. 1982), ABA (mem. banking law com. 1982). Office: 1330 Connecticut Ave NW Washington DC 20036-1704

COLLINS, JOHN W. nurse practitioner, lecturer; b. Chgo., Jan. 13, 1950; s. Joseph Theodore and Christine Pebble (Sisco) C.; m. Julia Marie Watson, July 20, 1984. BS in Civil Engring., U. Tex., 1973; ADN, San Antonio Coll., 1978; MSN, Vanderbilt U., 1983. RN; cert. diabetic educator; cert. adult and family nurse practitioner. Family nurse practitioner Cmty. Health Ctr., Alberta, Ala., 1984-86, Project Concern Internat., San Diego, 1986-87; nurse practitioner Encompass Med. Group, Inc., Kansas City, Mo., 1987-2000; clin. instr. in family nurse practitioner program U. Kans. Sch. Nursing, Kansas City, 1994—2003; lectr. in grad. nurse practitioner program U. Mo. Sch. Nursing, Kansas City, 1994-99, affiliated faculty, 1999—; asst. prof. in family nurse practioner program Ctrl. Mo. State U., 2001—. Contbr. articles to profl. jours. Vol. nurse practioner Duchesne Clinic, Kansas City, 2000--. Mem. ANA (nurses in advanced practice com.), Am. Acad. Nurse Practitioners (Nurse Practitioner of Yr. for State of Mo. 2000), Nat. Orgn. Nurse Practitioner Faculties. Avocations: Aikido, guitar. Office: CMSU Dept Nursing SHC 114 Warrensburg MO 64093 E-mail: jwcollins@cmsu1.cmsu.edu.

COLLINS, JOHN W., JR., retired military officer, technologist, educator; b. Lackawanna, NY, Jan. 27, 1958; m. Simona E Aschenbrenner, Apr. 12, 1980; children: Mary, John III. Basic Cert. in Mgmt., City Colls. Chgo., 1975—76; Assoc. in Sci., N.Y. Regents (now Excelsior) Coll., Albany, 1977—79; BA, Columbia College, Columbia, Mo., 1981—82; M in Pub. Adminstrn., U.Okla., Norman, 1984; Command and Gen. Staff Officer Diploma, U.S. Army Command and Gen. Staff Coll., Ft. Leavenworth, Kans., 1986; PhD, Calif.Coast U., Santa Ana, Calif., 1988; Logistics Exec. Devel.Diploma, U.S. Army Logistics Mgmt. Coll., Ft. Lee, VA, 1991; Air War Coll. Diploma, Air War Coll. Air U., Maxwell AFB, Ala., 1996; EdD, Seton Hall U., South Orange, NJ, 1999. Cert. K-12 Chief Sch. Administr. cert. eligibility 1999, K-12 Prin.and Supr. cert. eligibility 1999, K-12 Sch. Bus. Administr. cert. eligibility 1999, JROTC Mil. Tchr. standard cert. 1998. Enlisted U.S. Army, 1975, rose through ranks to sgt., 1978, commd. 2d lt., 1978, advanced through grades to lt. col., retired, 1998; faculty assoc. Seton Hall U., South Orange, NJ, 1998—; assoc. acad. dir. SetonWorldWide, Seton Hall U., South Orange, NJ, 1998—2001. Edn. tech. cons. Seton Hall U., South Orange, NJ, 1998—. Author: (National Essay Contest) Proud to Serve, 1991 (George Washington Freedom Foundation Medal, 1991), Ordnance Magazine (Bulletin), 1989 (Crimson Pen Award, 1989); contbr. articles to edn. and mil. logistics jours. Vol. Am. Overseas Schs., Germany, 1992—94. Recipient Legion of Merit, President U. S., 1988-1998, Cert. of Appreciation, President U.S., 1998, N. Y. State Conspicuous Svc. Cross (12 awards), Gov. of New York, 1999, N. Y. State Conspicuous Svc. Star (3 awards), Gov. N.Y., 2000, N.J. Meritorious Svc. medal, Gov. of N.J., 2003. Mem.: VFW, ASCD, N.J. Assn. Ednl. Tech., Internat. Soc. for Tech. in Edn., Am. Ednl. Rsch. Assn., Am. Assn. Adult and Continuing Edn., Am. Legion, Disabled Am. Vets. (life). Avocations: fishing, travel. Home: 12 Hunterdon Road West Orange NJ 07052-1604 Office: Seton Hall University 421 Kozlowski Hall 400 S Orange Ave South Orange NJ 07079 Personal E-mail: john.collins6@us.army.mil. Business E-Mail: collinjo@shu.edu.

COLLINS, JUDITH ANN, librarian; b. San Francisco, Aug. 12, 1941; d. Walter George and Dorothy Louise (Eisenhut) Petersen; m. Curtis Allan Collins, Dec. 22, 1962; children: Nathaniel Christopher, Hillary Victoria Collins Edwards. AA, Modesto Jr. Coll., 1962; BS, Oreg. State U., 1967; MS, Cath. U. Am., 1983. Libr. cons. World Bank, Washington, 1983—84; reference libr. Am. Bankers Assn., Washington, 1984—87; libr. cons. Monterey (Calif.) County Libr., 1987—; circulation libr. Nat. Rural Electric Coop. Assn., Washington, 1984—87; tech. svcs. libr. Zimmerman Assocs., Inc., Washington, 1986—87; substitute sch. libr. Fairfax County Schs., Va., 1986—87; media libr. Hartnell CC, Salinas, Calif., 1987—, instr., 1988—. Cons. AID, 1984—85. Election ofcl. Fairfax Electoral Bd. (Va.), 1980—87, Monterey County Electoral Bd., 1987—; ruling elder Presbyn. Ch., Springfield, Va., 1981—83. Mem.: ALA, Calif. Library Assn., Order Ea. Star. Home: 24010 Ranchito Del Rio Ct Salinas CA 93908-9652

COLLINS, JULIANNE SHEA, research scientist; d. Kenneth James and Rosalie Ann (Shea) Collins; m. Bryan Alan Wesson, Oct. 20, 2001. BS in Animal Sci., Calif. Poly. State U., 1992; MS in Genetics, Tex. A&M U., 1994; PhD in Med. Genetics, U. Ala., 2000. Asst. rsch. scientist Greenwood (SC) Genetic Ctr., 2000—. Adj. rsch. asst. prof. Clemson (SC) U., 2002—. Treas. Greenwood Women's Forum, 2001—02, sec., 2002—; vol. Hosts, Greenwood, 2002—. Mem.: Internat. Genetic Epidemiology Soc., Am. Soc. Human Genetics, Nat. Birth Defect Prevention Network. Democrat. Roman Catholic. Avocation: horseback riding. Office: Greenwood Genetic Ctr 1 Gregor Mendel Cir Greenwood SC 29646 Business E-Mail: julianne@ggc.org.

COLLINS, KATHLEEN, writer; b. Lowell, Mass., Nov. 10, 1953; d. John Joseph and Barbara Ann (McCarthy) C. BA, Mich. State U., 1975. Sr. rschr. Cen. States, S.E. and S.W. Areas Health & Welfare Fund, Chgo., 1976-79; steward Teamster Local 743, Chgo., 1978-79; tchr. religious edn. Roman Cath. Ch., Chgo., 1976-77, 81, eucharistic min., 1985—, data and info. coord. Schooley's Mt., N.J., 1980-84; English lang. tutor for fgn. students Mich. State U., East Lansing, 1971-74, entertainment and movie coord., 1972-74. Author: (with Mary E. Collins): A People Worth Saving, 1981, Treasures, 1983, Israel--Destroyed?, 1986, NOW, 1987, He's Coming, 1987, The Azume, 1991, Alexin and the Bear, 1992, Yatahay-Okay! 1993; co-author, editor booklets. Dem. election judge Washington Twp., N.J., 1985; election clk. 1984-88, election insp., 1988-89; advisor to bd. trustees Mich. State U., 1975; invited Patriot's Day marcher, Lexington, Mass., 1962-66; active Rep. Presdl. Task Force, 1995-97, Nat. Rep. Senatorial Com., 1995-98, Christian Def. League, 1997-98, Republican Presdl. Legion of Merit, Rep. Nat. Com., 1996—, campaign issues advisor, 1998; N.J. rep. to Presdl. Roundtable, 1997; hon. trustee Am. Indian Relief Coun., 1996; supporter Nat. Law Enforcement Officers Meml. Fund, 1996-98, WWII Meml., Washington, 1997-98; invited participant, advisor to Lincoln Inst. Honors. of Supreme Ct. Justice Clarence Thomas; church organist, East Brunswick, N.J., 1967-69. Named Hon. Citizen, Boys Town, 1996, 97, 98, Hon. Educator, Lakota Indians at St. Joseph's Indian Sch.; recipient Merit medal Rep. Presdl. Task Force, 1997-98. Mem.: DAR. Avocations: ceramic painting, real estate, wild-animal, fowl preservation. Home: 57 Nestlingwood Dr Long Valley NJ 07853-3528

COLLINS, KATHLEEN ANNE, artistic director; b. Elmira, N.Y., Dec. 20, 1951; d. James G. and Joyce (Balmer) C.; m. Andrew Stephon Elston, May 28, 1977; children: Megan, Kate. BA, SUNY, Albany, 1974; MA in Theatre, U. Wash., 1976, MFA in Theatre, 1979. Dir. edn. Seattle Children's Theatre, 1975-78; instr. drama Lakeside Sch., Seattle, 1978-79; artistic dir. Honolulu Theatre for Youth, 1979 83, Fulton Opera House, Lancaster, Pa., 1983-98; prof. Cornish Coll. of Arts, Seattle, 1999—. Guest lectr. U. Hawaii, Honolulu, 1981, U. Wash., Seattle, 2002—03; guest dir. Seattle Children's Theatre, 2002—03; adj. faculty Lesley U., 2000—. Contbg. author: Drama With Children, 1979. Bd. dirs. PTO, Lancaster, 1990-98. Mem. Am. Assn. Theatre Educators, Assn. and Soc. for Theatre and Children. Democrat. Roman Catholic.

COLLINS, KATHLEEN ELIZABETH, pharmaceutical company official; b. Rock Island, Ill., Jan. 14, 1951; d. A. Phillip and Henrietta (Zeis) C.; m. David Mark Hasenmiller, June 23, 1973 (div. June 1975). Fgn. student, U. Grenoble, 1970; student, Barat Coll., 1968-70, U. Wis., 1970-71; BA in French and English, St. Ambrose Coll., Davenport, Iowa, 1972; postgrad. secondary edn., Augustana Coll., Rock Island, 1975, U. Iowa, 1979, 84; M Counseling, Western Ill. U., 1996. Sales clk. Scharff's Dept. Store, Bettendorf, Iowa, 1970-72; teller Moline (Ill.) Nat. Bank, 1972-73; mgr. Music Box, Rock Island, 1973-74, Disc Records, Moline, 1974-75; with quality assurance dept. U.S. Army, Savanna, Ill., 1975-76; sales rep. Burroughs Wellcome Co., Research Triangle Park, N.C., 1976-81; vol. nutritionist Peace Corps, Niger, 1981-82; sales rep. Phil Collins Co., Rock Island, 1982-85; med. rep. Lederle Labs., Overland Park, Kans., 1985-88, Summit (N.J.) Pharms. Co. divsn. Ciba-Geigy, 1988-93, Circle of Excellence; profl. med. rep. Summit (N.J.) Pharms Co. div. Ciba-Geigy; pharm. purchasing specialist John Deere Health Care, Inc., Moline, 1994—96; market devel. assoc. Merck & Co., Inc., 1996—98; Shamanic counselor, 1998—; pharm. sales rep. PDI, Inc., 2001—. Vol. Big. Bros./Big Sisters, Moline, 1984-85, Pathway Hospice, Luth. Hosp., Moline, 1984-86, 88; vol. domestic violence/sexual assault advocacy Family Resources, Davenport, Iowa; vol. for parent support Network of the Child Abuse Counsel; disaster relief counselor ARC, 1998—. Mem. Quad Cities Pharm. Assn. (treas. 1978, 86, v.p. 1979, sec. 1987, sec./treas. 1988), Jr. League Quad Cities. Roman Catholic. Avocations: swimming, fashion modeling, scuba diving, piano, holistic medicine. Home and Office: 3649 Cedarview Ct Bettendorf IA 52722-2877

COLLINS, KEITH, federal executive; BS in Math., Villanova U., 1969; MS in Econs., U. Conn., 1973; PhD in Econs. and Stats., PhD in Econs. and Stats., N.C. State U., 1977. With USDA, Washington, 1978—, dir., econ. analysis staff, 1986-92, acting asst. sec. econs., 1993-95, chief economist, 1996—. Mem. Sr. Exec. Svc. Recipient Presdl. Rank award, 1990, 92, 96. Office: USDA Office Chief Economist Whitten Bldg Rm 112A Washington DC 20250-0001 E-mail: keith.collins@usda.gov.

COLLINS, KERRY, football player; b. Lebanon, Pa., Dec. 30, 1972; Student, Pa. State U. Quarterback Carolina Panthers, 1995-98, New Orleans Saints, 1998-99, N.Y. Giants, 1999—. Office: Giants Stadium East Rutherford NJ 07073

COLLINS, LARRY, author, journalist; b. Hartford, Conn., Sept. 14, 1929; s. John Laurence and Helen (Cannon) C.; m. Nadia Hoda Sultan, Sept. 17, 1966; children— John Lawrence III, Michael Kevin. Grad., Loomis Inst., Windsor, Conn., 1947; BA, Yale U., 1951. With advt. dept. Proctor & Gamble, Cin., 1951-52; With U.P.I., 1956-59, corr., 1957-59; Middle East editor Newsweek mag., 1959-61; chief Newsweek mag. (Paris bur.), 1961-64. Author: (with Dominique La Pierre) Is Paris Burning, 1965, Or I'll Dress You in Mourning, 1967, O, Jerusalem!, 1972, Freedom at Midnight, 1975, The Fifth Horseman, 1980, Mountbatten and the Partition of India, 1982, Fall from Grace, 1985, Maze, 1989, Black Eagles, 1993, Le Jour du Miracle: D Day Paris, 1994, Tomorrow Belongs to Us, 1998, The Road to Armageddon, 2003. With AUS, 1953-55, ETO. Recipient Lit. prize Deauville Film Festival, 1985, Mannesmann-Talley Lit. prize, 1989. Address: La Biche Niche 83350 Ramatuelle France

COLLINS, LINDA LOU POWELL, manager of contracts; b. Michigan City, Ind., May 6, 1957; d. Ronald Edward Powell and Betty Louise (Gruenberg) Will; m. Aug. 15, 1981 (div. May 18, 1983); m. Edward T. Collins, oct. 14, 1989; 1 child, Elizabeth Louise. BA in English, Purdue U., 1980; MBA, St. Francis Coll., Fort Wayne, Ind., 1988; postgrad., Ind. U., 1999. Cert. purchasing mgr., profl. contracts mgr. Head expeditor Graham Electronics, Ft. Wayne, Ind., 1981-82; expeditor solid state Raytheon Sys. Co. (formerly Magnavox Electronic Sys. Co.), Ft. Wayne, 1982-83, assoc. buyer, 1983-85, buyer, 1985-87, subcontract adminstr., 1987-88, sr. contract adminstr., 1988-93, contract mgr., 1993-96, mgr. contracts, 1996—2002, program mgr. of contracts, 2002—. Bus. writing instr. Ind.-Purdue U., Ft. Wayne, 1990-91; seminar instr. Nat. Contract Mgmt. Assn., 1991-92, 2000—. Active Civic Theater Dirs.' Cir., Ft. Wayne, 1989—; property trustee St. Joseph United Meth. Ch., Ft. Wayne, 1992, choir mem., 1993-95, liturgist, 2001-03; mentor Heart-to-Heart, 2002; vol. tutor Study Connection, 1995-97; troup leader Daisy Scouts, 2000-01; bd. dirs. Fort Wayne chpt. ARC, 2002—; liturgist Leo United Meth. Ch., 2003—. Recipient Woman of Achievement award YWCA, 1996. Fellow Nat. Contract Mgmt. Assn. (chptr. program chair 1990-91, v.p. 1991-92, mem. chair 1992-93, v.p. programs/facilities 1993-94, v.p./sec. 1994-95, regional mem. chair 1994-96, nat. functional dir. mem. retention 1994-95, v.p. membership 1995-96, nat. dir. 1996-97, 2003—, pres.-elect 1997-98, pres. 1998-99, North Ctrl. region nat. v.p. 2000-01, nat. v.p. membership 2001-02, nat. v.p. and sec. 2002-03, regional fellows chair 1996, James E. Cravens Mem. award 1993, 96, Blanch Witte Hon. Mention award 1996, Albert Berger Outstanding chpt. Leadership award 1999, Nat. Achievement award 2001, Women's Enterprise Ctr. adv. bd. 1999-2001); mem. Philips Electronics Credit Union (bd. dirs. 1997-2000), Purdue U. Alumni Assn. (life), Magna Health Club (v.p. 1990-91, mem. chair 1991-95, sec. 1995-96), Magnavox Mgmt. Club Ind. (facilities chair 1990-91, bd. dirs. 1993-96), Alpha Gamma Delta (altruism chair 1977-78). Republican. Avocations: reading, writing, fitness, boating. E-mail: poco@rexnet; po_collins@raytheon.com. Office: Raytheon Co 1010 Production Rd Fort Wayne IN 46808-4106

COLLINS, LYNN H. psychologist, educator, web site designer; BS, Duke U., Durham, N.C., 1980; MA, Ohio State U., 1984, PhD, 1988. Lic. psychologist Md., Pa. Asst. prof. U. Balt., 1995—98; assoc. prof. psychology LaSalle U., Phila., 1998—. Cons. editor Sex Roles, 2002—, Psychology of Women Quar., 2000—, Psychol. Assessment, 1994—. Co-editor: (book) Career Strategies for Women in Academe: Arming Athena, 1998, charting a New Course for Feminist Psychology, 2002; contbr. ; contbg. editor: Jour. of Genetic Psychology, 1992—, Genetic, Social and General Psychology Monographs, 1992. Fellow: Pa. Psychol. Assn. (internal pubs. com. 2000—, pub. info. and mktg. com. 2000—, media coord. com. 2002—), Md. Psychol. Assn. (PEA State Assn. rep. 1996—98, bd. sci. and ednl. affairs 1997—98, legis. com. 1997—98, web page task force 1998), Am. Psychol. Soc.; mem.: APA (internat. com. for womenn chair 2002—, conv. program chair internat. psychology divsn. 2003, site accreditation site visitor), New Eng. Psychol. Assn. (sec. 1992—95), Nat. Coun. of Schs. and Programs in Profl. Psychology (del. 1999—, webmaven 2002—, conf. com. 2003), Internat. Coun. Psychologists (co-chair gender rsch. interest group 1996—), Ea. Psychol. Assn. (dept. liaison 1995—, bd. dirs. 1998—2001), Assn. for Women in Psychology (book rev. editor 1992—94, officer, newsletter editor 1994—97, conf. coord. 1998), Balt. Psychol. Assn. (sec. 1996—97, liaison to Md. Psychol. Assn. 1997—98, pres. 1998, 1998), Phila. Soc. Clin. Psychologists (pres.-elect 2001—03, 2001—03, webmaven 2001—, sec. 1999—2001), Psi Chi (nat. cons. 1999—, regional steering com. mem. 1999—). Avocations: camping, art, renovation. Office: LaSalle Univ Dept Psychology 1900 W Olney Ave Philadelphia PA 19141

COLLINS, LYNN M. oncology clinical nurse specialist; b. St. Paul, Oct. 10, 1960; d. Bruce W. and Marianne (Palla) Baumann; m. Robert H. Collins Jr., Sept. 14, 1985. BSN, Winona State U., 1982; M in Nursing, UCLA, 1990. Cert. advanced oncology nurse. Staff clin. nurse II Baylor U. Med. Ctr., Dallas, supr., 1984-87; acting nurse mgr. Children's Hosp. of L.A., 1987-89; rsch. asst. UCLA Sch. Nursing; oncology clin. nurse specialist Sammons Cancer Ctr. Baylor U. Med. Ctr., Dallas, 1990-97; oncology nurse cons. Dallas, 1997—. Asst. editor for Clin. Practice, ONS, On-line, 1998-2002. Mem. Oncology Nursing Soc. (nat. Congress com. 1989, 90, nat. Fall inst. com. 1991, 92, chair nat. Fall inst. com. 1993), Leukemia Soc. Am. (N. Tex. chpt., bd. trustees 1995-99, chair patient svcs. com. 1997), Sigma Theta Tau. Home: 5365 Nakoma Dr Dallas TX 75209-5619 E-mail: lmcollin@swbell.net.

COLLINS, MARGARET HELEN, pathologist; b. Bronx, N.Y., July 5, 1950; d. Michael Robert and Catherine (Murray) C. BS cumma cum laude, Fordham U., 1972; MD, Georgetown U., 1977. Diplomate Am. Bd. Pathology. Intern in pathology Cornell U.-N.Y. Hosp., N.Y.C., 1977-78, resident in pathology, 1978-80; chief resident in pediatric pathology Columbia-Presbyn. Med. Ctr., N.Y.C., 1980-82, rsch. resident in pediatric pathology, 1982-83, asst. prof. clin. pathology, 1983-91; assoc. prof. pathology Ind. U., Indpls., 1991-95; pathologist Children's Hosp. Phila., Phila., 1995-98, Children's Hosp. Med. Ctr., Cin., 1999—; assoc. prof. pathology and pediats. U. Cin., 2000—. Contbr. rsch. articles to med. jours. Rsch. fellow N.Y. Lung Assn., 1983-85, Am. Lung Assn., 1985-87. Mem. AMA, AAAS, U.S.-Can. Acad. Pathology, Soc. Pediatric Pathology, Phi Beta Kappa. Democrat. Roman Catholic. Office: Children's Hosp Med Ctr 3333 Burnet Ave Cincinnati OH 45229-3026 E-mail: margaret.collins@uc.edu.

COLLINS, MARIBETH WILSON, foundation president; b. Portland, Oreg., Oct. 27, 1918; d. Clarence True and Maude (Akin) Wilson; m. Truman Wesley Collins, Mar. 12, 1943; children: Timothy Wilson and Terry Stanton (twins), Cherida Smith, Truman Wesley Jr. BA, U. Oreg., 1940. Pres. Collins Found., Portland, Oreg., 1964—. Dir. Collins Pine Co., Collins Holding Co., Ostrander Resource Co. Life trustee Willamette U., Salem, Oreg., also mem. campus religious life. Mem. Univ. Club, Gamma Phi Beta. Republican. Methodist. Home: 2275 SW Mayfield Ave Portland OR 97225-4400 Office: Collins Found 1618 SW 1st Ave Ste 505 Portland OR 97201-5708

COLLINS, MARTHA, English language educator, writer; b. Omaha, Nov. 25, 1940; d. William E. and Katheryn (Essick) C.; m. Theodore M. Space, Apr. 1991. AB, Stanford U., 1962; MA, U. Iowa, 1965, PhD, 1971. Asst. prof. N.E. Mo. U., Kirksville, 1965-66; from instr. to prof. English U. Mass., Boston, 1966—2002, co-dir. creative writing, 1979—2000; Pauline Delaney prof., co-dir. creative writing Oberlin (Ohio) Coll., 1997—. Author (poetry): The Catastrophe of Rainbows, 1985, The Arrangement of Space, 1991, A History of Small Life on a Windy Planet, 1993, Some Things Words Can Do, 1998; translator: The Women Carry River Water, 1997. Fellow Bunting Inst., 1982-83, Ingram Merrill Found., 1988, NEA, 1990; grantee Witter Bynner/Santa Fe Art Inst., 2001, Lannon Found. Residency, 2003; recipient Pushcart prize, 1985, 96, 98, Di Castagnola award, 1990, Lannan residency, 2003. Mem. Poetry Soc. Am., Assoc. Writing Programs. Democrat. Office: Oberlin Coll Rice Hall Oberlin OH 44074

COLLINS, MARTHA TRAUDT See ROLLE, MARTHA

COLLINS, MARY, management consultant, former Canadian legislator; b. Vancouver, B.C., Can., Sept. 26, 1940; d. Fredrick Claude and Isabel Margaret (Copp) Wilkins; children: David, Robert, Sarah. Student, U. B.C., Queen's U., Kingston, Ont., Can.; LLD (hon.), Royal Rds. Mil. Coll., 1994. Mem. Can. Ho. of Commons, 1984-93; pres., CEO B.C. Health Assn., 1994-97; pres. Amarok Holdings, Ltd. Mem. fed. cabinet Can., assoc. min. nat. def., 1989-92, min. Western econ. diversification, 1993, min. state environ., 1993, min. responsible for status of women, 1990-93, min. of health, 1993; dir. Can. Blood Svcs. Trustee Queen's U.; bd. dirs. Vancouver Libr., Vancouver Bd. Trade, A.C. Global Corp. Mem. Internat. Womens Forum. Mem. Progressive Conservative Party. Office: Amarok Holdings Ltd 1185 W 7th Ave Vancouver BC Canada V6H 1B5 E-mail: amarok@telus.net.

COLLINS, MELISSA ANN, oncological nurse; b. Wichita Falls, Tex., June 6, 1951; d. Foley D. Jr. and Pathea Jo (Thornton) C. BS, U. Tex., Austin, 1973. Cert. oncology nurse, med. radiologic technologist. Nurse technologist U. Tex. System Cancer Ctr. at M.D. Anderson Hosp., Houston; staff nurse, technologist Hermann Hosp., Houston; nurse/radiation therapist Park Plaza Hosp., Houston. Mem. Oncology Nursing Soc.

COLLINS, MICHAEL A. (MAC COLLINS), congressman; b. Flovilla, Ga., Oct. 15, 1944; m. Julie Watkins; 4 children. Owner Collins Trucking Co., 1962—; former chmn. Butts County Commn., 1977—81; mem. 2 terms Ga. State Senate, 1989—93; mem. Congress from 8th Ga. dist., 1993—; mem. House com. ways and means; mem. House com. on the budget; dep. majority whip Rep. leadership. Mem. House Com. on Ways and Means; dep. majority whip. Republican. Office: US House Representatives 1131 Longworth Bldg Washington DC 20515-1003*

COLLINS, MICHAEL HOMER, lawyer; b. Dallas, Apr. 26, 1949; s. William and Sheila (Peers) C.; m. Melissa Ringland, Aug. 11, 1956; children— Alexander, Valentina. B.A., Harvard U., 1971, J.D., 1977. Bar: Tex. 1977, U.S. Dist. Ct. (no. dist.) Tex. 1978, (so. dist.) Tex. 1993, (ea. dist.) Tex. 1989, U.S. Ct. Apls. (5th cir.) 1981. Briefing atty. Judge Robert Hill, U.S. Dist. Judge for No. Dist. Tex., Dallas, 1977-78; assoc. Locke, Purnell, Boren, Laney & Neely, Dallas, from 1978, now shareholder. Chmn. bd. mgmt. Town North YMCA, Dallas, 1983-85, bd. dirs. Dallas County Hist. Found., 1991—. Fellow ABA, Tex. Bar Found.; mem. Dallas Bar Assn. (chmn. legal ethics com. 1985). Home: 6207 Lakehurst Ave Dallas TX 75230-5126 Office: Locke Purnell Rain Harrell 2200 Ross Ave Ste 2200 Dallas TX 75201-6776

COLLINS, MICHAEL JOHN, dean; b. New York, Dec. 5, 1941; s. Michael John Collins and Marion Patterson; m. JoEllen Anne Giuliano, May 31, 1965; 1 child, Deanne. BSc, Forham Coll., 1963; MA, N.Y.U., 1964, PhD, 1973. Asst. dean coll. liberal arts Fordham U., N.Y.C., 1973-77; assoc. dean Fordham Coll., N.Y.C., 1977-81; dean sch. for summer and contg. edn. Georgetown U., Washington, 1981—. Bd. dirs. Shenandoah Shakespeare, Stauton, Va. Editor: Teaching Values and Ethics in College, 1983, Shakespeare's Sweet Thunder, 1997; co-editor: Text and Teaching: The Search for Human Excellence, 1991; publisher Shakespeare Mag. Capt. U.S. Army, 1965-68. Fellow Soc. Values in Higher Edn., The Royal Soc. Art; mem. Nat. Coun. Tchrs. English, Modern Lang. Assn. (del. assembly 2000-02), Shakespeare Assn. Am., Phi Beta Kappa. Office: SSCE Georgetown Univ Washington DC 20057

COLLINS, MICHAEL PAUL, secondary school educator, earth science educator, consultant; b. Chula Vista, Calif., Jan. 2, 1959; s. William Henry and Linda Lee (Capron) C.; children: Christopher M., Matthew R., Kyle P., Colby W. A in Gen. Studies, Clatsop Community Coll., Astoria, Oreg., 1983; BS in Sci. Edn., BS in Geology, Oreg. State U., 1987; postgrad., U. Alaska, Anchorage. Cert. tchr., Wash., Alaska. Emergency med. technician II, fireman Sitka (Alaska) Fire Dept., 1978-80; paramedic Medix Ambulance, Astoria, 1980-83; cartographer technician U.S. Geol. Survey, Grants Pass, Oreg., 1985; tchr. earth sci. Lake Oswego (Oreg.) Sch. Dist., 1987-88; tchr. sci. Gladstone (Oreg.) Sch. Dist., 1988-90; radon technician Radon Detection Systems, Portland, Oreg., 1988-90; dir. sales and mktg. Evergreen Helicopters of Alaska, Inc., Anchorage, 1990-91; tchr. math. and sci. Anchorage Sch. Dist., 1991—99; Alaska pharm. ter. bus. mgr. Ventiv Health/Bristol Myers Squibb Co., 1999—2001, Reliant Pharms, 2001—02; acct. mgr. RS Med., Inc., 2003—. Instr. geology Alaska Jr. Coll., Anchorage, 1992—93; cons. earth sci. edn. Project ESTEEM, Ctr. Astrophysics, Harvard U., Cambridge, Mass., 1992—95; field technician Water Quality divsn., City of Anchorage, 1993; cons., atmospheric ednl. resource agt. Project Atmosphere Am. Meteorol. Assn., 1994—99; cons. Ala. State H.S. Scis. Olympics, 1998; cons. Project MicroObs. Ctr. for Astrophysics Harvard U., 1995—98; coord. instr. Project DataStreme Am. Meteorol. Soc., 1996—99; cons. geologist Unocal Alaska, 1997; geologist II Shannon & Wilson, Inc., 1998; Alaska pharm. ter. bus. mgr. Ventiv Health/Bristol Myers Squibb Co., 1999—2001, Reliant Pharms., 2001—02; acct. mgr. RS Med., Inc., 2003—. Co-author: Merrill Earth Science Lab Activities, 1989. With USCG, 1977-81. Mem.: NEA, Alaska Pharm. Assn., Nat. Assn. Geosci. Tchrs. (pres. N.W. sect. 1996—99), Alaska Geol. Soc. Inc., Am. Meteorol. Soc., Am. Geol. Inst., Nat. Sci. Tchrs. Assn., Geol. Soc. Am., Am. Assn. Petroleum Geologists. Avocations: weight training, fishing, hiking, camping, real estate. Home and Office: 2340 Sentry Dr Apt 802 Anchorage AK 99507

COLLINS, MOIRA ANN, graphics and communications company executive, calligrapher; b. Dec. 16, 1942; d. Peter William and Louise (Carroll) Collins; m. Andrew Joseph Griffin, Aug. 21, 1965; children: Andrew Fitzgerald, Timothy Collins. BA, U. Toronto, Ont., Can., 1964; MA in Tchg., Northwestern U., 1965; MEd in Urban Studies, Northeastern U., Chgo., 1968; studied with profl. calligraphers, Haystack Mountain Sch., Deer Isle, Maine, 1973, U. Calif., Santa Cruz, 1973-74. Tchr. Chgo. Bd. Edn., 1965-68; freelance calligrapher, 1974-78; mem. publicity and promotional staff Swallow Press, Chgo., 1978-79; owner Letters, Chgo., 1979—. Pres. Astrogram, Chgo. 1986-99, Kiddygram, 2000-; intern Gestalt Inst. of Toronto & Oasis Ctr, Chgo., 1986-87. HEW fellow Northeastern U., 1967-68. Author, contbr.: Celebration: Anais Nin, 1975; contbr. to Goodfellow Rev. of Crafts, 1979; calligrapher: Erotica, 1976, Chgo. Rev., 1978. Chmn. fund raising Van Gorder Walden Sch., Chgo., 1979-80. Mem. Chgo. Calligraphy Collective (co-founder, chmn. 1976-77, pres. 1978-79, hon. mem.), Soc. Scribes N.Y., Soc. Scribes and Illuminators (Eng.), Friends Calligraphy Calif. Democrat. Roman Catholic. Home: 3920 N Lake Shore Dr Apt 9N Chicago IL 60613-3465 Office: 533 Lake Front Dr Beverly Shores IN 46301 E-mail: mac@moiracollins.com.

COLLINS, MONICA ANN, journalist; b. Rockville Center, N.Y. d. Louis Andrew and Eileen Ann Collins. BA, Vassar Coll. Writer, editor The Real Paper, Cambridge, Mass., 1975-79; TV critic Boston Herald Am., 1979-83, USA Today, Arlington, Va., 1983-89; columnist Boston Mag., 1983-85, TV Guide, 1989-93; TV critic, editl. page columnist Boston Herald, 1989—. Roman Catholic. Office: The Boston Herald 1 Herald St Boston MA 02118-2200 E-mail: mcollins@bostonherald.com.

COLLINS, NANCY WHISNANT, foundation administrator; b. Charlotte, N.C., Dec. 20, 1933; d. Ward William and Marjorie Adele (Blackburn) Whisnant; m. James Quincy Collins Jr., Apr. 25, 1959 (div. 1974); children: James Quincy III, Charles Lowell, William Robey; m. Richard F. Chapman, May 29, 1982. Student, Queens Coll., Charlotte, 1951-53; AB in Journalism, U. N.C., 1955, MS in Personnel Adminstrn., 1967; postgrad., Cornell U., 1955 56. Personnel asst. R.H. Macy & Co., Inc., N.Y.C., 1955; jr. exec. placement dir. Scofield Placement Agy., San Francisco, 1956-57; free-lance journalist, London, Paris, and Frankfort, Fed. Republic Germany, 1957-59; program dir. Girl Scouts U.S., Hampton, Va., 1959-61; dir. tour, Tokyo, Hong Kong, Singapore, 1965-66; asst. dir. Sloan Exec. Program, Stanford (Calif.) U., 1968-78; asst. dir. Hoover Instn., 1979-81; asst. to pres. Palo Alto (Calif.) Med. Found., 1981-2000; bd. dirs. Am. Healthway Systems. Author: Professional Women and Their Mentors, Women Leading: Making Tough Choices on the Fast Track, 1988, Love at Second Sight-A Guide to Midlife Dating; contbr. articles, short stories and poems to mags. and newspapers. Mem. coun. Trinity Episcopal Ch., Menlo Park Calif., 1975-80; fundraiser Cornell U., N.Y.C., 1975-81; exec. council Stanford area council Boy Scouts Am., 1980-81; mem. San Mateo County Charter Rev. Com.; mem. personnel bd. City of Menlo Park, 1979—; mem. women's program bd. Coro Found.; trustee Pacific Grad. Sch. Psychology; sec.-treas. Chapman Research Fund; bd. dirs. Santa Clara County council Girl Scouts U.S.; mem. leadership team Menlo Pk. Presbyn. Ch. Grantee Richardson Found., 1967; Cornell U. fellow. Mem. AAUW, Am. Mgmt. Assn., Peninsula Profl. Women's Network (adv. coun.), Nat. Alliance Profl. and Exec. Women (speakers' bank), Catalyst, Kappa Delta. Clubs: Overseas Press, Commonwealth. Home: 1850 Oak Ave Menlo Park CA 94025-5842

COLLINS, PAT LOWERY, writer, artist, educator; b. L.A., Oct. 6, 1932; d. Joseph Michael and Margaret Meyer Lowery; m. Wallace Curtis Collins; children: Christopher, Kimberly Jermain, Colleen, Cathlin Smith, Mathias. BA, U. So. Calif., 1953. Part time instr. Worcester (Mass.) Art Mus., 1998—. Author: I Am An Artist, 1992 (Reading Rainbow, 1994, 97), The Quiet Woman Wakes Up Shouting, 1998, Signs and Wonders (Children's Lit. Choice 2000), Just Imagine, 2001, Schooner, 2002, The Fattching Hut, 2003. Fellow in fiction N.H. State Coun. on Arts, 1991; recipient Children's Book of Yr. award Child Study Assn., 1993, 2000 Books for the Teenagers award N.Y. Pub. Libr., 2000, Children's Lit. Choice award, 2000; grantee writers in poetry Vt. Studio, 1997. Mem. Authors Guild, Soc. Children's Book Writers and Illustrators (regional advisor N.E. 1993), Concord Art Assn, Poets and Writers, Penn New England, Northshore Art Assn. Roman Catholic. Avocations: singing with chamber choir, swimming, tennis. Home: 3 Wauketa Rd Gloucester MA 01930 E-mail: patlc@earthlink.net.

COLLINS, PAUL DOUGLAS (DOUG COLLINS), former professional basketball coach; b. Christopher, Ill., July 28, 1951; Student, Ill. State U. Profl. basketball player Phila. 76ers, NBA, 1973-81; asst. basketball coach U. Pa., University, 1981-82, Ariz. State U., Tempe, 1982-84; basketball commentator CBS-TV, 1982-85; profl. basketball announcer Sta. WPHL, Phila.; head coach Chgo. Bulls, NBA, 1986-89; coach Detroit Pistons, 1995—98, Washington Wizards, 2000—03. Mem., capt. U.S. Olympic Basketball Team, 1972; Coll. All-Am., 1972-73; mem. NBA All-Star Team, 1976-79

COLLINS, PAUL JOHN, banker; b. West Bend, Wis., Oct. 26, 1936; s. Curtis Alvin and Adele (Stopenbach) C.; m. Carol Lee Hoffmann, May 8, 1965; children: Ronald Alvin, Julia Downing. BBA, U. Wis., 1958; MBA, Harvard U., 1961. With Citibank, N.Y.C., 1961-2000, investment analyst, portfolio mgmt., 1961-70, sr. v.p., chmn. investment policy com., 1970-75, sr. v.p., head corp. planning, 1976-77, sr. v.p., head fin. div., 1977-79, exec. v.p. acctg. and control, 1980-81, group exec. investment br., 1982-85, sr. corp. officer N.Am., 1985-88, vice chmn., 1988-98, also bd. dirs., Citigroup vice chmn., 1998-2000. Bd. dirs. Kimberly Clark Corp., Nokia Corp., BG Group. Bd. dirs. Glyndebourne Arts Trust, U. Wis. Found. Republican. Congregationalist. Home: 29 Wilton Crescent London SW1 X8SA England E-mail: pcollins@pjcpartners.com.

COLLINS, PAUL STEVEN, vascular surgeon; b. Portsmouth, Ohio, July 24, 1954; s. Paul Whitney and Geralda Pearl (Hoskins) C.; m. Cathy Ann McWicker, Jan. 17, 1981; children: Lauren Elizabeth, Paul McWicker, Andrew Steven. BS, Davidson Coll., 1976; MD, U. South Fla., 1979. Diplomate Am. Bd. Surgery, spl. qualifications in gen. vascular surgery and surg. critical care; diplomate Nat. Bd. Med. Examiners; lic. surgeon, Fla., Va. Commd. 2d lt. U.S. Army, 1979, advanced through grades to lt. col., 1990, resident in gen. surgery Walter Reed Army Med. Ctr., 1979-84, chief gen. surg. Würzburg, West Germany, 1984-86, fellow peripheral vasc. surgery Walter Reed Army Med. Ctr. Washington, 1986-87, chief vascular surgery Letterman Army Med. Ctr. San Francisco, resigned, 1992; pvt. practice St. Petersburg, Fla., 1990—; asst. clin. prof. surgery U. S. Fla., Tampa, 1995—. Asst. clin. prof. surgery Uniformed Svcs. U. Health Scis., Bethesda, Md., 1984—; chief of surgery St. Anthony's Hosp., St. Petersburg, 1998—2000, dir. vascular lab., 1994—97, chmn. dept. surgery, 1998—2000; profl. mem. Keystone, Tampa, Fla., 1993—97; pres. Bay Plaza Outpatient Surgery, 1994—2001; bd. dirs., trustee St. Anthony's Found.; team surgeon Tampa Bay Devil Rays Baseball Team, 1996—. Contbr. chpts. to books, articles to med. jours. Bd. dirs. St. Anthony's Found. Recipient Physicians Recognition award AMA, 1992, Sigvaris award Camp Internat., 1987. Fellow ACS (Regional Trauma award 1984), Internat. Soc. for Cardiovascular Surgeons; mem. So. Assn. for Vascular Surgery (Pres.'s award 1992), Fla. Vascular Soc., Fla. Med. Assn., Pinellas County Med. Soc. (bd. govs.). Avocations: golf, tennis, snow and water skiing, gardening. Office: 1201 5th Ave N Ste 200 Saint Petersburg FL 33705-1410 E-mail: sclpac@aol.com.

COLLINS, PHIL (PHILIP DAVID CHARLES COLLINS), singer, songwriter, drummer, record producer; b. London, Jan. 30, 1951; s. Greville and June Collins; m. Andrea Collins, 1975 (div. 1982); 1 child, Simon; step child, Joely; m. Jill Collins, 1984 (div. 1996); 1 child, Lily Jane; m. Orianne Cevey, July 24, 1999; 1 child: Nicholas. Drummer rock band Genesis, 1971-75, lead singer, songwriter, 1975—. Albums with Genesis include: Nursery Cryme, 1971, Foxtrot, 1972, Selling England by the Pound, 1973, Genesis Live, 1973, The Lamb Lies Down on Broadway, 1974, Trick of the Tail, 1976, Wind and Wuthering, 1977, Seconds Out, 1977, Spot the Pigeon, 1977, And Then There Were Three, 1978, Duke, 1980, Abacab, 1981, Three Sides Live, 1982, Genesis, 1983, Invisible Touch, 1986, We Can't Dance, 1991, The Way That We Walk Volume One: The Shorts, 1992, The Way That We Walk Volume Two: The Longs, 1993; solo albums include: Face Value, 1981, Hello, I Must be Going, 1982, No Jacket Required (Grammy award 1986), 1985, ...But Seriously, 1989, Serious Hits-Live, 1990, Both Sides, 1993, Dance into the Light, 1996, Hits, 1998, Big Band-A Hot Night in Paris, 1999, Testify, 2000; composer film: Against All Odds (Acad. award nomination), 1984, Buster, 1988, (voice) Balto, 1995; TV movie Hook, 1991, Frauds, 1993, Calliope, 1993, And the Band Played On, 1993. Winner Grammy award for Best Song (Against All Odds), 1985, Grammy award for Two Hearts, 1989, 5 others, 2 Silver Clef awards, 2 awards Variety Club of Gt. Britain, 1 Elvis award, Golden Globe for the song Two Hearts from the movie Buster, 1989, Oscar and Golden Globe for the song You'll be in my Heart from the movie Tarzan, 2000, numerous others, Star on the Hollywood Walk of Fame, 1999, Diamond award RIAA, 1999, City of Life award, 2002. Office: Atlantic Records 1290 Avenue Of The Americas New York NY 10104-0184

COLLINS, REY, financial analyst; b. Harrisburg, PA; m. Patricia Fanning, Sept. 25, 1970. Analyst Meriks Venture Capital Inc, Rapid City, SD, 1969—. Office: Meriks Venture Capital Inc 409 Kansas City St Box 2078 Rapid City SD 57709

COLLINS, RICHARD ANDREW, pathologist, biochemist; b. Norristown, Pa., Oct. 27, 1924; s. George W. and Blanche (Latshaw) C.; m. Carmen Portillo, Oct. 29, 1955 (dec.); children: Cynthia, Deborah, Daniel. BS, Pa. State U., 1948; MS, U. Wis., 1950, PhD, 1952; MD, Marquette U., 1962. Diplomate Am. Bd. Clin. and Anat. Pathology. Intern Mary Fletcher Hosp., Burlington, Vt., 1962-63; resident in pathology U. Vt., Burlington, 1963-65; pathologist Regional Med. Labs., Battle Creek, Mich., 1972-81, St. Luke's Med. Ctr., Milw., 1981-97; ret., 1997. 1st lt. USAF, 1943-46, PTO.

COLLINS, RICHARD AUGUSTINE, mechanical engineer; b. Plain City, Ohio, Oct. 13, 1933; s. John Bernard and Mildred Leona (Klein) C.; m. Rieta June Peterson, Aug. 3, 1963; children: Daphne Lynn, Andrew Douglas. BS in Mech. Engring., Ohio State U., 1956; MS in Mech. Engring., Ga. Inst. Tech., Atlanta, 1961. Chief engr. Solar Industries, Inc., Tempe, Ariz., 1967-68; sr. devel. engr. A. Rsch. Mfg. Co., Phoenix, 1968-79; asst. project engr. Garrett Engine Divsn., Phoenix, 1979-85; project engr. Allied Signal, Phoenix, 1985-91, mgr. II, 1991-93, prin. engr., 1993-98. Cons. Solar Designs & Sales, Tempe, 1976-98. Contbr. articles to profl. jours.; patentee in field. Founding pres. N. Tempe Homeowners Assn., 1975; mem., chmn. City Tempe Design Rev. Bd., 1975-81; nation chief Indian Guides, Tempe, 1981; mem., vice-chmn. Tempe Aviation Commn., 2001—. With Corp. Engrs., U.S. Army, 1957. Mem. ASME (dir. 1977-81, 93-97, Lifetime Svc. award 1996). Avocations: backpacking, golfing, fishing. Home: 1736 N Mcallister Ave Tempe AZ 85281-1406

COLLINS, RICHARD FRANCIS, microbiologist, educator; b. St. Paul, Minn., Jan. 22, 1938; s. Francis Bernard and Maude Roegene (Night) C.; m. Deanne Margaret Scafati, Dec. 28, 1960 (div. 1970); children: Lisa, Mark, Michael; m. Judy A. Wright, Feb. 15, 1978; children: Kristyn, Todd. AB, Shepherd Coll., 1962; MA, Wake Forest U., 1968; PhD, U. Okla., 1973. Tchr. Alexandria (Va.) Schs., 1962-66; instr. U. Okla., Oklahoma City, 1972-73; lab. dir. Infectious Disease Svc. U. Ill./Rockford Sch. of Medicine, 1974-80; asst. prof. U. Ill., Rockford, 1973-80; assoc. prof. U. Osteo. Medicine and Health Scis., Des Moines, 1980-85, faculty pres., 1990-91, pres.-elect, 1997-98, prof., dept. head, 1985-95; prof., divsn. head Midwestern U., Glendale, 1997—. Cons. U.S. EPA, Washington, 1975-81; mem. Nat. Bd. Podiatry Examiners, Princeton, N.J., 1983-96, Nat. Bd. Osteo. Med. Examiners, Des Plaines, Ill., 1994-97; participant mission project Christian Med. Soc., Dominican Republic, 1977. Mem. editorial bd. African Jour. Clin. Exptl. Immunology, 1979-83; contbr. articles to profl. jours. Vol. Blank Guild, Iowa Meth. Hosp., Des Moines,

1988-91. Recipient awards NSF, 1962-67, fellowship NIH, 1969-70, Gov.'s Vol. awards State of Iowa, 1988, 89. Mem. Am. Soc. for Microbiology, Am. Soc. Tropical Medicine and Hygiene, Sigma Xi (pres. 1987-90, 96-97, treas. 1990-91). Avocations: photography, auto restoration. Home: 4131 W Tierra Buena Ln Phoenix AZ 85053-3717 Office: Midwestern U Ariz Coll Osteo Medicine 19555 N 59th Ave Glendale AZ 85308-6813 E-mail: rcolli@midwestern.edu.

COLLINS, RICHARD LAWRENCE, magazine editor, publisher, author; b. Little Rock, Nov. 28, 1933; s. Leighton Holden Collins and Sarah Aloysia (Banks) Polk; m. Ann Terry Slocomb, Feb. 14, 1958; children— Charlotte, Sarah, Richard Jr. Chief pilot Ben M. Hogan Co., Little Rock, 1957-58; mng. editor Air Facts mag., Princeton, N.J., 1958-68; sr. editor Flying mag., N.Y.C., 1968-77, editor in chief, 1977-88; editor in chief, pub. Pilot, sr. v.p. Aircraft Owners and Pilots Assn., Frederick, Md., 1988-89; aviation cons., 1989—. Author numerous aviation books including: Flying Safely, 1977, Tips to Fly By, 1980, Thunderstorms and Airplanes, 1982, Flight Level Flying, 1985, Air Crashes, 1986, The Perfect Flight, 1988, Pilot Upgrade, 1989, Mastering the Systems, 1991; contbr. articles to mags. Chmn. Ark. Aero. Commn., Little Rock, 1976. Served with U.S. Army, 1955-57 Recipient Earl D. Osborn award Aviation Writers, 1978, Sherman Fairchild award Flight Safety Found., 1965, platinum wing award NBAA, 2000; named to Ark. Aviation Hall of Fame, 1988. Mem. Flying Physicians Assn. (hon.), Lawyer Pilots Bar Assn. (hon.), Civil Aeromed. Assn. (hon.) Clubs: Quiet Birdmen. Avocation: sailing. Office: 500 W Putnam Ave Greenwich CT 06830-6086

COLLINS, RICHARD STRATTON (DICK COLLINS), retired public relations executive; b. Smith Center, Kans., Dec. 11, 1929; s. Edgar Wesley and Rosina Ann (Allbert) C.; children: Ann Michelle, Jennifer Lee, Logan Reed. BA, U. Tex., 1952. Editor of Lookout Look Mag., N.Y.C., 1952-53, asst. circulation promotion mgr., 1953-57, circulation promotion mgr., 1957-64, pub. rels. mgr., 1964-67; v.p., dir. corp. pub. rels. Cowles Comm., N.Y.C., 1967-74; assoc. The Jonathan Rinehart Group, N.Y.C., 1974-76; dir. pub. rels. ABA, Chgo., 1976-80, dir. comms., 1980-89, dir. comms./pub. affairs, 1989-94, ret., 1994. Writer, prodr. audio/visual prodns. and speeches; writer mag. advts. (award of Excellence Communication Arts Mag. 1971); contbr. articles to jours., newspaper columnist. Bd. dirs., pres. Family Counseling Svcs., Bergen County, N.J., 1968-76. Recipient Silver Screen award U.S. Indsl. Film Festival, 1979, The Chris Plaque, Columbus Film Festival, 1979. Mem. Pub. Rels. Soc. of Am. (Silver Anvil award 1964). Avocations: golf, gardening, reading history, civil liberties organizations, recording for the blind.

COLLINS, RICHARD WAYNE, English literature educator; b. Eugene, Oreg., Sept. 4, 1952; s. Alva Corder and Reba Voneta (Tannehill) C.; m. Leigh Frances Guillory, June 6, 1992; children: Cyleste, Isabel. BA in English, U. Oreg., 1977; MA in English, U. Calif., Irvine, 1979, PhD in English, 1984. Asst. prof. La. State U., Baton Rouge, 1982-92; assoc. prof. Am. U. of Bulgaria, Blagoevgrad, 1995-97; prof. Xavier U., New Orleans, 1997—. Author: Foolscape, 1983, John Fante: A Literary Portrait, 2000; editor Xavier Rev., 2000—, Here and Now: Newsletter of the Am. Zen Assn., 2001—. Recipient Fulbright Rsch. Grant, London, 1980-81, Leverhulme Commonwealth-USA fellowship, Wales, 1984-85; named Fulbright Sr. Lectr., U.S. Info. Agy., Bucharest Romania, 1992-93, Timisoara, Romania, 1993-94. Office: Xavier U La 1 Drexel Dr New Orleans LA 70125 Home: 155 Pelican Ave New Orleans LA 70114-2343 E-mail: rcollins@xula.edu.

COLLINS, ROBERT ARNOLD, English language educator; b. Miami, Fla., Apr. 25, 1929; s. John William and Edna (Arnold) C.; m. Laura Virginia Roberts, June 3, 1960; 1 child, Judith. BA in English, U. Miami, Coral Gables, Fla., 1951; MA in English, U. Ky., 1960, PhD in English, 1968. Chair English Midway (Ky.) Jr. Coll., 1960-64; assoc. prof. English No. Ill. U., DeKalb, 1964-68, Morehead (Ky.) State U., 1968-69; from assoc. prof. to prof. English Fla. Atlantic U., Boca Raton, 1970—. Founder, dir. Internat. Conf. on the Fantastic in the Arts, Ft. Lauderdale, Fla., 1980—. Author: Thomas Burnett Swann: A Critical Biography, 1980, Science Fiction and Fantasy Book Review Annual, 1987-91; editor: Scope of the Fantastic, 1985, Modes of the Fantastic, 1995; editor Fantasy Rev., 1981-87; mng. editor Jour. of the Fantastic in the Arts, 1995—; contbr. articles to profl. jours. Recipient World Fantasy award World Fantasy Conv., New Haven, 1982, Balrog award Sword and Shield, 1982, 83. Home: 1320 SW 5th St Boca Raton FL 33486-4404 Office: Fla Atlantic U English Dept 777 Glades Rd Boca Raton FL 33431-6424 E-mail: collins@fau.edu.

COLLINS, ROBERT ELLWOOD, surgeon; b. Cottage City, Md., Aug. 4, 1932; s. Edward Clarence and Edith (Blough) C.; m. Barbara Kauffmann Murray, June 28, 1964; children: Garret, Randy, Robin, Bill, Bruce, Brad, Beth. BS, Ea. Mennonite Coll., 1954; MD, Med. Coll. Va., 1958. Diplomate Am. Bd. Orthopaedic Surgeons. Intern Washington Hosp. Ctr., 1958-59, orthopaedic resident, 1961-64; pvt. practice medicine Broadway, Va., 1959-60; resident in gen. surgery Med. Coll. Va., Richmond, 1960-61; pvt. practice medicine specializing in orthopaedic surgery Washington, 1964—. Acting orthopaedic chief Children's Hosp., 1970—72; chief orthopaedics Washington Hosp. Ctr., 1973—75, vice-chmn. dept. orthopaedics, 1975—80, bd. dirs., pres. med. and dental staff, 1981, 1983—85; assoc. prof. Georgetown U. Hosp., 1975—; courtesy staff Sibley Meml. Hosp.; pres. med. staff Nat. Rehab. Hosp., Washington, 1988—2001; bd. dirs. Medlantic Health Corp., Washington. Bd. dirs. Easter Seal Soc. of Washington and Md., 1986—, chmn. bd. dirs., 1990—92; bd. dirs. Nat. Orthopedic Hosp., Washington, 1990, Nat. Easter Seals Soc., 1995—2001. Recipient Teaching award Georgetown U., Washington, 1985; Children's Orthopaedic's fellow Children's Hosp., 1963, Cerebral Palsy fellow Children's Rehab. Inst. Johns Hopkins U., 1965. Fellow ACS (chmn. D.C. trauma com.), Am. Acad. Cerebral Palsy, Am. Acad. Orthopaedic Surgeons, Am. Acad. Orthopaedic Foot Surgeons; mem. Med. Soc. D.C. (pres. 1985-86), Washington Clin. Club (past pres.), Georgetown Club, Congl. Country Club (Bethesda, Md.). Presbyterian. Office: Drs Collins Johnson & Tozzi PC Tozzi PC 106 Irving St NW Ste 215 Washington DC 20010-2993 E-mail: grandbarrie.comn@aol.com.

COLLINS, ROBERT HOWARD, JR., oncologist; b. St. Louis, June 3, 1960; s. Robert Howard Sr. and Elsie (Alford) C.; m. Lynn Marie (Baumann); children: Andrew, James Michael. BA, U. Mo., 1983, MD, 1984. Diplomate Am. Bd. Internal Medicine, Am. Bd. Med. Oncology. Intern in internal medicine Baylor U. Med. Ctr., 1984-85, resident in internal medicine, 1985-87, asst. dir. bone marrow transplantation, 1989-98, assoc. attending, 1990-96, attending, 1996-98; fellow in hematology and oncology UCLA, 1987-89; pvt. practice, Dallas, 1989-98; assoc. prof. internal medicine U. Tex. Southwestern Med. Ctr., Dallas, 1998—2002, prof. internal medicine, 2002—, H. Lloyd and Willie V. Skaggs prof. med. rsch., 1999—, dir. bone marrow transplantation program, 1998—, Sydney and J.L. Huffines disting. chair in cancer rsch., 2001—. Mem. com. on radiation and isotopes Baylor U. Med. Ctr., 1989-92, transfusion com., 1991—, ethics com., 1992-93, instl. rev. bd., 1992—; mem. sci. subcom. and acquired non-malignant diseases Nat. Marrow Donor Program, 1993—; presenter in field. Contbr. numerous articles and abstracts to profl. and sci. jours. Curator's scholar U. Mo., 1979, Univ. scholar U. Mo., 1982, Flarscheim scholar; UCLA clin. oncology fellow Am. Cancer Soc., 1988. Fellow ACP; mem. AAAS, Am. Soc. Clin. Oncology, Am. Soc. Hematology, Am. Soc. for Blood and Marrow Transplantation, Tex. Soc. Med. Oncology, Dallas Med. Soc., Phi Kappa Phi. Avocations: reading, music. Home: 5365 Nakoma Dr Dallas TX 75209-5619 Office: U Tex Southwestern Med Ctr 5323 Harry Hines Blvd Dallas TX 75390-8852 E-mail: robert.collins@utsouthwestern.edu.

COLLINS, ROBERT OAKLEY, history educator; b. Waukegan, Ill., Apr. 1, 1933; s. William George and Louise Van Horsen (Jack) C.; m. Janyce Hutchins Monroe, Oct. 6, 1974; children by previous marriage: Catharine Louise, Randolph Ware, Robert William. BA, Dartmouth Coll., 1954; AB (Marshall scholar 1954-55), Balliol Coll., Oxford U., 1956, MA, 1960; MA (Ford fellow), Yale U., 1958, PhD, 1959. Instr. history Williams Coll., Williamstown, Mass., 1959-61; lectr. U. Mass. Extension, Pittsfield, 1960-61; vis. asst. prof. history Columbia U., N.Y.C., 1962-63; asst. prof. history Williams Coll., 1963-65; mem. faculty U. Calif., Santa Barbara, 1965—, prof. history, 1969-94, dir. Ctr. for Study Developing Nations, 1967-69, acting vice chancellor for research and grad. affairs, 1970-71, dean grad. div., 1971-80; prof. emeritus, 1994—; vis. sr. assoc. fellow St. Antony's Coll., Oxford U., Eng., 1980-81; Trevelyan fellow Durham U., 1986—. Dir. Washington Ctr. U. Calif., Santa Barbara, 1992-94; mem. Internat. Adv. Group for the Nile Basin, World Bank, 1997. Author: The Southern Sudan, 1883-1898, 1962, King Leopold, England and the Upper Nile, 1968, Problems in African History, 1968, The Partition of Africa, 1969, Land Beyond the Rivers: The Southern Sudan, 1898-1918, 1971, Europeans in Africa, 1971, An Arabian Diary, 1969, The Southern Sudan in Historical Perspective, 1975, Shadows in the Grass: Britain in the Southern Sudan, 1983, The British in the Sudan, 1898-56, 84, The Waters of the Nile: Hydropolitics and the Jonglei Canal, 1900-1988, 1990, Western African History, Eastern African History, Central and Southern African History, 1990, The Nile Waters: An Annotated Bibliography, 1991, Problems In African History, The Pre-Colonial Centuries, 1993, Requiem for the Sudan, 1994, Historical Problems of Imperial Africa, 1994, Problems in the History of Modern Africa, 1996, Africa's Thirty Years' War: Chad, Libya and the Sudan, 1963-1993, 1999, Historical Dictionary of Pre-Colonial Africa, 2001, Documents from the African Past, 2001, The Nile, 2002, Revolutionary Sudan: Hasan al-Turabi and the Islamist State, 1989-2000, 2003. Recipient Gold class award Order Scis. and Arts Dem. Republic of Sudan, 1980; John Ben Snow Found. prize, 1984; NDEA lang. fellow, 1960-61, Social Sci. Rsch. Coun. fellow, 1962-63; Rockefeller Found. scholar-in-residence Bellagio, Italy, 1979, 87; Ford Found. fellow, 1979-81; Fulbright sr. rsch. fellow, 1982, 90; Woodrow Wilson fellow, 1983; vis. fellow Trevelyan Coll. mem. Soc. Fellows Durham U., 1986, fellow Balliol Coll., Oxford U., 1986-87; fellow Am. Coun. Learned Soc. 1990. Fellow Am. Philos. Soc.; mem. Am. Hist. Assn., African Studies Assn., Western River Guides Assn., Sudan Studies Assn., Explorers Club, Phi Beta Kappa. Home: 735 Calle De Los Amigos Santa Barbara CA 93105-4438 Office: U Calif Dept History Santa Barbara CA 93106-9410

COLLINS, ROBERT T. publisher; Pres., pub. Cherry Hill (N.J.) Courier Post, Asbury Park Press, Neptune, NJ, 1997—. Office: Asbury Park Press/The Gannett Co PO Box 1550 3601 Hwy 66 Neptune NJ 07754-1551

COLLINS, RONALD LESLIE LEOPOLD, physician, neurosurgeon; b. Nov. 19, 1944; Came to U.S., 1979; MB BS, U. W.I., Kingston, Jamaica, 1968. Diplomate Am. Bd. Neurological Surgery, Am. Bd. Minimally Invasive Spinal Surgery. Intern Harlem Hosp. Ctr., 1979-80, resident, 1980-81, King/Drew Med. Ctr., 1985-88; fellow Cook County Hosp., 1984-85, Robert Wood Johnson U. Hosp., 1988-89; neurosurgeon N.Y.C., 1989—. Contbr. articles to profl. jours.; inventor in field. Fellow Royal Coll. Surgery (Edinburgh), Internat. Coll Surgeons, Masons. Home: 681 E 78th St Brooklyn NY 11236-3307 E-mail: rllcolins@aol.com.

COLLINS, RONALD WILLIAM, psychologist, educator; b. N.Y.C., Jan. 6, 1947; s. Edward H. Collins Jr. and Estelle Lott. BA, Rutgers U., 1969; MS, Nova U., 1987; EdD, Fla. Internat. U., 1990; PhD, Saybrook Inst., 1996. Diplomate Am. Bd. Psychol. Spltys.; lic. profl. counselor, Mont., mental health counselor, Fla., psychologist, Colo. Spl. agt., ret. U.S. Secret Svc., Miami, Fla., 1971-91; adj. prof. St. Thomas U., Miami, 1990-91; asst. prof. Ea. Mont. Coll., Billings, 1991-94, Mont. State U., Billings, 1994-95; psychol. intern Inst. for Psychol. Growth, Ft. Lauderdale, Fla., 1994-95; adj. prof. instrnl. analysis/design Fla. Internat. U., Ft. Lauderdale, 1995-96; psychologist Dept. Corrections, Canon City, Colo., 1998-99, in pvt. practice, Miami, 1999-2000; dept. chair gen. studies U. Phoenix, Ft. Lauderdale, Fla., 2000—00; prof. Am. Inter Continental U., 2001—. Pvt. cons., adj. prof. U. Phoenix, Nova Southeastern U., Ft. Lauderdale, Keiser Coll., 2001—. Author: Kabiroff Papers, 1988, Transfer of Learning, 1990, Psychological Perspectives on Security Issues, 2000; contbr. articles to profl. jours. Mem. Billings Family Violence Task Force, 1992. Mem. APA, Am. Coll. Forensic Examiners, Am. Ednl. Rsch. Assn., Mental Health Assn. Broward County. Episcopalian. Avocations: skiing, horseback riding, flying, fiction writing, jogging. Office: PO Box 2053 Fort Lauderdale FL 33303-2053 Fax: (954) 761-7119. E-mail: r.collins.phd@worldnet.att.net.

COLLINS, ROSE ANN, minister; b. Pittsburgh, Pennsylvania, July 5, 1935; d. Joseph and Rochelle (McCray) Covington; m. Frank Collins, June 30, 1960 (div. 1978); children: Gar Andre, Guy Tracy. BA, Ctrl. Bible Coll., Springfield, Mo., 1987; MDiv, Assemblies of God Theol. Sem., Springfield, Mo., 1989. Ordained to min., 1990. Assoc. min. Deliverance Temple World Outreach Ministries, Springfield, Mo., 1988-90, evangelist Springfield and Pitts., 1991-93; chaplain Western Ctr., Canonsburg, Pa., 1993-96; min. New Jerusalem Holiness Ch., Pitts., 2002—. Trustee Northside Ch. of God in Christ, Pitts., 1982-87, bd. dir., 1983-87. Vol., Ctr. for Victims Violent Crime; vol. mentor Lydins Pl., Pitts. Mem. Soc. Chaplains (Western chpt.), Pa. Coun. Chs., Ret. Enlisted Assn. (hon., Steel City chpt. 72 chaplain 1994-96). Avocations: reading, walking. Home: 6290 Auburn St Apt 622 Pittsburgh PA 15206-3136

COLLINS, SAMUEL W., JR., judge; b. Caribou, Maine, Sept. 17, 1923; s. Samuel Wilson Collins & Elizabeth Black C; m. Dorothy Small, 1952; children: Edward, Elizabeth, Diane. BA, U. Maine; JD, Harvard U. Lawyer, Rockland, Maine, 1947—; justice Supreme Jud. Ct., Portland, Maine. Trustee Rockland Sch. Dist, 1949-61; Maine State Senate Dist. 21, 1975-84, majority leader, 1981-82, minority leader, 1983-84. Recipient Disting. Svc. award Jaycees, 1978. Mem. Maine Bar Assn., Rotary, Phi Beta Kappa, Phi Kappa Phi, Delta Tau Delta. Unitarian Universalist. Republican. Office: Knox County Courthouse 62 Union St Rockland ME 04841-2836

COLLINS, SANDRA KAY, pianist, composer, music educator; b. Hillsdale, Mich. d. Gerald Ellison and Barbara Jean (Stanfield) Fish; m. Christopher Terry Collins, Feb. 1, 1986; 3 children. BA in Piano Performance, Ea. Mich. U., 1995, MA in Music/Piano Performance, 1997. Instr. piano Jackson (Mich.) C.C., 1988; owner/instr. Sandra Collins Piano Studio, Jackson, 1987-91, Ann Arbor, Mich., 1991—; prof. piano Washtenaw C.C., Ann Arbor, Mich., 1997-2000; dir. Ea. Mich. U. Cmty. Music Acad., 2001—02. Staff accompanist, instr. Ea. Mich. U., 2000-02; prof. of piano, Washtenaw C.C., 2002—. Author: Adult Piano Method for the College Classroom, 1999. Mem. Music Tchrs.' Nat. Assn., Mich. Music Tchrs.' Assn., Ann Arbor Piano Tchrs.' Guild. Avocation: sports and nutrition. E-mail: collinspiano@cs.com.

COLLINS, STEPHEN BARKSDALE, retired health care executive; b. Houston, Mar. 14, 1932; s. Ray George and Ruth Ella (Davis) C.; m. Katherine Jane Justice, June 6, 1955; children: Nancy Catherine, Rebecca Jane, Ruth Anne, Stephen Barksdale, Cynthia Marye. BA, Baylor U., 1954; M.H.A., Washington U., 1956. Asst. adminstr., adminstr. Good Samaritan Hosp., Vincennes, Ind., 1959-65; adminstr. Rosewood Gen. Hosp., Houston, 1965-72; chief exec. officer Lake Charles Meml. Hosp., La., 1972-85; v.p. shareholder rels. and membership VHA, Inc., Irving, Tex., 1985-97; ret., 1997. Bd. dirs. Better Bus. Bur. Served with USAF, 1956-59. Decorated Meritorious Service medal, Commendation medal. Fellow Am. Coll. Hosp. Adminstrs.; mem. C. of C. (dir.), Southeastern Hosp. Conf. (bd. dirs. 1981-82, exec. com. 1983, chmn.-elect 1984), La. Hosp. Assn. (chmn.-elect 1981, chmn. 1982), Am. Hosp. Assn. Clubs: Rotary. Baptist. Home: 1009 Inwood Ln Colleyville TX 76034-3848 E-mail: scollins@quixnet.net.

COLLINS, STEVEN M. lawyer; b. Atlanta, Oct. 22, 1952; s. E.B. and Judith (Morse) C.; divorced; 1 child, Erin M.; m. Anne Frances Garland, Oct. 31, 1987; 1 child, Timothy G. AB, Harvard U., 1974, JD, 1977. Bar: Ga. 1977, U.S. Dist. Ct. (no. dist.) Ga. 1977, U.S. Ct. Appeals (11th cir.) 1981, U.S. Dist. Ct. (mid. dist.) Ga. 1982, U.S. Tax Ct. 1984, U.S. Ct. Appeals (4th cir.) 1986, U.S. Ct. Appeals (6th cir.) 2001, U.S. Supreme Ct. 1994. Assoc. Alston & Bird, Atlanta, 1977-83, ptnr., 1983—. Editor-in-chief Ga. State Bar Journal, Atlanta, 1982-84. Mem. ABA, State Bar Ga., Atlanta Bar Assn. Office: Alston & Bird One Atlantic Ctr 1201 W Peachtree St NW Atlanta GA 30309-3424 E-mail: scollins@alston.com.

COLLINS, SUNNIVA REFSNES, metallurgist; b. Cleve., May 23, 1960; d. Sigvald Matthias Refsnes and Faith Corrigan; m. Michael James Collins, July 8, 1989; children: Kristina Venephe, William Arthur. BA, U. Mich., Ann Arbor, 1983; MSE, Case Western Res. U., Cleve., 1991, PhD, 1994. EIT, Ohio. Editor ASM Internat., Materials Park, Ohio, 1984-89; rsch. Case Western Res. U., Cleve., 1989-94; rsch. metallurgist Swagelok, Solon, Ohio, 1995—. Inventor/patentee; contbr. articles to profl. jours. Mem.: ASM Internat. (Cleve. chpt., tech. books com. 1994—2001, exec. com. 1996—, sec. 1997—98, treas. 1998—99, vice chair 1999—2000, chair 2000—01). Democrat. Roman Catholic. Avocations: knitting, reading, bicycling. Home: 2244 Maplewood Rd Cleveland Heights OH 44118-2816

COLLINS, SUSAN FORD, leadership consultant; b. N.Y.C., Dec. 8, 1939; d. Eugene Elwood and Mary Elizabeth Crighton Ford; m. Donald J. Collins, Sept. 9, 1962 (div. 1973); children: Catherine Lyn Rosenberg, Margaret Ann Chaneles. Student, Smith Coll., 1958-60; BA, U. Richmond, 1961. Rsch. psychologist NIMH, Bethesda, Md., 1962-64; rschr. success and leadership strategies Miami, Fla., 1964—. Creator The Technology of Success, The Leadership Relay; ptnr. Success Internat., Miami, 1985-86, co-dir., 1988-93; v.p. Winterstreet Corp. USA, Miami, 1986-88; pres. Our Children Are Watching, Inc., Miami, 1993—; cons. Arthur Andersen, CNN, Am. Express, Digital Equipment, Kimberley-Clar, Ryder Sys., Fla. Power and Light, IBM, Levitz Furniture, Coopers and Lybrand, City of Miami, City of Seaside, Fla., Palm Beach County, Fla.; spkr. in field. Author: (Book) The Me Book: A Manual for Being Human, 1963, Our Children Are Watching: Ten Skills for Leading the Next Generation to Success, 1995, Intuition at Work, 1996, The Joy of Success: 10 Essential Skills for Getting the Success You Want, 2003, (foreword) Women and Leadership, 1996; guest (TV and Radio Shows). Fellow The Leadership Trust; mem. Nat. Spkrs. Assn., Nat. Writers Assn., Phi Beta Kappa, Psi Chi, Pi Kappa Delta, Phi Kappa Phi. Address: Tech of Success Inc 12040 NE 5th Ave Miami FL 33161-6260 E-mail: susanfordcollins@msn.com.

COLLINS, SUSAN M. senator; b. Caribou, Maine, Dec. 7, 1952; BA in Govt. magna cum laude, St. Lawrence U., 1975. Prin. advisor bus. affairs U.S. Senator Bill Cohen; commr. Maine Dept. Profl. and Fin. Regulation; dir. New England ops. U.S. Small Bus. Adminstrn.; exec. dir. Ctr. Family Bus., Husson Coll., Bangor, Maine; U.S. senator from Maine, 1997—. Staff dir. Senate Subcom. on Oversight Govt. Mgmt., 1981-87; chair Cabinet Coun. on Health Care Policy, State of Maine; mem. U.S. Senate com. health, edn., labor and pensions, 1997—, subcom. on children and families, 1997—, subcom. on pub. health and safety, 1997—, com. on govtl. affairs, 1997—; chmn. permanent subcom. on investigations, 1997—; mem. spl. com. on aging. Rep. candidate for Gov., State of Maine, 1994. Recipient Outstanding Alumni award St. Lawrence U., 1992. Mem. Bangor Rotary Club, Phi Beta Kappa. Republican. Roman Catholic. Office: 172 Russell Sen Office Bldg Washington DC 20510*

COLLINS, THEODORE JOHN, lawyer; b. Walla Walla, Wash., Oct. 2, 1936; s. Robert Bonfield and Catherine Roselle (Snyder) C.; m. Patricia Spengler Pasieka, May 11, 1968; children: Jonathan, Caitlin, Matthew, Patrick, Flannary. BA, U. Notre Dame, 1958; postgrad., U. Bonn, Fed. Republic Germany, 1959; LLB, Harvard U., 1962. Bar: Wash. 1962, U.S. Supreme Ct. 1982, U.S. Ct. Appeals (fed. cir.) 1982, U.S. Dist. Ct. (ea. dist.) Wash. 1965, U.S. Dist. Ct. (we. dist.) Wash. 1962. Ptnr. Perkins Coie Law Firm, Seattle, 1962-86; v.p., gen. counsel The Boeing Co., Seattle, 1986-98, sr. v.p., gen. counsel, 1998-2000; of counsel Perkins Coie Law Firm, 2001—. Adj. prof. Seattle U. Law Sch. Mem. ABA, Wash. State Bar Assn., King County Bar Assn., Wash. Athletic Club. E-mail: tcoll10236@aol.com., collt@perkinscoie.com.

COLLINS, THOMAS HANSEN, coast guard officer; b. Quincy, Mass., June 25, 1946; s. Harley Hartford and Inger Dagmar (Hansen) C.; m. Constance Ann Monahan, June 7, 1968; children: Christine Ann, Kathryn. BS, USCG Acad., New London, Conn., 1968; MA in Liberal Studies, Wesleyan U., 1972; MBA, U. New Haven, 1976. Commd. 1st lt. USCG, 1968, advanced through grades to rear adm., 1994; comdg. officer USCG Cutter, Cape Morgan, Charleston, S.C., 1969-71; instr., prof. USCG Acad., 1972-76; mem. planning program, budget staff Office of R&D USCG Hdqs., Washington, 1976-80; dep. group comdr. USCG Group, St. Petersburg, Fla., 1980-83; mem. program rev. staff USCG Hdqs., Washington, 1983-87; group comdr. USCG Group L.I. Sound, New Haven, 1987-90; chief adminstrn. divsn. USCG Dist. 14, Honolulu, 1990-92; chief program divsn. USCG Hdqs., Washington, 1992-94, dep. chief of staff, 1994—98, chief office of acquisition, 1994—; comdr, Pac. area and 11th Coast Guard dist. U.S. Coast Guard, 1998—2000, vice-commandant, 2000—02, commandant, 2002—. Decorated Legion of Merit, Meritorious Svc. medal (2), Coast Guard Commendation medal (3). Mem. Am. Soc. Naval Engrs. (hon.). Avocations: golf, gardening, reading. Office: Comdt US Coast Guard 2100 2nd St SW Washington DC 20593*

COLLINS, THOMAS JOSEPH, English language educator; b. London, Ont., Can., Aug. 23, 1936; s. Joseph Benedict and Margaret Jean (Collins) C.; div.; children: Mark, Kristen, Brendan; m. 1985. BA, U. Western Ont., 1959, MA, 1961; PhD, Ind. U., 1965. Prof. English U. Western Ont., London, 1965—, chmn. dept., 1974-82, dean faculty arts, 1982-86, acad. v.p., provost, 1986-95. Author: Robert Browning's Moral-Aesthetic Theory: 1833-55, 1967; editor: Letters from the Brownings to the Tennysons, 1971, Letters of Robert Browning to the Rev. J.D. Williams, 1976, (with J. Pettigrew) Robert Browning: The Poems, 1981, (with R.J. Shroyer) Robert Browning: The Plays, 1988, Robert Browning: Centennial Issue of Victorian Poetry, 1989, (with R.J. Shroyer) Robert Browning Concordance, 7 vols., 1996, The Broadview Anthology of Victorian Poetry and Poetic Theory, 1999, The Broadview Concise Anthology, 2000, (with Richard D. Altick) Robert Browling: The Ring and the Book, 2001; mem. editl. bd. Victorian Poetry, 1974—, Victorian Studies, 1979—. Can. Council research grantee, 1974; grantee U. Western Ont. Acad. Devel. Fund, 1982, Social Sci. and Humanities Research Council, 1983. Mem. Can. Assn. U. Tchrs., MLA (exec. com. Victorian group 1972-75), Internat. Browning Soc. (bd. dirs. 1976), Com. Chairmen English Ont. (pres. 1979-81), Can. Assn. Chairmen English (pres. 1979-80), Council Deans Arts and Scis. Ont. (chmn. 1983-85), Ontario Assn. Triathletes. Office: Univ of Western Ont Dept English London ON Canada N6A 3K7 E-mail: collinst@uwo.ca.

COLLINS, THOMAS MICHAEL, surgeon; b. Oakland, Calif., 1943; BS, St. Mary's Coll. Calif., 1965; MD, Creighton U., 1969. Diplomate Am. Bd. Surgery. Intern Portsmouth Naval Hosp., 1969-70; resident in surgery Maine Med. Ctr., Portland, 1972-76; med. staff HD Goodall Hosp., Sanford, Maine; courtesy staff Mercy Hosp., Portland, So. Maine Med. Ctr., Biddeford, Maine Med. Ctr., Portland. Dir. New England div. Am. Cancer Soc. Fellow ACS; mem. AMA., New England Surg. Soc. Office: 25A June St Ste 5 Sanford ME 04073-2642

COLLINS, THOMAS WILLIAM, caterer, consultant; b. Lewiston, Idaho, Nov. 4, 1926; s. William James and Mary (Egan) C.; m. Mary Charlene Tracy, Aug. 1, 1947 (dec. Apr. 1984); children: Kathleen, William, Charles. Grad. high sch., Staples, Minn., 1944. Owner Collins Cafe, Park Rapids, Minn., 1947-63, Tom Collins Restaurant, Walker, Minn., 1963-83, Tom Collins Catering, Walker, 1983—. Author: Collins Cooking Secrets, 1981. Fundraiser DFL, 1976-83; adv. bd. Lake Country Food Bank, Mpls., 1981-86, bd. dirs., 1987-98. Served with USN, 1945-46, 51-52. Recipient Recognition award Mont. Gov., 1978, cert. of Spl. Congl. Recognition, 1995; Tom Collins Day proclaimed by Minn. Gov., 1977. Mem. Assn. Great Lakes Outdoor Writers, Am. Legion. Lodges: Masons (sr. warden 1958), Shriners. Avocations: hunting, fishing, photography. Home and Office: PO Box 33 Walker MN 56484-0033

COLLINS, TIMOTHY CLARK, holding company executive; b. Frankfort, Ky., Oct. 8, 1956; s. Frank Dane and Betty (Cunningham) C.; m. Andrea Shaffer, Jan. 15, 1983; children: Dane Andrew, Matthew Ramsey, Lucius Walker Bell. BA in Philosophy, DePauw U., 1978; MBA, Yale U., 1982. Assoc. Booz Allen & Hamilton, Chgo., 1981-84; v.p. Lazard Freres & Co., N.Y.C., 1984-90; sr. mgr. dir. Onex Corp., N.Y.C., 1990-95; CEO Ripplewood Holdings LLC, N.Y.C., 1995—. Bd. dirs. Shinsei Bank, WRC Media Inc., Western Multiplex Corp. Mem. bd. advisors Yale U. Div. Sch.; bd. dirs. Lennox Hill Neighborhood House. Mem. Siwanoy Country Club, Hollenbeck Club (Conn.), Bronxville Field Club. Presbyterian. Address: Ripple Wood nHoldings LLC 1 Rockefeller Plz Lbby 1 New York NY 10020-2002

COLLINS, TUCKER, pathologist, molecular biologist; b. Lorain, Ohio, Nov. 3, 1952; s. Robert James and Catherine (Meisner) C.; m. Mary Judith Whitley, June 15, 1985. BA, Amherst Coll., 1975, DSc (hon.), 1998; MD, PhD, U. Rochester, 1981. Diplomate Am. Bd. Pathology. Clin., rsch. fellow Brigham and Women's Hosp., Boston, 1981-85; from instr. to prof. pathology Harvard Med. Sch., Boston, 1985-98, prof. pathology, 1998—; Wolbach prof., chmn. dept.

pathology Children's Hosp., Boston, 1992-99. Staff pathologist Brigham and Women's Hosp., 1992-99; charter mem., chmn. pathology study sect. NIH. Author: Pathologic Basis of Disease, 1999; mem. editl. bd. Am. Jour. Pathology; contbr. articles to profl. jours. Scholar Pew Scholars Program, 1987-91; grantee NIH, 1985, 90, 93, 96, 97, 2002, Am. Heart Assn. Established Investigator, 1991-96; recipient Warner-Lambert/Parke-Davis award Am. Soc. for Investigative Pathology, 1994; assoc. master Francis Weld Peabody Soc. Mem. Am. Soc. Investigative Pathology (pres.), Am. Assn. Univ. Pathologists, N.Am. Vascular Biology Orgn., New England Soc. Pathologists (pres.), Acad. Harvard Med. Sch.. Achievements include research in the structure and regulation of SCAN family of transcription factors and of genes for leukocyte-endothelial adhesion molecules. Home: 120 Jerusalem Rd Cohasset MA 02025 Office: Children's Hosp Boston MA 02115 E-mail: tcoll02115@aol.com.

COLLINS, WALTER LLOYD GEORGE, editor; b. Broken Arrow, Okla., Dec. 6, 1917; s. Dow Otho and Myrtle Hester (Campbell) C.; m. Ruth Leona Hamilton, Sept. 3, 1935; children: Mary, Walter, Alvin, Shirley. *George and wife, Ruth, are both descendants of generations of pioneers. One of his great grandmother's sisters was Daniel Boone's wife. One great grandfather was a cousin of Lt. General Nathan Bedford Forrest. His grandfather built one of the early stone houses in Indian Territory. His father worked for Frank Phillips as he built his oil empire in the 1920s. Ruth's family, the Hamiltons, moved from Maryland to Missouri about 1780. He and Ruth have four children: Mary Ellen Moore, Walter Lewis, Alvin Lloyd and Shirley Marie Green. They have eighteen grandchildren, thirty-five great grandchildren, and two great, great grandchildren.* BA, Pan Am. U., 1966; MA, U. Tulsa, 1975. Aviation cadet USAAF, 1942; advanced through grades to maj. USAF, 1962; exec. in charge C-E Installation Project NATO, Europe, North Africa, Mid. East, 1956-57; sr. editor radar and missiles project USAFE, 1957-58; ops. officer C-E divsn. Def. Atomic Support Agy., Alburquerque, 1959-63; dir. comm.-elec., spacetrack NORAD, Colorado Springs, 1963-64; ret., 1964; gen. mgr. Desert Lodge, Moab, Utah, 1967-68; design engr. planner Beech Aircraft Corp., Wichita, Kans., 1968-72; dir. internat. student affairs Spartan Sch. Aeronautics, Tulsa, 1979-83; pres. R&W Internat., Tulsa, 1984-88, Alpha-Omega Press, Tulsa. Ponca City, Okla., 1990—. Adv. bd. Higher Edn. Com. Okla. Acad. State Goals, 1977-95. Author: On the Razor's Edge, 1990, Manner of Man, 2001. Mem. Kay County (Okla.) Rep. Com., 1993—; mem. Ponca City Traffic Commn., 1997-2000. Mem. Acad. Am. Poets, Nat. Author's Registry, Nat. Order Battlefield Commns. (charter mem.), Am. Air Mus. in Great Britain, Air Force Assn., Mil. Officers Assn. Am. Avocations: writing, editing, photography. Office: Alpha-Omega Press PO Box 2163 Ponca City OK 74602-2163

COLLINS, WAYNE DALE, lawyer; b. Portsmouth, Va., Dec. 23, 1951; s. Wayne D. Sr. and Mary L. (Higdon) C.; m. Mary Ann Bradshaw, Aug. 9, 1981; children: Laura, Melissa, Christopher. BS with honors, Calif. Inst. Tech., 1973, MS, 1974; JD, U. Chgo., 1978; postgrad., U. Minn., 1979. Bar: N.Y. 1979, U.S. Supreme Ct. 1983, D.C., 1991. Assoc. Shearman & Sterling, N.Y.C., 1978-81, 83-86, ptnr., 1987—; spl. asst. to V.P. George Bush, Washington, 1981-82; dep. asst. atty. gen. antitrust div. U.S. Dept. Justice, Washington, 1983. Vis. lectr. Yale Law Sch., 1991-95; vis. com. U. Chgo. Law Sch., 2003—. Co-author: Horizontal Mergers: Law and Policy, 1986, Non-Horizontal Mergers: Law and Policy, 1988, State Antitrust Practice and Statutes, 1991. White House fellow, 1981-82. Fellow Am. Bar Found.; mem. ABA (chmn. antitrust sect. subcom. on fin. markets and instns. 1983-87, chmn. pub. com. 1987-91, coun. mem. antitrust sect. 1991-94, officer antitrust sect. 1994-1999), Am. Law Inst., Assn. of Bar of City of N.Y., Am. Econ. Assn., Econometric Soc., Soc. for Advancement of Econ. Theory, Am. Coun. Nationalities Svc. (bd. dirs. 1988-1999). Republican. Roman Catholic. Office: 599 Lexington Ave New York NY 10022-6030 also: 801 Pennsylvania Ave NW Washington DC 20004-2615

COLLINS, WHITFIELD JAMES, lawyer; b. Dallas, Aug. 26, 1918; s. Jasper and Gertrude (James) C.; m. Beth Cooper, June 5, 1951 (dec. Aug. 1980); children: Whitfield James Jr., Kay, Cooper R. AA, Kemper Mil. Sch., 1936; BA, U. Tex., 1938, JD, 1940; LLM, Harvard U., 1941. Bar: Tex. 1940, U.S. Dist. Ct. (no. dist.) Tex. 1950, U.S. Ct. Claims 1978, U.S. Tax Ct. 1949, U.S. Ct. Appeals (5th cir.) 1981. Atty. Office Gen. Counsel Treasury Dept., Washington, 1941-42, Office Chief Counsel, IRS, Washington and N.Y.C., 1946-48; assoc. Cantey, Hanger, Johnson, Scarborough & Gooch, Ft. Worth, 1949-54; ptnr. Cantey & Hanger and predecessor firms, Ft. Worth, 1954-96, of counsel, 1996—. Sec., bd. dirs. Vol. Purchasing Groups, Inc., Bonham, Tex., 1968-95; pres. Fifth Ave. Found. and C.J. Wrightsman Ednl. Fund, 1980—; bd. dirs., treas. T.J. Brown and C.A. Lupton Found., Ft. Worth; bd. dirs. All Saints Health Found. Contbr. articles in field to profl. jours. Bd. dirs., past pres. Moncrief Radiation Ctr., Ft. Worth, Ft. Worth Art Assn., Arts Council Ft. Worth and Tarrant County, Ft. Worth Art Commn.; bd. dirs. Van Cliburn Found., Non-Profit Svc. Ctr.; Ft. Worth Opera Assn., Ft. Worth Symphony Orch. Assn. Served to lt. comdr. USNR, 1942-46. asst. adminstrv. aide to chief of naval ops., 1945-46. Recipient Spl. Recognition award West Tex. Legal Svcs., 1999, Heritage Philanthropist award All Saints Health Found., 2001. Fellow ABA (life), State Bar Tex. (chmn. taxation sect. 1964-65), Tex. Bar Found. (life), Tarrant County Bar Found. (life, bd. dirs. 2003—); mem. Tarrant County Bar Assn. (Blackstone award 1995). Episcopalian. Home: 6732 Brants Ln Fort Worth TX 76116-7202 Office: Cantey & Hanger 801 Cherry St Ste 2100 Fort Worth TX 76102-6898 E-mail: wcollins@canteyhanger.com.

COLLINS, WILLIAM EDWARD, aeromedical administrator, researcher; b. Bklyn., May 16, 1932; s. William Edward and Loretta Agnes (Brasier) C.; m. Corliss Jean Barnes, June 20, 1970; 1 child, Corliss Adora BS, St. Peter's Coll., 1954; MA, Fordham U., 1956, PhD, 1959. Lic. psychologist, Okla. Psychol. rsch. asst. Fordham U., 1954-56, tchg. fellow, 1958, grad. instr., 1958-59, rsch. asst., 1958-59; rsch. psychologist U.S. Army Med. Rsch. Lab., Ft. Knox, Ky., 1959-61; rsch. psychologist Aviation Psychology Lab. FAA Civil Aeromed. Inst., Oklahoma City, 1961-63, chief sensory integration sect., 1963-65, lab. supr., 1965-86, human resources rsch. br. mgr., 1986-88, dep. dir., 1988-89, dir., 1989-2001; adj. assoc. prof. psychology U. Okla., Norman, 1963-70, adj. prof., 1970-89; adj. assoc. prof. rsch. psychology dept. psychiatry and behavioral scis. U. Okla. Health Scis. Ctr., Oklahoma City, 1965 71, adj. prof., 1971 . Mem. Nat. Acad. Sci.-NRC Com. on Vision, 1963-82, mem. exec. coun., 1973-81; mem. Nat. Acad. Sci.-NRC Com. on Hearing, Bioacoustics and Biomechanics, 1963-87; appearances before House Sub-Com. on Pub. Health and Environ., 1971, House Sub-Com. on Investigations and Oversight, 1983, House Sub-Com. on Transp., Aviation and Materials, 1987, 88; judge Okla. Sci. and Engring. Fair, Ada, 1980, 81, 82; mem. Okla. Bd. Examiners Psychologists, 1981-84, chmn., 1982-84; evaluator proposals NSF, 1968-82, HEW, 1971-80; lectr. in field. Contbr. chpts., numerous articles to profl. publs.; numerous rsch. presentations in field. Served to capt. Med. Services Corps, U.S. Army, 1959-61 Recipient Disting. Career Svc. award FAA, 2001. Fellow AAAS, APA (abstractor Psychol. Abstracts 1962—, citation 1973), N.Y. Acad. Scis., Aerospace Med. Assn. (Raymond F. Longacre award 1971, presdl. exec. com. 1982-84, exec. coun. 1982-85, editl. bd. Aviation, Space and Environ. Medicine 1974-2000, assoc. editor 1980-2000, Pres.'s Citation 1993, Harry G. Moseley award 1998, Life Scis. and Biomed. Engring. Profl. Excellence award 1989, Pres.'s award 1999), Am. Psychol. Soc. (charter), Aerospace Human Factors Assn. (charter, Paul T. Hansen award 1998, William E. Collins ann. award for excellence in human factors established 2002); mem. Assn. Aviation Psychologists (pres. 1974-75), Okla. Psychol. Assn. (Disting. Psychologist award 1984), South African Soc. Aerospace and Environ. Medicine (Silver Medal award 1998), Nat. Mus. Am. Indian (charter mem. 1992-, cert. of appreciation 1995), So. Poverty Law Ctr., Nat. Campaign Tolerance (founding mem.). Achievements include William E. Collins Ann. award for Outstanding FAA Publs. in Aerospace Medicine named in his honor, 2003. Home: 8900 Sheringham Dr Oklahoma City OK 73132-4764 Office: Dept Psychiat Behavior Sci Okla U Health Sci Ctr Room 302-R PO Box 26901 Research Building Oklahoma City OK 73190-3048

COLLINS, WILLIAM F., JR., neurosurgery educator; b. New Haven, Conn., Jan. 20, 1924; MD, Yale U., 1947. Diplomate Am. Bd. Neurol. Surgery. Intern Barnes Hosp., St. Louis, 1947-49, asst. resident in neuro-surgery, 1951-52, resident, 1952-53; fellow neurophysiology Washington U., 1953-54; instr. neurosurgery Western Res. U., Cleve., 1954-55, sr. instr., 1955-57, asst. prof., 1957-60, assoc. prof., 1960-63; prof., chmn. div. neurosurgery Med. Coll. Va., 1963-67; prof. Yale U., New Haven, 1967—, chmn. sect. neurosurgery, 1967-86, chmn. dept. surgery, 1986-93, prof. neurosurgery, 1993-94, prof. neurosurgery emeritus, 1994—; clin. prof. neurosurgery U. Calif. Sch. Medicine, San Diego, 1997—. With M.C., U.S. Army, 1949-51. Office: Yale Sch Medicine Dept Neurosurgery PO Box 208082 New Haven CT 06520-8082 E-mail: william.collins@yale.edu., wfcollin@aol.com.

COLLINS, WILLIAM J. poet, educator; b. N.Y.C., Mar. 1941; Prof. English Lehman Coll., CUNY. Author: (books of poetry) Pokerface, 1977, Video Poems, 1980, The Apple That Astonished Paris, 1988, Questions About Angels, 1991 (Selected by Edward Hirsch for Nat. Poetry Series), The Art of Drowning, 1995 (finalist for Lenore Marshall Poetry Prize), Picnic, Lightning, 1998, Taking Off Emily Dickinson's Clothes, 2000, Sailing Alone Around the Room: New and Selected Poems, 2001, Nine Horses, 2002; contbr. poetry to profl. jours. and publs.; editor: Poetry 180: A Turning Back to Poetry, 2003; reader (recording) The Best Cigarette, 1997. Named a Literary Lion, N.Y. Pub. Libr., 1992; named U.S. Poet Laureate, 2001; recipient Oscar Blumenthal Prize, Bess Hokin Prize, Frederick Bock Prize, Levinson Prize; fellow, N.Y. Found. for the Arts, NEA, Guggenheim Found.*

COLLINS, WILLIAM THOMAS, retired pathologist; b. Omaha, Feb. 21, 1922; s. John Maurice and Bess (Ewing) C.; m. Ann E. Adams, May 30, 1942; children: William Thomas, Carol Ann, John Mark, Donald Brian. BS, U. Ky., 1942; MD, U. Mich., 1944. Diplomate Am. Bd. Pathology. Intern Good Samaritan Hosp., Cin., 1944-45; resident in pathology Cin. Gen. Hosp., 1945-46, asst. attending pathologist, 1948-51; pathologist, dir. labs Good Samaritan Hosp., Cin., 1952-56; fellow in exfoliative cytology Free Hosp. for Women, Brookline, Mass., 1949; assoc. pathologist Blodgett Meml. Hosp., Grand Rapids, Mich., 1956-57, Lima Meml. Hosp., Ohio, 1957-58, pathologist, dir. lab., 1958-87. Instr. in pathology Coll. Medicine, U. Cin., 1948-51, asst. prof. pathology, 1951-56; assoc. clin. prof. pathology Med. Coll. Ohio, Toledo, 1972-98; pres. med. staff Lima Meml. Hosp., 1968-70; chmn. adv. group Northwestern Ohio Regional Med. Program, 1970-71; exec. com. bd. dirs., sec.-treas. Gt. Lakes Regional Quality Assurance Assn.; cert. lab. assts. com. Nat. Accrediting Agy. for Clin. Lab. Scis., 1974-76; chmn. bd. dirs. Ohio Region III PSRO, 1977-80; mem. Ohio Statewide Profl. Standards Rev. Coun., 1980-81 Bd. dirs. Allen County chpt. ARC, pres., 1972-73; bd. dirs. Allen County unit Am. Cancer Soc., pres., 1973-75, mem. exec. com. Ohio divsn., sec., 1979-80, v.p., 1980-81, pres., 1981-82, nat. del., 1985-92; nat. dir. Am. Cancer Soc., 1992-95; bd. dirs., exec. com. Cancer Control Consortium Ohio, 1980-86; bd. dirs. Lima Symphony Orch., 1963-69, United Fund Greater Lima, 1970-72. Lt. (j.G.) M.C. USNR, 1946-48. Mem. Lima and Allen County Acad. Medicine (sec.-treas. 1972-79), Ohio Med. Assn., AMA, Ohio Soc. Pathologists (pres. 1970-71), Am. Soc. Investigative Pathology, Am. Soc. Clin. Pathologists, Coll. Am. Pathologists, Internat. Acad. Pathology,Rotary Lodge (pres. 1964-65), Sigma Xi. Republican. Presbyterian. Home: 4030 S Wapak Rd Lima OH 45806-9409

COLLINS, JR. ARISTIDE J. academic administrator; s. Aristide J. Collins, Sr. and Barbara Ann Collins. MPA, Calif. State U., Long Beach, 1995—98; BA in Polit. Sci., Calif. State U., Hayward, 1993. Cert. Specialist in Planned Giving Am. Inst. for Philanthropic Studies, Ednl. Mgmt. Calif. State U., Hayward. Exec. dir. of corp. rels. Calif. State U., Long Beach, 1993—99; dir. of devel. for u. projects The George Wash. U., 1999—2000; assoc. v.p. Calif. State U., Long Beach, 2000—. Mem. Coun. for Advancement and Support of Edn., Washington, Pi Alpha Alpha Nat. Honor Soc. for Pub. Adminstrn., Phi Delta Gamma Nat. Grad. Honor Soc., Nat. Soc. of Fund-raising Executives, Los Angeles, Calif. Bd. of trustees Goodwill Industries of Long Beach, 2001—; bd. dirs. Long Beach Cmty. Improvement League; field organizer and office mgr. Clinton/Gore '92, Calif. Dem. Party, Oakland, 1992—92. Mem.: Nat. Soc. of Fund-raising Executives, Coun. for Advancement and Support of Edn., Calif. Faculty Assn., AAUP, Phi Delta Gamma, Pi Alpha Alpha. Roman Catholic. Avocations: sports collectibles, music, writing, sports. Office: Calif State U Long Beach 1250 Bellflower Blvd BH387 Long Beach CA 90840-0116 Office Fax: 562-985-8109. E-mail: acollins@csulb.edu.

COLLINS-ADLER, CATHERINE KAY, social services professional; b. Aurora, Colo., May 3, 1964; d. Carroll Gail and Mary Kay Collins; m. John Thomas Adler, June 22, 1985. Student, S.D. State U., 1982-85. Tech. support specialist Gary Snow & Assocs., Pierre, S.D., 1988-91; co-owner Whistlestop, Pierre, 1992-93; program asst. S.D. Bankers Assn., Pierre, 1993-95; owner Simply Office Support, Pierre, 1989—; arts coord. Short Grass Arts Coun., Pierre, 1993—; exec. dir. Pierre-Fort United Way, 1991—. Mem. Healthy Starts Com. Healthy Communities/Healthy Youth Com., Pierre Area Charitable Orgns., Am. Red Cross Disaster Team, Pierre Econ. Devel. Corp., Ctrl. South Dakota Leadership Alumni Group; past mem. Nat. Historic Preservation Com., S.D. Archives Registered Rschr., Youth at Risk Big Sister, Pierre Fire Dept. Auxiliary and S.D. Arts. Coun., Hughes/Stanley Counties Families First Partnership, River Hills Vol. Ctr. Bd., South Dakota Planned Giving Coun., Adolescent Health Coalition, Retired Sr. Vol. Program Adv. Bd., I-3 Work Group for Free Immunization Clinics for Youths 0-6, Central Edn. Network for Tech. Tng., Youth Power Task Force, Gifts-in-Kind Am. Pres.'s Coun., Project Care Coalition, Pierre Assn. Vol. Leaders, Nat. Soc. Fundraising Execs., Pierre City Commn. Traffic Safety Bd., Pierre Postal Adv. Com., Mayor's Non-profit Task Force. Recipient Dottie Rosso scholarship, 1994, Gus Shea Meml. scholarship, 1996, Outstanding Young Woman award, 1997. Office: Pierre Fort Pierre United Way 221 S Central Ave Pierre SD 57501-2428

COLLINS BLOCK, CATHY, education educator, writer, educational consultant; b. Madison, Wis., Dec. 11, 1948; d. Charles Douglas and Jo Ann (Jiru) Zinke; m. Stanley Byron Block, June 31, 1991; 1 child, Michael Donegan. BS in Elem. Edn., Lamar U., 1970; M in Elem. Edn., U. North Tex., 1974; PhD in Curriculum and Instrn., U. Wis., 1976. Cert. tchr. Tex., Okla. Tchr. elem. sch. Beaumont (Tex.) Ind. Sch. Dist., 1970-71, Oklahoma City Ind. Sch. Dist., 1971-72, Azle (Tex.) Ind. Sch. Dist., 1972-74; grad. rsch. asst. U. Wis., Madison, 1974-76; asst. prof. edn. So. Ill. U., Carbondale, 1976-77; prof. edn. Tex. Christian U., Ft. Worth, 1977—. Ednl. cons. 300 sch. dists., U.S., Can., Poland, Russia, Hungary, Germany, Bahrain, Philippines, 1976—, Walt Disney Corp., Burbank, Calif., 1995—, Scholastic Inc., N.Y.C., 1997—. Author: Teaching Language Arts, 1999, 3d edit., 2003; contbr. 90 articles to profl. jours. including Scholastic, Inc., Walt Disney, Reading Rsch. Quar., The Reading Tchr. Bd. dirs. Nobel Edn. Dynamics, Media, Pa., 1996—. Mem. APA (mem. editl. adv. bd. Jour. Ednl. Psychology 1996—), Internat. Reading Assn. (pres. spl. interest group for gifted and creative readers 1991—, bd. dirs., 2002-05). Jewish. Avocations: running, piano. Office: Tex Christian U 2800 S University Dr PO Box 297900 Fort Worth TX 76129

COLLINSON, DALE STANLEY, lawyer; b. Tulsa, Okla., Sept. 1, 1938; s. Harold Everett and Charlotte Elizabeth (Bonds) C.; m. Susan Waring Smith, June 7, 1969; children: Stuart, Eleanor. AB in Politics and Econs. summa cum laude, Yale U., 1960; LLB, Columbia U., 1963. Bar: N.Y. 1963, U.S. Tax Ct. 1977. Law clk. U.S. Ct. Appeals (2d cir.), N.Y.C., 1963-64; law clk. to Justice Byron R. White U.S. Supreme Ct., Washington, 1964-66; asst. prof. Stanford (Calif.) Law Sch., 1966-68, assoc. prof., 1968-72; atty.-advisor Office of Tax Policy, U.S. Dept. Treasury, Washington, 1972-73, assoc. tax legis. counsel, 1973-74, dep. tax legis. counsel, 1974-75, tax legis. counsel, 1975-76; tax ptnr. Willkie Farr & Gallagher, N.Y.C., 1976-2000; spl. counsel fin. instns. and products IRS, Washington, 2000—. Panel mem. Practising Law Inst. programs, 1981, 82, 84, 86, 88, Am. Law Inst.-ABA program, 1984, Investment Co. Inst. programs, 1992, 94, 97. Contbr. articles to legal jours. Fellow Am. Coll. Tax Counsel; mem. ABA, N.Y. State Bar (chmn. tax sect. 1985), Assn. of Bar of City of N.Y. (tax coun. 1990-93, vice chmn. taxation of corps. com. 1990-93). Republican. Home: 5480 Wisconsin Ave Apt 920 Chevy Chase MD 20815 Office: IRS 1111 Constitution Ave Washington DC 20224 E-mail: dale.collinson.td.60@aya.yale.edu.

COLLINSON, VIVIENNE RUTH, education educator, researcher, consultant; b. Kitchener, Ont., Can., July 30, 1949; d. Earl Stanley and Mary Magdalena (Sauder) Feick; m. Charles L. Collinson, May 21, 1983. BA, Wilfrid Laurier U., Waterloo, Ont., 1974; MEd, U. Windsor, Ont., 1989; PhD, Ohio State U., 1993. Cert. adminstr. Tchr. Waterloo County Bd. Edn., 1969-84, Windsor Bd. Edn., 1984-89; vis. asst. prof. U.Windsor, 1989-90, U. Md., College Park, 1993-94, asst. prof. edn., 1994-98; assoc. prof. Mich. State U., 1999—. Author: Teachers As Learners, 1994, Reaching Students, 1996. Charter mem. Eleanor Roosevelt Found., 1989—; benefactor Stratford (Ont.) Shakespearean Festival Found. Recipient Ont. Silver medal for piano U. We. Ont. Conservatory of Music, 1965, McGraw-Hill awrd, 1969; Ont. scholar, 1968; Wilfrid Laurier U. grad. scholar. Mem. AAUW, Am. Ednl. Rsch. Assn., Fedn. Women Tchrs. Assn. Ont. (provincial resource leader 1988-94), Nat. Soc. for Study of Edn., Delta Kappa Gamma (Doctoral Dissertation award 1994), Phi Kappa Phi. Avocations: music, theatre, travel. Fax: 313-824-2949.

COLLIS, CHARLES, aircraft company executive; b. Bklyn., Aug. 6, 1920; s. Charles and Marie (Barnaby) C.; m. Margaret Howell, July 11, 1942; children: Jane, Joy. BSMechE, Brown U., 1942. V.p. Stratos div. Fairchild Hiller Corp., 1946-65, sr. v.p. Republic Aviation div., 1965-67, exec. v.p. corp., 1967-81; pres. Fairchild Hiller-F.R.G. Corp., 1966-69, Fairchild Republic Co., 1973-75, ret., 1981; mgmt. cons. Babylon, N.Y., 1982—. Mem. grad. mgmt. engring. adv. council C.W. Post Coll., L.I., 1965-66. Served as lt. USNR, 1942-45. Mem. AIAA, L.I. Assn. Commerce and Industry (bd. dirs. 1964-66), Babylon Yacht Club, Southward Ho Country Club. Home and Office: 116 Peninsula Dr Babylon NY 11702-3336

COLLIS, DAVID JOHN, management educator; b. Cardiff, Wales, June 15, 1955; arrived in U.S., 1976; s. Arthur Thomas Collis and Sheila Catherine Keith (Robson) Dodd; m. Jillian Kay Gapes, Nov. 20, 1982; children: William, Emma, Charlotte. BA, Cambridge (Eng.) U., 1976, MA, 1979; MBA, Harvard U., 1978, PhD, 1986. Cons. Boston Consulting Group, London, 1978—82; asst. prof. Columbia U., N.Y.C., 1985—86; assoc. prof. Harvard U., Boston, 1986—97, MBA Class of 1958 sr. lectr., 2002—; Frederick Frank prof. Yale U., New Haven, 1997—2002. Mem. adv. bd. Ocean Spray, Boston, 1999—2000, Webct, Boston, 1999—, MLX.com, 1999—, Folder Wave, 2003—; founder E-Edge, N.Y.C., 2001—, Ludlow Ptnrs., 2003—; mem. adv. bd. Vivaldi Ptnrs., 2001—. Author: Corporate Strategy, 1997, Strategy and the Business Landscape, 2000, Corporate Headquarters, 2001. Mem.: Acad. Mgmt., Strategic Mgmt. Soc. Home: 120 Sudbury Rd Concord MA 01742

COLLIS, DENNIS K. orthopedic surgeon; b. Wall Lake, Iowa, Mar. 2, 1937; s. Kennth O. and Blanche Marie Collis; m. Julie Ann Kellu, Oct. 27, 1962 (div. Dec. 1990); children: Randall, Amy; m. Jeanne Camicle Tyack, Aug. 28, 1994. BA in chem., biol., Grinnell Coll., 1959; MD, Wash. U. Sch. of Med., 1963. Lic. Mo., 1963, Iowa, 1967, Oreg., 1970, cert. Am. Bd. of Orthop. Surgery, 1971. Intern to resident Hennepin County Gen. Hosp., Mpls., 1963—65; orthop. surgeon U. Iowa, Iowa City, 1967—70; clin. instr. to sr. clin. instr. U. Oreg. Med. Sch., Dept of Orthop., Portland, 1971—78; adj. assoc. prof. U. Oreg., Phys. Edn. Dept., Eugene, 1972—78; asst. clin. prof. to assoc. clin. prof. Oreg. Health Scis. U., Dept. Orthop., Portland, 1978—. Cons. Letterman Gen. Hosp., 1977—79, Portland Vet. Admin. Hosp., Hip Clinic, 1984—; orthopedic surgeon Orthopedic Healthcare Northwest, Eugene, Oreg., 1971—. Contbr. articles various profl. jours., chapters to books various medical publications. Capt. USAF, 1965—67. Decorated Air Force Commendation medal. Fellow: Am. Coll. of Surgeons; mem.: AMA, Orthop. Rsch. and Edn. Found. (treas. 1994—95, chmn. of bd. 1995—98), Am. Orthop. Assn. (vp 1999—2000), Assn. of Bone and Joint Surgeons (2nd to 1st vp 1992—93, pres. 1994), North Pacific Orthop. Assn. (sec. treas. 1985), Russell Hibbs Soc. (pres. 1990), The Hip Soc. (chmn. 1990, pres. 1996), Oreg. Med. Assn., Lane County Med. Soc., Western Orthop. Assn. (pres. of Oreg. chpt. 1983), Am. Acad. Orthop Surgeons (chmn. 1986), Ctrl. Presbyn. Ch., Support Hult Ctr. Orgn. (pres. 1984—85), Eugene Arts Found. (bd of trustees 1984—86), Eugene Rotary Club, Eugene Country Club (bd. of dirs. 1989—92). Avocations: golf, racquetball, travel, spectator sports. Home: 3265 Riverplace Dr Eugene OR 97401 Office: Orthopedic Healthcare Northwest 1200 Hilyard St Ste 600 Eugene OR 97401

COLLIS, KAY LYNN, sales executive; b. Dallas, July 15, 1958; d. Martin Edward and Norma June C. AA, Tyler Jr. Coll., 1978; BBA, Sam Houston State U., 1982. Mgr. World Fin. Corp., Bryan, Tex., 1977-81; ops. analyst Republic Bank Dallas, 1983-85; asst. v.p. MBank, Dallas, 1985-87; v.p. Murray Fed. Savs., 1987-90; owner KC Enterprises, Las Vegas, 1990—. Sales dir., Mary Kay Cosmetics, 1994—; advisor Collis Cons. Co., Sulphur Springs, Tex., 1983-2001. Columnist Contemporary Singles Lifestyles, 1993-96; contbr. articles to mags. Vol. Spkr. Bur. Mem. NAFE, Fin. women Internat. (group pres. 1989-90, Tex. mktg./pub. rels. 1990-91), Las Vegas C. of C. (Mentor com. 1997—), Toastmasters Internat. (Disting. Toastmaster, divsn. gov. 1996-97). Republican. Episcopalian. Home and Office: 10801 Woodstream Ct Las Vegas NV 89135-1731 E-mail: kcollis@marykay.com.

COLLIS, SIDNEY ROBERT, retired telephone company executive; b. Oak Park, Ill., Mar. 24, 1924; s. Sidney John and Celia (Steele) C.; m. Lois E. Harding, Feb. 23, 1946 (dec.); children— Robert H., Elizabeth A., Gail M., April L. Student, Ill. Inst. Tech., 1941-43, U. Santa Clara, 1943-44; BS in Elec. Engring, Northwestern U., 1947. Registered profl. engr., Ill. With Ill. Bell Telephone Co., 1947-54, 60-61; with Am. Tel. & Tel. Co., 1954-60, 61-62, asst. v.p., 1968-83; v.p. Am. Tel. & Tel. Communications, 1984. Asst. v.p. N.Y. Telephone Co., 1962-63, v.p., 1963-68. Home: 70 Fieldstone Dr Basking Ridge NJ 07920-1607

COLLISON, JIM, business executive; b. Blue Earth, Minn., May 24, 1933; s. Elliott Eugene and Rosa Theresa (Whitcomb) C.; m. Valerie Ann Thul, Oct. 28, 1954; children: Judith, Michelle, Daniel, Michael, Rebecca, David. BA, St. John's Univ., 1955. Sports editor Blue Earth Post and Faribault County Register, 1953; staff writer St. Cloud Daily Times, Minn., 1953-55, Waterloo Courier, Iowa, 1955-57, Mason City Globe Gazette, Iowa, 1958-63; bus. and edn. cons. Jim Collison Assoc., Mason City, Iowa, 1963-77; exec. dir. Employers of Am., Mason City, Iowa, 1978-81, pres., 1981—; pres., pub. Sunburst Publ., Mason City, Iowa, 1990—. Co-founder Employers of Am., 1978; chmn. bd. ISBE Ins. Alliance, Mason City, 1986—, Select Advantage, Inc., ISBE Bus. Ins. Assn., ISBE Employer Benefits Assn.; pres. Am. Corp. Advisors, Inc.; workshop presenter. Author: Skill Building in Advanced Reading, 1968, Mental Power in Reading, 1970, Complete Employee Handbook Made Easy, 1994, 97, 2001, The Employer Protection Workshop, 1996, No-How Coaching, 2001, Complete Suggestion Program Make Easy, 2001; pub., sr. editor (e-newletter) HRmadeEasy. Asst. min. Orchard (Iowa) Congreg. Ch., 1985—; designer Adult Literacy and Employment Reading Training Program. Democrat. Avocations: flower gardening, hiking. Home: 310 Meadow Ln Mason City IA 50401-1717 Office: Employers of Am 1431 4th SW #305 Mason City IA 50401

COLLMAN, JAMES PADDOCK, chemistry educator; b. Beatrice, Nebr., Oct. 31, 1932; married. B.Sc., U. Nebr., 1954, MS, 1956; PhD (NSF fellow), U. Ill., 1958; Docteur Honoris Causa, U. Dijon, France, 1988, U. Borgogne, 1988; D (hon.), U. Nebr., 1988. Instr. chemistry U. N.C., Chapel Hill, 1958-59, asst. prof., 1959-62, asso. prof., 1962-67; prof. chemistry Stanford U., 1967—; George A. and Hilda M. Daubert prof. chemistry Stanford U., 1980—. Frontiers in Chemistry lectr., 1964, Nebr. lectureship, 1968; Venable lectr. U. N.C., 1971; Edward Clark Lee lectr. U. Chgo., 1972; vis. Erskine fellow U. Canterbury, 1972; Plenary lectr. French Chem. Soc., 1974; Dreyfus lectr. U. Kans., 1974; Disting. inorganic lectr. U. Rochester, 1974; Reilley lectr. U. Notre Dame, 1975; William Pyle Philips lectr. Haverford Coll., 1975; Merck lectr. Rutgers U., 1976; FMC lectr. Princeton, 1977; Julius Steiglitz lectr. Chgo. sect. Am. Chem. Soc., 1977; Pres.'s Seminar Series lectr. U. Ariz., 1980; Frank C. Whitmore lectr. Pa. State U., 1980; Plenary lectr. 3d IUPAC Symposium on Organic Synthesis, 1980, 2d Internat. Kyoto Conf. on New Aspects Inorganic Chemistry, 1982, Internat. Symposium on Models of Enzyme Action, Brighton, Eng., 1983, Internat. Symposium, Italy, 1984; Brockman lectr. U. Ga., 1981; Samuel C. Lind lectr. U. Tenn., 1981, Syntex Disting. lectr. Colo. State U., 1983; Disting. vis. lectr. U. Fla., 1983; vis. prof. U. Auckland, New Zealand, 1985; Nelson J. Leonard lectr. U. Ill., 1987; plenary lectr. Internat. Symposium on Activation of Dioxygen and Homogeneous Catalytic Oxygenations, Tsukuba, Japan, 1987; plenary lectr. 12th Internat. Symposium on Macrocyclic Chem., Hiroshima, Japan, 1987; lectr. Texas A&M, 1988; J. Clarence Karcher lectr. U. Okla., 1989; Musselman lectr. Gettysburg Coll., 1990; Davis lectr. U. New Orleans, 1991; PLU lectr. Okla. State U., 1991; lectr. 5th Internat. Fischer Symposium, Karlsruhe, Ger., 1991; lectr. Euchem Conf., 1991; Pratt lectr. U. Va., 1992, others; lectr. series Harvard/MIT, 1992, Yale U., 1993; invited speaker symposia, univs., confs. Recipient Disting. Teaching award Stanford U., 1981, Calif. Scientist of Year award, 1983, Allan V. Cox medal for excellence in fostering undergrad. rsch., 1988, LAS Alumni Achievement award Coll. Liberal Arts and

Scis. U. Ill., 1994, John C. Bailar Jr. medal, 1995, Joseph Chatt medal Royal Soc., 1998; named George A. and Hilda M. Daubert Prof. Chemistry (endowed chair, Stanford U.), 1980; Guggenheim fellow, 1977-78, 85-86, Churchill fellow, Cambridge, 1977—, Bing fellow, 1996. Fellow Calif. Acad. Sci. (hon.); mem. Am. Chem. Soc. (Calif. sect. award 1972, soc. award in inorganic chemistry 1975, Arthur C. Cope scholar 1986, Pauling award Puget Sound and Oreg. sect. 1990, Disting. Svc. award in inorganic chemistry 1991, Alfred Bader award in bioinorganic or bioorganic chemistry 1997, Joseph Chatt lectr. 1998, Marker lectr. medal 1999), N.Y. Acad. Sci. (Basolo medal 2000), Chem. Soc. (London), Nat. Acad. Sci., Am. Acad. Arts and Scis., Phi Beta Kappa, Sigma Xi, Phi Lambda Upsilon, Alpha Chi Epsilon. Office: Stanford U Dept Chemistry Stanford CA 94305

COLLMER, ROBERT GEORGE, English language educator; b. Guatemala, Central Am., Nov. 28, 1926; (parents Am. citizens); s. G. Russell and Constance Ethel (Cravener) C.; m. Linnie Maffett Burney, Jan. 5, 1948 (dec. 1979); children: Carol Linda Collmer McLaren, Mark Wesley; m. Alys Edney, July 4, 1981. BA, Baylor U., 1948, MA, 1949; PhD, U. Pa., 1953. Asst. instr. U. Pa., Phila., 1949-52; instr. Phila. Coll. of Bible, Phila., 1952-54; from assoc. prof. to prof., chmn. dept. English Hardin-Simmons U., Abilene, Tex., 1954-58, 61; Smith-Mundt vis. prof. Inst. Technologico, Monterrey, Mex., 1958-60; independent rschr. U. Leiden, The Netherlands, 1960; acad. dean, prof. Wayland Bapt. U., Plainview, Tex., 1961-66; Fulbright vis. prof. Universidad Nacional, Asuncion, Paraguay, 1966-67; prof. English Tex. Tech. U., Lubbock, 1967-73; prof., chmn. dept. English Baylor U., Waco, 1973-80, dean grad. studies and rsch., 1979-92, disting. English prof., 1992-97, emeritus disting. English prof., 1997—. Vis. English Prof. U. of Jordan, fall 1997. Editor: (with others) American Bypaths, 1980, The English Journals of Lodewijck Huygens, 1982, Bunyan in Our Time, 1989; contbr. articles to profl. jours. Served to cpl. U.S. Army, 1945-46. Fellow Rockefeller Found., 1958, Smith-Mundt, 1958-60, Fulbright-Hays, 1966-76, Hon. Rsch. fellow U. Glasgow, 1994; grantee Dutch Ministry Edn. Scis., 1981, Fulbright-Hays sr. rsch. grantee, 1982, Am. Philosophical Soc. grantee, 1976. Mem. Deans Conf. So. Assn. Bapt. Schs. (pres. 1963-64), S. Central Renaissance Conf. (pres. 1970-71), Assn. Tex. Grad. Schs. (pres. 1982-83), Conf. Christianity and Lit. (pres. 1982-85), Conf. Coll. Tchrs. of English (pres. 1983-84). Democrat. Avocations: traveling to Latin Am. and Europe, book collecting. Home: 2801 Wooded Acres Dr Waco TX 76710-1252 E-mail: rcol1017@aol.com.

COLLOMB, BERTRAND PIERRE, cement company executive; b. Lyon, France, Aug. 14, 1942; came to U.S., 1985; s. Charles and Helene (Traon) C.; m. Marie Caroline Wirth, July 1, 1967; children: Cedric, Alex, Stephanie. Engring. student, Ecole Poly., Paris, 1960—62; engring. degree, Ecole des Mines, Paris, 1966; law degree, U. Nancy, France, 1968; PhD in Mgmt., U. Tex., 1972. Mining engr. Ministry of Industry, France, 1967-74; spl. asst. to Minister of Edn. Paris, 1974-75; with Lafarge, 1975—; regional v.p. Ciments Lafarge, Paris, 1976-77, pres., 1978-82; pres., CEO Orsan, Paris, 1982-85; CEO Gen. Portland, Inc., Dallas, 1985-87, Lafarge Corp., Paris, 1987-88, chmn. bd. Reston, Va., 1989—; sr. v.p. Lafarge, Paris, 1988-89, CEO, 1989—, chmn., 1989—2003, chmn., CEO, 2003—. Bd. dirs. Total Fina Elf, Viven di Universal; adv. dir. Unilever; mem. supervisory bd. Allianz. Home: 4 rue de Lota 75116 Paris France Office: Lafarge 61 rue des Belles Feuilles 75116 Paris France also: Lafarge NAm 12950 Worldgate Dr Ste 400 Herndon VA 20170

COLLONS, RODGER DUANE, decision sciences educator; b. Glenn, Neb., Jan. 8, 1935; s. Rodger Bernard and Ethel Bernice (Littrel) C.; m. Cynthia Carolyn Dyer, May 6, 1961; children: Kevin Rodger, Theresa Rene. BCE, U. Tex., El Paso, 1957; JD, George Washington U., 1961; MBA, Ga. State U., 1965, DBA, 1967. Bar: Va. 1961, Ga. 1963; registered U.S. patent atty.; CLU. Patent examiner U.S. Patent Office, Washington, 1957-60; assoc. counsel Strauch, Nolan & Neale, Washington, 1960-61; asso. patent counsel Lockheed Ga. Co., Atlanta, 1961-64; teaching fellow Ga. State U., 1964-65; asst. prof. mgmt. Ga. So. Coll., 1965-66; asst. prof. quantitative analysis Ga. State U., 1966-68; dir. div. adminstrv. scis. Grad. Coll. W.Va., 1969-71; dean Coll. Bus. and Adminstrn., Drexel U., 1971-76, prof. decision scis., 1976—. James S. Bingay vis. prof. creative leadership Am. Coll., 1979-81. Author: (with Donald Del Mar) Classics in Scientific Management, 1976; editor: Decision Line, 1969-72; contbg. editor: Creative Leadership Rev., 1980-82; bi-monthly series Best's rev., 1980-83; patentee container closure, sealing method. Bd. dirs. Phila. Civic Ballet, 1974-86, pres. 1979-82; bd. dirs. Rosemont-Villanova (Pa.) Civic Assn., 1976—, pres., 1980-86. Recipient cert. of appreciation Allied Social Scis. Assns., 1976. Fellow Decision Scis. Inst. (Disting. Service award 1971, pres. 1972-73, dir. 1969-76, chmn. fellows 1979-81); mem. Middle Atlantic Assn. Colls. Bus. Adminstrn. (pres. 1975-76), Alpha Iota Delta (pres. 1971-72, 73-74, Disting. Svc. award 1976, dir. 1972—), Kiwanis (dir. Phila. club 1973-76). Home: 1909 Firethorn Ln Villanova PA 19085-1809 Office: Coll Bus and Adminstrn Drexel U Philadelphia PA 19102

COLLOPY, CHRISTOPHER STEPHEN, clothing company executive; b. San Francisco, Sept. 26, 1952; s. George Francis and Dorothy (Rose) C.; m. Mary Catherine Collopy, Apr. 26, 1986; children: Tristan Connor, Dillon O'Leary. BA, San Jose State U., 1977. With Brookhurst Inc. Counselor Options House, Hollywood, Calif., 1981-86. Instr. Jr. Achievement, Redondo Beach, Calif., 1982-86; coun. mem. Calif. State PTA, 1997-99 (hon. svc. award 1999); bd. commr. City of Redondo Beach; presiding officer Wildomar Mcpl. Adv. Coun., 1999-2000, 2001-02, vice presiding officer, 2000-01. Recipient Mater Dei award Archdiocese of San Fancisco, 1979, Vol. Svc. award City of L.A., 1984, Civic award City of Redondo Beach, 1989, Mem. Sierra Club. Democrat. Roman Catholic. Avocations: tennis, racquetball, rafting, climbing, hiking. Home: 40349 Corte Campem Murrieta CA 92562 Office: Brookhurst Inc 107 W Carob St Rancho Dominguez CA 90220-5206 E-mail: cirishman@aol.com.

COLLOTON, JOHN WILLIAM, university health care executive; b. Mason City, Iowa, Feb. 20, 1931; s. Harold and Miriam (Kelly) Colloton; m. Mary Ann Hagglund, Oct. 8, 1960; children: Steven, Laura, Ann. BA with high honors, Loras Coll., 1953; MA, U. Iowa, 1957. Hosp. relations rep. Hosp. Service Inc. of Iowa, Des Moines, 1957—58; with U. Iowa, Iowa City, 1958—; assoc. dir. U. Iowa Hosps. and Clinics, 1969—71, dir., asst. to univ. pres. for statewide health svcs., 1971—93; v.p. statewide health svcs. U. Iowa, 1993—. Bd. dirs. Baxter Internat., Inc., Nat. Med. Waste Inc., Iowa State Bank & Trust Co., MidAm. Energy Co., Premier Anesthesia, Atlanta, Assn. Health Svcs. Rsch.; cons. HIH; pres. adminstrv. bd. Assn. Am. Med. Colls. Coun. of Tchg. Hosps, 1979—80; mem. presdl. search com. Assn. Am. Med. Colls., 1984; mem. adv. bd. Duke U. Hosp., 1985; mem. task force on acad. health ctrs. Commonwealth Fund, chmn. selection com. exec. nurse leadership program, 1983; mem. prospective payment commn. Congl. Office Tech. Assessment, 1983; chmn. bd. dirs. Iowa-S.D. Health Svcs. Corp. (now Blue Cross/Blue Shield Iowa, Blue Cross S.D.), 1993—. Contbr. articles. Served with Fin. Corps U.S. Army, 1953—55. Fellow: Am. Coll. Hosp. Adminstrs.; mem.: U. Iowa Alumni Assn., Johnson County Med. Soc., Assn. Am. Med. Colls. (chmn. 1987—88, disting. svc. mem.), Am. Assn. Hosp. Planning, Iowa Hosp. Assn. (chmn. bd. trustees 1977—78, trustee 1978—), Am. Hosp. Assn. (coun. on financing 1977, med. edn. com. 1984—87), Inst. Medicine of NAS, Rotary. Roman Catholic. Office: U Iowa Hosps & Clinics 200 Hawkins Dr Ste 8820 Iowa City IA 52242-1009

COLLOTON, STEVEN M. judge; b. Iowa City, Jan. 9, 1963; m. Deborah Colloton. AB, Princeton U., 1985; JD, Yale Law Sch., 1988. Law clk to Hon. Laurence H. Silberman U.S. Ct. Appeals, DC cir., Washington, 1988—89; law clk. to Hon. William H. Rehnquist U.S. Supreme Ct., Washington, 1989—90; special asst. to Asst. Atty. Gen. Dept. Justice Office Legal Counsel, 1990—91; asst. U.S. Atty. No. Dist. Iowa, 1991—99; assoc. counsel Office Ind. Coun. Kenneth W. Starr, 1995—96; ptnr. Belin, Lamson, McCormick, Zumbach & Flynn, DesMoines, 1999—2001; U.S. Atty. so. dist. Iowa, 2001—03; judge U.S. Ct. Appeals, 8th cir., 2003—. Office: 455 US Courthouse Annex 110 E Court Ave Ste 286 Des Moines IA 50309-2053*

COLLUMB, PETER JOHN, communications company executive; b. Newark, July 29, 1942; s. Peter A. and Rose M. (Coffey) C.; 1 child, Alexandra Christine. BS in Indsl. Psychology, East Tex. State U. (now Tex. A&M U.), Commerce, 1967. Registered lobbyist. Dir. pers./labor rels. Roper Corp., Chattanooga, Tenn., 1969-71; v.p. human resources Nat. Sharedata Corp., Dallas, 1971-74; dir. pers./labor Dallas Times Herald, 1975-78; dir. econ. devel. divsn. Tex. Dept. Community Affairs, Austin, 1978-80; dep. exec. dir. Tex. Dept. Cmty. Affairs, 1978-81; legis./adminstrv. dir. U.S. Senator John G. Tower, Washington and Dallas, 1980-83; member U.S. Senate Armed Services Com., U.S. Senate Banking, Finance and Labor Com.; v.p. fin., sec.-treas. Diversified Packaging Co., Inc., Dallas, 1983-85; pres. N.Am. Systems, Inc., Dallas, 1981—; chmn. of bd., pres. Collumb, Hess, Navarro Pub. Rels., Dallas, Austin, Washington, Sacramento, 1991—; chmn., pres. Collumb Communications Co., Dallas, 1983—; chmn. Komatsu, Ashcraft and Collumb Inc.; personal envoy Ronald W. Reagan, Pres. of U.S., Washington, 1981-82. Adj. prof. Bishop Coll., Dallas; bd. dirs. Tex. Housing Agy., Govs. Coms. on Aging and Migrant Affairs; guest lectr. So. Meth. U., Dallas, 1988—; chmn. bd. D.S.P. Corp., Dallas, 1985-98, C.H.N. Internat., Washington, Geneva, London and Tokyo; advisor to U.S. Sec. of Labor, Houston Econ. Summit, 1990; labor cons. Kullman, Lange, Inman & Bee, New Orleans; dir. Drug Prevention and Treatment Divsn., Tex. Dept. Cmty. Affairs; city adminstr., City of Westminster, Tex. Author: Political Process, 1982. Bd. dirs. Plano Child Guidance Ctr., Collin County Mental Health-Mental Retardation Coun., Edna Gladney Ctr., Ft. Worth, 1979—, Free Shakespeare Festival, Dallas, 1978-85, v.p. finance; Outstanding Young Men Am., Atlanta, 1982—, Nat. Com. Adoption, 1986—, Ark. State Vocat./Tech. Schs., Ft. Worth State Sch. for the Retarded, Beautify Tex. Coun., 1980-85, Westminster Ind. Sch. Dist. Bd.; lobbyist, City of Fairview, Tex.; dir. advance staff Reagan/Bush Presdl. Campaign, Washington, 1978-85, Sam Johnson for Congress Campaign, 1991, Bush-Quayle 1992 Presdl. Campaign, Elizabeth Dole Senate Campaign, 2002, Lamar Alexander Senate Campaign, 2002; vice-chmn., dir. fin. Fair Housing Coun., 1988—; mem. community adv. coun. Coord. Bd. Tex. Colls. and Univs.; mem. Rep. Presdl. Task Force, 1984—; co-chair, parents counc., Mary Baldwin Coll., chmn. Fourth Border Conf. on Drug Abuse; candidate U.S. Ho. Reps., Dallas, 1982-84; del. White House Confs. on Aging, Small Bus. and the Family, Tex. Rep. Party Convs., 1984, 88, 92; pvt. advisor to Pres. U.S.: Ronald Reagan; exec. dir., receiver Dallas County Community Action Com.; cons. U.S. Can. Free Trade Commn., Washington, 1986-87, Plano Sister Cities, Inc., Big Brothers & Sisters, others; chmn., v.p. fin., v.p. devel. Tex. World of Children; chmn. Pres.'s Adv. Coun., HUD Tech. Adv. Coun., Hillcrest Acad. Found., 1986-91, George W. Bush Re-Election Campaign, 1994, George Bush Presidential Campaign, nat. fin. com., Marshall Program, Bush-Cheney Presdl. Campaign, Bush-Cheney Inaugural Com., 1999-2000, Hutchinson for U.S. Senate, 1994, Ralph Hall for Congress Re-Election Campaign, Welfare to Work Pilot Project, State of Tex., office of Gov. George W. Bush. Named to Outstanding Young Men Am., Jaycees, 1981, Amigo Extradonaire, Govt. of Mexico, 1984. Mem. Centros de Juv Mexico (chmn. 1980-84), North Dallas C. of C. (bus. resource, internat. affairs, govt. affairs com.), Dallas Coun. on World Affairs, Tex. Sheriffs Assn. (charter), Tex. A&M Commerce Alumni Assn., Stallion Club (pres.), Lions (v.p. Mena, Ark. 1976-77), Rotary, Lambda Chi Alpha (pres. 1967-69, chmn. alumni control bd., pres. alumni assn.). Republican. Presbyterian. Avocations: tennis, golf, reading, politics. Office: Collumb Communication Co 3404 Mission Ridge Rd Ste 100 Plano TX 75023-8115

COLLYER, MICHAEL, lawyer; b. N.Y.C., Feb. 5, 1942; s. Clayton Johnson and Heloise (Green) Collyer; m. Sandra Karen Schaum, July 28, 1979 (div. Aug. 1999); m. Susan Catherine Bruyn, Nov. 13, 1999; children: Sophie Marie, Matthew Michael Severyn;1 stepchild, Shelley Malia. BA, Williams Coll., 1963; LLB, Columbia U., 1966. Bar: N.Y. 1966. Assoc. Becker & London, N.Y.C., 1966—70; ptnr. Kay Collyer & Boose and predecessors, N.Y.C., 1970—2001, Cascone Cole & Collyer, N.Y.C., 2001—, Collyer & Schutte, 2001—; legal adviser NATAS, N.Y.C., 1978—, trustee, 1982—, nat. officer, 1982—, chmn., 1990—. Instr. bus. law Columbia U., N.Y.C., 1966—69; spkr. conv. Practicing Law Inst., 1977; mem. chpt. motion pictures and TV under new copyright statute, 78. Trustee George Heller Meml. Scholarship Fund; active N.Y.C. Mayor's Adv. Coun. Film and Broadcasting, 1993. With U.S. Army, 1966—71. Mem.: Internat. Coun. Nat. Acad. Arts and Scis. (bd. dirs.), Internat. Radio and TV Soc., N.Y. Bar Assn. (author TV sect. entertainment law 1995), Assn. of Bar of City of N.Y., N.Y. Yacht Club. Home: 25 Chester Ct Cortlandt Manor NY 10567-6361 Office: Cascone Cole & Collyer 711 3d Ave 15th FlPla New York NY 10017 E-mail: collyerlaw@aol.com.

COLLYER, ROBERT B. trade association administrator; b. Decatur, Ill., Oct. 16, 1932; s. Murray Gordon and Frances Mary (Evans) C.; m. Margaret Mary Hebel, Feb. 27, 1960; 1 son, Bryan. BA, Humboldt Coll., 1956. Cons. DeLeuw Cather & Co., 1957-59; claims and mgr. govt. relations Indsl. Indemnity Co. Calif., San Francisco, San Jose, Sacramento, 1960-73; exec. asst. UBA Inc., Washington, 1974-81; dep. under sec. Employment Standards Adminstrn. U.S. Dept. Labor, Washington, 1981-84; pres. The Collyer Co., 1984—; exec. dir. Internat. Assn. Indsl. Accident Bds. and Commns., 1990-96; exec. dir., sec.-treas. Internat. Workers' Compensation Found., 1990—; dean Internat. Workers' Compensation Coll., 1990-96. Co-founder, dir. Nat. Symposium Workers Compensation U. Maine, 1976-80; dir. Western States Self-Ins. Colloquim, Inc., Nat. Employers' Adv. Council on Workers Compensation; cons. Nat. Indsl. Council; mem. Nat. Adv. Commn. on State Workers Compensation Law Compliance U.S. Dept. Labor; mem. Nat. Adv. Commn. on Indsl. Rehab. Research and Tng. Program U. N.C.; mem. steering com. Nat. Workers Compensation Info. Exchange Group; mem. steering com. Permanent Disability Study Adv. Comm. NSF; mem. steering com. U.S. Longshoremen and Harbor Workers' Reform Group Pres. Marin county Republican Council, (Calif.), 1973; mem. Calif. Rep. Central Com., 1970-73; asst. county chmn. Com. to Re-elect Pres., 1972. Named Republican of Yr. Marin County, 1972 E-mail: tobobcollyer@aol.com.

COLMAN, CHARLES KINGSBURY, academic administrator, criminologist; b. Nashua, N.H., May 14, 1929; s. Charles David Colman and Lela (Bessey) Sproul; m. Marjorie Gertrude Bahe, Aug. 19, 1950 (dec. May 2003); children: Charles David, Cathleen Ann. Diploma, Yale U., 1961; BA, U. Md., 1963; MEd, Stetson U., 1972; EdD, Fla. Atlantic U., 1978. Spl. agt. USAF, U.S. Army, 1947-67; asst. prin. Satellite High Sch., Satellite Beach, Fla., 1969-81, dean acad. edn., 1981-85; ctr. dir. Brevard C.C., Patrick AFB, Fla., 1985-92, provost Palm Bay, Fla., 1992-94; pres. emeritus, 1994—. Mem. Fla. State Adv. Com. on Mil. Edn., Patrick AFB, 1985—; edn. rep. Semiconductor Mfg. Tech., Dallas, 1985—. Author: Formative Years, 1970; author computer software. Co-founder Boys Club Am., Melbourne, Fla, 1968. Grantee Fla. Dept. Edn., 1987, 89, 90, 91, U.S. Dept. Edn., 1991-92; recipient Ace award Fla. Dept. Edn., 1991. Mem. ASCD, Ret. Officers' Assn., Assn. Former Intelligence Officers (v.p. 1998-2000, pres. 2001—, Fla. chpt.), Assn. Former OSI Spl. Agts. (sec. 1998—, Space Coast chpt.), Phi Delta Kappa (chpt. pres. 1983-84). Avocations: golf, computer programming. Home: 1230 Seminole Dr Indian Harbor Beach FL 32937-4123 Office: Brevard Community Coll Palm Bay Campus 250 Community College Pky Palm Bay FL 32909-2206 E-mail: ccolman@cfl.rr.com.

COLMAN, RICHARD THOMAS, retired lawyer; b. Boston, Sept. 22, 1935; s. Albert Vincent and Marie Catherine (Henehan) C.; m. Marilyn Flavin, Dec. 1, 1962; children: Elizabeth B., Catherine B., Richard T. Jr., Patrick B. AB magna cum laude, U. Notre Dame, 1957; LLB cum laude, Boston Coll., 1962. Bar: Mass. 1962, D.C. 1966. Trial atty. Antitrust Div. U.S. Dept. Justice, Washington, 1962-66; ptnr. Howrey Simon Arnold & White LLP, Washington, 1970—2001; ret. Trustee Indian Mountain Sch., Lakeville, Conn., 1992-98; regional del. Boston Coll. Law Sch. Alumni Assn., 1992-99; adv. bd. Georgetown U. Law Ctr., Corp. Counsel Inst., 1999—2001; bd. overseers Boston Coll. Law Sch., 2001—. Mem.: ABA, DC Bar Assn., Beach Club, Wianno Club. Republican. Roman Catholic. E-mail: colmanr@howrey.com.

COLMAN, ROBERT WOLF, physician, medical educator, researcher; b. NYC, June 7, 1935; s. Jack K. and Miriam (Greenblatt) C.; m. Roberta Fishman, June 16, 1957; children: Sharon, David. AB summa cum laude, Harvard U., 1956, MD cum laude, 1960. Intern Boston City Hosp., 1960-61; resident Beth Israel, Brookline, Mass., 1961-62; clin. assoc. USPHS, NIH, 1962-64; resident Barnes Hosp., St. Louis, 1964-65, fellow in hematology, 1965-67; assoc. in medicine Harvard Med. Sch., Cambridge, Mass., 1967-69, asst. prof., 1969-73, assoc. prof., 1973, U. Pa., Phila., 1973-77, prof. medicine, 1977-78, Temple U. Sch. Medicine, Phila., 1978—, prof. thrombosis rsch., 1981—, prof. physiology, 1992—, dir. Sol Sherry Thrombosis Rsch. Ctr., 1979—, Sol Sherry prof. of medicine, 1989—. Hematology study sect. NIH, Bethesda, Md., 1977-81; parent com. to review SCORs in Ischemic Heart Disease; chemistry spl. emphasis panel to review SBIR, STTR grants, NIH, study sect. rev. therapeutic modulation angiogenisis disease, study sect. to rev. tng. grants and careeer devel. awards; invited lectr. Gordon confs., Internat. Congress Hemostasis and Thrombosis, Fedn. Am. Socs. Exptl. Biology; plenary lectr. and chair Gordon Conf. Internat. Soc. Kallikreins and Kinins, others. Editor: Hemostasis and Thrombosis, 4th edit., 2001; editor Platelet Jour.; mem. editorial bd. Jour. Clin. Investigation, Blood, Procs. Soc. Exptl. Biology, Thrombosis Rsch. Platelets, Thrombosis Hemostasis; contbr. numerous articles to profl. jours. Surgeon USPHS, 1962-64. Recipient Leon Resnick prize Harvard U., Career Devel. award NIH, Sr. Investigator award S.E. Pa. chpt. Am. Heart Assn., Disting. Career award Internat. Soc. Thrombosis and Hemostasis. Fellow ACP; mem. Assn. Am. Physicians. Am. Soc. Clin. Investigation, Am. Soc. Biochemistry and Molecular Biology, Internat. Soc. Hemostasis and Thrombosis (councillor 1989-95), Peripatetic Club, Interurban Clin. Club, Phi Beta Kappa, Sigma Xi, Alpha Omega Alpha. Office: Temple U Sch Medicine Sol Sherry Thrombosis Rsch Ctr 3400 N Broad St Philadelphia PA 19140-5104 E-mail: colmanr@temple.edu.

COLMANT, ANDREW ROBERT, lawyer; b. Bklyn., Oct. 10, 1931; s. Edward J. and Mary Elizabeth (Byrne) C.; children: Elizabeth, Carolyn, David (dec.), Stephen, Robert. BBA, St. Johns U., Jamaica, N.Y., 1957, LLB, 1959. Bar: N.Y. 1959, U.S. Dist Ct. (so. and ea. dists.) N.Y. 1961, U.S. Ct. Appeals (2nd cir.) 1969, U.S. Ct. Appeals (4th cir.) 1977, U.S. Supreme Ct. 1991. Assoc. Hill, Rivkins, Carey, Loesberg O'Brien & Mulroy and predecessor firms, 1959-73, ptnr., 1973-87; of counsel Jerrold E. Hyams, 1988-97, Peter F. Broderick, 1992. Proctor in admiralty; active USMC amphibious reconnaissance Army Gen. Intelligence Sch. Author: Outline of General Average. Interpretive vol. Sandy Hook Lighthouse and History House, Fort Hancock, NJ, Navesink Light Sta., Highland, NJ; active Conservation Coun. for Hawaii, Honolulu, St. Stephans Indian Sch., Am. Indian Mus. Natural History; founder Deep Cut Gardens, Middleton, NJ; vol. Twin Lighthouse, NJ, Highlands Hist. Soc., Highlands, NJ; VIP Nat. Park Svc.; vol. Sandy Hook Lighthouse, History House, Hancock, NJ, 2002—, Cmty. St. Benedict, Holmdel, NJ; rep., leader Bayshore Comty. Hosp., Holmdel, NJ, 1978—; min. of eucharist St. Benedict Parish, Holmdel, NJ; extraordinary min. Holy Eucharist Asssigned; Sunday contingent; mem., track chmn. Parish Coun., Fin. Funding, Constl. Lance cpl. USMC, 1952—54. Recipient Social Min. award, Diocese Trenton Bishop Riess, VIP award, Dept. Interior. Mem.: ACLU, ABA (torts and ins. and admiralty comm. on com.), St. John's Sch. Law Admiralty Soc., Social Security Com., Assn. Internationale de Droit des Assurances, Pacific Rim Maritime Law Assn., Asia Pacific Lawyers Assn., NY State Bar Assn. (admiralty), Maritime Law Assn. U.S. (life; proctor in admiralty 1960, carriage goods com.), NY County Lawyers Assn. (life; admiralty com. 1963,), Nat. Trust for Hist. Preservation, Nat. Maritime Hist. Soc., Navy League U.S., Amnesty Internat., Anti-defamation League, Nat. Park Conservation Assn., Twin Light Hist. Soc., Nat. Wildlife Fedn., ATLA (admiralty com. 1995), Sierra Club. Home: Bethany Manor 500 Broad St Apt 11Y Keyport NJ 07735-1640

COLN, C. DALE, pediatric surgeon, educator; b. Dallas, Dec. 23, 1934; s. Charlie Edward and Jessie Ruth (Enix) C.; m. Shirley Jane Kindberg, May 12, 1962; children: Sara, Eric, Lois, Ruth, Mary. BA, Baylor U., 1957; MD, Baylor Coll. Medicine, 1961. Med. intern Jefferson Davis Hosp., Houston, 1961-62; resident in surgery Parkland Meml. Hosp., Dallas, 1963-67; asst. prof. U. Tex. Southwestern Med. Ctr., Dallas, 1969-75, chmn. pediatric surgery, 1972-87, assoc. prof., 1975-93; dir. pediatric surgery Baylor U. Med. Ctr., Dallas, 1987—. Rsch. fellow in surgery U. Tex. Southwestern Med. Ctr., 1962-63, prof. surgery, 1993; fellow Red Cross War Meml. Hosp., Cape Town, S. Africa, 1971-72, L.A. Children's Hosp., 1978; founder and dir. pediatric trauma unit Parkland Meml. Hosp., 1982-89. Author numerous publs. on trauma in children, fluid and electrolyte abnormalities, shock, sepsis and pectus deformities; contbr. articles to profl. jours. Active Northwest Bible Ch., Dallas, 1972, Dallas Symphony Assn., 1984; mem. exec. com. Tex. Office for Prevention of Devel. Disabilities, 2003—. Sr. surgeon USPHS, 1967-69, Sitka, Alaska. Recipient Disting. Svc. award, Children's Med. Ctr., 2002. Fellow ACS (pres. North Tex. chpt. 1999-2000), Am. Acad. Pediats., Internat. Coll. Surgeons; mem. Am. Assn. Surgery Trauma, Am. Pediat. Surg. Assn., Parkland Surg. Soc. (founding 1982, pres. 1983), Tex. Pediat. Soc. (exec. com., chmn. injury and environ. hazards com., pres. 2000-2001). Evangelical. Avocations: gardening, watercolor, tennis. Home: 9 Turtle Creek Bnd Dallas TX 75204-1635 Office: Baylor U Med Ctr 3600 Gaston Ave Dallas TX 75246-1800 E-mail: dalecoln@swbell.net.

COLN, WILLIAM ALEXANDER, III, retired pilot; b. Los Angeles, Mar. 20, 1942; s. William Alexander and Aileen Henrietta (Shimfessel) C.; m. Lora Louise Getchel, Nov. 15, 1969 (div. July 1979); 1 child, Caryn Louise. BA in Geography, UCLA, 1966. Cert. airline transport pilot, flight engr. Commd. USN, Pensacola, Fla., 1966, pilot, officer Fighter Squadron 102, 1969-71, Port Mugu, Calif., 1975-77, USNR, Port Mugu, Calif., 1971-75, advanced through grades to lt. comdr., 1978, ret., 1984; capt. Delta Airlines, Inc. (formerly Western Airlines Inc.), L.A., 1972—2002; ret., 2002. Recipient Nat. Def. medal USN, 1966. Mem. Nat. Aero. Assn., Airline Pilots Assn., Aircraft Owners and Pilots Assn., UCLA Alumni Assn., Am. Bonanza Soc., Internat. Platform Assn., Santa Barbara Yacht Club. Clubs: Santa Barbara (Calif.) Athletic, Santa Barbara Yacht. Republican. Avocations: sailing, scuba diving, flying, computers, electronics. Home: 486 Cota Ln Montecito CA 93108-1210 E-mail: bcoln@silcom.com.

COLODNY, EDWIN IRVING, lawyer, retired air transportation executive; b. Burlington, Vt., June 7, 1926; s. Myer and Lena (Yett) Colodny; m. Nancy Dessoff, Dec. 11, 0965; children: Elizabeth, Mark, David. AB with distinction, U. Rochester, 1948; LLB, Harvard U., 1951; D in Comml. Sci. (hon.), Robert Morris Coll., 1985; LLD (hon.), Middlebury Coll., 1986; HHD (hon.), Kings Coll., 1988. Bar: N.Y. 1951, DC 1958. With Office Gen. Counsel, GSA, 1951-52, CAB, 1954-57, USAirways Inc. (formerly Allegheny Airlines Inc.), 1957-91; exec. v.p. mktg. and legal affairs USAirways, Inc. (formerly Allegheny Airlines Inc.), 1969-75, pres., 1975-90, CEO, 1975-91, chmn. bd. dirs., 1978-92; also chmn. USAirways Group, Inc., 1978-92; ret., 1992; of counsel Paul, Hastings, Janofsky and Walker, Washington, 1991—2002; chmn. Comsat Corp., 1997-2000. Interim pres. U. Vt., 2001—02; interim pres., CEO Fletcher Allen Health Care, Burlington, 2002—. Lt. U.S. Army, 1952—54. Recipient James D. McGill Meml. award, U. Rochester, Wright Bros. Meml. award, 1990, Tony Jannus award, 1990. Mem.: ABA, U. Vt. (bd. trustees), U. Rochester (bd. trustees). E-mail: eic8225@aol.com.

COLOGNE, GORDON BENNETT, lawyer; b. Long Beach, Calif., Aug. 24, 1924; s. Knox M. Cologne; m. Patricia Cologne; children: Steven J., Ann Maureen Meyer. BS, U. So. Calif., 1948; LLB cum laude, Southwestern U. Sch. of Law, L.A., 1951. Bar: Calif. 1951, U.S. Supreme Ct. 1961. Trial atty. U.S. Dept. of Justice, Jacksonville, Fla., 1951-52; pvt. practice Indio, Calif., 1952-61; mayor Indio City Coun., 1954; mem. state assembly Calif. Legis., Sacramento, 1961-65; mem. senate Calif. State Senate, Sacramento, 1965-72; justice Ct. of Appeal, San Diego, 1972-84; govt. rels. atty. Sacramento, 1984-99. With USN, 1944-46. Named one of Outstanding Young Men of Calif., Calif. Jr. C. of C., 1961; recipient Freedom Found. award, 1965.

COLOMB, CAMILLE MARIE, anesthesiologist; b. Houston, May 7, 1962; d. William Frederick and Shirley (Giddens) C. BS, Rhodes Coll., 1984; MD, LSU Sch. Medicine, 1988. cert. anesthesiologist, 1993. Intern Presbyn. Hosp., Dallas, 1988-89; residency anesthesiology U. Tex. S.W. Med. Sch., Dallas, 1989-92; fellow pediatric anesthesiology Ark. Childrens Hosp., Little Rock, 1992-93; anesthesiologist Tex. Children's Hosp., Houston, 1993—; asst. prof. Baylor Coll. Medicine, Houston, 1993—. Mem. AMA, Tex. Med. Assn., Tex. Soc. Anesthesiology, Am. Soc. Anesthesiology. E-mail: ccolomb@bcm.tmc.edu.

COLOMB, MARJORIE MONROE, investor, volunteer; b. New Orleans, Sept. 9, 1929; d. Joseph Percy and Mary Velma Monroe; m. Charles McConvill Hardie, June 6, 1953 (div. Nov. 1972); m. John Joseph Colomb, Jr., Sept. 28, 1983 (dec.). BA Art History, La. State U., 1973; BS Bus., U. New Orleans, 1982. Adv. bd. dirs. New Orleans Mus.; bd. dirs. Easter Seals La., New Orleans; trustee J.Edgar Monroe Found., New Orleans. Fellow: New Orleans Mus. Art; mem.: Raintree Svcs. (hon. bd. dirs.). Republican. Roman Catholic. Home: 302 Glorias Pl Mandeville LA 70471-1612

COLOMBI-MONGUIO, ALICIA DE, foreign language educator, poet; b. Buenos Aires; came to the U.S., 1967; d. Carlos and Rosa de Colombí; m. Luis Monguió, Aug. 8, 1979. BA in History, U. Santa Clara, 1969; MA in Spanish and Portuguese, Stanford U., 1971, PhD in Spanish and Humanities, 1973. Asst. prof. Spanish Mills Coll., Oakland, Calif., 1973-79; faculty Bennington (Vt.) Coll., 1979-82; prof. Spanish SUNY, Albany, 1982-84, 86-98, chair dept. Hispanic and Italian studies, 1986 90, rsch. prof. Hispanic and humanistic studies, 1998—; prof. Spanish U. Ariz., 1984-86. Chair divsn. letters Mills Coll., Oakland, 1975-79; chair fgn. langs. and lits. Bennington Coll., 1979-82; head dept. Spanish and Portuguese U. Ariz., Tucson, 1984-86; chair dept. Hispanic and Italian studies SUNY, Albany, 1986-90, rsch. prof. Hispanic and humanistic studies, 1998—. Author: De amor y poesia en la Espana Medieval, 1976, Petrarquismo Peruano, 1985, Del exe antiguo a nuestro nuevo polo, 2003, 3 books poetry; contbr. over 80 articles to profl. jours. Recipient Diploma de Honor, U. P.R., Mayagüez, 1981; Guggenheim fellow, 1978-79. Mem. MLA, Assn. Internat. Hispanistas, Renaissance Soc. Am. Avocations: gardening, travel. Office: Office VP Acad Affairs Ad Bldg 203 State U Albany Albany NY 12222

COLOMBO, JOHN ROBERT, poet, editor, writer; b. Kitchener, Ont., Can., Mar. 24, 1936; s. John Anthony and Irene (Nicholson) C.; m. Ruth Florence Brown, May 11, 1959. BA, U. Toronto, 1959, postgrad., 1959-60, DLitt (hon.), 1998. Editorial asst. U. Toronto Press, 1957-59; asst. editor Ryerson Press, Toronto, 1960-63; sr. adv. editor McClelland & Stewart, Toronto, 1964-70; publ. cons. Toronto, 1971—; editor Tamarack Rev., Toronto, 1960-82. Spl. instr. Atkinson Coll., York U., Toronto, 1965-68; mem. adv. arts panel Can. Council, 1968-70; advisor Ont. Council Arts, 1965-68 Author (over 130 books, including) ; author: Colombo's Canadian Quotations, 1974; author: (with Nikola Roussanoff) The Balkan Range: A Bulgarian Reader, 1976; author: Colombo's Canadian References, 1976, (anthology) The Poets of Canada, 1978, Other Canadas: An Anthology of Science Fiction and Fantasy, 1979, Colombo's Hollywood, 1979, 222 Canadian Jokes, 1981, Friendly Aliens, 1981, Selected Poems, 1982, Selected Translations, 1982, Songs of the Indians, 1983; author: (with George Faludy) Learn This Poem of Mine by Heart, 1983; author: Canadian Literary Landmarks, 1984, 1001 Questions about Canada, 1986, Colombo's New Canadian Quotations, 1987, (poetry) Off Earth, 1987, Mysterious Canada, 1988, Extraordinary Experiences, 1989, 999 Questions About Canada, 1989, Songs of the Great Land, 1989, Mysterious Encounters, 1990, Mackenzie King's Ghost, 1991, UFOs Over Canada, 1991, The Dictionary of Canadian Quotations, 1991, Worlds in Small, 1992, Dark Visions, 1992, The Little Blue Book of UFOs, 1992, Walt Whitman's Canada, 1992, The Mystery of the Shaking Tent, 1993, Colombo's All-Time Great Canadian Quotations, 1994, Ghost Stories of Ontario, 1995, Voices of Rama, 1995, Strange Stories, 1995, Shapely Places, 1996, Haunted Toronto, 1996, Ether, 1997, What is What, 1998, All about Us, 1998, Marvellous Stories, 1998, More Iron Curtains, 1998, Closer than You Think, 1998, Quotable Canada, 1998, Interspaces, 1999, Self-Schrift, 1999, Mysteries of Ontario, 1999, Ghosts in our Past, 2000, The UFO Quote Book, 2000; gen. editor: The Canadian Global Almanac, 1992—2000, Colombo's Famous Lasting Words, 2000, The Penguin Book of Canadian Jokes, 2001, Ghost Stories of Canada, 2001, Half Life, 2002, Only in Canada, 2002, Making Light, 2002, Say It Again, Sam, 2003, More or Less, 2003. Recipient Can. Centennial medal, 1967, Order Cyril and Methodius 1st class, Esteemed Knight of Mark Twain, lit. prize Harbourfront's Internat. Festival Authors, 1985 Mem. P.E.N., League Can. Poets (provisional coordinator 1966-67), Assn. Can. TV and Radio Artists. Home and Office: 42 Dell Park Ave Toronto ON Canada M6B 2T6 Fax: 1 (416) 782-0285. E-mail: jrc@ca.inter.net.

COLON, CARLOS WILDO, librarian; b. Shreveport, La., Apr. 23, 1953; s. Wildo Domingo and Mercedes (Alejandro) C.; m. Alma Maria Mutzi, June 17, 1979; 1 child, Gina Marie. BA in English, La. State U., Shreveport, 1975; MLS, La. State U., 1977. Ref. libr. Memphis-Shelby County Pub. Libr. and Info. Ctr., 1978-81; ref./reader's adv. supr. Shreve Meml. Libr., Shreveport, 1981—. Libr. practicum instr. La. State U., Shreveport, 1982—. Author: The Worst of Almira Gulch, 1984, Almira Gulch: Confessions of a Social Wallflower, 1987, Jiminy Limericks, 1991, 94, Blue Jay on a Bowling Pin, 1991, Mountain Climbing, 1993, Clocking Out, 1996; (with Alexis K. Rotella) Nothing Inside, 1996, (with Alexis K. Rotella) Sassy, 1998; editor: Shreve Memorial Library Public Service Statistics 1922-89, 1990, Voices and Echoes: Haiku Soc. of America Members' Anthology, 2001; sr. editor A Selective Index to the Shreveport Journal, 1985-91, A Selective Index to the Shreveport Times, 1985-96, The Best of the Electronic Poetry Network, 2000, (with Raffael de Gruttola) Circling Bats, 2001; co-editor: Area Agencies and Organizations Directory, 1985—; contbr. articles to profl. jours. Vol. disk jockey Sta. WEVL, Memphis, 1981; lit. panel chmn. Shreveport Regional Arts Coun., 1990—, bd. dirs., 1991—. Named Outstanding Young Man of Am., Outstanding Young Men of Am., 1986; recipient Pushcart Prize nomination, 1994; Shreveport Regional Arts Coun. lit. fellow, 2002. Mem. ALA, Acad. Am. Poets, La. Libr. Assn., Am. Contract Bridge League, Shreveport Bridge Assn., Poets & Writers, Haiku Soc. Am., Shreveport Writers Club, Yellow Bus Tour, LogJam. Roman Catholic. Home: 185 Lynn Ave Shreveport LA 71105-3523 Office: Shreve Meml Libr 424 Texas St Shreveport LA 71101-5452 E-mail: ccolon@shreve.net.

COLON, ELSIE FLORES, American and English literature educator; b. N.Y.C., Oct. 26; d. Juan and Rosa Catalina (Caban) Flores; m. Daniel Colon, July 16, 1977. BA magna cum laude, Hunter Coll., 1992; postgrad., Grad. Sch. and Univ. Ctr., N.Y.C., 1992—; MA, Queens Coll., 1998; M Philosophy, Grad. Sch. and Univ. Ctr., 1999. Cons. Clairol, Inc. Bristol-Myers Co., N.Y.C., 1983-91; tchr.-counselor Manhattan North Ctr. Assn. for Children with Retarded Mental Devel. Inc., N.Y.C., 1992. Adj. prof. Touro Coll., N.Y.C., 1993—. Scholar Estate of J. Raymond Gerberick, 1992-93, Jewish Found. for Women, 1992-94; rsch. fellow Columbia U., 1991; Mellon assoc. Mellon Found., 1990-92; Dean K. Harrison fellow CUNY Grad. Sch., 1999, 2000. Mem. MLA, AAUW, Nat. Coun. Tchrs. of English, Am. Mus. Natural History (assoc.). Avocations: writing, reading, painting, drawing, travel. Office: Touro Coll 240 E 123d St New York NY 10035

COLONEY, WAYNE HERNDON, civil engineer; b. Bradenton, Fla., Mar. 15, 1925; s. Herndon Percival and Mary Adore (Cramer) C.; m. Anne Elizabeth Benedict, June 21, 1950; 1 child, Mary Adore. B.C.E. summa cum laude, Ga. Inst. Tech., 1950. Registered profl. engr. and surveyor, Fla., Ga., Ala., N.C. Project engr. Constructora Gen. S.A., Venezuela, 1948-49, Fla. Rd. Dept., 1950-55; hwy. engr. Gibbs & Hill, Inc., Guatemala, 1955-57, project mgr., 1957-59; project engr., then assoc. J.E. Greiner Co., Tampa, 1959-63; ptnr. Barrett, Daffin & Coloney, Tallahassee, 1963-70; pres. Wayne H. Coloney Co., Inc., Tallahassee, 1970-78, chmn., bd. chief exec. officer, 1978-85; pres., sec. Tesseract Corp., 1975-85; dep. chmn. Howden Airdynamics Am., Tallahassee, 1985-90; pres. Coloney Co. Cons. Engrs., Inc., 1978—; v.p., dir. Howden Coloney Inc., Tallahassee, 1985-90; prin. Coloney-Von Soosten & Assocs. Inc., Tallahassee, 1990—2002, Aurora Mgmt. Ptnrs., Tallahassee, 2002—03. Chmn. adv. com. Area Vocat. Tech. Sch., 1965-78; pres. Retro Tech. Corp., 1983-93, Profl. Mgmt. Con. Group, 1983-87; pres., bd. dirs. Internat. Enterprises Inc., 1967-73; bd. dirs., exec. com. GTO, Inc., 1990—. Patentee roof framing system, dense packing external aircraft fuel tank, tile mounting structure, curler rotating device, bracket system for roof framing; contbr. articles to profl. jours. Pres. United Fund Leon County, 1971-72; bd. dirs. Springtime Tallahassee, 1970-72, pres., 1981-82; bd. dirs. Heritage Found., 1965-71, pres., 1967; mem. Pres.'s Adv. Council on Indsl. Innovation, 1978-79; bd. dirs. LeMoyne Art Found., 1973, v.p., 1974-75; bd. dirs. Goodwill Industries, 1972-73, Tallahassee-Popoyan Friendship Commn., 1968-73; mem. Adv. Com. for Hist. and Cultural Preservation, 1969-71, vice chmn. Govs. Commn. for Purchase from the Blind, 1980-2002. Served with AUS, 1943-46. Fellow ASCE, Nat. Acad. Forensic Engrs. (pres.); mem. NSPE, Am. Def. Industries Assn., Fla. Engring. Soc. (sr.), Fla. Inst. Cons. Engrs., Fla. Surveying and Mapping Soc., Anak, Koseme Soc., Fla. Small Bus. Assn. (pres. 1981), Gov.'s Club, Phi Kappa Phi, Omicron Delta Kappa, Sigma Alpha Epsilon, Tau Beta Pi. Episcopalian. Home: 1304 Hollow Oak Cir Tallahassee FL 32308 Office: Coloney Bell Engring Ste 200 1520 Killearn Center Blvd Tallahassee FL 32309 E-mail: whc@coloney.com.

COLONNA, WILLIAM MARK, accountant; b. Joliet, Ill., Jan. 18, 1956; s. William and Lorraine (Govednik) C. BA in Acctg., Lewis U., 1974-78. Cost acct., asst. acctg. mgr. Insta-Foam Products, Joliet, Ill., 1978-86; cost acct. Durkee Foods, Joliet, 1986-88; chief acct. mgr. Lennon Wallpaper Co., Shorewood, Ill., 1988-90; pres., owner William M. Colonna Acctg. and Tax Svc., Crest Hill, Ill., 1990—; contr. Whiteford Warehouse & Distbn., Joliet, 1992—, Midwest Motor Svc. Co. of Ill., Inc., Joliet, 1992—. Sec., Joliet St. Anne Credit Union, Crest Hill, Ill., 1980-99, also bd. dirs. Home: 1718 Dearborn St Joliet IL 60435-2550

COLONNIER, MARC LEOPOLD, neuroanatomist, educator; b. Quebec, Que., Can., May 12, 1930; s. Jean and Enilda (Bourguignon) C.; m. Lise De Gagne, Oct. 24, 1959; 1 son, Jean. BA, B.Ph., U. Ottawa, 1951, MD, 1959, MS, 1960; PhD, U. Coll. London, 1963. Asst. prof. anatomy U. Ottawa, 1963-65; asst. prof. dept. physiology U. Montreal, Que., Can., 1965-67; assoc. prof., assoc. fellow neurol. scis. group Med. Research Council Can., 1967-69; prof., head dept. anatomy U. Ottawa, 1969-76; prof. dept. anatomy Laval U., Quebec City, Que., 1976-91; ret., 1991. Recipient Lederle Med. Faculty award, 1966, Charles Judson Herrick award Am. Assn. Anatomists, 1967 Fellow Royal Soc. Can.; mem. Am. Assn. Anatomists; Mem. Soc. Neurosci.; mem. Can. Assn. Anatomists (pres. 1973-75) Clubs: Cajal.

COLONY, PAMELA CAMERON, medical researcher, educator; b. Boston, Apr. 18, 1947; d. Donald Gifford Colony and Priscilla (Adams) Pratley; m. E. Paul Cokely Jr., Apr. 26, 1986 (div. 2000); 1 child, Daniel Patrick Cokely; m. Richard M. Sparling, June 1, 2003; 1 child, John Travis Cokely. BA, Wellesley (Mass.) Coll., 1969; PhD, Boston U., 1976. Rsch. asst. sch. medicine Boston U., 1969-71, U. Hosp., 1971-73, Peter Bent Brigham Hosp., Boston, 1973-75; instr. dept. anatomy Harvard Med. Sch., 1975-77; assoc. staff in medicine Peter Bent Brigham Hosp., Boston, 1976-79; sr. fellow, instr. Harvard Med. Sch., Boston, 1979-81; asst. prof. anatomy and medicine Pa. State Coll. Medicine, Hershey, Pa., 1981-88; assoc. prof. rsch., pre-health advisor Franklin and Marshall Coll., Lancaster, 1988-91; adj. assoc. prof. of surgery Pa. State Coll. Medicine, Hershey, 1988-91, sr. rsch. assoc. dept. surgery, 1991-95; asst. prof. SUNY, Cobleskill, 1995-97, assoc. prof., 1997-99, program dir. histotech., 1995—, prof. biology, 1999—, co-dir. Women in Sci., 1996—. Bd. dirs. N.Y. State Histotechnol. Soc.; ind. assessor Nat. Health and Med. Rsch. Coun., Australia, 1985—; ad-hoc reviewer NIH, Nat. Cancer Inst., Bethesda, Md., 1986; lectr., adj. instr. Harrisburg Area Cmty. Coll., 1991—95. Contbr. articles to profl. jours. Fellow Nat. Found. Ileitis and Colitis, 1979-81; grantee Fed. Republic Germany, 1978, Cancer Rsch. Ctr., 1982-83, NIH, 1982-91. Mem.: AAAS, Nat. Soc. for Histotech., N.Y. Histotechnol. Soc. (bd. dirs. 2001—), Nat. Assn. Advisors Health Profls., Am. Gastroent. Assn., N.Y. Acad. Sci., Am. Soc. Cell Biology. Avocations: endurance and competitive trail riding, breeding and showing horses. Office: SUNY Cobleskill Dept Natural Scis Main St Cobleskill NY 12043 E-mail: colonyp@cobleskill.edu.

COLOSI, THOMAS R. educator, mediator; b. May 25, 1934; BS, Cornell U., 1958. Internat. rep. dist. 50 United Mine Workers Am., NY, 1958-61; commr. U.S. Fed. Mediation and Conciliation Svc., Buffalo, 1961-68; corp. dir. employee rels. Monogram Industries, L.A., 1968-71; v.p. alt. dispute resolution Am. Arbitration Assn., Washington, 1971-99; cons. appropriate dispute resolution The Colosi Group, 1999—. Cons. alternate dispute resolution. Home and Office: 1348 Hunter Mill Rd Vienna VA 22182-1303 Fax: (703) 757-7205. E-mail: TCOLOSI@aol.com.

COLOSIMO, MARY LYNN SUKURS, psychology educator; b. Chgo., Aug. 14, 1950; d. Charles Paul and Charlotte Pearl (Bartkus) S.; m. Ronald Alfred Colosimo, Nov. 26, 1977; children: Elizabeth Catherine, Victoria Carmella, Christina Charlotte, Diana Clare. BA, Bradley U., 1972, MA, 1974; PhD, U. Chgo., 1981. Cert. tchr., Ill. Tchr. Lincoln (Ill.) High Sch., 1973-75; counselor Lyle Elem. Sch., Bridgeview, Ill., 1975-78; prof. St. Xavier Coll., Chgo., 1984-86; prof. ednl. psychology, tchg. methods, coord. tchr. interns field placements Trinity Christian Coll., Palos Heights, Ill., 1988-99; dir. recruitment and cmty. rels. S.W. Chgo. Christian Schs., Palos Heights, Ill., 1999-2001; adj. prof. Trinity Christian Coll., 2001—. Pvt. practice as counselor, cons., Orland Park, Ill., 1983-90; educator women's ministry, retreat work; rsch. in gifted edn., gender equity, tchg. methods. Contbr. articles to profl. jours. Mem. ACA, ASCD, AAUW, Am. Edn. Rsch. Assn., Assn. Rsch. Value Issues in Counseling,, Assn. Christian Therapists, Am. Assn. Christian Counselors, Nat. Gifted Edn. Assn., Ill. Gifted Edn. Assn., Nat. Assn. Guidance Counselors, Ill. Assn. Guidance Counselors, Phi Kappa Phi. Avocations: tennis, swimming, downhill skiing. E-mail: mlcolosimo@aol.com.

COLP, NORMAN BARRY, photographic artist, curator; b. Bronx, NY, Sept. 3, 1944; s. Joseph Johnny Colp and Martha (Berman) Colp Levine; m. Marsha Stern, July 18, 1981. BA in Art, CUNY, 1967; postgrad., Pratt Inst., 1967, Parsons Sch. Design, 1971. Archtl. modelmaker Milton Glaser Inc., N.Y.C., 1978-80; assoc. curator Alternative Mus., N.Y.C., 1979-80; curator exhibits Ctr. for Book Arts, N.Y.C., 1980-83, exhbn. coord., 1983; instr. Pratt Graphics Ctr., N.Y.C., 1983-84, Sch. Visual Arts, N.Y.C., 1982-86, acad. advisor, 1984-87; photog. artist, curator N.Y.C., 1978—. Cons. curator Anchorage Mus. History and Art, 1990, Golden & Dresnin Design, Phila., 1990, Islip Art Mus., East Islip, N.Y., 1990, Boca Raton (Fla.) Mus. Art, 1991; cons. on book Exploring Color Photography, 1991, 97, The Girls' Guide to Hunting and Fishing, 1999-2000; artist-in-residence Pub. Sch. 1, Long Island City, N.Y., 1977-78, Cabin Creek Ctr. for Work and Environ. Studies, N.Y.C., 1979; workshop presenter-in-residence Mus. Holography, N.Y.C., 1985; cons. Artists Found., Inc., Boston, 1986, juror, 1989; lectr. in field. Author: Freud's Recipe, Crazy Hair, A Primer on Art Criticism, 1983; one-man shows include Victoria and Albert Mus., London, 1991, Islip Art Mus., 1993, UCLA, 1994, Coll. of Charleston, 1997, Hugo de Pagano Gallery, N.Y.C., 1998, The Tiny Cinema, Red Mills, Claverack, N.Y., 2001; exhibited in group shows at Mus. Modern Art Libr., Mus. Fine Arts, St. Petersburg, Fla., Boca Raton Mus., Corcoran Gallery of Art, Washington, U. Art Mus., U. Calif., Berkeley, Wadsworth Atheneum, Hartford, Conn., The Ralls Collection, Washington, FotoFest 2002, Houston, Art in Embassies Program, U.S. Dept. State, Havana, Cuba, 2003, Lima, Peru, 2003; represented in permanent collections Nat. Libr., Paris, Victoria and Albert Mus., Corcoran Gallery, Libr. Congress, Mus. Modern Art Libr., N.Y.C., N.Y. Pub. Libr., Queens Mus. of Art, Flushing, N.Y., Islip Art Mus., East Islip, N.Y., Bklyn. Mus. of Art, Archives of Am. Art, Smithsonian Instn., Washington, Whitney Mus. Am. Art, Internat. Ctr. Photography, N.Y.C. Grantee, Com. for Visual Arts, 1980, Met. Transit Authority, 1991, Fieldcrest Cannon Inc., 1991, The Merchant and Ivory Found., 2002, FotoFest, 2002. Avocation: collecting american art and japanese redware pottery and gutta-purcha frames. Home: 180 W End Ave Apt 3R New York NY 10023-4913

COLQUHOUN, JAMES S. physician; MD, Georgetown, 1996. Medicine cons. svc. U. Wash. Med. Ctr, Seattle, 1999—2002. Med. cons. Office: Univ Wash Med Ctr 1959 NE Pacific St Box 356166 Seattle WA 98195

COLQUHOUN, PETER LLOYD, artist, educator; b. N.Y.C., Dec. 1, 1955; s. Harvey Edward Colquhoun and Janet Olive Gurge. BFA, Pratt Inst., 1989. Tchr. painting New Bklyn. Sch., 1979-81, N.Y. Acad., N.Y.C., 1981-83, Centro del Arte Verrochio, Casole d'Elsa, Italy, 1985-86. Bd. dirs., columnist N.Y. Artists Equity, 1998-2002. Max Beckmann scholar Bklyn. Mus. Art Sch., 1974-76, Adolph & Esther Gottlieb Found. grantee, 1993, 2001, Helene Wurlitzer Found. residency, Taos, N.Mex., 2000, Pollock Krasner Found. World Trade Ctr. Emergency grantee, 2002; Md. Inst. sponsored resident, Rochefort en terre, Brittany. Mem. Audubon Artists (Giulia Palermo prize 1994), Orgn. Ind. Artists, Fedn. Modern Painters and Sculptors. Home: 105 Duane St #4C New York NY 10007

COLSKY, ANDREW EVAN, lawyer, mediator, arbitrator; b. Miami, Fla., Nov. 20, 1964; s. Jacob and Irene Vivian (Belen) Colsky. BA, U. Fla., 1986, JD, 1989; LLM in Litigation, Emory U., 1990. Bar: Fla. 1989, Ga. 1990, D.C. 1990, U.S. Dist. Ct. (no. dist.) Ga. 1990, U.S. Dist. Ct. (so. dist.) Fla. 1990, U.S. Ct. Appeals (D.C. cir.) 1990, U.S. Ct. Appeals (11th cir.); cert. mediator Fla. Supreme Ct. Pvt. practice, Miami, Fla., 1992-99; alt. dispute resolution atty. Resolve Employment Disputes Reach Equitable Solutions Swiftly program U.S. Postal Svc., 1999—; pres. The Am. Mediation Inst., Miami, Fla., 1995—; CEO Am. Conflict Mgmt. Inst., 1998—. Mem. trial team U. Fla., Gainesville, 1988-89, co-founder U. Miami Collaboration in Advanced Dispute Resolution Edn. program. Mem. Golden Key Honor Soc., Phi Delta Phi, Omicron Delta Kappa, Phi Kappa Phi, Alpha Lambda Chi (pres. 1985-86).

COLSON, EARL MORTON, lawyer, educator; b. Bklyn., Mar. 8, 1930; s. Abraham and Rebecca (Hecker) C.; m. Helen Theresa Austern, Apr. 24, 1960; children: Adam Thomas, Amy Esther, Deborah Austern. BS magna cum laude, Syracuse U., 1950; LLB magna cum laude, Harvard U., 1957. Bar: N.Y. 1958, D.C. 1960. Assoc. Chadbourne, Parke, Whiteside & Wolff, N.Y.C., 1957-60, Arent, Fox, Kintner, Plotkin & Kahn, Washington, 1960-68, partner, 1968—. Adj. prof. law Georgetown U., 1970 ; lectr on tax subjects. Author: Capital Gains and Losses, 1975; co-author: Federal Taxation of Estates, Gifts and Trusts, 1975. Bd. dirs. Washington Hebrew Congregation, 1979—, v.p., 1984-90, pres., 1990-92; trustee Kingsbury Ctr., 1978-81; mem. N.Y. bd. overseers Hebrew Union Coll., 1995-97; bd. dirs. D.C. chpt. Am. Jewish Com., 1995-98. Mem. ABA (chmn. estate and gift tax com. sect. taxation 1972-73), D.C. Bar Assn. (chmn. tax com. 1971-72, treas., bd. govs. 1974-76), Am. Law Inst., Assn. of Bar of City of N.Y., Cosmos Club Washington. Office: 1050 Connecticut Ave NW Washington DC 20036-5303

COLSON, ELIZABETH FLORENCE, anthropologist; b. Hewitt, Minn., June 15, 1917; d. Louis H. and Metta (Damon) C. BA, U. Minn., 1938, MA, 1940, Radcliffe Coll., 1941, PhD, 1945; D of Sociology, Brown U., 1979; D.Sc., U. Rochester, 1985, U. Zambia, 1992. Asst. social sci. analyst War Relocation Authority, 1942-43, research asst. Harvard, 1944-45, research officer Rhodes-Livingstone Inst., 1946-47, dir., 1948-51; sr. lectr. Manchester U., 1951-53; assoc. prof. Goucher Coll., 1954-55; research assoc., assoc. prof. African Research Program, Boston U., 1955-59, part-time, 1959-63; prof. anthropology Brandeis U., 1959-63, U. Calif.-Berkeley, 1964-84, prof. emeritus, 1984—; vis. prof. U. Zambia, 1987. Lewis Henry Morgan lectr. U. Rochester, 1973; vis. rsch. assoc. Refugee Studies Program Queen Elizabeth House, Oxford, 1988-89. Author: The Makah, 1953, Marriage and the Family Among The Plateau Tonga, 1958, Social Organization of the Gwembe Tonga, 1960, The Plateau Tonga, 1962, The Social Consequences of Resettlement, 1971, Tradition and Contract, 1974, A History of Nampeyo, 1992; jr. author Secondary Education and the Formation of an Elite, 1980, Voluntary Efforts in Decentralized Management, 1983, sr. author For Prayer and Profit, 1988, The History of Nampeyo, 1991; sr. editor: Seven Tribes of British Central Africa, 1951; jr. editor People in Upheaval, 1987. AAUW travelling fellow, 1941-42, fellow Ctr. Advanced Study Behavioral Scis., 1967-68, Fairchild fellow Calif. Inst. Tech., 1975-76. Fellow Am. Anthrop. Assn., Assn. Social Anthropologists of the Commonwealth, Royal Anthrop. Inst. (hon.); mem. Nat. Acad. Sci., Am. Acad. Arts and Scis., Am. Assn. African Studies (Disting. Africanist award 1988), Soc. Applied Anthropology, Soc. Woman Geographers, Phi Beta Kappa. Avocations: walking, opera, reading. Office: U Calif Dept Anthropology Berkeley CA 94720 0001

COLSON, KIRBY LEWIS, music educator; b. Dublin, Ga., July 25, 1945; d. Iris Keene Robertson and Kirby Romulus Lewis, Jack Barker Robertson (Stepfather); m. Oliver Kirby Colson, III, Jan. 27, 1968; children: Heather Ewing, Tierney Stutz, Eliza Lewis. BA, Brenau U., Gainsville, Ga., 1963—67; Grad. sch., U. of Ga., Athens, Ga., 1967—68; Grad. of Prep. Dept., The Peabody Conservatory of Music of John Hopkins U., Balt., MD, 1957—62. Nationally Certified Teacher of Music, Music Teachers Nat. Assn. Certification Bd., 1977, Music Teachers National Association Permanent Professional Certificate, Music Teachers Nat. Assn., 1997. Piano tchr., Wilmette and Highland Pk., Ill., 1976—93, Self Employed, St. Louis, 1993—; regional dir. The Worth Collection, New York, NY; divisional sales mgr. for MO, KS, OK, The Carlisle Collection, LTD, New York, NY, 1994—97. Judge North Shore Music Teachers Assn., Winnetka (Chicago's North Shore), Ill., 1977—93; profl. mem. Fashion Group Internat., New York (St. Louis Chpt.), NY, 1998—. Contbr. booklet; co-author (architecture book) An Arch. Album; Chicago's North Shore; contbr. cookbook. Bd. mem. and actress North Shore Cmty. Theater, Wilmette, Ill., 1979—84; mem. St. Louis Music Teachers Assn., St. Louis, 1993—2003; Capital Campaign Steering Com. The Jr. League of St. Louis, St. Louis, 1993—95; Bd. of Regents St. Louis U., St. Louis, 1993—99; co-chair of housing com.; guild bd. Opera Theater of St. Louis, St. Louis, 1998—2002; vestry, choir soloist, del. to Chgo. diocesan conv.; dir. youth music prog.; Trinity Episcopal Ch., Highland Pk., Ill., 1983—93; chalice bearer and lay reader, lic. by the bishop of mo, diocesan del., vestry, stewardship com. - St. Michael and St. George;; first v.p. (edn.) The Women's Soc. of Wash. U., St. Louis, 2003—; founded Project Prairie Rose Jr. League of Evanston, North Shore, Evanston, Ill., 1986—87; mktg. dir. of An Archtl. Album; Chicago's North Shore Jr. League of Evanston; North Shore, Evanston, Mo., 1977—93; judge for piano competitions and syllabus exams North Shore Music Teachers Assn., Winnetka, Ill., 1977—93; chair of concert for Children with Spl. Needs; chair of fund raising gala, co-chair - internat. string competition, co-chair - Rotogravure; St. Louis Symphony Vol. Assn., St. Louis, 1993—2001; mem. at large of exec. bd. The Women's Soc. of Wash. U., St. Louis, 2000—03; mem., mktg. chair, chair of opening night gala The Ravinia Women's Bd., Chgo., 1991—2002; cmty. v.p., founded task force for Hdqs., mktg. dir., chair-hist. preservation, Opera in Classroom chair, appraisal ch Jr. League of Evanston, North Shore, Evanston, Ill., 1979—93; mem. The Fortnightly of Chgo., Chgo. Recipient Vol. of the Yr., The Jr. League of Evanston; North Shore, 1989 - 1990, The Aerobic Woman of the Yr., The Mo. Athletic Club, 1996; scholar A. Paige Reed Meml. Scholarship, The Peabody Conservatory of Music of John Hopkins U.; prep dept., 1959 - 1962. Mem.: The Women's Soc. of Wash. U. (life; see above), The Fortnightly of Chgo. (assoc.), Mu Phi Epsilon, Delta Delta Delta. Episcopal. Avocations: travel, cooking, reading, art, painting, piano, guitar. Home: 10 Portland Place Saint Louis MO 63108

COLSON, ROSEMARY, music educator; b. Madison, Ind., July 15, 1937; d. Howard Paul and Mary Wilder Colson. Student, Georgetown Coll., 1955—56; MusB, George Peabody Coll., 1960; MusM, Yale U., 1965. Piano tchr. Wilmington (Del.) Music Sch., 1965—66, Settlement Music Sch., Phila., 1966—77, Chestnut Hill Acad., Phila., 1969—78, Acad. Cmty. Music, Ft. Washington, Pa., 1993—; pvt. piano tchr. Phila., 1967—; organist, choir master Grace Epiphany Episcopal Ch., Phila., 1987—2000. Contbr. articles to profl. jours. Treas. West Ctrl. Germantown Neighbors, Phila., 1981—83; bd. dirs. YWCA Germantown, Phila., 1990—94, Women's Sacred Music Project, 2003—. Mem.: Music Tchrs. Nat. Assn., Am. Guild Organists, Delta Omicron (advisor to U. Pa. chpt. 1963—64). Democrat. Presbyterian. Avocations: gardening, reading, travel. Home: 6021 McCallum St Philadelphia PA 19144

COLTEN, HARVEY RADIN, pediatrician, educator; b. Houston, Jan. 11, 1939; s. Oscar Aaron and Zina Mae (Radin) Colten; m. Susan J. Kaplowitz, July 29, 1959; children: Jennifer J., Lora, Charles Thomas. BA, Cornell U., 1959; MD, Western Res. U., 1963; MA (hon.), Harvard U., 1978. Diplomate Am. Bd. Allergy and Clin. Immunology, Am. Bd. Pediats. Intern Univ. Hosps., Cleve., 1963, resident in pediat., 1964—65, Children's Hosp. of D.C., Washington, 1968—69; rsch. assoc. Nat. Inst. Child and Human Devel., NIH, Bethesda, Md., 1965—67; asst. prof. pediat. George Washington U., 1969—70; from asst. prof. pediat. to prof. Harvard U., 1970—97; chief divsn. cell biology, dir. cystic fibrosis program Children's Hosp. Med. Ctr., Boston, 1976—86; pediatrician-in-chief Jewish Hosp., 1986—89; Harriet B. Spoehrer prof. pediat. Washington U. Med. Sch., St. Louis, 1986—97, chmn. dept. pediat., 1986—95; pediatrician-in-chief Children's and Barnes Hosps., 1986—95; dean, v.p. med. affairs Northwestern U. Sch. Medicine, Chgo., 1997—99; chief med. officer iMetrikus, Inc., Carlsbad, Calif., 2000—. Prof. pediat. and microbiology/immunology Northwestern U. Sch. Medicine, 1999—2000; clin. prof. pediat. U. Calif., San Francisco, 2001—02; pres., v.p. and sr. assoc. dean for transl. rsch. Health Sci. divsn. Columbia U., 2002—; past chmn. pediat. allergy Nat. Inst. Allergy and Infectious Disease Task Force on Asthma and Allergy; past mem. Nat. Inst. Child and Human Devel. Task Force on Cystic Fibrosis; past rsch. rev. com. Nat. Cystic Fibrosis Found.; past mem. pulmonary diseases adv. com. NIH. Assoc. editor Jour. Immunology, 1971—74, Immunochemistry, 1972—75, Jour. Allergy and Clin. Immunology, 1977—80, New Eng. Jour. Medicine, 1978—81, Jour. Clin. Investigation, 1982—85, Am. Jour. Respiratory Cell and Molecular Biology, 1988—91, New Insights into CF, 1993—94, editl. bd. Molecular and Cellular Biochemistry, 1983—87, Jour. Pediat., 1981—88, Jour. Clin. Immunology, 1985—89, Ann. Rev. Immunology, 1986—90, Clin. Immunology and Immunopathology, 1987—91, Blood, 1987—92, New Eng. Jour. Medicine, 1990—98, Jour. Biomed. Sci., 1992—, Proc. Assn. Am. Physicians, 1995—99, Ency. of Life Scis., 1997—; contbr. articles to profl. jours. Vice chmn. bd. dirs. Parents As Tchrs. Nat. Ctr.; bd. dirs. The Oasis Inst., Immtech Internat. Inc.; past mem. pediat. scientist program selection com. AMSPDC; sci. adv. coun. March of Dimes; mem. Nat. Heart, Lung, Blood Adv. Coun. NIH; past bd. mgrs. Ctrl. Inst. for Deaf. Recipient Spl. Faculty Rsch. award, Western

Reserve U., 1963, E. Mead Johnson award, 1979. Fellow: AAAS, Am. Acad. Pediat., Am. Acad. Allergy and Immunology; mem.: NAS (vice-chmn. coun. Inst. Medicine 1997—), Inst. of Medicine, Am. Soc. Biochem. and Molecular Biology, Am. Thoracic Soc., Am. Pediatric Soc., Soc. Pediatric Rsch., Hungarian Soc. Immunology (hon.), Assn. Am. Physicians, Am. Soc. Clin. Investigation, Am. Assn. Immunologists (past sec.-treas., Disting. Svc. award), E. Mead Johnson Award Program Com. (past chmn.), Fedn. Am. Socs. for Exptl. Biology. Address: 299 Hollow Hill Rd Tamworth NH 03886

COLTMAN, EDWARD JEREMIAH, communication executive; b. Boston, Aug. 20, 1948; s. Edward Philip and Eleanor (Dwyer) C. BA, Harvard U., 1969, M of City and Regional Planning, 1979. Reporter The Hartford (Conn.) Courant, 1970; asst. to Alfred G. Aronowitz, N.Y.C., 1970-72; reporter The Evening Capital, Annapolis, Md., 1973-74, The Sun, Balt., 1974-77; sr. assoc. Richard Grefé Assocs., Washington, 1979-83; dep. dir. policy Corp. for Pub. Broadcasting, Washington, 1983-89; dir., 1989-95; exec. dir. new media Corp. for Pub. Broadcasting, Washington, 1995-97, exec. dir. strategic planning, 1997-99, exec. dir. spl. projects, 1999—. Avocation: hand bookbinding. Home: 122 6th St SE Washington DC 20003-1132 Office: Corp for Pub Broadcasting 401 9th St NW Washington DC 20004-2129 E-mail: ted_coltman@post.harvard.edu., tcoltman@cpb.org.

COLTMAN, JOHN WESLEY, physicist; b. Cleve., July 19, 1915; s. Robert White and Louise (Tyroler) C.; m. Charlotte Waters Beard, June 10, 1941; children— Sally Louise, Nancy Jean. BS in Physics, Case Inst. Tech., 1937; MS, U. Ill., 1939, PhD in Physics, 1941. Rsch. scientist Rsch. Labs. Westinghouse Electric Corp., Pitts., 1941—49, mgr. electronics and nuc. physics dept., 1949—60, assoc. dir. rsch. labs., 1960—64, dir. rsch. math. and radiation, 1964—69, dir. rsch. industry, def. and pub. sys., 1969—74, dir. rsch. and devel. planning, 1974—80. Mem. adv. group on electron devices Dept. Def., 1958-62; mem. Naval Intelligence Sci. Adv. Com., 1971-73, NRC Commn. on Human Resources, 1977-80; privately sponsored rschs. on acoustics of the flute. Contbr. articles to profl. jours. Recipient Longstreth medal Franklin Inst., 1960; Roentgen medal Remscheid, W. Ger., 1970; Gold medal Radiol. Soc. N.Am., 1982 Fellow Am. Phys. Soc., IEEE; mem. Nat. Acad. Engring., Am. Musical Instrument Soc. Presbyterian. Achievements include inventing x-ray image amplifier, scintillation counter. Home: 3319 Scathelocke Rd Pittsburgh PA 15235-5122 E-mail: coltmanjw@worldnet.att.net.

COLTON, CLARK KENNETH, chemical engineering educator; b. N.Y.C., July 20, 1941; s. Sidney and Goldie (Chases) C.; m. Ellen Ruth Brandner, June 20, 1965; children: Jill Erin, Jason Adam, Michael Ross, Brian Scott. B of Chem. Engring., Cornell U., 1964; PhD, MIT, 1969. Asst. prof. chem. engring. MIT, Cambridge, 1969-73, assoc. prof., 1973-76, prof., 1976—, Bayer prof. chem. engring., 1980-85, dep. head dept. chem. engring., 1977-78, chmn. centennial chem. engring. edn., 1988. Cons. to NIH, FDA, various indsl. orgns.; mem. adv. bd. mil. personnel supplies NRC, 1971-75 Mem. editl. bd. Jour. Membrane Sci., 1975-81, 97, Jour. Bioengring., 1976-79, Preparative Chromatography, 1988-94, Isolation and Purification, 1994—, ASAIO Jour., 1985-94; mem. editl. bd. Cell Transplantation, 1991-94, 97, assoc. editor, 1997—; contbr. articles to sci. jours. Ford found. fellow, 1969-70; recipient Tchr./Scholar award Camille and Henry Dreyfus Found., 1972, Lifetime Contbn. award in bioartificial organs Engring. Found., 1998. Fellow AAAS; mem. N.Y. Acad. Scis., Am. Inst. Chem. Engrs. (dir. food, pharm. and bioengring. div. 1978-81 (food, Pharm. and Bioengring. div. award, 1999, Allan P. Colburn award 1977), Am. Soc. Artificial Internal Organs (editorial bd. 1978-84), Am. Diabetes Assn., Am. Soc. for Apheresis, Am. Soc. for Engring. Edn. (Curtis W. McGraw rsch. award 1980), North Am. Membrane Soc., Am. Heart Assn., Cell Transplantation Soc. (sec. 1994-2001, treas. 2001—), Internat. Soc. on Oxygen Transport to Tissue, Am. Chem. Soc., Am. Inst. Med. and Biological Engring., Internat. Soc. Articificial Organs, Internat. Soc. Blood Purification (Gambro award 1986), Biomed. Engring. Soc., Cornell Club, Sigma Xi, Tau Beta Pi, Phi Lambda Upsilon. Home: 279 Commonwealth Ave Chestnut Hill MA 02467-1012 Office: MIT Dept Chem Engring Cambridge MA 02139 E-mail: ckcolton@mit.edu.

COLTON, DAVID LEM, mathematician, educator; b. San Francisco, Mar. 14, 1943; s. Ellis and Myrl (Crowder) C.; m. Renate, Dec. 20, 1968; children— Claire, Natasha. BS, Calif. Inst. Tech., 1964; MS, U. Wis., 1965; PhD, U. Edinburgh, Scotland, 1967, DSc, 1977. Asst. prof. math. Ind. U., 1967-71, assoc. prof., 1972-74; prof. U. Strathclyde, Glasgow, Scotland, 1975-78, U. Del., Newark, 1978—, Unidel prof., 1996—. Vis. prof. McGill U., 1968-69, U. Glasgow, 1971-72, U. Konstanz, 1974-75 Author various rsch. monographs; rschr. numerous publs. in field. Mem. Soc. Indsl. and Applied Math. (assoc. editor jour.). Office: U Del Dept Math Newark DE 19716

COLTON, FRANK BENJAMIN, retired chemist; b. Bialystok, Poland, Mar. 3, 1923; came to U.S., 1934, naturalized, 1934; s. Rubin and Fanny (Rosenblat) C.; m. Adele Heller, Mar. 24, 1950; children: Francine, Sharon, Laura, Sandra BS, Northwestern U., 1945, MA, 1946; PhD, U. Chgo., 1949. Research fellow Mayo Clinic, Rochester, Minn., 1949-51; with G.D. Searle & Co., Chgo., 1951-86, asst. dir. chem. research, 1961-70, research advisor, 1970-86. Contbr. articles to profl. jours. Pioneer in organic and steroid chemistries. Patentee first oral contraceptive Recipient Discovery medal for first oral contraceptive Nat. Assn. Mfrs., 1965, Profl. Achievement award U. Chgo., 1978, Achievement award Indsl. Research Inst., 1978; inducted in Nat. Inventors Hall of Fame, 1988. Mem. Am. Chem. Soc., Chgo. Chemists Club. Home: 1419 Lorete Ln Northbrook IL 60062-5142 E-mail: fbcolton@aol.com.

COLTON, JAMES PATRICK, community college administrator; m. Margaret Hill; children: Rebecca, Barbara, William. AA, Weatherford (Tex.) Coll., 1976; BS cum laude, Tex A&M U., 1978, MEd, 1979. Grad. asst. Tex. A&M U., College Station, 1978, grad. fellow, 1978-79; agr. instr. Poolville (Tex.) H.S., 1979-80, Weatherford Coll., 1980-87, instnl. rsch. dir., 1987-93, dir. student devel., 1993-98, dean student devel., 1998—. Chmn. occupl. adv. bd. Aledo (Tex.) Ind. Sch. Dist., 1983-85; mem. rsch. com. North Tex. C.C. Consortium, 1988-92; presenter programs. Bd. dirs. Palo Pinto County Hosp. Dist., Mineral Wells, Tex., 1999—; del. Tex. Dem. State Conv., Austin, 1985; Pan Am. Exposition beef supt. State Fair Tex., Dallas, 1981-88; mem. Parker County Youth Com., chmn., 1981-83. Named Faculty Mem. of Yr., Weatherford Coll., 1984, Staff Mem. of Yr., 1991; named to Outstanding Young Men of Am., 1988. Mem. Weatherford Bus. and Profl. Men's Club (publicity chmn.), Phi Theta Kappa, Gamma Sigma Delta. Alpha Zeta. Avocations: computers, history, youth development, bassets. Office: Weatherford Coll 225 College Park Dr Weatherford TX 76086-6265 E-mail: colton@wc.edu.

COLTON, JOEL, historian, educator; b. N.Y.C., Aug. 23, 1918; s. Philip and Theresa (Cotler); m. Shirley Baron, May 8, 1942; children— Valerie Beth, Kenneth Richard. BA magna cum laude, CCNY, 1937, MS, 1938; MA, Columbia U., 1940; PhD, 1950. Lectr. history Columbia U., 1946-47; successively instr., asst. prof., assoc. prof., prof. history Duke U., 1947-89, prof. emeritus, 1989—, chmn. dept. history, 1967-74, chmn. acad. council, 1971-73; dir. for humanities Rockefeller Found., 1974-81. U.S. mem. Internat. Commn. on History of Social Movements and Social Structures, 1975—, v.p., 1980-85, co-pres., 1985-90, hon. pres., 1990—; vis. prof. U. Wis., Makerere U., Uganda; lectr. Cadi-Ayyad U., Morocco. Author: Compulsory Labor Arbitration in France, 1936-39, 1951, (Japanese transl. 1999), Léon Blum: Humanist in Politics, 1966 (French transl. 1968), rev. edit., 1987, Twentieth Century: Time-Life Great Ages of Man Series, 1968, rev. edit., 1980; co-author: (with R.R. Palmer) A History of the Modern World, 2d - 8th edits., 1956-95 (transl. into Arabic, Persian, Swedish, Finnish, Spanish, Italian and Chinese), (with R.R. Palmer and L. Kramer), 9th edit., 2002, Study Guide for A History of the Modern World, 9th edit., 2002; editor: The Humanities in an International Context, 1976, The Search for a Value Consensus, 1978, Toward the Restoration of the Liberal Arts Curriculum, 1979; co-editor: Technology, The Economy and Society, 1987; bd. editors: Jour. Modern History, 1967-70, Third Republic/Troisième République, 1975-85, French Hist. Studies, 1985-88; mem. adv. bd. Hist. Abstracts, 1981—; contbr. articles to profl. jours., encys., internat. conf. procs. and yearbooks. Mem. adv. bd. Duke U. Press, 1982-88; trustee Triangle Univs. Ctr. for Advanced Studies, N.C., 1982-85. U.S. Army, 1942-46, 1st lt. M.I., 1944-46, ETO. Recipient book award Mayflower Soc., 1967, Townsend Harris medal CCNY Alumni Assn., 1980, Disting. Tchg. award Duke U., 1986, award for contbns. to study and tchg. French history Western Soc. for French History, 1994; Guggenheim fellow, 1957-58, fellow Rockefeller Found., 1961-62, sr. fellow NEH, 1970-71. Fellow Am. Acad. Arts and Scis. elected 1979, Phi Beta Kappa (vis. scholar 1983-84), Phi Beta Kappa Soc.; mem. Am. Hist. Assn. (com. on internat. hist. activities 1980-85), So. Hist. Assn. (chmn. European sect. 1975-76), Soc. French Hist. Studies (v.p. 1972-73), PEN Am. Ctr. Home: 2701 Pickett Rd # 3044 Durham NC 27705 Office: Duke U Dept History Box 90719 Durham NC 27708-0719

COLTON, ROY CHARLES, management consultant; b. Phila., Feb. 26, 1941; s. Nathan Hale and Ruth Janis (Baylinson) C. BA, Knox Coll., 1962; MEd, Temple U., 1963. With Sch. Dist. of Phila., 1963-64; sys. analyst Wilmington Trust Co., 1967-69; exec. recruiter Atwood Consultants Inc., Phila., 1969-71; pres. Colton Bernard Inc., San Francisco, 1971—. Occasional lectr. Fashion Inst. Tech., Phila. Coll. Textiles and Scis. Served with AUS, 1964-66. Mem. San Francisco Fashion Industries, San Francisco C. of C., Calif. Exec. Recruiter Assn., Nat. Assn. Exec. Recruiters, Am. Apparel Mfrs. Assn., Am. Arbitration Assn. (panel arbitrators). Office: Colton Bernard Inc 870 Market St Ste 822 San Francisco CA 94102-2921 Fax: 415-399-0750. E-mail: rcolton@coltonbernard.com.

COLTON, STERLING DON, lawyer, business executive, missionary; b. Vernal, Utah, Apr. 28, 1929; s. Hugh Wilkins and Marguerite (Maughan) C.; m. Eleanor Ricks, Aug. 6, 1954; children: Sterling David, Carolyn, Bradley Hugh, Steven Ricks. BS in Banking and Fin., U. Utah, 1951; JD, Stanford U., 1953. Bar: Calif. 1954, Utah 1954, D.C. 1967. Ptnr. Van Cott, Bagley, Cornwall & McCarthy, Salt Lake City, 1957-66; vice chair, sr. v.p., gen. counsel, bd. dirs. Marriott Corp. and Marriott Internat., 1954-95. Pres. Can. Vancouver Mission Ch. of Jesus Christ of Latter Day Saints, 1995-98, Washington DC Temple, Ch. of Jesus Christ of Latter Day Saints, 1999-2002; v.p. Colton Ranch Corp., Vernal, 1987—; former bd. dirs. Megaherz Corp. and Dyncorp; former chmn. bd. dirs. Nat. Chamber Litigation Ctr. Former bd. dirs. Polynesian Cultural Ctr.; former chmn. nat. adv. coun. U. Utah, Ballet West, nat. adv. counsel; mem. adv. coun. The Nat. Conservancy; trustee So. Va. U., 2003—. Maj. JAG, U.S. Army, 1954-57. Mem. ABA, Calif. Bar Assn., Utah Bar Assn., D.C. Bar Assn., Washington Met. Corp. Counsel Assn. (former pres., dir.), Sigma Chi. Republican. Mem. Lds Ch. E-mail: sdercolton@aol.com.

COLTON SKOLNICK, JUDITH A. artist; b. Washington, Jan. 31, 1947; d. Bernard and Helen (Glick) Colton; 2 children. Student, Corcoran Sch. Art, 1964, 93-94; BA in Art and Art History with honors, U. Md., 1972; postgrad., Montgomery Coll., 1990-91. Tchr. faux painting workshop The Artful Framer, 1991, Craft Country, Olney, Md., 1991; artist guest lectr. Radford U., spring 1996; supr. painting Paint Out Aids Ea. Market, Washington, 1992; asst. to art cons. Capitol Arts, Washington, 1992-96; tech. illustrator Vitro Corp., 1981-86; artist assoc. Mary Anne Reilly, 1995; founder Unity in Diversity Women's Exhibn. Group; interviewer, active Va. Juvenile Detention Ctr., 1993; spkr., presenter in field. One-woman shows include Beltone Hearing Aid, Washington, 1963, New Trends, Springfield, Va., 1971, Artful Framer, Olney, Md., 1991, Kurz, Koch, Doland and Dembling, Washington, 1992, Heartland Cafe, 1992, "R" St. Gallery Jackson Sch., 1993, Franklin Ct. Gallery, 1994, Parish Gallery, 1995, Flossie Martin Gallery Radford U., Blacksburg, Va., 1996, Sunrise Gallery, Kilmarnock, Va., 1997, Nat. Press Club Bldg., Washington, 1997—98, Art Mine Agora Gallery, N.Y.C., 1998—2001, Very Spl. Arts Online Gallery, Washington, 1998—2001, Articulate Gallery, 1999, exhibited in group shows at The Artful Framer, 1991, Glen Echo (Md.) Park, 1991, The Montpelier Cultural Arts Ctr., Laurel, Md., 1991, 1994, Md. Arts Pl., Rockville, 1992, Emerson Art Gallery, McLean,Va., 1992, Mus. Latin and Hispanic Art, Miami, Fla., 1992, Willow St. Gallery, Washington, 1992—93, SODARCO, Montreal, 1993, Howard C.C., Columbia, Md., 1993, Feminist Expo, Balt., 2000, N.Y.C., 1993—94, Art Expo N.Y., 2000, Fresno (Calif.) Mus. Art, 1993, Agora Galleries, N.Y.C., 1992—2001, Santa Barbara (Calif.) Mus. Art, 1993, U. Md., Albin O. Kuhn Libr. and Gallery U. Md., Balt., 1994, Owen Patrick Gallery, Phila., 1994, D.C. Arts Ctr., 1994, Mus. Ams., Washington, 1994, Mus. Nacional Palacio Bellas Artes, Havana, Cuba, 1995, French Emb., Washington, 1995, Very Spl. Arts Gallery, 1996, Venable Neslage, Washington, 1996, Nat. Mus. Women in Arts, 1995, 1998, B'nai B'rith Klutznick Nat. Jewish Mus., Washington, 1997, Corcoran Mus. Art, 1999, King St. Stephen Mus., Hungary, 2000, Jemison-Carnegie Heritage Hall Mus., Ala., 2001, Attleboro (Mass.) Mus., 2001, The Music, Comune de Imola, Italy, 1999, Castel S. Pietro Terme, 1999—2003, Maison Francois de Bologne, Sung Kyun Kwan U., Seoul, Korea, CIA, McLean, Va., 1998, Amsterdam Whitney Gallery, NYC, 2002—03, Nat. Assn. Women Artists, 2002, others; (command murals, faux painting); contbr. to profl. mags. and pubs. Mem. Nat. Assn. Women Artists Inc., Nat. Mus. Women in Arts, Corcoran Sch. Art Alumni Assn. (presenter). Democrat. Jewish. Avocations: poetry, reading, walking, boating. Home: 2301 E St NW A1115 Washington DC 20037

COLUCCI, JACQUELINE STRUPP, interpreter, small business administration specialist, sculptor; b. Montevideo, Uruguay, July 24, 1963; d. Gunther and Silvia (Klemens) S.; children: Matias Camprubi-Soms, Mercedes Camprubi-Soms; m. John Michael Colucci, Sept. 6, 1997. BA with hons. cum laude, NYU, 1986. Customer svc. mgr. Games Mag./Mail Order, N.Y.C., 1984-86; treas., property mgr., asst. to chief exec. officer Hudson Properties, Lyndhurst, N.J., 1986-90; sales assoc. Bloomingdale's, Palm Beach Gardens, Fla., 1990-91, staff tng. supr. and pers. asst., 1991-92; legal asst., bookkeeper Gov.'s Bank and Bruce W. Keihner, Palm Beach, Fla., 1993; assoc. Ideas & Things, 1994-97; freelance bus. mgr., 1993—; personal and bus. coach, 1993-97; bus. mgr. MCR/Michael Colucci Race Engring., Inc., Jupiter, Fla., 1997—. Office: MCR/Michael Colucci Race Engineering Inc 1092 Jupiter Park Ln Ste 270 Jupiter FL 33458-6024

COLUCCIO, JOSEPHINE CATHERINE, primary and elementary school educator; b. Bklyn., Oct. 21, 1952; d. Dominic Anthony and Catherine (Pomponio) Ferone; m. Frank Anthony Coluccio, June 26, 1976; 1 child, Nancy Marie. BA in Edn. cum laude, Bklyn. Coll., 1974. Cert. nursery, kindergarten, and elem. tchr., N.Y., nursery and elem. tchr., N.J. Elem. math. and sci. tchr.-coord. Our Lady of Perpetual Help Sch., Bklyn., 1974-77; pub. rels. coord. McDonald's Corp., S.I., N.Y., 1977-78; day care group tchr. Congress of Italian Am. Orgns., Bklyn., 1979-80; elem. math. and sci. tchr.-coord. Resurrection Elem. Sch., Bklyn., 1980-83; owner, dir. Little Yellow House, Toms River, N.J., 1984-90, Little Explorers-An Ed U Care Program, Toms River, 1990—. Active Rep. Nat. Com., Washington, 1991—. Mem. ASCD, Nat. Assn. for Edn. Young Children, Am. Family Assn., Nat. Safety Coun., Soc. Children's Book Writers and Illustrators (assoc.), Assn. for Curriculum and Devel. Republican. Roman Catholic. Avocations: piano playing, bowling, arts and crafts, cooking, writing children's stories.

COLUMBUS, CHRIS, film director, screenwriter; b. Spangler, Pa., Sept. 10, 1958; s. Alex Michael and Mary Irene (Puskar) C., m. Monica Devereux, 1983. BFA, NYU, 1980. Writer: (films) Reckless, 1983, Gremlins, 1984, Goonies, 1985, Young Sherlock Holmes, 1985, Little Nemo, 1992, Daredevil, 2002; dir.: (films) Adventures in Babysitting, 1987, Home Alone, 1990, Home Alone 2: Lost in New York, 1992, Mrs. Doubtfire, 1993, Harry Potter and the Sorcerer's Stone, 2001 (Las Vegas Film Critics Award, 2001, Broadcast Film Critics Award, 2001); dir., writer: (films) Heartbreak Hotel, 1988, Only the Lonely, 1991; dir., writer, prodr.: Nine Months, 1995; dir., prodr.: Stepmom, 1998, Bicentennial Man, 1999; prodr.: Jingle All the Way, 1996. Democrat. Office: Creative Artists Agy c/o Beth Swofford 9830 Wilshire Blvd Beverly Hills CA 90212-1804

COLUMBUS, R. TIMOTHY, lawyer; b. West Bend, Wis., Mar. 17, 1949; s. Robert M. and Dena (Eggabean) C.; m. Penny G. Baker, June 16, 1979; children: Alexandra Baker, Robert Benjamin. BA, Harvard U., 1971; JD, U. Va., 1974. Bar: Va. 1974, D.C. 1975. Assoc. Collier Shannon Scott, PLLC, Washington, 1974-80, ptnr., 1980—. Home: 6011 Nevada Ave NW Washington DC 20015-2527 Office: Collier Shannon Scott PLLC 3050 K St NW Washington DC 20007-5108 E-mail: tcolumbus@colliershannon.com.

COLUMBUS, SHANNA S. advertising executive; With Price Weber Mktg. Comm. Inc., Louisville, Ky., 1979—, pres., CEO, chmn., 1988—. Office: Price Weber Mktg Comms Inc 2101 Production Dr Louisville KY 40299-2111

COLUSSY, DAN ALFRED, aviation executive; b. Pitts., June 3, 1931; s. Dan and Viola E. (Andreis) C.; m. Helene Graham, June 6, 1953; children: Deborah, Jennifer. BS U.S. Coast Guard Acad., 1953; MBA, Harvard U., 1965. Applications engr. Jet Propulsion div. Gen. Electric Co., 1956-63; dir. ops. Am. Airlines, N.Y.C., 1965-66; v.p. mktg. N.E. Airlines, Boston, 1966-69; v.p. Wells, Rich, Green Advt. Agy., N.Y.C., 1969-70; v.p. mktg. devel. Pan Am. World Airways, N.Y.C., 1970-72, v.p. passenger mktg., 1972-74, sr. v.p. passenger mktg., 1974, sr. v.p. field ops., 1974-75, sr. v.p. mktg. and services, 1975-76, exec. v.p. mktg. and services, dir., 1976-78, pres., chief operating officer, mem. exec. com., 1978-80; chmn., chief exec. officer Columbia Air, Balt., 1981-82; pres., CEO Can. Airlines Internat., Vancouver, B.C., 1982-84, chmn., 1985-86; bd. dirs., mem. exec. com. Can. Pacific Hotels, 1983-84; pres., chief exec. officer UNC Inc., Annapolis, Md., 1985-97, chmn. bd., chmn. exec. com., 1989-97; chmn. Gemini Capital, Palm Beach Gardens, Fla., 1997—. Mem. bd. visitors Coll. Bus. and Mgmt. U. Md.; pres. adv. bd. St. John's Coll.; mem. Johns Hopkins Medicine Bd. Visitors.; bd. dirs. Balt. Gas and Electric o., Hist. Annapolis Found.; chmn. Care First Inc. Mem. Campaign Cabinet, U.S. Naval Ist., Chesapeake Bay Found. (pres.' coun.), Larchmont Yacht, Annapolis Yacht, Harvard (N.Y.C.) Club, Old South Country Club, Wings Club (N.Y.C.), Econ. Club Washington, Met. Club Washington, Order of St. John (Can.), Chartwell Country Club, Ballen Isles Country Club. Office: 20 Saint Thomas Dr Palm Beach Gardens FL 33418-4598

COLVARD, DEAN WALLACE, emeritus university chancellor; b. Ashe County, N.C., July 10, 1913; s. W. P. and Mary (Shepherd) C.; m. Martha Lampkin, July 7, 1939; children: Carol Lampkin, Mary Lynda, Dean Wallace. BS, Berea Coll., 1935; MA, U. Mo., 1938; PhD, Purdue U., 1950, D.Agr., 1961; LHD (hon.), Belmont Abbey Coll., 1978; D of Pub. Svc., U. N.C., Charlotte, 1979; LHD, Berea Coll., 2003. Instr. agr., farm mgr. Brevard Coll., 1935-37; supt. N.C. Mountain Expt. Sta., 1938-46; prof. animal sci. N.C. State Coll., 1947-48, head dept. animal sci., 1948-53; dean agr., 1953-60; pres. Miss. State U., 1960-66; chancellor U. N.C., Charlotte, 1966-78, chancellor emeritus, 1978—. Mng. cons. Sci. Mus. of Charlotte, 1980-81; dir. Fed. Res. Bank of Richmond, 1955-60, dep. chmn., 1959-60; dir. Mut. Savs. & Loan, 1975-91; Spl. cons. ICA, Bangkok, Thailand, 1960; mem. Gov.'s Rsch. Triangle Devel. Coun., 1957-59; co-ordinator Agr. Rsch. Mission in Peru, S. Am., 1954-60; mem. agr. adv. com. W. K. Kellogg Found., 1954-60; chmn. Miss. Gov.'s Com. on Latin Am. Edn., 1961. Author: Mixed Emotions: As Racial Barriers Fell-A University President Remembers, 1985; co-author: (with W.L. Carpenter) Knowledge is Power, 1987, (with Orr and Bailey) University Research Park: The First Twenty Years, 1988; contbr. to publs. in animal sci., agrl. econs., ednl. adminstrn. Chmn. Miss. Rhodes Scholar Com., 1965-66; chmn. N.C. Rhodes Scholar Com., 1967, 78; mem. Miss. Jr. Coll. Commn., 1960-66; vice chmn. Dimensions for Charlotte-Mecklenburg, 1973-76; mem. N.C. Council on State Goals and Policy, 1972-76, So. Growth Policies Bd., 1977-85, Mecklenburg and Union Counties Health and Hosp. Council, 1967-76; chmn., 1974-76; bd. dirs., exec. com. U. Research Park, Charlotte, 1967-87, vice chmn., 1974-79; trustee Berea Coll., 1956-76, St. Andrews Coll., 1969-76, Cordell Hull Found. for Internat. Edn., 1961-67; chmn. bd. trustees N.C. Sch. Sci. and Math., 1978-83. Recipient Disting. Svc. award N.C. Farm Bur., 1956, Disting. Svc. award Miss. Farm Bur., 1965, Disting. Svc. award N.C. Grange, 1958, Outstanding Civilian award U.S. Dept. Army, 1966, Charlotte News Man of Yr. award, 1977, Disting. Alumnus award Berea Coll., 1980, U. N.C. Disting. Svc. award, 1989, N.C. Disting. Pub. Svc. award, 1990, Lifetime Achievement award Nat. 4H CLub Found., 1998; named Man of Yr. in Agr. in N.C., 1954. Mem. Nat. Assn. State Univs. and Land Grant Colls. (co-chmn. joint com. edn. for govt. svc. 1961-65, chmn. president's coun. 1966), Am. Coun. Edn. (commn. internt. edn. 1966-68, chmn. com. higher adult edn. 1966-68), Am. Assn. State Colls. and Univs. (bd. dirs. 1978), Charlotte C. of C. (bd. dirs. 1968-70), Charlotte Country Club, Blue Key, Sigma Xi, Omicron Delta Kappa, Phi Kappa Phi, Gamma Alpha, Alpha Gamma Rho, Gamma Sigma Delta, Alpha Zeta. Clubs: Charlotte Country, Charlotte Rotary (pres. 1978, hon. 1984—). Home: 3600 Cypress Club Dr Apt B403 Charlotte NC 28210-2478

COLVILLE, DAVID ALEXANDER, artist; b. Toronto, Aug. 24, 1920; s. David Harrower and Florence (Gault) C.; m. Rhoda Wright, Aug. 5, 1942; children: Graham, John, Charles, Ann. B.F.A., Mt. Allison U., 1942. One-man shows include Kestner Gesellschaft, Hanover, Germany, 1969, Marlborough Mus. Fine Art, London, 1970, Gemeentmuseum, Arnhem, Netherlands, 1977, Städtische Kuntsthalle, Düsseldorf, Germany, 1977, Fischer Fine Art, London, 1977, Mira Godard Gallery, Toronto and Montreal, 1978, Art Gallery Ont., Toronto, 1983, Staatliche Kunsthalle, Berlin, 1983, Mus. Ludwig, Cologne, Germany, 1983, Beijing Exhbn. Hall, China, 1984, Mus. U. Hong Kong, 1985, Telen Art Mus., Tokyo, Canada House, London, 1985, Drabinsky Gallery, Toronto, 1991, Montreal Mus. Fine Art, 1994, Mira Godard Gallery, Toronto, 1999, Nat. Gallery of Can., Ottawa, 2000; represented in permanent collections, Nat. Gallery Can., Mus. Modern Art, N.Y.C., Mussee National d'Art Moderne, Paris, Sammlung Ludwig, Aachen, Germany, Boymans-Van Beuningen Mus., Netherlands, Rotterdam, Montreal Mus. Fine Arts, Mus. Ludwig, Cologne, Germany, Art Gallery Ont.; vis. artist, U. Calif.-Santa Cruz, 1967, Berliner Kunstler Programm, 1971. Served with Canadian Army, 1942-46. Decorated companion Order of Can. Home and Office: Box 2135 Wolfville NS Canada B4P 1B1

COLVILLE, ROBERT E. judge; b. Pitts., May 23, 1935; s. John and Mary M. (Goldbronn) C.; children: Michael C., Robert J., Molly. B.A. Duquesne U., 1963, J.D., 1969. Bar: Pa. 1969, U.S. Dist. Ct. (we. dist.) Pa. 1969. Tchr., coach North Catholic High Sch., Pitts., 1959-64; patrolman, detective Bur. of Police, Dept. Pub. Safety, Pitts., 1964-68, police legal adviser, 1969-70, asst. dir. Dept. Pub. Safety, 1970-71, supt. Bur. of Police, Pitts., 1971-75; clk., detective Dist. Atty.'s Office of Allegheny County, Pitts., 1968-69, dist. atty., 1976-97; judge Allegheny County Ct. Common Pleas, 1998—; adj. prof. law Duquesne U. Sch. of Law, Pitts., 1976-78; instr. in labor law LaRoche Coll., Pitts., 1983-84. Contbr. articles to profl. jours. Past chmn. Joint Allegheny County Narcotics Task Force; chmn. Allegheny County Drug Initiative; mem. Pa. Democratic Com. Served with USMC, 1953-56; foremr trustee Community Coll. of Allegheny County. Recipient Dapper Dan award Pitts. Post Gazette, 1963, Disting. Service award County Detectives Assn., 1977, Service Recognition award Pitts. Community Crime Prevention Coalition, 1980; Law Enforcement award Dep. Sheriff's Assn. of Pa., 1983; Outstanding Grad., Duquesne U., 1969; Jr. C. of C. Man of Yr. in Law, 1973; Phi Alpha Delta Law Alumni of Yr., 1976; Outstanding Grad., Duquesne U. Century Club, 1978; Outstanding Law Alumnus Duquesne U. Law Alumni Assn., 1985. Office: 436 Grant St Pittsburgh PA 15219-2400

COLVIN, GRETA WILMOTH, entrepreneur; b. Odessa, Tex., Mar. 24, 1962; d. Charles Hayden and Sherry Beth (Browning) Wilmoth; m. Michael Anthony Colvin, Aug. 16, 1986; 1 child, Michael Anthony Jr. AA in Radio-TV-Film, San Antonio Coll.; BS, U. Tex.; grad., Dale Carnegie, 1993; postgrad., St. Mary's U., San Antonio, 1997—. Lic. broadcaster, paralegal, pvt. investigator. Various media positions W.M. Entertainment, San Antonio, 1978-86; co-owner Image Nightclubs, San Antonio, 1986-88; owner W.C. Advt., San Antonio, 1980-88; retail mgr. Hastings, San Antonio, 1989-94; pres. Paradigm Enterprises, Flagstaff, Ariz., 1994—. Democrat. Avocations: motorcycle racing, skiing, reading, rock scaleing, going to drag races. Address: 2800 Cerrillos Rd Santa Fe NM 87507-2313 also: 11623 Whisper Valley St San Antonio TX 78230-3737

COLVIN, HARRY WALTER, JR., physiology educator; b. Schellsburg, Pa., Dec. 5, 1921; s. Harry Walter and Maude Elizabeth (Girven) C.; m. Marie Catherine McNinch, Apr. 8, 1950; children: Sarah Lee, William McNinch. BS, Pa. State U., 1950; PhD, U. Calif., Davis, 1957. Instr. Okla. State U., Stillwater, 1955-57; assoc. prof. physiology U. Ark., Fayetteville, 1957-65; prof. U. Calif., Davis, 1965—. Cons. Pel-Freez Biologicals, Inc., Rogers, Ark., 1960-65. Assoc. editor Hilgardia, 1981-92; contbr. articles to profl. jours. Served with U.S. Army, 1942-45, ETO. Recipient Fulbright award CIES, Washington, 1972, 86. Mem. Am. Dairy Sci. Assn., Am. Soc. Animal Sci., Sigma Xi, Phi Kappa Phi, Alpha Zeta, Gamma Sigma Delta, Phi Sigma, Phi Eta Sigma. Clubs: El Macero (Calif.) Country. Republican. Avocations: golf, flying. Home: 1515 Shasta Dr Apt 3326 Davis CA 95616 Office: U Calif Davis Dept Neurobiology Physiol & Behavior Davis CA 95616

COLVIN, HERBERT, JR., (OTIS HERBERT COLVIN), musician, educator; b. El Dorado, Ark., Mar. 18, 1923; s. Otis Herbert and Irene (Hammons) C.; m. Mary Ila Ullom, June 18, 1948; children: Carol Kay Colvin Smith, Mary Edith Colvin Reitmeier, Susan Elizabeth Colvin White. BA, Baylor U., 1944, BMus, 1948; MMus, U. Colo., 1950; PhD, U. Rochester, 1958. Grad. asst. U. Colo., 1948-50; instr. music Tex. Tech. Coll., 1950-55; grad. asst. Eastman Sch. Music, 1955-57; asst. prof. piano Baylor U., 1957-62, chmn. dept., 1958-62, assoc. prof. theory, 1962-64, prof., 1964-93; prof. emeritus Baylor U. Sch. Music, 1993—; chmn. dept. Baylor U., 1962-76, coordinator theory div., 1976-85, dir. acad. studies, 1985-88, univ. carillonneur, 1988—. Concert accompanist, organist, 7th and James Bapt. Ch., 1969-99; editor choral compositions.; Composer: Organ Voluntaries Based on Early American Hymn Tunes, 1964, Short Pieces for Organ, 1971, For Sunday; six organ pieces based on modal melodies, 1972, Gloria; anthem for mixed voices and organ, 1974, Nine Hymn Settings for Organ, 1975, For Sunday Volume II; six organ pieces based on modal melodies, 1976, Sheep May Safely Graze; six organ-piano duets on compositions by Bach and Billings, 1977, Surely the Lord Is in This Place; anthem for mixed voices, accompanied, 1977, Four Madrigals; mixed-voice choral settings of A.E. Housman poems, 1978, They That Wait Upon the Lord, 1980, anthem for mixed voices, accompanied, Once in Royal David's City (anthem for mixed voices, children's choir, oboe and organ); editor choral compositions; contbr. articles to profl. jours. Served with USNR, 1944-46, CBI. Mem. Am. Guild Organists (dean Waco chpt. 1958-60, 68-69, 79-80, treas. 1990-92), Music Tchrs. Nat. Assn., Guild of Carillonneurs N.Am. (bd. dirs. 1996-99), Tex. Soc. Music Theory, Phi Mu Alpha Sinfonia, Pi Kappa Lambda, Masons (32 degree). Baptist. Office: Baylor U Sch Music Waco TX 76798

COLVIN, JAMES EDWARD, freelance journalist, publicist; b. Springfield, Mo. s. Hugh Patrick Colvin and Margaret Mary Irby; divorced; children: Timothy, Stephen. PhB, Loyola U., 1934; postgrad., U. Chgo., 1936—38, Harvard U., 1941—42. Reporter, editor Chgo. Daily News, 1934—43; writer, assoc. editor Popular Mechanics Mag., Chgo., 1943—44; publicist Campbell-Mithun Advt. Agy., Chgo., 1946; publicist, mem. editl. bd. Ency. Britannica, Chgo., 1946—62; v.p. advt., pub. rels. World Book, Chgo., 1962—73; freelance writer, publicist Greenville, SC, 1973—. Co-founder Great Books Found., Chgo., 1953; nat. v.p. Chgo. Press Club, 1946—50; creator Flying Short Courses in Photojournalism. Author, editor: World War II History, Navy Supply Corps, 1946; author: Words Most Often Mispronounced and Misspelled, 1963, Question on Catholicism, 1952; prodr.: (TV discussion) Great Books Speak to Today, 1962—64. Mem. staff U.S. Senator William B. Benton, Conn., 1952—54. Lt. USNR, 1943—46, historian Supply Corps USN, 1944—46. Named Nieman fellow, Harvard U., 1941—42; recipient Edom award, U. Mo. Sch. Journalism, 1961, award, Loch News Phenomena Investigation Bur., Scotland, 1976. Mem.: Nat. Press Photographers Assn. (life Sprague award 1961), Soc. Nieman Fellows.

COLVIN, O. MICHAEL, medical director, medical educator; b. Princeton, Ind., June 15, 1936; s. Jack Gene and and Evelyn Mae (Satkamp) C.; m. Arline Mae Lockerbie, Aug. 23, 1959; children: Michael Eric, Jennifer Susan, Kimberly Anne, Christopher Andrew. BA in Chemistry, Ind. U., 1957; MD, Washington U., St. Louis, 1961. Intern, resident Johns Hopkins Hosp., Balt., 1961-64; clin. assoc. Nat. Cancer Inst., Bethesda, Md., 1964-66; fellow in pharmacology Johns Hopkins U., Balt., 1966-68, physician, 1968-95, from asst. prof. to prof. medicine, 1968-95; dir. Duke Comprehensive Cancer Ctr. Duke U. Med. Ctr., Durham, NC, 1995—2002; Wm. Shingleton prof. cancer rsch. Duke U. Sch. Medicine, Durham, 2002—. Grant rev. study sect. Nat. Cancer Inst., Bethesda, 1968—. Recipient Career Devel. award Nat. Cancer Inst., 1975-80. Mem. AAAS, Am. Soc. Clin. Oncology, Am. Soc. Bone Marrow Transplantation, Am. Assn. Cancer Rsch. Home: 208 Arcadia Ln Chapel Hill NC 27514-1472 Office: Duke U Med Ctr 419 Jones Bldg PO Box 3843 Durham NC 27702-3843

COLVIN, ROBERT BARNES, pathologist, researcher; b. Columbus, Ohio, May 7, 1942; s. Robert M. and Ellen M. (Barnes) C.; m. Gatewood Warwick Wise, July 23, 1966; children: Jessica. BS, MIT, 1964; MD, Harvard U., 1968. Lic. anatomic and immunopathologist. Intern-resident/fellow Mass. Gen. Hosp., Boston, 1968-72, from asst. pathologist to pathologist, 1975-91, dir. immunopathology unit, 1980-91; chief Dept. of Pathology Mass. General Hosp., Boston, 1991—; maj. Walter Reed Army Inst. Rsch., Washington, 1972-75; from asst. prof. to prof. pathology Harvard Med. Sch., Boston, 1975-91, Benjamin Castleman prof. pathology, 1991—, master Holmes Soc., 1990-92; chief pathology svcs. Mass. Gen. Hosp., Boston, 1991—. Mem. test com. Nat. Bd. Med. Examiners, Phila., 1983-87, 89-90, Am. Bd. Pathology, Tampa, Fla., 1985-91. Editor: Diagnostic Immunopathology, 1996, Organ Transplantation in Children, 1989; contbr. over 200 articles to profl. jours. Maj. U.S. Army, 1972-75. Recipient Merit award NIH, 1987; grantee NIH, 1975—. Mem. Am. Assn. Pathologists, Am. Assn. Immunologists, Am. Soc. Nephrology, Transplantation Soc., Internat. Acad. Pathology. Episcopalian. Office: Mass Gen Hosp Dept Pathology Boston MA 02114

COLVIN, THOMAS STUART, agricultural engineer, farmer; b. Columbia, Mo., July 17, 1947; s. Charles Darwin and Miriam Elizabeth (Kimball) C.; m. Sonya Marie Peterson, Sept. 11, 1982; children: Christopher, Kristel. BS, Iowa State U., 1970, MS, 1974, PhD, 1977. Registered profl. engr., Iowa. Farmer, Hawkeye and Cambridge, Iowa, 1970—; rsch. assoc. Iowa State U., Ames, 1972-77; agrl. engr. USDA/Agrl. Rsch. Svc., Ames, 1977—. Cons. WillowCreek Cons., Manning, Iowa, 1978-85. Sgt. USAF, 1970-72, Vietnam. Recipient Air Force Commendation medal USAF, 1971. Mem. Am. Soc. Agrl. Engrs. (power machinery stds. com. St. Joseph, Mich. 1989—, Iowa sec., Young Engr. of Yr. 1986), Soil and Water Conservation Soc., Iowa Acad. Sci. (chair agrl. scis. sect. 1991-92), Sigma Xi, Alpha Epsilon (pres. 1978), Gamma Sigma Delta, Phi Mu Alpha. Achievements include design and development of first computer program to help farmers manage tillage and residue cover for erosion control. Office: Nat Soil Tilth Lab USDA ARS 2150 Pammel Dr Ames IA 50011-3120

COLVIS, JOHN PARIS, aerospace engineer, mathematician, scientist; b. St. Louis, June 30, 1946; s. Louis Jack and Jacqueline Betty (Beers) C.; m. Nancy Ellen Fritz, Mar. 15, 1969 (div. Sept. 16, 1974); 1 child, Michael Scott; m. Barbara Carol Davis, Sept. 3, 1976; 1 child, Rebecca Jo; stepchildren: Bruce William John Zimmerly, Belinda Jo Zimmerly Little. Student, Meramec Community Coll., St. Louis, 1964-65, U. Mo., 1966, 72-75, Palomar Coll., San Marcos, Calif., 1968, U. Mo., Rolla, 1968-69; BS in Math., Washington U., 1977. Assoc. system safety engr. McDonnell Douglas Astronautics Co., St. Louis, 1978-81; sr. system safety engr. Martin Marietta Astronautics Group-Strategic Systems Co., Denver, 1981-87; sr. engr. Martin Marietta Astronautics Group-Space Launch Systems Co., Denver, 1987-95, Lockheed Martin Astronautics Co.-Space Launch Sys., Denver, 1995—. Researcher in field. Lance cpl. USMC, 1966-68, Vietnam. Mem. VFW (post 4171), Math. Assn. Am., Colo. Home Educators' Assn. (pres. 1989), Khe Sanh Vet Incorp. Evangelical. Achievements include the quantum postulate; the quantum philosophy of science and mathematics; a complete and verifiable logic-quantum synthesis. Avocations: camping, hiking, swimming. Home: 4978 S Hoyt St Littleton CO 80123-1988 Office: Lockheed Martin Space and Strategic Missiles PO Box 179 Denver CO 80201-0179 E-mail: John.P.Colvis@lmco.com.

COLWELL, BRYAN YORK, private investor, philanthropist; b. Atlanta, Feb. 10, 1964; BA magna cum laude, Harvard U., 1983; MBA with distinction, Columbia U., 1986; postgrad., U. Pa. Wharton Sch., 1985. Strategic planner SmithKline Beckman Corp., Phila., 1983-85; v.p. Goldman, Sachs and Co., N.Y.C., 1986—2000; mng. dir., head of global power and utilities Corp. Fin. Group, ABN Amro Inc., N.Y.C., 2000—02; pres. Colwell Found., 2002—. Mem. bd. Archtl. Rev. and Planning for Tuxedo Pk., N.Y.C. Author: The Public-Private Partnership (Harvard University), 1983. Mem. dirs. coun. Mus. of City of N.Y.; bd. dirs., chmn. assocs. com. Lenox Hill Neighborhood House, 1994—; bd. dirs. Tuxedo Park Archtl. Rev. Bd., Nat. Hypertension Assn. Named Outstanding Young Am., WSB-Radio-TV Network, Atlanta, 1979; recipient Young Scholar award Harvard Club of Atlanta, 1979, Outstanding Student cup Atlanta Jour., 1979. Mem. Am. Fin. Assn. (v.p. 1985-86), Columbia Bus. Sch. Alumni Assn., Harvard U. Inst. Politics, World Affairs Coun., Harvard Architecture Soc. (pres. 1980), Brook Club, Links Club, Owl Club, Hasty Pudding Club (v.p. 1981-83, Cambridge chpt.), Harvard Club of N.Y., Racquet and Tennis Club, Tuxedo Club, Sea Island Club, Southampton Club.

COLWELL, GENE THOMAS, engineering educator; b. Chattanooga, Aug. 3, 1937; s. William Clarence and Mary Virginia (Smith) C.; m. Peggy Ann Fletcher, June 1, 1973. BSME, U. Tenn., 1959, MSME, 1962, PhD, 1966. Rsch. engr. Oak Ridge (Tenn.) Nat. Lab., 1959-62; instr. U. Tenn., Knoxville, 1962-65; rsch. engr. Oak Ridge Nat. Lab., 1965-66; asst. prof. Ga. Inst. Tech., Atlanta, 1966-71, assoc. prof., 1971-77, prof., 1977-95; prof. emeritus, 1995—; assoc. dir. Ga. Inst. Tech., Atlanta, 1984-87. Vis. prof. U. Carabobo, Venezuela, 1971; cons. in field. Patentee in field; contbr. articles to profl. jours. Recipient numerous Rsch. grants. Fellow ASME (life); mem. Sigma Xi, Pi Tau Sigma. Avocations: tennis, golf, hiking. Home: 9145 Prestwick Club Dr Duluth GA 30097-2442

COLWELL, HOWARD OTIS, advertising executive; b. New Rochelle, N.Y., Sept. 16, 1929; s. Robert Talcott and Louise (Otis) C.; m. Barbara Elaine Hrosenchik, Aug. 14, 1954; children: John Robert, Christian, Mary Louise. AB, Colgate U., 1953. Copy group head Batten, Barton, Durstine & Osborn, N.Y.C., 1953-59; v.p., creative dir. Tatham-Laird & Kudner, N.Y.C., 1959-68; sr. v.p., creative dir. William Esty Advt., N.Y.C., 1968-87; v.p., corp. creative dir. Combe, Inc., White Plains, NY, 1987-98, sr. creative cons., 1998—. Guest lectr. NYU, 1979-81, Pace U., 1980-84, adj. prof., 1982-83 Chmn. YMCA Indian Guides Norwalk-Wilton, 1966; chmn. Wilton Voice on Edn., 1972-75, Wilton Arts Council, 1980-83; v.p. bd. dirs. Wilton Orch., 1985—, pres., 1986-87. Mem. Phi Beta Kappa. Congregationalist. Office: 1101 Westchester Ave White Plains NY 10604-3503

COLWELL, JOHN EDWIN, retired aerospace scientist; b. Bellaire, Kans., Sept. 2, 1930; s. Clyde Theodore and Ida Mae (Swank) C. BS in Chemistry, Kans. State U., 1952; postgrad., Harvard U., 1952-53; PhD in Phys. Chemistry, U. Pa., 1958. Rsch. chemist Shell Oil Co., Wood River, Ill., 1952; staff scientist Rocketdyne divsn. N.Am. Aviation, Canoga Park, Calif., 1958-61; mem. tech. staff The Aerospace Corp., El Segundo, Calif., 1961-72, cons., 1972-73. Cons. NASA, 1970-72. Bd. dirs. Ctrl. Kans. Libr. System, Great Bend, 1977-81, 89-93; vice chmn. Smith County Rep. Ctrl. Com., 1986-90, 2000-02, chmn., 1990-94, 96-2000; alt. Kans. Republican Party State Com., 1996-98, 2000-02, del., 1998-2000; trustee Blaine Twp., Lebanon, 1981-98; treas. Smith County Hist. Soc., 1990-93. 1st lt. USAF, 1953-55. Fellowships Harvard fellow Harvard U., 1952-53, NSF fellow U. Pa., 1957-58. Mem. Am. Legion (post comdr. 1991-93), Sigma Xi, Phi Kappa Phi, Theta Xi. Republican. Avocations: music, gardening, fishing. Home: RR 2 Box 54 Lebanon KS 66952-9500

COLWELL, JOSHUA EDWARDS, astronomer, researcher; b. Deland, Fla., June 8, 1964; s. Charles Carter and Ann (Colwell; m. Anne-Marie Caubet, Dec. 31, 1985; 1 child, Aylia Monique. BS, Stetson U., 1985; PhD, U. Colo., 1989. Teaching lab. asst. dept. physics Stetson U., Deland, 1982-84; rsch. asst. U. Colo., Boulder, 1985-89, teaching asst., 1988, lectr., 0190—, rsch. assoc., 1989—. Fulbright sr. rsch. scholar, Toulouse, France, 1995—96. Contbr. articles to profl. jours. Recipient Grad. fellowship U. Colo., 1985-89. Mem. Am. Astron Soc. (div. planetary scis.), Am. Geophys. Union, Phi Beta Kappa, Sigma Pi Sigma, Omicron Delta Kappa. Democrat. Achievements include discovery of importance of topography on the thermal evolution of comet nuclei; research in origin and evolution of planetary rings; experimental studies of collisions in planet formation and planetary rings in microgravity.

COLWELL, RITA ROSSI, microbiologist, molecular biologist, federal agency administrator, medical educator; b. Nov. 23, 1934; BS in Bacteriology with distinction, Purdue U., 1956, MS in Genetics, 1958; PhD, U. Wash., 1961; DSc, Heriot-Watt U., Edinburgh, Scotland, 1987, Hood Coll., 1991, Purdue U., 1993, U. Surrey, Eng., 1995, U. Bergen, Norway, 1999, Coastal Carolina U., 1999, U. Md. Balt. County, 1999, St. Mary's Coll., 1999, Mich. State U., 2000, Washington Coll., 2000, U. Conn., 2000, Williams Coll., 2000, SUNY, Albany, 2000, U. Ancona, Italy, 2001, George Washington U., 2001, Mount Holyoke, 2001, Washington U., St. Louis, 2001, Calif. Poly. Inst., San Luis Obispo, 2001, Renssalaer Poly. Inst., 2001, U. Newcastle, U.K., 2001, Mercy Coll., 2002, U. Queensland, Australia, 2002, U. Glasgow, 2002, Weizmann Inst. Sci., Israel, 2002, Tuskegee Inst., 2003, U. Ill., 2003, Dartmouth Coll., 2003; LLD, Notre Dame Coll., 1994; DHL (hon.), U. Ala., 2001; LLD, U. Nebr., 2003. Rsch. asst. genetics lab. Purdue U., West Lafayette, Ind., 1956—57; rsch. asst. U. Wash., Seattle, 1957—58, predoctoral assoc., 1959—60, asst. rsch. prof., 1961—64; asst. prof. biology Georgetown U., Washington, 1964—66, assoc. prof. biology, 1966—72; prof. microbiology U. Md., 1972—, v.p. for acad. affairs, 1983—87; dir. Ctr. Marine Biotech., 1987—91; founder, pres. Md. Biotech. Inst. U. Md., 1991—98; dir. NSF, 1998—. Hon. prof. U. Queensland, Brisbane, Australia, 1988; mem. ocean scis. bd. NAS, 1977—80; hon. prof. Quindao U., China, 1995; cons. Washington area comms. media, congressman, legislators, 1978—; external examiner various univs. abroad, 1964—; vice chmn. polar rsch. bd. NAS, 1990—94; mem. Nat. Sci. Bd., 1984—90; mem. sci. adv. bd. Oak Ridge Nat. Labs., 1988—90, 1993—96; adv. com. FDA, 1991—92, food adv. com., 1993—96, sci. bd., 1996—; Koch lectr., Berlin, 2000. Author (manual numerical taxonomy): Collecting the Data, 1970; author: (with M. Zambruski) Rodina-Methods in Aquatic Microbiology, 1972; author: (with L.H. Stevenson) Estuarine Microbial Ecology, 1973; author: (with R.Y. Morita) Effect of the Ocean Environment on Microbial Ecology, 1973; author: (with A. Sinsky and N. Pariser) Marine Biotechnology, 1983; author: Vibrios in the Environment, 1985, Nucleic Acid Sequence Data, 1988; author: (with others) Marine Biotechnology, 1995; Microbial Diversity, 1996; author: Viable But Nonculturable Microorganisms in the Environment, 2000, others; mem. editl. bd.: Microbial Ecology, 1972—91, Applied and Environ. Microbiology, 1969—81, Oil and Petrochemical Pollution, 1980—91, Jour. Washington Acad. Scis., 1981—87, Johns Hopkins U. Oceanographic Series, 1981—84, Revue de la Fondation Oceanographique Ricard, 1981—, Estuaries, 1983—89, Zentralblatt fur Bacteriologie, 1985—, Jour. Aquatic Living Resources, 1987—, Sys. Applied Microbiology, 1985—2000, World Jour. Microbiology and Biotech., 1988—95, Environ. Microbiology, 2001—; contbr. articles; (Koch lecture) Anatomy Lesson, Amsterdam, 2002. Named Prof. Extraordinairo, U. Catolica Valparaiso, Chile, 1976, Scholar of Yr., Phi Kappa Phi, 1992; recipient Gold medal, Internat. Biotech. Inst., 1990, Purkinje Gold medal for achievment in sci., Czechoslavakian Acad. Sci., 1991, Civic award, Gov. Md., 1990, Woman of the Yr. award, Women Legis. of Md., 1996, Cert. of Recognition, NASA, 1984, Alice Evans award, Am. Soc. Microbiol., 1988, Andrew White medal, Loyola Coll., 1994, medal of distinction, Barnard Coll./Columbia U., 1996, Gold medal, Charles U., Prague, 2000, Gold medals, UCLA, 2000, Alumna Summa Laude Dignata award, U. Wash., 2000, Achievement award, AAUW, 2001, Carey award, Am. Assn. Adv. Sci., 2001, Thomas award, Explorer's Club Lowell, 2000. Fellow: AAAS (chmn. sect. biol. scis. 1993—94, pres. 1995, chmn. bd. 1996, Carey award 2001), Marine Tech. Soc. (exec. com. 1982—88), Washington Acad. Scis. (bd. mgrs. 1976—79, pres. 1996—98), Am. Acad. Microbiology (chmn. bd. govs. 1989—99), Can. Coll. Microbiologists, Grad. Women. Sci., Sigma Delta Epsilon; mem.: Am. Philos. Soc., Am. Acad. Arts and Sci., Am. Philos. Soc., Am. Acad. Arts and Scis., Soc. Gen. Microbiology, Internat. Coun. Sci. Unions, Am. Soc. Limnology and Oceanography, World Fedn. Culture Collections, Classification Rsch. Group Eng. (charter), Soc. Indsl Microbiology (bd. govs. 1976—79, Charles Thom award 1998), U.S. Fedn. Culture Collections (governing bd. 1978—88), Internat. Coun. Sci. Unions (exec. bd. 1993—96, gen. com.), Am. Inst. Biol. Scis. (bd. govs. 1976—82), Internat. Union Microbiol. Soc. (v.p. 1986—90, pres. 1990—94), World Fedn. Culture Collections, Royal Soc. Can., Nat. Acad. Sci., Australian Soc. Microbiology (hon.), Israeli Soc. Microbiology (hon.), French Soc. Microbiology (hon.), Bangladesh Soc. Microbiology (hon.; fgn.), U.K. Soc. Applied Microbiology (hon.), Am. Soc. Microbiology (hon.; various sci. coms. 1961—, pres. 1985, chmn. program com. REGEM-1 1988, Fisher award 1985), Explorers Club (Lowell Thomas award 2000), Omicron Delta Kappa, Phi Beta Kappa, Sigma Xi (nat. pres. 1991, Ann. Achievement award 1981, Rsch. award 1984), Delta Gamma (Delta Gamma Rose award 1989). Achievements include research in marine biotechnology; marine and estuarine microbial ecology; survival of pathogens in aquatic environments; ecology of Vibrio cholerae and related organisms; microbial systematics; marine microbiology; antibiotic resistance; environmental aspects of Vibrio cholerae in transmission of cholera; in global climate and cholera transmission. Office: NSF Office of the Dir 4201 Wilson Blvd Rm 1205 Arlington VA 22230-0001 E-mail: rcolwell@nsf.gov.

COLWILL, JACK MARSHALL, physician, educator, dean; b. Cleve., June 15, 1932; s. Clifford V. and Olive A. (Marshall) Colwill; m. Winifred Stedman, 1954; children: James F., Elizabeth Ann, Carolyn. BA, Oberlin Coll., 1953; MD (George Whipple scholar), U. Rochester, 1957. Diplomate Am. Bd. Med. Examiners, Am. Bd. Internal Medicine, Am. Bd. Family Practice (bd. dirs. 1998-2003). Intern Barnes Hosp., Washington U. Sch. Medicine, St. Louis, 1957—58; resident in medicine U. Washington Affiliated Hosps., Seattle, 1958—60; chief resident U. Hosp., 1960—61; instr. medicine, dir. med. outpatient dept. U. Rochester (N.Y.) Sch. Medicine and Dentistry, 1961—62, sr. instr. medicine, dir. med. outpatient dept., 1962—64; asst. dean, asst. prof. medicine, asst. prof. community health and med. practice U. Mo. Sch. Medicine, Columbia, 1964—67, assoc. dean, asst. prof., 1967—69, assoc. dean for acad. affairs, asst. prof., 1969—70, assoc. dean, assoc. prof., 1970—76, interim chmn. dept. family and community medicine, 1976—77, prof., 1976—97, prof. emeritus, 1999—, chmn. dept., 1977—97, interim dean, 2000. Cons. Bur. Health Manpower, NIH, 1969—75, Office Divsn. Dir. USPHS, 1977—; mem. Coun. on Grad. Med. Edn. Health Resources and Svcs. Adminstrn., 1990—96. Contbr. articles to profl. jours. Chair commn. on Gulf War and Health Inst. of Medicine, NAS, 1999—2003; dir. Robert Wood Johnson Found. Generalist Physician Initiative, 1991—2000. Mem.: AMA, Inst. Medicine NAS, Am. Acad. Family Physicians (commn. on govtl. legis. affairs 1984—87), Soc. Tchrs. Family Medicine (bd. dirs. 1978—82, 1983—87, pres.-elect 1987—88, pres. 1988—89), Assn. Med. Am. Colls. (chmn. Midwest-Gt. Plains Group on Student Affairs 1971—73, nat. vice chmn. group 1973—74, chmn. working group on non-cognitive assessment 1974—77, adv. to com. on admissions assessment 1974—77), Alpha Omega Alpha. Office: U Mo-Columbia Sch Medicine Dept Family And Medicine Columbia MO 65212-0001

COLWIN, ARTHUR LENTZ, biologist, educator; b. Sydney, Australia, Jan. 26, 1911; came to U.S., 1936, naturalized, 1942; m. Laura North Hunter, June 15, 1940. B.Sc., McGill U., 1933, M.Sc., 1934, PhD (NRC Can. fellow), 1935-36; Moyse Travelling fellow, Cambridge (Eng.) U., 1934-35; Seessel fellow, Yale, 1936-37, Royal Soc. Can. fellow, 1937-38. Mem. faculty Queens Coll., 1940-73, prof., 1957-73, emeritus, 1973; adj. prof. Rosenstiel Sch. Marine and Atmospheric Sci., U. Miami, Fla., 1973—. Fulbright research fellow Tokyo U., 1953-54; vis. scientist Nat. Inst. Med. Research, London, Eng., 1960 Mem. editorial bd. Jour. Exptl. Zoology, 1964-68, Jour. Morphology, 1964-68, Biol. Bull, 1969-73, Am. Zoologist, 1970-75; contbr. articles to profl. jours. Trustee Marine Biol. Lab., Woods Hole, Mass., 1962-72. Served to capt. USAAF, 1943-46. Fellow N.Y. Acad. Scis., AAAS; mem. Internat. Inst. Developmental Biology, Internat. Soc. Cell Biology, Am. Soc. Zoologists, Soc. Study Devel. and Growth, Soc. for Study of Reprodn., Electron Microscope Soc. Am. Asso. Achievements include spl. research fertilization, devel. biology, cell contacts and assn., membrane structure and behavior. Home: 320 Woodcrest Rd Miami FL 33149-1322 Office: U Miami Rosenstiel Sch Marine & Atmospheric Sci 4600 Rickenbacker Cswy Miami FL 33149-1031

COLY, LISETTE, foundation executive; b. N.Y.C., Apr. 6, 1950; d. Robert Raymond and Eileen (Lyttle-Garrett) C.; children: George Robert Damalas, Anastasia Eileen Damalas. BA cum laude, Hunter Coll., 1973. Sec. Parapsychology Found., Inc., N.Y.C., 1972-75, assoc. editor, 1975—, v.p., 1978—, exec. dir., 1999—. Assoc. editor Parapsychology Rev. and Procs. Ann. Internat. Parapsychology Found. Confs., 1978—; editor, conf. coord. Procs. Ann. Internat. Confs., 1989—; editor-in-chief Internat. Jour. Parapsychology. Office: Parapsychology Found Inc 228 E 71st St New York NY 10021-5136 E-mail: lisettecoly@parapsychology.org.

COLYER, DALE KEITH, agricultural economics educator; b. Albion, Ill., Dec. 22, 1931; s. Wallace C. and Louella (Walker) C.; m. Norma L. DeWind, Sept. 18, 1959; children: Claudia R., Wallace C. BS, U. Ill., 1954, MS, 1955; PhD, U. Wis., 1963. Rsch. asst. Fed. Res. Bank of Kansas City, Mo., 1958-60; asst. prof. U. Mo., Columbia, 1963-65, assoc. prof., 1965-70; prof. W.Va. U., Morgantown, 1970—2001, prof. emeritus, 2002—; interim assoc. dir. W.Va. Agrl. Exp. Sta., 2000. Fulbright lectr., Rosario, Argentina, 1968; dir. resource mgmt. divsn. W.Va. U., 1978-83; agrl. economist U.S. AID, Quito, Ecuador, 1984-87, cons., 1983, 88, 89, 90, 91, 93. Assoc. editor Rev. Agrl. Econs., 1991-93; contbr. articles to profl. jours. With U.S. Army, 1956-58. Benedum Disting. scholar W.Va. U., 1994. Mem. Am. Agrl. Econ. Assn. (Best Pub. Rsch. award 1968), N.E. Agrl. Econ. Coun. (editor 1977-81, pres. 1979-80, disting. mem. 1984), Internat. Assn. Agrl. Economists, Fulbright Assn. Home: 936 Riverview Dr Morgantown WV 26505-4634 Office: West Va U Agrl Scis PO Box 6108 Morgantown WV 26506-6108

COLYER, KIRK KLEIN, insurance executive, real estate investment executive; b. Fayetteville, N.C., Jan. 30, 1956; s. Joe Bill and Charlotte (Klein) C. Assoc. in Bus., SUNY, Albany, 1977; BBA in Polit. Sci., U. Incarnate Word, 1980; student, Leonard's Tng. Sch., 1985, Tex. Crime Prevention Inst., 1985. Lic. recording agt. Councilman City of Balcones Heights San Antonio, Tex., 1977-82, mayor, 1982-86, mayor emeritus, 1986; pres. Colyer Real Estate Investments, San Antonio, 1980—; pres., founder Colyer Ins. Agy., San Antonio, 1982—; pres. Colyer Oil Co., San Antonio, 1982—. Pres. Dominion Village, San Antonio, Tex., 1991—, ABC Colyer Nursery, 1999; adv. coun. U.S. Postal Svc., 1994, Nat. Consumers, 1998-99; campaign dir. Congl. Rep. nominee Carl Bill Colyer, San Antonio; campaign treas. Gerry Richkoff County Clk., Bexar County, 1994, Leon M. Hernandez; mem. dinner com. U.S. Congress Dist. 20 Charlie Gonzalez, 1998—. Featured extra (films) Miss Congeniality, 2000, speaking role Reason to Believe, 2001. V.p. Balcones C of C., San Antonio, 1978, San Antonio Young Reps., 1991; bd. mem. Beautify San Antonio, 1982, South Tex. Charities, 1998; pres. Tex. Mcpl. League Region 7, San Antonio, 1985; founder Bexar County Young Reps., 1995; bd. dirs. San Antonio March of Dimes, 1985; grad. Leadership San Antonio, 1985; pres. Lulac Coun. 602, 1998-2000; host. Com. for Nat. Rep. Conv. 2000 Bid for San Antonio, Tex.; campaign treas. Leon Hernandez Dem. Precinct, 2000—; treas. Hunters Creek North Homeowners Assn., 1995; bd. dirs. U.S. Postal Adv. Com., San Antonio, 1994; mem. raffle com. corp. donations San Antonio Stock Show, 2001. Named one of Outstanding Mems. of Am., U.S. Jaycees, 1977-91; Rey Feo XLIX, 1996-97. Mem. IHIO Corridor (founder, pres. 1984-86), San Antonio Ind. Car Dealers Assn. (founder, pres. 1993—), Tex. Auto Dealers Assn. (bd. dirs. 1994—), San Antonio City Club, San Antonio Plaza Club (life), Rey Feo '97, Distributive Edn. Clubs of Am. (life), Lions (bd. dirs. Balcones chpt. 1976-78), Tex. Jaycees (dist. bd. dirs. 1978, pres. Balcones Hts. chpt. 1977, Top Recruiter 1980), San Antonio Crime Stoppers (bd. dirs. 1984—), San Antonio Martini Found. (bd. dirs. 1988—), San Antonio Parrot Head Club, San Antonio P.A.R.T.I. Found. (bd. dirs. 1998—), South Tex. Charities, Shoppers Voice Consumer Product Survey Am. Avocations: fishing, hunting, hiking, jogging, roller blading. Home: 13290 Hunters View St San Antonio TX 78230-2032 Office: Colyer Ins Agy 4311 IHIOW San Antonio TX 78201 E-mail: kirkkcolyer@aol.com.

COMANOR, WILLIAM S. economist, educator; b. Phila., May 11, 1937; s. Leroy and Sylvia (Bershad) C.; m. Joan Thall; children: Christine, Katherine, Lauren, Gregory. Student, Williams Coll., 1955-57; BA, Haverford Coll., 1959; MA, PhD, Harvard U., 1963; postgrad., London Sch. Econs., 1963-64. Spl. econ. asst. to asst. atty. gen. Antitrust div. U.S. Dept. Justice, Washington, 1965-66; asst. prof. econs. Harvard U., Cambridge, Mass., 1966-68; assoc. prof. Stanford (Calif.) U., 1968-73; dir. bur. econs. FTC, Washington, 1978-80; prof. econs. U. Calif., Santa Barbara, 1975—, dept. chmn., 1984-87; prof. Sch. Pub. Health UCLA, L.A., 1990—. Author: National Health Insurance in Ontario, 1980, Advertising and Market Power, 1974, Competition Policy in Europe and North America, 1990, Competition Policy in the Global Economy, 1997; contbr. articles to profl. jours. Recipient Disting. fellow award, Indsl. Orgn. Soc., 2003. Mem.: Indsl. Orgn. Soc. (pres. 1991, Disting. Fellow award 2003), Am. Econ. Assn. Home: 519 S Arden Blvd Los Angeles CA 90020-4737 Office: U Calif Dept Econs Santa Barbara CA 93106 E-mail: comanor@ucla.edu.

COMAS, ALICE CUPRILL, lawyer; b. Weisbaden, Germany, Apr. 26, 1970; came to U.S., 1980; d. William M. Cuprill-Cuebas and Elsa Alicia Comas-Rivera; m. Richard M. Short, Aug. 12, 1994; 1 child, Alejandro Martin Comas Short. BA with honors, U. Tex., 1992; JD, Lewis and Clark Coll., 1995. Bar: Oreg. 1995, Tex. 1998. Atty. Tonkon Torp LLP, Portland, Oreg., 1995-98, Vinson & Elkins LLP, Austin, 1998—. Dir. Portland Creative Conf., 1997-98. Mem. Oreg. State Bar Assn. (affirmative action com. 1997-98), Tex. State Bar Assn., Hispanic Bar Assn. Office: Vinson & Elkins LLP 600 Congress Ave Ste 2700 Austin TX 78701-3248

COMBE, JOHN CLIFFORD, JR., lawyer; b. New Orleans, Jan. 5, 1939; s. John Clifford and Gladys Ann (Reine) C.; m. Lynne Wendel Watson, July 11, 1964; children: John, Wendy, Holly. BBA, Tulane U., 1960, LLB, 1965. Bar: La. 1965, U.S. Dist. Ct. (ea. and mid. dists.) La. 1965, U.S. Ct. Appeals (5th cir.) 1965, U.S. Supreme Ct. 1971, U.S. Ct. Appeals (11th cir.) 1981, U.S. Dist. Ct. (we. dist.) La. 1986. Assoc. Jones, Walker, Waechter, Poitevent, Carrere & Denegre, New Orleans, 1965—, ptnr., 1970—, sr. ptnr., 1989—. Editor: La. Bar Jour., 1975-77; contbr. articles to legal jours. Organizer, mem. Crestmont Pk. Improvement Assn.; organizer Greater New Orleans Law Explorer program Boy Scouts Am., 1974; mem. St. Catherine of Siena Parish Sch. Bd., 1976-89; trustee Acad. of Sacred Heart, 1993-96. Lt. (j.g.) USN, 1960-62. Fellow: ABA (mem. ho. of dels. 1982—88), La. State Bar Found., Am. Bar Found., Am. Coll. Trial Lawyers (state chair 1999—2000); mem.: La. Bar Assn. (mem. bd. govs. 1973—74, sec.-treas. 1975, mem. bd. govs. 1975—76, 1977—78, 1978—80, pres. 1979—80), So. Regional Conf. Bar Pres., Nat. Conf. Bar Pres., Def. Rsch. Inst., Am. Judicature Soc. (mem. bd. govs. 1982—86), La. Assn. Def. Counsel (bd. dirs. 1969—75, faculty trial acad. 2000—02), Internat. Assn. Def. Counsel (speaker 1989, mem. faculty trial acad. 1991), Stratford Club (pres. 1993—95), Boston Club, Metairie Country Club. Republican. Roman Catholic. Office: Jones Walker Waechter Poitevent Carrere & Denegre 201 Saint Charles Ave Ste 50 New Orleans LA 70170-5100

COMBEST, LARRY ED, retired congressman; b. Memphis, Tex., Mar. 20, 1945; s. Lawrence Nelson and Callie (Gunter) C.; m. Sharon McCurry, Sept. 10, 1981. BBA, W. Tex. State U., 1969; postgrad., Lubbock Christian U. Farmer, stockman, Memphis, 1965-71; county trainee Dept. Agr., Graham, Tex., 1971; spl. asst. Senator John Tower, Washington, 1971-78; owner Combest Distbg., Lubbock, Tex., 1978-85; mem. 99th-106th Congresses from 19th Tex. dist., Washington, 1985—2003; chmn. agriculture com.; ret., 2003. Recipient Santa Fe award Future Farmers Am., 1962, Gerald W. Thomas Outstanding Agriculturalists award for pub. svc., 1989, Lubbock Area Found. Hero of Yr. award, 1999. Mem.: Rotary, Lions. Republican. Methodist.

COMBS, ANN L. federal agency administrator; BA, U. Notre Dame, 1978; JD, George Washington U., 1981. Prin. William M. Mercer Cons.; deputy asst. sec. labor, 1987—2001; asst. sec. pensions and welfare benefits adminstrn. U.S. Dept. Labor, Washington, 2001—. Office: US Dept Labor 200 Constitution Ave NW Washington DC 20210

COMBS, CHARLES DONALD, academic administrator; b. Levelland, Tex., Mar. 28, 1952; s. Harold Bloyd and Emma Laura (Cole) C.; m. Pamela Quattlebaum, Mar. 31, 1983. BA with high honors, Tex. Tech U., 1972, MA, 1974; PhD, U. N.C., 1980, State Univ. Medicine and Dentistry, Moldova, 2003. Instr. polit. sci. Tex. Tech U., Lubbock, 1973-76, Elon (N.C.) Coll., 1975-76; instr. pub. adminstrn. N.C. Cen. U., Durham, 1976-77; sr. program assoc. Robert Wood Johnson Found., Chapel Hill, N.C., 1977-79; adminstr. Surry (Va.) Family Health Group, 1978-81; program dir. Ea. Va. Med. Sch., Old Dominion U., Norfolk, 1980-85; asst. v.p. adminstrn. and svcs. Ea. Va. Med. Sch., Norfolk, 1985-87; assoc. v.p. instl. advancement Med. Coll. Hampton Rds., Norfolk, 1987-88, v.p. instl. advancement, 1988-92; v.p. planning and program devel., 1992—. Cons. numerous health and human svc. orgns., Va., N.C., Tex., Kans., Eastern and Ctrl. Europe, Africa, Asia and C.Am.; chmn. exec. com. Va. Statewide Health Edn. Adv. Com., 1992-2000; chmn. Regional Perinatal Coordinating Coun., 1989—; treas. Women's Health Va., 1998-2000. Contbr. articles to profl. jours. Grantee City of Durham, 1976, Kresge Found., 1979, Dept. Health and Human Svcs., 1981-85, 90—, Champus Mental Health Demonstration Program, 1986-89; sr. fellow Naval Postgrad. Sch., 1996-2003; recipient Disting. Alumni award South Plains Coll., 1998. Mem. APHA, Am. Assn. Univ. Adminstrs., Am. Hosp. Assn., Am. Soc. Pub. Adminstrs., Hampton Rds. C. of C. (mem. regional legis. affairs com. and health care task force 1985-96), Assn. of Acad. Health Ctrs. (nat. program chair 1996). Methodist. Home: 7800 N Shore Rd Norfolk VA 23505-1735 Office: Ea Va Med Sch PO Box 1980 Norfolk VA 23501-1980 E-mail: combscd@evms.edu.

COMBS, JEROME THOMAS, pediatrician, consultant; b. Wallingford, Conn, July 11, 1933; s. Stanley M. and Mary L. (ArtKop) C.; m. Maureen K. Donner; children: Cynthia, Christopher, Craig, Charles, Curtis. BS, Yale U., 1955; MD, Johns Hopkins U., 1959. Diplomate Am. Acad. Pediats. Intern in pediats. U. Minn., Mpls., 1959-60, resident in pediats., 1962-64; fellow in pediats. Yale U., New Haven, 1964-66; physician Wallingford Pediat. Group, 1966-81; pvt. practice Wallingford, 1981—96, New Haven, 1996—2001, Meriden, 2001—. Patentee in field; contbr. articles to profl. jours. Lt. M.C., USNR, 1960-62. Mem. Am. Pediat. Assn., Soc. Ear, Nose, Throat Advances Childhood, Ambulatory Pediat. Assn., Alexander Graham Bell Assn. Deaf. Roman Catholic. Avocations: fishing, arts and crafts. Home: 37 Copper Hill Dr Guilford CT 06437 Office: 285 Broad St Meriden CT 06450 Fax: (203) 237-2162. E-mail: jcombs@proheathmd.com.

COMBS, LINDA MORRISON, federal agency administrator; b. Lenoir, N.C., June 29, 1946; d. Robert Hugh and Vera Ludema (Bryant) Morrison; m. David Michael Combs, June 20, 1970. AA, Gardner Webb Coll., 1966, PhD (hon.), 1985; BS, Appalachian State U., 1968, MA, 1978; EdD, Va. Poly. Inst. and State U., 1985. Tchr., adminstr. Winston-Salem (N.C.)/Forsyth County Schs., 1968-79, sch. bd. mem., 1980-82; exec. sec., dep. U.S. Dept. Edn., Washington, 1982-84, dep. under-sec., 1984-86; pub. edn. advisor State of N.C., Raleigh, 1986-87; owner Combs Group Cons., Winston-Salem, 1987; acting asst. dir. for mgmt. U.S. Dept. Vet. Affairs, Washington, 1987-89; asst. sec. for mgmt. U.S. Dept. Treasury, Washington, 1989—; chief financial officer EPA, Washington, 2002—. Gov.'s advocate Com. for Children and Youth, Winston-Salem, 1974-75; treas. Michael Britt for N.C. Senate, Forsyth County, 1976; v.p. Forsyth County Young Reps. Club, 1980-81. Recipient Honor and Outstanding Svc. award Combined Fed. Campaign, Washington, 1983, Alumnus of Yr. award Gardner Webb Coll., Boiling Springs, N.C., 1987, Disting. Alumnus of Yr. Appalachian State U., Boone, N.C., 1986. Mem. Forysth County Rep. Womens Club, Pres.'s Coun. on Mgmt. Improvement (vice chair, Outstanding Leadership award 1989), Phi Delta Kappa, Delta Kappa Gamma. Republican. Baptist. Avocations: running, cooking, tennis. Office: EPA Off of the Chief Financial Officer 1200 Pennsylvania Ave NW Washington DC 20460 Office Fax: 202-501-1714.

COMBS, ROBERT KIMBAL, museum director; b. Oklahoma City, Mar. 5, 1955; s. Harold Lee and Joanna Jane (Barton) Combs; m. Lynn Marie Robison, June 9, 1979 (div. 1984); 1 child, Caitlyn. BA in History, San Francisco State U., 1978; cert. in museology, U. Calif., Berkeley, 1979; MA in Museology, John F. Kennedy U., 1980. Curator San Mateo (Calif.) County Mus., 1978-79; intern Smithsonian Instn., Washington, 1979; San Francisco Fine Arts Mus., 1979-81; curator Presidio Army Mus., San Francisco, 1981-83; dir. U.S. Army Engr. Mus., Ft. Leonard Wood, Mo., 1983—2001; prof. history Columbia Coll., Ft. Leonard Wood, 1984—2001; dir. 2d Inf. Div. Mus., Republic of Korea, 2001—. Cons. Nat. Park Svc., San Francisco, 1978; dir. mus. educators forum, 1983-85; historian 2d Inf. Divsn., 1994-96; guest lectr. Kookmin U., Seoul, 1995. Editor: Fort Leonard Wood, 1941, 1991; contbr. articles and monographs to mags. and newspapers; appeared in numerous TV documentaries and programs. Bd. dirs. South Ctrl. Mo. Arts Coun., Rolla, 1991. Mem. Am. Assn. Mus., Am. Assn. State and Local History, Internat. Commn. on Mus., Commn. on Mil. Mus. in Am., Rolls Royce Owners Club. Avocations: travel, archaeology, theatre. E-mail: combsk@usfk.korea.army.mil.

COMBS, ROY JAMES, JR., analyst, researcher; b. Marion, Va., Dec. 11, 1954; s. Roy James and Mary Cathleen Mitchem C.; m. Eva Sue Smith, March 17, 1973 (div. Aug. 1991); children: Crystal Michelle, Mark Nicholas; m. Kathryn Michelle Howard, June 25, 1994. Student, U. Va., 1992-93; MPA, Harvard U., 1995; DPA, U. So. Calif., Washington, 2001. Analyst CIA, Washington, 1977-98; program mgr. Nat. Imagery and Mapping Agy., Bethesda, Md., 1998-2000, dir. enterprise svcs., 2000—. Asst. coach Fairfax (Va.) Police Youth Club, 1993-94; fund raiser Harvard Graduate Sch., Washington, 1998; vol. Christmas in April, Arlington, Va., 1995; sec., treas., Purple Sage Homeowners Assn., Reston, Va., 1995-2000. Mem. Am. Soc. Pub. Administrs. Avocations: sailing, rollerblading, biking, reading.

COMBS, STEPHEN PAUL, pediatrician, health facility administrator; b. Bristol, Tenn., Feb. 11, 1966; s. Paul Willis and Janis Rose C. BS, East Tenn. State U., 1988, MD, 1992. Diplomate Nat. Bd. Med. Examiners, Am. Bd. Pediat. (fellow), Am. Bd. Forensic Examiners (fellow), Am. Bd. Forensic Medicine. Resident in pediat. Duke U., Durham, N.C., 1992-95, asst. chief pediat. residents Duke Children's Hosp., 1994-95; ptnr. Mountain Region Pediats., Kingsport, Tenn., 1995-98, sec., 1998—; pediatrician Gray (Tenn.) Sta. Pediat., 1999—. Dir. pediat. intensive care Wellmont Health Sys., 1998—, chmn. pediat. critical care, 1996—; quality oversight com. Holston Valley Med. Ctr., Kingsport, Tenn., 1998—99; chmn. dept. pediat. Indian Path Med. Ctr., 1999—; mem. med. adv. bd. Am. Homepatient, Nashville, 1995—98; regional faculty PALS Tenn. chpt. AHA, 1995—; mem. child fatality rev. bd. jud. Dist. II State of Tenn., 1995—; bd. dirs. Wellmont Holston Valley Med. Ctr., 2000—; med. dir. clin. trials program Highlands Physicans Inc., 2001—, bd. dirs., mem. various coms.; assoc. clin. prof. pediatrics East Tenn. State U., 2002—. Contbr. articles to profl. jours. Recipient Forty Under 40 award, Bus. Jour., Health Care Hero award, 2003. Fellow AAP (resident rep. 1993-95, program chmn. Tenn. chpt. 2000, nominating chair Tenn. chpt. 2001); mem. AMA, Tenn. Med. Assn., N.C. Med. Assn., Duke Med. Alumni Assn., East Tenn. State U. Med. Alumni Assn. (rep. 1992—), History of Appalachia Soc., Alpha Omega Alpha. Republican. Baptist. Avocations: civil war, revolutionary war, gardening, snow skiing, golf. Home: 405 Westfield Pl Kingsport TN 37664-6410 Office: Gray Sta Pediat 2103 Forest Dr Ste 5 Gray TN 37615-8423

COMBS, STEVEN PAUL, orthopedic surgeon; b. Ft. Dodge, Iowa, Apr. 9, 1944; s. Eugene Charles and Marie Wilhelmina (Mack) C.; m. Penelope Ann Calvey, July 6, 1974; children: Patrick, Mary Katherine, Meaghan, Bridget. BS, U. Iowa, 1966, MD, 1970; MBA, Lake Erie Coll., 1991. Diplomate Am. Bd. Orthopedic Surgery; cert. physician exec. Intern Robert Packer Hosp., Sayre, Pa., 1970-71; resident in orthopedics Cleve. Clinic, 1971-75; orthopedic surgeon Drs. DeMarco & Irwin, Willoughby, Ohio, 1979—. Pres. med. staff Lake Hosp. Sys., 1998-02. Served to maj. USAF, 1975-79. Fellow ACS; mem. AMA, Am. Acad. Orthopedic Surgeons, Orthopedic Rsch. Soc., Coll. Physician Execs., Lake County Med. Soc. (pres. 1991), Lake Hosp. Found. (chmn. 1993-96), Ohio State Med. Assn. (alt. del. AMA 1997-2002, chmn. legis. com. 1997-2000, 5th dist. coun. 2000-03, pres.-elect, 2003—). Republican. Roman Catholic. Home: 8685 King Memorial Rd Mentor OH 44060-7960 Office: Lake Orthopaedic Assn 36100 Euclid Ave Ste 170 Willoughby OH 44094-4475 E-mail: stevencombs@hotmail.com.

COMBS, W(ILLIAM) HENRY, III, lawyer; b. Casper, Wyo., Mar. 18, 1949; s. William Henry and Ruth M. (Wooster) Combs; 1 child from previous marriage, J. Bradley. Student, Northwestern U., 1967—70; BS, U. Wyo., 1972, JD, 1975. Bar: Wyo. 1975, U.S. Dist. Ct. Wyo. 1975, U.S. Ct. Appeals (10th cir.) 1990, U.S. Supreme Ct. 1990. Assoc. Murane & Bostwick, Casper, 1975—77, ptnr., 1978—. Mem. com. resolution fee disputes, 1990—92. Mem.: ABA (tort and ins. practice sect., law office mgmt. sect.), U.S. Handball Assn., Nat. Bd. Trail Advocacy (cert.), Assn. Ski Def. Attys., Def. Lawyers Assn. Wyo., Am. Judicature Soc., Def. Rsch. Inst., Natrona County Bar Assn., Waterski USA, Porsche Club Am. Republican. Episcopalian. Avocations: handball, waterskiing, snow skiing, climbing, driving. Office: Murane & Bostwick 201 N Wolcott St Casper WY 82601-1922

COMEAU, CAROL SMITH, educator; b. Berkeley, Calif., Sept. 4, 1941; d. Floyd Franklin and Bessie Caroline (Campbell) Smith; m. Dennis Rene Comeau, Dec. 27, 1962; children— Christopher, Michael, Karen. BS in Edn., U. Oreg., 1963; M in Pub. Sch. Adminstrn., U. Alaska, 1985. Third grade tchr., Springfield, Oreg., 1963-64; elem. sch. tchr. Ocean View Elem. Sch., Anchorage, 1975-84, 2d-6th grade tchr.; 6th grade tchr. Spring Hill Elem. Sch., Anchorage, 1985-86; adminstrv. intern Tudor Elem. Sch., Anchorage, 1986-87; prin. Orion Elem. Sch., Anchorage, 1987-89; prin. Spring Hill Elem. Sch., 1989-90; exec. dir. elem. edn. Anchorage Sch. Dist., 1990-93; asst. supt. instrn., 1993-2000; supt., 2000—; community activist ednl. issues. Chair Alaska PTA Edn. Commn., 1987-88; sec. bd. Frontier (Alaska) State Credit Union, 1987-91; vice-chair Anchorage United Way, 2002--; bd. dirs. KAKM pub. TV, 1990-92, Alaska Ctr. Performing Arts. Named Tchr. of Yr., Anchorage Sch. Dist. PTA Coun., 1976, Top 25 Most Powerful Alaskans, 2002, Alaska Supt. of Yr., 2003. Mem. NEA, Nat. Assn. Elem. Sch. Prins., Alaska Assn. Elem. Sch. Prins., Anchorage Edn. Assn. (Tchr. of Yr. 1986), Phi Delta Kappa, Kappa Delta Pi. Democrat. Home: 13632 Jarvi Dr Anchorage AK 99515-3934 Office: Anchorage Sch Dist Adminstrn Bldg 4600 Debarr Rd Anchorage AK 99519-6614

COMEAU, LORENE ANITA EMERSON, real estate developer; b. Haverhill, Mass., Sept. 6, 1952; d. Russell Paul and Jeannette (La Course) Emerson; m. Peter Robert Comeau, May 6, 1950; children: Stephen David, Michelle Patricia. BA with honors, Northeastern U., 1975; MBA with high honors, Simmons Coll., 2002. Lic. real estate broker. Housing rep., pub. liaison U.S. Dept. HUD, Boston, 1975-78; devel. mgr. John M. Corcoran & Co., Milton, Mass., 1978-84, v.p., 1984-94; ptnr. Corcoran Realty Assocs., Milton, 1994-2000; co-owner, treas. Refrigeration Engring. & Contracting Co., Inc., 1995—. Bd. dirs. Stoneham Coop. Bank, bd. affairs com., 1992-93, security com., 1993—, chair bldg. com., 1997—; v.p. Merrimack Valley Housing Partnership, Lowell, Mass., 1986-89. Active Fessenden Sch. Parent's Orgn., 1995—97, Shady Hill Sch. Parents Coun., 1998—99; bd. dirs. Merrimack Valley YMCA, 1982—92, vice chair, 1988—90, chair, 1990—92; mem. Andover Fair Housing Com., 1982—87, Andover Housing Partnership Com., 1990—2001, vice-chair, 2000—01; mem. Andover Planning Bd., 1993—96, Andover Master Plan Com., 1982—84, chair com. housing component and master plan, 1989—90; assoc. mem. Andover Zoning Bd. Appeals, 1984—87; fin. com., cor. bd. Merrimack Valley YMCA, Lawrence, Mass., 1984—86, 1991—94, treas. corp. fin. com., 1992—94; low income housing subcom. corp. bd., 1992—99; vice-chair adv. bd. Caritas Cmtys., 1994—97, chair adv. bd., 1998—2000; treas. Merrimack Valley YMCA, Andover, Mass., 1986—88. Mem. LWV (fin. chair Andover chpt. 1981-83, budget chair 1983-84, 86-87), New England Women in Real Estate (seminars com. 1992, cmty. rels. com. 1992-97, program com. 1996-2000, chair 1998-2000, steering com. 1997-2001, spl. events com. 1999-2000, awards com. 1999-, v.p. 1999-2000, pres. 2000-01), Nat. Assn. Indsl. and Office Properties (pub. affairs com. 1992—, vice-chair land use com. 1999), past mem. Nat. Pvt. Developers Coun., Svc. Club of Andover, Sanborn Sch. PTO (curriculum enrichment com. 1988-95) West Mid. Sch. PAC (curriculum enrichment com., women's history month 1993-95). Republican. Episcopalian. Home: PO Box 4108 Andover MA 01810-0812 Office: RECCO 39 Commercial St Medford MA 02155 E-mail: lori_comeau@yahoo.com.

COMEAU, MATTHEW J. athletic training program director, educator; s. Roger L. and Linda A. Comeau; m. Denise D. Gabel, Oct. 12, 1996. BS in Exercise Sci., MS in Exercise Sci., U. Kans., PhD, 1988—2000. Cert. athletic trainer Nat. Athletic Trainers' Assn., 1993, strength and conditioning specialist Nat. Strength and Conditioning Assn., 1996. Asst. prof. Ark. State U., 1999—2002, assoc. prof./program dir., 2003—. Fin. sec. KC, West Memphis, Ark., 2002—03. Mem.: Nat. Athletic Trainers' Assn. Rsch. and Edn. Found. (dist. 6 chair 2002—), Nat. Strength and Conditioning Assn., Am. Coll. Sports Medicine, Nat. Athletic Trainers' Assn. R-Consevative. Roman Catholic. Office: Arkansas State U PO Box 240 State University AR 72467 Office Fax: 870-972-3096. Personal E-mail: mcomeau@midsouth.rr.com. E-mail: mcomeau@astate.edu.

COMEAU, SUSAN, bank executive; Grad., Colby Coll. Exec. v.p. State St. Corp., Boston, 1963—. Office: State St Corp 225 Franklin St Boston MA 02110-2804*

COMEAUX, ERICK J. chemical engineer; BSChemE, La. State U., 1997, postgrad., 2001—. Registered engr., La. Profl. Engring. and Land Surveying Bd., 1997. Rsch. assoc. macromolecular studies group La. State U., Baton Rouge, 1992—97; compound devel. engr. Ga. Gulf Corp., Plaquemine, La., 1997—99; process engr. Crompton Corp.-Uniroyal Chem. Co., Geismar, La., 1999—2000, prodn. supt., 2000—. Exec. treas. Soc. Plastics Engrs.-Gulf South Ctrl. Sect., Baton Rouge, 1997—99. V.p. Civic Assn., Baton Rouge, 1999—2002. Recipient Rsch. award, Soc. Plastics Engrs., 1995, First Pl. Rsch. award, Sigma Xi Rsch. Soc., 1996, Internat. Soc. Materials, 1997, Governor's Environ. Leadership award, State of La. Govs. Office, 1999; scholar, La. State U., 1992; La. Top 5% Honors scholar, State of La., 1992, Pegues scholar, La. State U. Coll. Engring., 1992, Svc. Award scholar, Lions Club, 1992, Achievement scholar, Svc. Mdse., 1992. Mem.: AIChE, NSPE, Am. Chem. Soc., Nat. Collegiate Hon. Socs., Gamma Beta Phi. Achievements include research in PVC fusion mechanisms. Office: Crompton Corp-Uniroyal Chemical Company PO Box 397 Geismar LA 70734

COMEGYS, ETHEL BLANCHE, brokerage house administrator; b. Balt., Sept. 11, 1961; d. Elmer Anthony and Ethel Blanche Weber; m. Mark Steven Comegys, Apr. 26, 1989. BA with honors, Johns Hopkins U., 1983. Bank teller Augusta Fed., Balt., 1984-89; from funds processing svc. rep. to client svc. rep. Legg Mason, Balt., 1992-98, client svc. asst. supr., 1999—. Active Nat. Trust, D.C., 1997, Balt. Preservation, Inc., 1998. Md. State Ho. of Dels. scholar, 1979. Democrat. Lutheran. Avocations: antiques, gardening, old house restoration.

COMER, BRENDA WARMEE, educator, real estate company executive; b. Lakewood, Ohio, May 14, 1938; d. Walter Byron and Annabelle (Broderick) Warmee; m. Gerald Edmund Comer, June 30, 1962; children: Brian, James, David, Kristen. BS, Kent State U., 1961; postgrad., Bowling Green State U., 1981, 82, 83-84; reading cert., Baldwin Wallace Coll., 1987. Elem. tchr. Lorain (Ohio) Bd. Edn., 1961-63, tchr. aux. svcs. remedial reading and math., 1979-87, tchr. Chpt. I reading program, 1987—. V.p. Warmee, Inc., real estate. Vice pres. Lakeland Woman's Club, Loraine, 1972, scholarship chmn., 1973-76. Mem. NEA, Ohio Edn. Assn., Loraine Edn. Assn., Internat. Reading Assn., Daniel T. Gardner Reading Coun., AAUW (v.p. Lorain 1981-82, scholarship chmn. 1986-90). Home: 1075 Archwood Ave Lorain OH 44052-1248

COMER, DEBRA RUTH, management educator; b. Phila., Apr. 11, 1960; d. Nathan Lawrence and Rita C.; m. James Michael Maloney; children: Rudy Gabriel Malcom and Jacob Eli Malcom (twins). BA, Swarthmore Coll., 1982; MA, Yale U., 1984, MPhil, 1985, PhD, 1986. Instr. Yale U., New Haven, 1983-84; orgnl. devel. cons. Port Authority of N.Y. & N.J., N.Y.C., 1984-87; asst. prof. mgmt. Hofstra U., Hempstead, N.Y., 1987-93, assoc. prof. mgmt., 1993-99, chairperson dept. mgmt. and GB, 1995-97, assoc. dean faculty devel. Sch. of Bus., 1997-98, prof. mgmt., 1999—. Co-author: Instructor's Manual: Developing Management Skills, 2002; contbr. articles to profl. jours. Yale U. fellow, 1982-86, Joshua B. Lippincott fellow Swarthmore Coll., 1982; Hofstra U. grantee, 1988-2000. Mem. APA, Acad. Mgmt., Ea. Acad. Mgmt., Orgnl. Behavior Teaching Soc. Jewish. Avocations: music, fitness, cooking, reading. Office: Hofstra U Dept Mgmt and Gen Bus 228 Weller Hl Hempstead NY 11549-1340

COMER, DONALD, III, investment company executive; b. N.Y.C., June 23, 1938; s. Donald and Isabel (Anderson) C.; m. Jane Stephens, May 4, 1962; children: Jason Legare, Luke McDonald, Carrie St. George. BS, U. Ala., 1962. With Cowikee Mills, Eufaula, Ala., 1962-82, plant mgr., 1965-66, v.p., 1966-68, pres., treas., dir., 1968-82; pres., dir. Aurizon Inc., 1982—; past pres., treas., dir. Avondale Mills., Sylacauga, Ala. Past chmn. Ala. Ethics Commn. Served with USAF, 1961-64. Mem.: Mountain Brook Country (Birmingham). Home: 3905 Hillock Dr Birmingham AL 35213-3223

COMER, EVAN PHILIP, manufacturing company executive; b. Cumberland Gap, Tenn., May 29, 1927; s. Evan Mitchell and Margaret Nola (Estep) C.; m. Mary Blanc, Aug. 28, 1948; children: Vivian, Jane. BA, Carson-Newman Coll., Jefferson City, Tenn., 1948; MA, Columbia U., 1949. Asst. prof. psychology, dir. student personnel and placement Furman U., Greensville, S.C., 1949-52; self-employed writer, 1952-53; supervisory conf. leader Union Carbide Nuclear Co., Oak Ridge, 1953-55; instr. in-plant tng. U. Tenn., Knoxville, 1955-56; with Foote Mineral Co., 1956-67, 69-84, v.p., gen. mgr. chems. and minerals div., 1970-80, pres., chief exec. officer, 1980-84, also bd. dirs.; pres., chief exec. officer, chmn. bd. Ashram Farm, Inc., Rutledge, Tenn., 1984-98. Mem. Pa. adv. bd. Liberty Mut. Ins. Co.; chmn. exec. com., dir. Phila. Mfrs. Mut. Ins. Co. Pres. Southeastern C.C., Whiteville, N.C., 1967-69; mem. adv. bd. Carson-Newman Coll.; bd. dirs. Pa. Sci. and Engring. Found.; mem. Pa. Gov's Sci. Adv. Com.; mem. adv. coun. Pa. Tech. Assistance Program, Pa. State U.; chmn. bd. Chester County Pvt. Industry Coun., 1983-84; mem. Jefferson County (Tenn.) Planning Commn., 1998—, Jefferson County Zoning Appeals Bd., 1998—; mem. regional resource stewardship coun. TVA, 2000—; pres. Jefferson County Hist. Soc., 2003—. With USNR, 1945-46. Mem.: AIME, Am. Mining Congress, Ferroalloys Assn. (chmn. bd. dirs. 1983—84), Mining Club (N.Y.C.). Republican. Baptist. Home: 1548 Smoky View Dr Dandridge TN 37725-6328 E-mail: PhilMary@att.net.

COMER, JAMES PIERPONT, psychiatrist, educator; b. East Chicago, Ind., Sept. 25, 1934; s. Hugh and Maggie (Nichols) C.; m. Shirley Ann Arnold, June 20, 1959 (dec. Apr. 1994); children: Brian Jay, Dawn Renee. AB, Ind. U., 1956; MD, Howard U., 1960; MPH, U. Mich., 1964; DSc (hon.), U. New Haven, 1977; LittD (hon.), Calumet Coll., 1978; LHD (hon.), Bank St. Coll., N.Y.C., 1987, Albertus Magnus Coll., 1989, Quinnipiac Coll., 1990, DePauw U., 1990; DSc (hon.), Ind U., 1991, Wabash Coll., 1991; EdD (hon.), Wheelock Coll., 1991; LLD (hon.), U. Conn., 1991; LHD (hon.), SUNY Buffalo, 1991, New Sch. for Social Rsch., 1991; D Pedagogy (hon.), R.I. Coll., 1991; DSc (hon.), Amherst Coll., 1991; LHD (hon.), John Jay Coll. Criminal Justice, 1991, Wesleyan U., 1991; DH (hon.), Princeton U., 1991; DSc (hon.), Northwestern U., 1991, Worcester Poly. Inst., 1991; LHD (hon.), U. Pa., 1992; DPD (hon.), Niagara U., 1992; LHD (hon.), Hamilton Coll., 1992; DSc (hon.), Brown U., 1992; LHD (hon.), U. Mass. at Lowell, 1992; DSc (hon.), Med. Coll. Ohio, 1992, Howard U., 1993, W.Va. U., 1993; LLD (hon.), Lawrence U., 1993; DSc (hon.), Morehouse Sch. Medicine, 1993; LLD (hon.), Columbia U., 1994, Boston Coll., 1994; LHD (hon.), Briarwood Coll., 1994, Cleve. State U., 1996; DSc (hon.), St. Mary's Coll., Md., 1996, Albion Coll., 1997, Conn. Coll., 1997, So. Conn. State Coll., 1998; D in Pediats., Long Island U., 1999; LHD (hon.), Ea. Mich. U., 2000; LHD (hon.), N.C.State Univ. Served with USPHS, Washington and Chevy Chase, Md., 1961-68; intern St. Catherine's Hosp., East Chicago, 1960-61; resident Yale Sch. Medicine, 1964-67; asst. prof. psychiatry Yale Child Study Center and dept. psychiatry, 1968-70, assoc. prof., 1970-75, prof., 1975-76, Maurice Falk prof. child psychiatry, 1976—; assoc. dean Yale Med. Sch., New Haven, 1969—. Dir. pupil svcs. Baldwin-King Sch. Project, New Haven, 1968-73; dir. sch. devel. program Yale Child Study Ctr., 1973-97, founder sch. devel. program adv. bd., 1997—; dir. Conn. Energy Corp., 1976—, Nat. Acad. Found. N.Y., N.Y.C., 1993—; co-dir. Black Family Roundtable Greater New Haven, 1986—; cons. Joint Commn. on Mental Health of Children, Nat. Commn. on Causes and Prevention of Violence, NIMH; mem. nat. adv. mental health coun. HEW; Henry J. Kaiser Sr. fellow Center for Advanced Study in the Behavioral Scis., Stanford, 1976-77. Author: Beyond Black and White, 1972, Black Child Care, 1975, 2d edit., 1992, School Power, 1980, 2d. edit., 1993, Maggie's American Dream, 1988, Rallying the Whole Village: The Comer Process for Reforming Education, 1996, Waiting For a Miracle: Why Schools Can't Solve Our Problems-And How We Can, 1997, Child by Child: The Comer Process for Change in Education, 1999; mem. editl. bd. Am. Jour. Orthopsychiatry, 1969-76, Youth and Adolescence, 1971-87, Jour. Negro Edn., 1973-83; guest editor Jour. Am. Acad. Child Psychiatry, 1985; columnist Parents mag.; contbr. articles to profl. jours. Bd. dirs. Field Found., 1981-88, Dixwell Soul Sta. and Yale Afro-Am. House; trustee Hazen Found., 1974-78, Wesleyan U., 1978-84, Nat. Coun. for Effective Schs., 1985—, Albertus Magnus Coll., 1989—, Carnegie Corp., 1990, Milton S. Eisenhower Found., Washington, 1991—, Conn. State U., 1991-94; bd. dirs., mem. profl. adv. bd. Children's TV Workshop, 1972-88; mem. profl. adv. coun. Nat. Assn. Mental Health; mem. ad. hoc adv. com. Conn. Rsch. Commn.; mem. adv. coun. Nat. Com. for Citizens in Edn.; mem. nat. adv. coun. Hogg Found. for Mental Health, 1983-86; mem. adv. com. adolescent pregnancy prevention Children's Def. Fund, 1985—; mem. adv. coun. Nat. Com. for Citizens in Edn., 1983—; mem. nat. adv. coun. Hogg Found for Mental Health, 1983-86; mem. edn. adv. bd., bd. dirs. (hon.) Kids Voting USA, 1997—; mem. nat. evaluation adv. coun. Kellogg Youth Initiative Partnerships W.K. Kellogg Found., 1997—. Recipient Child Study Assn.-Wel-Met Family Life book award, 1975, Howard U. Disting. Alumni award, 1976, Rockefeller Public Service award, 1980, Media award NCCJ, 1981, Cmty. Leadership award Greater New Haven C. of C., 1983, Disting. Fellow award Conn. chpt. Phi Delta Kappa, 1984, Elm and Ivy award New Haven Found., 1985, Disting. Svc. award Conn. Assn. Psychologists, 1985, Disting. Educator award Conn. Coalition of 100 Black Women, 1985, Outstanding Leadership award Children's Def. Fund, 1987, Whitney M. Young Jr. Svc. award Boy Scouts Am., 1989, Prudential Leadership award Prudential Found., 1990, Harold W. McGraw Jr. prize in Edn., 1990, James Bryant Conant award Edn. Commn. States, 1991, Charles A. Dana prize in Edn., 1991, Disting.

Svc. award Coun. Chief State Sch. Officers, 1991, Family Focus Nat. award, 1991, Charles A. Dana award for pioneering achievement in edn., 1991, Ind. U. Disting. Alumni Svc. award, 1992, Burger King Disting. Svc. to Edn. award, 1992, Conn. Assn. for Human Svcs. Pres. award, 1992, Golden Acorn award Bronx C.C., 1994, Presdl. citation Am. Ednl. Rsch. Assn., 1995, Health Trac Found. prize, 1996, Heinz Family award, 1996, Lehigh U. Outstanding Svc. to Coll. Edn. award, 1996, Ann Vanderbilt Achievement award for ednl. leadership, 1997, Great Friend to Kids award Assn. Youth Mus., 1997, Disting. Svc. medal Tchrs. Coll., 1997, Friends of the Family citation, Working Mother Mag., 1997, World of Children award Judge Baker Children's Ctr., 1997, Michael Bolton Lifetime Achievement award, 1997, Edn. award Inst. Student Achievement, 1999, Disting. Pub. Svc. award Conn. Bar Assn., 1999, Martin Luther Freedom award New Haven Chpt. NAACP; John and Mary Markle Found. scholar, 1969—; James Comer NIMH Minority Fellowship established in his honor, 1991.; Disting. Service Award, Covenant to Care, Inc., 2001. Mem. APA (Disting. Svc. award 1993), Am. Acad. Child Adolescent Psychiatry, Nat. Med. Assn., Nat. Mental Health Assn. (Lela Rowland Prevention award 1989), Am. Psychiat. Assn. (Agnes Purcell McGavin award 1990, Solomon Carter Fuller award 1990, Spl. Presdl. Commendation 1990, Disting. Svc. award 1993), Am. Orthopsychiat. Assn. (Vera S. Paster award 1990), Am. Acad. Child Psychiatry, Black Psychiatrists of Am., NAACP, Black Coalition of New Haven, Greater New Haven Black Family Roundtable (co-dir. 1986—), Alpha Omega Alpha, Alpha Phi Alpha. Avocations: photography, travel, sports fan. Office: Yale U Child Study Ctr PO Box 207900 New Haven CT 06520-7900 E-mail: james.comer@yale.edu. *As a black child, I sometimes had doubts about my future opportunities for success in our predominantly white country. My parents counselled me never to let the issue of race stand in my way; that the time of greater opportunity for blacks would come. They advised me to work hard, prepare myself, to strive to be the best or among the best in every undertaking, and at the same time be respectful of all people, regardless of their abilities, race, beliefs, or station in life. I have lived by this advice and it has served me well. I have learned not to strive for top position but to let my work take me where it will in line with my interests.*

COMER, JAMES R., JR., state representative; b. Carthage, Tenn., Aug. 19, 1972; BS, Western Ky. U., 1993. State pres. Ky. FFA Assn., 1990—91; chair Rep. Party of Monroe County, 1993—94; del. Rep. Nat. Conv., San Diego, 1996; pres. Monroe County C. of C., 1999—2000; state rep. Ky. State Legislature, 2001—. Co-owner Comer and Polston Ins., Inc., 1993—95, Comer Land and Cattle Co., 1994—; pres. CFB Foods, Inc., 2001—; dir. Deposit Bank of Monroe County, 2000—. Dir. Monroe County Farm Bur., 1996—; mem. Monroe County Inter-Agy. Coun., Ky. Cattleman's Assn., First Bapt. Ch. of Tompkinsville. Mem.: Lions Club of Tompkinsville. Republican. Baptist. Office: Capitol Annex Rm 432G Frankfort KY 40601*

COMER, NATHAN LAWRENCE, psychiatrist, educator; b. Phila., Nov. 10, 1923; s. Rubin L. and Fannie (Cassover) C.; m. Rita Ellis, June 19, 1949 (dec. Mar. 1978); children: Robert, Susan Comer Kitei, Debra R., Marc J. BA, U. Pa., 1944; MD, Hahnemann Med. Coll., 1949; postgrad., U. Pa. Diplomate Am. Bd. Psychiatry and Neurology, Am. Bd. Profl. Disabiligy Cons., Sr. Disability Analyst of Am. Bd. Disability Analysts, Am. Bd. Forensic Examiners, Am. Bd. Forensic Medicine. Intern Hahnemann Med. Coll., Phila., 1949-50; resident, NIMH fellow Inst. of Pa. Hosp., Phila., 1951-53, sr. attending psychiatrist, 1968—, resident in psychiatry, 1951-53; chief of psychiatry Ford Rd. campus Thomas Jefferson U. Hosp., Phila., 1978-94; clin. assoc. prof. psychiatry and human behavior Jefferson Med. Coll., Thomas Jefferson U., Phila., 1994—; clin. assoc. prof. psychiatry Drexel U. Coll. Medicine, Phila., 1978—; emeritus attending psychiatrist Hosp. Med. Coll. Pa., 2000—. Pres. med. staff Belmont Ctr. Comprehensive Treatment (formerly Phila. Psychiat. Ctr.), 1975—77, emeritus sr. attending physician, 1988—; pres. med. staff Inst. of Pa. Hosp., 1983—85. Contbr. articles to profl. jours. Bd. dirs. Temple Adath Israel of Main Line, Merion, Pa., 1958-78. Fellow Coll. Physicians Phila., Am. Psychiat. Assn. (disting. life); mem. AMA, Am. Soc. for Adolescent Psychiatry, Hahnemann Med. Coll. Alumni Assn. (pres. 1973-74), B'nai B'rith. Republican. Jewish. Home and Office: 1100 Hillcrest Rd Narberth PA 19072-1224 Fax: (610) 668-7417. *Do things to the best of your ability and be willing to go that extra mile. Alsobe willing to express your opinion if you think you're right even if you seem to be in the minority. Being respected is more important than being liked.*

COMERFORD, JOHN LEO, college official; b. Kenosha, Wis., Sept. 26, 1976; s. Leo Paul and Jonell Anne Comerford. BA in Polit. Sci., Western Ill. U., 1996; MS in Coll. Student Pers. Adminstrn., Ctrl. Mo. State U., 1998; student in Higher Edn. Adminstrn., U. Kans., 2003—. Residence hall dir. Ball State U., Muncie, Ind., 1998-2000; asst. dean students Mo. Western State Coll., St. Joseph, 2000—. Mem.: Am. Coll. Pers. Assn. (pres. 2003—). Roman Catholic. Avocations: public speaking, consulting. Office: Mo Western State Coll 4525 Downs Dr Saint Joseph MO 64507 Fax: 816-383-7106. E-mail: comerford@mwsc.edu.

COMERFORD, SUSAN MARIE, artist; b. Drain, Oreg., Mar. 6, 1933; d. Samuel Roy and Eleanor Ruth (Crandall) Ball; m. William Brown Comerford, Dec. 31, 1964 (dec. Jan. 1989); children: Anita, Kim Blodgett, Kelly Wadsworth; m. Frank Rusch, 1994. AA, Umpqua C.C., Roseburg, Oreg., 1974; BA, U. Oreg., 1979, MFA, 1983. Artist Best Sign Co., Las Vegas, Nev., 1962-64, Comerford Sign Co., Las Vegas, 1964-70; artist, owner Comerford Studio & Gallery, Roseburg, 1988—. Tchg. fellow U. Oreg., Eugene, 1982-83; mem. adv. bd. Umpqua C.C., 1976-78; mem. N.W. Print Coun., Portland, 1982-2001, Roseburg Mural Com., 1997-99. Exhibited works in various galleries in the Northwest. Initiator, artist mural program City of Roseburg, 1988-97. Recipient Disting. Svc. award City of Roseburg, 1994. Mem. Roseburg Area C. of C. (bd. dirs. 1997-2000, Beautification award 1995), Exec. Club (pres. 1998). Republican. Mem. Lds Ch. Avocations: gardening, travel, outdoor activities, music. Office: Comerford Studio 485 SE Kane St Roseburg OR 97470-4903

COMERFORD, WALTER THOMPSON, JR., lawyer; b. May 27, 1949; s. Walter Thompson and Mary Lou (Phetteplace) C.; m. Joyce Faye Call; children: Callison Taylor, Erin Elizabeth, Kristen Nicole. Student, U. Tenn., 1968-70; BA magna cum laude, Wake Forest U., 1972; JD cum laude, 1974. Bar: N.C. 1974, U.S. Dist. Ct. (mid. and we. dists.) N.C. 1974, U.S. Ct. Appeals (4th cir.) 1977. Ptnr. Petree, Stockton & Robinson, Winston-Salem, N.C., 1980—. Contbr. articles to profl. jours. Chmn. Wake Forest Law ALumni Coun. (pres. 2000-01). Recipient Disting. Achievement award Internat. Acad. Trial Lawyers, 1974. Mem. Am. Trial lawyers Assn., N.C. Acad. Trial Lawyers, Am. Bd. Trial Lawyers, ABA (vice chmn), N.C. Bar Assn., N.C. State Bar, Forsyth County Bar Assn., Aviation Ins. Assn., Pilot's Bar Assn. Home: 3500 Stonegate Ct Winston Salem NC 27104-1824 Office: Comerford & Britt 250 W First St Ste 300 Winston Salem NC 27101-2400 E-mail: wtc@comerfordbritt.com.

COMEROTA, ANTHONY JAMES, vascular surgeon, biomedical researcher; b. Newark, Aug. 4, 1948; s.Louis Anthony and Eleanor Dorothy (Dombroski) C.; m. Elsa Benavides, Aug. 18, 1973; children: Anthony James, Maya Christine, Mark Anthony. BA, Millikin U., 1970; MD, Temple U., 1974. Diplomate Am. Bd. Surgery. Surg. resident Temple U. Hosp., Phila., 1974 78; vascular surgery fellow Good Samaritan Hosp., Cin., 1979-81; from asst. prof. to prof. surgery Temple U. Hosp, Temple U. Sch. Medicine, Phila., 1981-88, prof. surgery, chief vascular surgery, 1988—2002; dir. Ctr. for Vascular Diseases Temple U. Hosp., Temple U. Sch. Medicine, Phila., 1995—2002; dir. Jobst Vascular Ctr., Toledo; clin. prof. U. Mich., Ann Arbor, 2002—. Editor: Thrombolytic Therapy for Peripheral Vascular Disease, 1995; co-editor: Prevention of Venous Thromboembolism, 1994. Fellow ACS, Royal Australian Coll. Surgeons; mem. Am. Surg. Assn., Soc. Vascular Surgery, Am. Assn. Vascular Surgery, Peripheral Vascular Soc. (pres. 1988-89), Am. Venous Forum (pres. 2000-01), Phila. Acad. Surgery (pres. 1996-97), Temple U. Sch. Medicine Alumni Assn. (pres. 1993-95), Alpha Omega Alpha. Office: Jobst Vascular Ctr 2109 Hughes Dr # 400 Toledo OH 43606

COMES, ROBERT GEORGE, research scientist; b. Bangor, Pa., July 7, 1931; s. Victor Francis and Mabel Elizabeth (Mack) C.; student U. Detroit, 1957-58, Oreg. State Coll., 1959-60, U. Nev., 1960, Regis Coll., 1961-62; m. Carol Lee Turinetti, Nov. 28, 1952; children: Pamela Jo, Robert G. II, Shawni Lee, Sheryl Lynn, Michelle Ann. Tech. liaison engr. Burroughs Corp., Detroit, 1955-60, mgr. reliability and maintainability engring., Paoli, Pa., 1962-63, Colorado Springs, Colo., 1963-67; sr. engr. Martin Marietta Corp., Denver, 1960-62; program mgr., rsch. scientist Kaman Scis. Corp., Colorado Springs, 1967-75; dir. engring. Sci. Applications, Inc., Colorado Springs, 1975-80; mgr. space def. programs Burroughs Corp., Colorado Springs, 1980-82; tech. staff Mitre Corp., Colorado Springs, 1982-85; dir. Colorado Springs opn. Beers Assoc., Inc., 1985; dir. space programs Electro Magnetic Applications, Inc., Colorado Springs, 1985-87; dir. Space Systems, Profl. Mgmt. Assocs., Inc., 1987-88; mgr. Computer Svcs., Inc., Colorado Springs, 1989—; dir. mktg. Proactive Techs., Inc., Colorado Springs, 1990—; chmn. Reliability and Maintainability Data Bank Improvement Program, Govt.-Industry Data Exch. Program, 1978-80—; cons. in field. Youth dir. Indian Guides program YMCA, 1963-64; scoutmaster Boy Scouts Am., 1972-73; chmn. bd. dirs. Pikes Peak Regional Sci. Fair, 1972-84. Served with USAF, 1951-55. Mem. AAAS, IEEE, Inst. Environ. Scis., Soc. Logistics Engrs., Am. Soc. Quality Control. Lutheran. Club: Colorado Springs Racquet. Author: Maintainability Engineering Principles and Standards, 1962. Inventor Phase Shifting aircraft power supply, 1957. Home and Office: Proactive Tech Inc 4309 Tipton Ct Colorado Springs CO 80915-1034

COMETTO-MUÑIZ, JORGE ENRIQUE, biochemist, researcher; b. Buenos Aires, May 31, 1954; came to U.S., 1988; s. Jorge Raul and Teresa (Muñiz) Cometto; children: Carolina S., Lucas M., Tomás P. Biochemist, U. Buenos Aires, 1977, D in Biochemistry, 1986. Lic. in clin. analysis. From rsch. fellow to assoc. investigator Nat. Coun. for Sci. & Tech., Buenos Aires, 1978-93; asst. prof. biolog. chemistry U. Buenos Aires, 1986-93; assoc. rsch. scientist Yale U., New Haven, 1988-94; asst. fellow John B. Pierce Lab., New Haven, 1991 94; assoc. scientist U. Calif., San Diego, 1994—2001, rsch. scientist, 2001—. Vis. asst. fellow John B. Pierce Lab., New Haven, 1988-91. Contbr. articles to Annals the N.Y. Acad. Sci., Pharmacology, Biochemistry & Behavior, Physiology & Behavior, Perception & Psychophysics. Mem. Soc. Sci. Argentina, Assn. for Chemoreception Sci., European Chemoreception Rsch. Orgn., Internat. Soc. Indoor Air Quality and Climate, Soc. of Toxicology. Office: U Calif Chemosensory Perception Lab 8950 Villa La Jolla Dr Ste C135 La Jolla CA 92037-1703

COMFORT, CLIFTON C. fraud examiner, management consultant; b. Dallas, 1943; BBA in Acctg. with honors, U. Tex., Arlington, 1964; MBA, U. Phoenix, 1989. CPA, Tex., Ariz.; cert. internal auditor, cost analyst, fraud examiner, Tex. Auditor U.S. Govt., Dallas, 1964-75, fin. mgr., 1975-78, audit mgr., 1978-83; mgmt. cons. C.C. Comfort Cons., Dallas, 1983-86, Scottsdale, Ariz., 1992—; dir. compliance Litton Industries, Tempe, Ariz., 1986-92; fraud examiner Maricopa County Attorney's Office, Phoenix, Ariz., 1999—. Mem. Fed. Exec. Bd., Dallas, 1979-82, Intergovtl. Audit Forum, Dallas, 1979-82; co. rep. to Electronic Industries Assn., Washington, 1986-92, Machinery and Alied Products Inst., Washington, 1986-92; presenter seminars in field. Contbr. articles to profl. jours. Bd. dirs. Assn. Govt. Accts., 1983-84; res. dep. sheriff Sheriff's Dept. Dallas, 1976-83; pres. U. Tex.-Arlington Alumni Assn., 1984-85. Recipient Cert. of Merit Sheriff's Dept. Dallas, 1980, Best Tech. Article award Assn. Govt. Accts., 1979. Mem. ABA, AICPA, Soc. for Advancement of Mgmt. (bd. dirs. 1984-85), Nat. Contract Mgmt. Assn. (v.p. 1994-95, bd. dirs. 2000-02), Assn. Cert. Fraud Examiners (bd. dirs. 1994-95, 2003—, officer 2000-02). Avocations: travel, hiking, reading, teaching. Office: CC Comfort 3370 N Hayden Rd # 123 Scottsdale AZ 85251-6632

COMFORT, KENNETH A. court official; b. Nov. 9, 1945; m. Ellen Draper, Oct. 31, 1980; 4 children. BA in Polit. Sci. cum laude, Jacksonville (Ala.) State U., 1991, MPA, 1995. Enlisted man U.S. Army, 1965, advanced through grades to 1st sgt., 1984; chief evaluations, dir. stds. and evaluations U.S. Army Mil. Police Sch., Ft. McClellan, Ala., 1981—84; with Co. E, 787th Mil. Police Bn., Ft. McClellan, Ala., 1984-87; ops. sgt. mgr. Office Provost Marshal, U.S. Army Western Command, 57th Mil. Police, 25th Inf. Div., 1987-88; ret., 1990; divsn. mgr. ea. divsn. U.S. Bankruptcy Ct. for No. Dist. Ala., Anniston, 1991—. Decorated Meritorious Svc. medal, Army Commendation medal, Army Achievement medal, Nat. Def. Svc. medal; recipient award of operational merit (life saving) USCG, 1998. Mem. Am. Soc. Mil. Comptrs. (v.p. 1993-95), USCG Aux. (flotilla comdr. 2002), Calhoun County C. ov C., Pi Sigma Alpha. Avocations: boating, woodwork, geneaology, history. Office: US Bankruptcy Ct 914 Noble St Rm 201 Anniston AL 36201-5628 E-mail: chriscraft481@excite.com.

COMFORT, PAUL WILLIAM, county administrator, lawyer, writer; b. Norfolk, Va., June 10, 1965; s. William Michael and Emma Shirley Comfort; m. Lisa Amy Will, Nov. 21, 1987; children: Joseph, Amanda, Carrie, Daniel. AA, Chesapeake Coll., 1985; BA, U. Md., 1987, JD, 1996. Radio personality WCTR-AM 1530, Chestertown, Md., 1986—; tranp. coord. Queen Anne's County, Centreville, Md., 1987-94; mktg. mgr. Laidlaw Transit Svcs., Arlington, Va., 1994-98; v.p. nat. contracts Yellow Transp., Balt., 1998—, gen. mgr., 1999—2003; county adminstr. Queen Anne's County, Md., 2003—. Author: over 40 songs; musical artist (album) Bloodlove, 1986. Mem. Md. State Ctrl. Com., Centreville, 1986-90; pres. Gov.'s Youth Adv. Com., 1983-84; mem. Gov.'s Transp. Coord. Coun., 1998—; Rep. nominee Queen Anne's County State's Atty. Mem. Cmty. Transp. Assn. Am. (state del. 1991-94, Best Small Bus. Transit Sys. in Am. 1991), Transp. Assn. Md. (pres. 1991-94, Transit Sys. of the Yr. 1989, 92). Republican. Avocations: periodical writing, playing piano, singing, politics, public speaking. Office: The Liberty Bldg 107 N Liberty St Centreville MD 21617 E-mail: pcomfort@qac.org.

COMFORT, PRISCILLA MARIA, retired college official, human resources professional; b. Ft Dix, NJ, Feb. 20, 1947; d. Jennie Rita (Manes) McGuire; children: James, Aimee. BS, Montclair State Coll., 1969; MEd, Trenton State Coll., 1980. Cert. tchr., guidance counselor, NJ. Tchr. Burlington Twp. and City Sch., NJ, 1969-72; employment svc. interviewer NJ Dept. Labor and Industry, 1972-74; career devel. specialist, pers. tech. princ. NJ Dept. Civil Svc., Trenton, 1974—79; dir., asst., assoc. v.p. Human Resources Richard Stockton Coll. NJ, Pomona, 1979—2003, spl. asst. to pres., 2003—. Mem. Pres.'s adv. coun. NJ Gov.'s Task Force on Sexual Harassment, 1993, pers. adv. bd., human resources coun., 2002. Mem.: NJ CUPA-HR (life; life). Roman Catholic. Avocations: reading, travel, collecting bells, books, candles. Office: Richard Stockton Coll NJ Jim Leeds Rd Pomona NJ 08240

COMFORT, ROBERT DENNIS, lawyer; b. Camden, N.J., Nov. 22, 1950; s. Joseph Albert Sr. and Elizabeth (Rogers) C.; m. Loretta Masullo, Aug. 24, 1974; 1 child, Adam. AB summa cum laude, Princeton U., 1973; JD magna cum laude, Harvard U., 1976. Bar: Pa. 1976, N.J. 1977, U.S. Dist. Ct. N.J. 1977, U.S. Dist. Ct. (ea. dist.) Pa. 1977, U.S. Ct. Appeals (3d cir.) 1977, U.S. Tax Ct. 1978, U.S. Claims Ct. 1983. Law clk. to Hon. James Hunter III U.S. Ct. Appeals 3d Cir., Phila., 1976-77; law clk. to Lewis F. Powell Jr. U.S. Supreme Ct., Washington, 1977-78; assoc. Morgan, Lewis & Bockius, Phila., 1978-82, ptnr., 1982-2000; v.p. tax and tax policy Amazon.com, Seattle, 2000—. Adj. prof. U. Pa. Law Sch., Rutgers-Camden Law Sch. Mem. ABA, Phila. Bar Assn. (vice chair tax sect. 1990-92, chair 1993-94). Avocations: golf, camping, music, history, fishing. Office: Amazon com PO Box 81226 Seattle WA 98108-1300

COMFORT, WILLIAM TWYMAN, JR., banker; b. Ellsworth, Kans., Aug. 3, 1937; s. William Twyman and Leoti Dora (Shackleford) C.; m. Nathalie Pierrepont, June 6, 1964; children: Nathalie Pierrepont, William Twyman III, James Theodore, Stuyvesant Pierrepont. BA, Okla. U., 1959, LLB, 1961; LLM, NYU, 1964. With W.E. Hutton & Co., N.Y.C., 1962-73, ptnr., 1969-73, sr. v.p., 1973-74, Citibank, N.Y.C., 1974—; exec. dir. Citicorp Internat. Bank Ltd., London, 1976-78; chmn. bd. dirs. 399 Venture Ptnrs. Inc., Citigroup Venture Capital, Ltd. Chmn. bd. dirs. CourtSquare Capital Ltd.; adj. prof. Columbia Bus. Sch., N.Y.C.; bd. dirs. I-Flex (India), Flender AG (Germany); trustee The John A. Hartford Found., Inc. Trustee NYU Law Ctr. Found.; former trustee Pine Mano Coll., Chest nut Hill, Mass.; advisor to bd. dirs. Old Westbury (L.I.) Gardens. With U.S. Army, 1961. Mem. N.Y. Bar Assn., Okla. Bar Assn., Piping Rock Club (Locust Valley, N.Y.), Jupiter Island Club (Hobe Sound, Fla.). Home: 340 Duck Pond Rd Locust Valley NY 11560-2404 Office: 14th Fl 399 Park Ave New York NY 10022-4600

COMFORT, WILLIAM WISTAR, mathematics educator; b. Bryn Mawr, Pa., Apr. 19, 1933; s. Howard and Elizabeth (Webb) Comfort; m. Mary Constance Lyon, Mar. 30, 1957; children: Martha Wistar, Howard III. BA, Haverford Coll., 1954; MS, U. Wash., 1957, PhD, 1958; MA ad eundem gradum, Wesleyan U., Middletown, Conn., 1969. Tchg. asst., rsch. asst. U. Wash., Seattle, 1954-58; B. Peirce instr. Harvard U., Cambridge, Mass., 1958-61; asst. prof. U. Rochester, N.Y., 1961-65; assoc. prof. U. Mass., Amherst, 1965-67; prof. math. Wesleyan U., 1967—, Edward Burr Van Vleck prof. math., 1982—, chmn. dept., 1969-70, 80-82, 96-97. Vis prof Univ Ark, 1965, McGill Univ, Montreal, Canada, 1970—71, Univ Heidelberg, 1974, Istituto Matematico Leonida Tonelli, Pisa, Italy, 1974, Athens Univ, Greece, 1978, Univ Nacional Autonoma de Mex, 1983, Univ São Paolo, 1983, 99, Vrije Univ, Amsterdam, The Netherlands, 1984, 95, Technische Hochschule Darmstadt, Germany, 1991, Univ Jaume I Castellon, Spain, 1995. Author (with S Negreponti s): (book) The Theory of Ultrafilters, 1974, (books) Continuous Pseudometrics, 1975, (book) Chain Conditions in Topology, 1982; mem ed bd: Procs Am Math Soc, 1972—75; editor (managing ed), 1974—75; mem ed bd: Topology Procs, 1976—, Am Math Monthly, 1983—86, Karachi Jour Math, 1984—, Scientiae Mathematicae, 1992—, Topology and Its Applications, 1993—; contbr. articles to prof jours. Bd mgrs Haverford Col, 1971—74; trustee Ind Day Sch, Middlefield, Conn., 1972—75. Recipient Excellence-in-Teaching Award, Univ Rochester, 1966. Mem.: AAUP, Asn Concerned Scientists, Conn Acad Sci and Eng, Am Math Soc (coun 1972—75, 1982—93, assoc secy eastern region 1982—93), Math Asn Am, Phi Beta Kappa. Mem. Soc. Of Friends. Office: Wesleyan U Math Dept Middletown CT 06459 0001 Home: 3 Ball Ln Old Lyme CT 06371 E-mail: wcomfort@wesleyan.edu.

COMINGS, DAVID EDWARD, physician, medical genetics scientist; b. Beacon, N.Y., Mar. 8, 1935; s. Edward Walter and Jean (Rice) C.; m. Shirley Nelson, Aug. 9, 1958; children: Mark David, Scott Edward, Karen Jean.; m. Brenda Gursey, Mar. 20, 1982. Student, U. Ill., 1951-54; BS, Northwestern U., 1955, MD, 1958. Intern Cook County Hosp., Chgo., 1958-59, resident in internal medicine, 1959-62; fellow in med. genetics U. Wash., Seattle, 1964-66; dir. dept. med. genetics City of Hope Med. Ctr., Duarte, Calif., 1966—. Mem. genetics study sect. NIH, 1974-78; mem. sci. adv. bd. Hereditary Disease Found., 1975—, Nat. Found. March of Dimes, 1978-92. Author: Tourette Syndrome and Human Behavior, 1990, Search for the Tourette Syndrome and Human Behavior Genes, 1996, The Gene Bomb, 1996; editor: (with others) Molecular Human Cytogenetics, 1977; mem. editorial bd.: (with others) Cytogenetics and Cell genetics, 1979—; editor in chief Am. Jour. Human Genetics, 1978-86. Served with U.S. Army, 1962-64. NIH grantee, 1967— Mem. Assn. Am. Physicians, Am. Soc. Clin. Investigation, AAAS, Am. Soc. Human Genetics (dir. 1974-78, pres. 1988), Am. Soc. Cell Biology, Am. Fedn. Clin. Research, Western Soc. Clin. Research, Council Biology Editors. Office: City Hope Med Ctr 1500 Duarte Rd Duarte CA 91010-3000

COMINI, ALESSANDRA, art historian, educator; b. Winona, Minn., Nov. 24, 1934; d. Raiberto and Megan (Laird) C. BA, Barnard Coll., 1956; MA, U. Calif., Berkeley, 1964; PhD with distinction, Columbia U., 1969. Tchg. asst. U. Calif., Berkeley, 1964, vis. instr., 1967; preceptor Columbia U., 1965-66, 67-68, instr., 1968-69, asst. prof., 1969-74; vis. asst. prof. So. Methodist U., summers 1970, 72, assoc. prof. art history, 1974-75, prof., 1975—, univ. disting. prof., 1983—. Alfred Hodder resident humanist Princeton U., 1972-73; disting. vis. lectr. Oxford U., 1996; vis. asst. prof. Yale U., 1973; vis. humanist various univs.; lectr. in English, German and Italian; keynote spkr. Gewandhaus Symposia, Leipzig, Germany, 1983, 85, 87, 89, Mahler Internat Congress, Amsterdam, 1988, 95, Hamburg, 1989, Oxford, 1996, Montpellier, 1996, Internat. Mahler Fest, Boulder, Colo., 1998; featured spkr. Purchase, N.Y., 1989, Leningrad, 1990, Stockholm, 1991, Berlin, 1993, Bethoven Extravaganza, Milw., 1994, Schiele Symposium, Indpls., 1994, Helsinki, 1996, Schubertiads at Curtis Inst., Phila., Reed Coll., Oreg. and So. Meth. U., 1997, Santa Fe Opera, 1997, 98, 99, 2000, 01, 02, Mozart Internat. Symposium U. Dublin, Ireland, 1999, San Diego Mus., 1999, 2000, 01, 02, 03; panelist NEH Mus. and Pub. Programs, 1978—; vis. scholar Kalamazzoo Coll., Mich., 1999. Author: Schiele in Prison, 1973, Egon Schiele's Portraits, 1974 (Nat. Book award nominee 1975, reissued 1990, Charles Rufus Morey Book award 1975), Gustav Klimt, 1975, reissued 1986, 90, 93, also German, French and Dutch edit., Egon Schiele, 1976, reissued 1986, 94, also German, French and Dutch edits., The Fantastic Art of Vienna, 1978, The Changing Image of Beethoven, 1987, Egon Schiele: Nudes, 1995; contbg. author: World Impressionism, 1990, Käthe Kollwitz, 1992, Egon Schiele, 1994, Violetta and her Sisters, 1994, Salome, 1996, By a Finnish Fireside: An Evening with Akseli Gallen-Kallela and Gustav Mahler, 1997, The Visual Wagner, 1997, Irony and Gustav Mahler, 2000, Toys in Friend's Attic, 2001, Beethoven and His World, 2000; contbr. numerous articles to Stagebill, Arts Mag., English Nat. Opera, Chgo. Lyric Opera; also author various catalogue and book introductions, also book revs. for N.Y. Times, Women's Art Jour. Awarded Grand Decoration of Honor for svcs. to Republic of Austria, 1990; recipient Charles Rufus Morey Book award Coll. Art Assn. Am., 1976, Laural award AAUW, 1979; named Outstanding Prof., 1977, 79, 83, 85, 86, 87, 88, 90, 98, 99, 2000, 01, 02, Laurence Perrine prize Phi Beta Kappa Gamma of Tex., 2003; AAUW travel fellow, 1966-87; NEH grantee, 1975; named Meadows Disting. Tchg. Prof., 1986-87, Tchr./Scholar of Yr., United Meth. Ch., 1996. Mem. ASCAP, Nat. Mus. for Women in the Arts (nat. bd. 1997—), Coll. Art Assn. Am. (bd. dirs. 1980-84), Women's Caucus for Art (bd. dirs. 1974-78, Life Achievement award 1995, Tex. Women's Hall of Fame 2002), Tex. Inst. Letters. Democrat. Home: 2900 McFarlin Blvd Dallas TX 75205-1920 Office: So Meth U Divsn Art History Dallas TX 75275

COMISKY, HOPE A. lawyer; b. Phila., Apr. 23, 1953; married; three children. BA with distinction, Cornell U., 1974; JD, U. Pa., 1977. Bar: Pa. 1977, U.S. Dist. Ct. (ea. dist.) Pa. 1978, D.C. 1979, U.S. Ct. Appeals (3d cir.) 1979, U.S. Supreme Ct. 1987, U.S. Dist. Ct. (mid. dist.) Pa. 1991, N.Y. 1993. Law clerk ea dist. U.S. Dist. Ct., Pa., 1977-78; assoc. Dilworth, Paxson, Kalish & Kauffman, Phila., 1978-84, ptnr., 1985-91, Anderson Kill & Olick, P.C., Phila., 1992-98, mng. ptnr. Phila. office, 1995-98; ptnr. labor & employment dept. Office of Pepper Hamilton, 1998—. Spkr. in field. Contbr. articles to profl. jours. Bd. dirs. Phila. Sch., 1989—, pres. 2001—; hon. bd. dirs. Fedn. Day Care Svcs., 1991-97, mem. exec. com., chmn. pers. practices com., 1985-91; bd. dirs. Ctr. for Literacy, 1996—; chmn. pers. com. 2000—, bd. dirs. Women's Law Project, 1998—; mem. Phila. Regional Employment Adv. Com. Am. Arbitration Assn., 1996. Mem. Am. Arbitration Assn. (comml. and employment arbitrator), Phi Beta Kappa, Mortar Bd. Office: Pepper Hamilton LLP 3000 Two Logan Sq 18th & Arch Sts Philadelphia PA 19103-2799

COMISKY, IAN MICHAEL, lawyer; b. Phila., Feb. 5, 1950; s. Marvin and Goldye (Elving) C. BS magna cum laude, U. Pa., 1971, JD, 1974; LLM in Taxation, U. Miami, 1984. Bar: Pa. 1974, Fla. 1976, D.C. 1976, U.S. Ct. Appeals (3rd and 11th cirs.), U.S. Ct. Claims, U.S. Tax Ct., U.S. Supreme Ct., U.S. Dist. Ct. (ea. dist.) Pa., U.S. Dist. Ct. (so. dist.) Fla., U.S. Dist. Ct. (mid. dist.) Fla. Law clk. to Hon. Alfred Luongo Jr. U.S. Dist. Ct. Pa., Phila., 1974-75; asst. dist. atty. Office of Dist. Atty., Philadelphia County, Phila., 1975-78; asst. U.S. atty. So. Dist. Fla., 1978-80; spl. asst. Office of Dist. Atty., So. Dist. Fla., 1980; ptnr., comml. litigation and white collar crime Blank Rome LLP, Phila., 1980—. Presenter various profl. confs. seminars, 1981—; guest TV and radio programs, 1990. Co-author: Tax Fraud and Evasion (2 vols.); contbr. articles to profl. pubs. Sec. Mann Music Ctr. Mem. ABA (past chmn. civil and criminal tax penalties com. tax sect., mem. CLE com. tax sect., vice chmn. COGS spl. projects, mem. various coms. criminal justice and litig. sect.), ATLA, Am. Law Inst., Am. Coll. Tax Counsel, Fed. Bar Assn., Pa. Bar Assn., Fla. Bar Assn. (bd. govs. 1998), D.C. Bar Assn., Phila. Bar Assn., Assn. Fellows and Legal Scholars or Ctr. for Internat. Legal Studies (hon.). Avocations: sailing, gardening, Karate, jogging.

COMISO, JOSEFINO CACAS, research scientist; b. Narvacan, The Philippines, Sept. 21, 1940, came to U.S., 1964; s. Severino Cacho and Silvestra (Cacas) C.; m. Diana Parreñas Jimenez, June 27, 1970; children: Glen Arnold, David Arnel, Melissa Jane. BS in Physics, U. The Philippines, Quezon City, 1962; MS in Physics, Fla. State U., 1966; PhD in Physics, UCLA, 1972. Scientist Philippine Atomic Rsch. Ctr., Quezon City, 1962-63; instr. U. The Philippines, Quezon City, 1963-64; asst. rsch. physicist UCLA, 1972-73; rsch. assoc. U. Va., Charlottesville, 1973-77; sr. mem. tech. staff Computer Scis. Corp., Greenbelt, Md., 1977-79; phys. scientist Goddard Space Flight Ctr. NASA, Greenbelt, 1979—. Co-author: Arctic & Antarctic Sea Ice, 1992; contbr. articles to profl. jours. Pres. Philippine-Am. Acad. Sci. and Engrs., Washington, 1987. Mem. Am. Geophys. Union, Am. Phys. Soc., Internat. Glaciol. Soc., Com. on Polar Meteorology and Oceanography, Electromagnetics Acad. Achievements include space based assessments and studies of surface temperatures, sea ice distributions, heat and salinity fluxes in polynyas, and phytoplank-

ton blooms in the polar regions and the development of satellite sensor algorithms. Home: 11013 Elon Dr Bowie MD 20720-3509 Office: NASA/GSFC Lab for Hydrospheric Processes Code 971 Greenbelt MD 20771-0001 E-mail: comiso@joey.gsfc.nasa.gov.

COMISSIONA, SERGIU, conductor; b. Bucharest, Romania, June 16, 1928; came to U.S., 1969; naturalized, 1976; s. Isaac and Jean L. (Haufrecht) C.; m. Robinne Florin, July 16, 1949. Studied with Constantin Silvestri and Eduoard Lindenberg, 1928; ed. music conservatoire, Bucharest; Mus.D. (hon.), Peabody Conservatory Music, 1972; LHD (hon.), Loyola Coll., Balt., 1973, Towson State U., 1980; D.F.A. (hon.), Washington Coll., Chestertown, Md., 1980, Western Md. Coll., 1977, U. Md., 1981, Johns Hopkins U., 1982; PhD (hon.), U. Bucharest, 2003. Operatic conducting debut in Faust at Sibiu, 1945, conducting debut Bucharest Opera Orch., 1946; violinist Bucharest Radio Quartet, 1946, Rumanian State Ensemble Orch., 1947, asst. condr., 1948, music dir., 1950-55; prin. condr. Rumanian State Opera, 1955-59, Asian Youth Orch., 1995; founder, condr. Ramat Gan (Israel) Chamber Orch., 1960-67; music dir. Haifa (Israel) Symphony, 1960-66, Israel Chamber Orch., 1960-67, Goteburg (Sweden) Symphony Orch., 1966-67, Balt. Symphony Orch., 1969-84, condr. laureate, 1995—; music dir. Houston Symphony Orch., 1983-88, N.Y.C. Opera, 1987-89, Helsinki Philharm. Orch. (also chief condr.), 1990-93, Vancouver Symphony, 1990—. Orquesta Sinfonica de RTVE, Madrid, 1990-97, Asian Youth Orch., 1995-2001, Vancouver Symphony Orch., 1990-2000; Am. debut with Phil. Orch., 1965; mus. adviser, condr. No. Ireland Orch., 1967-68; artistic dir. Temple U. Music Festival, 1976-80, music advisor, prin. condr., 1977-80; music dir., prin. condr. Chautauqua Symphony Orch. Summer Festival, 1976-80; music adviser Am. Symphony Orch., 1978-82; artistic advisor Houston Symphony Orch., 1980-83; permanent guest condr. Radio Philharm. Orch. of Netherlands, 1982-83, chief condr., 1983-89; with London Symphony, Stockholm Philharm., Swedish Radio Orch.; founder Joseph Meyerhoff Hall, Balt. Decorated Order Merit 2d Class Rumania; winner internat. competition for young condrs. Besancon, France, 1954; recipient Gold medal award City of Goteborg, 1973, Ditson Condr.'s award Columbia U., 1979. Mem.: Royal Swedish Acad. Music (hon.), Nat. Order of Romanian Star (comdr. 2003), Knight Order Arts Letters (France). Home: ICM Artists Classical Divsn 10 W 66th St Apt 20F New York NY 10023-6210 Office: Hemsing Assocs c/o Josephine Hemsing 401 E 80th St Apt 14H New York NY 10021-0650.

COMITAS, LAMBROS, anthropologist, educator; b. N.Y.C., Sept. 29, 1927; s. Dennis and Magdaline (Livanis) C.; m. Irene Mousouris. AB, Columbia U., 1948, PhD in Anthropology, 1962. Instr. anthropology Columbia U., N.Y.C., 1958-61, asst. prof., 1962-64, assoc. prof. anthropology and edn. Tchrs. Coll., 1965-67, prof., 1967-87, Gardner Cowles prof. anthropology and edn., 1988—, dir. div. philosophy, social scis. and edn., 1979-96, dir. Inst. Latin Am. and Iberian studies, 1977-84; dir. Rsch. Inst. study of man, 1985-2001; adminstr. Ruth Landes Meml. Rsch. Fund, 1991—; pres. Comitas Inst. Anthrop. Study, 2003—. Mem. drug abuse, clin., behavioral and psychosocial rsch. rev. com. Nat. Inst. Drug Abuse, 1977-81. Author books and articles in field. With U.S. Army, 1946-47. Office Edn. fellow, 1968-69, Guggenheim fellow, 1971-72; Fulbright grantee, 1957-58, Nat. Inst. Drug Abuse grantee, 1975-79. Mem. Soc. Applied Anthropology (pres. 1970-71), Am. Anthrop. Assn., Am. Ethnol. Soc., Nat. Acad. Edn. (chmn. com. anthropology and edn.), N.Y. Acad. Scis. Home: 1107 5th Ave New York NY 10128-0145 Office: Teachers Coll Columbia U New York NY 10027 E-mail: lc137@columbia.edu.

COMITER, CRAIG VANCE, urologist; b. N.Y.C., July 6, 1966; s. Paul and Marylyn Comiter; m. Linda Fresco, June 14, 1992; children: Jacqueline, Laurel. BA, Harvard Coll., 1988; MD, Harvard Med. Sch., 1992. Diplomate Am. Bd. Urology. Assoc. prof. Urology U. Ariz., Tucson, 1999—. Instr. Ob-Gyn. U. Ariz., Tucson, 2000—, chief Dept. Urology, 2002—. Author: Multiple Manuscripts, 1996—2002. Grantee, NIH, 2001—02. Mem.: Am. Urologic Soc., Internat. Continence Soc. Office: Univ Ariz Med Ctr 1501 N Campbell Ave PO Box 245077 Tucson AZ 85724

COMITO, FRANK JOSEPH, lawyer; b. Des Moines, Sept. 8, 1954; s. William J. and Joanne E. (Porto) C.; m. Margaret Katherine Beiter, Aug. 23, 1975. BS, Iowa State U., 1976; JD, Georgetown U., 1979. Bar: Iowa 1979, U.S. Dist. Ct. (no. and so. dists.) Iowa 1980, U.S. Tax Ct. 1984. Clk. to presiding justice Md. Ct. of Appeals, Annapolis, 1978-80; sole practice Carroll, Iowa, 1980—87; ptnr. Nei, Minnich, Comito & Neu, P.C., 1987—. Asst. county atty. Carroll County, 1981-83, magistrate, 1983-99. Pres. Carroll Arts Coun., 1982. Mem. ABA, Iowa State Bar Assn., Carroll County Bar Assn. (pres. 1984-89). Democrat. Roman Catholic. Office: Neu Minnich Comito & Neu PC 721 N Main St Carroll IA 51401-2327 E-mail: fjcomito@yahoo.com.

COMMANDAY, PETER MARTIN, educator; b. N.Y.C., Oct. 4, 1932; s. Joseph and Dorothy (Kaplan) C.; m. Susan Nancy Shair, Apr. 28, 1962; children: Lisa, Clifford. BS in Graphic Arts, Rochester Inst. Tech., 1959; MS in Adminstrv./Supr. Edn., Manhattan Coll., Riverdale, N.Y., 1967. Cert. peacemaking instr.; cert. crisis intervenor; cert. peace officer. Dean, tchr. N.Y.C. Bd. Edn., South Bronx, N.Y., 1964-79, coord. profl. tng. divsn. sch. safety, 1979-91; peacemaker, educator, dir. Commanday Peacemaking Inst. Corp., Congers, N.Y., 1991—; cons. and trainer on safety and crisis intervention Rockland County Office of Aging, Family Shelter of Rockland County. Calvary Christian Acad., Ft. Lauderdale, Fla.; cons. crisis intervention, resolution, prevention. Author: Peacemaking: The Management of Confrontation, 1979, Crisis Without Violence, 1980; appreared on Today Show, Geraldo Rivera Show, Phil Donahue Show, 20-20 Show, UN Radio. Trustee Solomon Schechter Sch., Rockland County, N.Y., 1972-84. With USAF, 1952-56. Recipient PONY award Fed. Govt., 1967. Home and Office: Commanday Peacemaking Inst 7 Greenfield Ter Congers NY 10920-2606

COMMANDAY, SUE NANCY SHAIR, English language educator; b. N.Y.C., Oct. 9, 1938; d. Leonard Allan and Sally (Bernstein) Shair; m. Peter Martin Commanday, Apr. 28, 1962; children: Lisa Robin Commanday Durow, Clifford Martin Commanday. BA cum laude, Syracuse U., 1959; MA with honors, Columbia U., N.Y.C., 1960; PhD with honors, NYU, N.Y.C., 1973. Adj. instr. English Rockland C.C., Suffern, N.Y., 1968-75, asst. coord., then coord. Israel and Judaic studies, 1975-93, coord. telecourses and distance learning, 1978-94, prof. English, 1994—, pres. faculty senate, 1999—2003, chair dept. English, 2000—. Sec., exec. com. faculty coun. SUNY, 1993-94; bd. trustees Consortium Distance Learning, N.Y.-N.J., 1990-94; planning and evaluation coms. Annenberg-funded telecourses; presenter and cons. in field. Contbr. articles on Henry James, English composition, internat. edn., telecourse and distance learning to profl. jours. Founding mem., sec. Solomon Schechter PTA, 1970-75; exec. com. Jewish Family Svc., 1993-95; trustee Jewish Fedn. Rockland County, 1985-95, exec. com., chair long-term planning, 1994-95; women's commn. Rockland County Legislature, 1987—, editor newsletter, editor com. reports, 1988—; mem. area Dem. com., N.Y.C., 1994-2001; co-coord. Gov. Mario Cuomo campaign in Rockland County, 1994; campaign writer N.Y. State Assemblyman Sam Colman, 1994, local legislator Harriet Cornell, Clarkstown, 1991-94; pub. rels. dir., writer for campaign of Bob Axelrod, Rockland County Legislature, 1997, others. Recipient SUNY Chancellor's award for Profl. Svc., 1991, Svc. to Students with Disabilities award, 1997; award for tchg. Nat. Inst. Staff and Orgnl. Devel., 1999. Mem. Delta Tau Kappa, Kappa Delta Pi, Pi Lambda Theta, Rho Delta Pi, Phi Kappa Phi, Eta Pi Upsilon. Avocations: knitting, beading, gardening. Office: Rockland Cmty Coll 145 College Rd Suffern NY 10901-3611

COMMANDER, CHARLES EDWARD, lawyer, real estate consultant; b. Jacksonville, Fla., Aug. 17, 1940; s. Charles Edward Jr. and Eleanor (Wood) C.; m. Victoria Coxe, Aug. 10, 1963; children: Eleanor, Charles IV, Christopher. BS in Commerce, Washington & Lee U., 1962; JD, U. Fla., 1965. Bar: Fla. 1966. Atty., assoc. ptnr. Mahoney, Hadlow, Chambers and Adams, Jacksonville, 1966-73; pres. Barnett Winston Properties, Jacksonville, 1973-74; founding ptnr. Commander, Legler, Werber, Dawes, Sadler & Howell, Jacksonville, 1974-91; ptnr., mgmt. com. Foley & Lardner, 1991—. Cons. First Union Nat. Bank Fla., Jacksonville, 1990-95; chmn. bd. dirs. First Nat. Bank, Jacksonville, 1979-84; chmn. Property Investment Svcs., Inc., Jacksonville, 1974—; bd. Alliance Capital Partners, First Alliance Bank FSB; trustee Builders Investment Group, King of Prussia, Pa. and Fullerton, Calif., 1977-80; dir. Koger Equity Inc., 1993-95, Computer Power, 1974-79, 86-92; bd. dir. U. Fla. Law Ctr. Assn. Editor Law Review U. Fla., 1964-65; reporter Fla. Law Revision Coun., 1975-76. Trustee The Bolles Sch., Jacksonville, 1980-90; pres. U. No. Fla. Found., 1994-97, Cummer Gallery of Art, 1993—2002; bd. dirs. Jacksonville Housing Authority, 1995—2003; vice chmn. Mus. Sci. and History, Jacksonville, 1968-73, Jacksonville Zool. Soc., 1972-76; pres. bd. dirs. The River Club, Jacksonville, 1977-84. Episcopalian. Avocations: fishing, hunting, boating, farming. Office: Foley & Lardner The Greenleaf Bldg PO Box 240 Jacksonville FL 32201-0240 E-mail: ccommander@foleylaw.com.

COMMIRE, ANNE, playwright, writer, editor; b. Wyandotte, Mich., Aug. 11, 1939; BS, Eastern Mich. U., 1961; postgrad., Wayne State U., NYU. Author: (plays) Shay, 1973, Transatlantic Bridge, 1977, Put Them All Together, 1978, Sunday's Red, 1982, Melody Sisters, 1983, Starting Monday, 1988; author: (with Mariette Hartley) (book) Breaking the Silence, 1990; editor: Something About the Author, 1970—90, Yesterday's Authors of Books for Children, 1977—78, Historic World Leaders, 1994, Women in World History: A Biographical Encyclopedia, 1999—2002 (Dartmouth medal, 2002). Recipient Eugene O'Neill Theatre award, 1973, 1978, 1988; grantee, Creative Artists Program, 1975; playwriting grant, Rockefeller Found., 1979. Mem.: PEN, Writers Guild Am., Dramatists Guild, Authors Guild. Home: 11 Stanton St Waterford CT 06385-1400

COMMONER, BARRY, biologist, educator; b. Bklyn., May 28, 1917; s. Isidore and Goldie (Yarmolinsky) C.; m. Lisa Feiner, 1980; children by previous marriage: Lucy Alison, Frederic Gordon. AB with honors, Columbia U., 1937; MA, Harvard U., 1938, PhD, 1941; DSc (hon.), Hahnemann Med. Coll., 1963; D.Sc. (hon.), Clark U., 1967, Grinnell Coll., 1968, Lehigh U., 1969, Williams Coll., 1970, Ripon Coll., 1971, Colgate U., 1972, Cleve. State U., 1980; LL.D. (hon.), U. Calif., 1974, Grinnell Coll., 1981; D.Sc. (hon.), St. Lawrence U., 1988; D.H.L. (hon.), Lowell U., 1990; DSc (hon.), Conn. Coll., 1992, Queens Coll., 2001. Asst. biology Harvard, 1938-40; instr. biology Queens Coll., 1940-42; asso. editor Sci. Illus., 1946-47; asso. prof. plant physiology Washington U., St. Louis, 1947-53, prof., 1953-76, chmn. dept. botany, 1965-69; dir. Washington U. (Center for the Biology of Natural Systems), 1965-81, Univ. prof. environ. sci., 1976-81; prof. dept. geology Queens Coll., Flushing, N.Y., 1981-87, prof. emeritus, 1987—, dir. Center for the Biology of Natural Systems, 1981-2000, sr. scientist, 2000—. Vis. prof. cmty. health Albert Einstein Coll. of Medicine, N.Y.C., 1981-87, disting. univ. prof. indsl. policy U. Mass., Lowell, 1992-95; pres. St. Louis Com. for Nuclear Info., 1965-66, bd. dirs., 1966; mem. Nat. Tb Commn. on Air Conservation, 1966-68; bd. dirs. Scientists Inst. Pub. Info., 1963—, co-chmn., 1967-69, chmn., 1969-78, chmn. exec. com., 1978—; chmn. spl. cons. group sonic boom Dept. Interior, 1967-68; mem. adv. coun. on environ. edn. Office Edn., HEW, 1971; mem. internat. sponsoring com. Chaim Weizmann Centenary Celebration, 1974-75; mem. adv. com. Coalition Health Communities, 1975; mem. sec.'s adv. coun. Dept. Commerce, 1976; mem. sci. adv. coun. on dioxin Vietnam Vets. Am. Found., 1985—; mem. sci. adv. N.Y. State Com. on Sci. and Tech., 1981—; mem. adv. bd. Com. for Responsible Genetics, 1983—. Author: Science and Survival, 1966, The Closing Circle, 1971 (Phi Beta Kappa award), (Internat. prize City of Cervia, Italy), La Technologia del Profitto, 1973, The Poverty of Power, 1976 (Premio Iglesias award, Sardinia, Italy 1978), Ecologia e Lotte Sociali, 1976, l'energia alternativa, 1978, The Politics of Energy, 1979 (Premio Iglesias award 1982), Se Scoppia La Bomba, 1984, Il Cerchio Da Chiudere, 1986, Making Peace With the Planet, 1990; editorial bd. World Book Ency., 1968-73, Environment mag., 1977; mem. adv. bd. Science Year, 1967-72; editorial adv. bd. Hon. Chemosphere, from 1972; bd. sponsors In These Times, 1976— . Bd. cons. experts Rachel Carson Trust for Living Environment, 1967— ; adv. com. Center for Devel. Policy, 1978; mem. bd. Univs. Nat. Anti-War Fund; adv. bd. Fund for Peace, 1978, Citizens Party candidate for pres. of U.S., 1980. Served to lt. USNR, 1942-46. Recipient Newcomb Cleveland prize AAAS, 1953; 1st Humanist award Internat. Humanist and Ethical Union, 1970; medal AIA, 1979; decorated comdr. Order of Merit Italy, 1977 Fellow AAAS (chmn. com. sci. in promotion of human welfare 1958-65, dir. 1967-74, chmn. com. on environ. alterations 1969-72), Am. Sch. Health Assn. (hon.); mem. Soc. Biol. Chemists, Soc. Gen. Physiologists, Am. Soc. Plant Physiologists, Sierra Club, Nat. Parks Assn. (trustee 1968-70), Soil Assn. Eng. (hon. life v.p.), Am. Chem. Soc., Am. Soc. Biol. Chemists, Fedn. Am. Scientists, Ecol. Soc. Am., Inst. Environmental Edn. (trustee), Phi Beta Kappa, Sigma Xi. Office: Queens Coll Ctr for Biol Natural Systems Flushing NY 11367 E-mail: commoner@cbns.qc.edu.

COMP, PHILIP CINNAMON, medical researcher; b. Kewanee, Ill., Feb. 28, 1945; s. Franklin Howard and Alberta (Cinnamon) C.; m. Carol Lee Winter, May 11, 1974; children: Vanessa Cinnamon, Justin Philip, Aubrie Elizabeth. BA, Reed Coll., 1967; MD, U. Wash., 1971; PhD, U. Okla., 1978. Intern, then resident U. Pa. Hosp., Phila., 1971-74; fellow allergy sect. U. Okla. Health Sci. Ctr., Oklahoma City, 1974-76, asst. prof. medicine, 1976-82, assoc. prof. medicine, 1982-88, prof. medicine, 1988—, dir. thrombosis/coagulant lab., 1979—99, dir. gen. clin. rsch. ctr., 2000—; attending physician med. svc. VA Med. Ctr., Oklahoma City, 1976—, assoc. chief of staff rsch., 1992—; dir. Adult sect. Okla. Comprehensive Hemophilia Treatment Ctr., Oklahoma City, 1980—. Mem. cardiovasc. biology rsch. program Okla. Med. Resident Found., Oklahoma City, 1988—; program dir. Gen. Clin. Rsch. Ctr., 2000—. Avocations: amateur mycology, breadmaking. Office: VA Med Ctr 921 NE 13th St (151) Oklahoma City OK 73104

COMPAGNON, ANTOINE MARCEL, French language educator; b. Brussels, July 20, 1950; came to U.S., 1985; s. Jean and Jacqueline (Terlinden) C. Ecole, Nat. des Ponts et Chaussees, Paris, 1975; D es Lettres, U. Paris VII, 1985. Rsch. attache Centre Nat. de la Recherche Scientifique, Paris, 1975-78; lectr. Ecole Poly., Paris, 1978-85, French Inst., London, 1980-81, U. Rouen, France, 1981-85; prof. Columbia U., N.Y.C., 1985—, Blanche W. Knopf prof., 1991—; vis. prof. U. Pa., Phila., 1986, 90; prof. U. Le Mans, France, 1989-90, U. Paris, Sorbonne, 1994—. Author: La Seconde Main, 1979, Ferragosto, 1985, Proust entre deux Siecles, 1989; editor: Marcel Proust, Sodome et Gomorrhe, 1988. Fellowship Found. Thiers, 1975-78, Guggenheim Found., 1988, All Souls Coll., Oxford U., 1994. Mem. Am. Acad. Arts and Scis. Office: Columbia U 517 Philosophy Hall New York NY 10027 E-mail: amc6@columbia.edu.

COMPAIN, RITA, librarian; b. N.Y.C., Dec. 4, 1926; d. Benjamin and Sara (Modell) Romer; m. Ernest A. Compain, Apr. 17, 1948 (div. 1987); children: Michael, Daniel, Andrew. BS, CUNY, 1947; MLS, L.I. U., 1963; Profl. Dipl., St. John's U., N.Y.C., 1975; postgrad., Columbia U., 1969-70, Lang. & Lit. Inst. Genosee, 1985. Children's librarian Bklyn. Pub. Library, 1947-49; library coordinator Oceanside (N.Y.) pub. schs., 1959-61; librarian Franklin Sq. (N.Y.) pub. schs., 1961-71; staff developer BOCES Nassau, Jericho, N.Y., 1974-76, BOCES Ulster County, N.Y., 1992-93; serials librarian Am. Mus. Natural History, N.Y.C., 1977-79; library cons. Rita Compain Agy., N.Y.C., 1980-85; project dir. "Open Sesame" Am. Reading Council, N.Y.C., 1985-88; staff developer library media Kingston (N.Y.) pub. schs., 1988-93. Asst. prof. L.I. U., Greenvale, 1969-75; libr. cons. Great Neck Pub. Schs., 1975-76; adj. prof. SUNY, New Paltz, 1988-94, U. South Fla., Sarasota, 1996-99; ednl. cons.; lectr. in field; mem. com. nassau county Jail Libr. Pilot Program, East Meadow, 1979. Contbg. author: Open Sesame Guide to Implementation, 1987; contbg. author, dir. video: Teacher Training Film, 1986; author: New Connections: An Integrated Approach to Literacy, 1994, Giants a Thematic Guide, 1992. Recipient Educator award, Young Playwrights Festival, 2001, 2002. Mem. Nassau-Suffolk Sch. Libr. Assn. (pres. 1969-70), Amnesty Internat., Delta Kappa Gamma. Avocations: tennis, golf, travel. Home: 7742 Whitebridge Gln University Park FL 34201-2244

COMPANS, RICHARD W. microbiology educator; b. Syracuse, N.Y., Sept. 15, 1940; m. Marian Merly Compans. BA magna cum laude, Kalamazoo Coll., 1963; PhD, Rockefeller U., 1968. Asst. prof. The Rockefeller U., 1969-73, assoc. prof., 1973-75; prof. dept. microbiology The U. Ala., Birmingham, 1975-92, prof. dept. biochemistry, 1985-92; prof., chmn. dept. microbiology and immunology Emory U., 1992—. Guest investigator Inst. Cancer Rsch., Villejuif, France, 1968; hon. fellow John Curtin Sch. Med. Rsch., Canberra, Australia, 1968-69; vis. scientist Nat. Inst. Med. Rsch., Mill Hill, U.K., 1998-99; vis. investigator Scripps Clinic and Rsch. Found., 1982; vis. prof. U. Geneva, 1988-89, U. Marburg, Germany, 1999; numerous univ. appointments including sr. scientist Cancer Ctr., U. Ala., 1975-92; dir. Electron Microscope Core Facility, 1975-92dir. Molecular Cell Biology Grad. Program, 1982-92, others; mem. various virology task forces. Editor: Virus Research, 1983—2002; mem. editl. bd. Jour. Gen. Virology, 1972—77, Jour. Virology, 1974—82, 1991—94, Intervirology, 1974—90, Virology, 1974—76, 1992—, CRC Handbook Series in Clin. Lab. Sci., Archives of Virology, 1980—83, Jour. Biol. Chemistry, 1983—88, Current Topics Microbiology and Immunology, 1985—; contbr. numerous articles to profl. jours. Recipient Wright A. Gardner award Ala. Acad. Scis., 1988, Alexander von Humboldt Rsch. award, 1999; grantee NIH, 1972—, others. Mem. Am. Acad. Microbiology, Am. Soc. Virology, Am. Soc. Biol. Chemists, Am. Soc. Cell Biology, Am. Assn. Immunologists, Soc. Gen. Microbiology, Am. Soc. Microbiology, Soc. Mucosal Immunology, Phi Beta Kappa. Office: Emory U Sch Med Dept Micro & Immunology Rm 3001 1510 Clifton Rd NE Atlanta GA 30322-4218 E-mail: rcompan@emory.edu.

COMPANYS, YOSEM EDUARDO, research scientist; b. San Juan, PR, Nov. 24, 1974; s. Jose Maria Companys and Doris Feliciano. BA in econ., Yale U., 1996; MPA in econ. devel., Harvard U., 2001; pre-doctoral in policy and strategy, Stanford U., 2001—. Rsch. scientist Gen. Motors, Warren, Mich., 2002; assoc. Goldman Sachs, London, 2000; acting brand mgr. Procter & Gamble, San Juan, PR, 1996—99; fin. analyst Merrill Lynch, NYC, 1995. Founder & co-chmn. Devel. Venture Capital Profl. Interest Coun., Cambridge, Mass., 2000—01; instr. Jr. Achievement, San Juan, PR, 1996—97; bd. of directors Casa Cultural Julia de Burgos, New Haven, 1994—96; founder & chmn. Latino Heritage Month, New Haven, 1995—96, Latino Heritage Festival, New Haven, 1995—96; dir. Gov. of PR Reception Com., New Haven, Hartford & Bridgeport, 1995—96. Recipient Julia de Burgos Leadership award, Yale U., 1996, Casa Otonal Leadership award, City of New Haven, 1996; Ford fellow, NRC, 2001—, 3D fellow, Stanford U., 2001—, Truman scholar, Harry S. Truman Found., 1996. Mem.: Assn. for the Study of the Cuban Economy, Am. Econ. Assn., INFORMS, Am. Sociol. Assn., Acad. of Mgmt., Nat. Soc. of Hispanic MBAs. Catholic. Home: 850 Roble Ave Apt B Menlo Park CA 94025 Office: Stanford University Terman Engineering Bldg Suite 425 Stanford CA 94305 Personal E-mail: ycompanys@hotmail.com.

COMPER, TONY, banker; b. Toronto, Ont., Can., Apr. 24, 1945; m. Elizabeth Comper. BA in English, U. Toronto, 1966; DHL (hon.), Mt. St. Vincent U. With Bank of Montreal, 1967—, with ops. and sys. group, 1971-82, sr. v.p. personal banking, 1982, sr. v.p., sr. ops. officer treasury group, 1982-84, sr. v.p., mgr. London br., 1984-86, sr. v.p., sr. mktg. officer corp. and govt. banking, 1986-87, exec. v.p. ops., 1987-89, pres., chief gen. mgr., COO, 1989-90, pres., COO, 1990-99, pres., CEO, 1999, chmn., CEO, 1999—, also bd. dirs., now CEO. Bd. dirs. Bank of Montreal and its subs., Harris Bankcorp, Inc., Harris Trust and Savs. Bank, BMO Nesbitt Burns Inc. Bd. dirs. C.D. Howe Inst., BMO Nesbitt Burns Inc., C.D. Howe Meml. Found., Catalyst, N.Y., Can. Club Toronto; hon. chair bd. govs. Yee Hong Ctr Geriatric Care; chair Capital Campaign U. Toronto; past chair governing coun. U. Toronto; past vice-chair St. Michael's Hosp. Recipient Human Rels. award Can. Coun. Christians and Jews, 1998. Avocations: golf, classical music, theater, art. Office: Bank Montréal 1st Canadian Pl 100 W King St Toronto ON Canada M5X 1A1

COMPONATION, PAUL JOSEPH, industrial and systems engineer, educator; b. Glendale, W.Va., June 9, 1959; s. Paul Joseph and Jean C.; m. Kimberly Marie LaPlante, Dec. 26, 1981; children: Justin, Seth, Ian. BS in industrial engr., W. Va. Univ., Morgantown, 1982; MS in mgmt., Troy State Univ., 1987; PhD in industrial engr., W. Va. Univ., 1995. Engring. officer U.S. Air Force, 1983-89; engr. Sonoco Products Co., Orlando, Fla., 1991-92; instr. W.Va. Univ., Morgantown, 1992-95; resident assoc. Ctr. for Engreprenurial Studies & Devel., Morgantown, W.Va., 1995-96; asst. prof. indsl. engr. Univ. Ala., Huntsville, 1996—2002, assoc. prof. indsl. engring., 2002—; sys. engring. resident rschr. NASA-MSFC, Huntsville, 2001—. Dir. Internat. Coun. Systems Engrs. Contbr. articles to profl. jours. Capt. U.S. Air Force, 1983-89. Decorated Air Force Commendation Medal, 1985; named Outstanding Young Men of Am., 1987, 88. Mem. Inst. Indsl. Engrs. (sr., Indsl. Engr. of Yr. 2000), Internat. Coun. of Systems Engrs. Office: Univ Ala Iseem Dept Th N134 Huntsville AL 35899-0001

COMPTE, MARIA EMILIA, physician, educator, administrator; b. Buenos Aires, Jan. 17, 1958; arrived in U.S., 1989, naturalized, 2002; d. Alberto J. Compte and Hilda M. Hostansky. MD, U. of Buenos Aires, 1984; MPH, TM, Tulane U., 1992. Cert. in tropical medicine and travel health Am. Soc. of Tropical Medicine and Hygiene, 2000, Ednl. Commn. for Fgn. Med. Graduates, 1995, lic. physician U.S. Med. Licensing Exam. Bd., 1997, Ministry of Health, Argentina, 1984. Pvt. med. practice, Buenos Aires, 1985—87; med. dir. & program adminstr. Dooley Found. -Intermed, Honduras, 1988—91; dep. med. dir. Item Home-Hosp. Corp., Buenos Aires, 1993—94; vol. program dir. Dooley Found.-Intermed Internat., N.Y.C., 1994—; dir. of cmty. medicine Mercy Coll., Dobbs Ferry, NY, 1998—, asst. prof., 1998—. Bd. dir. Intermed Internat.; adj. assoc. prof. St. John's U., N.Y.C., 1998—2000, CUNY, N.Y.C., 1998—2001, Adelphi U., Garden City, NY, 1999. Recipient Excellence in Vol. Med. Work award, Friends of the Americas, 1991; fellow, N.Y. Acad. of Medicine, 2002. Mem.: AAUP, APHA, Argentine-Am. Med. Soc., The Global Health Coun., Am. Com. on Clin. Tropical Medicine & Traveler's Health, Am. Soc. of Tropical Medicine & Hygiene, Soc. of Tchrs. of Family Medicine (assoc.), Infectious Disease Soc. of Am. (assoc.), Tulane Med. Alumni Assn., The Cornell Club, Tulane Club N.Y. Independent. Roman Catholic. Achievements include design, development, implementation, and evaluation of comprehensive rural health and emergency programs for refugees in Central America. Avocations: anthropology, tennis, trekking. Office: Dooley Found Intermed Internat 420 Lexington Ave Rm 2331 New York NY 10170

COMPTON, ALLEN T. retired state supreme court justice; b. Kansas City, Mo., Feb. 25, 1938; 3 children. BA, U. Kans., 1960; LL.B., U. Colo., 1963. Pvt. practice, Colorado Springs, 1963-68; staff atty. Legal Svcs. Office, Colorado Springs, 1968-69, dir., 1969-71; supervising atty. Alaska Legal Svcs., Juneau, Alaska, 1971-73; pvt. practice Juneau, 1973-76; judge Superior Ct., Alaska, 1976-80; justice Alaska Supreme Ct., Anchorage, 1980-98, state supreme ct. chief justice, 1995-97, ret., 1998.

COMPTON, ASBURY CHRISTIAN, state supreme court justice; b. Portsmouth, Va., Oct. 24, 1929; BA, Washington and Lee U., 1950, LLB, 1953, LLD, 1975. Bar: Va. 1957. Mem. firm May, Garrett, Miller, Newman & Compton, Richmond, 1957-66; judge Law and Equity Ct., City of Richmond, 1966-74; justice Supreme Ct. Va., Richmond, 1974-2000, sr. justice, 2000—. Trustee Collegiate Schs., Richmond, 1972-89, chmn. bd., 1978-80; former chmn. adminstrv. bd. Ginter Park United Meth. Ch., Richmond; former mem. adminstrv. bd. Trinity United Meth. Ch., Richmond; trustee Washington and Lee U., 1978-90. With USN, 1953-56, USNR, 1956-62. Decorated Letter of Commendation. Mem. Va. Bar Assn., Va. State Bar, Bar Assn. City Richmond, Washington and Lee U. Alumni Assn. (past pres., dir.), Omicron Delta Kappa, Phi Kappa Sigma, Phi Alpha Delta. Clubs: Country of Va. Office: Va Supreme Ct 100 N 9th St Richmond VA 23219-2335

COMPTON, CARNIS EUGENE, lawyer; b. Grundy, Va., June 20, 1948; s. Virginia (Compton) Hughart; m. Dollie McGlothlin, Aug. 24, 1966; children: Wade Trent, Nicholas Brian. BA, U. Va.-Clinch Valley, Wise, 1976; JD, Campbell Coll., 1979. Bar: Va. 1979, Fla. 1982, U.S. Dist. Ct. (we. dist.) Va. 1979, U.S. Supreme Ct. 1982, U.S. Ct. Appeals (4th cir.) 1984. Assoc. John L. Bagwell, P.C., Grundy, 1979; ptnr. Bagwell & Compton, P.C., Grundy, 1980-82, Watts & Compton, Deland, Fla., 1982; pvt. practice Honaker, Va., 1982-86; ptnr. Compton & Jessee, P.C., Abingdon and Honaker, Va., 1985—86; pvt. practice Honaker, 1986—88, Lebanon, Va., 1988—. Sec. Buchanan County Republican Party, Grundy, 1980; chmn. Reagan/Bush Com.-Buchanan County, Grundy, 1980; Republican candidate 40th State Senatorial Dist., Va., 1983; mem. Young Republicans of CVC, Wise, 1975. With USAF, 1967-73, Vietnam. Mem. ATLA, Va. Bar Assn., Va. Trial Lawyers Assn. (com. mem., dist. gov. 1995-96), Russell County Bar Assn. (pres. 1989), Fla. State Bar, Am. Legion. Avocations: bird dog field trials, reading history, horse back riding. Home: Rte 614 PO Box 1090 Lebanon VA 24266 Office: PO Box 1000 Lebanon VA 24266-1000 E-mail: gene@comptonlaw.net.

COMPTON, CHARLES DANIEL, chemistry educator; b. Elizabeth, N.J., Jan. 8, 1915; s. Charles Daniel and Janie (Little) C.; m. Ida Lightman, Dec. 19, 1953. AB cum laude, Princeton U., 1940; PhD in Chemistry, Yale U., 1943. Rsch. chemist Calco Chem. Co., 1943; instr. Princeton, 1944-46; rsch. assoc. Manhattan Dist. Project, Princeton, 1943-45; faculty Williams Coll., 1946—, prof., 1957—, chmn. chemistry dept., 1964-74, Halford R. Clark prof. natural

sci., 1966-72, Ebenezer Fitch prof. chemistry, 1972-77, Ebenezer Fitch prof. chemistry emeritus, 1977—. Lectr. chemistry New Coll., U. South Fla., 1979-81. Author: Introduction to Chemistry, 1958, Inside Chemistry, 1979, Japanese transl., 1982; contbr. articles to profl. jours. Allied Chem. and Dye Co. fellow, Yale U., 1942-43. Fellow AAAS; mem. Am. Chem. Soc., Phi Beta Kappa, Sigma Xi. Home: Apt H406 6401 21ST aVE w Bradenton FL 34209-5056

COMPTON, DALE LEONARD, retired space agency executive, consultant; b. Pasadena, Calif., June 18, 1935; s. John Leonard and Gladys Imnachuck (Foster) C.; m. Marilyn Doris Garland, June 21, 1959 (dec. Mar. 1997); children: David, Debora; m. Doris Bost Martin, Aug. 6, 2000. BSME, Stanford U., 1957, MS in Aero. Engring., 1958, PhD, 1969; MMS in Mgmt. Sci., MIT, 1975. Rsch. scientist NASA-Ames Rsch. Ctr., Moffett Field, Calif., 1957-72, Tech. asst. to dir., 1972-73, dep. dir. astronautics, 1973-74, chief space sci. div., 1974-80, mgr. IRAS Project, 1980-81, dep. dir. astronautics, 1981-82, dir. engring. & computer systems, 1982-85, dep. dir., 1985-88, dir., 1988-94; Sloan fellow MIT, Cambridge, Mass., 1974-75. Recipient NASA's Outstanding Leadership and Disting. Svc. medals, SES Presdl. Ranks of Meritorious and Disting. Exec. Fellow AIAA (named Outstanding Engr./Astro. 1983-84), AAAS; mem. Internat. Acad. Astronautics, Tau Beta Pi, Sigma Xi. Avocations: woodworking, reading, sailing, bird watching. Home: 22123 Stocklmeir Ct Cupertino CA 95014-2727 E-mail: dlcompton@worldnet.att.net.

COMPTON, DAVID BRUCE, software engineer; b. Dayton, Ohio, Sept. 27, 1952; s. Hall W. and Joan E. (Reinheimer) C.; m. Danielle M. Dufour, Apr. 19, 1986; children: Kyle Hall, Benjamin David, Zachary James. BS, No. Ariz. U., 1976; MBA in Internat. Mgmt., Am. Grad. Sch. Internat. Mgmt., 1977. Microsoft cert. profl.; Microsoft cert. solutions provider. Cons. Harris Graham and Ptnrs., London, 1978-81, Wyatt Co., Stamford, Conn., 1981-84; mgr. internat. benefits dept. Motorola, Inc., Chgo., 1984-86; dir. internat. benefits dept. Dart & Kraft, Chgo., 1986; dir. employee benefits dept. Premark Internat. subs. Dart & Kraft, Chgo., 1986-89, dir. internat. compensation and benefits dept., 1989—; pres., dir. HR Solutions, Inc., 1991-99; senior. tech. architect SBC, Hoffman Estates, Ill., 1999—. Active Boy Scouts Am. Avocations: guitars, cooking, tai chi, Aikido, computers. Office: Ameritech M/S 2B47B 2000 W Ameritech Dr Hoffman Estates IL 60196-0001 Home: 550 E Carpenter Dr Palatine IL 60074-3706 *Personal philosophy: Always strive for improvement and maintain honesty and integrity in everything you do.*

COMPTON, HAROLD F. retail executive; married; 2 children. Grad., U. of Fla. Exec. v.p. opers. and human resources HomeBase, Inc., 1989-93; exec. v.p. opers. CompUSA Stores, 1994-95, exec. v.p. and COO, 1995-96, exec. v.p. and pres., 1996—99, CEO, 2000—. Dir. JumboSports, Inc., Linens 'n Things, Inc., Stage Stores, Inc. Office: 14951 Dallas Pkwy Dallas TX 75254-7892*

COMPTON, JOHN CARROLL, accountant; b. Woodruff, S.C., July 3, 1941; s. Ligon Grant and Thelma (Blythe) C.; m. Monnie Digh, Jan. 7, 1967; children: Gillian Nicole, Jeanne Christen. BSBA in Acctg., U. N.C., 1963. CPA, N.C., Fla., S.C. Sr. acct. Peat, Marwick, Mitchell & Co., Greenville, S.C., 1963-64, supervising sr. acct., 1967-69; treas. Henderson Advt. Agy., Inc., Greenville, 1969-70; audit mgr. Cherry, Bekaert & Holland, Charlotte, N.C., 1970-71, ptnr., 1971-75, resident mng. ptnr., 1975-76, 1976-78, asst. dir. acctg. and auditing, 1978-80, resident mng. ptnr., 1980-85, dir. acctg. and auditing Greensboro, NC, 1985—99, dir. quality and compliance, 1999—. Treas., exec. com., chmn. fin. com. of bd. trustees All Children's Hosp.; vice-chmn., bd. dirs. All Children's Found.; past pres., exec. com., bd. dirs. Suncoast Ronald McDonald House, Inc.; sr. warden St. Thomas' Episc. Ch. Lt. (j.g.) USNR, 1963-67. Mem. AICPA (past mem. com. on banking, auditing stds. bd., ethics div. spl. taks force on firms performing govtl. grant audits, adv. bd. Nat. Sch. Banking), Fla. Inst. CPAs (practice rev. com., chmn. com. legis. policy, quality control com., pvt. cos., practice sect. com.), N.C. Assn. CPAs, Nat. Assn. Accts., Greensboro City Club. Republican. Office: 100 S Elm St Ste 500 Greensboro NC 27401-2639

COMPTON, JOHN JOSEPH, philosophy educator; b. Chgo., May 17, 1928; s. Arthur Holly and Betty Charity (McCloskey) C.; m. Marjorie Ann Yaple, July 8, 1950; children: Elizabeth Holly, Catherine Marchus, John Arthur. BA, Coll. of Wooster, 1949; MA, Yale U., 1951, PhD, 1953. Asst. prof. philosophy Vanderbilt U., Nashville, 1952-55, assoc. prof., 1955-68, prof., 1968-98, prof. emeritus, 1998—, chmn. or acting chmn. dept., 1966-73, 84-85, 88-89, 93-95. Vis. prof. Colo. Coll., Colorado Springs, 1977, Wesleyan U., Middletown, Conn., 1984. Contbr. articles to profl. jours. and chpts. in books. Mem. bd. advisers Matchette Found., 1968—; trustee Coll. of Wooster, Ohio, 1975—. Recipient Harbison award for disting. teaching Danforth Found., 1966; fellow Belgian-Am. Edn. Found., 1956-57, sr. fellow NEH, 1974-75, fellow Ctr. for Humanities, Wesleyan U., 1974-75. Mem. AAAS, AAUP, Am. Philos. Assn. (sec. ea. div. 1970-73, v.p. 1974), Metaphys. Soc. Am. (pres. 1979), Soc. for Phenomenology and Existential Philosophy, So. Soc. for Philosophy and Psychology, Philosophy of Sci. Assn., Soc. for Values in Higher Edn. (Kent fellow 1951), Phi Beta Kappa. Democrat. Avocations: hiking, camping, gardening, choral singing, cooking. Home: 3708 Whitland Ave Nashville TN 37205-2430 Office: Vanderbilt U Dept Philosophy Nashville TN 37235 E-mail: jjcompton@aol.com.

COMPTON, JOHN ROBINSON, retired rake company executive; b. Elmira, N.Y., Feb. 24, 1923; s. William Randall and Ada (Viele) C.; m. Jean Elinor York, Apr. 17, 1943; children— John York, Jan Elizabeth (Mrs. Harriss M. Ganey), Julie Ann (Mrs. William Cook). BS cum laude, Syracuse U., 1950. Acct., factory mgr. York Modern Corp., Unadilla, N.Y., 1947-51, pres., 1969-95; CEO, treas. bd. dirs., acct. Brewer-Titchener Corp., Binghamton, N.Y., 1951-52, chmn., 1996-99, retired, 1999; divsn. contr. Riegel Paper Corp., Riegelwood, N.C., 1953-65, corp. contr., 1966-69; pres. Mail-Print, Inc., 1970-99. Served to 2d lt. USAAF, World War II. Methodist. Home: 1681 County Road 39 Bainbridge NY 13733-4211

COMPTON, MARY BEATRICE BROWN (MRS. RALPH THEODORE COMPTON), public relations executive, writer; b. Washington, May 25, 1923; d. Robert James and Abia Eliza (Stone) Brown; m. Ralph Theodore Compton, Mar. 18, 1961. Grad. Thayer Acad., Chandler Sch., Leland Powers Sch. Radio, TV and Theatre, Boston, 1942. Radio program dir. Converse Co., Malden, Mass., 1942-45; head radio continuity dept. Sta. WAAB, Yankee Network, Worcester, Mass., 1945-46; asst. dir. radio Leland Powers Sch. Radio, TV and Theatre, Boston, 1946-49, dir., 1949-51; program asst. Sta. KNBH, Hollywood, Calif., 1951-52; v.p. Acorn Film Co., Boston, 1953-54; dir. women's communications, editor Program Notes, radio interviewer NAM, N.Y.C., 1954-61. Celebrities pub. rels. Nat. Citizens for Nixon, 1968, Kennedy Ctr. Pub. Info., 1985-89, Washington Nat. Cathedral Visitor's Svcs., 1989—2001. Mem. Soc. Old Plymouth Colony Descs., Magna Carta Dames, Congl. Country Club (Bethesda, Md.), White House Hist. Assn. Home: 15300 Wallbrook Ct Apt 3F Silver Spring MD 20906-1455

COMPTON, MICHAEL, music educator; s. Mary Jane Chaffee; m. Andrea Arnold, June 25, 1988; children: Ian, Nathan. MA, Calif. State U., Sacramento, 1993. Dir. music Galt (Calif.) H.S., 1990—95; dir. bands Barton County C.C., Great Bend, Kans., 1995—.

COMPTON, NORMA HAYNES, retired university dean, artist; b. Washington, Nov. 16, 1924; d. Thomas N. and Lillian (Laffin) Haynes; m. William Randall Compton, Mar. 27, 1946; children: William Randall, Anne Elizabeth. AB, George Washington U., 1950; MS, U. Md., 1957, PhD, 1962; D of Letters, Purdue U., 1996. Rschr. Julius Garfinckel & Co., Washington, 1955; tchr. Montgomery Blair High Sch., Silver Spring, Md., 1955-57; instr. U. Md., 1957-60, teaching and rsch. fellow Inst. Child Study, 1960-61, assoc. prof., 1962-63; psychology extern St. Elizabeths Hosp., Washington, 1962-63; assoc. prof. Utah State U., 1963-64, prof., 1964-68, head dept. clothing and textiles, 1963-68, dir. Inst. for Rsch. on Man and His Personal Environment, 1967-68; dean Sch. Home Econs. Auburn (Ala.) U., 1968-73; dean Sch. Consumer and Family Scis. Purdue U., 1973-87, prof. family studies, 1987-90; faculty The Edn. Ctr., Longboat Key, Fla., 1991-2000, mem. ednl. adv. bd., 1995-98. Cons. Burgess Pub. Co., Mpls., 1975-81, Nat. Advt. Rev. Bd., N.Y.C., 1978-82; bd. dirs. Armour & Co., Phoenix, 1976-82, Home Hosp., Lafayette, Ind., 1983-89; adv. com. Women's Resource Ctr. of Sarasota, Fla., 1992-96; chair Adv. Commn. Status Women, Sarasota, 1993-96; mem. advocates coun. Family Law Network Sarasota, 1994—; exec. bd. Sarasota-Manatee Phi Beta Kappa Assn., 1996-99; bd. trustees Plymouth Harbor, Inc., 2003—. Author: (with Olive Hall) Foundations of Home Economics Research, 1972, (with John Touliatos) Approaches to Child Study, 1983, Research Methods in Human Ecology/Home Economics, 1988; contbr. articles to profl. jours. Mem. exec. coun. Plymouth Harbor Residents Assn., Sarasota, 2001—, bd. trustees, 2003—. Recipient Woman of Impact Lifetime Achievement award, 1997. Mem.: PEO, AAUW, APA, Nat. League Am. Pen Women (v.p. Sarasota br.), Am. Assn. Family and Consumer Sci., Sigma Xi, Phi Beta Kappa, Psi Chi, Omicron Nu, Phi Kappa Phi. Congregational United Ch. Christ. E-mail: normahc@aol.com.

COMPTON, OLIN RANDALL, consulting electrical engineer, researcher; b. Parsons, W.Va., Apr. 12, 1925; s. Troy William and Strauda Belle (Robinson) C.; m. Patricia Ruth Osborne, June 3, 1947; children: Patricia Randall, Olin Bryan, Lisa Adrienne, Barry Christopher. BSEE, W.Va. U., 1949; Cert., Advanced Sch. Electric Utility Engring., Pitts., 1961. Registered profl. engr., Va. Jr. engr. Va. Electric & Power Co., Richmond, 1949-56, asst. supt elec. equipment, 1956-59, supt. elect. equipment, 1959-64, asst. substa. engr., 1965-79, elec. systems coord., 1979-83, corp. engring. advisor, 1983-85, prin. engr., 1985-91; pvt. practice cons., elec. rsch. Richmond, 1991—. Chmn. C76 Am. Nat. Standards Inst., Washington, 1968-72, C29, 1983-86; U.S. expert on transformers Internat. Electrochem. Commn., Geneva, Switzerland, 1982-86, on insulators, 1986-89. Contbr. 60 articles to profl. jours. Dir. Ctrl. Va. Ednl. TV Group, Richmond, 1972-79; commr. Tuckahoe Little League, Richmond, 1972-80; dir. United Meth. Lay Tng. Sch., Richmond, 1973-79; Native Am. Ministries coord., Va. Conf. United Meth. Ch., 1995—; chmn. State Spl. Edn. Adv. Com., Richmond, 1976-79; constrn. chmn., 1995-97, bd. mem. Richmond Metro Mabitat for Humanity, Inc., 1995—. 2d lt. USAAF, 1943-47. Fellow IEEE (chmn. substa. com. 1976-78, chmn. transformer com. 1985-88, Disting Svc. awards, best paper prizes 1948, 89). Republican. Avocation: bible study. Home and Office: 8423 Kalb Rd Richmond VA 23229-4133

COMPTON, RALPH THEODORE, JR., electrical engineering educator; b. St. Louis, July 26, 1935; s. Ralph Theodore and Ethel (Evans) C.; m. Lorraine Fielding, Nov. 9, 1957; children: Diane Marie, Ralph Theodore III, Richard Thomas. S.B., MIT, 1958; M.Sc., Ohio State U., 1961, PhD, 1964. Jr. engr. DECO Electronics, Leesburg, Va., 1958-59; sr. engr. Battelle Meml. Inst., Columbus, Ohio, 1959-62; asst. supr. Antenna Lab., Columbus, 1962-65; asst. prof. Case Inst. Tech., Cleve., 1965-67; fellow, guest prof. Tech. Hochschule, Munich, W. Ger., 1967-68; assoc. prof. Ohio State U., Columbus, 1968 78, prof. elec. engring., 1978-91; pres. Compton Rsch., Inc., Columbus, 1992—. Cons. to various orgns., U.S., Europe, Israel, 1969— Author: Adaptive Antennas-Concepts and Performance, 1988; contbr. chpts. to books, articles to profl. jours. Fellow Battelle Meml. Inst., 1961; NSF fellow, 1967; recipient Outstanding Paper awards Ohio State Electro-Sci. Lab., 1978, 80, 82, M. Barry Carlton award IEEE Aerospace and Electric Systems Soc., 1983, Sr. Research award Ohio State U. Engring. Coll., 1983 Fellow IEEE (assoc. editor Jour. Trans. on Antennas Propagation 1970); mem. Antenna and Propagation Soc. (chmn. Columbus chpt. 1971-72), Sigma Xi (sec.-treas. Case Inst. Tech. chpt. 1965-67), Pi Mu Epsilon Home and Office: 477 Poe Ave Worthington OH 43085-3036 E-mail: compton@ieee.org.

COMPTON, ROBERT, private school educator; b. Midland, Ontario, Canada, Sept. 25, 1952; s. Robert and Martha (Clark) Compton; m. Mary Jean Pertchack, Aug. 21, 1976; children: Mary Beth, Amy. BS, Bloomsburg U., 1974; MA, U. Delaware, 1976, EdD, 1995. Admin. Goldey Beacom Coll., Wilmington, Del., 1974—78, St. Joseph's U., Phila., 1978—83; prof., admin. Valley Forge Mil. Coll. Found., Wayne, Pa., 1983—. Coord. Delaware County Food Bank, Media, Pa., 1990—. With U.S. Army. Recipient Order of Anthony Wayne medal, Soc. of Anthony Wayne, Pa., 1991. Mem.: Am. Assn. U. Prof., Masons, Am. Legion. Avocations: ice skating, cross country skiing, swimming, bicycling. Office Fax: 610-989-1550. E-mail: rcompton@vfmac.edu.

COMPTON, STACY, race car driver; b. May 26, 1967; m. Vickie Compton. Race car driver Melling Racing, 2000—02, A.J. Foyt Racing, Mooresville, NC, 2002—. Named Champion, Late Model Stock Car Track/South Boston Speedway, 1994, Rookie of the Yr., NASCAR Craftsman Truck Series, 1997, Most Popular Driver, 1998. Avocations: golf, racquetball. Office: AJ Foyt Racing 128 Commercial Dr Mooresville NC 28115-7863

COMPTON, W. DALE, physicist, researcher, engineer; b. Chrisman, Ill., Jan. 7, 1929; s. Roy L. and Marcia (Wood) D.; m. Jeanne C. Parker, Oct. 14, 1951; children: Gayle Corinne, Donald Leonard, Duane Arthur. BA, Wabash Coll., 1949; MS, U. Okla., 1951; PhD, U. Ill., 1955; D.Eng. (hon.), Mich. Technol. U., 1976. Physicist U.S. Naval Ordnance Test Sta., China Lake, Calif., 1951-52, U.S. Naval Research Lab., Washington, 1955-61; prof. physics U. Ill. at Urbana, 1961-70, dir. coordinated sci. lab., 1965-70; dir. chem. and phys. scis., exec. dir. sci. research staff, v.p. research Ford Motor Co., Dearborn, Mich., 1970-86; sr. fellow Nat. Acad. Engring., 1986-88; disting. prof. indsl. engring. Purdue U., West Lafayette, Ind., 1988—, interim head Sch. Indsl. Engring., 1998-2001. Mem. Presdl. Commn. for Award of Medal of Sci., 1978—80; mem. vis. com. Nat. Bur. Stds., 1975—79, chmn. vis. com., 1979; mem. coun. Nat. Acad. Engrs., 1990—96, 2000—, home sec., 2000—; bd. govs. NRC, 1991—95, 2000—, mem. com. engring. and tech. sys., 1996—97, chmn., 1997—99. Author: (with J.H. Schulman) Color Centers in Solids, 1962; editor: Interaction of Science and Technology, 1969, Design and Analysis of Integrated Manufacturing Systems, 1988; co-editor (with J. Heim): Manufacturing Systems, Foundations of World Class Practice, 1992, Engineering Management: Creating and Managing World Class Operations, 1997. Mem. energy rsch. adv. bd. Dept. Energy, 1979—80; bd. dirs. Mich. Cancer Found., 1975—86; Coordinating Rsch. Coun., 1983—85; adv. com. Combustion Rsch. Facility Sandia Nat. Lab., 1983—86; bd. govs. Argonne Nat. Lab., 1983—86; mem. Coun. Energy Engring. Rsch., 1983—2001. Recipient M. Eugene Merchant Mfg. medal ASME/SME, 1999, Disting. Svc. award U. Ill. Coll. Engring. Alumni, 2002. Fellow AAAS, Am. Phys. Soc., Soc. Automotive Engrs., Engring. Soc. Detroit, IC2 Inst. U. Tex.; mem. NAE, Rsch. Soc. Am.

COMPTON, WILLIAM F. air transportation executive; m. Dreana Compton. Flight instr., 1966; pilot TWA, 1968; exec. v.p. ops. Trans World Airlines, Inc., St. Louis, 1996—, pres., COO, 1997—, now pres., CEO. Chmn. Air Lines Pilots Assn. TWA Master Exec. Coun., 1991-95, mem. exec. bd.; guest lectr. Stanford U. Grad. Sch. Bus./Law Sch., Midwest Acad. Mgmt. Office: Transworld Airlines Inc One City Ctr 515 N 6th St Saint Louis MO 63101-1842

COMPTON, WILLIAM THOMAS, real estate investor; b. Bedford, Ind., Dec. 1, 1945; s. Thomas Franklin and Dorothy Jane (Smith) C.; m. Nancy Marie Radocchia, Sept. 13, 1969 (div. Aug. 1994); children: Kimberly Dawn, Lindsay Ann; m. Kathleen Ann Berrigan, Feb. 14, 1997. BS in Mgmt., MIT, 1968, Postgrad., 1968-70. Cert. data processor. Sr. systems analyst First Nat. Bank Boston, 1970-73; systems analyst Gen. Computer Systems, Wellesley, Mass., 1973-76; bus. systems analyst Fram Corp., East Providence, R.I., 1976-78; v.p. Span Mgmt. Systems, East Providence, 1978; project leader Prime Computer Inc., Natick, Mass., 1979-81; owner Compton Software Solutions, Tiverton, R.I., 1981-88; prodn. foreman Tillotson Rubber Co., Inc., Fall River, Mass., 1988-89. Author several computer software programs, 1982-85. Loaned officer United Fund Boston, 1970. Mem. Data Processing Mgmt. Assn. (cert. data processing instr. 1985-86). Lodges: Kiwanis (local v.p. 1985, pres. 1985-86). Democrat. Methodist. Avocations: stained glass, model railroading. Home and Office: 250 Ash St Brockton MA 02301-4140

COMRIE, SANDRA MELTON, human resource executive; b. Plant City, Fla., Sept. 15, 1940; d. Finis and Estelle (Black) Melton; m. Allan Crecelius; children: Shannon Melissa, Colleen Megan. BA, UCLA, 1962, grad. exec. program, 1984. Div. mgr. City of L.A., 1973-77, asst. pers. dir., 1977-84; v.p. Transam. Life Cos., L.A., 1984-89; chief operating officer Treacy & Rhodes Consultants, Solana Beach, Calif., 1989-92; exec. dir. Reward Strategy Group, Inc., Del Mar, Calif., 1992-98. Bd. dirs. Found. for Employment and Disability, Sacramento, Clif.; mem. Asian Pacific Employment Task Force, Los Angeles, 1986-89. Bd. dirs. L.A. Urban League, 1985-92, Vols. of Am.-L.A., 1985-89; active United Way Downtown Bus. Consortium, Child Care Task Force, L.A., 1985-86; mem. adv. bd. L.A. City Child Care, 1987-89. Recipient Young Woman of Achievement award Soroptimists of Los Angeles, 1979. Mem. Internat. Pers. Mgmt. Assn. (mem. assessment coun., co-chair program com. for 1982 nat. conf., chair human rights com. 1983, pres. 1985), So. Calif. Pers. Mgmt. Assn., Planning Forum, Human Resource Planning Soc., Soc. for Human Resource Mgmt., Am. Compensation Assn., Am. Mgmt. Assn., L.A. C. of C. (human resources com. 1986-89). Democrat. Avocation: travel. Office: Reward Strategy Group Inc 9276 Scranton Rd Ste 120 San Diego CA 92121

COMSTOCK, CHRISTINE HOLADAY, obstetrician, gynecologist, radiologist, educator; b. Detroit, 1944; m. Robert Paul Lorenz, Feb. 3, 1973; children: Andrew Lorenz, David Lorenz. BS, U. Mich., 1967; MD, U. Chgo. - Pritzker Sch. Med., 1971. Diplomate Am. Bd. Ob-Gyn., Am. Bd. Radiology. Intern, rotating Northwestern U. Hosps., Chgo., 1971-72; resident in radiology Rush-Presbyn. St. Luke's, Chgo., 1972-73, U. Mich., Ann Arbor, 1973-75, resident in ob/gyn, 1977-79; resident in ob/gyn. Pa. State U., Hershey, Pa., 1979-81; dir. Divsn. Fetal Imaging William Beaumont Hosp., Royal Oak, Mich., 1984—; asst. prof. Wayne State U., 1984-99, assoc. prof., 1999—. Editor: The Fetal Brain, 1996, Survey Ob-Gyn. Ultrasound, 2000—; mem. editl. bd. Jour. Ultrasound in Medicine, 2000—. Fellow ACOG; mem. Radiol. Soc. N.Am., Am. Inst. Ultrasound Medicine (bd. govs. 1997-2000), Mich. Ultrasound Soc. (pres. 1996-98), Soc. Maternal Fetal Medicine, Ctrl. Soc. Obstetricians and Gynecologists (bd. dirs. 2000—). Office: William Beaumont Hosp 3601 W Thirteen Mile Rd Royal Oak MI 48073-6769 E-mail: ccomstock@beaumont.edu.

COMSTOCK, DALE ROBERT, mathematics educator; b. Frederic, Wis., Jan. 18, 1934; s. Walter and Frances (Lindroth) C.; m. Mary Jo Lien, Aug. 18, 1956; children— Mitchell Scott, Bryan Paul. BA, Ctrl. Wash. State Coll., 1955; MS, Oreg. State U., 1962, PhD, 1966. Tchr. math. Kennewick (Wash.) High Sch., 1955-57, 59-60; instr. Columbia Basin Coll., Pasco, Wash., 1956-57, 59-60; programmer analyst Gen. Electric Co., Hanford Atomic Works, Richland, Wash., 1963; prof. math. Cen. Wash. U., Ellensburg, 1964—, dean Grad. Sch. and Research, 1970-90; on leave as sr. program mgr. U.S. ERDA, also Presdl. interchange exec., 1976-77; mem. Pres.'s Commn. on Exec. Devel., 1976-77; bd. dirs. Council Grad. Schs. in U.S., 1981-84, dean in residence, 1984-85, Cons. Indian program NSF, 1968, 69, USIA, India, 1985, NSF, Saudi Arabia, 1986; mem. grant proposal rev. panels NSF, 1970, 71, 76, 77, 89, 90; pres. Western Assn. Grad. Schs., 1979-80, sec.-treas. 1984-90; pres. N.W. Assn. Colls. and Univs. for Sci., 1988-89; Russian exch. prof., St. Petersburg, 1993; vis. prof. U. Wash., 1990-91. With U.S. Army, 1957-59. NSF fellow, 1960-61; grantee, summer 1964 Mem. Am. Math Soc., Math. Assn. Am., Assn. Computing Machinery (exec. com.), Soc. Indsl. and Applied Math., Northwest Coll. and Univ. Assn. for Sci. (pres. 1980-83) Methodist. Office: Cen Wash U Dept Math Ellensburg WA 98926

COMSTOCK, REBECCA ANN, lawyer; b. Mpls., Mar. 13, 1950; d. Clark Franklin and Ruth Carolyn (Sundt) C. Student, Conn. Coll., 1968-70; BA summa cum laude, U. Minn., 1973; JD Order of St. Ives, U. Denver, 1977; MBA, Northwestern U., 2002. Bar: Minn. 1978, U.S. Dist. Ct. Minn., U.S. Ct. Appeals (8th cir.). Atty. Dorsey & Whitney, Mpls., 1982—. Bd. dirs. St. Paul Chamber Orch., 1996-2001, Big Bros./Big Sisters, Twin Cities, 2003—. Mem. ABA, Minn. Bar Assn., Hennepin County Bar Assn., Legal Aid Soc. Mpls. (bd. dirs. 1988-93), Nat. Assn. Women Bus. Owners, Licensing Exec. Soc. (USA and Can.), Environ. Law Inst. Avocations: skiing, biking, golf, music, theatre. Office: Dorsey & Whitney LLP 50 S 6th St Minneapolis MN 55402-1498 E-mail: comstock.becky@dorsey.com.

COMSTOCK, ROBERT DONALD, JR., real estate executive; b. Miami, Fla., Sept. 28, 1921; s. Robert Donald Sr. and Gertrude (Quigg) C.; m. Mary Evans, Oct. 12, 1949; children: Carol Frances, Robert Donald III (dec.). BS in Commerce, U. Miss., 1943. Lic. real estate broker. Acct. New Orleans Pub. Service Co., 1946-47; salesman, br. mgr. Capitol Records, Inc., New Orleans and Charlotte, N.C., 1948-51; regional v.p. Atlanta, 1952-57; owner, pres. Comstock Distbg. Co., Atlanta, 1957-74, Comstock and Assocs., Atlanta, 1968-74, Cartridge Control Corp., Atlanta, 1968-80, Comstock Properties, Atlanta, 1980—. Pres. Ctr. for Rehab. Tech., Ga. Tech. U., Atlanta, 1987-91, chmn. bd., 1991—. Mem. Atlanta Arts Alliance, 1970—, Atlanta Symphony, 1970—; bd. dirs. Christian Council Met. Atlanta, 1975-77; trustee So. Ctr. for Internat. Studies; mem. Atlanta Hist. Soc. Served to exec. officer USN, 1943-46, PTO. Named #1 Distbr. CBS Records, Columbia Broadcasting, N.Y.C., 1965, 69, Outstanding Distbr. Columbia Phonographs, Columbia Broadcasting, 1968, 70-72. Mem. Atlanta Bd. Realtors, Capital City Club, Commerce Club, Breakfast Club (pres. 1970-71), Trinity Presbyn. Ch. Men's Club (pres. 1977, Rotary (pres. Atlanta Midtown 1978-79), Omicron Delta Kappa. Avocations: golf, swimming, foreign affairs. Home: 3400 Ridgewood Rd NW Atlanta GA 30327-2418 Office: Ste 814 1447 Peachtree St NE Atlanta GA 30309-3029

COMSTOCK, ROBERT FRANCIS, lawyer; b. Lincoln, Ill., June 4, 1936; s. William Bryan and Mary Euceba (Durham) C.; m. Jean Joyce Herring, May 9, 1970; children: James, Michael, Kelly, Jennifer, Margaret. AB, Cath. U., 1958, LLB, 1964. Bar: U.S. Dist. Ct. 1965, U.S. Ct. Appeals (D.C. cir.) 1965, U.S. Tax Ct. 1971. Ptnr. Comstock & Reilly LLP, Washington, 1965—. Chmn. bd. dirs. Balt. Bancorp, 1991, Met. Fed. Savs. & Loan, Bethesda, Md., 1986-87, Met Holding Co., Bethesda, 1985-87, First Continental Bank, Silver Spring, Md., 1983-86; dir. Nat. Captial Bank Washington, 1999—. Trustee, vice chmn. bd. trustees Cath. U. Am., Washington, 1987—; bd. dirs. Cath. Cemeteries Washington, 1986—, Cath. Youth Orgn. Capt. USAF, 1958-61. Named Knight of St. Gregory, Knight of Holy Sepulchre, Papal Award of Holy See, to Athletic Hall of Fame, Cath. U., 1985. Mem. ABA, D.C. Bar Assn., Cath. U. Alumni Assn. (bd. govs.). Clubs: Columbia Country (Chevy Chase, Md.); Univ. Md. M. Roman Catholic. Avocation: sports. Home: 7707 Brookville Rd Bethesda MD 20815-3933 Office: Comstock & Reilly LLP Ste 300 5225 Wisconsin Ave NW Washington DC 20015-2014

COMUS, LOUIS FRANCIS, JR., lawyer; b. St. Marys, Ohio, Feb. 26, 1942; BA, Antioch Coll., 1965; JD, Vanderbilt U., 1968. Bar: N.Y. 1969, Ariz. 1973. Dir. Fennemore Craig P.C., Phoenix, 1975—. Notes editor Vanderbilt Law Rev., 1967-68. Fellow Am. Coll. Trust and Estate Counsel; mem. ABA, State Bar Ariz., Maricopa County Bar Assn., Order of Coif. Office: Fennemore Craig PC 3003 N Central Ave Ste 2600 Phoenix AZ 85012-2913 E-mail: lcomus@fclaw.com.

CONABOY, RICHARD PAUL, federal judge; b. Scranton, Pa., June 12, 1925; m. Marion Hartnett; children: Mary Ann, Richard, Judith, Conan, Michele, Kathryn, Patrick, William, Margaret, Janet, John, Nancy. BA, U. Scranton, 1945; LLB, Cath. U. Am., 1950. Bar: Pa. 1951. Ptnr. firm Powell & Conaboy, Scranton, 1951-54; dep. atty. gen., 1953-62; assoc. firm Kennedy O'Brien & O'Brien, 1954-62; judge Pa. Ct. Common Pleas, 1962-79, pres. judge, 1978-79; judge U.S. Dist. Ct. (mid. dist.) Pa., Scranton, 1980—, chief judge, 1989-93, now sr. judge. Pres. Pa. Joint Council on Criminal Justice System, 1971-79; mem. Nat. Conf. Juvenile Justice, Nat. Conf. Corrections. Contbr. articles to legal jours. Bd. dirs. Marywood Coll., U. Scranton; apptd. chmn. U.S. States Sentencing Commn., 1994. Mem. Pa. Conf. State Trial Judges (pres. 1976-77, v.p. 1973-76, sec. 1968-73), ABA, Pa. Bar Assn., Am. Judicature Soc. Office: US Dist Courthouse & Post Office Bldg PO Box 189 Scranton PA 18501-0189

CONAHAN, FRANK C. retired government executive, educator; b. Wilkes Barre, Pa., Sept. 4, 1933; s. Frank A. Conahan and Loretta A. Cantwell; m. Anne M. Corrigan; children: Frank, Tom, Nancy, Marguerite. BS in Acctg., King's Coll., 1955; postgrad., U. Mich., 1968, Harvard U., 1980; cert., Fgn. Svc. inst., 1972-73. Mem. exec. staff U.S. Gen. Acctg. Office, Washington, 1955-95, dir. European br., 1970s, dir. internat. divsn., 1980-83, asst. comptr. gen., nat. security and internat. affairs, 1983-95; sr. fellow Logistics Mgmt. Inst., Fairfax, Va., 1997-99; adj. faculty mem. Prince George's Coll., Largo, Md., 1997—. Testified at over 150 hearings before Congl. coms.; lectr. Brookings Inst., Def. Sys. Mgmt. Coll., Nat. Security Agy., Am. U., Ohio State U., U. Md., George Washington U., Ind. State U. Contbr. over 4,000 reports and testimonies to U.S. Congress. Tchr. Confraternity of Christian Doctrine, 1962-78; chmn. bd. external auditors Orgn. Am. States, 1982-85; sr. player Global War Games, Naval War Coll., 1990s. Served with USNR, 1951-58. Recipient Nat. Pub. Svc. award Nat. Acad. Pub. Adminstrn., 1991. Roman Catholic. Home: 12907 Clearfield Dr Bowie MD 20715

CONAN, ROBERT JAMES, JR., chemistry educator, consultant; b. Syracuse, N.Y., Oct. 30, 1924; s. Robert James and Helen M. (O'Brien) C. BS, Syracuse U., 1945, MS, 1947; PhD, Fordham U., 1950. Instr. Fordham U., N.Y.C., 1947-49; asst. prof. Le Moyne Coll., Syracuse, 1949-54, assoc. prof., 1954-58, prof. chemistry, 1958-89, prof. emeritus, 1990—. Cons. Carrier Corp., Syracuse, 1949-63, Owl Wire and Cable Co., Oneida, N.Y., 1952-62, Edison Audio Archives, Syracuse, 1972-86; rschr. U. Stockholm, Sweden, 1953, Swiss Fed. Inst. Tech., 1967, U. South Fla., 1988-90; mem. com. Onondaga Lake Sci. Coun., Syracuse, 1964-65; vis. prof. U. South Fla., 1991-2001. Contbr. over 50 articles to profl. jours. Recipient Plaque award Le Moyne Coll., 1989. Mem. Am. Chem. Soc. (chmn. Syracuse sect. 1958, 72, nat. councillor 1982-85, Unique Plaque Svc. award 1989, Spl. 50 Yr. Pin, life mem.), Tech. Club Syracuse (pres. 1981-82, plaque award). Republican. Roman Catholic. Avocations: music, irish genealogy. also: 263 Robineau Rd Syracuse NY 13207-1643 E-mail: conan@lemoyng.edu.

CONANT, ALLAH B., JR., lawyer; b. Waco, Tex., July 24, 1939; s. Allah B. and Frances Louise (James) C.; m. Sheila Conant; children: Heather Lee Arsham, Lisa Lynn, Leslie Marie Thorne; stepchild, Thomas R. Bone II. BA, N. Tex. State Coll., Denton, 1961; JD cum laude, Baylor U., 1963. Bar: Tex. 1963, U.S. Dist. Ct. (no. dist.) Tex. 1964, U.S. Dist. Ct. (so. dist.) Tex. 1969, U.S. Dist. Ct. (ea. dist.) Tex. 1986, U.S. Dist. Ct. (we. dist.) Tex. 1986, U.S. Ct. Appeals (5th cir.) 1970, U.S. Ct. Appeals (8th cir.) 1975, U.S. Ct. Appeals (4th and 7th cirs.)1978, U.S. Ct. Appeals (3d and 11th cirs.) 1981, U.S. Ct. Appeals (10th cir.) 1987, U.S. Tax Ct. 1963, U.S. Supreme Ct. 1971. Since practiced in, Dallas; ptnr. Shank, Irwin, Conant, Lipshy & Casterline, 1964-90; owner ABC Ranch, 1981-89; of counsel Whittenburg Whittenburg and Schachter, 1990; mem. Conant Whittenburg French & Schachter, Dallas, 1991-99; ptner. Conant French & Chaney, LLP, Dallas, 1999—. Contbr. to legal jours. Trustee St. John's Episcopal Sch., 1987-90. Fellow Am. Bar Found. (life), Tex. Bar Found. (life), Dallas Bar Found. (life); mem. ABA (coun. gen. practice sect. 1977-80, chmn. 1982-83, del. 1983-86), Dallas Bar Assn., State Bar Tex., Trial Attys. Am., Baylor Law Sch. Counsellors, Baylor Law Alumni Assn. (dir. 1979-82), Baylor Law Rev. Ex-Editors Assn., N.Tex. State U. Alumni Assn. (dir., v.p.), Sigma Phi Epsilon, Omicron Delta Kappa, Phi Delta Phi (historian 1962). Clubs: Petroleum (Dallas). Avocations: swimming, reading, travel, boating. Home: 98 Tanda Trail Trinidad TX 75163 Office: Conant French & Chaney LLP 1717 Main St Ste 3880 Dallas TX 75201-7311 E-mail: abconant@cfc-law.com.

CONANT, DAVID ARTHUR, architectural acoustician, educator, consultant; b. Biloxi, Miss., Dec. 22, 1945; s. Roger and Lillian Rose May (Lovell) C.; m. Nancy Hayes, June 17, 1972; children: Christopher, Tyler. BS in Physics, Union Coll., 1968; MA in Geology, Columbia U., 1972; BArch, MArch, Rensselaer Poly. Inst., 1975. Faculty fellow Lamont-Doherty Earth Obs., Palisades, N.Y., 1970-72; teaching asst. Rensselaer Poly. Inst., Troy, N.Y., 1973-76; asst. prof. dept. architecture Calif. State Poly. U., Pomona, 1976-78; sr. cons. Bolt Beranek Newman Inc., Canoga Park, Calif., 1977-87; prin. McKay Conant Brook, Inc., Westlake Village, Calif., 1987—. Cons. in field. Co-author: (textbook) Fundamentals and Abatement of Highway Traffic Noise, 1980; author computer software; Geffen Playhouse Expansion and Renovation, Westwood, Calif.,Renovation of Symphony Hall, Phoenix, Granada Theatre, Santa Barbara, Calif. sound stage prodn. and post prodn. facilities, Capetown, South Africa. Instr., vol. Upward Bound, Schenectady, N.Y., 1967-68; overseas vol. Am. Friends Svc. Com., Yugoslavia and Denmark, 1967. With U.S. Army, 1968-70. Recipient Honor award AIA, 1991, Merit award, 1997. Mem. ASHRAE, Acoustical Soc. Am. (archtl. acoustics tech. com.), Nat. Coun. Acoustical Cons. (bd. dirs.), Constrn. Specifications Inst., Sigma Xi (univ. chpts. lectr. physics). Republican. Presbyterian. Achievements include development of binaural/analog computer and psychoacoustic model to assess and predict degree of subjective "immersion" in auditorium sound fields. Home: 1504 Grissom St Thousand Oaks CA 91362-2010 Office: McKay Conant Brook Inc 5655 Lindero Canyon Rd Ste 325 Thousand Oaks CA 91362-4045 E-mail: dconant@mcbinc.com.

CONANT, DOUGLAS R. food products executive; BA, MBA, Northwestern U. With mktg. dept. Gen. Mills, 1976—86; mgmt. Kraft, 1986—92; with Nabisco, 1992—95; pres. Nabisco Food Co., 1995—2000; pres., CEO Campbell Soup Co., 2001—. Bd. dirs. Applebee's Internat. Inc., NJ Network. Bd. dirs. Safe Am. Found. Mem.: NJ C. of C. (bd. dirs.). Office: Campbell Place Camden NJ 08103-3878*

CONANT, HOWARD SOMERS, artist, educator; b. Beloit, Wis., May 5, 1921; s. Rufus P. and Edith B. (Somers) C.; m. Florence C. Craft, June 18, 1943; children: Judith Lynne Steinbach, Jeffrey Scott; m. Virginia E. Lusk, June 7, 1999. Student, Art Students League of N.Y., 1944-45; BS, U. Wis.-Milw., 1946; MS, U. Wis.-Madison, 1947; Ed.D., U. Buffalo, 1950. Instr. art, asst. head housefellow U. Wis., 1946-47; asst. prof. art SUNY, Buffalo, 1947-50, prof. art, 1950-55; chmn. dept. art and art edn. also chmn. art collection NYU, 1955-76; head dept. art U. Ariz., Tucson, 1976-86, prof. art, 1986-87; profl. artist, 1987—. Art edn. cons. NBC-TV, also Girl Scouts Am. TV series, 1958-60; field reader, also Title III program cons. U.S. Office of Edn.; adviser N.Y. State Council on Arts, 1962-63, Conn. Commn. on Arts, 1967-68; cons. Ford Found., 1973, Children's Theatre Assn., 1973, Getty Trust, 1985; examiner Internat. Baccalaureate Orgn., 1998. Moderator: weekly TV program Fun to Learn About Art, WBEN-TV, Buffalo, 1951-55; numerous one man shows; represented maj. group exhbns. pub. art mus. and coll. art collections; represented by Sol Del Rio Gallery, San Antonio, Art Source Inc., Tulsa, Ideas and Products, Tucson; executed mural Sperry High Sch., Henrietta, N.Y., 1971, Good Samaritan Med. Ctr., Phoenix, 1982, Valley Nat. Bank, Tucson, 1983; one-man retrospectives, Amarillo (Tex.) Art Mus., 1989, Tucson Jewish Cmty. Ctr., 1995, Sun City (Ariz.) Art Mus., Prescott (Ariz.) Fine Arts Assoc., 1996; author: (with Arne Randall) Art in Education, 1959, 63; author, editor: Art Workshop Leaders Planning Guide, 1958, Masterpieces of the Arts, New Wonder World Cultural Library, Vol. 4, 1963, Art Education, 1964, Seminar on Elementary and Secondary School Education in the Visual Arts, 1965, Lincoln Library of the Arts (2 vols.), 1973; art editor: Intellect, 1975-78, USA Today, 1978-85; assoc. editor Arts mag., 1973-75; contbr. articles profl. publs. Dept. State lectr., India, 1964; Dir. Waukesha County (Wis.) YMCA Art Program, 1946-48; pres., dir. Children's Creative Art Found., 1959-60; mem. adv. com. Coll. of Potomac, 1966; mem. cultural exchange mission to Mex., Ptnrs. of the Ams., 1988, 90; Lt. USAAF, 1943-46. Recipient 25th Ann. medal Nat. Gallery Art, 1966, Disting. Alumnus award U. Wis.-Milw., 1968, Purchase award Richard Florsheim Art Fund, 1992; Disting. fellow Nat. Art Edn. Assn., 1985, Nat. Endowment Arts sr. fellow in painting, 1985. Mem. Coll. Art Assn., Nat. Art Edn. Assn., Internat. Art Critics Assn., Alliance for Arts in Edn., Nat. Assn. Schs. Art and Design, AAUP, Nat. Com. Art Edn. (council, chmn. 1962-63), Inst. Study of Art in Edn. (bd. govs. 1965-72, pres. 1965-68) Clubs: Torch (N.Y.C.) (pres. 1965-66). Studio: 6954 E Cicada Ct Tucson AZ 85750-1395 *I have learned to freely follow my interests from one area of concern or involvement to another without feeling guilty about "putting off until tomorrow what one can do today." I have learned to be an innovator and an enjoyer, rather than a solemn plodder. I have learned how to do two or three things more or less at once, much like an organist handling contrapuntal melodies. As a result, I am a happy artist, author, lecturer and private human being whose multiple interests seem highly compatible and, indeed, essential to one another.*

CONANT, JAN ROYCE, artist; b. Boston, Sept. 14, 1930; d. Frank A. and Margaret (Newlin) Royce; m. Richard W. Conant, Mar. 22, 1952 (div. 1977); children: Peter Ames, Stephen Wright. Student, Milton Acad., 1948, Boston Mus. Sch., 1951; MFA, Cin. Art Acad., 1954. Lic. internat. judge combined tng. Fedn. Equestre Internationale. Owner, mgr. Tinker Hill Farm, Glastonbury, Conn., 1956-73, Stonefield Farm, East Haddam, Conn., 1973—; mng. dir. Chukka Cove Farm, Jamaica, W.I., 1982-84; owner Stonefield Farm and Studio LLC, East Haddam, 1985—. Author, illustrator: Half Pint & Others, 1962, Children of Light, 1998; illustrator The Winning Streak, 1962, Judge & Jr. Exhibitor, 1964; exhibited in solo shows at Chester Art Gallery, 1987, Lyman Allyn Mus., 1989, W. Graham Arader Gallery, N.Y.C., 1994, Mut. Life Gallery, Kingston, Jamaica, 1997; group show at Lyme Art Assocs. Trustee Lyme Art Assn.; friend Lyme Acad. Coll. Fine Arts. Mem. Allied Artists Am., Am. Acad. Equine Art (patron), Am. Horse Shows Assn. (lic.), U.S. Combined Tng. Assn., U.S. Pony Clubs Inc. (v.p. 1974-78, gov. 1966-78, nat. examiner 1968-78). Independent. Avocations: photography, animal behaviorist, racquetball. Home and Office: Stonefield Farm 23 Three Bridges Rd East Haddam CT 06423-1732

CONANT, RALPH WENDELL, educator, consultant, author; b. South Hope, Maine, Sept. 7, 1926; s. Earle Raymond Conant and Margaret Verrill (Long) Young; m. Audrey Florence Karl, Aug. 27, 1950 (dec. Feb., 2001); children: Beverlie Elaine, Lisa Audrey, Jonathan Arnold (dec.). BA, U. Vermont, 1949; MA, U. Chgo., 1954, PhD, 1959. Asst. prof. Mich. State U., E. Lansing, Mich., 1955-57; rsch. assoc. Nat. Mcpl. League, N.Y.C., 1957-59; asst. prof. U. Denver, 1960-62; asst. dir. Joint Ctr. for Urban Studies, Harvard U. and MIT, Cambridge, Mass., 1962-67; assoc. dir. Ctr. for Study of Violence, Brandeis U., Waltham, Mass., 1967-69; pres. S.W. Ctr. for Urban Rsch., Houston, 1969-75, Shimer Coll., Mt. Carroll, Ill., 1975-78, Unity (Maine) Coll., 1978-80, Conant Assocs., Winslow, Maine, 1980-87; dean Mercy Coll., Dobbs Ferry, N.Y., 1987-89; sr. fellow Phelps Stokes Fund, N.Y.C., 1989—. Author 15 books, including The Prospects for Revolution, 1971, The Conant Report, A Study of the Education of Librarians, 1980, Public Ends, Private Means, 1987, Toward a More Perfect Union: The Governance of Metropolitan America, 2002, (with Daniel J. Myers and Chandler E. Sharp) The Future of Poverty in American Cities, 2003; contbr. articles to profl. jours. Exec. dir. Citizens for Mich., 1959-60; trustee Shimer Coll., 1978—; chmn. Shimer Coll. Found., 1982—; candidate U.S. Congress, 1st Dist., Maine, 1982, 86; mem. Dem. State Com., 1984-92, Maine State Bd. Edn., 1985-90. Named Disting. Alumnus, U. Vt., Burlington, 1978. Home: PO Box 703 Trinidad CA 95570-0703 Office: Asgard Found 1326 Stagecoach Rd Trinidad CA 95570-9705

CONANT, ROBERT SCOTT, harpsichordist, music educator; b. Passaic, NJ, Jan. 6, 1928; s. Frederick Banks and Bessie Trimble (Scott) C.; m. Nancy Lydia Jackson, Oct. 10, 1959; children: Elizabeth Scott, Andrew Frederick. BA, Yale U., 1949, MusM, 1956. Recorded with various labels including: RCA Victor, CBS, Decca, Musurgia, Kapp, Ex Libris, FBM, 1958—; asst. prof. music Yale U., New Haven, 1961-66; fellow Silliman Coll., 1961-66, assoc. fellow, 1967-71; assoc. prof. music history and harpsichord Roosevelt U., Chgo., 1967-71, prof. music history and harpsichord, 1971-86, prof. emeritus, 1986—. Vis. artist Aspen Inst. Humanistic Studies, 1988-89, NC Sch. Arts, 1990. Concert harpsichordist NY Town Hall recital debut, 1953, ann. tours as recitalist, chamber music player, US, Europe, Can., 1953—; appeared with Pitts., Chgo., and Denver Symphonies, soloist, Casals Festival, 1963, lectr. performer numerous coll., univ., mem. Viola da Gamba Trio of Basel, 1968-94, Robert Conant Baroque Trio, 1987-99, Nova/Antiqua (new music trio) 1987—; author: (with others) Twentieth Century Harpsichord Music: A Classified Catalog, 1974; contbr. articles to profl. jour. Founder, pres. Found. for Baroque Music, Inc., Greenfield Center, NY, 1959—. Served with AUS, 1951-53. Recipient Lifetime Achievement award Saratoga County Arts Coun., 1992. Mem. Coll. Music Soc. (treas. 1971-74), Am. Musicol. Soc., Am. Mus. Instrument Soc. Clubs: The Cliffdwellers (Chgo.). Democrat. Avocations: photography, mountain climbing. Home and Office: Found for Baroque Music Inc 165 Wilton Rd Greenfield Center NY 12833-1704

CONANT, STEVEN GEORGE, psychiatrist; b. Elkhart, Ind., July 8, 1949; s. Hubert Eugene and Ruth (Weaver) C. BA in Zoology with distinction, DePauw U., 1971; MD, Ind. U., 1975. Diplomate Am. Bd. Psychiatry and Neurology. Intern Ind. U. Med. Ctr., Indpls., 1975-76, resident in psychiatry, 1976-78, asst. prof. psychiatry, 1978-80, asst. clin. prof. psychiatry, 1988-93; cons. psychiatry Gallahue Mental Health Ctr., Indpls., 1979-85; staff psychiatrist Metro Health, Indpls., 1983-97. Staff privileges at Meth. Hosp., Indpls., 1979—; cons. psychiatrist Ind. Prison Sys., 1986, Ctrl. State Hosp., 1992-94, Hamilton Ctr., 1994—. Represented in permanent collections Indpls. Mus. Art, DePauw U., Safeco Corp. Mem. Conductor's Cir. Indpls. Symphony, 1984-96, Indpls. Symphonic Choir Orch., 1976-83; life trustee Indpls. Mus. Art, 1988—. Recipient several prizes for abstract paintings. Mem. AMA, Am. Acad. Clin. Psychiatrists, Mensa, The Hoosier Group, Wash. DePauw Soc. Republican. Presbyterian. Avocations: european and american literature, classical piano, american modernist and contemporary art, early chinese ceramics.

CONARD, JOHN JOSEPH, financial official; b. Coolidge, Kans., June 30, 1921; s. Joseph Harvey and Jessie May (Shanstrom) C.; m. Virginia Louise Powell, Sept. 13, 1947; children— Joseph Harvey II (dec.), James Powell, Spencer Dean, John Joseph. BA, U. Kans., 1943, MA, 1947; D. Internat. Law, U. Paris, 1951. Instr. polit. sci. U. Kans., 1946-49, asst. to chancellor, 1970-75; spl. asst. U.S. Mut. Security Agy., Paris, France, 1951-54; editor, pub. Kiowa County Signal, Greensburg, Kans., 1955-70; exec. officer bd. regents State of Kans., Topeka, 1976-82; pres. Higher Edn. Loan Program of Kans., Inc., Overland Park, Kans., 1982-86; v.p. Higher Edn. Assistance Found., 1982-86; legis. liaison Gov. of Kansas, 1987-88. Dir. Haviland (Kans.) State Bank. Mem. Kans. Ho. of Reps., 1959-69; mem. State Fin. Council, 1961-69; speaker of House, 1967-69; exec. asst. to Gov. Kans., 1975-76; trustee William Allen White Found., 1959— . Served to ensign USNR, 1943-45. Summerfield scholar, 1939-42; Rotary Found. fellow, 1949-50 Mem. VFW, Rotary, Phi Beta Kappa, Sigma Delta Chi, Pi Sigma Alpha, Tau Kappa Epsilon. Republican. Methodist. Home: 904 Joseph Dr Lawrence KS 66049-3255 E-mail: jnvaparis@sunflower.com.

CONARD, REBECCA ANN, historian, educator; b. Ida Grove, Iowa, Aug. 10, 1946; d. Herbert John Wiegel and Patricia Mae Conard. BS, Calif. Poly. Inst., Pomona, 1973; MA, UCLA, 1976; PhD, U. Calif., Santa Barbara, 1984. Ptnr. PHR Assocs., Santa Barbara, 1982-92; co-prin. Tallgrass Historians L.C., Iowa City, 1993; asst. prof. Wichita (Kans.) State U., 1992-98; assoc. prof. Mid. Tenn. State U., Murfreesboro, 1998—2003, prof., 2003—. Author: Places of Quiet Beauty: Parks, Preserves, and Environmentalism, 1997 (Benjamin Shambaugh award 1998), Benjamin Shambaugh and the Intellectual Foundations of Public History, 2002; mem. editl. bd. Pub. Historian, 1999-01. Recipient Oustanding Hist. Restoration award Calif. Preservation Found., 1991, Throne-Aldrich award State Hist. Soc. Iowa, 1993. Mem. Nat. Coun. Pub. History (v.p. 2001-02, pres. 2002-03), Orgn. Am. Historians, Am. Soc. Environ. History, Am. Assn. State Local History (Cert. Commendation 1998), Calif. Coun. Promotion History (Spl. Commendation 1991). Avocations: swimming, gardening. Office: History Dept Box 23 Middle Tenn State U Murfreesboro TN 37132 Business E-Mail: rconard@mtsu.edu.

CONARROE, JOEL OSBORNE, foundation administrator, educator, editor; b. West Orange, N.J., Oct. 23, 1934; s. Elvin Hamn and Elizabeth (Lofland) C. BS, Davidson Coll., 1956, LHD (hon.), 1987; MA, Cornell U., 1957; PhD, NYU, 1966; LHD (hon.), Rhodes Coll., 1983; PhD (hon.), U. Md., 1989, Tulane U., 1996. Asst. prof. English U. Pa., 1966-71, assoc. prof., 1971-77, prof., 1977—, ombudsman, 1971-73, chmn. dept. English, 1973-77, master Van Pelt Coll. House, 1974-77, dean faculty arts and scis., 1983-85; pres. John Simon Guggenheim Meml. Found., 1985—2003, pres. emeritus, 2003—. Exec. dir. MLA, N.Y.C., 1978-83; mem. selection com. Commonwealth Award in Lit., 1980-83; v.p. Nat. Book Critics Circle, 1981-85; chmn. Nat. Book Award Fiction Jury, 1988, Pulitzer Prize Fiction Jury, 1989, 94, 97, 2000, 2002, Nat. Book Found., 1991-94; bd. dirs. PEN, pres. PEN Am. Ctr., 2002—, Am. Acad. Poets, Yaddo. Author: William Carlos Williams' Paterson: Language and Landscape, 1970, John Berryman: An Introduction to the Poetry, 1977, Six American Poets, 1992, Eight American Poets, 1994, essays and revs.; editor PMLA, 1978-83. With U.S. Army, 1957-58. Recipient Founders Day award NYU, 1966, Lindback Teaching award U. Pa., 1970, Disting. Alumni award NYU, 1995; Yaddo fellow, 1973, 76, Guggenheim fellow, 1977-78. Mem. MLA, Am. Acad. Arts Sci., Century Assn., Phi Beta Kappa. Office: 126 W 11 St New York NY 10011-1301

CONATON, MICHAEL JOSEPH, financial service executive; b. Detroit, Aug. 3, 1933; s. John Martin and Margaret Alice (Cleary) C.; m. Nancy D. Kelley, June 13; children: Catherine, Macaira (dec.), Michael, Margaret, Elizabeth. BS, Xavier U., 1955. Public accountant Stanley A. Hitter, C.P.A., Cin., 1956-58; controller The Moloney Co., Albia, Iowa, 1958-61; v.p. fin. The Midland Co., Cin., 1961-80, sr. v.p., chief fin. officer, 1980-83, exec. v.p., chief fin. officer, 1983-88, pres., chief operating officer, 1988—, also dir., vice-chmn., 1998—. Interim pres. Xavier U., 1990-91. City councilman, Albia, 1959-61; trustee, chmn. bd. Xavier U., 1983—. Served to lt. USMC, 1955-56. Mem. Fin. Execs. Inst., New Ohio Inst. (chmn.), Cin. Soc. Fin. Analysts, Athenaeum of Ohio (trustee), Met. Club (chmn. bd.). Home: 736 Elsinboro Dr Cincinnati OH 45226-1706 Office: The Midland Company PO Box 1256 Cincinnati OH 45201-1256

CONATSER, BRIAN KEITH, music educator, musician; b. Trumann, Ark., Aug. 11, 1958; s. James Russell and JoAnn Conatser; m. Lisa Renee Lindsey, Aug. 22, 1968. MusB in Piano Performance, Ark. State U., Jonesboro, 1980; MusM in Piano Performance, U. of Mo., 1983; DMA in Accompanying and Chamber Music, ABD, U. of Miami, Coral Gables, Fla., 1997. Cert. permanent cert. piano tchr. Ohio. Accompanist U. of Cen. Ark., Conway, 1989—93; music dir. Hispanic-Am. Lyric Theater, Miami, 1993—99; accompanist Linfield Coll. Opera Workshop, McMinnville, Oreg.; repetiteur Treasure Coast Opera Soc., Fort Pierce, Fla., 1997—99; music instr. New World Sch. of the Arts, Miami, 1999—2001; accompanist Oreg. State U., Corvallis, 2001—. Freelance musician Ark. State U., Jonesboro, 1985—89; adjudicator Oreg. Music Educators Assn., Salem, 2001—; faculty mem. Nat. Guild of Piano Tchrs., Tex., 1980. Composer: (Operas) Rosalinda; musician The Fowl Opera Trilogy, Sleeping Beauty, Albert Herring, La Pizza con Funghi. Spl. election judge Dem. Party, Trumann, Ark., 1986—87; organist Riverside United Meth. Ch., Miami, 1993—98; membership sec. Opera Theater Corvallis, 2002—03. Mem.: Phi Mu Alpha (life; pres.Omicron Omega chpt. 1979—80, Kans. City Alumni Chpt. scholarship 1983). Home: #4 430 SW 7th St Corvallis OR 97333-4567 Office: Oreg State U Music Dept Benton Hall Corvallis OR 97333 Personal E-mail: ortroubadour@hotmail.com.

CONAWAY, CHARLES ALAN, music educator; b. Anniston, Ala., Dec. 1, 1958; s. Audrey Jefferson and Carolyn Hope Conaway; m. Tawana Ann McGullion, Aug. 27, 1959; children: Alaina, Amber. EdD, U. Ala., 1996; EdS, Jacksonville State U., 1990; MS, U. Ala., 1986; BS, Jacksonville State U., 1980. Cert. Ednl. Adminstrn. N-12 1996, Music Ednl. Specialist AA 1990. Dir. band Alexandria H.S., Alexandria, Ala., 1998—; dir. choir Angel Grove Bapt. Ch., Jacksonville, Ala., 1988. Recipient Clay County Tchr. of Yr., WASZ Radio and First Nat. Bank of Ashland, Ala., 1993. Mem.: NEA, Ala. Assn. Tchrs. English, Nat. Assn. Tchrs. English, Ala. Music Educators Assn., Music Educators Nat. Conf., Ala. Assn. Secondary Sch. Prins., Nat. Assn. Secondary Sch. Prins., Ala. Edn. Assn. Baptist. Avocations: antique automobile collecting, running. Home: 50 E Glen Rd Alexandria AL 36250 Office: Alexandria High School 353 Stadium Dr Alexandria AL 36250

CONAWAY, CHARLES C. former retail company executive; Exec. v.p., chief operating officer Reliable Drug Stores, Inc., 1989-92; sr. v.p. pharmacy CVS Corp., Woonsocket, RI, 1992-95, exec. v.p., CFO, 1995-99, pres., chief operating officer, 1999-2000; chmn., CEO Kmart Corp., Troy, Mich., 2000—02. Bd. dirs. Linens 'n Things.

CONAWAY, CHARLES WILLIAM, information scientist, educator; b. Anniston, Ala., July 11, 1943; s. Ralph A. and Frances Marion Conaway; m. Frances Aidman Aidman, Oct. 18, 1973; children: Sandra Beth, Carla Marie. AB, Jacksonville State U., 1964; MSLS, Fla. State U., 1965; PhD, Rutgers U., 1974. Cert. archivist Acad. Cert. Archivists, 1999, public libr. State of N.Y., 1974. Assoc. prof. Fla. State U., Tallahassee, 1977—2002, prof. emeritus, 2002—. Fulbright sr. specialist CIES, Washington, 2002, Fulbright sr. lectr., 1975—76; cons. Computational Bibliographic Services, Tallahassee, 1977, OAS, 1985—, USAID, 1985—, Fla. Internat. Vol. Corps, 1985—. Contbr. articles to profl. jours. Com. mem. Brokaw-McDougall Ho. Adv. Bd., Tallahassee, 2002. Democrat-Npl. Avocations: travel, foreign work. Home: 3202 Adwood Ct Tallahassee FL 32312

CONAWAY, HERB(ERT) C., JR., assemblyman; b. Jan. 30, 1963; BA in Politics, Princeton U.; MD, Jefferson Med. Coll.; JD, Rutgers Law Sch. Assemblyman N.J. Gen. Assembly, 1998—; dep. spkr., 2002—. Physician Cooper Hosp. Capt. med. corps. USAF, 1992—96. Democrat. Office: Delran Profl Ctr Ste 125 8008 Rt 130 N Delran NJ 08075 E-mail: AsmConaway@njleg.org.*

CONAWAY, JANE ELLEN, elementary education educator; b. Fostoria, Ohio, July 9, 1941; d. Robert and Virginia C.. BA in Elem. Edn., Mary Manse Coll., Toledo, Ohio, 1966—67; MEd in Elem. Edn., U. Ariz., 1969; postgrad. in reading, U. Toledo, 1975—77; postgrad., U. Wis., 1987—. Cert. reading specialist in diagnostic and remedial reading Wis. Tchr. Sandusky pub. schs., Ohio, 1969—70; coord. 1st grade small group instrn. program St. Mary's Grade Sch., Sandusky, 1970—71; tchr. Chpt. I remedial reading Eastwood Local schs., Pemberville, Ohio, 1971—87; dist. dir. Right to Read program; reading specialist Middleton-Cross Plains (Wis.) Area Sch. Dist., 1987—. Mem.: Madison Area Reading Coun., Middleton Edn. Assn., Wis. Edn. Assn., NEA. Home: 1302 Wexford Dr Waunakee WI 53597-1842 Office: Middleton Cross Plains Sch Dist Sauk Trail Sch 2205 Branch St Middleton WI 53562-2840

CONAWAY, MARGARET GRIMES (PEGGY CONAWAY), library administrator; b. Minot, N.D., June 6, 1944; d. John Francis and Veronica Ann (McCarthy) Grimes; m. Steven L. Conaway, July 15, 1967 (div. July 1991); 1 child, Anne Marie. BS in Edn., Minot State Coll., 1966; MA in English, San Jose State U., 1978, MLS, 1988. Cert. secondary tchr., Calif.; cert. c.c. tchr., Calif. Instr. Boise (Idaho) Ind. H.S., 1966-67, Santa Maria (Calif.) Joint Union H.S. Dist., 1967-72; libr. asst. San Jose (Calif.) Pub. Libr., 1984-86, libr., 1986-89, sr. libr., 1989-97, divsn. mgr., 1997—2000; libr. dir. Los Gatos (Calif.) Pub. Libr., 2000—. Oper. design project mgr. San Jose Pub. Libr./San Jose State U. Joint Libr., 1998—2000; vice chmn. adminstrv. coun. Silicon Valley Libr. Sys., 2001—02, chmn. adminstrv. coun., 2002—03. Author: One Reference Service for Everyone?, 2000, (Ency. of Library and Info.Sci.) Shared Libraries, 2003. Recipient Helen Putnam award for excellence League of Calif. Cities, 1997. Mem. ALA, Calif. Libr. Assn., Pub. Libr. Assn., Libr. Adminstrn. and Mgmt. Assn. Avocations: writing, antiques, history, travel. Office: Los Gatos Pub Libr 110 E Main St Los Gatos CA 95030

CONBOY, KENNETH, lawyer, former federal judge; b. 1938; AB, Fordham Coll., 1961; JD, U. Va., 1964; MA in History, Columbia U., 1980. Asst. dist. atty., exec. asst. dist. atty. Manhattan Dist. Atty.'s Office, 1966-77; dep. commr., gen. counsel N.Y. Police, 1978-83; criminal justice dir. N.Y.C., 1984-86; N.Y.C. commr. of investigation, 1986-87; judge U.S. Dist. Ct. (so. dist.) N.Y, 1987-93; sr. litigation ptnr. Mudge, Rose, Guthrie, Alexander & Ferdon, N.Y.C., 1994-95; ptnr. Latham & Watkins, N.Y.C., 1995—. Summer faculty Cornell Law Sch.; adj. prof. of law Fordham Law Sch. Author: Grand Jury Examination of the Recalcitrant Witness, 1977; contbr. articles to profl. jours. Mem. N.Y. State Crime Control Planning Bd., N.Y. Sovern Commn. Capt. U.S. Army, 1964-66. Mem. Am. Soc. Legal History, N.Y. State Bar Assn., Assn. of Bar of City of N.Y., Fed. Bar Coun. Office: Latham & Watkins 885 3rd Ave Ste 1000 New York NY 10022-4834

CONBOY, ROY, playwright, educator; b. Lynwood, Calif., May 22, 1951; s. Roy Sr. and Josephine (Niño) C.; m. Teresa Elaine Conboy, Oct. 24, 1987; children: Miguel, Roy Cruz. BS, Ea. N.Mex. U., 1974; MFA, U. Calif., Irvine, 1976. Lectr. Santa Ana (Calif.) Coll., 1986-91; gen. mgr. Grove Shakespeare Festival, Garden Grove, Calif., 1988-90; artistic dir. Cucucuevez Multicultural Ensemble, Santa Ana, 1988-91; prof. theater arts and creative writing San Francisco State U., 1991—, chmn. theater arts, 1999—. Dramaturg Bay Area Playwrights Festival, San Francisco, 1999-2000; playwright Teatro Esperanza, San Francisco, 1992—; assoc. artist Cucucuevez Multicultural Ensemble, 1988-93. Playwright, performer: Drive My Coche, 1999; playwright: Dancing With the Missing, 1991, When El Cucui Walks, 1994, Suburban Canciones, 1997. Fellow Nat. Endowment for Arts, 1991; rsch. scholar, creative activity grantee San Francisco State U., 1996. Mem. Theatre Comms. Group, Theatre Bay Area. Office: San Francisco State U Dept Theater Arts 1600 Holloway Ave San Francisco CA 94132 E-mail: rconboy@sfsu.edu.

CONCANNON, JAMES M. law educator, university dean; b. Columbus, Ga., Oct. 2, 1947; s. James M. Jr. and Mary Jane (Crow) C.; m. Melissa P. Masoner, June 9, 1988. BS, U. Kans., 1968, JD, 1971. Law clk. Kans. Ins. Commn., Topeka, 1971; rsch. atty. Kans. Supreme Ct., Topeka, 1971-73; asst. prof. law Washburn U., Topeka, 1973-75, assoc. prof. law, 1976-81, prof., 1981—, dean, 1988-2001. Vis. prof. law Washington U., St. Louis, 1979; active Kans. Commn. on Pub. Understanding of Law, 1983-89, Task Force on Law Enforcement Consolidation, Topeka, 1991-92; mem. Nat. Conf. Commrs. on Uniform State Laws, 1998—, Pattern Instrns. for Kans.-Civil and Criminal Com., Kans. Jud. Coun., 2001—. Co-author: Kans. Appellate Practice Manual, 1978, Kansas Statutes of Limitations, 1988; sr. contbn. editor: Evidence in

America-Federal Rules in the States, 1987. Coord. Citizens to Keep Politics Out of Our Courts, Topeka, 1984; mem. bd. dirs. Kans. Legal Svcs. for Prisoners, 2003— ; co-reporter Citizens Justice Initiative, 1997-99; chmn. legal com. Concerned Citizens Topeka, 1995-99; bd. dirs. Mut. Funds Waddell and Reed, Inc., 1997—. Master: Topeka Am. Inn. of Ct. (pres. 2001—02); fellow: Kans. Bar Found., Am. Bar Found. (state chair 2002—, Kans. pres. 2002—); mem.: Assn. Am. Law Schs. (com. on bar admission, lawyer performance 1994—97), Kans. Bar Assn. (CLE com. 1976—2001, Outstanding Svc. award 1982, 2003), Washburn Law Sch. Alumni Assn. (life), Order of Coif. Office: Washburn U Law Sch 1700 SW College Ave Topeka KS 66621-0001

CONCANNON, THOMAS BERNARD, JR., lawyer; b. Newton, Mass., Nov. 10, 1939; s. Thomas Bernard and Anne Gertrude (Connolly) C.; m. Jeanne Ellen Twohig, Feb. 21, 1970; children— Kate Elizabeth, Maureen Anne. B.B.A., Boston Coll., 1961; M.Ed., State Coll. at Boston, 1962; J.D., Suffolk U., 1969. Bar: Mass. 1970, U.S. Dist. Ct. Mass. 1971. Assoc. Cohen & Concannon, Newton, 1970-76, Cohen, Concannon & Rosenberg, Newton, 1976-78, Concannon & Rosenberg, Newton, 1978-82, Concannon, Rosenberg & Freedman, Newton, 1982— ; sponsor Mass. Continuing Legal Edn., Inc. Mem. Newton Bd. Aldermen, 1970-78; chmn. Newton Democratic Citizens Com., 1978-82; bd. dirs. Newton Wellesley Weston Com. to Establish Residence for Retardates, 1983— . Named Outstanding Young Man in Newton, Jaycees, 1969. Mem. Mass. Bar Assn. (probate & family law sects.). Democrat. Roman Catholic. Home: 8 Bacon Rd Newton MA 02460-1304

CONCES, RORY JOSEPH, philosophy educator; b. East Chicago, Ind., Aug. 8, 1954; s. Dewey and Shirley Conces; m. Ann Marie C., May 28, 1977; children: Christopher D., Colin P., Daniel T. BA in Psychology and Philosophy, Creighton U., 1976; MA in Philosophy, DePaul U., 1980; PhD in Philosophy, U. Mo., Columbia, 1991. Instr. Columbia (Mo.) Coll., 1985, Moberly (Mo.) Area Jr. Coll., 1990; vis. asst. prof. U. Nebr., Omaha, 1992—; lectr. Creighton U., Omaha, 1994—2002. Vis. asst. prof. South China Normal U., Guangzhou, 2000, U. Sarajevo; program chair Nat. 3d World Studies Conf., Omaha, 1994—; coord. Nebr. Ctr. Critical Thinking, Omaha, 1994—; bd. dir. med. sci. bd. Alzheimer's Assn., Omaha, Nebr. Author: Blurred Visions: Philosophy, Science and Ideology in a Troubled World; editor: Internat. Third World Studies Jour. and Rv., 1994—. Fulbright scholar, Bosnia and Herzegovina, 2001. Mem. Am. Philos. Assn., Ctrl. States Philos. Assn., Soc. Social and Polit. Philosophy, Phi Beta Delta. Avocations: mountain climbing, travel, photography. Home: 12311 Wirt St Omaha NE 68164-2593 Office: U Nebr at Omaha Dept Philos and Religion 60th And Dodge Sts Omaha NE 68182-0265 E-mail: rconces@mail.unomaha.edu.

CONCORDIA, CHARLES, consulting engineer; b. Schenectady, N.Y., June 20, 1908; s. Francis G. and Susie Elizabeth (Decker) C.; m. Frances Butler, Dec. 18, 1948. ScD, Union Coll., 1971; ScD (hon.), Iowa State U., 1993. Reg. profl. engr., N.Y., Fla. With GE, Schenectady, 1926-73, in lab., 1926-31, participant, tchr. advanced engring. program, 1932-35, in power system engring. dept., 1936-73, applications engr., 1936-49, in aircraft devel., 1941-45, cons. engr., 1949-73; cons. electric power systems engring. Venice, Fla., 1973—. Lectr. various univs. Author: Synchronous Machines, 1951; contbr. over 130 articles to profl. jours.; patentee in field (6). Recipient Coffin award Gen. Electric Co., 1942, Steinmetz award, 1973. Fellow IEEE (Lamme medal 1961, Centennial award 1984, Power life award 1992, First chmn. of First Com. on Computing Devices, 1946, medal of hon. 1999Millennium medal 2000), ASME (chmn. profl. practice com., chmn. Schenectady sect. 1948), AAAS; mem. NAE, NSPE (Engr. of Yr. award 1963), Assn. Computing Machinery (founding mem., treas. 1953), Conf. Internationale des Grands Reseaux Electriques a Haute Tension (Philip Sporn award 1989), Sigma Xi, Tau Beta Pi. Clubs: Venice Yacht, Mohawk Golf. Republican. Presbyterian. Home and Office: 900 Tamiami Trl S Apt 316 Venice FL 34285-3625 E-mail: venice34285@yahoo.com.

CONDAYAN, JOHN, foreign service officer, diplomat, consultant; b. Addis Ababa, Ethiopia, Sept. 1, 1933; s. Vahram Hagop and Sirvart (Parthog) C.; m. Eileen Mary Ferguson, Nov. 6, 1965; children: Christopher Charles, Alicia Elizabeth BS, Bucknell U., 1955; MPA, Syracuse U., 1974; postgrad., Nat. Def. U., 1978. Mng. dir. V.H. Condayan & Co., N.Y.C., 1955-63; joined Fgn. Service, Dept. State, 1965; adminstrv. officer Am. embassy, Niamey, Niger, 1965-67, gen. services officer Manila, 1967-69; spl. asst. to dep. asst. sec. Dept. State, Washington, 1969-71; adminstrv. officer Am. embassy, Copenhagen, 1971-73, exec. dir. Office Fgn. Bldgs., 1974-75, spl. exec. dir. to asst. sec. of state for adminstrn., 1975-77, counselor of embassy Moscow, 1978-80, Bangkok, Thailand, 1980-82; exec. dir. Bur. E. Asian and Pacific Affairs, 1982-83; dep. asst. sec. for ops. bur. adminstrn. U.S. Dept. State, Washington, 1983-87, dir. office fgn. missions, 1987-89; minister-counsellor Am. Embassy, London, 1989-91; assoc. dir. for mgmt. USIA, Washington, 1991-94; pvt. cons., 1994—. Bd. dirs. Internat. Sch., Copenhagen, 1970-71, Anglo-Am. Sch., Moscow, 1978-80, Am. Employee Assn., Moscow, 1978-80, Am. Employee Support Orgn., Bangkok, 1980-82; mem. assets and liability com. State Dept. Fed. Credit Union, 1985, 92-93, bd. dirs., 1993-98, treas., 1994-95. Recipient Presdl. Humanitarian award (The Philippines), 1968, Meritorious Honor award Dept. State, 1975, Superior Honor award, 1985, 92, Presdl. Meritorious award, 1987, Dir.'s award for Superior Achievement, 1993. Mem. Armenian Orthodox Ch. Avocations: photography; reading; sports.

CONDE, MIGUEL A. hematologist, oncologist; b. 1958; MD, Columbia U., 1986. Diplomate Am. Bd. Internal Medicine, Am. Bd. Hematology, Am. Bd. Oncology. Resident medicine George Washington U. Hosp., Washington, 1986-89, fellow hematology and oncology, 1989-91; fellow rsch. FDA/Nat. Cancer Inst., 1991-93; mem. staff St. Barnabas Med. Ctr., Livingston, N.J., 1993—; clin. affiliate Meml. Sloan Kettering Cancer Ctr., 1996-2000. Mem. ACP, AMA, Assn. Medicine N.J., Am. Soc. Clin. Oncology, N.J. Med. Soc., Am. Soc. Blood and Marrow Transplantation, Am. Soc. Hematology, Soc. for Neuro-Oncology. Office: St Barnabas Cancer Ctr East Wing 2nd Fl Livingston NJ 07039 E-mail: mconde@sbhcs.com.

CONDE, YVONNE M. freelance journalist; b. Havana, Cuba, Oct. 28, 1950; came to the U.S., 1961; d. Pedro M. and Maria L. (de Quesada) C.; m. B. Loret de Mola, Apr. 10, 1989. BA in Communication, SUNY, N.Y.C., 1989; MA in Journalism, NYU, 1991. Freelance journalist various publs., N.Y.C., 1991—; columnist HOY Newspaper. Author: Operation Pedro Pan, 1999. Recipient award for best news and pub. affairs work Nat. Assn. Coll. Broadcasters, 1991. Mem.: Nat. Assn. Hispanic Journalists. Roman Catholic. Avocation: sporting clays. Home: 340 E 64 St Apt 23B New York NY 10021-7510 E-mail: nytropical@aol.com.

CONDEE, WILLIAM FARICY, theater educator, writer; b. State College, Pa., Feb. 17, 1954; s. Ralph Waterbury and Norma (Faricy) C.; m. Kathleen Dierkes, Mar. 16, 1985; children: Colin Johnson Dierkes, Austin Faricy Dierkes. BA, Vassar Coll., 1976, MA, 1980; PhD, Columbia U., 1987. Prof. theater Ohio U., Athens, 1986—, dir. Sch. Interdisciplinary Arts Athens. Vis. lectr. U. Leipzig (Germany); lectr. (hon.) U. Wales, Cardiff; vis. prof. Vassar Coll., Poughkeepsie, N.Y.; dramaturg Young Vic Theatre, London, 1987. Author: Theatrical Space, 1995; contbr. articles to jours. Faculty fellow Ohio U., 1994. Mem. Am. Soc. Theatre Rsch., Assn. Theater in Higher Edn., Actors Equity Assn., Literary Mgrs. and Dramaturgs of the Ams. Democrat. Avocations: birdwatching, playing flute, singing. Office: Ohio U Sch Interdisciplinary Arts 102 Lindley Athens OH 45701

CONDENI, JOSEPH ANTHONY, lawyer; b. Cleve., Nov. 21, 1956; s. Joseph George and Marie Dorothy Condeni; m. Maritza Acevedo, Aug. 29, 1987. BLS, Bowling Green U., 1979; JD, Cleve. State U., 1982. Bar: Ohio 1982, U.S. Dist. Ct. (no. dist.) Ohio 1983, U.S. Ct. Appeals (6th cir.) 1990. Assoc. Jerome and Smith, Cleve., 1982-88; ptnr. Jerome, Smith and Condeni, Cleve., 1988-92; prin. Smith and Condeni Co., LPA, Cleve., 1992—. Editor Cleveland State Law Rev., 1980-81, mng. editor, 1981-82. Mem. ATLA, Nat. Employment Lawyers Assn., Cleve. Bar Assn., Cuyahoga County Bar Assn., Cleve. Acad. Trial Lawyers, Cleve. Employment Lawyers Assn., Cleve. Acad. Employment Lawyers. Avocations: snow skiing, golf. Office: Smith and Condeni Co LPA 1801 E 9th St Ste 900 Cleveland OH 44114-3103 Fax: 216-771-3387. E-mail: joe@smith-condeni.com.

CONDER, JIMMIE LEE, commercial pilot, farmer; b. San Antonio, Nov. 24, 1934; s. William Thomas and Kathryn Louise Conder; m. JoNell Conder, Jan. 27, 1962 (div. Dec. 23, 1983); children: Laurie A., Troy E.; m. Bernice A. Conder, June 8, 1998. AA in Liberal Arts, Coll. So. Idaho, 1982. Lic. comml. pilot, multi-engine land, single engine land, instrument, DC-3. Commd. 2d lt. USAF, 1960, advanced through grades to maj., 1969; aerial gunner 90th Bomb Squadron, 1953; aviation cadet Air Tng. Command, Bainbridge, Ga., 1957-60; pilot, aerial tanker USAF Tactical Air Command, Biggs AFB, Tex., 1960-64; air commando pilot 315th Air Commando Group, Vietnam, 1964-65; pilot Mil. Airlift Command, Travis AFB, Calif., 1966-68; airlift coord./emergency actions officer 513th Tactical Airlift Wing, RAF Mildenball, Eng., 1968-70; civil air patrol liaison USAF, Twin Falls, Idaho, 1971-75; charter pilot Reeder Flying Svc., Twin Falls, Idaho, 1975-77; asst. safety and info. officer/pilot Idaho Bur. Aeronautics, Boise, 1977-79; corp. pilot Nielson, Twin Falls, 1983; safety and info. officer/chief pilot Idaho Bur. Aeronautics, Boise, 1984-88; pilot Corp. Air, Billings, Mont., 1988—; adminstr. Idaho Bur. Aeronautics, 1995-96. Pilot/program mgr. AirServ Internat., Ethiopia, 1991-92, 93, Sudan, 1995, Mozambique, Uganda and Congo, 1996-97, Uganda, Congo, 1998; airlift coord., pilot Flood Disaster Relief, Mozambique, 2000; Gt. Lakes Region program dir., pilot, Uganda and Congo, 2001, 02; pilot CorporateAir, 2002-2003. Decorated D.F.C., Meritorious Svc. Medal, 21 Air medals. Mem. Gideons, Alpha Eta Rho (hon.). Republican. Avocations: farming, antique clock restoration, political science. Home: Bird-in-Hand Farm 3623 N 2000 E Filer ID 83328-5667 E-mail: comet@filertel.com.

CONDICT, EDGAR RHODES, medical electronics, aviation instrument manufacturing and medical health care executive, inventor, mediator, pastor; b. Boston, Apr. 27, 1940; s. Clinton Adams and Elizabeth May (Lane) C.; m. Judith Pond, June 9, 1962; children: Edgar Rhodes Jr., Robert Adams, Carolyn Helen. Student, Bucknell U., 1962, U. Pa., NYU. Cert. lic. min., clin. pastoral edn. Chmn. bd., pres., founder Bio-Tronics Rsch., Inc., 1962—, Kearsarge Healthcare, Inc., 1978—, Condict Instruments, Inc., 1985—; cons. U. Tex. Med. Sch., 1968-70; pres. Medel Corp., patent devel. investment, 1965—; pres., chmn. bd. Erin Eye Clinics, 1998—. Cons. in med. electronics, electronics, biophysics, biofeedback, telecomm., environ. health and welfare; pastor 1st Bapt. Ch. Lyme (NH), 2002—. Author: A Theory of Anesthesia, 1962, Feedback Anesthesia, 1968, Electronic Pain-Killing Devices, 1970, Healing in 1993, 1993, How Your Brain Works, 1993, Your Temperament, 1993, Mediation and the Law, 1993, Healing in the '90's, 1992, We Need Religion-Now!, 1994, others. Patentee in med. electronics, telecommunications fields. Vol., bereavement coord. Lake Sunapee Hospice, 2001; tchr. ch. sch. Bapt. ch., 1962—97; supt., 1995—97; ABC Cert. Lay Minister program, 1996; trustee ABC/VTNH, 2002; bd. dirs. Lake Sunapee Area Mediation Program, 1988—90, pres., 1990; chmn. bd. World Mediators, 1990—. Recipient various grants in neuro-brain scis.; numerous med. awards from fgn. countries. Mem. Sigma Chi. Avocations: flying, amateur radio, computers. Address: PO Box 1110 New London NH 03257-1110

CONDIFF, DAVID WESLEY, clinical psychologist; b. St. Paul, Sept. 22, 1943; s. Howard Lee and Hazel Condiff; m. Lorraine Condiff, Aug. 28, 1965; children: Deborah, David Wesley. Student, U. Minn., 1961-62; BA in Social Scis., Bethel Coll., St. Paul, 1965; PhD in Clin. Psychology, Fuller Theol. Sem., Pasadena, Calif., 1972. Lic. psychologist, lic. marriage and family therapist, Calif. Group leader Fuller Theol. Sem., 1967-68; psychology intern Glendale (Calif.) Adventist Hosp., 1968-69, social worker asst., 1969-70; psychology asst. Foothill Psychiat. Med. Ctr., Glendora, Calif., 1971-73, clin. psychologist, 1973-75; dir. Live Oak Counseling Ctr., Glendora, 1973—. Profl. cons. to sr. pastor Glenkirk Presbyn. Ch.; profl. cons. to Glendora Police Dept.; mem. Human Svcs. Com. Assisting City Mgr., Glendora, 1987. Mem. choir Glenkirk Presbyn. Ch., 1975—; mem. choir for opening ceremonies XXIII Olympiad at Coliseum, L.A., 1984; coach Little League, San Dimas-La Verne, Calif. Mem. APA, Calif. State Psychol. Assn., Nat. Register Health Svc. Providers in Psychology, Pi Epsilon Mu. Democrat. Avocations: swimming, tennis, waterskiing, reading, singing. Office: Live Oak Counseling Ctr 1114 E Route 66 Glendora CA 91740-3771 E-mail: d.condiff.sr.@worldnet.att.net.

CONDINI, NED, translator; s. Enrico Condini and Bianca Marin; m. Marilyn Wojcik, May 20, 1942. PhD, Turin U., 1963. Tchr. Hudson County C.C., Jersey City, 1977—81, H.S., Westwood, NJ, 1985—2000; translator Bordighera Press, West Lafayette, Ind., 2002—. Author: Poetry Collections (Modesto Della Porta, 1972), (plays) Malcolm X, (short stories) Rattlers (Short Fiction First prize, Abiko, Japan., 1993); contbr. articles to profl. and popular publs.; author: (novels) Eldorado (PEN/Poggioli award, 1986), 1960-2002: A Testimony (Winning Writers award, 2002); translator: Andsongsongsonglessness (Bordighera prize, 2002), (plays) Plays by Ben Jonson. Fellow: People Ethical Treatment Animals; mem.: Sierra Club. Roman Catholic. Avocations: swimming, tennis, mountain climbing, jogging, music. Personal E-mail: fydor@juno.com.

CONDIT, DORIS ELIZABETH, retired historian; b. Balt. d. Harlan Whitney and Dorothy Elizabeth (Witte) Morgan; m. Kenneth W. Condit, Aug. 22, 1953; children: Caroline Walbridge, Victoria Whitney. Student, Johns Hopkins U., 1945-46; AB, George Washington U., 1949, MA, 1952. Historian U.S. Corps of Engrs. Hist. Divsn., Balt., 1949-51; ops. analyst Johns Hopkins U. Ops. Rsch. Office, Chevy Chase, Md., 1952-56; rsch. scientist, sr. rsch. scientist Am. Univ. Ctr. for Rsch. in Social Sys., Washington, 1956-69; sr. rsch. scientist Am. Inst. for Rsch., Kensington, Md., 1969-74; cons. Office of Sec. of Def., Washington, 1974-77, 85-87, contract historian, 1977-85. Cons. Braddock, Dunn & McDonald, 1973-74, Am. Insts. for Rsch., 1974, Ops. Rsch. Office, 1956-57; assoc. prof. rsch. Am. U., 1960-69; rsch. area chmn. Ctr. for Rsch. in Social Sys., 1966-70; mem. ad hoc group for Sci. and Tech. Info., 1962. Author: Allied Supplies for Italian Partisans During World War II, 1954, A System for Handling Data on Unconventional Warfare, 1956, Case Study in Guerrilla War: Greece During World War II, 1961, Modern Revolutionary Warfare: An Analytical Overview, 1973, The Test of War, 1950-53, History of the Office of the Secretary of Defense, Vol. II, 1988, (with Bert H. Cooper, Jr. and others) Challenge and Response in Internal Conflict, 3 vols., 1967-68, U.S. Military Response to Overseas Insurgencies, 1970, Strategy and Success in Internal Conflict, 1971, Population Protection and Resources Management in Internal Defense Operations, 1971. Recipient Gardiner G. Hubbard Meml. prize in Am. history George Washington U., 1949. Mem. Phi Beta Kappa. Episcopalian.

CONDIT, GARY ADRIAN, former congressman; b. Salina, Okla., Apr. 21, 1948; AA, Modesto Jr. Coll., 1970; BA, Calif. State Coll., 1972. Councilman City of Ceres, Calif., 1972-74, mayor, 1974-76; supr. Stanislaus County, Calif., 1976-82; assemblyman State of Calif., 1982-89; mem. U.S. Congress from 18th Calif. dist., 1989—2002; mem. agr. com. Democrat.*

CONDIT, LINDA FAULKNER, economist; b. Denver, May 30, 1947; d. Claude Winston and Nancy Isobel (McCallum) Faulkner; m. John Michael Condit, Dec. 20, 1970; 1 child, David Devin. BA, U. Ark., 1969; MA, U. Wis., 1970; postgrad., U. Minn., 1974-77. Rsch. asst. U. Wis., Madison, 1969-70; economist St. Louis Fed. Res. Bank, 1971-73; ops. analyst No. States Power co., Mpls., 1973-76; energy economist, 1976-78; from ecoomist to v.p. Pennzoil Co., Houston, 1978—95, v.p., 1995—98; v.p., corp. sec. Pennzoil-Quaker State Co., Houston, 1998—2002. Econ. cons. Jr. Achievement, 1983. Recipient Alumni award U. Ark., 1969. Mem. Internat. Assn. Energy Economists (pres., v.p., treas.), Nat. Assn. Bus. Economists, Internat. Bus. Coun. (v.p.), Am. Econ. Assn., N.Am. Soc. Corp. Planners, Am. Soc. Corp. Secs. (membership chmn.), Hits Theatre (bd. dirs.), Corp. Alliance To Eliminate Ptnr. Violence (bd. dirs.), Leadership Am., Harvard Discussion Group Indsl. Economists, Forst Club, River Oaks Women's Breakfast Club (v.p., pres.), Mortar Bd., Phi Beta Kappa, Kappa Alpha Theta. Home: 11822 Village Park Cir Houston TX 77024-4418

CONDIT, PHILIP MURRAY, aerospace executive, engineer; b. Berkeley, Calif., Aug. 2, 1941; s. Daniel Harrison and Bernice (Kemp) C.; m. Madeleine K. Bryant, Jan. 25, 1963 (div. June 1982); children: Nicole Lynn, Megan Anne; m. Janice Condit, Apr. 6, 1991. BS MechE, U. Calif., Berkeley, 1963; MS in Aero. Engring., Princeton U., 1965; MS in Mgmt., MIT, 1975. Engr. The Boeing Co., Seattle, 1965-72, mgr. engring., 1973-83, v.p., gen. mgr., 1983-84, v.p. sales and mktg., 1984-86, exec. v.p., 1986-89, exec. v.p., gen. mgr. 777 divsn., 1989-92, pres., 1992-96, chmn., CEO, 1996—. Adv. coun. Dept. Mech. and Aerospace Engring., Princeton (N.J.) U., 1984—; chmn. aero. adv. com. NASA Adv. Coun., 1988-92; bd. dirs. The Fluke Corp., Nordstom, Inc. Co-inventor design of a flexible wing. Active Mercer Island (Wash.) Utilities Bd., 1975-78; bd. dirs. Camp Fire, Inc., 1987-92; exec bd. chief Seattle coun. Boy Scouts Am., 1988-90; trustee Mus. of Flight, Seattle, 1990—. Co-recipient Laurels Award Aviation Week & Space Tech. magazine, 1990; Sloan fellow MIT, Boston, 1974. Fellow AIAA (Aircraft Design award 1984, Edward C. Wells tech. mgmt. award 1982, Wright Brothers Lectureship Aeronautics 1996), Royal Aero. Soc.; mem. NAE, Soc. Sloan Fellows (bd. govs. 1985-89), Soc. Automotive Engrs., Rainer Club, Columbia Tower Club (Seattle). Clubs: Rainier, Columbia Tower (Seattle). Office: The Boeing Co 7755 E Marginal Way S Seattle WA 98108-4000

CONDITT, MARGARET KAREN, research scientist, policy analyst; b. Mobile, Ala., Aug. 7, 1953; m. David Joseph Bruno, Feb. 13, 1988; 2 stepchildren: Josh, Holly. BS in Chemistry, U. Ala., Tuscaloosa, 1975; PhD in Chemistry, U. Colo., 1984. Field hydrologist U.S. Geol. Survey, Tuscaloosa, 1975; sci. aide II Geol. Survey Ala., Tuscaloosa, 1975-77; tchg. asst. U. Ala., Tuscaloosa, 1977-79; rsch. asst. U. Colo., Boulder, 1979-84; sr. scientist Procter & Gamble, Cin., 1984—. Reviewer sci. edn. grant proposals NSF, Washington, 1988; mem. water sci. and tech. bd. com. Nat. Acad. Scis., Washington, 1989-91. Author: (chpt.) Advanced Techniques in Synthetic Fuels Analysis, 1983; contbr. articles to profl. jours. Intern Colo. Gov.'s Sci. and Tech. Adv. Coun., 1981—83; appointee Liberty Twp. Bd. Zoning Appeal, 1994—97; elected trustee Liberty Twp., 1998—2001. Recipient fellowship Mining and Mineral Resources and Rsch. Inst., 1980, Rsch. fellowship U. Colo. Grad. Sch., 1981, Browns-Rickett grant AAUW, 1982. Mem. Am. Chem. Soc. Roman Catholic. Avocations: collecting antiques, boy scouts. Home: 6959 Rock Springs Dr Liberty Township OH 45011-9376

CONDLIFFE, PETER GEORGE, research scientist; b. Christchurch, New Zealand, June 30, 1922; arrived in U.S., 1926; s. John Bell Condliffe and Olive Grace Mills; m. Susa Hearst Condliffe, Oct. 22, 1942 (div. June 13, 1980); children: Katherine Margaret, Donald Peter, John Jacob; m. Eleanor Michelle Hart, Sept. 14, 1980. BA, U. Calif., Berkeley, 1947, PhD, 1952. Rsch. assoc. biochemistry dept. Cornell U. Med. Coll., N.Y.C., 1952—54; rsch. scientist Nat. Inst. Diabetes, Digestive and Kidney Diseases, NIH, Bethesda, Md., 1954—75; chief scholars program Fogarty Internat. Ctr., NIH, Bethesda, Md., 1975—88; scientist emeritus NIH, Bethesda, Md., 1988—. Hormone distbn. officer NIDDK, NIH, Bethesda, 1971—75. Contbr. articles to profl. jours.; co-editor: Ethical Issues in Human Genetics, Pharmacology and Pharmacokinetics, 1974, Chemical Synthesis and Sequencing of Peptides and Proteins, 1981. S/sgt. U.S. Army, 1942—46. Mem.: Cosmos Club. Democrat. Avocations: skiing, tennis, gardening. Home: 3939 Washington St Kensington MD 20895 Office: Lab Cellular and Devel Biology NIDDK NIH Bethesda MD 20892

CONDO, JAMES ROBERT, lawyer; b. Somerville, N.J., Mar. 2, 1952; s. Ralph Vincent and Betty Louise (MacQuaide) C. BS in Bus. and Econs., Lehigh U., 1974; JD, Boston Coll., 1979. Bar: Ariz. 1979, Colo. 2001, U.S. Dist. Ct. Ariz. 1979, U.S. Ct. Appeals (9th cir.) 1982, U.S. Supreme Ct. 1983, U.S. Ct. Appeals (D.C. cir.) 1989, U.S. Ct. Appeals (10th cir.) 1989, U.S. Ct. Appeals (6th cir.) 1991, U.S. Ct. Appeals (4th cir.) 1994. Assoc. Snell & Wilmer, Phoenix, 1979-84, ptnr., 1985—. Judge pro tem Ariz. Ct. Appeals. Active Ariz. Town Hall, 1985—. Fellow Ariz. Bar Found.; mem. ABA, State Bar Ariz., Maricopa County Bar Found., Defense Rsch. Inst. Office: Snell & Wilmer One Arizona Ctr Phoenix AZ 85004-2202 E-mail: jcondo@swlaw.com.

CONDON, CHARLES MOLONY, former state attorney general; b. Charleston, S.C., May 2, 1953; s. James Joseph and Harriet (Molony) Condon; m. Emily Yarbrough, June 21, 1980; children: Charles Molony Jr., Patrick Monaghan, Doreen Yarbrough, Emily Elliot. Student, Saltzburg (Austria) Summer Sch., 1972, U. Innsbruck, Austria, 1972—73; BA, U. Notre Dame, 1975; JD, Duke U., 1978. Bar: S.C. 1978, U.S. Dist. Ct. S.C. 1978, U.S. Ct. Appeals (4th cir.) 1987, U.S. Supreme Ct. 1988. Assoc. Nexsen, Pruet, Jacobs & Pollard, Columbus, SC, 1978—79; asst. solicitor S.C. 9th Jud. Cir., Charleston, 1979—80, solicitor, 1980—92; atty. gen. State of S.C., Columbia, 1995—2002. Lectr. med. U. S.C., 1982—83, Coll. Charleston, 1986, bd. visitors com., 1992—; panel mem. Nat. Inst. for Drug Abuse, Washington; prosecuter City of Isle Palms, SC, 1993—; cons. Nat. Consortium for Justice Info. and Stats.; profl. rep. So. Environ. Network, 1990—91. Sect. chmn. govtl. divsn. United Way; ex-officio mem. Friends of Charleston County Courthouse; com. mem. Charleston County Criminal Justice Task Force; bd. dirs. com. for drug free soc. Charleston County Sch. Dist., 1989, Children's Ctr., Charleston, SC, 1990—91, S.C. Commn. on Presecution Coord., 1991—92. Mem.: ABA, S.C. Law Enforcement Assn., S.C. Cir. Solicitors Assn. (v.p. 1987—88, pres. 1988—89), Richland County Bar Assn., S.C. Bar Assn., Silver Elephant Club, Notre Dame Club, Charleston Lawyers Club. Republican.

CONDON, DAVID BRUCE, lawyer; b. Tacoma, May 20, 1949; s. Lester Milo and Ruby Elizabeth (Elson) C.; m. Constance Lynn Montgomery, Aug. 27, 1971; children: Amy M., Anne E. BA, U. Wash., 1971; JD cum laude, Gonzaga U., 1974. Bar: Wash. 1974, U.S. Dist. Ct. (we. dist.) Wash. 1974, U.S. Ct. Appeals (9th cir.) 1976, U.S. Dist. Ct. (ea. dist.) Wash. 1989. Assoc. Griffin & Enslow, Tacoma, 1974-78; ptnr. Welch & Condon, Tacoma, 1978—. Examiner Wash. State Higher Edn. Pers. Bd., 1979-95. Bd. dirs. Bldg. A. Scholastic Heritage, pres., 1991-92; bd. dirs. Tacoma Art Mus., 1993-94. Law. ABA, Wash. State Bar Assn., Tacoma-Pierce County Bar Assn., Assn. Trial Lawyers Am., Wash. Trial Lawyers Assn., Nat. Assn. Social Security Claimants Reps. Avocations: running, swimming. Office: Welch & Condon PO Box 1318 Tacoma WA 98401-1318 E-mail: condond@harbornet.com.

CONDON, ELIZABETH M. education educator; b. Toledo, Ohio, Feb. 9, 1967; d. Richard J. and Joyce E. Condon. BS, univ. Toledo, Ohio, 1989; MS, Univ. Toledo, Ohio, 1991. Cert. sec. edn. Ohio. Math instr. Univ. Toledo, Toledo, 1991—96; high sch. math tchr. Springfield High Sch., Holland, Ohio, 1994—95; devel. math instr. Owens Cmty. Coll., Toledo, 1996—. Mem.: Am. Math. Assn., Nat. Assn. Devel. Edn., Ohio Assn Devel. Edn. Office: Owens Cmty Coll PO Box 10000 Toledo OH 43699

CONDON, FRANCIS EDWARD, retired chemistry educator; b. Abington, Mass., Oct. 12, 1919; s. Maurice Francis and Eva Isabel (Cole) C.; m. Mary Anna Medvetz, Jan. 9, 1943; children: Francis E., Mary Ellen Condon Laessig, John M., Arthur T., Dorothy A. Condon Waldt, James M., Rita C. Condon McCarthy. AB, Harvard, 1941, PhD, 1944. Research chemist Phillips Petroleum Co., Bartlesville, Okla., 1944-52; asst. prof. chemistry CCNY, 1952-61, assoc. prof., 1962-66, prof., 1967-82, ret., 1982, Louis J. Curtman prof., 1976-78; founder, chmn. Seven Siblings Found., Ltd., 1977-94. Vis. prof. Purdue U., 1960 Author: (with H. Meislich) Introduction to Organic Chemistry, 1960, Study Projects in Physical Chemistry, 1963, Chess monographs, 1992—, also articles; contbr. chpt. to Catalysis, 1958. Mem. planning bd. Borough of Bogota, N.J., 1963; Trustee, pres. Bogota Swim Club, Inc., 1967-71. Petroleum Research Fund grantee, 1967-70; NSF Sci. Faculty fellow U. So. Calif., 1964-65 Mem. Am. Chem. Soc. (dir. N.Y. sect. 1967-68), U.S. Chess Fedn. (life), Glen Rock (N.J.) Chess Club (pres. 1975-79, Washington Twp. (N.J.) Chess Club (pres. 1990-92), Dumont (N.J.) Chess Mates (sec. 1992-99), St. Joseph's Holy Name Soc. (pres. 1974-75, sec. 1992—), Alpha Chi Sigma, Sigma Xi. Home: 471 Larch Ave Bogota NJ 07603-1058

CONDON, GEORGE EDWARD, journalist; b. Fall River, Mass., Nov. 6, 1916; s. John Joseph and Mary Agnes (O'Malley) C.; m. Marjorie Philona Smith, May 9, 1942; children— Theresa, John, George, Katherine, Mary, Susan. BSc in Journalism, Ohio State U., 1940. Publicity dir. Mt. Union Coll., Alliance, Ohio, 1941; info. dir. Agrl. Adjustment Adminstrn. for Ohio, 1941-42; mem. staff Cleve. Plain Dealer, 1943-84; TV critic, 1948—62; gen. columnist Cleve. Plain Dealer, 1962-84; pres. George Condon & Assocs., Inc., 1985—. Author: Cleveland-The Best-Kept Secret, 1967, Laughter from the Rafters, 1968, Stars in the Water, 1972, Yesterday's Cleveland, 1976, Yesterday's Columbus, 1977, Cleveland: Prodigy of the Western Reserve, 1979, History of Ohio Farmers Insurance Company, 1985, Gaels of Laughter and Tears, 1995, The Man in the Arena, 1995. Recipient Ohioana Library Assn. Lit. award, 1975, Cleve. Women's City Club Lit. award, 1975, Emily Gray Burke Meml. award lit., 1979; award Cleve. Newspaper Guild; awards for public service, copy editing and column writing Press Club Cleve.; Disting. Service award Nat. Soc. Profl.

Journalists, 1980; named to Cleve. Journalism Hall of Fame, Press Club Cleve., 1990. Mem. Sigma Delta Chi, Pi Sigma Alpha. Home: The Waterford 12500 Edgewater Dr Lakewood OH 44107 E-mail: geocondon@msn.com.

CONDON, J. EMMETT, information technology executive; b. Phila., Apr. 17, 1960; s. James Patrick and Loretta Marie Condon; m. Edith M. France, Apr. 28, 2001. AAS Data Processing, Delaware County C.C., Media, Pa., 1981; BS Bus. Adminstrn. Computer Info. Sys., Western New England Coll., 1987; MBA, LaSalle U., Phila., 1995. PMP cert., Project Mgmt. Inst., 2002. Sr. sys. cons. Betz Labs., Trevose, Pa., 1987—2001; project mgr. e-Duction Inc., Blue Bell, Pa., 2001—02, Tenex Systems Inc., King of Prussia, Pa., 2003—. Adj. prof. LaSalle U., Phila., 1996—2002, U. Phoenix, 2002—. With USAF, 1981—85. Decorated Meritorious Svc. medal. Mem.: Northeast Regional Computer Users Group (bd. dirs. 1995—). Republican. Roman Catholic. Avocation: sailing. Home: 4268 Lawnside Rd Philadelphia PA 19154

CONDON, JOSEPH DENNIS, broadcasting executive; b. Albany, N.Y., Apr. 12, 1946; s. Joseph O. and Loretta (Halleran) C.; m. Kathleen M. Sullivan, Jan. 25, 1969; 1 child, Daniel J. Assoc. Degree in Bus. Adminstrn., Hudson Valley C.C., Troy, N.Y., 1966; BA in Mktg. and Acctg., Siena Coll., 1969; Degree in Pub. Rels., Albany Bus. Coll., 1975. Cert. TV prodn. specialist, USARNG, 1970. Announcer, disc jockey WTRY Kopps/Monahan Corp., Troy, 1963-67; announcer, news and weathercaster WAST-TV RKO Gen., Albany, 1967-68; announcer, disc jockey WABY Radio, Albany, 1967-69; announcer WTEN/WROW Capital Cities Comm., Albany, 1969-83; with WROW/WYJB Radio Albany Broadcasting, 1969—, pub. affairs dir., 1982—; owner Radio Albany.com, Albany, 2000—. N.E. corr. Voice of Am., Washington, 1983-87; owner radioalbany.com, 2000—; cons. in field, 1991—; owner, operator racioalbany.com comml. internet sta. Pub. rels. chmn. bicentennial com. St. Mary's Ch. Sgt. N.Y. Nat. Guard, 1969-75. Recipient first place for best pub. affairs show N.Y. State Broadcasters, Albany, 1995, second place Nori award Ad Club, Albany, 1995, Best Sta. Event award N.Y. State Broadcasters, Albany, 1996, Best Pub. Affairs Series, 1997, 1998, Best Pub. Affairs Show, 1998, awd. Albany Broadcasting Co., 1998, cmty. svc. award for pub. affairs Nat. Broadcast Assn., 1998, 99, Proclamation, N.Y. State Senate, 1999, Proclamation, N.Y. Senator Neil Breslin, 1999, nominee Marconi award 1997, 98, recipient awards N.Y. State Broadcasters, 1999, silver microphone nat. finalist award, 1999, Best Pub. Affairs show award, 2000, Best Pub. Affairs Series award, 2000. Mem. AFTRA, NAACP, Am. Broadcast Pioneers Broadcast Found., N.Y. State Broadcasters (advisor job fair com.), Holocaust Survivors and Friends, R.R. Hist. Soc., Ad Club, Nat. Music Found. Avocations: broadcast historian, wwii historian, photographer, railroad historian. Home: 48 Glenwood Rd Menands NY 12204-2407 Office: Albany Broadcasting 6 Johnson Rd Latham NY 12110-5638

CONDON, ROBERT EDWARD, surgeon, educator, consultant; b. Albany, N.Y., Aug. 13, 1929; s. Edward A. and Catherine (Kilmartin) C.; m. Marcia Jane Pagano, June 16, 1951; children: Sean Edward, Brian Robert. AB, U. Rochester, 1951, MD, 1957; MS, U. Wash., 1965. Diplomate Am. Bd. Surgery, Nat. Bd. Med. Examiners. N.Y. Bd. Regents scholar U. Rochester, 1957; intern King County Hosp., Seattle, 1957-58; resident dept. surgery U. Wash. Sch. Medicine (and affiliated hosps.), 1958-65; postdoctoral rsch. fellow Nat. Heart Inst., 1961-63; asst. prof. surgery Baylor Coll. Medicine, Houston, 1965-67; assoc. prof. surgery U. Ill. Coll. Medicine, Chgo., 1967-69, prof., 1969-70; prof., head dept. surgery U. Iowa Coll. Medicine, Iowa City, 1971-72; prof. surgery Med. Coll. Wis., Milw., 1972—98, prof. emeritus, 1998, chmn. dept. surgery, 1979-95; chief surg. svcs. Wood VA Hosp., Milw., 1972-81. Attending surgeon Froedtert Meml. Luth. Hosp., 1982-98; cons. Columbia Hosp., Milw., St. Joseph Hosp., Milw.; clin. prof. surgery U. Wash., 2000—. Author: (with others) Abdominal Pain: A Guide to Rapid Diagnosis, 2d edit., 1995, Manual of Surgical Therapeutics, 9th edit., 1996, Hernia, 4th edit., 1995, Surgical Care, 1980. Recipient sr. class award as Outstanding Faculty Member Baylor U. Coll. Medicine, 1966, Excellence in Teaching award Phi Chi, 1967, Cert. Appreciation U. Iowa Coll. Medicine, 1971, Tchr. of Yr. award U. Iowa Coll. Medicine, 1972, Tchr. of Yr. award Med. Coll. Wis., 1983, 95, Disting. Svc. award Med. Coll. Wis., 1993, Disting. Alumnus award U. Wash., 1998; rsch. fellow Guggenheim Found., 1963-64. Mem. ACS (bd. govs.), Am. Surg. Assn. (v.p.), Surg. Infection Soc. (pres.), Am. Assn. Surgery of Trauma, Internat. Soc. Surgery, Collegium Internationale Chirurgiae Digestivae (pres.), Assn. for Acad. Surgery, Cen. Surg. Assn. (pres.), So. Surg. Assn., Western Surg. Assn., Wis. Surg. Soc. (pres.), Milw. Surg. Soc. (pres.), Chgo. Surg. Soc., Soc. U. Surgeons, Soc. Clin. Surgery, Milw. Acad. Medicine, Soc. Surgery Alimentary Tract (v.p.), Milw. Acad. Surgery (pres.). Home and Office: 2722 86th Ave NE Clyde Hill WA 98004-1653 E-mail: rec@wolfenet.com.

CONDON, STANLEY CHARLES, gastroenterologist; b. Glendale, Calif., Feb. 1, 1931; s. Charles Max and Alma Mae (Chinn) C.; m. Vaneta Marilyn Mabley, May 19, 1963; children: Lori, Brian, David. BA, La Sierra Coll., 1952; MD, Loma Linda U., 1956. Diplomate Nat. Bd. Med. Examiners, Am. Bd. Internal Medicine, Am. Bd. Gastroenterology; recertified Nutritional Support Physician 2002. Intern L.A. County Gen. Hosp., 1956-57, resident gen. pathology, 1959-61; resident internal medicine White Meml. Med. Ctr., L.A., 1961-63, attending staff out-patient clinic, 1963-64; active jr. attending staff L.A. County Gen. Hosp., 1964-65; dir. intern-resident tng. program Manila Sanitarium and Hosp., 1966-71, med. dir., 1971-72; chief resident internal medicine out-patient clinic Loma Linda U. Med. Ctr., 1972-74; fellow in gastroenterology Barnes Hosp./Wash. U., 1974-76; attending staff, asst. prof. medicine Loma Linda U. Med. Ctr., 1976-91, assoc. prof. medicine, 1991—, med. dir. nutritional support team, 1984—. Contbr. articles to profl. jours. Capt. U.S. Army, 1957-59. Fellow: ACP; mem.: AMA, San Bernardino County Med. Soc., So. Calif. Soc. Gastroenterology, Calif. Med. Assn., Am. Gastroent. Assn., Am. Soc. for Parenteral and Enteral Nutrition. Republican. Seventh-day Adventist. Avocations: trombone, choral singing, camping, hiking, gardening. Home: 11524 Ray Ct Loma Linda CA 92354-3630 Office: Loma Linda U Med Ctr 11370 Anderson St Loma Linda CA 92354-3450

CONDON, THOMAS JOSEPH, university historian; b. New Haven, July 27, 1930; m. Ann Kathleen Gorman, 1962 (dec. June 2001); children: Katherine, Caroline, Gregory. BA, Yale U., 1952; MA, Boston Coll., 1953; PhD, Harvard U., 1962. Teaching fellow history Harvard U., 1959-62; asst. prof. history U. N.B. (Can.), Fredericton, 1962-66; exec. asso. Am. Council Learned Socs., N.Y.C., 1966-70; vis. asso. prof. history Ind. U., 1967-68, City U. N.Y., 1968-69; prof. history, dean of Arts U. N.B., 1970-77; prof. history, dean and v.p. U. N.B. (St. John Campus), 1977-79, acting pres., 1979-80, v.p., 1980-87, prof. history, 1977-96, v.p. emeritus, gov. emeritus, 1996—, acting v.p., 2001—03. Hon. rsch. fellow Inst. U.S. Studies, U. London, 1975-76; mem. Humanities Rsch. Coun. Can., 1972-73, Commn. on Fgn. Students Policy, Can. Bur. Internat. Edn., Ottawa, 1980-83, Maritime Provinces Higher Edn. Commn., 1982-85; chmn. adv. com. on arts in N.B. Min. of Youth, 1973-75; bd. govs. Rothesay Collegiate Sch., 1977-88, U. N.B., 1977-87, 90-96; chmn. engring. task force Maritime Provinces Higher Edn. Commn., 1977-78; chmn., pres. Bi-Capitol Project, Inc., 1982-91; chmn. Festival by the Sea, Sur Mer, 1985, Bi-Capitol Found., 1984—; bd. govs., exec. com. Can. Conf. Arts, 1988-94; bd. dirs. Writers Devel. Trust; bd. govs. Internat. Scholarship Found., 1996—. Author: New York Beginnings: The Commercial Origins of New Netherland, 1968; Mem. editorial bd.: Computers and the Humanities, 1969-70, Acadiensis, 1970— ; contbr. articles to profl. jours. V.p. St. John Can. Games, 1977-87. Served with USNR, 1953-57. Recipient Lescarbot award Can. govt., 1991, Commemorative medal for 125th anniversary of Confedn. of Can., 1992, Queen's Golden Jubilee medal, 2002; Can. Coun. grantee, 1964, 65. Mem. Am. Hist. Assn., Can. Assn. Am. Studies, Can. Hist. Assn. Home: 268 Princess St Saint John NB Canada E2L 1L3 Office: Box 5050 Saint John NB Canada E2L 4L5 E-mail: tjc@unbsj.ca.

CONDON, THOMAS JOSEPH, editor, writer; b. N.Y.C., Sept. 10, 1934; s. Thomas Joseph and Mary Josephine (Tully) C.; m. Teresa Elvira Garcia, Feb. 14, 1982. BS in Social Studies, Fordham U., 1962; MS in English Edn., Long Island U., 1977. Journalist Long Island Daily Press, Jamaica, N.Y., 1964-77; equal opportunity specialist U.S. EEOC, Washington, 1979-83; writer-editor office of the asst. sec., pub. affairs Dept. of Def., Rosslyn, Va., 1983-84, supr. writer-editor office of sec., Pentagon Washington, 1984-98; freelance writer-editor, 1999—. Author, editor: (manual) DoD Directives System Procedures, 1994. With USN, 1952-54. Mem. Nat. Press Club (affil.), KC (3d deg.). Democrat. Roman Catholic. Avocations: play writing, physical fitness, traveling, reading. Home: 512 Vivienne Dr Watsonville CA 95076-3563

CONDOOR, SRIDHAR S. information technology educator; b. Nellore, Andhra Pradesh, India, Jan. 14, 1967; arrived in U.S., 1990; s. Hanumantha Rao and Sumathi Condoor; m. Deepna Sarangam, June 21, 1995; children: Nishil, Amisha. BTech, Jawaharlal Nehru Technol. U.; MTech, Indian Inst. Tech., Bombay; PhD, Tex. A&M U., 1996. Lectr. Tex. A&M U., College Station, 1995—96; asst. prof. St. Louis U., 1996—2001, assoc. prof., 2001—. Author: (design book) Mechanical Design Modeling Using ProEngineer, 2001, Innovative Conceptual Design, 2001. Mem.: ASME (faculty advisor student orgn. 2000—), Am. Soc. for Engring. Edn. Achievements include development of parameter analysis - a conceptual design methodology; cognitive framework for the design process; unique mechatronics curriculum. Office: St Louis Univ 3450 Lindell Blvd Saint Louis MO 63103 E-mail: condoor@slu.edu.

CONDOS, BARBARA SEALE, real estate broker, developer, investor; b. Kenedy, Tex., Feb. 24, 1925; d. John Edgar and Bess Rochelle (Ainsworth) Seale; m. George James Condos, Dec. 24, 1955 (dec.); 1 child, James Alexander. MusB magna cum laude, U. Incarnate Word, San Antonio, 1946. Lic. real estate broker, Tex. Ptnr., CEO Mountain Top-V.I. Devel. Properties, V.I., 1977-85; pres. Investment Realty Co., L.C., San Antonio, 1978—. Choreographer, dancer San Antonio Symphony's Youth Concerts and Opera Festival; actress San Antonio Little Theatre-Patio-Players 1948—. Trustee San Antonio Little Theatre, 1953-76; trustee Incarnate Word Coll., 1977-89, vice chair, 1980-82, trustee emerita, 1989—; mem. coun. McNay Mus., 1986—, chmn. coun., 1987—, chair coun., 1988—, trustee, 1989-97, trustee emerita, 1997—; bd. dirs. San Antonio Performing Arts Assn., 1978—; mng. trustee Russell Hill Rogers Fund for Arts. Mem. Internat. Real Estate Fedn., Internat. Real Estate Inst., Nat. Assn. Realtors, Tex. Assn. Realtors, San Antonio Bd. Realtors, Tex. Watercolor Soc. (signature mem.), The Argyle Club. Avocation: painting. Home: 217 Geneseo Rd San Antonio TX 78209-5913 Office: Investment Realty Co 1635 NE Loop 410 San Antonio TX 78209-1625 E-mail: bsc@investmentrealty.com.

CONDOS, J. ALEXANDER, mortgage company executive; b. San Antonio, Tex., Nov. 19, 1959; s. George James and Barbara Seale Condos; m. Linda Sue Warner, Aug. 18, 1990 (div. Dec. 12, 2001); children: Elliot Warner, Alexa Nicole. BA with honors, U. Tex., 1981; MBA, U. Chgo., 1984. Lic. real estate broker Tex. and Ill. Sr. investment officer Lomas Fin. Corp., Chgo., 1984—88; owner Alexander Condos Real Estate, San Antonio, 1989—92; prin. Investment Realty Co., L.C., San Antonio, 1993—. Bd. dirs. N.E. YMCA/San Antonio & the Hill Country, 2002. Mem.: Tex. Assn. Realtors (comml. investment divsn. 1993—), Nat. Assn. Realtors, Real Estate Coun. of Austin, Real Estate Coun. of San Antonio (govt. affairs com. 1996—), Mortgage Bankers Assn. of Am. (capital markets com. 2000—), Rotary. Methodist. Avocation: running. Office: Investment Realty Co LC 1635 NE Loop 410 Ste 910 San Antonio TX 78209-1622

CONDRA, ALLEN LEE, lawyer, state official; b. Middlesboro, Ky., Apr. 11, 1950; s. Allen and Dorothy Dell (Douglas) C. BA, Western Ky. U., 1972; JD, No. Ky. U., 1978. Bar: Ky. 1979, U.S. Dist. Ct. (we. dist.) Ky. 1980. Staff atty. West Ky. Legal Services, Madisonville, 1979-81; dist. atty. Dept. Transp. Commonwealth of Ky., Madisonville, 1981—. Mem. Ky. Bar Assn., Hopkins County Bar Assn., Phi Alpha Delta. Lodges: Elks, Masons, K.T. Democrat. Methodist.

CONDRAN, CYNTHIA MARIE, gospel musician; b. Avon Park, Fla., Apr. 29, 1953; d. Kenneth Dale and Ruth Mae (Garber) Grubb; m. Lee Light Condran, July 3, 1971. Student, Lebanon Valley Coll., 1970—72. Piano tchr., Sebring, Fla., 1968-70, Annville, Pa., 1971—; gospel musician, writer, arranger Condran Music Co., Annville, Pa., 1972—, also recording engr. Writer comml. jingles. Sang by spl. invitation at Elipse of The White House, 1982; composer The Only Thing Holding You Back, 1977, Just A Few More Rivers, 1975, The Patchwork Quilt, 1978, Freedom, 1976, The Little Things, 1980, We're America, Heavens Fiesta, He's the Lord of Everyday, 1989, I've Never Known Such Love, 1990, I Just Want To Talk To You, 1990, Sweep Our Sins, 1990, Eternal Friends, 1991, The Precious Jewels At Christmas Time, 1992, Lost On My Way Back Home, 1993, I Believe in the Power of Love, 1993, To Speak Your Name, 1994, Forever, 1994, We Praise You Lord, 1994, R.D. #11, Heaven, 1996, Surprise, 1997, Patience, 1998, His Healing Blood, 1999, Back Door Blessings, 2000. Recipient Contemporary Country Artists of Yr. award Internat. Country Gospel Music Assn., 1995, Internat. Star Music award, 1997, Contemporary Country Duo of Yr. award, 1999, Entertainer of Yr. Silver Heart award, 1999, Female Vocalist of Yr. northeast region, 1999, Golden Heart award for the Nat. Female Vocalist of Yr., 1999; named Female Vocalist of the Yr., Country Gospel Music Assn., 1999, Reciter of the Yr., Country Gospel Music Assn., 2000, 2002. Mem. Gospel Music Assn., Broadcast Music Inc., Christian Bus. and Prof. Women (music chmn.), So. Gospel Music Guild. Republican. Avocations: skiing, golf, swimming, tennis, racquetball. Home: 935 N Route 934 Annville PA 17003-9803

CONDRATE, ROBERT ADAM, SR., spectroscopy educator; b. Jan. 19, 1938; s. Adam Vincent and Angela Marian (Talacka) C.; m. Judith Campbell, Aug. 13, 1960; children: Barbara Louise, Robert Adam, Laura Angela. BS, Worcester Poly. Inst., 1960; PhD, Ill. Inst. Tech., 1965. Rsch. assoc. U. Ariz., Tucson, 1966-67; from asst. prof. spectroscopy to assoc. prof. N.Y. State Coll. Ceramics, Alfred (N.Y.) U., 1967-78, prof., 1978—. Vis. prof. Los Alamos Sci. Lab., 1972, GTE, Towanda, N.Y., 1980; summer lectr. Korea Inst. Sci. & Tech., Seoul, 1989; cons. ceramic cos.; spectroscopy cons. Statue of Liberty/Ellis Island Found., 1984-86. Co-editor: Advances in Materials Characterization, 1983, Vol. II, 1985; mem. editl. bd. Nat. Forum, Asian Jour. Spectroscopy; assoc. editor Am. Ceramic Soc., 1989—; contbr. articles to profl. jours. Mem. parents adv. bd. secondary edn. Alfred-Almond Cen. Sch., 1975-80; Danforth Found. assoc. for higher edn, 1976-85. Recipient Spectroscopy award Chgo. Sect. Soc. Applied Spectroscopy, 1964, Scholes award Alfred U., 1972, commendation Statue of Liberty/Ellis Island Found., 1984-86; grantee Inland Steel-Ryerson Found., 1963-64, NSF, 1966-67, 84-86, 86-87, Coll. Ctr. Finger Lakes, 1969, Alfred U. Rsch. Found, 1975; NIH fellow, 1964-65; SUNY faculty exch. scholar, 1988—. Fellow: Can. Ceramic Soc., Am. Ceramic Soc., Royal Soc. Chemistry, Am. Inst. Chemists; mem.: AAAS, Materials Rsch. Soc., Clay Minerals Soc., N.Y. Acad. Scis., Coblentz Soc., Am. Phys. Soc., Soc. Applied Spectroscopy, Am. Chem. Soc., Internat. Lions Club, Masons, Sigma Xi, Keramos, Tau Beta Pi, Sigma Alpha Epsilon, Psi Lambda Upsilon, Phi Kappa Phi. Home: 5761 Random Rd Alfred Station NY 14803-9793 E-mail: fcondrate@alfred.edu.

CONDRON, BARBARA O'GUINN, metaphysics educator, school administrator, publisher; b. New Orleans, May 1, 1953; d. Bill Gene O'Guinn and Marie Gladys (Newbill) Jackson; m. Daniel Ralph Condron, Feb. 29, 1992; 1 child, Hezekiah Daniel. BJ, U. Mo., 1973; MA, Coll. Metaphysics, Springfield, Mo., 1977, DD, D in Metaphysics, 1979. Cert. counselor; ordained min. Interfaith Ch. Metaphysics. Field rep. Sch. Metaphysics, New Orleans, 1978-80; dir. Interfaith Ch. Metaphysics, 1884-89; pres. Nat. Hdqs., Sch. Metaphysics, Windyville, Mo., 1980-84, prof., 1989—, chmn. bd. dirs., 1991-98, mem. coun. elders, bd. govs. internat. edn., 1998—; CEO SOM Pub., Windyville, 1989-98. Guest lectr., instr. Wichita (Kans.) State U., 1977, U. New Orleans, 1979, La. State U., 1981, Am. Bus. Womens Assn., 1982, U. Mo., Kansas City, 1984, Unity Village, 1985, Kans. Dept. Social Svcs. Conf., Topeka, 1986, U. Mo., Columbia and St. Louis, 1986, Mo. Tchrs. Conf., St. Louis, 1991, U. Okla., Norman, 1988—89, Parliament of World's Religions, Chgo., 1993, Mo. Writers Guild Conf., 2001, many others; creator Sch. Metaphysics Assocs., 1992; initiator Universal Hour Peace, 1995; initiator, internat. coord. Nat. Dream Hotline, 1988—; radio and TV guest, 1977—; creator Maker's Dozen-Visionary Schs. Recognition, 1999, Taraka Yoga Psi Counseling Program; initiator Spiritual Focus Sessions, 1997—; internat. coord. Peace Dome dedication, 2003. Author: What will I do Tomorrow?, Probing Depression, 1977, Search for a Satisfying Relationship, 1980, Strangers in My Dreams, 1987, Total Recall: An Introduction to Past Life & Health Readings, 1991, Kundalini Rising, 1992, Dreamers Dictionary, 1994, The Work of the Soul: Past Life Recall & Spiritual Enlightenment, 1996, Uncommon Knowledge, 1996, First Opinion: 21st Century Wholistic Health Care, 1997, Spiritual Renaissance Elevating Your Conciousness for the Common Good, 1999, The Bible Interpreted in Dream Symbols, 2000, Every Dream is About the Dreamer, 2001, Remembering Atlantis: The History of the World Vol. 1, 2002, How to Raise an Indigo Child, 2002; author series When All Else Fails; editor-in-chief Thresholds Jour., 1990-2001; editor Wholistic Health and Healing Guide, 1992-2000; also numerous poems. Mem. Internat. Platform Assn., Am. Bus. Women's Assn., Interfaith Ministries, Kundalini Rsch. Network, Planetary Soc., Heritage Found., Mo. Writers Guild, Sigma Delta Chi. Office: Sch Metaphysics World Hdqs Windyville MO 65783

CONDRON, CHRISTOPHER (KIP CONDRON), investment company executive; b. Scranton, Pa. B Bus., U. Scranton. Sr. v.p. C.S. McKee & Co., Pitts.; founder Condron Assoc., 1978—85; founder, pres. Ayco, 1985—89; vice chmn. Boston Safe Deposit and Trust Co., 1989—92; exec. v.p. The Boston Co. (now Mellon Pvt. Asset Mgmt.), 1993; vice chmn. Mellon Bank, 1994—98, pres., COO, 1998—2001; vice chmn. Mellon Fin. Corp., 1994—98, pres., COO, 1998—2001; pres., CEO AXA Financial, 2001—. Dir., treas. Am. Ireland Fund, 1999. Former trustee U. Scranton, St. Sebastian's Country Day Sch., Needham, Mass. Mem. Fin. Svcs. Roundtable. Office: AXA Financial 1290 Avenue of the Americas New York NY 10104

CONDRON, DANIEL RALPH, academic administrator, metaphysics educator; b. Chillicothe, Mo., Jan. 30, 1953; s. Ralph Wesley and Rosa Irene (Garber) C.; m. Barbara Gail O'Guinn, Feb. 29, 1992; 1 child, Hezekiah Daniel. BS, U. Mo., 1975, MS, 1978; DDiv, Coll. Metaphysics, Springfield, Mo., 1982, D in Metaphysics, 1985. Cert. counselor; ordained to ministry Interfaith Ch. of Metaphysics. Dir. Sch. Metaphysics, Des Moines, 1980, Kansas City, Mo., 1981, regional dir., 1982-85, 1985-90, pres. bd. nat. hdqs. Windyville, Mo., 1988—; chancellor, prof. Coll. Metaphysics, Windyville, Mo., 1990—. Tchg. asst. U. Mo., Columbia, 1977; sales and mgmt. cons. Am. Media, Des Moines, 1980-83; spkr. in field including Parliament of the World's Religions, Chgo., 1993. Author: Dreams of the Soul, 1991, Permanent Healing, 1992, Universal Language of Mind, 1994, Understanding Your Dreams, 1994, Uncommon Knowledge, Seven Secret Keys to Prosperity and Abundance, 1996, Superconscious Meditation, 1997, The Four Stages of Growth, 2001, Remembering Atlantis: The History of the World, Vol. 1, 2002; pub. jour. Thresholds Quar., 1988-, Internat. radio and TV guest including BBC, Radio Hong Kong, Voice of Am., 1979-. Mem. Sch. Metaphysics Assocs. (pres.), Nat. Space Soc., Planetary Soc., Alpha Gamma Rho, Alpha Zeta. Republican. Achievements include implementer and designer of organic and bio-dynamic farming and agriculture at the 1500 acre College of Metaphysics campus, landscape designer and artist for 1500 acre college of metaphysics campus, discoverer and developer of the Universal language of mind as it applies to dreams, to the Bible and other holy works; discoverer of specific attitudes that cause specific disease and disorders in the body. Home: 163 Moon Valley Rd Windyville MO 65783 Office: Sch Metaphysics Nat Headquarters Windyville MO 65783

CONDRY, IAN, humanities educator; b. L.A., Mar. 6, 1965; s. John Charles and Sandra Condry; m. Margot Elise Stone, June 6, 1992; children: Nicholas, Jackson, Alec. BA, Harvard Coll., 1987; PhD, Yale U., 1999. Asst. English tchr. Japan Exch. and Tchg. Program, Kurikoma, Japan, 1988—89; rschr. Yomiuri Shimbun, Washington, 1990—92; asst. prof., anthropology Union Coll., Schenectady, NY, 1999—2001; fellow Reischauer Inst. Japanese Studies Harvard U., Cambridge, Mass., 2001—02; prof. Japanese cultural studies MIT Fgn. Lang. and Lit., Cambridge, 2002—. Recipient Fulbright fellowship, Japan-U.S. Ednl. Commn., 1995—97. Mem.: Am. Anthrop. Assn. Office: Foreign Lang and Lit Dept Mass Inst Tech Cambridge MA 02139 Office Fax: 617-258-6189.

CONDRY, ROBERT STEWART, retired hospital administrator; b. Charleston, W.Va., Aug. 16, 1941; s. John Charles and Mary Louise (Jester) C.; m. Mary Purcell Heinzer, May 21, 1966; children: Mary-Lynch, John Stewart. BA, U. Charleston, 1963; MBA, George Washington U., 1970. Asst. hosp. dir. Med. Coll. of Va., Richmond, 1970-73, assoc. adminstr., 1973-75; assoc. hosp. dir. McGaw Hosp., Loyola U., Maywood, Ill., 1975-84, hosp. dir., 1984-93, ret., 1993. Pres. Inter-Hosp. Planning Assn. of Western Suburbs, Maywood, 1983-93; bd. dirs. PentaMed, Inc., San Antonio. Bd. dirs. Met. Chgo. Healthcare Coun., 1985-93, mem. exec. com., 1989-93; bd. dirs. Cath. Hosp. Alliance, 1992, chmn. bd. dirs., 1992, mem. exec. com. 1988-94; mem. Ill. Gov.'s Adv. Bd. on Infant Mortality Reduction, 1988-93, Rev. Bd. on Emergency Medicine Svcs., 1989-93. With U.S. Army, 1964-66. Recipient preceptorship George Washington U., 1985, U. Chgo., 1984, St. Louis U., 1984, Tulane U., 1984, Yale U., 1991. Fellow Am. Coll. Healthcare Execs., Am. Acad. Med. Adminstrs.; mem. Am. Hosp. Assn., Cath. Hosp. Assn., Am. Mgmt. Assn. Republican. Roman Catholic. Avocations: golf, tennis, camping, travel. E-mail: carmelcondry@comcast.net.

CONE, CAROL LYNN, public relations executive; b. N.Y.C., June 7, 1950; d. William Addison Cone and Harriet (Gurney) Brown. BA, Brandeis U., 1972; MS, Boston U., 1978. Account exec. Newsome and Co., Boston, 1977-80; pres., CEO Cone Comm. Inc., Boston, 1980—. Mem. Gov.'s Entrepreneurial Adv. Council, Boston, 1982, Dukakis for Pres. campaign nat. fin. com., Boston, 1987. Named Outstanding Female Entrepreneur La Salle Jr. Coll., Newton, Mass., 1986, YWCA Achievement Entrepreneur, Boston, 1986, Entrepreneur of Yr. Arthur Young/Venture Mag., 1988; recipient Golden Quill award Internat. Assn. Bus. Communicators, 1987. Mem. Counselor's Acad. of Pub. Relations Soc. Am., Pub. Relations Soc. Am. (Silver anvil 1987), Am. Mktg. Assn. Avocations: skiing, windsurfing, walking. Office: Cone Inc 90 Canal St Boston MA 02114-2018

CONE, DAVID BRIAN, professional baseball player; b. Kans. City, Mo., Jan. 2, 1963; Baseball player Kans. City Royals, 1986—87, N.Y. Mets, 1987—92, Toronto Blue Jays, 1992, Kans. City Royals, 1992—94, Toronto Blue Jays, 1994—95, N.Y. Yankees, 1995—. Named to All-Star Team, Nat. League, 1988, Am. League, 1992, 1994, Am. League All-Star Team, Sporting News, 1994; recipient Cy Young award, Am. League, 1994. Achievements include sharing Nat. League single-game rec. most strikeouts; playing in World Series, 1992; playing a no-hit game (perfect) on July 18, 1999. Office: NY Yankees Yankee Stadium E 161st St and River Ave Bronx NY 10451

CONE, DENNIS ALLEN, music educator; b. Casper, Wyo., Jan. 8, 1951; s. Arvine Carl and LaVere Jean Cone; m. Lucy Anne Cone, June 1, 1974; 1 child, Molly May. MA, U. of Wyo., Laramie, Wyoming, 1986, BA Music, 1974. Educator Weston Co. Sch. Dist., Newcastle, Wyo., 1974—78, Fremont Co. Sch. Dist., Lander, Wyo., 1979—. V.p. Wyo. Music Edn. Assn., Wyo., 1978—79; pres. South Bighorn Music Edn., Wyo., 1992—93, treas., 1992. Mem.: Lander Edn. Assn., Wyo. Music Educators. Avocations: mountaineering, running, reading, traveling.

CONE, EDWARD TONER, composer, emeritus music educator; b. Greensboro, N.C., May 4, 1917; s. Julius Washington and Laura Barbara (Weill) C. AB, Princeton U., 1939, M.F.A., 1942; D.Mus. (hon.), U. Rochester, 1973, New Eng. Conservatory Music, 1984; D.F.A. (hon.), U. N.C.-Greensboro, 1983. Asst. prof. dept. music Princeton U., 1947-52, assoc. prof., 1952-60, prof., 1960-85, prof. emeritus, 1985—; Andrew D. White prof.-at-large Cornell U., 1979-85. Treas. Am. sect. Internat. Soc. Contemporary Music, 1950-52 Composer numerous compositions, 1 symphony, other works for piano, voice, chorus, orch., chamber combinations, 1939— . Author: Musical Form and Musical Performance, 1968, The Composer's Voice, 1974, Music: A View from Delft, 1989; co-editor: Perspectives of New Music, 1965-69, adv. editor, 1969-72. Guggenheim fellow in composition, 1947-48 Mem. AAUP, Am. Philos. Soc., Am. Acad. Arts and Scis. Clubs: Century.

CONE, FRANCES MCFADDEN, data processing consultant; b. Columbia, S.C., Oct. 20, 1938; d. Joseph Means and Francis (Graham) McFadden: m. Charles Cone Jr., May 1962 (div. Sept. 1964); 1 child, Deborah Ann Cone Craytor. BS, U. S.C., 1960, MEd, 1973, M Math., 1977. Systems svc. rep. IBM, 1960-62; programmer/analyst Ga. Power Co., Atlanta, 1964-68, S.C. Fin. and Data Processing, Columbia, 1968-69; instr., head dept. Midlands Tech. Coll., Columbia, 1969-75; tng. coord. S.C. Nat. Bank, Columbia, 1975-79; systems analyst S.C. Dept. Health and Environ. Control, Columbia, 1979-80; project analyst So. Co. Svcs., Atlanta, 1980-89; cons. George Martin Assocs., Atlanta,

1989-93; sr. sys. developer Emory U., Atlanta, 1993-97; sys. analyst Southland Life Ins. Co., Atlanta, 1997-99; team leader ING-Life of Ga., Atlanta, 1999—2002; ret., 2002. Adj. prof. Golden Gate U., Sumter, S.C., 1976-80. Vol. Ga. Wildlife Found., Save the Manatee Club, Names Project, Ellijay Wilflife Rehab. Sanctuary, 2000—02, Shepherd Spinal Ctr., 2000—01; chair Silver Polishing Daughters of the King Cathedral of St. Philip. Mem. Nat. Mgmt. Assn. (sec., treas., awards comn. 1981-89). Episcopalian. Avocations: reading, embroidery. E-mail: fcone@mindspring.com.

CONE, GEORGE WALLIS, lawyer; b. Augusta, Ga., Aug. 20, 1945; s. William Harry and Agnes M. (Hill) Cone; children: Jennifer Lee, Laura Katherine, David Willis. Student, Clemson Coll., 1963—64; BS in PHarmacy, U. Ga., 1967, JD, 1973. Bar: Ga. 73, SC 74. Pharmacist-in-charge Walterboro (SC) Drug, Inc., 1967—76; atty. firm McLeod, Fraser & Unger, Walterboro, 1976—84, McLeod, Fraser & Cone, Walterboro, 1985—; city atty. City of Walterboro, 1995—. Bd. dirs. Found. for Human Svcs., 1986—90, Bank of Walterboro, sec. corp., vice chmn.; sec. corp., vice chmn., bd. dirs. Communitycorp, 1995—. Notes editor: Ga. Jour. Internat. and Comparative Law, 1971—72, revs. and comments editor:, 1972—73. Mem. SC Bd. Pharmacy, 1981—87; chmn. SC Bd. PHarmacy, 1986—87; bd. dirs. SC Humane Assn., 1978—85, treas., 1979—84, PRES., 1984—85; bd. dirs. Colleton County SPCA, 1975—85, pres., 1975—77; mem. Colleton County Alcohol and Drug Abuse Com., 1979—81, chmn., 1980—81; bd. dirs. Pub. Defender Corp. Colleton County, 1978—, sec., 1979—; mem. Colleton County Bd. Voter Registration, 1982—84; bd. dirs. Nat. Assn. Bds. Pharm. Found./Bur. Voluntary Compliance, 1983—85, Low Country Cmty. Action Agy., Inc., 1980—85, sec., 1983—85; chmn. Colleton County Old Jail Restoration and Preservation Com., 1984—95; mem. City of Walterboro Downtown Rev. Bd. With SC Army NG, 1970—76. Mem.: ABA, Omar Temple A.A.O.N.M.S., 14th Dist. Pharm. Assn. (pres. 1980—82), SC Pharm. Assn., SC Bar Assn. (ho. of dels. 1975—76, 1977—78, 1979—85), State Bar Ga. (ho. of dels. 1985—89), Am. Soc. Pharm. Law, Colleton County Hist. Soc. (past pres.), Sertoma, Lowcountry Sertoma Club, Dogwood Hills Country Club (pres. 1979—81), Unity Lodge, A & A Scottish Rite Freemasonry, Coastal Shrine Club, Grand Lodge Masons, Phi Alpha Delta, Delta Chi. Democrat. Baptist. Office: PO Box 230 Walterboro SC 29488 Mailing: PO Box 233 Walterboro SC 29488 Personal E-mail: george@coneonline.com. Business E-Mail: gcone@lowcountry.com.

CONE, JAMES ELMER, physician; b. Eugene, Oreg., July 3, 1949; s. Elmer and Eleanor (Scott) C.; m. Blanche Grosswald, June 30, 1991. AB, Stanford U., 1971; MD, U. Calif., San Francisco, 1978; MPH, U. Calif., Berkeley, 1978. Internship/residency Cook County Hosp., Chgo., 1978-80; epidemic intelligence svc. Ctrs. for Disease Control, Cin., 1980-82; resident internal medicine Worcester (Mass.) Meml. Hosp., 1982-83; chief, Occupational Health Clinic San Francisco Gen. Hosp., 1983-91; dir. health effects Carpenters Health and Safety, Washington, 1992-93; asst. clin. prof. U. Calif., San Francisco, 1983—; acting chief Hazard Evaluation System and Info. Svc./State of Calif., Berkeley, 1994-98; chief Occupational Health Branch State of Calif., Oakland, 1999—2002; dir. environ. and occupl. disease epidemiology N.Y.C. Dept. Health and Mental Hygiene, 2002—. Med. cons. Assn. Flt. Attendants, Washington, 1991—. Editor: Problem Buildings, 1989, Occupational Medicine Secrets, 1999. Bd. dirs., pres. Assn. Occupational Health Clinics, Washington, 1992-93. With USPHS, 1980-82. Mem. Am. Pub. Health Assn. (chmn. sect. 1985-86). Avocation: sailing. Home: 201 S 2d Ave #1 Highland Park NJ 08904 Office: New York City Dept Health/Mental Hygiene 253 Broadway CN 34-C Rm 602 New York NY 10007 E-mail: jcone@igc.org.

CONE, JAMES HAL, theologian, educator, author; b. Fordyce, Ark., Aug. 5, 1938; s. Charlie M. and Lucy (Frost) Cone. BA, Philander Smith Coll., 1958; BD, Garrett Theol. Sem., 1961; MA, Northwestern U., 1963, PhD, 1965; DD (hon.), Garrett Evang. Theol. Sem., 2000. Asst. prof. religion and philosophy Philander Smith Coll., Little Rock, 1964-66; asst. prof. religion Adrian (Mich.) Coll., 1966-69; asst. prof. theology Union Theol. Sem., N.Y.C., 1969-70, asso. prof., 1970-73, prof., 1973-77, Charles A. Briggs prof. systematic theology, 1977-87, Briggs disting. prof., 1987—. Vis. prof. Afro-Am. history U. Pacific, Stockton, Calif., 1969; vis. assoc. prof. religion Barnard Coll., N.Y.C., 1969-71, 74; vis. prof. theology Drew U., Madison, N.J., 1973; lectr. systematic theology Woodstock Coll., N.Y.C., 1971-73; vis. prof. theology Princeton (N.J.) Theol. Sem., 1976, Notre Dame Sch. Theology, New Orleans, 1977, Candler Sch. Theology, Emory U., Atlanta, Howard U. Sch. Religion, Washington, 1980, Pacific Luth. Theol. Sem., Berkeley, Calif., Maryknoll (N.Y.) Sch. Theology, 1983, Inst. Justice and Peace; vis. prof., Diana Blabon Holt fellow Rollins Coll., Winter Park, Fla., 1989. Author: Black Theology and Black Power, 1969 (transl. into Dutch, 1970, German, 1971, Japanese, 1971, Korean, 1979), A Black Theology of Liberation, 1970 (transl. into Spanish, 1973, Italian, 1973, Japanese, 1974), The Spirituals and the Blues: An Interpretation, 1972 (transl. into German, 1973, Japanese, 1975, Korean, 1987), God of the Oppressed, 1975 (transl. into Japanese, 1976, Italian, 1978, Korean, 1979, German, 1982, Portuguese, 1985, French, 1989, Malayalam, 1993), My Soul Looks Back, 1982 (transl. into Japanese, 1987), For My People, 1984 (transl. into German, 1987), Speaking the Truth, 1986, Martin and Malcom and America: A Dream or a Nightmare, 1991, Risks of Faith: The Emergence of a Black Theology of Liberation, 1968-98, 1999, Black Faith and Public Talk: Critical Essays on James H. Cone's Black Theology and Black Power, 1999; contbr. articles to profl. publs.; mem. editorial bd.: Jour. Religious Thought, 1975—, Jour. Interdenominational Theological Ctr.; co-editor: Black Theology: A Documentary History, 1966-79, 1979, Black Theology: A Documentary History Vol. II, 1980-92, 1993; assoc. editor Henry McNeal/Sojourner Truth Series in Black Religion; mem. editl. bd. Sojourners mag. Recipient Am. Black Achievement award in Religion, Ebony Mag., 1992, theol. Scholarship and Rsch. award Assn. Theol. Schs., 1994; Rockefeller Found. grantee, 1973-74 Mem. Black Theology Project Theology in Ams., Am. Acad. Religion (Fund for Theol. Edn. award 1999), Soc. Study Black Religion, Ecumenical Assn. Third World Theologians. Mem. African Methodist Episcopal Ch. Office: Union Theol Sem 3041 Broadway New York NY 10027-5710

CONE, JOHN BAXTER, trauma surgeon, medical researcher; b. Jackson, Tenn., Jan. 20, 1950; s. Cleo Wilson and Wilma Fern (Saunders) C.; m. Sandra Lynn McCullough, Jan. 9, 1988. BS, Ark. Poly. Coll., 1971; MA, Rice U., 1974; MD, U. Ark., 1977. Resident surgery U. Ark., Little Rock, 1977-82, asst. prof. surgery, 1985-89, assoc. prof., 1989-94, prof., 1994—; lectr. biochemistry U. Pa., Phila., 1982-83; fellow critical care U. Pitts., 1983-84. Cons. Ark. State Health Dept., Little Rock, 1994—, med. dir. for trauma, 2002--; Claude H. Organ lectr. Southwestern Surg. Congress, 2001. Co-author: Oxford Textbook Critical Care, 1996; contbr. articles to profl. jours. Chair Gov.'s Com. Trauma Ark. State Dept. Health, 1994-2001. Fellow ACS (trauma ctr. site visitor 1994—, chair state com. trauma 1993-99), Am. Assn. Surgery Trauma, Am. Coll. Critical Care Medicine, Alpha Omega Alpha. Office: U Ark Dept Surgery Little Rock AR 72205

CONE, JUNE ELIZABETH, civic worker; b. Portland, Oreg., Sept. 29, 1918; d. Otto Warner and Signa Elizabeth (Johansson) Woldt; m. Edwin Earl Cone, Jan. 31, 1943; children: Barbara Jean, Richard Bruce, Susan Elizabeth (dec.), Douglas Earl, Gregory Paul. BA, Willamette U., 1942. Charter mem. Com. for Performing Arts, Eugene, Oreg., Assistance League Eugene; endowed chair sch. bus. adminstrn. U. Oreg., mem. libr. bd., chmn. steering com. Fgn. Student Friendship Found.; mem. bd. overseers Lewis and Clark Coll., Portland; mem. Pres.' Assocs., U. Oreg.; established Cone Scholarship Fund, Willamette U., Cone Fund, Oreg. Cmty. Found. Athletic field house, chapel named in honor of her and her husband Willamette U., Salem, Oreg.; orch. pit named in honor of her and her husband Hult Ctr. Performing Arts, Eugene; named One of Eugene Outstanding Women Yr., 1968; recipient Woman of Achievement for Yr. award Quota Club, 1969, Lestle J. Sparks Medallion Disting. Svc., Willamette U., 1992. Mem. Travelers Century Club, PEO Sisterhood (charter mem. chpt. DH), Eugene Fortnightly Club, Monday Book Club, Eugene Country Club, Delta Gamma. Republican. Methodist. Home: 2130 Olive St Eugene OR 97405-2838

CONE, ROBERT EDWARD, immunologist, educator; b. Bklyn., Aug. 18, 1943; s. Joseph and Ruth Cone; m. Michele Nash, Aug. 21, 1966; children: Jennifer, Laura. BS, CUNY, 1964; MS, Fla. State U., 1967; PhD, U. Mich., 1970. Postdoctoral fellow Walter and Eliza Hall Inst., Melbourne, Australia, 1971-73, Basel (Switzerland) Inst. Immunology, 1973-74; asst. prof. pathology Yale U., New Haven, 1974—79, assoc. prof., 1979-84, asst. prof. surgery, 1974-79, assoc. prof., 1979-84; prof. pathology U. Conn. Health Ctr., Farmington, 1985—. Histocompatability com. New Eng. Organ Bank, 1974-84; commr. Conn. Commn. on Medico-Legal Investigation, 1990—; reviewer in field. Recipient Rsch. award UpJohn, 1979, 82, Conn. Pub. Svc. award, 2003; Horace Rackham fellow, 1968-69, F.G. fellow, 1969-70, Damon Runyon fellow, 1971-72; grantee NIH, 1974-77, 81-91, 2000—, Am. Cancer Soc., Am. Heart Assn., 1998-2000, Nat. Multiple Sclerosis Soc., 1997-99. Office: U Conn Health Ctr Dept Pathology Farmington CT 06030-3105 E-mail: cone@uchc.edu.

CONELLI, MARIA ANN, art educator, dean, architectural historian; b. Bklyn., Nov. 1, 1957; d. Carmine S. and Mary Conelli; m. Kim J. Hartswick, May 11, 1990. BA, Bklyn. Coll., 1980; MA, NYU, 1983; PhD, Columbia U., 1992. Educator Met. Mus. of Art, N.Y.C., 1981—84; instr. Parsons Sch. of Design, N.Y.C., 1983—2001; chair Parsons/Smithsonian Inst., N.Y.C. and Washington, 1992—2001; dean Fashion Inst. Tech., N.Y.C., 2001—. Contbr. articles to profl. jours., books. Trustee Skyscraper Mus., N.Y.C., 1999—; mem. mus. com. Coll. Art Assocs., N.Y.C., 2003—. Pub. Works Challenge grantee, Nat. Endowment for the Arts, Washington, 2002—03, J. Paul Getty Postdoctoral fellow, 1997. Fellow: Am. Acad. in Rome (fellow 1987—88); mem.: AmColl. Art Assn. Roman Catholic. Office: Dean Sch Grad Studies E315 27th St & 7th Ave New York NY 10001 Fax: 212-217-5156. Business E-Mail: maria_conelli@fitnyc.edu.

CONERLY, EVELYN NETTLES, educational consultant; b. Baton Rouge, Aug. 25, 1940; d. Noel Douglas and Evelyn Elsie (Pratt) Nettles; children from previous marriage: Douglas Wayne, Kelee Lynne. BS, La. State U., 1962, MEd, 1965, PhD, 1973. Tchr. East Baton Rouge Parish Pub. Schs., 1962-67, elem libr., 1967-73, prin., 1973-81, 1983-84, elem. libr. supr., 1981-83; ednl. cons. Baton Rouge, 1984—. Co-owner Acad. Learning Ctr., 1986—92; dir. Libr. Power Project East Baton Rouge Parish, DeWitt Wallace-Reader's Digest Fund, 1992—96; vol. pub. sch.; with Nat. Libr. Power Program Network Cons., 1996—2000; program evaluator La. State Bd. Elem. and Secondary Edn., 1996—2002, program adminstr., 1998—99; supr. office field experiences Southeastern La. U. Coll. Edn., 1997—98. Co-author: (book) Principals' Pointers for Parents, 1985. Mem.: AASL, ALA, Inst. Reality Therapy (cert.), La. Libr. Assn., La. Reading Assn., Internat. Reading Assn., Assn. Tchr. Educators (pres. La. 1981—82), La. Ret. Tchrs. Assn., Delta Kappa Gamma, Phi Delta Kappa, Phi Kappa Phi. Presbyterian. Home and Office: 3727 Woodland Ridge Blvd Baton Rouge LA 70816-2772 E-mail: econerly@att.net.

CONERLY-PERKS, ERLENE BRINSON, retired chemist; b. Jackson, Miss., Nov. 16, 1938; d. Alvin Bryan and Erlene (Brinson) Conerly; m. Paul Allen Perks, May 4, 1991. BS, Millsaps Coll., 1959; MS in Tech. Mgmt., Am. U., 1978. Chemist NIH, Bethesda, Md., 1962-78; research biologist Dynamac, Rockville, Md., 1979-80; chemist EPA, Washington, 1980-94; ret., 1994. Democrat. Episcopalian. Avocations: madrigal singing, wildlife. E-mail: eperx@olg.com.

CONETTA, TAMI FOLEY, lawyer; b. Akron, Ohio, Aug. 29, 1965; d. Charles David and Roxanne (Onyett) Foley; m. Anthony Joseph Conetta, July 29, 1989 (div.); 1 child, Emory Elizabeth Conetta; m. Barry Frank Spivey, June 8, 2002. BA in Polit. Sci., Furman U., 1987; JD with honors, U. Fla., 1990. Bar: Fla. 1991; bd. cert. estates, trusts and wills Fla. Bar Bd. Legal Specialization. Ptnr. Gassman & Conetta, PA, Clearwater, Fla., 1990-98, Ruden, McClosky, Smith, Schuster & Russell, PA, Sarasota, Fla., 1998—. Contbr. articles to profl. jours. Mem. planned giving com. All Children's Hosp. Found.; bd. dirs. Literacy Coun. of Sarasota, Sch. Readiness Coalition of Sarasota County. Recipient Am. Jurisprudence awards in Estate Planning and Taxation of Gratuitous Transfers, 1990. Mem. Am. Bus. Womens Assn. (pres. Sunrise chpt. 2002-03, Woman of Yr. 2003), Sarasota County Bar Assn. (chair probate and estate planning sect. 2000-01), Clearwater Bar Probate Com. (chair 1996-98), Southwest Fla. Estate Planning Coun., Fla. Bar Assn. (chair probate rules com. 2003-2004, rules jud. adminstrn. com.). Avocations: golf, reading. Office: Ruden McClosky Smith Schuster & Russell PA 1549 Ringling Blvd Ste 600 Sarasota FL 34236-6772 also: PO Box 49017 Sarasota FL 34230-6017 E-mail: tami.conetta@ruden.com.

CONEY, AIMS C., JR., lawyer, labor-management negotiator; b. Cleve., Sept. 22, 1929; s. Aims Chamberlain and Elizabeth (Lee) C.; m. Rita Newbold Platt, Feb. 20, 1954; children: Aims C. III, Sylvia L., Anne F. BA, Yale U., 1951; JD, U. Pa., 1954. Bar: Pa. Assoc. Kirkpatrick, Lockhart, Johnson & Hutchison, Pitts., 1956-69; ptnr. Kirkpatrick & Lockhart, Pitts., 1969-89, of counsel, 1990—. Contbr. articles in field of union-management relations to profl. jours. Bd. dirs. Arthritis Found., Pitts., 1967—, pres., 1972-75; bd. dirs. Ellis Sch., Pitts., 1974-91, Freedom House Amb. Svc., 1968-75, Indian Lake (N.Y.) Zoning Commn., 1993-95, Transitional Svcs. Inc., 1992-98; bd. dirs. Pace Sch., Pitts., 1980-94, pres., 1990-91. With U.S. Army, 1954-56. Mem. Pa. Bar Assn. (co-chmn. ethics com. 1999-2001), Allegheny County Bar Assn. Republican. Home: 516 Glen Arden Dr Pittsburgh PA 15208-2809 Office: Kirkpatrick & Lockhart 535 Smithfield St Pittsburgh PA 15222-2312

CONEY, CAROLE ANNE, accountant; b. Berkeley, Calif., Aug. 11, 1944; d. Martin James and Ida Constance (Ditora) Skuce; m. David Michael Coney, June 20, 1964; children: Kristine Marie, Kenneth Michael. BS cum laude, Calif. State Poly. U., 1985, MBA, 1988. Tax cons., instr. H&R Block, Portland, Oreg., 1969-71; acct., asst. sec.-treas. Surety Ins. Co., La Habra, Calif., 1973-76; bookkeeper Homemakers Furniture, Downers Grove, Ill., 1976-79; office mgr., acct. Helen's Pl. Printing, Upland, 1979-80; bookkeeper Vanguard Cos., Upland, 1980-82; dir. acctg. Coll. Osteopathic Medicine of Pacific, Pomona, Calif., 1982-89; fiscal svcs. mgr. City of Ontario, Calif., 1989—. Pres. Brea/La Habra Newcomers, 1975; treas. Alta Loma (Calif.) Com. to Elect Robert Neufeld, 1981. Mem. NAFE, Nat. Assn. Coll. and Univ. Bus. Officers, Calif. Soc. Mcpl. Fin. Officers, Govt. Fin. Officers Assn., Assn. Coll. and Univ. Auditors, Coun. Fiscal Officers, Soroptomists, Ontario Kiwanis, Delta Mu Delta, Alpha Iota. Democrat. Roman Catholic. Avocations: fishing, crafts, sewing, golf. Home: PO Box 4910 24581 San Moritz Dr Crestline CA 92325 4910 Office: City of Ontario 303 E B St Ontario CA 91764-4196 E-mail: caconey@aol.com., cconey@ci.ontario.ca.us.

CONEY, ELAINE MARIE, English and foreign languages educator; b. Magnolia, Miss., Aug. 9, 1952; d. Allen Leroy and Katie Jane (McLeod) C. BA in Spanish, Millsaps Coll., 1974; MA in Spanish, U. Interam. Saltillo Coahuila, Mex., 1975, PhD, 1977; MEd, U. So. Miss., 1979, EdS in Higher Edn. Adminstrn., 1997. Tchr. fgn. langs. South Pike High Sch., Magnolia, Miss., 1977-91; tchr. English Amite County Schs., Liberty, Miss.; instr. Jackson (Miss.) State U.; GED instr. South Pike Schs., Magnolia, Miss.; instr. Spanish, French and English composition S.W. Miss. Community Coll., Summit, 1989—. Mem. NEA (del. conv. 1986, 88), MLA, Am. Coun. Tchrs. Fgn. Langs., Am. Assn. Tchrs. French, Am. Assn. Tchrs. Spanish and Portuguese, Miss. Assn. Educators (instructional profl. devel. com.), Nat. Coun. Tchrs. English, Miss. Fgn. Lang. Assn. (pres. 1991-93, Disting. Svc. award 1998), SPAE (treas.). Home: PO Box 208 Magnolia MS 39652-0208

CONEY, PONJOLA, dean, researcher, educator; MD, U. Miss. Med. Ctr.; resident, U. N.C. Prof., chmn. dept. obstet. and gynecology So. Ill. U. Sch. Medicine, 1995; dean medicine, sr. v.p. health affairs Meharry Med. Coll. Sch. Medicine, 2002—. Rschr. in field. Contbr. over 40 pubs. in med. lit. Mem.: Hedwig van Amerigen Exec. Leadership Acad. Medicine Program, Soc. Exec. Leadership in Acad. Medicine (founding dir.). Achievements include first to do an invitro-fertilization procedure in the state of Nebraska. Office: 1005 DB Todd Jr Blvd Nashville TN 37208

CONFER, ANTHONY WAYNE, veterinary pathologist, educator; b. Hot Springs, Ark., July 29, 1947; s. Edwin M. and Gloria V. (Parker) C.; m. Carolyn Gay Pope, Aug. 15, 1970; children: Andrew W., Aaron J., Michael E., Christina A. DVM, Okla. State U., 1972; MS, Ohio State U., 1974; PhD, U. Mo., 1978. Diplomate Am. Coll. Vet. Pathologists. Assoc. prof. La. State U., Baton Rouge, 1978-81, Okla. State U., Stillwater, 1981-85, prof., 1985—, dept. head, 1986-99, assoc. dean for rsch. Coll. Vet. Medicine, 1999-2001, Sitlington endowed chair food animal rsch., 1995—, regents prof., 2003—. Vis. prof. U. B.C., Vancouver, 1990-91; cons. Ft. Dodge (Iowa) Lab., 1987-92, 2003—, Baxter Healthcare Corp., Round Lake, Ill., 1988-89, Vet. Reference Lab., Dallas, 1988-89, Smith Kline Beechan Ltd., Lincoln, Nebr., 1990; mem. Conf. Rsch. Workers-Animal Diseases, 1981—; cons. Diamond Animal Health, Des Moines, 1994-98, Pfizer Animal Health, Lincoln, Nebr., 1997—. Mem. editl. bd. Am. Jour. Vet. Rsch., 1993—, Vet. Pathology, 1995-97. V.p. Stillwater Soccer Assn., 1987-91, pres., 1992-93; pub. rels. specialist Stillwater H.S. Soccer Club, 1990-96; cub master Cub Scout pack 22, Stillwater, 1987-89, Capt. USAF, 1974-76. Recipient Beecham award for rsch., SmithKline Beecham Lab., 1985, Norden Disting. Tchr. award, Pfizer, Inc., 1987, 2002. Mem. AVMA (Vet. Rsch. award 1992), Am. Coll. Vet. Pathologists (chair standing edn. com. 1994-96, program chair 1995), Morris Animal Found. (sci. advisor 1991-95), Sigma Xi (chpt. lectr. 1993). Mem. Lds Ch. Avocations: physical fitness, youth sports, guitar, cooking. Home: 2817 W 28th Ave Stillwater OK 74074-2212 Office: Okla State U Dept Vet Pathobiology Stillwater OK 74078-2007 E-mail: aconfer@okstate.edu.

CONFORTI, MICHAEL PETER, museum director, art historian; b. Bradford, Mass., Apr. 3, 1945; s. Sven and Cecile Conforti; m. Licia Peterson; children: Peter, Julia. BA, Trinity Coll., Hartford, Conn., 1968; MA, Harvard U., 1973, PhD, 1977. Cataloguer Sotheby & Co., London, 1968-69, dir. tng. program N.Y.C., 1969-71; curator sculpture and decorative arts Fine Arts Mus., San Francisco, 1977-80; chief curator, Bell curator decorative arts and sculpture Mpls. Inst. Arts, 1980-94; dir. Sterling and Francine Clark Art Inst., Wiliamstown, Mass., 1994—. Curated (exhibitions) Sweden: A Royal Treasury, 1988, The American Craftsman and the European Tradition, 1620-1820, 1989, Art and Life on the Upper Mississippi, 1890-1915, 1994, A Grand Design--The History of London's Victoria and Albert Museum, 1997, Organized Uncanny Spectacle: The Public Career of John Singer Sargent, 1997, organizer Impression: Painting Quickly in France 1820-1890, 2001, Gustav Klimt: Landscapes, 2002; contbr. articles. Trustee Am. Acad. in Rome, 2000—. Decorated Order of Polar Star (Sweden); recipient Robert Smith award, 1987, Charles Montgomery award, 1990; Bush fellow, 1985, Nat. Endowment Arts Mus. fellow, 1974, Am. Acad. in Rome fellow, 1975-77; Getty Guest scholar, 1988; Andrew Mellon fellow Ctr. for Advanced Study in the Visual Arts, Nat. Gallery of Art, 1993. Mem.: Am. Acad. of Rome (mem. 2000—), Assn. of Art Mus. Dirs. (mem. 2001—). Office: Sterling & Francine Clark Art Inst 225 South St Williamstown MA 01267-2878

CONGALTON, CHRISTOPHER WILLIAM, lawyer; b. N.Y.C., Apr. 8, 1946; s. William Alexander and Jacqueline Rose (Ryan) C.; m. Susan Tichenor, May 29, 1971. AB, Fairfield (Conn.) U., 1968; JD, Georgetown U., 1971. Bar: N.Y. 1972, U.S. Dist. Ct. (so. dist.) N.Y. 1974, U.S. Ct. Appeals (2d cir.) 1974, U.S. Supreme Ct. 1976, Ill. 1988, Colo. 1990. Assoc. Dunnington, Bartholow & Miller, N.Y.C., 1971-78; asst. gen. counsel Diamond Internat. Corp., N.Y.C., 1978-82; gen. counsel, v.p. Children's TV Workshop, N.Y.C., 1987-88; chmn. and ceo Moffitt Co., Schiller Park, Ill., 1988—. Mem. ABA, (corp. banking & bus. sect.), Am. Corp. Counsel Assn., N.Y. State Bar Assn., Assn. of Bar of City of N.Y., Chgo. Bar Assn., Eagle Springs Golf Club. Home: 1500 N Lake Shore Dr Chicago IL 60610-6657 Office: Moffitt Co 9347 Seymour Ave Schiller Park IL 60176-2206

CONGALTON, SUSAN TICHENOR, lawyer; b. Mt. Vernon, N.Y., July 12, 1946; d. Arthur George and M. Marjorie Tichenor; m. Christopher William Congalton, May 29, 1971. BA summa cum laude, Loretto Heights Coll., 1968; JD, Georgetown U., 1971. Bar: N.Y. 1972, Ill. 1986, Colo. 1990. Assoc. Reavis & McGrath (now Fulbright & Jaworski), N.Y.C., 1971-78, ptnr., 1978-85; v.p., gen. counsel, sec. Carson Pirie Scott & Co., Chgo., 1985-87, sr. v.p. fin. and law, 1987-89; mng. dir. Lupine LLC (formerly known as Lupine Ptnrs.), Chgo., 1989—; chmn. bd. dirs., prin. exec. officer Calif. Amforge Corp., 2002—. Bd. dirs. Harris Trust & Savs. Bank, Harris Bankcorp, Inc., Bankmont Fin. Corp.; chmn. Community Reinvestment Act Com., 1990-97, chmn. audit com., 1997—; bd. dirs. Pulitzer Inc., St. Louis; chmn. bd. Calif. Amforge Corp., 2002—. Mem. editorial staff Georgetown U. Law Jour., 1969-70, editor, 1970-71. Mem. bd. overseers Ill. Inst. Tech., Chgo., Chgo. Kent Coll. Law, 1985-89; mem. bus. adv. coun. Bus. Sch., U. Ill., Chgo., 1987-90; mem. planning com. Ann. Corp. Counsel Inst., 1986-89; bd. dirs. Ill. Inst. Continuing Legal Edn., 1992-95; mem. Chgo. Workforce Bd., 1995-98; chmn. Strategic Planning Task force, 1995-96, chmn. Performance Rev. Com., 1996-98. Mem. ABA, Nat. Assn. Corp. Dirs. (bd. dirs. Chgo. chpt. 2001—), Econ. Club Chgo., Chgo. Club (bd. dirs. 1996—, treas. 1999-02, sec. 2002—). Office: Lupine LLC 1520 Kensington Rd Ste 112 Oak Brook IL 60523-2140 E-mail: lupineLLC@aol.com.

CONGDON, CHARLES C. pathologist, researcher; b. Dunkirk, N.Y., Dec. 13, 1920; s. Charles C. and Jessie Goldie Congdon; m. Margaret Louise Ribble, Apr. 12, 1947 (div. Aug. 1967); children: Dune, Mary Dawn, Claudia, Kyle E., Lara Paige; m. Marjorie Ann Davis, Nov. 18, 1967. BA, U. Mich., 1942, MD, 1944, MS, 1950. Diplomate Am. Bd. Pathology. Intern Bellevue Hosp., N.Y.C., 1944—45; med. officer U.S. Army, 1944—47; instr. pathology U. Mich., Ann Arbor, 1948—51; vis. scientist, med. officer Nat. Cancer Inst., Bethesda, Md., 1951—55; group leader Oak Ridge (Tenn.) Nat. Lab., 1955—73; prof. pathology U. Tenn., Knoxville, 1966—83, prof. emeritus, 1983—. Contbr. articles and reports to profl. jours. Mem. Inst. Study of Human Knowledge, Los Altos, Calif.; bd. dirs. emeritus Gene Rsch. Access Corp., Oak Ridge; bd. dirs. Ea. Tenn. Alzheimer's Assn., 2000—01. Capt. U.S. Army, 1944—47, U.S. and Europe. Mem.: AMA (emeritus), Am. Assn. Cancer Rsch., Transplantation Soc., Internat. Soc. Hematology (emeritus), Internat. Soc. Exptl. Hematology (editor Exptl. Hematology 1st series 1957—70, emeritus), Soc. Exptl. Biology and Medicine (emeritus), FASEB (emeritus), Am. Soc. Investigative Pathology (emeritus), Am. Soc. Clin. Investigation (emeritus), Knoxville Acad. Medicine (emeritus), Tenn. Med. Assn. (emeritus), Sigma Xi. Home: 103 West Wind Dr Oak Ridge TN 37830

CONGDON, HOWARD KREBS, philosopher, clergyman, educator; b. Syracuse, NY, Dec. 13, 1941; s. Frank and Jean C.; m. Leigh Anne; 1 child, Kristine M. AB, Syracuse U., 1963; MDiv, Wesley Theol. Sem., Washington, 1966; MA, Pudue U., 1968, PhD, 1970. Ordained to ministry United Meth. Ch., 1966. Pastor Christian Temple of Balt., 1963-65, St. George Is. United Meth. Ch., Md., 1965-67, Aubia, Talbot and Locust Grove (Ind.) United Meth. ch., 1967-68; prof. philosophy Lock Haven U., Pa., 1970—. Author: The Pursuit of Death, 1977, Problems in Philosophy, 1995. Office: Lock Haven U Lock Haven PA 17745 E-mail: hcongdon@lhup.edu.

CONGDON, JOHN RHODES, transportation executive; b. Balt., Feb. 17, 1933; s. Earl Everett and Lillian Francis (Herbert) C.; m. Barbara Natalie Neblett, June 17, 1952; children: Susan Lee, John Rhodes, Jeffrey Whitefield. Student, U. Richmond, 1952-53. Driver Old Dominion Freight Line, 1951; founder, chmn. Old Dominion Truck Leasing, 1963—; vice chmn. Old Dominion Freight Line. Deacon River Rd. Ch., 1981; pres. Dorset Woods Civic Assn., 1973-74. With U.S. Army, 1953-55. Mem. Va. Hwy. Users Assn. (pres. 1976-78), River Rd. Citizens, Country Club of Va., Masons, Shriners. Home: Randolph Sq 112 W Square Dr Richmond VA 23233 Office: 7511 White Pine Rd Chesterfield VA 23832

CONGDON, JON HARVEY, music educator; b. Decatur, Ga., May 11, 1969; s. Frederick Voorhees Congdon and Katherine Elizabeth Bray, Rebecca Ann Congdon (Stepmother) and Roy Bray(Stepfather); m. Lesley Susan Day, Aug. 14, 1999; children: Kaitley Alexis, Ellie Margaret. Assoc. Fine Arts in Music, Brevard Coll., 1989; BS Music Edn., Ga. State U., 1995. Cert. K-12 music tchr. Ga. Beginning band dir. DeKalb County Bd. Edn., Decatur, Ga., 1996—98, mid. sch. band dir., 1998—2000, H.S. band dir., 2000—02, Hall County Bd. Of Edn., Gainesville, Ga., 2002—. Dist. elem. honor band coord. DeKalb County Bd. Edn., 1997—98, dist. mid. sch. large ensemble band festival coord., 1999—2000, dist. all-state audition coord., 2001—02, dist. chair, 2001—02. Mem.: Ga. Music Educator's Assn., Music Educators Nat. Conf. Avocations: golf, tennis, baseball. Home: 5188 Migration Point Gainesville GA 30506 Office: Flowery Branch HS 4950 Hog Mountain Rd Flowery Branch GA 30542 Personal E-mail: jlc814@yahoo.com.

CONGDON, ROGER DOUGLASS, theology educator, minister; b. Ft. Collins, Colo., Apr. 6, 1918; s. John Solon and Ellen Avery (Kellogg) C.; m. Rhoda Gwendolyn Britt, Jan. 2, 1948; children: Rachel Congdon Lidbeck, James R., R. Steven, Jon B., Philip F., Robert N., Bradford B., Ruth A. Mahner, Rebecca York Skones, Rhoda J. Miller, Marianne C. Potter, Mark Alexander.

BA, Wheaton Coll., 1940; postgrad, Eastern Bapt. Sem., 1940-41; ThM, Dallas Theol. Sem., 1945; ThD, Dallas Theology Sem., 1949. Ordained to ministry Bapt. Ch., 1945. Exec. sec., dean Altanta Bible Inst., 1945-49; prof. theology Carver Bible Inst., Atlanta, 1945-49; prof. Multnomah Bible Coll., Portland, Oreg., 1950-87; pastor Emmanuel Bapt. Ch., Vancouver, Wash., 1985—. Past dean of faculty, dean of edn., v.p., chmn. libr. com., chmn. achievement-award com., chmn. lectureship com., advisor grad. div. and mem. pres.'s cabinet Multnomah Bible Co.; chmn. Chil Evang. Fellowship of Greater Portland, 1978-97; founder, pres. Preaching Print Inc., Portland, 1953—. Founder, speaker semi-weekly radio broadcast Bible Truth Forum, KPDQ, Portland, Oreg., 1989—, DZAM, Manila, Philippines, 1996—, Radio Africa 2, 1998—; author: The Doctrine of Conscience, 1945. Chmn. Citizen's Com. Info. on Communism, Portland, 1968-75. Recipient Outstanding Educators of Am. award, 1972, Loraine Chafer award in Systematic Theology, Dallas Theol. Sem., 1949. Mem. Am. Assn. Bible Colls. (chmn. testing com. 1953-78), N.Am. Assn. Bible Colls. (N.W. rep. 1960-63), Near East Archaeol. Soc., Evang. Theol. Soc. Republican. Home: 16539 NE Halsey St Portland OR 97230-5607 Office: Emmanuel Bapt Ch 14810 NE 28th St Vancouver WA 98682-8357 *A base person's problems usually consist in selecting between overt evils. The average person chooses between the shady and the good. But the truly noble person, who follows Jesus Christ, never bothers with evils or shady acts; he ever seeks to discern the transcendent, to choose the best of all good choices.*

CONGEL, FRANK JOSEPH, federal agency administrator, physicist; b. Syracuse, N.Y., Mar. 6, 1943; s. Frank Richard and Emily (Crimi) C.; m. Mary Ellen Taylor, July 10, 1965; children: Karin, Suzanne, Frank A. BS, LeMoyne Coll., 1964; MS, Clarkson U., 1967, PhD, 1969. Postdoctoral fellow Argonne (Ill.) Nat. Lab., 1968-69; asst. prof. physics Macalester Coll., St. Paul, 1969-72; radiation physicist AEC, Washington, 1972-74; radiation physicist, tech. mgr. U.S. Nuclear Regulatory Commn., Washington, 1974-81, sr. tech. mgr., nuclear power reactors, 1981—. Cons. U.S. Govt. Response Commn. for Nuclear Emergencies. Washington, 1984—. Contbr. articles to profl. jours. Mem. U.S. Del. to Vienna to discuss the Chernobl nuclear accident, 1986. Mem. Health Physics Soc., Izaak Walton League (Damascus, Md.). Republican. Roman Catholic. Avocation: photography. Home: 7400 Cutty Sark Way Gaithersburg MD 20002 4301 Office: US Nuclear Regulatory Commn MS 0 11 E 9 Washington DC 20555-0001 E-mail: fjc@nrc.gov.

CONGER, HARRY MILTON, mining company executive; b. Seattle, July 22, 1930; s. Harry Milton Jr. and Caroline (Gunnell) C.; m. Phyllis Nadine Shepherd, Aug. 14, 1949 (dec.); children: Harry Milton IV, Preston George; m. Rosemary L. Scholz, Feb. 22, 1991. D in Bus. Adminstrn. (hon.), S.D. Sch. Mines and Tech., 1983; D. in Engring. (hon.), Colo. Sch. Mines, 1988, hon. degrees. Registered profl. engr., Ariz., Colo. Shift foreman Asarco, Inc., Silver Bell, Ariz., 1955-64; mgr. Kaiser Steel Corp. Eagle Mountain Mine, 1964-70; v.p., gen. mgr. Kaiser Resources, Ltd., Fernie, B.C., Can., 1970-73, Consolidation Coal Co. (Midwestern div.), Carbondale, Ill., 1973-75; v.p. Homestake Mining Co., San Francisco, 1975-77, pres., 1977-78, pres., chief exec. officer, 1978-82, chmn., pres., chief exec. officer, 1982-86, chmn., chief exec. officer, 1986-96, chmn., 1996-98, chmn., CEO emeritus, also bd. dirs., 1998, ret., 1998, PG& E Corp., 1982—2001, Baker Hughes Inc., 1987—97, Calmat Inc., 1986—97. Bd. dir., ASA Ltd., Apex Silver Mines; chmn. Am. Mining Congress, 1986—89, World Gold Coun., 1995—97. Trustee Calif. Inst. Tech. With C.E. U.S. Army, 1956. Recipient Disting. Achievement medal Colo. Sch. Mines, 1978, Am. Mining Hall of Fame, 1990, Disting. Svc. award Am. Mining Congress, 1995. Mem. NAE, Nat. Mining Assn. (hon. bd. dirs.), Am. Inst. Mining Engrs. (disting., Charles F. Rand gold medal 1990), Mining and Metallurgy Soc. Am., Mining Club, Bohemian Club, Commonwealth Club, Pacific Union Club, World Trade Club. Republican. Episcopalian.

CONGER, JOHN JANEWAY, psychologist, educator; b. New Brunswick, N.J., Feb. 27, 1921; s. John C. and Katharine (Janeway) Conger; m. Mayo Trist Kline, Jan. 1, 1944; children: Steven Janeway, David Trist. BA magna cum laude, Amherst Coll., 1943; MS, Yale U., 1947, PhD, 1949; DSc (hon.), Ohio U., 1981, Amherst Coll., 1983; DS (hon.), U. Colo., 1989. Asst. prof. psychology Ind. U., 1949—53; chief staff psychologist U.S. Naval Acad., 1951—52; mem. faculty U. Colo. Sch. Medicine, prof. psychology, 1957—88, assoc. dean, 1961—63, v.p. for med. affairs, 1963—70, dean, 1963—68, acting chmn. dept. psychiatry, 1983—84, acting chancellor, 1985—86, prof. emeritus, 1988—. V.p., dir. health program John D. and Catherine T. MacArthur Found., 1980—83, cons., 1983—85, NIH, VA, USPHS; vice chmn. Colo. Bd. Psychology Examiners, 1961—64; mem. Gov. Colo. Com. Mental Health, 1957; chmn. mental health adv. coun. Colo. Dept. Pub. Health, 1957—61; mem. tng. com. Nat. Inst. Mental Health, 1959—62; mem. Western coun. mental health rsch. & tng. Western Interstate Commn. Higher Edn., 1959—66; chmn. rsch. com. Pres.'s Com. Traffic Safety, 1960—63; vice chmn. nat. motor vehicle safety adv. coun. Dept. Transp., 1967—70; mem. inter-coun. com. constrn. univ.-affiliated facilities for mentally retarded Dept. Health, Edn. and Welfare, 1967—70, mem. sec.'s adv. com. traffic safety, 1966—69; coun. rsch. and planning Am. Hosp. Assn., 1965—68; nat. adv. mental health coun. USPHS, 1965—69; nat. adv. com. John F. Kennedy Ctr. Rsch. on Edn. and Human Devel., 1965—76, chmn., 1970—74; mem. adv. com. on undergrad. med. edn. AMA, 1969—70; adv. com. on casualty ins. Dept. Transp., 1970; mem. Pres.'s Task Force on Hwy. Safety, 1970, Pres.'s Commn. on Mental Health, 1977—78; mem. com. study nat. needs for biomed. and behavioral sci. rsch. personnel Nat. Acad. Scis., 1976—80; mem. Inst. Medicine/Nat. Acad. Scis., 1983—; bd. mental health and behavioral medicine, 1986—92; vis. scholar Inst. Human Devel. U. Calif., Berkeley, 1978. Author: Child Development and Personality, 7th edit., 1990, Readings in Child Development, 3d edit., 1984, Personality, Social Class and Delinquency, 1965, Adolescence and Youth: Psychological Development in a Changing World, 5th edit., 1997, The Shape of the Tree: Selected Poems, 1993, Basic and Contemporary Issues in Developmental Psychology, 1975, Contemporary Issues in Adolescent Development, 1975, Psychological Development: A Life-Span Approach, 1979, Essentials of Child Development and Personality, 1980; contbr. articles to profl. jours.; Applied and Preventive Psychology, 1991—. Lt. USNR, 1944—46, lt. USNR, 1951—52. Recipient Stearns Alumni medal for extraordinary svc., U. Colo., 1970, U. Colo. medal, 1986, disting. profl. achievement award, Am. Bd. Profl. Psychology, 1979; fellow, Ctr. Advanced Study in Behavioral Scis., Stanford, Calif., 1970—71; vis. scholar, Inst. Human Devel., U. Calif., Berkeley, 1978. Fellow: AAAS, APA (mem. policy and planning bd. 1967—70, rec. sec., dir. 1974—79, pres. 1980—82, award for disting. contbns. psychology in pub. interest 1986), Soc. Rsch. in Child Devel. (program chmn. 1975, fin. com. 1989—93, Disting. Contbns. to Pub. Policy for Children award 1995); mem.: Colo. Med. Soc. (Disting. Svc. award 1970), Colo. Psychol. Assn. (pres. 1959), Denver Med. Soc. (hon.), Am. Psychol. Found. (bd. dirs. 1982—86, pres. 1985—86), Sigma Xi, Phi Beta Kappa, Alpha Omega Alpha (hon.). Home: 130 S Birch St Denver CO 80246-1017

CONGER, ROBERT B. music educator; MusB in Edn., East Carolina U., 1975; M of Music, Northwestern U., 1976; DMA, U. North Tex., 1983. Band dir. Hartsville (S.C.) Pub. Schs., 1977—80, Orange County Pub. Schs., Orlando, Fla., 1984—2000; asst. prof. Ft. Hays State U., Hays, Kans., 2001—. Performer Brevard Symphony Orch., 1986—2001; mem. Hays Lions Club, Hays, Kans., 2001—02. Home: 110 W 34th St Hays KS 67601 Office: Fort Hays State U 600 Park St Hays KS 67601 Personal E-mail: rconger@fhsu.edu. E-mail: rconger@fhsu.edu.

CONGER, SUE ANN, computer information systems educator; b. Akron, Ohio, Nov. 6, 1947; d. Scott Stanley and Norma Marie (Bauknecht) Summerville; m. David Boyd Conger, July 3, 1971 (dec. June 1997); 1 child, Kathryn Summerville. BS, Ohio State U., 1970; MBA, Rutgers U., 1977; PhD, NYU, 1988. Programmer, analyst USDA, Washington, 1970-72; project leader Ednl. Testing Svc., Princeton, N.J., 1972-73; 2d v.p. Chase Manhattan Bank, N.Y.C., 1973-77; tech. dir. Lambda Technology, Inc., N.Y.C., 1977-80; sr. cons. Mobil Corp., N.Y.C., 1980-83; asst. prof. computer info. systems Ga. State U., Atlanta, 1988-90; asst. prof. Baruch Coll. CUNY, 1990-94; assoc. prof. So. Meth. U., Dallas, 1994-99; dir. electronic commerce Sewell Automotive Cos., Dallas, 1999—2001; assoc. prof., dir. IT program U. Dallas, Irving, 2001—. Freelance cons., educator, 1970—. Author: The New Software Engineering, 1994, Planning and Designing Effective Web Sites, 1998; contbr. articles to profl. jours. Grantee, U.S. Army Info. Systems Engring. Command, 1989, The CMI Group, 2002. Mem. IEEE, AIS, Assn. for Computing Machinery, Acad. of Mgmt. Avocations: reading, sports, cooking. Office: Univ of Dallas 1845 W Northgate Dr Irving TX 75062 E-mail: sconger@aol.com.

CONGER, VIRGINIA DAY, music educator, educator; b. Washington D.C., Oct. 21, 1931; d. William B. and Ruth Virginia Day; m. David B. Conger; children: Susan Wycoff, Bruce M., Carol Conger Wieting. BA, The Am. U., 1949—53. Tchr. Towson H.S., Towson, Md., 1953—56; piano tchr. Towson pub. sch., Towson, Md., 1958—2000. Recipient Mortar Bd., The Am. U., 1952. Home: 910 Copley Ln Silver Spring MD 20904-1315

CONGER, WILLIAM FRAME, artist, educator; b. Dixon, Ill., May 29, 1937; s. Robert Allen and Catherine Florence (Kelly) C.; m. Kathleen Marie Onderak, May 23, 1964; children: Sarah Elizabeth, Clarisa Lynn. Student, Art Inst. Chgo., 1954, 56-57, 60, 62; BFA, U. N.Mex., 1960; MFA, U. Chgo., 1966. Asst. prof. Rock Valley Coll., Rockford, 1966-71; vis. lectr. Beloit Coll., 1969; prof., chmn. dept. art DePaul U., Chgo., 1971-85; vis. artist U. Chgo., 1976, 83, Cornell U., 1980; Sch. Art Inst. Chgo., 1985, Univ. Iowa; adj. prof. So. Ill. U., 1984; chmn. dept. art theory and practice Northwestern U., Evanston, Ill., 1985-99, prof., 1985— ; numerous lectures; cons. Puresol. One man shows Burpee Mus., Rockford, Ill., 1971, Douglas Kenyon Gallery, Chgo., 1974, 75, Krannert Ctr. for Arts, Urbana, Ill., 1976, Zaks Gallery, Chgo., 1978, 80, 83, Roy Boyd Gallery, Chgo., 1985, 87, 90, 92, 94, 96, 97, 98, 99 Janus Gallery, Santa Fe, 1992, Tarbel Mus., Ill., 1993, Univ. Club Chgo., 1998, Jonson Mus., Albuquerque, 1998, Walters Art Ctr., Tulsa, 2000, 2001; group shows include Art Inst. Chgo., 1963, 71, 73, 78, 80, 84-85, Mus. Contemporary Art, Chgo., 1976, 96-97, Krannert Mus., Urbana, 1976, Ill. State Mus., 1978, 88-89, E.B. Crocker Gallery, Sacramento, 1977, Phoenix Mus., 1977, Mitchell Mus., 1980, Notre Dame U., 1981, Sonoma State U., 1983, Cowles Mus., 1983, Arts Club Chgo., 1983-97, Sheldon Meml. Gallery, U. Nebr., 1984, Anchorage Fine Arts Mus., 1985, Ark Art Ctr., 1985, Block Gallery, Northwestern U., 1986, 90, 96-97, Smart Mus., 1996; represented in permanent collections Art Inst. Chgo., Mus. Contemporary Art, Chgo., Smart Mus., U. Chgo., Ill. State Mus., Chgo., No. Ill. U., DePaul U., Jonson Mus., U. N.Mex., Block Gallery, others; also pvt. collections U.S. and worldwide; numerous catalogs, revs. and commentary in Arts mag., Art Forum, Art in Am., Ciamese, Art News, Art Criticism, Art & Antiques; others; author essays in Whitewalls, Chicago/Art/Write, Psychoanalytic Perspectives on Art, Psychoanalytic Studies of Biography, Critical Inquiry, other jours. Bd. dirs. Ox Bow Art Sch., 1982-86; adv. bd. Renaissance Soc., 1988—; bd. trustees St. Benedict H.S., Chgo., 1994—; referee NEH, 1989; interviewee TV and radio programs including Am. Art Forum. Recipient Bartels award Art Inst. Chgo., 1971; Clusmann award, 1973; Friedman awards U. Chgo., 1965, 66. Mem. Coll. Art Assn. Am., Phi Sigma Tau. Office: Northwestern U Dept Art Theory & Practice Rm 244 Kresge Hall Evanston IL 60201 Home: 3500 N Lake Shore Dr Chicago IL 60657-1815 Studio: 3711 N Ravenswood Chicago IL 60613 E-mail: w-conger@nwu.edu.

CONGLETON, CONLEY COLE, III, lawyer; b. N.Y.C., Sept. 17, 1945; s. Conley Cole and Gladys (Hale) C.; 1 child, Katharine Lindsay. BA, Eastern Ky. U., 1968; JD, U. Ky., 1971. Bar: Ky. 1973. Pvt. practice, Lexington, Ky., 1974-76, 88-89; with Begley Co., Richmond, Ky., 1976-88, v.p., sec., gen. counsel, 1980-88; asst. atty. gen. State of Ky., 1989—. Bd. dirs., treas. Bluegrass Boys' Ranch, Inc., Lexington, 1975-89, trustee, 1985-89. Capt. Transp. Corps, USAR, 1976. Democrat. Office: Capitol Bldg Ste 18 Frankfort KY 40601

CONIDI, DANIEL JOSEPH, private investigation agency executive; b. Chgo., Mar. 11, 1957; s. Joseph Frank and Gloria (Zimmerman) C. BS, SUNY, Albany, 1983; MA, Chgo. State U., 1987. Lic. pvt. detective, Ill. Owner, mgr. Conidi Enterprises, Chgo., 1979-81; pres. Daniel J. Conidi-Assocs., Chgo., 1981—; cons. Office Cook County Sheriff, Chgo., 1983-90. Freelance lectr., 1983—. Author: Professional Investigative Methods, 1984, Private Investigators Training Manual, 1986. Del. Cook County Rep. Conv., 1987. Recipient cert. of appreciation Boys Town, 1982; named Ky. col. State of Ky., 1987. Mem. World Assn. Detectives, Internat. Police Congress, Coun. Internat. Investigators, Nat. Assn. Investigations and Security, Fraternal Order Police, NRA (life), Navy League (life), Univ. Club, Masons, Shriners. Presbyterian. Avocations: flying, writing. Home: 500 Ashland Ave River Forest IL 60305-1825 Office: 734 N La Salle Dr Ste 1082 Chicago IL 60610-3530

CONIGILARO, PHYLLIS ANN, retired elementary education educator; b. Ilion, N.Y., Nov. 27, 1932; d. Gus Carl and Jennie Margaret (Marine) Denapole; m. Paul Anthony Conigilaro, July 16, 1983. BS cum laude, SUNY, Cortland, 1955; MA in Edn., Psychology, Cornell U., 1961. Cert. tchr., N.Y. Elem. classroom tchr. Mohawk (N.Y.) Central Sch., 1955-88. Contbr. articles to profl. jours. Bd. dirs. United Fund of Ilion, Herkimer, Mohawk and Frankfort, 1984-86, pres., 1986; pres. bd. edn. St. Mary's Parochial Sch., 1978; mem. Herkimer County Hist. Soc., 1988—, trustee, 1994-97; bd. dirs. local Federal Emergency Mgmt. Agy., 1987-96. Recipient Outstanding Elem. Tchrs. of Am. award, 1974, Outstanding Elem. Tchrs. of Am, 1974. Mem. N.Y. State United Tchrs., Mohawk Tchrs. Assn. (past pres.), AAUW (pres. Herkimer chpt. 1981-82), N.Y. State Ret. Tchrs. Assn. (past legis. chmn. Herkimer County chpt.), Rep. Women's Club, Kappa Delta Pi. Republican. Roman Catholic. Avocations: golf, travel, reading, music. Home: 137 7th Ave Frankfort NY 13340-3612 E-mail: pconigil@twcny.rr.com.

CONINE, ERNEST, newspaper commentator, writer; b. Dallas, Dec. 31, 1925; s. Ernest and Myrtle Eva (Elkins) C.; m. Phyllis Joan Hoyland, Nov. 28, 1953 (dec.); m. Ulla Fisher, Jan. 10, 1981. BS, So. Methodist U., 1948. Staff writer UPI, Dallas, 1948-51; Washington corr. Dallas Times Herald, 1952-55; successively Washington corr., Moscow corr., New Eng. mgr. Bus. Week mag., 1955-63; fgn. corr. L.A. Times, Vienna, 1963-64, public affairs columnist, mem. editorial bd., 1964-87, contbr., 1988-92. Mem. Ctr. Internat. and Strategic Affairs, UCLA, 1975-90, Internat. Inst. for Strategic Studies, 1984-98; mem. Calif. Seminar Internat. Security and Fgn. Affairs, 1970-93, L.A. Com. Fgn. Affairs, 1973-93. Contbr. articles to nat. magazines. Served with Army Air Corps, 1944-46, AUS, 1951-52. Mem. Soc. Profl. Journalists. Home and Office: 205 Dasher Dr Austin TX 78734-5040

CONINE, GARY BAINARD, lawyer, educator; b. Jackson, Miss., Nov. 26, 1947; s. Wallace Bainard and Mary Belle (Thompson) C.; m. Donna Sue Burnett, Sept. 2, 1982; 1 child, Joshua Wallace. B.A. in Econs., So. Meth. U., 1970; J.D., U. Okla., 1977. Bar: Tex. 1977. Assoc. Liddell, Sapp, Zivley & Brown, Houston, 1977-79; asst. prof. law U. Wyo., Laramie, 1979-80; assoc. Liddell, Sapp, Zivley, Brown & LaBoon, Houston, 1980-83; adj. prof. law South Tex. Coll. Law, Houston, 1982; ptnr. Liddell, Sapp & Zivley, Houston, 1984-87; adj. prof. law, advanced energy studies U. Houston Law Ctr., 1985-87. Contbr. articles to profl. jours. Served to 1st lt. USAF, 1970-74. Decorated Air Force Commendation medal; Leon J. York, Jr. scholar U. Okla., 1975, Rayburn L. Foster Meml. scholar 1975, George J. Fagin Mcpl. Law endowment scholar, 1976, William R. Bandy Meml. scholar 1977. Mem. ABA (vice chmn. oil com. 1981-83), Houston Bar Assn., State Bar Assn. Tex. (rsch. grantee 1987), Southwestern Legal Found. (planning com. annual inst. on oil and gas law and taxation 1985-88), Order of Barristers, Order of Coif, Houston C. of C. (govt. relations council 1983-87). Republican. Mem. Christian Ch.

CONINO, JOSEPH ALOYSIUS, lawyer; b. Hammond, La., Aug. 17, 1920; s. Dominic and Catherine (Tamborella) C.; m. Mae Evelyn Moragas, Feb. 27, 1943; children: Joseph Aloysius Jr., Robert Carl. BBA, Tulane U., 1950; JD, Loyola U., 1961; MBA, U. Pa., 1951. Bar: La. 1961, U.S. Dist. Ct. (ea. dist.) La. 1961, U.S. Ct. Appeals (5th cir.) 1972, U.S. Supreme Ct. 1989. Pvt. practice, Jefferson, La., 1961—. County judge State of La. Parish, Jefferson, 1970; del. State of La. Constnl. Conv., Baton Rouge, 1973-74; asst. atty. Parish of Jefferson, 1977—. With USN, 1942-45. Mem. La. Bar Assn. (ho. of dels. 1963-92, bd. dirs. 1981-83, 96-99), Jefferson Bar Assn. (pres.), New Orleans C. of C. (bd. dirs. 1974-77), Kiwanis (pres. Metairie, La. chpt.). Avocations: golf, swimming, tennis. Office: 1920 Jefferson Hwy Jefferson LA 70121-3816

CONISON, JAY, lawyer; b. Cin., Oct. 21, 1953; s. Allan Abraham and Theresa (Yudofsky) C.; m. Nancy Jo Kelber, Sept. 7, 1980; children: Alexander, David. BA, Yale U., 1975; MA, U. Minn., 1978, JD, 1981. Bar: Ill. 1981, U.S. Dist. Ct. (no. dist.) Ill. 1980, U.S. Dist. Ct. (ea. dist.) Wis. 1984, U.S. Dist. Ct. (no. dist. trial) Ill. 1985, U.S. Ct. Appeals (7th cir.) 1986, U.S. Dist. Ct. (we. dist.) Okla. 1990, U.S. Supreme Ct. 1990. Atty. Sonnenschein, Carlin, Nath & Rosenthal, Chgo., 1981-90; asst. prof. Oklahoma City U. Sch. Law, 1990-92, assoc. prof., 1992-94, prof., assoc. dean, 1994-97, interim dean, 1997-98; dean, prof. Valparaiso (Ind.) U. Sch. Law, 1998—. Chair employee benefits com. Assn. Am. Law Schs., 2002; mem. employee benefits adv. bd. John Marshall Law Sch., 2003—. Author: Employee Benefit Plans in a Nutshell, 1993, 2d edit., 1998. Bd. dirs. Jewish Fedn. of N.W. Ind., 2002—; mem. bd. visitors U. Minn. Law Sch., 1999—. Fellow Ind. Bar Found. (trustee 1998—); mem. ABA (Forum com. franchising, sect. on legal edn. and admission to the bar, co-chair sect. on legal edn. and admission to the bar, clin. skills edn. com. 2001—), Ill. Bar Assn., Ind. Bar Assn. (chair profl. legal edn. admission and devel. com. 2001-02, vice chair legal edn. conclave com. 2001—). Home: 2103 Chandana Trl Valparaiso IN 46383-2295 Office: Valparaiso U Sch Law Wesemann Hall Valparaiso IN 46383 E-mail: jay.conison@valpo.edu.

CONKEL, ROBERT DALE, lawyer, pension consultant; b. Oct. 13, 1936; s. Chester William and Marian Matilda (Ashton) Conkel; m. Elizabeth A. Cargill, June 15, 1958; children: Debra Lynn, Dale William, Douglas Alan; m. Brenda Jo Myers, Aug. 2, 1980; 1 child, Chelsea Ashton. BA, Mt. Union Coll., 1958; JD cum laude, Cleve. Marshall Law Sch., 1965; LLM, Case Western Res. U., 1972. Bar: Ohio 1965, U.S. Ct. Appeals (5th cir.) 1979, U.S. Tax Ct. 1974, U.S. Supreme Ct. 1974. Supr. Social Security Adminstrn., Cleve., 1958—65; trust officer Harter Bank & Trust Co., Canton, Ohio, 1965—70; exec. v.p. Am. Actuaries, Inc., Grand Rapids, Mich., 1970—73; mgr. plans and rsch. A.S. Hansen, Inc., Dallas, 1973—74; pvt. practice Dallas, 1973—; pension cons., southwest regional dir. Am. Actuaries, Inc., Dallas, 1974—88. Sr. cons. Coopers & Lybrand, Dallas, 1989; pres. Robert D. Conkel, Inc., 1989—; mem. devel. bd. Met. Nat. Bank, Richardson, Tex.; instr. Am. Mgmt. Assn., 1975, Am. Coll. Advanced Pension Planning, 1975—76; enrolled actuary Joint Bd. Enrollment U.S. Depts. Labor and Treasury. Contbr. articles to legal publs.; mem. editl. adv. bd.: jour. Jour. Pension Planning and Compliance, 1974—83. Mem. Zoning Bd. of Adjustments, City of Richardson, Tex.; sustaining mem. Rep. Nat. Com., 1980—88. Mem.: ABA (employee benefit com. sect. taxation), Am. Acad. Actuaries, Am. Soc. Pension Actuaries (dir. 1973—81), Dallas Bar Assn., Tex. Bar Assn., Ohio State Bar Assn. Office: 100 N Central Expy # 519 Richardson TX 75080-5332

CONKIN, PAUL KEITH, history educator; b. Chuckey, Tenn., Oct. 25, 1929; s. Harry Thomas and Dorothy (Staten) C.; m. Dorothy L. Tharp, 1954; 3 children. BA, Milligan Coll., 1951; MA, Vanderbilt U., 1953, PhD, 1957. Asst. prof. history U. Southwestern La., 1957-59; asst. prof., assoc. prof., prof. U. Md., 1959-67; prof. U. Wis., Madison, 1967-76, Merle Curti prof., 1976-79; disting. prof. history Vanderbilt U., Nashville, 1979—2000, emeritus, 2000—, chmn. dept. history, 1984-87. Author: The New Deal, 1967, F.D.R. and the Origins of the Welfare State, 1967, Puritans and Pragmatists, 1968, Self-Evident Truths, 1974, Prophets of Prosperity, 1980, Gone with the Ivy: A Biography of Vanderbilt U., 1985, Big Daddy from the Pedernales: Lyndon Baines Johnson, 1986, The Southern Agrarians, 1988, Cane Ridge: America's Pentecost, 1991, Four Foundations of American Government, 1994, The Uneasy Center: Reformed Christianity in Antebellum America, 1995, American Originals: Homemade Varieties of Christianity, 1997, When All the Gods Trembled: Darwinism, Scopes, and American Intellectuals, 1998, Requiem for the American Village, 2000, Peabocy College: From a Frontier Academy to the Frontiers of Teaching and Learning, 2002; co-author: The Heritage and Challenge of History, 1971; author: (with others) A History of Recent America, 1974; co-editor: New Directions in American Intellectual History, 1979. Guggenheim fellow, 1965-66; sr. fellow Nat. Endowment for Humanities, 1972-73, 90. Mem. Am. Hist. Assn. (Beveridge award 1958), Orgn. Am. Historians, So. Hist. Assn. (pres. 1996-97). Home: 1003 Tyne Blvd Nashville TN 37220-1026

CONKLIN, D(ONALD) DAVID, academic administrator; b. Waynesburg, Pa., Oct. 29, 1944; s. Donald David and Esther Louise (McCracken) C.; children: Donald David III, Elizabeth Ann. BA, Pa. State U., 1966, MEd, 1967; EdD, NYU, 1975. Asst. dean. instrn. SUNY, Farmingdale, 1970-72, exec. asst. to pres., 1972-78; spl. asst. N.J. Dept. Higher Edn., Trenton, 1978-80; dean for planning and devel. Mercer County Community Coll., Trenton, 1980-83, dean for adminstrn., 1983-86, dean for acad. affairs, 1986-92; pres. Dutchess Community Coll., Poughkeepsie, N.Y., 1992—. Cons. AAA of No. N.J., Morristown, 1984, Harrisburg Area C.C., 1983, Ednl. Testing Svc., Princeton, N.J., 1990, Educom Cons. Svcs., Princeton, 1985-90, Md. Higher Edn. Commn., 1992-95. Contbr. articles to profl. jours., chpts. to books. Chair Dutchess County Empire Zone Bd.; chmn. bd. dirs. United Way of Dutchess County; vice chmn., bd. dirs. St. Francis Hosp., Cmty. Fund of Dutchess County, Hudson Valley Philharm., Hudson Valley coun. Boy Scouts Am., Dutchess County Econ. Devel. Corp.; mem. SUNY Coun. of Pres.; chmn. Coll. Bd. CC Adv. Com. Recipient Adminstrs. award for excellence in aviation edn. FAA, 1989. Mem. Poughkeepsie C. of C., Rotary, Phi Theta Kappa, Alpha Mu Gamma, Phi Delta Kappa, The Club. Presbyterian. Avocations: tennis, golf, reading. Home: 57 Pendell Rd Poughkeepsie NY 12601-1512 Office: Dutchess CC Pendell Rd Poughkeepsie NY 12601 E-mail: conklin@sunydutchess.edu.

CONKLIN, DONALD RANSFORD, retired pharmaceutical company executive; b. Bound Brook, N.J., Sept. 10, 1936; s. Walter Ransford and Dorothy Ann (Haase) C.; m. Louise Sealey, July 13, 1960; children: Elizabeth, Edward. BA, Williams Coll., 1958; MBA, Rutgers U., 1961; grad. program for mgmt. devel., Harvard U., 1970. Dir. mktg. Schering Corp. U.S.A. (name changed to Schering-Plough 1971), Kenilworth, N.J., 1970-74; dir. mktg. Europe div. Schering-Plough, Lucerne, Switzerland, 1975-76, v.p. internat. mktg. Kenilworth, 1977-79, regional dir., sr. v.p. Latin Am. div. Miami, Fla., 1980 83, sr. v.p. internat. hdqrs. Kenilworth, 1984—, pres., 1985, group v.p. pharm. ops., 1986, exec. v.p. pharm. ops., 1987-89, pres. pharm. ops., 1989-94, pres. healthcare products, 1994-96; ret., 1996. Bd. dirs. Vertex Pharms., Ventiv Inc. Home: 120A Youngs Rd Basking Ridge NJ 07920

CONKLIN, ERIC LINWOOD, artist; b. Balt., Apr. 20, 1950; s. Vernon Linwood Conklin and Thelma Mae Helgoe; m. Victoria Lynn Davis, Apr. 21, 1984. Exhibited in group shows at Marr Gallery, Santa Fe, 2002, McBride Gallery, Annapolis, Md., 2002, Eleanor Ettinger Gallery, N.Y.C., 2002, Phoenix Art Mus., 2003, Leigh Yawkey Woodson Art Mus., Wausau, Wis., 2003. Master: Trompe l' Oeil Soc. Artists (rsch. historian 2001); mem.: Allied Artists Am., Md. Fedn. Art (artist mem. 1998), Delaplaine Visual Arts Ctr. (artist mem. 1999, Hon. Mention 2000), Md. Hall Sch. for Art's (artist mem. 2000). E-mail: eric@ericconklin.com.

CONKLIN, GEORGE HENRY, sociologist, educator; b. Dumont, N.J., Apr. 9, 1941; s. Richard Brown and Heloise Sealey Conklin; m. Verna Gibble, Aug. 21, 1966; children: Heather, Wendy;1 child, Dawn. AB, Colgate U., 1963; PhD, U. Pa., 1971. Asst. prof. Syracuse (N.Y.) U., 1969—74; assoc. prof. Sweet Briar (Va.) Coll., 1974—78; prof. sociology N.C. Ctrl. U., Durham, 1978—, chair faculty senate, 1999—2000. Vice chmn. faculty assembly U. N.C., 2002—03. Contbr. articles to profl. jours., chapters to books; editor: Sociation Today, 2003—. Airport commr. Raleigh-Durham Airport Authority, 1990—99; chair bd. of adjustment Durham County Planning Dept., 1984—90; planning commr. Durham City/ County Planning Dept., 2000—. Grantee Fulbright grantee, U.S. Ednl. Found. in India, 1963—64, rsch. grantee, Am. Inst. Indian Studies, 1968, Coll. Tchg. Improvement grantee, Fund for Improvment of Postsecondary Edn. (FIPSE), 1982—86, Computer-Based Instrnl. Materials grantee, NSF, Lilly Endowment, 1982—93. Mem.: Internat. Sociol. Assn., So. Sociol. Assn., N.C. Sociol. Assn. (pres. 1998—99, webmaster, Contbns. to Sociology award 1998). Liberal. Presbyterian. Avocation: collecting antique phonographs. Home: 2905 Scuppernong Ln Durham NC 27703-9264 Office: NC Ctrl U Fayetteville St Durham NC E-mail: george@ncsociology.org.

CONKLIN, GEORGE MELVILLE, retired food products executive; b. Roselle Park, N.J., Dec. 29, 1921; s. Melville Guy and Anna Elizabeth (McMahon) Conklin; m. Jean Austin Wiley, Feb. 19, 1944; children: Andrea(dec.), Blair. BS, Clarkson Coll. Tech., 1947; MS, Newark Coll. Engring., 1951; DSc (hon.), Clarkson U., 1987. Draftsman Babcock & Wilcox, N.Y.C., 1939-42; indsl. engr. Johns-Manville Co., Manville, NJ, 1947-48, Western Electric Co., Kearny, NJ, 1948-50, Gen. Ceramics, Keasby, NJ, 1950-51; indsl. engring. supr. Gen Electric Co., Bloomfield, NJ, 1951-52; with M & M/Mars, Hackettstown, NJ, 1952—, pres., 1968-78, chmn., 1980-82; group pres. Mars,

Inc., 1979-80; ret., 1982. Trustee Clarkson U., 1976—86. With inf. AUS, 1943—45. Decorated Combat Inf. badge; named Hon. Commodore, Lake Waco, Tex.; recipient Key to City of Cleveland, Tenn. Mem.: Tex. Rangers (hon.), Evergreen Club (Palm City, Fla.), Somerset Hill Golf Club (Bernardsville, N.J.), Tau Beta Pi. Home: Apt 2227 1221 SW Shoreline Dr Palm City FL 34990-4555 *Be a leader that most people do not notice so that when a job is done well, the people believe that they did it themselves.*

CONKLIN, HAL (HAROLD CONKLIN), public affairs director; b. Oakland, Calif., Dec. 11, 1945; s. Ralph Harold and Stella (Garabedian) C.; m. Barbara Elaine Lang, Mar. 25, 1972; children: Nathaniel, Joseph Lucas, Zachary. Student, Calif. State U., Hayward, 1967-71. Editor New Focus Mag., Santa Barbara, Calif., 1969-72; co-dir. Community Environ. Coun., Santa Barbara, 1972-82; pres. Santa Barbara Renaissance Fund, 1983-93; mem. Santa Barbara City Coun., 1977—93; mayor City of Santa Barbara, 1993-94. Dir. pub. affairs So. Calif. Edison, 1995--. Bd. dirs. Santa Barbara Redevel. Agy., 1978-94, Calif. Local Govt. Commn., Sacramento, 1979-94, Nat. League of Cities, 1987-94; chmn. Santa Barbara Civic Light Opera, 1998-2000; pres. Calif. Ctr. Civic Renewal; chmn. La Casa do Maria Retreat Ctr.; v.p. Nat. League of Cities, 1994. Mem. League of Calif. Cities (bd. dirs. 1986—, pres. 1991-92), Calif. Resource Recovery Assn. (pres. 1978-82). Free Methodist. Avocation: photography. Home: 214 El Monte Dr Santa Barbara CA 93109-2006

CONKLIN, HAROLD COLYER, anthropologist, educator; b. Easton, Pa., Apr. 27, 1926; s. Howard S. and May W. (Colyer) C.; m. Jean M. Morisuye, June 11, 1954; children: Bruce Robert, Mark William. AB, U. Calif.-Berkeley, 1950; PhD, Yale U., 1955. From instr. to assoc. prof. anthropology Columbia U., 1954-62; lectr. anthropology Rockefeller Inst., 1961-62; prof. anthropology Yale U., 1962-96, chmn. dept., 1964-68, Crosby prof. anthropology, 1990-96; curator of anthropology Yale Peabody Mus. Natural History, 1974-96, dir. divsn. anthropology, 1994-96, Crosby prof. emeritus, curator emeritus, 1996—. Mem. Inst. for Advanced Study, Princeton, N.J., 1972; fellow Ctr. for Advanced Study in Behavioral Scis., Stanford, Calif., 1978-79; field rsch. in Philippines, 1945-48, 52-54, 55, 57-58, 61, 62-63, 64, 65, 68-69, 70, 73, 80-81, 82-85, 90-91, 95, 2000-01, Malaya, Malaysia and Indonesia, 1948, 57, 83, Melanesia, 1987, N.Y., 1942, 48, 52, Calif., 1943, 48, 51, Guatemala, 1959, Peru, 1987; dir., com. problems and policy Social Sci. Rsch. Coun., 1963-70; bd. dirs. Survival Internat. USA, 1985-90; spl. cons. Internat. Rice Rsch. Inst., Los Baños, Philippines, 1962—; book rev. editor Am. Anthropologist, 1960-62; mem. Pacific sci. bd. Nat. Acad. Scis.-NRC, 1962-66. Author: Hanunóo Agriculture, 1957, Folk Classification, 1972, Ethnographic Atlas of Ifugao, 1980; other publs. on ethnol., linguistic and ecol. topics. Served with AUS, 1944-46. Guggenheim fellow, 1973; recipient Internat. Sci. prize Fyssen Foundation, 1983 Mem. NAS; Fellow Am. Acad. Arts and Scis., Am. Anthrop. Assn. (exec. bd. 1965-68), Royal Anthrop. Inst., N.Y. Acad. Scis. (sec. sect. anthropology 1956); mem. Am. Ethnol. Soc. (councilor 1960-62, pres. 1978-79), Koninklijk Inst. voor Taal- Land- en Volkenkunde, Conn. Acad. Arts and Scis., Linguistic Soc. Am., Kroeber Anthrop. Soc., Phila. Anthrop. Soc., Am. Geog. Soc., Am. Oriental Soc., Assn. Asian Studies, Classification Soc., Linguistic Soc. Philippines, Indo-Pacific Prehistory Assn., Soc. Econ. Botany, Internat. Assn. Plant Taxonomy, AAAS, Phi Beta Kappa, Sigma Xi. Home: 106 York Sq New Haven CT 06511-3625 Address: Yale Univ Dept of Anthropology PO Box 208277 New Haven CT 06520-8277

CONKLIN, JEFFREY T. director; b. Lansing, Mich., Oct. 18, 1954; s. Lloyd T. and Joyce M. Conklin(Stepmother); m. Connie May Hale, May 2, 1999; children: Lyndsey J Hyde, Justin Jeffrey Hyde. BS, Grand Valley State U., 1980; M. in Mgmt., Aquinas Coll., 1989; D in Edn., Western Mich. U., 2000. LCSW Mich., 1988. Asst. exec. dir. Riverview Residential Treatment Facilities, Lowell, Mich., 1985—90, exec. dir., 1990—93; spl. edn. program coord. Albany State U., Ga., 1999—2001, Columbus State U., Ga., 2001—. Mng. ptnr. Valeasco, Inc., Columbus, 1989—2003. State Improvement grant, State of Ga., Dept. of Edn., 2002—03. Mem.: Coun. Exceptional Children. Avocations: travel, motorcycling. Office: Columbus State Univ 4225 University Ave Columbus GA 31907 E-mail: conklin_jeffrey@colstate.edu.

CONKLIN, JOHN EVAN, sociology educator; b. Oswego, NY, Oct. 2, 1943; s. Evan Nelson and Susan Estelle (Brenner) C.; m. Ruth Tiffany Edmonds, July 10, 1965 (div. Oct. 1974); children: Christopher Perry, Anne Tiffany; m. Sarah Hubbard Belcher, Jan .2, 1982; children: Lydia Catherine, Gillian Jane. AB, Cornell U., 1965; PhD, Harvard U., 1969. Research assoc. Harvard U. Law Sch., Cambridge, Mass., 1969-70; asst. prof. sociology Tufts U., Medford, Mass., 1970-76, assoc. prof. sociology, 1976-81, prof. sociology, 1981—, chmn. dept. sociology, 1981-86, 90-91. Author: Robbery and the Criminal Justice System, 1972, The Impact of Crime, 1975, Illegal But Not Criminal, 1977, Criminology, 1981, 8th edit., 2004, Sociology: An Introduction, 1984, 2d edit., 1987, Art Crime, 1994, Why Crime Rates Fell, 2003; editor: The Crime Establishment, 1973, New Perspectives in Criminology, 1996. Mem. Am. Sociol. Assn., Am. Soc. Criminology. Avocations: collecting books, movie memorabilia. Office: Tufts U Dept of Sociology Eaton Hall Medford MA 02155 E-mail: john.conklin@tufts.edu.

CONKLIN, JOHN ROGER, retired electronics company executive; b. Poughkeepsie, N.Y., Dec. 20, 1933; s. Leland Thomas and Eleanor (Warren) C.; m. Catharine Becker, Dec. 28, 1956 (div. Apr. 1976); children: Thomas Stephen, Todd Roger; m. Nancy Plank, July 16, 1983. BS in Mil. Sci., U.S. Mil. Acad., 1956; postgrad., Xavier U., Cin., 1961-62, Northeastern U., 1974. Engr. Procter & Gamble Co., Cin., 1960-64; sales engr. Orville Simpson Co., Cin., 1964-67; various sales positions DeLaval Separator Co., Poughkeepsie, 1967-74, pres., 1974-78, Standard Gage Co., Poughkeepsie, 1979-86; pres., owner Discount Data Products, Inc., Poughkeepsie, 1988-97. Adv. bd. Dutchess divsn. Bank of N.Y., Poughkeepsie, 1974-98. Contbr. articles to profl. jours.; patentee basket centrifuge. Bd. dirs. Area Fund-Dutchess County, Poughkeepsie, 1975, Poughkeepsie C. of C., 1981-86, YMCA, Poughkeepsie, 1982; campaign chair United Way, Dutchess County, N.Y., 1986; dir., pres. West Point Soc. of Mid-Hudson Region, 2003. 1st lt. U.S. Army, 1956-60. Mem. D.C. Hist. Soc. Avocations: skiing, trout fishing, gardening, mycology. Home: 5 Dutchess Ter Rhinecliff NY 12574

CONKLIN, RICHARD ALLAN, management consultant; b. Syracuse, N.Y., Dec. 16, 1939; s. George William and Beatrice Anne (Weeks) C.; m. Rose Marquez, Feb. 14, 1991. BA, Pacific Coll., Fresno, Calif., 1964; postgrad., Cornell/Hofstra U., 1978-80. Asst. mgr. Weinstein Holding Corp., Commack, N.Y., 1967-73; ops. mgr. Allan Tire Ctrs., Selden, N.Y., 1973-77; zone mgr. Vogue Tire Co., Bayside, N.Y., 1977-81; personnel mgr. United Cerebal Palsy Assn., Roosevelt, N.Y., 1981-86; assoc. ptnr. R.J. Carroll Co., Springfield, Pa., 1986-88; dir. human resources Daughters of Jacob Geriatric Ctr., Bronx, N.Y., 1988—. Adj. prof. Cornell U.; instr. U. Pa., Hofstra U., N.Y. Inst. Tech.; cons. N.Y. State Senator Levy, Albany, 1980-86; Nassau County Bd. Cooperative Edn. Service, Westbury, N.Y., 1982-85; Inst. Internat. Med. Edn., N.Y.C., 1982-84; Goodwill Industries, L.I. City, N.Y., 1986—. Recipient Pres. Sports award, 1979; Repub. Pres. Task Force Medal of Merit, 1984. Mem. Research Inst. Am., Soc. Personnel Adminstrn., Am. Personnel Guidance Assn., Am. Arbitration Assn., Alpha Psi Omega (bd. dirs. 1976—). Roman Catholic. Home: 265 W Lido Promenade Lindenhurst NY 11757-6620

CONKLIN, ROBERT EUGENE, electronics engineer; b. Loveland, Ohio, Apr. 21, 1925; s. Charles and Alberta (Reynolds) C.; m. Virginia E. McCann, June 14, 1952; children: Carl Lynn, Jill Elaine Conklin Bradford. BSEd, BS in Sci., Wilmington Coll., 1949. Electronic scientist Electronic Technol. Lab. Wright-Patterson AFB, Ohio, 1951-55, electronic engr. AF Avionics Lab., 1956-60, supr. elec. engr., 1960-72; cons. electronic engr., 1972-78; supervisory electronic engr., 1978-82; electronic engr. VHSIC, 1982-84. Cons. engr. REC Electronics, Fairborn, Ohio, 1984—; mem. Inst. Nav., 1968-72. With USAAC, 1943-46. Mem. IEEE (H.V. Noble award for Achievements in Electronic Devices 1998), Lions (Fairborn). Republican. Mem. Soc. Of Friends. Home: 114 Wayne Dr Fairborn OH 45324-5228 Office: 47 N Broad St Fairborn OH 45324-4863 E-mail: recelect@earthlink.net.

CONKLIN, SUSAN JOAN, psychotherapist, educator, corporate staff developer, TV talk show host; b. Bklyn., Feb. 7, 1950; d. Joseph Thomas Hallek and Stella Joan (Kubis) Kuceluk; m. John Lariviere Conklin, July 25, 1981; children: Genevieve Therese, Michelle Therese. BA, CCNY, 1972; MSW, CUNY, 1975. Lic. ind. clin. social worker; cert. diplomat. Shop counselor Assn. for Help of Retarded Citizens, N.y.C., 1971-75; dir. social svcs., acting exec. dir. North Berkshire Assn. for Retarded Citizens, North Adams, Mass., 1975-77; project dir. Title XX tng. grant State of Mass., North Adams, 1978-79; pvt. practice psychotherapy, Williamstown, Mass., 1979—. Adj. asst. prof. Mass. Coll. Liberal Art, 1977—2000, Berkshire C.C., Pittsfield, Mass., 1985—86, Pittsfield, 1995; Therapeutic Touch practitioner, 1978—; talk show host Pub. Access TV, 1998—; vol. Salvation Army. WTC Disaster Relief Family Assistance Ctr., 2001, 9/11 United Svcs. Group, 2002; adj. faculty Springfield Coll. Sch. Social Work, 2002. Pres. Williamstown PTO, 1989-91; bd. dirs., edn. com., spl. events coord. Hospice No. Berkshire, Inc., 1989—. Named Mass. Social Worker of Yr., 2003. Mem. NASW (bd. dirs. 1981-83, regional coun. mem. 1980-83, 93—), LWV, Nurse Healers-Profl. Assn., Inc. (trustee 1981-83, rec. sec., editor-in-chief Coop. Connection newsletter 1983-88), Women of Vision Action. Democrat. Episcopalian. Home and Office: 85 Hawthorne Rd Williamstown MA 01267-2700 *I wish all human beings the ability to honor and respect each other especially during times of conflict.*

CONKLIN, THOMAS WILLIAM, lawyer; b. Chgo., Mar. 1, 1938; s. Clarence Robert and Ellen Pauline (Gleason) C.; children: Thomas William, Sarah Adrienne. BA, Yale U., 1960; JD, U. Chgo., 1963, Bar: Ill. 1964, Mich. 1997. Ptnr. Upton, Conklin & Leahy, Chgo., 1969-72, Conklin, Leahy & Eisenberg, Chgo., 1972-79, Conklin & Adler, Ltd., Chgo., 1979-87, Conklin & Roadhouse, Chgo., 1988-95; Rivkin, Radler & Kremer, Chgo., 1995-97; ptnr. Conklin, Murphy, Conklin & Snyder, Chgo., 1997—. Contbr. numerous articles to legal jours. With USAF, 1963-64. Mem. ABA, Fed. Bar Assn., Am. Arbitration Assn., Internat. Assn. Ins. Counsel, Chgo. Bar Assn., Maritime Law Assn., Mich. Bar Assn., Ill. State Bar Assn., Chgo. Bar Assn., Union League Club Chgo. Home: PO Box 189 Bangor MI 49013-0189 Office: Conklin Murphy Conklin & Snyder 53 W Jackson Blvd Ste 1150 Chicago IL 60604-3790 E-mail: tconk@msn.com.

CONKLIN, WILLIAM FRANK, writer; b. Cambridge, Mass., Apr. 8, 1926; s. Frank Alvin and Helen Pearl (Harvison) C.; m. Celia Bass, Aug. 13, 1948. Student, Bucknell U., U. Colo., U. Va. Lic. comml. pilot, FAA; master U.S. Merchant Marine. Enlisted USN, 1944, naval aviator, combat missions in Korea and Vietnam, 1947—68, exch. officer Fleet Air Arm, Royal Navy, 1956—58, ret. comdr., 1968; sys. analyst Ctr. for Naval Analyses, Rosslyn, Va., 1968-71; freelance writer various publs., 1971-80; capt. Am. Cruise Lines, Haddam, Conn., 1981; founder Conklin Marine Ctr. and Chesapeake Area Profl. Capts. Assn., Annapolis, Md., 1982-91; owner, writer BBC Comm., Naples, Fla., 1991—. Decorated 2 Disting. Flying Cross, Bronze Star, 17 Air medals.

CONKLING, ROGER LINTON, consultant, business administration educator, retired utility executive; b. Bloomington, Ill., July 12, 1917; s. Robert Edwin and Helen (Ricketts) C.; m. Meta Baskerville, Apr. 4, 1941; children—Mary Beth, Jane Linton, Roger Marc. BBA, Northwestern U., 1941; MA, U. Oreg., 1948; LLD, U. Portland, 1972. With Pub. Svc. Co. No. Ill., Chgo. and Joliet, 1936-42; economist Bonneville Power Adminstrn., Portland, Oreg., 1945-47, asst. to power mgr., 1948-51, chief system devel., 1952-53, chief customer svc., 1954, dir. budget and mgmt., 1955-56, asst. to adminstr., 1957; v.p., assoc. H. Zinder & Assocs., Inc., Washington, 1958-61; pres., cons. Conkling, Inc., Portland, 1962-67; v.p. N.W. Natural Gas Co., Portland, 1967-76, sr. v.p., CFO, 1976-82; ret., 1982. Adj. prof. bus. adminstrn. U. Portland, 1988—; former pres., dir. Pacific Western Pipeline Corp., Portland; mem. grad. faculty Oreg. System Higher Edn., Portland, 1946-56; cons. in field. Past pres., chmn. Oreg. United Appeal; pres. Delauney Inst. Mental Health, 1964; mem. Gov.'s Com. Child Care, 1964; bd. dirs. Cath. Charities, Inc., Portland, 1957-58, 61-64; pres. Oreg. State Soc., Washington, 1960; chmn. exec. com. Nat. Found., 1958-60; chmn. March of Dimes campaign, Portland, 1957; bd. dirs. Mental Health Assn., 1957-58, Cath. Services for Children, 1954-57, Oreg. Symphony Assn., NCCJ, 1980-82, Found. Oreg. Research and Edn., 1967-80; chmn. bd. regents U. Portland; trustee Providence Children's Center; chmn. ann. fund dr. Oreg. Symphony, 1981; mem. fin. council Archdiocese of Portland, 1988-98. With USNR, 1942-45. Recipient Distinguished Service award Dept. Interior, Arthur S. Fleming award Jr. C. of C., Papal honor, Benemerenti medal. Mem. Am. Econ. Assn., Western Econ. Assn., Fed. Govt. Accts. Assn., Am. Gas Assn., Pacific Coast Gas Assn., Assn. Wash. Gas Utilities (trustee, past pres.), Multnomah Athletic Club (Portland), Beta Gamma Sigma, Delta Mu Delta. Clubs: Multnomah Athletic (Portland). Home and Office: 2539 SW Hill Crest Dr Portland OR 97201-1749 E-mail: conkling@up.edu.

CONLEY, DARLENE ANN, actress; b. Chgo. d. Raymond and Melba (Manthey) C.; m. William Woodson, Oct. 1959 (div. 1966); 1 child, Raymond. Actress Broadway prodns. including: The Baker's Wife, The Night of the Iguana Actress feature films including: Tough Guys, Faces, Minnie and Moscowitz, Play it As it Lays, Lady Sings the Blues, Valley of the Dolls, The Birds; TV movies include: I Want to Live, The Fighter, The Choice, Return Engagement, The President's Plane is Missing; TV episodes include: Get Christie Love, Scarecrow and Mrs. King, Highway to Heaven, Murder She Wrote, Bill Cosby Show, Little House on the Prairie; continuing role on The Young and The Restless, 1980-88, The Bold and The Beautiful, 1989—. Emmy nominee for Outstanding Supporting Actress, 1991, 92; statue made for Madame Tussaud's Wax Mus., 1998. Office: Bell-Phillip TV Prodns Inc 7800 Beverly Blvd # 3371 Los Angeles CA 90036-2112

CONLEY, DAYSPRING LINDER, retired music educator; b. Houston, Mar. 20, 1977; d. Gary Anthony and Linda Lou Linder; m. Jeremie Lee Conley, Aug. 30, 1997; 1 child, Justice Lee. MusB(hon.), Centenary Coll. La., 1999. Cert. tchr. music in piano Music Tchrs. Nat. Assn., 2002, piano tchr. La. Music Tchrs. Assn., 1999. Owner Dayspring Piano Studio, Shreveport, La., 1999—2002. Mem.: Greater Shreveport Music Tchrs. Assn. (1st v.p. 2000—01, pres. 2001—02, immediate past pres. 2002—03), Sigma Alpha Iota (life). Republican. Avocations: travel, reading, fitness. Home: 742 Booth Dr Shreveport LA 71107

CONLEY, KATHERINE LOGAN, religious studies educator; b. Rutherford, N.C., Sept. 3, 1911; d. Claude Joseph and Mary (Beam) Logan; m. Jesse William Conley, Dec. 26, 1942. BS in Edn., Asheville (N.C.) Coll., 1936; postgrad., Presbyn. Ch. Christian Edn., Richmond, Va., 1939-40. Dir Christian edn. Presbyn. Ch., Spartanburg, S.C., 1940-41, Knoxville, 1941—. Chmn. bldg. com. Seventh-Day Adventist Ch., Rutherford, N.C., 1963; lay speaker United Meth. Ch., Rutherfordton, 1973-91. Mem. Genealogical Soc., DAR (regent 1976-78), Amnesty Internat., Am. Bible Soc. (silver). Democrat. Avocations: gardening, arts and crafts, hiking. Home: Restwell Home 401 US 221 Hwy S Rutherfordton NC 28139-9289

CONLEY, PATRICK, clinic administrator; b. Roby, Tex., Oct. 10, 1921; s. Boerne Lurl and Mary Esther (Barlow) C.; m. Lucy Ann Webster, Sept. 26, 1942; children: Christopher Redifer, Peter Lurl, Molly Catherine. BSEE, Rice U., 1942; MS in Comm. Engring., Harvard U., 1946, PhD in Applied Physics, 1948, MBA, 1955. V.p. Boston Consulting Group, vis. prof. Carnegie Mellon U., Pitts.; v.p. Westinghouse Elec., Pitts.; gen. mgr. Westinghouse Aerospace, Balt.; dir. devel. Westinghouse Def. Prodn., Balt.; mgr. electronics and nuc. physics Westinghouse Rsch. Labs.; dir., acting chmn. Am. Overseas Clinics Corp. Contbr. articles to profl. jours.; patentee in field. Pres. Friends of Manchester (Mass.) Trees, 1992, Manchester Hist. Soc., 1994. Lt. comdr. USN, 1942-46. Named Outstanding Engring. Alumnus, Rice U., Houston, 1988. Mem. Am. Orchid Soc. (accredited judge), Harvard Club Boston, Singing Beach Club, Manchester Yacht Club (bd. dirs. 1981-83). Avocations: gardening, orchid growing. Home: 510 Fearrington Post Pittsboro NC 27312-8568

CONLEY, PATRICK T. lawyer; b. Branford, Conn., June 22, 1938; s. William Lincoln Conley and Edith Mae De Stasio; m. Gail C. Cahalan-Conley, Dec. 30, 1994; m. Virginia M. Anderson (div.); m. Donna L. Arruda (div.); m. Ruth E. Trainor (div.); children from previous marriage: Patrick Jr., Kathleen, Carolyn, Sharon, Thomas, Colleen. AB, Providence Coll., 1959; JD, Suffolk U., 1973; MA, U. Notre Dame, 1963, PhD, 1970. Bar: R.I.; lic. real estate broker. Prof. history and constitutional law Providence Coll., 1963—88, dir. grad. rsch. Am. history, 1964—94, spl. lectr. history, 1988—94; spl. lectr. constitutional law Salve Regina Coll., 1972—81; tchr. LaSalle Acad., Providence, 1961—62; teaching asst. U. Notre Dame, 1962—63; mem. corp., law sch. adv. com., chmn. libr. adv. com. Roger Williams Coll.; proproetor P.T. Conley Books, 1963—97; ptnr. Foreseeable Devel., Providence. Pres. Phoenix Realty, Four Seas Realty, Hardscrabble Land Co., Sedona Assocs., Options Realty, Phoenix Gambino, Zeus Realty Co.; spkr. in field. Author: Democracy in DEcline: Rhode Island's Constitutional Development, 1776-1841, 1977, Rhode Island Profile, 1982, An Albun of Rhode Island History, 1986, First in War: Last in Peace: Rhode Island and the Constitution, 1786-1970, 1987, Liberty and Justice: A History of Law and Lawyers in Rhode Island, 1636-1998, 1998, Neither Seperate Nor Equal: Legislature and Executive in Rhode ISland Constitutional History, 1999, Rhode Island in Rhetoric and Reflection, 2002; co-author (with Matthew SMith): Catholicism in Rhode ISland: The Formative Era, 1976; co-author: (with Paul Campbell) Providence: A Pictorial History, 1982, Firefighters and Fires in Providence, 1954-1984, 1985; co-author: (with William MacKenzie Woodward and Robert Jones) The Statehouses of Rhode Isldna: An Architectural and Historical Survey, 1988; editor: Proceedings of Rhode Island Constitutional Concention of 1973, 1973; co-editor: The Constitution and the States, 1988, The Bill of Rights and rhe States, 1992; mem. editl. bd.: Rhode Island Bar Jour., 1980—81, 1985—88, 1990—93, 1998—; editor: R.I. Ethnic Heritage Pamphlet series (13 vols.). Bd. trustees Bicentennial Coun. Thirteen Original States, 1970—92, vice chmn., 1986—87; chmn. U.S. Constitution Coun., 1988—90; pres. Cath. Assn. Coll. Alumni, 1976; chmn. Cranston Historic Dist. Commn., 1970—72; mem. Gov.'s Justice Commn., 1967—69; chmn. Cranston Charter Rev. Commn., 1972—73; policy advisor Gov. Frank licht, Gov. Philip Noel, Lt. Gov. J. Joseph Garrahy, Atty. Gen. Herbert F. DeSimone, 1966—76; chmn. R.I. Bicentennial Commn. and Found., 1974—77; dir. Provicence Crime Commn., 1977—84; v.p. Human Rels. Commn. Diocese Providence, 1968—69; bd. trustees R.I. Hist. Soc.; chmn. libr. adv. com. Roger Williams Coll., 1990—93, mem. law sch. adv. bd., 1991—97; spl. asst., chmn. adv. coun. U.S. Congressman Robert O. Tiernan, 1967—74; sec., del. R.I. Constitutional Convention, 1973; spl. asst. to pres. R.I. Constitutional Conv., 1986; bd. dirs. Heritage Harbor Mus., 1999—. Mem.: Bristol Train Artillery Found. (bd. dirs. 2001—), Providence Maritime Heritage Found. (v.p., dir. 1998—), Bristol Statehouse Found. (founder, pres. 1995—99), R.I. Pubs. Soc. (chmn. 1981—), Bristol Hist. and Preservation Soc. (life), R.I. Hist. Soc. (life), Am. Hist. Assn. (life), Orgn. Am. Historians (life), Brahmin Soc. Bristol County, Rotary, Eagles, Elks, KC, The Squatum Assn., Delta Epsilon Sigma. Roman Catholic. Avocations: track and field, travel, interior decorating. Home: 1 bristol Point Rd Bristol RI 02809 Office: 1445 Wampanoag Trail Providence RI 02918 Fax: 401-273-1791.

CONLEY, PHILIP JAMES, JR., retired air force officer; b. Providence, May 22, 1927; s. Philip James and Lillian Loretta (Burns) C.; m. Shirley Jean Andrews, Jan. 26, 1956; children: Sharon, Kathleen, Anne, James. BS, U.S. Naval Acad., 1950; MS, U. Mich., 1956, Rensselaer Poly. Inst., 1963. Commd. 2d lt. USAF, 1950, advanced through grades to maj. gen., 1979; dep. chief staff, ops. Air Force Systems Command, Andrews AFB, Washington, 1974-75, chief staff, 1975-78; comdr. Air Force Flight Test Center, Edwards AFB, Calif., 1978-82; vice-comdr. Electronic Systems Divn. Hanscom AFB, Mass., 1983; ret., 1983. Decorated Disting. Svc. medal (2), Legion of Merit (2), Disting. Flying Cross, Bronze Star, Air medal (3). Mem. Air Force Assn., Order of Daedalians, U.S. Naval Acad. Alumni Assn., Am. Legion, Vikings Club (L.A.), Santa Barbara Yacht Club, Monticeto Country Club. Roman Catholic. Home: 930 Camino Viejo Santa Barbara CA 93108-1920

CONLEY, RAYMOND LESLIE, English language educator; b. Manhattan, Kans., Feb. 25, 1923; s. Orville Ray and Goldie Gladys (Wallack) C. AB with honors, Park Coll., 1947; postgrad., Nebr. U., 1948-50; MA, Northwestern U., Evanston, Ill., 1958; postgrad., Ol Dominion U., 1968. Cert. tchr. speech, English, social scis. Dep. county clk. Nemaha County, Auburn, Nebr., 1942-45; tchr., English, speech St. Edward (Nebr.) High Sch., 1948-50, Oakland (Nebr.) High Sch., 1950-52, Nebraska City (Nebr.) High Sch., 1952-56, Galesburg (Ill.) High Sch., 1956-58, Maine Twp. High Sch. East, Park Ridge, Ill., 1958-65; asst. prof. English, speech Meth. Coll., Fayetteville, N.C., 1966-77; English prof. Campbell U., Buies Creek, N.C., 1980-83, aux. faculty Fort Bragg, NC, 1978—2001. Coach Nebr. State Debate Champs, 1951, 52; judge Iowa State Speech Contest, 1952, 53; mem. Coun. Status of Women, Fayetteville, 1965-68; aux. faculty Campbell U., Pope AFB, N.C., 1985-2001; speech coach, judge local and sectional contests Toastmistress Club. Actor Fort Bragg Vietnam War Tng. Films. Precinct officer Dem. party, Fayetteville, 1964-68; coord. Congrl. Dist. Common Cause, 1978, mem. state program action com., state and gov. bd. 1976-78, 95-2000; dir. state governance bd. Common Cause, N.C., 1995-2000; mem. Congress Watch/Pub. Citizen, People for the Am. Way, ACLU, N.C. ACLU; conservation coord. Sierra Club, 1978; mem. Amnesty Internat.; vol. Fayetteville Mus. Art. Recipient Am. Legion Citizenship award, 1938. Mem. NOW, AAUP, Internat. Platform Assn., Fayetteville Fgn. Film Soc. (co-founder 1967), Inst. for So. Studies, World Future Soc., Found. For Nat. Progress, N.C. Alliance For Democracy, Amnesty Internat., Ams. United for Separation Ch. and State, Lambda Chi Alpha. Presbyterian. Home: 1076 Stamper Rd Fayetteville NC 28303-4191

CONLEY, SARAH ANN, health facility administrator; b. Richmond, Ind., Sept. 14, 1942; d. Harry Herbert and Mary Janet Kercheval; m. Philip Howard Conley, Apr. 5, 1963 (dec.); children: Christine L., Philip Douglas. BS, Purdue U., 1964; postgrad., U. Cin., 1965. Elem. tchr. Southwest Local Schs., Harrison, Ohio, 1964-66; svc. office mgr. Renault of Dayton (Ohio), 1970-73; mgr. Office of Charlotte Ames, Xenia, Ohio, 1974-77; bus. mgr. Radiol. Physicians, Inc., Dayton, 1977-79, Nat. Tractor Pullers Assn., Columbus, Ohio, 1979-85; HMO adminstr. Cen. Benefits Mutual Ins. Co., Columbus, 1985-90; adminstr. Orthopedic and Neurol. Cons., Columbus, 1990-97, Peripheral Vascular Surgery, Columbus, 1997-99; owner Conley Mgmt. Svc., Westerville, Ohio. Mem. Am. Coll. Med. Practice Execs. (cert.), Ohio Med. Group Mgmt. Assn. (pres. 1993-94), MidOhio Med. Mgmt. Assn., Med. Group Mgmt. Assn., Licking County Bus. and Profl. Women (pres. 1989-91). Democrat. Methodist. Avocations: piano, organ, church choir, teaching sunday school. E-mail: conleyserv.@cs.com.

CONLEY, TOM CLARK, literature educator; b. New Haven, Dec. 7, 1943; s. Walter Frederick and Hazel Mason (Hatch) C.; m. Verena Andermatt; children: David, Francine. BA, Lawrence U., 1965; MA, Columbia U., 1966; PhD, U. Wis., 1971. Prof. U. Minn., Mpls., 1971-95; prof. renaissance lit., cinema Harvard U., Cambridge, Mass., 1995—, dir. grad. studies in French. Vis. prof. U. Calif., Berkeley, 1978-79, CUNY Grad. Ctr., 1985-87, Miami U., Ohio, 1989, UCLA, 1995; instr. Folger Inst., 1998; summer seminar leader NEH, 1998; seminar leader Sch. Critical Theory, 2003. Author: Lectura de Bunuel, 1988, Film Hieroglyphs, 1991, Graphic Unconscious, 1992, Self-Made Map, 1995; translator 5 books, editor 2 books; editor jour. Lendemains, 1985—, Diacritics, 2000—; corr. jour. Litterature, 1988—; contbr. articles to profl. jours. Woodrow Wilson fellow, 1965-66, Fulbright fellow, 1968-69, study fellow Am. Coun. Learned Socs., 1975-76, summer fellow NEH, 1974, 89, Inst. for Rsch. in Humanities fellow, 1990, Newberry Libr. fellow, 1992, Soc. Humanities fellow, 1998, Harvard Cabot fellow, 2002, Guggenheim fellow, 2003—. Mem. MLA, Renaissance Soc. Am., Assn. Study Dada/Surrealism, Midwest MLA (mem. exec. com. 1977-80), Sixteenth Century Studies Soc. (exec. com. 1994—), Alpha Omega Alpha. Avocations: handball, fishing, mycology. Office: Harvard U Romance Langs 201 Boylston Hall Cambridge MA 02138 E-mail: tconley@fas.harvard.edu.

CONLEY RIEDY, MARY THERESE, peri-operative nurse; b. Sandusky, Ohio, Mar. 15, 1955; d. Elmer J. and Adelaide C. (Tremper) C. Diploma, Providence Hosp. Sch. Nursing, 1976; BSN cum laude (Ruth E. Kelly award), Bowling Green (Ohio) State U., 1986; MA in Pastoral Ministries summa cum laude, St. Mary's Coll. of Minn., Winona, 1990. RN, Ohio, CNOR. Nurse surgery dept. Providence Hosp. (now Firelands Regional Med. Ctr.), Sandusky, 1976—2002; surgery staff RN Magruder Hosp., Port Clinton, Ohio, 2002—; pacel staff Bellevue Hosp., Ohio, 2003. Active in parish music svcs. Mem. Assn. Oper. Rm. Nurses (past bd. dirs. Sandusky chpt., scholarship), Golden Key Nat. Honor Soc., Phi Kappa Phi, Phi Eta Sigma, Sigma Theta Tau (Zeta Theta chpt.), Assn. Nat. Pastoral Musicians.

CONLIN, LINDA MYSLIWY, federal agency administrator; b. Springfield, Mass. m. Joseph F. Conlin Jr.. Pres. Park-Main Travel Agy.; protocol visits officer U.S. Dept. State; from corp. liaison officer for US/USSR intiatives to assoc. dir. Office of Pvt. Sector Coms. U.S. Info. Agy.; asst. sec. commerce for mktg. U.S. Travel and Tourism Adminstrn., 1989—93; dir. Office Travel and

Tourism N.J. Commerce Dept., 1994—98; exec. dir. Office Travel and Tourism N.J. Commerce and Econ. Growth Commn., 0998—1999; dep. to program chmn. 2000 Rep. Nat. Conv.; sr. campaign coord. Bush/Cheney 2000-Southeastern Pa. Region; asst. sec. trade devel. Dept. Commerce, Washington, 2001—. Republican. Office: Dept Commerce Trade Devel 14th & Constution Ave Nw Washington DC 20230

CONLIN, ROXANNE BARTON, lawyer; b. Huron, S.D., June 30, 1944; d. Marion William and Alyce Muraine (Madden) Barton; m. James Clyde Conlin, Mar. 21, 1964; children: Jacalyn Rae, James Barton, Deborah Ann, Douglas Benton BA, Drake U., 1964, JD, 1966, MPA, 1979; LLD (hon.), U. Dubuque, 1975. Bar: Iowa 1966. Assoc. Davis, Huebner, Johnson & Burt, Des Moines, 1966-67; dep. indsl. commr. State of Iowa, 1967-68, asst. atty. gen., 1969-76; U.S. atty. So. Dist. Iowa, 1977-81; ptnr. Conlin, P.C., Des Moines, 1983—. Adj. prof. law U. Iowa, 1977-79; chmn. Iowa Women's Polit. Caucus, 1973-75, del. nat. steering com., 1973-77; cons. U.S. Commn. on Internat. Women's Year, 1976-77; gen. counsel NOW Legal Def. and Edn. Fund, 1985-88, pres., 1986-88; lectr. in field. Co-editor Westlaw's 6 Volume Atlas Litigating Plaintiff's Tort Cases; contbr. articles to profl. jours. Nat. committeewoman Iowa Young Dems.; pres. Polk County Young Dems., 1965-66; del. Iowa Presdl. Conv., 1972; Dem. candidate for gov. of Iowa, 1982; bd. dirs. Riverhills Day Care Ctr., YWCA; chmn. Drake U. Law Sch. Endowment Trust, 1985-86; bd. counselors Drake U., 1982-86; pres.. founder Civil Justice Found., 1986-88; pres. Roscoe Pound Found., 1994-97; chair Iowa Dem. Party, 1998-99. Named one of Top Ten Litigators, Nat. Law Jour, 1989, 100 Most Influential Attys., 1991, 50 Most Powerful Women Attys., Nat. Law Jour., 1998, 10 Most Influential Women Lawyers, 2002; recipient award, Iowa ACLU, 1974, Alumnus of Yr. award, Drake U. Law Sch., 1989, ann. award, Young Women's Resource Ctr., 1989, Verne Lawyer award as Outstanding Mem., Iowa Trial Lawyers Assn., 1994, Rosalie Wahl award, Minn. Women Lawyers, 1998, Marie Lambert award, 2000, Mary Louise Smith award, YWCA, 2001, lifetime achievement award, Des Moines Human Rights Commn., 2003; grantee scholarship established in her homor Kansas City Women Lawyers; scholar Reader's Digest scholar, 1963—64, scholar, Fishcher Found, 1965—66. Mem.: ATLA (chmn. consumer and victims coalition com. 1985—87, chmn. edn. dept 1987—88, parliamentarian 1988—89, sec. 1989—90, v.p. 1990—91, pres.-elect 1991—92, pres. 1992—93, lifetime achievement award 2003), ABA, NOW, Trial Lawyers Care (bd. dirs.), Inner Circle of Advocates, Higher Edn. Commn. Iowa (co-chmn. 1988—90), Iowa Acad. Trial Lawyers, Internat. Acad. Trial Lawyers, Assn. Trial Lawyers Iowa (bd. dirs.), Iowa Bar Assn., Chi Omega, Alpha Lambda Delta, Phi Beta Kappa. Office: Griffin Bldg 319 7th St Ste 600 Des Moines IA 50309-3826

CONLIN, THOMAS, conductor; b. Arlington, Va., Jan. 29, 1944; BMus, Peabody Conservatory Music, 1966, MMus, 1967; studied with Leonard Bernstein, Erich Leinsdorf, Sir Adrian Boult. Artistic dir. Chamber Opera Soc., Balt., 1966-72; assoc. condr. N.C. Symphony Orch., 1972-74; music dir. Queens (N.Y.) Orchestral Soc., 1974-76; condr. Amarillo (Tex.) Symphony Orch., 1976-84, W.Va. Symphony Orch., 1983-2001, condr. laureate, 2001—; prin. condr. Toledo Opera, 2002—. Asst. prof. mus. CUNY, 1974-76. Recipient Grammy award for Contemporary Classical Composition, 2001, Indie award nomination for Best Orch. Rec., 2002. Mem. Am. Symphony Orch. League, Nat. Opera Assn., Condrs. Guild, Opera America. Studio: 8440 Augusta Ln Holland OH 43528 E-mail: thconmusic@aol.com.

CONLON, BRIAN THOMAS, promotion executive; b. Oceanside, N.Y., Mar. 19, 1958; s. Thomas James and Joan Anna (Erickson) Conlon; m. Mary Jane Lewis, Nov. 12, 1988; children: Brendan Lewis, Ryan Bradshaw Erickson, Emily Rose Mary. BA in English, Hofstra U., 1979. Asst. account exec. DR Group, N.Y.C., 1981-82, account supr., 1982—83; account exec. D.L. Blair, Inc., Garden City, NY, 1983—85, v.p./account supr., 1985—90, sr. v.p., 1990—91, exec. v.p., 1991—2002, pres., 2002—. Roman Catholic. Office: DL Blair Inc 1051 Franklin Ave Garden City NY 11530-2931 E-mail: bconlon@dlblair.com.

CONLON, CYNTHIA KELLY, lawyer, educator; b. Ft. Knox, Ky., July 24, 1950; d. Charles Robert Kelly and Barbara Wood Leon; m. Robert Kevin Conlon, Nov. 2, 1984; children: Kevin Patrick, Caitlin Kelly, Molly Elizabeth. BS, Northwestern U., Ill., 1972; JD, U. of Pa., 1975; PhD, Northwestern U., Ill., 1979. Lic.: Ill. State Bar Assn. 1977. Assoc. prof. of law Loyola U., Chgo., 1980—91; docent Milw. Art Mus., 1999—2002; part-time faculty Northwestern U., Evanston, Ill., 2002—. Visual arts coord. St. Francis de Sales Parish Sch., Lake Geneva, Wis., 1994—2002. Author: (curriculum) St. Francis de Sales Visual Arts Curriculum, (textbook) Teachers and the Law. Bd. mem. Badger HS, Lake Geneva, Wis., 1986—88, St. Francis de Sales Parish, Lake Geneva, Wis., 1994—96. Recipient Outstanding Young Lawyer, Chgo. Bar Assn., 1980, Maurice Weigle award, Chgo. Bar Found., 1981, Erma Wensink Prof., Beloit Coll., 1989—90; fellow, Robert F. Kennedy Found., 1980—82. Mem.: Ill. State Bar Assn. Avocations: running, paddling, bicycling. Personal E-mail: conlon@genevaonline.com.

CONLON, EDWARD J. management educator; b. Patterson, N.J., Apr. 30, 1951; s. Francis and Cornelia (DeWitte) C.; m. Helene W. Conlon, Sept. 11, 1971; children: Amy Beth, Katherine, Megan, Laura. BS, Pa. State U., 1972; MS, Carnegie-Mellon U., 1975, PhD, 1978. Asst. prof. Ga. Inst. Tech., Atlanta, 1977-82; assoc. prof. U. Iowa, Iowa City, 1982-89, prof., 1989-92, U. Notre Dame, South Bend, 1992—. Contbr. articles to profl. jours. Recipient rsch. grant NSF, 1981, rsch. grant USAF Office of Sci. Inquiry, 1989. Mem. APS, Acad. Mgmt. Avocation: sailing. Office: Univ Notre Dame PO Box 399 Notre Dame IN 46556

CONLON, MICHAEL WILLIAM, lawyer; b. Wilkes Barre, Pa., Nov. 9, 1946; s. William Peter and Dorothy (Stone) C.; m. Alice Cario, June 14, 1969; children: Michele, Stacia. AB, Cath. U., 1968; JD, Duke U., 1971. Bar: Tex. 1971, D.C. 1993. Ptnr. Fulbright & Jaworski, Houston, 1978-93, 98—, ptnr. in charge Washington, 1993-98, co-head corp., banking and bus. practice dept., 1999—, co-ptnr. in charge Houston Office, 2001—. Office: Fulbright & Jaworski 1301 Mckinney St Houston TX 77010-3031 E-mail: mconlon@fulbright.com.

CONLON, PATRICK C. family nurse practitioner, pediatric nurse practitioner; b. Sioux City, Iowa, July 24, 1962; s. James Ambrose and Mary Lee Emily (Donahue) Conlon. Diploma in Nursing, St. Joseph Mercy Hosp., Sioux City, 1986; BA in Psychology, BSN, Briar Cliff Coll., Sioux City, 1988; MSN, U. N.Mex., 1998. Cert. FNP, PNP, BC-ADM gen. nursing practice; cert. diabetes educator; cert. BCLS; cert. case mgr. Staff nurse, charge nurse Marian Health Ctr., Sioux City, 1979-89; staff nurse Western Med. Svcs., Sioux City, 1987-89; asst. nurse mgr., orthopaedic nurse adminstr. Michael Reese Hosp. and Med. Ctr., Chgo., 1989-91; edn. dir. ADA Iowa Diabetes Childrens Camp, 1989-93; health team coord., nurse educator, teaching faculty Triangle D Childrens Diabetes Camp, No. Ill., 1990-93; dir., clin. coord. diabetes edn. Mt. Sinai Hosp., 1991-96; grad. tching. asst. U. N.Mex., Albuquerque, 1996-97; diabetes specialist St. Josephs Hosp/S.W. Endocrinology Assocs., Albuquerque, 1997; nurse practitioner Sinai Family Health Ctr., Chgo., 1998-2000, Alivio Med. Ctr., Chgo., 2000—02; dir. diabetes ambulatory care tng. and cmty. outreach devel. Sinai Med. Group, 2002—. Cons. obesity mgmt. program Roche Labs., 2000—. Manuscript reviewer Jour. of Care Mgmt., Jour. of Woman's Health in Primary Care, The Diabetes Educator, Women's Health in Primary Care, Jour. Care Mgmt. Mem. ANA (chmn. 1992-94, scope and stds. of practice sect.), ACNP (com. on practice), Am. Nurses Credentialing Ctr. (cert.), Am. Diabetes Assn. (bd. dirs., camp com. No. Ill. affiliate, peer reviewer of recognition program 1994-97), Iowa Nurses Assn. (nursing adminstrn. commn. 1993-97), Am. Coll. Nurse Practitioners, Am. Psychol. Soc. (charter), Nat. Nurses in Bus. Assn. (charter), St. Joseph Mercy Sch. Nursing Alumni Assn., Am. Assembly for Men in Nursing, Am. Assn. Diabetes Educators (manuscript reviewer jour.), Diabetes Educators Chgo. Area (v.p. 1991-92, pres.-elect 1992-93, pres. 1993-94, past pres./symposium chair 1994-95), Am. Acad. Nurse Practicioners, Ill. Nurses Assn. (mem. continuing edn. and competencies com. 1999-2003, mem. assembly on nursing practice 1999—), Ill. Coun. Advanced Practice Nurses (vice-chair 1999-2002), Sigma Theta Tau (Heritage com.), Alpha Tau Delta, Psi Chi. Home: 2059 Roundtable Rd Sergeant Bluff IA 51054-9743 Office: 2507 W Cermak Rd Chicago IL 60608

CONLON, RAYMOND JOSEPH, lawyer; b. Butler, Pa., Aug. 21, 1962; s. Hugh L. and Frances J. (Augustine) C.; m. Nance Lee Hirsch, Mar. 21, 1992. BA in Clownology, Barnum & Baileys Clown U., 1980; BA, Duquesne U., 1984; JD, Dickinson Sch. Law, 1987. Bar: Pa. 1987, U.S. Dist. Ct. (we. dist.) Pa. 1987. Assoc. Myer Darragh, Pitts., 1987-88; shareholder Zimmer Kunz, Pitts., 1988—. Author: The Search for Satchmo-An Archer's Lament; mem. bd. editors Dickinson Law Rev., 1986-87. Active Big Bros., Pitts., 1990-91; bd. dirs. Butler County chpt. Big Bros., 1996-02. Named Lord Mayor, Dublin, Ireland by George the Earl of Stewart; recipient Silver Medal World's Strongest Man Competition, Helsinki, Finland 2001, Oscar award for Shrek animation, 2002; named to Am.'s Best Dressed Lawyers, Mr. Blackwell, 2003. Mem. ABA, Pa. Bar Assn., Allegheny County Bar Assn., Maritime Law Assn., Assn. Transp. Lawyers, Butler Co. Bar Assn., Am. Arbitration Assn. (arbitrator), Moose. Republican. Roman Catholic. Played banjo at Grand Ol Opry during Minnie Pearl's Final performance. Office: Zimmer Kunz 3300 Usx Towers Pittsburgh PA 15219

CONLON, THOMAS JAMES, marketing executive; b. N.Y.C., July 30, 1935; s. Kenneth Charles and Catherine (Gavaghan) C.; m. Joan Anna Erickson, Jan. 19, 1957; children: Brian T., Michael K., Keith J.K. Ed., Art Students' League, N.Y.C., 1951-53, St. Peter's Coll., Jersey City, 1953-56. Staff artist N.Y. News, N.Y.C., 1953-57, spl. features writer-reporter, 1957-59; mktg. mgr. Tricolator Inc., Wantagh, N.Y., 1959-64; assoc. dir. promotion Benton & Bowles, N.Y.C., 1964-68; chmn. D.L. Blair Inc., Garden City, NY, 1968—, PMI, Inc., Atlanta, 1986—, DLB/W, Beverly Hills, Calif., 1987—; mng. dir./gerant Blair Europe, Paris, 1991-98; mng. ptnr. Conlon Holdings Inc., 1999—; pres. Conlon Assocs., LP, 1999—. Illustrator for various mags., 1952-53. Home: Wolver Hollow Rd Upper Brookville NY 11771-4301 Office: DL Blair Inc 1051 Franklin Ave Garden City NY 11530-2931

CONLY, JOHN FRANKLIN, engineering educator, researcher; b. Ridley Park, Pa., Sept. 11, 1933; s. Harlan and Mary Jane (Roberts) C.; m. Jeannine Therese McDonough, Apr. 14, 1967; children: J. Paul, Mary Ann. BS, U. Pa., 1956, MS, 1958; PhD, Columbia U., 1962. Instr. U. Pa., Phila., 1956-58; research asst. Columbia U., N.Y.C., 1959-62; asst. prof. engring. San Diego State U., 1962-65, assoc. prof., 1965-69, prof., 1969—, chmn. dept., 1971-74, 77-85, wind tunnel dir., 1978 [illegible] D. and F. Guggenheim fellow, 1958. Assoc. fellow AIAA (sect. chmn. 1970 best U.S. sect.) Republican. Episcopalian. Office: San Diego State U Dept Aerospace Engring San Diego CA 92182

CONN, ERIC EDWARD, plant biochemist; b. Berthoud, Colo., Jan. 6, 1923; s. William Elmer and Mary Anna (Smith) C.; m. Louise Carolyn Kachel, Oct. 17, 1959; children: Michael E., Kevin E. BA in Chemistry, U. Colo., 1944; PhD in Biochemistry, U. Chgo., 1950. Instr. biochemistry U. Chgo., 1950-52; instr. U. Calif., Berkeley, 1952-53, asst. prof., 1953-58, assoc. prof. Davis, 1958-63, prof., 1964—. Author: (with P.K. Stumpf) Outlines of Biochemistry, 1963, 5th edit., 1987; editor: (with P.K. Stumpf) (book series) Biochemistry of Plants, 1980-90. With U.S. Army, 1944-46. Fellow USPHS, 1960; Fulbright Rsch. grantee, 1965; recipient Pergamon Phytochemistry prize and cert., 1994. Mem. NAS, Phytochem. Soc. N.Am. (hon. life mem., pres. 1971-72, editor in chief 1984-89), Am. Soc. Plant Biology (pres. 1986-87, Charles Reid Barnes life mem.), Am. Soc. Biol. Chemistry, Phytochemistry Soc. Europe, Am. Soc. Pharmacognasy. Democrat. Avocations: gardening, philately. Office: U Calif Sect Molecular & Cellular Biol Davis CA 95616

CONN, GORDON BRAINARD, JR., lawyer; b. St. Louis, Dec. 20, 1944; BA, Macalester Coll., 1967; JD, U. Mich., 1970. Bar: Minn. 1970, U.S. Supreme Ct. 1986; cert. in bus. bankruptcy law Am. Bd. Certficiation. Law clk. to Chief Justice Minn. Supreme Ct., St. Paul, 1970-71; ptnr. Faegre & Benson, Mpls., 1971-99, Kalina, Wills, Gisvold & Clark, P.L.L.P., Mpls., 1999—. Mem. ABA, Am. Bankruptcy Inst., Minn. State Bar Assn., Comml. Law League Am., Nat. Assn. Bankruptcy Trustees. Office: # 560 6160 Summit Dr N Minneapolis MN 55430-2100

CONN, HAROLD O. physician, educator; b. Newark, Nov. 16, 1925; s. Joseph H. and Dora (Kobrin) C.; m. Marilyn Barr, May 2, 1951; children: Chrysanne, Steven A., Dorianne. BS, U. Mich., 1946, MD, 1950; MS, Yale U., 1972. Diplomate: Am. Bd. Internal Medicine. Intern Johns Hopkins Hosp., 1950-51; asst. resident Grace New Haven Community Hosp., 1951-52, chief resident, 1955-56; James Hudson Browne research fellow, 1952-53; dir. med. edn. Middlesex Meml. Hosp., 1956-57; clin. investigator VA, 1957-61; chief med. svc. VA Hosp., West Haven, Conn., 1959-60, chief hepatic rsch. lab., 1961-89; instr. Yale Sch. Medicine, 1955-58, asst. prof., 1958-66, assoc. prof., 1966-71, prof., 1971-91, prof. emeritus, 1991—, dir. continuing med. edn. program, 1988-91; clin. prof. surgery divsn. liver/intestinal transplantation U. Miami, 1986—; dir. continuing med. edn. program Yale Univ., 1988-91. Vis. assoc. prof. Washington U. Sch. Medicine, 1982-83; CEO, Med., Med.-Legal and Consultations; dir. Continuing Med. Edn. dept. medicine Yale U. Sch. Medicine, 1990-92. Author: (with M.M. Lieberthal) The Hepatic Coma Syndromes and Lactulose, 1979, (with J. Rodes M. Nevasa) Spontaneous Bacterial Peritonitis, The Disease, Pathogenesis and Treatment, 2000; co-author: (with G. Klatskin) Histopathology of the Liver, 1990; editor: Cyanidanol in Diseases of the Liver, 1981; (with J. Palmaz, J. Rösch, and M. Rössle) Transjugular Intrahepatic Partal-Systemic Stent-shunts: TIPS, 1995; mem. editl. bd. Gastroenterology, 1970-80, Italian Jour. Gastroenterology, 1977—, Jour. Internal Medicine, 1988-99; assoc. editor Hepatology, 1980-90; book editor: Hepatology, 1985-88; editor Hepatology, 1985-91; editor: (with J. Bircher) Hepatic Encephalopathology: Management with Lactulose and Related Carbohydrates, 1988, (with J. Bircher) Hepatic Encephalopathy: Syndromes and Therapies, 1994. Bd. dirs. Am. Liver Found., 1977-80. Ensign USNR, 1943-44; 1st lt. USAR, 1953-54, USAFR, 1954-55. Recipient Rorer award, 1973, William Beaumont award clin. rsch., 1974. Fellow ACP, Royal Coll. Physicians; mem. Assn. Am. Physicians, Am. Soc. Clin. Investigation, Internat. Assn. Study Liver, Sydenham Soc. (sec. 1968-88, mem. med. adv. bd. Seminars and Symposia 1974-80), Am. Assn. Study Liver Disease (v.p. 1971, pres. 1972), Am. Fedn. Clin. Rsch., Am. Gastroenterol. Assn. (councillor 1974-77, Hugh Butt-Miles and Shirley Fiterman award for clinical rsch. in hepatology 1990), Nat. Assn. Va. Physicians (bd. dirs. 1986-88, chmn. continuing med. edn. com. 1987-89); hon. mem. Australian Soc. Gastroenterology, Brazilian Assn. for Study of Liver, China Med. Assn. (Shanghai br.; Taiwan), Hungarian Gastroent. Soc. (hon.), Nominated for Distinguished Educator Awd., Amer. Gastro Assn., 1998, Hampton Beach Club (bd. dirs. 2002—). Home and Office: 1 Mansfield Grove Rd # 115 East Haven CT 06512 Home: 1800 S Ocean Blvd Apt 1109 Pompano Beach FL 33062-7919 E-mail: Marhal@aol.com. *It is among my professional goals to apply the principles of the laboratory to the bedside, to enhance and enliven medical writing and to introduce a modicum of humor into the somber realm of the medical literature.*

CONN, REX BOLAND, JR., physician, educator; b. Marengo, Iowa, Aug. 3, 1927; s. Rex Boland and Helena Dorothea (Schoenfelder) C.; m. Victoria Grace Sellens, Dec. 28, 1950; children: Elizabeth Marian, Victoria Anne, Mary Catherine. BS, Iowa State U., 1949; MD, Yale U., 1953; BSc, U. Oxford, Eng., 1955; MS, U. Minn., 1960. Prof. pathology, dir. clin. labs. W.Va. Med. Center, Morgantown, 1960-68; prof. lab. medicine, dir. dept. Johns Hopkins Med. Instns., Balt., 1968-77; prof. pathology and lab. medicine, dir. clin. labs. Emory U., Atlanta, 1977-87; prof. and vice chmn. dept. pathology and cell biology, dir. clin. labs. Thomas Jefferson U., Phila., 1987-97; prof. emeritus Jefferson Med. Coll., Phila., 1997—. Mem. pathology tng. com. NIH, 1972-73, mem. pathology A study sect., 1968-72; cons. Walter Reed Army Med. Center, 1972-77; cons. Armed Forces Inst. of Pathology, 1984-88. Editor: Current Diagnosis, 1997, Yearbook of Pathology and Clinical Pathology, 1980, Applied Laboratory Medicine, 1992. Served with USNR, 1945-46. Mem. Coll. Am. Pathologists, Am. Soc. Clin. Pathologists (dir. 1975-81, pres. 1993-94), Acad. Clin. Lab. Physicians and Scientists (pres. 1972). Office: Thomas Jefferson Univ Jefferson Alumni Hall 212 Philadelphia PA 19107 E-mail: rex.conn@mail.tju.edu.

CONN, RICHARD LEE, computer scientist, educator; b. Logansport, Ind., Apr. 11, 1954; s. Harry Richard and Forest Geneva Conn. BS in Computer Sci., Rose-Hulman Inst. Tech., 1976; MS in Computer Sci., U. Ill., 1978. Cert. instr., GE Aircraft Engines. Tech. cons. U.S. Army Satellite Comm. Agy., Ft. Monmouth, N.J., 1978-80; instr. Air Force Inst. Tech., Wright-Patterson AFB, Ohio, 1980-82; computer scientist U.S. Army Software Devel. and Support Ctr., Ft. Monmouth, 1982-84; software design engr. Tex. Instruments, Dallas, 1984-85; mgr. Ada Software Repository Project, White Sands, N.Mex., 1984-93; pvt. practice Plano, Tex., 1986; software engr. advanced engring. tech. dept. software engring. section GE Aircraft Engines, Cin., 1986-92; mgr. Mgmt. Assistance Corp. Am., White Sands Missile Range, 1987-91; with Defense Advanced Rsch. Projects Agy./Ada Joint Program Office, Washington, 1991-92; mem. fed. adv. bd. Ada Joint Program Office The Pentagon, Washington, 1992-93; mgr. Pub. Ada Libr. Monmouth Coll., West Long Branch, N.J., 1993-97; prof. software engring. dept. Monmouth U., 1995-97; sr. software process engr. Lockheed Martin Aeronautics, Marietta, Ga., 1997—2003; rsch. prof. info. sci. and tech. Monmouth Coll., West Long Branch, N.J., 1993-95; mem. tech. staff MITRE Corp., Eatontown, N.J., 1992-95; acad. liaison Microscoft, Atlanta, 2003—. Adj. prof. dept. elec. and computer engring. U. Cin., 1990-92; adj. prof. computer sci. and info. sys. Kennesaw (Ga.) State U., 1998—; adj. prof. computing and software engring. So. Polytech. State U., 2002—; instr. dept. elec. engring. Air Force Inst. Tech., Wright-Patterson AFB, 1980-82, human resources dept. GE Aircraft Engines, Cin., 1987-92; co-chair Assn. Computing Machinery/Spl. Interest Group Ada Edn. Working Group; mem. DoD Ada Awareness Group; mem. working group on Ada as design lang. IEEE; mem. Ada quality and style guide team Software Productivity Consortium. Author: ZCPR3: The Manual, 1985, The Ada Software Repository and the Defense Data Network: A Resouce Handbook, 1987; editor Walnut Creek Ada CDRom; editor, lead Ada and Software Engring. Libr. and CDRom. Capt. U.S. Army 1976-82. Capt. US Army Signal Corps, 1980—82, Wright-Patterson AFB, OH. Recipient 2 Army Commendation medals. Master: Software Devel. and Engring. SIG, Atlanta PC User's Group (lead 2001—02); mem.: IEEE, Am. Legion, Assn. Computing Machinery (edn. co-chair Spl. Interest Group in Ada 1984—95), Masons, Tau Beta Pi. Achievements include development of Created the ZCPR series of Operating and Software Development Systems; research in Performed funded research in software reuse; developed the ZCPR3, CSPARTS, SCATC, and DCS3 Domain Specific Software Development Kits; first to Played a role in the development of the Ada programming language; served on Federal Advisory Board for Ada; Reviewer for DoD Software Reuse Initiative; Awarded Outstanding Contributions to the Ada C; development of Wrote numerous courses distributed world-wide in the Public Ada Library, the Ada and Software Engineering Library, and the ACM Journal for Educational Resources in Computing. Avocations: chess, swimming.

CONNAIR, STEPHEN MICHAEL, financial analyst; b. Fredericksburg, Va., Sept. 10, 1950; s. Thomas Joseph Jr. and Wilma Melvina (McCarty) C.; m. Karen Lee Matusoff, Feb. 15, 1986. BA in Philosophy, Duns Scotus Coll., 1973; MA in Religious Studies, U. Dayton, 1976; PhL in Philosophy, Cath. U. Am., 1983; MPA, Va. Tech., 1992; grad., Air Command & Staff Coll., 1990, Naval War Coll., 1995, Nat. Def. U., 1996. Tchr. Cath. Sch. Sys., Cin., 1973-83; fin. analyst USAF The Pentagon, Washington, 1985—. Mem. Smithsonian resident assoc. program, Washington, 1987—; sec., bd. dirs. Arlington Run Homeowners Assn., 1990-92; v.p. Sleepy Hollow Woods Civic Assn., 1996-97, pres., 1997-98. Mem. Am. Soc. Mil. Comptrs. (Profl. award 1990, Outstanding Analysis and Evaluation award 1992), Soc. Cost Estimating and Analysis, Am. Cath. Philos. Assn., Air Force History Found., Air Force Assn., Naval War Coll. Found., Nat. Air and Space Soc., Wilson Ctr. Assn., Nat. Trust for Hist. Preservation, Am. Acad. Polit. Sci., Am. Soc. Pub. Adminstrn., Am. Econ. Assn., George C. Marshall Found., James Madison Inst., Nat. Hist. Soc., Va. Hist. Soc., Arlington County Hist. Soc., Fairfax County Hist. Soc., Soc. for Mil. History, Nat. Assn. Scholars, Libr. of Congress Assn., Civil War Round Table, Hon. Order of Ky. Cols., Pi Alpha Alpha. Roman Catholic. Avocations: civil war buff, american history, movies, reading. Home: 3808 Moss Dr Annandale VA 22003-1917

CONNALLY, MICHAEL W. lawyer; b. Long Beach, Calif., July 8, 1957; s. Jack Walton and Melba June (Renfro) C.; m. Mary Kathleen Tubbiola, June 11, 1977; children: Steven William, Lisa Marie, Amber Lynn. BA in History, Loyola Marymount U., Los Angeles, 1978; JD, Loyola Law Sch., Los Angeles, 1981. Bar: Calif. 1981. Assoc. Wolf & Leo, L.A., 1981-84, sr. assoc., 1984-88, ptnr., 1987-91, Lewis, Brisbois, Bisgaard & Smith LLP, Costa Mesa, Calif., 1991—. Faculty Calif. Mission Bapt. Inst., Bellflower, 1984-92. Youth assoc. Calif. Rep. State Cen. Com., 1976, assoc., 1977-86; deacon Hillcrest Missionary Bapt. Ch., Huntington Beach Calif., 1979-85, Grace Missionary Bapt. Ch., Anaheim, Calif., 1985-97; trustee Ctrl. Bapt. Ch., Huntington Beach, Calif., 1999—. Mem. Calif. State Bar, Orange County Bar Assn. Republican. Baptist. Avocations: white water rafting, bowling, chess, basketball, cooking. Office: Lewis Brisbois Bisgaard & Smith LLP 650 Town Center Dr Fl 14 Costa Mesa CA 92626-1989 E-mail: connally@lbbslaw.com.

CONNALLY, SANDRA JANE OPPY, retired art educator, artist; b. Crawfordsville, Ind., Feb. 10, 1941; d. Thomas Jay and Helen Louise (Lane) Oppy; m. Thomas Maurice Connally, Nov. 9, 1962; children: Leslie Erin Connally Hosier, Tyler Maurice. BS, Ball State U., 1963, MA, 1981. Freelance writer, Muncie, Ind., 1971-76; art/freelance, 1964-81; substitute tchr. Muncie (Ind.) Cmty. Schs., 1980—81, art tchr., 1981—2003; ret., 2003. Two women shows include Emens Auditorium, Ball State U., 1983; exhibited in group shows at Ball State U., 1964, Alford House/Anderson (Ind.) Fine Arts Ctr., 1979-81, Historic 8th St. Exhbn., 1981, Patrons Watercolor Gala, Oklahoma City, 1983, Whitewater Valley Annual Drawing, Painting and Printmaking Competition, Richmond, Ind., 1983; represented in pvt. collections; contbr. short stories to profl. publs. Grantee Container Corp. Am., 1981, Ball State U. Mus. Art/Margaret Ball Meml. Fund, 1992, Robert B. Bell, 1993-95; recipient Achievement award Ind. Dept. Edn., 1992-94, Nat. Gallery Videodisc Competition, 1993; named disting. UniverCitizen Ball State U., 1992, Tchr. Intergalactic Art First Place Ind. State winner, 1998. Mem. NEA, Ind. State Tchr. Assn., Muncie Tchrs. Assn., Nat. Art Edn. Assn. (del. nat. convention 1998, 2000-03), Art Edn. Assn. Ind. Republican. Methodist. Avocations: computer art, watercolor, interior design, arts, antiques and travel. Home: 1932 Bay Pointe Dr E Bloomington IN 47401-8136

CONNAUGHTON, JAMES L. federal agency administrator; m. Susanna Connaughton; children: Spencer, Grace. Grad., Yale U.; JD magna cum laude, Northwestern U. Law clk. U.S. Dist. Judge Marvin Aspen No. Dist. Ill.; U.S. negotiator ISO 14000, 1993—2001; ptnr. environ. practice group Sidley Austin Brown & Wood; chmn. Coun. on Environ. Quality Exec. Office of the Pres., Washington, 2001—. Lectr. in field. Coordinating articles editor: Northwestern U. Law Rev. Scholar Austin scholar, Northwestern U. Mem.: Order of the Coif. Avocations: sailing, singing, beach combing. Office: Exec Office of the Pres Coun on Environ Quality 730 Jackson Pl NW Washington DC 20503

CONNAUGHTON, JAMES PATRICK, psychiatrist; b. Dublin, Mar. 13, 1931; arrived in U.S., 1965; s. Patrick and Julia (Barrett) Connaughton; children: Bernadette, Eileen, James, Paul, John. MB, ChB, Univ. Coll., Dublin., 1956; MS in Bus. of Medicine, Johns Hopkins U., 2002. Diplomate Am. Bd. Psychiatry & Neurology, Am. Bd. Child & Adolescent Psychiatry. Intern Mater Univ. Hosp., Dublin, 1956-57; resident in psychiatry Seton Psychiat. Inst., Balt., 1958-61; sr. staff psychiatrist Milw. Psychiat. Hosp., 1961-65; fellow dept. child psychiatry, dept. pediatrics Johns Hopkins Hosp., Balt., 1965-67, sr. staff div. child psychiatry, 1967—. Family practice medicine, Manchester, England, 1957—58; psychiat. cons. VA Hosp., Wood, Wis., 1961—65, Peace Corps Tng. Projects, 1963—64; dir. adolescent program Milw. Psychiat. Hosp., 1961—65; cons. dept. medicine West Allis Meml. Hosp., Milw., 1962—65; ass.t prof. psychiatry Marquette U., 1962—65; treas. Milw. Psychiat. Clinic Chartered, 1963—64, v.p., 1964—65; dir. Dundalk Mental Health Clinic, Baltimore County, Md., 1966—67; cons. Assoc. Cath. Charities, 1966—81, Oldfields Sch., 1968—78, Children's Guild, 1969—78, John F. Kennedy Inst., 1971—, Villa Maria-Residential Treatment Ctr., 1981—, Francis Scott Key Cmty. Psychiatry Program, 1994—; dir. child in-patient neuropsychiatric unit and psychiatric unit Johns Hopkins U. Med. Sch., 1969—72, assoc. prof. psychiatry and pediat., 1972—, liaison-cons. svcs., children-adolescents, 1972—74, dir. psychiat. and mental health scis., 1972—82; dir. child & adolescent nueropsychiat. unit Johns Hopkins Hosp., 1969—73, assoc. dir. divsn. child psychiatry, 1971—, mem. child care com., 1971—73, bed utilization com., 1971—74, pediatric intern selection com., 1971—74; psychiat. svcs. and mental health svcs. Comprehensive Pediatric Child Care Clinic, 1973—81, mental health com., 1974—81, chmn. child abuse and neglect com. dept. pediats., 1975—80, directorate com. cmty. mental health programs, 1981—, dir. child and adolescent cmty. mental health program, 1981—93; psychiat. svcs. and mental health svcs. Children and Adolescent Mental Health Ctr., 1981—93, psychosomatic

clinic divsn. child adolescent psychiatry, 1993—. Mem. divsn. spl. edn. City of Balt. Dept. Edn.; directorate com. cmty. mental health programs City of Balt. Health Dept., 1981—, mem. children's mental health planning com.; mem. steering com. East Balt. Mental Health Ctr.; goals and objectives com. Villa Maria Children's Inst., med. adv. com. Fellow: Royal Coll. Psychiatrists, Am. Acad. Child Psychiatry, Am. Psychiat. Assn. (life Disting. Life Fellow); mem.: AAAS, Md. Psychiat. Soc., Balt. County Med. Soc. Roman Catholic. Home: 45 Thornhill Rd Luthervillc MD 21093-5806 Office: Johns Hopkins Hosp 600 N Wolfe St Baltimore MD 21287-0005

CONNAWAY, ROBERT WALLACE, artist, computer programmer; b. Dothan, Ala., Nov. 5, 1956; s. Charles Earl and Ina Lee (Wallace) C.; m. Catherine Coyne. B in Info. Sys. Tech., U. No. Fla., 1981; BA cum laude, Flagler Coll., 1978. Computer programmer Mgmt. Info. Sys. Group, 1981-83; computer analyst/programmer Grumman St. Augustine Corp., 1985-95; flight line attendant, free-lance artist Aero Sport Inc., St. Augustine, Fla., 1978-83; founder, prin. Aviation Art Works, St. Augustine, 1978—; owner connaway Gallery, 1996—. Ann. one-man show Profl. Artist of St. Augustine Gallery, 1988-95; airshow poster art work Today Show Sta. NBC TV, 1989; commd. 6 pieces artwork St. Augustine Psychiat. Ctr., 1992; commn. mural St. Augustine Mcpl. Airport, 1982; exhibited Fly-In art show Exptl. Aircraft Assn., 1980. Recipient Arts awards Sr. Honors Project, 1978; Honorable Mention awards Audubon Soc. Art Show, St. Augustine, 1978, 86, 87, 89, 1st Prize, 1987. Mem. St. Augustine Art Assn., Exptl. Aircraft Assn. Episcopalian. Home: 416 Arredondo Ave Saint Augustine FL 32080-3805 Office: Connaway Gallery 11 Aviles St # F Saint Augustine FL 32084-4457 E-mail: connaway@aug.com.

CONNEEN, JAMES THOMAS, lawyer, management consultant; b. Orange, N.J., June 1, 1939; s. Thomas J. and Mary Elizabeth (Doyle) C.; B.S. (scholar), St. Peter's Coll., 1961; J.D. (scholar), N.Y. U., 1964; m. Maureen C. Rielly, Aug. 24, 1963; children— Elizabeth, Sheila, Martin. Admitted to Pa. bar, 1964, N.Y. bar, 1967; law clk. to chief justice Pa., 1964-65; asso. firm Breed, Abbott & Morgan, N.Y.C., 1967-69; v.p., gen. counsel, dir. Posi-Seal Internat., Inc., North Stonington, Conn., 1969-70; asso. counsel Union Camp Corp., Wayne, N.J., 1970-72; v.p. Syncronamics, Inc., Englewood Cliffs, N.J., 1972-75; chmn. bd. A. T. Hudson & Co., Inc., Paramus, N.J., 1975—, also dir. Served to capt., M.I., U.S. Army, 1965-67. Decorated Army Commendation medal. Mem. Am. Bar Assn., N.Y. Bar Assn., Pa. Bar Assn. Republican. Roman Catholic. Club: Ridgewood (N.J.) Country. Home: 299 Highland Ave Ridgewood NJ 07450-4003

CONNEEN, MARI M. artist; b. Allentown, Pa., Dec. 21, 1946; d. Edward Charles and Margaret Florence (Reiter) Leidig; m. Joseph Lawrence Conneen Jr., Aug. 3, 1965; children: Christopher Joseph, Matthew Ward, Michael Walker. One-woman shows include 1st Fed. Savs. of Mid Fla., Deland, 1983, Brevard Art Ctr. and Mus., Melbourne, Fla., 1983, Fla. Frame House Gallery, Winter Pk., 1983, Cielo Gallery, Wellfleet, Mass., 1984, Galleries Internat., Winter Pk., 1986, Ctr. for the Arts, Vero Beach, Fla., 1986, Ormond Beach (Fla.) Meml. Art Gallery, 1986, Deland Art Mus., 1985, Naples (Fla.) Art Gallery, 1987, Seminole C.C., Sanford, Fla., 1988, The Hartley Gallery, Winter Pk., 1989, Herr Chambliss Gallery, Hot Springs, Ark., 1990, Hobe Sound (Fla.) Gallery, 1990, J. Lawrence Gallery, Melbourne, 1991-96, Brevard Mus. Art and Sci., Melbourne, 1997, Brevard Art Ctr. and Mus., 1997; exhibited in group shows at Adirondacks Nat. Exhibit of Am. Watercolors, Old Forge, N.Y., 1984-99 (numerous awards), Nat. Arts Club, N.Y.C., 1984, La. Watercolor Soc. Annn. Internat. Exhbns., 1985, 95 (awards), 1985, Orlando (Fla.) Mus. of Art, 1985, 90-91, Tampa Mus. of Art, 1986, Ky. Watercolor Soc., 1986, 92, 93, 95 (Grumbacher Gold medallion and award 1986, award 1992), San Diego Watercolor Soc., 1987, 93, Miss. Watercolor Soc., 1995 (Gold medallion), Fla. Watercolor Soc., 1979-97 (awards), Okla. Arts Ctr., 1987-95 (awards), Mus. Arts and Scis., Daytona Beach, Fla., 1988, Boca Raton (Fla.) Mus. Art, 1990, 91, 92, So. Watercolor Soc. Ann. Juried Exhbn., 1984-97 (awards), Springfield (Mo.) Art Mus., 1993 (honor soc.), Samford U., Birmingham, Ala., 1996 (award), Lafayette (La.) Art Gallery (award), numerous others; represented in numerous pub. and pvt. collections; contbr. art work to numerous publs., books in field. Recipient 2d pl. award Invitational Wildlife Exhbn., Atlanta, 1978, Best of Show award Artists Showcase, Miami, Fla., 1981, 1st pl. award Fla. Watercolor Soc. Ann. Juried Exhbn., 1982, Best of Show award, 1983, 2d pl. Festival of the Masters, Lake Buena Vista, Fla., 1982-83, 1st pl., 1987, Best of Show award Brevard Art Ctr. Ann. Juried Exhbn., Melbourne, 1983-84, Best of Show and 1st pl. awards Winter Pk. Art Festival, 1983, Best of Show award St. Stephens Arts Festival, Coconut Grove, Fla., 1983, Beaux Arts Festival of the Arts, Lowe Art Mus., Miami, 1983, Miami Beach Festival of the Arts, 1983, Coconut Grove Arts Festival, 1983, 1st pl., 1988, Artists Three award Orlando Mus. Art, 1985, Best of Show award La. Watercolor Soc. Ann. Juried Exhbn., New Orleans, 1985, Natural Resources award Adirondacks Nat. Exhbn. of Am. Watercolors, 1985, 99, award, 1988, Experts Choice award Artists Soc. Internat., San Francisco, 1987, Jurors award San Diego Watercolor Soc., 1987, 2d pl., Purchase award Nat. Watercolor Soc. Ann. Exhbn., 1993, 1st pl. award Fla. Artists Group, Mus. Arts and Scis., Daytona Beach, 1994, Purchase award Bank of Newport, Brea, Calif., 1994. Mem. Am. Watercolor Soc., Guild of Natural Sci. Illustrators, Am. Artist Profl. League, Nat. Watercolor Soc. (signature), Nat. Mus. Women in the Arts, Watercolor USA (honor soc.), Fla. Watercolor Soc. (signature), So. Watercolor Soc. (signature), Ky. Watercolor Soc. (signature), Ala. Watercolor Soc. (signature), Fla. Artists Group Inc., Miss. Watercolor Soc. (signature), Okla. Watercolor Soc., Brevard Mus. Art and Sci., Brevard Cultural Alliance. Democrat. Roman Catholic. Home: Apt C-14 441 N Harbor City Blvd Melbourne FL 32935-6844 E-mail: joemar@mindspring.com.

CONNELL, ALASTAIR MCCRAE, physician; b. Glasgow, Scotland, Dec. 21, 1929; came to U.S., 1970; s. Alex McCrae and Maud (Crawford) C.; m. Joyce Dethlefs, 1983; children: Stewart, Fiona, Alison, Iain, Andrew. BS, U. Glasgow, 1951, MB, ChB, 1954, MD, 1969. Intern Western Infirmary, Glasgow, 1954-55; resident in gastroenterology Cen. Middlesex and St. Mark's Hosp., London, 1957-60; practice medicine specializing in gastroenterology, 1960—; mem. med. staff Med. Rsch. Coun., 1960-64; sr. lectr. clin. sci. Queen's U., Belfast, No. Ireland, 1964-70; Mark Brown prof. medicine Med. Ctr., U. Cin., 1970-79, dir. div. digestive diseases, 1970-79, prof. physiology, 1972-79, assoc. dean, 1975-77; dir. Office Clin. Affairs, 1975-77; dean Coll. Medicine, U. Nebr. Med. Ctr., 1979-84, prof. internal medicine, 1979-84; v.p. health scis. Va. Commonwealth U., Richmond, 1984-88; scholar-in-residence Inst. Medicine, 1988-89; vice chancellor health scis. Ea. Carolina U., 1989-90; dir. Office Healthcare Inspections, Dept. Vets. Affairs, Washington, 1991-96; adj. prof. med. George Washington U., 1992-97. Vis. prof. dept. moral philosophy U. St. Andrews, Scotland, 1984-86; mem. sci. adv. bd. Nat. Found. for Ileitis and Colitis, 1974-80, chmn. rsch. devel. com., 1974-78; mem. Personal Health Com. Ohio, 1974-76; trustee Medco Peer Rev., 1974-79; adj. prof. health adminstrn. Va. Commonwealth U., 1996-2000; med. dir. Williamsburg Landing, 1999-2002. Author: Clinical Tests of Gastric Function, 1973; author: (with T. Wan) Monitoring the Quality of Health Care, 2002; assoc. editor Am. Jour. Digestive Diseases; contbr. articles to profl. jours. Served with M.C. Royal Army, 1955-57. Fellow Royal Coll. Physicians (Edinburgh), ACP; mem. Am. Assn. Home Care Physicians, Brit. Soc. Gastroenterology, Internat. Group for Study Intestinal Motility (past pres.). Address: 3523 Hollingsworth Dr Williamsburg VA 23188 E-mail: joycecon@bellatlantic.net.

CONNELL, CAROL MATHESON, corporate strategist, consultant; d. David Matheson and Marion Elizabeth Frances Connell. MBA in Mktg., Columbia U., 1992; PhD, U. Glasgow, Scotland, 2001. Dir. corp. comms. and rsch. Seagram Co. Ltd., N.Y.C., 1980-96; dir. mktg. and rsch. Juvenile Diabetes Found., N.Y.C., 1996-98; sr. strategy cons. IBM, Armonk, N.Y., 1998—. Author: A Business in Risk - Jardine Matheson and the Hong Kong Trading Industry, 2004. NDEA and Columbia U. fellow Columbia U. Grad. Faculties, 1971, 72. Mem. IEEE, AAAS, Airplane Owner and Pilot Assn. (assoc.). Roman Catholic. Avocation: aviation (private pilot). Office Fax: 914-499-6003. E-mail: templetuttle@aol.com.

CONNELL, CHARLES R. language educator; b. Waltham, Mass., Jan. 4, 1937; s. William J. and Joyce Mayne Connell; m. Felicitas Erzebet Klein, Dec. 28, 1962; children: Deirdre, Allegra, Alexander. BA, Brown U., 1958; MA, U. Chgo., 1961, MA, 1964, PhD, 1973. Instr. City Coll. Chgo., 1961—68; prof. Cornell Coll., Mt. Vernon, Iowa, 1968—. Editor: Iowa Fgn. Lang. Bull., 1972—77. Fellow, DAAD, Berlin, Germany, 1962, Fulbright Found., 1975; grantee, NEH, 1976—81, 1989—95. Republican. Episc.

CONNELL, DIANE JACOBS, education educator; b. Nashville, Apr. 26, 1951; d. Marvin Miller and Dorothy (Kaplan) Jacobs; m. James L. Connell, July 15, 1985; children: Jason, Robert. BA, Avilla Coll., 1974; MA, Columbia U., 1975; EdD, Boston U., 1980; postgrad., Northeastern U., 1988. Cert. sch. psychologist Mass., elem. tchr., spl. edn. tchr. Mo. Tchr. Vanguard Sch., Lake Wales, Fla., 1975-77; instr. Boston U., 1978-80; asst. prof. Northeastern U., Boston, 1980-89; assoc. prof., dir. grad. lang./learning disability and emotional and behavioral disorders programs Notre Dame Coll., Manchester, N.H., 1989—. Cons., presenter in field. Contbr. articles to profl. jours. Mem. Am. Psychol. Assn., Nat. Sch. Psychology Assn., Mass. Assn. Learning Disabilities (bd. dirs. 1985-86), Mass. Sch. Psychology Assn., Coun. Exceptional Children, Phi Delta Kappa. Office: River Coll 420 Main St Nashua NH 03060

CONNELL, EDWARD PEACOCK, SR., lawyer; b. Memphis, Apr. 8, 1936; s. Charles Willis, Sr., and Georgia (Peacock) C.; m. Ann Morris, Dec. 27, 1958 (div. 1966); m. Eva Badger, Nov. 23, 1968; 1 son, Edward P. Jr. Student Tulane U., 1954-55; B.B.A. with distinction, U. Miss., 1958, J.D. with distinction, 1961; postgrad, NYU, 1962. Bar: Miss. 1961, U.S. Supreme Ct. 1966. Part time adj. prof. law U. Miss., 1963-75; mem. Holcomb, Dunbar, Connell, Chaffin & Willard, Clarksdale, Miss., 1961—90 . Assoc. editor Miss. Law Jour., 1960-61. Fellow Am. Coll. Probate Csl. (state chmn. 1985-87); mem. ABA (exec. council young lawyers sect. 1966-68), Miss. State Bar (2d v.p. 1967-68, pres. young lawyers sect. 1966-67, chmn. com. on taxation 1973-74), Coahoma County Bar Assn. (pres. 1969-70), Lawyer Pilots Bar Assn., Phi Delta Phi, Phi Kappa Phi, Omicron Delta Kappa, Beta Gamma Sigma. Office: PO Box 368 152 Delta Ave Clarksdale MS 38614

CONNELL, EVAN SHELBY, JR., writer; b. Kansas City, Mo, Aug. 17, 1924; s. Evan Shelby and Elton (Williamson) C. Student, Dartmouth, 1941-43; AB, U. Kans., 1946-47; grad. study, Stanford U., 1947-48, Columbia U., 1948-49. Editor Contact mag., Sausalito, Calif., 1960-65. Author: The Anatomy Lesson and Other Stories, 1957, Mrs. Bridge, 1959, The Patriot, 1960, Notes From a Bottle Found on the Beach at Carmel, 1963, At the Crossroads: Stories, 1965, The Diary of a Rapist, 1966, Mr. Bridge, 1969, Points for a Compass Rose, 1973, The Connoisseur, 1974 (Calif. Literature Silver medal 1974), Double Honeymoon, 1976, A Long Desire, 1979, The White Lantern, 1980, St. Augustine's Pigeon, 1980, Son of the Morning Star: Custer and the Little Bighorn, 1984 (Nat. Book Critics Circle award nomination 1984, LA Times Book award 1985), The Alchymist's Journal, 1991, Mesa Verde, 1992, Collected Stories, 1996, Deus Lo Volt!: Chronicle of the Crusades, 2000, The Aztec Treasure House, 2001; editor: Jerry Stoll's I Am A Lover, 1961, Woman by Three, 1969. Served as naval aviator 1943-45. Eugene Saxton fellow, 1953, Guggenheim fellow, 1963; Rockefeller Found. grantee, 1967; recipient Am. Acad. Inst. Arts and Letters award, 1987, Lannan Foud. Award, 2000. Mem. AAAL

CONNELL, GEORGE EDWARD, former university president, scientist; b. Saskatoon, Sask., Can., June 20, 1930; s. James Lorne and Mabel Gertrude (Killins) C.; m. Sheila Harriet Horan, Dec. 27, 1955; children: James, Caroline, Thomas, Margaret. BA, U. Toronto, Ont., Can., 1951, PhD in Biochemistry, 1955; DSc, U. Toronto, 1993; LLD (hon.), McGill U., 1987. NSF postdoctoral fellow, 1956-57; asst. prof. biochemistry U. Toronto, 1957-62, assoc. prof., 1962-65, prof., chmn. dept. biochemistry, 1965-70, assoc. dean faculty of medicine, 1972-74, v.p. rsch. and planning, 1974-77, pres., 1984-90, U. Western Ont., London, 1977-84; chair Nat. Round Table on Economy and Environ., 1990-95; vice chair Environ. Assessment Bd., Ont., 1990-93. Chmn. TC207, Internat. Stds. Orgn., 1993-96; prin. adviser Commn. Inquiry on Blood Sys. Can., 1993-95; chmn. bd. protein engrng. Nat. Ctr. Excellence, 1995-97; chmn. Task Force on Funding and Delivery Med. Care in Ont., 1995-96; sr. policy advisor Can. Found. for Innovation, 1997; bd. dirs. Allelix Biopharms., Inc., 1994-99; mem. Ont. Press Coun., 1996-2002; trustee McLaughlin Found., 1996-2002; vice-chair Premier's Rsch. Excellence Awards, Ont., 1999-02; chair mgmt. com. Can. Prostate Cancer Rsch. Initiative, 2000-02; mem. rsch. adv. panel Walkerton Inquiry; bd. dirs. Lake Simcoe Region Conservation Found., 2001—, Energy Probe Found., 2002—. Recipient Order of Can., 1987. Fellow Chem. Inst. Can., Royal Soc. Can.; mem. Am. Soc. Biol. Chemists, Can. Biochem. Soc. (pres. 1973-74). E-mail: george.connell@sympatico.ca.

CONNELL, GROVER, food company executive; b. N.Y.C., Apr. 12, 1918; s. Grover Cleveland and Violet Regina Connell; m. Patricia Day, July 31, 1940; children: Ted, Terry, Toni. BSBA, Columbia, 1939. With The Connell Co. (formerly Connell Rice & Sugar Co., Inc.), Westfield, NJ, 1939—, pres., chmn. bd., 1950—. Lt. USNR, 1942—46. Democrat. Presbyterian. Home: 207 Watchung Fork Westfield NJ 07090-3813 Office: Connell Co 1 Connell Dr Berkeley Heights NJ 07922*

CONNELL, HUGH P. foundation executive; b. Bethlehem, Pa., May 7, 1931; s. Joseph B. and Mary A. (McFadden) C.; m. Susan Hobbs, July 2, 1965; children: Hugh Richardson, Andrew Warfield, Edward William. AB, Moravian Coll., 1953; JD, U. Pa., 1956; student, Hague (The Netherlands) Acad. Internat. Law, 1959; LLM, U. London, 1960. Bar: Pa. 1956, N.Y. 1963. Intelligence analyst AUS Counter Intelligence Corp., Berlin, 1956-58; lectr. internat. law Univ. London, 1960-62; with Coudert Bros. Law Firm, N.Y.C., 1962-65; gen. counsel J. Walter Thompson Co., N.Y.C., 1966, v.p., 1967, sec., 1972, sr. v.p., 1973, exec. v.p., dir., 1974, JWT Group Inc., N.Y.C., 1980-86; founder, owner Crosswoods Vineyards Inc., N. Stonington, Conn., 1981-90; pres., CEO, trustee Sea Rsch. Found. Inc., Mystic (Conn.) Aquarium, 1991—2001. Trustee, past chmn. bd., chmn. exec. com. Jackson Lab., Bar Harbor, Maine, 1978—. Mem. Pilgrims of U.S., Union Club, N.Y.C., Wadawanuck Club, Stonington, Conn.

CONNELL, JOHN GIBBS, JR., former government official; b. Atlanta, Sept. 26, 1914; s. John Gibbs and Vena Estelle (Turner) C.; m. Bernice E. Siewerdsen, Oct. 2, 1941 (dec. June 2001) children: Sharon Elaine, Candace Anne. AA, George Washington U., 1948, AB, 1952. With U.S. Civil Service Commn., 1935-38, U.S. Housing Authority, 1938-40; with War Dept. and Army Dept., 1940-79; personnel mgr. Office of Sec. Army, 1942-54, asst. for security and personnel, 1954-62, dep. adminstrv. asst. to sec. army, 1962-66, adminstv. asst. to sec. army, 1966-79. Chmn. Army Security Screening Bd., 1953-66; prin. adminstrv. officer Army Loyalty-Security Program, 1950-79; mem. Army Bd. Correction Mil. Records, 1947-62; Army Dept. rep. interdepartmental com. to study govt. employee security programs for Pres. Truman, 1951-52; Army rep. Exec. Officers Group, 1968-79; mem. Dept. Def. Concessions Com., 1966-79; Army rep. Fed. Exec. Bd., 1969-79; mem. adv. com. Nat. Archives and Records Service, 1973 Bd. dirs. Army-Air Force Civilian Welfare Fund, Youth Devel. Inst. Served to 2d lt. USAAF, 1943-45; 1st lt. OSS, 1945-46; maj. M.I. Army Res. Recipient Army Exceptional Civilian Svc. medal, 1973, 75, 79, 40-Yr. cert. of svc. award, 1975, Meritorious Civilian Svc. award, 1977, sculpture award Faculty-Student Show, Art League, Alexandria, Va., 1982, 89; hon. mention for sculpture Young at Art Exhbn., 1991, hon. mention, 1992, 93. Mem.: OSS Soc., Sculptor, Coun. Former Fed. Execs., Nat. Assn. Ret. Fed. Employees, Fed. Sr. Exec. Svc. (charter), Art League of Alexandria, Sigma Nu. Presbyterian (elder). Home: 302 Cloverway Dr Alexandria VA 22314-4818 *I try to govern my life so as to serve others as I would have them serve me. I believe in the inherent dignity of man as an individual.*

CONNELL, MARION FITCH, retired government official, management consultant; b. New London, Conn., May 4, 1940; d. Avery Williams and Marion Booth (Gammons) Fitch; m. Lawrence Connell, 1965 (div. 1988); children: Elizabeth Cunningham, Rachel Avery. AB, Mt. Holyoke Coll., 1962; MPA, U. Hartford, 1974. Program officer Peace Corps, Washington, 1962-65; social sci. advisor U.S. Dept. Labor, Women's Bur., Boston, 1974-76; exec. dir. Internat. Women's Yr. Coord. Com., Hartford, Conn., 1977; program analyst HUD, Washington, 1978-80, program officer Office Field Ops., 1980-86, dir. urban homesteading Office Urban Rehab., 1986-89, dir. programs div. Office Fair Housing Enforcement, 1989-90, program advisor Office Insured Single Family Housing, 1990-96; dir. Manufactured Housing & Standards Divsn., Washington, 1996-98; mgr. Real Estate Assessment Ctr., 1998—2003; exec. dir. Pub. Employees Roundtable, 2001—02. Adminstr. Expt. in Internat. Living, 1966-76; HUD rep. V.P.'s Nat. Partnership for Reinventing Govt., 2000. Commr. Town Planning and Zoning Commn., Glastonbury, Conn., 1973-77; rep. Regional Planning Commn., Hartford, 1974, Neighborhood Sch. Coun., Washington, 1979-80. Recipient Vice-President's Hammer award, 1998. Mem. Am. Soc. Pub. Adminstrn. (pres. Conn. chpt. 1976-77, bd. dirs. Nat. Capital Area chpt., 1993-95). Democrat. Unitarian Universalist. Avocations: tennis, music, travel.

CONNELL, PHILIP FRANCIS, food industry executive; b. Hamilton, Ont., Can., Jan. 20, 1924; s. Maurice W. and Kathleen (Richardson) C. BA, McMaster U., Can., 1946. Chartered acct. With Clarkson Gordon & Co. (Ernst & Young), Hamilton and Toronto, 1946-57; comptroller Canadian Westinghouse Co. Ltd., Hamilton, 1957-67; controller Domtar Ltd., Montreal, 1967-68; v.p. fin. George Weston Ltd., Toronto, Ont., 1968-75, Loblaw Cos., Ltd., Toronto, Ont., 1972-75; exec. v.p. Oshawa Group Ltd., Toronto, Ont., 1976-92, dir., 1976-97. Fellow Inst. Chartered Accts.; mem. Fin. Execs. Inst. (pres. Hamilton chpt. 1966-67), Ont. Inst. Chartered Accts., Hamilton Club, Nat. Club. Home: 400 Walmer Rd Apt 2510 Toronto ON Canada M5P 2X7 Fax: 416-920-3638.

CONNELL, SHIRLEY HUDGINS, public relations professional; b. Washington, Oct. 5, 1946; d. Orville Thomas and Mary (Beran) H.; m. David Day Connell, Dec. 13, 1980 (div. 1985). BA, U. R.I., 1968, MA, 1970. Lic. property, casualty broker, N.Y. Clk., editor MGM Studios, Culver City, Calif., 1970-72; scriptor, talent Monarch Records, Studio City, 1972-73; communications specialist U. So. Calif., L.A., 1973-81; dir. pub. rels. Six Flags Movieland, Buena Park, Calif., 1981-82, Donald J. Fager & Assocs., N.Y.C., 1982-93, dir. policy holder/pub. rels., 1993-99, asst. v.p., 1999—. Cons. Children's TV Workshop, N.Y.C., 1978; ind. beauty cons. Mary Kay Cosmetics, 1991—; instr. Princeton Rev., 1990-91. Editor: Coastal Ocean Space Utilization III, 1995; contbr. articles to profl. jours.; contbg. editor Greater N.Y. Doctor's Shopper mag., 1987—. Pres. bd. trustees Oaks at North Brunswick Condominium Assn., 1987-2000; founding mem. Mcpl. Svcs. Com., North Brunswick; mgr. Animal Rescue Force, 1988—; chair environ. com. Twp. of North Brunswick, 1990-2001, vice chair, 2001—; snuggler pediat. and neonatal units St. Peter's Hosp.; Blue Belt Tiger Schulmann's Karate, 1997; founding mem., trustee, bd. dirs. Lawrence Brook Watershed Partnership, 1998—. Mem. NAFE, Marine Tech. Soc. (vice chmn. 1980-81), Mensa (pub. rels. adv. com. 1989—, pub. rels. coord. Ctrl. N.J. chpt. 1992—, bd. dirs. 1992—), Oceanic Soc. (bd. dirs. 1979-81), Stony Brook Millstone Watershed Assn. (water qualification monitor 1994—), Ctrl. N.J. Mensa (trustee, chair pub. rels. 1990—). Avocations: photography, reading, swimming, wood finishing, writing. E-mail: sconnell@mlmic.com.

CONNELL, WILL, financial consultant; b. L.A., Nov. 24, 1935; s. Will James and Grace Allen Connell; m. Rolleen Spotkov, Aug. 18, 1962 (div. 1982); children: Eve Lorraine, Ian William; m. Judith Rae, Apr. 26, 1997. BA, U. Calif., Berkeley, 1958. Aerospace engr. MacDonnell Douglas, Monrovia, Calif., 1962—73; pvt. practice sculptor Grass Valley, Calif., 1969—; pvt. practice fin. cons., 1991—; pub. Edconco Press, Grass Valley, 1998—. Mem. advocacy bd. U. Calif. San Francisco Hosp., 2001—02. Author: Prostate Cancer Treatment, 1998. Lectr. to prostate cancer support groups and hosp. clinics, Calif., 1999—2002. Lt. (j.g.) U.S. Coast and Geodetic Survey, 1958—61. Democrat. Achievements include patents for optical device. Avocations: mountain climbing, Antarctic travel, literature, furniture creation, classical music. Office: Edconco Press PO Box 357 Grass Valley CA 95945

CONNELL, WILLIAM D. lawyer; b. Palo Alto, Calif., Apr. 1, 1955; s. Robert Charles and Audrey Elizabeth (Steele) C.; m. Kathy Lynn Mleko, Aug. 13, 1977; children: Hilary Anne, Andrew James. BA in Polit Sci. with honors, Stanford U., 1976; JD cum laude, Harvard U., 1979. Bar: Calif. 1979, U.S. Dist. Ct. (cen., no. and ea. dists.) Calif. 1979, U.S. Ct. Appeals (9th cir.) 1979. Assoc. Gibson, Dunn & Crutcher, L.A., 1979-80, San Jose, Calif., 1980-87, ptnr., 1988-97, GCA Law Ptnrs. LLP, 1997—. Mem. Christian Legal Soc. Mem. Stanford Alumni Assn. (life), Commonwealth Club Calif., The Churchill Club, U.S. Golf Assn., The Federalist Soc., Phi Beta Kappa. Republican. Avocations: photography, golf.

CONNELL, WILLIAM TERRENCE, lawyer, judge; b. Montclair, N.J., July 29, 1949; s. Raymond Charles and Kathryn (Hanley) C.; m. Honor Marilyn McMahon, July 19, 1975; children: Sean William, Heather Erin, Lauren Blythe. AB, Providence Coll., 1971; JD, Seton Hall U., 1976. Bar: N.J. 1977, D.C. 1979, U.S. Dist. Ct. N.J. 1977, U.S. Ct. Appeals (3d cir.) 1984; cert. trial atty. Investigator Comml. Union Ins. Co., West Orange, N.J., 1971, Essex County Prosecutors Office, Newark, 1971-77; mem. Dwyer, Connell & Lisbona, Montclair, NJ, 1977—, Fairfield, N.J., 1997—. Arbitrator Middlesex County Superior Ct., New Brunswick, N.J., 1984—; judge Mcpl. ct. Borough of Roseland, N.J., 1988—. Mem.: Def. Rsch. Inst., Trucking Ind. Def. Assn., Middlesex County Trial Lawyers Assn., Middlesex County Bar Assn., Essex County Bar Assn., N.J. Bar Assn., Am. Bd. Trial Attys. (adv.), Assn. Trial Lawyers Am., ABA, Bear Lakes Country Club (Fla.), Essex Fells Country Club (N.J.). Roman Catholic. Home: 18 Ford Ln Roseland NJ 07068-1456 also: 3360 S Ocean Blvd Palm Beach FL 33480 Office: Dwyer Connell & Lisbona Greenbrook Corp Ctr 100 Passaic Ave Fairfield NJ 07004-3508 E-mail: wconnell@dcllaw.com.

CONNELLAN, WILLIAM WESLEY, higher education educator; b. Detroit, Apr. 25, 1945; s. Thomas Kennedy and Florence Irene Connellan; m. Mary Emma Solonika Simms, Aug. 17, 1969 (div. Jan. 1979); 1 child, Brian Patrick; m. Catherine Joanne Marine, Oct. 12, 1985 (div. Dec. 2000). BA, Oakland U., Rochester, Mich., 1967; MA, U. Mich., 1971, PhD, 1981. Reporter Detroit News, 1965-70; acting v.p., assoc. provost, dir. pub. rels. Oakland U., 1970-2000, vice provost, 2000—; assoc. dean, sr. v.p. Detroit Metro. Convention Vis. Bur., 2002—. Vis. scholar U. Mich., Ann Arbor, 1987, Harvard U., 1999-2000; participant Inst. for Edn. Mgmt., Harvard U., Cambridge, Mass., 1993. Mem. exec. com. Met. Detroit Conv. and Visitors Bur., 1979-2001, sr. v.p., 2002—, chair, 1999-2000; mem. Rochester Hills (Mich.) Bldg. Authority, 1981-97; mem. Avon Twp. Charter Commn., Rochester Hills, 1982-84; active Habitat for Humanity. Mem. Am. Assn. Higher Edn., Earthwatch Inst., Detroit Econ. Club, Sigma Xi. Presbyterian. Avocations: international research projects, recreational sports. Home: 1267 Putnam Cir Rochester MI 48307-6045 Office: 211 W Fort St Ste 2000 Detroit MI 48226 E-mail: wconnellan@visitdetroit.com.

CONNELLY, COLIN CHARLES, lawyer; b. Hopewell, Va., Nov. 1, 1956; s. Charles Bernell and Doris Louise (Beasley) C.; m. Stephanie Paige Lowder, May 9, 1981. AA, Richard Bland Coll., 1977; BA, Va. Commonwealth U., 1979; JD, U. Richmond, 1983. Bar: Va. 1983, U.S. Ct. Appeals (4th cir.) 1983. Assoc. Tuck, Freasier, & Herbig, Richmond, Va., 1984-87; ptnr. Tuck & Connelly Profl. Assocs., Inc., Richmond, Va., 1988-95, Connelly & Assocs., P.C., Chester, Va., 1996—. Bd. dirs., v.p. Cen. Title Ins. Agy., Richmond, 1988—; agt. Chgo. Title Ins. Corp., Richmond, 1988—. Mem., assoc./counsel Home Builders Assn. South Side Va. Mem. ABA, Va. Bar Assn., Richmond Bar Assn., Southside Bd. Realtors (affiliate), Chester Jaycees, Omicron Delta Kappa, Phi Kappa Phi, Phi Alpha Delta (justice 1983-86). Baptist. Avocations: biking, racquetball, basketball. Home: 14206 Masada Ct Chesterfield VA 23838-8725 Office: Connelly & Assocs 4830 W Hundred Rd Chester VA 23831-1746

CONNELLY, DAVID O'BRIEN, art museum administrator, journalist; b. Canton, Ohio, Apr. 25, 1952; s. Harold O'Brien and Mary Louise (Wells) C. BA in English with honors, summa cum laude, Mt. Union Coll., 1974; MA in Coll. Student Pers., Bowling Green State U., 1975; MA in Latin Am. Studies, U. Tex., Austin, 1995, postgrad., 1977-78. Dir. men's housing Southwestern U., Georgetown, Tex., 1975-76; cmty. educator, publicist Planned Parenthood Assn. Summit County, Akron, Ohio, 1976-77; arts/entertainment editor Shreveport (La.) Jour., 1978-90; asst. grants dir. Mus. Fine Arts, Houston, 1991-93; pub. rels. dir. Mus. of Fine Arts, St. Petersburg, Fla., 1996—. Staff writer The Archer M. Huntington Art Gallery, U. Tex., Austin, 1993-95; staff rep. long-range plan and devel./mktg. coms. bd. trustees Mus. Fine Arts, St. Petersburg. Editor, chief writer Mosaic; arts critic The Daily Texan, 1977-78; contbr. articles to profl. jours. Organizing com. Inner City Soup Kitchen, Shreveport, 1986-87; organizing com., first sec. exec. com., grants writer N.W. La. AIDS Task Force, Shreveport, 1988-91. Harmon O. DeGraff Meml. scholar Akron YMCA, 1977; Emmett Walter fellow U. Tex., 1977-78, Music Critics Inst. fellow, 1980, Aspen

Summer Music Festival; named one of Outstanding Young Men of Am., 1989; grantee Tinker Found., 1994. Mem. Am. Assn. Mus., St. Petersburg Mus. Consortium, Blue Key, Phi Kappa Phi, Psi Kappa Omega. Democrat. Jewish. Avocations: reading, travel, swimming, film, the arts. Home: 5190 Salmon Dr SE Apt B Saint Petersburg FL 33705-6351 Office: Mus Fine Arts 255 Beach Dr NE Saint Petersburg FL 33701-3498 E-mail: david@fine-arts.org.

CONNELLY, DONALD PRESTON, retired electric and gas utility company executive; b. Newark, Del., Nov. 27, 1939; s. Walton Theodore and Edna Rocelia (Lee) C.; m. Margaret Burnetta Boylan, Oct. 29, 1940; children: Donald Preston Jr., Pamela Margaret. AS, U. Del., 1970, BS, 1980. Clk. Delmarva Power, Wilmington, Del., 1961-66, supr., 1966-67, spl. acct., 1967-72, sr. acct., 1972-73, gen. supr., 1973-76, coordinator customer info. system, 1976-79, mgr., 1979-85, mgr., asst. sec., 1985, corp. sec., 1985-88; corp. sec., ethics officer Delmarva Power Subs. Cos., Wilmington, Del., 1988-98, ret., 1998. 1st v.p. Civic League for New Castle County, Wilmington, 1985-86, treas., 1987-91; mem. Metroform Coun. Civic Assns., 1993-96, Churchman's Crossing Civic Assn., 1996—. With USN, 1957-60. Mem. Am. Soc. Corp. Secs. (nat. bd. dirs. 1994-97, exec. steering com. 1995-97, v.p. Mid Atlantic chpt. 1989-91, pres. 1991-92, adv. com. 1988-97), Ethics Officer Assn. Methodist. Avocations: hiking, coin collecting, photography. Home: 7 Greenridge Rd Newark DE 19711-6704

CONNELLY, ELIZABETH ANN, retired state legislator; b. N.Y.C. d. John Walter and Alice Marie (Mallon) Keresey; m. Robert Vincent Connelly; children: Alice, Robert, Margaret, Therese. Grad. H.S., Bronx; LLD (hon.), Wagner Coll., 1996. Telephone sales Pan Am. World Airways, N.Y.C., 1946-54; mem. N.Y. State Assembly, Albany, 1973-2000, chair com. on mental health, retardation/devel. disabilities, 1977-92, chair com. on standing coms., 1993-95, speaker pro tem, 1995-2000, chair intern com., 1995-2000; ret., 2000. Chair Legis. Women's Caucus, N.Y. State, 1993-95. Recipient over 350 awards and honors including S.I. Hosp. Vol. of Yr. award, 1972-73, Cert. Appreciation Willowbrook chpt. Benevolent Soc. Retarded Children, 1978, Legislator of Yr. award N.Y. State Coun. on Alcoholism, 1983, Woman of Yr. award Epilepsy Ctr., 1984, Disting. Humanitarian of Yr. award S.I. Ctr. Ind. Living, 1987, Alliance for Mentally Ill of N.Y. State award, 1988, Thomas G. Gilbert Meml. award N.Y. State Mental Health Soc., 1989, Nat. Barrier Awareness Found., 1990, Irish Am. Heritage Mus., 1991, N.Y. State Head Injury Assn. Pub. Policy award, 1994, N.Y. State Cath. Conf. Pub. Policy award 1996, St. John's U. Pres.' medal, 1998, Pres.' medal CUNY Coll. of S.I. Mem. Am.-Irish Legislators' Soc. (pres. 1999—). Democrat.

CONNELLY, GEORGE WILLIAM, lawyer; b. Charlottesville, Va., Nov. 27, 1945; s. George William and Margaret Mary (Shannon) Connelly; m. Elaine Helen Tylenda, Aug. 24, 1968; children: Allison Lynn, Devin Matthew. BSBA, Northwestern U., 1967, JD, 1971. Bar: Ill. 71, U.S. Tax Ct. 71, NY 79, U.S. Supreme Ct. 80, U.S. Ct. Appeals (5th cir.) 89. Spl. trial atty. Office of Chief Counsel, IRS, Buffalo, 1971—85; shareholder Chamberlain, Hrdlicka, White, Williams & Martin, Houston, 1986—. Instr. trial atty. tng., Washington, 1978—80; lectr. continuing profl. edn. North Atlantic region, N.Y.C., 1981—85; counsel appeals tracking sys., Washington, 1982—85. Moot ct. judge Albert R. Mugel Tax Competition SUNY, Buffalo, 1974—85, brief grader, 1974—80; lectr. U. Rochester Tax Planning Inst., NY, 1981, Tex. Soc. CPAs, 1986—, Erie County Bar Assn., Buffalo, 1979; panel mem. NY State Soc. CPAs, 1983. Sgt. USAR, 1969—75. Named Atty. of Yr., North-Atlantic region IRS, 1983; recipient James H. Markham Jr. Meml. award, Chief Counsel IRS, 1980. Roman Catholic. Office: Chamberlain Hrdlicka White Williams & Martin 1200 Smith St Ste 1400 Houston TX 77002-4401

CONNELLY, JENNIFER, actress; b. New York, NY, Dec. 12, 1970; m. Paul Bettany, 2003. Actress: appeared in Italian, Canadian, British, Argentinian, and U.S. films: Once Upon a Time in America, 1984, Phenomena, 1985, The Valley, 1985, Labyrinth, 1986, Seven Minutes in Heaven, 1986, Some Girls, 1988, Etoile, 1988, The Hot Spot, 1990, Career Opportunities, 1991, The Rocketeer, 1991, Higher Learning, 1994, Far Harbor, 1996, Mulholland Falls, 1996, Of Love and Shadows, 1996, Dark City, 1997, Inventing the Abbots, 1997, Waking the Dead, 2000, Requiem for a Dream, 2000, Pollock, 2000, Dario Argento Collection 1: Inferno/Phenomena, 2001, A Beautiful Mind, 2001 (Best Supporting Actress Acad. award 2001, Golden Globe, 2001, Am. Film Inst. award, Brit. Acad. award, Golden Satellite award, KCFCC award, OFCS award, SEFCA award and BFCA award 2001-2002, nominee Best Actress SAG award 2001, Featured Actor of Yr. Female Movies AFI Film award 2002), The Hulk, 2003; TV movies: The Heart of Justice, 1993; TV series: The $treet, 2000. Office: Internat Creative Mgmt 8942 Wilshire Blvd Beverly Hills CA 90211-1934*

CONNELLY, JOAN BRETON, archaeologist; BA, Princeton U., 1976, MA, 1979; PhD, Bryn Mawr Coll., 1984. Asst. dean undergrad. coll., lectr. in classical and Near Eastern archaeology Bryn Mawr Coll., 1984—86; assoc. prof. fine arts NYU, 1986—, Lillian Vernon chair for tchg. excellence, 2002—, dir. Yeronisos Island Excavations, 1990—. Mem. French Archaeol. Mission to Failaka, Kuwait U. de Lyon, 1985—; mem. Pres.'s Cultural Property Adv. Com. U.S. Dept. State, 2003—. Author: Votive Sculpture of Hellenistic Cyprus, 1988. Named hon. citizen, Republic of Cyprus, Municipality of Peyia, 2000; recipient MacArthur Genius award, 1996; Classical fellow and Norbert Schimmel fellow, Met. Mus. Art, 1982—84, Oxford U. vis. fellow, All Souls Coll., 1994—95, New Coll., 1997, Magdalen Coll., 1998, John D. and Catherine T. MacArthur Found. fellow, 1996—2001, Radcliffe Inst. for Advanced Study, Harvard U., 2000, vis. scholar, Phi Beta Kappa Soc., 2000—01. Fellow: Explorers Club, Royal Geog. Soc., Soc. Antiquaries of London; mem.: Soc. for Preservation of the Greek Heritage (trustee), Soc. Women Geographers. Office: NYU Dept Fine Arts 303 Main Bldg 100 Washington Sq E New York NY 10003-6688 E-mail: joan.connelly@nyu.edu.

CONNELLY, JOHN JAMES, retired oil company technical specialist; b. Lima, Ohio, Aug. 14, 1935; s. Robert Vincent and Helen Josephine (Hay) C.; m. Aug. 22, 1959 (dec. Aug. 1991); children: Thomas, Kathleen, Joseph, Patrick; m. Virginia Connelly, July, 1993. BSChemE, Ohio State U., 1958; MBA with honors, Baldwin Wallace U., 1975. Registered profl. engr., Ohio. Engr. Std. Oil of Ohio, Lima, 1958-63; rsch. assoc. Battelle Meml. Inst., Columbus, Ohio, 1963-65; tech. specialist Owens Corning Fiberglas, Granville, Ohio, 1965-67; sr. engr. Std. Oil of Ohio, Lima, 1967-71, tech. program analyst Cleve., 1971-74, linear program specialist, 1974-78, fed. affairs analyst, 1978-81; project leader Std. of Ohio/Brit. Petroleum Am., Cleve., 1981-92; tech. specialist BP Am., Cleve., 1992-95; retired, 1995; part time technical specialist Paramount Tech. Svcs., 1995—. Instr. Ohio State U., Lima, 1961-63. Advisor Jr. Achievement, Lima, 1960-62; treas. Harding Middle Sch. PTA, Lakewood, Ohio, 1975-77, Music Parents Assn., Lakewood, 1978-80, Sch. Bd. Candidate Treas., Lakewood, 1981; mem. Vols. for Internat. Tech. Assistance, 1988—. Mem. Soc. Of Friends. Avocations: reading, biking, needlework. Home: 23749 Wonneta Pkwy Westlake OH 44145-2733 E-mail: johnjconnelly@stratos.net.

CONNELLY, MARK, writer, educator; b. Phila., July 8, 1951; s. Edward James and Hilda Virginia (Pfleger) C. BA in English and History, Carroll Coll., 1973; MA in Creative Writing, U. Wis., Milw., 1974, PhD in English, 1984. Instr. English Milw. Area Tech. Coll., 1986—. Cons. Great Lakes Precision Products. Author: The Diminished Self: Orwell and the Loss of Freedom, 1987, The Sundance Reader, 1997, Orwell and Gissing, 1997, The Sundance Writer, 1999, Deadly Closets, 2000. V.p. Irish Cultural and Heritage Ctr. of Wis., 2000—. Recipient Ann. Fiction award Milw. Mag., 1982, 1st Place Fiction award Ind. Mag., 1982. Presbyterian. Avocations: reading, travel, Irish studies. Office: Milw Area Tech Coll 700 W State St Milwaukee WI 53233-1419 E-mail: markconn@earthlink.net.

CONNELLY, MARY JO, lawyer; b. Chgo., May 19, 1949; d. Joseph Anthony and Veronica Colette (Casey) C. BSN, Coll. St. Teresa, 1971; JD, DePaul U., 1980. Bar: Ill. 1980, U.S. Dist. Ct. (no. dist.) Ill. 1980, U.S. Dist. Ct. (ctrl. dist., no. dist.) Ill. 1990. Head nurse neurosurgery St. Mary's Hosp., Rochester, Minn., 1971-73; head nurse ambulatory care U. Calif., San Francisco, 1973-77; ptnr. Sweeney & Riman Ltd., Chgo., 1980-98. Mem. ABA, Women's Bar Assn. Ill., Ill. Bar Assn., Chgo. Bar Assn. (investigator hearing, bd. dirs. jud. evaluation com. 1984-89). Home: 340 W Diversey Pky Apt 618 Chicago IL 60657-6242 E-mail: maryjo.21stcentury@rcn.com.

CONNELLY, SHARON RUDOLPH, lawyer; b. Kingwood, W.Va. d. John E. and Lorene E. Rudolph; 1 child, John. BS, W.Va. State U., 1966; MBA, Ind. U., 1968; JD, Cath. Univ., 1976; LLM in Taxation, Georgetown U., 1995. Bar: Va. 1977. Mgr. IRS, Washington, 1969-76; asst. contr. Mfrs. Hanover, N.Y.C., 1976-77; compliance chief D.C. Dept. Labor, Washington, 1977-79; dir. compliance U.S. Dept. Commerce, Washington, 1979-82; asst. insp. gen. NASA, Washington, 1982-84; dir. insp. office Nuclear Regulatory Commn., Washington, 1984-89, spl. asst. internal controls, 1989-98. Owner, financier and property mgr., 1998—. Contbr. articles to profl. jours.

CONNELLY, TERRENCE JOHN, SR., television and cable station executive; b. Chgo., Aug. 23, 1947; s. Charles Bernard, Jr. and Margaret Agnes (Gilmore) C.; m. Andrea Susan Hahn, Feb. 12, 1972; children: Terrence John, Jr., Bridget Colleen. BS in Comms., U. Ill., 1970. Reporter WITI-TV, Milw., 1970-73, WRGB-TV, Schenectady, N.Y., 1973-74; news dir. WNYT-TV, Albany, N.Y., 1974-76, WDAF-TV, Kansas City, Mo., 1976-78; exec. news producer WMAQ-TV, Chgo., 1978-80; v.p. TV news Taft Broadcasting, Cin., 1980-86; v.p., gen. mgr. WCPO-TV, Cin., 1986-88, WKRC-TV, Cin., 1988-92, WSYX-TV, Columbus, Ohio, 1992-95; pres., gen. mgr. WJLA-TV, Washington, 1995-98; sr. v.p. programming and prodn. The Weather Channel, Atlanta, 1999—. Dir. teletext, Taft Broadcasting, Cin., 1981-86; mem. broadcast adv. bd. UPI, N.Y.C., 1983-85. Editor/gen. mgr.: WCPO TV news, 1987 (Peabody award for investigative report 1987). Bd. dirs. United Way, Washington, 1995-99, Easter Seals Bd., Washington, 1995-97, Muscular Distrophy Assn., Columbus, 1992-95; chmn. Neediest Kids, Inc., Washington, 1995-99. With U.S. Army, 1970-76. Mem. Soc. Profl. Journalists, Radio-TV News Dirs. Assn., Nat. Assn. TV Program Execs., Rotary. Roman Catholic. Office: The Weather Channel 300 Interstate North Pkwy SE Atlanta GA 30339-2403

CONNELLY, THEODORE SAMPLE, communications executive; b. Middletown, Conn., Oct. 15, 1925; s. Herbert Lee and Mabel Gertrude (Wells) C. BA, Wesleyan U., 1948, postgrad., 1951—52, U. Paris, 1950. Sec. nat. com. edn. Am. Trucking Assn., Inc., Washington, 1952-54; dir. pub. affairs Nat. Automobile Club, San Francisco, 1955-62; pres., chmn. Connelly Corp., San Francisco, 1963—. Treas. Ednl. Access Cable TV Corp.; dir. Mission Neighborhood Ctrs., Inc., Neighborhood Devel. Corp.; mem. adv. com. motor vehicle legis. Calif. Legis., 1955-62; mem. com. hwys. Calif. State C. of C., 1959-62; trustee, sec., v.p. Lincoln U.; sec. Lincoln U. Found., 1968-82; mem. USN Treasure Island Restoration Adv. Bd., 2000-02; bd. dirs. San Francisco Program for Aging; founder, dir. Comm. Libr., 1963—, Comm. Inst., 1977—; founding mem. Calif. Coun. UN U., 1976; organizer Internat. Child Art Collection; co-founder African Rsch. Commn., 1970; established Connelly Fund, 1981; mem. founding regents Am. Pan-Pacific U., 1991; co-established awds. for excellence in writing about comm., 1981—; mem. steering com. Mesopotamian Exhibit, 1993—; mem. steering com. Africa Week in San Francisco. Author/compiler: BCTV: Bibliography on Cabletelevision, 1975—, 13,500 References on cable-TV, 1975—, Electromagnetic Radiation, 1976; editor: An Analysis of Joint Ventures in China, 1982, CINCOM-2000: Worldwide Communications Courses and Degrees, 2000; developer bilingual Web site: www-.comlibrary.org, 2001; contbr. articles to profl. jours.; prodr., writer, dir. over 100 cable-TV programs; pub. hist. newspapers, 1964-69; complier of first survey of U.S. Coll. and Univ. offering motor transport cirricula, 1953. Co-founder Learning Ctr. for Srs., St. Francis Meml. Hosp., 1998; founder Cyber Rsch. Ctr., 2000; established work-study programs for internat. students, 2001. With USN, with USNR, 1943—54. Recipient cert. of merit San Francisco Jaycees, 1959, award of merit USPHS, 1980, citation U.S. Dept. H&HS, 1981, commendations U.S. Coun. World Comm., 1983, commendation Sabrung Radio and TV, Karachi, 1986. Mem. AAAS, AAUP, NAACP, SAR, Pub. Rels. Round Table San Francisco, Atlanta Hist. Soc., Asian Mass Comm. and Info. Ctr. (Singapore), UN Assn. USA, Dolphin Swimming and Boating Club (San Francisco), Golden Gate Swimmer, Hawaii Theatre Ctr. (Honolulu), Marine's Meml. Assn., Colonial Williamsburg. Achievements include Worked with Dr. Benjamin Spock and criminally insane; neurosurgical tech./plasma glue devel. with Dr. Thomas I. Hoen; direct descendent Brigidier Gen. (brevet) Jeremiah Mosher, Continental Army, Am. Revolution. Office: Marina Sta Lock Box 472139 San Francisco CA 94147-2139 E-mail: palmyraatoll@aol.com.

CONNELLY, THOMAS JOSEPH, lawyer; b. Kansas City, Kans., Jan. 31, 1940; s. Edward J. and Mary (McCallum) C.; m. Barbara Helen Marciniak, Aug. 1, 1964; children: Catherine, Jennifer. AB, U. Detroit, 1963, JD, 1968. Bar: Mich. 1969, U.S. Dist. Ct. (so. and ea. dists.) Mich. 1969, U.S. Ct. Appeals (6th cir.) 1969. Sr. ptnr. Connelly, Crowley, Groth & Seglund, Walled Lake, Mich., 1975—. Exec. bd. dirs. Oakland County (Mich.) Reps., 1979-82. Mem. Mich. Bar Assn. (rep. assembly 1978—), Oakland County Bar Assn., Internat. Arabian Horse Assn. (pres.), Mich. Arabian Horse Assn. (pres. 1986—), Am. Horse Shows Assn. (bd. dirs., exec. com. 1996—). Roman Catholic. Home: 1635 S Garner Rd Milford MI 48380-4127 Office: Connelly Crowley Groth & Seglund 2410 S Commerce Rd Walled Lake MI 48390-2129 E-mail: tjconnelly@ccgs-law.com.

CONNELLY, WARREN E. lawyer; b. Mt. Vernon, N.Y., Nov. 18, 1946; BA cum laude, Dartmouth Coll., 1968; JD, Georgetown U., 1973. Bar: D.C. 1973. Atty. Cost of Living Coun., 1973-74; mem. Akin, Gump, Strauss, Hauer & Feld L.L.P., Washington. Active NAFTA Binat. Panel. 1st lt. U.S. Army, 1968-70. Mem. D.C. Bar. Office: Akin Gump Strauss Hauer & Feld LLP 1333 New Hampshire Ave NW Washington DC 20036-1564

CONNER, CECIL C., JR., performing company executive; b. Greensboro, N.C. Student, U. Vienna, Austria; BA, U. N.C.; LLB, Columbia U. With Goldman Sachs & Co., N.Y., Simpson, Thacher & Bartlett, N.Y.; from mng. ptnr. to of counsel Mandelbaum, Schweiger & Conner, 1980-94; exec. dir. The Joffrey Ballet, N.Y.C., 1992-95; mng. dir. Houston Ballet, 1995—. Active Nat. Assn. Regional Ballet, Inc., N.Y.C., N.Y. State Coun. for the Arts, N.Y.C., Dance Consort Found., N.Y.C., Tornay Mgmt., N.Y.C.; bd. dirs., vice-chmn., sec., treas. Vol. Lawyers for the Arts, Inc., 1975-94. Co-author: Skeletons from the Opera Closet. Lt. USN (ret.). Office: Houston Ballet 1921 W Bell St Houston TX 77019-4801

CONNER, DAVID LEE, secondary educator; b. Hattiesburg, Miss., Mar. 16, 1934; s. Charlie Conner and Ernestine Blanks; m. Vilene Hundley, July 10, 1959 (dec. July 1977); children: Valoree Conner-Dye, Doreese Conner, Darin Van, David Lee Jr., Richard Vaughn. BS in Math., Alcorn State U., 1957. Tchr., coach Hattiesburg Pub. Schs., 1959-69, Milw. Pub. Sch., 1969-97; life jeep operator Pabst Brewery, Milw., 1975-81; mentor, coach U. Wis., Milw., 1975 summer, h.s. math. tchr., 1984 summer; shelter care counselor St. Charles Boys Homes, Milw., 1984-87. Grantee NSF, 1960-61, 63, 64, 65 summer; named Miss. Coach of Yr. for football and track Southeastern Athletic Conf. for Jr. H.S., 1964-68; named to Alcorn State U. Hall of Fame, 1999. Mem. Milw. Spartans Track Club (founder, Coach of Yr. 1998), Kappa Alpha Psi (vice polemarch Hattiesburg chpt. 1961-69). Avocations: bowling, flag football, tennis (city of hattiesburg recreational mens singles champion 1967), basketball. Home: 9099 N 75th St Milwaukee WI 53223-2066

CONNER, DEONDRA, education educator; s. Patricia Terry. PhD, Fla. State U., 1997—2002. Instr./doctoral student Fla. State U., 1997—2002; prof. Alcorn State U., Miss., 2002—. Author: (article) Jour. of Occupl. & Orgnl. Psychology, Jour. of Applied Mgmt. & Entrepreneurship. 1st. lt. U.S. Army, 1989—92. Mem.: Southwestern Acad. of Mgmt., So. Mgmt. Assn., Acad. of Mgmt. Office: Alcorn State U 1000 ASU Dr #90 Alcorn State MS 39096

CONNER, HEATHER J. music educator; b. Meadowbrook, Pa., Sept. 22, 1975; d. Richard Walter and Jeanne Sugalski Conner. MusB, Curtis Inst. Music, Phila., 1997; MusM, Yale U., 1999; Dr.Mus. Arts, Manhattan Sch. Music, N.Y.C., 2003. Asst. prof. piano U. Utah, Salt Lake City, 2001—. Concert pianist, chamber musician Weill Recital Hall, Carnegie Hall, N.Y.C., 2001; pianist, chamber musician Glenn Gould Studios, Toronto, Ont., Canada, 2001; soloist Midland Symphony Orch., Midland, Tex., 2000; pianist chamber music series Nova Chamber Music Series, 2002—; soloist Phila. Orch., 1992, 2000, 01. Recipient Kingsville Internat. Young Performer's competition Grand Prize, 1990, Hilton Head Island Internat. Piano Competition Grand prize, 1997, Helen cohn award, Manhattan Sch. of Music, 2003; scholar Presdl. scholar, Lancaster H.S., Pa., 1993. Mem.: Coll. Music Soc., Utah Music Tchrs. Assn., Music Tchrs. Nat. Assn. Avocations: tennis, hiking, running, crossword puzzles. Office: Univ of Utah 204 David P Gardner Hall 1375 E Presidents Cir Salt Lake City UT 84112

CONNER, JEANETTE JONES, elementary school educator; b. St. Charles, Va., Nov. 29, 1934; d. Luster and Georgia (Jessee) Jones; m. Samuel Barton Conner, Aug. 3, 1966. BS in Edn., Campbellsville Coll., 1979; MA in Edn., cert. sch. psychometrist, Western Ky. U., 1980, cert. in exceptional edn. K-12, 1981, cert. reading specialist, 1984, cert. elem. sch. supr., 1985, Edn. Specialist degree, 1986. Cert. tchr., Ky. Factory worker Lee Co. Garment Factory, Pennington Gap, Va., 1956-58; receptionist Harlan (Ky.) Appalachian Hosp., 1959-67; sec. Kemper & Assoc., Louisville, 1967-69, Murray (Ky.) State U., 1970-71, Greer & Assoc., Louisville, 1971-73, Cambellsville (Ky.) Coll., 1974-76; tchr. Taylor Co. Bd. Edn., Campbellsville, 1980—. Tchr. trainer Ky. Early Learning Profile Assessment System; citizen's ambassador People to People Program Del. to Perth 1994 Early Childhood Conf., People to People Del. to China 1999 Early Childhood Conf., 20th Trienniel Australian Early Childhood Conf.; mem. Campbellsville Woman's Club (beautification com.). Commd. Ky. Col., State of Ky., 1989. Mem. AAUW (pres. 1989-90), NEA, South Cen. Reading Coun. of the Internat. Reading Assn. (Pres. 1989-90, v.p. 1990-91), Ky. State Coun. of the Internat. Reading Assn. (bd. dirs. 1988-91), Taylor County Edn. Assn. (v.p. 1989-90, pres. 1990-91), Ky. State Reading Coun. (chair com. on parents and reading 1990-91, svc. awards for promoting reading 1989-90), Ky. Edn. Assn., Ky. Coun. New Tchr. Performance Standards, Ky. Early Childhood Task Force for Early Childhood Cert. Guidelines, Ky. Dept. Special Edn. Task Force (KEA instructional com.), Ky. Assn. Supervision and Curriculum Devel. (bd. dirs., exec. bd. dirs.), Taylor County Bus. and Profl. Women, Phi Delta Kappa. Republican. Baptist. Avocations: travel, reading, tennis, hiking. Home: 619 Shawnee Dr Campbellsville KY 42718-1643 Office: Taylor County Elem Sch Old Lebanon Rd Campbellsville KY 42718

CONNER, JOHN WALLACE, humanities educator; b. Indpls., Ind., June 27, 1938; s. John Wallace Conner and Anne Marie Hanley; m. Chintana Kanchanapach, Jan. 28, 1964; children: Christopher, Matthew. BA in English, U. Notre Dame, 1960; MA in English, Ind. U., 1965. Tchr. U.S. Peace Corps, Bangkok, 1963—65; instr. English Robert Morris Jr. Coll., Carthage, Ill., 1965—66, U. Hawaii, Honolulu, 1966—69; lectr. English U. Addis Ababa, Ethiopia, 1969—71; asst. prof., assoc. prof., prof. Lit. Leeward C.C. U. Hawaii, Pearl City, 1971—. Author: Pleiades Jour. U. Hawaii, 1988, Japan Studies Essays, 1992, Poems on Modern Japanese Authors, 2002—03. With U.S. Army, 1960—61. Recipient Award for Contbns. to Japan-Hawaii-U.S. Relations, Hawaii State Legis., 1986. Mem.: Assn. Lit. Scholars and Critics. Independent. Roman Catholic. Avocations: running, mountain climbing. Home: 2611 Ala Wai Blvd 701 Honolulu HI 96815 Office: Univ Hawaii Leeward CC 96-045 Alaike Pearl City Pearl City HI 96782*

CONNER, LELAND LAVON, Indian lorist; b. Logan, Ohio, May 9, 1930; s. Foster Everett and Ida May (Cullison) C.; m. Doris Ann Keller, 1953; children: Lavonna Sue, Gregory Lee, Kay Annette, Melinda Lou. Indian lore speaker Conner Indian Show, Logan, 1960—. Author: The Vengeance of Lewis Wetzel, 1980; contbr. articles to profl. publs. Pres. Hocking County Hist. Soc., Logan, 1977-78, 2002, v.p., 1975-76; chmn. ARC Blood Program, Logan, 1976-77. With U.S. Army, 1951-53. Recipient Schiele award for Excellence in Indian Lore Schiele Mus., Gastonia, N.C., 1987, Proclamation of Recognition Ohio Ho. Reps., 1988. Mem. Am. Indian Lore Assn. (nat. dir. 1988—, Catlin Peace Pipe award 1979), Continental Confederation of Adopted Indians (Continental chief 1988—), Pipestone Indian Shrine Assn. Avocations: camping, nature hiking, teaching wilderness survival, fossil hunting. Home and Office: Am Indian Lore Assn 960 Walhonding Ave Logan OH 43138-1868

CONNER, LEONARD WAYNE, association administrator, layworker; b. Kansas City, Mo., Aug. 5, 1944; s. Clyde Page and Daisy Marie (Clevenger) C.; m. Joanne Marie Di Bianca, Jan. 6, 1968; 1 child, Brett Page. BA, U. Mo., 1968; MBA, Widener U., 1975. V.p. Continental Bank, Norristown, Pa., 1971-85; adminstrv. v.p. First Pa. Bank, Phila., 1985-86; AVP Centerre Bank, Kansas City, Mo., 1986-88; v.p., cashier Bank of Lee's Summit, Mo., 1988-92; bus. adminstr., CFO, Assn. Gospel Rescue Missions, North Kansas City, Mo., 1992—95. Bd. dirs. Englewood Assembly of God, Independence, Mo., 1993-94. Squadron comdr. Kingsway Power Squadron, Cherry Hill, N.J., 1986; ministry deacon, bd. dirs. Englewood Assembly of God, Independence, Mo., 2000—. Capt. U.S. Army, 1968-70, Vietnam. Recipient Golden Telephone award Greater Phila. C. of C., 1972 Mem. Christian Mgmt. Assn. Avocations: fishing, weight lifting, power walking, re-modeling. Office: Assn Gospel Rescue Missions 1045 Swift Ave North Kansas City MO 64116-4127 E-mail: lconner@agrm.org.

CONNER, LESLIE LYNN, JR., lawyer; b. Oklahoma City, July 15, 1939; s. Leslie Lynn and Grace Dorothy (Hartnell) C.; m. Nancy Newblock, Sept. 9, 1960; children: Deborah Lynn, Lauren Elaine, Thomas Hartnell. BA, Okla. U., 1961, LLB, 1963. Bar: Okla. 1963, U.S. Dist. Ct. (we. dist.) Okla. 1963, U.S. Ct. Appeals (10th cir.) 1963, U.S. Dist. Ct. (no. dist.) Okla. 1967, U.S. Supreme Ct. Sole practice P.C., Oklahoma City, 1992—; ptnr. Conner & Little, Oklahoma City, 1966-92. Bd. dirs. First State Bank, Jones, Okla.; hearing examiner Okla. Ins. Dept., 1995—. Trustee Heritage Hall Sch., Oklahoma City, 1977-83, sec. bd. trustees, 1977-78, pres. bd. trustees, 1979-82; trustee, chmn. various coms., lay leader United Meth. Ch., Nichols Hills, Okla., 1963—; bd. dirs. Ctrl. Okla. United Meth. Retirement Facility, 1990-96. Served to capt. USAF, 1963-66, lt. col. res. ret. Mem. ABA (ho. of dels. 1978-81), Okla. Bar Assn. (bd. of govs. 1977-81, pres. 1980, chmn. various coms.), Am. Arbitration Assn. (bd. dirs. 1991-98, comml. arbitrator 1968-2000, mediator 1985-2000), Okla. County Bar Assn. (Outstanding Service award 1974). Democrat. Methodist. Avocations: reading fiction, woodworking. Home: 5812 Chestnut Ct Edmond OK 73003-2513 Office: PO Box 30426 Edmond OK 73003

CONNER, LEWIS HOMER, JR., lawyer; b. Chattanooga, Mar. 21, 1938; s. Lewis H. Sr. and Cleo (Johnson) C.; m. Ashley Whitsitt, June 1, 1960; children: Holland Ashley, Lewis Forrest. BA, Vanderbilt U., 1960, JD, 1963. Bar: Tenn. 1963, U.S. Dist. Ct. (all dists.) Tenn. 1963, U.S. Ct. Appeals (6th cir.) 1963, U.S. Ct. Mil. Appeals 1964, U.S. Supreme Ct. 1990; cert. mediator, Tenn. Founding ptnr., atty. Dearborn & Ewing, Nashville, 1972-80; judge Ct. Appeals Middle Dist., Nashville, 1980-84; sr. ptnr., atty. Waller Lansden Dortch & Davis, Nashville, 1985-89, Boult, Cummings, Conners & Berry, Nashville, 1989-96; of counsel Stokes & Bartholomew, Nashville, 1997—. Chmn. Willis Coroon, Tenn., 1996-99; spl. chief justice Supreme Ct. Tenn., 1980-81; lectr. law Vanderbilt U. Sch. Law, Nashville, 1984-93; life del. Sixth Cir. Ct. Appeals Jud. Conf. Mng. editor Vanderbilt Law Rev. Elder Westminster Presbyn. Ch.; bd. dirs. Tenn. Golf Assn., Nashville, 1965—, pres., 1985; chmn. Tenn. Golf Found., 1992-93, 96-97, 2000-01; fin. co-chmn. Alexander for Gov., 1974-78; chmn. Tenn. Rep. Fin. Com., 1975, Tenn. Corrections Overcrowding Commn., 1985-86; bd. dirs. Boys & Girls Club Middle Tenn., 1980—, pres., 1991-92; bd. govs., chmn. Tenn. State Mus., 1987-91; bd. govs.,chmn. Gaylord Music City Bowl, 1998-. Recipient Tennessean of Yr. award, Tenn. Golf Found., 2001, Nat. Lifetime Achievement award, Boys & Girls Club Mid. Tenn., 2003. Fellow Am. Acad. Matrimonial Lawyers, Am. Bar Found., Tenn. Bar Found., Nashville Bar Found.; mem. ABA, Am. Arbitration Assn. (bd. dirs. 1990-96, chmn. Tenn. large complex case panel 1992—, panel of arbitrators 1975—, panel of mediators 1995—), Tenn. Bar Assn., Tenn. Jud. Conf., Nashville Bar Assn. (pres. 1986-87, bd. dirs., 1984-87), Commn. on the Future of the Cts. in Tenn., Order of the Coif, PGA of Am. (hon. Tenn. sect.), The Golf Club Tenn. (founder, exec. com. 1991-2003), Richland Country Club (bd. dirs. 1976-79, pres. 1978-79), Belle Meade Country Club, The Honors Course, Naples Grande Golf Club, Nashville City Club, Nashville Cumberland Club, Nashville Stadium Club, Tenn. Golf Assn. (amateur player of yr., 1973). Republican. Avocations: golf, basketball, softball, politics. Home: 163 Charleston Park Nashville TN 37205-4703 Office: Stokes Bartholomew Evans & Petree PO Box 150039 Nashville TN 37215-0039 E-mail: lewconner@stokesbartholomew.com.

CONNER, LINDSAY ANDREW, investment banker; b. N.Y.C., Feb. 19, 1956; s. Michael and Miriam Conner. BA summa cum laude, UCLA, 1976; MA, Occidental Coll., 1978; JD magna cum laude, Harvard U., 1980. Bar: Calif. 1980, U.S. Dist. Ct. (cen. dist.) Calif. 1983. Assoc. Kaplan, Livingston, Goodwin, Berkowitz & Selvin, Beverly Hills, Calif., 1980—81, Fulop &

Hardee, Beverly Hills, 1982—83, Wyman, Bautzer, Kuchel & Silbert, L.A., 1983—86; ptnr., entertainment dept. head Hill Wynne Troop & Meisinger, L.A., 1986—93; screenwriter and prodr. 54 St. Prodns., L.A., 1994—99; COO, I-Drop, Inc., L.A., Calif., 1999—2001; investment banker, cons. Beverly Hills, Calif., 2001—. Author: (with others) The Courts and Education, 1977; editor: Harvard Law Rev., 1978-80. Trustee L.A. Community Coll., 1981-97, bd. pres., 1989-90; pres. Calif. Community Coll. Trustees, 1992-93. Mem. ABA, UCLA Alumni Assn. (life), Harvard-Radcliffe Club, Phi Beta Kappa. Office: 9601 Wilshire Blvd Ste 340 Beverly Hills CA 90210-4101

CONNER, NATALIE ANN, community health nurse specialist; b. Iowa City, May 6, 1962; d. Frederick Raymond and Sheila Ruth (Rapoport) Greenberg; m. Eric Lyle Conner, Sept. 12, 1987 (div. May 1995). BSN, U. Wash., 1984; MS, U. Calif., San Francisco, 1992. Cert. specialist cmty. health, pub. health nurse, State Calif., HIV counselor DHHS/ Oreg. State Health Divsn. Charge nurse Riverton Hosp. Care Unit., Seattle, 1985; community health nurse Sound Heart, Seattle, 1985-88; staff nurse Univ. Hosp., Seattle, 1986-88; nurse Portland (Oreg.) Indian Health Clinic, 1988-89; staff nurse San Francisco State U. Student Health Svc., 1989-92; clin. instr. U. California, San Francisco, 1992; staff nurse U. Wash. Med. Ctr., Seattle, 1992-99; nurse mgr. student health svc. U. Wash., 1999—. Nurse cons. job corps program Seattle region Dept. Labor, 1992—; sec. Grad. Nurses Student Coun., U. Calif., 1991-92, mem. commencement com., 1992; chairperson Nursing Peer Rev. Com. Student Health Svcs. San Francisco State U., 1991-92. Delegate Washington State Democratic Convention, Seattle, 1984. Mem. Am. Nurses Assn., Am. Coll. Health Assn., King County Nurses Assn. (membership com. 1986-88), Sigma Theta Tau. Democrat. Jewish.

CONNER, PATRICK W. literature educator; b. Crisfield, Md., July 31, 1946; s. Stanley F. and Janie Lee Conner; m. Vicki Lynn Windsor, Aug. 24, 1947; 1 child, Nathan Windsor. BA, U. Md., 1968, MA, 1970, PhD, 1975. Instr. dept. English, U. Md., College Park, 1970—76; lectr. dept. English, Goucher Coll., Towson, Md., 1975—76; asst. prof. dept. English W.Va. U., Morgantown, 1976—82, assoc. prof., 1982—90, prof., 1990—95, Eberly Centennial prof. English, 1995—, chair dept. English, 1994—2000. Dir. W.Va. U. Press, Morgantown, 1999—. Recipient Benedum Disting. Scholars award, W.Va. U. Found., 1992, Joe Wyatt Challenge to EDUCOM award, EDUCOM, 1991; NEH fellow, 1987. Mem.: MLA (all offices, exec. com., divsion of old english 1991—97), Internat. Soc. Anglo-Saxonists (exec. dir. 1991—97), Medieval Acad. Am. (mem. electronic resources com. 1991—99). Democrat. Episcopalian. Achievements include research in Anglo-Saxon culture and history; founding and editing of ANSAXNET, the first online discussion group dedicated to a humanities discipline, Anglo-Saxon and Early Medieval Studies; founding and coordinating of the Center for Literary Computing, West Virginia University. Avocations: travel, humanities computing. Office: W Va U PO Box 6295 44 Stansbury Hall Morgantown WV 26506-6295 Office Fax: 304-293-5380. Personal E-mail: pconner@wvu.edu.

CONNER, RUTH (EDONE), not-for-profit developer; b. N.Y.C., May 13, 1950; d. Anthony Charles and Ruth Natalie (Weireter) Edone; m. Michael E. Conner, 1985 (div. 1992); m. Noureddine Afsi, 2003. BA, NYU, 1972; MDiv, Union Theol. Sem., N.Y.C., 1976; student, U. Tuebingen, Germany, 1977. Tchr. various schs., N.Y.C., 1977-79; editor Book of the Month Club, N.Y.C., 1979-85; tech. writer AT&T, Freehold, NJ, 1985-87; editor grad. mktg. comm. Rutgers U., New Brunswick, NJ, 1987-89, dir. alumni comm., 1989-97; v.p. individual support Nat. Med. Fellowships, N.Y.C., 1997-99; dir. devel. Nat. Charities Info. Bur., N.Y.C., 1999-2000; pres. Clearstory LLP, Jersey City, 2000—. Adj. prof. English and humanities Hudson County CC. Author: (book) Getting Organized, 1981; contbr. articles to profl. jours. and trade mags. Bd. dirs. Union Sem. Libr. Friends, N.Y.C., 1992—94; v.p. Duncan Hill Block Assn., Jersey City, 1994—99. Recipient Woman of Distinction award, Mayor of Jersey City, 1997. Mem.: WID, APRA, AFT. Episcopalian. Avocation: oil painting. Office: Clearstory Jersey City NJ 07306-8132 E-mail: rconner@clearstorycommunications.com.

CONNER, STEWART EDMUND, lawyer; b. Louisville, Oct. 7, 1941; s. James Pleasant and Lucille (Winter) C.; m. Joan E. Fish, May 20, 1989; children: Shannon Lynn, Erin Eileen, Margaret Eisele; stepchildren: Hunt Rounsavall, Gibbs Rounsavall, Christine Rounsavall. BS, U. Louisville, 1963, JD cum laude, 1966. Bar: Ky. 1966, U.S. Dist. Ct. (ea. and we. dists.) Ky. 1966, U.S. Tax Ct. 1967. Assoc. Wyatt, Tarrant & Combs, Louisville, 1966-72, ptnr., 1972-90, chmn. gen. corp. sect., 1980-90, mng. ptnr., 1988-2001, chmn. exec. com., 1988—. Author, editor: Kentucky Business Practice Handbook, 1988; editor Kentucky Legal Forms, 1988; contbr. to U. Ky. Law Rev. Bd. dirs. Coun. on Higher Edn., 1992-95, Louisville Water Co., 1990—, Lincoln Heritage coun. Boy Scouts Am., 1989—, dePaul Sch., 1996—. With U.S. Army, 1968-69, Vietnam. Fellow Am. Bar Found., Ky. Bar Found.; mem. ABA (banking com. 1983), Ky. Bar Assn., Louisville Bar Assn. (chmn. ethics com. 1980), Ky. C. of C. (bd. dirs. 1992-96), Greater Louisville Inc. (bd. dirs. 1996-2001), Law Club, Harmony Landing Country Club, Louisville Boat Club. Republican. Office: Wyatt Tarrant & Combs 2800 PNC Plz Louisville KY 40202 E-mail: sconner@wyattfirm.com.

CONNER, WILLIAM CURTIS, judge; b. Wichita Falls, Tex., Mar. 27, 1920; s. D.H. and Mae (Weeks) C.; m. Janice Files, Mar. 22, 1944; children: William Curtis, Stephen, Christopher, Molly. BBA, U. Tex., 1941, LLB, 1942; student, Harvard, 1942-43, MIT, 1943. Bar: Tex. bar 1942, N.Y. State bar 1949. Asso., mem. firm Curtis, Morris & Safford (and predecessor firm), N.Y.C., 1946-73; judge U.S. Dist. Ct. (so. dist.) N.Y., White Plains, 1973—, now sr. judge. Editor Tex. Law Rev. Served to lt. USNR, 1942-45, PTO. Recipient Jefferson medal N.J. Patent Law Assn., Outstanding Pub. Svc. award N.Y Intellectual Property Law Assn. Mem. Am. Judicature Soc., N.Y. Patent Law Assn. (pres. 1972-73), St. Andrews Golf Club. Presbyterian (elder). Office: US Dist Ct US Courthouse 300 Quarropas St White Plains NY 10601-4140

CONNER, WILLIAM HERBERT, lawyer; b. Columbus, Ohio, Jan. 29, 1940; s. Herbert Lee and Beulah Doris C.; m. Julie Ann Katzan, Aug. 13, 1966; children: W. David, Kristen Ann. Student, Purdue U., 1960-61; AB magna cum laude, Miami U., Oxford, Ohio, 1964; JD cum laude, U. Mich. Law Sch., 1967. Bar: Ohio 1967, U.S. Dist. Ct. (no. dist.) Ohio 1967. Assoc. Squire, Sanders & Dempsey L.L.P., Cleve., 1967-77, ptnr., 1977—. Contbr. articles to profl. jours. Mem. ABA (tax exempt financing com. 1981--), Ohio Bar Assn. (chmn. taxation com. 1981-84), Cleve. Bar Assn. (chmn. gen. tax com. 1983-84), Nat. Assn. Bond Lawyers (bd. dirs. 1991, 94-99, treas. 1995-96, pres. elect 1996-97, pres. 1997-98, immediate past pres. 1998-99). Republican. Methodist. Home: 3139 Falmouth Rd Shaker Heights OH 44122-2844 Office: Squire Sanders & Dempsey LLP 4900 Key Tower 127 Public Sq Ste 4900 Cleveland OH 44114-1304

CONNER, WILLIAM J. diversified financial services company executive; s. William J. and Margaret M. Conner. AB, Dartmouth Coll., 1985; MBA, Amos Tuck Sch. of Bus. Adminstrn., 1987. Intern bd. govs. FRS, Washington, 1983—84; asst. v.p. True BASIC, Inc., Hanover, NH, 1984—87; internal cons. Prog. Corp., Tampa, Fla., 1986, product support specialist Mayfield Heights, Ohio, 1987—89, product mgr., 1990—91, Prog. Casualty Ins. Co. of Can., Toronto, 1991—97, pres., ceo & gen. mgr., 1997—99; sr. v.p. Associates First Capital Corp., Irving, 1999—2000, Citigroup, Inc., Irving, 2000—01; mng. dir. Trilogy, Inc., Austin, 2001—. Mem. Ont. com. Ins. Bur. of Can., Toronto, 1995—99. Contbr. preface to exhibition catalogue. Sponsor Art Gallery of Ont., Toronto, 1998—99. Recipient Alumni award, Brown U. Alumni Club, 1981; grantee, Rockefeller Endowment at Dartmouth, 1983—84. Mem.: IEEE (assoc.), La Cima CLub, Cum Laude Soc. (life), Dartmouth Ednl. Assn. (life). Achievements include invention of channel-independent all-risk auto insurance. Avocations: aviation, music, sailing, scuba diving, technology. Personal E-mail: wconner@sbcglobal.net.

CONNERLEY, MARY L. psychologist, educator; b. Iowa; BS, Iowa State U., 1987, MS, 1988; PhD, U. Iowa, 1993. Assoc. prof. Va. Tech., Blacksburg, 2000—, asst. prof., 1993—2000. Mem.: Am. Psychol. Soc., Soc. for Human Resource Mgmt., Soc. for Indsl. and Orgnl. Psychologists, Acad. Mgmt. Office: Virginia Tech 2007 Pamplin Hall Blacksburg VA 24061 Office Fax: 540-231-3076. Business E-Mail: maryc@vt.edu.

CONNERS, JOHN BRENDAN, insurance company executive; b. Boston, Oct. 6, 1945; s. Stephen Edward and Josephine (McMahon) Conners; m. Jean Marie McLean, June 15, 1968; children: James, Michael, Colleen. AB, Boston Coll., 1967. Cert. casualty actuary. Actuarial asst. Liberty Mut. Ins. Co., Boston, 1969-70, actuarial analyst, 1970-73, asst. actuary, 1973-75, assoc. actuary, 1975-79, asst. v.p., assoc. actuary, 1979-80, v.p., assoc. actuary, 1980, v.p., actuary, 1980-82, v.p., mgr. personal risks, 1982-83, sr. v.p., mgr. personal market, 1983-87, exec. v.p. personal market, 1987—. Bd. dirs. Hwy. Loss Data Inst., Washington, Advs. Hwy. and Auto Safety, Washington; mem. Ins. Rsch. Coun. Mem.: Casualty Actuaries New Eng. (pres. 1980), Casualty Actuarial Soc. (bd. dirs. 1983—85). Roman Catholic. Avocations: golf, gardening. Office: Liberty Mutual 175 Berkeley St Boston MA 02116-5066

CONNERS, PATRICIA A. lawyer; b. Patrick AFB, Fla., Nov. 10, 1958; d. Charles Patrick and Ella (Hardon) C. BS with distinction, U. Fla., 1979, JD, 1982. Bar: Fla., 1983. Law clerk Fifth Dist. Ct. Appeal, Daytona Beach, Fla., 1982-84; asst. atty. gen. criminal appeals Fla. Atty. Gen., Tallahassee, 1984-87, asst. atty. gen. antitrust, 1987-97, chief antitrust sect., 1997—. Southeast regional vice-chair Nat. Assn. Atty. Gen. Antitrust Task Force, Washington, 1996-98, nat.-vice-chair, 1999-2001, chair, 2001-. Mem. Fla. Supreme Ct. Com. on the Arts, Tallahassee, 1998—. Recipient Antitrust Sect. Davis Productivity award, Fla. Tax Watch, 1989, Economic Crimes Davis Productivity award Fla. Tax Watch, 1993. Mem. Am. Bar Assn. (antitrust sect., govt., pub. sector lawyers sect.), Fla. Bar (vice chair Antitrust Certification Comm. 2001—, govt. lawyers sect., bus. law sect., health law sect.), Am. Antitrust Inst. (adv. bd. 2002-), Fla. Assn. Women Lawyers, Tallahassee Womens Lawyers Assn., U.S. Supreme Ct., Eleventh Circuit Ct. Appeals, U.S. Dist. Ct. Northern Dist. Fla., U.S. Dist. Ct. Middle Dist. Fla., U.S. Dist. Ct. So. Dist. of Fla. Office: Atty Gen Office Antitrust Sect PL-01 The Capitol Tallahassee FL 32399-1050

CONNERS, PETER HAMILTON, writer; b. Rochester, N.Y., Sept. 11, 1970; s. Gary Hamilton and Gwenyth Francis C.; m. Karen Westervelt, July 18, 1998. BA, SUNY, Potsdam, N.Y., 1993; MS in Edn., Nazareth Coll., 1997. Founding dir. New Visions Programs, Rochester, NY, 2001—. Adj. prof. Rochester Inst. Tech. Author: (poetry) Burnt Offerings, 1999, (poetry and fiction) While In The World, 2003; co-editor: Double Room: A Journal of Prose Poetry and Flash Fiction. Mem.: Assn. Tchg. Artists (founding bd. dirs. Rochester region). Avocations: guitar, live music, travel. E-mail: phconners@hotmail.com.

CONNERY, SIR SEAN (THOMAS CONNERY), actor; b. Edinburgh, Scotland, Aug. 25, 1930; s. Joseph and Euphamia C.; m. Diane Cilento, 1962 (div.); 1 son, Jason; m. Micheline Roquebrune, 1975; 1 stepdaughter. D.Litt. (hon.), Heriot-Watt U., 1981, St. Andrews U., 1988. Founder Fountainbridge Films, Los Angeles, 1992—2002. First theater appearance in road show co. of South Pacific, Eng., 1953, also in Macbeth, Judith; films include: Let's Make Up, 1955, No Road Back, 1956, Action of the Tiger, 1957, Hell Drivers, 1957, Time Lock, 1957, Another Time, Another Place, 1958, Tarzan's Greatest Adventure, 1959, Darby O'Gill and the Little People, 1959, The Frightened City, 1961, Operation Snafu, 1961, The Longest Day, 1962, Woman of Straw, 1964, Marnie, 1964, The Hill, 1965, A Fine Madness, 1966, Shalako, 1968, The Molly Maguires, 1970, The Red Tent, 1971, The Anderson Tapes, 1971, The Offence, 1973, Zardoz, 1974, The Terrorists, 1974, Murder on the Orient Express, 1974, The Wind and the Lion, 1975, The Man Who Would be King, 1975, Robin and Marian, 1976, The Next Man, 1976, A Bridge Too Far, 1977, The Great Train Robbery, 1979, Cuba, 1979, Meteor, 1979, The Outland, 1981, Time Bandits, 1981, Sword of the Valiant, 1982, Wrong is Right, 1982, Five Days One Summer, 1982, The Name of the Rose, 1986, The Untouchables, 1987 (Acad. award for best supporting actor), The Presidio, 1988, Indiana Jones and the Last Crusade, 1989, Family Business, 1989, The Hunt for Red October, 1990, The Russia House, 1990, Highlander 2: The Quickening, 1991, Robin Hood: Prince of Thieves, 1991, Rising Sun, 1993, A Good Man in Africa, 1994, Just Cause, 1995, First Knight, 1995, The Rock, 1996, (voice) Dragon Heart, 1996, actor, co-exec. prodr.: Medicine Man, 1992; James Bond films include: Dr No, 1962, From Russia with Love, 1964, Goldfinger, 1964, Thunderball, 1965, You Only Live Twice, 1967, Diamonds are Forever, 1971, Never Say Never Again, 1983; TV appearances include Requiem For a Heavyweight, 1957, Anna Karenina, The Crucible; prodr., dir.: The Bowler and the Bonnet (film documentary), I've Seen You Cut Lemons (London stage); prodr.: Something Like the Truth, Playing by Heart, 1998, (narrator) Macbeth, 1999; actor, prodr., Entrapment, 1999, Finding Forrester, 2000, actor, exec. prodr. The Avengers, 1998, The League of Extraordinary Gentlemen, 2003. Served with Brit. Royal Navy. Named Star of the Yr., Nat. Assn. Theater Owners, 1987, Commander of Arts, France; recipient Tribute award Brit. Acad. Film and Television Arts, 1990, Cecil B. DeMille Golden Globe award Hollywood Fgn. Press Assn., 1996; recipient Lifetime Achievement award ShoWest Conv., 1999, Career Achievement award Nat. Bd. Rev., 1993. Office: Creative Artists Agy 9830 Wilshire Blvd Beverly Hills CA 90212-1804*

CONNETTE, EDWARD GRANT, III, lawyer; b. Nashville, Sept. 23, 1952; s. Edward G. and Elizabeth (Stone) C.; m. Jane V. Harper, Feb. 10, 1990. BA, Davidson Coll., 1974; JD, U. N.C., 1977. Bar: N.C. 1980, Conn. 1977, U.S. Dist. Ct. Conn. 1979, U.S. Dist. Ct. (we. dist.) N.C. 1980, U.S. Dist. Ct. (mid. dist.) N.C. 1981, U.S. Ct. Appeals (4th cir.) 1981, U.S. Supreme Ct. 1986. Atty. United Ch. of Christ, N.Y.C., 1977-78, Legal Aid Soc. Hartford County, Hartford, Conn., 1978-80; mng. atty. Legal Svcs. of S-. Piedmont, Inc., Charlotte, N.C., 1980-84; ptnr. Lesesne & Connette, Charlotte, N.C., 1984—. Mem. N.C. Bar Assn., N.C. Acad. Trial Lawyers. Democrat. Presbyterian. Office: Lesesne & Connette 1001 Elizabeth Ave # D Charlotte NC 28204-2234

CONNEY, ALLAN HOWARD, pharmacologist, researcher; b. Chgo., Mar. 23, 1930; s. Leo Younkers and Celia (Gasway) Conney; m. Diana Conney, Sept. 5, 1954; children: Michael Raymond, Steven Herbert. BS, U. Wis., 1952, MS, 1954, PhD, 1956. Research asst. McArdle Lab., Madison, Wis., 1952—56; guest investigator Nat. Heart Inst., Bethesda, Md., 1957—58, pharmacologist, 1958—60; head dept. biochem. pharmacology Burroughs Wellcome & Co., Tuckahoe, NY, 1960—70; dir. dept. biochemistry Hoffmann-La Roche Inc., Nutley, NJ, 1970—71, dir. dept. biochemistry and drug metabolism, 1971—83, assoc. dir. exptl. therapeutics, 1979—83, dir. lab. exptl. carcinogenesis and metabolism, 1983—85; head Lab. of Exptl. Carcinogenesis and Metabolism Roche Inst. Molecular Biology, Nutley, NJ, 1985—87; chmn. dept. chem. biology Rutgers U. Coll. Pharmacy, Piscataway, NJ, 1987—2002. Mem.: AAAS, NAS, Soc. Toxicology, Inc. (Arnold J. Lehman award), Am. Assn. Cancer Rsch. (G.H.A. Clowes award, DeWitt S. Goodman award), Am. Soc. Pharmacology and Exptl. Therapeutics (ASPET award), Am. Soc. Biol. Chemists. Office: Rutgers U Coll Pharmacy/Lab Canc Rsch 164 Frelinghuysen Rd Piscataway NJ 08854-8020

CONNICK, HARRY, JR., jazz musician, actor, singer; b. New Orleans, 1967; m. Jill Goodacre, April 16, 1994. Student, New Orleans Ctr. for the Creative Arts; studied with, Ellis Marsalis; student, Hunter Coll., Manhattan Sch. Music. Albums include Harry Connick Jr., 1987. 20, 1989, We Are in Love, 1991, Lofty's Roach Souffle, 1991, Blue Light, Red Light, 1991, Eleven, 1992, 25, 1992, When My Heart Finds Christmas, 1993, She, 1994, Star Turtle, 1996, To See You, 1997, Come By Me, 1999, 30, 2001, Songs I Heard, 2001, contributed music to soundtrack When Harry Met Sally; actor: (films) Memphis Belle, Little Man Tate, 1991, Copycat, 1995, Independence Day, 1996, Hope Floats, 1998, The Iron Giant, 1999, My Dog Skip, 2000; (TV films) South Pacific, 2001; appeared on PBS' Great Performances, band leader Harry Connick's Big Band. Recipient Grammy awards. Office: Wilkins Mgmt Inc 323 Broadway Cambridge MA 02139

CONNICK, ROBERT ELWELL, retired chemistry educator; b. Eureka, Calif., July 29, 1917; s. Arthur Elwell and Florence (Robertson) C.; m. Frances Spieth, Dec. 19, 1952; children: Mary Catherine, Elizabeth, Arthur, Megan, Sarah, William Beach. BS, U. Calif. at Berkeley, 1939, PhD, 1942. Mem. faculty U. Calif., Berkeley, 1942-88, researcher Manhattan project, 1942—46, asst. prof. then assoc. prof. chemistry, 1945-52, prof., 1952-88, chmn. dept. chemistry, 1958-60, dean Coll. Chemistry, 1960-65, vice chancellor acad. affairs, 1965-67, vice chancellor, 1969-71, acting dean Coll. Chemistry, 1987-88. Contbr. articles profl. jours. Guggenheim fellow, 1949, 59 Mem. Am. Chem. Soc., Nat. Acad. Scis., Phi Beta Kappa, Sigma Xi, Pi Mu Epsilon. Home: 50 Marguerita Rd Kensington CA 94707-1020 E-mail: connick@uclink4.berkeley.edu.

CONNOLA, DONALD PASCAL, JR., management consultant; b. New Brunswick, N.J., Sept. 25, 1948; s. Donald Pascal and Josephine (Montalbano) C. AB, Rutgers U., 1970, MBA, 1973; JD, Bklyn. Law Sch., 1977. Mktg. control analyst Gen. Foods Corp., White Plains, N.Y., 1973-74, product analyst, 1974, sr. fin. analyst, 1974-75, fin. assoc., 1975-79, fin. specialist, 1979, internal mgmt. cons., 1979-82, mgmt. cons., 1983—. Prof. mgmt. Fairleigh Dickinson U., Rutherford, N.J., 1983-86, dir. MBA program, dir. undergrad. student svcs., 1986-94; prof. bus. adminstrn. Concordia Coll., Bronxville, N.Y., 1995-97; team leader Verizon Comm., 2000—. Mem. N.J. State Bar Assn., Am. Soc. Tng. and Devel., Assn. MBA Execs., Soc. for Human Resource Mgmt. Home: 1220 Cellar Ave Apt 12 Clark NJ 07066-2044 Office: 1500 Teaneck Rd Teaneck NJ 07666

CONNOLLY, CARLA GARCIA, lawyer; b. San Antonio, Jan. 12, 1953; d. Gus C. Garcia and Eleanor (Rodriguez) McCusker; m. James M. Connolly, Nov. 1, 1985; children: Erin C., Cara A. BA, Tex. A&I U., 1974; JD, U. Tex., 1980. Bar: Tex. 1980, U.S. Dist. Ct. (we. dist.) Tex. 1991. Asst. dist. atty. Travis County Dist. Atty.'s Office, Austin, Tex., 1980—89; shareholder Wright & Greenhill, P.C., Austin, 1989—98; ptnr. Black & Connolly LLP, Austin, 1998—2001, Connolly & Castagna, L.L.P., Austin, 2001—. Mem. Am. Bd. Trial Advocates, Tex. Assn. Def. Counsel, Travis County Bar Assn. Office: Connolly & Castagna LLP 4611 Bee Caves Rd Ste 201 Austin TX 78746-5222

CONNOLLY, E. SANDER, JR., medical educator; BA, Dartmouth Coll., 1987; MD, La.State U., 1991. Assoc. prof. Columbia U., New York, 1997—. Office: Columbia U 710 W 168th St New York NY 10032

CONNOLLY, EDWARD S. neurological surgeon; b. Omaha, 1934; MD, Creighton U., 1960. Diplomate Am. Bd. Neurol. Surgery (pres. 1994). Intern U. Calif. Med. Ctr., 1960—61, resident in gen. surgery, 1961—62, resident in neurosurgery, 1962—67; neurol. surgeon Ochsner Clinic, New Orleans; prof. neurol. surgery La. State U. and Tulane U.; clin. prof.; pvt. practice. Fellow: ACS; mem.: AMA, Congress Neurol. Surgeons, Soc. Neurol. Surgeons, Am. Acad. Neurol. Surgeons, Neurol. Soc. Am., Am. Assn. Neurol. Surgeons. Office: 1514 Jefferson Hwy New Orleans LA 70121-2429

CONNOLLY, ELAINE ALEXANDER PATERSON, nurse; b. N.Y.C., May 22, 1961; d. George A.P. and Joan Elaine Wallace; m. Thomas J. Connolly, Aug. 10, 1991, Clancy, Katherine, Thomas. BFA, NYU, 1986; MS in Nursing, U. So. Maine, 1993. Staff nurse Maine Med. Ctr., Portland, 1989—96, breast health nurse educator, 1996—98; staff nurse H.D. Goodall Hosp., Sanford, Maine, 1998—2001, nursing supr., 2002—. Dir. Am. Nurses Assn. Bd. Dirs.; trustee Am. Nurses Found., 1998-2002; sec., 2000-2002; nurse vol. ARC, 2001-; care mem. Maine Disaster Health Svs. ARC, 2001-. Editl. adv. bd. Am. Jour. Nursing. Group organizer Citizen's Action Group, Sagamore Village, Portland, 1993; co-founder citizen's group Coalition for Direct Action at Seabrook, 1979; active Clinton/Gore Re-Election campaign, Maine State Dem. Party; nurse vol. ARC, 2001-, core mem. Maine Disaster Health Svcs., 2001-. ANA grantee, 1998. Mem.: ANA (Maine 2d v.p. 2001—02, chair legis. com. 2002—), Acad. Med. Surg. Nurses, Maine Women's Lobby, Sigma Theta Tau. Avocations: family, reading, art. Home: 417 Black Point Rd Scarborough ME 04074-9413

CONNOLLY, ELMA TROUTMAN, artist, contractor, designer; b. Middleburg, Pa., May 10, 1931; d. Benjamin F. and Eva Ellen (DeLong) Hollenback; m. Kenneth R. Troutman, Aug. 15, 1950; children: Kenneth, Linda, Robert, Terri; m. Jerome P. Connolly, Apr. 15, 1973. Student, Lock Haven State Tchrs. Coll., 1949. Profl. dancer, 1949—51; instr.; cons. for exceptions unit Pa. Tax Bur., Harrisburg; owner, founder, pres. Arts ETC Co., Sunbury, Pa.; owner Art Gallery, 1976-93. Bus. cons. Cohen, Danville, 1970-72; art restoration work, 1955-2001; art instr., Pa., Fla. and Idaho, 1959-2001. Murals (with Jerome Connolly): Nature Ctr., Winston Salem, N.C., 1974, South Am. Hall-Smithsonian Nat. History Mus., Washington, 1975, George Page Mus. of La Brea Discoveries, L.A., 1976, Makah Mus., Neah Bay, Wash., 1978, Woolly Mammoth Background Provincial Mus. B.C., Can., 1979, The African Hall Springfield (Mass.) Sci. Mus., 1980, Big Cypress Nature Ctr., Naples, Fla., 1982, Indian Hall Ill. State Mus., 1984, Edn. Ctr. Taipei, Taiwan, 1987, African Water Hole, American Kudu, Carnagie Mus. Nat. History, Pa., 1992, Alaskan Brown Bear, Carnagie Mus. Natural History, Pitts., 1994; sculpture, murals George Page Mus., Provincial Mus., Springfield Sci. Mus., Big Cypress Nature Ctr. Fla., Pa. State Univ., 2000, Pa. Messiah Coll. Oak Mus., 2001-02; sculpture The Foregrounds for Mass. Mus., Nature Ctr. Fla., Frazer Delta diorama Provincial Mus. Can., Page Mus., L.A. Pres. Susquehanna Art League, 1999. Named Woman of Yr., ABI, 1991; recipient Am. Women's award. Mem. NAFE, Sunbury Mchts. Coun. (pres.), C. of C. (govt. affairs com.), Susquehanna Art Soc. (pres.), Internat. Platform Assn. Republican. Avocations: sculpture, writing, civic affairs, art, bldg. contractor. Home: RR 2 Box 176n3 Selinsgrove PA 17870-9657 E-mail: murals051031@aol.com.

CONNOLLY, GERALD EDWARD, lawyer; b. Boston, Oct. 13, 1943; s. Thomas E. and Grace J. (Fitzgerald) C.; m. Elizabeth Heidi Eckert, Jan. 6, 1968; children: Matthew F., Dennis F., David D., Edward F. BS, Coll. of Holy Cross, 1965; JD, U. Va., 1972. Bar: Wis. 1972, U.S. Tax Ct. 1973. From assoc. to ptnr. Whyte & Hirschboeck S.C., Milw., 1972-78; ptnr. Minahan & Peterson S.C., Milw., 1978-91, Quarles & Brady, 1991—. V.p., bd. dirs., sec. Reinhart FoodService, Inc.; bd. dirs., sec. Reinhart Real Estate Group, Inc., Reinhart Retail Group; sec. Hometown Inc.; bd. dirs. Viterbo U., LaCrosse, Wis., Hatco Corp., Milw., Adaptive Engring. Lab., Inc., Diversatek, Inc., Medovations, Sunlite Plastics, Inc., Milw.; sec. The Medalcraft Mint, Inc., Radisson LaCrosse Hotel, Water Blasting. Trustee Emory T. Clark Family Charitable Found., D.B. Reinhart Family Found.; chmn. Circle of Care Children's Hosp. Wis.; bd. dirs. Children's Hosp. Wis. Found. Lt. USN, 1966-69. Mem. ABA, Milw. Club, Milw. Athletic Club, North Shore Country Club, Order of Coif. Home: 10134 N Range Line Rd # 27W Mequon WI 53092-5435 Office: Quarles & Brady 411 E Wisconsin Ave Ste 2550 Milwaukee WI 53202-4497 E-mail: gec@quarles.com.

CONNOLLY, JOHN EARLE, surgeon, educator; b. Omaha, May 21, 1923; s. Earl A. and Gertrude (Eckerman) C.; m. Virginia Hartman, Aug. 12, 1967; children: Peter Hart. John Earle, Sarah. AB, Harvard U., 1945, MD, 1948. Diplomate: Am. Bd. Surgery (bd. dirs. 1976-82), Am. Bd. Thoracic and Cardiovascular Surgery, Am. Bd. Vascular Surgery. Intern. in surgery Stanford U. Hosps., San Francisco, 1948-49, surg. research fellow, 1949-50, asst. resident surgeon, 1950-52, chief resident surgeon, 1953-54, surg. pathology fellow, 1954-55, 1957-60, John and Mary Markle Scholar in med. scis., 1957-62; surg. registrar professional unit St. Bartholomew's Hosp., London, 1952-53; resident in thoracic surgery Bellevue Hosp., N.Y.C., 1955; resident in thoracic and cardiovascular surgery Columbia-Presbyn. Med. Ctr., N.Y.C., 1956; from instr. to assoc. prof. surgery Stanford U., 1957-65; prof. U. Calif., Irvine, 1965—, chmn. dept. surgery, 1965-78; attending surgeon Stanford Med. Ctr., Palo Alto, Calif., 1959-65; chmn. cardiovascular and thoracic surgery Irvine Med. Ctr. U. Calif., 1968—; attending surgeon Children's Hosp., Orange, Calif., 1968—, Anaheim (Calif.) Meml. Hosp., 1970—. Vis. prof. Beijing Heart, Lung, Blood Vessel Inst., 1990, A.H. Duncan vis. prof. U. Edinburgh, 1984; Hunterian prof. Royal Coll. Surgeons Eng., 1985-86, Kinmonth lectr., 1987, Hume Lectr. Soc. for Clin. Vascular Surgery, 1998; King James IV lectr. Royal Coll. Surgeons Edinburgh, 2003; Dist. Prof. Lectr. Uniformed Svcs. U. Health Scis., Bethesda, 1998; adv. coun. Nat. Heart, Lung, and Blood Inst.-NIH, 1981-85; cons. Long Beach VA Hosp., Calif., 1965—. Contbr. articles to profl. jours.; mem. editl. bd.: Jour. Cardiovascular Surgery, 1974—, chief editor, 1985—; mem. editl. bd. Western Jour. Medicine, 1975—, Jour. Stroke, 1979—, Jour. Vascular Surgery, 1983—. Bd. dirs. Audio-Digest Found., 1974—, Franklin Martin Found., 1975-80; regent Uniformed Svcs. U. Health Scis., Bethesda, 1992—. Served with AUS, 1943-44. Recipient Cert. of Merit, Japanese Surg. Soc., 1979, 90. Fellow ACS (gov. 1964-70, regent 1973-82, vice chmn. bd. regents 1980-82, v.p. 1984-85), Royal Coll. Surgeons Eng., 1982 (hon.), Royal Coll. Surgeons Ireland, 1988 (hon.), Royal Coll. Surgeons Edinburgh, 1983 (hon.); mem. Japanese Surg. Soc. (hon.), Am. Surg. Assn., Soc. U. Surgeons, Am. Assn. Thoracic Surgery (coun. 1974-78), Pacific Coast Surg. Assn. (pres. 1985-86), San Francisco Surg. Soc., L.A. Surg. Soc., Soc. Vascular Surgery, Western Surg. Assn., Internat. Cardiovascular Soc. (pres. 1977), Soc. Internat. Chirurgie, Soc. Thoracic Surgeons, Western Thoracic Surg. Soc. (pres. 1978), Orange County Surg. Soc. (pres. 1984-85), James IV Assn. Surgeons (councillor 1983—), San Francisco Golf Club, Pacific Union Club,

Bohemian Club (San Francisco), Harvard Club (N.Y.C.), Big Canyon Club (Newport Beach, Calif.), Cypress Point Club (Pebble Beach), Pacific Union Club. Home: 7 Deerwood Ln Newport Beach CA 92660-5108

CONNOLLY, JOHN JOSEPH, health care company executive; b. Worcester, Mass., Feb. 4, 1940; s. Nicholas John and Margaret Anne (Flynn) C.; m. Ingrid Schlemminger, Apr. 11, 1964; children: Sean Timothy, Cheryl Lea. BS, Worcester State Coll., 1962; MA., U. Conn., 1963; EdD, Columbia U., 1972; LLD, Mercy Coll., 1980. Pres. Dutchess C.C., Poughkeepsie, N.Y., 1972-81; pres., CEO N.Y. Med. Coll., Valhalla, N.Y., 1981-92, Castle Connolly Med. Ltd., N.Y.C., 1992—. Bd. dirs. Mortons Restaurant Group, Charlie Browns Restaurant, Inc., Gradipore Inc.; chmn. Alpha Gene Inc. Chmn. Dutchess County Indsl. Devel. Agy., 1978—81; hon. chmn. Dutchess/Columbia br. Am. Lung Assn., 1993—; pres. Westchester Hist. Soc., 1985—88; mem. pres.'s adv. coun. United Hosp. Fund; mem. bd. advisors Whitehead Inst. for Biomed. Rsch.; mem. adv. com. Funding First, Inc.; dir. Profl. Exam. Svc., 1998—; bd. dirs. United Way of Dutchess County, pres., 1978; chmn. bd. trustees St. Francis Hosp., Poughkeepsie, 1976—80; trustee, chmn. acad. affairs Com. N.Y. Med. Coll.; trustee Culinary Inst. Am., 1976—2002, chair, 1996—98; trustee Poughkeepsie Area Fund, 1973—78, St. Agnes Hosp, White Plains, 1988—99; bd. dirs. Econ. Devel. Corp. Dutchess County, Westchester County Mental Health Assn., Lupus Found., Am. Lyme Disease Found., 1993—2001, founder, chair, 1994—99. Recipient Disting. Svc. award Poughkeepsie Jaycees, 1974, Marie Y. Martin award Assn. Community Coll. Trustees, 1978; named Man of Yr. Dutchess County Legislature, 1980, One of 100 Outstanding Young Leaders in Higher Edn. Change Mag., 1979. Fellow N.Y. Acad. Medicine; mem. N.Y. Acad. Sci., Assn. Colls. Mid-Hudson Area (pres. 1976-79), Friends of the Nat. Libr. Medicine (dir. 1994-96), Friends of Hudson Valley (chmn. 1990), Westchester County Assn. (bd. dirs. 1991-2001), Phi Delta Kappa. Roman Catholic. Office: Castle Connolly Med Ltd 42 W 24th 2nd Floor New York NY 10010

CONNOLLY, JOHN MATTHEW, philosophy educator, administrator; b. N.Y.C., Sept. 20, 1943; s. John Clement and Alice Agnes (Joiner) C.; m. Marianna P. Kaul, June 28, 1969; children: Fiona, Sabine. BA, Fordham Coll., 1965; MA, Oxford U., 1967; postgrad., Princeton U., 1967-69; PhD, Harvard U., 1971. Instr. philosophy Elms Coll., Chicopee, Mass., 1971-73; asst. prof. Smith Coll., Northampton, Mass., 1973-81, assoc. prof., 1981-88, prof., 1988—, chmn. philosophy dept., 1984-87, sec. of faculty, 1984-87, dir. Jr. Yr. in Germany, 1978-79, dean curriculum and faculty devel., 1992-94, dean of the faculty, 1994-2001, provost, 1998-2001, acting pres., 2001—02. Cons. FernUniversität Hagen, Germany, 1981-82. Author: Correspondence courses Handlungstheorie I, II, 1982, III, 1989; translator/editor: Absicht, 1986, Hermeneutics versus Science?, 1988; contbr. articles to profl. jours. Recipient Open Exhbn. award Brasenose Coll., Oxford, Eng., 1966; Presdl. scholar, 1961-65; Danforth fellow, 1965-71, Humboldt fellow, 1979-82. Mem. Am. Philos. Assn. Democrat. Avocations: music, hiking, reading, racquet sports. Home: 11 O'Neil Rd Haydenville MA 01039-9717 E-mail: jconnolly@smith.edu.

CONNOLLY, JOSEPH FRANCIS, II, educational executive, government consultant; b. Quincy, Mass., Feb. 15, 1944; s. Joseph Francis and Flora Frances C.; m. Donna M. Cameron, May 4, 1968; children: Jennifer S., Joseph F. III. BA magna cum laude, Park Coll., Parkville, Mo., 1971; LLB, Blackstone Sch. Law, Chgo., 1972, JD, 1977; postgrad., U. South Fla., 1977-79, Fla. Inst. Tech., Melbourne, Liberty U., Lynchburg, Va., Am. Mil. U., Manassas, Va.; MEd, Nat. Coll. Edn., 2000; MMA, Coll. of Higher Edn. for, Martial Arts, U.K., 2001; MS, Knightsbridge U., 2002. Cert. EMT, firefighter and law enforcement officer, Fla. Former coord. emergency med. svcs. City of Quincy, 1971-73; former EMT Boston Ambulance Squad, 1973-74; former coord. 14-community emergency med. svcs. program, 1974; formerly safety tng. coord., lead instr. Fire Tng. Acad. Orange County Pub. Schs., Fla., 1979-82; former dir. pub. safety Poinciana, Fla., 1985-86; sr. cons. Resource, Studies, and Devel. Internat., Inc., 1988-91; CEO Connolly, Hudson, Taylor & Assocs., Orlando, Fla., 1988-91; pres. Joseph F. Connolly II, P.A., Fla., 1982-95. Adj. faculty mem. Pikes Peak Community Coll., Valencia Community Coll., Fla. Inst. Tech., Nat. Fire Acad., So. Coll.; tng. counselor emeritus NRA; med. cons. State of Bahrain Def. Force; former mem. Health Planning Coun. Greater Boston; dir. Royal Nat. Lifeboat Instn., Ireland, U.K.; dir. U.S. Jujitsu Fedn. Mem. Orange County subcom. Health Systems Agy. of East Ctrl. Fla.; fire commr. Conway Fire control Dist. of Orange County, 1980-84; former combat lt., staff capt. reserve program Orange County Fire Dept.; com. chmn. Orange County Rep. Exec. Com., 1985-93; former Safety Tng. Coord. Orange County Pub. Schs., Fla., pres. Coun. of Vol. Coords., Orange County, 1987; mem. Rep. Presdl. Task Force, Natl. Rep. Senatorial Commn.; active Boy Scouts Am., 1954—; life mem. Nat. Eagle Scout Assn., ret. lt. col. CAP, 1989; USCG Auxiliary ret., 1999; chmn. bd. trustees Inst. of Mil. Arts, 1999—, Internat. Yudo Fedn., 2000—, U.S. Yudo Fedn., 1998—; col. Fla. Guard, 2003—. Master sgt. Sr. Forces U.S. Army, 1961—96, col. Fla. Nat. Guard, 2003—. Decorated Purple Heart with two oak leaf clusters, 24 other U.S. and fgn. mil. decorations or citations, Knight Sovereign Mil. Order St. John of Jerusalem (Austria); recipient Gill Robb Wilson award CAP, Aerospace Edn. Achievement award, 1987, Resolution of Tribute award Orange County Sch. Bd., 1989, Presdl. Sports award for martial arts, 1999, Pres.'s Leadership award and gold medal U.S. Ju-Jitsu Fedn., 2003; named Vietnam Vet. of the Yr., Vietnam Vets. Ctrl. Fla., Inc., 1988; named to Order Knights Templar, 1985; inducted into state, nat. and internat. martial art halls of fame. Fellow Soc. Martial Arts U.K. (founder); mem. Aircraft Owners and Pilots Assn., Boat/US, Sons of the Union Vets. of the Civil War, Ducks Unltd., VFW (life), DAV (life), Nat. Fire Acad. Alumni Assn. (pres. 1984-92), Internat. Assn. Counselors and Therapists, Nat. Eagle Scout Assn. (life), Legion of Frontiersmen of the British Commonwealth, Third Order St. Francis, Mil. Order of Purple Heart, Mensa, Masons, U.S. Judo Assn. (life, 8th degree black belt in jujitsu, 9th degree black belt in judo, inducted into World Martial Arts Hall of Fame, 1996), Asahi Internat. Dojo (pres.), Midori Yama Budokai, U.S. Yudo Assn. (founder 1998), Internat. Yudo Fedn. (founder 2000). Anglican Catholic. Office: PO Box 620395 Orlando FL 32862-0395

CONNOLLY, JUDITH, financial consultant; b. N.Y.C., Nov. 29, 1939; d. Alfred and Gladys Newman; m. Arthur Kessler (div. Apr. 1971); children: Scott, Todd; m. Gerald Connolly, May 25, 1971 (dec. Nov. 1982). BS, Cornell U., 1964. Tchr. N.Y.C. Pub. Schs., 1964-66, Linden Hill Sch., Hawthorne, N.Y., 1966-69, Lynbrook Pub. Schs., N.Y.C., 1969-79; v.p., sr. fin. cons. Merrill Lynch, N.Y.C., 1979—. Adv. mem. Senator Roy Goodman, N.Y. Avocations: reading, travelling. Office: Merrill Lynch 717 Fifth Ave 8th Fl New York NY 10022 E-mail: Judith_Connolly@ml.com.

CONNOLLY, K. THOMAS, lawyer; b. Spokane, Wash., Jan. 23, 1940; s. Lawrence Francis and Kathleen Dorothea (Hallahan) C.; m. Laurie Samuel, June 24, 1967; children: Kevin, Megan, Amy, Matthew. BBA, Gonzaga U., Spokane, Wash., 1962; JD, Gonzaga U., 1966; LLM in Taxation, NYU, 1972. Bar: Wash. 1966, U.S. Ct. Mil. Appeals 1967, U.S. Tax Ct. 1983. Assoc. Witherspoon, Kelley, Davenport & Toole, Spokane, 1972-77, ptnr./prin., 1977—. Assoc. prof. law Gonzaga Sch. Law, 1973-77. Bd. overseers Gonzaga Prep. Sch., Spokane, 1988-89; trustee Spokane Guild Sch. Neuromuscular Ctr., 1975-78, Wash. State U. Found. Bd., 1992-97, Whitman Coll. Planned Giving Coun., 1994-2001, Holy Family Adult Day Care Bd., 2001—. Capt. U.S. Army, 1966-70. Recipient Wall St. Jur. award, 1962; decorated Bronze Star medal. Mem. Wash. State Bar Assn. (founder, chmn. health law sect. 1989-92, health law coun. 1989-94, pres. state tax sect. 1987-88, mem. tax coun. 1984—), ABA (chmn. health care subcom. 1990-94). Republican. Avocations: tennis, astronomy. Office: Witherspoon Kelley Davenport & Toole 1100 US Bank Bldg Spokane WA 99201 E-mail: ktc@wkdtlaw.com.

CONNOLLY, KELLY ANN, secondary school educator; b. West Islip, N.Y., May 27, 1977; d. Stephen Karl and Sharon Bridget Connolly; m. Daniel A. Smith, Nov. 28, 2003. BA in English, SUNY, Stonybrook, 1994—97; MA in English, Hofstra U, 2002—. Cert. secondary edn.,english,provisional. Tchr., writer Dawnwood Elem. Sch., Centereach, NY, 1997; asst. media buyer Grey Direct, N.Y.C., 1997—98; media planner Goote, Cone & Belding, N.Y.C., 1998—2001; internal media cons. Cablevision Sys., Inc., Bethpage, NY, 2001—02; tchr. english West Babylon (N.Y.)H.S., 2002—. Recipient Pres. Scholar, SUNY Stonybrook, 1994, Honors Coll. Scholar, 1994. Mem.: N.Y. State United Tchrs., Nat. Council of Tchrs. of English, Modern Lang. Assn. (assoc.). Avocation: fitness. Home: 65 Jean Rd West Islip NY 11795 Office: West Babylon High School 500 Great East Neck Rd West Babylon NY 11704

CONNOLLY, KEVIN JUDE, lawyer; b. NYC, May 25, 1954; s. John William and Beatrice Joan (Fallon) C.; m. Audrey Mason, May 25, 1995; children: Shea Alexander, Ciaran Jude. BA cum laude, Fordham Coll., 1976; JD, Fordham U., 1985. Bar: NY 1990. Assoc. Stroock & Stroock & Lavan, NYC, 1985-89; pres. Imagetronics, Inc., Mineola, NY, 1989-92; counsel Schreiber, Simmons, MacKnight & Tweedy, NYC, 1992-94, Eaton & Van Winkle, NYC, 1994-97; assoc. Robinson, Silverman, Pearce, Aronsohn & Berman LLP, NYC, 1998—2001; ptnr. Duval & Stachenfeld LLP, NYC, 2001—. Vis. lectr. Sch. Visual Arts, NYC, 1996—2000; dir. Internet Soc., NYC chpt., 1997—2000; outside counsel Internet Policy Adv. Body, Geneva, 1997—99, Internet Coun. Registrars, Geneva, Hatewatch, Inc., 1998—2002; faculty mem. Practising Law Inst., 2003—. Author: Law of Internet Security and Privacy, 2003; contbr. Avocations: antiques, paintball. Home: 205 Blackheath Rd Lido Beach NY 11561-4838 Office: Duval & Stachenfeld LLP 300 E 42nd St New York NY 10017 Business E-Mail: kconnolly@dsllp.com.

CONNOLLY, THOMAS EDWARD, judge; b. Boston, Nov. 7, 1942; s. Thomas Francis and Catherine Elizabeth (Skehill) C. AB, St. John's Coll., Brighton, Mass., 1964; JD, Boston Coll., 1969. Bar: Mass. 1969. Assoc. Schneider & Reilly, Boston, 1969-73; ptnr. Schneider, Reilly, Zabin, Connolly & Costello, P.C., Boston, 1973-85, Connolly Leavis & Rest, Boston, 1986-90; judge Mass. Superior Ct., Boston, 1990—. Instr. law Northeastern Law Sch., Boston, 1975—76. Mem. governing coun. Boston Coll. Law Sch. Alumni Coun., 1980—82, 2001—03. Fellow Am. Coll. Trial Lawyers; mem. ABA (vice chmn. products liability sect. 1978-80), Trial Lawyers Assn. Am. (nat. gov. 1977-80), Mass. Acad. Trial Lawyers (gov. 1976-90), Univ. Club (Boston). Roman Catholic. Home: 253 Marlborough St # 4 Boston MA 02116-1731 Office: The Superior Ct Boston MA 02109

CONNOLLY, VIOLETTE M. small business owner; b. N.Y.C., Nov. 25, 1918; d. Gysbert Martens and Marie Therese dePont; m. Joseph Vincent Connolly Jr., Feb. 27, 1937 (dec.). BA, Hunter Coll., 1940; MS, Columbia U., 1941. Accredited Pub. Rels. Soc. Am. Analyst The Payne Fund, N.Y.C., 1941-53; ptnr. Elser & Assocs., N.Y.C., 1954-56, The J.V. Connolly Co., N.Y.C., 1957-64; cons. on pub. rels., radio and TV Assn. of the Jr. Leagues of Am., N.Y.C., 1964-72; asst. dir. N.Y. Assn. for Brain Injured Children, N.Y.C., 1973-74; circulation mgr. Plants and Gardens Bklyn. Botanic Garden, N.Y.C., 1974-82; adminstr. Nat. Broadcasting Co., N.Y.C., 1983-86; owner, mgr. The White House, Block Island, R.I., 1986—; clk. Town of New Shoreham, Block Island, 1986—. Bd. mem., publicist The Village Art Ctr., N.Y.C., 1944-54; pres. Washington Sq. Bus. and Profl. Women's Club, N.Y.C., 1953-55; founder, chair House and Garden Tours Com., Block Island Hist. Soc., 1971-96; pres. Block Island Gardeners, 1986-97. Capt. First Assembly Dist., Rep. Club, N.Y.C., 1945-57; mem. Bishop's com. St. Ann's Ch., 1995—. Republican. Avocations: oriental gardens, antique collecting, traveling. Home: The White House PO Box 447 Block Island RI 02807-0447

CONNOLLY, WILLIAM M. state supreme court justice; Undergrad., Creighton U., 1956—59, JD, 1963. Dep. atty. Adams County, 1964—66, atty., 1967—72; pvt. law practice Hastings, 1972—91; former judge Nebr. Ct. of Appeals, Lincoln, 1992—94; assoc. justice Nebr. Supreme Ct., Lincoln, justice, 1994—. Office: Nebr Supreme Ct PO Box 98910 2413 State Capitol Bldg Lincoln NE 68509 Office Fax: 402-471-3480.*

CONNOR, BERNADETTE YVONNE, retired writer; d. Richard Oscar Smith and Inez Patterson; m. Edsel Louis Connor, Jan. 16, 1971 (div. Mar. 23, 1983); children: Edsel Louis, Eros Lamaas, Erica Latice. Author: (novels) Damaged!, The Parcel Express Murders. Achievements include first psychological thriller written and published by an African American in the fiction genre. Office: Bee-Con Books Po Box 27708 Philadelphia PA 19118 Home Fax: 215-247-0680; Office Fax: 215-247-0680. Personal E-mail: byconnor@aol.com. E-mail: beeconbooks@aol.com.

CONNOR, CHRISTOPHER M. textiles executive; Grad., Ohio State U. Dir. advt. Sherwin-Williams' Paint Stores Group, 1983, pres., gen. mgr. western divsn., sr. v.p. mktg. group, pres., gen. mgr. diversified brands divsn., pres., 1997, vice chmn., CEO, 1999, also bd. dirs. Office: Sherwin-Williams Co 101 Prospect Ave NW Cleveland OH 44115-1075

CONNOR, DANIEL F. child and adolescent psychiatrist, researcher; b. Chgo., Feb. 9, 1953; s. Daniel and Joyce Rebecca (O'Brien) Connor; m. Sara N.B. Barber, Oct. 4, 1981; children: Charlotte Naismith, David Anderson. BA, Columbia U., 1976; MD, Northwestern U. Med. Sch., Chgo., 1982. Asst. prof. psychiatry U. Mass. Med. Sch., Worcester, 1987—97, assoc. prof. psychiatry, 1997—, co-dir. rsch. in child and adolescent psychiatry, 2000—; dir. ambulatory child and adolescent psychiatry U. Mass. Meml. Health Care, 2000—. Dir. pediat. psychopharmacology U. of Mass., Meml. Health Care, Worcester, 1994—. Author: (textbook) Aggression & Antisocial Behavior in Children and Adolescents: Rsch. and Treatment, New York: Guilford Press (2002). Rsch. in pediatric psychopharmacology and aggression, Pharm. Industry, 2002. Mem.: Am. Acad. of Child and Adolescent Psychiatry.

CONNOR, FRANCES PARTRIDGE, retired education educator; b. Bklyn., May 4, 1919; d. Horace K. and Sybil V. (Rafters) P.; m. Leo E. Connor, June 7, 1952. BA, St. Joseph's Coll., 1940; MA, Columbia U., 1948, EdD, 1953; LLD (hon.), Coll. New Rochelle, 1976. Cert. history, social studies tchr., spl. edn. tchr., N.Y. Tchr. history/econs. Haverstraw (N.Y.) Schs., 1940-42; tchr. N.Y. State Rehab. Hosp., West Haverstraw, 1942-49; lectr. Hunter Coll., CCNY, N.Y.C., 1946-54; tchr. spl. edn. Ramapo Ctrl. Schs., Suffern, N.Y., 1949-53; coord. spl. edn. U. Ga., Athens, summers 1952-53; rsch. assoc. U.S. Office of Edn., Washington, 1954-58; survey assoc. Tchrs. Coll., Columbia U., N.Y.C., 1953-54, prof., dir. Rsch. and Demonstration Ctr./Inst. for LD, 1955-87, dept. chair, 1962-85, Richard March Hoe prof. emeritus, 1989—. Mem. profl. adv. bd. Willowbrook Consent Decree, N.Y. State Dept. of Mental Retardation/Devel. Disabilities, Albany, 1977—; mem. bd. dirs. Family Resource Assocs., Shrewsbury, N.J. Author: Education of Homebound and Hospitalized Children, 1964, Experimental Curriculum for Young Mentally Retard Children, 1964; editor: Critical Issues for Low Incidence Populations, 1987. Mem. bd. trustees Mt. Saint Mary Coll., Newburgh, N.Y., 1970—, Human Resources Schs., Albertson, N.Y., 1984—; mem. Pres.'s Com. on Employment of Handicapped, Washington, 1972-89; del., mem. steering com. White House Conf. on the Handicapped, Washington, 1975-78; mem. Coalition of Disabled Women and Their Advocates, Ocean County, N.J., 1990—. Recipient Behavioral Sci. award Nat. Hemophilia Found., 1968, Pioneer in Spl. Edn. award Hofstra U., 1986. Fellow Am. Assn. on Mental Retardation; mem. Coun. for Exceptional Children (pres. 1964-65, Wallin award 1982, Outstanding Contbr. award 1992, R.P. MacKie award 1998), Com. Rehab. Internat. Roman Catholic. Avocations: choral/choir singing, swimming, writing. Home: 23343 Blue Water Cir Apt B113 Boca Raton FL 33433-7074 also: 200 4th Ave Spring Lake NJ 07762 E-mail: franleo@att.net.

CONNOR, GEOFFREY WARREN, wine merchant, wine writer; b. Balt., Oct. 23, 1946; s. Arthur Joseph and Sara Eugenia (Brown) C. BS, Rutgers U., 1968. Asst. mgr. Medco Fine Jewelry, East Brunswick, N.J., 1968-69; operating rm. orderly Robert Wood Johnson Univ. Hosp., New Brunswick, 1969-71; mgr. camera dept. Woolco, Union, N.J., 1971; mgr. Bottle King Liquors, Union and Hackensack, N.J., 1971-76; mgr. wine dept. Field's Pharmacy, Pikesville, Md., 1976-78; wine mgr. Wells Discount Liquors, Balt., 1978-80; wine salesman The Kronheim Co., Balt., 1980; pres. Calvert Discount Liquors, Hunt Valley, Md., 1981-93, 2002—, wine cons., 1994—2002, Total Beverage, Alexandria, Va., 1993-94. Author newspaper column From the Wine Cellar, 1989, Notes From the Wine Cellar, 1989-93, 97—. Advisor Am. Heart Assn. Fine Wine Auction, Balt., 1989—. Mem. Am. Wine Soc., Soc. Wine Educators. Libertarian. Deist. Avocations: meteorology, poetry, railroads, classical and popular music. Home: 14 Warren Lodge Ct Apt A Cockeysville MD 21030-2574 Office: Calvert Discount Liquors 10128 York Rd Cockeysville Hunt Valley MD 21030-3306 E-mail: winemang1@comcast.net.

CONNOR, JAMES RICHARD, retired foundation administrator; b. Indpls., Oct. 31, 1928; s. Frank Elliott and Edna (Felt) C.; m. Zoe Ezopov, July 7, 1954; children: Janet K., Paul A. BA with highest distinction, U. Iowa, 1951; MS, U. Wis., 1954, PhD, 1961. Asst. prof. history Washington and Lee U., 1956-57, Va. Mil. Inst., 1958-61; asst. dir. Salzburg Seminar in Am. Studies, 1961-62; joint staff mem. Wis. Coordinating Com. Higher Edn., 1962-63; dir. Inst. Analysis; asst. prof. history U. Va., 1963-66; assoc. prof. history, assoc. provost No. Ill. U., 1966-69; provost, acad. v.p., prof. history Western Ill. U., 1969-74; chancellor, prof. history U. Wis., Whitewater, 1974-91, chancellor, prof. emeritus, 1991. Exec. dir. James S. Kemper Found., Long Grove, Ill., 1991-99; assoc. dir. Va. Higher Edn. Study Com., 1964-65; intern acad. adminstrn. Am. Coun. Edn., Stanford U., 1965-66; staff dir. Study of Governance of Acad. Med. Ctr., Josiah Macy Jr. Found., 1968-70; mem. commn. on higher edn. North Ctrl. Assn. 1970-75, 79-84, cons.-examiner, 1972-91; chair adv. com. on alcohol and drug use U. Wis. System, 1984-85; mem. nat. adv. com. Woodrow Wilson Nat. Fellowship Found., 1990-96, trustee, 1996—; dir. Fairhaven Retirement Corp., 1994—. Author: Studies in Higher Education, 1965; contbr., Ency. Brit. Served with AUS, 1946-47, 51-53. Woodrow Wilson fellow, 1953-54; So. fellow, 1957-58 Mem. AAUP, Orgn. Am. Historians, Blue Key, Golden Key, Order of Omega, Phi Beta Kappa, Phi Eta Sigma, Phi Kappa Phi, Phi Delta Kappa, Beta Gamma Sigma, Phi Alpha Theta, Delta Sigma Pi. Home: N7447 Linden Dr Whitewater WI 53190-4357 E-mail: j31z29connor@webtv.net.

CONNOR, JOAN CAROL, literature educator; b. Holyoke, Mass., Jan. 21, 1954; d. Walker Frances Connor, Mary (Lyon) Connor; 1 child, Nils Walker Wessell. BA cum laude, Mt. Holyoke Coll., 1976; MA, Middlebury Coll., 1983; MFA, Vt. Coll., 1995. Asst. prof. Ohio U., Athens, 1995—2000, assoc. prof., 2000—. Author: We Who LIve Apart, 2001, Here On Old Route 7, 1997, History Lessons, 2002. Recipient Short Story award, Columbus Dispatch, 2001, Writer award, Ohio Writer, 1996, John Gilgun award, 2002. Mem.: New Eng. Writers Assn. (bd. dirs.), Young Writers Inst., AWP (Short Fiction award 2002). Home: 328 Carroll Rd Athens OH 45701 Office: Ohio Univ English Dept 327 Ellis Athens OH 45701

CONNOR, JOHN MURRAY, agricultural economics educator; b. Attleboro, Mass., July 7, 1943; s. John Murray Sr. and Victoria Rose (Moro) C.; m. Ulla Maija Niemelä, Apr. 3, 1972; 1 child, Timo. BA cum laude, Boston Coll., 1965; MA, U. Fla., 1974; MS, U. Wis., 1974, PhD, 1976. Vol. U.S. Peace Corps, Nigeria, Uganda, 1966-68; agrl. economist Econ. Rsch. Svc. USDA, Madison, 1976-79, head food mfg. rsch. Washington, 1979-83; assoc. prof. agrl. econs. Purdue U., West Lafayette, Ind., 1983-89, prof., 1989—, asst. dept. head, 1985-88. Adj. prof. Cath. U. Sacred Heart, Piacenza, Italy, 1991—; vis. prof. Åbo (Finland) Akademi U., 1994; cons. subcom. on multinats. U.S. Senate, Washington, 1974-76, select com. on nutrition, 1977-78, UN Ctr. on Transnats., 1981-82, U.S. Dept. Justice, 1999, Nat. Assn. Attys. Gen., 2000-03; chair Orgn. and Performance World Food Systems, 1988-93. Author: Market Power of Multinationals, 1977, Food Processing: An Industrial Powerhouse in Transition, 1988, 2d edit., 1997, Global Price Fixing, 2001; (with others) Food Manufacturing Industries, 1985; contbr. articles to profl. jours., chpts. to books. Grantee US Office Tech. Assessment, 1984-85, Inst. Food Technologists, 1986-88, 94-95, Ind. Dept. Commerce, 1987-91, Econ. Rsch. Svc., USDA, 1988-89, Coop. State Rsch. Svc., USDA, 1989—; recipient Antitrust Writing award Jerry S. Cohen Meml. Trust, 2003. Mem. AAUP (pres. Purdue U. chpt. 1988-90, exec. bd. ind. conf. 1990-94, nat. coun. 1991-92), Am. Agrl. Econs. Assn. (Policy award 1980, Quality of Comm. award 1985, 2002, Disting. Extension Program award 1993), Indsl. Orgn. Soc., Am. Econs. Assn., ACLU. Home: 4355 Creekside Pass Zionsville IN 46077-9292 Office: Purdue U Dept Agrl Econs West Lafayette IN 47907-1445

CONNOR, JOSEPH E. former international organization official; b. N.Y.C., Aug. 23, 1931; s. Joseph E. Connor; m. Cornelia B. Camarata, Apr. 17, 1958 (dec. Oct. 11, 1983); children: Anthony, Cornelia, David; m. Sally Howard Johnson, Dec. 27, 1992. AB summa cum laude, U. Pitts.; MS in Bus., Columbia U.; DHL (honoris causa), Georgetown U., 1989. Joined Price Waterhouse & Co., N.Y.C., 1956, ptnr., 1967-92, ptnr. in charge So. Calif., 1973-76, mng. ptnr. Western region, 1976-78, chmn. policy bd. U.S., 1978-88, chmn. World Firm, 1988-92, ret., 1992. Disting. prof. bus. Georgetown U., 1992-94; under-sec. gen. UN, N.Y.C., 1994—2002. Cons. fgn. direct investment program U.S. Dept. Commerce; project adv. rsch. study AICPA; lectr. in field.; mem. adv. coun. Columbia U. Grad. Sch. Bus.; bd. visitors U. Pitts. Grad. Sch. Bus., Georgetown U. Sch. Bus.; chmn. U.S. Coun. for Internat. Bus., 1987—; mem. Pres.'s Mgmt. Adv. Coun., Pres.'s Pvt. Sector Survey on Cost Control Contbr. articles to profl. lit. Trustee YMCA Greater N.Y.; bd. overseers Meml. Sloan Kettering Cancer Inst.; bd. dirs. Georgetown U., 1982-92; mem. coun. Brookings Instn. Served to 1st lt. U.S. Army, 1954-56. Mem. N.Y. State Soc. CPAs (chmn. internat. ops. com., mem. acctg. and auditing com., real estate acctg. com.), Calif. Soc. CPAs (legis. com.), Internat. C. of C. (exec. bd. 1989-94, pres. 1990-92), Melt. Club (Washington), Links Club, Univ. Club.

CONNOR, JOSEPH PATRICK, III, lawyer; b. Phila., Apr. 15, 1953; s. Joseph Patrick Jr. and Wanda Delores (Filipkowski) C.; m. Mary Margaret Kazanicka, Aug. 13, 1977; children: Cathleen Marie, Christopher Joseph, Christine Anne. BA in Polit. Sci., Villanova U., 1974; JD, St. Mary's U., San Antonio, 1974. Bar: Pa. 1977, U.S. Dist. Ct. (ea. dist.) Pa. 1977, U.S. Dist. Ct. (mid. dist.) Pa. 1997, U.S. Ct. Appeals (3d cir.) 1977, U.S Supreme Ct. 1982. Assoc. ptnr. Gibbons, Buckley, Smith, Palmer & Proud, Media, Pa., 1977-82; pres. Connor & Weber, P.C., Phila., Paoli, 1982—. Mem. ABA (tort & litigation sects.), Pa. Bar Assn., Pa. Def. Inst., Def. Research Inst., Pa. Trial Lawyers Assn., Chester County Bar Assn. Clubs: Overbrook County (Bryn Mawr). Republican. Roman Catholic. Avocations: flying, golf, swimming, traveling. Office: Connor & Weber PC 2401 Pennsylvania Ave Philadelphia PA 19130-3010 Address: 171 W Lancaster Ave Paoli PA 19301

CONNOR, JOSEPH ROBERT, editor; b. N.Y.C., Jan. 31, 1927; s. Joseph M. and Ethel May (Ball) Connor; m. Marie Louise Zolezzi, Sept. 6, 1952; children: Jeanne Marie, Robert Brian, Ellen Louise. BA, Hunter Coll., 1951. Copy editor sports desk N.Y. Mirror, N.Y.C., 1950-52; mng. editor Mechanix Illustrated Mag. div. Fawcett Publs., N.Y.C., 1953-70; editor in chief CBS Publs., N.Y.C., spl. interest publs., 1970-72; editor in chief Motor Mag. div. Hearst Corp., N.Y.C., 1972-77; editor Construction Contracting, 1978-79; editor in chief Graduating Engr. McGraw-Hill, Inc., 1979-81, 88-90; editor Bus. Week New Product Devel., 1981—, Bus. Week Almanac, 1981—; editor in chief Bus. Week Careers, 1982-87; editor-in-chief Graduating Engr., 1988-90; exec. editor Graduating Engr. Peterson's-Cog Publs., 1990-91; freelance writer, editorial cons., 1991—; editor MOTORScoop Mag., GRG Publs. Inc., 1995-96. Author: A Job With a Future in Automotive Mechanics, 1969; author: (with Heinz Ulrich) The National Job-Finding Guide, 1981; author: Cracking the Over-50 Job Market, 1992, Living with Your Bulldog, 2001; contbr. articles to popular mags. With AUS, 1945—46. Mem.: Am. Soc. Mag. Editors, Internat. Motor Press Assn. (pres. 1966—67). Home: 8 Woodvale Ln Huntington NY 11743-2324 E-mail: scoop09@aol.com.

CONNOR, LAURENCE DAVIS, lawyer, director; b. Columbus, Ohio, May 14, 1938; s. Laurence R. and Gladys C. (Davis) C.; m. Clare Elizabeth Hartwick, Aug. 8, 1964; children: Jeffrey H., Lynne D. Scoville. BA, Miami U., Oxford, Ohio, 1960; JD, U. Mich., 1965. Bar: Mich. 1966, U.S. Dist. Ct. (ea. dist.) Mich. 1966, U.S. Ct. Appeals (6th cir.) 1973, U.S. Supreme Ct. 1979. Assoc. Dykema Gossett, Detroit, 1965-73, ptnr., 1973—2002, mem. exec. com., 1984-90, dir. litigation sect., 1987-91. Mem. coun. sect. on alternative dispute resolution State Bar of Mich., 1992—, chairperson, 1996-97; pres. Vis. Nurse Assn. Met. Detroit, 1980-81, Vist. Nurse Corp., Detroit, 1986-88; asst. clin. prof. law U. Mich., 2002-. Mem. ABA, Am. Judicature Soc., Country Club Detroit, Detroit Athletic Club, Yondotega Club. Office: Dykema Gossett 400 Renaissance Ctr Ste 3500 Detroit MI 48243-1602 E-mail: lconnor@dykema.com.

CONNOR, LEO EDWARD, special education administrator; b. Phila., Sept. 5, 1922; s. Leo A. and Margaret (McMahon) C.; m. Frances Partridge, June 7, 1952. BA, LaSalle U., 1945; MA, U. Pitts., 1949; EdD, Columbia U., 1955. Cert. tchr. spl. edn., adminstr., audiologist. Tchr. Pitts. and Phila. schs., 1945-49; elem. prin., dir. elem. edn. Clarkstown Cen. Sch. Dist., New City, N.Y., 1950-57; ednl. dir. Lexington Sch. for the Deaf, N.Y.C., 1957-68, exec. dir., 1968-85, Lexington Ctr. for Hearing Impaired, N.Y.C., 1985-88. Chmn. N.Y.

Schs. for Deaf and Blind, Albany, N.Y., 1968-83, Coun. on Edn. of Deaf, Washington, 1976-78, Nat. Adv. Com. on Media for Handicapped, Washington, 1978-80; adj. prof. edn. Columbia U., N.Y.C.; instr. NYU, N.Y.C. Author: Administration of Special Education, 1960, History of Research, 1978, History of the Lexington School for the Deaf, 1988, Review of Oral Education, 1980; editor: Speech for the Deaf Child, 1971, Lexington Education Series, 1965-80; contbr. articles to profl. jours. Chmn. Bd. Zoning Adjustment, Borough of Spring Lake, N.J., 1989-96, chmn. lake com., 1990-95; trustee New Rochelle (N.Y.) Coll. Recipient annual award N.Y. Coun. Exceptional Children, Albany, 1988. Fellow Am. Speech/Hearing/Lang. Assn. (clin. cert. competency); mem. Alexander Graham Bell Assn. (Honors of the Assn. award 1986, pres. 1970-72), Coun. for Exceptional Children (pres. 1968-69). Roman Catholic. Home: 23343 Blue Water Cir Boca Raton FL 33433-7035 E-mail: franleo@att.net.

CONNOR, NANCY L. foundation executive; b. Chgo., Sept. 7, 1960; d. Edward Joseph and Bernadette Marie Cider; m. Martin David Connor, June 16, 1984 (div. Nov. 1987). BS, Towson State U., 1982. Sys. adminstr. Ballistics Rsch. Lab., Aberdeen, Md., 1982-84; programmer, documentation specialist Symbolics, Inc., Boston, 1984-86; pres., chmn. FTP Software, Inc., Boston, 1986-93; pres. Ringing Rocks Found., Phila., 1995—. *Previously a for profit executive, Ms. Connor founded and runs a non-profit foundation that specializes in publishing new research on indigenous healing methods. RRF also sponsors local events in communities as opportunities arise and makes small grants available on a yearly basis to other organizations working on health and cultural preservation projects in indigenous communities.* Co-chmn. discretionary fund Women's Way, Phila., 1995-2001. Mem. Internat. Soc. Study Subtle Energy and Energy Mgmt., Inst. Noetic Scis., James Smithson Soc. of Smithsonian Instn. Avocations: gardening, pottery, gliding. Office: Ringing Rocks Found PO Box 22656 Philadelphia PA 19110-2656

CONNOR, TERENCE GREGORY, lawyer; b. Chelsea, Mass., Dec. 28, 1942; s. Joseph Gerard Sr. and Rosalie Cecilia (Ryan) C.; m. Julie Kaye Berry, Dec. 18, 1971; children: Cormac, Kristin, Etain, Brendan. AB, Georgetown U., 1964; LLB, Seton Hall U., 1967; LLM, Georgetown U., 1975. Bar: D.C. 1968, U.S. Supreme Ct. 1976, Fla. 1980. Trial atty. U.S. Dept. Justice, Washington, 1973-76; labor counsel Nat. Airlines Inc., Miami, Fla., 1976-79; practicing atty. Morgan, Lewis & Bockius, Miami, 1979-96, mng. ptnr., 1996—2002. Mem. firm wide governing bd., 1996-2000. Chmn. Miami: Dade citizen com. for Observance Bicentennial of U.S. Constitution, 1986. Served to capt. JAG, USAF, 1968-73. Mem. Fla. Bar Assn. (chair labor and employment law sect. 1994-95, mem. exec. coun. 1986 93), Miami C. of C. (co-chair pers. and Labor mgmt. com. 1993-94) Home: 1517 San Rafael Ave Miami FL 33134-6241 Office: Morgan Lewis & Bockius Wachovia Fin Ctr 200 S Biscayne Blvd Ste 5300 Miami FL 33131-2333

CONNOR, WALTER DOWNING, political scientist, educator, researcher; b. Bay Shore, NY, Apr. 20, 1942; s. Edward Joseph and Mary Margaret (Downing) Connor; m. Eileen Mary Donohue, Oct. 22, 1966; children: Christine Marie, Elizabeth Catherine. AB, Holy Cross Coll., Worcester MA, 1963; MA, Princeton U., 1966, PhD, 1969. Asst. prof., assoc. chair dept. of sociology U. Mich., Ann Arbor, 1968—76; dir. Soviet and East European studies Fgn. Svc. Inst., US Dept. of State, Washington, 1976—84; prof. polit. sci., sociology and internat. rels. Boston U., 1983—, chair, dept. of polit. sci., 1987—92. Cons. fgn. area fellowship program Ford Found., 1969—71; cons. Internat. Rsch. Exchanges Bd., 1973—76, mem., program com., 1980—89; dep. coord. nat. targets project Nat. Coun. Fgn. Lang. Internat. Studies, 1980—81; vis. prof. sociology U. Va., Charlottesville, 1981—84; profl. lectr. govt. Georgetown U., Washington, 1982; vis. prof. polit. sci. Columbia U., NYC, 1989. Author: Deviance in Soviet Soc.: Crime, Delinquency and Alcoholism, 1972; co-author: Pub. Opinion in European Socialist Systems, 1977; author: Socialism, Politics and Equality: Hierarchy and Change in Ea. Europe and the USSR, 1979; mem. editl. bd.: Studies Comparative Communism, 1980—89, Ea. European Politics Socs., 1986—88; mem. editl. bd. Am. Sociol. Rvw., 1987—90; author: Socialism's Dilemmas: State and Soc. in the Soviet Bloc, 1988, The Accidental Proletariat: Workers, Politics and Crisis in Gorbachev's Russia, 1991; co-editor: Soviet Social Problems, 1991; contbr. articles to profl. jours.; co-editor: The Polish Rd. from Socialism, 1992; author: Tattered Banners: Labor, Conflict and Corporatism in Post-Communist Russia, 1996. Fellow Davis Ctr. Russian and Eurasian Studies, Harvard U., 1984—, Sr. fellow, Sociology, U. Pa., 1981—84, John Simon Guggenheim Found., 1986—87; grantee, Am. Coun. Learned Socs., 1973, 1975—76, Nat. Coun. Soviet and East European Rsch., 1986—87, 1992—93. Mem.: Boston World Affairs Coun. (bd. dirs. 1990—96), Am. Assn. Advancement Slavic Studies (treas., bd. dir. 2001—). Republican. Roman Catholic. Home: 26 Downing Rd Brookline MA 02445-2153 Office: Boston Univ Dept of Political Science 232 Bay State Rd Boston MA 02215 E-mail: wdconnor@bu.edu.

CONNOR, WILDA, government health agency administrator; b. Pleasantville, N.J., Apr. 9, 1947; d. Herman Smith and Rubina (Miraglilo) Cooney; m. James J. Connor Jr., Nov. 5, 1966; 1 child, James J. III. BSBA cum laude, Rowan U., 1985; MS, U. Pa., 1995. Employee services coord. Turning Point Drug Outpatient Program, Collingswood, NJ, 1976-78; mgmt. specialist Camden County Ctr. Addictive Diseases, Lakeland, NJ, 1978-87; adminstr. Family Practice Ctrs. Camden (N.J.) County Health Dept., 1988—; fiscal analyst Camden County Dept. Health & Human Svcs., Lakeland, NJ, 1995—2002; COO Med. One, Inc., Mays Landing, NJ, 2002—. Com. fund raiser Camden County Dem. Congl. Campaign, Stratford, N.J., 1986; mem. Solid Waste Adv. Coun., Camden County; mem. Coastal Resources Adv. Commn. Dept. Environ. Protection. Mem. N.J. Assn. Alcoholism Counselors, N.J. Substance Abuse Cert. Bd. (cert. 1987, 89 MSA), LWV, Solid Waste Adv. Council. Roman Catholic. Avocations: jogging, aerobics, skiing, travel. Home: 228 Vasey Ave Lindenwold NJ 08021-2249 Office: Medical One Inc 4622 Black Horse Pike Mays Landing NJ 08330 E-mail: wconnor@docisp.com.

CONNOR, WILLIAM ELLIOTT, physician, educator; b. Pitts., Sept. 14, 1921; s. Frank E. and Edna S. (Felt) C.; m. Sonja Lee Newcomer, Sept. 19, 1969; children: Rodney William, Catherine Susan, James Elliott, Christopher French, Peter Malcolm. BA, U. Iowa, 1942, MD, 1950. Diplomate Am. Bd. Internal Medicine, Am. Bd. Nutrition. Intern USPHS Hosp., San Francisco, 1950-51; resident in internal medicine San Joaquin Gen. Hosp., Stockton, Calif., 1951-52; practice medicine specializing in internal medicine Chico, Calif., 1952-54; resident in internal medicine VA Hosp., Iowa City, 1954-56; cons., 1967-75; mem. faculty U. Iowa Coll. Medicine, 1956-75, prof. internal medicine, 1967-75; acting dir., then dir. Clin. Research Center, 1967-75, dir. lipid-atherosclerosis sect., cardiovascular div., 1974-75. Vis. prof. Basic Sci. Med. Inst., Karachi, Pakistan, Ind. U., 1961-62, Baker Med. Rsch. Inst., Melbourne, Australia, 1982; vis. fellow clin. sci. Australian Nat. U., Canberra, 1970; prof. cardiology and metabolism-nutrition, dept. medicine, 1975-79, head sect. clin. nutrition, 1979-90, acting head, head div. endocrinology, metabolism and nutrition, 1984-90, prof. sect. clin. nutrition, 1990—, dir. lipid-atherosclerosis lab., assoc. dir. Clin. Rsch. Ctr., Oreg. Health Scis. U. Portland, 1975-94; chmn. heart and lung program project com. Contbr. numerous articles to med. jours.; editor Jour. Lab. and Clin. Medicine, 1970-73; mem. editorial bds., reviewer profl. jours. Mem. Johnson County (Iowa) Cen. Dem. Com., 1965-69; mem. nat. council Fellowship Reconciliation; nat., North Central and Pacific Northwest bds. Am. Friends Service Com. Served with AUS, 1943-46. Research fellow Am. Heart Assn., 1956-58; ACP traveling fellow Sir William Dunn Sch. Pathology, Oxford, Eng., 1960; recipient Career Devel. Research award Nat. Heart Inst., 1962-73, Discovery award Med. Research Found. Oreg. Mem. AAAS, ACP, AMA, AAUP (pres. U. Iowa chpt. 1968-69, pres. Oreg. Health Sci. U. chpt. 1978-79), Am. Diabetes Assn. (vice chmn. food and nutrition com. 1972-74), Am. Dietitic Assn. (hon.), Am. Fedn. Clin. Rsch., Am. Heart Assn. (chmn. coun. arteriosclerosis 1975-78, exec. com. coun. epidemiology 1967-70, exec. com. coun. cerebral vascular disease 1966-68, C. Lyman Duff meml. lectrue 1989), Am. Soc. Clin. Nutrition (pres. 1978), Nat. Acad. Sci. (food and nutrition bd. 1986-89), Am. Inst. Nutrition, Am. Oil Chemists Soc., Am. Physiol. Soc., Am. Soc. Clin. Investigation, Am. Soc. Study Arteriosclerosis, Assn. Am. Physicians, Ctrl. Soc. Clin. Rsch., Nutrition Soc., Soc. Exptl. Biology and Medicine (coun. 1971-72, pres. Iowa sect. 1971-72), Western Assn. Physicians, Western Soc. Clin. Rsch., Phi Beta Kappa, Sigma Xi, Alpha Omega Alpha. Achievements include research in nutrition, lipid metabolism, blood vessel diseases. Home: 2600 SW Sherwood Pl Portland OR 97201-2285 Office: Oreg Health Scis U L465 Portland OR 97201 E-mail: connorw@ohsu.edu.

CONNORS, CHRISTOPHER J. state legislator; b. Ridgewood, N.J., June 26, 1956; m. Deborah Connors, 1979; children: Christopher Jr., Kelly. BS, Stockton State Coll., 1978; MPA, Rutgers U., 1988. State assemblyman Dist. 9, 1989—; asst. majority leader N.J. State Assembly, 1992-93; mem. Lacey Twp. Com., 1985-90, mayor, 1986-89; mem. Rep. County com., 1984, 85. Mem. N.J. Conf. of Mayors, Air Force Assn., Lacey Twp. Italian Am. Club, K.C. Republican. Home: 620 W Lacey Rd Forked River NJ 08731-2244*

CONNORS, DONALD LOUIS, lawyer, land use planner; b. Boston, Mar. 25, 1936; s. Edward Joseph and Rosella (Adams) C.; m. Margaret Sheffield, June 15, 1957; children: Joan F., Brian E., Thomas M., Christopher Sean. BS cum laude, Boston Coll., 1957; JD, Suffolk U., 1967. Bar: Mass., U.S. Dist. Ct. Mass., U.S. Ct. Appeals (1st cir.). Legis. counsel Greater Boston C. of C., 1963-68; counsel pub. affairs New Eng. Telephone, Boston, 1968-71; prin., pres. Tyler & Reynolds, Boston, 1971-81; ptnr., chmn. land use and environ. law group Choate, Hall & Stewart, Boston, 1981-93; of counsel Foley, Hoag & Eliot, Boston and Washington, 1993-95; ptrn. Connors & Bliss P.C., 1996—. Lectr. Grad. Sch. Design, Harvard U., 1978-89; adj. lectr. in regional planning U. Mass., Amherst, 1984-89; counsel Cape Cod and Martha's Vineyard Commns.; counsel, bd. dirs. Environ. League Mass., Inc., Boston, 1989—, Cape Cod Ctr. for Environ. and Sustainable Devel., 1991—; chair counsel The Growth Mgmt. Inst., Washington, 1992—; founder, chair, dir. Environ. Bus. Coun. N.E., Boston, pres., 1993-95; chmn. environ. law curriculum adv. com. Mass. Continuing Edn. Inc., 1990-94; chmn. Internat. Environ. Bus. and Tech. Inst., Inc., 1993; mem. Environ. Bus. Practice Group; founder Pres. Environ. Bus. Coun. U.S., Inc., Internat. Environ. Bus. Tech. Inst., Inc.; chair adv. com. Southeastern Mass. Vision 2020, 1997-2002. Co-author: The Public Trust Doctrine, 1991; author, editor: State and Regional Planning, 1991; contbr. numerous articles to profl. jours. Mem. bd. advisors Sea Grant Coll., MIT, Cambridge, 1972-2002; chair, bd. dirs. Conservation Law Found. New Eng., Boston, 1976-79; chair com. adv. bd. Sta. WGBH Pub. Broadcasting, Boston, 1976-79; co-chair marine sci. policy adv. bd. U. Mass., Boston, 1991. Capt. U.S. Army, 1957-62; mem. environ. technol. trade adv. com. U.S. Dept. Commerce, Washington, 1994-96. Recipient award Assn. for Preservation Cape Cod, 1990, Pres. award for Environ. Leadership The Conte Inst., Mass., 1993, Environ. merit award U.S. EPA Region One, 1995. Mem. ABA, Mass. Bar Assn., Boston Bar Assn., AICP (cert.), Urban Land Inst. (co-chmn. policy forum on state and regional planning 1989-92), Cross and Crown Soc., Beta Gamma Sigma, Alpha Sigma Nu. Democrat. Roman Catholic. Avocations: hiking, canoeing, bicycling, travel. Office: Connors & Bliss PC 277 Dartmouth St Boston MA 02116-4002 E-mail: dconnors@adelphia.net.

CONNORS, DORSEY, television and radio commentator, newspaper columnist; b. Chgo. d. William J. and Sarah (MacLain) C.; m. John E. Forbes; 1 dau., Stephanie. BA cum laude, U. Ill. Fl. reporter WGN-TV Rep. Nat. Conv., Chgo., Dem. Nat. Conv., L.A., 1960. Conducted: Personality Profiles, WGN-TV, Chgo., 1948-49, Dorsey Connors Show, WMAQ-TV, Chgo., 1949-58, 61-63, Armchair Travels, WMAQ-TV, 1952-55, Homeshow, NBC,1954-57, NBC Today Show, Dorsey Connors program, WGN, 1958-61, Tempo Nine, WGN-TV, 1961, Society in Chgo, WMAQ-TV, 1964; writer: column Hi! I'm Dorsey Connors, Chgo. Sun Times, 1965—; Author: Gadgets Galore, 1953, Save Time, Save Money, Save Yourself, 1972, Helpful Hints for Hurried Homemakers, 1988. Founder Ill. Epilepsy League; mem. woman's bd. Children's Home and Aid Soc., mem. women's bd. USO. Named one of Am.'s Outstanding Irish Am. Women, World of Hibernia mag., 1995. Mem. AFTRA, NATAS (Silver Cir. award 1995), SAG, Mus. Broadcast Comm. (founding mem.), Soc. Midland Authors, Chgo. Hist. Soc. (guild com., costume com.), Chi Omega. Roman Catholic. Office: Chgo Sun Times 401 N Wabash Ave Chicago IL 60611-5642

CONNORS, EUGENE KENNETH, lawyer, educator; b. Dobbs Ferry, NY, Oct. 3, 1946; s. Edward Micheal and Eileen (Burke) C.; children: Kevin Patrick, Kathryn Margaret. BA in English, Holy Cross Coll., Worcester, Mass., 1968; JD, Columbia U., 1971. Bar: Pa. 1971. Assoc. Reed Smith Shaw & McClay, Pitts., 1971-76; ptnr. Reed Smith LLP (formerly Reed Smith Shaw & McClay), Pitts., 1977—. Adj. prof. St. Francis Coll. Grad. Sch., Loretto, Pa., 1975—; ski instr. Holiday Valley Ski Area, Ellicottville, N.Y., 1987—; bd. dirs. Green Garden Inc., 1985—, arbitrator, Am. Arbitration Assn. Contbr. articles to profl. jours. Bd. dirs. Sch. Vol. Assn. Pitts., 1973-78, Pitts. Human Resources Assn., 1988-95, TEC/Pa. Smallers Mfrs. Coun., 1993-94, Pitts. Pub. Theater, 1999—, exec. com., 2000—. Mem. ABA, Pa. Bar Assn., Allegheny County Bar Assn., Pitts. Human Resources Assn. (bd. dirs. 1988-95, treas. 1987-95), Tri-State Employers Assn. (bd. dirs. 1992-93), Profl. Ski Instrs. Am. Avocations: alpine (downhill) skiing, scuba diving, golf. Office: Reed Smith LLP PO Box 2009 435 6th Ave Pittsburgh PA 15219-1886

CONNORS, FRANK JOSEPH, lawyer; b. N.Y.C., Oct. 8, 1944; s. Frank Joseph and Nina Florence (Kirk) C.; m. Evelyn Noreen Mills, Oct. 14, 1983. BA, UCLA, 1965; MA, Columbia U., 1966; JD, Harvard U., 1969. Bar: N.Y. 1970, Fla. 1982, Mass. 1986, U.S. Supreme Ct. 1973. Assoc. Dewey, Ballantine, Bushby, Palmer & Wood, N.Y.C., 1969-75; asst. atty. gen. N.Y. State Spl. Prosecutor, N.Y.C., 1975-77; gen. atty. Am. Broadcasting Cos., Inc., N.Y.C., 1977-85; atty. Harvard U., Cambridge, Mass., 1985—; acting gen. counsel, 1992. Arbitrator N.Y.C. Civil Ct., 1980-85; comml. arbitrator Am. Arbitration Assn., N.Y.C., 1984-85. Bd. dirs. World Teach, Inc., 1992-2002. Mem. Am. Judicature Soc., N.Y. State Bar Assn. (copyright com. 1981-85), Assn. of Bar of City of N.Y. (profl. discipline com. 1983-85). Republican. Methodist. Office: Harvard U 1350 Massachusetts Ave Cambridge MA 02138-3846 E-mail: frank_connors@harvard.edu.

CONNORS, JACK, JR., advertising executive; m. Eileen Connors; 4 children. Grad., Boston Coll. Founding ptnr., chmn. Hill, Holliday, Connors, Cosmopulos, Inc., Boston, CEO. Bd. dirs. Navic Networks. Office: Hill Holliday 200 Clarendon St Boston MA 02116*

CONNORS, JAMES PATRICK, lawyer; b. N.Y.C., May 28, 1952; s. Joseph Patrick Connors and Edna Theresa Fitzgerald; m. Gloria Ann Ciccarelli, Jan. 12, 1974; children: Nicholas, Patrick, Jamie Cathleen. BA, Herbert H. Lehman Coll., 1974; JD, N.Y. Law Sch., 1977; LLM, NYU, 1985. Bar: N.Y. 1978, U.S. Dist. Ct. (so. and ea. dists.) N.Y. 1978. Assoc. Bower & Gardner, N.Y.C., 1978-80, Joseph W. Conklin, N.Y.C., 1980-82; ptnr. Jones, Hirsch, Connors & Bull, N.Y.C., 1982—. Lectr. NYU Sch. Medicine, 1983, N.Y. Law Jour., 1984, Bellevue Hosp., 1984, Hillcrest Gen. Hosp., 1984, Mt. Sinai Hosp., 1985, Am. Coll. Ophthalmologists, 1986—88. Contbr. Recipient Am. Jurisprudence award, Lawyers Pub. Coop., 1977. Mem.: ABA, Lawyer Pilot Bar Assn., Def. Assn. of N.Y., N.Y. County Bar Assn., N.Y. State Bar Assn. Home: 85 Mayflower Dr Yonkers NY 10710-3801

CONNORS, JIMMY (JAMES SCOTT CONNORS), former professional tennis player; b. East St. Louis, Ill., Sept. 2, 1952; s. James and Gloria (Thompson) C.; m. Patti McGuire; children: Brett David, Aubree Leigh. Student, UCLA. Joined World Championship Tennis, Inc., 1972; now in Men's Seniors' Circuit. Recipient Player of Year award, 1974; named All-Am., 1971; ranked number 1 male tennis player in U.S. and World, 1976; ranked number 1 in world, 1978; elected to Tennis Hall of Fame, 1998. Achievements include winning Australian Men's Singles, 1974, Wimbledon Men's Singles, 1974, 82, Wimbledon Men's Doubles (with Ilie Nastase), 1973, U.S. Pro Championship Men's Singles, 1973, Cologne Cup, 1976, U.S. Clay Ct. Championship-Men's Singles, 1974, 76, 78, 79, U.S. Open Men's Singles, 1974, 76, 78,82, 83, U.S. Indoor Open Men's Singles, 1973, 74, 75, 78, 79, 83, 84, Pro Indoor Men's Singles, 1976, 78, 79, 80, U.S. Open Men's Doubles (with Ilie Nastase), 1975, U.S. Indoor Men's Doubles (with Frew McMillan), 1974, (with Ilie Nastase), 1975, U.S. Clay Ct. Men's Doubles (with Ilie Nastase), 1974, S.African Men's Singles, 1973, 74, World Championship Tennis Singles, 1977, Grand Prix Masters Championship, 1978, U.S. Nat. Indoor Men's Singles, 1978, Australian Indoor Men's Singles, 1978, Suntory Cup, 1986, D.C. Tennis Classic, 1987, Olympia Open, Toulouse, France, 1987, Toulouse Grand Prix, 1989; mem. Davis Cup Team, 1976, 81, World Cup Team, 1976, 85(winning team). Office: Tennis Mgmt Inc 109 Red Fox Rd Belleville IL 62223-2242 also: RHB Ventures Ste 700 1250 Connecticut Ave NW Washington DC 20036-2657

CONNORS, JOHN MICHAEL, JR., advertising agency executive; b. Boston, June 9, 1942; s. John Michael and Mary (Horrigan) C.; m. Eileen Marie Ahearn; children: John, Timothy, Susanne, Kevin. Grad., Boston Coll., 1963. Mktg. rep. Campbell Soup Co., Boston, 1963-65; account exec. Batten, Barton, Durstine & Osborne, New York and Boston, 1965-68; chmn., CEO Hill, Holliday, Connors, Cosmopulos, Inc., Boston, 1968—. Bd. dirs. Am. Ireland Fund, John Hancock Mut. Life Ins. Trustee Boston Coll., 1979—; chmn. bd. trustees Brigham and Women's Hosp., Boston; bd. dirs. Boys and Girls Club Boston. Mem. Advt. Club Greater Boston (past pres.), New Eng. Broadcasting Assn. (past pres.), Sportsmen's Tennis Club (bd. dirs.), Braeburn Country Club, Oyster Harbors Country Club, Eastward Ho! Country Club. Roman Catholic. Office: Hill Holliday Connors Cosmopulos Inc John Hancock Tower 200 Clarendon St Boston MA 02116-5021

CONNORS, JOSEPH ALOYSIUS, III, lawyer; b. Washington, June 24, 1946; s. Joseph Aloysius Jr. and Charlotte Rita (Fox) C.; m. Mary Louise Bucklin, June 14, 1969. BBA, U. Southwestern La., 1970; JD, U. Tex., 1973. Bar: Tex. 1973, U.S. Dist. Ct. (so. dist.) Tex. 1975, U.S. Supreme Ct. 1976, U.S. Ct. Appeals (5th cir.) 1976, U.S. Dist. Ct. (ea., we. and no. dists.) Tex. 1981, U.S. Ct. Appeals (11th cir.) 1981, U.S. Ct. Appeals (3d, 4th, 6th, 7th, 8th, 9th, 10th and D.C. cirs.) 1986. Law clk. to assoc. justice Tex. Ct. Civil Appeals, Amarillo, 1973-74; assoc. Rankin & Kern, McAllen, Tex., 1974-76; asst. criminal dist. atty. Hidalgo County, Tex., 1976-78; pvt. practice, McAllen, 1978—. Faculty Criminal Trial Advocacy Inst., Huntsville, Tex., 1981-84; spkr. seminars State Bar Tex., 1980-81, 84; adj. prof. Reynaldo G. Garza Sch. Law, Edinburg, Tex., 1988-89. Contbg. editor Criminal Trial Manual, Tex., 1984-95; contbr. articles to profl. jours. Bd. dirs. Tex. Rural Legal Aid, 1991—, pres. bd. dirs., 1994-96. With USMCR, 1966-71. Mem. NACDL, State Bar Tex. (grievance com. 12B 1984-91, chmn. com. 1989-90, profl. enhancement program 1997-2000), Tex. Assn. Criminal Def. Lawyers (bd. dirs. 1982-89, Excellence award 1983, medal of honor 1987), Hidalgo County Bar Assn. (bd. dirs. 1981-83), Am. Soc. Writers on Legal Subjects, Hidalgo County Criminal Def. Lawyers Assn. (bd. dirs. 1991-98). Democrat. Roman Catholic. Home: 605 E Violet Ave Ste 3 Mcallen TX 78504-2469 Office: Law Offices Joseph A Connors III 605 E Violet Ave Ste 3 Mcallen TX 78504

CONNORS, KENNETH ANTONIO, retired chemistry educator; b. Torrington, Conn., Feb. 19, 1932; s. Peter Francis and Adeline (Gioia) C.; m. Patricia R. Smart, Dec. 30, 1972. BS, U. Conn., 1954; MS, U. Wis., 1957, PhD, 1959. Rsch. assoc. dept. chemistry Ill. Inst. Tech., Chgo., 1959-60, Northwestern U., Evanston, Ill., 1960-61; asst. prof. U. Wis. Sch. Pharmacy, Madison, 1962-65, assoc. prof., 1965-72, prof., 1972-97, prof. emeritus, 1997—, acting dean, 1991-93. Author: A Textbook of Pharmaceutical Analysis, 3d edit., 1982, Reaction Mechanisms in Organic Analytical Chemistry, 1973, Chemical Stability of Pharmaceuticals, 2d edit., 1986, Binding Constants, 1987, Chemical Kinetics, 1990, Thermodynamics of Pharmaceutical Systems, 2002. Served with U.S. Army, 1961. Fellow AAAS, Acad. Pharm. Scis., Am. Assn. Pharm. Scis.; mem. Am. Chem. Soc., N.Y. Acad. Scis. Office: U Wis Sch Pharmacy 777 Highland Ave Madison WI 53705-2222

CONNORS, LEONARD T. state legislator; b. Jersey City, Apr. 11, 1929; m. Lorraine G. Marine; children: Leonard T. III, Christopher J. Student, Rutgers Extension Univ. City councilman Surf City, N.J., 1963-65; tax assessor; mayor Surf City, N.J., 1966-; freeholder Ocean County, N.J., 1977-82, 1979-80; mem. N.J. Senate, Dist. 9, Trenton, 1982—; ranking mem. county and mcpl. govt. aging and vet. affairs; mem. spl. com. on automobile ins. reforms/legis. svc. com.; mem. tourism coun. and women's commn. Mem. K.C., Kiwanis, Air Force Assn., N.J. Conf. Mayors, Nat. Coun. on Alcoholism, Long Beach-So. Ocean County C. of C., United Way, Fraternal Order of Police. Home: 620 W Lacey Rd Forked River NJ 08731-2244 Office: NJ Senate State House Sec of the Senate CN-099 Trenton NJ 08625*

CONNORS, LINDA MARIE, community health nurse; b. Buffalo, Aug. 28, 1963; d. Joseph J. and Dolores Mary (Norgiel) Rodney; m. Michael E. Connors, Apr. 16, 1988; children: Chase Joseph, Michael Tobin, Matthew Ryan, Brett James, Alexander Bernard. BSN, D'Youville Coll., Buffalo, 1985. RN, N.Y. Office nurse pvt. physician's office, Gowanda, N.Y.; ICU staff nurse Tri-County Hosp., Gowanda, 1985-86; nurse I/nurse II Gowanda Psychiat. Ctr., Helmuth, N.Y., 1986-89, nurse adminstr., chair nursing policy and procedure com., 1989-91; nurse II Buffalo Psychiat. Ctr., 1991-93; infusion therapy nurse clinician Springville (N.Y.) Home, 1992—; home care nurse Staff Builders, 1993; dir. nursing Partnership of Springville Pharmacy Home Infusion, 1993—2002; gen. mgr. Optioncare, Inc., 2002—. Substitute sch. nurse, Springville, 1993-95; screener and assessor PRI. Mem. Intravenous Nursing Soc., Sigma Theta Tau (sec. 1984-85, treas. sr. honor soc. D'Youville sect. 1985), INS. Home: 9247 S Hill Rd Boston NY 14025

CONNORS, LOREN M. composer, guitarist; b. New Haven, Oct. 22, 1949; s. Joseph and Mary Mazzacane; m. Suzanne Y. Langille; 1 child, Jamie. BA in Art, So. Conn. State U., 1971; student, U. Cin., 1974—75. Composer, guitarist, New Haven, 1975—90, Bklyn., 1990—. Composer, guitarist: compact disc Departing of a Dream II, 2003, compilation CD Composers Recordings Inc. N.Y. Guitarists, 1995, composer, guitarist: various compact discs and albums. Recipient Lafcadio Hearn award, Haiku Soc. Am., 1986.

CONNORS, MARTY, political party administrator, small business owner; Fellow, J.F.K. Sch. Govt., 1993, Harvard U., 1993. Exec. dir. Ala. Republican Party, 1983—86; founder So. and New England Republican Exch. Policy Network, 1986; pres. M.J. Connors Consulting; chmn. Republican Exec. Com. of Ala., 2001—. Campaigner schs. USSR, Romania, Ukraine, 1990; spl. asst. Lamar Alexander, U.S. Dept. Edn., 1991; congl. candidate, 92. Republican. Office: PO Box 361784 Birmingham AL 35236*

CONNORS, ROBERT LEO, city official; b. Kings County, N.Y., June 11, 1940; s. John Leo and Emma Mae (Bayers) C.; children from former marriage: Anne, Laura, Kathleen; m. Sharon M. Skeels, Jan. 20, 1996; 1 child, Sarah. B. Profl. Studies, Pace U., 1974, MS in Indsl. Labor Relations, 1976. Police officer, trustee, fin. sec. exec., 1st v.p. Patrolmen's Benevolent Assn., N.Y.C. Police Dept., 1965-77; dep. commr., dir. labor relations Dept. Gen. Services City of N.Y., 1977-83; dir. personnel adminstrn. City of Fall River, Mass., 1984-85, city adminstr., 1985-2000; orgnl. cons., 2000—; cons. Bristol County Sheriff's Office, Dartmouth, Mass. Lectr. in field. Co-author: Comprehensive Reorganization of Municipal Government, 1986. Mem. Fall River Regional Task Force, 1984—. Served with USAF, 1957-61. Recipient Community Relations Service award, U.S. Justice Dept., Boston, 1985. Mem. Am. Mgmt. Assn., Nat. League of Cities, Internat. City Mgmt. Assn., Greater Fall River Personnel Council, Internat. Personnel Mgmt. Assn., Soc. of Profls. in Dispute Resolution. Lodges: Masons. Democrat. Avocations: golf, carpentry. Home: 26 Primrose Dr Seekonk MA 02771-5916 Office: Bristol County Sheriff's OPffice Dartmouth MA 02747

CONNORS, WILLIAM EDWARD, lawyer; b. Madison, Wis., Dec. 7, 1962; s. William James and Carol Mae (Nachtwey) C.; m. Joan Camille Sorteberg, Aug. 24, 1991; 1 child, Cara Brigid Sorteberg. BA in History, U. Wis., 1985, MA in Pub. Policy and Adminstrn., JD, 1989. Bar: Minn. 1989, Wis. 1989. Judicial law clk. U.S. Bankruptcy Ct., Mpls., 1989-91; assoc. lawyer Fredrikson & Byron, Mpls., 1991-95; legis. fiscal analyst Minn. Ho. of Reps., St. Paul, 1995-97; dir. tax increment fin. divsn. Office of the State Auditor, Minn., 1997—2003; city adminstr. City of Evansville, Wis., 2003—. Pres. Macalester-Groveland Cmty. Coun., St. Paul, 1997. Mem. Minn. State Bar Assn., State Bar Wis. Roman Catholic. Avocation: lacrosse. Home: 622 E Countryside Dr Evansville WI 53536 E-mail: billconnors@inwave.com.

CONNUCK, ERIC S. lawyer; b. Bklyn., Nov. 14, 1965; m. Wendy E. DiMarco, Aug. 23, 1991; children: Marc, David. BS, SUNY, Binghamton, 1986; JD, NYU, 1991. Bar: Conn. 1991, N.Y. 1992, U.S. Dist. Ct. (ea. and so. dists.) N.Y. 1992, U.S. Dist. Ct. (no. dist.) N.Y. 1998, U.S. Dist. Ct. Colo. 1998, U.S. Dist. Ct. (ea. and we. dist.) Ark. 1999, U.S. Ct. Appeals (2d cir.) 2000. Assoc. Rogers & Wells, N.Y.C., 1991-94, McCarrick, Finnerty & Mayer, N.Y.C., 1994-96, Piper Marbury Rudnick & Wolfe L.L.P., N.Y.C., 1996—2002; of counsel Piper Rudnick LLP, N.Y.C., 2002—. Office: Piper Rudnick LLP 1251 Ave of Americas New York NY 10020 E-mail: eric.connuck@piperrudnick.com.

CONOBY, JOSEPH FRANCIS, chemist; b. Albany, June 12, 1930; s. Joseph Francis and Helen Emma (Brucker) C.; m. Mary Joan A. Ryan, June 21, 1958; children: James Francis, Mark Joseph. BS, Union Coll., 1952. Sr. tech. svc. engr. Allied Chem. Corp., Syracuse, N.Y., 1956-66; rsch. chemist Conversion Chem. Corp., Rockville, Conn., 1966-69; environ. engr., indsl. hygienist Honeywell Bull, Billerica, Mass., 1969-87, mgr. environ. and health engring., 1969-87; mgr. environ. engring. Bull HN Worldwide Info. Sys., 1987-95; sr. scientist Concorp, Inc., Acton, Mass., 1996—. Adv. bd. Mass. Water Resources Authority Sewer Use (rules and regulations, policy and procedures, and facilities planning task forces); cons. exptl. project course Mass. Inst. Tech., 1977-78. Contbr. articles to profl. jours.; patentee in field. Lt. USN, 1952-56. Mem. Am. Indsl. Hygiene Assn., Nat. Assn. Environ. Mgmt. Home: 5 Samuel Parlin Dr Acton MA 01720-3206 Office: Concorp Inc PO Box 2766 Acton MA 01720-6766

CONOMIKES, GEORGE SPERO, management consultant executive, publisher; b. Canastota, N.Y., Oct. 8, 1925; s. Spero P. and Mary (Pappas) C.; m. Lynne Rowland; children: Melanie, Spero. AB with honors, Middlebury Coll., 1950; AM in Econs., U. Chgo., 1956. Rsch. assoc., project dir. Indsl. Relations Ctr., U. Chgo., 1951-55; dir. dept. commerce U. Chgo., 1955-57; pres. Bus. Forum, Inc., Chgo., 1958-70; chmn., CEO Conomikes Assoc., Inc., Greenwich, Conn., 1970-74, pres. L.A., 1974—. Lectr. econs. U. Chgo., 1955-58; guest lectr. Purdue U., NYU, Loyola U., Chgo., U. So. Calif., UCLA, U. Tex., Tufts U., U. P.R., U. Iowa, U. Tenn., U. Minn., Georgetown U., Marquette U., U. Md., Temple U., U. Oreg., Emory U.; presenter Practice Mgmt. series on Med. News Network, 1993-94. Contbg. editor: Stock Market Handbook, 1969; editor, pub. Conomikes Reports, 1982—, Conomikes Medicare Hotline, 1991—; author: Successful Practice Management Techniques, 1988, The Answer Book on Maximizing Practice Profits, 1998. With USAAF, 1943-45. Mem. Riviera Tennis Club (Pacific Palisades, Calif.). Republican. Home: 11687 Bellagio Rd Los Angeles CA 90049 Office: Conomikes Assocs Inc 12233 W Olympic Blvd Ste116 Los Angeles CA 90064

CONOSCENTI, CRAIG STEPHEN, physician; b. Jersey City, Jan. 11, 1955; s. Gerald Raoul and Constance Theresa (Niosi) C.; m. Rosanne Denise Scarpa, June 27, 1982; 1 child, Stephen Joseph. BS, Fordham U., 1977; MD, St. Georges U., 1981. Diplomate Am. Bd. Internal Medicine. Resident in internal medicine Meth. Hosp., Bklyn., 1981—82, Hackensack U. Med. Ctr., 1982—84, chief resident, 1984—85; fellow in pulmonary critical care medicine Norwalk (Conn.) Hosp., Yale U. Sch. Medicine, 1985—87, chief diving and hyperbaric medicine, 1991—, med. dir. comprehensive wound care, sr. attending physician pulmonary and critical care medicine; pvt. practice Norwalk, 1987—. Med. dir. Norwalk Hosp. Sch. Respiratory Therapy, 1987-90, med. dir. advanced cardiac life support program, 1986-90. Contbr. articles to profl. jours.; co-inventor Bronchoscopy Catheter; Probal Bronchoscopic Catheter. Orator Norwalk Sons of Italy, 1990-92, v.p., 1992-93, pres., 1993-97. Norman Brady Internat. fellow Brompton Chest Hosp., London, and Norwalk Hosp., 1986. Fellow: Am. Coll. Chest Physicians; mem.: ACP, Fairfield County Lung Assn. (bd. dirs. 1987—94), Conn. Thoracic Soc. (bd. dirs. 1994—, pres. 1997—), Undersea and Hyperbaric Med. Soc., Am. Lung Assn. (bd. dirs. Conn. chpt. 1994—), Am. Thoracic Soc. Avocation: boating. Office: Norwalk Hosp Dept Pulmonary and Critical Care Medicine Maple St Norwalk CT 06856

CONOVER, DOROTHY NANCY LEVER, medical practice administrator, nurse; b. Abington, Pa., Jan. 11, 1941; d. Charles Ambler and Dorothy Nancy (Greenway) Lever; m. Albert Paul Conover, Dec. 23, 1960 (div. Aug. 1981); 1 child, Hollie Marie. Degree in nursing, Phila. Gen. Hosp. Sch. Nursing, 1960. Staff and pvt. duty nurse Morton Plant Hosp., Clearwater, Fla., 1963; med. asst., sec. Office of E.E. Wilkison, MD, Tallahassee, 1966-69; med. sec. Urology Clinic Assocs., Houston, 1977-78; adminstr. Glenn A. Helwig, M.D.-Coastal Women's Ctr., Clearwater, 1979-98, Digestive Disease Assn. Clearwater, 1998-99, Northeast Family Practice, St. Petersburg, Fla., 1999—. Editor (newsletter) People with AIDS, 1995. V.p. Meadows Swim Team Booster Club, Stafford, Tex., 1974, Meadows Cmty. Improvement Assn., Stafford, 1975; ruling elder Presbyn. Ch., 1976—. Mem. Assn. Healthcare Mgrs., Profl. Assn. Healthcare Office Mgrs., Am. Acad. Procedural Coders (adv. bd. 1994-95), Med. Group Mgmt. Assn. (mem. ob-gyn. assembly, sec.-treas. 1996, pres.-elect 1997, pres. 1998, newsletter editor ob-gyn. assembly 1995-96, adv. bd. Ob Prac Mgmt Newsletter 1997-98, gastroenterology adminstrn. assembly 1998-99, Med. Group Mgmt. Assn. primary care assembly 1999—), Clearwater Bus. and Profl. Womens Club (treas. 1985-86), Am. Coll. Medical Practice Execs. Republican. Presbyterian. Avocations: gardening, needlepoint, depression era glassware. Home: 246 Temple Ln Belleair Bluffs FL 33770-1966 Office: Northeast Family Practice 8730 4th St N Saint Petersburg FL 33702-3186 E-mail: lever41@aol.com.

CONOVER, LLOYD HILLYARD, retired pharmaceutical research scientist and executive; b. Orange, N.J., June 13, 1923; s. John Howard and Marguerite Anna (Cameron) C.; m. Virginia Rogers Kirk, Aug. 24, 1944 (dec. Dec. 1988); children: Kirk Howard, Roger Lloyd, Heather Cameron, Craig Scott; m. Marie Strauss Solomons, Oct. 18, 1990 (dec. May 2003). BA, Amherst Coll., 1947; PhD, U. Rochester, 1950. Rsch. chemist, mgr. Chas. Pfizer & Co., Bklyn. and Groton, Conn., 1950—68; dir. chem. rsch. and chemotherapy Pfizer Cen. Rsch., Groton, 1968-71, rsch. dir. Europe, Sandwich, Eng., 1971-74, v.p. agrl. R & D Groton and Sandwich, 1975-84. Contbr. articles on antibiotics, anthelminics and animal health drugs to sci. jours.; patentee tetracycline and pyrantel Chmn. Waterford Planning, 1961-63. Lt. (j.g.) USNR, 1943-46, PTO. Recipient Eli Whitney award Conn. Patent Law Assn., 1983, Third Century award Found. Creative Am., 1990; inductee Nat. Inventors Hall of Fame, 1992. Fellow Royal Soc. Chemistry, Royal Soc. Arts; mem. Am. Chem. Soc., Phi Beta Kappa, Sigma Xi. Republican. Avocations: travel, gardening, genealogical research.

CONOVER, NANCY ANDERSON, retired secondary school counselor; b. Manhattan, Kans., July 8, 1943; d. Howard Julius and Wilma June (Katz) Anderson; m. Gary Hites Conover, Aug. 10, 1968; children: Chad Anderson, Cary Hites. BS in Edn., Kans. State U., 1965; MEd, Wichita State U., 1991. Cert. sch. counselor, tchr., Kans.; lic. profl. counselor, Kans. Tchr. Flint (Mich.) Sch. Dist., 1965-66, Unified Sch. Dist. 259, Wichita, Kans., 1967-68, Overland Park (Kans.) Sch. Dist., 1968-70; bus. mgr., sec.-treas. Gary Conover, D.D.S., Wichita, 1985-94; sch. counselor Unified Sch. Dist. 259, Wichita, 1991-94; secondary sch. counselor Unified Sch. Dist. 385, Andover, Kans., 1994—2002; ret., 2002. Mem. Am. Counselors Assn., Kans. Sch. Counselors Assn., Kans. Assn. Counselors, Mental Health Counselors Assn., Kans. Dental Aux. (sec. 1970-74), Wichita Dist. Dental Aux. (pres. 1970-75), Jr. League Wichita (adminstrv. v.p. 1978-82), Gamma Phi Beta, Phi Kappa Phi. Republican. Lutheran. Avocations: golf, reading. E-mail: gcon810000@aol.com.

CONOVER, NELLIE COBURN, retail furniture company executive; b. Lebanon, Ohio, Dec. 21, 1921; d. Frank C. and Isabel (Murphy) Coburn; student public schs.; m. Lawrence E. Conover, Jan. 11, 1941; children—Lawrence R., Carol, David C., Constance, Christina. Co-founder, 1949, since exec. sec.-treas. Larry Conover Furniture & Appliance, Inc., and predecessor, Milford, Ohio, also trustee co. pension fund. Mem. Milford C. of C., Cin. Hist. Soc., Milford Hist. Soc., DAR. Democrat. Roman Catholic. Address: 438 Main St Milford OH 45150-1128

CONOVER, RICHARD CORRILL, lawyer; b. Bridgeport, Nebr., Jan. 12, 1942; s. John Cedric and Mildred (Dunn) C.; m. Cathy Harlan, Dec. 19, 1970; children— William Cedric, Theodore Cyril. B.S., U. Nebr., Lincoln, 1965, M.S., 1966; J.D., Cornell U., 1969. Bar: N.Y. 1970, Mont. 1982, U.S. Dist. Ct. (so. and ea. dists.) N.Y. 1971, U.S. Supreme Ct. 1977, U.S. Ct. Customs and Patent Appeals 1979, U.S. Ct. Claims 1980, U.S. Dist. Ct. Mont. 1984, U.S. Tax Ct. 1986. Assoc. Brumbaugh, Graves, Donohue & Raymond, N.Y.C., 1969-73; assoc. Townley, Updike, Carter & Rodgers, N.Y.C., 1974-75; assoc. gen. counsel legal office Automatic Data Processing, Inc., Clifton, N.J., 1975-77; assoc. Nims, Howes, Collison & Isner, N.Y.C., 1977-81; sole practice, Mont., 1981— ; lectr. indsl. and mech. engring. dept. Mont. State U., 1981-97. Mem. Mont. Gov.'s Bd. Sci. and Tech., 1985-87. Mem. ABA, Assn. Bar City N.Y., Mont. Bar Assn., Am. Pat. Law Assn. Home: PO Box 1329 Bozeman MT 59771-1329 Office: 104 E Main St Ste 404 Bozeman MT 59715-4787

CONOVER, WILLIAM JAY, statistics educator; b. Hays, Kans., Dec. 6, 1936; s. William Joseph Conover and Viola Marie (Herman) Beishline; m. Patricia Louise Solomon, June 11, 1960 (div. Apr. 1994); children: Christopher Michael, Robert Andrew, Judith Ann, Therese Marie, William Joseph; m. Susan Theresa Mole, Dec. 27, 1996. BS, Iowa State U., 1958; MA, Cath. U., 1962, PhD, 1964. Asst. prof. stats. Kans. State U., Manhattan, 1964-67, assoc. prof. stats., 1967-73; vis. prof. stats. U. Zürich, Switzerland, 1970-71; prof. stats. Tex. Tech U., Lubbock, 1973-81, Horn prof., 1981—, area coord. of info. systems/quantitative scis., assoc. dean, 1978-88. Vis. prof. U. Calif., Davis, 1976-77; vis. staff mem. Los Alamos (N.Mex.) Sci. Lab., 1976—; cons. Sandia Lab., Albuquerque, 1979—. Author: Practical Nonparametric Statistics, 1971, 3rd edit., 1999, Modern Bus. Stat., 1983, 2d edit., 1989; co-author 9 textbooks on statistics; contbr. articles to profl. jours. Lt. (j.g.) USN, 1958-61. Recipient Rushing Faculty Rsch. award Tex. Tech Dad's Assn., 1983, Samuel Wilks award US Army, 1997. Fellow Am. Statis. Assn. (Don Owen award San Antonio chpt. 1986); mem. Inst. Math. Stats., Biometric Soc., Inst. Decision Scis. Roman Catholic. Avocations: chess, basketball. Office: Tex Tech U Coll Bus Adminstrn Lubbock TX 79409 E-mail: conover@ba.ttu.edu.

CONOVITZ, MYRON WILLIAM, physician, consultant; s. Harry Daniel and Ceil Warshaw Conovitz; m. Ellen Elgart, June 24, 1956; children: Amy Conovitz Lindsay, Jennifer Conovitz Russo. BA summa cum laude, Yale U., 1954; MD cum laude, Harvard U., 1958. Diplomate Am. Bd. Internal Medicine, 1966. Rsch. asst. divsn. biochemistry Brookhaven Nat. Lab., Upton, L.I., NY, 1955—55; summer fellow dept. biochemistry Harvard Med. Sch., Boston, 1956—56; med. intern Brigham and Women's Hosp., Boston, 1958—59, resident medicine, 1959—60, Mt. Sinai Med. Ctr., N.Y.C., 1960—61, Nat. Cancer Inst. fellow dept. hematology, 1961—62; active staff physician North Shore U. Hosp., Manhasset, NY, 1964—66, asst. attending physician, 1966—72, assoc. attending physician, 1972—83, attending physician, 1983—98, hon. attending physician, 1998—; attending physician medicine and hematology LI Jewish Med. Ctr., New Hyde Park, NY, 1964—98, hon. attending physician, 1998—; clin. instr. medicine Cornell U. Med. Coll., N.Y.C., 1971—74, clin. asst. prof. medicine, 1974—85, clin. assoc. prof. medicine, 1985—96, NYU Sch. Medicine, N.Y.C., 1996—; practitioner of internal medicine and hematology in med. partnership Norman Rosenthal, M.D., Mordecai A. Berkun, M.D. and Myron W. Conovitz, M.D., Great Neck, NY, 1964—77; pvt. practice internal medicine and hematology Great Neck, 1977—98; attending physician and cons. in hematology St. Francis Hosp., Roslyn, NY, 1974—96. Mem. peer rev. com. Nassau County Med. Soc., Garden City, NY, 1982—86; mem. various coms. and positions including sec.-treas. North Shore U. Hosp. Med. Staff, Manhasset, 1983—84; v.p. med. staff North Shore U. Hosp., Manhasset, 1984—85, pres. med. staff, 1985—86, chmn. med. staff fin. com., 1985—86, mem. ad hoc disciplinary com., 1991—91; founding mem. N.Y. State Task Force on Life and the Law, N.Y.C., 1984—97; mem. panel med. experts Physicians' Reciprocal Insurers, Manhasset, 1985—, Med. Liability Mut. Ins. Co., N.Y.C., 1996—, Group Coun. Mut. Ins. Co., N.Y.C., 1996—; cons. Validation Rev. Assocs., Inc., Great Neck, 1988—94. Co-author: (non-fiction book) The Determination of Death, 1986, Do Not Resuscitate Orders, 1986, (pamphlet) The Required Request Law, 1986, (non-fiction book) Life-Sustaining Treatment: Making Decisions and Appointing a Health Care Agent, 1987, Transplantation in New York State: The Procurement and Distribution of Organs and Tissues, 1988, Surrogate Parenting: Analysis and Recommendations for Public Policy, 1988, When Death is Sought: Assisted Suicide and Euthanasia in the Medical Context, 1994, (pamphlet) Fetal Extrauterine Survivability, 1988, (non-fiction book) When Others Must Choose: Deciding for Patients Without Capacity, 1992; contbr. articles to profl. jours. Pres. L.I. Regional Bd., Anti-Defamation League, East Meadow, NY, 1983—85, Gt. Neck Lodge B'nai B'rith, 1976—79; founding mem. N.Y. State Task Force on Life and the Law, N.Y.C., 1984—97. Capt. USAF, 1962—64. Fellow, Nat. Cancer Inst., 1961—62. Fellow: Royal Soc. Medicine London; mem.: AMA, Nassau County Med. Soc. (bd. censors 1986—), Med. Soc. of the State N.Y., N.Y. Soc. for the Study of Blood, Am. Soc. Hematology, Internat. Soc. Hematology, Boylston Med. Soc., Alpha Omega Alpha, Phi Beta Kappa, Sigma Xi (assoc.). Achievements include research in analysis of haptoglobinuria in renal disease; removal of iron from body by use of desferrioxamine; relation between glomerulonephritis and lupus erythematosus; relationship between renal erythropoietin and hematopoiesis; quantitative measurement of drive-strength of mating behavior in a male mammal; co-author of new state-wide Do Not Resuscitate regulation; co-author of proposed state law allowing designation of Health Care Agent; co-author of proposed state regulation for new definition of death. Avocations: travel, photography, computers. Office: 14 Bond St Great Neck NY 11021-2045

CONQUEST, (GEORGE) ROBERT (ACWORTH), writer, historian, poet, critic, journalist; b. Malvern, Worcestershire, Eng., July 15, 1917; s. Robert Folger Westcott and Rosamund Alys (Acworth) C.; m. Joan Watkins, 1942 (div. 1948); children: John, Richard; m. Elizabeth Neece, Dec. 1, 1979. Student, Winchester Coll., Eng., 1931-35, U. Grenoble, France, 1935-36, U. Oxford, 1936-39; MA, U. Oxford, Eng., 1972; DLitt, U. Oxford, 1975. First sec. H.M. Fgn. Svc., Sofia, Bulgaria, U.N., London, 1946-56; rsch. fellow London Sch. Econs., 1956-58; vis. poet U. Buffalo, N.Y., 1959-60; lit. editor The Spectator, London, 1962-63; sr. fellow Russian Inst. Columbia U., N.Y.C., 1964-65; fellow Woodrow Wilson Internat. Ctr., Washington, 1976-77; sr. rsch. fellow Hoover Inst., Stanford (Calif.) U., 1977-79, 81—. Disting. vis. scholar Heritage Found., Washington, 1980-81; adv. bd. Freedom House, N.Y.C., 1980—; rsch. assoc. Ukrainian Rsch. Inst. Harvard U., Cambridge, Mass., 1983—; adj. fellow Washington Ctr. Strategic Studies., 1984—. Author: Poems, 1955, A World of Difference, 1955, Common Sense About Russia, 1960, Power and Policy in the USSR, 1961, The Pasternak Affair, 1962, Between Mars and Venus, 1962, (with Kingsley Amis) The Egyptologists, 1965, Russia after Khrushchev, 1965, The Great Terror, 1968, Arias from a Love Opera, 1969, The Nation Killers, 1970, Where Marx Went Wrong, 1970, V I Lenin, 1972, Kolyma: The Arctic Death Camps, 1978, Coming Across, 1978, The Abomination of Moab, 1979, Forays, 1979, Present Danger: Towards a Foreign Policy, 1979, We and They: Civic and Despotic Cultures, 1980, (with Jon. M. White) What to do When the Russians Come, 1984, Inside Stalin's Secret Police: NKVD Politics 1936-39, 1985, The Harvest of Sorrow: Soviet Collectivization and the Terror-Famine, 1986, New and Collected Poems, 1988, Stalin and the Kirov Murder, 1988, Tyrants and Typewriters, 1989, The Great Terror: A Reassessment, 1990, Stalin: Breaker of Nations, 1991, Demons Don't, 1999, Reflections on a Ravaged Century, 1999. Capt. inf. Brit. Army, 1939-46, ETO. Decorated Officer Order of the Brit. Empire, London, 1955, Companion Order St. Michael and St. George, London, 1996; recipient Alexis de Tocqueville award, 1992, Light Verse award Acad. Arts and Letters, 1997; Jefferson lectr. humanities, Washington, 1993, Richard M. Weaver prize for scholarly letters, 1999; Royal Soc. Lit. fellow, 1972. Fellow Brit. Acad., Brit. Interplanetary Soc.; mem. Soc. for Promotion of Roman Studies. Clubs: Travellers (London). Home: 52 Peter Coutts Cir Stanford CA 94305-2506 Office: Stanford U Hoover Inst Stanford CA 94305-6010

CONRAD, ALAN JOHN, internist; b. N.Y.C., May 23, 1954; s. Francis Bernard and Joan Betty C.; m. Susan Lynn Caparosa, July 14, 1990; children: Samantha Elizabeth, Alison Nicole. BA, U. Vt., 1976; MD, N.Y. Med. Coll., 1981. Diplomate Am. Bd. Internal Medicine. Intern U. Calif., San Diego, 1981-82, resident, 1982-84; with emergency dept. Clairemont Hosp., San Diego, 1984—85; with Indsl. Med. Ctrs., San Diego, 1985—86, Smith Hanna Med. Group, San Diego, 1986—87; pvt. practice, Poway, Calif., 1987—. Chief of staff Pomerado Hosp., Poway, 2000-01. Mem. ACP, Am. Holistic Med. Assn., Am. Acad. Med. Acupuncture, Alpha Omega Alpha. Home: 10525 Quail Springs Ct San Diego CA 92131 Office: North County Internists 15721 Pomerado Rd Poway CA 92064 E-mail: ajcmd@san.rr.com.

CONRAD, ANGELA, humanities educator; b. Glen Ridge, N.J., Aug. 17, 1966; m. Roberto Osti, June 13, 1996; 1 child, Emilia Mirella Osti. BS in Langs., Georgetown U., Washington, 1988; M. Philosophy and English Lit., Drew U., Madison, N.J., 1997; PhD in English Lit., Drew U., 1999. Postdoctoral fellow Montclair State U., NJ, 1997—2000; asst. prof. humanities Bloomfield Coll., NJ, 2000—. Author: (book) The Wayward Nun of Amherst, 2000. Recipient Chamberlain Prize for Outstanding Doctoral Dissertation, Drew U., 1999. Fellow: Soc. for Values in Higher Edn.; mem.: MLA, Emily dickinson Internat. Soc. Office: Bloomfield Coll Dept Humanities Bloomfield NJ 07003

CONRAD, BETTE ANNE KESTER, lawyer, writer, minister; b. Chester, Pa., Oct. 27, 1944; d. Robert Howard Kester, Sr. and Grace Elizabeth Kester; m. Michael Allan Conrad; children: James David, Kristine Marie Conrad Connors. BBA, Columbia Coll., 1978; JD magna cum laude, U. Miami, 1987; DD, Am. Inst. Holistic Theology, 1999. SFC / Recruiter / Chief Data Analyst US Army & Army Reserve, 1975—93; spkr., cons. West Palm Beach, Fla., 1970—; author, 1975—; atty., shareholder Gunster, Yoakley & Stewart, P.A., West Palm Beach, 1988—; min., spiritual counselor, life coach United Christian Fellowship Ch., West Palm Beach, 2001—. Career and personal transition cons., 1981—. Author: The Tao of Legal Ethics, 2001, (poetry) The Golden Fishing Pole, 1997 (Internat. Soc. Poets Editor's Choice award, 1997); contbr. articles to profl. jours.; author: numerous poems. Vol. VISTA, Pompano Beach, Fla., 1974—75. Sgt. 1st class U.S. Army, 1975—91, Fla., Ind., Va., Pa. Decorated Achievement medal with 2 oak-leaf clusters U.S. Army; recipient Acad. Achievement in Adminstrv. Law award, Am. Jurisprudence, 1987, Acad. Achievement for Bankruptcy, 1987, Acad. Achievement for Profl. Mgmt., 1987. Mem.: Order of Coif. Office: Gunster Yoakley & Stewart PA 777 N Flagler Dr Ste 500-E West Palm Beach FL 33401 Home Fax: 561-753-6016; Office Fax: 561-835-1487. Personal E-mail: kitkanpro@aol.com. Business E-Mail: bconrad@gunster.com.

CONRAD, BRUCE PHILLIPS, mathematics educator; b. Ann Arbor, Mich., July 2, 1943; s. John P. and Charlotte (Merchant) C.; m. Rebecca K. Smith, Dec. 22, 1964; children: Clinton, Esther, Jessica, Rosemary. BS, Harvey Med. Coll., 1964; PhD, U. Calif., Berkeley, 1969. Asst. prof. math. dept. Temple U., Phila., 1969—73, assoc. prof., 1973—, sr. assoc. dean, Coll. Sci. & Tech., 1998—. Contbr. articles to profl. jours.; author: several mathematics textbooks. Mem. Am. Math. Soc., Math. Assn. Am., Soc. Indsl. and Applied Math., AAAS, Fedn. Am. Scientists. Democrat. Home: 147 Pelham Rd Philadelphia PA 19119-2661 Office: Temple U PO Box 038 16 Philadelphia PA 19146-0116

CONRAD, CHARLES A. neurologist, neuro-oncologist; b. San Antonio, Tex., June 12, 1961; BS, Tex. A&M U., 1984; MD, U. Tex. Med. Sch., 1988. Cert. bd. cert. Am. Bd. Psychiatry and Neurology, 1995, lic. Tex., Mo., Kans. Intern in internal medicine U. Tex. Med. Sch., Houston, 1988—89, resident in neurology, 1989—92; fellow in neuro-oncology U. Tex. MD Anderson Cancer Ctr., Houston, 1992—94, faculty assoc. dept. neuro-oncology, 1994—95; pvt. practice Cons. in Neurology, P.C., Kans. City, Mo., 1995—2000; assoc. prof. dept. neuro-oncology, ctr. med. dir. M.D. Anderson Cancer Ctr., Houston, 2000—. Rschr. in field. Contbr. articles, chapters to books. Recipient Fellowship award, Am. Cancer Soc., 1992—93, 1993—94. Mem.: AMA, Am. Assn. for Cancer Rsch., N.Am. Brain Tumor Consortium, Kans. City Round Table of Hematology/Oncology, Kans. City Neurology and Neurosurgery Soc., Am. Acad. Neurology, Soc. for Neuro-Oncology. Office: Univ Tex MD Anderson Cancer Ctr 1515 Holcombe Blvd Houston TX 77030

CONRAD, DANIEL EDWARD, physician; b. Chgo., Aug. 30, 1935; s. Benjamin Edward and Dorothy Elizabeth Esther (Sonne) C.; m. Jane Ellen Parker; children: Kristin Anne, Carol Patricia, Mary Catherine. BS in chem., Univ. Ill., 1956, MB, 1958, MD, 1960. Diplomate Am. Bd. Internal Medicine, Am. Bd. Preventive Medicine in Occupl. Medicine. Pvt. practice internal medicine Swedish Covenant Hosp., Chgo., 1966-78; medical dir. central region AT & T Long Lines, Chgo., 1971-81; corp. medical dir. GTE Automatic Elec., Northlake, Ill., 1981-84, West Suburban Hosp., Oak Park, Ill., 1984-86, Lockheed Martin Energy Systems, Oak Ridge, Tenn., 1986-97; ptnr. Conrad & Conrad Cons., Knoxville, Tenn., 1997—. Vice-chmn. dept. medicine Swedish Convenant Hosp., Chgo., 1973-79. Contbr. numerous articles to profl. jours. and news media. Pres. United Lutheran Ch., Oak Park, Ill., 1977-79, River Forest Tennis Club, 1977; mem., bd. dirs. Youth Svcs. Youth Haven, Oak Ridge, Tenn., 1991—, Knoxville Opera Co., 1995-2001; pres. Tenn. Coll. Occupational Medicine, 1990-91. Recipient First Annual Corp. Health Achievement award Am. Coll. Occupational & Environ. Medicine, 1997. Fellow Am. Coll. Occupational & Environmental Medicine (dir. 1981-84, sec. 1984-87), Am. Coll. Physicians, Am. Coll. Preventive Medicine, Ctrl. States Occupl. Med. Assn. (pres. 1982-83), Tenn. Coll. Occupl. Medicine (pres. 1990-91), Rotary Internat. Republican. Lutheran. Avocations: sailing, music, woodworking. Home: 11409 Berry Hill Dr Knoxville TN 37931-2804

CONRAD, DAVID L, music educator; b. Kankakee, Ill., Sept. 5, 1974; s. Cathy E. and Terry L. Conrad. B.S.M.E., U. of Ill., 1992—96; M.M.Ed., Ill. State U., 1997—99. Music tchr. El Paso Sch. Dist., 1996—98, Manteno Sch. Dist., 1998—. V.p. Cmty. Arts Coun. of Kankakee County, Ill., 2000—02; pres. Manteno Edn. Assn., Ill., 2002—. Composer: (choral arrangement) The Ship That Never Returned; dir.: (variety show) Manteno Showcase, (show choir) Manteno Magic; musician: (variety show) The Spice of Life, Kankakee Municipal Band; editor: (newsletter) Student Voice Electronic Newsletter. Arts advocacy Cmty. Arts Coun. of Kankakee County, Ill., 1998. Recipient Recognition of Something Extraordinary (R.O.S.E.), Manteno Bd. of Edn., 2002, Cert. of Honor, Music Educators Nat. Conf., 1995, Outstanding Vol. Award, Exploration Station.a children's mus., 1990—92. Mem.: Ill. Edn. Assn., NEA, MENC: The Nat. Assn. for Music Edn., Nat. Fedn. H.S. Music Assn., Voice Care Network (life). D-Conservative. Avocations: web page design, composing music, piano, trombone, photography. Home: 1050 Shawnee Ct Bourbonnais IL 60914 Office: Manteno Community Unit School District # 250 North Poplar Manteno IL 60950 Office Fax: 815-928-7158. Personal E-mail: dconrad@prodigy.net. E-mail: dconrad@manteno.k12.il.us.

CONRAD, DAVID PAUL, business broker, retired restaurant chain executive; b. Greensboro, NC, Jan. 11, 1946; s. Lucas Lee and Elizabeth Gertrude (Kincaid) Conrad; 1 child, Lucas Wilfong. BSBA, East Carolina U., 1970; cert. in real estate, Forsyth Tech. Coll., 1979. From cashier to cook Libby Hill Seafood, Greensboro, N.C., 1962-64; plant mgr. Libby Hill Seafood Restaurants, Inc., Greensboro, N.C., 1970-76, mgr. Winston-Salem, N.C., 1976-85, v.p., dir. ops. Greensboro, N.C., 1985-93, also bd. dirs., 1985-93; comml. real estate broker Allied Comml. Real Estate, Kernersville, N.C., 1993; franchise owner Swisher Maids of West Greensboro, N.C., 1994-99, regional dir., 1996-98; broker-in-charge VR Bus. Brokers, 1998—2000; owner Triad Bus. Brokerage, Star Videogames, Greensboro, High Point, NC, 2002—. Pvt. pilot. Mem. Greensboro Jaycees, 1973—81; vol. Wesley Long Hosp. Staff sgt. N.C. N.G, 1968—74. Mem.: Inst. Cert. Bus. Counselors, Masons. Republican. Methodist. Avocation: flying (pvt. pilot). Fax: 336-662-0505.

CONRAD, DAVID WILLIAMS, lawyer; b. St. Louis, Jan. 10, 1930; s. Lawrence Henry and Roberta (Williams) C.; m. Marilyn Russo, Sept. 26, 1959; children: Roberta Lucy, Philip Lloyd, Angela Beth. AB, Colgate U., 1951; JD, Harvard U., 1954. Bar: N.J. 1954, U.S. Supreme Ct. 1973. Assoc. McCarter & English, Newark, 1956-59; ptnr. Conrad & Jones, Montclair, N.J., 1964-71; pvt. practice Montclair, 1959-64, 71-93; ptnr. Conrad & Boutillier, Montclair, 1993—. Counsel Montclair State U. Found., 1959—, Homes of Montclair Ecumenical Corp., 1988—. Legis. candidate N.J. State Assembly, 1971; pres. N.J. Chamber Music Soc., 1984-86, Union Congl. Ch., Montclair, 1988-91. With U.S. Army, 1954-56. Mem. N.J. State Bar Assn., Montclair-West Essex Bar Assn., Essex County Bar Assn. Democrat. Congregationalist. Avocations: piano, music composition, travel. Home: 23 Hyde Rd Bloomfield NJ 07003-3018 Office: 31 S Fullerton Ave Montclair NJ 07042-3358

CONRAD, DONALD GLOVER, insurance executive; b. St. Louis, Apr. 23, 1930; s. Harold Armin and Velma Glover (Morris) C.; m. Stephania Shimkus, Feb. 8, 1980; 1 child, Christina; 1 stepchild, Alexa Sanzone Paolella; children by previous marriage: Marcy Conrad Tramont, Suzanne Conrad, Mark. Student, Wesleyan U., 1948-49; BS, Northwestern U., 1952; MBA, U. Mich., 1957. With Exxon Co., 1957-70; fin. adv. Exxon Co. (Esso Natural Gas), The Hague, Netherlands, 1965-66; treas. Exxon Co. (Esso Europe), London, 1966-70; sr. v.p. Aetna Life & Casualty Co., Hartford, Conn., 1970-72, exec. v.p., dir., 1972-88, ret., 1988; prin. owner, chmn. Hartford Whalers Hockey Club, 1988-92; sr. advisor to the pres. World Bank, Washington, 1995—. Bd. dirs. Chevy Chase (Md.) F.S.B.; founder Greater Hartford Arts Coun. Chmn. emeritus Am. Coun. for Arts N.Y., Greater Hartford Arts Coun. Lt. USNR, 1952-55. Mem. Watch Hill Yacht Club, The Club at Windermere, Bath and Tennis Club (Palm Beach), Teton Pines Country Club (Jackson Hole), Chevy Chase Club (Washington).

CONRAD, FLAVIUS LESLIE, JR., retired minister; b. Hickory, N.C., May 5, 1920; s. Flavius Leslie and Mary Wilhelmina (Huffman) C.; m. Mary Elizabeth Isenhour, Nov. 4, 1944; children: Ann Meisner (dec.), Susan Amis. AB, Lenoir Rhyne Coll., 1941; MDiv, Luth. Theol. So. Sem., 1944; MST, Temple U., 1955, STD, 1959. Ordained to ministry Evang. Luth. Ch. Am., 1944. Pastor St. Timothy Luth. Ch., Hickory, 1944-49, Holy Comforter Luth. Ch., Belmont, N.C., 1949-50; youth dir. United Luth. Ch. Am., Phila., 1950-60; pastor St. Luke's Luth. Ch., Richardson, Tex., 1960-86, pastor emeritus, 1986—. Dean Dallas and East Tex. dist. Luth. Ch. Am., 1973-77, mem. publ. bd., 1974-82; del. convs. Luth. Ch. Am., 1968, 74, 76; exec. sec. Luther League Am., 1950-60; mem. exec. bd. and gen. assembly Nat. Coun. Chs. of Christ in U.S.A., 1954-60. Author: A Study of Four Non-Denominational Youth Movements, 1955, Poetic Potshots at People and Preachers, 1977; pub. sermons for The Clergy Jour., worship materials for The Minister's Annual Manual, 1996-97; contbg. editor Ch. Mgmt. mag., 1966-74; corr. The Lutheran from S.W., 1962-76; contbr. sermons, articles and poems to various mags. V.p. Piedmont (N.C.) coun. Boy Scouts Am., 1948-49. Winner Nat. Poetry Contest, 1960. Home: 1108 Pueblo Dr Richardson TX 75080-2913

CONRAD, GEOFFREY WENTWORTH, archaeologist, educator; b. Boston, Dec. 24, 1947; s. Albert Austin and Ruth Wentworth (Cadieux) C.; m. Karen Ann Hildebrant, June 12, 1971; children: Matthew, Peter, Marc. AB, Harvard U., 1969, PhD, 1974. Curatorial asst. Smithsonian Inst., Washington, 1974-75; asst. prof. and asst. curator Harvard U., Cambridge, Mass., 1976-81, assoc. prof. and assoc. curator, 1981-83; dir. William Hammond Mathers Mus. Ind. U., Bloomington, 1983—, assoc. prof. anthropology, 1983-91, prof., 1991—, chair, 1991-95, assoc. dean faculties, 2003. Cons. Nat. Geog. Soc., Washington, 1982-83. Co-author: Religion and Empire, 1984, The Andean Heritage, 1982; co-editor: Ideology and Precolumbian Civilizations, 1992; contbr. articles to profl. jours.; mem. editl. bd. Jour. of Field Archaeology, 1986-96. Bd. dirs. Monroe County Hist. Soc., Bloomington, 1989-92. Grantee NSF, 1978, 85, Ind. Humanities Coun., 1983, 86, 88, 95, Wenner-Gren Found., 1987, Inst. Mus. and Libr. Svcs., 2000. Fellow AAAS; mem. Archaeol. Inst. Am. (pres. Ctrl. Ind. chpt. 1989-91, acad. trustee 1994-97), Soc. Am. Archaeology, Assn. for Field Archaeology, Internat. Assn. for Caribbean Archaeology, Am. Assn. Mus., Internat. Assn. for Caribbean Archaeology, Assn. Midwest Mus., Assn. Coll. and Univ. Mus. and Galleries (Midwest rep. 1990-91). Home: 3130 Saint James Ct Bloomington IN 47401-7105 Office: Mathers Mus Ind U 601 E 8th St Bloomington IN 47408-3812 also: Ind U Dept Anthropology Student Bldg Bloomington IN 47405 E-mail: conrad@indiana.edu.

CONRAD, GEORGE JOHN, retired design engineer, planner; b. N.Y.C., Apr. 24, 1943; s. George John and Bridget Anne (Kelly) C.; m. Marita Margaret Teuber, Apr. 24, 1971; children: Tracey Lynn, Kimberly Ann, Christopher George. BEE, Manhattan Coll., 1965. With Phila. Naval Shipyard, 1965-95, supr. field design, 1973-79, gen. engr., 1979-84, design br. head, 1984-85, asst. chief design engring., 1985-87, advance planning supr., 1987-90, waterfront supr., 1987-95, ret., 1995; transp. coord. Lakewood Pathology, 1998-2001; CEO Conrad Sr. Planning, 2002—. CEO Conrad Properties, Atco, N.J., 1973—. Coach Waterford Twp. Athletic Assn., 1987-94; founder Winslow Crossing Civic Assn., 1972. Mem. Fed. Mgrs. Assn. Roman Catholic. Avocations: hiking, canoeing. Home: 635 Raritan Ave Atco NJ 08004-1830 E-mail: atco400@aol.com.

CONRAD, HANS, materials engineering educator; b. Konradstahl, Germany, Apr. 19, 1922; came to U.S., 1926, naturalized, 1944; s. Henry K. and Martha Ann (Bader) C.; m. Emma Ann Bort, June 10, 1944; children— Sandra Joy, Roberta Lee, Gary Richard. Student, Washington and Jefferson Coll., 1940-42; BS in Metall. Engring, Carnegie Inst. Tech., 1943; M.Eng., Yale, 1951, D.Eng., 1956. Research metallurgist Chase Copper & Brass Co., Waterbury, Conn., 1953-55; supervisory engr. Westinghouse Research Labs., Churchill Boro, Pa., 1955-59; sr. research specialist Atomics Internat., Canoga Park, Calif., 1959-61; head dept. physics Aerospace Corp., El Segundo, Calif., 1961-64; tech. dir. Franklin Inst. Research Labs., Phila., 1964-67; prof., chmn. dept. metall. engring. and materials sci., assoc. dir. Inst. Mining and Minerals Research, U. Ky., Lexington, 1967-80; prof., head dept. materials engring., dir. minerals and materials research programs N.C. State U., 1981-85, prof., 1985—. Japan Soc. Promotion Sci. vis. prof. 1976; Disting. vis. prof. Am. U., Cairo, 1983, Soviet Acad. Scis, 1984; Ministry Metall. Industry, PRC, 1986. Contbr. articles to profl. jours. and books. Recipient Rsch. award U. Ky., 1971, U.S. Sr. Scientist award Alexander von Humboldt-Stiftung, 1974; Alcoa Rsch. award N.C. State U., 1985, Alumni Rsch. award, 1991; TMS 2000 Structural Matls. Disting. Scientist award, 2000. Fellow: Am. Soc. Materials; mem.: Rheol. Soc., Minerals, Metals and Materials Soc., Tau Beta Pi, Sigma Xi. Home: 205 Glasgow Rd Cary NC 27511-6517 E-mail: hans_conrad@mcsu.edu.

CONRAD, HAROLD AUGUST, retired religious pension board executive; b. Cleve., Dec. 18, 1928; s. August and Olga (Heise) C.; m. Anne (Chernosky) Conrad, July 10, 1948 (widowed Mar. 1956); children: Deborah Anne Hamer, Loren Harold Conrad, Rebecca Faith Towle; m. Naomi Ruth (Sweeny) Conrad, Dec. 31, 1960; 1 child, Paul Alan Conrad, MD. BA, Anderson U., Ind., 1952; MDiv, Christian Theo. Sem., Indpls., 1970; DD, Mid-Am. Bible Coll., Oklahoma City, 1975. Pastor Akron Ch. of God, Akron, Ind., 1952-63, First Ch. of God, Winchester, Ky., 1963-66, Glendale Ch. of God, Indpls., 1966-74; exec. sec. treas. Bd. of Pensions of Ch. of God, Anderson, Ind., 1974-93; ret., 1993. State chmn. Ind. Ministerial Assembly, Indpls., 1961-62; vice chmn. Ky. Ministerial Assembly, Winchester, Ky., 1965-66; bd. mem. Bd. of Pensions of Ch. of God, Anderson, Ind., 1964-74; bd. dirs. Exec. Coun. of Ch. of God, Anderson, Ind., 1976-84, 87-90. Mem. Nat. Ch. Pensions Conv. (pres. 1985). Republican. Mem. Ch. Of God. Avocations: stamp collecting, gardening, walking, reading, traveling. Home: 810 Northwood Dr Anderson IN 46011-1072 E-mail: conradhn@cs.com.

CONRAD, HAROLD THEODORE, psychiatrist; b. Milw., Jan. 25, 1934; s. Theodore Herman and Alyce Barbara Conrad; m. Elaine Marie Blaine, Sept. 1, 1962 (dec.); children: Blaine, Carl, David, Erich, Rachel. *Wife Elaine, deceased, was an accomplished musician. She studied piano in Rome and at Newcomb College. Son Blaine is a graduate in Economics and is currently studying computer applications for health data management. Son Carl is an attorney in private practice. Son David is an expert in environmental preservation and safety. He has a graduate degree in the field and works for a Native American group. Daughter Rachel is a physician. Son Erich is a physician.* AB, U. Chgo., 1954, BS, 1955, MD, 1958. Diplomate Am. Bd. Psychiatry. Intern USPHS Hosp., San Francisco, 1958-59, commd. sr. asst. surgeon, 1958, advanced through grades to med. dir., 1967, resident psychiatry Lexington, Ky., 1959-61, Charity Hosp., New Orleans, 1961-62; chief of psychiatry USPHS Hosp., New Orleans, 1962-67, clin. dir., 1967; dep. dir. div. field investigation NIMH, Chevy Chase, Md., 1968; chief NIMH Clin. Rsch. Ctr., Lexington, 1969-73; cons. psychiatry region IX USPHS, HEW, San Francisco, 1973-79; dir. adolescent unit Alaska Psychiat. Inst., Anchorage, 1979-81, supt., 1981-85; clin. assoc. prof. psychiatry U. Wash. Med. Sch., 1981-85; psychiatrist pvt. practice, Houma, La., 1985—. Contbr. articles to profl. jours. Recipient cmty. awards for contbns. in field of drug abuse and equal employment opportunity for minorities. Fellow: Royal Soc. Medicine; mem.: AMA, Am. Psychiat. Assn., Alpha Delta Phi, Alpha Omega Alpha. Office: 4608 Highway 1 Raceland LA 70394-2623

CONRAD, JOHN REGIS, lawyer, engineering executive, consultant; b. Bloomington, Ind., Feb. 23, 1955; s. John Francis and Patricia Ann (English) C.; m. Paula Jane Vessels, July 4, 1980; children: William Celestine Vessels, John Paul Vessels, M. Alexander Vessels, David Thomas Kelamalamalamanokeakua Vessels, Rachel Elizabeth Ho'ouluolaikeaouha Vessels. AB cum laude, Harvard U., 1977; MBA, JD, Ind. U., 1981. Bar: Hawaii 1981, Fla. 1994, Tex. 1994, N.C. 1995, U.S. Dist. Ct. Hawaii 1981, U.S. Ct. Appeals (9th cir.) 1981, U.S. Ct. Claims 1981, U.S. Tax Ct. 1981. Assoc. Cades, Schutte, Fleming & Wright, Honolulu, 1981-85, 89-90, Thompson & Chan, Honolulu, 1985-89; ptnr. Cades Schutte Fleming & Wright, Honolulu, 1991-94; regional bus. mgr. Kimley-Horn and Assocs., Inc., West Palm Beach, Fla., 1994-96, regional prodn. mgr., 1996-98, regional bus. mgr., sr. assoc., sr. v.p. Phoenix, 1999—. Lectr. law Kapiolani C.C., Honolulu, 1984-86; adj. prof. Richardson Sch. Law, U. Hawaii, 1989-90; webmaster Conrad-Vessels Genealogy. Author: A Conrad Genealogy, 1979, Hawaii Probate Sourcebook, 1985, rev. 1986, rev. 1992; co-author: Beyond the Basics: Hawaii Estate Planning & Probate, 1985, Hawaii Wills & Trusts Sourcebook, 1986, Hawaii Guardianship Sourcebook, 1988; editor HICLE Fin. and Estate Planning Manual, vol. II, 1989, vol. I, 1990. Planned giving com. Hawaii Heart Assn., Honolulu, 1983-86; arbitrator Hawaii Ct. Annexed Arbitration Program, 1989-94; sch. bd. Star of the Sea Sch., Honolulu, 1992-94, pres., 1993-94, chair Carnival, 1992; chair Cub Scout Pack Aloha Coun. Boy Scouts Am., den leader Cub Scout Pack, Gulf Stream Coun., Grand Canyon Coun.; lector Good Shepherd of the Hills Ch., Cave Creek, Ariz.; trustee St. Paul's Prep. Acad. (vice chair 2003-), Phoenix, 2002-. Fellow Am. Coll. Trust and Estate Coun.; mem. ABA, Am. Arbitration Assn., Hawaii Bar Assn. (chmn. estate and gift tax com. 1984-85, CFO probate and estate planning sect. 1989-90), Hawaii Bar Found. (bd. dirs. 1985-92, v.p. 1989, pres. 1989-91), Ancestral Trails Hist. Soc., Sons of Am. Legion, John T. Reilly Hist. Soc., Hawaii Estate Planning Coun. (bd. dirs. 1991-94, sec. 1993), Filson Club Hist. Soc. Roman Catholic. Avocations: genealogy, coin collecting. Office: Kimley-Horn and Assocs Inc 7600 N 15th St Ste 250 Phoenix AZ 85020-4335 Home: 33214 N 61st St Scottsdale AZ 85262-8206 E-mail: jrconrad@post.harvard.edu., john.conrad@kimley-horn.com.

CONRAD, JOSEPH HENRY, animal nutrition educator; b. Cass County, Ind., Dec. 7, 1926; s. Ferdinand M. and Marie E. (Hubenthal) C.; m. Frances Ash, June 18, 1950; children: Kenneth A., Leonard J., Carol Ann, Joseph C. BS, Purdue U., 1950, MS, 1954, PhD, 1958; prof. (hon.), Fed. U. Viçosa, Brazil, 1965. Asst. prof. Purdue U., West Lafayette, Ind., 1958-63, assoc. prof., 1963-68, prof., 1968-71; animal scientist Fed. U. Viçosa, 1961-65; prof., coord. tropical animal sci. programs U. Fla., Gainesville, 1971-95. Co-author: Swine Production, 1982; contbr. monographs and numerous articles on animal nutrition and tropical animal prodn. to profl. jours. Served with USN, 1944-46. Recipient Disting. Nutritional award Distillers Feed Rsch. Coun., 1964; Moorman fellow, 1989. Fellow Am. Soc. Animal Sci. (Internat. Animal Agrl. award 1985, Bohstedt award 1987, Internat. Mktg. award 1989); mem. World Assn. Animal Prodn. (v.p.), Latin Am. Soc. Animal Prodn., Sociedade Brasileira de Zootecnia, Purdue U. Alumni Assn. (life, pres.'s coun.), Sigma Xi, Gamma Sigma Delta. Republican. Lutheran. Home: 1824 NW 10th Ave Gainesville FL 32605-5312 Office: PO Box 110910 Gainesville FL 32611-0910 E-mail: joegogator@aol.com.

CONRAD, KELLEY ALLEN, industrial and organizational psychologist; b. N.Y.C., June 29, 1941; s. Allen and Dorothy Etta (McAtee) C.; m. Barbara Rae Bedessem, July 8, 1976. BS in Behavioral Science, Mont. State U., 1963; MA in Psychology, SUNY, Geneseo, 1970; PhD in Psychology, Iowa State U., 1973. Lic. psychologist Wis., Colo., cert. Assn. State and Provincial Psychology Bds. Cons. indsl. psychologist Humber, Mundie & McClary, Milw., 1973-96; v.p. Human Resources Devel. Ctr., 1988-95, pres., 1995-96, mgr., 1996-98, Conrad Cons. Internat., Inc., 1998—; pvt. practice indsl. and orgnl. psychology Naples, 1996-01, Ft. Collins, Colo., 2001—02. Contbg. author Learning by Experience—What, Why, How, 1978; co-editor: A Handbook of Psychological Assessment in Business, 1991; co-author: Current Perspectives in Industrial Organizational Psychology, 1998; contbr. articles to profl. jours. Mem. Naples Free Net, co-chmn. help desk, 1997-99, chmn. intership com., 1997-2000, mem. strategic planning com., 1997-98, bd. dirs., sec. 1998, pres., 1999-2001, mem. Home Organ Festival, newsletter editor, 1992-2001, co-dir., 1999-2000. Lt. USN, 1964-68, Vietnam. Recipient Eli Tash award Wis. Assn. for Children with Learning Disabilities, 1983, 93. Fellow Am. Psychol. Soc., Wis. Psychol. Assn. (sec. 1984-86, pres. indsl./organizational divsn. 1984-85); mem. APA, ASTD (bd. dirs. 1980), Nat. Psychol. Cons. to Mgmt. (pres. 1988-89, sec.-treas. 1990-96), Midwest Psychol. Assn., Colo. Psychol. Assn. (assoc.), Midwest Human Resources Planning Assn., Milw. Area Psychol. Assn. (pres. 1985-86), Coun. Police Psychol. Svcs., Acad. Mgmt., Kiwanis (bd. dirs. Milw. 1978-80, com. chmn. 1980, 91), Sigma Xi, Psi Chi. Congregationalist. Republican. Avocations: computer programming, music, jogging, sking, photography. Home and Office: 552 Wildridge Ln #40 Lafayette CO 80026 E-mail: kaconrad@naples.net.

CONRAD, KENT, senator; b. Bismarck, N.D., Mar. 12, 1948; m. Lucy Calautti, Feb. 1987; 1 child, Jessamyn Abigail. Student, U. Mo., 1967; BA, Stanford U., 1972; MBA, George Washington U., 1975. Asst. to tax commr. State of N.D. Tax Dept., Bismarck, 1974-80, tax commr., 1981-87; U.S. senator from N.D. Washington, 1987—. Mem. agr. nutrition and forestry com., mem. budget com. and fin. coms., ethics com., Indian affairs com., senate Dem. steering and coord. com., forestry com. Democrat. Office: US Senate 530 Hart Senate Office Bldg Washington DC 20510-0001*

CONRAD, MARCEL EDWARD, hematologist, educator; b. N.Y.C., Aug. 15, 1928; s. Marcel Edward and Lulu Marie (Geraghty) C.; m. Marcia Louise Grove; children: Marcel Edward, III, Mark E., Carol J., Erin E., Julia P. BS, Georgetown U., 1949, MD, 1953. Diplomate Am. Bd. Internal Medicine, Am. Bd. Hematology. Intern Walter Reed Gen. Hosp., Washington, 1953-54, resident, then chief resident in internal medicine, 1955-60; mem. staff Walter Reed Army Inst. Rsch., 1961-74, chief dept. hematology, 1965-74; chief clin. investigation svc. Walter Reed Army Med. Ctr., 1971-74; clin. asst. prof., then clin. assoc. prof. medicine Georgetown U. Med. Sch., 1964-74; prof. medicine U. Ala. Med. Sch., Birmingham, 1974-83, also dir. div. hematology and oncology, 1974-83; prof. medicine, pathology, dir. divsn. hematology, oncology U. South Ala., Mobile, 1983-2001, dir. USA Cancer Ctr., 1985-2001, disting. prof. medicine, 2001. Contbr. numerous articles to med. publs. Commd. 1st lt. M.C. U.S. Army, 1953; advanced through grades to col. 1968. Decorated Legion of Merit with oak leaf cluster; recipient Skinner medal U.S. Army, 1955, Hoff medal, 1962, John Shaw Billings award, 1967, William Beaumont award, 1972, Walter Reed award, 1974 Fellow Internat. Soc. Hematology, ACP (Laureate award 1989, named Disting. Prof. of Medicine, 2001); mem. AAAS, Assn. Am. Physicians, Internat. Soc. Hematology, Am. Soc. Clin. Investigation, Am. Physiol. Soc., Internat. Soc. Blood Transfusion, Am. Soc. Hematology, Am. Soc. Clin. Oncology, Am. Chem. Soc., Soc. Exptl. Biology and Medicine, So. Soc. Clin. Investigation, Am. Fedn. Clin. Rsch. Roman Catholic. Home: 28451 Perdido Pass Dr Orange Beach AL 36561-3602

CONRAD, MARIAN SUE (SUSAN CONRAD), special education educator; b. Columbus, Ohio, May 3, 1946; d. Harold Marion Griffith and Susie Belle (House) Goheen; m. Richard Lee Conrad, Jan. 23 1971. BS, Ohio State U., 1967. Tchr. spl. edn. West High Sch., Columbus, Ohio, 1967-70; spl. edn. work study coord. North High Sch., Columbus, 1974-79, Whetstone High Sch., Columbus, 1979-80, Briggs High Sch., Columbus, 1980-97, West High Sch., Columbus, 1970-97; ret., 1997. Bd. dirs. Jr. Div., The Columbus Symphony Club, 1972-79; vice chmn. Zoofari, Columbus, 1978-97; bd. dirs., life mem. Wazoo, Columbus, 1974-87; bd. dirs., chair coms. Jr. League, Columbus, 1982-99; vice chmn. devel. com. Dublin (Ohio) Counseling Ctr., 1987-97; trustee Columbus Zoo, 1991—. Recipient Mayors Award for Vol. Svc., Columbus, 1988. Mem. Am. Bus. Women's Assn. (v.p. 1979-80, bd. dirs., Woman of Yr. 1980), Coun. Exceptional Children (pres. 1988-89, Educator of Yr. 1989), Ohio Assn. Suprs. and Work Study Coords., Dublin Women in Bus. and Professions, Country Club at Muirfield, Dublin Women's Club, Iota Lambda Sigma. Republican. Methodist. Avocations: golf, gardening, travel, family, cooking. Home: 8039 Crossgate Ct S Dublin OH 43017-8432

CONRAD, PAUL ERNEST, transportation consultant; b. Hartford, Conn., June 11, 1927; s. Ernest and Agnes Anita (Eis) C.; m. Audrey Grace Lindner, June 17, 1947; children: Cynthia Dale, Robin Sue, Kristen Diane. BS, U. Conn., 1949. Hwy. engr. Fed. Hwy. Adminstrn., Southeast U.S., Conn. and N.Y., 1949-55; prin. assoc. Wilbur Smith & Assocs., Columbia, S.C., 1955-69, sr. v.p., 1969-72, exec. v.p., 1972-91, also bd. dirs. Bd. dirs. Spring Valley Homeowners Assn., 1976-77, 97-98, Enclave Comty. Assn., 1999—. With USN, 1945-46. Mem. NSPE, ASCE, Inst. Transp. Engrs., Am. Cons. Engrs. Coun., Spring Valley Country Club (bd. govs. 1993-96, v.p. house). Lutheran. Home: 103 Enclave Loop Columbia SC 29223-3260 E-mail: pauleconrad@aol.com.

CONRAD, PAUL FRANCIS, editorial cartoonist; b. Cedar Rapids, Iowa, June 27, 1924; s. Robert H. and Florence G. (Lawler) C.; m. Barbara Kay King, Feb. 27, 1954; children: James, David, Carol, Elizabeth. BA, U. Iowa, 1950. Editorial cartoonist Denver Post, 1950-64, L.A. Times, 1964-93; cartoonist L.A. Times Syndicate, 1973-2000, Tribune Media Svcs., 2000—. Richard M. Nixon chair Whittier Coll., 1977-78 Exhibited sculpture and cartoons, Los Angeles County Mus. Art, 1979, Libr. of Congress, 1999; author: The King and Us, 1974, Pro and Conrad, 1979, Drawn and Quartered, 1985, CONArtist: Thirty Years With The Los Angeles Times, 1993, Drawing The Line, 1999. Served with C.E. AUS, 1942-46, PTO. Recipient Editl. Cartoon award, Sigma Delta Chi, 1963, 1969, 1971, 1981—82, 1988, 1997, Pulitzer prize editl. cartooning, 1964, 1971, 1984, Overseas Press Club award, 1970, 1981, Journalism award, U. So. Calif., 1972, Robert F. Kennedy Journalism award 1st prize, 1985, 1990, 1992, 1993, Hugh M. Hefner 1st Amendment award, 1990, Lifetime Achievement award, Am. Assn. Editl. Cartoonists, 1998, Lifetime Pub. Svc. award, Edmund G. Brown Inst. Pub. Affairs, 2000; fellow sr. fellow, Sch. Pub. Policy and Social Rsch., UCLA, 2001—02. Fellow Soc. Profl. Journalists; mem. Phi Delta Theta. Democrat. Roman Catholic. Office: LA Times Syndicate 2121 Rosecrans Ave Ste 2370 El Segundo CA 90245-4745

CONRAD, PHILIP JEFFERSON, software development engineer; b. New Iberia, La., Nov. 30, 1957; s. Karl Donovan and Dolores Beatrice (Bienvenu) C.; children: Siobhan, Turner; m. Diane Tucker, Mar. 30, 1996 (div. 2000); stepchildren: Ryan, Ree. BSME, U. Southwestern La., 1979; postgrad., U. Okla., 1992-93. Commd. 2nd lt. USAF, 1979, advanced through grades to capt., 1983, structural engr., 1979-81, safety officer, investigator, specialist, 1983-89, A-10 pilot, 1983-84, RAF Bentwaters, U.K., 1984-87, E-3 pilot Oklahoma City, 1987-89, supv. Command Ctr., 1989-92; software engr. Texas Instruments, Dallas, 1993-96, DSC Comms. Co., Plano, Tex., 1996-98, Alcatel, Plano, 1998-99, Santera Systems Inc., Plano, 1999—2002, Rapport Techs. Inc., Carrollton, 2003—. Decorated Air medal. Avocations: bicycling, personal computers. Home: Apt 1812 701 Legacy Dr Plano TX 75023-2234 Office: Rapport Techs Inc 2833 Trinity Sq Ste 105 Carrollton TX 75006 E-mail: pjconrad@mail.com.

CONRAD, ROBERT DAVID, broadcast executive, educator; b. Kankakee, Ill., July 17, 1933; s. Clarence P. and Geneva (Beatty) C.; m. Jean Smith, July 11, 1959; children: Caroline, Allison, Christopher, Susan, Andrea. BS, Northwestern U., 1955; DFA (hon.), Baldwin Wallce Coll., 1983; MusD (hon.), Cleve. Inst. Music, 1998; DHum (hon.), Oberlin Coll., 2002. Announcer KULA, KAIM, Honolulu, 1956-57, WKAN, Kankakee, 1947-51; announcer, program dir. WEAW AM/FM, Evanston, Ill., 1951-54; announcer WFMT, Chgo., 1954-55, announcer, ops. mgr., 1957-60; program dir. WDTM, Detroit, 1960-62; v.p., program mgr. WCLV, Cleve., 1962-92, pres., broadcast mgr., 1992—. Prodr., commentator Cleve. Orch., 1965—; broadcasting instr. Cuyahoga C.C., Cleve., 1984-91; adj. prof. broadcasting Case Western Res. U./Cleve. Inst. Music, 1991—. Bd. dirs., trustee Cleve. Music Sch. Settlement, 1995—; bd. dirs. Rainey Inst., 2000—, Cleve. Sch. of the Arts, 1998—; bd. trustees Cleve. Orch., 2002—. Named Program Dir. of Yr., Billboard Mag., N.Y., 1982, Excellence in Broadcasting award Cleve. Assn. Broadcasters, 2001; named to No. Ohio Radio Hall of Fame, 1993, City Club Hall of Fame, 2000; recipient award of achievement Cleve. Radio Broadcasters Assn., 2000, Lifetime Achievement award Cleve. Achievement in Radio Awards, 2002. Mem. Concert Music Broadcasters Assn. (bd. dirs., pres. 1980-83), City Club Cleve. (past bd. dirs., v.p. 1975-78). Office: WCLV 26501 Renaissance Pkwy Cleveland OH 44128-5798 E-mail: rconrad@wclv.com.

CONRAD, STEPHEN EDWARD, secondary school educator; b. Phila., Jan. 27, 1948; married. BA, Gettysburg (Pa.) Coll., 1970; MA, Temple U., 1980, postgrad., 1997—. Cert. comprehensive secondary social studies Pa. Dept. Edn. Tchr. Sch. Dist. of Phila., 1973—79, Council Rock Sch. Dist., Richboro, Pa., 1979—. Vice chairperson Cheltenham Twp. (Pa.) Hist. Commn., 2003; lifeguard trainer ARC, Phila., 1966—2002; ward leader Cheltenham Twp. Rep. Orgn., 1992—2003; committeeman Montgomery County Rep. Com., Norristown, Pa., 1982—2003; trustee Unitarian Soc. of Germantown, Phila., 2001—03. Tchg. fellow, Athens (Greece) Coll., 1970—71. Mem.: NEA, Pa. State Edn. Assn., Council Rock Edn. Assn., Nat. Coun. Social Studies, Orgn. Am. Historians, Coast Def. Study Group. Republican. Unitarian Universalist. Avocations: historical research, travel, reading. Office: Council Rock HS - North 62 Swamp Rd Newtown PA 18940

CONRAD, STEVEN ALLEN, critical care and emergency physician, biomedical engineer, educator; b. St. Martinville, La., Aug. 23, 1953; s. Karl Donovan and Dolores Beatrice (Bienvenu) C.; m. Mona Theresa Hollier, Aug. 9, 1974; children: David, Lesley, Taylor. BS, U. S.W. La., 1974; MD, La. State U., Shreveport, 1978; MS, Case Western Reserve, Cleve., 1980, PhD, 1985; MS in Engring., La. Tech. U., 1981; MBA, La. State U., 2001, MS in Info. Sys. Tech., 2003. Diplomate Am. Bd. Internal Medicine, Critical Care Medicine, Am. Bd. Emergency Medicine; cert. nutritional support physician. Postdoctoral trainee in biomed. computing Case Western Res., 1979—80; resident internal medicine La. State U., Shreveport, 1981-84; fellow in critical care medicine Mayo Grad. Sch. Medicine, Rochester, 1984-86; from asst. prof. medicine to prof. La. State U. Med. Ctr., Shreveport, La., 1986—97, prof., 1997—, dir. critical care medicine tng. program, 1987—. Instr. computer sci. Winona State U., 1985—86; adj. prof. biomed. engring. La. Tech. U., Ruston, 1989—, adj. prof. human ecology, 1996—, prof. anesthesiology, 2002—; adj. prof. mech. engring. Inst. for Micromanufacturing, 1994—; cons. physician critical care VA Med. Ctr., 1986—, dir. extracorporeal life support program, 1993—, co-dir. nutritional support svc., 1994—, transplant intensivist Willis Knighton Regional Heart Transplant Program, 1994—, attending physician in pediat. ICU, 1994—; mem. emergency med. svcs. task force Shreveport Fire Dept., 1992—; prin. investigator in multiple device and drug trials. Editor: Pulmonary Function Testing: Principles and Practice, 1984; manuscript reviewer ASAIO Jour., Artificial Organs, Intensive Care Medicine, Critical Care Chest Medicine, Chest; abstract reviewer Critical Care Medicine; contbr. chpts. to books and articles to profl. jours. Grantee, Am. Heart Assn., NHLBI. Fellow ACP, Am. Coll. Crit. Care Med., Am. Coll. Chest Physicians, Am. Coll. Emergency Physicians; mem. IEEE (sr.), Biomed. Engring. Soc., Shock Soc., Am. Soc. Artificial Internal Organs, Internat. Soc. for Artificial Organs, Soc. for Acad. Emergency Medicine, Am. Soc. for Parenteral and Enteral Nutrition, Alpha Omega Alpha, Sigma Xi, Phi Kappa Phi, Beta Gamma Sigma, Sigma Iota Epsilon. Office: La State U Health Scis Ctr 1501 Kings Hwy Shreveport LA 71103-4228

CONRAD, WILLIAM MERRILL, architect; b. Sapulpa, Okla., Sept. 5, 1926; s. William Samuel and Lillian Lorraine (Strain) C.; m. Esther Marian Lenz, Nov. 8, 1952. BS in Architecture, U. Kans., 1950, BSBA, 1951. Lic. architect. Prin., architect William M. Conrad, F.A.I.A., Kansas City, Mo., 1956—; asst. prof., Sch. of Architecture and Urban Design U. Kans., Lawrence, 1956-59. Mem. adv. com. U. Kans. Sch. of Architecture and Urban Design, 1974-86; vis. Fulbright prof., U. Helsinki, 1958-59. Mem. Kans. City-St. Joseph Bldg. Commn., 1970-82; leader People to People Internat. Peace Mission Overseas Tours, 1994-2002. Recipient Patriotic Svc. award Dept. Army, 1974, 84, Nat. Friend of Park and Recreation award Nat. Assn. Park and Recreation Ofcls., 1982, Urban Design award Mcpl. Art Com., Kansas City, 1976, Disting. Alumnus award U. Kans. Sch. Arch. and Urban Design, 1993, Achievement award PTP Philippines, 1999, PTP Taiwan, 1999. Fellow AIA (treas. nat. conv. 1979, Kansas City chpt. pres. 1968, past sec., other offices, mem. numerous coms., Cmty. Svc. award 1990, numerous other awards); mem. SAR (Good Citizenship award 1997), Mo. Coun. Architects (past dir. and treas.), People to People Internat. (pres. Greater Kansas City chpt. 1972-74, chmn. Gt. Plains regional coun. 1974-77, chmn. bd. dirs., trustee 1985-89, internat. pres. 1988-91, Disting. Mem. award 1986, Eisenhower Lifetime Achievement award 1996), Optimists (past pres. Honor Club), Masons, Shriners (pres. 1990), Sertoma Kans. dist. gov. 1984-86, pres. Honor Club 1982-84, Sertoman of Yr. 1987, Outstanding Regional Sec. award 1995), Christian the Fourth Guild (hon. Denmark, 2000), Tau Beta Pi (life), Tau Sigma Delta. Methodist. Home: 6120 W 69th St Overland Park KS 66204-1411

CONRAD, WINTHROP BROWN, JR., lawyer; b. Detroit, May 26, 1945; s. Winthrop Brown and Dolores (Millard) C.; m. Ellen Rouse, May 12, 1973; children: Parker Rouse, Louisa Katherine, Frances Winthrop. AB, Yale U., 1967; JD, Harvard U., 1971. Bar: N.Y. 1972, U.S. Dist. Ct. (so. dist.) N.Y. 1975, U.S. Ct. Appeals (2d cir.) 1975. Ptnr. Davis, Polk & Wardwell, N.Y.C., 1979—, Paris Office, 1985-88. Bd. dirs. Found. for Joffrey Ballet, N.Y.C., 1985-86, British-Am. Ednl. Found.; former trustee Estate and Property of the Conv. of the Diocese of N.Y., Episcopal Diocese of N.Y., Ch. Pension Fund; trustee Vt. Studio Ctr.; dir., BAR Vermont Inc. Mem. ABA, Assn. of Bar of City of N.Y. Home: 1120 5th Ave New York NY 10128-0144 Office: Davis Polk & Wardwell 450 Lexington Ave Fl 31 New York NY 10017-3982 also: 856 Old Post Rd Bedford NY 10506-1215

CONRAD-ENGLAND, ROBERTA LEE, pathologist; b. Meriden, Conn., Aug. 25, 1950; d. Hans and Emma Ann (Bort) Conrad; m. Gary Thomas England, June 6, 1976; children: Eric Bryan, Christopher Ryan. BS in Microbiology, U. Ky., 1972, MD, 1976. Diplomate Nat. Bd. Med. Examiners, Bd. Am. Pathologists. Resident anatomic and clin. pathology Emory U. Affiliated Hosps., Atlanta, 1976-80; pathologist Western Bapt. Hosp., Paducah, Ky., 1980—. Cons. Marshall County Hosp., Benton, Ky., 1985—, chair infection control com., 1985—. Mem., com. chairperson PTA, Poducah, Ky., 1993-94; mother's asst. Boy Scouts Am., Poducah, 1991-94. Fellow Coll. Am. Pathologists, Am. Soc. Clin. Pathologists; mem. Ky. Med. Assn., Ky. Soc. Pathologists, Ky. Women Mentors in Sci., Alpha Omega Alpha, Phi Beta Kappa. Avocations: swimming, snorkeling, interior decorating.

CONRADER, CONSTANCE RUTH, artist, writer, librarian; b. Vandalia, Mo., Apr. 13, 1919; d. Gilbert Fordyce and Elizabeth Florence (Cleghorn) Stone; m. Jay Merten Conrader, Nov. 29, 1941 (dec. 1996). Student, Carroll Coll., 1938-40, North Park Coll., 1940-41. Cert. pub. libr. Artist, author, Oconomowoc, Wis., 1940—. Libr. Oconomowoc Pub. Libr., 1947-82, vol. 1982—; illustrator Turtox classroom charts Gen. Biol. Supply House, Chgo., 1940-60; manuscript critique Baha'i Pub. Trust, Wilmette, Ill., 1970-89, editor, 1988. Author, illustrator: Blue Wampum, 1958; co-editor: Tokens From the Writings of Baha'u'llah, 1973, Baha'i newsletter, 1997—; illustrator: Northwoods Wildlife Region, 1983; co-author, illustrator articles to profl. jours.; co-editor regional Baha'i Newsletter, 1997—. Chair UN Day, Oconomowoc, 1976-86. Avocations: gardening, music, reading, cooking. Home: 738 E Washington St Oconomowoc WI 53066-3110

CONRADI, JANET K. art educator; b. Iowa; MA, Iowa State U., 1986—88. Assoc. prof. of graphic design Ball State U., 1989—2000; prof. of graphic design SUNY Coll., Fredonia, NY, 2000—. Edn. editor Visual Arts Trends, N.Y.C., 2001—. Author: (design, typography and design edn.) Visual Arts Trends. Mem.: AIGA. Office: SUNY Coll at Fredonia Rockefeller Arts Center Fredonia NY 14063

CONRAN, JOSEPH PALMER, lawyer; b. St. Louis, Oct. 4, 1945; s. Palmer and Theresa (Bussmann) C.; m. Doria D. Conran, June 8, 1968; children: Andrew, Lisabeth, Theresa. BA, St. Louis U., 1967, JD with honors, 1970. Bar: Mo. 1970, U.S. Ct. Mil. Appeals 1971, U.S. Ct. Appeals (8th cir.) 1974. Assoc. Husch and Eppenberger, St. Louis, 1974-78, ptnr., 1978—, chmn. litigation dept., 1980-95, chmn. mgmt. com., 1995—. Mem. faculty Trial Practice Inst. Capt., JAGC, USAF, 1970-74. Mem. Bar Assn. Met. St. Louis (Merit award 1976, 77), Mo. Bar Assn. (bd. govs. 1987-92), Mo. Athletic Club (pres. 1986-87), Norwood Hills Country Club, St. Louis Club. Roman Catholic. Home: 53 Hawthorne Est Saint Louis MO 63131-3035 Office: Husch & Eppenberger 100 N Broadway Ste 1300 Saint Louis MO 63102-2789 E-mail: joe.conran@husch.com.

CONROY, RICHARD TIMOTHY, writer, retired foreign service officer; b. Copperhill, Tenn., Dec. 20, 1927; s. Edward Hubert and Elizabeth Lowry (Scruggs) C.; m. Sarah Jane Booth, Dec. 31, 1949; children: Camille Booth, Sarah Claire. BA, U. Tenn., 1950. Fgn. svc. officer U.S. Dept. State, Washington, 1956-72; fgn. affairs staff Smithsonian Instn., Washington, 1972-88; ret., 1988. Author: The India Exhibition, 1992, Mr. Smithson's Bones, 1993, Old Ways in the New World, 1994, Our Man in Belize, 1997, Our Man in Vienna, 2000. Mem. Nat. Press Club. Democrat. Avocations: painting, sculpting, making jewelry, architectural photography, piano. Home: 5016 16th St NW Washington DC 20011-3842

CONROY, ROBERT JOHN, lawyer; b. Newark, Feb. 17, 1953; s. Michael John and Frances (Goncalves) C.; m. Mary Catherine McGuire, June 7, 1975; children: Caitlin Michaela, Michael Colin. BS, St. Peter's Coll., 1977; M in Pub. Adminstrn., CUNY, 1981; JD, N.Y. Law Sch., 1981; MPH, Harvard U., 1985. Bar: N.Y. 1981, N.J. 1981, U.S. Dist. N.J. 1981, Calif. 1982, U.S. Dist. Ct. (so. and ea. dists.) N.Y. 1982, U.S. Dist. Ct. (we. dist.) Calif. 1990, U.S. Ct. Appeals (2d, 3d and 11th cirs.) 1982, Fla. 1984, D.C. 1984, U.S. Supreme Ct. 1984, Pa., 2000, U.S. Dist. Ct. (ea. dist.), Pa., 2001. Asst. corp. counsel City of N.Y., 1981-83, dep. chief med. malpractice unit, 1983, chief med. malpractice unit, 1984; assoc. Jones, Hirsch, Connors & Bull, N.Y.C., 1985-88; counsel Kern & Augustine, P.A., Morristown, N.J., 1988-90; prin. Kern Augustine Conroy & Schoppmann, P.C., Bridgewater, N.J., 1990—. Spl. counsel pro bono med. malpractice rsch. project, N.Y.C., 1985-88; gen. counsel Med. Soc. N.J., 2002—. Decorated knight of merit Sacred Mil. Constantinian Order St. George, 2002; Solomon scholar, NY Law Sch., 1979; recipient Bronze Pelican award Roman Cath. Archdiocese, Newark, 2000. Fellow: Coll. Law Practice Mgmt.; mem.: ABA (chmn. govt. mgmt. com. 1984—86, mgr. products media bd. 1985—92, chmn. document retrieval com. 1985—86, vice-chmn. ins. and malpractice com. 1986—88, co-chmn. glass ceiling task force 1992—95, vice-chmn. law practice mgmt. phb. bd. 1992—95, coun. mem. 1989—95, co-chmn. law practice mgmt. pub. bd. 1995—98, Foonberg award 1998), Am. Healthcare Lawyers Assn., N.Y. Bar Assn. (mem. health law sect. 1996—), Assn. of Bar of City of N.Y., Cmty. Health Law Project N.J., Inc. (trustee 1988—91), Westfield Sr. Citizens Housing Corp., Inc. (trustee 1994—, v.p. 1996—98, pres. 1998—), Soc. Health Care Risk Mgmt. N.J. (chmn. legis. com. 1987—96), N.J. Bar Assn. (dir., chmn. health hosp. sect. 1993—95, mem. com. health law litigation, mem. subcom. profl. licensing 1997—, del. gen. coun. adminstrn. sect. 1995—97), Mensa, Harvard Club. Home: 905 Pennsylvania Ave Westfield NJ 07090-3433 Office: Kern Augustine Conroy & Schoppmann PC 1120 Rt 22 E Bridgewater NJ 08807 E-mail: CONROY@DRLAW.COM.

CONROY, SARAH BOOTH, columnist, novelist, speaker; b. Valdosta, Ga., Feb. 16, 1927; d. Weston Anthony and Ruth (Proctor) Booth; m. Richard Timothy Conroy, Dec. 31, 1949; children: Camille Booth, Sarah Claire. BS, U. Tenn., 1950. Continuity writer Sta. WNOX, 1945-48; commentator, writer Sta. WATO, 1948-49; reporter, architecture columnist Knoxville News Sentinel, 1949-56; assoc. editor The Diplomat mag., 1956-58; columnist Washington Post, 1957-58, design editor, columnist, editor in chief Living in Style, 1970-82, feature writer, columnist, 1982-94, Chronicles columnist, 1986—; reporter, art critic Washington Daily News, 1968-70; regular contbr. N.Y. Times, 1968-70. Mem. adv. bd. Horizon mag., 1978-85 Author: Refinements of Love A Novel about Clover and Henry Adams, 1993. Recipient Raven award Mystery Writers Am., 1990, U. Tenn. Disting. Alumni award, 1995, Mortar Bd. award, 1997. Mem.: AIA (hon. first recipient Glenn Brown award 2000). Home: 5016 16th St NW Washington DC 20011-3842

CONROY, TAMARA BOKS, artist, special education educator, former nurse; b. Most, Bohemia, Czechoslovakia; came to U.S., 1947; d. Alois and Tatiana (Shapilova) Boks; m. John P. Conroy, Aug. 19, 1950 (dec. Oct. 1973); 1 child, Michael Thomas (dec.). Student, U. Graz, Austria, 1945-47; RN, New Rochelle (N.Y.) Med. Ctr., 1950; student, Coll. of William & Mary, 1958, 59, Cath. U. Am., 1960; BS in Nursing Edn., Columbia U., 1963, MA in Spl. Edn., 1965. RN, N.Y.; cert. spl. edn. tchr., N.Y. Nurse accident rm. New Rochelle Hosp./Med. Ctr., 1950-51; pub. health nurse Va. Dept. of Health, Richmond, 1958-59; tchr. spl. edn. Southern Westchester Bd. Coop. Edn. Svcs., Portchester, N.Y., 1965-83; freelance artist and painter N.Y.C. and Pelham, N.Y., 1969—. Asst. to chmn. math. dept. Columbia U., N.Y.C., 1975-76. Author math. program Learning Numbers-Step by Step, 1977. Pres., founder Classical Music Lovers' Exch., Pelham, N.Y., 1980-98. Mem. Am. Fedn. Tchrs., N.Y. State United Tchrs., BOCES Tchrs. Assn. (profl.), Women's Mus. Group, Mamaroneck Artists Guild, Silvermine Artists Guild, Westchester Musicians Guild (assoc.), Kappa Delta Pi. Avocations: flying, reading, music, fashion designing, painting and drawing.

CONROY, THOMAS FRANCIS, insurance company consultant; b. Chgo., Sept. 26, 1938; s. Thomas Francis and Eleanor Althea (Heatherly) C.; m. Mary Elizabeth Schaeffer, June 19, 1965; children: Alexandra B., Margaret E. BSc, De Paul U., 1959; MBA, U. Chgo., 1969. CPA, CDP. Mgr. Ernst & Whinney, Chgo., 1959-74; exec. v.p. fin., treas., contr. Security Life of Denver, 1974-93; prin. Ea. Hemisphere Trading Corp., Denver, 1990—; pres. Security Life Reins., 1993-99, ING Re Internat., 2000-01; mng. prin. Strategic Reins. Cons. Internat., Englewood, Colo., 2001—; ptnr. Mann Conroy Eisenberg & Assoc., LLC, Greensboro, 2002—; dir. Teton Petroleum Co., 2002—. Bd. dirs. Buffalo Mountain Met. Dist. Bd. trustees Denver Chamber Orch., 1988-93; bd. dirs. Denver Affiliate Susan G. Fonen Found. Capt. U.S. Army, 1960-62. Fellow Life Mgmt. Inst. Roman Catholic. Office: 3825 S Colorado Blvd Englewood CO 80110-4202 E-mail: tom-conroy@strategicre.com.

CONROY, WILLIAM B. retired university administrator; b. Malone, N.Y. m. Patricia Conroy; children: Kathryn, William Michael, David, Carol, Kevin. B in History magna cum laude, U. Notre Dame, 1953; MEd, Syracuse U., 1959, PhD in Social Sci., 1963. Tchr. U. Tex., U. Wash., Tex. Tech. U.; exec. v.p. N.Mex. State U., Las Cruces, 1985-97, interim pres., 1994-95, pres., 1997—2001, now pres. emeritus. Mem. Nat. Coun. Geog. Edn., Assn. Am. Geographers, Southwestern Social Sci. Assn. (past pres.), N.Mex. Coun. Univ. Presidents, Las Cruces C. of C. (bd. trustees town-gown com.). Office: NMex State U MSC 388 PO Box 30001 Las Cruces NM 88003-8001 Fax: 505-646-6344. E-mail: wconroy@nmsu.edu.

CONROY-LACIVITA, DIANE CATHERINE, city administrator; b. Niskayuna, N.Y., Aug. 22, 1965; d. William John and Bernice Mary (Paluch) Conroy; m. Joseph James LaCivita, Nov. 5, 1988; children: Frances Catherine LaCivita, Catherine Elizabeth LaCivita, Louis Philip LaCivita. BA, SUNY, Oswego, 1986; Master's degree, SUNY, Albany, 1991; postgrad., Russell Sage Grad. Sch., 2000—. Exec. dir. Shaker Heritage Soc., Albany, N.Y., 1988-92; asst. dir. tng. N.Y. State Martin Luther King Jr. Commn. & Inst., Albany, 1992-96; asst. exec. dir. Latham (N.Y.) Area C. of C., 1996-97; dep. town clk. Town of Colonie, N.Y., 1997—. Cons. N.Y. State Dept. Corrections, Albany, 1996-97. Past pres., mem. Friends of the Pruyn House, 1997—; mem. Latham Ridge PTA, 1996—, Colonie Youth Ctr. Ann. Dinner Com. and Kids Fest, 1998, 1999, 2000, 2001, 2002; steering com. Capital Leadership Class of 2000, 2000—02; bd. dirs., chair ann. dinner com. Regional Food Bank of Northeastern N.Y.; chair Give From the Heart Food Drive; active Colonie Women's Rep. Com., 1997—; mem. Govs. Capital Dist. Women's Adv. Coun. Mem. Shaker Heritage Soc. (bd. dirs.), Latham Rotary Club (bd. dirs.), Latham Area C. of C. (women in bus. coun.). Avocations: private pilot training, gardening. Office: Town of Colonie Memorial Town Hall 534 Loudon Rd Newtonville NY 12110-5316 E-mail: conroyd@colonie.org.

CONRY, THOMAS FRANCIS, mechanical engineering educator, consultant; b. West Hempstead, N.Y., Mar. 7, 1942; s. Thomas and Bridget Anne (Walsh) C.; m. Sharon Ann Silverwood, June 10, 1967; children: Christine Elizabeth, Carolyn Danielle, Anne Marie. BS, Pa. State U., 1963; MS, U. Wis.-Madison, 1967, PhD, 1970. Registered profl. engr., Wis., Ill. Engr. Gen. Motors Corp., Milw., 1963-66, sr. research engr. Indpls., 1969-71; asst. prof. gen. engring. U. Ill., Urbana, 1971-75, assoc. prof. gen. and mech. engring., 1975-81, prof. gen. and mech. engring., 1981—; co-dir. mng. engring. program Coll. Engring., Urbana, 1986-89, head dept. gen. engring., 1987-98, coord. program in tech. and bus., 1995-98. Sr. visitor U. Cambridge (Eng.), 1978; cons. Zurn Industries, 1974-83; staff cons. Sargent & Lundy, Engrs., 1977, 79; cons.-evaluator commn. on instns. of higher edn. North Ctl. Assn., 1983—; cons. indsl. firm on machine dynamics, optimization and tribology. NSF trainee, 1968-69; NASA/ASEE summer faculty fellow, 1974-75. Contbr. articles to profl. jours. Mem. Bd. Edn. St. Matthews Parish Roman Catholic Ch., Champaign, 1981-84. Fellow ASME (chmn. design engring. divsn. 1979-80, tech. editor Jour. Vibration, Acoustics, Stress and Reliability in Design, 1984-89, mem. bd. on comm. 1989-93, 96-2000, mem. com. on fin. and investment 1999—); mem. Am. Soc. Engring. Edn., Rotary, Sigma Xi, Lambda Chi Alpha, Phi Kappa Phi. Home: 3301 Lakeshore Dr Champaign IL 61822-5205 Office: 104 S Mathews Ave Urbana IL 61801-2925

CONSAGRA, SOPHIE CHANDLER, academy administrator; b. Radnor, Pa., Apr. 28, 1927; d. Alfred D. and Carol (Ramsay) Chandler; children: Maria, Pierluigi, Francesca, George. BA, Smith Coll., 1949; MA, Cambridge (Eng.) U., 1952. Exec. dir. Del. Arts Council, 1972-78; dir. visual arts and architecture N.Y. State Council Arts, 1978-80; dir. Am. Acad. in Rome, 1980-84, pres., 1984-88, pres. emerita, vice chmn./spl. projects, 1988-90. Cons. Nat. Endowment Arts. Recipient Smith Coll. award, 1986, Centennial medal Am. Acad. in Rome, 1995. Address: 955 Lexington Ave New York NY 10021-5128

CONSER, WALTER HURLEY, JR., religion and philosophy educator; b. Riverside, Calif., Apr. 4, 1949; s. Walter Hurley and Barbara Healy C.; m. Janet Gunter, June 7, 1986; 1 child, Emily. BA, U. Calif., Irvine, 1971; MA, Brown U., 1974, PhD, 1981. From vis. asst. prof. to prof. U. N.C., Wilmington, 1985—. Author: Church and Confession, 1984, God and the Natural World, 1993; editor: Experiences of the Sacred, 1992, Sacred Spaces, 1999; mem. adv. bd. Jour. So. Religion, 1997—. Mem. Am. Hist. Assn. Mem. Am. Acad. Religion. Office: Dept Philosophy and Religion U NC 601 S College Rd Wilmington NC 28403-5601

CONSEY, KEVIN EDWARD, museum administrator; b. N.Y.C., Jan. 15, 1952; s. Edward and Dorothy (Kemmann) C.; m. Susan Mary Kirsch, Aug. 26, 1972. BA, Hofstra U., 1974; M in Mus. Practice, MA, U. Mich., 1977. Dir. Emily Lowe Gallery, Hofstra U., Hempstead, N.Y., 1977-80, San Antonio Mus. Art., 1980-83; dir., chief exec. officer Newport Harbor Art Mus., Newport Beach, Calif., 1983-89, Mus. Contemporary Art, Chgo., 1989-2000; dir. art mus. and pacific film archive U. Calif., Berkeley, 2000—. Panelist profl. devel. Nat. Endowment for Arts, Washington, 1987-88, panelist challenge grant, 1988, panelist mus. program, 1989-90, panelist F.A.C.I.E., 1991-94. Hofstra U. scholar, 1970-74, Guggenheim Mus. intern, 1976; grantee Nat. Mus. Act, 1976-77. Mem. Assn. Art Mus. Dirs., Coll. Art Assn. Office: BAM/FFA U Calif Berkeley 2625 Durant Ave Berkeley CA 94720-2250

CONSIDINE, JOHN JOSEPH, advertising executive; b. Jersey City, N.J., Sept. 6, 1941; s. Joseph Patrick and Helen (Hrezak) C.; m. Catherine Christine Noone, Nov. 26, 1966; children: Elizabeth, Laura, Adam, Kate. BA, St. Peter's Coll., Jersey City, 1963. Rsch. analyst Prudential Ins. Co., Newark, 1964-66; asst. rsch. mgr. The Mennen Co., Morristown, N.J., 1966-68; rsch. mgr. The Gillette Co., Boston, 1968-69; rsch. dir. W. B. Doner & Co., Detroit, 1969-74, sr. v.p., corp. rsch. dir., 1974-82, exec. v.p., corp. dir. strategic planning, 1982-94, vice chmn., 1994—. Mem. Pine Lake Country Club (West Bloomfield, Mich.). Home: 3652 Erie Dr West Bloomfield MI 48324-1524 Office: W B Doner & Co 25900 Northwestern Hwy West Bloomfield MI 48075-1067

CONSIDINE, RUSSEL A. publisher, real estate consultant; b. New Hyde Park, N.Y., July 14, 1950; s. Howard and Dorothy M. Considine; m. Margaret A. Waters, May 28, 1983; children: Blake, Noelle. BA, Hofstra U., 1974. Investment officer TIAA-CREF, N.Y.C., 1977-88; pres., founder BMR Corp., Hastings-on-Hudson, N.Y., 1988-2000, NOELLeBooks.com Corp., Hastings-on-Hudson, N.Y., 2000—. Founder, CEO Considine Real Estate Adv. Group Inc., Hastings-on-Hudson, N.Y., 2001—; co-founder www.globalcalm.com., 2000—. Author, illustrator: Moonlight's Sleepy-Time Story, 2000 (Children's e-book cert. distinction, Writer's Digest, 2001); author: Armu-The King's Favorite Horse, 2000, Woofy & Noelle's Pocantico Hills Adventure, 1999. Coach Colts Youth Club, Yonkers, NY, 1996—99. Recipient Investor of Yr. award Interstate Mortgage Co., 1987. Avocations: golf, skiing, writing, hiking, reading. Home: 83 Rosedale Ave Hastings On Hudson NY 10706 Office: NOELLeBooks dot com Corp 83 Rosedale Ave Hastings On Hudson NY 10706 E-mail: russconsidine@considinerealestate.com., pax@globalcalm.com.

CONSIGLIO, HELEN, nursing educator and consultant; b. Wyandotte, Mich., June 21, 1962; d. Francis and Helen (Grabowski) Zgoda; m. Anthony Consiglio, Nov. 10, 1989. BSN, Madonna Coll., 1984; postgrad., U. Mich., Dearborn, 1984-85, Madonna Coll., 1987. RN, Mich. Student tutor Ctr. for Personalized Instrn., Madonna Coll., Livonia, Mich., 1981-84; nursing asst. Wyandotte (Mich.) Hosp. and Med. Ctr., 1983-84, staff nurse ICU/CCU, 1984-88, critical care instr., 1988-90; staff RN, SICU Henry Ford Hosp., Detroit, 1990-91; staff RN, cons. Nurses Plus, Inc., Wyandotte, Mich., 1991-98; staff nurse pre-op/post anesthesia care unit Oakwood Hosp. and Med. Ctr., Dearborn, Mich., 1996—. Spkr., rschr. in field; adj. clin. faculty Oakland C.C., Union Lake, Mich., 1992-94. Producer ednl. videotape. Mem. Am. Assn. Critical Care Nurses, Sigma Theta Tau.

CONSOLI, MARC-ANTONIO, composer; b. Catania, Italy, May 19, 1941; came to U.S., 1956, naturalized, 1967; s. Francesco Gabriele Settimio and Rosa (Puglisi) C. B.Mus., N.Y. Coll. Music, 1966; M.Mus., Peabody Conservatory, 1967; M.Mus. Arts, Yale U., 1971, D.Mus. Arts, 1977. Lectr. Bridgeport U.; vis. prof. U. Western Ont., 1975 Composer, works performed by Balt. Symphony Orch., N.Y. Philharm., Los Angeles Philharm., Louisville Orch.,, Ensemble Kontrapunkte, Vienna, Austria, Monday Evening Concerts, Los Angeles, Berkshire Music Center, Yale Players for New Music, Gaudeamus Festival, Netherlands, Royan Festival, France; commns. for Graz (Austria) radio sta., Royan Festival, others; performer, dir.-mem., Yale Players for New Music, 1969-71, The Experiment, 1974, Equinox I, 1967, Equinox II, 1968, Isonic, 1970, Interactions I-V, 1970-71, Profiles, 1972-73, Music for Chambers, 1974, Canti Trinacriani, 1975, Sciuri Novi I, 1974, Sciuri Novi II, 1975, Tre Canzoni, 1976, Odefonia, 1976, Vuci Siculani, 1979, Tre Fiori Musicali, 1979, Naked Masks, 1980, The Last Unicorn, 1981, Orpheus' Meditation, 1981, Saxlodie, 1981, Afterimages, 1982; String Quartet, 1983, Fantasia Celeste, 1983, Ancient Greek Lyrics, 1984, Musiculi II (summer), 1985, Reflections, 1986, Eyes of the Peacock, 1987, Sans Parole I and II, 1988, Cello Concerto, 1988, String Quartet II, 1989, Arie Mutate, 1990, Musiculi IV (winter), 1990/92, Musiculi III (autumn), 1992/94, Games for 2 and 3, 1994/95, Cinque Canti, 1995, Varie Azioni, Di-ver-ti-mento (Games for 4), 1995, Sciuri Novi III, 1997, Pensieri Sospesi, 1997, Rounds & Relays, 1997, Varie Azioni II, 1998, Varie Azioni III, 1999, Four Shades of Tango, 1999, Rounds' Separation, 1999, Passaggi Obbligati, 2000, Estratti Obbligati I, II and III, 2001, Night Whispers, 2002. Recipient award Nat. Inst.-Am. Acad. Arts and Letters, 1975; Guggenheim Found. fellow, 1971-72, 79-80; Fulbright fellow Poland, 1972-74; Creative Artists Pub. Service grantee, 1975; Nat. Endowment for Arts grantee, 1979, 81, 85. Mem. Broadcast Music Inc., Am. Composers Alliance, Am. Music Center.

CONSTABLE, JOHN, advertising executive; b. 1943; Pvt. practice, London, 1964-76; with Cramer Krasselt Co., Milw., 1976-78; ptnr. Laughlin/Constable Inc., Milw., 1978—, now v.p., sec., ptnr., creative dir., art dir., 1978—. Office: Laughlin/Constable Inc 207 E Michigan St Stop 1 Milwaukee WI 53202-4996

CONSTABLE, SIMON JAMES, hospital administrator; b. U.K., Mar. 4, 1968; s. John and Hilary Constable; m. Katherine Constable. MA in Econ., St. Andrews U., 1991; MBA Darden Grad. Sch. Bus. Adminstrn., U. Va., 1997. Rsch. assoc. Kidder, Peabody & Co., Inc., N.Y.C., 1992-94; rsch. analyst Rudolf Wolff & Co. Inc., N.Y.C., 1994-95; sr. treasury analyst GMC, N.Y.C., 1997-99; mgr. Delphi Automotive Sys., Troy, Mich., 1999—2001; dir. Can. Imperial Bank of Commerce, N.Y.C., 2001—03, N.Y. Presbyn. Hosp., N.Y.C., 2003—. Avocations: fly fishing, horseback riding, travel. Office: NY Presbyn Hosp 525 E 68th St Box 198 New York NY 10021 E-mail: constables97@alum.darden.edu.

CONSTANT, ANITA AURELIA, publisher; b. Youngstown, Ohio, Jan. 5, 1945; d. Sandu Nicholas and Erie Marie (Tecau) C. BA, Ind. U., 1967; postgrad., Northwestern U., Evanston, Ill., 1991. Sales rep. Economy Fin. Inc., St. Louis, 1967-69; recruiter Case Western U. Hosp., Cleve., 1969-70; sales rep. Internat. Playtex Inc., Chgo., 1970-71, John Wiley & Sons, Inc., Chgo., 1971-77; sr. product mgr. CBS Pub. Inc., The Dryden Press, Chog., 1977-80; exec. editor Dearborn Fin. Pub., Inc., Chgo., 1980-81, v.p., 1981-89, sr. v.p., prin., 1989-97; cons. to pub. industry, 1997-98; prin. Ea. European investment venture EUROTEC, 1997-99; sr. v.p., editor-in-chief Southwestern Coll. Pub. divsn. ITP Inc., 1988-94; sr. v.p. new bus. devel. South-Western/Thomson Learning, 2000—; v.p. devel. and contract mgmt. Riverside Pub. Divsn. Houghton Mifflin, 1995—. Bd. dirs. Romanian Heritage Ctr., Detroit, 1988—, Orthodox Brotherhood of Am., Detroit, 1985—. Mem.: Nat. Assn. Women Bus. Owners, Chgo. Book Clinic (bd. dirs. 1987—88, v.p. 1988—90, pres. 1990—91, past pres. 1991—92, Mary Alexander award 1995), Internat. Assn. Fin. Planners, Real Estate Educators Assn., Chgo. Women in Pub. Eastern Orthodox. Avocations: property development and renovation, hiking, bicycling. Office: 425 Springlake Dr Itasca IL 60143 E-mail: anita_constant@hmco.com.

CONSTANT, WILLIAM DAVID, chemical engineer, educator; b. Bunkie, La., May 15, 1954; s. Warren LeRoy and Montez Henning (Haas) C.; m. Donna Gail Hall, Nov. 14, 1987; 1 child, Justin Glen Germany. BSChemE, La. State U., 1977, MSChemE, 1980, PhD, 1984. Registered chem. and environ. engr., La. Lab. tech. U.S. Forest Svc., Pineville, La., 1973, 74; chem. engr. Ethyl Corp., Baton Rouge, 1977-78; Exxon fellow dept. chem. engring. La. State U., Baton Rouge, 1978-84, asst. prof. petroleum engring., 1984-88, asst. dir. hazardous waste rsch. ctr., 1988-91, dir. hazardous waste rsch. ctr., 1991-99, asst. dir. hazardous substance rsch. ctr. south and S.W., 1991—, assoc. prof. dept. civil & environ. engring., 1994-97, dir. La. water resources rsch. inst., 1989-99, prof. dept. civil and environ. engring., 1997—2003, Humphreys Turner prof. dept. civil and environ. engring., 2003—. Exec. dir. divsn. engring. rsch. La. State U., 1998-2000; cons. in field. Contbr. articles to profl. jours. Recipient numerous Rsch. grants, 1985—. Mem. ASME, AIChE, Soc. Petroleum Engrs., Univ. Coun. on Water Resources, Soc. Petroleum Engrs., Gamma Beta Phi, Tau Beta Pi, Pi Epsilon Tau, Phi Lambda Epsilon (chpt. pres. 1980-81). Republican. Methodist. Avocation: golf. Office: HSRC/S&SW 3221 CEBA Baton Rouge LA 70803 E-mail: hscons@lsu.edu.

CONSTANTELOS, DEMETRIOS JOHN, priest, educator; b. Spilia, Messinia, Greece, July 27, 1927; came to U.S., 1955; naturalized, 1958; s. John and Christine (Psilopoulos) C.; m. Stella Croussouloudis, Aug. 15, 1954; children: Christine, John, Eleni, Maria. BTh, Holy Cross Sch. Theology, 1958; ThM, Princeton Theol. Sem., 1959; MA, Rutgers U., 1963, PhD, 1965; DD, Hellenic C/Holy Cross, 1991. Ordained priest Greek Orthodox Ch., 1955. Pastor St. Demetrios, Perth Amboy, N.J., 1955-64, St. Nicholas Ch., Lexington, Mass., 1965-67; interim pastor St. Barbara Ch., Toms River, N.J., 1972-74, St. Anthony Ch., Vineland, N.J., 1975-82, Holy Trinity Ch., Egg Harbor Twp., N.J., 1982-89; prof. Holy Cross Sem., Brookline, Mass., 1965-71; prof. history Richard Stockton Coll. of N.J., Pomona, N.J., 1971-86, Charles Cooper Townsend Disting. prof., 1986-97, prof. emeritus, 1997—, disting. rsch. scholar in residence, 2001—. Mem. Orthodox-Cath. Theol. Consultation, 1965-84, New Rev. Standard Version Bible Com., 1974—, Anglican-Orthodox Theol. Consultation; vis. lectr. Boston Coll., 1967-68; vis. prof. religion, Onassis vis. prof. Hellenic studies NYU, spring 1991. Author: Byzantine Philanthropy, 1968, 2d edit., 1991, Understanding the Greek Orthodox Church, 1982, 4th edit., 2003, Poverty, Society and Philanthropy in the Late Mediaeval Greek World, 1992, Christian Hellenism, 1998; editor: Encyclicals, 1976, Orthodox Theology, 1981, Archbishop Iakovos, Visions and Expectations for a Living Church, 1998, Archbishop Iakovos: The Torch Bearer, vol. 1 1999, vol. II, 2001, Archbishop Iakovos, Paideia, 2002; editor Greek Theol. Rev., 1965-71, assoc. editor Jour. Ecumenical Studies, 1976—. Lane Cooper fellow Rutgers U., 1962, Jr. fellow Dumbarton Oaks, 1964. Mem. Orthodox Theol. Soc. (pres. 1968-71), Modern Greek Studies Assn., U.S. Nat. Com. for Byzantine Studies. Home: 304 Forest Dr Linwood NJ 08221-1511 Office: Richard Stockton Coll NJ Dept History Pomona NJ 08240 Office Fax: 609-652-4550. E-mail: djconstantelos@aol.com.

CONSTANTINE, KEVIN, professional hockey coach; Head coach Rochester (Minn.) USHL, 1987-88, Kansas City IHL, 1991-92, San Jose Sharks, 1993-94, 95-96; asst. coach Calgary Flames, 1996-97; head coach Pitts. Penguins, 1997—. Runner-up for Jack Adams award as NHL Coach of Yr., 1993-94, IHL Coach of Yr., 1991-92; career NHL coaching record (all with the Sharks) is 55-78-24; coached USHL championship team in 1987-88, and IHL championship team in 1991-92. Office: Pittsburgh Penguins/Civic Arena/66 Mario Lenieux Pl Pittsburgh PA 15219

CONSTANTINE, MICHAEL, actor; b. Reading, Pa, May 22, 1927; s. Theoharis and Andromache (Foteadou) Efstration; m. Juliana McCarthy, Oct. 5, 1953 (div. 1969); children: Thea Eileen, Brendan Neil. Actor, TV programs: Room 222, 1969-74; Sirotas Court, Hey Landlord, 1965; Murder She Wrote, 1988, 89; The Love Boat, 1983; Homicide, 1993; Law and Order, 1993,94; Judging Amy, 2002; My Big Fat Greek Life, 2003; films: The Hustler, 1959; If It's Tuesday This Must Be Belgium, Deadfall, 1993; My Life, 1993; The Juror, 1995; Steven King's 'Thinner,' 1995; World War III, 2000; My Big Fat Greek Wedding, 2000; plays: Inherit the Wind, 1955; The Egg, 1965; Compulsion, 1967; The Miracle Worker, 1969; Arturo VI, 1972; A Walk in the Woods, 1986; Three Sisters, 1991; Meshugah or Lost Souls, 1998. Recipient Emmy award for "Room 222", 1970, San Diego Drama Critics award, 1986, Dramalogue, Hollywood Fgn. Press, also numerous nominations.

CONSTANTINEAU, CONSTANCE JULIETTE, retired banker; b. Lowell, Mass., Feb. 18, 1937; d. Henry Goulet and Germaine (Turner) Goulet-Lamarre; m. Edward Joseph Constantineau; children: Glen Edward, Alan Henry. Student, Bank Adminstrn. Inst. and Am. Inst. Banking, 1975-87. Mortgage sec. The Ctrl. Savs. Bank, Lowell, 1955-57; head teller First Fed. Savs. & Loan, Lowell, 1957-59, Lowell Bank & Trust Co., Lowell, 1973-74; br. mgr. Century Bank & Trust Co., Malden, Mass., 1975-78; v.p. purchasing, mgr. support svcs. First Security Bank of N.Mex. (formerly First Nat. Bank Albuquerque), 1983-96; ret., 1996. Mem. planning purchasing mgr.'s conf. Bank Adminstrn. Inst., San Antonio, Orlando, Fla., New Orleans; treas. polit. action com. First Nat. Bank, 1986. Bd. dirs., historian Indian Pueblo Cultural Ctr., Albuquerque, 1986-89. Home: 13015 Deer Dancer Trl NE Albuquerque NM 87112-4831

CONSTANTINESCU, TIBERIU, mathematician; b. Bucharest, Romania, June 13, 1955; s. Stelian and Elena Constantinescu; m. Marie Ene, June 7, 1985; 1 child, Kristina Marie Reed. PhD, U. of Bucharest, 1980. Rsch. scientist INCREST, Bucharest, 1980—90, Inst. Math. of the Romanian Acad., Bucharest, 1990—99; assoc. prof. of math. U. of Tex. at Dallas, Richardson. Vis. rschr. Stanford U., Palo Alto, Calif., 1991—93. Author: (book) Schur's Algorithm and Several Applications, Schur parameters, dilation and factorization problems. Recipient Simion Stoilow Prize in Math., Romanian Acad., 2000. Office: U Tex at Dallas Box 830688 Richardson TX 75083-0688 E-mail: tiberiu@utdallas.edu.

CONSTANTINI, JOANN M. small business owner, consultant; b. Danbury, Conn., July 30, 1948; d. William J. and Mathilda J. (Ressler) C. BA, Coll. White Plains, N.Y., 1970; postgrad., Ctrl. Conn. State Coll., 1977-78, U. Hartford, 1985-88, U. Jacksonville, 1991; MS, Nova Southeastern U., 1996. Cert. records mgr., 1987; lic. realtor, N.C. Psychiat. social worker N.Y. State Dept. Mental Hygiene, Wassaic, 1970-73; with N.E. Utilities, Hartford, Conn., 1973-88, methods analyst, 1979-82, records and procedures mgmt. adminstr., 1982-88; document contr., mgr. Ralph M. Parsons Co., Fairfield, Ohio, 1990-91, St. Johns River Power Park, Jacksonville, 1991—2001; dir. Jacksonville Elec. Authority, 2001—03; owner Contantini & Assocs., 1988—, Family Threads, 1999—. Mem. faculty Ctrl. Piedmont C.C., 1989-90, Fla. C.C., Jacksonville, 1993-95. Bd. dirs. Meriden YWCA, Conn., 1978-79; vol. Queen City Friends, Charlotte, 1988-89, Cath. Charities AIDS Ministries, Jacksonville, 1996-99; mem. Greater Charlotte Bd. Realtors, 1989-91, First Coast Chorus, 1998-2002; mem. adv. coun. Greater Hartford C.C., 1986, Clermont Coll., Cin., 1990-91, Jacksonville C.C., 1991-94; mem. com. St. Augustine Diocesan Task Force Alternative Ministries, 1997—. Mem.: NACDLGM (nat. v.p. 1999—2001, bd. dirs. 1999—, mcm. human rights campaign 1999—, bd. dirs. Riverwoods HOA 2000—02, nat. pres. 2002—), AAUW, Jacksonville Small Bus. Network, Am. Platform Assn., Inst. Cert. Records Mgrs., Nat. Trust for Hist. Preservation, Coll. White Plains Alumnae Assn., Electric Coun. New Eng. (chair records mgmt. com. 1985—87), Assn. Configuration Data Mgmt., Women Bus. Owners, Assn. Image and Info. Mgmt. (dir. 1984—86), Assn. Record Mgmt. and Adminstrs. (sec. 1984—85, bd. dirs. 1984—86, chair industry action com. for pub. utilities 1986—89, internat. chair industry action program 1989—93, profl. issues com. 1997—99), N.E. Utilities Women's Forum Club (treas. 1983—88), Beta Sigma Phi. Democrat. Roman Catholic. Avocations: antiques, online auctions, travel, investing. Home: 11538 Jonathan Rd Jacksonville FL 32225-1314 E-mail: novaleo@yahoo.com.

CONSTANTINI, LOUIS O. financial consultant, stockbroker; b. Columbus, Ga., Jan. 12, 1948; s. Louis T. and Edna G. (Spears) C.; m. Mary Ann Jennings, Feb. 9, 1974; children: Rachel J., Emily J. BA, U. Fla., 1972. Cert. fin. mgr. Intelligence officer CIA, Washington and overseas, 1972-76; v.p., fin. cons. Merrill Lynch & Co., El Paso, Tex., 1976-84, fin. cons. Las Cruces, N.Mex., 1984—, v.p., 1988—. Chmn. El Paso Estate Planning Coun., 1982. Decorated Bronze Star, Combat Infantryman Badge, Cross of Gallantry with Gold Star (Republic of Vietnam). Mem. Sigma Phi Epsilon (Disting. Alumnus award 1999, dist. gov. s.w. dist.), Frederick A. Cook Soc. (bd. dirs.). Avocation: arctic exploration. Home: 5155 Hunters Chase Rd Las Cruces NM 88011-2553 Office: Merrill Lynch & Co 425 S Telshor Blvd Ste 101C Las Cruces NM 88011-8211 E-mail: Newmex@attglobal.net.

CONSTANTINO, BECKY, political organization administrator; State chmn. Wyo. Rep. State Ctrl. Com., 1999—. Mem. Rep. Nat. Com. Western State Chmn. Assn., 1999—. Office: 400 E 1st St Ste 314 Casper WY 82601-2561 also: PO Box 241 Casper WY 82601

CONSTANTINO, JOHN NICHOLAS, medical educator, researcher; b. St. Louis, Aug. 30, 1962; s. Henry Franklin and Julia Shamia Constantino; m. Michele Ann McDermott, July 18, 1963; children: Anna Marie, Benedict John, Celia Terese. BA, Cornell U., 1984; MD, Wash. U., 1988. Diplomate bd cert. pediatrics Am. Bd. Pediat., 1993, gen. psychiatry Am. Bd. Psychiatry and Neurology, 1999, subsplty. child and adolescent psychiatry Am. Bd. Psychiatry and Neurology, 2000. Asst. prof. psychiatry and pediat. Wash. U. Sch. Medicine, St. Louis, 1996—. Author: A Poor Man's Proof for the Existence of God; contbr. articles to profl. jours. Grantee, Nat. Inst. Child Health and Human Devel. Pub. Health Svc. Rsch., 2003; scholar, Cornell U., 1980. Office: Washington U Sch Medicine 660 South Euclid Ave Campus Box 8134 Saint Louis MO 63110 E-mail: constantino@psychiatry.wustl.edu.

CONSTANTINO, VALERIE, artist, writer, art educator; b. N.Y.C., Nov. 14, 1950; d. Anthony and Elizabeth (Jordan) Constantino. BFA, U. Arts, 1989; MFA, Sch. Art Inst. Chgo., 1991. Self-employed artist, writer, 1991—. Gallery dir. N.Y. Open Ctr., N.Y.C., 1992—94; adj. prof. Pima CC, Tucson, Md. Inst. Coll. Art, Balt., 1996—97, Sch. Art Inst. Chgo., 2001, lectr., Western Wash. U., Syracuse U., No. Ill. U., U. Arts. Exhibitions include nat. and internat. shows; author: (jours.) Fiberarts, Surface Design Jour. Vol. St. Joseph Ho., N.Y.C., 1994—96, God's Love We Deliver, N.Y.C., 1996. Fellow, Legihton Artist Colony, Banff, Alta., Can., 1985; scholar, Sch. Art Inst. Chgo., 1989—91; Rsch. and Writing grantee, Empire State Crafts Coun., 1994. Mem.: Coll. Art Assn., Sch. Art Inst. Alumni Assn., Univ. Arts Alumni Assn. Avocations: swimming, nature walks, travel. Home: 4500 N Via Entrada # 120 Tucson AZ 85718

CONSTANTINO-BANA, ROSE EVA, nursing educator, researcher, lawyer; b. Labangan Zamboanga delSur, Philippines, Dec. 25, 1940; came to U.S., 1964; naturalized, 1982; d. Norberto C. and Rosalia (Torres) Bana; m. Abraham Antonio Constantino, Jr., Dec. 13, 1964; children: Charles Edward, Kenneth Richard, Abraham Anthony III. BS in Nursing, Philippine Union Coll., Manila, 1962; MNursing, U. Pitts., 1971, PhD, 1979; JD, Duquesne U., Pitts., 1984. Lic. clin. specialist in psychiatric-mental health nursing; RN. Instr. Philippine Union Coll., 1963-65, Spring Grove State Hosp., Balt., 1965-67, Montefiore Sch. Nursing, Pitts., 1967-70, U. Pitts., 1971-74, asst. prof., 1974-83, assoc. prof., 1983—, chmn. Senate Athletic Com., 1985-86, 89-90, sec. univ. senate, 1991-92, v.p., 1993-95. Project dir. grant divsn. of nursing HHS, Washington, 1983-85; bd. dirs. Am. Jour. Nursing; prin. investigator NIH NINR, 1991-94; bd. dirs. Internat. Coun. on Women's Health Issues, 1986—. Author: (with others) Principles and Practice of Psychiatric Nursing, 1982; contbr. chpts. to books and articles to profl. jours. Mem. Presdl. Task Force, Washington, 1980, Rep. Senatorial Com., Washington, 1980. Fellow Am. Acad. Nursing, Am. Coll. Forensic Examiners; mem. ABA, ATLA, Allegheny County Bar Assn. (bd. cert. forensic examiner), Pa. Bar Assn., Women's Bar Assn., Am. Assn. Nurse Attys., Am. Nurses Assn., Pa. Nurses Assn. (sec. 1994-98), Nat. League Nursing, Pa. League Nursing (chairperson area 6), Allegheny County Bar Assn., U. Pitts. Sch. Nursing Alumni Assn., U. Duquesne Law Alumni Assn., Sigma Theta Tau, Phi Alpha Delta. Seventh Day Adventist. Avocations: cooking, piano. Home: 6 Carmel Ct Pittsburgh PA 15221-3618 Office: U Pitts Sch Nursing 4500 Victoria St Rm 415 Pittsburgh PA 15261-0001

CONSTINE, LOUIS SANDERS, III, pediatric oncologist, radiation oncologist; b. San Francisco, Feb. 4, 1948; s. Louis Sanders and Nancy Jane (Meyer) C.; m. Sally Joanne Baxter; children: Alysia, Joshua. BA, Stanford U., 1969; MD, Johns Hopkins U., 1973. Diplomate Am. Bd. Pediatrics, sub.-bds. Pediatric Hematology/Oncology, Therapeutic Radiology. Resident in pediatrics U. Calif., San Francisco, 1973-75, Stanford U., 1975-76, resident in radiation oncology, 1978-81; fellow in pediatric hematology/oncology U. Wash., Seattle, 1976-78; asst. prof. pediatrics and radiation oncology U. Rochester (N.Y.) Med. Ctr., 1981-87, assoc. prof., 1987-96, prof., 1996—. Author: Pediatric Radiation Oncology, 1989, 94, 99; editor: Survivors of Childhood Cancer, 1994. Mem. Phi Beta Kappa. Office: U Rochester Cancer Ctr PO Box 647 601 Elmwood Ave Rochester NY 14642-0001 E-mail: louis_constine@urmc.rochester.edu.

CONSTON, HENRY SIEGISMUND, lawyer; b. Dresden, Germany, Dec. 18, 1928; arrived in U.S., 1947, naturalized, 1952; BSBA, NYU, 1955, JD, 1958, LLM, 1961. Bar: N.Y. 1959. With Calif. Tex. Oil Corp., N.Y.C., 1947-61; sr. ptnr. Walter, Conston, Alexander & Green PC, N.Y.C., 1961—95; sr. counsel Alston & Bird$D, N.Y.C., 2001—. Contbr. Bd. dirs. Margaret Tietz Ctr. for Nursing Care, N.Y. Found. Nursing Homes, Inc. Office: 90 Park Ave New York NY 10016-1301

CONTA, RICHARD VINCENT, actuary; b. N.Y.C., Sept. 4, 1946; s. Antonio and Eugenia Theresa (Cavally) C.; m. Joanne Shultis, July 14, 1979 (div. 1990); children: Kerry, Gregory; m. Maureen Fitzgerald, June 8, 1991; 1 child, Tracy. BA, Fordham U., 1968. Pension clk. Tchrs. Retirement Sys., City of N.Y., 1968-69; actuarial student U.S. Life Ins. Co., N.Y.C., 1969-74; pension actuary Laiken, Siegel & Co., N.Y.C., 1974-75; enrolled actuary Guardian Life Ins. Co., N.Y.C., 1975-99; ptnr. Fitzgerald & Conta Pension Svcs., Bloomfield, N.J., 1990—. Mem. Am. Acad. Actuaries, Am. Soc. Pension Actuaries. Roman Catholic. Office: Fitzgerald & Conta Pension Svcs 104 Davis Ave Bloomfield NJ 07003-4140 Fax: 973-338-7834. E-mail: Fitzconta@aol.com.

CONTE, JOSEPH JOHN, II, meteorologist, management consultant; b. Mt. Vernon, N.Y., Dec. 11, 1932; s. John Salvatore and Eva (DeNardo) C.; m. Constance J. Schneider, June 11, 1955; children: Joseph John, Michael Louis, Mark Anthony, Richard Angelo, Vincent Edward, Celeste Maria. BS in Meteorology, St. Louis U., 1963; BA in Mgmt. summa cum laude, Nat. Louis U., 1992; postgrad., Shenandoah U., 1993—. Observer radar meteorology, aviation and local weather Weather Bur., St. Louis, 1955-64, severe weather forecaster Kansas City, Mo., 1965-66; USAF, chief severe weather unit-Europe Air Weather Svc., High Wycombe-Croughton, England, 1966-73, cmty. preparedness program mgr., 1973-74; weather radio program mgr. NOAA, Nat. Weather Svc., Silver Spring, Md., 1974-86; dir. confs., spl. events Office Legis. Affairs Nat. Oceanic/Atmospheric Adminstrn., Rockville, Md., 1986-90; pres., v.p. mgmt. cons. Tech. Adv. Group (TAG), Purcellville, Va., 1987—. Pres. Video Info. Bus. Electronic Sales, 1983—, C&W Enterprises, Inc., 1985-90; trade show mgr. Loudoun County C. of C., 1993; retail sales mgr. PCI Comm. Cellular-One, Leesburg, Va., 1993; acct. Kirby Constrn., Inc., 1993-95, Dunn Plumbing Co., Inc., 1994-95; sr. meteorologist, program mgr. Gen. Scis. Corp., 1995-2000; sr. project mgmt. planning specialist Lockheed Martin Tech. Svcs., 2000-01; rschr. Huthwaite, 2002-03; dep. program mgr., cons. Electronic Cons. Svcs., 2002—. Dir. parks and recreation Bluemont Cmty. Ctr., 1994-95. With USAF, 1951-55. Recipient Silver medal Dept. Commerce, 1979, 94-95. Mem. Futurist Soc., Internat. Platform Assn., Am. Meteorol. Soc., Am. Mgmt. Assn., NAt. Trust Hist. Preservation, Nat. Def. Exec. Res., VFW. Office: Technical Adv Group PO Box 324 Philomont VA 20131-0324 Home: PO Box 324 Philomont VA 20131 E-mail: con20132@yahoo.com., joe.conte@ecs.-federal.com.

CONTE, LOU, artistic director, choreographer; b. DuQuoin, Ill., Apr. 17, 1942; s. John and Floy Mae (Saunders) C. Student, Ellis DuBoulay Sch. Ballet, Chgo., 1961-68, So. Ill. U., 1960-62, Am. Ballet Theatre Sch., N.Y.C., 1964-66. Choreographer musicals Mame, 1972, Boss, 1973; choreographer Milw. Melody Top, 1966; dir. Lou Conte Dance Studio, Chgo., 1974—; artistic dir. Hubbard St. Dance Co., Chgo., 1977—; lectr. Mem. Actors Equity Assn., AFTRA. Office: Hubbard St Dance Co 1147 W Jackson Blvd Chicago IL 60607-2905

CONTE, SUSAN, secondary school counselor; b. N.Y. d. Anthony Robert and Laura Marie (Di Bartolomeo) C. MA, Fordham, 1974, M in Social Work, 1990; postgrad., NYU. Cert. social worker. Tchr. Archbishop Williams H.S., Braintree, Mass., 1974-76, Ursuline Sch., New Rochelle, N.Y., 1976-87; dir. Ursuline Companions in Mission, Bronx, 1987-92; dir. counseling Ursuline Sch., New Rochelle, 1992—. Bd. trustees Coll. New Rochelle, 1993-99. Mem. Order of St. Ursula Roman Union. Democrat. Roman Catholic. Home: 44 Liberty Ave New Rochelle NY 10801-7143

CONTESCU, CRISTIAN ION, chemist, researcher; b. Galati, Romania, Apr. 17, 1948; s. Nelu Marcel and Aurora C.; m. Adriana Ghitulescu, Aug. 22, 1971; 1 child, Corneliu Daniel. MS, Bucharest U., Romania, 1971; PhD, Bucharest Poly. Inst., 1979. Chemist Ctr. Phys. Chem., Bucharest, Romania, 1971-76; rsch. scientist Inst. Phys. Chem, Bucharest, Romania, 1976-82, sr. rsch. scientist, 1982-92; rsch. assoc. Syracuse U., Syracuse, NY, 1992-96, rsch. scientist, 1996-97; sr. scientist Hitco Carbon Composites, Inc., Gardena, Calif., 1999-2001, Material Methods LLC, Newport Beach, Calif., 2001—. Adj. assoc. prof. Syracuse U., 1997; cons. in field. Editor: Surfaces of Nanoparticles and Porous Materials, 1999; contbr. articles to profl. jours. Recipient Romanian Acad. Gheorghe Spacu award, 1991. Mem. Am. Chem. Soc. (co-chmn. symposia, 2001, 02), Am. Carbon Soc. Home: Apt 22 343 Palos Verdes Blvd Redondo Beach CA 90277 E-mail: ccontescu@juno.com.

CONTI, INDALICIO PALOMAR, accountancy educator; b. Dinas, Philippines, Dec. 22, 1953; s. Ismael Hernandez Conti and Irenea Demit Palomar.. BS in Mgmt., Philippine Coll. of Commerce, Manila, 1976, BSC in Acctg., 1977; LLB, U. of the East, Manila, 1985; MBA, Polytechnic U. of Philippines. CPA. Jr. acct. Gen. Textile Mills, Inc., Libis, Quezon City, Philippines, 1978; dir., acct. Supreme Traders, Inc., Manila, 1978-79; auditor PUP Credit Union, Manila, 1978-83; legal rschr. Polytechnic U. Philippines, Manila, 1992; prof. Coll. Accountancy, Polytechnic U. Philippines, Manila, 1993—; mgng. ptnr. Conti & Assoc. CPA's, Quezon City, Philippines. Fin. cons., bd. trustees Fieldridge Learning Ctr., Brgy. San Felipe, Batangas, 11999; tax cons., legal rschr. V.C. Ramirez Law Office, Quezon City, 1997—; external auditor N.F.K. Constrn., Merto Manila, 1998—, Vincent Mark Security Agy., Quezon City, 1998—, Psychol. Ext. Evaluation Rsch. Svcs., Quezon City, 1999—; assoc. prof. CBIBE Philippine Women's U., Manila, 1999; mem. faculty Colegio San Lorenzo Project 6, Quezon City, 2000—; CPA, tax practitioner, chief legal rschr., Fabella & Assocs. Law Office, Quezon City, 2002; profl. lectr., Trinity Grad. Sch. (Cmty. Outreach), 2000 Author: (textbooks) Income Taxation Law, 1984, Transfer and Business Taxes, 1986, Fundamentals of Transfer and Business Taxes, 1987, Fundamentals of Income Tax, 1988. Mem. PICPA, GACPA, CALFCI. Roman Catholic. Avocations: martial arts, dancing, playing chess, bowling, reading.

CONTI, JAMES JOSEPH, chemical engineer, educator; b. Coraopolis, Pa., Nov. 2, 1930; s. James Joseph and Mary (Smrekar) Conti; m. Concetta Razziano, May 13, 1961; children: Lori Ann, James Robert. B.Chem. Engring. summa cum laude, Poly. Inst. Bklyn., 1954, M.Chem. Engring., 1956, D. Chem. Engring., 1959. Sr. engr. Bettis atomic power divsn. Westinghouse Electric Corp., 1958—59; mem. faculty Polytech. U. N.Y., 1959—90, prof. chem. engring., 1965—90, chmn. dept., 1964—70, provost, 1970—78, v.p. ednl. devel., 1978—90; pres. Webb Inst. Naval Architecture, Glen Cove, NY, 1990—99, ret., 1999. Cons. in field. Contbr. articles to profl. jours.; patentee in field. Trustee Webb Inst. Naval Architecture, 1974—99. Fellow: AAAS, Am. Inst. Chemists; mem.: AIChE, Am. Soc. Engring. Edn., Omega Chi Epsilon, Phi Lambda Upsilon, Tau Beta Pi, Sigma Xi. Home: 26 Miami Rd Bethpage NY 11714-2229

CONTI, JOY FLOWERS, judge; b. Kane, Pa., Dec. 7, 1948; d. Bernard A. Flowers and Elizabeth (Tingley) Rodgers; m. Anthony T. Conti, Jan. 16, 1971; children: Andrew, Michael, Gregory. BA, Duquesne U., 1970, JD summa cum laude, 1973. Bar: Pa. 1973, U.S. Dist. Ct. (we. dist.) Pa. 1973, U.S. Ct. Appeals (3d cir.) 1976, U.S. Supreme Ct. 1993. Law clk. Supreme Ct. Pa., Monessen, 1973-74; assoc. Kirkpatrick & Lockhart, Pitts., 1974-76, 82-83, ptnr., 1983-96; shareholder Buchanan, Ingersoll, P.C., Pitts., 1996—2002; dist. judge U.S. Dist. Ct.(we. dist.) Pa., Pitts., 2002—. Prof. law Duquesne U., Pitts., 1976-82; hearing examiner Pa. Dept. State, Bur. Profl. Occupation and Affairs, 1978-82; chairperson search com. for judge U.S. Bankruptcy Ct. (we. dist.) Pa., 1987, 95; active Pa. Futures Commn. on Justice in 21st Century, 1995-97. Contbr. articles to profl. jours. Mem. disciplinary hearing com. Supreme Ct. Pa., 1982-88; v.p. Com. for Justice Edn., Pitts., 1983-84; mem. Leadership Pitts., 1987-88. Named One of Ten Outstanding Young Women in Am., 1981. Fellow Am. Bar Found. (Pa. state chair 1991-97); mem. ABA (ho. of dels. 1980-86, 91-97), Am. Law Inst., Am. Coll. Bankruptcy, Pa. Bar Assn. (gov. 1993-95, ho. of dels. 1978—, Am. Inns of Ct., Pitts. Chpt. 2002—, corp. banking and bus. law sect. coun. 1983-89, treas. 1991-93, v.p. 1993-95, chair-elect 1995-97, chmn. 1997-99, chmn. commn. comml. law 1990-93, co-chair 1995-2002, chair civil rights and responsibilities com. 1986-89, Achievement award 1982, 87, 99, Anne X. Alpern award 1995), Nat. Conf. Bar Pres. (exec. coun. 1993-96), Allegheny County Bar Assn. (adminstrv. v.p. 1984-86, 90, chairperson corp. banking and bus. law sect. 1987-89, treas. 1988-90, gov. 1991, pres.-elect 1992, pres. 1993), Internat. Women's Insolvency and Restructuring Confedn. (chair Tri-State Network 1996), Pa. Bar Inst. (dir. 1991-97), Duquesne Club. Roman Catholic. Office: US Dist Judge 936 US Courthouse 7th & Grant Sts Pittsburgh PA 15219

CONTI, LEE ANN, lawyer; b. Astoria, Oreg. BA with honors, So. Ill. U., 1970; JD summa cum laude, De Paul U., 1976. Bar: Ill. 1976, U.S. Dist. Ct. (no. dist.) Ill. 1976. Ptnr. Mayer, Brown & Platt, Chgo., 1983-94; assoc. gen. counsel Citizens Comm. Co., Stamford, 1994—2002. Contbr. articles to profl. jours. Mem. Bd. Edn. Cmty. Consol. Sch. Dist. 89, Du Page County, 1987-93. Recipient Am. Jurisprudence awards in Torts, Remedies. Mem. ABA, Am. Corp. Counsel Assn., Ill. State Bar Assn., Du Page County Bar Assn., Chgo. Bar Assn., Phi Kappa Phi, Pi Sigma Alpha, Phi Lambda Pi. Office: 635 S Park Blvd Glen Ellyn IL 60137-6977

CONTI, LISA ANN, epidemiologist, veterinarian; b. Amityville, N.Y., July 10, 1963; d. Daniel Desiderio and Lorraine Conti; m. Thomas Lee Seal, Oct. 21, 1989. BS, U. Miami, Coral Gables, Fla., 1984; DVM, U. Fla., 1988; MPH, U. South Fla., 1993. Diplomate Am. Coll. Vet. Preventive Medicine. Relief vet. various clinics, Tallahassee, 1988—; vet. epidemiologist Fla. Dept. Health, Tallahassee, 1988-89, epidemiologist, 1989-94, med. health care program analyst, 1994-97, program adminstr., 1997-98, state pub. health vet., 1998—, dir. divsn. environ. health, 2003—. Mem. rabies control adv. com. Fla. Dept. of Health, 1997—. Assoc. editor Fla. Jour. Pub. Health. Vol. Lit. Vols. Am., Tallahassee, 1995—. Mem. AVMA (pub. health rep. coun. pub. rels. 1997—), Nat. Assn. State Pub. Health Vets. (Psittacosis compendium com. 1996-98, Rabies compendium com. 1999—), Fla. Vet. Med. Assn. (pub. health chmn. 1994—), Big Bend Vet. Med. Assn. (pres. 1991-92). Avocations: stained glass, folk dancing, hiking. Office: Fla Dept Health Bin A-08 4052 Bald Cypress Way Tallahassee FL 32399-1720

CONTI, LOUIS THOMAS MOORE, lawyer; b. Phila., Aug. 31, 1949; s. Alexander and Yolanda (DiLorenzo) Conti; m. Christina M.S. Moore, May 1, 1982; children: Charles Alexander, Whitney Caroline. BS, LaSalle Coll., 1971; MBA, Drexel U., 1972; JD, Creighton U., 1975; LLM, Temple U., 1981. Bar: Pa. 1975, U.S. Claims Ct. 1975, U.S. Tax Ct. 1975, U.S. Dist. Ct. (ea. dist.) Pa. 1978, U.S. Ct. Appeals (3d cir.) 1979, U.S. Supreme Ct. 1981, Fla. 1982, U.S. Dist. Ct. (mid. dist.) Fla. 1988. Tax atty. Office Chief Counsel IRS, Washington and Phila., 1975-81; tax mgr. Touche Ross & Co., Phila., 1981-84; assoc. Saul, Ewing, Remick & Saul, Phila., 1984-87; shareholder Swann & Haddock, P.A., Orlando, Fla., 1987-89; ptnr., chmn. corp. tax and securities dept. Holland & Knight, Orlando, 1989—. Mem. fin. com. S.E. Pa. chpt. ARC, Phila., 1984—87; advisor Vol. Lawyers for Arts, Phila., 1984—87; bd. dirs. Fla. Hosp. Found., Ctrl. Fla. Planned Giving Coun., 1989—97, Cmty. Found. Ctrl. Fla. Inc., World Trade Ctr., Orlando, 1992—95; mem. internat. bus. adv. bd. Metro Orlando; grad. Leadership Orlando, 1994, Leadership Fla., 1996; chair recruiting com. East Ctrl. Region of Leadership Fla., 1997; bd. dirs. Orlando Performing Arts and Edn. Ctr., Inc., 1998—2001. Mem.: ABA (tax and bus. law sect., chmn. task force on drafting prototype ltd. liability co. operating ag 1998—, chmn. Fla. Bar drafting com. 1999), Orange County Bar Assn. (chmn. tax sect. 1990—91), Fla. Bar Assn. (tax and bus. law sect., chmn. drafting com. ltd. liability co. operating agreements 1998—, chair corps. and securities com., bus. law sect. 1999—2001, chair tax sect. 2001—02), Seminole County C. of C. (bd. dirs. 1994—97). Republican. Avocation: travel, skiing, golf, tennis, theatre. Home: 603 Genius Drive Winter Park FL 32779 Office: Holland & Knight PO Box 1526 Orlando FL 32802-1526 E-mail: lconti@hklaw.com.

CONTI, PAUL LOUIS, management consulting company executive; b. Utica, N.Y., Sept. 3, 1945; s. Louis Joseph and Dorothy Mae (Kellogg) C.; m. Lee Ann Scheuerman, Apr. 18, 1970; children: Meghan Elizabeth, Dawn Michelle. BA, So. Ill. U., 1972, MBA, 1974. Sr. cons. Lester B. Knight & Assocs., Chgo., 1974-76; dir. pers. Applied Info. Devel., Oak Brook, Ill., 1976-80; v.p. Comsi, Inc., Oak Brook, 1980-82; CEO Prestige Mgmt. Sys., Inc., Glen Ellyn, Ill., 1982-86; v.p. human resources Rand McNally & Co., Skokie, Ill., 1986-87; assoc. dir. Ernst & Young (formerly Ernst & Whinney), Chgo., 1987-93; regional v.p. Alexandria Alexander, Inc., Chgo., 1993-97; COO, sr. v.p. AON Corp., 1997-99; sr. v.p. Apropos Tech., Inc., Oak Brook, Ill., 1999—. Bd. dirs. So. Ill. U. Coll. Bus. Adminstrn. Lobbyist Invest in the Future, Invest in Edn., State of Ill., 1988; bd. dirs., exec. com. So. Ill. U.-Carbondale Found., 1991—, pres., 1994-97. Named to So. Ill. U. COBA Hall of Fame, 1988; named Cmty. Ambassador So. Ill. U., 1980. Mem. Soc. Human Resource Profls., Soc. Human Resources Mgmt., Human Resources Mgmt. Assn. of Chgo., Employment Mgmt. Assn., Pontikes Ctr. for Mgmt. Info. (bd. dirs. 1989—), So. Ill. U. Alumni Assn. (pres. 1986-88, bd. dirs. 1986—, exec. com. 1991—), Ideal Club (pres. 1986-88), McCullom Lake Club. Republican. Roman Catholic. Avocations: hunting waterfowl and upland game, golf, various participative sports, coaching women's fast pitch softball. Home: 635 S Park Blvd Glen Ellyn IL 60137-6977 E-mail: contip@msn.com.

CONTI, PETER SELBY, astronomy educator; b. N.Y.C., Sept. 5, 1934; s. Attilio Carlo and Marie (Selby) C.; m. Carolyn Safford, Aug. 26, 1961; children: Michael, Karen, Kathe BS, Rensselaer Poly. Inst., 1956; PhD, U. Calif-Berkeley, 1963; Honoris Causa degree, U. Utrecht, 1993. Rsch. fellow Calif. Inst. Tech., Pasadena, 1963-66; asst. prof. astronomy U. Calif./Santa Cruz, 1966-71; astronomer Lick Obs., Santa Cruz, 1966-71; prof., fellow Joint Inst. Lab. Astrophysics U. Colo., Boulder, 1971-99, chmn., 1989-90, chmn. dept. astrophys., planetary scis., 1980-86, prof. emeritus, 1999—. Chmn. bd. dirs. Assoc. Univs. for Rsch. in Astronomy Inc., Tuscon, 1983-86; vis. prof. U. Utrecht, The Netherlands, 1969-70, minnaert prof. U. Utrecht, 1995. Editor: Mass Loss and Evolution of O-type Stars, 1979, O Stars and Wolf Rayet Stars, 1988; contbr. over 200 articles to profl. jours. Served to lt. (j.g.) USNR, 1956-59 Recipient Gold medal U. Liege, Belgium, 1975; Fulbright fellow, 1969-70 Fellow AAAS (chmn. sect. D in astronomy 1980); mem. Am. Astron. Soc. (councillor 1983-86), Astron. Soc. of Pacific, Internat. Astron. Union (organizing com. 1983-85, v.p. 1985-88, pres. 1988-91, commn. 29 stellar spectra). Democrat. Home: 817 Racquet Ln Boulder CO 80303-2972 Office: U Colo-Boulder Joint Inst Lab Astrophysics Campus Box 440 Boulder CO 80309-0440

CONTI, RONALD SAMUEL, electronics engineer, fire prevention engineer; b. PItts., June 23, 1948; s. Eugene H. and Helen V. (Pietrzak) C.; m. Mary Ann Pagano, May 6, 1972; children: Ronald S. Jr., Ryan A., Renai L. BS in Electronics Engring., Point Park Coll., 1979. Fire prevention engr., supr. gen. engr. response group Pitts. Rsch. Lab. of NIOSH, 1970—. Mem. nat. mine rescue assn. Pa. Dept. Environ. Protection; PADEP adv. bd. of mine rescue subcom. coord. open industry briefings, seminars and workshops on mine fire preparedness and mine rescue team, fire brigade and smoke tng. simulations. Author: Combustion Science and Technology, 1991, also abstracts; patentee inflatable partition for fighting fires (spl. achievement award 1996), trigger device for explosion barriers (spl. achievement award 1980); contbr. over 50 articles to profl. jours. Pres. Brookline Youth Soccer Assn., Pitts., 1985-86; coach Little League, Pitts., 1980-89, BYSA Soccer, City League Soccer, Pitts., 1982-90, Brookline Boxing, Pitts., 1981-82. Sgt. USMC, 1968-70, Vietnam. Recipient PE 5 Star award Pollution Engring., Washington, 1982, Mine Rescue Tng. Team Honor award Ctr. for Disease Control/Agy. for Toxic Substances and Disease Registry, 1999, Rsch. Operational award Ctr. for Disease Control/Agy. for Toxic Substances and Disease Registry, 2001; named Tech. Transfer Person of Yr., Pitts. Rsch. Ctrs., 1992. Mem. Internat. Emergency Mgmt. Soc., Soc. Mining Engrs., Combustion Inst., Nat. Mine Rescue Assn., Pleasant Hill Hall Assn. (bd. dirs. 1984-90), Vietnam Vets Inc., Am. Legion, Pleasant Hills Guthrie Lodge (past master). Roman Catholic. Office: Pitts Rsch Lab NIOSH PO Box 18070 Pittsburgh PA 15236-0070 E-mail: RCont@cdc.gov.

CONTI, SAMUEL, federal judge; b. L.A., July 16, 1922; s. Fred and Katie C.; m. Dolores Crosby, July 12, 1952; children: Richard, Robert, Cynthia. BS, U. Santa Clara, 1945; LLB, Stanford U., 1948, JD. Bar: Calif. 1948. Pvt. practice,

San Francisco and Contra Costa County, 1948-60; city atty. City of Concord, Calif., 1960-69; judge Superior Ct. Contra Costa County, 1968-70, U.S. Dist. Ct. (no. dist.) Calif., San Francisco, 1970-88, sr. judge, 1988—. Mem. Ctrl. Contra Costa Bar Assn. (pres.), Concord C. of C. (pres.), Alpha Sigma Nu. Office: US Dist Ct 450 Golden Gate Ave Ste 36052 San Francisco CA 94102-3482

CONTI, TOM, actor, writer, director; b. Paisley, Scotland, Nov. 22, 1941; s. Alfonso and Mary (McGoldrick) C.; m. Kara Drummond Wilson, July 2, 1967; 1 child, Nina. Appeared in plays on London's West End, Jesus My Boy, 1998, Chapter Two, The Ride Down Mount Morgan, Savages, Other People, The Black and White Minstrels, Don Juan, The Devil's Disciple, Romantic Comedy, Chapter Two, Jesus My Boy: Broadway debut in Whose Life Is It Anyway, 1979 (Tony award), Jeffrey Bernard is Unwell, 1990; appeared in They're Playing Our Song, 1980; dir. Before the Party, 1980; dir., star Present Laughter, 1993; film appearances include Galileo, Eclipse, Merry Christmas Mr. Lawrence, Reuben, Reuben (Acad. Award nomination), 1983, American Dreamer, 1984, Saving Grace, Miracles, Heavenly Pursuits, Beyond Therapy, The Dumb Waiter, White Roses, Shirley Valentine, Someone Else's America, 1995, Sub Down, Something To Believe In, 1996, Don't Go Breaking My Heart, 1998, Out of Control, 1997, The Enemy, 2000; appeared in TV plays including the Beaux Strategem; appeared in American TV prodns. Princess and the Pea, Faerie Tale Theatre, the Beate Klarsfeld Story, The Quick and the Dead, Fatal Dosage, When Rabbit Howls, Wright Verdicts, The Inheritance, Friends, Deadline, Cinderella and Me, 2001, Donovan, 2003; appeared in Brit. TV prodns. The Glittering Prizes, Norman Conquests, Madame Bovary. Named Most Popular Actor for Last 20 Yrs., Theatre Goers of U.K., 2000. Mem.: Garrick Club (London). Address: Artists Ind Network 32 Tavistock St London WC2E 7PB England

CONTILLO, LAWRENCE JOSEPH, financial and computer company executive; b. Washington, Mar. 3, 1960; s. Lawrence and Kathleen Grace (O'Neill) C. BS in Acctg. and Fin., U. Md., 1981; MBA, George Washington U., 1982. CPA, Md. Financial analyst Fed. Home Loan Mortgage Corp., Washington, 1982-83; budget analyst Am. Security Bank, 1983-84; mgr. MCI, Arlington, Va., 1984-86; cons. Laventhol & Horwath, Washington, 1986-87; mgr. Watkins, Meegan, Drury & Co., Bethesda, Md., 1987-91; pres., founder, CEO Rennaisance Computing Ltd., Greenbelt, Md., 1991—.

CONTINO, ROSALIE HELENE, historian, playwright; b. Bklyn., Apr. 1, 1938; d. Nicholas and Domenica Helen (Nostro) C. EdB, Fordham U., 1959; MA in Ednl. Theater, NYU, 1980, PhD in Ednl. Theater, 1997. Tchg. fellow NYU Ednl. Theater Dept., N.Y.C., 1980-83. Resident costume designer TRG Prodn., N.Y.C., 1979-89, B.F.R. Prodn., N.Y.C., 1980-82, Studio Theatre, 1985-88, Unity Theatre Prodns., 1985-88; co-host Internat. Arts Festival, NYU. Assoc. prodr. : Art for All, Art for the Disabled, Channel 25/58 Cablevision; Telegram, My Grandmother's Garden; playwright: Ricky, Transitions, Kids, Kids, Kids, Twixt 'n' Tween; author: (creative non-fiction) Born to Create; playwright Three One Act Plays (Tree Talk, Is That All There Is?, The Reunion); author (poetry): The Day the Sun Forgot to Shine; author: (short stories) The Telegram, My Grandmother's Garden, Is That All There Is?; author: (poetry) Trees, Days of Future's Past, 1989, Life, The World of Poetry Anthology, 1991, (TV program) Sixteen Hours, Junior High Madness. Former mem. Ladies' Aux. Victory Meml. Hosp., Bklyn., 1964-74. N.Y. Times and N.Y. Sch. Continuing Edn. scholar, 1987; USITT grantee. Mem.: Theatre Libr. Assn., Costume Soc. Am. (region I rec. sec. 1999—2001), NYU Grad. Student Orgn. (treas. 1984—92), Dramatists Guild, U.S. Inst. Theater Tech. (grantee 2000), United Fedn. Tchrs., Am. Alliance for Theatre and Edn., Pi Lambda Theta (Rho chpt., exec. bd. 1987—2001, region I editor 1992—2000, treas. 2000—02). Roman Catholic. Avocations: tennis, bike riding, reading. Home: 74 Bay 10th St Brooklyn NY 11228-3412 E-mail: rhcphd@worldnet.att.net.

CONTOIS, JOHN HENRY, clinical chemist, researcher; b. Weymouth, Mass., July 24, 1959; s. Louis Joseph Contois and Mary A. Davidson; m. Liang-Ru Wen, June 7, 1995; 1 child, Stephanie Danielle. BS in Biology, U. Mass., 1983; MS in Nutritional Scis., U. Conn., 1987, PhD, 1994. Diplomate Am. Bd. Clin. Chemistry. Postdoctoral fellow in clin. chemistry Hartford (Conn.) Hosp., 1994-96; dir. sci. and quality SpectraCell Labs., Houston, 1996-97; cancer prevention fellow, rsch. assoc. U. Tex., M.D. Anderson Cancer Ctr., Houston, 1998; sr. rsch. scientist Bayer Corp., Tarrytown, N.Y., 1999-2000; dir. chemistry Quest Diagnostics, Teterboro, N.J., 2000—. Contbr. numerous peer-reviewed articles and book chpts. to profl. publs.; invited reviewer profl. jours. Hamilton Eaton fellow U. Conn., 1993-94, rsch. fellow Travelers Ctr. on Aging, U. Conn., 1990-91. Fellow Acad. Clin. Biochemistry; mem. Am. Assn. for Clin. Chemistry (Outstanding Spkr. award 1997), Assn. Clin. Scientists, Am. Soc. Preventive Oncology, Am. Assn. for Cancer Rsch., Gamma Sigma Delta, Phi Kappa Phi. Avocations: hiking, traveling, photography. Office: Quest Diagnostics Inc 1 Malcom Ave Teterboro NJ 07608-1070 Fax: (201) 462-4331. E-mail: john.h.contois@questdiagnostics.com.

CONTOS, PAUL ANTHONY, engineer, investment consultant; b. Chgo., Mar. 18, 1926; s. Anthony Dimitrios and Panagiota (Kostopoulos) C.; m. Lilian Katie Kalkines, June 19, 1955 (dec. Apr. 1985); children: Leslie, Claudia, Paula, Anthony. Student, Am. TV Inst., Chgo., 1946-48, U. Ill., 1949-52, 53-56, Ill. Inst. Tech., 1952-53, U. So. Calif., 1956-57. Engr. J.C. Deagan Co., Inc., Chgo., 1951-53, Lockheed Missile and Space Co., Inc., Sunnyvale, Calif., 1956-62, engrng. supr., 1962-65, staff engr., 1965-88; genealogy rsch. San Jose, Calif., 1970—; pres. PAC Investments, Saratoga, Calif., 1984-88, San Jose, Calif., 1988—, also advisor, cons., 1984—. Mem. Pres. Coun. U. Ill., 1994—. With U.S. Army, 1944-46, ETO. Decorated Purple Heart. Mem. DAV (life, commdr. Chgo. unit 1948-51), VFW (life), Pi Sigma Phi (pres. 1951-53). Republican. Greek Orthodox. Avocation: genealogy research. Home and Office: Paseo Villas No 407 130 E San Fernando Street San Jose CA 95112-7414 E-mail: paulacontos@illinoisalumni.org.

CONTRACTOR, DINSHAW N. civil engineer, educator; b. Bangalore, India, Apr. 23, 1933; came to U.S., 1958. s. Nariman C. and Goola N. (Engineer) C.; m. Hutoxy R. Hirjibehdin, Sept. 18, 1958; children: Rashna, Shernaz, Yasmin, Yazdi, Arnavaz. BE in civil engring., U. Baroda, India, 1956; MS, U. Iowa, 1959; PhD, U. Mich., 1963. Registered profl. engr., Ariz. Research scientist Hydronautics, Inc., Laurel, Md., 1963-68; asst. prof. Va. Poly. Inst. & State U., Blacksburg, 1968-75, assoc. prof., 1975-81; visiting prof. Water & Energy Res. Inst. Univ. Guam, 1980-81; prof. U. Ariz., Tucson, 1981—2003; ret., 2003. Cons. United Nations Dev. Program, Baroda, 1984. Contbr. articles to profl. jours. Mem. ASCE, ASME, Am. Geophys. Union, Am. Water Resources Assn. Democrat. Zoroastrian. Avocation: amateur astronomy. Office: U Ariz Dept Civil Engrng & Engring Mech Tucson AZ 85721-0001 E-mail: contract@u.arizona.edu., contract@dakotacom.net.

CONTRACTOR, FARHAD M. diagnostic radiologist, educator; b. Bombay, Apr. 22, 1946; came to U.S., 1971; s. Minocher K. and Dina M. (Udwadia) C.; m. Huty D. Randeria, Feb. 1, 1976; children: Laila, Cyra. MB, BS, U. Baroda, India, 1969, DMR, 1971. Diplomate Am. Bd. Radiology with added qualification in interventional radiology. Intern St. Francis Hosp., Pitts., 1971-72; resident Allegheny Gen. Hosp., Pitts., 1972-75, fellow, 1975-76; pvt. practice Pitts., 1976—; asst. prof. radiol. scis. Allegeny U. Health Scis., Pitts., 1990—. Sr. radiologist Allegheny Gen. Hosp., Pitts., 1980—. Fellow: Soc. Cardiovasc. and Interventional Radiology, Am. Coll. Radiology, Am. Heart Assn.; mem.: Tri-State Assn. Physicians from India (pres. 1995—96), Mammographers Soc. Pitts. (pres. 1998—99). Zoriastrian. Office: 320 E North Ave Pittsburgh PA 15212-4756 Fax: 412-359-6799. E-mail: fcontrac@wpahs.org.

CONTRACTOR, FAROK, business and management educator; b. Bombay, Dec. 24, 1946; came to U.S., 1967; s. Jamshed Phirozshaw and Hilla C. Contractor; children: Cyrus, Sahm, Eric. BSME, U. Bombay, 1967; MS in Indsl. Engring., U. Mich., 1968; MBA, U. Pa., 1977, PhD in Managerial Sci. and Applied Econs., 1980. Staff indsl. engr. Max Factor, Inc., L.A., 1969; rsch. fellow U. Mich., Ann Arbor, 1969-70; exec. officer, asst. to mng. dir. TATA Group subs. TATA Adminstrv. Svcs., India, 1970-74; asst. instr. bus. and mgmt. Wharton Sch. Bus., U. Pa., Phila., 1975-77, instr., 1977-80; assoc. prof. Grad. Sch. Mgmt., Rutgers U., Newark and Piscataway, N.J., 1980-90, prof. internat. bus., 1991—, chmn. internat. bus. dept., 1986-88, 90-93. Lectr. Wharton Sch. Bus., U. Pa., 1985-86; vis. scholar UN Ctr. on Transnat. Corps., N.Y., fall 1988; mem. Internat. Bus. Inst., Rutgers U., 1986—, rsch. dir. CIBER, 1997-99, com. mem., 1980-90; NSF reviewer, 1980, 84, 94; organizer, co-chmn. joint conf. on coop. ventures in internat. bus. Rutgers U. and Wharton Sch. Bus., U. Pa., 1986, co-chmn. conf. on coop. strategies and alliances, Lausanne, Switzerland, 2001; licensing and tech. transfer agreements cons.; Unilever Group vis. fellow, vis. prof. Indian Inst. Fgn. Trade, New Delhi, spring 1994; vis. prof. Copenhagen Bus. Sch., 1995, Lubin Sch. Pace U., 1997, Fletcher Sch. Law and Diplomacy, Tufts U., 2000; presenter in field. Author: International Technology Licensing: Compensation, Costs and Negotitation, 1981, Licensing In International Strategy: A Guide for Planning and Negotiation, 1985, Government Policies And Foreign Direct Investment, 1991, Cooperative Strategies in International Business, 1988, Economic Transformation in Emerging Countries: The Role of Investment, Trade and Finance, 1998, the Valuation of Intangible Assets in Global Operations, 2001, Cooperative Strategies and Alliances, 2003, others; co-author: Introduction to International Business, 1986. Esmee Fairbairn fellow U. Reading, Eng., 1982, Fulbright fellow, 1991-92; grantee The German Marshall Fund of U.S., 1986, Carnegie Bosch Found., 1996-98. Fellow Acad. Internat. Bus. (bd. dirs., sec.-treas. 1992-94); mem. Licensing Execs. Soc., Acad. Mgmt. (exec. bd. 1997—2002, pre-conf. workshop chair San Diego meeting 1998, program chmn. Chgo. meeting 1999, pres. internat. mgmt. divsn. 2000—), European Internat. Bus. Assn., Zoroastrian Assn. Greater N.Y., Internat. Trade and Fin. Assn. (bd. dirs. 1995-97). Avocations: antique restoration, skiing, trekking, canoeing, interior design. Office: Rutgers Univ Sch Mgmt 81 New St Newark NJ 07102

CONTRENI, JOHN JOSEPH, JR., humanities educator, educator; b. Savannah, Ga., Aug. 31, 1944; s. John Joseph Sr. and Elfriede Johanna (Hille) C.; m. Margarita Lee Partridge, July 3, 1986; children: Judith, Rachel, Daniel, Maureen, Jennifer Rogers, Paul Rogers. BA, St. Vincent Coll., 1966, HHD (hon.), 1996; PhD, Mich. State U., 1971. From asst. prof. to prof. history Purdue U., West Lafayette, Ind., 1971—, head dept. history, 1985-97, asst. dean Sch. Humanities, Social Sci. and Edn., 1981-85, interim head dept. fgn. langs. and lits., 1983-85. Pres. Midwest Medieval Conf., 1980-81. Author: The Cathedral School of Laon from 850 to 930: Its Manuscripts and Masters, 1978, (John Nicholas Brown prize 1982), Codex Laudunensis 468: A Ninth-Century Guide to Virgil, Sedulius, and the Liberal Arts, 1984; co-author: Glossae Divinae Historiae: The Biblical Glosses of John Scottus Eriugena, 1997; translator: Education and Culture in the Barbarian West, Sixth Through Eighth Centuries (Pierre Riché), 1976, Carolingian Learning, Masters, and Manuscripts, 1992; co-editor: Religion, Culture, and Society in the Early Middle Ages: Studies in Honor of Richard E. Sullivan, 1987, French Historical Studies, 1991-2000, word, Image, Number: communication in the Middle Ages, 2002; mem. editl. bd. Internat. History Rev., 2001—; contbr. articles to profl. jours. and chpts. to books. Pres., bd. trustees Brookston-Prairie Twp. Pub. Libr., 1995-01. Grantee Am. Philos. Soc., 1973, 76, 82, 86, NEH, 1973, 86, Am. Coun. Learned Socs., 1975, 77-79, 83, 89, Purdue U., 1973, 75-76, 81, 83, 89, 99. Mem. Soc. for Promotion Eriugenian Studies, Medieval Acad. Am. (councillor 1987-90, grantee 1973), Phi Beta Kappa. Home: 504 W 5th St Brookston IN 47923-8100 Office: Purdue Univ Dept of History Univ Hall West Lafayette IN 47907-1358 E-mail: contreni@purdue.edu.

CONTRERAS, MIGUEL ALBERTO, materials scientist, researcher; b. Rancagua, Chile, Nov. 19, 1959; s. Jose Miguel Contreras and Maria del Carmen Bustos; m. Barbara Burgess, Sept. 15, 1955; children: Luke Burgess, Sena Margaret. BSEE, U. Santiago, Chile, 1983; MSEE, U. of Wis., Madison, 1990; PhD, Colo. U., Golden, 1996. Rsch. asst. U. of Wis., Madison, 1988—90; scientist Nat. Renewable Energy Lab., Golden, Colo., 1990—94. Sr. scientist Nat. Renewable Energy Lab., Golden, 1995—. Author: (scintific journal publication) .Graded band-gap Cu(In, Ga)Se thin-film solar cell absorber with enhanced open-circuit voltage, (scientific journal publication) Progress Toward 20% Efficiency in Cu(In, Ga)Se2 Polycrystalline; contbr. articles to sci. jours. (Popular Sci. award in sci. and tech., 1993, Most Cited Physics Paper, Sci. Watch, 2001). Soccer coach Table Mountain Soccer Assn., Golden, 1995. Grantee, New Energy and Indsl. Tech. Devel. Orgn., Japan, 2002. Mem.: IEEE, Am. Solar Energy Assn., Materials Rsch. Soc. Achievements include research in polycrystalline thin-film solar cell efficiency. Office: Nat Renewable Energy Lab 1617 Cole Blvd Golden CO 80401 Office Fax: 303-384-6430. E-mail: miguel_contreras@nrel.gov.

CONTRERAS, THOMAS J., JR., career officer; b. Morenci, Ariz. m. Gloria Rachel Gutierrez, Sept. 4, 1965; children: Naomi, Thomas. BS in Chemistry and Secondary Edn., No. Ariz. U., 1967; MS in Phys. Organic Chemistry, U. Utah, 1969; PhD in Physiology, Uniformed Svcs. U. Health Sci., 1983. Commd. lt. (j.g.) USN, 1971, advanced through grades to capt.; prin. investigator Naval Blood Rsch. Lab., Boston, 1972-76, Armed Forces Radiobiology Rsch. Inst., Bethesda, Md., 1976-79, Naval Med. Rsch. Inst., Bethesda, 1982-85; rsch. area mgr. combat casualty care Naval Med. R&D Command, Bethesda, 1985-87; tech. area mgr. biomed. and chem./biol. warfare def. program Office of Naval Tech., Office of Chief of Naval Rsch., Arlington, Va., 1987-91, dep. dir. support technologies directorate, 1989-91; exec. officer Naval Health Rsch. Ctr., San Diego, 1991-95; comdg. officer Naval Med. Rsch. Inst., Bethesda, 1995-98, Naval Med. Rsch. Ctr., Forest Glen, Md., 1998-99, Naval Health Rsch. Ctr., San Diego, 1999-2001. Contbr. articles to profl. jours. Decorated Joint Svc. Commendation medal, Meritorious Svc. medal with 2 gold stars, Legion of Merit with gold star; recipient Hispanic Engrng. Nat. Achievement award for profl. achievement in govt., 1991, Hispanic Mag. Role Model of the Yr. award, 1992, Nat. Image Inc. Meritorious Svc. award, 1993, No. Ariz. U. Disting. Citizen award, 1995, Outstanding Alumnus award of Dept. Chemistry, 1995. Mem. Soc. Armed Forces Med. Lab. Scientists, Soc. for Advancement of Chicanos and Native Americans in Sci., Assn. Naval Svc. Officers. Office: Commanding Officer Naval Health Rsch Ctr PO Box 85122 San Diego CA 92186-5122 E-mail: co@nhrc.navy.mil.

CONVERSE, ELIZABETH, artist, writer; b. Springfield, Ill., Jan. 17, 1946; d. Frank Thomas and Frances Converse (Deal) Sheets; m. Daniel B. A. Richter, Apr. 12, 1979 (div. Mar. 1996); children: William, Joan Clair; m. Eddie Truman, June 2002. BA in Anthropology, Lake Forest Coll., 1964-67; student Writing Ctr., Sarah Lawrence Coll., N.Y.C., 1991; MA in Human Devel., Pacific Oaks Coll., 1999. Cert. multiple-subject tchr., Calif. Tchr., enrichment program Washington Accelerated Sch. Anthropol. field worker, interviewer NIMH, Chgo., 1967-70; v.p., creative dir. Prodn. Sys., Inc., N.Y.C., 1984-89; with The Light/Bright Project at youth activity ctrs.; exec. dir. Calif. Living Histories, 1999-2002; mem. We 7 Collaborative. Performer Absolute Reality Theatre, N.Y.C., The Bridge Collective, N.Y.C., The Performance Group, N.Y.C., 1971-78; dir. Whitney Counterweight, N.Y.C., 1971-78; dir. Uto Theatrical Experiment, N.Y.C., 1971-78; writer, dir., actor: (short film) Mercy, 1971-78; prodr., writer, actor: (ind. film) Alexyx, 1978-83; works included in publs. Artweek, Visions, Pasadena Weekly, L.A. Reader, mus. and galleries; author: (fiction) The Pursuit of Happiness, The Clearing, Imbroglio, Wild Thing, Dust and Gold, The Citadel, Stories for Our Times, Our Dream; exhibited in group shows Pierce Coll., Sierra Madre Libr., SouthBay Contemporary Mus., Restaurant Lozano, The Armory, Pasadena; commns. include Susan Chen, Above the Rest, Jim Grancich, Carol Tannenbaum, Judy Webb-Martin, Little Stuga, Eddie Truman, City of Sierra Madre, Dopkins Chapel, Lozano Restaurant; mural project for Mayor Riordan's Office, L.A., 2000. Chair Gooden Sch. Silent Auction, Sierra Madre, Calif., 1992, Harvest Ball Silent Auction, Greenwich, Conn., 1987. Avocations: bicycling, gardening, horse racing, traveling. Home: 823 Canyon Crest Dr Sierra Madre CA 91024-1313

CONVERSE, JAMES CLARENCE, agricultural engineering educator; b. Brainerd, Minn., Apr. 2, 1942; s. James L. and Doris E. (Beck) C.; m. Marjorie A. Swanson, Aug. 6, 1965; children— James, Julie, Mark, Katherine AA, Brainerd Jr. Coll, 1962; BS in Agrl. Engring., N.D. State U., 1964, MS in Agrl. Engring., 1966; PhD in Agrl. Engring., U. Ill., 1970. Asst. prof. agrl. engring. U. Wis., Madison, 1970-75, assoc. prof., 1975-80, prof., 1980—, chmn. dept., 1988-96. Fellow Am. Soc. Agrl. Engring. (Gunlogson countryside engring. award 1984). Roman Catholic. Avocations: scouts, soccer. Office: U Wis Dept Agrl Engring 460 Henry Mall Madison WI 53706-1533

CONVERSE, JOSEPH THOMAS, archivist, records manager; b. Glasgow, Ky., July 22, 1950; s. Henry Thomas and Betty Rue (Lee) C.; m. Myra Massey, June 21, 1974; 1 child, Emma Victoria. BA, U. Ky., 1972, MLS, 1978; postgrad. studies, U. Ga., 1972-74, U. Va., 1974-76. Br. chief Ky. State Archives, Frankfort, 1979-85; vice consul U.S. Embassy U.S. Dept. State, Guatemala City, Guatemala, 1986-88, U.S. Consulate Gen., Barcelona, Spain, 1989-90; consul U.S. Embassy, Managua, Nicaragua, 1990-91; chief libr. Nat. Archives, Washington, 1991-93; chief records mgmt. Inter Am. Devel. Bank, Washington, 1993—. Mem. Soc. Am. Archivists, Assn. Records Mgrs. and Adminstrs., Ky. Coun. on Archives, Acad. Cert. Archivists, Inst. Cert. Records Mgrs., Internat. Coun. Archives. Democrat. Unitarian Universalist. Avocations: reading, cooking, travel. Home: 2837 Sutton Oaks Ln Vienna VA 22181 Office: Inter Am Devel Bank 1300 New York Ave NW Washington DC 20577-0001

CONVERSE, PHILIP ERNEST, social science educator; b. Concord, N.H., Nov. 17, 1928; s. Ernest Luther and Evelyn (Eaton) C.; m. Jean Gilmore McDonnell, Aug. 25, 1951; children: Peter Everett, Timothy McDonnell. BA, Denison U., 1949, DHL (hon.), 1974; MA, State U. Iowa, 1950; cert., U. Paris, 1954; MA, U. Mich., 1956, PhD, 1958; DHL (hon.), U. Chgo., 1979. Asst. prof. sociology U. Mich., 1960-65, prof. sociology and polit. sci., 1965-89, Robert C. Angell Disting. prof., 1975-89. Asst. study dir. Inst. Social Rsch. U. Mich., 1956-58, study dir., 1958-65, program dir., 1965-82, dir. Ctr. for Polit. Studies, 1982-86, dir. Inst. Social Rsch., 1986-89; dir. Ctr. Advanced Study in Behavioral Scis., 1989-94; trustee Ctr. Advanced Study in Behavioral Scis., 1980-86, 94-2000, Russell Sage Found., 1982-92. Co-author: The American Voter, 1960, Elections and the Political Order, 1966, The Human Meaning of Social Change, 1972, The Quality of American Life, 1976, Political Representation in France, 1986; contbr. articles to profl. jours. Served with U.S. Army, 1950-52. Recipient Disting. Faculty Achievement award U. Mich., 1973; Fulbright fellow, 1959-60; NSF fellow, 1967-68; Guggenheim fellow, 1975-76; Ctr. Advanced Study in Behavioral Scis. fellow, 1979-80 Mem. AAAS, Am. Sociol. Assn., Am. Polit. Sci. Assn. (pres. 1983-84), Internat. Soc. Polit. Psychology (pres. 1980-81), Nat. Acad. Scis., Am. Acad. Arts and Scis., Am. Philos. Soc. Home: 9 Haverhill Ct Ann Arbor MI 48105-1406

CONVERTINO, VICTOR ANTHONY, physiologist, educator, research scientist, civil servant; b. Troy, N.Y., Apr. 26, 1949; s. Roger Orazio and Yolanda Ann (Trunfio) C.; m. Barbara Anne Bow, June 3, 1978; children: Laura, Pamela, Kevin, Brian. BA, San Jose State U., 1971, BS, 1972; MA, U. Calif.-Davis, 1974, PhD, 1981. Rsch. assoc. U. Calif.-Davis, 1977-78, exercise test supr., 1978-79; rsch. assoc. Stanford U., Palo Alto, Calif., 1979-82, lectr., 1982, cons., 1982-85; asst. prof. U. Ariz., Tucson, 1982-85; cons. NASA, Moffett Field, Calif., 1982-85; rsch. physiologist The Bionetics Corp., Kennedy Space Ctr., Fla., 1985-87; sr. rsch. physiologist NASA, Kennedy Space Ctr., Fla., 1987-93; rsch. physiologist USAF, Brooks AFB, Tex., 1993-98; sr. rsch. physiologist U.S. Army Inst. Surg. Rsch., Ft. Sam Houston, Tex., 1998—. Mem. editl. bd. Med. Sci. Sports Exercise, 1986, 2001, Jour. Applied Physiology, 1991; contbr. articles and chpts. to profl. publs. Chancellor's Patent grantee U. Calif., 1973. Fellow: Aerospace Med. Assn. (Ellingson Lit. award 1985), Am. Coll. Sports Medicine (trustee 1988, v.p. 1991, New Investigator award 1982, lectureship award 1984, 1990, 2002, vis. scholar award 1986); mem.: Am. Physiol. Soc. (travel grantee 1981, 1984), Nat. Space Biomed. Rsch. Inst. (extern adv. coun. 2000—02), Internat. Soc. Gravitational Physiology (trustee 2001). Office: US Army Inst Surg Rsch Bldg 3611 3400 Rawley E Chambers Ave Fort Sam Houston TX 78234

CONVERY, FREDRICK RICHARD, retired surgeon, orthopedist; b. Olympia, Wash., June 12, 1932; m. Martha Ann Minteer; children: Kristine Helen, Linda Lea, Mark Richard. BA, U. Wash., 1954, MD, 1958. Diplomate Am. Bd. Orthopaedic Surgery (examiner 1980-91). Intern Mpls. Gen. Hosp., 1958-59; resident U. Wash., Seattle, 1961-66; fellow in arthritis Rancho Las Amigos, Downey, Calif., 1966-67; instr. orthopedics U. Wash., Seattle, 1967-68, asst. prof., 1968-71, assoc. prof., 1971-72, U. Calif., San Diego, 1972-77, surgeon in residence, prof. surgery, 1977-97. Inventor prosthetic fixation technique. Mem. med. and sci. com. Western Wash. chpt. The Arthritis Found., 1968-72, San Diego chpt., 1973, chmn., 1977-78; mem. Calif. State Arthritis Coun., 1974-76. With USNR. Grantee Johnson & Johnson, 1994. Fellow Am. Acad. Orthopaedic Surgeons (exam. and evaluation com. 1974-82, Kappa Delta award 1972); mem. Am. Rheumatism Assn. (sect. arthritis, program com. 1973-75), Western Orthopaedic Assn. (Vernon P. Thompson award for Resident Rsch. 1964), Acad. Orthopaedic Soc., Am. Orthopaedic Assn. (resident guest 1966), Orthopaedic Rsch. Soc., Internat. Soc. of the Knee, Assn. for Arthritic Hip and Knee Soc., Wilson-Bost Interurban Club. E-mail: rcon725286@aol.com.

CONWAY, BERRY LESLIE, II, lawyer; b. Morganfield, Ky., Apr. 14, 1956; m. Darlene Conway; children: Michael, John, Nicole. BA with high distinction, U. Ky., 1979, JD, 1986. Bar: Va. 1987, U.S. Dist. Ct. (we. dist.) Va. 1987. Sr. assoc. Penn, Stuart, Eskridge, Abingdon, Va., 1987-93; ptnr. Conway Law Firm P.L.L.C., Abingdon, 1993—. Mem. Phi Beta Kappa. Avocation: breeding standardbred horses. Office: Conway Law Firm PLLC 165 W Main St Abingdon VA 24210-2837 E-mail: conwayattorneys@naxs.com.

CONWAY, BRIAN PETER, ophthalmologist, educator; b. N.Y.C., Dec. 20, 1942; s. Francis Xavier and Marie Theresa (Bohan) C.; m. Dora Linda Rubin, July 23, 1971 (div. Dec. 1995); children: Jennifer, Matthew, Michael; m. Gwyn DuVal Yardley, Sept. 6, 1998. AB in Econs., Georgetown U., 1964, MD, 1968. Intern Peter Bent Brigham Hosp., Boston, 1968-69, asst. resident in internal medicine, 1969-70; resident in ophthalmology Johns Hopkins Hosp., Balt., 1972-75, asst. chief of svc., 1976-77; asst. prof. Johns Hopkins U., Balt., 1977-78; prof. ophthalmic surgery, chmn. dept. U. Va. Med. Sch., Charlottesville, 1978—. Mem. data monitoring com. Nat. Eye Inst., Bethesda, Md., 1982—. Lt. cmdr. USPHS, 1970-72. Retinal disease fellow Bascom Palmer Eye Inst., Miami, Fla., 1975-76. Presbyterian. Office: Univ of Va Sch Medicine Dept of Ophthalmology PO Box 10009 Charlottesville VA 22906-0009

CONWAY, CONNIE ANNE See HELLYER, CONSTANCE

CONWAY, DANIEL EDWARD, management consultant; b. L.A., Nov. 5, 1940; s. Daniel Edward and Kathryn Lenora C.; children: Daniel E. III, Patrick A., Charlotte J. BA, U. Md., 1962, MA, 1964, postgrad., 1969; cert., U. Geneva, 1964; diploma, Ctrl. Am. Inst. Trade Union Studies, San Pedro Sula, Honduras, 1966. Spl. asst. to dep. dir. gen. adminstrn. Internat. Labor Orgn., Geneva, 1974-78; divsn. chief office of personnel Orgn. of Am. States, Washington, 1978-79; chief personnel Internat. Civil Aviation Orgn., Montreal, Can., 1979-83; head personnel svcs., spl. advisor to high commr. UN High Commr. for Refugees, Geneva, 1984-89, rep. Ankara, Turkey, 1989-91, Bangkok, Thailand, 1991-93, dir. human resources mgmt. Geneva, 1993-95; dir. ctrl. adminstrn. MIGA/World Bank Group, Washington, 1995-99; internat. cons. Conway Group Internat., Carlsbad, Calif., 1999—. Cons. Global Cons. Svc., N.Y.C., 1999—. Asst. inspector San Diego County Bd. Elections, Carlsbad, Calif., 1999. Grantee J. Frederick Brown Found., 1963, 65. Mem. Internat. Who's Who of Profl. Mgmt., Inst. for Internat. Human Resources, Assn. for Human Resources Mgmt. in Internat. Orgns., Acad. of Polit. Sci. Avocations: historical studies, model railroads, traveling. Home: 3211 Celinda Dr Carlsbad CA 92008 E-mail: conwaycgi@aol.com.

CONWAY, DAVID ANTONY, management executive, marketing professional; b. N.Y.C., Dec. 31, 1941; s. David A. and Elizabeth (Reidy) C.; m. Rosanne Kearney, July 30, 1966; children: Jennifer Stanton, Caroline Sloane. BS in Econs., Fordham Coll., 1963, MS in Econs., 1965. With Allied Chem. Corp., N.Y.C., 1967-68, CBS, Inc., N.Y.C., 1968-75, Goldman Sachs & Co., N.Y.C., 1975-76; v.p. adminstrn. Keene Corp., N.Y.C., 1976-86, KDI Corp., Cin., 1986-93; pres. Modern Edn. Svcs., N.Y.C., 1994-97; pres., CEO WaterChef, Inc., Glen Head, NY, 1998—, also chmn. bd. dirs. 1st lt. U.S. Army, 1965-67. Mem. Manhasset Bay Yacht Club (Port Washington, N.Y.). Republican. Roman Catholic. Office: WaterChef Inc 1007 Glen Cove Ave Glen Head NY 11545-1589

CONWAY, DOROTHY JEAN WILLIAMS, economist; b. Elizaville, Ky., Apr. 13, 1927; d. John Downing and Maud (Knight) Williams; m. Gene Farris Conway, Sept. 1, 1950; children: Lisa Ann Conway Allen, Janet Lee Conway Fleenor, Linda Knight Conway Hensley. Student, Ky. Wesleyan Coll., Winchester, 1945-46; BS, U. Ky., Lexington, 1949; student, Drexel Inst. Tech., Phila., 1952. Extension svc. agt. U. Ky., Maysville, 1949-52; tchr. home econ. Dayton (Ky.) H.S., 1952; therapeutic dietitian Doctor's Hosp., Phila., 1952-53; R&D lab. asst. Pillsbury Ballard, Louisville, Ky., 1953-54; home svc. adv. Indpls.

Power and Light, 1954, The Gas Svc. Co., Topeka, Kans., 1954-56; lectr. home mgmt. U. Cin., 1963. Bd. mem. Mary P. Shelton Pub. Libr., Georgetown, Ohio, 1979-93; bd. United Way. Allocations Com. Cin., 1985-94; bd. mem., chmn. Georgetown United Meth. Ch., 1981-87; mem., pres., sec. U. Cin. Women's Club, 1958-98. Mem. DAR, Am. Home Econ. Assn., Brown County Gen. Hosp. Aux., Cin. Women's Club, Phi Epsilon Omicron. Methodist. Home: 315 E State St Georgetown OH 45121-1416

CONWAY, DWIGHT COLBUR, chemistry educator; b. Long Beach, Calif., Nov. 14, 1930; s. Dee A. and Ruth (Mills) Conway; m. Diane Faye Coulter, Aug. 25, 1962; children: Kathleen Conway Jurell, Karyn Conway Hasselbrinck, Michael Dwight, Patrick Hugh. BS, U. Calif. at Berkeley, 1952; MS, U. Chgo., 1953, PhD, 1956. Postdoctoral student Purdue U., West Lafayette, Ind., 1956-57, asst. prof., 1957-63; assoc. prof. chemistry Tex. A.&M. U., College Station, 1963-67, prof., 1967—. Recipient Excellence in Tchg. award, Std. Oil Co. of Ind., 1969, Disting. Achievement award, Assn. of Former Students, 2003; fellow, U.S. Rubber Co., 1953—54; DuPont tchg. fellow, 1954—55. Mem. Am. Chem. Soc. (chmn.), Am. Phys. Soc., Am. Soc. Mass Spectrometry, Phi Beta Kappa, Sigma Xi (pres. local chpt.), Alpha Chi Sigma. Home: 1909 Bee Creek Dr College Station TX 77840-4871 Office: Tex A&M U Dept Chemistry College Station TX 77843-0001 E-mail: conway@mail.chem.tamu.edu.

CONWAY, E. VIRGIL, financial consultant, banker, lawyer; b. Southhampton, N.Y., Aug. 2, 1929; m. Elaine Wingate, June 28, 1969; children: Allison, Sarah. BA in Philosophy and Religion magna cum laude, Colgate U., 1951; LLB cum laude, Yale U., 1956; LLD (hon.), Pace U., 1990; LHD (hon.), SUNY, Stony Brook, 1998; LLD (hon.), Colgate U., 2002. Bar: N.Y. 1956. Assoc. firm Debevoise & Plimpton, N.Y.C., 1956-64; 1st dept. supt. Banks of State N.Y., 1964-67; sec. N.Y. State Banking Bd., 1964-67; exec. v.p. Manhattan Savs. Bank, N.Y.C., 1967-68; vice chmn., bd. dirs. Seamen's Corp., 1986-89; pres., chmn. The Seamen's Bank for Savs., 1969-88. Bd. dirs. Union Pacific Corp., chmn. exec. compensation com., mem. exec. com. 1978-2002; bd. dirs. J.P. Stevens & Co., Inc., 1974-88 ; trustee, mem. exec. com., chmn. audit com. mut. funds managed by Phoenix Funds; dir., mem. audit com. of mut. funds managed by Phoenix Duff & Phelps Funds; trustee, mem. exec. com., chmn. exec. devel. & comp. Atlantic Mut. Ins. Co., 1974-2002; trustee, mem. exec., chmn. exec. pers. and pension coms. Consol. Edison Co. of N.Y., 1970-2002; trustee, chmn. compensation com., mem. exec. com. Urstadt Biddle Property Co., 1989—; adv. dir. Blackrock BFM, Freddie Mac Securities Mortgage Fund, 1969-2001; N.Y. rep. Conf. of State Bank Suprs., 1970-77, mem. adv. coun., 1973-74, mem. adv. com. to N.Y. State Supt. Banks, 1967-70; chmn. Fin. Acct. Standards Adv. Coun., 1992-1995; adv. dir. Fund Directions; dir. chmn. comp. com. Trism, Inc., 1995-2001; dir., mem. exec. com., audit com., chmn. stock option com. Accuhealth, Inc., 1995-2002; N.Y. rep. Conf. State Bank Suprs., 1970-77, mem. adv. coun., 1973-1974. Editor: Yale Law Jour. Mem. Met. Transp. Authority, chmn. audit and cplnning and real estate coms., mem. Metro North and N.Y.C. Transit coms., 1992-95; chmn. Met. Transp. Authority, L.I. Railroad, Metro North, Transit Authority of City of N.Y., Triborough Bridge and Tunnel Authority, 1995-2001; chmn. Temporary State Commn. on Water Supply Needs of Southeastern N.Y., 1970-75; mem. Audit Com. N.Y.C., 1981-1996, chmn., 1990-1996, Mayor's Mgmt. Adv. Bd., N.Y.C., 1975-77; mem., chmn. meml. design com. N.Y.C. Korean Vets. Meml. Commn.; del. Rep. State Conv. N.Y., 1962, 66; pres. N.Y. Young Rep. Club, 1962-63; mem. adv. bd. N.Y. U. Real Estate Inst.; bd. dirs. Realty Found. N.Y.; bd. dirs., chmn. audit, fin., exec. coms. Josiah Macy, Jr. Found.; trustee, former vice chmn., mem. exec. com. Citizens Budget Commn.; life trustee N.Y.C. Police Found., Pace U., N.Y.C., Colgate U., 1970-76; trustee N.Y. coun. Boy Scouts Am.; hon. life trustee South Street Seaport Mus.; bd. govs., pres. Fed. Hall Meml. Assos., Inc., 1981-84; bd. dirs., vice chmn, treas., mem. audit and fin., compensation, project planning and pub. policy com., N.Y.C. Partnership, Inc., 1980-91, hon. ptnr., 1991—; elder Refored Ch. of Bronxville. Recipient Humanitarian award Jewish Hosp. and Rsch. Ctr., Denver, 1977, Good Scout award Greater N.Y. couns. Boy Scouts Am., 1980, Spl. Recognition award NAACP, 1980, Disting. Svc. to Higher Edn. medal Brandeis U., 1976, Urban Leadership award NYU, 1981, Hundred Yr. Assn. Gold Medal award, 1986, Eagle Scout award, 1988, Silver Beaver award Boy Scouts Am., 1989, Alexander Hamilton award Bowling Green Assn., Disting. Svc. award Bklyn. Bur. Cmty. Svc., 1995, Family of Yr. award Family Svc. Westchester, Inc., 1996, Norman Vincent Peale award, Insts. Religion and Health, 1998, Ellis Island medal of honor, Nat. Ethnic Coalition, 1998; Gov.'s Parks and Preservation award, 1999, March of Dimes Svc. to Humanity award, 2000, Urban Visionaries award, Cooper Union, 2002; named Man of Yr. Realty Found. N.Y., 1978. Mem. ABA, N.Y. State Bar Assn., Assn. of Bar of City of N.Y., Nat. Assn. Mut. Savs. Banks (past dir.), Savs. Banks Assn. N.Y. State (pres. 1978-79, past dir. and chmn. legis.), N.Y. C. of C. and Industry (bd. dirs., exec. com., sec.-treas. 1974-91, chmn. mission rev. com. 1985), Real Estate Bd. N.Y. (bd. govs. 1976-79), Econ. Club N.Y., Knights of St. Patrick (chmn. bd. dirs., co-chmn.), Union League Club, Links Club, Siwanoy Country Club, Phi Beta Kappa. Office: 101 Park Ave Rm 2500 New York NY 10178-3099

CONWAY, EARL CRANSTON, business educator, retired manufacturing company executive; b. Asbury Park, N.J., Nov. 14, 1931; s. Earl Cranston and Alda Evelyn (Hendrickson) C.; m. Nancy Lou Schucker, Oct. 23, 1954; children: Karen Marie, Anne Margaret, Earl Edward, Nancy Maureen. BA in Polit. Sci. and Internat. Rels., U. Pa., Phila., 1954. Sales-mktg. rep. Procter & Gamble, Phila., 1957-59, unit mgr. Balt. and Chgo., 1960-64, dist. mgr., 1964-69, divsn. mgr., nat. sales mgr., 1970-81, gen. sales mgr. Europe Brussels, 1981-85, corp. dir. world-wide quality Cin., 1985-92; pres., COO Innovative Food Technology, Inc., 1998-99. Co-chmn. U.S. Quality Coun. of Conf. Bd., N.Y.C., 1989-92; adj. prof. U. Cin., 1990—; adj. faculty Indian River C.C., Indian River County, Fla., 1996-99; lectr. quality and strategic planning Ministry of Light Industry, China, 1992—, Moscow and Kirov, Russia, 1994—; vis. lectr. bus. and engring. schs.; advisor quality mgmt. V.P. Gore, U.S. and Gov. Jim Hunt, N.C., 1992-93, 93-94. Vice chmn. nat. bd. dirs. Vols. of Am., New Orleans, 1991-96; mem., bd. trustees Ursuline Acad., Cin., 1992-93; mem. planning and zoning bd. City of Vero Beach, Fla., 1995-99; bd. dirs. Civic Assn., Indian River County, Fla., Vero Beach, Fla., 1995—; vice chmn., bd. dirs. Indian River Meml. Hosp., Indian River County, 1999—. 1st lt., inf. U.S. Army, 1955-56. Recipient Taguchi Quality Engring. award Am. Supplier Inst., 1989, Recognition by Ministry of Light Industry, People's Republic of China, Guangzhou and Wuxi, 1992-93. Mem. Am. Soc. Quality. Republican. Roman Catholic. Home: 1020 Olde Doubloon Dr Vero Beach FL 32963-2449

CONWAY, EDWARD GERALD, JR., university educational technology administrator; b. Bklyn., Aug. 10, 1948; s. Edward Gerald and Louise (McNamara) C.; m. E. Regina Harris, Nov. 8, 1998. AA, Valley Forge Mil. Acad. Coll., 1969; postgrad., Georgetown Coll., 1969, Bloomfield Coll., 1970, Rutgers U., 1971, Muhlenberg Coll., 1973, Marywood Coll., 1977; BS in Media, Comms. and Tech. cum laude, E. Stroudsburg U., 1983; MS in Instructional Tech., Marywood Coll., 1994. Various acctg. and fin. positions in large cos. in eastern U.S., 1970-77; fin. aid officer Valley Forge Mil. Acad., Wayne, Pa., 1977-80; pers. recruiting, cons. Va., Tex., 1980-87; media technician U. Scranton, Pa., 1987-89, coord. media broadcast, 1989-92, dir. office of instructional techs., prodn. & broadcasting, 1992-95; coord. ednl. affairs Media Svc., Ga. Perimeter Coll., 1995—. Mem. comm. adv. bd. Diocese of Scranton, Pa. 1993-96. Presenter, lectr. at profl. meetings. Mem. Consortium of Coll. and Univ. Media Ctrs., Assn. for Ednl. Comm. and Tech. Avocation: travel. E-mail: egconway@harris-conway.com.

CONWAY, EVELYN ATKINSON, accountant, financial analyst; b. Goose Creek, Tex., Aug. 14, 1921; d. George Henry and Sadie Ray (Bouldin) Atkinson; m. Lucian Gideon Conway, Nov. 2, 1945; children: Lucian Gideon Conway Jr., Karen Elizabeth Conway, Rebecca Annette Conway, Terri Ruth Conway, Jerry Andrew Conway, Priscilla Janice Conway. BS in Acctg., La. Tech. U., 1943; postgrad., New Orleans Bapt. Theol. Sem., 1949—51. Sr. acct. McGuire & Mazur CPAs, Houston, 1943—45; math. tchr. Enterprise Sch., Summit, Miss., 1953—54; sr. ptnr. Conley & Conway, Coushatta, La., 1955—56; office mgr. Annuity Bd. Rep. SBC, Alexandria, La., 1959—83; regional mgr., pers. fin. analyst Primerica Life & PFS Investments, Inc., Alexandria, La., 1984—. Auditor The Bapt. Message, Alexandria, 1962—64. Emergency evacuation officer Civil Def., Coushatta, 1955—57; treas. Dist. 8 La. Bapt. Missions, Coushatta, 1955—56. Named Hometown All Am., Alexandria Daily Town Talk, 1995. Republican. Baptist. Avocations: sewing, music. Home: 118 Pearce Rd Pineville LA 71360

CONWAY, FRENCH HOGE, lawyer; b. Danville, Va., June 11, 1918; s. Lysander Broadus and Mildred (Hoge) C.; BS, U. Va., 1942, JD, 1946; m. Louise Throckmorton, Feb. 3, 1961; children: French Hoge Jr., William Chenery, Helen (Mrs. Carlton Bedsole), Donna F. LeFevers. Bar: Va. 1942. Sole practice, Danville, 1942—; mem. firm Clement, Conway & Winston, 1950-60. Sec., Danville City Bd. Rev., 1985— ; v.p. Va. Election Bd. Assn., 1974. Served with USNR, 1942-46. Mem. ABA, Va. Bar Assn., Danville Bar Assn. (pres. 1985-86), Am. Trial Lawyers Assn., Va. Trial Lawyers Assn., Soc. Cincinnati in State of Va., Ret. Officers Assn., Boat Owners Assn. U.S. Lodges: Kiwanis, Masons. Home: 912 Main St Danville VA 24541-1810 Office: 105 S Union St Danville VA 24541-1113

CONWAY, GENE FARRIS, cardiologist; b. Cynthiana, Ky., 1928; s. Farris Lee and Cora Jane (Hall) C.; m. Dorothy Jean Williams, Sept. 1, 1950; children: Lisa Ann, Janet Lee, Linda Knight. BS, U. Ky., 1949; MD, U. Cin., 1952. Cert. in internal medicine, specialty in cardiovasc. disease. Intern Phila. Gen. Hosp., 1952-53; resident in medicine Louisville Gen. Hosp., 1953-54; resident in rsch. medicine Indpls. Gen. Hosp.; resident in medicine Cin. Gen. Hosp., 1957, 58-59, fellow in cardiology, 1959-61; with U. Hosp. Cin. Prof. med., assoc. dir. internal medicine U. Cin. Coll. Medicine, 1988—; mem. adv. com. Area Health Edn. Ctrs., Ohio Bd. Regents, Columbus, 1977-85; mem. adv. com. Regional Med. Planning, Cin., 1978-82; chair Adv. Group to VA on Cardiac Catheterization, Washington, 1973-75. Contbr. sci. papers to profl. jours. Vice chair Ohio Legis. Com. on Health Care, Columbus, 1994; mem. adv. com. geriatrics Ohio Bd. Regents, Columbus, 1978-80. Fellow Am. Coll. Cardiology, Coun. on Clin. Cardiology; mem. Am. Coll. Physician Execs., Am. Heart Assn., Ctrl. Soc. for Clin. Rsch., Cin. Soc. Internatl Medicine (pres. 1988-89), Soc. Sigma Xi Republican. Methodist. E-mail: Gene.Conway@uc.edu.

CONWAY, HEATHER, communications executive; Spl. asst. to fin. min. Michael Wilson, Parliament Hill, Ottawa, Canada, 1989; with Hill & Knowlton, TD Bank Fin. Group; exec. v.p., corp. and pub. affairs Alliance Atlantis Comms. Inc., Toronto. Office: Alliance Atlantis 121 Bloor St East Ste 1500 Toronto ON Canada M4W 3M5

CONWAY, HOWARD, geophysicist, educator; b. Hawera, Taranaki, New Zealand, Jan. 14, 1950;, U.S., 1987; s. Dorothy Betty and Barry Edward Conway; m. Leslie Blank, July 30, 1999. B Chem. Engring., U. Canterbury, Christchurch, New Zealand, 1973, PhD Chem. Engring., 1986. Rsch. ast. prof. geophysics U. Wash., Seattle, 1991—97, rsch. assoc. prof. geophysics, 1997—2002, rsch. prof. geophysics, 2002—. Snow and avalanche cons., Seattle, 1984—. Contbr. articles to profl. jours. Mem.: Am. Avalanche Profls., Am. Geophys. Soc., Internat. Glaciological Soc. Office: U Wash Dept Earth and Space Scis Seattle WA 98195

CONWAY, JAMES BERNARD, hospital administrator, consultant; b. Boston, Jan. 6, 1947; s. John J. and Nora M. (O'Leary) C.; m. Joanne M. Duffy, Nov. 30, 1969; children: Christopher, Kerry, Peter. BS, Boston State Coll., 1969; MA in Applied Mgmt., Lesley Coll., Cambridge, Mass., 1992. Diplomate Am. Coll. Healthcare Execs. Radiology adminstr. Children's Hosp., Boston, 1972-85, asst. to v.p. fin., 1985-87, dir. ops., 1987-95; COO Dana-Farber Cancer Inst., Boston, 1995—; pres. HCD Hospice; faculty Sch. of Mgmt. Lesley Coll., Cambridge, Mass., 1995—. Bd. dirs. Children's Hosp. Fed. Credit Union, 1973-80; speaker, presenter in field. Mem. editorial bd. Risk Mgmt. Found., Cambridge, 1991-95; author articles. Bd. dirs. Ronald McDonald House, 1992-2002, mem. hospitality program, 1992-2002; bd. dirs. Boy Scouts Am. Recipient Dist. award of Merit boy Scouts Am., 1984, Oliver Morrill award Mass. Soc. Radiologic Technologists, 1980, others. Fellow Am. Healthcare Radiology Adminstrs. (bd. dirs., chair 1978-85, Gold award 1982); mem. Am. Soc. for Quality Control, Healthcare Mgmt. Assn., Mass. Hosp. Assn. (bd. dirs.). Roman Catholic. Avocations: travel, gardening, genealogy, singing. Home: 8 Mt Pleasant St Woburn MA 01801-4311

CONWAY, JAMES CLAUDE, periodontist; b. Raven Run, Pa., June 24, 1920; s. Patrick Joseph and Maude (Hoats) C.; m. Elizabeth Jane Davenport, June 7, 1947; children: Timothy Patrick, Deborah Ann. BS in Edn., Kutztown (Pa.) U., 1943; DDS, Georgetown U., 1950; BS, Baylor U., 1957; MS in Edn., U. Pitts., 1977. Diplomate Am. Bd. Periodontology. Asst. assoc. prof. dept. periodontics U. Pitts., 1967-76, chmn. dept. periodontics, 1976-87, assoc. chmn. dept. periodontics, 1987-90, vol. faculty dept. periodontics, 1990—, prof. emeritus, 1991—. Cons. Coun. on Dental Edn., 1975-81, VA Hosp., Butler, Pitts., 1975-90, Commn. on Accreditation, Pitts., 1975-80. Contbr. articles to profl. jours. Lt. col. U.S. Army, 1942-45, 49-67. Fellow Am. Coll. Dentistry, Internat. Coll. Dentistry; mem. ADA, Am. Acad. Periodontology. Republican. Roman Catholic. Avocation: model building. Home: 4051 Tall Timber Dr Allison Park PA 15101-3043

CONWAY, JAMES JOSEPH, radiologist, educator; b. Chgo., July 1, 1933; s. Frank and Mary (Tuohy) Conway; m. Dolores Mazer, June 30, 1956; children: Laurie, John, Cheryl. BS, DePaul U., 1959; MD, Northwestern U., 1963. Asst. instr. U. Pa., 1964—68; assoc. in radiology McGaw Med. Ctr. Northwestern U., Chgo., 1968—71, asst. prof. to assoc. prof. radiology, 1974—80; attendant radiology Children's Meml. Hosp., Chgo., 1968—98, prof. radiology, 1980—. Contbr. articles over 110 to profl. jours. With U.S. Army, 1953—55. Recipient Gold medal, Chgo. Radiol. Soc., 1993. Fellow: Radiol. Soc. N.Am. (Scroll of Appreciation award 1983), Am. Coll. Radiology, Am. Coll. Nuc. Physicians, P.R. Soc. Nuc. Medicine (hon.); mem.: Soc. Nuclear Medicine (pres. 1994—95). Avocation: collector of Chicago memorabilia. Office: Childrens Meml Hosp 2300 N Childrens Plz Chicago IL 60614-3394 E-mail: nukedr@hotmail.com.

CONWAY, JAMES VALENTINE PATRICK, forensic document examiner, former postal service executive; b. Scottdale, Pa., July 16, 1917; s. James Aloysius and Mary Margaret (Yahner) C.; m. Mildred E. Garypie, Aug. 6, 1936; children: James W., Ruth A. Conway Masonek, Colleen L. Conway Weyland, Judith Conway Henderson. Student, St. Vincent Coll., Latrobe, Pa., 1931-34, Cambria-Rowe Bus. Coll., Greensburg, Pa., 1935-36. Diplomate Am. Bd. Forensic Document Examiners. With U.S. Postal Svc., 1939-80, regional chief insp., 1971-73; exec. asst. to Postmaster Gen., Washington, 1973-75; sr. asst. postmaster gen. for employee and labor rels., 1975-78; dep. Postmaster Gen., 1978-80, bd. govs., 1978-80; forensic document examiner Alameda, Calif., 1980—. Author: Evidential Documents, 1959; contbr. articles to profl. jours. Bd. dirs. Regional Civil Def. Bd., Santa Rosa, Calif., 1964-69. Recipient Benjamin Franklin award Postmaster Gen.'s. 1980; named Staff Man of Yr. Fed. Bus. Assn., San Francisco, 1957. Fellow Am. Acad. Forensic Scis. (chmn. document sect. 1960-61, chmn. adv. coun. 1960-61); mem. Internat. Assn. Chiefs Police (life), Internat. Assn. Identification (chmn. subcom. questioned document 1953-56), Am. Soc. Questioned Document Examiners (pres. 1988-90). Lodges: Elks. Democrat. Roman Catholic. Avocations: cantoring, tennis. *Professional competence is a must but necessarily subordinate to absolute personal integrity. Call things the way they are, not the way others, e.g., clients might wish them to be.*

CONWAY, JOHN BELL, health educator, university dean; b. Madison, Wis., Apr. 5, 1936; s. John Edward and Barbara (Bell) C.; m. Susan Jane Hawley, Sept. 1, 1961; children: Julie Anne, Steven Douglas. BS in Biology, San Diego State U., 1964, MS in Biology, 1967; MPH in Pub. Health, U. Minn., 1970, PhD in Environ. Biology, 1973. Asst. prof. bio. scis. Wright State U., Dayton, Ohio, 1972—76; asst. prof. bacteria and pub. health Wash. State U., Pullman, 1976—78, assoc. prof., 1978—81; prof. divsn. occupl. and environ. health Grad Sch. Pub. Health, San Diego State U., 1981—92, head divsn. occupl. and environ. health, 1984—87, assoc. dir., prof., 1987—92; assoc. dean, dir. profl. edn. program, prof. SUNY Sch. Pub. Health, Albany, 1993—97, prof. dept. environ. health and toxicology, 1993—2000, interim dean, 1998—2000; prof. allied health U. Tex., El Paso, 2001—, dean Coll. Health Scis., 2001—, Charles H. & Shirley T. Leavell endowed chair in nursing and health scis., 2001—. Cons. NBS/Lowry Engrs. and Planners, San Diego, 1984-95, Congressman Duncan Hunter, San Diego, 1991-92, Compliance Consultants, N.Y.C., 1993-95; pub. health officer Grand Teton Nat. Park, Moose, Wyo., summers, 1996, 97. Editl. reviewer Jour. Environ. Health, 1978— (Harry Bliss award 1985), Cancer Prevention Internat., 1994—. Recipient Outstanding Faculty award San Diego State U. Alumni, 1986. Mem. Nat. Environ. Health Assn. (chair air and water sect. 1979-80), Nat. Environ. Health Sci. and Protection Accreditation Coun. (chair 1994-96), Am. Pub. Health Assn. (Disting. Svc. award sect. on environ. 1997). Office: U Tex Coll Health Scis 1101 N Campbell El Paso TX 79902-0581 E-mail: jconway@utep.edu., sjanecon@cs.com.

CONWAY, JOHN E. federal judge; b. 1934; BS, U.S. Naval Acad., 1956; LLB magna cum laude, Washburn U., 1963. Assoc. Matias A Zamora, Santa Fe, 1963-64; ptnr. Wilkinson, Durrett & Conway, Alamogordo, N.Mex., 1964-67, Durrett, Conway & Jordon, Alamogordo, 1967-80, Montgomery & Andrews, P.A., Albuquerque, 1980-86; city atty. Alamogordo, 1966-72; mem. N.Mex. State Senate, 1970-80, minority leader, 1972-80; chief fed. judge U.S. Dist. Ct. N.Mex., Albuquerque, 1994—2000, sr. fed. judge, 2000—. Mem. Jud. Resources Com., 1995—98. 1st lt. USAF, 1956-60. Mem. 10th Cir. Dist. Judges Assn. (pres. 1995-98), Fed. Judges Assn. (bd. dirs. 1996-2001), Nat. Commrs. on Uniform State Laws, N.Mex. Bar Assn., N.Mex. Jud. Coun. (vice chmn. 1973, chmn. 1973-75, disciplinary bd. of Supreme Ct. of N.Mex. vice chmn. 1980, chmn. 1981-84, apptd. to fgn. intelligence surveillance ct. 2002). Office: US Dist Ct Chambers #740 333 Lomas Blvd NW Albuquerque NM 87102-2272 E-mail: jconway@nmcourt.fed.us.

CONWAY, JOHN S. history educator; b. London, Dec. 31, 1929; s. Geoffrey S. and Elsie (Philips) C.; m. Ann P. Jefferies, Aug. 10, 1957; children— David, Jane, Alison BA, Cambridge U., Eng., 1952; MA, Cambridge U., 1955, PhD, 1956. Asst. prof. U. Man., Can., 1955-57; asst. prof., assoc. prof., then prof. history U. B.C., Vancouver, 1957-94, prof. emeritus, 1995—. Mem. editl. bd. dirs. Holocaust and Genocide Studies, Kirchliche Zeitgeschichte; Smallman Disting. vis. prof. history U. Western On., 1998. Author: The Nazi Persecution of the Churches, 1968, 2d edit., 1997. Contbr. numerous articles on churches and the holocaust to topical publs. Pres. Tibetan Refugee Aid Soc., Can., 1971-81; chmn. Vancouver Coalition with World Refugees, 1982-84. Recipient Queen's Silver Jubilee medal, 1977. Mem. Can. Inst. Internat. Affairs, German Studies Assn., Can. Hist. Assn. Anglican. Home: 4345 Locarno Crescent Vancouver BC Canada V6R 1G2 Office: U BC Dept History East Mall Vancouver BC Canada V6T 1Z1

CONWAY, JOHN THOMAS, government official, lawyer, engineer; b. N.Y.C., May 10, 1924; s. John Joseph and Johannah (Stanley) C.; m. Priscilla Harris, Sept. 13, 1947 (div. 1978); children: John, Daniel, Sean, Thomas, Christopher, Johannah; m. Virginia McLaughlin, Mar. 17, 1989. B.N.S., Tufts U., 1945, BS in Engring., 1947; JD, Columbia U., 1949. Bar: N.Y. 1949, U.S. Supreme Ct. 1952. Spl. agt. FBI, Washington, 1950-56; asst. dir. U.S. Congress Joint Com. on Atomic Energy, Washington, 1956-62, exec. dir., 1962-68; exec. asst. to chmn. Consol. Edison, N.Y.C., 1968-78, exec. v.p., 1982-89; chmn. Def. Nuclear Facilities Safety Bd., Washington, 1989—. Pres. Am. Nuclear Energy Council, Washington, 1978-82, chmn. bd., 1983-89; bd. dirs. Empire State Energy Research Com., N.Y., 1970-76, Atomic Indsl. Forum, 1976-78; mem. oversight com. U.S. Com. Energy Awareness, Washington, 1982-89, safet bd., U.S. Def. Nucl. Facilities. Bd. dirs. Americans for Energy Independence, Washington, 1982-89, Youth for Energy Independence, Washington, 1982-89, Assn. For A Better N.Y., 1982-89, N.Y. Fire Safety Found., 1984-89; mem. N.Y.C. Mayor's Com. for Sci., 1969-76. Capt. j.g. USNR, 1943—52. Mem. Am. Legion (life), U.S. Army Ft. Meyer Officer Club, Democratic Club (Washington). Democrat. Roman Catholic. Office: Defense Nuclear Facilities Safety Bd 625 Indiana Ave NW Ste 700 Washington DC 20004-2909

CONWAY, JOHN W. manufacturing executive; Pres. Continental Can Internat. Corp., 1988; sr. v.p. Crown Cork & Seal (acquired Continental Can Internat. Corp.), Phila., 1991-93; exec. v.p., pres. internat. divsn. Crown Cork & Seal, Phila., 1993-96, pres., exec. v.p. Am. divsn., 1997-2001; chmn. bd., pres., CEO, 2001—. Bd. dirs. Crown Cork & Seal, Nat. Food Processors Assn., The West Co.; chmn. Can Mfrs. Inst. Office: Crown Cork & Seal 1 Crown Way Philadelphia PA 19154-4599

CONWAY, KEVIN, actor, director; b. N.Y.C., May 29, 1942; s. James John C. and Margaret O'Brien; m. Mila Quiros, Apr. 5, 1966. Broadway and Off-Broadway appearances include: Dinner at Eight, Elephant Man, Of Mice and Men, Moonchildren, Red Ryder, One Flew Over the Cuckoo's Nest, Life Class, Other Places, King John, Other People's Money, 1988 (Outer Critics Circle award for best actor, 1989), On the Waterfront, Lawyers; films include: Slaughterhouse Five, Portnoy's Complaint, FIST, Paradise Alley, The Funhouse, Flashpoint, Homeboy, Jesse, One Good Cop, Ramblin Rose, Jennifer 8, Gettysburg, Lawnmower Man II, Whipping Boy, The Quick and the Dead, Rage of Angels, The Scarlet Letter, The Deadliest Season, The Lathe of Heaven, Elephant Man, Something About Amelia, When Will I Be Loved, Breaking the Silence, (miniseries) Mark Twain, Gettysburg, Streets of Laredo, Flamingo Rising, Calm at Sunset, Sally Hemmings, Oz, (films) Black Knight, Gods and Generals, 13 Days, Looking for Richard, Mercury Rising, The Confession, Mystic River, (TV) Miami Vice, Law and Order, Jag, Equalizer; dir.: (plays) Off-Broadway and Lincoln Ctr. Mecca, Old Flames, Milk Train Doesn't Stop Here, Chgo. and L.A. prodn. Other Peoples Money, 1990; star, dir.: (feature film) The Sun and the Moon, 1985. Bd. dirs. Second Stage Co. Served with USN, 1960-62. Recipient Village Voice Obie award, 1973; recipient Drama Desk award, 1973-74. Mem. Screen Actors Guild (bd. dirs. 1979-81), Nat. Acad. TV Arts and Scis. Home and Office: 25 Central Park W New York NY 10023-7253 E-mail: gemicon@aol.com.

CONWAY, LOIS LORRAINE, piano teacher; b. Caldwell, Idaho, Oct. 20, 1913; d. William Henry and Auttie Arrola (Bierd) Crawford; m. Edward Owen Conway, June 23, 1934; children: Michael David, Judith Ann, Steven Edward, Kathleen Jean. Degree, Albertson Coll. of Idaho, 1960's; student, Shorwood Music Sch., Chgo., Coll. of Notre Dame, San Francisco. Pvt. piano tchr., Ontario, Oreg., 1940-74, Pendleton, Oreg., 19774-92; ret., 1992. Nat. Guild Piano Tchrs. adjudicator spring auditions Am. Coll. Musicians, Austin, Tex., 1972-96. Author: (poetry) Pacifica-The Voice Within (Semi-finalist 1995). Chmn. Nat. Guild Auditions, Ontario, Oreg., 1959-72, Pendleton, Oreg., 1972-80; v.p., publicity Community Concerts Assn., Ontario, 1960-72, membership work, 1972 75. Democrat. Avocations: gardening, playing piano, bridge, duplicate bridge, motor home travel. Home: 114 Shamrock Cir Santa Rosa CA 95403-1156

CONWAY, LOWAVA DENISE, data processing administrator; b. Galesburg, Ill., Mar. 27, 1958; d. Richard Eugene and Lowava Jeanine (Squire) Corbin; m. James Dean Rutledge, June 17, 1977 (div. May 1981); 1 child, Tiffany Michelle; m. Dennis Lane Conway, May 26, 1995. Computer operator cert., Carl Sandburg Coll., 1977, student, 1976-86, IBM Edn., Chgo., 1979-87. Keypunch operator Fin. Industry Systems, Galesburg, Ill., 1977-79; computer operator Solution Assocs., Peoria, Ill., 1979-80; programmer, data processing mgr. May Co., Galesburg, 1980-81; programmer Kirkendall Gen. Offices, Galesburg, 1981-82; MIS dir. Munson Transp., Monmouth, Ill., 1982-89; ind. contract programmer analyst Oklahoma City, Okla., 1989-92; product line mgr. Innovative Computing Corp., 1992-94; sr. programmer analyst, dir. info. resources Freymiller Trucking, Inc., Oklahoma City, 1994-96; ptnr. D&D Computers, Inc., 1996—. Mem. Cmty. Bible Ch. Address: 1793 Monroe St Galesburg IL 61401-3441

CONWAY, LYNN, computer scientist, electrical engineer, educator; b. Mt. Vernon, N.Y., Jan. 2, 1938; BS, Columbia U., 1962, MSEE, 1963; D (hon.), Trinity Coll., 1997. Rsch. staff IBM Corp., Yorktown Heights, N.Y., 1964-68; sr. staff engr. Memorex Corp., Santa Clara, Calif., 1969-73; rsch. staff Xerox Corp., Palo Alto, Calif., 1973-78, rsch. fellow, mgr. VLSI systems area, 1978-82, rsch. fellow, mgr. knowledge systems area, 1982-83; asst. dir. for strategic computing Def. Advanced Research Projects Agy., Arlington, Va., 1983-85; prof. elec. engring. and computer sci., assoc. dean U. Mich. Coll. Engring., Ann Arbor, Mich., 1985—. Vis. assoc. prof. elec. engring. and computer sci. MIT, Cambridge, Mass., 1978-79; sci. adv. bd. USAF, 1987-90. Co-author: textbook Introduction to VLSI Systems, 1980; contbr. articles to profl. jours.; patentee in field. Mem. coun. Govt.-Univ.-Industry Rsch. Roundtable, 1993-98; mem. corp. Charles Stark Draper Lab., 1993—; mem. bd. visitors USAF Acad., 1996-2000, presdl. appt.; mem. Air Force Sci. and Tech. Bd., Nat. Acads., 2000—. Recipient Ann. Achievement award Electronics mag., 1981, Harold Pender award U. Pa., 1984, Wetherill Medal Franklin Inst., 1985, Sec. of Def. Meritorious Civilian Svc. award, 1985. Fellow IEEE; mem. NAE, AAAS, Soc.

Women Engrs. (Ann. Achievement award 1990), Assn. Computing Machinery. Avocations: motocross racing, whitewater canoeing, natural landscaping. Office: U Mich 146 ATL Bldg Ann Arbor MI 48109-2110 E-mail: conway@engin.umich.edu.

CONWAY, M. MARGARET, political science educator, consultant; b. Terre Haute, Ind., May 14, 1935; d. Frank J. and Mary K. Conway. BS in Econs., Purdue U., 1957; MA in Polit. Sci., U. Calif., Berkeley, 1960; PhD in Polit. Sci., Ind. U., 1965. From lectr. to prof. U. Md., College Park, 1963—89; prof. U. Fla., Gainesville, 1989—98, disting. prof., 1998—2000, disting. prof. emeritus, 2000—. Mem. Am. Polit. Sci. Assn. (v.p. 1991-92, pres. women's causes sect. 1991-92, pres. polit. orgns. and parties sect. 1989-91), So. Polit. Sci. Assn. (pres. 1986-87). Office: U Fla Dept Polit Sci Gainesville FL 32611-7325

CONWAY, MARK ALLYN, lawyer; b. Dayton, Ohio, Dec. 13, 1957; s. Allyn Walter and Doris Jean (Wright) C.; m. Dawn Elizabeth Manning, July 31, 1982; children: Ashley Wright, Alexandra Mills. BA, Denison U., 1980; JD, Calif. Western Sch. of Law, 1983; LLM in Taxation, Georgetown U., 1984. Bar: D.C. 1983, U.S. Tax Ct. 1983, Calif. 1988, Ohio 1991. Ptnr. Thompson Hine LLP, Dayton, 1990—. Fellow Am. Coll. of Trust and Estate Counsel; mem. ABA (real property, probate and trust law sect.), D.C. Bar Assn., Calif. Bar Assn. (real property, probate and trust law sect. 1988—), Dayton Racquet Club. Republican. Presbyterian. Avocations: tennis, skiing, sailing. Home: 5712 Price Hill Pl Dayton OH 45459-1428 Office: Thompson Hine LLP 2000 Courthouse Plz NE Dayton OH 45402

CONWAY, MICHAEL MAURICE, lawyer; b. St. Joseph, Mo., Mar. 11, 1946; s. Michael Maurice and Genevieve (Hepburn) C.; m. Kathleen Stevens; children: Michael, Cara, Mary. BS in Journalism, Northwestern U., 1968; JD, Yale U., 1973. Bar: Ill. 1973, U.S. Dist. Ct. (no. dist.) Ill. 1973, U.S. Tax Ct. 1975, U.S. Ct. Claims 1976, U.S. Ct. Appeals (7th cir.) 1976, U.S. Ct. Appeals (1st cir.) 1979, U.S. Supreme Ct. 1980, U.S. Ct. Appeals (5th and 11th cirs.) 1981, U.S. Ct. Appeals (fed. cir. 1982). Ptnr. Hopkins & Sutter now Foley & Lardner, Chgo., 1979—. Counsel U.S. Ho. Reps. com. on judiciary impeachement inquiry Richard M. Nixon, 1974. Chmn. Ill. Lawyers Com. Clinton/Gore, Chgo., 1992; alt. del. Dem. Nat. Conv., 1992, del., 1996. Mem. Am. Coll. Trial Lawyers, Union League Club. Roman Catholic. Avocation: baseball coaching. Office: Foley & Larndner 330 N Wabash Ave Chicago IL 60611 E-mail: mconway@foleylaw.com.

CONWAY, NANCY ANN, newspaper editor; b. Foxboro, Mass., Oct. 15, 1941; d. Leo T. and Alma (Goodwin) C.; children: Ana Lucia DaSilva, Kara Ann Martin. Cert. in med. tech., Carnegie Inst., 1962; BA in English, U. Mass., 1976, cert. in secondary edn., 1978. Tchr. Brazil-Am. Inst., Rio de Janeiro, 1963-68; freelance writer, editor Amherst, Mass., 1972-76; staff writer Daily Hampshire Gazette, North Hampton, Mass., 1976-77; editor Amherst Bull., 1977-80, Amherst Record, 1980-83; features editor Holyoke (Mass.) Transcript/Telegram, 1983-84; gen. mgr. Monday-Thursday Newspapers, Boca Raton, Fla., 1984-87; dir. editorial South Fla. Newspaper Network, Deerfield Beach, 1987-90; pub., editor York (Pa.) Newspapers, Inc., 1990-95; metro editor Denver Post, 1995-96; exec. editor, v.p. Alameda Newspaper Group Oakland (Calif.) Tribune, 1996—2003; editor The Salt Lake (Utah) Tribune, 2003—. Bd. dirs. Math.: Opportunities in Engring., Sci. and Tech.-Pa. State, York, 1991-95. Recipient writing awards, state newspaper assns. Mem. Am. Soc. Newspaper Editors, Soc. Profl. Journalists. Avocations: literature, photography, communication, gardening. Office: Editor Salt Lake Tribune 143 S Main St Salt Lake City UT 84111 E-mail: nconway@angnewspapers.com.*

CONWAY, RICHARD ASHLEY, environmental engineer; BS, U. Mass., 1953; MS, MIT, 1957. Registered profl engr., W.Va.; Diplomate Am. Acad. Environ. Engrs. (trustee 1996-98, Kappe award 1999). Sr. corp. fellow Union Carbide Corp., South Charleston, W.Va., 1957-97; pvt. cons., 1997—. Cons. sci. adv. bd. EPA, chmn. environ. engring. com., 1988-93; sci. adv. bd. DOD Strategic Environ. R&D Program, 1992-98; mem. NRC Bd. Army Sci. and Tech. Author: Industrial Waste Disposal, 1980; editor: Hazardous Solid Waste Testing, 5 vols., 1981-87, Environmental Risk Analysis, 1982; patentee in field. Served to 1st lt. U.S. Army, 1954-56. Recipient Personal Achievement award in Chem. Engring., Chem. Engring. mag., N.Y.C., 1986, Kappe award Am. Acad. Environ. Engrs., 1999. Fellow ASCE (chmn. environ. engring. divsn. 1975, Hering medal 1974); mem. NAE, ASTM (Dudley medal 1984), Internat. Water Quality Assn. (governing bd. 1978-88), Soc. Environ. Chemistry and Toxicology (bd. dirs. 1983-86, Rachel Carson award 1997), Water Environ. Fedn. (Gascoigne medal 1967, Rudolfs medal 1974, 83). Avocations: tennis, walking. E-mail: conwayenv@aol.com.

CONWAY, RICHARD FRANCIS, investment company executive; b. Greenwich, Conn., Jan. 4, 1954; s. Francis Xavier and Marie (Bohan) C.; m. Greta Weil, Oct. 29, 1988; children: Signe Charlotte Weil, Anna Augusta Weil. BA, Harvard Coll., 1976; MBA, Yale U., 1981. Mgmt. trainee Citibank, N.Y.C., 1976-79; assoc. L.F. Rothschild, Unterberg, Towbin Inc., N.Y.C., 1981-83, v.p., 1983-86, prin., 1986-88; v.p. Salomon Bros. Inc., N.Y.C., 1988-90, Security Pacific Mcht. Bank, N.Y.C., 1990-91; sr. v.p. Needham and Co. Inc., N.Y.C., 1992-94; v.p. Smith Mgmt. Co., N.Y.C., 1994-97, Lone Star Securities Mgmt., Inc., N.Y.C., 1998-99; ptnr. Lampe, Conway & Co., LLC, N.Y.C., 1999—. Trustee Choate Rosemary Hall Sch., Wallingford, Conn., 1974-78; class com. Harvard Coll. Fund, Cambridge, Mass., 1991, 2001. Mem. Harvard Club (N.Y.C.), Knickerbocker Club (N.Y.C.), Georgica Assn. (Wainscott, N.Y.). Roman Catholic. Home: 1361 Madison Ave New York NY 10128-0713 Office: 680 5th Ave 12th Fl New York NY 10019 E-mail: richardconway@nyc.rr.com., conway@lampeconway.com.

CONWAY, RICHARD WALTER, computer scientist, educator; b. Milw., Dec. 12, 1931; s. Ralph Walter and Tennie May (Mitchell) C.; m. Edythe Davies, Aug. 29, 1953; children— Kathryn Dimiduk, Ralph, Evan. B.M.E., Cornell U., 1954, Ph.D, 1958. From instr. to prof. computer sci. Cornell U., Ithaca, N.Y., 1956-84, Emerson prof. mfg. Johnson Grad. Sch. Mgmt., 1984—. Sr. scientist DataWorks Corp. Author numerous books including: Theory of Scheduling, 1967; Introduction to Programming, 3d edit., 1979; Programming for Poets, 1979; XCELL Simulation System, 1986. Mem. Nat. Acad. Engring., Tau Beta Phi. Office: Cornell U Sage Hall Ithaca NY 14853-4201

CONWAY, ROBERT EDWARD, corporate executive; b. Waynesboro, Pa., Feb. 6, 1954; s. Gerald R. and Laura C. (Davis) C.; m. Carolyn Jean Hurd, Aug. 24, 1991. BA, Marquette U., 1976; MBA, U. Cin., 1980. CPA, Wis. Internal auditor Allis Chalmers Corp., Milw., 1977, supr. cost acctg. Cin., 1977-79; plant acct. Hazleton Systems, Inc., Cin., 1979-80, fin. analyst Aberdeen, Md., 1980-81; acct. mgr. Hazleton Labs. Washington, Vienna, Va., 1981-82; contr. fin. Hazleton Wis., Inc., Madison, 1982-83, contr. fin. and adminstrn., 1983-85, dir. life scis. div. and adminstrn., 1985-88, gen. mgr., 1988-89, corp. v.p., gen. mgr., 1989-96. Mem. bd. visitors Sch. Pharmacy, U. Wis., Madison. Mem. Madison C. of C. (1st vice chmn. 1992—). Roman Catholic. Home: 1167 Pintail Ct Boulder CO 80303-1466 Office: Array BioPharma Inc 3200 Walnut St Boulder CO 80301

CONWAY, ROBERT GEORGE, JR., lawyer; b. Albany, NY, Apr. 26, 1951; s. Robert George Sr. and Kathryn Ann (Kelly) C.; m. Lynda Rae Christenson, Dec. 15, 1979; 1 child, Phillip Christopher. AB, Dartmouth Coll., 1973; JD, Union U., 1976; diploma, U.S. Army JAGC Sch., 1986. Bar: Pa. 1978, U.S. Ct. Mil. Appeals 1978, N.C. 1983, U.S. Dist. Ct. (ea. dist.) N.C. 1983, U.S. Dist. Ct. (no. dist.) N.Y. 1998, U.S. Army Ct. Mil. Rev. 1986, U.S. Supreme Ct. 1986, U.S. Ct. Appeals (4th and fed. cirs.) 1987, N.Y. 1998; cert. USMC judge advocate. Commd. 2d lt. USMC, 1975, advanced through grades to maj., 1983, gen. staff sec., 1982-83, chief rev. officer, 1983-84, spl. asst. U.S. atty., 1984-85, dir. joint law ctr. air sta. Cherry Point, N.C., 1986-88, chief rsch. officer air sta., 1988, dep. asst. staff judge adv. to comdt. Washington, 1989; mil. justice officer Marine Corps Base, Quantico, Va., 1990-91; assoc. counsel for land use law Ea. Area Counsel Office USMC Dept. of Navy Office of Gen. Counsel, Camp Lejeune, N.C., 1991-96; ret. USMC, 1996; counsel, dep. commr. N.Y. State Divsn. Mil. and Naval Affairs, Latham, 1996—. Adj. faculty mem. Ga. Inst. Tech., 1993, Webster U., 1994-96; spkr. in field. Trustee Cath. student ctr. Aquinas House, Dartmouth Coll., Hanover, N.H., 1973-89, sec. Dartmouth class of 1973, 1994-2003. Recipient Legion of Merit, 1996. Mem.: ABA, Marine Corps Assn., U.S. Naval Inst., Dartmouth Lawyers Assn., Fed. Bar Assn. (contbg. author assn. news and jour. 1990), N.Y. Bar Assn., N.C. Bar Assn., Pa. Bar Assn., Dartmouth Club Ea. N.Y. (v.p. 1998—2001, pres. 2001—), KC (adv. 1984—85), Am. Legion. Roman Catholic. Home: 27 Manor Dr Glenmont NY 12077-3326 Office: NY State Divsn Mil and Naval Affairs Attn MNLA 330 Old Niskayuna Rd Latham NY 12110-3514

CONWAY, SAMUEL ANTHONY, retired chiropractor; b. Dallastown, Pa., Jan. 19, 1917; s. Clarence C. and Coletta Elizabeth (Smith) C.; m. Irene May Runkle, Feb. 6, 1944; 1 son, Samuel A. Student, Lebanon Valley Coll., 1947-48; DC, Nat. Coll. Chiropractic, 1951. Lic. nursing home adminstr., Pa. Gen. practice chiropractic medicine, Hanover, Pa., 1951-83. Chmn. bd., pres. Golden Age Nursing Home, Inc., Hanover, 1961-82; trustee Nat. Coll. Chiropractic, 1960-80, mem. exec. bd. dirs., 1969-80, ret., 1982, chmn. bldg. fund com. 1961-64; participant internat. profl. confs. With Signal Corps, U.S. Army, 1942-46. Recipient Disting. Svc. award Nat. Coll. Chiropractic, 1972. Mem. VFW, DAV, Nat. Coll. Alumni Assn., Am. Chiropractic Assn., Pa. Chiropractic Assn., Pa. Assn. Drugless Therapists (pres. 1968-69, bd. dirs., Disting. Svc. award 1969), Health Care Facilities of Pa., Am. Nursing Home Assn., York County (Pa.) Hist. Soc., Hanover Area Hist. Soc., Antique Automobile Club, Am. Legion, Hanover Area C. of C., Masons, Shriners, Elks. Democrat. Mem. United Ch. of Christ (trustee). Address: 434 Deerfield Dr Hanover PA 17331-5203

CONWAY, SEAN, legislative staff member; b. Denver, Sept. 16, 1959; BA, Ft. Lewis Coll., 1982. Staff dir. Office of U.S. Senator Williams Armstrong, Colo., 1982-90, south Colo. dir., 1982-85, north Colo. dir., 1986-89, state dir., 1989-90; campaign mgr. Office of Congressman Mike Strang, Colo., 1986; dist. area dir., press sec. Office of U.S. Rep. Wayne Allard, Colo., 1991-96; co. press sec. Office of Senator Wayne Allard, Colo., 1997-98, press sec., 1998—2002, chief-of-staff, 2002—. Chmn., campaign mgr. Wayne Allard for Senate exploratory com., 1995—. Mem.: AF Acad. Quarterback Club (Denver) (bd. dirs. 1988—95, pres. 1991—92). Office: 525 Dirksen Washington DC 20510-0001

CONWAY, WILLIAM GAYLORD, zoologist, zoo director, conservationist; b. St. Louis, Nov. 20, 1929; s. Frederick Eldridge and Alice Harriet (Gaylord) C. AB, Washington U., 1951, ScD (hon.), St. Lawrence U., 1979, Fordham U., 1981, Trinity Coll., 1984. Curator birds St. Louis Zoo, 1951-56, N.Y. Zool. Soc. (now The Wildlife Conservation Soc.), N.Y.C., 1956-72, assoc. dir., 1960-61, zoo dir., 1962-99, gen. dir., 1966-99, pres., 1992-99; sr. conservationist, 1999—. Mem. expdns. to Trinidad, Argentina, Chile, Bolivia, China; dir. Asa Wright Nature Ctr., Trinidad; advisor Fundación Patagonia Natural, Argentina. Contbr. articles to profl. jours. Decorated comdr. Order of the Golden Ark (The Netherlands); recipient Mayor's award of honor for arts and culture, 1979, Marlin Perkins award AAZPA, 1986, Disting. Achievement award Soc. for Conservation Biology, Disting. Svc. medal Am. Assn. Mus., 1998, Heini Hediger award World Zoo Orgn., 1999, Peter Scott medal IUCN-Survival Svc. Commn., 2001. Fellow: N.Y. Zool. Soc.; mem.: Wildlife Conservation Soc. (bd. dirs., Gold medal 2000), Soc. Conservation Biology (bd. dirs.), Internat. Crane Found. (bd. dirs.), Nat. Audubon Soc. (Audubon medal 1999), Am. Zoo and Aquarium Assn., Am. Assn. Zool. Pks. and Aquariums (past pres.), Am. Assn. Museums (medal 1998), Am. Conservation Assn. (bd. dirs.), Cultural Instns. Group (past pres.), Internat. Survival Svc. Commn. (Peter Scott medal 2000), Wilson Ornithol. Club, Brit. Avicultural Soc., Cooper Ornithol. Soc., Am. Ornithologists Union. Office: Wildlife Conservation Soc 2300 Southern Blvd Bronx NY 10460 E-mail: w.conway@wcs.org.

CONWAY DE MACARIO, EVERLY, immunologist, molecular biologist; b. Buenos Aires, Apr. 20, 1939; d. Delfin E. and Maria Gloria (Benatuil) Conway; m. Alberto J. L. Macario, Mar. 16, 1963; children: Alex, Everly. PhD in Pharmacy, Nat. U. Buenos Aires, 1960; PhD in Biochemistry, 1962. Rsch. fellow Nat. Acad. Medicine Argentina, Buenos Aires, 1962-63; head lab. oncology and immunology Argentinian Assn. against Cancer, Buenos Aires, 1966-67; chief immunology Sch. Medicine, Buenos Aires, 1967-68; rsch. fellow dept. tumor-biology Karolinska Inst., Stockholm, 1969-71; sr. rsch. scientist Lab. Cell Biology, NRC Italy, Rome, 1971-73; vis. scientists Internat. Agy. Rsch. on Cancer, WHO, Lyon, France, 1973-74, Brown U., Providence, R.I., 1974-76; rsch. scientist Wadsworth Ctr. N.Y. State Dept. Health, Albany, 1976—; prof. Sch. Pub. Health dept. biomed. scis., 1986—; mem. admission com., 1986-89; pers. com., 1989-91; curriculum com., 1991-94; nominations and elections com., 1994—. Grant referee in field. Co-editor: Monoclonal Antibodies against Bacteria, 1985-86, vols. I-III, Gene Probes for Bacteria, 1990; assoc. editor profl. jour. 1986—; mng. editor Frontiers on Biosci.; contbr. articles to profl. jours.; contbr. chpts. to books and encyclopedias. Recipient Prof. J.M. Mezzadra award Nat. U. Buenos Aires, 1969, Travel award to Eng., 2nd Internat. Immunolgy Congress, 1974, Gold medal Argentinian Soc. Biochemistry, 1980, Hans Osterman Found. grantee, Sweden, 1969, Sir Samuel Scott of Yews Trust grantee, Sweden, 1970, Winifred Cullis grantee Internat. Fedn. Univ. Women, 1972, NATO rsch. grantee, 1975, 81, U.S. Dept. Energy grantee, 1981, 84; Travel awardee to China, 1985, Spain, 1993, South Africa, 1994. Mem. Scandinavian Soc. Immunology, Italian Assn. Immunologists, French Soc. Immunology (travel award 1974), Am. Assn. Immunologists (chmn. com. on status of women 1980-86, edn. com. 1982-87, awards com. 1991-92, travel award to Australia 1977), Am. Soc. Microbiology (sr. editor Manual Clin. Lab. Immunology 4th-5th edits.), Internat. Soc. Microbial Ecology, Cell Stress Soc. Internat., Nat. Acad. Microbiology (chmn. Morrison Rogosa awards com. 2002—, chmn. internat. subcom. on taxonomy of methanogens). Achievements include patents for microcircle system, microsample holder and carrier; invention of ultrasensitive micro-immunoenzyamtic assay and multipurpose modular system for use in lab and field settings, of the antigenic fingerprinting method; creation of immunotechnology for rapid identification of microbes directly in samples of complex microbial mixtures; first to establish the antigenic cohesiveness of methanogenic and halophilic archaea and demonstrate clusters overlapping phylogenetic branches; sequenced for the first time archaeal transportes and chaperone genes; found new motphotype of methanosarcina; created an integration vector for transformation of methanogens; participated in the sequencing of the genomes of two methanogens; discovered an archaeon with the four main chaperoning systems. Home: 18 Carriage Rd Delmar NY 12054-3704 Office: Wadsworth Ctr Empire State Plz Albany NY 12201

CONWAY-GERVAIS, KATHLEEN MARIE, reading specialist, educational consultant; b. Bklyn., Apr. 18, 1942; d. John Joseph and Mary Josephine Conway; m. Stephen Paul Gervais, July 10, 1976; 1 child, John Joseph. BA, Coll. Mt. St. Vincent, 1970; MS, Hunter Coll. of N.Y.C., 1973, Reading Specialization, 1974. Cert. reading and social studies tchr., nursery and elem. ecuator, N.Y., N.J. Elem. tchr. Archdiocese of N.Y., N.Y.C., 1963-74; reading specialist Malverne (N.Y.) Union Free Sch. Dist., 1974-86, dist. reading, testing coord., 1986-91, reading specialist, 1992-95, East Meadow (N.Y.) Union Free Sch. Dist., 1995-96; reading cons., tchr. trainer, staff devel. team Uniondale (N.Y.) Union Free Sch. Dist., 1996—. Adv. bd. mem. Newsday in Edn., Melville, 1982—; adj. prof. Nassau C.C., Garden City, N.Y., 1995—, L.I. U. Grad. Sch., 2003. Active Getting Out the vote presdl. election, N.Y., 1992. Recipient Ambassador in Edn. award Newsday, Melville, 1982, Congruence Model Project award N.Y. State Dept. Edn., Albany, 1988, Elizabeth Ann Seton award Office of Cathechesis and Worship, Long Island, 1991. Mem. ASCD, Internat. Reading Assn., N.Y. State Reading Assn., Orton Dyslexia Soc. (del.), Nassau Reading Coun. (bd. dirs., treas., exec. bd.). Democrat. Roman Catholic. Avocations: travel, reading, theater, swimming, computer. Home and Office: 174 Nassau Blvd West Hempstead NY 11552-2218 E-mail: watcher@optonline.net.

CONWAY-WELCH, COLLEEN, dean, nurse midwife; b. Monticello, Iowa, Apr. 26, 1944; d. John Andrew and Lorraine (Digman) Conway; m. Ted Houston Welch, Mar. 31, 1985. BSN, Georgetown U., 1965; CNM, Catholic Maternity Inst., 1969; MSN, Catholic U., Washington, 1969; PhD, NYU, 1973. Staff nurse Georgetown U. Hosp., Washington, 1965; staff nurse labor & delivery Queens Med. Ctr., Honolulu, 1966; nurse cons. U. So. Calif. Med. Ctr., L.A., 1967; staff assoc. Nat. League Nursing, N.Y.C., 1969-70; asst. prof. Downstate Med. Ctr., Bklyn., 1970-74, Georgetown U., 1974-76, assoc. dean, 1975-76; assoc. prof. George Mason U., Fairfax, Va., 1976-78, Calif. State U., Long Beach, 1978-80; prof. nursing U. Colo., Denver, 1980-84; dean Vanderbilt Sch. Nursing, Nashville, 1984—. Mem. Presdl. Commn. on HIV Epidemic, Washington, 1988, adv. coun. NIH Nat. Ctr. Nursing Rsch., Washington, 1989-93, bd. trust Healthcare Leadership Coun., Washington, 1990; chair nursing leadership coun. Inst. Healthcare Improvement, 1992; bd. dirs. Diversicare, Franklin, Tenn., Nat. League Nursing Community Health Accreditation, N.Y.C., Commonwealth Fund Nurse Exch. Fellowship Program, N.Y.C. Contbr. articles to profl. jours. Bd. govs. United Way, Middle, Tenn., 1989; active Mayor's Task Force for Substance Abuse, 1990, JFK Adv. Com. on Arts, Washington, 1991, Jr. League, 1973—. Recipient Dempsey Humanitarism award St. Clare's Hosp. AIDS Ctr., 1989; commencement speaker, Columbia Sch. Nursing, 1991. Fellow Am. Acad. Nursing; mem. Soc. Advancement Women's Health Rsch. (bd. dirs. 1991—), Rotary Club, Cosmos Club, Sigma Theta Tau (bd. dirs. 1968—). Avocations: snow skiing, scuba diving, hiking, reading. Home: 109 Lynnwood Ter Nashville TN 37205-2911 Office: Vanderbilt U Sch Nursing 111 Godchaux 461 21st Ave S Nashville TN 37240-1104

CONWELL, ESTHER MARLY, physicist, researcher; b. N.Y.C., May 23, 1922; d. Charles and Ida (Korn) C.; m. Abraham A. Rothberg, Sept. 30, 1945; 1 son, Lewis J. BA, Bklyn. Coll., 1942; MS, U. Rochester, N.Y., 1945; PhD, U. Chgo., 1948; DSc, Bklyn. Coll., 1992. Lectr. Bklyn. Coll., 1946-51; mem. tech. staff Bell Telephone Labs., 1951-52; physicist GTE Labs., Bayside, N.Y., 1952-61, mgr. physics dept., 1961-72; vis. prof. U. Paris, 1962-63; Abby Rockefeller Mauze prof. M.I.T., 1972; prin. scientist Xerox Corp., Webster, N.Y., 1972-80, rsch. fellow, 1981-98. Adj. prof. U. Rochester, 1990—2001, prof., 2001—; cons., mem. adv. com. engring. NSF, 1978—81. Author: High Field Transport in Semiconductors, 1967, also research papers; mem. editorial bd. Jour. Applied Physics; Proc. of IEEE; patentee in field. Fellow IEEE (Edison medal 1997), Am. Phys. Soc. (sec.-treas. divsn. condensed matter physics 1977-82); mem. AAAS, NAS, NAE, Soc. Women Engrs. (Achievement award 1960). Office: U Rochester Dept Chemistry Rochester NY 14627

CONWELL, HALFORD ROGER, physician; b. Cin., Jan. 28, 1924; s. Halford Fredrick and Erma Pearl (Cornelius) C.; m. Margaret Ann King, Dec. 15, 1965; children: Mark A., Sherri L., John H. BA, U. Wooster, 1948; MA, U. Louisville, 1950; MD, U. Cin., 1955. ATP; diplomate crew coordination tng. Continental Airlines. Practice in aviation medicine, Huntsville, Tex., 1959—; mem. staff Huntsville (Tex.) Meml. Hosp., chief of staff, 1974-75, chief medicine, 1976-80, bd. trustees, 1991—. Sr. U.S. med. officer Brit. Caledonian Airways, 1977-89; cons. Aeromexico, chief flight surgeon Continental Airlines, 1996—; mem. Walker County Hosp. Dist., 1975-79, chmn., 1976-79; asst. dean of men, instr. psychology Heidelberg U., Tiffin, Ohio, 1950-51; instr. psychology Cin. Coll.; sr. med. examiner FAA; sr. examiner C.A.A. (U.K.), C.A.A. (Australia); newspaper columnist, 1992—. Trustee Biol. Analysis and Rsch. Found.; capt. (hon.) Tex. Internat. Airline; founder Bomber Command Mus. (R.A.F.) Lt. USNR, 1942-46. Recipient safe pilot award Nat. Pilots Assn., Pilot Proficiency award FAA, Profl. Svc. Citation. Fellow Aerospace Med. Assn. (John A. Tamisiea award 2000); mem. Brit. Assn. Aerospace Medicine, Latin Am. Aviation Med. Assn., Scottish Assn. Aviation Med. Examiners, Airline Med. Dirs. Assn., Civil Aviation Med. Assn. (v.p. 1968-80, dir. 1968—, pres. 1980-81, Award of merit 1994, 97), Mitchell Pediatric Soc., Academie Internationale de Medicine Aeronatque et Spatiale, Aircraft Owners and Pilots Assn. (med. adv. panel), Confederate Air Force (founding mem.), Air Transp. Assn. (med. com.), Order Ky. Cols., Quiet Birdmen, Masons, Psi Chi, Alpha Psi Omega (hon.). Office: 2800 Lake Rd Huntsville TX 77340-5632 E-mail: saxet@lcc.net.

CONWELL, JOHN FREDRICK, lawyer; b. Oklahoma City, Nov. 4, 1966; s. Fred Ern and Linda Louise C. BA in Polit. Sci., U. Okla., 1989; JD, Villanova U., 1993. Bar: Md. 1994, Pa. 1994, U.S. Dist. Ct. Md. 1996, U.S. Ct. Appeals (4th cir.) 1998. Assoc. Davis & Assocs. Law Offices, Towson, Md., 1993—97, 1998—2001; staff atty. FCC, 1997-98; legal and regulatory counsel Cable Telecomms. Assn. Md./Del./D.C., Annapolis, Md., 2001—. Mem. staff Villanova Environ. Law Jour. Mem. Fed. Comm. Bar Assn. Office: 2530 Riva Rd Ste 316 Annapolis MD 21401-7414 E-mail: john_conwell@hotmail.com.

CONWELL, THERESA GALLO, financial services representative; b. Utica, N.Y., Mar. 6, 1947; d. Ernest and Anna (Caiazzo) Gallo; m. Charles Ray Conwell, Aug. 19, 1978 (dec. Feb. 1997). BS in Edn., SUNY, Potsdam, 1968; MA in Edn., SUNY, Cortland, 1978. Cert. tchr., N.Y.; CLU; chartered fin. cons., registered rep.; ChFC. Tchr. pub. schs., Clinton, N.Y., 1969-78; supr. mktg. svcs. Phoenix Home Life Ins. Co. (now Phoenix Home Life Ins. Co.), Hartford, Conn., 1980-82, assoc. mgr. advt. tng., 1982-84, mgr. agt. tng., 1984-85, dir. agt./mgmt. devel., 1985-88, fin. svcs. rep., 1988—. Speaker to small bus. orgns., women's groups, N.Y., New Eng., 1986—. Mem. Am. Soc. CLU, Nat. Assn. Life Underwriters, Bus. and Profl. Women of Glastonbury (pres. 1995), Pres. Club (assoc. 1991). Democrat. Avocations: tennis, golf, swimming, aerobics, reading, competitive ballroom dancing. E-mal. Home: 2749 SeaPines Cir E Clearwater FL 33761 Office: Apt 111 2587 Countryside Blvd Clearwater FL 33761-3535 E-mail: tgconwell@aol.com.

CONWELL, VIRGINIA DONLEY, librarian; b. Carlsbad, N.Mex., Jan. 3, 1921; d. William Guy and Frances Acree (Guthrie) Donley; m. Robert E.M. Conwell, Aug. 8, 1943 (dec. 1958); children— Elizabeth Conwell Shapiro, Virginia Conwell Hall. AB, U. N.Mex., 1944; library credential U. So. Calif., 1962. Librarian, Montebello (Calif.) Unified Sch. Dist., 1962-86. Files chmn. Downey Alumnae Panhellenic, 1978—; del. Calif. Dem. Cen. Com., 1986—; Mem. AARP, Mortarboard, Downey Alumnae Panhellenic Club, Chi Omega (LA coord. coun.), Assistance League Downey, Phi Alpha Theta. Democrat. Episcopalian. Address: 8132 Primrose Ln Downey CA 90240-3217

CONYERS, JOHN, JR., congressman; b. Detroit, May 16, 1929; s. John and Lucille (Simpson) C.; m. Monica Estes; children: John Jr., Carl Edward. BA, Wayne State U., 1957, JD, 1958; LL.D., Wilberforce U., 1969. Bar: Mich. 1959. Legis. asst. to Congressman John Dingell, 1959-61; sr. ptnr. firm Conyers, Bell & Townsend, 1959-61; referee Mich. Workmen's Compensation Dept., 1961-64; mem. U.S. Congress from 14th Mich. dist., 1964—; former chmn. Govt. Ops. Com., former chmn. subcom. on legis. and nat. security; ranking mem. Judiciary Com. Past dir. edn. Local 900, United Auto Workers; mem. adv. council Mich. Liberties Union; gen. counsel Detroit Trade Union Leadership Council; vice chmn. nat. bd. Ams. for Democratic Action; vice chmn. adv. council ACLU; an organizer Mems. Congress for Peace through Law; bd. dirs. numerous other orgns. including African-Am. Inst., Commn. Racial Justice, Detroit Inst. Arts, Nat. Alliance Against Racist and Polit. Repression, Nat. League Cities. Sponsor, contbg. author: Am. Militarism, 1970, War Crimes and the American Conscience, 1970, Anatomy of an Undeclared War, 1972; contbr. articles to profl. jours. Trustee Martin Luther King Jr. Ctr. for Non-Violent Social Change. Served to 2d lt. U.S. Army, 1950-54, Korea. Recipient Rosa Parks award SCLC. Mem. NAACP (exec. bd. Detroit), Kappa Alpha Psi. Democrat. Baptist. Office: 2426 Rayburn Bldg Washington DC 20515-2214 also: District Office 669 Federal Building 231 W Lafayette Detroit MI 48226*

COOCH, EDWARD W(EBB), JR., lawyer; b. Wilmington, Del., Mar. 22, 1920; s. Edward Webb and Eleanor Bedford (Wilkins) C.;m. Sarah Rodney, June 12, 1946; children: Richard Rodney Cooch, Anne Bedford Cooch Doran. BA, U. Del., 1941; LLB, U. Va., 1948. Bar: Del. 1948, U.S. Dist. Ct. Del. 1949, U.S. Ct. Appeals (3d cir.) 1949, U.S. Supreme Ct. 1965. Law clk. to Hon. John Biggs Jr. chief judge U.S. Ct. Appeals (3d cir.), Wilmington, 1948-49; pvt. practice Wilmington, 1949-60; ptnr. Cooch and Taylor, Attys. at Law, Wilmington, 1960-81; pres. Cooch and Taylor, PA, Wilmington, 1981-94; of counsel, 1994—. Bd. dirs. Del. Wild Lands, Inc. Wilmington, 1962-02, past pres., 1980-86; trustee U. Del. Libr. Assocs., Newark, 1986—; pres. Christina Conservancy, Inc., Wilmington, 1991—; bd. dirs. Wilmington Trust Co., 1974-93. Maj. Coast arty. U.S. Army, 1941-46. Recipient U. Del. Merit award, 1986. Mem. ABA, Del. State Bar Assn. (sec. 1952-53, cmty. svc. award 1991), Wilmington Club. Democrat. Episcopalian. Avocations: farming, conservation, historical study. Office: Cooch and Taylor 824 Market St Ste 1000 Wilmington DE 19801-3027

COOCH, F. GRAHAM, ecologist, educator, ecologist, researcher; b. Winnipeg, Man., Can., Apr. 20, 1928; arrived in U.S., 1989; s. Angus Graham and Mylrea Elizabeth Cooch; m. Joan Needes Cooch, Sept. 6, 1958; children: Evan, Janice, Sandra. BA with honors, Queens U., Kingston, Ont., Can., 1951; MSc, Cornell U., 1953, PhD, 1958. Field technician Can. Wildlife Svc., 1947—53, arctic ornithologist, 1954—61, head toxic chems., 1961—70, chief surveys and

rsch., 1967—79, U.S. Fish and Wildlife Svc. liaison, 1967—88, sr. scientist, 1979—88; adj. prof. fisheries and wildlife N.Mex. State U., Las Cruces, 1988—. Contbr. chapters to books, articles to profl. jours. Recipient Speirs award, Can. Soc. Ornithologists, 1988. Fellow: AAAS, Arctic Inst., Am. Ornithologist Union. Episcopalian. Home: 665 Windmill Ct Las Cruces NM 88011

COOEY, WILLIAM RANDOLPH, economics educator; b. Wheeling, W.Va., Feb. 23, 1942; s. William Earl and Marguerite Ruth (Potts) C.; m. Linda Faye Whiteman, Aug. 11, 1973; children: William Justin, Crissa Kaye. BA, Bethany Coll., 1964; MS, W.Va. U., 1966; postgrad., Miss. State U., 1973-74. Prof. Bethany (W.Va.) Coll., 1966—, adminstrv. chair econs. dept., 2002—, John F. and Evelyn Cassey Steen chair in econs., 2002—. V.p., bd. dirs. Cooey-Bentz Co., Wheeling, 1986-90; part-time assoc. prof. Ohio U., St. Clairsville, 1967-86, W.Va. U., West Liberty, 1976-84; pvt. practice legal cons., Bethany, 1975—. Contbr. articles to publs. West Va. Commn. Higher Edn. Advisor Boy Scouts Am., Bethany, 1986-90; asst. coach Little League Baseball, Bethany, 1986-90. Mem. Midwestern Econs. Assn., Beta Beta Beta, Omicron Delta Epsilon, Gamma Sigma Kappa. Avocations: woodworking, making videos, computers. Home: 102 Pt Breeze Dr Bethany WV 26032 Office: Bethany Coll Morlan Hall Bethany WV 26032

COOGAN, FRANK NEIL, health and social services administrator; b. Watertown, Wis., June 14, 1929; s. Neil Christopher and Lilian (Nelson) C.; m. Mary Louise Block, Apr. 14, 1951; children: Michael, Thomas, Karen. BS, U. Wis., 1951, MSW, 1955. Psychiatric social worker VA, 1955-62; dist. mental health cons. Wis. State Div. Mental Hygiene, 1962-65; dir. Bur. Alcohol and Other Drug Abuse, Wis. Dept. Health, 1965-77; v.p. DePaul Health Corp., 1977-90; behavioral health cons. Corphealth, West Allis, Wis., 1990-94; psychotherapist Am. Behavioral Clinics S.C., Milw., 1994—. With U.S. Army, 1951-53. Fellow Am. Coll. Addiction Treatment Adminstrs.; mem. Alcohol and Drug Problems Assn. N. Am. (chmn. membership com.), Wis. Alcohol and Drug Treatment Providers Assn. (bd. dirs.), Wis. Assn. Alcohol and Other Drug Abuse (bd. dirs., Outstanding Profl. award 1990, Pres.'s award 1999), Am. Legion. Lutheran. Avocations: hiking, golf, fishing, cycling, cross country skiing. Home: 2127 S 99th St Milwaukee WI 53227-1452

COOGAN, MARY ELLEN, musician, educator; b. Yonkers, N.Y., Oct. 31, 1958; d. James Michael and Cecelia (Casserly) C. BA, Mount St. Mary's Coll., Newburgh, 1980; MSEd, SUNY, New Paltz, 1990. Cert. tchr. N.Y. Elem. sch. tchr. Sacred Heart, St. Francis Sch., 1980-95; musician Cherish the Ladies Music & Dance Ensemble, Yonkers, 1987—.

COOGAN, PHILIP SHIELDS, pathologist; b. Peoria, Ill., Feb. 13, 1938; s. Paul Mathew and Elizabeth Ann (Shields) C.; m. Carol Jean Gerlach, June 18, 1960 (div. 1985); children: Mary Brighid, Philip Gerlach, Joseph Baker, Clare Ann; m. Joan C. Storozynski, Dec. 24, 1987. Student, U. Notre Dame, 1955-58; MD, St. Louis U., 1962. Diplomate: Am. Bd. Pathology. USPHS summer research trainee pathology St. Louis U. Med. Sch., 1959-61; intern Presbyn.-St. Luke's Hosp., Chgo., 1962-63, resident, 1963-67; research pathologist, chief histopathology U.S. Air Force Sch. Aerospace Medicine, 1967-69; asst. prof. pathology Rush Med. Coll., Chgo., 1971-73, assoc. prof., 1972-75; assoc. prof. pathology Northwestern U., Chgo., 1974-78; dir. anatomic pathology Northwestern Meml. Hosp., Chgo., 1974-78; prof. pathology James H. Quillen Coll. Medicine, East Tenn. State U., Johnson City, 1978-99. Cons. FDA, 1972-81, USPHS, 1962-67 Assoc. editor: Year Book Pathology and Clinical Pathology, 1978-80. Served with USAF, 1967-69. Recipient Hektoen award Chgo. Path. Soc., 1969; named Outstanding Tchr. East Tenn. State U. Coll. Medicine, 1980, 81, 83, 84, 85 Mem. AMA, AAAS, U.S. and Can. Acad. Pathology, Am. Soc. Exptl. Pathology, Am. Soc. Clin. Pathology, Coll. Am. Pathology, Am. Soc. Investigative Pathology, Alpha Omega Alpha. Roman Catholic. Home: 3409 Stoneridge Dr Johnson City TN 37604-2182 Office: East Tenn State U Dept Pathology Johnson City TN 37614 *"Don't shoot the wounded." As a teacher of medical students and residents, it is advisable to treat those struggling under adversity with special care. They often become the most empathetic physicians.*

COOGLE, CONSTANCE L. gerontology educator, researcher; b. Richmond, Va., Sept. 27, 1954; PhD, Va. Commonwealth U., 1984. Asst. dir. for rsch. Va. Ctr. on Aging, Va. Commonwealth U., Richmond, 1989—; assoc. prof. of gerontology and psychology Va. Commonwealth U., Richmond, 1996—. Adminstr. Alzheimer's and Related Diseases Rsch. Award Fund, Richmond, 1997—; mem. Gov.'s Commn. on Alzheimer's Disease and Related Disorders, Va., 1999—. Author articles, book chpts., books. Past pres., bd. dirs. Greater Richmond chpt. Alzheimer's Assn., Richmond, 1992—. Fellow: Gerontol. Soc. Am.; mem.: So. Gerontol. Soc. (bd. dirs. 2000—, past sec. to the bd. 2000—02, Outstanding Svc. award 1997, Pres.'s award 1995). Achievements include research in aging research and training. Office: Virginia Commonwealth U PO Box 980229 Richmond VA 23298-0229

COOIL, BRUCE KIMO, mathematical statistician, statistics educator; b. Honolulu, Mar. 26, 1953; s. Bruce James and Drea Georgia (O'Connell) Cooil. BS with honors, Stanford U., 1975, MS, 1976; PhD, U. Pa., 1982. Biostatistician Inst. Health Rsch., San Francisco, 1976—78; rsch. and tchg. fellow Wharton Sch., Phila., 1978—82; asst. prof. stats. Owen Grad. Sch., Vanderbilt U., Nashville, 1982—88, assoc. prof., 1988—, dir. PhD program, 1988—92. Contbr. Recipient Bursk prize in stats., Wharton Sch., 1980, Dean's Award for Tchg. Excellence, 1991, 1994, 1995, 2000, 2002, AMA Lehmann award, NSF, 2001; fellow Dean's fellow, Wharton Sch., 1978—79; Vanderbilt U. grantee, 1984—. Mem.: AAAS, Inst. Mgmt. Sci., Inst. Math. Stats., Am. Statis. Assn. (grantee 2001—), Beta Gamma Sigma, Phi Beta Kappa. Unitarian. Office: Vanderbilt U Owen Grad Sch 401 21st Ave S Nashville TN 37240-1104

COOK, ALBERT THOMAS THORNTON, JR., financial advisor; b. Cleve, Apr. 24, 1940; s. Albert Thomas Thornton and Tyra Esther (Morehouse) C.; m. Mary Jane Blackburn, June 1, 1963; children: Lara Keller, Thomas, Timothy. BA, Dartmouth Coll., 1962; MA, U. Chgo., 1966. Asst. sec. Dartmouth Coll., Hanover, NH, 1972-77; exec. dir. Big Bros., Inc., NYC, 1977-78; underwriter Boettcher & Co., Denver, 1978-81; asst. v.p. Dain Bosworth Inc., Denver, 1981-82, Colo. Nat. Bank, Denver, 1982-84; pres. The Albert T.T. Cook Co., Denver, 1984—. Arbitrator Nat. Assn. Securities Dealers, NYC, 1985—, Mcpl. Securities Rulemaking Bd., Washington, 1987-98. Pres. Etna-Hanover Ctr. Cmty. Assn., Hanover, NH, 1974-76; mem. Mayor's Task Force, Denver, 1984; bd. dir. Rude Park Cmty. Nursery, Denver, 1985-87, Willows Water Dist., Colo., 1990—, pres., 1998-99, 2003-04; trustee The Iliff Sch. Theol., Denver, 1986-92; mem. Dartmouth Coll. Com. on Trustees, 1990-93. Mem.: Dartmouth Alumni Coun. (chmn. nominating and trustee search coms. 1987—89, exec. com.), Yale Club, Dartmouth Club of NYC, University Club (chmn. admissions com. 1997—98), Cactus Club, Lions (bd. dir. Denver chpt. 1983—85, treas. 1986—87, pres. Denver Found. 1987—88, 2d v.p. 2001—02, 1st v.p. 2002—03, pres. 2003—), Delta Upsilon. Congregationalist. Avocations: fly fishing, furniture making, running, skiing, backpacking. Home: 7099 E Hinsdale Pl Centennial CO 80112-1610 Office: One Tabor Ctr 1200 17th St Ste 960 Denver CO 80202-5835

COOK, ALEXANDER BURNS, museum curator, artist, educator; b. Grand Rapids, Mich., Apr. 16, 1924; s. Gorell Alexander and Harriette Florence (Hinze) C.; m. Marilyn Bierschwal Coffey, Aug. 11, 1992. BA, Ohio Wesleyan U., 1949; MS, Case Western Res. U., 1967. Editl. cartoonist, artist Cleve. Plain Dealer, 1949-55; account exec. Edward Howard & Co., Cleve., 1955-61; spl. art tchr. Cleve. Pub. Schs., 1964-88; curator exhibits Inland Seas Maritime Mus. (formerly Gt. Lakes Mus.), Vermilion, Ohio, 1970-78, curator, 1978—, chmn. mus. oper. com., 1977—. Contbr. editl. cartoons to Reid Cartoon Collection, U. Kans. Jour. Hist. Ctr., The Critique, 1975-88; editl. advisor, columnist Inland Seas Quar. Jour., 1957—, The Chadburn, 1976—; cover illustrations for Ohioana Quar., 1979—; book cover illustrations Dodd, Mead & Co., 1984; paintings represented in pvt. collections, 1960—; executed murals depicting Gt. Lakes shipping Gt. Lakes Mus., 1969, Great Lakes shipwreck Inland Seas Maritime Mus., 2001. Trustee Berkshire Condominium Owners Assn., 1981-83, pres., 1982-83; trustee Shaker Hist. Soc., 1999—. With AUS, 1943-45. Recipient award of honor Ohio Wesleyan U., 1955, Disting. Achievement award Gt. Lakes Hist. Soc., 1973, 1st pl. award for editl. cartoons Union Tchr. Comm. Assn., 1980, 81, 82, 87, Vermilion C. of C. Svc. Award, 2000, Disting. Mus. Profl. award Ohio Museums Assn., 2001. Mem. Gt. Lakes Hist. Soc. (exec. v.p. 1959-64, v.p. 1964-95, trustee, mem. exec. com. 1959—), Ohioana Libr. Assn., Art Inst. Chgo., Akron Art Mus., Cleve. Mus. Art, Am. Soc. Marine Artists (artist mem.), Assn. for Great Lakes Maritime History, Chgo. Maritime Soc., English Speaking Union, Ohio Acad. History, Northeastern Ohio Inter-Mus. Coun., Vermilion Boat Club, The Union Club,Delta Tau Delta, Pi Delta Epsilon, Pi Sigma Alpha. Republican. Episcopalian. Avocations: gardening, sailing, model railroading. Home: 2449 Saybrook Rd University Heights OH 44118

COOK, ANN JENNALIE, English language educator; b. Wewoka, Okla., Oct. 19, 1934; d. Arthur Holly and Bertha Mable (Stafford) C.; children: Lee Ann Merrick, Amy Ceil Leonard; m. Gerald George Calhoun, Apr. 1994. BA, U. Okla., 1956, MA, 1959; PhD, Vanderbilt U., 1972. Instr. English, U. Okla., 1956-57; tchr. English, N.C. and Conn., 1958-61; instr. So. Conn. State Coll., 1962-64; asst. prof. U. S.C., 1972-74; adj. asst. prof. Vanderbilt U., Nashville, 1977-82, assoc. prof., 1982-89, prof., 1990-98, prof. emeritus, 1999—. Exec. sec. Shakespeare Assn. Am., 1975-87; chmn. Internat. Shakespeare Assn., 1988-96, v.p. 1996—. Author: Privileged Playgoers of Shakespeare's London, 1981, Making a Match: Courtship in Shakespeare and His Society, 1991; assoc. editor Shakespeare Studies, 1973-80; contbr. articles to profl. jours. Trustee Folger Shakespeare Libr., 1985—90, Shakespeare Birthplace Trust (life); bd. mem. Friends of the Shakespeare Birthplace Trust, 2000—, patron, Nashville Symphony, 2000—, U. Sch. Nashvillle, 2000—, Nashville Opera Guild, 2000—, Nashville Shakespeare Festival, 2002—, Shakespeare on the Cumberland; pres. English-Speaking Union, 2003—. Recipient Letseizer award, 1956, Nat. Leadership award Delta Delta Delta, 1956; Danforth fellow, 1968-72, Folger summer fellow, 1973, Donelson fellow, 1974-75, fellow Rockefeller Found., 1984, Guggenheim Found., 1984-85; grantee Folger seminar NEH, 1992-93 Mem. Shakespeare Assn. Am., MLA, AAUP, Shakespeare Inst., Deutsche Shakespeare Gesellschaft, Renaissance Soc. Am. (bd. dirs.), Phi Beta Kappa. Episcopalian. Home: 114 Prospect Hl Nashville TN 37205-4721 Office: Vanderbilt U Dept English Nashville TN 37235

COOK, ANNE WELSH, lumber company executive; b. Hilo, Hawaii, July 9, 1948; d. Charles Edward and Charlotte Annabelle (Redfield) Welsh; m. Thomas Rollin Kramer, Sept. 12, 1970 (div. Dec. 1981); 1 child, Jeanne Elizabeth; m. Jeffrey Dean Cook, June 22, 1985; children: Julia Charlotte, Andrea Michelle, Daniel James Welsh. BS in Math., Duke U., 1970, MA in Math., Computer Sci., 1971; PhD in Stats., Am. U., 1983. Programmer, researcher Duke U. Hosp., Durham, N.C., 1969-71; math. statistician Bur. Census, Suitland, Md., 1971-73; sr. programmer, mgr. EG&G Mason REsearch, Rockville, Md., 1973-74, 75-78; project mgr. Price, Williams & Assocs., Silver Spring, Md., 1974-75; instr. Am. U., Washington, 1981-82; asst. prof. math. Pacific Luth. U., Tacoma, 1983-87; statis. cons. Donald Murtha, Washington, 1981-83, EPA, Washington, 1982-83. Cons. Fairchild, Puyallup, Wash.; elected mem. rank and tenure com. Pacific Luth U., 1984-86; majority stockholder, treas. Cook Lumber Co., Tacoma, 1991—. Newsletter editor St. Joseph/St. John's Episcopal Ch., Tacoma, 1989-91; treas. Northwest Investors Club, 1993-95, St. Frances Cabrini Parent's Assn., 2000-2002; mem. fin. com. Greater Lakes Mental Health, 2003—. Home: 7308 North St SW Lakewood WA 98498-5212 Office: 7308 North St SW Lakewood WA 98498-5212

COOK, AUGUST JOSEPH, lawyer, accountant; b. Devine, Tex., Sept. 25, 1926; s. August E. and Mary H. (Schmidt) C.; m. Matie M. Brangan, July 12, 1952; children: Lisa Ann, Mary Beth, John J. BS, Trinity U., 1949; BBA, U. Tex., 1954; JD, St. Mary's U., 1960. Bar: Tex. 1960, Tenn. 1975. Bus. mgr., corp. sec. Life Enterprises, Inc. and affil. cos., San Antonio, 1950-58, also bd. dirs.; mgr. Ernst & Young, San Antonio, 1960-69, ptnr., Memphis, 1970-84; ptnr. McDonnel Boyd, Memphis, 1984-91; of counsel Harris, Shelton, Dunlap and Cobb, Memphis, 1991-97, Pietrangelo Cook, Memphis, 1997—. Author: A.J. $ Tax Court, 1987; author newspaper column A.J.'s Tax Fables, 1983—; contbr. articles to profl. jours. Alderman City of Castle Hills, Tex., 1961-63, mayor, 1963-69; chmn. Bexar County Coun. Mayors, 1967-69; v.p. Tex. Mcpl. League, 1968-69; bd. dirs. San Antonio Met. YMCA. With U.S. Army, 1945-46, PTO. Mem. AICPA, Tex. Soc. CPAs, Tex. Bar Assn., Estate Planning Coun. San Antonio (pres. 1967), Tenn. Soc. CPAs, Tenn. Bar Assn. (chmn. tax, probate and trust sect., 1993-95), Estate Planning Coun. Memphis (pres. 1983-84), Toastmasters (pres. 1963), Delta Theta Phi, Kappa Pi Sigma, University Club (Memphis), Canyon Creek Country Club (San Antonio, bd. dirs.), Chicksaw Country Club, Optimists (bd. dirs.), Rotary (treas. 1978, 99, bd. dirs. 1986-87, 96-97). Home: 6785 Slash Pine Cv Memphis TN 38119-5617 Office: Pietrangelo Cook PLC 6410 Poplar Ave Ste 190 Memphis TN 38119-4841

COOK, B. THOMAS, lawyer; b. Dallas, July 15, 1946; s. Bryan Jennings and Winifred Texana (Tipps) C.; m. Nancy Illback, Nov. 8, 1969; children: Rachel Lynn, David Thomas, Hayden Paul. AB, Wheaton Coll., 1968; JD, U. Tex., 1971. Bar: Tex. 1974, U.S. Ct. Appeals (5th cir.) 1975, U.S. Dist. Ct. (so. dist.) Tex. 1975, U.S. Dist. Ct. (ea. dist.) Tex. 1981, U.S. Dist. Ct. (no. dist.) Tex. 1985, U.S. Dist. Ct. (we. dist.) Tex. 1990. Atty., ptnr. Bracewell & Patterson L.L.P., Houston, 1974—. Capt. U.S. Army, 1968-71. Named Disting. Military Grad. U.S. Army, 1968. Fellow: Tex. Bar Found., Houston Bar Found.; mem.: Tex. Bar Assn., Houston Club. Avocation: skiing. Office: Bracewell & Patterson LLP 711 Louisiana St Ste 2900 Houston TX 77002-2781

COOK, BARBARA ANN, lawyer; b. N.Y.C., Sept. 14, 1947; d. Paul J. and Mary (Doogan) McGuire; m. David S. Cook, Aug. 14, 1971; children: Peter James, Andrew David. AB, Manhattanville Coll., 1968; JD, Columbia U., 1971. Bar: N.Y. 1971, U.S. Dist. Ct. (so. and ea. dists.) N.Y. 1977. Assoc. Lynton, Klein, Opton & Saslow, N.Y.C., 1971-74; asst. gen. counsel McGraw-Hill, Inc., N.Y.C., 1974-85; sr. counsel and asst. sec. Phelps Dodge Corp., N.Y.C., 1986-87; regional counsel Cushman & Wakefield, Inc., N.Y.C., 1987-90; sr. counsel Grow Group, Inc., 1990-92; asst. gen. counsel Rheem Mfg. Co., 1992—. Contbr. articles to profl. jours. Mem. Assn. of Bar of City of N.Y. (comm. law com., lib. com.), N.Y. County Lawyers Assn. (corp. law com., environ. law com.). Home: 2 Stuyvesant Oval Apt Mg New York NY 10009-2144 E-mail: bcook@rheemny.com.

COOK, BERNADINE FERN, book publisher, writer; b. Saginaw, Michigan, Sept. 6, 1924; d. Luke C. and Evelyn Estella (Rands) Smith; m. George Cook, Jr., Oct. 25, 1942; (dec. Mar. 1964); children: George Daniel, Joan Louise, Marcie Ann, Lisë Dawn, Brian Lee. Corr., reporter Owosso Argus Press, Mich., 1960-62; freelance writer Durand, Mich., 1962-64; sec. Congl. Ch., Durand, Mich., 1964-68, 70-71; receptionist, copywriter WNEM-TV, Flint, Mich., 1968-69; bookkeeper, copywriter Rossano Assoc. Ad Agy., Flint, Mich., 1969-70, Comm. Ctr. Ad Agy., Flint, Mich., 1972; vol. coord., pub. info. officer Saginaw County Mental Health, Mich., 1973-78; pres., pub. Little Peoples' Press, Durand, Mich., 1994—2002. Author: Little Fish That Got Away, 1956; The Curious Little Kitten, 1956; Looking For Susie, 1959; Little Puppy That Lost It's Tail, 1995; Shorty and That Cat, 1999. Mem. Shiawassee Scribblers (pres. 1995-96). Avocations: genealogy, knitting, reading, gardening, travel. Home and Office: 10625 Garrison Rd Durand MI 48429-1814

COOK, BETH MARIE, writer, poet, volunteer; b. Electra, Tex., Jan. 4, 1933; d. Charles Bolivar Allen and Ida Marie (Nelson) Burton; m. William H. Cook, May 30, 1955 (div. Nov. 1981); children: David M., Dianne M. Gleason. Student, Rockmont Coll., 1951-54; BA, Antioch U. West, 1981. County coord. office econ. opportunity Upper Arkansas Coun., Salida, Colo., 1974-76; dir. area agy. on aging Upper Arkansas Coun./Dept. Social Svcs., State of Colo., 1976-80; specialist community devel. Mountain Plains Congress Sr. Orgns., Denver, 1980-82; sr. adminstrv. asst. Digital Rsch. Inc., Monterey, Calif., 1983-85, asst. to pres., 1985-87, retail rep., 1987-88; co-owner, ptnr. Scotia Gallery, Monterey, 1983-86; COO MiniSoft, Inc., Phoenix, 1988-89; property mgr. Parklane Arms Apts., 1989-92; exec. asst. Ft. Collins (Colo.) Housing Authority, 1989-92, occupancy specialist, 1992-95; vol. Peace Corps, Kingdom of Tonga, 1995-97, U.S. Dept. Commerce Census Bur., 1998-2000, 2002—. Hostess Sr. Sound-Off show, Sta. KVRH-AM/FM, Salida, 1978-80; cons. Devel. Assocs. Inc., Denver, 1982. Author: (poem) Jessie, 1989-90. Coord. crisis intervention line Chaffee County Cmty. Crisis Ctr., Salida, 1976-80; committeewoman Chaffee County Dem. Ctrl. Com., Salida, 1979-80; speaker, program com. Colo. Gov.'s Conf on Aging, Denver, 1980; docent Lincoln Ctr.; vol. food distbn. SHARE; youth Bible tchr., deacon Westminster Presbyn. Ch.; mem. bd. dirs. Fort Collins Housing Corp., Neighbor to Neighbor. Recipient Human Devel. Svc. award HHS, 1980, Golden Poet award, 1989; named Woman of Yr. Chaffee County Bus. and Profl. Women's Club, 1978. Mem. Am. Assn. Ret. Persons, Nat. Mus. Women in Arts. Presbyterian. Avocations: art, study of ancient mexican civilizations, travel.

COOK, BEVERLY, federal agency administrator; b. Wash. BA in Metallurgical Engring., U. Wash. Contractor Dept. Energy, various positions Office Nuc. Energy, prin. dep. dir., dir. Office Idaho Ops., 1999, asst. sec. environment, safety, and health, 2001—. Office: Dept Energy Environment, Safety, and Health 1000 Independence Ave SW Washington DC 20585-0001

COOK, BLANCHE WIESEN, history educator, journalist; b. N.Y.C., Apr. 20, 1941; d. David Theodore and Sadonia (Ecker) Wiesen. BA, Hunter Coll., 1962; MA, Johns Hopkins U., 1964, PhD, 1970; DHL (hon.), Russell Sage Coll., 1998. Instr. Hampton Inst., Va., 1963; instr. Stern Coll. for Women, Yeshiva U., N.Y.C., 1964-67; prof. history John Jay Coll., Grad. Faculty CUNY, 1968—; disting. prof., 1995—. Prodr., broadcaster program stas. WBAI and WKPFK Radio Pacifica, N.Y.C. and L.A., 1978—; vis. prof. UCLA, 1982-83; syndicated journalist; bd. dirs. Women's Fgn. Policy Adv. Coun., v.p., co-chair Fund for Open Info. and Accountability; mem. freedom to write com. PEN; elected univ.-wide union officer PSC-CUNY, 2000. Author: Crystal Eastman on Women and Revolution, 1978, Declassified Eisenhower, 1981 (N.Y. Times Notable Book), Biography of Eleanor Roosevelt, vol. 1, 1992 (L.A. Times Book award, N.Y. Times Notable Book), vol. 2, 1999, ER I, ER II (Best Books), Christian Sci. Monitor, 1999 (Notable Book award 1999); sr. editor: The Garland Library of War and Peace, 360 vols., 1970-80, Bella Abzug in Jewish Women's Encyclopedia, 1997; contbr. articles to various publs. Appointed to com. on documents for fgn. rels. U.S. Dept. State, 1986-90. Named Scholar of the Yr. N.Y. Coun. Humanities, 1996, Alumna of Yr. Hunter Coll. Hall of Fame, 1999; recipient Breakthrough award Women, Men and Media, 1992, Feminist of Yr. award Feminist Majority Found., 1992, Lambda Lit. Prize, 1992; faculty fellow CUNY, 1978, 84, 91. Mem. Orgn. Am. Historians (co-chair freedom of info. com.), Am. Hist. Assn. (v.p. for rsch. 1991-94), Coordinating Com., Women in Hist. Profession (pres. N.Y.C. chpt. 1969-71), Berkshire Women Historians, Soc. Historians Am. Fgn. Rels., Conf. on Peace Rsch. in History (bd. dirs., v.p.), Peace History Soc. Women's Internat. League for Peace and Freedom, Pi Sigma Alpha, Phi Alpha Theta. Office: CUNY John Jay Coll Dept History 445 W 59th St New York NY 10019-1104

COOK, BRADLEY JAMES, academic administrator; b. Ogden, Utah, Oct. 19, 1964; s. Gilbert Earl and Jerry Mae Cook; m. Terresa Jo Kerr; children: Sam, Cairo. BA, MA, Stanford U., 1990; PhD, U. Oxford, Eng., 2000. Spl. asst. to pres. Am. U., Cairo, 1990—91; govt. rels. specialist Bechtel Internat., Ahmadi, Kuwait, 1991—93; asst. to pres. Utah Valley State Coll., Orem, 1993—96; asst. prof. Brigham Young U., Provo, Utah, 1997—99; v.p. for coll. rels. Utah Valley State Coll., Orem, 1999—2002, v.p. acad. affairs, 2002—. Author: (book chpt.) Comparative Education for a New Millennium: Purposes, Problems and Potential, 2000; contbr. ency. entry, articles to profl. jours. Mem.: Orem/Provo C. of C. (bd. dirs. 1999—), Coun. for Advancement for the Support of Edn., Mid. East Assn., Comparative and Internat. Edn. Soc. Office: Utah Valley State Coll 800 W University Pkwy Orem UT 84058 Home Fax: 801-226-5207; Office Fax: 801-226-5207. Personal E-mail: cookbr@uvsc.edu. Business E-Mail: cookbr@uvsc.edu.

COOK, BRUCE LAWRENCE, research analyst; b. Chgo., Dec. 12, 1942; s. David Charles III and Anna Mae (Lawrence) C.; m. Carolyn Winslow Smith Hammock (div. Dec. 1972); 1 child, Steven Winslow; m. Eileen Clare McPeak, Jan. 3, 1973; children: Christopher David, Helen Clare, Bruce Michael. BA in Radio-TV, Ohio Wesleyan U., 1965; MA in Speech Arts, San Diego State U., 1967; PhD in Comm., Temple U., 1979. Trustee comm. rsch. David C. Cook Found., Elgin, Ill., 1972-83; dir. Ill. Mcpl. Inst., Dundee, 1983-88; mng. editor Sr. Am. Newspapers, Dundee, 1988-90; dir. Cook Comm., Dundee, 1990—; rsch. analyst Copley Chgo. Newspapers, Plainfield, 1995-2000; sr. rsch. analyst Reach Chgo., Hollinger Inc. Chgo. (Ill.) Sun-Times, Plainfield, Ill., 2000—. Instr. Columbia Coll., Chgo., 1989—, DeVry U./Keller Grad. Sch. Mgmt., Oak Brook, Ill., 1991—. Author: (monograph) Understanding Pictures in Papua, 1981, (booklet) Serving Mentally Impaired People, 1983; founder, editor website: author-me.com Trustee Village of Sleepy Hollow, Ill., 1983-87; alt. bd. rev. Kane County, Batavia, Ill., 1993-95; v.p. gen. edn. adv. bd. De Vry Inst. Tech., 1997—. Capt. USAF, 1967-72. Mem. Am. Legion. Republican. Home: 1211 Carol Crest Dr Sleepy Hollow IL 60118-2643 Office: Fox Valley Pubs 3101 N Us Highway 30 Plainfield IL 60544-9604 E-mail: cookcomm@gte.net.

COOK, BRYSON LEITCH, lawyer; b. Balt., Apr. 17, 1948; s. A. Samuel Cook. BA magna cum laude, Princeton U., 1970; JD cum laude, MBA, U. Pa., 1973. Bar: Md. 1974, U.S. Dist. Ct. Md. 1976, U.S. Tax Ct. 1977. Assoc. Alex Brown & Sons, Balt., 1973-75, Venable, Baetjer & Howard, Balt., 1975-81, ptnr., 1981—. Adj. prof. U. Md. Law Sch., Balt., 1981, Loyola U. Bus. Sch., Balt., 1980-82. Contbr. articles to legal jours.; author tax mgmt. portfolios. Trustee Balt. Ballet, 1980-83, Keswick Home for the Incurables, Balt., 1983—; bd. dirs. Balt. City Jail, 1980-82; counsel Md. Hist. Soc., Balt., 1981—. Recipient Gordon A. Block award U. Pa. Law Sch., 1973. Mem. ABA, Bar Assn. Balt. City, Md. State Bar Assn., Internat. Fiscal Assn., Order of Coif, Elkridge Club (Balt.). Republican. Methodist. Home: 201 Woodbrook Ln Baltimore MD 21212-1037 Office: Venable Baetjer & Howard LLP Mercantile Bank Trust Bldg 2 Hopkins Plz Ste 1800 Baltimore MD 21201-2971 E-mail: blcook@venable.com.

COOK, CAMILLE WRIGHT, retired law educator; b. Tuscaloosa, Ala. d. Reuben Hall and Camille Tunstall (Searcy) Wright; children: Sydney, Reuben, Cade, Camille. AB, U. Ala., 1945, JD, 1948. Bar: Ala. 1948. Asst. prof. law, Law Sch. Auburn (Ala.) U., 1968; mem. faculty Sch. Law U. Ala., 1968-93, assoc. dean, dir. continuing legal edn., prof. law, Law Sch., 1975-93, asst. acad. v.p., 1984-85; prof. emeritus, 1993—. Bd. dirs. U. Ala. Law Sch. Found., Am/South. Mem. Smithsonian Coun., Washington, 1972-78, Ala. Air Pollution Commn., 1971-81; vestry Christ Episcopal Ch. Recipient outstanding commitment to tchg. award U. Ala., 1990, disting. alumni award, 1996, Algernon Sydney Sullivan award, 1999. Fellow Am. Bar Found., Ala. Bar Assn. (award merit 1973); mem. ABA (Rawles Spl. Merit award 1983), Farrah Law Soc. (trustee 1972—, disting. alumnae award 1992), Am. law Inst. (coun., Rawles Spl. Merit award 1983). Episcopalian. Home: 32 Ridgeland Tuscaloosa AL 35406-1607 Office: PO Box 870382 Tuscaloosa AL 35487-0001

COOK, CATHERINE WELLES, state legislator; b. New London, Conn., Jan. 24, 1950; BA, Conn. Coll. Mem. Dist. 18 Conn. Senate, Hartford, 1993—. Chief dep. minority leader; mem. commerce and com.; ranking mem. appropriations com., human svcs. com.; mem. subcoms. on conservation and devel.; gov.'s appointee Conn. Bd. of Protection and Advocacy for Persons with Disabilities; mem. Pres.'s Commn. of Nat. Acad. of Mental retardation. Republican. Office: Conn State Senate State Capitol Rm 3400 Hartford CT 06106

COOK, CHARLES ADDISON, lawyer; b. N.Y.C., Mar. 31, 1952; s. Hugh F. and Lurana (Higgins) C.; m. Barbara Edgar, June 10, 1973; children: Ian Hugh, Alexander Charles. BA, U. Conn., 1974; M in Pub. Adminstrn., Northeastern U., 1976; JD magna cum laude, New Eng. Sch. Law, 1980. Bar: Mass. 1980, U.S. Dist. Ct. Mass. 1980, U.S. Ct. Appeals (1st cir.) 1980, (D.C. cir.) 1992, U.S. Supreme Ct., 1991. With Colonial Gas Co., Lowell, Mass., 1978—, dir. human resources, 1978-80, counsel, 1980-82, v.p., 1982-88, v.p., counsel, 1988-89. Mem. ABA, Mass. Bar Assn., Am. Gas Assn., New England Gas Assn., Bristol Yacht Club (commodore R.I. 1985-87), Eastern Yacht Club. Republican. Avocation: yacht racing. Office: Colonial Gas Co 40 Market St Lowell MA 01852-1806 Home: 25 Brookhouse Dr Marblehead MA 01945-1638

COOK, CHARLES DAVENPORT, pediatrician, educator; b. Mpls., Nov. 30, 1919; s. Henry W. and Ellen (Davenport) C.; m. Carolyn Crowther, June 12, 1976; 1 child, Deborah; children by previous marriage: Andrew D., Sheila D., Peter G., Charles Davenport II; stepchildren: Peter C. Brinzey, Christopher F. Brinzey. AB, Princeton U., 1941; MD, Harvard U., 1944; MA (hon.), Yale U., 1964. Intern U. Minn. Hosp., 1944-45; fellow Mayo Clinic, 1945-46; resident Mass. Gen. Hosp., 1948-49; chief resident Children's Hosp., Boston, 1949-51; assoc. clin. prof. pediatrics Harvard Med. Sch., 1963-64; prof., chmn. dept.

pediatrics Yale Sch. Medicine, 1964-74; vis. prof. U. Conn. Health Center, 1974-75; prof. pediatrics Downstate Med. Center, State U. N.Y., Bklyn., 1975-81, chmn. dept., 1975-81; Edward H. Townsend, Jr. emeritus prof. pediatrics U. Rochester, N.Y., 1990—; chief pediatrics Rochester (N.Y.) Gen. Hosp., 1982-90, Anthony Jordan Health Ctr., Rochester, N.Y., 1990-92; lectr. dept. pediatrics Yale Sch. Medicine, New Haven, 1992-2000, Yale Sch. Nursing, New Haven, 1995-99; pediatrician Hill Health Ctr., New Haven, 1993-94. Vis. scholar Japan Soc. Promotion Sci., Nagoya, 1974; vis. prof. Ben Gurion U. Negev, Beersheva, Israel, 1976, U. Hong Kong, 1989; pres. Monroe County Bd. Health, 1989-91; health dir. Town of Old Lyme, Conn., 1994-96. Served with M.C. AUS, 1945-47. Mem. Am. Pediatric Soc. (sec., treas. 1964-75) Achievements include research in med. care, med. edn. and quality assurance. Home: 3-1 Meetinghouse Ln Old Lyme CT 06371-1623 E-mail: davcookmd@juno.com. *On the basis of training as an academic pediatrician, my work for the past several decades has been directed to the development of techniques for the evaluation of physicians and for the assurance of quality care for children. While quality care for all is still a distant goal, third party payors and consumers are beginning to demand accountability and computers are beginning to facilitate the quality assurance programs we have developed, despite the mostly negative effect of H.M.O.'s.*

COOK, CHARLES DAVID, international lawyer, arbitrator, consultant; b. Saginaw, Mich., Apr. 5, 1924; s. Charles Christian and Grace (Robins) C.; m. Bobette Ringland, Oct. 30, 1947 (dec. 1984); children: Ian Ainsworth, Kendra. AB, U. Mich., 1947; LLB, MA in Internat. Affairs, Columbia U., 1950. Bar: N.Y. 1951, D.C. 1965, Fed. Dist. Ct. So. N.Y 1965, Supreme Ct. U.S 1967. Assoc. dir. Inst. World Affairs seminar, Twin Lakes, Conn., summer 1950; mem. U.S. Mission to UN, 1950-62, dep. counselor, chief polit. sect., 1956-60, counselor, 1960-62; ptnr. Barco, Cook, Patton & Blow, 1962-67; sr. counsel Gen. Tel. & Electronics Internat., 1967-72; v.p., gen. counsel, sec., dir. GTE Internat., 1972-78; gen. counsel, cons. Copadco Ltd., 1978-81, 85-95; of counsel Patton, Boggs & Blow, Washington, 1981-87; resident Law Office of Ismail S. Nazer, 1981-85. Adj. prof. internat. bus. transactions Bklyn. law Sch., 1980; mem. panel arbitrators Ministry Fgn. trade, Govt. of Poland, 1987—; arbitrator Internat. Ct. Arbritration, Internat. C. of C., Paris, 1989, World Intellectual Property Orgn., Geneva, 1993—; lectr. in field; counselor U.S. dels. UN Gen. Assemblies, 1958-61; accompanied Amb. Adlai Stevenson on Presdl. mission to S.Am., 1961; mem. U.S. del. disarmament com., Geneva, Switzerland, 1962; adviser U.S. del. WHO, Geneva, 1962; spl. cons. Pres. Nixon's Commn. for Observance of 25th Anniversary of UN; biographee Oral History Project on Eisenhower Yrs., Columbia U.; assoc. Inst. of World Affairs, Twin Lakes, Conn., 1993-2000. Chmn. bd. dirs. Maxwell Inst., Inc., Bronxville, N.Y., 1989-96; chmn. Bronxville Little Forum, 1987-89; trustee Bronxville Adult Sch., 1990-93, treas., 1992-93; mem. adv. bd. Maxwell Inst. of St. Vincent's Hosp. Westchester, Harrison, N.Y., 1996-2000, hon. mem., 2000—; mem. bd. mgrs. Music Mountain Inc., Falls Village Conn., 2002—. With USNR, 1943-46. Univ. seminar assoc. Columbia U., N.Y.C., 1961-73, 86— Mem. Assn. Bar City N.Y. (past com. on lawyers role in search for peace), Am. Arbitration Assn. (internat. arbitrator, panel arbitrators 1964—), Faculty House of Columbia U., Columbia Club N.Y., Univ. Club Litchfield County. Home: PO Box 506 181 Interlaken Rd Lakeville CT 06039-0506 Office: PO Box 506 Lakeville CT 06039-0506 E-mail: cdcook.esq@vmag.com.

COOK, CHARLES EDWARD, JR., editor, political analyst; b. Shreveport, La., Nov. 20, 1953; s. Charles Edward and Mary Elizabeth (Hudgens) C.; m. Lucy Gerald, Apr. 17, 1982. Student, Georgetown U., 1972-77. Rsch. dir. Dem. Senatorial Campaign Com., Washington, 1977-79; so. regional desk person Kennedy for Pres. Campaign, Washington, 1979-80; pub. opinion analyst, polit. cons. William R. Hamilton & Staff, Washington, 1980; asst. dir. for polit. affairs Nat. Assn. of Home Builders, Washington, 1981-82; mem. profl. staff Senate Dem. Policy Com., Washington, 1982-84; editor The Cook Polit. Report, Washington, 1984—. Election night analyst C-Span, 1986, 88, NBC News, 1988, CBS News, 1990, 92, NBC, 1994, 96, 98, 2000, 02; political analyst CNN, 1996-2002, NBC, 2002—. Columnist Roll Call, 1986-98, Nat. Jour., 1998—. Methodist. Home: 4002 E West Hwy Chevy Chase MD 20815-5915 Office: 1501 M St NW Ste 300 Washington DC 20005-1700

COOK, CHARLES FRANCIS, insurance executive; b. Hackensack, N.J., Mar. 23, 1941; s. John Cooper and Emily (Morse) C.; m. Barbara Ann Dotter, Sept. 8, 1962; children: Melanie, Cynthia. AB, Princeton U., 1963; MBA, St. Mary's of Tex., 1974. Asst. actuary Continental Ins. Cos., N.Y.C., 1965-68; actuary Gen. Accident, Phila., 1968-70; v.p., actuary USAA, San Antonio, 1970-75; sr. v.p. Am. Internat. Underwriters, N.Y.C., 1975-80, N.H. Ins. Co., Manchester, 1980-83; pres. Am. Universal Group, Providence, 1983-88; pvt. cons. practice in actuarial and ins. mgmt. Barrington, R.I., 1988-89; Bristol, R.I., 1989-90. Pres. The HuroCook Group, Inc., 1989-95, Ins. for Animals, Inc., 1989-95, MBA, Inc., 1991—, Cook Cons., Inc., 1990—, PetHealth, Inc., 1995. Contbr. articles to profl. jours. Pres. St. John and St. Matthew Emanuel Luth. Ch., Bklyn., 1978-80; bd. dirs. United Way S.E. New Eng., 1985-89; bd. dirs., stewardship chmn. St. James Evang. Luth. Ch., 1988-89; deacon Montville Reformed Ch., 1998—. Fellow Casualty Actuarial Soc. (bd. dirs. 1971-74, 85-88, gen. chmn. exam com., Woodward Fondiller prize 1968, Matthew Rodermund Svc. award 2000), Conf. Cons. Actuaries (bd. dirs. 1998—, v.p. casualty 1999-2000); mem. Am. Acad. Actuaries, Soc. CPCU's (cert.), Internat. Assn. Actuaries. Home: 9 Lakeview Ter Montville NJ 07045-9158 Office: 36 Midvale Rd Mountain Lakes NJ 07046-1330 E-mail: chapcook@mbainc.to.

COOK, CHARLES WILKERSON, JR., retired banker, former county official; b. Nashville, Sept. 10, 1934; s. Charles Wilkerson and Virginia (Jones) C.; m. Sally Randolph Frierson, June 24, 1961 (dec. May 2001); children: Charles Wilkerson III, John Stephenson Frierson; m. Mary Hawkins, Jan. 18, 2003. BS, Yale U., 1956; postgrad., Stonier Grad. Sch. Banking, Rutgers U., 1964-66. With Third Nat. Bank, Nashville, 1959-85, pres., 1979-83, chmn., 1983-85, also dir.; with Third Nat. Corp., Nashville, 1985-89, pres., chief exec. officer, 1985-87, chmn. bd. dirs., chief exec. officer, 1987-89, dir., 1983-90; exec. v.p. Sun Trust Banks, Inc., 1989-90; dir. fin. Met. Govt. of Nashville-Davidson County (Tenn.), Nashville, 1991-93; pres., CEO, dir. Union Planters Bank of Mid. Tenn., N.A., Nashville, 1993-99, chmn., bd. dirs., 2000—01; ret., 2001. Bd. dirs. Nashville Electric Power, chmn. bd. dirs., 1998-2002; bd. dirs. Quality Industries, Inc., Centennial Med. Ctr, 1993-99, Richland Place, Inc. Author: History of a Bank Merger, 1969. Mem. Nashville-Davidson County Govt. Social Svcs. Commn., 1970-85; sr. warden Christ Episcopal Ch., Nashville, 1970-71; pres. Episc. Churchmen of Tenn., 1974; mem. bishop and coun. Episc. Diocese of Tenn., 1979-81; chmn., bd. dirs. United Way Nashville, 1984-85, 1993-97; chmn. Project PENCIL, 1988-89, Jr. Achievement of Nashville, Bill Wilkerson Hearing and Speech Ctr., Nashville, 1970-80, Ensworth Sch., 1978-81, Better Bus. Bur. Nashville, 1980-83, Nashville Meml. Hosp., 1974-89, Tenn. Performing Arts Mgmt. Corp., 1985-89, vice-chmn., 1987-89, Tenn. State Mus. Found., 1986-89; mem. adv. bd. Salvation Army, Nashville, 1976-79; bd. dirs. Episcopal Ch. Found., 1991-92, St. Luke's Cmty. House, 1999—, chmn., 2002--; bd. dirs. Nashville Pub. TV Corp., 1998—, Nashville Cmty. Found., 2000—, Tenn. Hist. Soc., 2000—; campaign chmn. United Way Mid. Tenn., 1994. With USN, 1956-59; capt. Res., 1977-84. Mem. Nashville C. of C. (bd. govs. 1982-84, 95-2000), Belle Meade Country Club (bd. dirs. 1996-2000, pres. 1999-2000), Army-Navy Club (Washington), Yale Club NYC, Cumberland Club (Nashville). E-mail: cwcook@comcast.net.

COOK, CHARLES WILLIAM, aerospace engineer, consultant, educator; b. Yankton, S.D., Sept. 27, 1927; s. William O. and Kathryn S. (Eymer) C.; m. Virginia M. Fosness, May 30, 1950; children: Jennifer Cook Clark, William O. II, Amy Cook Lewandowski. AB summa cum laude, U. S.D., Dean Akeley fellow, 1951; MS, Calif. Inst. Tech., 1954, PhD, 1957. Head nuclear physics Convair Corp., San Diego, 1957-60; chief Ballistic Missile Def. br. Advanced Rsch. Project Agy., Washington, 1961; corp. dir. elec. rsch. and devel. No. Am. Aviation Inc., El Segundo, Calif., 1961-67; dep. div. chief. CIA, Washington, 1961-71; asst. dir. def. rsch. and engring. Dept. Def., Washington, 1971-74; dep. under sec. for space systems, acting dir. NRO Air Force, 1974-79, dep. asst. sec. for space plans and policy, 1979-88. Adj. prof. George Mason U., Fairfax, Va., 1988-90; cons. aerospace engring., plans and policy Inst. Def. Analyses, Alexandria, Va., Sys. Planning Corp., Arlington, Def. Sci. Bd., Pentagon, Global Outpost Inc., Alexandria, ANSER, Arlington, George Washington U., VEDA, Alexandria, Kistler Aerospace, Kirkland, Wash., McGraw-Hill Inc., 1988—. Contbr. articles to profl. jours., chpts. to books. With A.C. AUS, 1944-47. Decorated Air Force Exceptional Civilian Svc. award with three oak leaf clusters; named to Coyote Hall of Fame, U. S.D., 1976; recipient Meritorious Civil Svc. award, Sec. Def., 1974, Disting. Svc. award, 1976, Disting. Alumni award, U. S.D., 1982, cert. of appreciation, Intelligence R&D Coun., 1987, Disting. Svc. medal, NASA, 1988, Nat. Intelligence medal of achievement, 1988, Disting. Svc. award, Nat. Reconnaissance Office, 1998; fellow Dean Akeley, U. S.D., 1951, Dobbins, Calif. Inst. Tech., 1953, 1954—56. Fellow AIAA; mem. IEEE (sr.), Am. Phys. Soc., Am. Inst. Physics, Sigma Xi, Phi Beta Kappa, Sigma Pi Sigma. Achievements include determination of astrophysical significance of B12 with respect to element synthesis in stellar interiors. Home: 1180 Daleview Dr Mc Lean VA 22102-1540 Office: Inst for Def Analyses 4850 Mark Center Dr Alexandria VA 22311-1882 E-mail: ccook@ida.org, ccook@ioip.com.

COOK, CHARLES WILLIAM, JR., manufacturing executive; b. St. Louis, July 13, 1944; s. Charles William and Mildred (Bush) C.; m. Renee Marie Marre, May 10, 1969; children: Cynthia, Christina. BA in Economics, Denison U., 1966; MBA, Washington U., 1968. Various sales and mktg. positions Monsanto Co., St. Louis, 1968-82; dir. mktg. Avery Internat., Painesville, Ohio, 1983-84; v.p. Monsanto Electronic Materials, Tokyo, 1985-89; corp. v.p. MEMC Electronic Materials, St. Peters, Mo., 1990-98; chmn., CEO MEMC Pasadena, Inc., St. Peters, Mo., 1997-98; v.p., gen. mgr. electronic chems. divsn. Ashland Chem. Co., Dublin, Ohio, 1998—. Mem. adv. bd. Webster U. Bus. Sch. Exec. in residence U. Ill., Champaign, 1997. Mem. Washington U.-Olin Sch. Alumni Assn. (exec. com. 1997), Japan Am. Soc. St. Louis (bd. dirs. 1990-98, pres. 1994, 96), Bellerive Country Club, Hawk's Nest Golf Club, Country Club at Muirfield Village.. Avocations: golf, jogging, photography.

COOK, CHEQUETTA LYNN FAVORS, nurse; b. Kankakee, Ill., Mar. 24, 1959; d. Malcolm Melrose and Mary Lou (Land) Rabe; m. Kenneth Daniel Cook; 1 child, Desha Love. ADN, Edison C.C., 1988. RN N.C., Fla., cert. critical care nurse. Radiol. technologist Collier County Health Dept., Naples, Fla., 1984-88; staff nurse Naples Cmty. Hosp., 1988-93; clin. instr. L. Walker Vocat. Tech. Ctr., Naples, 1990-92, Edison C.C., Ft. Myers, Fla., 1992; home health nurse Able Care, Naples, 1992-93; transport nurse Nurses' Registry, Naples, 1993; ICU staff nurse, patient care coord. Margaret R. Pardee Meml. Hosp., Hendersonville, NC, 1993—99, nursing svc. dir., 1999—2001, ER staff nurse, charge nurse, 2001—. With ACLS, Hendersonville, 1989—2002; co-chair nursing policy, procedure and protocol com., nurse practice coun. utilization and ICU edn. coun. M.R. Pardee Hosp., 1996, program coord. advanced resuscitation edn. team, 1997—2001; provider, instr. PALS, 1999—, instr., ACLS provider, 1989—, PALS instr., 1999—2002, provider, 1999—, ENPC, 2002—. Co-leader Girl Scout Troop, Naples, 1987—88; co-advisor Med. Explorers Post, Hendersonville, 1996; sec.-treas. Supporters of Edneyville Libr., 2001—. Named Outstanding Young Women of Am., 1997. Mem.: AACN, Phi Theta Kappa. Republican. Avocation: Avocations: gardening, reading, sewing.

COOK, CHRISTINE L. endocrinologist, gynecologist, educator; b. Eugene, Oreg., Feb. 8, 1946; d. Wayne Vincent and Grace Louise (DuBois) Burt; m. Larry N. Cook, June 17, 1973; children: Brian D., Amelia L. BA in Microbiology, Oreg. State U., 1967; MD, U. Louisville, 1971. Cert. OB/GYN 1979. Instr. dept. ob-gyn., women's health U. Louisville, 1976-78, asst. prof., 1978-83, fellow reproductive endocrinology, 1980-82, assoc. prof., 1984—2001, prof., 2001—, vice chmn. dept. ob-gyn., women's health, dir. residency program; intern to resident U. of Louisville Hosps., 1971—76. Dir ob/gyn. residency program U. Louisville, 1984—89, 2003—; pres. U. OB/Gyn Assoc., 1998—2001. Author: (chpt.) Clinical Obstetrics & Gynecology, 1991, Dysmenorrhea & Premenstrual Tension, 1985. Fellow Am. Coll. Ob-Gyns; mem. Am. Soc. Reproductive Medicine, Am. Soc. Reproductive Surgeons, Soc. Asst. Reproductive Tech., Am. Andrology Soc., Assn. Profs. Ob-Gyn., Am. Assn. Gynecologic Laparoscopists, Am. Med. Women's Assn. Democrat. Methodist. Home: 2011 Woodford Pl Louisville KY 40205-1929 Office: Univ Louisville Deot Ob-gyn Women's Health Louisville KY 40292

COOK, CHRISTOPHER L. accountant; b. San Bernardino, Calif., Dec. 6, 1974; s. Lee and Gayle Cook. AA in Bus. Adminstrn., San Antonio Coll., 1994; BBA in Acctg. and Mgmt., U. Tex., San Antonio, 1996, MBA in Mgmt. Acctg., 2002. Contr. Boys and Girls Clubs of San Antonio, 1996-97; MIS product support specialist Columbia Industries, San Antonio, 1997-98; acctg. mgr. GW Plastics, San Antonio, 1998-99; acct. Columbia Industries, San Antonio, 1999—. Cons., contr. Boys and Girls Club of San Antonio, 1997—2001. E-mail: valla@worldnet.att.net.

COOK, CLARENCE EDGAR, research facility scientist; b. Jefferson City, Tenn., Apr. 27, 1936; s. Edgar Marion and Lillie Grey (Hodge) C.; m. Gail O'Connor McKee, June 1, 1957; children— David Grey, Lisa O'Connor Priebe, Kevin McKee. BS, Carson-Newman Coll., 1957; PhD, U. N.C., 1961; postdoctoral, U. Cambridge, Eng., 1961. Chemist, sr. chemist Rsch. Triangle Inst., Research Triangle Park, N.C., 1962-68, group leader, 1968-71, asst. dir. chem. life sci., 1971-75, dir. life sci. bioorganic chemistry, 1975-80, dir. bioorganic chemistry, 1980-85, research v.p., 1983-96, chief scientist, 1996—. Adj. prof. Sch. Pharmacy, U. N.C., Chapel Hill, 1985-96. Mem. editorial adv. bd. Drug Metabolism and Disposition, 1977-93; mem. editl. bd. Emerging Drugs: The Prospect for Improved Medicines, 1999-2003; contbr. articles to profl. jours., chpts. to books; patentee in field. Fellow N.Y. Acad. Scis.; mem. AAAS, Am. Chem. Soc., Am. Soc. Pharmacology and Exptl. Therapeutics, Coll. on Problems of Drug Dependence, Nat. Inst. on Drug Abuse (biomed. rsch. rev. com. 1985-89). Avocation: gardening. Office: Research Triangle Inst 857 Stingy Hollow Rd Staunton VA 24401

COOK, COLIN BURFORD, psychiatrist; b. London, Jan. 20, 1927; came to U.S., 1952, naturalized, 1975; s. Bertram William and Anna Marie (Forster-Jones) C. MD, London U., 1951. Diplomate Am. Bd. Psychiatry and Neurology. Rotating intern Bridgeport (Conn.) Hosp., 1952-53; resident Goodmayes Hosp., Warlingham Park Hosp., London, 1955-57; gen. med. practitioner London, 1960-66; resident in psychiatry Marquette Sch. Medicine, Wis., 1968-69, Cornell U., White Plains, N.Y., 1969-71; fellow Nat. Hosp. Neurol. Disease, U. London, 1973; practice medicine specializing in psychiatry, Stamford, Conn., 1975—. Prof. psychiatry Columbia U., N.Y.C., 1992-95; attending physician, psychiatrist Regional Network Programs, Inc., Conn., 1995-96. Author: (as Alan Phillips) Jazz Improvisation and Harmony, 1965, 4th edit., 1998. Served with Brit. Navy, 1953-55, 57-59. Fellow: Am. Soc. Psychoanalytical Physicians; mem.: AMA, Authors League, Masons (32 deg.). Address: 373 Strawberry Hill Ave Stamford CT 06902-2512 E-mail: ccookie3210@aol.com.

COOK, CYNTHIA ANN LOVELAND, health and mental health educator; b. Toledo, Oct. 29, 1945; d. Roy Frederick and Dorothy Helen (Aiken) C.; m. Jack W. Greer, May 25, 1991; children: Bryan Williams, Ron Greer, Jaime Greer. BS in Nursing, U. Ariz., 1968; MSW, U. Wash., 1974; PhD, U. Mich., 1986. Cert. social worker; RN, Wash. Nurse Mercy Hosp., Rockville Centre, N.Y., 1970, Northwest Hosp., Seattle, 1972; social worker VA Med. Ctr., Seattle, 1974-80; asst. clin. prof. U. Wash., Seattle, 1976-80; asst. study dir. Inst. Social Rsch., Ann Arbor, Mich., 1981-85; rsch. health sci. specialist VA, Ann Arbor, Mich., 1986-89; asst. prof. Wash. U., St. Louis, 1989-92; sr. rsch. health scientist VA, Indpls., 1992-95; dir. Ctr. Nursing Rsch. Barnes Jewish Hosp., St. Louis, 1995-98; assoc. prof. St. Louis Univ., 1998—. Cons. in field. Contbr. chpts. to books and articles to profl. jours. Lt. (j.g.) USN, 1968-69. Grantee Nat. Inst. Alcohol Abuse and Alcoholism, 1990-92, Robert Wood Johnson Found., 1992-95, Nat. Inst. Mental Health, 1999—. Mem. NASW, Coun. Social Work Edn., Sigma Theta Tau. Home: 227 S Main St Apt A Waterloo IL 62298-1365 Office: St Louis U 3550 Lindell Blvd Saint Louis MO 63103-1021 E-mail: cookca@slu.edu.

COOK, DAVID, editor; b. Boston, Dec. 28, 1946; s. Theodore N. and Charlotte M. (Stachelhaus) Cook; m. Linda Markarian, Dec. 19, 1981; children: Matthew D., Christopher E., Timothy T. BA, Principia Coll., 1969; postgrad., Columbia U., 1977, Mich. State U., 1979-81. Staff writer Christian Sci. Monitor, Boston and Washington, 1971-77, bus. corr. Boston, 1981-82, Washington corr., 1982-88; chief bur. McGraw Hill World News, Detroit, 1977-79, dep. chief Chgo., 1980-81; corr. Bus. Week Mag., Detroit, 1979-80; mng. editor Monitor TV, Boston, 1988-92; editor Monitor Radio, Boston, 1992-94, The Christian Sci. Monitor, Boston, 1994—2001, Washington bur. chief, sr. editor, 2001—. With U.S. Army, 1969—71. Christian Scientist. Avocation: reading. Office: Christian Sci Monitor Washington Bur 910 16th St Washington DC 20006 E-mail: cookd@csmonitor.com.

COOK, DEBBIE, lawyer, councilman; m. John Fisher; 1 child. BS, Calif. State U.-Long Beach; JD, Western State Coll. Law, 1994. Bar: Calif. Mayor City of Huntington Beach, Calif., 2000—01; mem. Huntington Beach (Calif.) City Coun., 2001—. Mem. Southern Calif. Assn. of Govt.'s Energy & Environ. Com., League of Cities' Admin. Policies Com., League Local Self Govt.'s Ethics Project Adv. Com.; dir. Orange County Sanitation Dist. Office: City Coun 2000 Main St Huntington Beach CA 92648 E-mail: hbdac@hotmail.com.*

COOK, DEBORAH L. judge, former state supreme court justice; b. Pittsburgh, Feb. 8, 1952; BA in English, U. Akron, 1974, JD, 1978, LLD (hon.), 1996. Ptnr. Roderick & Linton, Akron, 1976-91; judge 9th dist. Ohio Ct. Appeals, 1991-94; justice Ohio Supreme Ct., 1995—2003; judge U.S. Court of Appeals, 6th cir., Cincinnati, Ohio, 2003—. Bd. trustees Summit County United Way, Vol. Ctr., Stan Hywet Hall and Gardens, Akron Sch. Law, Coll. Scholars, Inc.; bd. dirs. Women's Network; vol. Mobile Meals, Safe Landing Shelter. Named Woman of Yr., Women's Network, 1991. Fellow Am. Bar Found.; mem. Omicron Delta Kappa, Delta Gamma (pres., Nat. Shield award). Office: 532 Potter Stewart US Courthouse 100 E Fifth St Cincinnati OH 45202-3988*

COOK, DON LLOYD, marketing educator, lawyer, consultant; b. Sacramento, July 7, 1962; s. Don Lloyd and Bonnie Mae Cook; m. Elizabeth Bampfield Jacoby, Aug. 21, 1992. D, U. Ark., 1988, MBA, 1994; PhD, Va. Poly. Inst. and State U., 2001. Bar: Ark. 1989. 0asst. prof. mktg. Ga. State U., Atlanta, 2000—; assoc. Lisle Law Firm, Springdale, Ark., 1992-93; asst. prof. La. Tech U., Ruston, 1999-2000. Am. Mktg. Assn.-Sheth fellow Va. Poly. Inst. and State U., 1998. Mem. ABA, Am. Mktg. Assn. (pres. doctoral spl. interest group 1997-98), Assn. for Consumer Rsch., Acad. Mktg. Sci., Decision Scis. Inst., Soc. for Consumer Psychology, Tech. Alliance Ga., Ga. Electronic Commerce Assn. Home: 110 Paisades Rd NE Atlanta GA 30309 Office: Ga State U Ste 1300 RCB University Plz Atlanta GA 30303-3083 Fax: 404-65104198. E-mail: doncook@gsu.edu., donlc@bellsouth.net.

COOK, DONALD CHARLES, lawyer; b. Marshalltown, Iowa, Sept. 29, 1943; s. Gerald E. and Alma Mae (Johnson) C.; m. Mary Lou Schroeder, July 30, 1973; 1 dau., Caillin Alice. B.A., Calif. State U.-Long Beach, 1973; J.D., Whittier Coll., 1976. Bar: Calif. 1976, U.S. (cen. dist.) Calif. 1977, U.S. Ct. Appeals (9th cir.) 1978. Sole practice, Los Angeles, 1976-81; assoc. firm Cook & Symonds, Los Angeles, Westwood and Thousand Oaks, Calif., 1981-83, Glenn E. Stern A Law Corp., West Covina, Calif., 1983-84, Stern, Cook & Naiditch, 1984— . Atty., Olympic Classes Regattas Organizing Com., Long Beach, 1981. Served with U.S. Army, 1962-65. Mem. Los Angeles County Bar Assn. Democrat. Club: Seal Beach Yacht (judge advocate 1980-83) (Long Beach).

COOK, DONALD E. pediatrician, educator; b. Pitts., Mar. 24, 1928; s. Merriam E. and Bertha (Gwin) C.; m. Elsie Walden, Sept. 2, 1951; children: Catherine, Christopher, Brian, Jeffrey. BS, Colo. Coll., 1951; MD, U. Colo., 1955. Diplomate Am. Bd. Pediat., 1961. Intern Fresno County Gen. Hosp., Calif., 1955-56; resident in gen. practice Tulare (Calif.) County Gen. Hosp., 1956-57; resident in pediatrics U. Colo., 1957-59; practice medicine specializing in pediatrics Aurora, Colo., 1959—64, Greeley (Colo.) Med. Clinic, 1964—86, Greeley Sports Medicine Clinic, 1988—93; med. adv. Centenniial Develop. Svcs., Inc., 1993-95; clin. faculty U. Colo., clin. prof., 1977—; pres. Am. Acad. Pediatrics, Elk Grove Village, Il., 1999-2000. Organizer, dir. Sports Medicine Px Exam Clinic for Indigent Weld Co. athletes, 1990—96; mem. adv. bd. Nat. Ctr. Health Edn., San Francisco, 1978—80; mem. adv. com. inmaternal and child health programs Colo. State Health Dept., 1981—84, chmn., 1981—84; preceptor Sch. Nurse Practitioner program U. Colo., 1978—88; affiliate prof. nursing U. No. Colo., 1996; vol. physician Monfort Children's Clinic, 2000—02. Mem. Weld County Dist. 6 Sch. Bd., 1973—83, pres., 1973—74, 1976—77, chmn. dist. 6 accountability com., 1972—73, mem. adv. com. dist. 6 teen pregnancy program, 1983—85; mem. Weld County Task Force on Teen-aged Pregnancy, 1986—89, Dream Team Weld County Task Force on Sch. Dropouts, 1986—92; mem.Weld County Interagy. Screening Bd., Weld County Cmty. Ctr. Found., 1984—89; mem. Weld County Task Force Spkrs. Bur. on AIDS, 1987—94, Weld County Task Force Adolescent Health Clinic, Task Force Child Abuse, C. of C.; bd. dirs. No. Colo. Med. Ctr., 1993—98, No. Colo. Med. Ctr. Found., 1994—; med. advisor Weld County Sch. Dist. VI-Nurses, 1987—; mem. Sch. Dist. 6 Health Coalition, Task Force on Access to Health Care; group leader neonatal group Colo. Action for Healthy People Colo. Dept. Pub. Health, 1985—86; co-founder Colorodians for Seatbelts on Sch. Buses, 1985—90; co-founder, v.p. Coalition of Primary Care Physicians Colo., 1986; mem. adv. com. Greeley Ctrl. Drug and Alcohol Abuse, 1984—86; bd. dirs. Rocky Mtn. Ctr. for Health Promotion and Edn., 1984—, v.p., 1992—93, pres., 1994—95; rep. coun. on med. specialty soc. AAP, 1988—89, mem. coun. pediat. rsch., AAP cons. to nat. PTA, 1990—94, mem. coun. on govt. affairs, 1989—90, rep. to coun. sects. mgmt. com., mem. search com. for new exec. dir.; med. cons. Sch. Dist. 6, 1989—; adv. com. bd. comm., membership and fin. AAP, 1990—95, com. govt. affairs, 1990—2001; mem. United Way Weld County, 1993—98; founder, med. dir. Monfort Children's Clinic, 1994—98; bd. dirs. Colo. Coll. Alumni Assn., 2003—. With USN, 1946—48. Recipient Disting. Svc. award, Jr. C. of C., 1962, Disting. Citizenship award, Elks, 1975—76, 2000—01, Svc. to Mankind award, Sertoma Club, 1972, Spark Plug award, U. No. Colo., 1981, Svc. award, Eta Sigma Gamma, 1996, Mildred Doster award, Colo. Sch. Health Coun. for Sch. Health Contbns., 1992, Citizen of Yr. award, No. Colo. Med. Ctr. Found., 1996, Humanitarian of Yr. award, Weld County United Way, 1996, Alfred Winchester Humanitarian award, Greeley/Weld Sr. Found., Inc., 1996, Silver and Gold award, U. Colo. Med. Alumni Assn., 1997, Franklin Geggenbach award, 1997, Denver Children's Hosp. Pediatric Alumni award, 1997, Benezet award, Colo. Coll., 2000. Mem.: AMA (chmn. sch. and coll. health com. 1980—82, James E. Strain Cmty. Svc. award 1987, 1994), Centennial Pediatric Soc. (pres. 1982—86), Colo. Med. Soc. (com. in sports medicine 1980—90, com. chmn. 1986—90, chmn. com. sch. health 1988—91, A.H. Robbins Cmty. Svc. award 1974), Weld County Med. Soc. (pres. 1968—69), Adams Aurora Med. Soc. (pres. 1964—65), Am. Acad. Pediat. (chmn. sch. health com. 1975—80, mem. taskl force on new age of pediatrics 1982—85, chmn. Colo. chpt. 1982—87, media spokesperson Speak Up for Children 1983—, Ross edn. and award com. 1985—86, alt. dist. VIII chmn. 1987—93, mem. coun. sects. mgmt. 1991—92, chmn. alt. dist. chmn. com. 1991—93, dist. chmn. dist. VIII 1993—98, mem. search com., exec. dir. candidate for pres. 1998, pres. elect 1998—99, v.p. AAP 1998—99, pres. 1999—2000, 1999—2000, immediate past pres. 2000—01, dist. VIII catch facilitator 2000—, tomorrows children's task force 2001—, reimbursement task force 2002—), Colo. Med. Soc. Sch. Health Com. (chmn. 1967—78), Rotary (bd. dirs. Greely chpt. 1988—91, chmn. immunization campaign Weld County 1994, mem. immunization com. 1994—, mem. adv. bd. Greeley Promises for Children 2001—, bd. dirs. Greeley chpt. 2003—, bd. dirs. Greely chpt. 2003—). Republican. Methodist. Office: Monfort Children's Clinic 100 N 11th Ave Greeley CO 80631 E-mail: dcook@aap.org.

COOK, DONALD EUGENE, retired orthopedist; b. Cromwell, Ala., Oct. 19, 1935; s. Frances Aubrey and Ethie Francis (Nicholson) C.; m. Myrna Nell Shadow, June 20, 1959; children: Janet Lynn, Donald Scott. Student, U. Miss., 1959, MD, 1963. Extern Miss. State Hosp., Whitfield, 1962-63; intern Mobile (Ala.) Gen. Hosp., 1963-64; resident U. Miss. Med. Ctr., Jackson, 1964-68, chief resident, 1967-68; cons. physician Miss. Crippled Children's Svc., Meridian, 1968-72; staff Riley Meml. Hosp., Meridian, 1968-76, Meridian Regional Hosp., 1968-89, Anderson Med. Ctr., Meridian, 1968-99; pres. East. Ctrl. Orthops., Ltd., Meridian, 1982-99; ret., 2000. CEO Astro Devel. Co., Meridian, 1986—92; pres., CEO Planetary Products, Inc., 1986—93. Patentee. Mem. bd. dirs. ARC, Meridian, 1978-80; team physician Meridian Boxing Club, 1980-95. With U.S. Army, 1954-57. Mem.: AMA, Miss. State Med. Assn., Shriners, Masons (32 degree). Baptist. Home: 6485 Highway 493 Meridian MS 39305-9281

COOK, DORIS MARIE, accountant, educator; b. Fayetteville, Ark., June 11, 1924; d. Ira and Mettie Jewel (Dorman) C. BSBA, U. Ark., 1946, MS, 1949; PhD, U. Tex., 1968. CPA, Okla., Ark. Jr. acct. Haskins & Sells, Tulsa, 1946-47;

instr. acctg. U. Ark., Fayetteville, 1947-52, asst. prof., 1952-62, assoc. prof., 1962-69, prof., 1969-88, Univ. prof. and Nolan E. Williams lectr. in acctg., 1988-97, emeritus disting. prof., 1997—. Mem. Ark. State Bd. Pub. Accountancy, 1987-92, treas., 1989-91, vice chmn. 1991-92; mem. Nat. Assn. State Bds. of Accountancy, 1987-92; appointed Nolan E. Williams lectureship in acctg., 1988-97; Doris M. Cook chair in acctg. U. Ark., Fayetteville, 2000. Mem. rev. bd. Ark. Bus. Rev., Jour. Managerial Issues, contbr. articles to profl. jours. Recipient Bus. Faculty of Month award Alpha Kappa Psi, 1997, Outstanding Faculty award Ark. Tchg. Acad., 1997, Charles and Nadine Baum Outstanding Tchr. award, 1997, Outstanding Leadership and Svc. award from several women's orgns. for Women's History Month, 1999, AAUW, others. Mem. AICPA, Ark. Bus. Assn. (editor newsletter 1982-85), Am. Acctg. Assn. (chmn. nat. membership 1982-83, Arthur Carter scholarship com. 1984-85, membership Ark. 1985-87), Am. Women's Soc. CPAs., Ark. Soc. CPA's (life, v.p. 1975-76, pres. N.W. Ark. chpt. 1980-81, sec. Student Loan Found. 1981-84, treas. 1984-92, pres. 1992-97, chmn. pub. rels. 1984-88, 93-95, Outstanding Acctg. Educator award 1991, Outstanding Com. Svc. award 1995, Student Loan Found. Bd. award 2001, 21 Yrs. Outstanding Svc. award 2001), Acad. Acctg. Historians (life, trustee 1985-87, rev. bd. of Working Papers Series 1984-92, sec. 1992-95, pres.-elect 1995, pres. 1996), Ark. Fedn. Bus. and Profl. Women's Clubs (treas. 1979-80), Fayetteville Bus. and Profl. Women's Clubs (pres. 1973-74, 75-76, Woman of Yr. award 1977) Mortar Bd., Beta Gamma Sigma, Beta Alpha Psi (editor nat. newsletter 1973-77, nat. pres. 1977-78, Outstanding Alumni in Edn. Iota chpt. 1999, Outstanding Svc. award 1999), Phi Gamma Nu, Alpha Lambda Delta, Delta Kappa Gamma (sec. 1976-78, pres. 1978-80, treas. 1989-2000), Phi Kappa Phi. Home: 1115 N Leverett Ave Fayetteville AR 72703-1622 Office: U Ark Dept Acctg Fayetteville AR 72701

COOK, EDWARD JOSEPH, college president; b. N.Y.C., July 8, 1925; s. Clinton J. and Catherine A. (Cullen) C.; m. Dorothy A. Collins, July 21, 1951; children: Barbara A., Thomas E., Patricia M. BS summa cum laude, Fordham U., 1949, PhD, 1958; MA, Columbia U., 1950. Assoc. prof., chmn. dept. econs. Sch. Bus., Fordham U., N.Y.C., 1950-62; asst. dean Sch. Bus., chmn. econs. dept. St. John's U., N.Y.C., 1962-64; prof. econs., dir. div. bus. C.W. Post Coll., Greenvale, N.Y., 1964-69, exec. dean Sch. Bus. Adminstrn., 1969-73; pres. C. W. Post Center, L.I. U., Greenvale, 1973-86. Mgmt. cons. to U.S. Navy and pvt. industry, 1969-73 Author: Causes of Commercial Bank Failures in New York State, 1958, (with R. Vizza) The Marketing Concept, 1968, (with A.F. Chapman) Peter Drucker, Contributions to Business Enterprises, 1970, (with J.N. Macri) Maternal Serum Alpha-Fetoprotein Patient-Specific Risk Reporting: Its Use and Misuse, 1990, (with J.N. Macri) Maternal Serum Down Syndrome Screening: Free Beta Protein, 1990. Chmn., L.I. Regional Planning Bd. Served with U.S. Army, 1942-45. Decorated Purple Heart. Mem. Am. Econ. Assn. Roman Catholic.

COOK, EUGENE AUGUSTUS, lawyer; b. Houston, May 2, 1938; s. Eugene A. and Estelle Mary (Stiner) C.; m. Sondra Attaway, Aug. 27, 1968; children: Laurie Ann, Eugene A. BBA, U. Houston, 1961, JD, 1966; LLM, U. Va., 1992. Bar: Tex. 1966, U.S. Dist. Ct. (so. dist.) Tex. 1967, U.S. Ct. Appeals (5th cir.) 1969, U.S. Supreme Ct. 1971, U.S. Ct. Claims 1972, U.S. Tax Ct. 1974, U.S. Ct. Appeals (11th cir.) 1982, U.S. Dist. Ct. (no., we. and ea. dists.) Tex. 1983. Ptnr. Butler & Binion, Houston, 1966-85; founding ptnr. Cook, Davis & McFall, 1985-88; justice Tex. Supreme Ct., Austin, 1988-93, chmn. jud. edn. exec. com., chmn. professionalism com., 1988-92; sr. ptnr. Bracewell & Patterson, Houston, 1993—. Adj. asst. prof. law U. Houston, 1971-72, 74. Editor in chief, contbg. author: Creditors Rights in Texas, 2d edit., 1981; bd. dirs. U. Houston Law Rev., 1978-79; contbr. articles to profl. jours. Vice-chmn. bd. YMCA, 1977; bd. dirs. Spl. Olympics, Tex., 1989-95, chmn. bd. dirs., 1994. Recipient Disting. Alumnus award U. Houston Law Ctr., 1990, Am. Inns of Ct.-Lewis F. Powell Jr. award, 1992. Fellow Am. Coll. Trial Lawyers, Am. Acad. Matrimonial Lawyers, Internat. Acad. Matrimonial Lawyers, Am. Bar Found., Tex. Bar Found. (Outstanding Pub. Svc. award 1990); mem. ABA, Am. Inns of Ct. (pres. Austin Inn 1990-91), Tex. Bar Assn. (chmn. grievance com. 1971-72, vice chmn. consumer law sect. 1976-77, chmn. consumer law sect. 1979-80, Presdl. Citation 1979, dir. family law sect. 1984-88, Presdl. Cert. Merit, 1983, 84, 86, Pres.'s award as most outstanding lawyer in Tex., 1989, chmn. pubs. com. 1981-82, Achievement award 1982, chmn. litigation sect. 1982-84, chmn. CLE, 1988-89), Houston Bar Assn. (seminar com. 1976-77, Chmn. of Yr. award, 1976-77, chmn. insts. com. 1977-78, Outstanding Svc. award 1977-78, chmn. CLE com. 1978-79, Pres.'s award, 1978-79, 96-97; chmn. consumer law sect. 1978-79, vice-chmn. family law sect. 1981-82, chmn. family law sect. 1982-83, Officers award 1983, chmn. staff and staffing com. 1985-86, chmn. Spl. Oympics Com. 1987-88, chmn. long range planning and devel. com. 1988-89, dir. 1984-86, 2d v.p. 1986-87, 1st v.p. 1987-88, pres. elect 1988-89, pres. 1989-90, chmn. profl. com. 1996-97), Texas Bd. Legal Specialization (cert.), Civil Trial and Family Law, Nat. Bd. Trial Advocacy (bd. cert. civil trial law), Tex. Assn. Cert. Civil Trial Law Lawyers, Gulf Coast Family Law Specialists Assn., Tex. Acad. Family Law Specialists, ABA, State Bar Tex., Phi Kappa Phi, Phi Theta Kappa (chmn. bd. dirs. 1966-71, 87-88, Most Disting. Alumnus in Nat. award, 1988), Omicron Chi Epsilon, Omicron Delta Kappa, Phi Rho Pi, U. Houston Alumni Assn. (bd. dirs. 1996—). Office: Bracewell & Patterson LLP S Tower Pennzoil Pl 711 Louisiana St Ste 2900 Houston TX 77002-2781

COOK, FERRIS, writer, illustrator; b. N.Y.C., Dec. 28, 1950; d. Norman and Nancy (Burge) C.; m. Kenneth L. Krabbenhoft Jr., Feb. 26, 1979; 1 child, Isaac. Student, Skowhegan (Maine) Sch. Painting and Sculpture, 1971; BA, Bennington Coll., 1972; MA, NYU, 1993. Author, illustrator: The Garden Trellis, 1996; illustrator, editor: Garden Dreams, 1991 (Quill & Trowel awards for illustration and book design 1991), Remembered Gardens, 1993, Odes to Common Things by Pablo Neruda, 1994, Odes to Opposites by Pablo Neruda, 1995 (Excellence in Graphics award New England Bookshow 1996), The Rose Window by R.M. Rilke, 1997, A Murmur in the Trees by Emily Dickinson, 1998, The Sonnets by William Shakespeare, 1998, The Poems of St. John of the Cross, 1999, Gifts of Love: A Selection of Unusual Love Poetry, 2000, Bark: A Selection of Poems about Dogs, 2000, Yowl: A Selection of Poems about Cats, 2001, Garden Nouveau: Two Blank Journals and Notecards, 2001, others; editor: Invitation to the Garden, 1992 (Quill & Trowel award for garden communication 1993). Avocations: painting, gardening, cello playing. Home: 438 Mohonk Rd High Falls NY 12440-5301 E-mail: fcook123@earthlink.net.

COOK, GARY RAYMOND, university president, clergyman; b. Little Rock, Ark., Sept. 27, 1950; s. Raymond C. and Vada (James) C.; m. Sheila Gayle Raymer, Dec. 28, 1974; children: David Daniel, Mark Andrew. BA, Baylor U., 1972; MDiv, So. Sem., Louisville, 1975; MA, U. North Tex., 1977; D in Ministry, Southwestern Sem., 1977. Pastor 1st Bapt. Ch., McGregor, Tex., 1976-78; dir. denomination and community rels. Baylor U., Waco, Tex., 1978-88; pres. Dallas Bapt. U., 1988—. Author: Retirees in Mission, 1977; co-editor: Abner McCall: One Man's Journey, 1981. Mayor pro tem City of Waco, 1983-84, mem. city coun., 1981-84; past bd. dirs. Tex. Dept. on Aging; past internat. bd. dirs. Habitat for Humanity. Recipient Humanitarian award Waco Conf. Christians and Jews, 1986, Disting. Alumnus award Southwestern Sem., 2000, Baylor U., 2003. Mem. Rotary (sustaining). Home and Office: 3000 Mountain Creek Pkwy Dallas TX 75211-6700

COOK, GEOFFREY ARTHUR, editor, writer; b. Cleve., Apr. 9, 1946; s. Arthur William and Donna Christy Cook. Student, Kenyon Coll., 1964-67; BA, U. Calif., Berkeley, 1982, MA, 1987. Cert. C.C. tchr. in ethnic studies, history and humanities, Calif. Contbg. editor Margins, Milw., 1975-78, Mus. Art Contemporary, San Francisco, 1977-81; corr. India Today, New Delhi, 1994-97; dir. G. Cook et al, Berkeley, 1998; editor Pakistan Weekly, Berkeley, 1998—. Bd. dir. Pakistan Edn. Found., Berkeley, G. Cook et al, Berkeley; lectr. in field. Author: Tolle Lege, 1974, Azrael, 1992, The Heart of the Beast, 1995. Mem. PEN/Am. Ctr., Nat. Writers Union, Assn. Asian Studies, Ind. Scholars South Asia, Am. Com. for So. Asian Art. Democrat. Mem. Anglican Ch. Avocations: computers and technology, human rights. Office: PO Box 4233 Berkeley CA 94704

COOK, GEORGE VALENTINE, lawyer, consultant; b. Glendale, N.Y., Feb. 14, 1927; s. Walter Preston and Ida Ruth (Smith) C.; m. Edith Wengler, Sept. 4, 1948 (dec. Dec. 2002); children: George V., James, Robert, Laura, Barbara, Mary, Walter, Elizabeth. BA, Columbia U., 1949, LL.B., 1952. Bar: N.Y. 1953, U.S. Dist. Ct. (so. dist.) N.Y. 1955, U.S. Dist. Ct. (ea. dist.) N.Y. 1955, U.S. Ct. Appeals (2d cir.) 1955, U.S. Ct. Appeals (3d cir.) 1982, US. Dist. Ct. (no. dist.) N.Y. 1987. Assoc. Dewey, Ballantine, Bushby, Palmer & Wood, N.Y.C., 1952-56; mem. legal staff N.Y. Telephone Co., N.Y.C., 1956-59, 60-61; atty. AT&T, N.Y.C., 1959-60, 61-65, v.p., 1973-76; v.p. regulatory matters Western Electric Co., Inc., N.Y.C., 1966-72, v.p. gen. counsel, 1976-83, also dir.; exec. v.p., gen. counsel AT&T Technologies, Inc., N.Y.C., 1984-85; counsel Hunton & Williams, 1985-90; cons., 1990—. Contbr. articles to profl. jours. Active alumni activities Columbia U. Served to 2d lt. U.S. Army, 1945-47. Fellow Am. Bar Found.; mem. ABA, N.Y. State Bar Assn., Assn. Gen. Counsel, Assn. of Bar of City of N.Y. Home: 127 Somerset Ave Garden City NY 11530-1348

COOK, GERALD, electrical engineering educator; b. Hazard, Ky., Oct. 31, 1937; s. Rudolph H. and Rose I. (Boyer) C.; m. Nancy Anne Gillespie, June 9, 1962; children: Gerald Boyer, Allan Binford. BS, Va. Poly. Inst., 1961; MS, MIT, 1962, ScD, 1965. Registered profl. engr., Va. Lectr. U. Colo., Colorado Springs, 1966-68; asst. prof. U.S. Air Force Acd., Colorado Springs, 1966-68; assoc. prof. U. Va., Charlottesville, 1968-73, prof., 1973-81; prof., chmn. dept. Vanerbilt U., Nashville, 1981-85; Earle C. Williams prof. elec. engring. George Mason U., Fairfax, Va., 1985—, chmn. dept. elec. and computer engring., 1990-98. Vis. prof. Tech. U. Denmark, 1979-80; vis. rschr. Night Vision Lab., Ft. Belvoir, 1998-99. Editor in chief IEEE Trans. on Indsl. Electronics, 1984-91. Recipient Outstanding Rsch. award USAF Office Aerospace Rsch., 1968, Cert. of Achievement, U.S. Army, 1981; NSF fellow, 1961-64. Fellow IEEE (life, pres. Indsl. Electronics Soc. 1981-83, Centennial medal 1984, Eugene Mittelmann Achievement award 1989), Am. Soc. Engring. Edn. (Outstanding Rsch. awrd S.E. sect. 1971), Sigma Xi, Eta Kappa Nu, Phi Kappa Phi, Tau Beta Pi. Home: 4821 Fox Chapel Rd Fairfax VA 22030-4508 Office: George Mason U Dept Elec Engring Fairfax VA 22030 E-mail: gcook@gmu.edu.

COOK, GLORIA HOUSTON, civic leader; b. Portland, Maine, Aug. 22, 1933; d. Ellwyn Kenelm and May Elvera (Delay) Houston; m. James Thomas Cook Jr., Jan. 28, 1952; children: Victoria Cook Leonhardt, Sheryl Ann. Student, U. Fla., 1950-52. Invitee, White House Conf. on Food, Nutrition and Health, 1969, cons. to Fla. conf., 1970; Gen. Synod del. from Fla., United Ch. of Christ, 1975-77; dir. pub. rels., trustee, chmn. nominating com., mem. pulpit com., tchr. Sunday sch., mem. stewardship bd., Seabreeze United Ch.; legis. appointee, sec. exec. bd., Volusia County Charter Rev. Commn., 1975-77; mem. Volusia County Pers. and Merit Bd., 1974-85, chmn., 1980-83; bd. counselors, Bethune-Cookman Coll., 1977-84; bd. dirs., Atlantic Ctr. for Arts, New Smyrna Beach, Fla.; pres., bd. dirs., exec. com. Meml. Health Care Systems, Ormond Beach, Fla., 1980-2000, mem. hosp. estate planning com., chmn., treas. pers. com., chmn. fin. com., v.p., CEO search, evaluation and compensation com.; hon. life dir. Volusia/Flagler Easter Seals, 1955—, fundraising capital campaign chmn., 1999—; past pres., v.p., sec. Fla. Easter Seals; past pres., v.p., chair, vice chmn. Ho. of Dels. Nat. Easter Seals; mem. nat. adv. child health and human devel. Coun. Nat. Insts. Health, 1990-94; past pres., sustaining mem. Jr. League Daytona Beach, Civic League Halifax Area. Recipient Meritorious Service and Outstanding Vol. Service awards Nat. Easter Seals, Humane Carer of Yr. Meml. Health Sys., 1991; named Layman of Yr., Fla. Med. Soc., 1985, one of 100 Outstanding Jr. League Mems. Internat. Jr. Leagues, named Vol. of Distinciton, Centennial Yr., 1995. Mem. Nat. League Am. Pen Women (patron), Highlands Country Club (N.C.), Hammock Dunes Country Club (Fla.). Republican. Avocations: collecting perfume bottles, photography. Home: 15 Madeira Ct Palm Coast FL 32137-2103 also: 78 S Sassafras Ct Highlands NC 28741-6635

COOK, HAROLD DALE, federal judge; b. Guthrie, Okla., Apr. 14, 1924; s. Harold Payton and Mildred Arvesta (Swanson) C.; children: Harold Dale II, Caren Irene, Randall Swanson; m. Kristen Elizabeth Ward; stepchildren: Kimberley Ward, Stephanie Ward, Erica Ward. BS in Bus., LLB, U. Okla., 1950, JD, 1970. Bar: Okla. 1950. Pvt. practice law, Guthrie, Okla., 1950; county atty. Logan County, Okla., 1951-54; asst. U.S. atty. Oklahoma City, 1954-58; assoc. Butler, Rinehart and Morrison, Oklahoma City, 1958-61; ptnr. Rinehart, Morrison and Cook, 1961-63; legal counsel and adviser to Gov. State of Okla., 1963-65; ptnr. Cook & Ming, Oklahoma City, 1965, Cook, O'Toole, Ming & Tourtellotte, Oklahoma City, 1966-68, Cook, O'Toole & Tourtellotte, 1969-70, Cook & O'Toole, 1971; gen. counsel Shepherd Mall State Bank, Oklahoma City, 1967-71, pres., 1969-71, chmn. bd., 1969-71; dir. Bur. of Hearings and Appeals, Social Security Adminstrn., HEW, 1971-74; judge U.S. Dist. Ct., Tulsa, 1974-79; chief judge U.S. Dist. Ct. (no. dist.) Okla., Tulsa, 1979-91, sr. judge, 1992—. Mem. legal adv. coun. Okla. Hwy. Patrol, 1969-70; mem. magistrates com. Jud. Conf. U.S., 1980-88; mem. indsl. adv. coun. Bur. Bus. and Econ.Rsch., U. Okla., 1970-71. First v.p. PTA, Sunset Elementary Sch., 1959-60; v.p. Parent-Tchrs. & Students Assn., John Marshall High Sch., Oklahoma City, 1970-71, pres., 1971; mem. Econ. Opportunity Com., Okla., 1963-65; tchr. Sunday sch. classes for coll., high sch. and adult ages Village Methodist Ch., Oklahoma City, 1959-65; mem. bd. of stewards First Meth. Ch., Guthrie, Okla., 1951-54. Served with USAAF, 1943-45. Recipient Secretary's Spl. Citation HEW, 1973 Fellow Am. Bar Found.; mem. ABA, Fed. Bar Assn., Okla. Bar Assn. (del. to state bar convs.), Oklahoma City C. of C. Clubs: So. Hills Country, Shriners, Masons, Tulsa, Order Eastern Star (past worthy patron Okla.). Republican. Office: Tulsa Fed Bldg Ste 241 224 S Boulder Ave Tulsa OK 74103-3026

COOK, HARRY CLAYTON, JR., lawyer; b. Washington, Mar. 25, 1935; s. Harry Clayton and Lillian June (A'harrah) Cook; m. Jane Clare Mellius, 1963 (div. 1974); children: Christianne Pier, Nicole, Harry Clayton III; m. Judith Ann Taber, 1994; children: Rebecca Lyeth Kelsey, Parker Burr Kelsey. BSChemE, Princeton U., 1956; LLB, U. Va., 1960. Bar: Colo. 1960, N.Y. 1961, Pa. 1966, D.C. 1973. Assoc. Sullivan & Cromwell, N.Y.C., 1960-63, Holme Roberts & Owen, Denver, 1964, Pepper Hamilton & Scheetz, Phila., 1965-69, ptnr., 1969-70, 73; on assignment as sr. tax counsel Sun Oil Co., Phila., 1970; ptnr. Cadwalader Wickersham & Taft, Washington, 1974-87, Bishop, Cook, Purcell & Reynolds, Washington, 1988-90; pvt. practice Langley, Va., 1991—2002; of counsel Bastianelli, Brown and Kelley, Washington, 1992—2002; ptnr. Mgmt. & Transp. Assoc., Inc., Essex, Conn., 2001—; sr. counsel Fulbright & Jaworski LLP, 2002—. Page to U.S. Sen. E. D. Millikin, Colo., 1950—52; gen. counsel Maritime Adminstrn.; mem. Maritime Subs. Bd., U.S. Dept. Commerce, Washington, 1970—73; U.S. del. to Soviet Union Maritime Agreement between U.S. and USSR, 1971—73; mem. Adminstv. Conf. U.S., 1980—90, chmn. com. jud. rev., 1982—88, sr. fellow, 1988—90; mem. Nat. Def. Exec. Res., U.S. Mil. Sealift Command, 1983—91, U.S. Office Tech. Assessment; mem. citizens adv. panel U.S. Maritime Ind., 1982—85, cargo policy workshop particpant, 1984—85. Mem. editl. bd.: Va. Law Rev., 1958—60, exec. editor:, 1959—60; contbr. articles to profl. jours. Dir. Com. on the Present Danger, 1978—87; bd. dirs. New World Inst., 2000—; bd. dir. Inst. Fgn. Policy Analysis, 1975—87. Mem.: ABA, Maritime Law Assn. U.S. (marine fin. com., proctor in admiralty), D.C. Bar Assn., Am. Law Inst. (life), Raven Soc., Univ. Club (N.Y.C.), Fishers Island Club (N.Y.), Chevy Chase (Md.) Club, Cosmos Club (Washington), Hay Harbor Club (N.Y.), Met. Club (Washington), Order of Colf, Phi Delta Phi. Home: 1011 Langley Hill Dr Mc Lean VA 22101-1709 Office: Ste 500 801 Pennsylvania Ave NW Washington DC 20004-2623 E-mail: plimsolldc@aol.com., ccook@fulbright.com.

COOK, HARVEY CARLISLE, law enforcement official; b. Cambridge, Md., June 19, 1936; s. John Morrison and Lula Arbelia (Warfield) C.; m. Shirley Marie Cox, Aug. 4, 1973; children: Brenda, Claudine, John, Anne. AA in Police Sci., Charles Ct. Community Coll., LaPlata, Md., 1973; BBA, U. Md., 1979, cert. in paralegal, 1980; cert. in criminal justice, FBI Nat. Acad., Quantico, Va., 1983. USCG Masters lic., 1988. Inspector Tidewater Fisheries Dept., Hughesville, Md., 1958-61, dist. inspector, 1962-64; lt. Md. State Marine Police, Hughesville, 1965-69, capt. LaPlata, 1970-72, Md. Natural Resources Police, LaPlata, 1973-75, maj. Annapolis, 1976-86, dep. supt., 1986-88; dir. Hovercraft tng. and ops. Hover Systems, Inc., 1988-93; dir. health & indsl. safety Mech. Constrn. Inc., 1994—; dir. marine & indsl. safety & security Cook & Assocs., 1995—. Liaison officer Emergency Mgmt. Agy., Pikesville, Md., 1974-86, USCG Aux., Balt., 1982-86. Bd. dirs. Charles County Fair, LaPlata, 1985. Recipient Ann. Safe Boating award USCG Aux., 1975, Instr. Svc. award, 2001, Pa. F & BC Instr. award, 2002; Disting. Svc. award Gov. of Md., 1987, C.G. Aux. Pub. Educator award, 1999, C.G. Sustained Aux. Svc. award, 2000; named Best Engring. Soldier Md. N.G. 121st Engr. Battalion, 1967, Disting. Citizen, Mass. Gov.'s Office, 1983; commd. Ky. Col., Gov. Ky., 1983. Mem. FOP, NRA (life), Nat. Police Officers Assn. Am. (charter), Hoverclub Am., U.S. Hovercraft Soc. Inc. (bd. dirs. 1987, v.p. 1990-92, pres. 1993), USCG Auxiliary (vice Flotilla comdr. 1996, comdr. 1997-98, Flotilla staff officer 1998-2002, Flotilla officer 2003), Chesapeake Bay Profl. Capts. Assn., Potomac River Pilots Assn., FBI Nat. Acad. Assocs., Dr. Samuel A. Mudd Soc. Inc. (treas. 1987), So. Md. Bd. Realtors, Md. Chiefs Police Assn., Charles County Cmty. Coll. Alumni Assn. (pres. 1984). Republican. Methodist. Avocations: hunting, fishing, power boating, antiques. Office: Cook & Assocs 408 Briarwood Rd Wallingford PA 19086-6503

COOK, IAN AINSWORTH, psychiatrist, researcher, educator; b. N.Y.C., May 1, 1960; s. Charles David and Bobette Cook. BS in Engring. magna cum laude, Princeton U., 1982; MD, Yale U., 1987. Diplomate Nat. Bd. Med. Examiners, Am. Bd. Psychiatry and Neurology. Resident in surgery U. Colo., Denver, 1987-88; resident in psychiatry Neuropsychiat. Inst. UCLA, 1991-94, chief resident in liaison psychiatry, 1993-94, instr. dept. psychiatry, 1995-96, assoc. dir. residency edn. dept. psychiatry, 1995-96, asst. prof psychiatry, 1996—; registrar Neuropsychiat. Inst., 1999—; dir. NPI Acad. Info. Tech. Core, 1999—; assoc. dir. Office of Profl. and Cmty. Edn., 1998—. Examiner Am. Bd. Psychiatry and Neurology, 1998—. Mem. editl. bd. Jefferson Jour. Psychiatry, 1992-94; contbr. articles to profl. jours. Rsch. fellow Nat. Inst. Mental Health, 1993-96; recipient Young Investigator award Nat. Alliance Rsch. Schizophrenia and Depression, 1995, 97. Mem. Am. Psychiat. Assn. (Burroughs-Wellcome fellow 1992, mem. com. of resident and fellows 1992-94, mem. steering com./practice guidelines 1994—), Nat. Eagle Scout Assn., Sigma Xi, Tau Beta Pi. Achievements include four patents in biomed. devices and methods. Office: UCLA Neuropsychiat Inst & Hosp 760 Westwood Plz Los Angeles CA 90095-8353

COOK, IVA DEAN, education educator; b. Palmero, W.Va., Jan. 13, 1927; d. Hobert and Elwa (Hill) Lovejoy; m. George William Cook, July 16, 1943; children: Brenda Sue Burford, Pamela Ann Marks. BA, Marshall U., 1963, MEd, 1967. Cert. in elem. and spl. edn., W.Va. Instr. Marshall U., Huntington, W.Va., 1966-67; spl. edn. tchr. Fairfield Spl. H.S., Huntington, 1963-65, 67-70; demonstration tchr. W.Va. Grad. Coll., Institute, 1969, asst. prof. spl. edn., 1970-79, assoc. prof., 1979-86, prof., mental retardation progrm coord., 1986-91, prof. spl. edn., 1970-91, prof. spl. edn. emerita, 1991—. Coord., adj. fculty orientation W.Va. Grad. Coll., 1992-94; mem. mental retardation task force W.Va. Dept. Edn., Charleston, 1984-88; cons. W.Va. Dept. Edn., 1970-91, U. Mo., Columbia, 1987-88. Author: Occupational Notebook Program, 1971; co-author: (5 books and 5 cassette tapes) Learning Through Reading, 1987; contbr. articles to profl. jours. Mem. adv. bd. W.Va. Senator Robert Holiday, 1987-88. Recipient awards for teaching and service. Mem. W.Va. State Coun. on Vocat. Edn., Coun. for Exceptional Children (past pres. div. on career devel.). Democrat. Presbyterian. Avocations: cooking, walking, writing, entertaining, volunteering.

COOK, JAMES IVAN, clergyman, religion educator; b. Grand Rapids, Mich., Mar. 8, 1925; s. Cornelius Peter and Cornelia (Dornbos) C.; m. Jean Rivenburgh, July 8, 1950; children: Mark James, Carol Jean, Timothy Scott, Paul Brian (dec.). BA, Hope Coll., 1948; MA, Mich. State U., 1949; BD, Western Theol. Sem., 1952; ThD, Princeton Theol. Sem., 1964. Ordained to ministry Reformed Ch. America, 1953. Pastor Blawenburg Reformed Ch., N.J., 1953-63; from instr. to asst. prof. bibl. langs. Western Theol. Sem., Holland, Mich., 1963-67, prof. bibl. langs. and lit., 1967-77, Anton Biemont prof. New Testament, 1977-95, prof. emeritus, 1995—; chmn. Theol. Commn., Reformed Ch. Am. N.Y.C., 1980-85; pres. Gen. Synod-Reformed Ch. Am., N.Y.C., 1982-83. Author: Edgar Johnson Goodspeed, 1981, Shared Pain and Sorrow: Reflections of a Secondary Sufferer, 1991, One Lord/One Body, 1991; editor Reformed Rev., 1987-2002; contbg. editor: Grace Upon Grace, 1975, Saved by Hope, 1978, The Church Speaks, 1985; founding editor Perspectives: A Jour. of Reformed Thought, 1986-90, The Church Speaker, vol. 2, 2002. Served with U.S. Army, 1943-45, ETO. Home: 1004 S Shore Dr Holland MI 49423-4539 Office: Western Theol Sem 101 E 13th St Holland MI 49423-3622

COOK, JAMES WESLEY, music educator; b. Fayetteville, NC, May 31, 1977; s. Jimmy Ray Cook and Wanda Sue Livengood. MusB in Edn., Appalachian State U., Boone, NC, 1999. Asst. adminstr. Fred J. Miller Inc., Dayton, Ohio, 1995—2001; dir. bands Jack Britt H.S., Fayetteville, NC, 2000—. Scholar Cratis Williams scholar, Appalachian State U. Mem.: NEA (assoc.), MENC (corr.), Theta Chi (assoc.). Avocations: music, swimming, movies. Home: 513-7 Meadowland Court Hope Mills NC 28348 Office: Jack Britt High School 7403 Rockfish Road Fayetteville NC 28348 Office Fax: 910-429-2810. Personal E-mail: cookjames@hotmail.com. E-mail: jamescook@ccs.k12.nc.us.

COOK, JANE HAMPTON, communications executive, consultant; b. Nurnberg, Bavaria, Germany, June 8, 1970; (parents Am. citizens); d. Larry Wayne and Judith Travis Hampton; m. John Kim Cook, Apr. 23, 1994. BA in Music, Baylor U., 1992; MS in Ednl. Adminstrn., Tex. A&M U., 1995. Spl. events coord. Tex. A&M U., Coll. Sta., Tex., 1995—98; internet comm. dir. and writer Office of the Gov. of Tex., Austin, Tex., 1998—2001; dep. dir. for internet news svcs. The White Ho., Washington, 2001—03; cons., spkr., writer Alexandria, Va., 2003—. Author: Maggie Houston: My Father's Honor, 2002. Spkr. Tex. Book Festival, Austin, 2002—02; vol. Rep. Nat. Conv., Phila., 2000—00; worship group leader McLean (Va.) Bible Ch., 2001—03. Fellow, White Ho. Hist. Assn. and Orgn. of Am. Historians, 2003—. Mem.: Soc. of Children's Book Writers and Illustrators (corr.), Orgn. of Am. Historians (assoc.). Achievements include design of first White House web site for President George W. Bush. Avocations: singing, writing, reading, crafts, walking.

COOK, JANICE ELEANOR NOLAN, retired elementary school educator; b. Middletown, Ohio, Nov. 22, 1936; d. Lloyd and Eleanor Lee (Caudill) Nolan; m. Kenneth J. Cook, May 16, 1980 (dec.); children: Gerald W. Fultz Jr., Jana Linn Perkins, Jennylee Heard. BSEd, Miami U., 1971; MEd, reading specialist cert., Xavier U., 1982, rank 1 cert., 1987, spl. edn. cert., 1988. Tchr. pre-sch. and elem. Middletown (Ohio) Pub. Schs., 1957-58, 71-80; tchr. Boone County Schs., Florence, Ky., 1980-99; ret., 1999. Resource tchr. Ky. Internship Program, 1985—95; substitute tchr. Lebanon City Schs. Fellow ABI Rsch. Assn. (life); mem. NEA, Nat. Assn. Edn. Young Children, Internat. Reading Assn., Nat. Coun. Tchrs. English, Ky. Edn. Assn., Boone County Edn. Assn., Assn. Childhood Edn. Internat., Nat. Coun. Tchrs. Math. Home: 926 Pineneedle Pl Maineville OH 45039-7019

COOK, JAY MICHAEL, accounting company executive; b. N.Y.C., Sept. 16, 1942; m. Mary Anne Griffith, July 11, 1964; children— Jennifer Lynn, Angela Marie, Jeffrey Thomas. BS in Bus. Adminstrn. cum laude, U. Fla., 1964. C.P.A., N.Y., Fla. Ptnr. Deloitte, Haskins & Sells, N.Y.C., 1974-81, ptnr.-in-charge Miami, 1981-83, mng. ptnr. N.Y.C., 1983-86, chmn., CEO, 1986-89, Deloitte & Touche, 1989-99; ret. Adv. com. Securities Regulation Inst., The Directorship Search Group; chmn. GAO Accountability Adv. Panel; bd. dirs. The Dow Chem. Co.; bd. dirs., chmn. audit com. Rockwell Automation, Internat. Flavors and Fragrances, Comcast Corp.; ind. trustee, bd. dirs. The Fidelity Group Mut. Funds. Bd. govs., past chmn. United Way Am.; chmn. emeritus Catalyst; mem. adv. com. Sch. Bus., U. Fla., Gainesville; past chmn. bd. trustees Fin. Acctg. Found. Recipient Disting. Alumnus award U. Fla., John McCloy award, 2001; named to Acctg. Hall of Fame, 1999. Mem. AICPA (mem. coun. 1983—, vice-chmn. 1985-86, chmn. 1986-87, John J. McCloy award 2001), Greenwich (Conn.) Country Club, Blind Brook Club. Republican. Presbyterian. Avocations: tennis, golf. Home: 980 Lake Ave Greenwich CT 06831-3032 E-mail: jmichaelcook@worldnet.att.net.

COOK, JEANNINE SALVO, library consultant; b. N.Y.C., Apr. 11, 1929; d. Ernest August and Edith Agatha (Lombardo) S.; m. Donald Carter Cook, June 9, 1962; 1 child, Carter Steven. BA, Hunter Coll., 1951; MLS, Columbia U., 1958, postgrad., 1973. Chemist Charles Pfizer and Co., Inc., Bklyn., 1951-56, lit. chemist, 1956-58; cen. med. librarian Am. Cyanamid, N.Y.C., 1958-60; sr. profl. adminstr. Engring. and phys. scis. library Columbia U., N.Y.C., 1960-62; assoc. librarian SUNY, Stony Brook, 1962-63; dir. Emma S. Clark Meml. Library, Setauket, N.Y., 1966-93; cons. Bro Dart, Williamsport, Pa., 1990—. Editorial adv. bd. Gale, Rsch. Pub., Detroit, 1989, adv. bd., 1986-88; design com. Gaylord Bros., Syracuse, N.Y., 1987. Pres. bd. dirs. 3 Village Community Youth Coun., Stony Brook, 1978-88; bd. dirs. Ministries Coun., Setauket, 1978-85, 3 V Schs.-Community Youth at Risk, Stony Brook, 1989—; co-chmn. edn. com. Assn. Community Univ. Cooperative, Stony Brook, 1973-80; v.p. Health House, 1991-93; bd. dirs. 3 Village Civic Assn., 1991-95; aux. mem.

Mather Meml. Hosp., 1991—, rec. sec., 2000—. Recognized for voluntarism Brookhaven Youth Bur., Setauket, 1984, for Outstanding Service Community Youth Services, Stony Brook, 1988; recipient Pub. Relations award Library Pub. Relations Coun., 1978. Mem. ALA (pub. relations award 1987), Brookhaven Library Dirs. (pres. 1976-80), Pub. Library Dirs. Assn. (exec. bd. 1976—), Spl. Library Assn., Med. Library Assn. Home and Office: 40 Seabrook Ln Stony Brook NY 11790-3328

COOK, JEFFREY ARTHUR, engineer; b. Port Clinton, Ohio, Feb. 5, 1951; s. Arthur George Cook and Fay Cecile Bush; m. Jane Marie Weekley, Feb. 16, 1974; 1 child, Adam Arthur. BS in mech. engring., Ohio State U., 1973; MS Electronics and Computer Control in electronics and computer control, Wayne State U., 1985. Staff tech. specialist Ford Motor Co. Fellow: IEEE. Achievements include 22 US patents on automotive control.

COOK, JENIK ESTERM (JENIK ESTERM COOK SIMONIAN), artist, educator; b. Rezaieh, Iran, July 7, 1940; came to U.S., 1964; d. Sameual Amijon and Nanajan (Amreh Sarkissian) Simonian; m. Carrol Ross Cook, Sept. 28, 1961; children: Fiona Gitana Cook Anderson, Herold H. Studied with Hossein Delrish, Iran, 1968-70; studied with Barbara Lae, Scotland, 1970-78; studied with Chalita Robinson, 1981-87, studied with Jake Lee, 1987-90, studied with Dr. Alex Vilumsons, 1988-94. Tchr. art. Resident artist Orlando Gallery, L.A.; art tchr. U. Judaism, Bel Air. One-woman shows include Pacific Design Ctr., L.A., 1996, Orlando Gallery, 1997, 98, Bakery Digital Post Prodn. Ctr., L.A., West Wood Fed. Bldg., L.A., 1999, Hilton Hotel, L.A., 1999; exhibited in groups shows at Orlando Gallery, 1998, L.A. Conv. Ctr., 1998. Rheinfelden (Germany) Town Hall, 1998, Gallery Merkel, Grenzack, Germany, 1998, L.A. Art Expo, 1998, MGM Conf. Ctr., 1999, Long Beach Conv. Ctr., 1999, Art 21, Las Vegas MGM Conv. Ctr., 1999, Art Expo, N.Y., 2000; set designer, scenic artist North Hollywood Ch. of Religious Sci., 1999. Office: Everywomans Village 5650 Sepulveda Blvd Van Nuys CA 91411-2981

COOK, JOHN GRANGER, religious studies educator, philosopher, educator; b. Miami, Fla., July 1, 1955; s. Walter Granger and Janet van de Erve Cook; m. Barbara Tyler Horton, June 14, 1980; children: Christopher Lee Horton-Cook, Elisabeth Granger Horton-Cook. BA, Davidson Coll., 1976; MDiv, Union Theol. Sem., Va., 1979, PhD, Emory U., 1985. Pastor Reems Creek Presbyn. Parish, Weaverville, NC, 1985—91; post doctoral rschr. Emory U., Atlanta, 1991—94; prof. religion and philosophy LaGrange (Ga.) Coll., 1994—. Author: (book) The Structure and Persuasive Power of Mark. A Linguistic Approach, 1995, The Interpretation of the New Testament in Greco-Roman Paganism, 2000; contbr. articles to profl. jours. Asst. scout master Boy Scouts Am., LaGrange, 2000—02. Mem.: Soc. Bibl. Lit., Phi Beta Kappa. Avocation: hiking. Office: LaGrange College 601 Broad St Lagrange GA 30240

COOK, JOHN ROSCOE, JR., insurance executive; b. Houston, Apr. 17, 1943; s. John Roscoe and Ruth Mildred (Spargo) C.; m. Loxi June Gumienny, Aug. 28, 1964 (dec. 1993); children: John T., Andrew J., Wesley A.; m. Crystal R.E. Grennan, May 6, 2000. BA, U. Houston, 1968. With Allstate Ins. Co., Houston, various states including, Pa., Tex., Ill. and Va., 1968-80; v.p. pub. affairs Am. Ins. Assn., Washington, 1980-85; sr. v.p. Ins. Inst. for Hwy. Safety, Washington, 1985-87, exec. v.p., 1987-89; sr. v.p., chief comm. officer USAA, San Antonio, 1989-97, Nationwide Ins. Enterprise, Columbus, Ohio, 1997—2003. Chmn. Walkamerica March of Dimes, Franklin County, Ins. Edn. Foun., Columbus Jazz Arts, Riverwalk, Live at the Landing, Buckeye Ranch Found. Fellow Pub. Rels. Soc. Am.; mem. Nat. Press Club, Capitol Hill Club, The Lakes C.C., The Capitol Club, Club Giraud. Home: 2433 Edington Rd Columbus OH 43221-3047

COOK, J(OHN) ROWLAND, lawyer; b. Dallas, July 20, 1942; s. John Hubbard and Nancy Eva Cook; m. April Beall, Dec. 24, 1966 (div. 1984); children: Matthew Rowland, Samantha, Joshua Malcolm, Abigail; m. Diane E. Ireson, Aug. 10, 1990; stepchildren: Eric Perlmutter, Lindsay Perlmutter. Student, Tex. A&M U., 1960, So. Meth. U., 1961; BBA, U. Tex., 1964, LLB, 1965. Tax law specialist IRS, Washington, 1965-66; adminstrv./legis. asst. U.S. congressman J. J. Pickle, Washington, 1966-69; spl. counsel, staff atty. div. corp. fin. SEC, Washington, 1969-76, chief, asst. dir. Office of Disclosure Policy and Proceedings div. corp. fin., 1976-79; asst. atty. gen. ins., banking and securities dept. State of Tex., Austin, 1979-80; from assoc. to ptnr. Salmanson, Smith & Mouer, Austin, 1980-81; ptnr., mem. Johnson & Wortley, P.C., Austin, 1981-95; ptnr. Jenkens & Gilchrist, P.C., Austin, 1995—. Bd. dirs., pres. Travis County Dispute Resolution Ctr., 1990-95. Contbr. articles to profl. jours. Bd. dirs. Peoples' Cmty. Clinic. Office: Jenkens & Gilchrist PC 2200 One American Center 600 Congress Ave Austin TX 78701-3238

COOK, JOHN WESLEY, foundation administrator; b. Mar. 1, 1933; m. Phyllis Carol Depp, Apr. 14, 1962; children: Stephanie, Clayton. BA, Baylor U., 1954; MDiv, Yale U., 1957, MPhil, 1973, PhD, 1975; LLD (hon.), Valparaiso U., 1995. Ordained minister United Ch. of Christ, 1963. Prof. religion and arts Yale U., New Haven, 1971-92, prof. emeritus, 1992—; pres. The Henry Luce Found., N.Y.C., 1992—. Lectr. in field; lectr. twentieth century art Lady Margaret Hall, Oxford, England, 1996; dir. Yale Inst. Sacred Music, New Haven, 1984-92, dir. religion and the arts program, 1978-84; minister 1st Congregational Ch., Derby, Conn., 1965-68, River Oaks Ch., Houston, 1963-65; cons. NEH, 1976, 77; vis. prof. Kalamazoo (Mich.) Coll., 1974, 76. Co-author: Conversations with Architects, 1973; contbr. articles to profl. jours. Fulbright fellow, 1970-71, NDEA fellow, 1968-70; recipient disting. alumnus award Baylor U., Waco, Tex., 1993; grantee The Henry Luce Found., 1977-80, Lilly Endowment, 1987-93, Menil Found., 1991; Rayzor scholar fellow, 1960-62. Office: The Henry Luce Found 111 W 50th St New York NY 10020-1202

COOK, JOSEPH V. physician; b. Brigham City, Utah, Sept. 7, 1935; s. Joseph Vernon and Berniece (Kimball) C.; m. Nancy Carlson, July 7, 1958; children: Joseph David, John Carlson, Paul Carlson. BS, Utah State U., 1959; MD, U. Utah, 1962. Diplomate Am. Bd. Family Practice. Med. intern U. Okla., 1963; pvt. practice San Mateo, Calif., 1967-89; chmn. Family Med. Clinics, San Mateo, 1982-89; sr. v.p., med. dir. Bay Pacific Health Plan, San Bruno, Calif., 1989-91; med. dir. Aetna Health Plan, San Bruno, 1991-93; v.p. med. affairs Medspan Inc., Hartford, Conn., 1993-98; chief med. officer Health Plan of the Redwoods, Santa Rosa, Calif., 1998—2001. Clin. faculty U. Calif., San Francisco, 1971-93, clin. prof., 1990-93, 1999-2003. Contbr. articles to profl. jour. Mission pres. Pa. Phila. Mission Ch. of Jesus Christ of Latter-day Saints, 2001—. Lt. USN, 1963-67. Recipient award of merit Am. Bd. Family Practice, 1995 Republican. Office: 300 W State St Ste # 107 Media PA 19063 E-mail: jvccook@aol.com.

COOK, JULIAN ABELE, JR., federal judge; b. Washington, June 22, 1930; s. Julian Abele and Ruth Elizabeth (McNeill) C.; m. Carol Annette Dibble, Dec. 22, 1957; children: Julian Abele III, Peter Dibble, Susan Annette. BA, Pa. State U., 1952; JD, Georgetown U., 1957, LLD (hon.), 1992; LLM, U. Va., 1988; LLD (hon.), U. Detroit, 1996, Wayne State U., 1997. Bar: Mich. 1957. Law clk. to judge, Pontiac, Mich., 1957-58; pvt. practice Detroit, 1958-78; judge U.S. Dist. Ct. (ea. dist.) Mich., Detroit, 1978, chief judge, 1989-96, sr. judge, 1996—. Spl. asst. atty. gen. State of Mich., 1968-78; adj. prof. U. Detroit Sch. Law, 1971-74; gen. counsel pub. TV Sta. WTVS, 1973-78; labor arbitrator Am. Arbitration Assn. and Mich. Employment Rels. Commn., 1975-78; mem. Mich. State Bd. Ethics, 1977-78; instr. trial advocacy workshop Harvard U., 1988—, trial advocacy program U.S. Dept. Justice, 1989-90; com. on fin. disclosure Jud. Conf. U.S., 1988-93, chmn., 1990-93; screening panel NYU Root-Tilden-Snow Scholarship Program, 1991, 96—; mem. U.S. Sentencing Commn. Judicial Adv. Group, 1996-98; mem. nat. bd. trustees Am. Inn Ct., 1996—; mem. adv. com. Nat. Publs., 1994-96, chmn. nat. nominations and election com., 1994-95; pres. chpt. XI, Master of Bench, 1984-95. Contbr. articles to profl. jours. Exec. bd. dirs. Child and Family Svcs. Mich., 1968-89, past pres., 1975-76; bd. dirs. Am. Heart Assn. Mich., 1968-89, Hutzel Hosp., 1984-95; chmn. Mich. Civil Rights Commn., 1968-71; co-chair exec. com. Walter P. Reuther Libr. Labor and Urban Affairs, Wayne State U.; mem. bd. visitors Georgetown U. Law Ctr., 1992—. With Signal Corps, U.S. Army, 1952-54. Recipient Merit citation Pontiac Area Urban League, 1971, Pathfinders award Oakland U., 1977, Svc. award Todd-Phillips Home, Inc., 1978, Disting. Alumnus award Pa. State U., 1987, Georgetown U., 1989, Focus and Impact award Oakland U., 1985; resolution Mich. Ho. of Reps., 1971, Outstanding Community Svc. award Va. Park Community Investment Assocs., 1992, 1st Ann. Trailblazers award D. Augustus Straker Bar Assn., 1993, Renowned Jurist award Friends of African Art, 1993, Brotherhood award Jewish War Vets. U.S., 1994, Paul R. Dean award Georgetown U. Law Sch., 1997; named Boss of Yr., Oakland County Legal Secs. Assn., 1974, one of Mich. Most Respected Judges, Mich. Law Weekly, 1990-91; named one of the Best Judges, Detroit Monthly, 1991; named Disting. Citizen of Yr., NAACP Oakland County, Mich., 1970. Fellow Am. Bar Found., Mich. Bar Found. (vice-chmn. 1992-93, chmn. 1993—); mem. NAACP (mem. state constl. revision and legal redress com. 1963, Disting. Citizen of Yr. 1970, Presdl. award North Oakland County, Mich. chpt. 1987), ABA, Fed. Bar Assn. (fed.-state ct. seminar lectr. Detroit chpt. 1981—), Mich. Bar Assn. (chmn. constl. law com. 1969, vice-chmn. civil liberties com. 1970, co-chmn. profl. devel. task force 1984-87, U.S. cts. com. 1988-95, com. on professionalism 1991—, Champion of Justice 1994), Mich. Tribunal Assn. (bd. dirs. 3rd cir. 1992-98), Detroit Bar Assn. (Bench-Bar award 1987), Oakland County Bar Assn. (chmn. continuing legal edn. com. 1968-69, jud. liaison Dist. Ct. com. 1977, unauthorized practice law com. 1977), Wolverine Bar Assn. (Bench-Bar award 1987, D. Augustus Straker award 1988), Mich. Assn. Black Judges, Am. Inn of Ct. (founder Met. Detroit chpt., pres., master of bench, chmn. 6th cir. com. on standard jury instructions 1986—), Am. Law Inst., Union Black Episcopalians (Detroit chpt., Absalom Jones award 1988), Justice Frank Murphy Honor Soc.

COOK, KARLA JOAN, elementary education educator; b. L.A., June 24, 1939; d. Charles Paul and Helen Barbara (Hamel) Belanger; m. John Rencoret, Aug. 1962 (div. 1964); 1 child, Renee; m. John Cook, Mar. 15, 1973 (div., 1983); children: Michael Donovan, Melody Marie. AB, Compton Jr. Coll., 1963; BA, Calif. State U., L.A., 1970. Cert. life tchr., Calif. Bookkeeper, asst. 1st Nat. Bank, N.Y.C., 1957-58; bookkeeper, vault teller 1st Western Bank, L.A., 1958-61; Blue-line operator County Sanitation, L.A., 1963-66; tchr. Long Beach (Calif.) Unified Sch. Dist., 1971-72, L.A. Unified Sch. Dist., Calif., 1974-94, 96—, Anaheim (Calif.) Sch. Dist., 1994-96; film background artist many casting cos., 1994—. Founder, dir. Crisis Intervention Resource and Referral Agy., South Gate, Calif., 1991-95; dir. Sunday sch. program Lynwood Ch. of God, 1995. Mem. Christian Blue Collar Workers (pres. 1990-91), United Tchrs. L.A. (chpt. chair 1990-91). Democrat. Avocations: painting, dancing, acting, poetry writing, sculpture. Home: 1602 E Harding St Long Beach CA 90805

COOK, KATHRYN ANNE, secondary school educator; b. Coral Gables, Fla., Dec. 5, 1951; d. Raymond Clarence Cook and Dorothea Pauline Glühr-Cook; 1 child, Kimberley Spinney. BA, Marquette U., 1973; diploma in German lang., Goethe Inst., Passau, Germany, 1973; EdM, Cambridge Coll., 1998. English tchr. Goethe Inst., Germany, 1973; liason officer Royal Embassy Saudi Arabia, London, 1973—76, Riyad, Saudi Arabia, 1973—76; adminstrv. asst. Dr. Kenneth G. Robbins, DDS, Springfield, Mass., 1988—96; computer tchr. Mount Carmel Sch., Springfield, 1989—95; telemarketer Media One, Springfield, 1991—98; tchr. City of Springfield Dept. Edn., 1996—. Tutor Mass Comprehensive Assessment Sys. Dept. Edn., Springfield, 2000—; tchrs. tutor City of Springfield, 2000—; athletes tutor Play It Smart, Springfield, 2001—. Author: Journey Through the Abyss, 2000. Mass. state advisor Rep. Nat. Com., Springfield, 2001. Mem.: Alumni Assn. Marquette, Phi Mu, Alpha Delta Kappa (historian elect 2000—). Republican. Lutheran. Avocations: writing, horseback riding, rowing, travel, cooking. Home: 151 White St Springfield MA 01108

COOK, KENNETH RAY, radiologist; b. Sublette, Kans., Sept. 16, 1953; s. Curtis Carl and Carmen Madonna (Countryman) Cook; m. Paula Rose Petryszyn, July 22, 1978; children: Erin Michelle, Leah Nicole, Tara Rachelle. AA, Hutchinson Community Coll., Kans., 1976; BA, U. Kans., 1979, MD, 1983. Diplomate Am. Coll. of Radiology. Resident in diagnostic radiology U. Kans. Med. Ctr., 1983-87; pvt. practice, Corpus Christi, Tex., 1987—; chmn. mgmt. com. Radiology Assocs., Corpus Christi, Tex., 1997—2002. Staff radiologist Spohn Meml. Med. Ctr., Columbia N.W., Corpus Christi, 1987-99; chief radiology Bay Area Med. Ctr., 1993-99, vice chmn., trustee, 1993-94, chmn., 1994-96; bd. dirs. BAMC, 1993-98, chief radiology Rehab. Hosp. South Tex., 1989-91; asst. clin. prof. family practice U. Tex., San Antonio; med. dir. Del Mar Coll. Ultrasound Technol. Sch.; chief Corpus Christi Med. Ctr., 1998-99. Recipient Resident Teaching award, Dept. Radiology, U. Kans., Kansas City, 1985-86, Resident Teaching award, Med. Ctr. Kans. U., 1986-87. Mem. AMA, Am. Coll. Radiology, Radiologic Soc. N. Am., Tex. Med. Soc., Tex. Radiologic Soc., Am. Inst. Ultrasound in Medicine, Nueces County Med. Soc. Republican. Roman Catholic. Avocations: fishing, hunting, camping, boating, golfing. Office: Radiology Assocs PO Box 5608 Corpus Christi TX 78465-5608 E-mail: kcook@xraydocs.com., kcook963@msn.com.

COOK, KIM DIANE, concert cellist; d. Willard Allen Cook and Doris Ann Powell. MusB, U. Ill., 1979; MusM, Yale U., 1981. Prin. solo cellist Wurzburg (Germany) Chamber Orch., 1980; faculty Sch. Music, Piracicaba, Brazil, 1982—83; prin. cellist Sao Paulo (Brazil) State Symphony, 1982—85; prof. cello U. St. Marcellina, Sao Paulo, 1983—84, U. Faculdade Mozarteum, Sao Paulo, 1983—84; asst. prof. music N.Mex. State U., Las Cruces, 1985—90; prof. music Pa. State U., University Park, 1991—. Pres. Gardiner/Cook Cello Endowment, State College, Pa., 2001—. Contbr. articles to profl. jours.; performer: (CD recordings) Trios by Brahms and Ravel, with Castalia Trio, 1994, Haydn Concertos with Dvorak Collegium, 1995, Solo Sonatas by Kodaly, Crumb and Hindemith, 1998, Dvorak Concerto, Bruch's Kol Nidrei, Pololanik's Capriccio, with Bohuslav Martinu Philharm., 2003. Named Artistic Amb., State Dept., Washington, 1996, Honored Musician, Jiangsu Opera and Dance Theater, Nanjing, China, 1997, Cultural Exch. Artists, Cleve. Ptnr. Cities/Volgograd, Russia, 1990—91, prize winner, Internat. Cello Competition, Brazil, 1982; recipient Achievement award, Women's Commn., 1998, selected as Roster Artist, Pen Performing Arts on Tour (PAT), Mid-Atlantic Arts Found., 2000—; grantee, Coll. Arts and Arch., 1995—2002, Inst. for the Arts and Humanities, 1995—2002, Pa. Performing Arts on Tour, 2001; Term fellow, Inst. for the Arts and Humanities, 1999—2001. Mem.: N.Y. Cello Soc., Chamber Music Am., Am. String Tchrs. Assn. (advisor Pa. state chpt. 1994—97, guest artist S.C. 2002, grantee 2002), Phi Kappa Phi, Pi Kappa Lambda. Office: Pa State Sch Music 233 Music Bldg University Park PA 16802

COOK, LARRY NORMAN, pediatrician, neonatologist, educator; b. Erie, Pa., Dec. 8, 1943; s. Charles Fremonst and Virginia June (Weinheimer) C.; m. Christine Louise DuBois, June 17, 1973; children: Kirk, Brian, Amelia. BS with honors, U. Louisville, 1964, MD with highest honors, 1968. Diplomate Am. Bd. Pediat., Am. Bd. Neonatal-Perinatal Medicine; cert. in neonatal advanced life support; cert. in controlled substances Drug Enforcement Adminstrn.; cert. in aspects of AIDS, Ky. Straight pediatric intern U. Colo. Med. Ctr., Denver, 1968, resident in pediat., 1969; fellow in neonatology U. Louisville Sch. Medicine, 1970-72, asst. clin. prof. pediat., 1972-74, asst. clin. prof. ob.-gyn., 1972-79, assoc. prof. pediat. and ob-gyn., 1979-84, prof. pediat., 1984—, billy F. Andrews prof., chmn. dept., 1994—, co-dir. divsn. neonatology, 1974-94; pvt. practice, Louisville, 1984—. Cons. on neonatology Ireland Army Hosp., Ft. Knox, Ky., 1974—, St. Joseph's Informary, Louisville, 1974-76; chief staff Kosair Children's Hosp., Louisvllle, 1994—; pres. Med. Sch. Fund, Louisville, 1994—; numerous presentations in field. Contbg. author: Fetal and Maternal Medicine, 1980, Management of High Risk Pregnancy, 1980, 85; contbr. over 200 articles and abstracts to med. jours., including Pediat., Am. Jour. Ob-Gyn., Am. Jour. Diseases of Children, Jour. Ky. Med. Assn., Archives Perinatal Medicine. Mem. med. adv. ad hoc com. Louisville area region ARC Blood Svcs., 1982-84; bd. dirs., mem. exec. com. Univ. Pediat. Found., Inc., Louisville, 1983—, acting pres., 1992-94, pres., 1995—; trustee Children's Hosp. Found., Alliant Health Sys., Louisville, 1991—; pres. Louisville Pediatric Found., Inc., 1993—. Maj. M.C., U.S. Army, 1972-74. Named Outstanding Young Man of Ky., Ky. Jaycees, 1977; recipient Lawrence Grever award Nat. Assn. Residents and Interns, 1993, Order of Merit award U. Louisville Alumni Assn., 1996, Roger J. Fox award Kosair Charities, 1998; alumni scholar U. Ky., 1964, summer rsch. scholar, 1965-67, Pfizer med. scholar, 1966, John Walker Moore scholar, 1967; Norman Joliffe med. student fellow, 1967; numerous grants, 1974—, including Burroughs Wellcome Co., WHAS Crusade for Children, Humana Inc., Univ. Health Care, Inc. Mem. AMA, Am. Acad. Pediat. (manuscript reviewer Pediat. 1991—), Assn. Am. Med. Colls., Assn. Med. Sch. Pediatric Dept. Chairmen (exec. com. 1993—), Extracorporeal Lif Support Orgn. (treas. 1989—), Am. Pediatric Soc., So. Perinatal Assn., So. Soc. for Pediatric Rsch., Ky. Pediatric Soc. (exec. com. 1993—), Ky. Med. Assn. (maternal and child health adv. bd. 1974—), Calif. Perinatal Assn., Jefferson County Med. Soc., Louisville Pediatric Soc., Med. Sch. Practice Assn. (pres. 1993—), Alpha Omega Alpha. Avocations: fly fishing, hiking, interior design. Office: U Louisville Dept Pediat 571 S Floyd St Ste 300 Louisville KY 40202-3829

COOK, LINDA KAY, critical care nurse; b. Olean, N.Y., Jan. 14, 1955; d. William Reese and Helen Cora (Torrey) Miller; m. B. Bruce Cook, May 23, 1981. Diploma in Nursing, Genesee Hosp. Sch. Nursing, Rochester, N.Y., 1976; AA, Monroe C.C., 1976; BSN, Alfred U., 1979; MS, U. Md., 1997, postgrad., 2001. Cert. CCRN; cert. ACLS instr.; cert. CCNS, ANCP, BC. Staff nurse Drs. Cmty. Hosp., Lanham, Md., 1979—86; patient care coord. Doctor's Cmty. Hosp. PG County, Lanham, 1986—94; coord. cardiac rehab. Drs. Cmty. Hosp., Lanham, 1994—98, clin. edn. specialist, 1998—2000, staff nurse critical care, 2001—, spl. project coord., 2002—; clin. nurse specialist Johns Hopkins Bayview Med. Ctr., Balt., 2000—01, Doctors Cmty. Hosp., 2002—. Mem. Nat. Assn. Clin. Nurse Specialists, Am. Assn. Critical Care Nurses, Nurse Practitioner Assn. Md., Heart Failure Soc. Am. Home: 7128 Cipriano Springs Dr Lanham Seabrook MD 20706-3835

COOK, LYNN J. nursing educator; b. Newark, Aug. 18, 1950; d. George Roy Cook and Jean Aileen (Wegner) Cook Ainsley; m. Troy Wagner Ray, Mar. 11, 1995. Diploma, Mass. Gen. Hosp. Sch. Nursing, 1971; BSN, U. Va., 1975; MPH, Boston U. Sch. Pub. Health, 1986. RN, Pa.; cert. neonatal nurse practitioner. From staff nurse newborn ICU to nursing dir. for neonatal transport and perinatal outreach edn. U. Va., Charlottesville, 1973-83, nat. coord. for the perinatal continuing edn. program, 1983—. Coord. perinatal edn. for Poland/Project HOPE, Millwood, Va., Krakow, Poland, 1986-89; lectr., gen. faculty U. Va. Sch. Medicine, 1992—; staff NICU Hosp. U. Pa., Phila., 1991-93; mem. Va. Perinatal Svcs. Adv. Coun. to Va. Dept. Health, 1979-83; fellow Project HOPE, Hangzhou, China, 1985. Author: Perinatal Continuing Education Program, 1978—; contbr. articles to profl. jours. Recipient outstanding instrnl. devel. award, Nat. Soc. Performance & Instrn., 1979. Mem. Assn. Womens Health, Obstet.-Neonatal Nursing (Excellence in Edn. award 2002), Nat. Assn. Neonatal Nurses, Nat. Perinatal Assn., Phila. Perinatal Soc., Del. Valley Assn. Neonatal Nurses. Office: Perinatal Continuing Edn Program U Va Health Sys Dept of Pediatrics PO Box 800386 Charlottesville VA 22908-0386

COOK, MARCELLA KAY, retired theater educator; b. Albuquerque, Dec. 22, 1949; d. Joseph Raymond and Vivian Francis (Mullinax) Murdick; m. James Rogers Cook, Mar. 25, 1975 (dec. Aug. 1991); 1 child, Amanda Kay. BA, U. Albuquerque, 1971; MA, Eastern N.Mex. U., 1973. Prof. theatre, speech Vernon (Tex.) Coll., 1973—2002; co-owner, publicity dir. Umpire Entertainment and Enterprise Records, 1998—2001; ret., 2002. Fine arts chair Vernon Regional Jr. Coll., 1982—87, 1997—2001; stage mgr. Columbia Cmty. Concert Series, 1976—91; actress, dir. Bill Fegan Attractions, Raton, N.Mex., 1974; costume designer Ea. N.Mex. U., Portales, 1972—73; head wardrobe mistres Cinegai Films, Rome, 1971, Paramount Studios, 1971. Writer, dir. : (plays) Waggoner Ranch's Entry Tex. Ranch Roundup, 1987, 1988, 1989. Named Outstanding Young Women Am., 1978; recipient Humanitarian Svc. award, Tex. Army N.G., 1979, Am. Coll. Theater Festival awards Excellence in Directing, 1987, 1997, Friends of Arts award, 2002; grantee, Stokes Found., Tex. Commn. Arts. Mem.: S.W. Theatre Assn., Tex. Ednl. Theatre Assn., Delta Psi Omega, Alpha Psi Omega, Phi Theta Kappa. Avocations: sculpting, travel, collecting classic cars, collecting classic rock and roll music. Home: 6309 Vista Montaro NW Albuquerque NM 87120

COOK, SISTER M(ARY) MERCEDES, educator, educational administrator; b. Hagerstown, Md., Dec. 18, 1939; d. Garland and Anita Rideoutt (Willis) C. Student, Fordham U.; BA, Ea. Conn. State U., 1974, MS, 1983; grad., Norwich Dicocesan Prins. Acad., Conn., 1991. Joined Sistes of Charity of Our Lady of Mother of the Ch., Roman Cath. Ch.; cert. tchr., Conn. Tchr., prin. St. Joseph Sch., Baltic, Conn., 1959-61; tchr. Sacred Heart Sch., Byram, Conn., 1961-63, Bloomfield, Conn., 1963-66, Taftville, Conn., 1966-67, Acad. of Holy Family, Baltic, 1967-84; tchr., vice prin. Assumption Sch., Manchester, 1984—; vice-prin., tchr., chair dept. English, guide counselor Acad. of the Holy Family, Baltic, Conn., 1990—2003; dir. Sacred Heart Ednl. Ctr., Baltic, 2003—. Mem.: Nat. Cath. Ednl. Assn., Math. Assn. Am., Nat. Coun. Tchrs. English. Republican. Avocations: reading, writing, painting, cooking, interior decorating.

COOK, MAURICE GAYLE, soil science educator, consultant; b. Frankfort, Ky., Dec. 26, 1931; s. Price Cash and Evelyn (Moore) C.; m. Eva Nancy Blalock, Aug. 27, 1966; 1 child, Stephen Price. BS, U. Ky., 1957, MS, 1959; PhD, Va. Poly. Inst., 1961. From asst. prof. to prof. N.C. State U., Raleigh, 1961-92, Alumni Disting. prof., 1975; ret., 1992. Spl. advisor Gov. N.C., 1999-2000. Author: Concepts in Soil Science, 1973; contbr. numerous articles to profl. jours. With U.S. Army, 1957; col. USAR, 1962-90. Named to Hall of Disting. Alumni, U. Ky., 2000. Fellow Soil Sci. Soc. Am., Am. Soc. Agronomy, Soil and Water Conservation Soc. (bd. dirs. 1979-88, pres. 1986-87), Nat. Assn. Colls. and Tchrs. Agr.; mem. Soil Sci. Soc. N.C. (Achievement award 1991), N.C. Divsn. Soil and Water Conservation (exec. dir. 1982-84), Am. Water Resources Assn., Internat. Erosion Control Assn., Gamma Sigma Delta (Merit award 1986), Epsilon Sigma Phi, Alpha Zeta (pres. 1976-85). Democrat. Baptist. Home: 3458 Leonard St Raleigh NC 27607-6827 Office: NC State U Dept Soil Science Raleigh NC 27695-0001 E-mail: mgcook@mindspring.com.

COOK, MERRILL A. former congressman, explosives industry executive; b. Phila., May 6, 1946; s. Melvin A. and Wanda (Garfield) C.; m. Camille Sanders, Oct. 24, 1969; children: Brian, Alison, Barbara Ann, David, Michelle. BA magna cum laude, U. Utah, 1969; MBA, Harvard U., 1971. Profl. staff cons. Arthur D. Little, Inc., Cambridge, Mass., 1971-73; mng. dir. Cook Assocs., Inc., Salt Lake City, 1973-78; pres. Cook Slurry Co., Salt Lake City, 1978—; mem. U.S. Congress from 2d Utah dist., 1997-2001. Patentee in field. Del. Rep. Nat. Conv., Kansas City, Mo., 1976, San Diego, 1996, Phila., 2000. Mem. Salt Lake City C. of C., Phi Kappa Phi. Republican. Mem. Lds Ch.*

COOK, MICHAEL ALLAN, social sciences educator; b. Newark, Eng., Dec. 24, 1940; s. John Manuel and Enid May (Robertson) Cook. BA, Cambridge (Eng.) U., 1963. Lectr. Sch. Oriental and African Studies U. London, 1966—84, reader, 1984—86; Cleveland E. Dodge prof. Near Ea. studies Princeton (N.J.) U., 1986—. Author: Early Muslim Dogma, 1981, Muhammad, 1983, The Koran, 2000, others. Fellow: Royal Asiatic Soc.; mem.: Am. Philos. Soc., Am. Oriental Soc. Office: Princeton Univ Dept Near Eastern Studies Princeton NJ 08544 E-mail: mcook@princeton.edu.

COOK, MICHAEL BLANCHARD, government executive; b. Buffalo, May 8, 1942; s. Gerhard Albert and Lura (Lincoln) C.; m. Le Thi Kim Oanh, Feb. 10, 1942; children: Arthur, Benjamin. BA, Swarthmore Coll., 1963; postgrad., Princeton U.; B in Philosophy, Oxford U., 1966. Field advisor Agy. for Internat. Devel., Saigon, Vietnam, 1966-68; model cities rep. HUD, Phila., 1968-70; consular officer Dept. of State, Udorn, Thailand, 1971-73; exec., Water Programs EPA, Washington, 1973-80, superfund dir., 1980-81, dep. dir. hazardous waste, 1981-85, dir. drinking water, 1985-91, dir. wastewater enforcement and compliance, 1991-94, dir. wastewater mgmt., 1994—2002, dir. superfund remediation and technology innovation, 2002—. Author numerous articles on sewage treatment, hazardous waste and drinking water. Rhodes scholar Rhodes Trust, Oxford U., Eng., 1964; recipient Meritorious Honor awards U.S. Dept. of State, 1967, 72, Gold, Silver, Bronze medals EPA, 1975-87, Disting. Exec. award, Pres. Ronald Reagan, 1987. Avocations: coaching wrestling, running marathons, triathlete. Home: 3406 Rose Ln Falls Church VA 22042-4015 Office: EPA Emergency and Remedial Response 5201G 1200 Pennsylvania Ave NW Washington DC 20460-4201 E-mail: cook.mike@epa.gov.

COOK, MICHAEL HARRY, lawyer; b. June 9, 1947; s. Leonard James and Ethel (Shapiro) C.; m. Michele Anne Reday, Apr. 21, 1979; children: Noah Reday, Megan Rose. Student, U. Wis., Madison, 1965-66; BA with honors cum laude, Temple U., 1969; JD, Villanova U., 1973. Bar: Pa. 1973, D.C. 1979, U.S. Dist. Ct. (no. dist.) Ill. 1977, U.S. Dist. Ct. D.C. 1981, U.S. Ct. Claims 1982, U.S. Ct. Appeals (3d cir.) 1982, U.S. Ct. Appeals (5th cir.) 1981, U.S. Ct. Appeals (9th cir.) 1979, U.S. Ct. Appeals (11th cir.) 1981, U.S. Ct. Appeals (7th cir.) 1984, U.S. Ct. Appeals (10th cir.) 1984, U.S. Ct. Appeals (fed. cir.) 1984,

U.S. Ct. Appeals (D.C. cir.) 1981, U.S. Supreme Ct. 1976. Atty. Gen. Counsel's Office U.S. Dept. Health and Human Svcs., Washington, 1973-80; assoc. Wood, Lucksinger & Epstein, Washington, 1981-85, ptnr., 1985-90, Katten, Muchin & Zavis, Washington, 1991-97; mem. Mintz, Levin, Cohn, Ferris, Glovsky and Popeo, P.C., Washington, 1997-98; shareholder Jenkens & Gilchrist, P.C., Washington, 1998—. Lectr. Am. Health Lawyers Assn., Aspen Sys., Inc., various state and nat. hosps. and long-term care assns. Lectr.: Am. Health Lawyers Assn., : Aspen Sys., Inc., : various state and nat. hosps. and long-term care assns., contbg. author: book Handbook of Subacute Health Care, 1994, Subacute Care: A Guide to Devel., Implementation and Mgmt., 1995, The Long Term Care Handbook: Regulatory, Operational, and Fin. Guideposts, 2000; contbr. articles to profl. health care jours. V.p. Taylor Run Citizens Assn., Alexandria, Va., 1982-84, pres., 1984-85, bd. dirs., 1985—. Named to 100 Most Influential People in Long Term Care, 1996; Pres.'s scholar Temple U., Phila., 1969. Mem.: ABA, Nat. Assn. for Support of Long Term Care, Assisted Living Fedn. Am. (former mem. task force on managed care, former mem. public policy force, leadership coun., mem. pres.'s coun., mem. legal task force), Sword Soc., Tau Epsilon Phi, Phi Eta Sigma. Democrat. Jewish. Home: 2724 King St Alexandria VA 22302-4009 Office: Jenkens & Gilchrist a Profl Corp Ste 600 1919 Pennsylvania Ave NW Washington DC 20006-3404 E-mail: mhcook@jenkens.com.

COOK, MICHAEL LEWIS, lawyer; b. Rochester, N.H., Mar. 5, 1944; s. Israel J. and Molly L. Cook; m. Roberta Tross, Feb. 25, 1995; children: Jonathan, Alexander. AB, Columbia U., 1965; JD, NYU, 1968. Bar: N.Y. 1968. Assoc. Weil, Gotshal & Manges, N.Y.C., 1970-75, ptnr., 1975-80, Skadden, Arps, Slate, Meagher & Flom, LLP, N.Y.C., 1980-2000; adj. prof. law NYU Sch. Law, 1975—2001; ptnr. Schulte Roth & Zabel LLP, N.Y.C., 2000—. Co-author: A Practical Guide to the Bankruptcy Reform Act, 1979, Creditors' Rights, Debtors' Protection and Bankruptcy, 1985, rev. edit., 1997; contbr.: Collier on Bankruptcy, 1979, rev. edit., 1999, Collier Bankruptcy Practice Guide, 2003; editor and contbg. author: Bankruptcy Litigation Manual, rev. edit., 2002. Bd. dirs. Goddard Riverside Cmty. Ctr.; bd. dirs., former chair Lawyers Alliance for N.Y. Fellow ABA, Am. Coll. Bankruptcy, Am. Bar Found.; mem. Assn. of Bar of City of N.Y., Practicing Law Inst. (mem. bankruptcy law adv. com.), Columbia Coll. Alumni Assn. (bd. dirs., v.p.). Home: 45 E 89th St New York NY 10128-1251 Office: Schulte Roth & Zabel LLP 919 3d Ave New York NY 10022

COOK, MICHELLE WESTERMAN, special education educator; b. Ft. Stockton, Tex., Feb. 17, 1959; d. Carl Anthony and Jacquelyn Cecil (Smith) Westerman; m. Bruce Duncan Cook, Aug. 11, 1984; children: Carl Gary, Ashley Rose. Student, St. Gregory's Jr. Coll., Shawnee, Okla., 1977-78; BSEd, Okla. U., 1985; postgrad., Tex. Tech. U., 1993—. Cert. tchr. lang. arts, spl. edn./secondary edn., visual impairments. Spl. edn. tchr. Springhill Jr. High, Longview, Tex., 1991—. Owner WCR, Inc., Longview, 1993. Author: (newsletter) The Ascension, 1994—; co-author: What America's Teachers Wish Parents Knew, 1993. Mem. United We Stand, Dallas, 1992. Tuition scholar Tex. Tech., Lubbock, 1993-95. Mem. Coun. Exceptional Children, Assn. Tex. Profl. Educators,Assn. for Edn. and Rehab. of Blind and Visually Impaired. Avocations: music, sailing, painting, yoga. E-mail: shellcook@aol.com.

COOK, NOEL ROBERT, manufacturing company executive; b. Houston, Mar. 19, 1937; s. Horace Berwick and Leda Estelle (Houghton) C.; children: Laurel Jane, David Robert. Student, Iowa State U., 1955-57; BS in Indsl. Engring., U. Mich., 1960. Registered profl. engr., Mich.; cert. Fluid Power Engr. Engr. in tng. Eaton Mfg., Saginaw, Mich., 1960-61; mgr. mfg. and contracting J.N. Fauver Co., Madison Heights, Mich., 1961-65; pres. Newton Mfg., Royal Oak, Mich., 1965—; sec. Indsl. Piping Contractors, Birmingham, Mich., 1969-75; pres. RNR Metal Fabricators, Inc., Royal Oak, 1974-78; chmn. bd. dirs. Kim Internat. Sales Co., 1978-88; pres. Newton Sales Co., Royal Oak, 1978-90, Power Package Windsor Ltd., Windsor, Ont., Can., 1981—. Patentee in field. With U.S. Army, arty. officer, 1960-61. Mem. ASME, Fluid Power Soc., Nat. Fluid Power Assn., Birmingham Jr. C. of C. (past bd. dirs.), Delta Tau Delta. Home: 4481 Cherry Hill Dr Orchard Lake MI 48323-1615 Office: Newton Mfg Co 4249 Delemere Blvd Royal Oak MI 48073-1897 E-mail: ncook@mindspring.com.

COOK, NORMA BAKER, consulting company executive; b. N.C. d. Charles and Mildred Baker. BA in Bus. and Econs., Meredith Coll.; postgrad., Alliance Francaise, N.Y.C., 1980-83, N.Y. Sch. Interior Design, 1983-84. Cert. tchr., N.C. Pres., owner John Robert Powers Sch. Fashion Careers, Raleigh, N.C., 1971-87, NBC of Raleigh, Inc., 1979—2001. Mem. adv. comm. N.C. Pvt. Bus.; Trade and Corr. Schs., 1986; bus. broker, 1991-93; instr. continuing edn. Meredith Coll., Raleigh, 1994—; pres. Fast Forward Concepts, 1996—. Author articles on fashion and success motivation and personal devel. Established Norma Baker Cook Art Scholarship at Meredith Coll., 1989; vice chmn. Meredith Coll. Bd. Assocs., 1991-92; charter mem. Meredith Coll. Heritage Soc., Raleigh. Recipient Svc. award Am. Cancer Soc., 1978. Mem. AFTRA, AAUW, The Fashion Group, Inc., Greater Raleigh C. of C. Avocations: art, writing, music.

COOK, PAMELA MARGARET, French educator; b. Gateshead, Eng., Apr. 11, 1955; came to U.S., 1983; d. John Andrew and Doreen Cook; m. Philip Edward Mirowski, June 14, 1986; 1 child, Alexander John Daniel Mirowski. BA with honors, U. Nottingham, Eng., 1977; MA, MPhil, PhD, Yale U., 1991. Tchr. Sawston Coll., Cambridge, Eng., 1978-83; asst. head dept. Hitchin Sch., Herts, Eng., 1983-85; part-time asst. prof. French St. Mary's Coll., Notre Dame, ind., 1990—. Mem. Hoosier Environ. Coun., Indpls., 1997—; mem. Ind. Opera North. Christine Jankowski fellow, 1984. Mem. MLA. Avocations: singing, flute, piano, theater.

COOK, PAUL CHRISTOPHER, engineering psychologist; b. Corpus Christi, Tex., Mar. 24, 1953; s. William Eckford and Nelle (Gladney)C. AA, Ocean City Coll., Md., 1973; BA, U. Ariz., Tucson, 1978; MA, U. Ariz., 1981, PhD, 1987. Oceanographer Dept. Natural Resources, State of Md., Annapolis, 1973-75; researcher Child Psychology Lab., Tucson, 1977-78; behavioral and video cons. Intermt. Ctrs. for Human Devel., Tucson, 1978-79; rsch. assoc. Family & Community Medicine Ariz. Health Sci. Ctr., Tucson, 1982-84, rsch. cons., 1989-98; rsch. and analysis assoc. U. Ariz., Tucson, 1980-87, rsch. cons. Coll. Medicine, 1989-98; sr. human factors engr. U.S. Army Electronic Proving Ground, Ft. Huachuca, Ariz., 1986-87; engring. psychologist U.S. Army Yuma Proving Ground, Ariz., 1988; cons. engr. Cook Enterprises, Tucson, 1989-91; pres. World Trade Assocs. Ltd. Sterling (Va.), Inc., Tucson, Lake Havasu, Ariz., 1991-97; pres., ptnr. Unicus Imports, Inc., 1997-2000; candidate, sr. exec. svcs., sr. rsch. scientist U.S. Navy Space and Naval Warfare Sys. Ctr., San Diego, 1999; ops. specialist, intelligence warfare test directorate commd Ft. Huachuca (Az.), Ft Hood (Tex.), 2000—01; ops. rsch. analyst intelligence electronic warfare Theatre Missle Def., Fort Huachuca, Ariz., 2000—00; ops. analyst U.S.A. Intelligence Electronic Warfare Reconnaissance, Spl. Projects, Ft. Huachuca, Ariz., 2001—02; intelligence officer U.S. Army Intelligence Ctr. and Ft. Huachuca, 2002—. Rsch. cons. Coll. Medicine Ariz. Health Scis. Ctr., U. Ariz., Tucson, 1989—; pres. World Trade Assocs. Ltd. of Sterling, Inc., Tucson, Sterling, Va. and Lake Havasu, Ariz., 1990-98. Scuba diver Pima County Sheriff's Dept., 1985-90; plank owner USN Meml., Washington. Mem. Navy League (life), U.S. Naval Inst., Human Factors Soc., Internat. Platform Assn., Profl. Assn. Diving Instrs., U.S. C. of C. Republican. Methodist. Home: 6537 E Santa Elena Tucson AZ 85715-3132 Office: Trail Dust Town #10 PO Box 10 6541 E Tanque Verde Rd Tucson AZ 85715-3813 E-mail: uexport@prodigy.net.

COOK, PAUL MAXWELL, technology company executive; b. Ridgewood, N.J. BSChemE, MIT, 1947. With Stanford Rsch. Inst., Menlo Park, Calif., 1948-53, Sequoia Process Corp., 1953-56, Raychem Corp., Menlo Park, Calif., 1957-95, founder, former pres., CEO, until 1990, chmn., bd. dirs., until 1995; chmn., CEO CellNet Data Sys., San Carlos, Calif., 1990-94; chmn., bd. dirs. SRI Internat., 1993-98; chmn. DIVA Sys. Corp., Menlo Park, Calif., 1995—, CEO, 1995-99; founder, CEO, Agile TV Corp., 2000—. Mem. exec. com. San Francisco Bay Area Coun., 1988-94, chmn., 1990-91. Recipient Nat. Medal Tech., 1988; named to San Francisco Bay Area Bus. Hall of Fame, 1999. Mem. NAE, Am. Acad. Sci., Environ. Careers Orgn. (past chmn., bd. trustees), MIT Corp. (life, emeritus). Office: Diva Sys Corp 800 Saginaw Dr Bldg 205 Redwood City CA 94063-4740 E-mail: pcook@agile.tv.

COOK, PETRONELLE MARGUERITE, writer; b. Plymouth, Devon, Eng., May 16, 1925;, naturalized, U.S., 1953; d. Harry Alfred and Ada Wood (Alford) Crouch; m. Philip R. Jr. Cook, July 20, 1949 (div. 1979); children: Philip R. III, Nicholas E. A., Alexandra M. L. BA with hons., Oxford U., Eng., 1946, diploma in anthropology/archaeology, 1947, MA, 1950. Profl. archaeologist U. Chgo., 1947-52, Ryerson fellow, 1952; lectr. anthropology and archaeology U. Md., Cape Cod C.C., 1972-90. Author (pen name Margot Arnold): (novels) The Officers' Woman, 1972, The Villa on the Palatine, 1975, Marie, 1979, Exit Actors Dying, 1979, The Cape Cod Caper, 1980, Zadok's Treasure, 1980, Death of a Voodoo Doll, 1982, Lament for a Lady Laird, 1982, Death on Dragon's Tongue, 1982, Affairs of State, 1983, Love Among the Allies, 1985, Desperate Measures, 1986, Sinister Purposes, 1987, The Menehune Murders, 1989, Toby's Folly, 1990, The Catacomb Conspiracy, 1992, The Cape Cod Conundrum, 1993, Dirge for a Dorset Druid, 1994; author: (pen name Petronelle Cook) The Queen Consorts of England, 1993, The Midas Murders, 1995, 1997, Survivors and Non-Survivors, 2002, The Wellman Chronicles, 2003, others. E-mail: margot@cape.com.

COOK, PHILIP JACKSON, economist, educator; b. Buffalo, N.Y., Oct. 15, 1946; s. Gerhard Albert and Lura (Lincoln) C.; m. Judith Walmsley, June 27, 1966; children: Elizabeth Camden, Brian Lincoln. BA, U. Mich., 1968; PhD, U. Calif., Berkeley, 1973. Prof. Duke U., Durham, N.C., 1973—, dir. Inst. Policy Scis., 1985-89, dir. Sanford Inst. Pub. Policy, 1997-99; rsch. assoc. Nat. Bur. Econ. Rsch. Vis. scholar Inst. Rsch. in Social Sci. U. N.C., Chapel Hill, 1980; expert Office Poly and Mgmt. Analysis, criminal div. U.S. Dept. Justice, 1982; mem. rsch. adv. com. U.S. Sentencing Commn., 1986—91, chair rsch. adv. com., 1986; mem. adv. bd. Injury Prevention Rsch. Ctr. U. N.C., 1990—; mem. adv. bd. H. John Heinz III Sch. Pub. Policy and Mgmt. Carnegie Mellon U., 1992—; mem. Ctr. Gun Policy Rsch. Johns Hopkins U., 1995—; cons. enforcement div. U.S. Dept. Treasury, 1999—2000; rsch. assoc. Nat. Bur. Econ. Rsch., 1996—. Author: Selling Hope, 1989, The Winner-Take All Society, 1995, Gun Violence, 2000, Evaluating Gun Policy, 2003. Recipient Kenneth J. Arrow award for best paper published in health econ., 1993; fellow Spl. Career, Ford Found., 1968—72; grantee, US Dept. Justice, Robert Wood Johnson Found. Fellow: Am. Soc. Criminology; mem.: NAS (inst. medicine 2001—), Am. Econ. Assn., Assn. Pub. Policy and Mgmt. (treas. 1985—93). Office: Duke Univ Inst Pub Policy PO Box 90245 Durham NC 27708-0245 E-mail: cook@pps.duke.edu.

COOK, QUENTIN LAMAR, lawyer, healthcare executive, church leader; b. Sept. 8, 1940; s. J. Vernon and Bernice (Kimball) C.; m. Mary Gaddie, Nov. 30, 1962; children: Kathryn Cook Knight, Quentin Laurance, Joseph Vernon III. BS, Utah State U., 1963; JD, Stanford U., 1966. Bar: Calif. 1966. Assoc. Carr, McClellan, Ingersoll, Thompson & Horn, Burlingame, Calif., 1966-69, ptnr., 1969-93; interim pres., CEO Calif. Healthcare Sys., San Francisco, 1993-94, pres., CEO, 1994-95; vice chmn. Sutter Health/Calif. Healthcare Sys., San Francisco, 1996; gen. authority LDS Ch., 1996—. City atty. Town of Hillsborough, Calif., 1982-93; mem. adv. bd. Utah State U., Logan, 1985-95; mem. bd. visitors Brigham Young U. Law Sch., Provo, 1994-96.

COOK, RALPH D. lawyer, retired state supreme court justice; Former judge Ala. Cir. Ct. (10th jud. dist.), Ala. Dist. Ct.; assoc. justice Ala. Supreme Ct., Montgomery, ret. assoc. justice, 2001; now attorney Hare, Wynn, Newell & Newton. Office: Hare Wynn Newell & Newton The Historic Massey Bldg 2025 3rd Ave N Birmingham AL 35203

COOK, REBECCA MCDOWELL, former state official; m. John Larkin Cook; children: Hunter, and Morgan. BA in Polit. sci., U. Mo., 1972, JD, 1975; D (hon.), Mo. We. State Coll., 1997. Former clk., assoc., ptnr. Limbaugh, Limbaugh, and Russell Law Firm, Cape Girardeau, Mo.; v.p. Oliver, Oliver, Waltz, and Cook Law Firm, 1979-92; del. to Mo. State Dem. Conv., 1980; mem. Mo. State Bd. Elem. and Sec. Edn., 1990-94; sec. of state State of Mo., 1994—2001. Mem. Future of South Commn., Dem. Nat. Com., 1995—. Recipient Order of Barristers Award., 1992, Woman of Achievement Award., Cape Girardeau Zonta Club, 1994, James C. Kirkpatrick Excellence in Governance Award; Henry Toll fellow. Mem. S.E. Mo. State U. Found., S.E. Mo. Hosp. Found., Nat. Assn. Secretaries of State (dir., exec. com.), Coun. Econ. Edn., Mo. K-16 Coalition, Lift Mo., Inc. Democrat. Presbyterian.*

COOK, RICHARD BORRESON, architect; b. Harvard, Ill., May 23, 1937; s. Ernest Keller and Clara Matilda (Borreson) C.; m. Shirley Jean Antrup,; children: Alan Blair, Elizabeth Ann, Rebecca Alica. BArch, U. Ill., 1962. Registered architect, Calif., Fla., Ill., Ind., Mich., Mo., N.D., N.Y., Ohio, Wis. Intern architect Skidmore, Owings & Merrill, Chgo., 1962-64, Ulrich Franzen & Assocs., N.Y.C., 1964-65; assoc. I.W. Colburn & Assocs., Chgo., 1965-70, Metz, Train, Olson & Youngren, Chgo., 1970-78; pres. Orput Assocs., Wilmette, Ill., 1978-81, Stowell Cook Frolichstein, Chgo., 1981—, Green Cook Ltd., Chgo., 1981. Bd. dirs., pres. Chgo. Archtl. Assistance Ctr., 1983; chmn. handicapped subcom. Mayor's Commn. Bldg. Code Amendments, Chgo., chmn. constrn. industry affairs com.; speaker, presenter papers in field. Prin. projects with Stowell Cook Frolichstein and Cook, Hiltscher Assoc. include Countryside Mall, Fla., Orange Park Mall, Fla., Trinity Evangel. Div. Sch., Rolfing Libr. addition and renovation, Deerfield, Ill, renovation main br. U.S. Postal Svc., Chgo., City Colls. of Chgo., Main St. Sq. Shopping Ctr., Downers Grove, Ill., Chgo. Bd. Edn.; with Orput Assocs. Kenosha (Wis.) County Pub. Safety Bldg., Burnham Terr. Apts. for Elderly, Rockford, Ill., addition and renovation Garrett-Evangel. Sem. Libr., addition Elmhurst (Ill.) Pub. Libr., addition Lake Forest (Ill.) Sch. Mgmt., apt. bldg. renovation Gt. Lakes (Ill.) Naval Sta., Hickory Hills (Ill.) Mcpl. Bldg.; with Metz Train, Olson & Youngren, Inc. office and computer ctr. Lumbermen's Mut. Casualty Co., Long Grove, Ill., Safeguards Analytical Lab. Bldg. Argonne (Ill.) Nat. Lab., Cancer Virus Rsch. Lab. U. Chgo., pub. bldg. commn. John Hope Middle Sch., Chgo.; with I.W. Colburn & Assocs. Geophys. Sci. Bldg. U. Chgo, Cathedral Christ the King, Kalamazoo, dormitory complex and dining facilities Bryn Mawr Coll, Pa., lab. and office bldg. Standard "T" Chem. Co., Lisle, Ill., Temple Jeremiah, Northbrook, Ill. Mem. plann commn. Evanston, 1997. Fellow AIA (dir. Ill. region 1988-89, chmn. T6B documents com., chmn. 1987 nat. conv., chmn. membership svcs. task force, mem. goals and grassroots '82 com.); mem. Ill. Council AIA (bd. dirs., pres., co-chmn. Midwest Regional Conf., mem. fin. and nominating coms.), Chgo. chpt. AIA (sec., v.p., 1st v.p., pres., mem. 1992 World's Fair Rev. Com., chmn. nominating com., mem. Logan Sq. Design Ctr.), Am. Arbitration Assn., Chgo. chpt. AIA Found. (pres.). Democrat. Congregationalist. Avocations: sculpture, photography. Home: 1330 Wesley Ave Evanston IL 60201-4141 Office: Stowell Cook & Frolichstein 33 W Grand Ave Chicago IL 60610-4306

COOK, RICHARD KELSEY, aerospace industry executive; b. White Plains, N.Y., Nov. 14, 1931; s. Albert James and Frances Elizabeth (Butler) C.; m. Marjorie S. Schellabarger, Sept. 10, 1959 (div.); children: Geoffrey, Patrick, Sarah, Catherine; m. Fleur Wales Baillie, Oct. 14, 1987. Postgrad., Stanford U., 1979; BA, George Washington U., 1958. Legis staff Am. Trucking Assn., 1959-61; adminstrv. asst. Rep. Edwin B. Dooley, 1961; legis. asst. Rep. Oliver P. Bolton, 1963-65; profl. staff mem. Banking and Currency Com., U.S. Ho. of Reps., Washington, 1965-69; spl. asst. to Pres. of U.S., Washington, 1969-71, dep. asst., 1971-73; v.p. Lockheed Corp., Washington, 1973-94, sr. v.p., 1994-95; pres. RKC Ltd., 1995—. Spl. adv. O'Connor & Hannan, Washington, 1995-98; cons. to major U.S. and South African Companies, with offices in Johannesburg and Washington, 1995-99; cons. telecom. cos. Thorlock Corp. Ltd., Australia, 1999—; registered lobbyist; pioneered internet lobbying with PanAmSat Corp., 1998-2000. Served with USAF, 1949-53. Mem. Aero. Club (pres. 1979), Met. Club, 116 Club (D.C.), Burning Tree Club (Bethesda, Md.), Captiva Island Yacht Club (Fla.), Inanda Club (Johannesburg, South Africa), Tau Kappa Epsilon. Office: 1201 Pennsylvania Ave NW Washington DC 20004-2436

COOK, RICHARD W. motion picture company executive; b. Bakersfield, Calif., Aug. 20, 1950; Ed., U. So. Calif. Saels rep. Disneyland, 1971-74, sales mgr., 1974-77; mgr. pay TV and non-theatrical releases Disney Studios, 1977-80; asst. domestic sales mgr. Buena Vista, 1980-81, v.p., asst. gen. sales mgr., 1981-84, v.p., gen. sales mgr., 1985-88, sr. v.p. domestic distbn., 1988-94; pres. Buena Vista Pictures Distbn., 1994; pres. worldwide mktg. Buena Vista Pictures Mktg., 1994-97; chmn. Walt Disney Motion Pictures Group, Burbank, Calif., 1997—2002, Walt Disney Studios, 2002—. Office: Walt Disney Studios 500 S Buena Vista St Burbank CA 91521-0006

COOK, ROBERT CROSSLAND, research chemist; b. New Haven, June 5, 1947; s. Russell C. and Tensia (Veazey) C. BS in Chemistry, Lafayette Coll., 1969; MPh in Phys. Chemistry, Yale U., 1971, PhD in Theoretical Chemistry, 1973. Mem. faculty Lafayette Coll., Easton, Pa., 1973-81; staff scientist Lawrence Livermore (Calif.) Nat. Lab., 1981—. Instr. Calif. State U., Hayward, 1985-86, 94, Chabot Coll., 1986-90, Las Positas Coll., 1990-92; mem. vis. faculty Dartmouth Coll., Hanover, N.H., 1977, 78, 79, Colo. State U., Ft. Collins, 1980. Contbr. articles to profl. jours. Grantee in field. Mem. Am. Chem. Soc., Am. Phys. Soc., Sigma Xi. Office: Lawrence Livermore Nat Lab L-481 PO Box 808 Livermore CA 94551-0808 E-mail: bobcook@llnl.gov.

COOK, ROBERT S., JR., lawyer; b. Syracuse, N.Y., 1940; m. Sally Williams. BA, Amherst Coll., 1962; LLB, Yale U., 1965. Bar: N.Y. 1966. Assoc. Hancock, Ryan, Shove & Hust, Syracuse, N.Y., 1965-68; urban renewal rep. HUD, N.Y.C., 1968-71; exec. dir. The Parks Coun., Inc., N.Y.C., 1972-73; v.p., co-founder Project for Pub. Spaces, Inc., N.Y.C., 1974-77; cons. N.Y.C., 1978-80; assoc. Tufo & Zuccotti, N.Y.C., 1981-86; assoc., then ptnr. Brown and Wood, N.Y.C., 1986-94; ptnr. DeForest & Duer, N.Y.C., 1995—2001, Anderson, Kill & Olick, P.C., NYC, 2002—. Author: Zoning for Downtown urban Design, 1980. V.p., bd. dirs. Citizens Housing and Planning Coun., 1985; cons. The Denver Partnership, 1981; mem. N.Y. State Freshwater Wetlands Appeals Bd., 1991-94. Design project fellow Nat. Endowment for Arts, Washington, 1978-79; Graham Found. for Advanced Studies in the Fine Arts fellow, Chgo., 1979. Mem. N.Y. State Bar Assn., Assn. Bar City N.Y. (com. environ. law 1979-82, com. land use planning and zoning, 1994-2000, chmn. 1997-2000, com. N.Y.C. affairs 2000-01). Office: Anderson Kill & Olick PC 1251 Ave of the Americas New York NY 10020-1182

COOK, ROBERTA LYNN, agricultural economist, educator; b. Oceanside, Calif., Feb. 27, 1954; d. Robert Merold and Wanda Eugenia (Wright) C.; m. José Canela-Cacho, May 12, 1999. BA, Mich. State U., 1976, MS, 1981, PhD, 1985. Grad. rsch. asst. Mich. State U., East Lansing, 1978-81, 84; cons. Banco de Mexico, Mexico City, 1981-84; ext. economist, prof. U. Calif., Davis, 1985—. Appointed to the Agricult. trade Adv. Com. (ATAC) for Fruits and Vegs. by the US Trade Rep., 1997—, bd. dirs. Calif. Kiwifruit Commn., Sacramento, chair, 1997-98; bd. dirs. Calif. Tomato Commn., 1993—, Fresno; mem. Internat. adv. coun. Produce Mktg. Assn., Newark, Del., 1994-97, Ag Bennet Round Table, 1997-2000; cons. OECD, Colombian Govt., Trade Bur., U.S. AID, World Bank, UN, others; chair S-222 Regional Rsch. Group on Fruits and Vegetables, 1991-93. Contbr. articles to profl. jours. Bd. dirs. Katalysis Found., Stockton, Calif., 1987-91; chair U. Calif./Legis. Task Force on Cooperatives, Davis, 1987-88. Recipient Grad. Inst./Coop. Leadership award U.S. Dept. Agr., U. Mo., Columbia, 1986, Affirmative Action award U. Calif., 1991. Mem. Food Dist. Rsch. Soc. (bd. dirs. 1995—, v.p. for programs 1997-98), Am. Agrl. Econs. Assn. (various coms. 1984—, fdn. gov. bd. 2001), Produce Mktg. Assn. (various coms. 1987—), United Fresh Fruit and Vegetable Assn. (various coms. 1987—), Internat. Soc. Hort. Sci. (v.p. econ. divsn. 1992-96). Avocations: travel, tango, cooking/wine, history. Office: U Calif Davis Dept Agr and Resource Econs Davis CA 95616 E-mail: cook@primal.ucdavis.edu.

COOK, ROBIN, author; b. N.Y.C., May 4, 1940; s. Edgar Lee and Audrey (Koons) C.; m. Barbara Ellen Mougin, July 18, 1979. BA, Weslyan U., 1962; MD, Columbia U., 1966. Resident in gen. surgery Queen's Hosp., Honolulu, 1966-68; resident in ophthalmology Mass. Eye and Ear Infirmary, Boston, 1971-75, mem. staff, from 1975; clin. instr. Harvard U. Med. Sch., 1972. Author: The Year of the Intern, 1972, Coma, 1977, Sphinx, 1979, Brain, 1981, Fever, 1982, Godplayer, 1983, Mindbend, 1986, Outbreak, 1987, Mortal Fear, 1988, Mutation, 1989, Harmful Intent, 1990, Vital Signs, 1990, Blindsight, 1991, Terminal, 1992, Fatal Cure, 1994, Acceptable Risk, 1995, Invasion, 1997, Chromosome 6, 1997, Toxin, 1998, Vector, 1999, Shock, 2001, Abduction, 2002, Seizure, 2003. Lt. comdr. USN, 1969-71. Avocations: skiing, surfing, painting, cooking. Home: 4601 Gulf Shore Blvd N # P4 Naples FL 34103-2221*

COOK, S. ALAN, lawyer, accountant; b. Bangor, Maine, Mar. 25, 1947; s. Harry George and Margaret (Black) C.; 1 child, Heather Alison. B.S., U. R.I., 1972; J.D., U. Ariz., 1978. Bar: Ariz. 1978, U.S. Dist. Ct. Ariz. 1978, U.S. Ct. Appeals (9th cir.) 1978, U.S. Supreme Ct., 1985; CPA, Ariz., R.I. Law clk. to chief judge U.S. Dist. Ct. Ariz., Phoenix, 1978-81; clk. of ct. Ariz. Supreme Ct., Phoenix, 1981-85; pvt. practice law Phoenix, 1985—; bd. visitors U. Ariz. Coll. Law, Tucson, 1983— . Editorial staff Appellate Ct. Adminstrn. Rev., 1982-83. Area chmn. Western region Nat. Eagle Scout Assn., 1983— . Served as chief warrant officer, U.S. Army, 1966-69, Vietnam; mem. Ariz. Army N.G. (capt. JAGC). Decorated Air medal with 29 clusters, Army Commendation medal. Mem. Nat. Conf. Appellate Ct. Clks. (chmn. various coms. 1981—), Am. Inst. C.P.A.s, U. Ariz. Law Coll. Assn. (exec. com. 1983—), Phi Kappa Phi, Beta Gamma Sigma, Beta Alpha Psi. Republican.

COOK, SAMUEL ROBERT, anthropologist, educator; b. Radford, Va., May 1, 1965; s. Thomas Eugene and Mary Arena Cook; m. Susan Ewing Fleming, Jan. 3, 1955. BA in History, Radford U., 1983; MA in Am. Indian Studies, U. of Ariz., 1992, PhD in Comparitive Cultural Studies, 1997. Rsch. asst. Am. Indian studies U. of Ariz., Tucson, 1990—92, adj. instr. Am. Indian studies, 1996; adj. prof. anthropology Radford U., Radford, Va., 1998; adj. prof. appalachian studies Va. Tech, Blacksburg, Va., 1999—2000, asst. prof. appalachian studies & Am. Indian studies, 2000—. Coord. Am. Indian studies Va. Tech, 2000—; cons. on Am. Indian exhibits Va. Mus. of Fine Arts, Richmond, Va., 2002—; rsch. & ednl. cons. Va. Indian Tribal Alliance for Life, Richmond, 2001—; cons. Ohio Valley Environ. Coalition, Huntington, W.Va., 1999—2002, Monacan Indian Ancestral Mus. Com., Bear Mountain, Va., 1996—, Monacan Indian Nation Fed. Recognition Project, Bear Mountain, 1997—. Author: Monacans and Miners: Native American and Coal Mining Communities in Appalachia, 2000 (Mooney award So. Anthropol. Soc., 2003); dir.: (video documentary) What it means to be a Virginia Indian in the 21st Century, 2001; editor: Red Ink Jour., 1993. Organizer Ohio Valley Environ. Coalition, Huntington, W.Va., 1999—2002, W.Va. Highlands Conservancy, Charleston, W.Va., 1999—2002. Recipient Outstanding Contbn. to Am. Indians award, Va. Coun. on Indians, 2002; grantee Millenium grant, Va. Tech Coll. of Arts & Sci., 1999—2000, Discretionary grant, Va. Found. for the Humanities, 2001, Edn. grant, Va. Coun. on Indians, 2001, Discretionary grant, Va. Found. for the Humanities, 2002, Edn. grant, Va. Coun. on Indians, 2002. Fellow: Soc. for Applied Anthropology; mem.: Appalachian Studies Assn., Assn. for Polit. and Legal Anthropology, Am. Anthrop. Assn. Office: Center for Interdisciplinary Studies vi 124 Lane Hall Blacksburg VA 24061 Office Fax: 540-231-7013. E-mail: sacook2@vt.edu.

COOK, SHARLA J. career officer; BS in Edn. with honors, Brigham Young U., 1971; disting. grad., Officer Tng. Sch., 1972; aircraft maintenance officer course, Chanute AFB, Ill., 1973; M in Logistics Mgmt., Air Force Inst. of Tech., 1977; grad., Air Command and Staff Coll., 1985; disting. grad., Indsl. Coll. of Armed Forces, 1993. Commd. 2d lt. USAF, 1972, advanced through grades to brigadier gen., 1998; wing job control officer U-Tapao Air Base, Thailand, 1975-76; aide-de-camp air logistics ctr. comdr. Sacramento Air Logistics Ctr., McClellan AFB, Calif., 1981-82, dep. br. chief inventory and scheduling br., 1982-84; comdr. 374th Orgnl. Maintenance Squadron, Clark Air Base, The Philippines, 1985-87; maintenance ops. officer 58th Tactical Tng. Wing, Luke AFB, Ariz., 1988-90, asst. dep. comdr. for maintenance, 1990-91; dep. comdr. 58th Support Group, Luke AFB, 1991-92; comdr. 8th Logistics Group, Kunsan Air Base, South Korea, 1993-94; chief maintenance engring. Hdqs. Pacific Air Forces, Hickam AFB, Hawaii, 1994-95, asst. dir. logistics, 1995-96; dir. aircraft directorate Ogden Air Logistics Ctr., Hill AFB, Utah, 1996-97; dir. logistics Hdqs. Air Edn. and Tng. Command, Randolph AFB, Tex., 1997—; comdr. 82d tng. wing Air Edn. and Tng. Command, Sheppards AFB, Tex., 1999—. Decorated Legion of Merit, Meritorious Svc. medal with 4 oak leaf clusters. Address: 82 TRW/CC Sheppard AFB TX 76311

COOK, STANTON R. media company executive; b. Chgo., July 3, 1925; s. Rufus Merrill and Thelma Marie (Borgerson) C.; m. Barbara Wilson, Sept. 23, 1950 (dec. Nov. 1994). BS in Mech. Engring., Northwestern U., 1949. With Shell Oil Co., 1949-51, Chgo. Tribune Co., 1951-81, v.p., 1967-70, exec. v.p. and gen. mgr., 1970-72, pres., 1972-74, pub., 1973-90, CEO, 1974-76, chmn., 1974-81; dir. Tribune Co., 1972-96, v.p., 1972-74, pres., 1974-88, chmn., 1989-92, CEO, 1974-90; chmn. Chgo. Nat. League Ball Club, Inc., 1990-94. Bd. dirs. AP, 1975-84, 2d vice chmn., 1979-84; bd. dirs. Newspaper Adv. Bur., 1973-92, Am. Newspaper Pubs. Assn., 1974-82; dep. chmn., bd. dirs. Fed. Res. Bank Chgo., 1980-83, chmn., 1984-85; bd. dirs. Robert R. McCormick Tribune Found., 1990-2001. Trustee Robert R. McCormick Trust, 1972-90, Savs. and Profit Sharing Fund of Sears Employees, 1991-94, U. Chgo., 1973-87, Mus. Sci. and Industry, Chgo., 1973—, Field Mus. Natural History, Chgo., 1973—, Gen. Douglas MacArthur Found., 1979—, Northwestern U., 1987—, Shedd Aquarium Soc., 1987—, Am. Newspaper Pubs. Assn. Found., 1973-82. Mem. Newspaper Assn. Am. (bd. govs. 1992), Chgo. Coun. Fgn. Rels. (bd. dirs. 1973-93), Comml. Club (past pres.), Econ. Club (past pres., life mem.), Glen Lake Assn. (pres. 2001-). Home: 224 Raleigh Rd Kenilworth IL 60043-1209

COOK, STEPHEN ARTHUR, mathematics and computer science educator; b. Buffalo, Dec. 14, 1939; s. Gerhard Albert and Lura C.; m. Linda Marie Craddock, May 4, 1968; children— Gordon, James. BS in math., U. Mich., 1961; S.M. in math., Harvard U., 1962, PhD in math., 1966. Asst. prof. U. Calif.-Berkeley, 1966-70; assoc. prof. U. Toronto, 1970-75, prof., 1975—, univ. prof., 1985—. Contbr. articles to profl. jours. E.W.R. Staecie Meml. fellow, 1977-78; Killam research fellow Can. Council, 1982-83; recipient ACM Turing award Assn. Computing Machinery, 1982, Killam prize Can. Coun., 1997. Fellow Royal Soc. Can., Royal Soc. London; mem. Nat. Acad. Scis., Am. Acad. Arts and Scis. Home: 6 Indian Valley Crescent Toronto ON Canada M6R 1Y6 Office: Dept Computer Sci U Toronto Toronto ON Canada M5S 3G4 E-mail: sacook@cs.toronto.edu.

COOK, STEPHEN BARTON, art educator, artist; b. Riverside, Calif., Oct. 9, 1959; s. Douglas N. and Joan B. Cook; m. Kristen Lynn Bentz, Apr. 28, 1993; 1 child, Tulliver. Student, Nat. Taiwan U., Taipei, 1982—83; BA, Pa. State U., 1985, MFA, Calif. Inst. Arts, 1992. ESL tchr. numerous cos., Taipei, 1982—87; radio tchr. ESL Modern Am. Lang. Program, Taipei, 1986—87; actor, stuntman Philippine film industry, 1984—85; actor, stuntman, cameraman, editor LA film industry, 1988—98; tchr. at-risk populations LA Office Edn., 1994—96; tchr. art Francis Parker Sch., San Diego, 1999—. Mem. adv. com. headmaster search Francis Parker Sch., San Diego, 2001, mem. adv. com. global citizenship curriculum devel., 01; faculty advisor East Meets West Club, 2001—03. Dir.: (documentaries) Desert Cave Painting, 1992; editor: Children's Understanding of False Belief and Mental State, 2000. Grantee, Kodak Film, 1991. Mem.: Am. Anthrop. Assn., Ceramic Artists San Diego, Nat. Coun. Edn. Ceramic Arts. Green Party. Zen Tao Animism. Avocations: Asian philosophy, Kung Fu, anthropology. Home: 4318 E Overlook Dr San Diego CA 92115 Office: Francis Parker Sch 6501 Linda Vista Rd San Diego CA 92111 E-mail: scook@francisparker.org.

COOK, STEPHEN CHAMPLIN, retired shipping company executive; b. Portland, Oreg., Sept. 20, 1915; s. Frederick Stephen and Mary Louise (Boardman) C.; m. Dorothy White, Oct. 27, 1945 (dec. Sept. 1998); children: Mary H. Cook Goodson, John B., Samuel D., Robert B. (dec.). Student, U. Oreg., 1935-36. Surveyor U.S. Engrs. Corp., Portland, Oreg., 1934-35; dispatcher Pacific Motor Trucking Co., Oakland, Calif., 1937-38; manifest clk. Pacific Truck Express, Portland, 1939; exec. asst. Coastwise Line, San Francisco, 1940-41, mgr. K-Line svc., 1945-56; chartering mgr. Ocean Svc. Inc. subs. Marcona Corp., San Francisco, 1956-75, ret., 1975. Cons., San Francisco, 1976-78. Author 1 charter party, 1957. Mem. steering com. Dogwood Festival, Lewiston, Idaho, 1985-92; sec. Asotin County Reps., Clarkston, Wash., 1986-88; adv. bd. Clarkston Pt. Commrs., 1989-92. Lt. USN, 1941-45, PTO; grand marshall Asotin Christmas Parade, 2000. Recipient Pres.'s award Marin (Calif.) coun. Boy Scouts Am., 1977, Order of Merit, 1971, 84, Skillern award Lewis Clark coun., 1982, Silver Beaver award 1987; Lewis-Clark Valley Vol. award, 1987, Youth Corps award Nat. Assn. Svc. and Conservation Corps, 1990, Pres.'s Spl. award Clarkston C. of C., 1983, Asotin Citizen of Yr. award, 1999. Mem. VFW, Asotin County Hist. Soc. (hon. life pres. 1982-83, bd. dirs.), Asotin C. of C. (v.p. 1994-95). Republican. Mem. Stand for United Ch. of Christ. Avocations: hiking, camping, stamp collecting.

COOK, STUART DONALD, physician, educator; b. Boston, Oct. 23, 1936; s. Martius and Nina (Schwartzman) C.; m. Josepha Emdin, June 26, 1960; children— Andrew, Peter, Jonathan. AB, Brandeis U., 1957; MS, U. Vt., 1959, MD, 1962. Diplomate: Am. Bd. Psychiatry and Neurology. Intern Upstate Med. Center, Syracuse, N.Y., 1962-63; resident in neurology Albert Einstein Coll. Medicine, Bronx, N.Y., 1965-67, chief resident, 1967-68, instr. dept. neurology, 1968-69; asst. prof. neurology Coll. Physician and Surgeons, Columbia U., N.Y.C., 1969-71; prof. medicine N.J. Med. Sch., Newark, 1971, chmn. dept. neuroscis., 1972-98, acting dean, 1987-89; chief neurology svc. VA Med. Ctr., East Orange, N.J., 1971-86; pres. U. Medicine and Dentistry N.J., 1998—. Vis. scientist div. virology Nat. Inst. Med. Research, London, 1977-78; vis. scientist Swiss Inst. for Cancer Research, 1985. Contbr. articles to profl. jours. Served with USN, 1963-65. Mem. Am. Acad. Neurology (S. Weir Mitchell award 1968), Am. Assn. Neuropathologists, AAUP, Am. Fedn. Clin. Research, Harvey Soc., Am. Neurol. Assn., Sigma Xi, Alpha Omega Alpha. Home: 26 Dogwood Dr Morristown NJ 07960-3310 Office: U Medicine and Dentistry Ste 1535 65 Bergen St Newark NJ 07107-3001

COOK, SUSAN FARWELL, associate director planned giving; b. Boston, Apr. 28, 1953; d. Benjamin and Beverly (Brooks) Conant; m. James Samuel Cook Jr., Aug. 17, 1985; children: Emily Farwell, David McKendree. AB, Colby Coll., 1975; MBA, Thomas Coll., 2002. Bank teller Boston 5 Cent Savs. Bank, 1975-76; asst. technician plan cost John Hancock Mut. Life Ins. Co., Boston, 1976-77, technician plan cost, 1977-78, sr. technician plan cost, 1978-79, asst. mgr. group pension plan cost, 1979-81; assoc. dir. alumni rels. Colby Coll., Waterville, Maine, 1981-86, dir. alumni rels., 1986-97, assoc. dir. planned giving, 1997—. Co-dir. adv. bd. women's studies Colby Coll., 1987-89, adv. women's group, 1987-89; bd. dirs. Maine Planned Giving Coun., 2001—, treas., 2002--. Bd. dirs., newsletter sec. Literacy Vols. Am., Waterville, 1986—89, 1991—92, v.p., 1995—97, pres., 1997—99; treas. Pitcher Pond Improvement Assn., 1988—95, Gagnon/100 Campaign, 1996, 1998; coach Waterville Area Youth Hockey Assn., 1997—2001; bd. dirs. Youth Hockey Assn., 2001—; treas. Gagnon for Senate, 2000, 2002; trustee Universalist-Unitarian Ch., Waterville, 2001—, v.p., 2003—; bd. dirs. Congress Lake Assns., Yarmouth, Maine, 1988—92, Waterville Youth Soccer Assn., 2001—, Kennebec Montessori Sch., 1999—2001; pres. Waterville Youth Soccer Assn., 2002—. Mem. AAUW (sec. Waterville br. 1989-91, pres. 1991-93, co-pres. 1993-95), Coun. Advancement and Support of Edn., CASE Dist. I (exec. bd. dirs. 1994-97, sec. 1996-97, nominating com. 1997-99). Avocations: skiing, sewing, golf. Home: 6 Pray Ave Waterville ME 04901-5339 Office: Colby Coll 4372 Mayflower Hl Waterville ME 04901-8843

COOK, SYBILLA AVERY, school library consultant; b. Buffalo, Aug. 20, 1930; d. Edward Carrington and Elizabeth (Boorum) Avery; m. John D. Cook, June 12, 1951; children: Harold John, Robert Sherman, Raymond Avery. BS, Northwestern U., 1951; MLS, Rosary Coll., River Forest, Ill., 1968; MA, U. Oreg., 1982. Cert. ednl. media tchr. and supr., Oreg., Ill. Tchr. Glenview (Ill.) Pub. Schs., 1951; librarian Deerfield (Ill.) Pub. Schs., 1968-69; media specialist Des Plaines (Ill.) Pub. Schs., 1969-76; librarian Dillard (Oreg.) Pub. Schs., 1976-78; libr. media specialist Glide (Oreg.) Pub. Schs., 1978-90; sch. libr. cons., Roseburg, Oreg., 1986—. Adj. instr. Western Oreg. State Coll., Monmouth, 1988-93; mem. libr. info. skills com. Oreg. Dept. Edn., 1987. Author: Instructional Design for Libraries, 1986, Walking Portland, 1998; author: (with Cheryl Page) Battles, and Bees, 1994; author: (with B. Fonnesbeck and F. Corcoran) Battle of the Books and More, 2001; contbr. articles to profl. jours. Recipient Gandalf award Douglas County Libr. System, 1994. Mem. ALA, AAUW (v.p. 1999-2003), Am. Assn. Sch. Librs., Author's Guild, Lane Douglas Regional Libr. Assn. (chmn. 1982-84), Oreg. Ednl. Media Assn. (exec. bd. 1987—, Tchr. of Yr. 1984), Soc. Children's Book Writers, Friends of the Libr. (pres. 2002—), Willamette Writers, Beta Phi Mu. Home and Office: 19 N River Dr Roseburg OR 97470-9473 E-mail: sybilla@rosenet.net.

COOK, TONY MICHAEL, legislative staff member; m. Joy Cook; children: Michael, Libby. BA, Wash. State U., 1970; JD, Stanford U., 1973. Bar: Wash. 1973. With Senate Rsch. Ctr., 1973, U. Wash.; mem. staff Utilities and Transp. Commn., 1977; counsel Wash. State Senate, 1991, sec., 1999—; counsel Legis. Ethics Bd., 1997. Office: Wash State Senate PO Box 40482 Olympia WA 98504-0482 Fax: 360-786-7520. E-mail: cook_to@leg.wa.gov.

COOK, VICTOR JOSEPH, JR., marketing educator, consultant; b. Durant, Okla., June 25, 1938; s. Victor Joseph and Athelene Ann (Arduser) C.; m. Linda Lee Potter, June 6, 1960 (div. 1971); children: Victor Joseph III, William Randall, Christopher Phelps; m. barbara Brainard, Dec. 29, 1989 (div. 1997). BA, Fla. State U., 1960; MS, La. State U., 1962; PhD, U. Mich., 1965. Rsch. assoc. Mktg. Sci. Inst., Phila., 1965-68; assoc. rsch. dir. Boston, 1968-69; asst. prof. U. Chgo., 1969-75; pres., dir. Mgmt. & Design, New Orleans, 1975-78; prof. Freeman Sch. Bus. Tulane U., 1978—. Pres. The Styjl Furniture, 1998—; cons. Ford Motor Co., Dearborn, Mich., 1964-67, IBM, N.Y.C., 1968-72, Sears, Roebuck & Co., Chgo., 1975-77, Internat. Computers Ltd., ICL, London, 1982-91, The DuPont Co., Wilmington, 1986—, The Bases Group, Cin., 1986-89. Author: Brand Policy Determination, 1967, Readings in Marketing Strategy, 1989; designer, patentee furniture, frameworks, 1976—. Mem. Am. Mktg. Assn., Am. Econ. Assn., Inst. for Ops. Rsch. and The Mgmt. Scis., Beta Gamma Sigma, Phi Beta Kappa. Republican. Office: Tulane U AB Freeman Sch Bus New Orleans LA 70118 E-mail: victor.cook@tulane.edu., vcook@thestyle.com.

COOK, WAYNE EVANS, music educator; b. Pearsall, Tex., Dec. 16, 1939; s. George Evans and Ruth Loreen Cook; m. Marlene Bruce Cook, Aug. 28, 1965; children: Julie, Sheri, Leslie. BMus, U. North Tex., 1962; MS in Music Edn., U. Ill., 1964; postgrad., Eastman Sch. Music, 1965. Instr. music Ind. State U., Terre Haute, 1964-66; asst. prof. music U. Wis., Milw., 1966-73, assoc. prof. music, 1973-79, prof. music, 1979-99, prof. music emeritus, 1999—[00fe]. Dir. grad. studies in music U. Wis., Milw., 1985—, assoc. dean sch. of fine arts, 1983-84, chmn. dept. of music, 1993-96; profl. trumpet performer Freel Artist in City, Milw., 1966—; mem. trumpet sect. Waukesha Symphony Orchestra, 1997—; mem. concert tours Ctrl. Am., S.Am., Mex., Europe, Australia; trumpet faculty Wis. Conservatory Music, 2002—. Dir. music Abiding Savior Luth. Ch., Milw., 1978-89; prin. trumpet Festival City Symphony, Milw., 1968-2001, utility trumpet Milw. Symphony Orch., 1966-80; prin. trumpet Skylight Opera Orch., Milw., 1970-84. Mem. Internat. Trumpet Guild, Nat. Assn. of Schs. of Music, Nat. Assn. of Coll. Wind and Percussion Instrs. Democrat. Congregationalist. Avocations: tennis, golf, gardening. Home: 4133 N Woodburn St Milwaukee WI 53211-1837 E-mail: wecook@csd.uwm.edu.

COOK, WILLIAM HOWARD, architect; b. Evanston, Ill., Dec. 19, 1924; s. Clare Cyril and Matilda Hermine (Schuldt) C.; m. Nancy Ann Dean, Feb. 1, 1949; children: Robert, Cynthia, James. BA, UCLA, 1947; BArch, U. Mich., 1952. Chief designer Fabrica de Muebles Camacho-Roldan, Bogota, Colombia, S.Am., 1949-52; assoc. architect Orus Eash, Traverse City, Mich., Ft. Wayne, Ind., 1952-60; ptnr. Cook & Swaim (architects), Tucson, 1961-68; project specialist in urban devel. Banco Interamericano de Desarrollo, Buenos Aires, Argentina, 1968-69; pres. Cain, Nelson, Wares, Cook and Assocs., architects, Tucson, 1969-82. Vis. lectr. architecture U. Ariz., 1980-89; coord. archtl. exch. with U. LaSalle, Mexico City, 1983, 85, 87, 89, 93. Lt. (j.g.) USNR, 1943-46. Served to lt. (j.g.) USNR, 1943-46. Fellow AIA (pres. So. Ariz. 1967); mem. Ariz. Soc. Architects (pres. 1970), Ariz. Soc. of AIA (Architect's medal 1981) Presbyterian. Home and Office: PO Box 347 Sonoita AZ 85637-0347 E-mail: fincadesonoita@theriver.com.

COOK, WILLIAM LESLIE, JR., lawyer; b. July 1, 1949; s. William Leslie and Mary Elizabeth (Roberts) C.; m. Mary Jo Dorr, July 17, 1976; children: Leslie Patton, William Roberts, Maribeth Dorr. BA, U. Miss., 1971, JD, 1974. Bar: Miss. 1974, U.S. Dist. Ct. (no. dist.) Miss. 1974, U.S. Dist. Ct. (we. dist.) Tenn. 1986. Assoc. Bailey & Trusty, Batesville, Miss., 1974-79; ptnr. Bailey, Trusty & Cook, Batesville, Miss., 1980-90, Bailey & Cook, Batesville, Miss., 1990-92, Bailey, Cook & Womble, Batesville, Miss., 1992—. Chmn., Miss. Coll. Rep. Clubs, 1973, Panola County March of Dimes, Batesville, 1976-78; Miss. chmn. Nat. Orgn. Social Security Claimants Reps., 1981-82; rep. Honor Coun., U. Miss. Sch. Law, 1974 King Batesville Jr. Aux. Charity Ball, 2000. Paul Harris fellow 1998—. Mem. ABA (torts and ins. practice sect. 1979—, vice chmn. com. on delivery of legal svcs. tothe disabled young lawyers divsn. 1983-85, gen. practice sect. 1985-86), ATLA, Miss. State Bar (state bd. bar admissions 1978-79, mem. ethics com. 1980-83, bd. dirs. Young Lawyers sect. 1980-83, chmn. com. on unauthorized practice of law 1983-86, workers compensation sect., mem. com. on Kid's Second Chance 1992), Panola County Bar Assn. (pres. 1979-80), Miss. Trial Lawyers Assn. (membership com. 1983-84), Ct. Practice Inst. (diplomate), Lawyer-Pilots Bar Assn., Lamar Soc. Internat. Law, Lamar Order-U. Miss., Batesville Jaycees (legal counsel 1975-77), Masons, Shriners, Rotary (pres. 1991-92, 96-97, asst. dist. gov. 1997-99, dist. gov. nominee 1999-2000, dist. gov. 2000-01, Paul Harris fellow, Four Aves. of Svc. Citation, Rotary Found. Dist. Svc. award, Dist. Found. chmn., del. Coun. on Legislation 2003—), Omicron Delta Kappa, Pi Sigma Alpha, Delta Theta Pi. Methodist. Home: 110 Shagbark Dr Batesville MS 38606-8470 Office: Panola Plz 118 Highway 6 W Batesville MS 38606-2507 E-mail: wlcook@panola.com.

COOK, WILLIAM STATON, medical researcher; b. Denver, July 2, 1970; m. Paula Rogers, Aug. 21, 1993; 1 child, William Samuel. BA, Baylor U., 1993; MS, Tex. Tech U., 1995; PhD, Northwestern U., 2001. Post doctoral fellow Touchstone Ctr. for Diabetes Rsch. U. Tex. Southwestern Med. Ctr., Dallas, 2001—. Contbr. articles to profl. jours. Mem.: Am. Diabetes Assn. Achievements include research in fat metabolism in mice and how it is controlled by the nuclear receptor protein ppark. Office: Touchstone Ctr Dept Internal Medicine Dallas TX 75390

COOK-BENNETT, GAIL, pension fund administrator; BA in Econ., Carleton U., 1962; MA in Econ., U. Mich.; PhD in Econ., U. Mich.i. Former acad. positions U. Toronto; former sr. exec. position C.D. Howe Inst.; vice-chair Bennecon Ltd., 1982—98; chairperson Can. Pension Plan Investment Bd., Toronto, 1998—. Bd. dirs. Groupe Transcontinental GTC Ltd., MacKenzie Finl. Corp., Manulife Finl. Corp., Petro-Can. Recipient Honour for Contbn. to Working Women, Montreal YWCA, 1977. Fellow: Can. Inst. Corp. Dirs. Office: Can Pension Plan Investment Bd Ste 2700 PO Box 101 1 Queen St E Toronto ON M5C 2W5 Canada Office Fax: 416-868-4760. E-mail: csr@cppib.ca.

COOK-DEEGAN, ROBERT MULLAN, science and health policy analyst, physician; b. Pitts., May 18, 1953; s. William Raymond Cook and Merry (Mullan) Low. BA in Chemistry, Harvard Coll., 1975; MD, U. Colo., 1979. Intern U. Colo., Denver, 1979-80, postdoctoral fellow, rsch. pathologist, 1980-82; sr. assoc. Office Tech. Assessment, U.S. Congress, Washington, 1982-88; acting exec. dir. biomed. ethics adv. com. U.S. Congress, Washington, 1988-89; expert Nat. Ctr. Human Genome Rsch., Bethesda, Md., 1989-90; dir. div. bio-behavioral scis. and mental disorders Inst. Medicine, NAS, Washington, 1991-94; sr. program officer NAS, 1994-96; Cecil and Ida Green fellow U. Tex., Dallas, 1996; dir. Nat. Cancer Policy Bd., 1996-2000, Robert Wood Johnson Health Policy Fellowship Program, 2001—. Sr. rsch. fellow Kennedy Inst. Ethics, 1986—; assoc. Johns Hopkins Sch. Hygiene and Pub. Health, Balt., 1988—; staff Allocating Federal Funds for Sci. and Tech., 1994-96. Author: The Gene Wars: Science, Politics, and the Human Genome, 1994. Bd. dirs. Physicians for Human Rights, Boston, 1987-96. Recipient Robert Johnson Health Policy Rsch. Investigator award, 1999—2002; grantee Alfred P. Sloan Found., Georgetown U., 1988—91, NSF, 1990—91, Nat. Cancer Inst. and Robert Wood Johnson, 1992—2000, Burroughs Wellcome Fund, 2000—01. Fellow AAAS. Achievements include research in history of human genome project, public policy in cancer, health policy, tobacco control, neurology, psychiatry, behavioral medicine, neuroscience and addiction; U.S. federal policy on Alzheimer's disease and other dementing disorders, public policy on human gene therapy and bioethics. Office: Kennedy Inst of Ethics Georgetown Univ Box 571212 Washington DC 20057-1212 E-mail: bcd@nas.edu.

COOKE, ALEXANDER HAMILTON, lawyer; b. Louisville, Ky., Jan. 25, 1941; s. Henry Thurston and Elizabeth Hamilton (Davis) C.; m. Genie Ray Warson, Aug. 8, 1964; children: Henry Thurston II, Katherine Watson. AB, Davidson (N.C.) Coll., 1963; JD, Vanderbilt U., 1968. Bar: Fla. 1968, U.S. Dist. Ct. (mid dist.) Fla. 1969; cert. wills, trusts and estates. Assoc. Mahoney, Hadlow, Chambers & Adams, Jacksonville, Fla., 1968-71, Adams & Adams, Jacksonville, 1972-74; sole practice Jacksonville, 1974; ptnr. Alexander, Spraker, Cooke & Hand, Jacksonville, 1975-78; ptnr., pres. Cooke, Hand, Carithers, Showalter & Mercier, Jacksonville, 1979-88; ptnr. Ulmer, Murchison, Ashby & Taylor, Jacksonville, 1988-92; ptrn., pres. Cooke & Meux, P.A. (formerly A. Hamilton Cooke, P.A., Jacksonville, 1993—2002, Cooke & Meux, P.A., 2003—. Chmn. Jacksonville Cmty. Rels. Commn., 1979; bd. dirs. Luth. Social Svcs., Inc., 1984-90; bd. dirs. Presbytery of St. Augustine, 1989—2001, pres., 1999—2001. 1st lt. U.S. Army, 1963-65. Mem. Fla. Bar Assn. (bd. govs. 1987-91, exec. coun. cir. rep. real property, probate and trust law sect. 1981-97), Jacksonville Bar Assn. (pres. 1982-83), Fla. Bar Found. (bd. dirs. 1991-2001, pres. 2000-01). Democrat. Presbyterian. Avocations: golf, camping, canoeing, traveling. Office: Cooke & Meux PA 1301 Riverplace Blvd Ste 2254 Jacksonville FL 32207-9036

COOKE, ALFRED ALISTAIR, correspondent, writer, broadcaster; b. Manchester, Eng., Nov. 20, 1908; naturalized, 1941; s. Samuel and Mary Elizabeth (Byrne) C.; m. Ruth Emerson; 1 child, John Byrne; m. Jane White Hawkes; 1 child, Susan Byrne. 1st class English Tripos, Jesus Coll., Cambridge, 1929, BA, 1930; Commonwealth Fund fellow, Yale, 1932-33, Harvard U., 1933-34; LL.D. (hon.), U. Edinburgh, 1969, U. Manchester, 1973; Litt.D. (hon.), St. Andrew's U., 1976, Cambridge U., 1988, Yale U., 1993. Film critic BBC, 1934-37, BBC commentator on Am. affairs, 1938—; London corr. NBC, 1936-37; spl. corr. Am. affairs London Times, 1938- 42; Am. feature writer London Daily Herald, 1941-43; UN corr. (Manchester) Guardian, 1945-48, chief U.S. corr., 1948-72; host PBS Series Masterpiece Theater, 1971-92. Scholar Jesus Coll., Cambridge, hon. fellow, 1986. TV emcee: Omnibus, 1952-61; writer, narrator: TV series America: A Personal History of the U.S, 1972-73; (4 Emmy awards 1973); Author: Douglas Fairbanks, 1940, A Generation On Trial, 1950, One Man's America, 1952, Christmas Eve, 1952, A Commencement Address, 1954, Talk About America, 1968, Alistair Cooke's America, 1973, reprinted 2002, Six Men, 1977, reprinted 96, The Americans: Fifty Letters from America on our life and times, 1979, Masterpieces, 1981, The Patient Has the Floor, 1986, America Observed, 1988, Fun and Games with Alistair Cooke, 1994, Memories of the Great and the Good, 1999; co-author: Above London, 1980; Editor: Garbo and the Night Watchmen, 1937, The Vintage Mencken, 1955, The Granta, 1931-32; narrator: March of Time, 1938-39; on-screen narrator: Three Faces of Eve, 1957. Recipient Peabody award for internat. news reporting, 1952, 73; Benjamin Franklin medal Royal Soc. Arts, 1973; Howland medal Yale U., 1977; Spl. Peabody award, 1983; decorated knight comdr. Brit. Empire, 1973 Mem.: The Links N.Y.C. (hon. life), Lotos Club (hon. life), Nat. Arts Club N.Y.C. (hon. life), Players Club (hon. life), San Francisco Golf Club (hon. life). Address: 1150 5th Ave New York NY 10128-0724

COOKE, CARLTON LEE, JR., mayor; b. Marion, Ala., July 12, 1944; s. Carlton Lee and Willie (Rinehart) C.; married; 1 child, Kimberly Ann. Student, U. Hawaii, 1962-65; BA, La. Tech. U., 1966; postgrad., U. Tex., 1970-72. Mfg. engr. Tex. Instruments, Austin, 1972-75, site personnel mgr., 1975-81, mktg. mgr., 1981-83; pres., CEO Greater Austin C. of C., 1983-87; mayor City of Austin, Austin, 1988—. CEO, pres. good2CU.com, Inc., 1999—2000; chmn., CEO Habitek Internat., Inc., 1991—, Tanisys Tech. Corp., 2002—03; pres., CEO U.S. Med. Systems, Inc., 1992—; bd. dirs. New Century Equity Holdings Corp., Bill Concepts Corp., U.S. Long Distance Corp., Sharps Compliance Corp., Med. Polymers Tech., Inc., CUville.com, Inc., FIData.com, Inc., The Staubach Co., Austin, Tanisys Tech. Corp.; participant U.S. Conf. Mayors, Washington, 1991; mem. Anthony Commn., U.S. Congress; bd. dirs. Stewart Title, Austin. Contbr. editor to mags. Mem. Austin City Coun., 1977-91, mayor pro tem, 1979; co-chmn. Jerry Lewis Telethon, Austin, 1986-87; chmn. United Negro Telethon, 1991, Tex. Housing Fin. Corp., 1992-94, Austin Charter Com., 1993-94, Tex. Walk of Stars, 1991-2003; mem. adv. bd. U. Miami Rosenstiel Sch. Ctr. for Sustainable Fisheries, 2001—. Capt. USAF, 1966-72. Decorated Bronze Star (Vietnam); recipient Carl Burnett Cmty. award, 1981, Disting. Austin Citizen's award, 1992, Excellence award Real Estate Coun. of Austin, 1992; named Jaycee of Yr. Austin Jaycees, 1976, one of Five Outstanding Young Texans Tex. Jaycees, 1979. Mem. Nat. League Cities (chair fin. steering com.), Tex. Mcpl. League (pres. 1991), Austin-San Antonio Corridor Coun. (pres. 1988, 91), VFW. Baptist. Avocations: travel, reading, civic work, movie history, art. Home: PO Box 50442 Austin TX 78763-0442 Office: Office of Mayor 2705 Bee Cave Rd Ste 160 Austin TX 78746 E-mail: usmedsys@austin.rr.com.

COOKE, CHRISTOPHER ROBERT, former state judge, lawyer; b. Springfield, Ohio, Dec. 23, 1943; s. Warren and Margaret Louise (Martin) C.; m. Margaret (Nick), July 1, 1970; children— Karen, Anastasia, Nicholas. B.A., Yale U., 1965; J.D., U. Mich., 1968. Bar: Ohio 1968, Alaska 1970, U.S. Dist. Ct. Alaska 1970. Atty., Alaska Legal Services Corp., Anchorage, 1968-71, supervising atty., Bethel, 1971-73; mem. firm Rice, Hoppner & Hedland, Bethel, 1973-76; superior ct. judge State of Alaska, Bethel, 1976-86; ptnr. Hedland, Fleischer, Friedman, Brennan & Cooke, Bethel and Anchorage, 1986—; chmn. Alaska Dem. Party, 1999-2001. Composer, singer Chris Cooke's Tundra Music, 1981. Bd. regents U. Alaska-Fairbanks, 1975-77; mem. com. Alaska Humanities Forum, Anchorage, 1979-86; adv. bd. Bethel Sch. Bd., 1982-83. Mem. ABA, Alaska Bar Assn. Home and Office: PO Box 555 Bethel AK 99559-0555 Address: Ste 300 1227 W 9th Ave Anchorage AK 99501 E-mail: LAW@hbhc.alaska.net.

COOKE, EDWARD STRONG, JR., art educator; b. Orange, N.J., Dec. 14, 1954; s. Edward Strong and Barbara Murray C.; m. Carol Ridgely Warner, Dec. 26, 1981; children: Benjamin Warner, Rachel Allison. BA, Yale U., 1977; MA, U. Del., 1979; PhD, Boston U., 1983. Adj. assoc. prof. Am. studies Boston U., 1985-92; assoc. curator Am. decorative arts Mus. Fine Arts, Boston, 1985-92; Charles F. Montgomery prof. Am. decorative arts Yale U., New Haven, Conn., 1992—. Author: New American Furniture, 1989, Making Furniture in Pre-Industrial America, 1996 (Montgomery prize 1996); co-author: Inspiring Reform: Boston's Arts and Crafts Movement, 1997; mem. editl. bd. Am. Furniture, 1993—. Bd. dirs. Vernacular Arch. Forum, 1994-97. Recipient Iris Found. award Bard Grad. Ctr., 2000. Mem. Decorative Arts Soc. (chair Montgomery Prize award com. 1991—), Furniture Soc. (trustee 1997—), Cambridge Boat Club, Prouts Neck Yacht Club. Avocations: sculling, woodworking. Home: 26 Lowell Ave Newtonville MA 02460-1612 Office: Dept History Art Yale U PO Box 208272 New Haven CT 06520-8272

COOKE, FRED CHARLES, real estate broker; b. Winchester, Tenn., Dec. 3, 1915; s. Warner Cleveland and Emma (Lancaster) C.; m. Pamela Burr, Dec. 27, 1942; children: Gary Donald, David Charles, Pamela Ann, Alexander Campbell. AB, Lincoln Meml. U., 1939; grad., Realtor's Inst., 1988. Commd. USAF, 1942, advanced through ranks to lt. col., project officer, R & D engr. specialist, 1951-53, resigned, 1953; realtor Ft. Walton Beach, Fla., 1956—. With USAF Res. Decorated DFC, Air medal with oak leaf cluster; inducted into Alumni Athletic Hall of Fame, 1987. Mem. Ft. Walton Beach Bd. Realtors (pres. 1959-60, 65), Fla. Assn. Realtors (dist. v.p. 1965, pres. Diamond Pin Club 1988), Nat. Assn. Realtors (bd. dirs. 1983-86, realtor emeritus 1993), Fla. Real Estate Exchangors (founder 1972), Greater Ft. Walton Beach C. of C. (chmn. waterways and reefs com. 1983-87, Award of Excellence), Fla. Waterways Adv. Bd., Ft. Walton Yacht Club (vice commodore 1984, commodore 1989, dir. 1990-95), Ft. Walton Power Squadron (commdr. 1972-73), Civitan (pres. 1961-62, dist. v.p. Birmingham 1963), Emerald Coast Sailing Assn. (founder 1992). Republican. Episcopalian. Home: 227 Alconese Ave SE Unit F Fort Walton Beach FL 32548-2803 Office: 79 Beal Pky NE Fort Walton Beach FL 32548-4822

COOKE, KENNETH LLOYD, mathematician, educator; b. Kansas City, Mo., Aug. 13, 1925; s. Sidney Kenneth and Mildred Blanche (Brown) C.; m. Margaret Sarah Burgess, Aug. 18, 1950; children: Catherine Sarah, Robert K., Susan E. BA, Pomona Coll., 1947; MS, Stanford, 1949, PhD, 1952. Instr., then asst. prof. math. State Coll. Wash., Pullman, 1950-57; mem. faculty Pomona Coll., 1957-93, Joseph N. Fiske prof. math., 1963—, chmn. dept., 1961-71, W.B. Keck disting. service prof., 1985-93. Cons. RAND Corp., 1956-65; mathematician Rsch. Inst. Advanced Studies, Balt., 1963-64; NSF sci. faculty fellow Stanford, 1966-67; Fulbright rsch. scholar U. Florence, Italy, 1971-72; vis. prof. Brown U., 1978-79, Inst. Math. Applications, U. Minn., 1983, Cornell

U., 1987; Fulbright lectr. U. São Paulo, Sao Carlos, Brazil, 1987. Author: (with Richard Bellman) Differential-Difference Equations, 1963, Modern Elementary Differential Equations, 2d edit., 1971, (with Richard Bellman and J.A. Lockett) Algorithms, Graphs and Computers, 1970, (with Donald Bentley) Linear Algebra with Differential Equations, 1973, (with Colin Renfrew) Transformations: Mathematical Approaches to Culture Change, 1979, (with Stavros Busenberg) Vertically Transmitted Diseases, 1993; co-editor: Differential Equations and Applications in Ecology, Epidemics, and Population Problems, 1981, Differential Equations and Applications to Biology and to Industry, 1995. Served with USNR, 1944-46. Mem.: AAAS, Soc. Math. Biology, Soc. Indsl. and Applied Math., Math. Assn. Am., Am. Math. Soc., Sigma Xi, Phi Beta Kappa. Mem. United Ch. Christ. Home: 654 N Northwestern Dr Claremont CA 91711-4149

COOKE, MARVIN LEE, sociologist, consultant, urban planner; b. Tulsa, Dec. 9, 1947; s. Marvin Joel and Mary Lee (Sleeper) C.; m. Sandra Pauline Creason, Dec. 23, 1967 (div. Mar. 1979); 1 child, Francis Wesley; m. Mary Lou Albitz, Nov. 25, 1981. BA summa cum laude, Cen. State U., Edmond, Okla., 1970; PhD, Okla. State U., 1993; M in Divinity summa cum laude, Phillips U., Enid, Okla., 1975. Ordained to ministry United Meth. Ch., 1972, withdrew, 1985. Pastor Carmen (Okla.) United Meth. Ch., 1973-75, Turley United Meth. Ch., Tulsa, 1975-78; assoc. dir. Tulsa Met. Ministry, 1978-82, exec. dir., 1982-88; planner urban devel. City of Tulsa, 1992-98; divsn. chair Tulsa Cmty. Coll., 1998-2001, assoc. dean instrn., 2001—. Recipient O.D. Duncan award, Rsch. Excellence award Okla. State U., 1993. Mem. Am. Planning Assn., Am. Sociol. Assn. Democrat. Episcopalian. Avocations: running, biking, hiking. Home: 2929 E 103rd St Tulsa OK 74137 E-mail: mcooke@tulsacc.edu., marvincooke@hotmail.com.

COOKE, MICHAEL, editor-in-chief; Former editor-in-chief The Vancouver Province, 2000; editor-in-chief Chgo. Sun Times, 2000—. Office: Chgo Sun Times 401 N Wabash Ave Chicago IL 60611 Office Fax: 312-321-3084.*

COOKE, R(ICHARD) CASWELL, JR., architect; b. Richmond, Va., Dec. 19, 1935; s. Richard Caswell and Caroline (Kellock) C.; m. Mary Gibson, June 6, 1962; children: Richard, Frederick, Gordon, Molly. BArch, U. Va., 1962; MArch, Yale U., 1967. Registered architect, Mass., Conn., Va., N.C., S.C., Ill., N.J., Pa., N.S., Colo., R.I. Project mgr. Clinch Crimp Brown & Fischer, Boston, 1962-64, Paul Rudolph Arch., New Haven, 1964-65; prin., dir. Geotactics, Inc., New Haven, 1965-82; gen. mgr. Gulf Consult Archs., Al Khobar, Saudi Arabia, 1982-86; prin. Fellows, Read, Loncavallo & Cooke, Princeton, N.J., 1986-89; v.p., dir. arch. Washington Group (formerly Raytheon Engrs. & Constructors), London, 1989—; pres. Washington Archs. LLC (formerly Raytheon Archs.), Princeton, Phila., London. Lectr. Quinnipiac Coll., New Haven, St. Paul's Ch., Kiwanis Club; juried design Yale U. Prin. works include design of Petromin Corp. Bldg., Riyadh, Saudi Arabia, Baxter Health Care Facility, Calif., Roche Carolina Campus, S.C., Can. Red Cross Facility, N.S., Derby (Conn.) Elderly Housing, The Mus. at Fort Bliss, El Paso, Tex. Chmn. New Haven Harbor Commn., 1976, Conn. Regional Planning Com., 1976; bd. dirs. Am. Businessmen's assn., Saudi Arabia, 1986; pres. Yale Alumni Assn. Sch. Architecture, 1978; past bd. dirs. Conn. Soc. Architects. Recipient Christchurch Sch. Alumni award, 1975, first design award Milford Yacht Club, 1977, Alpha Rho Chi award U. Va., 1962. Mem. AIA, N.J. Soc. Archs., Nat. Coun. Archtl. Registration Bds., Assn. of Yale Alumni, Yale Club of Princeton (past pres.), Constrn. Specification Inst., Illuminating Engrs. Soc., Am. Soc. Landscape Archs., Sons of the Revolution (N.J. bd. dirs.), Henry Found. for Bot. Rsch. Episcopalian. Office: Washington Architects LLC 510 Carnegie Ctr Princeton NJ 08543-5287 E-mail: caswell.cooke@wgint.com.

COOKE, RON CHARLES, science educator; b. Chico, Calif., Dec. 31, 1947; s. Charles Edgar and Sylvia Johnson Cooke; m. Lucy Jean Whittlesey; 1 child, Rhonda. BS, Calif. State U., Chico, 1970; MS, U. of the Pacific, Stockton, CA, 1972. Lab dir. Baileys Nursery, Lodi, Calif., 1975—78; tech. rep. Flow Laboratories, McLean, Va., 1978—81; instr. Calif. State University-Chico, Chico, Calif., 1981—. Author: (book) Online Searching Curriculum for Chemistry ; contbr. articles to profl. jour. Office: California State University Chemistry Dept Chico CA 95929-0210 Office Fax: 530-898-5234. E-mail: rcooke@csuchico.edu.

COOKE, THOMAS PAUL, education educator; b. Panama Canal, Oct. 12, 1948; s. Thomas Paul and Sarah Anne (Downing) C.; m. Sharon Anne Raver, Dec. 18, 1968 (div. June 1975); 1 child, James Mitchell; m. Marrianne McKinley, Apr. 14, 1990. BA, U. South Fla., 1970, MA, 1971; PhD, Vanderbilt U., 1974. Coord. spl. edn. Sonoma State U., Rohnert Park, Calif., 1982-88, prof. edn., 1983—, chmn. dept. edn., 1988-92, dept. chmn. ednl. leadership, spl. edn., 2001-. Author: Exceptional Children: Assessing and Modifying Social Behavior, 1976, Towards Excellence: Achievements in Residential Arrangements, 1980, Early Independence: A Curriculum System, 1981, Self Instructional Curriculum Development, 1981, A New Look at Guardianship, 1984; contbr. articles to profl. jours. Chmn. bd. Found. for Ednl. Devel., Napa, Calif., 1993-96. Avocations: sea kayaking, river kayaking, skiing.

COOKE, WALTA PIPPEN, automobile dealership owner; b. Shreveport, La., Oct. 18, 1940; d. Billy Burt and Eula (Heaton) Pippen; m. John William Cooke II, Dec. 20, 1958; children: Cheryl Cooke Williams, John William III. BA, Baylor U., 1963. Co-owner, sec.-treas. Pippen Motor Co., Carthage, Tex., 1972-80, owner, sec.-treas., 1980—. Bd. dirs. Sabine River Authority of Tex., 1993-99, pres. bd., 1996-97; past dir. Toledo Bend Joint Project; chmn. lower basin project com. Sabine River Authority Tex., 1999, mem. by-laws com., chmn. 50th ann. com., 1999. Pianist for sanctuary choir Ctrl. Bapt. Ch., Carthage, 1986—; chmn. 50th anniversary celebration com. Sabine River Authority of Tex., 1999; bd. dir. Panola Co. Heritage Found., 2000—, patron mem., mem. ednl. found. steering com., 2002—; mem. task force Groundwater Conservation, East Tex. Area.; founding dir. Carthage Ind. Sch. Dist. Edn. Found. Mem. Carthage 32 Club, Carthage Book Club (rec. sec. 1995-97), The Carthage Club. Avocations: reading, gardening, travel, music. Home: 200 Timberlane Dr Carthage TX 75633-2231 Office: Pippen Motor Co 1300 W Panola St Carthage TX 75633-2346

COOKE, WILLIAM L. lawyer; b. Aulander, N.C., May 19, 1925; s. Willie A. Cooke and Nina Parker; m. Betty Butler; 1 child, Elizabeth Leigh. AB, U. N.C., 1948, LLB, 1950. Bar: N.C. 1950, U.S. Dist. Ct. N.C., U.S. Supreme Ct. Atty. Pritchett & Cooke, Windsor, N.C., 1951-97; sole practitioner Windsor, 1997—. Lt. USNR, 1945-65. Mem. N.C. Bar Assn., Bertie County County and Dist. Bar Assn., Rotary (pres. 1958). Democrat. Baptist.

COOKE, WILLIAM ROBERT, minister, mayor; b. Cornelius, Oreg., Apr. 6, 1929; s. William Robert and Edna (Ivorine) C.; m. Doris Marie Cooke, June 1, 1953; children: Jan Robert, Jon Mario, Joan Marie. Grad., Life Bible Coll., L.A., 1951. Ordained min. Internation Ch. of Foursquare Gospel, 1951. Pastor Foursquare Ch., Dallas, Oreg., 1953-56, Nampa, Idaho, 1956, Redmond, Oreg., 1957-80, Tulare, Calif., 1980-2000. Contbr. articles to profl. publs. Mem. coun. City of Tulare, 1992-98, mayor, 1998-2002; bd. dirs. Love Inc. Tulare, Calif., 1990—, pres., 2002—; chair Citizen's Com. to Evaluate and Fin. Schs., Redmond, 1979; mem. Tulare Assn. Chs., 1980—; mem. Local Agy. Formation Commn. for Tulare County; mem. housing and econ. policy com. Calif. League of Cities, 1994—. Republican. Home: 320 N Blackstone St Spc 10 Tulare CA 93274-4451

COOKMAN, CLAUDE, journalist, educator; AB in Classical Greek (with hons.), Wheaton Coll., 1965; MS in Journalism, Columbia U., 1971; MFA in Art History, Princeton U., 1989, PhD in History of Photography, 1994. Reporter Anderson (Ind.) Herald, 1965, 1968—70; picture editor Assoc. Press, NYC, 1971—73; copy editor Herald-Jour., Syracuse, NY, 1973—74; picture editor Louisville Times, Louisville, 1974—81; graphics editor Miami Herald, 1981—84; copy editor Courier-Jour., Louisville, 1984—86; asst. instr. dept. art and archaeology Princeton (NJ) U., 1988—89; assoc. prof. journalism Ind. U., Bloomington, 1990—. Adj. instr. Western Ky. U., Bowling Green, 1979, Bowling Green, 1979, 80; vis. lectr. U. Iowa, 1981; adj. instr. Barry U., Miami, 1984. Contbr. articles to profl. publs. Co-recipient Pulitzer prize, 1976; fellow Gretchen Kemp Tchg. fellow, Ind. U., 1993. Mem.: Soc. Photographic Edn., Nat. Press Photographers Assn. (Robin F. Garland Educator award 1999), Soc. News Design, Assn. Edn. Journalism Mass Comm. Office: Sch Jour Ind Univ Ernie Pyle Hall 209 940 E 7th St Bloomington IN 47405-7108*

COOKSEY, JOHN CHARLES, former congressman, ophthalmic surgeon; b. Aug. 20, 1941; s. Henry Oscar and Ruth (Lee) C.; m. Dorothy Ann Grabill, Dec. 30, 1969; children: Karen, Carol Ann, Catherine. MD, La. State U., New Orleans, 1966; MBA, U. Tex., Austin, 1994. Mem. Congress from 5th La. Dist., 1996—, mem. agr. & internat. rels. coms.; practice medicine specializing in ophthalmology Monroe, La., 1972-96. Mem. teaching staff E.A. Conway Hosp., Monroe, 1972—; vis. lectr. Alton Ochsner Med. Found., New Orleans, 1978—; asst. clin. prof. La. State U. Med. Sch., New Orleans, 1979—. Republican. Address: 1310 N 19th St Monroe LA 71201

COOKSEY, RAY WAGNER, human resource management educator; b. Hamilton AFB, Calif., Aug. 30, 1954; arrived in Australia, 1982; s. James Wagner Cooksey and Jean Elizabeth (Blowers) Barrows; m. Christie Anne Christopher, Dec. 19, 1976; children: Sarah Anne, Aaron James. BSc, Colo. State Univ., 1976, MSc, 1978, PhD, 1981. Engring. psychologist Bendix Corp., Denver, 1981-82; lectr. in edn. Univ. New England, Armidale NSW, Australia, 1982-90, sr. lectr. in psychology, 1990-94, assoc. prof., 1994-99, prof., 2000—. Chair acad. bd. U. New Eng., 2001—; statistical cons. U.S. Dept. Agriculture, Ft. Collins, Colo., 1977-81; external assessor Australian Rsch. Coun. and Nat. Sci. Found., 1993—; editl. bd. mem. Jour. of Behavioral Decision Making, 1997—, Internat. Jour. Mgmt. Lit., 2000— Author: Judgment Analysis: Theory, Methods & Applications, 1996; contbr. articles to profl. jours. V.p., federal and state councillor UNE Tchr.'s Assn., Australia, 1986-88; electoral chair acad. bd. U. N.Eng., 2001—. Recipient Vice-Chancellor's award for Teaching Excellence, Univ. New Eng., 1996. Mem. The Brunswik Soc., System Dynamics Soc., Soc. Judgment and Decision Making, Australian and New Zealand Acad. Mgmt. treas. mem. nat. exec. com. 1999-2002, pres. 2003), Phi Beta Kappa. Avocations: reading science fiction, ten pin bowling, astronomy, fractal mathematics. Office: Univ New Eng New Eng Bus Sch 2351 Armidale Australia

COOKSON, ALAN HOWARD, electrical engineer, researcher; b. London, July 3, 1939; arrived in U.S., 1968; s. Joseph and Rachel Cookson; m. Elizabeth Rosamond Ritblat, Oct. 24, 1965; children: Richard Jonathan, Simon Charles. B.Sc. in Engring. with 1st class honors, Queen Mary Coll., London U., 1961, PhD in Elec. Engring., 1965. Chartered engr., Gt. Brit. Rsch. fellow Queen Mary Coll., London, 1964-65; rsch. officer Ctrl. Elec. Rsch. Labs., Leatherhead, England, 1965-68; sr. engr. Westinghouse R & D Ctr., Pitts., 1968-75; mgr. gas cable rsch. Westinghouse Power Circuit Breaker, Westborough, Mass., 1975-80; mgr. polymers, dielectrics and advanced batteries Westinghouse Sci. & Tech. Ctr., Pitts., 1980-92; dep. dir. Electronics and Elec. Engring. Lab. divsn. Nat. Inst. Stds. and Tech., Gaithersburg, Md., 1992—. U.S. rep. advanced materials for electro tech. com. Internat. Conf. Large Elec. Systems, 1996—; mem. US nat. com. Internat. Electrotech. Commn.; convener Working Group on Gas Insulated Cables, Internat. Conf. Large Elec. Systems, 1980-90. Editor: Digest of Literature on Dielectrics, 1970; contbr. articles to profl. jours.; patentee in field. Mem. adv. com. Miss. State U., 1983. Fellow IEEE (pres. Dielectrics and Elec. Insulation Soc. 1993-94), Inst. Elec. Engrs. London; mem. Phys. Soc., Inst. Physics London. Home: 15717 Bondy Ln Darnestown MD 20878-2114 Office: Nat Inst Standards/Tech Rm B358 Bldg 220 Gaithersburg MD 20899-0001 E-mail: alan.cookson@nist.gov.

COOKSON, ALBERT ERNEST, telephone and telegraph company executive; b. Needham, Mass., Oct. 30, 1921; s. Willard B. and Sarah Jane (Jack) C.; m. Constance J. Buckley, Sept. 10, 1949 (dec. July 1987); children: Constance J., William B.; m. Lorraine B. Hirsch, Dec. 29, 1987. BEE, Northeastern U., 1943; MEE, MIT, 1951; ScD, Gordon Coll., 1974. Group leader Research Lab. Electronics, Mass. Inst. Tech., 1947-51; lab. dir. ITT Fed. Labs., Nutley, N.J., 1951-59; v.p., dir. operations ITT Fed. Labs. (Internat. Elec. Corp. div.), Paramus, N.J., 1959-62; pres. ITT Intelcom, Falls Church, Va., 1962-65; dep. gen. tech. dir. Internat. Tel. & Tel. Corp., N.Y.C., 1965-66, v.p., tech. dir., 1966-68, sr. v.p., gen. tech. dir., 1968-84, ret., 1984; pres., chief exec. officer Richmond Properties, 1982—. Chmn. bd. ITT Interplan; pres., chmn. Comtexco Industries, 1980—; chmn. tech. adv. bd. U.S. Postal Svc., 1983-91; bd. dirs. Internat. Standard Electric, ITT Industries; mem. Def. Communications Satellite Panel; adviser research and engring. on def. communications satellite systems Dept. Def.; mem. indsl. panel sci. and tech. NSF; mem. Fairfax County Econ. and Indsl. Devel. Com., 1962-65; mem. nat. coun. Northeastern U.; mem. pride com. U. Hartford, 1973-76; elec. engring./computer adv. bd. MIT, 1977-82. Bd. dirs. Fundacion Chile, 1983-89. Served with USNR, 1943-46. Fellow IEEE; mem. Armed Forces Communications and Electronics Assn., Am. Mgmt. Assn., Am. Inst. Aeros. and Astronautics, Electronic Industries Assn., Sigma Xi, Tau Beta Pi. Achievements include patents in frequency search and track system.

COOL, MARY L. education specialist; b. Buffalo, Dec. 7, 1954; d. Paul G. and Dorothy R. (O'Brien) Wailand; m. Ronald J. Cool, June 23, 1979; children: Logan Elizabeth, Colin Jeffery. BS in Elem. Edn. cum laude, SUNY, Fredonia, 1976; MS in Ednl. Leadership, Nova Southeastern U., 1996. Cert. tchr., N.Y., Fla. Tchr. grade 1, Buffalo, N.Y., 1976-77; tchr. grade 5 Orange County, Orlando, Fla., 1979-85; tchr. grade 1, ESEA Title I head tchr. Manatee County, Myakka City, Fla., 1977-79; tchr. grade 5, media specialist Volusia County, Osteen, Fla., 1985-89; intermediate resource tchr. S.W. Volusia County, Fla., 1989-91; dist. elem. resource tchr., elem. tchr. specialist Volusia County Schs., Fla., 1991-97, staff devel. specialist, 1997-98, sch. improvement coord., 1998—2002; sch. improvement coord. initiative implementation Charter Sch. Dist., 2002—, elem. edn. coord., 2003—. Grade level chair, sci. chair, reading chair, facilitative leader, coop. learning trainer, tchr. coach, tech. edn. coach, tchr. asst. coord., student success team coord., tchr. induction coord. Volusia County Schs.; ednl. cons. Scholastic, Inc., Sports Illus. for Kids, Kids Discover, Marvel Comics, Time for Kids, UNICEF, Miami Mus. Arts and Scis. Mem. ASCD, AAUW, Nat. Coalition for Sex Equity in Edn., Nat. Staff Devel. Coun., Fla. Coun. Elem. Edn., Kappa Delta Pi. Home: 1566 Gregory Dr Deltona FL 32738-6159 Office: PO Box 2410 Daytona Beach FL 32115-2410

COOLEDGE, RICHARD CALVIN, lawyer; b. Charleston, S.C., Apr. 20, 1943; s. Russell Clarence and Lorena Ann (Weymouth) C.; m. Nancy Jean Western, June 15, 1965 (div. Dec. 1986); children: Dean Richard, Mark Alan, Jocelyn Joy; m. Jeanine Diana Smith, Apr. 12, 1989 (div. Nov. 1993). BA in Econs. with honors, U. Mo., Columbia, 1965; JD, U. Mich., 1968. Bar: Ariz. 1969, U.S. Dist. Ct. Ariz. 1969, U.S. Ct. Appeals (9th cir.) 1973, U.S. Supreme Ct. 1973. Mem. Brown & Bain P.A., Phoenix, 1968—. Contbg. editor: Banking and Lending Institutions Forms, Business Workouts Manual; contbr. articles to profl. jours. Fellow Ariz. Bar Found.; mem. Motorcycle Safety Found. (instr. 1994-), Harley Owners Group. Avocations: motorcycling, golf, music, aviculture. Office: Brown & Bain PA 2901 N Central Ave Fl 20 Phoenix AZ 85012-2700 E-mail: cooledge@brownbain.com.

COOLEN, PHYLLIS ROSE, community health nurse; b. Monterey, Calif., Oct. 13, 1950; BSN, U. Wash., 1973, MSN, 1981. Hospice clinician Providence Med. Ctr., Seattle, 1980-86; nursing cons. home health Dept. Social and Health Svc. Med. Asst. Adminstrn., Olympia, 1986, nursing care cons., 1987-87, nursing cons. advisor, 1987-93, nursing cons. adv., quality care coord., 1993-95, acting dir. divsn. utilization svcs., 1995-97; dir. divsn. health svcs. quality support Med. Assistance Adminstrn., Olympia, 1997—2001, dir. med. ops. div. med. mgmt., 2001—02, mgr. exception case mgmt., 2002—; NRS cons. advisor Dept. Social and Health Svcs., 2002—. Theory, clin. instr. fundamentals and advanced med.-surg. Kauai C.C., Lihue, Hawaii, 1983-85; clin. instr. advanced med.-surg. Seattle C.C., 1985-86; nursing cons. advisor. Home Health Phys. Medicine and Rehab., Medically Intensive Home Care Program, Dept. Social and Health Svcs., Med. Assistance Adminstrn. Lt. comdr. USNR, 1989—. Mem.: Nat. Assn. Surveillance and Utilization Rev. Svcs. Orgn., Wash. State Assn. for Health Care Quality, Cmty. Health Nurse Rsch. Home: 14040 Prairie Pkwy SW Olympia WA 98512-9267 Office: Med Assistance Adminstrn Divsn Med Mgmt PO Box 45506 Olympia WA 98504-5506

COOLEY, ANDREW LYMAN, corporation executive, former army officer; b. St. Louis, Oct. 14, 1934; s. Andrew L. and Algretta R. (Carr) C.; m. Joan Lynn Wheatley, Jan. 9, 1958; children: Cathleen Wheatley, Caroline Carr. BA, George Washington U., 1964, MA, 1967; MS, U.S. Army Command and Gen. Staff Coll., 1966; postgrad., U.S. Army War Coll., 1972-73. Commd. 2d lt. U.S. Army, 1955, advanced through grades to maj. gen., 1955-64; bn. adv. Vietnam, 1964-65; aide to chief of staff SHAPE, Belgium, 1967-69; tank bn. comdr. Germany, 1969-70; mem. staff Dept. of Army Pentagon, 1970-72; brigade comdr. and div. chief of staff Korea, 1975-77; exec. to comdr. in chief Pacific, 1978-79; asst. div. comdr. 101st Airborne Div., 1979-81; asst. dep. dir. for politico-mil. affairs, plans and policy directorate Joint Chiefs of Staff, Washington, 1981-83; mil. adviser Habib-Draper Mission, Lebanon, 1982-83; dir. strategy, plans and policy Dept. Army, Washington, 1983-85; comdg. gen. 24th Inf. Div. (Mech.) and Fort Stewart, Hunter Army Air Field, Fort Stewart, Ga., 1985-87; chief Office Military Cooperation, Cairo, 1987-89; ret., 1989; program mgr. Vinnell Brown Root, Turkey Base Maintenance Agreement, 1989-91; project mgr. ops. and maintenance Brown and Root Svcs. Corp., Houston, 1991-94; program mgr. Project Restore Hope Somalia, 1993. Ind. cons. with expertise in Africa, Croatia, Bosnia and Haiti, 1994-97; dir. ops. Dyncorp Internat. LLD Svcs., 1998—. Author: Diplomatic Significances of the Great White Fleet, 1966, Realistic Deterrence in NATO, 1973. Decorated Def. D.S.M. with oak leaf cluster, Legion of Merit with oak leaf cluster, Bronze Star, Air medal, others; Fed. Exec. fellow Brookings Instn., 1977-78; named to Officer Candidate Sch. Hall of Fame, 1979. Mem. Assn. U.S. Army, Armor Assn. Episcopalian. Home: 17202 De Chirico Cir Spring TX 77379-6269

COOLEY, DENTON ARTHUR, surgeon, educator; b. Houston, Aug. 22, 1920; s. Ralph C. and Mary (Fraley) C.; m. Louise Goldsborough Thomas, Jan. 15, 1949; children: Mary, Susan, Louise, Florence, Helen. BA, U. Tex., 1941; MD, Johns Hopkins U., 1944; Doctorem Medicinae (hon.), U. Turin, Italy, 1969; H.H.D. (hon.), Hellenic Coll., 1984, Holy Cross Greek Orthodox Sch. of Theology, 1984; DSc honoris causa, Coll. of William and Mary, 1987. Diplomate: Am. Bd. Surgery, Am. Bd. Thoracic Surgery. Intern Johns Hopkins Sch. Medicine, Balt., 1944-45, resident surgery, 1945-50; sr. surg. registrar thoracic surgery Brompton Hosp. for Chest Diseases, London, Eng., 1950-51; assoc. prof. surgery Baylor U. Coll. Medicine, Houston, 1954-62, prof. surgery, 1962-69; clin. prof. surgery U. Tex. Med. Sch., Houston, 1975—; founder, surgeon-in-chief Tex. Heart Inst., 1962—. Served as capt., M.C., 1946-48. Named one of ten Outstanding Young Men in U.S., U.S. C. of C., 1955, Man of the Yr. award Kappa Sigma, 1964; recipient Rene Leriche prize Internat. Surg. Soc., 1967, Billings Gold medal Am. Surg. Soc., 1967, Vishnevsky medal Vishnevsky Inst., USSR, 1971, Theodore Roosevelt Award, 1980, Presdl. Medal of Freedom, presented by Pres. Reagan, 1984, Gifted Tchr. award Am. Coll. Cardiology, 1987, Disting. Svc. award AMA, 1997, Nat. Medal of Tech., U.S. Dept Commerce, 1998 Hon. fellow Royal Coll. Physicians and Surgeons of Glasgow, Royal Coll. Surgeons of Ireland, Royal Australasian Coll. Surgeons, Royal Coll. Surgeons of Eng.; mem. ACS, Am. Surg. Assn., Internat. Cardiovascular Soc., Am. Assn. Thoracic Surgery, Soc. Thoracic Surgery, Soc. Univ. Surgeons, Am. Coll. Cardiology, Am. Coll. Chest Physicians, Soc. Clin. Surgery, Soc. Vascular Surgery, Western Surg. Assn., Tex. Surg. Soc., Halsted Soc. Achievements include performance of numerous heart transplants; implanted 1st artificial heart, 1969. Office: Tex Heart Inst PO Box 20345 Houston TX 77225-0345 *As a person progresses along the path of life, he may achieve certain goals he set for himself as a youth. But to be more completely fulfilled, he must forever extend hid goals to utilize his talents ans accomplishments more fully. Too often, a man receives recognition for his deeds early in life and contents himself prematurely with living in peace and self-satisfaction.*

COOLEY, FANNIE RICHARDSON, emeritus educator, consultant; b. Tunnel Springs, Ala., July 4, 1924; d. Willie C. Richardson and Emma Jean (McCorvey) Stallworth. BS, Tuskegee (Ala.) Inst., 1947, MS, 1951; PhD, U. Wis., 1969. Cert. counselor. Asst. inst. Tuskegee Inst., 1947-48, prof. counseling, 1969-2000, prof. emeritus, 2000—. Instr. Alcorn A&M Coll., Lorman, Miss., 1948-51; asst. prof. Ala. A&M Coll., Normal, 1951-62, assoc. prof., 1964-65; grad. fellow Purdue U., West Lafayette, Ind., 1962-64; house fellow U. Wis., Madison, 1965-69; cons. VA Med. Ctr. Tuskegee, 1969— . Mem. AAUW, AAUP, ASCD (bd. dirs., Disting. Svc. award 1985), Ala. Assn. Counseling and Devel. (pres. 1976-77, Svc. award 1978-79), Ala. Assn. for Counselor Edn. (pres. 1985-86), Aassn. Specialists in Group Work (pres. 1989-90, Career award 1998), Internat. Platford Assn., Chi Sigma Iota. Episcopalian. Home: 802-C Avenue A Tuskegee Institute AL 36088-2402 Office: Tuskegee Inst Dept Counseling and Student Devel Thrasher Hall Tuskegee Institute AL 36088

COOLEY, HILARY ELIZABETH, county official; b. Leesburg, Va., May 8, 1953; d. Thomas McIntyre and Helen Strong (Stringham) C. BA in Econs., U. Pitts., 1976; postgrad. in bus. adminstrn., Hood Coll., Frederick, Md., 1985-90. Mgr. Montgomery Ward, Frederick, 1976-80, merchandiser, 1980-82; asst. bus. mgr. Arundel Comm., Leesburg, 1982-84; bus. mgr. Loudoun Country Day Sch., Leesburg, 1984-85, bd. trustees, 1989-93, sec. bd. trustees, 1989-90, v.p., 1990-92; contr. Foxcroft Sch., Middleburg, Va., 1984-86, 91-92; corr. Loudoun Times Mirror, Leesburg, 1985-87; estate mgr. Delta Farm Inc., Middleburg, Va., 1988-98; cmty. ctr. mgr. County of Loudoun, 1998—. Area chmn. Keep Loudoun Beautiful, Middleburg, 1983-90, pres., bd. dirs. 1993-96; pres. Waterford (Va.) Citizens' Assn., 1985-86, Waterford Players, 1986-88; bd. dirs. Waterford Found., Inc., 1992-95, pres. 1995-98; bd. dirs. Loudoun Hist. Soc., Leesburg, 1987, Mt. Zion Ch. Preservation Assn., 1996-99; treas. Amendment 1 Inc., 1997-99, pres., 1999—. mem.bd.Loudoun County Arbor Day Commn. 2003- Mem. Penn Hall Alumnae Ann. (pres. 1987-92). Democrat. Episcopalian. Avocations: photography, music, drama, tennis. Home and Office: 171 Blue Ridge Acres Harpers Ferry WV 25425-9309

COOLEY, JAMES WILLIAM, retired executive researcher; b. N.Y.C., Sept. 18, 1926; s. William F. and Anna (Fanning) C.; m. Ingrid Uddholm, May 1, 1957; children: William, Anna-Carin, Lars. BA, Manhattan Coll., Riverdale, N.Y., 1949; MA, Columbia U., 1951, PhD, 1961. Programmer Inst. Advanced Study, Princeton, N.J., 1953-56; research staff Courant Inst., NYU, 1956-62; research staff mem. IBM Watson Research Ctr., Yorktown Heights, N.Y., 1962-91; with dept. elec. engring. U. R.I., Kingston, 1991-93; ret., 1993. Inventor fast fourier transform. Served with USAAF, 1945-46. Fellow IEEE (life, Third Millennium medal, Jack Kilby medal 2002); mem. NAE.

COOLEY, JOHN WAYNE, lawyer; b. St. Louis, Oct. 28, 1943; s. Clyde W. and Mary Angela (Brewer) Cooley; m. Maria L. Kenefick, Sept. 3, 1966; children: John Christopher, Christina Marie. BS, US Mil. Acad., 1965; JD, U. Norte Dame, 1973. Bar: Ill. 1973, Mo. 1973, US Dist. Ct. (no. dist.)/Ill. 1973, US Ct. Appeals (7th cir.) 1974, US Supreme Ct. 1982. Law clk. US Ct. Appeals (7th cir.), 1973—74; asst. US atty. No. Dist., Dept. Justice, Chgo., 1974—77; sr. staff atty. US Ct. Appeals (7th cir.), 1977—79; US magistrate US Dist. Ct. (no. dist.), Ill., 1979—81; ptnr. Stone, McGuire & Benjamin, Chgo., 1981—; lectr. law Loyola U., Chgo. Contbr. articles. Capt. arty. U.S. Army, 1965—70. Decorated Air medal, Bronze Star medal, Army Commendation medal with oak leaf cluster, Spl. Achievement award Dept. Justice. Mem.: North Suburban Bar Assn., Chgo. Bar Assn., Ill. Bar Assn., ABA, Alt. to Present Fed. Ct. System (chmn. subcom.), 7th Cir. Ad Hoc Com. to Study High Cost of Litig. Home: 2106 Orrington Ave Evanston IL 60201-2914 Office: 55 E Monroe St Rm 3740 Chicago IL 60603-5713

COOLEY, LORALEE COLEMAN, professional storyteller; b. Charleston, Ill., Jan. 17, 1943; d. Leland Henry and Lorene Madge (Carpenter) C.; m. Edwin Mark Cooley, July 1, 1967; foster children: Jenni, Gail, Bridgette, Carla, Shannon, Diana. BA, Ea. Ill. U., 1965; postgrad., So. Bapt. Theol. Sem., Ky., 1965-67, Ariz. State U., 1972-74; MA, Antioch U., 1994. Piano, music tchr. various schs., 1967-69; women's program dir. Sta. WDXB-AM, Chattanooga, 1969-70; tutoring svcs. coord. Newton Cmty. Ctr., Chattanooga, 1969-71; asst. editor New Age mag., Washington, 1971-72; publicity coord. Firebird Lake/Watersports World, Phoenix, 1975; asst. libr. Casa Grande (Ariz.) Pub. Libr., 1975-77; profl. storyteller Casa Grande, 1977-78, Richmond, Va., 1978-79, Atlanta, 1979-88, Anderson, S.C., 1988-94, Pampa, Tex., 1994—. Publicity dir. Callanwolde Fine Arts Ctr., Atlanta, 1987; toured Republic of Ga., Newly-Ind. States, started rsch. project on Georgian Folklore, 1989. Author: (juvenile novel) Huckle, Buckle, Beanstalk, 2000. Co-chmn. Casa Grande Bicentennial Com., 1974-76; bd. dirs. Genesis House, Pampa,1995-99, M.K. Brown Mcpl. Auditorium, Pampa, 1995-99, 2001—, chmn. bd. 1998-99, trustee, 1995-98; advisor Tribute to Woody Guthrie Ctr., Pampa, 2001, v.p., 2001—; mem. Panhandle Tourism and Mktg. Coun., 1998-2000. Named Miss Louisville, 1966 (preliminary to Miss Am. pageant). Mem. AAUW, Nat.

Storytelling Network, So. Order Storytellers (founder 1982), Pampa Fine Arts Assn. (bd., pres. 1996-97, coord. Artrain tour to Tex. Panhandle 1998), Tex. Women's Forum/Amarillo, DAR, Pampa C. of C. (com. on tourism 1999—). Democrat. Presbyterian. Avocations: travel, walking, cooking, reading. Home: 410 Buckler Ave Pampa TX 79065-6207 E-mail: lcooleystoryspinning@hotmail.com.

COOLEY, NICOLE RUTH, writer, educator; b. Iowa City, Oct. 1, 1966; d. Peter John and Jacqueline (Marks) C.; m. Alexander Laban Hinton, Jan. 9, 1994; 1 child, Meridian Iris. BA, Brown U., 1988; MFA, Iowa Writers Workshop, 1990; PhD, Emory U., 1996. Tchg. asst. Emory U., Atlanta, 1991-94, instr., 1994-96; asst. prof. Bucknell U., Lewisburg, Pa., 1997-99; assoc. prof. Queens Coll., CUNY, Flushing, 1999—. Author: Resurrection, 1996, (novel) Judy Garland Ginger Love, 1998; poetry and fiction pub. in lit. jours. Recipient Walt Whitman award Acad. Am. Poets, 1995, Nat. Endowment for Arts grantee for fiction, 1996. Mem. MLA. Democrat. Office: Queens Coll CUNY 65-30 Kissena Blvd Flushing NY 11367 E-mail: ncooley@qc.edu.

COOLEY, REGINA KAE, educational administrator; b. Dalhart, Tex., July 29, 1956; d. James Lee and Virginia Lee (Cagle) Ferguson; m. Danny Ray Cooley, Oct. 18, 1975; children: Keenan DeWaine, Kyle Lee. Grad. high sch., Dalhart; grad. tchr. aid, Internat. Corr. Schs., 1995. Tchr. aide Dalhart Elem. Sch., 1989—2990; libr. aide, hearing, vision and spinal screener Hartley (Tex.) Sch., 1990—. Saleswoman Alco Dept. Store, Dalhart, 1988; mgr. Photo Kwick, Dalhart, 1987. Vol. Phandle Cmty. Svcs. Avocations: reading, making jewelry, needlepoint. Office: Hartley Sch PO Box 408 Hartley TX 79904-0408 E-mail: kae.cooley@region16.net.

COOLEY, RICHARD EUGENE, lawyer; b. Flint, Mich., Apr. 28, 1935; s. Eugene J. and Helen Frances (Lumbert) C.; m. Wanda Lee Ford, Feb. 20, 1965; children: Scott Richard, Courtney Cooley Breaugh. AB, Albion Coll., 1957; JD, Duke U., 1960. Bar: Mich. 1960, U.S. Supreme Ct. 1970. Asst. pros. atty. Genesee County, Mich., 1962-64; ptnr. Bellairs, Dean, Cooley, Siler, Moulton & Smith, Flint, 1964—; spl. asst. atty. gen. State of Mich., 1975-81. City atty. City of Linden, Mich., 1964-89; twp. atty. Fenton (Mich.) Twp., 1970—; village atty. Village of Gaines, Mich., 1989-96. Past bd. dirs. Tall Pines coun. Boy Scouts Am., Fairwinds coun. Girl Scouts U.S.A.; past pres. Child and Family Svcs. Mich., Flint. Mem. State Bar Mich., Genesee County Bar Assn. (pres. 1977-78), Flint Estate Planning Coun. (pres. 1999-2000), Rotary, Masons. Republican. Presbyterian. Avocations: skiing, sailing, travel. Office: Bellairs Dean Cooley Siler Moulton & Smith 412 S Saginaw St Ste 300 Flint MI 48502-1810 Home: 906 E Kearsley St Flint MI 48503-6119

COOLEY, SIDNEY ELIZABETH ANN, engineer; b. Williamston, S.C., Dec. 20, 1953; d. Hilton Vance Gary Jr. and Elizabeth (Pruitt) C.; m. L. John Toumaras, June 22, 1991. BA, Furman U., 1976; MS, U. Va., 1978, Va. Poly. Inst. & State U., 1984. Tchr. The Brookstone Sch., Columbus, Ga., 1978-79; instr. Va. Poly. Inst. & State U., Blacksburg, 1979-84; engr. transmission systems AT&T Bell Labs., Holmdel, N.J., 1984-88, engr. switching systems, 1988-90, engr. data comms. svcs., 1990—95; project mgr. local network svcs. AT&T Labs., Middletown, NJ, 1995—98, program mgr. internet svcs. devel., 1998—2000, dist. mgr. internet svcs. devel., 2000—. Leader Explorer Boy Scouts Am., Columbus, 1978-79; clarinetist Bell Labs. Sinfonia, 1984-91; campaigner N.J. Dems., Long Branch, 1988, 89. James B. Duke scholar Furman U., 1971, Deering-Milliken Found. scholar, 1971. Mem. IEEE, Nat. Trust for Hist. Preservation, Sierra Club, Phi Beta Kappa, Phi Kappa Phi. Avocations: old house renovation, clarinet, photography, traveling, cooking. Office: AT&T Labs 200 S Laurel Ave Middletown NJ 07748

COOLEY, WILLIAM CROCKETT, mechanical engineer, retired educator; b. Lakeland, Fla., Dec. 19, 1924; s. Sumner Dewey Cooley and Kate Lilah Crockett; m. Anne Waterman, June 4, 1949 (div.); children: Jean, Brian, Stuart, Laura. ME, MIT, 1944, ScD, 1951; MS in Aeronautics, Calif. Inst. Tech., 1947. Student engr. on nuclear propulsion Fairchild project Nuclear Energy for Propulsion of Aircraft, Oak Ridge, Tenn., summer 1947; staff engr. Lexington project MIT, summer 1948; rsch. engr. N.Am. Aviation, L.A., 1951-53, 58-61; nuc. propulsion engr. GE, ANPD, Cin., 1953-58; chief space propulsion and aux. power program NASA, Washington, 1961-63; v.p., tech. dir. Exotech, Inc., Alexandria, Va., 1963-68; pres. Terraspace Inc., Rockville, Md., 1968-84; assoc. prof. engring. George Mason U., Fairfax, Va., 1985-91, ret., 1991. Patentee water jet tech.; contbr. articles to rsch. publs. Lt. USNR, 1952-61. Recipient Pioneer award U.S. Nat. Water Jet Conf., Pitts., 1985. Mem. ASME (life), Water Jet Tech. Assn. (opening lectr. 5th Pacific Rim Internat. conf. 1998). Democrat. Unitarian Universalist. Avocations: swimming, skiing, ballroom dancing, writing poetry. Home: 5480 Wisconsin Ave Apt 1101 Chevy Chase MD 20815-3519

COOLEY, WILLIAM EDWARD, regulatory affairs manager; b. St. Louis, Mar. 7, 1930; s. Charles Frederic and Lillian Marie (Williams) C.; m. Marion Grace Sherman, June 5, 1952; children: Charles, Marilyn, Harold, Noele. AB, Cen. Coll., 1951; PhD, U. Ill., 1954. Rsch. chemist Procter & Gamble Co., Cin., 1954-61, product devel. chemist, 1961-65, product devel. group leader, 1965-75, product devel. regulatory sect. mgr., 1975-90, regulatory affairs sect. mgr., 1990-91; worldwide regulatory coordination sect. mgr., 1991-94; pres. Cooley Cons., Inc., 1994—. Contbr. articles to profl. jours.; inventor, patentee in field. Mem. Am. Assn. Dental Rsch., Internat. Assn. Dental Rsch., Drug Info. Assn., Assn. Food Drug Ofcls., Regulatory Affairs Profl. Soc. (bd. editors 1990), Consumer Healthcare Products Assn. (bd. dirs. 1987-91), Food and Drug Law Inst. Republican. Avocations: music, motorcycling, railroading, flying, astronomy. Home and Office: Cooley Cons Inc 531 Chisholm Trail Wyoming OH 45215-2517

COOLEY-PARKER, SHEILA LEANNE, psychologist, consultant, educator; b. Oakland, Calif., July 25, 1956; d. Philips Theadore and Helen Ellene (Newbill) Cooley; m. Kenneth Louise Parker. BA, St. Leo Coll., 1979; MS, U. So. Miss., 1986; PhD, Miss. State U., 1990. Lic. psychologist Ky. Counselor Charter Counseling Ctr., Jackson, Miss., 1988—89; staff psychologist Rivendell Psychiat. Ctr., Bowling Green, Ky., 1989—90; program dir. MidSouth Hosp., Memphis, 1990—91; resource ctr. dir. MidSouth Resource Ctr., Ridgeland, Miss., 1991—92; partial hosp. dir. Pathways Partial Hospitalization, Ridgeland, 1991—92; edn. specialist, sr. position Miss. Dept. of Edn., Bur. Spl. Svcs., Jackson, Miss., 1993—94; psychologist Western State Hosp., Hopkinsville, Ky., 1994—99, Caring Connections, Hopkinsville, Ky., 1995; pvt. practice Hopkinsville, Ky., 1996—; chief psychology Ky. State Penitentiary, Eddyville, Ky., 1999—. Adj. prof. Hopkinsville C.C., 2001—, Murray State U., 2003—. Campaign organizer Dem. Mayor, Jackson, Miss., 1992. Mem.: APA, Ky. Psychol. Assn., Theta Pi Sigma, Psi Chi, Phi Delta Kappa. Baptist. Home: 4081 Singletree Dr Hopkinsville KY 42240-9191 Office: PO Box 5128 Eddyville KY 42038-5128

COOLIDGE, ARCHIBALD CARY, JR., English language educator, literature researcher; b. Oxford, Eng., June 9, 1928; s. Archibald Cary and Susan Thistle (Jennings) C.; m. Lillian Dobbel Merrill, June 29, 1951; children: Lillian, Emily, Sarah, Archibald, Anne, John, Alexander. BA, Harvard U., 1951; MA, Brown U., 1954, PhD, 1956. Instr. English, U. Iowa, Iowa City, 1956-59, asst. prof., 1959-65, assoc. prof., 1965-74, prof., 1974—2001, prof. emeritus, 2001—. Author: Charles Dickens as Serial Novelist, 1967, Beyond the Fatal Flaw: A Study of the Neglected Forms of Greek Drama, 1980, A Theory of Story, 1989, English Laws and American Problems, 1995, Political Metaphors, 2000, Hollywood Looks at Women, 2001. With USMC, 1945-46, CBI. Mem. U. Iowa Rsch. Club, Phi Beta Kappa. Avocations: fishing, movies. Home: 304 Brown St Iowa City IA 52245-5802 Office: U Iowa Dept English Iowa City IA 52242 E-mail: archibald-coolidge@uiowa.edu.

COOLIDGE, CHARLES H., JR., career officer; BS in Basic Sci., USAF Acad., 1968; student undergrad. pilot tng., Moody AFB, Ga., 1968-69; M in Physics, Air Force Inst. Tech., 1974; student, Air Command and Staff Coll., 1979, Nat. War Coll., 1988. Commd. 2d lt. USAF, 1968, advanced through grades to maj. gen., 1996, various pilot/instr. pilot assignments, 1969-72; instr. and assoc. prof. dept. physics USAF Acad., Colorado Springs, Colo., 1974-77, br. chief cadet parachute program airmanship div., 1977-78; KC-135 pilot 4017th Combat Crew Tng. Squadron, Castle AFB, Calif., 1979; stationed at 911th Air Refueling Squadron, Seymour Johnson AFB, N.C., 1979-83; various assignments USAF, 1983-87; vice comdr. then comdr. 301st Air Refueling Wing, Malmstrom AFB, Mont., 1988-91; asst. dep. chief staff requirements and test Hdqs. Strategic Air Command, Offutt AFB, Nebr., 1991-92; vice comdr. Tanker Airlift Control Ctr. Hdqs. Air Mobility Command, Scott AFB, Ill., 1992-93; various comdr. positions USAF, 1993-96; dir. plans and ops. then dir. ops. Hdqs. Air Edn. and Tng. Command, Randolph AFB, Tex., 1996-97; dir. ops. and logistics U.S. Transp. Command, Scott AFB, 1997—2000; vice comdr. HQ Air Force Materiel Commd., Wright-Patterson AFB, Ohio, 2000—. Decorated Legion of Merit with oak leaf cluster, D.F.C., Air medal with four oak leaf clusters, Rep. Vietnam Gallantry Cross with Palm.

COOLIDGE, DANIEL SCOTT, lawyer; b. Portland, Maine, Sept. 20, 1948; s. John Walter and Mary Louise (Arnold) C.; m. Carolyn Stiles, Nov. 23, 1984; children: Lillian Mae, Lydia Stiles. BS summa cum laude, U. Bridgeport, 1976; JD, Harvard U., 1980. Bar: Conn. 1980, N.H. 1982, Mass. 2001, U.S. Patent Office 1999, U.S. Ct. Appeals (1st cir.) 1983, U.S. Supreme Ct. 1985. Assoc. Cummings & Lockwood, Stamford, Conn., 1980-82, Sheehan, Phinney, Bass & Green PA, Manchester, N.H., 1982-87, ptnr., 1987—. Chmn. juvenile diversion com. Pittsfield (N.H.) Dist. Ct., 1982-85. Author: Survival Guide for Road Warriors, 1996; mem. editl. bd. Law Tech. News; columnist Law Office Computing, 1997—; patentee tel. test equipment. Chmn. Bradford Constitution Bicentennial Com.; mem. Pittsfield Planning Bd., 1984-85; treas., trustee First Congl. Ch., Pittsfield, 1984-85, First Bapt. Ch. Bradford; pres. Pittsfield Arts Coun., 1985; del. N.H. Constl. Conv., Concord, 1984-94; moderator Town of Bradford, N.H., 1999-, Kearsago Reg. Sch. Dist, 2002-; founding bd. dirs., officer U.S. Found. for Inspiration and Recognition of Sci. and Tech. Mem. ABA (environ. law sect., intellectual property law sect., acting chmn., chmn. computer and tech. divsn., vice-chmn. sys. and tools law practice mgmt. sect. 1994—, governing coun. 1996—, advisor UCC article 2B drafting com. 1995-99), N.H. Bar Assn. (vice-chmn. tech. sect. 1993-96, chmn. lex mundi intellectual property sect. 1992-93), Manchester Bar Assn. Avocations: computers, physics, fly fishing, hiking, machining. Home: 106 Bible Hill Ln Warner NH 03278-3701 Office: Coolidge and Graves 106 Bible Hill Ln Warner NH 03278 Personal E-mail: dancoolidge@yahoo.com. Business E-Mail: dancoolidge@ipbizlaw.com.

COOLIDGE, FRANCIS LOWELL, lawyer; b. Waltham, Mass., Aug. 4, 1945; s. Francis Lowell and Helen Read (Curtis) C.; m. Marylouise E. Redmond, July 7, 1984; children: Georgina Lowell, Lucy Read. BA cum laude, Harvard Coll., 1968; JD magna cum laude, Boston U., 1971. Bar: Mass. 1971. Assoc. Ropes & Gray, Boston, 1971-80, ptnr., 1980—. Sec., trustee Collage, Inc., Boston, 1974, Kodaly Musical Tng. Inst., Hartford, Conn., 1977, The Wayside Inn., 1989, sec., 1992—; trustee, adviser Colony Meml., Keene, N.H., 1977—; bd. dirs. Am. Cancer Soc., Inc., 1992—, sec., bd. dirs. Mass. Divsn. Am. Cancer Soc., 1981-86, 89—, chmn. bd. dirs., 1986-88; sec., bd. dirs. Boston Children's Service Assn., 1982, Bostonian Soc., 1984—, sec., 1991—; pres., bd. dirs. Ellis Meml. and Eldredge House, Boston, 1979—, The Hermes Found., Boston, 1984—; trustee Mus. Fine Arts, Boston, 1985-86, overseer, 1987-91; mem. bd. trustees Charity of Edward Hopkins, 1988—, sec.-treas., 1994—. Roman Catholic. Clubs: Somerset (sec. 1976—), Union Boat, Tavern, City Club Corp. (mgr. 1980-87, sec. 1987-94, pres. 1994—); Knickerbocker (N.Y.C.), Newport Reading Room (R.I.), Country Club (Brookline). Home: 62 Beacon St Boston MA 02108-3542 Office: Ropes & Gray One International Pl Boston MA 02110

COOLIDGE, MARTHA, film director; b. New Haven, Aug. 17, 1946; MFA, RISD, 1968; ed., Columbia U.; MA, NYU, 1971. Dir.: (films) Valley Girl, 1983, The City Girl, 1983, Joy of Sex, 1984, Real Genius, 1985, Plain Clothes, 1988, Rambling Rose, 1991, Crazy in Love, 1991, Boston Grace pilot episode, Introducing Dorothy Dandridge, 1999, (HBO) If these Walls Could Talk II, 2000, (PBS) The Ponder Heart, 2001, (HBO) Sex and the City, 2002; (documentaries) David; On and Off, 1972 (Am. Film Festival award), More Than A School, 1973 (Am. Film Festival award), Old Fashioned Woman, 1974 (Am. Film Festival award), Not A Pretty Picture, 1975 (Am. Film Festival award); (films) Angie, 1994, Lost in Yonkers, 1992, Out to Sea, 1997, Three Wishes, 1995, Flaming Rising, 2001. Recipient Best Dir. and Picture Rambling Rose, Independent Spriit Awards, nomination for If These Walls Could Talk II, Emmy awards. Mem.: Dir. Guild of Am. (pres. 2002—). Office: Lee Rae Leaver 11800 Osborne St Lakeview Terrace CA 91342

COOLIDGE, ROBERT TYTUS, deacon, historian, educator; b. Boston, Mar. 30, 1933; s. Lawrence and Victoria Stuart (Tytus) C.; m. Ellen Osborne, Sept. 10, 1960 (div.); children: Christopher, Miles, Matthew. Grad., Groton (Mass.) Sch., 1951; AB, Harvard U., 1955; MA, U. Calif. at Berkeley, 1957; BLitt, U. Oxford, Eng., 1966. Ordained deacon Episcopal Ch., 1967. Non-stipendiary min. Christ Ch. Cathedral, Montreal, Que., Can., 1967-69, 71—, dir. Montreal Fund for the Diaconate, 1984—; non-stipendiary min. St. Marylebone Ch., London Clin., 1969-71; mem. faculty Loyola Coll. (now Concordia U.), Montreal, 1963—, assoc. prof. history, 1968-88, adj. assoc. prof., 1988—2000, assoc. prof. emeritus, 2000—. Historian Monticello Assn., 1975—. Contbr. to hist. vols. Fellow Royal Hist. Soc.; mem. Am. Soc. Ch. History, Ecclesiastical History Soc., Medieval Acad. Am., Am. Hist. Assn., Soc. d'Histoire de l'Eglise de France, Oxford and Cambridge Club (London), Univ. Club (Montreal), Royal St. Lawrence Yacht Club. Home: POB 4070 Westmount QC Canada H3Z 2X3 *If you really want to help your fellow humans, don't think it is their fault if they refuse or reject your help. Look instead at how you react to help offered to you.*

COOLIO, (ARTIS IVEY JR.), popular musician; b. Los Angeles, Calif., 1963; Albums It Takes a Thief, 1994, Gangsta's Paradise, 1995, C U When U Get There, 1997, Straight Butta, 2000, El Cool Magnifico, 2002. Recipient World Wide Music award, 1995, Favorite Rap Artist Am. Music award, 1995, Billboard Music award, 1995, Grammy award Best Rap Solo Performance, 1996. Office: Crowbar Management PO Box 5147 Culver City CA 90231-5147*

COOMBE, GEORGE WILLIAM, JR., lawyer, retired banker; b. Kearny, NJ, Oct. 1, 1925; s. George William and Laura (Montgomery) Coombe; m. Marilyn V. Ross, June 4, 1949; children: Susan, Donald William, Nancy. BA, Rutgers U., 1946; LLB, Harvard U., 1949. Bar: NY 1950, Mich. 1953, Calif. 1976. Practice US Supreme Ct., NYC, 1949—53, Detroit, 1953—69; atty., mem. legal staff Gen. Motors Corp., Detroit, 1953—69, asst. gen. counsel, sec., 1969—75; exec. v.p., gen. counsel Bank of Am., San Francisco, 1975—90; ptnr. Graham and James, San Francisco, 1991—95; sr. fellow Stanford Law Sch., 1995—. Lt. USNR, 1942—46. Mem.: NYC Bar Assn., Los Angeles Bar Assn., San Francisco Bar Assn., Calif. Bar Assn., Mich. Bar Assn., Am. Bar Assn., Phi Gamma Delta, Phi Beta Kappa. Presbyn. Home: 2190 Broadway St Apt 2E San Francisco CA 94115-1312 Fax: 415-923-9266. E-mail: gwcoombe@aol.com.

COOMBE, V. ANDERSON, retired valve manufacturing company executive; b. Cin., Mar. 5, 1926; s. Harry Elijah and Mary (Anderson) C.; m. Eva Jane Romaine, Sept. 26, 1957; children— James, Michael, Peter. B.E., Yale, 1948. Asst. to pres. Wm. Powell Co., Cin., 1953-57, v.p., 1957-63, exec. v.p., 1963-69, pres., treas., 1969-91, chmn. bd., 1991—. Mem.: Cin. Country Club, Queen City Club (Cin.), Camargo Club (Cin.). Home: 6 Corbin Dr Cincinnati OH 45208-3302 Office: 2503 Spring Grove Ave Cincinnati OH 45214-1729

COOMBER, JAMES ELWOOD, English language educator; b. Freeport, Ill., Jan. 17, 1942; s. Elwood Lowell and Vi Anna Margaret (Schoonhoven) C.; m. Eleanor Ruth McKinnon, June 11, 1966; children: Sarah Ellen Suomala Coomber, Matthew James. BS, U. Wis., Platteville, 1964; MA, U. Wis., Madison, 1966, PhD, 1972; student, U. Ariz., 1989, student, 2003. Prof. English Concordia Coll., Moorhead, Minn., 1966—, chair dept. English, 1984—88, 1996—2001. Vis. prof. U. Calgary, Alta., Can., 1979, 81; adj. faculty Hamline U., St. Paul, 1982-98, ND State U., Fargo, 1972—; faculty mem. Prairie Writing Project, Moorhead, 1977-82; dir. Concordia Conf. on Reading and Writing, 1983-99; cons. to pub. sch., Minn., N.D. Co-author: The English Book, 1981, Macmillan Spelling, 1983, Vocabulary for College Reading and Writing, 1984, Words for Success, 1996, Magnificent Chruches on the Prairie: A Story of Immigrant Priests, Builders and Homesteaders, 1997, Teaching Vocabulary: An Internet Course for Teachers, 1998, Wordskills, 1990, 2000, Unwanted Bread: The Struggle of Farmers and Ranchers in North Dakota, 2000, Spelling for Writing: Instructional Strategies, 2001; contbr. articles to profl. jours. Active Bread for the World, Washington, 1988—. Nat. Teaching fellow U.S. Dept. Edn., 1969. Mem. Sierra Club. Democrat. Episcopalian. Avocations: canoeing, hiking, gardening, reading. Office: Concordia Coll Dept Of English Moorhead MN 56562-0001

COOMBES, DAVID HARRISON, health facility administrator; b. Washington, Apr. 14, 1939; s. David Russell and Christine (Spignul) C.; m. Mary Gaasterland, June 9, 1962; children: Karen Marie, David Harrison. BA, Duke U., 1962; MHA, U. Minn., 1969. Diplomate Am. Coll. Healthcare Execs. Exec. dir. Health Facilities Commn. State of Tenn., Nashville, 1973-75; exec. dir. Hosps. and Clinics U. Tenn., Memphis, 1975-80, vice chancellor, 1980-82; pres., CEO Diagnosticorp, Inc., Nashville, 1982-85, U. Minn. Clin. Assocs., Mpls., 1985-88; founder, co-ptnr. Medicant, Inc., Oklahoma City, 1988-96; pres., CEO Nat. Assn. Integrated Health Orgns., Fredericksburg, Va., 1996—2001; CEO Clin. Focus, Inc., Mt. Vernon, NY, 2001—. Asst. prof. U. Tenn., Memphis, 1975-80; dir. Medex Global, Inc. Timonium, Md., 1987—. Chmn. planning commn. Town Colonial Beach, Va., 1996-2002, councilman, 1992-2002. 1st lt. USAF, 1964-67. Mem. Am. Hosp. Assn., Am. Soc. Assn. Execs. Home: 1313 Irving Ave Colonial Beach VA 22443 Office: Clin Focus Inc 825 Gramatan Ave Mount Vernon NY 10552 E-mail: dhcoombes@3n.net.

COOMBS, EUGENE G. lawyer; b. Hutchinson, Kans., Mar. 17, 1911; s. Albertus J. and Sarah (Dorth) C.; m. Nancy Elizabeth Wilcox, July 13, 1932 (div.); m. Mary Alice Johnson Goeney, July 12, 1965; children: Eugene G., Russell M., Judith Coombs Schreiber, Sheley Goemey Bush. A.B., Wichita State U., 1933; LL.B., U. Kans., 1936. Bar: Kans. 1936. Assoc., Cowan, McCorkie & Nelson, Wichita 1936-37; spl. agent FBI 1937-43; sole practice, Wichita; now ptnr. Coombs and Durrett, Chartered, Wichita. Mem. Wichita Met. Planning Commn. 1960-73; bd. dirs. United Fund, Community Planning Council; active YMCA, Salvation Army; trustee Herbert Hoover Library, West Branch, Iowa. Served with USNR 1943-46. Mem. ABA, Kans. State Bar Assn., Wichita Bar Assn., Am. Bd. Trial Advocates, Phi Delta Phi. Republican. Methodist. Clubs: Wichita Country, Rotary, Mason. Office: PO Box 405 421 E 3rd St N Wichita KS 67202-2509

COOMBS, ROBERT HOLMAN, behavioral scientist, medical educator, therapist, writer; b. Salt Lake City, Sept. 16, 1934; s. Morgan Scott and Vivian (Holman) C.; m. Carol Jean Cook, May 29, 1958; children: Robert Scott, Kathryn, Lorraine, Karen Youn Jung, Holly Ann, Krista Ho Jung, David Jeremy. BS, U. Utah, 1958, MS, 1959; PhD, Wash. State U., 1964. Asst. prof. sociology Iowa State U., 1963-66; fellow Behavioral Sci. Ctr.-Bowman Gray Sch. Medicine/Wake Forest U, 1966, asst. prof., 1966-68; assoc. prof. Behavioral Sci. Center, Bowman Gray Sch. Medicine, Wake Forest U., 1968-70; career rsch. specialist Calif. Dept. Mental Hygiene, Camarillo, 1970-73; assoc. rsch. sociologist UCLA, 1970-77, assoc. prof. biobehavioral scis. Sch. Medicine, 1977-78, prof., 1978—; chief Camarillo Neuropsychiat. Inst., 1970-78; asst. dir. rsch. UCLA Neuropsychiat. Inst., Center for Health Scis., 1978-81; dir. Office Edn. of Neuropsychiat. Inst., 1980-90, UCLA Family Learning Center, Oxnard, Calif., 1977-84. Cons. World Fedn. for Med. Edn., 1990—92; dir. grief and bereavement program UCLA Neuropsychiat. Hosp., 1993—98; mem. internat. faculty Mediterranean Summer Inst. on Drug Use, Rome and Jerusalem, 2003. Author: Psychosocial Aspects of Medical Training, 1971, Junkies and Straights: The Camarillo Experience, 1975, Socialization in Drug Abuse, 1976, Mastering Medicine: Professional Socialization in Medical School, 1978, Making It in Medical School, 1979, Inside Doctoring: Stages and Outcomes in the Professional Socialization of Physicians, 1986, The Family Context of Adolescent Drug Use, 1988, Drug Testing: Issues and Options, 1991, Handbook on Drug Abuse Prevention, 1995, Drug-Impaired Professionals, 1997, Surviving Medical School, 1998, Addiction Recovery Tools: A Practical Handbook, 2001, Cool Parents, Drug-free Kids: A Family Survival Guide, 2002, Addictive Disorders: A Practical Handbook, 2003, Family Therapy Review, 2003, Addiction Counseling Review, 2003, The Addiction Counselor's Desk Reference, 2003; assoc. editor Family Rels., Jour. Applied Family and Child Studies, 1970—80, Clin. Sociololgy Rev., Jour. Clin. Sociology, Jour. marriage and the Family, 1982—86, Qualitative Health Rsch., 1990—94, Family Dynamics and Addiction Quar., 1990—94, corr. editor Med. Edn., Eng., contbg. editor Jour. Drug Issues, 1977, series editor Sage Book Series on Medical Student Survival, 1997—2000, Wiley Book Series on Treating Addictions, mem. editl. bd., sect. editor Substance Using Health Profls., Substance Use and Misuse; contbr. articles, chapters to books. Bishop Winston-Salem (N.C.) Ward, Ch. Jesus Christ of Latter-day Saints, 1969-70, Camarillo (Calif.) Ward, 1972-77; mem. Calif. Atty.-Gen.'s Commn. on Prevention of Drug and Alcohol Abuse, 1985-86; high risk youth prevention grant rev. com. USPHS, 1990—; com. to combat drug abuse World Fedn. Mental Health, 1989—. With U.S. Army, 1958-64. Grantee, NIMH, 1968—73, Nat. Fund Med. Edn., 1969—71, Nat. Inst. Justice, 1971—76, Nat. Inst. Drug Abuse, 1977—80, Calif. Dept. Alcohol and Drug Programs, 1977—78, Father Flanagan's Boys Home, 1977—79, CETA, Ventura County, Calif., 1978. Fellow: APS, AAAS, Am. Assn. Applied and Preventive Psychology; mem.: Am. Acad. Health Care Providers in Addiction Disorders (internat. adv. bd., cert. addiction specialist), Am. Group Psychotherapy Assn. (cert.), Assn. Am. Med. Colls., World Fedn. Mental Health (mem. com. to combat drug abuse), Internat. Sociol. Assn., Internat. Family Therapy Assn., Internat. Coalition of Addiction Studies Edn., Assn. for Addiction Profls., Am. Assn. Mariage and Family Therapists, APA, Sigma Xi, Phi Kappa Phi. Democrat. Office: UCLA Sch Medicine Dept Psychiatry Biobehavioral Scis 760 Westwood Plz Los Angeles CA 90095-8353 E-mail: rcoombs@mednet.ucla.edu. *I have surrounded myself with superior people, those whose specialized talents have enriched my thinking and productivity. I actively pursue the association and assistance of those whose skills exceed or compliment my own.*

COOMER, STEVEN ROBERT, music educator; b. Muncie, Ind., Dec. 23, 1946; s. Robert and Thelma Geneva Coomer; m. Jeannette Oyler, June 19, 1993; m. Pamela Ann Shaver, Aug. 12, 1978 (div. Apr. 23, 1993); m. Sharon Lynn Zimmerman, Nov. 26, 1969 (div. June 18, 1976); children: Stefanie Lynne Shultz, Stacie Roberta Dixon, Stephanie Lynne Brown. BS, Ball State U., Muncie, In., 1964—68. Band dir. Del. Cmty. Schs., Muncie, Ind., 1968—69, East Chgo. Pub. Schools, East Chicago, Ind., 1969—70; music dir. Crown Point Cmty. Schools, Crown Point, Ind., 1970—71; band & choral dir. Wash. Twp. Sch., Valparaiso, Ind., 1971—72; band dir. Franklin County Schools, Brookville, Ind., 1972—73; orch. dir. Anderson Cmty. Schools, Anderson, Ind., 1973—74; band dir. Brebeuf Prep. Sch., Indianapolis, Ind., 1975—76; free lance musician & educator Self-employed, Cary, Ill., 1976—88; band dir. Randolph Ea. Sch. Corp., Union City, Ind., 1988—89, Indpls. Pub. Schools, Indianapolis, Ind., 1989—; free lance musician Self-employed, Anderson, Ind., 1974—75. Coord. of all-city h.s. bands Indpls. Pub. Schools, Indianapolis, Ind., 1992—, mgr. marching band tournament, 2002—; dir. of bands Murat Shrine Temple, Indianapolis, Ind., 1996—2002; prin. trumpet Athenaeum Pops Orch., Indianapolis, Ind., 2000—, Scottish Rite Orch., Indianapolis, Ind., 1998—; founder Ind. All Star Masonic Band, Franklin, Ind., 1997—2001; pres. Shrine Band Assoc. of N.Am., Tampa, Fla., 2000—; dir. of bands Sahara Grotto, Indianapolis, Ind., 1995—98; assoc. band condr. Greenwood Cmty. Band, Greenwood, Ind., 1992—95; mem. Murat Shrine Band Bd. of Directors, Indianapolis, Ind., 1996—2002, Ind. Band Assn., Indianapolis, Ind., 1988—, Music Educator's Nat. Conf., Ann Arbor, Mich., 1988—, Ind. Music Educator's Assn., Muncie, Ind., 1988—; adjudicator band, orch., solo and ensemble Ind. State Sch. Music Assn.; mem. NEA, Washington, DC, 1988—, Ind. State Teacher's Assn., Indianapolis, Ind., 1988—; pvt. trumpet tchr. Self-employed, Indianapolis, Ind., 2000—; 2nd trumpet Ft. Wayne Philharm., Fort Wayne, Ind., 1968—69; 3rd trumpet Muncie Symphony Orch., Muncie, Ind., 1966—68; prin. trumpet Anderson Symphony Orch., Anderson, Ind., 1973—75; mem. Am. Fedn. of Musicians, Indianapolis, Ind., 1995—, Nat. Band Assn., Nashville, Tenn., 1988—. Mem. Indpls. 500 Festival Band Com., Indianapolis, Ind., 2001—, York Rite, Cary, Ill., 1988—; jr. deacon & mem. Cary Grove Masonic Lodge, Cary, Ill., 1987—; mem. Scottish Rite, Indianapolis, Ind., 1996—; dir. of bands & mem. Murat Shrine Temple, Indianapolis, Ind., 1995—. Mem.: Scottish Rite Valley of Indpls. (32nd degree trumpeter 1996—), York Rite, Dunkirk Masonic Lodge #275. Avocation: woodworking. Home: 1333 Shawnee Rd Indianapolis IN 46260

COON, DAREN ROSS, public administrator; b. Gooding, Idaho, July 11, 1953; s. William Joseph and Roberta Elaine (Gifford) C.; m. Kathleen M. Simer, Aug. 22, 1981; children: Heidi M., Heather E. BA, Boise State U., 1975, Micro

M in Bus. Adminstrn., 2002. Lic. real estate agt., Idaho; notary pub., Idaho. Asst. sec.-treas. Nampa & Meridian Irrigation Dist., Nampa, Idaho, 1976-89, info. tech. mgr., 1984--, sec. treas., 1989—, sec. bd. dirs., 1989—; fed. and state govt. lobbyist, 1990—. Sec., bd. dirs. Treasure Valley Fed. Credit Union, Caldwell, Idaho, 1976-80, Idaho div. Fed. Credit Union, Nampa, 1986-89; pres. Lincoln PTO, 1997-2000, Nampa Sr. H.S. Band Booster, 1999—; commr. Boise City Irrigation Commn., 1995—. Mem. Idaho Pub. Employees Assn. (bd. dirs. 1987-89), Digital Equipment Computer User Soc., Idaho Water Users Assn. (mem. legis. com. 1990—), N.W. Irrigators Ops. Conf., Idaho Irrigation Mgrs. Assn., Nat. Water Resource Assn., Family Farm Alliance. Avocations: swimming, camping, hunting, cooking. Home: 9 N Fairview St Nampa ID 83651 Office: Nampa & Meridian Irrigation 1503 1st St S Nampa ID 83651-4395

COON, PENNY K. human services administrator; b. Penn Yan, N.Y., May 21, 1959; d. Wilfred Orval and Marilyn Estelle (Wells) Knapp; m. Thomas Allen Gray, Aug. 30, 1980 (div. July 1990); m. David Charles Coon, May 23, 1992; 1 child, Rachel Mariah. BSW, Keuka Coll., 1980. Residence counselor Cath. Charities Residential Program, Penn Yan, 1981-82, residence mgr., 1982-92, residential supr., 1992-2001, quality and compliance dir., 2001—. Bd. dirs. Yates County (N.Y.) ARC, Penn Yan, 1993-98, mem. incident rev., 1989-2001; co chmn. Keuka Lake Conf. Com., Rochester, N.Y., 1986—; mem. Yates County Rep. Com.; mem. parent adv. coun. and bldg. level team Dundee (N.Y.) Ctrl. Sch., 1998—. Election insp. Yates County Bd. Elections, 1996—; mem. Yates County Rep. Com., Yates County Women's Rep. Club, Women of the Moose. Recipient Direct Care award N.Y. State Assn. Cmty. Residence Adminstrs. Mem. DAR, Daus. Am. Colonists. Avocations: reading, pets, camping. Home: 2599 Knapp Rd Dundee NY 14837-9730 Office: Cath Charities Community Services 1945 Ridge Rd E Ste 24 Rochester NY 14622

COON, ROBERT MORELL, JR., retired lawyer; b. Bronxville, N.Y., Nov. 17, 1930; s. Robert Morell Coon and Pearl Edna Weekley; m. Aileen Blanche Edwards, June 10, 1961 (div. Mar. 1978); 1 child, Charles Nicholas; m. Jean Hall Tuttle, Oct. 8, 1983. AB magna cum laude, Harvard U., 1952, JD, 1958. Bar: N.Y. 1958, U.S. Tax Ct. 1963. Assoc. Carter, Ledyard & Milburn, N.Y.C., 1958-65, O'Connor & Farber, N.Y.C., 1965-66, Putney, Twombley, Hall & Skidmore, N.Y.C., 1966-69; ptnr. O'Connor & Farber, N.Y.C., 1969-70; assoc. Fulton, Walter & Duncombe, N.Y.C., 1970-71, ptnr., 1971-77, Fulton, Duncombe & Rowe, N.Y.C., 1977-81, Farber & Childs, N.Y.C., 1981-86; pvt. practice Bronxville, 1986-93; ptnr. Fulton, Duncombe & Rowe, N.Y.C., 1994-96, Fulton, Rowe, Hart & Coon, N.Y.C., 1997—2002. Dir. Nat. Com. to Preserve Social Security and Medicare, Washington, 1987-97. Mem. Bronxville Rep. Com., 1966-73, chmn., 1971-73. Sgt. U.S. Army, 1952-55, Germany. Mem. N.Y. State Bar Assn., Assn. of Bar of City of N.Y., Bronxville Field Club., Phi Beta Kappa. Republican. Reformed. Home: 36 Pine Island Rd Hilton Head Island SC 29928 Office: Fulton Rowe & Hart 1 Rockefeller Plz Rm 301 New York NY 10020-2002

COONEY, CHARLES HAYES, lawyer; b. Nashville, Apr. 25, 1937; s. Robert G. and Annie Lee (Hayes) C.; m. Patsy M. Cooney, Dec. 25, 1986; children: Susan, Hayes Jr. BA, Vanderbilt U., 1959, JD, 1963. Bar: Tenn. 1963. Pvt. practice Cornelius & Collins, Nashville, 1963-67; chief def. atty. gen. State of Tenn., Nashville, 1967-80; ptnr. Watkins, McGugin, McNeilly & Rowan, 1980—. Staff mem. Vanderbilt U. Law Review, 1961-62. Capt. U.S. Army, 1959. Mem. ABA, Rotary, Tenn. Bar Assn. (pres. young lawyers sect., 1961), Nashville Bar Assn. (bd. dirs. 1985-87), Tenn. Bar Found., Nashville Bar Found. Presbyterian. Avocations: golf, travel. Office: Watkins McGugin McNeilly & Rowan 214 2nd Ave N Ste 300 Nashville TN 37201-1638

COONEY, JAMES PATRICK, lawyer; b. Texarkana, Ark., Feb. 22, 1944; s. James Raphael and Kathlyn Mary (Price) C.; m. Pamela Joy Pagano, July 15, 1967; children: Elena Valentine, Kathlyn Mary, Erin Joy, James Brennan. AB cum laude, U. Notre Dame, 1966, JD, 1969. Bar: Tex. 1969, U.S. Dist. Ct. (ea. dist.) Tex. 1969, U.S. Dist. Ct. (so. dist.) Tex. 1974, U.S. Ct. Appeals (5th cir.) 1971, U.S. Supreme Ct. 1976. Law clk. Hon. Lewis R. Morgan U.S. Ct. Appeals (5th cir.), Newnan, Ga., 1969-71; assoc. Powell, Goldstein, Frazen & Murphy, Atlanta, 1971-74, Royston, Rayzor, Vickery & Williams, Houston, 1974-77, ptnr., 1977—. Chmn. Southeastern Admiralty Inst., 1992-93. Editorial assoc. Notre Dame Lawyer, 1968-69. Bd. dirs. Houston Internat. Seafarers Ctr., 1992—; pres. Westheimer Ecumenical Social Ministry, 1994-96. Mem.: Maritime Law Assn. U.S. (proctor, chmn. com. on uniformity of maritime law 1998—2002, dir. 2001—, assoc. editor Am. Maritime Cases 1996—), Notre Dame Club Houston. Roman Catholic. Office: Royston Rayzor Vickery & Williams LLP 1001 McKinney 11th Flr Houston TX 77002 E-mail: patrick.cooney@roystanlaw.com.

COONEY, JOAN GANZ, broadcasting executive; b. Phoenix, Nov. 30, 1929; d. Sylvan C. and Pauline (Reardan) Ganz; m. Timothy J. Cooney, 1964 (div. 1975); m. Peter G. Peterson, 1980. BA, U. Ariz., 1951; degrees (hon.), Boston Coll., 1970, Hofstra U., Oberlin Coll., Ohio Wesleyan U., 1971, Princeton U., 1973, Russell Sage Coll., 1974, Harvard U., 1975, Allegheny Coll., 1976, Georgetown U., 1978, U. Notre Dame, 1982, Smith Coll., 1986, Brown U., 1987, Columbia U., 1991, NYU, 1991. Reporter Ariz. Republic, Phoenix, 1953—54; publicist NBC, 1954—55, U.S. Steel Hour, 1955—62; prodr. Sta. WNET, Channel 13, pub. affairs documentaries, 1962—67; TV cons. Carnegie Corp. N.Y., N.Y.C., 1967—68; exec. dir. Children's TV Workshop (producers Sesame Street, Electric Company, others), N.Y.C., 1968—70, pres., trustee, CEO, 1970—88, chmn., CEO, 1988—90, chmn. exec. com., 1990—. Bd. dirs. Johnson & Johnson; bd. dirs. Met. Life Ins. Co. Mem. Pres.'s Commn. on Marijuana and Drug Abuse, 1971—73, Nat. News Coun., 1973—81, Pres.'s Commn. for Agenda for 80's, 1980—81, Adv. Com. for Trade Negotiations, 1978—80, Carnegie Found. Nat. Panel on High Sch., 1980—82, Gov.'s Commn. on Internat. Yr. of the Child, 1979; Mus. TV and Radio; bd. dirs. Edison Schs.; trustee N.Y. Presbyn. Med. Ctr. Named to Hall of Fame, Acad. TV Arts and Scis., 1990; recipient numerous awards for Sesame Street and other TV programs including Nat. Sch. Pub. Rels. Assn. Gold Key, 1971, Disting. Svc. medal, Columbia Tchrs. Coll., 1971, Soc. Family Man award, 1971, Nat. Inst. Social Scis. Gold medal, 1971, Frederick Douglass award, N.Y. Urban League, 1972, Silver Satellite award, Am. Women in Radio and TV, Woman of Yr. in Edn. award, Ladies Home Jour., 1975, NAEB Disting. Svc. award, NEA Friends of Edn. award, Kiwanis Decency award, 5th Women's Achiever award, Girl Scouts U.S.A., Stephen S. Wise award, 1981, Harris Found. award, 1982, Ednl. Achievement award, AAUW, 1984, Disting. Svc. to Children award, Nat. Assn. Elem. Sch. Prins., 1985, DeWitt Carter Reddick award, Coll. Comm., U. Tex.-Austin, 1986, Emmy Lifetime Achievement award, Acad. TV Arts and Scis., 1989, Presdl. medal of Freedom, 1995. Mem.: NATAS, Am. Women in Radio and TV, Internat. Radio and TV Soc., Nat. Inst. Social Scis. Office: Children's TV Workshop 1 Lincoln Plz New York NY 10023-7129

COONEY, J(OHN) GORDON, JR., lawyer; b. Alexandria, Va., Mar. 22, 1959; s. John Gordon Sr. and Patricia Ruth (McEwen) C.; m. Gretchen Smith Millspaugh, July 17, 1999. BA, Wesleyan U., 1981; JD magna cum laude, Villanova U., 1984. Bar: Pa. 1984, U.S. Dist. Ct. (ea. dist.) Pa. 1986, U.S. Ct. Appeals (5th cir.) 1997, U.S. Ct. Appeals (3d cir.) 1988, U.S. Supreme Ct. 2002. Law clk. to hon. judge J. William Ditter Jr. U.S. Dist. Ct. (ea. dist.) Pa., Phila., 1984-86; assoc. Morgan, Lewis & Bockius, LLP, Phila., 1986-92, ptnr., 1992—. Adj. lectr. Villanova U. Law, 1993—, master Villanova U. Inn of Ct., 1999—; barrister U. Pa. Law Sch. Inn of Ct., 1994-96. Editor-in-chief Villanova U. Law Rev., 1983-84; mem. editl. bd. The Legal Intelligencer, 1997-2001. Trustee Rosemont Sch. of the Holy Child, 1997-, chmn., 2001-; alumni bd. mgrs. Episcopal Acad., 1996-2002; trustee Gesu Sch., 2002--. Mem. ABA (com. on class actions and derivative suits), Pa. Bar Assn., Phila. Bar Assn. (profl. guidance com., fed. cts. com.), Union League Phila., Merion Cricket Club, Pyramid Club, Wesleyan U. Alumni Assn. (pres. Phila. area 1993-96), Arthritis Found. (bd. dirs Ea. Pa. chpt. 1993-96), Order of Coif. Republican. Roman Catholic. Office: Morgan Lewis & Bockius LLP 1701 Market St Philadelphia PA 19103-2903

COONEY, JOHN PATRICK, JR., lawyer; b. Chgo., Oct. 18, 1944; s. John Patrick and Katherine (Rafferty) C.; m. Joan Oberbeck, Dec. 7, 1968 (div. 1990); children: John, Brian, Anne; m. Jane Elizabeth Hewett, Oct. 3, 1992; children: Luke, Nathaniel, Emma. BS, Ind. U., 1966; JD, Duke U., 1969. Assoc. Davis Polk & Wardwell, N.Y.C., 1969-72, 77-80, mem. firm, 1980—; asst. U.S. atty. U.S. Atty.'s Office for So. Dist. N.Y., N.Y.C., 1972-77, chief narcotics unit, 1976-77. Note editor Duke Law Jour., 1968-69. Fellow: Am. Coll. Trial Lawyers; mem.: Wong Sung Soc. San Francisco, Supreme Ct. Hist. Soc. (chmn. N.Y. chpt.), Knickerbocker Club, Am. Alpine Club. Roman Catholic. Home: 50 Hillside Rd Rye NY 10580-2013 Office: Davis Polk & Wardwell 450 Lexington Ave Fl 31 New York NY 10017-3982

COONEY, JOHN THOMAS, retired banker; b. Warren, Pa., Jan. 20, 1927; s. Willis Edward and Elaine (Blanden) C.; m. Clara Jean Ellberg, Dec. 22, 1950; children: John B., Michael T., Lisa J. BS in Bus., Gannon U., 1951. Asst. personnel mgr. Nat. Biscuit Co., Houston, 1951-52; v.p. Bank of Southwest, Houston, 1956-80, exec. v.p., and sr. trust officer, 1980-85; vice chmn. M Trust Corp., 1985-90, Ameritrust Tex. N.A., Houston, 1990-92. Adv. dir. Legacy Trust Co., 1993—; bd. dirs. Marine Safety Systems, Inc., 1996—; mem. SEI II Bd. of Trustees, 1994—. Pres. Mental Health Assn., Houston; bd. dirs. Am. Heart Assn., state treas., Tex.; established TBA Tex. Sch. of Trust Banking (chmn. 1978). Served as cpl. U.S. Army, 1945-46. Recipient Medal of Honor Gannon U., 1951. Mem. Tex. Bankers Assn. (trust divsn. chmn. 1982-83), Lakeside Country Club, The Houstonian Club. Republican. Roman Catholic.

COONEY, JOSEPH J. microbiologist, educator; b. Syracuse, N.Y., Jan. 16, 1934; s. Joseph Francis and Ethel (Nixon) C.; m. Margaret V. Hammerle, Aug. 10, 1957; children: Timothy J., Sheila A., Susan M., Joseph M. BS in Biology, LeMoyne Coll., 1956; MS in Bacteriology, Syracuse U., 1958, PhD in Microbiology, 1961. From asst. to assoc. prof. Loyola U., New Orleans, 1961-65; from assoc. to prof. U. Dayton, Ohio, 1965-76; prof., head lab. U. Md., Solomons, 1976-82; prof. environ. scis. program U. Mass., Boston, 1982-98, chmn. environ. coastal and ocean scis., 1982-88, 93-98, prof. emeritus, 1998—. Adj. prof. Nat. U. Ireland, Galway, 1995—; cons. in field. Editor-in-chief Jour. Indsl. Microbiology and Biotechnology; contbr. over 100 articles to profl. jours. Fulbright scholar Galway, Ireland, 1989. Fellow AAAS, Am. Acad. Microbiology, Am. Soc. Microbiology, Soc. Indsl. Microbiology (pres. 1992-93), Soc. Gen. Microblog. E-mail: jjc@capecod.net.

COONEY, MIKE, former secretary of state; b. Washington, Sept. 3, 1954; s. Gage Rodman and Ruth (Brodie) C.; m. Dee Ann Marie Gribble; children: Ryan Patrick, Adan Cecelia, Colin Thomas. BA in Polit. Sci., U. Mont., 1979. State rep. Mont. Legislature, Helena, 1976-80; exec. asst. U.S. Sen. Max Baucus, Butte, Mont., 1979-82, Washington, 1982-85, Helena, Mont., 1985-89; sec. of state State of Mont., Helena, 1988—2001; coord. Lewis & Clark Bicentennial Public Safety Project, 2001; ex. dir. Healthy Mothers/ Healthy Babies: The Montana Coalition, 2001—. Bd. dirs. YMCA; mem. adv. panel Fed. Clearinghouse. Mem. Nat. Secs. of State (pres.), Nat. Assns. Secs. of State (pres. 1997) Democrat. Office: 1235 Birch St, Ste 1 Helena MT 59601

COONEY, M(URIEL) SHARON TAYLOR, medical and surgical nurse; b. Edenton, N.C., Oct. 12, 1947; d. Howard Russell and Evelyn Louise (Phelps) Taylor (dec.); children: Michael James, Patrick Russell. BSN, East Carolina U., 1969; MS in Nursing, St. Louis U., 1972. Cert. orthopaedic nurse. Staff nurse Johns Hopkins Hosp., Balt., 1969-71, Barnes Hosp., St. Louis, 1971-72, Person County Meml. Hosp., 1989—99; cardiovascular clin. nurse specialist Jackson Meml. Hosp., Miami, 1973-74; instr. Shepherd Coll., Shepherdstown, W.Va., 1983-84, Piedmont Community Coll., Roxboro, N.C., 1989-90, Watts Sch. Nursing, Durham, N.C., 1990—; staff nurse N.C. Splty. Hosp., 2003—. Clin. instr., lectr. Shepherd Coll.; home health care supr., mgr. Coord. Coun. for Sr. Citizens, 1985. Mem. ANA, Nat. Assn. Orthopaedic Nurses, Nat. League for Nursing, Acad. Med.-Surg. Nursing, N.C. Alliance Hosp.-Based Schs. Nursing, N.C. Nurses Assn. (coun. of clin. specialists, med.-surg. coun., chmn. coun. nurse educators). Home: 4812 Bahama Rd Rougemont NC 27572-7241 E-mail: cooneyst@drh.duhs.duke.edu.

COONEY, PATRICIA RUTH, civic worker; b. Englewood, N.J. d. Charles Aloysius and Ruth Jeannette (Foster) McEwen; m. J. Gordon Cooney, June 8, 1957; 1 child, J. Gordon, Jr. Student, Fordham U., 1950-51; DHL honoris causa, Phila. Theol. Sem. St. Charles Boromeo, 1991. Blood bank chmn. Strafford Village Civic Assn., 1968-69, sec., 1970-71; vice chmn. Spl. Gifts Com. Cath. Charities Appeal of Archdiocese of Phila., 1980—, chmn., 1985. Mem. Coun. of Mgrs. Archdiocese of Phila., 1982-88, sec., exec. com., 1983-88; bd. dirs. Cath. Charities of Archdiocese of Phila., sec., exec. com., 1988-90, v.p., exec. com., 1991—; bd. dirs. Village of Divine Providence, Phila., sec., 1983-85, v.p. exec. com., 1990—; bd. dirs. St. Edmond's Home for Crippled Children, Phila., v.p. exec. com., 1990—; bd. dirs. Don Guanella Village of Archdiocese of Phila., v.p. exec. com., 1990—; v.p. exec. com. St. Francis Homes for Boys, 2000—, St. Joseph House for Boys, 2000--, St. Vincent Svcs. for Women and Children, 2000—, St. Joseph Cath. Home for Children, 2000—, St. Gabriel's Sys., 2000—, St. Vincent's Home, Tacony, 2003; mem. Archdiocesan Adv. Com. on Renewal, 1991-2000; Women's Com. Wills Eye Hosp., 1973—, mem.-at-large, 1st v.p.; mem. Women's Aux. St. Francis Country House, Darby, Pa., 1976—, treas., 1978-82; exec. com. United Way of Southeastern Pa., 1984-90, sec., 1986-88; bd. dirs. Chapel of Four Chaplains, 1984-89, Phila. Criminal Justice Task Force, 1989-90. Decorated Cross Pro Ecclesia et Pontifice, 1982, Lady Order St. Gregory the Gt., 1998. Republican. Avocations: reading, tennis, sailing. Home: 320 Gatcombe Ln Bryn Mawr PA 19010-3628

COONEY, PATRICK LOUIS, writer; b. Bellflower, Calif., Apr. 7, 1947; s. Jack William and Lauretta (Jenkins) C.; m. Rosemary Santana Cooney, Sept. 10, 1967; 1 child, Carl. BA in Sociology, Fla. State U., 1969; MA, PhD, U. Tex., 1976; MBA, Fordham U., 1979; cert. in Field Botany, N.Y. Bot. Garden, Bronx, 1993. Asst. prof. sociology Coll. Mount St. Vincent, Bronx, 1975-77; mktg. exec. pub. firms, 1980-89; Cert. in Field Botany. Spkr. Martin Luther King Jr. Inst. for Non-Violence, Westchester County, N.Y., 1994. Author: Discovering the Mid-Atlantic: Historical Tours, 1991, Seeing the United States as the South and the World Community of the North: Using the Approach of Martin Luther King Jr. to Invigorate the Next Civil Rights Movement, 1994, The Role of Multiculturalism in Establishing A New Period of Separate but Equal Segregation in the United States: A Comparison of the Periods After and First and Second Civil Wars, 1997, (with Henry W. Powell) The Life and Times of the Prophet Vernon Johns: Father of the Civil Rights Movement, 1998; editor: Witness to Civil Rights History: The Essays and Autobiography of Henry W. Powell, 2001. Civil rights activist. With Army Nat. Guard, 1966-73. Dissertation fellow Sweden-Am. Inst., N.Y.C., 1973-74. Mem. Torrey Bot. Club (chairperson field com.). Democrat. Mem. Soc. Of Friends. Home: 221 Mount Hope Blvd Hastings On Hudson NY 10706

COONEY, PATRICK RONALD, bishop; b. Detroit, Mar. 10, 1934; s. Michael and Elizabeth (Dowdall) C.. BA, Sacred Heart Sem., 1956; STB, Gregorian U., Rome, 1958, STL, 1960; MA, Notre Dame U., 1973. Ordained priest Roman Cath. Ch., 1959, ordained bishop Roman Cath. Ch., 1983. Assoc. pastor St. Catherine Ch., Detroit, 1960—62; asst. chancellor Archdiocese of Detroit, 1962—69, dir. dept. worship, 1969—83; rector Blessed Sacrament Cathedral, 1977—83; regional bishop Roman Cath. Ch., Detroit, 1983—89; apptd. bishop Diocese of Gaylord, Mich., 1989—. Office: Diocese of Gaylord Pastoral Ctr 611 W North St Gaylord MI 49735-8349*

COONEY, THOMAS EMMETT, lawyer; b. Portland, Oreg., July 16, 1931; s. Thomas M. and Ruth (Clune) C.; m. Janice Cooney; children: Jeff, Tom, Paul, Tracy, Eric. BA, U. Portland, 1953; JD, Willamette U., 1956. Bar: Oreg. 1956, U.S. Dist. Ct. Oreg. 1956, U.S. Ct. Appeals (9th cir.) 1956, U.S. Supreme Ct. 1980. Assoc. Maguire, Shields, Morrison, Bailey & Kester, Portland, 1956-60, ptnr., 1960-65, Morrison & Bailey, Portland, 1965-80, Cooney and Van Hoomissen, Portland, 1980-82, Cooney & Crew, Portland, 1982-88, 93—, Cooney, Moscato & Crew, Portland, 1988-93. Adj. instr. Coll. Law Lewis and Clark U., 1978-79. With USAF, 1951-52. Recipient Multnomal Bar Assn. Professionalism award, 1996; named Disting. Trial Lawyer of Yr. Fellow Am. Coll. Trial Lawyers, Nat. Health Lawyers Assn., Assn. Med. Soc. Attys., Oreg. Assn. Hosp. Attys.; mem. Oreg. Assn. Def. Counsel (past pres.), Am. Bd. Trial Advocates (diplomate), Internat. Assn. Def. Counsel, Def. Rsch. Inst., Oswego Lake Country Club, Elks. Address: 888 SW 5th Ave Ste 720 Portland OR 97204-2022

COONEY, WILLIAM J. lawyer; b. Augusta, Ga., July 31, 1929; s. John F. and Ellen (Joy) C.; m. Martha L. Whaley, May 1, 1971; children: William J. IV, Sarah C. BS, U. Notre Dame, 1951; JD, Georgetown U., 1954, LLM, 1955. Bar: Ga. 1963, Calif. 1961, D.C. 1954. Law clk. U.S. Ct. Appeals, Washington, 1954, U.S. Claims Ct., Washington, 1955; asst. U.S. atty. Washington, 1958-60, San Francisco, 1960-63; sole practice Augusta, 1963—. Capt. JAGC, U.S. Army, 1955-58. Mem. State Bar Ga., Spl. Master State Bar Ga., Augusta Bar Assn. (mem. exec. com.), Am. Arbitration Assn. (arbitrator). Roman Catholic. Office: 1 Habersham Sq 3602 Wheeler Rd Augusta GA 30909-1826 E-mail: cooney@knology.net.

COONLEY, CRAIG JOSEPH, internist, hematologist, oncologist; b. Schenectady, N.Y., Feb. 18, 1951; MD, Columbia U., 1977. Diplomate Am. Bd. Internal Medicine with subspecialties in oncology and hematology. Intern wilford Hall USAF Med. Ctr., San Antonio, 1977-78, resident in medicine, 1978-80; fellow in hematology and oncology Sloan-Kettering Cancer Ctr., N.Y.C., 1980; pvt. practice Oncology-Hematology Assocs., Clarksburg, W.Va., 1990—. Mem. ACP, AMA, Am. Soc. Hematologists, Am. Soc. Clin. Oncology. Office: Oncology-Hematology Assocs 300 Davisson Run Rd Clarksburg WV 26301-9304 Fax: 304-623-4941. E-mail: ccoonley@ma.rr.com.

COONS, BARBARA LYNN, public relations executive, librarian; b. Peoria, Ill., June 1, 1948; d. Harold Leroy and Norma (Brauer) C. BA, Stephens Coll., Columbia, Mo., 1970; MA, U. N.C., 1972; MLS, Cath. U., 1982. Rsch. asst. Am. Revolution Bicentennial Office Libr. of Congress, Washington, 1974-76, editl. asst., office of the Asst. Librarian, 1976-78; ednl. liaison specialist Libr. of Congress, Washington, 1978-82; dir. rsch. svc. Gray and Co., Washington, 1982-85, v.p., 1985-86; from v.p., dir. rsch. svcs. to sr. mng. dir. Hill and Knowlton Pub. Affairs Worldwide, Washington, 1986—2003; U.S. dir. rsch. svcs. Hill and Knowlton USA, 2003—. Pres. Library of Congress Profl. Assn., 1982. Mem. Spl. Libraries Assn., Stephens Coll. Alumnae Club of Greater Washington (pres. 1987). Lutheran. Home: 709 Arch Hall Ln Alexandria VA 22314-6208 Office: Hill & Knowlton Pub Affairs Worldwide 600 New Hampshire Ave NW Washington DC 20037-2403

COONS, RONALD EDWARD, historian, educator; b. Elmhurst, Ill., July 24, 1936; s. William A. and Madeline Louise (Theisen) C. BA, DePauw U., Greencastle, Ind., 1958; A.M., Harvard U., 1959, PhD, 1966. Teaching fellow history Harvard U., 1961-62, 63-66; research fellow Inst. Europäische Geschichte, Mainz, Germany, 1962-63; mem. faculty U. Conn., Storrs, 1966—2002, prof. history, 1979—2002, prof. emeritus, 2002—, dir. grad. studies, dept. history, 1983-87, 90-98, assoc. chmn., 1993—94, 2000—02, interim chmn., summer 1994. Author: Steamships, Statesmen and Bureaucrats: Austrian Policy Towards the Steam Navigation Company of the Austrian Lloyd, 1836-1848, 1975, I primi anni del Lloyd Austriaco, 1983; editor: Over Land and Sea. Memoir of an Austrian Rear Admiral's Life in Europe and Africa, 1857-1909 (Ludwig Ritter von Höhnel), 2000; mem. editl. bd. Austrian History Yearbook, 1992-94, 96-97, mem. adv. bd., 1994-96, also articles and revs. Mem. exec. com. St. Mark's Episcopal Ch., Storrs, 1976-82, 83-85, asst. organist, 1980-87; mem. exec. com. U. Conn. Friends of Soccer, 1989-98, v.p., 1993-95, pres. 1995-97; mem. exec. com. New Eng. Hosta Soc., 1989-92; co-chair interim com. St. Paul's Episcopal Ch., Willimantic, 1998-2001, mem. vestry, 2001—, archivist, 2003—. Nat. Endowment Humanities summer fellow, 1969; Am. Council Learned Socs. grantee, 1974, Am. Philos. Soc. grantee, 1974; NIH grantee, 1979; Gladys K. Delmas Found. grantee, 1983-84; Am. Council Learned Socs. grantee, 1985 Mem. AAUP, Am. Hist. Assn., Conf. Group Cen. European History, German Studies Assn., Soc. for Austrian and Habsburg History (exec. com. 1992-97, exec. sec. 1994-96), New Eng. Hist. Assn., Vienna Hist. Soc., Conn. Acad. Arts and Scis., Conn. Hort. Soc., Phi Beta Kappa (chpt. sec. 1976-86, v.p. 1987-88, 99-2000, pres. 1988-89, 2000-2001), Phi Alpha Theta, Phi Mu Alpha. Democrat. Office: U Conn Dept History 241 Glenbrook Rd Storrs Mansfield CT 06269-2103 Home: 1 Gin Still Ln West Hartford CT 06107-2647 E-mail: recoons@hotmail.com.

COONS, STEPHEN MERLE, lawyer; b. Indpls., May 27, 1941; s. Harold M. and Margaret L. (Richman) C.; children: Richard, Lori, Caroline. BA, Wabash Coll., 1963; JD, Ind. U., 1971. Bar: Ind. 1971, Ga. 1994, U.S. Dist. Ct. (so. dist.) Ind. 1971, U.S. Tax Ct. 1971, U.S. Dist. Ct. (no. dist.) Ind. 1980, U.S. Dist. Ct. (no. dist.) Ga. 1994, U.S. Ct. Appeals (7th cir.) 1980, U.S. Supreme Ct. 1978. Ptnr. Bradford & Coons, Indpls., 1971-72; assoc. Yockey & Yockey, Indpls., 1972-73; ptnr. Compton, Coons & Fetta, Indpls., 1973-78, Coons & Saint, Indpls., 1979-92, Coons, Maddox & Koeller, Indpls., 1993-95; exec. v.p., gen. counsel, sec. Standard Mgmt. Corp., Indpls., 1993—. Securities commr. State Ind., Indpls., 1978-83. Mem. ABA, State Bar Ga., Indpls. Bar Assn., Ind. State Bar Assn. Office: 9100 Keystone Xing Ste 400 Indianapolis IN 46240-2159 also: 1135 Brookhaven Ct NE Atlanta GA 30319-2867

COONTS, JANET RODMAN, education educator; b. Salem, Oreg., Feb. 17, 1942; d. Bruce E. Rodman and Margaret Louise (Mansfield) Samsel; m. Douglas M. Smith, Sept. 5, 1964 (div. Sept. 1986); 1 child, Christopher; m. Thomas E. Coonts, July 17, 1987. BA, Lewis and Clark Coll., Portland Oreg., 1960; postgrad., Ea. Wash. U., 1984—87. Cert. secondary edn. tchr., Idaho, Wash. G.E.D. instr. Columbia Basin Coll., 1978-86; tchr. English, chmn. dept. Kimberly (Idaho) H.S., 1987—. Recipient Tchr. of Yr. award U. Idaho, 1990, 93. Mem. Nat. Coun. Tchrs. English, Idaho Coun. Tchrs. English (bd. dirs. 1994). Republican. Avocations: running, reading, landscaping, antiques. Home: PO Box 125 Kimberly ID 83341-0125 E-mail: jtcoon@iglide.net.

COONTS, STEPHEN PAUL, novelist; b. Morgantown, W.Va., July 19, 1946; s. Gilbert Gray and Violet (Gadd) C.; m. Nancy Quereau, Feb. 19, 1971 (div. 1985); children: Rachael Diane Quereau, Lara Danielle Quereau, David Paul; m. Deborah Buell, Apr. 12, 1995. AB in Polit. Sci., W.Va. U., 1968; JD, U. Colo., 1979. Commd. ensign USN, 1968, with attack squadron 196, flight instr., asst. catapult arresting gear officer USS Nimitz; pvt. practice Hymes & Coonts Attys., Buckhannon, W.Va., 1980-81; in-house counsel Petro-Lewis Corp., Denver, 1981-86; freelance novelist, 1986—. Author: Flight of the Intruder, 1986 (Author of Yr. award U.S. Naval Inst. 1986), Final Flight, 1988, The Minotaur, 1989, Under Siege, 1990, The Cannibal Queen: An Aerial Odyssey Across America, 1992, The Red Horseman, 1993, The Intruders, 1994, War In the Air, 1996, Fortunes of War, 1998, Cuba, 1999. Trustee W.Va. Wesleyan Coll., 1990-98. Inductee Acad. of Dist. Alumni W.Va. U., 1992.

COOP, ANDREW, chemist, educator; PhD, U. of Bristol, 1994. Asst. prof. U. Md. Sch. Pharmacy, Balt., 1999—2003. Grantee NIH R01, NIDA, 2001—. Mem.: Coll. on Problems of Drug Dependence (biol. coord., dec 2000—03). Achievements include patents for Novel chemistry of opiates.

COOP, FREDERICK ROBERT, retired city manager; b. San Diego, Mar. 1, 1914; s. Ernest Frederick and Hazel (Angier) C.; m. Jean Haven, Feb. 11, 1939; children— Susan, Robert, Thomas, Elizabeth. AB, U. Calif. at Berkeley, 1935; MS in Pub. Adminstrn, U. So. Calif., 1937. Pers. technician Calif. State Pers. Bd., 1937-41; pers. dir. Pasadena, Calif., 1941-49; pers. cons. UN, 1947; city mgr. Inglewood, Calif., 1949-56, Fremont, Calif., 1956-58; chief pub. svcs. div. U.S. Ops. Mission to Yugoslavia, 1958-61; city mgr. Newport Beach, Calif., 1961-64, Phoenix, 1964-69; regional dir. HEW, San Francisco, 1969-71; dir. pub. adminstrn. svcs. Arthur D. Little, Inc., San Francisco, 1972-78; pres. Coop Mgmt. Svcs. Inc., 1978—91. Pres., bd. dirs. Pub. Svc. Skills Inc. Served to lt. comdr. USNR, World War II. Named Young Man of Yr., Pasadena Jr. C. of C., 1947. Mem. Internat. City Mgmt. Assn. (regional v.p. 1965-67, Disting. Svc. award 2000), Am. Soc. Pub. Adminstrn. (bd. dirs.), Nat. Acad. Pub. Adminstrn., League Calif. Cities (hon. life. city mgrs. dept.).

COOPER, ALAN MICHAEL, psychiatrist; b. Balt., Mar. 14, 1950; s. William I. and Barbara (Stein) C.; m. Elizabeth Ann Mumper, May 31, 1980; children: William, Leigh. SB, MIT, 1972; MD, Med. Coll. Va., 1976. Diplomate Am. Bd. Psychiatry and Neurology. Intern Med. Coll. Va., 1976—77, resident in psychiatry, 1977—78, U. Va. Hosps., 1978—79, fellow pain clinic, 1979—80, fellow child and adolescent psychiatry, 1981; instr. psychiatry Harvard Med. Sch., Boston, 1980—81; assoc. in anesthesia (psychiatry) Brigham & Women's Hosp., Boston, 1980—81; dir. diagnostic and evaluation unit David C. Wilson Hosp., Charlottesville, Va., 1982—84; clin. adminstr. psychiatry Va. Bapt. Hosp., Lynchburg, 1984—85; chief psychiatrist Ctrl. Va. Cmty. Svcs., Lynchburg, 1985—92, cons. psychiatrist, 1992—. Asst. prof. clin. family medicine U. Va. Sch. Medicine, Charlottesville, Va., 1997—2000; faculty Lynchburg Family Practice Residency Program, 1997—2000. Bd. dir. First Unitarian Universalist

Ch. of Lynchburg, past pres. MIT Nat. scholar, 1968. Mem. Am. Psychiat. Assn., Psychiat. Soc. of Va., Lynchburg Acad. Medicine, Nat. Assn. for the Dually Diagnosed. Office: Central Virginia Tng Ctr PO Box 1098 Lynchburg VA 24505-1098

COOPER, ALAN SAMUEL, lawyer, educator; b. June 13, 1942; s. Rudey and Rosalie (Schwartz) C.; m. Maxine Jacobs, Aug. 13, 1966 (dec.); children: Lauren K., Jennifer D.; m. Linda Morguelan Klein, April 18, 1999. BA, Vanderbilt U., 1964, JD, 1968. Bar: Tenn. 1968, D.C. 1969, U.S. Dist. Ct. D.C. 1969, U.S. Supreme Ct. Appeals (Fed. cir.) 1975, U.S. Supremem Ct. 1980. Law clk. U.S. Dist. Ct. (mid. dist.), Tenn., 1967-68; assoc. Browne, Schuyler & Beveridge and Browne, Beveridge & DeGrandi, Washington, 1968—72, Schyler, Birch, Swindler, McKie & Beckett, Washington, 1972-74; ptnr. Schyler, Banner, Birch, McKie & Beckett, Washington, 1974-94; mem. bd. dirs., shareholder Banner & Witcoff, Ltd., Washington, Chgo., Boston, 1995-97; ptnr. Shaw Pittman Potts & Trowbridge, Washington, N.Y.C., L.A., London, 1997—. Adj. prof. Georgetown U. Law Ctr., 1985—; adviser on trademark law to U.S. del. to Diplomatic Conf. on Revision of Paris Conv. for Protection of Indsl. Property, Nairobi, Kenya, 1981. Mem. ABA (faculty Nat. Insts. on Trademark Litigation 1978-79), Internat. Trademark Assn., D.C. Bar, Bar Assn. D.C., Tenn. Bar Assn., Bethesda Country Club. Jewish. Office: 2300 N St NW Washington DC 20037-1122

COOPER, ALCIE LEE, JR., entrepreneur, former insurance executive; b. Gadsden, Ala., Aug. 3, 1939; s. Alcie Lee and Jettie Merle (Farabee) C.; m. Audrey May MacAuslan, Sept. 3, 1976. AB, Asbury Coll., 1961; MDiv, St. Paul Sch. Theology, 1966; student, Workers Compensation Coll., 1979. CPCU, Am. Inst. Property and Liability Underwriters, 1991. Claims adjuster Sentry Ins. A Mut. Co., St. Louis, 1967-69, claim supr. Kansas City, Kans., 1969-72, regional claims supr. Dallas, 1972-77; home office workers compensation cons. Houston Gen. Ins. Co., Ft. Worth, 1977-79, asst. claims mgr., 1979-82, worker's compensation claims mgr., 1982-85, dir. Field Claim Ctr., asst. v.p. claims, 1986-93; ptnr. Al Cooper & Assocs., distbrs. Quixtar products, Ft. Worth, 1977—; br. mgr. Hammerman & Gainer, Inc., 1993-2000. Instr. Workers Compensation Sch., 1977-85; owner Alcieco Enterprises, 2000. Mem. Rep. Presdl. Task Force; bd. dirs. Am. Heart Assn., Tarrant County, Tex., 1983-89. Mem. CPCU Soc. (sec. Ft. Worth chpt. 1994-95, v.p. 1995-96, pres.-elect 1996-97, pres. 1997-98, bd. dirs. 1998-99), Quixtar Ind. Bus. Owners. Office: 4125 Alicante Ave Fort Worth TX 76133-5503 E-mail: acooper@flash.net.

COOPER, APRIL HELEN, family nurse practitioner; b. Evergreen Park, Ill., Dec. 24, 1951; d. Frank and Anne (Mirocha) Stevens; m. Michael Dennis, June 20, 1970; children: Christine Michelle, Brian Michael, Jeannette Michelle. AAS, Ohio U., 1981, BSN, 1996; MS, Wright State U., 2000. RN Ohio; cert. med./surg. nurse, ANCC, family nurse practitioner, ANCC. Supr. home health care Med. Pers. Pool, Cambridge, Ohio, 1989-91; primary nurse pediat. home care Primary Care Nursing Svcs., Dublin, Ohio, 1989-91; case mgr. Buckeye Home Health Svc., Zanesville, Ohio, 1990-91; with home health svcs. Genesis Home Care, Zanesville, 1981-98; family practice nurse practitioner Bucyrus Cmty. Hosp., 2001—. Mem. ANA, Golden Key. Phi Kappa Phi, Sigma Theta Tau, Gamma Pi Delta. Republican. Methodist. Avocations: reading professional journals, travel. Home: 3172 Oak Dr Bucyrus OH 44820-9654

COOPER, ARNOLD COOK, management educator, researcher; b. Chgo., Mar. 9, 1933; s. Millard and Sarah Ellen C.; m. Jean Phillips Lord, Sept. 12, 1959; children: Katherine Lord, David Andrew. BS in Chem. Engring., Purdue U., 1955, MS in Mgmt., 1957; D in Bus. Adminstrn., Harvard U., 1962. Engr. Proctor & Gamble, Cin., 1957-58; asst. prof. Harvard U., Cambridge, Mass., 1961-63; assoc. prof. Purdue U., West Lafayette, Ind., 1963-70, prof., 1970-84, Weil prof. mgmt., 1984—. Vis. assoc. prof. Stanford Univ., Palo Alto, Calif., 1967-68; vis. prof. Manchester (Eng.) Bus. Sch., 1972, IMEDE Mgmt. Devel. Inst., Lausanne, Switzerland, 1977-78; past dir. Grad. Profl. Programs, chmn. Mgmt. Policy Com., Purdue U., West Lafayette; mem. Ind. Employment Devel. Commn., 1982-89, Fed. Adv. Com. on Indsl. Innovation, 1978-79. Author: The Founding of Technologically Based Firms, 1971; co-author: Small Business Management, 1966, Technical Entrepreneurship: A Symposium, 1972, The Entrepreneurial Function, 1977, New Business in America, 1990; contbr. numerous articles to profl. jours. and bus. publs.; mem. editorial bd. Stategic Mgmt. Jour., 1979—, Jour. of Bus. Venturing, 1985—, Acad. of Mgmt. Jour., 1978-84, Jour. High Tech. Mktg., 1986-87. 2nd lt. U.S. Army, 1956. Recipient Honeywell Master Tchr. award, 1990, Disting. Scholar award, Intenat. Coun. on Small Bus., 1987, Ten Year Author award, Babson Entrepreneurship Conf., 1990, John S. Day Disting. Alumni Acad. Svc. award, 2001. Mem. Acad. Mgmt. (chmn. bus. policy and strategy divsn. 1978-79, Outstanding Paper award Entrepreneurship Divsn. 1991, 92, Coleman Entrepreneurship Mentor award, 1993), Soc. Fellows (Richard D. Irwin outstanding educator award, 1999, Internat. award for entrepreneurship and small bus. rsch. 1997), Internat. Coun. Small Bus., Strategic Mgmt. Soc. (bd. govs. 1984-86). Home: 616 Ridgewood Dr West Lafayette IN 47906-2367 Office: Purdue Univ Krannert Sch of Mgmt 1310 Krannert West Lafayette IN 47907-1310 E-mail: coopera@mgmt.purdue.edu.

COOPER, ARTHUR WELLS, ecologist, educator; b. Washington, Aug. 15, 1931; s. Gustav Arthur and Josephine (Wells) C.; m. Jean Farnsworth, Aug. 30, 1953; children: Paul Arthur, Roy Alan. BA, Colgate U., 1953, MA, 1955; PhD, U. Mich., 1958. Asst. prof. botany N.C. State U., Raleigh, 1958-63, assoc. prof., 1963-68, prof., 1968-71, prof. forestry, 1976—2001, prof. emeritus, 2001—, head dept. forestry, 1980-94, faculty athletics rep., 1990-2001. Asst. sec. N.C. Dept. Natural and Econ. Resources, Raleigh, 1971-76; mem. N.C. Coastal Resources Commn., Raleigh, 1976-89, N.C. Environ. Mgmt. Commn., Raleigh, 1989-91; chmn. Com. Scientists for Nat. Forest Mgmt. Act, Washington, 1977-79, 82, Govs. Task Force on Forest Sustainability, 1995-96; bd. dirs. N.C. Environ. Def. Fund, 1987-90, So. Environ. Law Ctr., 1987-90. Trustee N.C. Nature Conservancy, Chapel Hill, 1977-87; mem. coun. NCAA, 1995-96, mem. Divsn. I mgmt. coun., 1996-2001. Recipient Am. Motors Conservation award, 1972, Sol Feinstone award SUNY Coll. Environ. Sci. and Forestry, Syracuse, 1982, Outstanding Svc. to Forestry award N.C. Forestry Assn., 2002; named Conservationist of Yr., N.C. Wildlife Fedn., 1982. Fellow AAAS, Soc. Am. Foresters (chmn. N.C. chpt. 1984, Appalachian Soc. 1990, Gifford Pinchot medal 1999); mem. Ecol. Soc. Am. (cert. sr. ecologist 1982—, v.p. 1974, pres. 1981, Disting. Svc. award 1984), N.C. Acad. Sci. (pres. 1979), Assn. Southeastern Biologists. Democrat. Home: 719 Runnymede Rd Raleigh NC 27607-3103 Office: NC State U Dept Forestry Raleigh NC 27695-8008 E-mail: awcooper@earthlink.net., arthur_cooper@ncsu.edu.

COOPER, AUSTIN MORRIS, chemist, chemical engineer, consultant, researcher; b. Long Beach, Calif., Feb. 1, 1959; s. Merril Morris and Charlotte Madeline (Wittmer) C. BS in Chemistry with honors, Baylor U., 1981; BSChemE with honors, Tex. Tech U., 1983, MSChemE with honors, 1985. Solar energy researcher U.S. Dept. Energy, Lubbock, Tex., 1983-85; advanced mfg. and process engring. mgr. McDonnell Douglas Space Systems Co., Huntington Beach, Calif., 1986-87, chem.-process line mgr., 1987-89, prin. material and process engr., 1999—. Contbr. articles to profl. jours. Mem. AIChE, Am. Chem. Soc., Soc. Advancement of Materials and Process Engrs., SCV, SAR, Sigma Xi, Omega Chi Epsilon, Kappa Mu Epsilon, Beta Beta Beta.

COOPER, BYRON STANLEY, physician, educator; b. Washington, May 21, 1947; s. Joseph David and Ruth (Zeidner) C.; m. Jane Ann Kanter, Feb. 5, 1978; children: Joseph, Allison. BA, Johns Hopkins U., 1969; MD, Washington U., St. Louis, 1973. Diplomate in internal medicine and pulmonary medicine Am. Bd. Internal Medicine. Clin. prof. George Washington U., Washington, 1981—. Fellow Am. Coll. Chest Physicians; mem. AMA (alt. del. 2000--), ACP, D.C. Thoracic Soc. (pres. 1994), Med. Soc. D.C. (pres. 1998-99). Avocations: photography, computers, running. Office: Capital Pumonary Internists 2440 M St NW Washington DC 20037-1404

COOPER, CAROL DIANE, publishing company executive; b. Williamsport, Pa., Aug. 14, 1953; d. Ray Calvin and Norma Jane (Stiger) Cooper. BA, Colgate U., 1975; cert. in pub., Radcliffe Coll., 1975; MA, Syracuse (N.Y.) U., 1977. Editl. and promotion asst. St. Martin's Press, N.Y.C., 1977—78, sales rep., 1978—79; dir. sales, v.p. Clearwater Pub. Co., Inc., N.Y.C., 1979—80, dir. mktg., 1980—81, v.p., 1980—83; exec. v.p. K.G. Saur Inc., N.Y.C., 1983—87; v.p., pub. R.R. Bowker Co., N.Y.C., 1987—90; v.p. internat. pub. ops. Bowker, Martindale Hubbell, N.Y.C., 1990—92, Reed Reference Pub., New Providence, NJ, 1992—96, also bd. dirs., 1996; sr. v.p. pub. Martindale-Hubbell, New Providence, 1996—. Office: Martindale Hubbell 121 Chanlon Rd New Providence NJ 07974-1544

COOPER, CHARLEEN FRANCES, special and elementary education educator; b. Jamaica, N.Y., Oct. 23, 1948; d. Charles and Dolly (Oakes) Fells; m. Chris M. Cooper, June 23, 1969 (div.); children: Chris A., Scott F. BS in Spl. Edn. cum laude, Coll. of St. Joseph, Rutland, Vt., 1985; postgrad., The Provider; MA in Edn., Castleton State Coll., 1994. Cert. spl. and elem. edn. tchr., Vt.; cert. learning specialist/consulting tchr. spl. edn. Spl. edn. and resource rm. tchr. Rutland City Pub. Sch., 1985-88; tchr. spl. edn., multi-handicapped Rutland Cen. Supervisory Union, 1988-91; spl. edn. and resource rm. tchr. Addison-Rutland Supervisory Union, 1991-92; mktg. instr. Stafford Tech. Ctr., Rutland City Pub. Schs., 1992-93; vocat. rehab. employment facilitator State of Vt., 1995-96; chpt. 1 title 1 head instr. Bennington Sch., Inc., 1996-97; title 1 head instr. Catamount Elem., Bennington, Vt., 1997—2002, resource rm. tchr., 1998; tchr. resource rm. Poultney Elem. Sch., Poultney, Vt., 2002—. Coord. program, instr. Integration of Proctor High Sch. Students with Spl. Needs, 1989-91. Coll. of St. Joseph scholar. Avocations: gardening, motorcycling, flying. Home: PO Box 40 North Clarendon VT 05759-0040 Office: Pooultney Elem Sch Circle Poultney VT

COOPER, CHARLES DONALD, association executive, editor, retired career officer; b. Exeter, N.H., Dec. 19, 1932; s. Herbert Almon and Mildred (Pitcher) C.; m. Beverly Lorraine Hummel, May 18, 1957; children: Liane, Dale, Kristin. BS, Northwestern U., 1954; grad., Indsl. Coll. Armed Forces, Washington, 1975. Commd. 2d lt. USAF, 1954, advanced through grades to col., 1977, mem. ops. staff, 1955-76; dep. chief pub. affairs USAF Fifth AF, Yokota Air Base, Japan, 1975-77; dep. chief community rels. USAF, Washington, 1977-78, dep. chief media rels., 1978-80, chief media rels., 1980-82, dir. internal info., 1982-83; vol. community svc. Springfield, Va., 1984-86; exec. editor The Ret. Officer Assn., Alexandria, Va., 1986-88, dir. publs., 1988-96. Contbr. articles to mags. and newspapers in field. Trustee Messiah United Meth. Ch., Springfield, 1985-96, mem. adminstrv. bd., 1998—2002, asst. treas., 1999—, mem. fin. com., 1999—, alt. del. Va. United Meth. Ch. Conf., 2003—. Decorated Meritorious Svc. Medal, D.F.C., Air medal with five oak leaf clusters, Legion of Merit. Mem. Mil. Officers Assn. Am., Daedalians, Masons, Shriners. Avocations: gardening, snow skiing. E-mail: chukbev@erols.com.

COOPER, CHARLES GILBERT, toiletries and cosmetics company executive; b. Chgo., Apr. 4, 1928; s. Benjamin and Gertrude Cooper; m. Miriam Meyer, Feb. 11, 1951 (dec. Oct. 17, 1983); children: Debra, Ruth, Janet, Benjamin; m. Nancy Cooper BS in Journalism, U. Ill., 1949. With sales promotion dept. Maidenform Co., N.Y.C., 1949-51; with circulation promotion dept. Esquire mag., Chgo., 1951-52; with Helene Curtis Industries Inc., Chgo., 1953-96, pres. salon div., 1971-75, pres. consumer products div., 1975-82, corp. exec. v.p., 1982-85, exec. v.p., COO, 1985-93, sr. v.p., 1993-96; sr. ptnr. GCG Ptnrs.; adj. prof. Loyola U. CEO, pres. Coun. for Jewish Elderly. With AUS, 1952-53. Office: 225 W Wacker Dr Ste 1800 Chicago IL 60606-1274

COOPER, CHARLES GORDON, insurance consultant, former executive; b. Providence, May 31, 1927; s. Irving and Helen Christina (Skog) C.; m. Barbara Caroline Termohlen, June 17, 1950; 1 dau., Marie Suzanne. BA, Ohio Wesleyan U., 1949. C.L.U. Group rep. Washington Nat. Ins. Co., 1949-53, asst. mgr., 1953-58, mgr., 1958-63, dir. assn. field services, 1963-65, asst. sec., 1965-67, 3d v.p., 1967-72, 2d v.p., 1972-77, v.p., 1977-79, sr. v.p., 1979-83, exec. v.p., 1983-85, dir., mem. exec. com., 1979-85; sr. v.p.-mktg. Washington Nat. Corp., parent co. Washington Nat. Ins. Co., Evanston, 1983-85, cons., 1985—. Dir. Washington Nat. Trust Co., 1974-85, chmn. exec. com., 1979-85; chmn., dir. Washington Nat. Fin. Services, Inc., 1979-85; pres., dir. Washington Nat. Equity Co., 1973-85, chmn. bd., 1983-85 Bd. dirs. North Shore Assn. for Retarded, Evanston, 1983— . Served with USNR, 1945-46, PTO. Mem. Am. Coll. Life Underwriters, Chartered Life Underwriters, Nat. Assn. Life Underwriters, Chgo. Life Underwriters Assn., Nat. Assn. Health Underwriters, Chgo. Health Underwriters Clubs: Ivanhoe (Ill.). Lodges: Masons, Shriners. Republican.

COOPER, CHARLES HOWARD, photojournalist, newspaper publishing company executive; b. Clinton, N.C., July 17, 1920; s. John Howard and Ella Jane (Bass) C.; m. Nell Elizabeth Slaughter, Jan. 2, 1943; children: Charles Howard II, John Phillip. Grad., U.S. Air Force Sch. Photography, 1943. Chief photographer, mgr. photo dept. Durham Herald Co. (N.C.), 1945-85; pub. Durham Morning Herald, 1945, Durham Sun, 1945-85. Chmn. Miss Nat. Press Photographer Pageant, 1952, 53, 55 Mem. Citizens Safety Com., Durham, 1961-71. Served with USAAF, 1942-45, ETO. Mem. Nat. Press Photographers Assn. (life, exec. dir. 1963-2000, exec. dir. emeritus 2001—, Fellowship award, Joseph A. Sprague award 1961, Pres.'s medal 1964, 67, 2001, Merit award 1965, Joseph Costa award 1977, exec. dir. emeritus 1998, interim exec. dir. 2001), Carolinas Press Photographers Assn. (life, pres. 1952-54) Democrat. Baptist. Office: Nat Press Photographers 6 Lucerne Ln Durham NC 27707-3839 E-mail: chcscoop@aol.com.

COOPER, CHESTER LAWRENCE, research administrator; b. Boston, Jan. 13, 1917; s. Israel and Hannah (Levenson) C.; m. Orah Pomerance, July 23; children: Joan Laurence Gould, Susan Louise Cooper. BS, NYU, 1939, MBA, 1941; PhD, Am. U., Washington, 1960. Asst. dep. dir. CIA, Washington, 1947-62; sr. staff White House/NSC, Washington, 1962-66, U.S. Dept. State, Washington, 1966-70; dir. internat. div. Inst. Def. Analysis, Arlington, Va., 1970-72; fellow Woodrow Wilson Internat. Ctr. Scholars, Washington, 1972-75; dep. dir. Inst. Energy Analysis, Oak Ridge, Tenn., 1975-83; dep. dir., acting dir. Internat. Inst. Applied Systems Analysis, Laxenburg, Austria, 1983-85; coord. internat programs Resources for the Future, Washington, 1985-92; dep. dir. Battelle Pacific N.W. Labs., Washington, 1992-2001, emeritus dir., 2001; dep. dir. emeritus Joint Inst. for Rsch. on Global Change, U. Md./Pacific Northwest Nat. Lab., 2001—. Cons. Aspen Inst., Sci. Policy Assocs., Washington, Screenscope Films, Washington. Author: The Lost Crusade, 1971 (award 1971), The Lion's Last Roar, 1977; editor: Growth in America, 1976, Science for Public Policy, 1987. Fellow Woodrow Wilson, Internat. Ctr. for Scholars, 1972—75; scholar, Nat. War Coll., Washington, 1952—53, Internat. Inst. Applied Sys. Analyses, Laxemburg, Austria, 1986. Mem. Coun. Fgn. Rels., Poets, Essayists, Novelists, Cosmos Club. Avocations: fishing, gardening, sculpting, 18th Century furniture and silver. Home: 700 New Hampshire Ave NW Washington DC 20037 Office: Univ Md 8400 Baltimore Ave Ste 201 College Park MD 20740 E-mail: clcooper@pnl.gov.

COOPER, CHRIS, actor; b. Kansas City, Mo., July 9, 1951; s. Charles and Mary Ann Cooper; m. Marianne Leone, July 1983. Student, U. Mo., Columbia, Stephens Coll. Actor: (TV series) The Equalizer, 1985, Miami Vice, 1984, Lifestories, 1990, Law & Order, 1990; (films) Matewan, 1987; (TV films) Journey Into Genius, 1988; (TV miniseries) Lonesome Dove, 1989; (TV films) To the Moon, Alice, 1990; (films) Thousand Pieces of Gold, 1990; (TV films) A Little Piece of Sunshine, 1990, In Broad Daylight, 1991; (films) Guilty by Suspicion, 1991; (TV films) Darrow, 1991; (films) City of Hope, 1991; (TV films) Bed of Lies, 1992, Ned Blessing: The True Story of My Life, 1992; (films) This Boy's Life, 1993; (TV miniseries) Return to Lonesome Dove, 1993; (TV films) One More Mountain, 1994; (films) Money Train, 1995, Pharaoh's Army, 1995; (TV films) The Deliverance of Elaine, 1996; (films) Boys, 1996, Lone Star, 1996, A Time to Kill, 1996; (TV films) Breast Men, 1997, Alone, 1997; (films) Great Expectations, 1998, The Horse Whisperer, 1998, The 24 Hour Woman, 1999, October Sky, American Beauty, 1999, Me, Myself & Irene, 2000, The Patriot, 2000, Interstate 60, 2002, The Bourne Identity, 2002, Adaptation, 2002 (Acad. Award for Best Supporting Actor, 2002); (TV films) My House in Umbria, 2003; (films) Seabiscuit, 2003; contbr. Address: Paradigm Talent Agy Ste 2500 10100 Santa Monica Blvd Los Angeles CA 90067*

COOPER, CLEMENT THEODORE, lawyer; b. Miami, Fla., Oct. 26, 1930; s. Benjamin Leon and Louise (Bethel) C.; m. Nan Coles Cooper; children: Patricia, Karen, Stephanie, Bridgette, Jessica (dec.), Stacy. AB, Lincoln U., 1952; student, Boston U., 1954-55; JD, Howard U., 1958; PhD in Bus. Adminstrn. (hon.), Colo. Christian Coll. Bar: D.C. 1960, Mich. 1960, U.S. Ct. Appeals (3rd, 4th, 6th, 9th and 10th cirs.), U.S. Ct. Mil. Appeals,, U.S. Ct. Claims, U.S. Supreme Ct. 1963. Pvt. practice, Washington, 1960—. Adj. prof. Strayer U., Washington, 1991-98; former legal cons. No. Calif. Mining Assn.; arbitrator NY Stock Exch., NASD. Author: Sealed Verdict, 1964; contbr. articles to profl. jours. Adv. coun. D.C. Dept. Welfare, 1963-66; adv. bd. Com. on Irish Ethnicity, N.Y.C. Mem. ABA, ATLA, NASD, D.C. Bar Assn., Nat. Bar Assn., ACLU, Am. Judicature Soc., Rocky Mountain Mining Law Found., Internat. Platform Assn., Nat. Assn. Securities Dealers (arbitrator), Soc. King Charles Martyr, Am. Legion, Knights Templar (Knights fellow), Alpha Phi Alpha (life). Episcopalian. Home: 728 Dahlia St NW Washington DC 20012-1844 Office: PO Box 76135 Washington DC 20013-6135

COOPER, CORINNE, communications consultant, lawyer; b. Albuquerque, July 12, 1952; d. David D. and Martha Lucille (Rosenblum) C. BA magna cum laude, U. Ariz., 1975, JD summa cum laude, 1978. Bar: Ariz. 1978, U.S. Dist. Ct. Ariz. 1978, Mo. 1985. Assoc. Streich, Lang, Weeks & Cardon, Phoenix, 1978-82; asst. prof. U. Mo., Kansas City, 1982-86, assoc. prof., 1986-94, prof., 1994-2000, prof. emerita, 2000—; pres. Profl. Presence, Comm. Cons., Tucson and Kansas City, Mo., 2001—. Vis. prof. U. Wis., Madison, 1985, 91, U. Pa., Phila., 1988, U. Ariz., 1993, U. Colo., 1994. Author: (with Bruce Meyerson) A Drafter's Guide to Alternative Dispute Resolution, 1991; editor: The Portable UCC, 1993, 3d edit., 2001, Getting Graphic I and II, 1993, 94, The New Article 9, 1999, 2d edit., 2000; editor in chief Bus. Law Today, 1995-97; mem. editl. bd. ABA Jour., 1999—; contbr. articles to profl. jours., chpts. to books. Legal counsel Mo. for Hart campaign, 1984; dir. issues Goddard for Gov. campaign, 1990; bd. dirs. Com. for County Progress, Kansas City, 1985-95. Mem. ABA (mem. coun. bus. sect. 1992-96, uniform comml. code com., chmn. membership com. 1992-94, editl. bd. Bus. Law Today, 1991-97, sect. of bus. law pubs. 1998-2002, standing com. on strategic comm. 2001—), Am. Law Inst., Am. Assn. Law Schs. (comml. law 1982-2000), Ariz. Bar Assn., Mo. Bar Assn. (comml. law com.), Order of Coif, Phi Beta Kappa, Phi Kappa Phi. Democrat. Jewish. Office: Profl Presence 6412 Morningside Dr Kansas City MO 64113 also: 4558 N 1st Ave Tucson AZ 85718

COOPER, CYNTHIA, retired professional basketball coach, retired professional basketball player; b. Chgo., Apr. 14, 1963; Degree in phys. edn., U. So. Calif., 1986. Basketball player Segovia, Spain, 1986—87, Parma, Italy, 1987—94, 1996—97, Alcamo, Italy, 1994—96; basketball player Houston Comets Women's NBA, 1997—2000; head coach Phoenix Mercury, 2001—02. Mem. U.S. Goodwill Games, 1986, 90, World Championships, 1986, 90, Pan Am. Games, 1987. Named MVP, Women's NBA Championship, 1997, 1998; recipient Gold medal, Pan Am Games, 1987, U.S. Olympic Basketball, 1988, Bronze medal, 1992; mem. WNBA champion, Houston Comets, 1997, 1998, 1999.

COOPER, DANIEL L. federal agency administrator; Grad., U.S. Naval Acad., 1957; MPA, Harvard U., 1963. Commd. USN, 1959, advanced through grades to vice admiral, ret., 1991, served in amphibious force, with submarine svc. USS Trigger, 1959, on USS Haddo, exec. officer USS Simon Bolivar, comdg. officer USS Puffer, 1972—76, comdr. submarine squadron TEN, 1976—79, comdr. Atlantic fleet's submarine force, 1986—88; v.p., gen. mgr. nuclear svcs. divsn. Gilbert Commonwealth, Reading, Pa., 1991; mem. tech. adv. group Applied Physics Lab. Johns Hopkins U.; chmn. adv. bd. Applied Rsch. Lab. Pa. State U.; chmn. VA Claims Processing Task Force; dir. bd. USAA; under sec. benefits Dept. Vets. Affairs, Washington, 2002—. Bd. dirs. Exelon Corp., Chgo. Office: US Dept Vet Affairs Vets Benfits Adminstrn 810 Vermont Ave NW Washington DC 20420

COOPER, DAVID EARL KALEOIKAIKA, foundation executive; b. Honolulu, Aug. 12, 1941; s. Robert Lewis and Lucy Kapuakela (Kamaka_ C.; m. Katherine S. Arakaki, June 16, 1962; children: Troy A.K., Bradley H.K., Ethan Scott K.K. BA in English, U. Hawaii Manoa, Honolulu, 1963; MA in English Lit., U. Mo., Kansas City, 1974; MS in Counseling Psychology, L.I. U., 1976; postgrad., Harvard U., 1992. Cert. fin. planner. Commd. 2d lt. U.S. Army, 1963, advanced through grades to brig. gen., 1993, ret., 1993; pres. Pacific Am. Found., Washington, 1993—; CEO Hana Engring., Inc., Honolulu, 1994—, Pacific Nations Internat., Washington, 1997—. Contbr. articles to army mags. Chmn. Fed. Adv. Com. on Minority Vets., Washington, 1995—; bd. govs. Japanese Am. Nat. Mus., L.A., 1996—. Decorated Silver Star with oak leaf cluster, Combat Inf. badge; Coun. on Fgn. Rrels. fellow, 1985. Mem. U. Hawaii Alumni Assn. (pres. Nat. Capital Region chpt. 1997—), Kamehameha Alumni Assn. (dir. East Coast chpt. 1994—), Inst. for Cert. Fin. Planners, 173rd Soc., 25th Inf. Divsn. Soc., Phi Kappa Phi. Avocations: tennis, running, biking. Home: 1106 W Abingdon Dr Alexandria VA 22314-1201

COOPER, DAVID FREDERICK, poet, translator; b. Bronx, N.Y., Dec. 27, 1954; s. Alan and Vera Dorothy Cooper; m. Shoshana Cohen, Aug. 29, 1982. BA, Hunter Coll., 1979; M Internat. Affairs, Columbia U., 1980; MA, CCNY, 1992. Contbr. poems and translations to lit. jours., including Mass. Rev., Painted Bride Quar., Archipelago, Lit. Rev., numerous others (Acad. Am. Poets Coll. prize 1992). Democrat. Jewish. Avocations: fitness, walking, jazz, modern art.

COOPER, DAVID WAYNE, product engineer; b. Houston, Apr. 5, 1964; s. Cary Wayne and Carolyn Kay (McDonald) C.; m. Lee Jane Hong, Apr. 30, 1994; children: Cary Anthony Hong Cooper, Robert Alan Hong Cooper. BS, Tex. A&M U., 1988; MS, U. Houston, 1996. Engr. Rockwell Space Ops. Co., Houston, 1989-96, United Space Alliance, Houston, 1996-98, Sperry-Sun, Houston, 1998—.

COOPER, DAVIS A. city official; b. South Fort Mitchell, Ky., Mar. 8, 1956; s. Davis A. and Geneva A. (Rudd) C.; children: Clinton C., Stephanie L. BS in Acctg., Western Ky. U., 1980. Cert. govt. fin. officer, Ky. Treas. City of Bowling Green, Ky., 1980—2001, CFO, 2002—. Bd. dirs. United Way of So. Ky., Bowling Green, 1994-99, treas., 1996-97. Mem. Govt. Fin. Officers U.S.A., Ky. Govt. Fin. Officers (bd. dirs. 1982-90, treas. 1983-84, pres. 1985-86). Avocations: basketball, soccer, football, hockey, family. Office: City of Bowling Green PO Box 430 Bowling Green KY 42102-0430 E-mail: coopd14@bgky.org.

COOPER, DENNIS LAWRENCE, oncologist, educator; b. Chgo., Apr. 15, 1954; s. Marvin and Gwendolyn (Janowicz) C.; m. Jean Bolognia, Aug. 25, 1984. BS, Loyola, Chgo., 1975; MD, Rush Med. Coll., 1979. Diplomate Am. Bd. Internal Medicine, Am. Bd. Oncology. Intern internal medicine Yale-New Haven Hosp., 1979-80, resident internal medicine, 1980-82; chief resident internal medicine U. Pitts., 1982-83; fellow oncology Yale U., New Haven, 1983-86, asst. prof. internal medicine, 1986-93, assoc. prof., 1993—2002, prof., 2002—, dir. stem cell transplant program, 1994-97, clin. dir. bone marrow and stem cell transplant program, 1997—. Clinic chief Oncology Outpatient Svc., New Haven, 1995-98; dir. Oncology Fellowship Program, New Haven, 1993-97, Inpatient Svc. Oncology, New Haven, 1994—. Editl. bd. Cancer Investigation, 1993—, Cancer Therapeutics, 1998—; contbr. articles to profl. jours. Basketball coach Orange (Conn.) Recreation League, 1991-92. Mem. Internat. Soc. Hematotherapy and Graft Engring., Am. Soc. Clin. Oncology, Conn. Oncology Assn. Avocations: softball, baseball. Home: 140 Patten Rd North Haven CT 06473-2830 Office: Yale U Sch Medicine 333 Cedar St New Haven CT 06510-3289

COOPER, DONALD LEE, physician; b. Columbus, Kans., Aug. 11, 1928; s. Calvin M. and J. Pearl (Mullen) C.; m. Dona Faye Maddux, June 4, 1950; children— Donald Lee, Catherine Susan, Cheryl Lyn, Tad Houston. AB, Pittsburg State U., 1949; MD, U. Kans., 1953. Intern St. Mary's and Childrens Mercy hosps., Kansas City, Mo., 1953-54; pvt. practice medicine Manhattan, Kans., 1956-57; team physician, asst. dir. Health Center Kans. State U., 1957-60; dir. health service, team physician Okla. State U. Hosp. and Clinic, Stillwater, 1960-90, dir. athletic medicine, 1990-98, emeritus dir., 1998—. Vis. lectr. div. sportsmedicine, dept. orthopedic surgery Coll. Medicine U. Okla. Health Scis. Center, 1974— ; liaison officer Am. Coll. Health Assn. to Nat. Athletic Trainers Assn., 1963— ; Am. chmn. 1st Am.-Soviet Conf. on Student Health, Moscow, Russia, 1967; team physician U.S. Olympic Team, 1967-68; mem. Pres.'s Coun. Phys. Fitness and Sports, 1981-92, del. to Moscow to rev. phys. culture and olympic tng. sites in Russia, 1989; team physician U.S. Deaf Olympic Team, Los Angeles, 1985; elected chmn. Joint Commn. on Competitive Safeguards and Med. Aspects of Sports, 1986. Author: (with others) Standard Nomenclature of Athletic Injuries, 1966; Contbr. (with others) articles med. jours. Served to capt. USAF, 1954-56. Recipient Pres.'s Challenge

Sportsmedicine award Nat. Athletic Trainers Assn., 1974, Bill Coltrin Meml. award Western Athletic Conf. Sports Writers Assn., 1974, Edward Hitchcock award Am. Coll. Health Assn., 1975; named among 10 healthy American fitness leaders Nat. Jaycees, Pres.'s Coun. on Physical Fitness and Sports, Allstate Ins. Co., 1995; inductee Okla. Hall of Fame, 1998. Mem. AMA (chmn. com. med. aspects sports 1971-76, chmn. 1976-77, mem. coun. sci. affairs 1976-79), Nat. Collegiate Athletic Assn. (med. cons. to football rules com. 1969-75), Am. Coll. Health Assn. (past pres., exec. com.), Southwestern Coll. Health Assn. (past pres.), Nat. Athletic Trainers Assn., Alpha Omega Alpha, Nu Sigma Nu. Presbyterian (elder 1971—). Club: Lion. Home: 1001 W Liberty Ln Stillwater OK 74075-2113 Office: Okla State U Hosp & Clinic 1202 Farm Rd Stillwater OK 74078-0001 *We must realize and accept that life is neither fair nor unfair; one must accept it as a unique journey composed of all types of experiences. It is not so much what happens to us as we go along in life, it is how we react to what happens that is so very important.*

COOPER, DORIS JEAN, market research executive; b. N.Y.C., Dec. 17, 1934; d. James N. and Georgina N. (Cassidy) Breslin; m. S. James Cooper, June 17, 1956; 1 son, David Austin. Student, Sch. of Commerce, NYU, 1953-55, Hunter Coll., 1956-57. Asst. coding supr. Crossley S-D Surveys, N.Y.C., 1955-57; asst. field supr. Trendex, Inc., N.Y.C., 1957-59; coding dir. J. Walter Thompson Co., N.Y.C., 1960-63, Audits & Surveys, N.Y.C., 1964-65; pvt. practice cons. N.Y.C., 1965-73; pres. Cooper Svcs., Hastings-on-Hudson, N.Y., 1973—; pres., CEO computer tabulation and lang. manipulation Doris J. Cooper Assocs., Hastings-on-Hudson, 1989—. Cons. market rsch. Mem. Am. Mktg. Assn. (N.Y. chpt.), nat. Bus. Women Owners Assn., Am. Assn. Pub. Opinion Researchers (N.Y. chpt.), Acad. Health Svcs. Mktg., Hastings C. of C. Republican. Episcopalian. Office: Doris J Cooper Assocs Ltd 447 Warburton Ave Hastings On Hudson NY 10706-1542

COOPER, DOUGLAS KENNETH, lawyer; b. Ithaca, NY, June 6, 1947; s. Murray I. and Meta F. Cooper; m. Pamela A. Regan, Aug. 22, 1970; children: James, Sarah. BA, N.C. State U., 1970; JD, U. N.C., 1974. Bar: Ohio 1974, U.S. Dist. Ct. (no. dist.) Ohio 1974, U.S. Dist. Ct. (no. dist.) Mich. 1997. Assoc. Shapiro, Persky, Stone & Marken Co., L.P.A., Cleve., 1974-76; of counsel Leaseway Transp. Corp., Cleve., 1976-78, assoc. corp. counsel, 1978-82, corp. counsel, 1982-88, asst. gen. counsel, 1988-92, v.p. opers. law, 1992-96; exec. v.p., gen. counse., sec. Peregrine Inc., Southfield, Mich., 1997—2001; sr. v.p. law GDX Automotive, Farmington Hills, Mich., 2001—. Contbr. articles to law revs. Mem. Cleve. Citizens League, 1974—. Mem. ABA, Bar Assn. Greater Cleve., Ohio State Bar Assn., Mich. State Bar, Oakland County Bar Assn. Office: GDX Automotive 36600 Corporate Dr Farmington Hills MI 48331 E-mail: doug.cooper@gdxautomotive.com.

COOPER, EDWARD HAYES, lawyer, educator; b. Highland Park, Mich., Oct. 13, 1941; s. Frank Edward and Margaret Ellen (Hayes) C.; m. Nancy Carol Wybo, June 29, 1963; children: Lisa, Chandra. AB, Dartmouth Coll., 1961; LL.B., Harvard U., 1964. Bar: Mich. 1965. Law clk. Hon. Clifford O'Sullivan, U.S. Ct. of Appeals, 1964-65; practice law, Detroit, 1965-67; adj. prof. Wayne State U. Law Sch., 1965-67; assoc. prof. U. Minn. Law Sch., 1967-72; prof. law U. Mich. Law Sch., Ann Arbor, 1972-88, assoc. dean for acad. affairs, 1981-94; Thomas M. Cooley prof. of law, 1988—. Advisor Restatement of the Law, 2d Judgments, 1976-80, Complex Litigation Project, Restatement of the Law, 3d Torts-Apportionment, Fed. Jud. Code Project, Transnational Procedure Project, Internat. Jurisdiction Judgment; reporter fed. state jurisdiction com. Jud. Conf. U.S., 1985-91; mem. civil rules adv. com., 1991-92, reporter, 1992—; reporter Uniform Transfer of Litigation Act, 1989-91. Author: (with C.A. Wright and A.R. Miller) Federal Practice and Procedure: Jurisdiction, Vols. 13-19, 1975-81, 2d edit., 1984-2002, 3d edit., 1999—; contbr. articles to law revs. Mem. ABA, Mich. Bar Assn., Am. Law Inst. (council). Office: U Mich 330 Hutchins Law Sch Ann Arbor MI 48109-1215 E-mail: coopere@umich.edu.

COOPER, EDWARD SAWYER, cardiologist, internist, educator; b. Columbia, S.C., Dec. 11, 1926; s. Henry Howard and Ada Crosland (Sawyer) Cooper; m. Jean Marie Wilder, Dec. 2, 1951; children: Lisa Marie Cooper Hudgins, Edward Sawyer Jr.(dec.), Jan Ada, Charles Wilder. AB, Lincoln U., Pa., 1946; MD, Meharry Med. Coll., Nashville, 1949; MS (hon.), U. Pa., 1972. Diplomate Nat. Bd. Med. Examiners, Am. Bd. Internal Medicine. Intern Phila. Gen. Hosp., 1949-51, resident in medicine, 1951-54, NIH fellow in cardiology, 1956-57, pres. med. staff, 1969-71, co-dir. Stroke Rsch. Ctr., 1968-74, chief med. svc., 1973-76; prof. emeritus medicine U. Pa., Phila., 1996—. Bd. dirs. Independence Blue Cross. Trustee Am. Found. Negro Affairs, 1969—, Rockefeller U., 1992—. Served to capt. USAF, 1954—56. Master: ACP; fellow: Phila. Coll. Physicians (coun.); mem.: Am. Heart Assn. (chmn., bd. dirs., past nat. pres.), Alpha Omega Alpha. Democrat. Methodist. Achievements include research in stroke and hypertension. Home: 6710 Lincoln Dr Philadelphia PA 19119-3155 Office: University of Pa Hosp 3400 Spruce St Philadelphia PA 19104-4206 E-mail: ecoopmdphila@aol.com.

COOPER, EDWIN LOWELL, anatomy educator; b. Oakland, Tex., Dec. 23, 1936; s. Edwin Ellis and Ruthesther (Porché) C.; m. Helene Marie Antoinette Tournaire, Sept. 13, 1969; children— Astrid Madeleine, Amaury Tournaire. BS, Tex. So. U., 1957; MS, Atlanta, 1959; PhD, Brown U., 1963. UHPHS postdoctoral fellow UCLA, 1962-64, asst. prof. anatomy, 1964-69, assoc. prof., 1969-73, prof., 1973—. Vis. prof. Instituto Politecnico Nacional, Mexico City, 1966; Mem. adv. com. Office Sci. Personnel, NRC, 1972-73; mem. bd. sci. counselors Nat. Inst. Dental Research, 1973— Author: Comparative Immunology; Editor: Phylogeny of Transplantation Reactions, 1970, Invertebrate Immunology, 1974; founding editor: Internat. Jour. Developmental and Comparative Immunology, 1977— . Guggenheim fellow, 1970; Fulbright scholar, 1970; Eleanor Roosevelt fellow Internat. Union Against Cancer, 1977-78 Fellow AAAS (council 1971, chmn. sect. 1976); mem. Soc. Invertebrate Pathology (founding), Pan Am. Congress Anatomy (founding), Am. Assn. Anatomy, Transplantation Soc., Am. Assn. Immunologists, Am. Soc. Zoologists (program officer 1974—; founder div. comparative immunology 1975, pres.), Brit. Soc. Immunology, Societe d'Immunologie Francaise, Sigma Xi. Office: UCLA Sch Medicine Dept Neurobiology 10833 Le Conte Ave Los Angeles CA 90095-3075 *Aims must always be high, so that when fate is cruel, there is somewhere to fall. Aiming for the bottom leaves nowhere to fall.*

COOPER, ELAINE JANICE, physical therapist; b. Detroit, Apr. 26, 1937; d. Morris and Sally (Mack) Braverman; divorced; children: Jeffrey, Michael, Jonathan. BS, U. Mich., 1959; cert. in massage therapy. Supr. Rehab. Inst., Detroit, 1959-61; cons. Redford (Mich.) Community Hosp., 1963-73; cons. in field Detroit, 1970-78; asst. dir. William Beaumont Hosp., Royal Oak, Mich., 1979-81; pres., cons. Cooper Ctr. for Phys. and Massage Therapies, Inc., Farmington Hills, Mich., 1981—. Cons. Drs. Sobel & Castle, Detroit, 1965-66; peer reviewer ins. co. Mem. Am. Phys. Therapy Assn. (edn. com. 1969), Mich. Phys. Therapy Assn., Biofeedback Soc. Mich., Am. Massage Therapy Assn., Mich. Dance Assn., Mich. State C. of C. (health care com.), Brookfield Highlands Club (chmn. land devel., restrictions coms. 1979-85). Avocations: dance, running, aerobics, skiing, karate (black belt isshinryu karate). Office: Cooper Ctr for Phys & Massage Therapies 29805 Middlebelt Farmington Hills MI 48334 E-mail: ecsan@aol.com. *Personal philosopy: The greatest thing in the world is not so much where we stand, as in what direction we are moving. (Oliver Wendell Holmes).*

COOPER, ELVA JUNE, artist, writer; b. Wilmore, Ky., Mar. 18, 1933; d. Scott Combs and Rhoda Mae (Hundley) Bishop; m. Lowell Howard Cooper, Nov. 29, 1952; children: Lowell Scott, Linda Janet, Candace Lea, Connie Lynn, June Roxanne. Student, Georgetown Coll., 1952-53, Southwestern Jr. Coll., 1961, U. West Fla., 1994, Pensacola Jr. Coll., 1998. Owner June Bug Art and Gifts, Pensacola, Fla., 1973—2003, The Studio, Pensacola, Fla., 1986—. Cons. editor Church Recreation, 1993-95; contbr. articles to mags. Drama writer, dir. Myrtle Grove Bapt. Ch., Pensacola, Fla., 1977-96, artist in residence, 1973-96, discipleship tng. dir., 1973-79, 88-97; sec. Lillian (Ala.) First Bapt. Ch., 1984-95; writer Bapt. Sunday Sch. Bd., Nashville, Tenn., 1987-98; state recreation counselor Fla. Bapt. Conv., Jacksonville, 1994—; discipleship tng. dir. Pensacola Bay Bapt. Assn., 1994-96. Three time winner of Peggy award Popular Ceramics Mag., 1970; numerous other awards in art shows; inducted into Internat. Soc. Poetry as Disting. Mem.. Mem. Quayside Art Gallery (asst. publicity, 1984), Art Study Club. Baptist. Avocations: porcelain doll making, sewing, flower arranging, stained glass artist.

COOPER, ERLYNE S. social worker; b. Montreal, Jan. 12, 1931; came to U.S., 1946; d. William Stroll and Edna (Druyen) Luban; m. Leonard Cooper, Sept. 1, 1957; 1 child, Ward Ross. BA, UCLA, 1953; MSW, U. So. Calif., 1959; postgrad., Denver U., 1982-85. Bd. cert. in clin. social work Am. Bd. Examiners Clin. Social Work; lic. clin. social worker, Colo. Dir. Blind Children's Ctr., L.A., 1967-68, exec. dir., 1968-70; coord. svcs. Marianne Frostig Ctr. Ednl. Therapy, L.A., 1970-71; chief social worker L.A. Child Guidance Clinic, 1971-73; vis. clin. prof. Smith Coll. Sch. Social Work, 1974-97; adj. field prof. U. Denver Grad. Sch. Social Work, 1974-97; field instr. clin. assocs., prof. U. So. Calif. Sch. Social Work, L.A., 1972-73; coord. student social work tng. U. Colo. Health Sci. Ctr., Denver, 1973-87, dir. social wk. tng., 1987-97; pvt. practice clin. social work Denver, 1977—; clin. instr. dept. psychiatry Sch. Medicine, U. Colo. Health Sci. Ctr., Denver, 1998—; field liaison com. U. Denver Grad. Sch. Social Work, 1998—2000, field svcs. com., 1998—. Bd. dirs. Allied Housing, Denver, 1989—95; vol. Pro Bono Mental Health Project, Denver, 1988—91; founding mem. Colo. Clin. Social Work Soc., 1974. Named Outstanding Field Instr., U. Denver Grad. Sch. Social Work, 1995; recipient Recognition award, Colo. Clin. Social Work Soc., 1982—83. Mem.: Interdisciplinary Com., Colo. Child and Adolescent Psychiat. Soc., Acad. Cert. Social Workers, Nat. Assn. Social Workers (diplomate). Avocations: reading, travel.

COOPER, ERWIN, writer; b. Chgo., Apr. 24, 1920; s. William Compton Cooper and Eugenia Selina Fröhlich. BA, U. Calif., Berkeley, Calif., 1948. Documents translator Nuremberg War Crimes Trials Office of Chief of Counsel, 1945—47; info. officer State of Calif., 1950—87. Author: Aqueduct Empire: A Guide To Water In California, Its Turbulent History And Its Management Today, 1968, Understanding California Water, 1997, 2003. Home: 1607 Ridgebrook Way Chico CA 95928

COOPER, EUGENE BRUCE, speech, language pathologist, educator; b. Utica, N.Y., Dec. 20, 1933; s. Clements Everett and Beulah (Wetzel) C.; m. Crystal Silverman, Sept. 12, 1965; children: Philip Adam, Ivan Bruce. BS, SUNY, Geneseo, 1955; MEd, Pa. State U., 1957, DEd, 1962. Pathologist speech and lang. Franklin County Schs., Chambersburg, Pa., 1957-59; asst. prof. Ohio U., 1962-64, Pa. State U., 1964-66; program specialist U.S. Office Edn., 1966; exec. sec. sensory study sect., rsch. and demonstrations Rehab. Services Adminstrn., HEW, Washington, 1966-67; faculty U. Ala., Tuscaloosa, 1967-96, prof. speech-lang. pathology, 1969-96, chmn. dept. communicative disorders, dir. Speech and Hearing Ctr., 1967-96, prof., chair emeritus, 1996—; Disting. prof. comm. scis. and disorders Nova Southeastern U., 1997—. Chmn. Ala. Bd. Examiners Speech Pathology and Audiology, 1979; cons.-at-large Nat. Student Speech-Lang.-Hearing Assn., 1983-88. Author: Personalized Fluency Control Therapy, 1976, Understanding Stuttering: Information for Parents, 1979, revised edit., 1990; (with Crystal Cooper) The Cooper Personalized Fluency Control Therapy Program, 1985, 2d edit., 2003, Cooper Assessment for Stuttering Syndromes, 1995; contbr. articles to profl. jours. Fellow Am. Speech, Lang. and Hearing Assn. (legis. coun. 1971-72, 85-97), Divsn. Fluency and Fluency Disorders (steering com. 1993-99, divsn. coord. 1994-99), Am. Speech, Lang. and Hearing Found. (chmn. adv. and devel. bd. 1988-89, trustee 1989-94); mem. Coun. Exceptional Children (pres. divsn. children comm. disorders 1975-76), Nat. Coun. Grad. Programs in Speech, Lang. Pathology and Audiology (pres. 1978-80), Nat. Coun. State Bds. Examiners Speech-Lang. Pathology and Audiology (pres. 1980, 91, mem. exec. bd. 1988-91), Nat. Coun. Comm. Disorders (chmn. 1982), Nat. Alliance Prevention and Treatment on Stuttering (pres. 1985-86), Internat. Fluency Assn. (bd. dirs. 1991-96, pres. 2d world congress on fluency disorders 1997, chmn. specialty commn. on fluency disorders 1997-99).

COOPER, GARY ALLAN, lawyer; b. Bristol, Va., Feb. 3, 1947; s. Earl Clarence and Reba Evelyn (Jenkins) C.; chidlren: Drew Kelsey, Gavin Morgan. BS in Journalism, U. Tenn., 1969, JD, 1972. Bar: Tenn. 1972, U.S. Dist. Ct. (ea. dist.) Tenn. 1972, U.S. Supreme Ct. 1979, Fla. 1981. Assoc. Luther, Anderson & Ruth, Chattanooga, 1972-76; ptnr. Luther, Anderson, Cleary, Luhowiak & Cooper, Chattanooga, 1976-79, Luther, Anderson, Cleary & Cooper, Chattanooga, 1979-80, Anderson, Cleary & Cooper, Chattanooga, 1981, Fleissner & Cooper, Chattanooga, 1982, Fleissner, Cooper & Marcus, Chattanooga, 1983-88, Fleissner Cooper Marcus & Steger, Chattanooga, 1988-89, Fleissner Cooper Marcus & Quinn, Chattanooga, 1990-97, Franklin, Cooper & Marcus, PLLC, Chattanooga, 1998—. Author: Tennessee Forms for Trial Practice, 1977, 5th edit., 1999, Tennessee Law Office Adminstration, 1977, Tenesee Forms for Trial Practice-Damages, 1997. With USAR, 1972-79. Recipient Herman Hickman Postgrad. scholarship for Athletes U. Tenn., 1969. Mem. ABA, Chattanooga Bar Assn. (bd. dirs. 1984-86), Fla. Bar Assn. (mem. out-of-state practitioners com. 1983-86), Tenn. Bar Assn., Tenn. Def. Lawyers Assn. (chmn. amicus curiae com. 1987-89), Phi Delta Phi. Republican. Methodist. Avocations: golf, reading, boating. Office: Franklin Cooper & Marcus PLLC 837 Fortwood St Chattanooga TN 37403-2313 E-mail: garyacooper@mindspring.com.

COOPER, GEORGE KILE, business educator; b. Bushnell, Ill., Apr. 5, 1920; s. George Kile and Lula Belle (Robison) C.; m. June Anna Cardell, June 12, 1948; children: Kyle, Ernest, Ruth Anne, William, Jean, Andrew. BEd, Western Ill. State U., 1942; MBA, Ind. U., 1951; PhD, U. Mich., 1962. Cert. secondary sch. tchr., Ill. Bus. tchr. Reynolds (Ill.) Community High Sch., 1946-47; student teaching coordinator Western Mich. U., Kalamazoo, 1948-55, head bus. edn. dept., 1955-62; head bus. edn. and adminstrv. office mgmt. dept. Eastern Ill. U., Charleston, 1962-73, prof. bus. edn. and adminstrv. office mgmt., 1962-82, prof. emeritus, 1982—. Vis. research and devel. specialist Ctr. for Vocat. and Tech. Edn., Ohio State U., Columbus, 1973-74. Treas. Wesley United Meth. Ch., Charleston, 1983-93, trustee, 1994-97; chmn. Ill. Curriculum Coun., 1980-81. With AUS, 1942-46. Recipient Alumni Achievement award Western Il.. U., 1994; Cooper Hall named in honor, Ea. Ill., U., 1991. Mem. Ill. Bus. Edn. Assn. (pres. 1971-72, disting. svc. award 1975), Ill. Vocat. Asns. (treas. 1965-69), Ill. State U. Annuitants Assn. (pres.-elect 1986-87), Eastern Ill. U. Annuitants Assn. (pres. 1984-86), Pi Omega Pi (nat. pres. 1966-68), Delta Pi Epsilon (pres. chpt. 1960-61), Phi Delta Kappa (pres. chpt. 1980-81, alt. del. 1986-87). Home: 708 Taft Ave Charleston IL 61920-4135 E-mail: cooper@worthlink.net.

COOPER, GERALD RICE, clinical pathologist; b. Scranton, S.C., Nov. 19, 1914; s. Robert McFadden and Viola Lavender Cooper; m. Lois Corrina Painter, Mar. 9, 1946; children: Annetta, Gerald Jr., Rodney. AB, Duke U., 1936, MA, 1938, PhD, 1939, MD, 1950. Cert. Am. Bd. Clin. Chemistry. Intern Atlanta VA Hosp., 1950-51, resident, 1951-52; rsch. assoc. Duke U. Sch. Medicine, Durham, N.C., 1939-46; chief chemistry, hematology and pathology Ctrs. for Disease Control, Atlanta, 1952-72; rsch. med. officer Ctrs. for Disease Control, Nat. Ctr. Environ. Health, Atlanta, 1973—. Author (with others) books; contbr. articles to profl. jours. Col. USPHS. Decorated commendation medal, Superior Svc. award, Disting. Svc. medal, Asst. Sec. for Health award for exceptional achievement; recipient Hektoen Silver medal AMA, 1954, Fulton County Med. Achievement award, 1954, Billings Silver medal, 1956, Sigma Xi rsch. award, 1997, Lifetime Sci. Achievement award CDC, 2002. Mem. Am. Assn. for Clin. Chemistry (pres. 1984, bd. dirs. 1975-77, chmn. bd. editors of selected methods 1967-80, bd. editors Clin. Chemistry jour. 1970-76, Fischer award 1975, Dade Internat. award 1975, N.J. Gerulat award 1979, SE Sect. Meritorious Svc. award 1989, Outstanding Contbn. Clin. Chemistry award 1992), Internat. Fedn. Clin. Chemistry (apolipoprotein expert panel 1985), Am. Soc. Clin. Pathologists (chmn. clin. chemistry coun. 1974, Continuing Edn. award 1967, 77). Methodist. Home: 2165 Bonnevit Ct NE Atlanta GA 30345-4126 Office: Ctrs for Disease Control Chamblee 102/2319 F25 4770 Buford Hwy Atlanta GA 30341-3724 E-mail: grcl@cdc.gov.

COOPER, GLORIA, editor, press critic; b. Oak Park, Ill., Jan. 8, 1931; c. Sam and Madelyn (Brandt) Glaser; m. Wallace J. Cooper, June 3, 1950; children—Alison, Julie BA summa cum laude, Briarcliff Coll., 1970; MA, Columbia U., 1974. From asst. editor to mng. editor to dep. exec. editor Columbia Journalism Rev., N.Y.C., 1974—. Editor: Squad Helps Dog Bite Victim, 1980, Red Tape Holds Up New Bridge, 1987; contbr. articles, revs., editorials to Columbia Journalism Rev., 1974—. Mem. Soc. Prof. Journalists, Princeton Club (N.Y.C.). Home: 91 Long Hill Rd E Briarcliff Manor NY 10510-2611 Office: Columbia U Columbia Journalism Rev 207 Journalism Bldg New York NY 10027 E-mail: gc15@columbia.edu.

COOPER, GRANT, composer, conductor, music educator; b. Wellington, New Zealand; Degree in Pure Math., U. Auckland; fellow in trumpet study with Gerard Schwarz. Artistic dir. 2 summer festivals Bach and Beyond Festival, Anchorage Festival of Music in Alaska; commd. composer Cayuga Chamber Orch., Coloratura Soprano, Rap Singer; music dir. Fredonia Chamber Players, 1983—89, Penfield Symphony Orch., 1993—99; assoc. conductor Syracuse Symphony Orch., 1997, resident conductor, 2001—; artistic dir., composer, conductor W.Va. Symphony Orch., 2001—. Guest conductor Cayuga Chamber Orch., Philharmonic Orchs. Buffalo and Rochester, XIVth Commonwealth Games closing ceremonies, Mozart Wochen Heidelberger Schlossfestspiele; prof. music, dir. orchs. Ithaca Coll. Sch. Music, 1993—2003. Conductor (appearances) Syracuse Symphony Orch., conductor Skaneateles Fest., Spokane Symphony, Erie Philharmonic, Kansas City Symphony, millenium celebration with Auckland Philharmonia, (recordings) Delos Internat., Atoll, Ode, Mark, Kiwi Pacific, conductor (CD) premier recordings string music New Zealand composer, Douglas Lilburn, Points in a Changing Circle. Fellow Fund for Arts, Chautauqua County. Office: WV Symphony Orch PO Box 2292 Charleston WV 25328

COOPER, GREGORY SCOTT, epidemiologist, gastroenterologist, educator; b. Newark, July 14, 1960; s. Murray and Frances Cooper; m. Cathy Lynne Cooper, Feb. 3, 1991; children: Marissa, Ryan, Nicole. BA, MA, U. Pa., 1982, MD, 1986. Diplomate Am. Bd. Internal Medicine. Intern, resident in internal medicine Univ. Hosps., Cleve., 1986-89, chief resident, 1991-92, fellow in gastroenterology, 1989-91, 92-93; instr. medicine Case Western Res. U., Cleve., 1991-93, asst. prof. medicine, 1993-96, asst. prof. medicine and epidemiology, 1996-98, assoc. prof. medicine and epidemiology, 1998—, dir. cancer epidemiology-health rsch., staff investigator, 2000—. Tng. program dir. Case Western Res. U., 1997—; dir. disease mgmt. U. Hosps. Cleve., 1997-99. Contbr. chpts. to books, over 90 articles to profl. jours. Grantee Nat. Cancer Inst., 1996—. Fellow ACP (med. sch. rep.), Am. Coll. Gastroenterology; mem. Am. Fedn. Med. Rsch. (midwest coun.), Am. Cancer Soc. (rsch. project grants 1997—). Avocation: long distance running. Office: Univ Hosps Cleveland 11100 Euclid Ave Cleveland OH 44106-5066

COOPER, HAL, television director; b. N.Y.C., Feb. 23, 1923; s. Benjamin and Adeline (Raichman) C.; m. Mary Patricia Meikle, Dec. 21, 1944 (div. 1971); children: Bethami, Pamela; m. Marta Lucille Salcido, June 26, 1971; 1 child, James Benjamin. BA, U. Mich., 1946. Ind. TV dir., writer, producer various prodn. cos., 1948—. Performer Big Bro.'s Rainbow House, Mut. Network, 1936-41, asst. dir. Dock Street Theatre, Charleston, S.C., 1946-48; writer, prodr. TV Babysitter, DuMont TV Network, 1948-52, The Magic Cottage, 1950-56; dir., prodr. various daytime TV shows including Search For Tomorrow, others, 1950-57; prodr. stage play The Troublemakers, London, 1952; dir. numerous TV shows (various episodes) including Death Valley Days, 1965-67, Dick Van Dyke Show, 1962, Gilligan's Island, 1966, I Dream of Jeannie, 1965-69, I Spy, 1966, That Girl, 1967-69, Courtship of Eddie's Father, 1968-71, The Odd Couple, 1970-72, Mary Tyler Moore, 1972, All in the Family, 1972, (pilots) Hot L Baltimore, 1974, One Day At a Time, 1975, All's Fair, 1976, Nancy Walker Show, 1976, The Time of Their Lives, 1987; dir., exec. prodr.: TV shows including Maude, 1972-78, Phyl and Mikky, 1980, Love, Sydney, 1982-83, Gimme a Break, 1983-87, Empty Nest, 1988-89, Dear John, 1989-92, The Powers That Be, 1992-93. Served to lt. (j.g.) USNR, 1943-46, PTO. Mem. Writers Guild Am., ASCAP, Screen Actors Guild, AFTRA, Actors Equity Assn., Dirs. Guild Am. (mem. dirs. council, nat. bd. dirs.). E-mail: halcoop@aol.com.

COOPER, HAL DEAN, lawyer; b. Marshall County, Iowa, Dec. 8, 1934; s. Truman Braton and Golda Frances (Chadwick) C.; m. Constance Bellinger Simms, Dec. 31, 1960; children: Shannon, Charles, Ellen. Student, Neb. U., 1952-54; BS in Mech. Engring., Iowa State U., 1957; JD with honors, George Washington U., 1963. Bar: Iowa 1963, Ohio 1963, U.S. Supreme Ct. 1971. Assoc., ptnr. Fay & Fay, Cleve., 1962-67; ptnr. Meyer, Tilberry & Body, Cleve., 1967-69, Yount, Tarolli, Weinshenker & Cooper, Cleve, 1969-72; trial judge U.S. Ct. Claims, Washington, 1972-75; ptnr. Jones, Day, Reavis & Pogue, Cleve., 1975-95; owner Halco Enterprises, Ltd., Austinburg, Ohio, 1995—; pvt. arbitrator, mediator, 1996—. Served with AUS, 1957-59. Mem. Cleve. Intellectual Property Law Assn., Rowfant Club, Clifton Club, Rotary. Episcopalian. E-mail: halco@apk.net.

COOPER, HENRY FRANKLYN, engineering, technology and national security affairs consultant; b. Augusta, Ga., Nov. 8, 1936; s. Henry F. and Ruby (Harris) C.; m. Barbara Kays, Aug. 17, 1958; children: Laura, Cynthia, Scott. BSME with high honors, Clemson U., 1958, MSME, 1960; PhD in Mech. Engring., NYU, 1964. Instr. engring. mechanics Clemson (S.C.) U., 1958-60; mem. tech. staff Bell Telephone Labs, Whippany, N.J., 1960-64; sci. advisor Air Force Weapons Lab., Albuquerque, 1964-71; program mgr. R&D Assocs., Rosslyn, Va. and Marina Del Rey, Calif., 1971-79; dep. asst. sec. Air Force, Washington, 1979-82; dep. dir. nuclear effects divsn. R&D Assocs., Rosslyn, 1982-83; asst. dir. U.S. Arms Control Disarmament Agy. State Dept., Washington, 1983-85; amb., chief U.S. negotiator Def. and Space Talks, Geneva, 1985-90; sr. v.p. JAYCOR, Vienna, Va., 1990; dir. strategic def. initiative Office of Sec. of Def., Washington, 1990-93; pvt. practice as cons., 1993—; chmn. Applied Rsch. Assocs., Albuquerque, 1995—, High Frontier, Arlington, Va., 1996—. Mem. bd. advisors coll. engring. Clemson U., 1985-87; adj. prof. S.W. Mo. State U., Springfield, 1992—; sr. assoc. Nat. Inst. Pub. Policy, Fairfax, Va., 1993—; advisor nat. security Empower Am., Washington, 1993-96; vis. fellow Heritage Found., Washington, 1993—; mem. nat. def. panel Nat. Policy Forum, Washington, 1994-96; commr. Presdl. Commn. on Weapons of Mars Destruction, 1998—. Contbr. articles to profl. jours. 1st lt. USAF, 1964-67. Decorated Commendation medal; recipient Founders Day award NYU, 1967, Cert. of Achievement, Air Force, 1982, Superior Honor award U.S. Arms Control & Disarmament Agy., 1987, Disting. Svc. award Clemson U., 1989, Disting. Pub. Svc. medal Dept. of Def., 1993; scholar Owens Corning Fiberglass, 1957, 58. Mem. ASME, AAAS, U.S. Strategic Inst., Internat. Inst. Strategic Studies, Sigma Xi, Tau Beta Pi. Republican. Presbyterian. Office: Applied Rsch Assocs 2760 Eisenhower Ave Ste 308 Alexandria VA 22314-4569

COOPER, IVA JEAN, special education educator; b. Newark, Mar. 6, 1950; d. William Brady McClintock and Aleata Margaret Locke-McClintock; m. Jeffrey Lamont Cooper, Oct. 18, 1986; children: Brianna, Jasmine. BS Comms., Howard U., 1973; MA Comms., Mich. State U., 1976. Intern Crippled Children's Soc., Hollywood, Calif., 1979—80; speech & lang. therapist pediats. Sierra Permanente Med. Grp., Fontana, Calif., 1980—81; supr. speech & lang. pathology Head Start Devel. Coun., Stockton, Calif., 1981; spl. edn. educator Manteca Unified Sch. Dist., Calif., 1981—. Mem.: Internat. Soc. Poets, AAUW, Am. Speech Hearing & Lang. Assn. Home: 1928 W Bristol Ave Stockton CA 95204

COOPER, JACK ROSS, pharmacology educator, researcher; b. Ottawa, Ont., Can., July 26, 1924; came to U.S., 1948; s. Harry and Jean (Levine) C.; m. Helen Achbar, Aug. 14, 1951; children: Marilyn, Sheila, Nancy. BA, Queen's U. Kingston, Ont., 1948; MA, George Washington U., 1952, PhD, 1954; MA (hon.), Yale U., 1971. Instr. Yale U., New Haven, 1956—58, asst. prof. pharmacology, 1958—63, assoc. prof., 1963-71, prof., 1971—. Author: The Biochemical Basis of Neuropharmacology, 8th edit., 2003. Served with RCAF, 1944. Smith, Kline and French rsch. fellow, 1950-52; USPHS predoctoral fellow, 1952-54; postdoctoral fellow USPHS, 1954-56; spl. fellow USPHS, London, 1965-66. Mem. Am. Soc. Neurochemistry, Internat. Soc. Neurochemistry, Am. Soc. Pharmacology and Exptl. Therapeutics, Soc. Neurosci. Democrat. Jewish. Home: 11 Jenick Ln Woodbridge CT 06525-1935 Office: Yale U Sch Medicine 333 Cedar St New Haven CT 06510-3289

COOPER, JAMES HAYES SHOFNER (JIM COOPER), congressman; b. Nashville, Tenn., June 19, 1954; s. William Prentice Jr. and Hortense (Powell) C.; m. Martha Hays; children: Mary Argentine Adams, John James Audubon, Hayes Hightower. BA, U. N.C., 1975, Oxford U., 1977; JD, Harvard U., 1980. Atty. Waller, Lansden, Dortch & Davis, Nashville, 1980-82; mem. 98th-103rd Congresses from 4th Tenn. dist., Washington, 1983—95, mem. budget com., mem. energy and commerce com.; mng. dir. Equitable Securities, 1995-99; founder, ptnr. & chmn. bd. Brentwood Capital Adv. LLC, 1999—2002; mem. 108th Congress from 5th dist., Washington, DC, 2003—. Bd. dirs. Resources for the Future, 1997—. Rhodes scholar, 1975, Morehead scholar, 1972. Mem.

Phi Beta Kappa. Democrat. Episcopalian. Mailing: Wash Office Office Bldg 1536 Longworth Ho Office Bldg Washington DC 20515-1535 also: District Office 706 Church St Ste 101 Nashville TN 37203 E-mail: jim.cooper@brentwoodcap.com.*

COOPER, JAMES MELVIN, healthcare executive, consultant; b. Prescott, Ariz., Oct. 29, 1940; s. Audrey Louise Cooper; m. Marlene Kitay, Oct. 29, 1960; children: Jamie Lynn Hill, David Paul. BS in Adminstrn., George Washington U., 1976, MBA, 1979. Cert. healthcare exec. Enlisted USN, 1959, advanced through grades to capt.; officer-in-charge pers. support detachment Naval Hosp., San Diego, 1979-81, dir. for ambulatory care Camp Pendleton, Calif., 1981-83; manpower analyst The Pentagon, Washington, 1983-85; dir. for adminstrn. Naval Med. Clinics, San Diego, 1985-88; exec. officer Naval Hosp., Long Beach, Calif., 1988-91; comdg. officer U.S. Naval Hosp., Naples, Italy, 1991-93; ret. USN, 1993; v.p. Capital Health Svcs., San Diego, 1994-97. Treas. Ramona/Julian Health Care Adv. Coun., 1996—. Bd. dirs., chmn. Ramona (Calif.) Food and Clothes Closet, 1995—. Decorated Legion of Merit, Meritorious Svc. medal (3). Fellow Am. Acad. Med. Adminstrs.; mem. Am. Coll. Healthcare Execs. (diplomate), Am. Coll. Managed Care Execs., San Diego Women in Health Adminstrn., Fed. Health Care Execs. Inst. (life), DAV (life), Assn. Med. Svc. Corps Officers (chmn. mentoring com. 1996—), Kiwanis of Ramona (pres. 1996-97), VFW (life). Avocations: jogging, horseback riding, leather tooling. Address: 1221 Cook St Ramona CA 92065-3211

COOPER, JAMES MICHAEL, education educator; b. Steubenville, Ohio, July 29, 1939; s. James Stanley and Regina Marie (Coen) C.; m. Susan Callaway, Sept. 1, 1962 (div. June 1978); children: Jeffrey, Craig, Cynthia; m. Shamim Sisson, June 13, 1987. AB in History with distinction, Stanford U., 1961, AM in Edn., 1962, AM in History, 1966, PhD in Edn., 1967. Tchr. Jordan Jr. High Sch. of Palo Alto (Calif.) Unified Sch. Sys., 1961-63, Palo Alto High Sch., 1963-65; lectr. Stanford U. Sch. Edn., 1967; asst. prof. edn. U. Mass., Amherst, 1968-71; assoc. prof. U. Houston, 1971-74, prof., 1974-84; Commonwealth prof. U. Va. Curry Sch. Edn., Charlottesville, 1984—, dean, 1984-94. Chmn. U. Houston faculty senate, 1982; mem. exec. bd. dirs. Holmes Group, East Lansing, Mich., 1985-94; mem. unit accreditation bd. Nat. Coun. Accreditation of Tchr. Edn., Washington, 1986-90. Co-author: Those Who Can, Teach, 9th edit., 2001; editor: Developing Skills for Instructional Supervision, 1984, Classroom Teaching Skills, 7th rev. edit., 2003; co-editor: Kaleidoscope: Readings in Education, 10th edit., 2001. Recipient Florence B. Stratemeyer award Assn. for Student Teaching, Washington, 1967, Fulbright-Hays award Portugal Coun. Internat. Exch. Scholars, Washington, 1980, Outstanding Leader in Tchr. Edn. award Assn. Tchr. Educators, 1990. Mem.: ASCD, Raven Soc. (The Raven award 2001), Am. Assn. Colls. for Tchr. Edn. (bd. dirs. 1990—93), Am. Ednl. Rsch. Assn., Omicron Delta Kappa, Phi Delta Kappa. Democrat. Roman Catholic. Avocations: golf, traveling.

COOPER, JAMES NELSON, medical educator; b. Staten Island, N.Y., Aug. 6, 1938; s. Charles Sylvester and Ella (Sabine) C.; m. Carolyn Olverson; children: John Emerson, Charles Key, James Ashley, Catherine Quesenberry. BA, Columbia U., 1959; MD, NYU, 1963. Diplomate Am. Bd. Internal Medicine and Gastroenterology. Intern Georgetown U., 1963-65; resident Boston City Hosp., 1965-66; fellow gastoenterology U. Chgo., 1966-68; clin. assoc. prof. medicine Georgetown U., Washington, 1977-83, prof. medicine, 1983—, asst. dean Sch. Medicine, 1985—, dir. transitional residency program, 1985—2001; pres. med. staff Fairfax Hosp., Falls Church, Va., 1975-77, chief gastroenterology, 1971-82, chmn. dept. medicine, 1982—; dir. Inova Inst. Rsch. & Edn., 1991—. Cons. State Dept., Washington, 1970—74; affiliate prof. George Mason U., 2001—; prof. medicine Va. Commonwealth Univ., Sch. of Medicine, 2003—. Editor: Gastrointestinal and Hepatic Complications In Pregnancy, 1986. Served to maj. USAR, 1964-71. Fellow ACP (Laureate award 1997), ACG; mem. Am. Gastroent. Assn., Am. Assn. Study Liver Diseases, No. Va. Acad. Internal Medicine (pres. 1975), Cosmos Club, Sigma Xi. Office: Fairfax Hosp 3300 Gallows Rd Falls Church VA 22042-3300 E-mail: james.cooper@inova.com.

COOPER, JAMES ROBERT, III, computer software company executive, mobile communications consultant; b. Mobile, Ala., Nov. 21, 1938; s. James Robert Jr. and Mary Nell (McMichael) C.; m. Marion Griser (div.); m. Nina Jessica Dotterer; children: Jessie Cameron, Charles Dotterer. BS in Sociology and Psychology, Spring Hill Coll., 1965. With sales and mktg. Proctor & Gamble, 1963-69; cons. to marine industry, 1969-79; pres., founder BCI Utilities Constn., Clearwater, Fla., 1979-84; v.p. aviation and navigation, co-founder ComGrafix, Inc., Clearwater, 1984-94; pres. Satellite Data, LLC, Newport, RI, 1998—2001; CEO Cooper Rsch., SP, Newport, RI, 1994—. Former mem. com. Radio Tech Commn., Washington, Cooper Rsch.; mem. mgmt. systems coun. ATA, interstate truckload corriers conf. Patentee in field. Bd. dirs. Mus. Yachting, Ida Lewis Yacht Club, Seaman's Ch. Inst. With USAR, 1958-63. Fellow Royal Inst. Navigation; mem. Nat. Marine Election Assn., Wild Goose Assn., U.S. Yacht Racing Assn. (contbg. mem.). Republican. E-mail: Cooper@efortress.com.

COOPER, JAMES RUSSELL, retired law educator; b. New Kensington, Pa., July 21, 1928; s. John Edward and Isabella Bird (Bowen) C.; m. Carolyn Hocker, Sept. 21, 1953 (div. Dec. 1975); children: L. Rachel, Julia Anderoni, Evan Lloyd, Jennifer Meyer; m. Leigh Ann Brian, Feb. 25, 1995 (div. Nov. 1999). BS Econs., U. Pa., 1952, JD, 1955. Bar: D.C., 1955, U.S. Supreme Ct., 1964; ordained to ministry Universal Brotherhood Movement, Inc., Meeting House for Aspiring Spirits. Pres., chmn. Radio WKPA-AM, WYDD-FM, New Kensington, 1959-64; urban renewal dir. Redevelopment Authority, New Kensington, 1964-68; assoc. prof. U. Ill., Champaign-Urbana, 1968-74; prof. legal studies Ga. State U., Atlanta, 1974-94, emeritus prof., 1994—. Author: Twilights Last Gleaming, 1992, Real Estate Investments, 3d edit. 1992. Sgt. U.S. Army, 1946-48. Mem. Fed. Bar Assn., D.C. Bar Assn., Am. Real Estate Soc. (founder, dir.). Home: 976 Forrest Blvd Decatur GA 30032 E-mail: jrctaopwr@sbcglobal.net.

COOPER, JANE TODD (J. C. TODD), poet, writer, educator; b. Bklyn., Dec. 24, 1943; d. John Curtis and Margaret E. (Johnston) C.; m. William Hudson Shoff; children: Donald Charles Taylor, Eamon Robert Shoff, Savannah Elizabeth Cooper-Ramsey. BA in Liberal Arts, Duquesne U., 1965; MFA in Creative Writing, Warren Wilson Coll., 1990. Instr. H.S., Pitts., 1967-73; ednl. dir. drug and alcohol treatment facility Pa. Dept. Corrections, Camp Hill, 1974-78; project mgr. domiciliary care, boarding home provider tng. Pa. State Coll. Medicine, Hershey, 1979-80, 82; dir. primary health care project Elizabethtown Hosp., Pa., 1980-81; instr. creative writing Coll. N.J., 1993-94; instr. writing Bryn Mawr Coll., 1999—2003; instr. creative writing Kutztown (Pa.) U., 2003—. Cons. Pa. Coun. on Arts, 1979-91; creative writing instr. Coll. N.J., 1992-94; instr. creative writing, Kutztown U., 2003; bd. dirs. Poetry Ctr., Phila., 1990-97, dir., 1994-97; artist in residence N.J. State Arts Coun., Pa. Coun. on the Arts, 1982—. Author: Entering Pisces, 1985, Nightshade, 1995; contbg. editor: The Drunken Boat. Recipient Pa. Coun. on Arts Fellowship in Poetry award, 1998, Disting. Tchg. Artist award, N.J. State Arts Coun., 1999—2001, N.J. Gov.'s award for arts edn., 1999, Disting. Artist award, NEA, 1999—2000, Leeway Found. award, 2001; fellow fellow poetry, Va. Ctr. Creative Arts, 1997; lit. fellow, Geraldine R. Dodge Found., 1987—, Carroll scholar, 1964—65, Warner Lambert/Nat. Merit scholar, 1961—65, fellow poetry, Hambidge Ctr., 1991—93, VCCA Internat. exch. fellow, Schloss Wiepersdorf, Germany, 2002, Pa. Coun. on Arts Profl. Devel. grantee, 1999, 2000, 2002. Mem. Acad. Am. Poets, Poets and Writers, Poetry Soc. Am., Friends of Writers. Studio: 119 Herr St # A Harrisburg PA 17102-3303 Fax: 215-629-3656. E-mail: JCTODD66@aol.com.

COOPER, JANELLE LUNETTE, neurologist, educator; b. Ann Arbor, Mich., Dec. 11, 1955; d. Robert Marion and Madelyn (Leonard) C.; children: Lena Christine, Nicholas Dominic. BA in Chemistry, Reed Coll., 1978; MD, Vanderbilt U., 1986. Diplomate Nat. Bd. Med. Examiners; diplomate in neurology Am. Bd. Psychiatry and Neurology; registered med. technologist Am. Soc. Clin. Pathologists. Med. technologist Swedish Hosp. Med. Ctr., Seattle, 1978-80, U. Wash. Clin. Chemistry, Seattle, 1980-82, Vanderbilt U. Hosp., Nashville, 1983-84; intern medicine Vanderbilt U. Med. Ctr., Nashville, 1986-87, resident neurology, 1987-90; instr. neurology Med. Coll. Pa., Phila., 1990-91, asst. prof., clerkship dir., 1991—, mem. curriculum com., 1990-91, vis. asst. prof., 1991-95; neurologist Greater Ann Arbor Neurology Assocs., 1991-93; dir. neurol. svcs., med. dir. Indsl. Rehab. Program St. Francis Hosp., Escanaba, Mich., 1993-98; founder, dir. No. Neuroscis., Escanaba, 1993-98; pres. HolderLady, Ltd., 1996—; chmn. dept. medicine St. Francis Hosp., Escanaba, Mich., 1998-99; dir. Affinity Health Sys., Oshkosh, Wis., 1998—; med. dir. Memory Clinic of the Upper Peninsula, Escanaba, Mich., 1998—. Neurologist Affinity Med. Group, Oshkosh, Wis., 1998—; physician MCP Neurology Assocs., Phila., 1990-91; emergency rm. physician Tenn. Christian Med. Ctr., 1989-90. Contbr. articles to Annals of Ophthalmology, Ophthalmic Surgery. Vol. Rape and Sexual Abuse Ctr., Nashville, 1988-90; mem. adminstrv. bd. Edgehill United Meth. Ch., Nashville, 1989-90; mem. editorial bd. Nashville Women's Alliance, 1989-90; bd. dirs. Upper Peninsula Physicians Network, 1995-98; mem. adv. bd. Perspective Adult Daycare Ctr., 1996-99; founding dir. Memory Clinic of Upper Peninsula, 1998-00; profl. adv. com. NE Wis. Alzheimer's Assn., 1999—. Recipient Svc. award for outstanding contbns. Rape and Sexual Abuse Ctr., 1990; epilepsy minifellow Bowman Gray U., 1995. Mem. AMA (physician's Recognition award 1989—), AAAS, Am. Med. Women's Assn., Am. Acad. Neurology, Am. Psychol. Soc., Wis. State Med. Soc., N.Y. Acad. Scis., Upper Peninsula Neuro Assn. (v.p. 1998-99, trustee 1998-99), Upper Peninsula Physician Network (bd. dirs. 1995-98), Aircraft Owners and Pilots Assn., Women in Aviation Internat. (charter), Air Force Assn. (life patron). Methodist. Achievements include first synthesis of Difluoromethanedisulfonic Acid; research on neurobehavioral disorders; on neuroendocrinology of sexual development, identity and orientation; on the history of women in medicine on effects of dietary lipids on the etiology of Alzheimer's disease; clinical investigation trials for new medications for dementias and epilepsy. Home: 108 Country Club Ln Oshkosh WI 54902-7459 Office: Affinity Med Group Dept Neurology 2725 Jackson St Oshkosh WI 54901-1513 E-mail: jcooper@affinityhealth.org.

COOPER, JANIS CAMPBELL, retired public relations executive; b. Laurel, Miss., July 26, 1947; d. Clifton B. and Hilna Mae (Welch) Campbell; m. William R. Cooper, Sept. 18, 1971; 1 child, Emily Susanne. BS, U. So. Miss., 1969. Certified home economist. Staff home economist Maytag Co., Newton, Iowa, 1969-73, supr. home econs., 1973-81, mgr. consumer edn., 1981-86; mgr. corp. pub. affairs Maytag Corp., Newton, 1986-87, asst. dir. corp. pub. affairs, 1987-88, corp. dir. pub. affairs, 1988-89, corp. v.p. pub. affairs, 1989-96, dir. found. programs, 1996—2002; ret., 2002. Chmn. bd. trustees Newton Cmty. Edn. Found., 1992-95; campaign vice chmn. United Way, Newton, 1996, campaign chmn., 1997, bd. dirs., 1998—, pres., 1998, mem. exec. com., 1998-99; bd. dirs. YMCA, 1997-2000; mem. Newton Chamber Edn. Com. 1999—, chair 2000; edn. com. Newton Chamber Alliance, 1999—, chmn. 2000—. Mem. Assn. Family and Consumer Scis., Pub. Rels. Soc. Am., Home Economists in Bus. (nat. chmn. 1981-82, Disting. Svc. award 1986, Nat. Bus. Home Economist of Yr. 1991), Iowa Assn. Bus. and Industry (bd. dirs., mem. exec. com. 1990-96), Assn. Home Appliance Mfrs. (treas. 1988-89, 1st vice chmn. 1989-90, chmn. 1990-92, chmn. Major Appliance Divsn. Bd. 1993-95), Consumer Sci. Bus. Profls., Maytag Mgmt. Club (Cmty. Svc. award 1997), Kiwanis Internat. Avocations: golfing, reading, travel.

COOPER, JAY LESLIE, lawyer; b. Chgo., Jan. 15, 1929; s. Julius Jerome and Grayce (Wolkenheim) C.; m. Darice Richman, July 30, 1970; children: Todd, Leslie, Keith. JD, De Paul U., 1951. Bar: Ill. 1951, Calif. 1953, U.S. Supreme Ct. 1965, N.Y. 1987. Ptnr. Cooper, Epstein & Hurewitz (and predecessors), Beverly Hills, Calif., 1955-93; ptnr. Manatt, Phelps & Phillips, L.A., 1993—2001; shareholder Greenberg Traurig, LLP, 2002—. Guest lectr. Advanced Profl. Program Legal Aspects of Music and Rec. Industry, U. So. Calif., 1968, 70, 75, Entertainment Industry Conf., 1971, Harvard Law Sch., 1985; guest lectr. Calif. Copyright Conf., 1967, 71, 73, 75, 77, 97, v.p., 1975, pres., 1976-77; co-chmn. ann. program The Rec. Contract, UCLA, 1977—; lectr. Midem, 1977-95, 96-97; adj. prof. entertainment law Loyola U. Law Sch., Los Angeles, 1978-80; moderator UCLA Seminar, 1994. Profl. musician with, Les Brown, Charlie Barnet, Frank Sinatra, Los Angeles Philharm. others, 1945-55; editor: (with Irwin O. Spiegel) Record and Music Publishing Forms of Agreement in Current Use, 1971, Annual Program on Legal Aspects of Entertainment Industry, Syllabus, 1966-70; co-author: Talent in the New Millennium, 2001, The Work Made For Hire Conundrum, 2001. Named Entertainment Lawyer of Yr. Billboard mag., 1975, Best of the Best, 2000. Mem. ABA (chmn. forum com. on entertainment and sports industries 1983-86), NARAS (chpt. pres. 1973-75, nat. pres. 1975-77), Beverly Hills Bar Assn. (co-chmn. entertainment law com. 1972-75, Entertainment Atty. of Yr. 2003), Calif. Copyright Soc. (pres. 1976), Los Angeles County Bar Assn., Calif. Bar Assn., Ill. Bar Assn., L.A. Copyright Soc., Internat. Assn. Entertainment Lawyers (exec. com.). Office: Greenberg Traurig LLP 2450 Colorado Ave #400 E Santa Monica CA 90404

COOPER, JEAN SARALEE, judge; b. Huntington, N.Y., Mar. 7, 1946; d. Ralph and Henrietta (Halbreich) Cooper; stepchildren: Mitzi Concklin Prochnow, John Todd Concklin. BA, Sophie Newcomb Coll. of Tulane U., 1968; JD, Emory U., 1970. Bar: La. 1970, Ga. 1970, U.S. Dist. Ct. (ea. dist.) La. 1970, U.S. Ct. Appeals (5th cir.) 1972, U.S. Ct. Appeals (2d cir.) 1976, U.S. Ct. Appeals (4th cir.) 1977, U.S. Ct. Appeals (fed. cir.), U.S. Supreme Ct. 1974. Trial atty. Office of Solicitor, U.S. Dept. Labor, Washington, 1970-73, spl. projects asst., 1973, sr. trial atty., 1973-77; adminstrv. judge Bd. Contract Appeals, HUD, Washington, 1977—2003, acting chmn. and chief judge, 1980-81, vice chmn., 1983—2003; bd. mem. Coalition for Free Trade, 2005—. Cons.; lectr. Contbr. Recipient Moot Ct. award, Tulane Law Sch., 1968. Fellow: ABA (life; jud. divsn. 1979—, standing com. on jud. selection, tenure and compensation. 1992—95, vice chair debarment and suspension com. pub. contracts sect. 1992—97, sec. Nat. Conf. Adminstrv. Law Judges 1996—97, vice chmn. 1997—98, chair-elect 1998—99, standing com. on fed. jud. improvements 2000—01, adminstrn. law sect), Am. Bar Found. (life); mem.: Contract Appeals Judges Assn., Nat. Assn. Women Judges (founder), BCA Bar Assn., Am. Judicature Soc., Prettyman-Leventhal Am. Inn of Ct. (past pres., master of bench), Am. Inns of Ct. Found. (trustee 1992—98, leadership com. 1998—), Am. Law Inst., Fed. Bar Assn. (jud. divsn. leadership coun.), La. Bar Assn. Republican. Home: 2800 Flagmaker Dr Falls Church VA 22042-2200 E-mail: jeansaralee@cs.com. *My approach to life has been "anything is possible." That removed the boundaries in my mind, so that I could move past the boundaries that might hold me back. I firmly believe in mentoring young people so that they, too, will see past boundaries real and imagined.*

COOPER, JEFFREY TODD, music educator; b. Olean, Ny, Sept. 12, 1969; s. Theron Cooper; m. Stacey Robin Krapf, Nov. 6, 1999; 1 child, Laura Rose. BS in Music Edn., Ind. U. of PA, Indiana, PA, 1988—92; MA in Psychology, Marywood U., Scranton, PA, 1995—98. Instructional II Pa Dept. of Edn., 1997. Music tchr. JT Lambert Intermediate Sch., East Stroudsburg, Pa., 1992—2001, Colonial Mid. Sch., Plymouth Meeting, Pa., 2001—. Musical theater dir. Colonial Mid. Sch., Plymouth Meeting, Pa., 2001—; musical/artistic dir. vocal music JT Lambert Intermediate Sch., East Stroudsburg, Pa., 1999—2001, stage mgr., 1994—2001. Singer: (christian music concerts) Jeff Cooper and Friends, (music recording) CODA Jazz Mass. Mem.: NEA, Music Educator's Nat. Conf. (licentiate), Am. Choral Director's Assn. (licentiate). Independent. Achievements include research in Course-work research/relation of music and study time among middle school students. Avocations: hiking, travel, antiques, gardening. Office: Colonial Middle School 716 Belvoir Road Plymouth Meeting PA 19462 E-mail: jcooper@colonialsd.org.

COOPER, JEROME A. lawyer; b. Brookwood, Ala., Jan. 15, 1913; s. Marks Benjamin and Etta (Temerson) C.; m. Lois Harriet McMillen, Aug. 16, 1938; children: Ellen (Mrs. Benjamin L. Erdreich), Carol. AB cum laude, Harvard, 1933, LLB, 1936. Bar: Ala. 1936. Practice in, Birmingham, 1946—; law clk. U.S. Dist. Judge Davis, 1936-37, U.S. Supreme Ct. Justice Hugo L. Black, 1937-40; regional atty. Solicitors Office, Dept. Labor, 1940-41; ptnr. Cooper, Mitch & Crawford, 1950-98; of counsel Gardner, Middlebrooks, Fleming & Gibbons, PC, Birmingham, 1999—. Mem. Pres. Kennedy's Lawyers' Com. for Civil Rights Under Law, 1963—; pres. adv. coun. Pub. Radio Sta. WBHM, 1980—. Mem. editl. adv. bd. The Ala. Lawyer. Mem. Birmingham area Manpower Resource Devel. Planning Bd., 1969; chmn. cmty. devel. com. Operation New Birmingham; mem. Jefferson County Drug Abuse Coordinating Com., 1970-76; pres. Jefferson County Assn. Mental Health, Birmingham Jewish Cmty. Ctr., United Jewish Fund; mem. Southeastern regional adv. bd. Anti Defamation League, 1981; exec. bd. Birmingham Concentrated Employment Program; pres. Positive Maturity; sec., exec. bd. Jefferson County Com. Econ Opportunity; pres. Crisis Ctr., 1976; mem. Gov.'s Task Force on Unemployment, 1983; Democratic candidate for Ala. Senate, 1966; bd. dirs. Birmingham Symphony Assn., 1979-80, Ruffner Mountain Nature Ctr., 1985—, v.p., 1990, pres. 1991-93; bd. dirs. Friends of U. Ala. in Birmingham Psychiatry, 1987, Birmingham Civil Rights Inst., 1992—, adv. com. (HAER) Birmingham Hist. Soc., 1992—. Served to lt. comdr. USNR, 1942-45. Fellow Internat. Soc. Barristers, Coll. Labor and Employment Lawyers (emeritus); mem. Ala. Law Inst., Adminstrv. Conf. U.S., Birmingham Audubon Soc. (v.p. exec. com. 1989—), Disting. Fellow Birmingham-So. Coll., 1995. Jewish (trustee temple). Home: 42 Fairway Dr Birmingham AL 35213-4211

COOPER, JEROME MAURICE, architect; b. Memphis, Jan. 24, 1930; s. Samuel and Bessie (Phillips) C.; m. Jean Kanter, Dec. 29, 1957; children: David Franklin, Samuel Randolph, Beth Lauren. BS, Ga. Inst. Tech., 1952, BArch, 1955; postgrad., U. Rome, Italy, 1956-57. Fulbright fellow, Rome, 1956-57; pres. Cooper, Carry & Assocs., Inc., Atlanta, 1960—, chmn. Vis. artist Am. Acad. Rome. Prin. works include Coll. of Architecture bldg. Ga. Inst. Tech., Siemens Corp. Hdqrs., Nat. Svc. Industries Corp. Hdqrs., Adtraw Corp. Hdqrs., Huntsville, Ala., Sci. Atlanta Corp. Hdqrs, Lazarus Dept. Store, Pitts., Clin. Info. Mgmt. Ctr., Drake U. Med. Ctr., Sch. of Theology, Mercer U., Green Hill Mall (AIA design award), Heritage Village at Sea Pines, Underground Atlanta, C&P Hdqrs., No. Va., Rich's Dept. Store, Northpoint Mall, Atlanta, Jordan Marsh Dept. Store, Natick Mall, Boston. Trustee Nat. Bldg. Mus. Served to lt. (j.g.) USN, 1952-54. Recipient Rothschild medal, 1985, Silver medal Atlanta chpt. AIA, 1987. Fellow AIA (pres. chpt., nat. dir., task force on ethics, task force on certification, task force on long span buildings, Silver medal firm award Atlanta chpt. 1987), Nat. Jud. Coun. Home: 1070 Judith Way NE Atlanta GA 30324-2905 Office: Cooper Carry & Assocs Inc 3520 Piedmont Rd NE Ste 200 Atlanta GA 30305-1595

COOPER, JERROLD STEPHEN, historian, educator; b. Chgo., Nov. 24, 1942; s. Emanuel Cooper and Adele (Faberson) Smith; m. Elaine Abrams, Dec. 22, 1962 (div. 1969); children: Nina Lynn, Sari Jean; m. Carol Manson Bier, Nov. 18, 1982; 1 child, Jenny Alexandra. AB, U. Calif., Berkeley, 1963, MA, 1964; PhD, U. Chgo., 1969. Asst. prof. Johns Hopkins U., Balt., 1968-74, assoc. prof., 1974-79, prof., 1979—, chmn. dept. Near Eastern Studies, 1983-91; acting chmn. Near Eastern Studies, 1992-93; acting chmn. classics Johns Hopkins U., Balt., 1988-91. Vis. prof. UCLA, 1975, U. Calif., Berkeley, 1981, U. Padua, Italy, 1992, U. Rome, 1998. Author: The Return of Ninurta, 1979, The Curse of Agade, 1983, Sumerian and Akkadian Royal Inscriptions, 1985; assoc. editor Jour. of Cuneiform Studies, 1972-89. NEH grantee, 1980-86. Mem. Am. Oriental Soc. (dir. 1982-85), Am. Schs. of Oriental Rsch. (trustee 1987-97). Avocation: early music. Office: Johns Hopkins U Dept Near East Studies Baltimore MD 21218 E-mail: anzu@jhu.edu.

COOPER, JOEL, psychology educator; b. N.Y.C., Dec. 3, 1943; s. Samuel Cooper and Sarah Tobias; m. Barbara Orenstein, Dec. 17, 1966; children: Jason, Aaron, Grant. BS, CCNY, 1965; PhD in Social Psychology, Duke U., 1969. Asst. prof. psychology Princeton (N.J.) U., 1969-73, assoc. prof., 1973-78, prof., 1978—, chmn. psychology dept., 1985-92, dir. grad. studies dept. psychology, 1976-83. Chmn. Inst. Rev. Bd. Princeton U., 1974-81, 84-87, 96-99, com. appointments and advancements, com. on grad. sch.; sr. fellow East-West Population Inst., 1975. Author: Understanding Social Psychology, 1976, 5th edit., 1991, Social Psychology, 1999, Gender and the Computer: Understanding the Digital Divide, 2003; editor: Attribution Processes, Person, Perception, and Social Interaction: The Legacy of Edward E. Jones, 1998, Sage Handbook of Social Psychology, 2003; editorial bd. Jour. Personality, Jour. Exptl. Social Psychology, Social Psychology Quar.; contbr. chpts. to books in field, articles to profl. jours. Office: Princeton U Dept Psychology Green Hall Princeton NJ 08544

COOPER, JOHN, university football coach; b. Powell, Tenn., July 2, 1937; m. Helen Cooper; children: John Jr., Cindy. BS, Iowa State U., 1962. Freshman football coach Iowa State U., 1962-63; asst. football coach Oreg. State U., 1963-67; defensive coord. U. Kans., 1967-72; asst. coach U. Ky., 1972-77; coach U. Tulsa, 1977-84, Ariz. State U., 1985-87; head football coach Ohio State U., Columbus, 1987—. Coach East-West Shrine Bowl Game, Hula Bowl, Japan All-State games. Active civic orgns., Columbus, including Big Bros./Big Sisters, Alzheimer's Found., Arthur James Cancer Hosp., Children's Hosp. With U.S. Army. Named Nat. Coach of Yr., 1986; winner Rose Ball games with Pac-10 and Big Ten conf. teams. Mem. Am. Football Coaches Assn. (past pres.). Office: Ohio State U Athletic Dept St John Arena 401 Woody Hayes Dr Columbus OH 43210

COOPER, JOHN ALFRED, JR., community development company executive; b. Memphis, Sept. 13, 1938; s. John Alfred and Mildred (Borum) C.; m. Pat McInnis, Oct. 23, 1965; children: Mary Virginia, John Alfred III, Borum. Student, U. Ark., 1961. With Cherokee Village Devel. Co., Inc., 1962—, exec. v.p., 1967-68; pres. John A. Cooper Co., 1968-90, Cooper Communities Inc., 1972-90, vice chmn., 1990-91; chmn. Cooper Communities, Inc., 1991-97, pres., CEO, 1997—. Bd. dirs. 1st Nat. Bank of Sharp County, J.B. Hunt Transport Svcs., Inc. Mem.: Memphis Country, Little Rock Country. Office: Cooper Communities Inc 1801 Forest Hills Blvd Bella Vista AR 72715-2395

COOPER, JOHN ARNOLD, financial analyst; b. Detroit, Oct. 27, 1917; s. Gage Whitman and Helen Dorothy (Danger) C.; m. Sylvia Grace, Sept. 6, 1941 (div. 1977); 1 child, Maud Cooper Granzow; m. Virginia Bailey Svagr, Mar. 11, 1977 (dec. 1981); m. Anny Marion Van Dyke, Apr. 9, 1983. BA, Williams Coll., Williamstown, Mass., 1939; MBA, Mich. State U., 1968. CFA, Inst. Chartered Fin. Analysts. Treas. Cooper Supply Co., Detroit, 1941-44, sec., 1944-56, pres., 1956-67; v.p. Texas Industries, Inc., Dallas, 1963-67; pres. Cooper, Van Dyke Assocs. Inc., Birmingham, Mich., 1970—2000; mem. Cooper, Van Dyke LLC, 2000—. Pres. Transit Mixed Concrete Inst. Met. Detroit, 1952-53, 55-77, Constrn. Assn. Mich., 1967-68; trustee Fin. Analysts Seminar, 1980-82. Class agt. Williams Coll., 1989-94; chmn. preservation fund drive The Cmty. House, Birmingham, Mich., 1995-98, fin. com. mem., 1988—2001, bd. dirs. 1996-2000. Lt. (j.g.) USNR, 1944-46. Fellow Fin. Analysts Fedn.; mem. Mich. Trucking Assn. (mem. bd. govs. 1958-63), Am. Trucking Assn. (bd. dirs. 1961-63), Inst. Chartered Fin. Analysts, Investment Analysts Soc. Detroit (pres. 1980-81, chmn. profl. conduct/ethics com. 1988-99), Assn. Investment Mgmt. and Rsch.(trustee, fin. analysts sem. 1980-82), Williams Club N.Y., Beta Gamma Sigma. Republican. Episcopalian. Avocations: photography, hiking, gardening, traveling.

COOPER, JOHN BURTON, band director; b. Decatur, Ala., Dec. 22, 1964; s. George Albert and Lorraine Hunter C.; m. Melissa Halcomb, Sept. 2, 1970; children: Rachel, Ben. MusB in Edn., La. State U., Baton Rouge, La., 1987. Band dir. Brookhaven Mid. Sch., Decatur, Ala., 1987—92, Cedar Ridge Mid. Sch., Decatur, Ala., 1992—93, Benjamin Russell H.S., Alexander City, Ala., 1993—98, Austin H.S., Decatur, 1998—. Dist. coord. Ala. Conf. of Educators, Decatur, Ala., 2001—, bd. dirs., 2002—. Mem.: Decatur Assn. Profl. Educators (pres. 2001—03), Nat. Band Assn., Ala. Bandmasters Assn. (dist. chmn. 1992—93, 2003—), Pi Kappa Lambda, Phi Kappa Phi, Phi Mu Alpha Sinfonia (pres. 1986—87). Church Of Christ. Office: Austin High Sch Band 1625 Danville Rd SW Decatur AL 35601 Office Fax: 256-350-7802. Personal E-mail: johncooper@ahs.dcs.edu.

COOPER, JOHN BYRNE, JR., airline pilot; b. Balt., May 13, 1942; s. John Bryne and Mary Louise (Shaffer) C.; m. Virginia Johnson, Oct. 30, 1964 (div. 1974); children: John Byrne, Tracy Diane; m. Jane Marian Simpson, Apr. 1, 1977; children: Julie Allison, Scott David. B in Indsl. Engring., Ga. Inst. Tech., 1964. Pilot Delta Air Lines, Inc., Atlanta, 1970—2002, capt. B727, B767, L-1011 Internat., B777, 1986—, B727 line check pilot, 1988-92, lead B727 line check pilot, 1991-93, lead B767 line check pilot, 1994-99, B777 line check pilot, 1999—2002. Mem. exec. com. Homeowners Assn., Marietta, Ga., 1988, v.p. bd. dirs., 1995-96; soccer coach Metro North/East Cobb Soccer, Marietta, 1985-92. Decorated DFC, Air medals (23), Navy Commendation medal. Mem. U.S. Naval Inst., Assn. Naval Aviation, Naval Res. Assn., Tailhook Assn., Barefoot Sailing Club (fleet capt.), So. Sailing Club, Coronado 15 Nat. Assn. (bd. dirs. 1976), Beta Theta Pi. Lutheran. Avocations: tennis, sailing, skiing, golf.

COOPER, JOHN JOSEPH, lawyer; b. Vincennes, Ind., Oct. 20, 1924; s. Homer O. and Ruth (House) C.; m. Nathalie Brooke, 1945. AB, Stanford, 1950, LLB, 1951; LLM, U. So. Calif., 1964. Bar: Calif. 1952. Pvt. practice, San Francisco, 1951-54; counsel Shell Oil Co., L.A., 1954-61; gen. counsel, v.p. Varian Assocs., Palo Alto, 1961—90, sr. v.p., 1990, also bd. dirs. Speaker, lectr. Am. Law Inst., ABA, other legal orgns. Contbr. articles to law revs. and profl. jours. Aviator USNR, 1942-45. Mem. ABA, Calif. Bar Assn. Home: 191 Ramoso Rd Portola Valley CA 94028

COOPER, JOHN MADISON, philosophy educator; b. Memphis, Nov. 29, 1939; s. Marion Armon and Bernardine (Sheehan) C.; m. Marcia Louise Coleman, Aug. 21, 1965; children: Stephanie Coleman, Katherine Alexander. AB magna cum laude, Harvard U., 1961, PhD, 1967; BPhil, Corpus Christi Coll., Oxford, Eng., 1963. Asst. prof. philosophy and the classics Harvard U., Cambridge, Mass., 1966-71; assoc. prof. U. Pitts., 1971-76, prof., 1976-81, chmn. philosophy dept., 1977-81; prof. Princeton U., N.J., 1981—, chmn. philosophy dept., 1984-92, Stuart prof., 1998—. Author: Reason and Human Good in Aristotle, Seneca: Moral and Political Essays, Plato: Complete Works, Reason and Emotion; mem. editl. bd. Am. Philos. Quar., 1977-80, History of Philosophy Quar., 1983-86, The Monist, 1987—, Ratio, 1988, Archiv für Ges. d. Phil., 1994—; contbr. articles to profl. jours. Recipient Ctr. for Advanced Studies fellow U. Ill., 1969-70, NEH fellow, 1982-83, John Simon Guggenheim fellow, 1987-88, Ctr. for Advanced Study in the Behavioral Scis. fellow, 1992-93, Am. Coun. Learned Socs. fellow, 2002-03. Fellow Am. Acad. Arts and Scis.; mem. Am. Philos. Assn. (ea. divsn. exec. com. 1984-87, chmn. com. def. profl. rights 1983-88, ea. divsn. nominating com. 1991-94, chmn. ea. divsn. program com. 1980, v.p. 1998-99, pres. 1999-2000). Home: 182 Western Way Princeton NJ 08540-7208 Office: Princeton Univ Dept of Philosophy 1879 Hall Princeton NJ 08544-1006 E-mail: johncoop@princeton.edu.

COOPER, JOHN MILTON, JR., history educator, author; b. Washington, Mar. 16, 1940; s. John Milton and Mary Louise (Porter) C.; m. Judith Karin Widerkrantz, June 9, 1962; children: John Milton III, Elizabeth Karin Doyle. AB summa cum laude, Princeton U., 1961; MA, Columbia U., 1962, PhD, 1968. Instr. history Wellesley (Mass.) Coll., 1965-67, asst. prof., 1967-70; asst. prof. history U. Wis., Madison, 1970-71, assoc. prof., 1971-76, prof., 1976-87, William Francis Allen prof. history, 1987-99, E. Gordon Fox prof. Am. instns., 1999—, chmn. dept., 1988-91. Fulbright prof. Coun. Internat. Exch. Scholars, Moscow, 1987. Author: Vanity of Power, 1969, Walter Hines Page, 1977, Warrior and Priest, 1983, Pivotal Decades, 1990, Breaking the Heart of the World: Woodrow Wilson and the Fight for the League of Nations, 2001; editor: Causes and Consequences of World War I, 1971, The Wilson Era, 1991. Woodrow Wilson Found. fellow, 1961, NEH fellow, 1969, 91, Guggenheim Found. fellow, 1979. Mem.: Ctr. for Nat. Policy, State Hist. Soc. Wis. (bd. curators), Woodrow Wilson Birthplace Found. (hon. pres.), Coun. Fgn. Rels., So. Hist. Assn., Orgn. Am. Historians, Am. Hist. Assn., Rotary, Phi Beta Kappa. Democrat. Congregationalist. E-mail: jmcooper@facstaff.wisc.edu.

COOPER, JOHN WEEKS, lawyer; b. Newark, Feb. 5, 1930; s. Ralph Emerson and Ann Elizabeth (Weeks) C.; m. Mary Kathryn Niles, Nov. 4, 1961; children: Sarah Elizabeth, Edward Niles. AB, Bowdoin Coll., 1952; LLB, Columbia U., 1955. Bar: N.J. 1955, U.S. Dist. Ct. N.J. 1955. Assoc. McCarter & English, Newark, 1955-57, Moser, Griffin & Kerby, Summit, N.J., 1957-63; ptnr. Kerby, Cooper, Schaul & Garvin, Summit, 1963-90, Cooper, Rose & English, LLP, Summit, 1990—. Sec., gen. counsel Anchorage Hotel, Antigua, West Indies, 1976-87. Pres. Summit First Aid Squad, 1967, Family Svc. Assn., Summit, 1978, Summit Area Pub. Found.; trustee Oak Knoll Sch., Summit, United Way, Summit; pres. United Way, 1985-87. Named United Way Citizen of Yr., 1990. Fellow Am. Coll. Trust and Estate Coun.; mem. Summit Bar Assn. (pres. 1975), Union County Bar Assn. (probate com. 1975—), N.J. Bar Assn. (bd. consultors, real property and probate sect., chmn. dist. XII supreme ct. fee arbitration panel, chmn. probate early settlement panel program Union County), No. N.J. Estate Planning Coun. (pres. 1985), Beacon Hill Club (pres. 1972-74), Shrewsbury Sailing and Yacht Club (Oceanport N.J.). Republican. Episcopalian. Home: 80 Prospect St Summit NJ 07901-2406 Office: Cooper Rose & English LLP 480 Morris Ave Summit NJ 07901-1523

COOPER, JOSEPH, political scientist, educator; b. Boston, Sept. 10, 1933; s. Charles and Esther (Balder) Cooper; m. Frances Lorna Wollin, Aug. 24, 1965; children: Samuel Wollin, Meryl Charlotte. AB summa cum laude, Harvard U., 1955, AM, 1959, PhD, 1961. Asst. prof. govt. Harvard U., 1963-67; mem. faculty Rice U., Houston, 1967-91, prof. polit. sci., 1970-91, chmn. dept., 1967-72, Lena Gohlman Fox prof., 1978-89, dean Sch. Social Scis., 1979-88, Herbert S. Autrey prof. social scis., 1989-91, pres. Rice Inst. for Policy Analysis Sch. Social Scis., 1989-91; provost, v.p. for acad. affairs Johns Hopkins U., Balt., 1991-96, prof. dept. polit. sci., 1991—. Vis. Olin prof. polit. sci. Stanford U., 1988—89; staff dir. commn. adminstrv. rev. U.S. Ho. Reps., 1976—78; vis. prof. govt. Harvard U., 1984—85; mem. acad. adv. coun. Ctr. Congress Ind. U.; mem. editl. adv. bd. Ctr. Legis. Archives; bd. dirs. Dirksen Congl. Ctr., 1994—2000, 2002—, Consortium Social Sci. Orgns., 1994—97, Pub. Campaign, 1997—. Author: (book) The Origins of the Standing Committees and the Development of the Modern House, 1970, Congress and Its Committees, 1988; contbr. articles to profl. jours.; co-editor: (book) Sage Yearbook on Electoral Studies, 1975—82; mem. bd. editors: Congress and the Presidency, Ency. of U.S. Congress, Legis. Studies Quar., 1987—90, 2001—, assoc. editor: Ency. of Am. Legis. Sys., Congress of U.S. 1789-1989. Mem. adv. com. Records of Congress U.S. Congress and Nat. Archives, 1995—; bd. dirs. Balt. Hebrew U., 1994—2001. Recipient Press award, Congl. Quar., 1989; fellow Brookings Rsch., Harvard U., 1959—60, Sr., NEH, 1973. Mem.: D.C. Area Polit Sci. Assn. (mem. coun. 1993—94, v.p. 1994, pres. 1996), Midwest Polit. Sci. Assn., So. Polit. Sci. Assn., Southwestern Polit. Sci. Assn. (pres. 1977), Am. Polit. Sci. Assn. (sec. 1979, program chmn. 1985, nominations chmn. 1992, exec. com. legis. studies sect. 1999—), Asia Soc. (bd. dirs. 1990—92), Jefferson Davis Assn. (dir. 1980—91), Phi Beta Kappa, Sigma Xi. Office: Dept Polit Sci Johns Hopkins Univ Baltimore MD 21218-2685 E-mail: jcooper@jhu.edu.

COOPER, JOSEPHINE SMITH, trade association and public relations executive; b. Raleigh, N.C., Aug. 2, 1945; d. Joseph W. and Marie (Peele) S. BA in bus. and econs., Meredith Coll., Raleigh, 1967; MS in mgmt., Duke U., 1977. Program analyst Office of Air & Quality Planning and Standards EPA, Rsch., Triangle Park, N.C., 1968-78; environ. protection specialist Office of Rsch. and Devel., Washington, 1978-80; mem. profl. staff majority leader Howard H. Baker, Jr., U.S. Senate Com. on Environ. and Public Works, Washington, 1980-83; asst. adminstr. for external affairs EPA, Washington, 1983-85; asst. v.p. for environ. and health program Am. Paper Inst., Washington, 1985-86; sr. v.p. for policy Synthetic Organic Chem. Mfrs. Assn., Washington, 1986-88; sr. v.p., dir. environmental policy Hill & Knowlton, Inc., Washington, 1988-91; founder, dir. Capitoline Internat. Group, Ltd., Washington, 1991-92; v.p. environ. and regulatory affairs Am. Forest & Paper Assn., 1992-99; pres., CEO Alliance of Automobile Mfrs., Washington, 1999—. Treas. RTP Fed. Credit Union, 1969—72, pres., CEO, 1975; pres. Women's Coun. on Energy and Environment, 1986—88, Nat. Coun. on Clean Indoor Air, 1988—96; mem. nat. adv. environ. health scis. coun. NIH, 1990—94; mem. adv. com. EPA Clean Air Act, 1994—98; liaison mem. trade and environ. policy adv. com. USTR, 1994—2002; chmn. Nat. Urban Air Toxic Rsch. Ctr., 2003—. Bd. visitors Duke U. Nicholas Sch. Environ., 1994-2002; bd. dirs. Leland Nat. Urban Air Toxics Rsch. Ctr. Congl. fellow, 1979-80. Mem.: NAM (coun. bd. dirs. 2000—), Orgn. of Internat. Auto Assn. (pres.), Orgn. d'Internationale Constructeurs d'Automobiles (chmn. 2003—), Am. Soc. Assn. Execs. (bd. dirs. 2000—), U.S. C. of C. (Com. of 100 2000—), Women in Govt. Rels., Federally Employed Women (pres. 1972—77, treas.). Mem. Christian Ch. (Disciples Of Christ).

COOPER, KATHLEEN BELL, federal agency administrator; b. Dallas, Feb. 3, 1945; d. Patrick Joseph and Ferne Elizabeth (McDougle) Bell; m. Ronald James Cooper, Feb. 6, 1965; children: Michael, Christopher. BA in Math. with honors, U. Tex., Arlington, 1970, MA in Econs, 1971; PhD in Econs, U. Colo., 1980. Research asst. econs. dept. U. Tex., Arlington, 1970-71; corp. economist United Banks of Colo., Denver, 1971-79, chief economist, 1980-81; v.p., sr. fin. economist Security Pacific Nat. Bank, Los Angeles, 1981-83, 1st v.p., sr. economist, 1983-85, sr. v.p., economist, 1985-86, sr. v.p., chief economist, 1986-87, exec. v.p., chief economist, 1988-90; chief economist Exxon Corp., Irving, Tex., 1990-99; chief economist, mgr. econs. & energy divsn. corp. planning Exxon Mobil Corp., 1999-2001; under sec. for econ. affairs U.S. Dept. Commerce, Washington, 2001—. Trustee Scripps Coll., 1987-2001, Com. for Econ. Devel.1993-2001; mem. Coun. on Fgn. Rels., Internat. Women's Forum. Mem. Nat. Assn. Bus. Economists (past pres. Denver and L.A. chpts.; bd. dirs. 1975-78, pres. 1985-86), Nat. Bur. Econ. Rsch. (bd. dirs. 1987-2001, exec. com., vice-chair 1999-2001), Am. Bankers Assn. (econ. adv. com. 1979-81, 86-90, chmn. 1989-90), U.S. Assn. Energy Econs. (pres. 1996), Am. Econ. Assn., Conf. Bus. Economists (tech. cons. to bus. coun. 1993-94). Office: US Dept Commerce Rm 4848 14th and Constitution NW Washington DC 20230

COOPER, KATHY STEGALL, school counselor; b. Monroe, N.C., Oct. 23, 1959; d. Luther and Frances Stegall; m. Bill Cooper, June 7, 1995. BS, Wingate (S.C.) U., 1982; MS in Social Work, U. S.C., Columbia, 1984. Social worker Dept. Social Svcs., Monroe, NC, 1984—87; elem. sch. counselor Benton Heights Elem. Sch., Monroe, 1987—98; h.s. counselor Piedmont (N.C.) H.S., 1998—. Presenter Devel. Resources, Columbia, SC, 1997; presenter Workshops in 25 states. Author: Power Play: Quality Time for Quality Kids, Innovative Strategies for Unlocking Difficult Children, Innovative Strategies for Unlocking Difficult Adolescents, Ready Freddy. Spl. events dir. Weddington Comty. Ch., 2001; bd. dirs., pres.. Turning Point, 1988—90. Baptist. Avocations: hiking, reading, visiting.

COOPER, KELLI D. music educator; b. Ft. Smith, Ark., May 2, 1968; d. Kenneth Paul and Shelby Kirby Birdsong; m. Todd A. Cooper, Dec. 8, 2001. AA, Tyler (Tex.) Jr. Coll., 1988; BFA, U. Tex., Tyler, 1991; MME, U. Okla., Norman, 1994. Piano instr. Birdsong Studio, Tyler, 1984—91; grad. asst. in piano U. Okla., Norman, 1993—94; piano instr. Kowachuk-Lancaster Studio, Norman, 1993—94; music tchr. Cain Elem. Sch., Whitehouse, Tex., 1994—96; adj. piano faculty Tyler Jr. Coll., 1996—; piano instr. Kelli Cooper Studio, Tyler, 2003—. Recipient Young Musician of the Yr., Tyler Music Coterie, 1986. Mem.: Music Tchrs. Nat. Assn., Nat. Guild of Piano Tchrs., East Tex. Music Tchrs. Assn. Bapt. Home: 607 Beechwood Dr Tyler TX 75701-7735 E-mail: soonermusic@yahoo.com.

COOPER, KEN ERROL, retired management educator; b. Bryan, Ohio, Mar. 10, 1939; s. George Wayne and Agnes Anibel (Fisher) C.; m. Karen Cremean, June 17, 1961; children: Kristin, Andrew. BS, Bowling Green State U., 1961; MBA, Miami U., Oxford, Ohio, 1962; PhD, U. Minn., 1984. Instr. Miami U., 1962-63; lectr. U. Minn., 1965-67, 84-86; group v.p. Land O'Lakes, Inc., Mpls., 1967-82; v.p. fin. and adminstrn. Hamline U., 1982-84; dean Coll. Bus., Ohio No. U., Ada, 1986-90, prof., 1990-2000; prof., post chair for ethics and professions Am. Coll., Bryn Mawr, Pa., 1994-95, retired, 1995. Vis. prof. (on leave) Coll. of St. Thomas, St. Paul, 1981-82, vis. prof. of mgmt. U. San Diego, 2001-02, U. Evansville, 2002—. Trustee Westmar Coll., 1980-86; bd. dirs., sec.-treas. Acad. Mgmt., 1989-95; mem. Iowa Supreme Ct. Adv. Coun., 1972-75, North Ctrl. Devel. Found. Republican. Methodist. Office: Ohio No U Coll Bus Adminstrn Ada OH 45810

COOPER, KENNETH, harpsicordist, pianist, music educator, conductor, musicologist; b. N.Y.C., May 31, 1941; s. Rudolf and Florence (Buxbaum) Cooper; m. Josephine Luisa Mongiardo, June 1, 1969; 1 child, Nicholas Perry Mongiardo-Cooper. BA, Columbia U., 1962, MA, 1964, PhD, 1971. Instr. Barnard Coll., N.Y.C., 1967—71; artist-in-residence Columbia U., N.Y.C., 1983—; chmn. harpsichord dept. Manhattan Sch. Music, 1984—; dir. Baroque Aria Ensemble, 1984—. Vis. specialist Montclair State Coll., NJ, 1977—92, Peabody Conservatory, Balt., 1986—90; cons. Juilliard Repertory Project; music dir. Berkshire Bach Ensemble; co-dir. Our Bach Concerts; soloist Bach's Brandenburg No. 5 Live From Lincoln Ctr.; soloist, guest condr. Am. Symphony, Detroit Symphony, Ohio Chamber Orch., N.W. Chamber Orch., Mostly Mozart Festival; cons. NBC-News, Channel 4, 1985; condr. Handel: Acis Galatea, Semele, Alcina, Giulio Cesare, Eccles: The Judgment of Paris. Contbr. ; musician: (recordings) Bach's Gamba-Harpsichord Sonatas, Scarlatti Sonatas for Harpsichord, Bach Brandenburg Concerti, Goldberg Variations, numerous soundtracks, recordings; editor: Three Centuries of Music in Score, 1990, Monteverdi: Tirsi e Clori, 1967. Recipient Record of the Yr. award for Cousins, Stereo Rev., 1977. Home: 425 Riverside Dr New York NY 10025 Office: Manhattan Sch of Music Music History Dept 120 Claremont Ave New York NY 10027

COOPER, KENNETH BANKS, business executive, former army officer; b. Ft. Leavenworth, Kans., Nov. 12, 1923; s. Avery John and Ona Carey (Gibson) C.; m. Virginia Leah Adkins, Dec. 29, 1979; children by previous marriage: Kenneth, Robert. BS, U.S. Mil. Acad., 1944; MS, MIT, 1951. Commd. 2nd lt. U.S. Army, 1944; advanced through grades to lt. gen., 1975; World War II svc. in S. Pacific, 1944-46; assigned to Manhattan Project-Armed Forces Spl. Weapon Project, N.Mex., Eniwetok, and Washington, 1946-48; mem. nuclear weapons staff AEC, Washington, 1951-55; nuclear weapons planning officer SHAPE, Paris, 1955-58; project mgr., ballistic missile def. rsch. Advanced Rsch. Projects Agy., Washington, 1959-63; bn. comdr. Korea, 1963-64; dir. Army Nuclear Power Program, 1965-66; with Def. Com. Planning Group, 1966-68; exec. to Sec. of Army, 1968-70; brigade comdr., 1970-71; dep. dir. civil works Office Chief of Engrs., Washington, 1971-72, asst. chief engrs., 1972-75; dep. comdr.-in-chief U.S. Army, Europe, Heidelberg, Germany, 1975-77; dep. adviser to Sec. of Def., 1977-78; ret., 1978; gen. mgr. Svc. and Constrn. Group ITT, Nutley, N.J., 1978-79; dep. asst. sec. def. for plans and resources Office Asst. Sec. Def. C3I, Washington, 1980-81; pres. SPC Internat., Arlington, Va., 1981-84; cons. BMD (Ballistic Missile Def., formerly SDI), Alexandria, Va., 1985-88, Inst. Def. Analysis, 1988-99. Decorated Legion of Merit (2), D.S.M. (2), D.D.S.M. Mem. Soc. Mil. Engrs, Army Navy Country Club.

COOPER, KENNETH CARLTON, training consultant; b. St. Louis, May 2, 1948; s. George Carlton and Mary Frances (Kavanaugh) C.; m. Susan Ann Bujnak, Sept. 6, 1969; children: Jeffrey Carlton, Daniel, Stephen, Mara Elizabeth. BS, U. Mo., Columbia, 1970, MS in Indsl. Engring., 1971. Registered profl. engr., Mo.; cert. adminstrv. mgr.; cert. speaking profl. Mktg. rep. IBM, St. Louis, 1971—76; account exec. Downtowner Newspaper, St. Louis, 1976; pres. CooperComm., Chesterfield, Mo., 1976—. Adj. faculty St. Louis U., 1972-73, Columbia Coll., 1976-79, Webster Coll., 1977-79; spkr. in field. Author: Nonverbal Communication for Business Success, 1979, Spanish edit., 1982; (with Lance Humble) The World's Greatest Blackjack Book, 1980; Body Business, 1981; Kroppsspråket, 1981; Always Bear Left, 1982; Stop It Now, 1985; Effective Competency Modeling and Reporting, 2000, The Relational Enterprise, 2002. Mem. United Meth. Ch. Roy P. Hart Scholar-Athlete grantee, 1970-71. Mem. ASTD. Republican. Office: 16457 Wilson Farm Dr Chesterfield MO 63005-4525

COOPER, KENNETH EDWARD, artist, art educator; b. Grand Rapids, Mich., Aug. 12, 1947; s. Kenneth Q. and Dorothy Mitchell Cooper; m. Ruth Ann Cline, Nov. 23, 1966. BS, Western Mich. U.; MA, Ctrl. Mich. U. Art instr. Manistee (Mich.) Area Pub. Schs., 1971—98; instr. and lectr. art workshops Coopworks, Manistee, 1998—. Artist-in-residence Lea Green Sch., Matlock, England, 1993. Exhibitions include Ball State U., Muncie, Ind., 1971, South Bend (Ind.) Regional Mus. of Art, 1974, West Shore C.C., Scottville, Mich., 1974, Grand Rapids Jr. Coll., 1974, Ctrl. Mich. U., 1976, Manistee County (Mich.) Hist. Mus., 1984, Jesse Besser Mus., Alpena, Mich., 1987, 1991, Dudley Mus. and Art Gallery, West Midlands, Eng., 1988, 1990, 1992, 1994, 1996, Con Foster Mus., Traverse City, Mich., 1990, Himley Hall, West Midlands, 1995, 1996, Saltwells Hall, 1995, Calke Abbey, Derbyshire, Eng., 1996, 2001, Grand Rapids Art Mus., 1996, Clumber Park, Nottinghamshire, Eng., 1998, Buxton Mus. and Art Gallery, Derbyshire, 1999, Mac-a-Cheek Castle, West Liberty, Ohio, 1999, Burton Constable, Yorkshire, Eng., 1999, Workman & Temple Homestead Mus., L.A., 2001, Canons Ashby Ho., Northamptonshire, Eng., 2001, Hardwick Hall, Derbyshire, 2001, Manistee (Mich.) Art Inst., 2003, Mary's City of David hist. site, Benton Harbor, Mich., 2003. Democrat. Avocations: gardening, mandolin. Office: Cooperworks 6754 Old US 31 Rt 1 Manistee MI 49660 E-mail: cooperworks@yahoo.com.

COOPER, KENNETH STANLEY, principal, educator, finance company executive; b. Oxford, N.C., May 17, 1948; s. Stephen and Helen (Norman) Cooper; m. Nancy Robinson, June 26, 1971; children: Danielle Jamilla, Janine Kandyce. AS, Miami Dade CC, 1971; BS in Criminal Justice, Fla. Internat. U., 1973, MS in Adult Edn., 1974; postgrad., Fla. Atlantic U., 1976, Ind. U., 1978. Police officer City of Miami (Fla.) Police Dept., 1971-72; tchr. Dade County Pub. Schs., Miami, 1974-76, 80-83, adminstr., asst. prin., 1983-89, prin. intern exec. tng. program, 1987-88, asst. prin., 1983-90; grad. asst. dept. social studies U. Ind., Bloomington, 1976-78; pres. Cooper Williamson Auto Brokerage, Miami, 1978-80; prin. Jan Mann Opportunity Sch., Miami, 1990-92, Robert Renick Ednl. Ctr., Opa Locka, Fla., 1992-96, Pine Villa Elem. Sch., Goulds, Fla., 1996-97, Mays Mid. Cmty. Sch., Goulds, 1997—; pres. Cooper Fin. Group, Inc., 1999—. Guest columnist: Miami Times, 1988; contbr. articles to profl. jours. Mem. United Tchrs. Dade County, Miami, 1974—76, 1980—83; sec. bd. dirs. Cmty. Crusade Against Drugs, Miami, 1995—96; organizer, activist Young Dems. S. Fla., 1967—68. With U.S. Army, 1969—70. Named Adminstr. of the Yr., Dade County Assn. Counseling and Devel., 1993. Mem.: NAACP. Home: 12840 SW 187th St Miami FL 33177-3000 Office: Arthur and Polly Mays Mid Cmty Sch 11700 SW 216th St Goulds FL 33170-2935 Personal E-mail: kscooper35@hotmail.com.

COOPER, KRISTINE MARIE, internist; b. Elgin, Ill., Mar. 9, 1970; d. Gary Lee and Carol Ann C. BA, Wartburg Coll., 1992; DO, U. Osteo. Medicine & Health Scis., 1996. Cert. Diplomate Am. Osteopathic Bd. Internal Medicine 2002. Intern, resident Genesys Regional Med. Ctr., Grand Blanc, Mich., 1996-99. Mem. Am. Osteopathic Assn., Am. Coll. Osteopathic Internists. Home: 322 Morris St Pewaukee WI 53072 Office: Profl IM Svcs Profl Office Bldg 3070 N 51st St Ste 501 Milwaukee WI 53210

COOPER, LAMAR EUGENE, SR., academic administrator, minister; b. New Orleans, Jan. 8, 1942; s. Irwin Nelson and Hazel Heughan Cooper; m. Barbara Ann Agent, Dec. 8, 1963; children: Lamar Jr., Stephen, Ruth Ann, Christopher David. BA, La. Coll., 1963; ThM, New Orleans Bapt. Theol. Sem., 1969, ThD, 1975. Tchr. grades 5 and 6 Jefferson Parish Schs., Gretna, La., 1963—67; pastor Clifton Bapt. Ch., Franklinton, La., 1971—74, First Bapt. Ch., Madisonville, Tex., 1974—78; prof. OT and Hebrew The Criswell Coll., Dallas, 1978—89, dean Grad. Sch., 1980—89, exec. v.p., provost, 1997—, acting pres., 2003—; dir. denominational rels. The Christian Life Commn., So. Bapt. Conv., Nashville, 1989—95; v.p. acad. affairs Midwestern Bapt. Theol. Sem., Kansas City, Mo., 1995—97. Lectr. Ministry Sci. Russian Fedn., Obninsk, Russia, 1993—94. Author: New American Commentary, Vo. 17, 1994; contbr. articles to profl. jours. Mem. Rep. Nat. Com., 2000—. Mem.: Inst. Bibl. Rsch., Evang. Theol. Soc., Alpha Chi, Eta Sigma Phi (pres. 1962—63). Republican. Baptist. Home: 1693 Yellowstone Ave Lewisville TX 75077 Office: The Criswell College 4010 Gaston Ave Dallas TX 75246

COOPER, LARRY S. carpet industry consultant; b. Bklyn., June 14, 1957; s. Jack and Evelyn (Weinfeld) C.; m. Tryna Lee Giordano, Dec. 31, 1975; children: Jonathan, Jennifer, Jillian. Student, U. Colo., 1975-78. Cert. master cleaner, sr. level carpet insp. Inst. of Inspection, Cleaning and Restoration. Owner Cooper's Carpet Cleaners, Boulder, Colo., 1975-79; pres. Profl. Cleaning Network, Denver, 1979-97; owner Textiles Cons., Denver, 1986—, Textile Cleaners of Am. Inc., 2001—. Chmn. Broomfield (Colo.) Connection, 1988-90; mayor pro-tem City of Broomfield, 1988-99, mem. city coun., 1988-99. Named Cleanfax Man of Yr., Clean Fax Mag., 1990. Mem. Profl. Carpet and Upholstery Cleaners Assn. (pres. 1980-81, 84-86), Internat. Inst. of Carpet and Upholstery Cert. (v.p. 1984-85, pres. 1985-87, chmn. bd. dirs 1988, chmn. cert. bd. 1990-2002, chmn. water, mold, carpet and upholstery stds. coms. 2002--, hon. dir.). Avocations: snow-mobiling, fishing. Office: Textile Cons Inc PO Box 21373 Denver CO 80221-0373 E-mail: textilecon@aol.com.

COOPER, LAWRENCE ALLEN, lawyer; b. San Antonio, Feb. 1, 1948; s. Elmer E. and Sally (Tempkin) C.; 1 child, Jonathan Alexander. BA, Tulane U., 1970; JD, St. Mary's U., San Antonio, 1974; LLM, Emory U., 1980. Bar: Ga. 1975, Tex. 1975. Atty. pvt. practice, Atlanta, 1975—. Arbitrator Fulton Superior Ct.; mem. Ga. Bar fee dispute com. Mem. ABA, ATLA, Atlanta Bar Assn., Ga. Trial Lawyers Assn., Ga. Bar Assn., Tex. Bar Assn.. Office: Cohen Cooper & Estep LLC Ste 2220 3350 Riverwood Pkwy Atlanta GA 30339 Home: Unit 613 1735 Peachtree St NE Atlanta GA 30309-7028 E-mail: lacooperatty@mindspring.com.

COOPER, LEON N. physicist, educator; b. N.Y.C., Feb. 28, 1930; s. Irving and Anna (Zola) Cooper; m. Kay Anne Allard, May 18, 1969; children: Kathleen Ann, Coralie Lauren. AB, Columbia U., 1951, AM, 1953, PhD, 1954, DSc (hon.), 1973, U. Sussex, Eng., 1973, U. Ill., 1974, Brown U., 1974, Gustavus Adolphus Coll., 1975, Ohio State U., 1976, U. Pierre et Marie Curie, Paris, 1977. NSF postdoctoral fellow, mem. Inst. for Advanced Study, 1954—55; rsch. assoc. U. Ill., 1955—57; asst. prof. Ohio State U., 1957—58; assoc. prof. Brown U., Providence, 1958—62, prof., 1962—66, Henry Ledyard Goddard U. prof., 1966—74, Thomas J. Watson Sr. prof. sci., 1974—; dir. brain sci. program Inst. for Brain and Neural Sys., Providence, 1978—91; dir. Inst. for Brain and Neural Systems Brown U., Providence, 1991—. Lectr. pub. lectrs., internat. confs. and symposia; vis. prof. various univs. and summer schs.; cons. indsl., ednl. orgns.; sponsor Fedn. Am Scientists; mem. Def. Sci. Bd., 1989—93; co-chair Nester Inc.; assoc. Neurosci. Rsch. Program. Author: Introduction to the Meaning and Structure of Physics, 1968, Structure and Meaning, 1992, How We Learn, How We Remember: Toward an Understanding of Brain and Neural Systems, 1995; contbr. articles to profl. jours. Recipient Nobel prize (with J. Bardeen and J.R. Schrieffer), 1972, award of Excellence, Grad. Faculties Alumni of Columbia U., 1974, Descartes medal, Acad. de Paris, U. Rene Descartes, 1976, John Jay award, Columbia Coll., 1985, award for Disting. Achievement, Columbia U., 1990, Alexander Hamilton award, Columbia Coll., 1995; fellow Alfred P. Sloan Found. rsch., 1959—66, John Simon Guggenheim Meml., 1965—66. Fellow: AAAS, Am. Acad. Arts and Scis., Am. Phys. Soc.; mem.: NAS (Comstock prize with J.R. Schrieffer 1968), Internat. Neural Network Soc., Soc. Neurosci., Am. Philos. Soc., Sigma Xi, Phi Beta Kappa. Office: Brown U Box 1843 Dept Physics and Neurosci Providence RI 02912-1843

COOPER, LOUIS ZUCKER, pediatrician, educator; b. Albany, Ga., Dec. 25, 1931; s. Jacob Harrison and Cecile (Berman) C. BS, Yale U., 1954, MD, 1957. Intern in medicine Mass. Meml. Hosp., Boston, 1957-58; jr. asst. resident in medicine Boston VA Hosp., 1958 59; fellow in medicine (infectious disease) Tufts-New England Med. Ctr., Boston, 1961-64; from instr. to assoc. prof. Sch. Medicine, NYU, N.Y.C., 1964-73; prof. pediat. Coll. Physicians and Surgeons, Columbia U., N.Y.C., 1973—; dir. pediat. Roosevelt Hosp., N.Y.C., 1973-81, St. Luke's-Roosevelt Hosp. Ctr., N.Y.C., 1981—. Pres. Am. Acad. Pediatrics, 2001—. Capt. USAF, 1959-61. Office: St Luke's-Roosevelt Hosp 1000 10th Ave New York NY 10019-1192

COOPER, LYNDA SHEPARD, music educator; b. Savannah, Ga., May 31, 1956; d. Louis Harvey and Mary Clifford (Sherrod) Shepard; m. Dennis Clair Cooper. Piano, voice, Armstrong State Coll., 1974-79. Instr. music, Savannah, 1983—. Mem. Ga. Music Tchrs. Assn. (hospitality com., cert. instr.). Republican. Baptist. Avocations: landscaping, interior designing. Home: 111 W Welwood Dr Savannah GA 31419-2909

COOPER, LYNN DALE, retired minister, retired navy chaplain; b. Aberdeen, Wash., Aug. 11, 1932; s. Lindsay Monroe and Mattie Ann (Cattron) Cooper; m. Doris Marlene Aydelott, June 2, 1956; children: Kevin Dale, Kathy Cooper O'Briant, Karen Cooper Holton. Student, Gray's Harbor Coll., 1950-51; BTh, Northwest Christian Coll., 1955; MDiv, Phillips U., 1961, D Ministry, 1977. Ordained to ministry Christian Ch., 1954. Commd lt. (j.g.) USN, 1965, advanced through grades to comdr., 1988, ret., 1988; assoc. pastor First Christian Ch., Olympia, Wash., 1955-57, min. Aline, Okla., 1957-61, Sumner, Wash., 1961-66; chaplain U.S. Navy, 1966-88; min. Cen. Christian Ch., Prosser, Wash., 1988-97. Bd. dirs. Jubilee Ministries, Prosser, Wash., 1988-96. Recipient many Navy and Marine Corps awards and medals; decorated Bronze Star medal. Mem. Mil. Chaplains Assn. U.S.A. (life), Disciples of Christ Hist. Soc. (life), Navy League of U.S. (life), Mil. Officers Assn. (life), Kiwanis (past pres. Prosser, Wash. chpt.), De Molay (past master councillor 1950—). Avocations: hiking, snowshoeing, kayaking. Home: 1818 Benson Ave Prosser WA 99350-1547

COOPER, MARC LAWRENCE, food products company executive; b. Brookline, Mass., Mar. 10, 1945; s. Samuel I. and Elizabeth (Handlin) C.; m. Susan Rachel Lewis, July 9, 1947; children: Seth Lewis, Amanda Lewis. BSEE, U. Pa., 1966, MBA, 1968. Prodn. control mgr. equipment divsn. Raytheon

Corp., Waltham, Mass., 1968-73, mfg. planning and forecasting mgr., 1973-75, mgr. mfg. programs, 1975-78; dir. fin. and adminstrn. radiology dept. Mass. Gen. Hosp., Boston, 1978-83; pres., gen. mgr. Samarc, Inc. (doing bus. as Herrell's MicroCreamery), Watertown, Mass., 1983—. Contbr. articles to profl. publs. Chmn. U. Pa. Brookline Secondary Sch. Com., 1976-96; co-founder, bd. dirs. Brookline Civic Assn., 1988—; mem. town meeting Town of Brookline, 1984—, mem. fin. com., 1986-88; pres. U. Pa. Club of Boston, 1974-75; bd. dirs. Temple Sinai, 1994—, treas., 1994-2000, pres., 2000-03; chmn. Allston Village Main Sts. Com., 1995-99; bd. dirs. Allston Bd. of Trade, 1990—, 2d v.p., 1996-99, pres., 1999-2001. Recipient Best of Boston award for ice cream Boston Mag., 1983, 85, 88, 90, 91, 93, 94, 96, 99, 2001, 02, Disting. Svc. award Temple Sinai, 1999, Unsung Hero award Allston-Brighton Healthy Boston Coalition, 2001. Mem. IEEE, Jimmy Fund Bus. Buddies (pres. 1990-91, Bus. Buddy award 1992). Democrat. Jewish. Avocations: theater, family, travel. Home: 165 Winthrop Rd Brookline MA 02445-4442 Office: Samarc Inc 128 Arlington St Watertown MA 02472 E-mail: marc.l.cooper@verizon.net.

COOPER, MARK FREDERICK, artist, sculptor, art educator; b. Evansville, Ind., Oct. 5, 1950; s. I. Phillip and J. Janice (Crystal) C.; m. Danette English, Aug. 22, 1987; children: Alexandra Carrey, Jack English. BS, Ind. U., 1972; MFA, Tufts U., 1980. Asst. prof. art Boston Coll., Chestnut Hill, Mass., 1978—; mem. permanent faculty Sch. Mus. Fine Arts, Boston, 1978—. One-man shows include Howard Yezerski Gallery, Boston, 1990, 1995, 1999, New England Bio-Tech Gallery, 1990—91, Ctr. St. Studio Gallery, Boston, 1995, NAO Project Gallery, 2002, NAU Project Gallery, Boston, 2002, Miller-Geisler Gallery, NYC, 2003, exhibited in group shows at Northwest Mo. State U., Maryville, 1996, Bernard Toale Gallery, Boston, 1996, U. Hawaii, Honolulu, 1996, Cambridge Mulicultural Arts Ctr., 1996, 1999, Baum Fine Arts Galleries, U. Ctrl. Ark., Conway, 1997, Whitney Mus. Am. Art, 2000, Davis Mus., 2000, Peabody Essex Mus., 2000, New Bedford Mus., 2002, Butler Inst. Am. Art, 2002, Attelboro Mus., 2002, Mus. Fine Arts, Boston, 2002—03, others; artist (mus. exhbns.) Inst. Contemporary Art, Boston, 1994, Fuller Mus., Brockton, Mass., 1994, Kuntsmuseum, Cologne, Germany, 1992, 1996, Capital Children's Mus., Washington, 1995, 1996, Corcoran Mus. Art, 1995, N.D. Mus. Art, Grand Forks, 1996, Revolving Mus., Boston, 1997, Newhouse Ctr. Gallery, Snug Harbor Cultural Ctr., 2000, numerous others, (commns. include) First Night Boston, 1992—94, House of Blues Corp., 1994, Lyons Group, 1995, Cambridge Hosp., 2000, Pracies Pharmaceutical, 2001. Dir. Project Against Violence, Boston, Washington, N.Y.C., 1991—; bd. dirs. Creativity in the 21st Century. Grantee Ruth Mott Fund, 1995-96, Cafritz Found., 1994, NEA, 1993; recipient pub. svc. award Mayor of Boston, 1995; fellowship Open Soc. Inst., 1998-00, Mass Cultural Coun. sculpture award, 1999. Home: 52 Saint James Ave Somerville MA 02144-2930 Office: c/o Miller Geisler Gallery New York NY 10001

COOPER, MARY CAMPBELL, information services executive; b. Meadville, Pa., Aug. 14, 1940; d. Paul F. and Margaret (Webb) Campbell; m. James Nicoll Cooper, June 8, 1963; children: Alix, Jenny. BA, Mt. Holyoke Coll., 1961; MLS, Simmons Coll., 1963; MEd, Harvard U., 1965. Cert. museum adminstrn. With Harvard U. Libr., Cambridge, Mass., 1961-63, Carleton U. Libr., Ottawa, Can., 1965-85; archive cons. U.S., Can., 1985-86; info. mgr. Haley & Aldrich Inc., Cambridge, 1986-88, Tsoi/Kobus & Assocs., Cambridge, 1988-90; pres., founder Cooper Info., Cambridge, 1990—. Bd. dirs. Mass. Com. for Preservation of Archtl. Records, Boston. Author: Records in Architectural Offices, 1992, Records and Information Management: Meeting the Challenge, 1994, Records and Information Management: Order Out of Chaos, 1996. Bd. dirs. Berkshire Hist. Soc., Pitts., Mass. Travel grantee Nat. Hist. Pub. Records Commn., 1991. Mem. Spl. Librs. Assn., Am. Mus. Assn., Assn. Ind. Info. Profls., Assn. Moving Image Archivists, Assn. Records Mgrs. and Adminstrs. (nat. com. 1991—). Avocations: travel, tennis, swimming. Home and Office: 5 Ellery Pl Cambridge MA 02138-4200

COOPER, MARY LITTLE, federal judge, former banking commissioner; b. Fond du Lac, Wis., Aug. 13, 1946; d. Ashley Jewell and Gertrude (McCoy) Little. AB in Polit. Sci. cum laude, Bryn Mawr Coll., 1968; JD, Villanova U., 1972; LLD (hon.), Georgian Ct. Coll., 1987. Bar. N.J. 1972. Assoc. McCarter & English, Newark, 1972-80, ptnr., 1980-84; commr. N.J. Dept. Banking, Trenton, 1984-90; assoc. gen. counsel Prudential Property & Casualty Ins. Co., Holmdel, N.J., 1991-92; judge U.S. Dist. Ct. N.J., 1992—. Chmn. bd. Pinelands Devel. Credt Bank. Bd. trustees Exec. Commn. Ethical Standards, Trenton, 1984-90, Corp. Bus. Assistance, Trenton, 1984-91, N.J. Housing & Mortgage Fin. Agy., Trenton, 1984-90, N.J. Cemetery Bd. Assn., 1984-90, N.J. Hist. Soc., 1976-79., YMCA of Greater Newark, 1973-76; mem. Supreme Ct. N.J. Civil Practice Com., 1982-84, Supreme Ct. N.J. Dist. Ethics Com., 1982-84. Fellow Am. Bar Found.; mem. ABA, N.J. Bar Assn., Princeton Bar Assn., John J. Gibbons Am. Inn of Ct. Office: US Courthouse 402 E State St Ste 5000 Trenton NJ 08608-1507*

COOPER, MATTHEW MARC, cardiothoracic surgeon; b. Yonkers, N.Y., Jan. 6, 1957; s. Leon M. and Ida C.; m. Nina Irene Germaniuk, Aug. 25, 1985. BA in Math. and Biology magna cum laude, Franklin and Marshall Coll., 1979; MD with honors, NYU, 1983; student, Harvard U., 1997. Diplomate Am. Bd. Thoracic Surgery, Am. Bd. Surgery; cert. Nat. Bd. Med. Examiners. Surg. house officer numerous N.Y.C. Hosps., 1983—85; med. staff fellow surgery br. Nat. Heart, Lung, Blood Inst. NIH, Bethesda, Md., 1985—87; chief and sr. resident U. Iowa Hosps. and Clinics Iowa City (Iowa) VA Med. Ctr., 1987—89; chief resident and resident cardiothoracic surgery Columbia-Presbyn. Med. Ctr., Babies Hosp., N.Y.C., 1989—91; sr. registrar cardiothoracic surgery Hosp. for Sick Children, London, 1991—92; cardiothoracic surgeon various hosps., Las Vegas, 1994—, Peak Cardiovascular Surgery, Las Vegas, 1994—2001. Clin. asst. prof. dept. surgery U. Nev. Sch. Medicine, 1995—; chief cardiovasc. and thoracic surgery Mountain View Hosp., 1996-97, 1999, 2001—, chmn. dept. surgery, 1997—; vice chmn. dept. surgery Sunrise Hosp. and Med. Ctr., 1997-98, chief cardiovasc. and thoracic surgery, 1997-98, chmn. dept. surgery, 1999-2000; chmn. Las Vegas Cardiovasc. IPA, 1997; mem. med. adv. com., bd. dirs. Nev. Donor Network. Guest reviewer Annals Thoracic Surgery, 1992—, Jour. heart & Lung Transplantation; contbr. articles to profl. jours.; presenter in field. Mem. coun. on cardiothoracic and vascular surgery Am. Heart Assn., 1997—. Fellow ACS; mem. AMA, Internat. Soc. Cardiac Biol. Implants, Internat. Soc. Heart and Lung Transplantation, Andrew G. Morrow Soc. Cardiovasc. Surgeons (Traveling fellowship award 1988), The John Jones Surg. Soc., Soc. Thoracic Surgeons, Nev. State Med. Soc., Clark County Med. Assn., Wilderness Med. Soc., Phi Beta Kappa, Mu Upsilon Sigma. Republican. Jewish. Avocations: parrots, music-clarinet and saxophone, skiing, biking, scuba diving. Office: Peak Cardiovascular Surgery 7375 Peak Dr Las Vegas NV 89128 Fax: 702-367-3884. E-mail: cophud@aol.com.

COOPER, MAX DALE, pediatrician, researcher; b. Hazlehurst, Miss., Aug. 31, 1933; s. Ottis Noah and Lily (Carpenter) Cooper; m. Rosalie Lazzara, Feb. 6, 1960; children: Owen Bernard, Melinda Lee Cooper Holladay, Michael Kane, Christopher Byron. Student, Holmes Jr. Coll., 1951—52, U. Miss., 1952—54; postgrad., U. Miss. Med. Sch., 1954—55; MD, Tulane U., 1957. Diplomate Am. Bd. Pediat. Intern Saginaw (Mich.) Gen. Hosp., 1957—58; resident dept. pediat. Tulane Med. Sch., New Orleans, 1958—60; house officer Hosp. for Sick Children, London, 1960, rsch. asst. dept. neurophysiology, 1961; allergy fellow dept. pediat. U. Calif. Med. Ctr., San Francisco, 1961—62; instr. Tulane Med. Sch., New Orleans, 1962—63; med. fellow specialist U. Minn., Mpls., 1963—64, instr., 1964—66; asst. prof. dept. pediat. U. Ala., Birmingham, 1967—71, assoc. prof. dept. microbiology, 1967—71, dir. rsch. Rehab. Rsch. and Tng. Ctr., 1968—70, prof. dept. microbiology, 1971—, dir. Cell. Identification Lab., 1987—90, dir. Ctr. Interdisciplinary Rsch. in Immunological Diseases, 1987—95, dir. Divsn. Devel./Clin. Immunology, 1987—, prof. dept. medicine, 1987—, investigator Howard Hughes Med. Inst., 1988—. Sr. scientist Comprehensive Cancer Ctr., U. Ala., Birmingham, 1971—, Multipurpose Arthritis Ctr., Birmingham, 1979—, Cystic Fibrosis Rsch. Ctr., Birmingham, 1981—; dir. Cellular Immunobiology Unit of Tumor Inst. U. Ala., Birmingham, 1976—87; vis. scientist, tumor immunology unit, dept. zoology U. Coll. London, 1973—74, Inst. D'Embryologie Nogent-Sur-Marne and Inst. Pasteur, Paris, 1984—85. Co-author: Acute Hemiplegia in Childhood, 1962, Ontogeny of Immunity, 1967, Immunologic Incompetence, 1971, Immunodeficiency in Man and Animals, 1975, numerous others; editl. bd. Immunology Today, 1986, Immunodeficiency Revs., 1987—94, Clin. Immunology and Immunopathology, 1987—90, Internat. Immunology, 1988—, assoc. editor Jour. Immunology, 1972—76, 1977—79, Arthritis and Rheumatism, 1985—90, Jour. Clin. Immunology, 1979—83, co-editor Seminars in Immunopathology, 1988—91, editor Current Topics in Microbiology and Immunology, 1981—, contbr. 450 articles to profl. jours., —. Trustee Leukemia Soc. Am., 1983—88; faculty rsch. assoc. Am. Cancer Soc., 1966—71; bd. sci. advisors St. Jude Hosp., Memphis, 1981—84, 1991—, Becton-Dickinson Monoclonal Antibody Ctr., 1980—90; mem. med. adv. com. Immune Deficiency Found., 1981—99; bd. sci. counselors Nat. Cancer Inst., Bethesda, Md., 1982—86, Nat. Inst. Allergy and Infectious Diseases, 1978—82, 1990—95, Inst. Merieux, Lyons, France, 1985—90, Med. Biology Inst., La Jolla, Calif., 1986; mem. internat. sci. adv. bd. Basel (Switzerland) Inst. Immunology, 1987—91; mem NIH Immunobiology Study Sect., 1974—78. Recipient tchg. trainee award, Nat. TB Assn., 1962—63, Samuel J. Meltzer Founder's award, Soc. Exptl. Biology and Medicine, 1966, Life Scis. award, 3M, 1990, Sandoz prize for immunology, 1990, award for sci. leadership in immunology, Irvington Inst., 1999, award in clin. and diagnostic immunology, Am. Assn. Microbiologists/Abbott Labs., 2001; fellow postdoctoral rsch., USPHS, 1964—66. Mem.: AAUP, AAAS, NAS, Soc. Mucosal Immunology, Am. Acad. Arts and Scis., Inst. Medicine NAS, Am. Acad. Scis., Clin. Immunology Soc., Jefferson County Med. Assn., Ctrl. Soc. Clin. Rsch., So. Soc. Pediatric Rsch. (pres. 1975), Soc. Pediatric Rsch. (v.p. 1978), Soc. Francaise d'Immunologie (life Membre d'Honneur), Internat. Soc. Devel. and Comparative Immunology, Med. Assn. State Ala., Fedn. Am. Scientists, Am. Pediatric Soc., Am. Acad. Pediat., Am. Assn. Cancer Rsch., Am. Soc. Clin. Investigation, Am. Soc. Exptl. Pathology, Am. Assn. Microbiology (Abbot Labs. award in Clin. and Diagnostic Immunology 2001), Am. Assn. Immunologists (pres. 1988—89, councilor 1983—86, chmn. membership com. 1974—77, Lifetime Achievement award 2000), Sigma Xi, Alpha Omega Alpha. Achievements include research in developmental immunobiology with emphasis on B cell and T cell differentiation; clinical immunology with emphasis on immunodeficiency diseases and lyhmphoid malignancies. Office: Howard Hughes Med Inst U Ala Birmingham Birmingham AL 35294-0001

COOPER, MICHAEL ANTHONY, lawyer; b. Passaic, N.J., Mar. 29, 1936; BA, Harvard U., 1957, LL.B., 1960. Bar: N.Y. State 1961, U.S. Supreme Ct. 1969. With firm Sullivan & Cromwell, N.Y.C., 1960—, ptnr., 1968—2003, sr. counsel, 2004—. Pres. Legal Aid Soc., 1981-83, chair, pro bono net, 2000—. Co-chair Lawyers Com. for Civil Rights Under Law, 1993-95; bd. dirs. Equal Justice Works, Fund for Modern Cts., Vols. of Legal Svcs. Fellow: Am. Coll. Trial Lawyers (bd. regents 2000—, sec. 2002—03, treas. 2003—); mem.: ABA, Am. Judicature Soc., Am. Law Inst., Fed. Bar Coun. (trustee 1994—2000), Assn. Bar City N.Y. (chair exec. com. 1996—97, v.p. 1997—98, pres. 1998—2000), N.Y. State Bar Assn. Office: Sullivan & Cromwell 125 Broad St Fl 28 New York NY 10004-2489

COOPER, MICHAEL DAVID, information systems educator; b. L.A., Oct. 30, 1941; s. I. Earl and Bessie Cooper; m. Judith A. Baker. BA, UCLA, 1963; MS, U. So. Calif., L.A., 1965; PhD, U. Calif., Berkeley, 1971. Sys. engr. IBM Sweden, Stockholm, 1966-67; computer performance evaluation specialist U.S. Nat. Libr. of Medicine, Bethesda, Md., 1979; info. sys. cons. USIA, Washington, 1987-95; prof. Sch. Info. Mgmt. and Sys. U. Calif., Berkeley, 1971—. Cons. info. sys. Food and Agr. Orgn. of UN, 1998—. Mem. editl. bd. Jour. of Am. Soc. Info. Sci., 1995—; author: (monographs) Design of Library Automation Systems: File Structures, Data Structures and Tools, 1996, California's Demand for Librarians: Projecting Future Requirements, 1978, (with others) Library Human Resources: A Study of Supply and Demand, 1983; contbr. articles to profl. jours. U. Calif.-Berkeley doctoral fellow, 1968-71. Mem. Am. Soc. for Info. Sci., Assn. for Computing Machinery, Inst. for Ops. Rsch. and Mgmt. Sci. Avocations: backpacking, tennis, skiing, woodworking. Office: Univ of Calif Sch Info Mgmt and Sys 102 South Hall Berkeley CA 94720-4600

COOPER, MICHAEL R. dean; b. Bklyn., Mar. 8, 1946; s. Sam and Shirley (Boris) C.; m. Ruth Mines, Sept. 7, 1969; children: Carolyn S., Jordan D. BA, Hofstra U, 1968; PhD, Ohio State U., 1972; grad. Owners and Pres. Mgmt. Program, Harvard U., 1999. Lic. psychologist, Mass.; diplomate Am. Bd. Adminstrv. Psychology. Sr. ptnr. The Hay Group, Phila., Washington, 1980-89; pres. Hay Rsch. for Mgmt., 1985-89, Hay Strategic Mgmt. Assocs., 1987-89; also dir. Opinion Rsch. Corp., Princeton, N.J.; prin. Cooper Interests LLC, Princeton, 1998—; pres., CEO Tempest Software, Inc., N.Y.C., 2000; CEO Optimization Scis., San Francisco, 2001; dean Exec. Leadership Inst., Stevens Inst. Tech., Hoboken, NJ, 2002—. Bd. dirs. Xlibis, Patient Passport, Trade Web Srs., N.Y. Pvt. Placement Exch. Bd. trustees Mktg. Sci. Inst.; bd. dirs. European Info. Centre, Gordon Simmons Rsch. Group, Strategic Rsch. and Cons., Opinion Rsch. Corp.; mem. exec. bd. Sen. Evan Bayh, 1999-2000. Finalist, Entrepreneur of the Year, 1992; Eisenhower Commission: Consigned Full and Honorable Commission by President G. Ford, President R. Reagan and President G. Bush,1995. Mem. Am. Psychol. Soc., Psychologists in Mgmt. (bd. dirs. 1996-99). Office: Cooper Interests LLC 44 Coppervail Ct Princeton NJ 08540-7714

COOPER, MICHELE F. writer, editor, analyst; b. N.Y.C., Mar. 16, 1941; d. Philip I. and Helen (Davis) Delfin; children: Petrina, Jesse. BA, Queens Coll., 1962; MA, NYU, 1964; PhD, U.R.I., 1991. Exec. asst. prodn. World Publ. Co., N.Y.C., 1962-63; exec. asst. The Macmillan Co. Publ., N.Y.C., 1963-64; faculty Eng. dept. Queens Coll., Flushing, N.Y., 1964-79; free-lance writer, editor, 1968—; faculty Eng. dept. R.I. Sch. Design, Providence, 1976-80, Brown U. & R.I. Coll., 1982-88; sr. analyst and sr. editor Aquidneck Mgmt. Assocs., Middletown, R.I., 1988—; editor Senior Times, Middletown, R.I., 1992-94. Part-time faculty mem. English dept. U.R.I., 1982-92; tech. writer McLaughlin Rsch. Corp., 1980-82; lectr. Cosmos, Amsterdam, 1978, Progressive League, London, 1978, URI Oceanography Sch., 1992, 93, 94, Jung Inst. R.I., 1982, U. Edn. Assn., 1984; artist resident Va. Ctr. for Creative Arts, Vt. Studio Ctr. Author: The Urban Reader, 1976, The Freshman Writer, 1979; founding editor The Newport Rev., 1979—, Crone's Nest: Wisdom of the Elderwoman, 1995—, Premier Poets Chapbook Series, 1996—, 4X4 The Newport Review, 2001—; contbr. articles to profl. jours., poems, fictions, essays. Adv. com. R.I. State Coun. Arts., writer-in-residence, 1983-87; mem. R.I. Gov.'s Art award com., 1979. Recipient 2d prize Galway Kinnell Poetry competition, 1999, Hon. Mention Sacramento Poetry Ctr. competition, 1st place Tall Grass Writers Guild Poetry competition, 2002, Hon. Mention Emily Dickinson award for poetry, 2003. Mem. Soc. Tech. Comm. Mem. Soc. Friends. Office: Aquidneck Mgmt Assocs 28 Jacome Way Middletown RI 02842-5679

COOPER, MILTON, real estate investment trust executive; b. N.Y.C., Mar. 15, 1929; s. Aaron and Fannie (Liebowitz) Cooper; m. Shirley Mandelker, Sept. 9, 1950; children: Clifford, David, Matthew, Todd. BBA, CCNY, 1949; LLB, Bklyn. Law Sch., 1952. Bar: N.Y. 1952. Ptnr. Jaffin, Schneider, Kimmel & Galpeer, N.Y.C., 1952-66, Galpeer & Cooper, N.Y.C., 1966-70; chmn. Kimco Realty Corp., New Hyde Park, N.Y., 1966—. Bd. dirs. Getty Realty Corp., Blue Ridge Real Estate Co. Trustee Mass. Mut. Corp. Investors, Mass. Mut. Participation Investors, Springfield. Mem. Nat. Assn. Real Estate Investment Trusts (chmn. bd. govs.). Office: Kimco Corp 3333 New Hyde Park Rd New Hyde Park NY 11042-1205 E-mail: mc@kimcorealty.com.

COOPER, N. LEE, lawyer; m. Joy Clark; children: Clark, Catherine. BS, U. Ala., 1963, LLB, 1964. Pvt. practice, Birmingham, Ala., 1966—; founder Maynard, Cooper & Gale, P.C., Birmingham. Vice chair U.S. Congl. Commn. on Structural Alternatives for the Fed. Cts. of Appeals; dir. Lawyers Com. for Civil Rights. Articles and Notes editor Ala. Law Rev., 1962-64. Nat. bd. dirs. U. Ala.; trustee Ala. Law Sch. Found.; bd. overseers Rand Inst. for Civil Jusice. 1st lt. U.S. Army, 1964-66, capt. USAR. Fellow Am. Bar Found.; mem. ABA (chair, litig. sect. 1985-86, sec. litig. sect. 1976-78, Birmingham bar del. to ho. of deps. 1979-80, Ala. del. to ho. of dels. 1980-89, mem. drafting com. on model rules of profl. conduct 1982-84, mem. com. on professionalism 1985-87, chair select com. on ho. of dels. 1989-90, chair ho. of dels. 1990-92, pres.-elect 1995-96, pres. 1996-97), Am. Judicature Soc. (dir.), Am. Bar Endowment (dir.), Am. Law Inst. (coun., advisor project on restatement of law governing lawyers), Ala. Bar Assn. (pres. young lawyers sect. 1974-75, Merit award 1976), Birmingham Bar Assn. (sec.-treas. 1972). Office: AmSouth Harbert Plz 1901 6th Ave N Ste 2400 Birmingham AL 35203-4604

COOPER, NANCY M. lawyer; b. Boulder, Colo., July 11, 1958; d. John Douglas and Betty Mae (Locke) McCullen; m. Neal David Cooper, July 29, 1984 (dec. Sept. 1998). BS in Pub. Adminstrn., U. Ariz., 1980; JD, Lewis and Clark Coll., 1995. Bar: Oreg. 1995. Juvenile probation officer Gila County, Globe, Ariz., 1980-82, State of Alaska, Anchorage, 1983-92; founding mem. Steinman, Cooper, Wiscarson, LLC, Portland, 1995—2001; atty. Bullivant Houser Bailey PC, Portland, 2001—. Contbr. articles to profl. jours. Mem. progress bd. City of Gresham, Oreg., 1999-2002. Mem. ABA, Oreg. State Bar Assn. (mem. legal ethics com. 1999-2001, chmn. 2001, mem. svcs. com. new lawyer divsn. 1995-99, family law sect. 1995-2001, litig. sect. 1995—, employment law sect. 1995—, chmn. spl. legal ethics commn. on disciplinary rules, 2001—), Multnomah County Bar Assn. (professionalsm com. 2000-2003), Gus Solomon Inns of Court. Office: 300 Pioneer Tower 888 SW Fifth Ave Portland OR 97204 E-mail: nancy.cooper@bullivant.com.

COOPER, NORTON J. (SKY COOPER), liquor, wine and food company executive; b. Phila., Aug. 16, 1931; s. Maurice J. and Elsie (Goldstein) C.; m. Kim Muller, July 7, 2001; children from previous marriage: John Amos, Rob. BA, Cornell U., 1953. With Charles Jacquin et Cie Inc., Phila., 1955—, pres., CEO, prin. owner, 1979—, Chambord et Cie, France, Doumen Canton Liquer Co. Ltd., Guandong, People's Republic of China, St Dalfour et Cie, Marmande, France; pres. Lost Horizons Wines Pty, Capetown, South Africa. Author: off-Broadway prodn. Ballad of Jazz Street, 1959. Served to 1st lt. AUS, 1953-55. Decorated Ordre de Chevalier de Provence. Mem. Confrerie des Chevalier, du Tastevin

COOPER, PATRICIA GORMAN, management consultant; b. Medford, Mass., Mar. 15, 1946; d. Joseph Arthur and Marguerite Isabel (Sullivan) Gorman; m. Peter Vincent Cooper, Sept. 18, 1971; 1 child, Jonathan Gregory. BS, Northeastern U., Boston, 1973; MBA, Boston Coll., 1977. Asst. fin. statistician Fed. Res. Bank of Boston, 1964-71; mgr. retirement plans Investment Cos. Services Corp., Boston, 1971-80; mgr. sales Keystone Distbrs. Inc., Boston, 1980-82, asst. v.p., 1982-83, v.p., 1983-86, v.p. ops., 1986-87; v.p. client services Keystone Investor Resource Ctr., Cambridge, Mass., 1987-95; v.p. investor svcs. Evergreen Svc. Co., Boston, 1996-99; prin. Cooper Consulting, Boston, 2000—. Lectr. Bentley Coll., Waltham, Mass.; panelist Nat. Investment Cos. Services Assn., Boston; panelist Investment Cos. Inst., Washington; bd. dirs. Dove, Inc., Milton, Mass., Transition House, Cambridge, Mass.

COOPER, PAUL, retired mechanical engineer, research director; b. Mt. Holly, N.J., May 21, 1934; s. Frederick and Katherine Lena (Sixt) C.; m. Therese Adams, Apr. 11, 1959; children: Margaret Mary, Gregory, Timothy Richard, Peter Dunstan. BSME, Drexel U., 1957; MSME, MIT, 1959; PhD in Engring., Case Western Res. U., 1972. Registered profl. engr., Ohio. Rsch. asst. MIT, Cambridge, 1957-59; instr. Case Western Res. U., Cleve., 1968, 72; fluids engring. specialist TRW Inc., Cleve., 1959-77; rschr., sr. staff Ingersoll-Rand Rsch., Inc., Princeton, N.J., 1977-85; dir. hydraulic tech. Ingersoll-Rand Co., Phillipsburg, N.J., 1986-87, dir. R & D Pump Group, 1987-92; dir. advanced tech. Ingersoll-Dresser Pump Co., Phillipsburg, N.J., 1992-99. Mem. adv. bd. Internat. Pump Symposium, Tex. A&M U., 1983-99; bd. dirs. R&D Coun. N.J., 1987-92. Co-editor: Pump Hanbook, 3d edit., 2001; contbr. articles to profl. jours. Recipient George Stephenson Rsch. prize Instn. of Mech. Engrs., London, 1984. Fellow ASME (exec. com. fluids engring. divsn. 1982-87, fluid machinery design award 1992, Henry R. Worthington medal 1993, Robert Henry Thurston lectr. 1995, Fluids Engring. award 2002); mem. Soc. Petroleum Engrs., Sigma Xi, Pi Tau Sigma, Tau Beta Pi. Episcopalian. Achievements include patents relating to aircraft fuel pumps and commerical industrial pumps. Home: 415 Pennington Titusville Rd Titusville NJ 08560-2012 E-mail: paul.cooper1@att.net.

COOPER, PAUL DOUGLAS, lawyer; b. Kansas City, Mo., July 22, 1941; s. W.W. and Emma Marie (Ringo) C.; m. Elsa B. Shaw, June 15, 1963 (div. 1991); children: Richard, Dean; m. Kay J. Rice, Aug. 30, 1992; 1 child, Natanya. BA in English, U. Mich., 1963; LLB, U. Calif., 1966. Bar: Colo. 1966, U.S. Dist. Ct. Colo. 1966, U.S. Ct. Appeals (10th cir.) 1967, U.S. Supreme Ct. 1979. Dep. dist. atty., Denver, 1969-71; asst. U.S. atty. Dist. of Colo., 1971-73; ptnr. Yegge, Hall & Evans, Denver, 1973-80; pres., dir. Cooper & Kelley PC, Denver, 1980-94, Cooper & Clough PC, Denver, 1994—. Faculty trial practice seminar Denver U. Law Sch., 1982; spl. asst. U.S. atty. Dist. of Colo., 1973-75; spl. prosecutor Mar. 1977 term, Garfield County Grand Jury; pres. Bow Mar Owners, Inc., 1976-77; mem. English adv. bd. U. Mich., 2000—. Mem. English adv. bd. Univ. Mich., 2000—. Recipient Spl. Commendation award for outstanding svc., 1972. Mem. ABA, Am. Bd. Trial Advocates, Colo. Bar Assn. (interprofl. com., bd. govs.), Denver Bar Assn. (trustee, 1st v.p. 1982-83), Colo. Med. Soc. (chmn. interprofl. com., Denver bar liaison com), Internat. Assn. Def. Counsel (exec. com. 1989-92). Republican. Home: 11571 Eliot Ct Westminster CO 80234-1665 Office: 1512 Larimer St Ste 600 Denver CO 80202-1610 E-mail: pcooper@cooper-clough.com.

COOPER, PAULA, art dealer; b. Mass., Mar. 14, 1938; Student, Pierce Coll., Athens, Greece, Sorbonne, Paris, Goucher Coll., Inst. Fine Arts, NYU; DFA (hon.), R.I. Sch. Design, 1995. Asst. World House Galleries, N.Y.C., 1959-61; pvt. dealer, 1962-63; with Paula Johnson Gallery, N.Y.C., 1964-65; dir. Park Place Gallery, N.Y.C., 1965-67, Paula Cooper Gallery, N.Y.C., 1968—. Chmn. bd. dirs. Kitchen Ctr., N.Y.C., 1985-95. Named honoree, N.Y. Studio Sch., 2001; recipient Art Table award for disting. svc. to the visual arts, 2001. Mem.: Art Dealers Assn. Am. (bd. dirs. 1982—86, 1988—90, 1997—2000, v.p. bd. dirs. 1997—2000), Art Students League. Office: Paula Cooper Gallery 534 W 21st St New York NY 10011-2812

COOPER, PEGGY (MARY MARGARET), artist, educator, poet, composer, choreographer; b. Huntington, W.Va., Sept. 30, 1941; d. James Edwin and Lois Lucille (Sweeney) Hedger; m. Ralph Harold Gebhard, June 9, 1962 (div. July 1981); children: Stephan Marc, Timothy Michael, Peter Thomas, Christopher Todd; m. Earl Lee Cooper, Apr. 1, 1983. Student, Hamline U., St. Paul, 1960-63; BA cum laude, Drew U., Madison, N.J., 1965; MA, Pacific Oaks Coll., Pasadena, 1991; Waldorf Tchr. Cert., Antioch New Eng. Grad. Sch., 1996. Founding tchr. Creative Arts Workshop, Ill., 1968-75; artistic dir. Comedia Dance Co., 1968—84; artist-in-residence Colo. Coun. on Arts and Humanities, 1976-77; founding tchr. Holly/Lamar Sch. of the Arts, Colo., 1978-81; arts dir. Tom Sawyer, Pasadena, 1988-90; tutor Pasadena City Coll., 1984-90; founding tchr. Children's Garden, Madison, Wis., 1991—. Area coord. Joseph Chilton Pearce, So. Calif., 1986-91 Artist paintings: Goddess series, 1987 (gallery award), Eternal Madonna, 1988; composer children's opera: Luminous Pearl, 2000; composer, poet: Singing the Spiral, 2001; poet, illustrator: Colors are Children of the Sun, 2002. Audition com. Colo. Coun. on Arts and Humanities, Denver, 1978-80; vol. asst. Richards Inst. Ednl. Rsch., 1985-90; adv. bd. Chgo. Indian Village, 1972-75; gray lady ARC, 1958-70; vol. Children's Theater of Madison, 1993—, Elvhjem Mus. Art, 2000—; singer Madison Symphony Chorus, 1994—, Winds of So. Wis., 1998—; presenter Children's Mus. Peace Day, 1996-99; spkr., writer Waldorf Without Walls, 1996—; bd. dirs., singer Madison Chamber Choir, 1992—; singer, dancer Madison Early Music Festival, 2000—, Isthmus Vocal Ensemble, 2003—; mentor Oak Song Sch., Madison, Three Rivers Sch., La Cross, 2001-. Richards Inst. scholar, 1986, Pasadena Art Club scholar, 1988, Pasadena City Coll. scholar, 1988, recipient choral arts award, 1989; named Outstanding Young Woman, Colo., 1979. Democrat. Methodist. Avocations: gourmet cooking, gardening, felting, marionette craft, storytelling. Home and Office: 405 Stang St Madison WI 53704

COOPER, R. JOHN, III, lawyer; b. East Orange, N.J., Mar. 2, 1942; s. Russell John and Cynthia Rhe (Runser) C.; m. Unni Irene Langaanes, June 20, 1964; children: Kirsten Elizabeth, R. John IV. AB, Amherst Coll., 1964; postgrad., U. Oslo, 1965; JD, Harvard U., 1968. Chief law clk. Supreme Jud. Ct. Mass., Boston, 1968-69; assoc. Cravath, Swaine & Moore, N.Y.C., 1969-77; ptnr. Casey Lane & Mittendorf, N.Y.C., 1977-82; gen. counsel video group Time Inc., N.Y.C., 1982-84; exec. v.p., gen. counsel, sec. Young & Rubicam, Inc., N.Y.C., 1984-94, also bd. dirs.; of counsel Hogan & Hartson, LLC, N.Y.C., 1995-2000; exec. v.p., gen. counsel, mng. dir. N.Am. hdqrs. Havas S.A., Paris, 2000—. Bd. dirs. Dentsu Young & Rubicam Partnerships, N.Y.C., Tokyo, DWD, Tokyo, Y&R Sovero, Moscow. Editor: Cablespeech, 1983 Vestry Christ Ch., Short Hills, N.J., 1978-82, 1999-2002, lay min., 1980—; trustee N.J. Shakespeare Fest, 1986; chmn. Millburn-Short Hills Cable TV Com., 1986-94;

prof. Salzburg Seminars, Austria, 1986; pres. Juniper Point Village Improvement Soc., Boothbay Harbor, Maine, 1997-99. Amherst Coll. fellow, Oslo, Norway, 1964-65 Mem. ABA (governing com., forum com. on sports and entertainment industries 1983-86), Assn. Bar City N.Y. (mem. antitrust and trade regulation com. 1982-84, corp. law depts. com. 1986-92), Am. Assn. Advt. Agys. (govt. rels. com. 1986-94), Short Hills (N.J.) Club, Boothbay Harbor Yacht Club (Maine), Harvard Club. Republican. Episcopalian. Home: 9 East Ln Short Hills NJ 07078-3202 Office: Havas N Am Hdqtrs 430 Mountain Ave New Providence NJ 07974-2732

COOPER, REBECCA, art dealer; b. Phila., July 11, 1947; d. Frank N. Cooper and Bernice Silverstein; m. Michael J. Waldman, June 27, 1982. BA, MA, NYU; postgrad. Cert. appraiser. Owner Gallery Rebecca Cooper, Washington; pres. Rebecca Cooper Fine Art, N.Y.C., 1980s-90s. Hon. chairperson N.Y. Women Bus. Owners Art Roundtable, 1981; lectr. Resources Coun., 1983, N.Y. Mayor's com. on interior design and furnishings, 1983; sec. bd. assocs. Am. Craft Mus., lectr. Collectors Circle; nat. patron Am. Fed. Art., Ind. Curators Inc. Patron, Mus. Modern Art; benefactor New Mus. Dirs. Forum; exhbn. mem. dirs. coun. Whitney Mus.; art tours, cons. Mem. Am. Appraisers Assn. (assoc.), Dame de la Chaine des Rotisseurs, Women's 008 Investment Club, Pvt. Art Dealers Assn., Nat. Arts Club, Lotos Club, Guggenheim Mus. (internat. cir.).

COOPER, REGINALD RUDYARD, orthopedic surgeon, educator; b. Elkins, W.Va., Jan. 6, 1932; s. Eston H. and Kathryn (Wyatt) C.; m. Jacqueline Smith, Aug. 22, 1954; children: Pamela Ann, Douglas Mark, Christopher Scott, Jeffrey Michael. BA with honors, W.Va. U., 1952, BS, 1953, MD, Med. Coll. Va., 1955, MS, U. Iowa, 1960. Diplomate Am. Bd. Orthopedic Surgeons (examiner 1968-70). Orthopedic surgeon U.S. Naval Hosp., Pensacola, Fla., 1960-62; assoc. in orthopedics U. Iowa Coll. Medicine, Iowa City, 1962-65, asst. prof. orthopedics, 1965-68, assoc. prof. orthopedics, 1968-71, prof. orthopedics, 1971—, chmn. orthopedics, 1973-99. Rsch. fellow orthopedic surgery Johns Hopkins Hosp., Balt., 1964-65; exch. fellow to Britain for Am. Orthopedic Assn., 1969. Trustee Jour. Bone and Joint Surgeons, 1989-94, chmn. 1993-94. Trustee Nat. Easter Seals Rsch. Found., 1977-81, chmn., 1979-81. Served to lt. comdr. USNR, 1960-62. Mem. Iowa, Johnson County Med. Socs., Orthopedic Rsch. Soc. (sec.-treas. 1970-73, pres. 1974-75), Am. Acad. Orthopedic Surgeons (Kappa Delta award for outstanding rsch. in orthopedics 1971), Can. Orthopedic Assn., Am. Orthopedic Assn., N.Y. Acad. Sci., Assn. Bone and Joint Surgeons, AMA, Am. Rheumatism Assn., Am. Acad. Cerebral Palsy, Am. Acad. Orthopedic Surgeons (chmn. exams. com. 1978-82, sec. 1982, 2d v.p. 1985-86, 1st v.p. 1986-87, pres. 1987-88, ortho residency rev. com. 1989-95, chmn. 1993-95). Home: 201 Ridgeview Ave Iowa City IA 52246-1625 Office: U Iowa Hosps & Clinics 450 Newton Rd Iowa City IA 52242

COOPER, REID FRANKLIN, geoscience and materials science educator; b. Washington, Oct. 3, 1955; s. Franklin Dero and Mildred (Pivetz) C.; m. Martha Kay Doane, July 10, 1982; children: Matthew, Catherine. BS in Civil Engring., George Washington U., 1977; PhD in Materials Sci. and Engring., Cornell U., 1983. Sr. rsch. scientist Corning (N.Y.) Glass Works (now Corning, Inc.), 1983-85; prof. materials sci. and engring., geophysics U. Wis., Madison, 1986—2003; prof. geol. scis. Brown U., Providence, 2003—. Vis. prof. divsn. geol. and planetary scis. Calif. Inst. Tech., 1994. Contbr. over 90 articles to profl. jours. Pres. coun. Advent Luth. Ch., Madison, 2000-2001. Faculty rsch. fellow U. Wis., 1994-2000; recipient Presdl. Young Investigator award NSF, 1987-92. Fellow Mineralogical Soc. Am.; mem. Am. Ceramic Soc. (assoc. editor Jour. Am. Ceramic Soc. 1999—), Am. Geophys. Union (chair physical properties of earth materials com. 2001—), AAAS, Materials Rsch. Soc. Office: Brown U Box 1846 Providence RI 02912

COOPER, RICHARD ALAN, lawyer; b. Hattiesburg, Miss., July 19, 1953; s. H. Douglas and Elaine (Reece) C. BA, BS, U. Ark., Little Rock, 1976; JD, Washington U., St. Louis, 1979. Bar: Mo. 1979, Ill. 1980, U.S. Dist. Ct. (ea. dist.) Mo. 1980, U.S. Dist Ct. (so. dist.) Ill. 1988. Law clk. U.S. Dist. Ct., St. Louis, 1979-80; assoc. William R. Gartenberg, St. Louis, 1980-81, Danis, Reid, Murphy, Tobben & Cooper, St. Louis, 1983-87, ptnr., 1987-88, Law Office Terry Sharp, P.C., 1988-89; pvt. practice, 1989-90, 1999—; ptnr. Davnis & Boyce, 1990—93, Davnis, Cooper, Cavanagh & Hartweger, LC, 1994—98, CFO MedCard Am., Inc., 1997-99. Liaison to Washington U. Sch. Law, Mo. Assn. Trial Attys., St. Louis, 1983-85; presenter in field. Bus. mgr. Urban Law Jour., 1978-79; editor Bankruptcy Law Reporter, 1983-88, co-mgr., editor, 1984-88; co-author seminars including Debt Collection from Start to Finish in Mo., Planning for the Newly Married Couple, Collection Practice in Missouri from Start to Finish, Impact of Bankruptcy on Family Law, Advanced Consumer Bankruptcy and Fair Debt Collection Practices, Collecting Judgments and Non UCC Liens, Advanced Consumer Bankruptcy; author: supplement to Missouri Desk Book Civil Procedure, 2000; contbg. author: Missouri CLE Deskbook Civil Procedure on Rule 76, Executions.. Recipient Milton F. Napier trial award Lawyers Assn. St. Louis, 1979, Outstanding Sr. Bus. Major award Wall St. Jour., 1976. Mem. Mo. Bar Assn., Boulder Yacht Club (commodore 1998-99), Commonwealth Yacht Club. Avocation: sailing. Office: Law Offices Richard Alan Cooper 2379 Cedar Dale Ct Maryland Heights MO 63043 E-mail: richard@richardalancooperattorney.com.

COOPER, RICHARD ALAN, hematologist, college dean, health policy analyst; b. Milw., Sept. 23, 1936; s. Peter and Annabelle (Schlomovitz) C.; m. Jaclyn Koppel, June 22, 1958 (dec.); children: Stephanie, Jonathan; m. Andrea Pastor, Aug. 20, 1988. BS, U. Wis., 1958; MD, Washington U., St. Louis, 1961. Intern Harvard U. med. svcs. Boston City Hosp., 1961-63, resident in medicine, 1965-66, fellow in hematology Thorndike Meml. Lab., 1966-69; asst. prof. medicine Harvard U. Med. Sch., 1969-71; chief hematology divsn. Thorndike Meml. Lab. and Harvard Med. Svcs., Boston City Hosp., 1969-71; prof. medicine, dir. Cancer Ctr., chief hematology-oncology sect. U. Pa., Phila., 1971-85; prof. medicine, exec. v.p., dean Med. Coll. Wis., Milw., 1985-94, dir. health policy inst., 1992—. Mem. editl. bd. Blood, 1979-84, Lipid Research, 1983-84. Served with USPHS, 1963-65. NIH grantee. Mem. Am. Soc. Hematology, Am. Fedn. Clin. Rsch., Am. Soc. Clin. Investigation, Assn. Am. Physicians, Am. Clin. Climatol. Assn., Phi Beta Kappa, Alpha Omega Alpha. Office: 8701 W Watertown Plank Rd Milwaukee WI 53226-3548

COOPER, RICHARD CASEY, lawyer; b. Tulsa, Jan. 20, 1942; s. Winston Churchill and Frances Margaret (Coppinger) C.; m. Ireen Lysbeth Evans, Nov. 24, 1965; children: Christopher Casey, Kimberly Ireen. BSBA, U. Tulsa, 1965, JD, 1967. Bar: Okla. 1967, U.S. Dist. Ct. (no., ea. and we. dists.) Okla. 1967, U.S. Ct. Mil. Appeals 1967, U.S. Ct. Appeals (10th cir.) 1972. Assoc. Boesche, McDermott & Eskridge, Tulsa, 1972-76, ptnr., 1977-92, mng. ptnr., 1990—. Editor in chief Tulsa Law Jour., 1967. Counsel Tulsa Philharm. Orch., 1990-92; trustee Mervin Bovaird Found., Tulsa, 1991—, pres., 1995—; trustee The Philbrook Mus. Art, 1997—, Tulsa Opera, 2000—, Bacone Coll., 2001—. Lt. USNR, 1967-71, mil. judge JAGC, 1970-71. Villard Martin scholar U. Tulsa, 1967; recipient Order of the Curule Chair, 1967. Mem. ABA, Okla. Bar Assn., Tulsa County Bar Assn., So. Hills Country Club. Republican. Avocations: family activities, fly fishing, travel. Home: 2923 E 58th St Tulsa OK 74105-7453 Office: Boesche McDermott Eskridge 100 W 5th St Ste 800 Tulsa OK 74103-4291

COOPER, RICHARD LEE, newspaper editor, journalist; b. Grand Rapids, Mich., Dec. 8, 1946; s. Harold Ralph and Elizabeth (DeSchipper) C.; m. Carol Jean Bonjernoor, Sept. 5, 1968; children— Jason Adam, Jessica Lynne. Student, Grand Rapids Jr. Coll., 1965-67; BA, Mich. State U., 1969. Reporter Rochester (N.Y.) Times-Union, 1969-77; reporter Phila. Inquirer, 1977—, Neighbors editor, 1983—, asst. city editor, 1988-91, Main Line editor, 1991—; editor Main Line & Del. County Neighbors, 1993—, Main Line, Del. County and Chester County Neighbors, 1995—, asst. regional editor, 1997-99; editor News Innovations, 1999—; rsch. svcs. dir. Phila. Newspapers, Inc., 2001. Instr. journalism Temple U., 1980—. Recipient N.Y. State Asso. Press Spot News First Place award, 1972, 76; Pulitzer prize for gen. local reporting, 1972; Distinguished Alumni award Grand Rapids Jr. Coll., 1974; Outstanding Contbn. in Pub. Info. award N.Y. State Bar Assn., 1977; 1st prize for investigative reporting Gannett News, 1977; Mich. Journalism fellow, 1990—. Mem. Pen and Pencil Club, Swan Creek Sailing Assn., Chesapeake Bay Triton Fleet, Rock Hall Sailing Club, Sigma Delta Chi. Presbyterian. Office: Phila Inquirer 400 N Broad St Philadelphia PA 19130-4099

COOPER, RICHARD MELVYN, lawyer; b. Phila., Nov. 13, 1942; s. Arthur Martin and Sophia Phyllis (Gottlieb) C.; m. Sabina Abbe Karp, June 12, 1965 (div. 1978); children: Alexander, Stephanie; m. Judith Carole Areen, Feb. 17, 1979; children: Benjamin, Jonathan. BA summa cum laude, Haverford Coll., 1964; BA 1st class, Oxford U., 1966, MA, 1970; JD summa cum laude, Harvard U., 1969. Bar: D.C. 1970, U.S. Ct. Appeals (5th, 6th and 9th cirs.) 1988, U.S. Ct. Appeals (10th cir.) 1982, U.S. Ct. Appeals (11th cir.) 1984, U.S. Ct. Appeals (fed. cir.) 1985, U.S. Ct. Appeals (4th cir.) 1997, U.S. Supreme Ct. 1973. Law clk. to Justice William J. Brennan, Jr. U.S. Supreme Ct., Washington, 1969-70; sr. lectr. Law Devel. Ctr., Kampala, Uganda, 1970-71; assoc. Williams, Connolly & Califano, Washington, 1971-77; chief counsel FDA, Rockville, Md., 1977-79; ptnr. Williams & Connolly, LLP, Washington, 1980—; mem. exec. com. Williams & Connolly, Washington, 1983-84, 89-92. Sr. mem. Office Energy Policy and Planning, Exec. Office of Pres., Washington, 1977; adj. prof. Georgetown U. Law Ctr., Washington, 1987-92, 96; mem. Adminstrv. Conf. U.S., 1978-79, Jud. Conf. D.C., Washington, 1979; mem. Adv. Panel on Strategies for Med. Tech. Assessment, Washington, 1980-81; mem. coms. NAS, 1980-83, 87-90. Editor: Food and Drug Law, 1991; co-editor: Fundamentals of Law and Regulation, 1997; contbr. articles to profl. jours. Chief counsel credentials com. Dem. Nat. Conv., Washington and N.Y.C., 1976; bd. mgrs. Haverford Coll., 1997—. Rhodes Trust scholar 1964; recipient FDA Award of Merit, 1979. Jewish. Office: Williams & Connolly 725 12th St NW Washington DC 20005-5901 E-mail: rcooper@wc.com.

COOPER, RICHARD NEWELL, economist, educator; b. Seattle, June 14, 1934; s. Richard Warren and Lucile (Newell) C.; m. Carolyn Jane Cahalan, June 5, 1956 (div. 1980); children: Laura Katherine, Mark Daniel; m. Ann Lorraine Hollick, Jan. 1, 1982 (div. 1994); m. Jin Chen, Oct. 13, 2000; 1 child, William Chen. AB, Oberlin Coll., 1956, LLD (hon.), 1978; MSc, London Sch. Econs., 1958; PhD, Harvard U., 1962; MA (hon.), Yale U., 1966; D (hon.), U. Paris II, 2000. Sr. staff economist Coun. Econ. Advisers, 1961-63; asst. prof. econs. Yale U., 1963-65, prof., 1966-77, provost, 1972-74; dep. asst. sec. state internat. monetary affairs Dept. State, 1965-66, undersec. for econ. affairs, 1977-81; prof. econs. Harvard U., Cambridge, Mass., 1981—. Chmn. Fed. Res. Bank Boston, 1990-92; chmn. Nat. Intelligence Coun., 1995-97; bd. dirs. Phoenix Cos., Circuit City, Inst. Internat. Econs., Ctr. Naval Analysis; mem. Trilateral Commn. Author: Economics of Interdependence, 1968, Currency Devaluation in Developing Countries, 1971, Economic Policy in an Interdependent World, 1986, The International Monetary System, 1987, Economic Stabilization and Debt in Developing Countries, 1992; author: (with others) Boom, Crisis and Adjustment, 1993; author: Environmental and Resource Policies for the World Economy, 1994; editor, contbr.: A Reordered World, 1973, The International Monetary System under Flexible Exchange Rates, 1982, Can Nations Agree?, 1989, Trade Growth in Transition Economies, 1997, What the Future Holds, 2002; contbr. articles to profl. jours. Trustee Oberlin Coll., 1993-98. Fellow Am. Acad. Arts and Scis.; mem. Am. Econ. Assn., Coun. Fgn. Rels. Office: Harvard U Ctr for Internat Affairs 1033 Massachusetts Ave Cambridge MA 02138-3016 E-mail: rcooper@fas.harvard.edu.

COOPER, RICKEY EUGENE, medical transcriptionist, educator; b. Stockton, Calif., May 27, 1946; s. Robert Evertt and Barbara Louise Cooper. AA in Physics, San Joaquin Delta Jr. Coll., 1970; student, Calif. State U., Fresno, 1973. File and unit clk. Stockton (Calif.) State Hosp., 1974-75; billing unit supr. Divsn. Substance Abuse, Sacramento, 1976-78; bus. mgr. Nat. Socialist White People's Party, Arlington, Va., 1978-80; med. transcriptionist Georgetown U. Hosp., Washington, 1980-82, Silas B. Hays Army Cmty. Hosp., Ft. Ord, Calif., 1983-85, Hood River (Oreg.) Meml. Hosp., 1985-87, Columbia Gorge Orthopedics, Hood River, Oreg., 1986-88, Emanuel Hosp., Portland, Oreg., 1988-98, Webb & Assocs., Portland, Oreg., 98-99, Rodeer Sys., Portland, Oreg., 1999-2000, N.W. Mediscript, Kennewick, Wash., 2000—01. Spokesperson Nat. Socialist Vanguard. Sgt. USAF, 1964-68. Office: Nat Socialist Vanguard PO Box 328 The Dalles OR 97058 E-mail: rcooper@gorge.net.

COOPER, ROBERT ELBERT, state supreme court justice; b. Chattanooga, Oct. 14, 1920; s. John Thurman and Susie Inez (Hollingsworth) C.; m. Catherine Pauline Kelly, Nov. 24, 1949; children: Susan Florence Cooper Hodges, Bobbie Cooper Martin, Kelly Ann Smith, Robert Elbert Jr. BA, U. N.C., 1946; JD, Vanderbilt U., 1949. Bar: Tenn. 1948. Assoc. Kolwyck and Clark, 1949-51; ptnr. Cooper and Barger, 1951-53; asst. atty. gen. 6th Jud. Ct. Tenn., 1951-53; judge 6th Jud. Circuit Tenn., 1953-60, Tenn. Ct. Appeals, 1960-70, presiding judge Eastern divsn., 1970-74; justice Tenn. Supreme Ct., 1974-90, chief justice, 1976-77, 84-85. Chmn. Tenn. Jud. Coun., 1967-90; chmn. Tenn. Code Commn., 1976-77, 84-85; mem. Tenn. Jud. Standards Commn., 1971-77. Mem. exec. bd. Cherokee coun. Boy Scouts Am., 1960-64; bd. dirs. Met. YMCA, 1956-65, St. Barnabas Nursing Home and Apts. for Aged, 1966-69. With USNR, 1941-46. Recipient Nat. Heritage award Downtown Sertoma Club, Chattanooga, 1989. Mem. Am., Tenn., Chattanooga bar assns., Conf. Chief Justices, Phi Beta Kappa, Order of Coif, Kappa Sigma, Phi Alpha Delta. Clubs: Signal Mountain Golf and Country, Masons (33 deg.), Shriners. Democrat. Presbyterian. Home and Office: 196 Woodcliff Cir Signal Mountain TN 37377-3147

COOPER, ROBERT GORDON, lawyer; b. Roanoke, Va., July 2, 1953; s. Arthur Darrah and C. Jane (Redman) C.; m. Ruth K. Cathcart, June 7, 1975; 1 child, Kimberly Anne. BBA, Furman U., 1974; JD, U. S.C., 1977. Bar: S.C. 1977, U.S. Dist. Ct. S.C. 1977, U.S. Ct. Appeals (4th cir.) 1980, U.S. Supreme Ct. 1982. Assoc. Robinson, McFadden, Moore & Pope, Columbia, S.C., 1977-80; asst. city atty. City of Columbia, 1980—; pvt. practice Columbia, 1982-98. Advisor City of Columbia Police Dept. Mem. S.C. Bar Assn., Richland County Bar Assn. Home: 104 Old Ridge Ct Columbia SC 29212-1355 Office: PO Box 667 Columbia SC 29202

COOPER, ROBERT SHANKLIN, engineering executive, former government official; b. Kansas City, Mo., Feb. 8, 1932; s. Robert S. and Edna A. (Pobanz) C.; m. Benita A. Sidwell, Oct. 5, 1985; children: Jonathan A., James G. BS in Elec. Engring, U. Iowa, 1954; MS, Ohio State U., 1958; ScD, MIT, 1963, Sc.D. (Ford Found. postdoctoral fellow), 1965. Mem. staff elec. engring. dept. Mass. Inst. Tech., 1958-65; mem. staff Lincoln Lab., 1965-72; asst. dir. def. rsch. and engring. Dept. Def., 1972-75; dep. dir. Goddard Space Flight Ctr., Greenbelt, Md., 1975-76, dir., 1976-79; v.p. engring. Satellite Bus. Systems, McLean, Va., 1979-81; asst. Sec. Def. Washington, 1983-85; dir. Def. Adv. Rsch. Projects Agy., Arlington, 1981-85; pres., CEO, chmn. bd. Atlantic Aerospace Electronics Corp., Greenbelt, Md., 1985-99; pres. Titan Corp., Aerospace Electronics Div., 1999. Bd. dirs. BAE N.Am., Rockville, Md., Etenna Corp.; chmn. Trimble Navigation Ltd., Sunnyvale, Calif., 1989—, GEC-Marconi N.Am., Wayne, NJ, 1998—99; chmn. bd. dirs. Talarian Corp., Mountainview, Calif., 1989—99; mem. def. sci. bd. Office Sec. Def., 1996—; mem. strategic adv. group U.S. Strategic Command, 1982—99. Served with USAF, 1954-56. Westinghouse fellow, 1958; recipient Sec. Def. Meritorious Civilian Svc. award, 1975 Fellow AAAS, AIAA, IEEE; mem. Sigma Xi, Tau Beta Pi, Eta Kappa Nu. Office: Titan Corp Aerospace Electronics Division 6404 Ivy Ln Ste 300 Greenbelt MD 20770-1407 E-mail: cooper@dc.aaec.com.

COOPER, ROBERTA, mayor; b. Mar. 18, 1937; m. Jerrel Cooper. BA, MA. Ret. secondary sch. tchr.; mem. Hayward (Calif.) City Coun., 1988-92; mayor City of Hayward, 1994—. Former mem. Gen. Plan Revision Task Force, dir. League of Calif. Cities. Active Eden (Calif.) Youth Ctr., Literacy Plus, Hayward Edn. Assn. Democrat. Avocations: reading mysteries, gardening. Office: Mayors Office 777 B St Hayward CA 94541-5007*

COOPER, ROGER MERLIN, information technology executive, federal government official, school administrator; b. Scottsbluff, Nebr., Feb. 25, 1943; s. Dean P. and Bette Jane (Ward) C.; m. Erica Feuer: children: Gregory Joseph, Lisa Jane. BS, U. Utah, 1964; MSA, George Washington U., 1970; MBA, U. So. Calif., 1970; grad., Fed. Execs. Inst. U. Utah, 1980, Harvard U. Kennedy Sch. Govt., 1984. Masters's lic. USCG. Mgr. sys. programming Larwin Group, Beverly Hills, Calif., 1973-74; chief teleprocessing sect. U.S. CSC, Washington, 1974-76, chief info. tech. divsn., 1976-77; dir. Office Automated Sys. Devel., Macon, Ga., 1977-78; asst. dir. U.S. Office Pers. Mgmt., Washington, 1979-82; dir. med. info. resources mgmt. office VA, Washington, 1982-85; dep. asst. sec. for info. sys. U.S. Dept. Treasury, Washington, 1985-88; dep. adminstr. Farmers Home Adminstrn., Washington, 1988-91; dep. asst. atty. gen. info. mgmt. U.S. Dept. Justice, Washington, 1991-95; v.p. I-NET Inc., Bethesda, Md., 1995-96; dir. info. tech. Fairfax County Pub. Sch. Sys., Alexandria, Va., 1996—. CEO The Cooper Group, Ltd.; mem. Coun. of Prins., Nat. Comms. Systems, Coun. Sch. Networks; mem. adv. bd. FTS2000, Ethertica, Inc.; chmn. Nat. Computer Security and Privacy Bd.; exec. bd. Inter-agy. Coun. on Info. Resources Mgmt., Fed. Micro Adv. Bd.; active Fed. Info. Ctr. Adv. Coun., Fed. Info. Rsch. Policy Coun., Fed. Data Ctrs. Dirs. Conf.; bd. dirs. Naval Liaison Office; mem. Consortium for Sch. Networking. Lt. USN, 1964-69; capt. USNR. Recipient Dept. Def. Joint Svc. achievment medal, 1988. Mem.: Armed Forces Comms. and Electronics Assn. (bd. dirs.). Home: 2121 Jamieson Ave # 1602 Alexandria VA 22314 Office: Fairfax County Pub Sch Sys 3701 Franconia Rd Alexandria VA 22310-2129 E-mail: cooper_roger@alumni.ksg.harvard.edu., roger.cooper@fcps.edu.

COOPER, ROY ASBERRY, III, state attorney general, lawyer; b. Rocky Mount, N.C., June 13, 1957; s. Roy Asberry Jr. and Beverly (Batchelor) C.; m. Kristin Bernhardt, Mar. 28, 1992; children: Hilary Godette, Natalie Rose, Claire Kristin. BA, U. N.C., 1979, JD, 1982. Bar: N.C. 1982. Ptnr. Fields and Cooper, Rocky Mount, 1982—2001; atty. gen. State of N.C., 2001—. Mem. N.C. Ho. of Reps., 1987-91, chmn. jud. com., 1989-91; mem. N.C. Senate, 1991-2001, chmn. jud. com., 1991-2000. Morehead scholar U. N.C., 1975-79. Democrat. Presbyterian. Office: NC Dept Justice PO Box 629 Raleigh NC 27602*

COOPER, SAUL, film and TV producer, public relations executive; b. NYC, July 31, 1934; s. Joseph Matthew and Libby (Benson) C.; m. Karin Granath, June 23, 1957; children: Louis, Andrew, Michael, David, Elisabeth. BA, NYU, 1955; MS, Columbia U., 1957. Account exec. Lynn Farnol Group, N.Y.C., 1952-58; nat. publicity coordinator Paramount Pictures, N.Y.C., 1958-63; dir. mktg. Robert Rossen Prodns., N.Y.C., 1963-64; unit publicist 20th-Century Fox/MGM/Columbia Pictures, Rome, London, 1964-67; dir. prodn. publicity United Artists, London, Paris, 1967-70, dir. European film prodn. Paris, 1970-72; prodr. owner Les Films de la Seine S.A., Paris, 1972-76; mktg. supr. Eon Prodns., London, N.Y.C., 1976-77; v.p. internat. advt. and publicity United Artists, N.Y.C., 1978-80; v.p. worldwide publicity and promotion 20th Century-Fox, L.A., 1980-82; prodr., Contact French CBS-Fox Video, L.A., 1982-83; pub. rels. cons. Saul Cooper Consultancy, L.A., 1983-88; dir. internat. mktg. ITC Entertainment Group, Studio City, Calif., 1988; v.p. Warfield (James Bond) Prodns., Inc., Culver City, Calif., 1988-92. Author: Dillinger, Sex on Celluloid, Hatari!, The Jayhawkers, Paris When It Sizzles; editor: Rodgers & Hammerstein Fact Book, 2d edit.; prodr. Les Gaspards, L'Agression, La Messe Doree, L'Education Amoreuse de Valentin, Le Fuhrer en Folie, Une Femme Fatale; exec. prodr. Madeline, 2001 (Emmy award Outstanding Children's Animated Program 2002), over 50 animated shows, 1988—; prodr. film Madeline, 1998; exec. prodr. Madeline-Lost in Paris, 1999. Mem. Acad. Motion Picture Arts and Scis., Acad. T.V. Arts and Scis. Home: 2439 Santa Barbara St Santa Barbara CA 93105-3549

COOPER, SHARON KAY, school media specialist; b. Junction City, Kans., Jan. 9, 1952; d. Duane Harvey and Helen Lucille Gugler; m. Stevan Frank Cooper, Aug. 3, 1974; children: Susan Kay, Shelley Kay. BS in Home Econs., Ft. Hays State U., 1974; postgrad., Wichita State U., 1979, Kans. State U., 1983, Emporia State U., 1988; MS in Edn. Adminstrn., Ft. Hays State U., 1996. Home econs. tchr., libr. Brewster (Kans.) H.S., 1974—75; lang. arts tchr., libr. West Smith County Jr. and Sr. H.S., Kensington, Kans., 1975-77; home econs., vocational tchr. Little River (Kans.)-Windom H.S., 1977-80; home econs. tchr. Chase (Kans.)-Raymond Schs., 1980-88; library media specialist Quivira Heights H.S., Bushton, Kans., 1988-95, Quivira Heights K-12 Schs., Holyrood and Bushton, Kans., 1995—. Sch. library rep., vice chairperson Kans. Interlibrary Loan Bd. Dirs., Topeka, 1999—; chmn. Reading Is Fun, Quivira Hts. Elem./Jr. High, 1995—; chmn. Red Ribbon Week Quivira Hts. Pre K-12, 1995—. Troop leader Wheatbelt coun. Girl Scouts U.S., Chase, 1989-96, svc. unit mgr., 1995-97; mem. Smoky Hills Drug-Free Schs. Adv. Coun. Mem. NEA, Kans. Assn. Sch. Librs., Kans. Edn. Assn. (pres. local chpt. 1999-2000), Phi Delta Kappa. Methodist. Avocations: reading, cooking, sewing, snow skiing, travel. Home: 213 Cedar Chase KS 67524 Office: Quivira Heights Pre K-12 Schs 500 S Main St Bushton KS 67427-9749

COOPER, SHARON MARSHA, marketing, advertising executive; m. Steven Jon Cooper, children: Robin Eve, Erik Scott. BA, Northeastern Ill. U., Chgo., 1974; MEd, Loyola U., Chgo., 1977. Adj. asst. prof. Chgo. Med. Sch., North Chicago, Ill., 1974-79; edn./media coord. Humana Hosp., Aurora, Colo., 1980-82; v.p. Healthcare Mktg. Corp., Denver, 1982-84; pres. Sharon Cooper Assocs., Ltd., Englewood, Colo., 1984—. Cons./speaker Jason Pharms., Balt., 1988—; cons. Am. Soc. Bariatric Physicians; lectr. in field; guest lectr. U. Denver, 1988—; pres. The Food Bank of Rockies Guild 2003—. Illustrator: A Manual of Radiographic Positioning, 1973; contbr. articles to profl. jours. Bd. dirs., v.p. The Barre Assn./Colo. Ballet, Denver, 1989—; bd. dirs. Am. Diabetes Assn., Denver, 1983—, Am. Cancer Soc., Denver, 1988—, Hospice of St. John, Denver, 1986-90; mem. adv. bd. U. Colo. Denver Sch. of the Arts, 1997—; pres. Colo. Angels, 2001-03, Food Bank of the Rockies Guild, 2003—. Named Co-Woman of the Yr., Lerner Newspapers, Chgo., 1973, Silver Microphone award, 1988, Golden Leaflet award, Colo. Hosp. Assn., 1981, 84. Mem. Am. Hosp. Assn., Assn. Healthcare Pub. Rels. and Mktg. (reg. rep. 1987—), Colo. Soc. Health Care Pub. Rels., Pub. Rels. Soc. Am., Zonta, Toastmasters (sec. 1972-84). Avocations: writing, art, aerobics. Office: Sharon Cooper Assocs Ltd Ste E-200 16 Inverness Pl E Englewood CO 80112-5612

COOPER, SHELDON MARK, medical educator, immunology researcher, rheumatologist; b. N.Y.C., Dec. 5, 1942; s. Alex and Sylvia (Silverman) C.; m. Amy Diane Freedman, Nov. 23, 1966; 1 child, Jonas Eric. BS cum laude, Hobart Coll., 1963; MD, NYU, 1967. Diplomate Am. Bd. Internal Medicine, Am. Bd. Rheumatology. Intern, asst. resident in internal medicine King's County Hosp. Ctr., Bklyn., 1967-69; fellow rheumatic disease study unit NYU Med. Ctr., N.Y.C., 1970-72; asst. prof. medicine U. So. Calif. Sch. Medicine, L.A., 1974-80, assoc. prof., rsch. coord., 1980-82; assoc. prof. medicine, dir. rheumatology and clin. U. Vt. Coll. Medicine, Burlington, 1982-86, prof. medicine, dir. rheumatology and clin. immunology unit, 1986—. Mem. staff L.A. County U. So. Calif. Med. Ctr., 1974-82, Med. Ctr. Hosp. of Vt., Burlington, 1982—. Contbr. articles to profl. jours. Mem. exec. com. Vt. chpt. Arthritis Found., Burlington, 1982—, chmn., trustee, 1990—; mem. panel gen. and plastic surgery devices FDA. Maj. USAF, 1972-73. NIH fellow, 1971; grantee Nat. Cancer Inst., 1976, Nat. Inst. Arthritis Musculoskeletal and Skin Diseases, 1984—, NIH, 1984—. Mem. Am. Coll. Rheumatology, Am. Fedn. Clin. Rsch., Am. Assn. Immunologists, Reticuloendothelial Soc., Physicians for Social Responsibility, Union Concerned Scientists. Democrat. Jewish. Avocations: jogging, swimming, traveling, cinema. Home: Barstow Rd Shelburne VT 05482 Office: U Vt Given Bldg D301 Burlington VT 05405-0001 E-mail: scooper@uvm.edu.

COOPER, SHEROD MONROE, JR., retired English literature educator; b. Norristown, Pa., Jan. 28, 1927; s Sherod Monroe and Louise (Morley) C.; m. Janet Williams, June 27, 1953; children: Sherod M. III, Stephen O., David L., Elizabeth C. Judy. BS with honors, Temple U., 1951, MA, 1953; PhD, U. Pa., 1963. English tchr. Woodstown (N.J.) H.S., 1952-54, instr. English Westminster Coll., New Wilmington, Pa., 1954-56, U. Md., College Park, 1957-63, asst. prof. English, 1963-67, assoc. prof. English, 1967-89, assoc. prof. emeritus, 1995—. Author: The Sonnets of Astrophel and Stella, 1968, S.S. John W. Brown: Baltimore's Living Liberty, 1991, Liberty Ship: The Voyages of the John W. Brown, 1942-46, 1997. With U.S. Merchant Marine, 1945-46, U.S. Army, 1946-47. Mem. Project Liberty Ship (historian 1988—, bd. dirs. 1990—), Nat. Maritime Hist. Soc., Steamship Hist. Soc. of Am., Naval Inst., Civitan Internat. Home: 2563 Golfers Ridge Rd Annapolis MD 21401-6917

COOPER, SHIRLEY RUTH, artist, illustrator; b. Kansas City, Mo., June 6, 1945; d. Omer and Thelma Ruth (Gunn) Henderson; m. Melvin C. Monk, Aug. 30, 1986; children: Geoffrey Donovan Cooper, Jules Mason Cooper. AA in Comml. Art, Everett (Wash.) C.C., 1973; BA in Human Svcs., Western Wash. U., 1976; BFA in Design and Illustration, Cornish Coll. of the Arts, 1994. Counseling intern Children's Resource Ctr., Snohomish County Mental Health, Everett, 1975-76; tchrs. aide Everett Sch. Dist., 1976-79; home base educator Head Start, Everett, 1983-84; family adv. Snohomish County Head Start, Edmonds, Wash., 1984-86; south dist. dir. Pilchuck Area Coun. Campfire, Everett, 1986-87; family life instr. Everett C.C., 1988-91; pvt. practice artist and illustrator Everett, 1994—. With Earthworks Galleries, Oreg. Works exhibited

in shows at Artistree Gallery, Bothell, Everett Ctr. for the Arts, Greater Marysville Artists Guild, 1995, Artsplash '95, 1995, Evergreen State Fair, 1995, Spring Into Monroe, 1996, 97, Greater Marysville Artists Guild, 1996, N.W. Pastel Soc., 1996, Burien Gallery, 1997, Edmonds Arts Festival, 1997, Arts Coun. Snohomish County, 1997, Arts of the Terrace, 1997, others. Vol., gallery com. Snohomish County Arts Coun., Everett, 1994—. Mem. N.W. Pastel Soc. Avocations: plein air painting, teaching, gardening, reading, writing. Home: PO Box 1016 Belfair WA 98528-1016

COOPER, SIGNE SKOTT, retired nurse educator; b. Clinton County, Iowa, Jan. 29, 1921; d. Hans Edward and Clara Belle (Steen) Skott. BS, U. Wis., 1948; MEd, U. Minn., 1955. Head nurse U. Wis. Hosp., Madison, 1946-48; instr. U. Wis. Sch. Nursing, Madison, 1948-51, asst. prof., 1952-57, assoc. prof., 1957-62, prof., assoc. dean, 1948-83, prof. emeritus, 1983—. Prof. U. Wis. Extension, 1955-83. Contbg. author: American Nursing: A Biographical Dictionary, Vol. 1, 1988, Vol. 2, 1992, Vol. 3, 2000; contbr. articles to profl. jours. 1st Lt. U.S. Army Nurse Corps, 1943-46. Recipient NLN Linda Richards award, ANA Honorary Recognition award, Adult Edn. Assn. Pioneer award; named to Nursing Hall of Fame, 2000. Fellow Am. Acad. Nursing (named Living Legend 2003); mem. Am. Assn. for History Nursing, Wis. Nurses Assn. (pres.).

COOPER, STEPHEN HERBERT, lawyer; b. N.Y.C., Mar. 29, 1939; s. Walter S. and Selma (Herbert) C.; m. Linda Cohen, Aug. 29, 1965 (dec.); m. Karen Gross, Sept. 6, 1981; 1 child, Zachary Noel. AB, Columbia U., 1960, JD cum laude, 1965. Bar: N.Y. 1965. Assoc. Weil, Gotshal & Manges, LLC, NYC, 1966-73, ptnr., 1973—. Lectr. Nat. Inst. Securities Regulation U. Colo., Boulder, 1985, Practicing Law Inst. 25th Annual Nat. Inst. Securities Regulation, N.Y.C., 1993, Law Jours. Seminars, 1997, 98; adj. prof. law, N.Y. Law Sch., N.Y.C., 2002-. Served to lt. USNR, 1960-62. Fellow Am. Bar Found.; mem. ABA (com. fed. regulation securities, subcom. internat. securities matters, co-chmn. 1990—). Home: 1125 Park Ave New York NY 10128-1243 Office: Weil Gotshal & Manges LLP 767 5th Ave New York NY 10153-0119 E-mail: stephen.cooper@weil.com.

COOPER, STEVE NEIL, art gallery owner, photographer; b. N.Y.C., July 19, 1944; s. Felix Cooper and Sybil Koff. AAS, Rochester (N.Y.) Inst. Tech., 1964, BFA, 1966; cert. in filmmaking, NYU, 1992. Owner Steve Cooper Studio, N.Y.C., 1972—, Sybille Art Gallery, N.Y.C., 1985—. Recipient NE Pocket Billiards Champion NCAA, 1966, award Soc. Publ. Designers, 1975, N.Y.C. Art Dirs. Club award, 1978, Award of Excellence Decor Mag., 1987, Freddy award Picture Framing Mag., 1993, Frame of the Month, Decor Mag., 2000; N.Y. State Regents Coll. scholar, 1962. Mem. Am. Soc. Mag. Photographers, Assn. Ind. Video and Filmmakers. Jewish. Avocation: chess. Office: Sybille Gallery 5 W 31st St New York NY 10001-4414 E-mail: sncfnby@aol.com.

COOPER, STEVEN HAROLD, education educator; s. Harold Cooper. and Rose Ann Denman. BS in Criminal Justice, Calif. State U., Sacramento, 1994—96; MS in Criminology, Fla. State U., 1997—98. Mil. Customs Inspector U.S. Customs, 2001, Phys. Security Specialist U.S. Army, 2001, Mil. Police Instr. U.S. Army Mil. Police Sch., 2002. Mil. police officer/instr. U.S. Army, Irvine, Calif., 1989—; prof. Chapman U., Orange, Calif., 1999—. Cons. to law enforcement organizations. Editor Stand!: Crime and Criminology, Perspectives: Criminology. Nat. v.p. Nat. Criminal Justice Honor Soc., Miami, 1996—97. Staff sgt. U.S. Army, 1989. Mem.: Am. Soc. of Criminology, Acad. of Criminal Justice Sciences (life). Office: Chapman U One University Dr Orange CA 92866 E-mail: stcooper@chapman.edu.

COOPER, STEVEN JON, healthcare management consultant, educator; m. Sharon M.; children: Robin E., Erik S. BA, U. Calif., L.A., 1966; MEd, Loyola U., 1973; PhD, Union Sch., 1979. Ednl. coord. dept. radiology Mt. Sinai Hosp. Med. Ctr., Chgo., 1969-72; chmn. dept. radiol. scis. U. Health Scis., Chgo. Med. Sch., VA Hosp., North Chicago, 1972-79; v.p. C&S, Inc., Denver, 1980-81; pres. Healthcare Mktg. Corp., Denver, 1981-84; corp. officer, exec. v.p. Sharon Cooper Assocs. Ltd., Englewood, Colo., 1984—. Cons. HEW; lectr. in field. Contbr. articles to profl. publs. Pres. bd. dirs. Hospice of St. John, 1997—. With USAF, 1960-64, USAFR, 1964-66. W.K. Kellogg Found. grantee. Mem. AMA (com. on allied health edn. and accreditation), Am. Soc. Radiol. Tech. (mem. edn., curriculum rev. coms., task force), Ill. Soc. Radiol. Tech. (chmn. annual meeting 1976, program Midwest conf. 1977), Coll. Radiol. Scis., Am. Hosp. Radiology Adminstrs. (mem. edn. com., treas. Midwest region, nat. v.p.), Kiwanis Club Castle Rock (charter, pres., lt. govt. divsn. 15 1997-98), Sovereign Order of St. John of Jerusalem, Knights of Malta, Sigma Xi. Office: 16 Inverness Pl E Ste E200 Englewood CO 80112-5612

COOPER, STEVEN MARK, law educator, writer; b. N.Y.C., Apr. 9, 1947; s. Fred Morris and Martha (Tieger) C.; m. Kitty Munson, Oct. 29, 2000. BA, NYU, 1970; MS, N.Mex. Highlands U., 1973; MA, U. Calif., Santa Barbara, 1978; JD with honors, Rutgers U., 1985; LLM, Harvard U., 1990. Bar: N.J. 1985, U.S. Dist. Ct. N.J. 1985, N.Y. 1986. Pres., chief exec. officer RT, Inc., Bronx, N.Y., 1978-86; adj. prof. law sch. We. State U., San Diego, 1986-87, Nat. U., San Diego, 1988-89; assoc. prof. Tex. Wesleyan U. Sch. Law, Irving, Tex., 1990-97; prof. Appalachian Sch. Law, Grundy, Va., 1997-2000; corp. assoc. Paul, Weiss, Rifkind, Wharton and Garrison, N.Y.C., 1985-86. Articles editor Rutgers Computer & Tech., 1984-85; sr. editor Harvard Jour. Law and Pub. Policy, 1984-85. Sustaining mem. Rep. Nat. Com. Mem. ABA, Federalist Soc. (founder, pres. Rutgers chpt., 1984). Avocations: computers, walking, tournament bridge (nat. champion 2000). Home and Office: 801 Carlisle Blvd SE Albuquerque NM 87106-1532

COOPER, STUART LEONARD, chemical engineering educator, researcher, consultant; b. N.Y.C., Aug. 28, 1941; s. Jacob and Anne (Bloom) C.; m. Marilyn Portnoy, Aug. 29, 1965; children: Gary, Stacey. BS, MIT, 1963; PhD, Princeton U., 1967. From asst. prof. chem. engrng. to prof. U. Wis., Madison, Wis., 1967—89, Paul A. Elfers prof., 1989—93; dean, H. Rodney Sharp prof. Coll of Engrng. U. Del., Newark, 1993-98; v.p., chief acad. officer, P. Danforth prof. engrng. Ill. Inst. Tech., 1998-2001; provost, vice chancellor for acad. affairs N.C. State U., 2001—03, prof. chem. engrng., 2003—. Vis. assoc. prof. U. Calif.-Berkeley, 1974; vis. prof. Technion, Haifa, Israel, 1977; cons. in field; trustee Argonne Univs. Assn., Argonne Nat. Lab., 1975-81 Editor: Multiphase Polymers, 1979, Biomaterials: Interfacial Phenomena and Applications, 1982, The Vroman Effect, 1992, Polymer Biomaterials: In Solution as Interfaces and as Solids, 1995; author: Polyurethanes in Medicine, 1986, Polyurethanes in Biomedical Applications, 1998; contbr. numerous articles in field to profl. jours. Lady Davis fellow, 1977 Fellow AIChE (Charles M.A. Stine award 1987), AAAS, Am. Phys. Soc., Am. Inst. Med. and Biol. Engrs. (founding), Soc. for Biomaterials (pres. 1996-97, Clemson award for basic rsch. 1987); mem. Am. Chem. Soc. (best paper award 1976), Am. Soc. Artificial Internal Organs, Soc. Rheology, Soc. Plastics Engrs. Office: Dept Chem Engring NC State U Box 7905 Raleigh NC 27695 E-mail: scooper@unity.ncsu.edu.

COOPER, THOMAS ASTLEY, banking executive; b. Phila., July 19, 1936; s. Thomas Astley and Elmira (Betts) C.; m. Anita June Danenberger, Sept. 7, 1957; children: Aleta Cooper Bossert, Anita Cooper Barbato, Alane Cooper Inacker, Allison, Anne Cooper Fleming, Thomas Astley III. BA, Haverford Coll., 1957; BD, Drew U., 1960; postgrad., Pa. U., Wharton, 1972; Program for Mgmt. Devel., Harvard U., 1976. Pres. Girard Bank, Phila., 1978; vice chmn. Mellon Bank, Mellon Nat. Corp., Pitts., 1982; pres. Bank of Am., Bank Am. Corp., San Francisco, 1984; chmn. Investment Svcs. for America, Tampa, Fla., 1986-90; pres., CEO Goldome, Buffalo, 1986-90; prin. TAC Assocs., Buffalo, 1992-95; CEO Chase Fed. Bank, Miami, Fla., 1993-96; chmn. Flatiron Credit, Denver, 1997. Dir. Dela. No. Cos., Buffalo, Rennaisance Reins, Bermuda, Wheeling Island Gaming, Inc.; CEO TAC Assocs. Inc., BISYS, New York, N.Y.; advisor E.M. Warburg, Pincus & Co., LLC. Mem. Island Country Club, Brant Beach Yacht Club (N.J.), Marco Island Yacht Club. Office: 1291 Laurel Ct Marco Island FL 34145-2351

COOPER, THOMAS LOUIS, lawyer; b. Pitts., Mar. 16, 1938; s. Louis D. and Gertrude V. (Edmonds) C.; m. Leah Mary Meyers, Aug. 5, 1961; children: Marcia, Jeffrey, Daniel. BA, Dartmouth Coll., 1959; LLB, U. Pitts., 1962. Bar: Pa. 1962, U.S. Dist. Ct. (we. dist.) Pa. 1962, U.S. Ct. Appeals (3d cir.) 1962, U.S. Supreme Ct., 1962. Assoc. McArdle & McLaughlin, Pitts., 1962-69; ptnr. Gilardi & Cooper, Pitts., 1969—. Mem. civil procedural rules com. Pa. Supreme Ct., 1985-92, continuing legal edn. bd., 1992—, common pleas automation implementation team, 1990-92; adj. prof. U. Pitts. Sch. Law, 1986—. Contbr. articles to profl. jours. Fellow Am. Coll. Trial Lawyers; mem. Pa. Bar Assn. (v.p. 1989, pres.-elect 1990-91, pres. 1991-92, bd. govs., ho. of dels.), Allegheny County Bar Assn. (pres. 1984), Allegheny County Acad. Trial Lawyers (pres. 1982), Pa. Trial Lawyers Assn. (bd. govs.), Western Pa. Trial Lawyers Assn. (bd. govs.). Office: Gilardi Cooper & Lomupo 808 Grant Building Pittsburgh PA 15219-2200

COOPER, THOMAS LUTHER, retired printing company executive; b. Statham, Ga., Sept. 30, 1917; s. William Henry and Ovelia Jane (Arnold) C.; m. Helen Brown, Aug. 30, 1941; 1 son, Thomas Luther. Student, Ga. State U., 1938-39, High Mus. Art, Atlanta, 1946. With Constn. Pub. Co., Atlanta, 1936-50, head photoengraving and art dept., 1947-50; pres. So. Engraving Co., Atlanta, 1950-75, Photo Process Engraving Co., Atlanta, 1954-75; pres., gen. mgr. So. Photo Process Engraving Co., Atlanta, 1955-75; v.p., bd. dir. Perry Comms., 1976-90, Beck Engraving Co., Inc., Phila., 1968-75. Bd. dirs. J.M. Tull Metals Co., Inc. Mem. exec. bd. Atlanta Area coun. Boy Scouts Am., Silver Beaver award, 1972; trustee Shorter Coll., Rome, Ga.; mem. adv. coun. Ga. State U.; chmn. bd. Ga. State U. Found. Served as capt. USAAF, 1942-45. Recipient Craftsman of Year award Inland Printer and Am. Lithographer mag., 1961 Mem. Internat. Assn. Printing House Craftsmen (pres. 1959-60), Am. Photoengravers Assn. (exec. com. 1952-54), Southeastern Photoengravers Assn. (pres. 1951-52), Nat. Soc. Art Dirs., Printing Industry Assn. Ga., Advt. Club Atlanta, Mil. Order World Wars, Am. Legion, Capital City Club, Masons, Shriners, Rotary (pres. Atlanta 1975, dist. gov. Ga. dist. 6900 1981-82). Baptist. Home: 1002 Dunwoody Chace NE Atlanta GA 30328-6012

COOPER, THOMAS RANDOLPH, lawyer; b. Bath, Maine, July 8, 1953; s. Tommy Gene and Cecile Sunshine (Butler) C.; m. Twila Ann Pirkle, Sept. 15, 1984; 1 child, Kimberly Nicole. BS, U. Houston, 1975; JD, South Tex. Coll. Law, Houston, 1978. Bar: Tex. 1978, U.S. Dist. Ct. (so., no., ea. and we. dists.) Tex. 1987, U.S. Ct. Appeals (5th cir.) 1991. Gen. counsel Umm Al-Qaiwain Oil Consortium, United Arab Emirates, 1978-80; assoc. Hill & Spoliansky, Dubai, United Arab Emirates, 1979-81; gen. counsel, v.p. Unigulf Petroleum, Inc., Dubai, 1981; legal cons. Azzam Internat., Ltd., Sharjah, United Arab Emirates, 1982; assoc. Shoemake & Selwyn, Houston, 1982-85, Law Offices of David N. Williams, Houston, 1987-92; sole practitioner Houston, 1985-87, 92-00; gen. counsel, bd. dirs. Tramco Builders, Inc., 2000—, Cherokee Directional Drilling, Inc., 2000—. Bd. dirs. Hazard Assessment Leaders, Inc., Houston. Columnist What's On Mag., 1981-82. Sigma Nu ednl. grantee, 1975. Mem. Coll. of State Bar of Tex., Nat. Assn. Eagle Scouts, Masons, Scottish Rite, Omicron Delta Kappa. Republican. Methodist. Avocations: woodworking, photography. Home: 1158 Chantilly Ln Houston TX 77018-3240 Office: 1183 Brittmoore Rd Ste 300 Houston TX 77043 E-mail: tom@cherokeedd.com.

COOPER, WILLIAM ALLEN, banking executive; b. Detroit, July 3, 1943; BS in Acctg., Wayne State U., 1967. CPA, Mich. With Touche, Ross & Co., Detroit, 1967-71; chm. Minn. Rep Party. Sr. v.p. Mich. Nat. Bank of Detroit, 1971-72; sr. v.p. Mich. Nat. Corp., 1971-78; exec. v.p. Huntington Nat. Bank, Columbus, Ohio, 1978-83, pres., 1983-84; pres., Am. Savs. & Loan Assn. of Fla., Miami, 1984-85, also dir.; chmn. bd., chief exec. officer TCF Bank, FSB, Mpls., 1985—; chmn., TCF Fin. Corp., Mpls., from 1987, now chmn. bd., past chief exec. officer, bd. dirs. Mem. AICPA. Office: TCF Bank Office of Chmn Bd 801 Marquette Ave Minneapolis MN 55402-3475 also: Minn Rep Party 480 Ceder Street Ste 560 Castle Rock MN 55010

COOPER, WILLIAM COPELAND, public library director; b. Laurens, S.C., Aug. 3, 1946; s. James Lafayette Jr. and Dorothy (Copeland) C. Ba in History, Presbyn. Coll., 1968; MA in History, Wake Forest U., 1969; MS in Libr. Sci., U. N.C., 1971. Tchr. Wade Hampton H.S., Greenville, S.C., 1969-70; reference asst. U. N.C. Libr., Chapel Hill, 1970-71, reference libr., 1971-72; head reference dept. Greenville County Libr., 1972-74; dir. Laurens County Libr., 1974—. Contbr. articles to profl. jours. Treas. Laurens Hist. Soc., 1990-2003, Laurens County Arts Coun., 1994-97; preas. Cmty. Concert Assn., Clinton, 1980-82. Mem. ALA, Southeastern Libr. Assn., S.C. Libr. Assn., Piedmont Libr. Assn. (pres. 1998-99), Pub. Libr. Adminstrs. (pres. 1982, treas. 1997-2003), Laurens County C. of C., Kiwanis (preas. 1998). Avocations: piano and organ, running, swimming, historical houses. Home: PO Box 42 Laurens SC 29360-0042 Office: Laurens County Libr 1017 W Main St Laurens SC 29360-2663 E-mail: BCooper@LCPL.Org.

COOPER, WILLIAM EDWIN, university president, educator; b. Balt, Md, Mar. 20, 1951; s. William Daniel and Mildred (Hively) C.; m. Clarissa Holmes, July 5, 1984; children: Ashley, Courtney. AB magna cum laude, AM, Brown U., 1973; PhD, MIT, 1976. NIH postdoctoral fellow speech comm. group MIT Rsch. Lab. Electronics, Cambridge, 1976-78, rsch. affiliate, 1978-83; asst. prof. psychology Harvard U., Cambridge, 1978-81, assoc. prof. psychology, 1981-83; prof. psychology U. Iowa, Iowa City, 1983-89, assoc. dean for R&D Coll. Liberal Arts, 1987-89; prof. psychology Tulane U., New Orleans, 1989-96, dean Coll. Arts and Scis., 1989-91, dean faculty liberal arts and sci., 1991-96; prof. linguistics and psychology Georgetown U., Washington, 1996—98, exec. v.p. main campus, 1996-98; pres. U. Richmond, Va., 1998—. Fellow Newcomb Coll., 1989-96. Author: Speech Perception and Production: Studies in Selective Adaptation, 1979; co-author: Syntax and Speech, 1980, Fundamental Frequency in Sentence Production, 1981; editor: Cognitive Aspects of Skilled Typewriting, 1983; co-editor: Sentence Processing: Psycholinguistic Studies Presented to Merrill Garrett, 1979; contbr. articles to profl. jours. Recipient Harold Schlosberg Meml. award in psychology, 1973, Acoustical Soc. Am. Biennial award, 1986; NSF grad. fellow, 1973, John Simon Guggenheim fellow, 1983; Fulbright Sr. scholar U. Fed. de Minas Gerais, Belo Horizonte, Brazil, 1984. Mem. Phi Beta Kappa, Sigma Xi. Office: U Richmond Office of Pres Richmond VA 23173 E-mail: wcooper@richmond.edu.

COOPER, WILLIAM EWING, JR., retired army officer; b. Birmingham, Ala., June 19, 1929; s. William Ewing and Margaret (Tate) C.; m. Mary Jane Beers, Feb. 16, 1952; children: William Ewing III, Leslie Beers. BA in History, Citadel, 1951; MA in History, U. Miami, 1961; postgrad., Georgetown U., 1970-72, U.S. Army Command and Gen. Staff Coll., 1961-62, Armed Forces Staff Coll., 1966-67, Army War Coll., 1970-71. Commd. 2d lt. U.S. Army, 1951, advanced through grades to maj. gen., 1979, comdr. arty. group, 1972-73, sr. liaison officer to Brit. Army, 1973-75, comdg. gen. arty. brigade, 1976-79, chief of staff NORAD Peterson AFB, Colo., 1979-81, comdg. gen. 32d Army Air Def. Command Darmstadt, Fed. Republic Germany, 1981-83, dep. dir. Def. Intelligence Agy. Washington, 1983-85; ret., 1985; assoc. Burdeshaw Assocs. Ltd., Bethesda, Md., 1986-93; ret., 1993. Decorated D.S.M., Def. Superior Service medal with oak cluster, Legion of Merit, Bronze Star with V and 2 oak leaf clusters, Air medal with 3 oak leaf clusters, Army Meritorious Service medal; knights cross (Germany), Honor medal (Vietnam). Mem. Phi Alpha Theta, Phi Sigma Alpha Clubs: Fla. Citadel (v.p. 1976-78); Colo. Citadel (pres. 1980-81). Democrat. Presbyterian. Avocations: golf, skiing, hunting. Home: 4925 Old Creek Dr Sarasota FL 34233-3942

COOPER, WILLIAM JAMES, JR., history educator; b. Kingstree, S.C., Oct. 22, 1940; s. William James and Mamie (Mayes) C.; m. Patricia Holmes, Sept. 1, 1962; children: William James III, Michael Holmes. AB, Princeton U., 1962; PhD, Johns Hopkins U., 1966. Asst. prof. history La. State U., Baton Rouge, 1968-70, assoc. prof., 1970-78, prof., 1978—, dean Grad. Sch., 1982-89, Boyd prof., 1989—. Douglas Southall Freeman prof. U. Richmond, 2000. Author: The Conservative Regime: South Carolina 1877-1890, 1968, The South and the Politics of Slavery 1828-1856, 1978, Liberty and Slavery: Southern Politics to 1860, 1983, Jefferson Davis, American, 2000; co-author: The American South: A History, 1990, 3d edit., 2001; editor: Jefferson Davis, The Essential Writings, 2003, co-editor: A Master's Due: Essays in Honor of David Herbert Donald, 1985, Writing the Civil War: The Quest to Understand, 1998; editor: Social Relations in Our Southern States (Daniel Hundley), 1979, So. Biography Series, 1979-93; also articles. Served to capt. U.S. Army, 1966-68. Recipient Prize for Biography L.A. Times, 2001, Jefferson Davis award Mus. of Confederacy, 2001; sr. fellow Inst. So. History, Johns Hopkins U., 1971-72, rsch. fellow Charles Warren Ctr. Studies in Am. History, Harvard U., 1975-76, Guggenheim fellow, 1980-81, NEH fellow, 1988-89; named Disting. Rsch. Master La. State U., 1980. Fellow Soc. Am. Historians; mem. Am. Hist. Assn., Orgn. Am. Historians, So. Hist. Assn. Presbyterian. Home: 250 Amherst Ave Baton Rouge LA 70808-4603 Office: La State U Dept History Baton Rouge LA 70803-0001 E-mail: wcooper@lsu.edu.

COOPER, WILLIAM LEWIS, research librarian, lawyer, consultant; b. Highland Park, Mich., Sept. 11, 1944; s. Frank Edward and Margaret Ellen (Hayes) C.; m. Bonnie McIntyre Devine, June 7, 2002. AB, Dartmouth Coll., 1966; JD, U. Mich., 1972, AM in Library Sci., 1974. Bar: Mich. 1972, D.C. 1976. Assoc. Miller-Canfield, Detroit, 1972-74; reference libr. U. Pa., 1974-75; libr. Hogan & Hartson, Washington, 1975-77; dir. legal rsch. Dykema Gossett, Detroit, 1977-91, Williamsburg Assocs., Birmingham, Mich., 1991-95; rsch. libr. Coll. William and Mary, Williamsburg, Va., 1995-99; legal practice prof. U. Mich., 1999-2002; assoc. prof. John Marshall Law Sch., Atlanta, 2002—. Contbr. articles to profl. jours. With US Army, 1967-69. Mem. Mich. State Bar Assn. (legal econs. sect.), Detroit Bar Found. (treas. 1980-82, trustee 1979-85). Episcopalian. Home: 495 Valley St Scottsville VA 24590-0702 Office: 1422 W Peachtree St NW Atlanta GA 30309 Personal E-mail: wlcoop44@hotmail.com.

COOPER, WILLIAM MARION, physician; b. Pitts., Jan. 12, 1919; s. Lardin Monroe and Sophia Antoinette (Swartz) C.; m. Sara Georgia Thomas, Jan. 19, 1942; children: Mikell Lee Cooper Schenck, William Marion, Thomas L., George Robert. BS, Pa. State U., 1939; MD, Hahnemann Med. Coll., 1943; JD, U. Pitts., 1987. Diplomate Am. Bd. Internal Medicine, Am. Bd. Hematology; cert. in Geriatrics. Intern Shadyside Hosp., Pitts., 1943; resident U. Pitts. Sch. Medicine, 1946-48, Cleve. Clin. Found., 1948; practice medicine specializing in internal medicine and hematology Pitts., 1948—; mem. staff Presbyn.-Univ., Shadyside; chief dept. medicine Shadyside Hosp., 1980-91; mem. med. faculty U. Pitts., 1948—, clin. prof. medicine, 1958—, dir. div. continuing edn., 1970-80, assoc. dean continuing edn., 1974-80; dir. continuing edn. Univ. Health Center, Pitts., 1975-80; sr. asst. vice-chancellor Univ. Health Ctr. Pitts., 1979-80. Med. dir. Ctrl. Blood Bank, Pitts., 1951-60, Pitts. Skin and Cancer Found., 1958-65. Contbr. articles to med. jours. Served with M.C. U.S. Army, 1944-45. Mem. AMA, AAAS, ACP (master; bd. govs. 1965-71), Pa. Med. Soc., Allegheny County Med. Soc., Am., Internat. Socs. Hematology, Am. Soc. Internal Medicine, Am. Coll. Legal Medicine, Oakmont (Pa.) Country Club. Home: The Mews 302 Fox Chapel Rd Pittsburgh PA 15238-2335 Office: Shadyside Hosp Hallman Cancer Ctr 5230 Centre Ave Pittsburgh PA 15232-1381

COOPER, WILLIAM S. state supreme court justice; b. Sept. 15, 1941; BA, U. Ky., 1963, JD with high distinction, 1970. Ptnr. Collier, Arnett, Coleman & Cooper, 1970—79; judge Ky. 9th Judicial Cir., Div. 1, 1979—96; justice Ky. Supreme Ct., Frankfort, 1996—. Capt. USAF, 1963-67. Office: Hardin County Justice Ctr 120 E Dixie Ave Elizabethtown KY 42701-1469

COOPER, WILLIAM SECORD, information science educator; b. Winnipeg, Man., Can., Nov. 7, 1935; m. Helen Clare Dunlap, July 22, 1964. BA, Principia Coll., 1956; MSc, MIT, 1959; PhD, U. Calif.-Berkeley, 1964. Alexander von Humboldt scholar U. Erlangen, Germany, 1964-65; asst. prof. info. sci. U. Chgo., 1966-70; assoc. prof. info. sci. U. Calif., Berkeley, 1971-76, prof., 1976-94, prof. grad. sch., 1994-96, prof. emeritus, 1996—. Miller prof. Miller Inst., Berkeley, 1975-76. Hon. rsch. fellow Univ. Coll., London, 1977-78; ACM/SIGIR Triennial Rsch. award, 1994. Office: Univ Calif Sch Info Mgmt & Sys Berkeley CA 94720-0001 E-mail: wcooper@socrates.berkeley.edu.

COOPER, WILLIAM THOMAS, retired air force officer, writer, educator; b. Itta Bena, Miss., Feb. 3, 1938; s. Singleton Moore and Vera Ernestine (Bussell) C.; m. Janet Faye Johnston, Mar. 8, 1960 (div. 1984); children: William Thomas Jr., Teryl Catherine, Jonathan Gregory; m. Joan Ellen Schulhafer, Aug. 17, 1985. BA, La. Tech. U., 1962; MA in Polit. Sci., U. Louisville, 1970. Commd. 2d lt., 1962; advanced through grades to col., 1983; chief internal info. Hdqrs. SAC, Offutt AFB, Nebr., 1973-75, chief pub. affairs 3902nd Air Base Wing, 1975-78; dir. pub. affairs Hdqrs. Eighth Air Force, Barksdale AFB, La., 1978-81; special asst. for B-1 Bomber Pub. Affairs USAF, Pentagon, Washington, 1981-83, chief, media rels., 1983-84, dir. internal info., 1984-86; tchr. Montclair (N.J.) Kimberly Acad., 1987—; dean student life Montclair (N.J.) Kimberley Acad., 1991-92. Author: Triad of Knives, 1984, Warmoon, 1985. Decorated Legion of Merit, Meritorious Service medal with 1 oak leaf cluster, Commendation medal with 1 oak leaf cluster. Baptist. Avocations: art, photography.

COOPER, WILLIAM THOMAS, natural history artist; b. Adamstown, NSW, Australia, Apr. 6, 1934; s. William and Coral (Bird) C.; m. Wendy Elizabeth Price, June 25, 1979. One-man shows include Artarmon Galleries, Sydney, 1973, 1980, City of Newcastle Art Gallery, 1973, Represented in permanent collections, Woodhall Art Found., Australian Nat. Libr., Papua New Guinea Govt., Newcastle Art Gallery, Rockhampton City Art Gallery; work represented in A Portfolio of Australian Birds, 1968, Parrots of the World, 1973, The Birds of Paradise and Bowerbirds, 1977, Australian Parrots, 1980, Kingfishers and Related Birds vol. I, 1983, vol. II, 1985, vol. III, 1987, vol. IV, 1993, vols. V & VI, 1995, Fruits of the Rainforest, 1995, The Turacos, 1997, The Cockatoos, 2001, illustrator Fierce Encounter, 1970, The Birds of Paradise, 1998, Cockatoos: A Portfolio of All Species, 2001, designer (stamps), Papua, New Guinea, 1973; co-dir.:. Decorated Order of Australia, Australian Govt., 1994; recipient Gold medal Distinction, Natural History Art Acad. Natural Scis., Phila., 1992. Office: PO Box 314 Malanda 4885 Australia Fax: 07 40968 333.

COOPER, WILLIAM WAGER, business educator; b. Birmingham, Ala., July 23, 1914; s. William Wager and Rae (Rossman) C.; m. Ruth Fay West, Sept. 11, 1944. AB, U. Chgo., 1938; postgrad., Columbia U., 1940-42; DSc (hon.), Ohio State U., 1969; MA (hon.), Harvard U., 1976; DSc (hon.), Carnegie Mellon U., 1982; D (hon.), U. Alicante, Spain, 1995. Asst. to comptroller TVA, 1938-40; prin. economist Bur. Budget, 1942-44; asst. prof. econs. U. Chgo., 1944-46; asst. prof. to prof. Carnegie-Mellon U., 1946-68; dean Carnegie-Mellon U. (Sch. Urban and Pub. Affairs), 1968-75, univ. prof. mgmt. sci. and pub. affairs, 1975-76, research prof. mgmt. sci. and pub. policy, 1976—; Arthur Lowes Dickinson prof. accounting Grad. Sch. Bus. Adminstrn., Harvard U., 1976-80; prof. mgmt. and acctg., mgmt. scis. and info. systems, Grad. Sch. Bus. Adminstrn. U. Tex., Austin, 1980-94; Foster Parker prof. fin. and mgmt. emeritus Grad. Sch. Bus. Adminstrn. U. Tex., Austin, 1994—; chmn. mgmt. sci. and info. systems dept. U. Tex., 1986-88. Vis. disting. internat. lectr. acctg. Am. Acctg. Assn., 1986, dir. pubs., chmn., pubs. com., exec. com., 1987-89. Author: (with A. Charnes) Management Models and Industrial Applications of Linear Programming, (with H. Leavitt, M.W. Shelly) New Perspectives in Organization Research, (with others) Studies in Budgeting, (with A. Charnes and R. Niehaus) Studies in Manpower Planning, (with Y. Ijiri) Eric Louis Kohler: Accounting's Man of Principles, (with A. Charnes, A. Lewin and L. Seiford) Data envelopment Analysis: Theory, Methodology, Applications, (with A. Whinston) New Directions in Computational Economics, (with R.G. Thompson and R.M. Thrall) Extensions and New Developments in DEA: The Annals of Operations Research, A Comprehensive Text,, 2000; editor: Auditing: A Jour. Practice and Theory, 1978-81; editorial bd. Management Science, 1954-74, Naval Research Logistics Quarterly, 1957-74; contbr. articles to profl. jours.; co-editor (with Y. Ijiri) Kohler's Dictionary for Accountants, 6th edit. Co-recipient John Von Neumann theory prize, 1982; recipient award Am. Inst. Accts., 1945, Profl. Achievement citation U. Chgo. Alumni Assn., 1986, Outstanding Contbr. to Auditing award Am. Acctg. Assn., 1988, Outstanding Acctg. Educator award, 1990, Notable Contbns. to Lit. award in govtl. and non-profit acctg., 1991; named to U. Tex. Coll. Bus. Adminstrn. Hall of Fame, 1990, Acctg. Hall of Fame, 1996, Lifetime Contbns. to Mgmt. Acct. award 2002. Fellow Econometric Soc., AAAS; mem. Inst. Mgmt. Sci. (1st pres.), Ops. Research Soc. Am. (editorial bd. 1957-68) Office: U Tex CBA 4-202 Austin TX 78712-1174 Home: Apt 304 1034 Liberty Park Dr Austin TX 78746-6853

COOPER, WYLOLA, retired special education educator; b. Cleve., Feb. 12, 1926; d. William Wilkins and Leola Anderson; m. Henry J. Cooper, Apr. 4, 1948 (dec. May 1992); children: Henry J. Jr., Wylola Jr., Antigone, Yolanda Lee. BE, Chgo. State U., 1967; MA, Roosevelt U., 1974. Itinerant tchr. Dist. 117 Elem. Level, Hickory Hills, Ill., 1968-71; tchr. learning disabled, emotionally and behaviorally handicapped Conrady Jr. High Sch. Dist. 117, Hickory Hills, 1971-86, behavior disorders tchr., 1986-91, dept. chairperson spl. edn. dept., 1988-94, tchr. emotionally disturbed and behaviorally handicapped, 1988-94;

ret., 1994. Staff S.W. Coop. of Cook County for Spl. Edn., Oak Forest; mem. organizing com. Ill. Spl. Edn. Program, Springfield, 1971-72. Min. of care U. Children's Hosp.; vol. Midwest Workers in Chgo. Mem. Coun. Exceptional Children, Am. Fedn. Tchrs. Union, S.W. Coop. for Spl. Edn. Democrat. Roman Catholic. Avocations: swimming, counseling. Home: 1451 E 55th St Chicago IL 60615-5429

COOPER, WYN, poet, editor, songwriter; b. Detroit, Jan. 2, 1957; s. William Wendell and Maree Edith C. BA in English, U. Utah, 1979; MA in English, Hollins Coll., 1981. Editor-in-chief Quar. West, Salt Lake City, 1983—85; tchr., editor Bennington Coll., Vt., 1989—94; prof. Marlboro Coll., Marlboro, 1993—96; founder, owner Wyn Cooper Music, Brattleboro, 1995—; freelance writer, 1996—. Dir. reading series North Bennington Ind. Artist's Space, 1992-95, Marlboro Coll., 1993-97. Author: The Country of Here Below, 1987, The Way Back, 2000, Secret Address, 2002; composer: (songs) All I Wanna Do, 1993 (Grammy award, 1995); composer: (CD) (with Madison Smartt Bell) Forty Words for Fear, 2003. Recipient Snow Line award Pacific Internat., 1993; Writing fellow Ucross Found., 1988. Mem. ASCAP (Pop Music award 1996), Poetry Soc. Am., Acad. Am. Poets (assoc.). Home and Office: 45 Metcalf Ln Brattleboro VT 05301 E-mail: wcooper@sover.net.

COOPERMAN, ALVIN, television and theatrical producer; b. Bklyn. s. Nathan and Marietta (Steinmann) C.; m. Marilyn Frances Fisher; Children: Karen Lynn, Audrey Joan, Margot Jane. Exec. dir. booking Shubert Theatre Enterprises, N.Y.C., 1963-68; v.p. spl. programs NBC, N.Y.C., 1967-68; exec. v.p. Madison Sq. Garden Ctr., Inc., N.Y.C., 1968-72; pres. Madison Sq. Garden Prodns., N.Y.C., 1968-72; CEO Athena Comms. Corp., N.Y.C., 1972—. Developed and produced spl. program Wide Wide World, 1955; exec. prodr. Producer's Showcase, 1955-56, Big Event, 1976-77, Screen Gems, 1957-58; prodns. include Dodsworth, Rosalinda, Jack and the Beanstalk, Shirley Temple Storybook, 1956-57, The Untouchables, 1962-63, Bolshoi Ballet Romeo and Juliet (Emmy award nomination 1976), Pele's Last Game, Amahl and the Night Visitors, A Tribute to Toscanini (Emmy award 1980), An Evening with Jerome Robbins (Emmy award 1981), The Life of Pope John Paul II, Ain't Misbehavin, 1985 (Emmy award, Best Musical of the Year award NAACP), My Two Loves, 1986, Safe Passage, 1987, Family Album, 1987, Witness to Survival, 1988-90; prodr./writer animated spl. NBC-TV Fourth King, 1984; prodr./dir./writer TV spl. Mobs and Mobster, 1993; prodr. cable TV show The Higgins Boys and Gruber Show, 1993 (Ace award nominee), ABC movie: Follow the River, 1994; writer: (stage musical) Honky Tonk Heaven, 1995, (ABC spl.) Susan B. Anthony Slept Here, 1995 (Am. Women in Radio and TV Best Documentary award), (feature film) Charity Royall, 1997-98; (play) Thrall, 1999; creator, writer: (websites) The Stork Club, Platinum, 1996; writer, lyricist (musical) The Life and Adventures of Santa Claus, 1998, weathertainment.com, 1999; established Infotainment Internat., Inc., 1999; website developer (with Herman Rush) Weathertainment.com, 1999. Creative cons. Rep. Nat. Conv., 1972; mem., trustee Judy Holliday Meml. Com. for Am. Med. Ctr., Denver; chmn. N.Y. chpt. Arthritis Found.; pres. Broadway Walk Stars Found., 2000. Recipient Peabody award, 1957, Christopher award, 1957, Judy Holliday Humanitarian award, 1972. Mem. Newcomen Soc. N.Am., Am. Theatre Planning Bd., Players Club. Home: 146 Central Park W 4F New York NY 10023-2005

COOPERMAN, BARRY S. educational administrator, educator, scientist; b. N.Y.C., Dec. 11, 1941; married, 1963; 2 children. BA, Columbia U., 1962; PhD in Chemistry, Harvard U., 1968. NATO fellow biochemistry Pasteur Inst., 1967-68; from asst. prof. to assoc. prof. dept. chemistry U. Pa., 1968-72, prof. bioorganic chemistry, 1977—, vice provost for rsch., 1982-95. Dir. French Inst., 1993-2001. Trustee Assoc. Univs., Inc., 1983—, chmn. bd., 1989-91; mem. policy governing bd. Advanced Tech. Ctr. S.E. Pa., 1984-88; bd. mgrs. Morris Arboretum, 1985-91; bd. dirs. Wistar Inst., 1987-2001; internat. sci. adv. bd. Max-Planck Inst. for Molecular Genetics, 2001—. Mem. Am. Soc. Biol. Chemists, Am. Chem. Soc. Achievements include research in mechanism of phosphoryl transfer enzymes; ribosomes; serum serine protease inhibitors; ribonucleotide reductase. Office: Univ Pa Dept Chemistry 358 Chemistry Philadelphia PA 19104

COOPERMAN, MATTHEW B. language educator; b. New Haven, Conn., Apr. 8, 1964; s. Lawrence Rayfield and Sandra Jean Cooperman. BA, Colgate U., Hamilton, N.Y., 1986; MA, U. Colo., 1992; PhD, Ohio U., 1998. Instr. Ohio U., Athens, 1997—98; adj. prof., tchg. asst. Harvard U., Cambridge, Mass., 1999; instr., adj. prof. U. Colo., Boulder, 1999—2001; asst. prof. Cornell Coll., Mt. Vernon, Iowa, 2002—03; asst. prof. dept. English Colo. State U., Ft. Collins, 2003—. Editor, contbg. editor Quarter After Eight, Athens, 1993—. Author: (book) A Sacrificial Zinc, 2001 (Lena Miles prize, 2001), Surge (Wick prize, 1998). Mem. grants bd. Arts and Humanities Assembly of Boulder, 2001. Mem.: MLA, Acad. Am. Poets, Assn. of Writing Programs. Avocations: climbing, skiing, music. Home: 7 Eagle Hill Terr Redwood City CA 94062 Office: Colo State U Dept Engring 359 Eddy Bldg Fort Collins CO 80523

COOPERMAN, ROBERT N. lawyer; b. Bklyn., July 9, 1935; s. Albert J. and Edith Cooperman; m. Barbara F. Burger, Mar. 22, 1959; children: M. James, Tod D., Nancy D. BBA, CCNY, 1956; LLB, Columbia U., 1959; LLM in Taxation, NYU, 1964. Bar: N.Y. 1959, U.S. Dist. Ct. (so. and ea. dists.) N.Y. 1959, U.S. Tax Ct. 1968, U.S. Supreme Ct. 1968. Assoc. Arthur Richenthal, N.Y.C., 1960-65; pres. Cooperman, Levitt, Winikoff, Lester & Newman and predecessor, N.Y.C., 1966—2000. Pres. United Community Fund, Great Neck, N.Y., 1969; vice chmn. Great Neck Village Zoning Bd. Appeals, 1980-85; v.p. Temple Israel, Great Neck, 1975-81. Mem. ABA, N.Y. State Bar Assn., Tides Homeowners Assn. (pres.). Home: 25 Strathmore Rd Great Neck NY 11023-1035 Office: Cooperman Lester Miller LLP 800 3d Ave New York NY 10022-7604 also: 1129 Northern Blvd Manhasset NY 11030-3022 Address: PO Box 292 6 Mitchell Dunes Ln Amagansett NY 11930 E-mail: RCooperman@clmlaw.com.

COOPERMAN, SAUL, educational administrator; b. Newark, Dec. 18, 1934; s. Louis Frank and Lucille (Swarthberg) C.; m. Paulette Beth Koch, Aug. 17, 1958; children: Suzanne, Deborah, David. BS, Lafayette Coll., 1956; MEd, Rutgers U., 1961, EdD, 1969; DHL (hon.), Drew U., 1984. Tchr. North Plainfield H.S., N.J., 1960-64; prin. Belvidere H..S., N.J., 1964-68; rsch. asst. Rutgers U., New Brunswick, N.J., 1968-69; supt. schs. Montgomery Twp., N.J., 1969-74, City of Madison, N.J., 1974-82; commr. N.J. State Dept. Edn., Trenton, 1982-90. Pres. Educate Am., 1990-2000; chmn. edn. adv. panel New Am. Sch. Devel. Corp., 1990-97; sec., treas., New Am. Schs., 2000—. Author: How Schools Really Work: Practical Advice to Parents from an Insider; contbr. articles; columnist (newspaper) Star Ledger, 1999—. Pres. 10,000 Mentors, Newark, 1996-2000. Served with USNR, 1956-82 Avocations: reading; athletics; travel. Address: 181 Roundtop Rd Bernardsville NJ 07924-2106

COOPERMAN, SUSAN, educator; b. Charleston, W.Va. m. William Cooperman. BS, U. Cin., 1971; MEd, U. North Fla., 1974. Instr. Ctr. Coll., Charleston, W.Va., 1971-72, Garnet Career Ctr, Charleston, W.Va., 1972-73, 75-83; prof. Montgomery Coll., Rockville, Md., 1983—. Adj. prof. Fla. C.C., Jacksonville, 1973-74, U. Charleston, 1974-75. Author: Professional Office Procedures, edits. 1, 2 and 3, Microsoft Publisher, 2000, Microsoft Publisher 2002. Mem. AAUP, Nat. Bus. Edn. Assn., Md. Bus. Assn. Avocations: music, gardening, crafts, history, reading. Office: Montgomery Coll 51 Mannakee St Rockville MD 20850-1101 E-mail: scooperm@mc.cc.md.us.

COOPERRIDER, TOM S. botanist, educator; b. Newark, Ohio, Apr. 15, 1927; s. Oscar Harold and Ruth Evelyn Cooperrider; m. Miwako Kunimura, June 13, 1953; children: Julie Ann, John Andrew. BA, Denison U., 1950; MS, U. Iowa, 1955; PhD, 1958. Instr. biol. scis. Kent (Ohio) State U., 1958-61, asst. prof., 1961-65, assoc. prof., 1965-69, prof., 1969-93, emeritus prof., 1993—, curator herbarium, 1968-93, dir. bot. gardens, 1972-93; mem. editl. bd. Univ. Press, 1976-79; on leave as asst. prof. dept. botany U. Hawaii, 1962-63. NSF rschr. Mountain Lake Biol. Sta. U. Va., 1958; faculty mem. Iowa Lakeside Lab. U. Iowa, 1965; cons. endangered and threatened species U.S. Fish and Wildlife Svc., Dept. Interior, 1976—83; cons. Davey Tree Expert Co., 1979—85, Ohio Natural Areas Coun., 1983. Author: (book) Ferns and Other Pteridophytes of Iowa, 1959, Vascular Plants of Clinton, Jackson and Jones Counties, Iowa, 1962, The Dicotyledoneae of Ohio, Part 2, 1995; editor (co-author): Endangered and Threatened Plants of Ohio, 1983, Seventh Catalog of the Vascular Plants of Ohio, 2001. Personnel placement U.S. Census Bur., Washington, 1950—51; orderly VA Hosp., Iowa City, 1952—53; active YMCA-YWCA Students in Govt., Washington, 1950; Quaker Internat. vol. Germany, 1951. With U.S. Army, 1945—46. Named dedicatee Kent Bog State Nature Preserve, Ohio Dept. Natural Resources, 1995; recipient Osborn award, Ohio Biol. Survey, 1994, Alumni Citation award, Denison U., 2000; fellow NSF predoctoral, 1957—58. Fellow: AAAS, Ohio Acad. Scis. (chair Ohio flora com. 1969—97), Explorers Club; mem.: So. Appalachian Bot. Soc., Bot. Soc. Am., Internat. Assn. Plant Taxonomists, Wilderness Soc., Nature Conservancy, Blue Key, Sigma Xi. Home: 548 Bowman Dr Kent OH 44240-4512

COOPERSMITH, JEFFREY ALAN, real estate developer; b. NYC, Mar. 23, 1946; s. Jack J. and Anita S. (Selikoff) C.; m. Marjorie Myers, July 5, 1987; children: Jarred, Aubrey, Lorie, Julie. B in Mgmt. Engring., Rensselaer Poly. Inst., 1967; MBA, Ohio State U., 1979. Security arbitrage Arnhold and S. Bleichroeder, Inc., N.Y.C., 1967-70; with Pfizer, Inc., N.Y.C., 1970-72, asst. contr. Minerals, Pigments and Metals divsn.; with Distbn. Ctrs., Inc. subs. Distek, Inc., Westerville, Ohio, 1972-87, v.p., contr., 1975-77, v.p., treas., 1977-78, v.p. fin., 1978-80; exec.v.p. Distek, Inc., Westerville, 1980-83, pres., COO, 1983-87, also bd. dirs.; pres. Directel, Inc., 1981-93; pres., CEO Triplefin, Inc., 1993—2001, Core Properties Ltd., Columbus, Ohio, 2002—. Bd. dirs. First Cmty. Bank. Mem. World Pres. Orgn. (bd. dirs., chmn.), JCCA Assn. (bd. dirs.), Columbus Jewish Cmty. Ctr., Columbus Jewish Fedn., Columbus Jewish Found. Office: Core Properties Ltd 401 N Front St Ste 350 Columbus OH 43215

COOPERSTEIN, PAUL ANDREW, lawyer, management consultant; b. New Bedford, Mass., Dec. 16, 1953; s. Leon I. and Dorothea (Silverman) C.; m. Beverly S. Schultz, July 16, 1983. BS summa cum laude, Ithaca Coll., 1974; JD, Western New Eng. Coll., 1978; cert. in dispute resolution, Cornell U., 1996. Bar: Mass. 1978, U.S. Ct. Appeals (1st cir.) 1979. Assoc. Law Office Irving Sheff, Boston, 1976-77; ptnr. Prince & Cooperstein, Boston and Cambridge, Mass., 1977-79, Cooperstein & Cooperstein, Cambridge, 1979-83; gen. counsel Carlyle-Omni Realty Investors, Inc., Lexington, Mass., 1986-88; pvt. practice Cambridge, 1983-85, 89-92; pres. Strategic Intervention Assocs., Inc., Cambridge, 1992—; dir. bus. devel. New Eng. Stereo, Inc., Boston, 1997-98. Mem. Milton (Mass.) Conservation Commn., 1988-92; co-chmn. The Partnership Found., 1997-99; bd. dirs. Temple Shalom, Milton, 1997-88, 2002—, treas., 2000. Mem. ASTD, Am. Mgmt. Assn., Soc. for Intercultural Tng. and Rsch. Home: 107 Hillside St Milton MA 02186-5217 E-mail: siapal@aol.com.

COOPERSTEIN, SHERWIN JEROME, medical educator; b. N.Y.C., Sept. 14, 1923; s. Joseph and Bessie (Berger) C.; m. Alice Ruth Peskin, June 1, 1947; children— Rhonda Ann, Lawrence Alan. BS, Coll. City N.Y., 1943; DDS, NYU, 1948; PhD in Anatomy, Western Res. U., 1951. Instr. biology Coll. City N.Y., 1943, 46-48; research asso. physiology N.Y. U., 1946-48; instr. anatomy Western Res. U., 1948-49, fellow anatomy, 1949-51, sr. instr., 1951-52, asst. prof. anatomy, 1952-55, asso. prof., 1955-64, asst. dean, 1957-64; prof., head dept. anatomy U. Conn. Schs. Medicine and Dental Medicine, Farmington, 1964-92, prof. emeritus, acting head dept., 1992-94; prof. emeritus, 1994—. Mem. adv. panel on med. student research NSF, 1960-61; mem. anatomical scis. tng. com. Nat. Inst. Gen. Med. Scis., 1966-70; mem. spl. study sect. on diabetes centers NIH, 1973-75, mem. ad hoc study sect. on research tng. grants in systems and integrative biology, 1977; mem. adv. panel on research personnel needs in basic biomed. sci. Nat. Acad. Scis./NRC, 1976-83 Contbr. articles profl. jours.; editorial adviser: Diabetes Lit. Index, 1966-79. Served with AUS, 1943-44. Mem. AAAS, Am. Chem. Soc., Marine Biol. Lab., Am. Assn. Anatomists, Am. Soc. Biol. Chemists, Am. Diabetes Assn., Sigma Xi. Home: 10 Hillsboro Dr West Hartford CT 06107-1011 Office: U Conn Health Ctr Farmington Ave Farmington CT 06030-0001 E-mail: scoopers@neuron.uchc.edu.

COOPERSTOCK, FRED ISAAC, physics educator, researcher; b. Winnipeg, Man., Can., Aug. 20, 1940; s. Thomas and Sima (Lipen) C.; m. Ruth Claire Bellan, Aug. 26, 1962; children: Jeremy, Ramona. BSc, U. Man., Winnipeg, 1962; PhD, Brown U., 1966. Prof. physics U. Victoria, Can., 1967—. Can.-France sci. exch. visitor Inst. Henri Poincaré, Paris, 1973-74, 80-81; Lady Davis vis. prof. Technion, Haifa, Israel, 1987-88; vis. prof. Tata Inst., Bombay, 1995, U. del Pais Vasco, Bilboa, Spain, 1995. Co-editor Developments in Relativity, Astrophysics and Cosmology, 1990, Procs. of the 3rd Can. Conf. on Gen. Relativity and Relativistic Astrophysics World Sci., 1990; apptd. reviewer Math. Revs., 1997; contbr. articles to profl. jours. Rsch. grantee Natural Scis. and Engring. Rsch. Coun. Can., 1968—. Mem. Internat. Soc. on Gen. Relativity and Gravitation, Am. Phys. Soc., European Acad. Scis. Avocations: badminton, photography. Office: Dept Physics and Astronomy Univ Victoria Victoria BC Canada V8W 3P6 E-mail: cooperstock@phys.uvic.ca.

COOR, LATTIE FINCH, university president; b. Phoenix, Sept. 26, 1936; s. Lattie F. and Elnora (Witten) C.; m. Ina Fitzhenry, Jan. 18, 1964 (div. 1988); children: William Kendall, Colin Fitzhenry, Farryl MacKenna Witten; m. Elva Wingfield, Dec. 27, 1994. AB with high honors (Phelps Dodge scholar), No. Ariz. U., 1958; MA with honors (Univ. scholar, Universal Match Found. fellow, Carnegie Corp. fellow), Washington U., St. Louis, 1960, PhD, 1964; LLD (hon.), Marlboro Coll., 1977, Am. Coll. Greece, 1982, U. Vt., 1991, No. Ariz. U., 2002. Adminstrv. asst. to Gov. Mich., 1961-62; asst. to chancellor Washington U., St. Louis, 1963-67, asst. dean Grad. Sch. Arts and Scis., 1967-69, dir. internat. studies, 1967-69, asst. prof. polit. sci., 1967-76, vice chancellor, 1969-74, univ. vice chancellor, 1974-76; pres. U. Vt., Burlington, 1976-89, Ariz. State U., Tempe, Ariz., 1990—2002, prof. pub. affairs, pres. emeritus, 2002—; chmn., CEO Ctr. for Future of Ariz., 2002—. Cons. HEW; spl. cons. to commr. U.S. Commn. on Edn., 1971-74; chmn. Commn. on Govtl. Rels., Am. Coun. on Edn., 1976-80; dir. New Eng. Bd. Higher Edn., 1976-89; co-chmn. joint com. on health policy Assn. Am. Univs. and Nat. Assn. State Univs. and Land Grant Colls., 1976-89; mem. pres. commn. NCAA, 1984-90, chmn. div. I, 1989; mem. Ariz. State Bd. Edn., 1993-98; chmn. Pacific 10 Conf., 1995-96. Trustee emeritus Am. Coll. Greece. Mem. Nat. Assn. Stae Univs. and Land Grant Colls. (chmn. bd. dirs. 1991-92), New Eng. Assn. Schs. and Colls. (pres. 1981-82), Am. Coun. on Edn (bd. dirs. 1991-93, 2000-02), Kellogg Commn. on Future of State and Land-Grant Univs. Office: Ctr for Future of Ariz 541 E Van Buren Ave Ste B-5 Phoenix AZ 85004 E-mail: Lattie.Coor@asu.edu.

COORAY, ASANTHA ROSHAN, astrophysicist, researcher; s. John Lucian and Leena Stella Cooray; m. Djuna Sunlight Copley-Woods, June 30, 2001. BSc in Physics, Math and Earth, Atmospheric & Planetary Scis., MSc in Earth & Planetary Sciences, MIT, 1997; MSc in Astronomy & Astrophysics, PhD in Astrophysics, U. Chgo., 2000. Rsch. and tchg. asst. MIT, Cambridge, Mass., 1996—97, U. Chgo., 1997—2000, rsch. fellow, 2000—01; sr. rsch. fellow Calif. Inst. Tech., Pasadena, 2001—. Contbr. articles to profl. jours. (Nathan Sugarman Award for Excellence in Rsch., Enrioc Fermi Inst., 2000). McCormick fellow, U. Chgo., 1997, Chandra Sci. Ctr. fellow, NASA, 2001, Miller fellow, 2001, Leverhulme fellow, U. Oxford, 2001. Fellow: Royal Astron. Soc. (life); mem.: Am. Astron. Soc. (life), Sigma Pi Sigma, Sigma Xi. Achievements include discovery of Understanding The Nature And Evolution Of The Universe, The Distribution And Statistics Of Galaxies And The Large Scale Structure, Physical Properties Of Outer Planets; development of Numerical And Computational Tools To Understand The Nature And Evolution Of The Galaxy Distribution In The Early And Local Universe. Office: California Institute of Technology 130 33 Theoretical Astrophysics Caltech Pasadena CA 91104

COORS, PETER HANSON, beverage company executive; b. Denver, Sept. 20, 1946; s. Joseph and Holly (Hanson) C.; m. Marilyn Gross, Aug. 23, 1969; children: Melissa, Christien, Carrie Ann, Ashley, Peter, David. BS in Idsl. Engring., Cornell U., 1969; MBA, U. Denver, 1970. Prodn. trainee, specialist Adolph Coors Co., Golden, Colo., 1970-71, dir. fin. planning, 1971-75, dir. market research, 1975-76, v.p. self distbn., 1976-77, v.p. sales and mktg., 1977-78, sr. v.p. sales and mktg., 1978-82, div. pres. sales, mktg. and adminstrn., 1982-85, pres. brewing div.; pres. Coors Brewing Co., Golden, Colo., 1989—, Coors Distbn. Co., 1976-82, 1976-81, chmn., from 1981, dir., Adolph Coors Co., 1973—, asst. sec.-treas., 1974-76; dir. CADCO, 1975-85; exec. v.p. Adolf Coors Co., Golden, Colo., 1991—; vice-chmn., CEO Coors Brewing Co., Golden, Colo., 1991—. Bd. dirs. Nat. Wildlife Fedn., 1978-81, Wildlife Legis. Fund, 1987—; hon. bd. dirs. Colo. Spl. Olympics Inc., 1978—; trustee Colo. Outward Bound Sch., 1978—, Adolph Coors Found., Pres.'s Leadership Com., U. Colo., 1978— ; chmn. Nat. Commn. on the Future of Regis Coll., 1981-82, chmn. devel. com., 1983—, now trustee. Mem. Nat. Indls. Adv. Council, Opportunities Ctrs. of Am., Young Pres.' Orgn., Ducks Unlimited (nat. trustee 1979, sr. v.p., mem. mgmt. com., exec. com. 1982—, dir. Can. 1982—, pres. 1984-85, chmn. bd. 1986—) Clubs: Met. Denver Exec. (dir 1979, pres. 1981—). Office: Adolf Coors Co PO Box 4030 Golden CO 80401-0030

COORS, WILLIAM K. brewery executive; b. Golden, Colo., Aug. 11, 1916; BSChemE, Princeton U., 1938, grad. degree in chem. engring., 1939. Pres. Adolph Coors Co., Golden, Colo., 1956—2000, chmn. bd., 1970—. Chmn. ACX Techs., Inc. Office: Adolph Coors Co PO Box 4030 Golden CO 80401*

COOTER, DALE A. lawyer; b. Syracuse, N.Y., Aug. 28, 1948; s. Charles Henry and Mavis Elizabeth (Wagner) C.; m. Mary Kathryn Nolan, Oct. 8, 1977; children: John Andrew, Jessica Averie. BA cum laude, SUNY, Fredonia, 1970; JD, Georgetown U., 1975. Bar: Md. 1975, D.C. 1976, Va. 1984, U.S. Dist. Ct. Md. 1976, U.S. Dist. Ct. D.C. 1976, U.S. Ct. Appeals (4th and D.C. cirs.) 1976, U.S. Supreme Ct. 1979. Ptnr. Cooter, Mangold, Tompert & Wayson, LLP, Washington, 1976—. Adj. prof. law Georgetown U., Washington, 1985—. Editor Georgetown U. Law Jour., 1973-75. Served with N.G. Mem. ABA, Va. Bar Assn., Md. Bar Assn., D.C. Bar Assn. Home: 4675 Kenmore Dr NW Washington DC 20007-1914 Office: Cooter Mangold Tompert & Wayson LLP 5301 Wisconsin Ave NW Ste 500 Washington DC 20015-2015 E-mail: dcooter@cootermangold.com.

COOVER, DORIS DIMOCK, artist; b. Beaverdam, Wis., Aug. 8, 1917; d. Almon Crowe and Alma Josephine (Johnson) Dimock; m. Francis Merle Coover, Apr. 11, 1945; children: Cheryl, Danelle. Student in Fashion and Design, Woodbury U., 1937. One-woman shows include Chappqua (N.Y.) Pub. Libr., 1964-79, Katonah (N.Y.) Gallery, 1967-72, Briarcliff (N.Y.) Coll., 1969, Silvermine (Conn.) Guild of Artists, 1965-81, Am. Can Corp., Greenwich, Conn., 1971—, Village Gallery at Gallmofry, Croton, N.Y., 1974-81, Manhattan Savs. Bank N.Y.C.-White Plains, 1963-68; gallery artist Virginia Barrett, Chappqua, 1964-98; exhibited in groups shows at Okla. Art Ctr., Oklahoma City, 1959, Tex. Oil Industry, Dallas, 1958, Delgado Mus., New Orleans, 1958, Dallas Mus. art, 1958-59, Westchester Art Soc., White Plaine, N.Y., 1962-74, Silvermine Guild Artists, 1970-81, Crocker Art Mus. Art Auction, 1981-98, Neuberger Mus., Purchase, N.Y., 1985, Sacramento Fine Arts, 1985 and many others; cover artist Sci. and Tech. Mag., 1966; work included in Am. Refs., 1978, Who's Who in Am. Art, 1996-97, Rockport Pubs.-Painting Color, 1997, 98, Sketching and Drawing, 1998. Mem., historian Officers Club, L.A., 1940-45; artist judge No. Westchester chpt. Cancreare, Bedford Village, N.J., 1958. Recipient numerous awards for art, including Helbein award Western Colo. Watercolor Soc. Mem. Nat. Watercolor Soc. (assoc.), Am. Watercolor Soc. (assoc.), Nat. Mus. Woman in Arts (charter), Crocker Art Mem. Republican. Avocations: visiting galleries with friends, reading mysteries, experimenting with art.

COOVER, HARRY WESLEY, manufacturing company executive; b. Newark, Del., Mar. 6, 1919; s. Harry Wesley and Anna (Rohm) C.; m. Muriel Zumbach, Sept. 17, 1941; children— Harry Wesley, Stephen R., Melinda Coover Paul. BS in Chemistry (Southerland prize), Hobart Coll., Geneva, N.Y., 1941; MS, Cornell U., 1942, PhD, 1944. Rsch. chemist Eastman Kodak Co., Rochester, N.Y., 1944-49; sr. rsch. chemist Tenn. Eastman Co., Kingsport, 1949-54, rsch. assoc., 1954-63, head polymers div., 1963-65, dir. rsch., 1965-73, v.p., 1970-73, exec. v.p., 1973-81; v.p. Eastman Kodak Co., Kingsport, 1981-84; internat. mgmt. cons. Kingsport, 1984-85; pres. New Bus. Devel. Loctite Corp., Newington, Conn., 1985-88, Mgmt. Cons., Kingsport, Tenn., 1988—. Bd. dirs. Reilly Industries Inc. Author; patentee in field. Mem. NAE, N.Y. Acad. Scis., Internat. Union Pure and Applied Chemistry, Am. Chem. Soc. (So. Chemist award 1960, Speaker of Yr. award N.E. Tenn. sect. 1962, Earle B. Barnes award 1985, Chem. Pioneers award 1986), AAAS, Am. Inst. Chemists, Indsl. Rsch. Inst. (pres. 1981-82, medal award 1984, Holland award 1987, Achievement award 1999), Soc. Chem. Industry, Masons. Presbyterian. Office: 1201 Eastman Rd PO Box 3866 Kingsport TN 37664-0866

COPE, DERRIKE, race car driver; b. Spanaway, Wash., Nov. 3, 1958; m. Renee Cope. Named NASCAR Late Model Sportsman of Yr., 1980, NASCAR Winston West Series Rookie of Yr., 1984, winner, NASCAR Late Model Sportsman Series, 1980, Winston West 500, Riverside, 1982, Winston Cup Daytona 500, 1990, Dover, 1990, Budweiser 500, 1990, Daytona 500, 1990, winner 6 top-20s, Winston Cup Series, 1994. Avocations: golf, horses. Office: c/o Bahari Racing 208 Rolling Hill Rd Mooresville NC 28117-6845

COPE, GINNY, poet; b. Silver Spring, Md., May 21, 1953; Contbr. poems, (Editor's Choice award), (cert.). Recipient Editor's Choice award, Internat. Libr. Poetry, 2000, 2003. Avocations: collecting autographs, decorating, gardening, music. Home: 5336 White Settlement Rd # 62 Fort Worth TX 76114-3647

COPE, JAMES DUDLEY, retired trade association executive; b. Nelsonville, Ohio, Apr. 22, 1932; s. James Wesley Cope; m. Katherine Clark Bealle, July 9, 1994. BA, Denison U., 1954; student, Inst. Orgn. Mgmt., Yale U., 1959. Exec. dir. Ohio State Pharm. Assn., Columbus, 1957-61; corp. sec. Nonprescription Drug Mfrs. Assn., Washington, 1961-66, v.p., sec., 1966-67, exec. v.p., 1967-73, pres., 1973-99, name changed to Consumer Healthcare Products Assn., Washington, 1999; ret., 1999. Pres. Nat. Conf. Pharm. Orgns., Washington, 1975, 83, 88, 98; bd. dirs. First Am. Bank, Washington, 1986-92; bd. overseers U. Calif. Sch. Pharmacy, San Francisco, 1997-2000; exec. v.p. adv. com. Am. Assn. Colls. Pharmacy. Contbr. articles to profl. jours. Pres. Glen Mar Pk. Civic Assn., Bethesda, Md., 1963; pres. bd. trustees Faith United Meth. Ch., Rockville, Md., 1978; bd. dirs. Coun. on Family Health, N.Y.C., 1967-99, Children's Hosp., 1968-76. Cpl. U.S. Army, 1954-56. Recipient Achievement medal Alpha Zeta Omega, 1960, Alumni citation Denison U., 1979, FDA Commrs.'s spl. citation, 1987, 99, named Man of Yr., Am. Druggist, 1959. Mem.: Nat. Assn. Execs. (pres. 1984), World Self-Medication Industry (vice chmn. 1979—86, 1989—99), Greater Washington Soc. Assn. Execs., Am. Soc. Assn. Execs. (bd. dirs. 1979—82), Denison U. Alumni Assn., Met. Club (N.Y.C.), Sky Club (N.Y.C.), Congl. Country Club (Potomac, Md.), Met. Club (Washington). Republican. Home: 631 Findley Ct Estes Park CO 80517-9038

COPE, JEANNETTE NAYLOR, executive search consultant; b. Corpus Christi, Tex., Feb. 9, 1956; d. Glen R. and Jeannine (Withington) N.; m. John R. Cope, May 22, 1993. BA in Psychology and Sociology, Trinity U., 1978. Asst. fin. dir. Jim Baker for Atty. Gen. Campaign, Houston, 1978; fin. dir. Rep. Party of Tex., Austin, 1979-81; regional Eagle rep. Rep. Nat. Com., Washington, 1981-83; devel. officer Nat. Endowment for the Arts, Washington, 1983-87; sr. project mgr. Internat. Skye Assocs., Washington, 1988; spl. asst. to Pres. of U.S. The White House, 1989-90, dep. asst. to Pres. of U.S., dep. dir. of presdl. pers., 1990-93; pres. J. Naylor Cope Co., Washington, 1994—. NEA liaison Pres.' Com. on Arts and Humanites, Washington, 1985-87; dir. Internat. Skye Advisor, Washington, 1988; bd. dirs. Bush/Quayle Alumni Assn., TransTech. Corp.; mem. Officer Pers. Mgmt.'s Task Force on Exec. and Mgmt. Devel., Washington, 1990. Mem. Pres.'s Com. on the Arts and Humanities, 2001—; chmn. alumni admissions coun. Trinity U., Washington, 1986—87; mem. Bush Cheney Transition Team, 2001; vestrywoman St. John's Episcopal Ch., Washington, 1990—94, co-chmn. outreach com., 1991—94, chmn. search com. for 14th rector, jr. warden, 1994—97, sr. warden, 1998—2001; bd. dirs. The Compass Rose Soc. of the Anglican Communion, 1999—, exec. com., 2000—; bd. dirs. Coop. Urban Ministry Ctr., Washington, 1987—89, Pennsylvania Ave. Devel. Corp., 1993—96, Decatur House, Washington, 1998—, exec. com., 2000—, vice-chmn., bd. dirs., 2001—; bd. visitors Kanuga Confs., 2001—. Tex. Coun. of Ch. Related Colls. scholar, 1974. Mem. Am. Soc. Assn. Execs. (exec. recruiter), Tex. State Soc. (chmn. membership com. 1981), Nat. Trust for Hist. Preservation, Smithsonian Instn., Am. Film Inst., Mcpl. Art Soc. (N.Y.C.), 1925 F Street Club (chmn. mems. com.), President's Club, Columbia Country Club (Chevy Chase, Md.), Tex. Breakfast Club, Blue Key (sec. 1976-78), City Tavern Club, Chi Beta Epsilon (v.p. San Antonio coun. 1976). Republican. Episcopalian. Office: J Naylor Cope Co PO Box 40069 Washington DC 20016-0069 Business E-mail: jnc@jnaylorcopecompany.com.

COPE, JOHN R(OBERT), lawyer; b. San Angelo, Tex., May 30, 1942; s. Robert Lloyd and Meta (Young) C.; m. Jeannette L. Naylor; 1 child, Lloyd Chapman. BBA, U. Tex., 1964, JD, 1966; MTS summa cum laude, Wesley Theol. Sem., Washington, 2001. Bar: Tex. 1966, D.C. 1976. Ptnr. Bracewell & Patterson, Attys., Houston, 1966-76, Washington, 1976—, mem. adv. mgmt. com., 1987-90; sr. ptnr., 1994—. Vice chmn. bd. dirs., gen. counsel Century Nat. Bank, Washington, 1982-2001; bd. dirs., gen. counsel Columbia Nat. Bank, Washington, 1987-90; bd. dirs., v.p., gen. counsel Century Bancshares, Washington, 1985-2001; mem. fed. savs. and loan adv. coun. Fed. Home Loan Bank Bd., Washington, 1980-81; chmn., lectr. Practicing Law Inst. Seminars on Energy Litigation, Washington, 1980, 81; chief judge Wake Island Ct., Wake Island, North Pacific Ocean, 1989. Bd. govs., mem. exec. com., chmn. personnel and acad. affairs com. Wesley Theol. Sem., Washington, 1997—; mem. devel. bd. Lon Morris Coll., Lake Jackson, Tex., 1974-76; mem. Southwest U. Spl. Edn. Found., San Marcos, Tex., 1973-76; v.p., dir. Harris County Easter Seal Soc., Houston, 1972-76; bd. dirs., sec. Nemours Wildlife Found., Yemassee, S.C., 1993—; treas. Dem. Party Harris County, Houston, 1976-77; mem. nat. fin. coun. Dem. Nat. Com., Washington, 1976-80; cert. lay spkr. United Meth. Ch., dist. dir. lay speaking dist. Washington-Columbia. Mem. ABA (mem. litigation sect.), D.C. Bar Assn. (mem. litigation and govt. contracts sect.), Tex. Bar Assn. (mem. litigation sect.), Houston Bar Assn. (mem. gen. litigation sect.), Orton Soc. Republican. Office: Bracewell & Patterson 2000 K St NW Ste 500 Washington DC 20006-1872 E-mail: jcope@bracepatt.com.

COPE, JOSEPH ADAMS, lawyer; b. Summit, N.J., Jan. 15, 1945; s. Joseph H. and Eunice (Adams) Cope; m. Michele Zeleny, Sept. 25, 1982 (dec. Dec. 2001). BA, U. Colo., 1967, JD, 1976. Bar: Colo. 1967, Calif. 1985, U.S. Dist. Ct. Colo. 1976, U.S. Ct. Appeals (10th cir.) 1977, U.S. Claims Ct. 1984, U.S. Supreme Ct. 1984; cert. civil trial advocate NBTA, 2001. Assoc. Vranesh & Musick, Boulder, Colo., 1976—78; ptnr. Musick and Cope, Boulder, 1978—91; of counsel Frascona, Joiner, Goodman & Greenstein, P.C., Boulder, 1991—. Served to lt. USN, 1967-73. Mem. ABA, Colo. Bar Assn., Boulder County Bar Assn., State Bar Calif., Lawyer-Pilots Bar Assn., Order of Coif. Avocation: raising shire draft horses. Home: 8595 N 95th St Longmont CO 80504-7768 Office: Frascona Joiner Goodman & Greenstein PC 4750 Table Mesa Dr Boulder CO 80305-5500 E-mail: jaj@frascona.com.

COPE, KATHLEEN ADELAIDE, critical care and parish nurse, educator; b. Bethlehem, Pa., Sept. 12, 1926; d. Harry Raymond and Mabel Eva (Newhard) Stine; m. Robert Clayton Cope, Aug. 9, 1951; children: Debra Kathleen Howard, Terry Faye Cicero. BA in Psychology summa cum laude, Bellevue (Nebr.) Coll., 1972; diploma, St. Luke's Hosp., Bethlehem, 1951; student, Whitworth Coll., Spokane, 1989, Wash. State U., 1989. RN, Pa., Wash.; cert. nutrition support nurse; cert. critical care nurse, quality improvement, health promotion specialist. Pvt. duty nurse Exeter (N.H.) Hosp., 1957-60; nurse Red Cross Blood Mobile, Portsmouth area, N.H., 1961-65; staff nurse Clarkson Hosp., Omaha, 1966, asst. head nurse, 1966-67, head nurse, 1967-68, supr., organizer coronary care ctr., 1968-70; staff nurse ICU/critical care Sacred Heart Med. ctr., Spokane, 1973—; founder, dir. nutritional risk/identification network Health Improvement Partnership, Spokane, Wash., 1997—. Mem. adv. coun. edn. com. Nutrition Screening Initiative, Washington, 1992—, Nutrition Inst. La., New Orleans, 1993—; apptd. del. by U.S. Senate to White House Conf. on Aging, 1995; developer Body Mass Index awareness cmty. action project through Leadership Spokane Class, 1999; presenter Spokane's body mass index project U.S. Surgeon Gen.'s Inaugural Session on Obesity, 2001. Author: (manual) Malnutrition in the Elderly: A National Crisis, (resolution) Ensuring the Future of the Medicare Program presented to White House and Congress; contbr. articles to profl. jours. Apptd. Silver Senator by U.S. Senate for Wash. in Nat. Silver Haired Congress, 1997. Recipient Cmty. Leadership Recognition award, YWCA, Spokane, 1993, commendation for developing a model for nation from former U.S. Surgeon Gen., 1999, Spl. Recognition award for contrbn. to malnutrition awareness, U.S. Adminstrn. on Aging, 2000. Mem. ANA, Wash. State Nursing Assn., Nat. Coun. on Aging, Am. Soc. for Critical Care Nursing (founding), Am. Soc. for Parenteral and Enteral Nutrition, U.S. apptd. Silver Senator for Wash. State in Nat. Silver Haired Congress, Sigma Theta Tau. Avocations: reading, walking, hiking, bicycle, cooking, crafts. Home: 8315 N Lucia Ct Spokane WA 99208-9654 Fax: (509) 468-1026. E-mail: kcope@mindspring.com.

COPE, KENNETH WAYNE, chain store executive; b. Rifle, Colo., May 31, 1924; s. William Grant and Mary (Park) C.; m. Patricia Miller, Feb. 1, 1946; children: Kimberly Ann, Bradley Mark. BA, La Sierra Coll., Arlington, Calif., 1948; postgrad., U. Wash., 1948-50. CPA, Calif. From staff acct. to mgr. Price Waterhouse & Co., CPAs, L.A., 1950-58, resident mgr. Phoenix, 1959-63; regional contr. Lucky Stores, Inc., San Leandro, Calif., 1963-68, v.p., corp. contr., 1968-83, sr. v.p. adminstrn., 1984-86, v.p. corp. affairs, 1986-87, ret., 1987. Served with AUS, 1943-46. Mem. AICPA, Calif. Soc. CPAs, Fin. Execs. Inst. Republican. Episcopalian.

COPE, LEWIS, journalist; b. Sweetwater, Tex., June 24, 1934; s. Millard L. and Margaret Wallace (Kilgore) C.; m. Betty Joan Ball, June 28, 1958; children— Margaret, Elizabeth, Mary Amelia. BA, Washington and Lee U., 1955. Reporter Greenville (Tex.) Herald-Banner, 1957-60; copy editor Richmond (Va.) Times Dispatch, 1960-62; copy editor, news editor San Antonio Express, 1962-66; sci. reporter Mpls. Star and Tribune, 1966-95; freelance science writer, newspaper cons., 1995—. Bd. dirs. Coun. Advancement of Sci. Writing, 1996—; writer-in-residence Nat. Cancer Inst., 1976. Author: Save Your Life, 1979, (with Victor Cohn) News and Numbers, 2001. Served as officer AUS, 1955-57. Recipient Merit award Am. Assn. Blood Banks, 1974, Journalism award Am. Acad. Family Physicians, 1976, 79, Penney award lifestyle reporting U. Mo., 1977, Nat. Media award Am. Cancer Soc., 1977, Blakeslee award Am. Heart Assn., 1979, Cecil award Arthritis Found., 1982, Harvey award Am. Med. Writers Assn., 1993; Sci. Writing fellow Columbia U. Grad. Sch. Journalism, 1963-64. Mem. Nat. Assn. Sci. Writers (exec. com. 1982-93, treas. 1985-88, v.p. 1989-90, pres. 1991-92), Sigma Delta Chi (pres. Minn. chpt. 1973-74, dep. regional dir. 1974-86). Episcopalian. Home: 5217 W 91st St Minneapolis MN 55437-1819 E-mail: lcope@mn.rr.com.

COPE, MAURICE ERWIN, art history educator; b. Detroit, Feb. 4, 1926; s. Henry Erwin and Myragene (Mead) C.; m. Beatrice L. Everson, June 18, 1949 (div. Jan. 1975); children: Thomas M., Cynthia E.; m. C. Penelope Bass, Dec. 23, 1977 (div. Feb. 1981); 1 child, Nicholas M. MA in English, U. Chgo., 1949, PhD in Art History, 1965; postgrad., U. Florence, Italy, 1954-56. Instr. English, Valparaiso (Ind.) U., 1949-51; instr., asst. prof. humanities U. Chgo., 1954, 56-60; asst. prof. art history Pomona Coll., Claremont, Calif., 1960-65; assoc. prof., prof. Ohio State U., Columbus, 1965-72; prof. U. Del., Newark, 1972-97, prof. emeritus, 1997—. Dir. fund raising in ctrl. and south Ohio, Com. To Rescue Italian Art after Floods of 1966, 1966-67, rep. in Italy, 1967-68, rep. to UNESCO meeting on Venice, 1968; reader in art history Ednl. Testing Svc., Princeton, N.J., 1972-77. Contbg. author: The Friedrick W. Schumacher Collection, 1976; author: The Venetian Chapel of the Sacrament in the 16th Century, 1979, (catalogues) James Turrell: Jida, 1984, Philipp Fehl: Birds of a Feather, 1991; editor The Arts, Ohio State U., 1969-72. With USN, 1944-46. Fulbright fellow, Florence, 1954-56; rsch. fellow NEH, Florence and Venice, 1967-68, Delmas Found., Venice, 1986. Mem. Coll. Art Assn. (com. for 1964 meeting, session chmn. 1979), Renaissance Soc. Am., Italian Art Soc. Avocations: music, art and political collecting. E-mail. Home: 602 Delaware St New Castle DE 19720-5058 E-mail: mecope@udel.edu.

COPE, THOM K. lawyer; b. Bremen, Fed. Republic Germany, Feb. 26, 1948; came to U.S., 1960; s. Ray and Gabriele E. (Meyer) C.; m. Melba D. Van Hemert, Nov. 8, 1980. BA with honors, Syracuse U., 1969; JD, U. Nebr., 1972. Bar: Nebr. 1972, U.S. Dist. Ct. Nebr. 1972, U.S. Ct. Appeals (8th cir.) 1972, Calif. 1976, U.S. Dist. Ct. (no. dist.) Calif. 1976, U.S. Ct. Appeals (9th cir.) 1976, U.S. Supreme Ct. 1987, U.S. Claims Ct. 1988, U.S. Ct. Appeals (D.C. cir.) 1990. Agy. legal counsel Nebr. Workers' Compensation Ct., Lincoln, 1972-73; assoc. counsel Fireman's Fund Ins. Co., San Francisco, 1973-76; asst. gen. counsel Argonaut Ins. Co., Menlo Park, Calif., 1976-78; assoc. counsel Ins. Svcs. Office, N.Y.C., 1978-82; assoc. atty. Tate & Assocs., Nebr., 1982-83, Bailey, Polsky, Cada & Todd, Nebr., 1983-84; ptnr. Bailey, Polsky, Cope & Knapp, Lincoln, 1984-97, Polsky Cope Shiffermiller Coe and Monzon and predecessors, Lincoln, 1997—2002; v.p. human resources Beaudry Motor Co., 2002—. Judge Nebr. Commn. of Indsl. Rels., 1986-91; mem. Nebr. Supreme Ct. Gender Bias Task Force; mem. Nebr. Motor Vehicle Industry Licensing Bd.; mem. Nebr. Atty. Gen. Odometer Fraud Task Force; mem. Fed. Practice Adv. Com.; lectr. in field. Author: Executive Guide to Employment Practices, 1985, 3d edit., 1999. Bd. dirs. Friends of Elderly Found., Lincoln, 1986-90, Capital Humane Soc., Planned Parenthood Lincoln, 1997—, v.p., 1998, pres. 1999—2001; bd. dirs. Child Advocacy Ctr., 1995-97; bd. trustees Lincoln Bar Assn. Fellow Coll. Employment and Labor Law (cert. sr. profl. in human resources 2003); mem. Nat. Employment Lawyers Assn., Nebr. Bar Assn. (labor and employment sect., exec. com., sec.), Nebr. Trial Lawyers Assn., NOW (bd. dirs. 1999), Soc. Human Resource Mgmt. Avocation: golf. Home: 9343 N Sunflower Blossom Pl Tucson AZ 85743- Office: Beaudry Motor Co PO Box 12747 Tucson AZ 85732

COPE, THOMAS FIELD, lawyer; b. Oak Park, Ill., Feb. 29, 1948; s. Benjamin Thomas and Myra Norma (Lees) C.; m. Ann Wattis, Mar. 21, 1970; children: Elizabeth Ann, Philip Thomas. BA, U. Denver, 1970, MA, 1976, JD, 1974; PhD, U. Chgo., 2001. Bar: Colo. 1974, Ill. 1978, Wyo. 1996, D.C. 2001, U.S. Dist. Ct. Colo. 1974, U.S. Dist. Ct. D.C. 2001, U.S. Ct. Appeals (10th cir.) 1989, U.S. Ct. Appeals (D.C. cir.) 2001. Assoc. Holme Roberts & Owen, Denver, 1974-78, 81-83, ptnr., 1984—. Instr. IIT/Chgo.-Kent Coll. Law, 1980, Loyola U. Sch. Law, Chgo., 1980-81; chief of party ABA Ctrl. European and Eurasian Law Initiative, 2002—. Co-editor: Colorado Environmental Law Handbook, 1989, 4th rev. edit., 1996, Colorado Environmental Compliance Update, 1993-96; contbg. editor Oil & Gas Law and Taxation Rev., Oxford, Eng., 1987-93; mng. editor Shepard's Environ. Liability in Comml. Transactions Reporter, 1990-92; mem. bd. editors Denver Law Jour., 1972-74; contbr. articles to profl. jours. Bd. dirs. Colo. Fourteeners Initiative, 1996-2002. Mem. Am. Law Inst., Am. Soc. Legal History, Irish Legal History Soc., Selden Soc. (state corr. Colo. 1997—), Rocky Mountain Mineral Law Found. (mem. grants com. 1983-95, chmn. 1995-2002), Order St. Ives, Am. Alpine Club, Colo. Mountain Club (chair high altitude mountaineering sect. 2001-02). Democrat. Mem. Orthodox Ch. in Am. Avocations: mountaineering, history. Home: 2800 S University Blvd Unit 108 Denver CO 80210-6072 Office: Holme Roberts & Owen LLP 1700 Lincoln St Ste 4100 Denver CO 80203-4541 E-mail: tcope@hro.com

COPE, WENDY, poet; b. 1945; Tchr. Portway Jr. Sch., London, 1967-69, Keyworth Jr. Sch., London, 1969-73, Cobourg Primary Sch., 1973-81, Brindishe Primary Sch., 1984-86; writer, TV columnist The Spectator, London, 1986-90. Arts editor ILEA Contact Tchrs. Newspaper, 1982-84. Author: Across the City, 1980, Hope and the 42, 1984, Making Cocoa for Kingsley Amis, 1986, Poem from a Colour Chart of Housepaints, 1986, Men and Their Boring Arguments, 1988, Does She Like Word-Games?, 1988, Twiddling Your Thumbs, 1988, The River Girl, 1991, Serious Concerns, 1992, If I Don't Know, 2001; editor: Is That the New Moon?, Poems By Women Poets, 1989, The Orchard Book of Funny Poems, 1993, The Funny Side, 1998, The Faber Book of Bedtime Stories, 2000, Heaven on Earth: 101 Happy Poems, 2001; George Herbert: Verse and Prose (a selection), 2002. Recipient Cholmondeley award for poetry, 1987, Michael Braude award AAAL, 1995. Fellow Royal Soc. Lit. Office: Faber & Faber 3 Queen Sq London WC1N 3AU England

COPELAND, CAROLYN ABIGAIL, retired university dean; b. White Plains, N.Y., May 5, 1931; d. Robert Erford and Mary Terwillinger; m. William E. Copeland, Aug. 16, 1964; children: Rob Cameron, Diana Elizabeth Bosworth. BA, U. Mich., 1973, MA, 1979, postgrad., 1992—. With dean's office Coll. Lit., Sci. and Arts U. Mich, Ann Arbor, 1967-91, asst. dean, 1980-84, assoc. dean, 1984-91. Rschr. in Buddhist art history. Author: Tankas from the Koelz Collection, 1980. CEW scholar, Rackham grad. student scholar. Mem. Phi Beta Kappa (mortar bd., v.p. Alpha chpt. 1984-86, pres. Alpha chpt. 1986-88). Home: 1867 Morley St Simi Valley CA 93065 Office: U Mich Ann Arbor MI 48109 E-mail: cabby1867@aol.com.

COPELAND, CHRISTINE SUSAN, therapist; b. Milw., Jan. 8, 1949; d. Walter Horace and Doris Esther (Becker) C. BA in Psychology, Valparaiso (Ind.) U., 1971; MS in Psychology, U. Wis., 1974. Psychologist Curative Workshop, Green Bay, Wis., 1974-77, No. Wis. Ctr. for Developmentally Disabled, Chippewa Falls, Wis., 1977-86; behavior therapist Midelfort Clinic, Eau Claire, Wis., 1986-93, Systems Counseling and Cons., Inc., Eau Claire, 1994-95; pvt. practice, Chippewa Falls, Wis., 1995—. Ind. computer cons. The Computer Tutor, Chippewa Falls. Mem. APA (assoc.), Am. Assn. Mental Retardation, Assn. for Advancement of Behavior Therapy, Wis. Psychol. Assn., C.H.A.D.D., Beta Sigma Phi (officer Wis. chpt. 1977—, Woman of Yr. 1979). Home and Office: 645 Summit Ave Chippewa Falls WI 54729-8754 E-mail: chris@tctutor.com.

COPELAND, DAVID A. software engineer; b. Jasper, Ala., Dec. 4, 1942; s. Charles Newman and Irene (Dodd) C.; m. Helen Grace Stalcup, Aug. 26, 1967; children: Samantha Ann, Andrew David. BSChem, U. Ala., 1965, MA in Math., 1966; PhD in Chem. Physics, La. State U., 1970. Registered profl. engr., Ala. Undergrad. teaching asst. U. Ala., University, 1963-65, grad. teaching asst., 1965-66, La. State U., Baton Rouge, 1966-67, grad. rsch. asst., 1967-69, postdoctoral rsch. assoc., 1969-70; asst. prof. chemistry U. Tenn. at Martin, 1970-74, assoc. prof. chemistry, 1974-77; supr., analyst Ala. Power Co., Birmingham, 1977-92, info. resources coord., 1992-95, Southern Co. Svcs., Birmingham, 1995-96; dir. of application svcs. Just For Feet, Inc., Pelham, Ala., 1996; project mgmt. cons. MedPartners, Inc., Birmingham, 1997; software engr. So. Co. Svcs., Wilsonville, Ala., 2000—. Instr. Faulkner U., Birmingham, Ala., 1997—2000. Contbr. articles to profl. jours. Treas. Rotary Club, Martin, 1974-77; dist. roundtable commr. Boy Scouts of Am., Birmingham, 1991-95, asst. scoutmaster, 1988-96. Recipient Dist. award of merit Boy Scouts of Am., 1993; James E. West fellow Nat. Boy Scouts of Am., 1994. Mem. Nat. Eagle Scout Assn., Sigma Xi. Ch. of Christ. Achievements include rsch. on complete neglect of differential overlap of several transition metal complexes; structured analysis of the electron pair species for pure liquid ammonia solutions. Office: Power Sys Devel Facilities So Co Svcs Hwy 25 Wilsonville AL 35186

COPELAND, EDWARD JEROME, lawyer; b. Chgo., Oct. 29, 1933; s. Harvey and Lilyan (Rubin) C.; m. Ruth Caminer, Sept. 2, 1962; children: Ellyn, Bradley. BA, Carleton Coll., 1955; JD, Northwestern U., 1958. Bar: Ill. 1959, N.Y. 1981. Mem. Ill. Ho. of Reps., Springfield, 1967-71; ptnr. Foss, Schuman, Drake & Barnard, Chgo., 1971-86, Wood, Lucksinger & Epstein, Chgo., 1986-88, Shefsky & Froelich, Ltd., Chgo., 1988-89, Schuyler, Roche & Zwirner, Chgo., 1989—. Chmn. Bank of North Shore, Northbrook, Ill., 1976-81. Mem. Ill. Bd. Edn., 1975-83, chmn., 1981-83. Mem. ABA, Ill. Bar Assn., Chgo. Bar Assn. Republican. Office: One Prudential Plaza Ste 3800 Schuyler Roche & Zwirner 130 E Randolph St Chicago IL 60601-6312 E-mail: ecopeland@srzlaw.com.

COPELAND, EDWARD MEADORS, III, surgery educator; b. Augusta, Ga, Oct. 6, 1937; s. Edward Meadors Jr. and Louise (Leggitt) C.; m. Martha Patterson, Ar. 24, 1964; children: Edward Meadors IV, Catherine Leggitt. BA, Duke U., 1959; MD, Cornell U., 1963. Diplomate Am. Bd. Surgery (bd. dir. 1983-91, chmn. 1990-91). Intern in surgery U. Pa. Hosp., Phila., 1963-64, resident in gen. surgery, 1964-69; resident surg. oncology Anderson Hosp., Houston, 1971-72; asst. prof. to prof. U. Tex. Med. Sch., Houston, 1972-82, U. Tex. M.D. Anderson Hosp. and Tumor Inst., Houston, 1972-82; prof. U. Fla. Coll. Medicine, Gainesville, 1982—, chmn. dept., 1982—2003. Project dir. Nat. Large Bowel Cancer Project, Nat. Cancer Inst., Houston, 1981-82. Bd. dir. Sun Bank No. Ctrl. Fla., Ocala, 1987—. Maj. US Army, 1969-71, Vietnam. Decorated Bronze Star Rep. Vietnam; recipient Seale Harris award So. Med. Assn., 1984, Disting. Alumnus award M.D. Anderson Hosp. and Tumor Inst., 1987. Fellow Am. Surg. Assn., So. Surg. Assn. (pres. 1998-99); mem. ACS (chmn. bd. govs. 1995-96, bd. regents 1997—, vice chair 2002—), Assn. for Acad. Surgery (pres. 1978-79), Soc. Surg. Oncology (pres. 1998-99), Soc. Surg. Chmn. (pres. 1996-98), Halsted Soc. (pres. 1993), Southeastern Surg. Congress (pres. 2000-01), Soc. Univ. Surgeons, Gainesville Country Club. Avocations: fishing, golf, tennis. Home: 2605 NW 7th Rd Gainesville FL 32607-2600 Office: Univ Fla Coll Medicine Dept of Surgery PO Box 100286 Gainesville FL 32610-0286

COPELAND, EUGENE LEROY, lawyer, writer; b. Fairfield, Iowa, Mar. 5, 1939; BA, Parsons Coll., 1961; JD with distinction, U. Iowa, 1965. Admitted to Colo. bar, 1965, Iowa bar, 1965, U.S. Supreme Ct. bar, 1966. Individual practice law, Denver, 1965-66; sr. v.p., gen. counsel, sec. Security Life of Denver, Denver, 1966—; gen. counsel Nationale Nederlanden N.Am. Corp., Denver, 1986—. Lectr., speaker at legal and industry convs., seminars, meetings; participant contemporary issue program Today show NBC, 1980. Author: Preventive Law for Medical Directors and Underwriters, 1973; Underwriting in a New Age of Legal Accountability, 1978; Insurance Law, 1982; bd. editors Iowa Law Rev., 1965. Bd. dirs. Colo. Pub. Expenditures Coun., 1988—, Buffalo Mountain Met. Dist., Summit County, Colo., Friends Found. of Denver Pub. Libr., Denver Pub. Libr. Commn. Served with U.S. Army. Fulbright scholar (alt.). Mem. ABA, Colo. Bar Assn., Denver Bar Assn., Iowa Bar Assn., Assn. Life Ins. Council, Am. Council Life Ins. (state v.p. 1973-83, legis. com., reins. com., policyholder tax com., litigation com.), Colo. Life Conv. (pres. 1988-90, v.p. 1987-88, legis. chmn. 1973-86), Colo. Assn. Corp. Counsel, Denver Estate Planning Council, Colo. Assn. Life Underwriters (co-author learning guide 1978), Law Club Denver, Phi Kappa Phi. Unitarian Universalist. Office: Security Life Ctr 1290 Broadway Fl 6 Denver CO 80203-2122

COPELAND, HENRY JEFFERSON, JR., former college president; b. Griffin, Ga., June 13, 1936; s. Henry Jefferson and Emory (Drake) C.; m. Laura Harper, Dec. 21, 1958; children: Henry Drake, Eleanor Harper. BA, Baylor U., 1958; PhD, Cornell U., 1966. Instr. Cornell U., Ithaca, N.Y., 1965-66; asst. prof. history Coll. Wooster, Ohio, 1966-69, assoc. dean, 1969-74, dean, 1974-77, pres., 1977-95, prof. history, 1995-98. Woodrow Wilson fellow, 1960 Presbyterian.

COPELAND, JACK G. cardiac surgeon, researcher; b. Roanoke, Va., Mar. 13, 1942; s. Jack G. and Josephine (Keane) C.; m. Janice Ann Copeland, Oct. 9, 1983; children: Patrick, Jennifer. AB, Stanford U., 1964, MD, 1969. Intern straight medicine U. Calif. San Diego, 1969-70, resident, 1970-71; cardiac surgery fellow Nat. Heart, Lung and Blood Inst., 1971-73; fellow gen. surgery Stanford, 1975-77, fellow cardiothoracic surgery, 1973-75; prof. U. Ariz., Tucson, 1981—, Michael Drummond Disting. prof., 1988—, assoc. prof. cardiac surgery, 1977-81. Vis. prof. in China, Houston, London, Paris, Louisville, others, 1980—; assoc. dir. Univ. Heart Ctr., 1987—. Contbr. more than 300 articles to profl. jours. Mem. Internat. Soc. for Heart Lung Transplantation (founder and pres.). Avocations: tennis, bicycling. Office: U Ariz/Univ Med Ctr 1501 N Campbell Ave Tucson AZ 85724-0001

COPELAND, KARIN A. training director; b. New Britain, Conn., Dec. 5, 1961; d. Ovide Joseph and Emilie Albert; m. James Philip Copeland, Sept. 27, 1991; children: Taylor Jacqueline, Garrett Ovide. AS in Retail Mktg., Lasell Coll., 1982; BSBA, Cen. Conn. State U., 1984. Acctg. clk., pub. rels. asst. Constructive Workshops, Inc., New Britain, 1985-88; account mgr. Beekley Corp., Bristol, Conn., 1988-91, sales supr., 1991-92, asst. product mgr., 1992-94, acting sales mgr., 1994-95, continuous learning mgr., 1995-97, dir. continuous learning, 1997—. Mem. ASTD, Am. Teleservices Assn. Avocations: painting, writing. Office: Beekley Corp Prestige Ln Bristol CT 06010

COPELAND, PHILLIPS JEROME, former academic administrator, former air force officer; b. Oxnard, Calif., Mar. 22, 1921; s. John Charles and Marion (Moffatt) C.; m. Alice Janette Lusby, Apr. 26, 1942 (dec. April 1998); children: Janette Ann Copeland Bosserman (dec. Aug. 2000), Nancy Jo Copeland Briner; m. Joanne Barra Lankenau, July 9, 1999. Student, U. So. Calif., 1947-49; BA, U. Denver, 1956, MA, 1958; grad., Air Command and Staff Coll., 1959, Indsl. Coll. Armed Forces, 1964. Commd. 2d lt. USAF, 1943, advanced through grades to col., 1964; pilot 8th Air Force, Eng., 1944-45; various flying and staff assignments, 1945-51; chief joint tng. sect. Hdqrs. Airsouth (NATO), Italy, 1952-54; asst. dir. plans and programs USAF Acad., 1955-58; assigned to joint intelligence Washington, 1959-61; plans officer Cincpac Joint Staff, Hawaii, 1961-63; staff officer, ops. directorate, then team chief Nat. Mil. command Ctr., Joint Chiefs of Staff, Washington, 1964-67; dir. plans and programs USAF Adv. Group, 1967-68; prof. aerospace studies U. So. Calif., L.A., 1968-72, exec. asst. to pres., 1972-73, assoc. dir. office internat. programs, 1973-75, dir. adminstrv. svcs. Coll. Continuing Edn., 1975-82, dir. employee rels., 1982-84. Advisor Vietnamese Air Force, Vietnam, 1967-68. Decorated D.F.C., Bronze Star, Air medal with 3 clusters, Medal of Honor (Vietnam). Mem. Air Force Assn., Order of Daedalians.

COPELAND, RANDOLPH LEIGH, orthopedic surgeon; b. Dodge City, Kans., July 8, 1949; s. Everett Leigh Copeland and Marcia Marie (Young) Unruh; m. Maria D. Copeland, June 23, 1973; children: Everett, Teresa, Johannes, James. BA, Sterling (Kans.) Coll., 1971; MD, Tulane U., 1975. Diplomate Am. Bd. Orthopedic Surgery. Commd. 2d lt. U.S. Army, 1973, advanced through grades to col., 1992; staff orthopedic surgery USA MEDDAC, Nurnberg, Germany, 1980-81, chief orthopedic svc., 1981-83; fellowship in pediatrics Scottish Rite Hosp., Atlanta, 1983-84; chief orthopedic svc. Gorgas Hosp., Panama, 1984-86; pediatric orthopedist William Beaumont Med. Ctr., El Paso, Tex., 1986-95, chief orthopedic svc., 1995-98, residency program dir., 1996-98, chief edn. divsn., dir. med. edn., 1998—2001; staff orthopedic surgery Gallup (N.Mex.) Indian Med. Ctr., 2001—02, chief orthopedic surgery dept., 2002—. Contbr. articles to profl. jours. Asst. scoutmaster Boy Scouts Am., El Paso, 1988-2001, Order of the Arrow advisor, 1991-2000. Mem. Michael Hoke Soc., Soc. of Mil. Orthopedic Surgeons (sec. 1993-98), Pediatric Orthopedic Soc. N.Am., Am. Acad. Orthop. Surgeons. Roman Catholic. Avocations: hiking, cycling, archery, photography. Office: Orthopedic Surgery Dept Gallup Indian Med Ctr 516 E Nizhoni Blvd El Paso TX 87301

COPELAND, ROBERT BODINE, internist, cardiologist; b. Arab, Ala., Jan. 24, 1938; s. Haden Paul and Jimmie Alice (Bodine) Copeland; m. Virginia (Jenny) Ruth Trammell, June 26, 1960; children: Robert Theodore, Haden McTieyre. BS, Auburn U., 1960; MD, U. Ala., Birmingham, 1963. Diplomate Am. Bd. Internal Medicine, cert. internal medicine, cardiovasc. diseases and geriatrics. Intern then resident, clin. rsch. fellow in cardiology Mass. Gen. Hosp., Harvard Med. Sch., Boston, 1963-67; physician Clark Holder Clinic, LaGrange, Ga., 1967-77; founder, dir. Ga. Heart Clinic, LaGrange, 1972—; founder, pres. So. Cardiopulmonary Assocs., LaGrange, 1977—; clin. prof. med. U. Ala., Birmingham, 1980—, Emory U., Atlanta, 1980—. Bd. govs. Am. Bd. Internal Medicine, Phila., 1980—86, Joint Commn. on Accreditation of Healthcare Orgns., Chgo., 1991—97; bd. dirs. Gaston Laughlin Inc., Atlanta. Contbr. Trustee LaGrange Coll.; chmn. bd. trustees ACP-ASIM Found., 1999—2002. Recipient Disting. Alumni award, U. Ala., Birmingham, 1985. Fellow: ACP (gov. Ga. chpt. 1987—91, Master 1993, regent 1993, chair bd. regents 1998—99), Am. Coll. Cardiology, Royal Coll. Physicians; mem.: NAS, Inst. of Medicine, Am. Heart Assn. (pres. Ga. affiliate 1985—86). Office: 1551 Doctors Dr Lagrange GA 30240-4139

COPELAND, ROBERT GLENN, lawyer; b. San Diego, Mar. 15, 1941; s. Glenn Howard and Luella Louise (Schmid) C.; m. Harriet S. Smith, June 27, 1964 (div. Jan. 1977); children: Katherine Louise, Matthew Robert; m. Marcia Diane Cummings, Jan. 8, 1977 (div. June 1990); m. Lynne Newman, Oct. 10, 1993; 1 child, Zachary Newman. AB, Occidental Coll., 1963; JD, U. So. Calif., 1966. Bar: Calif. 1966, U.S. Dist. Ct. Calif. (so. dist.), 1967. Ptnr. Gray, Cary, Ware & Freidenrich, San Diego, 1966-95, Luce, Forward Hamilton & Scripps LLP, 1995—. Mem. ABA, Calif. Bar Assn. Republican. Avocations: shooting, fly fishing, hiking, racquetball. Office: Luce Forward Hamilton & Scripps LLP 600 W Broadway Ste 2600 San Diego CA 92101-3311 E-mail: rcopeland@luce.com.

COPELAND, ROBERT MARSHALL, music educator, department chairman; b. Douglas, Wyo., Jan. 30, 1945; s. Wilbur Clyde and Arvilla Estella (Walkinshaw) C.; m. Louise Margaret Edgar, June 10, 1966; children: Thomas Edgar, Anne Louise, Kathryn Elizabeth. BS, Geneva Coll., 1966; MM, U. Cin., 1970, PhD, 1974; postgrad., Westminster Choir Coll., 1981-82, Emory U., 1988. Asst. prof. to prof. music Mid-Am. Nazarene Coll., Olathe, Kans., 1971-81; prof. music, dir. choral activities Geneva Coll., Beaver Falls, Pa., 1981—, chmn. dept. music, 1981-99. Vis. lectr. U. Kans., Lawrence, 1977; trustee, sec. Ref. Presbyn. Theol. Sem., Pitts., 1981-93, vis. lectr., 1983-84; mem. Presbyn. and Ref. Joint Commn. on Chaplains and Mil. Pers., 1988—, sec., 1995—. Author: Spare No Exertions, 1986, Isaac Baker Woodbury: The Life and Works of an American Musical Populist, 1995; co-editor: The Book of

Psalms for Singing, 1973; contbr. articles to profl. jours. Dir. music Internat. Covenanter Conf., Northfield, Minn., 1970, 76, 80, 84; ruling elder Ref. Presbyn. Ch., 1973—; moderator, Synod of the Ref. Presbyn. Ch. of N.Am., 1995-97; mem. Rep. County Com., 1992—. With AUS, 1966-68. NDEA fellow, 1968-71. Mem. AAUP (v.p. Kans. Conf. 1980-81), Am. Musicological Soc. (v.p. Allegheny chpt. 1987-89, 97-99, pres. 1989-91, 99-2001, coun. mem. 1992-95), Sonneck Soc. for Am. Music (founding mem., program com. 1982), Am. Choral Dirs. Assn. (co-editor Pa. Newsletter 1983-85, editor 1985-90), Soc. for Ethnomusicology, Huguenot Fellowship (bd. dirs. 1987—), Presbyn. and Ref. Joint Commn. on Chaplains and Mil. Personnel (sec. 1995—). Republican. Home: 3111 5th Ave Beaver Falls PA 15010-3616 Office: Geneva Coll 3200 College Ave Beaver Falls PA 15010-3557 E-mail: rmc@geneva.edu.

COPELAND, SUZANNE JOHNSON, real estate executive; b. Chgo., Aug. 01; d. John Berger and Eleanor (Dreger) Johnson; m. John Robert Copeland, Aug. 1, 1971 (div. June 1976). Assoc. French Lang. and Culture, Richland Coll., Dallas, 1974; BFA, Ill. Wesleyan U., Bloomington, 1965. Commercial artist Barney Donley Studio, Inc., Chgo., 1966-69; art dir. Levines Dept. Store, Dallas, 1970-74; creative dir. Titche-Goettinger, Inc., Dallas, 1974-78; catering mgr. Dunfey Hotel, Dallas, 1978-82; regional dir. corp. sales Rayburn Country Resort, Austin, Tex., 1982-84; real estate sales assoc. Henry S. Miller, Dallas, 1984-86; v.p. Exclusive Properties Internat., Inc., Dallas, 1986—. Cons. North Tex. Commn., Dallas, 1988. Acquisitions editor: Unser, An American Family Portrait, 1988. Mem. The Rep. Forum, Dallas, 1983-94; vol. Stars for Children, Dallas, 1988, Soc. for Prevention of Cruelty to Animals, Dallas, 1973-92, Preservation of Animal World Soc., 1986-92, Sedona Acad., 1996—, Sedona Humane Soc., 1996—, Sedona Women, 2001—; charter mem. P.M. League Dallas Mus. Art.; mem. Keep Sedona Beautiful, 1999—. Mem. Nat. Assn. Realtors, Tex. Assn. Realtors, Greater Dallas Assn. Realtors (com. chmn., Summit award 1984, 85), North Tex. Arabian Horse Club (bd. dirs. 1975-76, Pres.'s award 1978), Dallas Zool. Soc., Humane Soc. Dallas County (v.p. 1973-74), Humane Soc. U.S./Gulf States Humane Edn. Assn. (bd. dirs. 1990-91), Am. Montessori Soc., Delta Phi Delta, Phi Theta Kappa. Lutheran. Avocations: arabian and thoroughbred horses, scuba diving, equitation instr. Office: Exclusive Properties PO Box 1973 Sedona AZ 86339 E-mail: azmtnlion@aol.com.

COPELAND, TATIANA BRANDT, accountant; b. Dresden, Germany; came to U.S., 1959, naturalized, 1967; d. Cyril Alexander and Maria (von Satin) Brandt; m. Gerret van Sweringen Copeland, May 12, 1979. BS summa cum laude, UCLA, 1964; MBA, U. Calif., Berkeley, 1966. Sr. tax cons. Price Waterhouse & Co., L.A., 1966-72; asst. tax mgr. Whittaker Corp., L.A., 1972-75; mgr. internat. dept. E.I. Du Pont de Nemours, Wilmington, Del., 1975-80; pres. Tebec Assocs., Ltd., Wilmington, 1980—. Co-owner, CFO, Bouchaine Vineyards, Inc., Napa, Calif.; owner The Wine & Spirit Co., Greenville, Del.; co-owner, v.p. Rokeby Realty Co., Wilmington. Bd. dirs. Del. Symphony, Grand Opera House, Nat. Symphony Orch., Washington; mem. President's Adv. Com. for Trade Negotiations, 1982-87. Mem. AICPA, Am. Woman's Soc. CPA's, Am. Soc. Women Accts., Internat. Fiscal Assn., Del. Soc. CPA's, Rodney Square Club (bd. dirs.) Phi Kepa Kappa. Home: 175 Brecks Ln Wilmington DE 19807-3008 Office: PO Box 3662 Wilmington DE 19807-0662

COPELAND, WILLIAM CHENERY, biochemist; b. Port Washington, NY, May 28, 1960; s. Douglas Robert and Virginia Murrell (Brokenbrough) C.; m. Valerie Andrea Moczydlowski, Feb. 21, 1995; children: Chaz Darwin, Sophia Valeria. BS, U. Fla., 1982; PhD, U. Tex., 1988; postgrad., Stanford U., 1988-92. Chemist, microbiologist Orlando (Fla.) Labs., Inc., 1980-83; rsch. tech. dept. chemistry U. Fla., Gainesville, 1982; fellow dept. pathology Stanford (Calif.) U., 1988-92, rsch. assoc. dept. pathology, 1992-93; prin. investigator Nat. Inst. Environ. Health Scis. NIH, Rsch. Triangle Pk., N.C., 1993—, DNA repair interest group, mem. structural biology faculty, 1996—. Editor: Methods in Molecular Biology, 2002; contbr. articles to profl. jours. Mem. AAAS. Office: Nat Inst Environ Health Scis PO Box 12233 Research Triangle Park NC 27709 E-mail: copelan1@niehs.nih.gov.

COPEN, MELVYN ROBERT, management educator, university administrator; b. N.Y.C., Jan. 23, 1938; s. Samuel L. Copen and Frieda (Kroun) Zucker; m. Linda B. Kopans, Feb. 17, 1960 (div. 1991); children: Erika Beth Ellingsen, Susan Andrea Holtey; m. Beverly Joyce Stein, Sept. 7, 1991. BS in Bus., Engring Adminstrn., MIT, 1958, MS in Indsl. Mgmt., 1959; DBA in Prodn., Internat. Mgmt., Harvard U., 1967. Various positions Gen. Elec. Co., various locations, 1959-61; program assoc., rsch. fellow Harvard Bus. Sch., Boston, Ahmedabad, India, 1961-67; assoc. dean, prof., dir. grad. studies U. Houston, 1967-71; dir. office mgmt. improvement automated decision sys. U.S. Dept. Agr., Washington, 1971-74; dir. strategic planning Westinghouse Corp., Pitts., 1974-75; dir. internat. planning Gould, Inc., Rolling Meadows, Ill., 1975-77; assoc. dean, dean grad. studies coll. bus. adminstrn. Ga. State Univ., Atlanta, 1977-80; v.p. acad. affairs Babson Coll., Wellesley, Mass., 1980-87; rector Ctrl. Am. Inst. Bus. Adminstrn., Alajuela, Costa Rica, 1987-91; dean sch. internat. mgmt. Internat. Univ. Japan, Urasa, Tokyo, 1991-94; chmn., CEO Global Enterprises, Atlanta, 1991—; sr. v.p. acad. affairs, prof. internat. mgmt. Am. Grad. Sch. Internat. Mgmt., Glendale, Ariz., 1995-98; exec. v.p. global ops. Am. InterContinental U., Atlanta, 1998-99; chmn. Copen Comms. Internat., Atlanta, 1991—. Membership chmn. audit com. Nat. Bank Ga.-1st Am., Atlanta, 1980-87 Co-author: International Manangement and Economic Development, 1971, Production Management, 1972; contbr. articles to profl. jours. Bd. dirs. White House Fellows Found., Washington, 1973-74, Epilepsy Found. Ga., Atlanta, 1979-80, Hemophilia Ga., Atlanta, 1978-80, Nat. Bank Ga., Atlanta, 1979088; chmn. Arts in Progress, Roxbury, Mass., 1985-87, Am. Coll., Atlanta, 1996-2001, U. of the Pacific, Ecuador, 1998—, China U.S. Bus. U., China, 1988—; mem. Greater Phoenix Econ. Coun., 1997-98; mem. bus. adv. bd. UN Office for Project Svcs., 2000—; mem. adv. bd. Cisco Learning Systems, 2001-. With USAR, 1960. Recipient Command Gen. Citation, U.S. Transp. Corps., 1960; White House fellow, 1970-71. Mem. Beta Gamma Sigma, Omicron Delta Epsilon. Avocations: tennis, travel, outdoor activities, flying. Home: 3870 Adams Rd Cumming GA 30041-4650 Office: Copen Comms Internat 3870 Adams Rd Cumming GA 30041-4650 E-mail: meleopen@hotmail.com.

COPENHAVER, MARION LAMSON, former state legislator; b. Andover, Vt., Sept. 26, 1925; d. Joseph Fenwick and Christine (Forbes) Lamson; m. John H. Copenhaver, June 30, 1946; children: John III, Margaret, Christine, Eric, Lisa. Student, U. Vt., 1945-46. Mem. N.H. Ho. of Reps., Concord, ranking Dem. health and human svcs. com., 1973-2000, mem. adminstrv. rules com., 1982-2000, mem. health and human svcs. oversight, 1990-2000; ret., 2000. Chair Grafton County Dems., 1986-91; assoc. supr. Grafton County Soil Conservation Dist., 1980-2002, supr., 2002—; mem. Hanover (N.H.) Dem. Town Com., 1992; mem.-at-large Dem. State Com., Concord, 1992; bd. dirs. Dartmouth Hitchcock Found., Hanover, 1991—; bd. incorporators Dartmouth Hitchcock Med. Ctr., Lebanon, N.H., 1984—; bd. dirs. Grafton County Sr. Citizens Coun., Inc., 1995-96, 2001, vice chair; bd. dirs. Outreach House, an Assisted Living Facility, 2001—, Friends of Norris Cotton Cancer Ctr., Women's Policy Inst. N.H. Named N.H. Legislator of Yr. N.H. Nurses Assn., 1989; recipient Meritorious award N.H. Women's Lobby, 1996, James A. Hamilton award N.H. Hosp. Assn., 1997. Mem. NOW, Bus. and Profl. Women's Club (Outstanding Mem. award 1990). Democrat. Unitarian Universalist. Avocations: golf, skiing. Home: 14 Woodcock Ln Etna NH 03750-4402

COPES, MARVIN LEE, college president; b. Connersville, Ind., Sept. 19, 1938; s. Kenneth Edward and Frances Gertrude (Bean) C.; m. Luretta Ann Grenard, Aug. 26, 1961; children: Bradley Alan, Brian Keith, Brent Lee. BS, Purdue U., 1961, MS, 1962, PhD, 1975; postgrad., Ind. State U., 1967-68, Ind. U.Southeast, 1967-68. Cert. pub. mgr., Ky. Grad. asst. agrl. edn. Purdue U., 1961-62, grad. instr., 1968-69; tchr. vocat. agriculture Tri-County Sch. Corp., Walcott, Ind., 1964-65; vocat. dir. Met. Sch. Dist. Vernon Twp., Crothersville, Ind., 1965-68; also dir. Ind. Vocat. Agriculture Demonstration Ctr., 1965-68; asst. exec. sec. Kappa Delta Pi Hdqrs., West Lafayette, Ind., 1969-70; dir. Blue River Vocat.-Tech. Ctr., Shelbyville, Ind., 1970-79; nat. curriculum devel. coord. ITT Ednl. Svcs., Indpls., 1979-80, nat. dir. edn., 1980-82; dir. ITT Tech. Inst., Ft. Wayne, Ind., 1982-83, Indpls., 1983-86, Am. Coll., Mobile, Ala., 1986-89; nat. dir. edn. Am. Career Educators, Charlotte, N.C., 1989, v.p. ednl. resources, 1989-91; pres. Treasure Wheel, Inc., Mobile, Ala., 1991-93; dean acad. affairs Phillips Jr. Coll., Mobile, Ala., 1992-96; v.p. acad. affairs Am. Inst. Commerce, Davenport, Iowa, 1993-96; dir. Ky. Tech. Jefferson State Campus, Louisville, 1996-98; pres. Jefferson Cmty. & Tech. Coll., 1998-2000, exec. dir. of occupl., tech. and apprenticeship programs, 2000—02, ceo, Special Programs, 2001—02; dir. Heritage Inst., Falls Ch., Va., 2002—. Chmn. profl. devel. com. Ky. Postsecondary Tchr. Credentialing Adv. Bd.; mem. Welfare Reform Task Force, Ky.; bd. dirs. Pvt. Ind. Coun., Future Connections Sch. to Work; organizer Advanced Tech. Skills Acad., Advanced Welding Tech. Ctr., Heritage Coll., Falls Ch., Va.; pres. CopeSkills Cons., Power Ptnrs. cons. Author: A Curriculum Guide for Training in Agricultural Supply, 1968, Student Handbook for Cooperative Programs in Agricultural Occupations, 1968, A Predictability of Career Choices of High School Seniors, 1975, Personal Awareness Handbook, 1989, Retention Handbook, 1989, Placement Handbook, 1990, Vocational Adjustment Handbook, 1990, Train The Trainer Handbook, 1990, Instructor Certification Handbook, 1990, Administrative Certification Handbook, 1990, Master Teacher, 1990, Wheel of Fortune Enterprise Training Manual, 1991, Instructor Training Manual, 1993, Faculty Inservice Training Manual, 1993, Disaster Plan, 1993, Contract Training, 1994, School-to-Work Training, 1994, Assessment Planning, 1995, Welfare Reform, 1996, Guidelines for Apprenticeship Training, 2002, Guidelines for Corporate College, 2002. Mem. ops. coun. Met. Coll.; pres. Loper PTO, 1974-76; leader 4-H, 1964-68; advisor Future Farmers Am., 1964-70; cubmaster Boy Scouts Am., 1976-80, commr., bd. dirs. Shelbyville coun., 1978-92; mem. vocat. gng. com. Futuring Project, N.Y. State Dept. Edn.; bd. dirs. N.E. India Christian Mission, 1974, Kentuckiana Works; chmn. Shelby County Youth for Christ; mem. Nat. Curriculum Focus Group, 1993-96; bd. dirs., treas. Accrediting Coun. for Ind. Colls. and Schs., 1994; deacon area So. Bapt. Ch., 1995; mem. Kentukiana Edn. and Workforce Inst., Louisville Area Workforce Devel. Coun., School-to-Work Partnership Coun., Louisville/Jefferson County Redevel. Authority; bd. dirs. Career Resources One Stop Shop/Job Link, Pvt. Ind. Coun.; Louisville/Jefferson County Workforce investment bd., N. Cen. Ky. Workforce Investment Bd.; mem. Louisville/Jefferson County Youth Coun., N. Cen. Ky. Youth Coun., chmn.; mem. Immigrant/Refugee Task Force, Kentuckiana Works Skilled Trades Roundtable. 1st lt. U.S. Army, 1962-64. Mem. ASCD, Am. Vocat. Assn., Ind. Vocat. Assn., Nat. Coun. Local Adminstrs., Ind. Coun. Local Adminstrs., Bus. Profls. Am., Nat. Bus. Edn. Assn., Soc. Mfg. Engrs., Ky. Vocat. Assn. (pres. region 13), Robotics Internat., Network Iowa Svc. Learning, Ind. Assn. Pvt. Career Schs. (bd. dirs.), Future Farmers Am. Alumni Assn., Shelby County C. of C., Prichard C. of C. (bd. dirs.), Pershing Rifles, Gideons Internat., Metro Scholars, Davenport C. of C., Masons, Kiwanis, Order Ea. Star, Alpha Tau Alpha, Kappa Delta Pi, Phi Delta Kappa, Delta Pi Epsilon. Home: 20147 Hardwood Terrace Ashburn VA 20147 Office: Heritage Institute 350 South Washington Falls Church VA 22046 E-mail: marvin.cope@aol.com. *Be a bridge for the life of others that they may cross on their life's journey. Education, motivation, goal setting and training are those bridges.*

COPES, PARZIVAL, economist, researcher; b. Nakusp, B.C., Can., Jan. 22, 1924; s. Jan Coops and Elisabeth Catharina Coops-van Olst; m. Dina Gusskeloo, May 1, 1946; children: Raymond Alden, Michael Ian, Terence Franklin. BA, U. B.C., 1949, MA, 1950; PhD, London Sch. Econs., 1956; D of Mil. Sci. (hon.), Royal Roads Mil. Coll., Victoria, B.C., Can., 1991; Dr. Philos. (hon.), U. Tromsö, Norway, 1993. Economist, statistician Dominion Bur. of Stats., Ottawa, Canada, 1953—57; from assoc. prof. to prof., head econs. dept. Meml. U. Nfld., St. John's, Canada, 1957—64; founding dir. econ. rsch. Inst. Social and Econ. Rsch. Meml. U. Nfld., St. John's, 1961-64; prof. Simon Fraser U., Burnaby, Canada, 1964—91, founding head dept. econs. and commerce, 1964-69, chmn. dept. econs. and commerce, 1972—75, founding dir. Ctr. for Can. Studies, 1978—85, founding dir. Inst. of Fisheries Analysis, 1980—94, prof. emeritus, 1991—. Governor Inst. Can. Bankers, Montreal, Que., 1967-71; dir. Can.-Fgn. Arrangements Project, Can. Govt. Dept. Environment, 1976; pres., chmn. Pacific Regional Sci. Conf. Orgn., 1977-85; spl. advisor to Minister of Fisheries, B.C., 1998. Author: The Statistical Measurement of Morbidity Frequency, 1957, St. John's and Newfoundland: An Economic Survey, 1961, The Backward-Bending Supply Curve of the Fishing Industry, 1970, The Resettlement of Fishing Communities in Newfoundland, 1972, Factor Rents, Sole Ownership and the Optimum Level of Fisheries Exploitation, 1972, A Critical Review of the Individual Quota as a Device in Fisheries Management, 1986, The Extended Economics of an Innate Common Use Resource: The Fishery, 1998, Equity and the Rights Basis of Fishing in Iceland and Canada: Reflections on the Icelandic Supreme Court Decision, 1999, Sharing the Fishery Resources of the North Pacific for Mutual Advantage: Toward an International Management Regime, 1999, Aboriginal Fishing Rights and Salmon Management in British Columbia: Matching Historical Justice with the Public Interest, 2000., Challenging ITQs: Legal and Political Action in Iceland, Canada and Latin America, 2001. Active Netherlands Resistance Army, 1942—45, attached Can. Army, 1945—46, lt. Can. Army, 1950—51. Fgn. fellow Acad. Natural Scis. of Russian Fedn., Moscow, 1992. Mem. Internat. Inst. Fisheries Econs. and Trade (exec. com. 1982-86, Disting. Svc. award 1996), Internat. Assn. for Study of Common Property, Can. Regional Sci. Assn. (pres. 1983-85), Can. Econs. Assn. (v.p. 1972-73), Assn. for Can. Studies, Western Regional Sci. Assn. (pres. 1977-78), Social Sci. Fedn. Can. (dir., v.p. 1979-83), Can. Assn. Univ. Tchrs., Internat. Arctic Sci. Com. Achievements include some of earliest research contributions to establish sub-discipline of fisheries economics; writing, speaking, research and international consulting in fisheries policy and resource management. Home: 2341 Lawson Ave West Vancouver BC Canada V7V 2E5 Office: Simon Fraser U Dept Economics Burnaby BC Canada V5A 1S6 E-mail: copes@sfu.ca.

COPLAN, DANIEL JONATHAN, lawyer, actor, writer, producer, director; s. Robert Saul and Constance Joan (Karl) C. BFA, NYU, 1977; JD, Southwestern U., Los Angeles, 1984. Bar: Calif., 1985. Exec. producer NCL Films, N.Y.C., 1975-77; ptnr. The Kizer/Coplan Co., N.Y.C., 1977-78; agt. Daniel J. Coplan Entertainment Entrepreneur, N.Y.C., 1979—; mgr., asst. film buyer Walter Reade Orgn., Inc., N.Y.C., 1979-81; bus. affairs intern Paramount Pictures, Los Angeles, 1982-84; of counsel Raymond L. Asher PC, Los Angeles, 1984-86; pvt. practice Los Angeles, 1986-97; mem. Sheldon & Mak, Inc., 1997—. Actor Madames Black Book, 1996, Man in the Iron Mask, 1997, Echos of Enlightenment, 2000; actor, writer, prodr. The Dragon Gate, 1994; actor in Hell Comes to Frogtown, 1987, Wish Man, 1991; exec. producer motion picture The Dream Factory, 1977; producer, writer motion picture Of Mirrors, The Mind and Time, 1973, The Incredibly Awful Dr. Sporgo, 1973 (Silver medal Atlanta Internat. Film Festival, 1974, Golden Image cert. L.I. Film Festival, 1975); agt. motion picture Just Before Dawn. Mem. Screen Actors Guild, State Bar Calif., ABA, Beverly Hills Bar Assn., So. Calif. Kendo Fedn. Avocations: kendo, writing, music. Office: 330 Washington Blvd Ste 400 Marina Del Rey CA 90292-5141

COPLEY, DAVID C. newspaper publishing company executive; s. Mrs. James S. Copley. BSBA, Menlo Coll., 1975. Pres., CEO, chmn. Copley Press, Inc., La Jolla, Calif., 1988—; chair, exec. com., chmn. sr. mgmt. bd. and bd. dir. The Copley Press, Inc., La Jolla, Calif.; pub. The San Diego Union-Tribune, 2001—, The Borrego Sun. Chair, pres. Copley N.W., Inc., Puller Paper Co.; pres. Copley News Svc.; trustee Copley Ohio Newspapers, The Peoria Jour. Star, Inc., The Gales. Print. and Publ. Co.; pres. Copley Northwest, Inc. and puller paper Co., others. Mem. editl. bd. San Diego Union-Tribune. Pres., trustee & pres. James S. Copley Found.; trustee Canterbury Sch., San Diego Crew Classic Found.; trustee emeritus La Jolla Playhouse, Am. Craft Coun., Mus. Photog. Arts; bd. dir. San Diego Mus. Art, St. Vincent de Paul Soc.; pres. assoc., pres. adv. com., exhibits com. Zool. Soc. San Diego; adv. bd. San Diego Automotive Mus.; pres. coun. Scripps Clinic and Rsch. Found., San Diego Kind Corp.; active Pres. Club U. San Diego, San Diego Aerospace Mus., San Diego Hall Sci., San Diego Maritime Mus., San Diego Coun. on Literacy. Mem. Nat. Newspaper Assn., U.S. Humane Soc., F.O.C.A.S., San Diego Hist. Soc., San Diego Humane Soc., Bachelor Club San Diego. Office: The Copley Press Inc PO Box 1530 La Jolla CA 92038-1530

COPLEY, EDWARD ALVIN, lawyer; b. Memphis, Jan. 17, 1936; m. Connie James Patterson, Nov. 17, 1990; children: Julie, Ward, Drew, Kelly, Zeke. BA, So. Meth. U., 1957, JD, 1960. Bar: U.S. Dist. Ct. (no. dist.) Tex., U.S. Ct. Claims 1962, U.S. Supreme Ct. 1963, U.S. Tax Ct. 1966, U.S. Ct. Appeals (5th cir.) 1968. Atty. U.S. Dept. Justice, Washington, 1960-64, Ft. Worth, 1964-66; assoc. Akin, Gump, Strauss, Hauer & Feld, Dallas, 1966-67, ptnr., 1968—. Fellow Am. Coll. Probate Counsel; mem. Internat. Acad. Estate Trust Law, Dallas Bar Assn. (tax sect.), Dallas Estate Coun. (pres. 1975-76), So. Meth. U. Law Sch. Alumni Assn. (pres. 1978-79), Salesmanship Club, Order of Woolsac, Barristers, Dallas Petroleum Club, Dallas Country Club, Phi Alpha Delta. Avocations: racquetball, photography, hunting, fishing, reading. Home: 3711 Shenandoah St Dallas TX 75205-2120 Office: Akin Gump Strauss Hauer & Feld Ste 4100 1700 Pacific Ave Dallas TX 75201-4675 E-mail: ecopley@akingump.com.

COPLEY, RALPH D., JR., lawyer; b. 1924; ED, Colo. Sch. Mines, 1948; LLB, U. Denver, 1951. Atty. Getty Oil Co., Los Angeles, Calif., 1958—64, div. atty. western exploration and prodn. div., 1964—65, atty. western div., 1965—66; ops. coord., assoc. chief counsel, prodn. div., 1964—65; chief counsel, 1971—73; corp. sec., chief counsel, 1973; v.p., sec., chief counsel, 1973—; atty. Tidewater Oil Co., 1958—64; dir. Nuc. Fuels Svc. Inc., Pacific Western Oil Corp. Served USNR, 1944—46, lt. USAFR, 1950—55. Office: Getty Oil Co 3810 Wilshire Blvd Los Angeles CA 90010-3204

COPLEY, STEPHEN JEAN, minister; b. Lawton, Okla., Oct. 13, 1961; s. Albert Jean and Mary Lou (Carnes) C.; m. Judith Ann Wallace, May 18, 1966. BA, U. Ctrl. Ark., 1984; MDiv, So. Meth. U., 1999; JD, U. Ark., 2003. Min. Lamar Circuit United Meth. Ch., Barnesville, Ga., 1985-86; youth dir. Nashville (Ark) U. Meth. Ch., 1986; min. Prestwich (Eng.) Whitefield Circuit, 1986-87; youth min. Woodstock (Ga.) United Meth. Ch., 1987-88; min. Lamar/Mount Olive United Meth. Ch., 1988-89; asst. dir. Luton Indsl. Coll., Luton, Eng., 1989-92; min. Horatio (Ark.)/Winthrop United Meth. Ch., 1992-95; dir., founder Ouachita Regional Enterprise Fund, 1995-96; min. Hampton Circuit United Meth. Ch., 1996-2000, Gillett/Campshed United Meth. Ch., 2000—; law clk. Pamela D. Walker Atty.-at-Law, 1999—2001. Bd. dirs. Atlanta Clergy and Laity Concerned, 1985-86, Inst. Indsl. and Comml. Ministries, 1988-89, Meth. Fedn. for Social Action, 1993; mem. Little Rock Conf.-United Meth. Ch. Bd. Global Ministries, 1993—, Little Rock Conf. comm., 2000— (coun. on ministries, 2000—); founder, bd, dirs. Ouachita Regional Enterprise Fund, 1995—; cons. United Meth. Ch. Concern for Worker's Task Force, 1997-98; polit. dir. Svc. Employees Internat. Union, 1998-99; pres. RC and Assocs., 1997—. Senator Ga. Jaycees Legislature, 1985; chair Ga. Jaycees-Multiple Sclerosis, 1985-86, Dem. Party. Com. Abroad, U.K., 1992; commr. Sevier County Housing Authority, 1993—; chaplain Little River Hist. Soc., 1992—, Sevier County Literacy Coun., 1992—, Horatio City Coun., 1995, Leadership Ark., 1995—, Ark. State Jaycees, 1993—; pres. Horatio Recreation Assn., 1993-95; chmn. Horatio Parks Commn.; dep. chair Dem. Party, Ark., 1994—; mem. social affairs com. Ark. Interfaith Conf., 1996, Ouachita River United Way; bd. dirs. Hogskin Holidays, Ark. South Tourism Assn., Little River C. of C., 1994, Ark. South Tourism Bd., Regional AIDS Interfaith Network, Single Parent Scholarship Fund, RAIN Ark., Ark. Single Parent Scholarship Fund; leader Leadership Ark., 1995-97; chair Ark. Jobs With Justice Religion-Labor Com., 1997—; sec. Ark. Interfaith Com., Trustee, Office and Professional Employees Internat. Union. Recipient Jaycees Young Outstanding Arkansas award, 1994; named Town and Country Pastor of Yr., United Meth. Rural Fellowship Hope Dist., 1993, 94; named to N.Mex. Mil. Inst. Alumni Hall of Fame, 1994. Mem. Am. Acad. Religion, Horatio Mchts. Assn., Sevier County C. of C., Little River C. of C., Horatio Lions Club (pres. 1994-95, zone chair 1995-97), Young Dems. of Ark. (v.p. fin.), DeWitt Rotary Club, Hampton/Calhoun County C. of C. (pres.), Phi Alpha Delta. Avocations: tennis, golf. Home: PO Box 88 Gillett AR 72055-0088

COPLEY, WILLIAM MCKINLEY, III, counselor, counseling administrator, consultant; b. Orlando, Fla., July 10, 1943; s. William McKinley Jr. and Dorothy (Rathbun) C.; m. Suzanne Howard Montgomery, June 14, 1985. BA, E. Carolina U., 1966; MA, Ball State U., 1971; AS, Fla. Community Coll., 1976. Nat. cert. counselor. Dir. aftercare Univ. Hosp., Jacksonville, Fla., 1972-80; exec. dir. Orange County Crisis Unit, Orlando, 1980-81, Hillcrest Ho., Inc., Orlando, 1981-83; dir. CSP Mental Health Svcs. Orange County, Orlando, 1983-85; mng. ptnr. Montgomery, Copley & Assocs. Inc., Jacksonville, 1985—. Mem. Jacksonville Cmty. Coun., 1986—, Leadership Jacksonville, 1987—88; bd. dirs. Vol. Jacksonville, 1988—90; mem. citizens adv. com. Long-Range Corridor/Park and Ride study Jacksonville Transp. Authority, 1990; mem. Youth Leadership Jacksonville selection com., 1991, 1993, Duval County Sch. Readiness Coalition, 2001, exec. com., 2002—04. With U.S. Army, 1967—70. Mem. ACA, Mental Health Assn. (bd. dirs. 1989, chmn. adv. com., treas. 1991), Fla. Counseling Assn., Am. Mental Health Counselor Assn. Republican. Episcopalian. Avocations: tennis, sailing, reading, golf. Office: Montgomery Copley & Assocs Inc 1812 Atlantic Blvd Jacksonville FL 32207-3404

COPLIN, MARK DAVID, lawyer; b. Balt., Dec. 1, 1928; m. Judith Charlotte Levinson, Jan. 27, 1991. BA, U. Md., 1949, LLB, 1952. Bar: Md. 1952. Law clk. presiding justice U.S. Ct. Appeals (4th cir.), 1952-53; assoc. Weinberg and Green, LLC, Balt., 1953-60, mem., 1960-98; sr. ptnr. Saul Ewing, Balt., 1998-2001, of counsel, 2001—. Pres. Md. chpt., Am. Jewish Congress, 1971-74, Balt. Jewish Coun., 1976-78; pres. HIAS of Balt., Inc., 1972-74; mem. adv. com. Md. Blue Sky, 1968-92; bd. dirs. Jewish Family Svc., 1992-98; chmn. bd. trustees Balt. Hebrew U., 1987-89; mem. bd. visitors Balt. City Coll., 1990-97, sec., 1992-97. Mem. ABA, Md. Bar Assn., Balt. City Bar Assn., Balt. Bar Found. (pres. 1991-93), Order of Coif, Omicron Delta Kappa, Jewish. E-mail: mcoplin@saul.com., mdc12128@aol.com.

COPMAN, LOUIS, radiologist; b. Phila., Jan. 17, 1934; s. Jacob and Eve (Snyder) C.; m. Avera Schuster, June 8, 1958; children: Mark, Linda. BA, U. Pa., 1955, MD, 1959. Diplomate Am. Bd. Radiology; Nat. Bd. Med. Examiners. Commd. ensign Med. Corps USN, 1958; advanced through grades to capt. M.C. USN, 1975; ret.; asst. chief radiology dept. Naval Hosp., Pensacola, Fla., 1966-69; chief radiology dept. Doctors Hosp., Phila., 1969-73; radiologist Mercer Hosp. Ctr., Trenton, N.J., 1973-75; chmn. radiology dept. Naval Hosp., Phila., 1975-84; chief. radiology dept. Naval Med. Clinic, Pearl Harbor, Hawaii, 1984-89; pvt. practice radiologist Honolulu, 1989-92. Cons. Radiology Services, Wilmington, Del., 1978-84, Yardley (Pa.) Radiology, 1979-84. Author: The Cuckold, 1974. Recipient Albert Einstein award in Medicine, U. Pa., 1959. Mem. AMA, Assn. Mil. Surgeons of the U.S., Royal Soc. Medicine, Radiol. Soc. N.Am., Am. Coll. Radiology, Photographic Soc. Am., Sherlock Holmes Soc., Phi Beta Kappa, Alpha Omega Alpha. Avocations: photography, hang-gliding, scuba diving. Home: PO Box 384767 Waikoloa HI 96738-4767 Office: 68-1771 Makanahele Pl Waikoloa HI 96738-5128 E-mail: louiscopman@earthlink.net. *Throughout one's life, one should choose his companions wisely.*

COPP, CINDY PIERCE, education educator; b. Philadelphia, Pa., USA, July 24, 1954; d. Arthur Raymond and Johanna W. Pierce; m. Charles F. Copp, June 23, 1973; children: Julie, Adam, Chad. B.S. Edn., Eastern Conn., 1990; EdM, Lynchburg Coll., 1997. Tchr. Amherst County, Amherst, Va., 1991—; adj. instr. Ctrl. Va. C.C., Lynchburg, Va., 2001—. Mentor faculty Sweet Briar Coll., SweetBriar, Va., 1995; lead tchr Amherst County, Amherst, Va., 1992. Grantee Curriculum Devel. Grant, Amherst County, 2001—02. Presbyterian. Achievements include Nat. Bd. Cert. Tchr. 2002. Home: 122 Gartin Place Madison Heights VA 24572 Office: Amherst County Schools 156 Davis St Amherst VA 24521 E-mail: CindyCopp@msn.com.

COPPA, ANTHONY PATRICK, consulting engineer; b. Phila., Mar. 22, 1927; s. Nicola and Felicia (Migliaccio) C.; B.M.E., Villanova U., 1948; M.S. in Engring. Mechanics, U. Pa., 1959, postgrad., 1959-62; m. Mary Concetta Cimorelli, July 4, 1952; children— Loretta, Clare, Nicholas, Anthony, Mary Ann, Joan, Jean, Felicia, David, Justin. Mech. devel. engr. Westinghouse Electric Corp., 1949-56; engr. GE Missile and Space divsn. GE Co., 1956-59, rsch. engr. GE Space Scis. Lab., 1959-67, cons. engr. structural sys. and materials, 1967-81; program mgr. Flywheel Rotor and Containment, 1979-83; tech. staff engr. GE space divsn., 1981-92; cons. rotor blade containment GE Aircraft Engine Group, 1967-78; cons. GE Corp. Rsch. and Devel. Lab., 1975; cons. Louis I. Kahn, Architect, 1968-70. Served with USNR, 1944-46. Recipient Silver Medallion Inventor's award GE Co., 1987, Ralph J. Cordiner award GE Co., 1962, also GE 100 award, 1979, also named to GE Co. One-in-thousand Club; Barnwell Gold pin Tau Beta Pi. Mem. AIAA, AAAS, Internat. Assn. Shell Structures, Elfun Soc., Nat. Geog. Soc., Men of Malvern. Roman Catholic. Contbr. articles to profl. jours. Patentee impact devices, fold structures, MHD equipment, erectable space trusses. Author: Songs and Shadows (poems), 1971. Home: 748 S Highland Ave Merion Station PA 19066-1610

COPPEL, LAWRENCE DAVID, lawyer; b. Washington, July 3, 1944; s. Albert and Anne (Gold) C.; m. Arlene Cohen, Aug. 10, 1968; children: Jennifer, Allison. BA, U. Md., 1966, JD, 1969. Bar: Md. 1969, U.S. Dist. Ct. Md. 1971, U.S. Ct. Appeals (4th cir.) 1976, U.S. Ct. Appeals (3d cir.) 1983. Law clk. Md. Ct. Appeals, Annapolis, 1969-70; assoc. Gordon, Feinblatt, Rothman, Hoffberger & Hollander, LLC, Balt., 1970-77, mem., 1977—. Fellow Am. Coll. Bankruptcy; mem. ABA, Md. State Bar Assn., Bankruptcy Bar Assn. Dist. Md. (pres. 1988-89), Balt. City Bar Assn. Office: Gordon Feinblatt Rothman Hoffberger & Hollander LLC 233 E Redwood St Baltimore MD 21202-3332 E-mail: lcoppel@gfrlaw.com.

COPPENBARGER, CECELIA MARIE, special education educator; b. Kansas City, Mo., Nov. 3, 1961; d. Theodore Francis Bowman, Jr., Betty Marie Bowman; m. Charles Loren Coppenbarger, Jr.; children: Charles Loren Coppenbarger, III, Craig James, Cliff Robert, Joshua Richard, Elena Marie. A in Liberal Arts, Longview C.C., 1983; BA in Secondary Edn., BA in Eng., U. Missouri, 1998; postgrad., Ctrl. Mo. State U. Cert. cross categorical spl. edn. tchr. K-12, secondary Eng.tchr. 9-12. Cross-categorical spl. edn. tchr. Raytown C-2 Sch. Dist., Raytown, Mo., 1998—. Sponsor Raytown Chpt. Mo. State Tchrs. Assn.-Future Tchrs. Am., 2000—. Active James Lewis Elem. PTA, 2002—; mem. Plaza Heights Bapt. Ch. Choir, Blue Springs, 1998—; tchr. Plaza Heights Bapt. Ch. Sunday Sch. and Spl. Needs Ministry, Blue Springs, 1999—; mem. Lucy Franklin Elem. Sch. PTA, Blue Springs, 1998—2001, Blue Springs H.S. Parent Tchr. Student Assn., 1998—2001, Brittany Hills Mid. Sch. Parent Tchr. Student Assn., 1998—2003; educator Raytown South H.S. Parent Tchr. Student Assn., Raytown, 1998—2001. Recipient Outstanding Scholastic Achievment and Excellence award, Golden Key Nat. Honor Soc., 1997, Outstanding Omer award, Odyssey of the Mind Program, 1997; scholar, U. Mo., Kansas City, 1997—98. Mem.: Mo. State Tchrs. Assn., Raytown Cmty. Tchrs. Assn., Coun. Exceptional Children, Pi Lambda Theta. Baptist. Home: 2114 NE 3rd St Blue Springs MO 64014 Office: Raytown South High Sch 8211 Sterling Raytown MO 64138 Personal E-mail: Coppen@DiscoveryNet.com. Business E-Mail: cecelia.coppenbarger@mail.raytown.k12.mo.us.

COPPENS, LAURA KATHRYN, special education educator; b. Hoddesdon, England, Jan. 12, 1948; d. Tomas Adriaan and Sylvia Helen Coppens; m. G. Lawrence McQueen (div. 1985); children: Isaac David, Sean Little Hawk. BA in Edn., John F. Kennedy Coll., Wahoo, Nebr., 1970; MEd in Spl. Edn., William Paterson U., 1976. Spl. edn. tchr. Bellmar (N.J.) Schs., 1970—71, N.J. Commn. for Blind, Teaneck, 1972—76; dir. Randolph County Learning Ctr., Roanoke, Ala., 1976—80; spl. edn. tchr. Lineville (Ala.) H.S., 1980—89, BOCES Alternative Program, Apalachin, NY, 1989—93, Owego (N.Y.) Apalachin Middle Sch., 1993—98, Owego Free Acad., 1998—. Dir. Youth Group, Owego, 2000—; co-coord. Inst. of Arts in Edn., Owego, 1996—; mentor tchr. Owego Apalachin Ctrl. Schs., 1999—. Pres. Randolph County Assn. for Retarded Citizens, Roanoke, 1980—83; lay reader St. Paul's Episc. Ch., Owego, 1998—. Recipient Outstanding Tchr. award, So. Tier Inst. of Arts, Binghamton, N.Y., 1998. Mem.: Broome Tioga Autism Soc. Am., Owego Apalachin Tchrs. Assn. (sec. 1998—), Coun. for Exceptional Children. Episcopalian. Achievements include creation of school for the handicapped in Roanoke; creation of first high school program for the multihandicapped in Lineville. Avocations: tenor recorder, reading, singing in church choir. Home: 412 Forest Hill Rd Apalachin NY 13732 Office: Owego Apalachin Ctrl Schs Talcott St Owego NY 13827 E-mail: lcoppens@oagw.stier.org.

COPPENS, PHILIP, chemist; b. Amersfoort, Holland, Oct. 24, 1930; s. Alexander and Sophie (Berkeley) C.; m. Marguerite Louise Anholt, Aug. 6, 1957; children: Alon, Eldad, Daniel David. PhD, U. Amsterdam, Netherlands, 1960; Dr. honoris causa, U. Nancy, France, 1989. Chemist Weizmann Inst. Sch., Rehoboth, Israel, 1957-60, 62-65, Brookhaven Nat. Lab., Upton, L.I., N.Y., 1960-62, 65-68; prof. chemistry SUNY, Buffalo, 1968—; adj. prof. applied physics and engring. sci. Cornell U., 1982-87; disting. prof. SUNY, Buffalo, 1992—, H. M. Woodburn chair chemistry, 1999—. Vis. prof. Fordham U., 1966-67, Aarhus U., Denmark, 1973, U. Grenoble, France, 1974-75, 87, U. Calif., Santa Barbara, 1992; gov. consortium of advanced radiation sources U. Chgo., 1994—; materials rsch. adv. com. NSF, 1980-82; exec. com. Nat. Synchotron Light Source User, 1983-85, adv. com. High Flux Beam Reactor Program, Brookhaven Nat. Lab., 1985-90; steering com. Advanced Photon Source Argonne Nat. Lab, 1991-94. Mem. editl. bd.: Crystallographic Engring. Comm., 2002—; co-editor Acta Crystallographica A, 2002—. Recipient Harker award Hauptman-Woodward Med. Inst., 1995, George Aminoff award Swedish Acad. Scis., 1996. Fellow AAAS; mem. Internat. Coun. of Sci. Unions (gen. com. 1996-99), Am. Crystallographic Assn. (v.p. 1977, pres. 1978, Buerger award 1994), Internat. Union Crystallography (exec. com. 1987-99, pres. 1993-96), Internat. Coun. Sci. Unions (gen. com. 1996-98), Am. Chem. Soc. (Schoelkopf award Western N.Y. sect. 1996), Materials Rsch. Soc., Royal Dutch Acad. Scis. (corr.). Office: Suny Dept Chemistry Buffalo NY 14260-0001

COPPERMAN, STUART MORTON, pediatrician, educator; b. Bklyn., June 5, 1935; s. Irving and Anne (Reisfield) C.; m. Renee Stein, Aug. 17, 1958; children: Beth, Alan, Cara. BA cum laude, Bklyn. Coll., 1956; MD, SUNY-Bklyn., 1960. Diplomate Am. Bd. Pediat. Rotating intern. L.I. Jewish Hosp., New Hyde Park, N.Y., 1960-61, resident in pediat., 1961-63; practice medicine specializing in pediat. Merrick, N.Y., 1965-2000; sr. med. cons. Med. Advisers, P.C., 2001—; mem. staff L.I. Jewish Hillside Med. Ctr., Schneider Children's Hosp., New Hyde Park, Nassau County Med. Ctr., East Meadow, Winthrop U. Hosp., Mineola, North Shore Univ. Hosp., Manhasset; clin. assoc. prof. pediat. SUNY Med. Sch., Stony Brook, 1972-2000; asst. prof. clin. health studies SUNY Sch. Allied Health, Stony Brook, 1977-2000; clin. instr. physicians asst. program Stony Brook Med. Ctr., 1972 2000; prof. pediat. St. George's Med. Coll., St. Vincent, W.I., acting chmn. pediat., 1979-80; healthcare security analyst, healthcare cons., 2000—; medico-legal expert, 2000—; physician exec. Health and Info. Svcs., 2001—02. Med. advisor Assn. Children with Downs Syndrome, 1971-98; mem. com. for handicapped Bellmore Sch. Dist., 1976-86; mem. ad hoc com. on cmty. as sch. Merrick-Bellmore Schs., 1976-90; bd. dirs. North Shore-L.I. Jewish I.P.O., L.I. Sch. Health Edn. Coalition, North Shore Physicians Orgn., North Shore - L.I. Jewish PHO; mem. Nassau County Sch. Health Edn. Commn., 1990-93; mem. ad hoc com. on prevention of birth defects March of Dimes; preceptor in pediat. Physicians Asst. Program, Cath. Med. Ctr.; mem. doctor's adv. com. Shaare Zedek Hosp., Jerusalem, 1974-98; med. cons. Matchbox Toys, 1985-88, Proctor & Gamble, 1988, Carnation Co., 1989-90, Disney Ednl. Svcs., 1990-95, vaccine divsn. Merck Corp., 1997—, Sepracor, 1999—; cons., mem. spkrs. bur. N.Y. State Med. Soc., N.Y. State Senate Com. Mental Hygiene, 1988—, Lederle Labs., 1989-95, Merck Labs., 1996—, Wallace Labs., 1996—, ucb Pharma, 1999—, Connaught, 1999—, Abbott Labs., 1996—, Pfizer, 1998—, Sepracor, 1999—; author, co-founder, pres., bd. dirs. Child Health Imagery Prodns., 1997—. Appearance TV shows on Downs Syndrome, learning disabilities, CPR, first aid, infant exercise programs, TV's effects on children, infectious disease, parent-infant bonding, immunizations, enuresis, toilet training, prevention of cigarette smoking among children, 1972—, also on HealthLinks (Life Time TV), 1990-93; mem. editl. adv. bd. Jour. Assn. for Physician Assts., 1987—; editl. cons. Jour. Pediat. Mgmt., 1991—; contbr. chpt. to Textbook Pediat. Sports Medicine; developer Babycise (infant parent interactive program in video tape and book form), 1985; rschr. on hetacillin, 1966, pyridoxine effect on serotonin level and performance in children with Down's Syndrome, 1970-75, Alice in Wonderland syndrome as presenting sympton of infectious mononucleosis, 1966-77, on transmission of group A Beta hemolytic strep infection from pet reservoirs to children, 1963-81; med. editor Air Fair Mag., 1991-93, L.I. Parent Mag., 1985-93, L.I. Family Mag., 1994-95; contbr. articles to profl. jours. Mem. sch. bd. Temple Beth Am., Merrick, 1972-78, mem. exec. com., 1973-74, chmn. com. Israel and World Affairs, 1976-78, mem. sch. com., 1976-78, mem. ritual com., 1976-93; mem. N.Y. State Senate com. on mental hygiene, 1990—; mem. profl. adv. bd. So. Shore divsn. YM-YWHA; benefactor Merrick Libr., 1992—. With U.S. Army, 1963-65. Recipient Physician Recognition award AMA, 1966—, testimonial dinner and plaque Assn. Children with Down Syndrome, 1972, Best Clin. Tchrs. of Pediat. award Nassau County Med. Ctr., 1981-82; named Merrick Profl. of Yr., 1994. Fellow Am. Acad. Pediat. (chmn. com. TV effects on children 1976—, mem. nat. com. comm. and pub. info. 1984-85, mem. nat. com. on substance abuse 1998-2001, media spokesperson 1988—, tobacco, alcohol and drug-free generation coord. 1988-98, chmn. substance abuse com. 1992—, N.Y. state chmn. substance abuse com. 1992-94, managed care com. chpt. 2 1993-95), Internat. Coll. Pediat.; mem. AMA, N.Y. State Med. Soc. (com. on alcohol 1997—), Nassau County Med. Soc. (com. on mental health 1980—, project assist 1992—, Nassau Acad. Medicine Pub. Health com. 1991—, libr. com. 1993—, chmn. pediat. sect. 1995—), Nassau Pediat. Soc. (mem. exec. bd. 1972—, chmn. com. on mental health 1972-88, v.p. 1994-95, pres. 1996-97). A Non-Smoking Generation Internat. (organizer, med. dir. Am. divsn.), Am. Lung Assn., Nassau-Suffolk Lung Assn. (life mem., dir. 1982-84), Am. Physicians Fellowship for Israel Med. Assn., Assn. Children with Learning Disabilities (mem. profl. adv. bd.), La Leche League, Latin Am. Parents Assn., L.I. Sch. Health Edn. Coun. (bd. dirs. 1989-92), Alpha Epsilon Pi (chancellor Phi Theta chpt. 1955-56), Phi Delta Epsilon (consul Zeta chpt. 1960), B'nai Brith. Office: 676 Balfour Pl Melville NY 11747 E-mail: smcmd@aol.com. *No one person can do everything - but every person can do something. If you want something done, give it to a busy person. We must live for today with an eye toward tomorrow. I'd like my epitaph to read "While alive, he lived."*

COPPERMAN, WILLIAM H. value engineer, consultant; b. Cleve., Dec. 4, 1932; s. Jack Jason and Ruth (Rollnick) C.; m. Rena June Dorn, Dec. 26, 1954; children: Randy Lee, David Marc. BS, Duquesne U., 1954; MBA, U. So. Calif., L.A., 1962; JD, U. San Fernando, 1977. Cert. value specialist. Corp. mgr., value engr. Hughes Aircraft Co., L.A., 1957-89; pres. Copperman Assocs. in Value Engring., Inc., L.A., 1983—. Bd. dirs. Miles Value Found., Washington; cert. bd. SAVE, Chgo., 1986-88. Author books, video tape series in value engring.; contbr. articles to profl. jours. Recipient Outstanding Achievement award U.S. Army, 1986, Value Engring. award Purchasing Mag., Washington, 1987, Achievement in Value Engring. U.S. Army, 1977, 78, 79, 80, 82. Mem. SAVE Internat., the Value Soc. (exec. v.p. 1975—). Avocations: computer programming, tennis, golf. Home and Office: Copperman Assocs Value Eng 78728 Sunrise Canyon Ave Palm Desert CA 92211 Fax: 760-200-9437. E-mail: caveine@worldnet.att.net.

COPPERSMITH, SAM, lawyer; b. Johnstown, Pa., May 22, 1955; m. Beth Schermer, Aug. 28, 1983; children: Sarah, Benjamin, Louis. AB in Econs. magna cum laude, Harvard U., 1976; JD, Yale Law Sch., 1982. Bar: Calif. 1982, Ariz. 1983. Fgn. svc. officer U.S. Dept. State, Port of Spain, Trinidad and Tobago, 1977—79; law clk. to Judge William C. Canby Jr. U.S. Ct. Appeals (9th cir.), Phoenix, 1982—83; atty. Sacks, Tierney & Kasen, P.A., Phoenix, 1983—86; asst. to Mayor Terry Goddard City of Phoenix, 1984; atty. Jones, Jury, Short & Mast P.C., Phoenix, 1986—88, Bonnett, Fairbourn & Friedman P.C., Phoenix, 1988—92; mem. 103d Congress from 1st Ariz. Dist., 1993—95; atty. Coppersmith Gordon Schermer Owens & Nelson PLC, 1995—. Former dir., pres. Planned Parenthood Ctrl. and No. Ariz.; former chair City of Phoenix Bd. Adjustment; former dir. Ariz. Cmty. Svc. Legal Assistance Found., 1986—89; trustee Devereux Found., 1997—; chair Ariz. Dem. Party, 1995—97. Mem. ABA, Maricopa County Bar Assn. Democrat. Office: Coppersmith Gordon Schermer Owens & Nelson PLC 2800 N Central Ave Ste 1000 Phoenix AZ 85004-1007 E-mail: sam@cgson.com.

COPPIE, COMER SWIFT, retired state official; b. Washington, Oct. 19, 1932; s. John Lee and Marion (Peck) C.; m. Judith Ann Wright, Apr. 29, 1961; children: Cynthia, Sean, Scott. AB, Hamilton Coll., 1955; M in Pub. Adminstrn., Syracuse U., 1959. Budget analyst Bur. of Budget, State of Md., Balt., 1958—62; exec. dir., trustee Md. State Colls., Balt., 1963—68; dep. budget dir. Govt. of D.C., Washington, 1968—69; dir. Office of Budget and Mgmt. Systems, Washington, 1969—78; exec. dir. N.Y. State Fin. Control Bd., N.Y.C., 1978—86; CFO U.S. Postal Svc., Washington, 1986—92; 1st dep. compt. Office of State Compt., Albany, NY, 1993—99; ret., 1999. Dir., pres. Homeless and Travelers Aid Agy., Albany; dir. Grand Ctrl. Social Svcs. Corp. (chmn. fin. com. 2000—), N.Y.C. Served with USN, 1955-57. Recipient Gold medal Fin. Officers Assn. of U.S. and Can., 1978. Mem. Cosmos Club (Washington). Episcopalian. Avocation: swimming.

COPPLESTONE, DAVID WESLEY, artist, business owner; b. Newton, Mass., Feb. 29, 1952; s. Wesley and Elizabeth (Winchell) C.; m. Margaret Carroll, Dec. 1996; children: Hannah E., Sarah E. Diploma, Art Inst. of Boston, 1975. Owner Landscape Design, Wellesley, Mass., 1967-73, Home Improvement Contractor, Wellesley, 1973—, Copplestone Artworks: Fine Art, Gifts, Games, Wellesley, 1975—. Product design, graphic artist Fun-N-Safe Inc., Natick, Mass., 1991; owner gourmetgames.com, 1998—. Inventor of games: Lots, C.A. Hoopster, Copplestone's Putting Rail, Pandemonium, Tick Tack Toes, Geronimo, Stackm, Meltdown, Peggotty, Jumbling, Dots. Mem. Mus. of Fine Art, Boston. Mem. Cambridge Art Assn., Copley Soc., Italo Am. Ednl. Club. Avocations: golf, tennis, windsurfing, classic films, billiards. Home and Office: 6 Shadow Ln Wellesley MA 02482-4311

COPPOCK, BRUCE, orchestra executive; m. Linda Marder. Cellist Boston Symphony Orch.; ops. & orch. mgr. St. Louis Symphony Orch., exec. dir., 1992-97; dep. dir. Carnegie Hall, N.Y.C., 1997-98; v.p. Am. Symphony Orch. League, Washington, 1998-99; dir. Orch. Leadership Acad., Washington, 1998-99; pres., mng. dir. St. Paul Chamber Orch., 1999—. Mem. Boston Chamber Music Soc. (founder). Office: St Paul Chamber Orch 408 Saint Peter St Saint Paul MN 55102-1130

COPPOCK, JANET ELAINE, mental health nurse; b. Tipton, Ind., June 2, 1954; d. Jack Donavon and Bonnie Ruth (Luse) Weismiller; divorced; children: Jonathan Andrew, Daniel Jason. Student, Ball State U., 1972-73; ASN, Ind. U., Kokomo, 1977. RN, Ind., Mich.; cert. psychiat./mental health nurse ANCC. RN charge staff and med.-surg. Tipton County Meml. Hosp., Ind., 1977-79; RN psychiat. staff Howard Cmty. Hosp., Kokomo, 1987-89; pvt. nurse Kokomo, 1989-95; RN psychiat. and addiction treatment, instr. Koala Hosp. & Counseling Ctr. Behavioral Healthcare Corp., Kokomo, 1995-98; RN psychiat. and addiction treatment Lafayette (Ind.) Behavioral Health System, 1998-99; RN psychiat. staff, patient care coord. Home Hosp. of Greater Lafayette Health Svcs., Inc., Lafayette, 1999—. Instr. parenting edn. Kinsey Youth Ctr., Kokomo, 1995-96; co-developer Koala Halfway House, Behavioral Healthcare Corp., Kokomo, 1996, house mgr., 1996-98. Author: Poetic Reflections, Expressions and Inspirations, 1986, Faithful Resolutions, 1993, Coming to Terms, 1998. Recipient Golden Poet award World Poetry Orgn., 1987, 88. Mem. Ind. State Nurses Assn., Internat. Platform Assn., Nurses Svc. Orgn., Writers' Ctr. Indpls., Ind. U. Alumni Assn. (life). Avocations: musical instruments, art, movies, basketball. Home: 2711 President Ln Kokomo IN 46902-3066

COPPOCK, MARK STEPHEN, not-for-profit fundraiser; b. Atlanta, July 9, 1948; s. Ernest Rozar and Sandra Elizabeth Coppock; 1 child, Jennifer Anne Campbell. MBA, Alemeda Coll., Phoenix, 2003. Chair, CEO MRT Distbn., Inc., Powells Point, NC, 1990—94; chief profl. officer New Hope Charities, Inc., West Palm Beach, Fla., 1994—. Author: (book on taxation) How to Estimate Federal Estate Taxes. Sec., treas. Glades Acad., Pahokee, Fla., 2001—03, Everglades Prep. Acad., Pahokee, Fla., 2002—03, The Imagine Sch., West Palm Beach, Fla., 2002—03; co-founder Qual Internat., Inc. Recipient The Jefferson award, U.S. Congress, 2002. Conservative. Baptist. Home: 333 Kelsey Park Cir Palm Beach Gardens FL 33410 Office: New Hope Charities Inc 626 N Dixie Hwy West Palm Beach FL 33401 Personal E-mail: copp2070@bellsouth.net. E-mail: mark_coppock@floridacrystals.com.

COPPOLA, EILEEN, philosopher, educator; b. Stamford, Conn., Aug. 23, 1961; d. Silvio Joseph Coppola and Jean Bogdan Tymula; m. Saleh A. Fawaz, June 14, 1990; children: Amani Latifa Fawaz, Kiyan Jean Fawaz. BA, Wesleyan U., 1985; MA, Columbia U., 1992; MEd, Harvard U., 1995, EdD, 2000. Lic. tchr. NY, 1992, cert. sch. prin. Mass., 1998, sch. supt. Mass., 1998. Lectr. Ctr. for Edn. Rice U., Houston, 2000—, rsch. scientist Ctr. for Edn., 2000—. Cons. Children's Mus. of Houston, 2002—. Author: Computers, Pedagogy, and the Culture of School. Fellow Feurstein fellow, Harvard U. Grad. Sch. of Edn., 1994—95, Herold Hunt fellow, 1998, 1998—99, Nat. Acad. of Edn., Spencer Found., 2002—; grantee Spencer Found. Rsch. Tng. grant, Harvard U. Grad. Sch. of Edn., 1998. Mem.: Am. Ednl. Rsch. Assn. Office: Rice University 6100 Main Street MS 147 Houston TX 77005

COPPOLA, ELAINE MARIE, librarian; b. Dunkirk, N.Y., Aug. 5, 1947; d. Henry Stanley and Althea May Hruby. BA, St. Bonaventure U., 1969; MLS, Syracuse U., 1979, MS Sc, 1989. Asst. mgr. manpower planning and devel. Oneida (N.Y.) Ltd., 1972-74, asst. mgr. pub. rels., 1974-78; libr. SUNY Inst. Tech., Utica, 1979; catalog libr. E.S. Bird Libr., Syracuse U., 1979-89, social scis. ref. bibliographer, 1989-99, head ref. dept., 1999—. Author: Political Science Annotations within the Supplement to the Guide to Reference Books, 1992, Political Science Annotations in Guide to Reference Books, 11th edit., 1996. Mem. Dem. com. Town of Manlius, town councilor, 1998-2001. Mem. ALA, N.Y. Libr. Assn., Assn. of Coll. and Rsch. Librs. (ea. N.Y. chpt. pres. 1992-93, v.p. 1991-92, sec. 1989-91, Libr. of the Yr. 1996), Manlius Hist. Soc. (bd. trustees 1999--, sec. 2002--), Beta Phi Mu. Home: 103 Kenny St Fayetteville NY 13066-1230 Office: ES Bird Libr Syracuse Univ Syracuse NY 13244-0001 E-mail: emcoppol@syr.edu.

COPPOLA, FRANCIS FORD, film director, producer, writer; b. Detroit, Apr. 7, 1939; s. Carmine Coppola; m. Eleanor Neil; children: Gian-Carlo(dec.), Roman, Sofia. BA, Hofstra U., 1958; Master of Cinema, UCLA, 1968. Pub. mag., San Francisco, 1975-76. Artistic dir. Zoetrope Studios.; dir. films including Dementia 13, 1964, You're a Big Boy Now, 1967, Finian's Rainbow, 1968, The Rain People, 1969, One from the Heart, 1981, Peggy Sue Got Married, 1986, Gardens of Stone, 1987, Tucker: The Man and His Dream, 1988, Bram Stoker's Dracula, 1992, The Rainmaker, 1997; writer films This Property Is Condemned, 1966, Reflections In a Golden Eye, 1967, The Rain People, 1969, Is Paris Burning, 1966, Patton, 1970, The Great Gatsby, 1974; co-writer, dir. The Cotton Club, 1984, Life Without Zoe (segment in New York Film Stories), 1990, writer, prodr., dir. The Godfather (Acad. awards for Best Screenplay and Best Picture, nominee for Best Dir., Film Dir.'s award Dirs. Guild Am. 1972), The Godfather, Part II, 1974 (Acad. awards for Best Screenplay, Best Dir. and Best Picture), The Conversation, 1974 (Golden Palm award Cannes Film Festival 1974), Apocalypse Now, 1979 (Golden Palm award Cannes Film Festival 1979), Rumble Fish, 1983, writer, dir. The Godfather: Part III, 1990, The Rainmaker, 1997, prodr., dir. (films) The Outsiders, 1983, Jack, 1996, The Rainmaker, 1997; prodr.(films): THX 1138, 1971, The Escape Artist, 1982, The Black Stallion Returns, 1983, Lanai-Loa, 1998, The Florentine, 1999, The Virgin Suicides, 1999, Grapefruit Moon, 2000; exec. prodr.(films): Black Stallion, 1979, Hammett, 1983, Lionhart, 1987, The Secret Garden, 1993, Mary Shelley's Frankenstein, 1994, My Family/Mi Familia, 1995, Don Juan DeMarco, 1995, Buddy, 1997, The Third Miracle, 1999, Goosed, 1999, Sleepy Hollow, 1999; co-exec. prodr. Mishima, 1985; dir. TV Movie The People; prodr. (TV series) White Dwarf, 1995, First Wave, 1998; exec. prodr. TV movie Dark Angel, 1996, Outrage, 1998; exec. prodr.: (TV mini-series) The Odyssey, 1997, Moby Dick, 1998; dir. (play) Private Lives, opera The Visit; appeared in TV movie Marlon Brando: The Wild One, 1996. Mem.: Dirs. Guild Am. Inc.

COPPOLA, JOHN FRANCIS, exhibits director; b. Hackensack, N.J., July 26, 1947; BA, Thiel Coll., 1969; MS, Northwestern U., 1970. Program mgr. Arts Am. U.S. Info. Agy., Washington, 1982-86, chief Bur. Internat. Expositions, 1986-91; dir. Office Exhibits Ctrl. Smithsonian Inst., Washington, 1991-95; curator, exhbn. developer Washington, 1995—. Cons. Mus. of Dominican Man, Nat. Mus., Bahrain, Qatar Sci. City, King Abdulaziz Hist. Ctr., Saudi Arabia, Smithsonian Instn., Md.-Nat. Capital Pk. and Planning Commn., Mus. Latin Am. Art, Long Beach, Calif., Nat. Bonsai Mus., Washington, Panama Canal Mus., Ethnographic Mus. U. Buenos Aires, Nat. Mus., San Jose, Costa Rica; lectr. U. Victoria, B.C., Can., Ricardo Palma U., Lima, Peru. Numerous one man and group shows. Mem. Am. Assn. Mus., Internat. Coun. Mus., Nat. Assn. for Mus. Exhbn., Nat. Artist's Equity Assn. and Fund. Home and Office: 229 13th St SE Washington DC 20003-1432 E-mail: jfcoppola@aol.com.

COPPOLA, JOSEPH ANGELO, computer professional, educator; b. Rome, Dec. 2, 1947; s. Frank and Barbara (Tombasco) C.; m. Elaine Marie Hruby, Aug. 15, 1981; 1 child, Richard McCoy. BT in Indsl. Engring., SUNY, 1985; MS in Computer Engring., Syracuse U., 1990, postgrad., 1992—. Mgr. audio/visual svcs. SUNY, Stony Brook, 1968-77; owner, operator Enchanted Frog Prodns., Port Jefferson, N.Y., 1977-79; customer svc. rep. Xerox Corp., Syracuse, 1979-85; software engr. Rome (N.Y.) Rsch. Corp., 1985-88; sr. adminstr. ops. Syracuse U., 1988-97; asst. prof. elec. tech. SUNY, Morrisville, 1997—, mem. faculty congress, 1998—. Mem. budget com. Vernon-Verona-Sherrill Sch. Bd., 1986-87; mem. engring. tech. adv. com. SUNY, Utica, 1987-88; treas. Fayette Manor Homeowners Assn., 1992-93. Innovation fund grant Syracuse U., 1993-95. Mem. N.Y. State Engring. Tech. Assn., Fayetteville/Manlius Sch. Bd. Com. on Gifted Edn., Order of the Engr., Mycroft Holmes Soc. of Syracuse (pub.), Baker St. Irregulars, Tech. Club. of Syracuse, Hounds of the Internet. Avocations: sherlock holmes, woodworking, radio drama, blacksmithing. Home: 103 Kenny St Fayetteville NY 13066-1230 Office: SUNY Sch of Sci & Tech Morrisville NY 13408 E-mail: coppolja@morrisville.edu.

COPPOLA, NICOLAS See CAGE, NICOLAS

COPPOLA, PHYLLIS GLORIA CECIRE, retired special education educator; b. Bklyn., Apr. 20, 1930; d. Marie Corigliano Cecire Manley; m. Ben J. Coppola, Nov. 4, 1950; children: Robert, Joseph, John, Karen. AAS, Nassau C.C., 1972; BA, St. Joseph's Coll., 1974; MS, L.I. Univ., 1978. Cert. tchr., spl. edn. tchr. Head bookkeeper Babylon (N.Y.) Nat. Bank (now Chase Bank), 1948-54; homemaker, 1955-74; tchr. North Babylon (N.Y.) Schs., 1975-78; spl. edn. educator West Islip (N.Y.) Schs., 1978-96. Advisor Udall Rd. Student Coun., West Islip, Beautification, West Islip; mem. sch. adv. bd. Udall Rd. Sch., West Islip; mem. advisory homeroom com. West Islip Sch. Dist.; spl. edn. cons., 1995-96; advisor lit. mag. West Islip Schs., 1994-96, tchr. cons. L.D. specialist, 1978-96. Life mem. Lindenhurst (NY) PTA, 1971, West Islip (NY) PTA, 1984. Recipient commendation United Cerebral Palsy Assn. Mem. AAUW, Orton Soc., Coun. for Exceptional Children, Lions, Coun. for Exceptional Students. Roman Catholic. Avocations: crewel work, cooking, gardening. Home: 333 No Atlantic Ave #312 Cocoa Beach FL 32931

COPPOLA, SARAH JANE, special education educator; b. Alton, Ill., Apr. 20, 1957; d. Howard Earl and Dorothy Elizabeth (Eads) Cox; m. Daniel Joseph Coppola Jr., June 26, 1977; children: Daniel Joseph III, Shawn Marie. BS, Trenton State Coll., 1979; M Counseling Edn., Kean Coll. of N.J., 1995. Cert. guidance counselor, substance abuse counselor, N.J., early childhood cert., CIE coop. coord. cert. 1998, WECEP cert. Substitute tchr. Dunellen (N.J.) Bd. Edn., 1979-87, Greenbrook (N.J.) Bd. Edn., 1979-87, Middlesex (N.J.) Bd. Edn., 1979-87, Bound Brook (N.J.) Bd. Edn., 1983-84; tchr. of handicapped Piscataway (N.J.) Bd. Edn., 1987—, prin. adv. bd., 1990-91, editl. yearbook advisor, 1998—. Youth group advisor Trinity Reformed Ch., North Plainfield, N.J., 1983-91, deacon, 1985-87, 2001—, elder, 1997-2001, head Christian Edn., 1997—, v.p. consistory, 2000. Mem. NEA, N.J. Edn. Assn., Piscataway Edn. Assn., Kean Coll. Alumni Assn. (vol. Fish Hospitality program). Avocations: reading, needlework, church choir. Home: 200 Barclay Ct Piscataway NJ 08854 Office: Piscataway Bd Edn 100 Behmer Rd Piscataway NJ 08854-4161

COPPRIDGE, ALTON JAMES, urological surgeon; b. Roanoke, Va., Dec. 8, 1926; s. William Maurice Coppridge and Ferrie (Patterson) Choate; m. Helen Allen Burnett, June 24, 1950; children: William Allen, Virginia Choate. BA, U. N.C., 1949; MD, U. Va., 1953. Diplomate Am. Bd. Urology. Intern N.C. Meml. Hosp., Chapel Hill, 1953-54; surg. resident State U. of Iowa, Iowa City, 1954-56; urology resident U. Mich., Ann Arbor, 1956-59; mem. Coppridge Urologic Group, P.A., Durham, N.C., 1959-89; dept. chmn. Durham County Gen. Hosp., 1978-84; asst. clin. prof. Duke Med Ctr., Durham, N.C., 1970-89; clin. instr. U. N.C. Med. Sch., Chapel Hill, 1960-75. Contbr. articles to urologic lit. Served with U.S. Army, 1944-46; Japan. Mem.: ACS, NRA, Carolina Urol. Soc. (pres. 1985), N.C. Med. Soc. (pres. sect. urology 1978), Am. Urol. Assn. (exec. com. S.E. sect. 1983—86), Safari Internat. Club (Tucson) (pres. N.C. chpt. 1979—80), Durham Pistol and Rifle Club. Democrat. Presbyterian. Avocations: hunting, shooting, farm work. Home: A213 - 2600 Croasdaile Farm Pky Durham NC 27705

COPPS, MICHAEL JOSEPH, federal agency administrator; b. Milw., Apr. 23, 1940; s. Edmund J. and Ruth E. (Klemm) C.; m. Elizabeth Miller, Sept. 5, 1970; children: Robert, Mary, Michael, William, Claire. BA, Wofford Coll., 1963; PhD, U. N.C., 1967. Asst. prof. history Loyola U., New Orleans, 1967-70; adminstrv. asst. to U.S. Sen. Ernest F. Hollings U.S. Senate, Washington, 1970-85; dir. govt. affairs Collins & Aikman Corp., Washington, 1985-89; sr. v.p. Am. Meat Inst., Washington, 1989-93; dep. asst. sec. Dept. Commerce, Washington, 1993-98, asst. sec. for trade devel., 1998-2001; commr. FCC, Washington, 2001—. Mem. Phi Beta Kappa, Pi Gamma Mu. Democrat. Avocations: reading, automobiles. Office: FCC Off of Comn 445 12th St SW Washington DC 20554 Office Fax: 202-418-4802. E-mail: mcopps@FCC.gov.

COPPS, SHEILA, Canadian government official; b. Hamilton, Ont., Can., Nov. 27, 1952; d. Victor Kennedy and Geraldine (Guthro) C.; m. Austin Thorne; 1 child, Danelle. BA in French, English with hons., U. Western Ont., London; postgrad., U. Rouen, France, McMaster U., Hamilton. Reporter Ottawa Citizen, 1974-76, Hamilton Spectator, 1977; asst. to Ont. Liberal leader Stuart Smith, Hamilton, 1977-81; mem. Legis. Assembly Ont., Toronto, 1981-84, House of Commons, Ottawa, 1984-97; apptd. dep. leader Liberal Party Can., Ottawa, Ont., 1990—; dep. prime min. Govt. of Can., Ottawa, 1993-97, min. environ., 1993-96, min. of Can. heritage, 1996—. Author: Nobody's Baby, 1986. Mem. Liberal Party. Office: c/o Kerry Edmonds Dept Can Heritage 12th Fl 15 Eddy St Hull QC Canada K1A OM5

COPSETTA, NORMAN GEORGE, real estate executive; b. Pennsauken, N.J., Mar. 11, 1932; s. Joseph J. and Mary P. (DeMello) C.; m. Patricia Fitzpatrick, Mar. 5, 1971; children: Gregory, Margaret, Andrew, Norman G. Jr.; stepchildren: Samuel Sassano, James Sassano. Cert. real estate, Rutgers U. Extension, Camden, N.J., 1952; AA, Internat. Accts. Soc. Schl. Acctg., Chgo., 1968. Lic. title insurance agent, N.J. Settlement clk. Market Street Title Abstract Co., Camden, 1949-53; settlement administrator West Jersey Title & Guaranty Co., Camden, 1953; title examiner, abstract adminstr. Realty Abstract Co., Cherry Hill, N.J., 1954-64; mcpl. treas., tax collector Borough of Somerdale, N.J., 1961-65; title examiner, legal adminstr. Davis, Reberkenny & Abramowitz, Cherry Hill, 1974-97; pres., title officer Cooper Abstract Co., Cherry Hill, 1974-99, chmn. bd., 1997—. N.J. fgn. commr. of deeds in and for Pa., 1959—2000; mem. faculty Title Acad. N.J., The Title Ins. Sch. Custodian of funds Somerdale Bd. Edn., 1960-64. Mem. N.J. Title Ins. Agts. Assn., Haddonfield (N.J.) Hist. Soc., Camden County Hist. Soc. Avocation: local history. Office: Cooper Abstract Co 401 Cooper Landing Rd Ste C6 Cherry Hill NJ 08002-2598

COQUILLETTE, DANIEL ROBERT, lawyer, educator; b. Boston, May 23, 1944; s. Robert McTavish and Dagmar Alvida (Bistrup) C.; m. Judith Courtney Rogers, July 5, 1969; children: Anna, Sophia, Julia. AB, Williams Coll., 1966; MA Juris., U. Coll., Oxford U., Eng., 1969; JD, Harvard U., 1971. Bar: Mass. 1974, U.S. Dist. Ct. Mass. 1974, U.S. Ct. Appeals (1st cir.) 1974. Law clk. Mass. Supreme Ct., 1971-72; to chief justice Warren E. Burger U.S. Supreme Ct., 1972-73; assoc. Palmer & Dodge, Boston, 1973-75, ptnr., 1980-85; assoc. prof. law Boston U., 1975-78; dean, prof. Boston Coll. Law, 1985-93, prof., 1993-96, J. Donald Monan prof. law, 1996—. Vis. assoc. prof. law Cornell U., Ithaca, N.Y., 1977-78, 84; vis. prof. law Harvard U., 1978-79, 84-85, 94-2001, overseers com., Lester Kissel vis. prof., 2001—; reporter com. rules and procedures Jud. Conf. U.S.; mem. task force on rules of atty. conduct Supreme Jud. Ct. of Mass., 1996-97. Author: The Civilian Writers of Doctors Commons, London, 1988, Francis Bacon, 1993, Lawyers and Fundamental Moral Responsibility, 1995, Working Papers on Rules Governing Attorney Conduct, 1997, (with Basile, Beston, Donahue) Lex Mercatoria and Legal Pluralism, 1999, The Anglo-American Legal Heritage, 1999, (with McMorrow) Federal Law of Attorney Conduct, 2001; editor: Law in Colonial Massachusetts, 1985, Moore's Federal Practice, 3d edit., 1997; bd. dirs. New Eng. Quar., 1986—; contbr. articles to profl. jours. Trustee, sec.-treas. Ames Found; bd. overseers vis. com. Harvard Law Sch.; treas. Byron Meml. Fund; propr., trustee Boston Athenaeum. Recipient Kaufman prize in English Williams Coll., 1966, Sentinel of the Republic prize in polit. sci. Williams Coll., 1965; Hutchins scholar, 1966-67, Fulbright scholar, 1966-68 Mem. ABA (com. on profl. ethics 1990-93), Am. Law Inst., Mass. Bar Assn. (task force on model rules of profl. conduct), Boston Bar Assn., Am. Soc. Legal History (bd. dirs. 1985-89), Mass. Soc. Continuing Legal Edn. (bd. dirs. 1985-89), Selden Soc. (state corr.), Colonial Soc. Mass. (v.p., mem. coun.), Anglo-Am. Cathedral Soc. (bd. dirs.), Mass. Hist. Soc., Am. Antiquarian Soc., Phi Beta Kappa. Democrat. Mem. Soc. Of Friends. Home: 12 Rutland St Cambridge MA 02138-2503 Office: Boston Coll Sch Law 885 Centre St Newton MA 02459-1148 E-mail: coquill@bc.edu.

COQUILLETTE, WILLIAM HOLLIS, lawyer; b. Boston, Oct. 7, 1949; s. Robert McTavish and Dagmar (Bistrup) C.; m. Mary Katherine Templeton, June 19, 1971 (div. Oct. 1984); 1 child, Carolyn Patricia; m. Janet Marie Weiland, Dec. 8, 1984; children: Benjamin Weiland, Madeline Marie, Elizabeth Charlotte. BA, Yale U., 1971, Oxford U., 1973; JD, Harvard U., 1975. Bar: Ohio 1976, Mass. 1976. Law clk. to presiding justice Mass. Supreme Ct., Boston, 1975-76; assoc. Jones Day, Cleve., 1976-83, ptnr., 1984—. Trustee Cleve. Foodbank, Playhouse Sq. Found., Greater Cleve. Com. on Hunger. Mem. Kirtland Club, Yale Club (N.Y.C.), Union Club (Cleve.), Cleve. Skating Club, Rowfant Club, N.Y. Yacht Club. Office: Jones Day 901 Lakeside Ave E Cleveland OH 44114-1190

CORACE, JOSEPH RUSSELL, automotive executive; b. Mt. Clemens, Mich., July 22, 1953; s. Joseph Anthony and Josephine (Coniglario) C.; m. Judith Agnes Cynowa, June 24, 1977; children: Christina Marie, Joseph R., Anthony Casmier. AA, Macomb Coll., 1973; BSME, Wayne State U., 1976; MBA, Mich. State U., 1980. Staff engr. GM Corp., Warren, Mich., 1976-81; mgr. Volvo Cars N. Am., Rockleigh, N.J., 1981-85; dir. Volvo Automated Sys., Sterling Heights, Mich., 1985-88; pres., CEO Inalfa Roof Sys., Auburn Hills, Mich., 1988-98; pres., CEO, owner Forum Motors Group, 1999—. Mem. Rockleigh Sch. Bd., 1986, Holy Name Ch., 1987; lector St. Fabian Ch. Recipient Disting. Engring. Alumnus award Wayne State U.; named to Wayne State U. Hall of Fame; Sloan fellow Volvo Cars N.Am., 1981. Mem. Soc. Automotive Engrs. (jour. contbr.), Soc. Mfg. Engrs., Young Pres. Orgn. (pres. East Mich. chpt. 1997, bd. dirs., officer), Legatus (bd. dirs., pres. Detroit chpt. 1998—), Oakland Hills Country Club, Engring. Soc. Detroit, Detroit Econ. Club, Am. Mgmt. Assn. (pres.'s coun.), Walnut Creek Country Club (bd. dirs., pres.), Rochester Racquet Club, Detroit Athletic Club, KC (officer Detroit 1979). Roman Catholic. Avocations: racquetball, golf, squash, harley davidson motorcycles, hunting. Home: 5658 Springbrook Dr Troy MI 48098-5351

CORALLO, N. RALPH, health care products design engineer; b. Paterson, N.J., Apr. 14, 1937; s. Ralph John and Sylvia (DeStefano) C.; m. Mary Ann Katherin Glasstetter, Sept. 7, 1959; children: Ralph Charles, Charles Joseph, Mary Ann Catherine. Assoc. Engring., N.J. Inst. Tech., Newark, 1958; BSME, Fairleigh Dickinson U., 1968, MBA in Mgmt. cum laude, 1972. Engring. asst. Curtiss Wright Co., Inc., Woodridge, N.J., 1956; mgr. sensor engring. Thermo Electric Co., Inc., Saddle Brook, N.J., 1958-68; dir. rsch. and devel. Becton Dickinson & Co., Inc., Franklin Lakes, N.J., 1968-94; pres. Corco Sys., Elmwood Park, N.J., 1994—. Session editor Human Comfort and Biological Thermometry, Sixth Symposium on Temperature, 1982. Mem. ASTM (vice chmn. E20 1980-83, Robert D. Thompson award 1981), Internat. Soc. Pharm. Engrs., Instrument Soc. Am., Parenteral Drug Assn. (com. mem. 1989—). Roman Catholic. Achievements include patent for spring loaded thermocouple.

CORAM, DAVID JAMES, gaming industry professional; b. San Diego, Oct. 17, 1962; s. Thomas Harry and Joan Catherine (Reuter) C.; m. Irma Elizabeth Aquino, Jan. 14, 1989 (dec. July 1991); children: Catherine May, Corinna Briann, Carston James, Caitlin Kay, m. Corinna Kay Ward, May 6, 1995. AS with honors, Miramar Coll., 1989; honor grad. sheriff acad. basic tng., Southwestern Coll., 1986. Computer oper. Cubic Data Systems, San Diego, 1981-83, Electronic Data Systems, San Diego, 1983-84; ct. svc. officer San Diego County Marshal, 1985-86, dep. marshal, 1986-2000, San Diego County sheriff, 2000-01; regulatory compliance adminstr. Harrah's Rincon Casino, 2001—; pres., CFO Eagle Country Gaming Cons. A Nevada Corp. Pres. Coram Cons Group, 1994—; owner franchise Fantastic Sams Hair Salon, 1998—. Mediator San Diego Community Mediation Ctr., 1990-2001; soccer coach Temecula Valley Soccer Assn., 1987-, dir. planning and devel., 1999-2000; soccer coach S.W. Soccer Club, Temecula, Calif., 2002--; mem. nominating com. Outstanding Young Women Am. Awarded Gold medal soccer Ariz. Police Olympics, 1990, 91, Silver medal, 1993, Marksmanship award San Diego Marshal, Outstanding Young Men Am. award, 1989; 2d pl. Mid. Weight San Diego Gold's Gym Classic, 1993, Bronze medal Bodybuilding Calif. Police Olympics, 1994. Mem. Calif. State Marshal's Assn. (dir. on state bd. 1994), San Diego County Marshal's Assn. (parliamentarian 1988, dir. 1989-91, 93-94), San Diego County Marshal's Athletic Fedn. (dir. 1993-95), Nat. Physique Com. (contest judge). Republican. Avocations: golf, baseball, camping, computers, weight lifting. Office: Coram Cons Group 45620 Corte Montril Temecula CA 92592-1206

CORAN, ARNOLD GERALD, pediatric surgeon; b. Boston, Apr. 16, 1938; s. Charles and Ann (Cohen) C.; m. Susan Myra Williams, Nov. 17, 1960; children: Michael, David, Randi Beth. AB, Harvard U., 1959, MD, 1963. Diplomate Am. Bd. Surgery, Am. Bd. Thoracic Surgery, Am. Bd. Pediat. Surgery. Intern in surgery Peter Bent Brigham Hosp., Boston, 1963-64, resident in general and thoracic surgery, 1964-69; resident in pediatric surgery Children's Hosp., Boston, 1966-68, chief pediat. surgery, assoc. prof. surgery U. South Calif. Med. Sch., L.A., 1972-74; chief pediat. surgery, prof. surgery U. Mich., Ann Arbor, 1974—; surgeon in chief C.S. Mott Childrens Hosp., Ann Arbor, 1981—. Contbr. articles to profl. jours. Lt. comdr. USN, 1970-72. Mem.: Am. Pediat. Surg. Assn. (pres. 2001—02). Avocations: skiing, golf, running. Home: 505 E Huron St Apt 802 Ann Arbor MI 48104-1553 Office: CS Mott Childrens Hosp Rm F3970 Ann Arbor MI 48109-0245

CORAN, JOSHUA D. mechanical engineer; b. Brookline, Mass., Aug. 14, 1946; s. Murray M. and Ruth W. Coran. SB in mech. engring., Mass. Inst. Tech., Cambridge, 1968; MBA, U. Pitts., 1972. Assoc. engr. Westinghouse Elec. Co., East Pitts., 1968—72; prodn. and oc engr. Ill. Ctrl. R.R., Chgo., 1972—75; mgr. of engrs. Rail Sys. Inc., Mira Loma, Calif., 1975—76; mgr. of mfg. engring. Pullman Std., Chgo., 1976—83; chief mech. engr. Alaska R.R., Anchorage, 1983—. Chmn. Nat. Assn. of R.R. Environ. Testing, Anchorage, 2002—. Trustee Congregation Beth Shalom, Anchorage; sec.-treas. Alaska Pet Palace, Anchorage, 1985—98. Jewish. Office: Alaska RR Corp 327 Ship Career Ave Anchorage AK 99501

CORASH, RICHARD, lawyer; b. N.Y.C., Mar. 31, 1938; s. Paul and Mildred (Spanier) C.; m. Carol A. McKevitt, Dec. 11, 1966; children: Richard Jr., Sharon, Peter, Amy. BA, Harpur Coll., SUNY, Bingamton, 1959; MA, Bklyn. Law Sch., 1966; JD, Rutgers U., 1963. Bar: N.Y. 1964, U.S. Dist. Ct. D.C. 1964, U.S. Supreme Ct. 1972. Pvt. practice, N.Y.C., 1964-77; pres. Corash & Hollender, P.C ., N.Y.C., 1977—. Pres. NEFM Trading Co., N.Y.C.; chmn. North Eastern Fiscal Mgmt. Co., N.Y.C.; pres. North Eastern Equities, L.L.C.; counsel Caywood Homeowners Assn. Mem. N.Y. State Bar Assn. (real estate and trust and estates sects.), N.Y. State Bar Assn. (chmn. grievance com.), Richmond County Bar Assn. Address: 81 Roxiticus Rd Far Hills NJ 07931-2225 E-mail: E-mailchlawnyc@aol.com.

CORATTI, JOHN EDWARD, judicial clerk; b. Jersey City, Nov. 17, 1950; s. Nicholas and Bernice (Johnson) C.; 1 child, Kathleen Mary. BA in English, Rutgers Coll., 1973; MA, Seton Hall U., 1981; postgrad., NYU, 1981-88, Trinity Coll., Dublin, Ireland, 1974; JD, U. Dayton, 1988; postgrad., Rutgers U., 1994. Pres. off-Broadway theater John a-Dreams Profl. Repertory Theatre, N.J., N.Y., 1973-84; instr. English Wright State U., Dayton, 1988, U. Dayton, 1986-88; legal adminstrv. asst. Ocean County Prosecutor's Office, N.J., 1988-91; jud. appellate clk. Superior Ct. Appellate Div., N.J., 1991—. Active Women Exploited by Abortion. Recipient Am. Jurisprudence award Lawyers Coop. Pub. Co., 1988, Award for Excellence, Italian Am. Bar Assn. Mem. Nat. Right to Life, Univ. Ctrs. for Rational Alternatives, Federalist Soc., Amnesty Internat., Am. Theatre Wing, Civil Liberties Union, Phi Theta Kappa. Democrat. Roman Catholic. Avocations: reading, travel, theatre, physics, boxing. Home: PO Box 695 Orange TX 77631- Office: Superior Ct of NJ Appellate Div 100 E Water St Toms River NJ 08753-7518

CORAZA, MARY CATHERINE, psychologist; b. Newton, N.J. d. Alfred J. and Alice (Reynolds) C. Student, Lehigh U., 1970. Psychologist Pa. Hosp., Phila., 1980—; asst. prof. Univ. Pa. Med. Sch., Phila., 1991—. Cons. Phila. Dept. of Welfare and Human Svcs. Bd. dirs. Fitler Square Improvement Assn., Phila., 1987—; vol. Phila. Mus. of Art. Mem. APA, Pa. Psychol. Assn., Phila. Soc. Clin. Psychologists (bd. dirs. 1997—), Phila. Soc. of Clin. Psychologist (bd. dirs.), Psi Chi. Home: 220 W Rittenhouse Sq Philadelphia PA 19103-5737

CORBALLY, JOHN EDWARD, adult education educator; b. South Bend, Wash., Oct. 14, 1924; s. John Edward and Grace (Williams) C.; m. Marguerite B. Walker, Mar. 12, 1946; children: Jan Elizabeth, David William. BS, U. Wash., 1947, MA, 1950; PhD, U. Calif., Berkeley, 1955; LLD, U. Md., 1971; LL.D., Blackburn Coll., 1972, Ill. State U., 1977, Ohio State U., 1980; Litt.D., U. Akron, 1979. Tchr. Clover Park High Sch., Tacoma, 1947-50; prin. Twin City High Sch., Stanwood, Wash., 1950-53; asst. prof., then assoc. prof. edn. Ohio State U., Columbus, 1955-60, prof., 1960-69, dir. pers. budget, exec. asst. to pres., 1960-64, v.p. adminstrn., 1964-66, provost, v.p. acad. affairs, 1966-69; chancellor, pres. Syracuse (N.Y.) U., 1969-71; pres. U. Ill., Chgo. and Urbana-Champaign, 1971-79, pres. emeritus, 1979—, disting. prof. higher edn., 1979-82, disting. prof. emeritus, 1982—; pres. John D. and Catherine T. MacArthur Found., 1979-89, dir., 1979—2002, chmn., 1995—2002; cons. Heidrick & Struggles, 1989-90. Chmn. Nat. Coun. Ednl. Rsch., Nat. Inst. Edn., 1973-79; trustee Mus. Sci. and Industry, Chgo., 1971-79; chmn. Commn. Curricular Outcome, Ill. Bd. Edn., 1985-88; chmn. Chgo. Sch. Reform Authority, 1988-89. Author: Introduction to Educational Adminstration, 6th edit, 1983, Educational Administration: The Secondary School, 2d edit, 1965, School Finance, 1962. Bd. dirs. U. Wash. Found., 1989-93, Ill. Ednl. Consortium, 1973-79, Zion Prep. Acad. (Seattle), 2000-2002, Greater Everett Cmty. Found., Rural Devel. Inst., 1995-03, Seattle, Exec. Svc. Corps of Wash., 1990-96, 98-2000, Snonet, Everett, Wash., 1994-2002. Lt. (j.g.) USNR, 1943-46. Recipient Centennial medal U. Calif. Alumni Assn. and Sch. Edn. Alumni Soc., 1976, Disting. Eagle award Boy Scouts Am., 1978, Van Miller award Ill. Assn. Sch. Adminstrs. and Ednl. Adminstrn. Alumni Assn. U. Ill., 1986, Humanitarian award No. Ill. U., 1986, Disting. Alumnus award U. Wash. Coll. Edn., 1987, Disting. Achievement award U. Wash. Coll. Arts and Sci., 1995; named Alumnus Summa Laude Dignatus, U. Wash., 1988, Laureate, Lincoln Acad. Ill., 1989. Mem. U. Ill. Alumni Assn. (life, Disting. Svc. award 1986), U. Wash. Alumni Assn. (life), Tavern Club, Wayfarers Club, Phi Beta Kappa. Home: 1507 151st Pl SE Mill Creek WA 98012-1591

CORBANI, CANDACE BEDFORD, antiques broker, political campaign consultant; b. Sellersville, Pa., Sept. 1, 1944; d. Harry Clay and Gwendolyn Murdoch Bedford; m. John Francis Corbani, July 3, 1963; children: Kim, Donna. BA in Sociology, U. Calif., Santa Barbara, 1968; AS in Hotel Restaurant Mgmt., Santa Barbara City Coll., 1977. Orgnl. cons. Party Makers, Santa Barbara, 1977-84; owner C&G Collection, Santa Barbara, 1981-90; owner, appraiser, cons. Candi Corbani & Collector's Resource Network, Santa Barbara, 1989—; owner EstatesaleSB.com, Santa Barbara, 1999—. Events coord. Brinkerhoff Mchts. Assn., Santa Barbara, 1985-90; cons. Wood Glen Hall, Santa Barbara, 2001. Author: Bright Ideas I, 1980, II, 1984; contbr. articles to jours.; prodr. (talk radio show) Collector's News Hour, 1989-91. Chair affirmative action com. Santa Barbara Sch. Dist., 1986-89; pres. Bus. Women Environment, Santa Barbara, 1995-2001; mem. Santa Barbara County Rep. Ctrl. Com., 1998-2001; pres. G.A.L.S. Federated Rep. Women, 1999; founding pres. Moderate Rep. Majority, Santa Barbara; del. Calif. Reps., Santa Barbara County. Recipient Women of Achievement award Calif. State Senate, Assembly & Santa Barbara County, 1987. Mem. Am. Soc. Appraisers, Assn. Online Appraisers, Santa Barbara Bus. & Profl. Women (v.p. 1988). Deist. Home and Office: 4760 Calle Camarada Santa Barbara CA 93110 E-mail: condicorbani@aol.com.

CORBATO, CHARLES EDWARD, geology educator; b. Los Angeles, July 12, 1932; s. Hermenegildo and Charlotte Carella (Jensen) C.; m. Patricia Jeanne Ferg, May 18, 1957; children: Steven, Barbara, Susan. BA, UCLA, 1954, PhD, 1960. Instr. geology U. Calif., Riverside, 1959, Los Angeles, 1959-60, asst. prof., 1960-66; assoc. prof. Ohio State U., Columbus, 1966-69, prof., 1969-92, chmn. dept. geology and mineralogy, 1972-80, assoc. provost office of acad. affairs, 1987-92, prof., assoc. provost emeritus, 1992—. Geophysicist U.S. Geol. Survey, 1966-74; dir. State Postsecondary Rev. Entity, Ohio Bd. Regents, 1994-95, dir. info. svcs., 1995-99. Fellow: Geol. Soc. Am.; mem.: Inst. Profl. Geologists, Am. Geophys. Union, Delta Tau Delta. Home: 2400 Buckley Rd Columbus OH 43220-4616 Office: Ohio State U 125 S Oval Mall Columbus OH 43210-1308 E-mail: corbato.1@osu.edu., ccorbato@columbus.rr.com.

CORBEILL, ANTHONY, classicist, educator; b. Detroit, Dec. 30, 1960; s. Wallace and Elsie Corbeill. PhD, U. Calif., Berkeley, 1990. Prof. U. Kans., Lawrence, 1991—2003. Editor Memoirs of the Am. Acad. in Rome, 1999—. Author: (book) Controlling Laughter: Political Humor in the Late Roman Republic, Nature Embodied: Gesture in Ancient Rome. Home: 1445 Jayhawk Blvd #2083 Lawrence KS 66045-7594

CORBET, DONALD LEE, audio and technology company executive, technical systems educator; b. Dayton, Ohio, Dec. 1, 1959; s. John Rodger and Barbara Lou (Timmerman) C.; m. Heidi A. Herschede, 1998; 1 child, Jessica Lea. Student, Wright State U., 1978-80, Capitol U., Columbus, Ohio, 1991—93. Cert. in NCR svc., comm. theory. Computer cons. Radio Shack, Dayton, 1981-82; computer service tech. Reynolds and Reynolds, Peoria, Ill., 1982-84, tech. systems instr. Dayton, 1984-91; sr. instr., 1991-94; team leader tech. tng., 1994-98; cert. repair, trainer Compaq Computers, Houston, Calif., 1995-97, tech. specialist, 1997-99; mgr. client network adminstrn. Cole-Layer-Trumble Co., 1999-2000; CIO Gaspricewatch.com, 2000—02; mgr. Open Source Bus. Solutions Team Linux Corp., 2000-01; pres. evolServ Techs., 2001—02; CIO D.L. Corbet and Assoc., LLC, Centerville, Ohio, 2002—. Owner D. L. Corbet Media Systems, Dayton, 1980—; career developer Success Motivation Inst., Waco, Tex., 1986-88; bd. dirs. Mgmt. Documentation Assn., Dayton; cons. SIGI Wittenburg U., Springfield, Ohio, 1982; spkr. various clubs and lodges; trainer, lectr. Team Linux Corp., 2000-01. Author: Understanding Customer Satisfaction, 1987; co-author: Everybody's Guide to P.C.'s, 1986; composer (recs.) Thunder Road Theme, 1985, Twister film soundtrack (Ind. U.), 1986, Chrysler Interactive Training Theme; prodr., engr.: (CD) Shake, Rattle and Humm, 1995, The Rejects Forever, 1999; prodr., dir. various ednl. computer videos; host (radio) Radio PC Review, WING-AM, 1998-2002; radio host On-Technology, WHIO-AM, 2002--. Recipient Dayton Music Link award Hands Across Am., 1986. Home: 1857 E Social Row Rd Centerville OH 45458-4730 E-mail: thelinuxguy@gemair.com.

CORBET, RICHARD HUGH, trade policy specialist, writer; b. Perth, Australia, Nov. 18, 1936; arrived in U.S., 1990; s. John Arthur and Freda Marian (Sherwood) Corbet; m. Rosalind Mary Willett Bevan, June 10, 1961 (div. Oct. 1978). BA, U. Adelaide, Australia, 1960; postgrad., U. Keele, Eng., 1990-93. Cert. journalist Brit. Inst. Journalists. Rsch. asst. Cazenove & Co., stockbrokers, London, 1961-62; rsch. asst. conservative backbench com. on European cmty. Brit. Ho. of Commons, London, 1962-63; econs. corr. Thomson Newspapers, London, 1963-65; specialist writer The Times, London, 1965-68; dir. Trade Policy Rsch. Ctr., London, 1968-89; mng. editor The World Economy, Boston and Oxford, England, 1977-89; guest scholar Woodrow Wilson Internat. Ctr. for Scholars and the Brookings Inst., Washington, 1990-92; sr. fellow Manhattan Inst., N.Y. and Washington, 1992-93; dir. trade policy program Sigur Ctr. for Asian Studies George Washington U., Washington, 1993-97; pres. Cordell Hull Inst., Washington, 1998—. Spl. advisor Opposition Spokesmen on Trade Brit. Ho. Commons, London, 1978—79; cons. on trade policy Internat. C. of C., Paris, 1979—83; mem. adv. com. on studies internat. trade policy U. Mich. Press, Ann Arbor, 1989—; mem. adv. bd. The World Economy, Oxford and Boston, 1990—2001; cons. European Inst. Japanese Studies, Stockholm, 1994—97, Swiss-Asia Found., Lausanne, Switzerland, 1996—99. Author: Beyond the Rhetoric of Commodity Power, 1974; co-author: (book) Trade Strategy for the Asia-Pacific Region, 1970, Opportunity of a Century to Liberalise Farm Trade, 2002; co-editor: Europe's Free Trade Area Experiment, 1970, Commonwealth Policy in a Global Context, 1971, In Search of a New World Economic Order, 1974, Reason vs. Emotion: Requirements for a Successful WTO Round, 1999, Labor Standards in an Integrating World Economy, 2003; rapporteur: various profl. reports including Economic Policy for the European Community, 1974; author: Trade Routes to Sustained Economic Growth, 1987, Public Scrutiny of Protection, 1987; contbr. articles to profl. jours. Office: Ste 115 2400 Pennsylvania Ave NW Washington DC 20037-1714 Office Fax: 202-338-0327. E-mail: hugh.corbet@cordellhullinstitute.org.

CORBETT, EUGENE C., JR., medical educator; b. Phila., Feb. 13, 1943; s. Eugene Charles Corbett Sr. and Dolores Marie (Hoffmann) Corbett; m. Susan Genevieve Houtman, Oct. 27, 1967; children: Roland Charles, Gabriel John, Cornelius Matthew. BA, Fla. State U., 1966; MD, U. Chgo., 1970. Diplomate Am. Bd. Internal Medicine. Intern SUNY, Syracuse, 1970—71; resident in internal medicine Balt. City Hosp., 1973—75; physician Ctrl. Va. Cmty. Health Ctr., Buckingham, 1971—73, 1975—79; pvt. practice Fork Union, Va., 1979—84; cons. asst. prof. medicine Stanford U., Palo Alto, Calif., 1984—85; assoc. prof. medicine U. Va., Charlottesville, 1985—. Faculty devel. program Stanford U., Palo Alto, 1987—; vis. faculty Harvard Macy Inst., Boston, 2000—; state coun. Va. Am. Coll. Physicians, 2002—. County coroner State Va. Med. Examiner, Fluvanna County, Va., 1976—. Scholar, Johns Hopkins U., 1973—75, Assn. Am. Med. Colls., 2002—03. Mem.: Alpha Omega Alpha. Avocations: farming, astronomy, cello, cooking. Office: Univ Va PO Box 800744 Charlottesville VA 22908 Office Fax: 434-924-1138. Business E-Mail: ecc9h@virginia.edu.

CORBETT, GORDON LEROY, minister; b. Melrose, Mass., Dec. 11, 1920; s. Winfield Leroy and Lalia Estey (Fiske) C.; m. Winifred Pickett, Sept. 7, 1946; children: Douglas Leroy, Christine, Patricia, Carolyn. AB, Bates Coll., 1943; MDiv, Yale U., 1948. Ordained to ministry Bapt. Ch., 1948. Pastor Montowese Bapt. Ch., North Haven, Conn., 1948-52; assoc. pastor First Presbyn. Ch., Glen Falls, N.Y., 1952-59; synod exec. Synod of Ky., Lexington, 1959-71; assoc. synod exec. for Alaska, 1971-84; interim synod exec. Synod of Lincoln Trails, Indpls., 1987-88; interim Presbyn. exec. Santa Barbara (Calif.) Presbytery, 1991-92. Trustee Appalachian Regional Hosps., Lexington, 1969-72, Sheldon Jackson Coll., Sitka, Alaska, 1972-84; chmn. chaplaincy com. Alaska Christian Conf., 1975-78, Alaska Pipeline Chaplaincy. Author: Thirteen Generations of Descendants of Robert Corbett, who died in Woodstock, Conn., 1695, 1995. Mem. Santa Barbara Presbytery; chmn., bd. dirs. Encina Royale, Inc., 1997-98. Dist. chmn. Rep. Party, Anchorage, 1974-78. 1st lt. USAAF, 1944-45, China. Recipient Christian Citizenship award Sheldon Jackson Coll., 1984. *"Since we are surrounded by so great a cloud of witnesses... let us run with perserverance the race that is set before us". (Hebrews 12:1).*

CORBETT, JAMES JOHN, neurologist, neuroophthalmologist; b. Chgo., July 2, 1940; s. Maxwell Melville and Rose Marie (Evanchak) C.; m. Joyce Roberta Zymali, Dec. 29, 1962; children: John Christopher, Jill Stephanie, Jennifer Sarah. BA in Biology, Brown U., 1962; MD, Chgo. Med. Sch., 1966. Diplomate Am. Bd. Neurology and Psychiatry. Intern, then med. resident R.I. Hosp., Providence, 1966-68; resident in neurology Univ. Hosps Cleve., 1968-71; instr., clin. asst. prof. Jefferson Med. Coll., Phila., 1973-77; pvt. practice Phila., 1973-77; asst. prof. neurology U. Iowa, Iowa City, 1977-80, assoc. prof., 1980-85, prof. neurology and ophthalmology, 1985-90; McCarty prof., chmn. dept. neurology, prof. ophthamology U. Miss., Jackson, 1991—. Lt. comdr. M.C., USNR, 1971-73. Fellow Am. Neurol. Assn., Am. Acad. Neurology, N.Am. Neuroophthalmology Soc.; mem. Alpha Omega Alpha. Democrat. Episcopalian. Home: 1402 Bay Vista Dr Brandon MS 39047-8654 Office: UMC 2500 N State St Jackson MS 39216-4500 E-mail: jcorbettmd@aol.com.

CORBETT, JAMES JOSEPH, retired computer programmer; b. Glens Falls, N.Y., Feb. 29, 1944; s. John Howard and Margaret Claire (Tupper) C.; m. Elaine Cecile Smith, Nov. 16, 1974. BA, Siena Coll., 1965; MA in Am. Studies, U. Md., 1967. Logistics intern U.S. Army Logistics Intern Tng. Ctr., Texarkana, Tex., 1967-68; supply specialist U.S. Army Electronics Command, Phila., 1968-70; computer programmer, analyst U.S. Army Logistics Systems Support Ctr., St. Louis, 1970-99. Contbr. articles to jours. Mem. Blueliners, Inc., St. Louis, 1970—, pres. 1983-85; mem. Bridge Line Hist. Soc., Albany, N.Y., 1990—; mem. choir Assumption Parish, 1994—; mem. Year 2000 Task Group, LSSC, 1996-99. Recipient Comdr.'s award for Civilian Svc., U.S. Army, 1987. Mem. Nat. Railway Hist. Soc. Roman Catholic. Avocations: railroad history, ice hockey, basketball, flags.

CORBETT, JOHN, actor; b. Wheeling, W.Va., May 9, 1961; s. Actor: (TV series) Northern Exposure, 1990; (films) Flight of the Intruder, 1991, Tombstone, 1993; (TV films) Innocent Victims, 1996, Don't Look Back, 1996; (films) Wedding Bell Blues, 1996; (TV films) The Morrison Murders, 1996; (films) Volcano, 1997; (TV series) The Visitor, 1997; (TV films) The Warlord: Battle for the Galaxy, 1998, The Sky's On Fire, 1998; (TV series) To Serve and Protect, 1999; (films) Desperate But Not Serious, 1999; (TV films) On Hostile Ground, 2000; (films) Dinner Rush, 2000; (TV films) Rocky Times, 2000, Private Lies, 2000; (TV series) Sex and the City, 1998; (films) Serendipity, 2001, Prancer Returns, 2001, My Big Fat Greek Wedding, 2002; (TV films) The Griffin and the Minor Cannon, 2002; (TV series) Lucky, 2003. Office: Creative Artists Agy 9830 Wilshire Blvd Beverly Hills CA 90212*

CORBETT, LENORA MEADE, mathematician, community college educator; b. Reidsville, N.C., Aug. 1, 1950; children: Kenneth Russell Johnson, Ralph Nathaniel Brown. AAS in Electromechanics, Tech. Coll. of Alamance, 1985, AAS in Electronics, 1986; BS in Indsl. Tech., Electronics, N.C. A&T State U., 1996. Cloth inspector Burlington (N.C.) Industries, 1971-74; electrician's helper Williams Electric, Greensboro, N.C., 1978, Nobility Mobile Homes, Reidsville, N.C., 1979; instr. math. and physics Alamance C.C., Graham, NC, 1985—2002, chmn. learning resources, 1993. Contbr. poems to profl. publs. (Golden Poet award 1991, Merit award 1990, 92). Mem. sr. choir Jones Cross Rd. Ch., Reidsville, 1988-94, pastor's aide mem., 1988-90, jr. Sunday sch. tchr., 1989-91, asst. choir sec., 1988-94; bd. dirs. Nu Generation Enrichment Program; mem. bd. Nu Generation Enrichment Ctr., Teach Tolerance Nat. Campaign Tolerance, 2002, 2003. Recipient Famous Poet, 1996, 2000, Editor's Choice Award, 1997, Famous Poets So. Recognition award, 1998. Mem. AAUP, AAUW, Alamance C.C. Alumni Assn., Golden Key, N.C. A&T State U. Alumni Assn. Baptist. Avocations: cooking, reading, writing poetry, drawing, singing.

CORBETT, LUKE R. energy executive; m. Becky Corbett; 1 child, Carrie. Grad., U. Ga., 1969. Geophysicist Amoco Prodn. Co., Mitchell Energy, Aminoil; with Kerr-McGee Corp., 1985—, pres., COO, 1995—97, CEO, 1997—, chmn., 1999—. Bd. dirs. Am. Petroleum Inst., Domestic Petroleum Coun.; chmn. adv. bd. Energy Geosci. Inst., U. Utah; bd. dirs. Devon Energy Corp., Okla. Gas Electric. Bd. dirs. Allied Arts Found.; United Way. Mem.: Oklahoma City C. of C. (bd. dirs.). Office: Kerr-McGee Corp 123 Robert S Kerr Ave Oklahoma City OK 73102*

CORBETT, MICHAEL ARTHUR, JR., business management consultant; b. Port Chester, N.Y., Feb. 23, 1965; s. Michael Arthur and Margaret Mary (Powell) Corbett; married; 3 children. B.E.E., Villanova U., 1987; MBA in Finance, Seton Hall U., 1997. Sr. engr. BOC Gases, Murray Hill, N.J., 1991-94; project mgr. Kline & Co., Little Falls, N.J., 1995-98, dir. electronic & advanced materials, 1999—. Contbr. articles to profl. jours. Soc. Automotive Engrs., I.E.E.E., Am. Vacuum Soc., Materials Rsch. Soc. Republican. Roman Catholic. Avocations: golf, reading, charities.

CORBETT, SUZANNE ELAINE, food writer, marketing executive, food historian; b. St. Louis, Jun. [illegible], 1950; d. George Edward and Opal Laverne (Duncan) Traxel; m. James Joseph Corbett, Jr., July 17, 1970 (div. 2000); 1 child, James J. III. BA, Webster U., 1994, MA in Media Comm., 1995. Cert. culinary profl., Internat. Assn. Culinary Profls. Tchr. Inst. Continuing Edn. St. Louis C.C., 1976—; tchr. cmty. edn. Lindbergh Sch. Dist. Pub. Schs., St. Louis, 1983-89; confectioner/caterer Suzanne Corbett Seasonal Confections, St. Louis, 1977-84; test baker Fleishman's Yeast, St. Louis, 1983; food stylist St. Louis, 1980—; rsch. cons./food mktg. and rsch. food/product history, 1994; rsch. cons. media prodn. PanCor Prodns., 1994—. Food historian, folklorist Jefferson Nat. Parks Assn., St. Louis County Parks and Recreation, Mo. Hist. Soc., St. Louis Art Mus., Colonial Dames of Am.; food media trainer Internat. Assn. Culinary Profls., 1990; ALFHM lectr. in field. Author: Cowpuncher's Provision, 1988, River Fare, 1990, Pharoh's Pheast-Food from the Nile, 1991, Tips from Missouri Win Country, 1993, Pushcarts & Stalls: The Souland Market History Cookbook, 1999; food writer, cookbook editor St. Louis Bugle food editor, 1991-96, columnist, 1991-96; columnist Sr. Circuit Newspaper; food writer, columnist News Weekly, Connoisseur; contbg. food editor St. Louis Home & Lifestyles, Achieve Mag. Bd. dirs. St. Louis South sect. Am. Heart Assn., Historyonics Theatre Co.; mem. Mo. Grape and Wine Adv. Bd. Recipient Folklife Greentree grant award Ralston Purina, 1989, grant award Commerce Bank, 1990, grant award Wetterau Foods, 1991. Mem. Women in Communications (pres. St. Louis chpt. 1996, Communication awards 1989, 90, 91, 92, 93, 94, 95, 96, 97, 98, 99), Nat. Fedn. Press Women (v.p. Mo. chpt.), Mo. Press Women (past pres., Communication award 1989, 96, 97, Communicator of Yr. 1993), Victorian Soc. Am. (past pres. St. Louis chpt.), James Beard Found. (charter), Am. Inst. Wine and Food, Internat. Assn. Culinary Profls. (cert., culinary historian Boston and Ann Arbor, internat. conf. com. 1990), Assn. Ind. Video and Filmmakers, St. Louis Press Club (former co-editor Courier, interim dir., Pres.' award, Press Club Charitable Fund pres. 1993-94), Nat. Fedn. Press Women (Communication and Writing awards), Nat. Trust for Hist. Preservation, St. Louis Culinary Soc. (sec., bd. dirs.), Order Eastern Star. Roman Catholic. Avocations: folklife crafts, gardening, travel, historic preservation. Home and Office: Apt B 12150 Queens Charter Ct Saint Louis MO 63146-5250 E-mail: corbettsuzanne@aol.com.

CORBETT, THOMAS WINGETT, JR., lawyer; b. Phila., June 17, 1949; s. Thomas Wingett and Mary Bernadine (Diskin) C.; m. Susan Jean Manbeck, Dec. 16, 1972; children: Thomas Wingett III, Katherine. BA, Lebanon Valley Coll., 1971; JD, St. Mary's U., 1975. Bar: Pa. 1976, U.S. Dist. Ct. (we. dist.) Pa. 1976, U.S. Ct. Mil. Appeals 1979, U.S. Supreme Ct. 1984. Asst. dist. atty. Allegheny County, Pitts., 1976—80; asst. U.S. atty. Office U.S. Atty. for Western Dist. Pa., Pitts., 1980—83; assoc. Rose, Schmidt, Hasley & DiSalle, Pitts., 1983—86, ptnr., 1986—89; U.S. atty. We. Dist. Pa., Pitts., mem. U.S. atty. gen.'s adv. com., 1991—, chmn., 1993; Atty. Gen. State of Pa., Harrisburg, 1995—97; ptnr. Thorp, Reed & Armstrong, Pitts., 1993—95, 1997—98; asst. gen. counsel for govt. affairs Waste Mgmt. Inc., Pitts., 1998—2002; owner Thomas Corbett & Assocs., 2002—. Pres. St. Mary's Parent-Tchr. Guild, Glenshaw, Pa., 1983-85; mem. Allegheny County Republican Com., 1985-89, 2002—; mem. Shaler Twp. Bd. Commrs., 1988-89; chmn. Pa. Commn. on Crime and Delinquency, 1995—. Mem. ABA, Pa. Bar Assn., Allegheny County Bar Assn. (judiciary com.). Roman Catholic. Avocations: skiing, golf, reading. Office: 1720 Gulf Tower 7th and Grant St Pittsburgh PA 15219

CORBETT, WILLIAM JOHN, government and public relations consultant, lawyer; b. Bklyn., Mar. 15, 1937; s. John Joseph and Mildred (Bauer) C.; m. Ann Virginia Teplitz, June 25, 1966; children: William John, Spencer Thomas, Sally Ann. BA, Hobart Coll., 1959; JD, Fordham U., 1965. Bar: N.Y. 1966, U.S. Dist. Ct. (fed. dist.) 1968, Customs Ct. 1968, U.S. Supreme Ct. 1990. Info. officer USAF, Greenville, S.C., 1959-62; trial lawyer Nassau County Legal Aid Soc., Mineola, N.Y., 1966-67; asst. dist. atty. County of Nassau, 1967-68; corp. dir. pub. rels. Avon Products, Inc., N.Y.C., 1968-84; v.p. comm. AICPA, N.Y.C., 1984-90; chmn. Corbett Assocs., Inc., 1990—. Pub. rels. advisor USIA, Washington, 1981-93; cons. status UN Office Info. and ECOSOC, N.Y.C., 1979-84, 90-93; pros. atty. Inc. Village of Floral Park, N.Y., 1975-84, acting village justice, 1984-98, adj. asst. prof. Iona Coll. Grad. Sch. Comm., 1990-2000. Mem. adv. bd. Pub. Rels. News (Leadership award 1984); mem. Commn. on Pub. Rels. Edn. Participant White House Conf. on Indsl. World Ahead, 1972, White House Mini Conf. on Consumer Elderly, 1979, White House Conf. on Small Bus., 1986, 95, White House Conf. on Librs. and Info. Svcs., 1991; staff mem. N.Y. State Senate, Albany, 1962-63. Capt. USAF, 1959-62. Decorated Air Force Commendation medal; recipient Legion of Honor Internat. Coun. Order DeMolay, 1982, Hobart Coll. Alumni award, 1984, N.Y. State Conspicuous Svc. medal, 1970, Pinnacle award, 1990; named to Hall of Fame, U.S. Dept. Def. Info. Sch., 1990. Fellow Internat. Pub. Rels. Assn. (bd. dirs. 1984-90, pres. 1990); mem. Pub. Rels. Soc. Am. (accredited, Fellow Pres. award 1985, 88), Pub. Rels. Soc. N.Y. (past pres.), Corp. Forum N.Y., Ctr. for Study Presidency (adv. bd.), Pub. Affairs Coun., Nat. Assn. Corp. Dirs. N.Y. (v.p. 1993-94), Nat. Commn. on Pub. Rels. Edn., Am. Legion (commdr. Floral Pk. chpt. 2001-02). Home: 102 Chestnut Ave Floral Park NY 11001-2421 Office: 111 S Tyson Ave Floral Park NY 11001-1822 E-mail: wjcorbett@corbettpr.com.

CORBIÈRE, PAUL, music educator; b. Hollywood, Fla., June 21, 1964; s. Paul Arthur and Mary Lou Corbière; m. Alicia Catherine Lancaster, Aug. 5, 1995; children: Phillip Jacob, Matthew Paul. MusM, Ohio State U., 1992; BFA, Fla. Atlantic U., 1989; AA, Broward C.C., Davie, Fla., 1986. Cert. Tchg. Fla., 1992. Music educator Palm Beach Sch. Dist., West Palm Beach, Fla., 1992—. Tchg. asst. World Music Drumming Project, 1998—. Mem.: Music Educator Nat. Conf. (assoc.). Democrat. Roman Catholic. Avocations: fishing, live music performance. Office: Freedom Shores Elem Sch 3400 Hypoluxo Rd Boynton Beach FL 33436 Personal E-mail: djembedad@aol.com.

CORBIN, DAVID P. counselor; b. Ripley, W.Va., Jan. 23, 1943; s. Oliver Paige and Catherine Elaine Corbin; m. Shirley Mae Francis, July 3, 1968; children: Max David, Beth Ann. AA in Speech, Potomac State Coll., 1962; BA in Speech, W.Va. U., 1965; MEd in Counseling, Ohio U., 1991. Lic. counselor Ohio. Contbr. articles to profl. jours. Pres. Sugar Lane Improvement Assn., Rivesville, W.Va., 1972, Neighborhood Watch, Little Hocking, Ohio, 1986. Corr. U.S. Army, 1966—67, Vietnam. Mem.: Ohio Counselors Assn., Mensa (winner fiction Region III 1994). Avocations: piano, writing, acting, walking, harmonica. Home: PO Box 68 Little Hocking OH 45742

CORBIN, DAVID R. state legislator; b. July 20, 1944; m. Betty Corbin. Mem. Kans. Ho. of Reps., Topeka, 1990-92; mem. from dist. 16 Kans. Senate, Topeka, 1993—. Chmn. energy and natural resources com., agrl. com.; mem. assessment and taxation coms.; farmer and commodity broker; market analyst Kans. Agrl. Network, 1983—. Mem. Farm Bur., Livestock Assn., Nat. Assn. Farmbroadcasters, El Dorado and Augusta C. of C., Lions, Kiwanis. Republican. Home: 5079 SW Fulton Rd Towanda KS 67144-9097*

CORBIN, DONALD L. state supreme court justice; b. Hot Springs, Ark., Mar. 29, 1938; BA, U. Ark., 1964, JD, 1966. Bar: Ark. 1966, U.S. Dist. Ct. (we. dist.) Ark. 1966. Lawyer Lewisville and Stamps, 1967-80; judge Ark. Ct. Appeals, 1981-87, chief judge, 1987-90; assoc. justice Ark. Supreme Ct., Little Rock, 1991—. State rep. Ark. Gen. Assembly, 1971-80. Served with USMC, 1955-59. Mem. ABA, Ark. Bar Assn., SW Ark. Bar Assn., Sigma Alpha Epsilon. Democrat. Avocation: duck hunting. Office: Supreme Ct Justice Bldg 625 Marshall St, 120 Justice Builiding Little Rock AR 72201-1054*

CORBIN, HERBERT LEONARD, public relations executive, director; b. Bklyn., Mar. 30, 1940; s. H. Dan and Lillian Corbin; m. Carol Heller, June 2, 1963; children: Jeffrey, Leslie Faith. BA, Rutgers U., 1961. Staff corr. Newark News, 1961-63; asst. dir. pub. rels. Rutgers U. News Svc., New Brunswick, N.J., 1963-65; account exec. A.A. Schechter Assocs., N.Y.C., 1965-66, Barkis & Shalit, Inc., N.Y.C., 1965-66; sr. account exec. Daniel J. Edelman, Inc., N.Y.C., 1967-69; founder, chmn., mng. ptnr. KCSA Pub. Rels. Worldwide, N.Y.C., 1969—. Chmn. pub. rels. com. AJC. Mem. nat. bd. govs., chmn. pub. rels. com. Am. Jewish Com., White Plains Pub. Access Cable TV Commn.; mem. mktg. adv. com. United Jewish Appeal-Fedn. N.Y. Mem.: Soc. Profl. Journalists, Pub. Rels. Soc. Asm. (counsellors Acad.), Old Oaks Country Club (bd. dirs., sec., sec.). Home: 31 Hathaway Ln White Plains NY 10605-3610 Office: KCSA Pub Rels Worldwide 800 2nd Ave New York NY 10017-4709 E-mail: hcorbin@kcsa.com.

CORBIN, PATRICK, dancer; b. Potomac, Md. Student, D.C. City Ballet, 1977, Washington Sch. Ballet, Sch. Am. Ballet. Dancer ABT II, Joffrey II, Joffrey Ballet, 1985—89, Paul Taylor Dance Co., N.Y.C., 1989—. Instr. Taylor Sch. Office: Paul Taylor Dance Co 552 Broadway 2d Fl New York NY 10012

CORBIN, SOL NEIL, lawyer; b. N.Y.C., Apr. 16, 1927; s. Nathan I. and Sarah (Kaiser) Corbin; m. Tanya Jacobs, Aug. 7, 1963; 1 child, David J. BS, Columbia U., 1948; JD cum laude, Harvard U., 1951. Bar: N.Y. 1952. Pvt. practice, N.Y.C., 1952—; law clk. Judge Charles D. Breitel, 1954-56; counsel Gov. of N.Y., 1962-65; ptnr. Corbin, Silverman & Sanseverino LLP, N.Y.C., 1970—96, sr. counsel, 1997—2001, Taylor, Colicchio & Silverman, LLP, N.Y.C., 2001—. Chmn. N.Y. State Commn. Constl. Conv., 1966—67, N.Y. State Crime Control Planning Bd., 1974—75; mem. N.Y. State Banking Bd., 1969—76, N.Y. State Commn. Local Govt. Powers, 1971—73; mem. chief judge's com. to recruit state ct. adminstr., 1973; trustee bankruptcy Franklin N.Y. Corp., 1974—90; spl. counsel to v.p. U.S., 1975; apptd. counsel to trustee BCCI, 1990—97. Trustee N.Y. Pub. Libr., 1977—; mem. chief judge's com. availability legal svcs., 1988—90. With USNR, 1945—46. Mem.: ABA, Am. Law Inst., New York County Bar Assn., Assn. Br. City of N.Y., Lotus Club. Home: 1100 Park Ave New York NY 10128-1202 Office: 99 Park Ave Ste 1703 New York NY 10016

CORBISIERO LOVE, ANGELA M. lawyer; b. N.Y.C., July 1964; d. Anthony and Mary Ann Corbisiero. BA in Polit. Sci., U. Pa., 1986, M in Govt. Adminstrn., 1992; JD, Rutgers U., Camden, 1989. Bar: N.J. 1989, Pa. 1989, D.C. 1991. Jud. law clk. to Hon. Martin L. Haines, Hon. Harold B. Wells, Mt. Holly, N.J., 1989-90; assoc. Parker, McCay & Criscuolo, Marlton, N.J., 1990-92, Archer & Greiner, Haddonfield, N.J., 1995-96; pvt. practice Sicklerville, N.J., 1996—; contract atty. Larrabe & Cunningham, Phila., 1997—. Mem. ABA, Am. Soc. Pub. Adminstrn., Nat. Italian-Am. Bar Assn., Order Sons Italy Am., N.J. State Bar Assn. Avocations: travel, foreign languages, cooking, politics. Home and Office: 62 Brearly Dr Sicklerville NJ 08081-4456

CORBITT, ANN MARIE, municipal official; b. Jersey City, N.J., Nov. 28, 1966; d. Andrew M. and Maria Gisondi; m. Frederick William Corbitt, Sept. 18, 1988; children: Frederick Francis, Benjamin Brandon. Cert. Tax Collector, Rutgers U., 1988. Cert. fire fighter. Work study program in tax office Twp. of Parsippany, N.J., 1983-84, acct. clk. tax office, 1984-87, sr. acct. clk., 1987-88, dep. tax collector, 1988-94; tax collector Twp. Morris, N.J., 1994-99, City of East Orange, N.J., 1999—. Vol. Denville Fire Dept., 1992—, firefighter, 1997—. Mem. Essex County Tax Collectors Assn., Tax Collectors and Treasurers N.J. Republican. Roman Catholic. Avocations: camping, fishing, outdoor activities. Office: 44 City Hall Plz East Orange NJ 07017-4104

CORBITT, DORIS ORENE, retired real estate agent, dietician; b. Warrior, Ala., Oct. 25, 1929; d. Olen J. and Begie Pernie (Motte) Florence; m. Wallace R. Cornett, Nov. 29, 1952 (div. 1980); children: Wallace R. Jr., Kris J., Brett T.; m. Weldon Plant Corbitt, Jr., Apr. 21, 1984. BS in Dietetics, Maryville Coll., 1950; postgrad., Duke U., 1950-51. Registered dietitian. Asst. dir. dietary St. Mary's Hosp., Knoxville, 1952-53; dir. dietary Soldier and Sailor Sch. for Children, Bloomington, Ill., 1966-68; tchr. Nashville Area Vocat. Sch., 1971-73; dir. dietary Westside Hosp., Nashville, 1973-79, Meml. Hosp., Tampa, Fla., 1980-85; realtor assoc. Coldwell Banker, Tampa, 1986—2000. Spkr. in field. Devel. original curriculum for Food Svc. Workers and Suprs., Tenn.; co-author first diet manual for Nashville Dietetic Assn. Sec. Galleria Homeowners Assn., Tampa, 1986-87; Sunday sch. tchr. Recipient Internat. Citizenship award, 1995; named The Honourable by Prince Kevin of Australia, 1996, Nobility status, 1996; named to 500 Notable Women Hall of Fame, 1998. Mem.: Tampa Bd. Realtors, Tampa Dietetic Assn., Am. Dietetic Assn., Red Hat Soc., Million Dollar Club. Republican. Mem. Ch. of Christ. Avocations: music, movies, reading, church work, walking. Home: 19410 Melody Fair Pl Lutz FL 33558-9216

CORBITT, EUMILLER MATTIE, education educator, special education educator; b. Detroit, Jan. 07; d. Harrison and Arnetha (Tatum) Jones; m. Luther Corbitt (div. Dec. 1976); children: Tonya, Stephen. BS, Wayne State U., 1969, MEd, 1976, EdS, 1995. Cert. elem. and secondary sch. tchr., cert. tchr. spl. edn. emotionally and mentally impaired, grades K-12, elem. secondary sch. and central office administration. Tchr. mentally impaired Detroit Pub. Schs., 1969-72, tchr. emotionally impaired, 1972-75, spl. edn. tchr. cons., 1975—, Title I tchr. math. and sci., summers 1993-96; mediator Spl. Edn. Mediation Svcs., Lansing, Mich., 1986-96, Spl. Edn. Mediation Svcs. State Project PL 94-142, Lansing, Mich., 1985—; spl. edn. hearing officer Mich. Dept. Edn., Lansing, 1985—. Developer at-risk program for emotionally impaired, socially maladjusted and ADHD students 12-17 yrs. Wolverine Human Svcs., Detroit, Mich. 1998—; mem. U.S. del. educators and attys. to South Africa for evaluation of schs. and govtl. agys. under leadership of Nelson Mandella Citizen Amb. program People to People, Spokane, Wash., 1996; mem. citizens alliance to uphold spl. edn. study adv. com. Emotionally Impaired Children in Mich./Lansing, 1986; mem. North Ctrl. Assn. accreditation com. Grand Rapids (Mich.) Pub. Schs., 1981; presenter profl. devel. conf. Detroit Fedn. Tchrs. and Detroit Pub. Sch. Adminstrs., 1996. Chairperson Met. Detroit chpt. March of Dimes, 1987; chairperson Women Who Dare to Care com. United Negro Coll. Fund, Detroit, 1987-89; gen. coord. Mus. African Am. History, Detroit, 1987; tutor, usher, chairperson Hartford Meml. Bapt. Ch., Detroit, 1979—. Recipient Mayor's award of merit for Cmty. Svc., City of Detroit, 1987, plaque and cert. March of Dimes, 1987; recognized as outstanding educator Detroit Tchr., Detroit Fedn. Tchrs., 1987, 94. Mem. Coun. for Exceptional Children (presenter nat. conv. 1983, cert. 1983), Soc. Profls. in Dispute Resolution, Wayne State U. Alumni Assn., Delta Sigma Theta (chairperson 1965—), Phi Delta Kappa (chairperson). Avocations: golf, writing poetry, racquetball, painting, reading. Home: 1249 Navarre Pl Detroit MI 48207-3014 Office: Detroit Pub Schs Office Specialized Std Svcs 5057 Woodward Ave Rm 1010 Detroit MI 48202-4050 E-mail: eumillercorbitt@aol.com.

CORBO, VINCENT J. textiles executive; b. Port Chester, N.Y. BS in Chem. Engring., Manhattan Coll., 1965; PhD in Chem. Engring., Princeton U., 1969. Rsch. engr., then rsch. supr., rsch. divsn. mgr. Hercules Inc., Wilmington, Del., 1969-82, dir. strategy, dir. project office R&D, 1983; dir. R&D Hercules Engineered and Fabricated Products Co., 1984, v.p., gen. mgr. fibers, 1986, v.p., gen. mgr. film, 1987-89; pres. Hercules Advanced Materials & Sys. Co., 1989; group v.p., pres. Hercules Food & Functional Products Co., 1993-95, sr. v.p. tech., 1995, exec. v.p. paper chem., fibers, worldwide tech. function, 1996, pres., COO, 1997—, COO, 1997-99, CEO, 1999, chmn., 2000—. Chmn. bd. dirs. Tastemaker, 1993—95, sr. v.p. tech., 1995; exec. v.p. paper chemicals and fiber worldwide tech. function, 1996. Mem. adv. bd. Ga. Tech. Coll. Scis; mem. adv. coun. dept. chem. engring., dept. mech. aerospace engring. Princeton U.; mem. Gov.'s Corp. Leaders Coun. Boys & Girls Clubs Del.; past pres. OperaDel; trustee, fin. com. Del. Symphony; mem. exec. com. Bus./Pub. Edn. Coun. Mem. Chem. Mfrs. Assn. (bd. dirs.), Soc. Chem. Industry (exec. com.), Bus. Roundtable. Office: Hercules Inc Hercules Plaza 1313 N Market St Fl 1 Wilmington DE 19894-0002

CORBOY, JAMES MCNALLY, investment banker; b. Erie, Pa., Nov. 3, 1940; s. James Thomas and Dorothy Jane (Schluraff) C. ; m. Suzanne Shaver, July 23, 1965; children: Shannon, James McNally. BA, Allegheny Coll., 1962; MBA, U. Colo., 1986. Mem. sales staff Boettcher & Co., Denver, 1964-70, Blyth Eastman Dillon, Denver and Chgo., 1970-74, William Blair & Co., Chgo., 1974-77; mgr. corp. bond dept. Boettcher & Co., Denver, 1977-79; ptnr. in charge William Blair & Co., Denver, 1979-86; first v.p. Stifel, Nicolaus & Co., Denver, 1986-88; pres., CEO SKB Corboy Inc., Denver, 1988-97, Century Capital Group Inc., 1997-98; ptnr. Corboy and Jerde, LLC, Englewood, Colo., 1999—; pres., CEO Sci. Cylinder Corp., 2002—. With USMC, 1962-67. Mem. Nat. Assn. Securities Dealers, Country Club at Castle Pines, Met. Club. Republican. Presbyterian. Home: Castle Pines Village 870 Homestake Ct Castle Rock CO 80108 Office: 7860 E Berry Pl Ste 150 Greenwood Village CO 80111 E-mail: corboy@corboyjerde.com.

CORBY, FRANCIS MICHAEL, JR., financial executive; b. Chgo., Feb. 2, 1944; s. Francis M. and Jean (Wolf) C.; m. Diane S. Orselli, Aug. 5, 1972; children: Francis Michael III, Brian A., Christopher S. BA, St. Mary of the Lake, 1966; MBA, Columbia U., 1969. With Chrysler Corp., 1969-80; treasury mgr. Chrysler Peru S.A., Lima, 1973-74; fin. dir. Chrysler Wholesale Ltd., London, 1974-76; mng. dir. Chrysler Comml. S.A. de C.V., Mexico City, 1976-77; v.p., treas. Chrysler Fin. Corp., Troy, Mich., 1977-80; treas. Joy Mfg. Co., Pitts., 1980-83, contr., 1983-86, v.p., 1984-86; sr. v.p. fin., CFO Harnischfeger Industries, Inc., Milw., 1986-94, exec. v.p. fin. and adminstrn., 1994-99; exec. v.p. Frederick & Co., 2000-2001; exec. v.p., CFO Guide Corp., Pendleton, Ind., 2001—. Bd. dirs. Ultra Visual Med. Sys., Inc., Magnasphere Corp. Mem.: Country Club Naples, Westmoor Country Club. Office: Guide Corp Tech Customer Ctr 600 Corp Dr TC26 Pendleton IN 46064

CORBY, JOHN MEADE, investment company executive; b. Santa Monica, Calif., Nov. 25, 1952; s. Grant White and Frances Irene (Meade) C. BS, Ariz. State U., 1974, U. Edinburgh, 1974. Account exec. Johnson & Higgins, L.A., 1977-81; sr. assoc. Korn/Ferry Internat., L.A., 1981-84; v.p. First Interstate Investment Svcs., L.A., 1984-86, Trust Svcs. Am., L.A., 1986-87; mng. dir. Provident Investment Coun., Pasadena, Calif., 1987—. Bd. dirs. L.A. Free Clinic, fin. com., investment com., 2000-01. Mem. Assn. Investment Mgmt. and Rsch., L.A. Soc. Fin. Analysts, Sigma Phi Epsilon. Avocations: golf, reading, travel. Office: 300 N Lake Ave Ph Pasadena CA 91101-4109 E-mail: jcorby@provnet.com.

CORCHIN, MARK ALAN, lawyer; b. Phila., Nov. 3, 1947; s. Jerome and Jean Edith (Mayerson) C.; m. Randi Beth Levy, June 4, 1978; children: Carolyn, Max, Daniel. BSBA, Villanova U., 1969; JD, N.Y. Law Sch., 1973; LLM in Trial Advocacy, Temple U., 1994. Bar: Pa. 1973, U.S. Dist. Ct. (ea. dist.) Pa. 1973, U.S. Ct. Appeals (3d cir.) 1981, U.S. Supreme Ct. 1982. Pvt. practice, Blue Bell, Pa., 1973-80; ptnr. Malis, Tolson, Meltzer & Corchin, Phila., 1980-83, Merirov, Gelman, Jaffe, Cramer & Jamieson, Phila., 1983-91, Mayerson, Munsing, Corchin & Rosato, Norristown, Pa., 1991-95, Corchin, Graham, Rosato & Mauer, Valley Forge, Pa., 1995-98, Corchin & Rosato, P.C., Valley Forge, 1998—. Fed. arbitrator U.S. Dist. Ct. for Ea. Dist. Pa., 1976-95, fed. mediator, 1991-93. Author: Medical Malpractice in Pennsylvania, 1991, Proving Damages in Pennsylvania, 1991; editor Lawyer-Pilots Bar Assn., 1975. Counsel Barren Hill Vol. Fire Co., Lafayette Hill, Pa., 1990. Recipient cert. of appreciation U.S. Dist. Ct. for Ea. Dist. Pa., 1982. Avocations: fishing, flying, football. Home: 4103 Fields Dr Lafayette Hl PA 19444-1531 Office: Corchin & Rosato PC PO Box 987-23 Ste 7 Valley Forge PA 19482 E-mail: corchinlaw@aol.com.

CORCORAN, CHRISTOPHER HOLMES, lawyer; b. Rochester, N.Y., Jan. 24, 1951; s. Victor F. and Merrill (Holmes) C.; m. Mary P. Fritschler, Aug. 1, 1992. AB, Princeton U., 1973; JD, Albany Law Sch. Union U., 1976. Bar: N.Y. 1977, U.S. Dist. Ct. N.Y. (so. dist.) 1977. Atty. Dunnington Bartholow & Miller, N.Y.C., 1976-78, Shearman & Sterling, N.Y.C., 1978-79, Harris Beach & Wilcox, Rochester, 1979-82; ptnr. Wiedman Vazzana Corcoran & Volta, Rochester, 1982—. Mem. Country Club Rochester. Avocations: golf, aviation, reading. Office: Wiedman Vazzana Corcoran & Volta 5 Fitzhugh St S Rochester NY 14614-1413

CORCORAN, CLEMENT TIMOTHY, III, lawyer; b. Kansas City, Mo., Dec. 18, 1945; s. Clement T. and Bette Lou (Hohl) C. BA, U. N.C., 1967; JD, U. Va., 1973. Bar: Fla. 1973, U.S. Dist. Ct. (mid. dist.) Fla. 1973, D.C. 1974, U.S. Dist. Ct. (no. and so. dists.) Fla. 1975, U.S. Supreme Ct. 1979, U.S. Ct. Appeals (11th cir.) 1981; cert. cir. mediator Fla. Supreme Ct. Law clk. U.S. Dist. Ct., Tampa, Fla., 1973-75; assoc. Carlton, Fields, Ward, Emmanuel, Smith & Cutler, P.A., Tampa, 1975-78, ptnr., 1978-89; judge Bankruptcy Ct. (mid. dist.) Fla., Orlando, 1989-93, Tampa, 1993—2003. Dir. Bay Area Legal Svcs., Inc., Tampa, 1983-89, v.p., 1987, pres., 1988; bd. dirs. Fla. Coun. Bar Pres., 1982-88, pres., 1986-87; arbitrator Ct. Annexed Arbitration Program, U.S. Dist. Ct. (mid. dist.) Fla., 1984-89; counselor U. Tampa, 1981-86, fellow, 1986-89. Co-author: Conflicts of Interest, 1984; contbr. articles to legal jours. Lt. USNR, 1967-70. Mem. ABA (litigation sect., coun. mem. 1999-2002, co-chair comm. com. 1990-92, chair book pub. bd. 1992-98, assoc. editor Litigation News 1982-87, mng. editor 1987, editor-in-chief 1988-90, 2002—, Nat. Conf. of Lawyers and Reps. of Media 1992-95, mem. adv. com. on nominations 1994-95, chair media-law roundtable 1994, chair sect. officers conf. com. on non-dues revenue 1995-96, mem. working group on ABA bus. plan for pub. 1995-96, standing com. on pub. oversight 1996-2002, ho. of dels. 2003—), Fla. Bar (chmn. voluntary bar liaison com. 1985-86, chmn. grievance com. 13-D 1986-88, chmn. legal edn. com. 1981-82, Most Productive Young Lawyer award 1981), Am. Judicature Soc., Hillsborough County Bar Assn. (Robert W. Patton Outstanding Jurist award 2002, Red McEwen award 1980, pres. 1982-83), Am. Inns of Ct. (Master of the Bench 1990-93, 96—). Roman Catholic. Office: 400 N Ashley Dr Ste 2540 Tampa FL 33602

CORCORAN, DAVID, newspaper editor; b. N.Y.C., July 22, 1947; s. William and Ruth (Brody) Diebold; m. Karrie Olick; children: Thomas, Daniel, Katie. BA, Amherst Coll., 1969; fellow journalism, Stanford U., 1976-77. Tchr. Rockland Country Day Sch., Congers, N.Y., 1969-70; reporter Hackensack (N.J.) Record, 1969-73, from editl. writer to asst. editor, 1973-77, editor editl. page, 1977-87, chief news editor, 1987-88; staff editor N.Y. Times, 1988—2001, asst. sci. editor, 2001—. Trustee Ctr. Analysis of Pub. Issues, 1983-91. Mem. Am. Soc. Newspaper Editors, Nat. Conf. Editorial Writers, Soc. Profl. Journalists (dir. N.J. chpt. 1980—, pres. N.J. chpt. 1983-84). Home: 437 Wildwood Rd Northvale NJ 07647-1221 Office: NY Times 229 W 43rd St New York NY 10036-3959 E-mail: corcoran@nytimes.com.

CORCORAN, DAVID, designer, artist; b. Seattle, Nov. 3, 1967; s. Paul John Corcoran, Patricia Bounds Corcoran. Diploma of Fine Arts, School of the Museum of Fine Arts, Boston Massachusetts, 1987—92. Furniture Designer Freelance, New York, NY, 1999—2002; Industrial Design Shop Technician Pratt institute, Brooklyn, NY, 2001; Freelance Theatrical Carpenter Several Boston area sceneshpos, Boston, 1995—99; Assistant Granite Sculptor Barre Sculpture Studios, Barre, VT, 1991; Stained Glass Artist Anderson Glass Arts, Boston, 1986—91; Apprentice Stained Glass Artist Lynn Hovey Studio, Cambridge, MA, 1985. Mural on exterior of Auto Showroom, "Transportation

Evolution" at US auto Exchange Boston Ma., 1998 (3'rd Largest mural in Boston area), Several Murals in Boston area, Enginehouse Studios: Depiction of historic Boston fire fighters. Great Wall of China, Quan's Kitchen Brookline Ma. Photo real 50's car on exterior of garage door, Brooklie,Ma. (Outdoors in restaurants and private homes), For Enviro Graphics, San Francisco CA., Assisted in painting murals for the MGM Grand Hotel, Las Vegas, Nevada., 1991, Exhibition of Paintings, Paintings of Coffee beans on paper using brewed and condensed coffee as paint, 1997, Several Murals in Boston area, Outdoors, in restaurants and in private homes, Exhibit of Paintings, 100% espresso on paper Borders Books and Music Boston Ma., 1998, Several paintings in private collections; furniture designer, pizza and popcorn table purchased by Warner Bros. and considered for use in film, Analyze That.

CORCORAN, MAUREEN ELIZABETH, lawyer; b. Iowa City, Feb. 4, 1944; d. Joseph and Velma (Tobin) C. BA in English with honors, U. Iowa, 1966, MA in English, 1967; JD, Hastings Coll. of Law, San Francisco, 1979. Bar: Calif. 1979, D.C. 1988, U.S. Ct. Appeals (9th cir.), 1979, U.S. Dist. Ct. (no. dist.) Calif., 1979, U.S. Dist. Ct. (cen. dist.) Calif., 1979, US. Ct. Appeals (D.C. cir.) 1983. Assoc. Hassard Bonnington Rogers & Huber, San Francisco, 1979-81; spl. asst. to gen. counsel HHS, Washington, 1981-83; assoc. Weissburg & Aronson, San Francisco, 1983-84; gen. counsel U.S. Dept. Edn., Washington, 1984-86; ptnr. Pillsbury Winthrop LLP (and predecessor firms), San Francisco, 1987-; bd. dirs. Hastings Coll. Law U. Calif., San Francisco, 1993—, chmn., 1998-2000. Chmn. Managed Health Care Conf., 1989; mem. AIDS adv. com. Ctrs. for Disease Control, 1989-91; spkr. health law mtgs. Author: (book) Managed Care Contracting: Advising the Managed Care Organization, 1996; contbr. articles on health law to profl. jours. Mem. U.S. delegation to 1985 World Conf. to Review and Appraise Achievements of UN Decade for Women, Nairobi, Kenya, 1985; mem. Adminstrv. Conf. U.S., Washington, 1985. Mem. ABA (sect. health law), Calif. State Bar Assn., Am. Health Lawyers Assn. Office: Pillsbury Winthrop LLP Ste 1004 50 Fremont St San Francisco CA 94105

CORCORAN, PHILIP E. wholesale distribution executive; b. 1954; Grad., St. Mary's, Winona, MN, 1976. CEO, co-founder, chmn. Comark, Inc., Bloomingdale, Ill., 1977—2002; vice chmn. Insight Enterprises Inc., Tempe, Ariz., 2002—.*

CORCORAN, ROBERT JOSEPH, fund raising executive; b. Boston, Dec. 1, 1929; s. John William and Mary Magdelen (Wall) C.; m. Edith Therese Fidler, Nov. 3, 1956 (dec. Feb. 1989); children: Robert J. Jr., Gerard J., Michael I.; m. Marie Murphy Clausen, May 31, 1991; children: Mark V., Jeanmarie Whittaker, Annmarie Bremser. AB in Econs. with honors, Boston Coll., Chestnut Hill, 1951; MA, Georgetown U., 1956. Cryptographer Nat. Security Agy., Washington, 1951-52; with bus. tng. program GE, Ashland, Mass., 1955-58; area dir. Mass. divsn. Am. Cancer Soc., Boston, 1958-63; v.p. The Lavin Co., Boston, 1963-70; sr. v.p. Instl. Fundraising Inc., Boston, 1970-71; pres. Robert J. Corcoran Co., Boston, 1971—. Lt. USN, 1952-55. Decorated knight Equestrian Order of the Holy Sepulchre of Jerusalem. Mem. Nat. Soc. Fund Raising Execs. (cert.), Boston Coll. Alumni Soc., Boston Latin Sch. Alumni Soc. Democrat. Roman Catholic. Avocations: reading, travel, golf, tennis, swimming. Home and Office: 5 Loew Cir Ste 150 Milton MA 02186-1043 E-mail: recorcor@aol.com.

CORCORAN, THOMAS A. metals and mining company executive; m. Claudia Corcoran; 2 children. Grad. mfg. mgmt. program, GE; B Engring., Stevens Inst. Tech. Various positions appliance bus. GE, 1967-83; various gen. mgmt. positions GE Aerospace, from 1983; gen. mgr. GE Aircraft Instruments, GE Comm. Sys.; v.p., gen. mgr. GE Govt. Electronic Sys., GE Ocean & Radar Sys., until 1991, GE Aerospace Ops., 1991-93; pres. electronics group Martin Marietta Corp., 1993-95; pres., COO electronics sector Martin Marietta Corp. (merger with Lockheed), 1995-98; pres., COO space and strategic missiles sector Lockheed Martin Corp., 1998-2000; chmn., pres., CEO, Allegheny Techs. Inc. (formerly Allegheny Teledyne), Pitts., 2000—. Bd. dirs. L-3 Comm. Holdings, Inc., Lincoln Electric Holdings, Inc., REMEC, Inc.; featured spkr. at numerous bus. and industry forums; guest lectr. bus. programs Worcester Poly. Inst., Dartmouth Coll., Stanford U. Trustee Worcester Poly. Inst., Stevens Inst. Tech.; active Am. Ireland Fund, corp. chmn. nat. gala, Washington, 1997, 98. Recipient Stevens honor award Stevens Inst. Tech., 1996; named to Bus. 100, Irish Am. mag., 1998. Avocations: golf, skiing, jogging. Office: Allegheny Techs Inc 1000 Six PPG Pl Pittsburgh PA 15222-5479

CORDARO, MATTHEW CHARLES, energy and utility executive, educator; b. N.Y.C., July 25, 1943; s. Matteo C. and Josephine (Picone) C.; m. Janet Chick, June 24, 1967; children: Anne-Marie, Allison; m. Martha Warnock, July 18, 1987; 1 child, Marie Elena. BS, C.W. Post Coll., 1965; MS in Nuclear Engring., NYU, 1967; PhD in Engring. and Physics, Cooper Union, 1970. Asst. engr. L.I. Lighting Co., Hicksville, NY, from 1966, successively assoc. engr., nuclear physicist, sr. environ. engr., mgr. environ. engring., v.p. engring., 1978-84, v.p. engring. and adminstrn., 1984-85, sr. v.p. ops. and engring., 1985-88; pres. Long Lake Cogeneration Corp., Melville, NY, 1988-93; sr. v.p. Long Lake Energy Corp., N.Y.C., 1988-93; pres. and CEO Nashville Electric Svc., 1993-99, Midwest Ind. Transmission Sys. Operator, 1999-2001; chmn. dept. pub. adminstr., dir. Ctr. for Mgmt. Analysis, Long Island U., Brookville, NY, 2001—. Cons. Bechtel, CMS, GE, Panhandle, Shoreham Project, 1992-93, R.J. Rudden Assocs., Hauppauge, N.Y.; guest rsch. assoc. Brookhaven Nat. Lab., 1968-71; adj. assoc. prof. nuclear engring. Poly. Inst. N.Y., 1979-80; adj. asst. prof. engring. C.W. Post Coll., 1968-72; former bd. dirs. ctr. for energy studies Adelphi U. Contbr. articles to profl. jours. Mem. Coun. overseers C.W. Post Coll., 1968-72; former mem. campaign coun. L.I. U., cmty. adv. bd. Sta. WLIW Pub. TV, Garden City, N.Y., Nashville C. of C., bd. dirs., Nashville Urban League, Nashville BBB, Nashville Jr. Achievement, Nashville Heart Assn., Tenn. Mcpl. Elec. Power Assn., Tenn. Valley Pub. Power Assn., Nature Conservancy of Tenn., corp. bd. Nashville Bapt. Hosp., adv. com. Nashville Girl Scouts; chmn. Mid. Tenn. U.S. Savs. Bond campaign, 1995-97; trustee Elec. Power Rsch. Inst. 1997-2001. AEC fellow, 1965-66 Mem. Am. Pub. Power Assn. (bd. dirs. 1994-00). Office: Post Campus Long Island University Greenvale NY 11548-1300 *One must try with all their heart to achieve anything of value on this earth. The tragedy of life is not giving your full effort for fear of failure. Never give up, never give in.*

CORDEIRO, ELIZABETH DALEIN, law enforcement training educator; b. New Bedford, Mass., Oct. 18, 1958; children: Vincent, Lisa. AS in Criminal Justice, Bristol C.C., 1979; BS in Adminstrn. of Criminal Justice, Roger Williams Coll., 1982. Court transp. officer New Bedford 3rd Dist. Ct., 1980-81; police officer U.S. Dept. Defense Police, Mass. and R.I., 1981-86; corrections officer S.E. Correctional Ctr., Bridgewater, Mass., 1986-87; police instr. Police Survival Def. Tactics Tng., New Bedford, 1987—. Specialized training include Training Rsch. Validation, 1989, Use of Force Reporting Systems, 1989, Monadnock PR-24 Police Baton instr., 1988, Court Room Survival, 1989, Edges Weapon Defense, 1989, Street Survival, 1982-87 and others. Author: Who's Who in Law Enforcement Collecting and Police Trainers, 1988; editor, pub.: Who's Who in Law Enforcement Institutes and Schools, Trainers, and Training Organizations, 1995, 2d edit., 1999—, Who's Who in Law Enforcement Trainers, 2d edit., 1999-2000. Office: Police Survival Def Tactics PO Box 6454 New Bedford MA 02742-6454

CORDELL, A(LFRED) ROBERT, cardiothoracic surgeon, educator; b. Union, S.C., Oct. 16, 1924; s. Carl Eugene and Ann Louise (Elsmore) C.; m. Dewitt Cromer, June 4, 1956 (dec. Feb. 1984); children: Alfred Robert Jr., Carl Dewitt, Mark Bynum. BS, U. N.C., 1945; MD, Johns Hopkins U., 1947. Diplomate Am. Bd. Surgery, Am. Bd. Thoracic Surgery. Intern Johns Hopkins U. Hosp., Balt., 1947—48; asst. resident in surgery Yale VA Surg. Svc., Newington, Conn., 1948—50; med. corps, surgeon USNR (1st M.A.S.H.), Korea and Va., 1950—52; asst. resident gen. and thoracic surgery N.C. Bapt. Hosp., Winston-Salem, 1952—55, resident gen. and thoracic surgery, 1955—56; asst. prof. surgery, assoc. prof. Wake Forest U.-Bapt. Med. Ctr., Winston-Salem, 1957—70, prof. surgery, 1970—79, Howard Holt Bradshaw Prof. Surgery, dept. chmn., 1979—91, emeritus prof., 1995—; vis. asst. prof. surgery U. Buffalo, 1956—57. Contbr. chpts. to books, articles to profl. jours. Bd. dirs. Piedmont Opera Theatre Inc., Winston-Salem, Triad Meth. Home, Winston-Salem, Centenary Meth. Ch., Winston-Salem, Winston-Salem Piedmont Triad Symphony; active United Way Forsyth County, Arts Coun. Winston Salem. Recipient Gold Heart Forsyth-Stokes-Davie County (N.C.) Heart Assn., 1997. Fellow Assn. Physician Assts. in Cardiovasc. Surgery (hon.); mem. ACS (bd. govs. 1983-89, pres.-elect 1999-00, pres. N.C. chpt. 2000-01, Surgeon of Yr. N.C. chpt. 1997), N.C. Stroke Assn. (bd. dirs., pres. 2000-02), Soc. Thoracic Surgeons, Am. Heart Assn. (chmn. mid-Atlantic region 1970-71, bd. dirs. 1966-67), Am. Assn. Thoracic Surgery, So. Thoracic Surg. Assn. (pres. 1971-72), N.C. Heart Assn. (pres. 1966-67, bd. dirs. 1956-75), So. Assn. Vascular Surgery (pres. 1984), Thoracic Surgery Found. (bd. dirs. 1994-2001). Methodist. Avocations: bonsai, opera, symphony. Home: 349 Arbor Rd Winston Salem NC 27104-1909 Office: Wake Forest U Sch Medicine Bapt Med Ctr Medical Center Blvd Winston Salem NC 27157-0001 E-mail: rcordell@wfubmc.edu.

CORDELL, BEULAH FAYE, special education educator; b. Clifty, Ark., Mar. 5, 1939; m. Jack Cordell; children: Dennis, Kevin. B in English and Social Studies, U. Ark., 1987, M in Spl. Edn. and Reading, 1994. Cert. tchr. K-12, Ark. Tchr. Benton County Alternative Sch., Rogers, Ark., 1988-90, Job Tng. Partnership Act at Fayetteville, Ark., 1990-91; reading and study skills tchr. N.W. Ark. C.C., Rogers, 1991-94; dir. spl. edn. tutoring The One-Room Sch., Springdale, 1993—; kindergarten tchr. Springdale, 1994-96; tchr. ESL and GED N.W. Tech. Inst., 1996—. Contbg. writer The Mailbox Mag., 1999—; author & illus. Pinky's Family, 2001, The Christmas Coloring Book, Pinky's Coloring Book, The Artist's Coloring Book, 2001. Bd. dirs. Ozark Literacy, Inc., Fayetteville, 1984-90; contbg. mem. Beaver Lake Lit., Inc., Rogers, 1994—. Recipient Tchg. Excellence award Gamma Beta Phi, 1993, Outstanding Achievement cert. Internat. Biog. Inst., Cambridge, Eng., 1998. Mem. Coun. for Exceptional Children, Am. Assn. Mentally Retarded, Poets and Writers Assn., Am. Biog. Inst. (rsch. bd. of advisors 1999). Avocations: oil painting, writing poetry and children's fiction. Home: 1100 N Monitor Rd Springdale AR 72764-9024 Office: 807 C Bailey St Springdale AR 72764-4247

CORDELL, BOBBIE B. music educator; b. Greenville, S.C., June 1, 1937; d. James Marvin Bishop and Allie Mae Moody; m. Ralph D. Cordell, Mar. 16, 1957 (dec. Oct. 1967); children: Ralph D. Jr., J. Gregory, Elizabeth G. Cottle. Student, Shorter Coll., 1955—57; BS, U. N.C., Greensboro, 1970, EdM, 1976. Min. music St. Martins Episcopal Ch., San Francisco, 1958—60; choir master, organist Army Chapels, Ansbach, Germany, 1961—63; min. music Sharpe Rd. Bapt. Ch., Greensboro, 1967—80, South East Bapt. Ch., Greensboro, 1981—88, organist, 1988—; pvt. piano and voice tchr. Greensboro, 1968—. Mem.: Nat. Fedn. Music Club, Nat. Assn. Music Tchrs., N.C. Assn. Music Tchrs., Greensboro Music Tchrs. (pres. 1983—85), Mil. Officers Assn. Am. (Piedmont chpt.), Greensboro Enterpe Club (first v.p. 1993—95). Avocations: bridge, travel.

CORDELL, FRANCIS MERRITT, instrument engineer, consultant; b. South Pittsburg, Tenn., Sept. 11, 1932; s. Lucien Hall and Sara Frances (Taliaferro) C.; m. Olivia Elizabeth West, June 17, 1950; 1 child, Francis Merritt Jr. LittB, Hamilton Coll., 1966; PhD in Physics, U. Del., 1973. Low speed code operator Dept. Army, Ft. Devens, Mass., 1949-52; materials tester TVA, Stevenson, Ala., 1952-53, instrument mechanic, 1953-57, sr. instrument mechanic, 1957-80, instrumentation supr., 1980-86; prin. restorer, telescope and observatory project U. of the South, Sewanee, Tenn., 1982—. Info. cons. South Pittsburg, 1980—; mem. Tenn. Vis. Scientists Program, Associated Univs. for the Tenn. Acad. Sci., Oak Ridge, 1989—. Contbng. writer Barnard Astronomical Soc. Jour., 1973—. Recipient Llewellyn Evans award Barnard Astronomical Soc., Chattanooga, 1983. Mem. AAAS, Barnard Astronomical Soc., Instrument Soc. Am., Tenn. Acad. Sci., Astronomical Soc. Pacific. Achievements include restoration of Alvan Clark & Sons refractor and observatory (renamed Cordell-Lorenz Obs.). Home: Medius Lodge Dogwood Trail South Pittsburg TN 37380 Office: Info Consulting 1018 Holly Ave South Pittsburg TN 37380

CORDELL, PHILIP GRANVILE, music educator, musician; b. Urbana, Ohio, Sept. 12, 1959; s. Granville Ogden and Pauline Davis Cordell; life ptnr. Don W Roush, Jan. 1, 2003; 1 child, Athena Roush. BMus in Piano Performance, Wittenberg U., 1981; MMus in Composition, Ohio U., 1982, MMus in Piano Performance/Pedagogy, 1984. Cert. tchr. of music in piano. Instr. The Ctr. for Musical Devel., Springfield, Ohio, 1977—86; accompanist dance dept. The Ohio State U., Columbus, 1987—89; lectr. Capital U., Bexley, Ohio, 1988—2001, instr., 2001—, orchestral pianist, theatre dept., 2003. Freelance musician, 1976—; pianist Ballet Met, Columbus, 1988—91; profl. accompanist Opera Columbus, 2001—. Composer: (piano solo) The Wonder of Love, (sacred music) Sacred Arrangements for Solo Piano and Solo Organ, (work for two violins) Dances for Two Violins; musician: (faculty rec.) Cmty. Music Sch. Faculty Concert, 1998, Conservatory of Music Faculty Concert, 1999; musician: (producer) (conservatory faculty concert) Conservatory Faculty Concert Rec., 2000. Super swimmer Ctrl. Ohio Diabetes Assn., Columbus, 1989—2003; organist/musician New Life United Meth. Ch., Columbus, 1987—2003; organist/pianist St. Paul's Luth. Ch., Westerville, Ohio, 2003—. Mem.: Midwestern Keyboard Hist. Soc. (life), Coll. Music Soc. (life), Nat. Fedn. of Music Clubs (life; profl. adjudicator 1979—), Music Tchrs. Nat. Assn. (life; profl. adjudicator 1981—, dist. festival co-chmn. 1991, condr. for pianorama 1991—, dist. festival judge com. 2000—01, time keeper 2001, graves piano competition door monitor 2003), Ctrl. Ohio Diabetes Assn. (life). Avocations: swimming, walking, playing piano, organ, harpsichord and other electronic keyboard instruments.

CORDELLA, TITO, economist; b. Parma, Italy, Dec. 17, 1964; s. Marco Cordella and Maria Grasselli; m. Ana Paula Fialho Lopes, Sept. 15, 1995. Degree in polit. sci., U. Bologna, Italy, 1988; MA, U. Catholique de Louvain, Louvain la Neuve, Belgium, 1990, PHD, 1993. Asst. prof. Pompeu Fabra U., Barcelona, 1994—97; Jean Monnet prof. U. Bologna, Forli, Italy, 1994—95; sr. economist IMF, Washington, 1995—. Contbr. articles to profl. jours. Fellow, Ecole Polytechnique, Paris, 1994—95; scholar, Consiglio Nazionale Delle Ricerche, 1991—92, European Union, 1992—94. Office: Internat Monetary Fund 700 19th St NW Washington DC 20431

CORDEN, WARNER MAX, economics educator; b. Breslau, Germany, Aug. 13, 1927; arrived in Australia, 1939; s. Ralph and Kate (Levy) C.; m. Dorothy Grace Martin, June 1, 1957; 1 child, Jane Margaret. BCom, U. Melbourne, Australia, 1949, MCom, 1953, DCom (hon.), 1995; PhD, London Sch. Econs., 1956; MA (hon.), Oxford (Eng.) U., 1967. Lectr. econs. U. Melbourne, Australia, 1958—61; professorial fellow Australian Nat. U., Canberra, 1962—67, prof. econs., 1977—88; Nuffield reader in internat. econs. Oxford U., 1967—76; sr. advisor IMF, Washington, 1986—88; prof. internat. econs. Paul H. Nitze Sch. Advanced Internat. Studies, Johns Hopkins U., Washington, 1989—2002, prof. emeritus, 2002—; prof. fellow U. Melbourne, 2002—. Vis. prof. Harvard U., 1986. Author: The Theory of Protection, 1971, Trade Policy and Economic Welfare, 1974, 2nd edit., 1997, Inflation, Exchange Rates and the World Economy, 1977, 3d edit., 1986, Protection, Growth and Trade, 1985, International Trade Theory and Policy, 1992, Economic Policy, Exchange Rates, and the International System, 1994, The Road to Reform, 1997, Too Sensational: On the Choice of Exchange Rate Regimes, 2002. Mem. Group of Thirty, 1982-90. Recipient Bernhard Harms prize U. Kiel, 1986. Fellow Acad. Social Scis. Australia, Brit. Acad.; mem. Am. Econ. Assn. (hon.), Econ. Soc. Australia and N.Z. (pres. 1977-80, dist. fellow 1995); Companion of the Order of Australia, 2001. Office: Univ Melbourne Dept Econ Melbourne VIC 3010 Australia

CORDER, BILLIE FARMER, clinical psychologist, artist; b. Sept. 12, 1934; d. Lee Kennith and Jimmy Louise (Hawkins) Farmer; m. Robert Floyd Corder, July 11, 1961. BS, Memphis State U., 1957; MA, Vanderbilt U., 1959; postgrad., Memphis Acad. Art, 1959, N.C. State U., 1971-75; EdD, U. Ky., 1966. Intern U. Tenn. Sch. Medicine, Memphis, 1959; staff psychologist Ea. State Hosp., Lexington, Ky., 1960-65, Child Guidance Clinic, Lexington, 1965-67; asst. prof. psychology Inter-Am. U., P.R., 1967-68; dir. psychology adolescent day care Area Cmty. Mental Health Ctr., Washington, 1968-70; dir. psychol. svcs. Alcoholic Rehab. Ctr., Butner, N.C., 1970-71; co-dir. psychol. svcs. in child psychiatry Dix Hosp., Raleigh, N.C., 1971—. Mem. adv. bd. Raleigh Developmental Evaluation Clnic, 1976-80; adj. faculty psychology dept. N.C. State U., Raleigh, 1975—, U. N.C. Sch. Medicine, 1975—. Contbr. articles to profl. jours.; dir. editl. bd. N.C. Jour. Mental Health, 1974—; adj. editl. rev. bd. Hosp. and Cmty. Psychiatry, Quar. Jour. Studies on Alcohol, Raleigh Acad. Women, 1993. Mem. Wake County Youth Adv. Bd., 1979-80; mem. adv. com. Raleigh Arts Commn., 1980-82; bd. dirs. Haven House for Children, 1980-85, Nazareth House for Children, 1980-85. Recipient best rsch. award N.C. Dept. Mental Health, 1965, cert. of appreciation Washington Tchrs. Assn., 1969, Outstanding Youth Svcs. award Wake Coun., 1991, Hargrove Rsch. award N.C. Mental Health Rsch. Found., 1995, numerous awards for art, including Purchase award N.C. Mus. Art, 1976, awards N.C. Watercolor Soc., 1978, 79; numerous rsch. grants. Mem. APA, AAUW, Southeastern Psychol. Assn., N.C. Psychol. Assn., Am. Assn. Psychiat. Svcs. for Children (program chmn. 1976-77), Raleigh Artists Guild (pres.), Raleigh Fine Arts Soc., N.C. Art Soc., Women's Equity Action League, N.C. Women's Polit. Caucus, Durham Artists Guild, N.C. Watercolor Soc. (v.p.), Wake Visual Artists Assn. (pres.). Office: Dix Hospital Child Psychiatry Clinic Raleigh NC 27611

CORDER, STEVEN LEE, non-profit organization executive; b. Sacramento, Sept. 24, 1958; s. Donald Leon and Betty Jean C.; m. Thea Marie, Feb. 4, 1960; children: Erica, Jamie. BSBA, U. Denver, 1981, MBA, 1982. Fin. reporting mgr. Norwest Banks, Denver, 1987-90; v.p., controller Christian Booksellers Assn., Colorado Springs, 1990-96; fin. mgr. Cook Comms., Colorado Springs, 1996-97; dir. fin. Focus on the Family, Colorado Springs, 1997—. Republican. E-mail: Steve.Corder@juno.com.

CORDERO, JOSE FERNANDO, pediatrician, federal agency administrator; b. Camuy, P.R., July 25, 1948; s. Fernando and Ana T. Cordero; m. Milagros J. Garcia, June 18, 1970; children: Jose F., Ana M., Joann M., Maria M. BS in Biology, U. P.R., Rio Piedras, 1969; MD, U. P.R., San Juan, 1973; MPH, Harvard U., 1979. Diplomate Nat. Bd. Med. Examiners, Am. Bd. Med. Genetics, Am. Bd. Pediatrics; lic. physician, Ga. Intern Boston City Hosp., 1973-74, jr. asst. resident dept. pediatrics, 1974-75; clin. and rsch. fellow pediatrics Mass. Gen. Hosp., 1975-77; pediatrician South End Cmty. Health Ctr., Boston, 1977-79; epidemiology intelligence svc. officer Bur. Epidemiology Ctrs. for Disease Control & Prevention, Atlanta, 1979-81, dep. chief birth defects and genetic diseases br., 1985-88, acting chief birth defects and genetic diseases bd., 1988-89, asst. dir. sci. divsn. birth defects and devel. disabilities, 1989-94, dep. dir. nat. immunization program, 1994—2001, dir. Nat. Ctr. on Birth Defects and Devel. Disabilities, 2001—. Clin. instr. pediatrics Children's Hosp., Boston, 1978-79; clin. asst. prof. pediatrics Emory U., 1982—. Co-editor jour. Teratology, 1983-86; mem. editl. bd. Birth Defects Ency., 1988; reviewer jours.; contbr. numerous articles and abstracts to publs. Mem. working group cancer chemotherapy Internat. Agy. Cancer Rsch., 1980; mem. task force on child health and related issues FDA, 1980-83; mem. rev. coms. NIH; coord. U.S. Govt. Task Force Premature Thelarche in P.R., 1982-85; trustee Calif. Birth Defects Monitoring Program, 1983-89; mem. adv. bd. TERIS, Seattle, 1986—, Fla. Teratogen Info. System, 1986-90; cons. WHO, Guatemala, 1990, 91, 92, Copenhagen, 1991; founding mem. Emmaus Community, 1992—; mem. troop 547 com. Boy Scouts Am., 1983-94. Recipient Arthur S. Flemming award, 1988, Physician's Recognition award AMA, 1980, 84, 88. Mem. APHA, Am. Soc. Human Genetics, Am. Bd. Med. Genetics, Am. Acad. Pediatrics (nutrition com. 1980, com. on drugs 1988-93, genetic com. 1985), Am. Epidemiology Soc., Mass. Med. Soc., Genetics Soc. Ga., Coalition of Spanish Speaking Mental Health and Human Svcs. Orgn., Teratology Soc., Soc. Pediatric Rsch. Roman Catholic. Avocations: bird watching, flying, painting, travel. Office: Ctrs for Disease Control & Prevention 4770 Buford Hwy, NW F34 Atlanta GA 30341-3724 E-mail: JFC1@cdc.gov.

CORDES, ALEXANDER CHARLES, lawyer; b. Buffalo, Aug. 14, 1925; s. Alexander J. and Margaret (Markens) C.; m. Jane Wells, Feb. 9, 1976; children by previous marriage: John J., Ann T., Susan A. BA, Yale U., 1947; LLB, U. Buffalo, 1950. Bar: N.Y. 1950. Assoc. Kenefick, Bass, Letchworth, Baldy & Phillips, 1950-54; asst. U.S. atty. Western Dist. N.Y., 1954-56; ptnr. Phillips, Lytle, Hitchcock, Blaine & Huber, Buffalo, 1956-90, of counsel, 1990—. Mem. Erie County Bd. Suprs., 1960-61 Trustee The Park Sch. Buffalo, 1993-96. With USNR, 1943-46. Fellow Am. Coll. Trial Lawyers, Am. Bar Found., N.Y. Bar Found. Presbyterian. Home: 470 Village Pl Apt 316 Longwood FL 32779-6031

CORDES, EUGENE HAROLD, pharmacy and chemistry educator; b. York, Nebr., Apr. 7, 1936; s. Elmer Henry and Ruby Mae (Hofeldt) C.; m. Shirley Ann Morton, Nov. 9, 1957; children: Jennifer Eve, Matthew Henry James. BS, Calif. Inst. Tech., 1958; PhD, Brandeis U., 1962. Instr. chemistry Ind. U., Bloomington, 1962-64, asst. prof., 1964-66, assoc. prof., 1966-68, prof., 1968-79, chmn., 1972-78; exec. dir. biochemistry Merck, Sharp and Dohme Research Labs., Rahway, N.J., 1979-84, v.p. biochemistry, 1984-87; v.p. R & D Eastman Pharms., Malvern, Pa., 1987-88; pres. Sterling Winthrop Pharms. Rsch. divsn. Sterling Winthrop Inc., Collegeville, Pa., 1988-94; prof. U. Mich., Ann Arbor, 1995—2002; chmn. bd. dirs. Concurrent Pharms., 2002—. Author: (with Henry Mahler) Biological Chemistry, 1966, 2d. edit., 1971, Basic Biological Chemistry, 1969, (with Riley Schaeffer) Chemistry, 1973; also articles. Recipient NIH Career Devel. award, 1966; Alfred P. Sloan Found. fellow, 1968. Mem.: AAAS, Am. Soc. Biol. Chemists. Home: 867 Lesley Rd Villanova PA 19085-1117

CORDES, LOVERNE CHRISTIAN, interior designer; b. Cleve., Feb. 13, 1927; d. Frank Andrew and Loverne Louise (Brown) Christian; m. William Peter Cordes, Nov. 14, 1959; children: Christian Peter, Carey Pomeroy. BS, Purdue U., 1949. Owner, mgr. Loverne Christian Cordes, Chagrin Falls, Ohio, 1967—. Tchr. John Carroll U., Cleve., 1976-77 Interior designer, Fred Epple Co., Cleve., 1949-67. Fellow AIA, Am. Soc. Interior Designers, Nat. Home Fashion League (past pres. Ohio chpt.), Am. Inst. Interior Designers (past pres. Ohio chpt., nat. bd. dirs. 1969-75, nat. v.p. East Central region 1972-75, nat. exec. bd. 1972-75, recipient 1st Presdl. citation 1973, '74, '75); mem. Soc. Collectors Dunham Tavern Mus. (bd. dirs. 1961-62), Dunham Dames (past pres.), Western Res. Hist. Soc., Cleve. Mus. Art, Cleve. Garden Center, Chagrin Falls Hist. Soc., Nat. Trust for Hist. Preservation, Internat. Platform Assn., Am. Furniture Collectors (bd. dirs. 1998—, decorative arts trust v.p. 1998), Audobon Soc., Confrérie de la Chaine des Rôtisseurs, Decorative Arts Trust Cleve. Cir.(pres. 2001-02), Wallkill Golf Club, Chagrin Valley Country Club, Dogwood Garden Club, Intown Club, Arcadian, Kappa Kappa Gamma. Republican. Congregationalist. Avocations: golf, cross country skiing, wine maker, calligraphy. Address: 60 S Franklin St Chagrin Falls OH 44022-3235 *We must never stop striving to make this world a more beautiful, healthful, safer place for all people and creatures to live and enjoy harmoniously.*

CORDLE, CHRISTOPHER T. immunologist, race boat driver; b. Columbus, Ohio, July 28, 1947; s. Harold P. and Jacqueline A. Cordle; m. Susan Palmer; 1 child, Andrew C. BS, Otterbein Coll., Westerville, OH, 1969; PhD, Johns Hopkins U., Balt., 1975. Lic. Private Pilot, Instrument FAA, 1967. Rsch. fellow Ross Products Divsn., Abbott, Columbus, Ohio, 1980—; driver John Shewbrooks Racing, Waverly, Ohio, 1998—. Advisor, cons., faculty Ohio State U., Columbus, Ohio, 1982—. Contbr. articles to 23 profl. jour. Advisor, collaborating scientist Nat. Ctr. for Food Safety and Tech., Chicago, Ill., 2000—02; mem. and past pres. Ohio Agrl. R & D Support Coun., Wooster, Ohio, 1982—2002; mem., food sci. adv. bd. Clemson U., Clemson, SC, 1988—98. Mem.: Mucosal Immunology Soc., Am. Assn. of Immunologists, Am. Powerboat Assn. (2001 World Champion, 2002 Nat. Points Champion 2001, 2002), Aircraft Owners and Pilots Assn., Exptl. Aircraft Assn., Lions Club (pres., sec./treas.), Sigma Xi Rsch. Honor Soc. (pres. 1999—2000). Achievements include patents for Holds 6 United States patents; 2001 World Champion, 2.5L modified inboard hydroplane; 2002 Nat. Points Champion, 2.5L modified inboard hydroplane. Avocations: aviation, boat racing, target shooting. Home: 92 S Preston St Box 16 Centerburg OH 43011-0016 Office: Ross Products Divsn Abbott Labs 625 Cleveland Ave Columbus OH 43215-1724 E-mail: chris.cordle@abbott.com.

CORDOBA, MIKE, food service executive; BBA, Simon Fraser U., 1988. From contr. to pres., COO Boston Pizza Internat., Richmond, Canada, 1988—. Office: Boston Pizza Internat 550 Parkwood Way Richmond BC Canada V6V 2M4

CORDOVA, ARMANDO, chemist; b. Sofia, Apr. 5, 1970; PhD, The Royal Inst. of Tech., 1995—98. Sr. rsch. assoc. The Scripps Rsch. Inst., La Jolla, Calif., 1999—2003; asst. prof. Stockholm U., 2003—. Sr. rsch. scientist The Swedish Pulp and Paper Rsch. Inst., Stockholm, 1998—99. Sniper Lapland Ranger Rgt. I22, 1991—92, Kiruna, Sweden. Wennergren found., 1999—2000, Skaggs Post Doctoral fellow, 2000. Mem.: The Am. Chem. Soc. Achievements include discovery of novel asymmetric reactions; research in design and synthesis of biodegradable materials; patents for lipase catalyzed transesterifi-

cation of B-Ketoesters; patents pending for enantioselctive synthesis of functional amino acids; first to regioselective polymerizations of dendrimers and sugars; the use of unmodified aldehydes in asymmetric Mannich-type reactions. Home: 7623 Eads Ave La Jolla CA 92037 Personal E-mail: acordova1a@netscape.net.

CORDOVA, RON, lawyer; b. L.A., Aug. 18, 1946; s. Reuben and Lya (Gruber) C.; m. Mariann Pehrson, June 2, 1970; children: Danielle, Andrea. AB, Dartmouth Coll., 1967; postgrad., Trinity Coll., Dublin, Ireland, 1966; JD, U. So. Calif., 1972. Bar: U.S. Dist. Ct. (ctrl. dist.) Calif., 1979, U.S. Dist. Ct. (so. dist.) Calif., 1989, U.S. Dist. Ct. (no. dist.) Calif., 1995, U.S. Dist. Ct. (we. dist.) Tex., 1996, Ariz., 1994, U.S. Dist. Ct. (ea. dist.) Mich., 1995, U.S. Dist. Ct. Colo., 1999. Dep. dist. atty. Orange County Dist. Atty., Santa Ana, Calif., 1973-76; legis. Calif. State Assembly, Sacramento, 1976-78; trial lawyer Newport Beach, Calif., 1979—. Adj. prof. U. Calif., Irvine, 1975-77, 81-84. Author: Orange County Bar Journal, 1975. Recipient Outstanding Young Men. Am. Jaycees, 1977, 78. Mem. Lincoln Club. Republican. Jewish. Avocations: travel, languages, photography. Office: 120 Newport Center Dr Newport Beach CA 92660-6922 Business E-Mail: advokaat@aol.com.

CORDTS, PAUL ROGER, surgeon; b. Cumberland, Md., Sept. 27, 1958; s. Harold J. and Jeanne (Moore) C.; m. Patricia Ann Matzoll, Nov. 14, 1996. BA, Johns Hopkins U., 1980; MD, USUHS, 1984. Diplomate Am. Bd. Surgery, Am. Bd. Surg. Critical Care, Am. Bd. Gen. Vascular Surgery. Commd. med. officer U.S. Army, 1980; intern, resident in surgery William Beaumont Army Med. Ctr., El Paso, Tex., 1984-89; staff surgeon Munson Army Community Hosp., Ft. Leavenworth, Kans., 1989-90; fellow in vascular surgery Boston U. Med. Ctr., Boston, 1990-92; chief vascular surgery sect. Tripler Army Med. Ctr., Honolulu, 1992-93, chief gen. surgery svc., tng. dir. surg. residency program, 1993—2001, chief, dept. surgery, 2002—. Fellow ACS (Hawaii chpt.); mem. AMA, Am. Coll. Phys. Execs., Am. Coll. Surgeons (exec. coun. Hawaii chpt.), Soci. for Mil. Vascular Surgery, Am. Assn. Vascular Surgery, Am. Med. Polit. Action Com., Uniformed Svcs. U. Health Scis. Surg. Assocs., Am. Venous Forum, Peripheral Vascular Surgery Soc., 38th Parallel Med. Soc., Soc. Critical Care Medicine, Soc. for Clin. Vascular Surgery, Assn. Mil. Surgeons U.S., Assn. for Acad. Surgery, Hawaiian Surg. Assn., Western Vascular Soc., Pacific Coast Surg. Soc., Pan Pacific Surg. Assn., Internat. Soc. Cardiovascular Surgery, Western Surg. Assn., Johns Hopkins U. Alumni Assn., Am. Legion (Farrady Post 24), Omicron Delta Kappa Nat. Leadership Soc. Home: 98-885 Ainanui Loop Aiea HI 96701-2764 Office: Tripler Army Med Ctr Dept Surgery MCHK-DS 1 Jarrett White Rd Tripler Army Medical Center HI 96859-5000 E-mail: paul.cordts@amedd.army.mil.

CORDUNEANU, CONSTANTIN C. mathematician, educator; b. Iasi, Moldavia, Romania, July 26, 1928; arrived in U.S., 1978; s. Costache and Aglaia (Anitoaie) Corduneanu; m. Alice Olga Vultur, July 23, 1949. Diploma in math., U. Iasi, 1951, DMath, 1956. From instr. to assoc. prof. U. Iasi, 1949—67, prof., 1968—78; prof. dept. math. U. Tex., Arlington, 1979—96, prof. emeritus, 1996—. Author: (book) Almost Periodic Functions, 1968, 1989, Principles of Differential and Integral Equations, 1971, 1989, Integral Equations and Stability of Feedback Systems, 1973, Integral Equations and Applications, 1991, Functional Equations with Causal Operators, 2002; assoc. editor: Math. Sys. Theory, 1967—75, Revue Roumaine Pure Applied Math, 1973—78, Jour. Integral Equations, 1979—91, Libertas Mathematica, 1981—, Differential and Integral Equations, 1988—95. With Romanian Army, 1952. Recipient Rsch. prizes, Ministry of Edn., Bucharest, 1965; Rsch. fellow, Inst. Math. Romanian Acad., Iasi, 1954—59, 1963—67. Mem.: Romanian Acad. (Rsch. prizes 1963), Am. Romanian Acad. Arts and Scis., Soc. Indsl. and Applied Math., Math. Assn. Am., Am. Math. Soc. Christian Orthodox. Office: U Tex Arlington S Cooper St Arlington TX 76019 Business E-Mail: cordun@uta.edu.

CORDWELL, ARTHUR GEORGE, not-for-profit fundraiser; b. Portage, Pa., Sept. 29, 1938; s. Jacob and Cora Cordwell; m. Mary Ann Cordwell, June 29, 1957; children: John, James, Toni. BSME, Point Park Coll., Pitts., 1985. Coord. econ. devel. svcs. Consol. Nat. Gas Co., Pitts., 1981-86; mgr. econ. devel. Peoples Natural Gas Co., Pitts., 1986-95; exec. dir. econ. devel. Comm. Devel. Corp. of Butler Co., Pa., 1996—. Chmn. Butler County Tourism, 1999; bd. dirs. Tri-County Pvt. Industry Coun., Butler, 1998-99, Pa. Econ. Devel. Coun., 1997-98; mem. Am. Econ. Devel. Coun. Mem. Butler County C. of C. (bd. dirs. 1998-99).

CORE, HARRY MICHAEL, psychiatric social worker, mental health therapist and administrator; b. Core, W.Va., Oct. 7, 1933; s. Earl Lemley and Freda Bess (Garrison) C.; m. Jane Ann Boggs, Oct., 1976; children: Kevin M., Brian D., Jennifer T. BS, W.Va. U., 1955; MSW, U. N.C., 1957. Psychiat. social worker Lake County Mental Health Ctr., Mentor, Ohio, 1960-67, asst. dir., 1967-72, exec. dir., 1972-87; psychiat. social worker Simon & Bertschinger MDs, Inc., Eastlake, Ohio, 1966-92; clin. assoc. Kent A. Young, PhD & Assocs., Mentor, Ohio, 1992—. Trustee Tri-Care, Inc., Westlake, Ohio, 1986-87. Trustee Western Res. Counseling, Inc., 1988-2001, emeritus, 2001—, Point One Behavioral Health Svcs., 1997-2000; mem. adv. bd. Lakeland C.C. Sch. Nursing, 1983—. 1st lt., U.S. Army, 1957-60. Fellow Am. Orthopsychiat. Assn. (life); mem. Acad. Cert. Social Workers, NASW, Ohio Coun. Cmty. Mental Health Agys. (trustee 1981-84, v.p. 1984). Democrat. Mem. Christian Ch. (Disciples Of Christ). Home: 6707 Stratford Rd Painesville OH 44077-1533 Office: Lake Ambulatory Care Ctr 9500 Mentor Ave Ste 320 Mentor OH 44060-8712

CORE, MARY CAROLYN W. PARSONS, health facility administrator; b. Valpariso, Fla., Dec. 8, 1949; d. Levi and Mary Etta (Elliott) Willey; m. Joel Kent Core, Aug. 3, 1979; 1 child, Candace W. Parsons. Student, Peninsula Gen. Hosp. Sch. Radiologic Tech., Salisbury, Md., 1969; student, U. Del., 1969-73, Del. Tech. C.C., 1973-79, St. Joseph's Coll., 1983-86, BSBA, 1987; M in Gen. Adminstrn., U. Md., 1995. Cert. profl. in healthcare info. and mgmt. sys. Technologist Peninsula Gen. Hosp., Salisbury, 1967-72; tech. dir. edn. Sch. Radiologic Tech., Salisbury, 1973-75; technologist Johns Hopkins Hosp., Salisbury, 1972-73, Nanticoke Meml. Hosp., Seaford, Del., 1975-79; adminstrv. chief technologist, imaging depts. Shady Grove Adventist Hosp., Rockville, Md., 1979-81; dir. dept. radiol. scis. Anne Arundel Diagnostics, Inc., Annapolis, Md., 1981-92; COO Anne Arundel MRI (Magnetic Resonance Imaging), Annapolis, Md., 1985-92; CEO Anne Arundel Diagnostics, Inc. and Anne Arundel MRI, Annapolis, Md., 1987-92; v.p. corp. svcs. Anne Arundel Healthcare Systems, Inc., 1992-2001, v.p. strategic planning, 2001—. Mem. Coun. Girl Scouts Am., Pres.'s award svc. team, 1989; bd. mem. Anne Arundel Trade Coun., 1996—98; adv. bd. YWCA; bd. dirs. Providence Ctr., 2001—, 2001—. Recipient twin award YWCA, 1988. Mem. NAFE, Md. Soc. Radiologic Technologists (pres. 1980-81, sr. bd. mem. 1982-83, various awards including 1st Pl. Essay awards 1974, 76, 84, 87), Am. Hosp. Radiology Adminstrs. (v.p. 1984-85, chmn. by-laws com. 1984-85, statis. resources com. 1985-86), Am. Mgmt. Assn., Radiology Bus. Mgrs. Assn., Ea. Shore Dist. Radiologic Technologists (pres. 1976-78), Md. Assn. Healthcare Execs., Project Mgrs. Inst., Leadership Anne Arundel, 1998—, Anne Arundel Trade Cncl., 1996-97, YWCA Careers, 1994-97, Phi Kappa Phi. Republican. Methodist. Home: 1907 Harcourt Ave Crofton MD 21114-2103 Office: 2001 Medical Pkwy Annapolis MD 21401 E-mail: ccore@aahs.org.

COREIL, RAYMOND CLYDE, English educator; b. Ville Platte, La., Nov. 29, 1939; s. Armand Bernard and Thelma (Perrodin) C.; m. Vivian Jr Yi Tsao, June 5, 1976. *Coreil was born and raised in the semi-rural Cajun Louisiana town of Ville Platte to parents of French ancestry. This background continues to exert a strong influence on his plays and short stories. With brothers Kern (who would become a physician) and Armand Bernard Jr., Coreil spent a lot of time camping and fishing at nearby Lake Chicot. He delivered newspapers by bicycle and worked as janitor at a variety store while attending Sacred Heart High, a Catholic school. After one semester in seminary, Coreil transferred to the University of Southwestern Louisiana and received a B.A. in English in 1961. During the war, Coreil taught in Vietnamese schools and universities. His grandmothers "Mamou" Perrodin and "Maman" Coreil and his sister Charlene helped shaped his character.* BA in English, U. S.W. La., 1961; MFA in Theatre, Carnegie-Mellon U., 1976; PhD in Linguistics, CUNY, 1992. Writer--journalist Daily Advertiser Newspaper, Lafayette, La., 1961-62, La. State U., Baton Rouge, 1963-67; tchr. English U. Hue, Vietnam, 1967-68, U. Abdulaziz, Jeddah, Saudi Arabia, 1968-69, 77-80, U. Saigon, Vietnam, 1970-74, New Jersey City Univ., 1981—. Founder Ctr. for Imagination in Lang. Learning, 1997, dept. chair, 1999—, founder certificates in Am. English Lang. and Am. Culture, 2000; keynote spkr. confs. on lang. and imagination Richmond (Va.) U., 2001, Simon Fraser U., Vancouver, B.C., 2003. *Coreil has three areas of specialization: creative writing, songwriting, and linguistics. He holds a Master of Fine Arts in theatre from Carnegie Mellon University in Pittsburgh where his teachers included Larry Carra and Leon Katz. Author of some 20 long plays, Coreil is recipient of a major grant from the National Endowment for the Arts. He has written 50 songs, most of which are incorporated in musical plays. From the City University of New York, he holds a Ph.D. in linguistics. He has coined the term "supralexicals," which designates recurring fixed phrases. His usage of the term is defined in his dissertation, which received the Edward Sapir Award in 1992 from the New York Academy of Sciences. Coreil maintains that grammar cannot account for language without placing great emphasis on preformulated structures.* Playwright numerous stageplays and screenplays; songwriter: (musical plays) Remembering Hue, 1998, Homelands, 1999; editor-founder Jour. Imagination, 1993—; editor anthology: Multiple Intelligences and New Methods in College Teaching: Articles by Howard Gardner and 41 Educators. Recipient Edward Sapir award N.Y. Acad. Scis., 1992; Fulbright grantee U.S. Govt., 1972; grantee Nat. Endowment Arts, 1976. Roman Catholic. Avocations: photography, music, painting, linguistics. Home: 17 Fuller Pl Brooklyn NY 11215-6006 Office: New Jersey City Univ 2039 Kennedy Blvd Jersey City NJ 07305-1527 Fax: (201) 200-2202. E-mail: ccoreil@njcu.edu., coreil@erols.com.

CORELL, MARCELLA ANNE, community worker, retired educator; b. Denver, Mar. 2, 1919; d. Berton Wilson and Marcella Jacobs; m. Allen Lawrence Corell, Sept. 25, 1950 (dec. June 1996); children: Michele Anne, Lawrence Robert. AA, Colo. Woman's Coll., 1939; BA, Denver U., 1948. Tchr. Kiowa Sch. Dist., Colo., 1939-40, Jefferson Co. Sch. Dist., Arvada, Colo., 1941-49, Dept. Edn. Hawaii, Spreckelsville, 1949-50, substitute tchr. Kihei, Wailuku, Kahului, 1962-72. Mem. adv. bd. Maui Cmty. Mental Health Ctr., Wailuku, 1968-72; coord. Crisis Phoneline, 1971-81; founder Mental Health Assn. Maui, 1972, pres., 1972-75, bd. dirs., 1975-81, chmn. membership com. 1978-99, edn. com. 1985—, hon. mem. bd. 1991. Recipient 1st Lady's Outstanding Vols. award Vols. in Paradise, Hawaii, 1974, 76, 84, vol. award Maui United Way, 1975, Golden Rule award J.C. Penney, Honolulu, 1994, 98, Jefferson award Honolulu Advertiser, 1987. Avocation: organic gardening. Home: 357 Auhana Rd Kihei HI 96753-8519

CORELL, ROBERT WALDEN, science administrator, educator; b. Detroit, Nov. 4, 1934; s. George W. and Grace (Hagland) C.; m. Billie Jo Proctor, June 16, 1956; children: Robert Walden, David Proctor, Beth Anne. BSME, Case Inst. Tech., 1956; MS, MIT, 1959, PhD, 1964. Engr. GE, Cleve., 1955, program engr., Lynn, Mass., 1956-57; instr. U. N.H., 1957-58, asst. prof., 1959-60, assoc. prof., 1964-66, prof., 1966-90, chmn. dept. mech. engring., 1964-72, dir. marine program, 1975-87; asst. dir. geoscis. NSF, Arlington, Va., 1987-2000; sr. rsch. fellow Belfer Ctr. Sci. for Science and Internat. Affairs, 2000; sr. rsch. fellow Kennedy Sch. Govt. Harvard U., 2000—; sr. fellow Am. Meterol. Soc., Wash., 2000—. Rsch. engr. Huggins Hosp., Wolfeboro, N.H., 1957-60, Highland View Hosp., Cleve., 1960-64; vis. investigator Woods Hole Oceanographic Inst., 1965; rsch. assoc., vis. prof. Scripps Instn. Oceanography, 1971-72; vis. prof. U. Wash., 1985; chair U.S. Global Change Rsch. Com. of U.S. Govt., 1987-2000; sr. rsch. fellownumerous positions as chair of interagy. sci. coms. and internat. bodies. Contbr. articles to profl. jours. Founding chair Internat. Group of Funding Agencies for Global Change Rsch., 1988-90; chair Implementation Com. for Inter-Am. Inst. for Global Change Rsch., 1992-95; dir. White House Conf. on Sci. and Econs. to Global Change Rsch., 1990. Fellow Sr. Rsch. fellow, Harvard U., 2000—, Sr. fellow, Am. Meteorol. Soc. Mem. AAAS, Am. Soc. Engring. Edn., IEEE, Marine Tech. Soc., Sigma Xi, Tau Beta Pi, Sigma Alpha Epsilon. Achievements include research in global change, climate and environmental research, medicine, medical engineering, ocean science and technology. Office: Am Meteorol Soc 1120 G St N W Ste 800 Washington DC 20005-737 E-mail: global@dmv.com.

COREN, JONATHON SILOW, science educator, researcher; b. Phila., Oct. 26, 1960; s. Benedict Emanuel and Harriet Selma Coren. PhD, Cornell U., Ithaca, NY, 1985—91. Rsch. technician Wistar Inst., Phila., 1984—85; grad. student Cornell U., Ithaca, NY, 1985—91; postdoctoral rschr. Thomas Jefferson U., Phila., 1991—93; vis. scientist DuPont Merck Pharmaceuticals, Wilmington, Del., 1993—97; adj. prof. St. Joseph's U., Phila., 1997—99; asst. prof. Southwestern Okla. State U., Weatherford, Okla., 1999—2002, Elizabethtown Coll., Elizabethtown, Pa., 2002. Grantee NIH R15 grant, Nat. Inst. Health, 2001—04. Mem.: AAAS, Sigma Xi. Jewish. Home: 418 Indian Rock Cir Elizabethtown PA 17022 Office: Elizabethtown Coll One Alpha Dr Elizabethtown PA 17022 Office Fax: 717-361-1243. Personal E-mail: corenj@etown.edu. E-mail: corenj@etown.edu.

COREN, LANCE SCOTT, consulting firm executive; b. Inglewood, Calif., Dec. 19, 1949; s. Melville and Shirley Ann (Ehrlich) C.; m. Susan Hodges; 1 child, Amy Elizabeth. BSBL, Van Norman U., L.A., 1973; cert. ins. law, UCLA, 1975; cert. comparative psychology, The Calif. Grad. Inst., 1975; MBA, Cal-Western U., 1976; cert. automotive impact nalysis, UCLA/SAE Traffic Inst., 1976. Cert. automotive expert, Calif., Nat. Inst. Automotive Svc. Elegance; cert. master appraiser Internat. Auto Appraisers Assn. Auto claims adjustor Gulf & Western Cos., L.A., 1974-77; western regional mgr., field ops. Guaranty Nat. Ins. Group, L.A., 1977-80; pres., chief exec. officer L.S.C. Enterprizes, Inc., Torrance, Calif., 1980—. Pres., CEO L.S.C. Ent., Inc./Corenco Corp., N.Y.C./Torrance, Calif., 1980—; ptnr. C&H Racing Team U.S.A., 1989—; bd. dirs. Capital Investment Trust, N.Y., L.S.C. Investment Co., L.A., N.Y.C., Palm Springs Ann. Rd. Races-Concours D'Elegance, Newport Invitiational Concours D'Elegance, Palos Verdes Concours D'Elegance; cons. Auto Assn. Am., L.A., 1984-88, State Farm Inst. Co., L.A., 1984-92, Guaranty Nat. Cos., 1993-96, U.S.A.A. Ins. Co. L.A., 1986-92, Inst. Inst. Hwy. Safety, 1987-92; mem. Internat. Orgn. of Experts to UN, 1992-1999; adv. bd. dirs. Nat. Automobile Dealers Assn., 2000-03, Cars of Particular Interest, 2001-2003, Kelley Blue Book, El Camino C.C., 2000-2003, Nat. Inst. Automotive Svc. Excellence. Author: The International Firm, 1976, Exotic Automotive Investments, 1985; mem. adv. bd.: Vehicle Values, 1999—2003, Vintage Racecar Jour., 2000—. Fund raiser Children's Hosp., Orange County, 1987, Soroptimist Internat., Newport Beach, 1983, Children's Hosp. Soc. of Calif., Fresno, 1985; mem. govs. coun. Ins. Practices, 1987-91, Carroll Shelby Heart Fund, L.A., 1990; vice chmn. The Coren Found., Fresno, Calif., 1998-2003, Marconi Children's Charities, 2000-2002, Chldren's Charities of Am., 1985-2000. Named One of Outstanding Young Men in Am., U.S. Jaycees, 1986; recipient Presdl. Sports award (skiing), Washington, 1973, Internat. Man of Yr. Automotive Internat. Fedn. of Automotive Analysts, London, 1992. Mem.Internat. Automotive Appraisers Assn.(master appraiser), Internat. Soc. Automotive Appraisers (pres. 1983-84), Am. Assn. Auto Appraisers (pres. 1984-85), Soc. Automotive Engrs., Internat. Soc. Automotive Analysis. Democrat. Jewish. Avocations: tennis, snow skiing, auto racing. Office: L S C Enterprizes Group Inc PO Box 429 Prather CA 93651-0429 E-mail: LSCENT@earthlink.net.

CORETH, JOSEPH HERMAN, investment advisor; b. San Antonio, Jan. 14, 1937; s. Rudolph C. and Eltha (Zipp) C.; m. Margaret Nowell Graham, June 18, 1960; 1 child, Elizabeth Coreth Bowden. BS, U.S. Mil. Acad., 1959; MA, Cornell U., 1966; JD, George Washington U., 1989. Bar: Md. 1989, Tex. 1990, D.C. 1990, N.H. 1991, U.S. Supreme Ct. 1993; registered investment advisor. Commd. 2d lt. U.S. Army, 1959, advanced through grades to maj., 1967; assoc. prof. English U.S. Mil. Acad., West Point, NY, 1966—69; chief plans officer 4th Inf. Divsn., An Khe, Vietnam, 1969—70; resigned U.S. Army, 1970; exec. v.p. Nat. Mortgage Corp., Washington, 1970—78; pres. Stannard's, Inc., Silver Spring, Md., 1979—84; v.p., trust officer Riggs Bank NA, Washington, 1985—2002; v.p. Farr, Miller and Washington, LLC, Investment Counsel, Washington, 2002—. Past trustee, assoc. Grads. U.S. Mil. Acad.; mem. Order of St. John. Mem.: Chevy Chase Club (Md.), Met. Club (Washington). Avocations: golf, birding. Home: 5508 Park St Chevy Chase MD 20815-7107 Office: 1020 19th St NW Ste 200 Washington DC 20036

COREY, BARRY MARTIN, lawyer; b. Louisville, Apr. 15, 1942; s. Joseph and Ann (Friedman) C.; m. Arlene Corey; children: David, Pamela; stepchildren: Vanessa Aldecoa, Sarah Rivera, Esther Rivera. BA, U. Colo., 1963; JD, Georgetown U., 1966. Bar: Ariz. 1967, US Dist. Ct. DC 1967, US Ct. Appeals (9th cir.) 1973, US Supreme Ct. 1990. Law clk. to chief judge U.S. Dist. Ct. for Ariz., Tucson, 1966-7; assoc. Schorr & Karp, P.C., Tucson, 1967-69; asst. city atty. City of Tucson, 1969-71; ptnr. Schorr, Karp & Corey, Tucson, 1971-73; pvt. practice Tucson, 1974-78; shareholder Corey & Kime, PC, Tucson, 1978—. Pres., co-founder Cmty. Food Bank, Inc., Tucson, 1980, bd. dirs. 1975—; bd. dirs. United Way Tucson, 1982-95, chmn. bd., 1990-91. Fellow Ariz. Bar Found.; mem. ABA, ATLA, Am. Judicature Soc., Ariz. Trial Lawyers Assn., State Bar Ariz. (chmn. pub. rels. com. 1987-89), Pima County Bar Assn. (bd. dirs. 1978-85, pres. 1983-84). Democrat. Jewish. Avocations: reading, hiking, music, golf. Office: Corey & Kime PC 711 Transamerica Bldg 177 N Church Ave Tucson AZ 85701-1119

COREY, CLAIRE, artist; b. Redondo Beach, Calif., Sept. 29, 1968; d. Frederick Constantine and Dorothy Lucille Corey; m. Ross Bryan Knight, May 2, 1992. BFA, UCLA. Contbr. ; one-woman shows include Christinrose Gallery, N.Y.C., 2000, Galerie Bugdahn und Kaimer, Dusseldorf, Germany, Plains Art Mus., Fargo, N.D., 2002, Ten in One Gallery, N.Y.C., 2003, exhibited in group shows at Visual Arts Mus., 1998, Circulo de Bellas Artes, Madrid, 1999, Triennal di Milano, Milan, 1999, DFN Gallery, N.Y.C., 1999, Christinerose Gallery, 2000—01, Robert Pearre Gallery, Tucson, 2000, The Aldrich Mus. Contemporary Art, Ridgefield, Conn., 2000, 2002, Vesceglia Gallery, N.J., 2001, Am. Acad. Arts and Letter, N.Y.C., 2001, Jay Grimm Gallery, 2001, Dumbo Arts Ctr., Bklyn., 2002, David Risley Gallery, London, 2002, Ace Gallery, N.Y.C., 2002, Artists Space, 2002, Ten in One Gallery, 2002, numerous others. Recipient Trustee's award, The Aldrich Mus. of Contemporary Art, 2001, Space Program award, Marie Walsh Sharpe Art Found., 1999; Pollock-Krasner Found. grantee, 2000.

COREY, DAVID THOMAS, invertebrate zoology specialist; b. Saratoga Springs, N.Y., Apr. 12, 1960; s. Raymond Roy and Eleanor Ann (Ahrens) C. AA, U. Cen. Fla., 1981, BS, 1982, MS, 1987; PhD, So. Ill. U., 1993. Sr. mgr. Davgar Restaurants Inc., Winter Park, Fla., 1981-86; rsch. asst. genetics lab. U. Cen. Fla., Orlando, 1984-86, biol. scientist II, 1986-88; rsch. asst. fisheries So. Ill. U., Carbondale, 1989, teaching asst., 1990-93; asst. aquarist Riverbanks Zool. Park and Bot. Gardens, Columbia, SC, 1997—. Adj. instr. John A. Logan Coll., 1993; full-time instr. Midlands Tech. Coll., Columbia, S.C., 1994—, Beltline sci. coord. 1996; presenter, manuscript reviewer, reviewer textbook chpts. in field; reviewer grant proposal for Nat. Geographic Soc. Contbr. articles to profl. jours. Recipient Padgett scholarship So. Ill. U. chpt. Sigma Xi, 1993; grantee Exline-Frizzell Fund for Arachnological Rsch., Calif. Acad. Scis., 1983, 87, Fla. Entomol. Soc., 1990, 93. Mem. Am. Arachnol. Soc., Brit. Arachnol. Soc., Lambda Chi Alpha. Avocations: tropical fish, model ship building, scuba diving, photography. Office: Sci Dept Beltline Midlands Tech Coll PO Box 2408 Columbia SC 29202-2408 E-mail: coreyd@midlandstech.com.

COREY, ELIAS JAMES, chemistry educator; b. Methuen, Mass., July 12, 1928; s. Elias and Tina (Hashem) Corey; m. Claire Higham, Sept. 14, 1961; children: David, John, Susan. BS, MIT, 1948, PhD, 1951; AM (hon.), Harvard U., 1959; DSc (hon.), U. Chgo., 1968; DSc (hon.), Hofstra U., 1974, Colby Coll., 1976; DSc (hon.), Oxford U., 1982, U. Liege, 1985; DSc (hon.), U. Ill., 1985, Kenyon Coll., 1989, Helsinki Coll., 1990, Ariz. U., 1990, Merrimac Coll., 1990, Hokkaido U., 1991, Boston Coll., 1992. From instr. to asst. prof. U. Ill., Champaign-Urbana, 1951—55, prof., 1955—59; prof. chemistry Harvard U., Cambridge, Mass., 1959—68, Sheldon Emory prof. of Chemistry, 1968—; mem. Microbia Scientific Advisory Bd., 2002—. Contbr. articles to profl. jours. Recipient Intrasci. Found. award, 1968, Ernest Guenther award in chemistry, 1968, Harrison Howe award, 1971, Ciba Found. medal, 1972, Evans award, Ohio State U., 1972, Linus Pauling award, 1973, Dickson prize in sci., Carnegie Mellon U., 1973, George Ledlie prize in sci., Harvard U., 1973, Nichols medal, 1977, Buchman award, Calif. Inst. Tech., 1978, Franklin medal in sci., Franklin Inst., 1978, Sci. Achievement award, CCNY, 1979, J.G. Kirkwood award, Yale U., 1980, C.S. Hamilton award, U. Nebr., 1980, Chem. Pioneer award, Am. Inst. Chemists, 1981, V.D. Mattia award, Roche Inst. Molecular Biology, 1985, Wolf prize in chemistry, Wolf Found., 1986, Silliman award, 1986, Japan prize, 1989, Nat. Med. Sci. award, 1988, Nobel prize in chemistry, 1990, Gold medal, AIC, 1990; fellow, Swiss-Am. Exch., 1957, Guggenheim Found., 1957—58, 1968—69, Alfred P. Sloan Found., 1956—59. Mem.: AAAS, Franklin Inst., Nat. Acad. Sci., Am. Acad. Arts and Scis., Chem. Soc. Japan (hon.), Am. Chem. Soc. (hon. award in synthetic chemistry 1971, Pure Chemistry award 1960, Fritzche award 1968, Remsen award 1974, Arthur C. Cope award 1976, Roger Adams award organic chemistry 1993, Madison Marshall award 1985), Sigma Xi. Office: Harvard U Dept Chemistry Rm 319 12 Oxford St Dept Cambridge MA 02138-2902*

COREY, ELIZABETH B. poet; b. Orlando, Fla., Oct. 26, 1962; d. Arthur E. and Margaret Fannie (Dinsfelder) Corey. English dept. cons. Trinity Prep. H.S., Winterfield, Fla. Fellow: Mensa. Democrat. Jewish. Avocations: fencing, surfing, diving, swimming, weightlifting. Home: Apt 4V 2385 Barker Ave Bronx NY 10467-7786

COREY, JUDITH ANN, retired educator; b. Peoria, Ill., Dec. 1, 1937; d. Lyle William and Eileen A. (Zigrang) Springston; m. Thomas W. Corey, Aug. 12, 1961; children: John William, Jeffrey Michael, Gregory Lyle, Mark Andrew. BA in Bus., English, Marycrest Coll., 1960; MA in Counseling, Bradley U., 1972. Lic. tchr. K-12, Ill.; lic. clin. profl. counselor. Tchr. Riverview Sch., Spring Bay, Ill., 1960-61, Lincoln Sch., East Peoria, Ill., 1963-64; counselor Bradley U., Peoria, 1972-73; clin. psychologist intern Zeller Zone Ctr., Peoria, 1973; dean students Morton (Ill.) High Sch., 1974-85; tchr. Jefferson Sch., Morton, 1985—2002. Contbr. poem to Worlds Greatest Contemporary Poems, 1981 (Hon. Mention). Campaign work Grace Bunn Lievens Ill. Rep., 89th Dist. Ill., Morton, 1994; mem. exec. bd. Ill. State Deans' Assn., 1980-84, historian, 1980-82, membership com., 1982-84. Named to Outstanding Young Women in Am., 1973. Mem. NEA, Ill. Edn. Assn., Morton Edn. Assn. (newsletter editor 1987-90, mem. exec. com. and maj. negotiator, 1987-2000, v.p. 1993-95), Assn. Play Therapy, Phi Kappa Phi (life), Kappa Gamma Pi, Pi Lambda Theta. Roman Catholic. Avocations: reading, writing, photography, music, nature. Home: 20432 Tennessee Ave Morton IL 61550-9777

COREY, KAY JANIS, business owner, designer, nurse; b. Detroit, Aug. 22, 1942; d. Alexander Michael Corey and Lillian Emiline (Stanley) Kilborn; divorced; children: Tonya Kay, William James, Jason Ronald. Student, C.S. Mott Community Coll., 1960-62, Mich. State U., 1962-64; AA, AS in Nursing, St. Petersburg Jr. Coll., 1978; student, U. South Fla., 1985-86. RN; cert. perioperative nurse; cert. varitypist. Mgr. display Lerner Shops, Flint, Mich., 1960-62; layout artist Abdulla Advt., Flint, 1966-67; varitypist, artist City Hall Print Shop, Flint, 1967-70; nurse Suncoast Hosp., Largo, Fla., 1976-78; nurse, coord. plastic surgery svc., perioperative staff nurse Largo Med. Ctr. Hosp., 1978-81, 84-90; assoc. dir. nursing Roberts Home Health Svc., Pinellas Park, Fla., 1982-84; co-owner Sand Castle Resort, White Bay, Jost Van Dyke, Brit. Virgin Island, 1990-95; perioperative nurse Columbia Gulf Coast Surgery Ctr., 1995-99; perioperative nurse, surg. nurse Blake Med. Ctr. Hosp., 2000—. Designer, artist K.J. Originals clothing line, 1990-95, The Magic Needle clothing line, 1998; insvc. edn. instr., dir. video edn., team leader oncology dept. Largo Med. Ctr. Hosp., 1980-81; designer, mfr. Haelan Jewelers--Fine Custom Jewelry, 1999. Editor, illustrator: (book) Some Questions and Answers About Chemotherapy, 1981, Thoughts for Today, 1981; illustrator (cookbooks) Spices and Spoons, 1982, Yom Tov Essen n' Fressen, 1983; various brochures and catalogues; art work in permanent collection of C.S. Mott Jr. Coll., Flint, 1962; artist, designer of casual and hand painted clothing for children and adults. Historian Am. Businesswomen's Assn., Flint, 1968-73 (scholarship 1976); outreach chmn. Temple B'nai Israel, Clearwater, Fla., 1981-85; regional outreach coord. Union of Am. Hebrew Congregations, N.Y.C., 1983-85. Mem. Assn. of Oper. Rm. Nurses, Phi Theta Kappa. Republican. Jewish. Avocations: sailing, scuba diving, tennis, original teddy bear making, golf. Address: 4080 Kingsfield Dr Parrish FL 34219 E-mail: bubbeKay@msn.com.

COREY, KENNETH EDWARD, urban planning and geography educator, researcher; b. Cin., Nov. 11, 1938; s. Kenneth and Helen Ann (Beckman) C.; m. Marie Joann Fye, Aug. 26, 1961; children: Jeffrey Allen, Jennifer Marie. BA with honors, U. Cin., 1961, MA, 1962, M of Cmty. Planning, 1964, PhD, 1969. Instr. U. Cin., 1962-65, asst. prof. cmty. planning, 1965-69, assoc. prof., 1969-74, prof., 1974-79, head grad. comty. planning and geography, 1969-78;

assoc. prof. cmty. planning and geography U. R.I., 1966-67; prof. geography, planning, chmn. dept. geography, dir. urban studies U. Md., 1979-89; prof. geography and urban and regional planning, dean Coll. Social Sci. Mich. State U., East Lansing, 1989-99, sr. rsch. advisor to v.p. for rsch. and grad. studies, 1999—. Vis. prof. geography Univ. Wales, Aberystyth, 1974-75, Peking U., 1986; chmn. Cin. Model Cities Bd., 1974; Fulbright rsch. scholar Inst. S.E. Asian Studies, Singapore, 1986, Fulbright group study abroad, Sri Lanka, 1983; trustee Met. Washington Housing Planning Assn., 1980-82. Author: The Local Community, 1968, Community Internships for Undergraduate Geography Students, 1973, The Planning of Change, 3d edit., 1976, Information Tectonics, 2000. Bd. dirs. Potomac River Basin Consortium, Washington, 1982-85. Recipient Svc. award Cmty. Chest and Coun. Cin., 1979; recipient Svc. award Planning Divsn., 1979, Svc. award Coalition of Neighborhoods, Cin., 1979, 83, medal of city Mayor of Seoul, South Korea, 1980. Fellow Royal Geog. Soc.; mem. Am. Inst. Cert. Planners, Am. Planning Assn., Assn. Am. Geographers (award spl. group on planning and regional devel. 1985), Assn. Asian Studies, Asia Soc., Pacific Rim Coun. on Urban Devel., World Future Soc. Democrat.

COREY, MARK, historic site director; b. DeKalb, Ill., Aug. 3, 1950; BA, U. Miss., Oxford, 1972. Supt. Ocmulgee Nat. Park, Macon, Ga., 1988-92, Andrew Johnson Nat. Hist. Site, Greenville, Tenn., 1992—. Office: Andrew Johnson Nat Hist Site College and Depot Sts Greeneville TN 37743 also: PO Box 1088 Greeneville TN 37744-1088

COREY, ORLIN RUSSELL, publisher, editor; b. Nowata, Okla., May 4, 1926; s. Lue A. and Nada Gladys (Patton) C.; m. Irene Lockridge, Aug. 25, 1949 (div. 1974); m. Shirley Trusty, Nov. 27, 1975. BA, Baylor U., 1950, MA, 1952; cert. of directing and acting, Ctrl. Sch. Speech and Drama, London, 1956. Drama dir., asst. prof. Georgetown (Ky.) Coll., 1952-59; drama dir., assoc. prof. Centenary Coll., Shreveport, La., 1960-68; dir. Everyman Players, Pineville, Ky., 1958-80; pub., editor Anchorage Press, Inc., New Orleans, 1977-2000, editl. advisor, 2000—. Guest dir. U. N.H., Durham, 1968; lectr. Ohio State U., also other univs., 1968—75; prodr. John F. Kennedy Ctr., Washington, 1973—75; pres. Children's Theatre Found., Inc., Greensboro, NC, 1977—2001; mem. exec. com. Nat. Theater Conf., 1985. Author: Theatre for Children, 1973, Towers of the Brazos, Theatre for Children—Kid-Stuff or Theatre?, 1974, An Odyssey of Masquers: The Everyman Plwyers, 1990, Religious Drama: A Classic Quartet, 1999; adaptor dor drama of book of Job, 1960; prodr. La. World Expo, World Theatre Festival, New Orleans, 1984. Bd. dirs. New Orleans Ctr. Creative Arts, 1975—, Nat. Theatre Conf. With USN, 1944-46, PTO. Recipient religious drama award Nat. Cath. Theater Assn., 1968, Radius, London, 1974. Fellow Am. Theatre (dean Coll. Fellows 1994-96, Jennie Heiden award 1970); mem. Children's Theater Assn. Am. (pres. 1971-73), Am. Alliance for Theatre and Edn. Avocations: photography, cooking, reading. Office: Childrens Theatre Found Am PO Box 8067 New Orleans LA 70182-8067

COREY, STEPHEN DALE, magazine editor, poet, educator; b. Buffalo, N.Y., Aug. 30, 1948; s. Dale Burton and Julienne Barbara (Holmes) C.; m. Mary Elizabeth Gibson, Jan. 28, 1970; children: Heather, Miranda, Rebecca, Catherine. BA, SUNY, Binghamton, 1971, MA, 1974; PhD, U. Fla., Gainesville, 1979. Instr. English U. Fla., 1979-80, asst. prof. English U. S.C., Columbia, 1980-83; asst. editor The Ga. Rev. U. Ga., Athens, 1983-86, assoc. editor, 1986—. Author: The Last Magician, 1981, Synchronized Swimming, 1985, All These Lands You Call One Country, 1992, Mortal Fathers and Daughters, 1999, Greatest Hits, 2000; editor: Necessary Fictions, 1986, Keener Sounds, 1987, Spreading the Word: Editors on Poetry, 2001, There is No Finished World, 2003. Ga. Coun. Arts literary grantee, 1985-86, 88-89; lit. fellow S.C. Arts Commn., 1981-82; named Author of Yr. Poetry Ga. Writers, Atlanta, 1992, 93, 2000. Mem. South Atlantic Modern Lang. Assn., Assoc. Writing Programs. Home: 357 Parkway Dr Athens GA 30606-4951 Office: The Georgia Rev U Ga Athens GA 30602-9009 E-mail: scorey@uga.edu.

CORICH, CHRISTOPHER BLAZE, airport planner; b. Dallas, Feb. 21, 1953; s. Bernard Paul and Mary (Delayne) C.; m. Eleanora Denise Kleim, Aug. 11, 1985; children: Aaron Christopher, Paige Eleanora. BAB in Fin., Tex. A&M U., 1975, M in Urban Planning, 1977. Assoc. city planner City of Salem (Oreg.) Planning Dept., 1980-85; noise abatement specialist Portland Internat. Airport, 1985-86, airfield ops. supr., 1986-87, aviation planner, 1987-90, sr. aviation planner, 1998—; gen. aviation airports mgr. Port of Portland, 1990-91; airport planning mgr.-Oreg. W&H Pacific, Beaverton, 1991-98, sr. aviation planner, 1998—2001; gen. mgr. ops. and maintenance Portland Internat. Airport, 2001—. Fundraising co-chair, bd. dirs. Fruit & Flower Child Care, Portland, 1989. Mem. Am. Inst. Cert. Planners (cert.), Am. Planners Assn., Aircraft Owners and Pilots Assn., Oreg. Airport Mgrs. Assn., Oreg. Nordic Club (pres. Salem chpt. 1983-85), Tex. A&M U. Sports Car Club (pres. 1974-75). Avocations: aviation, photography, camping, nordic skiing, private pilot. Office: Portland Internat Airport 7000 NE Airport Way Fl 3D Portland OR 97218-1009

CORK, DONALD BURL, electrical engineer; b. Terre Haute, Ind., Aug. 10, 1949; s. Clay Jr. and Margaret M. (Ellis) C.; m. Carolyn R. Lewis, Nov. 18, 1978. BSEE, U. Evansville, Ind., 1971. Owner Ellcor Electric, West Union, Ill., 1971-73; test engr. Zenith Radio, Paris, Ill., 1973-78, mfg. engr., 1978-81; design engr. TRW Electronics, Marshall, Ill., 1981-84, electrical engr. coord., 1984-88, program mgr., 1988—2001, Indigo Systems, Goleta, Calif., 2002—. Mem. West Union (Ill.) Fire Dept., 1969—2002, trustee, 1995—2002; elder Christian Ch., West Union, 1991—2001. Mem. Eta Kappa Nu, Ea. Ill. Hamateurs (pres. 1971-73), West Union Firemans Assn. (v.p. 1977-78, treas. 1989), Old Nat. Trail Firefighters'. Republican. Avocation: amateur radio. Home: 7220 Davenport Rd # 206 Goleta CA 93117 Office: Indigo Systems 50 Castilian Dr Goleta CA 93117

CORK, ROBERT LANDER, lawyer; b. Central, S.C., Oct. 27, 1927; s. James Walter and Lila (Mitchell) C.; m. Anne McNeill Ward, Oct. 11, 1952; children: Leah, Robert Jr. (dec.), Travis, Patrick. AB, U. Ga., 1952, LLB, 1953. Bar: Ga. 1951, Fla. 1958, S.C. 1989, U.S. Dist. Ct. (mid. dist.) Ga. 1951, U.S. Ct. Appeals (11th cir.) 1981, U.S. Dist. Ct. (mid. dist.) Fla. 1983. Ptnr. Cork & Gaines, Athens, Ga., 1951-53; pvt. practice law Valdosta, Ga., 1954-83; ptnr. Cork & Cork, Valdosta, 1983—. Gen. counsel Warrior Cattle Co., Sylvester, Ga., 1964-70; legal draftsman charter and mcpl. code Town of Dasher, Ga., 1967; counsel Truman Arnold Co., Texarkana, Ark., 1995—, Internat. Petroleum, Inc., Jacksonville, Fla., 1990—, Strasburg and Assocs. (Petroleum), Waco, Tex., 1996—. County co-chmn. campaign Goldwater for Pres., Valdosta, 1964, county chmn. campaign Wallace for Pres., Valdosta, 1968; precinct chmn., del. to state Rep. Conv., Valdosta, 1983, 84, 87-88, 89, 91, 92, 94, 96, 98, 99, 2000; alt. del. Nat. Rep. Conv., 2000. With AUS, 1953-54. Mem. Am. Legion, Shriners, Masons, St. John the Baptist, Delta Theta Phi. Republican. Methodist. Home: Sunnyside Lake Francis Lake Park GA 31634 Office: Cork & Cork 700 N Patterson St Valdosta GA 31601-4527

CORKERY, JAMES CALDWELL, retired Canadian government executive, mechanical engineer; b. East Orange, N.J., June 23, 1925; S. Kirk James and Helen May (Caldwell) C.; m. Jane Woodruff, Sept. 19, 1953; children— Kirk, Candace BA Sc., U. Toronto, Ont., Can., 1948, MA Sc., 1950. Registered profl. engr., Ont. Plant mgr. Can. Gen. Electric, Montreal, Que., 1956-61, plant mgr. Oakville, Ont., 1961-68, mng. mfg. Toronto, 1968-70; regional gen. mgr. Can. Post, Toronto, 1970-77, dep. postmaster gen. Ottawa, Ont., 1977-82. Pres. Royal Can. Mint., Ottawa, 1982-86, chmn. bd., 1986-95; pres. Gold. Inst., 1986-88 Chmn. bd. Oakville Trafalgar Hosp., 1968-72; chmn. Easter Seal Campaign, Ottawa, 1985; chmn. bd. Ottawa Children Treatment Hosp., 1986-89. With RCAF, 1943-45. Mem. Profl. Engrs. Ont., Mint Dirs. Conf. (sec. 1984-86). Lodges: Rotary. Anglican. Avocations: furniture refinishing; antiques; gardening.

CORKINS, MARK R. physician, pediatric gastroenterologist; b. St. Joseph, Mo., Feb. 17, 1962; s. Charles R. and Virginia R. Corkins; m. Linda E. Eime, May 21, 1983; children: Christopher M., Charity E., Abigail M. BA, U. Mo., 1984, MD, 1989. Bd. cert. pediats. Am. Bd. Pediat., 1992, cert. pediat. gastroenterology subboard Am. Bd. Pediat., 1997. Asst. prof. pediat. Creighton Univ./Univ. Nebr. Med. Ctr., Omaha, 1995—99, Riley Hosp. for Children/Ind. Univ., Indpls., 1999—. Pres.-elect Ind. Soc. for Parenteral and Enteral Nutrition, 1999—2000, pres., 2000—01. Editor: (pediatric nutrition handbook) Pediatric Nutrition in Your Pocket; contbr. articles to profl. jours. Ch. bd. Abundant Life Ch., Indpls., 2000—02. Mem.: Crohns and Colitis Found. Am., N.Am. Soc. for Pediat. Gastroenterology, Hepatology and Nutrition, Am. Gastroent. Assn., Am. Acad. Pediat., Am. Soc. for Parenteral and Enteral Nutrition (sec. 2000—01, chmn.-elect pediat. sect. 2001—), Soc. for Pediat. Rsch., Alpha Chi Sigma. Office: Riley Hospital for Children/Indiana Univ 702 Barnhill Drive ROC 4210 Indianapolis IN 46202

CORKRAN, VIRGINIA B. retired realtor; b. N.Y.C., Feb. 13, 1924; d. Stuart H. and Bessie (Moses) Bowman; m. Sewell H. Corkran, Jr., June 15, 1946; children: Sewell H. III, Leslie C. Price. BA, Conn. Coll., 1945. Tchr. Low-Heywood Sch., Stamford, Conn., 1946-47; editor North Shore Calendar, Winnetka, Ill., 1955-59; real estate assoc. Lodge McKee Realty Inc., Naples, Fla., 1969-2001; ret., 2001. Elected Naples City Coun., 1974-78; pres. Old Naples Assn., 1995-97; past bd. dirs. Big Cypress Nature Ctr., Naples, The Conservancy, Inc., Collier County LWV, Southwest Heritage, Inc., Naples; active Naples Garden Club (legis chmn.), Collier Co. Audubon; bd. mem. S.W. Heritage, Inc., Naples (hon. bd. mem., 2002). Recipient Guy Bradley award Collier County Audubon, ONA award Old Naples Assn., 1998.

CORLE, FREDERIC WILLIAM, II, marketing professional; b. Phila., June 20, 1945; s. Frederic William and Marjorie (Dudley) Corle; m. Pamela Gaus White, Apr. 16, 1983 (div. May 1987); children: Alison Gaus, Louise Armour; m. Morrell T. Taggart, Dec. 9, 1995. BA, Marietta Coll., 1967; MBA, U. Denver, 1973. Supply mgmt. officer Fed. Deposit Ins. Corp., Washington, 1970-72; program analyst Exec. Office of Pres., Washington, 1973-77; dir. Commn. on Budget U.S. Ho. of Reps., Washington, 1977-78; v.p. City Sports Mgmt., Inc., Washington, 1978-82; asst. to adminstr. White House, Washington, 1983-84; dir. mktg. Interand Corp., Washington, 1984-85; spl. asst. Dept. of Interior, Washington, 1985-86; regional dir. fed. mktg. Datapoint Corp., Washington, 1987-89; CEO Mktg. Solutions Internat., Inc., Washington, 1989—; bd. dirs., dir. fed. mktg. Sun Microsystems Fed. Inc., Washington, 1991-96; ptnr. Potomac Rsch. Group, Washington, 1996-98; pres. Spatial Techs. Industry Assn., Washington, 1996—. Lt. (j.g.) USN, 1967—70. Mem.: Army Navy Country Club. Republican. Episcopalian.

CORLE, JAMES THOMAS, lawyer; b. Jay County, Ind., Dec. 28, 1927; s. Herbert R. and Mary M. (Reitenour) Corle; m. Jean Polhemus, July 16, 1950; children: James Thomas, Sarah Corle Thomas, Kenneth D. BS Engring. Law, Purdue U., 1955; JD, Ind. U., Bloomington, 1955. Bar: Ind. 1955, DC 1964. With E.I. DuPont de Nemours & Co., Wilmington, Del., 1955; patent counsel Washington, 1967—70; sr. supervising patent counsel, legal dept., 1970—85; corp. counsel, legal dept., 1986—92; intellectual property cons., 1993—. Lt. col. USAR, 1946—52. Mem.: Del. bar Assn., Phila. Patent Law Assn., Am. Patent Law Assn., ABA. Republican. Meth.

CORLESS, DOROTHY ALICE, nurse educator; b. Reno, Nev., May 28, 1943; d. John Ludwig and Vera Leach (Wilson) Adams; children: James Lawrence Jr., Dorothy Adele Carroll. RN, St. Luke's Sch. Nursing, 1964. Clinician, cons., educator, grant author, adminstr. Fresno County Mental Health Dept., 1991—94; instr. police sci. State Ctr. Tng. Facility, 1991-94; pvt. practice, mental health cons., educator, 1970—; sr. assoc. guidance distbn. response, disaster svcs. ARC, 2003—. Res. asst. officer ARC, Disaster Mental Health Svcs., 1993-2003. Maj. USAFR, 1972-94. Mem. NAFE, Forensic Mental Health Assn. Calif., Calif. Peace Officer's Assn., Critical Incident Stress Found. Office: 3401 38th St NW # 304 Washington DC 20016 E-mail: dorothydmh@aol.com.

CORLETT, CLEVE EDWARD, government administrator; b. Boise, Idaho, July 19, 1940; s. Edward John and Bertha (Wagner) C.; m. Ruth Ann Augspurger, Dec. 26, 1961; children: Christopher Sean, Gregory Cleve. Student, Coll. of Idaho, 1958-60; BA, George Washington U., 1963. Reporter UPI, Washington, 1960-64; Washington corr. Fed. Publs., Washington, 1964-68; press sec. to Senator Frank Church, U.S. Senate, Washington, 1968-75, 76-81, press sec. to Senator Joseph R. Biden, 1975-76, press sec. to Senator John H. Chafee, 1981-87; dir. pub. affairs GAO, Washington, 1987-95, dir. external affairs, 1996-2000; ret., 2000. Pub. affairs cons. to corps. and non-profit orgns. Episcopalian. Avocations: photography, cooking.

CORLETT, EDWARD STANLEY, III, retired lawyer; b. Miami, May 28, 1924; s. Edward Stanley Jr. and Marjorie (Cook) C.; m. Jeanne Sherouse, Mar. 27, 1948; children: Karen Marie Corlett McCammon, Edward S. AA, U. Fla., 1946, LLB, 1949. Bar: Fla. 1949, U.S. Dist. Ct. (so. dist.) Fla. 1949, U.S. Ct. Appeals (5th cir.) 1949, U.S. Ct. Appeals (11th cir.) 1981. Sole practice, 1949-58; sr. ptnr. Sherouse and Corlett and successor Corlett, Killian, Hardeman, McIntosh and Levi, P.A., Miami, 1958-96. Chmn. bd. Internat. Oceanographic Found.; pres. Miami Met. Fishing Tournament, 1973-80; mem. Fed. Jud. Nominating Panel. Served with USN, 1942-44. Recipient Henry Hyman trophy, 1974. Fellow Am. Coll. Trial Lawyers; mem. ABA, Fla. Bar Assn., Dade County Bar Assn., Fedn. Ins. Counsel (pres. 1978-79, testimonial award 1979), Fla. Def. Lawyers Assn. (pres. 1970), Def. Rsch. Inst. (dir. 1978-79, testimonial award 1979), Internat. Assn. Ins. Counsel, Miami Rod and Reel Club, Riviera Country Club, Bankers Club. Republican. Presbyterian. E-mail: ecorl82673@aol.com.

CORLEW, JOHN GORDON, lawyer; b. Dyersburg, Tenn., July 13, 1943; s. Emmett Atkins and Margaret Elizabeth (Swann) C.; m. Elizabeth Lee Scott, July 8, 1967; children: John Scott, William Heath, Carey Elizabeth. BA, U. Miss., 1965; JD, Vanderbilt U., 1968. Bar: Miss. 1968. Clk. to judge U.S. Dist. Ct. (so. dist.) Miss., 1968-69; assoc., then ptnr. Megehee, Brown, Williams & Corlew, Pascagoula, Miss., 1969-74; sole practice Pascagoula, 1975-78; ptnr. Corlew, Krebs & Hammond, Pascagoula, 1978-84, Watkins & Eager, Jackson, Miss., 1984. Mem. Miss. State Senate, 1974-80, chmn. appropriations com., 1979, chmn. constn. com., 1975-79, chmn. legis. audit com., 1978; chmn. Miss. State Bd. Pub. Welfare, 1980-84. Mem. ABA, Miss. Bar Assn., Hinds County Bar Assn., Miss. Bar Found., Order of Coif, Phi Delta Phi. Democrat. Methodist. Home: 2124 Eastover Dr Jackson MS 39211-6719 Office: Emporium Bldg 400 E Capitol St Jackson MS 39201-2610

CORLEY, ALTON L. music educator; b. Odessa, Tex., Aug. 31, 1955; s. Luther Ralph and Argie Ree Corley; m. Paula Beck, Aug. 14, 1984. MM, So. Meth. U, 1984; PhD, Univ. N. Tex., 2003. Teaching Certificate Tex., 1978. Dir. of bands Plano Sr. HS, Plano, Tex., 1984—98; lectr. U of North Tex., Denton, 1998—2002. Dir. of bands Mars Hill Coll., Mars Hill, NC, 2002—. Mem.: Phi Beta Mu. Office: Mars Hill Coll Music Dept Mars Hill College Mars Hill NC 28754 E-mail: acorley@mhc.edu.

CORLEY, CAROL LEE, retired school nurse; b. Waco, Tex., Feb. 2, 1943; d. Henry Lee (dec.) and Irma Geraldine (King) Cranfill; m. Thomas Lane Corley, May 22, 1965; 1 child, Christopher Lyn. ADN, McLennan C.C., 1974; BSN, U. Tex.-Arlington, 1983. Staff nurse ICU Providence Health Ctr., Waco, Tex., 1974; sch. nurse Crawford (Tex.) Ind. Sch. Dist., 1975—79, Midway Ind. Sch. Dist., Waco, 1979—2000, coord., 1994—2000; ret., 2000. Mem. ANA, Tex. Nurses Assn. (dist. 10 pres. 1992-94, past v.p.), Tex. Assn. Sch. Nurses (dist. 12 pres. 1990), Tex. Sch. Nurses Administrs. Assn., Sigma Theta Tau. Home: 8930 Raven Dr Waco TX 76712-3453 E-mail: ccorley@hot.rr.com.

CORLEY, JENNY LYND WERTHEIM, elementary education educator; b. Lincoln, Ill., June 18, 1937; d. Robert Glenn and Nancy Lynd (Hoblit) Wertheim; m. William Gene Corley, Aug. 9, 1959; children: Anne Lynd Corley Baum, Robert William, Scott Elson. BS in Music Edn., U. Ill., 1959, MS in Music Edn., 1961; postgrad., U. Ill., Loyola U., 1985—. Tchr. choral music Mahomet (Ill.)/Seymour K-12, 1959-61; supr. music Fairfax County (Va.), 1961-63; tchr. music Highland Park (Ill.) 107, 1969, dir. gifted edn., 1969-70; tchr. music Glenview (Ill.) 34, 1981—2003. V.p. Corley Agroleum Properties, 1993—2003; water safety instr./trainer ARC; lifeguard instr./trainer Cmty. First Aid & Safety, 1995. Dir. mid-Am. bd. ARC, Chgo., 1980-86; mem. Chgo. Symhony Orch. Chorus, 1965-75. Recipient Heart of Gold United Way, 1992, Cmty. Svc. award Ill. Park & Recreation Assn./Ill. Assn. Park Dists., 1994, Disting. Svc. award Boys and Girls Swimming Ofcl., Ill. High Sch. Assn., 1994, also 25 yr. recognitiuon as swimming ofcl. Mem. Music Edn. Nat. Conf., North Shore Music Tchrs. Assn. (treas. 1987-90), Jr. League Chgo. (treas. 1978-81), Sigma Alpha Iota, Phi Delta Kappa (found. chmn. 1994—), U. Ill. Music Alumnae (pres. bd. dirs. 1995-97). Presbyterian. Home: 744 Glenayre Dr Glenview IL 60025-4411 E-mail: corley@corleywg.com.

CORLEY, JOHN D. W. military officer; BS in Engring., USAF Acad., 1973; grad., Squadron Officer's Sch., 1978; MBA, U. of The Philippines, Manila, 1984; grad., Air Command and Staff Coll., 1985, Naval Command and Staff Coll., 1986; M in Nat. Security and Strategic Studies, 1986; grad., Army War Coll., 1992. Commd. 2d lt. USAF, 1973, advanced through grades to col., 1994; instr. pilot, flight examiner 64th Flying Tng. Wing, Reese AFB, Tex., 1974-78, 49th Tactical Fighter Wing, Holloman AFB, N.Mex., 1979-82; flight comdr. 26th Aggressor Squadron, chief Aggressor Ops., Clark Air Base, The Philippines, 1982-85; analyst advanced tactical fighter Air Force Ctr. for Studies and Analyses, Washington, 1986-88; analyst comdr.'s action group Tactical Air Command, Langley AFB, Va., 1988-90; ops. officer 7th Fighter Squadron, comdr. 8th Fighter Squadron, 49th Fighter Wing, Holloman AFB, N.Mex., 1990-92; comdr. 33d Ops. Group, 33d Fighter Wing, Eglin AFB, Fla., 1993-95; chief Western Hemisphere divsn. Directorate of Strategic Plans and Policy, J-5 Joint Staff, 1995-97; comdr. 355th Wing, Davis-Monthan AFB, Ariz., 1997—; dir. studies and analysis HQ USAF Europe, Ramstein AFB, Germany, 1999—. Decorated Def. Superior Svc. medal, Def. Meritorious Svc. medal, Meritorious Svc. medal with 4 oak leaf clusters. Office: 355 WG/CC Ramstein AFB Unit 3050 Box 1 Apo AE 09094-0001

CORLEY, ROSE ANN MCAFEE, government official; b. Lawton, Okla., Aug. 21, 1952; d. Claude James and Mary Margaret (Holman) McAfee; m. Gary Michael Griffin, Feb. 14, 1973 (div. Oct. 1984); m. Terry Joe Corley, July 31, 1988 (div. Oct. 2002); stepson Troy Justin Corley. BS, Cameron U., Lawton, Okla., 1970; diploma, Army Command and Staff Coll., Ft. Leavenworth, Kans., 1989; MCJA, Oklahoma City U., 1990; cert., Army Mgmt. Staff Coll., Ft. Belvoir, Va., 1991. Cert. in Distbn. Mgt. Supply clk. Dept. of Army, Ft. Sill, Okla., 1972-80, supply mgmt. asst., 1980-82, supply systems analyst Ft. Lee, Va., 1982, supply tech. Ft. Sill, Okla., 1982-83, supr. inventory mgmt. specialist, 1983-86, manprint program mgr., 1986-91; weapon system advisor Def. Logistics Agy., San Antonio, 1991-96, customer svc. rep. Robins AFB, Ga., 1996-98; dir. supply mgmt. NIH, Rockville, Md., 1998—2002, dir. divsn. logistics serviced, 2002—. Equal employment counselor USA Field Artillery Sch., Ft. Sill, Okla., 1976-82; mentor Fed. Women's Program, Kelly AFB, Tex., 1991-96. Active Md. Citizen Foster Care Rev. Bd., 1999—. Recipient Cert. of Appreciation, Sec. of Def., Washington, 1981, Cert. of Appreciation, Director of Engring. and Housing, Ft. Sill, 1986; decorated Order of St. Barbara, U.S. Army Arty. Sch., Ft. Sill, 1991. Mem. Fed. Women's Program, Soc. Logistics Engrs., Fed. Mgrs. Assn., Kelly Mgmt. Assn., World Affairs Coun. of San Antonio, Internat. City Mgmt. Assn., Tex. Corvette Assn. Avocations: autocrossing, reading, golf, crafts. Home: 45 Nipetown Rd Martinsburg WV 25401 Office: NIH Office Logistics Mgmt 6011 Executive Blvd Rockville MD 20852-3804 E-mail: corleyr@od.nih.gov.

CORLEY, WILLIAM GENE, engineering research executive; b. Shelbyville, Ill., Dec. 19, 1935; s. Clarence William and Mary Winifred (Douthit) C.; m. Jenny Lynd Wertheim, Aug. 9, 1959; children: Anne Lynd, Robert William, Scott Elson. BS, U. Ill., 1958, MS, 1960, PhD, 1961. Lic. profl. engr., Ill., Va., Wash., Calif., Miss., Fla., La., Pa., Ala., Hawaii, Tenn., Tex., Utah, Mich., Mo., S.D., S.C., Kans., Ohio, N.Y.; lic. structural engr., Ill.; chartered structural engr., U.K. Devel. engr. Portland Cement Assn., Skokie, Ill., 1964-66, mgr. structural devel. sect., 1966-74, dir. engring. devel. divsn., 1974-86; sr. v.p. Constrn. Tech. Labs., Inc. (formerly Portland Cement Assn.), Skokie, 1986—. Adv. panels NSF; prin. investigator, Bldg. Performance Study Okla. City Bombing; team leader, WTC Bldg. Performance Study. Contbr. articles to profl. jours. Pres. caucus Glenview (Ill.) Sch. Bd., 1971-72; elder United Presbyn. Ch., 1975-79; sec. bd. dirs. Assn. Ho., Chgo., 1976, treas., 1977, pres., 1978-79; chmn. bd. dirs. North Cook dist. ARC, bd. dirs. Mid-Am. chpt., chmn. North Region Coun., 1988-92; mem. Gov.'s (Ill.) Earthquake Preparedness Task Force. Recipient Wason medal for rsch., 1970, Nat. Acad. Engring., 2000; Martin Korn award Prestressed Concrete Inst., 1978, Authur J. Boase award Reinforced Concrete Rsch. Coun., 1986. Fellow: Inst. Structural Engrs., Am. Concrete Inst. (hon.; bd. dirs. 1994—97, Bloem award 1978, Reese Structural Rsch. award 1986, Henry C. Turner award 1988, Ferguson lectr. 1991, Henry Crown award 1997, Lindau award 1999, Alfred E. Lindau award 2000); mem.: NAE, ASCE (hon. T.Y. Lin award 1979, lifetime achievement award 1994, Chgo. Civil Engr. of Yr., Pres.'s award 2003), NSPE, Nat. Coun. Structural Engrs. Assns. (pres. 1996—97, Best Paper award 1999, Disting. Svc. award 1999), Post-Tensioning Inst., Nat. Coun. Examiners Engring. and Surveying (v.p., bd. dirs. 2002—, Disting. Svc. award 2000), Structural Engrs. Assn. Ill. (pres. 1986—87, meritorious publ. award 1993, 1997, John Parmer award 1997), Internat. Assn. Bridge and Structural Engring., Earthquake Engring. Rsch. Inst. (chpt. sec.-treas. 1980—82, chmn. 1984—86), Reunion Internat. des Laboratoires d'Essais et Rsch. sur Materiaux Constrn., Bldg. Seismic Safety Coun. (vice-chmn. 1983—85, sec. 1985—87), Chgo. Com. High-Rise Bldgs. (vice-chmn. 1978—82, chmn. 1982—84). Presbyterian. Home: 744 Glenayre Dr Glenview IL 60025-4411 Office: Construction Tech Labs Inc 5420 Old Orchard Rd Skokie IL 60077-1053

CORLISS, JOHN OZRO, zoology educator; b. Coats, Kans., Feb. 23, 1922; s. Clark L. and Catharine (Smith) C.; children: Susan Elizabeth, Joan Alison, Kimberley Ann, Jennifer Sara, Catharine Megan Corliss; m. Yuemei Geng, June, 1992. BS, U. Chgo., 1944; BA, U. Vt., 1947; PhD, NYU, 1951; DSc (hon.), Universite de Clermont, France, 1973. Postdoctoral fellow AEC, Coll. de France, Paris, 1951-52; instr. zoology Yale, 1952-54; asst. prof. to prof. zoology U. Ill., Urbana, 1954-64, prof., head dept. biol. scis. Chgo. Circle, 1964-69; dir. systematic zoology NSF, 1969-70; prof., chmn. dept. zoology U. Md., College Park, 1970-87, prof., 1987-89, emeritus prof., 1989—. Adj. prof. U. N.Mex., Albuquerque, 1988-96; hon. rsch. assoc. zoology Univ. Coll., London, 1960-61; vis. prof. zoology U. Exeter, Eng., 1961-62; vis. prof. protozoology, Shanghai, China, 1980, 86, Geneva, 1980; mem. panel systematic biology NSF, 1966-69; active Nat. Com. Internat. Biol. program, 1966-68; mem. Internat. Commn. on Zool. Nomenclature, 1972-96, mem. corp. Marine Biol. Lab., Woods Hole, Mass. Author: The Ciliate Protozoa, 1961, 2d edit., 1979; joint editor 5 books on protistology, 1984-91; contbr. articles on protozoology/protistology to profl. jours. Served to capt. USAAF, 1943-46. Fellow AAAS, Am. Inst. Biol. Scis., Am. Acad. Microbiology; mem. Soc. Protozoologists (past pres, mem. editl. bd., past editor), Am. Micros. Soc. (past editor, past pres.), Am. Zool. Soc. (hon.), French Zool. Soc. (hon.), Spanish Zool. Soc. (hon.), Mexican Zool. Soc. (hon.), Italian Zool. Soc. (hon.), Coun. Biology Editors (past chmn., CBE Meritorious award 1982), Am. Soc. Zoologists (past pres.), Soc. Systematic Zoology (past pres.), Am. Soc. Parasitologists, Am. Soc. Microbiology (U.S. Fedn. Culture Collections/J. Roger Porter award 1994), Internat. Congress Systematic and Evolutionary Biology (convenor 1970-74, 76-80), Internat. Union Biol. Scis. (chmn. U.S. nat. com. 1971-73), numerous others. Home: 730 Yale Rd Bala Cynwyd PA 19004-2116 Address: PO Box 2729 Bala Cynwyd PA 19004-6729 E-mail: jocchezmoi@aol.com.

CORMAN, EUGENE HAROLD, motion picture producer; b. Detroit, Sept. 24, 1927; s. William and Anne (High) C.; m. Nan Chandler Morris, Sept. 4, 1955; children: Todd William, Craig Allan. BA, Stanford U., 1948. Vice-pres. Music Corp. Am., Beverly Hills, Calif., 1950-57; owner, operator Corman Co., Beverly Hills, 1957—; pres. Penelope Prodn. Inc., Los Angeles, 1965—, Chateau Prodn. Inc., Los Angeles, 1972—; v.p. 20th Century Fox TV, Beverly Hills; exec. v.p. 21st Century Film Corp. of Worldwide Prodn. Producer: The Big Red One, 1978-79, F.I.S.T, 1977-78. Recipient Emmy award for A Woman Called Golda, Cath. Christopher award for A Woman Called Golda Mem. Acad. Motion Picture Arts and Scis., TV Acad. Arts and Scis., Los Angeles County Mus. Art (patron), Beverly Hills Tennis Club, Theta Delta Chi. Roman Catholic. Office: 20th Century Fox TV PO Box 900 Beverly Hills CA 90213-0900

CORMAN, LOURDES C. physician, educator; b. Havana, Cuba, Dec. 29, 1944; m. Norman Ackerman, Jan. 3, 1977; children: Tiffany, Anthony. MD, Woman's Med. Coll. Pa., 1970. Diplomate Am. Bd. Internal Medicine, Am. Bd. Rheumatology, Am. Bd. Geriatrics. Asst. prof. dept. medicine U. Fla., Gainesville, 1979-86, assoc. prof., 1986-95; prof., vice chair dept. medicine U. Louisville, 1995-99; prof., dir. divsn. internal medicine U. Ala.-Birmingham,

Huntsville, 1999—. Recipient award Alpha Omega Alpha, 1970. Fellow ACP, Am. Coll. Rheumatology. Office: UAB Sch Medicine Huntsville Regional Med Campus 301 Governors Dr SW Rm 389 Huntsville AL 35801-4326 E-mail: spicerj@uasomh.uab.edu.

CORMAN, RANDY, lawyer; b. El Paso, Tex., Sept. 24, 1960; s. Theodore Howard and Joan (Golaszewski) C.; m. Kathleen Glynn, July 27, 1996; children: William Joseph, Justin Ryan, Bridget Alexandra, Maura Elizabeth. BA, Rutgers U., 1982; JD, Rutgers U., Newark, 1985. Bar: N.J. 1985. Assoc. counsel State Senate Rep. Staff, Trenton, N.J., 1986-92; state senator N.J. Senate, Trenton, 1992-94; of counsel Donington, Karcher, Salmond, Ronan and Rainone, Edison, N.J., 1994-95, Karcher and Rainone, Sayreville, 1996-97; dir. law N.J. Turnpike Authority, New Brunswick, 1997—2002; exec. dir. Sayreville Econ. and Redevelopment Agency, 2002—. Counsel Perth Amboy City Coun., 1995-96; borough atty. Borough of Spotswood, 1996-97; vice chmn. Senate Environment Com., 1992-94; spl. counsel Howell Twp., 2002-; adj. prof. Berkeley (Calif.) Coll., 2002—. Mem. Bd. of Edn., Sayreville, N.J., 1980-84; councilman Borough of Sayreville, 1985-92; chmn. Sayreville Rep. Com., 1986-87, 94-98; trustee St. Stanislaus Kostka Roman Cath. parish, 1998—. Decorated knight comdr. Order of Merit of St. Angilbert, knight comdr. Order of Noble Companions of the Swan, knight Order of Merit of the Bear of Alabona. Mem. Phi Beta Kappa. Republican. Roman Catholic. Office: Sayreville Econ & Redevelopment Agency 167 Main St Sayreville NJ 08872

CORMAN, ROGER WILLIAM, motion picture producer, director; b. Detroit, Apr. 5, 1926; s. William and Anne C.; m. Julie Ann Halloran, Dec. 26, 1970; children: Catherine Ann, Roger Martin, Brian William, Mary Tessa AB, Stanford, 1947; postgrad., Oxford (Eng.) U., 1950; D in Fine Arts (hon.), Am. Film Inst., 1998. Founder, pres. New World Pictures, 1970-83, Concorde-New Horizons Corp., 1983—. Prodr.: Carnosaur, The Fantastic Four, I Never Promised You a Rose Garden, St. Jack, Battle Beyond the Stars, Deathrace 2000, Piranha, Avalanche, Munchies, Crime Zone, The Terror Within, Black Scorpion, others; dir.: Five Guns West, 1955; prodr., dir.: The Intruder, Fall of the House of Usher, Masque of the Red Death, Machine Gun Kelly, Little Shop of Horrors, The Trip, The Man with X Ray Eyes, Von Richthofen and Brown, Frankenstein Unbound, 1980, others; distbr.: Cries and Whispers, Autumn Sonata, Amarcord, Small Change, The Tin Drum, Cabeza de Vaca, others; films shown at numerous film festivals; prodr., dir., screenwriter: Roger Corman's Frankenstein Unbound; exec. prodr.: Hollywood Boulevard, Rock and Roll High School, Avalanche Alley, Firefight, Fire OVer Afghanistan; actor Silence of the Lambs, The Godfather, Part II, Philadelphia, Apollo 13, Looney Tunes-Back in Action. Recipient Grand prize Venice Film Festival, 1979, Lifetime Achievement award L.A. Film Critics, 1997, 1st Prodrs. of Century award Cannes Film Festival, 1998, Lifetime Achievement award Am. Film Market, 2001. Mem. Producers Guild Am., Dirs. Guild Am. Office: Concorde-New Horizons Corp 11600 San Vicente Blvd Los Angeles CA 90049-5102

CORMIER, JEAN G. communications company executive; b. Campbellton, N.B., Can., May 3, 1941; s. Simon and Leona (Arsenault) C.; m. Helen Morrison, Sept. 9, 1965; children: Paul, Michel. BA in Philosophy, Bathurst Coll., N.B., 1963; postgrad., McMaster U., Hamilton, Ont., Can., 1963-64. Dir. pub. affairs Dofasco, Hamilton, 1970-75; v.p. pub. rels. Can. Nat., Montreal, Que., Can., 1975-79; pres. CN Hotels and Tower, Montreal, 1979-81; sr. v.p. corp. affairs B.C. Resources Investment Corp., Vancouver, Can., 1981-86; pres. Cormier Communicators, Inc., Vancouver, 1986—. Contbr. articles to profl. jours. Fellow Internat. Assn. Bus. Communicators (bd. dirs. 1983-89, past chmn. 1987-88); mem. Can. Pub. Rels. Soc. (accredited), Vancouver Club, Marine Dr. Golf Club (pres. 1999, 2000). Roman Catholic. Avocation: photography. Office: Cormier Communicators Inc 1050 W Pender St Ste 910 Vancouver BC Canada V6E 2N7

CORN, MILTON, academic dean, physician; b. Berlin, Jan. 17, 1928; came to U.S., 1934; m. Gilan Akbar Tocco; children: Stephanie, Sarah, Paul, Rhoya Tocco. BS with highest honors, Yale U., 1952, MD with highest honors, 1955. Diplomate Nat. Bd. Med. Examiners, Am. Bd. Internal Medicine, Am. Bd. Hematology. Intern then resident Peter Bent Brigham Hosp., Boston, 1955-58; fellow in hematology Johns Hospkins Sch. Med., Balt., 1958-60; asst. prof. medicine Seton Hall Coll. Medicine, 1960-63; from asst. to assoc. prof. medicine George Washington U., 1963-72, prof. medicine, 1972-73; chief of hematology D.C. Gen. Hosp. div. George Washington U., 1963-73, chief of medicine, 1970-73; dir. blood bank and emergency dept. Geogetown U., Washington, 1973-78; dir. clerkship jr. medicine, dir. med. residency tng. program Georgetown U., Washington, 1978-84, also vice chmn. medicine, 1978-84, assoc. dean hosp. liaison, 1984, med. dir. hosp., 1984-85; dean Sch. Medicine, Georgetown U., Washington, 1985-89; dir. Office of Clin. Informatics Georgetown U. Med. Ctr., Washington, 1989-90; spl. cons. to dir. Nat. Libr. Medicine, 1990—, assoc. dir. extramural programs, 1990—. Dir. med. edn., hematologist St. Michael's Hosp., Newark, 1960-63; cons. hematology FDA, 1978—; chief physician Cath. Relief Svcs. Refugee Capt, Thailand, 1981, 83; regional dir. rev. courses CX ACP, 1981-87; mem. UN Relief and Works Agy. Inspection Team for Palestinian Refugee Camps, 1984; guest lectr. U. Southampton, Eng., 1981; keynote speaker India Med. Soc., New Delhi, 1985. Co-editor Hematology Revs., 1984— ; contbr. articles to profl. publs. Recipient Golden Apple award Georgetown U. Student Med. Assn., 1971, 83, Teaching award Kaiser Permanente, 1983, Maimonides award Anti Defamation League, 1989. Home: 6404 Goldleaf Dr Bethesda MD 20817-5830 Office: Nat Libr Medicine NIH Biomed Comms Bethesda MD 20894-0001

CORN, MORTON, environmental engineer, educator; b. N.Y.C., Oct. 18, 1933; s. Julius and Sophie (Haber) C.; m. Jacqueline Karnell, Aug. 21, 1955; children: Matthew Irwin, Frederick Eliot. BS in Chem. Engring., Cooper Union, 1955; MS, Harvard U., 1956, PhD, 1961. Asst. san. engr. USPHS, Cin., 1956-58; rsch. assoc. Harvard, 1960-61; asst. prof. U. Pitts., 1962-65, assoc. prof., 1965-66, prof. Grad. Sch. Pub. Health and Sch. Engring., 1967-79; prof. and divsn. head environ. health engring. Sch. Hygiene and Public Health, Johns Hopkins U., Balt., 1980-97; prof. emeritus Johns Hopkins U., Balt., 1997—; pres. Morton Corn; Assocs., Cons. Engrs., 1977—. Cons. divsn. biology and medicine AEC, 1965—74; chmn. air pollution rsch. grants com. EPA, 1968—71, mem. sci. adv. bd., 1978—84; mem. com. no biol. effects air pollution NAS, 1971, mem. com. risk assessment, 1982—83; mem. expert panel occupl. health WHO, 1973—98; asst. sec. labor for occupl. safety and health U.S. Dept. Labor, 1975—77; mem. Allegheny County Air Pollution Adv. Com., 1967—72; mem. nat. adv. com. health vital stats. Dept. HHS, 1979—81; mine health rsch. adv. com. Nat. Inst. Occupl. Safety and Health, 1986—89, GM/UAW joint health and safety adv. com., 1988—92; chmn. OTA Commn. Preventing Injury and Illness in the Workplace, 1982—84; chmn. tech. adv. bd. Clean Sites, Inc., Alexandria, Va., 1984—87; trustee Assoc. Univ., Inc., 1991—93; mem. Hanford tank adv. panel DOE, 1993—99; cons. Health, Safety and Environment, 1993. Chmn. Gov. of Md.'s Toxic Coun., 1986-89. NSF postdoctoral fellow U. London, 1961-62; WHO fellow, 1970; Guggenheim fellow, 1972 Fellow APHA; mem. Am. Soc. Safety Engrs., Am. Indsl. Hygiene Assn. (bd. dirs. 2000-03), Am. Conf. Govt. Indsl. Hygienists (chmn. 1983-84). Home and Office: Morton Corn Assocs Inc 3208 Bennett Point Rd Queenstown MD 21658-1126 E-mail: mjcorn@friend.ly.net.

CORNABY, KAY STERLING, lawyer, former state senator; b. Spanish Fork, Utah, Jan. 14, 1936; s. Sterling A. and Hilda G. Cornaby; m. Linda Rasmussen, July 23, 1965; children: Alyse, Derek, Tara, Heather, Brandon. AB, Brigham Young U., 1960; postgrad. law, Heidelberg, Germany, 1961-63; JD, Harvard U., 1966. Bar: NY 1967, Utah 1969, U.S. Patent and Trademark Office 1967. Assoc. Brumbaugh, Graves, Donahue & Raymond, N.Y.C., 1966-69; ptnr. Mallinckrodt & Cornaby, Salt Lake City, 1969-72; sole practice Salt Lake City, 1972-85; mem. Utah State Senate, 1977-91, majority leader, 1983-84; shareholder Jones, Waldo, Holbrook & McDonough, Salt Lake City, 1985—. Mem. Nat. Commn. on Uniform State Laws, 1988-93; mem. adv. bd. U. Mich. Ctr. for Study of Youth Policy,1990-93; mem. Utah State Jud. Conduct Commn., 1983-91, chmn., 1984-85; bd. dirs. KUED-KUER Pub. TV and Radio, 1982-88; bd. dirs. Salt Lake Conv. and Visitors Bur., 1985—. Mem. N.Y. Bar Assn., Utah Bar Assn., Utah Harvard Alumni Assn. (pres. 1977-79), Harvard U. Law Sch. Alumni Assn. (pres. 1995—). Office: Jones Waldo Holbrook & McDonough Ste 1500 170 S Main St Salt Lake City UT 84101-1644

CORNACCHIO, JOSEPH VINCENT, engineering educator, computer researcher, consultant; b. N.Y.C., Dec. 27, 1934; s. Vincent and Elena (Vuolo) C.; m. Carole Ester Taber, Aug. 27, 1960; children: Karen Marie, Kevin Joseph. BSEE, Pa. State U., 1956; MEE, Syracuse U., 1959, PhD, 1962. Adv. engr. IBM, Endicott, N.Y., 1962-72; postdoctoral fellow, 1965; assoc. prof. engring. SUNY, Binghamton, 1972-74, prof., 1974—, dept. chmn., 1981=84. Cons. ptnr. Usability Svcs,m Binghamton, 1982—; cons. N.Y. Dept. Commerce, Albany, N.Y., 1978-80, N.Y.-Pa. Health Plan, Binghamton, 1975-76. Editor, author Sys. Complexity Jour., 1976; contbr. articles to profl. jours.; patentee in field. Bd. dirs. Am. Arthritis Assn., Binghamton, 1980—. Grantee SUNY, 1971, State of N.Y., 1977-78. Mem. IEEE (chpt. pres. 1974-75), Assn. for Computing Machinery, Mark Tawin Soc., Danforth Found. (assoc.). Home: 3120 Belmont Ave Vestal NY 13850-2802 Office: SUNY Dept Engring Binghamton NY 13901 E-mail: jvc@binghamton.edu.

CORNATZER, WILLIAM EUGENE, retired biochemistry educator; b. Mocksville, N.C., Sept. 23, 1918; s. William Pinkston and Stella Augusta (Vogler) C.; m. Margaret Virginia Freeman, Mar. 30, 1946; children— Nancy Freeman, MD, William Eugene, MD. Student, Mars Hill Coll., 1935-37; BS, Wake Forest Coll., 1939; MS, U. N.C., 1941, PhD, 1944; postgrad., Oak Ridge Inst. Nuclear Studies, 1948; MD, Bowman Gray Sch. Medicine, 1951; DSc (hon.), Univ. N. Dak., 1992. Student asst. zoology Wake Forest Coll., 1937-38, Wake Forest Coll. (phys. chemistry), 1938-39; grad. and student asst. biol. and food chemistry U. N.C., 1939-41, Fels Research fellow, 1941-45; asst. prof. biochemistry Bowman Gray Sch. Medicine, 1946-51; prof., head dept. biochemistry med. sch. U. N.D., Grand Forks, 1951-83, Chester Fritz disting. prof., 1973—, Univ. prof., 1983, prof. emeritus, 1983—; also dir. Ireland Rsch. Lab. Mem. biochem. test com. Nat. Bd. Med. Examiners; mem. White Ho. Com. for Orgn. Conf. on Food, Nutrition and Health, 1969 Mem. bd. editors: Jour. Clin. Chemistry, 1971-81; mem. editorial bd.: Jour. Nutrition, 1975-79; author: Clinical Significances of Laboratory Tests, 1986, The Role Of Nutrition In Health And Disease, 1989; contbr. articles sci. jours. Recipient Frank Billing award for original investigation; Silver medal AMA, 1951; Nat. Scis. Travel award to Internat. Congress Biochemistry Paris, 1952; Nat. Scis. Travel award to Internat. Congress Biochemistry Tokyo, 1967; travel award Internat. Congress Cancer, London, Eng.; travel award Am. Assn. for Cancer Research, 1958; travel award to 1st Internat. Congress Pharmacology Stockholm, 1961; travel award to Internat. Union Physiol. Sci.; NSF Travel award to 7th Internat. Congress Biochemistry, Tokyo, 1967; travel award 8th Internat. Congress Nutrition; travel award Am. Inst. Nutrition, Prague, 1969; travel award 9th Congress, Mex., 1972; Distinguished Service award U. N.C., 1970; Outstanding Sci. Research award U. N.D. chpt. Sigma Xi, 1970; Distinguished Alumnus award Bowman Gray Med. Sch., 1976 Fellow ACP, N.Y. Acad. Scis., Am. Inst. Chemists, AAAS; mem. Am. Assn. Oil Chemists, Nat. Acad. Clin. Chemistry, Am. Bd. Clin. Chemistry (dir.), Am. Assn. Clin. Chemists (nat. exec. com. 1957), Am. Assn. for Study of Liver Disease, Ctrl. Soc. for Clin. Rsch., Radiation Rsch. Soc., Am. Chem. Soc., Am. Soc. Biol. Chemistry, So. Soc. for Clin. Rsch., Am. Fedn. for Clin. Rsch., Soc. Exptl. Biology and Medicine, AAUP, Am. Inst. Nutrition, Elisha Mitchell Sci. Soc., N.D. Acad. Scis. (pres. 1956), N.D. Diabetic Assn., Royal Soc. Medicine. Baptist. Achievements include research in properties of proteins, quinine metabolism, anti-malarial testing, phospholipide metabolism, radioactive isotopes, biol. effects of radiation. Home: 1810 Edgemere Ct SE Huntsville AL 35803-3634 *Faith in yourself and your Creator/Positive thinking/High Objectives/Hard work.*

CORNELISON, FLOYD SHOVINGTON, JR., retired psychiatrist, former educator; b. San Angelo, Tex., Apr. 30, 1918; s. Floyd Shovington and Nannie Lee (Brewer) C.; m. Erwina Ladelle Bode, Aug. 30, 1940 (div. 1966); 1 child, Ann Brewer; m. Ruth Reeder Williams, Sept. 17, 1966. BA, Baylor U., 1939; postgrad., Northwestern U., 1939-40, Columbia U., 1943-45; MD, Cornell U., 1950; MS, Boston U., 1958. Diplomate Am. Bd. Psychiatry and Neurology. Intern Grasslands Hosp., Valhalla, N.Y., 1950-51; resident in psychiatry Mass. Meml. Hosp., Boston U. Sch. Medicine, also Boston State Hosp., 1951-54; from asst. in psychiatry to instr. Boston U. Sch. Medicine, 1951-58; lectr. psychology Tufts Coll., 1954-56; successively asst. prof., assoc. prof., cons. prof. psychiatry U. Okla. Sch. Medicine, 1958-64; prof. psychiatry Jefferson Med. Coll., Thomas Jefferson U., Phila., 1962-83, hon. prof., 1983—, chmn. dept., 1962-74; past mem. staff numerous hosps.; med. staff Wilmington Med Center; cons. area hosps., 1962—. Med. dir. Freedom From Fear, Inc., 1980-83; dir. Marka T. du Pont Inst. Human Behavior, Wilmington, Del., 1971-75; initiated self-image experience, photog. confrontation technique in psychiat. rsch. Author articles; prodr. films in field. Fellow psychiat. films Med. Audio-Visual Inst., Assn. Am. Med. Colls., 1951-53; candidate Boston Psychoanalytic Inst., 1954-58 Fellow Am. Coll. Psychiatrists (emeritus), Am. Psychiat. Assn. (life), Royal Australian and New Zealand Coll. Psychiatrists (hon.); mem. AMA, Del. Psychiat. Soc., Del. County Med. Soc., New Castle County Med. Soc., Sigma Xi. Home and Office: 16 Stone Hill Rd Wilmington DE 19803-4411

CORNELISON, SALLY J. art historian; b. Columbia, Mo., Sept. 11, 1965; d. Wilson Dale Cornelison and Joan Marie Hathman. BA, U. of Mo., 1983—88; MA, Syracuse U., 1988—92; PhD, Courtauld Inst.of Art, 1994—98. Asst. prof. Va. Tech, 2000—02, U. of Kans., 2002—. Contbr. chapters to books, articles to profl. jours. Humanities Summer grant, Coll. of Arts and Sciences, Va. Tech, 2000, Postgraduate studentship (scholarship), Courtauld Inst. of Art, 1995, 1996, 1997, Florence fellowship, Syracuse U., 1988—89. Mem.: SE Coll. Art Conf., Renaissance Soc. of Am., Italian Art Soc., Coll. Art Assn.

CORNELISSEN, GERMAINE, physicist, educator; BS in Physics, Free U., Brussels, 1969, MEd in Sci., MS in Physics, Free U., Brussels, 1971, PhD in Physics, 1976. Tchr. Lycée Emile Max, 1971—73; rsch. fellow IRSIA, U. Brussels, 1974—76; internat. visitor U. Minn., Mpls., 1975, vis. rsch. fellow Chronobiology Labs./Ctr., 1976—79, rsch. fellow, 1979—82, rsch. assoc., 1982—91, asst. prof., 1987—92, assoc. dir., 1987—92, sr. rsch. assoc. dept. lab. medicine and pathology, 1992—93, sr. rsch. assoc. dept. pediats., 1994—, dir. biometry, chronobiology labs. dept. lab. medicine and pathology, 1992—93, 1994—. Coord. Internat. Womb to Tomb Chronome Initiative Group; sec. N.Am. br. Internat. Soc. for Rsch. on Civilization Diseases and the Environment, 1987—, mem. sci. coun., 1987—; bd. dirs. Underlab Project, Pioneer Frontier Explorations and Rsch. s.r.l., Ancona, Italy. Mem. editl. bd. Chronobiologia, 1989—91; co-editor: Chronobiologia, 1991—94; mem. editl. bd. Il Policlinico, 1991—96, assoc. editor Procs. Workshop on Computer Methods on Chronobiology and Chronomedicine, 1990; contbr. Recipient Chronobiologia award, 1983. Mem.: IEEE, AAAS, Acad. Integrative Anthropology, Cardiac Electrophysiology Soc., Internat. Soc. for Study of Comparative Oncology, Am. Statis.. Assn., Biometric Soc., Soc. for Indsl. and Applied Math., Am. Phys. Soc., Internat. Soc. Chronobiology (bd. dirs. 1985—95), Groupe d'Etude des Rythmes Biologiques, Societé Belge de Physique, Sigma Xi. Office: Univ of Minnesota Halberg Chronobiology Ctr Minneapolis MN 55455

CORNELIUS, ALETA, artist, designer, restorer, educator, judge; b. Pittsburgh, PA, Mar. 21, 1922; d. James Alvin and Ethel Aleta (Lewis) Cornelius; children: Ethel Aleta, James Alvin; m. Walter S. Eastman, Oct. 1992. Stud. in painting & design, Carnegie Mellon Univ., Pittsburgh, PA. Sec., dir. PIttsburgh Associated Artists, Pittsburgh, PA, 1948-53; tchr. (painting) YWCA, Pittsburgh, PA, Providence, RI; art tchr. Rocky Hill Country Day, East Greenwich, RI; owner Pvt. Art Gall., Providence; curator Hyannis Art Assn., Cape Cod, MA; art dir. Dahl, Orresman, Morgan, Mousey, RI, 1963-72; freelance painter & restorer Aleta Cornelius Studio, Flagler beach, Fla., 1972—. Chartered pres., hon. mem. Flagler County Counc. for the Arts, 1989; logo designer, catalog designer, Fla. Artists Grp., judge, art shows, restoration and appraisals, Grps. in South and North East, 1954-90, 1970—, appointed grant panel, Fla. Arts Counc., Tallahassee, 1991-92, served as judge and juror for many art exhbns. Designer, (book cover) Little Brown, Kind Hearted Tiger, 1955, (catalog and layout) Fla. Artists Grp., 1979, (logo) numerous grps., 1985, 93; one man shows: Attleboro Mus., MA, Providence Art Club, Cape Cod Art Assn. Gall., Gal. Internat., NY; exhibitions: Am. Acad. of Arts and Letters, NY, Whitney Annual, NY, Metropolitan Mus., NY, Carnegie Inst., Pittsburgh, PA, Carnegie Inst. summer show, Pitsburgh, PA, Attleboro Mus., Attleboro, MA; juried shows: Corcoran, Wash., D.C., Pepsi-Cola, Nat. Acad. of Design, NY, (Achievement award), Butler Art Mus., OH, Boston Arts Festival, Rhode Island Arts Festival (1st prize), Nat. Acad. of Design, New England Artists - Jordan Marsh, Fla, Artists Grp.; contbr. articles to profl. publications. Mem. Presdl. Task Force, Republican Party, Wash., 2000, Nat. Com., Republican Party, Wash., 2000, Senatorial Com., Republican Party, Wash., 2000, Fla. and Flagler County, Republican Party, Wash., 2000; apptd. grant arts coun. Sec. of State of Fla., 1991-92. Recipient Kappa Kappa Gamma Pi Timne Achievement Awd., Hot Spgs., VA, 1952, Childe Hassam Purchase Awd., Am. Acad. of Arts & Letters, NY, 1960, First Prize R.I. Art Festival, Providence Jour. and City, R.I., 1960, Life Mag. 19 Am. Artists, Life Mag., 1951-52, many awards Pitts. Assn. Artists shows, Purchase award 100 Friends of Pitts. Art, many others; named Hon. Alumnus Carnegie Mellon U., 2000. Mem. (hon.), charter pres., Flagler County Coun. for the Arts (life), 1989-2000, Kappa Kappa Gamma. Republican. Baptist. Home: 2017 N Daytona Ave Flagler Beach FL 32136-2835

CORNELIUS, JACQUELYN H. high school principal, educator; b. Jacksonville, Fla., Feb. 26, 1948; d. Jack Allen and Dorothy Mae Henson; m. Carey Michael Cornelius, May 21, 1982; children: Amber, Heather. BA, U. Fla., 1970; MEd, U. No. Fla., 1984. Eng. tchr. Forrest High Sch., Jacksonville, 1970-84, asst. prin., 1984-87; arts dir. Douglas Anderson Sch. of the Arts, Jacksonville, 1988-95, prin., 1996—. Vis. evaluation team mem. So. Accreditation of Colls. and Schs., 1989—; dir. Fla. Edn. Found., 1991-95; spkr. in field; bd. dirs. Fla. Women's Consortium, Duval County Assn. Secondary Sch. Adminstrs., Fla. Fedn. Bus. and Profl. Women, Inc., The Fla. Women's Alliance. Choreographer, host pub. TV. programs Inside Your Schs., The Hearing Impaired: The Creative Tchr., Testing: Pros and Cons. Active Jacksonville Symphony Edn. com., 1999—, Theatre Jacksonville, 1991—; mem. Mayor's Insight com., 1993-94, Mayor's Task Force on Domestic Violence, 1997-98; bd. dirs. Gateway Girl Scout Coun., 1991-94, Youth Leadership Jacksonville, 1992-94, Cultural Coun. Greater Jacksonville, 1998—. Recipient Excellence award Fla. Commr. of Edn., 1988, Arts Educator award Jacksonville Arts Assembly, 1995. Mem. Nat. Network of Performing and Visual Arts Schs. (treas., nominating chair arts advocacy com., arts achievement chair, southeast regional publicity chair), Nat. Assn. Secondary Sch. Prins. (Fla. chpt.), Jacksonville Women's Network, Bus. and Profl. Women's Club (First Coast, River City chpts., pres. 1995, vol. chair, jr. civitan com., mem. chair, program chair, ace com.), Jacksonville Rotary (internat. edn. chair, publicity com., charity com.). Avocations: travel, reading. Home: 4103 Cedar Rd Orange Park FL 32065-6903 Office: Douglas Anderson Sch of Arts 2445 San Diego Rd Jacksonville FL 32207-3699 E-mail: cornelius@educationcentral.org.

CORNELIUS, JEFFREY MICHAEL, music educator; b. Chgo., Apr. 26, 1943; s. George Edward and Helen (Benjamin) C.; m. Betty Wallace, June 10, 1967; children: Benjamin Michael, Lisa Louise. BA, King Col., 1965; B in Music magna cum laude, Westminster Choir Col., 1970; M in Music, Temple U., 1972, EdD, 1986. Tchr. Bristol Tenn. Sch. Sys., 1965-68; adj. music instr. Mercer County C.C., Trenton, N.J., 1970-71; music instr. La Salle Col., Phila., 1971-72; music prof. Temple U., Phila., 1972—, dean Esther Boyer Coll. Music, 1993-2001. Condr., adjudicator Music Educators Assn., Eastern States, 1989—; adv. bd. Phila. Ave. Arts, 1993—2001, Sta. WRTI, Pa., 1994-96 Choral singer with numerous major orchs. including Phila. Orch., N.Y. Philharmonic, L.A. Philharmonic, Am. Symphony Orch., 1968—; contbr. articles to profl. jours. Cons. City of Phila., 1992; panel member City of Phila. Cultural Fund, 1993-96; bd. dirs. Singing City, Phila., 1987-90, The Presser Found., 2003—. Recipient Cert. of Merit Temple U. Alumni Assn., 1981. Mem. Am. Choral Dirs. (Pa. chpt., pres. 1984-86), Music Educators Nat. Conf., Musical Fund Soc. Phila. (v.p. 1999-2001), Nat. Assn. Schs. Music (evaluator 1994-2001), Nat. Soc. Sci. Honor Soc., Pi Kappa Lambda. Avocations: photography, travel, history. Office: Temple U Esther Boyer Coll Music Philadelphia PA 19122

CORNELIUS, PETER KLAUS, economist; b. Hannover, Germany, June 10, 1960; s. Guenter and Ursula (Wallossek) C.; m. Heike Hoefer, Sept. 19, 1997. Vordiplom, U. Hannover, Fed. Republic Germany, 1981; student, London Sch. Econs., 1983; diploma in econs., U. Goettingen, Fed. Republic Germany, 1985; D. in Polit. Sci., U. Goettingen, 1987. Trainee UN Indsl. Devel. Orgn., Vienna, 1982; economist German Coun. Econ. Experts, Wiesbaden, Fed. Republic Germany, 1987-89, IMF, Washington, 1989-96; chief internat. economist Deutsche Bank, Frankfurt, Germany, 1996-99; vis. scholar Harvard U., Cambridge, 1999-2000; adj. prof. Brandeis U., 2000; dir. Global Competetiveness Program World Econ. Forum, 2000—03; head econ. rsch. Shell Internat., London, 2003—. Vis. lectr. Wissenschaftliche Hochschule fuer Unternehmens Fuehrung Sch. Mgmt., Koblenz, Germany. Author: Das Prinzip der Konditionalitaet, 1988; co-author: The Impact of the EC's Internal Market on the EFTA; co-editor: Ukraine-Transition to Market, 1997, European Monetary Union, Emerging Markets, and Econometric Issues in International Finance, 2000, Africa Competitiveness Report, 2000, Global Competitiveness Report, 2000, 01, Global Information and Communication Technology Report, Latin American Competitiveness Report, 2001, Arab World Competitiveness Report, Corporate Governance and Capital Flows in a Global Economy; contbr. articles to profl. jours. Mem. London Sch. Econs. Soc., Am. Econ. Assn., Am. Fin. Assn., Verein Fuer Social Politik. Lutheran. Avocations: tennis, squash. Home: North End House 129 Fitzjames Ave London W14 0RZ England Office: Shell International Shell Centre London England E-mail: peter.cornelius@shell.com.

CORNELIUS, RICHARD MEREDITH, English language educator; b. Phila., May 18, 1934; s. Frederick Meredith Cornelius and Elizabeth Marie Yahraes; m. Donna Jean Black, Aug. 15, 1959; children: Craig Alan, Crista Lynn. BA, William Jennings Bryan Coll., 1955; MA, U. Tenn., 1961, PhD, 1971. Tchr. Beulah Beal Elem. Sch., Jacksonville, Fla., 1957-58; prof. English William Jennings Bryan Coll., Dayton, Tenn., 1961-99, W.J. Bryan/Scopes trial liaison, archivist, 1978—, prof. English emeritus, 1999—. Adj. prof. Chattanooga State Tech. C.C., 2000-01, chmn. English dept. William Jennings Bryan Coll., Dayton, 1962-76, 91-99, chair divsn. lit. and modern langs., 1974-76, 90-91, faculty chmn., 1979-80; guest lectr. U. Tenn., Knoxville, 1991, The Citadel, Charleston, S.C., 1991, Natchez (Miss.) Nat. Literary Celebration, 2000, Maryville (Tenn.) Coll., 1998, Conf. Am. Coll. Family Trial Lawyers, New Orleans, 1998, Cedarville (Ohio) U., 2002, Jilin U., Changchun, China, 2002; exhibit designer U. Tenn. Theater, Knoxville, 2001, Cedarville Univ. Theater, 2002, Bryan Coll., 1986—; presenter and cons. in field. Author: Christopher Marlowe's Use of the Bible, 1984, (booklet) Understanding William Jennings Bryan and the Scopes Trial: A Study Guide, 1998; editor: (books) Dandilines, 1971-87, Legacy of Faith: The Story of Bryan College, 1995, Selected Orations of William Jennings Bryan, 1996, 2000; editor, author: (book) Impact: The Scopes Trial, 2000, (booklet) Selected, Annotated Bibliography of William Jennings Bryan, the Scopes Trial, Creation, and Evolution, 1993, 4th edit., 2001; TV appearances include The History Channel, 1998, Sta. WTCI-TV 45 (PBS), 2001, Coral Ridge Ministries, 1988; contbr. articles to profl. publs. and chpts. to books. Co-founder, mem. Scopes Trial Festival Com., Dayton, 1988—; co-chmn. Scopes Trial Festival Symposia, Dayton, 1995-98, 2000, 02; dir. Scopes Trial Trail Markers Project, Dayton, 1995—; mem. bd. elders Grace Bible Ch., Dayton, 1962-99, 2000-03; mem. Rhea County Hist. and Geneal. Soc.; mem. Southeastern Conf. on Christianity and Lit., 1979—, chmn., 1979-80. Summer workshop grantee Christian Coll. Coalition/NEH, 1983, 88, 89, Tenn. Assn. Museums/Humanities Tenn., 2003. Mem. MLA, Nat. Coun. Tchrs. English, South Atlantic MLA, Tenn. Assn. Museums. Republican. Evangelical Christian. Avocations: creative writing, photography. Home: 311 Cedar Ln Dayton TN 37321-6234 Office: Bryan Coll Box 7591 721 Bryan Dr Dayton TN 37321-7000 E-mail: cornelri@bryan.edu.

CORNELIUS, WAYNE ANDERSON, electrical and computer engineering consultant; b. Russellville, Ky., Nov. 8, 1923; s. Eldon and Mabel Ruth (Gentle) C.; m. Elizabeth Grider (dec. Sept. 1946); children: Johanna Vastola, Keith, John(dec.); m. Linda Brady, Apr. 27, 1985; stepchildren: Pam Gondzur, Mark Smith, Todd Smith, Allison Stines. BS, U. Ky., 1953, EE, 1966; MS, U. Louisville, 1962; ABD, U. Cin., 1972. Elec. engr. U.S. Naval Ordnance Sta., Louisville, 1953-66, dir. engring. electronics lab., 1973-85; rsch. assoc. Pa. State U., State College, 1966-67; prof. engring. tech. Miami U., Oxford, Ohio, 1967-72; elec. engr. System Devel. Corp., Dayton, Ohio, 1972-73; chmn. dept. electronics tech. Ivy Tech. Coll., Sellersburg, Ind., 1985-90. Adj. prof. elec. engring. tech. Purdue U., New Albany, 1992-95, U. Louisville, 1976-84; adj. prof. math. Bellarmine Coll., Louisville, 1964-66, Ind. U., New Albany, 1990-91. With USN, 1942-45. Named to Honorable Order of Ky. Cols., 1963. Mem. NSPE, Am. Soc. for Engring. Edn., Phi Delta Kappa. Democrat. Presbyterian. Office: 9005 Lethborough Dr Louisville KY 40299-1437 E-mail: lbcwac@prodigy.net.

CORNELL, CARL ALLIN, civil engineering educator; b. Mobridge, S.D., Sept. 19, 1938; s. Homer Carl and Opal Loss (Allinson) C.; m. Elizabeth Ann Peabody, Dec. 30, 1959 (div. 1979); children— Eric Allin, Robert Aaron, Joan Elizabeth; m. Marie-Elisabeth Pate, Jan. 4, 1981; children— Phillip Edouard, Ariane Ilse. BA in Pre-Architecture, Stanford U., Calif., 1960, MS in Civil Engring., 1961, PhD, 1964. Asst. prof. engring. Stanford U., Calif., 1963-64; asst. prof. to prof. engring. MIT, Cambridge, 1964-83; research prof. civil engring. Stanford U., Calif., 1983—. Cons. engr. CAC Inc., Portola Valley, Calif., 1981— ; sr. v.p. Cygna Inc., San Francisco, 1984-85. Co-author: Probability, Statistics and Decision for Civil Engineers, 1970. Contbr. articles to profl. jours. Fulbright Found. and Guggenheim fellow, 1974-75. Mem. Nat. Acad. Engring., ASCE (Huber Research award 1971, Norman medal 1983, Moissieff award 1977, Fruedenthal medal 1988), Seismol. Soc. Am. (v.p. 1985-86, pres. 1986-87), Earthquake Engring. Research Inst., Phi Beta Kappa Democrat. Office: Stanford U Dept Civil Engring Stanford CA 94305-4020

CORNELL, ERIC ALLIN, physics educator; s. Allin and Elizabeth (Greenberg) Cornell; m. Celeste Landry; 1 child, Eliza. BS in Physics with honors, Stanford U., 1985; PhD in Physics, MIT, 1990. Tchr. English as Fgn. Lang. Taichung YMCA, Taiwan, 1982; rsch. asst. Stanford (Calif.) U., 1982—85; tchg. fellow Harvard Ext. Sch., 1989; postdoctoral Rowland Inst., Cambridge, Mass., 1990; postdoctorate Joint Inst. Lab. Astrophysics, Boulder, Colo., 1990—92; asst. prof. adj. dept. physics U. Colo., Boulder, 1992—95; staff scientist Nat. Inst. Stds. and Tech., Boulder, 1992—; fellow JILA U. Colo and Nat. Inst. Stds. and Tech., Boulder, 1994 ; prof. adj. dept. physics U. Colo., Boulder, 1995—. Contbr. over 30 articles to profl. jours.; patentee in field. Recipient Grad. fellowship, NSF, 1985—88, Undergrad. Rsch. award for Excellence, Firestone, 1985, Samuel Wesley Stratton award, 1995, Newcomb-Cleveland prize, 1995—96, Carl Zeiss award, 1996, Fritz London prize in low temperature physics, 1996, Gold medal, Dept. Commerce, 1996, Presdl. Early Career award in sci. and engring., 1996, I.I. Rabi prize in atomic, molecular and optical physics, Am. Phys. Soc., 1997, King Faisal Internat. prize in sci., 1997, Alan T. Waterman award, NSF, 1997, Benjamin Franklin Medal in Physics, 1999, The Nobel Prize in Physics, 2001. Fellow: Optical Soc. of Am., 2000 (R.W. Wood Prize, 1999); mem.: Am. Phys. Soc., 1997 (fellow), Royal Netherlands Acad. of Arts & Sci. (Lorentz Medal, 1998), NAS, 2000. Achievements include first to successfully complete Bose-Einstein condensation, 1995. Office: Univ Colo JILA Campus Box 440 Boulder CO 80309-0440*

CORNELL, JOHN ROBERT, lawyer; b. Boston, Nov. 7, 1943; s. Robert Cole Cornell and Thelma Marjorie (Bassett) Strout; m. Susan Lindsay Jordan, June 11, 1966; children: Jared, Joshua, Alexandra, Margaret. AB, Colby Coll., 1965, MA, 1997; JD, Georgetown U., 1968; LLM in Taxation, NYU, 1972. Bar: N.Y. 1969, Maine 1972, U.S. Dist. Ct. Maine 1972, Ohio 1982, U.S. Tax Ct. 1990. Assoc. Dewey Ballantine, N.Y.C., 1968-72; from assoc. to ptnr. Drummond, Woodsum & MacMahon, Portland, Maine, 1972-81; ptnr. Jones Day, Cleve., 1981-98, Atlanta, 1998-2000, former tax group coord. for S.E., ptnr. N.Y.C., 2001—. Former chmn. tax group's employee benefits sect. Jones Day; lectr. in field. Overseer Colby Coll., 1992-97, trustee, 1997-2003; trustee Cleve. San Jose Ballet, 1994-98, treas., 1995-98. Mem. ABA, Maine Bar Assn. (chmn. tax sect. 1980-81), Colby Coll. Alumni Assn. (chmn. 1979-82), Cleve. Yachting Club (Rocky River, Ohio), Anglers Club (N.Y.C.), Megantic Club (Eustis, Maine), DKE Club (N.Y.C.). Republican. Avocations: sailing, bicycling, skiing, fly fishing. Office: 222 E 41st St New York NY 10017 E-mail: jrcornell@jonesday.com.

CORNELL, KENNETH LEE, lawyer; b. Palo Alto, Calif., Feb. 23, 1945; s. Clinton Burdette and Mildred Lucy (Sheafer) C.; m. Barbara J. Smith, June 26, 1966; children: Melinda Lee Van Hise, Geoffery Mark. BBA, BA in Social Sci., Pacific Union Coll., 1966; JD, U. Wash., 1971. Bar: Wash. 1971, U.S. Dist. Ct. (we. dist.) Wash. 1971, U.S. Supreme Ct. 1974. Ptnr. Keller & Rohrback, Seattle, 1971-75, Richard, Rossano & Cornell, Seattle, 1975-77, Moren, Lageschulte (now Cornell, Hansen, Bugni & McConnell), Seattle, 1978-87, Cornell, Hansen, Bugni & McConnell PS (firm name change), 1995-98; pvt. practice Seattle, 1998—. Cons. atty. Town of Clyde Hill, Wash. 1980-87. Editor Wash. U. Law Rev., 1970-71. Bd. dirs. Kirkland (Wash.) Seventh Day Adventist Sch., 1972-78, Auburn (Wash.) Acad., 1974-80, Western Wash. Corp. Seventh Day Adventists, Bothell, 1974-80. Mem. Wash. State Bar Assn., Wash. State Trial Lawyers Assn., Order of Coif. Democrat. Avocations: skiing, reading, gardening. Office: 11320 Roosevelt Way NE Seattle WA 98125-6228 E-mail: kbcornell@yahoo.com.

CORNELL, PETER MCCAUL, economic consultant, former government official; b. Thunder Bay, Ont., Can., Nov. 28, 1926; s. Maurice Leo and Jeanette Ethel (McCoy) C.; m. Kathryn Elizabeth Griffin, Sept. 7, 1949 (dec. May 1984); children— Allison, Ellen, Peter G.; m. Judith May Fagan, Sept. 14, 1991; stepchildren: Andrew Slater, Kathryn Slater. BA in Econs., Queen's U., Kingston, Ont., Can., 1951, MA in Econs., 1952; PhD in Econs., Harvard U., 1956. Research officer Bank of Can., Ottawa, Ont., Can., 1956-66; economist, project dir. Econ. Council of Can., Ottawa, Ont., Can., 1966-81, dir., 1981-86. Author monographs, also articles in profl. jours. Comdr. Can. Navy, 1943-68. Mem. Ottawa Econs. Assn., Naval Officers Assn. Can., Royal Mil. Colls. Club of Can., Harvard U. Club Ottawa. Avocations: skiing, golf, fishing. Home: 20 Cherrywood Dr Ottawa ON Canada K2H 6G7 E-mail: pmcornell@aol.com.

CORNELL, RALPH LAWRENCE, JR., publishing executive; b. Albany, NY, Nov. 26, 1951; s. Ralph Lawrence and Madeline (Hitchcock) C. Student, Purdue U., 1986-87; Diploma in Environ. Sci./Conservation, Stratford Sch., 2000. Cert. wildlife habitat naturalist. Food svcs. supr. Univ. Aux. Svcs. SUNY, Albany, 1981-89, 95-99; owner, editor R.C. Publs., Albany, 1988—; supr. SoDexHo-Marriott @ SUNYA, 1999-2000, Chartwells SUNY, 2000—. Author: The Moods of Madness, 1985, 3d edit., 1999, Mindless Wanderings, 1986, Tales of the Streets, 1993, Silent Death, 2000; editor poetry newsletter Ralph's Rev., Opportunity Digest, RC's Stamp Hotline, Notre Dame Scrapbook, 1993; editor UAS News, 1997-98. With USN, 1971-74. Named Internat. Poet of Merit, World of Poetry, 2002; recipient Golden Poet award, 1993. Mem.: Hudson/Mohawk Bird Club, Federated N.Y. State Bird Clubs. Roman Catholic. Avocations: bicycling, stamp collecting, old books, oil painting. Home and Office: RC Publs 129A Wellington Ave Albany NY 12203-2637 E-mail: rcpub@juno.com.

CORNELL, RICHARD GARTH, biostatistics educator; b. Cleve., Nov. 18, 1930; s. Russell Gervas and Grace (Garlick) C.; m. Valma Yvonne Edwards, June 3, 1961; children: Sharon Cornell Murray, Russell Glenn, Carol Elizabeth Wheelock. BA, U. Rochester, 1952; MS, Va. Poly. Inst., 1954, PhD, 1956. Statistician, Nat. Communicable Disease Center, Atlanta, 1956-58, chief lab. and field sta. stats. unit, 1958-60; asso. prof. stats. Fla. State U., 1960-68, prof. stats., 1968-71; prof., biostats. U. Mich., Ann Arbor, 1971-96, prof. emeritus biostats., 1996—, chmn. dept., 1981-84, 90-93, interim dean pub. health, 1993-95. Cons. to govt. and industry. Served with USPHS, 1956-58. Mem. Biometric Soc. (program chmn. 1968, 71, pres. Eastern N.Am. region 1975, council 1978—), Am. Statist. Assn. (chmn. biometrics sect. 1973, program chmn. ann. meeting 1981), Phi Beta Kappa, Sigma Xi, Phi Kappa Phi, Pi Mu Epsilon. Baptist (deacon 1962—). Achievements include research, publs. in biometrics to sci. jours. Home: 6149 Water Works Rd Saline MI 48176-8811

CORNELL, ROBERT ARTHUR, retired international government official, consultant; b. Mineola, N.Y., Sept. 8, 1936; s. Herbert and Clara (Lange) C.; m. Nadine E. Dittmer, May 4, 1962 (div. June 1993); children: Robert Arthur Jr., James E., Suzanne N.; m. Catherine Rescoussie, Aug. 29, 1995. AB, Columbia U., 1958, postgrad., 1965-66, Pacific Luth. U., 1960-61, Am. U., 1964-65; MBA, NYU, 1963. With Grace Nat. Bank, N.Y.C., 1961-63, U.S. Govt., Washington, 1963-69, IBM World Trade Corp., 1970, S.J. Rundt & Assocs., N.Y.C., 1970-71; dep. dir. Office Econ. Research U.S. Internat. Trade Commn., Washington, 1971-76, dir. Office Trade and Industry, 1976-77, dep. dir. ops., 1977-79; asst. dir. for stockpile trans. GSA, Washington, 1979-80; dep. asst. sec. for internat. trade and investment policy U.S. Treasury Dept., Washington, 1980-88; dep. sec.-gen. OECD, Paris, 1988-95; cons., writer, editor France, 1995—. Mem. faculty U. Md., 1968; pvt. cons. in econs. and fin. Contbr. articles to profl. jours. With USN, 1958-61. Recipient Arthur S. Flemming award, 1974. Mem. Am. Econ. Assn., Western Econ. Assn., Nat. Economists Club, Nat. Assn. Bus. Econs. Lutheran. E-mail: 106035.1767@compuserve.com.

CORNELL, ROBERT WITHERSPOON, engineering consultant; b. Orange, N.J., Aug. 16, 1925; s. Edward Shelton and Helen Lauretta (Lawrence) C.; m. Patricia Delight Plummer, June 24, 1950; children: Richard W., Delight W. Cornell Dobby, Elizabeth Cornell Wilkin, Roberta Shelton Wolfe. BSME, Yale U., 1945, MSME, 1947, D in Engring., 1950. Registered profl. engr., Conn., N.Y. Instr. math. New Haven Jr. Coll., 1947-48; analytical engr. Pratt & Whitney Aircraft, East Hartford, Conn., 1947; with Hamilton Standard, Windsor Locks, Conn., 1948-87, chief applied mechanics and aerodynamics, 1961-87; instr. engring. Hillyer Coll., Hartford, 1955; pres. Cornell Cons., 1973—2000, Cornell Enterprises, West Hartford, 1984—2000. Adj. prof. Yale U., 1985, 90. Contbr. articles to profl. jours.; patentee in field. Bd. dirs., treas. Yale Sci. and Engring. Assn., 1969-2001, Conn. State Taxpayers Assn., Stratford, 1984-86; past pres., bd. dirs. West Hartford Taxpayers Assn., 1972-97, 2002--; Rep. state senatorial candidate 5th dist. State of Conn., 1988, 94, state Rep. candidate 18th dist., 1990; mem. Svc. Corps Ret. Execs., 1989—, chmn., 1998-2000; dir. Agawam Coun., 1993-99. With USN, 1943-46. Fellow ASME; mem. Yale Club of Hartford, Hartford Golf Club, Sigma Xi, Tau Beta Pi. Avocations: tennis, squash, jogging, swimming, gardening. Home and Office: 40 Belknap Rd West Hartford CT 06117-2819 E-mail: cornellrp@aol.com.

CORNELL, SUZANNE, youth services executive; b. West Chester, Pa., Mar. 2, 1962; d. Robert Alfred and Margaret Loughery Price; m. Craig Alan Cornell, Jan. 26, 1961; children: Erik, Autumn. BS in Edn. Health/Phys. Edn., West Chester U., 1988. Program dir. Southern Chester County YMCA, West Grove, 1989—93, sr. dir., 1993—98, assoc. exec. dir., 1998—2001, exec. dir., 2001—. V.p. Oxford (Pa.) Area Civic Assn., 1998—99. Recipient award for excellence, Assn. Profl. Dirs., 1998. Mem.: Southern Chester County C. of C. (bd. dirs. 2001—04). Office: Southern Chester County YMCA 880 W Baltimore Pike West Grove PA 19390

CORNELL, THOMAS CHARLES, peace activist, writer; b. Bridgeport, Conn., Apr. 11, 1934; s. Thomas Charles Cornell and Ann (Caruso) Cornell Rice; m. Monica Mary Ribar, July 7, 1964; children: Thomas Christopher, Deirdre Ann. AB in English, Fairfield U., 1956; MS in Secondary Edn., U. Bridgeport, 1962; diaconate, St. Thomas Sem., 1988; DLH (hon.), Fairfield U., 1990. Ordained deacon Roman Catholic Ch., 1988. Instr. English and Latin pub. schs., Brookfield, Conn., 1959-62; mng. editor The Catholic Worker, N.Y.C., 1962-64; program dir. Fellowship of Reconciliation, Nyack, N.Y., 1965-79; nat. sec. Cath. Peace Fellowship, N.Y.C., 1965-01; freelance writer and lectr., 1979-81; instr. English and Latin pub. schs., Conway, N.H., 1981-82; soup kitchens dir. Waterbury Area Coun. Churches, Conn., 1982-92; coord. Peter Maurin Cath. Worker Farm, Marlborough, N.Y., 1993—. Adj. prof. religion, Mercy Coll., Dobbs Ferry and Peekskill, N.Y., 1979-81, St. Joseph Sem., Yonkers, N.Y., 1997—; contbg. editor, The Catholic Worker, 1994—; del. Third World Congress Laity, 1967, Bishops' Bicentennial Call to Action, Detroit, 1976, Fourth World Congress Laity, Rome, 2000. Editor: (with James H. Forest) A Penny a Copy: Readings from The Catholic Worker, 1968, expanded edit. (with R.E. Ellsberg and J.H. Forest), 95; contr. articles to profl. jours. and newspapers. Mem. exec. com. War Resisters League, 1970-72; co-founder and mem. Pax Christi, USA, organized first pub. demonstration against U.S. participation in Vietnam, 1963, first group act resistance against Vietnam draft, 1965, imprisoned, Danbury Fed. Correctional Inst., 1968, pardoned by Pres. Jimmy Carter, 1978. Recipient Cath. Peace Fellowship award, 1985, Liberty Bell award Waterbury Bar Assn., 1986. Democrat. Home: Peter Maurin Farm 41 Cemetery Rd Marlboro NY 12542 Office: Catholic Peace Fellowship 55 E 3d St New York NY 10003-9003 E-mail: tomcornell1934@aol.com.

CORNELL, WILLIAM DANIEL, mechanical engineer; b. Valley Falls, Kans., Apr. 17, 1919; s. Noah P. and Mabel (Hennessy) C.; m. Barbara L. Ferguson, Aug. 30, 1942; children: Alice Margaret, Randolph William. BS in Mech. Engring., U. Ill., 1942. Registered profl. engr., N.Y. Rsch. engr. Linde Air Products Co., Buffalo, 1942-48, cons. to Manhattan Dist. project, 1944-46; project engr. devel. of automatic bowling machine Am. Machine and Foundry, Buffalo, 1948-55; cons. Gen. Electric Co., Hanford, Wash., 1949-50; project engr. devel. of automatic bowling machine Brunswick Corp., Muskegon, Mich., 1955-59, mgr. advanced engring., 1959-72; mgr. advanced concepts and tech. Sherwood Med. Industries divsn. Am. Home Products Corp., St. Louis, 1972-85; mem. faculty Coll. Engring., U. Buffalo, 1946-47; cons. Cornell Engring., St. Louis, 1985—; mem. faculty Coll. Engring. Washington U., St. Louis, 1993-94. Patentee numerous inventions, including automatic golf and bowling game apparatus, med. instruments; developer new method of measuring hemoglobin and new method of counting platelets in whole blood. Recipient Navy E award, 1945, Manhattan Project Recognition award, 1945, Merit award Maritime Commn., 1945. Republican. Presbyterian. Home and Office: 907 Camargo Dr Ballwin MO 63011-1506

CORNELL, WILLIAM HARVEY, clergyman; b. Pitts., May 27, 1934; s. Floyd Anderson and Audrey Fern (Wasson) C.; m. Betty Jean Yates, July 24, 1954; children: Deborah Jean, William Mark, Darla Ruth. AA, Central (S.C.) Wesleyan Coll., 1953; AB in Religion, Ind. Wesleyan U., 1956. Ordained to ministry Wesleyan Meth. Ch., 1958. Clergyman Wilgus Wesleyan Meth. Ch., Gypsy, Pa., 1956-59, Wolf Summit (W.Va.) Wesleyan Meth. Ch., 1959-63, Canal Wesleyan Meth. Ch., Utica, Pa., 1963-73, Greenville (Pa.) Wesleyan Meth. Ch., 1973-76, Salem (Ohio) Wesleyan Meth. Ch., 1976-78, Sagamore (Pa.) Wesleyan Meth. Ch., 1963-68, 78-95, Niles (Ohio) Wesleyan Meth. Ch., 1995-2000, ret., 2000—. Mem. mission bd. Allegheny Wesleyan Meth. Connection, 1965—2003, sec., 1973-98, editor ann. jour., 1973-98, mem. adv. bd., 1978-98; sec. N.W. Indian Bible Sch., Alberton, Mont., 1969—. Republican. Avocations: hunting, travel. Home and Office: PO Box 115 7695 Rte 85 Beyer PA 16211

CORNELSON, GEORGE HENRY, IV, retired textile company executive; b. Spartanburg, S.C., July 12, 1931; s. George Henry Cornelson III and Elizabeth Marshall (Woodward) Cornelson; m. Ann Martin Shaw, Oct. 6, 1956; children: George Henry Cornelson V, Martin Shaw, Scott Montgomery, Elizabeth Woodward. Student, Davidson Coll., 1949-51; BS in Textiles, N.C. State U., 1953; postgrad. in Bus. Adminstrn., Harvard U., 1953—54; DHL (hon.), Presbyn. Coll., 2003. With indsl. engring. dept. Clinton (S.C.) Mills, Inc., 1954-55, 57-58, from v.p. to pres., 1958—86, CEO, 1985—86; v.p. Clinton Mills Sales Corp., N.Y.C., 1958—86. Bd. dirs. Elastic Fabrics of Am., N.C. Textile Found., exec. com.; mem. S.C. Gov.'s Trade Mission to Far East, Hong Kong; pres. Clinton Investment Co., 1985—86; bd. dirs. Clinton Mills of Geneva, past pres., dir.; vice chmn. bd. dirs. Bailey Fin. Corp., 1996—99; bd. dirs. Anchor Bank, Myrtle Beach, SC, 1999—2000; mem. S.C. Gov.'s Trade Mission to Far East, Singapore, 1979, Kuala Lumpur, 79, Taiwan, 79, Malaysia, 79. Trustee Presbyn. Coll., Clinton, 1959—68, 1994—, Davidson (N.C.) Coll., 1992—95, bd. visitors, 1986—91; trustee Ind. Coll. and Univs. S.C., 1971—92, life trustee, 1993—; trustee Thornwell Home for Children, Clinton, 1968—76, exec. com., 1973—74, sec. bd. trustees, 1974; organizing chmn. Greater Clinton Planning Commn., 1967; pres. Cmty. Chest and United Fund, 1963—64; chmn. Laurens County dist. Boy Scouts Am., 1973, exec. bd. Blue Ridge coun., 1974; chair adv. com. Bailey Found., 1969—; dir. S.C. State Mus. Found., 1986—89; expansion com. mem. Carolina's NFL, 1988—92; bd. dirs. Columbia Theol. Sem., Decatur, Ga., 1990—93; trustee Laurens County Health Care Sys., 1996—2000, chmn., 1997—99; deacon 1st Presbyn. Ch., Clinton, 1959—67, elder, 1967—73, 1976—81, 1983—87, 1988—93. Served USAF, 1955—57. Recipient Disting. Svc. award, Clinton Jr. C. of C., 1962, Outstanding Young Alumnus award, N.C. State U., 1965, Disting. Alumnus award, McCallie Sch., 1989, N.C. State U., 1999. Mem.: S.C. Textile Mfrs. Assn. (bd. dirs. 1973—82, pres. 1979—80), Am. Textile Mfrs. Inst. (exec. com., rsch. and tech. svcs. com. 1964—71, vice chmn. Crafted With Pride in USA com. 1985—87, vice chmn. edn. com. 1975—76, cotton com. 1981—82, safety and health com. 1981—82), Clinton C. of C. (bd. dirs. 1959—61, 1966, v.p. 1968, pres. 1969), S.C. C. of C. (bd. dirs., exec. com. 1975—79), Musgrove Mill Golf Club (founder, bd. dirs.), Lions Club, Kappa Alpha, Phi Psi. Home: Merrie Oaks 1644 Hwy 56 S Clinton SC 29325

CORNETT, BRADLEY WILLIAMS, lawyer; b. Maryville, Tenn., Apr. 15, 1970; s. Billy Kenneth and Wilda Cornett; m. Wendy Leigh Love, Apr. 27, 1996. BS, U. Tenn., 1991; JD, U. N.C., 1995. Bar: Ala. 1995, U.S. Dist. Ct. (no. dist.) Ala. 1996, U.S. Ct. of Appeals (11th cir.), 2002. Atty. Ford, Howard & Cornett, P.C., Gadsden, Ala., 1996—. Mem. Ala. Def. Lawyers Assn., Def. Rsch. Inst., Am. Inns of Court. Office: Ford Howard & Cornett PC PO Box 388 Gadsden AL 35902-0388 E-mail: cornettb@bellsouth.net.

CORNETT, CATHY G. TURNER, consulting company executive, artist; b. Richmond, Va., Aug. 3, 1949; d. Beauregard Jr. and Margaret Catherine Turner; m. Willie Edward Cornett, Jan. 4, 1974. Student, Va. Commonwealth U., 1967-68. With acctg. dept. Massey Concrete Corp., Richmond, 1968-70, State Tractor & Equipment, Inc., Orlando, Fla., 1970-72; sr. acctg. clk. S & K Famous Brands, Inc., Richmond, 1972-74; bookkeeper North Bay Village, Tampa, Fla., 1975-76; acct., corp. officer for subs. cos. Elmer J. Krauss Orgn., Inc., Tampa, 1976-78; pres. C. G. Cons., Inc., Brooksville, Fla., 1978—. Exhibited in group shows Woodstock (N.Y.) Sch. Art, 25th Anniversary Exhbn., Spring Hill (Fla.) Art League, 1998, City of Brooksville and Hernando Fine Arts Coun. Exhbn. City Art Gallery; co-author: (book) Jenkins Art Workshop Series 11, 1997; edtl. asst.: (books) Jenkins Art Workshop Series 8, 1995, Series 9, 1995, Series 10, 1996. Finalist Internat. Art Contest, 2002; recipient Golden Webmaster award, 2002, Angelfire Gold award, 2002, A Woman's Touch Silver award, 2002. Mem. Nat. Mus. Women in Arts, Calif. Art Club (patron), Spring Hill Art League, Plein Air Fla., Internat. Plein Air Painters. Avocation: old art books.

CORNETT, DONNA J. counselor, alcohol moderation administrator; b. Calif., Jan. 26, 1949; d. L.D. and Shirley A. Cornett. BA in Psychology, San Jose State U., 1972, MA in Psychology, 1973. Founder dir., Drink/Link Alcohol Moderation Programs, Products, and Svcs., Santa Rosa, Calif., 1987—. Founder, dir. The Responsible Drinking Inst. Am., Santa Rosa, 1994 ; developer first at home alcohol abuse prevention program The Sensible Drinking Sys. Author: 7 Weeks to Safe Social Drinking: How to Effectively Moderate Your Alcohol Intake, 1996; copyrighted moderate drinking program developer, 1987. Mem. Calif. State Psychol. Assn. Avocations: writing, gardening, moderate drinking, psychology. Office: Moderate Drinking Programs & Products PO Box 5441 Santa Rosa CA 95402-5441

CORNETT, GREGG, newspaper publisher, newspaper editor, computer company executive; b. Dayton, Ohio, May 12, 1954; PhD in Computer Sci. Pres. Computer Commuter, Batesville, Ark., 1982-87, Gregg Cornett Assocs., Batesville, Bald Knob, Searcy, Ark., 1984—; pub., editor Bald Knob Banner, 1987—; CEO G.C.A. Computer Svcs., 1993—; v.p. Wood Nursery, Inc., 1995-96; systems analyst Arkansas Pub., 1996—. Police photographer Bald Knob Police Dept., 1988—; computer cons. Gregg Cornett Assocs., 1984—, freelance journalist, Bald Knob, 1987—. Author (booklet) Neighborhood Crime Prevention, 1989; contbr. articles to newspapers. Area coord. City Crime Prevention, Bald Knob, 1988—; assoc. KARK-TV Community Network, Little Rock, 1990—; acting city clk. City of Bald Knob, 1991; rural community cons. City of Bald Knob, 1988—; founding bd. dirs. Rsch. Internat., Aruba. Recipient Better Newspaper Advt. award Ark. Press Assn., 1988; Gregg Cornett Day proclaimed by City of Bald Knob, 1990. Fellow Rotary; mem. C. of C. (bd. dirs. 1988—). Avocations: writing, photography, electronics.

CORNETT, HOWARD, state representative; b. Harlan, K.Y., Mar. 11, 1953; m. Jackie Cornett; children: Marc, Mike, Cody. State rep., Ky., 1999—. Owner WDXC Radio Inc., 1990—, Mountain Top Mkt., Inc., 1999—. Mem.: Oleika Shrine Temple, Whitesburg Masonic Lodge. Republican. Baptist. Office: Capitol Annex Rm 432H Frankfort KY 40601*

CORNETT, LLOYD HARVEY, JR., retired historian; b. Seminole, Okla., Aug. 29, 1930; s. Lloyd Harvey and Edna Lee (Walker) C.; children from previous marriage: Lloyd Harvey III, Rosemary Lynne, Carlton Wayne, Curtis Lee; m. Sarah Frances Missildine, Apr. 15, 1992. BA, U. Okla., 1951, MA, 1954; postgrad., U. N.Mex., 1965, Auburn U., 1977. Asst. dir. command history 2d Air Force, U.S. Air Force, 1955-57; historian Air Def. Command, 1957-58; asst. dir. command history Continental Air Def. Command, 1958-59; asst. dir. command history N.Am. Air Def. Command, 1959-61; ctr. historian Air Force Missile Devel. Ctr., 1961-70; historian Air Force Spl. Weapons Ctr., 1970-72; command historian Aerospace Def. Command, 1972-73; command historian Air Tng. Command, 1973-74; dir. U.S. Air Force Hist. Rschr. Ctr., Maxwell AFB, Ala., 1974-89; prin. Ind. Hist. Rsch./Adv. Svc., Montgomery, Ala., 1989—. Mem. Gov.'s Com. for Ala. Conf. on Libr. and Info. Svcs.; bd. advisors Ala. Hist. Commn. Co-editor: Alabama History: An Annotated Bibliography, Vol. of Am. Astronautical Soc. Hist. and (sch. text) Hist. of Ala., 1998; contbr. to hist. jours. Committeeman Boy Scouts Am., 1963-70, 75-79; mem. at large adminstrv. bd. Meth. Ch., 1978-81. Served with USMCR, 1951-53. Mem. AIAA (chmn. tech. com. on history 1983-96), Am. Astronautical Soc. Hist. Com., Western History Assn., Soc. for History in Fed. Govt. Democrat. Home and Office: 3751 Marie Cook Dr Montgomery AL 36109-1509

CORNETT, PAUL MICHAEL, SR., lawyer; b. Chgo., Jan. 24, 1949; s. Paul Elvon and Phyllis (Pedone) C.; m. Marianne Elizabeth Hofer, Aug. 14, 1971; children: Paul Michael Jr., Matthew Charles, Nicholas Robert. BBA, Western Mich. U., Kalamazoo, 1971; JD, Marquette U., Milw., 1974. Bar: Wis. 1974. Officer, capt. legal asst. USAR, Green Bay, Wis., 1974-87; assoc. atty. Mazza Law Offices, New Berlin, Wis., 1974-75; pvt. practice Shawano, Wis., 1975-77; asst. dist. atty. Shawano County, Menominee County, Wis., 1977-78; dist. atty. Shawano and Menominee County, Wis., 1978-82; assoc. Direnzo and Bomier, Neenah, Wis., 1982-84; ptnr. Van Hoof, Van Hoof and Cornett Law Offices, Little Chute, Wis., 1984-93, 1993—. Pro bono atty. Legal Svcs. N.E. Wis., Appleton, 1990—; atty. Village of Combined Locks (Wis.) 1984—, Darboy (Wis.) Sanitary Dist., 1984—, Town of Buchanan, Wis., 1984—; lawyers in the classroom State Bar of Wis., 1974—; judge Mock Trial Competition, Appleton, 1993—. Bd. dirs., 1989—, chmn. bd., 1995-96, Heart of Valley C. of C., Kaukauna, Wis.; pres. Little Chute (Wis.) Businessman's Assn., 1994-95, bd. dirs., 1989—; mentor Outagamie County PAL Program, Appleton, 1994—, Outagamie County Juvenile Offender Program, Appleton, 1995—, Little Chute Elem. Sch., 1998—; bd. dirs., chmn. bd., big brother Big Bros. and Big Sisters of Shawano County, Wis., 1976-82; 2d lt. U.S. Army, 1974. Recipient Dedication award Shawano and Menominee Counties, Wis., 1982, Army Commendation medal, 1987, Army Achievement medal, 1985, USAR, Washington; named Vol. of Yr. PAL Program, 2001. Mem. State Bar of Wis., Outagamie County Bar Assn. Republican. Roman Catholic. Avocations: fishing, travel, camping, woodworking. Home: 2963 Creek Valley Ln Appleton WI 54914-1557 Office: Van Hoof Van Hoof & Cornett Law Offices 200 E Main St Little Chute WI 54140-1834 E-mail: cruiser1221@wmconnect.com.

CORNETT, RICHARD ORIN, research educator, consultant; b. Driftwood, Okla., Nov. 14, 1913; s. Grover Cleveland and Essie (Richardson) C.; m. Lorene Huston, May 26, 1943; children: Linda, Robert, Stanley. BS, Okla. Baptist U., 1934; MS, U. Okla., 1937; postgrad., U. Ill., 1938-39; PhD, U. Tex., 1940; DSc, Hardin-Simmons U., 1954; LittD, Jacksonville U., 1964; LLD, Belknap Coll., 1967. Instr. physics Okla. Bapt. U., 1935-37, assoc. prof., 1940-41, prof., 1941; asst. supr. physics Pa. State Engring., Sci., Mgmt., Def. Tng. Program, 1941-42; lectr. electronics Harvard U., 1942-45; spl. rsch. assoc. OSRD, 1945; asst. to pres. Okla. Baptist U., 1945-46, v.p., 1946-47, exec. v.p., 1947-51; exec. sec. Edn. Commn., So. Bapt. Conv., 1951-58, So. Assn. Bapt. Colls. and Schs., 1951-58; editor So. Bapt. Educator, 1951-58; specialist for coll. and univ. orgn. and adminstrn. U.S. Office Edn., 1959, exec. asst. to dir. div. higher edn., 1959-61, acting asst. commr., dir., 1961-64, dir. div. ednl. orgn. and adminstrn., 1964-65; v.p. Gallaudet Coll., Washington, 1965-75, rsch. prof., dir. cued speech programs, 1976-84; prof. emeritus Gallaudet U. (formerly coll.), 1985—. Prin. investigator field test of wearable electronic lipreading aid for deaf, 1988 89; mem. U.S. del. UNESCO Conf. on Devel. Higher Edn. in Africa, 1962; dir. Ann. Inst. on Coll. and Univ. Planning, Soc. for Coll. and Univ. Planning, 1975-77; nat. lectr. Sigma Xi, 1983-85. Author: (with White, Weber, Manning) Practical Physics, 1943, Algebra, A Second Course, 1945, Electron Tubes and Circuits, 1947, Cued Speech lessons in 34 langs., Cued Speech Handbook for Parents, 1971, Cued Speech Resource Book for Parents of Deaf Children, 1992, 2d edit., 2000. Recipient Disting. Svc. award Nat. Coun. on Communicative Disorders, 1992. Republican. Baptist. Achievements include originator of Cued Speech communication method for deaf, adapted to 59 languages and major dialects as of Nov. 2000; originator, co-developer electronic lipreading aid for deaf; author of recorded lessons in cued speech in 33 languages and major dialects; patentee in field. Home: 8702 Royal Ridge Ln Laurel MD 20708-2458 *If one is to be included in the company of those who give their very best, he must be able to create within himself a vision of success*

and have the courage to follow that vision. Two kinds of men follow visions: those who are fools and those who do great things. The man who sees a vision and has the impulse to follow it is not permitted to know in advance which he will turn out to be.

CORNETT, ROBERT ARNOLD, philosophy educator; b. Jackson County, Ky., Apr. 9, 1920; s. Marion Hall Cornett and Eva Gabbard; m. Barbara Ann Schamberger, Aug. 17, 1946; children: Robert Jr., Kathryn, Donald, Virginia. BA, Butler U., 1944; BDiv, Princeton (N.J.) Theol. Sem., 1946; PhD, U. Ill., 1953. Prof. philosophy Berea (Ky.) Coll., 1953—58, Randolph-Macon Womans Coll., Lynchburg, Va., 1958—90, prof. philosophy emeritus, 1990—. Contbr. articles to profl. jours. Fulbright grantee. Mem. Am. Philos. Assn. Democrat. Avocations: old books, minerals, rivers and mountains activities, writing. Home: 1542 Club Dr Lynchburg VA 24503 E-mail: cornett25@msn.com.

CORNFELD, DAVE LOUIS, lawyer; b. St. Louis, Dec. 24, 1921; s. Abraham and Rebecca (David) C.; m. Martha Herrmann, May 30, 1943; children: Richard Steven, James Allen, Lawrence Joseph. AB, Washington U., St. Louis, 1942, LLB, 1943. Bar: Mo. 1943. Practice law, St. Louis; ptnr. Husch & Eppenberger, 1954—2001, of counsel, 2001—. Adj. prof. Washington U., 1966-87. Co-author: Missouri Estate Planning, Will Drafting and Estate Administration, 2 vol., 1988, supplement, 2002; editor Law Quar. 1943. Bd. dirs. Jewish Fedn., St. Louis, 1977-80, 83-88, Jewish Ctr. for Aged, 1981-88; mem. adv. com. U. Miami Inst. Estate Planning, 1979—. Served with AUS, 1945-46. Mem. ABA (past chmn. com. taxation income estates and trusts, vice chmn. sect. taxation 1977-80, editor-in-chief Tax Lawyer 1977-80, sr. assoc. editor Probate and Property), St. Louis Bar Assn. (past chmn. taxation com), Am. Law Inst., Am. Coll. Trust and Estate Counsel (regent 1984-90), Am. Coll. Tax Counsel (regent 1980-88), Internat. Acad. Estate and Trust Law, Order of Coif. Jewish (trustee temple 1967-91). Club: Masons. Home: 834 Oakbrook Ln Saint Louis MO 63132-4812 Office: Husch & Eppenberger LLC 190 Carondelet Plz Ste 600 Saint Louis MO 63105-3441 E-mail: dave@cornfeld.net., dave.cornfeld@husch.com.

CORNFIELD, MELVIN, lawyer, university institute director; b. Chgo., June 5, 1927; s. Harry and Annabelle (Maltz) C.; m. Edith Pauline Haas, June 24, 1951; children: Daniel Benjamin, Deborah S. Cornfield Alexander. AB, U. Chgo., 1948, JD, 1951. Bar: D.C. 1951, N.Y. 1958. Atty. durable goods divsn. Office Price Stblzn., Washington, 1951-53; atty., advisor Chief Counsel's Office IRS, Washington, 1953-58; assoc. Willkie, Farr, Gallagher, Walton & FitzGibbon, N.Y.C., 1958-63; dir. taxes NBC, Inc., 1963-66; staff v.p. tax affairs RCA Corp., N.Y.C., 1966-76, v.p., treas., 1976-82, v.p. tax affairs, 1982-85; dir. NYU Tax Inst., 1985-94. With USAAF, 1946-47. Home: 4703 Iselin Ave Bronx NY 10471-3323

CORNFORTH, SIR JOHN WARCUP, chemist; b. Sydney, Australia, Sept. 7, 1917; s. John William and Hilda (Eipper) Cornforth; m. Rita H. Harradence, Sept. 27, 1941; children: Brenda Osborne, John, Philippa Horder. BSc, U. Sydney, 1937, MSc, 1938; DPhil, Oxford U., 1941, DSc (hon.), 1976; DSc (hon.), E.T.H. Zurich, 1975, Trinity Coll., Dublin, Univs. Liverpool, Warwick, Aberdeen, Hull, Sussex, Kent and Sydney. Mem. sci. staff Med. Rsch. Coun., London, 1946—62; dir. Milstead Lab. Chem. Enzymology, Shell Rsch. Ltd., Sittingbourne, England, 1962—75; Royal Soc. rsch. prof. U. Sussex Sch. Chemistry and Molecular Scis., Brighton, England, 1975—82. Contbr. articles to profl. jours. Decorated comdr. Brit. Empire, knight, Companion of the Order of Australia; recipient Stouffer prize, 1967, Prix Roussel, 1972, Nobel prize in chemistry, 1975. Fellow: Am. Chem. Soc. (Ernest Guenther award 1969), Royal Soc. Chemistry (Corday-Morgan medal 1953, Flintoff medal 1966), Royal Soc. (Davy medal 1968, Royal medal 1976, Copley medal 1982); mem.: NAS (assoc.), Netherlands Acad. Sci., Biochem. Soc. (CIBA medal 1966), Australian Acad. Sci. (corr.), Am. Soc. Biol. Chemists (hon.), Am. Acad. (hon.). Achievements include research in chemistry of penicillin, synthesis of steroids and other biologically active natural products, chemistry of heterocyclic compounds, biosynthesis of steroids, enzyme chemistry. Home: Saxon Down Cuilfail Lewes BN7 2BE England Office: U Sussex Sch Chemistry Physics & Environ Sci Falmer Brighton BN1 9QJ England

CORNGOLD, STANLEY ALAN, German and comparative literature educator, writer; b. Bklyn., June 11, 1934; s. Herman and Estelle (Bramson) C.; m. Marie Josephine Brettle, July 29, 1961 (div. May 1969); 1 child, Isabel Anna; m. Regine Schmidt-Üllner, Feb. 18, 1995. AB, Columbia U., 1957; postgrad., Sch. Oriental and African Studies-U. London, 1957-58; MA, Cornell U., 1963, PhD, 1969; postgrad., U. Basel (Switzerland), 1965-66. Instr. English U. Md. European div., 1959-62; teaching asst. English Cornell U., 1963-64; teaching asst. French Cornell U, 1964-65; asst. prof. German Princeton U., 1966-72, assoc. prof., 1972-79, assoc. prof. German and comparative lit., 1979-81, prof., 1981—, dir. grad. studies dept. German, 1979-82, 85, 93-95, 96-97. Author: The Commentators' Despair, 1973, The Fate of the Self, 1986, 2d edit., 1994, Franz Kafka: The Necessity of Form, 1988, Complex Pleasure: Forms of Feeling in German Literature, 1998; co-author: Borrowed Lives, 1991; editor: Ausgewählte Prosa by Max Frisch, 1968, Aspekte der Goethezeit, 1975, Thomas Mann, 1875-1975, Norton Critical Edition of the Metamorphosis (Franz Kafka), 1996; translator, editor: The Metamorphosis (Franz Kafka), 1972; translator: essays Walter Benjamin, Selected Writings, 1996. Served with U.S. Army, 1955-57. Named Am. Coun. Learned Socs. fellow, 1965-66, NEH fellow, 1973-74, Guggenheim Found. fellow, 1977-78, Fulbright fellow, 1986, Hölderlin Residence fellow, 1990, 98, Literarisches Colloquium, Berlin fellow, 1990, Hooker disting. vis. scholar McMaster U., 2003, hon. fellow Princeton U., 2003; recipient Festschrift Lit. Paternity, Lit. Friendship, 2002. Mem. PEN, MLA (exec. com. divsn. on philos. approaches to lit. 1993-97, past chair, pub. com. 1993-95), Acad. Lit. Studies, N.Am. Nietzsche Soc., Kafka Soc. Am. (past pres. 1989-92), Heidelberg Club Internat. Home: 51 Ridgeview Cir Princeton NJ 08540-7603 Office: Princeton U Dept German 208 Bobst Hall 83 Prospect Ave Princeton NJ 08540

CORNICK, MICHAEL F(REDERICK), accounting educator; b. Evansville, Ind., Apr. 15, 1940; s. Isadore John and Belle (Wigdor) C.; m. Charlotte Bozovich, Mar. 2, 1985; children; Elizabeth Ann, Ann Elliott. BS in Indsl. Mgmt., Purdue U., 1963; MBA, U.N.C., Chapel Hill, 1970, PhD, 1980. CPA, N.C. Stockbro. Thomson and McKinnon, Winston-Salem, N.C., 1965-68; bank officer 1 st. Nat. Atlanta, 1970-72; assoc. prof. acctg. U. N.C., Charlotte, 1985—2002, Winthrop U., 2002—. Adv. Internat. Bus. Club, Charlotte, 1987—; leader Internat. Acctg. Overseas, Fed. Rep. Germany, London, 1988—. Author: Bank Accounting, 1984: contbr. articles to profl. jours. Mem. British Am. Bus. Coun. 1st lt. U.S. Army, 1963-65. Recipient cert. appreciation, Retarded Citizens Greensboro, 1983. Mem. AICPA, Inst. Mgmt. Accts. (dir. 1985-88), Am. Acctg. Assn., N.C. Soc. CPAs, Charlotte World Trade Assn. Avocations: reading, tennis, basketball. Home: 1409 Biltmore Dr Charlotte NC 28207-2556 Office: Winthrop Univ Rock Hill NC 29733

CORNIES, LARRY ALAN, journalist, educator; b. Leamington, Ont., Can., Apr. 4, 1953; s. William Walter and Helen Louise (Rempel) C.; m. Jacquelyn Ann Brown, Aug. 17, 1974; children: Darryl, Graeme, Andrew, Natalie. BA in Religious Studies, U. Waterloo, 1975; postgrad., Wichita State U., 1981-84; MA in Journalism, U. Western Ontario, 1986. Comm. officer Conrad Grebel Coll., Waterloo, Ont., 1974-75; secondary sch. tchr. United Mennonite Ednl. Inst., Leamington, 1975-80; assoc. editor The Mennonite, Newton, Kans., 1980-84; comm. dir. Mennonite Ch. Hdqs., Newton, 1984-85; mng. editor London (Ont.) Mag., 1986-88; arts and entertainment editor The London Free Press, 1989-93, cluster editor, 1993-97, asst. city editor, 1997-98, Forum editor, 1998-2000, assoc. editor, 2000, editor, 2000—. Adj. prof. faculty info. and media studies U. Western Ont., 1987-97; corr. World Report, Washington, 1983-85, Ecumedia News, N.Y.C., 1982-85; bd. govs. Conrad Grebel Coll., U. Waterloo, Ont., 1994-97. Author: Essays in Journalism, 1986. Bd. dirs. divsn. gen. svcs. Gen. Conf. Mennonite Ch., Newton, Kans., 1995-2002. Recipient Derose-Hinkhouse award Religious Pub. Rels. Coun., 1985, Western Ont. Newspaper awards, 1997, 2002; fellow Knight Ctr. for Specialized Journalism, U. Md., 2001. Mem. Coun. Ch. and Media (chmn. 1991-93). Avocations: music, baseball. Home: 759 Barclay Rd London ON Canada N6K 1K4 Office: London Free Press 369 York St London ON Canada N6A 4G1 E-mail: lcornies@lfpress.com.

CORNING, JOY COLE, former state official; b. Bridgewater, Iowa, Sept. 7, 1932; d. Perry Aaron and Ethel Marie (Sullivan) Cole; m. Burton Eugene Corning, June 19, 1955; children: Carol, Claudia, Ann. BA, U. No. Iowa, 1954; hon. degree, Allen Coll. Nursing. Cert. elem. tchr., Iowa. Tchr. elem. sch. Greenfield (Iowa) Sch. Dist., 1951-53, Waterloo (Iowa) Cmty. Sch. Dist., 1954-55; mem. Iowa Senate, Des Moines, 1984-90, asst. Rep. leader, 1989-90; lt. gov. State of Iowa, Des Moines, 1991-99. Past chmn. Nat. Conf. Lt. Govs. Bd. dirs. Inst. for Character Devel.; mem. policy bd. Performing Arts Ctr., U. No. Iowa, also trustee UNI Found.; bd. dirs. Nat. Conf. Cmty. and Justice, Des Moines Symphony, Planned Parenthood of Greater Iowa. Named Citizen of Yr., Cedar Falls C. of C., 1984; recipient ITAG Disting. Svc. to Iowa's Gifted and Talented Students award, 1991, Pub. Svc. award Iowa Home Econs. Assn., 1994, Friend of Math. award Iowa Coun. Tchrs. of Math., 1995, Iowa State Edn. Assn. Human Rights award, 1996, Govs. Affirmative Action award, Spl. Recognition award Nat. Foster Parent Assoc., Des Moines Human Rights Commn. award, Pub. Svc. award Coalition for Family and Children's Svcs in Iowa, Friends of Iowa Civil Rights, Inc. award, Martin Luther King Jr. Lifetime Svc. award, 1999, Svc. award Des Moines Area Religious Coun., 2002, NCCJ Brotherhood-Sisterhood award, 2003, Senator Barry Goldwater award Planned Parenthood Fedn. Am., 2003; recognized for Extraordinary Advocacy for Children of Iowa chpt. Nat. Com. for Child Abuse, award for leadership Early Care and Edn. Congress, Alumni Achievement award U. No. Iowa; named among YWCA Women of Achievement, 2000, Woman of Influence, Bus. Record, 2003; Nat. Coun. for Commty. Justice honoree, 2003. Mem. AAUW, LWV, PEO, Nat. Assn. for Gifted Children (mem. adv. bd. 1991-99), Rotary Club, Delta Kappa Gamma, Alpha Delta Kappa. Republican. Mem. United Ch. Of Christ. Home: 4323 Grand Ave No 324 Des Moines IA 50312-2443 E-mail: corningj@aol.com.

CORNING, NICHOLAS F. lawyer; b. Seattle, Nov. 8, 1945; s. Frank C. and Jessie D. (Weeks) C.; m. Patricia A. Tomlinson, Dec. 14, 1968; children: Kristen Marie, Lauren Margaret. BCS cum laude, Seattle U., 1968; JD, U. Wash., 1972. Bar: Wash. 1972, U.S. Ct. Appeals (9th cir.) 1972, U.S. Dist. Ct. (we. dist.) Wash. 1973, U.S. Supreme Ct. 1976, U.S. Ct. Claims 1981. Assoc. Jennings P. Felix, Seattle, 1972-75; ptnr. Lagerquist, McConnell & Corning, Seattle, 1975-77; pres., ptnr. Treece, Richdale, Malone, Corning & Abbott, Inc., P.S., Seattle, 1977-90; atty. Corning Law Firm, Seattle, 1990—. Pres. Windermere Corp., Seattle, 1988, also bd. dirs. Recipient Am. Jurisprudence award in Criminal Law U. Wash., 1971. Mem.: ATLA, King County Bar Assn. (spkrs. bur. 1983—85, chmn. pub. info. com. 1985—87, chmn. judiciary and cts. com. 2001—), Wash. State Trial Lawyers Assn. (pres. 1994—95, bd. dirs.), Wash. State Bar Assn., Nat. Inst. Trial Advocacy, Ballard C. of C. (bd. dirs., pres. 1989—92), Beta Gamma Sigma (Key award 1968). Home: 5640 NE 55th St Seattle WA 98105-2835 Office: The Corning Law Firm 5301 Ballard Ave NW Seattle WA 98107-4061 E-mail: corninglawfirm@seanet.com.

CORNISH, DANTÉ ANTHONY, employee development specialist; b. Balt., Sept. 21, 1971; BS in Bus. Mgmt., Hampton (Va.) U., 1993; MA in Adminstrv. Mgmt., Bowie (Md.) State U., 1997; M in Pub. Adminstrn., U. Balt., 1999. Employee devel. asst. Dept. of Navy, Arlington, Va., 1995-97, employee devel. specialist, 1997-98, U.S. SBA, Washington, 1998—. Active NAACP, Inc., Rockville, Md., 1997—, Reid Temple A.M.E. Ch., Lanham, Md., 1999—; mem. Pres.'s Task Force on Fed. Tng. Tech., Washington, 1999—. Mem. Hampton U. Alumni Assn., Bowie State U. Alumni Assn., U. Balt. Alumni Assn., Prince Hall Freemasons, Kappa Alpha Psi, Alpha Epsilon Lambda. Democrat. Roman Catholic. Avocations: mentoring, reading, travel, swimming, basketball. Office: US SBA 409 3D St SW Washington DC 20416-0001

CORNISH, EDWARD SEYMOUR, magazine editor; b. N.Y.C., Aug. 31, 1927; s. George Anthony and Elizabeth Furniss (McLeod) C.; m. Sally Woodhull, Oct. 12, 1957 (dec. Mar. 1992); children: George Anthony, Jefferson Richard Woodhull, Blake McLeod. Diplome d'etudes, U. Paris, France, 1948; AB, Harvard U., 1950. Copy boy, cub reporter Evening Star, Washington, 1950-51; staff corr. U.P. Assn., Richmond, Va., 1951-52, Raleigh, N.C., 1952-53, London, 1953-54, Paris, 1954-55, Rome, 1956; staff writer Nat. Geog. Soc., 1957-69; founder, pres. World Future Soc., Washington, 1966—; creator, editor The Futurist Mag., 1966—; editor World Future Soc. Bull., 1968-77. Cons. to govt., bus. and ednl. orgns. Author: The Study of the Future, 1977; editor: Resources Directory for America's Third Century, 1977, The Future: A Guide to Information Sources, 1977, 1979: The World of Tomorrow, 1978, Communications Tomorrow, 1982, Global Solutions, 1984, The Computerized Society, 1985, Careers Tomorrow, 1988, The 1990s and Beyond, 1989, Exploring Your Future: Living, Learning and Working in the Information Age, 1996, The Opportunity Society, 2000, Futuring: The Exploration of the Future, 2003; editl. cons. Nat. Goals Rsch. Staff, 1970, White House Report Toward Balanced Growth, 1970, Russian Acad. Forecasting, 1999—, UNESCO Coun. on the Future, 1999—. Bd. dirs. World Watch Inst., 1974-2000; adv. bd. Inst. for Alternative Futures. Mem. Russian Future Studies Acad. (hon.). Home: 5501 Lincoln St Bethesda MD 20817-3723 Office: World Future Soc 7910 Woodmont Ave Bethesda MD 20814-3002

CORNISH, ELIZABETH TURVEREY, stockbroker; b. Ionia, N.Y., Dec. 31, 1919; d. Clifford Dwight and Mildred Althea (Spicer) T.; m. Louis Joseph Cornish, June 21, 1941 (div. June 1955); 1 child, Carol Cornish Reeves. BS, Cornell U., 1941. Lic. stockbroker N.Y. Stock Exch., Prin. Reg. Options Prin., Commodity prin., Insur. prin. Teletype operator, sec. to mgr. Carl M. Loeb Rhoades & Co., Ithaca, N.Y., 1955-65, reg. rep., 1962-75; br. mgr. Loeb, Rhoades & Co., Ithaca, 1975-82; registered rep. Shearson Loeb Rhoades, Shearson Am. Express, Ithaca, 1982-86, Hutton, Shearson, Ithaca, 1986-88, First Albany Corp., Ithaca, 1988-91; registered rep., br. office mgr. A.G. Edwards & Sons, Inc., Ithaca, 1991-97, investment broker, 1998—. Charter mem. Nuveen Adv. Coun., 1984, 85, 86; instr. stock market and various br. office jobs for coll. interns; bd. dirs. McGraw House, 1996—. Mem. Planning Com. Downtown Mall, Ithaca, N.Y., 1972-75; chmn. campaign United Way Tompkins County, Ithaca, 1983, dir., 1983-89; bd. dirs. Ithaca Neighborhood Housing, Leadership Tompkins, 1986-88; pres. Friends of Ithaca Coll., 1985-86; mem. adv. coun. Ithaca Coll., 1986—; comdr. Ithaca Squadron of U.S. Power Squadron, 2003—. Mem. Downtown Bus. Women (pres. 1971-72), Tompkins County C. of C. (bd. dirs. 1974-77, 83-86, v.p. 1980-81, pres.-elect 1989, pres. 1990, ambs. coun. 1997—), Ithaca Yacht Club (bd. dirs. 1988-90). Republican. Episcopalian. Avocations: boating, reading, letter writing, coach of cornell women's rifle team, 1942-55. Office: A G Edwards & Sons Inc 2 Graham Rd W Ithaca NY 14850-1055

CORNISH, GEOFFREY ST. JOHN, golf course architect; b. Winnipeg, Man., Can., Aug. 6, 1914; came to U.S., 1947, naturalized, 1955; m. Carol Burr Gawthrop, Mar. 31, 1951 BSA., U. B.C., Can., 1935; MS, U. Mass., 1952, Dr. Sci. (hon.), 1987. Golf course architect Thompson-Jones & Co., Toronto, Ont., Can., 1935-47; instr. U. Mass., 1947-52; pvt. practice golf course architecture Amherst, Mass., 1952—. Vis. lectr. U. Mass. Co-author: The Golf Course, 1981, rev. edit., 1987, The Architects of Golf, 1993, Golf Course Design, 1998, Eighteen Stakes on a Sunday Afternoon, 2002, Classic Golf Hole Design, 2002; subject of Interview mag., Apr. 1987; contbr. articles to profl. jours. Served to maj. Can. Army, 1940-45 Recipient Disting. Svc. award Golf Course Supts. Am., 1981; named Can. Golf Hall of Fame, 1996. Mem. Am. Soc. Golf Course Architects (pres. 1975, Donald Ross award 1982), Brit. Assn. Golf Course Architects (hon.), Soil Sci. Soc. Am., Sigma Xi, Phi Kappa Phi Episcopalian Home and Office: Fiddlers Grn 1030 S East St Amherst MA 01002-3078

CORNISH, RICHARD JOSEPH, international affairs consultant, retired diplomat; b. Omaha, Nov. 7, 1925; s. Lebbeus Morrison and Lydia Christine (Hermann) Cornish; m. Beverly Anne Cormier, July 28, 1958; children: Pamela Anne, Allyson Juillette, Carolyn Lydia. BA, Yale U., 1949; MA, Am. U., 1965; diploma, U.S. War Coll., 1976. Commd. fgn. svc. officer Dept. State, 1959; 2d sec., vice consul U.S. Embassy, Rangoon, Burma, 1959—62, 2d sec., consul Lome, Togo, 1964—66; regional dir. AID, Savannakhet and Vietiane, Laos, 1967—71; polit. advisor Dept. Def., Frankfurt, Germany, 1973—75, dir. mil. assistance Addis Ababa, Ethiopia, 1975—77; 1st sec. for polit. and econ. affairs U.S. Embassy, Yaounde, Cameroon, 1979—81, 1st sec. polit. affairs London, 1981—85; ret., 1985. Cons. London Diplomatic Assn., 1985—87, The Parvus Co., 1985—90, Trefoil Partnership, Ltd., London, 1987—90, CIA, 1991—98; chmn. bd. dirs. Cornish Assocs., 1987—. Author: The Development of Nationalism in Burma, 1966, The National Decision Making Process, 1975, Deployment of Military Forces, 1975. With USAAF, 1944—46, PTO, lt. col. USAFR, 1949—77. Mem.: Royal Commonwealth Soc., Assn. Asian Studies, Am. Fgn. Svc. Assn., Diplomatic and Consular Officers Ret., RAF Club, Kipling Soc., Rotary (bd. dirs. 1976—77), Yale Club, Univ. Club, Travellers Club, Chevy Chase Club, Masons.

CORNISH, RICHARD POOL, lawyer; b. Evanston, Ill., Sept. 9, 1942; s. William A. and Rita (Pool) C.; children: William Darby, Richard Gordon. BS, Okla. State U., 1964; LLB, U. Okla., 1966. Bar: Okla. 1966, U.S. Dist. Ct. (ea. dist.) Okla. 1969, U.S. Supreme Ct. 1979. Ptnr. Baumert & Cornish, McAlester, Okla., 1967-71, Cornish & Cornish, Inc., McAlester, 1971-77; magistrate U.S. Dist. Ct. for Ea. Dist. Okla., McAlester, 1976—2000; prin. Richard P. Cornish, Inc., McAlester, 1977—. Bd. dirs. McAlester Boys Club, 1970-80, pres., 1974. Capt. JAGC, USAR, 1966-78. Mem. Okla. Bar Assn. (legal aid to servicemen com., legal specialization com.), Pittsburg County Bar Assn., McAlester C. of C. (bd. dirs. 1973-75). Roman Catholic. Home: 611 E Creek Ave Mcalester OK 74501-6929 Office: PO Box 1106 Mcalester OK 74502-1106 E-mail: cornish@cwis.net.

CORNISH, THELBERT BERNARD, JR., internet service provider executive; b. Atlanta, Nov. 1, 1974; s. Thelberg Bernard Cornish and Kathleen Ross Henderson; stepfather, William L. Fentress; m. Marta Marie Rush, Apr. 22, 1996; children: Thelberg B. III, Solomon R., Jade B., Ashani L. Degree in multidisciplinary studies, N.C. State U., 1995. Cert. Apple server engr., svc. tech., solutions expert. Pres., CEO Eternal Computing, Inc., Raleigh, N.C., 1997-2000, chmn., 2000—; pres., CEO Subspace Wave Corp., Raleigh, 2000—. Musician, disc jockey radio broadcasting Underground 88, WKNC-FMN, 1995. USAF scholar, 1991; N.C. leadership fellow N.C. State U., 1992. Mem. Greater Raleigh C. of C., Coun. for Entrepreneurial Devel. Avocations: reading, design, inventing, wrestling, computers. Office: Subspace Wave Corp 900 S Wilmington St Ste 115 Raleigh NC 27601-1865

CORNUEJOLS, GERARD PIERRE, operations research educator; b. Meknes, Morocco, Nov. 16, 1950; came to U.S., 1974; s. Jean and Renee (Floch) C.; m. Chantal Fourgeaud, June 18, 1983 (dec. June 1994). Cert. civil engr., Nat. Sch. Bridges and Roads, Paris, 1974; PhD in Ops. Rsch., Cornell U., 1978. Asst. prof. ops. rsch. Carnegie Mellon U., Pitts., 1978-81, assoc. prof., 1981-87, prof., 1987—, IBM chair, 2000—, u. chair, 2002—. Author: Combinatorial Optimization, 2001; contbr. articles to profl. jours., including Math. of Ops. Rsch., Jour. Combinatorial Theory, Ops. Rsch. Mem. Inst. for Ops. Rsch. and Mgmt. Sci. (chmn. optimization sect. 1999-2000), Math. Programming Soc. Avocation: painting. Office: Carnegie Mellon U GSIA 5000 Forbes Ave Pittsburgh PA 15213 E-mail: gc0v@andrew.cmu.edu.

CORNWALL, JOHN MICHAEL, physics educator, consultant, researcher; b. Denver, Aug. 19, 1934; s. Paul Bakewell and Dorothy (Zitkowski) C.; m. Ingrid Linderos, Oct. 16, 1965. AB, Harvard U., 1956; MS, U. Denver, 1959; PhD, U. Calif., 1962. NSF postdoctoral fellow Calif. Inst. Tech., Pasadena, 1962-63; mem. Inst. Advanced Study, Princeton, N.J., 1963-65; prof. physics UCLA, 1965—. Vis. prof. Niels Bohr Inst., Copenhagen, 1968—69, Inst. Physique Nucléaire, Paris, 1973—74, MIT, 1974, 87, Rockefeller U., N.Y.C., 1988; cons. Inst. Theoret. Physics, Santa Barbara, Calif., 1979—80; assoc. Ctr. Internat./Strategic Affairs UCLA, 1987—; cons. MITRE Corp., Aerospace Corp., RAND Corp., Inst. Def. Analysis, John D. and Catherine T. MacArthur Found.; dir.'s adv. com. Lawrence Livermore Labs., 1991—, chmn., 2002—; cons. Ctr. Def. Info., 2002—; mem. Def. Sci. Bd., 1992—93, mem. task force, 1996; chmn. external rev. com. accelerator oper. and technol. divsn. Los Alamos Nat. Labs., 1995—97, cons., rev. com. advanced hydrodynamics facility, 2001—; adv. bd. Los Alamos Neutron Scattering Ctr., 2000—; chmn. external rev. com. Ctr. Internat. Security and Arms Control Stanford U., 1996; adv. commn. Accelerator Prodn. Tritium Project, 1997—2000; prof. sci. and policy analyis RAND Grad. Sch., 1998—; sci. and tech. panel Def. Threat Reduction Agy., 2000; rev. com. Advanced Accelerator Applications, 2001—02; mem. Missile Def. Agy. Countermeasures White Team, 2001—; tech. adv. group Integrative Grad. Edn. Rsch. and Tng. program in pub. policy and nuc. threat U. Calif., 2003—. Author: (with others) Academic Press Ency. of Science and Technology, Union of Concerned Scientists Report on Nat. Missile Def., other encys. and books; contbr. numerous articles to profl. jours. With U.S. Army, 1956-58. Grantee Dept. Energy, NSF, NASA, Dept. Edn.; pre and postdoctoral fellow NSF, 1960-63, A.P. Sloan fellow, 1967-71. Fellow AAAS; mem. Am. Phys. Soc., Am. Geophys. Union, N.Y. Acad. Sci. Avocations: jogging, bicycling, golf, bridge. Office: UCLA Dept Physics Los Angeles CA 90095-0001 E-mail: cornwall@physics.ucla.edu.

CORNWELL, DAVID GEORGE, biochemist, educator; b. San Rafael, Calif., Oct. 8, 1927; s. John Nevius and Nora (Jonasen) C.; m. Normagene Coon, Mar. 14, 1959; children: Karen Sue, David Andrew. BA (hon.), Coll. Wooster, 1950; MA, Ohio State U., 1952; PhD, Stanford U., 1955. NRC fellow Harvard U., 1954-56; faculty Ohio State U., 1956-92, prof. molecular and cellular biochemistry, 1963-92; part-time prof., 1993—; chmn. dept. medical biochemistry Ohio State U., 1965-80, assoc. dean acad. affairs Coll. Medicine, 1979-92, prof. and assoc. dean emeritus, 1992—; mem. nutrition study sect. NIH, 1966-70, nutrition sci. tng. rev. sect., 1970-73; hon. prof. Tongji Med. U., Wuhan, China, 1993—. Mem. editl. bd. Jour. Lipid Rsch., 1962-66, 88-95, Jour. Nutrition, 1969-72; mem. adv. bd. Jour Lipid Rsch., 1974-78, Chem. Abstracts, 1979-84; contbr. articles to profl. jour. Trustee Children's Hosp. Rsch. Found., Columbus, 1982-93. With AUS, 1946-47. Co-recipient hon. mention for rsch. 6th Internat. Congress Hematology, 1956. Mem. Am. Chem. Soc., Am. Soc. Biol. Chemists, Am. Oil Chemists Soc., Am. Inst. Nutrition, Alpha Omega Alpha, Sigma Xi. Presbyterian (elder). Home: 2290 Middlesex Rd Columbus OH 43220-4646 E-mail: cornwell.1@osu.edu.

CORNWELL, DAVID JOHN MOORE See LE CARRÉ, JOHN

CORNWELL, GIBBONS GRAY, III, physician, medical educator, retired; b. West Chester, Pa., Jan. 17, 1933; s. Gibbons Gray and Eva Chambers (Parke) C.; m. Mary Helen Fortmiller, Sept. 13, 1958; children: Gibbons Gray IV, Heidi Cornwell Trout, Holly Fortmiller. BS, Yale U., 1954; MD, U. Pa., 1963; MA (hon.), Dartmouth Coll., 1993. Diplomate Am. Bd. Internal Medicine, Am. Bd. Hematology. Resident in medicine Hosp. U. Pa., Phila., 1963-64, 65-66; research fellow Cambridge U., Eng., 1964-65; hematology fellow Hosp. U. Pa., Phila., 1966-68; biochemistry fellow Dartmouth Med. Sch., Hanover, N.H., 1968-70, asst. prof. medicine, 1971-74, assoc. prof., 1974-80, prof., 1980-95, prof. pathology, 1990-95, prof. emeritus medicine and pathology, 1995—, assoc. dean student and acad. affairs, 1973-76, chmn. sect. hematology-oncology, 1977-84. Vis. prof. Inst. Immunology, Oslo, 1976-77; dir. clin. rsch. Norris Cotton Cancer Ctr., Hanover, 1978-91; bd. dirs. Cancer and Leukemia Group B, Boston, 1978-91; trustee, chmn. Hitchcock Found., Hanover, 1978-90; staff bd. govs. Mary Hitchcock Meml. Hosp., Hanover, 1981-88; vis. scientist Inst. Pathology/Swedish Med. Rsch. Coun., Uppsala, Sweden, 1987. Contbr. articles to profl. jours. Bd. dirs. Upper Valley Hospice, Lebanon, N.H., 1980; mem. sch. bd. Town of Lyme, N.H., 1973-76, health officer, 1970-74, mem. conservation com., 1970-74, budget com., 1996—; trustee Lyme (N.H.) Found., Lyme, 1998—, chmn., 2000—. Capt. USAF, 1955-59. Clin. rsch. grantee NIH, 1978-91. Fellow ACP; mem. Am. Fedn. Clin. Rsch. (emeritus), Am. Soc. Hematology, N.H. Med. Soc. Republican. Episcopalian. Avocations: cycling, stamp collecting, whale watching, computer animation, scuba. Home: 1 Orfordville Rd Lyme NH 03768-3305

CORNWELL, ILENE JONES, writer, editor; b. Spartanburg, S.C., Sept. 27, 1942; d. Thurmond G. and Elizabeth (Furber) Jones; m. James H. Cornwell, Mar. 2, 1963 (div. 1977); children: James David, Robert Grant. Student, U. Tenn., 1975, Tenn. State U., 1987-88, Cumberland U., 1990—, Nashville Travel Inst., 1991. Pub. info. officer Tenn. Hist. Commn., Nashville, 1974-78; publs. editor, pub. info. officer Vanderbilt U. Med. Ctr., Nashville, 1978-81; writer, editor, owner So. Resources Unlimited, Nashville, 1981-92; copy editor, editorial cartoonist West Nashville Digest, 1993-94; contbg. editor and ptnr. New South Archtl. Press, Richmond, Va., 1993-98; gen. editor, writer Serviceberry Press, Memphis, 1993—98; adminstrv. asst. tchr. edn. and Pew retention program Fisk U., Nashville, 1995-97; pubs. designer and typesetter Typography 2000, Nashville, 1995—; webmaster, HTML writer WebText 2000, 1995—2002; webmaster, exec. dir. West Nashville Founders' Mus., Nashville, 2002—; gen. editor, writer Serviceberry Press, 2002—. Speaker, panelist

Women in Media Com., Saginaw State U., Mich., 1990; speaker, workshop leader Elderhostel, 1990, Austin Peay State U., 1990; asst. to coord. cmty. edn. Cohn Adult Learning Ctr., Nashville, 1992-93, program co-chair statewide women's history conf. Shaping A State: The Legacy of Tenn. Women, Nashville, 1995; planning com. The Perfect 36 Exhibit Fisk U.; compiler spl. exhibit on 4 black suffragists; founder Tenn. Womens Network, 1997, webmaster; spkr. in field. Author: Footsteps Along the Harpeth, 1970, 76, Travel Guide to the Natchez Trace Parkway, 1984; Biographical Directory of the Tennessee General Assembly, 1987-91, Ruskin!, 1972; (with Jim Leeson) The Old Trace in Tennessee, 1972; (screenplays) Early Travels on the Natchez Trace, 1974, Natchez Trace: Pathway to Parkway, 1986 (nominated Nashville's Emmy 1988); compiler: (selected bibliography) The Legacy of Tenn. Women, 1995; editor: The Perfect 36: Tennessee Delivers Woman Suffrage, 1998, The Essence of Mertie Buckman, 1998; editor Nat. Assn. Coll. Deans, Registrars, and Admission Officers News, 1998-99; collections include Ilene Jones-Cornwell Collection of Paul Adam's photographs, Great Smoky Mts. Regional Project Hodges Libr. U. Tenn., Knoxville, 2000; contbr. articles to profl. jours. Charter mem. West Nashville Founders' Mus., Nashville, 1987, bd. dirs., 1989-99; founding chmn. Richland Creek Campaign, West Nashville Community Coun., 1989-90; founder Bellevue-Harpeth Hist. Soc., 1970, 3-term pres.; Natchez Trace program presenter Internat. Conf. on Pkwys., Riverways, and Greenways Asheville, N.C., 1989; chair Natchez Trace Adv. Com., Tenn., 1990—; activist Natchez Trace Pky.: Doomed to Become an Interstate Hwy.?, 1990—; state judge Voice of Democracy student essay and scholarship contest, VFW, 1992, Tenn. Dept. Edn., Pencil student essay contest, 1994, history essay Tenn. students Tenn. Hist. Commn., 1989—; program co-chair Tenn. women's history symposium com. Vanderbilt U. Women's Ctr., 1993-95; mem. Mayor Bill Purcell's Neighborhood Hist. Preservation Com., 1999—. Recipient Vintage award Internat. Assn. Bus. Communicators, 1980, MacEachern award Am. Hosp. Assn., 1981, Pres. award Natchez Trace Pkwy. Assn., 1989, Outstanding Svc. and Leadership award West Nashville Cmty. Coun., 1989, Cert. of Merit, Unsung Am. Woman Essay competition Nat. Women's History Project, 1994, 1st pl. publs. Nat. Fedn. of Press Women Comm. Contest, 1999; named Tenn. Outstanding Young Woman, 1975; Lawlor scholar Cumberland U., 1990-91. Mem. Nat. League of Am. Pen Women (Nashville br., former pres., v.p., state conv. chair), Tenn. Woman's Press and Authors Club (affiliate of Nat. Fedn. of Press Women, pres. 1978, past v.p. and chair state conv.), White Bridge Neighborhood Assn. (charter, bd. dirs.), Tenn. Environ. Coun., Am. Biog. Inst. Rsch. Assn. (selected assoc. and mem. adv. bd. 1990), Friends of Richland Creek (charter), Nat. Women's History Project, Nat. Mus. of Women in the Arts (charter), Tenn. Native Plant Soc., Hypertext Markup Lang. (HTML) Writers Guild, U. S. Caroliniana Soc., Piedmont Hist. Soc., Old Pendleton Dist. Soc. Home: 5632 Meadowcrest Ln Nashville TN 37209-4631

CORNWELL, JIMMY LEE, fundraising executive, retired air force officer; b. Willitts, Calif., Jan. 11, 1933; s. Virgil Lee and Millicent Mae C.; m. Margaret Jane, Jan. 14, 1967; m. Peggy Joyce Tanner, July 27, 1956 (dec. Jan. 26, 1966); children: Cindy Lee, James Nolan. AA, Modesto Jr. Coll., 1952; BS, Ball State U., 1972, MBA, 1974; grad. with honors, Indsl. Coll. Armed Forces, 1974-75. Cert. fundraising exec. Flight comdr., chief trng. USAF, Vietnam, 1969—70, squadron comdr., wing dir. opers., 1971—73; chief nuc. policy Office Joint Chiefs of Staff, Pentagon, Washington, 1975—78; ret. USAF, 1978; sr. v.p., 2d chief tng. Kennedy Sinclaire, Inc., North Haledon, NJ, 1979—89; pres. Cornwell and Assocs., Granite Bay, Calif., 1989—; chief devel. officer U. Calif. Davis Med. Ctr., Sacramento, 1994—98, chief devel. officer, donor asset planning, 1999—2001; ret., 2001. Pres. Planned Giving Forum, Sacramento, 1987-89; mem. planned giving com. McGeorge Sch. Law, Sacramento, 1989-94, Sutter Hosp. Found., Sacramento, 1987-92; presentation spkr. Sons in Retirement (SIRS), 1995-2000, Rotary Club, 1995-2000, Kiwanis Club, 1995-2000, Non-Profit Resource Ctr., Sacramento, 1990-2000. Author: The Planned Giving Guide, 1991; contbr. to newsletter. Mem. adv. bd. Logstar, McClellan AFB, Sacramento, 1997-99. Recipient Outstanding Fundraising Exec. Yr., Nat. Soc. Fundraising Execs., 1997. Mem. Nat. Soc. Fundraising Execs. (trustee, Outstanding Fundraising Exec. of Yr. 1997), Nat. Com. Planned Giving, Air Force Assn., Aircraft Owners and Pilot Assn., Ret. Officers Assn. Republican. Protestant. Avocations: flying, boating, public speaking, bowling, fishing. Home and Office: 8512 Hidden Lakes Dr Granite Bay CA 95746 Office Fax: 916-791-3030. E-mail: jim.cornwell1@earthlink.net.

CORNWELL, LINDA LEE, media specialist; b. Milw., Sept. 4, 1944; d. Charles Robert and Leona Dorothy (Bennett) C. BS in secondary edn., Butler U., 1967, MS in edn., 1975. Cert. Sch. Libr. Media Specialist Endorsement Butler U., 1975. Tchr. Westfield Wash. Sch. Corp., Ind., 1973—76, M.S.D of Wash. Twp., Indpls., 1975—85; cons. Ind. Dept. Edn., Indpls., 1985—99, program mgr., 1987—95, dir., 1998—99; coord. Ind. State Tchrs. Assn., office sch. quality, profl. improvement, 1999—2000, Ind. Dept. Edn., Fed. Goals 2000, 1999—2001; assoc. dir. Scholastic, Inc., N.Y.C., 2001—. Staff developer Devel. Studies Ctr., 1990—2000; mem. to facilitator Ind. Profl. Standards Bd. Early Adolescent Generalist Adv. Group, 1994—96; reading cons. Children's Press and Franklin Watts, 1995—; co-pres. Ind. Staff Devel. Coun., 2001—03. Mem. NEA Reading Task Force, 2000, Am. Assn. of Sch. Librs., Task Force, 1994—96, Am. Assn. of Sch. Librs., Tchg. Learning Com., 2001, Am. Assn. of Sch. Librs., Reading for Understanding Com., 2002—03, Young Hoosier Book Award Com., 1988—2000, Am. Assn. of Sch. Librs., Seventh Nat. Conf. Com., 1992—94; chair Am. Assn. of Sch. Librs., Spl. Literacy Task Force, 1992—94, Ind. Staff Devel. Leadership Coun., 1999—2001; bd. mem. Butler U. Bd of Dist. Visitors, Coll. of Edn., 2001—, Ball State U. Bd. of Dist. Visitors, Coll. of Edn., 1999—2001; mem. Newbery Com., 1998; editl. bd. mem. Am. Libr. Assn., 1998—2002; mem. Grolier Pubs. Classroom Adv. Bd., Libr. Adv. Bd., 1995—2001; chair Am. Assn. of Sch. Librs., Sixth Nat. Conf. Com., 1989—92; bd. mem. Mid. Grades Reading Network's Adv. Bd., 1994—98. Mem. AASL (conf. chmn. Balt. chpt. 1990—), Delta Kappa Gamma. Avocations: traveling, reading, theater.

CORNWELL, PATRICIA DANIELS, writer; b. Miami, Florida, June 9, 1956; Grad., Davidson Coll. Police reporter Charlotte (N.C.) Observer, 1979-81; computer analyst Office Chief Med. Examiner, Richmond, Va., from 1985. Author: (biography) A Time for Remembering, 1983, (novels) Postmortem, 1990 (Edgar Award, 1991), Body of Evidence, 1991, All that Remains, 1993, Cruel and Unusual, 1993 (Gold Dagger Award, 1993), From Potter's Field, 1995 (One of Top 15 Bestsellers for 1995 Pubs. Weekly), Hornet's Nest, 1997, Unnatural Exposure, 1997, Ruth, A Portrait, 1997, Point of Origin, 1998, Black Notice, 1999, Last Precinct, 2000, Southern Cross, 1999, Isle of Dogs, 2001, Portrait of a Killer: Jack the Ripper--Case Closed, 2002; prodr. A.T.F., 1999. Vol. police officer. Address: ICM 40 W 57th St Fl 16 New York NY 10019-4001 also: Cornwell Enterprises PO Box 5235 Greenwich CT 06831-0504

CORNYN, JOHN, senator; b. Feb. 2, 1952; married; 2 children. BA, Trinity U., 1973; JD, St. Mary's U., 1977; postgrad., U. Va. Cert.: Tex. Bd. Legal Specialization (personal injury trial law). Assoc., ptnr. Groce, Locke & Hebdon, San Antonio, 1977—84; judge 37th Dist. Ct., Bexer County, 1985—90; presiding judge 4th Adminstrv. Jud. Region, 1989—92; justice Supreme Ct. Tex., Austin, 1991—98; atty. Thompson & Knight; atty. gen. State of Tex., Austin, 1999—2002; U.S. senator from Tex., 2003—. Bd. vis. Trinity U., Pepperdine U. Sch. Law; Tex. Supreme Ct. liaison Bd. Law Examiners, 1991—, Gender Bias Task Force, 1993—95; lectr. CLE programs. Fellow: San Antonio Bar Found., Tex. Bar Found.; mem.: Robert W. Calvent Inn of Ct. (pres. 1994—95), William Sessions Inn of Ct. (master bencher 1988—90, pres. 1989—90), Am. Law Inst. Republican. Office: US Senate Washington DC 20510*

CORO, EDYS, music educator; b. Santiago, Cuba, Oct. 11, 1935; d. Jose Antonio and Altagracia de la Estrella (Gonzalez) Coro; m. Raul Puig (annulled); m. Francisco Vazquez; stepchildren: Rosy, Francisco Jr. BS, Inst. Santiago, 1954; cert. in sec. tng., Greenbrier Coll., 1957; cert. in translation & interpretation, Miami Dade C.C., 1989; dipl., Inst. Children Lit., 1994. Sec. to mgr. Banco Nunez, Santiago, 1959—66; sec. to consul Brit. Consulate, Santiago, 1966—69; sec. to pres. Agencia La Nao, Javea Alicante, Spain, 1971—72; sec. to v.p. Chase Manhattan Bank NA, N.Y.C., 1972—79, adminstrv. asst. Miami, 1988—91, Family Counseling Svcs., Miami, 1979—87; owner, pres. Tu Grocery, Inc., Miami Beach, Fla.; music tchr., 1996—. Cmty. coord. City of Miami Beach, Fla., 1994—95. Mem.: Internat. Soc. Poets, Fla. Music Tchrs. Assn., Nat. Guild Piano Tchrs. Roman Catholic. Avocations: reading, bicycling, yoga, writing, drawing. Home: 4260 SW 84th Ave Miami FL 33155

CORODEMUS, STEVEN JAMES, state legislator, lawyer; b. Newark, Jan. 14, 1952; m. Michele Russell; 2 children. BA, Rutgers U., 1974; JD, Seton Hall U., 1979. Bar: N.J. 1979, Calif. 1981. Councilman Borough of Atlantic Highlands, 1986-88; vice-chmn. Monmouth County Planning Bd., 1989-92; mem. N.J. Gen. Assembly, 1991—; ptnr. Corodemus & Corodemus, Metuchen, N.J. Republican. Greek Orthodox. Office: PO Box 266 40 1st Ave Atlantic Highlands NJ 07716-1243 E-mail: asmcorodemus@njleg.state.nj.us.*

CORONADO, IRASEMA, political scientist, educator; b. Nogales, Sonora, Mex., Aug. 22, 1959; arrived in U.S., 1959; d. Gonzalo and Guadalupe Coronado; 1 child, Marissa Fernbaugh. BA in Polit. Sci., U. S. Fla., 1983; MA in Latin Am. Studies, U. Ariz., 1989, PhD in Polit. Sci., 1998. Prof. U. Incarnate Word, San Antonio, 1994—99, U. Tex., El Paso, 1999—. Mem. good neighbor environ. bd. U.S. EPA, Washington, 1998. Mem.: Am. Polit. Sci. Assn. Home: 5508 Fernwood Cir El Paso TX 79932 Office: U Tex El Paso Dept Polit Sci El Paso TX 79968 Office Fax: 915-747-5400. Business E-Mail: icoronado@utep.edu.

CORONADO, SANTIAGO SYBERT (JIM CORONADO), judge; b. Laredo, Tex., Nov. 12, 1951; s. Bill Gee and Lucia (Coronado) Sybert; m. Dawn Dittman, Apr. 27, 1996. BA cum laude, U. Tex., 1974, JD, 1978. Bar: Tex. 1978. Pvt. practice, Austin, Tex., 1979-89; mcpl. judge City of Austin, 1989-91, City of Kyle, Tex., 1989-91; magistrate judge Travis County Dist. Ct., 1991—. At large minority dir. State Bar Tex., 2003—. Bd. dirs. Am. Heart Assn., Austin, 1990; state pres. Mex. Am. Bar Assn., Tex., 1988-89; pres. Capital Area Mex. Am. Lawyers, Austin, 1986-87. Recipient Lifetime Achievement award Hispanic Issues Sect. State Bar of Tex., 1995, Presdl. citation for disting. svc., 1999. Mem.: Master Robert Calvin Inn of Ct., Travis County Bar Assn. (dir. 1995—2003, pres. 2001—02), State Bar of Tex. (at-large minority dir.), Hispanic Nat. Bar Assn. (regional pres. 1989—90, nat. v.p. 1991—92). Democrat. Home: 5602 Palisade Ct Austin TX 78731-4508 Office: Travis County Ct House Austin TX 78701

CORONEL, RAUL ANGULO, sculptor; b. Mexicali, Mex., Feb. 26, 1926; s. Jose Agapito and Emilia Angulo Coronel; m. Leanore Burden Cobb, Nov. 17, 1951 (dec. Oct. 1999). BS, U. Calif., Berkeley, 1951; BA, La. State Coll., 1954; cert. gemologist, GIA Santa Monica, Calif., 1984. Pres. Stoneware Design Inc., L.A., 1966—70; cons. designer Winbrook China, Santa Monica, 1970—80, Arch Pottery, L.A., 1970—80, Westwood Ind., NJ, 1980; treasure craft designer Calif., 1980—81. One-man shows include Paul Rivas Gallery, 1962, Represented in permanent collections U.S. Info. Ctr., Montevideo, Uruguay, Lytton Savs. & Loan, Palo Alto, Calif., Bank of Commerce, Ft. Worth. With USMCR, 1944—46. Recipient awards, Cal. State Fair, 1955—61, Young Ams., N.Y., 1955. Republican. Baptist. Avocations: painting, writing, gemology, music. Home: 1942 N Deer Park Dr # 44 Fullerton CA 92831

CORONITI, FERDINAND VINCENT, physics educator, consultant; b. Boston, June 14, 1943; s. Samuel Charles and Ethel Marie (Havlik) C.; m. Patricia Ann Smith, Aug. 30, 1969; children: Evelyn Marie, Samuel Thomas. AB, Harvard U., 1965; PhD, U. Calif.-Berkeley, 1969. Rsch. physicist UCLA, 1967-70, asst. prof. physics, 1970-74, assoc. prof., 1974-78, prof. physics and astronomy, 1978—. Cons. TRW Systems Contbr. articles to sci. jours. NASA grantee, 1974, NSF grantee, 1974—. Fellow Am. Geophys. Union, Am. Phys. Soc.; mem. Am. Astron. Soc., Internat. Union Radiol. Sci. Home: 10475 Almayo Ave Los Angeles CA 90064-2301 Office: UCLA Dept Physics & Astronomy 405 Hilgard Ave Los Angeles CA 90095-1547 E-mail: coroniti@astro.ucla.edu.

COROTIS, ROSS BARRY, civil engineering educator, academic administrator; b. Woodbury, N.J., Jan. 15, 1945; s. A. Charles and Hazel Laura (McCloskey) C.; m. Stephanie Michal Fuchs, Mar. 19, 1972; children: Benjamin Randall, Lindsay Sarah. SB, MIT, Cambridge, 1967, SM, 1968, PhD, 1971. Lic. profl. engr., Ill., Md., Colo., structural engr., Ill. Asst. prof. dept. civil engring. Northwestern U., Evanston, Ill., 1971-74, assoc. prof. dept. civil engring., 1975-79, prof. dept. civil engring., 1979-81, Johns Hopkins U., Balt., 1981-82, Hackerman prof., 1982-83, Hackerman prof., chmn. dept. civil engring., 1983-90, Hackerman prof., assoc. dean engring., 1990-94; dean Coll. Engring. and Applied Sci. U. Colo., Boulder, 1994-2001, Denver Bus. Challenge prof., 2001—. Mem. bldg. rsch. bd. Nat. Rsch. Coun., Washington, 1985-88; mem. steering com. Natural Disasters Roundtable, NRC, 2002—; lectr. profl. confs. Editor in chief Internat. Jour. Structural Safety, 1991-2000; contbr. articles to profl. jours. Mem. Mayor's task force City of Balt. Constrn. Mgmt., 1985. Recipient Engring. Tchg. award Northwestern U., 1977, Disting. Engring. Alumnus award U. Colo. Coll. Engring. and Applied Scis., 2000; named Md. Engr. of Yr., Balt. Engrs. Week Coun., 1989; rsch. grantee NSF, Nat. Bur. Stds., U.S. Dept. Energy, 1973-96. Fellow ASCE (chmn. safety bldgs. com. 1985-89, chmn. tech. adminstrv. com. structural safety and reliability 1988-92, chmn. probabilistic methods com. 1996-98, v.p. Md. chpt. 1987-88, pres. 1988-89, Walter L. Huber rsch. prize 1984, Civil Engr. of Yr. award Md. chpt. 1987, Outstanding Educator award Md. chpt. 1992); mem. Internat. Assn. for Structural Safety and Reliability (chair exec. bd. 1998-2001), NAE, Am. Soc. for Engring. Edn. (mem. pub. policy com. 1998-2001, mem. deans exec. bd. 1998-2001), Am. Concrete Inst. (chmn. structural safety com. 1986-88), Am. Nat. Stds. Inst. (chmn. live loads com. 1978-84), Nat. Inst. Stds. and Tech. (panel on assessment 1999—, vice chair panel on bldg. and fire rsch. lab. 2002—), Nat. Inst. Bldg. Scis. (affiliate, mem. multihazard mitigation coun. 2002—). Office: U Colo Coll Engring & Applied Sci PO Box 428 Boulder CO 80309-0428

CORPORON, JOHN ROBERT, broadcasting executive; b. Arcadia, Kans., Mar. 1, 1929; s. George William and Portteus (Stephens) C.; m. Harriett Sloan; children: John Robert Jr., David Sloan. BS in Journalism, U. Kans., 1951, MA in Polit. Sci., 1953. Reporter Pitts. Sun, 1950, UP, New Orleans, 1955, bur. chief Baton Rouge, 1956, New Orleans, 1956-58; correspondent Sta. WDSU-TV, New Orleans, Washington, 1958-60, 1960-62; news dir. Sta. WDSU-TV-AM, New Orleans, 1962-66; v.p., news dir. Sta. WNEW-TV, Metromedia, N.Y.C., 1967; v.p. news Metromedia TV, N.Y.C., Los Angeles, Washington and Kansas City, 1967-68; v.p., gen. mgr. Sta. WTOP-TV, Washington, 1968-71; exec. prodr. Newsweek Broadcast Svc., 1971-72; v.p., news dir. Sta. WPIX, N.Y.C., 1972-83, sr. v.p., 1983-96. Founding pres. Ind. TV News Assn., 1980; co-founder Ind. Network News, 1980. Spl. reporter London Economist, Washington Post, 1960's. Mem. Park Slope Civic Assn.; trustee William Allen White Found., U. Kans., 1994—; mem. adv. bd. Pew Charitable Trust Project, 1997—; v.p. Overseas Press Club Found., 2000—. Served with U.S. Army, 1953-55. Recipient Nat. Emmy award Acad. Arts and Scis., 1965. Mem. N.Y. State Associated Press Broadcasters (bd. dirs. 1984-96, pres. 1986-87), Radio TV News Dirs. Assn. (bd. dirs. 1988-91), Nat. AP Broadcasters (bd. dirs. 1989-2000, pres. 1995-97), Deadline Club, Overseas Press Club (pres. 1996-98). Democrat. Avocations: jogging, swimming, reading. Home: 671 10th St Brooklyn NY 11215-4501 Office: Overseas Press Club 40 W 45th St New York NY 10036-4202

CORPORON, MARY CAROLINE, lawyer; b. Oroville, Calif., May 9, 1956; d. Leonard and Leola (Seeds) C.; m. Gary W. Ott, May 8, 1983. B.A. in English, U. Utah, 1977, J.D., 1980. Bar: Utah 1980, U.S. Dist. Ct. Utah 1980, U.S. Ct. Appeals (10th cir.) 1983, U.S. Supreme Ct. 1984. Founder, ptnr. Corporon & Williams, Salt Lake City, 1980— . Tchr., BICEP, Salt Lake City, 1980— . Mem. Women Lawyers of Utah, Salt Lake C. of C., Mortar Bd. Office: Corporon & Williams 808 E South Temple Salt Lake City UT 84102-1305

CORPREW, HELEN BARBARA, mental health services professional; b. N.Y.C., Sept. 20, 1928; d. Charles August Shipley and Florence Lillian Musgrave-Shipley; m. Gerald Wilson Corprew, June 3, 1953 (div. May 1974); 1 child, Gerald Wilson Jr. BSW, Temple U., Phila., 1971; MSW, Temple U., 1980. LCSW. Tng. supr. Bell Telephone of N.Y., N.Y.C., 1947—70; dir. girls' day care Wissahickon Boys/Girls Social Programs Cmty. Club, Phila., 1970—73; dir. juvenile justice spl. svcs. programs Phila. Family Ct., 1973—; SCOH program supr. Sleighton Sch., Lima, Pa., 1991—; clin. therapist Harmony Mental Health, Phila., 1989—. Cons. home assignment Sleighton Sch., Phila., 1995—. Mem. cmty. recourse devel. com. Summit Presbyn. Ch., Phila., 1990—93, bd. deacons, 1972—78, bd. mem. elders session, 1979—87; cmty. coord. resources Wissahickon Boys and Girls Club, Phila., 1972—75. Recipient Disting. Outstanding Svc. award, Ct. Judges, Phila., 1986. Mem.: NASW, Acad. of Clin. Social Workers. Presbyterian. Avocations: travel, camping, dancing, reading, swimming. Mailing: 6701 Wissahickon Ave Philadelphia PA 19119

CORR, EDWIN GHARST, ambassador; b. Edmond, Okla., Aug. 6, 1934; s. E.L. and Rowena C.; m. Susanne Springer, Nov. 24, 1957; children: Michelle Ruth, Jennifer Jean, Phoebe Rowena. BS, U. Okla., 1957, MA, 1961, U. Tex., 1969. Fgn. svc. officer Dept. State, Washington, 1961-62; assigned to Mex., 1962-66; Peace Corps dir., 1966-68; Panama desk officer Dept. State, 1969-71; program officer Inter Am. Found., 1971; exec. asst. to amb. Am. Embassy, Bangkok, 1972-75, counselor polit. affairs Quito, Ecuador, 1976, dep. chief of mission, 1977-78; dep. asst. sec. internat. narcotics matters Dept. State, 1978-80; U.S. Amb. to Peru Lima, 1980-81; U.S. Amb. to Bolivia La Paz, 1981-85; U.S. Amb. to El Salvador San Salvador, 1985-88; Dept. State diplomat-in-residence U. Okla., 1988-90, prof. polit. sci., 1990-96; dir. Energy Inst. Ams., 1996—2002; assoc. dir. Internat. Programs Ctr., 1996—. Author: The Political Process in Colombia, 1971; co-editor: Low-Intensity Conflict: Old Threats in a New World, 1992, The Middle East Peace Process: Vision vs. Reality, 2002; co-author: The Search for Security: The U.S. Grand Strategy in the 21st Century, 2003; contbr. to books and profl. jours. Served to capt. USMC, 1957-60. Mem. Am. Fgn. Service Assn. Home: 1617 Jenkins Ave Norman OK 73072-6508

CORR, JAMES VANIS, furniture manufacturing executive, investor, lawyer, accountant; b. Selma, Ala., June 28, 1922; s. Mark Stroud and Julia (Dozier) C.; m. Judith Ann Hackney, Feb. 3, 1971; children by previous marriage: James Jr., William V., Emily S., Julia D. BS, U. Ala., 1948, LLB, 1951. CPA, Ala., Ga. Ptnr. Dent & Corr, CPA's, Birmingham, Ala., 1954-61; exec. v.p. Buck Creek Industries, Inc., Atlanta, 1961-70, pres., 1970-77, also bd. dirs.; v.p. Sperry & Hutchinson Co., N.Y.C., 1976-78, group v.p. furnishings divsn. Atlanta, 1976-78. Pres. JVC Enterprises, Inc., Atlanta, 1978—; speaker tax clinic U. Ala., 1954—. Bd. dirs. Met. YMCA, Birmingham. With AC, USMCR, 1944-46 Decorated D.F.C., Air medal with 2 oak leaf clusters. Mem. Ala. Soc. CPAs (past chmn. Birmingham chpt.), Ga. Soc. CPAs, ABA, Ala. Bar Assn., Am. Inst. CPAs, Ala. Textile Assn., Ga. Textile Assn., Exch. Club (Birmingham), Mountain Brook (Ala., past pres.). Home: 545 River Chase Pt NW Atlanta GA 30328-3555

CORRADA DEL RIO, ALVARO, bishop; b. Santurce, P.R., May 13, 1942; Joined Soc. of Jesus; ordained priest Roman Cath. Ch., 1974. Pastoral coord. Northeast Cath. Hispanic Ctr., N.Y., 1982-85; titular bishop of Rusticiana and aux. bishop Washington, 1985—; bishop, 2001—. Apostolic adminstr. Diocese of Caguas, P.R. Roman Catholic. Office: Bishop of Tyler 1015 ESE Loop 323 Tyler TX 75701-9663

CORRADINI, DEEDEE, mayor; Student, Drew U., 1961-63; BS, U. Utah, 1965, MS, 1967. Adminstrv. asst. for public info. Utah State Office Rehab. Svcs., 1967-69; cons. Utah State Dept. Cmty. Affairs, 1971-72; media dir., press sec. Wayne Owens for Congress Campaign, 1972; press sec. Rep. Wayne Owens, 1973-74; spl. asst. to N.Y. Congl. Rep. Richard Ottinger, 1975; asst. to pres., dir. cmty. rels. Snowbird Corp., 1975-77; exec. v.p. Bonneville Assocs., Inc., Salt Lake City, 1977-80, pres., 1980-89, chmn., CEO, 1989-91; mayor Salt Lake City, 1992—2000; pres. Corradini & Co., Salt Lake City, 2000—. Pres. U.S. Conf. of Mayors, 1998—, mem. unfunded fed. mandates task force, mem. crime and violence task force; chair Mayor's Gang Task Force; mem. interngovtl. policy adv. com. U.S. Trade Rep., 1993-94, 99—; mem. transp. and comm. com. Nat. League of Cities, 1993-94. Bd. trustees Intermountain Health Care, 1980-92; bd. dirs., exec. com. Utah Symphony, 1983-92, vice chmn., 1985-88, chmn., 1988-92; dir. Utah chpt. Nat. Conf. Christians and Jews, Inc., 1988; bd. dirs. Salt Lake Olympic Bid Com., 1989—; chmn. image com. Utah Partnership for Edn. and Econ. Devel., 1989-92; co-chair United Way Success by 6 Program; pres. Shelter of the Homeless Com., active Sundance Inst. Utah Com., 1990-92; disting. bd. fellow So. Utah U., 1991; v.p. Internat. Women's Forum, co-chair program com.; trustee Am. Comm. Sch., Beirut; vice-chair 2012 Bid Selection Com., U.S. Olympic Com.; active numerous other civic orgns. and coms. Fellow Disting. sr. fellow in Urban Studies, Richard Riley Inst. Govt., Politics and Pub. Adminstrn., Furman U., 2000—. Mem. Salt Lake Area C. of C. (bd. govs. 1979-81, chmn. City/County/Govt. com. 1976-86). Democrat. Office: 426 S 1000 East #606 Salt Lake City UT 84102

CORRADO, FRED, food company executive; b. Mt. Vernon, N.Y., May 20, 1940; s. Anthony Edward and Rose (Capone) C.; children: David, Paul, Christopher. BBA in Acctg., Manhattan Coll., 1961; grad. Advanced Mgmt. Program, Harvard U., 1983. CPA, N.Y. Sr. auditor Arthur Andersen & Co., N.Y.C., 1961-65; contr. Romney Cosmetics Co. divsn. Pfizer Co., Stamford, Conn., 1966-68; with ITT Corp., 1968-69, Kenton Corp., 1969-73, Nabisco Brands USA (formerly Stds. Brands Inc.), 1973-86; pres. Planters divsn. Nabisco Brands USA (name formerly Std. Brands Inc.), East Hanover, N.J., 1980-84; exec. v.p., COO Nabisco Brands Ltd., Toronto, Ont., Can., 1984-85, pres., COO, 1985-86, also bd. dirs.; vice chmn. fin. and adminstrn., CFO, bd. dirs. Great Atlantic and Pacific Tea Co., Inc., Montvale, N.J., 1987—. Bd. dirs. Covenant House, N.J. Performing Arts Ctr. Mem. AICPA, Fin. Execs. Inst. (vice chmn. CFO adv. com.), N.Y. State Soc. CPAs. Office: Gt Atlantic & Pacific Tea Co Inc 2 Paragon Dr Montvale NJ 07645-1718

CORRALES, JESÚS, dancer; b. Havana, Cuba, 1969; Student, Cuban Sch. Ballet. Mem. Nat. Ballet Cuba, 1987; soloist Royal Winnipeg Ballet, 1998—99, prin. dancer, 1999—. Guest dancer Nat. Co. of Dance, Mexico, 1995, Royal Opera of Wallonie, Belgium, 1995; dancer Nat. Ballet of Cuba Festival Cervantino, Mexico, Art Festival of Edinburgh, Scotland, Festival Krannoyarsk, Russia. Dancer (ballets) Romeo and Juliet, Royal Opera of Wallonie, Belgium, The Earth, Carmina Burana, Dracula, Royal Winnipeg Ballet, Tchaikovsky Pas de Deux, Impromptu Pas de Deux, Grand Pas Classique. Recipient Gold medal Best Dancer at a competition, Brazil, 1988, Bronze medal, IV Internat. Competition, N.Y.C., 1993, Gold medal, Nat. Competition, Guadalajara, Mex., 1994. Office: Royal Winnipeg Ballet 380 Graham Ave Winnipeg MB Canada R3C 4K2

CORREA, GALO A. construction executive; b. Ecuador; arrived in U.S., 1966; s. Leonidas and Piedad Correa; m. Cristina Correa, Dec. 31, 1965; children: Galo A. Jr., Tyrone. Student, Montgomery Coll. With VOB Datson Dealership, 1967—72; owner Car-Rite, 1972—; pres., CEO Rockville Autotech, Inc., Ecuabol Import and Export; pres, gen. mgr. Correa Gen. Contractors. Pres., founder Hispanic United, Rockville; founder Spanish Tng. Inst.; bd. dirs. Montgomery County Cmty. Partnership, Md. Ethnic Polit. Coalition; mem. adv. com. Montgomery County Police; active Lincoln Park Assn.; founder, pres. Latino Civil Task Force, Capital Area Latino Coalition. Home and Office: 422 N Stongstreet Ave Rockville MD 20850

CORREA, LOU, state official; m. Esther Correa; children: Alejandro, Andres, Adan, Emilia. BA in Econs., Calif. State U., Fullerton; MBA, JD, UCLA. Businessman; educator; candidate Dist. 69 Calif. State Assembly, 1996, state assembly mem. Dist. 69, 1999—. Mem. appropriations com.; mem. banking and fin. com.; chair bus. and professions com.; mem. ins. com.; mem. pub. employees, retirement and social security com. Democrat. Mailing: Rm 6025 PO Box 942849 Sacramento CA 94249 Office: Rancho Santiago CC Ste 225 2323 N Broadway Santa Ana CA 92706

CORREA-VILLASEÑOR, ADOLFO, epidemiologist, physician; b. Mazatlán, Sinaloa, Mex., Mar. 2, 1946; arrived in U.S., 1961; s. Adolfo and Estela (Villaseñor) Correa; m. Ana Isabel Alfaro, June 2, 1978. MS, U. Calif., San Diego, 1970, MD, 1974; MPH, Johns Hopkins U., 1981, PhD, 1987. Diplomate Am. Bd. Pediatrics, Am. Bd. Preventive Medicine. Intern San Francisco Gen. Hosp., San Francisco, 1974—75; resident in pediatrics U. Calif., San Francisco, 1975—77, chief resident in pediatrics, 1977—78; epidemic intelligence service officer Ctr. for Disease Control, Atlanta, 1978—80; resident in preventive medicine Johns Hopkins Sch. Hygiene and Pub. Health, Balt., 1980—83, asst.

prof. epidemiology, 1987—95, assoc. prof. epidemiology, 1995—98, asst. prof. pediatrics, 1988—92, asst. prof. population dynamics, 1990—95, assoc. prof. population dynamic, 1995—98; chief epidemiology and surveillance sect. Birth Defects and Pediat. Genetics/Nat. Ctr. Environ. Health, Atlanta, 1998—2001; med. officer Nat. Ctr. Birth Defects and Devel. Disabilities, Atlanta, 2001—. Vis. rsch. prof. Sch. of Pub. Health of Mex., 1993. Mem. Soc. for Epidemiologic Rsch., Teratology Soc., Internat. Soc. Environ. Epidemiology. Home: 840 Starlight Dr NE Atlanta GA 30342-2832 Office: Nat Ctr on Birth Defects & Devel Disabilities CDC MS E 86 1600 Clifton Rd Atlanta GA 30333 E-mail: acorrea@cdc.gov.

CORREDOR, MARY B. language educator, consultant, translator; b. Fairbury, Ill. d. Agnes K. Runyon; 1 child, Erik. MA, Ill. State U., 1976; MA TESOL, Am. U., Washington, 1996. Lectr. Spanish, ESL, and pedagogy Sul Ross State U., Alpine, Tex., 1996-98; dept. chair fgn. lang. and ESL, Austin (Tex.) C.C., 1998—. Freelance translator, Austin, 1999—. Mem. TESOL, Austin Translators and Interpreters Assn., Am. Assn. Tchrs. of Spanish and Portuguese. Home: 6303 B Okner Ln Austin TX 78745 Office: Austin CC-Rio Grande Campus 1212 Rio Grande Austin TX 78701 E-mail: mcorredo@austin.cc.tx.

CORREIA, ALBERTO ABRANTES, management executive; b. Milford, Mass., Nov. 16, 1956; s. Alberto Filipe and Julia Abrantes (Simones) C.; m. Sharon Ann Haaf; children: Alexis Abrantes, Emily Elizabeth. BS, Coll. Holy Cross, Worcester, Mass., 1978. With Waters, Milford, Mass., 1976-77; sales rep. Waters Assocs., Milford, Mass., 1978-79, sales mgr., 1980; dir. sales Millipore, Paris, 1981-84, Xydex Inc., Bedford, Mass., 1985-87; dir. product mgmt. Genex Co., Gaithersburg, Md., 1988-89; Zymark, Hopkinton, Mass., 1990-91, dir. engring., 1991-92, dir. sales, 1992-93; v.p. world wide sales and svc. Unisyn Techs., Tustin, Calif., 1993-96; v.p. ops. Unisyn, Hopkinton, Mass., 1996—2002; v.p. Velquest, Hopkinton, Mass., 2002—. Home: 3 Leah Ln Milford MA 01757-1276 E-mail: ACorreia@attbi.com.

CORREIA, ROBERT, state legislator; b. Fall River, Mass., Jan. 3, 1939; s. Manuel and Mary Perreira (Gomes) C.; m. Patricia Fogarty; children: Robert, Susan, Mark. BSBA, U. Mass., Dartmouth, 1962; MEd, Bridgewater State Coll., 1968; DPA (hon.), U. Mass., Dartmouth, 1989. Founding charter mem., bd. dirs., treas., mgr. Our Lady of Angels Fed. Credit Union, Fall River, 1962-92; tchr. math & sci. Henry Lord Jr. High Sch., Fall River, 1962-77; state rep. Commonwealth of Mass., Boston, 1977—. Mem. Dem. City Com., Fall River, 1979—; legis. liaison Sr. Senate of Mass., Fall River, 1979—; mem. U. Mass.-Dartmouth Labor Edn. Ctr., 1985-93. Served with USMC, 1962. Awarded Order of Prince Henry/rank of Knight Comdr., Portuguese Govt. Democrat. Roman Catholic. Office: 1290 Plymouth Ave Fall River MA 02721-2534 E-mail: robert.correia@hou.state.ma.us.

CORRELL, ALSTON DAYTON, JR., (PETE CORRELL), forest products company executive; b. Brunswick, Ga., Apr. 28, 1941; s. Alston Dayton and Elizabeth (Flippo) Correll; m. Ada Lee Fulford, June 23, 1963; children: Alston Dayton, Elizabeth Lee. BSBA, U. Ga., 1963; MS in Pulp and Paper Tech., U. Maine, 1966, MS in Chem. Engring., 1967. Tech. svc. engr. Westvaco, 1963—64; instr. U. Maine, Orono, 1964—67; various pulp and paper mgmt. positions Weyerhaeuser Co., 1967—77; pres. paperboard divsn. Mead Corp., Dayton, Ohio, 1977—80, group v.p. paperboard, 1980, group v.p. paper, 1981, group v.p. forest products, 1981—83, sr. v.p. forest products, 1983—88; sr. v.p. pulp and printing paper Ga.-Pacific Corp., Atlanta, 1988—89, exec. v.p. pulp and paper, 1989—91, pres., COO, 1991—93, pres., CEO, 1993, CEO, chmn. bd. and pres., 1993—. Bd. dirs. SunTrust Banks, Atlanta, SunTrust Banks, Inc., SunTrust Banks Ga., Inc., Mirant Corp., Norfolk Southern Corp.; chmn. Inst. Paper Sci. and Tech., Inc.; bd. councilors The Carter Coun. Trustee U. Ga. Found., Robert W. Woodruff Arts Ctr.; mem. Atlanta coun. Boy Scouts Am.; mem. Atlanta Action Forum; mem. exec. com. Nat. Coun. Paper Industry for Air and Stream Improvement, Inc., past chmn. bd.; bd. dirs. Miami Valley (Ohio) Boy Scouts, Nature Conservancy, Keep Am. Beautiful Inc.; Ga. Rsch. Alliance; chmn. United Negro Coll. Fund, vice chmn. Atlanta Campaign; bd. dirs. Ctrl. Atlanta Progress, chmn., 1995—97. Named CEO of Yr., Atlanta Bus. League, 1998, Exec. Papermaker of Yr., PaperAge, 1999; named one of 100 Most Influential Georgians, Ga. Trend Mag., 1994, 1995, 25 Most Influential Georgians, 1996, 1997, 1998; recipient Nat. Brotherhood award, 1991, Disting. Alumnus award, U. Ga., Terry Coll. Bus., 1994, Salute to Greatness award, The King Ctr., 1999. Mem.: Am. Forest and Paper Assn. (bd. dirs., forest resource product group exec. com.), Atlanta C. of C. (bd. dirs., Forward Atlanta Policy Group, chmn. 1997—98), Ga. C. of C. (bd. dirs.), Commerce Club (bd. dirs. Atlanta chpt.). Republican. Presbyterian. Office: Ga-Pacific Corp PO Box 105605 133 Peachtree St NE Fl 51 Atlanta GA 30303-1808

CORRELL, JANET MOORE, music educator; b. East Saint Louis, Ill., Sept. 2, 1942; d. John McCabe and Virginia (Killene) Moore; m. David Henry Correll, Aug. 21, 1965. BS in Music, U. Ill., 1964, MS in Music Edn., 1965. Cert. permanent tchg. Music K-12 Ill., 1965, Tchg. N.Y., 1977. Tchr. Music Homer Sch. Dist., Ill., 1965—66, Bloomington Pub. Schs., Ind., 1966—67; asst. dir. Music Program Belleville Pub. Schs., Ill., 1967; tchr. elem. music San Antonio Pub. Schs., 1968—70; tchr. Music Union Springs/Weedsport Schs., Union Springs, Weedsport, NY, 1970—72, Weedsport Pub. Schs., 1973—75; prof. Music Cayuga C.C., Auburn, NY, 1978—. Organist Westminster Presbyn. Ch., Auburn, 1978—93; organist, choir dir. United Ministry of Aurora, NY, 1993—94; organist Presbyn. Ch., Geneva, 1995—; adjudicator N.Y. State Sch. Music Assn., 1974; instr. Organ Am. Guild Organists, 2000. Author: The Organists Companion, 1986, Discover the Basics Series, 1998, Flowers of the Orient, 1994. Recipient Disting. Svc. award, Cayuga County Arts Coun., 1995. Mem.: Am. Guild Organists. Independent. Presbyterian. Avocations: reading, yoga, knitting, jewelry making, harp playing. Home: PO Box 293 Aurora NY 13026 Office: Cayuga Cmty Coll Franklin St Auburn NY 13021*

CORRERO, ANTHONY JAMES, III, lawyer; b. Monroe, La., Dec. 15, 1941; s. Anthony James Jr. and Robbie Lee (Pace) C.; m. Margaret Aline O'Meara, May 30, 1966; children: Margaret Hollis, Edward Thomas Eliot, Marshall Alan. BA, N.E. La. U., 1962; LLB, La. State U., 1965. Bar: La. 1965, U.S. Supreme Ct. 1968. Spl. asst. atty. gen. State of La., Baton Rouge, 1965-68; assoc. Jones, Walker, Waechter, Poitevent, Carrere & Denegre, New Orleans, 1968-72, ptnr., 1972-94, Correro, Fishman & Casteix, LLP, New Orleans, 1994-96, Correro Fishman Haygood Phelps Walmsley & Casteix, LLP, New Orleans, 1996—. Adj. prof. law La. State U., Tulane U., Loyola U.; bd. dirs. T.L. James & Co., Inc., Ruston, La., La. Partnership for Tech. 1st lt. USAR, 1965-71. Mem. ABA, La. Bar Assn. (chmn. sect. corp. and bus. law 1978-79), Am. Law Inst. Democrat. Roman Catholic. Office: Correro Fishman et al 201 Saint Charles Ave New Orleans LA 70170-4600 E-mail: acorrero@cfhlaw.com.

CORRIERE, JOSEPH N., JR., urologist, educator; b. Apr. 3, 1937; m. Evelyn Pavia Mossey, June 25, 1960 (div. July 1984); children: Joseph N., Christopher John, Gregory James, Evelyn Anne; m. Eileen Doyle Brewer, Oct. 17, 1987. BA, U. Pa., 1959; MD, Seton Hall Coll. Medicine, 1963. Diplomate Am. Bd. Urology (trustee). Intern Pa. Hosp., Phila., 1963—64; asst. instr. surgery, fellow Harrison Dept. Surgery Rsch. Hosp. U. Pa., Phila., 1964—65, asst. instr. urology, 1965—68, USPHS urol. rsch. trainee, 1967—68, instr. urology, 1968—69, assoc. in urology, 1969—71, asst. prof. urology, 1971—74; veneral disease trainee Phila. Dept. Pub. Health, 1965; radioisotope trainee William H. Donner Ctr. for Radiology, Phila., 1965—66; prof., dir. divsn. urology, dept. surgery U. Tex. Med. Sch., Houston, 0974—1993, interim chmn. dept. surgery, 1980—82, assoc. chmn. dept. surgery, 1984—86; chief urology svc. Hermann Hosp., 1974—93, Tex. Med. Ctr., Houston. Cons. residency rev. com. in urology Lyndon Baines Johnson Hosp., 1993—99, M.D. Anderson Cancer Ctr.; cons. NASA. Contbr. numerous articles to profl. jours. Maj. USAF, 1969—71. Mem.: ACS, Am. Assn. for Surgery of Trauma, Am. Assn. Genitourol. Surgery, Soc. Univ. Urologists, Soc. Univ. Surgeons (sec.-treas. 1984—86, pres. 1987—88, 1987—88), Am. Urol. Assn. (dir. edn. 1993—2002). Roman Catholic. Home: 7511 Morningside Dr Houston TX 77030-3619 Office: MD Anderson Cancer Ctr Box 333 1515 Holcombe Blvd Houston TX 77030-4009

CORRIGAN, E(DWARD) GERALD, investment banker; b. Waterbury, Conn., 1941; BS, Fairfield U.; MA, PhD, Fordham U. Group v.p. mgmt. and planning Fed. Res. Bank of N.Y., 1976-80; spl. assignment to chmn. bd. govs. Fed. Res. Sys., 1979-80; pres. Fed. Res. Bank of Mpls., 1981-84, Fed. Res. Bank of N.Y., N.Y.C., 1985-93; chmn. internat. advisors Goldman, Sachs & Co., N.Y.C., 1994-96, mng. dir., 1997—. Co-chair The Bretton Woods Com., The Per Jacobsson Found., The Group of Thirty, The Inst. for Fin. Stability, Bank for Internat. Settlements, The Trilateral Commn., Aspen Inst. Program on the World Economy, Internat. Adv. Panel of Monetary Authority of Singapore. Mem. Aspen Inst. (co-chmn.), Econ. Club of N.Y. Office: Goldman Sachs and Co 85 Broad St New York NY 10004-2456

CORRIGAN, FAITH, journalist, educator, historian; b. Cleve., Oct. 16, 1926; d. William John and Marjorie (Wilson) C.; m. Sigvald Matias Refsnes, Sept. 18, 1957 (dec. Feb. 1994); children: Marjorie Refsnes, Sunniva Collins, Stephen Refsnes. BA, Ohio State U., 1948; MAT, Kent State U., 1987. Cert. tchr. English, reading, Ohio. Staff writer women's news N.Y. Times, N.Y.C., 1953-57; investigative reporter Cleve. Plain Dealer, 1962-66; dir. pub. info. Cuyahoga County Bd. Commrs., Cleve., 1966-69; dir. news, publs. Huron Rd. Hosp., East Cleveland, Ohio, 1970-73; lectr. II U. Akron, Ohio, 1990-91; adj. prof. Kent State U., North Canton, Ohio, 1996-97, Kent State U., Ashtabula br., Geauga/Twinsburg, Ohio, 1999—. Lectr. Fordham U., N.Y.C., 1956; expert witness U.S. Senate Medicare Hearings, Cleve., 1965; mgr. Cuyahoga County Welfare Levy Campaign, Cleve., 1966. Author: First Generation, 2002, Bread Glass and History, 2003; contbr. articles to newspapers. TESOL, Lit. Vols. Am.; mem. bd. mgrs. Eleanor B. Rainey Meml. Inst., Cleve., 1966-78; officer, trustee Lake County Cmty. Svcs. Coun., 1984-90; mem. adv. bd. Lake Geauga Legal Aid Soc., Painesville, Lake County, 1984-87; chair Initiative Petition Campaign on Environ. Waste Plant Issue, Willoughby, Ohio, 1991; officer, founder Ohio State U. chpt. Am. Newspaper Guild, 1947-48; del. rep. assembly N.Y. Newspaper Guild, 1954-57; poll judge Lake County Bd. Elections, 1984-98; field rep. U.S. Census Bur., 1989—; recruiter, crew leader U.S. Census 2000. Recipient award of achievement Press Club of Cleve., 1964, Pulitzer nominee Cleve. Plain Dealer, 1964, 1st in state Ohio Newspaper Women's Assn., 1964, 1st in state Pub. Contest of Am. Heart Assn., 1972, 1st pl. publs. award Internat. Assn. Bus. Communicators, 1971-72. Mem. VFW (Ladies Aux.), Willoughby Hist. Soc. (trustee, v.p. 1997-2002, Heritage chmn. 2003-), Ohio Bicentennial Hist. Markers Rsch., Early Am. Pattern Glass Soc. Democrat. Roman Catholic. Avocations: expert on american china, glass, american labor history. Home: 37550 Euclid Ave Willoughby OH 44094-5622

CORRIGAN, HELEN GONZALEZ, retired cytologist; b. San Diego, Tex., Sept. 30, 1922; d. Rodrigo Simon and Eva Ruby (Corrigan) Gonzalez. BS, Our Lady of Lake, San Antonio, 1943. Registered cytologist Internat. Acad. Cytology. Tchr. San Diego H.S., 1943-45; microbiologist Nix Hosp. Profl. Lab., San Antonio, 1952-59; med. technologist Tucson Med. Ctr., 1959-60; cytologist in charge Jackson-Todd Cancer Detection Ctr., San Antonio, 1961-64; cytologist in charge cytology sect. Pathology Lab. 4th and 5th U.S. Army Ref. Area Lab., Fort Sam Houston, Tex., 1964-78; instr. trouble shooters, quality control analyst cytology sect. Brooks Med. Ctr., Fort Sam Houston, 1978-81; owner Corrigan Enterprises, San Diego, 1981-91; ret., 1997. Cytologist Waco (Tex. Med. Lab. Svc., 1988-89, Nat. Health Lab., San Antonio, 1989-90, Internat. Cancer Screening Lab., San Antonio, 1990-91; head cytologist Dr. R. Garza & Assocs., Weslaco, Tex., 1992—. Adv. bd. mem. EEO, Ft. Sam Houston, 1972-74. Mem. NAFE, Am. Soc. Clin. Pathologists (registered cytologist, registered med. technologist, assoc.), Greater San Antonio Women's C. of C. Republican. Roman Catholic. Avocations: fishing, hunting, tennis, skiing, dancing. Home: 149 Perry Ct San Antonio TX 78209-6211

CORRIGAN, JAMES JOHN, JR., pediatrician, dean; b. Pitts., Aug. 28, 1935; s. James John and Rita Mary (Grimes) C.; m. Carolyn Virginia Long, July 2, 1960; children: Jeffrey James, Nancy Carolyn. BS, Juniata Coll., Huntingdon, Pa., 1957; MD (hon.), U. Pitts., 1961. Diplomate Am. Bd. Pediats. (hematology-oncology). Intern, then resident in pediat. U. Colo. Med. Ctr., 1961-64; trainee in pediat. hematology-oncology U. Ill. Med. Center, 1964-66; assoc. in pediat. Emory U. Med. Sch., 1966-67, asst. prof., 1967-71; mem. faculty U. Ariz. Coll. Medicine, Tucson, 1971-90, prof. pediat., 1974-90; chief sect. pediat. hematology-ongology, also dir. Mountain States Regional Hemophilia Ctr., U. Ariz., Tucson, 1978-90; chief of staff U. Med. Ctr. U. Ariz., Tucson, 1984-86; prof. pediat., vice dean for acad. affairs Tulane U. Sch. Medicine, New Orleans, 1990-93, interim dean, 1993-94, dean, 1994-2000, v.p., 2000—02, prof. emeritus pediat., 2002—. Assoc. editor Am. Jour. Diseases of Children, 1981-89, 90-93, interim editor, 1993; contbr. numerous papers to med. jours. Grantee NIH, Mountain States Regional Hemophilia Ctr., Ga. Heart Assn., GE, Am. Cancer Soc. Mem. Am. Acad. Pediatrics, Am. Soc. Hematology, Soc. Pediatric Rsch., Western Soc. Pediatric Rsch., Am. Heart Assn. (coun. thrombosis), Internat. Soc. Thrombosis and Haemostasis, Am. Pediatric Soc., World Fedn. Hemophilia, Pima County Med. Assn. (v.p., 1986—, pres. 1988—), Alpha Omega Alpha. Republican. Roman Catholic. Office: Tulane U Health Scis Ctr Dept Pediat 1430 Tulane Ave New Orleans LA 70112-2699 E-mail: jcorrig@tulane.edu.

CORRIGAN, JAMES JOSEPH, II, retired lawyer; b. Providence, Feb. 17, 1943; s. Francis Vincent and Mary Catherine (Goggin) C.; m. Mary Katherine Fogle, Apr. 17, 1971 (div. Mar. 1984); children: Eileen, Leigh; m. Elaine Dennis, May 19, 1990 (div. June 1997); m. Anne Gerardi, Jan. 14, 2002. AB, Providence Coll., 1964; JD, Cath. U., 1968; LLM, George Washington U., 1974. Bar: Va. 1968, U.S. Supreme Ct. 1974. Mem. legis. office FDA, Washington, 1964-74; mem. consumer office White House, Washington, 1968; assoc. dir. Bur. Health Care Delivery and Assistance, Washington, 1968-86, dir. grants and procurement divsn., 1986-96, assoc. adminstr., 1996—2002. Lectr. George Mason U., Fairfax, Va., 1983-95, Keller Grad. Sch. Mgmt., 1996; adj. prof. Old Dominion U., 2003—; bd. dir. Portsmouth (Va.) Cmty. Health Ctr. Contbr. articles to profl. jours. Mem. ABA (subcom. govt. legislation and pub. interest food, drug and cosmetic law com. 1968-80). Roman Catholic. Home: 1450 E Ocean View Ave Norfolk VA 23503-2309 E-mail: jjoey@corrigan.com.

CORRIGAN, JOHN EDWARD, JR., banker, lawyer; b. Chgo., Sept. 26, 1922; s. John Edward and Veronica (Mulvey) C.; m. Eileen Williams, Nov. 4, 1950 (div. 1979); m. Sylvia Dennison McElin, Sept. 24, 1983. BA, Harvard U., 1943, JD, 1949. Bar: Ill. 1950. With First Nat. Bank Chgo., 1949-79, asst. v.p., 1960-61, v.p., 1961-72, sr. v.p., 1972-79; prin. Hedberg, Tobin, Flaherty & Whalen P.C., Chgo., 1980-87; of counsel Hedberg, Tobin, Flaherty & Whalen Inc., Chgo., 1988-92. With AUS, 1943-46, 51-52. Home: 560 Greenwood Ave Kenilworth IL 60043-1024

CORRIGAN, MARY KATHRYN, theater educator; b. Mpls., July 11, 1930; d. Arthur Joseph Kolling and Hazel (Pierce) Colp; children: Michael Edward, Timothy Patrick. BA, U. Minn., Mpls., 1965, MA, 1967. Advisor, counselor Coll. Liberal Arts U. Minn., Mpls., 1964-65, instr. dept. theatre, 1966-69, asst. prof. dept. theatre, 1969-73; assoc. prof. dept. theatre Fla. State U., Tallahassee, 1973-75, U. Calif., San Diego, 1975-89, 92-96, prof. emeritus, 1996—, faculty dir. edn. bd., 1997—; assoc. dir. U. Calif. Study Ctr. U.K., Ireland, 1989-91; faculty dir. ednl. bd. U.C., San Diego, 1997-2001; faculty dir. Brit. Am. Drama Acad. Balliol Coll., Oxford, England, 1987—2002. Master tchr. Brit. Am. Drama Acad., Balliol Coll., Oxford U., Eng., summers, 1987-2002, chmn. undergrad. and intermediate programs midsummer, 1992-2001, BADA, Oxford, Eng., 2003, U. San Diego, 2003; actress, San Diego, 2000. Actress nat. pub. radio Chopin, 1984, video film Ultrasonography, 1986; author: (with others) The Vocal Vision, 1997. Mem. adv. com. United Ministeries, Mpls., 1968-73, Mpls. Sch. Bd., 1968-72; vol. KPBS Reading Svc.; vol. dir. for Actors Alliance; mediator work with juvenile offenders. Recipient Tozier Found. award, Eng., 1967, Best Actress award Globe Theatre, San Diego, 1979, NEH award Folger Shakespeare Theatre, 1992-93; grantee Rockefeller Found., 1968, McMillan grantee U. Minn., Eng., 1968, U. Calif.-San Diego, 1982-87, NEH grantee Folger Inst., Washington, 1993-94, Stanford U., summer 1994, Creativity LaJolla Conf., 1995, 2000, Am. U., Cairo, 1996, U. Richmond, Va., 1997, Edn. Abroad Program U. Calif., 1997—. Mem. Am. Theatre Assn. (exec. com., v.p. performance tng. 1984-86), Voice and Speech Theater Assn. (bd. dirs. 1986-89), Play Actors Alliance (dir. 2001). Democrat. Avocations: hiking, theatre, reading, art. Home: 2645 Gobat Ave San Diego CA 92122-3127 Office: U Calif San Diego Theatre Dept La Jolla CA 92093-0344

CORRIGAN, MAURA DENISE, judge; b. Cleve., June 14, 1948; d. Peter James and Mae Ardell (McCrone) Corrigan; m. Joseph Dante Grano, July 11, 1976 (dec.). BA with honors, Marygrove Coll., 1969; JD with honors, U. Detroit, 1973; LLD (hon.), No. Mich. U., 1999, Mich. State U., 2003; JD (hon.), Mercy Law Sch., 2002. Bar: Mich. 1974. Jud. clk. Mich. Ct. Appeals, Detroit, 1973-74; asst. prosecutor Wayne County, Detroit, 1974-79, asst. U.S. atty., 1979-89, chief appellate divsn., 1979-86, chief asst. U.S. Atty., 1986-89; ptnr. Plunkett & Cooney PC, Detroit, 1989-92; judge Mich. Ct. Appeals, 1992-98, chief judge, 1997-98; justice Mich. Supreme Ct., Detroit, 1999-2001, chief justice, 2001—. Vice chmn. Mich. Com. to formulate Rules of Criminal Procedure, Mich. Supreme Ct., 1982-89; mem. Mich. Law Revision Commn., 1991-98; mem. com. on standard jury instrns., State Bar Mich., 1978-82; lectr. Mich. Jud. Inst., Sixth cir. Jud. Workshop, Inst. CLE, ABA-Cin. Bar Litigation Sects., Dept. Justice Advocacy Inst.; v.p. Conf. Chief Justices, 2003. Contbr. chpt. to book, articles to legal revs. Vice chmn. Project Transition, Detroit, 1976-92; mem. citizens Adv. Coun. Lafayette Clinic, Detroit, 1979-87; bd. dirs. Detroit Wayne County Criminal Advocacy Program, 1983-86; pres., bd. dirs. Rep. Women's Bus. and Profl. Forum, 1991. Recipient award of merit Detroit Commn. on Human Rels., 1974, Dir.'s award Dept. Justice, 1985, Outstanding Practitioner of Criminal Law award Fed. Bar Assn., 1989, award Mich. Women's Commn., 1998, Grano award, 2001, U.S. Dept. HHS award for child support, 2002; named Disting. Alumna, Margrove Coll., 2003. Mem. Mich. Bar Assn., Detroit Bar Assn., Fed. Bar Assn. (pres. Detroit chpt. 1990-91), Inc. Soc. Irish Am. Lawyers (pres. 1991-92, Achievment award 2001), Federalist Soc. (Mich. chpt.). Office: Mich Supreme Ct 8-500 3034 W Grand Blvd Detroit MI 48202

CORRIGAN, ROBERT ANTHONY, academic administrator; b. New London, Conn., Apr. 21, 1935; s. Anthony John and Rose Mary (Jengo) C.; m. Joyce D. Mobley, Jan. 12, 1975; children by previous marriage: Kathleen Marie, Anthony John, Robert Anthony; 1 stepdau., Erika Mobley. AB, Brown U., 1957; MA, U. Pa., 1959, PhD, 1967; LHD (hon.), 1995. Researcher Phila. Hist. Commn., 1957-59; lectr. Am. civilization U. Gothenburg, Sweden, 1959-62, Bryn Mawr Coll., 1962-63, U. Pa., 1963-64; prof. U. Iowa, 1964-73; dean U. Mo., Kansas City, 1973-74; provost U. Md., 1974-79; chancellor U. Mass., Boston, 1979-88; pres. San Francisco State U., 1988—. Author: American Fiction and Verse, 1962, 2d edit., 1970, also articles, revs.; editor: Uncle Tom's Cabin, 1968. Vice chmn. Iowa City Human Rels. Commn., 1970-72, Gov.'s Commn. on Water Quality, 1983-84; mem. Iowa City Charter Commn., 1972-73; chmn. Md. Com. Humanities, 1976-78, Assn. Urban Univs., 1988-92; mem. Howard County Commn. Arts, Md., 1976-79; bd. dirs. John F. Kennedy Libr.; trustee San Francisco Econ. Devel. Corp., 1989-92, Adv. Coun. of Calif. Acad. Scis., Calif. Hist. Soc., 1989-92; chmn., bd. dirs. Calif. Compact, 1990—; mem. exec. com. Campus Compact, 1991—, chmn., 1995—; Mayor's Blue Ribbon Commn. on Fiscal Stability, 1994-95; chmn. Pres. Clinton's Steering Com. of Coll. Pres. for Am. Reads and Am. Counts, 1996—. Smith-Mundt prof., 1959-60; Fulbright lectr., 1960-62; grantee Std. Oil Co. Found., 1968, NEH, 1969-74, Ford Found., 1969, Rockefeller Found., 72-75, Dept. State, 1977; recipient Clarkson Able Collins Jr. Maritime History award, 1956, Pa. Colonial Soc. Essay award, 1958, 59, William Lloyd Garrison award Mass. Ednl. Opportunity Assn., 1987; Disting. Urban Fellow Assn. Urban U., 1992. Mem. San Francisco C. of C. (bd. dirs.), San Francisco World Affairs Coun. (bd. dirs.), Pvt. Industry Coun. (bd. dirs.), Boston World Affairs Coun. (1983-88), Greater Boston C. of C. (v.p. 1987-89), Fulbright Alumni Assn. (bd. dirs. 1978-80), Univ. Club, World Trade Club, Commonwealth Club (bd. dirs. 1995-99), Phi Beta Kappa. Democrat. Office: San Francisco State U 1600 Holloway Ave San Francisco CA 94132-1722

CORRIGAN, WILFRED J. computer company executive; b. 1938; Divsn. dir. Motorola, Phoenix, 1962-68; pres. Fairchild Camera & Instrument, Sunnyvale, Calif., 1968-80; chmn. bd., CEO LSI Logic Corp., Milpitas, Calif., 1980—, also dir. Office: LSI Logic Corp 1551 Mccarthy Blvd Milpitas CA 95035-7451

CORRIGAN, WILLIAM THOMAS, retired broadcast news executive; b. Bridgeport, Conn., Sept. 18, 1921; s. Thomas F. and Anna M. (Callan) C.; m. Harriett Bell, Sept. 1, 1951; children: Kevin, Brian. BS, Am. U., 1948. Reporter Bridgeport Herald, sports broadcaster sta. WUST, Washington, 1947; writer, reporter, prodr. NBC News, 1948-51; prodr., editor NBC-TV (newsreel), 1951-52; assignment editor NBC-TV News, 1952-53; Washington mgr. CBS Newsfilm, Washington bur. chief, 1953-59; dir. news and pub. affairs Sta. KNXT-TV, West Coast bur. chief CBS TV News, 1959-61; Am. Networks prodr./editor Eichmann Trial, Jerusalem, Israel, 1961; mgr. Washington bur. NBC News, 1962; prodr. Huntley Brinkley Report, Wash., 1963-65; dir. news ops. NBC, N.Y.C., 1965-68; gen. mgr. ops. NBC News, N.Y.C., 1968-73, gen. mgr., 1973-79, dir. broadcast svc., 1979-81. Staff sgt. USAAF, World War II. Decorated D.F.C., Air medal. Mem.: Soc. Profl. Journalists, Nat. Press Club, Radio-TV Corrs. Assn., White House Photographers Assn., Radio-TV News Dirs. Assn., Bath Club (Nokomis), Phi Sigma Kappa. Home: 710 Bird Bay Dr W Venice FL 34292-4031 E-mail: harbil4@juno.com.

CORRIGAN-MAGUIRE, MAIREAD, peace worker; b. Belfast, Northern Ireland, Jan. 27, 1944; d. Andrew and Margaret C.; m. Jackie Maguire, Sept. 8, 1981; children: John Francis, Luke; stepchildren— Mark, Joanne, Marie-Louise. Grad., Miss Gordon's Comml. Coll., 1967; LL.D. (hon.), Yale U., 1976. Various secretarial positions in Belfast, 1959-76. Co-founder Community of Peace People (No. Ireland Peace Movement), Belfast, 1976, chmn., 1980-81; hon. chair Peace People. Lay mem. Legion of Mary, Roman Cath. Ch., 1959—. Co-recipient Nobel prize for peace, 1976; recipient Carl von Ossietzky medal for courage, 1976. Office: care Community of the Peace People 224 Lisburn Rd Belfast BT9 6GE Northern Ireland Fax: 01232 683 947. E-mail: peacepeople@gn.apc.org.

CORRIHER, SHIRLEY, food writer; b. Atlanta, Feb. 23, 1935; d. A.J. and Clide (Mann) Ogletree; m. Theodore Hecht, 1958 (div. 1970); children: Terron Jan, Sherron Ann, Theodore Jr. BA in Chemistry cum laude, Vanderbilt U., 1956. Cert. culinaryn profl. Rsch. biochemist Vanderbilt Med. Sch., Nashville, 1956-58; co-founder, tchr. Brandon Hall, 1959, food svc. mgr., 1959-69; a founder First Montessori, 1963; traveling tchr., writer and cons., 1975—. Cons. DK's Desserts, Fine Cooking, Cook's Illus., others. Regular columnist, contbg. editor Fine Cooking, 1994—; author: CookWise, 1998; contbr. articles to Food and Wine, Ladies Home Jour., Fine Cooking, Martha Stewart Living, The Phoenix, Jour. Biol. Chemistry, others. Trustee Cooking Advancement, Rsch. and Edn. Found., 1984, chair, 1985. Recipient Best Reference Book of Yr. award, James Beard Awards, 1998, Best Tchr. of Yr. award, Bon Apetit's Food and Entertaining Awards, 2001. Mem. Internat. Assn. Cooking Profls. (bd. dirs. 1982, 83-84), Les Dames d'Escoffier, Inst. Food Technologists, Am. Inst. Wine and Food, Am. Assn. Cereal Chemists Home: 3152 Andrews Dr NW Atlanta GA 30305-2013

CORROTHERS, HELEN GLADYS, criminal justice official; b. Montrose, Ark., Mar. 19, 1937; d. Thomas and Christene (Farley) Curl; m. Edward Corrothers, Dec. 17, 1968 (div. Sept. 1983); 1 child, Michael Edward. AA in Liberal Arts magna cum laude, Ark. Bapt. Coll., 1955; BS in Bus. Adminstrn. Mgmt., Roosevelt U., 1965; grad. officer leadership sch., WAC Sch., 1965; grad, Inst. Criminal Justice, Exec. Ctr. Continuing Edn., U. Chgo., 1973; postgrad., Calif. Coast U., 1981—. Enlisted U.S. Army, 1956, advanced through grades to capt., 1969, chief mil. pers., 1965-67; dir. for housing Giessen Support Ctr., Germany, 1967-69; resigned, 1969; social interviewer Ark. Dept. Corrections, Grady, 1970-71, supt. women's unit Pine Bluff, 1971-83; commr. U.S. Parole Commn., Burlingame, Calif., 1983-85, U.S. Sentencing Commn., Washington, 1985-91; fellow U.S. Dept. Justice, Washington, 1992-95; criminal justice cons., 1996—. Instr. women & crime U. Md., College Park, 1994; instr. corrections U. Ark.-Pine Bluff, 1976-79; mem. bd. visitation Jefferson County Juvenile Ct., Pine Bluff, 1978-81; bd. dirs. Vols. in Cts., 1979-83, Vols. Am., 1985-94; mem. Am./Can. study team Mex. penal system Am. Correctional Assn., Islas Marias, Mex., 1981; mem. Ark. Commn. Crimes and Law Enforcement, 1975-78; mem. U.S. Atty. Gen.'s Correctional Policy Study Team, 1987. Mem. Ark. Commn. on Status of Women, 1976-78; bd. dirs. Com. Against Spouse Abuse, 1982-83; mem. nat. adv. bd. dept. criminal justice Xavier U., Cin., 1993-97; bd. dirs. Bapt. Mission Found. of Md./Del., Columbia, Md., 1993-98. Recipient Ark. Woman of Achievement award Ark. Press Women's Assn., 1980, Human Rels. award Ark. Edn. Assn., 1980, Outstanding Woman of Achievement award Sta. KATV-TV, Little Rock, 1981, Correctional Svc. award Vols. Am., 1984, William H. Hastie award Nat. Assn. Blacks in Criminal Justice, 1986, Outstanding Victim Advocacy award Nat. Victim Ctr., 1991, Appreciation cert. Dept. Justice Office for Victims of Crime, 1994; recipient testimonial for svc. to fed. judiciary Adminstrv. Office of Cts., 1991. Mem.: NAFE, Am. Soc. Criminology, Nat. Coun. on Crime and

Delinquency, Ark. Law Enforcement Assn., N.Am. Assn. Wardens and Supts., Am. Correctional Assn. (treas. 1980—86, v.p. 1986—88, pres.-elect 1988—90, pres. 1990—92, mem. Del. Assembly 1993—, chmn. rsch. coun. 1997—2000, chmn. Correctional awards com. 2001—, E.R. Cass Correctional Achievement award 1993), Ark. Sheriff's Assn. (hon.), Delta Sigma Theta (local sec. 1976—79, local parliamentarian 1983). Baptist. Avocations: reading, music. Office: Am Correctional Assn 4380 Forbes Blvd Lanham Seabrook MD 20706-4863

CORRY, CHARLES ELMO, geophysicist, consultant; b. Salt Lake City, May 15, 1938; s. Elmo Leigh Corry and Sylvia Birch; children: Christopher Charles, Matthew Lee. BS in Geology, Utah State U., 1970; MS in Geophysics, U. Utah, 1972; PhD in Geophysics, Tex. A&M U., 1976. Electronic missile checkout GD Convair-Astronautics, San Diego, 1960-64; rsch. assoc. Scripps Inst. Oceanography, La Jolla, Calif., 1965-68, Woods Hole (Mass.) Oceanographic Inst., 1968; mgr. geophys. rsch. AMAX, Golden, Colo., 1977-82; v.p. Nonlinear Analysis, Inc., Bryan, Tex., 1982-84; vis., adj., assoc. prof. geophysics Tex. A&M U., College Station, 1983-87; assoc. prof. geophysics U. Mo., Rolla, 1984-89; coord. world ocean circulation experiment Woods Hole Oceanographic Inst., 1990—95, cons., 1995—2001; database cons. Denver, Colorado Springs, 1995—2001, pres. Equal Justice Found. Author: Laccoliths, Mechanics of Emplacement and Growth, 1988, Geology of the Solitario, Trans-Pecos Texas, 1990, Domestic Violence Against Men, 1999, (award); contbr. articles to profl. jours. and conf. procs., including Trans. Am. Geophys. Union, Jour. Applied Geophysics, others. Cpl., USMC, 1956-59, Calif.; pres. Equal Justice Found., 2001—. Fellow Geol. Soc. Am.; mem. IEEE, ACLU, Am. Geophys. Union, Soc. Exploration Geophysicists, Marine Corps League. Buddhist. Achievements include overturning of paradigm that had existed for over 150 years, regarding galvanic current flow in ore bodies; discovery that ore minerals are commonly ferroelectrics and that ore bodies behave as a polarized dielectric medium, or solid plasma, in electrical surveys; development of the controlled source audiomagnetotelluric method for electrical exploration; field and theoretical studies of magmatic intrusions; terrestrial heat flow studies in the North Pacific; coordination of hydrographic program of World Ocean Circulation Experiment; relational database design and data modeling; civil liberties. Home: 455 Bear Creek Rd Colorado Springs CO 80906-5820 E-mail: ccorry@ejfi.org.

CORRY, DALILA BOUDJELLAL, internist, educator; b. El-Arrouch, Algeria, July 7, 1943; came to U.S., 1981; MD, U. Algiers, 1974. Diplomate in internal medicine and nephrology Am. Bd. Internal Medicine. Intern Hosp. Mustapha Algiers, 1972-73; resident Hosp. Tenon, Paris, 1975-79; fellow in nephrology UCLA, 1981-83; chief renal divsn. Olive View-UCLA Med. Ctr., Sylmar, Calif., 1983—; from asst. prof. to prof. clin. medicine UCLA, 1993, prof. clin. medicine. Assoc. prof. clin. medicine UCLA. Fellow Am. Heart Assn. Office: Olive View-UCLA Med Ctr Dept Medicine 2B182 14445 Olive View Dr Sylmar CA 91342-1437

CORRY, EMMETT BROTHER, librarian, educator, researcher, archivist; b. N.Y.C. s. Patrick Joseph and Bridget Corry. BA, St. Francis Coll., N.Y.C., 1960; MS, Columbia U., 1962; PhD, NYU, 1977. Tchr. Franciscan Bros. Schs., Bklyn., 1960-69; libr. St. Francis Coll., Bklyn., 1970-71, St. Anthony's H.S., Smithtown, N.Y., 1971-77; prof. divsn. libr. and info. sci. St. John's U., Jamaica, N.Y., 1977-94; archivist Franciscan Bros., 1994—; dir. St. John's U., Jamaica, N.Y., 1988-93. Cons. N.Y.C. Bd. Edn., 1984-88, St. Francis Coll., 1996—. Author: Grants for Libraries, 1982, 2d edit., 1986, History of the Franciscan Brothers of Brooklyn in Ireland and America, 2003. Pres. N.Y. Irish History Roundtable, 1994-96. Mem. Cath. Libr. Assn. (pres. 1989-91, Libr. of Yr. 1991), N.Y. Irish History Roundtable (pres. 1994-96). Avocations: classical music, history of the Irish in N.Y.C. Home: Our Lady of Angels Friary 344 73rd St Brooklyn NY 11209 Office: St Francis Monastery 135 Remsen St Brooklyn NY 11201-4212

CORRY, JAMES MICHAEL, insurance executive, educator; b. N.Y.C., Apr. 27, 1947; s. Patrick Joseph and Bridget (Cosgrave) C.; m. Maureen Patricia Grogan; children: Matthew, Michael. BS, Manhattan Coll., 1968; MS, CUNY, 1971; PhD, U. Oreg., 1975. Health specialist N.Y.C. Bd. Edn., 1968-71; tchg. asst. U. Oreg., Eugene, 1971-73; asst. dir. health Oreg. Bd. Edn., Salem, 1973-74; asst. prof. Worcester (Mass.) State Coll., 1974-76, U. North Tex., Denton, 1976-81; dir. health edn. dept. Mt. Sinai Med. Ctr., N.Y.C., 1981-88; dir. health and fitness programs Met. Life Ins. Co., N.Y.C., 1988—. Cons. Tex. Dept. Edn., Austin, 1975-76; grant dir., rschr. State of Tex. Rsch. Fund, Denton, 1976-80. Author: Consumer Health: Facts, Skills and Decisions, 1983, Drugs: Facts, Alternatives, Decisions, 1984, Implementing Health/Fitness Programs, 1986; contbr. articles to profl. jours. Bd. dirs. Silvermine Community Assn., New Canaan, Conn., 1981-83, Mid Fairfield Hospice, Norwalk, Conn., 1982-84; trustee The Floating Hosp., N.Y.C., 2001—. Diocese of Bklyn. and U. of Oreg. scholar, 1964, 71. Democrat. Roman Catholic. Avocations: sailing, skiing, running, tennis. Home: 7 Peter Cooper Rd Apt 2F New York NY 10010-6606 Office: Met Life Ins Co 1 Metlife Plaza Long Island City NY 11101-4015 E-mail: JCorry@metlife.com.

CORRY, ROBERT EMMETT, lawyer; b. Mobile, Ala., Dec. 22, 1935; s. Robert Emmett and Rachel Christine C.; m. Anne Young; children: Robert, Megan, Peter. AB, U. Ala., 1957; JD with honors, George Washington U., 1964. Bar: Ga. 1964, U.S. Dist. Ct. Ga. 1964, U.S. Ct. Appeals (5th and 11th cirs.) 1964. Ptnr. Nall, Miller, Cadenhead & Dennis, Atlanta, 1964-70, Dennis & Fain, Atlanta, 1970-75, Dennis, Corry, Webb & Carlock, Atlanta, 1975-85, Dennis, Corry, Porter & Smith LLP, Atlanta, 1985—. Adj. prof. law Emory U. Law Sch., Atlanta, 1970-73. Co-author, co-editor: Motor Carrier Laibility, 1998; contbr. articles to profl. jours. Capt. USAF, 1957-60. Mem. Ga. Def. Lawyers Assn., Internat. Assn. Def. Counsel, Trucking Industry Def. Assn. (Ann. Svc. award 1996). Avocations: reading, gardening, cooking, hiking. Home: 1692 Rainwater Tr Tiger GA 30575 E-mail: rec@dcplaw.com.

CORSARO, FRANK ANDREW, theater, musical and opera director; b. N.Y.C., Dec. 22, 1924; s. Joseph and Marie (Quarino) C.; m. Mary Cross Bonnie Lueders, May 30, 1971; 1 child, Andrew. Grad. in Drama, Yale, 1947. Tchr. pvt. acting class for singers; artistic dir. Julliard Opera Ctr., Julliard Sch. Head music drama div. opera/music theatre Inst. N.J.; trustee Nat. Opera Inst. Dir.: Broadway prodn. A Hatful of Rain, 1955-56, The Night of the Iguana, 1961-62, Treemonisha, 1975, Cold Storage, 1978, Whoopee, 1979, Knockout, 1979, It's So Good to be Civilized, 1987; off-Broadway prodn. Master Class, 1986; dir.: N.Y.C. Opera, 1958—, Washington Opera Soc., 1970-74, St. Paul Opera, 1971, Houston Grand Opera, 1973-77, assoc. artistic dir., 1977—, Glyndebourne Festival, 1982-85, Deutsches Oper, Berlin, 1983, Chgo. Lyric Opera, 1984, 96, Covent Garden, 1984, Met. Opera, 1984, Spitalfields Festival, London, 1985, Den Norske Opera, Oslo, 1985, Australian Opera, 1986. appeared in: Broadway prodn. Mrs. McThing, 1951; film Rachel, Rachel, 1967; author: adaptation L'Histoire du Soldat, 1974, Memoir Maverik, 1978, Love for Three Oranges Glyndebourne Version, 1985, Kunma, 2003; dir. (double bill) Where the Wild Things Are, Higgeldy Piggelby Pop, 1985, Los Angeles Opera, 1986, Amsterdam Netherlanders Opera, 1986, Montreal Opera, 1986 Ravel: L'enfant et les Sortileges, L'heure Espagnol, Glyndebourne Festival, 1987, Hansel and Gretel, Houston Can. Opera Co., Rigoletto, 2001, Traviata, 2003; (libretto) Heloise and Abelard. Mem. Dirs. Guild Am., Soc. Stage Dirs., Choreographers, Am. Guild Mus. Artists. Home: 33 Riverside Dr New York NY 10023-8012

CORSAW, ARDITH, geriatrics nurse, administrator; b. Decatur, Ill., Sept. 10, 1950; d. Everette Eugene and Norma L. (Swarm) Kirkman; m. David Corsaw, Dec. 19, 1971; children: Adam, Tara, Karen. Diploma, Decatur Meml. Hosp., 1971. RN. Pvt. duty nursing, charge nurse med.-surg. unit Graham Hosp., Canton, Ill., 1972-82; nurse Hooper-Holmes Port-A-Medic, Peoria, Ill., 1982-83; office nurse family practice physician's office, Cuba, Ill., 1982-87; factory first-aid sta. relief nurse Caterpillar, Inc., Mapleton, Ill., 1986-88; nursing supr., insvc. dir. Heartland of Canton, Health Care and Retirement Corp., 1988-91, DON, 1991-92, quality assurance coord., rehab. coord., 1992; DON Sprucewood Health Care, Macomb, Ill., 1992-96, Ill. River Correctional Ctr., Canton, 1996—. Supr. nursing, clin. support br. chief ambulatory svcs. McDill AFB, 1991. Ill. Air N.G. Nurse Exec., 1971-95, comdr. med. squadron, 1995-96. Mem.: Assn. Air N.G. Nurses. Home: 8442 E Beaver Pass Rd Smithfield IL 61477-9427

CORSE, JOHN DOGGETT, university official, lawyer; b. Jacksonville, Fla., Mar. 16, 1924; s. Herbert Montgomery and Carita Ann (Doggett) C.; m. Margaret Murchison, Aug. 4, 1951; children: Carita Doggett, Cameron Murchison, John Doggett, Margaret Murchison. BS, U.S. Naval Acad., 1946; LLB, U. Va., 1957. Bar: Fla. 1957, Ga. 1974. Commd. ensign U.S. Navy, 1946, advanced through grades; resigned, 1954; ptnr. Ulmer, Murchison, Ashby & Ball, Jacksonville, 1957-75, Powell, Goldstein, Frazer & Murphy, Atlanta, 1975-92; sr. dir. devel. U. Va. Law Sch. Found., Charlottesville, 1992—. Pres. Gt. Am. Mgmt. Corp., Atlanta, 1972-75, chmn. bd., 1975; sr. v.p., dir. UniCapital Corp., Atlanta, 1972-75; mng. trustee Gt. Am. Mortgage Investors, 1972-75 Editor-in-chief: Va. Law Rev, 1956-57. Mem.: ABA, Ga. Bar Assn., Va. Bar Assn., D.C. Bar Assn., Fla. Bar Assn., Farmington Country Club (Charlottesville). Office: 3588 Richmond St Jacksonville FL 32205

CORSELLO, LILY JOANN, minister, counselor, educator; b. Newark, Mar. 30, 1953; d. Joseph DiFalco and Antonietta (Gandolfo) C. BA, Fla. State U., 1974; MEd, Fla. Atlantic U., 1977; MA, Southwestern Bapt. Theol. Sem., 1987; D of Ministry, Luther Rice Sem., 2003. Lic. profl. counselor, Tex.; lic. mental health counselor, Fla. Lang. arts tchr. Broward County (Fla.) Pub. Schs., 1974 80, guidance counselor, 1980-85; min. of single adults Park Pl. Bapt Ch., Houston, 1985-87; founder, exec. dir. SinglePlus, Inc., Flower Mound, Tex., 1989-96; guidance counselor Palm Beach and Broward County Pub. Schs., 1996-99; pastor Maranatha Ch., Pompano Beach, Fla., 2000—01. Writer, lectr. singles ministry and Christian Single mag. So. Bapt. Conv., Nashville, 1979-89. Mem.: Tex. Christian Counselors Assn., Nat. Assn. Single Adult Leaders, Am. Assn. Christian Counselors, Women's Club of Flower Mound (pres. 1989—90), Pilot Club of Ft. Lauderdale (chaplain 1982—83), Phi Delta Kappa, Lambda Iota Tau. Democrat. Home and Office: PO Box 811 Pompano Beach FL 33061-0811

CORSER, DAVID HEWSON, pediatrician, retired; b. Mpls., Aug. 4, 1930; s. John and Mary (Griswold) C.; m. Bettyrose Nerlich, June 10, 1954; children: William, Diana, Joan, Carolyn, Bonnie, Jennifer. AB, Washington U., 1951, MD, 1954. Diplomate Am. Bd. Pediat. Intern Mpls. Gen. Hosp., 1954-55; resident M U. Minn. Hosps., Mpls., 1955-57; practice medicine specializing in pediat. Skemp Walk In Clinic, LaCrosse, Wis., 1959-95; clin. asst. prof. pediat. U. Wis., Madison, 1959-95; ret., 1995. Mem. staff St. Francis Hosp. Served with U.S. Army, 1957-59. Mem. AMA, Am. Acad. Pediat., LaCrosse County Med. Assn., Wis. Med. Assn., Optimist Club. Roman Catholic. Home: 621 S 9th St La Crosse WI 54601 9102

CORSER, MAUREEN SLAGG, librarian, media specialist; b. Seattle, July 8, 1942; d. Maynard Owen and Bertha May (Bunnell) Slagg; m. George Albert Corser, Apr. 8, 1962; children: George Patrick, John Kevin, Carin Glendyne Corser Lang. BA in Econs., Wash. State U., Pullman, 1964; AM in LS, U. Mich., 1976. Cert. tchr., Mich. Media specialist Carman-Ainsworth Sch., Flint, Mich., 1972-79; libr., media specialist Flint Cmty. Schs., 1979—. Mem. Genesee County Adv. Bds. on Media, coun. chair 1999-2001, mem. Tech., Math./Sci., Microcomputers, 1980-98. Editor Media Spectrum, 1995—. Officer, chair voter svc., budget chair LWV of Mich., 1965—. Mem. LWV (pres. Saginaw County 2002—), Mich. Edn. Assn. (rep.), Mich. Assn. for Media in Edn. (sec. 1984-85), Phi Delta Kappa (v.p. 1983), Delta Kappa Gamma, Phi Chi Theta, Phi Beta Mu. Unitarian Universalist. Home: 5151 Laramie Rd Bridgeport MI 48722-9525 Office: Flint Cmty Schs G2138 W Carpenter Rd Flint MI 48505-1977

CORSI, PHILIP DONALD, lawyer; b. N.Y.C., Oct. 11, 1928; s. Edward and Emma Catherine (Gillies) C.; m. Marcia Munro, June 3, 1953 (div. 1976); children: Martina Jane O'Donnell, Charles Edward, Philip Munro, Christopher Matthew; m. Lois Joann Cobb, July 20, 1983. AB, Princeton U., 1950; LLB, Columbia U., 1953. Bar: N.Y. 1955, U.S. Dist. Ct. N.Y. 1970. Assoc. Willkie Farr & Gallagher, N.Y.C., 1955-69, ptnr., 1969-88, ret., 1988. Bd. dirs., pres. emeritus LaGuardia Meml. House, N.Y.C., 1964—. With U.S. Army, 1953—55. Mem. Garden City Golf Club, Black Diamond Club. Republican. Avocations: golfing, reading, history. Home: 3210 N Pinelake Village Pt Lecanto FL 34461-8140

CORSIGLIA, ROBERT JOSEPH, electrical construction company executive; b. Chgo., Jan. 22, 1935; s. John Robert and Marie Virgina Corsiglia; m. Patricia Ann Ryan, Jan. 26, 1960 (div. Jan. 1984); children: Nancee, Thomas, Karen; m. Emilie Joe Clementz, Sept. 10, 1989. BSEE, Ill. Inst. Tech., Chgo., 1963. Registered profl. engr., Ill., Ind., Calif., Tex., Fla. CEO, pres. Hyre Electric Co. Ind., Highland, 1970-90, JWP/Hyre Electric Co. Ind., Highland, 1990—; CEO Midwestern region JWP Mech./Elec. Svcs. Inc., Oak Brook, Ill., 1991-93; chmn. C & H Engring. Co., Inc., Highland, 1984-90; sec.-treas. Adventures in Travel, Highland, 1984-95. Bd. dirs. Bank One, Highland. Bd. dirs. No. Ind. Arts Assn., Munster, 1989-93, v.p. devel., 1990; bd. dirs. N.W. Ind. United Way, Highland, 1985, Chgo. Engring. Found., 1991-97; bd. dirs. IIT Alumni Bd., Chgo., 1985, v.p. adminstrn., 1986; mem. IIT Pres.' Coun., 1985—; mem. Legacy Found. Inc. Lake County, Griffith, Ind., 1993—; mem. exec. bd. Boy Scouts of Am. Calumet Coun., 1993—; pres. Nat. Elec. Contractors Assn., 1975, 76, 77. Served with U.S. Army, 1964-70. Mem. Internat. Brotherhood of Elec. Workers (hon.), Chgo. Pres. Orgn., Young Pres. Orgn., World Pres. Orgn., Union League Club. Republican. Roman Catholic. Avocations: collecting, golf. Home: 8701 Northcote Ave Munster IN 46321-2726

CORSO, FRANK MITCHELL, lawyer; b. N.Y.C., July 28, 1928; s. Joseph and Jane (DeBenedetto) C.; m. Dorothy G. McVeety, Apr. 7, 1951; children: Frank, Elaine, Patricia, Dorothy. LLB, St. John's U., 1952. Bar: N.Y. 1954, D.C. 1981, U.S. Ct. Mil. Appeals 1954, U.S. Supreme Ct. 1960. Ptnr. Corso & Ferrig, 1957-61, Corso & Petito, 1966-69, Corso & Landa, Jericho, N.Y., 1971-73, Corso & Engelberg, 1973-82; sr. ptnr. Frank Mitchell Corso, P.C., Westbury, N.Y., 1982—. Bd. dirs. UN Devel. Corp. by N.Y. Gov., N.Y. Mcpl. Bond Bank Agy.; lectr. St. John's U. Sch. of Law; U.S. congl. candidate, N.Y.; trustee WLIW pub. TV channel. Contbr. articles to legal jours.; TV commentator legal topics. With U.S. Army, 1951-53. Decorated Knight of Holy Sepulchre (Vatican City); named Man of Yr., Am.-Italians of L.I., 1966. Mem. ABA, ATLA, N.Y. State Bar Assn., Nassau Bar Assn., Internat. Bar Assn., World Assn. Lawyers (founding mem.). Home: 1 Southdown Ct Huntington NY 11743-2548 Office: 350 Jericho Tpke Jericho NY 11753-1317 E-mail: fmc28@aol.com.

CORSO, JOHN ANTHONY, management consultant, educator; s. Vero R. and Rita Jane Corso; m. Maria Lourdes Cano, Sept. 8, 1990; children: Sara Susan children: Mary Bridget, Bernadette Jane. BS, U. Md., 1980; MS in Adminstrn., Ctrl. Mich. U., 1991; MPA, DPA, U. So. Calif., L.A., 2001. Cert. charter cert. Myers-Briggs type indicator profl. Consulting Psychologists Press, 2001, profl. contracts mgr. Nat. Contract Mgmt. Assn., 1995. Mgmt. cons. Booz, Allen, & Hamilton, McLean, Va., 1992—92; contract specialist U.S. Dept. Vet. Affairs, Washington, 1992—97, 1993—99, sr. procurement analyst, 1997—99, mgmt. and program analyst, 1999—. Program dir./adj. prof. Georgetown U. Ctr. for Profl. Devel., Washington, 2001—. Contbr. articles to profl. jours. Eucharistic min. St. Raphael's Cath. Parish, Rockville, Md., 1996—2002. Lt. USN, 1983—92, Various, ret. comdr. USNR, 2002. Decorated Navy Expeditionary Medal USN, Navy Commendation Medal. Mem.: ASPA, Soc. Cath. Social Scientists, Acad. Mgmt., KC (outside guard 1976—76). Roman Catholic. Home: 12601 Orchard Brook Terr Potomac MD 20854 Office: US Dept Vets Affairs 810 Vermont Ave NW Washington DC 20420 Home Fax: 301-251-1013. Personal E-mail: corsojohn@aol.com.

CORSON, J. JAY, IV, lawyer; b. Richmond, Va., May 19, 1935; s. John Jay III and Mary Turner (Tilman) C.; children: John Jay V, Catherine Anne, Clare Tilman, Jennifer Page. BA, U. Va., 1957, LLB, 1960. Bar: Va. 1960. Assoc. Davis, Polk, Wardwell, Sunderland & Kiendl, N.Y.C., 1960, Boothe, Dudley, Koontz & Blankingship, Fairfax, Va., 1963-68; ptnr. McGuire, Woods, Battle & Boothe & predecessor firms, McLean, Va., 1968-2000. Capt. USAF, 1960-63. Fellow Am. Coll. Trial Lawyers, Am. Bar Found., Va. Law Found.; mem. Va. Assn. Def. Attys. (pres. 1981-82), Va. State Bar (pres. 1988-89, del. ABA 1989-96). Episcopalian. Avocations: golf, skiing, fishing, gardening. Home: 3137 Trenholm Dr Oakton VA 22124-1329 Office: McGuire Woods LLP 1750 Tysons Blvd Ste 1800 Mc Lean VA 22102-4231

CORSON, THOMAS HAROLD, manufacturing company executive; b. Elkhart, Ind., Oct. 15, 1927; s. Carl W. and Charlotte (Keyser) C.; m. Dorthy Claire Scheide, July 11, 1948; children: Benjamin Thomas, Claire Elaine. Student, Purdue U., 1945-46, Rennsselaer Poly. Inst., 1946-47, So. Meth. U., 1948-49. Chmn. bd. dirs. Coachmen Industries, Inc., Elkhart, 1965-97, chmn. emeritus, dir., 1997—. Bd. dirs. Middlebury, R.C.R. Sci. Inc., Goshen, Ind., Micrology Labs., Inc., Goshen, Morristown, N.J., Elkhart County Econ. Devel. Corp., Elkhart, Ind.; chmn., sec. Greenfield Corp., Middlebury. Adv. coun. U. Notre Dame; past trustee Ball State U.; dir., past trustee, past vice chmn. Interlochen (Mich.) Arts Acad. and Nat. Music Camp. With U.S. Naval Air Force, 1945-47. Mem. Ind. Mfrs. Assn. (past dir.), Elkhart C. of C. (past bd. dirs.), Ind. C. of C. (past bd. dirs.), Ind. Hist. Soc. (past dir.), Royal Poinciana Golf Club, Elcona Club (past bd. dirs.), 33 Degrees, Mason, Shriners. Methodist. Home: PO Box 340 Middlebury IN 46540-0340 Office: Coachmen Industries Inc PO Box 3300 Elkhart IN 46515-3300

CORTES, CAROL SOLIS, school system administrator; b. N.Y.C., N.Y., Aug. 16, 1944; d. Jesus and Dora Solis; m. Fernando Miranda, June 25, 1964 (div. Apr. 1978); children: Christopher, Christina Guerra; m. Jose Cortes (div. Nov. 1, 1983). BEd with hon., U. Miami, 1970; MSc, Fla. Internat. U., 1974. Cert. in Social Sci. & Adminstrn. Supr. From tchr. to dep. supt. Miami-Dade County Pub. Sch., Miami, Fla., 1970—96, dep. supt., 1996—. Exec. bd. Gender Equity Network. Exec. bd. Women's C. of C., Miami, Fla., 2000—01. Recipient Hispanic Educator award, Nova U., 1999, Cervantes Outstanding Educator award, 1999, Educator of Yr. award, 1999. Mem.: Phi Delta Kappa. Avocations: travel, dominoes. Home: 2105 SW 123rd Court Miami FL 33175 Office: Miami Dade Pub Schs 1450 NE 2nd Ave Miami FL 33132-1308

CORTES, ENGRACIO PADILLA, oncologist; b. Iloilo, Philippines, Jan. 9, 1938; came to U.S., 1965; s. Felix Francisco and Ofelia (Ledesma) Padilla; m. Lilia Serrano Gonzales June 7, 1969; children Carl, Marissa, Alfonso. BA, U. San Agustin, Iloilo City, 1958; MD, Far Eastern U., Manila, 1964. Diplomate Am. Bd. Internal Medicine, Am. Bd. Med. Oncology. Internship Cambridge (Mass.) City Hosp., 1965-66; residency in internal medicine Lemuel Shattuck Hosp., Boston, 1966-68; fellowship in medical oncology Roswell Park Meml. Inst., Buffalo, N.Y., 1969-71; physician-in-charge med. oncology Queens (N.Y.) Med. Ctr., 1972-81; clin. coord. cancer program L.I. Jewish Med. Ctr., New Hyde Park, N.Y., 1975-81; chmn. edn. com. Am. Cancer Soc., Queens, 1985-92; dir. oncology rsch. N.Y. Hosp. Queens, 1998—; clin. assoc. prof. medicine Weil Med. Coll. Cornell U., 2001—. Assoc. clin. prof. medicine Albert Einstein Coll. Medicine, NYC, 1983—2002. Contbr. articles to profl. jours., chpts. to books. Pres. N.Y. Cancer Soc. Fellow ACP; mem. Assn. Am. Cancer Rsch., Am. Soc. Clin. Oncology, N.Y. State Hematology-Oncology Soc., N.Y. State Med. Soc., Philippine Med. Assn. Am. (Best Philipine Physician 1975), Assn. Philippine Physicians N.Y. (pres. 1995-97). Avocations: playing tennis, classical guitar, ballroom dancing. Office: 200-20 44th Ave Bayside NY 11361

CORTESE, ALFRED WILLIAM, JR., lawyer, consultant; b. Phila., Apr. 2, 1937; s. Alfred William and Marie Ann (Coccio) C.; m. Rosanna S. Zimmerman, Aug. 18, 1962 (div. Aug. 1981); children: Aline Elizabeth, Alfred William III, Christina Nicole. BA cum laude, Temple U., 1959; JD, U. Pa., 1962. Bar: Pa. 1963, U.S. Supreme Ct. 1972, D.C. 1977. Assoc., ptnr. Pepper, Hamilton & Scheetz, Phila., 1962-71; asst. exec. dir. FTC, Washington, 1972-73; assoc. Dechert, Price & Rhoads, Phila., 1974-76; ptnr. Clifford & Warnke, Washington, 1977-81; chmn., CEO Cortese & Loughran Inc., Washington, 1982-84; ptnr. Kirkland & Ellis, Washington, 1985-94, Pepper Hamilton, LLP, Washington, 1994-98; mng. mem. Cortese PLCC, Washington, 1999—. Cons. Gen. Motors Corp., Detroit, 1985—. Lt. U.S. Army, 1959-60. Mem. ABA, Am. Law Inst., Pa. Bar, D.C. Bar Assn., Def. Rsch. Inst., Lawyers for Civil Justice (mem. exec. com., bd. dirs.), Racquet Club (Phila.), Univ. Club, Capitol Hill Club. Avocations: vintage automobile racing and restoration, art & antique collecting, cooking. Home: 113 3rd St NE Washington DC 20002-7313 Fax: 202-637-9797. E-mail: awc@cortesepllc.com.

CORTESE, EDWARD, marketing and public relations executive; Grad., Fordham U. Sr. v.p. mktg. and pub. rels. Lefrak Orgn Inc, Rego Park, N.Y.; tchr. English Tulane U.; sr. v.p. mktg. Levitt and Sons; mktg., advt. exec. Loew's-MGM. With USN. Office: Lefrak Orgn Inc 97-77 Queens Blvd Rego Park NY 11374

CORTESE, JOSEPH SAMUEL, II, lawyer; b. Des Moines, Aug. 17, 1955; s. Joseph Anthony and Kathryn Mary (Marasco) C.; m. Diane Caniglia, Aug. 5, 1978; children: Joseph III, James David, Kathryn Elizabeth. BA, Ind. U., 1977; JD with honors, Drake U., 1980. Bar: Iowa 1981, U.S. Dist. Ct. (no. and so. dists.) Iowa 1981, U.S. Ct. Appeals (8th cir.) 1984. Assoc. Jones, Hoffman & Huber, Des Moines, 1981-85; ptnr. Huber, Book, Cortese, Happe & Lanz, P.L.C., Des Moines, 1985—. Ordained permanent deacon Diocese Des Moines Roman Cath. Ch., Iowa, 1997. Mem. ABA, ATLA, Iowa State Bar Assn., Polk County Bar Assn., Def. Rsch. Inst., Iowa Trial Lawyers Assn. Roman Catholic. Home: 2915 Sherry Ln Urbandale IA 50322-6813 Office: Huber Book Cortese Happe & Lanz PLC 317 6th Ave Ste 200 Des Moines IA 50309-4127 Fax: 515-243-5481. E-mail: jcortese@desmoineslaw.com.

CORTESE, RICHARD ANTHONY, computer company executive; b. New London, Conn., Dec. 4, 1942; s. Anthony John and Winifred Silvia (Beebe) Cortese; m. Cindy Sue Folsom, Feb. 9, 1983; children: Cynthia Ann, Jennifer Lynn; m. Susan Louise Turner, Feb. 13, 1965 (div. 1973). BS, U. So. Calif., 1965, MBA, 1967. Fin. dir. Nat. Semiconductor Corp., Santa Clara, Calif., 1973-78; fin. control dir. TRW Corp., L.A., 1978-79; v.p. fin. No. Telecom Sys. Corp., Minn. and Calif., 1979-80; v.p., gen. mgr. Gen. Automation Inc., Anaheim, Calif., 1980-82; pres., CEO Alpha Microsystems, Santa Ana, Calif., 1982-87, also bd. dirs.; pres., CEO Hugin Sweda, Pine Brook, N.J., 1987-89; pres., CEO, vice-chmn. BOD, 1990-96; pres., CEO Racotek, Burnsville, Minn., 1990-96; pres. RMB Assocs., Durango, Colo., 1996—. Active Young Pres.'s Orgn., N.J. Named All-Am. in track and field NCAA, 1964, All-Am. in track and field AAU, 1964. Mem. Computer Communication Industry Assn. (mem. exec. com. 1983—), SoCal 10 (founding mem., bd. dirs. 1983—). Clubs: Chancellor's. Avocation: reading.

CORTEZ, EDWARD S. mayor; Mayor City of Pomono, Calif., 1993—. Office: City of Pomona 505 S Garey Ave Pomona CA 91766-3320 Mailing: PO Box 660 Pomona CA 91769*

CORTEZ, HERNAN GLENN, lawyer; b. Harlingen, Tex., Nov. 12, 1934; s. Hernan and Laura (Howell) C.; m. Carole Elaine DuBois, Jan. 29, 1958 (div. Aug. 1976); children: Vicky Foss, Marta Stephens, Jill Hubach, Ingrid Smith, H. Glenn Jr.; m.Carole Jean Simms, Dec. 31, 1976; 1 child, Troy Dillinger. BA, U. Tex., 1956, JD, 1962. Bar: Tex. 1962, U.S. Dist. Ct. (we. dist.) Tex. 1970, U.S. Ct. Appeals (5th cir.) 1981; bd. cert. pers. injury trial law Tex. Bd. Legal Specialization. Asst. atty. City of Austin, Tex., 1962-69, assoc. atty., 1969, atty., 1969-70; sole practice Austin, 1971-97; adminstrv. law judge State of Tex., 1997—. Atty. City of Manor, Tex., 1972-90, City of Rollingwood, Tex., 1972-86, City of Pflugerville, Tex., 1974-93, City of Sunset Valley, Tex., 1980-86, City of Granite Shoals, Tex., 1983-86. Served as capt. U.S. Army, 1957-59, USAR. Mem.: Travis County Bar Assn., Tex. Bar Assn. Home: 4701 Fieldstone Dr Austin TX 78735-6309 Office: 150 E Riverside Dr Austin TX 78704-1202

CORTEZ, JOSEPH ANTHONY, retired surgeon; b. Detroit, 1925; MD, St. Louis U., 1951. Diplomate Am. Bd. Surgery. Intern, then resident in surgery Mt. Carmel Mercy Hosp., Detroit, 1951-57; mem. staff Grace Hosp., Detroit; ret., 1990.

CORTEZ, RICARDO LEE, investment management executive; b. N.Y.C., Mar. 9, 1950; s. Eddie Adam and Marian Ruth (Lee) C.; children: Vanessa, Natalie, Rebecca; m. Harriet Anne Howard, Jan. 16, 1993. BA cum laude, CUNY, 1971; postgrad., Columbia U., 1971-73; cert. investment mgmt. analyst, U. Pa., 1993. Sr. stock market analyst Merrill Lynch, N.Y.C., 1971-76; exec. v.p. Trident Investment-Grace Capital, N.Y.C., 1976-78; pres. Liberty Capital Mgmt., N.Y.C., 1978-84, Cortez Capital Mgmt., N.Y.C., 1984-89, v.p., dir. fixed income Summit (N.J.) Trust Co., 1985-86; 1st v.p., dir. programs and communications Prudential Securities, N.Y.C., 1989-96, nat. sales dir. investment

mgmt. svcs., 1996—; No. divsn. dir. Prudential Investments, 1998—, nat. dir. investment mgmt. svcs. divsn.; v.p. global multi-mgr. strategies, mgr. Goldman Sachs, N.Y.C., 2000, program mgr., v.p., 2000-01; pres. pvt. client group Torrey Assocs., N.Y.C., 2001—. Lectr. stock market analysis N.Y. Inst. Fin., N.Y.C., 1973—75; bd. advisors Investment Mgmt. Cons. Assn., 1998—. Author: (with Edson Gould) Industry and Stock Forecast, 1976. Named Spkr. of Yr., Mcpl. Treas.'s Assn. Calif., 1981. Avocations: former lead guitar for mitch ryder, jay and the americans, coasters, other musical rock groups. Office: Torrey Assocs 505 Park Ave New York NY 10022 E-mail: rcortez@thetorreyfunds.com.

CORTI, LILLIAN ZELL, humanities educator, writer; b. Clinton, Okla., Dec. 18, 1942; d. Samuel Gordon Somers and Susie Mae Mote; children: Anna, Miriam, Paul. PhD in Comparative Lit., CUNY, 1984. Asst. prof. French and comparative drama Tulsa (Okla.) U., 1984—89; assoc. prof. English, world lit. and women's studies U. Alaska, Fairbanks, 1991—, prof., 2002—. Chair vis. spkrs. program U. of Alaska Statewide Women's Rsch. Consortium, Fairbanks, 2001—02. Translator: (book) The Fire of Origins (translation of Le Feu des Origines by Emmanuel Dongala, 2001; author: The Myth of Medea and the Murder of Children, 1998; contbr. anthology of essays, articles to profl. jours. Faculty advisor student br. Amnesty Internat., Fairbanks, 1999—2002. Recipient Fulbright Tchg./Rsch. award, Coun. for Internat. Exch. of Scholars, Brazzaville, The Congo, 1990, associateship, Five Coll. Women's Studies Rsch. Ctr., 2000; grantee Summer Inst. on Homer and Oral Traditions, U of Ariz., Tuscon, NEH, 1994. Mem.: MLA. Avocations: travel, gardening, cycling, swimming. Office: U Alaska PO Box 755720 Fairbanks AK 99775 Office Fax: 907-474-5247. E-mail: fflzc@uaf.edu.

CORTIJO, ANTONIO, education educator; b. Madrid, Aug. 3, 1967; arrived in U.S., 1993; s. Antonio Cortijo and Carmen Ocaña; m. Julie Spencer-Rodgers, Mar. 27, 1997. Lic. Spanish, Lic. classical language, Univ. Complutense, Madrid, 1989; PhD classical language, Univ. Allala, Spain, 1992; PhD romanca lanuage, Univ. Calif., Berkeley, Calif., 1997. Asst. prof. Univ. Calif., Santa Barbara, 1997—99, assoc. prof., 1999—2001, full prof., 2001—. Mem.: Am. Philos. Soc. Office: Dept of Spanish & Portugese Univ Calif Santa Barbara CA 93106

CORTINEZ, VERONICA, literature educator; b. Santiago, Chile, Aug. 27, 1958; came to U.S. 1979; d. Carlos Cortinez and Matilde Romo. Licenciatura en Letras, U. Chile, 1979; MA, U. Ill., Champaign, Ill., 1981, Harvard U., 1983, PhD, 1990. Tchg. asst. U. Chile, Santiago, 1977-79, U. Ill., Champaign, 1979-80; tchg. fellow Harvard U., 1982-86, instr., 1986-89; assoc. prof. colonial and contemporary Latin Am. lit. UCLA, 1989—. Fgn. corres. Caras, Santiago, 1987—. Author: Memoria Original de Bernal Diaz del Castillo, 2000, Cine a la chilena: Las peripecias de Sergio Castilla, 2001; editor: Albricia: La novela chilena del fin de siglo, 2000; mem. editl. bd. Mester/Dept. Spanish and Portuguese of UCLA, 1989—; editor Plaza mag., 1981-89, Harvard Rev., 1983-89; contbr. articles to profl. jours. Recipient award for Tchg. Excellence Derek Bok Ctr., Harvard U., 1982, 83, 84, 85, 86, Tchg. prize Romance Lang. Dept., Harvard U., 1986, Disting. Tchg. award UCLA, 1998; Whiting fellow. Mem. Cabot House, Phi Beta Phi. Avocations: reading, classical films, writing. Office: UCLA Dept Spanish & Portuguese 5310 Rolfe Hl Los Angeles CA 90095-0001

CORTNER, HANNA JOAN, research scientist, educator; b. Tacoma, Wash., May 9, 1945; d. Val and E. Irene Otteson; m. Richard Carroll Cortner, Nov. 14, 1970. BA in Polit. Sci. magna cum laude with distinction, U. Wash., 1967; MA in Govt., U. Ariz., 1969, PhD in Govt., 1973. Grad. tchg. and rsch. asst. dept. govt. U. Ariz., Tucson, 1967-70, rsch. assoc. Inst. Govt. Rsch., 1974-76, rsch. assoc. forest-watershed and landscape resources divsns. Sch. Renewable Natural Resources, 1975-82, adj. assoc. prof. Sch. Renewable Natural Resources, 1983-89; exec. asst. Pima County Bd. Suprs., 1985-86; adj. assoc. prof. renewable natural resources, assoc. rsch. scientist Water Resources Rsch. Ctr. U. Ariz., Tucson, 1988-89, prof., rsch. scientist Water Resources Rsch. Ctr., 1989-90, prof., rsch. scientist, dir. Water Resources Rsch. Ctr., 1990-96, prof., rsch. scientist Sch. Renewable Natural Resources, 1997-2000; rsch. prof., assoc. dir. Ecol. Restoration Inst. No. Ariz. U., Flagstaff, 2001—. Program analyst USDA Forest Svc., Washington, 1979-80; vis. scholar Inst. Water Resources, Corps of Engrs., Ft. Belvoir, Va., 1986-87; com. arid lands AAAS, 1986-89; com. natural disasters NAS/NRC, 1988-91, com. on planning and remediation of irrigation-induced water quality impacts, 1994-95; rev. com. nat. forest planning Conservation Found., Washington, 1987-90; chair adv. com. renewable resources planning techs. for pub. lands Office of Tech. Assessment U.S. Congress, 1989-91; mem. policy coun. Pinchot Inst. Conservation Studies, 1991-93; co-chair working party on evaluation of forest policies Internat. Union Forestry Rsch. Orgns., 1990-95, chair working party on forest instns. and forestry adminstrn., 1996; vice chair Man and the Biosphere Program, Temperate Directorate, U.S. Dept. State, 1991-96; bd. dirs. 7th Am. Forest Congress, 1994-96, mem. cmtys. com. steering com., 1996--, rsch. com., 1996-97; mem. sci. adv. com. Consortium for Environ. Risk Evaluation, 1996-97; cons. Greeley and Hansen, Cons. Engrs., U.S. Army Corps Engrs., Ft. Belvoir, U.S. Forest Svc., Washington, Portland, Oreg., Ogden, Utah. Assoc. editor Society and Natural Resources, 1992-94; book reviewer Western Polit. Sci. Quar., Am. Polit. Quar., Perspectives, Natural Resources Jour., Climatic Change, Society and Natural Resources, Jour. of Forestry, Environment; mem. editl. bd. Jour. Forest Planning, 1995—, Forest Policy and Econs., 1999-2002; co-author: The Politics of Ecosystem Management, 1999; co-editor: The State and Nature, 2002; contbr. articles to profl. jours. Bd. dirs. Planned Parenthood So. Ariz., 1992-94, mem. planning com., 1992, mem. bd. devel. and evaluation com., 1994; bd. dirs. N.W. Homeowners Assn., 1982-83, v.p., 1983-84, pres., 1984; vice chmn., chmn. Pima County Bd. Adjustment Dist. 3, 1984; active Tucson Tomorrow, 1984-88; mem. water quality subcom. Pima Assn. Govts., 1983-84, mem. environ. planning adv. com., 1989-90, chmn., 1984, mem. Avra Valley task force, 1988-90; bd. dirs. So. Ariz. Water Resources Assn., 1984-86, 87-95, sec., 1987-89, mem. com. alignment and terminal storage, 1990-94, mem. CAP com., 1988-92, chairperson, 1989-90, mem. basinwide mgmt. com., 1983-86, chairperson, 1992-93; active Ariz. Interagy. Task Force on Fire and the Urban/Wildland Interface, 1990-92; mem. wastewater mgmt. adv. com. Pima County, 1988-92, mem. subcom. on effluent reuse Joint CWAC-WWAC, 1989-91, mem. citizens water adv. com. Water Resources Plan Update Subcom., 1990-91; bd. dirs. Ctrl. Ariz. Water Conservation Dist., 1985-90, mem. fin. com., 1987-88, mem. spl. studies com., 1987-88, mem. nominating com., 1987; mem. Colo. River Salinity Control, 1989-90; chairperson adv. com. Tucson Long Range Master Water Plan, 1988-89; active water adv. com. City of Tucson, 1984. Travel grantee NSF/Soc. Am. Foresters; Rsch. grantee US Geol. Survey, US Army Corps of Engrs., USDA Forest Svc., Soil Conservation Svc., Utah State U., Four Corners Regional Commn., Office of Water Rsch. & Tech.; Sci. & Engrng. fellow AAAS, 1986-87; recipient Copper Letter Appreciation cert. City of Tucson, 1985, 89, SAWARA award, 1989. Mem. Am. Water Resources Assn. (mem. nat. award com. 1987-90, mem. statues and bylaws com. 1989-90, tech. co-chairperson ann. meeting 1993), Am. Forests Assn. (mem. forest policy ctr. adv. coun. 1991-95), Soc. Am. Foresters (mem. task force on sustaining long-term forest health and productivity 1991-92, mem. com. on forest policy 1994-96, sci. and tech. bd. 2001—), Am. Polit. Sci. Assn., Western Polit. Sci. Assn. (mem. com. on constrn. and bylaws 1976-80, chairperson 1977-79, mem. exec. coun. 1980-83, mem. com. on profl. devel. 1984-85, mem. com. on status of women 1984-85), Nat. Fire Protection Assn. (mem. tech. com. on forest and rural fire protection 1990-94), Phi Beta Kappa. Democrat. Achievements include research in political and socioeconomic aspects of natural resources policy, administration, and planning, water resources management, ecosystem management, wildland fire policy and management. Home: 4445 Savannah Cir Flagstaff AZ 86004 Office: Ecological Restoration Inst Northern Arizona U Flagstaff AZ 86011-5017 E-mail: hanna.cortner@nau.edu.

CORTNER, JEAN ALEXANDER, retired physician, educator; b. Nashville, Nov. 10, 1930; s. Roy Alexander and Ruth Elizabeth (McGaw) C.; m. Jean Gibson Morgan, Mar. 24, 1956; children: John Alexander, Ruth Morgan, Stephen Lee. BA in Chemistry, Vanderbilt U., 1952, MD, 1955. Diplomate Am. Bd. Pediat. Intern Vanderbilt Hosp., Nashville, 1955-56; resident in pediat. Babies Hosp., Columbia U., N.Y.C., 1956-58; chief resident, instr. Vanderbilt U., Nashville, 1958-59; NIH vis. fellow depts. pediat. and biochemistry Babies Hosp., Columbia U., N.Y.C., 1961-63; guest investigator, asst. physician dept. human genetics Rockefeller Inst., N.Y.C., 1962-63; chief dept. pediat. Roswell Pk. Meml. Inst., Buffalo, 1963-67; asst. rsch. prof. pediat. SUNY, Buffalo, 1963-67, prof., chmn. dept. pediat., 1967-74; physician-in-chief Children's Hosp. of Buffalo, 1967-74; prof., chmn. dept. pediat. U. Pa. Sch. Medicine, Phila., 1974-86; physician-in-chief Children's Hosp. of Pa., Phila., 1974-86; prof. pediat. in human genetics U. Pa. Sch. Medicine, Phila., 1975-89; dir. lipid-heart rsch. ctr. Children's Hosp. Phila., 1980—, dir. nutrition ctr., 1985—. Contbr. articles to med. and sci. jours. Hon. rsch. fellow dept. human genetics and biometry Galton Lab., U. Coll., London, 1972-73. Fellow Am. Acad. Pediatrics, Coll. Physicians Phila.; mem. Am. Soc. Human Genetics, AAAS, Am. Fedn. for Clin. Rsch., Soc. for Pediatric Rsch., John Morgan Soc., Assn. Med. Sch. Pediatric Dept. Chmn., Am. Pediatric Soc. Home: 6455 Snake River Ranch Rd Wilson WY 83014-9684 Office: Children's Hosp Phila Off of Dir of Nutrition Ctr 34th And Civic Center Blvd Philadelphia PA 19104

CORTO, DIANA MARIA, lyric-coloratura, producer, educator; b. N.Y. d. Samuel and Margaret C.; 1 child, Christian Miles Stomsvik. BA, CUNY, 1977, MA, 1984; studied drama, Am. Place Theatre; studied voice with Maria Kurenko, studied ballet with Maria Nevelska, Bolshoi Theatre, Moscow. Founder, dir. Am. Opera Musical Theatre Co., Inc., 1995—. Prof. drama for musical theatre Pace U., N.Y.C.; mem. voice faculty Calif. State U., L.A., also stage dir. opera program; founder, dir. Am. Opera/Mus. Theatre Co. Starred as Maria in West Side Story in numerous opera houses in Spain, Germany, Switzerland, Austria, 1984; appeared on Broadway in Her First Roman, Status Quo Vadis, Thirteen Daughters, West Side Story Revival, Stop the World, I Want To Get Off; concert tours in U.S., S.Am., Moscow, 1989-91; lead singer City of Angels Opera, Met. Studio; lyric-coloraturist in operas in U.S. and Europe; road tours include King and I, Man of La Mancha, Kismet; prodr. (N.Y. debut performance) The Jewel Box by Mozart/Griffiths; co-prodr. The Jewel Box with N.J. State Opera, Dmitiri Shostakovich concert with Fedn. of Russia, La Bohéme, and others; prodr., dir. Am. premiere of La Molinara by Paisiello at Town Hall, La Boheme; prodr.: Iolanta by Tchaikowski at Town Hall, Embassy of Russian Fedn., La Boheme, Rigoletto, Nat. Performing Arts Ctr. Taiwan. E-mail: corto@mindspring.com.

CORTOR, ELDZIER, artist, printmaker; b. Richmond, Va., Jan. 10, 1916; s. John and Ophelia (Twisdale) C.; m. Sophia Schmidt, Aug. 20, 1951; children: Michael, Mercedes, Stephen, Miriam. Student Art Inst. Chgo., 1936-41, Inst. Design, 1942, 43, 47, Columbia U., 1946. Painting instr. Centre D'Art, Port au Prince, Haiti, 1949-51; printmaker Pratt Inst., Bklyn., 1972-74. One-man shows include Le Museè de Peuple Haitien, Port-au-Prince, Haiti, 1950, Ctr. d'Art, Port-au-Prince, 1950, Elizabeth Nelson Gallery, Chgo., 1951, James Whyte Gallery, Washington, 1953, exhibited in group shows at Met. Mus. Art, N.Y.C., 1950, Studio Mus. Harlem, 1973, 1982, Boston Mus. Fine Arts, 1975, Museo de Arte Moderno La Pertulia, Cali, Colombia, 1976, Columbia Mus. Art, S.C., 1980, Kenkeleba Gallery, N.Y.C., 1988, Taipei Fine Arts Mus., 1988, San Antonio Mus. Art, 1994, Michael Rosenfeld Gallery, N.Y.C., 1995, 1996, 1997, 1998, 1999, Mus. Contemporary Art, Chgo., 1996—97, M. Rosenfeld Gallery, 1998—2003, Schomburg Ctr., N.Y.C., 1998, Flint (Mich.) Inst. Arts, 1999, Kenkeleba Gallery, N.Y.C., 2000, Represented in permanent collections Smithsonian Inst., Washington, Am. Fedn. Art, N.Y.C., Mus. Modern Art, IBM Corp., Portland (Oreg.) Art Mus., Art Inst. Chgo., Mus. Fine Arts, Boston. Recipient Bertha A. Florsheim award Art Inst. Chgo., 1945; recipient William H. Bartels award, 1946, Carnegie Inst. award, 1947; Julius Rosenwald fellow, Chgo., 1945-47; John Simon Guggenheim fellow, N.Y.C., 1949-50. Home: 35 Montgomery St Apt 19E New York NY 10002-6531

CORTRIGHT, BARBARA JEAN, writer; b. Oxford, Miss., Dec. 29, 1927; d. Lewis Stephen and Lucile (Chevalier) Grandy; m. Lem R. Cortright, Aug. 19, 1946; children: Lewis Stephen, Clyde Kenneth, Eric Allen, Barbara Edith. BFA with honors, Ariz. State U., 1949, MA in Humanities, 1977, MA in German Lang., 1979; PhD in Art History, U. N.Mex., Albuquerque, 1993. Instr. in art history Scottsdale (Ariz.) Coll., 1974-78; newsletter editor Heard Mus., Phoenix, 1978-79; lectr. in non-fiction Ariz. State U., Tempe, 1979-80; publicist O.K. Harris West Gallery, Scottsdale, 1981-84. Author: The Reach of Solitude, 1984; contbr. articles to profl. jours. NEA fellow, 1976. Mem. Phi Kappa Phi, Alpha Mu Gamma. Democrat. Episcopalian. Home: 516 E Erie Dr Tempe AZ 85282-3713 E-mail: GreenPer@aol.com.

CORTRIGHT, INGA ANN, accountant; b. Silver City, N.Mex., Sept. 30, 1949; d. Lester Richard and Claudia Marcella (Huckaby) Lee; m. Russell Joseph Cortright, June 25, 1986 (dec. Jan. 2000). BS in Acctg., Ariz. State U., 1976, MBA, 1978; postgrad., Walden U., 1995. CPA, Ariz., Tex. Sole practice cert. pub. acctg., Ariz., 1981—. Cons. in field. Mem. AICPA. Republican. Episcopalian. Avocation: travel. Office: Box HCR91 Morristown AZ 85342 E-mail: icortright@aol.com.

CORTRIGHT, LEWIS STEPHEN, elementary educator; b. Agana, Guam, Jan. 22, 1950; s. Lem Rouselle and Barbara Jean Cortright; m. Margarita Cortright Diaz, June 10, 1989; chldren: Lewis Stephen Jr., Paz Alejandra Cortright Diaz. BA, Ariz. State U., 1974. Cert. tchr. K-8 ESL. Tchr. Picacho (Ariz.) Elem. Sch. Dist., 1985-94, tchr., ESL dir., 1994—. Sch. coord. Hands Across the Border, Picacho, 1996—. Mem. Ariz. Edn. Assn. (local pres. 1993—), Am. Quarter Horse Assn. Democrat. Episcopalian. Avocations: horse training and breeding, musician. Home: PO Box 142 Picacho AZ 85241-0142 Office: Picacho Elem Sch Dist #33 PO Box 8 Picacho AZ 85241-0008

CORTRIGHT, LOUISE VERA, retired medical technologist, small business owner; b. Buffalo, Apr. 22, 1938; d. Asa Lawrence and Mary Lois (Ward) C. BS (hon.), Fairleigh Dickson U., 1960; postgrad., Rutgers U., 1965-67. Nationally registered med. technologist. Bacteriology supr. Middlesex Gen. Hosp., New Brunswick, N.J., 1963-64; hematology supr. Princeton Hosp., Princeton, N.J., 1964-65; tchg. supr. Somerset Med. Ctr., Somerville, N.J., 1965-67, chief technologist, 1966-79; owner, operator Aurora Kennel, Bridgewater, N.J., 1973-92. Cons. N.J. State Dept. of Health, Trenton, 1979-80. Treas., v.p. Bridgewater Twp. Bd. of Health, 1974, 1975; chmn. Regional Animal Shelter, 1978-81. Mem. Morris Hills Dog Training Club (founding mem. 1961), North Jersey Shetland Sheepdog Club (founding mem. 1965). Avocations: organic gardening, cross-country skiing, sewing, reading, participating in earth watch and habitat for humanity projects.

CORTS, PAUL RICHARD, college president; b. Terre Haute, Ind., Sept. 15, 1943; s. Charles H. and Hazel Corts; m. Diane Stevens, May 29, 1965; children: Kenneth Stevens, Daniel Paul, Susan Diane. BA, Georgetown Coll., 1965; MA, Ind. U., 1967, PhD, 1971. Assoc. prof. speech communication Western Ky. U., Bowling Green, 1968-78, dir. internat. edn., 1973-76, dir. univ. honors program, 1972-78, asst. dean for instrn., 1973-78, assoc. v.p. for instrn., 1978; exec. v.p., chief adminstrv. officer Okla. Bapt. U., Shawnee, 1978-83; pres. The Corts Co., Shawnee, 1983, Wingate (N.C.) Coll., 1983-91, Palm Beach Atlantic Coll., West Palm Beach, Fla., 1991—. Cons. bd. govs. U. N.C., Chapel Hill, 1987-88. Co-author: Fundamentals of Effective Group Communication, 1979, Let's Talk Business, 1983. Pres. coun. pres.' Carolinas Intercollegiate Athletic Conf., 1986-88; mem. edn. com. Bapt. World Alliance, McLean, Va., 1990—; bd. dirs. United Way Cen. Carolinas, Monore and Charlotte, 1984-91. Mem. Am. Assn. Pres. Ind. Colls. and Univs. (bd. dirs., pres. 2000-01), Charlotte Area Ednl. Consortium (pres. 1987-88), Am. Coun. Edn., Ind. Colls. and Univs. Fla. (chmn. 2000—), Williamsburg Pres. Colloquy (chmn. 1990), Palm Beach Lit. Soc. (pres. 1992-2000), Coun. Christian Colls. and Univs. (bd. dirs. 1999—), Fla. Coun. 100, Gov.'s Club (bd. dirs. 2000-), Good Samaritan Med. Ctr. (gov. bd. 2002-), Rotary. Office: Palm Beach Atlantic Coll Office of Pres PO Box 24708 West Palm Beach FL 33416-4708

CORTS, THOMAS EDWARD, university president; b. Terre Haute, Ind., Oct. 7, 1941; s. Charles Harold and Hazel Louise (Vernon) C.; m. Marla Ruth Haas, Feb. 15, 1964; children: Jennifer Ruth Corts Fuller, Rachel Anne Corts Wachter, Christian Haas BA, Georgetown (Ky.) Coll., 1963; MA, Ind. U., 1968, PhD, 1972; DLitt (hon.), Georgetown Coll., 1991; DHL (hon.), Campbell U., 1995, U. Ala., 2002. Asst. to pres. Georgetown Coll., 1963-64, 67-69, asst. prof., 1967-69, exec. dean, 1969-73, exec. v.p., 1973; coord. Higher Edn. Consortium, Lexington, Ky., 1973-74; pres. Wingate (N.C.) Coll., 1974-83, Samford U., Birmingham, Ala., 1983—. Bd. dirs. Samford U. Found., 1990—, Found. Ind. Higher Edn., 1988-92; chmn. Ala. Commn. on Sch. Performance and Accountability, 1993-94. Contbr. articles to profl. jours. Bd. dirs. Birmingham chpt. ARC, 1983-89, Ala. Citizens for Constl. Reform, 2000--; mem. adv. bd. Salvation Army, 1987—; mem. exec. coun. Boy Scouts Am., Birmingham, 1984—; bd. dirs. Leadership Birmingham, 1984-95, Exec. Com. Birmingham Better Bus. Bur., 1996—, Birmingham Summerfest, 1984—, Birmingham Area Consortium on Higher Edn., Ala. Poverty Project, Inc. Recipient Outstanding Alumnus award Georgetown Coll., 1987, Jefferson award Downtown Action Com., Birmingham, 1988, Outstanding Educator award Ala. Assn. Coll. and Univs.-Ala. Assn. Women, Birmingham, 1989, Good Shepherd award Assn. Bapt. for Scouting, 1990, Citizen of Yr., 1990, Most Supportive Pres. award Am. Assn. of Colls. for Tchr. Edn., 1991. Mem. Am. Assn. Pres. of Ind. Colls. and Univs. (v.p. 1990-92, pres. 1992-95, bd. dirs. 1989-2002), Coun. for Advancement of Pvt. Colls. in Ala. (past pres.), Ala. Assn. Ind. Colls., Nat. Fellowship Bapt. Educators (pres. 1988-89), Assn. So. Bapt. Colls. and Schs. (v.p. 1988-89, pres. 1990-91), So. Assn. Colls. and Schs. (trustee 1991-98, mem. commn. on colls., vice chmn. 1991, chmn. exec. coun. 1992-94, pres. 1996), Coun. Higher Edn. Accreditation (bd. dirs. 1995-97), Assn. Governing Bds. (pres.'s commn., chmn. 2001--), Birmingham Area C. of C. (bd. dirs.)Ala. Acad. Honor, Country Club Birmingham, The Club, The Summit Club, Rotary. Democrat. Office: Samford U 800 Lakeshore Dr Birmingham AL 35229-0002 E-mail: tecorts@samford.edu.

CORTY, ANDREW P. publishing executive; b. Wilmington, Del., June 16, 1952; s. Claude and Susanne Corty; m. Betty L. Wallace, Apr. 30, 1983; children: Robert Wallace, Edward Wallace. AB, Harvard U., 1974; MBA, Stanford U., 1978. Copy editor The Morning News, Wilmington, 1974—75; reporter The Record, Havre de Grace, Md., 1975—76; asst. to pub. The St. Petersburg (Fla.) Times, 1978—80; pub. Fla. Trend mag., St. Petersburg, 1981—85; gen. mgr. Washington Post mag., 1985—89; mktg. dir. St. Petersburg Times, 1989—91; v.p., sec., bd. dirs. Times Pub. Co., St. Petersburg, 1991—; vice chmn. Congrl. Quar., Inc., Washington, 1991—; pres. Fla. Trend, St. Petersburg, 1991—. Trustee Salvador Dali Mus., St. Petersburg, Fla. Office: St Petersburg Times PO Box 1121 Saint Petersburg FL 33731-1121

CORUJO, MARLENE, urologic surgeon; b. Bronx, N.Y., June 23, 1966; d. Norma Corujo. BA summa cum laude, CUNY, 1988; MD, Yale U., 1992. Diplomate Am. Bd. Urology. Resident in surgery Yale-New Haven Hosp., 1992-94, resident in urology, 1994-97; fellow in neuro-urology L.I. Jewish Med. Ctr., New Hyde Park, N.Y., 1997-98; asst. prof. urology Beth Israel Med. Ctr., N.Y.C., 1998—. Contbr. articles to profl. jours. Saik scholar, 1988, William and Charlotte Cadbury scholar, 1992. Mem. AMA, Am. Urologic Assn., Women in Urology, Soc. Urodynamics and Female Urology, Phi Beta Kappa. Avocations: writing poetry, music. Office: Beth Israel Med Ctr 10 Union Sqauare E New York NY 10003

CORUN, RONALD LEWIS, asphalt refining executive; b. Balt., Nov. 17, 1952; s. John Grebe and Cleo Hazel (Cornwell) C.; m. Mary Ann Hack, July 9, 1977; children: Mary Frances, Ronald Lewis. BSCE, U. Md., 1974. V.p., gen. mgr. Corun & Gatch, Inc., Fallston, Md., 1965-94; v.p. T.C. Simons, Inc., Fallston, Md., 1994-96; mgr. tech. support Citgo Asphalt Refining Co., Blue Bell, Pa., 1997—; pres. RLC Cons., Inc., Fallston, 1997—. Mem. Harford County Environ. Adv. Bd., Bel Air, Md., 1982-95. Recipient Sheldon G. Hayes award Nat. Asphalt Pavement Assn., 1994. Mem. Assn. Asphalt Paving Techs. Republican. Lutheran. Avocations: golf, skiing, fishing. Office: Citgo Asphalt PO Box 3220 Ocean City MD 21843

CORVINO, ERNESTA, ballet dancer; b. Bklyn., Feb. 27, 1952; d. Alfredo Alfonso and Marcella (Rubin) C. AA in English with honors, Manhattan C.C., 1972. Soloist Md. Ballet Co., Balt., 1966-68; mem. corps de ballet Met. Opera Ballet, N.Y.C., 1970-71, Radio City Music Hall, N.Y.C., 1972-74; dir., prin. dancer Ernesta Corvino's Dance Cir. Co., N.Y.C., 1981—. Co-dir., tchr. Dance Cir., N.Y.C., 1968-93; tchr. ballet Sarah Lawrence Coll., Bronxville, N.Y., 1993-94; artist-in-residence U. Nev., Las Vegas, 1995—; guest artist Randolph-Macon Woman's Coll., Lynchburg, Va., 1987-91, N.Y. Baroque Dance Co., N.Y.C., 1991-95, Danspace, Oakland, Calif., 1990—; workshops throughout U.S. and Europe; pres. Dance Cor Inc., N.Y.C., 1989—. Choreographer (ballets) Charlie & Co., 1981, Holmes Sweet Holmes, 1984, Somnus, 1987, Sujets d'Art, 1997, The Gallery, 1981, Derby, 1985, The Mummy Returns, 1986, Joie de Vivaldi, 1986, Handel with Care, 1988, Cycles, 1991, Jai Ma, 1991, The Revenant, 1994, Early Morning Hours of the Hard Moon, 1994, The Emerald Concerto, 1995, Sujets d'Art, 1997, Sundances, 2002.

CORVO, WILLIAM KENNETH, writer; b. Berwyn, Ill., July 26, 1959; s. Robert H. and Wilma D. Corvo; m. Renee Marie Lekan, Mar. 19, 1995. A, Coll. of DuPage, 2001. Author: (novel) Seduction for Hire, (self-help book) 112+ Used Car Buying Tips and Then Some. Recipient Poetic Achievement award, 2003. Avocations: drawing, cartoon drawing.

CORWIN, BERT CLARK, optometrist; b. Rapid City, SD, Oct. 4, 1930; s. Meade and Adeline (Clark) C.; m. Lydia M. Forehand; children: B. Clark II, Kelley Linette Fromm. AS, S.D. State U., 1952; BS, Ill. Coll. Optometry, Chgo., 1956, OD, 1957. Pvt. practice, Rapid City, 1957—. Projects chmn. S.D. Lions Sight and Svc. Found., 1964; chmn. med. adv. com. to S.D. Dept. Pub. Welfare, 1968-76; mem. S.D. Adv. Coun. for Regional Med. and Health Planning, 1971; cons. S.D. Dept. Human Svcs., 1989—; adv. bd. S.D. Dept. of Svc. to Visual Impaired; bd. dirs. Super 8 Motel Developers, Rapid City Regional Airport, v.p., 1999-2000, pres., 2000—; chmn. bd. dirs. Transaction Network, Inc., 1997—, Terry Peak Lodge, 2001-; mng. ptnr. Tight Line Lake, 1999-2002. Contbr. articles to profl. jours. Pres. Cleghorn PTA, Rapid City, 1968-70; bd. dirs. Am. Optometric Found., 1989-90, v.p., 1990-94, pres., 1994-96; chmn. bd. dirs. Terry Peak Condominiums, 001—. Recipient Presdl. medal of honor Pres. of Ill. Coll. of Optometry, 1999, 2002, Spl. honor Am. Optometric Found. Fellow Am. Acad. Optometry (diplomate contact lens sect., sec.-treas. 1985-86, pres.-elect 1987-88, pres. 1988-90, chmn. 1st internat. meeting 1992, nom. com. 2000-02); mem. Am. Optometric Assn. (exec. com. 1974-76, Am. Optometrist of the Yr. 1993), S.D. Optometric Soc. (pres. 1970-71), North Ctrl. State Optometric Conf. (bd. dirs. 1970-71), Black Hills Optometric Soc. (sec.-treas. 1958-69), S.D. State Bd. Examiners (pres. 1982-85), Nat. Acad. Practice Optometry (sec.-treas. 1990-94, Disting. Practitioners award, co-chmn. 1994-96). Clubs: Black Hills Water Ski (pres. 1963). Lodges: Masons, Elks, Lions (pres. Rushmore chpt. 1961-62, Robert Tyler award 1998). Republican. Methodist. Avocations: skiing, water skiing, hunting, piloting, public speaking. Home: 5048 Carriage Hills Dr Rapid City SD 57702 Office: 2800 3rd St Rapid City SD 57702-2520 E-mail: bccorwin@juno.com.

CORWIN, GREGG MARLOWE, lawyer; b. Mpls., May 4, 1947; s. Gerald Sidney Corwin and Shirley Mae (Nathenson) Nadler; m. Frances Gail Shapiro, mar. 21, 1971; children: Mitchell, David. BA summa cum laude, U. Minn., 1969, JD cum laude, 1972. Bar: Minn. 1972, U.S. Dist. Ct. Minn. 1972, U.S. Ct. Appeals (8th cir.) 1976, U.S. Supreme Ct. 1977. Assoc. Fred Burstein Law Firm, Mpls., 1972-77; ptnr. Cortlen Cloutier, Mpls., 1977-78; pvt. practice, Mpls., 1978—. Capt. USAF. Mem. ABA, Minn. Bar Assn., Hennepin County Bar Assn., Phi Beta Kappa. Democrat. Jewish. Avocations: reading, music, sports. Office: 1660 Hwy 100 Ste 508 E Minneapolis MN 55416-1534 E-mail: GCorwin@GCorwin.com.

CORWIN, HAL MICHAEL, neurologist; b. Indpls., June 24, 1953; s. Hyman S. and Ann Jane (Rabinowitz) C.; m. Jean Sirowatka, Jan. 12, 1955; children: Jenna Nicole, Jonathon Marc. BA in Biol. Sci., Math., Ind. U., 1974, MD, 1978. Diplomate Am. Bd. Psychiatry and Neurology, Am. Bd. Electrodiagnostic Medicine. Intern dept. internal medicine Ctr. for Health Scis., U. Tenn., Memphis, 1978-79; resident neurology U. Va., Charlottesville, 1979-82; fellow neurology & epilepsy U. Minn., Mpls., 1982-83, attending physician dept. neurology, 1982-83; pvt. practice neurology Neuroscience Assocs., P.S.C., Louisville, 1983—, pres., 1987-92; v.p. Neuroscience Ctr. Excellence at Humana Hosp. Audubon, Louisville, 1988-89; pres., 1990-91; sec. Spinoscopy of Louisville P.S.C., 1991-96. Med. expert in neurology for ANSI Z-365 Med. Mgmt. sub-com. on cumulative trama disorders; examiner Am. Bd. Psychiatry and Neurology, 2002-03. Co-author: Hand Clinics, 1986, Occupational Medicine, 1989; contbr. articles to profl. jours. Vice chmn., chmn. regulation Muscular Dystrophy Dance for Those Who Can't fundraiser, Bloomington, Ind., 1972; participant Jewish Welfare Fedn. Fundraising Drive, Bloomington, 1973; profl. adv. bd. Epilepsy Assn. Louisville, 1986. Pub. Health Svc. fellow Pub. Health Svc. Ind., 1975, Epilepsy fellow comprehensive epilepsy program U. Minn., 1982-83; recipient Founders Day High Scholastic Achievement

award Ind. U., 1972-74, Honors award dept. pediatrics Ind. U. Sch. Medicine, 1978, Citation of Merit Hooverwood Jewish Day Home, Indpls., 1971, Nat. Merit Scholarship Program Letter of Commendation, 1970, Earl Montgomery Sportsmanship award Jewish Community Ctr, Indpls., 1969-71; Merit scholar Ind. U., 1972-73. Mem. Am. Assn. Electrodiagnostic Medicine, Am. Epilepsy Assn., Am. Acad. Neurology, Am. Soc. Surgery of Hand, Ky. Med. Assn., Jefferson County Med. Soc., MENSA, Bnai Brith. Jewish. Avocations: running, hist. reading, tennis. Office: Neuroscience Assocs PSC 6400 Dutchmans Pkwy Ste 140 Louisville KY 40205-3342

CORWIN, JAMES A. radiation oncologist; b. Southampton, N.Y., Feb. 14, 1946; s. Richard Fifthion and Florence Elizabeth C.; m. F. Georgia, Dec. 22, 1984; children: Katherine, Emily. AB, Duke U., 1967; MS, Tufts U., 1970, MD, 1972. Diplomate Am. Bd. Radiology. Radiation oncologist Wilford Hall USAF Hosp., San Antonio, 1978-87, Allison Cancer Ctr., Midland, Tex., 1987—. Med. dir. Hospice of Midland, 1987—. Col. USAF, 1967-87. Episcopalian. Home: 4516 Robin Ln Midland TX 79707-2219 Office: Allison Cancer Ctr 301 N N St Midland TX 79701-6404

CORWIN, JOYCE ELIZABETH STEDMAN, construction company executive; b. Chgo. d. Cresswell Edward and Elizabeth Josephine (Kimbell) Stedman; m. William Corwin, May 1, 1965; children: Robert Edmund Newman, Jillanne Elizabeth McInnis. Pres. Am. Properties, Inc., Miami, Fla., 1966-72; v.p. Stedman Constrn. Co., Miami, 1971—. Owner Joy-Win Horses, Gray lady ARC, 1969-70. Guidance worker Youth Hall, 1969-70; sponsor Para Med. Group of Coral Park H.S., 1969-70; hostess, Rep. presdl. campaign, 1968; aide Rep. Nat. Conv., 1972. Mem. Dade County Med. Aux. (chmn. directory com. 1970), Marion County Med. Aux., Fla. Psychiat. Soc. Aux., Fla. Morgan Horse Assn., Fla. Thoroughbred Breeders Assn. Clubs: Coral Gables Jr. Women's (chmn. casework com.), Heritage, Royal Dames of Ocala. Home: Windrift Farm 8500 NW 120th St Reddick FL 32686-4513

CORWIN, JULES ARTHUR, civil servant; b. N.Y.C., June 9, 1946; s. Irving and Mary Corwin; m. Judith Hoffman, Oct. 4, 1969; 1 child, Oliver. AB, Dartmouth Coll., 1968; JD, Columbia U., 1971. Bar: N.Y. 1974. Legal officer devel. program UN, N.Y.C., 1971-73, adminstrn. officer, 1973-80, dep. exec. sec., 1980-85, exec. sec., adv. com. adminstrv. and budgetary questions, 1985—. Avocations: collecting rare books and prints, antiques. Home: 333 E 30th St Apt 3J New York NY 10016-6466

CORWIN, MELANIE S. lawyer; b. Cin., July 9, 1962; BA, Ea. Ky. U., 1984; JD, No. Ky. U., 1990. Bar: Ohio 1990, Ky. 1998, U.S. Dist. Ct. (so. dist.) Ohio 1991, U.S. Ct. Appeals (6th cir.) 1992. Assoc. Brown, Cummins & Brown Co., L.P.A., 1990-97, ptnr., 1998—2002; atty. Waite, Schneider, Bayless & Chesley Co. LPA, Cin., 2002—. Mem. ABA, Ohio Bar Assn., Ky. Bar Assn. Office: Waite Schneider Bayless & Chesley Co LPA 1513 4th and Vine Tower One W 4th St Cincinnati OH 45202

CORWIN, NORMAN, writer, director, producer; b. Boston, May 3, 1910; s. Samuel H. and Rose (Ober) C.; m. Katherine Locke, Mar. 1947; children: Anthony, Diane. Student, Boston, also Winthrop, Mass.; LittD, Columbia Coll., 1967, LHD, 1978; D in Lit. Arts, Lincoln Coll., 1990; LHD (hon.), Calif. Luth. U., 1996. Writer, producer, dir. CBS; vis. prof. U. So. Calif., 1981—; Patten Meml. lectr. Ind. U., 1981. Dir. creative writing Idyllwild (Calif.) Sch. Music and Art, 1970—; mem. LaGuardia One World Meml. Commn. to Europe, 1948; trustee L.A. Internat. Film Expn.; film adv. bd. L.A. County Mus. Art; adv. bd. Inst. for Readers Theatre, Poetry Therapy Inst.; lectr. in field. Wrote, produced radio broadcasts; commemorative broadcasts: We Hold These Truths, on 150th anniversary of Am. Bill of Rights, 1941, Bill of Rights: 200, 1991; chief spl. projects, UN Radio; wrote films for, RKO, MGM, 20th-Century Fox, UN; writer, dir., prod.: 26 By Corwin, 1941, This is War, 1942, An American in England, 1942, Columbia Presents Corwin, 1944-45; writer, dir.: (stage plays) The Hyphen, The Rivalry, The World of Carl Sandburg, Together Tonight--Jefferson, Hamilton and Burr; writer for: films Scandal at Scourie, Lust for Life (Oscar nominee), The Blue Veil, The Story of Ruth; producer, host: TV series Norman Corwin Presents for Westinghouse Group W, 1972; author: TV spl. The Ct. Martial of the Tiger of Malaya, 1974; writer, host: TV series Academy Leaders, 1979, radio series More by Corwin, 1996-97. Author: They Fly Through the Air With the Greatest of Ease, 1939, Thirteen by Corwin, 1942, More by Corwin, 1944, On a Note of Triumph, 1945, Untitled and Other Dramas, 1945, Dog in the Sky, 1952, The Plot to Overthrow Christmas, 1952, The World of Carl Sandburg, 1961, Overkill and Megalove, 1963, Prayer For the 70s, 1969, Jerusalem Printout, 1978, Holes in a Stained Glass Window, 1978, Greater than the Bomb, 1981, A Date with Sandburg, 1981, Trivializing America, 1988, Years of the Electric Ear, 1994, Norman Corwin's Letters, 1994; plays Cervantes, 1973; stage play The Rivalry (produced as Hallmark TV spl.); contbr. articles to mags.; writer: text of Human Rights Cantata, Yes Speak Out Yes (commd. by UN), text CONartist (cartoons of Paul Conrad), 1993; Norman Corwin's Letters, 1993, Years of the Electric Ear, 1994. Recipient Page One award Am. Newspaper Guild, 1944-45, award UCLA Ctr. Aging, 2001, Ray Bradbury award, 2001, Distinguished Merit award NCCJ, 1945, UCLA Icon award, 2001, Calif. Hist. Soc. Cmty. Enrichment award, 2003; Unity award Interracial Film and Radio Guild, 1945; citation Nat. Council Tchrs. English, 1945; citation Assn. Tchrs. Social Studies of N.Y., 1945; award Am. Schs. and Colls. Assn., 1946; first place in nat. poll radio editors Billboard mag., for On a Note of Triumph, 1946; co-winner 1st prize Met. Opera awards for new Am. opera, The Warrior, produced Jan. 1947; Freedom award telecast Between Americans, 1951; hon. grant Am. Acad. Arts and Letters; Valentine Davies award Writers Guild Am., 1972; Artists award U. Judaism, 1972; Pacific Pioneer Broadcasters' Carbon Mike award, 1974; Preceptor's award San Francisco State U., 1979; PEN award for body of work, 1986, Friends of Old Time Radio award, 1990, Byron Kane medal SPERDVAC, 1990, Gold medal Internat. Radio Festival, 1992, Lifetime Achievement award N.Y. Festival, 1992, Lifetime Achievement award League of Women Voters, 1993, Alfred I. duPont-Columbia U. award for 50 Yrs. after 14th Aug. commemorating surrender of Japan, 1997. Fellow Radio Hall of Fame; mem. Acad. of Motion Picture Arts and Scis. (chmn. documentary awards com. 1967-82, 85-92, co-chmn. scholarship com., bd. govs. 1979-86, 1st v.p. acad. 1988, sec. Acad. Found. 1983-88), Aspen Film Conf. (steering com.), Authors League Am., Dramatists Guild, Writers Guild Am. (dir.), Dirs. Guild Am., ASCAP, Internat. Documentary Assn. (bd. dirs.), Soc. Preservation of Radio Drama, Variety and Comedy. Wendell Willkie One World Flight award (flew around world, recording speeches leaders of state, artists and scientists, June-Oct. 1946), first award Inst. for Edn. by Radio, 1946; prod. and narrated One World Flight, 1947. Home: 1840 Fairburn Ave Los Angeles CA 90025-4958

CORWIN, SHERMAN PHILLIP, lawyer; b. Chgo., June 29, 1917; s. Louis C. and Becky (Goodman) Cohen; m. Betty C. Corwin (dec. Jan. 1998); children: Susan M. Rothberg, Laurie L. Grad. valedictorian, Wilson Jr. Coll., 1937; BA, U. Chgo., 1939, JD cum laude, 1941. Bar: Ill. 1941, Mich. 1946, Colo. 1946. Assoc. Lederer, Livingston Kahn & Adsit, Chgo., 1941-43; assoc. Sonnenschein Nath & Rosenthal, Chgo., 1946 60, ptnr., 1960—, head estate planning and probate group, 1970-88. Editor: Estate Planning Handbook for Lawyers, 6th edit., 1976, 7th edit., 1980 Bd. dirs., officer North Suburban Synagogue Beth El, Highland Park, Ill., 1959-80; bd. dirs. Congregation Moriah, Deerfield, Ill., 1980-84; chmn. profl. adv. com. (estate planning) Jewish Fedn. Met. Chgo., 1985-87. Served to 1st lt. U.S. Army, 1944-46 Fellow Am. Coll. Trust and Estate Counsel; mem. Chgo. Bar Assn. (chmn. trust law com. 1970, chmn. Am. citizenship com. 1955), Chgo. Estate Planning Coun. (pres. 1983), Nu Sigma Kappa (past pres. local chpt.), Nu Beta Epsilon (past pres. local chpt.). Home: 400 E Ohio St Apt 2104 Chicago IL 60611-4615 Office: Sonnenschein Nath Et Al 8000 Sears Tower 233 S Wacker Dr Ste 8000 Chicago IL 60606-6491

CORWIN, STANLEY JOEL, book publisher; b. N.Y.C., Nov. 6, 1938; s. Seymour and Faye (Agress) C.; m. Donna Gelgur; children: Alexandra, Donna, Ellen. AB, Syracuse U., 1960. Dir. subsidiary rights, v.p. mktg. Prentice-Hall, Inc., Englewood Cliffs, N.J., 1960-68; v.p. internat. Grosset & Dunlap, Inc., N.Y.C., 1968-75; founder, pres. Corwin Books, N.Y.C., 1975; pres., pub. Pinnacle Books, Inc., L.A., 1976-79; pres. Stan Corwin Prodns. Ltd., 1980—; pres., CEO Tudor Pub. Co., N.Y.C. and L.A., 1987-90. Lectr. Conf. World Affairs U. Colo., 1976, U. Denver, 1978, Calif. State U., Northridge, 1980, The Learning Annex; participant Pubmart Seminar, N.Y.C., 1977, UCLA, 1985, 93, 98; guest lectr. U. So. Calif., 1987—, iVillage Internet Chat Room, 1999—2001; expert witness nat. media trials; columnist Buddhascape Internet Network. Author: Where Words Were Born, 1977, How to Become a Best Selling Author, 1984, 3rd edit., 1999, The Creative Writer's Companion, 2001; contbr. articles, ; prodr.: (films) Remo Williams-The Adventure Begins, 1986, (video) How to Golf with Jan Stephenson, 1987; exec. prodr.: The Elvis Files TV Show, 1991, The Marilyn Files, 1993; pub.: The Movie Script Libr., 1994. Mem. Pres. Carter's U.S. Com. on the UN, 1977. Served with AUS, 1960. Nat. prize winner short story contest Writers' Digest, 1966 Mem. Assn. Am. Pubs., PEN. Home and Office: 114 N Wetherly Dr Beverly Hills CA 90211-1813

CORWIN, STEVEN, hospital administrator; BS, Northwestern U., 1977; MD summa cum laude, Northwestern U. Sch. Medicine, 1979. Bd. cert. in internal medicine and cardiology. Intern and resident Columbia-Presbyn. Med. Ctr., N.Y.C., 1979—82, chief med. resident, dept. medicine, 1982—83; asst. prof. clin. medicine Coll. Physicians and Surgeons, Columbia U., N.Y.C., 1986—98, assoc. prof. clin. medicine, 1998—; med. dir. Milstein Hosp. Columbia-Presbyn. Med. Ctr., N.Y.C., 1997—98, dir. critical care svcs., 1991—97, dir. cardiac intensive care unit, 1986—91; chief med. officer N.Y. Presbyn. Hosp., N.Y.C., 1998—, sr. v.p., 1999—. Office: 161 Fort Washington Ave New York NY 10032

CORWIN, VERA-ANNE VERSFELT, small business owner, consultant; b. Glen Ridge, NJ, Nov. 12, 1932; d. Porter LaRoy and Vera Anna (Price) Versfelt; m. John M. Corwin, Apr. 9, 1955; children: Gail Elizabeth Corwin Bayne, Gregory John, Lynn B. Corwin Byers. BS, Upsala Coll., 1954; MEd, Wayne State U., 1972, PhD, 1977. Instr. Wayne (N.J.) Sch. Dist., 1954-55; engr., spec., analyst Chrysler Corp., Highland Park, Mich., 1955-56, 78-85; instr. Royal Oak (Mich.) Sch. Dist., 1968-78; sr. systems engr. Electronic Data Systems, Troy, Mich., 1985-87; owner, pres. Unique Solutions, Inc., Royal Oak, 1987—. Adj. prof. U. Mich., Dearborn, 1989, Wayne State U., 1989; expert cons. Teltech, Inc., Mpls., 1990—. Author: (tng. manuals) Statistical Process Control Philosophies and Tools, 1988, Design of Experiments Philosophies and Tools, 1989. Pres. Arlington Pk. Homeowners Assn., Royal Oak, 1984—85, rd. commr., 1984—90; sec. bd. dirs. Cmty. Concert Assn. Troy, 1996—99, 3rd v.p. bd. dirs., 1999—2002, 2d v.p. bd. dirs., 2002—; vol. Oakland County Mobile Meals, 1996—; trustee First Presbyn. Ch. Royal Oak, 1990—93, sec., 1993, Presbies sec., 1994, choir, 1958—72, 1997—, ch. children's computer lab. cons., instr., 1997—, Christian edn. com., 2000—, adult computers instr., 2001—. N.J. scholar, 1950-51. Fellow Am. Soc. for Quality (standing rev. bd. 1996—); mem. Soc. Automotive Engrs. (trainer 1991—), Automotive Industry Action Group (chmn. design expts. subgroup 1988 94), Soc. Mfg. Engrs. (sr., trainer 1987-91), Am. Statis. Assn. Avocations: skiing, piano, travel. Office: Unique Solutions Inc PO Box 1711 Royal Oak MI 48068-1711 E-mail: corwinvj@aol.com.

CORWIN, WILLIAM, psychiatrist; b. Boston, Oct. 28, 1908; m. Frances M. Wetherell (dec.); m. Joyce S. Newman, 1965. MD, Tufts Coll., 1932. Diplomate Am. Bd. Psychiatry and Neurology, Am. Bd. Forensic Psychiatry. Intern Wesson Meml. Hosp., Springfield, Mass., 1932-33; physician Met. State Hosp., Waltham, Mass., 1933-37, asst. supt., 1937-42; rsch. fellow Harvard, 1937-46; practice medicine, specializing in psychiatry Springfield, Mass., 1946-54, Miami, Fla., 1954-88, Ocala, Fla., 1988—. Mem. staff Ocala Regional Med. Ctr.; instr. psychiatry Boston U., 1937—46, Tufts Coll., 1941—46; clin. assoc. prof. psychiatry U. Miami, 1955—70, clin. prof., 1970—88. Contbr. articles on physiology of schizophrenia to profl. pubs. Past mem. State Fla. Adv. Com. on Mental Health; agy. ops. com. United Fund; bd. dirs. Family and Childrens Svcs. Miami. Served to lt. col. M.C., USAAF, 1942-46. Fellow: Am. Coll. Psychiatrists, Am. Psychiat. Assn. (life); mem.: AMA, Fla. Psychiat. Soc.

CORY, CHARLES JOHNSON, lawyer; b. Coulee Dam, Wash., Jan. 30, 1941; s. James Murdock and Margaret Mary (Johnson) C.; m. JoAnne Frances Freeman, 1965; children— Brian, Kevin. A.B. cum laude, Gonzaga U., 1963; J.D., Stanford U., 1966. Bar: Calif. 1970, U.S. Dist. Ct. (no. dist.) Calif. 1970. Atty., SBA, San Francisco, 1966; claims adjustor Allstate Ins. Co., San Jose, Calif., 1968-69, claims supr., 1969-70; assoc. Miller, Morton, Caillat & Nevis, San Jose, 1970-75, ptnr., 1975—; sec., dir. Mai Industries, Inc., San Jose, 1982-84; v.p., dir. Mai V, San Jose, 1982-83, Mai-Cory Devel. Co., San Jose, 1982-83; judge pro tem, arbitrator Santa Clara County Superior Ct., San Jose, 1975—; lectr. in field. Coach Little League, Babe Ruth, AYSO, Sunnyvale and Los Altos, Calif., 1976-82; planning commr. Sunnyvale Planning Commn., 1976-78; commr. Los Altos Cable TV Citizens' Adv. Com., 1984—. Served to capt. arty. U.S. Army, 1966-68. Mem. Assn. Trial Lawyers Am., Calif. Trial Lawyers Assn., ABA, Calif. Bar Assn., Santa Clara County Bar Assn., Phi Delta Phi. Democrat. Lutheran. Clubs: Mid-Peninsula Tennis Patrons (pres. 1981-82) (Los Altos); Sunnyvale Tennis (pres. 1978). Lodge: Masons. Office: Miller Morton Caillat & Nevis 50 W San Fernando St Ste 1300 San Jose CA 95113-2434

CORY, CHRISTOPHER THAYER, communications executive; b. Englewood, N.J., Aug. 29, 1940; s. David Cleveland and Constance (Thayer) C.; m. Laura Page Williams (div.); children— Caroline Thayer, David Williams; m. Susan B. Lytle, Jan. 28, 1984 (div.); 1 child, Robert William; m. Helen Seldon Rattray; BA, Yale U., 1962. Corr., Time mag. Time, Inc., N.Y.C., 1962-65, chief Boston bur., 1965-67, assoc. editor, 1967-72; articles editor Learning mag., Palo Alto, Calif., 1973-75; dir. pub. affairs Carnegie Council on Children, N.Y.C., 1975-78; mng. editor Psychology Today, N.Y.C., 1978-83; mgr. editorial services Philip Morris Inc., N.Y.C., 1983—91; dir. coll. rels. Conn. Coll., 1991-96; univ. dir. pub. rels. L.I. U., 1996-2001; dir. comms. Internat. Longevity Ctr., 2001-02; dir. pub. info. Pace U., 2002—. Author: (with Joel Fort) American Drugstore, 1975. Pres., Horizon Concerts Inc., N.Y.C., 1977—83; trustee Pub. Edn. Assn. N.Y.C., 1985-90 ; bd. dirs. N.Y. Revels Inc., N.Y.C., 1984—91. Profl. journalism fellow Stanford U., 1972. Assoc. mem. Nat. Assn. Sci. Writers; mem. Coun. for Advancement and Support of Higher Edn. (nat. issues task force 1992-95). Democrat. Presbyterian. Avocations: sailing; folk guitar; choral music. Office: Pace U 1 Pace Plz New York NY 10039-1598 E-mail: ccory@pace.edu., cchristophert@nyc.rr.com.

CORY, DAVID H. museum administrator, former real estate broker; b. N.Y.C., May 16, 1930; s. David Munroe and Mina Haug Cory; m. Nancy G. Cory, Aug. 18, 1973; 1 child, David Denton. BMS, N.Y. State Maritime Coll., 1950. Ship's officer U.S. Lines Inc., N.Y., 1950-85; real estate broker F. Robertson Realty, Sag Harbor, N.Y., 1985-98; pres. Sag Harbor Whaling and Hist. Museum, 1998—. Mem. Coun. Am. Master Mariners, Internat. Orgn. Masters, Mates and Pilots. Democrat. Presbyterian. Avocations: local history, ship model building. Home: 19 Cove Dr Sag Harbor NY 11963

CORY, EDWARD WILLIAM, JR., underwriting executive; b. LaGrange, Ill., Sept. 29, 1964; s. Edward William and Joan Ellen (Hefele) C.; m. Amy Ruth Clemmens, July 1, 1995; children: Amy Anderson, Hadley Clemmens. BBA, U. Iowa, 1987. Assoc. in underwriting; assoc. in risk mgmt.; accredited adviser in ins.; assoc. in ins. svcs.; assoc. in surplus lines ins.; cert. profl. ins. agt. Underwriter Atlantic Mut., Chgo., 1989-91, Midwest Gen. Underwriters Group, Chgo., 1991-92, Agora Syndicate, Chgo., 1992-94; ptnr. Agora Ltd. Lyndicate, Chgo., 1994-97; v.p. Agora Syndicate, Chgo., 1994—. V.p. Walton Ins. Svcs., Chgo., 1994-98; v.p. Walton Risk Svc., Chgo., 1994-99, underwriting mgr., 1996-97, sr. v.p., 1999—. Instr. Project Literacy U.S., Chgo., 1990-92. Named Hon. State Senator, La. State Senate Dist. 7, 1993, Ky. Col., Gov. Paul Patton, Ky., 1996, Outstanding People of the 20th Century, 1999, 1000 Leaders of World Influence, 1999. Mem. Surplus Lines Assn. Ill., Ins. Soc. Chgo. Republican. Avocations: golf, travel, reading, sailing. Home: 166 Lookout Farm Dr Crestview Hills KY 41017-2287

CORY, JEFFREY, television, film, stage, event and creative director; b. Johannesburg, Rep. of South Africa, Oct. 10, 1945; came to U.S., 1990; s. Isaac and Flora (Moshal) Kwitz. BS, Jerusalem U., 1967. Freelance stage and event dir., U.K. and Israel, 1963-68; dir. ITC TV Sta., Israel, 1969-74; CEO, dir. Jeffricory Prodns., Israel, 1974-75; CEO San Hill Prodns., Rep. of South Africa, 1975-78; founder, exec. dir. Performing Arts Workshop Coll., Rep. of South Africa, 1983-87; CEO Screen Machine Prodns., Rep. of South Africa, 1978-90; pres., dir. Scene Internat., N.Y.C., 1990—. Recipient Israels Citizen's award for TV, 1971, over 70 awards for film and TV and pub. svc. Mem. Meeting Planners Internat., S.A. Film and TV Technicians Union, WIZO (hon. life), Graphic Artists Guild, Am. Inst. of Graphic Artists, Art Dirs. Guild. Jewish. Avocations: music, theatre, art, travel. Office: Scene Internat 300 W 55th St Ste 4J New York NY 10019-5163

CORY, WALLACE NEWELL, retired civil engineer; b. Olympia, Wash., Mar. 10, 1937; s. Henry Newell and Gladys Evelyn (Nixon) C.; m. Roberta Ruth Matthews, July 4, 1959; children: Steven Newell, Susan Evelyn Cory Carbon. BS in Forestry, Oreg. State U., 1958, BSCE, 1964; MSCE, Stanford U., 1965. Registered profl. engr., Idaho, Oreg. Asst. projects mgr. CH2 M/Hill, Boise, Idaho, 1965-70; environ. mgr. Boise Cascade Corp., 1970-78, dir. state govt. affairs, 1978-82; dir. indsl. group JUB Engrs., Boise, 1982-84; chief engr. Anchorage Water & Wastewater, 1984-90; dir. pub. works City of Caldwell, Idaho, 1990-92; prin. engr. Montgomery Watson, Pasadena, Calif., 1992-95; adminstr. Idaho Divsn. Environ. Quality, Boise, 1995-98; planning and assessment leader Alexandria Wastewater Project Chemonics Internta., 1998-99. Precinct committeeman Idaho Rep. Com., Boise, 1968-72, region chmn., 1973-77. Capt. USAF, 1958-62. Fellow ASCE; mem. NSPE, Idaho Soc. Profl. Engrs. (pres. 1976-77, Young Engr. of Yr. award 1971), Air Pollution Control Assn. (chmn. Pacific N.W. sect. 1977-78), Idaho Assn. Commerce and Industry (chmn. environ. com. 1974-75). Avocations: hunting, fishing, shooting. Home: 7247 Cascade Dr Boise ID 83704-8635

CORYELL, GLYNN HEATH, financial services executive; b. Lexington, Ky., May 8, 1929; s. Glynn Lawrence Coryell and Allie May (Heath) C.; m. Diane Garnett Dobyns, Dec. 27, 1955 (div. Aug. 1981); children: Heather Diane, Holly. Grad., Culver (Ind.) Summer Cavalry Sch., 1947; AB, Harvard U., 1951; student, Harvard Law Sch., 1951-52, 54-55; MBA, Northwestern U., 1957. Supr. cost acctg. Procter & Gamble Co., Cin., 1957-60; sr. fin. analyst Socony Mobil Oil Corp., N.Y.C., 1961-62; dir. corp. profit planning, corp. economist Libby, McNeill & Libby, Chgo., 1962-67; treas. Lyntex Corp., N.Y.C., 1968-69; asst. treas. Std. Brands, Inc., N.Y.C., 1969-71; v.p. adminstr. and ops. Std. Brands Foods Co., N.Y.C., 1971-73; fin. v.p. Grand Union Co., Elmwood Park, NJ, 1973-76; exec. v.p., CFO, dir. Cramer Electronics, Inc., Newton, Mass., 1976-79; sr. v.p., CFO, dir. Kuhn's-Big K Stores Corp., Nashville, 1979-81; v.p. fin. and adminstrn., sec. Sunmark, Inc., St. Louis, 1981-83; corp. fin. cons. Lemoyne, Pa., 1984-88; pres. Glynn H. Coryell & Assocs. Inc. doing bus. as Travel Agts. Internat., Falls Church, Va., 1988-94; corp. fin. cons. Alexandria, Va., 1994—. Mem. Rep. Nat. Com.; vol. USO; mem. John Harvard Soc. With intelligence U.S. Army, 1953—54. Mem.: Ind. Soc. of Washington, Ky. Soc. of Washington, Culver Edn. Found., Civil War Preservation Trust, World Affairs Coun., Ky. Hist. Soc., Ind. Hist. Soc., Korean War Vets. Assn., Alexandria Consumer Affairs Commn., Alumni Assn. Kellogg Grad. Sch. Mgmt. Northwestern U. Republican. Baptist. Home and Office: 1105 Quaker Hill Ct Alexandria VA 22314-4742

CORZEALIOUS, FORREST LEE, entrepreneur; b. Lower Peach Tree, Ala., Feb. 7, 1961; s. William Lee and Ethel Pearl Corzealious. BS magna cum laude, Ala. State U., 1983. Rschr. Nat. Data Reteriver, Atlanta; PBX operator Marriott Hotel, Atlanta, telephone operator; pvt. practice writing and inventing. Contbr. Mem.: Omega Phi Psi. Achievements include patents pending for. Avocations: hunting, fishing, writing, gardening, horseback riding. Home: 34706 Hwy 43 N Thomasville AL 36784

CORZINE, JON STEVENS, senator, former investment banker; b. Taylorville, Ill., Jan. 1, 1947; s. Roy Allen and Nancy June (Hedrick) C.; m. Joanne Dougherty, Sept. 8, 1968 (div.); children: Jennifer, Joshua, Jeffrey. BA, U. Ill., 1969; MBA, U. Chgo., 1973. Bond officer Continental Ill. Nat. Bank, Chgo., 1970-73; asst. v.p. BancOhio Corp., Columbus, 1974-75; with Goldman, Sachs & Co., N.Y.C., 1975—99, v.p., 1977, pntr., 1980, mem. mgmt. com., 1985-94, co-head fixed income divsn., ptnr., 1985-94, chmn., CEO, 1994-99; senator NJ, 2001—. Bd. dirs. N.J. Performing Arts Ctr., 1993-94, chmn. coun. trustees, 1995—; bd. dirs. N.Y. Philharmonic, 1996. Mem. Pub. Securities Assn. (vice chmn. 1985, chmn. 1986) Democrat. Office: US Senate Washington DC 20510 also: One Gateway Center, 11th Floor Newark NJ 07102 also: 208 White Horse Pike, Suite 18 Barrington NJ 08007 Fax: 856-546-1526; Office Fax: 973-645-0502.*

COSBEY, ROGER B. federal magistrate judge; b. 1950; BA, Western Mich. U., 1972; JD, U. Toledo, 1975. Bar: Ind. 1975. With Heckner & Assocs., Ligonier, Ind., 1975-81; judge Superior Ct., Noble County, Ind., 1982-90; magistrate judge U.S. Dist. Ct. (no. dist.) Ind., Ft. Wayne, 1990—. Presenter in field. Contbr. articles to profl. jours. Maj. JAGC, USAR, 1972-92. Fellow Allen County Bar Assn.; mem. Ind. State Bar Assn., Allen County Bar Assn., Fed. Magistrate Judges Assn., Am. Judicature Soc., Benjamin Harrison Am. Inns of Ct. (pres. Fort Wayne Ind. chpt. 1995-96), Supreme Ct. Historical Soc. Office: 1130 Adair Federal Bldg 1300 S Harrison St Fort Wayne IN 46802-3495

COSBEY, TED, water transportation executive; b. Buffalo, June 26, 1944; s. Edward Cosbey Jr. and Elsie Cosbey; m. Sally Bowden, Feb. 9, 1990; 1 child, Nora. Student, Ithaca, 1963—64, C.W. Post Coll., 1964—66. Master U.S. Coast Guard. Mate, tankerman Poling Transp., N.Y.C., 1992—95, Eklof Marine Corp., N.Y.C., 1995—97, Poling & Cutler Marine Corp., N.Y.C., 1998—2001, capt., mate & tankerman, 2002; capt. Circle Line Cruises, N.Y.C., 2001. Home: 41 E 1st St New York NY 10003

COSBY, BILL, actor, entertainer; b. Phila., July 12, 1937; s. William Henry and Anna C.; m. Camille Hanks, Jan. 25, 1964; children: Erika Ranee, Erinn Chalene, Ennis William (dec.), Ensa Camille, Evin Harrah. Student, Temple U.; MA, U. Mass., 1972, EdD, 1977. Pres. Rhythm and Blues Hall of Fame, 1968—. Appeared in numerous night clubs, including The Gaslight, N.Y.C., Hungry I, San Francisco, Shoreham Hotel, Washington, Basin St. East, N.Y.C., Hilton, Las Vegas, Nev., Harrah's Lake Tahoe; guest appearances on numerous TV shows, including The Electric Co., 1972, Capt. Kangaroo; co-star: TV show I Spy, 1965-68; star TV show The Bill Cosby Show, 1969-71, The New Bill Cosby Show, 1972-73, (host, voices) Fat Albert and the Cosby Kids, 1972-79, Cos, 1976, (host, voices) The New Fat Albert Show, 1979-82, The Cosby Show, 1984-92, The Cosby Mysteries, 1994-95, Cosby, 1996-2000; host, TV game show You Bet Your Life, 1992-93, Kids Say the Darndest Things, 1998-2000, Jack Paar "As I Was Saying...", 1997; interviewee 4 Little Girls (TV), 1997; exec. prodr. TV show A Different World, 1987-93, Here and Now, 1992-93; TV movies include I Spy Returns, 1994, The Bill Cosby Mystery Movies, 1994; recs. include: Revenge (Grammy award Nat. Acad. Performing Arts and Scis. 1967), To Russell, My Brother, With Whom I Slept, 1968 (Grammy award), Why Is There Air, 1965 (Grammy award), Wonderfulness, 1966 (Grammy award), It's True, It's True, Bill Cosby is a Very Funny Fellow...Right, 1963, I Started Out as a Child, 1964 (Grammy award), Reunion, 1982, Bill Cosby-...Himself, 1983 (dir., prodr.), Those of You With or Without Children, You'll Understand, (jazz albums) Where You Lay Your Head, 1990, My Appreciation, 1991, Hello Friend: To Ennis With Love, 1997; films include Hickey and Boggs, 1972, Man and Boy, 1972, Uptown Saturday Night, 1974, Let's Do It Again, 1975, Mother, Jugs and Speed, 1976, A Piece of the Action, 1977, California Suite, 1978, (voice) Aesop's Fable, 1978, Devil and Max Devlin, 1979, Bill Cosby...Himself, 1985, Leonard: Part VI, 1987, Ghost Dad, 1990, The Meteor Man, 1993, Jack, 1996; recipient 4 Emmy awards 1966, 67, 68, 69, 8 Grammy awards, named number 1 in comedy field Top Artists on Campus Poll (album sales) 1968; author: The Wit and Wisdom of Fat Albert, 1973, Bill Cosby's Personal Guide to Power Tennis, Fatherhood, 1986, Time Flies, 1988, Love and Marriage, 1989, Childhood, 1991. Served with USNR, 1956-60. Recipient Bob Hope Humanitarian award, Academy of Television Arts & Sciences, 2003. Achievements include setting concert attendance record Radio City Music Hall, 1986.*

COSBY, JOHN CANADA, retired lay worker; b. Greensboro, N.C., Nov. 24, 1929; s. John Canada and Mildred Bernice (Cooper) Cosby; m. Mary-Stuart Parker, June 5, 1954; children: J. Stuart, Williams C., Ellen Parker, Laura Elizabeth. BS, Furman U., 1951; postgrad., Episcopal Div. Sch., Cambridge, Mass., 1980-81. Cert. camp dir. Reporter, copy desk staff Greenville (S.C.) News, 1951-58; dir. Miramar Conf. Ctr., Newport, R.I., 1958-61; exec. sec. spkrs. bur. Episcopal Ch., N.Y.C., 1961-64, dir. diocesan press svc., 1964-67; asst. ecumenical officer Episcopal Ch. Ctr., N.Y.C., 1967-71; dir. Bement Camp & Conf. Ctr., Charlton Depot, Mass., 1972-81; exec. dir. Summit Conf. Ctr., Browns Summit, N.C., 1981-82. Exec. dir. Huston Camp & Conf. Ctr., Gold

Bar, Wash., 1983—88; mgr. Wash. Mktg. Group, Inc., Monroe, 1990—93; chmn. religious affiliated camps, 1988—92; asst. to the pres. Coun. Christian Unity Indpls. Christian Ch., 1994—98; mem. staff testing room Chateau Morrisette Winery, 2001—. Trustee Augustine Fellowship, 2003—; bd. dirs. Cmty. Found. New River Valley, 1995—, Sex Abuse Treatment Alliance, Inc., 1998—. Recipient Vol. of the Yr. award, Wash. State Reformatory, 1993, Patron of Christian Unity award, Christian Ch. (Disciples of Christ), 1998; fellow Proctor, Episcopal Divinity Sch., 1980—81. Mem.: Am. Camping Assn. (bd. dirs. 1988—90), Lions. Episcopalian. Avocations: music, theater, art, cooking, travel. Home: PO Box 539 Floyd VA 24091-0539 E-mail: jc@swva.net.

COSBY, LYNWOOD A. electrical engineer; b. Richmond, Va., June 11, 1928; s. Roscoe Roy and Ida Madeline Cosby; m. Maria Luisa Caban; children: Catherine, Andrew, Teresa, Ann, Michael, Patricia, Bryan. BS in Physics, U. Richmond, Va., 1949; MS in Indsl. Physics, Va. Poly. Inst. and State U., 1951. Instr. physics Va. Mil. Inst., Lexington, Va., 1951—52; electronic scientist U.S. Naval Rsch. Lab., Washington, 1952—84; cons. Teledyne, Inc., Arlington, Va., 1984—86; pres. E.W. System and Devel., Inc., Front Royal, Va., 1986—; cons. Inst. Def. Analyses, Alexandria, 1986—, System Planning Corp., Arlington, 1986—, Symmetron Inc., Fairfax, Va., 1986—. Mem. panel, chair Air Force Sci. Adv. Bd., Arlington, 1980—94; mem. adv. group electronic devices Dept. Def., Arlington, 1990—92; integrated apertures study rschr. ONR/USN, Arlington, 1996—97; chpt. editor Dept. of Def. Handwook, 1980. Treas., rds. chmn. Pointn o Woods Owners Assn., 1988—; ward rep. Cmty. Civic Govt., 1975—84. Recipient Outstanding Def. award, Dept. of Def., Dept. Navy, 1958. Fellow: IEEE (study chair 1951—2003); mem.: Am. Assn. Naval Engrs. (life Gold Medal 1969), Assn. Old Crows (life; pres., bd. dirs. 1952—2003). Achievements include development of of construction of unique hardware in loop simulation facility. Avocations: live steam locomotives, narrow gage railroads. Home: 100 Lakewood Dr Front Royal VA 22630

COSBY, RITA KAREN, newscaster; b. Bklyn., Nov. 18, 1964; d. Richard Roger and Adda Otilia (Arenfeldt) C. Honors degree, Conn. Sch. Broadcasting, 1983; BA in Broadcast Journalism, Spanish, U. S.C., 1989. Nat. sales mgr. Basic Wallpaper, Inc., Stamford, Conn., 1983-86; bus. cons. Lin-Gor, Inc., Clifton, N.J., 1986-89; announcer, control operator Sta. WACH-TV, Columbia, S.C., 1989; intern, asst. CBS Evening News, N.Y.C., 1989; anchor, reporter Sta. KERO-TV, Bakersfield, Calif., 1989-92, Sta. WBTV-CBS, Charlotte, N.C., 1992-95; sr. corr. Fox News, Washington, 1995—2001, host Foxwire with Rita Cosby, 2001—. News anchor S.C. Pub. Radio, Columbia, 1988-89; host, interviewer, prodr. Bus. and Fin. Shows, Bakersfield, 1989-92; host, interviewer Community Affairs Show, Bakersfield, 1989-92, Take One Prodns., N.Y.C., 1989—, Spanish Cable TV Show, Charlotte, 1993-95. News editor (newspaper) The Gamecock, 1987-89; writer (newspaper) The State, 1988-89; columnist (Hispanic newspaper) El Progreso Hispano, 1993—. Mem. adv. bd. Youth Involvement Coun., Charlotte, 1992-95; host, fundraiser United Negro Coll. Fund, Charlotte, 1993-95, Children's Miracle Network Telethon, Charlotte, 1993-95, Muscular Dystrophy Assn., Bakersfield, 1990-92; spkr., reader Charlotte-Mecklenburg Schs., Charlotte, 1992-95; vol., spkr. Girl Scouts U.S., 1989—; motivational spkr. anti-drug program DARE. Recipient Outstanding Sr. award U. S.C., 1989, Best Reporting award Kern County Press Club, 1991. Mem. NATAS (Emmy 1992, 95, listed as Outstanding Young Am. 1989, mem. nominating bd. 1997—), L.Am. Coalition (spkr. 1993—), L.Am. Women's Assn. (spkr. 1994—), Soc. Profl. Journalists (student pres. 1987—), Alpha Epsilon Rho (pub. info. officer 1987-89), Omicron Delta Kappa. Avocation: foreign languages. Office: Fox Network News 400 N Capitol St NW Ste 550 Washington DC 20001-1502

COSBY, STEPHANIE BENNETT, health services professional; b. Boynton Beach, Fla., Apr. 26, 1967; d. David Hendrie Cosby and Carolyn Clem Fant; m. Gary Merrill Brown, Aug. 21, 1956. BS, U. of Fla., 1987—89; BSN, Emory U., 1994—96. RN Ga., 1996, S.C., 1999. Staff nurse Emory U. Hosp., 1996—97; travel nurse Travcorps, LA, 1997—98, Mission St. Joseph's Hosp., Asheville, NC, 1998—99; sch. nurse Haywood Co. Health Dept., Waynesville, NC, 1999—2001; regional svc. coord. for the best chance network Am. Cancer Soc., Charleston, SC. Prodr., co-director, co-editor Haywood Active Youth Unlimited, Waynesville, NC, 2000—01; cons. Haywood County Domestic Task Force Resource Video, Waynesville, SC, 2001—01. Prodr.(co-director, co-editor): (video) H.A.Y.U. Health Promotion Video Project (Aegis Award, 2001); editor (consultant): (video) Fear Factor-Orientation Video for Waynesville M.S. (Aegis Award, 2001); editor: (director) You Are Not Alone-Resource Video for the Haywood Co. Domestic Task Force; author: (manual) Operation V.Y.D.E.O.-Health Promotion Video Projects; singer: (compact disc) Music of the Baha'i World Congress, 1992; singer: (soloist) (choir) Voices of Baha; singer: (concert at carnegie hall). Mem.: Womens Cancer Coalition. Independent. Baha'I Faith. Avocations: sailing, singing, travel. Personal E-mail: sailaway2k@earthlink.net.

COSCIA, ROBERT LINGUA, surgeon, educator; b. Memphis, Feb. 16, 1937; s. Louis and Anne (Lingua) C.; m. Joan K. Kingsbury, Dec. 27, 1964 (div. Jan. 1981); children: Paul, Matthew, Lori; m. Karen Kaye Kennedy, June 1, 1989. BS, Tex. A&M U., 1959; MD, U. Tenn., 1962. Intern Parkland Meml. Hosp., Dallas, 1963-64, resident, 1965-69; rsch. fellow dept. surgery U. Tex. Southwestern Med. Sch., Dallas, 1964-65; pvt. practice, Bryan, Tex., 1971-73, Springfield, Mo., 1973-99; asst. clin. prof. U. Mo., Kansas City, 1986-99; trauma med. dir. Brackenridge Hosp., Austin, Tex., 1999—. Bd. dirs. Mo. chpt. Am. Cancer Soc., Springfield, 1975-83; instr. advanced trauma life support, 1982—; del. Mo. State Med. Assn., Jefferson City, 1984; chmn. sub-com. adv. coun. Pediatric EMS, Jefferson City, 1991-94; mem. state adv. coun. EMS, Jefferson City, 1991-94; cons. Mo. Patient Rev. Found., Jefferson City, 1986—. Maj. USAF, 1969-71. Recipient EMS Leadership award Mo. Dept. Health, Jefferson City, 1994, Trauma Achievement award ACOS, Chgo., 1994. Mem. ACS (chmn. Mo. dist. 3 com. on applicants 1987-94, mem. 1978-94, chmn. com. on trauma Chgo. 1989—, chmn. Mo. com. on trauma 1989-95, chmn. region VII com. on trauma 1995—, site visitor 1993—), N.Am. Limousin Found. (bd. dirs. 1986-92, pres. 1990), Internat. Limousin Coun. (pres. 1990-92). Baptist. Avocation: farming. Home: 3801 W Quail HOllow Dr Fort Hall ID 83203 Office: 999 N Curtis Rd Ste 515 Branson MO 83706 E-mail: Roblc44@aol.com.

COSCO, JOHN ANTHONY, health care executive, educator, consultant, author; b. Cin., July 13, 1947; s. Adolph John and Pasqualina Marie (Saluppo) C.; m. Anne Patricia Ward, Aug. 5, 1978; children: Stephen Ward, Justin Thomas. BS, Xavier U., Cin., 1969, MEd, 1972, MBA, 1975; postgrad., U. Cin., 1972; PhD in Health Svcs. and Mgmt., Columbia-Pacific U., 1986. Asst. dir. edn. and staff devel. Jewish Hosp., Cin., 1972-77; exec. dir. Region IX Peer Rev. Systems, Inc., Portsmouth, Ohio, 1977-78, Region II Med. Rev. Corp., Dayton, Ohio, 1978-81; asst. adminstr., sr. v.p. Mercy Hosp., Tiffin, Ohio, 1981-87; adminstr. Grafton (W.Va.) City Hosp., 1987-89; sr. v.p., COO The St. Francis Acad., Inc., Salina, Kans., 1989—. Bd. dirs. Sunflower Network, Inc., Salina, Kans.; ptnr. Hos-Con & Assocs., 1974-79; pres., CEO, Hale Foster and Stunning, 1993—; mem. oun. exec. advisors Gerson-Leherman; adj. assoc. prof. bus. and health svcs. adminstrn. Kans. Wesleyan U., 1997—; book reviewer Health Adminstrn. Press. Lt. AUS, 1969-71. Fellow Am. Coll. Healthcare Execs. (mem. Kans. regnets adv. coun.). Roman Catholic. Office: St Francis Academy Inc 509 E Elm St Salina KS 67401-2348

COSENTINO, PATRICIA BYRNE, English educator, poet; b. Boston, June 6, 1927; d. Charles E. and Patricia (McDermott) Byrne; m. E. McDonough (div. 1953); 1 child, Peter E. McDonough; m. Kenneth Rosenfield, Aug. 29, 1954 (div. 1968); 1 child, R. Noah Rosenfield; m. David Cosentino, June 28, 1990. AS, Newton (Mass.) Jr. Coll., 1967; BS, Boston U., 1972; MA, Regis Coll., 1984. Dir. learning lab. Newton (Mass.) Jr. Coll., 1965-70; asst. to dir. MAT Sch. Edn. Harvard U., Cambridge, Mass., 1970-72; tchr. Wellesley (Mass.) High Sch., 1972-90. Cons. East-West Nexus/Prota, 1987—; writing tchr. Mt. Wachusett C.C., Gardner, Mass., 1999, instr., chair adv. bd. LIFE program, writing and poetry. Author: Cat in the Mirror, 1970, Whetstone, 1990, (poetry) Always Being Born, 2002, 03; editor: Tapestries, An Anthology, 2002; translator Arabic Poetry. Sec., treas. North Ctrl. (Mass.) Assn. Small Bus., 1991—; sec. Gardner-Athol (Mass.) Area Mental Health Assn., 1994—; chair gala Gardner Area League Artists. Recipient Mary F. Lindsley award N.Y. Poetry Forum, 1972. Mem. Am. Acad. Poets, Poetry Soc. Am., Gardner Cultural Coun., New Eng. Poetry Club (treas.). Avocations: golf, music, travel, education, theater. Home: 33 Leo Dr Gardner MA 01440-1211 Office: Reliable Fin & Antiques 177 West St Gardner MA 01440-2121 E-mail: alanahb@earthlink.net.

COSENTINO, PAUL JOHN, civil engineering educator; b. Pitts., Oct. 5, 1956; s. Erminio and Carmela (Russo) C.; m. Wendy Gay Crise, Sept. 15, 1987; children: Lauren Marie, Matthew Paul. BSCE, U. Pitts., 1978, MSCE, 1982; PhD, Tex. A&M U., 1987. Teaching asst. U. Pitts., 1980-82; adj. lectr. C.C. Allegheny County, Pitts., 1983; teaching asst., rsch. asst. Tex. A&M U., College Station, 1984-87; asst. prof. civil engring. Tex. Tech. U., Lubbock, 1987-90; prof. civil engring. Fla. Inst. Tech., Melbourne, 1990—. Geotech. engr. GAI Cons., Inc., Monroeville, Pa., 1978-82, Dravo Corp., Pitts., 1981-82; project engr. A.M. Richardson and Assocs., Pitts., 1982-83, Nus Corp., Pitts., 1983-86; cons. and lectr. in field. Contbr. articles to jours. Geotech. Engring., ASCE Jour., others. Judge IBM's Odyssey of the Mind, Lubbock, 1990, Melbourne Sci. Fair, 1990. Grantee NSF, Fla. Soclar Energy Ctr., Fla. Dept. Transp., FAA. Mem. ASCE, Chi Epsilon, Tau Beta Pi. Achievements include patent for Disclosure for Fiber Optic Pore Pressure and Lead Senser. Office: Fla Inst Tech 150 W University Blvd Melbourne FL 32901-6975

COSENZA, ARTHUR GEORGE, opera director; b. Phila., Oct. 16, 1924; s. Luigi and Maria (Piccolo) C.; m. Marietta Muhs, Sept. 16, 1950; children: Louis John, Arthur William, Maria. Student, Ornstein Sch. Music, Phila., 1946-48, Berkshire Music Festival, 1947, Am. Theater Wing, N.Y.C., 1948-50. Asso. prof. Coll. Music, Loyola U. of South, 1954-84, dir. opera workshop, 1954-84; dir. Opera Program for City of New Orleans, 1955-73 Appeared in maj. opera houses throughout U.S., Can.; baritone New Orleans Opera, 1954-70, prodr., 1960-74, dir., 1965-98, dir. emeritus, 1998- Served with AUS, 1943-45. Decorated Purple Heart medal; cavaliere Order Star Italian Solidarity; cavaliere Ufficiale dell' Ordine al Merito Italy; officier Ordre des Arts et des Lettres. Mem. Am. Guild Mus. Artists (hon. life), Blue Key.

COSENZA, VINCENT JOHN, accountant; b. Bklyn., Aug. 12, 1962; s. Vincent James and Rosalie Theresa (Ferraro) C. BS in Acctg., NYU, 1984. CPA, N.Y. Mgr. fin. adminstrn. Jr. Achievemnt N.Y. Inc., N.Y.C., 1984-85; staff acct. Rosenshein, Neiman & Weiss, CPA's, N.Y.C., 1985-87; sr. acct., mgr. Pepper, Gelbord, Roth & Co. LLP, N.Y.C., 1987-99; mgr. Diamond, Wohl, Fried, Roth & Co. PC, N.Y.C., 2000—; assoc. acct. Sheldon Plotnick, Bklyn., 1986-88; assoc. Avner Kanfi CPA, 1996—. Mem. AICPA, N.Y. State Soc. CPAs. Democrat. Roman Catholic. Avocations: stamp collecting, volleyball, reading, travel. Home: 1393 E 53rd St Brooklyn NY 11234-3226 Office: Diamond Wohl Fried Roth & Co 1775 Broadway Ste 419 New York NY 10019-1996

COSETTI, JOSEPH LOUIS, federal judge; b. Youngstown, Ohio, May 8, 1929; s. Raymond and Mary Cosetti; m. Marilyn Sullivan; children: Maura Kelly, John Sullivan. BS, Ohio State U., 1951, MBA, 1953; JD, Duquesne U., 1975. Bar: Pa. 1975, U.S. Dist. Ct. (we. dist.) Pa. 1975. Analyst U.S. Steel Corp., Pitts.; mgr. market rsch. Virginia-Carolina Chem. Corp., Richmond, Va., 1958-59; prin. economist Jones & Laughlin Steel Corp., Pitts., 1959-70; city treas. City of Pitts., 1970-77; atty. Titus, Marcus & Shapiro, Pitts., 1978-80; bankruptcy judge U.S. Bankruptcy Ct. we. dist. Pa., Pitts., 1980—, chief bankruptcy judge, 1985-94. Bd. dirs. Consumer Credit Counseling of Western Pa., Pitts. Col. ret., USAR. Mem. ABA, Allegheny County Bar Assn., Pa. Bar Assn., Am. Bankruptcy Inst., Am. Coll. Bankruptcy. Republican. Baptist. Avocation: skiing. Office: US Bankruptcy Ct 600 Grant St Ste 5436 Pittsburgh PA 15219-2805

COSGRIFF, JAMES ARTHUR, physician; b. Lamberton, Minn., Mar. 18, 1924; s. James Arthur and Elsie Ann (Forster) C. BS summa cum laude, Coll. St. Thomas, 1944; MD, U. Minn., 1946. Intern St. Mary's Hosp., Duluth, Minn.; pvt. practice Olivia, Minn., 1949—. With USN, 1947-49. Fellow Am. Acad. Family Physicians; mem. Minn. Acad. Family Physicians (pres. 1963, Merit award 1964), Alpha Omega Alpha. Roman Catholic. Avocations: travel, photography, reading, music. Home: 802 E Park Ave Olivia MN 56277-1361 Office: Olivia Clinic 619 E Lincoln Ave Olivia MN 56277-1349

COSGRIFF, STUART WORCESTER, internist, consultant, medical educator; b. Pittsfield, Mass., May 8, 1917; s. Thomas F. and Frances Deford (Worcester) C.; m. Mary Shaw, Jan. 23, 1943; children: Mary, Thomas, Stuart, Robert. BA cum laude, Holy Cross Coll., 1938; MD, Columbia U., 1942, D Med. Sci., 1948. Diplomate Am. Bd. Internal Medicine. Intern Presbyterian Hosp., N.Y.C., 1942-43; asst. resident in medicine, 1943, 46-47; chief resident, 1947-48; instr. in medicine Columbia U., N.Y.C., 1948-50, clin. asst. prof. medicine, 1951-63, clin. assoc. prof., 1963-73, clin. prof. medicine, 1973-83, clin. prof. emeritus, 1983—; attending physician Presbyn. Hosp., N.Y.C., 1948-83, cons. emeritus, 1984—; individual practice medicine, specializing in internal medicine and vascular diseases, 1948—. Cons. in medicine to dir. Selective Svc., N.Y.C., 1957-73, N.Y. Giants Baseball Club, 1951-57, San Francisco Baseball Club, 1958-61; dir. thrombo-embolic clinic Vanderbilt Clinic, N.Y.C., 1948-83. Contbr. articles to med. jours. Served to capt. M.C., U.S. Army, 1943-45, ETO. Fellow ACP, Pan Am. Med. Assn.; mem. Am. Heart Assn., N.Y. Heart Assn., Alpha Omega Alpha Clubs: Knickerbocker Country (Tenafly, N.J.). Roman Catholic. Home and Office: 11 Park St Tenafly NJ 07670-2217 Office: 161 Ft Washington Ave New York NY 10032-3713

COSGROVE, CAMERON, insurance company executive; b. Arcadia, Calif., July 25, 1957; s. Joseph Patrick Jr. and Marion (Barrons) C.; children: Christopher Farley, Steven Patrick; m. Patricia Marabello, 2001. BS in Mgmt., Calif. State U., Long Beach, 1980. V.p., chief info. officer Pacific Life Ins. Co., Newport Beach, 1982—. Co-author city ordnance Regulation of Ozone, Depleting Compounds, 1989-90; contbr. articles to newspaper. Fin. commr. City of Irvine, Calif., 1983-87, planning commr. 1987-88, city councilman, 1988-90; bd. dirs. Irvine Transp. Authority, 1988-90.; founding advisor Irvine Conservancy, advisor, 1986-88, Irvine Infrastructure Authority, 1988-90; founder San Joaquin Marsh Adv. Com., chair 1988-90. Recipient Sea and Sage Audubon Conservation award, 1990. Mem. Life Office Mgmt. Assn. (tech. and mgmt. com. 1990-96). Republican. Avocation: environmentalist. Office: Pacific Life Ins 700 Newport Center Dr Newport Beach CA 92660-6307 E-mail: ccosgrove@pacificlife.com.

COSGROVE, DENIS EDMUND, geographer, writer; b. Liverpool, Eng., May 3, 1948; arrived in US, 2000; s. Peter Cyril and Gwendoline Brenda Cosgrove; divorced; children: Emily Jocelyn, Isla Rose; m. Carmen Patricia Mills, Dec. 2, 1989; 1 child, Leon Richard. BA with honors, Oxford U., 1969, DPhil, 1977; MA, U. Toronto, 1971. From lectr. to prin. lectr. Oxford Poly., 1972—80; from lectr. to reader cultural geography Loughborough U., England, 1980—93; prof. human geography Royal Holloway U. London, 1994—99; Alexander von Humboldt prof. geography UCLA, 2000—. Author: Social Formation & Symbolic Landscape, 1984, The Palladian Landscape, 1993, Apollo's Eye, 2001; contbr. articles to profl. jours. Recipient Back medal, Royal Geog. Soc., 1988. Avocations: hiking, 16th century maps, gardening. Home: 1029 N Fairfax Ave Los Angeles CA 90046 Office: UCLA Dept Geography 405 Hilgard Ave 1170 Bunche Hall Los Angeles CA 90095 Business E-Mail: cosgrove@geog.ucla.edu.

COSGROVE, GREGORY PATRICK, information scientist; s. Leo Francis and Margaret Ann Cosgrove; m. Linda Sue Galins, Apr. 26, 1997; 1 child, Riley William. BS, James Madison U., Harrisonburg, Va., 1991. Diplomate Hahnemann U. Sch. of Medicine, 1995. Medicine resident Thomas Jefferson U., 1995—98, chief med. resident, 1998—99; pulmonary fellow U. of Colo. Health Scis. Ctr., 1999—2002; instr. Nat. Jewish Med. and Rsch. Ctr., Denver, 2002—. Fellow Parker B. Francis Pulmonary Fellow, Francis Families Found., 2002—. Office: Nat Jewish Med and Rsch Ctr 1400 Jackson St Denver CO 80206 Office Fax: 303-270-2240. E-mail: cosgroveg@njc.org.

COSGROVE, HOWARD EDWARD, JR., utility executive; b. Phila., Apr. 12, 1943; s. Howard Edward and Margaret C. (May); m. Roberta Joyce Olewine, Apr. 19, 1965; children: Pamela Joyce, Susan Ann. BS in Mech. Engring., U. Va., 1966; MBA, U. Del., 1970. Registered profl. engr., Del. With Delmarva Power Co., Wilmington, Del., 1966—, mgr. fin., 1979, v.p., chief fin. officer, 1979—, exec. v.p., 1984-92, chmn., CEO, 1992—; now chmn., pres. & CEO Conectiv, Wilmington, Del. Mem.: Fin. Execs. Inst., Nat. Soc. Profl. Engrs. Home: PO Box 197 Rockland DE 19732-0197 Office: Delmarva Power & Light Co 800 N King St Wilmington DE 19801-3518

COSGROVE, JOHN FRANCIS, lawyer, state legislator; b. Coral Gables, Fla., July 1, 1949; s. Francis Freheil and Vivian Adair (Rafferty) C.; m. Bernardine Elizabeth Cosgrove, Dec. 19, 1981; children: Michael, Tiffany, Colleen. AA, U. Fla., 1969, BS in Journalism, 1971; JD, Cumberland Sch. Law, 1975. Bar: Fla., U.S. Dist. Ct. (so. dist.) Fla., U.S. Ct. Appeals (5th cir.), U.S. Supreme Ct. Assoc. Hall & Hedrick, Miami, Fla., 1975-80; sole practice Miami, 1980—. Mem. Fla. Ho. of Reps., 1981-84, 1986—; gen. counsel Biscayne Coll.; columnist Miami Rev.: Juris Conspectus, 1975—; chair Nat. Conf. State Legislatures Com. on Commerce and Comm.; chair property and casualty com., mem. exec. com. Nat. Conf. Ins. Legislatures. Chmn. Coral Gables Code Enforcement Bd.; mem. Coral Gables Econ. Devel. Bd.; mem. Jr. Orange Bowl Com.; chmn. Metro-Dade Econ. Devel. Bd., Miami Budget Rev. Com.; mem. South Miami Hosp. Assocs. Mem. ABA, Fla. Bar Assn. (Jud. Selection, Adminstrn. and Tenure Com., vice chmn. jud. nominating com.), Dade County Bar Assn. (3d v.p.), Am. Judicature Soc., ATLA, Pvt. Industry Coun. Dade County, Emerald Soc. South Fla., Miami Springs-Hialeah C. of C., Coral Gables C. of C., Grtr. Miami C. of C., Blue Key, Serra Club, Viscayans Civic Club, Le Lega Civic Club, Grtr. Miami Leadership Prayer Breakfast Club, KC (grand knight Coral Gables; pres. Dade County chpt.), Kiwanis, Knight of Malta, Phi Kappa Tau. Democrat. Roman Catholic (chmn. Cath. Svc. Bur.-50th anniversary). Home: 8230 SW 192nd St Miami FL 33157-8013 Office: 201 W Flagler St Miami FL 33130-1510

COSGROVE, JOHN PATRICK, editor; b. Pittston, Pa., Sept. 25, 1918; s. Raymond Patrick and Alice (Gilroy) C.; m. Patricia Ellen O'Hara, Mar. 26, 1951. Ed. pub. schs., Pa. Reporter, Wilkes-Barre (Pa.) Record, 1936-37, AP, Washington, 1938-40; writer, research Nat. Republican Congl. Com., Washington, 1940; exec. asst. U.S. Senator Hiram W. Johnson, 1941-42; free lance writer, 1946-48; dir. publs. Broadcasting Publs., Inc. (pubs. Broadcasting Businessweekly, Television monthly, Broadcasting Yearbook), Washington, 1948-68. Author: The Gendreau Story: War History of DE 639; editor: SHRDLU-An Affectionate Chronicle of the first fifty years of the Nat. Press Club, 1959. Publicity dir. Honor Am. Day Celebration, 1970; exec. dir. Am. Hist. and Cultural Soc., Inc., 1970-88; sec. Nat. Christmas Pageant of Peace, 1974—, v.p., 1985—, mem. com. to light nat. Christmas tree; Washington rep. Nat. Com. Neurol. Disorders and Stroke, 1972-78, R.R. Task Force for Northeast Region, 1973-75; bd. dirs. Am. Irish Found., 1967-87, pres., 1971-73; bd. dirs. Washington chpt. Nat. Multiple Sclerosis Soc., 1962-70, Am. Ireland Fund, 1987—; mem. bd. dirs. USN Meml. Found., Washington, 1986—, sec. and chmn. dedication com., 1987; bd. dirs. Ellis Island Restoration Commn., N.Y., 1989—, Destroyer-Escort Hist. Mus., 1993—; vice chmn. Am. Fedn. Irish Heritage, 1988—; bd. dirs. Internat. Svc. Agys., 1992-99. Served with USNR, 1942-46; assigned Office Censorship, Washington 1942; U.S.S. Gendreau 1944-46. Named Gael of Yr., Washington D.C. St. Patrick's Parade, 1999. Mem. VFW (life), White House Corrs. Assn. (hon.), Soc. Profl. Journalists, Destroyer-Escort Sailors Assn. (life, bd. dirs. 1981-96), Am. Legion (life), Nat. Press Club (Post no. 20, comdr. 1999—), Soc. Friendly Sons of St. Patrick (life, bd. dirs. 1976-82), Nat. Headliners Club (Atlantic City), Circus Saints and Sinners Club (exec. v.p., dir. P.T. Barnum tent 1973-89, pres. 1989-91), Nat. Press Club (Washington) (bd. govs. 1956-59, v.p. 1960, pres. 1961, chmn. awards com. 1974, chmn. election com. 1978). Roman Catholic. Home: 7906 Jensen Pl Bethesda MD 20817-4671 Office: 1124 National Press Building Washington DC 20045-2101

COSGROVE, WILLIAM JAMES, business educator, researcher; b. Chgo., Mar. 3, 1946; s. William Joseph and Adeline C.; m. Julia Fukuda, July 23, 1973; 1 child, Joseph. BS, Benedictine U., 1968; MS, Wash. U., St. Louis, 1970; PhD, U. Nebr., 1984. Secondary sch. instr. Jennings (Mo.) Sch. Dist., 1970-73; bus. mgr. U. Nebr., Lincoln, 1973-80; acting asst. prof. mgmt. U. Okla., Norman, 1981-84; asst. prof. mgmt. sci. and info. systems U. Colo., Boulder, 1984-89; assoc. prof. ops. mgmt. Calif. Polytech. U., Pomona, 1989-92; vis. prof. ops. mgmt. Rajabhat Inst.-Suan Dusit, Bangkok, 1998-99; prof. tech. and ops. mgmt. Calif. Poly. U., Pomona, 1992—, project dir. Thailand Task Force, 2000—. Cons. Boeing Co., Canoga Park, 2000—. Contbr. articles to profl. publs. Sprk. Am. C. of C., 2000. Rsch. fellowship Calif. State U., 1993, 95. Mem. The Decision Scis. Inst., Calif. State U. Prodn. and Ops. Mgmt. Soc. Avocations: running, swimming, amateur radio. Office: Calif Polytech U Coll Bus Adminstrn Pomona CA 91768 E-mail: wcosgrove@csupomona.edu.

COSIER, RICHARD A. dean, business educator, consultant; b. Jackson, Mich., May 18, 1947; s. Roy A. and Wilma M. (Braund) C.; m. Rae L. Pettelle, June 14, 1969 (div. Feb. 1985); children: Jeffrey R., Nathan R.; m. Lynn M. Hays, Aug. 30, 1986; children: Courtney M., Kelsey L. BS, Mich. State U., 1969; MBA, Loyola U., 1972; PhD, U. Iowa, 1976. From asst. to assoc. prof. mgmt. Ind. U., Bloomington, 1976-86, prof. mgmt., 1986-92, chairperson, prof. mgmt., 1983-90, assoc. dean for acads., prof. mgmt., 1990-92; dean, Fred E. Brown chair U. Okla., Norman, 1993-99; dean and Leeds prof. mgmt. Purdue U., 1999—; dir. Burton D. Morgan Ctr. Entrepreneurship Purdue U., 2002—; with faculty U. Notre Dame. Cons. in field. Contbr. over 75 articles and book chpts. to profl. jours.; co-author mgmt. textbook; contbr. book chpts.; inventor patented packaging technique. Active with United Way Am.; mem. exec. com. Greater Lafayette Cmty. Devel. Corp., 2001; chmn. United Way campaign Purdue U., 2003—. Fellow Richard D. Irwin . Mem.: Acad. Mgmt. Republican. Office: Krannert Sch Mgmt Rm 122 Purdue U West Lafayette IN 47907-1310 Home: 3523 Chancellor Way West Lafayette IN 47906-8808 E-mail: rcosier@mgmt.purdue.edu.

COSING, ARTHUR PAUL, JR., writer, artist; b. Miami, Fla., May 11, 1926; s. Arthur Paul Cosing Sr. and Ruby Myrtledean Ogorek; m. Shirley Mae Baumann, Oct. 16, 1954 (dec. June 7, 1997); 1 child, Arthur Paul III. BS, U. Md., 1950. Artist Washington Post, Washington, 1950—52; visual info. specialist NIH, Bethesda, Md., 1952—55, pub. info. specialist, 1955—60; speech writer Office Surgeon Gen. USPHS, Washington, 1960—63; pub. info. officer Bur. Family Svcs. HEW, Washington, 1963—67; asst. chief Office Comm. NIMH, Rockville, Md., 1967—78, chief tech. svcs., 1978—88; ret. Contbr. articles to profl. jours. and lit. publs.; co-author paperback book of humor. With U.S. Army, 1944—45, ETO. Decorated Combat Badge, Purple Heart, Bronze Star; recipient award, NIH, 1958, HHS, 1985. Mem.: Omicron Delta Kappa, Pi Delta Epsilon, Theta Chi. Avocations: sketching, writing, travel, golf. Home: 3693 Persimmon Cir Fairfax VA 22031 E-mail: apc1@erols.com.

COSKRAN, KATHLEEN ANNE, principal; b. L.A., Oct. 22, 1943; d. Walter and Bettie (McClintock) Johnson; m. Charles Edmund Coskran, Jan. 20, 1968; children: Anna, John, Alexander Sosa. BA, Agnes Scott Coll., Decatur, Ga., 1965; MA, U. Minn., 1988. Vol. Peace Corps, Addis Ababa, Ethiopia, 1965-67; tchr., founder Nokomis Montessori, Mpls., 1975-79; tchr. Lake Country Sch., Mpls., 1979-86, prin., 1995—; adj. faculty U. Minn., Mpls., 1989-95, Hamline U., Mpls., 1989-95. Author: The High Price of Everything, 1985 (Minn. Book award 1988), Tanzania on Tuesday, 1996 (Minn. Book award 1996), An Inn Near Kyoto, 1997 (Paul Cowan Non-fiction award 1999). Bd. pres. First Universalist Ch., Mpls., 1994. Fellow Bush Found., 1988, Nat. Edowment for the Arts, 1991, Artist fellow Minn. State Arts Bd., 1990, 93. Mem. Assn. Montessori Internat. Avocations: walking, running. Office: Lake Country School 3755 Pleasant Ave Minneapolis MN 55409 E-mail: kcoskran@lakecountryschool.org.

COSLET, BRUCE N. professional football coach; b. Oakdale, Calif., Aug. 5, 1946; s. James A. and Mae C. (Coon) C.; m. Kathleen Joseph; children: Jonathan James, Amy Kathleen. BA, U. of Pacific, 1968. Player Edmonton (Alta., Can.) Eskimos, CFL, 1968; player, capt. Cinn. Bengals, NFL, 1969-76, coach spl. teams, 1981-83, coach wide receivers, 1984-85, coach, offense coord., 1986-89, 95-96; coach spl. teams San Francisco 49ers, 1980; head coach N.Y. Jets, 1990-93, Cincinnati Bengals, 1996—2001; offense coord. Dallas Cowboys, 2002—. Owner Coslet Devel., Stockton, Calif., 1977-80. Author: Youth Passing and Receiving, 1989 Named to Pacific Sports Hall of Fame U. Pacific, 1984, Oakdale (Calif.) Sports Hall of Fame, (charter) 1987. Mem. Lds Ch. Avocations: golf, fishing, reading, music. Office: Dallas Cowboys 1 Cowboys Pkwy Irving TX 75063

COSMAN, BARD CLIFFORD, surgeon, educator; b. N.Y.C., Mar. 1, 1963; s. Bard and Madeleine (Pelner) C.; m. Pamela Caren Feldman, Mar. 26, 1989; children: Benjamin, Rafael, Gilead, Ilan. AB magna cum laude, Harvard U., 1983; MPH, MD, Columbia U., 1987. Diplomate Nat. Bd. Med. Examiners, Am. Bd. Surgery, Am. Bd. Colon and Rectal Surgery. Resident in surgery Stanford (Calif.) U., 1987-89, postdoctoral fellow, 1989-91; fellow spinal cord injury svc. Palo Alto (Calif.) VA Med. Ctr., 1989-91; resident in surgery Stanford U. Hosp., 1991-94; resident in colon and rectal surgery U. Minn., 1994-95; asst. clin. prof. surgery U. Calif., San Diego, 1995—2001, assoc. prof. clin. surgery, 2001—; sect. chief Halasz gen. surgery sect., surg. svc. VA San Diego Healthcare Sys., 2000—. Contbr. articles to profl. jours. NRSA Tng. grantee Nat. Cancer Inst., Bethesda, 1990; Giannini Found. Postdoctoral Rsch. fellow Bank of Am., San Francisco, 1990. Home: 8708 Nottingham Pl La Jolla CA 92037-2128 Office: VA Med Ctr Surgical Svc 112E 3350 La Jolla Village Dr San Diego CA 92161-0002

COSMAN, FELICIA, endocrinologist, educator; b. N.Y.C., June 12, 1958; BA with distinction, Cornell U., 1979; MD, Stony Brook Med. Sch., 1983. Diplomate Am. Bd. Internal Medicine, Am. Bd. Internal Medicine, Endocrinology and Metabolism, Nat. Bd. Med. Examiners. Intern dept. medicine Columbia Presbyn. Med. Ctr., N.Y.C., 1983-84, resident, 1984-86; NIH fellow divsn. endocrinology Columbia Coll. Phys. and Surg., N.Y.C., 1986-88; assoc. prof. clin. medicine Columbia Coll. Phys. and surg., N.Y.C., 1996—; endocrinologist, osteoporosis specialist Helen Hayes Hosp., West Haverstraw, N.Y., 1988—. Clin. dir. Nat. Osteoporosis Found., 1996—. Author: What Your Doctor May Not Tell You About Osteoporosis; co-editor Osteoporosis; mem. editl. bd. Osteoporosis Internat.; contbr. articles to profl. jours., chpts. to books. NIH grantee, 1993—, Dept. Def. grantee, 1998—, Multiple Sclerosis grantee, 1997—. Mem. ACP (assoc.), Am. Soc. Bone and Mineral Rsch. Office: Helen Hayes Hosp West Haverstraw NY 10993

COSMAN, FRANCENE JEN, former government official; b. Windsor, Ont., Can., Jan. 14, 1941; d. John Douglas and Dorothy Mae (Machel) McCarthy; m. David Killam Cosman, July 25, 1964 (div.); children: Lara Machel, Andrea Leigh; m. Aza Avramovitch, June 27, 1998 (dec.). Diploma in Nursing, St. John Gen. Hosp., N.B., 1962; postgrad. diploma, Margaret Hague Hosp., Jersey City, 1963. RN Can. Various nursing positions, 1963-68; county councillor County of Halifax, N.S., 1976-79; mayor Town of Bedford, N.S., 1979-82; pres. Adv. Coun. on Status of Women, N.S., 1982-86; exec. dir. N.S. Liberal Party, 1989-93; mem. Legis. Assembly, House of Assembly of N.S., Halifax, 1993-99, dep. spkr., min. comty. svcs., 1995-99; ret. Chair Sr. Citizens Secretariat, 1997-99; min. responsible administn. Adv. Coun. Status Women Act, 1997-99; min. Cmty. Svcs., 1997-99; min. responsible Disabled Persons Commn. Act, 1997-99; mem. Healing Touch Ministry, 2000—. Contbr. numerous reports, brief, documents to provincial and fed. levels of govt.; opinion col. writer Chronicle Herald Newspaper, 1987-88. Liberal. Mem. United Ch. Avocations: artist, writing poetry, swimming, healing touch practitioner. E-mail: fjc@eastlink.ca.

COSME, LUKE GEORGE, retired structural engineer; b. Chgo., Dec. 1, 1911; s. Luke Cosme and Patricia Kerstenic; m. Margaret Smith, Apr. 12, 1939 (dec. Apr. 1977); children: Richard, James, Carol; m. Betty Lee Martin, July 22, 1978. BSCE, Armour Inst. Tech., 1934; cert. in soil mechanics, Northwestern U., 1960; cert. in advanced steel and tall bldg. design, Ill. Inst. Tech., 1953—55. Profl. engr., State of Ill., cert. structural engr., State of Ill. Draftsman, surveyor Chgo. Surface Lines, 1930—31; draftsman Chgo. Park Dist., 1935—39, sr. draftsman, 1939—49, structural designer, 1949—54, structural engr., 1954—60, engr. design and contract, 1960—78, design engr. 1st Spl. Olympics at Soldier Field, 1968, cons. engr., 1978—94; ret., 1994. Archtl. adv. bd. Village of Crete, Ill., 1954—60; bd. dirs. State of Ill. Structural Engrs. Assn., 1972—76; cons. engr. Rehab. Chgo.'s Lake Front, 1978—94, Friends of the Parks, Chgo., 1992—93; mem. Com. to Rehab. Northerly Island. Mem.: ASCE, Am. Concrete Inst. Avocations: art, photography, stained glass. Home: 785 St Andrews Dr Crete IL 60417 E-mail: LGC785@juno.com.

COSNER, CHRISTOPHER MARK, engineer; b. Balt., July 26, 1961; s. Donald Lester and Shirley Marie Cosner. BS with highest distinction, U. Va., 1983; MSME, U. Calif., Berkeley, 1990. Mem. tech. staff Calif. Inst. Tech. Jet Propulsion Lab., Pasadena, 1983-88; sr. scientist Boeing Space Systems, L.A., 1990—. Contbr. articles to IEEE Robotics and Automation Jour., AIAA Aerospace Controls Systems Jour.; patentee in field. Regents fellow U. Calif., Berkeley, 1988-89; named Outstanding Aerospace Student Sigma Gamma Tau, 1983; recipient Jefferson Scholar award U. Va. Alumni Assn., Charlottesville, 1979-83, Achievement award NASA, Washington, 1989-90, Hughes Tech. Achievement award 1993, 98, Hughes Space and Comms. Superior Performance award 1994, 97, Hughes Tech. Excellence award, 1995; Boeing Tech. fellow, 2001. Mem. AIAA (student chpt. pres. 1983), Tau Beta Pi. Achievements include patents for repetitive control of thermal shock disturbance and space vehicle configuration. Office: Boeing Space Systems W/S70/708 PO Box 92426 Los Angeles CA 90009-2426

COSPOLICH, JAMES DONALD, electrical engineering executive, consultant; b. New Orleans, Dec. 19, 1944; s. Clarence James and Olga Marie C.; m. Shirley Patricia Knipper, Feb. 4, 1967; children: Brian James, Jeffery Donald, Stephen William. BEE, La. State U., 1967, MEE, 1972. Registered profl. engr., La., Calif., Tex. Geophysicist Pan Am. Petroleum Corp. subs. AMOCO, New Orleans, La., 1967; elec. engr. Waldemar S. Nelson & Co., New Orleans, 1967-74, asst. v.p., mgr. elec. engring., 1974-83, v.p., mgr. elec. engring., 1983-85, sr. v.p. ops., 1985-91, exec. v.p., 1991—. Mem. Nat. Elec. Code Panel 14. Mem. Rep. Nat. Com., Washington, 1988; v.p. Ormond Civic Assn., Destrehan, La., 1985, pres., 1986; mem. representing St. Charles Parish, New Orleans Internat. Airport Noise Abatement Com. With USCGR, 1964-72. Mem. NFPA (nat. elec. code com.), IEEE, NSPE, Instrument Soc. Am. (sr., mem. various coms. 1975—), Am. Petroleum Inst. (com. recommended practice stds.), Gas Processors Assn., La. Engring. Soc., Ormond Country Club, The City Energy Club of New Orleans. Republican. Roman Catholic. Avocations: fishing, tennis, golf, skiing, boating, woodworking. Home: 61 Rosedown Dr Destrehan LA 70047-2529 Office: Waldemar S Nelson & Co Inc 1200 Saint Charles Ave New Orleans LA 70130-4334

COSS, JOHN EDWARD, retired archivist; b. Spring Valley, Ill., Apr. 2, 1947; s. Edward Francis and Doris (Leonard) C.; m. Sherry Lee Ushman, June 4, 1973 (div. May 1979); 1 child, Stephen John; m. Brenda Lynn Gibson, May 30, 1981; 1 stepchild, Anthony Robert. AA, Ill. Valley C.C., 1967; BA, Northwest Mo. State U., 1970. Sr. archivist Ill. State Archives, Springfield, 1971—2002; ret., 2002. Mem. Ill. Fedn. Archivists, Archival Technicians & Photographers, Springfield Trades & Labor Coun. (del.). Methodist. Avocations: music, reading, golf. Home: 10470 E State Route 54 Buffalo IL 62515-7148 E-mail: jcoss@springnet1.com.

COSS, ROCKY ALAN, lawyer; b. Dayton, Ohio, Apr. 6, 1951; s. Vernon F. and Necia Lea (Shaw) C.; m. Cheryl Sue Kelch, Sept. 9, 1972; children— : Tracey, Derek. B.A., Ohio State, 1973, J.D., 1976. Bar: Ohio, 1976, U.S. Supreme Ct., 1979, U.S. Dist. Ct. (so. dist.) Ohio 1982, U.S. Ct. Appeals (6th cir.) 1983. Sole practice, Hillsboro, Ohio, 1976-81; ptnr. Coss & Greer, Hillsboro, 1982— ; pros. atty. Highland County, Ohio, 1977— . Mem. Steering com. City of Hillsboro, 1980-85; county chmn. Highland County Fund Drive; pres. Highland County Soc. Crippled Children and Adults, 1985-86; mem. enrollment com. Highland County Boy Scouts Am., 1977-78. Fellow Ohio State Bar Found.; mem. Ohio State Bar Assn., Highland County Bar Assn. (pres. 1982), Ohio Pros. Atty's. Assn. (v.p.), Nat. Dist. Atty's. Assn., ABA, Ohio Council Sch. Bd. Attys., Nat. Council Sch. Bd. Attys., Hillsboro Jaycees (v.p. 1978-83). Democrat. Methodist. Lodges: Rotary (pres. 1983-84), Masons, Elks. Home: PO Box 258 Hillsboro OH 45133-0258 Office: 14612 E Main St Hillsboro OH 45133

COSS, RONALD ALLEN, radiation biologist, cell biologist; b. Long Beach, Calif., Apr. 24, 1947; s. Claude Leonard and Helen Elaine (Stevens) C.; m. Ingrid Lenore Valey, July 21, 1979; children: Nicholas Pieter Valey Coss, Elliott Benjamin Valey Coss. BA in Zoology, U. Calif., Riverside, 1969; PhD in Cell Biology, U. Colo., 1974. Postdoctoral fellow Rockefeller U., N.Y.C., 1974-76, Colo. State U., Ft. Collins, 1976-79, rsch. assoc., 1979-81, asst. prof., 1981-82, Thomas Jefferson U., Phila., 1982-87, assoc. prof., 1987-93, prof., 1993—. Contbr. articles to profl. jours. Mem. exec. bd. Phila. Cancer Rsch. Assn., 1983-90, pres., 1988-90. Numerous grants Nat. Cancer Inst., Dept. Health and Human Svcs., 1979—. Mem. AAAS, Am. Assn. for Cancer Rsch., Am. Soc. Cell Biology, Radiation Rsch. Soc., N.Am. Hyperthermia Soc., Sigma Xi (chpt. pres. 1995-97). Avocations: sports, fishing. Office: Thomas Jefferson Univ Dept Radiation Oncology 111 S 11th St Philadelphia PA 19107-5097 E-mail: ronald.coss@mail.tju.edu.

COSSA, DOMINIC FRANK, baritone; b. Jessup, Pa., May 13, 1935; s. Domenico and Pasquina (Stella) C.; m. Janet Edgerton, Dec. 26, 1956; children: Francine, Gian-Antonio. BS in Psychology, U. Scranton, Pa., 1959; MA, U. Detroit, 1961; postgrad., Detroit Inst. Mus. Arts, 1960-61, Phila. Acad. Vocal Arts, 1961-63; LHD (hon.), U. Scranton, 1982. Leading baritone N.Y.C. Opera, 1961—, San Francisco Opera, 1970, Met. Opera, N.Y.C., 1970-76. Prof. of voice, chair voice/opera dept. U. Md., College Park; former mem. voice faculty Manhattan Sch. Music; hon. life bd. mem. Am. Guild Mus. Artists, trustee Am. Guild Mus. artists pension fund, 1985—. Debut, N.Y.C. Opera, 1961, Met. Opera, N.Y.C., 1970, San Francisco Opera, 1970; rec. artist for, London Records, Elixir of Love, Les Huguenots, RCA Victor, Julius Caesar; appeared in title role in: world premiere of Gian Carlo Menotti's The Hero, 1976. Recipient Liederkranz award; Met. Nat. Coun. 1st pl. prize; winner Am. Opera Auditions; winner WGN Auditions; inducted into Great Am. Singers Hall of Fame, Phila. Acad. Vocal Arts; Rockefeller grantee. Republican. Roman Catholic. Avocations: antiques, wine collecting, gardening, collecting early american pressed glass. *One must keep a sense of balance and proportion. Whenever thoughts of success and career become foremost in my mind, I try to place it in a larger perspective. There are certainly issues of greater importance in life than my success or failure. In a word, I try to be honest with myself even if it's painful.*

COSSÉ, R. PAUL, realty company executive; b. Nashville, July 11, 1956; s. Xavier B. and Irene E. (Amburgey) C.; 1 child, Michelle Reneé. Student, Belmont Coll., 1974-75, Aquinas Jr. Coll., 1975-76, U. Tenn., Knoxville, 1976—, Middle Tenn. State U., 1980-81. Mktg. dir. First Tenn. Bank, Murfreesboro, Tenn., 1980-83; exec. v.p. First Federal, Columbia, Tenn., 1983-88; exec. v.p., mng. officer Security Trust Fed., Knoxville, 1988-89; pres., CEO Prudential Vol. Realty, 1989-98; pres. Home Mortgage Brokers, Inc., Knoxville, 1990-98; pres., CEO Fin. Investor Svcs. of Tenn., Inc., Knoxville, 1992-98, Ins. and Fin. Svcs. Group, Inc., Knoxville, 1992-98; realtor Realty Execs., 2000—. Pres./CEO Southeastern Holdings of Tenn., Inc., 1995-98; bd. dirs. YMCA, Knoxville; realtor, Prudential Vol. Realty, 1998-2000, Realty Execs., 2000—; cons. in field. Pres. Big. Bros. and Big Sisters Maury County, Columbia, Tenn., 1987-88; bd. dirs. YMCA, Columbia, 1988; chmn. Saturn Run, Columbia, 1987-88; chmn. realtor divsn. Am. Heart Assn. and United Way, Knoxville. Mem. Tenn. League Savs. (leadership bd., publicity com.), Exch. Club. Republican. Avocations: golf, tennis. Office: Realty Execs PO Box 647 Powell TN 37849-0647 E-mail: prutenn@aol.com.

COSSINS, EDWIN ALBERT, biology educator, academic administrator; b. Havering, Eng., Feb. 28, 1937; came to Can., 1962; s. Albert Joseph and Elizabeth H. (Brown) C.; m. Lucille Jeannette Salt, Sept. 1, 1962; children: Diane Elizabeth (dec. 1995), Carolyn Jane. BSc, U. London, 1958, PhD, 1961, DSc, 1981. Rsch. assoc. Purdue U., Lafayette, Ind., 1961-62; from asst. prof. to prof. U. Alta., Edmonton, Can., 1962-96, acting head dept. botany, 1965-66, assoc. dean of sci., 1983-88, prof. biol. scis. emeritus, 1996—. Mem. grant selection panel Natural Scis. and Enging. Research Council, Ottawa, Ont., Can., 1974-77, 78-81 Author: (with others) Plant Biochemistry; 1980, 1988, Folates and Pterins, 1984. Assoc. editor Can. Jour. Botany, 1969-78. Contbr. numerous articles to profl. jours. Recipient Centennial medal Govt. of Can., 1967 Fellow Royal Soc. Can. (life); mem. Can. Soc. Plant Physiologists (western dir. 1968-70, pres. 1976-77, gold medal 1998), Faculty Club (U. Alta.), Derrick Golf and Winter Club. Clubs: Faculty (U. Alta.), Derrick Golf and Winter. Avocations: gardening, golf, curling, cross-country skiing. Home: 99 Fairway Dr Edmonton AB Canada T6J 2C2 E-mail: ecossins@ualberta.ca.

COST, FRANCIS HOWARD, JR., physician; b. Hagerstown, Md., Sept. 24, 1938; s. Francis Howard and Mary Elizabeth C. AB, Gettysburg Coll., 1962; MD, U. Md., 1966. Diplomate Am. Bd. Internal Medicine, Am. Bd. Cardiovascular Disease, Am. Bd. Pulmonary Disease. Resident in internal medicine USPHS, S.I., 1967-68, U. Hosp., Balt., 1969-70, fellow in cardiology, 1970-72; fellow in pulmonary disease Temple U. Hosp., Phila., 1972-73; fellow in nuclear medicine/nuclear cardiology Johns Hopkins Hosp., Balt., 1984-85, fellow in med. ICU, 1986-88. Lt. comdr. USPHS, 1967-69. Fellow Am. Coll. Chest Physicians; mem. Am. Coll. Cardiology, Am. Coll. Physicians, Laennec Soc. Phila. Avocations: sailing, music. Home: 1101 Potomac Ave Hagerstown MD 21742-3439

COSTA, DANIEL LAWRENCE, architect; b. Providence, R.I., Feb. 16, 1953; s. Dimas and Laurinda (Diogo) C.; m. Shepley Patterson Metcalf, May 31, 1980 (div. Mar. 1988); 1 child, Hilary Metcalf. AB, Brown U., 1974; MArch, Harvard U., 1980. Architect Archtl. Resources Cambridge (Mass.), Inc., 1980-87, Shepard/Quraeshi Assocs., Watertown, Mass., 1987-88; prin. Costa/Flenniken Assocs., Boston, 1988-90, Dan Costa AIA, Boston, 1990—. Mem. Somerville (Mass.) Design Rev. Bd., 1988; bd. dirs. Somerville Hist. Preservation Commn., 1991-96. Recipient Home of Yr. award Met. Home Mag., 1997, Best in Am. Living award Profl. Builder Mag., 1995, Southern Home award So. Living Mag., 1995. Mem. AIA, Boston Soc. Architects. Office: 368 Congress St Fl 4 Boston MA 02210-1864

COSTA, ERMINIO, pharmacologist, cell biology educator; b. Cagliari, Italy, Mar. 9, 1924; s. Oreste and Gigina (Murgia) Costa; divorced; children: Max, Robert Henry, Michael John; m. Ingeborg Hanbauer, July 13, 1973. MD, U. Cagliari, 1947, PhD in Pharmacology, 1953; PhD in Biol. Sci. (hon.), U. Cagliari, Italy, 1986; DSc (hon.), Georgetown U., 1992; MD (hon.), U. Tampere, Finland, 1992. Asst. prof., assoc. prof. U. Cagliari, 1948—54, prof. pharmacology, 1954—56; physician II, med. rsch. assn. Thudichum Psychology Rsch., Galesburg, Ill., 1956—60; vis. scientist NIH, Bethesda, Md., 1960—61; dep. chief lab. chem. pharmacology Nat. Heart Inst., Bethesda, 1961—63, head sect. clin. pharmacology, 1963—65; assoc. prof. pharmacology Columbia U., N.Y.C., 1965—68; chief lab. preclin. pharmacology St. Elizabeth's Hosp., Washington, 1968—85; dir. Fidia-Georgetown Inst. for the Neuroscis. Georgetown U., Washington, 1985—94, 1996—; McDonnel vis. prof. neurology Washington U. Sch. Medicine, St. Louis, 1994—; sci. dir., prof. biochemistry in psychiatry U. Ill. at Chgo. Psychiat. Inst., 1996—. Editor Neuropharmacology, 1967, Advanced Biochem. Psychopharmacology, 1968, contbr. 915 articles to profl. jours. Recipient Bennet award and Gold medal, Soc. Biol. Psychiatry, 1990, Gold medal Fed. II Univ., Naples, 1990, Premio Fiuggi award, Fiuggi Rsch. Found., 1988. Mem.: NAS, Am. Soc. Biol. Chemistry and Molecular Biology, Am. Soc. Physiology, Am. Soc. Pharmacology and Exptl. Therapeutics, Academia Nazionale Lincei, Peripatetic Club, Cosmos Club. Office: Psychiatric Ins Univ of Illinois at Chicago 1601 W Taylor St Chicago IL 60612-4310

COSTA, GUSTAVO, Italian studies scholar; b. Rome, Mar. 21, 1930; came to U.S., 1961; s. Paolo and Ida (Antonangelo) C.; m. Natalia Zalessow, June 8, 1963; 1 child, Dora L. Maturità Classica, Liceo Virgilio, Rome, 1948; PhD cum laude, U. Rome, 1954. Asst. Istituto di Filosofia, Rome, 1957-60; instr. Italian Univ. de Lyon, Lyons, France, 1960-61, U. Calif., Berkeley, 1961-63, asst. prof., 1963-68, assoc. prof., 1968-72, prof., 1972-91, prof. emeritus, 1991—, chmn. dept. Italian, 1973-76, 88-91. Vis. prof. Scuola di Studi Superiori, Naples, 1984, Inst. Philosophy, U. Rome La Sapienza, 1992, Scuola Europea di Studi Avanzati, Naples, 2003; reviewer RAI Corp., Rome, 1982-89. Author: La critica Omerica di Thomas Blackwell (1701-1757), 1959, La leggenda dei secoli d'oro nella lett. ital., 1972, Le antichità germaniche nella cultura italiana, 1977, Il sublime e la magia da Dante a Tasso, 1994, Vico e l'Europa: Contro la boria delle nazioni, 1996, Malebranche y Vico, 1998, Vico e l' Inquisizione, 1999, Malebranche e Roma, 2003; mem. editl. bd. Nouvelles de la République des Lettres, New Vico Studies, Cuadernos sobre Vico. Inst. Italiano Studi Storici fellow, Naples, Italy, 1954-57, Guggenheim Meml. Found. fellow, N.Y.C., 1977; grantee French Govt., Paris, 1956, Belgian Govt., Brussels, 1956, Targa d'oro Apulia, Italy, 1990. Mem. Am. Assn. Tchrs. Italian, Am. Soc. for Eighteenth-Century Studies, Renaissance Soc. Am., Am. Soc. for Aesthetics, Dante Soc. Am., Faculty Club (Berkeley). Avocations: gardening, stamp collecting. Office: U Calif MC 2620 Dept Italian Studies Berkeley CA 94720-0001

COSTA, KELLI ANN, anthropologist, educator, archaeologist; d. George and Marion G. Woleck; m. William G. Costa, Apr. 16, 1988. BA, Goddard Coll., 1991; MA, U. Mass., 1993, PhD, 1998. Asst. prof. anthropology Franklin Pierce Coll., Rindge, NH, 1996—. Author: (book) The Brokered Image, 2001; contbg. author: book Situating Identities in Modern Celtic Europe, 2002. Fellow Alpine Studies fellow, Am. Alpine Club, 1995, Marion and Jasper A Whiting Rsch. fellow, Whiting Found., 2002, Austro-American fellow, Austrian Am. Found., 1996. Mem.: Assn. Feminist Anthropology (mem. exec. bd. and editor 2000—02), Ulster Archeol. Soc., Soc. Anthropology of Europe (mem. exec. bd. and jour. editor 1999—2002), Am. Anthrop. Assn. Office: Franklin Pierce Coll Anthropology Crestview 334 Rindge NH 03461 Personal E-mail: costaka@fpc.edu.

COSTA, TERRY ANN, principal; b. Huntington, W.Va., Jan. 9, 1951; d. Hobart G. and Beatrice (Chaput) Owens; m. Joseph M. Costa, June 5, 1970; children: Carrie Lynn, Anthony Martin. BA, Marshall U., 1972, MA, 1979; EdS, Nova U., 1988. Cert. specific learning disabilities, mentally and emotionally handicapped, varying exceptionalities, ESOL, speech tchr., coach, ednl. leadership, Fla. Tchr. spl. edn. Cabell County Sch. System, Huntington, 1973-77, 80-86, coach, 1980-86; adj. instr. Marshall U., Huntington, 1979-80; tchr. spl. edn., dept. chmn. Palm Beach County Sch. Sys., West Palm Beach, Fla., 1986-94, coord. exceptional student edn., dept. chairperson, coach, 1989-94; chmn. tng. and devel. Palm Beach County Sch. System, West Palm Beach, Fla., 1988-89; asst. prin. Loggers' Run Cmty. Mid. Sch., Boca Raton, Fla., 1994-98; prin. Christa McAuliffe Cmty. Mid. Sch., Boynton Beach, Fla., 1998—. Chmn. exceptional student edn. instructional materials coun. for math. and sci. Fla. Dept. Edn., West Palm Beach, 1988, clin. educator, 1986-91. Coord., vol. Spl. Olympics, Cabell County, 1974-76; religious tchr., coord. Diocese of Wheeling-Charleston, W.Va., 1980-86; leader Girl Scouts U.S.A., W.Va., 1984-86; sch. campaign chmn. United Way, Palm Beach County, 1988-89. Mem. ASCD, Nat. Assn. Secondary Sch. Prins., Coun. for Exceptional Children (sec. W.Va. 1973-74, corr. sec. 1992-93, Palm Beach County Tchr. of Yr. award chpt. 200, 1989, grantee 1988-90, 92), Fla. Assn. Sch. Adminstrs., Palm Beach County Sch. Adminstrs. Assn. (exec. bd. sec. 1996-2000), Palm Beach County Prins. Assn. (sec., chair tech. com.), Boynton Beach C. of C., Boynton Beach Kiwanis Internat. (treas. 1999-2001, pres. 2003—), Phi Delta Kappa (v.p. membership, Kappan of Yr. 1999-2001). Democrat. Roman Catholic. Avocations: tennis, water skiing, running, fishing, needlecrafts. Home: 880 SE Degan Dr Port Saint Lucie FL 34983- Office: Christa McAuliffe Cmty Mid Sch 6500 Le Chalet Blvd Boynton Beach FL 33437-2304 E-mail: costa@palmbeach.k12.fl.us.

COSTA, THOMAS CHARLES, priest; b. Queens, N.Y., Nov. 16, 1950; s. James B. and Catherine M. (Pensa) C. BA in English magna cum laude, Cathedral Coll., Douglaston, N.Y., 1972; MDiv, Immaculate Conception Sem., Huntington, N.Y., 1977; cert. in cross-cultural ministry studies, Cath. Theol. Union., Chgo., 1995. Ordained priest, Roman Catholic Ch., 1978. Customer svc. rep. Wallach's, Garden City, N.Y., 1972-73; assoc. pastor St. Boniface Ch., Elmont, N.Y., 1978-82, St. Rose of Lima Ch., Massapequa, N.Y., 1982-84, St. Ignatius Loyola Ch., Hicksville, N.Y., 1984-88; co-pastor St. John of God Ch., Central Islip, N.Y., 1988-94; assoc. pastor for ethnic ministry St. Brigid Ch., Westbury, N.Y., 1994-98; pastor St. Patrick Ch., Glen Cove, N.Y., 1998—. Mem. dea Founding sch. bd. pres. Our Lady of Providence Regional Sch., Central Islip, 1991-94; chmn. corp., All Saints Regional Sch., Glen Cove, 1998—; NE Rep. NCOD Exec. bd. 2002-. mem. deafness adv. bd. Cath. Charities, Rockville Centre, N.Y., 1988-92; nat. deaf vocat. adv. bd. DePaul Project, Yonkers, N.Y., 1992—; adv. bd. Haitian Civic Assn., Central Islip, 1988-94; mem. continuing edn. bd. Diocese of Rockville Centre, 1995-98; dir. spirituale Comitato Italiano Della Comunita, Westbury, N.Y., 1994-98; dir. espiritual Consejo Pastoral, Westbury, 1994-98; assoc. diocesan chaplain for the deaf Diocesan Deaf Apostolate, Rockville Centre, 1978—; procurator-adv. Diocesan Marriage Tribunal, Diocese of Rockville Centre, N.Y., 1981—; mem. Presbyn. Senate, 2002—; mem. Pastor's Forum for Edn., 2003—; pastoral worker Nat. Cath. Office of the Deaf. Capt. USAFR, 1982-88. Mem. Am. Legion (life), K.C. (trustee 1994-98, past grand knight Sign of Cross Coun. 1993-94), Internat. Cath. Deaf Assn. (life). Republican. Office: Saint Patrick Roman Cath Ch 235 Glen St Glen Cove NY 11542-3059 E-mail: ThomRev@aol.com., ThomRev@MSN.COM.

COSTA-GAVRAS, (CONSTANTIN GAVRAS), director, writer; b. Athens, Greece, Feb. 13, 1933; naturalized French citizen; m. Michele Ray, Sept. 12, 1968; children: Alexandre, Helene, Romain. Student, U. Sorbonne, Paris. Diplomate Inst. Higher Cinematic Studies. Ballet dancer, Greece; asst. to film dirs. Yves Allegret, Jacques Demy, Rene Clair, Rene Clement, Jean Giorno. Pres. Cinematheque francaise, 1982—. Dir., screenwriter films : The Sleeping Car Murders, 1964; Z, 1969 (Acad. awaard for best fgn. lang. film, 70, Jury prize, Cannes Film Festival, 69, Raoul-Levy prize, 69, Golden Globe award, 70); Missing, 1982 (Golden Palm award Cannes, 82, Acad. Award for best screenplay, 82); dir.: (films) Un Homme de Trop, 1966 (Moscow Film Festival prize), L'Aveu, 1970 (The Confession), State of Siege, 1973 (Cannes Film Festival award, 75), Special Section, 1975, Madame Rosa (also actor), 1978, Clair de Femme, 1979, Hanna K, 1983, Conseil de Femme, 1986, Betrayed, 1988, Music Box, 1990 (Golden Bear award Berlin film festival, 90), Little Apocalypse, 1992, Mad City, 1996; (Operas) Il Mondo Dela Luna (Joseph Haydn), 1994, Mad City, 1997; co-dir. : A Propos de Nice, 1995; Lumiere and Compagnie, 1995; Amen, 2001 (named Best European movie, 2002, Globo D'oro Assn. Fgn. Press, 2002); dir.: (theater musical show) All Around is Light, 2003. Named Best Dir., Cannes Film Festival 1975, Officier Ordre National du Merite; decorated Comdr. Arts and Letters, France, Chevalier Legion d'Honneur; recipient Life Achievement award De l'Academie Francaise, 1998, Gold medal of Bellas Artes King of Spain. E-mail: kgprod@wayadou.fr.

COSTAGLIOLA, FRANCESCO, former government official; b. Cranston, R.I., Aug. 24, 1917; s. Luigi and Rose (Lubrano) C.; m. Agnes Mary Ross, June 14, 1952 (dec.); children: Francesca Danieli, Marisa Costagliola, Antonia Burns, Roseanne Rubin. Student, U. R.I., 1935-37; BSEE, U.S. Naval Acad., 1941; postgrad., Naval Postgrad. Sch., 1946-47, MIT, 1947-49, Cath. U. Am., 1967-71; MBA, Am. U., Washington, 1974. Commd. ensign USN, 1941, advanced through grades to capt., 1960, served in U.S.S. Phoenix in 24 ops. PTO, 1941-46; commdg. officer U.S.S. Halsey Powell, Republic of Korea, 1951-52; various positions naval sea and shore assignments involving atomic energy USN, 1952-64; mil. asst. to asst. to Sec. Def. for atomic energy, 1964-67; ret., 1968; commr. AEC, 1968-69; engr. RCA, 1974-76; staff mem. Joint Congl. Com. on Atomic Energy, Washington, 1967-68, 69-71, 76-77, Office of Sec. of Senate, Washington, 1977-86. Mem. Md. Radiation Control Adv. Bd., 1973-81. Contbr. articles to profl. jours. Treas. Class of '41 U.S. Naval Acad., 1997—. Decorated Legion of Merit, Bronze Star with Combat V (2). Mem. AAAS, Inst. Ops. Rsch. and Mgmt. Scis., Am. Nuc. Soc., U.S. Naval Inst., Pearl Harbor Survivors Assn. (rep. Vets. Day nat. com. 1990—, pres. No. Va. chpt. 1991-1993, 2003—), Naval Acad. Alumni Assn., Mil. Order World Wars, Mil. Order Carabao, Army and Navy Club (Washington). Roman Catholic. Home: 307 Gibbon St Alexandria VA 22314-4129 E-mail: costagliola@starpower.net.

COSTANTINO, HENRY RAYMOND, chemical engineer, researcher; s. Henry Raymond and Jacqueline Costantino; m. Frances Alida Griffith, May 26, 2002. BS in chem. engring., The Johns Hopkins U., 1984—88; MS in chem. engring., The Johns Jopkins U., 1988—89; PhD in chem. engring., Mass. Inst. of Tech., 1989—95. Post-doctoral fellow MIT, Cambridge, Mass., 1995—95; rsch. scientist Genentech, Inc., South San Francisco, 1995—98. Assoc. dir. Alkermes, Inc., Cambridge, Mass., 1989. Contbr. articles to profl. jours. Mem.: Am. Chem. Soc., Am. Assn. of Pharm. Scientists. Achievements include patents for method of producing sub-micron particles of biologically active agents and uses thereof; saccharification enzymes from hyperthermophilic bacteria and processes for their production; patents pending for composition for the delivery of live cells and methods of use. Office: Alkermes Inc 88 Sidney St Cambridge MA 02139 Office Fax: 617-494-9263. E-mail: rick.costantino@alkermes.com.

COSTANZI, MARIANNE, retired music teacher; b. St. Paul, Dec. 19, 1923; d. Edward J. and Anna Marie (Klein) Ritter; m. Nello Dominic Costanzi, Nov. 4, 1944; children: Barry, Annette, Maureen, Victor, Christopher, Francine. Student, U. Minn., 1941-43. Music tchr. parochial schs., St. Paul, 1941-45; ski patrol Afton (Minn.) Alps, 1977-99; choir dir. St. John's Ch., St. Paul, 1959-83, St. Patrick's Ch., St. Paul, 1983-92. Dir. Marian Choral Club. Republican. Roman Catholic. Avocations: skiing, chamber music, swimming. Home: 790 Summit Ave Saint Paul MN 55105-3352

COSTANZO, HILDA ALBA, retired banker; b. Newark, Feb. 04; d. Smeraldo Luigi and Giovanna Marianna (Mancuso) Costanzo. Pub. rels. cert., Princeton U., N.J. Bankers Assn. Sch., 1965; pre-std. cert., Am. Inst. Banking, 1967, std. cert., 1972; BA in English summa cum laude, Caldwell Coll., 1992. Various positions Howard Savs. Bank, Newark, 1943-66, asst. sec., 1966-74, asst. to pres., 1974-76, corp. sec., 1976-80, v.p., corp. sec., 1980-87, ret., 1987. Mem. Nat. Assn. Bank Women, Zonta (v.p. 1973-74), Alpha Sigma Lambda, Kappa Gamma Pi. Republican. Roman Catholic. Avocations: reading, music, travel.

COSTANZO, NANCI JOY, art educator; b. New Britain, Conn., June 2, 1947; d. Edward Francis and Vivian Evelyn (Allen) Sarisley; m. Joseph Paul Costanzo, Apr. 10, 1974; 1 child, Ashley Allen Bailey. BA, Cen. Conn. State U., New Britain, 1973; MAE, R.I. Sch. Design, 1979; cert. advanced grad. study in Expressive Art Therapy, European Grad. Sch., Leuk, Switzerland, 1999. Assoc. prof. art Elms Coll., Chicopee, Mass., 1985—, also chair dept. visual arts. Exhibited at Western New Eng. Coll., 1977, Springfield Art League Show, 1978, Zone Gallery, 1981, Westfield State Coll., 1985, Valley Women Arts Show, 1980, 83, 85-89, New Britain Mus. Am. Art, 1987-90, Borgia Gallery Elms Coll., 1989-92, Hampden Gallery at U. Mass., 1990, Sino-Am. Women's Conf., Beijing, People's Republic of China, 1990, Monson Arts Coun., 1995, Elms Coll., 1997, European Grad. Sch., Switzerland, 1998-99, Dane Gallery, 2001-02, NY Am. Mus. Illustrators, 2002, Yorktown Mus., NY, 2002, others; one woman shows include Thronja Art Gallery, 1979-80, Elms Coll., 1992, 2002, Dane Gallery, 2001-02; represented in pvt. collections in Mass., RI, Wash., NY, Italy, corp. collections in RI and Conn.; creator Cmty. Art Exhibit for 9-11; contbr. articles to profl. jours.; lectr. Greece, Mex. and China. Recipient Outstanding Arts Educator in Mass. award Mass. Alliance for Arts Edn., 1985, New Britain Mus. Am. Art, 1987, 88; Nat. Endowment for Humanities grantee, 1987, 88; Faculty Devel. grantee, Beijing, 1989, 90. Mem. Nat. Art Edn. Assn., Valley Women Artists, Mass. Art Edn. Assn. (mem. coun. 1984-86, v.p. 1986-88), Nat. Mus. of Women in the Arts, Coll. Art Assn., Nat. Women's Studies Assn., Internat. Soc. for Edn. through Art, Women's Caucus for Art. Avocations: painting, reading, gardening, skiing, sailing. Office: Elms Coll 291 Springfield St Chicopee MA 01013-2837

COSTA-ZALESSOW, NATALIA, foreign language educator; b. Kumanovo, Macedonia, Dec. 5, 1936; came to the U.S., 1951; d. Alexander P. and Katarina (Duric) Z.; m. Gustavo Costa, June 8, 1963; 1 child, Dora. BA in Italian, U. Calif., Berkeley, 1959, MA in Italian, 1961, PhD in Romance Langs. and Lits., 1967. Tchg. asst. U. Calif., Berkeley, 1959-63; instr. Mills Coll., Oakland, Calif., 1963; asst. prof. San Francisco State U., 1968-74, assoc. prof., 1974-79, prof., 1979-98, coord. Italian program, 1992-98, prof. emerita, 1998—. Author: Scrittrici italiane dal XIII al XX secolo, Testi e critica, 1982; editor: Anima, 1997; transl.: Her Soul, 1996; contbr. articles to profl. publs. Sidney M. Ehrman scholar U. Calif., Berkeley, 1957-58, Gamma Phi Beta scholar U. Calif., Berkeley, 1958, Herbert H. Vaughan scholar U. Calif., Berkeley, 1959-60, Advanced Grad. Traveling fellow in romance lang. and lit. U. Calif., Berkeley, 1964-65. Mem. MLA, Am. Assn. Tchrs. Italian, Renaissance Soc. Am., Dante Soc. Am., Croatian Acad. Am. Roman Catholic. Avocations: swimming, hiking, opera, symphony, gastronomy. Office: San Francisco State U Dept Fgn Lang and Lit San Francisco CA 94132

COSTEL, DANIEL EUGENE, financial analyst; b. Homestead, Pa., July 23, 1966; s. Eugene Nicholas and Agnes (Ribar) C. BSBA in Econs. and Internat. Bus., Duquesne U., 1988, MBA, 1990, Advanced Cert. in Acctg., 2002. Statis. analyst Kaufmann's Credit Divsn., Pitts., 1988-90; fin. analyst Equibank N.A., Pitts., 1990-91; asst. examiner Office of Thrift Supervision/U.S. Treasury, Pitts., 1991-93, examiner I, 1993-94, examiner II, 1994-97; sr. fin. analyst, asst. officer Mellon Fin. Corp., Pitts., 1997-99, prin. fin. analyst, officer, 1999—2002, asst. v.p., 2002—. Piano accompanist Mellon Bankers on Broadway, Pitts., 1999—; bd. dirs., mus. chair Bulgarian-Macedonian Nat. Ctr., West Homestead, Pa., 2000—, Pitts. Folk Festival, 2000—; piano and organ accompanist St. Elizabeth-Ann Seton Children's Choir, North Huntingdon, Pa., 2000—; organist Christ United Presbyn. Ch., North Huntingdon, 2002—, Tamburitzan Performing Ensemble, 1984-88; active St. Paul Roman Cath. Cathedral, Pitts., 1993—. Mem. World Affairs Coun. Pitts., Pitts. Chamber Music Soc., Alumni of Duquesne U. Tamburitzans (past treas.), Homestead/Mifflin Twp. Hist. Soc. Democrat. Roman Catholic. Avocations: pianist, classical music, balkan music and dance, travel, sacred music. Home: # 304 5 Grandview Ave Pittsburgh PA 15211 Office: Mellon Fin Corp One Mellon Ctr 44th Fl Pittsburgh PA 15258 E-mail: costel.de@mellon.com.

COSTELLO, AMELIA FUSCO, educator; b. Schenectady, Apr. 12, 1946; d. Alfonso and Adele (D'Andrea) Fusco; m. Thomas Michael Costello, July ll, l98l; 1 stepchild, Jason Sean. BA in English, Russell Sage Coll., 1971, MS in Elem. Edn., 1974. Cert. tchr., N.Y. Tchr. English, theater arts Averill Park (N.Y.) Ctrl. Schs., 1971—; assisting in adminstrn. Averill Park H.S., 1996, asst. prin., 1997-98, tchr., mentor, 1996—2002. Contbr. articles to profl. jours. Sec. Troy (N.Y.) Charter Revision com., 1978; active Rensselaer Dem. Com., Troy, 1978-82; class agt. vol. Russell Sage Coll., sch. ombudsman, 2001-02; Averill Park Ctrl. Shared Decision Making Dist. Com., 1994-97; bd. dirs. Cath. Charities Sunnyside, 2003—. Named Labor Person of Yr., Troy Labor Coun., 1982; Filene fellow to Harvard U. Mem. AFL-CIO (pres. Troy area labor coun. 1980-82), LWV (pub. rels. chair 1981), Am. Fedn. Tchrs., N.Y. State United Tchrs. (del. 1999-2003), Averill Park Tchrs. Assn. (v.p. 1989-94, grievance com. 1990-94, 2001-03, pres. 2001-02), Russell Sage Troy Club (v.p. 1977-78), Russell Sage Alumni (admissions vol. 1992—), Capitol Dist. Assn. Women Adminstrs. (co-chair 1997-99, Spl. award 1999), Phi Delta Kappa (exec. bd. dirs.), Alpha Kappa Gamma. Roman Catholic. Avocations: reading, writing, antique collecting, church work. Office: Averill Park HS 146 Gettle Rd Ste 2 Averill Park NY 12018-9799

COSTELLO, ANDREW F. newspaper editor; b. Norwood, Mass., Sept. 18, 1947; BEngring, BA, U. Mass., 1969. Exec. editor Boston Herald, 1994—. Office: Boston Herald 1 Herald St PO Box 2096 Boston MA 02106-2096*

COSTELLO, CAROLINE, epidemiologist; b. Solihull, Eng., Dec. 23, 1973; d. Alan John and Margaret Mary Costello. BA, Agnes Scott Coll., 1995; MPH, U. Ala., 1997. HIV epidemiologist U. Ala., Birmingham, 1997—99; epidemiologist, CDC on-site contractor TRW, Inc., Atlanta, 1999—. Spkr. in field. Contbr. articles to profl. jours. Achievements include research in HIV, AIDS and female gynecological subjects.

COSTELLO, DANIEL BRIAN, lawyer, consultant; b. Arlington, Va., Apr. 23, 1950; s. James Russell and Hazel Virginia (Caudle) C.; m. Margaret Ruth Dow, June 13, 1970; children: James Brian, Rebecca Ruth, Kathleen Marie. BA, U. Va., 1972; JD, Coll. of William and Mary, 1975. Bar: Va. 1975, U.S. Dist. Ct. (ea. dist.) Va. 1979, U.S. Ct. Appeals (4th cir.) 1979, U.S. Bankruptcy Ct. (ea. dist.) Va. 1979, D.C. 1984. Reporter Globe Newspapers, Vienna, Va., 1965-68; freelance journalist Williamsburg, Va., 1972-73; news dir. Sta. WMBG, WBCI-FM, Williamsburg, 1973-76; spl. asst. atty. gen. Commonwealth of Va., Suffolk, Va., 1976-78, asst. atty. gen. Richmond, Va., 1978-80; ptnr. Dameron, Costello & Hubacher, Alexandria, Va., 1980-89, Costello & Hubacher, Alexandria, 1989-99; pvt. practice Springfield, 1999—; corp. sec., gen. counsel Olivares U.S.A., Inc., Fairfax, Va., 1999-2000, pres., 2000—. Press rels. cons. Va. Bar Assn.; spl. commr. in chancery Alexandria Cir. Ct. Author: Land Use Planning and Eminent Domain, 1997, 2d edit. 1999, Foreclosure in Virginia, 1991; co-editor, co-author The Layman's Guide to Virginia Law, 1977; editor night news Sta. WINA, 1969-72; contbr. articles to profl. jours. Mem. Va. State Bar, D.C. Bar, Soc. Alumni Coll. of William and Mary, U. Va. Alumni Soc., Rolling Hills Club. Presbyterian. Avocations: hunting, fishing, coin collecting. Office: Ste A-210 8136 Old Keene Mill Rd Springfield VA 22152-1843 E-mail: dbriancostello@att.net.

COSTELLO, DANIEL WALTER, retired bank executive; b. Mich., June 17, 1930; s. Walter William and Rose Angela (Dimond) C.; m. Sylvia Michael; children: Michael Joseph, Colleen Marie. BS in Engring. Sci, Purdue U., 1952. Various sales, mktg. and real estate positions Shell Oil Co., 1955-63; dir. real estate and constrn., planning mgr. Ford Motor Co., U.S. and Can., 1963-71; dir. real estate devel. and constrn. Ford Land Devel. Corp., Dearborn, Mich., 1971-75; chmn. Am. Express Realty Mgmt. Co., N.Y.C., 1975-82; corp. sr. v.p. real estate and gen. svcs. Am. Express Co. and subs., N.Y.C., 1975-82; exec. v.p. corp. real estate div. Bank of Am., San Francisco, 1982-95, ret. 1995. Commdr. U.S. Army, 1952-55; Korea. Mem. Nat. Assn. Rev. Appraisers (bd. dirs.), Internat. Real Estate Inst. (bd. govs.), Urban Land Inst., Nat. Assn. Corp. Real Estate Execs. (cert. master corp. real estate), Bldg. Owners and Mgrs. Assn., Meadow Club, Country Club, San Francisco Bankers Club, Theta Xi.

COSTELLO, DONALD FREDRIC, lawyer; b. Tacoma, Wash., Nov. 8, 1948; s. Bernard Peter and Ada Harriet (Morrill) C.; 1 child, Don Eric. BA, Calif. State U.-San Francisco, 1970; JD, U. Calif.-Hastings Coll., 1974. Bar: Calif. 1974, U.S. Supreme Ct. 1980. Assoc. Frolik-Filley & Schey, San Francisco, 1974-78; mem. Salomon & Costello, 1978-80; mem. law offices Donald F. Costello, Palo Alto, Calif., 1980-84, Santa Cruz, Calif., 1984—; lectr. Stanford U., 1983, U. Santa Clara, 1980; faculty Hastings Coll. Trial Advocacy, 1988—; expert witness on medical malpractice law, Calif. Senate Jud. Com., 1987. Mem. Planning Commn., City of Belmont (Calif.), 1976. Mem. ABA, Assn. Trial Lawyers Am., Calif. Trial Lawyers Assn. (contbr. articles to Forum), Am. Soc. Law and Medicine, Million Dollar Advocates Forum. Office: PO Box 8483 Santa Cruz CA 95061-8483

COSTELLO, EDWARD J., JR., arbitrator, mediator, lawyer; b. N.Y.C., Apr. 18, 1939; m. Karin Bergstrom, Aug. 21, 1981; 1 child, Catharine A. AB, Fordham U., 1961; JD, NYU, 1964. Bar: Fla. 1965, N.Y. 1967, Calif. 1969, U.S. Supreme Ct. 1973. Assoc. Donovan, Leisure, Newton & Irvine, N.Y.C., 1962-64; spl. agt. FBI, Washington, 1964-67; assoc. O'Melveny & Myers, Los Angeles, 1963, 68-72; ptnr. Costello & Walcher, Los Angeles, 1972-85, Proskauer, Rose, Los Angeles, 1985-89; professional neutral Santa Monica, Calif., 1989—. Adj. assoc. prof. law, evidence and criminal procedure Southwestern U. Sch. Law, Los Angeles, 1970-73, internat. bus. trans. U. So. Calif. Law Ctr., Los Angeles, 1973-75; judge pro tem Los Angeles Mcpl. Ct., 1971—; chmn. bd. dirs. Year Labs. Inc., Los Angeles; instr. arbitration/mediation Loyola Law Sch.; dispute resolution lectr. Am. Arbitration Assn., ABA, Calif. Continuing Edn. of the Bar, Ctr. for Profl. Edn., U. Calif. Editorial bd. mem. NYU Law Review; author: Controlling Conflict: Alternative Dispute Resolution for Business, 1996; author: (with others) Dispute Resolution Alternatives 1994, Insurance Alternative Dispute Resolution Manual, 1994. Chmn., trustee Brentwood Sch., Los Angeles, 1986-87. Root-Tilden scholar NYU. Mem. ABA (litigation and internat. law construction forum sects.), Calif. Bar Assn. (bar examiners com. 1985-86), N.Y. State Bar Assn., Fla. Bar Assn., Los Angeles County Bar Assn. (past mem. juvenile ct. and judiciary coms., trial lawyer sect.), Am. Arbitration Assn. (mem. large complex case panel, specialty panels in construction, employment, healthcare, intellectual property). Office: 620 E Channel Rd Santa Monica CA 90402-1316 E-mail: info@edcostello.com.

COSTELLO, ELVIS (DECLAN PATRICK MCMANUS), musician, songwriter; b. London, 1954; s. Ross McManus; m. Cait O'Riordan, 1986; 1 child. Composer: (songs) Alison, 1977, Watching the Detectives, 1977, (I Don't Want To Go To) Chelsea, 1979, Radio Radio, 1978, 1978; : (songs) Crawling to the USA, 1978, Radio Radio, 1978, Stranger in the House, 1978, Girls Talk, 1979, Oliver's Army, 1979, Boy With a Problem, 1982, Every Day I Write the Book, 1983; (albums) My Aim is True, 1977, This Year's Model, 1978, Armed Forces, 1979, Get Happy!!, 1980, Trust, 1980, Almost Blue, 1981, Taking Liberties, Imperial Bedroom, 1982, Goodbye Cruel World, Punch the Clock, 1984, The Best Of, 1985, Blood and Chocolate, King of America, 1986, Spike, 1989, Girls, Girls, Girls, 1990, Mighty Like a Rose, 1991, (with Steve Nieve, Pete Thomas, Bruce Thomas and Nick Lowe albums) Brutal Youth, 1994, (with the Brodsky Quartet albums) The Juliet Letters, 1993, (albums) The Very Best of Elvis Costello and the Attractions, 1994, Kojak Variety, 1995, All This Useless Beauty, 1996, Extreme Honey, 1997, Painted From Memory, 1998 (Grammy, 1999); When I Was Cruel, 2002 (nominated for 3 Grammy awards); appears in concert U.S. and Eng., 1978—, appeared in film Americathon, 1979—; actor(appeared in): Austin Powers 2: The Spy Who Shagged Me, 1999; recorded (with Burt Bacharach): I'll Never Fall in Love Again. Inducted into Rock and Roll Hall of Fame, 2003. Address: care Island Records 825 8th Ave New York NY 10019*

COSTELLO, FRANCIS WILLIAM, lawyer; b. Cambridge, Mass., Apr. 16, 1946; s. Frank George and Anna M. (Sinnott) C. BA, Columbia U., 1968, JD, 1973. Bar: N.Y. 1974, Calif. 1977. Assoc. Whitman & Ransom, N.Y.C., 1973-74, Anderson, Mori & Rabinowitz, Tokyo, 1974—76, Whitman & Ransom, L.A., 1976-82, ptnr., 1982-93, Whitman, Breed, Abbott & Morgan, L.A., 1993-2000, Holland & Knight, LLP, L.A., 2000—, mem. dirs. com., 2001—. Bd. dirs. Sunritz Corp., L.A., Japan Travel Bur. Internat., L.A. Served with U.S. Army, 1968-70, Vietnam. Mem. ABA, State Bar Calif., State Bar N.Y., L.A. County Bar Assn., Pumpkin Ridge Golf Club (Oreg.), Wilshire Country Club (L.A.), Calif. Club (L.A.). Home: 415 Knight Way La Canada Flintridge CA 91011-2725 E-mail: fcostell@hklaw.com.

COSTELLO, JAMES JOSEPH, retired electrical manufacturing company executive; b. Boston, Feb. 15, 1930; s. James Joseph and Jennie Theresa (Boyle) C.; m. Mary Virginia Bird, May 7, 1960; children: James, Susan, Maureen, Thomas, Daniel. BSBA, Northeastern U., 1953. With GE, various locations, 1956-71, fin. mgr. AC Motor divsn. Schenectady, 1971-76, fin. mgr. components and materials group Pittsfield, Mass., 1976-77, staff exec. tech. systems and materials sector Fairfield, Conn., 1977-79, v.p., compt., 1979-92; ret., 1992. Trustee Sacred Heart U., Fairfield, Conn.; dir. nat. coun. Northeastern U., Boston. Officer USN, 1953-56. Mem. Fin. Execs. Inst.

COSTELLO, JERRY F., JR., congressman, former county official; b. Sept. 25, 1949; County bd. chmn. St. Clair County, Ill.; dir. ct. svcs. and probation 20th Jud. Cir. Campaign; chmn. Heart Assn., Belleville, Ill., 1983; vice chmn. Ill. div. United Way, 1984, chmn., 1985; mem. U.S. Congress from 21st (now 12th) Ill. Dist., 1988—; former mem. budget com.; mem. transp., infrastructure and sci. coms. Bd. dirs. Ill. Ctr. for Autism; active St. Clair County Big Bros./Big Sisters, Belleville Women's Crisis Ctr., Children's Ctr. for Behavioral Devel.; helped establish St. Clair County chpt. Vets. Outreach Info. Ctr.; mem. East St. Louis Econ. Opportunity Commn., Ill.; vice chmn. Southwestern Ill. Bus. Devel. Fin. Corp., 1985—; bd. dirs. So. Ill. Leadership Council; pres. Urban Counties Council of Ill. Recipient cert. of Appreciation, Bus. and Profl. Women's Assn., 1985; honored Citizens League for Adequate Social Services; 1985 AAHMES Court #84, Daus. ISIS Ann. Humanitarian award, Gene Hughes award Ill. Ct. Services and Probation Assn. Democrat. Office: US Ho of Reps 2454 Rayburn House Off Bldg Washington DC 20515-1312*

COSTELLO, JOHN, military officer; b. Pottsville, Pa., Apr. 24, 1947; s. Samuel J. and Blanche (McAndrew) C.; m. Michele Marie Vonnegut, Jan. 25, 1970; children: Patrick M., Adrienne. BA in Polit. Sci., Citadel, 1969; MA in Fgn. Affairs, U. Va., 1975; M of Mil. Arts and Sci., Command and Gen. Staff Coll., Ft. Leavenworth, Kans., 1982; ed. program for sr. execs., Harvard U., 1996. Commd. 2nd lt. U.S. Army, 1969, advanced through grades to lt. gen., 1998; comdr. 1st bn. 59th Air Def. Arty., Schwabach, Germany, 1984-86; chief materiel and logistics Combat Devels., Ft. Bliss, Tex., 1987-88; comdr. 35th Air Def. Arty. Brig., Ft. Lewis, Wash., 1988-90; chief of staff 32nd Army Air Def. Command, Darmstadt, Germany, 1990-92, comdg. gen., 1992-93; asst. divsn. comdr. 1st Armored Divsn., Germany, 1993; dir. roles and missions Office of Dep. Chief of Staff Ops., Washington, 1994; comdg. gen. U.S. Army Air Def. Ctr., Ft. Bliss, 1995-98; comdr. U.S. Army Space and Missile Def. Command, Arlington, Va., 1998-99, lt. gen., 1998—. Contbr. articles to mil. publs. Decorated D.S.M., Legion of Merit with 2 bronze oak leaf clusters; recipient Star award El Paso (Tex.) C. of C., 1997. Mem. Citadel Alumni Assn., Rotary (El Paso), El Paso Citadel Club (v.p.). Avocations: reading, tennis. Address: USA/SMDC Crystal Mall 4 1941 Jefferson Davis Hwy Arlington VA 22202

COSTELLO, JOHN H., III, business and marketing executive; b. Akron, Ohio, June 2, 1947; s. John H. Jr. and Lia Costello; children from previous marriage, Michael, Jeffrey, Matthew. BS in Indsl. Mgmt., Akron U., 1968; MBA, Mich. State U., 1970. Mktg. dir. Procter & Gamble Co., Cin., 1971-84; sr. v.p. Pepsi-Cola USA, Purchase, N.Y., 1984-86; exec. v.p. Wells, Rich, Greene, Inc., N.Y.C., 1986-88; pres., chief oper. officer Nielsen Mktg. Rsch. U.S.A., Chgo., 1988-93; sr. exec. v.p. Sears, Roebuck & Co., Hoffman Estates, Ill., 1993-98; pres. Auto Nation, Inc., Ft. Lauderdale, Fla., 1999—; CEO MVP.com, 1999—, Bombay Co. Sr. mktg. execs. panel Conf. Bd., N.Y.C., 1985-87; industry speaker on bus. trends and issues, 1985—; bd. dirs. The Quaker Oats Co, Sears Can. Mem. exec. bd. N.E. Ill. coun. Boy Scouts Am., 1993-97; trustee Multiple Sclerosis Soc., Chgo., 1990—, vice chmn., 1995—; bd. dirs. Nat. Multiple Sclerosis Soc., 1989—, chair fundraising, 1990-94, mem. exec. com., 1990—, chair nominating com., 1996—. Mem. Assn. Nat. Advertisers (bd. dirs. 1995—, vice chmn. 1998, chmn. 1999), Direct Ad Coun. (bd. dirs. 1996—, vice chmn. 1998), Direct Retail Advt. and Mktg. Assn. (bd. dirs. 1995—, Retail Mktg. Hall of Fame 1997), Lake Forest Club, Econ. Club Chgo., Conway Farms Golf Club. Episcopalian. Avocations: skiing, golf, travel. Home: 860 Gloucester Xing Lake Forest IL 60045-4902 Office: Republic Industries Auto Nation Inc 110 SE 6th St Fort Lauderdale FL 33301-5000

COSTELLO, JOHN WILLIAM, lawyer; b. Chgo., Apr. 16, 1947; s. William John and June Ester (O'Neill) C.; m. Maureen Grace Matthews, June 13, 1970; children— Colleen, William, Erin, Owen. BA, John Carroll U., 1969; JD, DePaul U., 1972. Bar: U.S. Dist. Ct. (no. dist.) Ill. 1982. Assoc. Arvey, Hodes, Costello & Burman, Chgo., 1972-76; ptnr., 1976-90, ptnr. Wildman, Harrold Allen & Dixon, 1990—. Co-author: (manual) The Bankrupcy Reform Act of 1978, 1981. Served to capt. U.S. Army, 1972-73. Mem. ABA (bus. bankruptcy com., jurisdiction and venue and secured creditors subcoms.), Ill. State Bar Assn. (former vice chmn., chmn. comml. banking and bankrupcy law sect. 1979-81), Am. Bankruptcy Inst., Turnaround Mgmt. Assn. (former bd. dirs. Midwest sect.). Democrat. Roman Catholic. Office: Wildman Harrold Aller & Dixon 225 W Wacker Dr Chicago IL 60606-1224

COSTELLO, JOSEPH MICHAEL, lawyer; b. N.Y.C., Feb. 28, 1925; s. Michael J. and Mary J. Costello; m. Marianne K. Costello, Oct. 26, 1957; children: Michael, Kelly, J. McGarry, Patrick, Irene, Brendan, Marianne. BBA, Iona Coll., 1948; LLD, Fordham U., 1951. Bar: N.Y. 1952, U.S. Dist. Ct. (ea. and so. dists.) N.Y. 1954, U.S. Supreme Ct. 1958. Assoc. William H. Morris, N.Y.C., 1952-55; ptnr. Hanrahan & Costello, N.Y.C., 1955-60; sr. ptnr. Costello, Ward, Tirabasso & Shea, N.Y.C., 1960-65, D'Amato, Costello & Shea, N.Y.C., 1965-78, Costello & Shea, N.Y.C., 1978-96, Costello, Shea and Caffney, N.Y.C., 1996—. With U.S. Army, 1943-45. Fellow Am. Coll. Trial Lawyers; mem. ABA, N.Y. County Lawyers Assn., N.Y. State Bar Assn. (chmn. trial lawyers sect. exec. com.). Office: Costello Shea & Caffney 44 Wall St Fl 11 New York NY 10005-2401

COSTELLO, KELLY LYNN, lawyer; b. Cin., Nov. 30, 1973; d. Patrick and Vicki Costello. BS magna cum laude, Boston U., 1995; JD with honors, George Washington U., 1998. Bar: Ill. 1998, Calif. 2001. Assoc. Katten Muchin Zavis Rosenman, L.A., 1998—. Mem. ABA, L.A. Co. Bar Assn., Irish Am. Bar Assn. Office: Katten Muchin Zavis 2029 Century Park East Ste 2600 Los Angeles CA 90067

COSTELLO, KENNETH R., lawyer; m. Janet Costello: children: Quinn, Ian. BA, Loyola U., L.A., 1975; JD magna cum laude, U. Santa Clara, 1978. Ptnr. Thelen, Marrin, Johnson & Bridges, L.A., 1986-92, Loeb & Loeb LLP, L.A., 1992-98, Jenkens & Gilchrist, L.A., 1998—. Spkr. in field. Co-author: Franchising Law: Practice and Forms, 1996, Franchising: Legal Compliance Check-Ups: Business Clients, 1985; contbr. articles to bus. and profl. jours.; mem. bd. editors Law Rev., U. Santa Clara, 1978. Office: Jenkens & Gilchrist LLP 12100 Wilshire Blvd Fl 15 Los Angeles CA 90025-7120

COSTELLO, ROBERT JOSEPH, lawyer; b. N.Y.C., Jan. 4, 1948; s. Peter John and Barbara Theresa (Sheeran) C.; m. Alice Boyle, Aug. 31, 1975 (dec. 1990); children— Robert Ian, Maura Alison, Megan Ailish; m. Maureen Kearns, May 3, 1993. B.A., Fordham U., 1969, J.D., 1972. Bar: N.Y. 1973. Assoc., Dewey, Ballantine et al, N.Y.C., 1972-75; asst. U.S. atty. So. Dist. N.Y., N.Y.C., 1975-80, dep. chief criminal div., 1980-81; ptnr. Lumbard & Phelan, N.Y.C., 1981-82, Phelan & Costello, N.Y.C., 1982-94, Gibney, Anthony & Flaherty L.L.P., N.Y.C., 1994—. Mem. ABA, N.Y. State Bar Assn., Assn. Bar City of N.Y. Roman Catholic. Home: 233 Chapel Rd Manhasset NY 11030-3728 Office: Gibney Anthony & Flaherty LLP 665 5th Ave New York NY 10022-5305

COSTELLO, THOMAS JOSEPH, bishop; b. Camden, N.Y., Feb. 23, 1929; s. James G. and Ethel A. (Dupont) C.. Lic. in Sacred Theology, Cath. U. Am., 1954, JCB, 1960. Ordained priest Roman Cath. Ch., 1954. Sec. Diocesan Tribunal, Diocese of Syracuse, 1958; supt. schs. Cath. Diocese of Syracuse, 1960—75; pastor Our Lady Lourdes Ch., Syracuse, NY, 1975—78; aux. bishop Syracuse, 1978—. Roman Catholic. Home: 1515 Midland Ave Syracuse NY 13205-1447 Office: PO Box 511 240 E Onondaga St Syracuse NY 13201

COSTENBADER, CHARLES MICHAEL, lawyer; b. Jersey City, Dec. 9, 1935; s. Edward William and Marie Veronica Costenbader; m. Barbara Ann Wilson, Aug. 1, 1959; children: Charles Michael Jr., William E., Mary E. BS in Acctg., Mt. St. Mary's Coll., 1957; JD, Seton Hall U., 1960; LLM in Taxation, NYU, 1968. Bar: N.J 1960; U.S Tax Ct. 1961, U.S. Ct. Appeals (3d cir.) 1973, U.S. Supreme Ct. 1983. Trial atty. office regional counsel IRS, N.Y.C., 1961—69; tax assoc. Shanley & Fisher, Newark, 1969—76; tax ptnr. Stryker, Tams & Dill, Newark, 1976—98; spl. counsel McCarter & English, Newark, 1998—. Mem. N.J. State and Local Expenditure and Revenue Commn., 1985-88. Mem. ABA, N.J. Bar Assn. (chmn. taxation sect. 1984-85), N.J. State C. of C. (chmn. tax coun. com. 1988—), Am. Coll. Tax Counsel. Republican. Roman Catholic. Avocations: gardening, reading, sports. Home: 8 Neptune Pl Colonia NJ 07067-2502 Office: Gateway Four Ctr 100 Mulberry St Newark NJ 07102-4056 E-mail: ccostenbader@mccarter.com.

COSTES, NICHOLAS CONSTANTINE, aerospace technologist, university educator, retired government official; b. Athens, Greece, Sept. 20, 1926; came to U.S., 1948, naturalized, 1959; s. Constantine Nicholas and Anna (Papadopoulou) C.; m. Polytime Andros, Nov. 22, 1958; children: Constantine Nicholas, Anna Amalia, Christina Smaragtha. Diploma, Sci. Sch., Athens Coll., 1945; student, Athens Nat. Tech. U, 1945-48; AB, Darthmouth Coll., 1950, MSC.E. (George W. Davis scholar), 1951; A.M., M.E.N., Harvard U., 1962; MS, N.C. State U., 1955, PhD (Ford Found. fellow), 1965. Registered profl. engr., N.C., Ill. Teaching fellow dept. civil engring. N.C. State U., Raleigh, 1951-53, instr., 1962-63; materials engr. N.C. State Hwy. and Pub. Works Commn., Raleigh, 1953-56; research civil engr. U.S. Army Cold Regions Research and Engring. Lab., Hanover, N.H., 1956-62; sr. research scientist space sci. lab Marshall Space Flight Center, NASA, Huntsville, Ala., 1965-98, team leader Apollo II Soil Mechanics Investigation Sci. Team, co-prin. investigator Apollo 12, 13 Lunar Geology Experiment, Apollo 14-17 Soil Mechanics Expt., 1991—, prin. investigator, co-investigator, project scientist Mechanics of Granular Materials Microgravity Expt., 1991—. Cons. geotech. engring., 1965—; adj. prof. U. Colo., Boulder, 1998. Contbr. articles and tech. reports to profl. jours. Recipient Dartmouth Soc. Engrs. prize, 1951; recipient NASA awards including cert. of appreciation, 1970, Group Achievement award Lunar Roving Vehicle Team, 1971, invention award, 1971, Astronauts' Silver Snoopy award, 1972, dirs. commendation achievement, 1973, Group Achievemnt award Flow Process Modeling Space Shuttle Main Engine, 1985, Group Achievement awards Environs Definition of Space Shuttle Solid Rocket Motor Team, Challenger Incident, 1986, Mechanics of Granular Materials (MGM) Microgravity Expt. Fellow ASCE (life, Norman medal 1972, chmn. program com. aerospace council 1973-75, exec. com. aerospace div. 1976-82, chmn. 1980-81, profl. coordination com. 1982—), AIAA (assoc. fellow, dir. Ala./Miss. sect. 1976-79, Outstanding Aerospace Engr. award 1976, Martin Schilling award 1979, Herman Oberth award 1998); mem. NSPE, AAAS, Am. Geophys. Union, Dartmouth Soc. Engrs., Soc. Harvard Engrs. and Scientists, Assn. Civil Engrs. Greece (hon.), N.Y. Acad. Scis., Am. Men and Women of Sci., Sigma Xi, Phi Kappa Phi, Chi Epsilon Greek Orthodox. Home: 4216 Huntington Rd SE Huntsville AL 35802-1144

COSTIGAN, CONSTANCE FRANCES, artist, educator; b. Hoboken, N.J., July 3, 1935; d. Charles Francis and Joan Aletta (Visser) C.; m. John Francis Christian, June 6, 1959 (div. 1972); m. Michael Krausz, May 14, 1976. BS, Simmons Coll. and Boston Mus. Sch. Fine Arts, 1957; MA, Am. U., 1965; postgrad., U. Calif.-Berkeley, 1971, U. Va.-Fairfax, 1968-69, U. D.C., 1972-73. Cert. tchr. Va. Designer Smithsonian Instn., Washington, 1957-59, mus. svcs. staff mem., 1962-68, drawing and design instr., 1971-76; art and crafts instr. Arlington County (Va.) Pub. Schs., 1970-75; prof. fine arts George Washington U., Washington, 1976—2002, prof. fine arts emeritus, 2003—; curator Arlington Art Ctr., Va., 1980; disting. vis. prof. Am. U. in Cairo, 1980-81; vis. prof. in drawing Haystack Mt. Sch. Crafts, Deer Isle, Maine, 1990. Jurist and judge art show D.C. area, 1975, 76, 90, 82, area show Del. Ctr. for Contemporary Arts, 1985; judge art show Sussex County Arts Coun. Mems. Show, 1991. Author: Leonardo, 1982, Elements of Art: Line, 1980; one-woman shows Visual Arts Gallery, Habitat Ctr. for the Arts, Dehli India, 2003, Lavinia Ctr., Milton, Del., 2003; group shows Corkran Gallery, Rehoboth Art League, Del., 1998, Soho 20 Gallery, N.Y.C., 1997, Hampshire Coll. Gallery Hampshire Coll., Amherst, Mass., 1996, Dimock Gallery, George Washington U., 1987, Franz Bader Gallery, Washington, 1985, 90, No. Va. C.C., Alexandria, 1983, Barbara Fiedler Gallery, Washington, 1979, 82, Phillips Collection, Washington, 1977, Gulbenkian Gallery, U. Kent, Canterbury, Eng., 1975, Talbot Rice Arts Ctr., Edinburgh, Scotland, 1974, Design Ctr. Gallery, Cleve., 1974, Annenburg Arts Ctr., Phila., 1973; represented pub. collections Hirschhorn Mus. and Sculpture Garden, Washington, Phillips Collection, Washington, U. Iowa Mus., Iowa City, Dimock Gallery, George Washington U., Del. Mus. Art, others; included in numerous pvt. collections USA and abroad. Sec. steering com. Del. chpt. Nat. Mus. for Women in the Arts, Newark, 1997—01. Named to Nat. Mus. for Women in Arts to represent Del., 1998; fellow, Macdowell Colony, 1977, Ossabaw Island project, 1980; grantee, Lester Hereward Cooke Found., 1978—79, GSAS Facilitating Fund, 1990. Fellow Royal Soc. Arts; mem. Am. Craft Coun., Coll. Art Assn. Home: 210 NE Market St Lewes DE 19958-1574 Office: 210 NE Market ST Lewes DE 20037-2515

COSTIGAN, EDWARD JOHN, investment banker; b. St. Louis, Oct. 31, 1914; s. Edward J. and Elizabeth Keane; m. Sara Louise Guth, Mar. 30, 1940 (dec. Nov. 1988); children: Sally, Edward John, James (dec.), Betsy, Robert, David, Louise; m. Mildred F. Fabick, Dec. 27, 1995. AB, St. Louis U., 1935; MBA, Stanford U., 1937. Analyst, v.p. Whitaker & Co., St. Louis, 1937-43; ptnr. Edward D. Jones & Co., 1943-72; sr. v.p. Stifel Nicolaus & Co., Inc., St. Louis, 1972-74, pres., 1974-79, vice chmn., 1979-83, emeritus, 1983, ret., 2001. Gov. Nat. Assn. Securities Dealers, 1967-70, Investment Bankers Assn., 1968-69, Midwest Stock Exch., Chgo., 1962-64; bd. dirs. 12 cos. Trustee Calvary Cemetery Assn., St. Louis, 1956— Mem. St. Louis Soc. Fin. Analysts (pres. 1956), Harvard Club St. Louis (pres. 1955), Bellerive Country Club, Mo. Athletic Club, Old Warson Country Club, Noonday Club, University Club. Republican. Roman Catholic. Office: 501 N Broadway Fl 8 Saint Louis MO 63102-2102

COSTIGAN-KERNS, LOUISE E. musician; arrived in U.S., 1971; d. Thomas John Costigan and Beatrice Mary Trono; m. John S. Breen, Aug. 20, 1983 (div. Nov. 1991); m. Ralph Charles Kerns, Sept. 4, 1994; children: Stephen James, Jacqueline Victoria. MusB in Piano Performance, New Eng. Conservatory Music, 1975, MusM in Piano Performance, 1977. Cert. Music Tchr.'s Nat. Assn. Piano faculty preparatory divsn. New Eng. Conservatory, Boston, 1975—94, chairperson, musical dir. opera studio ext. divsn., 1978—94; opera coach Opera San Jose, 1995—96; part-time chorus accompanist San Francisco Symphony, 2000—. Opera coach/coord. opera dept. Boston U., 1983—84; piano prof. Phillips Exeter (N.H.) Acad., 1988—93; mem. long range planning com. New Eng. Conservatory Music, 1988—90; artist in residence Brandeis U., Waltham, Mass., 1990—94; freelance concert pianist and accompanist, San Francisco, 1994—; opera coach San Francisco Internat. Summer Music Festival, San Francisco Conservatory Music, 2000—. Grantee, Boston Arts Lottery, 1985, 1986. Mem.: New Eng. Piano Tchrs. Assn. (bd. mem. 1989—92), Nat. Opera Assn. (gov. New Eng. 1990—94, gov. Calif. 1995—98), Pi Kappa Lambda. Home: 890 Regent Ct San Carlos CA 94070 Office: Music Tchr's Nat Assn Carew Tower 441 vine St Ste 505 Cincinnati OH 45202-2811

COSTIKYAN, EDWARD N. lawyer; b. Weehawken, N.J., Sept. 14, 1924; s. Mihran Nazar and Berthe (Muller) C.; m. Frances Holmgren, 1950 (div. 1975); chldren: Gregory, Emilie; m. Barbara Heine, Mar. 6, 1977. AB, Columbia U., 1947, LLB, 1949. Bar: N.Y. 1949, U.S. Dist. Ct. (so. dist.) N.Y. 1950, U.S. Ct. Appeals (2d cir.) 1950, U.S. Supreme Ct. 1964. Law sec. to judge Harold R. Medina U.S. Dist. Ct., N.Y.C., 1949-51; ptnr. Paul, Weiss, Rifkind, Wharton & Garrison, N.Y.C., 1960-93, of counsel, 1994—. Spl. advisor to mayor on sch. and borough governance City of N.Y., 1994-96, chairperson mayor's investigative commn. on sch. safety, 1995-96; mem. Commn. on Integrity in Govt., N.Y.C., 1986, mem. joint com. on jud. adminstrn., 1985-92; adj. fellow Ctr. for Edn. Innovation, 1997—. Author: Behind Closed Doors: Politics in the Public Interest, 1966, How to Win Votes: The Politics of 1980, 1980; co-author: Re-Structuring the Government of New York City, 1972, New Strategies for Regional Cooperation, 1973; rsch. editor Columbia Law Rev.; mem. editl. bd. City Jour., 1992—; mem. bd. editors N.Y. Law Jour., 1976—; contbr. articles on legal and polit. subjects to profl. publs. Chmn. N.Y. State Task Force on N.Y.C. Juristiction and Structure, 1971-72; vice chmn. State Charter Revision for N.Y.C., 1972-77; county leader New York County Dem. Com., 1962-64; Dem. presdl. elector, 1964, 88; trustee, mem. exec. com., chmn. alumni adv. bd. Columbia U., 1981-93, trustee emeritus, 1993—; bd. dirs., mem. coun. Mcpl. Art Soc., 1993-98; chmn. bd. dirs. N.Y. Found. for Sr. Citizens, 1993—. 1st lt. inf. U.S. Army, 1943-46. Recipient William J. Brennan Jr. award for Outstanding Cont. to Pub. Discourse, 1997. Fellow Am. Coll. Trial Lawyers; mem. Assn. of Bar of City of N.Y. (mem. exec. com. 1986-90), Century Club. Unitarian Universalist. Home: 50 Sutton Pl S New York NY 10022-4167 Office: Paul Weiss Rifkind Wharton & Garrison Ste 12J 1285 Avenue Of The Americas Fl 21 New York NY 10019-6028

COSTIN, J(OSEPH) LAURENCE, JR., information services executive; b. Chgo., Mar. 14, 1941; s. Joseph Laurence and Maribel (Cummings) C.; m. Joan Gayley, June 20, 1964 (dec. June 1998); children: Jennifer, Michael. BA, U. Chgo., 1966. Divsn. mgr. Marshall Field and Co., Chgo., 1967-81; sr. v.p. Seligman and Latz, Inc., N.Y.C., 1981-83; exec. v.p. CCC Info. Svcs., Inc., Chgo., 1983-93, vice-chmn., 1993—. Lifetime trustee emeritus ICAR Edn. Found.; mem. vis. com. on the coll. U. Chgo.; trustee Omega chpt. Psi Upsilon Fraternity; immediate past pres. bd. dirs. Westmoreland Country Club Scholarship Found. With Ill. Army N.G., 1963—69. Mem.: Am. Ins. Svcs. Group (com. automobile phys. damage), Contemporary Arts Coun., East Bank Club, Chgo. Curling Club, Westmoreland Country Club (bd. dirs.). Roman Catholic. Avocations: golf, curling, contemporary art, urban history. Office: World Trade Ctr Chgo 444 Merchandise Mart Plz Chicago IL 60654-1005

COSTIN, REA-SILVIA, civil engineer; b. Salonika, Greece, Oct. 24, 1946; d. Stefan and Steliana Costin. MS in Civil Engring., Faculty of Hydrotech. Constrn., Bucharest, 1969; PhD cand., U. Fla., 1985. Registered profl. engr., Fla. Design engr. Inst. of Mining, Bucharest, Romania, 1969—75; project engr. Machine Constrn., Bucharest, 1975—80; engr. III Fla. Dept. Environ. Regulation, Jacksonville, 1981—83; design engr. Aikenhead Engring., Jacksonville, 1983—88; project engr. Smith & Gilespie Engrs., Jacksonville, 1988—90; project mgr. City of Jacksonville, 1990—. Author: Short Stories: The Story of a Refugee, 1997, poetry to poetry.com web site (Best Poets of 2001, Best Poets of 2002), (poetry) Hoble House Leader, 2003. Named Poet Laureate, The Internat. Libr. Poetry, 2002; recipient Editors Choice award, Poetry.com, 2001, 2002, Pres'. award for Lit. Excellence, Nat. Authors Registry, 2003. Fellow: Fla. Engring. Soc.; mem.: NSPE, Am. Pub. Wks. Assn. Avocations: reading, writing, running, weightlifting, skiing. Home: 1645 Flagler Ave Jacksonville FL 32207-3119

COSTLEY, BILL (BILL COSTLEY), poet, writer; b. Salem, Mass., May 21, 1942; s. William and Mary (Stefania) K.; m. Joan Helen Budyk, June 6, 1964 (div. Sept. 1985); children: Maya, Alex William; life ptnr. Carolin Combs. AB, Boston Coll., 1963. Pub. rels. dir. Wellesley (Mass.) Symphony Orch., 1986—. Author: (poetry) KNOSH I CIR, 1964-75, R(A)G(A)S, 1978, A(Y)S(H)A, 1989, TERRAZO, 1986, SICILICONIA, 1995; prodr., host: Poetry Corner, AT&T Comcast Cable TV. Co-founder Lynn (Mass.) Voices Collaborative, 1979--, Wellesley Peace Group, Mass., 1987--; mem. Wellesley Cultural Coun., 2002—. Recipient poetry performance/presentation award Mass. Cultural Coun. through Wellesley Cultural Coun., 2000. Mem. Robinson Jeffers Assn., Nat. Writers Union. Avocation: travel. Home: One Sunset Rd Wellesley MA 02482-4670 E-mail: billcostley@yahoo.com.

COSTNER, CHARLES LYNN, retired civil engineer; b. Banner, Miss., Aug. 15, 1928; s. Charles Arthur and Clyde Margarite (Head) C.; m. Sara Lynn McGuire, May 26, 1951; 1 child, Jeffrey Lynn. BSCE, U. Miss., 1951, postgrad., 1955. Registered profl. engr., Miss., Tex. Engr. E.I. Dupont, Wilmington, Del., 1951-53, Farnsworth & Chambers, Baton Rouge, 1953—54, Ross E. Cox, Baton Rouge, 1955—65, Brown & Butler Cons. Engrs., Baton Rouge, 1965—83; pres., ptnr. Brown & Butler Inc., Baton Rouge, 1983—98; ret., 1998. Contbr. articles to mags. Airport Services Management, Ports 83, ASCE. With U.S. Army, 1946-48, Korea. Republican. Baptist. Home: 114 Hillside Dr Oxford MS 38655-5443 E-mail: omclc@bellsouth.net.

COSTNER, KEVIN, actor; b. L.A., Jan. 18, 1955; m. Cindy Silva (div.); children: Annie, Lily, Joe. Degree in mktg., Calif. State U., Fullerton, 1978. Owner prodn. co. TIG Prodns. Film appearances include Sizzle Beach U.S.A., 1974, Shadows Run Black, 1981, Chasing Dreams, 1981, Frances, 1982, Night Shift, 1982, Table for Five, 1983, Stacy's Knights 1983, The Gunrunner, 1983, The Big Chill, 1983, American Flyers, 1985, Fandango, 1985, Silverado, 1985, The Untouchables, 1987, No Way Out, 1987, Bull Durham, 1988, Field of Dreams, 1989, Revenge (also exec. prodr.), 1990, Dances with Wolves (also co-prodr., dir.) 1990 (Acad. award for best dir. 1991, Star of Tomorrow award Nat. Assn. Theatre Owners 1987, Hasty Pudding Man of Yr., Harvard U. 1990, Acad. award for best picture, 1991, Acad. award nominee best actor 1991, Dir's. Guild Am. award Best Dir. Feature Film 1991), Robin Hood: Prince of Thieves, 1991, JFK, 1991, Truth or Dare, 1991, The Bodyguard (also co-prodr.) 1992, A Perfect World, 1993, Wyatt Earp, 1994, The War, 1994, Waterworld (also co-prodr.), 1995, Tin Cup, 1996, The Postman (also prodr., dir.) 1997, Message in a Bottle (also prodr.), 1999, For Love of the Game, 1999, Play It to the Bone, 1999, Thirteen Days, 2000 (also prodr.), 3000 Miles to Graceland, 2001, Dragonfly, 2002, Open Range, 2003 (also prodr., dir.); host, exec. prodr. (TV series) 500 Nations; co-prodr. China Moon, 1993; exec. prodr. Rapa Nui, 1994; TV movies include Testament (PBS) 1983. Office: TIG Prodns 4000 Warner Blvd Bldg 5 Burbank CA 91522-0001*

COSTON, BRENDA MARIA BONE, language arts educator; b. Pensacola, Fla., Sept. 25, 1961; d. Marvin Ralph and Irmgard Maria (Minna) Bone; m. Glen Howard Coston, Dec. 21, 1994. AA in Tchr. Edn., Pensacola Jr. Coll., Fla., 1981; BA in English and Comm. Arts, U. West Fla., 1983, MA in English, 1984; MS in Counseling and Human Devel., Troy State U., Pensacola, 1994. Cert. K-12 counseling, tchr. 6-12 English, tchr. 5-9 social sci. Tchr. 8th grade English Warrington Middle Sch., Pensacola, Fla., 1992—93; adj. instr. English Pensacola Jr. Coll., 1995—. Recipient Tchg. Excellence (Golden Apple) award, Pensacola Jr. Coll., 1999—2000, Award of Support for Student Support Svcs., 2002. Mem.: Phi Theta Kappa. Avocations: reading, writing, poetry, feeding wild animals. Home: 3022 N 14th Ave Milton FL 32583-5885

COSUE, LAMBERTO GUTIERREZ, III, internist; b. Manila, May 8, 1964; arrived in U.S., 1992; s. Lamberto C. Jr. and Celeste (Gutierrez) C. BS in Med. Tech. cum laude, U. Santo Tomas, Manila, 1985, MD, 1989. Cert. in internal medicine. Intern Luth. Med. Ctr., Bklyn., 1992-93, resident in internal medicine, 1993-95; med. staff North Sunflower County Hosp., Ruleville, Miss., 1995—. Dir. emergency rm. dept. North Sunflower County Hosp., Ruleville, 1997—98, chief of med. staff, 2000—01. Mem. ACP, AMA, Miss. State Med. Assn. Office: North Sunflower County Hosp PO Box 369 840 N Oak Ave Ruleville MS 38771-3227

COSULICH, PAOLO ULISSE, shipping company executive, consultant; b. Buenos Aires, May 5, 1916; s. Antonio N. and Maria (Gerolimich) C.; m. Matatia Luisella, July 10, 1946; children: Elisabetta, Elena, Augusto, Giovanna. DSc in Econs., U. Trieste, 1940. Co-founder Fratelli Cosulich Shipping Agts., 1946—; chmn. Cosulich A.G., Zurich, Switzerland, 1976; consul of Malta Genoa, 1970—; chmn. Irital Shipping, 1992, Link Trading Co., 1997, Coscos Shipping Agy., 1997. Bd. dirs. Voltri Terminal Europa, Genoa, Mulitport Ship Agys. Network, London. Capt. Italian Navy, 1940-45. Mem. Propeller Club (bd. dirs.), Rotary (bd. dirs.). Avocation: gardening. Home: Via Causa 6-2 16145 Genoa Italy Office: 41 Ponte Morosini 16126 Genoa Italy E-mail: management@ge.cosulich.it.

COSUMANO, JOSEPH, military officer, government agency administrator; b. Shreveport, La. BS in Indsl. Tech., MS in Indsl. Tech., Northwestern State Coll., Natchitoches, La.; grad., Army Aviation Sch., Air Command and Staff Coll., Def. Systems Mgmt. Coll., Indsl. Coll. of Armed Forces; grad. Mgmt. Exec. Course, Yale U. Commd. 2d lt. U.S. Army, advanced through grades to lt. gen.; comdr. 1st Armored Divsn., Germany, Hqrs. Battery and Hawk Battery, Korea, 1st Bn., 55th Air Def. Artillery, 5th Mechanized Divsn., Ft. Polk, La., 1984—86, 108th Air Def. Artillery Brigade, 32d Army Air Def. Command, U.S. Army Europe, 1990—92; dep. commdg. gen. U.S. Army Air Def. Artillery Ctr. and Sch., Ft. Bliss, Tex.; program mgr. Nat. Missile Def. Joint Program Office; asst. dep. chief of staff for ops. and plans Force Devel., U.S. Army, Washington; dir. task force objective force; commdg. gen. U.S. Army Space and Missile Def. Command and U.S. Army Space Command, Arlington, Va., 2001—. Decorated Legion of Merit with 2 oak leaf clusters, Army Commendation medal with 3 oak leaf clusters. Office: US Army Space and Missile Def PO box 15280 Arlington VA 22215-0280

COTA, JOHN FRANCIS, utility executive; b. Mason City, Iowa, Oct. 28, 1924; s. Sylvester D. and Ina (McAlpine) C.; m. Margaret Louise Allen, Oct. 22, 1945; children— David J., Julie A., Daniel A., Kim F. Student, Drake U., 1942; BS, Iowa State U., 1947. Cadet engr. Iowa Power & Light Co., Des Moines, 1948, project mgr., 1949, chief gas engr., 1954-57; v.p., gen. mgr. Winnebago Natural Gas Corp., Kaukauna, Wis., 1957-58; pres., dir. Natural Gas Distbrs., Inc., Madison, Wis., 1958; asst. v.p. Wis. Gas Co., Milw., 1960-64, v.p. ops., 1964-69, exec. v.p., 1969-75; dir., 1968-75; v.p., asst. to chmn. Am. Natural Resources, Detroit, 1975-78; v.p. engring. and constrn. Mich. Wis. Pipe Line Co., Detroit, 1978-86; cons. ANR Pipe Line Co., 1984; ret., 1986; pres. Marjac Investments, Inc., San Diego, 1993—. Served with USNR, 1942-45. Mem. Am., Midwest gas assns., Mich. Utilities Assn. Clubs: Bernardo Heights Country, Rancho Bernardo Swim and Tennis (San Diego). Home: 13193 Polvera Ave San Diego CA 92128-1147

COTCHETT, JOSEPH WINTERS, lawyer, author; b. Chgo., Jan. 6, 1939; s. Joseph Winters and Jean (Renaud) C.; children— Leslie F., Charles P., Rachael E., Quinn Carlyle, Camilla E. BS in Engring., Calif. Poly. Coll., 1960; LLB, U. Calif. Hastings Coll. Law, 1964. Bar: Calif. 1965, DC 1980. Ptnr. Cotchett, Pitre, Simon & McCarthy, Burlingame, Calif., 1965—. Mem. Calif. Jud. Coun., 1975-77, Calif. Commn. on Jud. Performance, 1985-89, Commn. 2020 Jud. Coun., 1991-94; select com. on jud. retirement, 1992—. Author: (with R. Cartwright) California Products Liability Actions, 1970, (with F. Haight) California Courtroom Evidence, 1972, (with A. Elkind) Federal Courtroom Evidence, 1976, (with Frank Rothman) Persuasive Opening Statements and Closing Arguments, 1988, (with Stephen Pizzo) The Ethics Gap, 1991, (with Gerald Uelmen) California Courtroom Evidence Foundations, 1993; contbr. articles to profl. jours. Chmn. San Mateo County Heart Assn., 1967; pres. San Mateo Boys and Girls Club, 1971; bd. dirs. U. Calif. Hastings Law Sch., 1981-93. With Intelligence Corps, U.S. Army, 1960-61; col. JAGC, USAR, ret. Fellow Am. Bar Found., Am. Bd. Trial Advs., Am. Coll. Trial Lawyers, Internat. Acad. Trial Lawyers, Internat. Soc. of Barristers, Nat. Bd. Trial Advs. (diplomate civil trial adv.), State Bar Calif. (gov. 1972-75). Clubs: Commonwealth, Press (San Francisco). Office: 840 Malcolm Rd Burlingame CA 94010-1401 also: 9454 Wilshire Blvd Ste 907 Beverly Hills CA 90202

COTE, DAVID EDWARD, state legislator; b. Nashua, N.H., Oct. 28, 1960; s. Edward David and Dorothy Eliza (Soucy) C. Mem. N.H. Ho. of Reps., Concord, 1982-88, 89—, asst. Dem. whip, 1991-92, dep. Dem. whip, 1992-96; mem. House Dem. Leadership, 1996—2003. Del. N.H. Constl. Conv., 1984, N.H. Dem. Convs., 1982—; memmem. platform com. N.H. Dem. Com., 1984; chmn. Nashua City Dem. Com., 1985-86; active various Dem. campaigns. Home: 96 W Hollis St Nashua NH 03060-3146 Office: NH Ho of Reps N State St Rm 306 Concord NH 03301-3229 Business E-Mail: david.cote@leg.state.nh.us.

COTE, DAVID M. diversified technology and manufacturing company executive; BS in Bus. Adminstrn., 1976, LLD (hon.) Pepperdine U., 2001. With GE, 1974—99, corp. sr. v.p., and pres., CEO appliances divsn., 1996—99; chmn., pres., CEO TRW, Cleve., 1999—2002; pres., CEO, chmn. Honeywell, 2002—. Appointed mem. Nat. Security Telecommunications Adv. Com. Office: 101 Columbia Rd Morristown NJ 07962

COTÉ, KATHRYN MARIE, psychotherapist, stress management educator; b. Oceanside, Calif., May 31, 1953; d. Richard Alfred Kauth and Carole Maxine Brue Potter; m. Dennis Malcolm Coté, Dec. 23, 1983; children: Claire Marie, Simone Gloria, Jesse Patrick. BA, St. Norbert Coll., DePere, Wis., 1975; MSSW, U. Wis., 1977. Lic. clin. social worker, Calif.; cert. clin. social worker, N.H. Psychiat. social worker Napa (Calif.) State Hosp., 1977-79, team leader, 1979-80; supr. adolescent clin. svcs. Solano County Mental Health, Vallejo, Calif., 1980-83; sect. head of residential svcs. for children and adolescents London Borough of Camden, 1983-84; mental health program mgr. Solano County Mental Health, Fairfield, Calif., 1985-87; clin. social worker, county liaison West Ctrl. Cmty. Svc. Ctr., Montevideo, Minn., 1987-90; pvt. practice as psychotherapist and stress mgmt. educator Berlin, N.H., 1990—; outpatient therapist N.E. Kingdom Human Svcs., St. Johnsbury, Vt., 2000—. Profl. cons. North Bay Suicide Prevention and Stressline, Napa, 1985-87. Bd. dirs. Coos County Family Health, Berlin, 1990—. Recipient Cert. of Appreciation, Solano County Mental Health Adv. Bd., 1987. Democrat. Roman Catholic. Avocations: hiking, travel, bicycling, cooking, reading.

COTE, LOUISE ROSEANNE, creative director, designer; b. Quincy, Mass., Sept. 16, 1959; d. John Anthony and Theresa Janet (Oriola) Burke; m. Robert Andrew Cote, Aug. 6, 1983. BA, Bridgewater State Coll., 1981. Advt. asst. Dunnington Super Drug, Brockton, Mass., 1978-81; bus. forms and graphic design artist Shawmut Bank of Boston, N.A., 1981-86; artist AlliedSignal Inc., East Providence, R.I., 1986-92, adminstr. creative svcs., 1992-94, supr. creative svcs., 1992-94, supr. computer graphics svcs., 1994-95; owner, design dir. Katmandu Studio, North Attleborough, Mass., 1995—. Active Town of North Attleborough Charter Commn., 2002—. Mem.: Advt. Club Southeastern New Eng., Southeastern Regional Alumni Assn. (vice-pres.), Downtown Assocs. North Attleborough (pres. 2003), North Attleborough and Plainville C. of C. (bd. dirs. 1997—, chmn. 2000—). Roman Catholic. Avocations: knitting, music, crafts. Office: Katmandu Studio PO Box 3064 North Attleborough MA 02761-3064 *The best advice I was ever given was: "Choose a profession you really like and you'll never have to work a day in your life." More than twenty years later, I still believe it.*

COTE, MICHAEL RICHARD, bishop; b. Sanford, Maine, June 19, 1949; Student, Our Lady of Lourdes Sem., Cassadaga, N.Y., St. Mary's Sem. Coll., Balt., Gregorian U. Rome, Cath. U. Washington; JCL, Cath. U., 1981. Ordained priest Roman Cath. Ch. 1975. Asst. SS Athanasius & John, Rumford, Maine, 1975—78; assoc. Holy Rosary, Caribou, 1978—79; notary Vice-Officialis Diocesan Tribunal, Portland, 1980—89; sec. Apostolic Nunciature, Washington, 1989—94; pastor Sacred Heart, Auburn, Maine, 1994—95; titular bishop Diocese of Cebarades, 1995—; aux. bishop Diocese of Portland, 1995—2003; bishop Diocese of Norwich, Conn., 2003—. Office: 274 Broadway Norwich CT 06360-4353

COTÉ, RALPH WARREN, JR., mining engineer, nuclear engineer; b. Berkeley, Calif., Oct. 5, 1927; s. Ralph Warren and Clara Maria (Neves) Coté; m. Lois Lydia Maddox, Aug. 8, 1950; children: Ralph Warren III, Michele Marie. BSME, N.Mex. Inst. Mining and Tech., 1952. Registered nuclear profl engr, Calif, grad, Realtor Inst. Resident engr. Am. Smelting and Refining Co., Page, Idaho, 1952-54; shift boss Bunker Hill Mining Co., Kellogg, Idaho, 1954-57, gen. mine foreman, 1958-60; project engr. Union Carbide Nuc. Co., Grand Junction, Colo., 1957-58; nuc. shift supr. GE, Richland, Wash., 1960-63, Vallecitos, Calif., 1963-66, nuc. maintenance mgr., 1966-67, nuc. start-up shift supr. San Jose, Calif., 1967-71; nuc. project start-up mgr. Bechtel Power Corp., San Francisco, 1971-89; realtor for retirement resort real estate Re/Max Integrity, Realtors, Sun City West, Ariz., 1989—. Mem.: VFW, President's Roundtable, Am Legion. Republican. Home: 14610 W Sky Hawk Dr Sun City West AZ 85375-5925 Office: Re/Max Integrity Realtors 13940 Meeker Blvd # 119 Sun City West AZ 85375-4428 E-mail: ralphcote@msn.com.

COTE, RICHARD JAMES, pathologist, researcher; b. L.A., May 10, 1954; s. Richard Patrick and Kathrine C.; m. Anne Louise Foxen, Feb. 8, 1992; children: Nicholas Foxen, Juliet Anne, Grace Elizabeth. BS in Biology, BA in Chemistry, U. Calif., Irvine, 1976; MD, U. Chgo., 1980. Diplomate Am. Coll. Pathologists. Intern in surgery U. Mich. Hosp., Ann Arbor, 1980-81; rsch. fellow, immunology Meml. Sloan-Kettering Cancer Ctr., N.Y.C., 1981-83; rsch. assoc., immunology Meml. Sloan-Kettering Hosp., N.Y.C., 1983-85, fellow, pathology, 1987-88, chief fellow, pathology, 1988-90; resident, pathology Cornell U. Med. Ctr., N.Y.C., 1985-87; asst. prof., pathology Keck Sch. Medicine, U. So. Calif., L.A., 1990-95, assoc. prof., 1995-99, prof., 1999—; attending pathologist Kenneth Norris Cancer Ctr., L.A., 1990—; dir. genitourinary program Keck Sch. Medicine, U. So. Calif./Norris Cancer Ctr., 1997—. Founder, dir. IMPATH, Inc., N.Y.C., 1987—; sci. dir. John Wayne Cancer and Rsch. Inst., Santa Monica, Calif., AVIVA Biosystems, San Diego, 2001—; mem. numerous nat. and internat. adv. bds.; sci. cons. MD Anderson Cancer Ctr., Houston, 2001—, Sidney Kimmel Cancer Ctr., San Diego, 2001—, U. Calif., L.A., 2002—, San Francisco, 2002—. Author: Immunomicroscopy, 1994; editor Modern Surg. Pathology; assoc. editor Applied Immunohistochemistry; contbr. articles to profl. jours., book chpts. Patentee in field. Am. Cancer Soc. fellow, 1988; recipient rsch. grants, awards NIH, ACS, others, 1981—. Mem.: Am. Assn. Cancer Rsch., Phi Beta Kappa. Avocations: golf, photography, skiing, writing. Office: U So Calif Keck Sch Medicine 1441 Eastlake Ave Los Angeles CA 90089-0112 E-mail: cote_r@norsur.hsc.usc.edu.

COTE, STEEVE D. biologist; b. Rimouski, Que., Can., Nov. 14, 1970; s. Desy Cote and Denise Belzile. PhD in Biology, U. Sherbrooke, Can., 1999. Rsch. asst. U. Laval, Ste-Foy, Que., 1991-93, asst. prof., 2001—; biologist U. Sask., Saskatoon, Can., 1993, Landcare Rsch., Dunedin, Otago, New Zealand, 1994; rsch. scientist CNRS, Strasbourg, France, 1997-98, Ctr. for Ecology and Hydrology, Banchory, U.K., 2000-2001; lectr. U. Sherbrooke, 1995-99. Contbr. more than 20 articles to profl. jours. Scholar Govt. of Can., 1990-93, Natural Scis. and Engring. Rsch. Coun. Can., 1994-98, Fonds pour la Formation de Chercheurs et Aide a la Recherche, 1996-99, Fondation Desjardins, 1991-92; FCAR Overseas Fellowship grantee, 1997-98; recipient Can.-U.K. Millennium Rsch. award Natural Scis. and Engring. Rsch. Coun. Can., 2000-2001, Gov. Gen. of Can. award, 1988, 90, 93; NSERC fellow, 2000-2001. Mem. Am. Soc. Mammalogists, Can. Soc. Zoologists (Helen Battle Award, 1995 and Cas Lindsay Book prize 1999), Internat. Soc. Behavioral Ecology, Wildlife Soc., Soc. Quebecoise pour l'Etude Biologique du Comportement. Avocations: travel, outdoor activities, mountaineering. Office: Dept Biology U Laval Saint-Foy Quebec QC Canada GIK 7P4 Fax: 418-656-2043. E-mail: steeve.cote@bio.ulaval.ca.

COTE, THOMAS JACQUES, lawyer; b. Ste-Foy, Quebec, Can., Oct. 26, 1951; came to U.S., 1970; s. Andre and Virginia C.; m. Josee L. Bourbeau, Aug. 29, 1987; children: Christine J., Julie M. BA, Suffolk U., 1972, JD, 1975. Bar: N.H. 1975. Pvt. practice, Gorham, N.H., 1976—. Former mem. faculty Sch. for Life Long Learning, Berlin. Past pres. United Way, Berlin. Avocations: skiing, hockey, piano, tennis, hiking. Office: 74 Main St Gorham NH 03581-1622

COTE-BEAUPRE, CAMILLE YVETTE, artist, educator; b. Worcester, Mass., May 21, 1926; d. Harvey and Blanche (Trahan) Cote. BA cum laude, Am. Internat. Coll., 1949; cert. in fine arts, Walker Studio Group, 1952; MS, U. Bridgeport, 1967. Dir. arts and crafts South End Cmty. Ctr., Springfield, Mass., 1955-58; art tchr. YWCA, Springfield, 1958-61; dir. workshops Hall Neighborhood House, Bridgeport, Conn., 1961-64, Jewish Cmty. Ctr., Bridgeport, 1964-69; tchr., chmn. art dept. Notre Dame H.S., Fairfield, Conn., 1970-95; chmn. art dept. Kolbe Cathedral H.S., 1995-98, Discovery Mus., 1998—.

One-woman shows: Bridgeport Cath. Center, 1978, Creative Mind Gallery, Stratford, Conn., 1978, Burroughs Library, Bridgeport, 1979, Trumbull (Conn.) Library, 1981, St. Vincent's Hosp., Bridgeport, 1981, St. Joseph Manor, Trumbull, 1981, Kellogg Environ. Ctr., Derby, Conn., 1999, Derby Environ. Ctr., 2001; group shows include: Stamford (Conn.) Mus., 1977, Slade Mus., Norwich, Conn., 1975, Mus. Sci. and Industry, Bridgeport, 1974, Sacred Heart U., Bridgeport, 1979, Fairfield (Conn.) U., 1979, 56th Grand Nat. Am. Artists Profl. League, Ho. of Reps., Washington, 1993, Nat. Arts Club, 1996, Creative Graphics Internat. Competition, 1997, others; represented in permanent collections: Eastern Conn. State Coll., Trumbull Libr. Assn., St. Vincent's Hosp., St. Joseph's Manor. Mem. Am. Artists Profl. League, Conn. Classic Arts, Am. Portrait Soc., Acad. Artists Assn., Nat. Arts Club, Conn. Pastel Soc. Home: 12 Melon Patch Ln Monroe CT 06468-1120

COTHERMAN, AUDREY MATHEWS, management and policy consultant, administrator; b. St. Paul, May 20, 1930; d. Anthony Joseph and Nina Grace (Harmon) Mathews; m. Richard Louis Cotherman, Dec. 30, 1950 (div. 1973); children: Steven, Michael, Bruce, Gen Elizabeth. BA, Hamline U., 1952; MA, U. Wyo., 1973, EdD, 1977. Communications coord. Natrona Sch. Dist., Casper, Wyo., 1968-69; hostess TV program KTWO-TV, Casper, 1970-71; exec. dir. United Way, Casper, 1971-73, Wyo. Coun. Humanities, Laramie, 1973-79; dep. state supt. Wyo. Dept. Edn., Cheyenne, 1979-90; devel. officer Coll. Edn. U. Wyo., Laramie, 1990-91; pres. Connections: Mgmt. and Policy Cons., Casper, 1991—; spl. asst. U.S. Dept. Edn. Region VIII, 1996-99; asst. dir. U. Wis. Comprehensive Ctr., 1999—2000; dir. U. Wis. Comprehensive Ctr., 2001—. Exec. sec. Wyo. Bd. Edn., 1979-90; dir. comty. programs HSS, Cheyenne, 1986-90; cons. Wyo. Atty. Gen., Cheyenne, 1990; dealer Profiles, Internat. Dem. precinct chair, Laramie, 1986-90. State exec. policy fellow U.S. Dept. Edn., 1985. Mem. LWV (past pres. local chpts., Wyo. chpt.), Am. Assn. Pub. Adminstrs. (pres. 1987-88), Wyo. Assn. Pub. Adminstrs. (Pub. Adminstr. of Yr. 1982), Phi Delta Kappa. Presbyterian. Avocations: writing, spending time with grandchildren, reading, antique hunting. Home: 8530 Greenway Blvd Apt 214 Middleton WI 53562-4605

COTHORN, JOHN ARTHUR, lawyer; b. Des Moines, Dec. 12, 1939; s. John L. and Marguerite (Esters) C.; m. Connie Cason, Aug. 6, 1996; children: Jeffrey, Judith. BS in Math., BS in Aero. Engring., U. Mich., 1961, JD, 1980. Bar: Mich. 1981, U.S. Dist. Ct. (ea. dist.) Mich. 1981, U.S. Ct. Appeals (6th cir.) 1981, U.S. Dist. Ct. (we. dist.) Mich. 1986, U.S. Supreme Ct. Exec. U.S Govt., 1965-78; asst. prosecutor Washtenaw County, Ann Arbor, Mich., 1981-82; ptnr. Kitch, Saurbier, Drutchas, Wagner & Kenney P.C., Detroit, 1982-94, Meganck & Cothorn P.C., Detroit, 1994-97, Meganck, Cothorn & Stanczyk P.C., Detroit, 1997-98, Cothorn & Stanczyk, P.C., Detroit, 1998-2000, Cothorn & Braceful, Detroit, 2000—02, Cothorn & Assocs., P.C., Detroit, 2002—. Served to capt. U.S. Army, 1961-65. Mem. ABA, Nat. Bar Assn. (numerous fed. and state coms.), Soc. Automotive Engrs., Assn. Def. Trial Counsel, Phi Alpha Delta. Republican. Avocations: bridge, golf. Office: 535 Griswold St Ste 530 Detroit MI 48226-3696

COTHRAN, DAN ALLEN, political scientist, educator; b. Carlisle, Ark., Feb. 24, 1941; s. Walter Marvin and Retha (Bentley) Cothran; m. Cheryl Cole; children: Leslie Danielle, Amanda Nicole. BA, U. Calif., Berkeley, 1963; MA, Claremont (Calif.) Grad. Sch., 1972; PhD, Cornell U., 1979. Asst. prof. polit. sci. U. B.C., Vancouver, Canada, 1977—81; prof. polit. sci. No. Ariz. U., Flagstaff, 1982—. Author: Political Stability and Democracy in Mexico, 1994; contbr. articles to profl. jours. Mem. Coconino County Planning and Zoning Commn., 1982—87, Flagstaff Planning and Zoning Commn., 1997—2001. Mem.: Am. Polit. Sci. Assn., Friends of Flagstaff's Future. Democrat. Avocations: hiking, reading history. Home: 214 N Bonito St # 1 Flagstaff AZ 86001 Office: No Ariz U PO Box 15036 Flagstaff AZ 86011

COTLER, JEROME MARVIN, orthopaedic surgeon; b. Bridgeton, N.J., July 26, 1928; s. Mitchell George and Elizabeth (Shapiro) C.; m. Florence, Aug. 19, 1951; children: Howard Bruce, Michelle Gail. BS, Ursinus Coll., 1948; MD, Jefferson Med. Coll., 1952. Intern Jefferson Med. Coll. Hosp., Phila., 1952-53, resident, 1953-57; orthop. surgeon pvt. practice, Bridgeton, N.J., 1957-73; instr. orthop. surgery Jefferson Med. Coll., Phila., 1957-70, clin. asst. prof., 1970-73; orthop. surgeon Jefferson Orthop. Assocs., Phila., 1973-95; clin. prof. Jefferson Med. Coll., 1973-81, prof., 1981—, Dr. Everett J. and Marian Gordon prof., 1991—; orthop. surgeon Jefferson Orthops., Phila., 1995—. Co-editor: Spinal Fusion: Science and Techniques, 1990, Spinal Instrumentation, 1992; contbr. articles to profl. jours. Mem. Union League Phila., 1974—. Fellow ACS (mem. bd. govs. 1985-90, 93-99, mem. adv. coun. 1985-90, 93-99), Am. Acad. Orthop. Surgeons (bd. dirs. 1972-76); mem. Am. Orthop. Assn. (v.p. 1993-94), Masons. Home: 4 E Kings Hwy Haddon Heights NJ 08035-1430 Office: 1025 Walnut St G4 Philadelphia PA 19107-5233

COTLEUR, MARK A. hospital administrator; b. Cleve., July 31, 1964; s. Neil Edward and Ruth L. (Cordiak) C.; m. Laurie J. Liss, Oct. 22, 1994 (div. June 1997). BA in History and Philosophy, Borromeo Sem. Coll., 1986; MA in Theology, Marquette U., 1993. Theology tchr. St. Peter Chanel H.S., Bedford, Ohio, 1986-90; prospect rsch. mgr. Children's Hosp. Wis., Milw., 1993-97, Children's Hosp., Boston, 1997-2000; asst. dir. devel. Univ. Hosps. Cleve., 2001—. Rsch. cons. Abbey Group Ltd., Milw., Northeast Health Found., Beverly, Mass., 2002—. Asst. editor Foundation Directory, Foundations in Wisconsin, 1992. Mem. planning com. No. Ohio Planned Giving Coun.; mem. edn. comm. St. Peter Chanel High Sch. Mem. Assn. Profl. Rschrs. for Advancement (bd. dirs. 2000-02, mem. nominating com. 2003--, media rels. advisor 2003--, v.p. Wis. chpt. 1995-96, pres. 1996-97), New Eng. Devel. Rsch. Assn. Avocations: golf, cooking, reading, computers. Office: 11100 Euclid Ave Cleveland OH 44106-1736

COTLOVE, ELAINE WOLF, psychiatrist, psychoanalyst; b. N.Y.C., Mar. 29, 1921; BA, Barnard Coll., 1942; MD, NYU, 1944; grad., Washington Psychoanalytic Inst., 1982. Diplomate Am. Bd. Neurology and Psychiatry. Resident in psychiatry George Washington U. Med. Ctr., Washington, 1971-74; cons. psychiatry Nat. Naval Med. Ctr., Bethesda, Md., 1977—; tchg. analyst Washington Psychoanalytic Inst., 1994—; clin. prof. psychiatry George Washington U. Med. Ctr., 1989—. Recipient Hornbook award for disting. svc. in pub. edn. Md. State Tchrs. Assn., 1967, 5th Ann. Roeske award for excellence in med. student tchg. Am. Psychiat. Assn., 1995. Office: Elaine W Cotlove MD 10310 Drumm Ave Kensington MD 20895-2736

COTMAN, JOHN MARTIN, accountant; b. Cleve., June 10, 1953; s. John Joseph and Gertrude Irene (Tomosko) C.; m. Joyce Ann Bill, Aug. 6, 1977. BBA, Cleve. State U., 1975, MBA, 1979, M in Accountancy and Fin. Info. Systems, 1981. CPA, Ohio; cert. mgmt. acct.; cert. bus. mgr. Sr. acct. N.E. Ohio Areawide Coordinating Agy., Cleve., 1977-79; fin. analyst Am. Parking Co. of Am., Cleve., 1979-80; asst. dir. Greater Cleve. Hosp. Assn., Cleve., 1981-86; fin. mgr. Univ. Hosp., Cleve., 1986-89, dir. acctg., 1989-99; fin. project cons. Parson Group, North Olmsted, Ohio, 2000; fiscal adminstr. Cleve. Clinic Found., 2000—01; dir. fin. planning Ohio Aerospace Inst., 2001—. Cons. Ctr. Hosp. Svcs., Cleve., 1984-88, Hosp. Fin. Corp., Cleve., 1985-88. Mem. allocations panel Children and Youth Svcs., United Way, Cleve., 1987-89. Mem. AICPA, Inst. Mgmt. Accts. Republican. Roman Catholic. Avocations: computers, sports, travel, music, scuba diving. Home: 5070 Hampton Dr North Olmsted OH 44070-3083 E-mail: cotmanj@aol.com.

COTNER, DOUGLAS MONROE, provost, mathematics and environmental science educator; b. Hawthorne, Calif., Sept. 15, 1942; s. Monroe and Vergie Jeanette Cotner; m. Peggy Ann Whyte, Aug. 15, 1967 (div. May 1984); children: Margaret Lyn, David Morrison. BA, Calif. State U., 1967; MA, Columbia Pacific U., 1995; ScD with honors, Am. Inst. Urban and Regional Affairs, 1997. Cert. sustainable devel. practitioner World Coun. Sustainable Devel. Supr. mcpl. code enforcement divsn. Culver City (Calif.) Fire Dept., 1989-93; tchr. phys. and environ. sci. Compton (Calif.) Unified Sch. Dist., 1996-97; sustainable devel. curriculum developer Montgomery C.C./Am. Inst. Urban and Regional Affairs, Montgomery Village, Md., 1995-97; curriculum developer U. Econ. Activity/Am. Inst. Urban and Regional Affairs, Warsaw, Montgomery Village, 1995-97; doctoral dissertation adv. coop Grad. Sch. Sustainable Devel Am. Inst. Urban and Regional Affairs, Montgomery Village, 1997—, exec. dir., provost academic affairs, 1998—; tchr. math. geology and environ. sci. Brooks Coll., Long Beach, Calif., 1998—. Author: (poetry) Now We Have It - An Urban Allegory, 1997; author monograph. Avocations: reading, shooting, yachting, travel. Home: 3516 hathaway Ave # 410 Long Beach CA 90815 Office: Brooks Coll 4825 E Pacific Coast Hwy Long Beach CA 90804-3289 E-mail: doctorcotner@earthlink.nr., dmcotner@yahoo.com.

COTON, CARLOS DAVID, finance manager; b. Havana, Cuba, Dec. 29, 1950; arrived in US, 1960; s. Jose Manuel Coton and Guillermina (Guitian) Coton Lopez; m. Susana M. Muriel, May 18, 1997; children: Alexandra Beatriz, David Alexander, Sean Stephen. AA, Miami Dade C.C., 1971; BA, Fla. Internat. U., 1973, MS, 1983; PhD in Internat. Bus., Kennedy Western U., 1992. Supr. trainee Richards Dept. Store, Miami, Fla., 1967-68, supr., 1968-73, mgr. distbn., 1973-76; dir. ops. Bassett Furniture Mfg., 1976-79; asst. dir. Fla. Internat. U., Miami, 1979-82; dir. Luth. Ministries Projects, Miami, 1982-84; fin. mgr. Emery Worldwide, Miami, 1984-90; v.p. fin. Transworld Computers, Miami, 1989—; v.p. Carinter Miami, 1991-95; v.p. ops. Internat. Sys. and Electronics, Miami, 1995—. Substitute tchr. Dade County Pub. Schs., Miami, 1973—; adj. prof. Fla. Internat. U., 1980—; pres. CDC Cons.; cons. in field. Author: (poetry book) ... And Other Poems, 1973; contbr. articles to profl. jours. Mem. Council on Laraza, Calif., 1980; mem. Dade County United Way. Mem.: Nat. Soc. Tax Profls., Am. Inst. Profl. Bookkeepers, Ecuadorian Inter-Am. C. of C., Nat. Coun. Tchrs. English, Acad. Internat. Bus., Am. Mgmt. Assn., Miami=Santiago Sister Cities Program, Am. C. of C., Cuban-Am. Orgn., Fla. HS Activities Assn. (ofcl.), Greater Miami Football Ofcls. Assn., Greater Miami C. of C. (mentor STAR/HOPE, hispanic com. mem., S.Am. com. mem.W. Dade com. mem.), Greater Miami Basketbal Ofcls.Assn., Miami Ofcls. club, Phi Delta Kappa. Democrat. Roman Catholic. Avocations: football referee, basketball referee. Home: 1320 SW 91st Ave Miami FL 33174-3130 E-mail: cdc@ise-corp.com., cdc1229@concentric.net.

COTROS, CHARLES H. food products company executive; b. 1937; Grad. Christian Brothers Coll., 1960. Exec. v.p, pres.. food svc. ops. Sysco Corp., Houston, 1988—95, COO, 1995—2000, pres., 1999—2000, chmn., CEO, 2000—02; ret., 2002. Bd. dirs. AmerisourceBergen Corp. Office: Sysco Corp 1390 Enclave Pkwy Houston TX 77077-2099

COTRUBAS, ILEANA, opera singer, retired lyric soprano; b. Galati, Romania; d. Vasile C. and Maria C. m. Manfred Ramin, 1972. Student, Scoala speciala de Musica, Bucharest, Ciprian Porumbescu Conservatory, Musikakademie, Vienna, Austria. Tchr. master-classes, interpretation and operatic roles. Debut as Yniold in Pelleas et Melisande, Bucharest Opera, 1964; appeared with Frankfurt (Fed. Republic Germany) Opera, 1968-71, Staatsoper, Vienna, 1970—, Covent Garden, London, 1971—, Staatsoper, Munich, 1973—, Lyric Opera Chgo., 1973-75, 83—, Opera Paris, 1974—, La Scala, Milan, 1975—, Met. Opera, N.Y.C., 1977—, San Francisco Opera, 1978, Ehrenmitglied Vienna Staats oper, 1991; major roles include: Zerlina, Susanna, Pamina, Norina, Gilda, Violetta, Elisabetta (Don Carlos), Mimi, Tatyana, Micaela, Manon, Antonia, Melisande; ret., 1990; author: Truth About Opera, 1998. Recipient 1st prize Internat. Singing Competition, Hertogenbusch, Netherlands, 1965; 1st prize Munich Radio Competition, 1966; Kammersängerin Vienna Staatsoper, 1981; Great Officer of the Order Sant' Iago da Espada, Portugal, 1990, Great Officer of Star of Romania, 2000.

COTRUVO, JOSEPH ALFRED, environmental and public health consultant; b. Toledo, Aug. 3, 1942; s. Nicholas and Angela (Campanale) C.; m. Karen Shrum, June 18, 1983; 1 child, Joseph Alfred Jr. BS in Chemistry, U. Toledo, 1963; PhD, Ohio State U., 1968; postgrad., U. Bologna, Italy, 1969. Mgr. R & D ChemSampCo, Columbus, Ohio, 1970-72; programs analyst EPA, Washington, 1973-76, dir. drinking water criteria and stds. divsn., 1976-90, dir. health and environ. rev. divsn., 1990-92; dir. risk assessment divsn., 1992-96; sr. regulatory exec. NSF Internat., Washington, 1996-98. V.p. environ. health scis. NSF Internat., 1998—2000; coun. pub. health cons. Nat. Sanitation Found., Ann Arbor, Mich., 1980—96; dir. NSF Internat./WHO Collaborating Ctr. for Water Safety and Tech., 1996—2002; adj. prof. environ. scis. Am. U., 1997; mem. rsch. adv. bd. Nat. Water Rsch. Inst.; mem. sci. adv. bd. Santa Ana River Water Quality and Health; ind. adv. bd. Tampa Water Resource Reuse Panel, 1997—98; pres. J. Cotruvo Assocs. Environ. Health Cons.; mem. sci. adv. bd. Cal-Fed Delta Water Quality Project; rsch. adv. bd. Water Reuse Found.; sci. panel on water sys. security rsch. NAS, 2003. Co-editor: Ozone/Chlorine Dioxide, 1978, Water Chlorination, 1983, Procs. Safe Drinking Water in Small Sys.: Tech., Ops. and Econs., 1999; chmn., editor book series NATO/CCMS Drinking Water Pilot, 1980; contbr. articles to jours. in field. Recipient Environ. Leadership award Nat. Sanitation Found., Ann Arbor, 1988, Donald R. Boyd award Assn. Met. Water Agys., 1990; named Meritorious Exec., Pres. U.S., 1983. Mem. NAS (mem. panel on water sys. security rsch. 2003), Am. Chem Soc., Am. Water Works Assn. (hon. life, mem. editorial adv. bd. Jour., 1987-90), Water Reuse Found. (dir. at large 2000-2002, v.p. 2003-), Interamerican Assn. of Sanitary and Environ. Engring. Roman Catholic. Avocations: woodworking, light construction.

COTSAKOS, CHRISTOS MICHAEL, former internet financial services company executive; b. Paterson, N.J., July 29, 1948; s. Michael John and Lillian (Scoulikas) C.; m. Hannah Batami Fogel, July 1, 1973; 1 child, Suzanne Renee. BA in Communications and Polit. Sci., William Paterson Coll., 1972; MBA, Pepperdine U., 1984. Tour guide Universal Studios, Burbank, Calif., 1973; courier Fed. Express Corp., Burbank, 1973-74, sales rep. Long Beach, Calif., 1974, sta. mgr. San Jose, Calif., 1974, we. dist. mgr., 1974, region engring. mgr., 1975, mng. dir. Chgo., 1975-80, v.p. Sacramento, 1980-92; pres., COO Nielsen, Europe, Middle East, Africa, 1992-93; pres., CEO Nielsen Internat., 1993-95; pres., co-CEO, COO, dir. A.C. Nielsen, Inc., 1995-96; CEO, chmn. E*TRADE Group, Inc., Palo Alto, Calif., 1996—2003. Instr. Consumers River Coll., Placerville, Calif., 1985-86; bd. dirs. Airlifeline, Sacramento, Nat. Processing, Inc., Louisville, Forté Software, Inc., Oakland, 4th Comms. Network, San Jose, Datacard, Mpls. Author: (book) It's Your Money: The E*Trade Step by Step Guide to Online Investing, 2000. Served as sgt. U.S. Army, 1967-70, Vietnam. Decorated Bronze Star, 1967, Purple Heart, 1967. Mem. World Econ Forum (Davos, Switzerland), Sutter Club, Comstock Club.

COTSONAS, NICHOLAS JOHN, JR., physician, medical educator; b. Boston, Jan. 28, 1919; s. Nicholas John and Louise Catherine (Lapham) C.; m. Betty Borge, Nov. 21, 1970; children by previous marriage: Nicholas III, Bruce, Elena. AB, Harvard, 1940; MD cum laude, Georgetown U., 1943. Intern D.C. Gen. Hosp., Washington, 1944, resident in chest diseases, 1946-47, asst. med. resident, 1947-48, chief med. resident, 1948-49; asst. prof. medicine Georgetown U. Sch. Medicine, 1949-53; chief med. officer, med. divsn. D.C. Gen. Hosp., 1951-53; asst. prof. medicine U. Ill. Coll. Medicine, Chgo., 1953-57, assoc. prof., 1957-62, prof., 1962-70; dean, prof. medicine Peoria Sch. Medicine, U. Ill., 1970-79; prof. medicine U. Ill., Chgo., 1979-90, prof. emeritus, 1989—, assoc. vice chancellor for acad. affairs, 1979-82. Mem. Bradley Assocs., 1972-79; bd. dirs. Ill. Heart Assn., 1972-79, pres., 1976-77; bd. dirs. Ill. Ctrl. Health Sys. Agy., 1976-79, Planned Parenthood Assn. Greater Peoria Area, 1971-79; mem. Statewide Health Coordinating Council, 1978-79; bd. dirs. Chgo. Heart Assn., 1980-82, Inst. Religion and Medicine, 1980; mem. task force on older women Ill. Council on Aging, 1985-86; chmn. Commn. on Health Resources Allocation, Peoria, Ill., 1985-87. Asst. editor: Disease-A-Month, 1960-77; asso. editor, 1977-80, editor, 1980-86, emeritus, 1987. Served to capt. AUS, 1944-46. Recipient Raymond Allen award U. Ill. Coll. Medicine, 1955, Faculty of Yr. award, 1978 Fellow ACP, Am. Heart Assn. (coun. clin. cardiology 1963), Am. Coll. Cardiology, Inst. Medicine Chgo., Am. Geriatrics Soc.; mem. Am. Fedn. Clin. Rsch., Chgo. Soc. Internal Medicine, Harvard Soc. Chemists, Sigma Xi, Alpha Omega Alpha.

COTTAM, KEITH M. librarian, educator, administrator; b. St. George, Utah, Feb. 13, 1941; s. Von Bunker and Adrene (McArthur) Cottam; m. Laurel Springer, June 16, 1961 (div. Feb. 4, 2000); children: Mark Patrick, Lisa Diane, Andrea Jill, Brian Lowell, Heather Dawn; m. Mary Bultena Albertson, Oct. 5, 2001. BS, Utah State U., 1963; MLS, Pratt Inst., 1965. Trainee Bklyn. Pub. Libr., 1963-65, asst. instr. reading improvement program, 1964-65, adult services libr., 1965; asst. social scis. libr., instr. So. Ill. U., Edwardsville, 1965-67; head, social sci. libr., instr. asst. prof. Social Scis. Libr., Brigham Young U., Provo, Utah, 1967-72; supr., inst. Libr. Technician Program Brigham Young U., Provo, Utah, 1969-72; head undergrad. libr., assoc. prof. U. Tenn., Knoxville, 1972-75, asst. dir. librs., assoc. prof., 1975-77; asst. dir. for pub. svcs. and employee rels. Vanderbilt U. Libr. (formerly Joint Univ. Librs.), Nashville, 1977-80, assoc. dir., 1980-82, acting dir., 1982-83; dir. libraries, prof. U. Wyo., Laramie, 1983-2000, dean univ. librs., 2001; assoc. dean outreach sch., dir. U. Wyo./Casper Coll. Ctr., Casper, 2001—. Cons. tng. program Assn. Rsch. Librs., 1979—80; active Leadership Wyo. Tng. Program, 2002—03. Author: Writer's Research handbook, 1977, 2d edit., 1978; editor Utah Libraries jour., 1971-72; mem. editl. bd. RQ jour., 1980-84; contbr. articles to profl. jours. Fellow Coun. Libr. Resources, 1975-76; sr. fellow UCLA Grad. Sch. Libr. Info. Sci., 1985-86. Mem.: ALA, Wyo. Libr. Assn. (pres. 1998—99), Phi Kappa Phi, Beta Phi Mu. Republican. Mem. Ch. of Jesus Christ of Latter-day Saints. Avocations: bicycling, racing and touring, free-lance writer, gardening. Home: 1751 W Coffman Ave Casper WY 82604-3453 Office: 125 College Dr Casper WY 82601 E-mail: kcottam@uwyo.edu.

COTTEN, ANNIE LAURA, psychologist, educator; b. Oxford, N.C., Nov. 18, 1923; d. Leonard F. and Laura Estelle (Spencer) Cotten; children: Hollis W., Rebecca Ann, Laura Cotten. Diploma, Hardbarger Bus. Coll., 1944; AB, Duke U., 1945; MEd, U. Hartford, 1965; PhD, The Union Inst., 1979. Diplomate Am. Bd. Sexology, lic. Am. Assn. Marriage & Family Therapists, 87. Asst. to pres. So. Meth. U., 1953; rsch. asst. Duke U., 1947-49; exec. sec. Ohio Wesleyan U., 1955-56, Conn. Coun. Chs., 1958-60; adj. prof. U. Hartford, 1976-78, 1976-78; clin. pastoral counselor Hartford Hosp., 1962-65; asst., then assoc. dir. social svcs. Hartford Conf. Chs., 1965-67; tchg. fellow U. N.C., 1970-71; assoc. prof. Ctrl. Conn. State U., New Britain, 1967-93, adj. prof., 1994—2002. Adj. prof. St. Joseph Coll., 1986-96; clin. intern Montefiore Med. Ctr., 1995; dir. elderhostel programs Ctrl. Conn. State U., 1989-93, organizer ctr. adult learners, 1991-93; cons. Somers Correctional Ctr., Conn., 1980-81, instr./rschr., 1980-81; cons. Conn. Life Ins. Mktg. Rsch., 1981-1982; amb. to China, spring, 1986; presenter 3d Internat. Interdisciplinary Cong. on Women, 1987; vis. prof., scholar Duke U., 1989; adj. prof. health and human svcs. Ctrl. Ch. St. U., 1995-2002; vis. prof. Conn. Coll., New London, 1990; mem. clin. faculty, Am. Bd. Sexology, 1994; land developer N.C. Triangle, 1995—. Cons. editor: Jour. Feminist Family Therapy, 2000—. Fellow: Clin. Sexologists (founder, clin. faculty 1994—), Nat. Coun. Family Rels.; mem.: APA (chair divsn. 1987—91), AAUW, Am. Assn. Sex Educators, Counselors and Therapists, Conn. Assn. Marital & Family Therapists (bd. dirs. 2000—02), Sex Info. & Edn. Coun. of Conn. (bd. dirs. 1994—2002, human sexuality leader of yr. 1997), Conn. Psychol. Assn., Am. Assn. Sex Educators Counselors & Therapists (cert. outstanding svc. 1996, disting. svc. award 1998), Am. Assn. Marriage & Family Therapists, Conn. Coun. Chs. (dir.), Hartford Women's Network.

COTTEN, SAMUEL RICHARD, fisheries consultant, former state legislator; b. Juneau, Alaska, July 16, 1947; s. Samuel L. Cotten and Kathryn Russell; m. Martha Tillion, June 16, 1984; children: Samuel Tillion, Augustus O'Dwyer Russell. AA, U. Alaska, 1971. Rep. Alaskan Ho. of Reps., Juneau, 1975-82, 85-91, speaker, 1989-91; senator Alaska State Senate, Juneau, 1991-93; chmn. Alaska Pub. Utilities Commn., 1995—99; fisheries cons., 1999—. Spl. advisor Intergovtl. Consultative Com. to North Pacific Fisheries Adv. Bd., 1989-92; advisor Internat. North Pacific Fisheries Commn., 1984-90; bd. dir. Fire Lake Recreational Ctr., Eagle River, Alaska. Co-chmn. Alaska Criminal Code Revision Commn., Juneau, 1976; mem. Anchorage Planning and Zoning Commn., 1983-84; candidate for Gov. Alaska, 1994—. Recipient Nat. Def. award Vietnam Svc. (2); named Outstanding Vietnam Vet. No Greater Love Found., 1976. Mem. Cook Inlet Seiners Assn., Navy League, Elks, VFW (life), Anchorage Ski Club. Democrat. Avocations: fishing, skiing, bowling. Home: PO Box 770296 Eagle River AK 99577-0296 E-mail: samc.er@gci.net.

COTTER, DANIEL A. diversified company executive; b. Duluth, Minn., Dec. 26, 1934; BA, Marquette U., 1957; MBA, Northwestern U., 1960. With Truserv Corp., Chgo., 1959-99, chmn., CEO; retired, 1999. Office: Truserv Corp 8600 W Bryn Mawr Ave Chicago IL 60631-3579

COTTER, DOUGLAS ADRIAN, healthcare executive; b. Brockport, N.Y., Aug. 15, 1943; s. Adrian Edwards and Rita Elizabeth (Marshall) C.; m. Rosalyn DeVaughn, June 12, 1965 (div.); children: Elizabeth D., Anne R.; m. Anne Holmes Thompson, Oct. 4, 1986. BS, Duke U., 1965; MS, N.C. State U., 1967, PhD, 1970. Rsch. engr. Corning Glass Works, Raleigh, N.C., 1966-69, mgr. R & D, 1970-78; bus. devel. mgr. Corning Med. Europe, Halstead, Essex, England, 1978-80; portfolio mgr. Corning (N.Y.) Glass Works, 1980-83; dir. info. sys. Corning Med., Medfield, Mass., 1984-85; pres. Healthcare Decisions Inc., Norwood, Mass., 1986-96; v.p. Decision Resources Inc., Waltham, Mass., 1996-98; pres. Healthcare Decisions, Inc., Walpole, Mass., 1998-2000, 2002—; sr. v.p. Leerink Swann and Co., Boston, 2000—02. Adj. prof. Boston U., 1985—, N.C. State U., 1973-76; dir. Respironics Inc., Murrysville, Pa., 1989—; dir. Applied Microbiology, Tarrytown, N.Y., 1995-96. Inventor/patentee in field. Mem. Inst. Elec. Engrs. (sr. mem.), Nat. Assn. Corp. Dirs. Avocations: sailing, tennis. Office: Healthcare Decisions Walpole MA E-mail: dacotter@aol.com.

COTTER, JAMES MICHAEL, lawyer; b. Providence, May 12, 1942; s. James Henry and Marguerite Louise (Clark) C.; m. Melinda Irene Tighe, Feb. 6, 1971; children: Elizabeth, Heather, Kathryn. AB, Fairfield U., 1964; LLB, U. Va., 1967. Bar: N.Y. 1967. Assoc. Simpson Thacher & Bartlett, N.Y.C., 1967-75, ptnr., 1975—. Trustee Fairfield U., 1995-2001; bd. dirs. M.G.A. Found., 1990—, chmn., 1990-92. Mem. ABA, N.Y. State Bar Assn., N.Y. Law Inst. (bd. dirs. 1984—, chmn. exec. com. 1993-98, pres. 1997—), Met. Golf Assn. (bd. dirs. 1974—, pres. 1990-92), Greenwich Conn. Country Club, Hudson Nat. Golf Club. Office: Simpson Thacher & Bartlett 425 Lexington Ave Fl 15 New York NY 10017-3954

COTTER, JOHN BURLEY, ophthalmologist, corneal specialist; b. Zanesville, Ohio, Sept. 14, 1946; s. John Burley and Evelyn Virginia (Ross) C.; m. Perrine Abauzit, Aug. 17, 1977; children: Neils John, Jeremy Pierre. BA, U. Kans., 1968; med. degree, U. Kans., Kansas City, 1968-72. Ophthalmology resident U. Mo., Kansas City, 1976-79; family practice Ashland (Kans.) Hosp., 1973-74; emergency room physician Providence-St. Margaret Hosp., Kansas City, Kans., 1974-75; family orthopedic practice Mountain Med. Assocs., Vail, Colo., 1975-76; ophthalmologist, pvt. practice Duluth, Minn., 1979-82; surgeon-chief out-patient clinic King Khaled Eye Specialist Hosp., Riyadh, Saudi Arabia, 1983-90, mem. exec. com., 1985-90; asst. clin. prof. King Saud U., Riyadh, Saudi Arabia, 1985-90; corneal splst., refractive surgeon in assn. Greensboro, NC, 1990—. Seminar chmn. Status of Refractive Surgery, Riyadh, 1986; active Nat. Survey Eye Disease and Ea. Province Survey Coun., Saudi Arabia, 1984, 90. Author: (booklet) Radial Keratotomy, 1986; contbr. articles to profl. jours. Rsch. grantee Contact Lens Assn. of Ophthalmology, 1981, Lasers Steering Com. King Khalid Eye Hosp. at Hosp. Hotel Dieu, Paris, 1988; ORBIS fellow Baylor U., Houston, 1982. Fellow Am. Acad. Ophthalmology; mem. AMA, Internat. Assn. Ocular Surgeons, Internat. Soc. Refractive Keratoplasty, Societe Francaise D'Ophthalmologie, Saudi Ophthalmologist Soc., Am. Soc. Cataract and Refractive Surgery. Avocations: wind surfing, scuba diving, running, math games. Office: 719 Green Valley Rd Ste 105 Greensboro NC 27408-7013

COTTER, JOSEPH FRANCIS, retired hotel and bank executive; b. Brockton, Mass., May 18, 1927; s. Joseph and Sarah (Thornell) C.; m. Catherine Florence Sullivan, 1950 (dec.); m. Barbara Tribou Salter, 1986; 14 children/stepchildren. BS cum laude, Boston Coll., 1949. CPA, Mass., N.Y. Accountant Price Waterhouse & Co., N.Y.C., 1949-67; v.p., contr. Howard Johnson Co., Braintree, Mass., 1967-70; exec. v.p., comptr., dir. Sheraton Corp., Boston, 1970-85, exec. v.p. planning and devel., 1985-87; ret., 1987-89; exec. Bank of Boston, 1989-95; ret., 1995. Former vice chmn. bd. trustees Boston Coll.; former chmn. bd. dirs. Greater Boston YMCA.; former v.p., bd. dirs. Greater Boston C. of C.; trustee for life Dana-Farber Cancer Rsch. Inst.; former bd. dirs. United Way of Mass. Bay. Mem. AICPA, N.Y. Soc. CPAs, Mass. Soc. CPAs, Boston Coll. Alumni Assn. (past pres.), Jonathan's Landing Golf Club (Jupiter, Fla.; past pres.). Home: 11 Running Tide Rd Cape Elizabeth ME 04107-2933

COTTER, LAWRENCE RAFFETY, management consultant; b. Albany, Calif., Aug. 13, 1933; s. Malcolm Thompson Cotter and Una Elyse Raffety. AA, U. Calif., Berkeley, 1953, BA in Astronomy, 1956; MS in Bus. Adminstrn., The George Washington U., 1967; CPhil in Mgmt. Theory, UCLA, 1972, PhD, 1977. Commd. 2nd lt. USAF, 1956, advanced through grades to col., 1975, ret., 1982, orbital analyst, network contr. Project Space Track, 1958-61; staff scientist Hdqs. N.Am. Air Def. Command, Colorado Springs, Colo., 1962-66, Hdqrs. USAF, Washington, 1967-70; dir. test and deployment DEF. Support

program USAF, Los Angeles, 1975-76, commdr. detachment 1 Electronic Systems Div. Tehran, Iran, 1976-78, sys. program dir. Electronic Sys. divsn. Bedford, Mass., 1978-79, dep. commdr. network plans and devel. AF Satellite Control Facility Sunnyvale, Calif., 1979-82; mgmt. cons. Berkeley, 1982—. Adminstrv. asst. Arnold Air Soc., Washington, 1959-72. Co-author: The Arnold Air Soc. Manual, 1956; (computer program) SPACE, 1970; editor: The Arnold Air Soc. Manual 1964-72. Recipient Department Citation U. Calif. Berkeley, 1955, Citation of Honor, Arnold Air Soc., 1967. Fellow Royal Soc. for Encouragement of Arts, Manufactures and Commerce; mem. Air Force Assn., The RAF Club, Beta Gamma Sigma. E-mail: seaotter6@aol.com.

COTTER, MICHAEL WILLIAM, retired ambassador, business consultant; b. Madison, Wis., Aug. 1, 1943; s. Patrick William and Lois Katherine (Schaus) Cotter; m. Joanne Marie Miller, Aug. 30, 1974. BSFS, Georgetown U., 1965; JD, U. Mich., 1968; MS, Stanford U., 1976. Polit.-mil. affairs officer Am. Embassy, Ankara, Turkey, 1980-82; sr. Turkish desk officer U.S. Dept. State, Washington, 1982-84; polit. officer Am. Embassy, Kinshasa, Zaire, 1984-86, polit. counselor, 1986-88; mgmt. analyst sec. of mgmt. U.S. Dept. State, 1988-90, office dir. politico-military affairs, 1990-92; dep. chief of mission Am. Embassy, Santiago, Chile, 1992-95; U.S. amb. to Turkmenistan, 1995-98; internat. bus. cons., 1999-2001; internat. bus. cons., lectr. Chapel Hill, NC, 2001—. V.p., assoc. publ. Am. Diplomacy Publs., Chapel Hill, NC, 2001—. Mem.: Am. Fgn. Svc. Assn. (secy 1989—91, bd govs 1988—89). Home and Office: 685 Fearrington Post Pittsboro NC 27312-8713 E-mail: mwcotter@hotmail.com.

COTTER, PATRICIA O'BRIEN, state supreme court justice; b. South Bend, Ind., 1950; m. Michael W. Cotter, 1979; 2 children. BS in Polit. Sci. and History with honors, We. Mich. U, 1972; JD, Notre Dame, 1977. Pvt. practice, South Bend, 1977—83, Great Falls, Mont., 1984; ptnr. Cotter & Cotter, Great Falls, 1985—2000; justice Mont. Supreme Ct., 2001—. Office: Rm 323 PO Box 203003 Helena MT 59620*

COTTER, WILLIAM DONALD, former state commissioner, former newspaper editor; b. Hartford, Conn., June 5, 1921; s. William Joseph and Alice I. (Murphy) C.; m. Alice K. Liller, Jan. 22, 1944; children: Carol A., Mary L., Alice E., William J., James D., Donald W. BA, Fordham U., 1943; postgrad. Polit. Sci., St. John U., 1956-57, Syracuse U., 1958. Reporter L.I. Star-Jour., Long Island City, 1947-51; night city editor Nassau Rev., Rockville Centre, N.Y., 1952-53; night editor Jersey Jour., Jersey City, 1954; mag., Sunday editor L.I. Press, Jamaica, N.Y., 1955-58; city editor Syracuse Herald-Jour./Am., 1958-66, editor, 1966-83; chmn. N.Y. State Energy R & D Authority, 1983-92; commr. N.Y. State Energy Office, 1983-92, N.Y. State Pub. Svc. Commn., 1992-96. Trustee N.Y. Power Authority, 1989-92; instr. journalism Syracuse U., 1960-66. Former bd. dirs. Cmty. Gen. Hosp., Boys Town of Italy, Erie Canal Mus.; past chmn. communications com. LeMoyne Coll.; chmn. Onondaga County Energy Com., 1975-83. Served with USNR, 1943-46. Mem. N.Y. State Soc. Newspaper Editors (pres.), Auburn Golf and Country Club (dir.). Roman Catholic. Home: 55 Shadow Wood Way Ballston Lake NY 12019-1213

COTTER, WILLIAM RECKLING, foundation president; b. Detroit, Mar. 9, 1936; s. Fred Joseph and Esther Jean (Reckling) C.; m. Linda Jane Kester, June 14, 1959; children: David Andrew, Deborah Anne, Elizabeth Anne. BA in Polit. Sci. magna cum laude, Harvard U., 1958, JD cum laude, 1961; LHD (hon.), Bowdoin Coll., 1987, West Brook Coll., 1995, U. New Eng., 2000, Colby Coll., 2000. Bar: N.Y. 1962, U.S. Supreme Ct. 1965. Law clk. to U.S. Fed. Judge, N.Y.C., 1961-62; MIT fellow in Africa Nigeria, 1962-63; assoc. firm Cahill, Gordon, Sonnett, Reindell & Ohl, N.Y.C., 1963-65; White House fellow Washington, 1965-66; Ford Found. rep. to, 1966-70; pres. African-Am. Inst., N.Y.C., 1970-79, Colby Coll., 1979-2000, Oak Found., Boston and Geneva, Switzerland, 2000—, chair adv. com., 1997—. Contbr. articles on fgn. policy and edn. to profl. jours. Bd. dirs. Pvt. Agys. Collaborating Together, 1975-81, Waterville ARC, 1980-87, Kennebec Valley Regional Health Agy., 1982-88, Mid-Maine Econ. Devel. Corp.; chmn. bd. trustees Oyster Bay-East Norwich (N.Y.) Pub. Libr., 1975-79; trustee African-Am. Inst., 1970-2001; bd. dirs. Maine Pub. Broadcasting, 1979-2000; chair bd. dirs. Waterville Regional Arts and Cmty. Ctr., 1996-2000; chmn. bd. visitors Baxter Sch. for the Deaf, 1982-87; chmn. com. for study ct. structure, probate and family law matters, 1985; bd. advisors Carrabassett Valley Acad., 1981-91; chair com. on pub. disclosure New Eng. Assn. Schs. and Colls., 1987; trustee Westbrook Coll., 1986-92; past mem. exec. com. South African Edn. Program; past mem. commn. on govt. rels. Am. Coun. on Edn.; commr. State of Maine Edn. Commn.; mem. Nat. Commn. on Responsibilities for Financing Postsecondary Edn., 1991-93; bd. visitors U. Maine Sch. Law; past chair and dir. Nat. Assn. Ind. Colls. and Univs.; trustee Colby Coll., 1979—; trustee Olin Coll., 2002—. Named Educator of Yr. The Washington Ctr., 1993, Leader of Yr., Equity Inst. Maine, 1996, Disting. Citizen Waterville C. of C. 1998. Mem. Nat. Assn. Ind. Colls. and Univs. (past chair and dir.), Coun. Fgn. Rels., Harvard Club (N.Y.C.), Harvard Club (Boston). Office: 47 Winter St Boston MA 02108-4706

COTTER-SMITH, CATHLEEN MARIE, art educator, artist; b. Dallas, 1950; d. Robert Jay and Betty Ann Cotter; 1 child, Ryan Patrick Holt; m. Jack Glendon Smith, Jr., 1991. BS, East Tex. State U., 1974; MS, Tex. A&M U., Commerce, 1977. Freelance artist, Garland and Plano, Tex., 1976—; assoc. prof. art Grayson County Coll., Dennison, Tex., 1981-85; prof. art Collin County C.C., Plano, Tex., 1986—, coord. art dept., 1986-97. Cons. on book Equine Images, 1992. One-woman shows include Cultural Art Ctr., Plano, 1990, Collin County C. C. Gallery, Plano, 1994; exhibited in group show S.W. Watercolor Soc., Dallas, 1990, juried show Southwestern Watercolor Soc. (signature status), 2000, Invitational Water Media Show, 2001, Western Fedn. Watercolor Exhbn., 2003; represented in permanent collection Farmerville C. of C.; illustrator for nat. card line, 1997-2000. Mentor Boles Children's Home, Quinlan, Tex., 1996—2003. Recipient award S.W. Watercolor Soc. Mem.: Southwestern Watercolor Soc. (signature mem., award in group 1999). Republican. Mem. Ch. of Christ. Avocation: nature lover. Office: Collin County CC 2800 E Spring Creek Pkwy Plano TX 75074-3300

COTTING, JAMES CHARLES, manufacturing company executive; b. Winchester, Mass., Oct. 15, 1933; s. Edward L. and Mary Ellen (Worrell) C.; m. Marjorie A. Kirsch, Feb. 8, 1963; children: James Charles, Steven Robert, Brenda Ann-Marie. BA cum laude, Ohio State U., 1955. Acctg. supr. U.S. Steel Corp., Pitts., 1959-61; mgr. profit analysis Ford Motor Co., Dearborn, Mich., 1961-63; mgr. devel. planning A.O. Smith Corp., Milw., 1963-66; asst. contr. Gen. Foods Corp., White Plains, N.Y., 1966-71; v.p. planning Internat. Paper Co., N.Y.C., 1971-76, v.p., contr., 1976-79; sr. v.p. fin. and planning, CFO Navistar Internat. Corp., Chgo., 1979-82, exec. v.p. fin., 1982-83, vice chmn., CFO, 1983-87, chmn., CEO, 1987-95, chmn. bd., 1995-96. Mem. Pres. Reagan's Task Force on Mkt. Mechanisms; bd. dirs. USG Corp., Chgo. Stock Exch. Dir. Jr. Achievement of Chgo.; trustee Adler Planetarium. Lt. USN, 1955-58. Mem. Chgo. Coun. on Fgn. Rels., Comml. Club Chgo., Econ. Club Chgo., Montclair Golf Club, Barrington Hills Country Club, Chgo. Club, Phi Beta Kappa, Alpha Tau Omega.

COTTINGHAM, BARBARA J. music educator; b. Macon, Ga., Oct. 16, 1950; d. William Harold and Eunie Mae Cook; m. Theodore Joseph Cottingham, Jan. 8, 1977; children: Amy Elizabeth, Christopher Clair. B in Music Edn., Oral Roberts U., 1977. Pvt. piano tchr., Tulsa, Okla., 1982—. Mem.: Broken Arrow Music Tchrs. Assn. (treas.), Tulsa Accredited Music Tchrs. Assn., Am. Coll. Musicians, Okla. Music Tchrs. Assn., Music Tchrs. Nat. Assn. Home and Office: 2139 E 56 Tulsa OK 74105

COTTINGHAM, RICHARD SUMNER, paper company executive; b. Columbus, Ohio, May 7, 1941; s. Robert E. and Lee Alice (Gasaway) C.; m. Sheila L. Robertson, Dec. 20, 1980. BA in History, Ohio State U., 1964. Pres. Cottingham Paper Co., Columbus, 1968—. Bd. dirs. Network Svcs. Co., 1984-90, chmn., 1986-88. Served as lt. (j.g.) USN, 1964-67, Vietnam. Recipient Ernst & Young Master Entrepreneur of Yr. award for Columbus and Ctr. Ohio, 1998, Bus. First Fast Fifty award, 2001, 02; named among Columbus Bus. First Fast Fifty Cos., 2001, 02; named Family Firm of Distinction, Weatherhead Sch. Mgmt., 2001. Mem. Nat. Paper Trade Assn. (young exec. com. 1976), Am. Mgmt. Assn., Nat. Assn. Wholesale Distbrs., Internat. Sanitary Supply Assn., Chief Exec. Bds. Columbus, Econ. Club Columbus, Columbus C. of C., Worthington Country Club. Republican. Address: Cottingham Paper Co 324 E 2d Ave PO Box 163579 Columbus OH 43216-3579 E-mail: rcottingham@cottinghampaper.com.

COTTINGHAM, STEPHEN KENT, real estate development executive, researcher, minister, educator; b. Denver, Dec. 28, 1951; s. Miles Dixon and Ruth (Skeen) C. Student, So. Oreg. Coll., 1970-71; BBA, So. Meth. U., 1974; ThM, Dallas Theol. Sem., 1984; postgrad., So. Meth. U. V.p. Cottingham Constrn. Co., Dallas, 1974-79; project mgmt. Avery Mays Constrn. Co., Dallas, 1981-82; asst. v.p. Pacific Realty Corp., Dallas, 1983-85, v.p., 1985-86, exec. v.p., 1986-88; v.p. Paragon Group, Dallas, 1988-91; regional v.p. The Prime Group Inc., San Antonio, 1991-93; pres. Brock Investment Group, Inc., San Antonio, 1993-95; chairman, pres. SKCI, Inc., San Antonio, 1995—; founder, chmn., pres. Theol. Edn. Found., Internat., 1996—; pres. Princeton Resources, Inc., 1992—; founder, chmn., pres. Cottingham Devel. Corp., San Antonio, 1997—; with planning and devel. divsn. San Antonio River Authority, 2000—; pastor, tchr. Univ. United Meth. Ch., San Antonio, 2002—. Adj. tchr. N.W. Bible Ch. Coll. Class, Dallas, 1981-83; student leader, counselor Young Life Internat., Dallas, 1974-76; chmn. Boyd Ministries, Norfolk, Va., 1996—; bd. dirs. Harvester Ministries, Plano, Tex. Charter mem. Rep. Nat. Com., Washington, 1985—; tchr. Christ Episcopal Ch., San Antonio, chmn. adult edn., exec. com.; founder, pres. Theol. Edn. Foun., Internat., San Antonio, 1996—. Named one of Outstanding Young Men of Am., Montgomery, Ala., 1986; So. Meth. U. Scholar, 1972-74. Mem. Internat. Right of Way Assn., Urban Land Inst. (assoc.), Evang. Theol. Soc., Phi Gamma Delta (treas.), Phi Beta Lamda. Avocations: skiing, antique restoration, cycling, writing, travel, missionary work. Office: Univ United Meth Ch 5084 De Zavala Rd San Antonio TX 78249

COTTLE, HAROLD RANSON, pathologist, laboratory owner; b. Bklyn., Dec. 7, 1925; s. Kenneth Raymond and Katharine Habershon (Blelloch) C.; m. Betty Lowell, July 15, 1950; children: David Lowell, Andrew Geoffrey, Susan Elizabeth. Student, Bard Coll., 1942-43, Dartmouth Coll., 1943-44; MD, N.Y. Med. Coll., 1948. Diplomate Nat. Bd. Med. Examiners; cert. Am. Bd. Pathology. Intern Meth. Hosp., Bklyn., 1948-49, resident in pathology, 1949-50, Kings County Hosp., Bklyn., 1952-54; asst. pathologist Kings County Hosp., SUNY, 1954-55, asst. to dir. of labs., 1955-56, chief autopsy svc., 1956-60, chief surg. pathology, 1960-62, vis. pathologist, 1962-70; clin. assoc. prof. SUNY, Downstate Med. Ctr., Bklyn., 1970-85; dir. Harold R. Cottle, M.D. Lab., 1975—. Asst. instr. SUNY, 1953-54, instr., 1954-56, asst. prof., 1956-62, prof., 1956-62, clin. asst. prof., 1962-70; assoc. dir. labs. Maimonides Hosp., Bklyn., 1962-66; dir. anatomic pathology Bklyn.-Cumberland Med. Ctr., 1966-70; pathologist Altoona (Pa.) Hosp., 1970-72, dir. lab. svcs., 1972-74, mem. exec. com., 1972-74; dir. lab. medicine Indiana (Pa.) Hosp., 1974-84; cons. pathologist VA Hosp., Altoona, 1973-89; coroner's pathologist various counties, Pa.; cons. staff Mercy Hosp., Altoona; mem. staff Conemaugh Valley Meml. Hosp. Contbr. articles to profl. jours. Chair Bklyn. chpt., bd. N.Y. State ACLU, 1956-70; various offices Sheepshead Bay Meth. Ch., 1950-70, 1st United Meth. Ch., Altoona, 1971-80; mem. Human Rights Commn., 1971-74. Lt. USNR, 1944-45, 50-52. Fellow Coll. Am. Pathologists, Am. Soc. Clin. Pathologists; mem. AMA, AAAS, AAUP, Pa. Med. Soc., Blair County Med. Soc., N.Y. Path. Soc., N.Y. State Soc. Pathologists, N.Y. State Assn. Pub. Health Labs., Pitts. Pathology Soc., Pitts. Comparative Pathology Soc., Ctrl. Pa. Regional Soc. Pathologists, Pa. Assn. Pathologists, Internat. Assn. Coroners and Med. Examiners, Pa. Assn. Coroners and Med. Examiners. Avocations: outdoor sports, firearms, books. Home and Office: 25 Sylvan Dr Hollidaysburg PA 16648-2718

COTTLE, THOMAS JOSEPH, sociologist; b. Chgo., Jan. 22, 1937; s. Maurice Hiam and Gitta Gradova (Weinstock) C.; BA, Harvard, 1959; MA, U. Chgo., 1963, PhD, 1968; m. Kay Mikkelsen, June 28, 1964; children— Claudia Mari, Jason Edwin, Sonya Ruth. Asst. prof. sociology Harvard, 1965-69; fellow Center for Advanced Study U. Ill., 1969-70; mem. div. edn. and dept. psychiatry Mass. Inst. Tech., Cambridge, 1970-73; researcher, writer Children's Def. Fund of Washington Research Project, 1973-75; psychologist Harvard Med. Sch., Cambridge, 1975—. NIMH fellow, 1962-64, Guggenheim fellow, 1975. Recipient Young Psychologist award Am. Psychol. Assn., 1966. Mem. Am. Sociol. Assn., PEN, Author's Guild, Soc. for Study Social Problems, Mass. Psychol. Assn., Nat. Soc. Lit. and Arts. Author: Time's Children, 1971; The Present of Things Future (with Stephen Klineberg), 1974; The Prospect of Youth, 1972; (with Craig Eisendrath and Laurence Fink), Out of Discontent, 1972; The Abandoners, 1973; The Voices of School, 1973; Perceiving Time, 1976; Black Children, White Dreams, 1974; A Family Album, 1974; Busing, 1976; Barred from School, 1976. Editorial bd. Social Problems, Urban Edn., Sch. Rev. Contbr. articles to profl. publs. Licensed clin. psychologist Mass. Home: 12 Beaconsfield Rd Brookline MA 02445-3305

COTTNER, DONALD, pathologist; b. Wichita, Mar. 26, 1937; s. Edward Floyd and Augusta Mae Cottner; m. Joreen Smith, Sept. 6, 1974 (div. June 1994); children: Dereck, Regina, John; m. Karolynne Kelly Cottner, June 12, 1996; stepchildren: Greg, Michael, Laquinta, Clifford. BA, Wichita State U., 1961; M of Religious Edn., Midwestern Sem., 1966; PhD, Southeastern U., 1982; D of Min., Evangel. Bible Sem., DDiv, U. Ctrl. Am., 1984. Janitor Dunbar Elem. Sch., Wichita, 1958—61; lawn cutter Ctrl. Bapt. Theol. Sem., 1961—62; agt. Western So. Life Ins., 1962—63; ins. cons. MEt. Life Ins., 1964—66; counselor Todd Phillips Home for Boys, Detroit, 1967; instr. Wolverine Bapt. Assn., 1967—68; counselor Neighborhood Youth Corps, Kansas City, 1968—69, exec. dir., 1969—70; with Operation Mainstream, 1970—72; tng. officer, counselor Neighborhood Youth Corp.s, 1972—73; dir. bus. inst. Black Econ. Union, 1973—78; psychotherapist pvt. practice, Kansas City, 1978—85; ret. Grant writer Eastside Ctr., St. Joseph, Mo., 1973—74; adj. prof. Penn Valley C.C., Kansas City, 1974. Mem.: Charles F. Menninger Soc. Republican. Baptist. Avocations: reading, writing. Home: 3201 N Kinley Ave Fort Worth TX 76106

COTTON, BARBARA JEAN, systems analyst; b. Cleve., Feb. 10, 1965; d. Eugene and Mamie Wilson; m. Robert Eugene Hunter, Feb. 19, 1991 (div. May 1993); 1 child, Robert Eugene Hunter,Jr.; m. David Cotton, Nov. 27, 1997. AAB in Computer Studies, Cuyahoga C.C., Cleve., 1995; postgrad., Cleve. State U., 1995—96; Diploma, Capital U., Cleve., 2003. Sec. Analex Corp., Brookpark, Ohio, 1984—89; data modeler NASA Tech. Mgmt., Brookpark, 1989—97; documentation specialist NASA Software Engring., Brookpark, 1992—, data systems analyst, 1994—. Motivational spkr. NASA Spkrs.'s Bur., Cleve., 1989—. Author: (book) Eugene - A Biography of a Sad Lonely Boy Growing Up in the South, 1997. Sec. Women's Adv. Group, Cleve., 2000—02. Recipient Cmty. award, Bus. Profl. Women of Cleve., 2001, Fed. Women Exec. award, Women's Adv. Group Cleve., 2001, Spl. Recognition, High Speed Rsch., Cleve., 1997, Cert. of Appreciation, Spkr.'s Bur., numerous certs. of appreciation various orgns. Mem.: Nat. Tech. Assn. (career awareness coord. 1989—). Jehovah'S Witness. Avocations: dancing, golf, writing. Office: NASA Glenn Research Ctr 21000 Brookpark Rd Brookpark OH 44135

COTTON, FRANK ALBERT, chemist; b. Phila., Apr. 9, 1930; s. Albert and Helen (Taylor) Cotton; m. Diane Dornacher, June 13, 1959; children: Jennifer Helen, Jane Myrna. Student, Drexel Inst. Tech., 1947—49; AB, Temple U., 1951, DSc (hon.), 1963; PhD, Harvard U., 1955; Dr. rer. Nat. (hon.), Bielefeld U., 1979; DSc (hon.), Columbia U., 1980, Northwestern U., 1981, U. Bordeaux, 1981, St. Joseph's U., 1982, U. Louis Pasteur, 1982, U. Valencia, 1983, Kenyon Coll., 1983, Technion-Israel Inst. Tech., 1983, U. Cambridge, 1986, Johann Wolfgang Goethe Universität, 1989, U. S.C., 1989, U. Rennes, 1992, Lomonosov U., 1992, Fujian Inst. Rsch., Chinese Acad. Scis., 1993, U. Pisa, Italy, 1994, U. Zaragoza, 1994, Cleve. State U., 1995, U. Crete, 1996, Mich. State U., 1996, U. Pierre and Marie Curie, 1997, U. Palermo, 1997, U. Jaume I, 2000, N.C. State U., 2000, Ohio State U., 2001, Hebrew U. Jerusalem, 2002, Drexel Univ., 2002. Instr. chemistry MIT, 1955—57, asst. prof., 1957—60, assoc. prof., 1960—61, prof., 1961—71; Robert A. Welch Distinguished prof. chemistry Tex. A&M U., 1971—, dir. Lab. for Molecular Structure and Bonding, 1983—. Cons. Am. Cyanamid, Stamford, Conn., 1958—67, Union Carbide, N.Y.C., 1964—94; Todd prof. Cambridge U., 1985—86. Author (with G. Wilkinson and P.L. Gaus): Basic Inorganic Chemistry, 1995; author: Chemical Applications of Group Theory, 1990; author: (with L. Lynch and C. Darlington) Chemistry, An Investigative Approach, 1969; author: (with G. Wilkinson, C.A. Murillo, M. Bochmann) Advanced Inorganic Chemistry, 1999; author: (with R.A. Walton) Multiple Bonds Between Metal Atoms, 1992; editor: Progress in Inorganic Chemistry, 1959—68, Inorganic Syntheses, 1971; editor: (with L.M. Jackman) Dynamic Nuclear Magnetic Resonance Spectroscopy, 1975; editor: (with R.D. Adams) Catalysis by Di- and Polynuclear Metal Atom Clusters, 1998. Recipient Michelson-Morley award, Case Western Reserve U., 1980, Nat. medal of Sci., 1982, King Faisal prize, 1990, Paracelsus medal, Swiss Chem. Soc., 1994, prize, Welch Found., 1994, Polyhedron medal, 1995, Gold medal, Am. Inst. Chemists, 1998, Lavoisier medal, French Chem. Soc., 2000, John Scott medal, City of Phila., 1997, Wolf Found. prize, State of Israel, 2000, hon. fellow, Robinson Coll., Cambridge (Eng.) U. Mem.: NAS (chmn. phys. scis. 1985—88, coun. 1991—94, gov. bd. NRC 1992—94, Cosepup 1992—94), Chinese Acad. Scis. (fgn.), Inst. de France Acad. des Scis. (fgn. mem.), Royal Soc. London (fgn. mem.), Am. Philos. Soc., Göttingen Acad. Scis. (Gaus Lectr. 2002), Am. Acad. Arts and Scis., Am. Chem. Soc. (award 1962, 1974, Baekeland medal N.J. sect. 1963, Nichols medal N.Y. sect. 1975, Pauling medal Oreg. and Puget Sound sect. 1976, Kirkwood Medal N.Y. sect. 1978, Gibbs medal Chgo. sect. 1980, Richards medal N.E. sect. 1986, Priestley medal 1998, F.A. Cotton medal Tex. A&M sect. 1995), Acad. Europea (hon.), Royal Soc. Edinburgh (hon.), Indian Acad. Scis. (hon.), Italian Chem. Soc. (hon.), Royal Danish Acad. Scis. and Letters (hon.), Royal Soc. Chemistry (hon.), N.Y. Acad. Scis. (life). Home: 4101 Sand Creek Rd Bryan TX 77808-8337 Office: Tex A&M Univ Dept Chemistry College Station TX 77843-0001

COTTON, JOSEPH L, music educator; b. Winnfield, La., 1955; s. Richard Newton and Charlene Verdale Bryant Cotton. B.M.E., Northwestern St. U., Natchitoches, La., 1976. Vocal music St. Charles Parish, Luling, La., 1978—82, St. Tammany Parish, Covington, La., 1982—2002. Mem.: Am. Choral Directors Assn. (assoc.), La. Music Edn. Assn. (assoc.), Music Edn. Nat. Conf. (assoc.). Home: 61224 Richard Avenue Slidell LA 70460 Personal E-mail: jicrdb@bellsouth.net.

COTTON, JOYCE E. DOHERTY, mental health nurse; b. Stoneham, Mass., Sept. 4, 1952; d. Joseph Francis and Anne M. (Bickford) Doherty; m. Paul Briggs Cotton, Oct. 28, 1979; children: Katherine Anne, Abigail Briggs 1 stepchild, Charlotte. Diploma, Lawrence Gen. Hosp. Sch. Nsg., 1973; BA in Psychology cum laude, Salem State Coll., 1978, MEd in Counseling, 1981. Cert. advanced practice RN, Maine, 1996. Team leader med.-surg. unit Lawrence (Mass.) Gen. Hosp., 1973-75; head nurse adolescent day treatment program Mass. Dept. Mental Health, Danvers (Mass.) State Hosp., 1976-78; psychiat. nurse, case mgr. adolescent aftercare program Greater Lawrence Area Office Mass. Dept. Mental Health, 1978-80, aftercare nurse day treatment ctr., 1980-81, coord. adult aftercare program, 1981-82; dir. aftercare clinic Greater Lynn (Mass.) Cmty. Mental Health Ctr., 1982-85; psychiatric nurse Jackson Brook Inst., Maine, 1985-86; clin. nurse specialist Androscoggin Home Health Svcs., Auburn, Maine, 1986-87, clin. nurse specialist cons., 1987—; clin. nurse specialist Western Maine Counseling Svc., Brigton, 1987-90, clin. dir., 1990-91; asst. dir. nursing Jackson Brook Inst., South Portland, Maine, 1991-95, dir. ambulatory care svcs., 1995-99; dir. clin. svcs. Shoreline Cmty. Mental Health Ctr., Brunswick, Maine, 1999-2000; v.p. clin. ops. and quality Sweetser, Portland, Maine, 2000—02; assoc. chief nursing and clin. svcs. Spring Harbor Hosp., South Portland, Maine, 2002—. Bd. dirs. Western Maine Counseling Svc., Solstice Adolescent Treatment Program, Office for Children in Lawrence. Recipient cert. of appreciation Greater Lynn Mental Health and Retardation Assn., 1984, North Shore Coll., 1985. Mem. ANA (cert. clin. nurse specialist in adult psychiat. and mental health nursing), Maine Assn. Clin. Nurse Specialists, 1993—, Sigma Theta Tau. Home: 10 Christopher Rd Kennebunk ME 04043-6715 Office: Spring Harbor Hosp 175 Running Hill Rd South Portland ME 04103

COTTON, LARRY, ranching executive; Pres. Cotton & Assocs., Howell, Mich. Office: Cotton and Assocs 131 Robin Ct Howell MI 48843-8776

COTTON, RICHARD, lawyer; b. Washington, July 1, 1944; s. Eugene and Sylvia Ruth (Glickstein) C.; m. Patricia B. Fellner, Oct. 11, 1981; children: Rachel, Jonathan. AB, Harvard Coll., 1965; LLB cum laude, Yale U., 1969. Bar: N.H. 1971, Calif. 1974, D.C. 1980, U.S. Ct. Appeals (D.C. cir.) 1984, U.S. Supreme Ct. 1980. Law clk. to judge J. Skelly Wright U.S. Ct. Appeals D.C. Cir., 1969-70; law clk. to justice Wm. J. Brennan Jr. U.S. Supreme Ct., 1970-71; mng. atty. N.H. Legal Assistance, Concord, 1972-73; lectr. in law U. Calif., Berkeley, 1973-74; staff atty. Nat. Resources Def. Coun., Palo Alto, Calif., 1974-77; exec. sec. U.S. Dept. HEW, Washington, 1978-79; ptnr. Califano, Ross & Heineman, Washington, 1981-83, Dewey, Ballantine, Washington, 1983-86; pres., chief exec. officer HCX, Inc., Washington, 1987-89; exec. v.p., gen. counsel NBC, N.Y.C., 1989—; chair bd. dirs. N.Y. Primary Care Devel. Corp., 1993—. Lectr. in law U. Calif., Berkeley, 1973-74. Office: NBC 30 Rockefeller Plz Fl 52 New York NY 10112-0002

COTTON, ROBERT BELL, pediatrician, neonatologist, researcher; b. Danville, Va., Feb. 19, 1940; s. Robert Bell and Gonia (Scott) C.; m. Anne Walker, June 12, 1965; children: Elizabeth Cotton Matsui, William Scott. BA, U. Va., 1961, MD, 1965. Diplomate Am. Bd. Pediats., Sub-Bd. Neonatal-Perinatal Medicine. Intern pediats. Vanderbilt U. Hosp., Nashville, 1965-66, chief nurseries dept pediats., 1978-92, assoc. prof. dept. pediats., 1981-86; resident pediats. U. Va. Hosp., Charlottesville, Va., 1966-67, chief resident pediats., 1967-68; chief dept. medicine SEATO Med. Rsch. Laboratory U.S. Army Med. R&D Command, Bangkok, 1968-72, rsch. internist, 1969-72; cons. pediatrician Whittaker Corp., Pertamina Med. Sys., Jakarta, Indonesia, 1973; rsch. assoc., fellow neonatology Vanderbilt U. Sch. Medicine, Nashville, 1972-75, instr. pediats., 1974-75, asst. prof. dept. pediats., 1975-81, prof. dept pediats, 1986—, divsn. head divsn. neonatology, 1989—, dir. newborn clin. rsch. core, 1981—96, dir. Mid. Tenn. Regional Newborn Ctr., 1985—, dir. tng. program neonatal-perinatal medicine, 1989—2001. Mem. AAAS, AMA, Internat. Collegium Neonatal Intensive Care, Nat. Perinatal Soc., Am. Thoracic Soc., Am. Pediat. Soc., Am. Acad. Pediats. (exec. com. Perinatal sect. 1988-94, program chmn. ann. meeting 1989, also Tenn. chpt., founder Orgn. Neonatology Training Program Dirs.), Am. Lung Assn. Tenn. (bd. dirs, chmn. Children's Lung Com., profl. edn. rsch. com. program and budget com.), So. Soc. Pediat. Rsch., So. Perinatal Soc., Tenn. Med. Assn., Davidson County Pediat. Soc., Nashville Acad. Medicine, Soc. Pediat. Rsch., Phi Beta Kappa. Office: Vanderbilt U Med Ctr 21st & Garland Rm A 0126 Mcn Nashville TN 37232-0001 E-mail: robert.cotton@mcmail.vanderbilt.edu.

COTTON, WILLIAM ROBERT, retired dentist; b. Miami, Fla., Nov. 29, 1931; s. Robert Lee and Mamie Bell (Daniel) Cotton; m. Marye Ruth Hartz; children: Caroline Ruth, William Robert Jr., David Michael, Lynn Cathryn. DDS, U. Md., 1955; MS, Northwestern U., Chgo., 1963; MA, Roosevelt U., 1973; EdS, George Washington U., 1980. With USN, 1955-81, commd. capt., 1973, ret., 1981; asst. dental officer Marine Corps Schs. and USS F.D. Roosevelt CVA 42, Quantico, Va. and Mayport, Fla., 1957 61; head exptl. pathology div. Naval Med. Rsch. Inst., Bethesda, Md., 1963-67; dental officer USS Fulton AS-11, New London, Conn., 1967-69; chief histopathology div. Naval Dental Rsch. Inst., Great Lakes, Ill., 1969-72, exec. officer, 1972-73, dep. comdg. officer, 1973-76; chmn. dental scis. dept. Naval Med. Rsch. Inst., Bethesda, Md., 1976-79; dir. Casualty Care Rsch. Program Ctr., Naval Med. Rsch. Inst., Bethesda, Md., 1979-81; assoc. prof. dept. operative dentistry Temple U., Phila., 1981-83; prof., chmn. dept. operative dentistry Georgetown U., Washington, 1983-90; pvt. practice Rockville, Md.; ret., 1999. Mem. adv. com. dental tech. program So. Ill. U., Carbondale, 1976—85; cons. Naval Dental Rsch. Inst., Great Lakes, 1981—85, Dentsply Internat., York, Pa., 1984—88; mem. spl. study sect. NIH, Washington, 1984, Washington, 87. Contbg. author: book Biology Dental Caires, 1968, Dental Clinics of North America, 1986, editl. bd.: Jour. Dental Rsch., 1976—86, 1988, Jour. Operative Dentistry, 1986—92. Fellow: Internat. Coll. Dentists (life), Am. Coll. Dentists (life); mem.: ADA (life), D.C. Dental Soc. (life; bd. dirs. 1986—89). Democrat. Presbyterian. Home: 11816 Winterset Ter Potomac MD 20854-2846 E-mail: wmrc@comcast.net.

COTTRELL, DAVID MILTON, sound recording engineer; b. Ft. Dodge, Iowa, Mar. 27, 1961; s. Milton and Evelyn Cottrell. AA in Counseling, Iowa Ctrl. Coll.; BS in Counseling, Almeda Coll. Music pub. My Friend Music, Hollywood, Calif., 1975—76; recording engr., prin. Super Sound, Ft. Dodge,

1986—97, Soul Survivor Sound, Lemars, Iowa, 2000—. Singer: (albums) Mr. Fingers, 1971, I Want You I Need You, 1981, Can You Rock Me, 1989, Good Gosh, 2002. Independent. Episcopalian. Home: 414 First St SE Le Mars IA 51031

COTTRELL, G. WALTON, manufacturing executive; b. Auburn, N.Y., Sept. 26, 1939; s. George H. and Eleanor H. (Day) C.; m. Jean H. Springer, June 15, 1963; children: Lisa, Lori. BSME, Cornell U., 1962, MBA, 1963. Various positions Owens-Ill., Inc., Toledo, 1965-85, treas., 1980-83, v.p. corp. planning, 1984-85; dir. fin. Europe Owens-Ill. Internat., Geneva, 1976-80; v.p. fin. The Allen Group, Inc., Melville, NY, 1986; v.p., treas. Squibb Corp., Princeton, N.J., 1987-88; sr. v.p. fin., CFO Carpenter Tech. Corp., Reading, Pa., 1989-2001, sr. v.p. strategic planning, 2001; ret., 2001. Dir. Andersen Labs., Inc., Bloomfield, Conn., 1992-98. Bd. dirs. Jr. Achievement N.W. Ohio, Toledo, 1980-86, Planned Parenthood N.W. Ohio, Toledo, 1982-86, United Way Berks County, 1990-97, Berks County Cmty. Found., 1999—; mem. coun. Cornell U., 1985-95. Lt. USNR, 1963-65. Mem. Fin. Execs. Inst. (bd. dirs. 1982-85), Nat. Assn. Corp. Treas. (pres. 1997-98, chair bd. dirs. 1998-99). Republican. United Ch. of Christ. Home: 4 Forest Rd Mohnton PA 19540-9300

COTTRELL, JANET ANN, controller; b. Berea, Ohio, Dec. 2, 1943; d. Carmen and Hazel (French) Volpe; m. Melvin M. Cottrell, Mar. 2, 1963; children: Lori A., Gregory C. Student, Los Angeles State Coll., 1961-63. Lic. ins. agt., Calif. Loan processing Eastern Lenders, Covina, 1962-64; asst. bookkeeper Golden Rule Discount Stores, Rosemead, Calif., 1964-66; acctg. supr. Walter Carpet Mills, Industry, Calif., 1967-69; co-owner Motorcycle Specialties Co., Industry, 1969-78, Covina (Calif.) Kawasaki, 1978-84; v.p., contr. M.C. Specialties Inc., Covina, 1984—, Aviation Communications Inc., Covina, 1992—. Active various coms. relating to promotion, safety and advancement of the recreational vehicle and auto industry, So. Calif., 1981—. Mem. com. Miss Covina Pageant, 1986—, presdl. task force, nat., 1982—, Rep. nat. com., 1986—. Mem. Covina C. of C., Calif. Motorcycle Dealers Assn., Nat. Auto Dealers Assn., Internat. Jet Ski Boating Assn. Republican. Avocations: traveling, gourmet cooking. Office: Aviation Comm Inc 1025 W San Bernardino Rd Covina CA 91722-4106

COTTRELL, JEANNETTE ELIZABETH, retired librarian; b. Buffalo, Dec. 10, 1923; d. Benjamin Birch and Mary Jeannette (Ashdown) Milnes; m. William Barber Cottrell, Jan. 21, 1944 (dec.); children: Karen Jean, Susan Marie, William Milnes, Scott Barber, Stephen Ashdown. BA in Sociology, U. Tenn., 1970, MS, 1976; student, Alfred U., 1940-43. Cert. tchr. libr., Tenn. Nursery sch. tchr. Concord Meth. Ch., Knoxville, Tenn., 1964-65; libr. City Sch. Sys., Knoxville, Tenn., 1971-84, ret., 1984. Author: (with husband) An American Family in the 20th Century, 1987; recorder textbooks for the blind, 1983—. Libr. Concord United Meth. Ch., Knoxville, 1975—, curriculum chair spl. studies class, 1989—, reading chair Suzanna Wesley Circle. Mem. AAUW, Phi Kappa Phi, Beta Phi Mu. Republican. Methodist. Avocations: singing, bridge, cooking, travel, reading. Home: 308 Camelot Ct Knoxville TN 37922-2076

COTTRELL, MARY-PATRICIA TROSS, bank executive; b. Seattle, Apr. 24, 1934; d. Alfred Carl and Alice-Grace (O'Neal) Tross; m. Richard Smith Cottrell, May 17, 1969 (dec. 1995). BBA, U. Wash., 1955. Sys. svc. rep. IBM, Seattle, Endicott, NY, 1955-58, customer edn. instr. Endicott, 1958—65; cons. data processing Stamford, Conn., 1965-66; asst. treas. Union Trust Co., Stamford, 1967-68, asst. v.p., 1969-76, v.p., 1976-78, v.p., head corp. svcs., 1978-83; v.p. corp. fin. svcs. Citytrust, Bridgeport, Conn., 1983-90, sr. v.p. cash mgmt. svcs., 1990-91; v.p. cash mgmt. Chase Manhattan Bank Conn., N.A., 1991-92, Centerbank, New Haven, 1992-95; v.p. corp. svcs. Lafayette Am. Bank, Bridgeport, 1995-97; sr. v.p. corp. svcs. Union Savs. Bank, Danbury, Conn., 1997—. Chmn. Family and Children's Agy., 1986—87, bd. dirs., 1982—; vice chmn. Gaylord Hosp., 1991, chmn. devel. com., 1992—, New Eng. Network, Inc., Bank Mktg. Assn., 1988—91; bd. trustees Norwalk Seaport Assn., 1997—2001; bd. dirs. Danbury Vis. Nurse Assn., 2003, Bridgeport Housing Svcs., 1985—91, Stamford Rehab. Ctr., 1996—; chmn. Stamford Rehab., 2003; bd. dirs. Gaylord Hosp., 1986—92, 1999—, Danbury Cemetery Assn., 2002—. Mem.: New Eng. Automated Clearing House Assn. (bd. dirs. 1995—97), Danbury Vis. Nurse Assn. (bd. dirs. 2003—), Fairfield County Bankers Assn. (dir., pres. 1984—85), Electronic Funds Transfer Assn. (vice chmn., bd. dirs., chmn. bd. dirs. 1983—84), Phi Beta Kappa, Beta Gamma Sigma. Republican. Roman Catholic.

COTTRELL, PAUL (WILLIAM COTTRELL), lawyer, educator; b. Penns Grove, N.J., Nov. 5, 1951; s. Arvil Earl and Gudbjorg (Gudmundsdottir) G.; m. Carolyn Anne Pokoyski, May 25, 1974; children: Jonathan Paul, Elizabeth Constance. BA magna cum laude, U. Del., 1975; JD, U. Chgo., 1978. Bar: Ill. 1978, U.S. Dist. Ct. (no. dist.) Ill. 1978, U.S. Ct. Appeals (7th cir.) 1980, U.S. Tax Ct. 1982, Pa. 1985, U.S. Dist. Ct. (ea. dist.) Pa. 1985, U.S. Ct. Appeals (3d cir.) 1985, Del. 1985, U.S. Dist. Ct. Del. 1986, Md. 1987. Assoc. Karon, Morrison & Savikas, Ltd., Chgo., 1978-81, Fohrman, Lurie, Sklar & Simon, Ltd., Chgo., 1981-84; assoc. dir. Constrn. Law Inst., Chgo., 1982-85; prin. Tighe, Cottrell & Logan, Wilmington, Phila., Balt., Woodstown, N.J., 1987—. Co-editor: Corporate Directors and Officers: Liability, Insurance and Risk Management, 1989; contbr. chpt. to Ill. Election Law, 1983, articles to profl. jours. Treas. Citizens Coalition, 1973-75; bd. dirs. Saxony Ct. Condominium Assn., Chgo., 1981-82. Named Outstanding Young Man of Am., Jaycees, 1983. Mem. Chgo. Bar Assn. (mem. exec. com. Young Lawyers sect. 1981-85, co-chmn. Fed. Trial Bar task force), ABA (vice chairperson com. on liaison Young Lawyers Div., 1982-84, mem. exec. com., health care law com., 1982-84, del. ABA conv. 1983, editor-in-chief law practice notes Barrister 1985-88), Del. Alumni Assn. (Chgo. area coord. 1987-85), Phi Kappa Phi, Omicron Delta Kappa, Pi Sigma Alpha. Democrat. Unitarian. Office: Tighe Cottrell & Logan P A First Fed Pla PO Box 1031 Wilmington DE 19899-1031

COTTRELL, THOMAS SYLVESTER, pathology educator, university dean; b. Chgo., Feb. 2, 1934; s. Sylvester Vincent and Cleo (Medley) C.; m. Jane Chichester, July 3, 1959; children: Matthew Thomas, Anne Medley, Sarah Jane. AB, Brown U., 1955; MD, Columbia U., 1965. Diplomate Am. Bd. Pathology. Asst. prof. N.Y. Med. Coll., Valhalla, 1968-79; assoc. prof. pathology SUNY Sch. Medicine, Stony Brook, 1979—, assoc. dean clin. affairs, 1979-88, exec. assoc. dean, 1988-97; interim exec. dir. U. Hosp. SUNY, Stony Brook, 1983-84, interim chmn. dept. ob-gyn. Sch. Medicine, 1991-92, interim chmn. dept. surgery Sch. Medicine, 1996, vice dean, 1997—2001. Lt. USNR, 1957-60. Scholar John and Mary R. Markle Found., 1969-73. Fellow Coll. Am. Pathologists, N.Y. Acad. Medicine; mem. AAAS. Home: PO Box 1292 3775 Skunk Ln Cutchogue NY 11935-1541 E-mail: skunkln@yahoo.com.

COTTY, WILLIAM FRANK (BILL COTTY), lawyer, state legislator; b. Aug. 9, 1946; s. William O. and Marie (Frank) C.; m. Amelia Dunlap, Dec. 26, 1969; children: William D., Mary K., Anne Marie. BA, Erskine Coll., Due West, S.C., 1969; JD, U. S.C., 1974. Bar: S.C. 1974. Adminstrv. asst. Congressman Tom Gettys, Washington, 1969-71; atty., legis. liaison S.C. Wildlife Dept., Columbia, 1974-77; assoc. atty. Ratchford & Eleazer, Columbia, 1977-81; sole practitioner Columbia, 1981-95; with Cotty & Jonas, 1995—; mem. S.C. Ho. of Reps., 1994—. Trustee Richland County Sch. Dist. Two, Columbia, 1986-94. Lt. col. S.C. Army NG. ret. Recipient Legis. Conservationist of the Yr. award S.C. Wildlife Fedn., 1971. Republican. Presbyterian. Home: 324 Valley Springs Rd Columbia SC 29223-6934 Office: 1328 Blanding St Columbia SC 29201-2903

COUCH, DANIEL MICHAEL, healthcare executive; b. Chgo., July 1, 1937; s. Arthur Daniel and Helen Margret (Kreamer) C.; m. Marilee Hermon, Sept. 12, 1958; children: Laura Ann, Mark Allen, Kristina Lynn, Michelle Louise, Daniel Michael Jr. BS in Bus., Ind. U., 1958; MBA, Butler U., 1977. Field examiner Ind. State Bd. Accounts, Indpls., 1959-61; controller Community Hosp., Anderson, Ind., 1961-67; field rep. Am. Hosp. Assn., Chgo., 1967-68; treas./controller Health & Hosp. Corp. of Marion County, Indpls., 1968-71; assoc. adminstr. Winona Meml. Hosp., Indpls., 1971-78; pres. Huntington (Ind.) Meml. Hosp., 1978-80; dep. exec. dir. Truman Med. Ctr., Kansas City, Mo., 1980-99. Bd. dirs. Nat. Pub. Health and Hosp. Inst., Washington, 1987-90, chmn., 1989. Bd. dirs, mem. exec. com. Labor-Mgmt. Coun., Kansas City, Mo., 1982—, co-chmn, 1991—97; bd. dirs. Greater Kans.City Mental Health Found., 1984—93, pres., 1992—93; bd. dirs. Kans. City Care Ctr., 1990—, treas., 1999—; bd. dirs. Resource Devel. Inst., Kans. City, 1998—; pres., 2002—; bd. dirs. Vis. Nurse Home Care Svcs, Kans. City, 1991—98; chmn., 1993—98. 1st lt. USAR, 1958—67. Fellow Am. Coll. Healthcare Execs. (life fellow, nominating com. 1995-99); mem. Am. Hosp. Assn. (ho. of dels. and Regional Policy Bd. 7 1989-92, governing coun. sect. met. hosps. 1990-93, chmn. 1993), Nat. Assn. Pub. Hosps. (bd. dirs. 1981-99, chmn. 1989), Kansas City Area Hosp. Assn. (bd. dirs. 1990-96), Greater Kansas City C. of C. (various coms. 1985-99), Healthcare Fin. Mgmt. Assn. (advanced), Kansas City Care Network (bd. dirs. 1995-99, pres. 1995-99), Family Health Ptnrs. (bd. dirs. 1995-99), Masons, Rotary. Episcopalian. Avocations: golf, bowling, reading. *While into life a little rain must fall, I like to dwell on the fact that into every life a little joy must come.*

COUCH, JAMES RUSSELL, JR., neurology educator; b. Bryan, Tex., Oct. 25, 1939; married; 2 children. BS, Texas A&M U., 1961; MD, Baylor U., 1965, PhD in Physiology, 1966; fellow, Lab of Neuropharmacology, NIMH, 1967-69; postgrad., Nat. Inst. Neurol. Diseases and Stroke, 1969-72. Diplomate Am. Bd. Psychiatry and Neurology, subspeciality clin. neurophysiology, 1992, recert., 2002; lic. physician, Tex., Md., Kans., Mo., Ill., Okla. Intern Barnes Hosp., St. Louis, 1966-67; resident in neurology Washington U. Sch. Medicine, St. Louis, 1969-72; mem. staff Kans. U. Med. Ctr., Kansas City, asst. prof. div. neurology, 1972-76, assoc. prof., 1976-79; prof., chief divsn. neurology So. Ill. U. Sch. Medicine, Springfield, 1979-92, acting chmn. dept. medicine, 1988-89; staff VA Hosp., Kansas City, Mo., Marion, Ill., Oklahoma City, St. Joseph (Mo.) Hosp., Kansas U. Med. Ctr., Atchison (Kans.) Hosp., Kansas City Gen. Hosp., Meml. Med. Ctr., Springfield, dir. EEG lab., muscular dystrophy clinic, cons. speech and hearing lab., 1979-92; staff St. John's Hosp., Springfield; prof., chmn. dept. neurology Okla. U. Coll. Med. and Health Sci. Ctr., Oklahoma City, 1992—; staff Presbyn. Hosp., Oklahoma City, Univ. Hosp., Oklahoma City, Childrens Hosp. of Okla. Investigator Mental Retardation Rsch. Ctr. Kans. U. Med. Ctr., Kansas City, 1972—79; bd. dirs. postgrad. neurology course Continuing Med. Edn. Kans. U. Med. Ctr.; examiner Am. Bd. Psychiatry and Neurology, 1975—77, 1979, 1984—85, 1989—98, 2000—01, Am. Bd. Neurosurgery, 1977; cons. Richland Meml. Hosp., Olney, Ill., 1981—85, Abraham Lincoln Meml. Hosp., Lincoln, Ill., 1981—92; staff cons. Lincoln Devel. Ctr., Outpatient Clinics, Lincoln, 1981—92; vis. prof. Northwestern U., Chgo., 1982, Chgo. 93 U. Nebr. 1992, Wayne State U. Med. Sch., 1992, Ind. U. Med. Sch., 1992, U. Rochester, 1992, U. Ala., Birmingham, 1994, U. W.Va., Morgantown, 1995, U. Mo., Columbia, Med. Sch. Kans. U., 1996, 2001, R.I. Hosp., Providence, 1996, Med. Coll. S.C., 1996, U. So. Fla., 1996, 99, Med. Sch. Brown U., 1996, U. Md., 1997, U. Minn., 1997, U. North Tex., 1997, L.I. Jewish Hosp., 1998, So. Ill. U. Med. Sch., 1999, U. Calif., Irvine, 2000; com. mem. med. sch. Kans. U., 1972—79, So. Ill. U., 1980—92, 1997, U. Nebr., Omaha, 1999, Washington U., St. Louis, 2001, Henry Ford Hosp., Detroit, 2001, Penn State Med. Sch., 2003. Mem. editl. bd. Headache, 1979-92, Jour. Stroke & Cerebrovascular Disease, 1995—; contbr. articles to profl. jours. Med. adv. bd. Lincoln Land Epilepsy Assn., 1980-92; exec. bd., chmn. edn. com. Am. Soc. Neurorehab., 1990-95. Fellow Nat. Heart Inst., 1965-66, NIH, NIMH, 1967-69; recipient numerous grants for neurology rsch., 1969—. Fellow Am. Acad. Neurology (bd. dirs. asst. sec.-treas. 1984-86, sec.-treas. 1986-88, chmn. sect. neurorehab. 1996-98, pres.-elect headache sect. 2001—, dir. 2001—, chair headache sect., 2003—), Stroke Coun. of Am. Heart Assn.; mem. AMA, Am. Neurological Assn. (elected), Am. Assn. for Study of Headache (exec. com. ad hoc 1983-85, winter headache course, membership com. 1983-85, chmn., 1994-96, faculty continuing med. edn. courses 1982—, edn. com. 1983—, achievement recognition com., publs. com. 1986—, bd. dirs. 1983-92, treas. 1992-94, sec. 1994-96, pres.-elect 1996-98, pres. 1998-2000), Am. Geriatric Soc., Am. Assn. Univ. Profs. Neurology (chmn. undergrad. edn. com, sec.-treas. 1992-96, chmn. VAMC com. 1997-2001) Am. Soc. Neurorehab. (chmn. edn. com. 1989-95, bd. dirs. 1990-98), Neurosci. Soc. (sec. Kansas City chpt. 1976-77, pres. 1977-78, pres. Sangamon County chptr. of Neurosci. 1982-92, pres. 1986-87), Consortium of Neurology (program dir., chair 2003—); Ill. Med. Soc., Sangamon County Med. Soc., Okla. State Med. Soc., Okla. County Med. Soc., Baylor U. Med. Alumni Assn., Washington U. Med. Alumni Assn., Sigma Xi, Alpha Omega Alpha, Phi Eta Sigma, Phi Kappi Phi. Home: 1616 Queenstown Rd Oklahoma City OK 73116-5523 Office: U Okla Health Sci Ctr Dept of Neurology PPOB209 PO Box 26901 Oklahoma City OK 73190-0001 E-mail: james-couch@ouhsc.edu.

COUCH, JESSE WADSWORTH, retired insurance company executive; b. Atlanta, Mar. 2, 1921; s. Jesse Newton and Laura (Day) W.; m. Charlotte Lucretia Collins, Jan. 13, 1945 (dec.); children: Robert Collins (dec.), Laura W.; m. Charlotte H. Gran, Oct. 17, 1997. AB, Princeton, 1947. With 1st Nat. Bank Houston, 1947-51; assoc. Wray Assocs., Houston, 1951-60; ptnr. Wray, Couch & Elder, Houston, 1960-69; v.p. Marsh & McLennan, Inc., 1969-83; pvt. cons., 1983-95. Mem. exec. bd. Episcopal Diocese of Tex., 1965-67, 68-71; trustee St. Luke's Episcopal Hosp., 1971-76; bd. dirs. Houston-Harris County YMCA, 1969-74, Houston Soc. Prevention Cruelty to Animals, 1974— ; Bd. dirs. Tex. divsn. Am. Cancer Soc., mem. exec. com., 1982-91; chmn. Am. Cancer Soc. Greater Houston, 1981-83; trustee Mus. Fine Arts, Houston, 1970-74. Served to capt. USAAF, 1943-46. Mem.: Houston C. of C. (aviation com. 1965—75), Allegro Club, Bayou Club, Houston Country Club, Rod & Gun Club, Eagle Lake. Home: 6015 Pine Forest Rd Houston TX 77057-1431 Office: 800 Bering Dr Ste 125 Houston TX 77057-2130 E-mail: jcouch@pdq.net.

COUCH, JOHN ALEXANDER, SR., biomedical researcher; b. Washington, Feb. 12, 1938; s. Raymond Carl and Rubye Frances (Wates) C.; m. Carolyn Susan Barrett, July 3, 1963; children: Catherine Susan, John Alexander Jr. BS, U. Ala., Tuscaloosa, 1961; MS, Fla. State U., 1964, PhD, 1971. Rsch. biologist U.S. Dept. Interior, Oxford, Md., 1964-71, U.S. EPA, Gulf Breeze, Fla., 1971-87, br. chief pathobiology, 1985—90, sr. rsch. scientist, 1987-96. Contbr. 90 articles to profl. jours. Mem. Am. Men & Women of Sci. Home: 4703 Soule Pl Gulf Breeze FL 32563-9271

COUCH, REX DEE, pathologist, medical executive; b. Fairmount, Ind., July 7, 1930; s. James Alva and Velma Elizabeth (Briles) C.; m. Patricia Alice Hynes, Feb. 19, 1955; children: Denis, Philip, Meredith, Patrick, Marie, Brian. AB, Ind. U., 1952; MD, Ind. U., Indpls., 1956. Diplomate Am. Bd. Pathology; cert. anatomic and clin. pathology, forensic pathology. Intern Upstate Med. Ctr. SUNY, Syracuse, 1956-57; resident instr. Med. Ctr. Ind. U., Indpls., 1957-58, 60-62; chief of lab. svc. Ft. Sill, Lawton, Okla., 1958-60; asst. to assoc. prof. Coll. of Med. U. Vt., Burlington, Vt., 1962-68; pvt. practice Christie-Couch Profl. Assn., Lancaster, N.H., 1968-75; dir. of lab. G.N. Wilcox Meml. Hosp., Lihue, Hawaii, 1975-96, also bd. dirs.; med. dir. Kauai Med. Group, Lihue, 1989-92, also bd. dirs. Bd. dirs. G.N. Wilcox Hosp. Editor Am. Soc. Clin. Pathologists Summary Report, Chgo., 1968; contbr. articles to profl. jours; researcher emporiatric pathology, sudden cardiac death. Mem. and soloist Kauai Chorale, Lihue, 1975-82; bd. dirs. Hale Opio Children's Home, 1975-82, Mayors Task Force Substance Abuse, 1984-86, Kauai Community Players, 1975-85. Capt. M.C., U.S. Army, 1958-60. Student fellow Nat. Polio Found., 1954, clin. fellow Am. Cancer Soc., 1960-61: named best actor Kauai Community Players, 1980. Fellow Am. Soc. Clin. Pathologists (bd. dirs. 1970-73, disting. svc. award 1979), Coll. Am. Pathologists, Nat. Assn. Med. Examiners; mem. Hawaii Soc. Pathologists (pres. 1981), Kauai 200. Avocations: amateur theater, music, big band jazz, poetry, bridge. E-mail: placerstwo@tscnet.com.

COUCH, ROBERT BARNARD, physician, scientist, educator; b. Guntersville, Ala., Sept. 25, 1930; s. Ezekiel Harvey and Frances Jane (Barnard) C.; m. Katherine Frances Klein, Apr. 23, 1955; children: Robert Steven, Leslie Ann, Colleen Frances, Elizabeth Lee. BA, Vanderbilt U., 1952, MD, 1956. Diplomate Am. Bd. Internal Medicine. Intern Vanderbilt U. Hosp., Nashville, 1956—57, resident in medicine, 1959—60, chief resident in medicine, 1960—61; clin. assoc. NIH, Washington, 1957—59, sr. investigator, 1961—65, head clin. virology sect., 1965—66; assoc. prof. Baylor Coll. Medicine, Houston, 1966—71, dir. influenza research center, 1974—91, prof. microbiology and immunology and medicine, 1971—2000, Disting. prof., 1995—, head infectious diseases sect. medicine, 1987—92, chmn. dept. microbiology and immunology, 1989—2000, dir. acute viral respiratory diseases unit, 1991—96, dir. respiratory pathogens rsch. unit, 1996—, dir. Ctr. for Infection and Immunity Rsch., 1999—, prof. molecular virology & microbiological med., 2000—. Mem. rsch. rev. panels infectious diseases; cons. NIH, Dept. Def., FDA. Contbr. articles to profl. jours. Served to sr. surgeon USPHS, 1957-66. Mem. ACP, AAAS, Soc. Exptl. Biology and Medicine, Am. Soc. Microbiology, Infectious Diseases Soc. Am., Am. Assn. Immunologists, Am. Fedn. Clin. Rsch., Am. Soc. Clin. Investigation, So. Soc. Clin. Investigation, Am. Assn. Physicians, Am. Soc. Epidemiology, Am. Soc. Virology. Office: Baylor Coll Medicine 1 Baylor Plz Houston TX 77030-3411 E-mail: rcouch@bcm.tmc.edu.

COUCHMAN, ROBERT GEORGE JAMES, human services consultant; b. Toronto, Ont., Can., Feb. 21, 1937; s. Robert George and Mary (Bigelow) C.; m. Jane Barker (div. 1985); children: Barbara, Stephen; m. Carolyn Moore; 1 child, Michael. BA, Queen's U., Kingston, Ont., 1965; MEd, U. Toronto, 1969. Tchr. Scarborough (Ont.) Bd. Edn., 1957-63; dir. student svcs. Etobicoke (Ont.) Bd. Edn., 1963-74; exec. dir. Family Svc. Assn. Met. Toronto, 1974-89; pres. Donner Can. Found., Toronto, 1989-93; assoc. Re Think Group, 1993; dir. Terra Nova, 1995-97; chmn. Outward Bound Can., 1989-95; found. cons. Atlin, 1995—. Co-chmn. U.N. Can. Com. Internat. Yr. of Family, 1993-94; patron Outward Bound Can., 1995-99; mem. nat. adv. com. Fed. Minister of Health on Rural Health. Author: Reflections on Canadian Character, 2003; contbr. 40 articles to profl. jours., 1984-87. Chmn. Outward Bound Wilderness Sch., 1987-88; pres. Can. Mental Health Assn., Ont., 1971-73; dir. White Ribbon Found. of Can.; bd. dirs. Addiction Rsch. Found., Ont., 1980-86, Metro Toronto Housing Co., 1982-88, United Way Metro Toronto, 1994-96; vice chmn. Vanier Inst. of the Family, 1988-90; chmn. Atlin Big Water Soc.; gov., Grey Owl Nature Trust, 1997-2000, advisor Can. Arctic Resources Com. Mem.: Yukon Family Svcs. Assn. (exec. dir. 1999—2001), Ont. Assn. Profl. Social Workers (hon.), Rorary (com. chmn.). Anglican. E-mail: bcouchman@yknet.ca.

COUDERT, DALE HOKIN, real estate executive, marketing consultant; b. Chgo., Nov. 29, 1941; d. Sidney and Ruth (Brower) Manowitz; m. Frederic R. Coudert (div.); children Dana, Alexandra. BA, Northwester U., 1964. V.p. Cross & Brown, N.Y.C., 1975-86; dir., sec. First Women's Bank, N.Y.C., 1980-87; head bus. devel., office of pres. 1st N.Y. Bank for Bus., 1988-91; mktg. dir. Lafer Mgmt., N.Y.C., 1993-94; pres., CEO Coudert Assocs. Ltd., N.Y.C., 1991—; broker Brown Harris Stevens Palm Beach Real Estate, Pal, 1999—. Dir. Hosp. Tak Co., L.I., NY, 1979—98; creator, chmn., CEO Coudert Inst. for Enlightened Dialogue at Villa Dei Fiori, Palm Beach, Fla., 2001—. Pub., editor: (book) Business and Pleasure, 1986-87. Bd. dirs. Women's Rep. Club, N.Y.C., 1994, N.Y. Drama League, N.Y.C., 1975—; mem. nat. bd. dirs. Aspen Art Mus., [illegible], Colo., 1996-98; trustee, treas. Zoo of the Palm Beaches at Dreker Park 1996-98, bd. dirs., 1996—; regent St. John the Divine, N.Y.C., 1988. Fellow Aspen Inst. (life); mem. Internat. Womens Forum, Met. Opera Club, Women's Forum Fla. Avocations: piano, voice, dance, golf, tennis. Home: 485 Park Ave New York NY 10022-1228 also: 163 Seminole Ave Palm Beach FL 33480-3732 also: Brown Harris Stevens Palm Beach Real Estate Ste 329 340 Royal Poinciana Plz Palm Beach FL 33480-4048 Office: 163 Seminole Ave Palm Beach FL 33480-3732 E-mail: dal1129@aol.com.

COUFOUDAKIS, VAN, political science educator; b. Athens, Greece, May 27, 1938; came to U.S., 1955. s. Fotios and Helen (Voutopoulos)C.; m. Marion Mason, Dec. 26, 1964; 1 child, Helen. BA in Pub. Adminstrn., Am. U. of Beirut, 1962; MPA, U. Mich., 1964, PhD in Polit. Sci., 1972; DHL (hon.), Ind. U., 2002. Prof. Polit. Sci. Ind. U./Purdue U., Ft. Wayne, 1967—, interim dean Sch. Bus., 1983-94, interim dean Sch. Edn., 1994-95, dean Sch. Arts & Scis., 1996—2002; rector Intercollege, Nicosia, Cyprus, 2002—. Assoc. vice chancellor for acad. affairs, Ind. U./Purdue U. Ft. Wayne, 1986-96. Editor: (book) Greece and the New Balkans, 1999; contbr. articles to profl. jours. Chair Found. for Hellenic Studies, Washington, 1995—, AHEPA Ednl. Found., Washington, 1999—. Recipient Comdr. of Order of Phoenix pres. of the Greek Republic, 1998; hon. consul Republic of Cyprus Govt. Republic of Cyprus, 1985-2002. Mem. Modern Greek Studies Assn. (pres. 1995-99). Greek Orthodox. Avocations: classical music, stamp collecting. Home: 109 Garfield Dr #302 Sarasota FL 46805 E-mail: coufouda@ipfw.edu., coufoudakis.v@intercollege.ac.cy.

COUGHENOUR, KAVIN LUTHER, career officer, military historian; b. New Kensington, Pa., Mar. 1, 1947; s. Roy Edgar and Anna Louise (Coleman) C.; m. Kathryn Mary Domurat, May 17, 1969; 1 child, Stacey Anne. BA in Social Scis., Ind. U. of Pa., 1969; MA in Pers. Mgmt., Ctrl. Mich. U., 1979; diploma, U.S. Army War Coll., 1990. Commd. 2d lt. U.S. Army, 1969, advanced through grades to col., 1991, adj., 1973-75, adj. gen. 79th Res. Command Willow Grove, Pa., 1976-79, adj. 5th Spl. Forces Group Ft. Bragg, N.C., 1979-82, adj. gen. 3d Armored Divsn. Frankfurt, Germany, 1985-86, commdg. officer U.S. Mil. Entrance Processing Sta., Dept. Defense Chgo., 1986-88, tng. officer Spl. Forces Sch. Ft. Bragg, 1988-89, spl. forces br. chief Pers. Command Alexandria, Va., 1990-92, dep. comdr. Ctr. Mil. History Washington, 1992-95; lic. battlefield guide Gettysburg (Pa.) Nat. Mil. Park, 1995—. Decorated Legion of Merit; recipient Gold medal, Nat. Hon. Soc. Pershing Rifles, 1968, Supts. award of Excellence, Gettysburg Nat. Mil. Park, 2001. Mem. Spl. Forces Assn., Soc. Mil. History, U.S. Army Coll. Alumni Assn., Nepoleonic Alliance, Assn. Lic. Battlefield Guides. Republican. Methodist. Avocation: civil war history. Home: Lake Heritage 964 Johnson Dr Gettysburg PA 17325-8970

COUGHLAN, GARY PATRICK, pharmaceutical company executive; b. Fresno, Calif., Feb. 14, 1944; s. Edward Patrick and Elizabeth Claire (Ryan) C.; m. Mary Cary Kelley, Dec. 21, 1967; children: Christopher, Sarah, Laura, Claire, Moira. BA, St. Mary's Coll., 1966; MA in Econs., UCLA, 1967; MBA, Wayne State U., 1971. Sr. fin. analyst Burroughs Corp., Detroit, 1969-72; with Dart Industries, L.A., 1972-81, group v.p. field services, 1978-81, v.p. ops. services, 1981, Dart & Kraft Inc., Northbrook, Ill., 1981-82, v.p. fin., contr., 1984-85, sr. v.p. fin. affairs, 1985-86, sr. v.p., CFO, 1986; v.p. fin. retail food group Kraft Inc., Glenview, Ill., 1982-84, sr. v.p., CFO, 1986-88; sr. v.p. fin. Kraft Gen. Foods, Glenview, 1989-90; sr. v.p. fin., CFO Abbott Labs., Abbott Park, Ill., 1990-2001, ret., 2001. Instr. prof. fin. ext. program UCLA, 1974—80; bd. dirs. Arthur J. Gallagher, Itasca, Ill., Hershey (Pa.) Corp., Chgo. Hort. Soc., Glencoe, Ill.; mem. adv. coun. Coun. Fgn. Rels., Chgo. Com. Mem. Fin. Execs. Inst. Republican. Roman Catholic. Home: 1135 Central Rd Glenview IL 60025-4432 Office: Abbott Labs 1200 Central Ave Ste 306 Wilmette IL 60091 E-mail: gcoughlan@earthlink.com.

COUGHLAN, KENNETH L. lawyer; b. Chgo., July 8, 1940; s. Edward James and Mary Virginia (Lewis) C.; m. Therese Koziol, Oct. 11, 1981; 1 child, Kevin Edward. BA, U. Notre Dame, 1962; JD, Northwestern U., Chgo., 1966. Bar: Ill. 1967. Trust officer Am. Nat. Bank & Trust Co., Chgo., 1969-72; sec. bd., sr. v.p., gen. counsel, cashier Ctrl. Nat. Bank., Chgo., 1972-82; sec., gen. counsel Ctrl. Nat. Chgo. Corp., 1976-82; sr. v.p., gen. counsel Exch. Nat. Bank, Chgo., 1982-83; gen. counsel Exch. Internat. Corp., Chgo., 1982-83; chmn. bd., pres. Union Realty Mortgage Co., Inc., Chgo., 1981-83; shareholder DeHaan & Richter P.C., 1983-2000; mem. Kelly, Olson, Michod, DeHaan & Richter, L.L.C. Capt. U.S. Army, 1966-68. Fellow Ill. Bar Found.; mem. ABA, Ill. State Bar Assn. (chmn. sect. on comml., banking and bankruptcy law 1981-82), Chgo. Bar Assn. (chmn. fin. instns. com. 1980-81, chmn. comml. fin. com. 1979-80), Lawyers Club (Chgo.). E-mail: kcoughlan@komdr.com.

COUGHLAN, PATRICK CAMPBELL, lawyer, mediator; b. Orange, N.J., May 28, 1940; s. Gerald Noel and Carter (Van Schaick) C.; m. Joyce Miskuf; children: Kimberly Campbell,Devon Gerald, Carter Turner. BA, Duke U., 1962, JD, 1965. Bar: Fla. 1965, U.S. Supreme Ct. 1968, Calif. 1974, Maine 1985. Assoc. Alley, Maass, Rogers & Lindsay, Palm Beach, Fla., 1969-72, ptnr., 1972-74; judge Mcpl. Ct., Ocean Ridge, Fla., 1970-72; assoc. firm Richards, Watson & Gershon, Los Angeles, 1974-75, ptnr., 1975-84; city atty. City of Rancho Palos Verdes, Calif., 1975-82, City of San Fernando, Calif., 1977-82, City of Seal Beach, Calif., 1978-84, City of La Habra Heights, Calif., 1979-84, 1981-84, Rolling Hills, Calif., 1981-84, Westlake Village, Calif., 1981-84; chair bd. appeals Raymond, Maine, 1985-98; pres. Kingsley Pines, Inc.; prin. Coughlan Assoc., 1987-88; pres. Resolve Disputes, Inc. N.Am., Portland, Maine, 1989-92, Conflict Solutions, Portland, Oreg., 1992—, Naples, Fla., 1992. Pres. No. Pines, Inc., 1980-86; ptnr. Atlanean Ptnrs.; trustee, sec. Gulf Stream Sch. Found., Inc., 1970-85; bd. dirs. Mountains Restoration Trust, 1981-82; trustee North Yarmouth Acad., 1984-93, pres., 1985-89; treas., trustee Natural Resources Coun. Maine, 1989-93; pres. parish coun. Our Lady of Perpetual Help, 1983-85; pres. World Affairs Coun. of Maine, 1986-89, trustee, 1985-93; trustee Portland Stage Co., 1989-93, sec., 1990-91, v.p., 1991-92; trustee Maine Youth Camps Assn., 1989-96, sec., 1990, v.p., 1990-93, pres., 1993-95; trustee Susan Curtis Found., 1991-96; dir. Pvt. Adjudication Ctr. Duke U., 1994-2002, mediator 1998-2002; dir. The Club at La Peninsula, 1997-98.

Capt. USAF, 1965-68. Fellow Internat. Acad. Mediators (bd. dirs. 1999—, v.p. 2001—); mem. ABA, State Bar Calif., Fla. Bar, Maine State Bar, Soc. Profls. in Dispute Resolution, Maine Assn. Dispute Resolution Profls. (pres. 1990-92), Am.Coll. Civil Trial Mediators, Woodlands Country Club,Falmouth, ME, Windstar Country Club (Naples, Fla.). Roman Catholic. Home: 47 Coughlan Cove Rd Raymond ME 04071-6274 Home and Office: 1540 Star Pointe Ln Naples FL 34112 E-mail: coglan@aol.com., pat@conflictsolutionsinc.com.

COUGHLIN, CAROLINE MARY, library consultant, educator; b. Bronx, N.Y., Dec. 6, 1944; d. Daniel Anthony and Antoinette (Aponte) C.; m. William Martin Weinberg, Oct. 3, 1981; 1 child, Nora Harie Weinberg. BA, Mercy Coll., 1966; MLS, Emory U., 1967; PhD, Rutgers U., 1976. Reference libr. First Nat. City Bank, N.Y.C., 1967-68; instr. Emory U., Atlanta, 1968-71; teaching asst. Rutgers U., New Brunswick, N.J., 1971-74; children's libr. Phillipsburg (N.J.) Pub. Libr., 1972-73; asst. prof. libr. sci. Simmons Coll., Boston, 1974-78; asst. dir. libr. Drew U., Madison, N.J., 1978-86, dir., 1986-94, assoc. prof. bibliography and rsch., 1986-94. Vis. lectr. Further Edn. Cen., Tampere, Finland, 1994, 96, Tallin, Estonia, 2000; cons. to librs., 1974—; team membership for site visits Mid. State Assn., 1979-94; chair libr. dir.'s group Assn. Ind. Colls. and Univs. of N.J., 1987-92; bd. dirs. Ctr. for Rsch. Librs., Chgo., 1987-92; vis faculty mem. Rutgers U., 1988, 90, 93—2003; vis. prof. Internat. Libr. Sch. U. Coll. Wales, 1992; evaluator HEA Office of Edn. and IMLR, 1987-2000. Co-author: Lyle's Administration of College Library Text Bd. dirs. Womens Project of N.J., 1984—. Recipient Outstanding Alumnae award Mercy Coll., 2001. Mem. ALA (councillor 1977-81), Assn. Libr. and Info. Sci. Edn. (various coms.), Archons of Colophon, N.J. Libr. Assn. (pres. coll. and univs. librs. sect. 1974-75, Disting. Svc. award 1993, Rsch. award 1993), Soc. for History of Authorship, Reading and Publ. (treas. 1994-96), Beta Phi Mu. Democrat. Avocations: reading, rug making, travel. Home: 304 Grant Ave Highland Park NJ 08904-1828

COUGHLIN, CHRISTOPHER J. financial executive; With Ernst & Young (formerly Arthur Young), Sterling Winthrop, Inc., 1982-96, CFO, bd. dirs., 1993-96; exec. v.p., CFO Nabisco Internat., 1996—98, Pharmacia & Upjohn, Inc., Peapack, NJ, 1998—2003; COO Interpub. Group Cos., Inc., N.Y.C., 2003—. Office: Interpub Group Cos Inc 1271 Ave of Americas New York NY 10020*

COUGHLIN, CORNELIUS EDWARD, accounting company executive; b. Boston, Sept. 9, 1927; s. Cornelius Stephen and Mabel Josephine (McMahon) C.; m. Rosemarie Toppi, Sept. 5, 1954; children: William, Brian, Stephen, Christopher, Maureen, Michael. BBA with honors, Northeastern U., 1956; student, Bentley Coll., 1948-50. Office mgr. Trim Alloys, Inc., Boston, 1952-57; contr. Form-A-Lite Inc., Northbridge, Mass., 1957-59; sales adminstr. Reiss Assocs., Inc., Lowell, Mass., 1959-61; ops. mgr. GPS Instrument Co., Newton, Mass., 1961-65, Computer Products, Newton, 1965-67; ptnr. McShane & Coughlin, Milton, Mass., 1967-74; owner, mgr. C.E. Coughlin & Co., Acton, Mass., 1974-78; pres. Coughlin, Sheff & Assocs., Acton, 1979—. Mem. audit com. Town of Acton. Served with USN, 1945-48, 50-51. Mem. AICPA, Mass. Soc. CPAs, Mass. Assn. Pub. Accts. (pres. 1989—), Inst. Mgmt. Accts., Small Bus. Assn. New Eng., Acton Rotary (pres. 1983-984). Democrat. Roman Catholic. Home: 98 Summer St Acton MA 01720-2223 Office: Coughlin Sheff & Assocs 40 Nagog Pk Acton MA 01720-3425 E-mail: conniec@csa-pc.com.

COUGHLIN, FRANCIS RAYMOND, JR., surgeon, educator, lawyer; b. N.Y.C., Feb. 22, 1927; s. Francis Raymond and Isabel (Archibald) C.; m. Barbara Ann Blunt, June 9, 1951; children: Hilary, Mary, Patricia, Christopher Francis, Geoffrey Blunt, Daniel Taylor, Isabel, David Carleton. BS, Fordham U., 1948; MD, Yale U., 1952; MS, McGill U., Montreal, Que., Can., 1955, diploma in surgery, 1959; JD, U. Bridgeport, 1988. Bar: N.Y., Conn., D.C., U.S. Supreme Ct.; diplomate Am. Bd. Surgery, Am. Bd. Thoracic Surgery. Intern N.Y. Hosp., N.Y.C., 1952-53; resident McGill U. Teaching Hosp., Montreal, 1953-57, Overholt Thoracic Clin., Boston, 1958-60; mem. staff Stamford (Conn.) Hosp., 1960—; practice medicine specializing in thoracic surgery Stamford, 1960—88; medico-legal cons., 1988—. Dir. thoracic and vascular surgery St. Josephs Hosp., Stamford, 1970-73, 80-85, assoc. chief surgery, 1971-73, chief surgery, 1973-77; assoc. prof. clin. surgery N.Y. Med. Coll., 1981-2002; mem. staff Norwalk Hosp., 1965-89, Standford Hosp., 1960—; vice chair Conn. State Commn. Medicolegal Investigations, 1990-2002. With U.S. Maritime Svc., 1945-46. Recipient Encaenia award Fordham U., N.Y.C., 1958; Teaching fellow Harvard U., 1958. Fellow ACS (sec.-treas. Conn. chpt. 1966-70), Royal Coll. Surgeons (Can.), Am. Coll. Cardiology, Am. Coll. Chest Physicians, Royal Soc. Medicine; mem. Soc. Thoracic Surgeons (founding mem.), N.Y. Acad. Medicine, Conn. Heart Assn. (dir. 1961-64), Conn. Lung Assn. (dir. and exec. com. 1963-69, v.p. 1967-69), Lung Assn. So. Fairfield County (pres. 1963-68, dir. 1960-70), Soc. Med. Jurisprudence (v.p. 1992-93, pres. 1995-97), English-Speaking Union, Scottish-Am. Found., Can. Soc. N.Y., Yale Club N.Y., Army Navy Club (Washington), Yale Med. Sch. Alumni Assn. (v.p. 1999-2001, pres. 2001-03). Republican. Office: 20 Mead St New Canaan CT 06840-5701 E-mail: fcoughlinmd@att.net.

COUGHLIN, JACK, printmaker, sculptor, art educator; b. Greenwich, Conn., Feb. 19, 1932; s. John J. and Gabrielle S. (Jones) Coughlin; m. Joan M. Hopkins, July 5, 1958; children: Maura, Molly. Student, Art Students League, N.Y.C., 1950-52; BFA, R.I. Sch. Design, 1954, MS, 1961. Asst. prof. art U. Mass., Amherst, 1964-68, assoc. prof., 1968-73, prof., 1973-94, prof. emeritus, 1994—. Hendriks Gallery, Dublin, Ireland, 1971, one-man shows include, 1974, 1976, 1978, 1980, 1983, 1987, Harvard U., 1974, Associated Am. Artists, N.Y.C., 1977, Dublin Writers Mus., 1993, Brandeis U., 1995, exhibited in group shows at 17th Biennial Am. Printmaking, Bklyn., 1970, Davidson Nat. Print Show, 1973, NAD, 1974—2003, Represented in permanent collections Met. Mus. Art, N.Y.C., Mus. Modern Art, Nat. Collection Arts, Washington, commd. regularly, The New Republic. With U.S. Army, 1954—56. Recipient numerous awards, prizes for work, Nat. Inst. Arts and Letters, 1969, prize for drawing 158th Nat. Exhbn., NAD, 1983, 33d N.D. Print and Drawing Ann., 1991, 34th Nat. Pring Exhbn., Hunterdon Art Ctr. Mem.: NAD (academician), Soc. Am. Graphic Artists. E-mail: jackjr@art.umass.edu.

COUGHLIN, JAMES PATRICK, mathematician, educator; s. Patrick and Mary Ellen (Duffy) Coughlin. BS, Fordham Coll., 1960; MA, Columbia U., 1961; PhD, U. Colo., 1973. Instr. Arlington (Tex.) State Coll., 1962, Rockhurst Coll., Kans. City, Mo., 1962—63, Regis Coll., Denver, 1963—65; prof. math. Towson (Md.) U., 1979—. Physicist US NSWC, Dahlgren, Va., 1960—83. Co-author: Neural Computation From The Hopfield Net To The Boltzmann Machine, 1995. Mem.: Math. Assn. Am., Sigma Xi. Avocations: history, cryptography, bridge. Home: 16 Overhill Road Catonsville MD 21228 Office: Mathematics Dept Towson 8000 York Road Towson MD 21252

COUGHLIN, JOAN HOPKINS, artist, educator; b. Jamaica, West Indies, July 4, 1936; parents Am. citizens; d. John Leroy and Marion (Baier) Hopkins; m. John J. Coughlin, July 5, 1958; children: Maura, Molly. BFA in Illustration, R.I. Sch. Design, 1958, BS in Art Edn., 1962; MFA in Painting, U. Mass., 1969. Painting tchr. Castle Hill Ctr. for the Arts, Truro, Mass., 1976—; dir. of family art gallery Golden Cod, Wellfleet, Mass., 1964—. Curator Wellfleet Hist. Soc. Mus., 1990—. Recipient Gold medal for painting, Grumbacher, George Walter Smith Mus. Show, Springfield, Mass./67th Nat. Art League Exhbn. Episcopalian. Office: Wellfleet Hist Soc Main St Wellfleet MA 02667

COUGHLIN, TIMOTHY CRATHORNE, bank executive; b. Evanston, Ill., June 1, 1942; s. Laurence and Mary (Crathorne) C.; m. Laura Jane Philipp, June 10, 1967; children: Elisabeth A., Timothy C. Jr., Mary Blair, John C. BA, Brown U., 1964; MBA, NYU, 1969. Special devel. program Chase Manhattan Bank, N.Y.C., 1964—67, asst. treas., v.p. dist. exec., 1967—78; sr. v.p., dept. gen. mgr. Banque Paribas, N.Y.C., 1978—83; exec. v.p. Riggs Bank, Washington, 1983—85; pres. Riggs Bank N.A., Washington, 1985—92, Riggs Nat. Corp., Washington, 1992—. Chmn. Riggs Investment Mgmt. Corp., 2001--. Bd. dirs. Boys and Girls Clubs Greater Washington, 1986—, Greater Washington Bd. Trade, 2002—; trustee Corcoran Gallery Art, 1993—, Fed. City Coun., 1998—, Colby-Sawyer Coll., 1999—; treas. John F. Kennedy Ctr. for Performing Arts, 1984-88; chpt. mem. Protestant Episc. Cathedral Found., 1989-97. Mem. Brit. Am. Bus Assn. (chmn. 1995—), Fin. Svcs. Roundtable (treas. 1992—), Columbia Country Club, Skytop Club, Soc.. of the Friendly Sons of St. Patrick (bd. dirs., pres. 2000), Alfalfa Club. Episcopalian. Avocations: tennis, long-distance running, reading. Office: Riggs Nat Corp 800 17th St NW Washington DC 20006-3906 E-mail: Tim_coughlin@riggsbank.com.

COUGHLIN, TOM, former professional football coach; b. Waterloo, N.Y., Aug. 31, 1946; m. Judy Coughlin; children: Keli, Katie, Tim, Brian. BA Educ., Syracuse U.; MA Educ. Grad. asst. Syracuse U., 1969; head coach Rochester Inst. Tech., 1970-73; offensive backfield coach Syracuse U., 1974-76, offensive coord., 1977-80, Boston Coll., 1981-83; wide receivers coach Philadelphia Eagles, 1984-85; receivers coach Green Bay Packers, 1986-87, N.Y. Giants, 1988-90; head coach Boston Coll., 1991-93, Jacksonville Jaguars, 1994—2002; founder The Jay Fund Found. Avocations: reading, running, golf.

COUGHRAN, JANE NORA, writer, editor, researcher; b. Visalia, Calif., Feb. 3, 1939; d. Tom Bristol and Florence Pogue (Montgomery) Coughran. AB, Stanford U., 1960. Exhibit mgr. Olivetti Corp. Am., N.Y.C., 1966-72; rschr. Time-Life Books, N.Y.C., 1973-76; editor Time-Life Inc., Alexandria, Va., 1976-98, cons., freelance writer, 1998—. Author: The Cabins of Mineral King, 1998; picture editor 55 books for 10 series of Time-Life Books, 1977-97. Bd. dirs. Mineral King Dist. Assn., Tulare County, Calif., 1999. Mem. Am. Soc. Picture Profls. Avocations: travel, theatre, ballet. E-mail: CoughranJN@aol.com.

COUGHRAN, WILLIAM M., JR., management consultant, researcher; s. William M. Coughran, Sr. and Marianne Coughran; m. Bridget A. McGuire, Sept. 2, 1972; children: Megan J., Brendan W. BS, MS, Calif. Inst. Tech., 1975, Stanford U., 1977, PhD, 1980. V.p. Computing Scis. Rsch. Ctr., Bell Labs, Murray Hill, NJ, 1996—99; sr. v.p. Bell Labs Rsch. Silicon Valley, Palo Alto, Calif., 1998—2000; CEO, founder Entrisphere, Inc., Santa Clara, Calif., 2000—02; prin. Coughran Consulting, Palo Alto, 2003—. Bd. dirs. nSolutions, Inc., Santa Clara, Calif.; mem. tech. adv. bd. Hammerhead Systems, Inc., Mountain View, Calif., 2002—. Home: 820 Arroyo Ct Palo Alto CA 94306 Personal E-mail: bill@coughran.net.

COUGILL, ROSCOE MCDANIEL, mayor, retired air force officer; b. Charleston, Ill., Oct. 24, 1941; s. Oral Wilson and Malora Emaline (Vaughn) C.; m. Sallie Anne Carrow, Feb. 15, 1969; children: Christopher McDaniel, Andrew Ashby. BS in Edn., Ea. Ill. U., 1963; MS in Guidance and Counseling, Troy (Ala.) State U., 1976; postgrad., Air Command and Staff Coll., Maxwell AFB, Ala., 1976, Army War Coll., Carlisle, Pa., 1981. Commd. 2d lt. USAF, 1964, advanced through grades to brig. gen., 1989, ret., 1992; staff and exec. officer Hdqrs. USAF, Washington, 1976-80, dir., 1985-86, dep. asst. chief staff, 1988-89; comdr. 2179th Command Group, Patrick AFB, Fla., 1981-83; exec. officer internat. mil. staff NATO, Brussels, 1983-85; chief staff Air Force Comm. Command, Scott AFB, Ill., 1986-88; dir. command and control, comm. and computer sys. Hdqrs. U.S. Cen. Command, MacDill AFB, Fla., 1989-92; mayor City of Charleston, Ill., 1993—. Decorated DSM, Legion of Merit, Def. Superior Svc. medal.

COUKIS, PETER GEORGE, musician, composer; b. Waterbury, Conn., Jan. 15, 1955; s. George Peter and Antoinette (Kachulis) C.; m. Lucrecia Monje, Aug. 20, 1998; 1 child: George Joshua. BA, Western Conn. State U., 1978; AS, Mattatuck C.C., Waterbury, 1987. Musical arranger, composer Waterbury Children's Found., 1977-78; arranger, songwriter Youth Theatre Ensemble, Watertown, Conn., 1985-87; prodr., performer Laurel Cablevision, Litchfield, Conn., 1988-91; solo recording artist Waterbury, Wallingford, Conn., 1990—; founder Blue Plum Records, 1993—, Weird Garden Records. Composer, keyboardist The Nutmeg Ballet, Torrington, Conn., 1988; songwriter World Star Prodns., New Haven, 1988; keyboardist South Mich. Ave, Wolcott, Conn., 1980-86; synthesizer player Angels and Co. (Nunsense), N.Y.C. and Waterbury, 1989; artist, prodr. cable In Performance, 1988, Repertoire, 1989 (Laurel award 1989), Kaleidoscope, 1991, 13-week cable series, 1991, cable spl., 1992; released cassette single Girl, 1992; rec. artist Stick Bride, 1994, Strange Beauty, 1995, Believe in Me, 1995, Midgetmajority, 1997, Tournament, 1997, Stephania in Orange, 1997, Blossoms of Beauty, 1999, (15 CD set) Archive of Tracks, 2000, The Orchard, 2001, Harp, 2001, Curtains of Autummn, Organ Symphony No.1, 2002, Songs for Eluthera, 2003. Talk show guest Barbara Davitt's Coffee Break, Sta. WATR, Waterbury, 1990; feature guest Lifestyles with Dr. Kotler, Sta. WCAT-13, Waterbury, 1990. Mem. NARAS, Conn. Songwriters Assn. (3-yr. award 1985, 5-yr. award 1987). Democrat. Avocations: reading, traveling, outdoors, environmental awareness. E-mail: b.plum@worldnet.att.net.

COULET DU GARD, DONNA M. language educator; BS, Shippensburg State U., 1973; MA in French Lit., U. Del., 1989. Instr. French U. Del., Newark, 1989—, coord. French 107, 1997—2001, coord. French 106, 2001—. Co-organizer Francophone Day, Newark, 1999—2001. Mem.: Alliance Française, Del. Coun. on Tchg. Fgn. Langs., Am. Assn. Tchrs. French. Office: Dept Fgn Langs Univ Del Newark DE 19716

COULLARD, CHAD, information systems specialist; b. Bridgeport, Conn., Oct. 23, 1947; s. John B. and Elizabeth F. (Orfanello) C. BSc, Syracuse U., 1969; postgrad., U. Md.; MBA, Nichols Coll., 1986. Sys. analyst Am. Chem. Soc., 1969-73; sr. programmer analyst Amherst (Mass.) Coll., 1973-77; programmer analyst, sys. analyst Spalding Divsn. Questor Corp., 1977-79; spl. projects coord. Gerber Sci., Inc., Hartford, Conn., 1979-98; info. tech. mgr. Barco, Inc., South Windsor, Conn., 1998—2002. Mem. Assn. Computing Machinery.

COULOMBE, CHARLES AQUILA, writer, educator; b. N.Y.C., Nov. 8, 1960; s. Guy Joseph Coulombe and Patricia Jaye Collins. Student, N.Mex. Mil. Inst., 1978-80, Calif. State U., 1980-82. Reviewer West Coast Rev. of Books, Hollywood, Calif., 1982-85; contbg. editor Nat. Cath. Register, L.A., 1989-96; reporter L.A. Lay Mission, 1995—; mem. rsch. bd. Almanach De Gotha, London, 1998—. Cons. Cath. Treasures, Monrovia, Calif., 1985—; L.A. corr. Fidelity of Australia, Melbourne, 1989-94, Creole mag., LaFayette, La., 1991-97, Bourbons mag., Paris, 1996—; mem. adv. bd. Almanach de Bruxelles, Brussels, 1996—; bd. dirs. Can. Royal Heritage Trust, Toronto. Author: Everyman Today Call Rome, 1987, The White Cockade, 1990, Puritans Progress, 1996, The Musein in the Bottle, 2002, Vicars of Christ: A History of the Popes, 2003; contbg. author: Tolkein: A Celebration, 1999. Mem. Monarchist League Can., Toronto, 1989—; West Coast del. Monarchist League, London,, 1993—. Recipient Christ the King Journalism award Christian Law Inst., El Paso, Tex., 1992. Mem.Cath. Writers Guild, Authors Guild, Drones Club, Weisse Rose (Vienna), Royal Stuart Soc. (London), Acad. Am. Poets, Nat. Trust for Historic Preservation, Irish Georgian Soc. (Dublin), Assn. Can.-Ams., The Green Rm. Club, City Tavern Club. Roman Catholic. Avocations: poetry, ballroom dancing, drinking. Home: PO Box 660771 Arcadia CA 91066-0771

COULOMBE, JOSEPH LOUIS, literature educator; b. Lafayette, Ind., Dec. 5, 1966; s. Michael Joseph and Theresa McInerny Coulombe; m. Michele Lee Gable, July 6, 2002. BA, U. St. Thomas, St. Paul, 1989; MA, U. Del., Newark, 1994; PhD, U. Del., 1998. Prof. U. Tenn., Martin, 1998—2001; prof. dept. English Rowan U., Glassboro, NJ, 2001—. Author: (book) Mark Twain and the American West, 2003; contbr. Mem.: MLA, Western Am. Lit. Assn. Avocations: hiking, bicycling, guitar, bassist, drummer. Home: 627 Kimball St Philadelphia PA 19147 Office: Rowan University Dept English Glassboro NJ 08028

COULSON, ELIZABETH ANNE, physical therapy educator, state representative; b. Hastings, Nebr., Sept. 8, 1954; d. Alexander and Marilyn (Marvel) Shafernich; m. William Coulson, Feb. 14, 1986. Student, Wellesley Coll., 1972-73; BS in Edn., U. Kans., 1976; cert. in phys. therapy, Northwestern U., Chgo., 1977; MBA, Keller Grad. Sch. Mgmt., 1985; postgrad., U. Ill., 1991. Lic. phys. therapist, Ill. Assoc. prof. dept. phys. therapy Chgo. Med. Sch., North Chicago, Ill., chmn. dept. phys. therapy, 1993-96. Contbr. articles to profl. jours. Trustee Northfield Twp., Ill., 1993-97; Ill. state rep. 17th dist., 1997—. Mem. APHA, Am. Phys. Therapy Assn. (Ill. del. 1986-93, chief del. 1991-93), Ill. Phys. Therapy Assn. (chmn. jud. com. 1989-91). Home: 1701 Sequoia Trl Glenview IL 60025-2022

COULSON, ROBERT, retired association executive, arbitrator, author; b. New Rochelle, N.Y., July 24, 1924; s. Robert Earl and Abby (Stewart) C.; m. Cynthia Cunningham, Oct. 16, 1961; children: Cotton Richard, Dierdre, Crocker, Robert Cromwell, Christopher. BA, Yale U., 1949; LLB, Harvard U., 1953; DSc in Bus. Adminstrn. (hon.), Bryant U., 1985; LLD (hon.), Hofstra U., 1987. Bar: N.Y. 1954, Mass. 1954. Assoc. Whitman, Ransom & Coulson, N.Y.C., 1954-61; ptnr. Littlefield, Miller & Cleaves, N.Y.C., 1961-63; exec. v.p. Am. Arbitration Assn., N.Y.C., 1963-71, pres., 1971-94; ret., 1994. Cons. N.Y. State Div. Youth, 1961-63; pres. Youth Consultation Service of N.Y., 1970 Author: How to Stay Out of Court, 1968, Labor Arbitration: What You Need to Know, 1973, Business Arbitration: What You Need to Know, 1980, The Termination Handbook, 1981, Fighting Fair, 1983, Arbitration in Schools, 1985, Business Mediation, 1987, Alcohol and Drugs in Arbitration, 1988, Empowered at Forty, 1990, Police Under Pressure, 1993, ADR in America, 1994, Family Mediation, 1996; editor: Racing at Sea, 1958; contbr. articles to profl. jours. Bd. dirs. Fedn. Protestant Welfare Agys., pres., 1982-84, chmn. 1985-87; adv. com. Internat. Coun. for Comml. Arbitration. Mem. N.Y. Yacht Club, Cruising Club Am., Riverside Yacht Club. Avocations: sailing, travel, writing. Home: 9 Reginald St Riverside CT 06878-2522 E-mail: coulfamily@aol.com.

COULSON, WILLIAM ROY, lawyer; b. Waukegan, Ill., Oct. 5, 1949; s. Robert E. and Rose (Stone) C.; m. Elizabeth A. Shafernich, Feb. 14, 1986. AB, Dartmouth Coll., 1969; JD, U. Ill., 1972. Bar: Ill. 1972, U.S. Dist. Ct. (no. dist.) Ill. 1974, U.S. Supreme Ct. 1976. Law clk. to judge U.S. Dist. Ct., East St. Louis, Ill., 1972-74, Chgo., 1975; asst. U.S. atty. U.S. Dept. Justice, Chgo., 1975-88, supr. criminal divsn., 1980-88; mng. ptnr. Cherry & Flynn, Chgo., 1988-99, Gold & Coulson, 1999—. Faculty Atty. Gens. Adv. Inst., Washington, 1980-88, Ill. Inst. for Continuing Legal Edn., Springfield, 1983-88, Fed. Law Enforcement Tng. Ctr., Glynco, Ga., 1983-86; co-chmn. U.S. Magistrate Merit Selection Panel, 1989-91. Author: Federal Juvenile Law, 1980; contbg. author Animation mag., 1993—. Served to 2d lt. Ill. N.G., 1965-66. Finalist U.S. Senate Jud. Selection Panel, 1996. Mem. ABA, Chgo. Bar Assn. (jud. evaluation com. 1987-89, vice chair 1990-91), Fed. Bar Assn. (pres. 1991-92), Dartmouth Club. Office: 11 S La Salle St Chicago IL 60602-2590

COULSON, ZOE ELIZABETH, retired consumer marketing executive; b. Sullivan, Ind., Sept. 22, 1932; d. Marion Allan and Mary Anne (Thompson) C. BS, Purdue U., 1954; AMP, Harvard U., 1983. Asst. dir. home econs. Am. Meat Inst., Chgo., 1954-57; acct. exec. J. Walter Thompson Co., Chgo., 1957-60; creative consumer dir. Leo Burnett Co., Chgo., 1960-64; mag. editor-in-chief Donnelley-Dun & Bradstreet, N.Y.C., 1964-68; food editor Good Housekeeping, N.Y.C., 1968-75; dir. G H Inst., 1975-81; corp. v.p. Campbell Soup Co., Camden, N.J., 1981-91. Bd. dir. Rubbermaid Inc., 1982-96, mktg. cons., Internat. Exec. Svc. Corp., 1998-99. Author: Good Housekeeping Cookbook, 1972, Good Housekeeping Illustrated Cookbook, 1981. Trustee Cooper Hosp./Univ. Med. Ctr., 1982-91; elder Old Pine Presbyn. Ch., 1992-96; vol. exec. Internat. Exec. Svcs. Corp., 1998—. Named Disting. Alumni Purdue U., 1971. Mem. Women's Econ. Bus. Alliance (bd. govs. 1987-91), Food and Drug Law Inst. (food bd. dirs. 1979-81), Harvard Bus. Sch. Club (Phila. v.p. budget 1994-95, mem. program com. 1993—, bd. dirs.), Purdue Club Phila. (pres. 1999—), Friends of Old Pine (sec. 1995—), Kappa Alpha Theta (pres. house corp. Beta Eta chpt. 1991-2000). Republican. Avocation: Meso-Am. archaeology. Home: 220 Locust St Apt 18B Philadelphia PA 19106-3931 Fax: (215) 922-4233. E-mail: zcoulson@aol.com.

COULT, NICHOLAS ASHTON, mathematician, educator; BA in Math., Carleton Coll., Northfield, Minn., 1993; PhD in Applied Math., U. of Colo., 1997. Postdoctoral fellow Inst. for Math. and its Applications, Mpls., 1998—2000; asst. prof. of math. Augsburg Coll., Mpls., 2000—. Indsl. cons. GeoEnergy, Inc., Tulsa, 1998—. Contbr. NSF grantee, 2003—. Achievements include patents pending for Algorithms for processing geophysical data. Office: Augsburg College 2211 Riverside Ave Minneapolis MN 55454

COULTAS, EDWARD OWEN, lawyer; b. Huntington Pk., Calif., May 17, 1946; s. Stanely S. and Josephine E. (Buckley) Coultas; m. Wanda Jean Viebig, June 22, 1968; children: Amy, Todd, Mark. BA, So. Meth. U., 1968; MS, Ind. State U., 1971; JD, So. Meth. U., 1974. Bar: Tex. 1974, Colo. 1975. Assoc. Gorsuch, Kirgis, Campbell, Walker & Grover, Denver, 1974—77, Strasburger & Price, Dallas, 1977—78; asst. dean So. Meth. U. Sch. Law, Dallas, 1978—80, assoc. dean, 1980—82; exec. dir. State Bar Tex., Austin, 1982—86; pres. Small, Craig & Werkenthin, P.C., Austin, 1986—. Office: Small Craig & Werkenthin PC 100 Congress Ave Ste 1100 Austin TX 78701-4042

COULTER, BARBARA CLARE, information services company executive; b. N.Y.C., Nov. 10, 1950; d. Francis Thomas and Mary Catherine (Hall) C.; m. Jay E. Pultz; May 7, 1978; children: Jude Elliott, Mary Margaret Anna Coulter-Pultz. BS in Physics and Math., Georgian Ct. Coll., 1972; MS in Ops. Rsch., Poly. Inst. N.Y., 1977; MBA, Pace U., 1984. Rsch. asst. Oak Ridge (Tenn.) Nat. Labs., 1971; sr. tech. asst. Bell Labs., Whippany and Holmdel, N.J., 1972-74, mem. tech. staff Holmdel, 1974-78; staff mgr. tariffs and costs AT&T, Basking Ridge, N.J., 1978-79, dist. mgr. fin. planning, market planning and strategic planning Morristown, N.J., 1980-85, product mgr. Spirit Comm. Sys. Parsippany, N.J., 1985-87, head facsimile strategic bus. unit, 1987-92, gen. mgr. DEFINITY product mgmt. Bridgewater, N.J., 1990-95; v.p. mktg. and strategy AT&T Solutions, Florham Park, N.J., 1995-97; v.p. bus. continuity and disaster recovery AT&T, Liberty Corner, N.J., 1997-98; COO Creditek Corp., Parsippany, NJ, 1999—2001; v.p. ops. Xebro Comms., South Plainfield, NJ, 2001—. Office: One Cragwood Rd South Plainfield NJ 07080 E-mail: bcoulter@xebeo.com.

COULTER, CHAD W. lawyer, insurance company executive; b. 1962; BA, Haverford Coll.; JD, U. Pa. Bar: Pa. 1987. V.p., gen. counsel Delphi Capital Mgmt., Inc., Wilmington, Del. Office: 1105 N Market St Ste 1230 Wilmington DE 19801-1216

COULTER, CHARLES ROY, lawyer; b. Webster City, Iowa, June 10, 1940; s. Harold L. Coulter and Eloise (Wheeler) Harrison; m. Elizabeth Bean, Dec. 16, 1961; 1 child, Anne Elizabeth. BA in Journalism, U. Iowa, 1962, JD, 1965. Bar: Iowa 1965. Assoc. Stanley, Bloom, Mealy & Lande, Muscatine, Iowa, 1965-68; v.p. Stanley, Lande & Hunter, Muscatine, 1969—, also bd. dirs. County fin. chmn. Leach for Congress, 1980-96; county coord. George Bush for Pres., 1980, 88, Reagan-Bush Campaign, 1984. Fellow Coll. of Law Practice Mgmt. (dir. 1994-, pres. 2001-), Am. Bar Found., Iowa State Bar Found., Am. Coll. Trust and Estate Counsel; mem. ABA (mem. coun. law practice mgmt. sect. 1984-88, sec. 1988-89, vice chair 1989-90, chair 1991-92, chair coord. commn. legal tech. 1994-97, mem. standing com. on tech. and info. sys. 1997-98), Iowa Bar Assn., Muscatine County Bar Assn., Thirty-Three Club (pres. 1981), Rotary, Order of Coif. Episcopalian. Avocation: tennis. Office: Stanley Lande & Hunter 301 Iowa Ave Ste 400 Muscatine IA 52761-3881 E-mail: chuckcoulter@slhlaw.com.

COULTER, DAVID CRESWELL, research engineer; b. Fargo, N.D., Apr. 4, 1928; s. John Lee and Phoebe Frost Coulter; m. Winifred Alice Russell, Apr. 4, 1952; children: Douglas Lee, Ann Claire, James Russell. BS in Physics/Math., Am. U., Washington, 1951. Electronic scientist U.S. Naval Rsch. Lab., Washington, 1951-54, electronic engr., 1966-84, Melpar, Inc., Falls Church, Va., 1954-66; rsch. engr. Gallaudet U., Washington, 1987-90; prs. Coulter Assocs., Inc., Fairfax, Va., 1978—; co-founder Metavox, Inc., Fairfax, 1983—, CEO, 1987-98. Cons., engr. Gallaudet U., Washington, 1990-95. Contbr. articles to profl. jours. Deacon Grace Presbyn. Ch., Springfield, Va., 1956-58. Mem. IEEE (sr. mem.), Acoustical Soc. Am. Republican. Achievements include patents for method and apparatus for improving binaunal hearing, method and system for speech compression, system for determining consonant formant loci, frequency, amplitude, time plotter with simulated three dimensional display; co-patentee instantaneous detection of human speech pitch pulses. Home: 9613 Pembroke Pl Vienna VA 22182-1443 Office: Coulter Assocs Inc Ste 140 45915 Maries Rd Sterling VA 20166-9280

COULTER, ELIZABETH JACKSON, biostatistician, educator; b. Balt., Nov. 2, 1919; d. Waddie Pennington and Bessie (Gills) Jackson; m. Norman Arthur Coulter Jr., June 23, 1951; 1 child, Robert Jackson. AB, Swarthmore Coll., 1941; A.M., Radcliffe Coll., 1946, PhD, 1948. Asst. dir. health study Bur. Labor Stats., San Juan, P.R., 1946; research asst. Milbank Meml. Fund, N.Y.C., 1948-51; economist Office Def. Prodn., 1951-52; research analyst Children's Bur.-HEW, 1952-53; from statistician to chief statistician Ohio Dept. Health,

1954-65; lectr. econs., then clin. asst. prof. preventive medicine Ohio State U., 1954-65; asst. clin. prof. biostats. U. Pitts. Sch. Pub. Health, 1958-62; assoc. prof. biostats. U. N.C., Chapel Hill, 1965-72, assoc. prof. econs., 1965-78, biostats. prof., 1972-90; adj. assoc. prof., hosp. adminstr. Duke U., 1972-79; assoc. dean undergrad. pub. health studies U. N.C., Chapel Hill, 1979-86, prof. biostats. emerita, 1990—. Contbr. articles to profl. jours. Mem. AAAS, AAUP, APHA (governing coun. 1970-72), Am. Econ. Assn., Am. Statis. Assn., Am. Acad. Polit. and Social Sci., Biometric Soc., Am. Evaluation Assn., Assn. for Health Svcs. Rsch., Sigma Xi, Delta Omega. Methodist. Home: 1825 N Lakeshore Dr Chapel Hill NC 27514-6734

COULTER, JACK BENSON, JR., financial planner; b. Louisville, Jan. 30, 1947; s. Jack Benson and Mary Belle (Roby) C.; m. Mary Llew Browne, July, 1977. BS, Fla. State U., 1967, MBA, 1969. CPA, Fla. Staff acct. Arthur Andersen & Co., Miami, Fla., 1971-73; sales rep. Commerce Clearing House, Inc., Miami, 1973-80; pres. First Fin. Planners, North Palm Beach, Fla., 1980-92, Coulter Fin. Advisors, Inc., Juno Beach, 1992—. Capt. U.S. Army, 1969-71. Mem. Inst. CFPs (nat. bd. dirs. 1986-89), Fla. Assn. CFPs (chmn. 1989-91), Fin. Planning Assn., Fla. Inst. CPAs. Republican. E-mail: ben@coulterfinancial.com.

COULTER, JAMES BENNETT, state official; b. Vinita, Okla., Aug. 2, 1920; s. Robert Leslie and Louise (Robinson) C.; m. Norma R. Brink, June 1, 1942; children: Linda Coulter Prandoni, James Bennett. BS in Civil Engring, U. Kans., 1950; MS, Harvard U., 1954; DSc (hon.), Washington Coll., 1979. Registered profl. engr., Md., Kans. Commd. officer USPHS, 1950-66; asst. commr. environ. health Md. Dept. Health, Balt., 1966-69; sec. Md. Dept. Natural Resources, Annapolis, 1969-82. Mem. vis. com. Sch. Engring. and Applied Physics, Harvard U.; mem. adv. com. Sch. Engring., U. Kan., Civitan. Bd. dirs. Blue Shield Md.; trustee Chesapeake Research Consortium; mem. exec. bd. Md. Save Our Streams. Served with C.E. AUS, 1940-45. Decorated Bronze Star Mem. APHA, NAE, Am. Acad. Environ. Engrs. (Gordon M. Fair award 1971, pres. 1978), Am. Water Works Assn. (Fuller award 1987), Water Pollution Control Fedn., Tau Beta Pi, Sigma Tau. Home: 778 Eastern Point Rd Annapolis MD 21401-6945

COULTER, JEAN WALPOLE, lawyer; b. Oklahoma City, Apr. 10, 1953; d. George C. and Frances Helen (Covelle) Walpole; m. Patrick William Coulter, Apr. 20, 1987; children: Jay Thomas, Courtney Covelle. BS, U. Tulsa, 1975, JD, 1981. Bar: Okla. 1981, U.S. Dist. Ct. (no. dist.) N.C. 1981, U.S. Dist. Ct. Okla. 1981, U.S. Tax Ct. 1981. Assoc. Waddel & Buzzard, Tulsa, 1981-84; shareholder Jean C. Walpole & Assoc., Inc., Tulsa, 1984-89, Pray, Walker, Williamson & Marlar, P.C., Tulsa, 1989-95, Jean Walpole Coulter & Assocs., Inc., Tulsa, 1995—. Tax instr. PDI, Denton, Tex., 1984-89. Trustee Univ. of Tulsa, 1990-91; dir. Big Bros./Big Sisters, Tulsa, 1983-89, Univ. Tulsa Alumni Assn., 1984-92, U. Tulsa Golden Hurrican Club, 1989-92. Mem. ABA (tax sect., labor sect.), Tulsa Employee Benefits Group. Episcopalian. Office: 1638 S Carson Ave Ste 1107 Tulsa OK 74119-4261 Fax: 918-583-6398. E-mail: jeancoult@aol.com.

COULTER, JOHN ARTHUR, academic administrator; b. Buffalo, N.Y., July 24, 1944; s. William David and Myra Elizabeth (Murray) C.; m. Ann Ahrens, July 4, 1966; children: Jennifer, Kelly, Amanda. BS, SUNY, Buffalo, 1967, MBA, 1975. Asst. to chmn. dept. physics SUNY, Buffalo, 1967-69, asst. dean Sch. of Pharmacy, 1969-73, asst. dean/adminstr./dir admissions, 1973-75, asst./assoc. dean medicine, 1975-79; asst. v.p. health scis. U. Wash, Seattle, 1979-83, assoc. v.p. health scis., 1983-92; exec. dir, health scis adminstn./assoc. v.p. for med. affairs U. Wash., Seattle, 1992—. Bd. dirs. Cmty. Health Plan of Suffolk, N.Y., 1978-79, Wash. Assn. for Biomed. Rsch., Seattle, 1988-96, Nat. Assn. for Biomed. Rsch., 1996-99, Poison Control Ctr., Seattle, 1994—; active United Way Leadership Tomorrow, C. of C., Seattle, 1985. Mem. Am. Assn. Med. Colls., Assn. Acad. Health Scis. Ctrs. Avocations: sailing, skiing. Office: Univ Wash Health Scis Ctr PO Box 356355 Seattle WA 98195-6355

COULTER, JUDY MARIE, writer; b. N.Y.C., July 3, 1928; d. Herbert and Margaret Mary (Harrington) Levy; m. Jerry Ross, Aug. 28, 1949 (dec. Nov. 1955); 1 child, Janie; m. Elliott Coulter, July 27, 1957 (dec. Oct. 1987); children: Julie, Matthew. BA in Edn., CUNY, 1949; postgrad., SUNY, 1970-75, New Sch., 1975-80, Manhattanville Coll., 1980-90. Cert. tchr. N.Y. Elementary sch. tchr. Bd. Edn., N.Y.C., 1949-52; columnist Spotlight Mag., N.Y.C., 1983-87; v.p. J & J Ross Co., N.Y.C., 1957—. Mem. Writer's Workshop, Scarsdale, N.Y., 1983—; pub., owner Musical Estate of Jerry Ross, 1955—. Contbr. essays to N.Y. Times, 1985-88, Reader's Digest, 1988-92, Gannett Chain, 1988—, Scarsdale Inquirer, 97—. Mem. ASCAP, LWV, AmSong, Songwriters Guild, MTI, Girl Scouts of Am. Home: 248 Sterling Rd Harrison NY 10528-1318

COULTER, MICHAEL L, political scientist, educator; b. Grove City, Pa., June 16, 1969; s. Ronald Coulter, Vernie Coulter; m. Laura Gold; children: Claire, Caroline, Joseph, Georgia. PhD, U. Dallas, 1999. Assoc. prof. Grove City (Pa.) Coll., Pa., 1995—. V.p. Shenango Inst. Pub. Policy, Grove City, 1999—. Contbr. articles. Mem.: Soc. Cath. Social Scientists (Web Page editor 2001—), Am. Polit. Sci. Assn., Grove City Area Hist. Soc. (bd. dirs. 1999—2002). Office: Grove City Coll 100 Campus Dr Grove City PA 16127

COULTER, MYRON LEE, retired academic administrator; b. Albany, Ind., Mar. 21, 1929; s. Mark Earl and Thelma Violet (Marks) C.; m. Barbara Bolinger, July 21, 1951; children: Nan and Benjamin (twins). BS, Ind. State Tchrs. Coll., 1951; MS, Ind. U., 1956, EdD, 1959; HLD (hon.), Coll. Idaho, 1982. Tchr. English Reading (Mich.) Pub. Schs., 1951-52; tchr. elem. grades Bloomington (Ind.) Pub. Schs., 1954-56; instr. edn. Ind. U., Bloomington, 1958-59; asst. prof. Pa. State U., 1959-64, asso. prof., 1964-66; vis. prof. U. Alaska, Fairbanks, 1965; asso. dean edn., prof. edn. Western Mich. U., Kalamazoo, 1966-68, v.p. for adminstrn., prof. edn., 1968-76, interim pres., 1974; pres. Idaho State U., Pocatello, 1976-84; chancellor Western Carolina U., Cullowhee, N.C., 1984-94, chancellor emeritus, 1994—. Del. Israeli Univs., 1976, Am. Assn. State Colls. and Univs. to People's Republic of China, 1981, Swaziland Coll. Tech., 1985, People's Republic China, 1985, 87, 88, 90, Jamaica, 1986, 89, 91, 94, Thailand, 1987, 90, The Netherlands, 1991; mem. U.S. Panama Canal Treaty Com., 1977-79 Author school textbooks. Bd. dirs. Kalamazoo C. of C., 1975-76, Pocatello Jr. Achievement; bd. dirs., chair N.C. Arboretum, 1994—; bd. dirs. WNC Pub. Radio, WNC Devel. Assn., WNC Tomorrow, Joint PVO/Univ. Rural Devel. Ctr., WNC Commn. Found., Friends of Great Smoky Mountain Nat. Park, 1994—, Inter-Regional Ctr., 2001—; lay leader Kalamazoo Meth. Ch., 1971-74; mem. Gov.'s Task Force on Aquaculture, 1988, N.C. Bd. Sci. and Tech., 1993—, Commn. for Competitive N.C., 1993—; chair N.C. Indian Gaming Cert. Commn., 1994—; trustee Bronson Hosp., Kalamazoo, 1975-76, N.C. Ctr. Advancement Tchg., C.J. Harris Cmty. Hosp.; chmn. Cherokee Preservation Found., 2001—. With U.S. Army, 1952-54. Named Disting. Alumnus, Ind. State U., 1975, Ind. U., 1994; recipient award Western Mich. U. Alumni Assn., 1974, resolution of tribute Mich. State Legislature, 1976, N.C. Order of the Long Leaf Pine, 1994. Mem. Internat. Reading Assn., Am. Assn. State Colls. and Univs. (bd. dirs. 1981-84, exec. com. 1981-84, sec.-treas. 1984-87, found. bd. dirs. 1987—, chmn. 1988-89), Nat. Soc. Study of Edn., N.C. Assn. Colls. and Univs. (bd. dirs.), Western Coll. Assn., Pocatello C. of C. (bd. dirs. 1977-80), Asheville C. of C. (bd. dirs. 1985-86), Cherokee Hist. Assn., Ind. U. Coll. Edn. Alumni Assn. (Disting. Alumnus award 1994), Phi Delta Kappa, Omicron Delta Kappa, Phi Kappa Phi, Beta Gamma Sigma. Office: Western Carolina Univ Office Chancellor Emeritus 61 Hunter Cullowhee NC 28723 E-mail: mcoulter@wcu.edu.

COULTER-HARRIS, DEBORAH MARCELLA, government analyst; b. Fitchburg, Mass., May 10; d. John Edward and Charlotte Germaine (Aubuchon) C.; m. Anthony V. Harris, Mar. 11, 1983. BA in English, Fitchburg State Coll., 1970; diploma in Russian, DLIFLC Presidio of Monterey, Calif., 1983; MS in Bus. and Human Rels. magna cum laude, Abilene Christian U., Garland, Tex., 1980; MA in English, U. Toledo, Ohio, 1993, PhD in Brit. Lit., 1995. Actress, poetess Theaters in Dublin, Ireland, 1970-77; speechwriter to CEO Mostek Corp., Carrollton, Tex., 1979-81; Russian analyst U.S. Army, Ft. Leonard Wood, Mo., Monterey, Calif., 1981-83, instr., 1985; Russian translator Soviet Army Studies Office, Ft. Leavenworth, Kans., 1986; founder, dir. and prodr. Rosary Cathedral Sch.-Performing Arts, Toledo, 1987-89; GTA and lectr. U. Toledo, 1990-94. Prof. Montgomery County Coll., Pa., 1999; Russian translator Churches of Christ, Montgomery, Ala., 1987-88; dir. Rosary Sch. of Performing Arts, Toledo, 1987-89; prof. Niagara U., 1996-97. Author, performer: (radio show RTE) Poet's Choice, 1977; author: (books) The Dirt Road, 1976, The Decline and Fall of the American Educational System, 1980, To Trace the Kindred Vices: Crabbe's Moral Instructions, 1995, The Moralist, 1997, Letters From the Tower, 1998. Mem. city com., pub. rels. Rep. Party, Niagara Falls, N.Y., 1995, religious meditations for TV NBC, CBS, ABC affiliates, Toledo, 1987-89; lector Rosary Cathedral, Toledo, 1987-89. Mem. MLA. Republican. Roman Catholic. Avocations: weight lifting, poetry writing, interior decorating, reading, gardening. Home: 11915 Winterthur Ln Ph 1 Reston VA 20191-1943 E-mail: drdcharris@aol.com.

COUNCILL, WILLIAM THOMAS, III, computer engineer, consultant; b. Hickory, N.C., May 9, 1950; s. William Thomas Jr. and Billie (Fulenwider) C.; m. Carol Frith, Sept. 19, 1987; 1 child, Aaron Todd Smith. BA with honors, U. N.C., 1972; MS, Nova U., 1975; JD, Birmingham Law Sch., 1990. Lic. profl. counselor. Dir. outpatient program Hill Crest Hosp., Birmingham, Ala., 1986-87; clin. ops. dir. Ala. Total Health Found., Inc., Birmingham, 1987-88; counselor AGAPE Ctrl. Ala., Birmingham, 1988-90; pres. Health Planning Assocs., Birmingham, 1990-93, PenKnowledge, Inc., Birmingham, 1991-95; v.p. product devel. Millbrook Corp., Dallas, 1995-96; program mgr. TERUS, Inc., Grapevine, Tex., 1996-97; sys. and process mgr. Mannatech, Inc., Coppell, Tex., 1997-99. Cons. Tech. Builders, Inc., Atlanta, 1997-99; mem. adv. bd. SELECT Software Tools, Irvine, Calif., 1998-99; lectr. U. Tex, Dallas. Co-editor: Component-Based Software Engineering, 2001; contbr. articles to profl. jours. Mem. N.C. Bd. Registered Practicing Counselors, Raleigh, 1984, Ala. Mental Health Bd., 1980-82; chair acute care com. Ala. Statewide Health Coord. Coun., Montgomery, 1986-88. Mem. IEEE, Assn. Computing Machinery. Avocations: writing, researching wyatt earp and doc holliday. Home and Office: TQC 4253 Hunt Dr Apt 1507 Carrollton TX 75010-3216 Fax: 972-939-7860. E-mail: bcouncil@cbseng.com.

COUNCILMAN, RICHARD ROBERT, product development engineer; b. L.A., Apr. 25, 1922; s. Frank Dwight and Gladys Vera (Clark) C.; m. Louise Perry Spalding (div.); children: Richard Martin, Robert Gordon; m. Barbara McCollough (div.); 1 child, Scott Richard; m. Shirley Ann DeVries, Apr. 25, 1964; 1 child, Marc Wayne. Chief draftsman USN, Pasadena & China Lake, Calif., 1944-49; engring. supr. USAF, Edwards AFB, Calif., 1949-51; sr. design specialist Bill Jack Sci. Inst., Solana Beach, Calif., 1951-52; head optical mech. rsch. Hughes Aircraft Flight Test, Culver City, Calif., 1952-56; group supr. R & D LTV Elecs., Garland, Tex., 1956-64; sr. engring. specialist R & D Conductron Divsn. McDonald Douglas, St. Louis, 1965-68; sr. project engr. Sr. Scientist Lab. Brunswick Corp., St. Louis, 1968-75; dir., chmn. bd. Imperial Gen. Life Ins. Co., St. Louis, 1970-75; sr. project R & D Brunswick Corp., Tulsa, 1975-87; pvt. practice pvt. practice, Collinsville, Okla., 1987—. Cons. in field. Fellow Internat. Soc. Optical Engring., Soc. Photo-Optical Instrumentation Engrs. (founding pres. 1955-56). Achievements include patentee in field. Home: 17001 N 137th East Ave Collinsville OK 74021-4415

COUNSELMAN, FRANCIS L. emergency medicine physician, educator; b. Washington, Apr. 8, 1957; s. Francis M. and Ann Counselman; m. Elizabeth Hanna Counselman, Dec. 19, 1987. MD, Ea. Va. Sch. Medicine, 1983. Cert. advanced trauma life support instr., ACLS instr., pediatric advanced life support instr. Intern internal medicine Ea. Va. Med. Sch., Norfolk, 1983-84, resident emergency medicine, 1984-86, disting. prof. emergency medicine, 2000—, dir. emergency medicine residency program, 1990—, chmn. dept. emergency medicine, 1992—. Editl. bd. Emergency Medicine. Recipient Residency Dir. award, Emergency Medicine Residents Assn., 2003. Mem.: Seaboard Med. Assn., Assn. of Acad. Chairs of Emergency Medicine (pres. 2002—03), Norfolk Acad. Medicine (pres. 1998—99), Soc. for Acad. Emergency Medicine, Va. Coll. Emergency Physicians (pres. 1995—96, Career Achievement award 2001, EMRA Residency Dir. of Yr. award 2003), Am. Coll. Emergency Physicians (residency rev. com. EM 2000—), Alpha Omega Alpha. Home: 7320 Shirland Ave Norfolk VA 23505-2940

COUNSIL, WILLIAM GLENN, electric utility executive; b. Detroit, Dec. 13, 1937; s. Glenn Dempsey and Jean Beverly (Rzepecki) C.; m. Donna Elizabeth Robinson, Sept. 10, 1960; children: Glenn, Craig. Student, U. Mich., 1955-56; BS, U.S. Naval Acad., 1960; Advanced Mgmt. Program, Harvard U., 1991. Ops. supr., asst. plant supt., sta. supt. N.E. Nuclear Energy Co., Waterford, Conn., 1967-76; project mgr., v.p. nuclear engring. and ops. N.E. Utilities, Hartford, Conn., 1976-80, sr. v.p. nuclear engring. and ops., 1980-85; exec. v.p. nuclear engring. and ops., electric-generating div. Tex. Utilities Generating Co., 1985-88; vice chmn. Tex. Utilities Electric Co., 1989-93; mng. dir. Wash. Pub. Power Supply System, Richland, 1993-96. With USN, 1956-67. Recipient Outstanding Leadership award ASME, 1986. Republican. Presbyterian. E-mail: wcounsil@aol.com. *My goal has been to improve our quality of life first through service in the United States Navy and second by ensuring an adequate and safe energy supply for our country.*

COUNTRYMAN, DAYTON WENDELL, lawyer; b. Sioux City, Iowa, Mar. 31, 1918; s. Cleve and Susie (Schaeffer) Countryman; m. Ruth Hazen, Feb. 2, 1941 (dec.); children: Karen, Joan, James, Kay. BS, Iowa State Coll., 1940; LLB, State U. Iowa, 1948, JD, 1969. Bar: Iowa 1948. Practiced in, Nevada; ptnr. Hadley & Countryman, Nevada, Iowa, 1949-64; mem. Countryman & Zaffarano P.C., 1984-87, Dayton Countryman Law Offices, P.C., 1987—; county atty. Story County, Iowa, 1950-54; atty. gen. State of Iowa, 1954-56. Candidate for U.S. Senate, 1956, 1960, 68. Air Force Res. pilot USAAF, 1941-46. Mem. ABA, Iowa Bar Assn., Story County Bar Assn., VFW, Am. Legion, Iowa State U. Alumni Assn. (pres. 1970-71), Iowa 2B Jud. Dist. Assn., Masons, Lions (pres. 1975-76). Methodist. Office: PO Box 28 Nevada IA 50201-0028 E-mail: dcountryman@midiowa.net.

COUNTRYMAN, EDWARD FRANCIS, historian, educator; b. Glens Falls, N.Y., July 31, 1944; s. Edward Francis and Agnes (Alford) C.; m. Evonne von Heussen, 1987; children: Karon Samantha, Kirstein Dawn; 1 son from previous marriage, Samuel Robert. BA, Manhattan Coll., 1966; MA, Cornell U., Ithaca, N.Y., 1969; PhD, Cornell U., 1971; LHD, Manhattan Coll., 1999. Lectr. in history U. Canterbury, N.Z., 1970-74; lectr. U. Warwick, Eng., 1975-83, sr. lectr., 1983-88, reader, 1988-91; prof. So. Meth. U., Dallas, 1991-99, disting. prof., 1999—. Vis. lectr. U. Cambridge, Eng., 1979-80, Mellon vis. sr. scholar, 1999; vis. scholar NYU, N.Y.C., 1980-81; Cardozo vis. prof. Yale U., spring 1989; coun. mem. Omohundro Inst. Early Am. History and Culture, 1999—. Cons. editor Radical History Rev., 1982—; author: A People in Revolution, 1981 (Bancroft prize 1982), The American Revolution, 1985, rev. edit. 2003; (video) American Independence 1776, 1989, Americans: A Collision of Histories, 1996; co-author: Who Built America, 1990, Shane, 1999; editor: How Did American Slavery Begin?, 1998, What Did the Constitution Mean to Early Americans?, 1998; co-author: The Empire State, 2001. Active civil rights movement, U.S., 1965-68; spokesperson Anti-War Movement, N.Z., 1970-73; active Campaign for Nuclear Disarmament, Eng., 1981—. Woodrow Wilson fellow, 1966-67, Danforth fellow, 1966-71, Samuel Foster Haven fellow, 1983; Mellon vis. sr. scholar U. Cambridge, 1998. Home: 5454 Anita St Dallas TX 75206-5336 Office: So Meth U Dept History Dallas TX 75275-0001 E-mail: ecountry@mail.smu.edu.

COUNTRYMAN, GARY LEE, insurance company executive, director; b. South Bend, Wash., July 30, 1939; s. William T. and Vernela K. (Stewart) C.; m. Sally Ann Mathews, Aug. 16, 1958; children: Christopher John, Susan Michelle, Sherry LeeAnn, Stefanie May. BS, U. Oreg., 1961, MS, 1963. With Liberty Mut. Ins. Co., Boston, 1963—, pres., 1981-86, pres., chief exec. officer, 1986-91, chmn., pres., CEO, 1991-92, chmn., 1992-99, CEO, 1998; pres. Liberty Fin. Co., Inc., Boston, 1999-2000, chmn., pres., CEO, 2000—. Bd. dirs. Liberty Mut. Ins. Group, Bank of Boston Corp., 1st Nat. Bank Boston, Boston Edison Co., Harcourt Gen., Inc., Alliance Am. Insurers; chmn. bd. dirs. Boston Mgmt. Consortium, Inc. Bd. dirs. Inst. Civil Justice, Jobs for Mass., Inc., Com. for Econ. Devel.; trustee Northeastern U., U. New Eng., Mus. Sci., Sudbury Valley Trustees; chmn. bd. Dana-Farber Cancer Inst.; bd. overseers Mass. Gen. Hosp. H.T. Miner fellow, 1962-63 Mem. NAM, Am. Inst. Property and Liability Underwriters (bd. dirs.), Algonquin Club. Office: Liberty Fin Co Inc 600 Atlantic Ave Boston MA 02210-2214

COUNTRYMAN, JAMES NELSON, English language educator; b. Albert Lea, Minn., July 25, 1956; s. Thomas Merritt and Margaret (Nelson) C. BA, St. John's U., Collegeville, Minn., 1978; PhD, U. Minn., 1999. Asst. prof. U. Minn., Morris, 2000—02, instr. Mpls., 1996-2000, 2002—. Mem. MLA, Medieval Acad. Am. Avocation: numismatics. Home: 3300 Fremont Ave S Minneapolis MN 55408

COUNTRYMAN, THOMAS ARTHUR, lawyer; b. Cleve., Mar. 14, 1957; s. Ralph Lyon Jr. and Dorothy Jean (Doherty) C.; m. Jean Millard Judson, June 7, 1980; children: Matthew Judson, Rachel Marie, Stephen Anthony. BS in Criminal Justice summa cum laude, Tex. Christian U., 1979; JD, Baylor U., 1982. Bar: Tex. 1982, U.S. Ct. Appeals (5th cir.) 1983, U.S. Dist. Ct. (we. dist.) Tex. 1984, U.S. Dist. Ct. (so. dist.) Tex. 1994, U.S. Dist. Ct. (ea. dist.) Tex. 1995. Assoc. Cox & Smith, Inc., San Antonio, 1982-88, shareholder, v.p., 1989-91; asst. gen. counsel Chuska Energy Co., 1991-92; of counsel Fulbright & Jaworski L.L.P., 1992-98, sr. counsel, 1999—. Spkr. San Antonio Legal Secs. Assn., San Antonio, 1984-86, U. Tex. Sch. Law. Annual Sch. Law Conf., 1998, U. Houston Law Found., 2001, others. Founder, dir., producer Univ. Players Drama Guild, San Antonio, 1983—; chmn. coun. on ministries U. United Meth. Ch., San Antonio, 1987-88; mem. bd. mgmt. YMCA, 1995-97. Named Vol. of Yr. YMCA, 1996. Mem. ABA, State Bar Tex. (moot ct. com. 1990), 5th Cir. Bar Assn., Def. Counsel San Antonio (sec. 1992), San Antonio Young Lawyers Assn. (mock trial com. 1986), Nat. and Tex. Assns. Sch. Bd. Attys., Tex. Bar Found. Republican. Avocations: drama, running, tennis, golf, softball. Home: 114 Fawn Dr San Antonio TX 78231-1515 E-mail: tcountryman@fulbright.com.

COUNTS, MARY LOU, retired telephone company executive; b. Prescott, Ark., June 14, 1933; d. Claude L. and Katie Gertrude (Bagwell) Barker; m. Eugene Counts, June 21, 1950; children: Brenda Kay, Jeanne Lou. Operator Southwestern Bell, Dallas, 1951-52, Hot Springs, Ark., 1952-62, clk., 1962-80, supr., 1980-83, mgr. Little Rock, 1983-88; ret., 1988. Pres. Ark. Chpt. Telephone Pioneers, Little Rock, 1986-87; co-chmn. State Pioneer Assembly, Ft. Smith, Ark., 1988-89. Vol. Nat. Park Svc., Hot Springs, 1989; pres. Jones PTA, Hot Springs, 1962-63; mem. Pub. Sch. Curriculum Study, 1963-64, Friends of the Fordyce, Hot Springs, 1989, Garland County Dem. Com.; co-chmn. State Pioneer Assembly, Hot Springs, 1989-91; active Virginia Clinton Kelley Dem. Women's Club of Garland County, Salvation Army Women's Aux.; bd. dirs. Jonestown Cmty. Assn. Named Mrs. Ark. Pioneer, 1987. Mem. Telephone Pioneers (life, rep. Ark. chpt. 1991-93, chairwoman state assembly 1994, 96), Belles Ext. Homemakers Club, Rock Gardeners Horticulture Club, Garland County Coun. Garden Clubs (sec. 1993-94), Grow and Show Garden Club, Mrs. Ark. (life), Century Club, United Meth. Women Circle #5, Vanilla Investment Club, Red Hat Soc. Democrat. Methodist. Home: 513 2nd St Hot Springs National Park AR 71913-3629 E-mail: mlcounts@swbell.net.

COUNTS, STANLEY THOMAS, aerospace consultant, retired naval officer, retired electronics company executive; b. Okfuskee County, Okla., July 3, 1926; s. Claud Curtley and Thelma (Thomas) C.; m. Bettejan Heft, Nov. 18, 1949; children:Ashlie Heft Jenkins. BS, U.S. Naval Acad., 1949; BS in Elec. Engring, U.S. Naval Postgrad. Sch., 1954, MS in Elec. Engring, 1955. Commd. ensign U.S. Navy, 1949, advanced through grades to rear adm., 1972; comdg. officer USS Bronstein, 1963-64; comdg. officer USS Towers, 1966-68; project mgr. NATO Seasparrow Surface Missile System, 1968-70; comdg. officer USS Chgo., 1970-71; dir. ships, weapons, electronics and asso. systems Office Asst. Sec. Def. for Installations and Logistics, 1971-73; dep. comdr. Naval Ordnance Systems Command, 1973-74; comdr. (Naval Ordnance Systems Command), 1974; vice comdr. Naval Sea Systems Command, 1974-76; comdr. Cruiser-Destroyer Group 5, 1976-78; ret., 1978; exec. Hughes Aircraft Co., Fullerton, Calif., 1979-89; ret., 1989; aerospace cons., chief exec. officer Bjan Enterprises, La Jolla, Calif., 1989-99. Chmn. Seasparrow steering com. NATO, 1973-76. Bd. dirs. San Diego chpt. Freedoms Found. at Valley Forge, 1992-94, 97-98; bd. dirs. Greater La Jolla Meals on Wheels, Inc., 1998—, pres., 2000—01. Decorated Legion of Merit with three oak leaf clusters, Bronze Star with combat distinguishing device. Mem. VFW, Surface Navy Assn. (life, bd. dirs. 1985-93), U.S. Naval Inst. (life), DAV (life), Ret. Officers Assn. (life), Navy League, USNA Alumni Assn. (life), Am. Legion, Rest and Aspiration Club San Diego. Home: 856 La Jolla Rancho Rd La Jolla CA 92037-7408 E-mail: okkid001@aol.com.

COUPER, RICHARD WATROUS, foundation executive, educator; b. Binghamton, NY, Dec. 16, 1922; s. Edgar W. and Esther (Watrous) C.; m. Patricia Pogue, Sept. 24, 1946; children: Frederick Pogue, Thomas Hayes, Margaret Couper Haskins. AB, Hamilton Coll., Clinton, NY, 1947, LLD (hon.), 1969; AM in Am. History, Harvard U., 1948; LLD (hon.), St.Joseph's Coll., 1982, Wesleyan U., 1986; LHD (hon.), NYU, 1974, William Paterson Coll., 1985, St. Lawrence U., 1986, Hartwick Coll., 1987. With Couper-Ackerman-Sampson, Inc. (and predecessor), Binghamton, NY, 1948-62, treas., 1957-60, v.p., 1960-63; adminstrv. v.p. Hamilton Coll., 1962-65, v.p., 1965-66, acting pres., 1966-68, v.p., provost, 1968-69, trustee, 1959—92; life trustee, 1992—; dep. commr. higher edn. State Edn. Dept., NY, 1969-71; pres., CEO Pub. Libr., NYC, 1971-81, pres. emeritus, 1981—; pres. The Woodrow Wilson Nat. Fellowship Found., Princeton, NJ, 1981-90, pres. emeritus, 1990—. Bd. dir. Archives Partnership Trust. Chmn. Episc. Fund for Human Needs. Capt. US Army, 1942-46. Mem. Orgn. Am. Hist., Am. Hist. Assn., NY State Hist. assn. (trustee 1979-97), Harvard Club, Century Assn., Lotos Club (NYC), Ft. Schuyler Club (Utica, NY), Nassau Club (Princeton, NJ), Grolier Club (NYC), Phi Beta Kappa Fellows. Office: Hamilton Coll Burke Libr Clinton NY 13323

COUPER, WILLIAM, bank executive; b. N.Y.C., May 3, 1947; s. John Lee and Margery (Beemer) Couper; m. Elise Marie Palma, Oct. 4, 1969; children: Elise, Margery, Dorothy. BS in Commerce, U.Va., 1968; cert., Coll. Fin. Planning, 1986. Trainee Am. Security Bank, N.A., Washington, 1972, asst. treas., asst. br. mgr., 1972-76, asst. v.p., mgr. main office, 1976-77, v.p., regional mgr., 1977-80, v.p. strategic planning, 1981-83, v.p. retail banking devel., 1983-84, sr. v.p. retail banking, 1984-89; sr. v.p. Md. Nat. Bank, Greenbelt, 1989-92; vice chmn. Va. Fed. Savs. Bank, 1991-93; exec. v.p. Am. Security Bank, Md. Nat. Bank, Washington, 1993-94; pres. Bank Am., Balt., 1994-2000, Washington, 2000—. Chmn. United Way Nat. Capital Area, Washington; bd. dirs. Greater Washington Bd. Trade, Fed. City Coun. Greater Washington Initiative. Mem.: Md. C. of C., Chartwell Golf and Country Club, Ctr. Club Balt. Republican. Episcopalian. Home: 1114 Bellevista Ct Severna Park MD 21146-4846 Office: Bank of Am 730 15th St NW Washington DC 20005 E-mail: william.couper@bankofamerica.com.

COUPEY, SUSAN MCGUIRE, pediatrician, educator; b. Montreal, Que., Can., June 29, 1942; came to U.S., 1978; d. Clarence Herbert and Paulette (Lefevre) McGuire; m. Pierre M.L. Coupey, July 1964 (div. 1981); children: Marc M.R., Ariane S.; m. James R. English III, Nov. 23, 1988. BA, Queen's U., Kingston, Ont., Can., 1962; postgrad., McGill U., Montreal, 1962-63; MD, U. B.C., Vancouver, Can., 1975. Diplomate Am. Bd. Pediatrics, subboard in adolescent medicine. Devel. chemist Merck, Sharp & Dohme, Ltd., Montreal, 1963-64; rotating intern Montreal Gen. Hosp., 1975-76; resident in pediatrics Montreal Children's Hosp., 1976-78; fellow in adolescent medicine Montefiore Med. Ctr., Bronx, N.Y., 1978-79, attending pediatrician, 1980—; rsch. asst. Cancer Rsch. Ctr., U. B.C., 1967-72; instr., asst. prof. pediatrics Albert Einstein Coll. Medicine, Bronx, 1979-85, assoc. prof., 1985-93, prof., 1993—, assoc. dir. div. adolescent medicine, 1984—2001, course dir. introduction to clin. medicine, 1989—, mem. faculty senate, 1983-84, 88-90, chief adolescent medicine, 2002—. Attending pediatrician North Ctrl. Bronx Hosp., 1979-97; cons. in adolescent medicine Flushing (N.Y.) Hosp. and Med. Ctr., 1982-96; Maricopa-Pima vis. prof. U. Ariz., 1989; vis. prof. Children's Hosp. Ea. Ont., U. Ottawa and Ea. Can. chpt. Soc. for Adolescent Medicine, 1990; vis. prof. Philippine Children's Med. Ctr., U. Philippines Coll. of Medicine, 1997; chmn. health svcs. adv. com. Children's Aid Soc., 1985—, bd. trustees, 1993—; mem. adv. bd. Office Substance Abuse Ministry, Archdiocese of N.Y., 1983-85; spkr. Hosp. Italiano, Buenos Aires, Argentina, 1999, Israeli Soc. Adolescent Medicine, Jeruseleum, Israel, 2000, Greek Soc. Adolescent Med., Athens, Greece, 2000. Editor: Primary Care of Adolescent Girls, 2000; assoc. editor Adolescent Medicine: State of the Art Revs., 1990—; assoc. editor Jour. Devel. & Behavioral Pediatrics, 1992-96, editl. bd., 1996—2000; assoc. editor Jour. Pediat. & Adolescent Gynecology, 1992-98, editl. bd. 1998—; editl. bd. Jour. of

Youth and Adolescence, 1998—; contbr. articles to med. jours., also chpts. to books and monographs. Fellow Am. Acad. Pediatrics (exec. com. sect. on adolescent health 1993-96); mem. Soc. for Adolescent Medicine (nominations com. 1984-85, chmn. jour. adv. com. 1987-97, program com. 1991-93, awards com. 1992-95, bd. dirs. 1997-2000), Am. Pediat. Soc. (abstract review com. 1999—2001), Soc. for Behavioral Pediatrics, N.Am. Soc. Pediat. and Adolescent Gynecology (bd. dirs. 1993-96, sec. 1996-2001, chair publs. com. 1996—, pres.-elect 2001-2002, pres. 2002-03), Ea. Soc. Pediat. Rsch., Soc. Rsch. in Adolescence, Sex Info. and Edn. Coun. U.S., Am. Acad. Physicians and Patients, Albert Einstein Coll. Medicine Alumni Assn. (v.p. pediatrics 1983-84, pres. 1984-85). Office: Albert Einstein Coll Medicine Montefiore Med Ctr 111 E 210th St Bronx NY 10467-2401 E-mail: coupey@aecom.yu.edu.

COUPLES, FREDERICK STEVEN, professional golfer; b. Seattle, Oct. 3, 1959; m. Thais; 2 children: Gigi, Oliver. Student, U. Houston. Mem. U.S. Ryder Cup golf team, 1989, 91, 93, 95, 97; mem. nat. teams USA vs. Japan, 1984, Asahi Glass Four Tours World Championship of Golf, 1990, 91, Dunhill Cup, 1991, 92, 93, 94, World Cup, 1992, 93, 94, 95, Pres.'s Cup, 1994, 96, 98. Named All-Am., 1978, 79; winner numerous golf tournaments including Kemper Open, 1983, Tournament Players Championship, 1984, Byron Nelson Golf Classic, 1987, French PGA, 1988, Nissan L.A. Open, 1990, 92, Tournoi Perrier de Paris, 1991, B.C. Open, 1991, Federal Express St. Jude Classic, 1991, Johnnie Walker World Championship, 1991, Nestle Invitational, 1992, The Masters, 1992, (with Jan Stephenson) J.C. Penney Classic, 1983, (with Mike Donald) Sazale Classic, 1990, (with Raymond Floyd) RMCC Invitational, 1990, Buick Open, 1994, World Cup, 1994, Dubai Desert Classic, 1995, Johnnie Walker Classic, 1995, The Player's Championship, 1996, Bob Hope chrysler Classic, 1998, Memorial Tournament, 1998; recipient Vardon trophy, 1991, 92; named PGA Player of Yr. Golf World Mag., 1991, 92, Golf Writers Assn., 1991, 92, PGA Tour Player of Yr, 1993, 94. Achievements include being the leading money winner PGA, 1992. Address: c/o PGA Tour 100 Ave of The Champions PO Box 109601 Palm Beach Gardens FL 33410

COURAGE, THOMAS ROBERTS, lawyer; b. New Haven, Conn., Apr. 22, 1947; s. Jack Haldane and Margaret Smith (Hirschberg) C.; m. Hollie Uong, May 27, 1972; children: Michael, Peter. AB, Harvard U., 1970; JD, U. Pa., 1973. Assoc. Hinckley, Allen, Salisbury & Parsons, Providence, 1973-79; ptnr. Hinckley, Allen & Snyder, Providence and Boston, 1979-98; v.p., gen. counsel Care New Eng. Health Sys., Providence, 1998—. Trustee Hattie Ide Chaffee Home, East Providence, R.I., 1987—. Treas. Greater Providence Youth Hockey Assn., 1988-91; trustee Interfaith Healthcare Ministries, Providence, 1992-93. Mem. Am. Health Lawyer's Assn., Healthcare Fin. Mgmt. Assn., Agawam Hunt, Harvard-Radcliff Club R.I. (pres. 1992-94), Carnegie Abbey Club. Avocations: golf, hiking, squash, photography. Office: Care New Eng Health Sys 45 Willard Ave Providence RI 02905-3218

COURANT, ERNEST DAVID, physicist, educator; b. Goettingen, Germany, Mar. 26, 1920; came to U.S., 1934, naturalized, 1940; s. Richard and Nina (Runge) C.; m. Sara Paul, Dec. 9, 1944; children: Paul N., Carl R. BA, Swarthmore Coll., 1940; MS, U. Rochester, 1942, PhD, 1943; MA (hon.), Yale U., 1962; DSc (hon.), Swarthmore Coll., 1988. Scientist Atomic Energy Project, Montreal, Que., Can., 1943-46; rsch. assoc. physics Cornell U., 1946-48; staff Brookhaven Nat. Lab., 1947—, sr. physicist, 1960-89, disting. scientist emeritus, 1990—; Brookhaven prof. physics Yale U., 1962-67, vis. prof., 1961-62; prof. physics and engring. SUNY, Stony Brook, 1967-85. Vis. asst. prof. Princeton, 1950-51; cons. Gen. Atomic divsn. Gen. Dynamics Corp., 1958-59; vis. physicist Nat. Accelerator Lab., 1968-69; vis. prof. U. Mich., 1989—; cons. Superconducting Supercollider Lab., Dallas, 1990-93; hon. prof. U. Sci. and Tech. of China, Hefei, 1994. Co-originator strong-focusing particle accelerators Fulbright Rsch. fellow Cambridge (Eng.) U., 1956; recipient Fermi award U.S. Dept. of Energy, 1986. Fellow Am. Phys. Soc. (R.R. Wilson prize 1987), AAAS; mem. Nat. Acad. Scis., N.Y. Acad. Scis. (Boris Pregel prize 1979). Home: 40 W 72nd St New York NY 10023-4104 E-mail: ecourant@msn.com.

COURANT, PAUL NOAH, economist, educator, academic administrator; b. Ithaca, N.Y., Jan. 5, 1948; s. Ernest David and Sara (Paul) Courant; m. Katherine Olive Johnson, Sept. 21, 1969 (dissolved 1984); children: Ernest Mendel, Noah Albert; m. Marta Anne Manildi, Jan. 30, 1988; 1 child, Samuel Robinson Manildi. BA, Swarthmore Coll., 1968; MA, Princeton U., 1972, PhD, 1973. Jr. economist Coun. Econ. Advisers, Washington, 1969—70, sr. economist, 1979—80; asst. prof. econs., pub. policy U. Mich., Ann Arbor, 1973—78, assoc. prof., 1978—84, prof. econs. and pub. policy, 1984—, dir. Inst. Pub. Policy Studies, 1983—87, 1989—90, chmn. econs. dept., 1995—97, assoc. provost, 1997—2001, provost, exec. v.p. acad. affairs, 2002—. Mem. task force long-term econ. growth State of Mich., 1983—84; cons. Mich. Dept. Commerce, Lansing, 1984—85, Congl. Budget Office, Washington, 1988—89; bd. dirs. Mich. Future. Author: (book) America's Great Consumption Binge, 1986; co-author: Economics, 12th edit., 1999; contbr. articles to profl. jours. Bd. dirs. Ctr. Watershed and Cmty. Health, Eugene, Oreg., 1997—. Grantee, NSF, 1976—77, 1979—81, 1994—97, Rockefeller Found., 1985—87, Nat. Cancer Inst., 1992—95. Mem.: Nat. Tax Assn., Assn. Pub. Policy Analysis and Mgmt. (mem. policy coun. 1994—98), Am. Econ. Assn. Avocations: sailing, skiing, tennis, hiking, clarinet. Office: Univ Mich 3074 Fleming Bldg Ann Arbor MI 48109-1340 E-mail: pncourant@netscape.net.

COURET, KEIRON LEIGH, performing arts presenter; b. New Orleans, June 29, 1970; d. William Earl Couret Jr. and JeanMarie Boudreaux. BA in Mgmt., Southeastern La. U., 1993, MBA, 1994. Grad. asst. Southeastern La. U., Hammond, 1993-94; asst. mgr. Internat. Mktg. Sys., Metairie, La., 1995; adminstrv. asst. Shared Med. Sys., Metairie, La., 1995-96; asst. dir. Fanfare, Southeastern La. U., Hammond, La., 1996—2001; assoc. dir. programming Columbia Theatre/Fanfare, Hammond, 2001—. Active Hammond Rep. Women, 1997-99, Hammond C. of C., 1996—. Mem.: AAUW, NAFE, Assn. Performing Arts Presenters, Am. Bus. Women's Assn. (Woman of Yr. award 1999). Republican. Avocations: attending cultural events, cooking. Office: Columbia Theatre Fanfare SLU 10797 Hammond LA 70402-0001 E-mail: kcouret@selu.edu.

COURIC, KATIE (KATHERINE COURIC), broadcast journalist; b. Arlington, Va., 1957; m. Jay Monahan; children: Elinor Monahan, Caroline Monahan. Grad. in Am. Studies, U. Va. Began career with reporting and producing jobs NBC affiliates, Miami, Washington; joined NBC Network News, 1989; former nat. corr. Today, NBC, Washington, co-anchor, 1991—; co-host Now with Tom Brokaw and Katie Couric, NBC, 1993—94. Contbg. anchor Dateline NBC. Address: NBC TV Today Show 30 Rockefeller Plz Fl 2 New York NY 10112-0002*

COURNIOTES, HARRY JAMES, academic administrator; b. Chicopee Falls, Mass., Aug. 13, 1921; s. James Harry and Chrisanthe (Gardekas) C.; m. Annette R. Giguere, Sept. 4, 1945; children: James H., Gregory H. BS, Boston U., 1942; Indsl. Adminstr. with high distinction, Harvard U., 1943, MBA with high distinction, 1947; DCS, Western New Eng. Coll., 1976. CPA, Mass. Asst. prof. Am. Internat. Coll., Springfield, Mass., 1946-52, assoc. prof., 1952-58, prof., 1958—, dean Sch. Bus. Adminstrn., 1960-69, v.p., 1964-69, pres., 1969—. Trustee, mem. investment com. Springfield Inst. Savs., 1974-95, vice chmn. bd.,mem. exec. com., 1993-95; trustee Springfield Neighborhood Housing Svc., 1988-92; corporator Springfield Libr. and Mus. Assn., 1997—, former corporator, Springfield Boys Club, 1972-76. Mem. adv. bd. World Affairs Coun., 1970; corporator Springfield Girls Club, 1970—, Wing Meml. Hosp., 1976—; trustee Econ. Edn. Coun. Mass., 1971—; com. mem. United Negro Coll. Fund, 1971; mem. exec. com. Springfield Adult Edn. Coun., 1972-74; mem. exec. com., bd. dirs. Jr. Achievement Western Mass., 1975-76; bd. dirs. Springfield Ctrl. Bus. Dist., 1976-79; mem. bd. adv., N.E. Congl. Inst., 1980; trustee Econ. sponsor Laughing Brook project Mass. Audubon Soc. Lt. AUS, 1943-46. Named Acct. of Yr., Nat. Assn. Cost Accts., 1970; recipient Nat. Human Rels. award NCCJ, 1984, Henry A. Butova Meml. award Western Mass. chpt. Football Found. and Hall of Fame, 1989, Tree of Life award Jewish Nat. Fund, 1993, Disting. Citizen award Pioneer Valley Boy Scouts Am., 1998. Mem. AICPA, Mass. Soc. CPAs (Outstanding Educator for 1991), Fin. Exec. Inst. (chmn. edn. com. 1964-65), Assn. Ind. Colls. and Univs. Mass. (mem. exec. com. 1972-74, 81-84), Greater Springfield C. of C. (dir. 1974-77), Colony Club (Springfield), Harvard Club (Boston), Longmeadow Country Club (Mass.). Home: Cote Rd Monson MA 01057 Office: 1000 State St Springfield MA 01109-3151

COURSEY, SHARON MARTIN, adult education educator, consultant; b. Erie, Pa., Apr. 19, 1955; d. John Henry and Alicia Malinowski Martin; m. Aug. 2, 1986. BA in Polit. Sci., Webster U., 1977; MA in Internat. Edn., Am. Univ., 1986; PhD in Edn. Policy Planning & Adminstrn., Univ. Md., 2001. Edn. splist. animal plant health inspection svc. USDA, Hyattsville, Md., 1986-90, dep. dir. internat. tng. Riverdale, Md., 1990-93, dir. orgnl. and profl. devel., 1993-97; chief of staff, vet. svcs. USDA/APHIS, Washington, 2000—. Tutor ptnrship. for edn. USDA. Author: (with others) Workforce Preparation: AN International Perspective, 2000. Vol. U.S. Peace Corps., West Africa, 1977-79, supr. placement splist., Washington, 1984-86, U.N. High Commn. for Refugees, Bataan, The Philippines, 1980-81. Mem. Phi Kappa Phi. Avocations: piano, gardening, cooking. Home: 10400 Stansfeild Rd Laurel MD 20723

COURSON, JOHN EDWARD, state legislator, insurance company executive; b. Aug. 21, 1944; s. James W. and Mary C. (Harris) C.; m. Elizabeth Poinsett Exum, Apr. 1973; children: James Poinsett, Elizabeth Boykin, Harris Russell. BA, U. S.C., 1968. Sr. v.p. Keenan & Suggs. Field dir. S.C. Republican Party, 1969—75, sec., 1976—80; nat. committeeman for S.C. Rep. Nat. Committee, 1980—88; chmn. campaign '80 for S.C.; Presdl. elector Rep., 1980, 1984; mem. S.C. Senate, 1984—; co-chmn., treas. Re-elect Thurmond Com., 1990—95. With USMCR, 1968—74. Named Young Agt. of Yr., Ind. Ins. Agts. S.C., 1981; recipient Mounted Gold Elephant, S.C. Republican Party, 1975, 1980, 1982, Order of Palmetto. Mem.: Am. Legion, Marine Corps League, Palmetto Club, Columbia Ball Club, Forest Lake Club, Tarantella Club, Sigma Chi. Episcopalian. Avocations: tennis, politics. Office: 401 Gressette Senate Office Bldg PO Box 142 Columbia SC 29202 E-mail: siv@scsenate.org.

COURSON, MARNA B.P. public relations executive; b. Waynesboro, Pa., Feb. 22, 1951; d. Eugene Perry ( ) and Charlotte Mae (Sherman) Roschli; m. Sydney E. Courson, May 24, 1982 (dec. 1999); 1 child, Sydney Alexandra; m. David W. Bowen, Oct. 14, 2001. BA, Franklin and Marshall Coll., 1973; postgrad., U. Kans., Kansas City. Reporter Beach Haven Times/The Beacon, Manahawkin, N.J., 1973-74, Dailey Observer Newspaper, Toms River, N.J., 1974-76; comm. mgr. Frick India Ltd., New Delhi, 1976-77; reporter, dictationist UPI, Washington, 1978-80, reporter Richmond, Va.; reporter, editor AP, Balt., 1980-84; comm. coord. St. Luke's Hosp. Found., Kansas City, Mo., 1986-88; exec. v.p. pub. rels. Spaw and Assocs., Inc., Overland Park, Kans., 1988-89; exec. v.p. CCI Pub. Rels. & Mktg. Comm., Inc., Shawnee Mission, Kans., 1990-92, pres. Kansas City, Mo., 1992—. Former bd. dirs. Wonderscope Children's Mus., Ctr. for Mgmt. Assistance; active Kansas City Downtown Coun.; bd. dirs. and former exec. com. Mid Am. Youth Aviation Assn. Recipient Prism award for fund raising, numerous awards and honors for reporting, 1973-80; also pub. rels. awards, 1988-2003. Mem.: Nat. Assn. Women Bus. Owners, Pub. Rels. Soc. Am. (Pres.'s award with GKC), Internat. Assn. Bus. Communicators, World Futurists Soc., Greater Kans. City C. of C., Sertoma. Office: Ste 800 934 Wyandotte Kansas City MO 64105 E-mail: marna@cci-pr.com. *Every step in my career has been building on my accumulated experience skill and knowledge, providing the basis for creativity and learning for the next stage. In almost every case, I've found that for me the process is as important as achieving the goal.*

COURT, LEONARD, lawyer, educator; b. Ardmore, Okla., Jan. 11, 1947; s. Leonard and Margaret Janet (Harvey) C.; m. JoAnn Dilleshaw, Sept. 2, 1967; children: Chris, Todd, Brooke. BA, Okla. State U., 1969; JD, Harvard U., 1972. Bar: Okla. 1973, U.S. Dist. Ct. (we. dist.) Okla. 1973, U.S. Dist. Ct. (no. dist.) Okla., 1978, U.S. Dist. Ct. (ea. dist.) Okla. 1983, U.S. Ct. Appeals (10th cir.) 1980, U.S. Ct. Mil. Appeals 1973. Assoc. Crowe & Dunlevy, Oklahoma City, Okla., 1977-81, shareholder, dir., 1981—. Adj. prof. Okla. U. Law Sch., Norman, 1984-85, 88-89, 99—, Okla. City U. Law Sch., 1998—; planning com. Ann. Inst. Labor Law, S.W. Legal Found., Dallas, 1984—. Contbg. author: (supplement book) The Developing Labor Law, 1978, Corporate Counsel's Annual, 1974, Labor Law Developments, 1993, Employment Discrimination Law, Supplement, 1998, 2000. Chmn. bd. elders Meml. Christian Ch., Oklahoma City, 1980, 98-2000; cubmaster Last Frontier coun. Boy Scouts Am., 1984, co-chmn. sustaining fund raising drive Oklahoma City Downtown YMCA, 1989, mem. bd. mgmt., 1994-96; participant Leadership Oklahoma City, 1987-88, bd. govs. Okla. State U. Found., 1990-2002; Oklahoma City Ronald McDonald House, 1990-93, mem. exec. com. 1991-93; co-chmn. ann. teleparty fundraising drive Am. Heart Assn., Okla. City, 1996-98, bd. dirs., 1996-98. Capt. USAF, 1973-77. Fellow Am. Coll. Labor and Employment Lawyer; mem. Am. Employment Law Coun., U.S. C. of C. (mem. labor rels. com. 1997—, chmn. fair labor stds. act subcom. 1999—, mem. steering com. 1999—), Oklahoma City C. of C. (mem. sports and recreation com. 1982-85, indsl. devel. com. 1986), Okla. State U. Alumni Assn. (nat. bd. dirs. 1989—, nat. exec. com., 1992-97, pres. 1995-96, chmn. alumni ctr. task force 1998—, Disting. Alumni award 1998), Okla. County Alumni Assn. (bd. sec. 1987-88, treas. 1988-89, v.p. 1989-90, pres. 1990-91), Harvard Law Sch. Assn., ABA (labor and employment law sect. com. on devel. of law under Nat. Labor Rels. Act, com. on EEO law, lititgation sect./employment and labor rels. law com.), Okla. Bar Assn. (labor and employment law sect. coun. 1978-83, 85-87, chmn. 1986), Okla. County Bar Assn., Fed. Bar Assn., U.S. Tennis Assn. (life). Office: Crowe & Dunlevy Mid America Tower 20 N Broadway Ave Ste 1800 Oklahoma City OK 73102-8273

COURTAUD, BERNARD JEAN-JACQUES, human resource consulting executive; b. Massy, France, June 22, 1945; s. Paul and Simone (Mustel) C.; children: Sebastien, Alexandre, Stanilas, Paul. Engring. degree, Ecole Centrale, Paris, 1968; MBA, Insead, Fontainebleau, France, 1972. Cons. Commissariat a l'energie Atomique, 1968—72; cons. Port N.Y. Authority, N.Y.C., 1970-71, Peat Marwick Mitchell & Co., 1972-74; chmn. Groupe Courtaud, Paris, 1974-98, H.R. Cons. Network, 1998—. Chmn. Insead Alumni Assn., France, 1983-88. Office: HR Cons Network 25 Rue François 1 75008 Paris France E-mail: cmi-fie@wanadoo.fr, courtaud@wanadoo.fr.

COURTEAU, GIRARD ROBERT, retired prosecutor; b. St. Paul, Minn., Aug. 21, 1942; s. Robert William and Laura Gertrude Courteau; m. Mary Linda Lucas, Apr. 3, 1964 (div. May 1997); m. Susan Frances DeBaca, Aug. 8, 1997; children: Steven, Girard, Devin, Heather. AA, Coll. Marin, 1965; BA, U. Calif., Berkeley, 1967; JD, U. Calif., 1970. Bar: Calif. 1971, U.S. Dist. Ct. (ctrl. dist.) Calif. 1971, U.S. Dist. Ct. (no. dist.) Calif. 1983. Dep. dist. atty. Monterey County, Calif., 1971, Marin County, San Rafael, Calif., 1972-2001; ret., 2001. Mem. editl. bd. Hasting's Law Jour., 1970; editor Marin Law Enforcement Newsletter, 1974-89. Named Prosecutor of the Yr., Marin County Dist. Attys. Office, San Rafael, Calif., 1987. Mem. Order of the Coif, Thurston Soc., Corvettes of Sonoma County, Palm Springs Corvettes Team ZR-1. Roman Catholic. Avocations: gardening, reading, corvettes. Home: 1307 Park St Santa Rosa CA 95404-3542 E-mail: courvettes@sbcglobal.net.

COURTEAU, JOANNA, foreign language educator; d. Ryszard Wojtowicz; m. Richard Courteau (div. Sept. 1976); two children: m. Charles Gratto, June 29, 1977; four stepchildren. BA cum laude, U. Minn., 1960; MA, U. Wis., 1965, PhD, 1970. Lab. technician dept. anatomy U. Minn., Mpls., 1958-60; grad. fellow U. Wis., Madison, 1960-63, 66-67; instr. Sullins Coll., Bristol, Va., 1963-65; asst. prof. U. Ark., Fayetteville, 1967-71; asst., assoc., full prof. Iowa State U., Ames, 1971-99, univ. prof., 1999—. Dir. summer riding acad. Rimrock Sch. Horsemanship, Elkins, Ark., 1972-76; vis. prof. U. Warsaw, Poland, 1979. Author: The Poetics of Rosalia de Castro's Sombra Negra, 1995; editor: Mujer, Sexo y Poder en la Literatura Femenina del S. XIX, 1999; assoc. editor Hispania, 1992-2002; contbr. numerous articles on modernist theory, feminist studies, and nat. identity to profl. jours. and essay collections. Activist Amnesty Internat., Ames, 1976—, Iowans Against the Death Penalty, Ames, Des Moines, 1995—; pres. Planned Parenthood, Ames, 1981-83, UN Assn. Am., Ames, 1999-2001; del. county, dist. and state convs., mem. rules com. Dem. Party. Recipient Fish award City of Ames, 1985, Human Rels. Recognition award City of Ames, 1989, Wilton Park Internat. award, 1997; fellow Ford Found., São Paulo and Rio de Janeiro, 1967, fellow Gulbenkian Found., Lisbon, Portugal, 1988, 93. Mem. AAUP (exec. bd. 1993-96), MLA, NOW, Am. Portuguese Studies Assn. (founder, pres. 1996-98, past pres.), Am. Assn. Tchrs. Spanish and Portuguese (exec. bd. 1992-95), Internat. Assn. Lusitanists (exec. bd. 1987-93), Women's Studies Assn., Women's Internat. League for Peace and Freedom, Archie C. and Nancy A. Martin Found. (founder, pres. 2000-). Office: Iowa State U Dept Fgn Langs & Lit 300 Pearson Hall Ames IA 50011 also: PO Box 1158 Ames IA 50014 Office Fax: 515-294-9914. E-mail: courteau@iastate.edu.

COURTENAY, LISA A. paralegal, foundation administrator; b. Melrose, Mass., Oct. 17, 1962; d. Joseph C. and Angelé S. Surette; m. Michael F. Courtenay, Sept. 20, 1992; children: Andrea Keene, Michael Keene, Ryan. BA, Newbury Coll., 2000. Paralegal Nigro, Pettepit & Lucas, Wakefield, Mass., 1995—; adminstr. Angel Fund Inc., Wakefield, 1999—. Roman Cath. Avocations: camping, travel, writing. Office: Nigro Pettepit & Lucas 649 Main Street Wakefield MA 01880

COURTENAY, WILLIAM JAMES, historian, educator; b. Neenah, Wis., Nov. 5, 1935; s. Walter Rowe and Emily (Simpson) C.; children: Elizabeth Spire, William Todd. AB, Vanderbilt U., 1957; STB, Harvard U., 1960, PhD, 1967. Instr. history Stanford (Calif.) U., 1965-66; asst. prof. U. Wis., Madison, 1966-69, assoc. prof., 1969-71, prof., 1971—, C.H. Haskins prof., 1988—. Vis. scholar Am. Acad. in Rome, 1995, 97, 98, assesseur du BureauSociéte international pour l'etude de la philosophie médiévale, 1997—. Author: Adam Wodeham, 1978, Covenant and Causality, 1984, Schools and Scholars in 14th Century England, 1987, Capacity and Volition. A History of the Distinction of Absoluate and Ordained Power, 1990, Parisian Scholars in the Early Fourteenth Century: A Social Portrait, 1999; editor: Rotuli Parisienses. Supplications to the Pope from the University of Paris, vol. I: 1316-1352, 2002; also over 60 scholarly articles; co-editor (4 vols.) Gabriel Biel, Canonis Misse Expositio, 1963-67; mem. editorial bd. Jour. the History Ideas, 1976—, Vivarium, 1990—, Medieval Acad. Am., 1978-82; sr. editor series: Education and Society in the Middle Ages and Renaissance, 1990—. Recipient Younger Scholar award NEH, Washington, 1968-69, 83; fellow Alexander von Humboldt Stiftung, Germany, 1975-76, 79-80, Guggenheim Found, 1980, NEH, Newberry Libr., Chgo., 1983, Humboldt Preis, 1988, Inst. for Advanced Study, Princeton, N.J., 1989, Herzog August Bibliothek fellow, 1997, 2002, 2003, Am. Coun. Learned Socs. fellow, 1995-96. Fellow Medieval Acad. Am. (mem. coun. 1974-77, 2002—), Am. Acad. Arts and Scis., Royal Hist. Soc. (London); mem. Am. Soc. Ch. History (councillor 1982-85, pres. 1988), Am. Hist. Assn., Societe internationale pour l'etude de la philosophie medievale, University Club. Avocation: sailing.

COURTER, JEANNE LYNN, materials scientist; b. Flushing, N.Y., May 7, 1953; d. Harry Melvin Jr. and Ruth Jane (Rieben) C. B in Engring. Sci., SUNY, Stony Brook, 1975; PhD in Materials Sci., MIT, 1981. Rsch. scientist Am. Cyanamid Co., Stamford, Conn., 1981-83, materials section projects mgr., 1983-90, quality asst. to divsn. dir., 1990-94; sr. prin. rsch. scientist Cytec Industries, Inc., Stamford, 1994-2000, automotive applications mgr., 2000—02, mgr. applications and tech. svc., coatings chems., 2002—. Inventor epoxy resin compound; patentee in field (with others), 1978-86. Pres., bd. dirs. Stamford Cross Road Residences, Inc. Recipient Elias Singer Best Paper award 23rd Ann. Internat. Waterborne, High Solids, and Powde Coatings Symposium, European Coatings award for best paper 5th Nürnberg Congress. Mem. ASTM, Am. Chem. Soc., N.Am. Guild Change Ringers, N.Y. Soc. for Coatings and Tech., Tau Beta Pi. Methodist. Avocation: perennial gardening. Office: Cytec Industries Inc PO Box 60 1937 W Main St Stamford CT 06904-0060

COURTER, ROBERT J., JR., air force officer; b. N.J., Aug. 1, 1945; BS in Indsl. Engring., Rutgers U., 1968; student, Squadron Officer Sch., 1971; M in Indsl. and Bus. Mgmt., Ctrl. Mich. U., 1974; student, Air Command and Staff Coll., 1975, Air War Coll., 1978, Nat. Def. U., 1987, U. N.H., 1992. Registered profl. engr., Tex. Commd. 2d lt. USAF, 1968, advanced through grades to maj. gen., 1998; chief indsl. engring. 3510th Civil Engring. Squadron, Randolph AFB, Tex., 1968-70; command indsl. engr., dep. chief staff civil engring. Hdqs. Air Tng. Command, Randolph AFB, Tex., 1970-72; chief engring. and constrn. then chief ops. and maintenance 635th Civil Engring. Squadron, U-Tapao Airfield, Thailand, 1972-73; assoc. prof. and course dir. Sch. Engring. Air Force Inst. Tech., Wright-Patterson AFB, Ohio, 1973-77; engring. mgmt. officer ops. and maintenance div., others Hdqs. USAF, Washington, 1977-82; comdr. 67th Civil Engring. Squadron, Bergstrom AFB, Tex., 1982-84, 1st Civil Engring. Squadron, Langley AFB, Va., 1984-86; dir. readiness and force devel., dir programs Hdqs. Tactical Air Command, Langley AFB, Va., 1987-90, dep. chief staff engring. svcs., 1987-90; dep. chief staff civil engring. Hdqs. Air Force Logistics Command, Wright-Patterson AFB, 1990-92; command civil engr. Hdqs. Air Force Material Command, Wright-Patterson AFB, 1992-95; comdr. 37th Tng. Wing, Lackland AFB, Tex., 1995-97; dir. plans and programs Hdqs. Air Force Material Command, Wright-Patterson AFB, 1997-99, dir. defense commissary agy., 1999—. Decorated Disting. Svc. medal, Legion of Merit, Bronze Star with V device and oak leaf cluster, Rep. Vietnam Gallantry Cross with Palm, Rep. Vietnam Campaign medal. Fellow Soc. Am. Mil. Engrs. (former mem. nat. bd.). Office: Def Commissary Agy 1300 E Ave Fort Lee VA 23801-1800

COURTÉS, JOSEPH JEAN-MARIE, humanities educator, writer, semiotician; b. Hérault, France, Feb. 6, 1936; s. Jean and Marthe (Carles) C.; m. Annie Joullié, June 22, 1974; children: Sophie, Jean-Noël, Benoît. Lic., Paris U., 1964, doctorate, 1965, doctorate, 1971, doctorate, 1983. Dir. Internat. Ctr. Semiotics and Linguistics, Urbino, Italy, 1971-73; asst. prof. Ecole de Hautes Études en Scis. Soc., Paris, 1973-84; prof. semiotics Toulouse (France) U., 1985—. Pres. of commn. of semiotics and linguistics Toulouse U., 1986-92, 98—; internat. cons. EHESS, 1985—; mem. Sci. Coms. of Revs., France, 1986—. Author: Lévi-Strauss et les contraintes de la pensée mythique, 1973, Introduction à la sémiotique narrative et discursive, 1976, Sémiotique, dictionnaire raisonné de la théorie du langage, vol. I, 1979, vol. II, 1986, Le conte Populaire: poétique et mythologie, 1986, Sémantiques de l'énoncé, 1989, Sémiotique du discours: de l'énoncé à l'énonciation, 1991, Du signifié au signifiant, 1992, Sémiotique narrative et discursive, 1993, Du lisible au visible: analyse sémiotique d'une nouvelle de Maupassant, d'une bande dessinée de B. Rabier, 1995, Éthnolittérature, rhétorique et sémiotique, 1995, Stratégies d'écriture et instabilité du sens, 1996, Des motifs ethno-litleraines aux to poi, 1997, L'énonciation comme acte sémiotique, 1998, Sémiotique du langage, 2003. Mem. Assn. for Devel. Semiotics (pres. 1988—), Semio-Linguistics Soc. Ctr. (pres. 1991-93). Office: Toulouse II Univ 31058 Toulouse France E-mail: joseph.courtes@wanadoo.fr.

COURTICE, THOMAS BARR, academic administrator; b. Dayton, Ohio, Oct. 31, 1943; s. Allyn J. and Mary Louise (Barr) C.; children: Heather, Ryan, Lindsey; m. Lisa Schweitzer. BS, U. Pitts, 1965; MBA, Ind. U., 1967; PhD, U. Minn., 1974; cert. Inst. Edn. Mgmt., Harvard U., 1977. Dir. placement, instr. Econs. Hamline U., St. Paul, 1967-69, asst. to pres., 1969-75, v.p. for univ. affairs, 1975-77; pres. Westbrook Coll., Portland, Maine, 1977-86, W.Va. Wesleyan Coll., Buckhannon, 1986-94, Ohio Wesleyan U., Delaware, 1994—. Accreditation evaluator North Ctrl. and New Eng. Assn. Schs. and colls., 1980—; mem. exec. com. Found. for Ind. Higher Edn., 1994—, NCAA Pres. Commn. Divsn. III, 1998-2002; bd. dirs. Ednl. and Instnl. Ins. Adminstrs., Inc. Trustee Wayneflete Sch., Portland, 1980-86, Portland Symphony Orch, 1982-86, Delaware Cmty. Found., 1996— Bush Found. summer fellow, St. Paul, 1977. Mem. Nat. Assn. Ind. Colls. and Univs. (bd. dirs. and exec. com. 1993), Nat. Assn. Schs. and Colls. of the United Meth. Ch. (bd. dirs., pres. 1996-97), Appalachian Coll. Assn. (pres. 1992-94). Home: 135 Oak Hill Ave Delaware OH 43015-2519 Office: Office of Pres Ohio Wesleyan Univ Delaware OH 43015 E-mail: tbcourti@cc.owu.edu.

COURTNEY, ANN M. lawyer; b. 1951; BA, Bridgewater State Coll.; JD, Western New Eng. Coll. Bar: Maine 1989. Pvt. practice, Portland, Maine; asst. V.P. & Litigation counsel Unumprovident Corp. Mem. ABA, Maine State Bar Assn. (pres. 1999). Office: 517 Summit St Portland ME 04103 also: Unumprovident Corp 2211 Congress St Portland ME 04102*

COURTNEY, CAROLYN ANN, school librarian; b. Plainview, Tex., Aug. 1, 1937; d. John Blanton and Geneva Louise (Stovall) Ross; m. Moyland Henry Courtney, Aug. 17, 1957; 1 child, Constance Elaine. BA summa cum laude, Wayland Bapt. Coll., 1969; MEd, W. Tex. State Coll., 1976; MLS, U. North Tex., 1990. Cert. elem., secondary, libr. tchr. 5th grade tchr. Hale Ctr. (Tex.) Ind. Sch. Dist., 1970-77, libr., 1977—. Bd. dirs. Plainvierw Cmty. Concerts, 2000—. Mem. LWV (bd. dirs. 1970-75), DAR (Good Citizen chair 1981-85), Tex. State Tchs. Assn. (life), Tex. Classroom Tchrs. Assn. (sec. 1983-85), Tex. Libr. Assn.,

Delta Kappa Gamma (rsch. chair 1975-77, publs. chair 1984-86, pres. 2002--, scholarship 1975). Methodist. Avocations: genealogy, travel. Home: 209 S Floydada St Plainview TX 79072-6665 Office: Hale Center Ind Sch Dist PO Box 1210 Hale Center TX 79041 E-mail: ccourtlibr@hotmail.com.

COURTNEY, EDWARD, retired classics educator; b. Belfast, Northern Ireland, Mar. 22, 1932; came to U.S., 1982; s. George and Kathleen (Nicholson) C.; m. Brenda Virginia Meek, Dec. 18, 1962; children: Richard Marcus, Adam Matthew. BA, Trinity Coll., Dublin, Ireland, 1954; MA, Oxford U., 1957. Research lectr. Christ Ch., Oxford, 1955-59; lectr. in classics King's Coll., London, 1959-70, reader in classics, 1970-77, prof. Latin, 1977-82; prof. classics Stanford U., Calif., 1982-93, Ely prof. humanities, 1986-93; Gildersleeve prof. classics U. Va., Charlottesville, Va., 1993—2002, prof. emeritus, 2002—. Author: Commentary on the Satires of Juvenal, 1980, The Poems of Petronius, 1991, The Fragmentary Latin Poets, 1993, 2d edit., 2003, Musa Lapidaria, A Selection of Latin Verse Inscriptions, 1995, Archaic Latin Prose, 1999, A Companion to Petronius, 2002; editor: Valerius Flaccus, Argonautica, 1970, Juvenal, The Satires, A Critical Text, 1985, Statius, Silvae, 1990; joint editor: Ovid, Fasti, 1978, 4th edit., 1997. Mem. Am. Philol. Assn. Avocation: chess. E-mail: Edcourt2@cs.com.

COURTNEY, EUGENE WHITMAL, computer company executive; b. East St. Louis, Ill., Jan. 3, 1936; s. Eugene and Goldie Genell (Mitchell) C.; m. Barbara Ann Beckwith, Aug. 1, 1959; children: Kevin Eugene, Kyle Patrick. BSEE, Princeton U. with honors, 1957. Exec. v.p., gen. mgr., dir. Digital Sci. Corp., San Diego, 1970-75, pres., CEO, 1975-79; dir. Digital Sci./Europe, 1975-79; v.p. corp. devel. Topaz, Inc., San Diego, 1979, Nat. Computer Sys., Mpls., 1980-81, v.p., gen. mgr. scanning divsn., 1981-83, group v.p., 1983-88; exec. v.p., COO, dir. HEI Inc., Victoria, Minn., 1988-90, pres., CEO, 1990-99; dir., 1989-2000; prin. and dir. Triangle Industries, Inc., 1988—; pres., CEO RSI Sys., Edina, Minn., 1999-2001; prin. E.W. Courtney & Assocs., 2001—. Chmn. bd. dirs. Datakey, Inc., Mpls.; mem. Minn. Software Tech. Com., 1985-86; dir. Waters Instruments, Inc., Mpls. Contbr. articles to profl. jours. Trustee, v.p. engring. San Diego Hall of Sci., 1974-79; mem. State of Calif. gov.'s task force on edn. and industry, 1977-78; mem. Rancho Santa Fe (Calif.) Park and Recreation Bd., 1978; mem. tech. adv. bd. Minn. Dept. Corrections, Shakopee, 1985-86. Am. Electronics Assn. (nat. bd. dirs., chmn. San Diego coun. 1976-79, chmn. Minn. coun. 1993-96), Princeton Club (N.Y.C.). Republican. Avocation: print collecting. Home and Office: 7312 Claredon Dr Minneapolis MN 55439-1722

COURTNEY, JAMES EDMOND, real estate developer; b. Meadville, Pa., Dec. 28, 1931; s. Alexis James and Marian (Winans) C.; m. Eileen Patricia Alman, Nov. 2, 1970; children: Alison M., David E. AB in Econs., Dartmouth Coll., 1953, MBA in Fin. Analysis and Acctg., 1954; LLB, Harvard U., 1959. Bar: Ohio 1960. Assoc. Jones, Day, Reavis & Pogue, Cleve., 1959-62, ptnr., 1963-74; v.p. internat. M.A. Hanna Co., Cleve., 1974-78, sr. v.p. corp. devel., 1978-79, exec. v.p., 1981-90, also bd. dirs., vice chmn., 1989-90; pres. The Mariner Group, Ft. Myers, Fla., 1992-95. Chmn. First Cmty. Bank of S.W. Fla., Ft. Myers, Robb & Stuckey, Ltd., Ft. Myers. Served to lt. USN, 1954-56. Home: 11804 Oakmont Ct Fort Myers FL 33908-3427

COURTNEY, PETER C. state legislator; b. Phila., June 18, 1943; m. Margie Courtney; 3 children. BA, U. R.I., 1965, MPA, 1966; JD, Boston U., 1969. Legal aid atty., 1974-75; hearings officer, 1975-80; pvt. practice, 1981-83; asst. to pres. Western Oreg. State Coll., 1983-; mem. Oreg. State Sen., Salem, 1998—, mem. edn. com., mem. info. mgmt. and tech. com., vice chair jud. com., senate pres., 2003—. Bd. dirs. YMCA, Salem United Soccer; coach Boys and Girls Club. Democrat. Democrat. Roman Catholic. Home: 2925 Island View Dr NE Salem OR 97303-6522 Office: State Capitol Rm 330 Salem OR 97310*

COURTNEY, SHERYL, rehabilitation nurse, consultant; b. Meadville, Pa., Mar. 6, 1947; d. Russell A. and Mary (McMaster) Courtney; children: Darren Warren, Heidi Warren. Diploma, Meadville City Hosp., 1970; BSN, USNY, Albany, 1988. Cert. in nursing adminstrn. and rehab. nursing and case mgmt. Adminstr. Whole Person Home Health Care, Inc., Erie, Pa.; dir. Pvt. Duty Care, Inc., Erie; med. svcs. cons. Crawford & Co. Health and Rehab. Svcs., Erie; mgr., owner Med. Case Mgmt., Greenville, Pa. Recipient Florence Nightingale and med. awards.

COURTNEY, WILLIAM HARRISON, business executive; b. Balt., July 18, 1944; s. Wilbur Harry Courtney and Mary Lee (Mitchell) Fleming; ; m. Laryssa Lapychak Courtney; children: William Jr., Mary Alison. BA in Econs., W.Va. U., 1966; PhD in Econs., Brown U., 1980. Fgn. svc. officer Dept. State, Washington, 1972-99; dep. exec. sec. NSC, The White House, Washington, 1987-88; dep. U.S. negotiator U.S.-Soviet Def. and Space Talks, Geneva, 1988-91; amb. Nuclear Testing & Nuclear Weapons Safety, Security, and Dismantlement,ACDA, Washington, 1991-92; amb. to Kazakhstan, 1992-95; amb. to Georgia, 1995-97; spl. asst. to pres. for Russia, Ukraine and Eurasia, White House, Washington, 1997-98; sr. advisor Fgn. Affairs Reorgn., U.S. Dept. State, Washington, 1998-99; sr. advisor U.S. Commn. Security & Coop. in Europe, 1999; sr. v.p. nat. security programs DynCorp, Alexandria, Va., 2000—. Pres. U.S. Com. for the Nat. Labs. Mem. Coun. Fgn. Rels. Home: 3722 48th St NW Washington DC 20016-3213 Office: 6101 Stevenson Ave Alexandria VA 22304-3540 E-mail: courtneywmh@mindspring.com.

COURTOIS, BERNARD ANDRE, communications executive; BA, U. Mont., 1965, LLB, 1968. Bar: Que. 1969, Ont. 1984. Exec. counsel BCE and Bell Can., Ottawa, Canada. Office: Bell Canada 110 O'Connor St F-14 Ottawa ON Canada K1P 1H1 E-mail: bernard.courtois@bell.ca.

COURTOIS, JEAN-PHILIPPE, information technology executive; DECS, The Ecole Superieure de Commerce, Nice, France. Product mgr. Memsoft; channel sales rep. Microsoft France, 1984—86, So. Europe sales mgr., head mktg. dept., 1986—89, dep. gen. mgr., gen. mgr. sales and mktg.; v.p. Worldwide Customer Mktg., Microsoft, Redmond, Wash., CEO Europe, Mid. East and Africa, 2000—; sr. v.p. Microsoft Corp. Office: Coeur Defense Tour B La Defense 4 100 Esplanade du Gen de Gau 92932 Paris France

COURTSAL, DONALD PRESTON, manufacturing company executive, financial consultant; b. New Haven, Dec. 30, 1929; s. Frederick Joseph and Viola (Schiffel) C.; m. Frances L. Chase, May 22, 1954; children: Lyle Donald, Charles Francis. BS in Mech. Engring, U.S. Coast Guard Acad., 1951; MS in Naval Architecture and Marine Engring, MIT, 1956. With shipbldg. div. Bethlehem Steel Co., Quincy, Mass., 1956-64; with Dravo Corp., 1965-85, gen. mgr. engring. works div., corp. v.p., 1976-82, treas., corp. v.p., 1982-83, group officer mfg. group, sr. v.p. corp., 1983-85; fin. cons. Allegheny Fin. Ltd., 1986-99. Mem. ship research com. Nat. Acad. Scis., 1979-81 Author papers in field. Served with USCG, 1951-54. Fellow Soc. Naval Architects and Marine Engrs. (v.p. 1979-90, v.p. (hon.) 1991—, exec. com. 1974-77, 80-88, coun. 1974—, chmn. adv. pub. svc. com. 1978-88, chmn. audit com. 1991-99). Clubs: Pymatuning Yacht. Unitarian Universalist. Home: 1208 Woodland Rd Pittsburgh PA 15237-4359

COURTWRIGHT, DAVID TODD, history educator, author; b. Kansas City, Mo., Apr. 10, 1952; s. Robert Thomas and Elizabeth Beatrice (Brown) C.; m. Shelby Marie Miller, Dec. 29, 1976; children: Andrew Miller, Paul Miller. BA in English, U. Kans., 1974; PhD in History, Rice U., 1979. Asst. prof. history U. Hartford, West Hartford, Conn., 1979-85, assoc. prof., 1985-88, chmn. dept., 1979-88; prof. history U. North Fla., Jacksonville, 1988—, chmn. dept., 1988-95. Mem. substance abuse com. Inst. Medicine, Washington, 1988-90. Author: Dark Paradise, 1982, rev. edit., 2001, Addicts Who Survived, 1989, Violent Land, 1996, Forces of Habit, 2001. Trustee Mark Twain Meml., Hartford, 1982-88. Recipient Coll. on Problems of Drug Dependence Media award, 2002; NEH fellow, 1991, 98-99, Am. Coun. Learned Socs. fellow, 1993-94; NASA/AHA fellow, 2002. Mem. Am. Hist. Assn., Orgn. Am. Historians, Am. Assn. for History Medicine, So. Hist. Assn., Phi Beta Kappa Assn. N.E. Fla. (pres. 1992-93, v.p. 1994-97). Roman Catholic. Avocation: running. Home: 3871 Arrow Point Trail W Jacksonville FL 32277 Office: U North Fla Dept History 4567 St Johns Bluff Rd S Jacksonville FL 32224-2645 E-mail: dcourtwr@unf.edu.

COUSER, G(RIFFITH) THOMAS, literature educator; b. Melrose, Mass., Sept. 22, 1946; s. William Griffith Couser and Ann Van Stelten; m. Barbara Beth Zabel, Dec. 29, 1984. BA, Dartmouth Coll., Hanover, N.H., 1964—68; PhD in Am. Civilization, Brown U., Providence, R.I., 1977. Asst. prof., English Conn. Coll., New London, 1976—82; prof., English Hofstra U., Hempstead, NY, 1982—. Author: (monograph) American Autobiography: The Prophetic Mode, Altered Egos: Authority in American Autobiography, Recovering Bodies: Illness, Disability, and Life Writing, Vulnerable Subjects: Ethics and Life Writing. Fellow, Nat. Endowment for the Humanities, 1986—87, 1995—96, 2001—02. Mem.: Soc. for Disability Studies, Am. Studies Assn., MLA. Liberal. Avocations: travel, kayaking. Office: Hofstra Univ Hempstead Tpke Hempstead NY 11549

COUSER, WILLIAM GRIFFITH, medical educator, academic administrator, nephrologist; b. Lebanon, N.H., July 11, 1939; s. Thomas Clifford and Winifred Priscilla (Ham) C. BA, Harvard U., 1961, MD, 1965; B.MS, Dartmouth Med. Sch., 1963. Diplomate Am. Bd. Internal Medicine. Intern Moffitt Hosp./U. Calif. Med. Ctr., San Francisco, 1965-66, 66-67; resident Boston City Hosp., 1969-70; asst. prof. medicine U. Chgo., 1972-73; asst. prof. Boston U., 1972-77, assoc. prof., 1977-82; prof., head div. nephrology U. Wash., Seattle, 1982—2002, Belding Scribner prof.medicine, 1995—. Mem. sci. adv. bd. Kidney Found. Mass., Boston, 1974—82; mem. rsch. grant com. Nat. Kidney Found., N.Y.C., 1981—86; mem. rev. bd. for nephrology VA, Washington, 1981—84; mem. exec. com. Coun. on Kidney in Cardiovasc. Disease, Am. Heart Assn., Dallas, 1982—85; mem. pathology A study sect. NIH, chmn., 1988—89; subsplty. bd. in nephrology Am. Bd. Internal Medicine, 1988—92; dir. George M. O'Brien Kidney Rsch. Ctr. U. Wash., 1993—2003. Co-editor: Immunologic Renal Diseases, 1997, 2d edit. 2001; contbr. numerous articles, chpts., abstracts to profl. publs.; mem. editl. bd. Kidney Internat., 1982-96, Am. Jour. Kidney Diseases, Am. Jour. Nephrology, Jour. Am. Soc. Nephrology, editor-in-chief, 2001—. Served to capt. U.S. Army, 1967-69, Vietnam. Recipient Rsch. Career Devel. award NIH, 1975-80, Method to Extend Rsch. in Time award, 1991-97; fellow Nat. Kidney Found., 1971, NIH, 1973; grantee, 1974—. Fellow: ACP, AAAS, Western Assn. Physicians (coun.), Am. Assn. Exptl. Nephrology, Internat. Soc. Nephrology (coun. 1999, v.p. 2001—03, pres.-elect 2003), Am. Soc. Nephrology (coun. 1991—94, pres. 1996), Am. Assn. Physicians, Am. Soc. Clin. Investigation (v.p. 1983—84). Avocation: boating. Office: U Wash Box 356521 1959 NE Pacific St Seattle WA 98195-0001

COUSINEAU, MADELEINE, sociologist, educator; b. Woonsocket, Ri, Mar. 14, 1947; d. Edmond and Charlotte (Tanguay) Cousineau; m. Jonathan Campbell, Jan. 6, 2001; m. Francis Adriance, Aug. 25, 1973 (div. June 0, 1994); children: Elizabeth DuPré, David Adriance. B.A., Emmanuel Coll., Boston, MA, 1967—70; M.A., Boston U., Boston, MA, 1971—73, Ph.D., 1973—84. Prof. of sociology Mt. Ida Coll., Newton Center, Mass., 1984—, chair of the social sci. dept., 2001—; lectr. in sociology U. of Mass. at Boston, Boston, Mass., 1976—2001; vis. prof. Universidade Fed. de Pernambuco, Recife, Brazil, 1993—93, Merrimack Coll., North Andover, Mass., 1990—91. Author: (book) Opting for the Poor: Brazilian Catholicism in Transition; contbr. scholarly journal, edited volume, encyclopedia, edited volume; author: (book) Promised Land: Base Christian Communities and the Struggle for the Amazon; translator: Rio Maria: Song of the Earth; editor: Religion in a Changing World: Comparative Studies in Sociology; contbr. scholarly journal. U.s. coord. Rio Maria Com., Acton, Mass., 1991—2003. Grantee Fulbright Lecture/Rsch. Award for Brazil, US Info. Svc., 1993, Fund for the Advancement of the Discipline, Am. Sociol. Assn./Nat. Sci. Found., 1993, Fichter Grant, Assn. for the Sociology of Religion, 1991 and 1998, Rsch. Grant, Soc. for the Sci. Study of Religion, 1989 and 1990, Faculty Devel. Grant, Mt. Ida Coll., 1990, 1993, 1997, 1998. Mem.: Am. Sociol. Assn. (sect. coun. mem. 1996—99), Soc. for the Sci. Study of Religion (exec. coun. mem. 1990—93), Latin Am. Studies Assn., Assn. for the Sociology of Religion (exec. coun. mem. 1986—89). Avocations: yoga, languages, music; writing. Office: Mount Ida College 777 Dedham Street Newton Center MA 02459-3310 Personal E-mail: mcousineau@mountida.edu.

COUSINEAU, PHILIP ROBERT, writer, filmmaker; b. Columbia, S.C., Nov. 26, 1952; s. Stanley Horace and Rosemary Marie (La Chance) C.; 1 child, Jack Philip Blue Beaton-Cousineau. BA cum laude, U. Detroit, 1974. Writer-in residence Shakespeare and Co. Bookstore, Paris, 1987; script judge Bay Guardian Scriptwriting Contest, 1987-89; judge Nat. Ednl. Film and Video Festival, 1990; mem. adv. bd. Joseph Campbell Archives and Libr., 1991—; documentary film judge Emmy Awards, 1992; dir. mythological tours Joseph Campbell Found., 1993-96; documentary judge San Francisco Film Festival, 1993-95. Author: Deadlines: A Rhapsody on a Theme of Famous Last Words (Recipient award Nat. Assn. Ind. Pubs.), 1991, UFOs: Manual for the Millenium, 1995, German edit., 1997, Soul Moments: Marvelous Stories from the World of Synchronicity, 1997, Spanish edit., 1998, Korean edit., 2001, retitled edit. Coincidence or Destiny: Stories of Synchronicity that Illuminate Our Lives, 2002, The Art of Pilgrimage: The Seeker's Guide to Making Travel Sacred, 1998, Korean edit., 1998, Portuguese edit., Spanish edit., 1999 (Quality Paperback Book Club selection 1998), The Book of Roads: Travel Stories, 2000, Once and Future Myths: The Power of Ancient Stories in Modern Times, 2001, The Olympic Odyssey: Rekindling the True Spirit of the Great Games, 2003; editor: The Hero's Journey: Joseph Campbell on His Life and Work, 1990, Portuguese edit., 1995, rev. edit., 1999, The Soul of the World, 1993 (Quality Paperback Book Club selection 1993, Book of Yr. award Contemporary Photography 1994), Soul: An Archaeology, 1994, Chinese edit., 1997, Turkish edit., 1999, Prayers at 3 A.M., 1995, Design Outlaws, 1997, Riddle Me This: A World Treasury of Folk Riddles, 1999, Spanish edit., 2000, Chinese edit., 2000, Italian edit., 2002, retitled edit. A World Treasury of Riddles, 2001, The Soul Aflame, 1999, The Way Things Are: Conversations with Huston Smith on the Spiritual Life, 2003; contbr. to 19 other books; co-dir., screenwriter documentary films: The Peyote Road, 1993 (best documentary award Gt. Plains Film Festival, Cine Golden Eagle award, Bronze Telly award, Silver award Chgo. Film Festival, award Mill Valley Film Festival), A Seat at the Table: Fighting for American Indian Religious Freedom, 2003; screenwriter: The Presence of the Goddess, 1987, Ecological Design, 1994 (Golden Gate award, Cine Golden Eagle award, Sundance Film Festival), A Seat at the Table: Struggling For American Indian Religious Freedom, 2003 (Amnesty Internat. Film Festival); co-writer: Wayfinders: A Pacific Odyssey, 1999 (Gold Apple, Nat. Ednl. Media Network Festival, Hawaii Film Festival); co-writer The Red Road to Sobriety, 1995 (Cine Golden Eagle award 1995, Gold award Red River Film Festival 1998); co-writer Your Humble Serpent: The Legacy of Reuben Snake, 1996 (Silver Apple award Nat. Ednl. Film Festival, Gold award Red Earth Film Festival), Gold Apple, Nat. Ednl. Media Network Festival, Hawaii Film Festival; co-writer: The 1932 Ford V8, 1986; co-writer Eritrea: A Portrait of the Eritrean People, 1989; co-writer (video) Wiping the Tears of Seven Generations, 1991 (Best Video award Am. Indian Film Festival, Silver Telly award, Gold Apple award Nat. Ednl. Film Festival; co-writer, assoc. prodr. The Hero's Journey: The World of Joseph Campbell, 1987 (Silver Apple award Ednl. Film and Video Festival); co-writer film Forever Activists: Stories from the Veterans of the Abraham Lincoln Brigade, 1990 (Acad. Award nomination, jury prize San Francisco Film Festival). Trustee Native Land Found., 1993-96. Fellow Calif. Inst. Integral Studies, 1991-95. Avocation: travel. Office: Harper San Francisco Pubs 353 Sacramento St San Francisco CA 94111-3620 E-mail: phil@philcousineau.com., soulcous@aol.com.

COUSINO, JOE ANN, sculptor; b. Toledo, Nov. 17, 1925; d. George Carl and Lucille Caroline (Kocher) Bux; m. (div.); children: Paula Rene, Richard Nils. BA in Art, U. Toledo, 1947; stud., U. of Mex., 1948, U. So. Ill., 1953; attended, Internatl. Wkshp., Pietra Santa, Italy, 1980. Art tchr. Ctrl. YMCA & YWCA, Toledo, 1945-47; sculpture tchr. U. Tex. Jr. Coll., Gainesville, 1965, Defiance (Ohio) Coll., 1970, Bowling Green (Ohio) State Univ., 1971; profl. sculptor worldwide, 1963—. Founder, pres. Toledo Potters Guild, 1951—55; Ohio rep. Am. Craft Coun., N.Y.C., 1960—62; pres. Fed. Art Socs. North Ohio, 1965—67, trustee, 1963—; co-chair midwest Kefauver com. Art in the Embassies Program, Dept. State, Washington, 1966; guest sculptor U. So. Calif., Berkley, 1981. One-woman shows include Toledo Mus. Art, Frank Ryan Gallery, Chgo., Forsythe Gallery, Mich., Mount St. Joseph Gallery, Cin., Arndt Mus. Art, Elmira, N.Y., Button Gallery Ltd., Saugatuck, Mich., Bowling Green State Univ. Grad. Ctr. Gallery, Ohio State Gallery, Kent State Univ. Gallery, Toledo Mus. Westgate Gallery, 2003, Exhbn. Bangkok, 1990, Sculpture In the Garden, Toledo Bot. Garden (sculpture honorarium), 2000; prin. sculptures include Rio de Janeiro Brazil Dept. of Commerce, 1963, the John Leslie Stevens Meml., Oak Harbor, Ohio, Mame Gordon Meml., United Ch., Sylvania, Ohio, Greek Orthodox Holy Cathedral, Christ the King Ch., Toledo Hosp., Riverside Hosp., Toledo, Univ. Toledo, Med. Coll. Ohio, Toledo Botanical Gardens, U. Toledo Student Union Bldg., 1994, Way Libr., Perrysburg, Ohio, 1986, U. Toledo McMaster Astronom Bldg., 1989, Sister of St. Francis, Mother House Commons, Tiffon, Ohio, 1999, Toledo Opera Sculpture Honor Opera Condrs. Presentation, 1999, Schedel Arboretum and Gardens, Elmore, Ohio, 2001, Eagle Pitcher Bearing divsn. Bunting Brass of U.S.A., Engring. Soc. Ohio; works featured in numerous mags. and jours. including The Blade Newspaper, Toledo, 7/2000, Ceramics Monthly Internat., 1965, Featured spkr. UNICEF, Madras, India, 1984; recipient Woman of Toledo civic award, 1987; bd. dirs. Toledo Arts Commn., 1978-84; pres. Toledo Women's Art League, 1950-51. Recipient Outstanding Svc. in Field of Art award Fedn. of Arts, Toledo, 1967, Touchstone nomination award Press Club of Toledo, 2000, Lifetime Achiever award, 2000; named Outstanding Intellectual of 21st Century, Internat. Biog. Ctr., London, 2001. Mem. Internat. Sculpture Ctr., Pan Pacific S.E. Asia Women's Assn., Scandinavian Club of Toledo, Sister Cities Internat. Episc. Avocations: internat. travel, folk dancing, jazz, photography, lectr. on art. Home: 3717 Indian Rd Toledo OH 43606-2408

COUSINS, ROBERT JOHN, nutritional biochemist, educator; b. N.Y.C., Apr. 5, 1941; s. Charles Robert and Doris Elizabeth (Sifferlen) C.; m. Elizabeth Anne Ward, Jan. 25, 1969; children: Sarah, Jonathan, Allison. BA, U. Vt., 1963; PhD, U. Conn., 1968. NIH postdoctoral fellow biochemistry U. Wis., 1968-70; asst. prof. nutrition Rutgers U., 1971-74, assoc. prof., 1974-77, prof. nutritional biochemistry, 1977-79, prof. II (disting. Prof.), 1979-82, dir. grad. program in nutrition, 1976-82, mem. grad. programs in biochemistry, nutrition and toxicology; Boston family prof. human nutrition and biochemistry U. Fla., Gainesville, 1982—, eminent scholar chair, 1982—; dir. Nutritional Sci. Ctr., U. Fla., 1987—, grad. coun., 1990-93. Mem. nutrition study sect. NIH, 1980-84; mem. USDA Expt. Sta., dir. subcom. on human nutrition, 1987-2001; J.L. Pratt vis. prof. Va. Poly. Inst. and State U., 1980; Wellcome vis. prof. Auburn U., 1986; C. Malcolm Trout vis. scholar Mich. State U., 2003; mem. NAS, Inst. of Med. Commn. on opportunites in nutrition and food scis., 1991-93, Food & Nutrition Bd., 1997-2002, Dietary Reference Intakes Sci. Evaluation Commn., 1999—2001, Ad Hoc Bionutrition Commn., NIH, 1993; lectr. in field.. Assoc. editor Jour. Nutrition, 1990-96; mem. editl. com. Ann. Revs. Nutrition, 1985-90, 96-99, assoc. editor, 1999—; contbg. editor Nutrition Revs., 1980-88; mem. editl. bd. FASEB Jour., 1994-99, Biol. Trace Element Rsch., 1982-2003; contbr. articles in nutritional biochemistry to profl. jours., chpts. to books. Recipient Mead Johnson award in nutrition, 1979, Osborne and Mendel award for basic rsch. in nutrition, 1989, U. Conn. Disting. Alumnus award, 1991, Merit award NIH, 1992, USDA Sec.'s Honor award, 2000, Am. Coll. Nutrition Rsch. award, 2003, Bristol-Myers Squibb/Mead Johnson award for disting. achievement in nutrition rsch., 2003; Future Leader grantee Nutrition Found., Inc., 1973, NIH grantee, 1972—, Am. Coll. Nutrition Rsch. award, 2003. Mem. AAAS, NAS (elected mem. 2000), Am. Soc. Biochem. and Molecular Biology, Am. Soc. Nutrition Sci. (chmn. nominating com. elected officers 1983, coun. 1986-89, pres.-elect 1995-96, pres. 1996-97), Biochem. Soc. U.K., Soc. Exptl. Biology and Medicine (edit. bd. Proc. 1980-86), Am. Chem. Soc., Soc. Toxicology, Fedn. Am. Socs. Exptl. Biology (vice chmn. summer conf. 1985, chmn. summer conf. 1989, bd. dirs. 1989—, v.p. 1990-92, pres., chmn. bd. 1991-92, chmn. subcom. consensus conf. biomed. funding 1991-94, chmn. pub. affairs exec. com. 1992-93), Sigma Xi, Phi Kappa Phi, Gamma Sigma Delta (U. Conn. Disting. Alumni). Home: 4510 NW 20th Pl Gainesville FL 32605-3441 Office: U Fla Ctr for Nutritional Sciences 201 Food Sci & Human Nutr Bldg Gainesville FL 32611 E-mail: cousins@ufl.edu.

COUSINS, WILLIAM, JR., retired judge; b. Swiftown, Miss., Oct. 6, 1927; s. William and Drusilla (Harris) C.; m. Hiroko Ogawa, May 12, 1953; children: Cheryl Akiko, Noel William, Yul Vincent, Gail Yoshiko. BA, U. Ill., 1948; LLB, Harvard U., 1951. Bar: Ill. 1953, U.S. Dist. Ct. (no. dist.) Ill. 1961, U.S. Supreme Ct. 1975. Title examiner Chgo. Title & Trust Co., 1953-57; asst. state's atty. Cook County, Ill., 1957-61; sole practice Chgo., 1961-67; judge Circuit Ct. Cook County, Chgo., 1976-92; justice Ill. Appellate Ct., 1992—2002. Chair exec. com. 1st Dist. Appellate Ct., 1997-98; lectr. DePaul Law Sch., Chgo.; bd. dirs. Nat. Ctr. State Cts., 1996-2002; faculty advisor Nat. Jud. Coll., 1987; mem. exec. com. Ill. Jud. Conf., 1983-2002, former chmn. exec. com.; liaison assoc. judge coordinating com.; former chmn. Ill. Jud. Coun. Bd. dirs. Ind. Voters Ill., 1964-67, Ams. for Dem. Action, 1968, Operation PUSH, 1971-76, Nat. Ctr. for State Cts.; mem. Chgo. City Coun., 1967-76; del. Dem. Nat. Conv., 1972; asst. moderator United Ch. of Christ, N.Y.C., 1981. Served with U.S. Army, 1951-53. Decorated Army Commendation medal; named Judge of Yr., John Marshall Law Sch., Chgo., 1980; recipient Thurgood Marshall award Ill. Jud. Coun., 1992, Earl Burris Dickerson award Chgo. Bar Assn., 1998, C. Francis Stradford award, 2001. Mem. ABA, Nat. Bar Assn. (jud. coun., Raymond Pace Alexander award 1999, Hall of Fame 1994), Ill. Bar Assn. IAccess to Justice award 2002), Cook County Bar Assn. (former bd. dirs., Edward N. Wright award 1968, William R. Ming award 1974, Hall of Fame 1997), Alpha Kappa Alpha (Monarch award for Statesmanship 1995), Kappa Alpha Psi, Sigma Pi Phi, Delta Sigma Rho. Home: 1745 E 83rd Pl Chicago IL 60617-1714 Fax: 773-374-4316. E-mail: wmcousins1@ameritech.net.

COUTEAU, MARIE-JOSÉ, sociologist; b. Pecquencourt, Nord, France, Mar. 15, 1961; d. Renè and Cécile (Lukaszewski) C.; m. Max Chlebowski. B in Philosophy and Sociology, U. Nanterre, 1983, M in Philosophy and Sociology, 1984, D.E.A. in Sociology, 1985. Sociologist Agy. Nat. de Recherche sur Le Sida Centre Nat. de la Recherche Scientifique, Paris, 1990-94; sociologist CERSES-CNRS, Paris, 1994—. Contbr. articles to profl. jours. Laureate of Vocation's Found., Sociologist of Med. Ethics, 1988. Fellow Recherche en Scis. Sociales. Office: CNRS 59 rue Pouchet 75849 Paris 17 France E-mail: couteau@iresco.fr.

COUTO, JAMES ROBERT, medical association director; b. Wichita Falls, Tex., Nov. 18, 1952; s. Robert L. Couto and Patricia Barck; m. Nancy Marie Grimes, Oct. 15, 1989; children: James, Kathryn, Kristin. BSBA, Wayne State Univ., 1988, MA in edn. adminstrn., 1990. Edn. coord. Wayne State Univ., Detroit, 1988-90, Am. Acad. Pediat., Elk Grove Village, Ill., 1990-93; acct. rep. Wyeth-Lederle Vaccines & Pediats., Elk Grove Village, 1995-98; dir. hosp., surgical svcs. Am. Acad. Pediats., Elk Grove Village, 1998—. Mem. Am. Soc. of Assn. Execs., Alliance for Continuing Med. Edn., Assn. Forum of Chgo., Roman Catholic. Avocations: jogging, golf, reading. Office: Amer Acad Pediatrics 141 NW Point Blvd Elk Grove Village IL 60007-1098 Fax: (847) 434-8000. E-mail: jcouto@aap.org.

COUTO, NANCY VIEIRA, poet, literary consultant; b. New Bedford, Mass., June 11, 1942; d. Edward and Angelina (Vieira) C.; m. Joseph Anthony Martin, Aug. 13, 1988. BS in Edn., Bridgewater State Coll., 1964; MFA, Cornell U., 1980. Secondary rights asst. Cornell U. Press, Ithaca, N.Y., 1981-82, subsidiary rights mgr., 1982-94; cons., proprietor Leatherstocking Literary Svcs., Ithaca, 1994—. Juror literature fellowship program Pa. Coun. Arts, Harrisburg, 1994; mem. selection com. fellowships Am. Antiquarian Soc., Worcester, Mass., 1995. Author: The Face in the Water, 1990 (award), various poems; assoc. editor Epoch, 1979-82, The Laurel Review, 1992-2000; poetry editor Epoch, 2000—. Artist ptnr. Cmty. Arts Partnership of Tompkins County. Creative Artists Pub. Svc. fellow N.Y. State, 1982-83, NEA fellow, 1987, 99, Creative Performing Artists and Writers fellow Am. Antiquarian Soc., 1995; Constance Saltonstall Found. for the Arts grantee, 1998; recipient Gettysburg Review award, 1994. Mem. Associated Writing Programs. Democrat.

COUTTS, LAWRENCE ROBERT, publisher; b. La Crosse, Wis., Oct. 9, 1948; s. Robert Samuel and Margaret Yvonne (Hougen) C.; m. Linda Lee Florio, May 23, 1970; children: Melissa, Marcia, Michelle, Michael. BS in political science, Carroll Coll., Waukesha, Wis., 1970; MBA, U. Wis., Milw., 1976. Advt. mgr. The Ansul Co., Marinette, Wis., 1970; mgr. comm. and advt. Will Ross Inc., Milw., 1970—74; advt. specialist Med. Systems divsn. GE, Waukesha, Wis., 1974—77; mgr. advt. and promotion Pfizer Med. Systems Inc., Columbia, Md., 1977—78; mktg. svcs. dir. Extrocorporeal Med. Spec., King of Prussia, Pa., 1978—80; pres. Coutts Enterprises LLC, Scottsdale, Ariz., 1980—; pub. Nephrology News and Issues, Lansdale, Pa., 1986—; co-founder, pres. Med. News & Issues, Inc., Medalnews.com., Inc., HON&I, Inc. and NN&I, Inc., 2001—. Chmn. dialysis mktg. subcom. Health Industry Mfrs. Assn., Washington, 1979-80; patient advocacy task force, Am. Kidney Fund, 2000—; pubs. adv. com., BPA Internat., Inc., 2001—. Recipient Bell Ringer

award with direct mail campaign Bus./Profl. Advt. Assn. Milw., 1978, NKF Pub. Svc. award, 1988, 90. Republican. Presbyterian. Avocations: golf, tennis, bridge, gardening, horseback riding. Home: PO Box 7288 Cave Creek AZ 85327-7288 Office: Medical News & Issues 13880 N Northsight Blvd Ste 101 Scottsdale AZ 85260-3666

COUTU, CHARLES ARTHUR, deacon; b. Central Falls, R.I., Oct. 3, 1927; s. Charles Arthur and Aldea Alma (Laliberte) C.; m. Yvette Rhea Dery, Nov. 26, 1953. AA, Our Lady of Providence Sem., 1949; Etudes Speciales de Philosophies, Sem. Philosophy, Montreal, Que., Can., 1951; A in Casualty Claims Law, Am. Ednl. Inst. N.J., 1966. Ordained deacon Roman Cath. Ch., 1978. Master of ceremonies Bishop Tracy, Lafayette, La., 1958-59; tchr. St. Teresa's High Sch., Decatur, Ill., 1964-65, Pitts., 1964-68, Holy Family Ch., Dale City, Va., 1971-97; ret., 1997; permanent diaconate commn. mem. St. Peter's Mission, Washington, Va., 1998, dir. religious edn., 1998—; defender of the bond Tribunal, Arlington, Va., 1992. Subrogation mgr. United Svcs. Automobile Assn., Reston, Va., 1976—; advocate Tribunal, Arlington, 1976—; chmn. Arbitration Com., Washington, 1975-88; mem. Diaconal Coun. Exec. Com., 1987-90; vice-chmn. evangelization commn. Diocese of Arlington, 1979-80, chmn. diaconal coun., 1999. Religious emblem counselor Cath. Com. on Scouting and Campfire, 1990. Sgt. 1st class U.S. Army, 1952-55. Mem. KC. Home: 328 Pine Dr Amissville VA 20106-9611 E-mail: cacoutu@earthlink.net., deachas@msn.com. *I want to try to develop and nurture a deeper love and respect for God through His Mother, the Blessed Virgin Mary.*

COUTURE, ARMAND, civil engineer; b. Quebec Central City, Can., 1930; BSc in Civil Engring., Laval U., Quebec, Can., 1953, MSc in Structures and Found., 1955; postgrad., U. Calif., Berkeley, 1958; Doctorate honoris causa, U. Quebec à Montréal. Structural engr. Nat. Ports Coun., Ottawa, Ont., Can., 1953-55, Fenco, Montreal, 1955-61; ptnr., dir., then chmn. and CEO Gen. Engring. Co., Ltd., Montreal, 1962-67; ptnr., dir. tech. and econ. studies Lamarre Valois Internat. Lavalin, Montreal, 1967-72, v.p., mem. mgmt. com., 1972-85, pres., CEO Shawinigan Lavalin Inc., 1983-87, sr. group v.p., 1988-91; sr. v.p. SNC-Lavalin, Inc., Montreal, 1991-92; pres., COO Hydro-Quebec, Montreal, 1992-96; chmn., bd. dirs. Societe D'Energie de la Baie James, Montreal, 1992-96; pres. La Soc. Bedelmar Ltee, Laval, Quebec, 1996—. Chmn. bd. dirs. Inst. Nat. de la Rsch. Scientifique, 1998—; pres. Bur. de Transition Fin., 2003—. Decorated Order of Can., officer Order of Quebec; recipient Can. Commemorative 125 medal, 1992, Julian C. Smith medal Engring. Inst. Can., 1995, Golden Jubilee medal, The Queen of England, 2002. Mem. Ordre des Ingenieurs du Quebec, Assn. Profl. Engrs. Ont., Can. Inst. Profl. Engrs., Can. Acad. Engring., Club Saint-Denis, Club de Golf Laval-sur-le-Lac. Home: Apt 106 1400 Croissant Merit Mount Royal QC Canada H3P 3N6 Office: Office 2100 1200 McGill Coll Montreal QC Canada N3P 3N6

COUTURE, JEAN G. retired surgeon, educator; b. Quebec City, Que., Can., July 1, 1924; Student, Jesuits Coll., Quebec City, 1936-44; MD, Laval U., 1944-49. Postgrad. New Rochelle Hosp., NYU, Bellevue Med. Ctr., N.Y.C., 1949-54; attending surgeon Hôpital du Saint-Sacrement, Que., 1954—, surgeon-in-chief, 1967-78, head dept. surgery, 1969-75, dir. oncology unit, 1981—; asst. prof. Faculty of Medicine, Laval U., Que., 1963-70, prof. surgery, 1970-2000, emeritus prof. surgery, 2000—, chmn. dept. surgery, 1981-89, dir. postgrad. programs, 1973-79, asst. dean for postgrad. studies, 1975-79. V.p. med. bd. St. Sacrement Hosp., Que., 1967-68; med. advisor Regional Council for Health and Welfare, Quebec City, 1978-81; vis. prof. McGill U., 1977, Hôpital Henri Mondor, Paris, 1978, U. Ottawa, 1980, U. Calgary, 1984; mem. com. on accreditation Royal Coll., 1974-78, chmn. area 4 regional adv. com., 1977-80; bd. govs. Profl. Corp. Physicians and Surgeons Can., 1976—; lectr. in field. Mem. editorial bd. Can. Jour. Surgery, 1974-81; contbr. articles to profl. jours. Pres. Jesuits Coll. Alumni Assn., Que., 1957, Alumni Assn. Laval U., 1969-70. Named Alumni of Yr., Laval U., 1996. Fellow Royal Coll. Surgeons Can., ACS (bd. govs. 1980-86, exec. bd. govs. 1981-85, chmn. Que. Province adv. com. 1976-82), Australasian Coll. Surgeons (hon.), Coll. Surgeons South Africa (hon.), Royal Coll. Surgeons of Eng. (hon.), Order of Can. (hon.); mem. Royal Coll. Physicians and Surgeons Can. (bd. examiners 1958-66, pres. bd. examiners 1964-66, sci. program in surgery 1968-71, pres. program com. in surgery 1970-71, chmn. com. on accreditation 1980-82, chmn. com. on credentials 1982-84, council 1976-80, v.p. 1978-80, pres. 1984-86), Can. Assn. Gen. Surgeons (pres. Eastern div. 1985-86, chmn. edn. com. 1980-83, nat. pres. 1989-90), Can. Coun. on Health Facilities Accreditation (pres. 1992-93), Assn. Clin. Surgeons Can., Can. Med. Assn., Am. Surg. Assn., Assn. des Médecins de Langue Française du Can., Que. Surg. Soc. (sec. 1966-70, pres. 1972-73), Assn. Française de Chirurgie, Internat. Surg. Soc., Que. Med. Soc., James IV Assn. Surgeons, Internat. Surg. Group, l'Académie de Chirurgie de Paris, l'Assn. Française de Chirurgie (hon.). E-mail: jean.couture@chg.ulaval.ca.

COUTURE, JEAN GUY, bishop; b. Quebec, Que., Can., May 6, 1929; s. Odilon and Eva (Drolet) C. BA, PhB, Laval U., Quebec, 1949, L.Theol., 1953, L.Sc.Phys., 1959. Ordained priest Roman Cath. Ch., 1953. Prof. math. and scis. St. Georges H.S. and Coll., Beauce, Que., 1953-65, adminstr. coll., 1961-68; mem. adminstrn. Roman Cath. Diocese Quebec, 1968-75; bishop of Hauterive Que., 1975-79; of Chicoutimi, 1979—. Mem. Order of Can., Order of Red Cross (officer). Roman Catholic. Home and Office: 602 E Racine Chicoutimi QC Canada G7H 1V1 E-mail: diocese.chicoutimi@videotron.net.

COUTURE, RONALD DAVID, art administrator, design consultant; b. Ware, Mass., Dec. 1, 1944; s. Roy and Thelma Mary (Ledger) C.; m. Sandra Elaine Sharpe, Sept. 28, 1968; children: David, Meredith. Diploma, Butera Sch. Art, Boston, 1966. Graphic designer Sta. WGBH-TV Ednl. Found., Cambridge, Mass., 1970-73; promotion art dir. The Boston Globe, 1973-74, editl. design dir., 1974-77; asst. mng. art dir. N.Y. Times, 1977-78, assoc. mng. art dir., 1978-79, mng. art dir., 1979-84, dep. dir./editl. art, 1984-86, mng. dir./editl. art, 1986-88; owner, pres. Newsvision Inc., Mt. Kisco, N.Y., 1988-95. Owner Riverbend Design, 1996-2002, Riverbend Gallery and Workshop, 2003—; design cons. for Web and corp. pub.; design cons. Met. Cultural Alliance, Boston, 1972-77, IBM Corp. Pubs., 1991-93; guest lectr. Boston U. Sch. Comm., 1977; judge 62d and 64th Ann Exhibit, The Art Dirs. Club of N.Y., 1983; internat. editl. design Internat. Editl. Design Forum, N.Y.C., 1983. Contbr. articles in field to profl. jours. Mem. Westborough Planning Bd., Mass., 1977; apptd. regional rep. Ctrl. Mass. Regional Planning Bd., Westborough, 1977; apptd. chmn. Archtl. Rev. Bd., Mount Kisco, N.Y., 1978, 81, 84, 86, 89, 92, 95; mem. task force Labor Market Info. Network of N.Y. Labor Dept. and N.Y.C. Dept. Employment, 1979; bd. dirs. Blanchard Means Found., 1997; mem. Brookfield Hist. Commn., 1999. Recipient Gold medal set design New England Theater Conf., 1974; recipient Gold medal newspaper design Soc. Newspaper Design, 1980 Mem. Soc. Newspaper Design (Gold medal chart design 1981, bd. dirs., nat. conf. dir. 1987-90), Art Dirs. Club N.Y., Am. Inst. Graphic Artist, Art Dirs. Club Boston, Nat. Computer Graphics Assn., Soc. Publ. Design Roman Catholic. Home: 44 Lake Rd Brookfield MA 01506-0537 Office: PO Box 537 9 S Maple St Brookfield MA 01506-1600

COUTURIAUX, CLAY JAMES, musician; b. Atlanta, June 5, 1972; s. Helen Ruth Moore and Paris Couturiaux; m. Desiree Danielle DuBose, July 15, 1995. D in Musical Arts, U. North Tex., 2000. Asst. condr. East Tex. Symphony Orch., Tyler, 1998—2002; asst. dir. orchestras U. North Tex., Denton, 2000—. Cellist East Tex. Symphony Orch., Tyler, 1994—. Mem.: Conductors Guild, Pi Lambda. Office: Univ North Tex PO Box 311367 Denton TX 76203 Office Fax: 940-565-2002. E-mail: ccoutur@music.unt.edu.

COUTURIER, GORDON WAYNE, computer information systems educator, consultant; b. Sparta, Mich., Sept. 14, 1942; s. Clifford Charles and Edith (Reyburn) C.; m. Sylvia Jean Hatch, Mar. 21, 1964; children: Andrew Scott, Laura Couturier Shepard. BSEE, Mich. State U., 1964, MSEE, 1965; PhD, Northwestern U., 1971. Tech. staff Bell Telephone Labs., Naperville, Ill., 1965—72; engr. project leader ITT, Des Plaines, Ill., 1972-80; dir. engr. GTE Subscriber Equipment Group, St. Petersburg, Fla., 1980-82, Paradyne, Largo, Fla., 1982-87; cons. C & C Cons., Tarpon Springs, Fla., 1987—; prof. U. Tampa, 1988—2000. Engr. adv. coun., guest U. Fla. engr. dept., 1985-2001; v.p. prof. devel. ASTD, Clearwater, 1987-90. Contbr. articles to profl. jours.; inventor. Councilman City of St. Charles, Ill., 1971-75; fin. chair Heritage Meth. Ch., Clearwater, Fla., 1982-88; mem., tng. and pub. staff officer USCG Aux., Palm Harbor, Fla., 1993-97. Recipient Men of Achievement award, 1989. Mem.: AIS, Decision Sci. Inst., Lake Tarpon Sail and Tennis Club (sec. 1999—2002, pres. 2003—, treas. 2002—). Avocations: travel, coin collection, philately, tennis. Home: 90 S Highland Ave Apt 2 Tarpon Springs FL 34689-5368 Office: U Tampa UT Box 131F 401 W Kennedy Blvd Tampa FL 33606-1490 E-mail: gcouturier@ut.edu.

COUZENS, LINDA LEE ANDERSON, oncology nurse; b. Alpena, Mich., May 10, 1957; d. Roy James and Celia Jeanette (Swartzinski) Anderson; m. Frank Couzens, Jr., Nov. 1, 1997. ADN, Lake Superior State U., Sault Ste. Marie, Mich., 1977; BSN, Wayne State U., 1980; MS, U. Mich., 1988. Advanced oncology cert. nurse, cert. clin. nurse specialist. Staff nurse Alpena Gen. Hosp., 1977-79, U. Mich. Med. Ctr., Ann Arbor, 1980-81, Catherine McAuley Health Ctr., Ann Arbor, 1981-89; case mgr. Harper Hosp., Detroit Med. Ctr., Detroit, 1989-91; clin. nurse specialist McLaren Regional Med. Ctr., Flint, Mich., 1991-93; nurse practitioner Harper Hosp., Detroit Med. Ctr., Detroit, 1993-96, Oakwood Hosp. and Med. Ctr., Dearborn, Mich., 1996-98; oncology nursing cons., 1998—. Co-editor chpt. Oncology Nursing, 3d edit., 1997. Mem. ANA, Oncology Nursing Soc. (sec. Detroit chpt. 1994-95), Ann Arbor Bicycle Touring Soc., St. Paul Altar Soc. (sec. 2001-02, pres. 2002—). Roman Catholic. Avocations: walking, cross stitch, reading, movies, home decoration. Home: 66 Lothrop Rd Grosse Pointe Farms MI 48236-3621 E-mail: Lroyceland@aol.com.

COVALT, ROBERT BYRON, chemicals executive; b. Chgo., Nov. 8, 1931; s. Byron L. and Thelma A. (Adams) C.; m. Virginia, Aug. 17, 1952; children: Karen Elizabeth Ryberg, David Byron. BSChemE, Purdue U., 1953, DEng (hon.), 1992; MBA, U. Chgo., 1967. Devel. engr. B.F. Goodrich Chem. Co., Avon Lake, Ohio, 1953-54; with Morton Chem. div. Morton Thiokol, Inc., 1956—, v.p. engring. and mfg., 1973-78, group v.p., 1978-79, pres., 1979-87; pres. specialty chems. group, group v.p. Morton Thiokol, Inc., 1987-89; pres. splty. chems. group, group v.p. Morton Internat. Inc., 1989-90, exec. v.p., 1990-94; chmn., pres. and CEO Sovereign Specialty Chems., Inc., 1994—2002, dir., 2003—. Bd. dirs. CFC Internat. Served as 1st lt. USAF, 1954-56. Recipient Disting. Engring. Alumnus award Purdue U. Mem. AIChE, Am. Chem. Soc. Home: 7517 Bull Valley Rd Mchenry IL 60050-7493 Office: Sovereign Splty Chems Inc 225 W Washington St Ste 2200 Chicago IL 60606-3408 *Success in business is truly based upon teamwork and the accomplishment of all members working in concert toward a common goal. In the end, it is the result of what you do with your people, not what you do to your people.*

COVARRUBIAS-LUGO, IRMA, physician; b. Tijuana, Bajo Co., Mexico, June 10, 1959; d. Manuel and Josefina (Hernandez) Covarrubias; m. Eduardo Limon Lugo, Dec. 19, 1981; children: Sabrina, Yolanda, Teresa, Christina. BA in Biology, U. Calif., San Diego, 1981; MD, U. Calif., San Francisco, 1985. Family practice resident U. N.Mex. Hosp., Albuquerque, 1988; staff Kaiser Permanente, San Diego, 1988—. Vol. clin. faculty UCSD Sch. Med. Office: Kaiser Permanente 3955 Bonita Rd Bonita CA 91902-1230

COVAULT, CRAIG, editor; b. Dayton, Ohio, 1949; BS in Journalism, Bowling Green State U., 1971. Writer Urbana Citizen, 1971—72; sr. space editor Aviation Week & Space Tech., Washington, 1972—92, chief Paris bur., 1992—96, sr. editor, 1996—. Office: Aviation Week & Space Tech Cape Canaveral Bureau 449 Turtle Cir Satellite Beach FL 32937-3806

COVELL, CHRISTOPHER GREENE, management executive; b. Providence, R.I., Apr. 14, 1947; s. Walter Howard and Harriette Francis (Tabakin) C. Founding pres. Ballet Who, Inc., N.Y.C., 1987—; resident fellow, CEO Abuse Rsch. Inst., N.Y.C., 1985—. Pub. Music-To-Go, 1984—. Composer-lyricist various songs. Mem. ASCAP.

COVEN, ALYSA LOUISE, advertising/marketing professional; b. Leesburg, Fla., Dec. 29, 1978; d. Michael Lamar and Peggy Lynn Coven. BS in Comm., Fla. State U., 2000. Pub. rels. intern Fla. Ins. Coun., Tallahassee, 2000, Gov.'s Office, State of Fla., Tallahassee, 2000; advt., mktg. intern So. Progress Corp., Birmingham, Ala., 2001—. Mem.: Soc. Profl. Journalists, Alpha Chi Omega. Republican. Baptist. Avocations: fishing, scuba diving, reading, writing.

COVEN, ROBERT MICHAEL, secondary school educator, researcher, writer; b. Detroit, Aug. 9, 1959; s. Sorrel Maurice and Barbara Rose (Farber) C.; 1 child, Madeline Anne. BA, U. Calif., Berkeley, 1980; MArch, U. Wis., Milw., 1984; MA in History, U. Del., 1990; postgrad., U. Chgo., 1990—. Corp. energy mgr., assoc. store planner Ohrbach's, N.Y.C., 1981-82; design and project mgmt. cons. Wells Fargo Bank, San Francisco, 1984-85; office mgr. House & House Archs., San Francisco, 1985-86; preceptor social scis. U. Chgo., 1993-95; chmn. dept. history and social scis. Foxcroft Sch., Middleburg, Va., 1996—2001, coord. interdisciplinary studies, 2001—. Computer cons. U. Chgo., 1991-96; panelist regional planning com. Met. Planning Coun. Chgo., 1995. Co-author: America's History: Reader, 1993; editor AIA, 1985-86; contbr. articles to profl. jours.; presenter at profl. confs. Mem. William H. Ray Elem. Curriculum Com., Chgo., 1995-96. Fellow U. Chgo., 1995-96, U. Del., 1988-90. Mem. Am. Hist. Assn., Orgn. Am. Historians, Nat. Coun. for History Edn., Nat. Forensic League, Orgn. History Tchrs., Phi Kappa Phi, Cum Laude Honor Soc. Democrat. Jewish. Avocations: photography, natural science, reading. Office: Foxcroft School PO Box 5555 Middleburg VA 20118-5555

COVENEY, RAYMOND MARTIN, JR., educator; b. Marlboro, Mass., Oct. 15, 1942; s. Raymond Martin and Rita Marie (Brani) C.; m. Anne Marie Keating, Feb. 22, 1965; children: Christine, Maureen, David. BS in Geology, Tufts U., 1964; MS in Geology, U. Mich., 1968, PhD in Geology, 1972. Asst. geologist N.J. Zinc Co., Hanover, N.Mex., 1968; geologist Dickey Exploration Co., Alleghany, Calif., 1969-70; grad. tchg. asst. U. Mich., Ann Arbor, 1966-70; from asst. prof. to prof. dept. geosci. U. Mo., Kansas City, 1971—, interim dean Coll. Arts and Scis., 1992-93, chair dept. geoscis., 1996—, dir. environ. studies. Cons. ProSoCo., Inc., Kansas City, 1986-92, Midwest Rsch. Inst., Kansas City, 1986-91, Woodward Clyde, Kansas City, 1981, Hunt Midwest, 1997. Contbr. articles to profl. jours. Lt. (j.g.) USNR, 1964-66. Rackham Predoctoral Rsch. fellow, U. Mich., 1970-71; NSF Rsch. grantee, 1981-85, 90-93, 95-98; recipient N.T. Veatch award, 1988. Fellow Geology Soc. Am., Soc. Econ. Geologists (councilor 1993-96, trustee 1992-96, chair pubs. com. 1995-2001); mem. AAAS, Geol. Soc., Am. Geophys. Union. Roman Catholic. Achievements include research in metal-rich black shales and related deposits of molybdenum, zinc, platinum. Home: 5405 Locust St Kansas City MO 64110-2443 Office: U Mo 5100 Rockhill Rd Kansas City MO 64110-2481 E-mail: coveneyr@umkc.edu.

COVENTRY, DEBRA ANN, mathematician, educator; b. Little Rock, Sept. 3, 1968; d. JC and Imogene Bryant; m. Jeffrey Raymond Coventry, Aug. 18, 1990; 1 child, Samuel Armistead. BSE, Henderson State U., 1989, MSE, 1991; PhD, Okla. State U., 1998. Grad. asst. Henderson State U., Arkadelphia, Ark., 1990—91, instr., 1991—98, asst. prof., 1998—2002, assoc. prof., 2002—; tchr. Arkadelphia H.S., 1991—92; tchg. asst. Okla. State U., Stillwater, 1992—96, assessment of math. placement, 1994—94, corr. instr., 1996—98, calculus tutor evaluator, 1997—97, rsch. assoc., 1996—98. Author: (multimedia education materials) Maple Picture Book; dir.(author): (high school course development) Functional Mathematics. Fin. officer Mothers of Preschoolers, Arkadelphia, 2000. Grantee Multimedia OSU, NSF, 1996—99. Mem.: Math. Assn. Am. (2nd vice chair 2000—00, 1st vice chair 2001—01, Okla.-Ark. sect. chair 2002—02). Office: Henderson State Univ 1100 Henderson St Arkadelphia AR 71999-0001 Office Fax: 870-230-5531. E-mail: coventd@hsu.edu.

COVERDALE, WATSON SHALLCROSS, JR., communications company executive; b. Milw., Nov. 22, 1932; s. Watson Shallcross and Ada Marguerite (Sheridan) C.; student Washington and Lee U., 1951-52, Ursinus Coll., 1956-61; m. Carolyn Lucille Mumby, Apr. 6, 1963; children: Watson Shallcross III, Carter Sheridan. Regional mgr. fed. mktg. Mohawk Data Scis., Washington, 1971-72, dist. mgr., N.Y.C., 1977-81; dir. nat. sales, product and systems div. Lockheed Electronics, Plainfield, N.J., 1972-74; br. mgr. Four Phase System Co., Rochelle Park, N.J., 1974-77; regional mgr. OEM sales WICAT Systems, N.Y.C., 1981-83; Eastern regional mgr. Xerox Imaging Systems, 1983-90; dir. sales TranSwitch Corp., 1990-98, v.p. internat. sales, 1998—; pres. TranSwitch Asia Ltd., 2002--. First v.p. bd. dirs. Haystack Ski Ednl. Found., 1978-80; bd. dirs. Chimney Hill Owners Assn., 1981-87. Served with USMC, 1952-56. Mem. Md. Soc. of Pa. (bd. of govs. 1985—). Episcopalian. Club: Downtown (Phila.). Home: 9-1 Riverbend Rd Old Lyme CT 06371-1428 Office: 3 Enterprise Dr Shelton CT 06484-4694

COVERT, EUGENE EDZARDS, aerospace engineer, physics educator; b. Rapid City, SD, Feb. 6, 1926; s. Perry and Eda (Edzards) C.; m. Mary Solveig Rutford, Feb. 22, 1946; children: David H., Christine J., Pamela M., Steven P. BS, U. Minn., 1946, MS, 1948; ScD, MIT, 1958. Registered profl. engr., Mass.; chartered engr., U.K. Preliminary design group USNADC, Johnsville, Pa., 1948-52; mem. staff MIT Aerophysics Lab., 1952-63, assoc. dir., 1963-75, assoc. prof. aeronautics and astronautics, 1963-68, prof., 1968—97, T. Wilson prof. aeronautics, 1993-96, head dept. aeronautics and astronaut., 1985-90; T. Wilson prof. of aeronautics emeritus, 1997—. Cons. Bolt, Beranek & Newman, Inc., Boeing Co., CACI, Inc., Govt. Israel, Pratt and Whitney Aircraft divsn. United Tech., Hercules, Inc., MIT Lincoln Lab., Sverdrup Tech., U.S. Army Rsch. Office, Rand Corp.; chief scientist USAF, 1972—73; mem. panel Naval Aeroballistic Adv. Com., 1965—75; mem. NASA Aeronautical Adv. Com., 1985—89, Aeronautics and Space Engring. Bd., 1986—92, chmn., 1992; mem., chmn. USAF Sci. Adv. Bd., 1975—86, 1990—94; chmn. Power, Energet. and Propulsion panel Adv. Group for Aerospace R&D NATO, 1982—86; aero. policy com. Office Sci. and Tech. Policy, 1976—92; mem. Pres. Commn. for Investigation of Space Shuttle Accident. Mem. Blue Ribbon Com. on the Osprey, 2001. Served with USNR, 1943—47. Recipient Exceptional Civilian Sci. award USAF, 1973, 86, 94, Univ. Educator of Yr. award, Am. Soc. Aerospace Edn., 1980, Tech. Leadership award U. Minn. Alumni Assocs., 1993, Pub. Svc. award NASA, 1991, von Karman medal Adv. Group for Aerospace R & D, 1980, Wright Brothers Lectureship Aeronautics AIAA, 1997. Fellow AAAS, Royal Aero. Soc., fellow AIAA (hon.; bd. dirs., Ground Testing award 1990, W.F. Durand lectureship for pub. svc. 1992, Wright Bros. lectr. 1997); mem. NAE, N.Y. Acad. Scis., Sigma Xi. Office: MIT 77 Massachusetts Ave Rm 9-466 Cambridge MA 02139-4307

COVERT, MICHAEL HENRI, healthcare facility administrator; b. Chgo., Apr. 7, 1949; s. Leonard and Shirley Gladys (Jeffe) C.; m. Janie Sibley; children: Madison, J. Ben, Brienn. BS in Bus., Washington U., St. Louis, 1970, M in Health Adminstrn., 1972. Adminstrv. asst. St. Agnes Hosp., White Plains, N.Y., 1969; adminstrv. resident Hillcrest Med. Ctr., Tulsa, 1971-72, asst. adminstr., 1972-73, adminstr., 1973-80; exec. v.p., chief operating officer St. Francis Regional Med. Ctr., Wichita, Kans., 1980-85; CEO Ohio State Univ. Hosps., Columbus, 1985-88; sr. v.p. Physician Corp. of Am., Wichita, Kans., 1988-89; ind. mgmt. cons. Wichita, 1989-91; acting dir. community health Wichita/Sedgwick County, Wichita, Kans., 1991-92; pres., CEO Sarasota (Fla.) Meml. Hosp., 1992—2000; pres. Washington Hosp. Ctr., Washington, 2000—02; CEO, pres. Palomar Pomerado Health Sys., 2003—. Pres.-elect Franklin County Hosp. Coun., Columbus, 1987-88; adj. faculty Ohio State U., 1985—, Washington U., St. Louis, 1992—; bd. dirs. Voluntary Hosp. Am., Fla., 1998-00, exec. com., 1999-00. Bd. dirs. United Way Sarasota, 1993—2000, campaign chair, 1996—97, chair, 1998—99; bd. visitors Georgetown Sch. Nursing and Health Adminstrn., 2001—02; del. Am. Hosp. Assn., State of Fla., 1996. Fellow Am. Coll. Healthcare Execs. (mem. accreditation commn. grad. edn. in health care adminstrn. 1988-94, chair commn. 1991-94, regent west ctrl. Fla. ACHE 1997-00); mem. Fla. Hosp. Assn. (bd. dirs. 1995-97), Assn. Cmty. Hosps. and Health Sys. Fla. (chair 1998-99), D.C. Hosp. Assn. (treas. 2001-02), Healthcare Alumni Assn. (chair Washington U. 1994-95), Sarasota C. of C. (chair 1995-96), Univ. Club (v.p. 1996, chair-elect 1997-99, chair 1998-99). Office: Palomar Pomerado Health Sys 15255 Innovation Dr Ste 204 San Diego CA 92128

COVEY, HERBERT CECIL, social services administrator, sociologist; b. Montezuma, Kans., July 29, 1949; s. Harold Junior and Barbara Joan Covey; m. Martha Ann Conner, May 22, 1971; children: Christopher Lee, Kelly Hye. BA in Sociology, Colo. State U., 1971; MA in Sociology, U. Nebr., 1975; PhD in Sociology, U. Colo., 1979. Rschr. Colo. Divsn. Criminal Justice, Denver, 1979—81; sr. auditor Colo. State Auditor's Office, Denver, 1981—91; adminstr. Colo. Dept. Human Svcs., Denver, 1991—. Part time instr. U. Colo., Boulder, 1991—; vice chair Colo. State Juvenile Parole Bd., Denver, 1992 ; mem. com. Colo. Senate 94 Com., Denver, 1999—, Multisystemic Therapy, Denver, 1999—. Author: Images of Older People in Western Art and Society, 1991, A History of the Social Perception of People with Disabilities, 1998; co-author: Juvenile Gangs, 1997, Street Gangs Throughout the World, 2003; contbr. articles to profl. jours. Co-chair Cmty. Svc. Com., Denver, 2001—. Avocations: skiing, tennis, writing. Home: 1030 W 15th Ave 80020 Office: Colo Dept Human Svcs 1575 Sherman St Denver CO 80203

COVI, LINO, psychiatrist, educator; b. Trento, Italy, Mar. 19, 1926; came to U.S., 1956, naturalized, 1965; s. Giuseppe and Giuseppina (Mariotti) C.; m. Beverly A. Yeutsy, Dec. 30, 1958 (dec.); children: Lisa Martina, Michelle Peppina, Gina Albina, Tina Maria. Student in philosophy, U. Florence, Italy, 1945-47, Sch. Social Work, Trento and Rome, 1949-51; MD, U. Rome, 1955. Asst. U. Rome Neuropsychiat. Clinic, 1955-56; intern Albert Einstein Med. Ctr., Phila., 1956-57; resident fellow psychiatry Johns Hopkins Hosp., Balt., 1957-60, dir. outpatient clin. rsch. unit, 1968-83, dir. Cognitive Therapy Clinic, 1982-98, dir. treatment assessment rsch. unit, 1983-94. Assoc. clin. prof. U. Md. Med. Sch., Balt., 1986-92; instr. psychiatry Johns Hopkins U., 1960-67, asst. prof., 1967-72, assoc. prof., 1972—; vis. psychiatrist Balt. City Hosp., 1960-80; vis. scientist Nat. Inst. Drug Abuse-Addiction Rsch. Ctr., Balt., 1988-94, guest rschr., 1994—; psychiatrist Francis Scott Key Med. Ctr.-Hopkins Bayview Med. Ctr., Balt., 1988-99; med. dir. Friends Health Svcs., 1994-97; cons. Friends Rsch. Inst. Epoch Ctrs., Balt., 1997-2000; staff psychiatrist Patuxent Instn., Jessup, Md., 1960-62; chief out-patient dept. Gundry Hosp., Balt., 1962-86, pres. bd. dirs., 1972-84, rsch. dir., 1973-86; mem. bd. govs. Cen. Md. Health Systems Agy., 1978-83; rsch. psychiatrist NIMH Collaborative Studies, 1962-64, co-prin. investigator, 1964-65, prin. investigator, 1965-83, prin. investigator clin. trials of new drugs for depression and anxiety, 1970-94, studies of group cognitive therapy in depression, 1980-94; tchg. assoc. Sheppard and E. Pratt Hosp., 1973-79; cons. Pharm. Rsch. Labs., 1971-96, Centro Psicologia Clinica, Milan, 1981-98; mem. inst. rev. bd. Friends Rsch. Inst., 1999—. Editor: The Md. Psychiatrist, 1974-80, Today's Psychiatry, Md. Med. Jour., 1985-95; contbr. articles to profl. jours. Mem. human rights com. Coop. Studies Program, VA, 1981-84. Fellow: Acad. Cognitive Therapy; mem.: AMA (profl. staff drug evaluation coun. on drugs 1968—71), Collegium Internat. Neuropsychopharmacologium, Balt. Med. Soc., Md. Med. Soc., Johns Hopkins Med. Soc., World Fedn. Mental Health, Am. Soc. Clin. Psychopharmacology, Am. Psychiat. Assn. (nat. coms., dep. rep. Md., Newsletter award 1977), Md. Psychiat. Soc. (coms.), Am. Coll. Neuropsychopharmacology (coms.), Italian-Am. Hist. Assn. Democrat. Roman Catholic.

COVIELLO, FRANK JOSEPH, lawyer; b. Washington, Dec. 27, 1940; s. Francis George and Mary Louise (Martini) C. BA, Western Car. U., 1966; LLB, U. Balt., 1969. Bar: Md. 1971, U.S. Dist. Ct. (4th cir.) 1971, U.S. Dist. Ct. D.C. 1985, U.S. Ct. Appeals (4th cir.) 1985. Law clk. Circuit Ct. for Montgomery County, Rockville, Md., 1969-71; asst. state's atty. Montgomery County, Rockville, 1971-73; pvt. practice, 1974-84; ptnr. Bivona & Cohen, Rockville, 1984-89, Gilberg & Kurent, Gaithersburg, 1989-90; pvt. practice Gaithersburg, 1990—. With U.S. Army, 1961-64. Mem. Montgomery County Bar Assn., D.C. Bar Assn. Roman Catholic. Avocations: tennis, skiing, scuba diving. Fax: 301-208-9063. E-mail: fjcoviello_esq@surfmk.com.

COVIELLO, ROBERT FRANK, retail executive; b. Hartford, Conn., Dec. 20, 1941; s. James Joseph Coviello and Ann Frances (Links) Leary; m. Anne Elizabeth Lomasney, Oct. 22, 1966; 1 child, Michael James. Student, U. Conn., 1960-61, U. Madrid, 1961-62; grad., Machine Accts. Tng., 1963; student, Northeastern U., Boston, 1969. Data processing mgr. Chadwick-Miller, Inc., Boston, 1964-66; systems design analyst nat. accts. KeyData Corp., Watertown, Mass., 1969-70, systems designs mgr. N.Y.C., 1970-72, western regional mgr. Chgo., 1972-73; pres. Gallery of Gifts Shoppes, Inc. (doing bus. as Kitchen Etc.), Hampton, N.H., 1973-93; co-founder, exec. v.p. merchandising Kitchen Etc., N.H., Vt., Mass., Conn., 1993-95; pres., founder Housewares Tabletop Internat., 1995—; founder, pres. HTI Buying Group, Inc., N.H., 1998—. Chmn. Downtown Bd. of Trade, Dover, N.H., 1975-77, 82-83; pres. Merchants Assn. of Lilac Mall, Rochester, N.H., 1982-83. Dir. C. of C., Dover, 1983-86. With U.S. Army, 1966-68. Recipient Buyer's award of recognition Housewares Club

New Eng., 1986, Potter's Club award Pfaltzgraff Co., 1986, 89. Mem. Retail Mchts. Assn. N.H. (past pres. 1985-87, dir. 1980-96, named Retailer of Yr. 1988), Am. Mgmt. Assn. (pres.'s Assn divsn. club), Gift Assn. Am. (dir. 1981-95), World Cup (St. Paul). Avocations: cooking, travel, flying, railroads, deep sea sports fishing. Office: HTI 47 Charles St Rochester NH 03867-2927 E-mail: hti@nhinternet.com.

COVIN, CAROL LOUISE, computer consultant; b. Chgo., July 2, 1947; d. Raymond Lincoln and Elizabeth Day (Notley) Frederick; m. David William Covin, Jan. 24, 1968; children: David William Jr., Jonathan Michael. BA, George Washington U., 1972. Data base adminstr. USN, Alexandria, Va., 1973-77; cons. Data Base Mgmt., Inc., Springfield, Va., 1977-79, 82-87; pres. Covin Assocs., Falls Church, Va., 1987-90; cons. Electro-Tech. Internat., Annandale, Va., 1990-91, Abacus Tech., Chevy Chase, Md., 1991-93, Tech. Internat., Fairfax, Va., 1993-95; sr. cons., dir. mktg. Xybernaut Corp., Fairfax, 1995-2000. Mem. MIT Enterprise Forum, 2000—, v.p. Washington/Balt. chpt., 2003. Author: The Computer Professional's Job Guide to Washington, D.C., 1989, Covin's New England Computer Job Guide, 1991, Covin's Washington Computer Job Guide, 1993, Covin's Midwest Computer Job Guide, 1995, Covin's Southeast Computer Job Guide, 1998, Best Computer Jobs in America: 20 Minutes from Home, 2002. Mem. Assn. Systems Mgmt. (pres. 1990-92, v.p. 1992-93, treas. 1993-96), Data Adminstrn. Mgmt. Assn., Washington Apple Pi.

COVIN, THERON MICHAEL, psychotherapist; b. Repton, Ala., Feb. 27, 1947; s. Fisher Burt Covin and Doris (Salter) Knight; m. Charlotte R. Covin, June 13, 1981; children: Caroline, Michelle. MS, Troy State U., 1971; specialist in Edn., U. Ala., Tuscaloosa, 1973; EdD, U. Sarasota, Fla., 1975. Diplomate Am. Bd. Med. Psychotherapists. Instr. psychology Troy (Ala.) State U., 1971-75, Lomax Hannon Jr. Coll., Greeville, Ala., 1975-78; asst. prof. Auburn U., Montgomery, Ala., 1978-80; staff psychologist S.E. Ala. Youth Svcs., Dothan, Ala., 1978-81; with Ctr. for Counseling and Human Devel., Ozark, Ala., 1981—2002. Contbr. articles to profl. jours. Mem. Am. Counseling Assn., Am. Assn. Family and Marriage Therapy, Rotary (Paul Harris fellow 1987). Office: 111 Katherine Ave Ozark AL 36360-1976

COVINGTON, ANN K. former state supreme court justice; b. Fairmont, W.Va., Mar. 5, 1942; d. James R. and Elizabeth Ann (Hornor) Kettering; m. James E. Waddell, Aug. 17, 1963 (div. Aug. 1976); children: Mary Elizabeth Waddell, Paul Kettering Waddell; m. Joe E. Covington, May 14, 1977. BA, Duke U., 1963; JD, U. Mo., 1977. Bar: Mo. 1977, U.S. Dist. Ct. (we. dist.) Mo. 1977. Asst. atty. gen. State of Mo., Jefferson City, 1977-79; ptnr. Covington & Maier, Columbia, Mo., 1979-81, Butcher, Cline, Mallory & Covington, Columbia, Mo., 1981-87; justice Mo. Ct. Appeals (we. dist.), Kansas City, 1987-89, Mo. Supreme Ct., 1989—2001, chief justice, 1993-95. Bd. dirs. Mid Mo. Legal Services Corp., Columbia, 1983-87; chmn. Juvenile Justice Adv. Bd., Columbia, 1984-87. Bd. dirs. Ellis Fischel State Cancer Hosp., Columbia, 1982-83, Nat. Ctr. for State Cts., 1998—; chmn. Columbia Indsl. Revenue Bond Authority, 1984-87; trustee United Meth. Ch., Columbia, 1983-86, Am. Law Inst., 1998—. Recipient Citation of Merit, U. Mo. Law Sch., 1993, Faculty-Alumni award U. Mo., 1993; Coun. of State Govt. Toll fellow, 1988. Fellow Am. Bar Found.; mem. ABA (jud. adminstrv. divsn., mem. adv. com. on Evidence Rules, U.S. Cts.), Mo. Bar Assn., Boone County Bar Assn. (sec. 1981-82), Am. Law Inst., Acad. Mo. Squires, Order of Coif (hon.), Mortar Bd. (hon.), Phi Alpha Delta, Kappa Kappa Gamma. Home: 1201 Torrey Pines Dr Columbia MO 65203-4825 Office: 101 High St Jefferson City MO 65101

COVINGTON, DONALD KINGSLEY, JR., plywood sales executive; b. Newport News, Va., May 28, 1920; s. Donald Kingsley and Jessie Alexandria (MacNeill) C.; m. Minnie Virginia Seay, Mar. 13, 1943; children: Donald Kingsley III, Duncan Seay. BS in Aero. Engring., Parks Coll. St. Louis U., 1941; postgrad., U. Md., 1942. Lic. aircraft mechanic, pvt. pilot; cert. sales exec. Sales exec., engring. draftsman to project flight test engr. Glenn L. Martin Co., Balt., 1942-48; with Harbor Sales Co., Inc., Balt., 1948—, successively asst. sales mgr., sales mgr., gen. sales mgr., dir. and sec., pres., chmn. bd., chmn. emeritus, 2002—. Bd. dirs. YMCA Greater Balt. Area, 1963-78; trustee Md. Masonic Homes, 1982-85, 88-93; pres. Sales Exec. Coun. of Balt. Assn. Commerce, 1958; trustee Sales and Mktg. Execs. Accredition Inst., 1988—, SMEI Acad. Achievement. Mem. AIAA, Sales and Mktg. Execs. Internat. (cert. sales exec. Accreditation Inst., v.p., dir., trustee, Outstanding Svc. award 1981, 86, dir. emeritus 1991), Sash and Door Jobbers Assn. (dir.), Forest Products Rsch. Soc., Exptl. Aircraft Assn., Sales and Mktg. Execs. Balt. (hon.), Sales Execs. Coun. Balt. (past pres.), Rsch. Inst. Am. (charter), So. Sash and Door Jobber Assn. (past dir.), Ponderosa Pine Woodwork Assn., Plywood Pioneers Assn., Inst. Aero. Scis. (past sec. Balt. sect.), Balt.-Washington Lumber Sales Club, York Rite K.T., Shiners, Masons (past master, past pres. Knights of Mecca, sr. grand warden Grand Lodge of Md., 33 degree, grand rep. to Australia), Salmagundi Club. Office: 1000 Harbor Ct Sudlersville MD 21668-1818

COVINGTON, GEORGE MORSE, lawyer; b. Lake Forest, Ill., Oct. 4, 1942; s. William Slaughter and Elizabeth (Morse) C.; m. Shelagh Tait Hickey, Dec.28, 1966 (div. May 1995); children: Karen Morse, Jean Tait, Sarah Ingersoll Covington; m. Barbara Schilling Trentham, Dec. 19, 1998. AB, Yale U., 1964; JD, U. Chgo., 1967. Assoc. Gardner, Carton & Douglas, Chgo., 1970-75, ptnr., 1976-95; atty. pvt. practice, Lake Forest, Ill., 1995—. Lectr. in field. Contbr. articles to profl. jours. Active Grant Hosp. of Chgo., 1974-95, chmn. of bd. 1990-95; bd. dirs. Grant Healthcare Found., 1995—, chmn. 1999—; trustee Chgo. Acad. Sci., 1974-85, pres., 1980-82; trustee, chmn. Ill. chpt. Nature Conservancy, Chgo., 1974-88; bd. dirs. Latin Sch Chgo., 1979-80, Open Lands Project, Chgo., 1972-86, Chgo. Farmers, 1994-96; bd. dirs., sec. Lake Forest Open Lands Assn., 1984—; bd. dirs., sec., treas. Les Cheneaux Found., 1978—; bd. dirs. Student Conservation Assn., 1996—, Little Traverse Conservancy, 1998—, vice chmn., 1999-2002, chmn., 2002—; mem. Bd. Fire and Police Commrs., Village of Lake Bluff, Ill., 1991—. With U.S. Army, 1967-69. Mem. ABA, Ill. Bar Assn., Lake County Bar Assn., Chgo. Bar Assn., Univ. Club (bd. dirs. 1985-88), Commonwealth Club, Legal Club, Shoreacres (Lake Bluff, Ill.), Les Cheneaux Club (Cedarville, Mich.), Lambda Alpha. Office: 500 N Western Ave Ste 204 Lake Forest IL 60045-1955

COVINGTON, GERMAINE WARD, municipal agency administrator; BS in Social Work, Ind. State U., 1966; MA in Urban Studies, Occidental Coll., 1972; postgrad., Harvard U., 1998. Budget analyst City of Seattle, Office Mgmt. and Budget, 1978-87; cmty. affairs mgr. City of Seattle, Engring. Dept., 1987-90, property and ct. svcs. mgr., 1990-91, dir. exec. mgmt., 1993-94, acting dir. drainage and wastewater utility, 1993-94; dep. chief staff City of Seattle, Mayor's Office, 1991-93; dir. office for civil rights City of Seattle, 1994—. Office: Seattle Office for Civil Rights 700 3rd Ave Ste 250 Seattle WA 98104-1827 E-mail: germaine.covington@seattle.gov.

COVINGTON, JAMES EDWIN, government agency administrator, psychologist; b. Wadesboro, N.C., June 26, 1943; s. James Edwin and Louise (Memory) C.; m. Linda Doreen Davis, May 31, 1971 (div. Feb. 1982); children: James Edwin III, Bradley Davis. BA, Duke U., 1965; MSc, N.C. State U., 1977, PhD, 1981. Lic. psychologist, N.C. Commd. 2d lt. U.S. Army, 1967, advanced through grades to col., 1989, ret., 1992; spl. advisor for arms control and chem. demilitarization Dept. of Def., Washington, 1993—. Psychol. cons., Alexandria, Va., 1992—; first prof. mil. sci. Duke U., Durham, N.C., 1983; primary planner for retrograde U.S. Chem. Weapons from Germany, 1989; del. 1st U.S. visit to former Soviet Chem. Weapons Sites in Russia, 1990; mem. U.S. delegation for negotiation of worldwide Chem. Weapons Conv., Geneva, 1992; advisor U.S. Delegation to Chem. Weapons Preparatory Commn., The Hague, 1993; mem. oversees prog. to destroy all U.S. chem. weapons by year 2007. Decorated Def. Superior Svc. medal, Purple Heart with oak leaf cluster, Bronze Star, Air Medal with 7 oak leaf clusters, Army Commendation Medal with valor device, 5 oak leaf clusters, others; decorated for heroism at Hamburger Hill, Vietnam, 1969. Mem. APA, Va. Psychol. Assn. Methodist. Avocations: military history, music, physical fitness. Home: 5909 Dawes Ave Alexandria VA 22311-1116 Office: Office of Asst Sec of the Army 2511 Jefferson Davis Hwy Arlington VA 22202-3926 Fax: 703-607-5827. E-mail: james.covington@saalt.army.mil., nedcovington@aol.com.

COVINGTON, MARLOW STANLEY, retired lawyer; b. Langhorne, Pa., Apr. 25, 1937; s. Marlow O. and Madalyn L. (Johnson) C.; m. Laura Aline Wallace, Aug. 28, 1965; children: Lisa M., Scott, Eric (dec.). BS, Bloomsburg U., 1959; postgrad., Rutgers U., 1960; JD, Howard U., 1965. Bar: D.C. 1971, U.S. Dist. Ct. D.C. 1971, U.S. Supreme Ct. 1975, U.S. Dist. Ct. Md. 1981, Md. 1985. Tchr. Pub. Schs., Long Branch, N.J., 1959-62; referee N.J. Dept. Labor, Newark, 1965-66; claim examiner Allstate's Ins. Co., Verona, N.J., 1966-71, house counsel Washington, Greenbelt, Md., 1971-97; sr. trial atty. Allstate Ins. Co., Greenbelt, Md., 1989-96; ret., 1996. Mem. adv. bd. Inverness Custom Plastics, Inc., Barrington, Ill., 1990—. Recipient cert. of recognition Balt.-Washington area Fellowship Christian Athletes, 1981. Mem. ABA (com. ins. negligence and compensation sect.), D.C. Bar Assn. (com. ins. and compensation sect.), Nat. Bar Assn., Bloomsburg U. Alumni Assn. (bd. dirs. 1977-80), Sigma Delta Tau, Gamma Theta Upsilon. Avocation: collecting antique pocket knives. Home: 16001 Amina Dr Burtonsville MD 20866-1039 Fax: 301-421-4329. E-mail: SCoving104@aol.com.

COVINGTON, MARSHA ELAINE, communications consultant; b. Ft. Monmouth, N.J., Jan. 1, 1950; d. Carroll M. and Carolyn (Shell) C.; m. Dean Agee, Aug. 1, 1971 (div. May 1976); 1 child, Carolyn Celeste. BA in Broadcast Comms., Calif. State U., Sacramento, 1977; MEd in Adult and Higher Edn., Mont. State U., 1992, EdD in Adult and Higher Edn., 1997. Radio announcer, pub. svc. dir. KZAP Radio, Sacramento, 1969-73; bus. mgr., journalism Pepperdine U., Malibu, Calif., 1982-84; corp. comms. mgr. Environ. Industries, Calabassas, Calif., 1986-89; pubs. editor Mont. State U., Bozeman, 1989-92; comms. trainer Americorps, Bozeman, 1994-96; dir. of edn., pub. rels. Credit Counselors of Am., Phoenix, 1990-97; instr. curriculum designer U. Calif., Berkeley, 1997—; owner, trainer Scribes & Sages Inst., Bozeman, 1989—; sr. corp. comms. specialist Synenergy, Sacramento, 1997-99; dir. mktg. and outreach programs Bloch Med., Evanston, Ill., 1999-2001; comm. mgr. Accenture People Enablement, 2001—; dir. mktg. and edn. Sr. Svcs. Assn., Elgin, Ill., 2002—. Adj. instr. speech comms. Mont. State U., 1990-91; adj. instr. Sch. Edn., Capella U., Mpls., 2001--; comms., edn. advisor Freelife Internat., Milford, Conn., 1997—; ednl. advisor, speech coach Linda Chae Internat., Denver, 1996—, dir. edn., pub. rels. Credit Counselors, Phoenix, 1990-97; writer, tchr. Ann Louise Gittleman/Nutritional Author, Bozeman, 1994-96 Editor-in-chief: Sword and Pen newsletter, 1994-97; designer curriculums in comms. Co-dir. Bozeman Cmty. Tchg. Ctr., 1995-97, v.p., 1994-95; ednl. advisor Gallatin County Sheriff's Office, Bozeman, 1992-93; literacy assessor JTPA Coun., Bozeman, 1992-94. Named Best Spkr. in Sacramento, Lyon's Club, 1967. Mem. Pub.'s Mktg. Assn. Avocations: writing, public speaking, teaching, swimming, solo and choral singing.

COVINGTON, PATRICIA ANN, university administrator; b. Mt. Vernon, Ill., June 21, 1946; d. Charles J. and Lois Ellen (Combs) C.; m. Burl Vance Beene, Aug. 10, 1968 (div. 1981). BA, U. N.Mex., 1968; MS in Ed., So. Ill. U., 1974, PhD, 1981. Tchg. asst. So. Ill. U., Carbondale, 1971-74, prof. art, asst. dir. Sch. Art, 1974-88, asst. dir. in admissions and records, 1988-95, assoc. dir. in admissions and records, 1995—2003, emerita assoc. dir., 2003—; cons. to Univ., 2003—. Mem. Am. Coun. on Edn., Nat. Com. for Army, Registry Transcript, AARTS SMART (Sailor, Marines Registry Transcript); mem. tech. com. Ill. Atriculation Initiative, Ill. Bd. Higher Edn.; vis. curator Mitchell Mus., Mt. Vernon, 1977-83, judge dept. conservation; mem. panel Ill. Arts Coun., Chgo., 1982; faculty advisor European Bus. Seminar, London, 1983; edn. cons. Ill. Dept. Aging, Springfield, 1978-81, Apple Computer, Cupertino, Calif., 1982-83; mem. adminstrv. profl. coun. Soc. Ill. U., 1989-93; presenter in field. Exhibited papercastings in nat. and internat. shows in Chgo., Fla., Calif., Tenn., N.Y. and others, 1974—; author: Diary of a Workshop, 1979, History of the School of Art at Southern Illinois University at Carbondale, 1981, Guidelines of Transcripts & Records, 2003; co-author: Transcript and Reel Guide, AACRAO Transcript and Record Guide, 2003; reviewer Mayfield Pub., Random House, William C. Brown, Holt, Reinhart & Winston. Bd. dirs. Humanities Couns. John A. Logan Coll., Carterville, Ill., 1982-88; mem. Ill. Higher Edn. Art Assn., chmn. bd. dirs., 1978-88; mem. Post-Doctoral Acad., 1981-95; sec. adminstrv. profl. coun., 1989-90; lifetime mem. Girl Scouts U.S.A., 1988—, del. 1992-93, 97—, bd. dirs., mgmt. com., fin. com., bldg. com., devel. com., nominating com., Shagbark Coun., treas., 2003, chair assessment com., 2003—. Grantee Kresge Found., 1978, Nat. Endowment for the Arts, 1977, 81, Ill. Bd. Higher Edn. HECA grantee, 1994, 95; named Outstanding Young Woman of Yr. for Ill., 1981, Woman of Distinction Girl Scouts U.S.A. Fellow Ill. Ozarks Craft Guild (bd. dirs. 1976-83); mem. Am. Assn. Coll. Registrars and Admissions Officers (task force on transcript guidelines 2001-03), Ill. Assn. Coll. Registrars and Admissions Officers (chair so. dist., exec. com. 1992-93, nominating com. 1993-94), Spinx (hon.), Rhen Soc., Chancellor's Coun., Phi Kappa Phi. Presbyterian. Home: 389 Lake Dr Murphysboro IL 62966-5955 Office: So Ill U Carbondale IL 62901 E-mail: mmouse@siu.edu.

COVINGTON, SHARON NICKEL, social worker, psychotherapist; b. Chgo., Feb. 27, 1948; d. Henry Carlyle and Shirley Skiff (Jannotta) N.; m. Barry Truitt Covington, July 11, 1970; children: Michelle, Brendan, Laura. BS, U. Md., 1970, MSW, 1973. cert. social worker, Md. Social worker Montgomery County Dept. Ofcl. Svcs., Rockville, Md., 1973-76; pvt. practice Rockville, Md., 1976—; clin. asst. prof. dept. ob/gyn. Georgetown U. Sch. Medicine, 1989—. Group therapist Cmty. Psychiat. Clinic, Wheaton, Md., 1976—81; dir. psychol. support svcs. Shady Grove Fertility Reproductive Sci. Ctr., Rockville, 1986—; bd. dirs. Nat. SHARE, St. Charles, Mo.; chmn. bd. Mercy Health Clinic, 2000—. Author: Silent Birth...If Your Baby Dies, 1986, Infertility Counseling: A Comprehensive Handbook for Clinicians, 1999. Founder MIS (miscarriage, infant death and stillbirth), Washington, 1981—. Fellow Am. Othopsychiat. Assn.; mem. NASW, Am. Soc. Reproductive Medicine (chair mental health profl. group 1989-90), Clin. Social Work Soc. (cert.). Roman Catholic. Avocations: fox hunting, sport fishing. Home: 12912 Three Sisters Rd Potomac MD 20854-6333 Office: 15001 Shady Grove Rd Ste 340 Rockville MD 20850-6352 E-mail: sharon.covington@integramed.com.

COVINGTON, STEPHANIE STEWART, psychotherapist, writer, educator; b. Whittier, Calif., Nov. 5, 1942; d. William and Bette (Robertson) Stewart; children: Richard, Kim. BA cum laude, U. So. Calif., 1963; MSW, Columbia U., 1970; PhD, Union Inst., 1982. Diplomate Am. Bd. Sexology, Am. Bd. Med. Psychotherapists. Pvt. practice Inst. for Relational Devel., La Jolla, Calif., 1981—; co-dir. Ctr. for Gender and Justice, La Jolla, Calif., 1981—. Instr. U. Calif., San Diego, 1981—, Calif. Sch. Profl. Psychology, San Diego, 1982-88, San Diego State U., 1982-84, Southwestern Sch. Behavioral Health Studies, 1982-84, Profl. Sch. Humanistic Psychology, San Diego, 1983-84, U.S. Internat. U., San Diego, 1983-84, UCLA, 1983-84, U. So. Calif., L.A., 1983-84, U. Utah, Salt Lake City, 1983-84; co-dir. Inst. Relational Devel.; cons. L.A. County Sch. Dist., N.C. Dept. Mental Health, Nat. Ctrs. Substance Abuse Treatment and Prevention, Nat. Inst. Corrections, others; designer women's treatment, cons. Betty Ford Ctr.; presenter and lectr. in field; addiction cons. criminal justice sys. Author: Leaving the Enchanted Forest: The Path from Relationship Addiction to Intimacy, 1988, Awakening Your Sexuality: A Guide for Recovering Women, 2000, A Woman's Way Through the Twelve Steps, 1994, Helping Women Recover: A Program for Treating Addiction (with spl. edit. for criminal justice sys.), 1999, A Womans Way Through the Twelve Steps Workbook, 2000, Beyond Trauma: A Healing Journey for Women, 2003; contbr. articles to profl. jours. Mem. NASW (diplomate), Am. Assn. Sex Educators, Counselors and Therapists, Am. Pub. Health Assn., Am. Assn. Marriage and Family Therapy, Assn. Women in Psychology, Calif. Women's Commn. on Alcoholism (Achievement award), Am. Soc. Criminology, Western Soc. Criminology, Internat. Coun. on Alcoholism and Addictions (past chair women's com.), Kettil Brun Soc. (Finland), San Diego Soc. Sex Therapy and Edn., Soc. for Study of Addiction (Eng.). Avocations: reading, theater, raising orchids. Office: 7946 Ivanhoe Ave Ste 201B La Jolla CA 92037-4517 E-mail: sscird@aol.com.

COVINGTON, TAMMIE WARREN, elementary education educator; b. Columbia, S.C., Dec. 20, 1960; d. Charles Larry and Betty Joyce (Collum) Warren; m. Terry Lee Covington, Dec. 22, 1979; 1 child, Matthew Lee. BA in Elem. Edn., U. S.C., 1982, M in Elem. Edn., 1989; M in Ednl. Adminstrn., Troy State U., 2001. Tchr. Ridge Spring (S.C.)-Monetta Elem. Sch., 1982-90, W. Wyman King Acad., Batesburg, S.C., 1991-92, North (S.C.) Elem. Sch., 1992-94, Batesburg (S.C.) Leesville Mid. Sch., 1994—. Mem. Lexington Sch. Dist. 3 Tchr. Forum. Mem. S.C. Edn. Assn., S.C. Mid. Sch. Assn., S.C. Coun. Tchrs. Math., Delta Kappa Gamma. Office: Batesburg-Leesville Mid Sch 425 Shealy Rd Leesville SC 29070

COVINGTON, VERONICA PRO, librarian, educator; b. Laredo, Tex., Nov. 14, 1949; d. Gilberto and Herminia (Esquivel) Pro; m. Billy C. Covington, Jan. 3, 1980; children: Christina, Jennifer, Elizabeth. BS in Edn., Tex. A&I U., 1971; MEd, Sam Houston State U., 1986; PhD in Curriculum and Instruction, Tex. A&M U., 1996. English tchr. Martin H.S., Laredo, Tex., 1970-73; English tchr., chair Dunbar H.S., Lubbock, Tex., 1973-75; asst. dir. Upward Bound Tex. Tech. U., Lubbock, 1975-77; English tchr. Matthews Jr. High, Lubbock, 1977-80; English tchr., chair Mance Park Jr. High, Huntsville, Tex., 1980-90; head libr. Huntsville H.S., 1990-95; coord., testing and program evaluation Huntsville Ind. Sch. Dist., 1995-98; libr. Austin Ind. Sch. Dist., 1998—. Cert. translator Tex. Dept. Criminal Justice, Huntsville, 1989—; adj. prof. children's lit. U. Tex., Austin, 2000-. Contbr. articles to profl. jours. Active Huntsville Leadership Inst., 1996-97; ambassador Huntsville-Walker County C. of C., 1997-98; mentor at-risk students Huntsville Ind. Sch. Dist., 1985-97. Elected del. The White House Conf. on Libr. and Info. Svcs., Washington, 1991. Mem. Nat. Assn. for Bilingual Edn., Tex. Assn. for Bilingual Edn., Tex. Assn. of Sch. Adminstrs., Coun. for Exceptional Children, Nat. Assn. for Gifted Children, Tex. State Tchrs. Assn. (pres. 1986-89), Delta Kappa Gamma (bd. dirs. com. chair 1985). Avocations: reading, travel, writing. Office: Austin Ind Sch Dist Baily Mid Sch 4020 Lost Oasis Holw Austin TX 78739-5501

COVINO, CHARLES PETER, chemicals executive; b. West New York, N.J., Dec. 9, 1923; s. Isaac L. and Rose (Luongo) C.; m. Sylvia A Covino, Dec. 27, 1947; 1 child, Candida. Student, U. Ala., 1941-43; BBA, Manhattan Coll., 1951; MBA, NYU; DHL (hon.), Philathea U., Can., 1963; DS (hon.), Manhattan Coll., 1995. Chmn. bd., CEO Gen. Magnaplate Corp., Linden, N.J. Mem. Hoover Inst. Coun. for Global Polit. and Econ. Transition, 1994; lectr. in field. Contbr. over 28 articles to profl. jours. Bd. dirs. Peoples Bankcorp, 1990. Recipient Air Force Assn. N.J. Wing award for space contbns., 1960, Royal Cross Austria Prince Rudolph, 1964, Eloy Alfaro Found. of Panama award, 1965, Manhattan Coll. Outstanding Alumni award, 1972, Vaaler award Chem. Engring. Inst., 1976, Indsl. Rsch. 100 award for Material Devels. of Yr., 1964, 68, 78, ASM award for Disting. Svc. and Contbns. to Metals Industry, 1967, Cookware Design of Yr. award Housewares Mfr.'s Assn., 1967, award of yr. Packaging Inst., 1967-68, Outstanding New Product award Popular Sci. mag., 1967, Packaging Design award Design Inst., 1968, Outstanding USA Design award U.S. Info. Agy., 1968, Italian-Am. Man of Sci. award 1978, Churchill Medal of Wisdom award, 1995, Heros of Chemistry award Am. Chem. Soc., 1996, Am. Chem. Soc. award, 1996, Thomas Alva Edison award for best N.J. invention of Yr., 1999; named to N.J. Inventors Hall of Fame, 1994-95, Manhattan Coll. Athletics Hall of Fame, 1998, N.J. Corp. Inventors Hall of Fame, 1999; named Internat. Scientist of Yr. Internat. Biog. Ctr., Cambridge, 2002. Achievements include over 101 patents and trademarks; invention of non-destructive testing method for thick lead shielding in nuclear reactors, ultrasonic test method for nuclear tubing used for condensors, various metal surface enhancement processes, low-cost (permanent composite) mold form by plasma spray method; featured in Guinness World Book of Records for world's slipperiest solid lubricant. Office: Gen Magnaplate Corp 1331 Route 1 & 9 N Linden NJ 07036

COVINO, JENNIFER KATHRYN, freelance/self-employed writer; b. Ridgewood, N.J., Mar. 28, 1973; d. John James and Jean Marie Brennan; m. Robert Paul Covino Jr., Apr. 29, 2000. BA in Comm., Loyola Coll., Balt., 1995. Staff writer Patuxent Pub., Towson, Md., 1995—98; reporter The Hour Newspapers, Norwalk, Conn., 1998—99, The Advocate, Stamford, Conn., 1999—2000; freelance writer, editor New Canaan, Conn., 2000—. Part time publ. writer Fairfield Univ. Contbr. articles to mags. Named Outstanding New Journalist, Soc. Profl. Journalists, Balt., 1995. Mem.: Nat. Fedr. of Press Women (Feature Story Award 2002), Conn. Press Club (Feature Story of the Yr. 2002, 2002), Phi Beta Kappa, Summa Cum Laude.

COVINO, PAUL FRANCIS XAVIER, religious executive, college chaplain, consultant; b. Methuen, Mass., Aug. 3, 1958; s. Benjamin Gene and Lorraine Mary (Gallagher) C.; m. Anne Elizabeth Hallisey, Apr. 23, 1983. BA, Georgetown U., 1980; MA, U. Notre Dame, 1981. Mem. staff Diocesan Office for Worship, Worcester, Mass., 1980; assoc. dir. Georgetown Ctr. for Liturgy, Spirituality and Arts, Washington, 1981-89; pvt. practice liturgical resource cons., 1989—; asst. chaplain, dir. liturgy Coll. of Holy Cross, Worcester, Mass., 1993-97, assoc. chaplain, dir. liturgy, 1997—. Dormitory min. in residence Georgetown U., Washington, 1981-83; mem. Rite of Christian Initiation of Adults steering com. Office of Permanent Diaconate adv. bd. Diocese of Worcester; mem. Order of Marriage adaptations task force U.S. Bishops' Com. on Liturgy; mem. Cath. Common Ground Initiative com. Editor: Celebrating Marriage: Preparing the Wedding Liturgy, 1987, rev. edit., 1994; contbr. articles to profl. jours. Mem. N.Am. Acad. Liturgy, Nat. Conf. on Environ. and Art for Cath. Worship. Roman Catholic. Office: Coll of Holy Cross Office Coll Chaplains 1 College St # 16A Worcester MA 01610-2395 E-mail: pcovino@holycross.edu.

COVINTREE, GEORGE E. retired anesthesiologist; b. Camden, N.J., Apr. 18, 1913; s. Clarence C. and Jessie E. (Snyder) C.; m. Laura Claye Fraley, July 11, 1942 (dec.); children: George Edward Jr., David Elwood, Ruth Ann. AB, Temple U., 1935; MD, Hahnemann U., 1941. Diplomate Am. Bd. Anesthesiology. Intern Deaconess Hosp., Cin., 1941-42; resident West Jersey Hosp., Camden, Berlin, Voorhees, 1947-49, mem. staff, 1956—, chief dept. anesthesiology, 1957-78, emeritus chief dept. anesthesiology, 1979—; fellow in anesthesiology Hahnemann Med. Coll., Phila., 1949-50; mem. staff Hahnemann Hosp., Phila., 1950-56; cons. anesthesiology Vets. Hosp., Phila., 1953-58; instr. anesthesiology Hahnemann Med. Coll., 1950-52, asst. prof. anesthesiology, 1952-56. Founder Annual N.J. Postgrad. Anesthesia Seminar, 1959. With U.S. Army Med. Corps., 1942-46. Fellow Am. Coll. Anesthesiologists; mem. AAAS, AMA, Am. Soc. Anesthesiologists, Internat. Anesthesia Rsch. Soc., Med. Soc. N.J., N.J. State Soc. Anesthesiologists (Disting. Svc. award 1981), N.Y. Acad. Scis. E-mail: doccovintree@att.net.

COVITZ, CARL D. state official, real estate and investment executive; b. Boston, Mar. 31, 1939; s. Edward E. and Barbara (Matthews) C.; m. Aviva Habert, May 15, 1970; children: Philip, Marc. BS, Wharton Sch., U. Pa., 1960; MBA, Columbia U., 1962. Product mgr. Bristol-Myers Co., N.Y.C., 1962-66; dir. mktg. Rheingold Breweries, N.Y.C., 1966-68; nat. mktg. mgr. Can. Dry Corp., N.Y.C., 1968-70; v.p. mktg., dir. corp. devel. ITT/Levitt & Sons, Lake Success, N.Y., 1970-73; owner, pres. Landmark Communities, Inc., Beverly Hills, Calif., 1973-87, pres., 1989-91; undersec. HUD, Washington, 1987-89; sec. bus., transp. and housing State of Calif., Sacramento, 1991-93; pres. Landmark Capital, Inc. (formerly Landmark Communities, Inc.), 1993—; chmn. bd. Century Housing Corp., 1995-2000. Bd. dirs. Arden Realty Group, chmn. acquisition com.; chmn. bd. Fed. Home Loan Bank, San Francisco, 1989-91, Century Housing Corp., 1995—; trustee SunAmerica Annuities Funds, 2000—, Kane Andersobn Mut. Funds, 2000—. Exec. com. Presl. Commn. Cost Control and Efficiency (Grace Commn.); co-chmn. Dept. Def. Task Force; past chmn. ops. com. Mus. Contemporary Art Los Angeles; chmn. L.A. County Delinquency and Crime Commn.; dir. Columbia U. Grad. Bus. Sch. Alumni Assn. Mem. Young Pres. Orgn.; chmn. L.A. Housing Authority Commn., 1989-91. Home: 818 Malcolm Ave Los Angeles CA 90024-3104 Office: 9595 Wilshire Blvd Beverly Hills CA 90212-2512 E-mail: cdc@landmarkcapital.com.

COWAN, ALVIN RANDALL, lawyer; b. N.Y.C., Jan. 9, 1907; s. Meyer and Matilda (Abrams) C.; m. Shirley P. Cowan, June 27, 1932 (dec.); children—Michael N., Nancy E. A.B., Cornell U., 1927; J.D., Fordham U., 1930. Bar: N.Y. 1931, U.S. Dist. Ct. (ea. and no. dists.) N.Y., U.S. Ct. Appeals (2d cir.), U.S. Tax Ct., U.S. Ct. Appeals (9th cir.), U.S. Supreme Ct. Ptnr. Abrams and Cowan, N.Y.C., 1955—. Mem. N.Y. County Bar Assn. Democrat. Home: 2109 Broadway New York NY 10023-2106 Office: 66 W Lakeshore Dr Rockaway NJ 07866-1026

COWAN, ANDREW GLENN, television writer, producer, performer; b. Phila., Dec. 24, 1951; s. Raymond Harold and Audrey Rene (Federman) C. BA in Psychology, The Am. U., 1973; MS in Broadcasting, Boston U., 1975. News reporter, writer Sta. WLYH-TV, Lancaster, Pa., 1975; announcer, news reporter Sta. WHUM, Reading, Pa., 1975; comedy performer various clubs, nationwide, 1976-81; talent coordinator, writer, performer, segment producer The Merv Griffin Show, Paris, L.A., N.Y.C., Atlantic City, and Las Vegas, 1981-86; freelance writer TV series Cheers Paramount, L.A., 1985-87; host, writer L.A. Singles, Group W Cable, L.A., 1985-86; freelance writer TV series Throb Taft Entertainment, L.A., 1986; story editor TV series Take Five Imagine Entertainment, CBS, L.A., 1987; freelance writer TV series Family Ties Paramount, L.A., 1988; staff writer, performer The Pat Sajak Show, CBS, L.A., 1988-90; staff writer Into the Night ABC, 1990; staff writer My Talk Show Second City Entertainment, 1990; freelance writer for Jay Leno The Tonight Show, NBC, L.A., 1990; Walt Disney Prodns., 1991; creator, writer TV pilot Howie Republic Pictures, L.A., 1991; staff writer TV pilot Only Human CBS Entertainment, 1991-92; freelance writer TV series Seinfeld Castle Rock Entertainment, L.A., 1994, then program cons., 1994-95; story editor TV series Double Rush Shukovsky-English Entertainment, L.A., 1994; exec. cons. TV series 3rd Rock from the Sun Carsey-Werner Co., L.A., 1995-96; exec. prodr., co-creator, writer, host tv pilot Evening Stew, 1996-97; writer, tv pilot Barely Fitz, 1999, Outer Child, 2000, Howie, 2001. Vocalist various clubs and venues, L.A., 1987—; vocalist pilot theme song Life As We Know It, Second City Entertainment, 1990; voice-over announcer Aerospace Ednl. Svcs., L.A., 1985-89, Cutler Prodns., CBS Morning Zoo, L.A., 1990; host, writer, prodr., co-dir. video short Six Minutes, Showtime, The Movie Channel, Bravo, PBS, 1989-91. Voice-over actor Seinfeld, 1994, 3rd Rock from the Sun, 1995, Best Damn Sports show Period, 2002, Time-Warner Audio Books, Lucas Films, Star Wars-Dark Empire, The Audio Drama, 1994, Star Wars-Dark Empire 2, 1995; writer, co-host (on internet) Up & Down Guys, 2000; contbr. articles to profl. jours. Recipient CableAce award for best short-form programming spl., 1991; named one of 50 Creatives to Watch, Variety, 1996. Mem. AFTRA, Writers Guild Am. West. Avocations: cartooning, playing keyboards. *You're better off creating your own opportunities, rather than waiting for someone to create them for you. Ignore the naysayers. And if you listen to conventional wisdom, develop a serious case of amnesia afterwards.*

COWAN, BARTON ZALMAN, lawyer; b. Cleve., Mar. 3, 1934; s. Milton Jerome and Clara (Umans) Cowan; m. Teri Anne Thomas, June 25, 1961; children: Pamela B., Cynthia R. Stewart, Susan L. Kraft. AB with honors, U. Mich., 1955; JD cum laude, Harvard U., 1958. Bar: Ohio 1958, Pa. 1962, U.S. Dist. Ct. (we. dist.) Pa., U.S. Ct. Appeals (3d, 4th and DC cirs.), U.S. Supreme Ct. Assoc. Eckert Seamans Cherin & Mellott, Pitts., 1961-67; mem. Eckert Seamans Cherin & Mellott LLC, Pitts., 1968-1999, spl. counsel, 2000—. Chmn. lawyers com., mem. policy com. Atomic Indsl. Forum, Washington, 1981—87; chmn. lawyers com. Nuc. Mgmt. and Resource Coun., Washington, 1988—90; vis. prof. law W.Va. U. Coll. Law, 2001—. Bd. dirs. Union Am. Hebrew Congregations; life trustee Pitts. chpt. Am. Jewish Com.; life trustee, past pres. Rodef Shalom Congregation, Pitts.; mem. bd. overseers Hebrew Union Coll., Jewish Inst. Religion, Pitts. Symphony Soc.; bd. dirs. ARZA/World Union N.Am. 1st lt. USAF, 1958—61. Recipient Clyde A. Lilly award, Atomic Indsl. Forum, Inc., 1985, award for leadership, Hebrew Inst. Pitts., 1991, award for dedication and commitment to Jewish edn., Jewish Edn. Inst., 1992, State of Israel bonds award, 1993, 2002, award, Am. Jewish Com. Human Rels., 1996. Mem.: ABA (chmn. energy resources law com. tort and ins. practice sect. 1986—87), Internat. Nuc. Law Assn., Allegheny County Bar Assn., Pa. Bar Assn., Duquesne Club. Republican. Office: Eckert Seamans Cherin & Mellott LLC 600 Grant St Ste 44th Pittsburgh PA 15219-2702 E-mail: bzc@escm.com., teribart61@aol.com.

COWAN, CHARLES GIBBS, lawyer, corporate executive; b. Cannington, Ont., Can., Nov. 13, 1928; s. Charles Gibbs and Jean Clarke (Macfarlane) C.; m. Susan Mary Tidy, Sept. 24, 1954; children: Julia Mary Cowan Soong, James Charles Strathy, Stuart Philip Gibbs. Student, Upper Can. Coll.; BA, U. Toronto, 1950; LLB, York U., Toronto, 1954. Bar: Ont. 1954; apptd. Queen's Counsel 1966. Ptnr. Holden, Murdoch & Finlay, Toronto, Ont., 1960-90; sec. Hollinger Consolidated Gold Mines, Ltd., 1961. V.p., sec., bd. dirs. Hollinger Inc., Argus Corp. Ltd., The Ravelston Corp. Ltd. Maj. Queen's Own Rifles of Can., Militia, 1947-63. Recipient Can. Forces decoration; Armiger. Mem. Can. Bar Assn., Toronto Club. Anglican. Home: 8 Powell Ave Toronto ON Canada M4W 2Y7 also: The Maples Cannington ON Canada L0E 1E0 Office: 10 Toronto St Toronto ON Canada M5C2B7

COWAN, DALE HARVEY, internist, lawyer; b. Cleve., Jan. 25, 1938; s. Milton Jerome and Clara (Umans) jC.; m. Deborah Wolowitz, Jan. 28, 1967; children: Rachel, Morris Benjamin, William Ezra. AB, Harvard U., 1959, MD, 1963; JD, Case Western Res. U., 1981. Diplomate Am. Bd. Internal Medicine with subspecialty cert. in hematology and med. oncology. Bar: Ohio 1981. Intern Cleve. Met. Gen. Hosp., 1963-64, resident, 1964-65, 67-70; practice medicine specializing in internal medicine, hematology and oncology; dir. hematology and oncology Marymount Hosp., Cleve., 1982-2001; asst. prof. medicine Case Western Res. U., Cleve., 1970-75, assoc. prof., 1975-84, clin. prof. environ. health scis., 1985—; assoc. Health Sys. Mgmt. Ctr., 1982-90; of counsel Burke, Haber & Berick, 1984-86; pres. med. staff Parma (Ohio) Cmty. Gen. Hosp., 1997-98; med. dir. Cmty. Oncology Group Cleve. Clinic Found., Cleve., 1999—. Spl. cons. President's Commn. on Bioethics, Washington, 1981-82; mem. nat. adv. coun. Nat. Heart Lung and Blood Inst., Bethesda, Md., 1982-85. Author: Preferred Provider Organizations, 1984; co-editor: Human Organ Transplantation, 1987; contbr. articles to profl. jours. Bd. dirs. Bur. Jewish Edn., 1977-87, Northeast Ohio affiliate Am. Heart Assn., 1982-86; pres. Ohio/W.Va. Oncology Soc., 1990-94; trustee No. Ohio Cancer Resource Ctr., 1998-2001, chmn. 1999-2001. Lt. comdr. USPHS, 1965-67. Fellow ACP, Am. Coll. Legal Medicine (bd. govs. 2001—); mem. AMA, Am. Soc. Hematology, Am. Soc. Clin. Oncology, Am. Assn. for Cancer Rsch., Am. Health Lawyers Assn. (bd. dirs. 1988-94), Am. Soc. Law and Medicine, Acad. Medicine Cleve. (pres. 1997-98), Cleve. Med. Libr. Assn. (pres.-elect 2003—), Ohio State Bar Assn., Greater Cleve. Bar Assn. Home: 19600 Shaker Blvd Cleveland OH 44122-1830 Office: 6100 W Creek Rd Ste 15 Cleveland OH 44131-2133 E-mail: cowand@ccf.org.

COWAN, DOUGLAS LEO, lawyer; b. L.A., May 22, 1943; s. Douglas L. and Mildred R. (Zimmerman) C.; m. Bettina VanDeCamp, Sept. 12, 1964 (div. Jan. 1972); 1 child, Kristina; m. Corinne Ellen Crawley, July 21, 1973; children: John, Greg. BA, Wash. State U., 1965; JD, U. Wash., 1968. Bar: Wash. 1968, U.S. Dist. Ct. (we. dist.) Wash. 1969. Ptnr. Shafer, Mitchell & Cowan, Seattle, 1969-74, Kinzel, Cowan & Allen, Bellevue, Wash., 1978-87; pros. atty. City of Bellevue, 1974-78; ptnr. Cowan Hayne & Fox, Bellevue, 1988-98; founder The Cowan Law Firm, Bellevue, 1998—. Pres. Wash. Found. for Criminal Justice, Bellevue, 1987—. Mem. Nat. Coll. for DUI Def. (founder, dean 1996-97), Wash. Assn. Criminal Def. Lawyers (bd. govs. 1987-88), East King County Bar Assn. (pres. 1979). Office: 3805 108th Ave NE Ste 204 Bellevue WA 98004-7613

COWAN, EDWARD, journalist, editor; b. Bklyn., Nov. 14, 1933; s. Marcy Hamilton and Jennie (Taleisnik) C.; m. Ann Louise Wrubel, July 1, 1962; children: Jeffrey Wrubel, Emily Martha, Rachel Jennifer. BA, Columbia Coll., 1954; MA in Econs., Johns Hopkins U., 1960. With UPI, 1957-62; with N.Y. Times, 1962-86, banking reporter, 1963-65, Benelux corr., 1965-66, corr. London bur., 1966-67, corr. Toronto (Can.) Bur., 1967-72, Washington corr., 1972-83, Washington econs. editor, 1983-86; Washington mgr. Ried, Thunberg and Co., Inc., 1986-99; assoc. editor Am. Enterprise Inst., 2002—02; pres. Editorial Svc., 2003—. Instr. econs. Johns Hopkins, 1956-57; cons. U.S. Bur. Budget, 1963; co-founder Chronicle, Barton, Vt., 1974. Nat. Inst. of Standards and Tech. 2001. Congressional Budget Office 2003. Author: Oil and Water: The Torrey Canyon Disaster, 1968; contbr. to The Economist, 1977-90, op-ed pages Washington Post, L.A. Times, New Eng. Regional Rev., Jour. Commerce, Indonesnian Daily News, Jakarta Post. Treas., dir. Anne Frank House, 1987-90. Served with AUS, 1954-56. Fellow Knight Internat. Press; recipient Chanler Hist. Essay prize Columbia, 1954, Gerald R. Loeb Found. award for fin. reporting, 1971. Mem. Nat. Econs. Club (v.p. programs 1989-90, pres. 1990-91, chmn. 1991-93). Home: 3924 Harrison St NW Washington DC 20015

COWAN, FAIRMAN CHAFFEE, lawyer; b. Wellesley Hills, Mass., Apr. 22, 1915; s. James Franklin and Hortense Victoria (Fairman) C.; m. Martha Logan Allis, Apr. 24, 1943; children: Douglas Fairman, Frederick Allis, Leonard Chaffee. AB magna cum laude, Amherst Coll., 1937; LLB, Harvard U., 1940; AMP, Harvard Bus. Sch., 1963. Bar: Mass. 1940. Assoc. Goodwin, Procter & Hoar, Boston, 1940-41; ptnr. Goodwin, Proctor & Hoar, 1952-54; gen. counsel, clk., sec., v.p., dir. Norton Co., 1955-79; counsel Bowditch & Dewey, Worcester, Mass., 1979-90. Mem. Citizen Plan E Assn. Worcester, 1957-87; vice chmn. Worcester Civic Ctr. Commn., 1977-79; chmn. Pvt. Industry Coun., Worcester Area CETA Consortium, 1979-83; bd. dirs. Legal Assistance Corp. of Ctr. Mass., 1982-86, Social Svc. Planning Corp., 1975-88, Worcester Mcpl. Rsch. Bur., Inc., 1986—, Mass. Job Tng. Inc., 1983-92, Elder Home Care Svcs. of Worcester, Inc., 1987-92, Daybreak, Inc., 1993-96; incorporator Alliance for Edn., 1986—2003, Worcester Dynamy, Inc., 1992—, Worcester YWCA, 2001—, Worcester Hist. Mus., 1995—, YOU, Inc., 1983—, ARC Ctrl. Mass., 2000—; mem. State Job Tng. Coordinating Coun., 1985-87, Worcester Housing Partnership, 1986-93; trustee Clark U., 1964-76, 79—, Meml. Hosp., Worcester, 1967-86, United Way Ctrl. Mass., 2000—; mem. bd. overseers Planned Parenthood League Mass., 1992-2001, mem. adv. bd. Mass. Coastal Resource Bd., 1992— . Lt. USNR, 1942-45.2003 Recipient Isaiah Thomas award, 1995. Mem. Am. Antiquarian Soc., Mass. Civic League (v.p. 1947), Worcester Club, Worcester Com. on Fgn. Rels., Phi Beta Kappa, Alpha Delta Phi. Home: 48 Berwick St Worcester MA 01602-1443 E-mail: fcowan1059@aol.com.

COWAN, FREDERIC JOSEPH, lawyer; b. N.Y.C., Oct. 11, 1945; s. Frederic Joseph Sr. and Mary Virginia (Wesley) C.; m. Linda Marshall Scholle, Apr. 28, 1974; children: Elizabeth, Caroline, Allison. AB, Dartmouth Coll., 1967; JD, Harvard U., 1978. Bar: Ky. 1978, U.S. Dist. Ct. (we. dist.) Ky. 1979, U.S. Ct. Appeals (6th cir.) 1984, U.S. Supreme Ct. 1989. Vol. Peace Corps, Ethiopia, 1967-69; assoc. Brown, Todd & Heyburn, Louisville, 1979-83; ptnr. Rice, Porter, Seiller & Price, Louisville, 1983-87; atty. gen. Commonwealth of Ky., 1988-92; counsel Lynch, Cox, Gilman & Manan P.S.C., 1992—. Ky. State Rep., 32d legis. dist., 1982-87; chair Ky. Child Support Enforcement Commn., 1988-91, Ky. Sexual Abuse and Exploitation Prevention Bd., 1988-91; bd. dirs. Ky. Job Tng. Coordinating Council, Frankfort, Louisville Bar Found., 1986. Vice chmn. judiciary criminal com. Ky. Ho. of Reps., 1985-87; chmn. budget com. on justice Judiciary and Corrections Ky. Ho. of Reps., 1985-87, Leadership Ky., 1985; U.S. del. election mission to Namibia Nat. Dem. Inst. for Internat. Affairs, 1989; U.S. del. dem. instns. seminar Nat. Dem. Inst. for Internat. Affairs, Slovenia, 1992; electoral supr. Orgn. for Security and Cooperation in Europe, Bosnia and Herzogovina, 1996; adv. com. Samara Oblast, Russia, 2001. Mem. ABA (adv. com. east european law initiative 2001), Ky. Bar Assn., Louisville Bar Assn., Ky. Acad. Trial Attys. Methodist. Home: 1747 Sulgrave Rd Louisville KY 40205-1643 Office: 400 W Market St Ste 2200 Louisville KY 40202-3354

COWAN, GEORGE ARTHUR, chemist, bank executive, director; b. Worcester, Mass., Feb. 15, 1920; s. Louis Abraham and Anna (Listic) C.; m. Helen Dunham, Sept. 9, 1946. BS, Worcester Poly. Inst., 1941, degree (hon.), 2002; DSc, Carnegie-Mellon U., 1950, DSc and Tech. (hon.), 2002; DHL (hon.), Coll. of Santa Fe, 2003. Rsch. asst. Princeton U., 1941-42, U. Chgo., 1942-45; mem. staff Columbia U., N.Y.C., 1945; mem. staff, dir. rsch., sr. fellow Los Alamos (N.Mex.) Sci. Lab., 1945-46, 49-88, sr. fellow emeritus, 1988—; tchg. fellow Carnegie Mellon U., Pitts., 1946-49. Chmn. bd. dirs. Trinity Capital Corp., Los Alamos, 1974-95; pres. Santa Fe Inst., 1984-91; mem. The White House Sci. Coun., Washington, 1982-85, cons., 1985-90, Air Force Tech. Applications Ctr., 1952-88; chmn. Los Alamos Nat. Bank, 1965-94. Contbr. sci. articles to profl. jours. Bd. dirs. Santa Fe Opera, 1964-79; treas. N.Mex. Opera Found., Santa Fe, 1970-79; regent N.Mex. Inst. Tech. Socorro, 1972-75; bd. dirs. N.Am. Inst., Santa Fe Inst., Los Alamos Nat. Lab. Found., Adv. Bd. Ctr. for Neural Basis of Cognition, Carnegie-Mellon U. Recipient E.O. Lawrence award, 1965, Disting. Scientist award N.Mex. Acad. Sci., 1975, Robert H. Goddard award Worcester Poly. Inst., 1984, Enrico Fermi award, Presdl. Citation, Dept. Energy, 1990; Los Alamos Nat. Lab. disting. fellow Santa Fe Inst., 2003, Los Alamos Nat. Lab. medal, 2003. Fellow AAAS, Am. Phys. Soc., Am. Acad. Arts and Scis.; mem. Am. Chem. Soc., N.Mex. Acad. Sci., Sigma Xi. Avocations: skiing, fly-fishing. Home: 721 42nd St Los Alamos NM 87544-1804 Office: Santa Fe Inst 1399 Hyde Park Rd Santa Fe NM 87501-8943 E-mail: gac@santafe.edu.

COWAN, GEORGE D. literature educator; s. Curtis Emmet and Eileen Ostrander Cowan; m. Diane Kay Hobert, Oct. 16, 1948; children: Sean Curtis, Kimberly Diane. BA, U. Mont., Missoula, 1970, MA, U. No. Iowa, Cedar Falls, 1985. Cert. tchr. Mont. Office of Pub. Instrn., 2000. Drama/English tchr. Bozeman H.S., Mont., 1970—73; drama/speech/English tchr. Flathead H.S., Kalispell, Mont., 1973—2000; English tchr. Dayspring Acad., Whitefish, Mont., 2000—01; drama/speech/English adj. tchr. Flathead Valley C.C., Kalispell, Mont., 1986—. Children's theatre cons. Mont. Office of Pub. Instrn., Helena, 1976—77. Master: Masons (worshipful master 1991—92); mem.: Elks (Elk of the Yr. 1991). Avocations: thinking, fishing, hunting, musician, writing. Home: 3240 Airport Rd Kalispell MT 59901 Personal E-mail: cowan@centurytel.net. E-mail: gcowan@fvcc.edu.

COWAN, GEORGE SHEPPARD MARSHALL, JR., surgeon, educator, research administrator; b., June 6, 1938; m. Anne Cowan; children: Scot Peter George, Katherine Beatrice, George Sheppard Marshall III. BA, Columbia Coll., 1959; MD equivalent with honors, MB, ChB, U. Aberdeen, Scotland, 1964. Diplomate Am. Bd. Surgery, Cert. Bd. Nutrition Specialists. Intern Aberdeen Royal Infirmary, 1964—65; resident in surgery Thomas Jefferson Med. U. Hosp., Phila., 1965—68, chief resident in surgery, 1968—70; commd. 1st lt. U.S. Army Med. Corps, 1966; advanced through grades to col. U.S. Army, 1982, resigned with honorable discharge, 1982; from assoc. prof. to prof. of surgery U. Tenn., Memphis, mem. staff Wm. F. Bowld Med. Ctr., 1982—2002; mem. staff City of Memphis Hosp., 1982—2002; mem. active staff Bapt. Meml. Hosp., Memphis, 1982—2002; jr. staff Meth. Hosp., Memphis, 1982—2001. Cons. VA Med. Ctr., 1982—83, 2000—02, surg. staff, 1983—2000; secretariat, sci. com. Internat. Bariatric Surgery Symposium, London, 1989, Japan, 90; mem. organizing com. Annual Obesity Surgery Symposium, L.A., 1988—91; chief obesity wellness ctr. and surg. endoscopy tchg. svc. U. Tenn. Sch. Medicine, 1982—2002; mem. U. Tenn. Memphis Planning Com., 1993—96; exec. U. Tenn. Faculty Senate, pres., 1994—95; faculty advisor to pres. U. Tenn., 1993—96; bd. dirs. Am. Coll. Nutrition, pres.-elect, 2002—03, pres., 2003—, chair program com., 2003; founder, chair TennSens, 1994—95; bd. dirs. Cert. Bd. Nutrition Specialists, 2000—; mem. adv. panel Medscape Endocrinology, 2000—; co-chair Nat. Nutrition Alliance, 2000—. Editor: Intravenous Hyperalimentation, 1972, (chpt.) The Essence of General Surgery, 1975; co-editor: Bariatric Surgical Stapling, 1989, Update: Surgery for the Morbidly Obese Patient, 2000, Surgical Stapling, 1987; co-founder, co-editor-in-chief: Obesity Surgery Jour., 1990—; bd. editors: The am. Surgeon, 1977-87, Jour. Nutritional Support Svcs., 1984-87, assoc. editor, 1987-88; reviewer Jour. Parenteral and Enteral Nutrition, 1987—; contbr. more than 250 articles to profl. jours.; inventor of surg. instruments, developer surg. products. Mem. Pub. Edn. com. Am. Cancer Soc., Mo., 1980-82. Capt. M.C., USNR, 1983-98, ret. Recipient Shepherd Gold medal in surgery, 1964; Surgeon Gen.'s rsch. fellow Cardiovasc. Rsch. Inst., U. Calif., San Francisco, 1971-73. Fellow: Am. Coll. Nutrition (bd. editors Jour. Am. Coll. Nutrition 1995—, chair program com. 2003, pres. 2003—, bd. dirs., chair exec. dir. search com.); mem.: AAUP (Claxton award 1996), N.Am. Fedn. for the Surgery of Obesity (sci. rev. com. 2001—), Memphis Surg. Soc. (sec.-treas. 1992—94, v.p. 1994—95, pres. 1995—96), Internat. Fedn. for the Surgery of Obesity (sec.-treas. 1995—97, pres. 1997—99, chair bd. trustees 1999—, Gold medal 2000), Am. Fedn. Clin. Rsch., Am. Heart Assn. (bd. dirs. 1974—80), Am. Trauma Soc., Memphis-Shelby County Med. Soc. (comms. com., legis. com.), Tenn. Med. Assn. (del., alt. del. 1990—, comms. com. 1999—), S.E. Surg. Congress, Am. Soc. Parenteral and Enteral Nutrition (membership com. 1994—96), Soc. Am. Gastro-Enterologic Surgeons, Am. Soc. Bariatric Surgery (pres. 1990—91, del. to Svcs. and Splty. Soc. of AMA 1991—, sec.-treas. 1993—96, allied health scis. sect. 2000, Golden Circle award), Memphis Econs. Club, Bachelor's Barge Club (Phila.), Sigma Xi. Office: U Tenn 956 Court Ave Ste A310 Memphis TN 38103-2814 E-mail: owcinc@mindspring.com.

COWAN, GEORGIANNE, dancer, educator, writer; b. Suffern, N.Y., Dec. 26, 1954; d. Julian Barker Cowan and Marcelle Weyl; m. Charles Bernstein, May 1, 1994; 1 child, Serina Bernstein; m. Steve Roach, Nov. 28, 1986 (div. June 1989). Student, Penland Sch., 1971—77. Photographer pvt. practice, L.A., Calif., 1979—, dance tchr., 1980—93; program dir. Earthways Found., Malibu, Calif., 1989—95. Dir.(photographer): (video) Earth Dreaming; author (editor): The Soul of Nature; contbr. articles. Recipient Stanfield Scholarship Award, Unitarian Universalist Assn., 1977. Avocations: hiking, poetry, art appreciation, dancing, nature. Home: 2120 Balsam Ave Los Angeles CA 90025-5910

COWAN, IRVING, real estate owner, developer; b. Irvington, N.J., Apr. 27, 1932; s. Jospeh and Adele (Goldman) Cohen; m. Marjorie Friedland, Dec. 29, 1956; children: Debra Jean, Cynthia Ann, Jonathan David. Student, U. Miami, 1949-50. Owner Sea Air Towers, Presdl. Towers Assn., Hollywood, Fla., 1960—2001; gen. ptnr. Indian Trail Groves, West Palm Beach, Fla., 1959—; owner, breeder Cowan Thoroughbred Racing Stable, Hollywood. Bd. dirs. City Nat. Bank, Miami, Fla.; owner Shelborne Hotel, South Miami Beach, Fla. With USCG, 1950-53. Mem. Com. of 100, Founders Club Mt. Sinai Hosp. (Miami, Fla.), Capitol Club, 200 Club of Greater Miami. Jewish. Home: 1615 Diplomat Pky Hollywood FL 33019-2233 Office: Sea Air Towers 3725 S Ocean Dr Hollywood FL 33019-2926

COWAN, JOHN JAMES, physicist, educator, astronomer, educator; b. Washington, Apr. 3, 1948; s. John Robert and Anna V. Cowan; m. Linda Elaine Demetry, May 24, 1971. BA, George Washington U., 1970; MS, Case Inst. Tech., 1972; PhD, U. Md., 1976. Postdoctoral fellow Harvard U., Cambridge, Mass., 1976—79; asst. prof. U. Okla., Norman, 1979—84, assoc. prof., 1984—89, prof. physics and astronomy, 1989—, S.R. Noble Presdl. prof., 1998—2002, David Ross Boyd prof., 2002—; rsch. fellow U. Tex., 2002. Mem. rev. panel NASA, Washington, 1987; vis. rsch. assoc. Harvard U., Cambridge, 1987—88; vis. prof. Columbia U., N.Y.C., 1991—92; mem. com. visitors NSF, Washington, 2002; lectr. in field. Reviewer: Astrophys. Jour., 1976—; contbr. articles to profl. jours. Grantee, NASA, 1994—, NSF, 1997—. Mem.: Am. Astron. Soc., Phi Beta Kappa. Achievements include co-discoverer of gold in one of the oldest stars in the universe. Avocations: racquetball, physical fitness. Office: Univ Okla 440 W Brooks St Norman OK 73019

COWAN, JOHN JOSEPH, retired lawyer; b. Chester, Pa., Nov. 14, 1932; s. John Joseph and Helen Marie (Frame) C.; m. Hilary Ann Gregory, Dec. 29, 1960; children: Daniel, Patrick, Meg, Jennifer. AB, LaSalle Coll., 1954; JD cum laude, U. Pa., 1959. Bar: D.C. 1960, Ohio 1964, W.Va. 1968, U.S. Supreme Ct. 1971. Tchg. fellow Stanford U., Palo Alto, Calif., 1959-60; trial atty. civil divsn. U.S. Dept. Justice, Washington, 1960-63; assoc. Taft, Stettinius & Hollister, Cin., 1963-67; gen. atty. Chesapeake & Potomac Tel. Co. of W.Va., Charleston, 1968-79; ptnr. Sullivan & Cowan, Charleston, 1979-82; sole practice Charleston, 1982-98; ret., 1998. Sr. adv. editor U. Pa. Law Rev., 1958-59. Served to 1st lt. AUS, 1954-56. Mem. ABA. Home and Office: 300 Sweetbriar Rd Greenville SC 29615

COWAN, ROBERT JENKINS, radiologist, educator; b. Greensboro, N.C., Apr. 22, 1937; s. John Columbus and Edith (Jenkins) C.; m. Leila Caroline Sikes, June 18, 1960; children: Caroline Cowan Morris, Barbara Cowan Scott. AB, U. N.C., 1959, MD, 1963. Diplomate: Am. Bd. Radiology (guest examiner), Am. Bd. Nuclear Medicine. Intern in medicine Presbyn. Hosp., Columbia-Presbyn. Med. Center, N.Y.C., 1963-64, resident, 1966-67; resident in radiology N.C. Bapt. Hosp., Winston-Salem, 1967-70; instr. radiology Bowman Gray Sch. Medicine, Wake Forest U., Winston-Salem, 1970-71; asst. prof. Wake Forest U. Sch. of Medicine, 1971-74, assoc. prof., 1974-79, prof., 1979-98; prof. emeritus Wake Forest U. Sch. Medicine, 1998—; dir. nuclear medicine N.C. Bapt. Hosp., Winston-Salem, 1977-98; med. dir. nuclear med. tech. tng. program Forsyth Tech. Coll., Winston-Salem, 1977-98. Contbr. articles to profl. jours. Adv. bd. Stone Mountain State Park, 1994—. Served to capt., M.C. U.S. Army, 1964-66. Decorated Bronze Star medal; Am. Cancer Soc. fellow, 1969-70; James Picker scholar, 1970-73; recipient James Quinn M.D. Teaching Excellence award, 1983, 97. Fellow Am. Coll. Radiology, Am. Coll. Nuclear Physicians; mem. AMA, Soc. Nuclear Medicine (coun. Southeastern chpt. 1972-84, pres. 1978, trustee 1983-84), Radiol. Soc. N.Am., N.C. Radiol. Soc., Med. Soc. N.C., Alpha Omega Alpha. Methodist.

COWAN, WALLACE EDGAR, lawyer; b. Jersey City, Jan. 28, 1924; s. Benjamin and Dorothy (Zunz) C.; m. Ruth Daitzman, June 8, 1947; children: Laurie, Paul, Judith. BS magna cum laude, NYU, 1947; JD cum laude, Harvard U., 1950. Ptnr. Stroock, Stroock & Lavan, N.Y.C., 1950-93, of counsel, 1994—. Dir. Ametek, Inc., Paoli, Pa., 1982-93, sec., 1969-93, sec. H.S. Stuttman, Inc., Westport, Conn., to 1996; adv. bd. Hackensack River Greenway, Teaneck, N.J. Mem. Teaneck (N.J.) Adv. Bd. on Parks, Playgrounds and Recreation, 1966—, chmn., 1974—; pres. No. Valley Commuters Assn.; past pres., life trustee Congregation Beth Sholom, Teaneck; mem. Forum adv. bd. Sch.-Based Youth Svcs. Project, 1998-2003. 1st lt. USAF, 1942-45, ETO. Decorated Air medal with silver cluster; recipient Vol. in the Parks award Bergen County, N.J., 1993, Disting. Svc. award Bergen County, N.J., 1994, Disting. Achievement award Bergen County, N.J., 2001. Mem. Beta Gamma Sigma. Home: 499 Emerson Ave Teaneck NJ 07666-1927 Office: Stroock Stroock & Lavan 180 Maiden Ln New York NY 10038-4937

COWAN, WILLIAM MAXWELL, neurobiologist; b. Johannesburg, Sept. 27, 1931; s. Adam and Jessie Sloan (Maxwell) C.; m. Margaret Sherlock, Mar. 31, 1956; children: Ruth Cowan Eadon-Rainer, Stephen Maxwell, David Maxwell. B.Sc., Witwatersrand U., Johannesburg, 1951, B.Sc. (hon.), 1952; D.Phil., Oxford U., 1956, BM, BCh, 1958, MA, 1959; DSc (hon.), Emory U., 1995, Northwestern U., 1995, Cold Spring Harbor, 2001; DLitt (hon.), Kalamazoo Coll., 2001. From demonstrator to univ. lectr. anatomy Oxford U., 1953-66; fellow Pembroke Coll., 1958-66; vis. prof. anatomy Washington U. Med. Sch., St. Louis, 1964-65; assoc. prof. U. Wis. Med. Sch., Madison, 1966-68; prof., chmn. dept. anatomy and neurobiology Washington U. Med. Sch., 1968-80; research prof., dir. Weingart Lab. Devel. Neurobiology, Salk Inst. Biol. Studies, La Jolla, Calif., 1980-86; v.p. Salk Inst. Biol. Studies, 1982-86; provost and exec. vice chancellor Washington U., St. Louis, 1986-87; v.p., chief sci. officer Howard Hughes Med. Inst., Chevy Chase, Md., 1988-2000. Mem. Inst. Medicine, Nat. Acad. Scis., 1978; fgn. assoc. Nat. Acad. Scis., 1981, disting. adj. prof. neurosci. Johns Hopkins Sch. Medicine, 1988-2000; Disting. adj. prof. neurosci. U. TEx. Southwestern Med. Ctr.. Editor-in-chief Jour. Neurosci., 1980-87; editor: Ann. Revs. Neurosci. Hon. fellow Pembroke Coll., Hertford Coll. Fellow Am. Acad. Arts and Scis., Royal Soc. (London); fgn. mem. Royal Soc. South Africa; mem. AAAS, Am. Philos. Soc., Soc. Neurosci. (pres. 1977-78), Norwegian Acad. Sci. (fgn.), Sigma Xi, Alpha Omega Alpha, Phi Beta Kappa. Home: 6337 Windermere Cir Rockville MD 20852-3550 E-mail: wmaxcowan@aol.com.

COWARD, DAVID HAND, physicist, researcher; b. Buffalo, Nov. 16, 1934; m. Doris Dickerson, June 4, 1960 (dic. Sept. 1991); 3 children; m. Diane Barbour, Jan. 8, 2000. B of Engring. Physics, Cornell U., 1957; MS in Physics, Stanford U., 1958, PhD in Physics, 1963. Exptl. physicist Stanford (Calif.) Linear Accelerator Ctr., 1963-99; physicist emeritus Stanford U., 1999—. Sci. assoc. European Orgn. for Nuclear Research (CERN), Geneva, 1976-77, 86-87, 89-90, Inst. Physics, U. Mainz, Germany, 1993-94; lectr. U. Colo., 1998—; cons. MITRE Co., McLean, Va., 1976. Fellow: Am. Phys. Soc. Office: Stanford Linear Accelerator Ctr Stanford U 2575 Sand Hill Rd Menlo Park CA 94025 E-mail: dhc@slac.stanford.edu.

COWARD, JAMES KENDERDINE, chemist; b. Buffalo, Oct. 13, 1938; s. Harold Wilbur and Ethel Rae (Hand) C.; m. Maria Adelaide Durso, June 7, 1975; 1 son, Robert. AB, Middlebury Coll., 1960; MA, Duke U., 1964; PhD, SUNY-Buffalo, 1967. Asst. prof. pharmacology Yale U., 1969-74, assoc. prof., 1974-79; assoc. prof. chemistry Rensselaer Poly. Inst., 1979-82, prof., 1982-86; prof. medicinal chemistry and chemistry U. Mich., Ann Arbor, 1987—, chmn. dept. medicinal chemistry, 1998—. Vis. prof. Salk Inst., 1977-78. Contbr. articles to profl. jours. NIH fellow, 1966-68; recipient various grants Mem. AAAS, Am. Chem. Soc., Chem. Soc. (London), Am. Soc. Biol. Chemists, Sigma Xi. Home: 6 Haverhill Ct Ann Arbor MI 48105-1407 Office: U Mich Depts Chemistry/Medicinal Chemistry Ann Arbor MI 48109

COWART, T(HOMAS) DAVID, lawyer; b. San Benito, Tex., June 12, 1953; s. Thomas W. Jr. and Glenda Claire (Miller) C.; children: Thomas Kevin, Lauren Michelle, Megan Leigh; m. Greta E. Gerberding, Aug. 12, 1995. BBA,

U. Miss., 1975, JD, 1978; LLM in Taxation, NYU, 1979. CPA Tex., Miss.; bar: Miss. 1978, Tex. 1979. Assoc. Dossett, Magruder & Montgomery, Jackson, Miss., 1978, Strasburger & Price, Dallas, 1979-87; ptnr., assoc., shareholder Johnson & Gibbs, Dallas, 1988-90; shareholder Jenkens & Gilchrist, Dallas, 1991—. Adj. prof. law So. Meth. U. Sch. Law, 1988; mem. key dist. adv. coun. IRS, Dallas, 1989—95, chmn., 1990—93; mem. Coll. State Bar Tex.; lectr. in field. Mem. editl. bd.: Flexible Benefits, 1993—, 401k Advisor, 1994—, COBRA, 1996—. Mem. adv. com. Goals for Dallas, 1984-85; vol. Children's Med. Ctr., 1992-96. Recipient Best Lawyer in Am. award, 2001—02, 2003—, Best Lawyer in Dallas award, 2003, Best Lawyer award, Corp. Coun., 2003, Tex. Super Lawyer award, 2003. Mem.: ABA (sect. taxation, employee benefit com., vice-chmn. 1995—97, chmn. elect 1997—98, chmn. 1998—99, sect. 83 issues task force, chmn. health plan designs issues subcom. 1992—95, health care task force 1991—98, chmn.-designate joint com. on employee benefits 1997—99, chmn. joint com. employee benefits 1999—2000), Dallas Bar Found., Am. Law Inst., Phi Alpha Phi, Dallas Benefits Soc. (co-moderator 1991—92, bd. dirs. 1991—93), S.W. Benefits Assn. (bd. dirs. 1994—97), Dallas Bar Assn. (lectr. 1985—, coun. mem. employee benefits sect. 1989—92, treas. 1992, sec. 1993, v.p. 1994, pres. 1995), State Bar Tex. (sect. taxation, com. compensation and employee benefits, fed. legislation, regulations and revenue rulings subcom. 1986—87, chmn. fiduciary stds. for trustees subcom. 1987—88), Am. Coll. Employee Benefits Counsel (1st chair, charter mem.), Beta Alpha Psi, Omicron Delta Kappa. Office: Jenkens & Gilchrist 1445 Ross Ave Ste 3200 Dallas TX 75202-2785 E-mail: dcowart@jenkens.com.

COWDEN, JOHN WILLIAM, lawyer; b. Springfield, Mo., June 3, 1945; s. John Marshall and Laura Alice (Lemmon) C.; m. Carol Jean Avery, Jan. 27, 1968; children: Jennifer, John. BA, Southwest Mo. State U., 1967; JD, U. Mo., 1970. Bar: Mo. 1970, U.S. Dist. Ct. (we. dist.) Mo. 1971, U.S. Ct. Appeals (8th cir.) 1980, U.S. Supreme Ct. 1982. Asst. atty. gen. State of Mo., Jefferson City, 1970-71; assoc. Morrison, Hecker, Curtis, Kuder & Parrish, Kansas City, Mo., 1971-76, ptnr., 1976-89, Baker, Sterchi & Cowden, Kansas City, 1989—. Co-author: Missouri Evidence Restated. Chmn. human devel. bd. YMCA, Kansas City; bd. dirs. Gt. Am. Basketball League, Johnson City, Kans., 1986-88. Mem. ABA, Mo. Bar Assn., Kansas City Bar Assn., Lawyers Assn. Kansas City, Am. Bd. Trial Advs., Am. Coll. Trial Lawyers, Internat. Assn. Def. Counsel, Def. Rsch. Inst., U. Mo. Law Soc., Indian Hills Country Club, Univ. Club. Avocations: golf, travel. Home: 6827 Linden St Prairie Village KS 66208-1427 Office: 2400 Pershing Rd Kansas City MO 64108-2504

COWDEN, ROGER HUGH, II, systems engineer; b. Dayton, Ohio, Jan. 26, 1955; s. Roger Hugh and Beverly Eileen Cowden. BS in Systems Engring., Wright State U., 1979. Engr. Steve R. Rauch Inc., Dayton, 1979—. Mem. Dayton Inventors Coun., 1994—. Mem. NSPE, Heartland Vintage Thunderbird Club. Achievements include patent for secondary containment for underground storage tanks. Home: 9985 Ainsworth Ct Miamisburg OH 45342-4571 Office: 1550 Soldiers Home West Car Rd Dayton OH 45418-2146

COWDERY, ROBERT DOUGLAS, consulting geologist; b. Lyons, Kans., Aug. 20, 1926; s. Herman Rayburn and Blanche (Charles) C.; m. Mary Sue Barlow, Oct. 9, 1954; children:; Craig Douglas, Patricia Lynn. BS in Geology, Kans. State U., 1949; postgrad., U. Denver, 1953-54, Colo. Sch. Mines, 1963-64, U. Colo., 1963-71, Wichita State U., 1979-98. Geologist Cities Svc. Oil Co., Oklahoma City-Gt. Bend, Kans., 1949-51; staff geologist Petroleum Inc., Wichita, Kans., 1951-53, dist. geologist Denver, 1953-56, div. geologist, 1956-57, Rocky Mountain exploration mgr., v.p., 1967-75, exploration mgr., v.p. Wichita, 1975-85, pres., dir. exploration, 1985-88; ret., 1988; cons. geologist, 1988—. Mem. adv. coun. dept. geology Kans. State U., downtown campus Wichita State U., Mus. Anthropology Wichita State U. Pres. bd. dirs. Episcopal Social Svcs. S.W. Convocation, Wichita, 1989-90; bd. dirs. Breakthrough Club, 1999-2000, 2002—, also pres. bd. Sgt. AUS, 1944-46. Recipient Disting. Svc. award Kans. State U. Coll. Arts and Scis., 1991; inducted into Kans. Oilmen's Hall of Fame, 2002. Fellow Geol. Soc. Am. (sr.); mem. Am. Assn. Petroleum Geologists (cert., hon., v.p. 1983-84, v.p. divsn. profl. affairs 1987-88, pres.-elect 1990-91, pres. divsn. profl. affairs 1991-92, pres., Disting. Svc. award divsn. profl. affairs 1994, pres.-elect 1995-96, pres. 1996-97), Am. Inst. Profl. Geologists (cert.), Rocky Mountain Assn. Geologists (hon., pres. 1973), Kans. Geol. Soc. (hon., pres. 1986, Presdl. citation 1977, Spl. award 1998, Disting. Svc. award 2001), Kans. Geol. Found. (pres. 1990—, bd. dirs. 1999—, Disting. Svc. award 1991, 2002 Pres.'s award 1993, Edn. award 1997), Soc. Ind. Profl. Earth Scientists (hon., Kans. chpt. chmn., bd. dirs. 1995— nat. sec. 1996-97, v.p. natural resources 1997-98), Am. Geol. Inst. (rep. of AAPG on the mem. coun., earth sci. com.), Archaeol. Assn. South Ctrl. Kans. (v.p. 1988-89, pres. 1990-93, program chair 1998-99), So. Am. Archaeologists, Wyo. Geol. Soc., Oklahoma City Geol. Soc., West Tex. Geol. Soc., Panhandle Geol. Soc., Petroleum Club (bd. dirs. 1988-91, sec. 1991), Phi Kappa Phi, Sigma Gamma Epsilon, Beta Theta Pi. Avocations: archaeology, karate (6th deg. black belt Tae Kwon Do). Home: 7520 E 21st St N Unit 10 Wichita KS 67206-1086 Office: 107 N Market St Ste 1007 Wichita KS 67202-1811 E-mail: sbc@southwind.net.

COWELL, JENNIFER M. music educator; b. Casper, Wyo., May 11, 1975; d. Walter Thomas and Janice Lee Cowell; m. Gary John DePaolo, July 19, 1997; 1 child, Alexis Ruth DePaolo. BMus, DePaul U., Chgo., 1993—97; MMus, U. Oreg., Eugene, 1997—2000. Suzuki violin instr. U. Oreg., Eugene, 1999—2001; strings prof. Casper Coll., Wyo., 2001—, dir., summer strings, 2002—; pvt. Suzuki violin instr. Casper, Wyo., 2001—. Dir. Summer Strings, Casper, Wyo., 2001—. Violinist Equinox String Quartet, Casper, Wyo., 2003—. Mem.: Music Educator's Nat. Conf., Suzuki Assn. of Am., Am. String Tchr.'s Assn. (pres.-elect, Wyo. chpt. 2001—). Avocations: fly fishing, hiking, cooking. Office: Casper Coll 125 College Dr Casper WY 82601 Office Fax: 307-268-3023. Business E-Mail: jcowell@caspercollege.edu.

COWELL, MARION AUBREY, JR., lawyer; b. Wilmington, N.C., Dec. 25, 1934; s. Marion Aubrey and Alice Saunders (Hargett) C.; m. Norma Hearne; children: Lindsay G., Mark P., Kathryn Huffman, Graham Shannonhouse, Elizabeth Shannonhouse, Mary Robbins Whisnant. BSBA, U. N.C., 1958, LLB, 1964. Bar: N.C. 1964. Pvt. practice law, Durham, N.C., 1964-72; assoc. Bryant, Lipton, Bryant and Battle, 1964-69, ptnr., 1971-72; pvt. practice law Durham, 1969-70; gen. counsel Cameron Brown Co., Raleigh, N.C., 1972-78; exec. v.p., gen. counsel, sec. First Union Corp., Charlotte, N.C., 1978-99, Kilpatrick-Stockton LLP, Charlotte, N.C., 1999—. Office: Kilpatrick Stockton LLP 214 N Tyron St Ste 2500 Charlotte NC 28202-6001 Office Fax: 704-371-8279.*

COWEN, EDWARD S. lawyer; b. N.Y.C., Mar. 3, 1936; s. Michael and Edith (Cohen) C.; m. Lesley J. Hoffman, Nov. 16, 1958; children: Adrienne, Justine. BS, Syracuse U., 1957; JD, NYU, 1961. Bar: N.Y. 1962, U.S. Dist. Ct. (so. dist.) N.Y. 1965, U.S. Ct. Appeals (2d cir.) 1965, U.S. Supreme Ct. 1967, U.S. Dist. Ct. (ea. dist.) N.Y. 1979. Law clk. to judge U.S. Dist. Ct. (so. dist.) N.Y., 1961-62; ptnr. Seligson & Morris, N.Y.C., 1963-69, Robinson, Silverman, Pearce, Aronsohn & Berman, N.Y.C., 1975-90, Kirkland & Ellis, N.Y.C., 1991-96; of counsel Pillsbury Winthrop, LLP, N.Y.C., 1996—2001. Cons. Poorman-Douglas Corp., 2002—; mem. faculty Practicing Law Inst. Author: Bankruptcy in Joint Venture Partnerships, Practicing Law Institute, 1985, Enforcing Liens Postpetition, Bankruptcy Strategist, 1998. With USAF, 1958. Named Honoree of Yr. Fedn. N.Y. Lawyers Divsn. Mem. ABA, N.Y. State Bar Assn., Assn. Bar City N.Y. (chmn. bankruptcy and corp. reorgn.), Harmonie Club. Home: 860 Fifth Ave New York NY 10021-5856 E-mail: ecowen@verizon.net.

COWEN, EUGENE SHERMAN, broadcasting executive; b. N.Y.C., May 2, 1925; s. Jacob M. and Shirley (Sherman) C.; m. Phyllis L. Wallach, Jan. 29, 1948; children: James Sherman, Stephanie Jane. BA magna cum laude, Syracuse U., 1949, MA, 1954. Reporter Syracuse Herald-Jour., 1948-52, Newhouse News Bur., Washington, 1952-53; press sec. Rep. Frances P. Bolton, Washington, 1953-56; info. officer HEW, Washington, 1956-58; v.p. Standard Pub. Rels., Washington, 1958-59; chief staff Senator Hugh Scott, 1959-69; spl. asst., dep. asst. to pres. White House, 1969-71; v.p.-Washington Capital Cities/ABC, Inc., 1971-90; cons. in field Washington, 1990—. Author: (book) My Life, A Novel, 2003. Legis. affairs dir. Svc. Corps Ret. Execs. With USAAF, 1943-46. Decorated Air medal. Mem. Phi Beta Kappa. Home: 2700 Calvert St NW Washington DC 20008-2621

COWEN, LENORE JENNIFER, mathematician, educator, computer scientist; b. N.Y. C., Apr. 10, 1967; d. Robert H. and Ilsa R. Cowen; m. William J. Bogstad, July 5, 1997. BA, Yale U., 1987; PhD, MIT, 1993. Postdoctoral fellow U. Minn., Mpls., 1993, Rutgers U., Piscataway, NJ, 1994; from asst. to assoc. prof. Johns Hopkins U., Balt., 1994—2001; sci. fellow Radcliffe inst. for advanced study Harvard U., Cambridge, Mass., 1999—2000; assoc. prof. Tufts U., Medford, Mass., 2001—. Recipient Young Investigator award, Office of Naval Rsch., 1996—99. Office: Tufts University Halligan Hall 161 College Ave Medford MA 02155 E-mail: cowen@eecs.tufts.edu.

COWEN, ROBERT E. federal judge; b. Newark, N.J., Sept. 4, 1930; s. Saul and Lillie (Selzer) C.; m. Toby Cowen, Dec. 21, 1973; children: Shulie, Eve. BS, Drake U., 1952; LLB, Rutgers U., 1958. Assoc. Schreiber, Lancaster & Demos, Newark, 1959-61; asst. prosecutor Essex County, N.J., 1969-70; dep. atty. gen. organized crime Criminal Justice Dept., N.J., 1970-72, dir. Div. Ethics and Profl. Svcs., 1972-78; magistrate U.S. Dist. Ct. N.J., Newark, 1978-85, judge Trenton, 1985-87, U.S. Ct. Appeals (3d cir.), Trenton, 1987-98, sr. judge, 1998—. Pvt. practice, Newark, 1961-69. Office: Clarkson S Fisher Jud Complex 402 E State St Rm 207 Trenton NJ 08608-1507*

COWEN, ROBERT NATHAN, lawyer; b. N.Y.C., July 6, 1948; s. Arthur S. and Elsie (Smerling) C.; m. Ann Barbara Goldberg, May 20, 1979; children: Elizabeth Rebecca, Alexandra Lee, Joanna Lindsay. AB, Cornell U., 1969, JD, 1972; LLM, NYU, 1979. Bar: N.Y. 1973. Law clk. Chief Judge State of N.Y., N.Y.C., 1972-74; assoc. Cleary, Gottlieb, Steen & Hamilton, N.Y.C., 1974-79, Proskauer, Rose, Goetz & Mendelsohn, N.Y.C., 1979; sec. Overseas Shipholding Group, Inc., N.Y.C., 1982—, gen. counsel, 1989-95, sr. v.p., 1993—, bd. dirs., 1993—; exec. v.p. Overseas Discount Corp., N.Y.C., 1979—. Office: Overseas Discount Corp 511 5th Ave New York NY 10017-4903

COWEN, ROY CHADWELL, JR., language educator, educator; b. Kansas City, Mo., Aug. 2, 1930; s. Roy Chadwell and Mildred Frances (Schuetz) Cowen; m. Hildegard Bredemeier, Oct. 6, 1956 (dec.); 1 child, Ernst Werner (dec.). BA, Yale U., 1952; PhD, U. Gottingen, Federal Republic of Germany, 1960. Instr. U. Mich., Ann Arbor, 1960-64, asst. prof., 1964-67, assoc. prof., 1967-71, prof., 1971—, chmn. dept. Germanic langs., 1979-85. Author: (book) Christian Dietrich Grabbe, 1972, Naturalismus Kommentar zu einer Epoche, 1973, Hauptmann Kommentar zum dramatischen Werk, 1981, Poetischer Realismus: Kommentar zu einer Epoche, 1985, Das deutsche Drama im 19. Jahrhundert, 1988, Christian Dietrich Grabbe-Dramatiker ungeloester Widersprueche, 1998. With USN, 1952—56. Decorated Sr. Officer's Cross Federal Republic of Germany; recipient Williams Tchg. award, U. Mich., 1967; fellow Sr., NEH, 1972—73. Mem.: MLA, Internationale Vereinigung fur Germanistik. Democrat. Methodist. Home: 2874 Baylis Dr Ann Arbor MI 48108-1764 Office: U Mich Dept Germanic Langs/Lits Ann Arbor MI 48109 E-mail: rcowen@umich.edu.

COWEN, SCOTT S. academic administrator; m. Marjorie Cowen; 4 children. BS, U. Conn., 1968; MBA, George Washington U., 1972, DBA in Fin., 1975. Asst. prof. mgmt. Bucknell U., 1974—76; faculty Case Western Res. U., Cleve., 1976—98, dean, Albert J. Weatherhead III prof. mgmt., 1984—98; pres. Tulane U., New Orleans, 1998—, Seymour S Goodman Meml. prof. bus. A.B. Freeman Sch. Bus., 1998—, prof. econs. Faculty of Liberal Arts and Scis., 1998—. Eleanor F. and Philip G. Rust vis. prof. Colgate Darden Grad. Sch. Bus. Adminstrn., U. Va., 1982—83; bd. dirs. Newell Rubbermaid, Inc., Am. Greetings Corp., Jo-Ann Stores, Inc., Forest City Ent., Inc.; cons. in field. Co-author: Introduction to Business: Concepts and Applications, 1981, Information Requirements of Corporate Boards of Directors, 1983, Accounting Today: Principles and Applications, Innovation in Professional Education: Steps on a Journey From Teaching to Learning, 1995; contbr. articles to profl. jours. Bd. dirs. New Orleans Bus. Coun., Com. for a Better New Orleans, New Orleans Regional C. of C., United Way Greater New Orleans. With U.S. Army, 1968—71. Co-recipient award of Achievement in Edn., No. Ohio Live Mag., 1991; named Disting. Alumni, George Washington U., 1998—99; named to, Sch. Bus. Adminstrn. Hall of Fame U. Conn.; recipient Torch of Learning, Hebrew U., Torch of Liberty, Anti-Defamation League, Leadership Cleve. award, Greater Cleve. Growth Assn., 1987—88; fellow, Ernst & Whitney, Cleve., 1978, 1979. Mem.: Nat. Assn. Ind. Colls. and Univs. (bd. dirs.), Am. Coun. Edn. (bd. dirs.), Am. Assembly of Collegiate Schs. Bus. Office: Tulane University 218 Gibson 6823 Saint Charles Ave New Orleans LA 70118-5698 Fax: 504-865-5202. E-mail: scowen@tulane.edu.

COWEN, WILLIAM B. government agency administrator; children: Halle, Lindsay, William Jr. BA in math, Case Western Reserve U., 1976; JD, Cleveland-Marshall Coll. of Law, Cleveland State U., 1979. Atty. Thompson and Hutson, 1985—92; counsel to bd. mem. Howard Jenkins, Jr. Nat. Labor Rels. Bd., 1979—85; ptnr. Coleman, Coxson, Penello, Foglemand & Cowen, P.C., 1992—96; founding mem Cowen and Assoc., McLean, Va., 1996—98; prin. atty. Inst. Labor Advisors, LLC, 1997—2002. Mem.: Nat. Labor Rels. Bd. Office: Franklin Court Bldg 1099 14th St NW Washington DC 20570-0001

COWEN, WILSON, judge; b. nr. Clifton, Tex., Dec. 20, 1905; s. John Rentz and Florence Juno (McFadden) Cowen; m. Florence Elizabeth Walker, Apr. 18, 1930; children: W. Walker, John E. LLB, U. Tex., 1928. Bar: Tex. 1928. Pvt. practice, Dalhart, Tex., 1928—34; judge Dallam County, Tex., 1935—38; Tex. dir. Farm Security Adminstrn., 1938—40, regional dir., 1940—42; commr. U.S. Ct. Claims, Washington, 1942—43, 1945—59, chief commr., 1959—64, chief judge, 1964—77, sr. judge, 1977—82; sr. judge fed. cir. U.S. Ct. Appeals, Washington, 1982—98. Asst. adminstr. War Food Adminstrn., 1943—45; spl. asst. to sec. agr., 1945; mem. Jud. Conf. U.S., 1964—77. Mem.: FBA, ABA, State Bar Tex., Cosmos Club (Washington), Delta Theta Phi, Order of Coif. Presbyterian. Home: 2512 Q St NW Apt 205 Washington DC 20007-4310 Office: US Ct Appeal Federal Circuit 717 Madison Pl NW Washington DC 20439-0002

COWENS, DAVID WILLIAM (DAVE COWENS), professional basketball coach, insurance executive, retired professional basketball player; b. Newport, Ky., Oct. 25, 1948; m. Deborah Cmaylo; children: Meghan, Samantha. BS, Fla. State U., 1970. Basketball player Boston Celtics, 1970-80, head coach (68 games), 1978-79; player Milw. Bucks, 1983; owner, pres., dir. David W. Cowens Basketball Sch., Inc., Needham, Mass., 1972—; pres. Survivors Income Option, Inc. (life ins.), 1987—; head coach Charlotte Hornets, 1996-98; assist. coach Denver Nuggets, 1998-99, head coach, 1999-2000, Golden State Warriors, 2000—. Athletic dir. Regis Coll., Weston, Mass., 1981-82; coach Bay State, Continental Basketball Assn., 1984-85; chmn. bd. New Eng. Sport Mus. Named Rookie of Yr. 1970-71, NBA Most Valuable Player, 1972-73; mem. NBA All Star teams, yearly 1971-77, NBA Championship team, 1974, 76; honored by having his number retired; inducted into Naismith Meml. Basketball Hall of Fame, 1990. Office: Golden State Warriors 1011 Broadway Oakland CA 94607-4027 also: 530 Oakshire Pl Alamo CA 94507-2325

COWETT, EVERETT R, retired agronomist; b. Ashland, Maine, Mar. 6, 1935; s. Linwood A Cowett and Amelia Rioux; m. Valentina W Wojciechowski, Aug. 13, 1960; children: Daniel A, Alexander M, Thomas J, Martha Ann, John Everett. BS, U. Maine, 1957, MS, 1958; PhD, Rutgers U., 1961. Prof. agronomy U. NH, Durham, 1961—63; rsch. rep. Geigy Chem. Co., Ardsley, NY, 1963—65, herbicide specialist, 1965—67, rsch. mgr., 1967—79, mgr. biol. rsch., 1969—71; dir. tech. svc. Ciba-Geigy, Greensboro, NC, 1971—91; owner, agronomist Everett Cowett Co., Greensboro, 1991—2000; retired, 2000. Pres. Greensboro Civitan Club, 2001—02, mem., 1996—2002; exec. dir. Rhythm Bones Soc., Greensboro, NC, 1996—2002. Pvt. 1st class USAR, 1955—62. Achievements include patents for Triazine Herbicide synergists. Home: 1822 New Garden Rd Greensboro NC 27410

COWGER, PHYLLIS, nurse; b. San Antonio, Sept. 12, 1944; d. Russell and Mildred Marie (Hamilton) Austin; m. Robert F. Cowger, Dec. 31, 1964; children: Rhonda, Teresa, Russell, Phillip, Robert II. Diploma in Nursing, Cochise Coll., Douglas, Ariz., 1985, AA in Gen. Studies, 1989. LPN, Ariz. Nurse Benson (Ariz.) Hosp., 1985-86; charge nurse Life Care Sierra Vista, Ariz., 1986-87; nurse Sierra Vista Care Ctr., 1987-89, Raymond W. Bliss Army Hosp., Ft. Huachuca, Ariz., 1989—. Com. mem. Sierra Vista council Boy Scouts Am. Nursing dept. grantee Cochise Coll., 1986. Democrat. Presbyterian. Avocations: reading, sewing, swimming. Home: 771 N Tacoma Pl Sierra Vista AZ 85635-1349

COWGILL, URSULA MOSER, biologist, educator, environmental consultant; b. Bern, Switzerland, Nov. 9, 1927; came to U.S., 1943, naturalized, 1945; d. John W. and Mara (Siegrist) Moser. AB, Hunter Coll., 1948; MS, Kans. State U., 1952; PhD, Iowa State U., 1956. Staff MIT, Lincoln Lab., Lexington, Mass., 1957-58; field work Doherty Found., Guatemala, 1958-60; research assoc. dept. biology Yale U., New Haven, 1960-68; prof. biology and anthropology U. Pitts., 1968-81; environ. scientist Dow Chem. Co., Midland, Mich., 1981-84, assoc. environ. cons., 1984-91; environ. cons., 1991—. Mem. environ. measurements adv. com. Sci. Adv. Bd. EPA, 1976-80; Internat. Joint Commn., 1984-89. Contbr. numerous articles on ecology, biology and minerology to sci. publs. Trustee Carnegie Mus., Pitts., 1971-75. Grantee NSF 1960-78, Wenner Gren Found., 1965-66, Penrose fund Am. Philos. Soc., 1978; Sigma Xi grant-in-aid, 1965-66 Mem. AAAS, Am. Soc. Limnology and Oceanography, Internat. Soc. Theoretical and Applied Limnology. Home and Office: PO Box 1329 Carbondale CO 81623-1329

COWHER, BILL, professional football coach; b. Pitts., May 8, 1957; m. Kaye Cowher; children: Meagan Lyn, Lauren Marie, Lindsay Morgan. Degree in edn., N.C. State. Football player Cleve. Browns, 1980-82, spl. teams coach, 1985-86, secondary coach, 1987-88; football player Phila. Eagles, 1983-84; def. coord. Kansas City Chiefs, 1988-91; head coach Pitts. Steelers, 1992—. Office: 3400 S Water St Pittsburgh PA 15203-2349

COWHEY, PETER FRANCIS, international relations educator, consultant; b. Chgo., Sept. 28, 1948; s. Eugene F. and Vivien (High) C.; m. Mary Pat Williams, July 1973 (div. June 1978); m. M. Margaret McKeown, June 29, 1985; 1 child, Megan. BS in Fgn. Svc., Georgetown U., 1970; MA, PhD, U. Calif., Berkeley, 1976. Lectr. U. Calif., Berkeley, 1975-76; from asst. to assoc. prof. polit. sci. U. Calif. San Diego, La Jolla, 1976-88, prof. polit. sci. & internat. rels., 1989—, dir. Inst. Global Conflict Coop., 1999—, dean grad. sch. internat. rels. and Pacific studies, 2002—; sr. counselor internat. coop. and competition policy FCC, Washington, 1994-97, chief internat. bur., 1997. Market planner AT&T Internat., Basking Ridge, N.J., 1985-86; advisor Telemation Assocs., Washington, 1987-88; mem. telecom. adv. bd. A.T. Kearney, Chgo., 1988-91; co-dir. project on internat. and security affairs U. Calif., San Diego, 1990-94; rsch. scholar Berkeley Roundtable on the Internat. Economy, 1992-94; vis. prof. Juan March Inst., Madrid, 1992; rsch. prof. Inst. of Oriental Culture, U. Tokyo, 1993; U.S. del. G-7 Ministerial, 1995, U.S. del. Asian Pacific Econ. Cmty. Ministerial, 1995; mem. sec. gen. Internat. Telecomm. Union Expert Group on Acctg. Rates, 1997-98; internat. adv. bds. Silicon Wave, SkyFlow, UN Devel. Program, Agy. for Internat. Devel. Author: Problems of Plenty, 1985; co-author: Profit and the Pursuit of Energy, 1983, When Countries Talk, 1988, Managing the World's Economy, 1993; co-editor: Structure and Policy in Japan and the United States, 1994; mem. editl. bd. Internat. Orgn., 1989-94. Mem. adv. bd. Project Promothee, Paris, 1985-94, Ctr. on Telecom. Mgmt., Lincoln, Nebr., 1988-92; com. mem. NRC, 1992-93. Rockefeller Found. internat. affairs fellow, 1984-87. Mem. Am. Polit. Sci. Assn., Coun. Fgn. Rels. (internat. affairs fellow 1985-86), Internat. Studies Assn. Democrat. also: UC San Diego 9500 Gilman Dr La Jolla CA 92093-5004 Home: 2447 Ardath Rd La Jolla CA 92037-3501 E-mail: pcowhey@ucsd.edu.

COWHILL, WILLIAM JOSEPH, retired naval officer, consultant; b. Bklyn., May 29, 1928; s. Joseph Henry and Lucy Rose (Foppiano) C.; m. Jennifer Jackson, Apr. 16, 1955; children Robin, Joseph, Beth, Michael, Douglas. BS, Northwestern U., 1950. Commd. ensign USN, 1950, advanced through grades to vice adm., 1979, comdg. officer USS Dace and USS Will Rogers, 1965-68, PCO instr., div. Naval Reactors, AEC, 1968-70, comdg. officer USS Holland, Rota, Spain, 1970-72, nuclear power program mgr. Bur. Naval Personnel, 1972, comdr. tng. command, U.S. Atlantic Fleet, 1973-75, asst. dep. chief naval ops. for submarine warfare, Office Chief Naval Ops., Washington, 1975-77, comdr. submarine force, U.S. Pacific Fleet, 1977-79, dep. chief ops. for logistics, office chief naval ops., 1979-83, dir. logistics, joint chiefs of staff, 1983-85, ret.; pvt. cons. Washington, 1985—. Decorated Def. D.S.M., Navy D.S.M., Legion of Merit. Home and Office: 1336 Elsinore Ave Mc Lean VA 22102-2753

COWIE, NORMAN EDWIN, credit manager; b. Balt., Nov. 24, 1958; s. Graham Norman Cowie and Jane Ardythe (Wertzler) Seekman; m. Sandra Jo Twaddle, Oct. 19, 1985; children: Samantha Lynn, Lauren Alexandra. AA, Kalamazoo Valley (Mich.) C.C., 1978; BBA magna cum laude, Western Mich. U., 1980. Cert. credit exec. Nat. Assn. Credit Mgmt. Mgr. Assocs. Fin. Co., Mich., Ill., 1980-85; region credit supr. Westinghouse Electric Supply, Elmhurst, Ill., 1985-89; v.p. fin., corp. credit mgr. Evergreen Oak Electric Sales and Supply, Crestwood, Ill., 1989—. Chmn. Elec. Distbrs. Credit Group, Park Ridge, Ill., 1990-92; bd. dirs. Chgo. Midwest Credit Mgmt. Assn., Park Ridge, 1993-96; spkr. Nat. Elec. Contractors Assn., DuPage, Ill., 1991, Chgo. Plumbing & Heating Wholesalers Credit Group, Oak Brook, Ill., 1994; moderator Roundtable Discussion Ill. Mechanic's Lien Law, Park Ridge, 1994, Ill. Mechanic's Lien Seminar, Rosemont, Ill., 1995; spkr. Understanding Constrn. Bonds and Mechanics Liens, Des Plaines, Ill., 1998, NACM/Chgo. Midwest Credit Leadership Conf. and Expo, 1999, 2001, 2002-2003; bd. dir. NACM/Chgo.-Midwest; spkr. in field; spkr. NACM-Chgo. Midwest Credit Conf., 2002. Author: (comic) Short Circuit, 1992; contbr. articles to profl. jours. Mem. steering com. New Lenox Park Dist., 2002—03. Mem. Nat. Assn. Credit Mgmt./Chgo. Midwest (collection activities task force com. 1996, nominating com. 1999, chmn. membership com. 2002-03), Nat. Assn. Credit Mgmt. Chgo.-Midwest (nominating com., 1999, 2000, improved constn. practices com., chmn. Ill. chpt. 1993—), Assn. Credit Execs. (spkr. 2001), Chgo. Midwest Credit Mgmt. Legis. Com. (chmn. 1992-95), U.S. Masters Swimming, Mystery Writers Am. Avocations: comic artist, swimming. Home: 2822 Hawkshead Dr New Lenox IL 60451-2709 Office: Evergreen Oak Electric Supply 13400 Cicero Ave Crestwood IL 60445-1460 E-mail: ncowie@evergreenoak.com.

COWIN, JUDITH A. state supreme court judge; m. William; 3 children. Grad., Wellesley Coll., Harvard U. Prosecutor, Norfolk County; judge Mass. Superior Ct.; assoc. justice Mass. Supreme Judicial Ct., Boston, 1999—. Office: Mass Supreme Judicial Ct 1300 New Courthouse Pemberton Sq Boston MA 02108

COWIN, STEPHEN CORTEEN, biomedical engineering educator, consultant; b. Elmira, N.Y., Oct. 26, 1934; s. William Corteen and Bernice (Reidy) C.; m. Martha Agnes Eisel, Aug. 10, 1956; children: Jennifer Marie, Thomas Burrows. BCE, Johns Hopkins U., 1956, MCE, 1958; PhD in Engring. Mechanics, Pa. State U., 1962. Registered profl. engr., La. Prof. mech. engring. Tulane U., 1969-77, prof. mechanics dept. biomed. engring., 1977-85, adj. prof. orthopedics, 1978-88, prof.-in-charge Tulane-Newcomb Jr. Yr. Abroad program, 1974-75, chmn. applied math. program, 1975-79, prof. applied stats., 1979-88, Alden J. Laborde prof. engring., 1985-88; disting. prof. CUNY, 1988—, chmn. dept. biomed. engring., 2002—03; dir. N.Y. Ctr. for Biomed. Engring., 2000—03. Sci. Rsch. Coun. Gt. Brit. sr. vis. fellow U. Strathclyde, 1974, 80; vis. research prof. Instituto de Matematica, Estatistica e Ciencia de Computanao, Universidade Estadual de Campinas, Brazil, 1978; participant U.S. Nat. Acad. Scis. interacad. exch. program with Bulgaria, 1983; fellow Japan Soc. for the Promotion Sci., 1987. Editor: (with M. Satake) Continuum Mechanical and Statistical Approaches in the Mechanics of Granular Materials, 1978, Mechanics Applied to the Transport of Granular Materials, 1979, (with M.M. Carroll) The Effects of Voids on Material Deformation, 1976, Bone Mechanics, 1988, Bone Mechanics Handbook, 2001, Cardiovascular Soft Tissue Mechanics, 2001; assoc. editor: Jour. Applied Mechanics, 1974-82, Jour. Biomech. Engring., 1982-88; editl. adv. bd. Handbook of Materials, Structures and Mechanics, 1981—, Handbook of Bioengineering, 1981, Acta Biomechanica, 1986—; editl. bd. Annals Biomed. Engring., 1985—; editl. cons. Jour. Biomechanics, 1988—. Served to capt. U.S. Army, 1957-64 Rsch. grantee NSF, NIH, NASA, U.S. Army Rsch. Office, Edward G. Schlieder Found.; sr. internat. rsch. fellow Fogarty Internat. Ctr., Amsterdam, 1996-97, Johns Hopkins U. fellow, 1958; Md. state scholar, Ambrose Howard Carner scholar. Fellow AAAS, ASME (Melville medal 1993, Lissner medal 1999), Am. Inst. Med. and Biol. Engring., European Soc. Biomechanics (Rsch. award 1994), Am. Acad

Mechanics; mem. Orthopedic Rsch. Soc., Soc. Rheology, Soc. Natural Philosophy (treas. 1977-79), Soc. Engring. Sci., Math. Assn. Am., N.Y. Acad. Scis., Sigma Xi. Home: 2166 Broadway Apt 12D New York NY 10024

COWLES, CHARLES, art dealer; b. Santa Monica, Calif., Feb. 7, 1941; s. Gardner and Jan (Streate) C. Student, Stanford, 1963. Assoc. pub. Artforum mag., San Francisco, 1964-65; pub., pres. Artforum, Inc., Los Angeles, 1965-67, pub., pres., chmn. N.Y.C., 1967-75, pres., chmn., 1975-79; chmn. Collegiate Press, N.Y.C., 1968-71; curator modern art Seattle Art Mus., 1975-79; pres. Charles Cowles Gallery, N.Y.C., 1980—. Mem. Fine Arts Council Fla., 1972-75; Trustee Studio Mus. in Harlem, N.Y.C., 1967-75, Miami Art Ctr., 1973-75, San Francisco Art Inst., 1978-80, Cowles Charitable Trust, 1983— ; mem. internat. council Mus. Modern Art, N.Y.C., 1967-79. Mem. Seattle Arts Commn., 1976-79; trustee Wolfsonian F.I.U., Miami Beach, 1995—, Laueier Sculpture Pk. St. Louis, 1996—, Am. Fedn. of the Arts, N.Y., 2000—, Alliance for the Arts, 2001--; trustee N.Y. Studio Sch., 1985-2003, chmn., 1987-95; trustee com. for librs. Mus. of Modern Art, N.Y., 2000—. With USCG, 1962—63, with USCGR, 1963—70. Mem. Art Dealers Assn. Am. (bd. dirs. 1988-90, 93-96). Office: Charles Cowles Gallery 537 W 24th St New York NY 10011-1104 Fax: 212-925-3501. E-mail: charlie@cowlesgallery.com.

COWLES, CHARLES EUGENE, JR., medical educator; b. Houston, Apr. 19, 1968; s. Charles Eugene Cowles Sr. and Carol Janice Wood. BA in Health Mgmt., U. Tex., Galveston, 1994; BS in Sports Medicine, U. Houston, 1998; ADN, SUNY, Albany, 1998. RN, paramedic Nat. Registry EMTs, Tex. Paramedic City of Baytown, Tex., 1989, City of Beaumont, Tex., 1989-95; prof., clin. coord. San Jacinto Coll., Pasadena, Tex., 1995—. Clin. instr., cons. NASA, Johnson Space Ctr., Houston, 1995—; advisor Internat. Assn. Fire Chiefs, Miami, 1994; ACLS CTC coord. Am. Heart Assn. Chmn. CPR task force Am. Heart Assn., Pasadena, 1998; liaison Internat. Assn. Fire Fighters, Beaumont, 1993. Named Paramedic of Yr., Am. Trauma Soc., 1988. Mem. AMA, Am. Soc. Anesthesiologists, Tex. Med. Assn. Republican. Baptist. Avocations: aquarium science, dining out, rollerblading, off road vehicles. Home: 3331 Luella Blvd La Porte TX 77571-3680 Office: San Jacinto Coll PO Box 7832 Pasadena TX 77508-7832 Fax: (281) 478-2754. E-mail: Charles.E.Cowles@uth.tmc.edu.

COWLES, JOE RICHARD, biology educator; b. Edmonson County, Ky., Oct. 29, 1941; s. Otis Wilson and Mamie E. (Rountree) C.; m. Barbara Sutton, June 5, 1965; children: Richard William, Daniel Morgan. BS, Western Ky. U., 1963; MS, U. Ky., 1965; PhD, Oreg. State U., 1968. Postdoctoral fellow Purdue U., West Lafayette, Ind., 1968-69, U. Ga., Athens, 1969-70; asst. prof. U. Houston, 1970-75, assoc. prof., 1976-81, chmn. biology dept., 1981-90, prof., 1982-90; head biology Va. Tech. U., Blacksburg, 1990—2002, prof., 1990—. Contbr. more than 40 articles to profl. jours. Grantee NASA, NSF, Dept. Energy, USDA. Mem. Am. Soc. Plant Physiology, Sigma Xi. Democrat. Baptist. Avocation: sports. Office: Virginia Tech U Dept Biology Blacksburg VA 24061 E-mail: cowlesjr@vt.edu.

COWLES, JOHN, JR., publisher, women's sports promoter; b. Des Moines, May 27, 1929; s. John and Elizabeth (Bates) C.; m. Jane Sage Fuller, Aug. 23, 1952; children: Tessa Sage Flores, John, Jane Sage, Charles Fuller. Grad., Phillips Exeter Acad., 1947; AB, Harvard U., 1951; LittD (hon.), Simpson Coll., 1965. With Cowles Media Co. (formerly Mpls. Star and Tribune Co.), 1953-83, v.p., 1957-68, editor, 1961-69, pres., 1968-73, 79-83, editorial chmn., 1969-73, chmn., 1973-79, dir., 1956-84; pres. Harper's Mag., Inc., 1965-68, chmn. bd., 1968-72; dir. Harper & Row, Pubs., Inc., N.Y.C., 1965-81, chmn., 1968-79. Dir. Des Moines Register & Tribune Co., 1960-84, Farmers & Mechanics Savs. Bank, Mpls., 1960-65, Cowles Comms., Inc., N.Y.C., 1960-65, Equitable Life Ins. Co. Iowa, Des Moines, 1964-66, 1st Bank Systems, Inc., Mpls., 1964-68, A.P., N.Y.C., 1966-75, Midwest Radio-TV, Inc., Mpls., 1967-76; fitness instr. Sweatshop Fitness Ctr., St. Paul, 1989-93; guest artist Bill T. Jones/Arnie Zane & Co., 1990-92; vice chmn. Women's Pro. Softball League LLC, Denver, 1994-2002, chmn. Pro Softball Founders LLC, 2002—; ptnr. St. Anthony Films LLC, 1998—, "Herman USA", 2001; investor Block E Hotel Capital LLC, 2000—. Mem. adv. bd. on Pulitzer Prizes, Columbia U., 1970-83; campaign chmn. Mpls. United Fund, 1967; bd. dirs. Guthrie Theatre Found., 1960-71, pres., 1960-63, chmn., 1964-65, arch. selection com., 2000-01, endowment campaign steering com., 1987-91; trustee Phillips Exeter Acad., 1960-65; bd. dirs. Walker Art Ctr., 1960-69, 87-92, Minn. Civil Liberties Union, 1956-61, Urban Coalition Mpls., 1968-70, Mpls. Found., 1970-75, German Marshall Fund U.S., 1975-78; bd. dirs. Am. Newspaper Pubs. Assn., 1975-77, mem. govt. affairs com., 1976-79. Served to 2d lt. AUS, 1951-53. Named one of Ten Outstanding Men of Yr. U.S. Jr. C. of C., 1964. Mem. Greater Mpls. C. of C. (dir. 1978-81, chmn. stadium site task force 1977-82). Clubs: Minneapolis (Mpls.). Office: 123 N 3rd St Ste 804 Minneapolis MN 55401-1668

COWLES, LOIS ANNE FORT, retired social worker; b. Providence, Dec. 26, 1933; d. Charles M. and Rebecca Parker (Latham) Fort. AB in Philosophy, Ind. U., 1955, MA in Sociology, 1964; MSW, Ind. U., Indpls., 1966; PhD, U. Wis., 1990. Social worker Meth. Hosp., Indpls., 1963-67, Community Svc. Coun., Indpls., 1967-69, Indpls. Pub. Schs., 1969-74, Middleton (Wis.) Pub. Schs., 1974-75; rsch. asst. Wis. HHS, Madison, 1976-77, 80-81; rsch. assoc. U. Wis., 1981-83, tchg. asst., 1983; ind. rschr., 1983-89; asst. prof. social work Ind. State U., Terre Haute, 1989-93; assoc. prof. social work Idaho State U., Pocatello, 1993—2003; ret., 2003. Author: Social Work in the Health Field: A Care Perspective, 2000, 2d edit., 2003; contbr. articles to profl. jours., poetry to anthologies. Mem. NASW, ACSW, Am. Pub. Health Assn., Coun. on Social Work Edn., Soc. Social Work Leadership in Health Care, Phi Kappa Phi. Home: 2921 E Southport Rd Indianapolis IN 46227 E-mail: cowllois@isu.edu.

COWLES, ROGER E. computer consultant; b. Boston, Feb. 9, 1950; s. S. Edwin C. and Irene M. Woodard. BA in Internat. Econs. with honors, Ohio Wesleyan U., 1974. Network cons. LAN Sys., Inc., N.Y.C., 1988-91, Network Alternatives, Inc., Washington, 1991-92, dir. network syss. Quad Microsystems, Inc., Southampton, Pa., 1992-93; network cons. Integrated Microcomputer Syss., Inc., Rockville, Md., 1993-95; sys. cons. Emtec, Inc., Mt. Laurel, N.J., 1995—; prin., owner DINET Corp., 1998—. Cons. World Bank, Washington, 1992, Judge Tech. Svcs., Bala Cynwyd, Pa., 1997; sr. cons. Chem. Bank, N.Y.C., 1995-96; sr. network cons. Arco Chem. Co., 1998—; founder Transcend Media Corp., 1998, Agora Devel. Corp., 1998. Mem. IEEE, Assn. Sys. Mgmt. Avocations: reading, politics, economics, sports, travel. Home: 2101 Chestnut St Philadelphia PA 19103-3108 E-mail: rcowles@sprintmail.com.

COWLES, RONALD EUGENE, church administrator; b. Ottumwa, Iowa, Jan. 30, 1941; s. Fred Howard and Bertha Ilela (Sammons) C.; m. Rowena Rae Miller, Apr. 30, 1959; children: Richard Eric, David Allen, Rebecca Ruth. BA, Ottawa (Kans.) U., 1963; BD, MDiv, Ctrl. Bapt. Theol. Sem., Kansas City, Kans., 1966; D of Ministry, U. Bibl. Studies, 1991. Pastor Dry Ridge Bapt. Ch., Uniontown, Kans., 1961-63, First Bapt. Ch., Easton, Kans., 1963-66, Renwick (Iowa)-Corwith Parish, 1966-72, First Bapt. Ch., Pella, Iowa, 1972-86; assoc. exec. min. S.D. Bapt. Conv., Sioux Falls, 1986-91; exec. min. Am. Bapt. Chs. Dakotas, Sioux Falls, 1991—. Bd. trustees Sioux Falls Coll., Ctrl. Bapt. Theol. Sem., Kansas City. Mem. Lions (pres. 1971), Rotary (bd. dirs. 1980-82). Baptist. Avocations: fishing, hunting, photography, canoe camping. Office: Am Bapt Chs 1524 S Summit Ave Sioux Falls SD 57105-1632

COWLES, WALTER CURTIS, naval architect; b. Chgo., Aug. 25, 1919; s. Harry Samuel and Blanche Lee (Gates) C.; m. Betty Ann McDuff, July 28, 1945; children: Mark Allan, Garry Stephen, Kent Edward, Joy Elizabeth. BS in Engring., U. Mich., 1942. Draftsman Am. Ship Bldg. Co., Cleve., 1942-51, chief hull draftsman, 1951-57, naval architect, 1951-63; marine designer Esso/Exxon, N.Y.C. and Morristown, N.J., 1963-84; ret., 1984. Contbr. paper to Transactions of Soc. Naval Architects and Marine Engrs., 1980; coord. publ. of centennial hist. vol., 1993; pub. Antrim Steamers A Brief History of Steam Navigation on the Inland Lakes of Antrim County Michigan, 1997. Mem. Soc. Naval Architects (life), U.S. Naval Inst. (life), Am. Soc. Naval Engrs. Home: 710 N Bridge St PO Box 283 Bellaire MI 49615

COWLES, WILLIAM STACEY, newspaper publisher; b. Spokane, Wash., Aug. 31, 1960; s. William Hutchinson 3rd and Allison Stacey C.; m. Anne Cannon, June 24, 1989. BA in Econs., Yale Coll., 1982; MBA in Fin., Columbia U., 1986. With The Spokesman Rev., Spokane, Wash., 1989—, pres., pub., 1992—. Office: Cowles Publishing Co PO Box 2160 Spokane WA 99210-2160

COWLEY, GERALD DEAN, architect; b. Great Bend, Kans., Oct. 2, 1931; s. Stone Oden and Elizabeth (Lillich) C.; m. Lois Ester Traudt, Aug. 10, 1957 (div. 1983); children: Tara Elizabeth, Craig Stone; m. Frances Leach, Dec. 28, 1986. BArch, Kans. State U., 1960. Lic. architect, Colo. Architect James H. Johnson Architect, Lakewood, Colo., 1963-74, James H. Johnson & Assocs. Architects, Lakewood, 1963-74; architect, ptnr., prin. Johnson Hopson & Ptnrs., Denver, 1974-82, JHP Architecture Interior Design and Planning, Denver, 1982—. Prin. works include Rocky Mountain Energy Headquarters Bldg., others. Sgt. USAF, 1951-55. Mem.: AIA, Constrn. Specifications Inst. Republican. Avocations: golf, sailing, skiing, watercolor. Home and Office: JHP Architecture 645 E Ylae Pl Englewood CO 80110

COWLEY, JOHN MAXWELL, physics educator; b. Peterborough, South Australia, Feb. 18, 1923; came to U.S., 1970; s. Alfred Ernest and Doris (Milway) C.; m. Roberta Joan Beckett, Dec. 15, 1951; children: Deborah Suzanne, Jillian Patricia. BS, U. Adelaide, Australia, 1942, MS, 1945, DSc, 1957; PhD, Mass. Inst. Tech., 1949. Research officer Commonwealth Sci. and Indsl. Research Orgn., Melbourne, Australia, 1945-62, chief research officer, head crystallography sect., 1960-62; prof. physics U. Melbourne, Australia, 1962-70; Galvin prof. physics Ariz. State U., Tempe, 1970-94, Regents' prof., 1988-94, regents prof. emeritus, 1994—. Mem. U.S. Nat. Com. for Crystallography, 1973-78, 84-86. Author: Diffraction Physics, 1975; editor: (with others) Acta Crystallographica, 1971-80; contbr. (with others) articles to profl. jours. Fellow Australian Acad. Sci., Inst. Physics (London), Australian Inst. Physics, Royal Soc. (London), Am. Phys. Soc.; mem. Internat. Union Crystallography (mem. exec. com. 1963-69, chair commn. on electron diffraction 1987-93, Ewald Prize 1987), Am. Inst. Physics, Am. Crystallographic Assn., Electron Microscope Soc. Am. (dir. 1971-75). Home: 2625 E Southern Ave Unit C90 Tempe AZ 85282 Office: Ariz State U Dept Physics & Astronomy Tempe AZ 85287 E-mail: cowleyj@asu.edu.

COWLEY, JOSEPH GILBERT, writer; b. Yonkers, N.Y., Oct. 9, 1923; s. Joseph Gilbert and Gertrude Hersey Cowley; m. Ruth Muriel Wilson, Feb. 28, 1948; children: Barbara, Charles, Jennifer, Joseph. BA with honors, Columbia U., 1947, MA, 1948. Ptnr. Writing-Editing Svcs., N.Y.C., 1946-47; instr. English, Cornell U., Ithaca, N.Y., 1948-49; salesman Allyn & Bacon, N.Y.C., 1949-54; sales promoter Home Life Ins. Co., N.Y.C., 1954-56; editor, then mng. editor Rsch. Inst. Am., N.Y.C., 1956-82; ret., 1982. Author: The Executive Strategist, 1969, The Chrysanthemum Garden, 1981, The Stargazers, 1991, Dust Be My Destiny, 1999, Home by Seven, 2000, The House on Huntington Hill, 2000, The Night Billy Was Born and Other Love Stories, 2002. 2nd lt. USAAF, 1943-45, ETO. Avocation: reading. Home: 69430 Main Rd Greenport NY 11944-2801 E-mail: jgcowley@suffolk.lib.ny.us.

COWLEY, ROBERT WILLIAM, editor, writer, lecturer; b. NYC, Dec. 16, 1934; s. Malcolm and Muriel (Maurer) C.; m. Blair Phillips (div.); children: Elizabeth Blair Roberts, Miranda Phillips Heller; m. Edith Pray Lorillard, June 24, 1978; children: Olivia Lorillard, Savannah Caroline Lorillard. AB, Harvard U., 1956. Assoc. editor Am. Heritage, N.Y.C., 1956-64; mng. editor Sky, N.Y.C., 1964; asst. editor The Reporter, N.Y.C., 1965-66; assoc. editor, mng. editor Horizon, N.Y.C., 1966-72; co-editor The Saturday Review of the Arts, N.Y.C. and San Francisco, 1972-73; sr. editor, exec. editor Houghton Mifflin, Boston, 1973-77; sr. editor Random House, N.Y.C., 1977-84, Henry Holt, N.Y.C., 1984-88; founding editor, editor-in-chief MHQ: The Quarterly Jour. of Military History, N.Y.C., 1988-98; cons., writer, 1998—2003. Author: The Rulers of Britain, 1982; editor, introducer, contbr.: Experience of War, 1992, The Great War, 2003; co-editor: (with Malcolm Cowley) Fitzgerald and the Jazz Age, 1966; (with Geoffrey Parker) The Reader's Companion to Military History, 1996; (with Thomas Guinzburg) West Point: Two Centuries of Honor and Tradition, 2002; contbg. author: A Weekend with the Great War: Proceedings of the Fourth Annual Great War Inter-Conf. Sem., 1997, To the Best of My Ability: The American Presidents, 2000, editor, contbr. What If?: The World's Foremost Military Historians Imagine What Might Have Been, 1999; editor, introducer No End Save Victory, 2001, With My Face to the Enemy, 2001, What If? 2, 2001. Fellow Soc. Am. Historians; mem. Soc. Mil. History. Democrat. Episcopalian. Avocations: jazz collecting, military archaeology. Home: PO Box 268 Sherman CT 06784-0268 Office: Am Hist Publications 37 W 39th St New York NY 10018-3886 E-mail: cowleyrw219@aol.com.

COWLISHAW, MARY LOU, government educator; b. Rockford, Ill., Feb. 20, 1932; d. Donald George and Mildred Corinne (Hayes) Miller; m. Wayne Arnold Cowlishaw, July 24, 1954; children: Beth Cowlishaw McDaniel, John, Paula Cowlishaw Rader. BS in Journalism, U. Ill., 1954; DHL, North Ctrl. Coll., 1999; DHL (hon.), Benedictine U., 2000. Mem. editorial staff Naperville (Ill.) Sun newspaper, 1977-83; mem. Ill. Ho. of Reps., Springfield, 1983—2003, chmn. elem. and secondary edn. com., 1995—97, vice-chmn. pub. utilities com., 1995—2003, mem. joint Ho.-Senate edn. reform oversight com., 1985—97; assoc. Ctr. for Govtl. Studies No. Ill. U., 2003—; adj. prof. North Ctrl. Coll., Naperville, Ill., 2003—. Mem. Ill. Task Force on Sch. Fin., 1990-96; vice chmn. Ho. Rep. Campaign Com., 1990—; co-chair Ho. Rep. Policy Com., 1991-2003; chmn. edn. com. Nat. Conf. State Legislatures, 1993-97; mem. Joint Com. Adminstrv. Rules, 1992-2003; commr. Edn. Commn. of the States, 1995-2002; chair, Ill. Women's Agenda Task Force, 1994—; mem. Nat. Edn. Goals Panel, 1996—, bd. govs. Lincoln Series for Excellence in Pub. Svc., 1996—. Author: This Band's Been Here Quite a Spell, 1983; columnist Ill. Press Assn., 2003—. Mem. Naperville Dist. 203 Bd. Edn., 1972-83; co-chmn. Ill. Citizens Coun. on Sch. Problems, Springfield, 1985-2003. Recipient 1st pl. award Ill. Press Assn., 1981, commendation Naperville Jaycees, 1986, Golden Apple award Ill. Assn. Sch. Bds., 1988, 90, 92, 94, Outstanding Women Leaders of DuPage County award West Suburban YWCA, 1990, Activator award Ill. Farm Bur., 1996, 1998, Bd. of Dirs. award Little Friends, Inc., 1998, Honor award Ill. Math. and Sci. Acad., 2002, Pub. Svc. award West Suburban Higher Edn. Consortium, 2002; named Best Legislator, Ill. Citizens for Better Care, 1985, Woman of Yr., Naperville AAUW, 1987, Best Legislator, Ill. Assn. Fire Chiefs, 1994, Outstanding Edn. Advc. Indian Prairie Sch. Dist. 204, 1994, Legislator of Yr., Ill. Assn. Pk. Dists., 1995; commr. Edn. Commn. of the States, 1994-2002; Mary Lou Cowlishaw Elem. Sch. named in her honor, 1997, Legislator of Yr., Ill. Assn. Mus., 1998. Mem. Am. Legis. Exch. Coun., Conf. Women Legislators, Nat. Fedn. Rep. Women, DAR, Naperville Rep. Women's Club (pres. 1994—), Jr. League of Greater DuKane (cmty. adv. bd. 1997—). Methodist. Avocation: the violin. Home: 924 Merrimac Cir Naperville IL 60540-7107 Office: North Central Coll 30 N Brainard St Naperville IL 60540-4690

COWLISHAW, MICHAEL FREDERIC, electronic engineer; b. Bath, Eng., Aug. 27, 1953; s. Mervyn George and Hilda Antonia Elizabeth (Gil) B.; m. Kittredge Cary, Dec. 31, 1982; 1 child, Mark. BSc in Electronic Engring., U. Birmingham, Eng., 1974. Chartered engr., U.K. Electronic engr. IBM U.K., Hursley, 1974-81; scientist IBM U.K. Sci. Centre, Winchester, 1982-85; programmer IBM U.K., Hursley, 1986-89, IBM Fellow, 1990—. Cons. Oxford (Eng.) English Dictionary, 1987—; vis. prof. U. Warwick, 1999—. Author: The Rexx Language, 1985, 90, The NetRexx Language, 1997. Fellow Instn. Elec. Engrs., Brit. Computer Soc., Royal Acad. Engring. Achievements include patents for color display apparatus and decimal encoding. Avocations: hiking, programming, curiosity, caving, potholing. Office: IBM UK Ltd PO Box 31 Birmingham Rd Warwick CV34 5JL England E-mail: mfc@uk.ibm.com.

COWPERTHWAIT, LINDLEY MURRAY, lawyer; b. Abington, Pa., Mar. 13, 1933; s. Lindley Murray Cowperthwait and Ruth Bronde Nicholas; m. Suzanne Dewees, Nov. 26, 1955 (div. July 1976); children: Murray, Mary Ruth, Edward, Linda, Tom, Suzanne; m. Karin Schmid Cowperthwait, Apr. 1, 1989. BA, Calif. State U., 1957; LLB, U. Pa., 1960, JD, 1970. Assoc. Wisler, Pearlstine, Talone Craig & Garrity, Norristown, Pa., 1960-68, ptnr., 1968-80; pvt. practice Norristown, 1980-96; of counsel High, Swartz, Roberts & Seidel, LLP, Norristown, 1997—. Prodr., author, dir. (video) Medicine for Lawyers, 1980-93; author: Damages-Delay and Punitive 1999, 2000, 2001, Scrivener Med-Leg Code of Ethics, 1960, 75, 94, 2001. Bd. dirs. ARC, Norristown, 1993-95, Big Bros./Big Sisters, Norristown, 1985-92. Recipient Citizenship award Big Bros./Big Sisters, 1992. Mem. Pa. Trial Lawyers Assn. (pres. 1974-75), Montgomery County Trial Lawyers (founder, sec. 1965-74), Assn. Trial Lawyers of Am., Pa. Bar Assn., Pa. Soc. Republican. Episcopalian. Avocation: sailing. Office: High Swartz Roberts & Seidel LLP 40 E Airy St Norristown PA 19401-4803

COWSER, DANNY LEE, lawyer, mental health specialist; b. Peoria, Ill., July 7, 1948; s. Albert Paul Cowser and Shirley Mae (Donaldson) Chatten; m. Nancy Lynn Hatch, Nov. 11, 1976; children: Kimberly Catherine Hatch Cowser, Dustin Paul Hatch Cowser. BA, No. Ill. U., 1972, MS, 1975; JD, DePaul U., 1980. Bar: Ill. 1980, Wis. 1981, U.S. Dist. Ct. (no. dist.) Ill. 1981, U.S. Ct. Appeals (7th cir.) 1983, U.S. Dist. Ct. (ea. and we. dists.) Wis. 1984, U.S. Supreme Ct. 1984, Ariz. 1985, U.S. Ct. Appeals (9th cir.) 1987, U.S. Dist. Ct. Ariz. 1989, U.S. Tax Ct. 1990, U.S. Ct. Claims 1990, Colo. 2000. Adminstr. Ill. Dept. Mental Health, Elgin, 1972-76, psychotherapist, 1976-79; assoc. Slaby, Deda & Henderson, Phillips, Wis., 1982-83; ptnr. Slaby, Deda & Cowser, Phillips, 1983-86; asst. atty. City of Flagstaff, Ariz., 1986-88; pub. defender Coconino County, Flagstaff, 1988-89; pvt. practice Flagstaff, 1989-97. Atty. City Park Falls, Wis., 1982-86; spl. dep. Mohave County capital def., 1989-90; instr. speech comms. No. Ariz. U., 1992-93; adminstrv. law judge Ariz. Dept. Econ. Security, 1997—. Bd. dirs. DeKalb County (Ill.) Drug Coun., 1973-75, Counseling and Personal Devel., Phillips, 1985-86, Northland YM-WYCA, 1990-91. Reginald Heber Smith fellow, 1980-81, C.J.S. legal scholar, 1979. Mem. NRA, Nat. Assn. Criminal Def. Lawyers, Ariz. Bar Assn., State Bar Ariz. (cert. specialist in criminal law 1993-98), State Bar Wis., Nat. Assn. of Criminal Def. Lawyers. Democrat. Avocations: skiing, photography, bicycling. Office: PO Box 22329 Flagstaff AZ 86002-2329

COX, ALBERT EDWARD, retired pastor; b. Turtle Creek, Pa., Oct. 30, 1935; s. Albert Earl and Naomi (Page) C.; m. Ruth Lynne Gray, July 5, 1958; children: Lynne Ellen Cox Chenot, Lisa Diane Shutt. BS, Houghton, 1957; BS in Mission, St. Paul Bible, 1958. Ordained to ministry Christian and Missionary Alliance, 1966 and in United Meth. Ch., as deacon, 1971, as elder, 1983. Pastor C&MA, Pa., 1963-68, Ctrl. Pa. Conf. United Meth. Ch., 1968-99; ret., 1999. Republican. Home: Williamsport, Pa. Died Feb. 26, 2003.

COX, ALBERT HARRINGTON, JR., economist; b. St. Louis, Oct. 13, 1932; s. Albert Harrington and Hildegarde (Raab) C.; m. Frances Marie French, Apr. 12, 1960; children: Cynthia, Bruce Harrington. BBA, U. Tex., 1954, MBA, 1956; PhD, U. Mich., 1965. Asst. prof. finance So. Meth. U., Dallas, 1959; economist First Nat. City Bank, N.Y.C., 1960-61; sec. research com. Am. Bankers Assn., N.Y.C., 1962-64; v.p., economist First Nat. Bank, Dallas, 1965-68; spl. asst. to chmn. Pres.'s Council Econ. Advs., Washington, 1969-70; exec. v.p., chief economist, dir. Lionel D. Edie & Co., N.Y.C., 1970-75; sr. econ. adv. Merrill Lynch, Pierce, Fenner & Smith, Inc., N.Y.C., 1970-75; pres. Merrill Lynch Econs., Inc., N.Y.C., 1976-81, chmn., 1982-84; chief economist Merrill Lynch & Co., 1976-81. Mng. dir. Merrill Lynch Capital Markets Group; dir. Merrill Lynch Capital Fund; mem. econ. adv. bd. Dept. Commerce, 1974-76; dir., sr. econ. adviser BIL Trainer, Wortham Inc. (Bank in Liechtenstein, A.G.), 1985-90; sr. econ. adviser Trainer Wortham, Inc., 1991; portfolio cons. The Seibels Bruce Ins. Cos., Columbia, S.C., 1993-94, dir., 1994-97; chief economist Danzell Investment Mgmt., Inc., Hilton Head, S.C., 1999—; mem. Pres.'s Inflation Policy Task Force, 1980; disting. lectr. in bus. and econs. U. S.C., Hilton Head, 1988-90. Author: Regulation of Interest Rates on Bank Deposits, 1966; contbg. economist Coast Business, 1997-99, Bankers Monthly mag., 1970-88; bus. columnist Hilton Head News, 1990-98; contbr. articles to profl. jours. Mem. Nat. Assn. Bus. Economists (past dir.), Securities Industries Assn. (chmn. econ. adv. com. 1979-80), Am. Econ. Assn., Beta Gamma Sigma, Beta Theta Pi, Phi Eta Sigma. Republican. Mem. Reformed Ch. Home: 2002 Claudette Cv Biloxi MS 39531-2426 E-mail: acox@iopener.net.

COX, ALBERT REGINALD, academic administrator, physician, retired; b. Victoria, B.C., Can., Apr. 18, 1928; s. Reginald Herbert and Marie Christina (Fraser) C.; m. Margaret Dobson, May, 1954; children: Susan Margaret, David John, Steven Fraser. BA, U. B.C., 1950, MD, 1954. Intern Vancouver Gen. Hosp., 1954-55, resident, 1955-59; fellow in cardiology U. Wash., 1959-61; asst. prof. medicine U. B.C., 1962-65, assoc. prof., 1966-69; prof., chmn. medicine Meml. U., St. John's, Nfld., Can., 1969-74, dean medicine, 1974-87, v.p. Health Scis. and Profl. Sch., 1988-90, v.p. acad., pro-vice chancellor, 1990-91; ret., 1991. Decorated mem. Order of Can. Fellow ACP, Royal Coll. Physicians and Surgeons Can., Am. Coll. Cardiology; mem. Nfld. Med. Assn., Can. Med. Assn., Can. Soc. Clin. Investigation, Assn. Can. Med. Colls. (pres. 1980-81), Coun. of Royal Coll. Physicians and Surgeons (v.p. medicine 1990-91), Alpha Omega Alpha. United Ch. Home: 1275 Campbell Rd Cobble Hill BC Canada V0R 1L0

COX, ALLAN JAMES, management consultant; b. Berwyn, Ill., June 13, 1937; s. Brack C. and Ruby D. C.; m. Jeanne Begalke, 1961 (div. 1966); 1 child, Heather; m. Bonnie Lynne Welden, 1966 (div. 1990); 1 child, Laura; m. Cheryl Patric, 1991. BA, No. Ill. U., 1961, MA, 1962; postgrad., McCormick Theol. Sem., Chgo., 1962-63, Alfred Adler Inst. of Chgo., 1965-67, Gestalt Inst. of Chgo., 1994-96. Instr. Wheaton (Ill.) Coll., 1963-65; assoc. Case and Co., Inc., Chgo., 1965-66, Spencer Stuart & Assos., Inc., Chgo., 1966-68; v.p. Westcott Assos., Inc., Chgo., 1968-69; founder, pres. Allan Cox & Assocs., Inc., 1969—; chmn. Berryman Comm. Co., Chgo., 1994-98; chmn. of the bd. Amateur Baseball, Inc., Chgo., 1992-96, CEO, 1996-98; chmn., CEO Assn. for Internat. Youth Sports, Inc., Chgo., 1998-99. Adj. staff Ctr. for Creative Leadership, Greensboro, N.C., 1985-90; mem. vis. com. U. Chgo. Div. Sch.; chancellor's associate Univ. Calif., San Diego. Author: Confessions of a Corporate Headhunter, 1973, Work, Love and Friendship, 1974, The Cox Report on the American Corporation, 1982, The Making of the Achiever, 1985, The Achiever's Profile, 1988, Straight Talk for Monday Morning, 1990, Redefining Corporate Soul: Linking Purpose and People, 1996; columnist L.A. Times Syndicate, 1986-90; contbr. articles to profl. jours. Chmn. bd. Ctr. for Ethics and Corp. Policy, 1987-92; Elder Fourth Presbyn. Ch. of Chgo. Mem. Am. Sociol. Assn., N.Am. Soc. Adlerian Psychology, Midwest Human Resources Planners Group, Human Resources Planning Soc., Chgo. Club, Alpha Kappa Delta. Presbyterian. Office: 45 East Bellevue Pl Chicago IL 60611-1133 E-mail: allan@allancox.com.

COX, AMIE C. publisher; b. 1956; BA, Auburn U., 1979; MA, U. West Fla., 1981. Editl. intern Nat. Geog. Soc., Washington, 1980; asst. to pub. Hyatt Regency Mag., New Orleans, 1981-82; assoc. editor Scuba Times Mag., Pensacola, Fla., 1982-83; graphic artist Dodson Craddock & Born Advt., Pensacola, 1983-85; mng. editor, art dir. Marlin Mag. of Marlin Internat., Pensacola, 1985-86; owner Pre-Press Svc. for Publs., Pensacola, 1986-87; art dir. Bassmaster Mag., Montgomery, Ala., 1987-89, Dutchess Mag. and Orange Mag. for Dutchess & Orange Counties, N.Y., 1989-92; owner VERSA Publs. and Coxswain Press, Hudson, N.Y., 1992—. Vol. coord. Cmty. Garden Horticulture Classes, Hudson, Environ. Rsch. Projects, Hudson. Recipient Columbia County N.Y. Good Earth Keeping award Environ. Mgmt. Coun. Mem. Sigma Tau Delta, Tau Sigma Delta. Address: 400 Pickens Ave # 119 Pensacola FL 32503-6459

COX, ANNA LEE, retired administrative assistant; b. Knoxville, Tenn., Feb. 18, 1931; d. Carter Calloway and Fairy Belle (Byers) Bayless; m. William Smith Cox, Sept. 4, 1952; 1 child, Catherine Anne Cox Faust. Grad. high sch., Knoxville. Sec. Am. Mut. Liability Ins. Co., Knoxville, 1948-53; flight procedures clk. FAA, Atlanta, 1963-66; legal sec., paralegal U.S. Atty.'s Office for Dist. S.C., Greenville, 1972-79; sec. criminal investigation div. IRS, Knoxville, 1981-84; sec., adminstrv. asst. CIA, Knoxville, 1984-88; adminstrv. asst. U.S. Dept. Def., Knoxville, 1988-91, ret., 1991. Tutor Greenville Literacy Assn., 1977-79; founder, dir. NATO Womens Chorus, Izmir, Turkey, 1969-71; choir dir., pres. United Meth. Women, Stephenson Meml. United Meth. Ch., Greenville, 1972-79; bd. dirs. Fountainhead Conservatory Music, Knoxville, 1983-85, 92-95, sec. of bd. dirs., 1994-95; singer Knoxville Choral Soc., 1955-56, Atlanta Symphony Chorus, 1971, Greenville Civic Chorale, 1973-79; vol. Ch. and Knoxville Mus. Art, 1992—. Republican. Avocations: music, drama. Home: 619 Farragut Commons Dr Knoxville TN 37922-1673 also: 18304 Gulf Blvd Apt 614 Redington Shores FL 33708-1055

COX, ARCHIBALD, JR., investment company executive; b. Wayland, Mass., July 13, 1940; s. Archibald and Phyllis (Ames) C.; children: Suzanne, Archibald III, Christopher. Pres., CEO The First Boston Corp., N.Y.C., 1990-93; chmn. Sextant Group, Inc., N.Y.C., 1993—; pres., CEO Magnequench, Inc., Indpls., 1995—. Bd. dirs. Hutchinson Tech. Inc., Builders Info. Group, Magnequench, Inc. Bd. dirs. Claremont McKenna Coll., 1992-97. Mem.: Harvard Club of Boston, Links Club N.Y.C., NY Yacht Club. Avocations: bicycling, sailing, hiking. Office: c/o Magnequench Inc 9775 Crosspoint Blvd Indianapolis IN 46256 also: Sextant Group Inc PO Box 489 Scotch Plains NJ 07076-0489 E-mail: acox@mqii.com.

COX, ARCHIBALD, lawyer, educator; b. Plainfield, N.J., May 17, 1912; s. Archibald and Frances Bruen (Perkins) C.; m. Phyllis Ames, June 12, 1937; children— Sally, Archibald, Phyllis. AB, Harvard U., 1934, LL.B., 1937, LL.D. (hon.), 1975, Loyola U., Chgo., 1964, U. Cin., 1967, U. Denver, 1974, Amherst Coll., 1974, Rutgers U., 1974, Mich. State U., 1976, Wheaton Coll., 1977, Northeastern U., 1978, Clark U., 1980; L.H.D. (hon.), Hahnemann Med. Coll., 1980, U. Mass., 1981, Georgetown U., 1988. Bar: Mass. 1937. Gen. practice law Ropes, Gray, Best, Coolidge & Rugg, Boston, 1938-41; atty. Office of Solicitor Gen., U.S. Dept. Justice, 1941-43, solicitor gen., 1961-65; assoc. solicitor Dept. Labor, 1943-45; lectr. law Harvard U., 1945-46, prof. law, 1946-61, Williston prof. law, 1965-76, Carl M. Loeb U. prof., 1976-84, prof. emeritus, 1984—; vis. prof. Boston U., 1985-97. Spl. investigator cases Mass. Legislature, 1972; dir. Office Watergate Spl. Prosecution Force, Washington, 1973; Co-chmn. Constrn. Industry Stblzn. Com., 1951-52; chmn. Wage Stablzn. Bd., 1952 Author: Cases on Labor Law, 1948, 12th edit., 1976, 11th edit. (with Derek C. Bok, Robert Gorman and Mathew W. Finkin), 1981, Law and the National Labor Policy, 1960, (with Mark DeWolfe Howe, J.R. Wiggins) Civil Rights, the Constitution and the Courts, 1967, The Warren Court, 1968, The Role of the Supreme Court in American Government, 1976, Freedom of Expression, 1981, The Court and the Constitution, 1987. Mem. bd. overseers Harvard U., 1962-65. Mem. ABA, Am. Acad. Arts and Scis., Common Cause (chmn. 1980-92), Health Effects Inst. (chmn. 1985-2001). Office: Harvard Law School Cambridge MA 02138

COX, BARBARA CLAIRE, costume designer, educator; b. Lock Haven, Pa., Apr. 4, 1939; d. Albert Clair and June Anna (Hutchins) Shultz; m. Richard Joseph Cox, Aug. 28, 1960 (div. 1970). BA, SUNY, Albany, 1961; student, Brandeis U., 1968, Cornell U., 1961-68; MFA, Carnegie-Mellon U., 1970. Mem. faculty Stanford U., Palo Alto, Calif., 1970-73; costume dir. Utah Shakespearean Festival, Cedar City, Utah, 1970-81; costume designer Alley Theatre, Houston, 1973-76; mem. faculty dept. theatre arts Calif. State U., Long Beach, 1976-81; costume designer South Coast Repertory Theatre, Costa Mesa, Calif., 1978-82; mem. faculty dance and theatre arts U. North Tex., Denton, 1988—; costume designer Dallas Shakespeare, 1991, Theatre L'Homme Dieu, 1997, Grand Canyon Shakespeare Festival, 1998. Owner Barbara C. Cox Designs, 1978—. Costume dir. Circle Theatre, Ft. Worth, 1989—. Bd. dirs. Denton Civic Ballet, 1989—, pres., 1998—2002, Music Theatre Denton, 1998—. Recipient Excellence in Costume Design award Los Angeles Drama Critics Circle, 1982, Costume Design awards Drama Logue, Los Angeles, 1982-88, LA Weekly, 1985-88, Excellence in Costume Design award The Column, 2000, 01, 02. Mem. AAUP, AAUW, U.S. Inst. Theatre Tech., Costume Soc. Am., United Scenic Artists. Avocations: reading, gardening, needlework, photography, cats. Home: 716 Thomas St Denton TX 76201-2447 Office: Univ N Tex Dept Dance Theatre Arts Denton TX 76203 E-mail: bcox@unt.edu.

COX, BOBBY (ROBERT JOE COX), professional baseball manager; b. Tulsa, Okla., May 21, 1941; m. Pamela Cox; children: Kami, Keisha, Skyla. Student, Reedley Jr. Coll., Calif. Player Calif. League, Reno, Nev., 1960, Northwest League, Salem, Oreg., 1961-62, Texas League, Albuquerque, 1963-64, Pacific Coast League, Salt Lake City, 1965, Tacoma, Wash., 1966, Internat. League, Richmond, Va., 1967, New York Yankees, N.Y.C., 1968-69, Internat. League, Syracuse, N.Y., 1970, Fla. State League, Ft. Lauderdale, 1971, mgr., 1971, Ea. League, West Haven, Conn., 1972, Internat. League, Syracuse, 1973-76; 1st base coach New York Yankees, N.Y.C., 1977; mgr. Atlanta Braves, 1978-81, Toronto (Ont., Can.) Blue Jays, 1982-85, Atlanta Braves, 1990—. Nat. League Championship Team, 1991-92, 95, World Series Championship Team, 1995. Named Maj. League Mgr. of Yr., Baseball Writers' Assn. Am., 1985, Nat. League Mgr. of Yr., 1991; Maj. League Mgr. of Yr. Sporting News, 1985, Nat. League Mgr. of Yr., 1991, 93. Office: care Atlanta Braves PO Box 4064 Atlanta GA 30302-4064

COX, BUFORD E. music educator; b. Atlanta, Jan. 3, 1956; s. Buford E. Cox, Sr. and Barnelle B. Cox; m. Judith L. Sturgill, Sept. 20, 1980; children: Jonathan, Jeremy, Jordan. BMus, Shorter Coll., Rome, Ga., 1978; MCM, So. Bapt. Theol. Sem., Louisville, 1980; PhD, Auburn U., Ala., 2000. Minister of music and edn. Corinth Bapt. Ch., London, Ky., 1980—82; minister of music and youth Arlington Bapt. Ch., Arlington, Ga., 1982—92; assoc. prof. piano Bapt. Coll. of Fla., Graceville, 1992—; minister of music First Bapt. Ch., Graceville, 2000—. Accompanist Sons of Jubal, Atlanta, 1985—92; clinician Ga. Bapt. Conv., Atlanta, 1985—92; accompanist Fla. Bapt. Conv. Sr. Adult Ministries, Jacksonville, 1992—; clinician Fla. Bapt. Conv., Jacksonville, 2000—. Chmn. Graceville Dixie Youth Baseball League, 1996. Mem.: So. Bapt. Ch. Music Conf., Music Tchrs. Nat. Assn., Am. Choral Dirs. Assn. (life), Optimist (program chmn. 1997—98), Pi Kappa Lambda, Phi Kappa Phi. Baptist. Avocation: gardening. Home: 1084 12th Ave Graceville FL 32440 Office: Baptist College of Florida 5400 College Dr Graceville FL 32440 Office Fax: 850-263-7506. Personal E-mail: bjcox@bellsouth.net. Business E-Mail: becox@baptistcollege.edu.

COX, CAROLE BETH, social worker, educator; b. L.A. d. Morris and Esther Bebe Abramson; m. Colin Roy Cox; children: Amanda, Susannah. BA, U. Calif., Berkeley; Diploma Social Adminstrn., London Sch. Econs., 1967; MSW, Va. Commonwealth U., 1975; PhD, U. Md., 1980. Rsch. asst. Addiction Rsch. Found., Toronto, Canada, 1969—71; tech. officer WHO, Geneva, 1972—73; cmty. health educator Md. State Dept. Health, Balt., 1976—77; asst. prof. San Jose State U., Calif., 1980—86; asst. to assoc. prof. Cath. U. Am., Washington, 1987—97; prof. Fordham U., N.Y.C., 1997—. Cons. Alzheimers Assn., Chgo., 1995—2000, Nat. Acad. on Aging, Washington, 1995, Nat. Coun. on Aging, Washington, 1994—95, Am. Assn. Ret. Persons, Washington, 1986—90. Author: (book) Home Care: An International Perspective, 1991, The Frail Elderly: Problems, Needs, Community Resources, 1993, Ethnicity and Social Work Practice, 1998, Empowerment Training for Custodial Grandparents, 2000; editor: To Grandmother's House We Go to Stay: A Perspective on Custodial Grandparents, 2000; contbr. Mem. pub. policy bd. Citizens Com. on Aging, N.Y.C., 1999—2001; commr. Commn. on Aging, Howard County, Md., 1989—95; bd. dirs. KinCare Task Force, N.Y.C., 1999—; adv. bd. Coun. on Aging, Santa Clara County, 1983—84. Postdoctoral fellow, NIMH, 1984—85, Mental Health fellow, 1978—79, Resident scholar, Nat. Inst. Social Work, London, 1995. Mem.: NASW, Am. Soc. on Aging, Gerontol. Soc. Am. Avocations: theater, painting, yoga, running. Office: Fordham Univ 113 W 60th St New York NY 10023

COX, CATHY, state official; b. Bainbridge, Ga. A.Agr., Abraham Baldwin Agrl. Coll., 1978; BJ summa cum laude, U. Ga., 1980; JD magna cum laude, Mercer U., 1986. Newspaper reporter The Times, Gainesville, 1980-82, Post-Searchlight, Bainbridge, 1982-83; atty. Hansell & Post, Atlanta, 1986-88, Lambert, Floyd & Conger, Bainbridge, Ga., 1988-95; mem. Dist. 160 Ga. Gen. Assembly, 1993-96; asst. sec. of state State of Ga., Atlanta, 1996-98, sec. of state, 1999—. Editor Mercer U. Law Rev. Named Conservation Legislator of the Yr., Ga. Wildlife Fedn., 1994, Woman of Courage award Woman's Policy Group, 1995, Woman of Yr., Ga. Commn. on Women, 2000. Democrat. Methodist. Office: Office of Sec of State 214 State Capitol SW Atlanta GA 30334-1600 E-mail: sosweb@sos.state.ga.us.*

COX, CHAPMAN BEECHER, lawyer, corporate executive; b. Dayton, Ohio, July 31, 1940; s. Charles Benjamin and Jewel Lorene (Nicholson) C.; m. Jeannette Gail Korody, Aug. 28, 1964; children: Charles Benjamin, Andrew David. BA, U. So. Calif., 1962; JD, Harvard U., 1965. Bar: Calif. 1966, Colo. 1972, U.S. Ct. Mil. Appeals 1966, U.S. Supreme Ct. 1986. Assoc. Adams, Duque & Hazeltine, Los Angeles, 1968-72, Sherman & Howard, Denver, 1972-74, ptnr., 1974-80, mng. ptnr., 1980-81, ptnr., 1987-90; dep. asst. sec. U.S. Dept. Navy, Washington, 1981-83, asst. sec., 1983-84; gen. counsel Dept. Def., Washington, 1984-85, asst. sec., 1985-87; pres., CEO United Svc. Orgns., Inc., 1990-96; sr. v.p. Lockheed Martin IMS, 1996-2000; ret., 2000. Vis. lectr. U. Colo. Sch. Law, Boulder, 1977-78; mem. def. policy bd. U.S. Dept. Def., 1988-90; mem. comml. space transp. adv. com. U.S. Dept. Transp., 1989-91; chmn. Colo. Commn. Space Sci. and Industry, 1988-90. Gen. counsel Colo. Reps., Denver, 1977-81; del. U.S. Dept. State cultural exch. mission to Syria and Jordan, 1979; ruling elder Presbyn. Ch., 1976—; bd. dirs. United Svc. Orgns., 1985-96, Colorado Springs Symphony Orch., 1988-90, MicroLithics Corp., 1989-91, Presbyn. Ch. U.S.A. Found., 1990-99, Freedoms Found., 1994-99, Fund for Am. Studies, 1995—, New Covenant Trust Co., 1996-99, Presbyn. Lay Com., 1997-2000, Alliance Def. Fund, 2002—, Lions Svcs. Inc., 2003-; bd. govs. Army-Navy Club Washington, 1998-2000. Col. USMCR, 1962-93, ret. Fellow: Am. Coll. Trust and Estate Counsel; mem.: ABA (standing com. law and nat. security 1988—2002), Colo. Bar Assn. (bd. govs. 1977—79, chmn. probate and trust law sect. 1978—79), Calif. Bar Assn., Army-Navy Club of Washington. E-mail: chapmancox@att.net.

COX, CHARLES SHIPLEY, oceanography researcher, educator; b. Paia, Hawaii, Sept. 11, 1922; s. Joel Bean and Helen Clifford (Horton) C.; m. Maryruth Louise Melander, Dec. 23, 1951; children: Susan (dec.), Caroline, Valerie, Ginger, Joel. BS, Calif. Inst. Tech., 1944; PhD, U. Calif., San Diego, 1955. From asst. rschr. to prof. U. Calif., San Diego, 1955—. Rschr. in field. Fellow AAAS, NAS (Alexander Agassiz medal 2001), Am. Geophys. Union (Maurice Ewing medal 1992), Royal Astron. Soc. Democrat. Office: U Calif San Diego Scripps Inst Oceanography La Jolla CA 92093-0213 E-mail: cscox@ucsd.edu.

COX, CHRISTOPHER (CHARLES COX), congressman; b. St. Paul, Oct. 16, 1952; s. Charles C. and Marilyn A. (Miller) C.; m. Rebecca Gernhardt; children: Charles, Kathryn, Kevin. BA, U. So. Calif., 1973; MBA, JD, Harvard U., 1977. Bar: Calif. 1978, D.C. 1980. Law clk. to judge U.S. Ct. Appeals (9th cir.), 1977-78; assoc. Latham & Watkins, Newport Beach, Calif., 1978-82; lectr. bus. adminstrn. Harvard U., 1982-83; ptnr. Latham & Watkins, Newport Beach, Calif., 1984-86; sr. assoc. counsel to the Pres. The White House, Washington, 1986-88; mem. U.S. Congresses from 48th dist. Calif. (formerly 47th), Washington, 1989—; mem. energy and commerce com., steering com.; mem. fin. svcs. com.; chmn. house policy com., homeland sec. com.; mem. Bipartisan Commn. on Entitlement and Tax Reform, Washington, 1994—. Prin., founder Context Corp., St. Paul, 1984-88. Editor Harvard Law Rev., 1975-77. Republican. Roman Catholic. Office: US Ho Reps 2402 Rayburn Ho Office Bldg Washington DC 20515 also: 1 Newport Place Dr Ste 420 Newport Beach CA 92660-2412*

COX, CLAIR EDWARD, II, urologist, medical educator; b. Lawrenceville, Ill., Sept. 2, 1933; s. Clair Edward and May E. (Judy) C.; m. Clarice Wicks, Aug. 23, 1958; children— Clair Edward III, Daniel Paul, Kevin Christopher, Kenneth Harold. Student, U. Mich., 1951-54, MD, 1958. Diplomate Am. Bd. Urology. Intern U. Colo. Med. Center, Denver, 1958-59, surg. resident, 1959-60; resident urology U. Cal. Med. Center at San Francisco, 1960-63; mem. faculty Bowman Gray Sch. Medicine, Wake Forest U., Winston Salem, N.C., 1963-72, assoc. prof., 1967-70, prof. urology, 1970-72; prof., chmn. dept. urology U. Tenn. Med. Sch., Memphis, 1972—. Contbr. profl. jours. Fellow ACS; mem. AMA, Am. Assn. Genito-Urinary Surgeons, Am. Urol. Assn., Internat. Soc. Urology, N.Y. Acad. Scis., Infectious Disease Soc. Am., Soc. Univ. Urologists, Am. Assn. Med. Colls., Am. Soc. Microbiology. Achievements include research in urinary tract infectious disease. Home: 6011 Sweetbriar Cv Memphis TN 38120-2514

COX, CLIFFORD LAIRD, retired academic administrator; b. New Kensington, Pa., Jan. 30, 1935; s. James Howard and Clara Pearl (Alderton) C.; m. Joanne Hill, Aug. 9, 1958; children: Lisa McKay, Bethany Jennings. BS in Music Edn., Indiana U., 1956, MEd, 1958, MusM, 1968; postgrad., SUNY, Buffalo, 1968-79. Tchr. Indiana Pub. Schs., 1956-68; prof. music U. Pa., Edinboro, 1968-82, dean sch. music, 1982-83, assoc. v.p., 1983-86, exec. asst. to pres., 1986—2002; ret., 2002. Chmn. bd. dirs. Nat. Bank NE, Pa., dir. N.E. Bankcorp Univ. Svcs. Inc., Edinboro; musician throughout U.S., 1956—; guest conductor Shandong Provincial Symphony Orch., Jinan, China. Composer: The Cynic (opera), 1956, PSI, 1961. Danforth Found. assoc., St. Louis, 1976; recipient Excellence in Teaching award Commonwealth of Pa., Harrisburg, 1979. Mem. Am. Fedn. Musicians. Republican. Presbyterian. Avocations: reading, aviation. Home: 222 Fairway Dr Edinboro PA 16412-2442

COX, CLIFFORD ERNEST, information systems consulting executive, former school administrator; b. Chgo., Apr. 28, 1942; s. Clifford Ernest and Beulah May (Lynn) C.; m. Scenobia Butler, June 20, 1964; children: Clifford, Fred, Sean. BA, U. Chgo., 1964, MBA, 1966; postgrad., No. Ill. U., 1988—. Cert. in data processing. Sr. systems engr. IBM, Chgo., 1966-69; v.p. MIS Golden Fifty Pharm., Chgo., 1969-71; sr. mgr. Arthur Andersen & Co., Chgo., 1971-79; pres. Cenox Systems, Inc., Chgo., 1979-81, 97—; chief info. officer Chgo. Pub. Schs., 1981-92; deputy supt. Detroit Pub. Schs., 1992-97; pres. Cenox Sys. Am., Cleve., 1998—. Lectr. Keller Grad Sch. Mgmt., 1986-89; del. Ill. Regional White House conf., 1990. Contbr. articles to profl. jours. Bd. dirs. Assn. House, Chgo., 1991; mem. Chgo. Assembly. Office: Cenox Sys 3357 W 85th St Chicago IL 60652 E-mail: cliffcox@cenox.com.

COX, COURTENEY, actress; b. Birmingham, Ala., June 15, 1964; d. Richard Lewis and Courteney (Bass-Copland) C.; m. David Arquette, June 12, 1999. Appearances include (music video) Bruce Springsteen's Dancing in the Dark, 1984; (TV series) Murder, She Wrote, 1984, Misfits of Science, 1985-86, Family Ties, 1987-88, Dream On, 1990, Seinfeld, 1990, The Larry Sanders Show, 1992, The Trouble with Larry, 1993, Friends, 1994—; (TV pilots) Sylvan in Paradise, 1986; (TV movies) If It's Tuesday, It Still Must Be Belgium, 1987, A Rockport Christmas, 1988, Roxanne: The Prize Pulitzer, 1989, Judith Krantz's Till We Meet Again, 1989, Curiosity Kills, 1990, Morton and Hays, 1991, Topper, 1992, Sketch Artist II: Hands That See, 1995; (feature films) Down Twisted, 1986, Masters of the Universe, 1987, Cocoon: The Return, 1988, Mr. Destiny, 1990, Blue Desert, 1990, Shaking the Tree, 1992, The Opposite Sex (and How to Live with Them), 1993, Ace Ventura, Pet Detective, 1994, Scream, 1996, Commandments, 1996, Scream 2, 1997, The Runner, 1999, Alien Love Triangle, 1999, Scream 3, 2000, 3000 Miles to Graceland, 2001. Office: c/o John Fogelman, Gaby Morgerman & Jeff Gorin William Morris Agency One William Morris Place Beverly Hills CA 90212*

COX, CYNTHIA A. art education specialist; b. Cleve., Mar. 29, 1957; d. Jerry L. and Lynn (Hargrove) C. BFA, Kent State U., 1979; MSEd with all honors, Lake Erie Coll., 1996. Cert. visual arts K-12, edn. specialist, Ohio. Art edn. specialist East Cleveland Schs., 1980-86, Kenston Schs., Chagrin Falls, Ohio, 1987—. Instr. profl. devel. grad. program Lake Erie Coll., Painesville, Ohio, 1996, in-svc. spkr. Kenston Schs., Chagrin Falls, Ohio, 1993, East Cleveland Schs., 1981; spkr. U.S. Joint Conf. on Edn., Beijing, 1992; vis. tchr. J.F.K. Schule, Berlin; Am. spkr. 1994 Commemorative Ceremony for Tearing Down Berlin Wall, 1994; apptd. del. leader People to People, Japan, 1999. Author, designer: Building Bridges: An International Approach to the Fine Arts, 1996; author: A Social, Cultural and Political Comparison Study of Children's Art Work from China, Germany, Bosnia and the United States, 1996. Elder Lake Shore Christian Ch., 1986-93. Mem. Ohio Art Edn. Assn., Ohio Edn. Assn., Internat. Assn. Edn. Through Art, Dwight D. Eisenhower Citizen Ambassador Program, Am. Acad. Disting. Students, Internat. Assn. of Asian Studies (presenter conf. 2000). Office: Kenston Schs 9421 Bainbridge Rd Chagrin Falls OH 44023-2703

COX, DAVE, state legislator; b. Fair Oaks, Calif., Feb. 20, 1938; m. Margaret Cox; children: Cathleen, Mary Margaret, Sarah. BA, U. San Diego, 1961; MSA, Golden State U., 1986. Pres. Integrated Benefits and Ins. Svcs.; bd. dirs. Sacramento Mcpl. Utility Dist., 1988—92, Sacramento County Bd. Suprs., 1992—98; mem., dist. 5 Calif. State Assembly, 1998—; mem. Sacramento Transp. Authority, South Placer Policy Com. Bd. dirs. Area Four Agy. Aging Commn. on State Mandates; chair KVIE-Channel 6, 1982; mem. Sacramento Area Coun. Govts., Sacramento Area Flood Control Agy., Sacramento Ballpark Authority, Sacramento Met. Air Quality Mgmt. Dist.; former dist. dir. Sacramento Municipality Utility, Sacramento Pub. Libr. Authority, Sacramento Regional Transit Dist. Former mem. Easter Seals; mem. Sacramento Sports Commn.; sr. warden St. Francis Episcopal Ch., Fair Oaks; bd. dirs. ARC. Mem.: Sacramento C. of C. (former bd. dirs.), Rotary (Sacramento). Republican. Episcopalian. Mailing: PO Box 942849 Rm 3104 Sacramento CA 94249 Office: 4811 Cheppendale Dr Ste 501 Sacramento CA 95841*

COX, DAVID LEON, telecommunications company executive; b. Lima, Ohio, Sept. 8, 1952; s. Leon Hamiln and Mildred Marie (Johnson) C.; m. Carolle Marie Mallette, July 17, 1978; children: Paul David, Elizabeth Christine. BS in Chemistry, Mich. State U., 1975, BS in Computer Sci., 1976; MBA in Telecomms., Parkwood U., London, 2001. Registered profl. engr., Va. 76asst. v.p. engring. KollMorgan Corp., Newburgh, NY, 1975; staff mgr. AT&T, Bedminster, N.J., 1976-79; asst. v.p. Satellite Bus. Systems, McLean, Va., 1979-83; devel. mgr. MCI, Washington, 1983-84; chief engr. Harris Corp., Melbourne, Fla., 1984-95; asst. dir. GTE, Rockville, Md., 1997-2000, dir. Irving, Tex., 1998-2000; exec. dir. engring. Parsons Brinkerhoff, Dallas, 2000; dir. Sprint PCS, Flower Mound, Tex., 2001. Mem. Pres.'s Commn. on Crit. Infrastructure Protection, advisor, 1996—2002 Pres.'s Nat. Security Telecomms. adv. com., cons., 1995-2002; bd. dirs. GTE, Irving, Tex. Contbr. articles to profl. jours. Active Friends of the Palm Bay (Fla.) Libr., Space Coast Sci. Ctr., 1000 Friends of Fla., Tallahassee, Turkey Creek Homeowners Assn., Turkey Creek Santuary Bd., Palm Bay PTA; vice chmn. pub. rels. Boy Scouts of Am., 1991-95, dist. com. mem., 1991-95, unit commr., 1990-95, troop com. mem., 1992-95, park com. mem., 1987-95; mem. Comprehensive Plan Com., Palm Bay, Fla., 1986-87. Mem. IEEE, Am. Chem. Soc., Am. Inst. Plant Engrs., Mensa, Assn. for Computing Machinery, N.Y. Acad. Sci., Nat. Fire Protection Assn., Building Industry Cons. Svc. Internat., Am. Radio Relay League, Nat. Eagle Scout Assn. (life), Nat. Coun. Boy Scouts of Am., Mich. State U. Alumni Assn., Lyman Briggs Coll. Alumni Assn., Mason (3d deg.), Orlando Scottish Rite (32nd deg., Master of Royal Secret), Alpha Phi Omega (Beta Beta chpt.). Republican. Presbyterian. Achievements include 7 patents in integrated svcs. digital network tech., signaling system 7, and surveillance technologies. Home: 5417 Colonial Ct Flower Mound TX 75028-2506 Office: Sprint PCS 2128 Lakeway Terr Flower Mound TX 75028-7526

COX, DAVID JACKSON, biochemistry educator; b. N.Y.C., Dec. 22, 1934; s. Reavis and Rachel (Dunaway) C.; m. Joan M. Narbeth, Sept. 6, 1958 (dec. Oct. 8, 1982); children: Andrew Reavis, Matthew Bruce, Thomas Jackson; m. Tamara L. Compton, Nov. 26, 1983. BA, Wesleyan U., 1956; PhD, U. Pa., 1960. Instr. biochemistry U. Wash., 1960-63; asst. prof. chemistry U. Tex., 1963-67, assoc. prof., 1967-73; prof., head dept. biochemistry Kans. State U., 1973-89; prof. chemistry Ind. U./Purdue U., Ft. Wayne, 1989-2000, prof. emeritus, 2000—. Vis. prof. U. Va., 1970-71; dean arts scis. Ind. U./Purdue U., Ft. Wayne, 1989-96. NSF predoctoral fellow, 1956-59; NSF sr. postdoctoral fellow, 1970-71 Mem. AAAS, Am. Soc. Biol. Chemists, Am. Chem. Soc., Phi Beta Kappa, Sigma Xi. Democrat. Presbyterian. Home: 309 Crown Ln Bellingham WA 98229-5929 E-mail: moody@gte.net.

COX, DAVID R. geneticist, educator; BS Brown U.; MD, PhD Genetics, U. Washington; Res. Fell., U. Calif - San Francisco. Prof. genetics, pediatrics sch. of medicine Stanford U., 1993—; co-dir. Stanford Human Genome Center. Mem.: Inst. Medicine. Office: Stanford U Sch Medicine Dept Genetics M-344 300 Pasteur Dr Stanford CA 94305-5120

COX, DONALD C. economics educator; b. Lawrence, Mass., Jan. 6, 1954; s. Donald C. and Mary T. Cox. BS in Econs., Boston Coll., 1975; MA in Econs., Brown U., 1977, PhD in Econs., 1980. Economist Fed. Res. Bank of N.Y., 1980-81; fellow Hoover Inst./Stanford (Calif.) U., 1984-85; asst. prof. Wash. U., 1981-87; assoc. prof. Boston Coll., 1987-95, prof., 1995—. Presenter confs. in field; cons. The World Bank, 1986—. Contbr. articles to profl. jours., publs.; referee profl. jours. Grantee NIH, 1989-91, 96-2000, NSF, 1986-89, U.S. Wis. Inst. for Rsch. on Poverty, 1986, Dept. Labor, 1979, Instl. Reform and the Informal Sector, 1994, Nat. Coun. for Soviet and E. European Rsch., 1995. Home: 17 Fairview Ter West Newton MA 02465 E-mail: donald.cox@bc.edu.

COX, DONALD CLYDE, electrical engineering educator; b. Lincoln, Nebr., Nov. 22, 1937; s. Elvin Clyde and C. Gertrude (Thomas) C.; m. Mary Dale Alexander, Aug. 27, 1961; children: Bruce Dale, Earl Clyde. BS, U. Nebr., 1959, MS, 1960, DSc (hon.), 1983; PhD, Stanford U., 1968. Registered profl. engr., Ohio, Nebr. With Bell Tel. Labs., Holmdel, N.J., 1968-84, head radio and satellite systems rsch. dept., 1983-84; mgr. radio and satellite systems rsch. divsn. Bell Comm. Rsch., Red Bank, NJ, 1984-91, exec. dir. radio rsch. dept., 1991-93; prof. elec. engring. Stanford (Calif.) U., 1993—, Harald Trap Friis Prof. Engring., 1994—, dir. telecomms., 1993-99. Em. comms. U.S. nat. com. Internat. Union of Radio Sci.; participant enbanc hearing on Personal Comm. Sys., FCC, 1991; mem. rsch. visionary bd. Motorola Labs., 2002. Contbr. articles to profl. jours.; patentee in field. 1st lt. USAF, 1960-63. Recipient Guglielmo Marconi prize in Electromagnetic Waves Propagation, Inst. Internat. Comm., 1983, Alumni Achievement award U. Nebr., 2002; Johnson fellow, 1959-60. Fellow IEEE (Morris E. Leeds award 1985, Alexander Graham Bell medal 1993, Millenium medal 2000), AAAS, Bellcore 1991, Radio Club Am.; mem. NAE, Comm. Soc. of IEEE (Leonard G. Abraham Prize Paper award 1992, Comms. Mag. Prize Paper award 1990), Vehicular Tech. Soc. of IEEE (Paper of Yr. award 1983), Antennas and Propagation Soc. of IEEE (elected mem. adminstrn. com. 1986-88), Sigma Xi. Achievements include rsch. in wireless communication systems, cellular radio systems, radio propagation. Home: 924 Mears Ct Stanford CA 94305-1029 Office: Stanford U Dept Elec Engring Packard 361 Stanford CA 94305-9515

COX, EMMETT RIPLEY, judge; b. Cottonwood, Ala., Feb. 13, 1935; s. Emmett M. Jr. Cox and Myra E. (Ripley) Stewart; m. Ann MacKay Haas, May 16, 1964; children: John Haas, Catherine MacKay. BA, U. Ala., 1957, JD, 1959. Bar: Ala. 1959, U.S. Ct. Appeals (5th, 8th and 11th cirs.), U.S. Supreme Ct. Assoc. Mead, Norman & Fitzpatrick, Birmingham, Ala., 1959—64; assoc. then ptnr. Gaillard, Wilkins, Smith & Cox, Mobile, Ala., 1964—69; ptnr. Nettles, Cox & Barker, 1969—81; judge U.S. Dist. Ct. (so. dist.) Ala., Mobile, 1981—88, U.S. Ct. Appeals (11th cir.), Mobile, 1988—2000, sr. judge, 2000—. Mem. def. svcs. com. Jud. Conf. U.S., 1992—98, chair, 1995—98, mem. jud. br. com., 2001—. Mem.: FBA, Maritime Law Assn. of the U.S., Mobile Bar Assn., Ala. Bar Assn., Alpha Tau Omega (past pres.), Phi Delta Phi, Omicron Delta Kappa. Office: US Courthouse 11th Circuit 113 Saint Joseph St Ste 433 Mobile AL 36602-3624 also: 56 Forsyth St NW Atlanta GA 30303

COX, FRANK, advertising executive; Grad., Hendrix Coll. Copywriter; brodcast prodr., assoc. creative dir.; account supr. Cranford Johnson Robinson Woods, Little Rock, Ark., 1987, v.p., assoc. dir. account svcs., 1991-93, dir. account svcs., 1993-96, pres., CEO, 1996—. Bd. dirs. Ark. Children's Hosp. Miracle Network Telethon; co-founder Little Rock chpt. Parents for Pub. Schs.; mem. Fifty for the Future. Named Advt. Person of the Yr. Ark. Advt. Fedn., 1997. Mem. Am. Mktg. Assn., Young Pres. Orgn. Office: CJRW 303 West Capitol Ave Little Rock AR 72201

COX, FRANK D. (BUDDY COX), oil company executive, exploration consultant; b. Shreveport, La., Dec. 20, 1932; s. Ohmer M. and Beulah O. (Scott) Cox; m. Betty Jean Hand, June 19, 1956; children: Cynthia Cox Sanford, Carolyn Cox Patton, Frank D. Jr. BS in Bus. Adminstrn., La. Tech. U., 1956; postgrad., Centenary Coll., 1958-59. Cert. profl. landman; lic. real estate, Fla. Various positions Exxon Corp., Houston, 1955-86, chief landman, v.p. coal resources, 1980-86; pvt. practice Houston, 1986-89; sr. v.p. Energy Exploration Mgmt. Co., Houston, 1989-94; v.p., mgr. T-Bar-X Ltd. Co., Houston, 1994-2000; v.p., dir. Power Exploration Internat., Houston, 1994-2000; ptnr. East Tex. Reef Fund, Ltd., 1994—; land mgr. Thomson-Barrow Corp., 1994-2000, Tecolotita, Inc., 1994-2000; exploration cons. Houston, 2000—. Active Second Bapt. Ch., Houston. Capt. USAF, 1956-58. Named disting. mil. grad. La. Tech. U., Ruston, 1955. Mem. Am. Assn. Profl. Landmen, Houston Assn. Profl. Landmen, W. Houston Assn. Profl. Landmen, W. Houston Exxon Annuitant Club, 100 Club of Greater Houston, La. Tech. U. Found., Crimestoppers Inc., Pi Kappa Alpha Ednl. Found., Omicron Delta Kappa Found., Delta Sigma Pi. Republican. Avocations: golf, tennis, amateur radio. Home and Office: 14830 Carolcrest St Houston TX 77079-6312

COX, FREDERICK MORELAND, retired university dean, social worker; b. L.A., Dec. 8, 1928; s. Frederick Alfred Edward and Ethel (Moreland) C.; m. Gay Campbell, June 1951 (dec. June 1991); children: Lawrence, Elizabeth,

Sherman. BA, UCLA, 1950, MSW, 1954; DSW, U. Calif., Berkeley, 1968. Caseworker child welfare L.A. Bur. Public Assistance, 1952-53; mental health counselor L.A. Superior Ct., 1953; caseworker Family Service Bur., Oakland, Calif., 1954-57; program dir. Easter Seal Soc., Oakland, 1957-60; asst. prof. to prof. social work U. Mich., Ann Arbor, 1964-76; prof., dir. Sch. Social Work, Mich. State U., East Lansing, 1976-80; prof., dean Sch. Social Welfare, U. Wis., Milw., 1980-89, ret., 1989. Author: As We See It: Men's Stories About Their Experiences with Prostate Cancer, 1999; sr. co-editor: Cmty.-Action Planning Development, A Casebook, 1974, Tactics and Techniques of Community Practice, 1977, 2d edit., 1984, Strategies of Community Organization, 4th edit, 1987; co-editor: Families in Trouble (5 vols.), 1988. Pres. Wis. Coun. Human Concerns, 1985-86. Spl. Rsch. fellow NIMH, 1960-63. Mem. NASW (v.p. Wis. chpt. 1984-86), Acad. Cert. Social Workers, Nat. Deans and Dirs. Schs. Social Work (sec.-treas. 1985-87), Coun. Social Work Edn. (bd. dirs. 1985-89). Home: 11300 First Ave NE # 221 Seattle WA 98125-6038 E-mail: fredmcox@hotmail.com.

COX, GARY WALTER, political science educator; b. Patuxent River, Md., Sept. 23, 1955; s. Dale William and Patricia Broadway Cox; m. Diane Christine Lin, June 18, 1988 (dec. Jan. 1999); 1 child, Dylan Gregory. BS, Calif. Inst. Tech., 1978, PhD, 1982. From asst. prof. to assoc. prof. U. Tex., Austin, 1982-86; assoc. prof. U. Calif., La Jolla, 1986-90, prof., 1990—. Author: (books) The Efficient Secret, 1987 (George Hallet prize 2002), Making Votes Count, 1997 (Woodrow Wilson Found. award 1998; co-author: (books) Legislative Leviathan, 1993 (Fenno prize 1994), Elbridge Gerry's Salamander, 2002. Guggenheim fellow, 1995, Am. Acad. Arts and Scis. fellow, 1996. E-mail: gcox@weber.ucsd.edu.

COX, GLENDA JEWELL, retired elementary school educator; b. Caruthersville, Mo., Mar. 6, 1938; d. Gladys Lee and Vera Lee (Malugen) Malone; m. Samuel Joseph Cox, Sept. 3, 1958; children: Cassandra Ann, Leslie Alexandria, Jonathan Paul, Peter Matthew. BS in Elem. Edn., Charleston (S.C.) So. U., 1975; MA, Maryville U., St. Louis, 1990; prin. cert., U. Mo., St. Louis, 1995. Cert. tchr., gifted, elem. edn. K-12, principal Mo., 1995. Tchr. 2nd/3rd grade combination Midland Park Elem., Charleston, 1975-76; tchr. 2nd grade Summerville (S.C.) Sch. Dist. II, 1978; tchr. 2nd grade, 5th grade math. Mascoutah (Ill.) Dist. 19, 1980-82; 6th grade tchr. Francis Howell Sch. Dist., St. Charles, Mo., 1985-91, gifted facilitator, 1991-97, asst. prin. Ctrl. Elem. Sch., 1997-98, prin., 1998-2000; ret. Mem. curriculum com. Francis Howell Sch. Dist., St. Charles, 1989-90, pilot mentor/mentor, 1988-95, dist. site support team, 1993-96; cooperating tchr. Becky-David Elem., St. Charles, 1986-88; site based team chmn./co-chmn., 1992-96, Odyssey of the Mind coord., 1991-96, tech. com., 1993—, cluster tchr. instr., 1993-97, prins. selection com., 1993. English conversation tchr. Bapt. Ch., Fuchu, Japan, 1969-71, vacation Bible sch. dir., 1970-71; PTA parent vol. chmn. Newington Elem., Summerville, 1977-78; chmn. Cystic Fibrosis Found., Summerville, 1977. Mem. NEA, Gifted Assn. Mo. (dist. A 1994-96, co-dir. 1994-96, dist. A registration chmn. 1992-94, state conf. registration chmn. 1995, 96), St. Louis Assn. Gifted Edn. Baptist. Avocations: bridge, bowling, learning. Home: 14344 Rainey Lake Dr Chesterfield MO 63017-2933 E-mail: gmcox6@hotmail.com.

COX, GLENN ANDREW, JR., petroleum company executive; b. Sedalia, Mo., Aug. 6, 1929; s. Glenn Andrew and Ruth Lonsdale (Atkinson) C.; m. Veronica Cecelia Martin, Jan. 3, 1953; children: Martin Stuart, Grant Andrew, Cecelia Ruth. BBA, So. Meth. U., 1951. With Phillips Petroleum Co., Bartlesville, Okla., 1956-91, asst. to chmn. oper. com., 1973-74, v.p. mgmt. info. and control, 1974-80, exec. v.p., 1980-85, dir., 1982-91, pres., COO, 1985-91. Bd. dirs. BOK Fin. Corp., Bank of Okla., The Williams Co.'s, Inc., Helmerich and Payne, Tulsa, Union Tex. Petroleum Holdings, Houston, Thermon Industries, Inc., San Marcos, Tex., Cimarex Energy, Inc., Denver. Pres. Cherokee Area coun. Boy Scouts Am., 1977-82, South Ctrl. region, 1987-90, mem. nat. exec. bd., 1987-94; mem. bd. curators Ctrl. Meth. Coll., Fayette, Mo., 1984-88, 1997—; trustee Philbrook Mus. Art, 1987-92, So. Meth. U., Dallas, 1988-96; bd. dirs. Okla. United Meth. Found.; mem. Okla. State Regents for Higher Edn., 1990-96. Mem. Am. Petroleum Inst. (bd. dirs. 1982-91), Nat. Assn. Mfrs. (bd. dirs. 1985-91), Bartlesville Area C. of C. (pres. 1978), Hillcrest Country Club. Methodist. Office: Reda Bldg 401 S Dewey Ave Ste 318 Bartlesville OK 74003-3545

COX, GREGORY ALLEN, musician; b. Seattle, Wash., Oct. 8, 1949; s. Kenneth Allen and Nona Fumerton Cox; m. Marian Turner; 1 child, Carolyn Violet. BA, Eastman Sch. of Music, Rochester, NY, 1971. Second trombone NC Symphony, Raleigh/Durham, NC, 1971—76; trombone instr. NC Sch. of the Arts, Winston-Salem, NC, 1972—76; brass instr. & coach Vancouver Acad. of Music, Vancouver, Canada, 1976—; trombone instr. U. of BC, Vancouver, Canada, 1982—; trombone affiliate Western Wash. U., Bellingham, Wash., 1984—; principle trombone & instr. Ea. Music Festival, Greensboro, NC, 1974—; second trombone Vancouver Symphony Orch., Vancouver, British Columbia, 1976—. Exec. bd. mem. Am. Fedn. of Musicians, Vancouver, Canada, 1976. Mem.: Nat. Assn. of Coll. Wind and Percussion Instruments, Am. Assn. of U. Profs., Internat. Trombone Assn., AFM Local 500. Avocations: travel, cooking, gardening. Office: 250 H St Pmb #242 Blaine WA 98231

COX, HEADLEY MORRIS, JR., lawyer, educator; b. Mt. Olive, N.C., July 25, 1916; s. Headley Morris and Frank (English) C.; m. Irene Todd, June 26, 1940; children: John Morris, Deborah English, Thomas Headley; m. Elizabeth Shelton Smith, Dec. 30, 1994. AB, Duke, 1937, AM, 1939; postgrad., U. Colo., 1944-45; PhD, U. Pa., 1958; JD, U. S.C., 1984. Successively instr., asst. prof., assoc. prof., prof. English Clemson (S.C.) U., 1939-82, head dept., 1950-69, dean Coll. Liberal Arts, 1969-80; of counsel Olson, Smith, Jordan & Cox, P.A., 1984—. Sr. Fulbright lectr. in Am. lit. Universitat Graz, Austria, 1958-59 Served with USNR, 1944-46. Mem. Phi Beta Kappa. Methodist. Home: 213 Riggs Dr Clemson SC 29631-1427 Office: PO Box 1633 Clemson SC 29633-1633

COX, HELEN ADELAIDE (HOLLY COX), artist, writer; b. El Paso, Tex., Oct. 17, 1932; d. Eugene Bonfanti and Anna Margaret (Lind) Thurston; m. Sanford C. Cox Jr., Sept. 27, 1958; children: Sanford C. III, Christopher Thurston. BA, Tex. Western Coll., El Paso, 1954. Tchr. Chavez Acad., El Paso, 1954-56; tchr. art El Paso Pub. Schs., 1956-58; artist El Paso, 1958—. Co-author: Eugene Thurston, 1996, Index to Early El Paso Artists, 1998. Bd. dirs. Matrix Soc., U. Tex., El Paso, 1991-93, El Paso Mus. of Art Guild, 1988; com. chmn. Kermezaar Art Fair, El Paso, 1990-93; bd. dirs., libr. St. Clements Episcopal Ch., El Paso, 1975-80; bd. dirs. Ctr. for Advancement and Study of Early Tex. Art, 2002—. Recipient McQuinn award Mesilla Valley Fine Arts, Las Cruces, N.Mex., 1995. Mem. Nat. Soc. Arts and Letters (bd. dirs., treas. 1996-98), Tex. Watercolor Soc., Tex. Fine Arts Assn., Internat. Assn. Visual Arts, El Paso Art Assn. (life, pres. 1971, 1st pl. 1997, Joseph A. Moore award 1994), Rio Bravo Watercolorists (signature, bd. dirs. 1994-95, Grumbacher award 1993). Avocations: collecting regional art, books. Home: 112 Vista Del Rey Dr El Paso TX 79912-4821

COX, HENRY, research company executive, research engineer; b. Phila., Mar. 7, 1935; s. Henry Robert and Helen (Kane) C.; m. Mary Ann Shaw, Sept. 3, 1960 (dec.); children: James, Daniel, Michael, Diane. BS, Coll. Holy Cross, 1956; ScD, MIT, 1963. Analyst Office Sec. of Def., 1970-72; research assoc. Scripps Instn. Oceanography, LaJolla, Calif., 1972-73; officer in charge Naval Underwater Systems Ctr., New London, Conn., 1973-76; div. dir. Def. Advanced Research Projects Agy., 1976-78; project mgr. Naval Electronic Systems Command, Arlington, Va., 1978-81; divisional v.p. BBN Systems and Tech. Corp., Arlington, 1981-91; chief tech. officer, sr. v.p. Orincon Corp., Arlington, 1991—. Contbr. articles to tech. jours. Served to capt. USN, 1956-81. Decorated Legion of Merit; decorated Meritorious Service medal, Navy Commendation medal; recipient Def. Superior Service medal Dept. Def., 1978 Fellow Acoustical Soc. Am., IEEE (Disting. Tech. Achievement award Oceanic Engring. Soc. 1991); mem. Am. Soc. Naval Engrs. (hon. Gold medal), Nat. Acad. Engring., U.S. Naval Inst. Roman Catholic. Home: 6513 Waterway Dr Falls Church VA 22044-1328 Office: Orincon Corp 4350 Fairfax Dr Arlington VA 22203-1695

COX, HILLERY LEE, retired primary school educator; b. Akron, Ohio, Nov. 2, 1946; d. Ellwood Lester Jr. and Leonide Juanita (Williams) Cosper; m. William R. Cox Jr., Apr. 2, 1966; 1 child, Geoffrey William. Student, Ohio U., 1964-65; BS in Edn., U. Akron, 1967, MS in Edn., 1980. Cert. tchr., Ohio; cert. reading specialist, Ohio. Tchr. Copley (Ohio) Fairlawn Schs., 1967-69; presch. tchr. Northminster Coop. Nursery Sch., Cuyahoga Falls, Ohio, 1974-75; ednl. math. aide Stow (Ohio) City Schs., 1975-76; grad. tchg. asst. U. Akron, 1976-77; tchr. Cloverleaf Local Schs., Lodi, Ohio, 1977—2002. Adj. prof. workshop presenter Ashland (Ohio) U., 1992-98; cons. The ABC's of Whole Lang., Copley, 1988—; insvc. presenter various sch. sys. in Ohio, 1988-2002. Contbr. articles to profl. jours. Vol. Doggie Brigade, Children's Med. Ctr. of Akron, 1992-98; driver substitute Mobile Meals, Copley, 1981-84; sec. Copley All Sports Boosters, 1984-88. Named Medina County Tchr. of Yr., 1993; grantee Ohio Dept. Edn., 1978-79, 79-80, Martha Holden Jennings grants, 2001-02.; Martha Holden Jennings Found. scholar, 1994 Mem. NEA, ASCD, Ohio Edn. Assn., Internat. Reading Assn. (pres. Lizotte coun. 1994-95, 97-97, spkr. Great Lakes conf. 1993), Ohio Coun. Tchrs. English and Lang. Arts (presenter 1987, 88, 89), Cloverleaf Edn. Assn. (bldg. rep. 1977—), Nat. Campers and Hikers and Family RVers (pres. local chpt.), Order Eastern Star (acdre officer Ellsworth chpt. 1991—, Worthy Matron 1996), Delta Kappa Gamma. Avocations: camping, crafts, traveling, quilting. Home: 649 S Medina Line Rd Copley OH 44321-1162

COX, HOWARD ELLIS, JR., venture capitalist; b. NYC, Feb. 1, 1944; s. Howard Ellis and Anne Delafield (Finch) C.; m. Julia Bolton Dempsey, Oct. 31, 1970. BA, Princeton U., 1964; JD, Columbia U., 1967; MBA, Harvard U., 1969. Bar: NY 1967. Ptnr. Greylock, Boston, 1971—. Bd. dir. Greylock Mgmt. Corp., Boston, Stryker, Kalamazoo, In-Q-Tel, Washington, Landacorp, Atlanta; mem. investment com. Ptnr. Healthcare. Bd. dir. Nat. Venture Capital Assn., Washington, 1997—, chmn., 2002; trustee Dana Farber Cancer Inst., 1987—; v.p., trustee Assn. Relief of the Elderly, NYC; overseer Mus. Fine Arts; mem. bd. fellow Harvard Med. Sch. Capt. US Army, 1969-71; bd. dir. Boston Pub. Libr. Found. Mem.: Nat. Venture Capitol Assoc. (chmn. 2002—03), Coun. Fgn. Rels., Bus. Assoc. Club Boston (pres. 1979—80), New Eng. Venture Capital Assn. (pres. 1986—88), Comml. Club Boston. Episcopalian. Home: 225 Sargent Rd Brookline MA 02445-7517 Office: Greylock 880 Winter St Waltham MA 02451

COX, J. ARTHUR, minister; b. Utica, N.Y., Aug. 5, 1940; s. James F and Margaret (Craig) Cox; m. Mahaillie Tillson, Dec. 29, 1962; children: Deborah Jean, James Andrew. AAS, Mohawk Valley C.C., 1961; BTh, Concordia Sem., 1975; D Ministry, Faith Sem., Tacoma, 1991. Cert. Ordained to ministry Luth Ch-Mo Synod, 1975. Pastor Grace Luth. Ch., Bradford, Pa., 1975-2000; pres. devel. leaders for ministry Mo. Synod, 2000—. Del. Synodical Conv., Dallas, 1977; counselor Cattaraugus Ctr., Bradford, 1982; chmn. Dist Open House, Bradford, 1982, Dist. Ext. Fund, Buffalo, 1982—85; chmn. ea. dist., bd. dirs. mission svcs. Alive in Christ, 1982—88, mem. evangelism com. ea. dist., 1992—97, bd. dirs.; chmn. dist. bd. Congl. Svcs., 1997—2002; counselor Cattanaugus Ct., 2002—. Chmn. bd. Excell Personnel Svcs., Inc., 1999—; bd dirs Evergreen Hylands, 1979, Am Cancer Soc, 1980, Vis Nurse Asn, 1980—86, Bradford Hosp, 1985—. Mem.: Rotary (bd dirs 1978—82, pres 1982—83). Republican. Home: 465 Interstate Pky Bradford PA 16701-2733 E-mail: jacox@penn.com. *Life is a sequence of God-given opportunities to serve Him and His people. The excitement is derived from accepting His call to service and experiencing His magnificent power working through you to accomplish His purpose.*

COX, JAMES CARL, JR., chemist, researcher, lexicographer, consultant; b. Wolf Summit, W.Va., June 17, 1919; s. James Carl and Maggie Lillian (Merrells) C.; m. Alma Lee Tenney, Sept. 8, 1945; children: James Carl III, Joseph Merrells, Alma Lee, Elizabeth Susan Cox Unger, Albert John. BS summa cum laude, W.Va. Wesleyan Coll., 1940; MS in Organic Chemistry, U. Del., 1947, PhD in Phys. Organic Chemistry, 1949; postgrad. in law, Am. U., summer 1953, George Washington U., summer 1954; JD with honors, U. Md., 1955. Bar: Md. 1955; registered profl. sanitarian, Tex. Rsch. chemist E.I. duPont de Nemours Corp., Belle, W.Va., 1940-43; grad. instr. chemistry U. Del., Newark, 1946-49; prof. chemistry, head dept. chemistry Wesleyan Coll., Macon, Ga., 1949-51; prof. U.S. Naval Acad., Annapolis, 1951-55, 1951-55; prof., rsch. dir. Lamar U., Beaumont, Tex., 1955-65; prof., head dept. chemistry, dir. div. sci. and math. Oral Roberts U., Tulsa, 1965-68; prof., head dept. chemistry Wayland Baptist U., Plainview, Tex., 1968-76; v.p., rsch. dir. Agrl. & Indsl. Devel., Inc., Plainview, 1976-79; environ. health expert Tex. Dept. Health, Plainview, 1979-84. Mem. U. Tex indsl. planning commn., commdr. 19th dist. Dept. Tex.; field rep. Bureau of Census, 1990-92; cons., quality assurer Agri-Search Corp.; lectr. U. London, U. Dublin, Heidelberg U., summer 1976, U. Glasgow; cons. in field; vis. prof. organic chemistry Middle Tenn. State U., Murfreesboro, summer 1950, U. Baghdad, Iraq, 1956-57; quality assurer Agri-Search, Inc., 1992—. Author: George WAshington, Farmer, 1941, Lives of Splendor, 1971; Patterson's German-English Chemical Dictionary, rev. edit., 1985; editor The Condenser, 1957-65; contbr. articles to profl. jours., also abstracts. Precinct chmn. Hale County Rep., Plainview, 1983-84; bd. dirs. Plainview chpt. ARC, 1969-73, United Way, Plainview, 1972-75. Served to cpl. Combat Engrs., U.S. Army, 1943-45, ETO; field rep. Bureau Labor Stats., 1992—. Named Outstanding Prof., Lamar U., 1963-64, Wayland Bapt. U., 1971-74; fellow DuPont Endowment Found., 1947-48, Carnegie Found., 1948-49, Phillips fellow, 1949-50, State of Tex., 1957-59. Fellow Tex. Acad. Sci.; mem. AAAS, AAUP, DAV (chmn. Americanism, judge adv., vice commdr., commdr.), VFW (vice commdr., commdr., quartermaster), Am. Chem. Soc., Tex. Pub. Health Assn., Tex. Environ. Health Assn. (governing coun. 1982-84), Am. Legion (adj.), Rotary (pub. rels. officer 1969-84), Confederate Air Force (col.). Methodist. Current work: Novel fuels for industry; agricultural chemicals. Subspecialties: Organic chemistry; Polymer chemistry.

COX, JAMES D. law educator; b. 1943; JD, U. Calif. Hastings Sch. Law, 1969; LL.M., Harvard U., 1971; D in Mercature (hon.), U. South Denmark, 2001. Bar: Calif. 1970. Atty.-adv. Office Gen. Counsel FTC, Washington, 1969-70; teaching fellow Boston U., 1970-71; asst. prof. U. San Francisco, 1971-74; assoc. prof. U. Calif. Hastings Sch. Law, 1974-75; vis. assoc. prof. Stanford U., 1976-77; prof. U. Calif. Hastings Sch. Law, 1977-79; vis. prof. Duke U. Sch. Law, spring 1979, prof., 1979-2000, Brainerd Currie prof. law, 2000—. Mem. com. on corps. State Bar Calif., N.C. bus. corp. act. draft com., N.C. nonprofit corp. draft com.; E.T. Bost rsch. prof., fall 1980, 96; mem. legal adv. com. N.Y. Stock Exch., 1995—; mem. legal adv. bd. NASD, 1999—. Author: Financial Information, Accounting and the Law, 1980, Sum and Substance of Corporations, 5th edit., 1988, (with Hillman and Langevoort) Securities Regulation: Cases and Materials, 3d edit., 2001, (with Hazen) Corporations, 2d edit., 2003. Sr. Fulbright Rsch. fellow, Australia, 1989. Mem. Am. Law Inst., Order of Coif, Phi Kappa Phi Office: Duke U Sch Law Durham NC 27706

COX, JAMES TALLEY, lawyer; b. Temple, Tex., Sept. 22, 1921; s. George Allan and Jane (Talley) C.; m. Alice Tarver, Jan. 12, 1945; children: Martha Cox Daniels, Louise Cox McGuire, Anne Cox, Allan. BBA, U. Tex., 1943; LL.B., 1947. Bar: Tex. 1947, U.S. Supreme Ct. 1951. Spl. atty. Justice Dept., Washington, 1947-48; staff atty. Tax Ct. U.S., Washington, 1948-50; trial atty. Treasury Dept., Phila., 1950-51; tax counsel Schlumberger Well Services, Houston, 1951-65; ptnr. Hoover, Cox & Shearer, Houston, 1965-86; sole practice Houston, 1986-90; pres. James T. Cox, P.C., Houston, 1990—, Advent Trust Co., 1991-99. V.p., bd. dirs. Westchase Travels, Inc., 1972-82; bd. dirs. Paradigm Valve Svcs. Inc., Embedded Sys. Products Inc. Contbr. articles to profl. publs. Bd. dirs. Houston Met. YMCA, 1972-78, Pin Oak Charity Horse Show Assn., 1972—, Retina Rsch. Found., 1977—. Served to lt. USNR, 1943-46. Mem. Am., Tex., Houston Bar Assns., Tax Rsch. Assn. (exec. com. 1950-67), Delta Theta Phi, Phi Kappa Psi. Republican. Presbyterian. Home: 11701 Forest Glen St Houston TX 77024-6433 Office: 908 Town and Country Blvd Ste 225 Houston TX 77024

COX, JANSON L. museum administrator; MA in History Museology, Cooperstown Grad. Sch., 1967. Chief historian State of S.C., 1968-73; mgr. Charles Towne Landing 1670, Charleston, S.C., 1973-98; exec. dir. S.C. Cotton Mus, Bishopville, 1998—. Office: SC Cotton Mus 121 W Cedar Ln Bishopville SC 29010-1454 E-mail: sccottonmus@ftc-i.net.

COX, JEROME ROCKHOLD, JR., electrical engineer; b. Washington, May 24, 1925; s. Jerome R. and Jane (Mills) Cox; m. Barbara Jane Lueders, Sept. 2, 1951; children: Nancy Jane Cox Battersby, Jerome Mills, Randall Allen. SB, MIT, 1947, SM, 1949, ScD, 1954. Faculty Washington U., St. Louis, 1955—61, prof. elec. engring., 1961—2000, dir. Biomed. Computer Lab., 1964—75, prof. biomed. engring. in physiology and biophysics, Sch. Medicine, 1965—2000, chmn. computer labs., 1967—83, program dir. tng. program tech. in health care, 1970—78, chmn. dept. computer sci., 1975—91, prof. biomedicine, Inst. for Biomed. Computing, 1983—2000, Harold and Adelaide Welge prof. computer sci., 1989—98, dir. Applied Rsch. Lab., 1991—95, sr. prof., 1999—; v.p. Growth Networks, 1999—2000. Co-chmn. computers in cardiology conf., 1974—88; cardiology adv. com. Nat. Heart and Lung Inst., 1975—78; epidemiology biostatistics and bioengring. cluster Pres.'s Biomed. Rsch. Panel, 1975—76; chmn. divsn. computer rsch. and tech. rev. com. NIH, 1983—96, PROPHET adv. com., 1983—88; adv. com. Harvard-MIT Health Scis. and Tech., Boston, 1988—92; nat. neural circuitry database com. Inst. of Medicine, NAS, 1989—91; mem. Nat. Adv. Coun. Human Genome Rsch., 1990—95; adv. com. John Hopkins Biomed Engr, 2000—. Mem. editl. bd.: Computers and Biomed. Rsch., 1967—2000, Applied Mathematics Letters, 1987—96. Bd. dirs. Ctrl. Inst. Deaf, 1993—, Mass Sensors, Inc., 2000—. With U.S. Army, 1943—44. Fellow: IEEE (mem. editl. bd. Trans. Biomed. Enring. 1969—71), St. Louis Acad. Sci. (bd. dirs. 1997—99), Am. Coll. Med. Informatics, Acoustical Soc. Am.; mem.: Inst. Medicine, Tau Beta Pi, Eta Kappa Nu, Sigma Xi. Achievements include patents for air traffic control; computerized tomography; medical display technology; network traffic pacing; design of. Office: Washington U Dept Computer Sci Campus Box 1045 One Brookings Dr Saint Louis MO 63130-4899 E-mail: jrc@cse.wustl.edu.

COX, JOHN CURTIS, healthcare and educational administrator; b. Lovington, N.Mex., July 27, 1947; s. Samuel Spurgeon and Monah LaJoyce (Perry) King; m. Mary Margaret King, May 27, 1967; children: Melissa Lynn Ewing, Melinda Leanne Field. BBA, Hardin-Simmons U., Abilene, Tex., 1969; MHA, Baylor U., 1978; PhD, Tex. A&M U., 1988. Commd. 2d lt. U.S. Army, 1969, advanced through grades to lt. col.; chief Ft. Hood Health Facility Project Office, Office Surgeon Gen., 1978-85; assoc. dir., mgr. field office, health facilities planning U.S. Army Med. Command, Stuttgart, Germany, 1988-89, dir. health facilities planning Heidelberg, Germany, 1989-90; chief programming div. Def. Med. Facilities Office, Office Asst. Sec. Def., Washington, 1990-91; ret. U.S. Army, 1991; adminstrv. asst. Garland (Tex.) Ind. Sch. Dist., 1991-93, exec. dir. sch. facilities, 1993-95; planning & cons. coord. HED Baylor Health Care Sys., 1995-98; adminstrv. dir. support svcs. Baylor Med. Ctr., Grapevine, Tex., 1997-98; project dir. Med. Cities Inc., Dallas, 1998-2001. Owner Cox Cons., 2001—. Editl. adv. bd. Facility Care; contbr. articles to profl. jours. Trustee Belton (Tex.) Ind. Sch. Dist., 1981-84; mem. pub. sch. bd. mems. adv. com. Tex. State Bd. Edn., 1982-84; fund raiser Garland br. Dallas YMCA, 1992-94. Decorated Legion of Merit, Bronze Star medal, Meritorious Svc. medal with 2 oak leaf clusters, Army Commendation medal, others; recipient Svc. Citation award Tex. Fellow Am. Coll. Healthcare Execs., Am. Soc. Healthcare Engrs., Phi Kappa Phi, Alpha Chi. Baptist. Avocations: woodworking, antiques, fitness.

COX, JOHN FRANCIS, retired cosmetic company executive; b. Chgo., Sept. 25, 1929; s. Roland Francis and Vera Pauline (Paisley) C.; m. T. Joanne Brown, Nov. 27, 1954 (dec.); children: James O., Thomas B., Paul A. BJ, U. Ill., 1951; MS in English and Edn., Western Ill. U., 1954. Reporter Galesburg (Ill.) Register Mail, 1954-56; staff writer pub. rels. United Airlines, Chgo., 1956-58; press rels. mgr. Kiekhaefer Corp., Fond du Lac, Wis., 1958-60, Internat. Minerals and Chems. Corp., Skokie, Ill., 1960-67, Heublein Inc., Hartford, Conn., 1967-69, v.p. pub. affairs Farmington, Conn., 1981-83; v.p. pub. rels. and advt. Warner Nat. Corp., Cin., 1969-72; v.p. franchising and pub. rels. Ky. Fried Chicken, Louisville, 1972-81; group dir. pub. rels. R. J. Reynolds Industries, Inc., Winston-Salem, N.C., 1983-84; sr. v.p. comm. Avon Products, Inc., N.Y.C., 1984-91. Staff sgt. U.S. Army, 1951-53. Mem.: Soc. Profl. Journalists.

COX, JOHN THOMAS, JR., lawyer; b. Shreveport, La., Feb. 9, 1943; s. John Thomas and Gladys Virginia (Canterbury) C.; m. Tracey L. Tanquary, Aug. 27, 1966; children: John Thomas, III, Stephen Lewis. BS, La. State U., 1965; JD, 1968. Bar: La. 1968, U.S. Dist. Ct. (we., mid. and ea. dist.) La., U.S. Dist. Ct. (ea. dist.) Tex., U.S. Ct. Appeals (5th and 8th cir.), U.S. Tax Ct., U.S. Supreme Ct. Assoc. Sanders, Miller, Downing & Keene, Baton Rouge, 1968-70, Blanchard, Walker, O'Quin & Roberts, Shreveport, La., 1970-71; ptnr., 1971—. Tchr. bus. law Centenary Coll. La., La. State U., Shreveport. Lt. USAR, 1963—69. Recipient George Washington Honor medal Valley Forge Freedoms Found. Mem. ABA, La. Bar Assn., Caddo parish Bar Assn., Am. Assn. Def. Counsel, La. Assn. Def. Counsel, Com. of 100, Shreveport Club. Presbyterian. Address: 555 Dunmoreland Dr Shreveport LA 71106-6124 E-mail: jcox@bwor.com.

COX, JOSEPH LAWRENCE, judge; b. Trenton, Mo., Dec. 7, 1932; s. Forrest Curtis and Lillian Judson (Ritzenthaler) C.; m. Lois Marie Hubble, May 20, 1956; children: Margaret Marie Cox Jarvis, Martha Mae Cox Anderson. BA, U. Mo., Kansas City, 1961, JD, 1965. Bar: Kans. 1965, U.S. Supreme Ct. 1970. Ptnr. Cox, Anderson & Covell, Mission, Kans., 1965-70; pvt. practice Tonganoxie, Kans., 1968-90; city atty., 1967-73, Linwood, Kans., 1972-78; mcpl. judge Mission, 1969-80, Tonganoxie, 1983-90, Topeka, 1990—2002. V.p. Sertoma Found. With USAF, 1952—54. Mem. Kans. Bar Assn., Kans. Mcpl. Judges Assn. (bd. dirs. 1975-79, pres. 1977-78), Topeka Bar Assn., Masons, Shriners, Sertoma (gov. Kans. dist. 1998-99, found. trustee), Topeka Evening Sertoma (pres. 1995-96), Jayhawk Sertoma (pres. 1973-76). Avocations: photography, boating, travel. Home: 910 SE 43rd St Topeka KS 66609-1620 Office: 214 E 8th St Topeka KS 66603 E-mail: jcox@topeka.org.

COX, JOSEPH WILLIAM, former academic administrator, education educator; b. Hagerstown, Md., May 26, 1937; s. Joseph F. and Ruth E. C.; m. Regina M. Bollinger, Aug. 17, 1963; children: Andrew, Matthew, Abigail. BA, U. Md., 1959, PhD, 1967; Doctor (hon.), Towson State U., 1990. Prof. dept. engring. & tech. mgmt. Portland State U.; successively instr., asst. prof., assoc. prof., prof. history Towson (Md.) State U., 1964-81, dean evening and summer programs, 1972-75, acting pres., 1978-79, v.p. acad. affairs and dean of univ., 1979-81; prof. history, v.p. acad. affairs. No. Ariz. U., Flagstaff, 1981-87; pres. So. Oregon U., Ashland, 1987-94; chancellor Oreg. Univ. Sys., Eugene, 1994—2002, Disting. Pub. Svc. prof. Author: Champion of Southern Federalism: Robert Goodloe Harper of South Carolina, 1972, The Early National Experience: The Army Corps of Engineers, 1783-1812, 1979; mem. bd. editors Md. Hist. Mag., 1979-89; columnist So. Oreg. Hist. Mag., 1989-94; contbr. articles to profl. jours. Bd. dirs. Oreg. Hist. Soc., Oreg. Shakespearean Festival, 1989-95, So. Oreg. Econ. Devel. Bd., 1988-94, Jackson/Josephine Co., Western Bank, 1993-97, Portland Ctr. Stage, 1999. Mem. AAUP, Am. Assn. Higher Edn., Am. Assn. State Colls. and Univs., Phi Kappa Phi, Omicron Delta Kappa. Episcopalian. Home: 3845 Spring Blvd Eugene OR 97405 Office: Portland State U PO Box 751 Portland OR 97207-0751

COX, JOY DEAN, business executive; b. Oklahoma City, Sept. 13, 1940; d. Wordy John Neely and Ethel (Russell) Neely Biggs; m. Sidney Lee Johnson, Sept. 10, 1958 (div. 1963); m. Ronald Gene Cox, Sept. 22, 1964; children: Beverly Kay, Jeffrey Wilson; 1 stepchild, Ronald D. Student pub. schs., Oklahoma City. Long-distance operator S.W. Bell Tel. Co., Oklahoma City, 1958-59, L.A., 1959-60; clk. John Pilling Shoes, Oklahoma City, 1960-62; cashier Dial Fin. Co., Houston, 1966; file clk., typist N.Am. Ins. Co., Oklahoma City, 1966-67; bookkeeper, co-owner farm and ranch ops. Dewey County, Okla., 1968—78, Panola, Okla., 1977-2001, Co-op R&J Farms-Ranch, Dewey County, 1991—. Co-owner, operator Apco Svc. Sta. and Bulk Fuel Plant, Taloga, Okla., 1972-76, D&R Svc. & Supply Co., Panola, 1979-89, Eufaula, Okla., 1989-95, Taloga, 1993—; co-owner, operator Panola Store, 1980-85; dealer, co-owner Cox Chevrolet, Wilburton, Okla., 1985. Contbr. articles to newspapers and jours. Pres. Taloga Ext. Homemakers, 1971-73, sec.-treas. 1973-75; entertainer Dewey County Rest Homes, 1969-78, Latimer County Rest Homes, Wilburton, 1978-88, County of McIntosh, Eufaula, 1990-93; leader, contbr. funds to drug abuse program Latimer County 4-H, Wilburton, 1979-89; fund raiser ARC, Am. Heart Assn., Girl Scouts U.S., Panola PTA, Drug Abuse Program, Panola 4-H, Latimer County, 1979-89, Salvation Army Donations, Pittsburg County, 1977-91, Am. Cancer Soc., Taloga, 1968-78, Panola, 1978-88, McIntosh Co., Eufaula, 1988-92, Nat. Help Hospitalized Vets., 1978-90; contbr. funds to drug abuse program Wilburton, Quinton and Okla. Police Dept., McIntosh County 4H; bd. dirs. Latimer County Pick-A-Star, 1985, Clown for Eufaula and Stigler Christmas Parade, Okla., 1989-93; clown,

singer McIntosh Rest Homes, 1989-93; participant Paradeentry Desert Storm Support Day, 1991; singer Eufaula Arts and Crafts Festival, 1991-93, entertainer, 1991-92; clown, singer 4th July Parade and Arts Festival, Eufaula, 1992-93; fundraiser Dewey County Hist. Jail House Mus., 1993— (past pres. 2000); singer Pittsburg County Ann. Masons Widows Banquet, 1993. Recipient Leadership award Latimer County 4-H, 1983, Citizen of Yr. award Com. to Keep and Bear Arms, 1986. Mem. Lake Eufaula Assn. (bd. dirs. 1990-91, entertainer ann. fund raiser 1989, Friendly Lake Eufaula Area Supporters (entertainer ann. fleas Christmas parties and talent show 1991-92), Lake Eufaula Area Flying Coun. (pub. rels. rep.), Taloga Kiwanis Club (v.p. 1999-2000, pres. 2000-01). Republican. Avocations: biking, sewing, swimming, walking, reading.

COX, KENNETH ALLEN, lawyer, communications consultant; b. Topeka, Dec. 7, 1916; s. Seth Leroy and Jean (Sears) C.; m. Nona Beth Fumerton, Jan. 1, 1943; children— Gregory Allen, Jeffrey Neal, Douglas Randall. BA, U. Wash., 1938, LL.B., 1940; LL.M., U. Mich., 1941; LL.D., Chgo. Theol. Sem., 1969. Bar: Wash. bar 1941. Law clk. Wash. Supreme Ct., 1941-42; asst. prof. U. Mich. Law Sch., 1946-48; with firm Little, LeSourd, Palmer, Scott & Slemmons (and predecessor), Seattle, 1948-61, partner, 1953-61; spl. counsel com. interstate and fgn. commerce charge TV inquiry U.S. Senate, 1956-57; chief broadcast bur. FCC, Washington, 1961-63, commr., 1963-70; counsel to comm. law firm Haley, Bader & Potts, 1970-99; sr. v.p., dir. MCI Comm. Corp., 1970-87; cons. MCI, 1987—2000. Lectr. U. Washington Law Sch., part-time 1954, 60; adj. prof. Georgetown U. Law Center, 1971, 72. Vice pres. Municipal League Seattle and King County, 1960, Seattle World Affairs Council, 1960; pres. Seattle chpt. Am. Assn. UN, 1957; chmn. one of five citizen subcoms. Legis. Interim Com. Edn., 1960; Bd. dirs. Nat. Pub. Radio, 1971-80; bd. dirs. Nat. Advt. Rev. Bd., 1971-74, chmn. bd., 1976-96 . Served to capt. Q.M.C. AUS, 1943-46, 51-52. Recipient Alfred I. duPont award in broadcast journalism Columbia U., 1970; Everett C. Parker award, the Minortiy Media and Telecommunications Coun., 2003. Mem. Am., Fed. Communications, Wash. State, D.C. bar assns., Order of Coif, Phi Beta Kappa, Phi Delta Phi. Democrat. Congregationalist. Home: 5836 Marbury Rd Bethesda MD 20817-6076 Office: MCI Comm Corp 1133 19th St NW Washington DC 20036 E-mail: coxk1o@cs.com, 100-4689@mcimail.com.

COX, KEVIN MONTEREY, school administrator; b. New London, Conn., Nov. 30, 1965; s. Carroll Monterey and Barbara Freeman Cox. BS, U. S.C., Spartanburg, 1987; MEd, Converse Coll., 1990, EdS, 1993. Tchr. Clinton (S.C.) H.S., 1990-96; asst. prin. Bell St. Middle Sch., 1996—97; adminstrv. asst. Clinton (S.C.) H.S., 1997—2001; asst. prin. Lewisville H.S., Richburg, SC, 2001—. State sponsor S.C. Beta Club, 1999—; adj. prof. Lander U., Greenwood, S.C., 1998—. Recipient S.C. Ambassador of Acad. Excellence award S.C. State Dept. Edn., 1992. Mem. ASCD, S.C. Sci. Coun., Exch. Club Clinton (pres. 1996-97), Phi Delta Kappa. Methodist. Avocations: movies, reading, music. Home: 625 Britt Ln Richburg SC 29729 Office: 3971 Lewisville High School Rd Richburg SC 29729 E-mail: coxkm_lhs@chester.k12.sc.us.

COX, LARRY D. airport executive; With Memphis Internat. Airport, Tenn., 1972—84, pres., CEO, 1985—. Mem.: Am. Assn. Airport Execs. (chmn. 2001—). Office: Memphis Internat Airport Memphis-Shelby County Airport Authority 2491 Winchester Rd Ste 113 Memphis TN 38116-3856

COX, LINDA SMOAK, real estate broker; b. Yonges Island, S.C., Sept. 5, 1943; d. Ryan Lanier Smoak and Frances Lapish Bock. Grad., Kings Coll., Charlotte, N.C., 1962. Lic. real estate broker, relocation specialist, new homes specialist. Exec. sec. Charlotte Observer Transp. Co., 1963-65; various positions Eastern Airlines, Charlotte, 1965-88; real estate salesperson Allen Tate Realtors, Charlotte, 1990—. Program dir. Delta Investment, Charlotte, 1984-88; mem. Bd. Realtors, Charlotte, 1990—; mem. Bd. Realtors, Rock Hill, S.C., 1993—. Troop leader Girl Scouts U.S., Charlotte, 1964; mem., vol. U.S. Humane Soc., Charlotte, 1964, 96—; co-founder, vol. Midway Meth. Ch. Libr., Kannapolis, N.C., 1958; mem. coun. River Hills Cmty. Ch., Lake Wylie, S.C., 1980-82, chair fellowship com., 1979-80, mem. edn. com., 1984-85, bd. trustees, 2002—; founding mem., vol. Stowe Bot. Gardens, Belmont, N.C., 1994—. Mem.: Charlotte Regional Realtor Assn., N.C. Assn. Realtors. Avocations: water sports, snow ski race team, sailing, gardening. Home: PO Box 240173 Charlotte NC 28224-0173 E-mail: lindacox1@aol.com.

COX, LOUIS ANTHONY, JR., telecommunications executive; b. Washington, Aug. 7, 1957; s. Louis Anthony and Frances McKee Cox; m. Christine Anne Cox, Sept. 8, 1979; 1 child, Emeline Dickinson. AB, Harvard U., 1978; SM, MIT, 1985, PhD, 1986; postgrad., Stanford U., 1993. Sr. rsch. assoc. Am. Inst. for Rsch., Washington, 1978-79; mgr. ops. rsch. Arthur D. Little, Inc., Cambridge, Mass., 1980-86; pres. Cox Assocs., Denver, 1986—; sr. dir. U.S. West Advanced Techs., Boulder, Colo., 1987-96. Hon. full prof. math. U. Colo., Denver, 2000—; clin. prof. preventive medicine and biometrics U. Colo. Health Scis. Ctr., 2000—; counselor Ops. Rsch. Soc. Am. Spl. Interest Group-Telecomm., 1992-94. Co-author: Beyond Probation: Juvenile Corrections and the Chronic Delinquent, 1979; contbr. articles to profl. jours., chpts. to books; co-editor: New Risks: Issues and Management, 1990, Jour. Heuristics, 1995; patentee in field. Fellow Soc. Risk Analysis (life, sec., co-founder New Eng. chpt. 1985-86); mem. Am. Statis. Inst., Inst. Ops. Rsch. and Mgmt. Scis., N.Y. Acad. Scis. Office: Cox Assocs 503 Franklin St Denver CO 80218 Fax: (303) 388-0609.

COX, LYNETTA FRANCES, neonatal nurse practitioner; b. Bethlehem, Pa., Oct. 11, 1945; d. LeRoy Evan and Gloria Essie (Lee) Sell; m. Henry George Fromhartz, June 4, 1967 (div. May 1984); 1 child, Deborah Suzanne; m. Steven David Cox, Sept. 10, 1989. BS in Chemistry, Moravian Coll., 1967; diploma, Pottsville Hosp. Sch. Nursing, 1981; BSN summa cum laude, Armstrong State Coll., 1992; M Nursing in Neonatal Nurse Practitioner summa cum laude, Emory U., 1994. RN, Ga.; cert. neonatal nurse practitioner; cert. instr. BCLS and neonatal resuscitation program; cert. RN in neonatal intensive care. Rsch. chemist Water Pollution Control Dept., City of Phila., 1967-70; quality control chemist Just Born Candy Co., Bethlehem, Pa., 1971-72; neonatal staff nurse Geisinger Med. Ctr., Danville, Pa., 1981-84, Meml. Med. Ctr., Savannah, Ga., 1984-96, Egleston Children's Hosp., Atlanta, 1993-94; neonatal nurse practitioner Savannah Neonatology PC, 1995-96, Phoebe Putney Meml. Hosp., Albany, Ga., 1996—2000, Northside Hosp., Atlanta, 2000—. Mem.: Acad. Neonatal Nursing, Ga. Perinatal Assn., Nat. Perinatal Assn., Sigma Theta Tau. Avocations: needlework, reading, trombone, piano. Home: 2551 Andorra Dr Hephzibah GA 30530 Office: Northside Hosp SCN 1000 Johnson Ferry Rd NE Atlanta GA 30342

COX, MARSHALL, lawyer; b. Cleve., Nov. 17, 1932; s. Marshall H.C. and Mary (Bateman) Mills; m. Nancy Huntley, Aug. 3, 1957 (div. Oct. 1994); 1 child, Vanessa; m. Nathalie Menapace, Jan. 3, 1997. BA, Vanderbilt U., 1954; JD, Ohio State U., 1958. Bar: D.C. 1974, N.Y. 1959. Assoc. Cahill Gordon & Reindel, N.Y.C., 1959-67, ptnr., 1968-97. Served to 1st. lt. U.S. Army, 1955-57, Korea. Republican. Episcopalian.

COX, MARVIN MELVIN, JR., finance executive, corporate officer; b. Kingman, Kans., Nov. 19, 1953; s. Marvin M. Sr. and Willa J. (Huddleston) C.; m. Barbara J. Bodecker, Oct. 6, 1979; 1 child, Andrew Michael. BSBA, U. Kans., 1975. Mem. dept. acctg. First Securities Co. Kans. Inc., Wichita, 1975-76, cashier, 1975-76, account rep., 1976-92, v.p., 1982-87, v.p., corp. sec., 1984-87, exec. v.p., corp. sec., 1987-92, also bd. dirs.; v.p. Shearson Lehman Bros., Wichita, 1992-93, Smith Barney, Inc., Wichita, 1993—. Bd. dirs. Heartspring, 1993—, Wichita Found., Sr. Svcs., Inc.; mem. Wichita Art Assn. Mem. U. Kans. Alumni Assn., Crestview County Club.

COX, MELVIN MONROE, lawyer; b. Omaha, Jan. 31, 1947; s. Monroe M. Cox and Wilma Grace (Prickett) McPherson. BA with high honors, U. Wyo., 1969; JD, Harvard U., 1972. Bar: Pa. 1972, U.S. Dist. Ct. (we. dist.) Pa. 1972, N.J. 1987, U.S. Dist. Ct. (N.J.) 1987. Assoc. Rose, Schmidt & Dixon, Pitts., 1972-78; atty. Chgo. Pneumatic Tool Co., N.Y.C., 1978-81, asst. sec., 1981-88; asst. gen. counsel Sun Chem. Corp., Ft. Lee, N.J., 1989-93, asst. gen. counsel and asst. sec., 1993-97, v.p., gen. counsel, sec., 1997—. Adj. prof. engring. law The Cooper Union, N.Y.C., 1984-91; asst. sec. DIC Ams., Inc., Ft. Lee, 1993-97; mng. dir. Sun Chem. B.V., Soest, The Netherlands; bd. dirs. Polychrome Corp., Ft. Lee, Kodak Polychrome, Graphics Co. Ltd., Barbados; bd. visitors U. Wyoming, Coll. Arts and Scis., 1997—, vice chmn., 1998-2001. Bd. dirs. Good Shepherd Cmty. Svcs., Inc., Ft. Lee, 1999-2001; bd. trustees U. Wyoming Found., 2001-. Recipient Outstanding Alumnus award, U. Wyo., 2002. Mem. ABA, Am. Corp. Counsel Assn., Phi Beta Kappa, Phi Kappa Phi. Office: Sun Chem Corp 222 Bridge Plz S Fort Lee NJ 07024-5703

COX, MIKE, state attorney general; m. Laura Cox; 4 children. BA in Polit. Sci. with distinction, U. Mich., 1986, JD, 1989. Asst. pros. atty. Office Pros. Atty. Oakland County, Pontiac, Mich., 1989—90; asst. pros. atty. spl. crimes sect. Office Pros. Atty. Wayne County, Detroit, 1990—2001, dep. chief homicide unit, 2001—03; atty. gen. State of Mich., Lansing, 2003—. With USMC, 1980—83. Mem.: Inc. Soc. Irish/Am. Lawyers, State Bar Mich. (criminal law sect.), Pros. Attys. Assn. Mich. (instr. Basic Sch.). Republican. Office: G Mennen Williams Bldg 7th Fl PO Box 30212 525 W Ottawa St Lansing MI 48909*

COX, MITCHEL NEAL, editor; b. Portsmouth, Ohio, Sept. 8, 1956; s. Walter Eugene and Mary Agnes (Orlett) Cox; m. Lisa Renee LaLonde, Sept. 8, 1979 (dec. May 2001); children: Harmony, Leigh Ann, Katie. BS in Journalism, Ohio State U., 1985. Mng. editor The Puller, Columbus, Ohio, 1984-87; editor Bicycles Today, Columbus, 1985-87, Fur-Fish-Game, Columbus, 1987—. Mem. Outdoor Writers Assn. Am. Office: Fur-Fish-Game 2878 E Main St Columbus OH 43209-2698 E-mail: ffgcox@ameritech.net.

COX, PAT, artist; b. Pasadena, Calif., Mar. 6, 1921; d. Walter Melville and Mary Elizabeth (Frost) Broadway; m. Dale William Cox Jr., Feb. 19, 1946; children: Brian Philip, Dale William III, Gary Walter. BA, Mills Coll., 1943, MA, 1944. Graphic artist Pacific Manifolding Book Co., Emeryville, Calif., 1944-45; tchr. art to adults China Lake, Calif., 1957-63; tchr. art to children Peninsula Enrichment Program, Rancho Palos Verdes, Calif., 1965-67; graphic artist Western Magnum Corp., Hermosa Beach, Calif., 1970-80; tchr. art workshop Art at Your Fingertips, Rancho Palos Verdes, 1994-95. One-woman shows include Palos Verdes Art Ctr., Rancho Palos Verdes, Calif., 1977, 79, 83, 92, Thinking Eye Gallery, L.A., 1988, Ventura (Calif.) Coll. Art Galleries, 1994, Mendenhall Gallery, Whittier (Calif.) Coll., 1995, The Gallery at Stevenson Union, So. Oreg. U., Ashland, 1996, Fresno Art Museum, Fresno, Calif., 1999; two person exhibits Laguna Art Mus., Laguna Beach, Calif., 1971, Creative Arts Gallery, Burbank, Calif., 1993; group exhibits include Long Beach Mus. Art, Art Rental Gallery, 1979, L.A. County Mus. Art, Art Rental Gallery, 1979, Palm Springs Mus. Art, 1980, Laguna Art Mus., 1981, N.Mex. Fine Arts Gallery, 1981, Pacific Grove Art Ctr., 1983, Phoenix Art Mus., 1983, Riverside Art Mus., 1985, Laguna Art Mus., 1986, Zanesville Art Ctr., Ohio, 1987, The Thinking Eye Gallery, L.A., 1987, 89, Hippodrome Gallery, Long Beach, 1988, N.Mex. State Fine Arts Gallery, 1988, Newport Harbor Art Mus., 1988, Downey Mus. Art, 1990, 92, Internat. Contemporary Art Fair L.A., 1986, 87, 88, 92, U. Tex. Health Sci. Ctr., 1992, Long Beach Arts, 1991, 92, 93, Young Aggressive Art Mus., Santa Ana, 1993, U. Ark. Fine Arts Gallery, Fayetteville, 1994, Laura Knott Art Gallery, Bradford Coll., Mass., 1994, Bridge Street Gallery, Big Fork, Mont., 1994, St. John's Coll. Art Gallery, Santa Fe, 1995, L.A. Harbor Coll., Calif., 1995, Walker Art Collection, Garnett, Kans., 1995, San Francisco State U., 1996, Coleman Gallery, Albuquerque, 1996, Loyola Law Sch., L.A., 1996, San Bernardino County Mus., 1996, Prieto Gallery, Mills Coll., Oakland, Calif., 1996, U. So. Calif. Hillel Gallery, L.A., 1997, The Stage Gall. Merrick, NY, 1999, Nabisco Gall., E. hanover, NJ, 2000, California State U., Los Angeles, 2001, Pasadena Historical Mus. Gallery, Calif., 2002, Schneider Mus. Art So. Oreg. U., Ashland, Oreg., 2003. Trustee L.A. Art Assn., 1972-79; bd. dirs. Palos Verdes Art Ctr., 1966-70, 87-89, chair exhbn. com., 1982-85, co-chair Art for Fun(d)s Sake, 1966; judge Tournament of Roses Assn., Pasadena, 1975; mem. strategic planning Palos Verdes Art Ctr., 1988; mem. Pacific Pl. Planning Commn. Percent for Art, San Pedro, Calif., 1989; juror Pasadena Soc. Artists, 1973, 81, Women Painters West, 1984-85. Recipient Silver Pin award Palos Verdes Art Ctr., 1988, Calif. Gold Discovery award V.I.P. Jury Panel, L.A., 1994. Mem. Nat. Watercolor Soc. (juror 1981, 1st v.p. 1980, 4th v.p. 1984), Nat. Mus. Women in the Arts, Oakland Mus. Art, Mus. Contemporary Art, L.A. County Mus. Art, Palos Verdes Cmty. Art Assn. (cert. appreciation 1981). Avocations: gardening, reading.

COX, PAUL ALAN, ethnobotanist, educator; b. Salt Lake City, Oct. 10, 1953; s. Leo A. and Rae (Gabbitas) C.; m. Barbara Ann Wilson, May 21, 1975; children: Emily Ann, Paul Matthew, Mary Elisabeth, Hillary Christine, Jane Margaret. BS, Brigham Young U., 1976; MSc, U. Wales, 1978; AM, Harvard U., 1978, PhD, 1981; DSc (hon.), U. Guelph, Can., 2000. Teaching fellow Harvard U., Cambridge, Mass., 1977-81; Miller research fellow Miller Inst. Basic Research in Sci., Berkeley, Calif., 1981-83; asst. prof. Brigham Young U., Provo, Utah, 1983-86, assoc. prof., 1986-91, prof., 1991—, dean gen. edn. and honors, 1993-97; King Gustav XVI prof. environ. sci. Swedish Biodiversity Ctr., 1997—; dir. Nat. Tropical Botanical Garden, Kalaheo, Hawaii, 1998—. Disting. prof. Brigham Young U., Hawaii, 2000—; ecologist Utah Environ. Coun., Salt Lake City, 1976; project ecologist Utah MX Coordination Office, Salt Lake City, 1981. Mem. editorial bd. Pacific Studies. Recipient Bowdoin prize, The Goldman Environ. prize, 1997; Danforth Found. fellow, 1976-81, Fulbright fellow, 1976-77, NSF fellow, 1977-81, Linnaen Soc. fellow, Melbourne Univ. fellow, 1985-86; named NSF Presdl. Young Investigator, 1985-90, Hero of Medicine, Time Mag., 1997. Mem. AAAS, Brit. Ecol. Soc., Internat. Soc. Ethnopharmacology (former pres.), Am. Soc. Naturalists, Assn. Tropical Biology, Soc. Econ. Botany (former pres.), Seacology Found. (founder and chmn.). Mem. Lds Ch. Office: Dir Nat Tropical Botanical Gardens 3530 Papalina Rd Kalaheo HI 96741-9599

COX, RICHARD GARNER, music educator; b. Rocky Mount, NC, Dec. 12, 1928; s. Richard Benjamin and Grace Willye (Garner) C.; m. Mary Alicia Carey, Dec. 19, 1959; children: David, John, Anna. BA, U. N.C., 1949, MA, 1951; diploma in voice, Paris Conservatory, 1952; PhD, Northwestern U., Evanston, Ill., 1963. Asst. prof. music High Point (N.C.) Coll., 1953-58; from instr. to prof. U. N.C., Greensboro, 1960—2002. Choral dir. Ea. Music Festival, Greensboro, 1977—, Greensboro Opera Co., 1981-96; choirmaster Holy Trinity Episcopal Ch., Greensboro, 1963—. Author: A Singer's Manual of German and French Diction, 1970, Singing in English, 1990; editor Rsch. Reports column Choral Jour., 1978-87; editor choral edits. Univ. N.C. Greensboro Choral Series, 1980, 82, 87. Recipient Fulbright award U.S. Govt., 1951. Mem. Am. Choral Dirs. Assn. (pres. So. divsn. 1967-71, pres. NC chpt. 1983-85, So. Divsn. Choral Excellence award 2002), Music Educators Nat. Conf., Phi Beta Kappa, Phi Mu Alpha. Episcopalian.

COX, RICHARD HORTON, civil engineering executive; b. Paia, Hawaii, Oct. 10, 1920; s. Joel B. and Helen Cliford (Horton) C.; m. Hester Virginia Smith, Dec. 12, 1942 (dec. Aug. 12, 1995); children: Millicent, Janet, Lydia, Evelyn, David, Samuel (dec.). BS, Calif. Inst. Tech., 1942, MS, 1946. Registered profl. engr., surveyor, Hawaii. Supr. rocket range Calif. Inst. Tech., Pasadena, 1942-46; civil engr. McBryde Sugar Co., Eleele, Hawaii, 1946-56; land mgr. Alexander & Baldwin, Honolulu, 1956-71, v.p., 1971-86; engring. cons. Honolulu, 1986—. Mem. State Commn. on Water Resource Mgmt., 1987-94, 95-99. Fellow ASCE; mem. AAAS, NSPE, Am. Geophys. Union. Mem. Soc. Of Friends. Home and Office: 1951 Kakela Dr Honolulu HI 96822-2156

COX, RICHARD JOSEPH, former broadcasting executive; b. Bklyn., Aug. 21, 1929; s. Harry Joseph and Rosemary Magdelene (Broderick) C.; m. Ray Louise Bradley, Oct. 2, 1954 (dec. 1996); children: Christopher Bradley, Cynthia Anne, John Anthony, Claudia Claire. Student, Fordham U., 1947-49. With Young & Rubicam Inc., N.Y.C., 1949-66, v.p. in charge radio and TV, 1963-66; v.p. in charge TV programming Doyle Dane Bernbach, 1966-71; v.p. in charge program devel. Tomorrow Entertainment Inc., 1971-73; pres. Y&R Ventures, Inc., N.Y.C., 1974-78; pres. subs. DCA Prodns. Inc., N.Y.C., 1974-78; owner, pres., exec. prodr. DCA TV, Inc., 1978-81; pres. CBS Cable div. CBS Inc., 1981-83; owner, pres. DCA TV Inc., 1983—. Co-producer off-Broadway play Orlando Furioso, 1970 (spl. Obie award 1971). Mem. Pres.'s Com. on Drug Abuse, 1969-70. Served with Psychol. Warfare Group, U.S. Army 1951-53. Mem.: Players, Burke Hollow, Vets of 7th Regt., Four Seasons. Republican. Roman Catholic. Home: 623 B Onondaga Ln Stratford CT 06614 E-mail: onondaga@sbcglobal.net.

COX, ROBERT GENE, management consultant; b. Liberal, Kans., June 3, 1929; s. Clarice Eldon and Margaret Verene (Jones) C.; m. Eileen Frances Hinshaw, July 10, 1953; children: Ann Rebecca Cox Taylor, Allan Robert. BA with honors, U. N.Mex., 1951, JD, 1955; grad., Fgn. Service Inst., 1956, Harvard Bus. Sch., 1978, 79. Joined Fgn. Svc., 1956; 3d to 2d sec. Am. Embassy, Panama, 1956-58; Am. Consul, Caracas, Venezuela, 1959-61; Korea desk officer Dept. State, Washington, 1961-62, chief of staff mgmt. planning, 1963-65, officer in charge Mission to Israel, 1965; staff asst. to President U.S. The White House, 1966-68; ptnr. William H. Clark Assos., N.Y.C. and Chgo., 1968-71; sr. staff officer UN Secretariat, Vienna and N.Y.C., 1971-72; pres. Hennes & Cox, Inc., N.Y.C., Washington and Los Angeles, 1972-75; prin., nat. dir. human resource systems Ernst & Ernst, Cleve., 1975-78; ptnr., mng. dir. Arthur Young & Co., N.Y.C., 1979-83; pres. PA Exec. Search Group, N.Y.C., 1983-86; chmn. PA Computers and Telecommunications NA, N.Y.C., 1985-86; mng. dir. A.T. Kearney, Inc., 1987-90, 93-96; exec. v.p. Oxford Analytica, Inc., N.Y.C., 1990-92; exec. dir. Oxford Analytica Ltd., Eng., 1990-92; pres. Nelson O'Connor & Cox, Tucson, Ariz., 1996—. Mem. history faculty Fla. State U., 1958; cons. Commn. U.S.-Latin-Am. Rels., 1974; sr. advisor Commn. Orgn. of Govt. for Conduct of Fgn. Policy, 1974-75; expert witness on mil. value of Panama Canal U.S. Ho. of Reps., 1977; ITT lectr. Georgetown U., 1981. Author: Defense Department Diplomacy in Latin America, 1964, Choices for Partnership or Bloodshed in Panama, 1975, The Canal Zone: New Focal Point in U.S.-Latin American Relations, 1977, The Chief Executive, 1980, Planning for Immigration: A Business Perspective, 1981, Selection of the Chief Executive Officer, 1982. Mem. Pacific Coun. Internat. Policy; bd. dirs. cmty. drug control program, Glen Ridge, N.J., 1971-72, Unitarian-Universalist Christian Fellowship, 1987-90; dep. to county chmn. Albuquerque Dem. Party, 1954; advisor on exec. selection to transition staff of Pres.-elect Carter, 1976-77; mem. bd. advisors Georgetown U. Program in Bus. Diplomacy, 1985-95; bd. dirs. Coun. on Econ. Priorities, 1982-86, LeRoy Industries, Inc., 1984-87, 89-91, Alden Owners, Inc., 1986-88; trustee Meadville Theol. Sch. U. Chgo., 1986-92; gov. Manchester Coll. Oxford U., 1991-96, councillor, 1992-96, hon. gov. 1996—; trustee Unitarian Ch. of All Souls, N.Y.C., 1980-84, sec., 1979-80, pres., 1983-84, deacon, 1985-92; lay preacher Manchester Coll. Chapel, Oxford U., 1990-96; mem. vestry St. Philip's Episc. Ch., Tucson, 1996—, sr. warden, 1997—. Mem. Jonesville (Mich.) Heritage Assn., Coun. Fgn. Rels. (chmn. study group on immigration and U.S. fgn. policy 1978), Royal Econ. Soc. (Eng.), Am. Soc. Internat. Law, Unitarian Hist. Soc. Eng., Martineau Soc. Eng., Internat. Assn. Religious Freedom, SAR. Episcopalian. Office: 712 W 12th St Silver City NM 88061-4204

COX, ROBERT RIPLEY, JR., wildlfe research biologist; b. Mar. 1, 1959; BS in Forest Resources, U. Ga., 1987; MS in Fisherier and Wildlife, Utah State U., 1993; PhD in Wildlife and Fisherier Sci., La. State U., 1996. Ecologist No. Prarie Sci. Ctr., Jamestown, N.D., 1995-97, statistician, 1997-2000, wildlife rsch. biologist, 2000—. Office: Northern Prairie Wildlife Rsch Ctr 8711 37th St SE Jamestown ND 58401-9736 E-mail: rrcox@valleytel.net., robert_cox@usgs.gov.

COX, RODY P(OWELL), medical educator, internist; b. New Brighton, Pa., June 24, 1926; s. Raymond James and Hazel (Powell) C.; m. Jane Beverly Birks, Sept. 5, 1953 (dec. Apr. 1995); children: Shelley Lea, Rody Powell, Sue Ellen; m. LaVaun Jeanne Sears, Mar. 1, 1997. Student, Franklin and Marshall Coll., 1946-48; MD, U. Pa., 1952. Diplomate Am. Bd. Internal Medicine. Intern U. Mich., 1952-53, resident in medicine, 1953-54, U. Pa., Phila., 1953-57, asst. prof. medicine, 1957-60; rsch. assoc. U. Glasgow, Scotland, 1960-61; prof. medicine NYU, N.Y.C., 1961-79, prof. pharmacology, 1972-79, chief div. human genetics, 1972-79; prof., vice chmn. dept. medicine Case-Western Res. U., Cleve., 1979-88; chief med. svc. VA Med. Ctr., Cleve., 1979-88; dean Med. Sch. U. Tex. Southwestern Med. Ctr., Dallas, 1988-89, prof. internal medicine, 1988—. Mem. metabolism study sect. NIH, 1970-74, chmn. genetics study sect., 1978-79, chmn. mammalian genetics study sect., 1979-81; mem. panel on clin. scis. NRC, 1976-86. Editor: Cell Communication, 1974; co-editor: Epithelial Cell Culture, 1981; contbr. articles to profl. publs. Sgt. U.S. Army, 1944-46, NATOUSA. Fellow ACP; mem. Am. Soc. Clin. Investigation (emeritus), Assn. Am. Physicians, Ctrl. Soc. Clin. Rsch., John Morgan Soc. U. Pa., Harvey Soc., Am. Clin. Climatol. Assn., Am. Soc. Human Genetics, Interurban Clin. Club, Alpha Omega Alpha (councillor NYU chpt. 1970-76). Home: 5 Connaught Ct Dallas TX 75225-2459 Office: U Tex Southwestern Med Ctr 5323 Harry Hines Blvd Dallas TX 75390-8889 E-mail: rcox@mednet.swmed.edu.

COX, ROGER FRAZIER, lawyer; b. Phila., Sept. 11, 1939; s. Roger Newcomb and Ethel May (Frazier) Cox; m. Lucy Jakstas, June 24, 1967. BA, Amherst Coll., 1962; LLB, U. Pa., 1966. Bar: DC 1967, Pa. 1967, Calif. 1970. Law clk. to presiding judge U.S. Dist. Ct., N.Y.C., 1966-67; asst. dist. atty. Phila. Dist. Atty.'s Office, 1967-69; staff atty. Alameda County Legal Aid Soc., Oakland, Calif., 1969-71; from assoc. to ptnr. Blank Rome LLP, Phila., 1971—. Mem.: ABA, Phila. Bar Assn., Pa. Bar Assn., Am. Judicature Soc., Order of Coif. Home: 303 Delancey St Philadelphia PA 19106-4208 Office: Blank Rome LLP One Logan Sq Philadelphia PA 19103-6998 E-mail: cox@blankrome.com.

COX, RON DEAN, non-commissioned officer, educator, psychologist; b. Miami, Fla., June 26, 1939; s. Fred Raymond and Wilbour Handy C.; m. Sue James, Aug. 8, 1964; 1 child, Victor. AA, Gulf Coast Cmty. Coll., 1984; BS in Psychology, Fla. State U., Panama City, 1986, MS in Applied Psychology, 1988. Enlisted USAF, 1957, advanced through grades to master sgt., 1974, ret., 1978; adj. prof. Gulf Coast Cmty. Coll., Panama City, Fla., 1988-95, ret., 1995. Chair ad-hoc com. computer selection City of Callaway, Fla., 1982. Designer of modifications for B-52 Flight Simulator, 1969, 70. Asst. campaign mgr. Mayor, Callaway, 1984. Mem. Phi Beta Kappa. Republican. Baptist. Avocations: reading, aviation history, politics. Home: 6521 Hiwassee St Panama City FL 32404-8020

COX, SANFORD CURTIS, JR., lawyer; b. El Paso, Tex., July 31, 1929; s. Sanford Curtis Sr. and Iva M. (Richardson) C.; m. Helen A. Thurston, Sept. 27, 1958; children: Sanford Curtis III, Christopher Thurston. BA, Tex. Western Coll., 1951, MA, 1952; LLB, U. Tex., 1957. Bar: Tex. 1957, U.S. Dist. Ct. (we. dist.) Tex. 1960, U.S. Ct. Appeals (5th cir.) 1964, U.S. Ct. Appeals (D.C. cir.) 1975. Assoc. Andress, Lipscomb, Peticolas & Fisk, El Paso, 1957-61; ptnr. Lipscomb, Fisk & Cox, El Paso, 1961-74, Fisk & Cox, El Paso, 1974-79; sole practice El Paso, 1979-81; pres./shareholder Sanford C. Cox Jr. P.C., El Paso, 1981-93, mem., 1993—. Mem. bd. editors U. Tex. Law Rev. Mem. adv. bd. Booth Meml. Home, 1963-79, Pleasant View Home, 1979-91. Served with U.S. Army, 1952-54. Mem. ABA, Tex. Bar Assn. (admissions com. 17th dist. 1976), El Paso Bar Assn. (ethics com. 1965-69, fee arbitration com. 1973-75), Order of Coif, Phi Delta Phi. Republican. Episcopalian. Office: 6006 N Mesa St El Paso TX 79912-4659

COX, TERI P. public relations executive; b. Pitts., May 21, 1952; d. Meyer and Faye Helen (Tischler) Polack; m. William R. Cox, Jan. 1, 1982. BA, U. Pitts., 1974; MBA in Mktg., NYU, 1989. Info. dir. United Mental Health; prodr., host weekly PA radio program; pub. rels. dir. Atlanta Merchandise Mart; mktg. rsch., pub. rels. cons. Pfizer Inc., NYU Stern Sch. Bus.; acct. supr. Burson-Marsteller; mng. ptnr. Cox Comms. Ptnrs., Lawrenceville, N.J., 1992-98, sr. mng. ptnr., 1998—. Bd. dirs. ea. divsn. Am. Cancer Soc.; mem. N.J. Cancer Coun., Advocacy Leadership Team. Recipient Capitol Dome award Nat. Am. Cancer Soc., 1997. Mem.: NAFE, Women Execs. in Pub. Rels., Healthcare Business-women's Assn. (past pres. bd. dirs.), Pub. Rels. Soc. Am. Office: Cox Comms Ptnrs 2 Roseberry Ct Lawrenceville NJ 08648-1058

COX, WALTER CLAY JR. lawyer, real estate broker; b. Danville, Ky., Nov. 9, 1922; s. Walter Clay Cox and Blanche Marie Phillips; m. Mary Lee Engle, Dec. 20, 1943 (dec. Dec. 1975); children: Mary Eugenia Cox Wakefield, Rebecca Lee Cox Woods; m. Pam G. Collis, July 3, 1988; 1 child, Walter Clay III. JD, U. Ky., 1948. Bar: Ky. 1948, U.S. Supreme Ct. 1970, U.S. Dist. Ct. Ky. 1953, U.S. Ct. Appeals 1953, Korea Supreme Ct. 1952. Police judge City of Lancaster, 1949-52; ptnr. Walker & Cox, Lancaster, Ky., 1948-52, Bell & Cox, Lexington, Ky., 1953—55, Fowler, Measle & Bell, Lexington, Ky., 1855—1988, of counsel, 1988—; assoc. broker Paul Semonin, Lexington, 1990—95; broker Realty Depot, Lexington, 1997—. Author: Commercial Collections, 1986. Capt. inf. U.S. Army, 1943-46, ETO, judge advocate, 1951-52, Korea. Mem. Ky. Bar Assn. (sr. counselor 1997), E. 70th Infantry

Divsn. Assn. (v.p. 1978-86, Ky. coord. 1996—), Civil War Roundtable, Lancaster Kiwanis Club (pres. 1949), Lexington Kiwanis Club (pres. 1976), Bluegrass Sportsmans Club (bd. dirs. 1993-94), Lexington Country Club (v.p. 1993-96). Republican. Greek Orthodox. Avocation: golf. Home: 4830 Wyndhurst Rd Lexington KY 40515-1251 Office: Fowler Measle & Bell 300 W Vine St Ste 600 Lexington KY 40507-1809 Fax: 859-255-3735. E-mail: walter@fmblaw.com., walter.cox2@verizon.net.

COX, WARREN JACOB, architect; b. N.Y.C., Aug. 28, 1935; s. Oscar Sydney and Louise Bryson (Black) C.; m. Claire Christie-Miller, July 1, 1975; children: Alexandra Louise, Samuel Oscar. BA magna cum laude, Yale U., 1957, MArch, 1961. Ptnr. Hartman-Cox Architects, Washington, 1965—. Vis. archtl. critic Yale, 1966, Cath. U. Am., 1967, U. Va., 1976; lectr. Works include master plan, dormitory and chapel, Mt. Vernon Coll., EURAM bldg. Nat. Perm. Bldg., Folger Shakespeare Libr. addition, Washington, Immanuel Presbyn. Ch., Nat. Humanities Ctr., Raleigh, Am. Embassy, Malaysia, HEB corp. hdqrs., San Antonio, Chrysler Mus. remodeling, Norfolk, Dumbarton Oaks remodeling, Monroe Hall and Rouss Hall addition, U. of Va., Charlottesville, Sumner Sq., 1001 Pa. Ave., Market Sq., Franklin Sq., Georgetown U. Law Ctr. Libr. and Residence Hall, Washington, John Carter Brown Libr. addition, Providence, Winterthur New Exhbn. Bldg., Wilmington, Del., Tulane Law Sch., New Orleans, Law Sch. Libr. Univ. Conn., Hartford, Law Sch. Washington U., St. Louis, Libr. Case We. Res. U., Cleve., Fed. Courthouse, Corpus Christi, Tex., Concert Hall remodeling Kennedy Ctr. for Performing Arts, Washington, New Dist. and Cir. Courthouses, Lexington, Kennedy Warren Apts. addition, Lincoln and Jefferson Memls. restoration, Patent Office Bldg. renovation, Nat. Archives Bldg. renovation, Washington, Jefferson Libr., Monticello and spl. collections libr., U. of Va., Charlottesville. Mem. Georgetown Commn. Fine Arts, 1971-75; chmn. Friends of Folger Shakespeare Libr., 1987-88; bd. dirs. Ctr. for Palladian Studies in Am., 1982—, D.C. Preservation League, 1987-89. Recipient over 110 nat. and regional design awards including Louis Sullivan Prize (1972), six AIA Nat. Honor awards, and the AIA Archtl. Firm award, 1988. Fellow AIA. Home: 3111 N St NW Washington DC 20007-3420 also: PO Box 1 Church Hill MD 21623-0001 Office: Hartman Cox Architects 1074 Thomas Jefferson St NW Washington DC 20007-3832

COX, WILFORD DONALD, retired food company executive; b. Marion, Ill., Sept. 5, 1925; s. James Roy and Mamie (Stahlhut) C.; m. Helen Eunice Turner, Sept. 8, 1945; 1 child, James Dexter. Grad. high sch., Crab Orchard, Ill. Asst. plant mgr. Std. Brands Inc., San Antonio, 1956-60; plant mgr. Dallas, 1960-64; asst. div. mgr. Kansas City, Mo., 1964-70; div. mgr., 1972-78; v.p. procurement N.Y.C., 1978-81; v.p. Cal-Maine Foods, Jackson, Miss., 1970-72; v.p. commodities Nabisco Brands Inc., East Hanover, N.J., 1981-84; v.p. oil procurement Kraft Inc., Glenview, Ill., then Memphis, 1984-90, ret., 1990. Mem. Nat. Inst. Oilseed Processors, Nat. Soybean Processors Assn., Nat. Assn. Purchasing Mgrs., Colonial Country Club (Memphis). Republican. Avocation: golf.

COX, WILLIAM ANDREW, cardiovascular thoracic surgeon; b. Columbus, Ga., Aug. 3, 1925; s. Virgil Augustus and Dale Jackson C.; m. Nina Recelle Hobby, Jan. 1, 1948; children: Constance Lynn Cox Rogers, Patricia Ann Cox Brown, William Robert, Janet Elaine Cox Sidewater. Student, Presbyn. Coll., 1942, Harvard U., 1944-45, Cornell U., 1945; BS, Emory U., 1950, MD, 1954; MS in Surgery, Baylor U., 1961. Diplomate Am. Bd. Surgery, Am. Bd. Thoracic Surgery. Active duty USN, 1943-46; lt. (j.g.) USNR, 1946-54; commd. 1st lt. M.C. U.S. Army, 1954, advanced through grades to col., 1969; intern Brooke Army Med. Ctr., San Antonio, 1954-55, resident gen. surgery, 1956-60; resident cardiovasc. thoracic surgery Walter Reed Army Med. Ctr., Washington, 1960-62, staff cardiothoracic surgeon, 1962; asst chief cardiothoracic surgery Letterman Gen. Hosp., San Francisco, 1962-65; chief dept. surgery and cardiothoracic surgery 121 Evaculation Hosp, Seoul, Korea, 1965-66; cons. cardiothoracic surgery Korean Theatre, 1965-66; asst. chief cardiothoracic surgery Brooke Army Med Ctr., 1966-69, chief, 1969-73, bd. dirs. thoracic surgery residency programs, 1966-73, ret., 1973. Brooke Tower, on call for Pres. Lyndon B. Johnson when he visited his Tex. Ranch, 1967-72; clin. prof. cardio-thoracic surgery U. Tex. Sch. Medicine, San Antonio, 1971—; practice specializing in cardiovasc. thoracic surgery, Corpus Christi, Tex., 1973-93; cons. cardio-thoracic surgery Brooke Army Med. Ctr., San Antonio, 1977—; chief staff Meml. Med. Ctr., 1980; dir. disaster med. care region 3A Tex. State Dept. Health, 1973-88, mem. Coastal Bend Coun. Gov.'s Emergency Med. Svc. Commn., 1979-88; mem. adv. bd. on congenital heart disease Tex. Dept. Health, 1980-88; participant joint confs. on cardiovasc. surgery and thoracic surgery Am. People Amb. Program, Leningrad, Moscow, Bucharest, Romania, Belgrade, Yugoslavia, Prague, Czechoslovakia, 1987; del. Vanderbilt U. Joint conf. vascular surgery Dublin, Ireland, Edinburgh, Scotland, London, 1986; participant joint confs. cardiovasc. surgery and thoracic surgery Am. Amb. People to People Program, Singapore, Kuala Lumpur, Malaysia, Hanoi, Vietnam, DaNang, Vietnam, Hue, Vietnam, Saigon, Vietnam, Hong Kong, 1992, People to People Am. Amb. Program, Eng., Scotland, Wales, 1996, 13th worldwide conf., Chester, England, 1998, 14th worldwide conf., Hong Kong, 2000, Denton A. Cooley Cardiovasc. Surgery Soc. mtg. Coeur d'Alene, Idaho, 2000; spkr. symposium Controversies in Cardiology, Dr. Willis Hurst, Holland Am. Lines Veendam, 1997; invited spkr. on open heart surgery 780 Bomb Squadron, Gainesville, 2001 Contbr. numerous articles to profl. jours. Ruling elder Presbyn. Ch., 1960—. Decorated Legion of Merit, Army Commendation medal; recipient A Prefix award Surgeon Gen. U.S. Army, commendation Surgeon Gen. South Korea, commendation Eighth U.S. Army Commdg. Gen. for Emergency Surgery on Adm. Blackburn U.S. Negotiator for Peace, Pan mun jom, North Korea; named hon. citizen Phila. by Mayor Edward G. Rendell, 1995. Fellow Am. Coll. Chest Physicians; mem. AMA, Soc. Thoracic Surgeons, Denton A. Coley Cardiovasc. Surgery Soc., Tex. Med. Assn. (del. conf. infectious diseases Bangkok, Hong Kong, Beijing, Shanghai, 1983), So. Thoracic Surgery Assn., Nueces County Med. Soc., Corpus Christi Surg. Soc., 38th Parallel Med. Soc., U.S. Power Squadron, People to People Internat., Internat. Platform, USN League (life), Retired Officers Assn. (life), Navy Meml. Yacht Club (past commodore presidio San Francisco), T-Bar-M Racquet Club, Corpus Christi Country Club, Corpus Christi Athletic Club, Corpus Christi Town, Ft. Sam Houston Officers Club. Republican. Home: 5214 Wooldridge Rd Corpus Christi TX 78413-3833

COX, WILLIAM DONALD, JR., lawyer; b. Haverhill, Mass., Nov. 26, 1957; s. William Donald, Sr. and Beatrice Mary (Denzin) Cox. BA, Bradford Coll., 1979; postgrad., Am. U., 1979-80; JD, New Eng. Sch. Law, 1987. Bar: Mass. 1987, U.S. Dist. Ct. Mass. 1989, Maine 1990. Pers. dir. City of Haverhill, 1984-88; asst. dist. atty. Dist. Atty.'s Office County of Essex, Salem, Mass., 1988; pvt. practice Haverhill, 1988—; asst. city solicitor City of Haverhill, 1994—. Chmn. Haverhill Dem. City Com., 2002—. Mem.: ABA, Essex County Bar Assn., Boston Bar Assn., Mass. Bar Assn., Bradford Coll. Alumni Assn. (treas.). Avocation: politics. Home: 8 Richmond St Haverhill MA 01830-6010 Address: 145 S Main St Bradford MA 01835-7438

COX, WILLIAM FREDERICK, hospital executive; b. Richmond, Ind., Mar. 20, 1962; s. Leon Thompson and Donna Eloise (Mitchell) C.; m. Laurie Ann DeTore, July 25, 1992. BA, Earlham Coll., 1984; MD, Case Western Res. U., 1988. Diplomate Am. Bd. Psychiatry and Neurology. Gaughan fellow in forensic psychiatry Harvard Med. Sch., Cambridge, Mass., 1993—94; staff psychiatrist Carney Hosp., Boston, 1994—96; preceptor Boston U. Sch. Medicine, 1994—96; assoc. med. dir. Fuller Hosp., Attleboro, Mass., 1996-98; assoc. in psychiatry U. Mass. Med. Sch., 1999—2000; staff psychiatrist VA Med. Ctr., Albany, NY, 2000—; instr. in psychiatry Albany Med. Coll., 2001—. Republican. Avocations: bicycling, chess, basketball, canoeing. E-mail: thesaltbox@juno.com.

COX, WILLIAM JACKSON, retired bishop; b. Valeria, Ky., Jan. 24, 1921; s. Robert Lee and Ora Ethel (Lawson) C.; m. Betty Drake, Dec. 20, 1941; children: Sharon Lee, William Richard, Michael Colin Student, U. Cin., 1939-40, George Washington U., Washington, 1945-46, U. Md. overseas extension, London, 1951-53, Va. Theol. Sem., Alexandria, 1957, D.Div. (hon.), 1974, Episcopal Theol. Sem. Ky., Lexington, 1980. Ordained priest Episcopal Ch., 1957. Pres., gen. mgr. McCook Broadcasting Co., McCook, Nebr., 1947-49; rector Church of the Holy Cross, Cumberland, Md., 1957-72; suffragan bishop of Md. Episcopal Ch., Frederick, Md., 1972-80, asst. bishop Okla. Tulsa, 1980—88; ret., 1988. Pres. Appalachian Peoples Service Orgn., Blacksburg, Va., 1974-80; chmn. Standing Com. on the Church in Small Communities, N.Y.C., 1976-82 Pres., Nursing Home Bd. of Allegany County, Cumberland, Md., 1965-72; pres. Episcopal Ministries to the Aging, Balt., 1973-80. Served to lt. col. U.S. Army, 1942-46, 1949-54; ETO. Episcopalian. Avocation: private pilot. Home: 6130 S Hudson Pl Tulsa OK 74136-2703 Office: St Johns Ch 4200 S Atlanta Pl Tulsa OK 74105-4331

COX, WILLIAM MARTIN, lawyer, educator; b. Bernardsville, NJ, Dec. 26, 1922; s. Martin John and Nellie (Fotens) Cox; m. Julia Sebastian, June 14, 1952; children: Janice Cox Trautman, William Martin, Joann Cox Cahoon, Julieann Cox Allen. AB, Syracuse U., 1947; JD, Cornell U., 1950. Bar: N.J. 1950, U.S. Dist. Ct. 1950. Mem. Dolan & Dolan, Newton, NJ, 1950—; mem. faculty, tchr. zoning adminstrn. Rutgers U., New Brunswick, NJ, 1968—98. Gen. counsel emeritus N.J. Planning Ofcls.: pres. N.J. Inst. Mcpl. Attys., 1982—84; mem. Land Use Law Drafting Com., 1970—, chmn., 1993—98; dir. Equip, Inc., Marion, NC; bd. dirs. Newton Cemetery Co., v.p., 2000—. Author: Zoning and Land Use Administration in New Jersey, 22nd edit., 2003. With U.S. Army, 1943—45. Named Citizen of Yr., Town of Newton, 2002; recipient Resolution of Appreciation award, N.J. Senate and Gen. Assembly, 1994, Pres.'s Disting. Svc. award, N.J. League Municipalities, 1999, Excellence in Land Use Law award, N.J. Inst. Mcpl. Attys., 1999. Mem.: NJ Bar Assn., Sussex County Bar Assn., NJ Planning Ofcls., Am. Planning Assn., VFW, Rotary (pres. 1978—79, Vocat. award 1996), Monarchist League, Am. Legion. Baptist. Office: 1 Legal Ln Newton NJ 07860-1827

COX, WILLIAM VAUGHAN, lawyer; b. Jersey City, Nov. 12, 1936; s. Walter Miles and Emily (McNenney); divorced; children: Millicent S., Jennifer V. BA, Princeton U., 1958; LLB, Yale U., 1964. Bar: Colo. 1965, N.Y. 1974. Law clk. Holland & Hart, Denver, 1963; atty. Conoco Inc., Denver, 1966-72, asst. to v.p., gen. counsel Stamford, Conn., 1972-73; v.p., gen. counsel Stromberg-Carlson Corp., Rochester, N.Y., 1974-78; mng. ptnr. Bader & Cox, Denver, 1979-86, of counsel, 1986-88; pres. William V. Cox, P.C., Denver, 1988—2003, also bd. dirs.; project and planning dir. Interwest Comm. Corp., 1995-97. Pres., bd. dirs. New West Indies Trading Co., Denver, 1984—; pres. Coll. Football Ltd., Denver, 1990—. Sportswriter/editor: Colorado Springs (Colo.) Free Press, 1960-61. Football coach Cheyenne Mountain H.S., Colorado Springs, 1961; founder, bd. dirs., v.p., com. chmn., editor Colo. chpt. Nat. Football Found., 1992-2001; mem. adv. bd. Downtown Denver Dist., 1991-93; bd. dirs., com. chmn. Downtown Denver Residents, 1990-93; pres., bd. dirs. Barclay Towers Condominiums, Denver, 1990-92, sec., bd. dirs., 1998-99, pres. bd. dirs., 1999-2000, 2001—, sec. bd. dirs., 2000-2001; dist. capt. Rep. Com., Cherry Hills, Colo., 1980-85; bd. dirs. Monroe County Humane Soc., Rochester, 1975-78. With inf., intelligence USAR, 1959—65. Mem.: Am. Arbitration Assn. (arbitrator 2002—), Denver Bar Assn., Colo. Bar Assn., Law Club Denver (com. chmn. 1971), Princeton Rocky Mountain Club (com. chmn. 1972), Univ. Club Denver (bd. dirs. 1997—2000), Am. Legion, Corbey Ct., Phi Delta Phi. Roman Catholic. Avocations: running, politics, college football history, military history, animal rights. Office: 1625 Larimer St Ste 2707 Denver CO 80202-1538 E-mail: wvcsq@mduonline.net.

COXE, TENCH CHARLES, lawyer; b. Asheville, N.C., Dec. 9, 1925; s. Tench Charles and Frances Kinloch (Huger) C.; m. Frances James Marbury, May 26, 1956; children— Tench, Molly. B.S., Yale U., 1949; J.D., U. N.C., 1953. Bar: Ga. 1954, U.S. Dist. Ct. (no. dist.) Ga. 1954, U.S. Ct. Appeals (5th cir.) 1956, U.S. Supreme Ct. 1960. Assoc. Troutman Sams Schroder & Lockerman, Atlanta, 1954-56, ptnr., 1956-71; ptnr. Troutman, Sanders, Lockerman & Ashmore, Atlanta, 1972-92; ptnr., Troutman, Sanders, (formerly Troutman, Sanders, Lockerman & Ashmore), Atlanta, 1992—; dir. Turner Broadcasting System, Atlanta, Munich Am. Reassurance Co., Atlanta. Served to 1st lt. AUS, 1944-53; ETO; Korea. Mem. Lawyers Club of Atlanta (pres. 1969), Atlanta Bar Assn., Ga. Bar Assn., ABA, Atlanta Lawyers Found. (treas. 1974—). Episcopalian. Clubs: Piedmont Driving, Commerce, Ashford (Atlanta). Home: 600 Peachtree St NE Ste 5200 Atlanta GA 30308-2231 Office: Troutman Sanders 5200 NationsBank Plz 600 Peachtree St NE Ste 5200 Atlanta GA 30308-2216

COX-KLACZAK, KAREN MICHELLE, marketing educator, computer company official; b. Drexel Hill, Pa., Oct. 16, 1963; d. Robert Harold and Margaret Ellen (O'Brien) Cox; m. Robert John Klaczak, June 4, 1994; children: Joshua Robert, Philip Christopher. BSBA, Drexel U., 1985; MBA, Villanova U., 1994. Fin. analyst Spectacor, Wynnewood, Pa., 1987-89; project mgmt. analyst Wyeth Ayerst Labs., Radnor, Pa., 1990-95; prof. mktg. Villanova (Pa.) U., 1995—. Cons. on advt. Mercia Grassi Assocs., Phila., 1984; cons. on strategy Villa St. John Hosp., Downingtown, Pa., 1992; cons. on new bus. devel. IBM, Wayne, Pa., 1995—. Mem. NAFE, Am. Mktg. Assn., Beta Gamma Sigma. Avocations: photography, collecting sea shells, travel, hiking, design. Home: 612 Thorncroft Dr West Chester PA 19380-6442 Office: Villanova U Mktg Dept 800 Lancaster Ave Villanova PA 19085-1603

COY, CHRISTOPHER JAMES, architect; b. Hackensack, NJ, Dec. 19, 1950; s. James Joseph and Evelyn Theresa (Popitti) Coy; m. Joann Owen, June 25, 1983; 1 child, Camille Violet. BArch, CCNY, 1986. Registered arch., NY. Prin. Barnes Coy Archs., Bridgehampton, NY, 1993—. Mem.: AIA. Office: Barnes Coy Archs 1936 Montauk Hwy Bridgehampton NY 11932 Office Fax: 631-537-0558. Business E-Mail: christopher@barnescoy.com.

COY, CRAIG P. airport terminal executive; Degree, U.S. Coast Guard Acad.; MBA, Harvard U. Various sr. level positions Fed. Govt., 20 yrs; v.p., gen. mgr. Lear Siegler Svcs. Inc., 1992-97; CEO HR Logic, Waltham, Mass., 1997—2001, Mass. Port Authority, 2001—. Past bd. dirs. White House Fellows Assn., U.S. Coast Guard Acad. Office: Mass Port Authority One Harborside Drive Ste 200S East Boston MA 02128-2909 E-mail: info@hrlogic.com.*

COY, CURTIS L. federal official; b. Ft. Belvoir, Va., Aug. 12, 1952; s. Malcolm L. and Beverly J. Coy; m. Denise Coy, Mar. 4, 1989; stepchildren: Bryan Carter, Justin Carter; m. Kathleen M. McGuire (div. Nov. 1986); children: Jaime, Matthew. BS, U.S. Naval Acad., 1975; MS in Logistics, MS in Acquisition/Contract, Naval Postgrad. Sch., Monterey, Calif., 1986. Cert. profl. contracts mgr. Commd. ensign USN, 1971, advanced through grades to comdr., 1990; ASW officer/nuclear weapons officer/navigator USS Fanning, San Diego, 1977—80; supply officer USS Waddell, San Diego, 1980—82, Naval Ordnance Sta., Indian Head, Md., 1982—84; bus./fin. mgr., contracting officer Naval Air Systems Command, Washington, 1986—90; asst. supply officer U.S. Naval Acad., Annapolis, Md., 1990—93; asst. comdr. for contracting Naval Supply Systems Command, Washington, Md., 1993—94; ret., 1994; with PricewaterhouseCoopers Cons., Fairfax, Va., 1994—2000; dir. sr. exec. svc. Program Support Ctr., U.S. HHS, Washington, 2000—. Adj. assoc. prof. U. Md.; lectr. in field; bd. dirs. Nat. Coop. Adminstrv. Support Units; mem. adv. bd. Surgeon Gen.'s Policy Adv. Bd.; dep. asst. sec. Adminstrn. Children and Families, 2002—. Contbr. Past mem. Charles County Bd. Econ. Devel., Md. Decorated Navy Commendation medal, numerous others; recipient Activity EEO award, Spl. Act Svc. award, Surgeon Gen.'s Medallion, 2002. Fellow: Nat. Contracts Mgmt. Assn. (past mem. nat. edn. and policy rev. bd., past chmn. nat. com. for CPCM recognition, past chpt. pres.); mem.: Am. Legion, U.S. Naval Acad. Alumni Assn., Commd. Officers Assn., Nat. Def. Transp. Assn., Am. Def. Preparedness Assn., Am. Logistics Assn., Am. Soc. Quality Control, Am. Soc. for Pub. Adminstrn., Nat. Assn. Purchasing Mgrs. Home: 525 Wintersweet Ct Annapolis MD 21401 Office: US Dept Health/Human Svcs Aerospace Bldg 370 L'enfant Promenade SW Washington DC 20447

COY, PATRICIA ANN, special education director, consultant; b. Beardstown, Ill., Apr. 2, 1952; d. Ben L. and Dorothy Lee (Hubbell) C. BS in Elem. and Spl. Edn., No. Ill. U., 1974; MS in Spl. Edn., Northeastern Ill. U., 1976, MA in Spl. Edn., 1978; MEd in Spl. Edn., Northeastern U., 1984; postgrad., No. Ill. U., 1988—. Cert. elem. and spl. edn. tchr.; cert. counselor. Mental health supr. Waukegan (Ill.) Devel. Ctr., 1974-77; ednl. therapist Grove Sch. and Residential Program, Lake Forest, Ill., 1977-78; dir. residential svcs. N.W. Suburban Aid for the Retarded, Park Ridge, Ill., 1978-83; exec. dir. The Learning Tree, Des Plaines, Ill., 1983—; dir. residential svcs. Augustanan Ctr. Luth. Social Svcs. of Ill., Chgo., 1984-86, dir. planning and evaluation, 1986-93, dir. cmty. svc., 1993-95; CEO Visions Network (formerly Blare House Inc.), Des Plaines, Ill., 1995—. Behavior advisor Habilitative Systems, Inc., Chgo., 1985-88; program coord. Human Resource Devel. Inst., Chgo., 1986-89; project dir. Support Svcs. Ill., Inc., Chgo., 1987-91; dir. TranSteps Inc. Steps for Success for Adults with Learning Differences, 1991—. Contbr. articles to profl. jours. Mem. Coun. for Exceptional Children, Am. Assn. Mental Deficiency, Chgo. Assn. Behavioral Analysis, Behavior Analysis Soc. Ill., Assn. for Supervision and Curriculum Devel., Nat. Rehab. Assn., Coun. for Disability Rights, Assn. for Learning Disability, Profls. in Learning Disabilities, Cwens, Echoes, Mortar Bd., Kappa Delta Pi. Democrat. Mem. United Ch. of Christ. Home: 8936 N Parkside Ave Apt 118 Des Plaines IL 60016-5517 Office: 7144 N Harlem Ave Ste 344 Chicago IL 60631-1005 also: The Visions Network 960 Rand Rd Ste 214 Des Plaines IL 60016-2355 E-mail: coycondo@aol.com.

COYAN, MICHAEL LEE, art and performing arts educator; b. Dayton, Ohio, Dec. 31, 1954; s. Eugene and Wilma Arlene (Surface) C. BA, Miami U., Oxford, Ohio, 1982, MA, 1985; postgrad., Ohio U., Athens, 1989-92. Asst. to producer, dir. pub. rels. Miami U. Summer Theatre, 1974-78; asst. to pub. rels. dir., box office and house mgr. Cin. Playhouse in the Park, 1977-80; drama dir., tchr. Lebanon (Ohio) H.S., 1980-83; dir., instr., advisor Miami U., 1984-86, vis. instr. interdisciplinary studies, 1993—94; instr., tchg. assoc. Ohio U., Athens, 1989—92; dir. pub. rels. Cin. Commn. on the Arts, 1986-88; grant writer, cons. M.L. Coyan & Assocs., Cin., 1986—; instr. art Sinclair C.C., Dayton, Ohio, 1992—; assoc. prof. theatre Wright State U., Dayton, 1997—2000. Artistic dir. Actors Repertory Theatre, Middletown, Ohio, 1999-2001; exec. dir. Lebanon Regional Arts Coun., 1977-79; chmn. mini-festivals Cin. Symphony Orch., 1977-83; allocations com.-project pool Cin. Fine Arts Fund, 1983-93; lectr. Pratt Inst. Venice Program, 1996; adj. prof. theatre Wright State U., Dayton, Ohio, 1998-2000. Author: The Lebanon Opera House, 1877-82, 1984; playwright: To Touch The Hem of Heaven, 2001, The Gentle Art: An Evening with Mr. Whistler, 2002, contbr. articles to profl. jours. Mem. City Coun., City of Lebanon, 1993-99; theatre dir. Bicentennial Commn., Lebanon, 1975-76; trustee, treas. Friends of the Libr., Lebanon, 1978-83. Recipient Svc. award Miami U., 1984; Hazen Trust Fund grantee, 1973, 77. Fellow Inst. for Edwardian Studies (co-founder), Soc. for a Brit. Theatre Inst.; mem. Coll. Art Assn., Theatre Comms. Group, Ohio Theatre Alliance, Integrative Studies Inst., Phi Kappa Phi. Democrat. Episcopalian. Avocations: antique collecting, gardening, painting, classical piano, travel. Home: 318 N Broadway Lebanon OH 45036-1717

COYKENDALL, ABBY LYNN, literature educator; b. Tucson, Jan. 21, 1971; d. Joe Garret and Sandra Coykendall. BA, U. Ariz., 1992; Ma, SUNY, Buffalo, 1997, PhD, 2002. Grad. instr. SUNY, Buffalo, 1993—99, adj. lectr., 1998—2002; assoc. instr. Daemon Coll., Buffalo, 2002; asst. prof. Ea. Mich. U., Ypsilanti, 2002—. Regents scholar, U. Ariz., 1989—93. Mem.: MLA (Florence Howe award 2001), Am. Soc. for 18th Century Studies, Aphra Behn Soc. Office: Ea Mich U Dept English Lang and Lit 612 Pray Harrold Hall Ypsilanti MI 48197

COYKENDALL, JAMES B. mathematician; b. Knoxville, Tenn., Sept. 16, 1966; s. James B. and Anne D. Coykendall; m. Kathleen A. Macko, Dec. 5, 1992; children: Ashley Ellen, Logan Joseph, Emily Anne. BS (hons.), Calif. Inst. of Tech., 1989; PhD, Cornell U., 1995. C. C. Hsiung vis. prof. of math. Lehigh U., Bethlehem, Pa., 1995—96; asst. prof. of math. N.D. State U., Fargo, 1996—2002, assoc. prof. of math., 2002—. Editl. bd. Internat. Jour. of Commutative Rings, 1999—, Rocky Mountain Jour. of Math., 2002—; bd. dirs. Rocky Mountain Math. Consortium, 1999—; reviewer Am. Math. Soc., Providence, 1999—. Editl. bd. Internat. Jour. of Commutative Rings, 1999—2003, Rocky Mt. Jour. of Math., 2002—03, rsch. math. (over 20 articles publ. in jours.) Jour. of Algebra, Jour. of Pure and Applied Algebra, Jour. of Number Theory, Comms. in Algebra, Proce .of the Am. Math. Soc. and others. Rite of Christian initiation of adults Holy Cross Cath. Ch., West Fargo, ND, 1998—2003, lay ministry, 1999—2003. Recipient E.T. Bell prize for Undergrad. rsch., 1989; grantee Hutchinson Fellowship, Cornell U., 1995; ND-EPSCOR grant, NSF, 1997, Grant, ND State U. Rsch. Devel. Found., 1998, Grant in Aid, ND State U., 2000. Master: Math Club, NDSU (sponsor 1996—2003); mem.: Math. Assn. of Am., Am. Math. Soc., Page Ho. (Caltech) (pres. 1988—89), Page Ho. (Caltech) (v.p. 1987—88). Liberal. Roman Catholic. Avocations: working out, racquetball, hiking, sports, camping. Home: 2802 39th Ave SW Fargo ND 58104 Office: Dept of Math ND State Univ Fargo ND 58105-5075 Office Fax: 701-231-7598. E-mail: jim.coykendall@ndsu.nodak.edu.

COYLE, CHARLES A. marketing educator; b. Phila., June 13, 1931; s. Charles A. and Roseanne (McPeake) C.; m. Suzanne B. McCann, Sept. 28, 1963; children: Suzanne, Christopher, Kevin, Timothy. BSBA, LaSalle U., 1955; postgrad., US Army Intelligence Ctr., Md., 1956; MBA, Drexel U., 1967; EdD with distinction, Temple U., 1974; postgrad., Mary Immaculate Sem., 1990-95. Sales rep. IBM, SCM, Diebold, Inc., R.E. Lamb, 1958-67; spl. agt. U.S. Dept. Treasury; asst. prof. mktg. and mgmt., curriculum supr. Phila. C.C., 1967-70; asst. prof. mktg. Phila. U., 1970-74; tchr., coord. distributive edn. Middle Bucks (Pa.) AVTS, 1974-76; prof., chmn. mktg. Kutztown (Pa.) U., 1976-2000; prof. emeritus Kutztown Coll. Bus. Chmn. mktg. adv. com. Lehigh Valley Vocat. Tech. Sch., 1984-94; adj. prof. Temple U., La Salle U., St. Josephs U., DeSales U.; presenter in field. Contbr. articles to profl. jours. Mgr., soccer and baseball coach Warminster Little League, 1973—79, Grandlawn Baseball Assn., 1987—88; founder, treas. Deerfield Cmty. Assn., 1983; pres., treas. LaSalle U. Student Congress, 1954—55; prefect min. St. Francis Third Order; ordained permanent deacon Allentown Diocese, 1995—; resource leader Nat. Conf. on New Strategies for Learning, 1969. Sgt. counter-intelligence corps U.S. Army, 1956—58, Tokyo. Recipient award Dale Carnegie Found., Phila., 1967, Outstanding Svc. award Distributive Edn. Clubs Am., 1975, 86, 88, 91, award Lehigh Valley Vocat.-Tech. Sch. Adv. Com., 1993; Direct Mktg. fellow, 1989. Mem. AAUP, Am. Acad. Advt., Sales and Mktgs. Execs., Am. Mktg. Assn., Direct Mktg. Assn., Assn. Pa. Univ. Bus. and Econ. Faculty (bd. dirs. 1989-91), Sales and Mktg. Execs., Am. Mgmt. Assn., Cross Keys, KC (4th degree), Faculty and Adminstrn. Club (pres. Kutztown U. 1988-90, v.p. 1986-88), Sons Union Vets. of the Civil War, CrossKeys Honor Soc., Phi Delta Kappa, Phi Kappa Phi, Alpha Epsilon, Epsilon Delta Epsilon. Home: 1236 Buck Trail Rd Allentown PA 18104-2019

COYLE, DENNIS PATRICK, lawyer; b. Detoit, Aug. 29, 1938; s. Myron Patrick and Vernice Beatrice (Smith) Coyle; children: Ian Patrick, Sean Patrick. BA, Dartmouth Coll., 1960; JD, Columbia U., 1964. Bar: NY 1965, Fla. 1971. Assoc. Breed, Abbott & Morgan, NYC, 1964—70, Courshon & Courshon, Miami Beach, Fla., 1970—74; mng. trustee First Mortgage Investors, Miami Beach, Fla., 1974—79; ptnr. Steel Hector & Davis, Miami, Fla., 1979—89; gen. counsel FPL Group, Inc. Fla. Power & Light Co., 1989—; dir. Fla. Power and Light Co., 1991—, Adelphia comms. Corp., 1995—. Mem.: ABA, Miami Beach C. of C. (hon. lifetime trustee). Office: FPL Group Inc PO Box 14000 700 Universe Blvd North Palm Beach FL 33408-2657 Home: 2455 Snook Trl West Palm Beach FL 33410-1270

COYLE, EDWARD J. physical education coordinator; b. Phila., July 8, 1949; s. Edward J. and Josephine (Orgilio) C. BS, West Chester U., 1973; MEd, Temple U., 1980; PhD, U. N.Mex., 1987. Cert. health edn. tchr., Pa.; cert. health, phys. edn. and recreation tchr., N.Mex. and Pa. Prog. dir. Sensitivity and Awareness progs. Phila. Sch. Dist., 1979-81; teaching asst. U. N.Mex., 1982-84; phys. edn. instr. Albuquerque Pub. Schs., 1982-88; cons. to phys. therapy dept. Grad. Health System, Phila., 1988-89; coord. adapted phys. edn. Norristown (Pa.) Area Sch. Dist., 1989—. Coord. Sun Co.'s "Someone Spl. Prog.", Olympic Sports Prog., 1990; vol. conditioning coach, football, U. N.Mex., 1981-86; prog. coord. in gymnasium, Slaten Farmer's Sch., 1980, 82, 90, coord. spl. events, 1980-82; others. Named to Pa. Sports Hall of Fame, Delaware County, 1990; hon. capt. Del. County Hero Bowl Football Game, 1989; Delaware County Athletic Hall of Fame, Pa. chpt., 1988; named to Outstanding Young Men of Am., 1984; U.S. rep. to Olympic Games, two gold medals, 1 silver medal in weight lifting, 1972, 76, 80, 3 world championship gold medals, 1973, 74, 75, 4 Pan Am. gold medals, 1971, 73, 75, 79, 10 nat. champsionships,; recipient Father Washington medal for Outstanding Citizenship, Nat. Cath. War Vets. award, 1980, Rotary Achievement award, Balt. Pike/Clifton Heights, Pa., 1978, award Pa. Sports Hall of Fame, 2001; numerous other awards. Mem. Nat. Strength and Conditioning Assn., Internat. Olympic Com., U.S. Olympic Com., AAHPERD, Fedn. Internat. Edn. Physique, Nat. Corrective Therapy Assn., U.S. Master Swimming Assn., Am. Coll. Sports Medicine, N.Mex. Phys. Educators Assn., Amateur Athletic Assn., Internat. Fedn. Power Lifting, Pa. State Phys. Edn. Assn., lst Marine Div. Assn., 3rd Marine Div. Assn., British Officers Club

of Phila., 5th and 14th Def. Bn. Assn., USMC, Marine Corps., Upland, Pa.; trustee Four Chaplains Assn., Phila., Pa., Sturzebecker Found. West Chester U., Delaware County Athletics Hall of Fame Commn. Home: 1078 Putnam Blvd Media PA 19086-6747

COYLE, JOSEPH THOMAS, psychiatrist; b. Chgo., Oct. 9, 1943; s. Joseph Thomas and Mercedes (Sartor) Coyle; m. Genevieve Sansoucy, Aug. 19, 1968; children: Andrew, Peter, David. AB, Coll. of the Holy Cross, 1965; MD, Johns Hopkins U., 1969; MA (hon.), Harvard U., 1991. Diplomate Am. Bd. Psychiatry and Neurology. Asst. prof. pharmacology Johns Hopkins Sch. of Medicine, Balt., 1974—76, asst. prof pharmacology and psychiatry, 1976—78, assoc. prof pharmacology and psychiatry, 1978—80, prof of neurosci., psychiatry and pharmacology, 1980—91, dir. divsn. child psychiatry, 1982—91, Disting. Svc. prof. of child psychiatry, 1985—91; Eben S. Draper prof. of psychiatry and neurosci. Harvard U., Boston, 1991—; chair consol. dept. psychiatry Harvard Med. Sch., Boston, 1991—2001. Co-dir. outpatient pharmacotherapy clinic Johns Hopkins Hosp., Balt., 1977—82; mem. sci. adv. bd. Pfizer Scholars Program, N.Y.C., 1989—94, John F. Merck Found., Boston, 1990—2000, Abbott Pharms., North Chicago, Ill., 1990—, Guilford Pharms., Balt., 1992—98. Contbr. articles to profl. jours.; editor: Archives of General Psychiatry, 2002—. Mem. adv. bd. NIMH, Washington, 1990—94. Recipient AE Bennett award, 1978, Gold Medal award, 1991, EA Strecker award, Inst. Pa. Hosp., 1993, Thomas Salmon medal, N.Y. Acad. Medicine, 1993. Fellow: Am. Acad. of Arts and Scis., Am. Psychiat. Assn. (Found. Fund prize 1985, Adolph Meyer award 1994, Kemp Fund award 1996); mem.: Inst. of Medicine of the Nat. Acad. Sci. (Pasarow Found. award 1997), Am. Soc. Pharmacology and Exptl. Therapeutics (John Jacob Abel award 1979), Am. Acad. Child and Adolescent Psychiatry, Am. Coll. Neuropsychopharmacology (pres. 2001, Effron award 1982), Soc. Neurosci. (pres. 1991—92, Spl. Achievement award 2001). Avocations: reading, fishing. Office: Harvard Med Sch Dept Psychiatry 115 Mill St Belmont MA 02478-1041 E-mail: joseph_coyle@hms.harvard.edu.

COYLE, KEVIN FRANCIS, planner; b. Dover, Del., Nov. 15, 1960; s. Francis S. and Mary E. (Kellenberg) Coyle; m. Laureen Jean Coyle, Oct. 26, 1996; children: Derek Richard White, Andrea Maria Reyes, Brendan Francis. BA in Program of Liberal Studies, U. Notre Dame, 1982; MPA in Pub. Adminstrn., U. So. Calif., 1995. Rsch. asst. Kent County (Del.) Levy Ct., 1987-90, planning project coord., 1990-93, sr. planner, 1993-96, asst. dir. planning, 1996-99; planner IV Del. Dept. Natural Resources and Environ. Control, Dover, 1999—2002, prin. planner, 2002—. Capt. U.S. Army, 1982-86. Recipient Pub. Svc. scholarship Pub. Employees Roundtable, Washington, 1993, Ides of March scholarship U. So. Calif. Sch. Pub. Adminstrn., 1993-95. Mem. Am. Inst. Cert. Planners (cert.), Am. Soc. Pub. Adminstrn., Am. Planning Assn., Nat. Eagle Scout Assn., Pi Alpha Alpha, Phi Kappa Phi. Roman Catholic. Avocations: travel, music, reading, sports, movies. Home: 410 Commons Ln Camden Wyoming DE 19934-1269 Office: Del Dept Natural Resources and Environ Control Office of Sec 89 Kings Hwy Dover DE 19901-7305 E-mail: kevin_coyle@hotmail.com., Kevin.Coyle@state.de.us.

COYLE, MARIE BRIDGET, retired microbiology educator, laboratory director; b. Chgo., May 13, 1935; d. John and Bridget Veronica (Fitzpatrick) C.; m. Zheng Chen, Oct. 30, 1995 (div. Aug. 2000). BA, Mundelein Coll., 1957; MS, St. Louis U., 1963; PhD, Kans. State U., 1965. Diplomate Am. Bd. Med. Microbiology. Sci. instr. Sch. Nursing Columbus Hosp., Chgo., 1957-59; research assoc. U. Chgo., 1967-70; instr. U. Ill., Chgo., 1970-71; asst. prof. microbiology U. Wash., Seattle, 1973-80, assoc. prof., 1980-94, prof., 1994-2000; ret., 2000. Assoc. dir. microbiology labs Univ. Hosp., Seattle, 1973-76; dir. microbiology labs Harborview Med. Ctr., Univ. Wash., 1976—; co-dir. Postdoc Training Clinic Microbiology, Univ. Wash., 1978-96; dir. postdoctoral tng. clin. microbiology, 1996-2000. Contbr. articles to profl. jours. Recipient Pasteur award, Ill. Soc. Microbiology, 1997, Profl. Recognition awards, Am. Bd. Med. Microbiology, Am. Bd. Med. Lab. Immunology, 2000. Fellow Am. Acad. Microbiology; mem. Acd. Clin. Lab. Physicians and Scientists (sec.-treas. 1980-83, exec. com. 1985-90), Am. Soc. Microbiology (chmn. clin. microbiology divsn. 1984-85, coun. policy com. 1996-99, bd. govs. 2000—, recipient bioMerieux Vitek Sonnenwirth Meml. award 1994), Kappa Gamma Pi. Avocations: hiking, skiing, cycling.

COYLE, MARTIN ADOLPHUS, JR., lawyer, consultant; b. Hamilton, Ohio, June 3, 1941; s. Martin Adolphus and Lucille (Baird) C.; m. Sharon Sullivan, Mar. 29, 1969 (div. Dec. 1991); children: Cynthia Ann, David Martin, Jennifer Ann; m. Linda J. O'Brien, July 31, 1993 (div. July 1996); m. Sandra C. Lund, July 1998. BA, Ohio Wesleyan U., 1963; JD summa cum laude, Ohio State U., 1966. Bar: N.Y. 1967, Ohio 1966. Assoc. Cravath, Swaine & Moore, N.Y.C., 1966-72; chief counsel securities and fin. TRW Inc., Cleve., 1972-73, sr. counsel, asst. sec., 1973-75, asst. gen. counsel, asst. sec., 1976, asst. gen. counsel, sec., 1976-80, v.p., gen. counsel, sec., 1980-89, exec. v.p., gen. counsel, sec., 1989-97, exec. v.p., 1997-99; sec. TRW Found., Cleve., 1975-80, trustee, 1980-88. Sec. TRW Found., 1975-80, trustee, 1980-98. Co-inventor voting machine. Pres. Judson Retirement Cmty., 1986-88, trustee, 1986-90; chmn., sec. Martin A. Coyle Found.; trustee Berea Coll. 1989—, Chautauqua Found., 1999-, Chautauqua Inst., 1990-2000, Ohio Wesleyan U., 1992-2001, Gebbie Found., 2001-. Mem. ABA, Am. Soc. Corp. Secs. (pres. Ohio regional group 1978-80, nat. dir. 1981-87, nat. chmn. 1985-86), Assn. Gen. Counsel (exec. com. 1992-99, pres. 1995-97), Harbour Club. Home: 26 Cormorant Island Ln Kiawah Island SC 29455-5808 E-mail: coyle@cecomet.net.

COYLE, MICHAEL LEE, lawyer; b. Mechanicsburg, Pa., Oct. 2, 1944; s. Patrick G. and Bertha M. C.; m. Kathleen J. West, July 15, 1967; children: Patrick M., Darren W. BS in Acctg., Utica Coll., 1966; JD, Syracuse U., 1971; LLM in Taxation, Georgetown U., 1975. Bar: N.Y. 1972, Conn. 1975, U.S. Tax Ct. 1975. Acct. Peat, Marwick, Mitchell & Co., Syracuse, N.Y., 1966, tax acct., 1969-71; atty., adviser interpretive div. Office Chief Counsel IRS, Washington, 1971-73; atty. adviser to judge U.S. Tax Ct., Washington, 1973-75; mem. firm Reid & Riege, P.C., Hartford, Conn., 1975—. Trustee U. Hartford Tax Inst., 1982-86; bd. dirs. adv. coun. Nat. Inst. State & Local Taxation, Old Lyme, Conn., 1987—. Mem., v.p., pres. St. Paul's Luth. Ch. Coun., Wethersfield, Conn., 1976-82, 87-92, 97-2000; bd. dirs. Children's Home Cromwell, Inc., Conn., 1980-88; mem. leadership Greater Hartford, 1978, Conn. Task Force Corp. Taxation; pres. Wethersfield Bus. & Civic Assn., 1978-80. With U.S. Army, 1966-68. Named one of Best Lawyers in Am., 1987—. Mem. ABA (chmn. sales and fin. transaction com., tax sect. 1983-85), Conn. Bar Assn. (tax exec. com., ltd. liability subcom. 1991—), Conn. Bus. & Industry Assn. (tax com. 1987—), Hartford Tax Study Group, Tax Club Hartford (pres.). Avocations: tennis, reading. Home: 144 Stonehill Dr Rocky Hill CT 06067 Office: Reid & Riege PC 1 State St Ste 18 Hartford CT 06103-3185 E-mail: mcoyle@reidandriege.com.

COYLE, ROBERT EVERETT, federal judge; b. Fresno, Calif., May 6, 1930; s. Everett LaJoya and Virginia Chandler C.; m. Faye Turnbaugh, June 11, 1953; children— Robert Allen, Richard Lee, Barbara Jean BA, Fresno State Coll., 1953; JD, U. Calif., 1956. Bar: Calif. Ptnr. McCormick, Barstow, Sheppard, Coyle & Wayte, 1958-82; chief judge U.S. Dist. Ct. (ea. dist.) Calif., 1990-96, sr. judge, 1996—. Former chair 9th Cir. Conf. of Chief Dist. Judges, chair 9th Cir. space and security com., mem. com. on state and fed. cts. Mem. Calif. Bar Assn. (exec. com. 1974-79, bd. govs. 1979-82, v.p. 1981), Fresno County Bar Assn. (pres. 1972). Office: US Dist Ct 5116 US Courthouse 1130 O St Fresno CA 93721-2201

COYLE, TERENCE, artist; b. Williamstown, Mass., Sept. 7, 1925; s. Terence Francis and Leona (Eichelser) C.; m. Anne Costello, Nov. 1975. Student, Columbia U., 1946-48, Hunter Coll., 1950. Instr. oil painting Art Students League, N.Y.C., 1974—; instr. NYU, 1979; lectr. artistic anatomy Nat. Acad. Design Sch. Fine Arts, NYC, 1979—98. Instr. figure portrait painting Scottsdale (Ariz.) Artists Sch. annual workshop, 1985. Exhbns. include Mus. City of N.Y., Fordham U., N.Y.C., N.Y. Mus. Performing Arts Billy Rose Collection, N.Y. State Mus., Albany, Chubb & Son, Inc., N.Y.C., Am. Artists Profl. League, N.Y.C., Nat. Arts Club Gallery, N.Y.C., Astor Gallery, N.Y.C., NAD, N.Y.C., Sharon (Conn.) Creative Arts Found. Gallery, Rosequist Gallery, Tucson, Loring Gallery, Sheffield, Mass., Sundance Gallery, Bridgehampton, N.Y., Jo-An Fine Art, N.Y.C. Gallery ; represented in permanent collections Helen Hayes Collection; author: Master Class in Figure Drawing, 1985; co-author: Anatomy Lessons from the Great Masters, 1977, Albinus on Anatomy, 1979. Recipient graphic design award, Am. Inst. Graphic Design, 1979. Home: 305 E 72nd St New York NY 10021-4683

COYNE, CHARLES COLE, lawyer; b. Abington, Pa., Dec. 3, 1948; s. James Kitchenman Jr. and Pearl (Black) Coyne; m. Paula J. Latta, May 15, 1976; 1 child, Anna Elizabeth. BS in Econs., U. Pa., 1970; JD, Temple U., 1973. Bar: Pa. 1973, U.S. Supreme Ct. 1982, N.J. 1985. Intern Gen. Svcs. Adminstrn., Washington, 1971; counsel Hepburn Willcox Hamilton & Putnam, Phila., 1994—. Bd. dirs. George S. Coyne Chem. Co., Inc., Croydon, Pa., sec., 1973—, chmn., 2000—; dir. Kitchenman Terminal Co. LLC; mng. dir. Cygnet Leasing Co. LLC. Assoc. editor: Temple Law Rev., 1972—73, columnist: Life in the Country, Ledger Newspaper Group, 1993—99. Chester County (Pa.) rep. Delaware Valley Regional Planning Commn., 1982—; mem. Chester County Health and Edn. Facilities Authority, 1982—, chmn., 1996—2000; bd. suprs. East Fallowfield Twp., Chester County, 1982—83; mem. panel U.S. Bankruptcy Trustees, 1991—93; mem. Chester County Pk. and Recreation Bd., 1998—; mem. racing com. Pa. Hunt Cup, 1992—; chmn. Greater Phila. Young Reps., 1975—76; Rep. candidate Pa. State Legislature, 1976; Phila. Rep. City Policy Com., 1975—77. Recipient Disting. Young Rep. award, 1976; Assn. Internat. Etudantes Scis. Econ. Comml., U. Melbourne, Australia, 1968. Mem.: ABA, S.R. (bd. mgrs. 2000—03), Nat. Steeplechase Assn., Phila. Bar Assn., Pa. Bar Assn., Pa. Soc., U. Pa. Gen. Alumni Soc. (exec. bd. organized classes, pres. class of 1970), Temple Law Sch. Alumni Assn. (chmn. 10th reunion com.), Quaker City Farmers Club, Union League, Capitol Hill Club, Lawyers Club Phila., Masons (master), Kappa Alpha Soc. Home: Sycamore Run Farm PO Box 155 Unionville PA 19375-0155 Office: Hepburn Willcox Hamilton & Putnam 1100 One Penn Ctr 1617 John F Kennedy Blvd Philadelphia PA 19103-1979 E-mail: cccoyne@aol.com.

COYNE, EDWARD JAMES, SR., international business educator; b. St. Louis, Sept. 25, 1930; s. Horace John and Bessie (Stinebaker) C.; m. Kathleen (Hayman), Sept. 9, 1952 (dec. April 1985); children: Edward James, Kevin Patrick, Shawn Thomas, Colin Mark, Kathleen Patrice (dec. Feb. 1968); m. Beulah (Shelton), April 19, 1986. BS, La. State U., 1952; MBA, Nova U., 1992; PhD, U. Bradford (Yorkshire, U.K.), 1994; LHD (hon.), Nova U., 1980. Gen. mgr., dir. Comalco Products, Pty., Sydney, Australia, 1966-73, pres. Kaiser Bauxite Co., Discovery Bay, Jamaica, 1974—86; v.p., gen. mgr., Rod, Bar, Wire Kaiser Aluminum & Chem., Oakland, Calif., 1986-90; exec., residence Nova U., Ft. Lauderdale, Fla., 1991-93; dir. MIBA program Nova Southeastern U., Ft. Lauderdale, 1993-96; acad. dean Am. Coll. Dublin, Dublin, 1997-98; vis. prof. Samford U., Birmingham, Ala., 1999—; CFO Connexxia, LLC, 2001—. Adv. bd. Inst. Internat. Edu., Southeastern Region, 1983-86, Ctr. Internat. Bus., U. Leeds, U.K., 1995—; vis. fellow U. Bradford, U.K., 1996—. Author: Targeting the Foreign Direct Investor, 1995, (chapt.) International Business Org., 1999; contbr. articles to profl. jours. Vice-chmn. Agr. Mktg. Corp., Jamaica, 1981-86; chmn. Discovery Bay Water Co., Jamaica, 1974-80; vice-chmn. Aboukir Edu. & Industl. Inst., Jamaica, 1976-85; adv. bd. World Trade Council Ft. Lauderdale, 1995-96. Recipient Comdr. Order of Distinction, Govt. Jamaica, 1980; Sports Hall of Fame, Jackson-Madison County, Tenn., 1997. Mem. Acad. Internat. Bus., HR Devel. Internat. Jour. Republican. Roman Catholic. Avocations: reading, travel, teaching. Home: 2752 Berkeley Dr Birmingham AL 35242-4105 Office: Sch Bus Samford U 800 Lakeshore Dr Birmingham AL 35229-0001 E-mail: ebcoyne@aol.com., ed.coyne@connexxia.com.

COYNE, JOHN MICHAEL, artist, educator; b. St. Stephen, N.B., Can., May 23, 1950; s. John Joseph and Marie Eleanor (Dennison) C. BFA, Mt. Allison U., 1975; MFA, U. Regina, 1977. Prof. visual arts Sir Wilfred Grenfell Coll., Meml. U. Nfld., 1991—. Lectr. Acadia U., 1977-78, asst. prof., 1978-84, assoc. prof., 1984-86, head dept. art, 1983-86, senate mem., 1981-84, bd. govs., 1985-86, art gallery adv. bd., 1978-86; founding head dept. visual arts Sir Wilfred Grenfell Coll., Meml. U. Nfld., 1986-92, assoc. prof., 1986-91, prof., 1991—, senate mem., 1991-92, 98-2002, head Divsn. of Arts, 1999-2000; mem. art procurement com. Govt. Nfld. and Labrador, 1986-92. One-man shows include Owens Art Gallery, Mt. Allison U., 1983, U. Coll. Cape Breton Art Gallery, 1983, St. Mary's U. Art Gallery, 1983, Acadia U. Art Gallery, 1983, 84, U. N.B. Art Ctr., 1984, Sir Wilfred Grenfell Coll., 1987, 89, Meml. U. art Gallery, 1990, Emma Butler Gallery, St. John's, 1990, Arts and Culture Ctr. Corner Brook, 1997; group exhbns. include Mackenzie Gallery, 1978, Newfoundland Artists, Gallery 78, 1978, Art Gallery N.S., 1980, Edmonton Art Gallery, 1984, U. N.B. Art Ctr., 1985, Mira Godard Gallery, 1985, 91, Fredericton, N.B., 1988, Meml. U. Art Gallery, 1994; represented in permanent collections Govt. Nfld. and Labrador, Art Gallery N.S., Mt. Allison U., N.S. Art Bank, U. Regina, St. Mary's U. Art Gallery, Sir Wilfred Grenfell Coll., Husky Oil, Labatt's Breweries, Bank N.S., Midland-Doherty, Placer Dome, Inc., Davies, Ward and Beck, Xerox Can., Faskin-Colvin, Abitibi-Price, Toshiba Can., Air Can. and pvt. collections. Greenshields Found. grantee, 1976. Avocations: reading, photography, digital imaging, running. Home: 31 Central St Corner Brook NF Canada Office: Meml Univ Nfld Corner Brook NF Canada A2H 6P9 E-mail: mcoyne@swgc.mun.ca.

COYNE, MARY DOWNEY, biologist, endocrinologist, educator; b. Lynn, Mass., Jan. 17, 1938; d. James Edward and Mary Kate (Martin) Downey; m. John Andrew Coyne, June 24, 1961; children: Carolyn Marie, John Andrew Jr. AB, Emmanuel Coll., 1959; MA, Wellesley Coll., 1961; PhD, U. Va., 1964. Instr. physiology U. Va. Med. Sch., Charlottesville, 1966-67, asst. prof., 1967-68, La. State U. Med. Sch., New Orleans, 1968-70, clin. asst. prof., 1970-72; asst. prof. Wellesley (Mass.) Coll., 1970-74, chmn. biol. scis. dept., 1975-78, 82-84, prof. biol. scis., 1980—2002, prof. emerita, 2002—. Vis. lectr. in pharmacology Harvard Med. Sch., 1978-79; vis. scientist grad. dept. biochemistry Brandeis Waltham, Mass., 1985-86, Worcester Found. for Exptl. Biology, 1991-92, U.S. Army Rsch. Inst. for Environ. Medicine, 1998-99; mem. endocrinology study sect. NIH, 1989-92; cons., reviewer high sch. biology texts, jour. articles in field. Presenter sci. papers to profl. confs. Bd. dirs. Citizens for Wellesley Pub. Edn., 1985-88; chmn. Com. on Sci. Edn. of Wellesley, 1986-88. NIH fellow, 1964-66; grantee NSF ROA, 1985-86, 92-93, Rsch. Corp., 1980-82, NIH, 1967-73, 93-97. Mem. AAAS, Endocrine Soc., Sigma Xi. Home: 21 Tennyson Rd Wellesley MA 02481-5231

COYNE, NANCY CAROL, advertising executive; b. Washington, Mar. 14, 1946; d. John David and Gloria Louise (Davie) Druckenbrod; 1 child, Kathleen Louise. BS, NYU, 1968. Dir. visitor svcs. Lincoln Ctr., N.Y.C., 1968-71; dir. advt. Sta. WRVR Radio, N.Y.C., 1971-74; creative dir. Blaine Thompson Inc., N.Y.C., 1974-77; chief exec. officer Serino, Coyne Inc., N.Y.C., 1977—. Adj. prof. Yale U., New Haven, Conn., 1980—; bd. dirs. Actors Fund, Williamstown Theatre Festival. Office: Serino Coyne Inc 1515 Broadway Fl 36 New York NY 10036-8901

COYNE, PATRICK IVAN, physiological ecologist; b. Wichita, Kans., Feb. 26, 1944; s. Ivan Lefranz and Ellen Lucille (Brown) C.; m. Mary Ann White, Aug. 22, 1964; children: Shane Barrett, Shannon Renee. BS, Kans. State U., 1966; PhD, Utah State U., 1970. R & D coord. U.S. Army Cold Regions Rsch. and Engring. Lab., Hanover, N.H., 1970-72; asst. prof. forestry U. Alaska, Fairbanks, 1973-74; plant physiologist, environ. scientist Lawrence Livermore (Calif.) Nat. Lab., 1975-79, cons., 1980—; rsch. plant physiologist USDA/Agrl. Rsch. Svc., Woodward, Okla., 1979-85; prof., head Agrl. Rsch. Ctr. Kansas State U., Hays, 1985-94, prof., head Western Kans. Agrl. Rsch. Ctrs., 1994—. Mem. adv. coun. Kans. Geol. Survey, Lawrence, 1986-91. Contbr. 33 articles to profl. jours. Capt., U.S. Army, 1970-72. Mem. AAAS, Am. Soc. Agronomy, Soil Sci. Soc. Am., Crop Sci. Soc. Am., Soc. Range Mgmt., Coun. Agriculture Sci. and Tech., Hays Area C. of C. (bd. dirs. 1988-90), Rotary, Phi Kappa Phi, Gamma Sigma Delta, Sigma Xi. Republican. Mennonite Brethren Ch. Office: Kans State U Agrl Rsch Ctr 1232 240th Ave Hays KS 67601-9228

COYNE, THOMAS JOSEPH, economist, finance educator; b. Dec. 24, 1933; s. Thomas Joseph and Mary Germaine (Fox) C.; m. Patricia Anne Smith, June 8, 1957 (div. June 1986); children: Kathleen, Karen, Kevin, Kenneth, Thomas. BBA, Marshall U., 1958; MBA, Kent State U., 1961; PhD, Case Western Res. U., 1967; postgrad., U. Chgo., 1968, U. Mich., summers, 1972, 73. With B.F. Goodrich Co., Akron, Ohio, 1959-61, Robinson Clay Products Co., Akron, Ohio, 1961-63, C&O-B&O Ry., Cleve., 1963-65; instr. econs. Kent (Ohio) State U., 1963-67, instr. money and fin. mgmt., 1967—; asst. prof. econs., chmn. dept. Marshall U., Huntington, W.Va., 1967-69; prof. bus. econs. U. Akron, 1969-81; prof. fin. John Carroll U., Cleve., 1981-95. Owner The Coyne Trust, 1986-91; pres. Coyne & Assocs., Akron, 1980—, Coyne Pub. Co., 1991—; pub. The Coyne Quar., 1990—; corp. valuations, acquisitions; cons. in field; presenter seminars in fin. engring. and mgmt., Zagreb, Croatia Stock Exch., 1993; leader 1st del. in fin. to USSR, 1989; arbitrator Am. Arbitration Assn., Fed. Mediation and Conciliation Svc., 1968—, pres. 1979-81; pres. Summit Petroleum Corp., Akron; founder, pres. Cosntn. Endl. Assn., Inc., 2000—. Author: Understanding Managerial Economics, 1975, Managerial Economics: Analysis and Cases, 5th edit., 1984, Readings in Managerial Economics, 5th edit., 1992, License To Lie, 1997, 2000, How to Take Charge of Yourself, Your Money, Your Government, 1999; also articles and monographs; host half-hour weekly radio show, 1994; host one hour weekly radio show, 2001—; pub. (econ. commentaries) Coyne Quar., Online. V.p. rsch. Akron Regional Devel. Bd., 1975-78, chmn. taxation and legis. com., 1975-78, spkr. in field; candidate U.S. Senate, Ohio, 1994—. Served with inf., U.S. Army, 1952-54, Korea. Nat. City Bank Cleve. fellow, 1963-65. Mem. Nat. Assn. of Securities Dealers Pub. Arbitrators, Sigma Phi Epsilon. Home: 535 Haskell Dr Akron OH 44333-2810 E-mail: tom@coyne-assoc.com. *When God has given you a great deal, He expects a great deal of you. If you achieve everything you set out to achieve, you probably did not set out to achieve enough in the first place.*

COYNE, WILLIAM J. retail executive; b. Chgo., Aug. 10, 1956; m. Maryann C. Coyne, May 28, 1983; children: Patrick, Jonathan, Robert. BS in Fin./Econs., U. Ill., 1978; JD, U. So. Calif., 1981. Bar: Calif. 1981, Minn. 1989, U.S. Dist. Ct. (so., ctrl., ea. and no. dists.) Calif., U.S. Ct. Appeals (9th cir.). Assoc. Overton, Lynan & Prince, L.A., 1981-85, Diepenbrock, Wulff, Plant & Hannegan, Sacramento, 1985-89, ptnr., 1990-97; gen. counsel Raley's, Sacramento, 1997—2002; COO Raley's, Inc., Sacramento, 2002, pres., COO, 2002—. Office: Raleys 500 W Capitol Ave West Sacramento CA 95605-2696

COYNE, WILLIAM JOSEPH, former congressman; b. Pitts, Aug. 24, 1936; s. Phillip and Mary (Ridge) C. BS, Robert Morris Coll., 1965. Mem. Pa. Ho. of Reps., 1970-72; mem. Pitts. City Council, 1973-80, U.S. Congress from 14th Pa. dist., Washington, 1981—2002; mem. budget com.; mem. ways and means com. With AUS, 1955-57. Democrat. Roman Catholic.

COYNE, WILLIAM R. advertising executive; b. Pitts, July 10, 1935; s. Patrick and Marie Anne Coyne; m. Dolly Coyne. With Tempo Studios, Pitts., Vic Maitland & Assoc., Ft. Lauderdale, Fla., 1968-69; pvt. practice, 1969-89; CEO Coyne Beahm Inc., Greensboro, N.C., 1989—. With USMC, 1954-56, Korean War. Office: Coyne Beahm Inc 6522 Bryan Blvd Greensboro NC 27409

COYNER, EUGENE CASPER, chemist, consultant, economist; b. Conover, Nc, Dec. 25, 1918; s. Martin Henry and Lucia Caroline Coyner; m. Ailie Miriam Hurley, Dec. 25, 1943 (dec. Nov. 29, 1987); children: Sandra, Sharon, Martin. BS Chemistry, Univ. Ill., Urbana, IL, 1940; PhD, Univ. Minn., Minneapolis, MN, 1944. Rsch. chemist E.I. DuPont De Nemours, Wilmington, Del., 1944—45; asst. prof. chemistry Univ. Tenn., Knoxville, 1946—48; rsch. group leader Mallinckrodt Chem. Works, St. Louis, 1948—54; rsch. supr. E.I. DuPont De Nemours, Wilmington, 1954—69, sales devel. assoc., 1962—69, bus. analysis assoc., 1969—79; sr. indsl. economist Stanford Rsch. Inst., Menlo Park, 1979—81; cons. S.R.I. Internat., Menlo Park, Calif., 1980—81. Contbr. articles to profl. jours. Mem.: Am. Chem. Soc. Achievements include invention of U.S. Patents fluorochemicals, 1962-present. Avocations: hiking, traveling. Home: 837 Seaview Drive El Cerrito CA 94530-3008 Personal E-mail: ecoyner@aol.com.

COZ, STEVE, editorial director; b. Grafton, Mass., Mar. 26, 1957; s. Henry and Mary Coz; m. Valerie Virga, 1987. Honors degree, Harvard U., 1979. Freelance writer various U.S. publs., 1979-82; reporter Nat. Enquirer, Lantana, Fla., 1982—; Am. celebrity analyst BBC Radio, 1995-96. Named one of 25 Most Influential People in Am., Time Mag., 1997; recipient Edgar Hoover Meml. award for disting. pub. svc., 1996, Haven House Award of Excellence for outstanding reporting on domestic violence issues, 1996, Citation of Recognition, Mass. Senate, 1997; recognized for award winning news coverage N.Y. Times, 1994, Columbia Journalism Rev., 1995, L.A. Times Mag., 1995, MediaWeek, 1995, L.A. Times, 1997, ABC's Nightline. Mem. Harvard Club Palm Beach. Avocations: sport fishing, boogie boarding, scrimshaw collecting. Office: American Media Inc 5401 NW Broken Sound Blvd Boca Raton FL 33487

COZBY, RICHARD SCOTT, electronics engineer, military officer; b. Las Cruces, N.Mex., Apr. 13, 1961; s. Scott Dempsey and Elizabeth Ann (Carroll) Cozby; m. Maria (Jo) Blackwell, Dec. 28, 1984; children: Brenton Blackwell, Bradford Carroll. B in Engring., Vanderbilt U., 1983; diploma, U.S. Army Command Coll., 1994; MSA, Ctrl. Mich. U., 2002; diploma, Def. Sys. Mgmt. Coll., 2002. Enlisted USAR, advanced through grade to lt. col.; comm. engr. U.S. Army Signal Corps, 1983-88; electronics engr., chief, simulation and tech. divsn. Army Testing and Evaluation Command, Aberdeen Proving Ground, Md., 1988—, chief tech. mgmt. divsn., 1998—. U.S. Army prin. Mutli-Svc. Test Investment Rev. Com., Washington, 1990—95; bd. dirs. N.E. Md. Tech. Coun. Author: (book) Army GPS Test Results, 1984, Aquilla RPV Test Results, 1985. Chmn. Hickory Recreation Coun., Bel Air, 1998—; mem. outreach com. St. Margaret Parish, Bel Air, Md., 1989—95. Mem.: IEEE, Internat. Testing and Evaluation Assn. (chpt. pres. 1993, chpt. dir. 1994—), Harford Leadership Alumni Assn. (bd. dirs. 1996—, v.p. 1997—). Roman Catholic. Avocation: stamp collecting. Office: CSTE-DTC-TT-M Aberdeen Proving Ground MD 21005 E-mail: rcozby@netzero.net.

COZZARIN, JAMES ROBERT, editor, writer; b. Cleve., June 23, 1964; s. Eugene L. and Marlene C. Cozzarin; 1 child, Susan Marie. BSEd, Kent State U., 1988. Tchr. English, Holy Cross Elem. Sch., Euclid, Ohio, 1988—90, Telshe Yeshiva HS, Wickliffe, Ohio, 1989—93; asst. editor Banks-Baldwin Law Pub., Cleve., 1990—94; project coord. Pro ED COMM, INC., Beachwood, Ohio, 1994—95, copy editor, 1995—98, sr. copy editor staff writer, 1998—. Author: (manual) In-House Style Guidelines; contbr. articles to profl. jours.; author: poetry. Mem. PTA Bellflower Elem. Sch., Mentor, Ohio, 2001—03. Fellow: Am. Med. Writers Assn. (Ohio Valley chpt. pres. 1997—98, Ohio Valley chpt. del. to bd. dirs. 1997—2000, budget and fin. com. 1998—2000, adminstr. devel. 2001—03, adminstr. ann. conf. 2004); mem.: Coun. of Sci. Editors, Bd. of Editors in Life Scis. Office: Pro ED COMM INC 25101 Chagrin Blvd Ste 230 Beachwood OH 44122 Office Fax: 216-595-7927. E-mail: cozzarin-j@proedcom.com.

COZZI, RONALD LEE, antiquarian book seller, rare book appraiser; b. Wellsville, N.Y., Dec. 29, 1943; s. Glenn Murray Cozzi and Almina (Rogers) Thornton; m. Marilee Ann Banas, Apr. 8, 1989; 1 child: Deborah Ann, stepchildren: Charles F. Banas III, William D. Banas. Diploma in acctg., Bryant Stratton Bus. Inst., Buffalo, 1972-73. Technician IBM, Buffalo, 1967-69, A-M Corp., Buffalo, 1969-71; with U.S. Post Office, Buffalo, 1971-75; owner, pres. Old Editions Book Shop, Buffalo, 1976—. Active Buffalo and Erie County Hist. Soc. Decorated knight Imperial Constantinian Mil. Order of St. George, 1991. Mem. Antiquarian Booksellers Assn. Am. Republican. Methodist. Avocations: chess, book collecting, travel. Office: Old Editions Book Shop 74 E Huron St Buffalo NY 14203

CRABBE, JOHN CROZIER, telecommunications consultant; b. Pomona, Calif., July 3, 1914; s. Arthur and Louise A. (Wiley) C.; m. Bobbin Gay Peck, June 17, 1940; children— John Crozier, William Charles, Barbara Gay. Student, Modesto (Calif.) Coll., 1931-34, Fresno (Calif.) State Coll., 1934-36; BA, Coll. Pacific, 1937, MA, 1940; postgrad., U. Iowa, 1938, N.Y. U., 1940, Stanford U., 1951, Ohio State U., 1951-52. Dir. broadcasting activities Coll. of Pacific, 1937-58; lectr. radio edn. Stanford U., summer 1951; asst., office radio-TV edn. Ohio State U., 1951-52; exec. sec. Delta-Sierra Ednl. TV Corp., 1953; dir. radio and TV Nat. Music Camp, Interlochen, Mich., 1954-55; program asso. Ednl. TV and Radio Center, Ann Arbor, Mich., 1955-56; exec. sec. Central Calif. Ednl. TV, 1955-58; gen. mgr. Sta. KVIE, 1958-69; spl. cons. radio edn., schs. central Calif.; chmn. TV Adv. Com. State Calif., 1967-69; cons. in broadcasting (East Africa) RTV Internat., N.Y., 1964; pres. Western Ednl. TV Network, 1967-69 mem. interim mgmt. group Corp. for Pub. Broadcasting Network Operation 1969; cons. in pub. broadcasting, 1969-73; cons. Joint Com. on Telecommunications Calif. Legislature, 1973-74; asso. Arthur Bolton Assos., 1972-73; gen

mgr. Tel-Vue Stockton, Inc., Calif., 1972; dir. telecommunications, gen. mgr. KTSC-TV U. So. Colo., Pueblo, 1976-81, ret., 1981; cons., from 1981. Bd. dirs. Rocky Mountain Corp. for Public Broadcasting; bd. govs. Pacific Mountain Network. Contbr. articles to profl. publs. Served as lt. USNR, 1943-46. Mem. Assn. for Ednl. Radio-TV (pres. 1950-53), Western Radio TV Conf. Home: Carmichael, Calif. *I have always cherished a commitment to a concept that change is exciting and good. Keeping abreast of and adjusting to change - change in goals, thoughts, ideas, principles of conduct - keeps one flexible and demands continuing accommodation to new developments. Forecasting benchmarks of human conduct and, by indirection, leading others toward predictable behaviour makes me an active participant in the process of change. This preoccupation makes it impossible to become sedentary - physically or intellectually.* Died Aug. 9, 2001.

CRABBS, ROGER ALAN, publisher, consultant, small business owner, educator; b. Cedar Rapids, Iowa, May 9, 1928; s. Winfred Wesley and Faye (Woodard) C.; m. Marilyn Lee Westcott, June 30, 1951; children: William Douglas, Janet Lee Crabbs Turner, Ann Lee Crabbs Menke. BA in Sci., State U. Iowa, 1954; MBA, George Washington U., 1965, DBA, 1973; M Christian Leadership, We. Sem., 1978. Commd. 2nd lt. USAF, 1950, advanced through grades to lt. col., 1968, Ret., 1972; prof. mgmt. U. Portland, Oreg., 1972-79; prof. bus. George Fox Coll., Newberg, Oreg., 1979-83; pres. Judson Bapt. Coll., The Dalles, Oreg., 1983-85. Pres. Host Pubs. Inc., pres., chmn. various corps., 1974-86; past chmn. nat. adv. bd. Travelhost, Inc.; cons. in field. Author: The Infallible Foundation for Management-The Bible, 1978, The Secret of Success in Small Business Management-Is in the Short Range, 1983; co-author: The Storybook Primer on Managing, 1976. Past pres. English Speaking Union, 1994-96, bd. dirs., 1994-97; bd. dirs. Christ Cmty. Ch., Conv. and Vis. Bur. of Washington County, 1986-2001, Oakhills Townhouse Assn., v.p., 1991-95; mem. Minority Conv. Tourism Adv. Coun., Oreg. Decorated Air Force Commendation medal with oak leaf cluster, Meritorious Service medal Dept. Def.; rated Command Air Force Missileman; recipient Jack Rosenberg Cmty. Svcs. award, 2000, regional, dist. and nat. awards SBA, Bonnie Hays Tourism award, 2001. Mem.: Soc. Advancement of Mgmt., Svc. Corps Ret. Execs., Am. Arbitration Assn., Acad. Mgmt., Assn. Atomic Vets., 51st Fighter Interceptor Wing Assn., Air Force Assn., Lang Syne Soc. of Portland, Portland Officers Club, Rotary (past pres.), Masons, Phi Mu Alpha, Delta Epsilon Sigma, Alpha Kappa Psi. Republican. Office: Host Publs Inc PMB #173 822 NW Murray Blvd Portland OR 97229-5868 E-mail: leecrabbs@everdream.com. *A positive attitude, sincere interest in others and a sense of humility have been the building blocks of my personal philosophy. They have served me well through my three careers - professional military, university professor and publisher.*

CRABTREE, BEN C. neuromuscular therapy clinic director; b. Las Vegas, Sept. 11, 1964; s. Ben C. and Jaynelle (Felix) C.; m. Virginia Kathryn Vance, Feb. 7, 1988 (div. Nov. 1989); m. Tania Oylan Tason, May 5, 1992; children: Greta, Bryan. AS, Panama Canal Coll., La Boca, Rep. of Panama, 1993, Austin Peay State U., 1995; BBA, Our Lady of the Lake U., 1995. Cert. firearms instr.; registered massage therapist; cert. neuromuscular therapist; lic. massage therapy instr.; cert. neuromuscular therapy instr. Software tech., adminstr. asst. Ace Personal Health Care, Inc., San Antonio, 1994-95; dir. info. systems River City Fin. Health Group/Home Health Care Solutions, San Antonio, 1995; chief fin. officer, alt. adminstr. A&E Quality Home Health Care, San Antonio, 1996-99; pres. Oylan, Inc., San Antonio, 1997-99; pres., owner Antonian Bodyworks, 1999-2001; instr. neuromuscular therapy Neuromuscular Therapy Ctr. N.Mex., 2000—. Profl. adv. com. Silver Days Home Health Care, San Antonio, 1996-97, Responsive Health Svcs., 1997-99. Mem. Dist. 128 State Budget Adv. Com., San Antonio, 1995. Ssgt. U.S. Army, 1984-92. Mem.: Internat. Massage Assn., Intenrat. Defensive Pistol Assn., Tex. Action Shooting Club, U.S. Practical Shooting Assn. Avocations: practical shooting, web page design. Office: Massage By Ben 11120 Wurzbach Ste 200 San Antonio TX 78230 E-mail: ibenunot@hotmail.com.

CRABTREE, BEVERLY JUNE, retired college dean; b. Lincoln, Nebr., June 22, 1937; d. Wayne Uniack and Frances Margaret (Wibbels) Deles Dernier; m. Robert Jewell Crabtree, June 1, 1958; children: Gregory, Karen. BS in Edn., U. Mo., 1959, MEd, 1962; PhD, Iowa State U., 1965. Tchr. home econs. area pub. schs., Pierce City and Sarcoxie, Mo., 1959-61; mem. faculty home econs. Mich. State U., East Lansing, 1964-67; assoc. prof. U. Mo., Columbia, 1967-72, coord. home econs. edn., 1967-73, prof., 1972-73, assoc. dean home econs., dir. home econs. extension programs, 1973-75; dean Coll. Home Econs. Okla. State U., Stillwater, 1975-87; dean Coll. Family and Consumer Scis. Iowa State U., Ames, 1987-97, ret., 1997. Mem. faculty Family Impact Seminar Inst. Ednl. Leadership, George Washington U., 1976-82, Cath. U. Am., 1982-87; mem. nat. panel cons. for Vocat. Ednl. Pers. Devel., 1969-70; mem. nat. com. on future of coop. extension USDA and Nat. Assn. State Univs. and Land Grant Colls., 1982; mem. joint coun. on food and agrl. scis., 1987-91. Contbr. articles in field to profl. jours. Gen. Foods fellow, 1963-64; recipient Centennial Alumni award Coll. Home Econs. Iowa State U., 1971, Alumni Citation of Merit, Coll. Home Econs. U. Mo., 1976, Profl. Achievement award Iow State U., 1983. Mem. Am. Home Econs. Assn. (pres. 1977-78, chmn. adv. coun. Ctr. for Family 1982-83, mem. coun. profl. devel. 1980-83, a leader to commemorate 75th anniversary 1984, pres. found. 1987-88, chair Coun. for Certification 1991-92, chair Coun. for Accreditation 1997-98, Disting. Svc. award 1993), Okla. Home Econs. Assn. (Profl. Achievement award 1983), Nat. Assn. State Univs. and Land Grant Colls. (mem. commn. home econs. 1981-84), Assn. Tchr. Educators, Home Econs. Edn. Assn., Nat. Coun. of Adminstrs. of Home Econs., Am. Ednl. Rsch. Assn., Am. Assn. Higher Edn., Nat. Assn. Tchr. Educators for Home Econs. (pres. 1969), Nat. Coun. on Family Relations, Mortar Bd., Golden Key, Omicron Nu, Phi Upsilon Omicron, Phi Delta Kappa, Omicron Delta Kappa, Pi Lambda Theta, Phi Kappa Phi, Gamma Sigma Delta. Methodist. Home: 3113 Rosewood Cir Ames IA 50014-4589

CRABTREE, DAVIDA FOY, minister; b. Waterbury, Conn., June 7, 1944; Alfred and Davida (Blakeslee) Foy; m. David T. Hindinger Jr., Aug. 28, 1982; stepchildren: Elizabeth Anne, David Todd. BS, Marietta Coll., 1967; MDiv, Andover Newton Theol. Sch., 1972; D of Ministry, Hartford Sem., 1989. Ordained to ministry United Ch. of Christ, 1972. Founder, exec. dir. Prudence Crandall Ctr. for Women, New Britain, Conn., 1973-76; min., dir. Greater Hartford (Conn.) Campus Ministry, 1976-80; sr. min. Colchester (Conn.) Federated Ch., 1980-91; bd. dirs. Conn. Conf. United Ch. of Christ, Hartford, 1982-90; conf. min. So. Calif. Conf., United Ch. of Christ, Pasadena, 1991-96, Conn. Conf., United Ch. of Christ, Hartford, 1996—. Rsch. assoc. Harvard Div. Sch., Cambridge, Mass., 1975-76. Author: The Empowering Church, 1989 (named one of Top Ten Books of Yr. 1990); editorial advisor Alban Inst., 1990-98. Bd. dirs. Hartford region YWCA, 1979-82, Christian Conf. of Conn., 1997—; trustee Cragin Meml. Libr., Colchester, 1980-91, Hartford Sem., 1983-91, Sch. of Theology at Claremont, 1993-96, Andover Newton Theol. Sch., 1997—; founder Youth Svcs. Bur., Colchester, 1984-89; pres. Creative Devel. for Colchester Inc., 1989-91; coun. Religious Leaders of L.A., 1991-96; v.p. Hope in Youth Campaign, 1992-96; dir. UCC Ins. bd., 1993-2000; bd. dirs. Amistad America, 1998—; trustee UCC Cornerstone Fund, 2000—. Named one of Outstanding Conn. Women, UN Assn., 1987; recipient Antoinette Brown award, Gen. Synod, United Ch. of Christ, 1977, Conf. Preacher award, Conn. Conf. United Ch. of Christ, 1982, Woman in Leadership award, Hartford region YWCA, 1987, Pres.'s award, Conn. Coalition Against Domestic Violence, 1997, Somos Uno award, United Neighborhood Orgn., 1995. Mem. Nat. Coun. Chs. (bd. dirs. 1969-81), Christians for Justice Action (exec. com. 1981-91). Mem. United Ch. Of Christ. E-mail: dfc@ctucc.org.

CRABTREE, JOHN DAVID, manufacturing company executive; b. Evansville, Ind., Apr. 13, 1947; s. George B. and Lucille (Barnhart) C.; m. Teresa Jean Whitsitt, June 15, 1968; children: John David Jr., Katherine Suzanne. BS in Indsl. Econs., Purdue U., 1969. Tool and die engr. Willow Run Hydramatic, Ypsilanti, Mich., 1974-75, foreman, 1975-77, gen. foreman plant 3, 1977-78, upt. plant 3, 1978-80, gen. supt. mfg., 1980-83, gen. supt. maintenance and process engring., 1983-85; plant mgr. Toledo Powertrain div. GM Corp., 1985-91, plant mgr. Flint V8 engine, 1991-99, plant mgr. Flint Engine South, 1999—. Mem. governing bd. Edison Indsl. Systems Ctr., Toledo 1987-88; coun. advisors ctr. for bus. and industry U. Toledo, 1988. Constable Saline Twp., 1985-88, mem. bd. tax rev., 1985-88; bd. dirs. Jr. Achievement, Toledo, 1986-88; governing bd. Working Coun. for Employee Involvement, NW Ohio, 1989, mem., 1990-91. Mem. Soc. Automotive Engrs., The Forum (Toledo), Toledo Leadership (com. of 100 1990-93), Am. Legion, Kiwanis. Republican. Methodist. Avocations: flying, private pilot. Home: 2423 Pepperidge Trl Brighton MI 48114-8956 E-mail: john.crabtree@gm.com.

CRABTREE, JOHN MICHAEL, college administrator, consultant; b. Fostoria, Ohio, Nov. 11, 1949; s. John Dwight and Opal Marie (Tate) C.; m. Cheryl Lynn Wallace, July 6, 1974. AA in Music Edn., Mt. Vernon Nazarene Coll., 1970; B of Music Edn., So. Nazarene U., 1972, MA in Edn., 1976; postgrad., U. Okla., 1976. Sports info. dir. So. Nazarene U., Okla., 1971-80, dir. pub. rels., 1974-80, assoc. dean student devel., 1974-78, dir. alumni and media rels., 1980-89, adminstrv. asst. to pres., 1989-90, dir. univ. advancement, 1989, exec. dir., 1990-91, v.p., 1991-98, asst. to pres., 1998—. Adj. prof. mktg. So. Nazarene U., 1979-82; bd. rsch. advisors Governing Bd. Editors and Pub. Bd. The Am. Biographical Inst. Editor The Perspective, 1981-89. Chmn. United Fund Drive, Bethany, 1983; pub. rels. dir. B.U.I.L.D. (Bethany United Improvement League Downtown); mem. exec. bd. Bethany Main St.; exec. sec. Nazerene Officers Instl. Advancement, 1989-90; pres. Nazarine Offices Instl. Adv., 1996-2000; bd. dirs. Mabel Fry Meml. Libr., Yukon,. Okla., 1990-94, So. Nazerene U. Found., 1993—; mem. Okla. Friends of Libr., Okla Civic Music Assn., exec. bd. dirs.; mem. Oklahoma City Friends Eng., exec. bd. dirs.; mem. Real Effective Action Leadership. Mem.: Oklahoma City Orch. League, Okla. Ind. Coll. Found., Okla. City C. of C. (pub. rels. and econ. devel. bds.), Sports Info. Dirs. Am. (ethics com. 1978—80, job attrition bd. 1980), Okla. Civic Music Assn. (bd. dirs.), Coun. Advancement and Support of Edn., Okla. Coll. Pub. Rels. Assn., Bethany C. of C., Assn. Fundraising Profls., Bethany Hist. Soc. (life), Oklahoma City Audubon Soc. (pub. rels. dir. wildlife film series 1974—93), Oklahoma City W. Rotary, Kiwanis, Sigma Delta Tau. Republican. Avocations: photography, philately, antique book collector. Office: So Nazarene U 6729 NW 39th Expy Bethany OK 73008-2605 E-mail: mcrabtre@snu.edu.

CRABTREE, LOREN WILLIAM, chancellor, academic administrator, history educator; b. Aberdeen, S.D., Sept. 2, 1940; s. Benjamin Forrest and Harriet Caroline (Zempel) C.; m. Sheila Ann Volz, Aug. 25, 1961 (div. May 1987); children: Christopher, Kathryn, Paul; m. Monica Sue Christen, 1987. BA, U. Minn., 1961, MA, 1965, PhD, 1969. Instr. Bethel Coll., St. Paul, 1965-67; from instr. to prof. history Colo. State U., Ft. Collins, 1967—, dean Coll. Liberal Arts, 1991-97, provost, acad. v.p., 1998-2001; v.p. and provost Univ. Tenn., Knoxville, 2001—. Vis. assoc. prof. U. Colo., Boulder, 1980; vis. prof., dean semester at sea program U. Pitts., 1986, 91; faculty affiliate Nat. Faculty, Atlanta, 1988—. Author: The Lion and the Dragon, 1970; co-author: Civilizations: A Cultural Atlas, 1994; contbr. articles to profl. publs. Trustee Am. Bapt. Ch., Ft. Collins, 1970-74; bd. deacons First Christian Ch., Ft. Collins, 1984-86. NDFL Chinese Lang. fellow Harvard U., 1964. Mem. Assn. for Asian Studies (pres. western conf. 1983-84), Coun. Colls. of Arts and Scis., Golden Key, Mortar Board, Phi Beta Kappa, Phi Alpha Theta. Democrat. Avocations: hiking, mountain climbing, court sports, furniture building. Home: 665 Oak Chase Blvd Lenoir City TN 37772 Office: Vp and Chancellor 810 Andy Holt Tower Univ Tenn Knoxville TN 37996 E-mail: lcrabtrl@utk.edu.

CRABTREE, VALLERI JAYNE, real estate executive, lawyer; b. Columbus, Ohio, Feb. 22, 1957; d. Ralph Dale and Ida Mae (Call) C. BS in Bus. Adminstrn., Ohio State U., 1979; JD, Capital U., 1983. Bar: Ohio 1983; lic. real estate broker, Ohio, Fla.; CLU; FLMI. Various mgmt. positions Nationwide Life Ins. Co., Columbus, 1980-87, dir. group annuity underwriting, adminstr., 1987-91; pvt. practice Columbus, 1991-95, 99—; real estate salesperson Metro II Realty, Henderson Realty, Columbus, 1991-94; pres., broker Onyx Real Estate Svcs., Inc., Columbus, 1994—2003, Condos to Castles Realty, Inc., 2003—; atty., owner Crabtree & Assocs., Attys. at Law, Columbus, 1995-99; owner Crabtree Jocularities, 2002—, Quixtar IBO, 2003—. Mem. adj. faculty Columbus State C.C., 1995-2002; instr. IFREC, 2003—; mem. equal opportunity com. Columbus Bd. Realtors, 1996-98, 2000-2002. Chair various coms. Welsh Hills Sch. Parent Orgn., 2000—02; asst. leader Brownie Girl Scout Troop 72, 2002—03; pres. Royal Ballet Parents Orgn., 2002—; trustee Unity Ch. Christianity, Columbus, 1991—94, 1999—2000, usher, 1990—2000, chair devel. com., 1996—99; vol. bus. mgr. Light in the Woods Ch., 2000—02; bd. dirs. Royal Celebration Ballet, Inc., 2003—. Mem. AAUW, ACLU, Nat. Assn. Realtors, Ohio Assn. Realtors, Columbus Bd. Realtors, Osceola County Assn. Realtors, Fla. Assn. Realtors, Rotary. Democrat. Avocation: toy collecting. Office: Condos to Castles Realty Inc 215 Celebration Pl Ste 500 Celebration FL 34747

CRACCO, ROGER QUINLAN, medical educator, neurologist; b. June 1, 1934; s. Frederick A. and Ruby Ann (Quinlan) C.; m. Joan Marie Bender, June 9, 1962. AB, Cornell U., 1956; MD, N.J. Med. Sch., 1960. Diplomate Am. Bd. Psychiatry and Neurology, Am. Bd. Electrodiagnostic Medicine, Am. Bd. Clin. Neurophysiology (bd. dirs. 1984-88). Intern Phila. Gen. Hosp., 1960-61; resident in neurology Jersey City Med. Ctr., 1961-64; fellow in neurophysiology Mayo Grad. Sch., Mayo Clinic, 1964-66; asst. prof. neurology Jefferson Med. Coll., Phila., 1968-71, assoc. prof., 1971-73; prof. neurology SUNY Health Sci. Ctr. at Bklyn., 1973-80, prof., chmn. neurology, 1980—. Head neurology service State U. Hosp.-Kings County Hosp. Ctr., Bklyn., 1980— ; vice dean Coll. Medicine SUNY Health Sci. Ctr., Bklyn., 1997—; mem. program project rev. com. Nat. Inst. Neurology, Communicative Disease and Stroke, NIH, USPHS, 1984-88, chmn. 1987-88. Editor: (with I. Bodis-Wollner) Evoked Potentials, 1986; mem. editl. bd. Ann. Neurology, Electroencephalography Clinical Neurophysiology, Muscle and Nerve jour., others; contbr. articles to profl. jours. Capt. M.C., U.S. Army, 1966-68. NIH grantee, 1970-86. Fellow Am. Acad. Neurology; mem. Am. Am. Neurol. Assn., Am. Neurophysiol. Soc. (pres. 1981-82), Ea. Assn. Electroencephalography (pres. 1979-80), Am. Assn. Electromyography and Electrodiagnosis, Am. Epilepsy Soc., Soc. for Neurosci., Assn. U. Profs. of Neurology, Am. Clin. Neurophysiologic Soc. (Herbert A. Jasper award for lifetime achievement 2002), Am. Acad. Clin. Neurophysiology (pres. 1987-89), Alpha Omega Alpha. Office: SUNY Health Sci Ctr Bklyn Dept Neurology 450 Clarkson Ave Dept Brooklyn NY 11203-2056 E-mail: roger.cracco@downstate.edu.

CRACKEL, THEODORE JOSEPH, historian, consultant; b. Urbana, Ill., Sept. 10, 1938; s. Orville Lee and Aleta (Smith) C.; m. Kay Knight, Sept. 2, 1961 (div. 1972); children: Todd, Dana; m. Mai Thi Nguyen, Oct. 14, 1972 (div. 1991); children: John, Robert; m. Mary-Jo Kline, May 23, 1998. AB, U. Ill., 1962; MA, Rutgers U., 1971, PhD, 1985. Commd. 2nd lt. U.S. Army, 1962, advanced through grades to lt. col., 1978, tank unit comdr., 1963-66, advisor, 1966-67, 71-72; weapons sys. analyst Combat Devels. Command, Ft. Knox, Ky., 1967-69; asst. prof. history U.S. Mil. Acad., West Point, N.Y., 1972-75, 78-81; instr. Dept. Strategy U.S. Army Command and Gen. Staff Coll., 1975-77; dir. mil. history and strategy studies U.S. Army War Coll., Carlisle Barracks, Pa., 1981-83, ret., 1983; sr. fellow The Heritage Found., Washington, 1983-85; sr. cons. GE Co., Washington, 1985-87; exec. dir. Papers of the Comdg. Gens., 1988-93; dir., editor Papers of the War Dept. 1784-1800, 1993—. Vis. prof. history dept. U.S. Mil. Acad., West Point, N.Y., 2001—. Author: The Army Additional Duty Guide, 1970, Mr. Jefferson's Army, 1987, The Illustrated History of West Point, 1991, History of the Civil Reserve Air Fleet, 1993, electronic edit., 1999, West Point: A Bicentennial History, 2002; contbr. articles on mil. and polit. history, def. orgn. reform to profl. jours. Mem. Assn. Documentary Editors, Orgn. Am. Historians, Soc. Historians of Early Am. Republic, Army and Navy Club (Washington), Chi Psi. Republican. Office: East Stroudsburg U Papers Of War Dept 1784-1800 East Stroudsburg PA 18301

CRACRAFT, JOEL, curator; BS in Zoology, U. Okla.; MS in Zoology, La. State U.; PhD in Biology, Columbia U. Curator in charge divsn. vertebrate zoology-ornithology Am. Mus. Natural History, N.Y.C. Adj. prof. Ctr. for Environ. Rsch. and Conservation., Columbia U., NY; adj. profl. biology CUNY. Office: Am Mus Natural History Devsn Vertibrate Zoology-Ornithology Central Park West at 79th St New York NY 10024

CRACROFT, RICHARD HOLTON, English literature educator; b. Salt Lake City, June 28, 1936; s. Ralph and Grace Darling (White) C.; m. Janice Marie Alger, Sept. 17, 1959; children: Richard Alger, Jeffrey Ralph, Jennifer Cracroft Lewis. BA, U. Utah, 1961, MA, 1963; PhD in English and Am. Lit., U. Wis., 1969. Student instr. U. Utah, Salt Lake City, 1961-63; instr. English Brigham Young U., Provo, Utah, 1963-66; grad. instr. U. Wis., Madison, 1966-69; from asst. prof. English to assoc. prof. English Brigham Young U., Provo, 1969-74, prof. English, 1974-2001, prof. emeritus English, 2001—, dept. chair English, 1975-80, dean Coll. Humanities, 1981-86, Nan Osmond Grass Prof. English, 1999-2001. Dir. Ctr. for Study of Christian Values in Lit., Brigham Young U., Provo, 1993-2001; bd. judges David Evans Biography Prize, Logan, Utah, 1983-2001, Orton Prize for Mormon Letters, Salt Lake City, 1991-2001. Author: Washington Irving: The Western Works, 1974; co-editor: A Believing People: The Literature of the Latter-day Saints, 1974, 1979, 22 Young Mormon Writers, 1975, Voices From the Past: (LDS) Journals, Diaries, Autobiographies, 1980, My Soul Delighteth in the Scriptures, 1999; editor: Dictionary of Literary Biography: 20th Century American Western Writers, vols. 206, 212, 256, 1999—2002, (jour.) Lit. and Belief, 1993—2002; founding assoc. editor: The Carpenter, 1966—70, assoc. editor: Dialogue, 1969—73, We. Am. Lit., 1973—86, mem. editl. bd.: BYU Studies, 1981—86, This People, 1996—2000; contbr. articles. Bishop, stake pres., mission pres. LDS Ch. Democrat. Avocations: reading, writing, gardening, leading tours of western europe. Home: 43 N 550 E Orem UT 84097-4800 Office: Brigham Young U Dept English 3146 Jesse Knight Hum Bldg Provo UT 84602-2724 E-mail: cracroftr@emstar2.net.

CRADDICK, THOMAS RUSSELL, speaker of state house of representatives; b. Beloit, Wis., Sept. 19, 1943; s. Russell Francis and Beatrice Eleanor (Kowalik) C.; m. Nadine Nayfa, Sept. 6, 1969; children: Christi Leigh, Thomas Russell Jr. BBA, Tex. Tech. U., 1965, MBA, 1966. Owner Craddick Properties, Midland; owner, pres. Craddick Inc., Midland; sales rep. Mustang Mud, Midland; state rep. Tex. Legis., Austin, 1968—. Chmn. Rep. Legis. Caucus, Austin, 1988-98, mem. legis. budget bd., Austin, 1992-98, legis. audit com., 1992-98, mem. state affairs com., 1999-2002, mem. house ways and means com., 1992-2002, chmn. house ways and means com., 1992-98; spkr. of the house, 2003—. Bd. dirs. Tex. Tech. U. Found., Lubbock. Recipient Disting. Eagle Scout award Boy Scouts Am., 1990, Hats Off award Tex. Ind. Roy. Owners Assn., 1988, Energy award for govt. svc. Midland Reporter-Telegram, 2002, Hope award Nat. MS Soc., 2002, Energy award for govt. svc., Midland Reproter-Telegram, 2002; Paul Harris fellow Rotary Found., 1991. Mem. Lions Club. Republican. Roman Catholic. Avocations: sports, hunting, fishing. Home: 3108 Stanolind Ave Midland TX 79705-8240 Office: Craddick Properties 500 W Texas Ave Ste 880 Midland TX 79701-4217

CRADDOCK, CAMPBELL (JOHN CAMPBELL CRADDOCK), geologist, educator; b. Chgo., Apr. 3, 1930; s. Alice Phillips; adopted by John and Bernice (Campbell) C.; m. Dorothy Dunkelberg, June 13, 1953; children: Susan, John, Carol. BA, DePauw U., 1951; MA, Columbia U., 1953, PhD, 1954. Geologist Shell Oil Co., N.Mex., Tex., Colo., Wyo., 1954-56; asst. prof. U. Minn., Mpls., 1956-60, assoc. prof., 1960-67; prof. geology U. Wis., Madison, 1967-96; prof. emeritus, 1996—; chmn. dept. U. Wis., 1977-80; leader Antarctic geologic field rsch. programs, 1959-69, geologist, 1980; leader Alaskan Range field rsch. programs, 1968-81; leader Svalbard field rsch. programs, 1977-86. Cons. C.E. AUS, 1957—58, N. Star Rsch. Inst., 1965—68, Dept. State, 1976, Phillips Petroleum Co., 1980, Texaco, 1985; vis. scientist N.Z. Geol. Survey, 1962—63; lectr. Nanjing (China) U., 1981, Beijing U., 1981; chmn. panel polar geology and geophysics NRC, 1967—71, com. on polar rsch., 1967—71, mem. polar rsch. bd., 1978—82; U.S. mem. working group on geology Sci. Com. on Antarctic Rsch., 1967—81, chmn. group, 1973—80; co-chief scientist Leg 35 Deep Sea Drilling Project, 1974; chmn. Antarctic panel Circum-Pacific Map Project, 1979—90. Editor: Antarctic Geoscience, 1982; co-editor: Geologic Maps of Antarctica, Folio 12, Antarctic Map Folio Series, 1970, Initial Reports of the Deep Sea Drilling Project, Vol. 35, 1976, Geology and Paleontology of the Ellsworth Mountains, Antarctica, Geol. Soc. of Am. Memoir 170, 1992; contbr. articles to profl. jours. Higgins fellow, 1951-52, NSF fellow, 1952-53; Rsch. grantee, 1957-95; recipient U.S. Antarctic Service medal, 1968, Bellingshausen-Lazarev medal Soviet Acad. Scis., 1970, Alumni citation DePauw U., 1976 Fellow AAAS (steering com. geology and geography sect. 1996-98), Geol. Soc. Am. (chmn. North Ctrl. sect. 1982-83, chmn. structural geology and tectonics divsn. 1983-84, books editor 1982-88, Disting. Svc. award 1988); mem. Internat. Union Geol. Scis. (commn. on structural geology 1968-76, mem. commn. on tectonics 1976-85, del. Sci. Com. on Antarctic Rsch. 1974-87, mem. commn. on geologic map of world 1974-91, commn. v.p. for Antarctica 1979-91), Am. Geophys. Union, Am. Assn. Petroleum Geologists, Groupe Francais d'Etude de Gondwana (hon.), Phi Beta Kappa, Sigma Xi. Office: U Wis Dept Geology and Geophysics 1215 W Dayton St Madison WI 53706-1600

CRADDOCK, ELAINE, religious studies educator; b. Denver, Jan. 17, 1960; d. Lane Dale and Norma Jean Craddock. BA, Smith Coll., 1982; MA, U. Calif. Berkeley, 1986, PhD, 1994. Asst. prof. Southwestern U., Georgetown, Tex., 1994—2000, assoc. prof., 2000—. Contbr. Grantee, Fulbright Found., 1989—90. Mem.: AAUW, Assn. Asian Studies, Am. Acad. Religion. Avocations: travel, piano, hiking.

CRAFT, BARBARA J. state representative; b. Junction City, Kans., Nov. 23, 1942; m. Rod Craft; children: David, Christine. BA, U. Kans., 1964. Medtech, dir. blood bank Irwin Army Hosp., 1966—70; owner, mgr. Craft's Pharmacy, 1993—99; mem. Kans. Ho. of Reps., 2003—. Leader, trainer Girl Scouts, 1973—86; bd. edn. USO 475, 1987—; elder, deacon, tchr. First Presbyn. Ch.; bd. dirs. Food Pantry Geary County, 1990—93, Kans. for Strong Ft. Riley, 1999—. Republican. Office: 181-W State Capital 300 SW 10th Ave Topeka KS 66612*

CRAFT, CHERYL MAE, neurobiologist, anatomist, researcher; b. Lynch, Ky., Apr. 15, 1947; d. Cecil Berton and Lillian Lovelle (Ellington) C.; m. Laney K. Cormney, Oct. 14, 1967 (div. Sept. 1980); children: Tyler Craft Cormney, Ryan Berton Cormney; m. Richard N. Lolley (dec. Apr. 2000). BS in Biology, Chemistry and Math., Valdosta State Coll., 1969; cert. in tchg. biol. and math., Ea. Ky. U., 1971; PhD in Human Anatomy and Neurosci., U. Tex., San Antonio, 1984. Undergrad. rsch. asst. Ea. Ky. U., Richmond, 1965-67; tchg. asst. dept. cell-structural biology U. Tex. Health Sci. Ctr., San Antonio, 1979-84; postdoctoral fellowship lab. devel. neurobiology NICHD and LMDB/NEI, Bethesda, Md., 1984-86; instr. dept. psychiatry U. Tex. Southwestern Med. Ctr., Dallas, 1986-87, asst. prof., 1987-91; dir. lab. Molecular Neurogenetics, Schizophrenia Rsch. Ctr., VA Med. Ctr., Dallas, 1988-94; dir. Lab. Molecular Neurogenetics Mental Health Clinic Rsch. Ctr., U. Tex. Southwestern Med. Ctr., 1990-94; assoc. prof. U. Tex. Southwestern Med. Ctr., 1991-94; Mary D. Allen prof. Doheney Eye Inst. U. So. Calif. Keck Sch. Medicine, L.A., 1994—, chmn. dept. cell and neurobiology, 1994—. Ad hoc reviewer NEI/NIH, Bethesda, 1993—; reviewer Molecular Biology, NSPB Fight for Sight Grants, 1991-94; STAR-sci. adv. bd. U. So. Calif./Bravo Magnet H.S., L.A., 1995—. Contbr. author: Melatonin: Biosynthesis, Physiological Effects, 1993; exec. editor Exptl. Eye Rsch. jour., 1993—; editor Molecular Vision. Recipient Merit award for rsch. VA Med. Ctr., 1992, 93, 94, nomination for Women in Sci. and Engring. award Dallas VA, 1992, 93; NEI fellow, 1986, NICHD/NIH fellow, 1986. Mem. AAAS, AAUW, Assn. for Rsch. in Vision and Ophthalmology (chair program planning com. 1991-94), Am. Soc. for Neurochemistry (Jordi Folch Pi Outstanding Young Investigator 1992), Sigma Xi (sec./treas. 1986-93, pres. 1993-94). Avocations: reading, travel. Home: 1191 Brookmere Rd Pasadena CA 91105-3301 Office: Keck Sch Medicine 1333 San Pablo St Rm 401 Los Angeles CA 90089-0111 E-mail: ccraft@hsc.usc.edu.

CRAFT, DOUGLAS DURWOOD, artist; b. Greene, N.Y., Oct. 20, 1924; s. Harry Benjamin and Phoebe (Hotchkiss) C.; m. Elizabeth Louise Harms, Sept. 8, 1951. BFA, U. Chgo. and Art Inst. Chgo., 1950; MA in Painting, U. N.Mex., 1953. Grad. asst. U. N.Mex., 1951-52; assoc. prof. fine arts Sch. Art Inst., Chgo., 1957-65, Carnegie-Mellon U., Pitts., 1966-69; prof. fine arts Coll. New Rochelle, N.Y., 1970-91. Vis. artist in residence U. Ky., 1964, Cooper Union, N.Y.C., 1969-71, Sch. Visual Arts, N.Y.C., 1988; 1st Am. exch. prof., artist in residence Royal Coll. Art, London, 1964-65; guest artist curator Selected Women, Painters Castle Gallery, Coll. New Rochelle (N.Y.), 1982, Of Paper, Pigment and Glass, Castle Gallery, New Rochelle, 1987. One-man shows include Kasha Heman Gallery, Chgo., 1963, 61, U. N.Mex., 1964, 52, U. Ky., 1964, Travers Festival Gallery, Edinburgh, Scotland, 1965, Royal Coll. Art, London, 1964, Carnegie Mellon U., 1968, Mus. Art, Carnegie Inst., Pitts., 1968, Fischbach Gallery, N.Y.C., 1973, Jersey City Mus., 1978, 55 Mercer Gallery, N.Y.C., 1980, Bratton Gallery, Inc., N.Y.C., 1989, Coll. Ctr. Art Gallery, Coll. New Rochelle, 1989, Rosefsky Studio Art Gallery SUNY Binghamton, 1993, retrospective Butler Inst. Am. Art, Youngstown, Ohio, 1993, Paul McCarron Gallery, N.Y.C., 1995, Delaware Valley Arts Ctr., Narrowsburg, 1996, retrospective traveling exhbn. Makee Gallery, Canton, Mo., Gray Gallery, Quincy,

Ill., Keokuk Art Ctr., Iowa, 1997, Paul McCarron Gallery, N.Y.C., 1996, 98, Del. Valley Arts Ctr., Narrowsburg, 2001, Gorshow Arch., N.Y.C., 2000, others; exhibited in group shows at Rose Fried Gallery, N.Y.C., 1968, Montclair (N.J.) Art Mus., 1984, Traverse Gallery, Edinburgh, 1984, Studio K., Long Island City, N.Y., 1985, Castle Gallery, New Rochelle, N.Y., 1985-86, Jersey City Mus., 1987, Montclair Art Mus., 1987, Robeson Gallery, Rutger's U., Newark, 1987, N.A.M.E. Gallery, Chgo., 1988, Bratton Gallery, Inc., N.Y.C., 1988-89, Schick Art Gallery Skidmore Coll., 1995, Del. Arts Ctr. Gallery, 1995, Pavel Zoubok Gallery, N.Y.C., 2001-02, others; represented in permanent collections Smithsonian Instn., Washington, Art Inst. Chgo., U. Ky., Mus. Modern Art, N.Y.C., Whitney Mus. Am. Art, N.Y.C., U. N.Mex., Gill Libr. Coll. New Rochelle, Butler Inst. Am. Art, Youngstown, Ohio, Meml. Art Gallery, Rochester, N.Y., others; corp. collections; pvt. collections in U.S.A, Can., Eng. Scotland, France, Saudi Arabia, Japan. Bd. dirs. Castle Gallery, New Rochelle. Served with USNR, 1943-46. Recipient Logan bronze medal Art Inst. Chgo., 1966, Harry Allison Logan meml. award Chautauqua Art Assn., 1963, jury award in painting Carnegie Inst., 1968; Carr scholar U. Iowa, 1942-43; Carl Loeb fellow Syracuse U., 1950; grantee Richard A. Florsheim Art Fund, 1993. Home: PO Box 245 Jeffersonville NY 12748-0245 Studio: 21 Jefferson Ave Jeffersonville NY 12748

CRAFT, EDMUND COLEMAN, retired automotive parts manufacturing company executive; b. Plainfield, N.J., Dec. 23, 1939; s. Edmund Coleman and Ruth Irene (Morrell) C.; m. Gail Christensen; children: Edmund Coleman III, Elisabeth Gordon, William Todd. BS, Lycoming Coll., 1963; postgrad., Syracuse U., 1963-64; grad. exec. program, U. Minn., 1984. With Borg-Warner Corp., Detroit, adminstrv. asst. to chmn. Chgo., 1969-70; with Borg-Warner Ltd., Letchworth, Hertfordshire, Eng., 1970-75; v.p. hydraulics div. Borg-Warner, Wooster, Ohio, 1975-79; dir. hydraulics div. Donaldson Co. Inc., Mpls., 1979-83, v.p., 1983-2000; sr. advisor Global Aftermarket, 2000-2001; ret., 2001. Bd. dirs. Jr. Achievement of Upper Midwest Inc., 1993-2000, mem. exec. com., 1994-2000; divsn. chmn. United Way, Wooster, 1974. Mem. Automotive Filter Mfrs. Coun. (vice chmn. 1985-89, chmn. 1989-91, bd. dirs. 1991-2000), Dataw Island Club, Dataw Island Yacht Club. Republican. Presbyterian. Avocations: golf, power boating.

CRAFT, KAY STARK, real estate company executive; b. Yoakum, Tex., Oct. 15, 1945; d. Jesse James and Leona Charlotte (Manchen) Stark; m. Michael Joseph Grogan IV, May 31, 1969 (div. June 1974); 1 child, Michael Joseph V; m. Roger Dale Craft, Apr. 1, 1983. AA, Victoria (Tex.) Coll., 1964; BS, S.W. Tex. State U., 1966, Broadway Sch. Real Estate, Hot Springs, Ark., 1985. Lic. real estate broker, Ark. Tchr. Victoria Ind. Sch. Dist., 1966-68, Pasadena (Tex.) Ind. Sch. Dist., 1968-85; real estate agt. Coldwell Banker, Hot Springs Village, Ark., 1985-88; prin. broker-owner Cross Roads Realty, Inc., Hot Springs Village, Ark., 1988—, pres., bd. dirs., 1991—, v.p., 1988-91; sec., bd. dirs. Craft Classic Homes, Inc., Hot Springs Village, Ark., 1987—2002. Mem. DAR, Colonial Dames of 17th Century, Nat. Soc. Magna Carta Dames, Nat. Assn. Realtors, Ark. Realtors Assn. (Million Dollar Club 1991—, Lifetime Million Dollar Prodr. award 1997, 2002, Multi Million Dollar Prodr. award 1993, 94, 96-2002, cert. Grad. Realtors Inst. 1992), N.W. Garland Bd. Realtors (treas. 1992, Million Dollar Prodr. award 1990-98), Woman's Coun. Realtors, Residential Sales Coun. (cert. residential specialist 1993). Republican. Methodist. Avocations: genealogy, travel, reading. Home: 45 Gerona Way Hot Springs National Park AR 71909-2762 Office: Cross Roads Realty Inc 4136 N Highway 7 Hot Springs National Park AR 71909-9564

CRAFT, ROBERT HOMAN, JR., lawyer; b. N.Y.C., Sept. 24, 1939; s. Robert Homan and Janet Marie (Sullivan) C.; m. Margaret Jamison Ford, Feb. 6, 1971; children: Robert H. III, Gerard Ford. AB, Princeton U., 1961; BA, Oxford U., 1963; LLB, Harvard U., 1966. Bar: N.Y. 1973, U.S. Dist. Ct. (so. and ea. dists.) N.Y. 1977, U.S. Ct. Appeals (D.C. cir.) 1977, U.S. Dist. Ct. D.C. 1978, U.S. Ct. Appeals (2nd cir.) 1974, U.S. Supreme Ct. 1977. Assoc. Sullivan & Cromwell, N.Y.C., 1966-74; spl. asst. to under sec. of state for security assistance U.S. Dept. State, Washington, 1974-76; exec. asst. to chmn. SEC, Washington, 1976; ptnr. Sullivan & Cromwell, Washington, 1977—. Bd. trustees Washington Opera, 1978—, pres. 1992-98; dir. Coun. for Excellence in Govt., 1989—. Mem. ABA, D.C. Bar Assn., N.Y. State Bar Assn., Assn. Bar City of N.Y., Am. Soc. Internat. Law, Met. Club (Washington), Chevy Chase (Md.) Club. Home: 5010 Millwood Ln NW Washington DC 20016-2620 Office: Sullivan & Cromwell 1701 Pennsylvania Ave NW Washington DC 20006-5866

CRAFT DAVIS, AUDREY ELLEN, writer, educator; b. Vanceburg, Ky., June 9, 1926; d. James Elmer and Lula Alice (Vance) Gilkison; m. Vernon Titus Craft, Nov. 5, 1943 (dec. Aug. 1979); children: James Vernon Craft, Alice Ann Craft Schuler; m. Louis Amzie Davis, Oct. 22, 1986. PhD, Ohio U., 1964; Dr. of Metaphysics, Coll. Divine Metaphysics, 1968; DD, Ohio U., 1971; postgrad., St. Petersburg Jr. Coll., 1975; DD (hon.), Assoc. Minister, Coll. Metephysical Studies, 1998. Owner beauty salon Audrey Craft Enterprises, Tampa Bay, Fla., 1970-83, owner cosmetic co. Portsmouth, Ohio, 1958-70; owner, distbr. Nightingale Motivation, Tampa Bay, Fla., 1960—; tchr., counselor Bus. Coll. U. Tampa Bay, 1965—; ins. staff Investors Heritage & Wabash, Portsmouth, 1967-70; ins. broker Jackson Nat. & Wabash, Tampa Bay, 1971-91; pres. The Gardens 107, Inc., Tampa Bay, 1987—. Travel writer, counselor Cruises/Travel & Etc., Fla., 1981—. Author: (poetry) Pathways, 1990, Metaphysical Techniques That Really Work, 1994, (Spanish translation), 2nd edit., 2002, Metaphysical Encounters, 1992, How to Stay Secure in a Chaotic World, 1993, Metaphysics Encounters of a Fourth Kind, 1995, How to Safeguard Your World and Avoid Becoming a Target, 1996, Angel Trails, 2002, Hidden Truths and Unusual Events of the Bible, 2002; contbr. articles to profl. jours. Bd. dirs. The Gardens Domicurculums, Cmty. Coun., 1987—; bd. dirs. State Bd. Cosmetology, Columbus, Ohio, 1962-63, Bus. and Profl. Women, Portsmouth, 1967-69, Sci. Rsch., Portsmouth, 1965-69, Tampa Bay, 1972-74. Recipient Key to Miami, Office of Mayor Claude Kirk, 1969, Million Dollar trophy Lt. Gov. John Brown Ohio; commd. Ky. Col. by Gov. Edward T. Breathitt, 1968, Gov. Wendell Ford, 1969. Mem. AARP, S.E. Writers Assn., Christian Writers Guild, Writers Digest Book Club, Nat. Assn. Retired Fed. Employees (assoc.), Am. Heart Assn. (chmn. Seminole area 1994). Democrat. Avocations: writing, lectures, counseling, travel, meditation. Home and Office: 102 Saint Petersburg Dr W Oldsmar FL 34677-3620

CRAFTON-MASTERSON, ADRIENNE, real estate company executive; b. Providence, Mar. 6, 1926; d. John Harold and Adrienne (Fitzgerald) Crafton; m. Francis T. Masterson, May 31, 1947 (div. Jan. 1977); children: Mary Victoria Masterson Bush, Kathleen Joan, John Andrew, Barbara Lynn Harrison Student, No. Va. C.C., 1971-74; A in Biblical Studies, Christ to World Bible Inst., Jacksonville, Fla., 1992; A in Pastoral Leadership, Calvary Bible Inst., Jacksonville, Fla., 1993. Mem. staff Senator T.F. Green of R.I., Washington, 1944-47, 54-60, with U.S. Senate Com. on Campaign Expenditures, 1944-45; asst. chief clk. Ho. Govt. Ops. Com., 1948-49; clk. Ho. Campaign Expenditures Com., 1950; asst. appointment sec. Office of Pres., 1951-53; with Hubbard Realty, Alexandria, Va., 1962-67; owner, mgr. Adrienne C. Masterson Real Estate, Alexandria, 1968-82; pres. Adrienne Investment Real Estate (AIRE) Ltd., Alexandria, 1982-91; devel. staff writer Calvary Internat., Jacksonville, Fla., 1992-93; Adrienne Crafton-Masterson Real Estate, Winchester, Va., 1993-94, owner, prin., broker Haymarket, Va., 1994—. Pres. AIRE-Merkli developers, 1988-92; founder AIHRE USA, Inc., 1993—. Mem. adv. panel Fairfax County (Va.) Coun. on Arts, 1987-88; founder, pres. Mt. Vernon/Lee Cultural Ctr. Found., Inc. 1984-92; mem. Haymarket (Va.) Hist. Commn., 1994-95, 97-2001, chmn., 1999-2001. Fellow Internat. Biog. Ctr. (dep. dir. gen.); mem. Internat. Orgn. Real Estate Appraisers (sr.), Nat. Assn. Realtors, No. Va. Assn. Realtors (chmn. comml. and indsl. com. 1982-83, cmty. revitalization com. 1983-84, pres. land comml. indsl. mems. 1985, v.p. land comml. and indsl. mems. 1989), Greater Piedmont Area Assn. Realtors, Prince William Assn. Realtors, Fairfax Affordable Housing Inc. (sec. 1990-91), Haymarket-Gainesville (Va.) Busl. and Profl. Assn. (bd. dirs. 1996-99, sec. 1998-99), Alexandria C. of C., Mt. Vernon/Lee C. of C., Friends of Kennedy Ctr. (founder), Optimist Club Gainesville-Haymarket (charter, bd. dirs. 1997-99). Office: Haymarket Profl Ctr PO Box 305 6611 Jefferson St Haymarket VA 20168-0305 Fax: 703-754-1170. E-mail: aihrecraft@earthlink.net.

CRAGIN, CHARLES LANGMAID, lawyer; b. Portland, Maine, Oct. 9, 1943; s. Charles Langmaid and Ruth (Meriam) C.; m. Maureen Patricia Ford, Oct. 8, 1994; children: Christine, Jean, Cathleen. BS, U. Maine, 1967, JD, 1970. Bar: Maine 1970, U.S. Dist. Ct. Maine 1970, U.S. Supreme Ct. 1974, U.S. Ct. Appeals (D.C. cir.) 1989, U.S. Ct. Vet. Appeals 1997. Assoc. Verrill & Dana, Portland, Maine, 1970-74, ptnr., 1974-90; chmn. U.S. Bd. of Vet.'s Appeals, Washington, D.C., 1991-97; counselor to undersec. U.S. Dept. VA, 1997, prin. dep. asst. sec. of def., Res. affairs, 1997-98, acting asst. sec. of def., res. affairs, 1998-2001; prin. dep. under sec. defense, personnel & readiness U.S. Dept. Defense, 1998-2001, acting under sec. def., personnel and readiness, 2001; ptnr. Blank Rome LLP, Washington, 2001—03; sr. v.p. nat. intelligence, security and response Sys. Planning Corp., Arlington, Va., 2003—. Contbr. articles to legal publs. Rep. candidate for gov. Maine, 1982; bd. dirs., v.p. Margaret Chase Smith Found., Skowhegan, Maine, 1986—, Potomac divsn. AAA, 1992—; chmn. budget com. Rep. Nat. Com., 1984-90; mem. MaineCommn. on Govt. Ethics and Elections, 1986-88, Def. Adv. Com. on Women in Svcs.,1986-88; bd. dirs. U.S. Navy Meml. Found., 1989—, vice chmn., 2002--. Capt. USNR; ret. Decorated Legion of Merit; named Outstanding Young Man Maine, Maine Jaycees, 1976; recipient Disting Svc. award U. So. Maine Alumni Assn., 1986, Exceptional Svc. award U.S. Dept. Vets. Affairs, 1997, Disting. Pub. Svc. award USCG, 2000, Nat. Pres.'s award Naval Res. Assn., 2000, Minuteman award Res. Officers Assn., 2000, Outstanding Svc. award Nat. Mil. Family Assn., 2000, Disting. Pub. Svc. medal Dept. Def., 2001, Decoration for Exceptional Civilian Svc., USAF, 2001, U.S. Army, 2001, Disting. Pub. Svc. medal U.S. Navy, 2001. Fellow Am. Acad. Hosp. Attys. (bd. dirs. 1979-82); mem. ABA, Maine Bar Assn. (Disting. Svc. award 1986), DC Bar Assn., Capitol Hill Club (Washington), Army and Navy Club (Washington). Roman Catholic. Avocations: skiing, wine collecting, ham radio, gardening. Office: Sys Planning Corp 1000 Wilson Blvd 30th Fl Arlington VA 22209-2211 E-mail: ccragin@sysplan.com.

CRAGNOLIN, KAREN ZAMBELLA, real estate developer, lawyer; b. Boston, May 19, 1949; d. John T. Zambella and Corrine M. (Feeney) Zenga; m. Robert Louis Cragnolin, Sept. 8, 1974; 1 child, Nikki Josephine. BA, Georgian Ct. Coll., 1971; JD, New Eng. Sch. Law, 1974. Bar: N.Y. 1974, D.C. 1981. Sr. tax editor Prentice-Hall, Englewood Cliffs, N.J., 1974-76; dir. pub. affairs Am.-Arab Affairs Coun., Washington, 1981-83; founder, dir. Am. Bus. Coun., Dubai, United Arab Emirates, 1983-86; dir. River Link, Inc., Asheville, N.C., 1987—. Bd. trustees Clean Water Mgmt. Trust Fund, WNC Tommorrow. Pres. Young Dems., Georgian Court, N.J., 1970-71, chair Greenway Commn., Asheville, N.C., 1990—; pres., bd. dirs. Leadership Asheville, 1993—, Asheville Area C. of C., 1992-96; bd. dirs. Hand Made Am., Asheville, 1994—, Handi-Skills, Asheville, 1986-90, chmn., 1986-88. Recipient Downtown Hero award Asheville Downtown Assn., 1991, Cir. Excellence Leadership Asheville, 1995, Friend of River award Land Regional Coun., 1995, Athena award Asheville C. of C., 1999. Mem. D.C. Bar Assn., N.Y. Bar Assn. Avocations: gardening, cooking, paddling. Home: 7 Cedarcliff Rd Asheville NC 28803-2905 Office: RiverLink Inc PO Box 15488 Asheville NC 28813-0488 E-mail: Karen@riverlink.org.

CRAGNOLINO, GUSTAVO ADOLFO, research scientist; b. Marcos Juarez, Cordoba, Argentina, July 23, 1940; arrived in US, 1976; s. Roberto Clemente and Maria Antonia (Ferrer) Cragnolino; m. Aida Apter, Aug. 16, 1966; children: Ana, Ernesto. Licenciado in Chem. Scis., U. Buenos Aires, 1966, D in Chem. Scis., 1975. Rsch. assoc. Atomic Energy Commn., Buenos Aires, 1968—76; sr. rsch. scientist Commn. Atomic Energy, Buenos Aires, 1988—90; rsch. scientist Ohio State U., Columbus, 1976—86; assoc. scientist Brookhaven Nat. Lab., Upton, NY, 1986—88; prin. scientist S.W. Rsch. Inst., San Antonio, 1990—95, staff scientist, 1995—2003, inst. scientist, 2003—. Lectr., adv. Internat. Atomic Energy Agy., Vienna, 1994; presenter in field. Co-editor: Accelerated Corrosion Tests for Service Life Prediction of Materials, 1994, Scientific Basis for Nuclear Waste Management XXV, 2002; co-author: ASME Handbook on Water Technology for Thermal Power Systems, 1998; contbr. articles to profl. jours. Fellow: Nat. Assn. Corrosion Engrs. Internat. (chmn. tech. com. 1996—98); mem.: ASTM Internat., Am. Nuc. Soc., Electrochem. Soc. Office: SW Rsch Inst 6220 Culebra Rd San Antonio TX 78238-5166 Business E-Mail: gcragno@swri.org.

CRAHAN, ELIZABETH SCHMIDT, librarian; b. Cleve., Oct. 6, 1913; d. Edward and Margaret (Adams) Schmidt; m. Kenneth Acker, 1938 (div. 1968); children: Margaret Miller, John Acker, Steven Acker, Charles Acker; m. Marcus E. Crahan, Dec. 16, 1968. Student, Wellesley Coll., 1931—32; BArch, U. So. Calif., 1937, MLS, 1960. Reference libr. Los Angeles County Med. Assn., L.A., 1960—61, head reference libr., 1961—67, asst. libr., 1967—78, dir. libr. svcs., 1978—90. Mem.: George Dock Soc. History of Medicine, Med. Libr. Group So. Calif. and Ariz., Med. Libr. Assn., Spl. Librs. Assn., Friends of the UCLA Libr. (founder, pres. 1977—79, sec. 1978—97), Am. Inst. Wine and Food, Zamorano Club.

CRAHAN, JACK BERTSCH, retired manufacturing company executive; b. Peoria, Ill., Aug. 24, 1923; s. John F. and Ann B. (Bertsch) C.; m. Peggy Furey, Sept. 9, 1944; children: Patrick Michael, Colleen Mary, Kevin Furey. BS, U. Minn., 1948. With Flexsteel Industries, Inc., Dubuque, Iowa, 1948—50, plant mgr., 1950-54, gen. mgr., v.p., 1955-70, exec. v.p., 1970-84, pres., 1985-89, vice-chmn., COO, 1989-90, chmn., CEO, 1990-99; ret., 1999. Bd. dirs. Dubuque Racing Assn.; trustee United Steel Workers Am. Pension Fund, 1960-99. Bd. regents Loras Coll., 1967-80, 81— ; bd. dirs. Xavier Hosp., 1969-78, Boys Club Am., 1981-99 . Served with USNR, 1942-43; with USMC, 1943-46, 51-52. Decorated D.F.C. (1), Air medal (4). Mem. Am. Furniture Assn. (bd. dirs. 1967-74). Republican. Roman Catholic. Home: 1195 Arrowhead Dr Dubuque IA 52003-8594 Office: Flexsteel Industries Inc Brunswick Indsl Block PO Box 847 Dubuque IA 52004-0847

CRAIB, KENNETH BRYDEN, resource development executive, physicist, economist; b. Milford, Mass., Oct. 13, 1938; s. William Pirie and Virginia Louise (Bryden) C.; m. Gloria Faye Lisano, June 25, 1960; children: Kenneth Bryden, Judith Diane, Lori Elaine, Melissa Suzanne. BS in Physics, U. Houston, 1967; MA in Econs., Calif. State U., 1982; postgrad., Harvard U., 1989. Aerospace technologist NASA, Houston, 1962-68; staff physicist Mark Sys., Inc., Cupertino, Calif., 1968-69; v.p. World Resources Corp., Cupertino, 1969-71; dir. resources devel. divsn. Aero Svc. Corp., Phila., 1971-72; dir. ops. Resources Devel. Assocs., Los Altos, Calif., 1972-80, pres., CEO Diamond Springs, Calif., 1980-85; owner Sand Ridge Arabians, 1980-98; chmn., dir. Resources Devel. Assocs., Inc., 1982-86, Devel. Support Internat. Inc., Placerville, Calif., 1981-86; pres., chn., dir. RDA Internat., Inc., 1985-96, 2000chmn., CEO, dir., 1995; mgr. acad. affairs U. Phoenix, Sacramento, 2001—02, chmn. Coll. Undergrad. Bus. and Mgmt. Ft. Lauderdale, Fla., 2002—, prof., 2002—. Bd. dirs. Transatlantic Fisheries, Inc.; adj. prof. Sacramento City Coll., 1996—2001; prof. U. Phoenix, Sacramento, 1997—2002. Contbr. articles to profl. jours. Served with USAF, 1957-61. Recipient Sustained Superior Performance award NASA, 1966; NASA grantee, 1968. Mem. Am. Soc. Photogrammetry, Soc. Internat. Devel., Agrl. Rsch. Inst., Calif. Select Com. Remote Sensing, Internat. Assn. Natural Resources Pilots, Remote Sensing Soc. (coun.), Am. Soc. Oceanography (charter), Aircraft Owners and Pilots Assn., Gulf and Cribbean Fisheries Inst., Placerville C. of C., Harvard Alumni Assn., Exptl. Aircraft Assn., Asian Fisheries Soc. Office: U Phoenix Ft Lauderdale Campus 600 N Pine Island Rd Ste 500 Fort Lauderdale FL 33324 Mailing: 900 SW 74 Terr Plantation FL 33317 *What you do is not as important as how you do it, and the people whose lives you touch in the process.*

CRAIG, ANNA MAYNARD, financial educator, consultant; b. Columbus, Ohio, Sept. 2, 1944; d. David Stuart and Ann (Armstrong) C.; m. John D. Hogan, Nov. 26, 1976. BA cum laude, Smith Coll., 1966; MA, U. Wis., 1970, PhD, 1972. Chartered fin. analyst; enrolled Treasury agt. Asst. prof. U. Ill., Chgo., 1971-75; vis. asst. prof. Ohio State U., Columbus, 1974-76; asst. prof. Cen. Mich. U., Mt. Pleasant, 1976-79; cons. Am. Productivity Ctr., Houston, 1979-81; adj. prof. Houston Bapt. U., 1980-86, Jones Grad. Sch. Adminstrn., Rice U., Houston, 1984; adj. prof. dept. fin. U. Ill., Champaign-Urbana, 1987-91; adj. faculty Goizueta Bus. Sch. Emory U., Atlanta, 1992—; faculty exec. and concentrated MBA program Ga. State U., 1992—93; faculty MBA program Poznan (Poland)/Ga. State U., 1997—; chief economist Encore Bank, Houston, 2001—. Bd. advisors Assn. for Internat. Exch. Students in Econs. and Commerce, U. Ill., 1987-91; advisor U. Ill. FMA Nat. Honor Soc., Fin. Club, enrolled treasury agt. IRS. Editor: (with John D. Hogan) Dimensions of Productivity Research, vol. 1, 1980, vol. II, 1981. Bd. dirs. Champaign-Urbana Symphony, 1987-91; trust mgmt. com. Univ. YWCA, Champaign, 1987-91. Ford fellow, U. Wis., 1970-72, NSF fellow, Stanford U., 1972; Fulbright scholar, 1966-67; named Outstanding Prof. Fin. U. Ill. Commerce Coun., 1987-88. Mem Am. Econ. Assn., Atlanta Soc. Fin. Analysts (trustee), Assn. for Investment Mgmt. and Rsch., Fin. Mgmt. Assn., Smith Coll. Alumnae Assn. (chmn. spl. gifts 1983-86, class fund agt.), Fulbright Alumni Assn., Phi Beta Kappa, Beta Gamma Sigma. Office: Emory Univ Goizueta Business School Atlanta GA 30322-0001

CRAIG, BRADFORD, retired secondary school educator; b. Highland Park, Ill., Nov. 12, 1926; s. Arthur Bane and Anna Elizabeth (Anderson) Craig; m. Mary Louise Slaughter, Dec. 24, 1950; children: Stephen Scott, Susan Elaine, Alan Bradford. BS, Bradley U., 1951, MA, 1960; postgrad., Ill. State U. Cert. secondary edn. tchr. Ill. Tchr. Bartonville (Ill.) Grade Sch., 1951—52, Peoria (Ill.) Pub. Schs., 1952—85; ret. Treas. Peoria Edn. Assn., 1956. Author, editor: A Poor Man's Journey, 1996. Election judge Peoria Election Commn., 1986—2001; sec., treas., pres. Homeowners Assn., North Peoria, 1989—2002; mem. steering com. Sr. Net, Peoria, 1989—2002; adult reading literacy tchr., 1987—89; deacon Presbyn. Ch., 1998—2000, 2002—; bd. dirs. Peoria Area Friends of Internat. Students, Bradley U., 1983—86. Sgt. USAF, 1944—47. Mem.: Local, State, Nat. Ret. Tchrs. Assn (mem. various offices 2002), Peoria County Geneal. Soc., VFW. Avocations: genealogy, elder hostel travel, reading and studying WWII, amateur (ham) radio, trained and showed Kerry Blue terriers.

CRAIG, CAROL MILLS, marriage, family and child counselor; b. Berkeley, Calif. BA in Psychology (hon.), U. Calif., Santa Cruz, 1974; MA in Counseling Psychology, John F. Kennedy U., 1980; doctoral student, Calif. Sch. Profl. Psychology, Berkeley, 1980-87, Columbia Pacific U., San Rafael, Calif., 1987—. Psychology intern Fed. Correction Inst., Pleasanton, Calif., 1979-81, Letterman Army Med. Ctr., San Francisco, 1980-82, VA Mental Hygiene Clinic, Oakland, Calif., 1981-82; instr. Martinez Adult Sch., 1983, Piedmont Adult Edn., Oakland, 1986; biofeedback and stress mgmt. cons. Oakland, 1986—; child counselor Buddies-A Nonprofit, Counseling Svc. for Persons in the Arts, Lafayette, Calif., 1993—; founder Chesley Sch., 1994, Healing with Music for People and All Animals, 1996, Music Therapy for animals, 1998—. Rsch. asst. Irvington Pubs., N.Y.C., 1979, Little, Brown and Co., Boston, 1983; music therapist for people and animals, 1998—. Mem. Calif. Scholarship Fedn. (life). Avocations: music-guitar, violin, folk and opera singing, song writing, art.

CRAIG, CHARLES SAMUEL, marketing educator; b. Atlantic City, May 6, 1943; s. Charles Hays and Catherine Sara (McMullen) C.; m. Elizabeth Anne Coyne, Aug. 10, 1985; children: Mary Catherine, Caroline Elizabeth. BA, Westminster Coll., 1965; MS, U. R.I., 1967; PhD, Ohio State U., 1971. Mktg. rep. IBM, Providence, 1966—68; asst. dir. Mechanized Info. Ctr., Columbus, 1971—73; asst. prof. lib. adminstrn. Ohio State U., Columbus, 1971—73, asst. prof. mktg., 1972—74; asst. prof. mktg. Grad. Sch. Bus. and Pub. Adminstrn. Cornell U., Ithaca, NY, 1974—77, assoc. prof., 1977—79; from assoc. prof. mktg. Stern Sch. of Bus. to prof. NYU, 1979—, dir. entertainment, media and tech. program, 1999—, Catherine and Peter Kellner prof., 2001—. Bd. dirs. P&R Pub. Co., Phillipsburg, NJ; mem. exec. bd. Jour. Retailing, 1985—. Co-author: Consumer Behavior: An Information Processing Perspective, 1982; International Marketing Research, 1983, 2d edit., 2000, Global Marketing Strategy, 1995; co-editor: Personal Selling: Theory, Research and Practice, 1984, The Development of Media Models in Advertising, Repetition Effects over the Years, The Relationship of Advertising Expenditures to Sales, 1986; mem. editl. bd. Jour. Mktg. Rsch., 1978-85, Jour. Retailing, 1980-85, Jour. Advt. Rsch., 1994—, Internat. Jour. of Advt., 1997—; contbr. articles to profl. jours. NDEA fellow, 1969-71. Mem. Am. Mktg. Assn., Assn. Consumer Rsch., Acad. Internat. Bus., Phi Kappa Phi, Omicron Delta Epsilon, Psi Chi. Presbyterian. Home: 100 Bleecker St Apt 28D New York NY 10012-2207 Office: NYU 44 W 4th St New York NY 10012-1106

CRAIG, CYNTHIA MAE, mathematics educator; b. Brownsville, Tex., Jan. 22, 1951; d. Richard Virgil and Mae Margaret (Phillips) Cole; m. Daniel Baxter Craig, Jan. 15, 1971; children: Tammy Michelle Craig Black, Heather Elizabeth Craig Rios. BA, Augusta (Ga.) Coll., 1985, MEd, 1989, specialist in edn., 1993. Cert. devel. specialist; cert. tchr., Ga. Tchr. 5th-6th grade tchr. Blessed Sacrament Sch., El Paso, Tex., 1981-82; tchr. 4-8th grade honors math. St. Mary on the hill Cath. Sch., Augusta, Ga., 1985-87; tchr. Aquinas H.S., Augusta, 1987-88; asst. prof. of math. in learning support Augusta State U., 1989—, assoc. chair dept. learning support, 1998—. Presenter at profl. confs. in field. Contbr. articles to profl. jours. Mem. ASCD, Ga. Assn. of Devel. Educators, Nat. Assn. for Devel. Edn., Phi Delta Kappa (newsletter editor 1990-93, v.p. membership 1993-94, newsletter editor 1989-92, 94-96, 97-98, found. rep. 1996-97, newsletter editor 1997-98, rsch. rep. 1998—). Avocations: reading, educational research, travel. Office: Augusta State U Learning Support 2500 Walton Way Augusta GA 30904-4562 E-mail: ccraig@aug.edu.

CRAIG, DAVID CLARKE, financial advisor; b. Ft. Smith, Ark., Oct. 23, 1955; s. Earl Lewis Craig and Shirley Ann (Clarke) Shepherd; m. Dana Jane Thompson, Dec. 19, 1980; children: Lauren Elizabeth, Erin Jane. BBA, U. Ark., 1978, MBA, 1979; postgrad., U. Tex., 1983-88, U. Ark., 1988—. Registered fin. advisor. Mktg. officer Merchants Nat. Bank, Ft. Smith, 1979-81; instr. fin. and econs. Westark C.C. (now U. Ark. at Ft. Smith), 1981-2000, faculty chairperson, 1987-88; asst. to pres. Richland Coll., Dallas, 1985; fin. advisor Paul Manners & Assocs., Ft. Smith, Ark., 1991—. Adj. instr. John Brown U., 1995—; bd. dirs., sec. Ark. Student Loan Authority, 1989-98, chmn. 1998—. Pres. Am. Cancer Soc. Ft. Smith, 1988-89, co-residential chmn. 1985-87, v.p. local bd. 1987-89, active Pub. Awareness Com. Ft. Smith, 1985-91; pres. Interfaith Comty. Ctr., Ft. Smith, 1982-84; vol. Ft. Smith Art Ctr. Auction, 1987, treas. 1995—; sponsor Harding U. Invitational Bus. Games, 1986-91; bd. dirs. Old Fort Mus., 1989-91; mem. class of 1990 Leadership Ft. Smith, elder, clk. of session 1st Presbyn. Ch., 1991-94; bd. ch. visitors U. Ozarks, Clarksville, Ark., 1996, 98; bd. dirs. Hobson Presch. and Kindergarten, 1993-95, Ft. Smith Pub. Libr. Endowment Fund; treas. Sebastian County Humane Soc., 2001-02; v.p. Ft. Smith Area Cmty. Found., 2002— (chmn. 2003-). Recipient Whirlpool Master Tchr. Awd., Westark Coll., 1999. Mem. Nat. Bus. Edn. Assn., Ark. Tchrs. of Bus. and Econs., Am. Inst. Banking (v.p. Ft. Smith chpt. 1981), Ark. Two Yr. Coll. Assn., East Side Baptist Ch., 1999—, Ft. Smith C. of C. (ednl. com. 1987—), Blue Key, Kappa Delta Pi, Alpha Kappa Psi (sec. 1977-78), Phi Delta Kappa (Kappan of Month 1985), Phi Beta Lambda (co-advisor univ. ctr. 1986-95). Office: Paul Manners & Assocs Inc 318 No Greenwood Ave Fort Smith AR 72904-7362

CRAIG, DAVID JEOFFREY, retired manufacturing company executive; b. Wyandotte, Mich., Sept. 29, 1925; s. Geoffrey F. and Catherine R. Craig; m. Shirley M. Lemhagen, Mar. 3, 1945; children: Susan Craig Noyes, Janice Craig Maggi, Sandra, Jeffrey Allan. BS in Physics, U. Detroit, 1950, MS summa cum laude, 1951; postgrad., U. Mich., 1952-53. With The BOC Group, Murray Hill, N.J., 1956-90; dir. corp. planning and devel., 1970-71; group v.p., 1971-79; dep. group mng. dir. BOC Group plc, Surrey, Eng., 1979-83; mng. dir. engring. and tech., 1983-90; dir. The BOC Group, Inc., BOC Group plc. Mem. Ticonderoga Country Club, Hobe Sound Golf Club. Home: 11430 SE Plandome Dr Hobe Sound FL 33455-7901

CRAIG, DAVID W. judge, author; b. Pitts., Feb. 17, 1925; s. David and Ella (Williamson) C.; m. Ella Van Kirk, July 15, 1945; children: Linda Marie Craig Mooser, Muriel Jean Craig Lagnese. AB, U. Pitts., 1948, JD, 1950. Bar: Pa. 1950. Rsch. asst. U. Pitts. Law Sch., 1950-51; ptnr. Moorhead & Knox, Pitts., 1952-61; city solicitor City of Pitts., 1961-65, dir. pub. safety, 1965-69; ptnr. Baskin, Sachs & Craig, 1962-78; judge Commonwealth Ct. Pa., 1978-90, pres., judge, 1990-94. Adj. prof. Carnegie-Mellon U., 1970-94; adj. asst. prof. U. Pitts., 1965-69; vis. lectr. Yale U., 1961-64. Author: Pennsylvania Building and Zoning Laws, 1951. Chmn. City Planning Commn., Pitts., 1960-61; mem. Home Rule Commn., Pitts., 1976. 1st lt. USAAF, 1943-45, ETO. Decorated D.F.C. Mem.: Inst. Jud. Adminstrn. (seminar faculty 1986—91), Am. Planning Assn. (pres. 1963—64), Pa. Bar Inst. (pres. 1987—88). Avocations: sailing, running. Office: Ste 905 1812 Foxcroft Allison Park PA 15101-3261

CRAIG, EDWARD VINCENT, orthopaedic surgeon, educator; b. Bklyn., May 5, 1947; s. Edward Vincent and Lorraine (Youngkin) C.; m. Kathryn Ann Davis, July 4, 1982. BA, Princeton U., 1969; MD, Columbia U., 1973. Diplomate Am. Bd. Orthopaedic Surgery. Intern Columbia-Presbyn. Med. Ctr.,

N.Y.C., 1973-74, resident in internal medicine, 1975-76, resident in orthopaedic surgery, 1977-80, fellow in shoulder surgery, 1980-81, fellow in hand surgery, 1981-82; attending surgeon U. Minn. Hosp., Mpls., 1982-94, Hosp. Spl. Surgery, N.Y.C., 1994—, New York Hosp., N.Y.C., 1994—; prof. clin. surgery Cornell Med. Coll., N.Y.C., 1994—. Cons., designer Biomet Atlas Total Shoulder Replacement Sys., Warsaw, Ind., 1985—; cons. Minn. Twins Baseball Club, 1993-94. Author: The Shoulder, 1995, Clinical Orthopaedics, 1999, The Unstable Shoulder, 1999; contbr. articles to profl. jours. Bd. dirs. Waveny Day Care Ctr., New Canaan, Conn., 1996, New Canaan Country Sch., 2002, Juvenile Diabetes Found. Fairfield County, New Canaan Basketball Assn. Fellow Am. Acad. Orthopaedic Surgeons; mem. AMA, Am. Shoulder and Elbow Surgeons (pres. 1985—), Am. Orthopaedic Soc. for Sports Medicine (rsch. grantee 1995), Am. Soc. Surgery of the Hand, Am. Orthopaedic Assn. (ABC Traveling fellow 1980). Republican. Roman Catholic. Avocations: piano, skiing, golf, tennis, running. Office: Hosp Spl Surgery 535 E 70th St New York NY 10021-4872 also: 143 Sound Beach Ave Old Greenwich CT 06870 E-mail: craige@hss.edu.

CRAIG, ELIZABETH COYNE, marketing executive; b. N.Y.C., Jan. 7, 1956; d. John Thomas and Mary Ellen (O'Sullivan) Coyne; m. Charles Samuel Craig, Aug. 10, 1985; children: Mary Catherine, Caroline Elizabeth. BS in Occupl. Therapy, NYU, 1980, MBA, 1986. Occupl. therapist Jacobi Hosp., N.Y., 1980-81, St. Vincent's Hosp., N.Y., 1981-85; mktg. intern worldwide consumer banking Citibank U.S. and Europe Consumer Bank, Citicorp Ins., N.Y.C., 1985-86, mgmt. assoc., 1986-87, asst. mgr., 1987-88, mktg. mgr. new product devel., 1988-90, asst. v.p. life acquisitions and relationship mktg., 1990-93, v.p. life and health acquisitions and relationship mktg., 1993-94, v.p. 3d party direct response, retail ins. sales pilots, 1994-96, v.p. annuity product mgmt., 1996-99; sr. v.p. e-commerce investment and ins., product mgr. Citi fi Interactive Fin. Network, Long Island City, N.Y., 1998-99; v.p., internet customer relationship mgr. Citibank Online, Long Island City, 1999—2001; v.p. protection products Citi Credit Cards, 2001—. Bd. dirs. First Citicorp Life Ins. Co. Mem. Am. Occupl. Therapy Assn., Fin. Women's Assn., Direct Mktg. Assn. Avocations: antiques, bicycling. Office: Citibank One Court Sq Long Island City NY 11120 E-mail: elizabeth.craig@citigroup.com.

CRAIG, FIONA ELIZABETH, pathologist; b. Farnborough, Hants., May 30, 1961; arrived in U.S., 1986; d. Stanley and Ann Marshal Craig; m. Stephen Allen Harvey; children: Adam Harvey, Emma Harvey. BSc, St. Bartholomew's U., London, 1985; M.B.B.S., St. Bartholomew's U., 1985. Staff pathologist U. Tex. Health Sci. Ctr., San Antonio, 1992—2001; hematopathologist U. Pitts. Med. Ctr./Presbyn. Hosp., 2001—. Office: UPMC-Presbyterian Hosp Rm C604 200 Lothrop St Pittsburgh PA 15213

CRAIG, GEORGE DENNIS, economics educator, consultant; b. Sept. 14, 1936; s. George S. and Alice H. (Childs) C.; m. Lelah Price, Aug. 21, 1984; children: R. Price Coyle, R. Nolan Coyle, Deborah L. Craig, W. Sean Coyle. BA, Wheaton Coll., 1960; MS, U. Ill., 1962, PhD, 1968. Asst. prof. econs. La. State U., Baton Rouge, 1965-69; assoc. prof. sch. bus. No. Ill. U., DeKalb, 1969-82; prof. econs., chmn. Oklahoma City U., 1982—. Cons. AT&T, Oklahoma City, 1984—. Contbr. articles to profl. jours. Mem. Am. Econs. Assn., So. Econs. Assn., Nat. Assn. Bus. Economists, Internat. Inst. Forecasting. Avocations: duplicate bridge, tennis. Home: 6915 Avondale Ct Oklahoma City OK 73116-5008 Office: 6421 Avondale Dr Ste 208 Oklahoma City OK 73116-6429 E-mail: craigg784@aol.com.

CRAIG, GORDON ALEXANDER, historian, educator; b. Glasgow, Scotland, Nov. 26, 1913; came to U.S., 1925; s. Frank Mansfield and Jane (Bissell) C.; m. Phyllis Halcomb, June 16, 1939; children: Susan, Deborah Gordon, Martha Jane, Charles Grant. BA, Princeton U., 1936, MA, 1939, PhD, 1941, DLitt (hon.), 1970; BLitt (Rhodes Scholar), Oxford U., Eng., 1938; DPhil (hon.), Free U. Berlin, 1983; HHD (hon.), Ball State U., 1984; DHL (hon.), Wake Forest U., 1988. Instr. history Yale U., New Haven, 1939-41; from instr. to prof. history Princeton U., N.J., 1941-61; prof. history Stanford U., Calif., 1961—, J.E. Wallace Sterling prof. humanities, 1969-79, J.E. Wallace Sterling prof. humanities emeritus, 1979—; prof. history Free U. Berlin, 1962—. Author: The Politics of the Prussian Army, 1640-1945, 1955, From Bismarck to Adenauer: Aspects of German Statecraft, 1958, Europe Since 1815, 1961, Europe Since 1815, 6th edit., 1983, The Battle of Königgrätz, 1964, War, Politics and Diplomacy: Selected Essays, 1966, Treitschke's History of Modern Germany, 1975, Economic Interest, Militarism and Foreign Policy: Essays of Eckart Kehr, 1977, Germany, 1866-1945, 1978, The Germans, 1982, Force and Statecraft: Diplomatic Problems of Our Times, 1983, The End of Prussia, 1984, Geld und Geist: Zürich im Zeitalter des Liberalismus, 1830-1896, 1988, The Triumph of Liberalism: Zürich in the Golden Age 1830-1869, 1989, Die Politik der Unpolitischen: Deutsche Schriftsteller und die Macht, 1770-1870, 1993, The Politics of the Unpolitical: German Writers and the Problem of Power, 1770-1871, 1995, Ueber Fontane, 1997, Theodor Fontane, Literature and History in the Bismarck Reich, 1999, Politics and Culture in Modern Germany: Essays From The New York Review of Books, 1999; assoc. editor, contbr.: Makers of Modern Strategy, 1943, Makers of Modern Strategy from Machiavelli to the Nuclear Age, 1986; joint editor, contbr.: The Diplomats, 1919-1939, 1953, The Diplomats, 1939-79, 1994; contbr. Geneva, Zurich, Basel: History, Culture and National Identity, 1994. Hon. mem. Berlin Hist. Commn., 1975—; polit. analyst Office Strategic Svcs., Dept. State, Washington, 1941-43; pub. mem. Fgn. Svc. Selection Bd., 1948-49; cons. U.S. Arms Control and Disarmament Agy., 1964-68; adv. coun. USAF Acad., 1968-73; adv. bd. USMC Hist. Sect., Washington, 1972-74. Capt. USMC, 1944-46. Named Hon. fellow, Balliol Coll., Oxford U., 1989; recipient Historikerpreis, Stadt Münster, Fed. Republic Germany, 1982, comdr.'s cross Legion of Merit, Fed. Republic Germany, 1984, Goethe medal, Goethe Inst., Fed. Republic Germany, 1987, Polit. Book prize, Ebert Stiftung, 1988, Max Geilinger prize, Max Geilinger Found., Zurich, 1991, Benjamin Franklin/Wilhelm von Humboldt prize, German-Am. Acad. Coun., 1999; fellow Guggenheim Found., 1969—70, 1982—83. Fellow Ctr. for Advanced Study in the Behavioral Scis., Bayerische Acad. Schönen Künste, Brit. Acad.; mem. Am. Acad. Arts and Scis., Am. Philos. Soc., Am. Hist. Assn. (pres. 1983), Internat. Com. Hist. Scis. (1st v.p. 1975-85), Coun. of Scholars of Libr. of Congress, Order pour le Merite fur Wissenschaften und Kunste (Germany), Phi Beta Kappa. Democrat. Presbyterian. Home: 451 Oak Grove Ave Apt B-2 Menlo Park CA 94025-3269 E-mail: professorgacraig@earthlink.net.

CRAIG, GREGORY BESTOR, lawyer, government official; b. Norfolk, Va., Mar. 4, 1945; s. William Gregory and Lois (Bestor) C.; m. Margaret Davenport Noyes, July 27, 1974; children: William Eliot, Eliza Noyes, Margaret Bestor, Mary Duncan, James Gregory. AB magna cum laude, Harvard Coll., 1967; diploma in historical studies, Cambridge U., 1968; JD, Yale U., 1972. Bar: D.C. 1972, U.S. Ct. Appeals (D.C., 2d, 3d, 4th, 6th, 7th and 11th cirs.), U.S. Supreme Ct. Assoc. Williams Connolly & Califano, Washington, 1972-74; asst. fed. pub. defender U.S. Dist. Ct. Conn., 1974-76; assoc. Williams & Connolly, Washington, 1977-78, ptnr., 1979-84; sr. advisor on fgn. policy and def. Sen. Edward M. Kennedy, Washington, 1984-88; ptnr. Williams & Connolly, Washington, 1989-97; dir. Office of Policy and Planning Dept. of State, 1997—98, asst. to pres. and spl. counsel, 1998—99; ptnr. Williams & Connolly, Washington, 1999—. Tchr. trial practice Yale Law Sch., 1975-76, Harvard Inst. Trial Advocacy, 1980-84; chmn. Internat. Human Rights Law Group, 1989-96. Trustee Overseas Devel. Coun., 1993-96; vice chmn. Carnegie Endowment for Internat. Peace, 1990-97, 99—, Robert F. Kennedy Meml., 1989-97, 99—, Fgn. Student Svc. Coun., 1990-96, Mexican-Am. Legal Def. and Edn. Fund, 1995-97. John Harvard scholar, 1967. Mem. ABA, Phi Beta Kappa. Avocations: mountain climbing, hiking. Office: Williams & Connolly 725 12th St NW Washington DC 20005-5901

CRAIG, HAROLD KENT, mechanical contracting executive, systems analyst; b. Columbus, Ohio, Nov. 21, 1956; s. Harold Harding and Mildred Annie (King) C.; m. Cathy M. Preslar, Nov. 19, 1979 (div. Sept. 2000); 1 child, Brian Scagel; m. Liann Craig Tabor, Oct. 24, 2000. Student, Goddard Coll., 1979. Lic. plumbing, boiler making, air conditioning, forced warm air heating; spl. elec. lic.; cert. exam proctor. V.p., project mgr. Craig Plumbing Co., Inc., Raleigh, N.C., 1972-95; v.p., project mgmt., sys. analyst Confluence Tech., Raleigh, NC, 1976—; sr. systems analyst Datasonix Inc., Smithfield, NC, 1980—83; heating, ventilation, air cond., plumbing and mech. cons. Valley Constrn. Co., Inc., Koslusco, Miss., 1985-86; sr. project mgr. and estimator Sneeden Mechanical Contractors, Inc., Wilmington, N.C., 1986-88; U.S. bus. agent The Circle Group, Arusha, Tanzania, 1974—; sr. estimator Bay Mech. Inc., Raleigh, N.C., 1996-97; sr. project mgr., estimator Atlantic Coast Mech., Inc., Raleigh, 1997-98; sr. estimator, project mgr. Superior Plumbing & Mech., Inc., Wilson, NC, 1998—. Sys. cons. Consulting, Tech., and Design, Inc., Research Triangle Park, N.C., 1988-94. Author: Yes, the Sun Will Rise, 1979; editor (periodical) Joe's Bozart mag., 1978; assoc. editor: (periodical) In the Steps, 1976-81; contbr. articles to profl. jours.; contbg. editor, Contractor mag., 1998—. Mem. bd. adjustments Town of Cary (N.C.), 1981; mem. bd. Raleigh Artists' Cmty., 1974-79. Mem.: Am. Humanists Assn. (Humanists N.C. chpt. bd. dirs. 1974—81, editor The Tarheel Humanist newsletter 1975—78, named Humanist Adv. 1979). Home: 6725 Hillsboro St Raleigh NC 27606-116 Mailing: PO Box 4153 Cary NC 27519-4153 E-mail: hkcraig@yahoo.com.

CRAIG, HERBERT EUGENE, language educator; b. Chardon, Ohio, Dec. 13, 1946; s. Herbert Eugene Craig II and Lois McMillen Craig; m. Barbara Emrys, Sept. 16, 1995. BA in Spanish, Ohio State U., 1969; MA in Spanish, U. Wis., 1972, PhD in Spanish, 1983; MA in French, U. Ill., 1985. Asst. prof. Spanish and French Bethany Coll., Lindsborg, Kans., 1979—89; asst. to assoc. prof. Spanish U. Nebr. at Kearney (formerly Kearney State Coll.), 1989—. Corr. Ctr. Proustian Rsch., the Sorbonne, Paris, 1996—. Editor: Concordance, by Javier Nunez Caceres, 1994, Emblems, by Javier Nunez Caceres, 1999; author: Marcel Proust and Spanish America, 2002. Mem.: Phi Beta Kappa. United Methodist.

CRAIG, HURSHEL EUGENE, agronomist; b. Chrisman, Ill., May 18, 1932; s. Thomas Hurshel and Letha Mac (Short) C.; m. Zada Pauline Honnold, Dec. 29, 1954; children: Toni Jane, Tina Jean. Student, Ea. Ill. U., 1951, Ill. State U., 1956; BS, U. Ill., 1958, MS, 1970, postgrad., 1974. Mgr. Lime Svc. Co., Chrisman, Ill., 1959-61; br. mgr. Remole Soil Svc., Inc., Potomac, Ill., 1961-64, home office mgr., 1966-67; ptnr., agronomist Harris Fertilizer, Inc., Farmer City, Ill., 1967-69; farm cons. Gifford (Ill.) State Bank, 1964-66; instr. agr. Danville (Ill.) Area Community Coll., 1970-80; agronomy cons. and ptnr. C & S Pro-Farm Svcs., Ridge Farm, Ill., 1977-80; agronomy cons. Ag-Vantage, Westerville, Ohio, 1980-85; soils analysis sales CLC Labs Ind., West Lafayette, 1985-90, agronomy cons., 1987—2003; soil and plant tissue analysis sales Cal-Mar Soil Testing Lab., West Lafayette, 1990—. Co-author: Career Awareness Test for Agriculture Students and Prospective Spouses, 1974. Chmn. adminstrv. coun. Bismarck (Ill.) United Meth. Ch., 1989-91, chmn., 2000—. With U.S. Army, 1952-54. Mem. Ill. Fertilizer and Chem. Assn., Profl. Crop Cons. Ill. (pres. 1992). Methodist. Avocations: reading, gardening. Home and Office: 16916 E 2690 North Rd Danville IL 61834-6067 E-mail: genecrag@cooketec.net.

CRAIG, JAMES HICKLIN, fine arts consultant; b. Chester, S.C., July 23, 1937; s. John Edward and Una Bee (Martin) C. Student, U. S.C., 1955-56, Cin. Coll. Conservatory Music, 1956-59, Juilliard Sch. Music, 1960, Paris, 1960. Curator decorative arts N.C. Dept. Archives & History, Raleigh, 1962-64; grantee writing book on N.C. decorative arts Mus. So. Decorative Arts, 1964-65; prin. James Craig Fine & Decorative Arts, 1965-69; pres. Craig & Tarlton, Inc., Raleigh, 1969-85; fine arts cons. Independence, Va., 1985—. Bd. dirs. Raleigh Chamber Music Soc., N.Y.C. Chamber Opera Theater, Mint Mus. of Art, Charlotte, trustee 2000—; cons. to N.C. Gov.'s Mansion bd.; mem. acquisitions com. Author: The Arts and Crafts in North Carolina 1699-1840, 1965 (listed by Montgomery as part of 100 best in field). Avocations: collecting Am. art and antiques, violins and related material, gardening. Office: James Craig Fine Arts PO Box 397 Independence VA 24348-0397

CRAIG, JAMES LYNN, physician; b. Columbia, Tenn., Aug. 7, 1933; s. Clifford Paul and Maple (Harris) C.; m. Suzanne Anderson, July 20, 1957; children: James Lynn, Margaret; m. Roberta Anne, May 17, 1980. Ed., Mid. Tenn. State U., 1953; MD, U. Tenn., 1956; MPH, U. Pitts., 1963. Diplomate Am. Bd. Preventive Medicine, Am. Bd. Family Practice. Intern U. Tenn. Meml. Hosp., Knoxville, 1957; resident in occupl. medicine U. Pitts., 1962-64, TVA, Chattanooga, 1964-65, physician, 1966-69, chief med. officer, 1969-74; corp. med. dir. Gen. Mills Corp., Mpls., 1974-76, v.p. corp. med. dir., 1976-80, v.p., dir. health and human svcs., 1980-98; adj. clin. prof. U. Minn., Mpls., 1979—, chmn. cmty. adv. com. Ctr. for Environ. and Health Policy, 1994-97, mem. adv. coun. health in scis., 1992-95, chmn. adv. bd. Ctr. for Environ. and Health Policy, 1994-97; pres. Family and Preventive Health Svcs., Inc., Mpls., 1998. Clin. instr. U. Tenn., Memphis, 1970-74, Meharry Med. Sch., Nashville, 1972-74; mem. adv. bd. to dir. Ctr. Disease Control and Prevention, 1996-99; nat. adv. bd. Internat. Health and Media Awards, 1996—. Contbr. articles to profl. jours. Bd. dirs. Mpls. Blood Bank, 1976-88, Minn. Bible Coll., Rochester, 1978-83, Minn. Safety Coun., 1981-90, Minn. Heart Assn., Mpls., 1976-87, Children's Heart Fund, 1976-88, Meth. Hosp. Found., 1979-87, Park Nicolett Med. Found., 1987-93, Altcare, 1983-95, Meth. Hosp. Health Assn., 1987-93, Minn. Wellness Coun., 1986-91, Health Sys. Minn. Assocs., 1993-94; bd. dirs. Health Systems Minn. Inst. for Rsch. and Edn., 1996-2000, chmn., 1997-2000, chmn. Park Nicollet Inst., 2000-01; trustee Minn. Med. Found., 2001—. Named Legacy Laureate, U. Pitts., 2000; recipient Cmty. Svc. award, Park Nicollet Med. Ctr., 1995, Knudsen award in occupl. medicine, Am. Coll. Occupl. and Environ. Medicine, 2000. Fellow: Am. Acad. Family Practice, Am. Acad. Occupl. Medicine (treas. 1982—83, sec. 1983—84, v.p. 1984—85, pres. 1986—87), Am. Occupl. Medicine Assn. (bd. dirs. 1974—78); mem.: AMA (alt. del. Ho. Dels. 1990—92, del. 1992—96, Recognition award 1975, 1978, 1981, 1985, 1989, 1993, 1996, 1999, 2002), Minn. Med. Found. (bd. dirs. 2001—), Emergency Physicians Assn. (bd. dirs. 1984—92), Mpls. Acad. Medicine (sec. 1983—85, pres. 1985—86), Minn. Acad. Medicine, North Ctrl. Occupl. Medicine Assn. (pres. 1977), Occupl. Health Inst. (chmn. 1983—84). Home: 10008 S Shore Dr Minneapolis MN 55441-5011 Office: PO Box 270330 Minneapolis MN 55427-6330 E-mail: jimlcraig@aol.com. *The activities of my life are based on a balance between quality and acceptance.*

CRAIG, JAMES WILLIAM, physician, educator, university dean; b. West Liberty, Ohio, Jan. 23, 1921; s. J. Frank and Clara Helen (Scarborough) C.; m. Helen Catherine Lang, Sept. 18, 1948 (dec.); children: Maribeth, Jon, William, Barbara; m. Wendy Burnip Johnson, June 23, 1972; stepchildren: Steven, Barbara, Philip, Laura Johnson. BS, Western Res. U., 1943, MD, 1945. Intern, asst. resident in medicine Presbyn. Hosp., N.Y.C., 1945-46, 48-50; fellow in medicine Western Res. U. Sch. Medicine, Cleve., 1950-52, from instr. to assoc. prof. medicine, 1952-72; assoc. dean Sch. Medicine U. Va., Charlottesville, 1972-89, prof. medicine, 1972-90, prof. emeritus, 1991—. Condr. research; contbr. articles on diabetes mellitus and intermediary metabolism to publs. Served with AUS, 1946-48. Recipient Lederle med. faculty award, 1962-64 Mem. Am. Inst. Nutrition, Ctrl. Soc. for Clin. Rsch., Med. Soc. Va., Phi Beta Kappa, Sigma Xi, Alpha Omega Alpha. Home: 101 Indian Spring Rd Charlottesville VA 22901-1019 E-mail: jwc9e@virginia.edu.

CRAIG, JOHN BRUCE, ambassador; BS, American U. With Sr. Fgn. Svc., dep. chief of mission, with Bur. Near Eastern Affairs, dir. jr. officer divsn. Bur. of Pers., dir. Office of Arabian Peninsula Affairs, amb. Sultanate of Oman, 1998—. Office: US Embassy PO Box 202 Code #115 Medinat Qaboos Oman

CRAIG, JOHN TUCKER, economist, consultant; b. Bklyn., June 17, 1926; s. Clarence Tucker and Rena (Stebbins) C.; m. Ruth Doris Weiler, Aug. 5, 1950; children: Daniel, Thomas, Andrew, Paul. BA, Oberlin Coll., 1948; MPA, Princeton U., 1950; postgrad., Tufts U., 1966-67. With AID, 1950-80, program officer, 1967-68, Kathmandu, Nepal, 1968-71, internat. rels. officer Latin Am. Bur. Washington, 1971-74, program officer Port-au-Prince, Haiti, 1974-78, asst. dir. Georgetown, Guyana, 1978-80; cons. Silver Spring, Md., 1980-83; economist for agr. survey U. Md./Rwanda Agrl. Ministry, Kigali, Rwanda, 1983-86; chief party Assocs. in Rural Devel., Proje Sove Te, Burlington, Vt. and Camp Perrin, Haiti, 1988-90; cons. Washington, 1986-88. Part-time employee Freedom of Info., State Dept., 1990—. Editor: Haiti: Development Assistance Program, 1976, Guyana: Country Development Strategy Statement, 1980. With USN, 1944-46. Recipient Superior Honor award AID, 1980. Mem.: Am. Econ. Assn. Methodist. Avocations: hiking, swimming. Home and Office: Apt 120 4200 Massachusetts Ave NW Washington DC 20016-4753

CRAIG, JOYCE KRUTICK, judge; b. Bklyn., Mar. 26, 1946; d. Sidney and Esther (Stone) Krutick; 1 child, Ian Lewis; married, July 4, 1999. BA, L.I. U., 1966; JD, Bklyn. Law Sch., 1969; LLM, Seton Hall U. Schl of Law, 2001. Bar: N.Y 1969, Fla. 1975, N.J. 1976. Assoc. Sabbatino & Todarelli, N.Y.C., 1969-70; assoc. atty. div. criminal def. Legal Aid Soc., N.Y.C., 1970-73; pvt. practice N.Y.C., 1973-81; U.S. judge adminstv. law SSA, Newark, N.J., 1981-2001; chief judge Hartford Office of Hearings and Appeals, 2001—02. Faculty SSA/OHA Jud. Coll. Alt. del. to jud. conf. state of N.Y., 1970-71. Recipient Hantman award N.Y. Soc. Sec. Bar Assn. Mem. ABA, Assn. Adminstrv. Law Judges (bd. dirs. 1986-90), Fla. Bar Assn., Iota Alpha Pi. Office: SSA-OHA 135 High St Rm 331 Hartford CT 06103-1100

CRAIG, KARA LYNN, children's home administrator; b. Portland, Oreg., Nov. 29, 1962; d. Raymond L. and Donna J. (Telford) Spencer. BA in Communication, Boise State U., 1985; MA in Psychology, Pepperdine U., 1990. Office mgr. Ustick Chiropractic Clinic, Boise, Idaho, 1983-85; comm. asst. First Interstate Bank Idaho, Boise, 1985-87; dir. Golden Gate U., Irvine, Calif., 1988-91, adj. prof., 1990-91; case mgr. Big Bros./Big Sisters of S.W. Idaho, Boise, 1992-94; CEO Children's Home Soc. of Idaho, Boise, 1994—. Adj. prof. Boise State U., 1992—2000. Pub. rels. com. Sounds of Music (cmty. choir), Boise, 1987—88; mem. Leadership Boise, 1996—97, S.W. Idaho Planned Giving Coun. Mem.: MENSA, Downtown Boise Rotary Club (named Rotarian of Yr. 2003, Rotarian of the Yr. 2003), Psi Chi. Avocations: playing piano and flute, ballroom dancing. Home: 12345 W Mercedes St Boise ID 83713-0501 Office: Children's Home Soc Idaho 740 Warm Springs Ave Boise ID 83712-6420 E-mail: kcraig@childrenshomesociety.com.

CRAIG, KAREN LYNN, accountant, controller; b. Detroit, Mar. 17, 1959; d. John and Corinne (Legel) C.; m. Robert A. Steshetz, May 3, 1986; children: Kamden, Kara. AS in Commerce, Henry Ford C.C., 1980; BS in Bus. and Acctg., Wayne State U., 1982. CPA, Mich., Calif. Cost and staff acct. Wilson Dairy Co., Detroit, 1982-83; sr. acct. Coopers & Lybrand, Detroit, 1984-86, supr. acct. Newport Beach, Calif., 1987-89; corp. contr. J.F. Shea Co., Inc., Walnut, Calif., 1989-99, AccentCare, 1999—. Mem. Mich. Assn. CPAs, Calif. Soc. CPAs. Avocations: music, hockey, photography, baseball. Office: 135 Technology Ste 150 Irvine CA 92618 E-mail: kcraig@accentcare.com.

CRAIG, KERN WILLIAM, political science educator; b. Grand Island, Nebr., Jan. 19, 1946; s. Arthur E. and Marian E. Craig; m. Stacy J. Hazle, June 27, 1981; 1 child, Daniel A. BSc, Calif. State U.; MBA, Fairleigh Dickinson U.; PhD, U. Miss. Lic. contractor, ins. agt., Calif; registered Nat. Assn. Securities Dealers. With bus. mgmt. depts. various banks and oil cos., Calif., 030with; with Dept. Def.; mem. faculty U. Ark., Fayetteville, U. Miss., Oxford, U. Nebr., Omaha, U. No. Ala., Florence. Author: Empirical Tests of Dependency Theory, 1996, Policy Studies and Developing Nations, Vol. 6, 1999. Mem. Am. Polit. Sci. Assn., Soc. Exploration Geophysicists, Nat. Assn. Life Underwriters, ACLU, NRA, Profl. Assn. Diving Instrs., Am. Quarter Horse Assn., Am. Paint Horse Assn., Amnesty Internat. Libertarian. Episcopalian. Avocations: scuba diving, water skiing, caribbean sailing, riding horses, playing tennis. Office: Wesleyan Coll Dept of Bus and Econ 4760 Forsyth Rd Macon GA 31210

CRAIG, L. CLIFFORD, lawyer; b. Ohio, Aug. 29, 1938; Student, Stanford U., 1957-59; BA, Duke U., 1961, LLB, 1964. Bar: Ohio. Ptnr. Taft, Stettinius & Hollister, Cin., 1971—. Fellow Am. Coll. Trial Lawyers; mem. ABA, Ohio Bar Assn., Cin. Bar Assn. Office: 425 Walnut St Ste 1800 Cincinnati OH 45202-3957

CRAIG, LARRY EDWIN, senator; b. Council, Idaho, July 20, 1945; s. Elvin and Dorothy Craig. BA, U. Idaho; postgrad, George Washington U. Farmer, rancher, Midvale area, Idaho; mem. Idaho Senate, 1974-80, 97th-101st Congresses from 1st Dist. Idaho, 1981-90, U.S. Senate, 1990—, mem. com. on judiciary, com. energy and natural resources, spl. com. on aging, vets. affairs, appropriations, chmn. subcom. on forests and pub. land mgmt., chmn. subcom. water and power. Chmn. Idaho Rep. State Senate Races, 1976-78, chmn. senate steering com.; mem. joint econ. com., com. veterans' affairs, subcom. energy R & D. Pres. Young Rep. League Idaho, 1976-77; mem. Idaho Rep. Exec. Com., 1976-78; chmn. Rep. Ctrl. Com. Washington County, 1971-72; advisor vocat. edn. in pub. schs. HEW, 1971-73; mem. Idaho Farm Bur., 1965-79. Served with U.S. Army N.G., 1970-72. Mem. NRA (bd. dirs. 1983—), Future Farmers of Am. (v.p. 1965). Republican. Methodist. Office: US Senate 520 Hart Senate Office Bldg Washington DC 20510-0001

CRAIG, MARY LAURI, accountant; b. Helena, Mont., Jan. 19, 1936; d. Henry and Hilma (Newman) Lauri; m. William Craig (div. 1982); children: Nona Marie, Lauri Sue. BS cum laude, Rocky Mtn. Coll., 1973. CPA. Acct. various firms, Billings, Mont.; sole practice CPA Billings, 1973-78; dir. Mont. Dept. Revenue, Helena, 1979-81; sole practice CPA Helena, 1982—. Commr.'s adv. group IRS, Washington, 1994-96; exec. com. Multi-State Tax Commn., Denver. Co-author: Adventure Bound in Montana. Mem. Am. Soc. Women Accts. (pres. chpt. 100 1976), Mont. Soc. CPAs. Avocations: fly fishing, gold mining, woodworking, watercolors, music. Home and Office: 408 Washington Dr Helena MT 59601-3911

CRAIG, PAUL MAX, JR., retired lawyer; b. Munich, Aug. 8, 1921; came to U.S., 1941; naturalized, 1944; s. Paul Max and Helen A. Craig; m. Leonie R. Hildebrand, June 26, 1962; children: Anthony P., Claudine A., Stephen P. BS in Elec. Engring., Worcester (Mass.) Poly. Inst., 1946; LLB, Georgetown U., 1950; LLM, George Washington U., 1952. Bar: D.C. 1950. Patent examiner U.S. Patent Office, Washington, 1946-50; patent advisor Office Chief Ordnance, Dept. Army, Washington, 1950-52; pvt. practice Washington, 1952—; ptnr. Craig & Antonelli (and predecessor firm), Washington, 1967-82, Craig & Burns, Washington, 1982-86, Barnes & Thornburg, Washington, 1986-88, Paul M. Craig, P.C., Washington, 1989-97; of counsel Dow, Lohnes & Albertson, 1989-92, affiliated with, 1992-95; of counsel Birch, Stewart, Kolasch & Birch, Falls Church, Va., 1995-97; pvt. practice Silver Spring, Md., 1998—. With USNR, 1944-46. Mem. Am., Inter-Am. bar assns., Am. Patent Law Assn., Assn. Internat. Pour la Protection de la Propriete Indsl., Licensing Execs. Soc., Am. Soc. Internat. Law, Assn. Trial Lawyers Am. Home: 207 Quaint Acres Dr Silver Spring MD 20904-2715 Fax: 301-622-6546. E-mail: pmcraig@starpower.net.

CRAIG, ROBERT GEORGE, dental science educator; b. Charlevoix, Mich., Sept. 8, 1923; s. Harry Allen and Marion Ione (Swinton) C.; m. Luella Georgine Dean, Sept. 29, 1945; children: Susan Georgine, Barbara Dean, Katherine Ann. BS, U. Mich., 1944, MS, 1951, PhD in Phys. Chemistry, 1955; MD (hon.), U. Geneva, Switzerland, 1989. Rsch. chemist Linde Air Products Co., Tonawanda, N.Y., 1944-50, Texaco, Inc., Beacon, N.Y., 1954-55; rsch. assoc. U. Mich. Engring. Rsch. Inst., 1955-57; faculty dept. dental materials Sch. Dentistry, U. Mich., Ann Arbor, 1957-87, asst. prof., 1957-60, assoc. prof., 1960-64, prof., 1964-87, chmn. dept., 1969-87, prof. biologic and material sci., 1987-93, Marcus Ward prof. dentistry, 1990-93, prof. emeritus, 1993—; dir. Specialized Materials Sci. Ctr. Nat. Inst. Dental Rsch., Ann Arbor, 1989-93; exec. com. Sch. Dentistry, U. Mich., Ann Arbor, 1972-75; budget priorities com. U. Mich., Ann Arbor, 1978-81, chmn. budget priorities com., 1979-81. Sci. adv. com. Dental Rsch. Inst., U. Mich., Ann Arbor, 1980-89, chmn., 1984-89; cons. Walter Reed Army Hosp., 1969-75; assessor for Nat. Health and Med. Rsch. Coun., Commonwealth Australia; mem. adv. bd. Dental Advisor, 1984—. Co-author (with K.A. Easlick, S.I. Seger and A.L. Russell): Communicating in Dentistry, 1973; co-author: (with W.J. O'Brien, J.M. Powers) Dental Materials-Properties and Manipulation, 6th edit., 1966; co-author: (with J.M. Powers, J.C. Wataha) Dental Materials-Properties and Manipulation, 8th edit., 2004; co-author: (with J.M. Powers) Workbook for Dental Materials, 1979; contbr. ; editor (with J.M. Powers): Restorative Dental Materials, 11th edit., 2002; mem. editl. bd.: Mich. State Dental Jour., 1973—77, Oral Implantology Jour., 1988—, editl. assoc.: Jour. Oral Rehab., 1999—. Prin. investigator specialized material Scis. Rsch. Ctr. (funded by Nat. Inst. Dental Rsch. 1989-94). Rsch. grantee Nat. Inst. Dental Rsch., 1965-76, 84-94, Nat. Scis. Res. Svc. Tng., 1976-93; Rsch. fellow E.I. du Pont, 1952-53. Mem. ADA (cons. coun. on dental materials and devices 1983-95), Am. Nat. Stds. Inst. (chmn. spl. com. 1968-77, subcom. with ADA on mouth protectors and materials 1996—), Internat. Assn. Dental Rsch. (pres. dental materials group 1973-74, Wilmer Souder award in dental materials 1975), Am. Assn. Dental Schs. (chmn. biomaterials sect. 1977-79), Am. Chem. Soc. (life), Soc. Biomaterials (Clemson award for basic rsch. in biomaterials 1978, program chmn. 1983, fellow 1994, 96), Acad. Operative Dentistry (George Hollenbach Meml. prize 1991), Sigma Xi (sec. U. Mich chpt. 1978-81), Phi Kappa Phi, Phi Lambda Upsilon, Omicron Kappa Upsilon. Home: 1503 Wells St Ann Arbor MI 48104-3914 Office: U Mich Sch Dentistry 1011 N University Ave Ann Arbor MI 48109-1078

CRAIG, ROBERT MARK, III, lawyer, educator; b. Mpls., Sept. 21, 1948; s. Robert Mark Jr. and Shirley A. (Collier) C.; m. Suzanne Bartlett, Aug. 22, 1970; children: Shannon Michelle, Scott Collier. BA in Journalism, Tex. Christian U., 1970; JD, U. Va., 1973. Bar: Va. 1973, U.S. Ct. Mil. Appeals 1974, Tex. 1975, U.S. Dist. Ct. (no. dist.) Tex. 1976, U.S. Dist. Ct. (so. dist.) Tex. 1980, U.S. Dist. Ct. (we. dist.) 1985, U.S. Ct. Appeals (5th and 11th cirs.) 1981, U.S. Supreme Ct. 1981, U.S. Ct. Appeals (9th and 10th cir.) 1984. Assoc. Judin, Ellis & Barron, McAllen, Tex., 1979—80, ptnr., 1980—81; sr. atty. Tenneco Oil Co., Houston, 1981—88; sr. v.p., assoc. gen. counsel First City, Tex., Houston, 1988—93; assoc. gen. counsel Am. Gen. Corp., Houston, 1993—99; v.p., gen. counsel A.G. Fin. Svc. Ctr., Inc., Evanville, Ind., 1999; assoc. gen. counsel Waste Mgmt., Inc., Houston, 1999—. Staff atty. Presdl. Clemency Bd., Washington, 1975; mem. faculty Vernon Regional Jr. Coll., Sheppard AFB, 1975-76; instr. paralegal tng., Houston, 1982-85; instr. USAF Acad., 1976-77, asst. prof. law, 1977-79; councilman City of Oak Ridge North, Tex., 1988-94, also mayor pro tem; dir. Oak Ridge N.Mcpl. Utility Dist., 1994-96; pres. Oak Ridge N.Econ. Devel. Corp., 1994-96, 2003—. Vice pres. Upper Rio Grande Valley Heart Assn., McAllen, 1980-81; ruling elder Timber Ridge Presbyn. Ch., 1983-88; pres. Montgomery County Assn. for Gifted and Talented, Conroe, Tex., 1985; chmn. Permanent Jud. Commn., New Covenant Presbytery, 1986-92; legal counsel Tex. Jaycees, 1981-82. Capt. USAF, 1973-79. Mem.: ABA (vice chair com. corp. counsel litigation sect. 1999—2003, co-chmn. litigation section com. corp. coun. 2003—), Internat. Assn. Def. Coun., Tex. Bar Found., Tex. Bar Assn. (coun. mem. antitrust and bus. litig. sect. 1999—2002), Va. Bar Assn. (assoc.), Clark Soc. and Alumni Bd. of Tex. Christian U., McAllen Jaycees (sec., bd. dirs. 1979—81). Republican. Avocation: golf. Home: 27122 Wells Ln Conroe TX 77385-9080 Office: Waste Mgmt Inc 1001 Fannin St Ste 4000 Houston TX 77002-6711 E-mail: rcraig@wm.com., rmcraig@swbell.net.

CRAIG, ROY PHILLIP, writer, educator, rancher; b. Durango, Colo., May 10, 1924; s. Philip Howard and Anna Dorothea Craig. BA, U. Colo., 1948; MS, Calif. Inst. Tech., 1950; PhD, Iowa State U., 1952. Group leader Dow Chem. Co., Denver, 1952-60; assoc. prof., coord. phys. scis. U. Colo., Boulder, 1961-66, rsch. assoc. UFO study, 1966-67; vis. prof. U. Hawaii, Honolulu, 1968-69; writer, lectr., rancher La Plata County, Colo., 1969—. Cons. Dow Chem. Co., Midland, Mich., 1959; vis. prof. Clarkson Coll. Tech., Potsdam, N.Y., 1962-65, Colo. Coll., Colorado Springs, 1979, State of Ponape, 1981; curriculum cons. U. Hawaii, Honolulu, 1969; spkr. Foresters, Soil Conservationists, Cattlemen's Assn., Bur. Indian Affairs, Colo. LWV, Colo. Edn. Assn., 1971-84; pres. Four Corners Rsch. Inst., Durango, 1975-86. Co-author: Scientific Study of UFOs, 1969; author: UFOs: An Insider's View of the Official Quest for Evidence, 1995; contbr. articles to profl. jours. Pres. La Plata County Landowners Assn., 1974-92. With U.S. Army, 1943-46, ETO. Mem. Four Corners Llama/Alpaca Owners Assn., Phi Beta Kappa, Sigma Xi. Avocations: skiing, white-water rafting, chess. Home and Office: PO Box 335 23808 Hwy 172 Ignacio CO 81137

CRAIG, STEPHEN JOHN, urban planner; b. Darby, Pa., Jan. 3, 1954; s. Robert Frank and Mary Elizabeth (McCarthy) C. BA, John Carroll U., 1976; MA in Urban Planning, George Washington U., 1979. Planning cons. Gladstone Assocs., Washington, 1978, Knight Assocs., Washington, 1977-79, Ednl. Futures, Inc., Phila., 1978-79; project planner Charles County Office Planning, LaPlata, Md., 1979-81; planner, economist Virgin Islands Planning Office, St. Croix, 1982-84; cons. William A. Taylor, Arch., St. Croix, 1983-84; dir. Lawrence County Planning, New Castle, Pa., 1984—2001. Pres. Lawrence County Hist. Soc., New Castle, 1985-86; founder bd. dirs. New Visions for New Castle. Co-author Frederiksted Preservation, 1983. Mem. Am. Inst. Cert. Planners (cert.), Am. Planning Assn., Nat. Trust Hist. Preservation, Pa. Planners Assn., Ptnrs. Livable Places (assoc.). Clubs: Alfa Owners (Calif.), Watts Bay Marina and Country (Lake Arthur, Pa.), YMCA. Democrat. Roman Catholic. Home: 134 E Leasure Ave New Castle PA 16101-2372

CRAIG, SUSAN LYONS, library director; b. Barksdale Air Force Base, La., Feb. 23, 1948; BA, Trinity Coll., Washington, 1971; MSLS, Fla. State U., 1976; MBA, Rosary Coll., 1989. Pub. svcs. libr. St. Mary's Coll., Moraga, Calif., 1976-79; head pub. svcs. Hood Coll., Frederick, Md., 1979-85, Dominican U. (formerly Rosary Coll.), River Forest, Ill., 1985-87; dir. libr. Aurora (Ill.) U., 1987-97; dir. libr. and acad. info. svcs. Trinity Coll. Libr., Washington, 1997—. Adj. assoc. prof Rosary Coll. Grad. Sch. Libr. and Info. Sci., 1990-97. Mem. ALA, Assn. Coll. and Rsch. Librs. (nat. adv. com., rep. Ill. chpt. 1991-95), Pvt. Acad. Librs. of Ill. (pres. 1994-96), Ill. Libr. Assn. (del. pre-White House Conf., Chgo., 1989-90), Beta Phi Mu, Phi Eta Sigma (hon.). Office: Trinity Coll Libr 125 Michigan Ave NE Washington DC 20017-1091

CRAIG, VICKI RENE, lawyer; b. Selma, Ala., Sept. 14, 1957; BS, U. Ala., 1979; JD, Howard U., 1987; LLM in Taxation, Georgetown U., 1991, cert. in employee benefits law, 1992. Bar: Pa. 1989, D.C. 1989, U.S. Dist. Ct. D.C. 1991, U.S. Claims Ct. 1991, U.S. Tax Ct. 1991, U.S. Ct. Appeals (D.C. and fed. cirs.) 1991, U.S. Supreme Ct. 1992. Tax atty. IRS, Washington, 1987—94; head ERISA dept. Leftwick & Douglas, Washington, 1994—95. Rsch. asst Am. Jour. Tax Policy, Tuscaloosa, Ala., summer 1986. Author: Almighty God! An Insightful Look Within, Thinking About God: Spiritual Soup for the Mind! Unlocking the Mind, Thinking About God: Spiritual Soup for the Mind: Thinking Outside of the Box, Thinking About God: Spiritual Soup for the Mind! Spiritual Food for Thought, Regarding God: A Believers Thoughts, Regarding God: A Believer's Thoughts (teen edit.), Out of the Mouth of Babes (children's edit.), Out of the Mouth of Babes (teen edit.), Excel: Hope will Never Fail! (adult edit.), Excel: Hope Will Never Fail! (teen edit.); contbr. Mem. Smithsonian Assocs., Washington, 1989, NAACP, Washington, 1989; founder, dir. English tutorial program Shiloh Bapt. Ch., Washington. Named Outstanding Young Woman in Am.; recipient Lay Person of the Yr. award, Phi Delta Kappa, 1994. Mem. ABA, Nat. Bar Assn. (Greater Washington Area chpt., women lawyers' divsn.), Fed. Bar Assn., D.C. Bar Assn., Nat. Polit. Congress of Black Women, Pa. Bar Assn., Assn. Trial Lawyers Am., Alpha Kappa Alpha, Delta Theta Phi.

CRAIG, WILLIAM, philosopher, educator; b. Nuremberg, Bavaria, Germany, Nov. 13, 1918; s. Walter Krakenberger and Alice Craig; m. Julia Rebecca Wilson, Aug. 20, 1949; children: Ruth, Walter, Sarah, Deborah. BA, Cornell U., 1940; PhD, Harvard U., 1951. Asst. prof. math. Pa. State U., State College, 1951—60; prof. philosophy U. Calif., Berkeley, 1961—89, prof. emeritus philosophy, 1989—. 1st lt. Signal Corps U.S. Army, 1943—45. Mem.: Am. Philos. Assn. (pres. Pacific divsn. 1979), Assn. Symbolic Logic (pres. 1965—68). Office: U Calif Berkeley Dept Philosophy Berkeley CA 94720-2390

CRAIGHEAD, RODKEY, banker; b. Pitts., July 24, 1916; s. Ernest S. and Florence L. (Rodkey) C.; m. Carol M. Price, June 26, 1943 (dec. June 1978); children: Rodkey, Virginia, Corinne; m. La Verne Hastings, Mar. 1979. BS, U. Pitts., 1942; postgrad., Grad. Sch. Banking, U. Wis., 1959-61. With Mellon Nat. Bank, Pitts., 1936-41; with Detroit Bank & Trust Co., 1946—, v.p., 1961-67, sr. v.p., 1967-69, exec. v.p., 1969-73, dir., 1971—, pres., 1974—, chmn., CEO, 1977—; pres., dir. Detroitbank Corp., 1974-81, chmn., CEO, 1977-81. Served to capt. AUS, 1942-46. Mem. Collier County Forum Club, Royal Poinciana Golf Club, Naples Athletic Club. Presbyterian. Home: 100 Glenview Pl #607 Naples FL 34108

CRAIGO, CHRISTINA ILA, artist, educator; b. Charleston, W.Va., Apr. 10, 1965; d. Oshel B. and Joanna (Parkins) C.; m. Charles Patrick Swarts, May 14, 1994; 1 child, Anna Craigo Swarts. BFA, Temple U., 1988; MFA, Sch. Visual Arts, N.Y.C., 1990. Adj. painting instr. U. Colo. Divsn. Continuing Edn., Boulder, Naropa U., Boulder. Solo exhbns. include Studio 602 Gallery, Charleston, W.Va., 1988, Coalition of Ind. Artists, Bklyn., 1990, Am. Ctr., Madras, India, 1993, Max & Roebling, Bklyn., 1996, St. Peter's Ch., N.Y.C., 1997, Naropa U., 2003; group exhbns. include Studio 602 Gallery, 1989, Coalition of Ind. Artists, 1989, 90, Visual Arts Gallery, N.Y.C., 1989-90, Hunter Coll., N.Y.C., 1990, Hunter Coll., N.Y., 1990, Artists Space, N.Y.C., 1992, Herron Test Site, Bklyn., 1992, N.Y. SoHo Biennial, N.Y.C., 1995, Karen McCready Fine Art, N.Y.C., 1999, Jan Abrams Fine Art, N.Y.C., 1999, First Nat. Fate Exhbn., Harmony Pk. Gallery, Fort Collins, Colo., 1999, Boulder Mus. Contemporary Art, 2000, Dairy Ctr. for the Arts, Boulder, Colo., 2001, Naropa U., 2002. Rsch./travel grantee Fulbright Found., India, 1992. Mem. Coll. Art Assn. Mem. Green Party. Home: PO Box 296 Jamestown CO 80455-0296

CRAIGUE, LESLIE J. systems analyst; b. Leominster, Mass., Sept. 26, 1951; s. Leslie John and Muriel Gertrude Craigue; m. Cheryl Suzanne Cammer, June 21, 1981 (div. Jan. 2003); children: Orion Daniel, Orpheus Simon. BS in Math., Rensselaer Poly. Inst., 1973. Programmer/analyst NY State Taxation & Fin., Albany, 1985—89; computer sys. programmer NY State Workers' Compensation Bd., Albany, 1989—2003. Co-chmn., facilities com. Averill Pk. Sch. Dist., Sand Lake, NY, 2001—02. Recipient Citizen of the Month, Town of Sand Lake, NY, 1991. Mem.: NY Acad. of Sci. Democrat. Avocations: writing, physics, artisan. Home: 6 Zoar Ave Albany NY 12203-5742 Office: NY State Workers' Compensation Bd 100 Broadway - Menands Albany NY 12241 Personal E-mail: LCraigue@nycap.rr.com. Business E-Mail: Leslie.Craigue@wcb.state.ny.us.

CRAIN, ALAN RAU, JR., lawyer, oil company executive; b. Washington, June 20, 1951; s. Alan Rau and Florence Carol (Clemmer) C. B.S., Rensselaer Poly. Inst., 1973, M.S., 1973; M.B.A., Syracuse U., 1976, J.D., 1976. Bar: D.C., Md., Tex. 1977, U.S. Dist. Ct. (so. dist.) Tex. 1980, U.S. Ct. Appeals (5th cir.) 1983, U.S. Ct. Internat. Trade 1983, U.S. Supreme Ct. 1983. Assoc. Glaser, Fletcher & Johnson, Washington, 1976; Successively counsel, sr. counsel, prin. counsel El Paso Co., Houston, 1976-81; chief counsel-internat. and research Pennzoil Co., Houston, 1981-88; successively counsel, asst. gen. counsel, v.p., gen. counsel Union Tex. Petroleum Holdings, Inc., Houston, 1988—; arbitrator N.Y. Stock Exchange, Houston, 1984— ; pres. Houston World Affairs Coun., 1997; mem. adv. bd. Inst. for Transnat. Arbitration, 1992—, South Tex. Coll. of Law, 1991—. Mem. Internat. Bar Assn., Tex. Bar Assn., Houston Bar Assn. (chmn. internat. law sect. 1987-88), State Bar of Tex. (chmn. 1989-90, corp. counsel 1996-97), Briar (Houston) Club. Office: Union Tex Petroleum Holdings Inc 1330 Post Oak Blvd Houston TX 77056-3031 Home: 3049 Locke Ln Houston TX 77019-6201

CRAIN, BARBARA JEAN, pathologist, educator; b. Long Beach, Calif., Sept. 18, 1950; d. Gerald Clough and Reya Jean (Dahms) C.; m. Michael Joseph Borowitz, Dec. 29, 1978; children: Jeffrey Adam, David Douglas. BS, U. Calif., Irvine, 1972; PhD, Duke U., 1978, MD, 1979. Diplomate Am. Bd. Neuropathology. Asst. prof. pathology and neurobiology Duke U. Med. Ctr., Durham, N.C., 1983-92; asst. clin. prof. pathology, asst. rsch. prof. neurobiology, 1992-93; assoc. prof. pathology Johns Hopkins Sch. of Medicine, Balt., 1993—. Cons. John Unstead State Hosp., Butner, N.C., 1989-93; neurobiology merit rev. bd. VA, Washington, 1989-93; staff physician VA Hosp., Durham, 1983-93. Contbr. articles to profl. jours. Pharmacology-morphology fellow Pharm. Mfrs. Assn., 1982; NIH Ctr. grantee, 1990. Fellow Coll. Am. Pathologists (neuropathology com.); mem. Am. Assn. Neuropathologists, U.S.-Can. Acad. Pathology, Soc. Neurosci. Office: Johns Hopkins Sch Medicine Dept Pathology 720 Rutland Ave Baltimore MD 21205-2109 E-mail: bcrain@jhmi.edu.

CRAIN, FRANCES UTTERBACK, retired dietitian; b. Crawfordsville, Ind., Dec. 28, 1914; d. Chelsey Chalmers and Margaret Myrtle (Henderson) Utterback; m. James William Crain, Sept. 13, 1937 (div. July 1944); children: James Michael, Patrick Desmond. BA, U. Ill., 1935; postgrad., Purdue U., 1945-46. Dietetic intern Indpls. City Hosp., 1935-36, therapeutic dietitian, 1936-37; dietitian Home Lawn Mineral Springs, Martinsville, Ind., 1937-38; WPA project dietitian Ill. Soldiers & Sailors Children's Home, Normal, 1939; chief dietitian Providence Hosp., Kansas City, Kans., 1939-40, Alexian Bros. Hosp., St. Louis, 1940-41; dietitian Ill. State Dept. Pub. Welfare, Springfield, 1943-45; exec. dir. Memphis Dairy Coun., 1947-61; program cons. Nat. Dairy Coun., Chgo., 1961-68; dietitian War on Poverty Com., Memphis, 1968-69, Shelby County Hosp., Memphis, 1969-74, Shelby County Penal Farm, Memphis, 1969-80; chief dietitian Oakville Health Care Ctr., Memphis, 1974-80. Dietitian feeding programs Salvation Army, 1982-93. Writer food feature column. Comml. Appeal, 1952-61; author: To Your Taste-Butter, 1957, Of Weeds and Views, 2000. Mem. speakers and path. coms. Memphis in May Internat. Festival, 1983, 84, 85. Named Career Women of Yr., Pilot Club of Memphis, 1955, Tenn. Outstanding Dietitian of Yr., 1976; recipient Spl. Svcs. award Salvation Army, 1983; Frances Crain Book Fund named in her honor MANC/MDDA, 2003. Mem.: Memphis Dist. Dietetic Assn. (pres. 1949—50, editor bull. 1958—59, Frances Crain Book Fund named in her honor 2003), Memphis Area Nutrition Coun. (pres. 1973—74), Tenn. Dietetic Assn. (life; pres. 1951—52), Am. Dietetic Assn. (life), Shelby County Retirees Orgn. (pres. 1987—89). Democrat. Avocations: reading, computers, cooking, Scrabble. Home: 255 N Avalon St Memphis TN 38112-5101 E-mail: fran255@aol.com.

CRAIN, J. LESTER, JR., corporate lawyer; b. 1929; BA, Southwestern U., Georgetown, Tex., 1951; LLB, Harvard U., 1954. Sole practice, 1958-77; v.p., gen. counsel Malone & Hyde Inc., Memphis, 1977-79, v.p., sec., gen. counsel, 1979—. Served to lt. comdr. USN, 1954-58.

CRAIN, JOHN WALTER, historian, educator; b. Amarillo, Tex., July 11, 1944; s. John Clyde and Roma (McDowell) C.; m. Mary Hemingway, Aug. 18, 1973; children: John Matthew, Sarah Hemingway, Margaret Aileen. BA, U. Tex., Austin, 1966; MA, S.W. Tex. State U., 1970; cert. arts adminstrn., Harvard U., 1975; cert. mus. mgmt., U. Calif.-Berkeley, 1979. Dir. Star of the Republic Museum, Washington-on-the-Brazos, Tex., 1971-76, Dallas Hist. Soc., 1976-90; chmn. Dallas County Hist. Commn., 1993-95. Cons. in field. Exec. dir. Summerlee Commn. on Tex. History, 1990-91; v.p., bd. dirs. program History Summerlee Found., Tex., 1990—; bd. dirs. Dallas County Hist. Found., Friends of Gov.'s Mansion. Mem. Tex. State Hist. Assn. (hon., coun. 1994, exec. com., pres.), Conf. of S.W. Founds. (bd. dirs.), Tex. Map Soc. (bd. dirs.). Methodist. Office: 5956 Sherry Ln Ste 610 Dallas TX 75225-8017

CRAIN, JOHN KIP, school system administrator; b. Urbana, Ohio, June 14, 1956; s. William Frederick and Patricia Ann (Bumgardner) C.; m. Rebecca Ann Ireland, July 11, 1980; children: Amanda Ann, Tiffany Kay, Kelly Jo. BS in Edn. summa cum laude, Ohio State U., 1985, MA, 1987; postgrad., Bowling Green State U., 1992—. Cert. tchr., supr. dir., prin., asst. supt., supt., Ohio. Drafter, office mgr. Crain Bldgs., Mechanicsburg, Ohio, 1974-82; tchr. drafting Springfield (Ohio)-Clark County Joint Vocat. Sch., 1982-86; supr. Eastland Vocat. Schs., Groveport, Ohio, 1986-91; dir. Oregon (Ohio) City Schs., 1991—. Bd. dirs. Ohio Indsl. Tng. Program, Toledo; co-chair skill olympics Ohio Vocat./Indsl. Clubs Am., Columbus, 1987-89; presenter in field. Author and editor catalog Eastland Vocat. Schs., 1987. Vol. St. Charles Hosp. Emergency Rm., 1991—; Ohio dist. chair Young Children Priority One, 2002-2003; bd. dirs. Ea. Comty. YMCA, Toledo, 1992-94. Pres.'s sr. scholar Ohio State U., 1984. Mem. Assn. Career Tech. Edn. (life), Ohio Career Tech. Adminstrs. (exec. bd. 1996-99, pres. 1999-2000), Ohio Assn. Career-Tech. Educators (exec. bd. 2000-2001, adminstrv. divsn. pres. 2000-2001), Ohio Assn. Secondary Sch. Adminstrs., Bay Area Jr. C. of C. (state dir. 1991-94), Oregon Area C. of C., Kiwanis (bd. dirs. 1991-95, pres. 1995-96, 98-99, East Toledo chpt., Disting. Svc. award 1996, Divsn. 1N lt. gov. 2001—), Ohio Vocat. Indsl. Club Am. (regional advisor 1984-86, asst. dir. summer leadership camp 1985-86, chmn. state skill olympics 1986-87, author and editor program guidelines 1985, local advisor notebook 1986), Phi Delta Kappa, Pi Lambda Theta, Omicron Tau Theta. United Methodist. Home: 2036 Coe Ct Perrysburg OH 43551-5600 Office: Oregon City Schs 5721 Seaman St Oregon OH 43616-2631

CRAIN, MARY ANN, elementary school educator; b. Dallas, Tex, Sept. 5, 1951; d. Robert Lee and Mary Ann (T.) Crain. MusB education, Fla. State U., 1973; MusM, Ohio State U., 1974; EdS, U. Ga., 1998. Cert. Ga. Profl. Std. Commn., Tchg. T-6, Music P-12, Early Childhood P-5, Mid. Grades 4-8, Ednl. Leadership P-12 Univ. Ga., 2001. First clarinet Vienna Kursalon Orch., Vienna, 1975—77; band dir. Sch. Bd. of Broward County, Ft. Lauderdale, Fla., 1977—78; teller Fla. Coast Bank, Coral Springs, Fla., 1978—79; strings tchr., grades 6-7 DeKalb County Bd. of Edn., Decatur, Ga., 1979—82, band tchr., grades 6-7, 1982—86, classroom tchr., grades 4-7, 1986—96, math specialist, grades 2-5, 1996—2000, early intervention math and reading specialist, grades 2-5, 2000—02; math. specialist, grades 1-5 Bethesda Elem. Sch., Lawrenceville, Ga., 2002—. Office: Bethesda Elem Sch 525 Bethesda Sch Rd NW Lawrenceville GA 30044

CRAIN, MARY TOM, volunteer; b. Vernon, Tex., Aug. 27, 1918; d. Samuel Asa Leland and Mary Verna (Johnson) Morgan; m. David Rasco, Dec. 24, 1941 (dec. Apr. 1955); children: Sarah M. Rasco Thomas, Mary Prudence Rasco Courtney; m. Sam H. Crain, Sept. 17, 1975 (dec. June 1980). Student, Stephens Coll., 1936-38, U. Tex., 1938-39; BS, U. Wis., 1941. Tchr. Williams Bay (Wis.) Schs., 1941; reporter Amarillo (Tex.) Globe News, 1957-65; exec. sec. Potter-Randall County Med. Soc., Amarillo, 1960-69; ret., 1969. Mem. lay adv. bd. St. Anthony's Hosp., Amarillo, 1957; mem. devel. bd. High Plains Hosp., 1995; coun. pres. Girl Scouts U.S., Amarillo, 1953-55; pres. Jr. League, Amarillo, 1956; bd. dirs. Amarillo Symphony, Art Mus., Panhandle Plains Hist. Soc., Amarillo Area Found., 1945—, Llano Cemetary; mem. City of Amarillo Park and Recreation Commn.; bd. dirs. Amarillo Coll. Found., Amarillo Pub. Libr., Art Force. Named Amarillo's Woman of yr., Beta Sigma Phi, 1955; named to Amarillo H.S. Hall of Fame, 1971. Methodist. Home: 3206 Amberwood Ln Amarillo TX 79106

CRAIN, RICHARD CHARLES, school district music director, retired; b. Christine, Tex., Apr. 22, 1934; s. Richard Clyde and Florence (Martin) C.; m. Gayle Ruth Albert, June 24, 1961; children: Richard Scott, Roy Christopher, Steven Guy. B in Music, Trinity U., San Antonio, 1956; postgrad., Vandercook Coll., 1958; MEd, U. N. Tex., 1969. Band dir. Mercedes (Tex.) H.S., 1956-60, Lamar Jr. H.S., Temple, Tex., 1960-64, Belton (Tex.) H.S., 1964-79, Spring H.S., Houston, 1979-81, Westfield H.S., Houston, 1981-82; dir. music Spring Ind. Sch. Dist., Houston, 1982-2000, ret., 2000. Coord. Nat. Concert Band Festival, Chgo., 1991—; bd. dirs. Midwest Internat. Band and Orch. Clinic, Chgo., 1991—. Mem. Tex. Bandmasters Assn. (Tex. Bandmaster of Yr. 1994), Nat. Fedn. Sch. Activities Assn. (Outstanding Music Educator award 1994), Univ. Interscholastic League (exec. sec. region IX 1994—), Phi Beta Mu Internat. Fraternity (exec. sec. 1977—). Home: 7 Surrey Run Pl The Woodlands TX 77384-4786

CRAINE, THOMAS KNOWLTON, non-profit administrator; b. Utica, N.Y., Apr. 19, 1942; s. Donald Holmes and Marjorie (Knowlton) C.; m. Susan Lynda Moseley, Dec. 21, 1966; children: Matthew Moseley, Tish Marjorie. BA, U. Rochester, 1964; MEd, SUNY, Buffalo, 1966, EdD, 1972. Dir. architecture and planning SUNY, Buffalo, 1968-72, asst. to pres., 1972-76, clin. assoc. prof., 1975-83, asst. v.p. acad. affairs, 1976-79; exec. v.p., assoc. prof. D'Youville Coll., Buffalo, 1979-83; pres. Loretto Heights Coll., Denver, 1983-88; v.p. instl. advancement and planning Iliff Sch. Theology, Denver, 1988-98; pres./CEO YMCA Met. Denver, 1998—2002, pres. emeritus, 2002—03; dir. N. Am. Urban Group of YMCA, 2003—. Evaluator North Cen. Assn. Instns. Higher Edn., 1984—, Assn. Theol. Schs., 1993—; cons. in strategic planning, bd. devel., fund raising. Mailing: YMCA of the USA 101 N Wacker Dr Chicago IL 60606 E-mail: tom.craine@ymca.net.

CRAKES, GARY MICHAEL, economics educator; b. Southington, Conn., July 2, 1953; s. Harry Fremont and Frances Katherine (Koth) C.; m. Deborah Jean MacArthur, Aug. 14, 1976; children: Andrew David, Jeffrey Alan, Timothy Scott. BA in Econs., Ctrl. Conn. State U., 1975; MA in Econs., U. Conn., 1976, PhD in Econs., 1984. Rsch. asst. Health Ctr. U. Conn., Farmington, 1976-79, vis. prof. Health Ctr., Sch. Dental Medicine, 1988, instr. Hartford, 1979-80; asst. prof. So. Conn. State U., New Haven, 1980-85, assoc. prof., 1985-89, prof., 1989—, chmn. dept. econs. and fin., 1991-96. Pres. Maher, Crakes & Assocs., Cheshire, Conn., 1987—; econ. expert witness. Contbr. articles to profl. jours. Mem. State of Conn. Sr. Economist Exam. Com., Hartford, 1987. Richard D. Irwin fellow Irwin Publ. Co., Homewood, Ill., 1983-84, U. Conn. fellow, 1983; recipient Univ. Tchr. of the Yr. award, 1987, Schs. of Bus. Outstanding Tchg. award, 1998. Mem. Am. Econ. Assn., Ea. Econ. Assn. Nat. Assn. Forensic Econ., AAUP, Omicron Delta Epsilon (chpt. advisor). Democrat. Avocations: family activities, golf, fishing. Home: 860 Ward Ln Cheshire CT 06410-3363 Office: So Conn State U 501 Crescent St New Haven CT 06515-1330

CRALL, AARON H. restaurant company executive, artist; s. Jack Crall and Carol Hellman; m. Kim R. Hoot. BFA, S.W. Mo. State U., 1995. Microsoft cert. profl., Computing Tech. Industry Assn. A+. Graphic designer, mktg. asst. Am. Poolplayers Assn., Saint Louis, 1995—97; digital svc. dir. Copy USA, Saint Louis, 1997—98; computer support technician Pyramid Tech., Belleville, Ill., 1998—2000; adminstr. JDC Restaurants Inc., Saint Louis, 2000—. Mem.: St. Louis Artists Guild (assoc.). E-mail: aaron@cjmuggs.com.

CRAM, REGINALD MAURICE, retired air force officer; b. Northfield, Vt., Apr. 29, 1914; s. Archie Rice and Beatrice (Cleveland) C.; m. Kathryn E. Mosher, June 29, 1937; children: Robin (Mrs. Paul Lualdi), Marilyn Jane (Mrs. Vcevold Strekalovsky). BS, Norwich U., 1936, D in Mil. Sci. (hon.), 1974; postgrad., Boston U. Law Sch., 1937-38, Air Force Intelligence Sch., 1943, U.S. Army Command and Gen. Staff Coll., 1944, Nat. Art Sch., 1949, Armed Forces Staff Coll., 1951, State Dept. Fgn. Service Inst., 1961; MA, U. Md., 1963. With Office Adj. Gen. Vt., 1938-41; asst. U.S. property and disbursing officer State of Vt., 1946-47; commd. 2d lt. Cav., 1936; advanced through grades to col. USAF, 1952; with anti-submarine campaign USAAF, 1941-42; Asiatic-Pacific Theatre with USMC, 1943-45; plans and operations officer Hdqrs. USAF, 1947-51; sec. Can./U.S. Regional Planning Group, NATO, 1951-54; dir. plans 3d USAF, Eng., 1954-55; with Supreme Hdqrs. Allied Powers, Europe, 1955-57; comdr. Orientation Group USAF, 1957-61; with Orgn. Joint Chiefs of Staff, 1961-64; ret., 1964; elected adj. gen. Vt. with rank maj. gen. ANG, 1967—81. Dep. adj. gen. Vt., 1964-66, adj. gen., 1967-81 Past pres. Long Trail council Boy Scouts Am.; trustee Norwich U. Decorated D.S.M., USAF, Legion of Merit, USAF and U.S. Army, Air medals USN and U.S. Army, Joint Commendation medal, Army Commendation medal, Commendation medal, Selective Svc. Sys. Commendation medal USAF, Vt. WWII Victory medal; recipient Vt. Disting. Svc. medal, Disting. Alumni award Norwich U., 1972. Mem. N.G. Assn. U.S. (Disting. Svc. medal, Am. Cancer Soc. St. George medal), Soc. Colonial Wars (war cross), Ret. Officers Assn., VFW, Vt. Hist. Soc., The Hillard Soc., U.S. Biathlon Hall of Fame, Ethan Allen Inst., Theta Chi, Pi Sigma Alpha, Masons (33 deg.), Scottish Rite, Rotary Club (past dist. gov.). Congregationalist. Home: 936 S Prospect St Burlington VT 05401-6169 E-mail: regcram@aol.com.

CRAMBLETT, HENRY GAYLORD, pediatrician, virologist, educator; b. Scio, Ohio, Feb. 8, 1929; s. Carl Smith and Olive (Fulton) C.; m. Donna Jean Reese, June 16, 1960; children: Deborah Kaye, Betsy Diane. BS, Mt. Union Coll., 1950; MD, U. Cin., 1953. Diplomate Am. Bd. Pediatrics, Am. Bd. Microbiology, Am. Bd. Med. Specialists. Intern in medicine Boston City Hosp., Harvard Med. Svc., 1953-54; resident in pediatrics Children's Hosp., Cin., 1954-55; clin. rsch. assoc. Nat. Inst. Allergy and Infectious Diseases, Clin. Ctr., Bethesda, Md., 1955-57; chief resident, instr. dept. pediat. State U. Iowa, Iowa City, 1957-58, faculty, 1957-60, asst. prof., 1958-60; faculty Bowman Gray Sch. Medicine, 1960-64, prof. pediat., 1963-64, dir. virology lab., 1960-64; prof. pediat. Ohio State U., Columbus, 1964-95, prof. med. microbiology, 1966-95, exec. dir. Children's Hosp. Rsch. Found., 1964-73, chmn. dept. med. microbiology, 1966-73, dean Coll. Medicine, 1973-80, acting v.p. for med. affairs, 1974-80, v.p. health scis., 1980-83, Warner M. and Lora Kays Pomerene chair in medicine, 1982-95, assoc. to v.p. health svcs., to dean and prof. emeritus, 1984-95. Mem. Ohio State U. bd. trustees Cancer Hosp. Oversight Com., 1991-96, mem. Ohio Med. Bd., sec. 1984-92, past pres.; hosp. surveyor Joint Com. on Accreditation of Health Care Orgns., 1985-95; chmn. com. on cert., subcert. and recert. Am. Bd. Med. Specialists; mem. coms. on written exam., comprehensive qualifying evaluation program Nat. Bd. Med. Examiners; mem. Accreditation Coun. Continuing Med. Edn., chmn., 1980-83, 93-94, also mem. fin. com., 1993—, mem. strategic plan implementation com., 1993—, mem. external monitoring com., 1993—; mem. adv. com. on undergrad. med. evaluation; mem. Fedn. State Med. Bds., pres., 1976-82 (mem. Flex bd. 1983-91, chmn. 1985-91), mem. fin. audit com., 1991; chmn. Fed. Exam. Bd., 1991-92, cons., 1992—; mem. composite com. Fedn. of State Med. Bds. and Nat. Bd. of Med. Examiners, U.S. Med. Licensing Exam., 1990-96; Fedn. of State Med. Bds. observer Clin. Skills Assessment Alliance, 1990-95; bd. dirs. Ohio State U. Hosp., 1979-80; dir. med. and postgrad. med. edn. King Faisal Specialist Hosp., Riyadh, Saudi Arabia, 1983-84; mem. strategic planning task force CSAA, 1992-94; med. dir. Columbus Health Plan, 1995—. Trustee Children's Hosp. Rsch. Found., 1973-84, Children's Hosp., 1973-84, Children's Hosp., Inc., 1982-84. Recipient Hoffheimer prize U. Cin., 1953, Eben J. Carey award in anatomy, 1950, Rsch. Career Devel. award NIH, 1961-63; Henry G. Cramblett chair in medicine established at Ohio State U., 1988; Henry G. Cramblett Hall dedicated at Ohio State U., 1999. Fellow Am. Acad. Microbi-

ology, AAAS; mem. So. Soc. Pediatric Rsch. (past pres.), Soc. Pediatric Rsch., Am. Pediatric Soc., Am. Acad. Pediat., Midwest Soc. Pediatric Rsch., Soc. Exptl. Biology and Medicine, Am. Soc. Microbiology, Alpha Omega Alpha. Achievements include research, publs. on medical licensure, medical staff hospital standards, etiologic assn. virus infections in illnesses of infants and children, estimation of importance of various viruses in morbidity and mortality in pediatric age group. Home: 2480 Sheringham Rd Columbus OH 43220-4274 Office: Ohio State U 1024 Cramblett Hall 456 W 10th Ave Columbus OH 43210-1240

CRAMER, ALLAN P. lawyer; b. Norwich, Conn., Mar. 8, 1937; s. E.L. and Dorothy N. (Pasnik) C.; children: Peter Alden, Alison Jane. BA cum laude, U. Pa., 1958; JD, U. Conn., 1964. Bar: Conn. 1964, U.S. Dist. Ct. Conn. 1965, U.S. Ct. Appeals (2d cir.) 1965. Atty. HEW, Washington, 1964-65; ptnr. Cramer & Ahern, Westport, Conn., 1966— . Chmn. Westport Dem. Town Com., 1972-73; J.P., Town of Westport, 1973-77; bd. dirs. Westport Pub. Libr., 1975-82; mem. Westport Zoning Bd. Appeals, 1984-88 . Mem. Conn. Bar Assn., Westport Bar Assn. Home: Yankee Hill Rd Westport CT 06880 Office: Cramer & Ahern 38 Post Rd W Westport CT 06880-4207 Business E-Mail: cramer.ahern@snet.net.

CRAMER, BETTY F. life insurance company executive; b. Indpls., Dec. 9, 1920; d. Frank E. and Ethelyn L. (Jackson) C. BA, Butler U., 1943. Sec. to head pers. dept., payroll acct. Am. United Life Ins. Co., 1943-51; Sec. to v.p. and treas. Indpls. Life Ins. Co., 1951-69, supr. bond and stock acctg., 1969-75, securities asst., 1975-81, sec.-treas., 1981-89, ret., 1989. Advisor Jr. Achievement, Indpls., 1959-60; campaign chmn. United Way, 1980 Mem. Nat. Assn. Corp. Treas., Life Ins. Women's Assn. Indpls. (past v.p., pres.) Republican. Roman Catholic. Avocations: swimming, reading, traveling. Home: 5158 N Central Ave Indianapolis IN 46205-1060

CRAMER, BRIAN STARKWEATHER, electrical engineer; b. Phila., Aug. 15, 1955; s. Arthur A. and Mary S. (Starkweather) C.; m. Colette C. Kolondra, May 20, 1979; children: Brian Alex, Arielle Nicole, Corinne Elizabeth. BSEE, Lehigh U., 1977. Registered profl. engr., Ill. Engr. AIL Sys., Deer Park, N.Y., 1977-81; sr. engr. Lockheed Electronics, Plainfield, N.J., 1981-84; pres. EPP, Inc., Plainfield, Ill., 1984-90; prin. engr. ComEd, Chgo., 1991-96, tech. expert inductive coordination and elec. effects, 1996—2002; project mgr. Electric Power Rsch. Inst., Palo Alto, Calif., 2002—. Contbr. articles to profl. jours. Youth soccer coach Manhattan (Ill.) Soccer Assn., 1992-96; asst. scoutmaster Boy Scouts Am., Manhattan, 1996—; 1st lt. CAP, 2001--. Mem. IEEE (sr., mem. power engring. soc. corona and field effects subcom. 1998—), Am. Railroad Engring. & Maintenance-of-way Assn. (assoc., consulting mem. comm. & signal subcom. #38 1994—), Conference Internationale des Grands Reseaux Electriques a Haute Tension. Address: 12410 W Manhattan Monee Rd Manhattan IL 60442-9560 E-mail: bcramer@epri.com.

CRAMER, CHERYL QUAVE WILSON, not-for-profit developer, consultant; b. New Orleans, La., July 14, 1944; d. Commodore Waddell and Mildred Louise Quave Wilson; m. David Nelson Cramer, Aug. 18, 1979; children: Damon Earl Murray, Daniel Nelson. BA, Howard U., 1962—66. Fgn. svc. res. officer US Dept. of State, Washington DC, 1969—76; asst. to the mayor City of New Orleans, New Orleans, 1978—86. Elected mem. Orleans Parish Sch. Bd., New Orleans, 1991—98. Mem. YWCA, New Orleans, La., 1999—2001. Mem.: Assn. of Fund Raising Professionals, Local Ch. Ministries of the UCC (pres. 1999—2003), Delta Sigma Theta, Inc. A Pub. Svc. Sorority (life). United Ch. Of Christ. Office: Southern University at New Orleans 6400 Press Dr New Orleans LA 70126 Office Fax: 504-284-5537. E-mail: ccramer@suno.edu.

CRAMER, DALE LEWIS, retired economics educator; b. Dixon, Ill., June 25, 1924; s. Ray C. and Rebecca (Levan) C.; m. Hula Jean Bond, Aug. 30, 1946; children: Becky Cramer McCarn, Craig Alan, Randall Scott. BS, Bradley U., 1949, MA, 1951; PhD, La. State U., 1958. Asst. prof. econs. La. State U., 1953-54, U. Tex.-El Paso, 1955-57, assoc. prof., 1957-58; assoc. prof. econs. U. Ala., 1958-63, prof., 1963-88, prof. emeritus econs., 1988—, head dept., 1968-72, acting head dept., 1981-82. Contbr. articles to profl. jours., books. Served with AUS, 1943-46. Earhart Found. fellow, 1954-55 Mem. Am., So. econ. assns., AAUP, Omicron Delta Epsilon, Beta Gamma Sigma. Home: 103 Riverdale N Tuscaloosa AL 35406-1818

CRAMER, EDWARD MORTON, lawyer, music company executive; b. N.Y.C., May 27, 1925; s. Israel and Elsie (Neuman) C.; m. Henrietta Pantel, 1973 (div.); children: Evin Joyce, Marjorie Sue Cramer Gmelin, Charles Harris; m. Ethel Metzger, June 13, 1982. BA, Columbia U., 1947; LLB with distinction, Cornell U., Ithaca, N.Y., 1950; LLM, NYU, 1953; HHD (hon.), Lincoln (Ill.) Coll., 1982; LHD (hon.), Five Towns Coll., N.Y., 1998. Bar: N.Y. 1950, U.S. Supreme Ct 1953. Teaching fellow NYU Sch. Law, 1950-51; assoc. Rosenman & Colin, N.Y.C., 1951-58; ptnr. Cramer & Hoffinger, N.Y.C., 1958-68; pres., CEO, Broadcast Music, Inc. (BMI), 1968-86; pvt. practice, N.Y.C., 1986—. Treas. Copyright Soc. U.S., 1963-68, 78-79, bd. editors bull., 1953-63; former mem. Peabody Awards Selection Com.; editor Cornell Law Quar. Trustee Congregation Adas Emuno; former trustee Tony Martell Found., Ford's Theater. lt. USNR, 1943-46 Recipient Spl. award Songwriters Guild Am., 1986, Spl. award Am. Composers Alliance, 1987, Spl. Peabody award, 1991; named Personality of Yr. Nat. Arts Club, 1972; Ed Cramer Day named in his honor, N.Y.C., 1979. Mem.: ABA (copyright com.), Practising Law Inst., Nat. Acad. Popular Music (trustee, bd. dirs. 1969—93, founding mem. Songwriters Hall of Fame, adv. com.), Internat. Confedn. Authoral Socs. (adminstrv. coun.), Broadcast Pioneers (pres. 1984, officer, bd. dirs. 1984—97), Nat. Music Coun. (v.p. 1968—86), Assn. Bar City NY (copyright com.), B'nai B'rith (pres. 1989—90, trustee, officer, pres. music and performing arts unit, Man of Yr. award 1979), Order of Coif. Jewish. Home: 254 Chestnut St Englewood NJ 07631-3134 Office: 110 E 59th St New York NY 10022-1304 *I'm not a creatively talented person but working with people who are, has given me a sense that I have shared their accomplishments.*

CRAMER, ESTHER RIDGWAY, author, historian, retired supermarket executive; b. La Habra, Calif., Jan. 17, 1927; d. Claude Arthur and Ida Alma Ridgway; m. Stanley Edward Cramer, June 17, 1948; children: Cynthia Ann Cramer Freeman, Melinda Cramer Ching, Janet Cramer Esguerra Buddle. BA, Pomona Coll., Claremont, Calif., 1948; postgrad., U. So. Calif., 1949, Calif. State U., Fullerton, 1960-67. Cert. secondary sch. tchr., Calif. Supr. phys. edn. Fullerton Schs., 1948-51; city historian City of La Habra, Calif., 1965—; v.p. cmty. rels. Alpha Beta Co., La Habra, 1979-86, dir. consumer affairs, 1973-79; author, historian Orange County, Calif., 1965—. Mem. Orange County Hist. Commn., Santa Ana, Calif., 1973—; commr. USDA Meat and Poultry Inspection Bd., Washington, 1982-84; v.p. Orange County Centennial, Santa Ana, 1987-89. Author: La Habra, The Pass Through the Hills, 1970, The Alpha Beta Story, 1973, Brea, The City of Oil, Oranges and Opportunity, 1992, A Bell in the Barranca, 1996; editor: A Hundred Years of Yesterdays, 1989, 2d edit., 2003, Early Business History of Orange County, 1992, others; oral histories in collection at Calif. State U., Fullerton. Adv. bd. Orange County coun. Boys and Girls Club, 1978—, past pres.; adv. bd. La Habra Children's Mus., 1980—, La Habra Boys and Girls Clubs, 1987—, past pres. Recipient Donald Pfleuger award Hist. Soc. So. Calif., 1992, Outstanding Author award U. Calif., Irvine, 1970, Outstanding Contbn. award Orange County Hist. Conf., 1999, Women Helping Women award Brea/La Habra Soroptimists, 2000, Cmty. Svc. award Calif. State U. History Alumni, 2002; named to Hall of Fame, So. Calif. Grocers, 1985, Fullerton Union H.S. Wall of Fame, 1994, Citizen of Yr., City of La Habra, 1978, Cmty. Grand Marshal, La Habra Corn Festival Parade, 2000, Women and Youth award Boys & Girls Clubs, LaHabra/Brea, 2003. Mem. Orange County Hist. Soc. (pres. 1971-72), Orange County Pioneer Coun. (pres. 1993-94), La Habra Old Settlers Hist. Soc. (historian 1973—), Mortar Board, Phi Beta Kappa. Republican. Methodist. Avocations: writing, travel. Home: 600 Linden Ln La Habra CA 90631-3124

CRAMER, FRANK BROWN, engineering executive, combustion engineer, systems consultant; b. Long Beach, Calif., Aug. 29, 1921; s. Frank Brown and Clara Bell (Ritzenthaler) C.; m. Hendrika Van der Hulst, 1948 (div. 1962); children: Frieda Hendrika, Eric Gustav, Lisa Monica, Christina Elena; m. Paula Gil, Aug. 3, 1973; children: Alfred Alexander, Consuelo F., Peter M. BA, U. So. Calif., 1942, postgrad., 1942-43, 46-51. Rsch. fellow U. So. Calif., L.A., 1946-51; supr. engring. Rocketdyne, Canoga Park, Calif., 1953-63; pres. Multi-Tech, Inc., San Fernando, Calif., 1960-69; systems cons. Electro-Optical Systems, Pasadena, Calif., 1969-70, McDonnell-Douglas Astronautic, Huntington Beach, Calif., 1971-72; pres. Ergs Unltd. Inc., Mission Hills, Calif., 1973-89, Acquisition, Mission Hills, 1988—, sr. prin. in applied tech. assoc., 1999—; sr. prin. Assocs. for Technology Advancement, 2000—. Instr. engring. stats. U. So. Calif., L.A., 1955-57, sys. cons. dept. medicine, 1959-68; sys. cons. Jet Propulsion Lab., Pasadena, 1964-68; mem. coun. Realtors Coun. Comml. and Investment Brokers. Author: Statistics for Medical Students, 1951, Combustion Processes/Liquid Rocket Engring., 1968; contbr. articles to profl. jours.; patentee in field. Committeeman Libertarian Party, San Fernando Valley, Calif., 1966, Rep. Party, Mission Hills, 1967-68; dir. realtor's com. on the air quality mgmt. plan So. Calif. Air Quality Control Dist., treas. realtor com. for air quality, 1994-95, vice chmn., 1996; pres. San Fernando Rep. Club, 1967-68; dir., mem. exec. com. Los Angeles County Bd. Realtors. Office: Acquisition 14800 Alexander St Mission Hills CA 91345-1210 *We, the children of the universe - glorify this relationship.To the laws of nature and the universe - we are accountable.Let us earn our bread each day.Let us admit to our ignorance - that we may learn.Let us hide, neither from ignorance nor accountability - that we may survive.*

CRAMER, GAIL LATIMER, economist; b. Walla Walla, Wash., Sept. 27, 1941; s. Lawrence Theodore and Myrtle Pauline (Latimer) C.; m. Marilyn Jean Karlenberg, Aug. 31, 1963; children: Karilee, Bruce. BS, Wash. State U., 1963; MS, Mich. State U., 1964; PhD, Oreg. State U., 1968. Asst. prof. Mont. State U., Bozeman, 1967-72, assoc. prof., 1972-76, prof., 1976-86; L.C. Carter prof. U. Ark., Fayetteville, 1987-2000; prof., dept. head La. State U., 2000—. Vis. prof. Harvard U., Cambridge, 1974-75, Winrock Internat., Morrilton, Ark., 1980-81, U. Calif. Berkeley, 1993, Ohio State U., Columbus, 1994; bd. dirs. Internat. Agrl. Mgmt. Assn. Co-author: Grain Marketing, 1993, Agricultural, Economics and Agribusiness, 1997; editor Am. Agrl. Econs. Assn. Jour., 1999-2002. Bd. dirs. ARC, Bozeman, 1982-83, Bozeman Kiwanis Club, 1972-86 (Disting. Pres. 1983); mem. White House Agrl. commn. Washington. Recipient E.G. Nourse award, Am. Inst. Coop., Washington, 1968, Communication award, Am. Agrl. Econs. Assn., 1980, Rice Rsch. award, Tech. Workers, Little Rock, 1992, 1998, SAEA Lifetime Achievement award, 2002. Fellow: IAMA; mem.: Nat. Assn. Agrl. Econ. Administrators (v.p. 2003—). Avocations: basketball, running, writing. Office: La State U Dept Agrl Econs Baton Rouge LA 70808 Home: 13735 Clarendon Dr Baton Rouge LA 70810-3584 E-mail: gcramer@agcenter.lsu.edu.

CRAMER, H. R. financial officer; CFO, Mobil Oil Corp., Fairfax, Va., until 2000. Office: Mobil Oil Corp 3225 Gallows Rd Fairfax VA 22037-0002

CRAMER, HAROLD, lawyer; b. Phila., June 16, 1927; s. Aaron Harry and Blanche (Greenberg) C.; m. Geraldine Hassuk, July 14, 1957; 1 dau., Patricia Gail. AB, Temple U., 1948; JD cum laude, U. Pa., 1951. Bar: Pa. 1951. Law clk. to judge Common Pleas Ct. No. 2, 1953; mem. law faculty U. Pa., 1954; assoc. firm Shapiro, Rosenfeld, Stalberg & Cook, 1955-56, ptnr., 1956-67, Mesirov, Gelman, Jaffe & Levin, 1967-74, Mesirov, Gelman, Jaffe & Cramer, Phila., 1974-77, Mesirov, Gelman, Jaffe, Cramer & Jamieson, Phila., 1977-89, of counsel, 1996-2000; ret. ptnr. Schnader, Harison Segal & Lewis, 2000—; CEO Grad. Health System, Phila., 1989-96. Instr. Nat. Inst. Trial Advocacy, 1970-78; pres. Jewish Exponent, 1987-89, Times., 1987-89. Co-author: Trial Advocacy, 1968; contbr. articles to profl. jours. Chmn. bd. Eastern Pa. Psychiat. Hosp., 1974-81, Grad. Hosp., 1975-91; trustee Fedn. Jewish Agys., Jewish Publ. Soc., pres., 1996-98, chmn., 1998-2001. 1st lt. U.S. Army, 1951-53. Decorated Bronze Star. Fellow Am. Bar Found.; mem. ABA, Am. Law Inst., Pa. Bar Assn. (ho. of dels. 1966-75, 78—, bd. govs. 1975-78), Phila. Bar Found. (pres. 1988, trustee, pres. elect), Phila. Bar Assn. (bd. govs. 1967-69, chmn. 1969, vice chancellor 1970, chancellor 1972, editor The Shingle 1970-72), U. Pa. Law Alumni Soc. (bd. mgrs. 1959-64, pres. 1968-70), Order of Coif (past chpt. pres., nat. exec. com. 1973-76), Tau Epsilon Rho (chancellor Phila. grad. chpt. 1960-62), Philmont Country Club, Pyramid Club, Greate Bay Golf Club. Home: 728 Pine St Philadelphia PA 19106-4005 Office: Schnader Harrison Segal & Lewis 1600 Market St Ste # 34 Philadelphia PA 19103-7501 E-mail: hcramer@schnader.com.

CRAMER, HARVEY M. cytopathologist; b. L.A., June 28, 1954; MD, U. Man., 1980. Diplomate Am. Bd. Pathology with subspecialty in cytopathology. Clin. asst. prof. pathology U. Western Ont., London, Can., 1987-91; assoc. prof. pathology Ind. U. Sch. Medicine, Indpls., 1991—. Contbr. articles to profl. jours. Mem. Am. Soc. Cytopathology, Am. Soc. Clin. Pathologists, U.S. Acad. Pathologists, Papanicolaou Soc. of Cytopathology. Office: Wishard Meml Hosp 1001 W 10th St Indianapolis IN 46202-2879 E-mail: hcramer@iupui.edu.

CRAMER, HOWARD ROSS, geologist, environmental consultant; b. Chgo., Sept. 17, 1925; s. Don William and Esther Natalia (Johnson) C.; m. Ardis V. Lahann, Dec. 15, 1950 (dec. 1980); m. Themis Poulos, Dec. 5, 1982 BS (with honors), U. Ill., 1949, MS, 1950; PhD, Northwestern U., 1954. Registered geologist, Ga. Mem. faculty Franklin and Marshall Coll., 1953-58; asst. prof. geology Emory U., Atlanta, 1958-62, assoc. prof., 1962-76, prof., 1976-87, chmn. dept., 1981-87; cons. geology Ga. State U., Atlanta, 1988-91. Chmn. Ga. Bd. Registration Geologists, 1977-79; mem. Ga. Natural Areas Council, 1968-72. Contbr. articles to sci. jours., chpts. to books on geology. Served with AUS, 1943-46, to lt. USAR, 1948-53. Decorated Bronze Star; recipient Holgate prize Northwestern U., 1953, Cert. Commendation, Am. Assn. State and Local History, 1974, Honor award Am. Fedn. Mineralogy and Lapidary Socs., 1986. Fellow Geol. Soc. Am.; mem. Am. Assn. Petroleum Geologists, Nat. Assn. Geology Tchrs. (pres. Southeastern sect. 1971-73), Ga. Acad. Sci. (pres. 1964-65), Lambda Chi Alpha. Lodges: Ahepa. Greek Orthodox. Home: 2047 Deborah Dr NE Atlanta GA 30345-3917 E-mail: hcramer@emory.edu.

CRAMER, JAMES PERRY, management consultant, architectural firm executive, educator; b. Aberdeen, S.D., Aug. 7, 1947; s. Harry John and Carol B. (Bickel) C.; m. Corinne M. Aaker, Dec. 21, 1969; children: Ryan James, Austin Michael. BS, No. State U., Aberdeen, 1969; MA, St. Thomas U., St. Paul, 1974; planning cert., U. Minn., Mpls., 1976; bus. mgmt. cert., Wharton Sch. Bus., U. Pa., 1987. Dir., teaching faculty U. Minn., Mpls., 1974-76; dir. St. Louis Park Community Svcs., Minn., 1976-78; exec. v.p. Minn. Soc. Architects, Mpls., 1978-82; pres., chief exec. officer AIA Svc. Corp., Washington, 1982-86, also bd. regents; pres. Greenway Comms. Inc., 1994—. Pres. Am. Archtl. Found. and Octagon Mus., Washington, 1986-89; CEO AIA, Washington, 1989-94; group pub. Architecture Mag., 1982-88, pub. chmn., 1990-94; with Archtl. Tech. Mag., 1983-89; chmn. The Greenway Group; pres. Greenway Comm. Inc., 1994—; adj. prof. U. Hawaii Sch. Arch., 1999—. Pres. Coun. Archtl. Components, Washington, 1980-81; pres. Greenway Civic Assn., McLean, Va., 1986-88; trustee Nat. Bldg. Mus., Washington, 1989-94; chmn. Washington div. United Way Assn., 1992; White House liaison, 1988-95. Recipient Disting. Alumnus award No. State U., 1992, medal of Distinction, U. Minn., 1994; Richard Upjohn fellow. Mem. AIA (hon.; chmn. 1981-82, CEO 1989—, Spl. award 1982), Am. Soc. Assn. Execs. (cert. assn. exec.), Mag. Pubs. Am., Octagon Soc. (life hon.), Am. Archtl. Found. (life; pres. 1986-89, regent 1981-82, 86—), Am. Design Coun. (founder, bd. dirs. 1988-95), Soc. Archtl. Historians (bd. dirs. 1994-97), Design Futures Coun. (chmn. 1994—). Avocations: gardening, tennis, antiquarian books, design. Home: 2320 Littlebrooke Dr Dunwoody GA 30338-3156 Office: 30 Technology Pkwy S Ste 200 Norcross GA 30092-2925

CRAMER, JANET FRENCH, social worker, marriage and family therapist; b. Balt., Oct. 10, 1935; d. Robert Bruce and Helen (French) Thompson; m. John Austin Knauth, June 8, 1957 (div. Sept. 1987); children: Jennifer Elizabeth Lord, Alison Lara Mott, Marianna Mott Newirth; m. Alfred Anthony Cramer, June 18, 1888. AB, Bryn Mawr Coll., 1957; MS, Columbia U., 1988. Lic. ind. clin. social worker, Vt., Mass. Supr., case mgr. Franklin County Home Care Corp., Turners Falls, Mass., 1988-89, social worker in adult family care program, 1989-92; social worker White River Junction (Vt.) VA Med. Ctr., 1992-99; marriage and family therapist Cramer Family Therapy, Brattleboro, Vt., 1989—. Mem. adv. bd., adj. prof., field instr. U. New Eng. Sch. Social Work, Biddeford, Maine, 1998-99; adj. prof., field instr. Smith Coll. Sch. Social Work, Northampton, Mass., 1995-97. Chmn. bd. dirs. Coun. on Aging for S.E. Vt., 2000—02, sec., 2002—; trustee Marlboro Coll., 1983—2000; bd. dirs. S.E. Vt. Area Health Edn. Coun., 2001, v.p., 2002—; pres. Hotline for Help, Brattleboro, 1990—92; mem. Vt. Dept. Aging and Disabilities Adv. Bd., 2001—; clk. Marlboro Meetinghouse, 1996—99. Mem.: LWV, NASW, Am. Soc. Aging, Am. Assn. for Marriage and Family Therapy. Democrat. Episcopalian. Avocations: reading, handwork, gardening. Home: 47 Morningside Commons Brattleboro VT 05301-0116 Office: Cramer Family Therapy 14 Park Pl Ste 3 Brattleboro VT 05301-6796

CRAMER, JEFFREY ALLEN, lawyer; b. Kansas City, Mo., Mar. 16, 1951; s. Robert Donald and Betty Jane (Leventhal) C.; m. Melinda Gail Segal, Nov. 18, 1993. BA, Vanderbilt U., 1972; JD, U. Fla., 1974. Bar: Fla. 1975, U.S. Dist. Ct. (no. dist.) 1975, U.S. Dist. Ct. (so. dist.) Fla. 1980, U.S. Dist. Ct. (mid. dist.) Fla. 1981, U.S. Ct. Appeals (5th cir.) 1975, U.S. Ct. Appeals (11th cir.) 1981. Assoc. Levin, Warfield, Middlebrooks, Graff, Mabie & Rosenbloum, Pensacola, Fla., 1975-76; mem. Carlton, Fields, Ward, Emmanuel, Smith & Cutler, Pensacola and Tampa, Fla., 1976-84; prin. Law Offices of Jeffrey A. Cramer, P.A., Pensacola, 1984-93; pvt. practice The Cramer Law Firm, Jacksonville, Fla., 1993—. Mem. Leadership Pensacola, 1985-86; pres. Five Flags Sertoma, Pensacola, 1985-86; dist. gov., Gulf Coast Dist. Sertoma Internat., 1986-87; bd. dirs. Speech-Hearing Bd. Bapt. Health Care Found., Pensacola, 1987, Etz Chaim Synagogue, 2002-. Mem. Fla. Bar Assn., Am. Bd. Trial Advocates (N.W. Fla. chpt. sec. 1990, v.p. 1991, pres. 1992, nat. bd. dirs. 1993-94), Escambia-Santa Rosa Bar Assn. (treas. 1988-89, v.p. 1989-90, pres.1990-91), Fla. Bar (cert. civil trial lawyer, workers' compensation lawyer, cir. ct. mediator). Office: 1 Independent Dr Ste 3300 Jacksonville FL 32202-5027 E-mail: cramerlf@bellsouth.net.

CRAMER, JOHN MCNAIGHT, lawyer; b. Lewistown, Pa., Sept. 23, 1941; s. John Mumma and Elaine Elizabeth (McNaight) C.; m. Susan Oakman, Nov. 26, 1966 (div. Mar. 1989); children: Natalie, Daniel, Melinda; m. Kay Stephenson, Apr. 8, 1989; children: Julia, Maria. AB, Juniata Coll., 1963; LLB, Harvard Law Sch., 1966. Bar: Pa. 1968. Law clk. U.S. Dist. Ct. So. Dist. N.Y., 1966-67; assoc. Reed Smith Shaw & McClay, Pitts., 1967-76, ptnr., 1976—2002, of counsel, 2002—. Advocacy fellow Dickinson Sch. Law, Pa. State U., Carlisle, Pa., 1987-2002. Mem. editl. staff: Harvard Law Rev. Trustee Juniata Coll., Huntingdon, Pa., 1981—, sec., 1983—96, vice chair, 1996—97, chair, 1997—2001; bd. dirs. Ctrl. Pa. Food Bank, 1996—2001. Mem. ABA, Cumberland County Bar Assn. Democrat. Home: Box 17 Old Trail Rd New Buffalo PA 17069 E-mail: crmfrm@aol.com.

CRAMER, JOHN SCOTT, retired banker; b. Charlotte, N.C., Dec. 10, 1930; s. Stuart Warren Jr. and Julia (Scott) C.; m. Nancy Arnott, Aug. 9, 1952; children: Julia Baxter Smith, Alice Arnott Tolson. AB, U. N.C., 1953. With Wachovia Bank & Trust Co., Charlotte, 1955—, asst. v.p., 1958-61, v.p., 1961-64, sr. v.p., bd. mgrs., 1964-71, exec. v.p., head banking div. Winston-Salem, N.C., 1971-74, vice chmn. bd., head fiduciary divsn., 1974-88, also bd. dirs., ret., 1989; vice chmn. bd., bd. dir. The Wachovia Corp., ret., 1989; exec. v.p. First Wachovia Corp., 1986, ret., 1989; pres. First Wachovia Trust Svcs., Inc., 1987-89, ret., 1989; dir. Linville Resorts, Inc. Former trustee N. C. Sch. of the Arts; trustee Salem Acad. and Coll., N.C. chpt. Nature Conservancy; active other civic, edn. and svc. orgns. 1st lt. USAF, 1953—55. Mem. Linville Golf Club (N.C.), Old Town Club, Twin City Club, Sigma Alpha Epsilon. Home: 16 Graylyn Pl Winston Salem NC 27106 Office: 420 A-2 West 4th St Winston Salem NC 27101

CRAMER, KATHRYN ELIZABETH, editor, writer; b. Bloomington, Ind., Apr. 16, 1962; d. John Gleason and Pauline Ruth (Bond) Cramer; m. David Geddes Hartwell, Mar. 29, 1997; children: Peter Henry Cramer Hartwell, Elizabeth Constance Cramer Hartwell. BA in Math., Columbia U., 1987, MLS in Am. Studies, 1992. Writing instr. Harvard U. Summer Sch., Cambridge, Mass., 1989—93; hypertext fiction editor Eastgate Systems, Watertown, Mass., 1993—94. Author: Walls of Fear; editor: (hypertext novel) In Small & Large Pieces, 1994, The New York Review of Science Fiction; co-editor (with David Hartwell): Year's Best Fantasy, 1999, Year's Best SF, 2000—, The Hard Science Fiction Renaissance, 2003; co-editor: (with Peter Pautz) The Architecture of Fear (World Fantasy award, 1988); co-editor: (with David Hartwell) The Ascent of Wonder, 1994; mem. editl. bd. The Little Mag.

CRAMER, KENNETH LEE, protective services official, consultant; b. Muskegon, Mich., Jan. 13, 1939; s. Ellsworth Leroy Cramer and Anna Elizabeth Walters; m. Judy Wilson Cramer, June 6, 1959; children: Craig Steven, Christine Suzanne Cramer Fisher. AS, St. Petersburg (Fla.) Coll., 1980; cert., Havard U., 1989, Nat. Fire Acad., Emmitsburg, Md., 1988. Cert. firefighter, fire officer, fire insp., vocat. edn. tchr. Printer Niles (Mich.) Daily Star, 1957-64; printer, foreman Elkhart (Ind.) Truth, 1964-66; printer Tampa Tribune, 1966-72; vol. firefighter, lt. Seminole Park Vol. Fire Dept., Largo, Fla., 1966-68; firefighter Pinellas Park (Fla.) Vol. Fire Dept., 1968-74; firefighter, lt. dep. fire chief Largo Fire Dept., 1972-78; fire chief City of Pinellas Park, 1978—. Cons. JTS & Assocs., Bradenton, Fla., 1993—; co-owner Cramer's Crafts. Contbr. articles to profl. jours. Mem. adv. bd. St. Petersburg Jr. Coll., 1980—2000, chmn. adv. bd., 2000—; mem. adv. bd. Pinellas Tech. Edn. Ctr., Fla., 1980—2000; bd. trustees Met. Gen. Hosp., 1996—2000. Named Outstanding Vet. Firefighter, City of Largo, 1974. Mem.: Fla. Fire Chiefs Assn., Internat. Assn. Fire Chiefs, Nat. Fire Protection Assn., Pinellas County Fire Chief Assn. (pres. 5 terms), Kiwanis. Address: PO Box 1100 Pinellas Park FL 33780-1100 Office: City of Pinellas Park Fire Dept 5095 93d Ave N Pinellas Park FL 33782 E-mail: ken-fire@ij.net.

CRAMER, MARK CLIFTON, lawyer; b. St. Petersburg, Fla., July 20, 1954; s. WIlliam Cato and Alice J. Cramer; m. Carol Blankenship, Aug. 6, 1977; children: Ryan Albert, Philip Rogers. BA, U. N.C., 1976; JD, U. Va., 1979. Bar: D.C., 1979, Fla. 1982, N.C. 1986. Assoc. Cramer & Lipsen, 1979-80; ptnr. Cramer & Cramer, 1980-81; dir. congl. rels. U.S. Govt. Printing Office, Washington, 1981, dep. gen counsel, 1981-83; gen. counsel, 1983-85; vice pres., gen. counsel Blankenship-Cramer Devel. Corp., Charlotte, NC, 1985—; legis. cons. N.C. Drug Cabinet, 1990; pvt. practice, 1991—. Sec. N.C. Global TransPark Authority, 1991-03; vice pres. Found. for Transp. Trade and Commerce, 1998-03, v.p. Counsel Inst. for Defense and Bus., 2003—; exec. dir. Real Estate and Bldg. Industry Coalition, 1995—; program counsel Ctr. of Excellence in Logistics and Tech., 2000 03; asso. dir. Ctr. of Excellence in Logistics and Tech., 2003—, sec. Ctr. for Air Commerce Studies, 2001-02, sec., treas. Piedmont Pub. Policy Inst., 2003—. Editor: Legislative Histories of the Laws Affecting the U.S. Govt. Printing Office as Codified in Title 44 of the U.S. Code. Liaison mem. Adminstrv. Conf. U.S., 1984-85; mem. Mecklenburg County Zoning Bd. of Adjustment, 1986-92, chair, 1991-92; commr. N.C. Gen Statutes Commn., 1988-93; mem. East Mecklenburg Planning Dist., 1989, Charlotte Mecklenburg Consolidation Charter Study Commn., 1990, Mecklenburg County Redistricting Com., 1991; Transp. Commn. of 100, 1994; Charlotte Mecklenburg Citizens Transit Advisory Group, 1999-2003; Surface Water Improvement & Mgmt. Task Force, 1997-99; Charlotte Mecklenburg Smart Growth Task Force, 1999-2001; vice chmn. Mecklenburg County Reps., 1989-93; founder, moderator Rep issues Forum; co-chmn. Mecklenburg County Com. to re-elect Gov. Jim Martin, 1988; elector U.S. Presdl. Electoral Coll., 1992. Recipient Pub. Printer's Gold medal for disting. svc., U.S. Govt. Printing Office, Long Leaf Pine award Gov. State of N.C. Mem. N.C. Bar Assn. Mecklenburg County Bar Assn., Urban Land Inst., N.C. Citizens for Bus. and Industry, Phi Beta Kappa, Sigma Nu (recipient Sr. Scholarship award 1976). E-mail: cramer@usa.com.

CRAMER, MICHAEL WILLIAM, insurance executive; b. London, Feb. 14, 1924; came to U.S., 1939; s. William and Belle (Klauber) C.; m. Martha Lorena Deckman, Jan. 20, 1951; 1 child, Bruce Edward. BSBA, Washington U., St. Louis, 1947. CLU. Clk., group claims Gen. Am. Life Ins. Co., St. Louis, 1947-51; inventory control clk. Fred Campbell Auto Supply Co., St. Louis, 1951-55; sales and planning rep. AXA Advisors LLC, St. Louis, 1955—. Active St. Louis Artists Guild, 1990; pres. Permanent Endowment Found., 1991-94, chmn. spl. funds com., 1994-99, pres. council 1995-98; bd. dirs. City of University City (Mo.) C. of C., 1994-99. Recipient Disting. award of merit for Keystone Dist., Greater St. Louis coun. Boy Scouts Am., 1996, 65 Yr. Vets. award, Nat. Office Boy Scouts Am., 2002. Mem. Nat. Assn. Ins. and Fin. Advisors (St. Louis chpt.), Life Underwriters Assn. St. Louis (bd. dirs. 1972-78, award 1987, nominee Life Underwriter of Yr. 1994), Estate Planning Coun. St. Louis, Assn. CLU and ChFC (bd. dirs. St. Louis chpt., chmn. student sponsorship com. through 1993, Meritorious Svc. award 1993), Soc. Fin. Svc. Profls. (Greater St. Louis chpt.), IW Club Varsity Athletics Alumni Washington

U. (mem. exec. com. 1991—). Avocations: travel, hiking, music, stamps, photography. Home: 8600 Delmar Blvd Apt 8H Saint Louis MO 63124-2206 Office: 8235 Forsyth Blvd Ste 800 Saint Louis MO 63105

CRAMER, OWEN CARVER, classics educator; b. Tampa, Fla., Dec. 1, 1941; s. Maurice Browning and Alice (Carver) C.; m. Rebecca Jane Lowrey, June 23, 1962; children: Alfred, Thomas, Ethan, Benjamin AB, Oberlin Coll., 1962; PhD, U. Tex., 1973. Spl. instr. U. Tex., Austin, 1964-65; instr. in classics Colo. Coll., Colorado Springs, 1965-69, asst. prof. classics, 1969-75, assoc. prof. classics, 1975-84, M.C. Gile prof. classics, 1984—, dir. comparative lit., 1993—2002. Cons. humanist Colo. Humanities Program, Denver, 1982-83; vis. prof. U. Chgo., 1987-88; reader Advanced Placement Latin Exam., 1995-99. Editorial asst. Arion, 1964-65; contbr. papers, articles on Greek lang. and lit. to profl. publs., 1974— ; contbr. classical music revs. to Colorado Springs Sun, 1984-86. Chorus tenor Colo. Opera Festival, Colorado Springs, 1976-82; mem. El Paso County Dem. Ctrl. Com., Colo., 1968-88; ordained elder Presbyn. Ch., 1992; mem. alumni coun. Oberlin Coll., 1992-2002. Hon. Woodrow Wilson fellow, 1962; univ. fellow U. Tex., Austin, 1962-64 Mem. Am. Philol. Assn. (campus adv. svc. 1989, chmn. com. on smaller depts. 1979-80), Am. Comparative Lit. Assn., Classical Assn. Middle West and South, Modern Greek Studies Assn., Colo. Classics Assn., Round Table (Colorado Springs) Club,. Phi Beta Kappa. Home: 747 E Uintah St Colorado Springs CO 80903-2546 Office: Colo Coll Dept Classics Colorado Springs CO 80903 E-mail: ocramer@coloradocollege.edu.

CRAMER, PHEBE, psychologist; b. San Francisco, Dec. 30, 1935; children: Mara, Julia. BA, U. Calif., Berkeley, 1957; PhD, NYU, 1962. Clin. psychologist Malmonides Hosp., Bklyn., 1962-63; asst. prof. Psychology Barnard Coll., N.Y.C., 1963-65; vis. asst. prof. Psychology U. Calif., Berkeley, 1965-70; assoc. prof. Psychology Williams Coll., Williamstown, Mass., 1970-73, prof. Psychology, 1973—. Pvt. practice in clin. psychology, Williamstown, 1970—; chief psychologist Berkshire Mental Health Ctr., Pittsfield, Mass., 1978-86. Author: (books) Word Association, 1968, Understanding Intellectual Development, 1972, The Development of Defense Mechanisms, 1991, Story-telling, Narrative, and the Thematic Apperception Test, 1996; mem. editl. bd. Jour. of Personality, 1987-96, assoc. editor, 1991-96; mem. editl. bd. Jour. of Personality Assessment, 1989—, European Jour. Personality, 2000—, Jour. Rsch. Personality, 2003—. Judge U.S. Figure Skating Assn., 1989—. Mem.: APA, Soc. Personality and Social Psychology, Soc. for Personality Assessment. Office: Williams Coll Dept Psychology Bronfman Sci Ctr Williamstown MA 01267 Home: 20 Forest Rd Williamstown MA 01267-2029 E-mail: phebe.cramer@williams.edu.

CRAMER, RICHARD CHARLES, artist, educator; b. Appleton, Wis., Aug. 14, 1932; s. Joseph S. and Mildred (Kuck) C.; m. Carol Markel, Apr. 4, 1970. B.F.A., Layton Sch. Art, 1954; BS, U. Wis.-Milw., 1960; MS, U. Wis., Madison, 1961, M.F.A., 1962. Art instr. U.S. Army Spl. Services, Ft. Huachuca, Ariz., 1955-57; grad. instr. U. Wis., Madison, 1960-62; asst. prof. art Elmira Coll., N.Y., 1962-66; prof. painting Tyler Sch. Art, Temple U., Phila., 1966—. Vis. artist SUNY-Oswego, 1982, U. Wis.-Milw., 1982, Washington U., St. Louis, 1986, U. N.Mex., Albuquerque, 1989. One-man shows Arnot Art Mus., Elmira, N.Y., 1964, Pa. Acad. Fine Arts, Ohila., 1978, New Gallery Contemporary Art, Cleve., 1980, Eric Makler Gallery, Phila., 1981, GHJ, N.Y.C., 1983, Space 504 N.Y.C., 1997, Caelum Gallery, N.Y.C., 2000; exhibited in group shows Contemporary Drawings, Phila. Mus. Art, 1979, Smithsonian, Inst. traveling exhibit, 1979, Phila. Coll. Art, 1980, Inst. Contemporary Art, Boston, 1981, Cranbrook Acad. Art Mus., 1981, Louis Meisel Gallery, N.Y.C., 1985, Steinbaum Krauss Gallery, N.Y.C., 1994, Glasgow (Scotland) Sch. Art, 1995. Recipient prize Munson-Williams Proctor Inst., 1965. Mem. AAUP, Coll. Art Assn.

CRAMER, ROBERT E., JR., (BUD CRAMER), congressman; b. Huntsville, Ala., Aug. 22, 1947; BA, U. Ala., 1969, JD, 1972. Former dist. atty. Madison County, Ala., 1981—91; mem. U.S. Congress from 5th Ala. dist., 1991—. Mem. appropriations com. U.S. Ho. of Reps., subcom. on HUD, VA and IA, on the Interior, NASA. Served in U.S. Army, 1972, served in USAR, 1976—78. Democrat. Methodist. Office: US House of Reps 2367 Rayburn Ho Office Bldg Washington DC 20515-0105*

CRAMER, ROBERT VERN, retired college administrator, consultant; b. Fayetteville, Ark., Jan. 6, 1933; s. Paul and Fern (Way); m. M. Joan Sullivan, Sept. 6, 1953; children: Paula Jo, Melinda Kay, John Aaron. BA, Monmouth Coll., Ill., 1954; MA, U. Conn., 1964, PhD, 1965; LHD (hon.), Ill. Coll., 1985, Carroll Coll., 1988. Tchr. Monmouth Jr. H.S., 1954-56; prin. Vandalia Elem. Sch., Ill., 1956-57; dir. publicity and publs. Monmouth Coll., 1957-59; dir. publs. and pub. info., also instr. journalism Millikin U., Decatur, Ill., 1959-61; v.p. Old Sturbridge Village, Mass., 1961-64; asst. dean, instr. Sch. Edn., U. Conn., 1964-65; v.p. Hanover Coll., Ind., 1965-68; pres. Northland Coll., Ashland, Wis., 1968-71, Carroll Coll., Waukesha, Wis., 1971-88, pres. emeritus, 1988—. Pres. Brunswick Pub. Charitable Found., Inc., Skokie, Ill., 1985-88; v.p. Wis. Found. Ind. Colls., 1969-71, pres., 1971-73, treas., 1973-76, sec., 1979-83; commr. Commn. Instns. Higher Edn., North Central Assn., 1972-76; v.p. Wis. Assn. Ind. Colls. and Univs., 1973-75, pres., 1985-87; bd. dirs. Payco Am. Corp., 1988-91; Council Ind. Colls, sec. 1979-81, vice chmn., 1981-83, chmn. 1983-85. Contbr. articles to profl. jours. Bd. dirs. Waukesha United Way, 1975-78, Waukesha Symphony, 1972-76, Waukesha Meml. Hosp., 1973-82, Lad Lake Residential Treatment Ctr. for Emotionally Disturbed Boys, 1974-78, Wis. Coun. on Econ. Edn., 1976-79; bd. dirs. Milw. chpt. ARC, 1973-81, vice chmn., 1978-80; mem. nexus com. Presbyn. Coll. Union, 1973-83; bd. dirs. Am. Coun. Edn., 1985-88; sec. Presbyn. Coll. Union, 1977-79, pres., 1979-81; trustee Columbia Coll. of Nursing, 1983-88, Hist. Preservation Soc. Durham, 1993-94; active Durham County Nursing Home Adv. Com., 1991-95, commr. Durham Hist. Preservation Com., 1992-97, Glaxo Welcome Instnl. Animal Care and Use Com., 1992-99. Recipient Outstanding Young Alumnus award Monmouth Coll., 1968, Disting. Alumnus award, 1980; named Ky. Col., 1975. Mem. Wis. Assn. Higher Edn. (exec. com., sec. 1972-73, pres. 1973-74), Delta Sigma Nu, Phi Delta Kappa, Theta Chi. E-mail: rvc-mjc@webtv.net.

CRAMER, STANLEY HOWARD, psychology educator, author; b. NYC, Oct. 1, 1933; s. Louis and Sophie (Zimmerman) C.; m. Rosalind Faber, Nov. 26, 1959; children: Elizabeth, Lauren, Matthew. BA, U. Mass., 1955; MA, SUNY, Albany, 1957; EdD, Columbia U., 1963. Prof. counseling psychology SUNY at Buffalo, Amherst, 1965-2000. Author: (with E.L. Herr) Critical Issues in the Helping Professions, 1987, Career Guidance and Counseling Through the Lifespan, 1972, 5th edit., 1996, (with J.C. Hansen and R.H. Rossberg) Counseling: Theory and Process, 1994. Home: 1676 Starling Dr Sarasota FL 34231

CRAMER, WILLIAM ANTHONY, biochemistry and biophysics researcher, educator; b. N.Y.C., June 11, 1938; s. Robert and Sylvia (Blumstein) C.; m. Hanni Aebersold, Sept. 11, 1964; children: Rebecca, Jean-Marc, Gabrielle, Nicholas. BS, MIT, 1959; MS, U. Chgo., 1960, PhD, 1965. NSF post doctoral fellow U. Calif., San Diego, 1965-67, rsch. assoc., 1967-68; asst. prof. dept. biol. scis. Purdue U., West Lafayette, Ind., 1968-73, assoc. prof., 1973-78, prof., 1978—, assoc. head dept., 1984-86, Henry Koffler prof. biol. scis., 1995-2001, Henry Koffler Disting. prof. biol. scis., 2001—. Head panel predoctoral fellowships in biophysics and biochemistry NSF, 1979, mem. molecular biology panel, 1980-82, mem. cellular biochemistry panel, 1989-91; mem. panel competitive grants USDA, 1983-84; chmn. Gordon Confs. on Photosynthesis, 1990, Bioenergetics, 2001; mem. phys. biochemistry study sect. NIH, 1991-95. Author textbook on bioenergetics; editor: Archives Biochemistry and Biophysics, 1979—91, Biochem. Biophys. Acta, 1983—2003, Photosynthesis Rsch., 1989—98, Jour. Bioenergetics Biomembranes, 1991—, Biophys. Jour., 1999—, Biochem. Jour., 2001—, Jour. Biol. Chemistry, 2002—; Bioenergetics sect. of Biophysics Textbook on-line (Biophysical Soc.), —; contbr. articles to profl. jours.; co-editor: Biophysics Textbook. Recipient Rsch. Career Devel. award, NIH, 1970—75, H.N. McCoy award for sci. achievement, Purdue U., 1988, Charles F. Kettering award, Am. Soc. Plant Physiologists, 1996; sr. EMBO fellow, U. Amsterdam, 1974—75, Alexander von Humboldt fellow, Max-Planck Inst., Frankfurt, 1992, John Simon Guggenheim fellow, 1992—93. Mem.: Biophys. Soc. (chmn. bioenergetics subgroup 1989—92, organizing com. "Biophys. Discussions" 1992, program chair 40th ann. meeting 1996, coun. 1997—2001, exec. coun. 1999—2001, rep. Fedn. Am. Socs. Exptl. Biology com. ethical issues genetic rsch. 1998, pub. policy com. 1999—), Protein Soc., Am. Soc. Biol. Chemists. Office: Purdue U Dept Biol Sci Lilly Hall of Life Sciences West Lafayette IN 47907

CRAMES, RENEE KARAS, management consultant; b. N.Y.C., Nov. 21, 1934; d. Valentine Naftali, Irene Naftali; m. Donald Arthur Karas, Feb. 16, 1956 (div. Mar. 1986); children: Jon Michael Karas, Robin Ann Karas, Steven Brett Karas, James Edward Karas; m. Charles Franklin Crames, Jan. 6, 2001. BS, Simmons Coll., 1956; MS, Columbia U., 1976. Cert. psychoanalysis Postgrad. Ctr. N.Y.C., 1982. Psychoanalyst Postgrad. Ctr., N.Y.C., 1977—84, White Plains, NY, 1982—. Cons. Leadership Devel., White Plains, 1990—2001; pres. Winning At Work, White Plains, 1990—2000. Bd. mem. Bus. and Profl. Divsn. UJA, N.Y.C., 1982—90. Mem.: Fin. Womens Assn. Avocation: Avocations: gardening, competitive bridge. Home: 12 Westfield Rd White Plains NY 10605

CRAMOND, RICHARD, JR., structural and systems engineer, diversified aerospace company executive; b. Mpls., June 30, 1945; s. Richard Sr. and Emelia Hilma (Lundstrom) C.; m. Helen A McNelis, Feb. 28, 1987; 1 child, Lindsay M. AS, Long Beach (Calif.) City Coll., 1966; BSE cum laude, Calif. State U., Long Beach, 1968; MSCE, U. N.Mex., 1970; PhD in Structural Engring., U. Ill., 1974. Registered profl. civil engr., Calif. Naval architect Long Beach Naval Shipyard, 1968; research asst. E.H. Wang Civil Engring. Research Facility, Albuquerque, 1968-70, A. H-S Ang, Cons. Engr., Urbana, Ill., 1972-73; from mem. tech. staff to sr. project mgr. TRW Corp., Reston, Va., 1973—97, sr. project mgr. hardening tech., 1997—2002; project mgr. Nat. Launch System, 1992-93; sr. project mgr. Northrop Grummann Mission Systems, 2002—. Mem. U. Ill. Pres.'s Council. Mem. ASCE, AIAA (presenter conf. paper), Soc. Exptl. Stress Analysis (sec.-treas. 1969), Internat. Assn. for Structural Safety and Reliability, Internat. Coun. on Sys. Engring. (chpt. dir., pres.), Tau Beta Pi, Chi Epsilon, Phi Kappa Phi. Democrat. Roman Catholic. Avocations: hiking, fishing. Home: 3217 Latigo Ct Oakton VA 22124-2309 Office: Northrop Grumman Mission Systems 12011 Sunset Hills Rd Reston VA 20190

CRAMP, JOHN FRANKLIN, lawyer; b. Ridley Park, Pa., Mar. 14, 1923; s. Alfred Charles and Mildred Frances (Cummins) C.; m. Suzanne Surrick, Sept. 15, 1951 (div.); children: John F., Catherine T., David B., Andrew H., Daniel E.; m. Gloria C. Maddox, Jan. 29, 1972. BS, Pa. Mil. Coll. (now Widener U.), 1943; LLB, Dickinson Sch. Law, 1948. Bar: Pa. 1949, U.S. Dist. Ct. (ea. dist.) Pa. 1951, U.S. Ct. Appeals (3d cir.) 1951. Assoc. Hodge, Hodge & Balderston, Chester, Pa., 1949-53; sr. ptnr. Cramp, D'Iorio, McConchie & Forbes, P.C., Media, Pa., 1973—75, pres., 1975-90; founding counsel Beatty, Cramp, Kauffman & Lincke, 1996—. Gen. counsel, bd. dirs. Bryn Mawr Group (name now Dixon Ticonderoga Inc.), 1965-79, pres. 1973-74; gen. counsel Widener U., 1968-91; bd. dirs. Phila. Subtransp. Co. Trustee Williamson Sch., 1968-91; bd. dirs., chmn. Crozer Chester Med. Ctr.; Elwyn Inst.; bd. dirs. Chester Hosp., Crozer-Keystone Health System; chmn. bd. dirs. Am. Inst. Mental Studies, Jerusalem Elwyn, Can. Friends of Elwyn; Rep. county chmn., 1957-61; del. Rep. Nat. Conv., 1960; state chmn. Citizens for Scranton, 1962. Mem. ABA, Del. County Bar Assn., Pa. Bar Assn., Internat. Soc. Barristers, Nat. Assn. Coll. and Univ. Attys., Def. Rsch. Inst., Wildcat Run Country Club, Masons. Episcopalian. Office: 215 N Olive St Media PA 19063-2810

CRAMP, LORI ANGELL, finance executive; b. Kansas City, Mo., Apr. 17, 1955; d. William Greenleaf and Arline (Mullaney) Angell; m. John Stitzer, Aug. 13, 1977; children: Jeffrey William, Chelsea Angell, Trevor John. BA, Franklin & Marshall Coll., 1977; MBA, Harvard U., 1979. Mgmt. cons. Coopers & Lybrand Co., Washington, 1979-80, supr. mgmt. cons., 1980-81; supr. internal cons. Marriott Corp., Washington, 1981-82, mgr. internal cons., 1982-83, mgr. corp. fin., 1983-85, dir. corp. fin., 1985-86, v.p. corp. fin., 1987-89; v.p. project fin., 1990-92; sr. v.p. corp. and project fin. Coded Communications Corp., Carlsbad, Calif., 1994; sr. v.p., treas. Host Marriott Svcs. Corp., Bethesda, Md., 1995-99. Treas. Churchill Sq. Homeowners Assn., Falls Church, Va., 1983; treas. Painted Rock PTA, 1993-94; mem. Painted Rock Sch. Site Coun., 1992-94, dist. rep. sch. site coun., 1993-94, mem. dist. math. adv. bd. 1994-95; bd. dirs. Marriott Employees Fed. Credit Union, 1996-99; pres. adv. sch. bd. Our Lady of Mercy Sch., 2001—; bd dirs. office youth ministry Cath. Youth Orgn., Archdiocese Wash. Mem. Phi Beta Kappa, Pi Gamma Mu. Avocations: skiing, tennis, in-line skating.

CRAMPON, JEAN ELAINE, librarian; b. Richmond, Calif., Nov. 9, 1947; d. John Edward and Betty Jane (Shade) Poast; m. William Jacques Crampon, Aug. 5, 1972; 1 child, Michael William. BA, San Diego State U., 1969; MS in LS, U. N.C., 1971. Libr. San Diego Pub. Libr., 1972—73, So. Ill. U. Sch. Medicine, Springfield, 1974-87, instr., 1974-81, asst. prof., 1981-87; head libr. Hancock Libr. Biology and Oceanography, U. So. Calif., L.A., 1987-98, curator Hancock Meml. Mus., 1997-98, libr. Sci. Ctr. and Engring. Libr., 1998—. Contbr. articles to profl. jours., including Online, Database, Libr. Jour. Elder Presbyn. Ch. USA, Long Beach, Calif., 1994-98, deacon, 2002–. Recipient cert. of recognition Midwest Health Sci. Libr. Network, Chgo., 1981, 82. Mem. PEO, Spl. Librs. Assn. (editor, treas. biol. and life scis. divsn. 1983-98, sect. chmn. info. tech. divsn. 1998-99, v.p., pres., treas., exec. or adv. bds. So. Calif. chpt. 1993-95, 98-2001), Internat. Assn. Aquatic and Marine Sci. Librs. and Info. (resource sharing com. 1999-2001). Office: U So Calif Sci and Engring Libr University Park Los Angeles CA 90089-0481 Fax: 213-740-0558. E-mail: crampon@usc.edu.

CRAMPTON, GEORGE HARRIS, neuroscientist, retired army officer; b. Spokane, Wash., Nov. 20, 1926; s. George M. and Anne (Carmody) C.; m. Willene Ann Fellows, Apr. 6, 1947; children: William Andrew, Colleen Ann. BS, Wash. State U., 1949, MS, 1950; PhD, U. Rochester, 1954. Enlisted U.S. Army Res., 1944; advanced through grades to col. U.S. Army M.S.C., 1969; ret. U.S. Army, 1971; prof. Wright State U., Dayton, Ohio, 1971-86, prof. emeritus, 1987—. Recipient Legion of Merit. Mem. Soc. for Neurosci. Home: 790 SW Dawnview Ter Oak Harbor WA 98277-8145

CRAMPTON, REBEKAH JEAN, judge, educator; b. New Marlborough, Mass., Jan. 26, 1938; d. John and Marion Caroline (Jones) Somes; m. Harold W. Crampton Jr., July 9, 1966; children: Kate, Gregory, Stephen. BS cum laude, U. Mass., 1959; JD magna cum laude, Western New Eng. coll., 1978. adj. prof. Western New Eng. Coll. Sch. Law, Springfield, 1980-85; spl. asst. atty. gen. sect. lead poisoning prevention Dept. Pub. Health, Commonwealth of Mass., 1981-84. Tchr. Apponequet High Sch., East Freetown, 1959-61, 65-66; dean, tchr. Amrikan Kiz Koleji, Izmir, Turkey, 1961-65; tchr. West Springfield (Mass.) H.S., 1966-67; assoc. Walder & Pepyne, Greenfield, Mass., 1978-81; ptnr. Crampton, Dion & Johnston, PC, Springfield, 1979-86; assoc. justice Trial Ct. Juvenile Dept., Springfield, 1986—98, 2003—; first justice Hampden County (Mass.) Juvenile Ct., Mass., 1998—2003. Adj. prof. Western New Eng. Coll. Sch. law, Springfield, 1980-85; spl. asst. atty. gen. sect. lead poisoning prevention Dept. Pub. Health, Commonwealth Mass., 1981-84. Bd. dirs Springfield Mentoring Partnership, 1999—, Open Pantry Inc., Springfield, 1982-2002, CASA of Springfield, 1988-95 (Vol. appreciation award 1994), Hampden County Civil Liberties Union, Springfield, 1983-85, Cmty. United Way, 1995-2003, Mass. Judge's Conf., 1994-2003. Named Alumni of the Yr., Dept. Consumer Svcs., U. Mass., 1996; recipient Jud. Excellence award, Mass. Judge's Conf., 1999, Cmty. Svc. award, Child and Family Svcs., 1993, Appreciation award, Dispute Resolution Svcs., 1999, Exec. Com. award, Women and Criminal Justice Conf., 2002. Mem. ABA, Nat. Women Judges Assn. (regional dir. 1990-91), Hampden Young Lawyers Assn. (treas. 1981-82, asst. chmn. 1982-83, chmn. 1983-84), Mass. Bar Assn., Hampden Bar Assn. (exec. bd. 1983-84). Home: 215 Maynard Rd Wilbraham MA 01095-1212 Office: Hampden County Juvenile Ct 80 State St Springfield MA 01102-0559 E-mail: crampton_r@jud.state.ma.us.

CRANDALL, EARLE ELLSWORTH, neurosurgeon, educator; b. Chgo., Feb. 17, 1933; s. Theodore Anton and Jeanette Crandall; m. Arlette Louise Passy, Oct. 6, 1963; children: Phillip Reddington, Carolyn Janet, Marc Stephen. BS, U. Ill., Chgo., 1955, MS, MD, U. Ill., Chgo., 1956; PhD, U. Minn., 1967. Diplomate Am. Bd. Neurol. Surgery. Intern U. Ill. Hosps., 1956-57; neurosurgery fellow Mayo Found., 1957-62; chief of neurosurgery St. Vincent Med. Ctr., L.A., 1990—; mem. staff Cedars Sinai Med. Ctr., L.A., 1965—. Assoc. clin. prof. depts. neurosurgery and neurobiology UCLA Med. Sch. Bd. dirs. South Calif. Regional Organ Procurement Agy., U. So. Calif. Friends of Sch. Fin. Arts. Lt. comdr. USN, 1963-65, Vietnam. Spl. NIH Brain Rsch. fellow Coll. of France, Paris, 1962-63; recipient Nat. Rsch. award Am. Acad. Neurosurgery, 1964; named Officer Order of Acad. Palms, France. Office: 8920 Wilshire Blvd Ste 430 Beverly Hills CA 90211-2004

CRANDALL, ELIZABETH WALBERT, home economics educator; b. Columbus, Kans., Jan. 18, 1914; d. Stanley Giltner and Edna Maude (Daniel) Walbert; m. Robert Dalton Crandall, Aug. 3, 1946 (dec. Sept. 1999). BS, Kans. State Coll., 1935, MS, 1939; EdD, Boston U., 1962. Tchr. Cedar Point (Kans.) H.S., 1935-36, Ellsworth (Kans.) H.S., 1936-38; instr., asst. prof. home econs. Mich. State Coll., East Lansing, 1939-46; instr., asst. prof., assoc. prof. home econs. R.I. State Coll., Kingston, 1946-62; prof. home econs., dept. chair U. R.I., Kingston, 1962-73, acting dean, Coll. Home Econs., 1973-76, dean, Coll. Home Econs., 1976-77, prof. emerita, 1977—. Vice chair R.I. Consumer Adv. Com., Office Price Stabilization, Providence, 1952-53; mem. adv. com. R.I. Office Vocat. Rehab., Providence, 1962-64, Cmty. Homemaker Svcs. R.I., Inc., Providence, 1965-79; mem. various coms., U. R.I., 1961-77. Co-author (coll. textbooks): Home Management in Theory and Practice, 1946, Management for Modern Families, 1st edit., 1954, 2d edit., 1963, 3d edit., 1973, 4th edit., 1980. Mem. So. Poverty Law Ctr., Montgomery, Ala., 1974—, Equal Rights for Maine Coalition, Augusta, 1984; citizen lobbyist, Maine Women's Lobby and Women's Devel. Inst., Hallowell, 1989—; legis. chair Maine Home Econs. Assn., rep. Women's Legis. Agenda Coalition, Augusta, 1984-93, rep. Maine Choice Coalition, Augusta, 1990-93; mem. campaign com. for Hon. Sophia Pfeiffer's election to Maine Ho. of Reps., 1990; adv. com. Bath-Brunswick Child Care Svcs., Inc., 1994-95; various other civic activities. Recipient Presdl. award for courage, svc. and integity, Maine Lesbian/Gay Polit. Alliance, Augusta, 1987; recipient Maine Women's Hall of Fame award Maine Fedn. Bus. & Profl. Women's Clubs and U. Maine, 1996. Mem. AAUW (hon. life mem.; pres. R.I. divsn. 1977-79, rep. New England Energy Task Force 1978-79, 79-81, mem. exec. bd. 1982-90, 92-95, chair legis. program 1984-86, chair women's issues com. 1986-88, chair legal advocacy fund 1992-95; Elizabeth "Liz" W. Crandall Rsch. & Projects Endowment, AAUW of Maine, 1996), LWV (exec. bd. Brunswick, Maine league 1981-93, pres. 1983-85), NOW, Family Planning Assn. Maine, Phi Kappa Phi, Phi Upsilon Omicron, Omicron Nu (nat. editor 1953-55, nat. pres. 1957-59). Democrat. Episcopalian. Avocations: philanthropy, feminism, physical fitness, social action, wildflowers. Home: 34 Belmont St Brunswick ME 04011-3051

CRANDALL, IRA CARLTON, consulting electrical engineer; b. South Amboy, N.J., Oct. 30, 1931; s. Carlton Francis and Claire Elizabeth (Harned) C.; m. Jane Leigh Ford, Jan. 29, 1954; children— Elizabeth Anne, Amy Leigh, Matthew Garrett BS in Radio Engring., Ind. Inst. Tech., 1954, BS in Elec. Engring., 1958; BS in Electronics Engring., U.S. Naval Postgrad. Sch., 1962; PhD, U. Sussex, 1964; MA, Piedmont U., 1967, DSc (hon.), 1968; LLB, Blackstone Sch. Law, 1970; DLitt, St. Matthew U., 1970; EdD, Mt. Sinai U., 1972; Assoc. Bus., LaSalle U., 1975, B in Computer Sci., 1986; D. Internat. Rels., Australian Inst. for Coordinated Rsch., 1991. Tchr. Madison Twp. Pub. Schs., N.J., 1954-55; commd. ensign U.S. Navy, 1955, advanced through grades to lt. comdr., 1965, released to inactive duty, 1972; engring. cons. Concord, Calif., 1972—. Pres. 7C's Enterprises, Concord, 1972-96; v.p. Dickinson Enterprises, Concord, 1972-77, Williamson Engring., Inc., Walnut Creek, Calif., 1974-82; pres., chmn. bd. I.C. Crandall and Assocs., Inc., Concord and Westminster, Calif., Tigard, Oreg., 1976-82; pres. Internat. Rsch. Assocs., Concord, 1982-98; v.p. Gayner Engring. Inc., San Francisco, 1982-92; sr. engr. Ajmani Assoc., San Francisco, 1992-99, Syska and Hennesy, L.A., 1999-02. Vice pres. PTA, Concord, 1969; tribal organizer Mt. Diablo YMCA Indian Guide Program, 1971-74; pres. Mt. Diablo Unified Schs. Interested Citizens. Decorated Vietnamese Cross of Valor Fellow Am. Coll. Engrs.; mem. IEEE, U.S. Naval Inst. Am. Naval Assn., Assn. Elec. Engrs., Am. Inst. Tech. Mgmt. (sr.), Soc. Am. Mil. Engrs., Nat. Model Ry. Assn., Assn. Old Crows, Concord Homeowners Assn., Concord Chamber Singers, Concord Blue Devils, Scottish-Am. Military Soc., Am. Legion, Order of the Knights (knight), Templar of Jerusalem, Lofsensic Ursinius Order (knight commdr. 1991—), Pi Upsilon Eta, Gamma Chi Epsilon, Alpha Gamma Upsilon Republican. Methodist (adminstrv. bd. ch. 1971-76). Clubs: Navy League, Century. Lodge: Optimists (pres.) Home and Office: 5754 Pepperridge Pl Concord CA 94521-4821 E-mail: ccrandall@yahoo.com.

CRANDALL, JOHN LYNN, insurance consultant, retired insurance company executive; b. Chgo., Apr. 17, 1927; s. Paul Bertram and Olga (Bleich) C.; m. Irene Anze Ruenne, Dec. 26, 1973; children by previous marriage: Deborah Crandall Kulchar, Jeffrey, Lynne Crandall Blais; stepchildren: George Ruenne, Helgi Ruenne. BS in Fire Protection Engring., Ill. Inst. Tech., 1951. CPCU; cert. in gen. ins. Highly protected risk insp. FIA, Chgo., 1951-53, asst. engr. supr., 1953-56, engring. supr., 1956-59, underwriting supr., spl. agt., 1959-65; HPR engr., underwriter Kemper Group, Chgo., 1965-67, HPR sales specialist, 1967-71; asst. to dir. underwriting Protection Mut. Ins. Co., Park Ridge, Ill., 1971-73, v.p. underwriting, 1973-78, v.p., dir. underwriting, 1978-90; cons. Served with USN, 1945-46. Mem. Soc. Fire Protection Engrs. (charter), Soc. CPCU (chpt. pres. 1980-81, nat. dir. 1987-90, ethics com. 1990-97, sr. resource com. 1997-2000, chmn. sr. rsch. com. 2000-02, v.p. ch. coun. 1992-95). Home: 10 Black Oak Trail Galena IL 61036-8518 also: Cypress Lakes 10000 US Hwy 98 N Lot 913 Lakeland FL 33809-8083 E-mail: JLC913@juno.com.

CRANDALL, MARGARET ELIZABETH, editor; b. Marietta, Ohio, Mar. 9, 1978; d. James Rider and Dianne Farley Crandall. BS in Journalism cum laude, Ohio U., 2000. Editor, paginator Lancaster (Ohio) Eagle-Gazette, 2000—. Avocations: reading, gardening, astronomy, camping, hiking. Office: Lancaster Eagle-Gazette 138 W Chestnut St Lancaster OH 43130

CRANDALL, OLIVER PERRY, lawyer, poet; b. R.I., Nov. 6, 1927; s. Harry Franklin Crandall and Lillian Mae Dinstel, Harry Franklin Crandall. AA, Boston U., 1949, JD, 1952. Bar: R.I. 1953, Conn. 1980. Pvt. practice, Old Lyme, Conn. Mem. RI Real Estate Commn., Providence, 1957—61; probate judge Probate Ct., Westerly, RI, 1956—58. With USCG, 1945—46. Republican. Episcopalian. Avocations: hiking, nature. Home: 249 Boston Post Rd # 3 Old Lyme CT 06371 Office: 249 Boston Post Rd Old Lyme CT 06371-1318

CRANDALL, STEPHEN HARRY, engineering educator; b. Cebu, Philippines, Dec. 2, 1920; s. William Harry and Julia Josephine (Kuenemann) C.; m. Patricia Estelle Stickel, Jan. 21, 1949; children: Jane S., William S. M.E., Stevens Inst. Tech., 1942; PhD, MIT, 1946. Registered profl. engr. Mem. staff radiation lab MIT, Cambridge, 1942-43, instr. math, 1944-46, asst. prof. mech. engring., 1947-51, assoc. prof., 1951-58, prof., 1958—, Ford prof. engring., 1975-91, prof. emeritus, 1991—, head div. applied mechanics, 1957-59, 61-67, head. div. mechanics and materials, 1968-71. Vis. prof. Marseille, France, 1960, U. Nat. Autonoma Mex., Mexico City, 1967, Ecole Nat. Superieure de Mecanique, Nantes, France, 1978, Fla. Atlantic U., 1993, Korean Advanced Inst. Sci. and Tech., 1996; exch. prof. Imperial Coll., London, 1949; NSF sci. faculty fellow, vis. scholar U. Calif., Berkeley, 1964-65; hon. rsch. assoc. Harvard U., 1971-72; Lady Davis vis. prof. Technion, Israel, 1987. Author: Engineering Analysis, 1956, Random Vibration in Mechanical Systems, 1963, (with others) Dynamics of Mechanical and Electromechanical Systems, 1968; editor: Random Vibration vol. 1, 1958, Random Vibration vol. 2, 1963, (with others) Mechanics of Solids, 1959, author (with others), 3d edit., 1978; contbr. artcles to profl. jours. Recipient ASCE Von Karman medal, 1984, Freudenthal medal, 1996, Alexander von Humboldt sr. U.S. scientist award, 1989; Fulbright fellow, London, 1949. Fellow AAAS, ASME (Worcester Reed Warner medal 1971, v.p. 1978-80, hon. mem. 1988, Timoshenko medal 1990, Den Hartog award 1991), Am. Acad. Arts and Scis., Am. Acoustical Soc. (Trent-Crede medal 1978), Am. Acad. Mechanics (pres. 1997, Disting. Svc. medal 1993); mem. NAS, NAE, NSPE, Soc. Indsl. and Applied Math., Am. Math. Soc., Am. Soc. for Engring. Edn., Internat. Union Theoretical and Applied Mechanics (chmn. U.S. del. 1974), Russian Acad. Engring. (fgn. mem.). Home: 25 Tabor Hill Rd Lincoln MA 01773-2905 Office: MIT/3-360 Dept Mech Engring Cambridge MA 02139

CRANDALL, TERRENCE LEE, counseling administrator; b. Watertown, S.D., Feb. 15, 1951; s. Howard Lee Crandall and Laurel Lynn (Overbaugh) Havelock; m. Catherine Dunn, Aug. 6, 1974; children: David, Caitlin, Alexander. BS, Dakota State U., 1974; MA, U. S.D., 1979. English tchr. Irene (S.D.) Pub. Schs., 1975-78, counselor, 1978-80, Yankton (S.D.) Sr. High,

1980—. Supr. Ednl. Testing Svc., Princeton, NJ, 1985—. Pres., bd. dirs. Yankton Riverboat Days, 1987—2001, hon. capt., 2003; pres., bd. dirs. Yankton Centennial Bd.; pres. Fed. Prison Adv. Bd., Yankton, 1988—91; mem. S.D. Acad. Achievement Testing Adv. Coun.; commr. City of Yankton Commn., 1986—96, 2000—; mayor City of Yankton, 1993—96, 2001—. Named one of Outstanding Young Men of Am., 1981, 1984, 1989. Mem.: NEA (Outstanding Young Educator 1984), ACA (cert., lic. profl. counselor), Yankton Edn. Assn. (pres. 2000—01), S.D. Mental Health Counselors, S.D. Counseling Assn. (pres. 1987—88, S.D. Counselor of Yr. 1992), Am. Mental Health Counselors Assn., Elks (various offices, Outstanding Svc. award 1988, S.D. Elk of the Yr. 1995), KC, Phi Delta Kappa. Democrat. Roman Catholic. Avocations: music, politics, sports, theater. Home: 809 E 19th St Yankton SD 57078-2426 Office: Yankton Sr High 1801 Summit St Yankton SD 57078-1908 E-mail: tcrandall@ysd.k12.sd.us.

CRANDALL HOLLICK, JULIAN BERNARD HUGH, radio producer; b. Oxford, Eng., Oct. 10, 1947; came to U.S., 1977; s. Harry Bernard and Margaret Francesca (Purcell) Hollick; m. Martine Lutece Crandall, Apr. 7, 1974; children: Jerome Francois, Margot Lutece. MS, London Sch. Econs., 1975. Lectr. New U. of Ulster, Coleraine, Northern Ireland, 1976; adminstr. Ministry of Defence, London, 1976-77; freelance journalist, Boston, 1977-80; radio prodr. for NPR, CBC, BBC, WBUR, Ind. Broadcasting Assocs., Inc., Littleton, Mass., 1980—. Author, prodr.: (radio shows) The World of Islam, 1984, The Fall of Berlin, 1985, United Nations at 40, 1985, Passages to India, 1987, 89, Living on the Edge, 1990, Imagining America, 1990, Islam Revisited, 1991, Letters From Jitvapur, 1992, Apna Street, 1995, 97, Trespass, 1996-98, Living Islam, 1995—, Monsoon, 1997, 99, Ganga, 2000—, others; exbhn. Gamv: Life in An Indian Village, Boston, 1985-90. Grantee NEH, 1981, 85, 89, 90, 97, 98-2001, Rockefeller Found., 1986, Carnegie Corp., 1987, Ford Found., 1987, 89, 93, 95, 98—, NSF, 2001; recipient Corp. for Pub. Broadcasting Radio award, 1985, 91, Cindy award, 1985, 89, 91, 92, 95, 97, 98, 99, NCCJ award, 1985, Armstrong award, 1986, 90, Gabriel award, 1989, 90, Ohio State award, 1989, 90, Presdl. End Hunger award, 1990, Grand prize N.Y. Internat. Radio Festival, 1991, 93, 94, 96, 98, Commonwealth award, 1995. Mem. Royal Inst. Internat. Affairs, Tocqueville Soc., Inst. Charles de Gaulle, WorldView Internat., Annotator Les Editions Tahra France. Hindu. Avocations: classical music, squash, tennis. Home and Office: 111 King St Littleton MA 01460-1527 E-mail: iba@ibaradio.org., jululuiba@aol.com.

CRANDELL, K(ENNETH) JAMES, management and strategic planning consultant, entrepreneur; b. Ajax, Ont., Can., July 12, 1957; s. James Bauder Butterill and Barbara Joy Gillard; m. Christine Josephine McElhenney, July 28, 1984. B in Adminstrn. and B in Commerce, U. Ottawa, 1980; MBA, Fla. Atlantic U., 1982. CPA, Fla., Calif. Assoc. dir. entrepreneurial svcs. div. Ernst & Young, Ft. Lauderdale, Fla., 1982-88; founder, chmn., CEO NBS Cons. Group, Inc. (now New Bus. Strategies), Los Gatos, Calif., 1988—. Guest lectr. State Univ. System. Writer, co-producer TV series Florida Business Advisor, 1988; contbr. articles to mags. Recipient Up and Comer award, 1988. Mem. AICPA, Fin. & Adminstrn. Mgmt. in Entertainment, Fla. Inst. CPAs, Calif. Soc. CPAs, Am. Assn. Accts. (MAS divsn. 1980-93), Inst. Mgmt. Accts. (bd. dirs. Ft. Lauderdale 1983—, pres. 1988-89, bus. planning com. 1987-89), Can.-Am. C. of C. (co-founder), U. Miami Venture Coun. Forum, Gold Coast Venture Capital Club (v.p., bd. dirs. 1987-91, treas. 1987-88, co-editor newsletter 1987-89), Ft. Lauderdale C. of C. (chmn. venture capital activities 1986-88, small bus. coun. 1985-90), others. Avocations: ice hockey, published songwriter, reading. Office: NBS Cons Group Inc PMB #J 245 Mount Hermon Rd Ste M Scotts Valley CA 95066-4045 also: 14125 Capri Dr Ste 7 Los Gatos CA 95032-1516 E-mail: James.Crandell@newbizs.com.

CRANDLEMERE, ROBERT WAYNE, engineering executive; b. South Weymouth, Mass., Mar. 5, 1947; s. Robert Winton and Elizabeth Mildred (Smith) C.; m. Cynthia Robin Stoddard, May 18, 1980; children: Donna Marie, Raina Lee. A.E. in Chem. Tech., Franklin Inst. Boston, 1967; BS in Chemistry, Suffolk U., 1970, MS in Analytical Chemistry, 1975. V.p., chief chemist, lab. dir., dir. Briggs Engring. & Testing Inc., 1973-83; founder, prin., pres., CEO Cert. Engring. & Testing Co., Weymouth, Mass., 1983-92, R.W. Crandlemere & Assocs., Inc., Weymouth, Mass., 1993—2002; sr. mgr. Green Environ., Inc., Quincy, Mass., 2002—03; mgr. R.W. Crandlemere, LLC, Holbrook, Mass., 2003—. Former instr. environmental and phys. chemistry Suffolk U. Contbr. articles to profl. jours. Memm. ASTM (com. E50 on envrion. assessment, risk mgmt. and corrective action), Nat. Inst. Bldg. Scis. (com. on asbestos ops. and mgmt. programs). Home: 423 S Franklin St Holbrook MA 02343-1855 Office: 423 South Franklin St Holbrook MA 02343

CRANE, BARBARA BACHMANN, photographer, educator; b. Chgo., Mar. 19, 1928; d. Burton Stanley and Della (Kreeger) Bachmann; children: Elizabeth, Jennifer, Bruce. Student, Mills Coll., 1945-48; BA in Art History, NYU, 1950; MS in Photography, Inst. Design, Ill. Inst. Tech., 1966. Prof. photography Sch. Art Inst. Chgo., 1967-93, prof. emeritus, 1993—; vis. prof. Phila. Coll. Art (now Univ. of the Arts), 1977, Sch. Mus. Fine Arts, Boston, 1979, Cornell U., Ithaca, N.Y., 1983; represented by Revolution Gallery, Ferndale, Mich., Troyer Gallery, Washington, N.C.E. Photographie Contemporaine, Paris, Stephen Daiter Gallery, Chgo., Flatfile Photography Gallery, Chgo. Vis. prof. Bezalel Acad. Art and Design, Jerusalem, 1987. Author: (retrospective monograph) Barbara Crane: 1948-80, (exhbn. catalog) Barbara Crane: The Evolution of a Vision, 1983, Barbara Crane: Chicago Loop, 2002, Barbara Crane Urban Anomalies: Chicago, 2002. Fellow Photography fellow, NEA, 1975, 1988, Guggenheim Meml. fellow in photography, 1979—80; grantee, Polaroid Corp., 1979—95, Ill. Arts Coun., 1985, 2001. Mem.: Friends of Photography (Carmel, Calif.), Soc. Photog. Edn. (Nat. Honored Educator award 1993). Studio: 1015 W Jackson Blvd Chicago IL 60607-2918 *Many of my photographic ideas have grown from chance or accident, both visually and technically, or from the subject matter itself. I welcome any unaccountable occurrence stemming from combinations of shutter speed, subject changes, technical happenings, or my mistakes. When such unpredictable pictures appear, I try to harness the visual episode by taking pictures that will allow the new experience to happen with intent. Fortunately, this way of working seems to expand my ideas and to continuously generate new visual experiences.*

CRANE, BARRY D. federal agency administrator; Grad., USAF Acad.; PhD in Physics, U. Ariz. With Air Force Studies and Anaylses Chief Tactical Br. USAF, 1983—86; specialist for decision svcs. Office of the Dir. of Def. Rsch. and Engring., 1987—91; project leader operational evaluation divsn. Inst. for Defense Analysis; dep. dir. for supply reduction Office Nat. Drug Control Policy Exec. Office of the Pres., Washington, 2002—. Col. USAF, 1991. Office: Exec Office of the Pres Office Nat Drug Control Policy 750 17th St NW Washington DC 20503

CRANE, BENJAMIN FIELD, lawyer; b. Holden, Mass., May 5, 1929; s. Frederick Turner and Gertrude (Stange) C.; m. Sarah Anne Molloy, Feb. 8, 1959; children: Michael Turner, Elizabeth Loring, Susan Field. BA, U. Iowa, 1951; LL.B., NYU, 1954. Bar: N.Y. 1955. Assoc. Cravath, Swaine & Moore, N.Y.C., 1954-63, ptnr., 1963-94. Served with U.S. Army, 1946-47. Mem. Assn. of Bar of City of N.Y. Office: Cravath Swaine & Moore LLP Worldwide Plz 825 8th Ave New York NY 10019-7475

CRANE, BONNIE LOYD, art gallery owner, director, author; b. Mpls., Aug. 24, 1930; d. Frank Riley and Evelyn (Davis) Loyd; m. David Alford, Oct. 23, 1954 (div. May 1992); children: Melinda Crane Engel, Matthew Loyd, Lauren Amanda. BA, Sweet Briar (Va.) Coll., 1950; MA, Bryn Mawr (Pa.) Coll., 1972. Lectr. Kinkaid Sch., Houston, 1975-76, Mus. Fin. Arts, Sch. of Arts, Houston, 1975-76, Rice U., Houston, 1976; tchr. Cairo Am. Coll., 1978-79; curator Clark Gallery, Lincoln, Mass., 1980-82; curatorial asst., dir. edn. Brockton (Mass.) Art Mus., 1982; freelance dealer Dedham and Dover, Mass., 1983-84; owner, dir. Crane Collection Gallery, Boston, 1985-96, Wellesley, Mass., 1996—. Author: Blanche Ames, Artist & Activist, 1982, The Gentle Art of Still Life, 1989, Russian Light, 1995. Donor, mem. Channel 2 Auction, Boston, 1985—; active Newbury St. League, Boston, 1985—; tour guide Trinity Ch., Boston, 1988-89; spl. gifts solicitor United Way, Back Bay, Boston, 1988-2002; bd. dirs. Handel and Haydn Soc., Boston, 1988-2002; v.p. bd. dirs. Friends of Art Sweet Briar Coll., 1992-97. Mem. Archives of Am. Art, Internat. Art Gallery Assn., New Eng. Appraisers Assn., St. Botolph Club. Episcopalian. Avocations: painting, traveling. Office: Crane Collection 564 Washington St Wellesley MA 02482-6409 E-mail: cranecollection@conversent.net.

CRANE, DAVID, producer; With Bright-Kauffman-Crane Prodns., Burbank, Calif. Creator, prodr. Dream On, 1990—; creator, exec. prodr. Friends, 1994— (Emmy nominee 1995, 96); creator, exec. producer Veronica's Closet, 1997—; exec. producer Jesse, 1998—. Office: Bright Kauffman Crane Prodns 4000 Warner Blvd Bldg 160 Burbank CA 91522-0001

CRANE, EDWARD HARRISON, III, institute executive; b. Los Angeles, Aug. 15, 1944; s. Edward Harrison Jr. and Mary Barbara (Greene) C.; m. Kristina Knall; children: Geoffrey Harrison, Kathleen Wilder, Mary Adams. BS, U. Calif., Berkeley, 1967; MBA, U. So. Calif., 1968. Chartered fin. analyst. Portfolio mgr. Scudder, Stevens & Clark, Los Angeles, 1969-73; v.p. Alliance Capital Mgmt. Corp., San Francisco, 1973-75; nat. chmn. Libertarian Party, Washington, 1974-77; pres. Cato Inst., Washington, 1977—. Bd. Nat. Taxpayers Legal Fund, 1978-82. Pub. Inquiry mag., 1977-81, Regulation mag., 1990—; editor: Beyond the Status Quo, 1984, An American Vision, 1988, Market Liberalism, 1993; contbr. articles to profl. jours. Bd. dirs. Inst. for Rsch. on the Econs. of Taxation, 1988-92, U.S. Term Limits, 1993—; bd. advisors Am. Inst. of Bus. and Econs. in Moscow. Inst. Chartered Fin. Analysts, Mont Pelerin Soc. Avocation: rowing. Home: 6213 Waterway Dr Falls Church VA 22044-1314 Office: Cato Inst 1000 Massachusetts Ave NW Washington DC 20001-5400

CRANE, FAYE, small business owner; b. Amery, Wis., Dec. 2, 1947; d. Vaemond Hall and Irene C. (L'Allier) C.; 1 child, Camille Mills Seifert. Grad. high sch., Milltown, Wis. Premiums statis. clk. State Farm Ins., St. Paul, 1968-73; pension adminstrn. asst. Mut. Svc. Ins., St. Paul, 1973-78; dist. dir. Avon Products, Inc., Morton Grove, Ill., 1978-79; sales rep. Midwest Bus. Sys., Duluth, Minn., 1979-84, REM's Inc., Grand Rapids, Minn., 1984; pres. prodn. Presto Print, Grand Rapids, 1984—. Mem. Grand Rapids Planning Commn., 1990—94, 2001—03; commr. Grand Rapids Econ. Devel. Authority, 1994—. Mem. NAFE, Nat. Fedn. Bus. and Profl. Women (treas. nat. conv. 1992, found. com. 1998-99, treas. nat. conv. 2000), Minn. Fedn. Bus. and Profl. Women (mem. promotion com. 1982-92, emblem chmn. 1982-83, found. chmn. 1983-84, exec. dir., chmn. 1984-85, editor 1987-90, v.p. 1992-93, pres.-elect 1993-94, pres. 1994-95, parliamentarian 2000-01, 03—, fin. com. 2001-03), Grand Rapids Bus. and Profl. Women (pres. 1985-86), Minn. Bus. and Profl. Women's Found. (trustee 1995 96, leadership chmn. 1996-98), Nat. Mus. Women in Arts. Home: PO Box 404 Grand Rapids MN 55744-0404 Office: Presto Print 1235 S Pokegama Ave Grand Rapids MN 55744-4208

CRANE, GARY WADE, mathematician, physicist; b. Austin, Tex., Apr. 7, 1957; s. John Watson and Marjorie Lorania (Haas) C. BS, Southwest Tex. State U., 1983, MS, 1986. Engring. asst. Lower Colorado River Authority, Austin, Tex., 1975-81; teaching asst. S.W. Tex. State U., San Marcos, 1982-86; rsch. scientist assoc. III Applied Rsch. Labs., U. Tex., Austin, 1986-88; engring. technician IV Tex. Dept. Hwys. and Pub. Transp., Austin, 1988-90; actuary Tex. Dept. Human Svcs., Austin, 1990-94; statis. cons., actuary II Tex. Dept. Health, Austin, 1994; chief strategy and analysis Tex. Workers' Compensation Commn., Austin, 1994; statis. cons. Tex. Dept. Human Svcs., Austin, 1994-98; mathematician, actuarial cons. Health and Human Svcs. Commn., Austin, 1998—. Instr. astronomy, physics and math. Austin C.C., 1993—. Home: 14902 Yellowleaf Trl Austin TX 78728-5423

CRANE, HEWITT DAVID, science advisor; b. Jersey City, Apr. 27, 1927; m. Suzanne Gorlin, June 20, 1954; children: Russell Philip, Douglas Mitchell, Daniel Bruce. BSEE, Columbia U., 1947; PhD, Stanford U., 1960. With IBM, N.Y.C., 1949-51, Inst. for Advanced Study, Princeton, N.J., 1952-55, RCA Labs., Princeton, 1955-56; sr. sci. advisor SRI Internat., Menlo Park, Calif., 1956—. A founder Ridge Winery, Cupertino, Calif., 1959-86, Comm. Intelligence Corp., 1981. Author: (with D. Bennion and D. Nitzan) Digital Magnetic Logic, 1969, The New Social Marketplace: Notes on Effecting Social Change in America's Third Century, 1980; contbr. over 70 articles to profl. jours.; patentee in various fields. With USN, 1945-46. Recipient award NASA, 1970, numerous others. Fellow IEEE, Optical Soc. Am. Home: 25 Cordova Ct Menlo Park CA 94028-7908 Office: SRI Internat Sensory Scis & Tech Ctr 333 Ravenswood Ave Menlo Park CA 94025-3453

CRANE, HORACE RICHARD, physicist, educator; b. Turlock, Calif., Nov. 4, 1907; s. Horace Stephen and Mary Alice (Roselle) Crane; m. Florence Rohmer LeBaron, Dec. 30, 1934; children: Carol Ann(dec.), George Richard. BS, Calif. Inst. Tech., 1930, PhD, 1934. Rsch. fellow Calif. Inst. Tech., 1934—35; mem. faculty U. Mich., Ann Arbor, 1935—, prof. physics, 1946—, chmn. dept. physics, 1965—72, George P. Williams Univ. prof., 1972—78, emeritus, 1978—. Rsch. assoc. (radar) MIT, 1940—41; physicist Carnegie Inst., Washington, 1941; project dir., proximity fuse project U. Mich., 1941—43, project dir., atomic energy project, 1943—45; cons. NDRC, 1941—45; mem. standing com. on controlled thermonuc. rsch. AEC, 1969—72; v.p. Midwestern Univs. Rsch. Assn., 1956—56, pres., 1957—60; mem. policy bd. Argonne Nat. Lab., 1957—67; bd. govs. Am. Inst. Physics, 1964—71, chmn., 1971—75; mem. Commn. on Human Resources, 1977—80; mem. Coun. for Internat. Exch. of Scholars, 1977—80. Author: (monthly series) How Things Work in the Physics Teacher, 1983—, How Things Work, 1992, Exhibits Guide, 1992, How to Build It, 1994; inventor, designer exhibits for hands-on type museums, 1981—; contbr. articles to profl. mags.; actor:. Recipient Davisson-Germer prize, 1967, Disting. Alumni medal, Calif. Inst. Tech., 1968, Disting. Svc. award, U. Mich., 1957, Nat. medal of Sci., 1986, Can-Doer award, Mich. Tech. Coun., 1993, Harris award, Rotary Internat., 1963, Henry Russel lectr., 1967. Fellow: AAAS, Am. Acad. Arts and Scis., Am. Phys. Soc.; mem.: NAS, Am. Assn. Physics Tchrs. (Oersted medal 1977, Melba Newell Phillips award 1988, pres. 1965), Sci. Rsch. Club (v.p. 1946—47, pres. 1947—48), Rsch. U. Mich. Club (pres. 1956—57), Sigma Xi. Achievements include invention of Race Track, a modified form of synchrotron for nuclear studies, 1946; early discoveries in field of artificially produced radioactive atoms, 1934-39; measurements of magnetic moment of free electron, 1950. Home: 830 Avon Rd Ann Arbor MI 48104-2738*

CRANE, JOHN S. architectural firm executive; BArch, Tex. Tech. U., 1968; MArch and Urban Design, Wash. U., 1971. Pres. and CEO FKP Arch., 1985—. Coach Little League; mem. pres. adv. coun. Greater Houston Partnership; bd. dirs. Houston br. Prevent Blindness Tex. Mem.: Am. Coll. Healthcare Archs. (founding mem.), Am. Assn. Hosp. Planning (mem. com. on architecture for health), Chief Exec. Network. Avocations: golf, hunting, fishing, cooking. Office: 8 Greenway Plz Ste 300 Houston TX 77046-0899*

CRANE, KAREN R. retired library director; BA, Ind. U., 1970, MLS, 1971. Dir. Alaska State Librs., Archives and Mus., Juneau, 1986—2002, ret., 2002—. Office: Alaska State Libr PO Box 110571 Juneau AK 99811-0571 also: 333 Willoughby Ave Juneau AK 99801-1770

CRANE, LAURA JANE, research chemist; b. Middletown, Ohio, Nov. 2, 1941; d. David R. and Frances T. (Watkins) Scott; m. Robert K. Crane, Apr. 13, 1972. BS, Carnegie Inst. Tech., 1963; MS, Harvard U., 1964; PhD, Rutgers U., 1972. Postdoctoral fellow Roche Inst. Molecular Biology, 1972-74, rsch. assoc., 1974-75; analytical chemist Eastman Kodak Co., Rochester, N.Y., 1962; asst. scientist Warner-Lambert Co., Morris Plains, N.J., 1965, 67-68; English tchr. Am. Sch., Manila, 1966; assoc. scientist W.R. Grace & Co., Clarksville, Md., 1969; sr. scientist diagnostic enzymology Warner-Lambert Co., 1975, group leader coagulation rsch., 1976-79; mgr. lab. products rsch. J.T. Baker Inc., Phillipsburg, N.J., 1979, asst. dir. R&D, 1980-85, dir. R&D, 1986-92; sr. dir. new product innovation Schering-Plough Health Products, Inc., Memphis, 1992-93, sr. dir. adv. products rsch. and new product innovation, 1993—. Mem. faculty Seton Hall U., 1979; participant profl. symposia; mem. R&D coun. N.J., state sci. adv. coun. Rutgers U. Contbr., editor sci. articles and books. US Dregsage Federation Bronze Medalist, 2003m, Armco Corp. scholar, 1959-63; Women's Dormitory Coun. scholar; William Connelly scholar: nat. Merit scholar; NSF fellow; DuPont fellow; NDEA fellow, 1969-72, others. Mem. AAAS, Am. Chem. Soc., U.S. Dressage Fedn., Arabian Horse Registry Assn., Al Khamsa Arabian Horse Breeders Assn. (pres.). Home: 7155 Highway 194 Williston TN 38076-3511 Office: Schering-Plough Health Products Inc 3030 Jackson Ave Memphis TN 38112-2020 E-mail: laura.crane@spcorp.com.

CRANE, MARK, lawyer; b. Chgo., Aug. 27, 1930; s. Martin and Ruth (Bangs) C.; m. Constance Bird Wilson, Aug. 18, 1956; children: Christopher, Katherine, Stephanie. AB, Princeton U., 1952; LLB, Harvard U., 1957. Bar: U.S. Dist. Ct. (no. dist.) Ill. 1957, U.S. Ct. Appeals (7th cir.) 1968, U.S. Ct. Appeals (9th cir.) 1972, U.S. Supreme Ct. 1978, U.S. Ct. Appeals (10th cir.) 1982, U.S. Ct. Appeals (fed. cir.) 1983, U.S. Ct. Appeals (6th cir.) 1995, U.S. Ct. Appeals (8th cir.) 1998. Assoc. Hopkins & Sutter, Chgo., 1957-63, ptnr., 1963-2001; of counsel Foley & Lardner, Chgo., 2001—. Adj. prof. Loyola U. Law Sch., 2000—; comml. arbitrator, mediator complex case panel Am. Arbitration Assn., Chgo., 1997—. Served to lt. (j.g.) USNR, 1952-54. Fellow Am. Bar Found., Am. Coll. Trial Lawyers (chmn. upstate Ill. com. 1997-99); mem. ABA (chmn. antitrust sect. 1986-87), Ill. Bar Assn. (chmn. fed. jud. appointments com. 1978-79, chmn. antitrust sect. 1970), Chgo. Bar Assn., 7th Cir. Bar Assn. (pres. 1984-85). Republican. Episcopalian. Home: 520 Hoyt Ln Winnetka IL 60093-2623 Office: 321 N Clark St Chicago IL 60610

CRANE, MARTHA BEAVERS, music educator; b. Loesburg, Va., Sept. 23, 1956; d. Dudley Norwood and Anna Manning Beavers; m. Stephen Jeffrey Crane, July 11, 1981; children: Matthew Norwood, Stephanie Helen. B of Music Edn., James Madison U., 1978. Music specialist Va. Beach Pub. Schs., Va., 1978—85; tchr. pvt. practice, Dublin, 1986—90, Rocky Mt., NC, 1990—96; mgr. consignment shop Classy Attic, 1992—96; tchr. music Hampton Pub. Schs., Va., 1998—. Pianist Dublin Bapt. Ch., 1986—90; pianist, choir accompanist Proctor's Chapel Bapt. Ch., Rocky Mt., 1991—96, Calvary Bapt. Ch., Newport News, Va., 1998—. Contbr. articles to profl. jours. Republican. Baptist. Avocations: antiques, music, sewing, cooking, Bible study. Home: 704 Prescott Cir Newport News VA 23602

CRANE, PATRICIA SUE, probation services administrator, social worker; b. Rockway, N.Y., Jan. 17, 1948; d. Herbert Milton and Miriam (Rosenblum) Brager; m. Marvin J. Crane, May 2, 1971; 1 child, Elizabeth A. BA, U. Wis., 1969; MS in Criminal Justice with honors, Wayne State U., 1984. Cert. social worker. Dir. probation svcs. 52d dist. ct. 1st divsn. State of Mich., Novi, 1979—. Jewish. Avocations: marathon runner, athlete. Home: 5042 Meadowbrook Dr West Bloomfield MI 48322-1570 Office: 52nd Dist Ct 1st Divsn 48150 Grand River Ave Novi MI 48374-1222 E-mail: trissiec@aol.com.

CRANE, PHILIP MILLER, congressman; b. Chgo., Nov. 3, 1930; s. George Washington III and Cora (Miller) C.; m. Arlene Catherine Johnson, Feb. 14, 1959; children: Catherine Anne, Susanna Marie, Jennifer Elizabeth, Rebekah Caroline, George Washington V, Rachel Ellen, Sarah Emma, Carrie Esther. Student, DePauw U., 1948-50; BA, Hillsdale Coll., 1952; postgrad., U. Mich., 1952-54, U. Vienna, Austria, 1953, 56; MA, Ind. U., 1961; PhD, 1963; LLD, Grove City Coll., 1973, Nat. Coll. Edn., 1987; Doctor en Ciencias Politicas, Francisco Marroquin U., 1979. Advt. mgr. Hopkins Syndicate, Inc., Chgo., 1956-58; tchg. asst. Ind. U., Bloomington, 1959-62; asst. prof. history Bradley U., Peoria, Ill., 1963-67; dir. schs. Westminster Acad., Northbrook, Ill., 1967-68; mem. 91st-108th Congresses from 13th, 12th (now 8th) Ill. Dist., Washington, 1969—, vice chmn. ways and means com.; mem. Joint Com. on Taxation. Author: Democrat's Dilemma, 1964, The Sum of Good Government, 1976, Surrender In Panama: The Case Against the Treaty, 1978; contbr.: Continuity in Crisis, 1974, Crisis in Confidence, 1974, Case Against the Reckless Congress, 1976, Can You Afford This House?, 1978, View from the Capitol Dome (Looking Right), 1980, Liberal Cliches and Conservative Solutions, 1984. Dir. rsch. Ill. Goldwater Orgn., 1964; mem. nat. adv. bd. Young Ams. for Freedom, 1965—; bd. dirs. Am. Conservative Union, 1965-82, chmn., 1976; bd. dirs., chmn. Intercollegiate Studies Inst.; bd. advisors Ashbrook Ctr., Ashland U., 1983—, univ. trustee, 1988-93; founder Rep. Study Com., 1972—, chmn., 1984; commr. Commn. on Bicentennial U.S. Constn., 1986-91; trustee Hillsdale Coll. Recipient Distinguished Alumnus award Hillsdale Coll., 1968, Independence award, 1974, William McGovern award Chgo. Soc., 1969, Freedoms Found. award, 1973; named Ill. Statesman's Father Yr., 1979. Mem. ASCAP, VFW (award 1978), Am. Hist. Assn., Orgn. Am. Historians, Acad. Polit. Sci., Am. Acad. Polit. and Social Scis., Am. Legion, Phila. Soc., B'nai B'rith (award 1978), Phi Alpha Theta, Pi Gamma Mu. Republican. Office: US Ho of Reps 233 Cannon House Bldg Washington DC 20515-0001*

CRANE, ROBERT KENDALL, engineering educator, researcher, consultant; b. Worcester, Mass., Dec. 9, 1935; s. Kendall Buck and Marjorie Armitage (Miller) C.; m. Emma Ruth Freeman, June 15, 1957; children: Garry Robert, Susan Emma Crane Jennings, Katherine Anne Crane Kulas, Cynthia Elizabeth. BSEE, Worcester Poly. Inst., 1957, MSEE, 1959, PhD, 1970. Staff engr. MITRE Corp., Bedford, Mass., 1959-64; staff mem. Lincoln Lab. MIT, Lexington, 1964-76, cons., 1976-88; divsn. sr. scientist, dep. divsn. mgr. Environ. Rsch. and Tech., Inc., Concord, Mass., 1976-81; rsch. prof. Thayer Sch. Engring. Dartmouth Coll., Hanover, N.H., 1981-91; prof. meteorology, elec. engring. Coll. Geoscis. U. Okla., Norman, 1992-2000, prof. emeritus meteorology, elec. engring., 2000—. Cons. Raytheon Corp., Sudbury, Mass., 1981-87, Tech. Svc. Corp., Silver Spring, Md., 1988, Norden Sys., Melville, N.Y., 1988, Globalstar, San Jose, Calif., 1995-97, Applied Data Trends, Inc., 1996—, Teledesic Corp., 1997-99, Triton Network Sys., Inc., 1999, Hughes Network Sys., 1999-2000, Boeing Satellite Sys., 2001-02. Contbr. over 100 tech. papers, reports to profl. jours. and other publs. Fellow IEEE (Disting. lectr. Antenna and Propagation Soc. 1988-91, adminstrv. com. 1985-87, wave propagation stds. com. 1971-92, assoc. editor Trans. Antennas and Propagation 1972-74), Internat. Sci. Radio Union (chmn. commn. F. 1987-90, vice comm. F. 1984-87), U.S. Nat. Com. Internat. Sci. Radio Union (chmn. 1985-87); mem. Am. Meterorol. Soc. (cert. cons. meterorologist, com. on radar meteorology 1981-83), Sigma Xi, Eta Kappa Nu. Avocations: hiking, skiing, photography. Home: 404 Road Round the Lake Grantham NH 03753 also: 51 Island Rd Fryeburg ME 04037 also: PO Box 536 Fryeburg ME 04037-0536 E-mail: bcrane@ou.edu.

CRANE, ROBERT MEREDITH, health care executive; b. Phila., Apr. 5, 1947; s. Frederick Barnard and Roberta Futhey (Phillips) C.; m. Susan Gail Dewald, May 5, 1973; 1 child, Alexis Meredith. BA, Coll. of Wooster, 1969; M Pub. Adminstrn., Cornell U., Ithaca, N.Y., 1971. Health planning specialist U.S. Dept. Health, Edn. and Welfare, Rockville, Md., 1971-73, tech. assistance bur. chief, 1973-76, regulatory methods bur. chief, 1976-77; sr. staff assoc. U.S. Ho. of Reps., Washington, 1977-79; dep. commr. N.Y. State Health Dept., Albany, 1979-82; dir. N.Y. State Office Health Sys. Mgmt., Albany, 1982-83; v.p. govt. rels. Kaiser Found. Health Plan, Oakland, calif., 1983-88, sr. v.p. nat. accts. and pub. rels., 1988-92, sr. v.p. quality mgmt., 1992-94, sr. v.p., chief adminstrv. officer, 1994-99; sr. v.p., rsch. and policy devel., dir. Inst. for Health Policy, Oakland, Calif., 1999—. Bd. dirs. Acad. Health Svcs. Rsch. and Health Policy, 2000—; mem. Nat. Acad. Social Ins., 2000—. Campaign cabinet United Way Bay area, 1989-90; steering com. Bay Area Econ. Forum, 1988-94, Bay Area Coun., 1991—; selection judge, preceptor Coro Found., San Francisco, 1985-86; chmn. bd. Alpha Ctr., 1992-98; co-chair conf. bd. Coun. of Shared Bus. Svcs. Execs., 1996—; trustee Employee Benefits Rsch. Inst. Sr. exec. fellow Harvard U., 1981. Mem. APHA (chmn. cmty. health planning sect. 1983-84, bd. govs. 1979-81), Am. Health Planning Assn. (bd. dirs. 1986-92). Presbyterian. Avocations: tennis, golf. Office: Kaiser Found Health Plan 1 Kaiser Plz Oakland CA 94612-3610

CRANE, ROGER RYAN, JR., lawyer; b. Washington, Mar. 28, 1946; s. Roger Ryan Crane and Jeanette (Hurlbut) Rosar. AB, Coll. of Holy Cross, 1968; JD, Fordham U., 1973; LLM, NYU, 1980. Bar: N.Y. 1974; U.S. Dist. Ct. (so. and ea. dist.) N.Y. 1974; U.S. Ct. Appeals (2nd cir.) 1974, (1st cir.) 1994. Assoc. Dunnington Bartholow & Miller, N.Y.C., 1973-79, Trubin Sillcocks Edelman, N.Y.C., 1979-81, ptnr., 1981—84; ptnr., head litig. dept. Bachner Tally Polevoy & Misher, N.Y.C., 1984-2000; co-mng. ptnr. N.Y. office McCarter & English, N.Y.C., 2000—02; ptnr. Nixon Peabody LLP, N.Y.C., 2003—. Contbr. articles to profl. jours. Mem. N.Y.C. Bar Assn. (prof. discipline com. 1996-99), Univ. Club N.Y., Tuxedo Club. Avocations: golf, tennis, fly fishing, riding. Office: Nixon Peabody 437 Madison Ave New York NY 10022 E-mail: rcrane@nixonpeabody.com.

CRANE, STEPHEN CHARLES, professional society administrator; b. Waterbury, Conn, Oct. 4, 1946; s. Homer and Edna Crane; children: Russell, Elizabeth. BA, Princeton U., 1969; MPH, U. Mich., 1973, PhD, 1981. Legis. analyst, mgmt. intern Office of the Dir., NIH, Bethesda, Md., 1969; project dir. Columbia Rsch. Assocs., Inc., Cambridge, Mass., 1970; program analyst Office Asst. Sec. for Planning & Evaluation U.S. Dept. Health, Edn. and Welfare, 1972; grad. rsch. fellow Program Health Planning U. Mich.-Sch. Pub. Health, 1973, sr. rsch. assoc., rsch. assoc., grad. rsch. fellow, 1973-79, lectr. program and bur. hosp. adminstrn., 1979-80, asst. prof., lectr. dept. med. care orgn., 1980-83; asst. prof. Sch. Pub. Health Boston U., 1984-93, dep. chief health svc. sect. Sch. Pub. Health, 1988, asst. acad. v.p. for health affairs, 1986-88, dir. ednl. programs Health Policy Inst., 1983-90; v.p. Assn. for Health Svc. Rsch. & Found. for Health Svc. Rsch., Washington, 1990-93; program dir. Robert Wood Johnson Found. Investigator Awards in Health, 1992-93; exec. v.p. Am. Acad. Physician Asst., Alexandria, Va., 1993—. Investigator and presenter in field. Contbr. articles to profl. jours. Staff Mich. Pub. Health Statue Revision Project, 1975-78; cons. Spkr.'s Office, Mich. Ho. of Reps., Lansing, 1975-81; mem. adv. com. Mercy Coll. Physician Asst. Program, Detroit, 1979-83, Western Mich. Physician Asst. Program, Kalamazoo, 1981-85; staff Boston Mayor's Com. on Access to Health Care, 1984-86; mem. task force on access to health care Divsn. Alcoholism, Mass. Dept. Pub. Health, 1985-86; health care cons. Mass. Com. for the Medically Uninsured, 1985-86; cons. Gen. Assembly Task Force on Health Cost/Policies, Nat. Presbyn. Ch., 1985-91; corporator Milton Med. Ctr., 1988-90; mem. Commn. on Future of U. Detroit/Mercy. McConnell fellow Woodrow Wilson Sch., Princeton U., 1968; USPH Svc. fellow, 1972-73; Grad. Rsch. fellow Bur. Hosp. Adminstrn., Sch. Pub. Health, U. Mich., 1973-74; hon. fellow Mich. Acad. Physician Assts., 1977; recipient commendation Pub. Health Statue Revision Commn., 1979; Faculty Devel. grantee Ctr. for Rsch. on Learning and Teaching, U. Mich., 1982, John H. Romani Disting. Alumni award Mich. Sch. Pub. Health, 1996. Office: Am Acad Physician Asst 950 N Washington St Alexandria VA 22314-1534

CRANEFIELD, PAUL FREDERIC, physiology educator, physician, scientist; b. Madison, Wis., Apr. 28, 1925; s. Paul Frederic and Edna (Rothnick) C. Ph.B., U. Wis., 1946, PhD, 1951; MD, Albert Einstein Coll. Medicine, 1964. Fellow biophysics Johns Hopkins U., 1951-53; from instr. to assoc. prof. physiology State U. N.Y. Downstate Med. Center, N.Y.C., 1953-60; research fellow psychiatry Albert Einstein Coll. Medicine, 1960-64. Exec. sec. com. publs. and med. information, editor bull. N.Y. Acad. Medicine, 1963-66; adj. assoc. prof. pharmacology Columbia Coll. Physicians and Surgeons, 1964-75, adj. prof., 1975-96; assoc. prof. Rockefeller U., 1966-75, prof., 1975-96, prof. emeritus, 1996—. Author: (with Hoffman) The Electrophysiology of the Heart, 1960, Paired Pulse Stimulation of the Heart, 1968, (with C. McC. Brooks) The Historical Development of Physiological Thought, 1959, The Way In and the Way Out, 1974, The Conduction of the Cardiac Impulse, 1975, Claude Bernard's Revised Edition of his Introduction à L'Étude de la Médicine Expérimentale, 1976, (with Aronson) Cardiac Arrhythmias, The Role of Triggered Activity and Other Mechanisms, 1988, Science and Empire: East Coast Fever in Rhodesia and the Transvaal, 1991, Born Wanderer: The Life of Stanley Portal Hyatt, 1995; also numerous articles; editor: Two Great Scientists of the Nineteenth Century, 1982, Jour. Gen. Physiology, 1966-96; mem. editorial bd.: Circulation Research, Spl. Collections, Jour. of Electrocardiology; cons. editor: Internat. Microform Jour. Legal Medicine, 1969-77. Chmn. bd. dirs. LaMama Exptl. Theatre Club, 1965-69; chmn. bd. dirs. Circle Repertory Co., 1970-76, The Working Theatre; trustee Milton Helpern Library Legal Medicine. Recipient Einthoven medal U. Leiden, 1983, Disting. Scientist award N.Am. Soc. Pacing and Electrophysiology, 1994. Fellow N.Y. Acad. Medicine (medal 1988), Internat. Acad. History of Medicine; mem. Am. Physiol. Soc., Biophys. Soc., Am. Assn. History Medicine, Bibliog. Soc., Episcopal Actors Guild (mem. coun. 1990-92), Century Club, Players Club, Nat. Arts Club, Grolier Club, Coffee House Club, Cosmos Club (Washington), Savile Club (London). Home: 310 E 9th St New York NY 10003-7901

CRANER, LORNE WHITNEY, federal official; b. Bitburg, Fed. Republic Germany; came to U.S., 1960; s. Robert Roger and Audrey Evelyn Craner. BA, Reed Coll., 1982; MA, Georgetown U., 1986. Staff asst. Congressman John McCain, Washington, 1983-84; legis. asst. Congressman Jim Kolbe, Washington, 1985, Congressman John McCain, Washington, 1986-87; staff Senate Cen. Am. observer Group, Washington, 1987-89; dep. asst. sec. state Dept. State, Washington, 1989—92; dir. Asian Affairs Nat. Security Coun., Washington, 1992—93; vpres. prog. Int. Rep. Inst., Washington, 1993—95, pres., 1995—2001; asst. sec. for democracy, human rights and labor U.S. Dept. State, Washington, 2001—. Mem. Aspen Inst. Indochina Forum, 1988-89; mem., speaker Coun. Fgn. Rels. Project on Cen. Am., 1989. Staff asst. George Bush for Pres., Alexandria, Va., 1980; mem. campaign staff John McCain for Senate, Phoenix, 1986. Republican. Office: US Dept State Democracy, Human Rights & Labor 2201 C St NW Washington DC 20520 Office Fax: 202-647-5283.

CRANFORD, PAGE DERONDE, lawyer; b. West Chester, Pa., Nov. 20, 1935; s. Joseph D. and Dorothy (Griffith) C.; m. Virginia Langen, Nov. 21, 1965; children: Elizabeth, Courtenay. BS, Washington and Lee U., 1958; JD, George Washington U., 1964; postgrad. in banking, Rutgers U., 1981. Bar: Md. 1964, D.C. 1965, Va. 1974, U.S. Ct. Appeals (D.C. cir.) 1965. Asst. v.p. Nat. Bank Washington, 1958-65; staff counsel U.S. Comptr. of Currency, Washington, 1965-66, regional adminstr. nat. banks Richmond, Va., 1966-72; sr. v.p., sec., gen. counsel Fidelity Am. Bank, Lynchburg, Va., 1972-75; assoc. Boothe, Prichard & Dudley, Fairfax, Va., 1975-76; corp. gen. counsel Va. Nat. Bankshares, Norfolk, Va., 1976-89; exec. v.p., gen. counsel Sorvan Fin. Corp, Norfolk, 1989-90, sr. exec. v.p., gen. counsel, 1990-91; sr. exec. v.p., gen. counsel, sec. C&S/Sovran Corp., Norfolk and Atlanta, 1990-92; ptnr. McGuire Woods Battle & Boothe, Norfolk, 1992-99, ptnr. in charge, 1992-96; of counsel McGuire Woods LLP, Norfolk, 2000—. Adj. prof. Sch. Law Regent U., Va. Beach, 1995-99, Sch. Law Coll. William and Mary, Williamsburg, Va., 1997-98. Trustee Richmond Montessori Sch., 1970-72, Lynchburg Montessori Sch., 1972-75, James River Day Sch., Lynchburg, 1973-75, Va. Symphony, Norfolk, 1984— . Served to capt. U.S. Army, 1958-66 Recipient Arthur S. Fleming award Jaycees, 1972 Mem. ABA (banking law subcom, corp. counsel subcom., bus. law sect.), Va. Bar Assn., Md. Bar Assn., D.C. Bar Assn., Town Point Club (Norfolk). Republican. Episcopalian. Office: McGuire Woods LLP 9000 World Trade Ctr 101 W Main St Ste 9000 Norfolk VA 23510-1655

CRANFORD, STEVEN L. lawyer; b. Oakland, Calif., Aug. 22, 1951; s. Leon B. and Dixie Lee (Hammond) C. AA, Cowley County Community Coll., Arkansas City, Kans., 1971; BS, Pittsburg State U., Kans., 1974; JD, Washburn U., 1977. Bar: Kans. 1977, U.S. Dist. Ct. Kans. 1977, U.S. Supreme Ct. 1987, DC 1989. Assoc. Wheeler and Mitchelson, Pittsburg, Kans., 1977-78; staff counsel S.E. Kans. Community Action Program, Girard, 1978-79; gen. counsel Distbn. Cos. Am. Inc., Houston, 1979-80; sole practice Winfield and Arkansas City, Kans., 1980-83; dep. county atty. Cowley County, Kans., 1981-82; spl. prosecutor Butler County, Kans., 1982—83; asst. sec., asst. gen. counsel Rent-a-Ctr., Inc., Wichita, Kans., 1984—91; chmn., CEO TumbleDrum, Inc., Wichita, 1992—2001; CEO Ironweed Strategy, Newport Beach, Calif., 2001—. Vis. instr. bus. and comml. law St. Johns Coll., Winfield, 1983. Staff aide Don Allegrucci for Congress Com., 1978, standing credentials com. mem. from Kans., Dem. Nat. Conv., 1988; selected mem. Leadership Kans., 1990; chmn. Wichita Pub. Bldg. Commn., 1991-95. Named Outstanding Young Alumnus, Pittsburg State U., 1991. Democrat. Home: 15 Coventry Newport Beach CA 92660-6810 Office: Ironweed Strategy PO Box 8642 Newport Beach CA 92658

CRANG, RICHARD FRANCIS EARL, plant and cell biologist, research center administrator; b. Clinton, Ill., Dec. 2, 1936; s. Richard Francis and Clara Esther (Cummins) Crang; m. Linda L. Crang, Aug. 10, 1958 (div.). BS, Eastern Ill. U., 1958; MS, U. S.D., 1962; PhD, U. Iowa, 1965. Asst. prof. biology Wittenberg U., 1965-69; assoc. prof. biol. sci. Bowling Green State U., 1969-74, prof., 1974-80; prof. plant biology U. Ill., Urbana-Champaign, 1980—2002, assoc. head dept. plant biology, 1995-97, faculty fellow in acad. adminstrn., 1997-99, dir. Ctr. Elec. Microsci., 1980-92, prof. emeritus, 2002—. Adj. prof. anatomy Med. Coll. Ohio, 1974—80; summer rsch. prof. Lehman Coll., CUNY, Bronx, vis. prof. biol. sci., 1999—2003; vis. scientist in botany Cambridge U., England, 1978—79, Komarov Bot. Inst., Warsaw U., Poland, 1993; rschr., collaborator in fungal adhesion Kaohsiung Med. Coll., Taiwan, China, 1988—90; lectr., China, 1990. Author: (with A. Vassilyev) CD-ROM Text on Plant Anatomy, 2003; rschr., contbr. numerous publs. in field of air pollution effects on plant, fungal, and lichen ultrastructure, 1967—; early developer asynchronous learning techs. by means of networked computers on World-Wide Web, 1995—. Mem. Statewide Democratic Support Group, Ill. Recipient Outstanding Faculty Rsch. Recognition awards Bowling Green State U., 1973, 75; grantee Paint Rsch. Inst., 1976-83, NSF, 1981-83, EPA, 1984-86, USDA, 1986-89, Internat. Plant and Pollution Lab., 1993-98; lifetime assoc. fellow Clare Hall, Cambridge, Eng. Mem. AAAS, Bot. Soc. Am., Internat. Soc. Environ. Botanists (advisor, life mem., inaugurated 1st internat. meeting, Lucknow, India, 1996), Microscopy Soc. Am. (nat. chmn. cert. bd. 1982-89, dir. USA local affiliates 1990-93, Disting. Svc. award 1994, Cecil Hall award for outstanding rsch. in biology with analytical microscopy 1994), Sigma Xi. Mem. Christian Ch. (Disciples Of Christ). Home: 1095 Baytowne Dr # 25 Champaign IL 61822-7971 Office: U Ill Plant Biology 505 S Goodwin Ave 665 Morrill Hall Urbana IL 61801-3707 E-mail: r-crang@life.uiuc.edu.

CRÂNGANU, CONSTANTIN, engineer; s. Sterian and Ioana Crânganu; m. Veturia Stamatin; children: Dan, Andreea. MS, U. Bucharest, Romania, 1971—76, PhD, 1990—93, U. Okla., Norman, 1994—97. Geotechnical engr. Vaslui County, Romania, 1976—81; asst. prof. Iasi, Romania, 1981—93; rschr. U. Okla., Norman, 1997—2001; assoc. prof. CUNY, Bklyn Coll., 2001—. Fulbright vis. scientist U. Okla., Norman, 1993—94; asst. dir. Inst. for Exploration and Devel. Geoscis., Norman, Okla., 1998—2000; grad. dep. chair CUNY, Bklyn Coll., 2003—. Achievements include patents pending for Method for Producing Natural Gas from Gas Hydrates. Office: Bklyn Coll 2900 Bedford Ave Brooklyn NY 11210

CRANGLE, ROBERT D. lawyer, management consultant, entrepreneur, manufacturing executive; b. Putnam, Conn., May 5, 1943; s. Dale E. and Libbie S. (Krepela) C.; m. S. Jeanne Rose, June 6, 1968; children: Rob, Scott, Elenor, Bill, Kimball, Susan, Sara, Paul, Hally. BS in Nuclear Engring., Kans. State U., 1966; JD, Harvard U., 1969. Bar: Mass. 1969, Ill. 1974, Kans. 1987, U.S. Dist. Ct. Kans. 1987. Sr. v.p. Harbridge House, Inc., Boston, 1969-84; pres., dir. Rose & Crangle, Ltd., Lincoln, 1984—; dir. Helisys Inc., L.A., 1985-99; ptnr. Metz and Crangle, Chartered, Lincoln, Kans., 1987—2003; elected Lincoln County Atty., 1997—2001; atty. Crangle Law Office, Lincoln, 2003—. Mem. faculty Bus. Sch., Ill. Inst. Tech., Chgo., 1984-87, dir. Ctr. Rsch. on Indsl. Strategy and Policy, Chgo., 1984-87. Bd. dirs. Lake Bluff (Ill.) Sch. Bd., 1982-87, Farmers Nat. Bank, 1992—; mem. Kans. Sci. and Tech. Coun., 1992-96; mem. Natural History Mus. Bd., 1995-98, Kans. Geol. Survey Adv. Com., 1995-2002. Recipient Meritorious Pub. Service award NSF, 1985. Fellow AAAS; mem. ABA, Kans. Bar Assn. (officer bus. law sect. 1993-97), N.W. Kans. Bar Assn., Kans. Math and Sci. Edn. Coalition (bd. dirs.), Inst. Mgmt. Cons. (cert. 1980). Republican. Mem. Soc. Of Friends. Avocations: science policy, entrepreneurship. Office: Crangle Law Office, Chtd 117 N 4th PO Box 285 Lincoln KS 67455-0285 also: Rose & Crangle Ltd PO Box 285 102 E Lincoln Av Lincoln KS 67455-0285 Office Fax: 785-524-3130. E-mail: mcc@nckcn.com.

CRANK, PAT, state attorney general; m. Anna Crank; children: Abbigail, Jerry, Zachary, Noah. B in Acctg., U. Wyo., 1982, JD, 1985. With Wyo. Atty. Gens. Office, 1985—86, Natrona County Dist. Attys. Office, 1987—90, U.S. Attys. Office for Dist. Wyo., 1990—2002; atty. gen. State of Wyo., Cheyenne, 2003—. Democrat. Avocations: hunting, fishing, camping. Office: Atty Gens Office 123 Capitol Bldg 200 W 24th St Cheyenne WY 82002*

CRANKSHAW, JOHN HAMILTON, mechanical engineer; b. Canton, Ohio, Aug. 29, 1914; s. Frederick Weir and Mary (Lashels) C.; m. Wilma Chaffee Thurlow, June 5, 1940; children: Wilma Jean, John H., Geoffrey Thurlow. BSME, MIT, MS, 1940. Registered profl. engr., Pa. Rotating engr. GE, 1940-41; sect. engr. mech. design sect. Motor Engr. divsn. Locomotive Car Equipment, Erie, Pa., 1946-52; exec. engr. J.A. Zurn Mfg. Co., Am. Flexible Coupling Co., 1952-54, v.p. engring., 1954; exec. v.p., dir. Zurn Industries, Inc., mng. dir. R & D divsn., until 1957; pres. Dynetics, Inc., Erie, 1957—, Dynetic Sys., Inc., Erie, 1970—. Expert witness numerous product liability cases. Contbr. articles to profl. jours. Mem. adv. coun. Gannon U.; chmn. Erie Sewer Authority. Maj. Ordnance Dept., AUS, 1941-46. Fellow ASME; mem. ASTM, Soc. Automotive Engrs., Assn. Iron and Steel Engrs., Soc. Exptl. Stress Analysis, Soc. Naval Archs. and Marine Engrs., Am. Soc. Metals, Am. Soc. Lubricating Engrs., Pa. Soc. Profl. Engrs., Erie Engring. Socs. Coun., MIT Club (N.Y.C.), Sigma Xi. Achievements include 25 U.S. and 5 foreign patents; invention and design of main propulsion couplings and clutches for nuclear powered submarines and Navy and Coast Guard surface ships. Home and Office: Dynetics Inc 439 Shawnee Dr Erie PA 16505-2433

CRANMER, THOMAS WILLIAM, lawyer; b. Detroit, Jan. 13, 1951; s. William Eugene and Betty Lee (Orphal) C.; children: Jacqueline, Taylor, Chase. BA, U. Mich., 1972; JD, Ohio No. U., 1975. Bar: Mich. 1975, U.S. Dist. Ct. (ea. dist.) Mich. 1978, U.S. Ct. Appeals (6th cir.) 1978, U.S. Supreme Ct. 1982, U.S. Tax Ct. 1986. Asst. pros. atty. Oakland County, Mich., 1975-78; asst. atty. U.S. Dist. Ct. (ea. dist.) Mich., 1978-80, asst. chief criminal div., 1980-82; assoc. Miro, Miro & Weiner, Bloomfield Hills, Mich., 1982-84, ptnr., 1984—. Mem. faculty Atty. Gen's. Adv. Inst., Washington, 1980-82, Nat. Inst. Trial Adv., Northwestern Chicago, Ill., 1987—, trial adv. workshop Inst. Continuing Legal Edn., 1988—, local rules adv. com. U.S. Dist. Ct. (ea. dist.) Mich., 1989-92; hearing panelist Atty. Discipline Bd., 1987—. Fellow Am. Coll. Trial Lawyers, Oakland County Bar Found. (charter, trustee 1994—, pres. 2002—), Mich. State Bar Found., Internat. Acad. Trial Lawyers, Internat. Soc. Barristers; mem. ABA (chair litigation sect., Detroit graphic subcom. of com. on complex crimes litigation 1990), FBA (exec. bd. dirs. Detroit chpt. 1988-96, pres. 1995-96, Leonard R. Gilman award 1995), Am. Bd. Trial Advocates, Am. Arbitration Assn. (mem. hearing panel 1990), State Bar Mich. (rep. assembly 1986-92, mem. grievance com. 1990—, chair 1993-97, bd. commrs. 1998—, treas. 2001-02, sec. 2002-03, v.p. 2003—), Oakland County Bar Assn. (chair CLE com. 1992, bd. dirs. 1994—, Disting. Svc. award 1996, chair membership com. 1997). Republican. Presbyterian. Office: Miro Weiner & Kramer PC 38500 Woodward Ave Ste 100 Bloomfield Hills MI 48304-5047 Home: 4739 Sandpiper Ln West Bloomfield MI 48323-2063 E-mail: tcranmer@mirolaw.com.

CRANNA, CHRISTINA M. social services specialist; b. Poughkeepsie, N.Y., May 27, 1975; d. Charles Francis and Mary M. Lauria. BS in Psychology, St. Thomas Aquinas Coll., 1997; MSW, Adelphi U., 2001. Mental health worker Rockland County Dept. Mental Health, Pomona, NY, 1997—98; svc. coord. Ulster-Green ARC, Kingston, NY, 1998—; social worker Aster Home for Children, 2000—. Mem.: NASW. Roman Catholic. Avocations: crafts, crocheting, swimming, traveling, history. Home: 44 Old Rte 199 Red Hook NY 12571

CRANNEY, MARILYN KANREK, lawyer; b. Bklyn., June 18, 1949; d. Sidney Paul and Aurelia (Valice) Kanrek; m. John William Cranney, Jan. 22, 1970 (div. June 1975); 1 child, David Julian. BA, Brandeis U., 1970; MA in History, Brigham Young U., 1975; JD, U. Utah, 1979; LLM in Tax Law, NYU, 1984. Bar: N.Y. 1980, U.S. Dist. Ct. (so. and ea. dists.) N.Y. 1992. Assoc. Cravath Swaine & Moore, N.Y.C., 1979-81; 1st v.p., asst. gen. counsel Morgan Stanley Investment Advisors Inc., N.Y.C., 1981—. Mem. Order of the Coif. Democrat. Jewish. Avocations: travel, reading. Office: Morgan Stanley Investment Advisors Inc 22nd Fl 1221 Ave of the Americas New York NY 10020 E-mail: marilyn.cranney@morganstanley.com.

CRANSTON, HOWARD STEPHEN, lawyer, management consultant; b. Hartford, Conn., Oct. 20, 1937; s. Howard Samuel and Agnes (Corvo) C.; m. Karen Youngman, June 16, 1962; children: Margaret, Susan. BA cum laude, Pomona Coll., 1959; LLB, Harvard U., 1962. Bar: Calif. 1963. Assoc. MacDonald & Halsted, L.A., 1964-68; ptnr. MacDonald, Halsted & Laybourne, L.A., 1968-82, of counsel, 1982-86; pres. Knapp Comm., L.A., 1982-87, S.C. Cons. Corp., 1987—. Bd. dirs. Boys Republic. Author: Handbook for Creative Managers, 1987. 1st lt. U.S. Army, 1962—64. Republican. Episcopalian. Office: 1613 Chelsea Rd # 252 San Marino CA 91108-2419 E-mail: hscran@earthlink.net.

CRANSTON, JOHN WELCH, historian, educator; b. Utica, N.Y., Dec. 21, 1931; s. Earl and Mildred (Welch) C. BA, Pomona Coll., 1953; MA, Columbia U., 1964; PhD, U. Wis., 1970. Asst. prof. history West Tex. State U., 1970-74, U. Mo., Kansas City, 1974, Rust Coll., Holly Springs, Miss., 1974-80, assoc. prof., 1980-83; historian U.S. Army Armor Ctr., Ft. Knox, Ky., 1983-95; ret., 1995. Adj. prof. history and govt. Elizabethtown C.C., Ft. Knox, 1988-2002. Contbr. history articles to profl. lit. With U.S. Army, 1953-55. NEH fellow, summers 1976, 81. Mem. Am. Hist. Assn., Orgn. Am. Historians. Democrat. Episcopalian. Home: 900 E Harrison Ave Apt D-61 Pomona CA 91767

CRAPARO, JOHN S. information technology executive; b. N.Y.C., Sept. 3, 1959; s. Francis Xavier Craparo, Jane Constance Licciardi. BA, Iona Coll., New Rochelle, N.Y., 1981; MS in Mgmt., Poly. U., Bklyn., 1990. Sr. v.p., chief tech. officer GE Capital Corp., Stamford, Conn., 1989—98; v.p. global info. tech. ops. Dell Computer Corp., Round Rock, Tex., 1998—; CIO Dell Fin. Svcs., Round Rock, 2002—. Assoc. prof. Pace U., White Plains, NY, 1990—; chancellor Continental U., Lemmon, SD, 1999—. Editor: (jour.) Journal of Continuing Professional Development, 1999; author: (book and software program) Trunkalculator: the telecommunications management tool, 1989. Torchbearer Salt Lake City Olympic Games, 2002; bd. dirs. and mentor Jr. Achievment of Ctrl. Tex., Austin, 1990—; mem. adv. bd. Pace U., White Plains, NY, 1997—; ofcl. U.S. agt. U. of South Africa, Pretoria, South Africa, 1998—; mem. Catholic Hospitalier Order of the the Knights of Malta - Brotherhood of the Blessed Gerard, Mandeni, South Africa, 1998—. Fellow Internat. Mgmt. Ctrs., 1999, N.Y.C. Sci. Found. fellow, Medgar Evers Coll. of CUNY, 1986—89; scholar N.Y. State Regent's scholar, SUNY, 1977—81. Fellow: Royal Soc. Arts; mem.: Assn. of Computing Machinery. Republican. Roman Catholic. Avocations: Swimming, boat building. Home: 5808 Misty Hill Cove Austin TX 78759

CRAPO, MICHAEL DEAN, senator, former congressman, lawyer; b. Idaho Falls, Idaho, May 20, 1951; s. George Lavelle and Melba (Olsen) C.; m. Susan Diane Hasleton, June 22, 1974; children: Michelle, Brian, Stephanie, Lara, Paul. BA Polit. Sci. summa cum laude, Brigham Young U., 1973; postgrad., U. Utah, 1973-74; JD cum laude, Harvard U., 1977. Bar: Calif. 1977, Idaho 1979. Law clk. to Hon. James M. Carter U.S. Ct. Appeals (9th cir.), San Diego, 1977-78; assoc. atty. Gibson, Dunn & Crutcher, L.A., 1978-79; atty. Holden, Kidwell, Hahn & Crapo, Idaho Falls, 1979-92, ptnr., 1983-92; mem. Idaho State Senate from 32A Dist., 1984-93, asst. majority leader, 1987-88; pres. Pro Tempore, 1989-92; congressman U.S. House of Reps., 2d Idaho dist., Washington, 1992-98; mem. commerce com., new mem. leader 103rd Congress, sophomore class leader 104th Congress, co-chair Congl. Beef Caucus, dep. whip western region U.S. House of Reps., Washington, vice chair energy and power subcom., strategic planning leader House Leadership 105th Congress, mem. house resources com., mem. commerce com., mem. resources com.; senator from Idaho U.S. Senate, 1999—, dep. whip 108th congress, chmn. subcom. on fisheries, wildlife and water, Senate environ and pub. works com., chmn. subcom. on forestry, conservation and rural revitalization, Senate agr. com., mem. banking, housing and urban devel. com., mem. small bus. com. Precinct committeeman Dist. 29, 1980-85; vice chmn. Legislative Dist. 29, 1984-85; Mem. Health and Welfare Com., 1985-89, Resources and Environ. Com., 1985-90, State Affairs Com., 1987-92; Rep. Pres. Task Force, 1989. Leader Boy Scouts Am., Calif., Idaho, 1977-92; mem. Bar Exam Preparation, Bar Exam Grading; chmn. Law Day.; Bonneville County chmn. Phil Batt gubernatorial campaign, 1982. Named one of Outstanding Young Men of Am., 1985; recipient Cert. of Merit Rep. Nat. Com., 1990, Guardian of Small Bus. award Nat. Fedn. of Ind. Bus., 1990, 94, Cert. of Recognition Am. Cancer Soc., 1990, Idaho Housing Agy., 1990, Idaho Lung Assn., 1985, 86, 89, Friend of Agr. award Idaho Farm Bur., 1989-90, medal of merit Rep. Presdl. Task Force, 1989, Nat. Legislator of Yr. award Nat. Rep. Legislators Assn., 1991, Golden Bulldog award Watchdogs of the Treas., 1996, Thomas Jefferson award Nat. Am. Wholesale Grocers Assn.-Ind. Food Distbrs. Assn., 1996, Spirit of Enterprise award U.S. C. of C., 1993, 94, 95, 96. Mem. ABA (antitrust law sect.), Idaho Bar Assn., Rotary. Republican. Mem. Lds Ch. Avocations: sports, backpacking, hunting, skiing. Office: US Senate 239 Dirksen Senate Ofc Bldg Washington DC 20510-0001

CRAPOL, EDWARD P. history educator; b. Buffalo, N.Y., Sept. 29, 1936; s. Paul H. and Emmi H. (klinger) C.; m. Jeanne Zeidler, Aug. 1, 1973; children: Heidi, Jennifer, Paul, Andrew. BA, SUNY, Buffalo, 1960; MS, Univ. Wis., 1964, PhD, 1968. Tchr. Amherst Ctrl. Jr. High Sch., Amherst, N.Y., 1961-63; instr. history Wis. State Univ., Eau Claire, Wis., 1966-67; asst. prof. history Coll. William and Mary, Williamsburg, Va., 1967-71, assoc. prof. history, 1971-77; exchange prof. history Univ. Exeter, Exeter, England, 1976-77; prof. history dept. Coll. William and Mary, Williamsburg, Va., 1978—, chmn. history dept., 1981-84, acting chmn. history dept., 1986-87; chancellor prof. history, 1994-99; William E. Pullen prof. Am. history, 1999—. Vis. faculty Utah State U., summer, 1972; reviewer grant proposals NEH, 1983-95; lectr. in field. Author: James G. Blaine: Architect of Empire, 1999; editor: Women and American Foreign Policy: Lobbyists, Critics, and Insiders, 1987, 1992, America for Americans: Economic Nationalism and Anglophobia in the Late Nineteenth Century, 1973; reviewer manuscripts for Diplomatic History, Journal of the Early Republic, Alfred A. Knopf, Scholary Recources, Greenwood Press, Kent State Univ. Press, D.C. Health, Univ. N.C. Press. Va. Found. for Humanities and Pub. Policy grant, 1983, NEH grant, 1984, 1986, Internat. Studies Curriculum Devel. grant Coll of William and Mary, 1987; Univ. Humanities fellow Coll. William and Mary, 1988; Thomas A. Graves Jr. award for Sustained Excellence in Teaching William and Mary Coll., 1991, Thomas Jefferson award Coll. William and Mary, 1992. Mem. Soc. Historians Am. Fgn. Rels., Orgn. Am. Historians, Am. Hist. Assn., Soc. Historians Early Am. Republic. Home: 148 Mimosa Dr Williamsburg VA 23185-4004

CRAPON DE CAPRONA, COUNT NOËL FRANÇOIS MARIE, lawyer, retired United Nations official, historian; b. Chambery, Savoie, France, May 23, 1928; s. Denys and Eleanor Worthington (Mather) Crapon de Caprona; m. Barbro Sigrid Wenne, 1954; children: Guy, Yann. BA, Coll. St. Martin, Pontoise, France, 1946; LLB, U. Paris, 1952; diploma, Inst. Comparative Law, 1951; postgrad., Sch. Polit. Scis., 1952—54. Asst. mgr. Sta. Catalina Estancias, Argentina, 1947—48; editor dept. gen. affairs and info. FAO, UN, Rome, 1954—57; liaison officer for UN and various orgns. FAO Office Dir. Gen., 1957—65, chief reports and records, 1966—72, chief conf. ops. br., 1972—74; sec. gen. FAO Conf. and Coun., 1974—78; dir. FAO Conf., Coun. and Protocol Affairs, Rome, 1974—83. Author: The Longobards, A Tentative Explanation, 1995. Served with French Army, 1944. Recipient 25 Years of Svc. award, Silver medal, FAO, 1979, Medal of Honor, City of Salon de Provence, 1992. Mem.: Soc. in France of SAR, Alumni Assn. Ecole des Sciences Politiques, Alumni Assn. Coll. St. Martin. Roman Catholic. Achievements include research in early medieval history, especially Longobards. Address: Lojovägen 73 S-18147 Lidingö Sweden also: Palais Hadrien Pl dei Tres Mast 83600 Port-Fréjus France

CRARY, MINER DUNHAM, JR., lawyer; b. Warren, Pa., Sept. 8, 1920; s. Miner D. and Edith (Ingraham) C.; m. Mary Chapman, Jan. 23, 1943; children: Edith Crary Howe, James G., Laura Crary Hall, Harriet Crary, Miner A. BA, Amherst Coll., 1942; MA, Harvard U., 1943, LLB, 1948. Bar: N.Y. 1949. Assoc. Curtis, Mallet-Prevost, 1949-61, ptnr., 1961-96, coun., 1996—. Trustee Am. U. in Cairo, 1959—, Heckscher Art Mus., Huntington, N.Y., 1968—; trustee Sterling and Francine Clark Art Inst., Williamstown, Mass., 1974—; bd. dirs. Robert Sterling Clark Found., N.Y.C., 1972—; chmn. exec. com. alumni coun. Amherst Coll., 1961-68; chmn. Huntington Bd. Edn. and Ctrl. Sch. Dist. 2, 1961-67; acting village justice Village of Asharoken, Northport, N.Y., 1987-2002. Lt. USNR, 1942-45. Mem. ABA (real property and probate com.), N.Y. State Bar Assn. (taxation and estate com. 1973), Assn. of Bar of City of N.Y. (surrogate ct. com. 1969-73), Union League Club, Century Assn. Club. (N.Y.C.), Huntington Country Club. Office: Curtis Mallet-Prevost Colt 101 Park Ave Fl 34 New York NY 10178-0061 E-mail: mdcrary@aol.com., mcrary@cm-p.com.

CRASEMANN, BERND, physicist, educator; b. Hamburg, Germany, Jan. 23, 1922; came to U.S., 1946, naturalized, 1955; s. Pablo Joaquin and Hildegard Carlota (Vorwerk) C. AB, UCLA, 1948; PhD, U. Calif.-Berkeley, 1953. With Lavadora de Lanas S.A., Viña del Mar, Chile, 1941-46; asst. prof. physics U. Oreg., Eugene, 1953-58, assoc. prof., 1958-63, prof., 1963-89, prof. emeritus, 1989—, chmn. dept., 1976-84, dir. Chem. Physics Inst., 1984-87. Guest assoc. physicist Brookhaven Nat. Lab., Upton, N.Y., 1961-62; vis. prof. U. Calif., Berkeley, 1968-69, Université Pierre et Marie Curie, Paris, 1977; vis. scholar Stanford U., 1983; cons. Lawrence Radiation Lab., 1954-68, physicist, 1968-69; mem. com. on atomic and molecular sci. NRC/Nat. Acad. Scis., 1976-82;

vis. scientist NASA Ames Rsch. Ctr., 1975-76; mem. panel on radiation rsch. NRC, 1985-87, chair bd. on assessment of NIST programs panel on atomic molecular and optical physics, 1989-90; chair exec. com. Advanced Light Source Users, 1984-88, sci. policy bd., 1989-92; chair adv. bd. Basic Energy Scis. Synchrotron Radiation Ctr. Argonne Nat. Lab, 1991-93; mem. U. Chgo. Review Com. for Argonne Nat. Lab. Physics Divsn., 1993-98; U.S. advisor in physics U.S.-Mex. Found. for Sci., 1994-97. Author: (with J.L. Powell): Quantum Mechanics, 1961; editor: Atomic Inner-Shell Processes, 1975, Atomic Inner-Shell Physics, 1985, Phys. Rev. A., 1992—; mem. editl. bd.: Phys. Rev. C, 1978-, Atomic Data and Nuc. Data Tables, 1982-, mem. publs. bd.: Am. Inst. Physics, 1992—2000; contbr. articles to sci. jours. Mem. region XIV selection com. Woodrow Wilson Nat. Fellowship Found., 1959-61, 62-68. Recipient Ersted award for distinguished teaching U. Oreg., 1959; NSF research grantee, 1954-64; U.S. AEC grantee, 1964-72; NASA grantee, 1972-79; AFOSR grantee, 1979-86; NSF grantee, 1986-95. Fellow AAAS, Am. Phys. Soc. (chmn. div. electron and atomic physics 1981-82, councillor 1983-86, mem. com. on internat. sci. affairs 1997-2000, chmn. 2000); mem. ACLU, Am. Assn. Physics Tchrs. (pres. Oreg. sect. 1956-57), Croatian Acad. Scis. and Arts (corr. mem.), Sierra Club, Phi Beta Kappa. Office: U Oreg Dept Physics Eugene OR 97403-1274 E-mail: berndc@uoregon.edu.

CRASSWELLER, ROBERT DOELL, retired lawyer, writer; b. Duluth, Minn., Sept. 17, 1915; s. Arthur Hallifax and Mary Elizabeth (Doell) C.; m. Mildred Elizabeth Clarke, Mar. 21, 1942; children: Peter, Karen Farbman, Pamela Baldino. BA, Carleton Coll., 1937; LLB, Harvard U., 1941. Bar: Minn. 1941, N.Y. 1960. Pvt. practice, Duluth, Minn., 1942-43; econ. warfare posts U.S. Dept. State, Washington, 1943-45; ptnr. McCabe, Gruber, Clure, Donovan & Crassweller, Duluth, Minn., 1946-51; mining exec. West Indies Mining Corp., San Juan, P.R., 1951-53; counsel Pan Am. Airways, N.Y.C., 1954-67; vis. fellow Coun. Fgn. Rels., N.Y.C., 1967-70; vis. prof. Bklyn. Coll., Sarah Lawrence, N.Y.C., 1969-70; staff atty. ITT, N.Y.C., 1970-74, gen. coun. Lat. Am., 1975-81. Author: Trujillo: Life and Times of a Caribbean Dictator, 1966, The Caribbean Community, 1972, Perón and the Enigmas of Argentina, 1986; reviewer (books) for Fgn. Affairs, 1968-81. Dir. Forum for World Affairs, Stamford, Conn., 1986-87. Mem. Internat. Assn. Torch Clubs (Chapel Hill Club v.p. 1994-95), Soc. Automotive Historians. Republican. Avocations: gardening, travel, reading, writing, antique cars. Home: 101 York Pl Chapel Hill NC 27517-6521 E-mail: rrdcrass@aol.com.

CRATE, DARRELL, political organization administrator; b. N.Y., 1968; Fin. chair Lt. Gov. Kerry Healey's campaign; chmn. Mass. Rep. Party, 2003—; exec. v.p. Affiliated Mgrs. Group, Inc. Office: Mass Rep Party Ste 309 27 Water St Wakefield MA 01880

CRATE, STEPHEN CHURCH, vocational rehabilitation specialist, consultant, author, politician; b. Doylestown, Pa., Aug. 2, 1952; s. Douglas Willits and Sally (Alexander-Church) C.; m. Allison Catherine Ferris, Aug. 23, 1975; children: Matthew Stephen, Daniel Church. Assoc., U. Me., Augusta, 1977; BA, U. Me., Farmington, 1980; postgrad., Northeastern U., 1981, Thomas Coll., 1991 . Cert. rehab. counselor, vocat. evaluation specialist, case mgr. Counselor Halcyon House Emergency Shelter, Hinckley, Maine, 1978-80; activities dir. Hinckley Home Sch. Farm, 1980-82; employment, tng. specialist Maine Dept. Labor, Skowhegan, 1982-83; vocat. evaluator Waterville (Maine) Sch. Dept., 1983-85; CEO Employee Devel. Corp. New Eng., Waterville, 1986-99, Maine Vol. Connection, Inc., Bangor, 2000—. Adj. instr. Kennebec Valley Tech. Coll., Fairfield, Maine, 1997—; rehab. specialist Maine Dept. Labor, Bur. Rehab. Svcs., 2001—. Co-author: I Lost My Job, Now What Do I Do?, 1990; syndicated columnist The Changing Workplace, Allied Feature Syndicate. Mem. Waterville City Coun., 1994-95, chmn. coun., 1995—; past v.p. Opera House Assn.; trustee Kennebec Water Dist., v.p., 1997-2001; adv. Ctr. for Consensual Democracy; dir. youth devel. and vol. svcs. Waterville Boys and Girls Club and YMCA, 2000—; elected mem. Waterville Sch. Bd., 2000—. Mem. Nat. Rehab. Assn. (pres. pvt. sector div. 1994-95), Better Bus. Bur. (consumer div.), Rotary Internat. Office: ME-DOL Bur Rehab Svcs 2 Anthony Ave Augusta ME 04333-0073 E-mail: Stephen.C.Crate@maine.gov.

CRATER, TIMOTHY ANDREWS, internist; b. Winston-Salem, N.C., Aug. 27, 1966; s. John Lee Crater and Nancy Denton Crater; m. Debra Marie Schuh, Feb. 14, 1992; children: Reed Brooks, Zoe Emerson, Grace Warren, Isabelle Holton. BA in History magna cum laude, Wake Forest U., 1989; student field arty. officers basic course, Ft. Sill Arty. Sch., Okla., 1990; officer's tng., U.S. Army Airborne Sch., Ft. Benning, Ga., 1990, 1st Infanty Divsn., 1991; MD, U. Kans., 1998. Commd. 2d lt. U.S. Army, 1989, advanced through grades to 1st lt., 1992, fire support officer hdqs. battery 1/5 field arty., 1990-91, fire direction officer bravo battery 1/5 field arty., 1991-92, targeting officer hdqs. battery 1/5 field arty., 1992-93; resigned, 1993; resident in internal medicine U. Ala. Birmingham Hosp., 1998-2001; staff physician internal medicine Hutchinson (Kans.) Clinic, 2001—; asst. med. dir. Harry Hynes Meml. Hospice, 2002—03; clin. asst. prof. internal medicine U. Kans. Sch. Medicine, Wichita, 2002—; asst. med. dir. Reno County Hospice, 2003—. History of medicine fellow U. Kans., summer 1995. Decorated Bronze Star medal, Army Commendation medal, Army Achievement medal with oak leaf cluster. Mem. AMA, ACP, VFW, Kans. Soc. SAR, Am. Mensa, Am. Legion, Officers of the 1st Divsn., Rotary, Phi Beta Kappa, Phi Alpha Theta, Alpha Omega Alpha. Republican. Avocations: reading, leading bible study group. Home: 3504 Thunderbird Dr Hutchinson KS 67502 Office: Hutchinson Clinic PA 2101 N Waldron Hutchinson KS 67502 E-mail: cratermd@aol.com.

CRAVEN, CHARLES WARREN, lawyer; b. Johnstown, Pa., Dec. 5, 1947; s. Warren Grant and Constance (Galardie) C.; B.A. in Polit. Sci., St. Joseph's U., Phila., 1969; J.D., Temple U., 1973. Bar: Pa. 1973, U.S. Dist. Ct. (ea. dist.) Pa. 1973, U.S. Ct. Appeals (3d cir.) 1976, U.S. Supreme Ct. 1976. Assoc. Marshall, Dennehey, Warner, Coleman & Goggin, Phila., 1973-83; ptnr., 1983— . Mem. ABA, Pa. Bar Assn., Phila. Bar Assn. Office: Marshall Dennehey Warner Coleman & Goggin 1845 Walnut St Philadelphia PA 19103-4708

CRAVEN, FRANK JOHN, actor, writer; b. N.Y.C., Sept. 19, 1955; s. John and Dorothy (Langan) Craven; m. Fedora di Eugenio, June 12, 1991. At, HB Studio, NYC. Summer stock apprentice Corning Summer Theatre, 1981; drama coach Actors Youth Fund; columnist Streetnews, NYC. Prodr.: (documentaries) Conversatio about Picasso, Free Leonard Peltier Now! (Houston Film Festival Silver award, 1992, writer/dir. Bronze, Worldfest, 2001, 2002), WTC RIP (Judges award, Hometown Video Fest, 1998, 1999); (TV series) What's Ailing/Healing US Am.; (TV films) The Clothes Make the Man (NY Film & Video Fest Best Costume award, 2001, Internet Cities Streamed TV award, 2001, Bronze Telly award, 00, 01, 02);, author plays, composer songs; actor: (TV series); (films); (plays);, performer (m.c.) cabaret; model : prodr.: (screen plays) Authority Vs. Majority (silver- comedy screenplay Worldfest Houston, 92); (plays) Am. Theater of Actors, 1982, 1989. Mem.: AEA, AFTRA, SAG. Avocations: flamenco guitar, blues harmonica, painting, cartooning. Office: Authority vs Majority Prod 307 E 81st St New York NY 10028 E-mail: autvsmaj@aol.com.

CRAVEN, GEORGE W. lawyer; b. Louisville, Mar. 11, 1951; s. Mark Patrick and Doris Ann Craven; m. Jane A. Gallery, Aug. 16, 1980; children: Charles, Francis. Student, Sophia U., Tokyo, Japan, 1970-71; BA, U. Notre Dame, 1973; JD, Harvard U., 1976. Bar: Ill. 1976, U.S. Dist. Ct. (no. dist.) Ill. 1976, U.S. Tax Ct. 1977. Assoc. Sidley & Austin, Chgo., 1976—80; ptnr. Ogden & Robertson, Louisville, 1980—81; assoc. Mayer, Brown, Rowe & Maw, Chgo., 1981—82, ptnr., 1983—. Sec., United Way, Chgo., 1997—, bd. dirs., 2001-. Mem. ABA (sect. taxation), Coun. on Fgn. Rels. (Chgo. com. 1996—), Econ. Club Chgo. Roman Catholic. Office: Mayer Brown Rowe & Maw 190 S La Salle St Ste 3100 Chicago IL 60603-3441 E-mail: gcraven@mayerbrown.com.

CRAVEN, JAMES MICHAEL, economist, educator; b. Seattle, Mar. 10, 1946; s. Homer Henry and Mary Kathleen Craven; 1 child, Christina Kathleen Florindo-Craven. Student, U. Minn., 1966-68; BA in Sociology, BA in Econs., U. Manitoba, Winnipeg, Can., 1971, MA in Econs., 1974. Lic. pilot; cert. ground instr. Instr. econ. and bus. Red River C.C., Winnipeg, 1974-76; lectr. rsch. methods of stats. U. Manitoba, Winnipeg, 1977-78; instr. econ. and bus. Big Bend C.C., Moses Lake, Wash., 1980-81; planning analyst Govt. P.R., San Juan, 1984; prof. econs. and bus. Interam. U. P.R., Bayamon, 1984-85; instr. econs., lectr. history Green River C.C., Auburn, Wash., 1988-92; prof. dept. chair econs. Clark Coll., Vancouver, Wash., 1992—. Vis. prof. St. Berchman's U., Kerala, India, 1981, 83, 86, 91; instr. econs. Bellevue (Wash.) C.C., 1988-92; cons. Bellevue, 1988—, Irwin Pubs., 1995—. Inventor in field; contbr. articles to profl. jours. Platform com. mem. Wash. State Dem., Seattle, 1992; cons. Lowry for Gov. Campaign, Seattle, 1992; mem. (assoc.) Dem. Party Nat. Com., 1994-99; mem. Nat. Steering Com. for Re-election of Pres. Clinton, 1995-96; mem. Pres.'s Second Term Com., 1996-99; tribunal judge Inter-Tribal Tribunal on Residential Schs. in Can., Vancouver, 1998; mem. Blackfoot Nation. With U.S. Army, 1963-66. Recipient pilot wings FAA, 1988-92; Govt. Can. fellow, 1973-74. Mem. Assn. Northwest Econ. Educators, Wash. Edn. Assn., Assn. Nat. Security Alumni, Blackfoot Confederacy. Syrian Orthodox. Avocations: flying, languages, tennis, hiking. Home: 904 NE Minnehaha St Apt C9 Vancouver WA 98665-8732 Office: Clark Coll Dept Econs 1800 E Mcloughlin Blvd Vancouver WA 98663-3598 E-mail: jcraven@clark.edu., blkfoot5@earthlink.net.

CRAVEN, ROBERTA JILL, educator in literature and film; b. White Plains, N.Y., Feb. 4, 1962; d. Robert James and Norma Eleanor (Page) Craven; m. Keith M. Stinchcomb, Sept. 16, 2000; 1 child, Sara Page Stinchcomb. BS in Math., U. N.C., 1984, PhD in Comparative Lit., 1999. Account systems engr. IBM Nat. Fed. Mktg., Bethesda, Md., 1984-86, account mktg. rep., 1986-89; telecomm. mktg. support rep. IBM, Research Triangle Park, N.C., 1990; instr. U. N.C., Chapel Hill, 1990-99; asst. prof. film Millersville U. of Pa., 1999—, asst. chair dept. English, 2003—. T.J. Watson Nat. Merit scholar IBM, Armonk, N.Y., 1980, Hon. Regents scholar N.Y. Bd. Regents, 1980, Frank Porter Graham Grad. Hon. Soc., 1993, Dissertation fellow U. N.C., 1997, Sr. fellow, 1998; grantee Commn. on Cultural Diversity, 2002; recipient Women's Issue Endowment award, 2002, Acad. Climate and Cultural Enrichment award, 2002. Mem. MLA, Southern Comparative Lit. Assn., Soc. Cinema & Media Studies, Phi Beta Kappa, Phi Eta Sigma. Avocations: skiing, film, writing. Office: Dept English Chryst Hall PO Box 1002 Millersville U Pa Millersville PA 17551-0302

CRAVEN, STEPHEN M. retired research chemist; b. Salem, N.J., July 30, 1944; s. John Richard and Helen Barbara (Orlowski) C.; m. Laura A. Blizzard, Mar. 6, 1971 (div. July 1984); children: Edward Marion, Theresae Marie. BA in Chemistry, Rutgers U., 1966; PhD in Phys.-Analytical Chemistry, U. S.C., 1970. Rsch. scientist Miami U., Wright-Patterson AFB, Ohio, 1970-72, rsch. assoc. Oxford, Ohio, 1972-73; sr. analytical chemist Akzona, Enka, N.C., 1973-75; rsch. assoc. Ohio U., Athens, 1975-76; sr. analytical chemist Monsanto Rsch. Corp., Miamisburg, Ohio, 1976-86; retired, 1986. Co-patentee in field. Mem. Cobletz Soc., Soc. for Applied Spectroscopy. Achievements include co-patent disclosure for new class of high electrical conducting (possible superconductor), and thermisters, low thermal conducting materials, new class of catalyst and new class of Lasant materials.

CRAVENS, GARY DEAN, informaticist, physician; b. Phila., Oct. 18, 1953; s. Robert Walker and Mary Edna Cravens. BA, Ind. U., 1975, MS, 1979, MS, 1984, MS, 1992, MD, 1997. Computer programmer analyst Naval Surface Warfare Ctr., Crane, Ind., 1984—85; mathematician USAF Sch. Aerospace Medicine, San Antonio, 1985—87; advanced discipline specialist Vanguard Tech. Corp., Crane, 1987—88; resident Mayo Clinic, Rochester, Minn., 1999—2000; sr. informaticist Ingenix Health Intelligence, Eden Prairie, Minn., 2000—02; bioinformaticist Ind. U., Indpls., 2002—. Contbr. articles to profl. jours. 2d lt. USAF, 1975-77. Med. Informatics fellow Ind. U., 1997-99. Mem. Am. Med. Informatics Assn. (reviewer 1998-99), World Future Soc., Alpha Omega Alpha. Avocations: travel, reading. Home: 516 Magdalene Ln Apt H Indianapolis IN 46224 Office: Ind U Sch Informatics 525 N Blackford St Indianapolis IN 46202

CRAVENS, HAMILTON, history educator; b. Evanston, Ill., Aug. 12, 1938; s. Charles Turner and Flora Hamilton C.; m. Carole Davis Kazmierski, July 22, 2000; children from previous marriage: Heather Lee, Christopher Hamilton. BA in History, U. Wash., 1960, MA in History, 1962; PhD in History, U. Iowa, 1969. Instr. history Ohio State U., Columbus, 1965-68; from instr. to assoc. prof. history Iowa State U., Ames, 1968-80, prof. history, 1980—. Vis. prof. history U. Md., 1971-72, U. Calif., Davis, 1991, hist. cons., 1999—, chair edit. bd. Am. Studies Jour., U. Kans., 1972-97; vis. scholar Stanford Humanities Ctr., 1986, U. Calif., 1990-92; prin. investigator, NSF, 1978-81. Author: Triumph of Evolution, 1978-88, Before Head Start, 1993, 2002, Technical Knowledge, 1996, Health Care Policy, 1997, Social Sciences Go to Washington, 2003. George Bancroft prof. Fulbright Kommission, Goettingen, Germany, 1988-89, J.W. Fulbright Disting. Prof., Bonn, Germany, 1997; fellow Stanford Humanities Ctr., 1986, Max Planck Inst. History, Germany, 1997. Mem. History Sci. Soc. (chair COP, 1990-92), Am. Studies Assn. (chair CB, 1986-88), Orgn. Am. Historians (chair 1990-92, Merle Curti prize com.), Mid-Am. Studies Assn. (pres. 1975-77). Democrat. Unitarian Universalist. Avocations: reading, writing, poetry, travel, music. Office: Iowa State U Dept History 603 Ross Hall Ames IA 50011

CRAVENS, RAYMOND LEWIS, retired political science educator; b. St. Bernard, Ohio, Dec. 5, 1930; s. R.L. and Ethel (Hammonds) C.; m. Ann Powell, Aug. 11, 1956; children: Andrea Lee, Alicia. AB, Western Ky. State Coll., 1952, MA, 1955; PhD, U. Ky., 1958. Prof. govt. Western Ky. U., 1958—, dean of coll., 1959-64, dean of faculty, 1964-66, v.p. acad. affairs, dean faculties, 1966-77, dean pub. service and internat. programs, 1977-80, dir. Coop. Ctr. for Study in Britain, 1982-89. Chmn. Ky. Coun. Acad. V.P.s; pres. Ky. Coun. on Internat. Edn., 1973-81; mem. adv. com. on tchr. edn. Ky. Coun. on Pub. Higher Edn. Served as 1st lt. USAF, 1952-54. Named one of 3 outstanding young men in state Ky. Jr. C. of C., 1964; named Ky. Internat. Educator of Yr., 1993; Ky. Rsch. Found. fellow U. Ky., 1957; Haggin scholar U. Ky., 1955-57. Mem. ASPA, So. Acad. Deans, So. Assn. Colls. (commn. on colls., chmn. com. admissions to membership), Masons. Baptist. Home: 1106 Southpark Dr Bowling Green KY 42103 E-mail: rlcravens@worldnet.att.net.

CRAVENS, STANLEY H. software development manager; b. San Francisco, Jan. 17, 1948; s. Homer A. and Virginia F. (Ference) C.; m. Debra Sargent, June 17, 1976. BA in History, U. N.H., 1974, MA in History, 1976. Project mgr. State of Wis., Madison, 1978—. Advisor: (film) A Vision Shaped in Stone, 1986. Sgt. U.S. Army, 1966-70. Decorated Bronze Star, U.S. Army, Viet Nam, 1970. Mem. Kiwanis (pres. Downtown Madison club 1990-91, lt. gov. 1992-93, gov. Wis. and Upper Mich. 1997-98, Circle K dist. adminstr. 2000--). Home: 3814 Sunhill Dr Madison WI 53718-6283 E-mail: scravens@execpc.com.

CRAVER, DIANE SUE, writer, educator; b. Bluffton, Ohio, Nov. 21, 1949; d. Horace Clifton and Laoma Gail Wilson; m. Thomas Philip Craver, Aug. 2, 1975; children: Sara Theresa, Christina Diane, April Marie, Bartholomew Thomas, Emily Catherine, Amanda Jean. BS, Ohio State U., Columbus, Ohio, 1968—72. Provisional Tchg. Cert. Ohio, 1972. Tchr. Ohio Soldiers and Sailors Orphans Home, Xenia, Ohio, 1972—73, Wabash Jr. HS, Wabash, Ind., 1973—74, Liberty-Benton HS, Findlay, Ohio, 1974—75; substitute tchr. Clermont County Schools, Batavia, Ohio, 1975—76, 1999—2000; author self-employed, Batavia, Ohio, 2001—; homemaker and educator Batavia, Ohio, 1975—. Author: (novel) The Christmas of 1957 (The Midwest Book Rev. - 5 stars, 2002), (e-book) How To Run A Profitable Preschool Without The Hassle. Recipient The Midwest Book Rev. - 5 stars, Oreg., Wis., 2002. R-Consevative. Catholic. Achievements include I have promoted literacy in schools. My topic in my book, The Christmas of 1957, deals with the topic of illiteracy. Avocations: reading, bicycling, swimming, sewing, gardening. Home and Office: 2633 Jackson Pike Batavia OH 45103

CRAVER, JAMES BERNARD, lawyer; b. Morristown, N.J., July 20, 1943; s. Herbert Seward and Anne (Brady) C.; m. Elinor Ladd, Aug. 27, 1966; children: Elisabeth Ladd, Amy Richmond. AB cum laude, Harvard U., 1965; JD, U. Pa., 1970. Bar: N.Y. 1970, Mass. 1974, Ohio 1980. Assoc. Sullivan & Cromwell, N.Y.C., 1970-73; asst. counsel, asst. sec. Mass. Fin. Svcs. Co., Boston, 1973-76; gen. counsel, sec. Anchor Corp., Elizabeth, N.J., 1976-79; sec., sr. corp. counsel B.F. Goodrich Co., Akron, Ohio, 1979-84; ptnr. Baker & Hostetler, Columbus, 1984-90; sr. v.p., gen. coun. Signature Fin. Group, Inc., Boston, 1991-95; mng. dir. Eagle Instl. Fin. Svcs., Inc., Dover, Mass., 1995-2000; ptnr. Burns & Levinson, Boston, Mass., 2000—. Mem. N.Y. State Bar Assn., Mass. Bar Assn., Ohio Bar Assn., Boston Bar Assn., Sakonnet Golf Club (Little Compton, R.I.), Harvard Club of Boston, Harvard Club of Akron, Dedham (Mass.) Country and Polo Club. Home: PO Box 811 Dover MA 02030-0811 Office: Burns & Levinson 125 Summer St Boston MA 02110-1624 Fax: 617-345-3299. E-mail: jcraver@burnslev.com.

CRAVEY, PAMELA J. librarian; b. Washington, Mar. 6, 1945; d. Jack M. and Marjorie M.W. Bristow; m. G. Randall Cravey; 1 child, Christopher B. BA, Baldwin Wallace Coll., 1967; MS, Fla. State U., 1968; PhD, Ga. State U., 1989. Libr., instr. Fla. State U., Tallahassee, 1968-69, U. Ga., Athens, 1969-72; asst. then assoc. libr. U. Ctrl. Fla., Orlando, 1973-75; asst. then assoc. prof., libr. Ga. State U., Atlanta, 1975-2000; pvt. practice $D, Decatur, 2000—. Author: Protecting Library Staff, Users, Collections, and Facilities, 2001; contbr. articles to profl. jours. and books. Libr. Svc. Enhancement Program grantee Coun. Libr. Resources; personal grantee Coun. Libr. Resources. Mem. ALA, Assn. Coll. Rsch. Librs. Home: 2413 Harrington Dr Decatur GA 30033-4903 Office: #308 2103 N Decatur Rd Decatur GA 30033-5305 E-mail: pamelajcravey@mindspring.com.

CRAW, FREEMAN (JERRY), graphic artist; b. East Orange, N.J. s. Stanley Reston and Mildred (Godfrey) C.; m. Janet Secor Johnson (dec.); children: Peter (dec.), Stephanie (dec.). Grad., Cooper Union, hon. degree, 1967. Artist Am. Colortype, Clifton, N.J., 1940-44; art dir. Tri-Arts Press, N.Y.C., 1944-65, art dir., v.p., 1956-65; prin. Freeman Craw Design, N.Y.C., 1965-81; mgr. graphics and prodn. Rockefeller U. Press, N.Y.C., 1981-86; prin. Freeman Craw, graphist, Millburn, NJ, 1986—2001; pvt. practice Tinton Falls, NJ, 2001—. One-man shows include: Am. Type Founders, U. Ala., BBDO, N.Y.C., Carnegie-Mellon U., Cooper Union, Royal Coll. Art, London, Soc. Typog. Designers, London, Soc. Typog. Arts, Chgo., Rochester Inst. Tech., N.Y.; represented in permanent collections: Mus. Modern Art., N.Y.C., Cooper-Hewitt Mus., Smithsonian Instn., N.Y.C.; created 10 type faces. Mem. alumni adv. bd. Cooper Union, 1969-71 Recipient Goudy award Rochester Inst. Tech., 1981, Type Dirs. Club medal, 1988, Lernhardt award, 1966. Mem. Type Dirs. Club (bd. dirs. 1983-86), Art Dirs. Club, Guttenberg Mus. (hon.), Essex Skating Club (West Orange, N.J., hon.). Avocations: japanese prints, lectures.

CRAWFORD, B. lawyer; b. Tulsa, June 29, 1922; s. Burnett Hayden and Margaret Sara (Stevenson) C.; m. Carolyn McCann, June 5, 1946 (div.); m. Virginia Baker, July 23, 1970 (dec. June 1994); m. Melanie Crowley, Dec. 24, 1994; children: Margaret Louise Crawford Brucks, Robert Hayden. BA, U. Mich., 1944, JD, 1949. Bar: Okla. 1949, U.S. Dist. Ct. (no. dist.) Okla. 1949, U.S. Supreme Ct. 1954, U.S. Ct. Appeals (10th cir.) 1954, U.S. Dist. Ct. (so. dist.) Ill. 1959, U.S. Ct. Mil. Appeals 1959, U.S. Ct. Appeals (fed. cir.) 1959, U.S. Dist. Ct. (we. and ea. dists.) Okla. 1960, U.S. Tax Ct. 1967. Law clk. to chief judge U.S. Dist. Ct. (no. dist.) Okla., 1950-51; asst. city prosecuter City of Tulsa, 1951-52, alt. mcpl. judge, 1952-54; U.S. atty. No. Dist. Okla., 1954-58; asst. dep. atty. gen. U.S. Dept. Justice, 1958-60; sole practice Tulsa, 1960-77; sr. ptnr. Crawford Crowne and Bainbridge, Tulsa, 1981-96, The Law Office of B. Hayden Crawford, Tulsa, 1996—. Lectr. in field. Rep. nominee U.S. Senate from Okla., 1960, 62, Okla. mem. adv. com. U.S. Ct. of Appeals (10th circuit); active civic and mil. orgns. Served to Rear Adm. USNR, 1942-78. Decorated Legion of Merit, Purple Heart, Disting. Pub. Svc. medal, Dept. Def. Disting. Svc. award; recipient Okla. Minute Man award 1974. Fellow Am. Assn. Matrimonial Lawyers; mem. ABA, Okla. Bar Assn., Tulsa County Bar Assn., Assn. Trial Lawyers Am., Okla. Trial Lawyers Assn., U.S. Res. Officers Assn. (nat. pres. 1973-74), Phi Delta Theta, Phi Delta Phi, Tulsa Summit Club, Army and Navy Club (Washington), Garden of Gods Club (Colorado Springs, Colo.), So. Hills Country Club (Tulsa), Masons, Kiwanis (pres. 1969). Presbyterian. Home: 2300 Riverside Dr Tulsa OK 74114-2400 Office: 240 Mid-Continent Tower 401 S Boston Ave Tulsa OK 74103-4016

CRAWFORD, BERNARD K., JR., thoracic surgeon, educator; b. Newark, Jan. 10, 1950; s. Bernard Keating and Clara Beatrice Crawford; m. Anne Elizabeth Whitehead, Aug. 25, 1979 (div. Sept. 1999); m. Angela Maria Atusmendy, June 2, 2002; children: Jessica, Maya. BA, Wesleyan U., Middletown, Conn., 1972; MD, George Washington U., 1980. Asst. prof. surgery NYU Med. Ctr., 1987—. Fellow: Am. Soc. Thoracic Surgeons, Am. Coll. Chest Physicians; mem.: ACS (cert.), Am. Coll. Thoracic Surgeons (cert.). Office: NYU Med Ctr 530 1st Ave 9V New York NY 10016 Office Fax: 212-263-6572.

CRAWFORD, BETTY ELIZABETH, English and computer science educator; b. Whittemore, Mich., Dec. 6, 1942; d. Kenneth Arnold and Ona Belle (Allen) St. John; m. Franklin Speaker Crawford, Dec. 29, 1968 (dec. Oct. 1994); 1 child, Tina. BS, Bob Jones U., 1965; MA in Tchg., Oakland U., 1980; cert. of journalism, Newspaper Inst., 1985. Cert. tchr., Mich. Computer coord., tchr. Faith Christian Schs., Clinton Twp., Mich., 1980—; English prof. Macomb C.C., Warren, Mich., 1988—. Spkr. in field. Editor: Computer Science, 1990. Mem. Mich. Assn. Christian Schs., Am. Assn. Christian Schs. Avocations: reading, surfing the web, church, singing, piano. Office: Faith Christian Schools 23130 Remick Dr Clinton Township MI 48036-2735 E-mail: FaithLab@juno.com.

CRAWFORD, BRUCE EDGAR, advertising executive; b. West Bridgewater, Mass., Mar. 16, 1929; s. Harry Ellsworth and Nancy (Morrison) C.; m. Christine Amelung, Feb. 1, 1958; 1 son, Robert Bosworth. BS in Econs., U. Pa., 1952. With Benton & Bowles, Inc., N.Y.C., 1954-58; v.p. Ted Bates & Co., N.Y.C., 1958-61; advt. dir. Chesebrough Ponds Inc., N.Y.C., 1961-63; with Batten, Barton, Durstine & Osborn, Inc., N.Y.C., 1963-85, pres., from 1978, BBDO Internat., N.Y.C., 1975-83, chief exec. officer, 1977-85, chmn., 1985; dir. Met. Opera Assn., from 1976, v.p., 1981, pres., 1984-85, gen. mgr., 1986-88; pres., chief exec. officer Omnicom Group, N.Y.C., 1989-97; chmn. Omnicom Group, Inc., N.Y.C., 1997—. Served with U.S. Army, 1947-48. Mem.: Racquet and Tennis (N.Y.C.); Turf and Field. Republican. Office: Omnicom Group Inc 437 Madison Ave New York NY 10022-7001 Also: Met Opera Assn Lincoln Ctr New York NY 10023

CRAWFORD, CAREN LEE, computer engineer; b. Maywood, Calif., Sept. 1, 1954; d. Charles Earl and Wilma May (Flom) Hillhouse; m. Jimmie Crawford, Aug. 6, 1983. BA, Adams State Coll., 1976; AA, Western Nev. CC, 1980. CRP planner Bently Nev. Corp., Minden; MRB and source inspection coord. Apple Computer, Cupertino, Calif., 1981-83; quality assurance specialist Convergent Tech., San Jose, Calif., 1983-88; sr. project coord. Sun Microsystems, Mountain View, Calif., 1988-90, quality engr., 1990, sr. quality engr., 1991-97; s/w process engr. KLA-Tencor Corp., San Jose, 1997-98; sr. quality assurance analyst NET Delivery Corp, San Jose, 1999-00; sr. cons. DATATREND Info. Sys., Chgo., 2000; quality program mgr. Qwest Comms., Inc., Denver, 2000-01; br. office admin. Edward Jones, 2002—. Mem.: APICS, Am. Soc. Quality Control (cert.), White Shine Jerusalem (worth shepardess 1981, Ruth 1972), Order Eastern Star. Home: 14871 Mariposa Ct Broomfield CO 80020-8742

CRAWFORD, CARL BENSON, retired civil engineer, government research administrator; b. Dauphin, Man., Can., Oct. 2, 1923; s. Arthur Benson and Eileen Agnes (Einarson) C.; m. Adah May Shanks, Sept. 6, 1948; children: Nora, Henry, Margaret, Blair. BSc in Civil Engring., Queen's U., Kingston, Ont., Can., 1949; MSc in Soil Engring, Northwestern U., 1951; D.I.C. in Soil Engring, U. London, 1957; LLD, Concordia U., 1984. Rsch. officer soil mechanics sect. Bldg. Rsch. divsn. Nat. Rsch. Coun. Can., Ottawa, Ont., 1949-53, head soil mechanics sect., 1953-69, asst. dir., 1969-74, dir., 1974-85; ret., 1985. Vis. prof. U. B.C., 1985—. Contbr. articles to tech. publs. Served with RCAF, 1943-45. Recipient Robert F. Legget award Can. Geotech. Soc., 1977, R.M. Quigley award, 1996. Fellow Can. Acad. Engring.; mem. ASTM (Hogentogler award 1961, Spl. Svc. award 1968, hon. mem. 1977—, dir. Inst. for Stds. Rsch., bd. dirs. 1990-92), ASCE, Engring. Inst. Can. (Julian C. Smith medal 1989), Internat. Soc. Soil Mechanics and Found. Engring. (v.p. N.Am. 1981-85), Stds. Coun. Can. (Jean P. Carriere award 1990), Assn. Profl. Engrs. Ont. Home: 108-2556 Highbury St Vancouver BC Canada V6R 3T3

CRAWFORD, CAROL GLORIA, mathematician, educator; b. Wilkes-Barre, Pa., Dec. 8, 1951; d. Harry H. and Gloria P. Crawford. BA in Math., Misericordia Coll., 1973; MA in Math., Georgetown U., 1975, PhD in Math. with distinction, 1979. Prof. math. LeMoyne Coll., Syracuse, NY, 1979—81, U.S. Naval Acad., Annapolis, Md., 1981—. Mem. rev. panels NSF, 1997—99, 2003; v.p. faculty senate U.S. Naval Acad., 2001—03; presenter in field.

Author: Math Without Fear, 1981; contbr. articles to profl. jours.; assoc. editor Am. Math. Monthly, 1984—86. Named rsch. fellow, USN, 1982, NASA, 1984; recipient Civilian Meritorious Svc. award and medal, USN, 1998; fellow, Inst. for Combinatorics, Winnipeg, Can., 1990; grantee, FBI, 1994—96, Office of Naval Rsch., 1994—96, NASA, 1994—96, David Taylor Rsch. Ctr., 1994—96, Carderock Divsn., 1994—96, Naval Air Warfare Ctr. Mem.: Math. Assn. Am. (regional chair, vice chair 1998—2000). Office: US Naval Acad Dept Math Annapolis MD 21402 Business E-Mail: cgc@usna.edu.

CRAWFORD, CAROL TALLMAN, law educator; b. Mt. Holly, N.J., Feb. 25, 1943; m. Ronald Crawford; children: Timothy, Jeffrey, Richard. BA, Mt. Holyoke Coll., 1965; JD magna cum laude, Washington Coll. Law, Am. U., 1978. Bar: Va. 1978, D.C. 1979. Legis. asst. to Senator Bob Packwood, Washington, 1969-75; assoc. firm Collier, Shannon, Rill & Scott, Washington, 1979-81; exec. asst. to chmn. FTC, Washington, 1981-83, dir. bur. consumer protection, 1983-85; assoc. dir. Office of Mgmt. & Budget, Washington, 1985-89; asst. atty. gen. legis. affairs U.S. Dept. Justice, Washington, 1989-90; commr. U.S. Internat. Trade Commn., 1991-2000; disting. vis. prof. law George Mason U., Arlington, Va., 2000-01. Bd. dirs. European Inst., Ind. Women's Forum, Smithfield Foods, Inc., Casals and Assocs. Trustee Barry Goldwater Chair of Am. Instns., Ariz. State U., Phoenix, 1983—; chair internat. trade and investment subcom. Federalist Soc., 1998—99, chair internat. and nat. security sect., 1999—2003. Republican.

CRAWFORD, DAVID L. astronomer; b. Tarentum, Pa., Mar. 2, 1931; s. William Letham and A. Blanche (Livingstone) C.; m. Mary Louise Mueller, Aug. 16, 1940; children: Christine, Deborah, Lisa. PhD, U. Chgo., 1958. Rsch. asst. Yerkes Obs., Chgo., 1953-57; asst. prof. Vanderbilt U., Nashville, 1957-59; staff astronomer Kitt Peak Nat. Obs., Tucson, 1960-96, emeritus astronomer, 1997—. Rsch. asst. McDonald Obs., 1955-57; project mgr. Kitt Peak Nat. Obs., 1963-73, assoc. dir. rsch., 1970-73, head office univ. rels., 1984-85, head office of tech. transfer, 1993-95; exec. dir. Internat. Dark-Sky Assn., 1987—, pres. bd. dirs. GNAT, Inc., 1993—. Recipient outstanding svc. award Astron. League, 1992. Fellow AAAS (coun. 1986-89, com. on coun. affairs 1986-88), Illuminating Engring. Soc. N.Am. (roadway lighting com., outdoor environ. lighting impact com., sports lighting com.); mem. Am. Astron. Soc. (coun. 1972-75, Van Briesbrock award 1997), Astron. Soc. Pacific (bd. dirs. 1970-76, nominating com., publs. com.), Internat. Astron. Union (active numerous commns., exec. coms., past chmn. working group on amateur/profl. rels.). Avocations: travel, reading, teaching, trout fishing, photography. Office: IDA 3225 N First Ave Tucson AZ 85719 E-mail: crawford@darksky.org.

CRAWFORD, DEWEY BYERS, lawyer; b. Saginaw, Mich., Dec. 22, 1941; s. Edward Owen and Ruth (Wentworth) C.; m. Nancy Elizabeth Eck, Mar. 24, 1973. AB in Econs., Dartmouth Coll., 1963; JD with distinction, U. Mich., 1966. Bar: Ill. 1967, U.S. Dist. Ct. (no. dist.) Ill. 1969. Assoc. Gardner, Carton & Douglas LLP, Chgo., 1969-74, ptnr., 1975—. Adj. prof. law, ITT, Kent Sch. Law, 1992—. Contbr. articles to profl. jours. Chmn. Winnetka (Ill.) Caucus Coun., 1988-89; governing mem. Chgo Symphony, Chgo. Bot. Garden. With U.S. Army, 1966-68, Vietnam. Mem. ABA, Chgo. Bar Assn., Am. Coll. Investment Counsel, Lawyers Club Chgo., Exec. Club Chgo. Republican. Congregationalist. Avocations: running, reading, music. Office: Gardner Carton & Douglas LLP 191 N Wacker Dr Ste 3700 Chicago IL 60606-1698 E-mail: dcrawford@gcd.com.

CRAWFORD, DONALD WESLEY, philosophy educator, university official; b. Berkeley, Calif., July 30, 1938; s. Arthur Loyd and Josephine (Gareffa) C.; m. Sharon Dee Messenger, Nov. 5, 1960; children: Kathryn, Alison. BA, U. Calif., Berkeley, 1960; PhD, U. Wis., 1965. From teaching asst. to dean U. Wis., Madison, 1962—89, dean Coll. Letters and Sci., 1989-92; asst. prof. U. Sask., Saskatchewan, Can., 1965-68; vice chancellor acad. affairs U. Calif., Santa Barbara, Calif., 1992-93, exec. vice chancellor, 1993-98, dir. London Ctr. for Edn. Abroad program, 1998-2000, dep. assoc. provost, 2001—. Author: Kant's Aesthetic Theory, 1974; editor Jour. Aesthetics and Art Criticism, 1989-93. Bd. dirs. Meriter Hosp., Madison, 1989-92, Santa Barbara Bot. Garden, 1993-98, U. Calif. Santa Barbara Found., 1992-98, U. Calif. Trust (U.K.), 2000—. NEH fellow, 1974. Mem. Am. Philos. Assn., Am. Soc. for Aesthetic, Brit. Soc. for Aesthetic. Office: U Calif Dept Philosophy South Hall Santa Barbara CA 93106 E-mail: crawford@philosophy.ucsb.edu.

CRAWFORD, EDWARD E. retired psychologist; b. Lawton, Ky., July 31, 1929; s. Thurmon Ray and Hazel Mae (Johnson) C.; m. Patricia Ann Dulin, Sept. 4, 1954; children: Scott, Susan. AB, W.Va. U., 1956, MA, 1958; postgrad., U. Pa., 1956-57; PhD, Cath. U. Am., 1969. Clin. psychologist Rosewood State Hosp., Owings Mills, Md., 1957-67; sr. staff psychologist Montrose Sch. for Girls, Reisterstown, Md., 1967-71; psychol. cons. Md. Dept. Health and Mental Hygiene, Balt., 1971-74; dir. psychol. and devel. svcs. Md. Preventive Medicine Adminstrn., Balt., 1974-76; chief psychology programs Md. Dept. Health and Mental Hygiene, Balt., 1976-80; chief psychology svcs. Md. Adminstrn. Chronically Ill and Aging, Balt., 1980-81; chief psychologist Henryton (Md.) Ctr., 1981-84; co-owner Psychol. Assessment & Therapy, Owings Mills, Md., 1984-86; pvt. practice psychology Md., 1984-98; now ret. Psychol. cons. Wicomico County (Md.) Health Dept., 1958-60, Anne Arundel County (Md.) Pub. Schs., 1965-66, Kernan Crippled Children's Hosp., Balt., 1972, The Chimes, Inc., Md., 1985-98. With AUS, 1948-52, VA trainee, 1956-57. Mem. APA, Masons, Scottish Rite, Shriners. Methodist.

CRAWFORD, EDWIN MAC, health facilities executive; b. 1949; Grad., Auburn U., 1971. With Salem Nat. Corp., 1977—78, Arthur Young & Co., 1971—77, GTI Ltd., 1981—85, Oxylance Corp., 1985—86, Mulberry St. Investment Co., 1986—90; exec. v.p. hosp. ops. Charter Med. Corp., Atlanta, 1990—92; pres., COO Magellan (formerly Charter Med. Corp.), Atlanta, 1992—93, chair., pres., CEO, 1993—97; pres., CEO MedPartners, Inc., Birmingham, 1997—98; chair., pres., CEO Caremark Rx, Inc. (formerly MedPartners), Birmingham, 1998—; with Arthur Young & Co., 1978—81, GTI Ltd., 1986. Office: Caremark Rx Inc 3000 Galleria Towers Ste 1000 Birmingham AL 35244-2359 Address: Caremark Inc 2211 Sanders Rd Northbrook IL 60062-6150

CRAWFORD, FELIX CONKLING, dentist; b. Jan. 11, 1938; DDS, U. Tex. Dental Br., Houston, 1963. Pvt. practice, Plainview, Tex. Pres. Rotary, Plainview, 1971-72, Plainview Country Club, 1973-74, Plainview C. of C., 1984; chmn. Tex. Dental Found., 1990-92. Named Outstanding Alumnus, U. Tex. Dental Br., 1996. Fellow: Internat. Coll. Dentists; mem.: ADA (chmn. ADPac 1994—95, vice chmn. coun. govt. affairs 1999—2000, 2d v.p. 2001—02), Tex. Dental Assn. (chmn. DenPac 1982—85, pres. 1988, Pres. award 1991, Disting. Svc. award 1994), Am. Coll. Dentists (chmn. Tex. sect. 1994), Acad. Gen. Dentistry. Office: 2615 W 24th St Plainview TX 79072-1809

CRAWFORD, FRANKLIN DAVID, publishing company executive; b. Denver, Aug. 9, 1928; s. Clifford Theodore and Sarah Ann (Fergeson) C.; m. Ruth Emilia Dallenbach, Oct. 19, 1957; children— Mark Franklin, Grant Robert. BA, Alma White Coll., 1953. Retail exec. Saks Fifth Av., N.Y.C., 1954-56, Federated Dept. Stores, N.Y.C., 1956-58, Allied Stores Corp., N.Y.C., 1958-61, J.C. Penney Corp., N.Y.C., 1961-63; owner, pres. Princeton Microfilm Corp., N.J., 1963—. Pres. Nat. Library Service Co., Princeton, 1974—. Chmn. bd. U.S. Hist. Documents Inst., Washington, 1970— ; cons. Alma White Coll., Zarephath, N.J.; v.p., bd. dirs. Weaver Found., St. Louis, 1966— ; mem. Internat. Tennis Found. and Hall of Fame, Inc. Served with USAF, 1946-49, 53-54. Mem.: Nassau, Beadensbrook, West Side Tennis. Republican. Home: PO Box 7006 Princeton NJ 08543-7006 Office: PO Box 2073 Princeton NJ 08543-2073 E-mail: fdc@princetonmicro.com.

CRAWFORD, FRED LEE, public affairs officer; b. Spartanburg County, S.C., Aug. 30, 1928; s. Fred and Missouri (Plemmons) C. BA, Furnam U., 1957; MA, NYU, 1958; PhD with distinction, 1965; JD, U. S.C., 1970. Bar: S.C. Adminstr. Profl. Counseling Placement Lighthouse Internat., N.Y.C., 1962-66; commn. adminstr. S.C. Commn. for the Blind, Columbia, 1966-73; social security adminstr. supplemental security income planning specialist Social Security Adminstrn., Balt., 1973—, now sr. advisor to assoc. commr. for external affairs. Chmn., 1st pres. The Alliance Inc., Baltimore County, Md., 1979-83. Author: Career Planning for the Blind, 1965; co-author: (with Sidney Lirtzman) Counseling and Placement of Blind Persons in Professional Occupations, Practice and Research, 1965. Pres. Lions, Catonsville, Md., 1977-94. Baptist. Avocations: reading, volunteering in community, investments, business. Home: 908 Southridge Rd Baltimore MD 21228-1324 Office: Social Security Adminstrn 6401 Security Blvd Baltimore MD 21235-0001 E-mail: fred.l.crawford@ssa.gov.

CRAWFORD, GLADYS PAULINE, microbiologist, educator; b. Krum, Tex., Apr. 12, 1927; d. John Franklin and Willa M. Hudgins; m. William Al Crawford, Jr., Sept. 5, 1953; children: Kala, Kal, Kurt. BSc, No. Tex. State Tchrs. Coll., 1946; MSc, No. Tex. State Coll., 1949. Cert. tchr. Tex., 1949. Instr. Our Lady of Victory Coll., Ft. Worth, 1946—47, St. Joseph Hosp. Sch. Nursing, Ft. Worth, 1946—47; tchg. asst. No. Tex. State Tchrs. Coll., Denton, Tex., 1947—49; instr. No. Tex. State Coll., Denton, 1949—70; asst. prof. U. No. Tex., Denton, 1970—. Workshop dir. Tex. Coordinating Bd., Denton, 1989—95. Author: Biology, Chemistry, Physics, 1975, General Biology, 1996; editor: various biology texts. Vol. Homeless Soup Kitchen, Denton, 1998—; Sunday sch. tchr. Bapt. Ch., Denton, 1960—85. Mem.: Delta Kappa Gamma (com. chmn. 1956—). Avocations: jogging, aerobics, camping, gardening, travel. Home: 519 Mimosa Drive Denton TX 76201 Office: University of North Texas Chestnut Street Denton TX 76203

CRAWFORD, HOWARD ALLEN, lawyer; b. Stafford, Kans., Aug. 4, 1917; s. Perry V. and Kate (Allen) C.; m. Millie Houseworth, Oct. 9, 1948; children: Catherine, Edward BS, Kans. State U., 1939; JD, U. Mich., 1942. Bar: Kans. 1942, Mo. 1943, U.S. Ct. Appeals (8th, 10th and D.C. cirs.), U.S. Supreme Ct. Mem. firm Lathrop and Gage, Kansas City, Mo., 1950-91; mng. ptnr. Lathrop and Norquist, Kansas City, Mo., 1970-85, ret., 1991. Dir. various cos. Mem. coun. City of Mission Hills, Kans., 1965-70 Mem. Lawyers Assn. Kansas City, Kansas City Club, Mission Hills Country Club. Home: 3103 W 67th Ter Shawnee Mission KS 66208-1857 Office: Lathrop and Gage 2345 Grand Blvd Fl 25 Kansas City MO 64108-2603

CRAWFORD, HUNT DORN, JR., retired military officer, educator, diplomat; b. Louisville, Dec. 25, 1948; s. Hunt Dorn Sr. and Carrol Frank (Watson) C.; m. Kate Kerr Delano, Aug. 1, 1970; children: Scott Holden, Carolyn Hunt. BS, U.S. Mil. Acad., 1970; MA and MS, Stanford U., Palo Alto, Calif., 1978; MPh, Columbia U., 1980; MMAS, Command & Gen. Staff Coll., 1985. Commd. 2d lt. U.S. Army, 1970, advanced through grades to lt. col., 1987; staff officer, comdr. 1st Inf. Div. Forward, Augsburg, Germany, 1970-73; staff officer Hdqrs. III Corps, Ft. Hood, Tex., 1974-75; from instr. to asst. prof. U.S. Mil. Acad., West Point, N.Y., 1978-81; staff prin. 1st Inf. Div. Forward, Goppingen, 1981-84; instr. Command & Gen. Staff Coll., Ft. Leavenworth, Kans., 1985-88; strategic analyst U.S. Army Concepts Analysis Agy., Bethesda, Md., 1988-91; ret. U.S. Army, 1992; polit./mil. affairs advisor U.S. Arms Control & Disarmament Agy., Washington, 1991-99, U.S. Dept. of State, Washington, 1999—. Mem. NATO arms control analysts group SHAPE Tech. Ctr., Hague, Netherlands, 1988-90; mem. conv. arms control work group Ctr. for Strategic and Internat. Studies, Washington, 1989-90; mem. arms control ad hoc study group Carnegie Endowment for Internat. Peace, Washington, 1990-92; mem. conventional arms control project Ford Found., 1993-96; adj. prof. polit. sci. U. Louisville, 1995—. Author: Conventional Armed Forces in Europe (CFE): A Review and Update of Key Treaty Elements, ann. 1991—; contbr. articles to profl. jours. and books. Decorated ACDA Meritorious honor award, Def. Superior Svc. medal, 5 M.S.M. awards. Mem. AAAS, Am. Polit. Sci. Assn., Acad. Polit. Sci., Internat. Inst. Strategic Studies, Internat. Studies Assn., Mil. Ops. Rsch. Soc. (bd. dirs. 1991-98, exec. coun. 1995-98), Inst. Ops. Rsch. and Mgmt. Scis., Phi Kappa Phi. Republican. Episcopalian. Avocations: cycling, racquetball, aquaria. Home: 932 Audubon Pkwy Louisville KY 40213-1365 Office: US Dept of State 2201 St NW Washington DC 20520 E-mail: crawforddo@t.state.gov., dorncrawford@aol.com.

CRAWFORD, JACKIE R. retired federal agency administrator; m. Frances Lindsey; children: Jessica, Andrea, Katrina. BBA, Fla. State U., 1967; M in Acctg., Bowling Green State U., 1974; postgrad., Fed. Exec. Inst., Charlottesville, Va., 1988, Harvard U., 1991. CPA, Fla. Auditor Air Force Audit Agy., Eglin AFB, Fla., 1967-72, audit mgr. Wright-Patterson AFB, Ohio, 1972-77, supr. auditor L.A. AFB, 1977-79, Robins AFB, Ga., 1980-82, assoc. dir. weapon sys. audits Wright-Patterson AFB, Ohio, 1982-86, assoc. dir. acquisition, 1986-87, asst. auditor gen. acquisition and logistics audits, 1988-93; dir. acquisition support programs Dept. Def., Arlington, Va., 1987-88; auditor gen. of the Air Force The Pentagon, Washington, 1993—2001. Office: Dept Air Force 1120 Air Force Pentagon Washington DC 20330-1120

CRAWFORD, JAMES G. director; b. Salem, Ohio, May 15, 1949; s. Kim Herbert and Helen Guy Crawford; m. Sharon Lynn Hickman, Jan. 20, 1968 (div. June 1992); children: Laura, Rachael, Adam, Peter; m. Linda Sue Emert, Dec. 30, 1993. Student, Harvard U., 1987; BA in Orgnl. Comm., Youngstown State U., 1996; MA in Profl. Comm., Duquesne U., 1997; PhD in Orgnl. Comm., Ohio U., 2002. Dir. pers. and tng. The Florsheim Shoe Co., Chgo., 1972—84; v.p. product Milgram Kagan Corp., South Holland, Ill., 1984—88; CEO Kushins of Calif., Hayward, 1988—89, Stellar Tech., San Ramon, Calif., 1990—94; dir. Ctr. for Devel. Ohio U., Ironton, 1999—. Mem. edn. com. Ohio Valley Regional Devel., Waverly. Pres. Ohio U. Grad. Students, Athens, 1999. Avocations: computers, reading. Home: 2940 Thornhill Dr Flatwoods KY 41139 Office: Ohio Univ So 1804 Liberty Ave Ironton OH 45638

CRAWFORD, JAMES WELDON, psychiatrist, educator, administrator; b. Napoleon, Ohio, Oct. 27, 1927; s. Homer and Olga (Aderman) C.; m. Susan Young, July 5, 1955; 1 child, Robert James AB, Oberlin Coll., 1950; MD, U. Chgo., 1954, PhD, 1961. Intern Wayne County Hosp. and Infirmary, Eloise, Mich., 1954-55; resident Northwestern U., Chgo., 1958-59, Mt. Sinai Hosp./Chgo. Med. Sch., 1959-60; practice medicine specializing in occupational, individual and family psychiatry Chgo., 1961—. Mem. staff Mt. Sinai Hosp., Chgo., St. Lukes-Presbyn. Med. Ctr.; clin. assoc. prof. dept. psychiatry Sch. of Medicine, U. Ill. at Chgo., 1970—; chair and assoc. prof. dept. psychiatry Ravenswood Hosp. Med. Ctr., 1973-79; chmn. J.W. Crawford Assocs., Inc., 1979-82; assoc. prof. depts. psychology and psychiatry Rush Med. Co.. Contbr. articles to profl. jours. Bd. dirs. Pegasus Player, Chgo., 1978—, chmn. bd. dirs., 1979-84; bd. dirs. Bach Soc., 1985-98; adv. Ill. Masonic Med. Ctr.; mem. health adv. com. Cook County (Ill.) Commr., 2003—; del. to Russia and the Ukraine with People-to-People Internat., 1993, del. to Kenya, Africa, 1995, del. to China, 1998 NIH Inst. Neurol. Diseases postdoctoral fellow, 1955-59 Fellow Am. Psychiat. Assn. (life; disting. fellow), Am. Orthopsychiat. Assn.; mem. AAAS, AAUP, Assn. Am. Med. Colls., Nat. Coalition Mental Health Profls. and Consumers, Ill. Coalition Mental Health Profls. and Consumers (steering com.), Inc. Psychiat. Soc., Chgo. Assn. for Psychoanalytic Psychology, Nat. Coun. on Family Rels., Sigma Xi. Lodges: Rotary (various coms. profl. rep.). Home and Office: 2418 Lincoln St Evanston IL 60201-2151 E-mail: sjcrawf@aol.com.

CRAWFORD, JEAN ANDRE, clinical therapist; b. Chgo., Apr. 12, 1941; d. William Moses and Geneva Mae (Lacy) Jones; m. John N. Crawford Jr., June 28, 1969. Student, Shimer coll., 1959-60; BA, Carthage Coll., 1966; MEd, Loyola U., Chgo., 1971; postgrad., Nat. Coll. Edn., Evanston, Ill., 1971-77, Northwestern U., 1976-83. Lic. profl. counselor, Mich., Ill.; cert. sch. counselor Nat. Bd. Cert. Counselors, elem. edn., spl. edn. and pupil personnel svcs., Ill. Med. technologist, Chgo., 1960-62; primary and spl. edn. tchr. Chgo. Pub. Schs., 1966-71, counselor maladjusted children and families, 1971-88, counselor juvenile first offenders, 1968-88, post-secondary vocat. counselor, 1988-93; tchr. transition coord. Cook County Dept. Corrections Alternative H.S., Chgo., 1993-94; clin. therapist St. Mary of Nazareth Hosp. Ctr., Adolescent Partial Hosp., Chgo., 1994—. Vol. Sta. WTTW-TV; vol. counselor deaf/hearing impaired children and their families; vol., mem. cmty. devel. bd. New City YMCA, 1987-92; mem. scholarship com. Chgo. Urban League. Mem.: AACD, Coun. Exceptional Children, Ill. Mental Health Counselors Assn., Am. Mental Health Counselors Assn., Ill. Sch. Counselors Assn., Ill. Assn. Counseling and Devel., Am. Sch. Counselors Assn., Shimer Coll. Alumni Assn. (sec. 1982—84), Coord. Coun. Handicapped Children, Phi Delta Kappa. Home: 601 E 32d St Apt 1200 Chicago IL 60616-4205 Office: 2233 W Division St Chicago IL 60622-3043 E-mail: j412@webtv.net.

CRAWFORD, JENNIFER, mathematician, secondary school educator; d. Margaret Ippolito; m. Patrick Francis Crawford, Feb. 16, 2002. BA in Math., Hofstra U., 1995, MEd with hons., 1999. Tchr. St. Francis Prep., Fresh Meadows, NY, 1995—2000, Garden City (N.Y.) Pub. Schs., 2000—. Instr. Upward Bound Program NYU, N.Y.C., 1996—.

CRAWFORD, JERRY LEE, economics educator; b. Vanndale, Ark., Sept. 11, 1935; s. Lee R. and Lottie L. (Cockrell) C.; m. Shirley Bradford, Oct. 31, 1959; children: Deedra, Laura. BS, Ark. State U., 1957; MA, U. Miss., 1958; PhD, U. Ark., 1969. Instr. econs. Tenn. Tech. U., Cookeville, 1958-63, U. Ark., Fayetteville, 1963-66; prof. econs. Ark. State U., Jonesboro, 1966—, chmn. bus. adminstrn. and econs. dept., 1984—95. Mem. Am. Econ. Assn., Mid South Acad. Econs. and Fin. (pres. 1991-92), Southwestern Soc. Econs. (sec.-treas. 1992-95, pres. 1996-97). Home: 1401 Twin Oaks Ave Jonesboro AR 72401-5633 Office: Ark State U PO Box 239 State University AR 72467-0239

CRAWFORD, JOHN EDWARD, geologist, scientist; b. Richmond, Va., June 6, 1924; s. James Henry and Loretta Ellen (Bankerd) C.; m. Mary Elizabeth Ayres, May 15, 1948; children: Michelle Lorraine, Caprice Lizette. BA, Johns Hopkins, 1947. Reg. geologist, Calif. Geologist uranium exploration program U.S. Geol. Survey, 1948-51; nat. stockpile materials specialist Munitions Bd., Office Sec. Def., 1951-53; prodn. engr. AEC, 1953-54; specialist on source, feed, fissionable materials Bur. Mines, 1954-57, nuclear tech. adviser to dir., 1957-60, chief nuc. engr. for atomic rsch. programs, 1960-63; dir. Marine Mineral Tech. Ctr., Tiburon, Calif., 1963-66; pres., founder Crawford Marine Specialists, Inc., San Francisco, also Suva, Fiji, 1966-76; pres. Earth Tech. Corp., San Rafael, 1973-77; mgr. geothermal rsch. programs and Salton Sea sci. drilling project U.S. Dept. Energy Ops. Office, Oakland, Calif., 1977-89; mgr. ops. and prin. geologist Western Geologic Resources, Inc., San Rafael, Calif., 1989-90; cons. geothermal and environ. affairs, 1990—; assoc., regional mgr. Western Ops. Earth Resources Internat., L.C., Carson City, Nev., 1994-2000. Author: Facts Concerning Uranium Exploration and Production, 1956; contbr. articles to govt. and profl. jours., Leaders in Am. Sci. Vol. VIII, 1968-69. Mem. Calif. Gov.'s Commn. Ocean Resources, 1966-67, Calif. Gov.'s Small Hydro Task Force, 1981-82. Served with AUS, 1943-46. Mem. Internat. Marine Minerals Soc. (Moore medal for excellence in devel. of marine minerals 1998), Geol. Soc. Am., Marine Tech. Soc. (past chmn. marine mineral resources com., past chmn. marine resources div.), Delta Upsilon. Home and Office: 1510 Valencia Ct Carson City NV 89703-2333

CRAWFORD, JUDY CAROL, energy services company executive; b. Lubbock, Tex., June 1, 1955; d. George Washington and Frances Louise (Hughes) Hopper; m. Joe Earl Crawford, May 31, 1975; children: Susan, Joshua, Bruce. Pres. Nice Guy Registry, Crane, Tex., 1995-97; adminstrv. sec. County of Crane, Crane, 1996-98; v.p. Maranatha Energy Svcs., Crane, 1997—; county and dist. clk. County of Crane, Crane, 1999—. Mem. Family and Consumer Sci. Com., Crane, 1997—; mem. site-based com. Crane Mid. Sch., 2000-01. Baptist. Home and Office: Maranatha Energy Svcs Inc PO Box 476 Crane TX 79731-0476 E-mail: crawfordjc@prodigy.net.

CRAWFORD, KATHRINE NELSON, special education educator; b. Springfield, Mass., June 5, 1954; d. Merrill William and Elizabeth (Hanor) Nelson; m. Michael David Crawford, June 19, 1993; 1 child, Cody M. BS in Phys. Edn. cum laude, U. N.C., Greensboro, 1979. Cert. tchr. phys. edn. K-12, learning disabled K-12, emotionally mentally handicapped K-12, Behavior emotionally handicapped K-12, N.C. Day care dir. Assn. for Retarded Citizens and United Way, Greensboro, 1979-82; behavioral self-contained instr. Guilford County Schs., Greensboro, 1982-88, EMH self-contained instr., 1988—, spl. olympic coach, 1988—. Advisor Action Mag., Scholastic, Inc., N.Y.C., 1999-2002. United Way campaign coord. Guilford County Schs., 1994-98. Recipient Cert. of Recognition for outstanding svc. BEH/Willie M., Guilford County Schs., 1987; named Tchr. of Yr., Eastern Guilford Mid. Sch., 2001-02; Guilford County Schs. grantee, 1990, 96. Mem. Assn. for Retarded Citizens of Greensboro. Republican. Lutheran. Avocations: bowling, camping, cross-stitch, folk guitar, fishing. Home: 3257 Saw Mill Dr Elon College NC 27244-9576 Office: Eastern Guilford Middle Sch 435 Peeden Dr Gibsonville NC 27249-8724 E-mail: crawfok@guilford.k12.nc.us.

CRAWFORD, KENNETH CHARLES, educational institute executive, retired government official; b. Nokomis, Ill., Oct. 31, 1918; s. Charles Bryant and Blanche Dora (Gates) C.; m. Madge Marie Douglas, Aug. 23, 1942; 1 son, James Douglas. BA, Ill. Coll., 1946, S.JD (hon.), 1970; JD, U. Va., 1951; grad., Command and Gen. Staff Coll., 1957, Army War Coll., 1962; MA, George Washington U., 1962. Bar: Va. 1951, Ga. 1967, Korean 1965, U.S. Supreme Ct. 1970, D.C. 1977. Commd. 2d lt. U.S. Army, 1942, advanced through grades to col., 1962; served in (F.A. and JAG Corps); tchr. legal subjects U. Md., U. Ga., Ga. State U., Nat. U., Washington, 1957-67; comdr. JAG Sch., 1967-70; ret., 1970; pres., CEO Ken Crawford Ednl. Inst., Inc., 1986-89. Editor: Laws of the Republic of Korea, 1964. Assoc. dir. edn. Southwestern Legal Found., Dallas, 1970-71, Atty. at Law, 1990-92; dir. edn. and tng. Fed. Jud. Ctr., Washington, 1971-86; cons. Fed. Jud. Ctr., 1986-87. Decorated Legion of Merit with 2 oak leaf clusters, Soldiers medal, Bronze Star, Belgian Fourragere, Disting. Citizen citation Ill. Coll., 1993. Mem. State Bar Va., Korean Bar, Order of Coif. E-mail: crawfordk286@aol.com.

CRAWFORD, LAWRENCE ROBERT, aviation and aerospace consultant; b. Ft. Lewis, Wash., May 4, 1936; s. Richard G. and Olive O. (Ericksen) C.; m. Yvonne G. Thompson, Nov. 8, 1957; children: Scott D., Robin L., Crawford Lafrankie. BS in Indsl. Engring., Ga. Inst. Tech., 1959; MS in Mgmt. with honors, Rensselaer Poly. Inst., 1965. Lic. comml. pilot. Commd. ensign USN, 1959, advanced through grades to lt. comdr., hon. discharge, 1968; airline pilot Pan Am, San Francisco, 1968-70, dir. corp. budgets N.Y.C., 1970-73; dir. methods and standards Am. Airlines, N.Y.C., 1973-75, sr. dir. reservations, 1975-79; v.p. mktg. Ransome Airlines, Phila., 1979-83; sr. v.p. mktg. and planning Empire Airlines, Utica, N.Y., 1983-85; founder, pres., CEO Avitas, Inc., Reston, Va., 1985-98; founder, chmn., CEO Avitas Engring., Inc., Miami, Fla., 1991-98; founder, pres., CEO Spectrum Aviation Svcs. Inc., Reston, 1998—. Exec. adv. bd. EDS Fin. Corp., Dallas, 1987-90; v.p. Det Norske Veritas, Oslo, 1992-98; frequest spkr. at aircraft fin. confs. Contbr. articles to profl. jours. Bd. dirs. Internat. Aviation Found., 1996—. Mem. AIAA, Exptl. Aircraft Assn. (builder 1987), U.S. Ultralight Flying Assn., Am. Aero. Soc., Internat. Soc. Transport Aircraft Trading, Nat. Aeronautics Assn., Royal Aeronautics Soc., Sr. Aerospace Execs. Assn., Stearman Restorers Assn., Wings Club, Washington Aero Club, Culpeper Aero Squadron (founder). Republican. Methodist. Achievements include devel. of the comml. aviation industry's first aircraft tech. monitoring product to ensure condition and value of leased aircraft; founded and devel. Avitas into world's largest appraiser and inspector of comml. aircraft. Home: 10031 Scenic View Ter Vienna VA 22182-1367 Office: Spectrum Aviation Svcs Inc 11951 Freedom Dr Reston VA 20190 E-mail: lcrawford@starpower.net.

CRAWFORD, LESTER MILLS, JR., veterinarian; b. Demopolis, Ala., Mar. 13, 1938; s. Lester Mills and Susan Doris (Mitchell) C.; m. Catherine Walker, July 27, 1963; children: Catherine Leigh, Mary Stuart. D.V.M., Auburn U., 1963; PhD, U. Ga., 1969; MDV. (hon.), Budapest U., Hungary, 1987. Pvt. practice vet. medicine, Meridian, Miss. and Birmingham, Ala., 1963-64; R & D staff agrl. divsn. Am. Cyanamid Co., Princeton, N.J., 1964-66, cons.; assoc. dean Coll. Vet. Medicine, U. Ga., 1970-75, head dept. physiology-pharmacology, 1980-82; dir. Bur. Vet. Medicine, FDA, HEW, Rockville, Md., 1978-80, 82-85; assoc. adminstr. food safety and inspection svc. USDA, Washington, 1986-87, adminstr., 1987-91; exec. v.p. sci. affairs Nat. Food Processors Assn., Washington, 1991-93; exec. dir. Assn. Am. Vet. Med. Colls., Washington, 1993—97, 2001—02; dir. Ctr. Food and Nutrition Policy, Georgetown U., Washington, 1997-2001; dir. Ctr. Food and Nutrition Policy Va. Tech., 2001—02; dep. commr. FDA, 2002—. Cons. pharm. industry, agribus. FDA, WHO; mem. Health Professions Commn., Pew Meml. Trust, 1990-93; bd. dirs. Embrex Inc.; mem. sci. adv. bd. Inst. Food Tech., 1999-2002. Contbr. sci. articles to profl. jours. Vice chmn. Codex Alimentarius Commn., 1991-93; bd. dirs. Food and Drug Law Inst., 1988-2002; expert advisor food safety WHO, com. scientific freedom & responsibility. Recipient A.M. Mills award, 1979, K.F. Meyer award, 1980, U.S. Presdl. Rank award of Meritorious Exec., 1988, Disting. Alumnus award, Auburn U., 1989, Wooldridge Meml. medal, Brit. Vet. Assn., 1991, Commrs. Spl. citation FDA, award of merit, 1983; fellow, Royal

Soc. Medicine, 2000, Internat. Acad. Food Sci. and Tech., 2001. Mem. AAAS, AVMA (Aux. award), Nat. Acad. Practice, D.C. Vet Med. Assn., French Acad. Vet. (hon.), Fedn. Am. Sch. Health Professions (pres. 1997), Cosmos Club (Washington), Sigma Xi, Phi Zeta, Phi Kappa Phi. Republican. Home: 5815 Highland Dr Chevy Chase MD 20815-5531 Office: FDA (14-71) (HF-1) 5600 Fishers Ln Rockville MD 20857 E-mail: deputy.commissioner@fda.gov. *I have always predicated my own life on the certain knowledge that God is still at work in the world. I believe that every person carries a divine spark, and that the function of leadership is to ignite that spark. I furthermore believe that a Franciscan love of and respect for animals is a prerequisite for membership in the human race. And I believe that the true rewards in life are to be found in communion with family, friends and colleagues.*

CRAWFORD, LINDA SIBERY, lawyer, educator; b. Ann Arbor, Mich., Apr. 27, 1947; d. Donald Eugene and Verla Lillian (Schenck) Sibery; m. Leland Allardice Crawford, Apr. 4, 1970; children: Christina, Lillian, Leland. Student, Keele U., 1969; BA, U. Mich., 1969; postgrad., SUNY, Potsdam, 1971; JD, U. Maine, 1977. Bar: Maine 1977, U.S. Dist. Ct. Maine 1982, U.S. Ct. Appeals (1st cir.) 1983. Tchr. Pub. Sch., Tupper Lake, N.Y., 1970-71; asst. dist. atty. State of Maine, Farmington, 1977-79, asst. atty. gen. Augusta, Maine, 1979-95; prin. Litigation Consulting Firm, N.Y.C. & Hallowell, Maine, 1986—, Linda Crawford and Assoc. Law Firm, Hallowell, Maine, 1995-2000. Legal adv. U. Maine, Farmington, 1975; legal counsel Fire Marshall's Office, Maine, 1980-83, Warden Svc., Maine, 1981-83, Dept. Mental Health, 1983-90, litigation divsn. 1990-95; mem. tchg. team trial advocacy Law Sch., Harvard U., 1987—; lectr. Sch. Medicine Harvard U., 1991; counsel to Bd. of Registration in Medicine, 1994-95; chmn. editl. bd. Mental and Physical Disability Law Reporter, 1993-95; arbitrator Am. Arbitration Assn., 1995—; facilitator Nat. Constrn. Task Force, St. Louis, 1995. Contbg. editor: Med. Malpractice Law and Strategy, 1997—, Managed Care Law Strategist, 1999—2002. Bd. dirs. Diocesan Human Rels. Coun., Maine, 1977-78, Arthritis Found., Maine, 1983-88; atty. expert commn. experts UN War Crime Investigation in the former Yugoslavia, 1994. Named one of Outstanding Young Women of Yr. Jaycees, 1981. Mem. ABA (com. on disability 1992-95), Nat. Assn. State Mental Health Attys. (treas. 1984-86, vice chmn. 1987-89, chmn. 1989-91), Nat. Health Lawyers Assn. Home and Office: 1643 Cambridge #77 Cambridge MA 02138 also: 45 Rockefeller Plz Fl 20 New York NY 10111-2099 E-mail: lscrawford@aol.com.

CRAWFORD, MARC, professional hockey coach; Head coach Quebec Nordiques, 1994-95, Colo. Avalanche, 1995-97, Vancouver Canucks, Vancouver, 1998-. Recipient Louis A.R. Pieri Meml. award, 1992-93, Jack Adams award, 1994-95; named NHL Coach of Yr. The Sporting News, 1994-95. Office: Vancouver Canucks 800 Griffiths Way Vancouver BC Canada V6B 6G1

CRAWFORD, MARIA LUISA BUSE, geology educator; b. Beverly, Mass., July 18, 1939; d. William Theodore Buse and Barbara (Kidder) Aldana; m. William A. Crawford, Aug. 29, 1963. BA, Bryn Mawr Coll., 1960; postgrad., U. Oslo, 1960-61; PhD, U. Calif., 1965. Asst. prof. Bryn Mawr (Pa.) Coll., 1965-73, assoc. prof., 1973-79, prof., 1979-92, prof. environ. studies and sci., 1992—, William R. Kenan Jr. prof., 1985-92, chmn. dept. geology, 1976-88, 98—; mem. U.S. Nat. Com. Geology, 1994-97. Chmn. women geoscientists com. Am. Geol. Inst., 1976-77; mem. U.S. Nat. Com. Geochemistry, 1980-82; organizing com. 28th Internat. Geol. Cong., 1987-89. MacArthur fellow, 1993-98; grantee NASA, 1973-76, NSF, 1967—. Fellow Geol. Soc. Am. (councillor 1982-85), Mineral Soc. Am. (councillor 1989-92);mem. Mineral Assn. Can. (councilor 1985-87), Am. Geophys. Union, Norwegian Geol. Soc., Phila. Geol. Soc., Assn. Women in Sci. Office: Bryn Mawr Coll Dept Geology Bryn Mawr PA 19010 E-mail: mcrawfor@brynmawr.edu.

CRAWFORD, MARIA LYNN, technical support analyst; b. Jacksonville, Fla., June 11, 1975; d. Linda Peterson Crawford. BS in MIS, U. South Fla., 1997. Help desk/desktop support technician Bellsouth Mobility, Jacksonville, 1998—99; tech. support analyst Equisys, Inc., Atlanta, 2000—. Author: Three Generations, 1995, Here I Am, 1999. Address: 6274 Barry Dr W Jacksonville FL 32208

CRAWFORD, MARK HARWOOD, technology and energy journalist, analyst; b. Washington, Aug. 2, 1950; s. Sterling and Patricia (Moore) Lee; m. Jean Burke, Feb. 2, 1974; 1 child, Emily Lee. BA in Polit. Sci. and Comm., The Am. U., 1973. Reporter Suffolk Life, Westhampton, N.Y., 1974-75; assoc. editor Fairfax Jour., Springfield, Va., 1975-77; mng. editor Coal Week, Washington, 1978-81; assoc. editor Inside Energy, Washington, 1981-83; corr. McGraw Hill World News, Washington, 1983-85; sr. writer Science Mag., Washington, 1985-90; freelance reporter Washington, 1990; sr. reporter New Tech. Week, Washington, 1991-99; corr. The Energy Daily, Washington, 1991-99; sr. trade/industry analyst Office Strategic Industries & Econ. Security U.S. Dept. Commerce, 1999—; ind. writer, 1999—. Co-editor, developer (book) Federal Coal Leases, 1981. Bd. dirs. Hillbrook-Tall Oaks Civic Assn., Annandale, Va., 1991-93. Recipient Nat. Press Club award for Best Exclusive Story Nat. Press Found., 1998, Commendation letter Fairfax (Va.) Police Dept., 1976, 1st place for investigative reporting Va. Press Assn., 1977. Mem. Soc. Profl. Journalists (v.p. Washington chpt. 1989-90, bd. dirs. 1990-96).

CRAWFORD, MICHAEL HOWARD, cardiologist, educator, researcher; b. Madison, Wis., July 10, 1943; s. William Henry and A. Kay (Keller) C.; m. Janis Raye Kirschner, June 23, 1968; children: Chelsea Susan, Dinah Jaye, Stuart Michael. AB, U. Calif., Berkeley, 1965; MD, U. Calif., San Francisco, 1969. Diplomate Am. Bd. Internal Medicine and sub-bd. Cardiovascular Disease. Med. resident U. Calif. Hosps., San Francisco, 1969-71; sr. med. resident Beth Israel Hosp., Boston, 1971-72; teaching fellow Harvard Med. Sch., Boston, 1971-72; cardiology fellow U. Calif. Hosps., San Diego, 1972-74; asst. prof. medicine U. Calif. Sch. Medicine, San Diego, 1974-76, U. Tex. Health Sci. Ctr., San Antonio, 1976-78, assoc. prof. medicine, 1978-82, prof. medicine, 1982-89; Robert S. Flinn prof. cardiology U. N.Mex. Sch. Medicine, Albuquerque, 1989—2001; prof. medicine Mayo Med. Sch., Minn., 2001—03, U. Calif., San Francisco, 2003—. Asst. dir. Ischemic Heart Disease Specialized Ctr. of Rsch., San Diego, 1975—76; adj. scientist S.W. Found. for Biomed Rsch., San Antonio, 1980—89; co-dir. div. cardiology U. Tex. Health Sci. Ctr., San Antonio, 1983—89; chief div. cardiology U. N.Mex. Sch. Medicine, Albuquerque, 1989—2001; cons. cardiovasc. diseases Mayo Clinic, Scottsdale, Ariz., 2001—03; chief clin. cardiology U. Calif. San Francisco Med. Ctr., 2003—. Editor: Current Diagnosis and Treatment in Cardiology, 1995, 2d edit., 2003, Cardiology, 2001; editor Clin. Cardiology Alert newsletter, 1990—; cons. editor (periodical) Cardiology Clinics, 1989—; mem. editl. bd. Circulation jour., 1990-99, Jour. Am. Coll. Cardiology, 1992-95. Pres. Am. Heart Assn., San Antonio, 1981, Austin, Tex., 1987, chmn. coun. clin. cardiology, Dallas, 1989, pres., Albuquerque, 1995-96. Recipient Paul Dudley White award, Assn. Mil. Surgeons of U.S., 1981, Merit Review grant, Dept. VA, 1985, Rsch. Tng. grantee, Nat. Heart Lung and Blood Inst., 1993—2001. Fellow: Am. Soc. Nuclear Cardiology, Am. Coll. Physicians, Am. Coll. Cardiology (bd. trustees 1998—2003); mem.: Assn. Profs. Cardiology, Western Assn. Physicians, Assn. Univ. Cardiologists, So. Soc. Clin. Investigation, Am. Soc. Physician Execs., Am. Soc. Echocardiography (bd. dirs. 1980—83). Avocation: skiing. Office: U Calif Box 0124 505 Parnassus Ave San Francisco CA 94143-0124

CRAWFORD, MURIEL LAURA, lawyer, author, educator; d. Mason Leland and Pauline Marie (Deslets) Henderson; m. Barrett Matson Crawford, May 10, 1959; children: Laura Joanne, Janet Muriel, Barbara Elizabeth. BA with honors, U. Ill., 1973; JD with honors, Ill. Inst. Tech., 1977; cert. employee benefit splst., U. Pa., 1989. Bar: Ill. 1977, Calif. 1991, U.S. Dist. Ct. (no. dist.) Ill. 1977, U.S. Dist. Ct. (no. dist.) Calif. 1991, U.S. Ct. Appeals (7th cir.) 1977, U.S. Ct. Appeals (9th cir.) 1991; CLU; chartered fin. cons. Atty. Washington Nat. Ins. Co., Evanston, Ill., 1977-80; sr. atty., 1980-81; asst. counsel, 1982-83; asst. gen. counsel, 1984-87; assoc. gen. counsel, sec., 1987-89; cons. employee benefit splst., 1989-91; assoc. Hancock, Rothert & Bushoft, San Francisco, 1991-92. Author: (with Beadles) Law and the Life Insurance Contract, 1989, (sole author) 7th edit., 1994, Life and Health Insurance Law, 8th edit., 1998; co-author: Legal Aspects of AIDS, 1990; contbr. articles to profl. jours. Recipient Am. Jurisprudence award Lawyer's Coop. Pub. Co., 1975, 2nd prize Internat. LeTourneau Student Med.-Legal Article Contest, 1976, LOMA FLMI Ins. Edn. award, 1999. Fellow Life Mgmt. Inst.; mem. Ill. Inst. Tech./Chgo.-Kent Alumni Assn. (bd. dirs. 1983-89, Bar and Gavel Soc. award 1977). Democrat.

CRAWFORD, NEIL ROBERT, mechanical engineer, researcher; s. Donald Robert and Sharon Rita Crawford; m. Michelle Mignon Paz Soldán; children: Elise Michelle Crawford-Paz Soldán, Esmé Simone Crawford-Paz Soldán. BSChemE, U. Calif., Berkeley, 1988; MS Bioengineering, Ariz. State U., Tempe, 1992, PhD Bioengineering, 1996. Rsch. scientist Barrow Neurol. Inst., Phoenix, Ariz., 1993—. Office: Barrow Neurol Inst 350 W Thomas Rd Phoenix AZ 85013 E-mail: ncrawfo@chw.edu.

CRAWFORD, NORMAN CRANE, JR., academic administrator, consultant; b. Newark, Oct. 30, 1930; s. Norman Crane and Anna (Wares) C.; m. Garnette Bell, June 25, 1955; children: Sally Jean, Ellen Ann. BS in Edn., Rutgers U., 1951, MEd, 1957; PhD, Northwestern U., 1966. Dir. scholarships Nat. Merit Scholarship Corp., Evanston, Ill., 1957-62; asst. dean arts and sci., asst. to provost U. Del., 1962-66, 67-70; acting dir. exams. Coll. Entrance Exam. Bd., N.Y.C., 1966-67; pres. Salisbury (Md.) State Coll., 1970-80, Drury Coll., Springfield, Mo., 1981-83; v.p. ops. Council for Advancement and Support Edn., Washington, 1985-87; interim pres. U. Maine, Farmington, 1987-88; v.p. pub. affairs Thomas A. Edison State Coll., 1989-91; cons. higher edn. Berlin, 1992—. Lt. j.g. USN, 1951-55. Joint recipient Higher Edn. Leadership award Gov. Del., Gov. Md., Gov. Va., 1974; named hon. trustee Ward Found. Wildfowl Art Museum, 1977. Mem. Phi Delta Kappa. Episcopalian. Home and Office: 108 Ocean Pkwy Ocean Pines MD 21811-1644 E-mail: nccrawford@salisbury.edu.

CRAWFORD, PATRICIA ALEXIS ANN, social justice advocate, writer; b. N.Y.C., July 17, 1952; d. Alexander James and Dorothy Patricia (Mudzinski) C. BA in Polit. Sci., East Carolina U., 1974; JD, Bklyn. Law Sch., 2003. With Naval Air Rework Facility, Dept. Navy, Norfolk, Va., 1973; news prodn. editor, fin. writer Media Gen. Fin. Weekly, Richmond, Va., 1974-75; editor, med. writer United Feature Syndicate, N.Y.C., 1975-79; asst. mng. editor United Feature Syndicate, Newspaper Enterprise Assn. and Ind. News Alliance, N.Y.C., 1979-86. Bd. dirs. Integrity/N.Y., v.p., 1998-99, pub. rels. dir., 1999-2000; dir. Integrity/Bklyn., 2000—. Mem. AIDS com. N.Y. Episc. Diocese. Recipient Spl. Achievement award Dept. of Navy, 1973. Mem.: Anti-Defamation League, Interfaith Ctr. of N.Y., N.Y. State Labor Religion Coalition, N.Y. State Dispute Resolution Assn., Interfaith Alliance, Episcopal Women's Caucus, Anglican Soc., Human Rights Campaign, Nat. Writers Union, Episcopal Pub. Policy Network, Soc. Profl. Journalists, Am. Constitution Soc., Am. Scottish Found. Episcopalian. Avocations: public health, social justice. Address: PO Box 90-022 Brooklyn NY 11209-0022 E-mail: exaudi@justice.com.

CRAWFORD, PATRICIA ANN, education educator; b. Pitts., Dec. 5, 1963; d. James F. and Patricia T. (Madden) C. BS in Elem. Edn., Indiana U. of Pa., 1986, MEd in Elem. Edn., 1991; PhD in Curriculum and Instrn., Pa. State U., 1995. Kindergarten and 1st grade tchr. Indiana (Pa.) Area Sch. Dist., 1986-91; grad. asst., instr. Pa. State U., University Park, 1991-94; asst. prof. elem. edn., literacy edn. U. Maine, Farmington, 1994-96; asst. prof. edn. U. Ctrl. Fla., Orlando, 1996—2002, coord. early childhood edn. program, 1999—2001, assoc. prof. edn., 2002—. Co-editor: Fla. Ednl. Leadership, 2002—; contbg. editor: Tchg. and Learning Lit., 1995—98. Tchr. edn. grantee Learning Disabilities Assn., 1997, faculty devel. grantee for tech. U. Ctrl. Fla., 1997. Mem. Nat. Coun. Tchrs. English, Internat. Reading Assn. (mem. editl. bd. 1997-99), Nat. Assn. for Edn. of Young Children (mem. editl. bd. 1997-2000), Assn. for Childhood Edn. Internat. (mem. editl. bd. 1995—, editor internat. newsletter Focus 1997-2000, publ. com. chair 2000-02, column editor Tchg. and Learning Lit. 1995-98). Office: U Ctrl Fla Coll of Edu Dept Of Tchg and Learning Principles Orlando FL 32816-1250

CRAWFORD, R. GEORGE, investment manager, educator; b. Mpls., Oct. 30, 1943; s. Robert John and Agnes C.; m. M. Holly Shissler, May, 17, 1980; 1 child, Katherine Barnes. BA, Harvard U., 1965, JD, 1968. Bar N.Y. 1974, DC 1970, Calif. 1972, Ohio, 1969. Law clk. to Hon. Byron R. White U.S. Supreme Ct., Washington, 1968-69; staff asst. to President Washington, 1970-72; v.p. Archon, Inc., L.A., 1972—74; chair pvt. capital sect. Jones Day Reavis & Pogue, L.A., 1974—93; prof. Stanford U., Calif., 1993—2001; pres. Ilex Group, Greenwich, Conn., 1997—. Rsch. fellow Hoover Instn., Stanford, Calif., 1994-97. Author: Derivatives for Decision Makers, 1996; contbr. articles to profl. jours. Pres. Fiduciary Found., Greenwich, Conn., 1992—; mem. supr. coun. Internat. Ctr. Not-for-Profit Law, Washington, 1998—. Mem. Internat. Corp. Governance Network (London) (com. on governance stds. 1997—). Address: 1117 E Putnam Ave # 330 Riverside CT 06878 Fax: 775-832-9772. E-mail: gc@fifo.org.

CRAWFORD, RICHARD BRADWAY, biologist, biochemist, educator; b. Kalamazoo, Feb. 16, 1933; s. Kenneth and Alma (Smith) C.; m. Betty J. Jacobs, Jan. 30, 1954; children: Kathleen, Christine, Kevin, Nancy. AB, Kalamazoo Coll., 1954; PhD in Biochemistry, U. Rochester, 1959. Postdoctoral fellow U. Rochester, N.Y., 1959; instr. to assoc. prof. U. Pa., 1959-67; assoc. prof. to prof. biology Trinity Coll., Hartford, Conn., 1967-98, prof. emeritus, 1998—, chmn. dept., 1978-87, resuming chmn., 1996-97. Asst. dir., trustee Mt. Desert Island Biol. Lab., Salsbury Cove, Maine, 1966-82; vis. scientist Jackson Lab., Bar Harbor, Maine, 1988; vis. prof. biology U. Warwick, Eng., 1988; vis. prof. marine biology U. Calif. San Diego, 1974; vis. prof. U. Edinburgh, 1996; mem. faculty and curriculum com. Acadia Sr. Coll., 2000—, v.p. bd. dirs.. Contbr. articles to profl. jours. Mem. Inlands, Wetlands and Water Courses Commn., Wethersfield, Conn., 1976-81, Wethersfield Conservation Commn., 1995-98; bd. dirs. Mt. Desert Island Hist. Soc., sec., 2001—. Mem. Rotary Club Hartford (pres. 1994-95), Mount Desert Island Rotary. Democrat. Congregationalist. Home: PO Box 826 Mount Desert ME 04660-0826

CRAWFORD, RICHARD EBEN, JR., former investment advisor; b. Lake Forest, Ill., Dec. 24, 1930; s. Richard Eben Crawford and Alice B. (Appleton) Smith; m. Caroline Hellen Kelley, June 20, 1952 (div. 1980); children: Wes, John, J.D., Lindsay, Richard; m. Debbie Sum Chan, Feb. 1, 1985; children: Alexandra, Jessica. BA, Trinity Coll., Hartford, Conn., 1953; MBA, U. Pa., 1976. Various positions Minn. Natural Gas Co., St. Louis Park, Minn., 1957-69, pres., chief exec. officer, 1969-74; pres. Minn. Natural div. Minn. Gas Co., St. Louis Park, 1974-77; underwriter Conn. Gen. Life Ins. Co., Mpls., 1978-79; pres. Crawford Assocs., Tucson, 1980—, Crawford Meml. Cemetery, Emlenton, Pa., 1986-90, 99—; founder Crawford Entrepreneurial Studies, LLC, 2002. Co-author: The Crawfords from Venango County, Pennsylvania, 1999. Area and state judge Career Devel. Conf. Ariz. Distbv. Edn. Clubs Am., 1986; vol. Mobile Meals program, Tucson, 1984-90; trustee St. Andrews Presbyn. Ch., Tucson, 1992-93, pre-sch. adv. bd., 1993; chartered mem. Presbyn. Ch. Am., 1998—; Rep. committeeman, 1992-94. Capt. USAF, 1955-57. Mem. SAR (treas. Tucson chpt. 1991, 2d v.p. 1992, 1st v.p. 1994), Tucson C. of C. (com. mil. affairs 1983-90), Pres.'s Club U. Ariz. Found., Skyline Country Club (tennis com. 1988-90), Wharton Club Ariz. (founder, pres. 1986-90), Greater Tuscon Econ. Coun. (agy. com. 1992-95), Toastmasters (pres. Aztec club 1984, 92, area gov. 1986-87, chmn. speechcraft com. 1987-88, Disting. Toastmaster, Catalina Foothills H.s. youth leadership pub. spkg. counselor 1995-96), Rotary (dist. treas. 1988-89, chmn. various coms.), Alpha Delta Phi. Avocations: genealogy, family history, tennis, fishing. Home and Office: 6550 N St Andrews Dr Tucson AZ 85718-2616 E-mail: rcrawfprd@aol.com.

CRAWFORD, ROBERT JOHN, credit company executive; b. Cleve., Mar. 8, 1942; s. Robert John and Jean (Holmes) C.; m. Edna Jean Parker, June 14, 1975. AA, U. Alaska, Fairbanks, 1967, BE, 1971; HHD (hon.), London Inst. of Applied Rsch., 1975; BA/BS, SUNY, 1978. Pres. World Credit Corp., Wilmington, Del., 1972—; rep. in U.S. Hillcrest Worldwide Devel. Corp., S.A., Panama, 1988—; mediator Summit Ct. Sys., Akron, Ohio, 1994—. With U.S. Army, 1961-64. Mem. Mensa, Intertel, Interter Corp. Assigned Names and Numbers. Libertarian. Avocations: computers, real estate speculation. Home: 74 Maplewood Ave Akron OH 44313-6898

CRAWFORD, ROBERT W., JR., furniture rental company executive; b. Yonkers, N.Y., Oct. 19, 1938; BS, Dickinson Coll., 1960; MBA, U. Pa., 1963. Founder, chmn., CEO Brook Furniture Rental, Inc., Lake Forest, Ill. Trustee Field Mus. Inductee Chicagoland Entrepreneurial Hall of Fame, 1998. Mem. Nat. Recreation Found. (chmn., trustee), Internat. Furniture Rental Assn. (chmn., bd. dirs.), Chicagoland C. of C. (chmn. bd. dirs.), The Chgo. Club, The CEO Club, Execs. Club Chgo., Comml. Club Chgo., Econ. Club Chgo., Phi Kappa Sigma (Alumnus of Yr. award). Office: Brook Furniture Rental Inc 100 Field Dr Ste 220 Lake Forest IL 60045 E-mail: rwc@bfr.com.

CRAWFORD, ROBERTA, association administrator; b. Richmond, Ind. d. Melvin Lee and Vida Ellen (Halstead) Smith; m. Melvin Barfield, Dec. 3, 1940 (div.); 1 child, Stephen; m. Charles Britt, Feb. 2, 1949 (div.); 1 child, Alan; m. Vernon Crawford, Aug. 29, 1970 (dec.). Radio engr. WLBC, Muncie, Ind., 1942; announcer, engr. WMAN, Mansfield, Ohio, 1943; dispatcher WPDH, Richmond, 1944; continuity dir. WPTW, Piqua, Ohio, 1945, WCAV, Norfolk, Va., 1947; writer, announcer WKBV, Richmond, 1950; continuity dir., announcer WSAL, Logansport, Ind., 1951; continuity dir. WAVE-TV, Louisville, Ky., 1953; sales-svc. mgr. WPTV, Palm Beach, Fla., 1954; copywriter WQXT, Palm Beach, 1962; city desk asst. Palm Beach Times, West Palm Beach, 1971; women's editor The Stuart (Fla.) News, 1973-77; founder, pres. Iron Overload Diseases Assn. Inc., North Palm Beach, Fla., 1980—. Author: The Iron Elephant, 1990, 2d edit., 2000, "tick... tick ... tick...", 1995. Avocation: barbershop singing. Office: Iron Overload Diseases 433 Westwind Dr North Palm Beach FL 33408-5123 E-mail: iod@ironoverload.org.

CRAWFORD, ROBIN YVETTE, county caseworker; b. Buffalo, N.Y., Sept. 13, 1954; d. Robert Lee and Sylvia Caroline Crawford. A in Specialized Tech., Art Inst. Pitts., 1986; BA, Carlow Coll., 2001. Campus min. Coalition for Christian Outreach, Pitts., 1986—94; assistance dir. Covenant Ch. Pitts., 1994—95; infant care baby holder The Childrens Home Pitts., 1997—98; dir. program Bethany Bapt. Ch., Pitts., 1999; residential counselor Three Rivers Youth, Pitts., 1999—2002; vol. outpatient group Western Psychiat. Inst. and Clinic, Pitts., 1999—2002; county caseworker Allegheny County Children and Youth Svc., Pitts., 2002—. Creator (with others) Nat. Tribute Quilt documenting September 11, 2001. Adv. com. Pitts. Action Against Rape, 2002—03; bd. dirs. Carlow Coll. Alumnae Assn., 2002—03. Recipient Aliquippa Embraces Art award; grantee, Pa. Coun. on Arts, Pitts., 1999, Multi-Cultural Arts Initiative, Pitts., 2001. Mem.: Quilt Co. East Quilter's Guild, Nat. Quilting Assn., Nat. Assn. Negro Bus. and Profl. Women. Baptist. Avocations: travel, jazz, performing arts, museums. Home: 1027 North Negley Ave # 11 Pittsburgh PA 15206

CRAWFORD, ROY EDGINGTON, III, lawyer; b. Topeka, Dec. 23, 1938; s. Roy E. and Ethel Trula (Senne) C.; children: Michael, Jennifer. BS, U. Pa., 1960; LL.B., Stanford U., 1963. Bar: Calif. 1964, U.S. Ct. Mil. Appeals 1964, U.S. Tax Ct. 1969, U.S. Dist. Ct. (no. dist.) Calif. 1971, U.S. Ct. Claims 1974, U.S. Supreme Ct. 1979. Assoc. Brobeck Phleger & Harison, San Francisco, 1967-73, ptnr., 1973—2003; spl. counsel Heller, Ehrman, White & McAuliffe, San Francisco, 2003—. Bd. dirs. Sqauw Valley Ski Corp. Contbr. chpts. to books; bd. editors: Stanford U. Law Rev., 1962-63. Served to capt. AUS, 1964-67. Recipient award of merit U.S. Ski Assn., 1980 Mem. ABA (chmn. com. on state and local taxes 1979-81), Calif. State Bar Assn., San Francisco Bar Assn., Calif. Trout (bd. dirs. 1970-1992, v.p. 1975-94, sec.-treas. 1994-2001), The Nature Conservancy of Idaho (bd. dirs. 1994—), Yosemite Inst. (bd. dirs. 1997—), Beta Gamma Sigma. Office: Heller Ehrman White & McAuliffe 333 Bush St San Francisco CA 94104

CRAWFORD, SANDRA KAY, lawyer; b. Sept. 23, 1934; d. Obie Lee and Zilpha Elizabeth (Ash) Stalcup; m. William Walsh Crawford, Dec. 21, 1968; children: Bill, Jonathan, Constance, Amelia, Patrick. BA, Wellesley Coll., 1957; LLB, U. Tex., 1960. Bar: Tex. 1960, U.S. Supreme Ct. 1965, Colo. 1967, Ill. 1974. Asst. v.p.-legal Hamilton Mgmt. Corp., Denver, 1966—68; v.p., gen. counsel, sec. Transamerica Fund Mgmt. Corp., L.A., 1968; cons. to law dept. Met Life Ins. Co., N.Y.C., 1969—71; counsel Touche Ross & Co., Chgo., 1972—75; v.p., assoc. gen. counsel Continental Ill. Bank, Chgo., 1975—83; sr. div. counsel Motorola, Inc., Schaumburg, Ill., 1984; sr. counsel, asst. sec. Sears Roebuck & Co., 1985—90. Mem.: ABA, Tex. Bar Assn., Colo. Bar Assn., Ill. State Bar Assn., River Club (N.Y.C.), Beach Club (Palm Beach), Everglades Club. Home: 100 Royal Palm Way Apt G5 Palm Beach FL 33480-4270

CRAWFORD, SARAH CARTER (SALLY CARTER CRAWFORD), broadcast executive; b. Glen Ridge, N.J., Oct. 3, 1938; d. Raymond Hitchings and Katherine Latta (Gribbel) Carter; m. Joseph Paul Crawford III, Sept. 10, 1960 (dec. 1966). BA, Smith Coll., 1960. Media dir. Kampmann & Bright, Phila., 1961-64; sr. media buyer Foote, Cone & Belding, N.Y.C., 1964-69; assoc. media dir. Grey Advt., L.A., 1969-75; account exec., research dir. Sta. KHJ-TV, L.A., 1975-76; mgr. local sales Sta. KCOP-TV, L.A., 1977-82; gen. sales mgr. Sta. KTVF-TV, Fairbanks, Alaska, 1982-96; nat. sales mgr. KTVF, KTVA, Fairbanks, 1996-97; gen. sales mgr. Sta. KYES-FM, Anchorage, 1997-2000; sta. and gen. sales mgr. Sta. KATN, Fairbanks, 2000—; owner Crawford Commns. of Ala., 2003—. Mem. adv. com. Golden Valley Electric Corp., Fairbanks, 1984-86; mem. coun. UAF Tanana County Campus, 1989-96, 2000—. Chmn. Fairbanks Health and Social Svc. Commn., 1986—96; vice chmn. Fairbanks North Star Borough Health and Social Svc. Commn., 1993—96; pres. Fairbanks Meml. Hosp. Aux., 1988—90, creator trust fund, 1990—94, chmn. fin. com., 1990—94; mem. Fairbanks Health Ctr. Coalition; mem. search com. UAF Tanana Valley Campus Dir.; mem. Tesoro (Alaska) Citiznes Adv. Coun., 1999; pub. rels. chair Kids Vote Anchorage; mem., chmn. mktg. com. Gov.'s Coun. on Youth Substance Abuse Prevention, 1999—2003; mem. Fairbanks Chamber Membership Com., 2000—02; bd. dirs. Breast Cancer Detectio Ctr.; mem. Intercollegiate Athletic Coun., 2002—; promotions com. Fairbanks Downtown Assn., 2000—; mem. sports commn. FCVB, 2003—; mktg. coord. UNID Eskimo Indian Olympics, 2003; mem. Fairbanks Sports Commn., 2003—; bd. dirs., vol. Fairbanks Downtown Assn., 1984—87; bd. dirs. Interior Regional Health Corp.; bd. dir. Breast Cancer Detection Ctr., 2002—. Recipient Vol. of Yr. award, Fairbanks Downtown Assn., 2002. Mem.: Alaska Broadcasters Assn. (bd. dirs. 1995—, pres. 2001—02, Broadcaster of the Yr. 2001). Avocations: weightlifting, stock and real estate investments, running, motorcycling. Home: 107 Maple Dr Fairbanks AK 99709-2956

CRAWFORD, SHEILA JANE, elementary education librarian, reading consultant; b. Beckley, W.Va., Mar. 1, 1943; d. Roger and Ruth (Ashworth) Crawford; m. Lloyd E. Johnston, June 4, 1966 (dec.); 1 child, Jacqueline; m. Troy Thomason, June 28, 2000. BA, Tenn. Tech. U., 1963; MA in Christian Edn., Seabury Western Theol. Sem., 1965; MS in Curriculum and Instrn., U. Tenn., Martin, 1989; EdD in Instrn. and Curriculum Leadership, U. Memphis, 1994; postgrad., San Jose State U., U. Calif., Berkeley, U. Utah, Tex. Woman's U. Cert. tchr. Tenn. Dir. Christian edn. St. Luke's Episcopal Ch., Rochester, Minn., 1965-66; elem. tchr. Santa Catalina Sch. Girls, 1967-69, Rowland-Hall St. Mark's Sch., Salt Lake City, 1968-69, Union City (Tenn.) Christian Sch., 1984-87; libr. Dept. Edn. U. Tenn. at Martin, 1987-89; rsch. asst. U. Memphis, 1989-92, adj. prof., 1996; prof., edn. dept. chair Lane Coll., Jackson, Tenn., 1992-94; reading tchr., drama club sponsor Ashland (Miss.) Mid. Sch., 1994-95; workshop presenter Jackson, Tenn., 1989-96; ednl. cons. Delta Faucet of Tenn. divsn. Masco Corp., Jackson, 1995—; homebound tchr. Jackson-Madison County Schs., 1996-97; instr., libr. LaGrange-Moscow (Tenn.) Sch., 1997-99; libr. Lauderdale Sch., Memphis. Mem. campus All Stars, Honda, Jackson, Tenn., 1992—93; cons. in field. Contbr. articles to profl. jours. Mem. AAUW, DAR, Nat. Libr. Assn., Ch. and Synagogue Libr. Assn., Order Eastern Star (worthy matron 1980-81), Sch. Libr. Assn., Sigma Tau Delta, Kappa Delta Pi. Anglican. Achievements include research in the effect of chess on predicting and summarizing skills. Home: 3207 Thirteen Colony Mall Apt 1 Memphis TN 38115-2972 E-mail: sheil101@cs.com.

CRAWFORD, STEPHEN S. financial services executive; Mgmt. investment banking divsn. Morgan Stanley Dean Witter, N.Y.C., 1986-98, mng. dir., 1998, chief strategic and adminstrv. officer, pres., CFO, 2001—. Office: Morgan Stanley Dean Witter 1585 Broadway New York NY 10036

CRAWFORD, SUSAN, library director, educator, author; b. Vancouver, B.C., Can. d. James Y. and S. Young; m. James Weldon Crawford, July 5, 1955; 1 son, Robert James. BA, U. B.C., 1948; MA, U. Toronto, 1950, U. Chgo., 1954, PhD,

1970. With bur. libr. and indexing svc. ADA, 1954-56; with office exec. v.p. AMA, Chgo., 1956-60, dir. divsn. libr. and archival svcs., 1960-81; assoc. prof. Sch. Libr. Sci., Columbia U., N.Y.C., 1972-75; prof., dir. Sch. Medicine Libr. and Biomed. Comm. Ctr. Washington U., 1981-92; adj. prof. U. Ill., Chgo., 1994—. Author over 155 books and articles; mem. editl. bd. Med. Socioecon. Rsch. Sources, Index to Sci. Revs., Jour. Am. Soc. Info. Sci., Med. Libr. Assn. News, Health and Info. Librs. (Budapest), Health Librs. Rev. (London), Health Info. and Librs. Jour. (U.K.); assoc. editor Jour. Am. Soc. Info Sci., 1979-82, editor Med. Info. Sys., 1988-90; editor-in-chief Jour. Med. Libr. Assn., 1982-88, 91-92. Bd. regents Nat. Libr. Medicine, NIH, 1971-75; mem. bd. overseers for univ. librs. Tufts U., 1988-89. Janet Doe hon. lectr., 1983; recipient Disting. Alumni award U. Toronto, 1987, Grad. medal U. Toronto, 1989. Fellow AAAS (chmn. coms.), Med. Libr. Assn. (life, Eliot award 1976, chmn. com. on surveys and stats. 1966-75, publs. panel 1977-80, chmn. consulting editors panel 1981-88, 91-92, spl. award to editor of bull. 1988, Noyes award 1992, pres.'s award 1992, Centennial award), Med. Libr. Assn. (100 Most Notable 1998); mem. ALA, Soc. Social Studies of Sci., Assn., Am. Soc. Info. Sci. (chmn. med. info. sys. 1987-88, outstanding specialty group award 1988, 89, bd. and program chair Chgo. chpt. 1993-95), Am. Med. Informatics Assn., Acad. Health Info. Profls. (disting. mem.), European Assn. Health and Info. Librs. (U.S. rep. 1989-94), Sigma Xi (chmn. coms.). Home: 2418 Lincoln St Evanston IL 60201-2151 E-mail: sjcrawf@aol.com.

CRAWFORD, SUSAN ALICE, realtor, artist; b. Phila., May 10, 1942; Student, The Shipley Sch., 1960; BA, Hollins U., 1964; CHC, Inst. Transformational Studies, 1994. Tchr. Mass., Conn., 1964—71; retail buyer, mgr. Norwegian Craft Shop/Lucretia L. Interiors, Farmington, Conn., 1971-78; owner Frog Pond, Farmington, Canton, Conn., 1978—; artist, 1978—; realtor Realty Execs., 1996—2002, Q Real Estate, 2002—. Artist mem. So. Vt. Arts Ctr. Exhibitions include Gallery on the Green, 2003, Canton Libr., 2003. Art curator Canton Pub. Libr., 2001—; mem. Pk. and Recreation Commn., Canton, 1993—95, Econ. Devel. Commn., Canton, 1995—98; founder, mem. Sam Collins Day Commn., 1995—; mem. adv. bd. Canton Artists' Guild, 2003; mem. Dem. Town Commn., Canton, 1997—. Recipient Platinum award, Realty Execs., 2000, 2001, 2002, Dale Rector award, 2002. Mem. Conn. Women Artists, Canton Artists Guild (bd. dirs., pres. 1984-86, 97-2001, v.p. 2001—, 2 jurors awards for mixed monotype prints), Canton C. of C. (Bus. Person of the Yr. 1995), Art Guild Farmington (bd. dirs.). Avocations: crafts, theater, music, reading, collectibles.

CRAWFORD, SUSAN JEAN, federal judge; b. Pitts., Apr. 22, 1947; d. William Elmer Jr. and Joan Ruth (Bielau) C.; m. Roger W. Higgins; 1 child, Kelley S. BA, Bucknell U., 1969; JD, New Eng. Sch. Law, 1977. Bar: Md. 1977, D.C. 1980, U.S. Ct. Appeals for Armed Forces 1985, U.S. Supreme Ct. 1993. Tchr. history, coach Radnor (Pa.) H.S., 1969-74; assoc. Burnett & Eiswert, Oakland, Md., 1977-79; ptnr. Burnett, Eiswert and Crawford, Oakland, 1979-81; prin. dep. gen. counsel U.S. Dept. Army, Washington, 1981-83, gen. counsel, 1983-89; insp. gen. U.S. Dept. Def., Arlington, Va., 1989-91; judge U.S. Ct. Appeals for the Armed Forces, Washington, 1991-99, chief judge, 1999—. Asst. states atty. Garrett County, Md., 1978-79; instr. Garrett County C.C., 1979-81. Del. Md. Forestry Adv. Commn., Garrett County, 1978-81, Md. Commn. for Women, Garrett County, 1980-83; chair Rep. State Cen. Com., Garrett County, 1978-81; trustee Bucknell U., 1988—, chair bd. trustees, 2003—; trustee New England Sch. Law, 1989—. Mem. FBA, Md. Bar Assn., D.C. Bar Assn., Edward Bennett Williams Am. Inn of Ct. Presbyterian. Office: US Ct Appeals Armed Forces 450 E St NW Washington DC 20442-0001

CRAWFORD, TIMOTHY PATRICK, lawyer, accountant; b. Racine, Wis., Aug. 23, 1948; s. Marcus and Margaret C.; m. Jeanne Drager, May 27, 1972; children: Amy, Ryan. BS, Marquette U., 1970, JD, 1972. Bar: Wis. 1972, U.S. Dist. Ct. (ea. and we. dists.) Wis. 1972; bd. cert. elder law atty. 1996; CPA, 1975. Ptnr. Stewart, Peyton & Crawford, Racine, 1981—. Pres. Racine Jaycees, 1979-80. Mem. Rotary (Paul Harris fellow 1988). Avocation: travel. Office: 840 Lake Ave Ste 200 Racine WI 53403-1566 E-mail: tpc@execpc.com.

CRAWFORD, TOMMY F. career officer; AA, N.Mex. Mil. Inst., 1970; BA, N.Mex. State U., 1972; student pilot tng., Laughlin AFB, Tex., 1972-73; student, Squadron Officer Sch., 1976, Air Command and Staff Coll., 1978, Air War Coll., 1994; MS in Computer Info. Sys., Boston U., 1994. Commd. 2d lt. USAF, 1972, advanced through grades to brig. gen., 1998; pilot 390th Tactical Fighter Squadron, Mountain Home AFB, Idaho, 1973-75, various positions, 1977-81; pilot 429th Tactical Fighter Squadron, Nellis AFB, Nev., 1975-77; instr. pilot, weapons and tactics officer 4450th Tactical Group, Nellis AFB, Nev., 1981-84; air staff spl. projects officer Hdqs. USAF, Washington, 1984-88; stationed at RAF Lakenheath, Eng., 1988-91, Taif, Kingdom Saudi Arabia, 1990-91; chief spl. weapons sect., mil. asst. Supreme Allied Comdr. Europe Supreme Hdqs. Allied Powers Europe, Mons, Belgium, 1991-93; pilot, dir. combat ops. and dep. comdr. 607th Air Ops. Group, Osan Air Base, S. Korea, 1994-95, pilot, comdr., 1995-97; insp. gen. Hdqs. Pacific Air Forces, Hickam AFB, Hawaii, 1996-97; comdr. 354th Fighter Wing, Eielson AFB, Alaska, 1997—. Decorated D.F.C. with oak leaf cluster, Legion of Merit, Air medal with oak leaf cluster. Office: Westfield Bldg 14675 Lee Rd Chantilly VA 20151-1708 Also: 4C1045 3000 Joint Staff Pentagon Washington DC 20318-3000

CRAWFORD, VINCENT PAUL, economist, educator; b. Springfield, Ohio, Apr. 6, 1950; s. Bennett and Marjorie Piga Crain; m. Zoe Marie Clark, Dec. 19, 1985. AB summa cum laude in Economics, Princeton U., 1972; PhD in Economics, MIT, 1976. Asst. and assoc. prof. econs. U. Calif., La Jolla, 1976—85, prof. econs., 1985—. Mem. econ. adv. panel NSF, Arlington, Va., 1996—98, mem. spl. emphasis panel for sci. and tech. ctrs., 1998—98; mem. coun. Game Theory Soc., Tilburg, Netherlands, 2001—; mem. editl. bd. Games and Econ. Behavior, 1988—; mem. exec. bd. Calif. Social Sci. Exptl. Lab., L.A., 1999—; professeur invite Ecole des Hautes Etudes en Sciences Sociales, Paris, 1998; vis. prof. econs. Princeton U., NJ, 1985—86. Author: (monograph) Essays in Economic Theory, International Lending, Long-Term Credit Relationships, and Dynamic Contract Theory; assoc. editor: Jour. Econ. Theory, 1986—, Jour. Econ. Behavior and Orgn., 2001—; contbr. articles to profl. jours. Fellow, Australian Nat. U.,Canberra, 1988, vis. Erskine fellow, U. Canterbury, New Zealand, 1991, 2003, John Simon Guggenheim Meml. Found., 1997—98; grantee, NSF, 1979—94, 1997—. Fellow: Am. Acad. Arts and Scis., Econometric Soc. (mem. and chair nominating com. fellows 2001—02); mem.: Game Theory Soc. (coun. mem., program co-organizer first world congress 2000). Office: U Calif 9500 Gilman Dr La Jolla CA 92093-0508

CRAWFORD, WALT, systems analyst; b. Modesto, Calif., Sept. 14, 1945; s. Charles D. and Mary (Gruenig) C.; m. Linda A. Driver, Jan. 1, 1978. BA, U. Calif., Berkeley, 1968. Programmer, analyst U. Calif., Berkeley, 1968-72, sr. programmer, analyst, 1972-76; mgr., programmer, analyst Rsch. Librs. Group, Stanford, Calif., 1979-86, sr. analyst Mountain View, Calif., 1986-95, access svcs. officer, 1995-97, info. architect, 1997—2000, sr. analyst, 2001—. Author: MARC for Library Use, 1984, Patron Access: Issues for Online Catalogs, 1987, Being Analog: Creating Tomorrow's Libraries, 1999, First Have Something to Say, 2003; co-author: Future Libraries: Dreams, Madness and Reality, 1995 (ALCTS/Blackwell scholar, 1997); columnist Online Mag., 1995— (Excellence in Info. Authorship award, 1998), Econtent mag., 1997—, Am. Librs., 2002—; contbg. editor: Am. Librs., 1999—2001; editor, pub. Cites & Insights, 2001—. Mem. ALA, Libr. and Info. Tech. Assn. (Outstanding Comm. 1995). Office: RLG 2029 Stierlin Ct Ste 100 Mountain View CA 94043-4684 E-mail: wcc@notes.rlg.org.

CRAWFORD, WILLIAM DAVID, office equipment company executive; b. Tuscaloosa, Ala., Jan. 19, 1947; s. Clarence W. and Louise (Hatcher) C.; m. Elaine Randall, July 21, 1977; 1 child, John Samuel. BS in Indsl. Mgmt., U. Ala., 1971; MBA, Jacksonville State U., 1974. Prodn. supr. Goodyear Tire & Rubber Co., Gadsden, Ala., 1971-77; mgmt. instr. U. Ala., Gadsden, 1975-77; various positions Mead-Hatcher, Inc., Buffalo, 1977-85, v.p., 1985-91, pres., CEO, 1991—; founder, pres. ErgoTeam, Ltd., 1999—. Bd. dirs., treas. Christian Found. for Performing Arts, 1992-99; bd. dirs. Athletes-in-Action, Buffalo, 1995-2001, Youth for Christ, Buffalo, 1996-2001; host com. Super Bowl Breakfast 2000, 01; bd. dirs. Oakbrook Condominium, Williamsville, N.Y., 1978-80, 87-90, pres., 1989-90. With USNR, 1964-80, Vietnam, 1967-68. Mem. Bus. Products Industry Assn. (various coms. 1983-2000, treas. 1997, vice chair 1998, chair 1999, bd. dirs. 1994-2000), Office Products Mfrs. Assn. (bd. dirs. 1986-96, treas. 1990-91, v.p. 1992, pres. 1993-94), Sons of Amer. Revolution, U. Ala. Alumni Assn., Delta Chi. Republican. Protestant.

CRAWFORD, WILLIAM DAVID, real estate broker, consultant; b. Abbeville County, S.C., Aug. 13, 1945; s. Jesse David and Elizabeth Virginia (Ashley) C.; m. Gail Eileen Watkins, June 9, 1967 (div. Aug. 1985); 1 child, Merritt Caitlin; m. Dawn P. Lantz, June 10, 1995; stepchildren: Chelsea Lantz-Cashman, Devon Lantz-Cashman. BA, Wofford Coll., 1967; MS, Tex. A&M U., 1974; MBA, U. New Orleans, 1977. Lic. real estate broker, S.C., N.C., Ga., Tex., Tenn.; lic. comml. aircraft pilot; cert. comml. investment mgr. Comml. Investment Real Estate Inst., cert. internat. property specialist, Comml. Investment Real Estate Inst., cert. realtor Nat. Assn. Real Estate Cons. Gen. mgr. Ramada Inn, New Orleans, 1973-74; rschr. divsn. bus. and econ. rsch. U. New Orleans, 1975-77; exec. asst. to pres. LaSalle Properties, New Orleans, 1977-81; v.p. Doerring Devel. Co., Austin, Tex., 1981-84; project mgr. Street-Martin Cos., Austin, 1984; pres. TriSource Corp., San Antonio, 1985-86; v.p. Merritt Properties, Inc., Greenville, S.C., 1986-87; pres. Crawford & Assocs. LLC, Greenville, 1986—. Author: Louisiana Business Survey, 1977, Application of Travel Economic Impact Model to New Orleans, 1977. Chmn. Paris Mountain Water Dist., Greenville, 1990—. Capt. C.E., U.S. Army, 1968-71. Mem. Comml. Investment Real Estate Inst., Nat. Assn. Real Estate Cons., Nat. Assn. Realtors, Greenville Bd. Realtors, Comml. Bd. Realtors, Greenville C. of C., Gamma Sigma Delta, Beta Gamma Sigma. Mem. Unity Ch. Avocations: hiking, snow skiing, scuba diving, flying. Home: 2 Persimmon Ln Greenville SC 29609-6511 Office: PO Box 3625 Greenville SC 29608-3625

CRAWFORD, WILLIAM WALSH, retired consumer products company executive; b. Clearwater, Fla., Oct. 7, 1927; s. Francis Marion and Frances Marie (Walsh) C. BS, Georgetown U., 1950; LL.B., Harvard, 1954. Bar: N.Y. 1955, Ill. 1972. Assoc. Sullivan & Cromwell, N.Y.C., 1954-58; counsel Esso Standard Oil, N.Y.C., 1958-60; ptnr. Alexander & Green, N.Y.C., 1960-71; v.p., gen. counsel Internat. Harvester Co., Chgo., 1971-76, v.p., gen. counsel, sec., 1976-80; sr. v.p. gen. counsel Kraft, Inc., Glenview, Ill., 1980-81; sr. v.p., gen. counsel, sec. Dart & Kraft, Inc., 1981-86, Kraft, Inc., 1986-88, sr. v.p., sec., 1988-89, ret., 1989. Mem. ABA, Ill. Bar Assn., Assn. Bar City N.Y., Am. Judicature Soc., Am. Law Inst., Assn. Gen. Counsel, Chgo. Club, River Club (N.Y.C.), Beach Club, Everglades Club, Old Guard Soc. Palm Beach Golfers.

CRAWFORD, WYNNE, physician, educator; b. Dec. 30, 1957; BS cum laude, U. Ala., 1978, MD cum laude, 1982. Diplomate Am. Bd. Internal Medicine. Intern U. Ala. Hosps., Birmingham, 1982-83, resident, 1983-85, fellow in cardiovasc. disease, 1985-88, mem. staff divsn. cardiovasc. disease, 1987-88; co-dir. coronary care unit Med. Coll. Ga., Augusta, 1989-91; cons. Augusta VAMC, 1989-91; asst. prof. medicine and pediats. Med. Coll. Ga., 1988-91; physician Montgomery Cardiovasc. Assocs., 1991—. Mem. staff Bapt. Med. Ctr., Montgomery, Bapt. Med. Ctr. East, Montgomery, Jackson Hosp. and Clinic, Inc., Montgomery, Edge Regional Med. Ctr., Troy, Ala. Contbr. articles to profl. jours. including Oxford Health Care, Am. Jour. Medicine, So. Med. Jour. Grantee NIH, 1988-91, Wyeth Ayerst Labs., 1989-90, DuPont Pharms.; recipient scholarship Am. Med. Women's Assn. Fellow Am. Coll. Cardiology, N.Am. Soc. Pacing and Electrophysiology, ACP, Am. Coll. Chest Physicians; mem. Am. Heart Assn. (coun. clin. cardiology), AMA, Med. Assn. State Ala., Montgomery County Med. Soc., Alpha Omega Alpha. Achievements include research in clin. electrophysiology, silent myocardial ischemia, pacemakers, implantable cardiac defibrillators, and anti-arrhythmic medications. E-mail: mca009@aol.com.

CRAWFORD-HARRIS, PATRICE ANN, accountant, financial consultant; d. Andrew Donald and Patricia Ann Crawford; children: Jolie LesTrice Harris, Brittany Shannell Harris, Breyon LaVelle Harris, Jeffery Harris, Patric Charles Harris. Cert. acct., Nat. Career Inst., 1988. Owner, operator Patrice Harris Acctg. and Income Tax Svc., Virginia Beach, Va., 1980—, Harris Family Daycare, Virginia Beach, 1992—. Cons. Liberty Income Tax, Virginia Beach, 2000—. Recipient Cert. Of Excellence for Daycare for children with spl. needs, Mayor City of Buffalo, NY, 1992. Mem.: NAFE, Nat. Assn. Tax Practitioners. Home: 2916 Old Glory Rd Virginia Beach VA 23456 Office: Patrice Harris Acctg and Income Tax 2916 Old Glory Rd Virginia Beach VA 23456 Personal E-mail: patriceharrisincometax@hotmail.com.

CRAWFORD-MASON, CLARE WOOTTEN, television producer, journalist; b. Durham, N.C., July 22, 1936; d. Charles Thomas and Clare (Erly) Wootten; m. Robert Watts Mason; children: Victor Lawrence Crawford Jr., Charlene Elizabeth Crawford; stepchildren: John Mason, Robert Mason 3d. BA, U. Md., 1958. Reporter, columnist Washington Daily News, 1961-72; columnist Washington Star News, 1972-74; Washington bur. chief People mag., 1974-82; reporter, sr. prodr. NBC-TV, 1969-80; pres. CC-M Prodns. Inc., Washington, 1981—, managementwisdom.com. Prodr. 1st network documentary on spouse abuse NBC-TV, 1975 (blue ribbon San Francisco Film Festival), 1st network documentary on child sexual abuse NBC, TV 1977, People of the Year (CBS), 1982, If Japan Can, Why Can't We, 1980 (Dupont award Columbia U. Sch. Journalism), It's Up to the Women, 1984, The Issues Hit Home, 1986, Windows on Women, 1986, How To Fix Up a Little Old American Town, 1987, Work Worth Doing, 1987 (Golden Eagle award Coun. on Internat. Non-theatrical Events), The Deming Library: Vols. I-27, Implementing Deming, vols. 1-4; co-author: Thinking About Quality, Progress, Wisdom and the Deming Revolution, 1995; prodr., dir. documentary series Quality of Else, 1991, W. Edwards Deming: The Prophet of Quality, 1994; co-author: Quality or Else: The Revolution in World Business, 1991; prodr. How Everyone Wins: Joy, Meaning and Profit in the Workplace, 1997, The Enneagram Nine Paths to a Productive and Fulfilling Life, 1999. Recipient Bill Pryor Meml. award, 1st prize Washington Newspaper Guild, 1966; Disting. Pub. Affairs Reporting award Am. Polit. Sci. Assn., 1967; Nat. Assn. Broadcasters award, 1971, 2 Emmy awards Nat. Acad. TV Arts and Scis., 1972, award for broadcast investigative reporting AAUW, 1972, award for investigative reporting Chesapeake Press Assn., 1971, Douglas Southall Freeman award for pub. service Va. Assn. Press Broadcasters, 1972; Washington Newspaper Guild award, 1974, Blue Ribbon Am. Film Festival, 1977, 1st place award Nat. Edn. Film Festival, 1985, documentary award Am. Women in Radio and TV, 1986, Golden Eagle award, 1986, 87, Award of Excellence Soc. Tech. Communication, 1988. Mem. AFTRA, SAG. Democrat. Roman Catholic. Office: 7755 16th St NW Washington DC 20012-1460 E-mail: cc-m@cc-m.com.

CRAWLEY, CHERYL K. school system administrator; b. Stanley, Wis., Aug. 14, 1943; d. Donald Arthur and Margaret Banderob Schultze; m. Edward Todd Marckx, Mar. 23, 1996; 1 child, Damara Leanne Crawley Griffith. BS, Mont. State U., Bozeman, 1965; MA, Calif. State U., Hayward, 1976; CPhil, U. Calif., Berkeley, 1983. Cert. K-12 supt. Oreg., Mont. Dir. programs Hardin-Crow Agency-Ft. Smith Schs., Mont., 1978—82; asst. supt. Hardin-Crow Agency Ft. Smith Schs., Mont., 1983—86; dir. student svcs. Salem-Keizer Sch. Dist., Oreg., 1986—94; supt. Pub. Schs., Joseph, Oreg., 1994—97; supt. sch. The Dalles, Oreg., 1997—. Mem. gov.'s task force Devel. Disabilities Svcs., Oreg., 1987—88; keynote spkr. Mont. Assn. for Bilingual Edn., 1987; mem. Horace Mann Soc. Pub. Edn., 1995—; chmn. resolutions com. Confederation Oreg. Sch. Adminstrs., 2002—03; bd. dirs. numerous non-profit orgns. Bd. examiners Baldridge Nat. Quality Award, Dept. Commerce, Washington, 2001—; fellow Leadership Am., Washington, 1997—, Leadership Mid-Columbia, Columbia Gorge, Oreg., 1998; govt. affairs com. C. of C., The Dalles, Oreg., 1999—; Oreg. econ. summit Oreg. Bus. Coun., 2002. Named Woman of Distinction, The Dalles Chronicle, 2001; recipient various grants, 1978—86. Mem.: NAFE, Am. Anthropol. Assn., Am. Assn. Sch. Adminstrs., Boardroom Bound, Rotary (The Dalles pres. 1998—99, Dist. 5100 area rep. 2001—, Paul Harris fellow 2002, Presdl. Citation 1999). Avocations: photography, travel, environment, child advocacy. Office: The Dalles Sch Dist 1413 E 12th St The Dalles OR 97058

CRAWSHAW, RALPH, psychiatrist; b. N.Y.C., July 3, 1921; AB, Middlebury (Vt.) Coll., 1943; MD, N.Y. U., 1947. Diplomate: Nat. Bd. Med. Examiners, Am. Bd. Psychiatry and Neurology. Intern Lenox Hill Hosp., N.Y.C., 1947-48; resident Menninger Sch. Psychiatry, Topeka, 1948-50, Oreg. State Hosp., Salem, 1950-51; practice medicine specializing in psychiatry Washington, 1954; staff psychiatrist C.F. Menninger Meml. Hosp., Topeka, 1954-57; asst. chief VA Mental Hygiene Clinic, Topeka, 1957-60; staff psychiatrist Community Child Guidance Clinic, Portland, Oreg., 1960-63; founder, clinic dir. Tualatin Valley Guidance Clinic, Beaverton, Oreg., 1961-67; pvt. practice medicine, specializing in psychiatry Portland, 1960—2001; mem. staff Holladay Park Hosp., 1961—73. Lectr. dept. child psychiatry Med. Sch. U. Oreg., 1961-63, clin. prof. dept. psychiatry, 1976; lectr. Sch. Social Work, Portland State U., 1964-67; founder Banjamin Rush Found., 1968, pres., 1968—; founder Friends of Medicine, 1969, Ct. of Man, 1970, Club of Kos, 1974, Oreg. Health Decisions, 1983, Am. Health Decisions, 1989, Health Vol. Overseas, 1984; Sonian Machanic vis. prof. South African Coll. Medicine, 1993. Contbr. editor: AMA Jour. of Socio-Econs, 1972-75; Columnist: Prism mag, 1972-76, The Pharos, 1972—, Portland Physician, 1975, Western Jour. Medicine, 1980—; Contbr. articles to med. jours. Cons. Bur. Hearings and Appeals, HEW, 1964-90; cons. Albina Child Devel. Center, Portland, 1965-75, HEW Region 8 Health Planning, 1979; mem. Inst. Medicine, Nat. Acad. Sci., 1978, Oreg. Health Coordinating Council, 1979; Mem. Gov.'s Adv. Com. on Mental Health, 1966-72; ad hoc com. Nat. Leadership Conf. on Am. Health Policy, 1976, Gov.'s Adv. Com. on Med. Care to Indigent, 1976—; trustee Millicent Found., 1964-67, Multnomah Found. for Med. Care, 1977; pres. Bull Run Heritage Found., 1996; vis. scholar Center for Study Democratic Instns., 1969, Jack Murdock Charitable Trust, 1977, U.S.-USSR exchange scholar, 1973; founder Bull Run Heritage Found., 1996. Served with AUS, 1943-46; to lt., M.C. USN, 1951-54. Named Oreg. Dr./Citizen of Yr., 1978; U.S.-USSR rsch. scholar, 1973, 79; recipient I.N. Piragou medal for humanitarian Svcs., Russian Govt., 1992; Ralph Crawshaw Ann. Lectr. in Civic Medicine named in honor by Oreg. Found. for Med. Excellence, 1987. Fellow Am. Psychiat. Assn.; mem. AMA, APA, AAAS, Nat. Med. Assn., Oreg. Med. Assn. (trustee 1972—), Multnomah County Med. Soc. (pres. 1975), Royal Soc. Medicine, Inst. of Medicine of NAS, North Pacific Soc. Neurology and Psychiatry, Soc. for Psychol. Study Social Issues, Western European Assn. Aviation Psychology, Am. Med. Writers Assn., Portland Psychiatrists in Pvt. Practice (pres. 1971), Russian Acad. Natural Scis. (fgn. mem.), Alpha Omega. Home: 2884 NW Raleigh Portland OR 97210

CRAYNE, LARRY RANDOLPH, lawyer; b. Waynesburg, Pa., Aug. 5, 1942; s. Robert Woodruff and Grace Louise (Ankrom) C.; m. Donna Lee Worley, Aug. 3, 1973; children: Jennifer, David, Stephanie. BA California U. Pa., 1967; JD, U. Pitts., 1971. Bar: Pa. 1971, U.S. Dist. Ct. (we. dist.) Pa. 1971, U.S. Supreme Ct. 1977. Assoc. atty. Duquesne Light Co., Pitts., 1971-72, atty., 1972-74, sr. atty., 1974-77, corp. atty., chief counsel, 1977—. Mem. Pa. Bar Assn., Allegheny County Bar Assn. Republican. Home: 238 Johnston Rd Pittsburgh PA 15241-2556 Office: Duquesne Light Co 301 Grant St Pittsburgh PA 15219-1407

CRAYPO, CHARLES, labor economics educator; b. Jackson, Mich., Jan. 3, 1936; s. Norman Laverne and Ann Marie (Bogdan) C.; m. Mary Louise Vaclavik, Sept. 6, 1958; children: Jack, Carrie, Susan. BA in Econs., Mich. State U., 1959, MA in Econs., 1961, PhD in Econs., 1966. Asst. prof. econs. U. Maine, Orono, 1966-67; assoc. prof. Mich. State U., East Lansing, 1967-72, Pa. State U., University Park, 1972-78, U. Notre Dame, Ind., 1978-82, prof., 1984-2000, prof., chmn. dept. econs., 1984-93; prof. Cornell U., Ithaca, N.Y., 1982-84. Bd. dirs. Bus. Devel. Com., South Bend, Ind.; dir. Bur. Workers Edn., U. Maine, Orono, 1966-67, Higgins Labor Rsch. Ctr., U. Notre Dame, 1993; mem. acad. evaluating com. Labor Studies Ctr., Empire State Coll., SUNY, 1980; mem. labor studies dept. Ramapo Coll., 1981; mem. indsl. rels. dept. LeMoyne Coll., Syracuse, N.Y., 1983, Bur. of Labor Edn., U. Maine, Orono; external rev. mem. Divsn. Labor Studies Ind. U., 1998-99; mem. Labor Rsch. Adv. Coun., Bureau Labor Statistics, U.S. Dept. Labor, 2000; lectr. in field; expert witness. Author: Economics of Collective Bargaining, 1986, Grand Designs, 1993; mem. editl. bd., bus. mgr. Labor Studies Jour., 1976-80, chmn. editl. bd., 1980-85; mem. editl. bd. Contbns. to Labor Studies, 1989—; internat. mem. editl. bd. Indsl. Rels. Jour., 1989—; contbr. articles to profl. jours. Mem. acad. adv. com. Divsn. Labor Studies Ind. U., 1978-82, 84-92, 95-96. Served with USMC, 1953-55. Recipient Lilly Endowment, 1992, D. Dority Labor Rsch. Fund, Ganey Rsch. award, 2002; grantee NEH, 1981, Rsch. grant, Dept. Commerce, 1984. Mem.: Indsl. Rels. Rsch. Assn. Home: 50600 Sorrel Dr Granger IN 46530-8506

CREAGAN, JAMES FRANCIS, diplomat, academic administrator; b. Elyria, Ohio, Dec. 28, 1940; s. James Malcolm and Mareta Creagan; m. Cherry Gwyn Jonsson, Jan. 29, 1966; children: Kevin James, Sean Malcolm Alan. BA in History, U. Notre Dame, 1962; PhD in Polit. Sci., U. Va., 1965. Asst. prof. govt. St. Mary's U., San Antonio, 1965-66; asst. prof. polit. sci. Tex. A&M U., Bryan, Tex., 1970-71; joined fgn. svc. Dept. State, Washington, 1966; labor and polit. officer Am. Embassy, Mex., 1967-69, labor attache, 1969-70, 2nd sec., labor officer Rome, 1971-74, 1st sec. Lima, Peru, 1974-77; U.S. consul Am. Consulate Gen., Naples, 1977-80; officer-in-charge, Italian and Vatican affairs U.S. Dept. of State, 1980-82; polit. counselor Am. Embassy, Lisbon, 1982-86, Brasilia, 1986-88; dep. chief of mission Am. Embassy to the Holy See, 1988-91; consul gen. Am. Consulate Gen., Sao Paulo, 1991-92; sr. advisor for Latin Am. U.S. Mission to UN, 1992; dep. chief mission Am. Embassy, Rome, 1993-96; Am. amb. to Honduras, 1996-99; pres. John Cabot U., Rome, 1999—. Mem. adv. coun. U. Notre Dame. Mem. Am. Fgn. Svc. Assn., Coord. Coun. Internat. Univs. (bd. govs.), Cosmos Club, InterAm. Dialogue Club. Roman Catholic. Avocations: tennis, biking. Office: John Cabot Univ Via Lungara 233 00165 Rome Italy

CREAGER, JOE SCOTT, geology and oceanography educator; b. Vernon, Tex., Aug. 30, 1929; s. Earl Litton and Irene Eugenia (Keller) C.; m. Barbara Clark, Aug. 30, 1951 (dec.); children: Kenneth Clark, Vanessa Irene; m. B. J. Wren, Sept. 5, 1987 (dec.); m. Eva R. Milligan, Mar. 18, 2001 (div.). BS, Colo. Coll., 1951; postgrad., Columbia, 1952-53; MS, Tex. A&M U., 1953, PhD, 1958. Asst. prof. dept. oceanography U. Wash., Seattle, 1958-61, assoc. prof., 1962-66, prof. oceanography, 1966-91, prof. geol. scis., 1981-91, prof. emeritus, 1991—, asst. chmn. dept. oceanography, 1964-65, assoc. dean arts and scis. for earth and planetary scis., 1966-95, assoc. dean for rsch., 1966-91, divisional dean emeritus, 1995—; program dir. for oceanography NSF, 1965-66; chief scientist numerous oceanographic expdns. to Arctic and Sub-arctic including Leg XIX of Deep Sea Drilling project, 1959-91. Vis. geol. scientist Am. Geol. Inst., 1962, 63, 65; U.S. Nat. coord. Internat. Indian Ocean Expedition, 1965-66; vis. scientist program lectr. Am. Geophys. Union, 1965-72; Battelle cons., advanced waste mgmt., 1974; cons. to U.S. Army C.E., 1976, U.S. Depts. Interior and Commerce, 1975; exec. sec., exec. com., chmn. planning com. Joint Oceanographic Insts. Deep Earth Sampling, 1970-72, 76-78; mem. evaluation com. Northwest Assn. Schs. and Colls., 1989-99. Mem. editorial bd. Internat. Jour. Marine Geology, 1964-91; assoc. editor Jour. Sedimentary Petrology, 1963-76; asst. editor Quaternary Research, 1970-79; contbr. articles to profl. jours. Skipper Sea Scout Ship, Boy Scouts Am., Bryan, Tex., 1957; coach Little League Baseball, Seattle, 1964-71, sec., 1971; cons. sci. curriculum Northshore Sch. Dist., 1970; mem. Seattle Citizens Shoreline Com., 1973-74, King County Shoreline Com., 1980. Served with U.S. Army, 1953-55. Colo. Coll. scholar, 1949-51; NSF grantee, 1962-82; ERDA grantee, 1962-64; U.S. Army C.E. grantee, 1975-82; Office of Naval Research grantee; U.S. Dept. Commerce grantee; U.S. Geol. Survey grantee. Fellow Geol. Soc. Am., AAAS; mem. Internat. Assn. Quaternary Research, Am. Geophys. Union, Internat. Assn. Sedimentology, Internat. Assn. Math. Geologists, Soc. Econ. Paleontologists and Mineralists, Marine Tech. Soc. (sec.-treas. 1972-75), Sigma Xi, Beta Theta Pi, Delta Epsilon. Home: 7449 NE 118th Pl Kirkland WA 98034 Office: U Wash PO Box 353765 Seattle WA 98195-3765 E-mail: bjnjoe@comcast.net.

CREAGER, MARK ALAN, cardiologist; b. Phila., May 26, 1949; MD, Temple U., 1974. Diplomate Am. Bd. Internal Medicine. Intern Univ. Hosp., Boston, 1974-75, resident, 1975-76; fellow in cardiovasc. medicine Boston U. Med. Ctr., 1976-79; staff Brigham & Women's Hosp., Boston. Mem. Am. Coll. Cardiology, Am. Fedn. Clin. Rsch., Am. Heart Assn., Am. Physiology Soc., Am. Soc. for Clin. Investigation, Soc. for Vascular Medicine and Biology. Office: Brigham & Women's Hosp 75 Francis St Boston MA 02115-6106

CREAMER, BRUCE CUNNINGHAM, retired safety educator, property manager; b. Champaign, Ill., Oct. 27, 1941; s. Carl Moore and Eunice (Cunningham) C.; m. Judith Ann Pride, June, 1968 (div. Apr. 1972). BS in Indsl. Edn., U. Ill., Urbana, 1964, MS in Libr. Sci., 1972, CAS in Libr. Sci., 1975. Auditorium mgmt. U. Ill. Assembly Hall, Urbana, Ill., 1968-70; documents libr. U. Ill. Library, Urbana, Ill., 1972-74; property mgr. Creamer Interests, Champaign, Ill., 1975-97; instr. motorcycle rider program U. Ill., Urbana, Ill., 1977-81, project coord. motorcycle rider program, 1982-93. Chmn. Curriculum

Com., Ill. Cycle Rider Training Program, Springfield, Ill., 1982-86. Co-author: Motorcycle Rider Program, 1982. Bd. dirs. Orpheum Children's Sci. Mus. 1st lt. USAF, 1964-67. Mem. Pres. Coun. U. Ill., U. Ill. Alumni Assn., Air Force Assn., Am. Motorcyclist Assn., Civil Air Patrol, Loyal Order of Moose, Res. Officers Assn. Avocations: military history, local history, family history, historic preservation. Home: 1015 W Daniel St Champaign IL 61821-4517

CREAMER, ROBERT ALLAN, lawyer; b. Sept. 25, 1941; m. Joy A. Blakslee. BA, Northwestern U., 1963; LLB, Harvard U., 1967. Bar: Ill. 1967, U.S. Dist. Ct. (no. dist.) Ill. 1967, U.S. Ct. Appeals (7th cir.) 1969, U.S. Supreme Ct. 1976. Assoc. Keck, Mahin & Cate, Chgo., 1967—73, ptnr., 1974—93; v.p., loss prevention counsel Attys.' Liability Assurance Soc., Inc., Chgo., 1994—. Adj. prof. John Marshall Law Sch., Chgo., 1969—75, Northwestern U. Sch. Law, Chgo., 2000—. Mem.: ABA, Am. Law Inst., Ill. Bar Assn. (chmn. standing com. profl. conduct 1990—91, 1997—98), Chgo. Bar Assn., Northwestern U. Alumni Assn. (pres. 1990—94), Univ. Club (Chgo.), Cliff Dwellers Club (Chgo.), Lawyers Club Chgo. Democrat. Episcopalian. Home: 1500 Oak Ave Evanston IL 60201-4279 Office: Attys' Liability Assurance Soc Inc 311 S Wacker Dr Ste 5700 Chicago IL 60606-6629 Fax: 312-697-6901. E-mail: racreamer@alas.com.

CREAMER, TIMOTHY J. astronaut; b. Ft. Huachuca, Ariz., Nov. 15, 1959; s. Edmund J. Creamer Jr. and Mary E. Creamer; m. Margaret E. Hammer; 2 children. BS in Chemistry, Loyola Coll., 1982; MS in Physics, MIT, 1992. Commd. 2d lt. U.S. Army, 1982, advanced through grades to lt. col., army aviator, 1983, varioius assignments, 1983—87, commdr. 82nd airborn divsn.; asst. prof. dept. physics U.S. Military Acad.; space ops. officer Army Space Commd., Houston; space shuttle vehicle integration test engr. NASA, Houston, 1995—98, astronaut candidate tng., 1998—2000, with space sta. branch astronaut office, 2000—. Decorated Meritorious Svc. medal with 2nd Oak Leaf Cluster U.S. Army, Army Achievement medal with 1st Oak Leaf Cluster, Nat. Def. Svc. medal. Mem.: Assn. U.S. Army, Army Aviation Assn. Am., Brit.-Am. Project, Sigma Pi Sigma, Phi Kappa Phi, Alpha Sigma Nu. Avocations: tennis, running, reading, scuba diving, information technologies. Office: Astronaut Office CB NASA Johnson Space Ctr Houston TX 77058

CREAMER, WILLIAM HENRY, III, retired insurance company executive; b. Narberth, Pa., Mar. 24, 1927; s. William Henry and Stella Elizabeth (McShane) C.; m. Anne Tyson Greer, Sept. 20, 1952 (dec. Mar. 1996); children: William Henry IV, Anne McSherry Creamer Devine, Mary Greer Conyack; m. Nancy Ann Falk, July 10, 1997. BS in Econ., Villanova U., 1951. C.L.U. With N.Y. Life Ins. Co., 1951-89, gen. mgr., 1957-60, regional supt. tng., 1960-62, gen. mgr., 1962-66, Arlington, Va., 1966-69, supt. agencies N.Y.C., 1969-70, regional v.p. Mpls., 1970-74, v.p. N.Y.C., 1974-83, sr. v.p., 1983-85, in charge office fed. affairs, 1986-88; ret., 1988. Past chmn. Navisank River Municipality Com. Served with USN, 1945-46. Mem. Nat. Assn. Life Underwriters, Am. Soc. CLUs, U.S. Power Squadron (past comdr. Shrewsbury squadron), Estate Planning Coun. (past dir.), Shrewsbury River Yacht Club, George Town Club, Capital Hill Club, Beacon Hill Country Club, Root Beer and Checker Club (past pres.), Kiwanis (past pres. Scranton chpt., past dir.), K. of C. (past grand knight Red Bank coun.). Republican. Roman Catholic. Home: 3 Wardell Ave Rumson NJ 07760-1036

CREAN, HUGH, art educator; BA, Nat. U. Ireland, 1974; MA, U. Calif., Davis, 1978; PhD, CUNY, 1990. Lectr. N.Y. Sch. Interior Design, N.Y.C., 1976—, Met. Mus. Art, N.Y.C., 1976—; chair restoration dept. Fashion Inst. Tech., N.Y.C., 1986—. Cons. in field. Prodr.(dir.): (films, documentary) Area of Glory, 2000. Mem.: Decorating Arts Soc., Coll. Art Assn., Nat. Arts Club. Office: Fashion Inst Tech 7th Ave at 27th St New York NY

CREAN, PETER THOMAS, lawyer; b. N.Y.C., Feb. 14, 1955; s. Thomas D. and Dorothy (Barry) C.; m. Stefanie Lewand, May 26, 1979; children: T.R., Patrick, Rosemary. AB in Politics, U. Mass., 1977; JD, Fordham U., 1981. Bar: N.Y. 1982, U.S. Dist. Ct. (ea. and so. dists.) N.Y. 1982, U.S. Supreme Ct. 1995. Ptnr. Martin, Clearwater & Bell, N.Y.C., 1981—. Bd. trustees St. Agnes Hosp., White Plains, NY. Mem. N.Y. State Bar Assn., Assn. Bar City N.Y., Def. Rsch. Inst., Am. Health Lawyers Assn., Assn. Healthcare Risk Mgrs. Office: Martin Clearwater & Bell 220 E 42nd St New York NY 10017-5806

CREASEY, DAVID EDWARD, physician, psychiatrist, educator; b. Santa Barbara, Calif., Aug. 26, 1944; s. Edward Louis Aja and Ruth (Bryan) Creasey; m. Beverly Dewolfe, Apr. 8, 1972. BA cum laude, Tufts U., 1966, MD, 1970. Diplomate Am. Bd. Psychiatry and Neurology, Am. Coll. Forensic Medicine. Surg. intern, then OB/GYN resident Tufts-New Eng. Med. Ctr., Boston, 1970-72; gen. med. officer Newport (R.I.) Naval Hosp., 1972-74; resident in psychiatry Boston VA Hosp., Boston, 1974-77; fellow in psychiatry Mt. Auburn Hosp., Cambridge, Mass., 1977-78; staff psychiatrist Westwood (Mass.) Lodge Hosp., 1978-79, Mass. Mental Health Ctr., Boston, 1979-97; psychiat. dir. New Eng. Psychiat. Rehab. Tng. program, Cambridge, Mass., 1978—. Cons. Mass. Rehab. Com. and Com. for the Blind, Boston, 1984—; adj. assoc. prof. Boston U., 1986-00, clin. assoc. prof., 2000—; assoc., pre-med. adv. North House Harvard U., 1982—; ind. med. reviewer, Metlife, 1994—. Contbr. articles to profl. jours.; reviewer Am. Jour. Psychiatry, Hosp. and Cmty. Psychiatry, Jour. Clin. Neuropsychiatry; author interactive videodisc tchg. program, 1985; med. editor Ency. Disability and Rehab. Mem. various comty. orgns. Lt. cmdr. USN, 1972-74. Recipient Am. Psychiat. Assn. Physician's Recognition award, 1978, 82, 85, 88, 91, 94, 97, 2000, Excellence in Media award Nat. Rehab. Assn., 1996. Avocations: hiking, raquetball, chess, marathoning, roadracing. Office: 1101 Beacon St Fl 8 Brookline MA 02446-5587

CREASIA, DONALD ANTHONY, toxicologist, researcher; b. Milford, Mass., Mar. 28, 1937; s. Dominic and Minnie (Bufalo) C.; m. Joan La Belle, June 29, 1963; children: Karen Joan, Tracey Dawn. BS in Biology, U. Vt., 1961; MS, Harvard U., 1967; PhD, U. Tenn., 1981. Rsch. assoc. Sch. Pub. Health, Harvard U., Cambridge, Mass., 1963-69; toxicologist Oak Ridge (Tenn.) Nat. Lab., 1970-77; program dir. Frederick (Md.) Cancer Rsch. Ctr., 1977-83; rsch. chemist U.S. Army R&D, Frederick, 1983-98; cons. Knoxville, Tenn., 1998—. Cons. toxicology. Author: (chpts. in books with others) Internat. Symposium on the Biological Effects of Ozone and Related Photochemical Oxidents, 1983, Trycothecine Mycotoxicosis: Pathophysiological Efffects, 1989; contbr. over 120 articles to profl. jours. NSF scholar, 1965-67; NRC fellow, 1981-83. Mem. AAAS, Soc. Toxicology, Am. Coll. Toxicology, Soc. Govt. Toxicologists, Internat. Soc. Toxicology, Sigma Xi. Achievements include patents for use of castor bean protein as an immunological adjuvant and discovery that insulin is equally effective in lowering blood glucose when inhaled into deep lung as when it is administered intramuscularly; patents pending for nose-only and body plethismograph animal holder used in inhalation toxicology studies; discovery that insulin is equally effective in lowering blood glucose when inhaled into deep lung as when it is administered intramuscularly. Home: 605 Scotswood Cir Knoxville TN 37919-7457 E-mail: dcreasia@aol.com.

CREASY, DANA EUGENE, communications educator; b. Phila., Mar. 22, 1957; s. Daniel DeFebo and A. June Creasy; life ptnr. Gwendolynne J. Rocchi. BA, Bloomsburg U., 1990—90; MA, Temple U., 2002. Prodr., assoc. dir. CNBC, Fort Lee, NJ, 1990—93; mgr. info. svcs. Request TV, Denver, 1993—95; dir. compliance and ops. PrimeTime 24, NYC, 1996—2000; adj. prof. comm. Passaic County C.C., Paterson, NJ, 2000; lectr. Albright Coll., Reading, Pa., 2002—. Cons. Paravant Corp., Catawissa, Pa., 1987—90, Universal Bus. & Edn. Consortium, Harrisburg, Pa., 2000—01. Prodr.: (television program) The Truth About Signal Strength; actor: (stage play) The Hostage (Best Supporting Actor, 1984); prodr.: (television program series) U.S. News Annual Guides Series; author: (academic conference paper presentation) Television Signal Strength as a Measurement of Broadcast Reception Picture Quality; prodr.: (radio program) JFK: 20 Years Later, (radio public service series) Kids and the Danger of Summer. Aux. officer Passaic (NJ) Police Dept., 1991—93; vol. Carter-Mondale Campaign, Washington, 1975—76; coord. north ctrl. region Rendell for Gov., Phila., 2002; mem. Columbia County Dem. Com., Bloomsburg, Pa., 1986—88; mem. coun. All Saints Luth. Ch., Aurora, Colo., 1994—95. Mem.: AAUP, Assn. Fed. Comm. Consulting Engrs. (assoc.), Broadcast Edn. Assn. (assoc.), Columbia County Dem. Exec. Bd. (hon.), NAm. Am. Fishing Club (life). Avocations: painting, fishing, reading, writing. Office: Albright College Reading PA Personal E-mail: deecee22@ptdprolog.net.

CREASY, RICHARD ALAN, anesthesiologist; b. Oak Park, Ill., 1947; BA in Biology, U. Va., 1969, MD, 1973. Diplomate Am. Bd. Anesthesiology. Intern Med. U. S.C., Charleston, 1973-74; resident in anesthesiology U. Va., Charlottesville, 1974-76, fellow in anesthesiology, 1976-77; pvt. practice Winchester Anesthesiology Inc., Winchester, Va., 1977—; mem. staff Winchester Med. Ctr. Mem. AMA, Am. Soc. Anesthesiologists, Internat. Anesthesia Rsch. Soc., Soc. Cardiovasc. Anesthesiologists. Office: Winchester Anesthesiology Inc 878 Fox Drive Winchester VA 22601-2807

CREATES, MARLENE RUTH, artist; b. Montreal, Que., Can., Apr. 18, 1952; d. Sydney Leslie and Margaret Isabel (Layte) C. BA in Art Edn., Queen's U., 1974. Tchr. visual arts dept. Algonquin Coll., 1975-82, U. Ottawa, 1982-85. Program dir. photography Banff Ctr. for the Arts, summer 1991, N.S. Coll. Art and Design, 1998; vis. artist, guest lectr. various univs., art schs. and galleries, Can., Glasgow (Scotland) Sch. Art, U. Oxford, Eng. Solo and group exhbns. Can., Eng., Scotland, Ireland, France, Denmark and USA; represented in permanent collections Meml. U. Nfld., St. John's, Can., Can. Coun. Art Bank, Ottawa, Can. Mus. Contemporary Photography, Ottawa, City of Montreal, Air Canada, Montreal, Can. Mus. Civilization, City of Ottawa, Nat. Gallery Can., Ottawa, Can. Dept. Fgn. Affairs, Govt. of Nfld. and Labrador, Mt. St. Vincent U., Halifax, N.S., numerous others; pub. commns. include Art Gallery Meml. U., St. John's, 1982, So. Alta. Art Gallery, Lethbridge, 1993, McMichael Can. Art Collection, Kleinburg, 1997, Mt. St. Vincent U. Art Gallery, Halifax, 1998, Gallery 101, Ottawa, 2000, Art Gallery Hamilton, 2000, Art Gallery Greater Victoria, 2000, Edmonton Art Gallery, 2001, Health Care Corp. of St. John's, 2001; author: The Diary Exhibition/Journaux Intimes, 1987, City and Sea, 1988, Don Wright 1931-1988: A Retrospective, 1990, Nature is a Verb to Me, 1992, Language and Land Use, Alberta, 1993, 94, The Distance Between Two Points is Measured in Memories, 1988, 99, Marlene Creates: Landworks, 1979-91, 1993, Language and Land Use, Newfoundland, 1994, Places of Presence, Newfoundland, 1989-1991, 1997. Co-founder, mem. bd. dirs. Ea. Edge Gallery, St. John's, 1986-94. Named Artist of Yr., Nfld. and Labrador Arts Coun., 1996. Mem. Royal Can. Acad. Arts. Home: 15 Blast Hole Pond Rd Portugal Cove NF Canada AIM 2J6 E-mail: marlene.creates@nf.sympatico.ca.

CREATH, CURTIS JANSSEN, pediatric dentist; b. Lynwood, Calif., Mar. 10, 1958; s. Ronald J. and Madelyn W. (Chryst) C.; m. Deborah Ann Lipari, June 23, 1990; 1 child, Andrew. Student, UCLA, 1976-81; DMD, Oral Roberts U., 1985; MS, U. Ala., 1988. Asst. prof. Sch. Dental Medicine SUNY, Stony Brook, 1988-91, Sch. Dentistry U. Ala., Birmingham, 1991-94; staff pediat. dentist Family Cental Care Assocs., Cin., 1994-95; pvt. practice Milford, Ohio, 1995—. Team leader dental mission trips to Mex., Jamaica, Peru, 1982-84. Contbr. chpt. to: Special and Medically Compromised Patients in Dentistry, 1989, Clark's Clinical Dentistry, Vol. 2, 1994; contbr. articles, revs. on tobacco control, pediat. dentistry, and preventive medicine to profl. jours. Semi-finalist E.H. Halton award Internat. Assn. Dental Rsch., 1985. Mem. ADA, Am. Acad. Pediat. Dentistry (mem. edn. com.), Am. Assn. Dental Schs. (v.p. 1986-88), Ala. Soc. Pediat. Dentistry (sec.-treas. 1992-94), Christian Med. and Dental Soc., Omicron Kappa Upsilon. Republican. Presbyterian. Avocations: vocal music, preaching, missionary work, woodworking, gardening. Home: 6514 Tulip Ct Liberty Township OH 45044-9726 Office: 1106-C Main St PO Box 267 Milford OH 45150-0267 E-mail: curtjcre@aol.com.

CRECELIUS, DANIEL NEIL, history educator; b. St. Louis, Jan. 15, 1937; s. Wilson John and (Imhof) R.; m. Anahid Tashjian, July 21, 1963; 1 child, Gia Maria. BA, Colo. Coll., 1959; MA, Princeton U., 1962, PhD, 1967. From asst. prof. to prof. emeritus Calif. State U., L.A., 1964—2001, assoc. prof., 1968-73, prof. emeritus, 2001—, chairperson, 1980-83, 98-01. Vis. lectr. UCLA, 1966-67, Colo. Coll., 1990, Cairo U., 1992. Author 2 books, editor 11 books; contbr. numerous articles to profl. jours., chpts. to 12 books. Trustees' scholar Colo. Coll., 1955-59; Woodrow Wilson Nat. fellow, 1959-60, Princeton U. Near East fellow, 1961-62; grantee U. Mich., 1960, Princeton U., 1961, Fulbright Found., 1962-63, 91-92, 92, 95-96, 96, Nat. Def. Fgn. Lang. grantee, 1963-64, Am. Rsch. Ctr., 1972, 79, 96, Am. Philos. Soc., 1975, 80, 89, Social Sci. Rsch. Coun., 1973, Dept. HEW Office Edn., 1973, Calif. State U., L.A., 1975, NEH, 1980-82, 83-84, 87, 91-92, 92, Calif. State U. L.A. Found., 1979, 81, others; Joseph P. Malone fellow, 1998. Mem. Mid. East Studies Assn., Turkish Studies Assn., Phi Beta Kappa, Pi Gamma Mu. Lutheran. Avocations: travel, hiking, bird watching. Address: Calif State U LA 5151 State University Dr Los Angeles CA 90032-4226 E-mail: dncrecelius@aol.com., dcrecel@calstatela.edu.

CREECH, HUGH JOHN, chemist, researcher; b. Exeter, Ont., Can., June 27, 1910; came to U.S., 1938, naturalized, 1945; s. Richard Newton and Edith (Sanders) C.; m. E. Marie Hearne, July 10, 1937; children: Richard Hearne, Joan Marie. BA, U. Western Ont., 1933, MA, 1935; PhD (rsch. fellow), U. Toronto, 1938; postgrad., Harvard U., 1938-41. Asst. prof. U. Md., 1941-43, assoc. prof., 1943-45; lectr. Bryn Mawr (Pa.) Coll., 1945-47; immunochemist Inst. for Cancer Rsch. and Lankenau Hosp. Rsch. Inst., Phila., 1945-47, head dept. chemotherapy, 1947-57, chmn. div. chemotherapy, 1957-70, sr. mem., 1949—; chmn. adminstrv. com. Inst. Cancer Rsch., 1947-54; mem. U.S. nat. com. Internat. Union Against Cancer, 1957-60, 80-84. Antimalarial rsch. U. Md. with OSRD, Washington, 1943-45; expert cons. to Surgeon Gen. U.S. Army, 1947-49 Recipient numerous awards for rsch. NIH Am. Cancer Soc. Mem. Am. Assn. Cancer Rsch. (hon., sec.-treas. 1952-77, v.p. 1977-78, pres. 1978-79, archivist 1983-99). Home: Fort Washington, Pa. Died Jan. 18, 2003.

CREECH, JOHN LEWIS, retired scientist, consultant; b. Woonsocket, R.I., Jan. 17, 1920; s. Edward and Bessie (Faulkner) C.; m. Amy Elizabeth Wentzel, Feb. 14, 1942 (dec. Apr. 1984); children: Diane, Victoria, John; m. Elaine E. Godden Innes, July 10, 1984 (dec. July 2003). BS in Horticulture, U. R.I., 1941; MS in Horticulture, U. Mass., 1947; PhD in Botany, U. Md., 1953. Instr. horticulture U. Mass., Amherst, 1946-47; horticulturist Office Plant Exploration, Agrl. Rsch. Svc. USDA, 1947-50, asst. chief new crops rsch. br. Agrl. Rsch. Svc., 1958-66, chief br. Agrl. Rsch. Svc., 1966-72, scientist nat. program staff Agrl. Rsch. Svc., 1972-73; dir. U.S. Nat. Arboretum, Washington, 1973-80, N.C. Arboretum, 1987-88. Sr. adviser Internat. Bd. for Plant Genetic Resources; negotiator Bicentennial gift of Nat. Bonsai Collection from people of Japan; developer Nat. Herb Garden; program dir. for conservation of plant genetic materials Internat. Biol. Program, NAS; mem. panel FAO, 1966-74; preparer U.S. position paper for Stockholm Conf. on the Environment; adj. prof. biology U. N.C., Asheville; bd. dirs. N.C. Arboretum, Asheville, interim dir., 1986-87; U.S. judge Internat. Flower & Garden Expo, Japan, 1990; leader 9 plant expeditions Japan, China, Taiwan, USSR, Nepal, 1955-78; co-chmn. Genetic Resource Team, China, 1974; rev. nat. gen. resource program USDA, NAS, 1988-92; cons. Time-Life Books for Children, 1993; cons. in horticulture; leader hort. tours. Author: The Bonsai Saga, 2001; co-author: Brocade Pillow, 1984, Garden Shrubs and Their Histories, 1992. Capt. U.S. Army, 1941-45, prisoner of war, ETO. Decorated Silver Star, Bronze Star; recipient Gold medal Scott Found., Gold medal Garden Club Am., Gold Seal medal Nat. Coun. State Garden Clubs, Thomas Roland medal Mass. Hort. Soc., Silver medal FAO-UN, Hort. medal Fedn. Garden Clubs N.Y., Norman J. Colman award Am. Nurserymans Assn., Hutchinson medal Chgo. Bot. Garden/Chgo. Hort. Soc., 1987, Gold medal and cert. of merit City of Kurume, Japan, 1988, Veitch Meml. medal Royal Hort. Soc., U.K., 1992, Award of Merit, Am. Assn. Bot. Gardens and Arb., 2000, Prs. award U. R.I., 2002; grantee Merrill Found., 1976, Nat. Geog. Soc., 1978, Japan Found., 1982; selected to give Morrison Meml. lecture. Mem. Am. Genetics Assn. (bd. dirs., Meyer medal), Am. Hort. Soc. (pres. 1954-56, profl. citation, Liberty Hyde Bailey medal 1989), Internat. Dendrology Soc. (v.p. 1989—), Sigma Xi, Phi Kappa Phi, Pi Alpha Xi. Republican. Episcopalian. Achievements include introduction of several plant varieties. Fax. E-mail: jlcreech@teleplex.net.

CREECH, SHARON, children's author; b. South Euclid, Ohio; d. Arvel and Ann Creech; m. Lyle Rigg; children: Rob, Karin. BA, Hiram Coll.; MA, George Mason U. Editl. asst., indexer Congl. Quarterly, Washington; rschr. Libr. Congress. Author: Recital, Nickel Malley, Walk Two Moons, 1994 (School Library Journal Best Book of 1994, ALA Notable Children's Book Award, 1995, John Newbery medal 1995), Absolutely Normal Chaos, 1995, Pleasing The Ghost, 1996, Chasing Redbird, 1997, Bloomability, 1999, The Wanderer, 2000, Fishing in the Air, 2000. Office: care HarperCollins Children's Bks c/o Author Mail 1350 Ave of the Americas New York NY 10019

CREECH, WILBUR LYMAN, retired career officer; b. Argyle, Mo., Mar. 30, 1927; s. Paul and Marie (Maloney) C.; m. Carol Ann DiDomenico, Nov. 20, 1969; 1 son, William L. Student, U. Mo., 1946-48; BS, U. Md., 1960; MS, George Washington U., 1966; postgrad., Nat. War Coll., 1966. Commd. 2d lt. U.S. Air Force, 1949; advanced through grades to gen.; fighter pilot 103 combat missions USAF, North Korea, 1950-51; pilot USAF Thunderbirds, 1953-56; comdr., leader Skyblazers, Europe aerial demo team USAF, 1956-60; dir. Fighter Weapons Sch., Nellis AFB, Nev., 1960-61; advisor to comdr. Argentine Air Force, 1962; exec., aide to comdr. Tactical Air Command, 1962-65; dep. comdr. fighter wing, 177 combat missions in F-100 fighters and asst. dep. chief staff for ops. 7th Air Force, Vietnam, 1968-69; comdr. fighter wings USAF in Europe, Spain and W.Ger., 1969-71; dep. for ops. and intelligence Air Forces Europe, 1971-74; comdr. Electronic Systems Div., Hanscom AFB, Mass., 1974-77; asst. vice chief of staff HQS Air Force, Washington, 1977-78; comdr. Tactical Air Command, Langley AFB, Va., 1978-85. Lectr., internat. mgmt. expert; cons. in field. Author: The Five Pillars of TQM, 1994. Decorated D.S.M. with three oak leaf clusters, Silver Star medal, Legion of Merit with two oak leaf clusters, D.F.C. with three oak leaf clusters, Air medal with 14 oak leaf clusters, Air Force Commendation medal with two oak leaf clusters, Army Commendation medal; Spanish Grand Cross. Home and Office: 20 Quail Run Rd Henderson NV 89014-2147

CREED, GERALD W. anthropologist, educator, researcher; b. Winston-Salem, N.C., Mar. 6, 1958; s. Raleigh Columbus and Ruby Speer Creed. BA, Duke U., 1980; PhD, CUNY, 1992. Asst. prof. CUNY Hunter Coll., N.Y.C., 1992—97; assoc. prof. CUNY Hunter Coll. and Grad. Ctr., N.Y.C., 1998—. Author: Domesticating Revolution, 1998; co-editor, contbg. author: Knowing Your Place, 1997, mem. editl. bd.: Slavic Rev., 2001—. Fellow, Am. Coun. Learned Socs., 1996, Agrarian Studies Program, Yale U., 2000, Howard Found., Brown U., 2000. Mem.: Am. Assn. for the Advancement Slavic Studies, Am. Ethnological Soc., Am. Anthropol. Assn., Coun. for European Studies (exec. com. mem. 2000—). Office: CUNY Hunter Coll Dept Anthropology 695 Park Ave New York NY 10021

CREED, ROBERT PAYSON, SR., retired literature educator; b. Phila., Apr. 22, 1925; s. Edward E. and Blanche H. (Southerland) Creed; m. Catherine Hilton, Oct. 9, 1987; children from previous marriage: Mary Louise, Robert Payson. BA, Swarthmore Coll., 1948; MA, Harvard U., 1949, PhD, 1956. Instr. Smith Coll., Northampton, Mass., 1952-56; from asst. prof. to assoc. prof. Brown U., Providence, 1956—65; assoc. prof. SUNY, Stony Brook, 1965-67, prof., 1967-69; prof. English U. Mass., Amherst, 1969-97, prof. emeritus, 1997—, dir. grad. studies in English, 1969-72, prof. English and comparative lit., 1980-90, chmn. comparative lit. dept., 1980-85. Cons. G&C Merriam Co., Springfield, Mass., 1955—56; featured storyteller Ann. Nat. Storytelling Festival, Jonesborough, Tenn., 1985, Jonesborough, 92; nat. vis. prof. Paul Valery U., Montepellier, France, 1987; disting. faculty lectr. U. Mass., Amherst, 1993—94. Writer, chief performer Beowulf, Sta. WNYC pub. radio, 1979 (award Corp. Pub. Broadcasting); author: (book) Reconstructing the Rhythm of Beowulf, 1990; featured performer Asheville (N.C.) Poetry Festival, 1994. Bd. dirs. Arcadia Players Baroque Orch., Chorus and Chamber Ensemble, Northampton, Mass., pres., 1995—98; mem. Corp. Boston Early Music Festival, 2002—. With USNR, 1943—46, served to lt. (j.g.) USNR, 1949. John Simon Guggenheim fellow, 1962—63, NEH fellow, Yugoslavia, 1976, Inst. Advanced Studies Humanities fellow, Edinburgh U., 1976, Am. Coun. Learned Soc. grantee, 1978. Mem.: AAAS, MLA (life), Archaeol. Inst. Am. (exec. coun. Western Mass. Soc. 1996—), European Soc. Study Cognitive Sys., Lang. Origins Soc., Nat. Storytelling Assn., N.Y. Acad. Scis., Internat. Soc. Anglo-Saxonists. Home: 5 Kinder Ln Shutesbury MA 01072-9762 E-mail: creed@english.umass.edu. *Though a professor of literature, I have become more and more deeply concerned with oral traditions. Behind surviving traditions-indeed, behind literature-lie tens of thousands of years of what we may call Memorable Speech, some of which survives embedded in early texts. Back of Memorable Speech lies the origin of human language. Through the study of (sound-) patterned Memorable Speech, I am trying to work back towards the beginning of language, our most adaptive and humanizing invention.*

CREED, WAYNE J. writer; b. Lineville, Ala., Jan. 17, 1931; s. Arney Preston and Lois Gerone (Hobbs) Creed; m. Rose Marie Falcone, Aug. 1, 1958; children: Wayne Preston, Gina Marie. Surveyor U/S. Coast and Geodetic Survey, Washington, 1949—69; adminstr. U.S. C.G., Portsmouth, Va., 1971—86, ret., 1986; substitute tchr. Clay County Pub. Schs., Ashland, Ala., 1994—; writer Lineville, 1994—. Author: Caney Head, 2001, The Little Boy & His Grandpa, 2002. V.p. Clay County Hist. Soc., Ala., 1993—2003; commr. Clay County, 1996—2000. With U.S. Army, 1951—53. Mem.: Shriners (pres. 1987—88). Republican. Mem. Ch. Of Christ. Avocations: golf, fishing. Home: 630 Blue Ridge Rd Lineville AL 36266

CREEKMORE, DAVID DICKASON, lawyer, educator; b. Knoxville, Tenn., Aug. 8, 1942; s. Frank Benson and Betsey (Beeler) C.; 1 child, Walton N. LLB, U. Tenn., 1965, JD, 1966; grad, Judge Adv. Gen.'s Sch., 1979, Army Command Gen. Staff Sch., 1985. Bar: Tenn. 1966, U.S. Supreme Ct. 1970, U.S. Ct. Mil. Appeals 1985. Law clk. Gen. Session Ct. Knox County, Knoxville, Tenn., 1963-66; judge divsn. II, Gen. Sessions Ct. Knox County, Knoxville, 1972-86; asst. county atty. Knox County, Knoxville, 1966-70; ptnr. Creekmore, Thomson & Hollow, Knoxville, 1966-72, Walter, Regan & Creekmore, Knoxville, 1993-97; pvt. practice Knoxville, 1986-93, 97-98; dep. law dir. Knox County, Knoxville, 1998—. Instr. criminal law and evidence Walters State Coll., Morristown, Tenn., 1974-80, U. Tenn., 1982-89. Committeeman Knox County Rep. Com., 1970—; active Tenn. Hist. Assn., Blount Mansion Assn. Lt. Col. JAGC, USAR, 1997. Mem. ABA, FBA, Tenn. Bar Assn., Tenn. Judges Conf. (v.p. 1976-78), Knox Bar Assn., Res. Officers Assn. (pres. 1989-91), Am. Legion (post judge adv. 1984-87), Studebaker Drivers Assn. (pres. 1992-97), Masons, Shriners, Elks, Eagles, Lions. Home: 11530 Midhurst Dr Knoxville TN 37922-4768 Office: Knox County Law Dept 612 City-County Bldg 400 W Main St Knoxville TN 37902-2405

CREEKMORE, JOSEPH R. pharmacist, researcher; s. Raymond Lee and Carol Lewis Creekmore; m. Lisa Marie Hall, Mar. 7, 1981; children: Joseph Richard Jr., Bengamin Clyde. BS in pharmacy, U. NC, 1980, MS in pharmacy, 1982; PhD in pharmacy, U. Iowa, 1986. Registered pharmacist NC, VA, DE. Sr. rsch. pharmacist AH Robins Co., Richmond, Va., 1986—89; pharmacist The Colonial Pharmacy, Mechanicsville, Va., 1987—89, Rite Aid Pharmacy, Wilmington, Del., 1989—2000, Saveway Pharmacy, New Castle, Del., 1992—2001, Happy Harry's Discount Pharmacy, New Castle, 2001—; mgr. formulation devel. Astra Zeneca Pharm., Wilmington, 1989—. Program com. Phila. Pharm. Forum, 1992—. Mem.: Internat. Soc. of Pharm. Engrs., Am. Assn. of Pharm. Achievements include patents for dry powder layering process for Zafirluleast; stabilization of Rosuvastatr by a multivalent cationic tribase phosphate salt. Office: Astra Zeneca Pharm 1800 Concord Pike Wilmington DE 19850 E-mail: richard.creekmore@astrazeneca.com.

CREEKMORE, VERITY VEIRS, media specialist; b. Cin., May 13; d. Noble L. and Maxine (Wright) Veirs; m. Kenneth L. Creekmore, Nov. 23, 1961; 1 child, Kenneth L. Jr. BS in Edn. magna cum laude, S.C. State U., 1975; MLS, U. S.C., 1978. Cert. libr. media specialist, S.C. Media specialist John Ford High Sch., St. Matthews, S.C., 1976-77, St. John High Sch., Cameron, S.C., 1977-82, St. John Elem./Mid. Sch., Cameron, 1982-86, Sheridan Elem. Sch., Orangeburg, S.C., 1986—. Directed libr. U. S.C., Columbia, 1997—; adj. tch. instr. S.C. State Dept. Edn., 1997—. Rep. S.C. Sci. Hub. Sys. Operator Sheridan Sch. Local Area Computer Network: Trainer Laubach Literacy Program, Orangeburg, 1990—. Recipient IMAGEMAKER award SCASL, 1999. Mem. NEA, ALA, S.C. Assn. Sch. Librs., Nat. Assn. Storytelling, S.C. State Coun. Internat. Reading Assn., So. Assn. Colls. and Schs. (evaluator), S.C. Edn. Assn. (dist. rep. 1991-93, IPD rep. 1993-97), Hon. Order Ky. Cols., Order Ea. Star, Alpha Kappa Mu. Avocations: reading, church work, travel. Home: 1172 Caw Caw Hwy Saint Matthews SC 29135-8300 Office: Sheridan Elem Sch 1139 Hillsboro St NE Orangeburg SC 29115

CREEL, HAROLD JENNINGS, JR., federal commission administrator, lawyer; b. Florence, S.C., July 1, 1957; s. Harold Jennings Sr. and Dorothy Louise (Fenters) C. BA in Polit. Sci., Wofford Coll., 1979; JD, U. S.C. Law Sch., 1982. Bar: La. Assoc. Courtenay, Forstall, Grace & Hebert, New Orleans,

1982-83; atty./advisor NOAA, Washington, 1983-89; sr. counsel subcom. of com. on commerce, sci. and transp. U.S. Senate - Mcht. Marine Subcom., Washington, 1989-94; commr. Fed. Maritime Commn., Washington, 1994-96, chmn., 1996—2002, commr., 2002—. Mem. La. State Bar Assn. Democrat. Avocations: fishing, gardening. Office: Fed Maritime Commn 800 N Capitol St NW Washington DC 20211-0001

CREEL, LUTHER EDWARD, III, lawyer; b. Huntsville, Ala., Sept. 23, 1937; s. Luther Edward and June (Oldacre) C.; m. Nan Dee McHalek, Apr. 11, 1974; children by previous marriage: Scott Mitchell, Todd Oldacre. AB in Psychology, George Washington U., 1959; JD, So. Methodist U., 1963. Bar: Tex. 1963. Pvt. practice, Dallas, 1963—; chmn. Creel & Atwood (and predecessors), Dallas, 1971-96; of counsel Malouf, Lynch, Jackson, Kessler & Collins, Dallas, 1996-98; chmn. Creel, Susman & Moore, Dallas, 1998—. Pres., chmn. The Pines Camp, 1999—2001; lectr. in bankruptcy and reorgn. law. Contbr. articles to profl. jours. Chmn. Ford Debtor Assistance Program, 1995-98. Mem. Dallas Bar Assn. (chmn. bankruptcy sect. 1972), State Bar Tex. (cert. bus. bankruptcy specialist 1989-2003, chmn. bankruptcy com. 1979-81), Am. Bankruptcy Inst. (co-founder, pres. 1982-87, vice-chmn. 1987-96, bd. dirs. 1982-2000, chmn. 1996-98, chmn. emeritus 1998-2000), Am. Coll. Bankruptcy (co-founder, fellow, pres. 1996-97), John C. Ford Inn of Ct. (master, exec. com. 1999—), Park Cities Club, GTG Tex. Longhorn Assn. (pres. 1998-2000), Internat. Tex. Longhorn Assn. (bd. dirs.). Republican. Baptist. Home: 7214 Desco Dr Dallas TX 75225-2003 Office: Creel Susman & Moore 8235 Douglas Ave Ste 1100 Dallas TX 75225-6011

CREEL, SCOTT, adult education educator, researcher; b. Hammond, Ind., June 25, 1962; s. Roger and Joan Creel; m. Nancy Marusha, Aug. 16, 1984; children: Andie Marusha, Bridget Marusha. PhD, Purdue U., 1987—91, MS, 1984—86; BS, Bowling Green State U., 1980—83. Postdoctoral rschr. Oxford U., England, 1992—93; rsch. scientist Frankfurt Zool. Soc., Germany, 1992—96, Smithsonian Instn., Conservation & Rsch. Ctr., Front Royal, Va., 1993—94; asst. prof. Rockefeller U., N.Y.C., 1995—96; assoc. prof. Mont. State U., Bozeman, Mont., 1997—2002. Author: (nonfiction book) The African Wild Dog: Behavior, Ecology and Conservation; contbr. articles to various profl. pubs. Mem. U.S. Nat. Biathlon team, 2000—02; mem. Rossignol Nordic Ski Racing team, 2002—02. Grantee NSF-NATO Fellowship, NATO, 1992. Democrat. Avocations: parenthood, running, nordic skiing, coaching. Office: Montana State University Dept of Ecology Bozeman MT 59717

CREEL, THOMAS LEONARD, lawyer; b. Kansas City, Mo., June 21, 1937; s. Thomas Howard and Elizabeth Alberta (Sharon) C.; m. Carol M. Plaisted, Nov. 26, 1992; children: Charles, Andrew, Andrea, Thomas. BS, U. Kans., 1960; LLB, U. Mich., 1963. Bar: Mich. 1963, N.Y. 1967, D.C. 1983, U.S. Supreme Ct. 1973, Ct. Mil. Appeals, 1964, U.S. Patent and Trademark Office 1965. Assoc. Kenyon and Kenyon, N.Y.C., 1966-74, ptnr., 1974-92, Kaye, Scholer, Fierman, Hayes & Handler, N.Y.C., 1992—2001, Goodwin Procter LLP, N.Y.C., 2001—. Faculty lectr. Columbia U. Sch. Law, N.Y.C., 1984-2001. Editor: Guide to Patent Arbitration, 1987. Capt., U.S. Army, 1963-66. Mem. ABA, Fed. Bar Coun., N.Y. Intellectual Property Law Assn. (past pres.), Am. Intellectual Property Assn. Home: 104 Cedar Cliff Rd Riverside CT 06878-2606 Office: Goodwin Procter LLP 599 Lexington Ave New York NY 10022

CREELEY, ROBERT WHITE, author, English educator; b. Arlington, Mass., May 21, 1926; s. Oscar Slade and Genevieve (Jules) C.; m. Ann MacKinnon, 1946 (div. 1956); children: David, Thomas, Charlotte; m. Bobbie Louise Hall, Jan. 27, 1957 (div. 1976); children: Kirsten, Leslie, Sarah, Katherine; m. Penelope Highton, 1977; children: William, Hannah. BA, Black Mountain Coll., 1954; MA, U. N.Mex., 1960, LittD (hon.), 1993. Instr. Black Mountain Coll., 1954-55; vis. lectr. English U. N.Mex., Albuquerque, 1961-62, lectr., 1963-66, vis. prof., 1968-69, 78-80, SUNY, Buffalo, 1966-67, prof. English, 1967—, Gray prof. poetry and letters, 1978-89, Capen prof. poetry and humanities, 1989—, dir. poetics program, 1991-92. Lectr. U. B.C., Vancouver, 1961-63; lectr. creative writing San Francisco State Coll., 1970-71; vis. prof. SUNY-Binghampton, spring 1985, 86; Bicentennial chair Am. studies, Fulbright award, U. Helsinki, Finland, 1988, Fulbright award U. Auckland, New Zealand, 1995. Author: Le Fou, 1952, The Immoral Proposition, 1953, The Kind of Act of, 1953, The Gold Diggers, rev. edit, 1965, All That is Lovely in Men, 1955, If You, 1956, The Whip, 1957, A Form of Women, 1959, For Love, Poems, 1950-60, 1962, The Island, 1963, Poems, 1950-65, 1966, Words, 1967, The Finger, rev. edit, 1970, The Charm, 1968, Numbers, 1968, Pieces, 1969, A Quick Graph, 1970, A Day Book, 1972, Listen, 1973, A Sense of Measure, 1973, Contexts of Poetry, 1973, Thirty Things, 1974, Backward, 1975, (with Marisol) Presences, 1976, Selected Poems, 1976, rev. edit., 1991, Mabel: A Story, 1976, Myself, 1977, Hello, 1978, Was That a Real Poem & Other Essays, 1979, Later, 1979, Robert Creeley and Charles Olson: The Complete Correspondence, Vols. 1 and 2, 1980, Vol. 3, 1981, Vol. 4, 1982, Vol. 5, 1983, Vol. 6, 1985, Vols. 7 and 8, 1987, Vol. 9, 1990, Vol. 10, 1996, Mother's Voice, 1981, Echoes, 1982, Collected Poems, 1945-1975, 1983, Mirrors, 1983, Collected Prose, 1984, Memory Gardens, 1986, The Company, 1988, Window, 1988, Collected Essays, 1989, (with Francesco Clemente) It, 1989, Windows, 1990, Places, 1990, Autobiography, 1990, The Old Days, 1991, Gnomic Verses, 1991, Tales Out of School, 1993, Echoes, 1994, Life & Death, 1998; I So There, poems, 1976-83, 1998, Just in Time Poems, 1984-94, 2001, Day Book of a Virtual Poet, 1998; editor: Black Mountain Rev., 1954-59, New American Story, 1965, (with Donald M. Allen) The New Writing in the U.S.A, 1967, Selected Writings of Charles Olson, 1967, Whitman: Selected Poems, 1973; Robert Burns, The Essential Burns, 1989, Charles Olson, Selected Poems, 1993. With Am. Field Svc., 1944-45. Recipient Levinson prize Poetry mag., 1960, Blumenthal-Leviton award, 1965, Union League Civic and Arts Found. prize Poetry mag., 1967; D.H. Lawrence fellow, 1969; Guggenheim fellow, 1964, 71; Rockefeller grantee, 1965; Shelley Meml. award Poetry Soc. Am., 1981; Premis Speciale, Leone d'Oro, Venice, 1985; Frost medal Poetry Soc. Am., 1987; Walt Whitman citation of merit and named N.Y. State Poet by State of N.Y., 1989-91; Disting. prof. award SUNY, Buffalo, 1989, Horst Bienek Preis fur Lyrick, Munich, 1993, The America award for Poetry, Washington, 1995, Lila Wallace Reader's Digest Writers' award, 1996—; Bollingen Prize, 1999, Chancellor's medal, SUNY, Buffalo, 1999, Am. Book award Beyond Columbus Found., 2000, Golden Rose award New Eng. Poetry Club, 2001, Lannan Literacy Lifetime Achievement award 2001; NEA grantee, 1982, DAAD grantee, 1983, 87. Mem. AAAL, Acad. Am. Poet (chancellor 1999—). Office: SUNY/Buffalo 313 Clemens Buffalo NY 14260-0001 E-mail: creeley@acsu.buffalo.edu.

CREEL MIRANDA, SANTIAGO, secretary of the interior for Mexico; b. Mexico City, Dec. 11, 1954; Grad., U. Nacional Autónoma Mex., Mexico City; postgrad., U. Mich. Bar: (Mex.). Lawyer, Mexico; prof. Autonomous Technol. Inst. Mex.; sec. Vuelta periodical; founder Este País mag.; citizen advisor Gen. Coun. Fed. Electoral Inst., 1994—96; fed. dep. LVII Legislature, 1997; 1st chmn. Com. Govt. and Constitutional Issues; joined Nat. Action Party (PAN), 1999, cand. to head of govt. of Fed. Dist., 1999; std. bearer Alliance for Change; sec. of the interior Govt. of Mex., Mexico City, 2000—. Nat. and internat. election overseer; organizer plebiscite, 1993. Mem.: Coll. Lawyers, Lawyer's Com. Human Rights, Assn. Unity Our Am., Mexican Acad. Human Rights. Office: Abraham Gonzalez 48 PB Col Juraz 06699 Mexico City Mexico*

CREENAN, KATHERINE HERAS, lawyer; b. Elizabeth, N.J., Oct. 7, 1945; d. Victor Joseph and Katherine Regina (Lederer) Petervary; m. Edward James Creenan; 1 child, David Heras. BA, Kean Univ., 1968; JD, Rutgers U., 1984. Bar: N.J. 1984, Maine, 1996, U.S. Dist. Ct. N.J. 1984, U.S. Ct. Appeals (3d cir.), 1998. Various tchg. positions including, Union and Stanhope, N.J., 1968-81; law clk. to presiding judge Superior Ct. of N.J. Appellate Div., Newark, 1984-85; assoc. Lowenstein, Sandler, Kohl, Fisher & Boylan, Roseland, N.J., 1985-88, Kirsten, Simon, Friedman, Allen, Cherin & Linken, Newark, 1988-89, Whitman & Ranson, Newark, 1989-93; sr. atty. Whitman Breed Abbott & Morgan LLP, Newark, 1993-99; assoc. Skadden, Arps, Slate, Meagher & Flom LLP, Newark, 1999—. Mem. ABA, N.J. State Bar Assn. Office: Skadden Arps Slate Meaghar & Flom LLP 1 Newark Ctr Newark NJ 07102-5297 E-mail: kcreenan@skadden.com

CREER, THOMAS LASELLE, psychologist, educator; b. Lund, Idaho, Nov. 2, 1934; s. Laselle Lewis Creer and Naomi Johanna Jones; m. Patricia P. Plummer, July 7, 1961; children: Jennifer, Matthew. BS, Brigham Young U., 1956; Master's, Utah State U., 1961; PhD in Psychology, Fla. State U., 1997. Lic. psychologist Colo. Prof. psychology Ohio U., Athens, 1980—96; pres. Creer Sys., Inc., Provo, Utah, 1995—. Co-exec. dir. Nat. Asthma Ctr., Denver, 1977—80. Author: (book) Chronically-Ill and Handicapped Children, 1976, Asthma Therapy: A Behavioral Health Care System for Respiratory Disorders, 1979, Self-Management of Chronic Disease, 1986, Psychology of Adjustment, 1997, Respiratory Disorders and Behavioral Medicine, 2002; contbr. more than 50 chpts. to books. Bd. dirs. Am. Lung Assn. Ohio, Columbus, 1983—93, Am. Lung Assn. Utah, 2002—, pres.-elect, 2003—04. With U.S. Army, 1956—58. Recipient Pre-doctoral Internship award, VA, 1966—67; fellow Pre-doctoral fellow, U.S. Pub. Health Svc., 1963—66. Mem.: Am. Coll. Allergy, Asthma and Immunology. Liberal. Avocation: reading. Home: 144 E 4620 N Provo UT 84604 Office: Creer Sys Inc 144 E 4620 N Provo UT 84604 Home Fax: 801-434-7731; Office Fax: 801-434-7731. Personal E-mail: tcreer@comcast.net.

CREGAN, FRANK ROBERT, financial executive, consultant; b. Jersey City, July 27, 1940; s. Frank Vincent and Maurie Geraldine (Kennedy) C.; m. Joan Marie Swancer, July 19, 1969; children: Christina Eileen, Darren Michael, Keith Francis. BBA, Manhattan Coll., 1962; MBA, St. John's U., Jamaica, N.Y., 1972. CPA, N.Y. Supr. KPMG Peat Marwick, N.Y.C., 1962-68; dir. taxes DuPont Glore Forgan, Inc., N.Y.C., 1968-73; v.p. taxes Marsh & McLennan Cos., Inc., N.Y.C., 1973-78; ptnr. Deloitte & Touche, Parsippany, N.J., 1978-83; v.p. fin. Madison Resources, Inc., N.Y.C., 1983-86; v.p., treas. WSGP Internat., Inc., Morristown, N.J., 1986-89; mng. dir. William E. Simon & Sons, L.L.C., Morristown, 1989—. Fin. planning cons., Morristown, N.J., 1962—. Fundraiser, United Way of Essex and West Hudson Counties, Newark, 1978, Morristown-Beard Sch., 1990-92, Colonial Touchdown Club, Morristown, 1991-94; bd. dirs. Better Bus. Bur. Greater Newark, 1981-83; team mgr. Morristown Nat. Little League, 1982-86; leader Boy Scouts Am., Morristown, 1984-95, fin. advisor Morris/Sussex coun., Denville, N.J., 1991-92; mem. adv. bd. St. Joseph Sch., Bronx, N.Y., 1991—, Resurrection Sch., N.Y.C., 1996—; treas. Morristown H.S. Booster Club, 1992-94; beautification com. Twp. of Morris, 1998-, Kiwanis Club of Morristown, 1998-2002. Mem.: Coun. N.J. Grantmkers, Fin. Execs. Inst., N.J. Soc. CPAs, AICPA, Friendly Sons of St. Patrick of Morris County. Avocation: golf. Home: 14 Kissel Ln Morristown NJ 07960-3613 Office: William E Simon & Sons LLC PO Box 1913 Morristown NJ 07962-1913 E-mail: fcregan@wesandsons.com.

CREGIER, DON MESICK, historian, educator, researcher, consultant; b. Schenectady, N.Y., Mar. 28, 1930; s. Harry Mesick and Marion (Shovea) C.; m. Sharon Kathleen Ellis, June 29, 1965. BA, Union Coll., 1951; MA, U. Mich., 1952; PhD, Columbia Pacific U., 1999. Instr. history U. Tenn., Knoxville, 1956-57; asst. prof. history Baker U., Baldwin City, Kans., 1958-61, Keuka Coll., Keuka Park, N.Y., 1962-64, St. John's U., Collegeville, Minn., 1964-65, St. Dunstan's U., Can., 1966-69; assoc. prof. history U.P.E.I., Charlottetown, 1969-85, prof., 1985-96, adj. prof., 1996—2002. Salvage editor, rsch. cons., 1996—. *Author of over 150 articles and reviews, Cregier continues his research into early twentieth-century British and Irish history, and is canvassing a possible venture into fiction. His current writing project is a biography of Frederick E. Guest (18975-1937), cousin and friend of Sir Winston Churchill, British army officer in the Boer War and World War I, political advisor to Prime Minister David Lloyd George between 1917 and 1921, and air minister in 1921-22. Based in rural Prince Edward Island, Cregier keeps in touch with colleagues, clients, and the wider world through the Internet.* Author: Bounder from Wales: Lloyd George's Career before the First World War, 1976, Novel Exposures: Victorian Studies Featuring Contemporary Novels, 1979, Chiefs Without Indians: Asquith, Lloyd George and the Liberal Remnant (1916-1935), 1982, The Decline of the British Liberal Party: Why and How?, 1985, Freedom and Order: The Evolution of Liberalism and the Liberal Party in Great Britain Before 1868, 1988; co-author: The Rise of the Global Village, 1988; editor Quest for Edn., 1966-67; fgn. book rev. editor Can. Rev. Studies in Nationalism, 1996-98; abstracter ABC-Clio Info. Svcs., 1978—; assessor Internat. Rev. Periodical Lit., 1988-89; contbr. articles to profl. jours. Social Scis. and Humanities Rsch. Coun. Can. grantee, 1984-86; Mark Hopkins fellow, 1965-66, Can. Coun. fellow, 1972-73. Mem.: Soc. Acad. Freedom and Scholarship, Nat. Assn. Scholars, Nat. Coalition Ind. Scholars, Can. Assn. Univ. Tchrs., Am. Hist. Assn., Assn. Contemporary Historians, The Hist. Soc. N.Am. Conf. on Brit. Studies, Mark Twain Soc., Internat. Churchill Soc., Oxford Club, Pi Gamma Mu, Phi Kappa Phi, Phi Beta Kappa, Phi Sigma Kappa. Office: PO Box 1100 Montague PE Canada COA 1RO E-mail: dcregier@upei.ca.

CREHAN, JOSEPH EDWARD, lawyer; b. Detroit, Dec. 8, 1938; s. Owen Thomas and Marguerite (Dunn) C.; m. Sheila Anderson, Nov. 6, 1965; children: Kerry Marie, Christa Ellen. AB, Wayne State U., Detroit, 1961; JD, Ind. U., 1965. Bar: Ind. 1965, Mich. 1966, U.S. Supreme Ct. 1984. Pvt. practice, Detroit, 1966-68; assoc. Louisell & Barris (P.C.), 1968-72; ptnr. Fenton, Nederlander, Dodge, Barris & Crehan (P.C.), 1972-74, Barris & Crehan (P.C.), 1975-88; pvt. practice Bloomfield Hills, Mich. and Naples, Fla., 1977—. Mem. Am. Trial Lawyers Assn. Roman Catholic. Home and Office: 827 Bentwood Dr Naples FL 34108-8204

CREHORE, CHARLES AARON, lawyer; b. Lorain, Ohio, Sept. 15, 1946; s. Charles Case and Catherine Elizabeth Crehore; 1 child, Charles Case II. BA, Wittenberg U., 1968; postgrad., U. Mich., 1968-69, Cleve. State U., 1972-73; JD, U. Akron, 1976; diploma mgmt. mgrs. program, Pa. State U., 1983. Bar: US Patent Office 1975, Ohio 1976, US Dist Ct (no dist) Ohio 1976, US Ct Appeals (DC cir) 1977, US Tax Ct 1977, US Supreme Ct 1980, US Ct Appeals (fed cir) 1982. Assoc. chemist B.F. Goodrich Co., Akron, 1969-70, chemist, 1970-72, sr. chemist, 1972, patent atty. trainee, 1972-74, sr. patent atty. trainee, 1974-75, patent assoc., 1975-76, patent atty., 1976-79; atty. regulatory affairs The Lubrizol Corp., Wickliffe, Ohio, 1979-81, corp. counsel environment, health and safety, 1981-85, sr. corp. counsel, 1985-94, counsel, 1994-99; patent atty. Hudak and Shunk Co., L.P.A., 2000; of counsel Ulmer & Berne, LLP, 2000—. Guest lectr, moot ct judge Case Western Res Univ, 1983—; spkr. Calif Inst Bus Law, Ohio, 1991, Northeast Ohio Software Asn, 2001—. Lakeland Cmty. Coll., 2001—, Media Profls. Conf., 2002—; adv bd applied environ mgmt program Lake Erie Col, 1991—94. Grantee, Kennedy Found, 1968—69; scholar, Delta Sigma Phi Found, 1968—69. Mem.: ABA, Cleve. Intellectual Property Law Assn., Am. Intellectual Property Law Assn., Greater Cleve. Intellectual Lawyers Group, Phi Alpha Delta. Home: PO Box 466 Wickliffe OH 44092-0466 Office: Penton Media Bldg 1300 E 9th St Ste 900 Cleveland OH 44114 E-mail: ccrehore@aol.com.

CREIGH, THOMAS, JR., utility executive; b. Evanston, Ill., Jan. 3, 1912; s. Thomas and Frances (Connor) C.; m. Dorothy Claire Weyer, July 17, 1948; children: Mary Elizabeth, Thomas III, John, James. Grad., Mercersburg (Pa.) Acad., 1929; AB, Wabash Coll., 1933. With No. Natural Gas Co., 1933-36; with KN Energy, Inc. (formerly Kans.-Nebr. Natural Gas Co., Inc.), 1936-86; v.p. KN Energy, Inc., 1951-61, pres., 1961-78, chmn. bd., 1978-85, chmn. emeritus, 1985-93, also dir.; v.p., dir. Excelsior Oil Corp., 1955-68, pres., 1968-84; pres., dir. Western Gas Corp., 1967-84. V.p., dir. Helium, Inc., 1960-85; sec., dir. Western Plastics Corp., 1953-69; dir. Dunne Gardner Drilling Co., City Nat. Bank, Hastings, Western Alfalfa Corp., Cap-Con Internat Inc., Cape Constrn. Co., Energy Transmission System, Inc., Advanced Fuel Systems, Inc., Slurry Transport Assos.. Mem. Nebr. Gov.'s Task Force for Govt. Improvemenet, 1980-82, Nebr. Bd. Ednl. Lands and Funds, 1987-91; trustee Hastings Coll., Inst. Gas Tech., U. Nebr. Found., Nebr. State Hist. Found.; bd. dirs. Nebr. Art Collection, Nebr. chpt. Nature Conservancy, Nebraskans for Pub. TV, 1994—; mem. Nebr. Hist. Preservation Bd., 1991—, Adams County Hist. Soc., Nebr. Ind. Coll. Found., Crane Meadows Nature Ctr. Mem. Am. Gas Assn. (dir. 1969-73), Midwest Gas Assn. (dir. 1965-68), Interstate Natural Gas Assn. (dir. 1967-71, 74-82), Nebr. Assn. Commerce and Industry (past pres.), Nebr. Coun. Econ. Edn. (chmn. 1967-70), Nebr. State Hist. Soc. (exec. bd. 1990-91). Presbyterian (trustee). Office: Ste 204 Burlington Ctr 747 N Burlington Ave Hastings NE 68901

CREIGHTON, JOANNE VANISH, academic administrator; b. Marinette, Wis., Feb. 21, 1942; d. William J. and Bernice Vanish; m. Thomas F. Creighton, Nov. 9, 1968; 1 child, William. BA with honors, U. Wis., 1964; MA, Harvard U., 1965; PhD, U. Mich., 1969. From instr. to prof. English Wayne State U., Detroit, 1968—85, assoc. dean liberal arts, 1983—85; dean arts and scis., prof. English U. N.C., Greensboro, 1985—90; v.p. acad. affairs, provost, prof. English Wesleyan U., Middletown, Conn., 1990—94, interim pres., 1994—95; prof. English, pres. Mt. Holyoke Coll., South Hadley, Mass., 1995—. Author: William Faulkner's Craft of Revision, 1977, Joyce Carol Oates, 1979, Margaret Dabble, 1985, Joyce Carol Oates: Novels of the Middle Years, 1992. Grantee, Am. Coun. Learned Socs. Mem.: Phi Kappa Phi, Phi Beta Kappa. Home: 45 College St South Hadley MA 01075-1403 Office: Mount Holyoke Coll Office of Pres 50 College St South Hadley MA 01075-1423*

CREIGHTON, JOHN WALLIS, JR., novelist, publisher, former management educator, consultant; b. Yeung Kong, China, Apr. 7, 1916; s. John Wallis and Lois (Jameson) C.; m. Harriet Harrington, June 30, 1940; childrn: Carol (Mrs. Brian LeNeve), Joan (Mrs. Robert Nielsen). Student, Wooster Coll., 1933-36; BS in Forestry, U. Mich., 1938; AB, Hastings Coll., 1939; PhD in Wood Tech. and Indsl. Engring., U. Mich., 1954. Operator, sawmill, Cuyahoga Falls, Ohio, 1939—41; mem. staff U.S. Bd. Econ. Warfare, Ecuador, 1941—44; asst. gen. mgr. R.S. Bacon Veneer Co., Chgo., 1944—45; gen. mgr., v.p. Bacon Lumber Co., Sunman, Ind., 1944—45; faculty Mich. State U., Lansing, 1945—54, prof. wood tech., 1945—54; asst. to gen. mgr., v.p. Baker Furniture Inc., Grand Rapids, Mich., 1954—58; pres. Creighton Bldg. Co., Santa Barbara, Calif., 1958—65; prof. mgmt. Colo. State U., Ft. Collins, 1965—67, U.S. Naval Post grad. Sch., Monterey, Calif., 1967—86, chmn. dept., 1967—71, dir. fed. exec. mgmt. program, 1974—82, emeritus prof., 1986. Cons. in field. Assoc. editor, co-founder Jour. Tech. Transfer, 1975-88; fiction writer, 1986–; author: Waring's War, 2001, Aira in Red, 2002; contbr. articles to profl. jours. Former mem. Forestry Commn., Carmel, Calif., 1986-95. Recipient numerous Rsch. grants. Mem. Tech. Transfer Soc., Writer's Internat. Network, Calif. Writer's Club. Presbyterian. Home: 8065 Lake Pl Carmel CA 93923-9514

CREIM, JERRY ALAN, lawyer; b. Chattanooga, Oct. 20, 1956; s. James Mond and Claire Sylvia Creim; m. Sarah McNeel Hrobsky, Mar. 25, 1983; children: Daniel, Elizabeth. BA, Emory U., 1978; JD cum laude, U. Puget Sound, Tacoma, 1981. Bar: Wash. 1981, U.S. Dist. Ct. Wash. 1984, U.S. Ct. Appeals (9th cir.) 1984. Law clk. to chief judge Wash. State Ct. Appeals, Seattle, 1981-83; assoc. Williams, Kastner & Gibbs PLLC, Seattle, 1983-89, ptnr., 1990—. Named Top Lawyer, Seattle Mag., 2003, Wash. Super Lawyer, Wash. Law and Politics, LLC, 2003. Fellow Am. Coll. Mortgage Attys.; mem. Bldg. Owners and Mgrs. Assn. (assoc. bd. trustees, course instr. 1993-95, trustee 2002—). Avocations: fly fishing, fly tying, golf. Office: Williams Kastner & Gibbs PLLC 601 Union St Ste 4100 Seattle WA 98101-1368

CREIM, WILLIAM BENJAMIN, lawyer; b. Seattle, May 12, 1954; s. Conrad Creim and Marjorie (Ross) Rosanoff; m. Linda Carol Denison, June 19, 1977; 1 child, Michael David. BA in Polit. Sci. summa cum laude, UCLA, 1976; JD, U. So. Calif., 1979. Bar: Calif. 1979, U.S. Dist. Ct. (cen. dist.) Calif. 1979, U.S. Ct. Appeals (9th cir.) 1980, U.S. Dist. Ct. (no. dist.) Calif. 1985, U.S. Supreme Ct. 1985, U.S. Dist. Ct. (ea. and so. dists.) Calif. 1987. Assoc. Fine, Perzik & Friedman, L.A., 1979-83; assoc. Dennis, Juarez, Reeser, Shafer & Young, L.A., 1983-85; ptnr. Dennis, Juarez, Shafer & Young, L.A., 1985-87; mng. ptnr. Dennis, Shafer, Fennelly & Creim, L.A., 1988-92, Bronson, Bronson & McKinnon, L.A., 1992-99; ptnr. Creim, Macias & Koeniz LLP, L.A., 1999—. Editor: Southern Calif. Law Rev., 1978-79, contbr., 1979; mem. editl. adv. bd. Credit Today. Recipient Am. Jurisprudence award, 1978. Mem. ABA (antitrust law sect., corp., banking and bus. law sects.), Calif. Bar Assn., L.A. County Bar Assn. (antitrust, bus. and corps. sect., comml. law and bankruptcy sect.), Century City Bar Assn. (bankruptcy and creditor's rights sect.), Conf. Fin. Lawyers, Order of Coif, Legion Lex (bd. dirs. 1992—), Phi Beta Kappa, Pi Gamma Mu, Phi Delta Phi. Democrat. Home: 26509 Sunbird Ct Valencia CA 91355-3505 Office: Creim Macias & Koeniz LLP 16th Flr 611 W 6th St Fl 16 Los Angeles CA 90017-3101

CREMEANS, JAMES L. minister; b. Rayland, Ohio, Dec. 22, 1939; s. Leroy and Waneda (Montgomery) C.; m. Mary McCormick, Oct. 4, 1956; children: James, David, Jeffery, Diane, Janet. DD (hon.), Internat. Bible Sem., 1985. Ordained to ministry 1st Tabernacle Ch., Ironton, Ohio, 1967. Pastor City Mission Ch., Ironton, 1967—; exec. dir. City Welfare Mission, Ironton, 1967—. Dir. corr. sch. Evangelistic Outreach, Pedro, Ohio, 1982—, v.p., 1975—, also bd. dirs. Mem. Lawrence County (Ohio) Welfare Adv. Bd., 1980-82, Home Health Care Bd., Ironton, 1980—, Lawrence County Youth Coun., 1988—; mem. bd. biomed. ethics River Valley Hosp., 1998—; bd. dirs. Ironton/Lawrence County Cmty. Action Orgn., 2002. Named Citizen of Yr., Cmty. Betterment Club, Lawrence County, 1979, Ironton Tribune, 1993. Mem. Lawrence County Ministerial Assn. (chmn. radio and TV 1975-80, sec.-treas. 1995—, chmn. chaplancy com. 1993—). Home: 365 Township Road 150 Pedro OH 45659-8928 Office: City Mission Ch 710 N 5th St Ironton OH 45638-1306 E-mail: jimmaryc@cloh.net.

CREMER, LEON EARL, federal agent, lawyer; b. Cin., Dec. 30, 1945; s. Walter H. and Beatrice (Campbell) C. BS, Calif. State U., 1973; MA, George Washington U., 1976; JD, Rutgers U., 1982. Bar: Pa. 1982. Officer U.S. Secret Svc., Washington, 1975-77; spl. agt. U.S. Bur. Alcohol Tobacco and Firearms, U.S. Dept. Treasury, Phila., 1977-83, FBI, U.S. Dept. Justice, N.Y.C., 1983—. With U.S. Army, 1968-69. Mem. ABA, FBI Agts. Assn., Phila. Bar Assn., Pa. Bar Assn., Am. Trial Lawyers Assn., Internat. Platform Assn., Am. Mensa Soc. Avocations: yachting, aviation, skiing, tennis, long-distance running. Office: FBI 26 Federal Plz New York NY 10278-0127

CREMER, RICHARD ELDON, marketing professional; b. Detroit, Apr. 13, 1928; s. Eldon Grant and Mildred Odessa (Williams) C.; m. Bernadine Ann Beaugrand, Aug. 21, 1948; children: Susan Marie, David Grant. AA in Acctg., USMC Inst., 1947. Br. mgr. Household Fin. Corp., Detroit, 1948-51; collection mgr. Internat. Harvester Co., Detroit, 1951-53; credit mgr. Montgomery Ward Co. Inc., Detroit, 1953-54, dist. credit mgr. for Mich., 1954—56, store ops. mgr. Livonia, Mich., 1956-61, corp. credit contr. Chgo., 1961-64, regional credit mgr. east region Balt., 1964-66, gen. credit mgr. Chgo., 1966-72; pres., chief exec. officer The Signature Group (M.W. subs.), Schaumburg, Ill., 1970-85; exec. dir. consumer divsn. Bally Fitness Products Inc., Irvine, Calif., 1985-88; pres., CEO Richard E. Cremer and Assocs., Kerrville, Tex., 1985—. Entered the congressional record as tribute to free enterprise sys., 1981. Exec. com. Columbia U. Arden House Cons. Credit Conf., 1965-75; spl. adviser Pres. Coun. Phys. Fitness and Sports, 1973-85, 92—, Ill. Gov.'s Coun. Health and Fitness, 1975-85; co-chmn. capital fund YMCA, Evanston, Ill., 1983. With USMC, 1945-48. Recipient Direct Marketer of Yr. award N.Y. Direct Mail Day, 1981. Mem. Direct Mktg. Assn. (bd. dirs. exec. com. 1974-80), Chgo. Assn. Direct Mktg. (Direct Marketer of Yr. award 1992), Econ. Club Chgo. Avocations: flying, golf, running. Office: 2180 Bandera Hwy Kerrville TX 78028-6629 Home (Winter): 37770 Alissa Dr Zephyrhills FL 33542-5672 Fax: 813-779-4399. E-mail: rcremer@up.net.

CREMIN, SUSAN ELIZABETH, lawyer; b. Chgo., July 2, 1947; d. William Amberg and Rosemary (Brennan) C. AB cum laude, Vassar Coll., 1969; JD, Northwestern U., Chgo., 1976. Bar: Ill. 1977. Assoc. Winston & Strawn, Chgo., 1976-83, ptnr., 1983-93, capital ptnr., 1993—. Co-author: Registration and Reporting Under the Exchange Act, 1995, 2nd edit., 1996. Trustee The Shedd Aquarium, Chgo., The Masters Sch., Dobbs Ferry, N.Y. Office: Winston & Strawn 35 W Wacker Dr Ste 4200 Chicago IL 60601-1695

CREMINS, JAMES SMYTH, political party official, lawyer; b. Washington, June 11, 1921; m. Mary Louise Gallagher (dec.); 5 children. AB with honors, U. Mo., Columbia, 1943; JD, U. Va., 1949. Asst. gen. counsel CSX Corp., Richmond, Va., 1980-85. Treas. Dem. Party Va., 1977-89. Contbr. articles to legal jours. Lay min. St. Mary's Ch., Richmond, 1968-85; bd. visitors U. Va., 1984-88, Pres.'s Roundtable JMU, 1985-90; mem. adv. bd. St. Gertrude H.S., Richmond, 1984-88; past instnl. rep. Robert E. Lee coun. Boy Scouts Am.; mem. fin. coun. Richmond Cath. Diocese, 1978—; trustee Commonwealth Cath. Charities, 1981—; bd. dirs. Maymont Found., 1976-89; mem. State Dem. Steering Com., 1972-89, State Dem. Ctrl. Com., 1972-89. Lt. USNR, 1943-46. Recipient Brotherhood award, Nat. Conf. Christians and Jews, 1985. Mem.: KC (4th degree Knight equesteian Order of the Holy Sepulchre of Jerusalem 1998), ABA, Am. Judicature Soc. (bd. dirs. 1973—77), Richmond Bar Assn. (chmn. corp. counsel sect. 1964—65), Va. Bar Assn., Ancient Order Hibernians (charter mem. Maj. James Dooley Divsn. 1), Nat. Soc. SAR (trustee 1989—90), Va. Soc SAR (pres. 1988—89), Navy League U.S. (Judge adv. Richmond coun 1985—89), Phi Delta Phi, Omicron Delta Kappa (hon.), Alpha Tau Omega.

CREMINS, WILLIAM CARROLL, lawyer; b. Virginia Beach, Va., Nov. 13, 1957; s. James Smyth and Mary Louise (Gallagher) C.; m. Kelly Robin Knapp, July 6, 1985; children: William Carroll Jr., Robert Gallagher. BA, BJ, U. Mo., 1980; JD, St. John's U., 1984. Bar: Tenn. 1984, N.Y. 1985, U.S. Dist. Ct. (ea. dist.) Tenn., U.S. Ct. Appeals (6th cir.). Assoc. Law Offices of J.D. Lee, Knoxville, Tenn., 1984-85; pvt. practice, Knoxville, 1986—. Dep. nat. organizer Ancient Order of Hibernians in Am., Inc., Tenn., 1985, pres. James Dardis divsn., 1997, 98; bd. dirs. Florence Crittenton Agy. of Knoxville, Inc., 1989-96, 2002—, pres., 1995; Little League baseball coach, 1993-97, football coach, 1987, 1993-94, soccer coach, 1992, 1995. Recipient Pro Bono award Knoxville Bar Assn. Vol. Legal Assistance Program, 1992. Mem. ATLA (Advocate recognition 1994), ABA, Tenn. Bar Assn., Knoxville Bar Assn., Tenn. Trial Lawyers Assn. Roman Catholic. Home: 710 Saint John Ct Knoxville TN 37922-1556 Office: 810 Henley St Knoxville TN 37902-2901 Fax: 865 546-7151. E-mail: wmcremins@aol.com.

CRENNER, JAMES T. poet, communications educator; b. Pitts., Feb. 10, 1938; s. James A. and Mae Connors Crenner; m. Kate Lybarger Blackburn, Nov. 14, 1959 (div. Feb. 1973); children: Christopher, Belle Mary, Timothy. BA in English, St. Vincent Coll., Latrobe, Pa., 1959; MA in Modern Lit., U. Iowa, 1961; MFA in Poetry, U. Iowa Writers Workshop, 1962; PhD in Am. Lit., U. Iowa, 1967. Instr. English St. Vincent Coll., Latrobe, 1962—64; grad. tchg. asst. U. Iowa Writers Workshop, Iowa City, 1964—67; asst. prof. English Hobart and William Smith Colls., Geneva, NY, 1967—72, assoc. prof. English, 1972—78, prof. English, 1978—, The John Milton Potter prof. English, 2000—, The Harter chair in humanities, 1992—94, The John Milton Potter chair, 2000—. Co-founder, editor The a Rev., 1970—83. Author: (book of poems) The Aging Ghost, 1964, My Hat Flies on AgainThe Aging Ghost, 1980. Woodrow Wilson Found. fellow, 1959. Mem.: The Acad. of Am. Poets. Democrat. Avocations: gardening, bicycling, birdwatching. Home: 4911 E Lake Rd Romulus NY 14541 Office: Hobart and William Smith Colls Pulteney St Geneva NY 14456

CRENSHAW, ALBERT BURFORD, journalist; b. Lexington, Va., Oct. 4, 1942; s. Ollinger and Marjorie (Burford) C.; m. Margaret Alice Price, Aug. 11, 1973; children— David Ollinger, Caroline Abbey AB, Harvard U., 1964; MS, U. Va., 1966; MS in Journalism, Columbia U., 1967. Reporter Washington Daily News, 1969-71, asst. city editor, 1971-72; asst. nat. editor Washington Post, 1972-76, night nat. editor, 1977-82, real estate editor, 1982-85, asst. fin. editor, 1985-88, fin. reporter, columnist, 1988—. Served with U.S. Army, 1967-69 Mem.: Harvard (N.Y.C.); Nat. Press (Washington). Home: 321 E Capitol St SE Washington DC 20003-3808 Office: Washington Post 1150 15th St NW Washington DC 20071-0002

CRENSHAW, ANDER, congressman; b. Jacksonville, Fla., Sept. 1, 1944; m. Kitty, 1971; children: Sarah, Alex. BA, U. Ga., 1966; JD, U. Fla., 1970. Investment banker, 20 yrs.; served Fla. House Rep, 1972, Fla. Senate, 1972, Florida Senate, 1986, pres., 1992; mem. U.S. Congress from 4th Fla. Dist., 2001—. Mem. Congressional com. Armed Svcs., Budget, Veterans' Affairs, Rep. policy, subcom. Mil. Rsch. and Devel., Mil. Installations and Facilities, Health, Benefits; appt. Asst. Majority Whip; rep. to House of GOP leadership. Mem. Fla. Ethics com., Fla. Constitution Revision com. Republican. Mem. Grace Episc. Ch. Office: 127 Cannon House bldg Washington DC 20515-0904*

CRENSHAW, BEN, professional golfer; b. Austin, Tex., Jan. 11, 1952; m. Julie Ann; children: Katherine Vail, Claire Susan, Anna Riley. Grad., U. Tex. Mem. U.S. World Amateur Cup Team, 1972; mem. U.S. Ryder Cup, 1981, 83, 87, 95; profl. golfer, 1973—; U.S. team capt. Kirin Cup, 1988; team capt. Ryder Cup Team, 1999. Winner San Antonio Open, 1973, Western Amateur open match and medal plan champion, 1973, Bing Crosby Nat. Pro-Am., Ohio Kings Island Open, Hawaiian Open, 1976, Colonial Nat. Invitational, 1977, NCAA Championship, 1971, 72, 73, Irish Open, 1976, Phoenix Open, 1979, Walt Disney World Team Championship, 1980, AnheuserOBusch Classic, 1980, Tex. State Open winner, 1980, Ryder Cup, 1981, 83, 87, Byron Nelson Classic, 1983, Masters tournament, 1984, PGA Sr. Event Jeremy Ranch Shoot-Out teameed with Miller Barber, 1985, Buick Open, 1986, Vantage Championship, 1986, USF&G, 1987, Doral Ryder Open, 1988, World Cup, 1988, Western Open, 1992, Masters winner Augusta Nat. Golf Club, 1995, Masters Tournament, 1995, Ryder Cup, 1999. Mem. Profl. Golfers Assn. Am. Office: PO Box 50568 Austin TX 78763-0568

CRENSHAW, FRANCIS NELSON, retired lawyer; b. Washington, Dec. 9, 1922; s. Russell Sydnor and Sally Nelson (Robins) C.; m. Jane Elizabeth Treadwell, Aug. 20, 1949 (dec. June 1993); children: Elizabeth, Page, Marian; m. Anne Bolling Alfriend, July 12, 1997. Grad., St. George's Sch., 1939; BA, U. Va., 1943, LLB, 1948. Bar: Va. 1948. Ptnr. Baird, White & Lanning, Norfolk, 1952-55, Baird, Crenshaw & Lanning, Norfolk, 1955-60, Baird, Crenshaw & Ware, Norfolk, 1960-68, Crenshaw, Ware & Johnson, Norfolk, 1968-89, Crenshaw, Ware & Martin, Norfolk, 1989-99; ret., 1999. Mem. Va. Bd. Bar Examiners, 1973-90, pres., 1983-90. Mem. Norfolk City Sch. Bd., 1955-64, chmn., 1962-64; bd. visitors Old Dominion U., 1968-76, rector, 1972-76; mem. bd. commrs., Ea. Va. Med. Authority, 1966-68. Served with USNR, 1943-46. Decorated Bronze Star. Fellow ABA, Va. Law Found.; mem. Va. Bar Assn. (chmn. exec. com. 1988-89), Va. State Bar (chmn. sr. lawyers sect. 1998-99; editor sr. lawyers newsletter 1999-2002), Norfolk-Portsmouth Bar Assn. (pres. 1967), Maritime Law Assn. Home: 305 Brooke Ave Unit 208 Norfolk VA 23510 Office: 1200 Bank Am Bldg Norfolk VA 23510

CRENSHAW, PATRICIA SHRYACK, sales executive, consultant; b. Kansas City, Mo., Oct. 7, 1941; d. George Randolf and Velma Irene (Carroll) Shryack; m. Paul Burton, Mar. 24, 1961 (div. 1971); m. Peter Frederick Schmidt, Jan. 21, 1989. Student, William Jewell Coll., 1959-60, S.W. Mo. State U., 1960-61; BEd, U. Mo., 1967; postgrad., Cen. Mo. State U., 1971-73. Cert. tchr. secondary edn. and history, Mo. Tchr. Lillis H.S., Kansas City, 1967—69, Park Hill H.S., Kansas City, 1969-73; terr. mgr. Hollister, Inc., Kansas City, 1973-75, field trainer, 1974-75, sales edn. mgr. Chgo., 1975; dist. sales mgr. Detroit Mich., 1976-81; regional sales mgr. Chgo., 1981-84; dir. contract sales Chgo. Serta, Inc., 1984-86, nat. dir. contract sales divsn., 1987-89, v.p. nat. contract sales, 1989-90; area v.p. B G Industries, Northridge, Calif., 1990-91, v.p. sales, 1992-95, v.p. internat. sales, 1995-97, v.p. clin. svcs., 1998—2002; ret., 2002. Mem. women's com. Young Reps., Kansas City, 1962. Mem. NOW, U.S. Golf Assn., Lake Barrington Shores (Ill.) Golf Club. Republican. Avocations: golfing, skiing, scuba diving, racquetball, reading, gardening. Home: 101 E Ocean Dr Key Colony Beach FL 33051

CRENSHAW, TENA LULA, librarian; b. Coleman, Fla., Dec. 15, 1930; d. Herbert Joseph Crenshaw and Nellie (Wicker) Cox. BS, Fla. So. Coll., 1951; postgrad., U. Fla., 1952-55; MLS (Univ. scholar), U. Okla., 1960. Tchr. pub. schs., Coleman, Fla., 1952-55, St. Petersburg, Fla., 1955-57, Houston, 1957-59; tech. libr. Army Rocket & Guided Missile Agy., Redstone Arsenal, Huntsville, Ala., 1960-61; acquisitions libr. Martin Marietta Corp., Orlando, Fla., 1961-64; reader svcs. libr. John F. Kennedy Space Ctr., NASA, Fla., 1964-66; rsch. info. analyst, specialist Lockheed Missiles and Space Co., Palo Alto, Calif., 1966-68; head svcs. to pub. A.W. Calhoun Med. Libr. Emory U., Atlanta, 1969-78; dep. dir. Louis Calder Meml. Libr. U. Miami (Fla.) Sch. Medicine, 1979-80; head edn. libr. U. Fla., Gainesville, 1980-84; libr. Westinghouse Electric Corp., Orlando, 1984-86; chief libr. tech. info. ctr. U. Ctrl. Fla., Orlando, 1986-87, libr. contracts and grants, 1987-88; libr. cons. Coleman, Fla., 1988-89; sch. libr., 1989-90; libr. Kennedy Space Ctr., Fla., 1990-91, Patrick Air Force Base, Fla., 1992-94, Coleman Pub. Libr., 1995—. Chmn. Fla. State Adv. Coun. on Librs. Mem. Spl. Librs. Assn. (treas. S. Atlantic chpt. 1970-72, chmn. membership com. 1973, v.p. 1973-74, pres. 1974-75, mem. resolutions com. 1975-76, nominating com. biol. scis. divsn. 1974-75, chmn. 1977-78), Med. Libr. Assn. (mem. conf. planning com. So. regional group 1973-74, membership com. 1977-79, by laws rev. com. 1979-80), Southeastern (mem. new directions com. 1972-74, chmn. spl. librs. sect. 1974), Ga. (careers in librarianship com. 1974-77), Fla. Libr. Assn., DAR, Alpha Delta Pi, Kappa Delta Pi. Democrat. Methodist. E-mail: Colemanlibrary@cfl.rr.com.

CREPAZ, MARKUS MICHAEL LEOPOLD, political scientist, educator; m. Nicole Yowen Chen, Aug. 4, 1997. MA, Bowling Green (Ohio) State U., 1986; PhD, U. of Calif., San Diego, Calif., 1992. Assoc. prof. The U. of Ga., Athens, Ga., 1993—. Contbr. articles to profl. jours. Mem.: Am. Polit. Sci. Assn. (assoc.). Achievements include research in constitutional determinants of politico-economic outcomes. Avocations: soaring, soccer, travel. Office: University of Georgia Sch Pub Internt Affairs Candler Hall Athens GA 30602 Home: 1171 Founder's Lake Dr Athens GA 30606

CREPEAU, DEWEY LEE, lawyer, educator; b. Richmond Heights, Mo., June 3, 1956; s. Dewey Lee and Floy Evelyn (Lacefield) Crapo; m. Susan Jane Stonner, July 15, 1978; children: Elizabeth, Courtney, Luke. AB, U. Mo., 1977, JD, 1980. Bar: Mo. 1980, U.S. Dist. Ct. (we. dist.) Mo. 1980, U.S. Ct. Appeals (8th cir.) 1984, U.S. Tax Ct. 2000. Assoc. William Johnson, P.C., Versailles, Mo., 1980-81; asst. prosecutor Morgan County, Mo., 1980; legal aid atty. Mid-Mo. Legal Services Corp., Columbia, 1981; pvt. practice Columbia, 1982—. Adj. prof. criminal justice Columbia Coll., 1983-84; adj. prof. bus. law U. Mo., 1988-90. Active Christian Fellowship of Columbia. Mem. Nat. Lawyers Assn., Mo. Bar Assn., Boone County Bar Assn., Nat. Orgn. Social Security Claimants' Reps., Order Barristers. Home: 212 Bright Star Dr Columbia MO 65203-0279 Office: 2501 W Ash St Columbia MO 65203-4609

CREPS, PHILP LLOYD, child psychiatrist; b. Bowling Green, Ohio, Dec. 16, 1951; s. Wayne Leroy and Elsie Marie (Frank) Creps; m. Barbara Dawn Keller, Dec. 11, 1976 (div. Mar. 1991); children: Jesse Jean, Sarah Marie; m. Diane Ruth Cook Bostwick, Nov. 11, 1993. BS, Bowling Green (Ohio) State U., 1973; BA, U. Toledo, 1980; AS, Aurora (Colo.) C.C., 1986; DO, Mich. State U., 1991. Cert. psychiatry, child and adolescent psychiats. Am. Coll. Neurology and Psychology. Rsch. project dir. Mich. State U., East Lansing, 1984-85; instr. Lansing C.C., 1984-85; environ. scientist Ohio EPA, Bowling Green, 1985; rsch. chemist Fitzsimmons Med. Ctr., Aurora, 1985-86; quality assurance chemist Pine Bluff (Ark.) Army Arsenal, 1986-89; extern Coll. Osteo. Medicine Mich. State U., Okemos, 1989-91; intern Riverside Osteopathic Hosp., Trenton, Mich., 1991-92; resident in psychiatry Case Western Reserve U., Cleve., 1992-95; fellow in child psychiatry Ind. U., Indpls., 1995-97; child psychiatrist Otis R. Bowen Ctr., Warsaw, Ind., 1996-2000; pres., CEO Creps Med. Corp., South Bend, Ind., 1997—; child psychiatrist Madison Ctr. Counseling Assoc., Warsaw, Ind., 2000; psychiatrist Madison Ctr. for Children, South Bend, Ind., 2000—03; pharmaceuticals adv. panel for Zyprexa and Strattera Eli Lilly, 2002—. Chemist Pine Bluff Arsenal SMCPB, Quality Assurance Lab., 1986—89; mem. Practice Rsch. Network Am. Psychiat. Assn., 1997—; mem. spkrs. bur. Shire Pharms., 2001—, prin. investigator LADD-CAT Stage III pre-market trial, 2001—02; mem. spkrs. bur. Forest Pharms., 2002—, Novartis Pharms., 2003—; prin. investigator Stage III pre-market trial Bristol-Myers Squibb Pharms., 2002—03; prin. investigator OPTIMAL Stage IV complications of Lamictal Glaxo Smith Kline Pharmaceuticals, 2003. Sec. Citizen's Coun. # 3, Lansing, Mich., 1980—83; youth dir. Assembly of God Ch., Fostoria, Ohio, 1969—71; mus. dir. 1st Assembly of God Ch., Toledo, 1977—79. With USN, 1980—83. Recipient Alfred award, South Counties Coun., Newport, R.I., 1981, Mayor's Commendation, City of Toledo, 1980, Alexis Coquillard award, United Way of South Bend, 2001—03, Glenn Harris Soc. for svc. to Madison Ctr., 2001—03, Topaz award, United Way of St. Joseph County, Ind., 2002, Sapphire award, United Way, 2003; grantee, Shire Pharm., 2001—02, Bristol-Meyers-Squibb, 2002—03. Mem.: AMA, APA, Charles F. Meninger Soc., Tri-State Group Psychotherapists, Initiative Social Anxiety Assessment Care, Practice Rsch. Network, Am. Acad. Clin. Psychiatrists, Am. Group Psychotherapy Assn., Am. Assn. Social Psychiatry, Cranial Acad., Am. Acad. Osteopathy, Am. Assn. Cmty. Psychiatrists, Assn. Osteopathic Physicians and Surgeons (Mich., Ind. chpts.), Am. Coll. Osteopathic Neurologists and Psychiatrists, Am. Acad. Child Adolescent Psychiatrists, Am. Assn. Orthopsychiatry, Am. Osteopathic Assn., Am. Chem. Soc., Beta Beta Beta, Psi Chi, Alpha Epsilon Delta. Republican. Avocations: dairy farming, gardening, singing. Home: 214 Ashbury Ct South Bend IN 46615 E-mail: pcrep1@onetzero.com.

CRESCENZ, VALERIE J. music educator; b. Bethlehem, Pa., Mar. 8, 1956; d. George Henry and Florence Showers; m. Joseph Martin Crescenz, July 26, 1980; children: Monica Lynn, Melanie Jane. BS in Music Edn., West Chester (Pa.) State Coll., 1978, MusM in Piano Performance, 1980. Music instr. West Chester State Coll., 1979—80, Delaware County C.C., Media, Pa., 1990—95; composer Hinshaw Music, Inc., Chapel Hill, NC, 1994—; music tchr., dir. Downingtown (Pa.) Sch. Dist., 1995—. Composer (choral music): various titles, including 3 written with composer James Green of Durham, N.C. ; composer: (commd. works) Durham Sch. Arts, 2002. Mem.: Music Educators Nat. Conf., ASCAP, NEA, Pa. State Edn. Assn., Pa. Music Educators Assn. (commn. 2001, 2002). Home: 10 Juniata Dr Coatesville PA 19320 Office: West Bradford Elem Sch 1475 Broad Run Rd Downingtown PA 19335

CRESHEVSKY, NOAH EPHRAIM, composer, music educator; b. Rochester, N.Y., Jan. 31, 1945; m. Joseph and Sylvia (Goldman) Cohen; m. Marianna Rosett, May 31, 1969 (div. June 1975). BFA, SUNY, Buffalo, 1966; MS, Juilliard Sch., 1968. Mem. faculty Juilliard Sch., N.Y.C., 1968-70; prof. music Bklyn. Coll., CUNY, 1969-2000, dir. Ctr. for Computer Music, 1995-2000. Vis. prof. Princeton (N.J.) U., 1987-88. Recordings include Circuit, In Other Words, Great Performances, Chaconne, Portrait of Rudy Perrez, Highway, Sonata, Celebration, Drummer, Strategic Defense Initiative, Man and Superman, Auxesis/Who; compositions include Three Wordless Songs, 1988, Electric String Quartet, 1988, Memento Mori, 1989, Electric Partita, 1990, Talea, 1991, Cantiga, 1992, Borrowed Time, 1992, Private Lives, 1993, Twice, 1993, Coup d'etat, 1994, Gone Now, 1995, Who, 1995, Sha, 1996, Breathless, 1997, Independence Day, 1997 Ossi di morte, 1997, Chamber Concerto, 1998, Et Puis, 1998, Credo, 1999, Novella, 2000. Nat. Endowment for Arts fellow, 1981-82; grantee N.Y. State Coun. on ARts, Meet the Composer. Mem. ASCAP (composers award 1982—). Home: 301 W 45th St Apt 10L New York NY 10036-3831

CRESPI, IRVING, public opinion and market research consultant; b. Bklyn., May 8, 1926; s. Joseph and Esther (Crespi) C.; m. Joan Striefling, Aug. 4, 1968; children: Robert Joseph, Judith Lofton. BSS., CCNY, 1945; MA, State U. Ia., 1946; PhD, New Sch. for Social Research, 1955. Instr. sociology Triple Cities Coll., Endicott, N.Y., 1948-50; instr. sociology Harpur Coll., SUNY, 1950-51, 53-55, asst. prof. sociology, 1955-56; v.p. Gallup Orgn., Inc., Princeton, N.J., 1958-70, exec. v.p., 1970-76; v.p. Mathematica Policy Rsch., 1976-77, sr. v.p., 1977-78, sr. fellow, 1978-79; v.p. Roper Orgn., 1979-81; owner Irving Crespi & Assos., Princeton, 1981-89; prof. mktg. Baruch Coll.-CUNY, 1986-88; dir. media and pub. affairs rsch. Total Rsch. Corp., 1989-91, v.p. quality, 1991-94; part-time mkt. rsch. cons. Princeton, 1994—. Author: (with H. Mendelsohn) Polls, Television and New Politics, 1971; Pre-Election Polling: Sources of Accuracy and Error, 1988, Public Opinion, Polls and Democracy, 1989, The Public Opinion Process: How The People Speak, 1997; contbr. articles to profl. jours. Trustee Paul F. Lazarsfeld Fund, 1977-79. Served with USAF, 1951-53. Mem. Am. Assn. Pub. Opinion Rsch. (v.p. 1975-76, pres. 1976-77, chmn. standards com. 1966-68, conf. chmn. 1970, award for exceptionally disting. achievement 1997), Am. Sociol. Assn., Am. Mktg. Assn. (dir. 1970-72), World Assn. for Pub. Opinion Rsch. (v.p. 1974-76, pres. 1976-78), Market Rsch. Coun. Jewish. Home: 9 Orchard Cir Princeton NJ 08540-3025

CRESPI, TED, lawyer; b. Bklyn., Oct. 23, 1959; s. Charles and Annette Crespi; m. Jodi Crespi, June 20, 1981; children: Candace, Craig. AS in Criminal Justice, Broward C.C., Davie, Fla., 1979; BA, Fla. Atlantic U., 1981; JD, U. Miami, 1984. Bar: Fla. 1984, U.S. Dist. Ct. (so. dist.) Fla. 1985. Police officer Hallandale (Fla.) Police Dept., 1979-84; atty. Broward County States Atty.'s Office, Ft. Lauderdale, Fla., 1983-85; pvt. practice Plantation, Fla., 1985—. Mem. ATLA, Fla. Bar, Fla. Trial Lawyers Assn., Fla. Criminal Def. Lawyers Assn., Broward County Bar. Avocations: coaching youth sports, sports, fishing, travel. Office: Ste 218 1776 N Pine Island Rd Plantation FL 33322 E-mail: tcrespi@aol.com.

CRESS, CECILE COLLEEN, retired librarian; b. Colorado Springs, Colo., Feb. 26, 1914; d. John Leo and Elizabeth Veronica (Rouse) Haley; m. Arthur Henry Cress, May 8, 1937 (div. 1960); children: Ronnie Lou Kordick, Dan, Elaine. BA, Adams State Coll., 1936; MA in English, Colo. Coll., 1964; MLS, Denver U., 1970. 5th grade tchr. Westcliffe (Colo.) Elem., 1953-56; English tchr. Penrose (Colo.) H.S., 1956-59; English-social studies tchr. Excelsior Jr. H.S. Dist. 70, Pueblo, Colo., 1959-64; libr. Pueblo County H.S. Dist. 70, Pueblo, 1964-80, Nat. Coll./Pueblo Br., 1980-91; cataloger in libr. Pueblo C.C., 1992-95. Tutor adult literacy program South Cen. Bd. Coop. Svcs., 1991. Recipient Ace of Clubs award Am. Contract Bridge League, 1988, 89. Mem. Pueblo Ret. Sch. Employees (v.p. 1990-92, pres. 1982-84, state bd. 1982-86, sec. 1995-97), Colo. Libr. Assn., Unit 367 Am. Contract Bridge Assn., Irish Club Pueblo (pres. 1995-96), Welsh Terrier Club Colo., Alpha Delta Kappa (Pueblo chpt., pres. 1976-78, state historian 1980-82, state bd. 1980-82, rec. sec. 1994-98), Am. Contract Bridge League (v.p. unit 367 1998-2000). Democrat. Roman Catholic. Avocations: duplicate bridge, welsh terriers, travel. Home: 901 Jackson St Pueblo CO 81004-2425 E-mail: ccress@cs.com.

CRESSY, DAVID SARRAT, lawyer; b. New Orleans, July 6, 1937; s. Louis Villere and Nellie Marie C.; m. Barbara Mequet, Apr; 4, 1964 (div. Jan. 35, 1984); children: David, Andree Landry, Paul, Suzanne Brown; m. Laura Sutis Cressy, June 28, 1984; children: Nicolas Villere, Jordan Cheval. BS, U. Southwestern La., Lafayette, 1963; JD, Loyola U., New Orleans, 1967. City atty. City of New Orleans, 19687-78; pvt. practice Mandeville, New Orleans, 1978-96; city atty. City of Mandeville, La., 1996—. Trustee Wisner Found., New Orleans, 1972-76, New Orleans Mus. Art, 1975-76; commr. City park Bd. Commrs., New Orleans, 1973-76. With USAF, 1957-59. Fellow La. Law Found., La. State Bar Assn. Democrat. Avocations: sailing, horseback riding. Home: 132 Coffee St Mandeville LA 70448 Office: City of Mandeville 3101 East Causeway Mandeville LA 70448

CRESWELL, DONALD CRESTON, business executive; s. Carroll Creston and Verna Moore (Taylor) C.; m. Terri Sue Tidwell; 1 child, Creston Lee. Student, Johns Hopkins U.; MBA, U. Dayton; postgrad., Stanford U. Cons. engr. A.D. Ring & Assocs., Washington; sales and mktg. mgr. Ampex Corp., Redwood City, Calif.; dir. mktg., magnetic products divsn. RCA Corp., N.Y.C.; staff v.p. sales and advt. Pan Am. World Airways, N.Y.C.; prin. mgmt. cons., dir. mktg. svcs. Stanford Rsch. Inst., Menlo Park, Calif.; v.p., gen. mgr. Decisions Sys.; gen. mgr. R&D Decision Quality Assocs.; dir. practice devel. Strategic Decisions Group/SDG, Menlo Park, 1987-2000; co-founder, v.p. Smart Org, Inc., Menlo Park, 2000—. Mem. mgmt. com. Jets Cybernetics, 1987-94; lectr. planning and mktg. mgmt. Am. Mgmt. Assn., 1968-69; program chmn. Grad. Bus. Assn., 1965; rep. to Electronics Industries Assn., 1968-71, to Internat. Air Transport Assn., 1971-74. Bd. dirs. Peninsula Youth Soccer Club, 1981-82; nat. dir. referee assessment, mem. referee com. U.S. Soccer Fedn., 1986-88; regional chief referee San Carlos Am. Youth Soccer Orgn., 1981-85; state dir. assessment Calif. Soccer Assn., 1982-85; mem. L.A. Olympics Organizing Com., 1983-84; nat. referee assessor, 1987—; ofcl. N.Am. Soccer League, 1983-84, World Cup, 1994; sponsor Silicon Valley Roundtable. Mem. Am. Mktg. Assn. (exec. com.), Am. Theatre Organ Assn. (bd. dirs. 1978-79), Nat. Intercollegiate Soccer Ofcls. Assn. (World Cup video inspector 1994), Charles Lindbergh Fund, U.S. Soccer Fedn. (cert. nat. assessor, USSF referee inspector), Silicon Valley Roundtable, The Churchill Club, Stanford Jazz Com. Republican. Home: 8 Pyrola Ln San Carlos CA 94070-1532 Office: Smart Org Inc 2440 Sand Hill Rd Menlo Park CA 94025-6900 E-mail: dcreswell@smartorg.com.

CRESWELL, DOROTHY ANNE, computer consultant; b. Burlington, Iowa, Feb. 6, 1943; d. Robert Emerson and Agnes Imogene (Gardner) Mefford; m. John Lewis Creswell, Aug. 28, 1965. AA, Burlington C.C., 1963; BA in Math., U. Iowa, 1965; MS in Math., Western Ill. U., 1970; postgrad., Iowa State U., 1974—. Computer programmer Mason & Hanger, Silas Mason Co., Inc., Burlington, 1965-74; systems programmer Contractor's Hotline, Ft. Dodge, Iowa, 1974; dir. data processing Iowa Cen. C.C., Ft. Dodge, 1975-80; systems programming mgr. Norand Corp., Cedar Rapids, Iowa, 1980-82; spl. svcs. mgr. Pioneer Hi-Bred Internat., Inc., Cedar Rapids, 1982-87; owner, pres. D.C. Cons., Inc., Ankeny, Iowa, 1987—. Computers-in-edn. del. to China, People to People Internat., Kansas City, Mo., 1987. Contbr. articles, papers to profl. publs. Mem. Data Processing Mgmt. Assn. (bd. dirs. 1986-87, v.p. 1988, 91-93, pres. 1993-94), Adminstrv. Mgmt. Soc. (sec. 1985-86, v.p. 1986-90, Merit award 1987), Assn. Computing Machinery, Hawkeye Pers. Computer Users, DEC Users Group (v.p. Ea. Iowa chpt. 1981-82), Ind. Computer Cons. Assn. (mem. editl. bd. 1989-96, chpt. pres.-at-large 1993-95). Democrat. Methodist. Avocations: jogging, traveling. Office: DC Cons Inc PO Box 195 Ankeny IA 50021-0195

CRETAN, DONNA, neonatal nurse, lactation consultant; b. Mpls., May 18, 1939; d. Howard Robert and Frances E. (Warner) Bjerke; m. Nestor Nicholas Cretan, Jan. 24, 1959; children: Colette, John, Christopher, Bernadette. ADN, Contra Costa Coll., 1973; BSN, Sacred Heart U., Fairfield, Conn., 1986. RN Conn. Nurse mgr., cons. St. Joseph Med. Ctr., Stamford, Conn., 1974-89; staff nurse Cmty. Hosp., Santa Rosa, Calif., 1989-93, Greenwich (Conn.) Hosp., 1993—2002, Mark Twin St. Joseph Hosp., San Andreas, Calif., 2002—. ESL tutor LVA, 1997—. Host parent A Better Chance, New Canaan, Conn., 1982-84, Am. Field Svc., 1983-84, Calif., 1991-93, Cultural Homestay, Cohasset, Mass., 1991-95, People Link, Petaluma, Calif.; sec. Hist. Soc., Sebastopol, Calif., 1989-92; vol. nurse Americares Free Clinic Norwalk, 1994—; literacy vol. ESL Inst., 1997-98. Mem.: ANA, Internat. Lactation Cons. Assn. (cert.), Neonatal Network, Obstetrics and Neonatal Nurses, Assn. Women's Health. Avocations: lactation promotion, photography. Home: 20526 Charlotte Ct Soulsbyville CA 95372 Office: Mark Twain St Joseph Hosp San Andreas CA

CRETIN, SHAN, activist; b. New Orleans, La., Dec. 5, 1946; d. Theodore David and Rosemary Mamie (Lombardino) C.; m. Burns Woodward, June 15, 1968 (div. July 1976); 1 child: Mikala Marie; m. Emmett Brown Keeler, Sept. 26, 1976; children: Lauren Shan, Alexis Marie. SBME, MIT, 1968; MPH, Yale U., 1970; PhD in Ops. Rsch., MIT, 1975. Rsch. assoc. Yale U., New Haven, 1970-71; asst. prof. Harvard U., Cambridge, Mass., 1974-76, UCLA, 1976-81, assoc. prof., 1981-88, prof., 1988-90; pres. Shan Cretin and Assoc., Santa Monica, Calif., 1990-98; regional dir. Am. Friends Svc. Com., Pasadena, Calif., 2003—. Cons. Rand, Santa Monica, Calif., 1977-98, sr. scientist 1998-2003; cons. Agy. for Health Care Policy and Rsch., Bethesda, Md., 1980-92, World Bank, Washington, 1984-96. Author: Cholesterol, Children, and Heart Disease, 1980; contbr. articles to profl. jours. Mem. Sigma Xi, Pi Tau Sigma, Delta Omega. Mem. Religious Soc. of Friends. Avocations: woodworking, guitar, square dancing, Chinese. Home: 402 15th St Santa Monica CA 90402-2232 E-mail: scretin@afsc.org.

CREUHERAS, SANTIAGO, social scientist; b. Guadalajara, Jalisco, Mex., June 30, 1974; s. Santiago Creuheras and Maryger Diaz. BA in Econs., U. Americas, Puebla, Mex., 1997; M in Liberal Arts in History, Harvard U., 2000, grad. cert. spl. studies in mgmt., M in Liberal Arts in Govt., Harvard U., 2001. Internat. affairs intern Embassy of Mex., Washington, 1997; legis. intern Rep. Joseph J. Kennedy's Office, Washington, 1997; rsch. asst. J.F.K. Sch. of Govt., Harvard U., Cambridge, 2000—; internat. internship program dir. David Rockefeller Ctr., Harvard U., Cambridge, 2000—01; regional econ. devel. dir. Ministry of Econ. Devel., Puebla, Mexico, 2001—, regional econ. devel. gen. coord., 2002—. Mem. Harvard U. Mex. Assn. (sr. mem.), Harvard Club of Boston, Acad. of Polit. Sci. Roman Catholic. Avocations: swimming, traveling, opera, golf. Office: Ministry of Econ Devel 4 Oriente #806 Puebla Mexico Home: 35 Sur #3901 Puebla Mexico E-mail: screuheras@post.harvard.edu.

CREUTZ, EDWARD CHESTER, physicist, museum consultant; b. Beaver Dam, Wis., Jan. 23, 1913; s. Lester Raymond and Grace (Smith) C.; m. Lela Rollefson, Sept. 13, 1937 (dec. Feb. 1972); children: Michael John, Carl Eugene, Ann Jo Carmel Creutz Cosgrove; m. Elisabeth B. Cordle, Oct. 5, 1974. BS, U. Wis., 1936, PhD, 1939. From rsch. assoc. to instr. physics Princeton U., 1939-41; physicist NDRC, 1941-42; physicist metall. lab. U. Chgo., 1942-44; physicist Manhattan Project, Los Alamos, 1944-46; assoc. prof. Carnegie Inst. Tech., Pitts., 1946-49, prof., head dept. physics, dir. Nuc. Rsch. Ctr., 1948-55; dir. John Jay Hopkins Lab. for Pure and Applied Sci., 1955-59; dir. rsch. Gen. Atomic Divsn. Gen. Dynamics Corp., San Diego, 1955-59, v.p. R&D, 1959-67, Gulf Gen. Atomic, San Diego, 1967-70; asst. dir. NSF, Washington, 1970-77, acting dep. dir., 1976-77; dir. Bernice Pauahi Bishop Mus., Honolulu, 1977-84, cons., 1984—. Mem. sea water conversion com. Water resources Ctr., U. Calif.-Berkeley, 1958-68; adv. com. office Sci. Pers. NRC, 1960-63; mem. exec. coun. Argonne Nat. Lab. (1946-51); cons. NSF, 1950-68; scientist-at-large Project Sherwood divsn. rsch. AEC, 1955-56; mem. com. sr. reviewers Dept. Energy, 1972-79, fusion power coordinating com., 1971-79; cons. Oak Ridge Nat. Lab., 1946-58; adv. panel gen. scis. Dept. Def., 1959-63; rsch. adv. com. electrophysics NASA, 1964-71, tech. adv. com., 1971-77; adj. prof. physics and astronomy U. Hawaii, 1977-87; adj. prof. physics U. Calif., San Diego, 1987—. Co-editor: Handbuch der Physik, vols. 14, 15; mem. editl. bd. Ann. Rev. Nuclear Sci., 1961-66, 72-75, Handbook of Chemistry and Physics, 1961-71;

mem. editorial bd.: Interdisciplinary Science Reviews, London, 1976— ; editl. adv. com. ann. revs.: Nuclear Sci. and Engring., 1959-72. Bd. dirs. San Diego Hall Sci. and Planetarium, v.p., 1956-70; v.p. San Diego Industry-Edn. Coun., 1956-65; mem. adv. coun. Dept. Edn. San Diego County. Fellow AAAS, Am. Phys. Soc. (NRC rep. 1956-57), Am. Nuclear Soc.; mem. NAS, Am. Assn. Physics Tchrs., Phys. Soc. Pitts. (pres. 1949), Am. Inst. Physics (dir.-at-large bd. govs. 1965-68) Home: PO Box 2757 Rancho Santa Fe CA 92067-2757

CREVELT, DWIGHT EUGENE, computer company executive; b. Kansas City, Mo., Jan. 16, 1957; s. James Robert and Louise Gwendolynn (Wolchek) C.; m. Jean Anne Cassens, Aug. 11, 1979; children: William Michael, Michelle Anne, Matthew Henry, Megan Louise. Student, U. Las Vegas, 1973-74, U.S. Naval Acad., 1975-77; BS in Computer Engring., Iowa State U., 1979. Computer engr., cons., Las Vegas, Nev., 1972-73; software engr. Gamex Industries, Las Vegas, 1973-74, United Audio Visual, Las Vegas, 1977; computer engr. Sircoma, Las Vegas, 1979-80; dir. research Mills-Jennings, Las Vegas, 1981; pres., chmn. Crevelt Computer, Las Vegas, 1977—; mgr. spl. projects Electronic Data Techs., 1988-91; dir. engring., quality assurance mgr. Internat. Game Techs., 1991-96; ptnr. Footraffic Promotional Gaming LLC, 1998—. Lobbyist Nev. Legis. Author: (computer programs) CDC160/NCR310 Disassembler, 1971, Computer Networking, 1983, Telephone Access Control, 1984, Fiber Optic Network, 1984; co-author: Slot Machine Mania, 1987, Video Poker Mania, 1991. Former corr. sec. Clark County Rep. Cen. Com.; mem. U.S. Congl. Adv. Bd. Mem. NRA, Eagle Scout Assn., Soc. Naval Engrs., Am. Philatic Soc., U.S. Naval Acad. Alumni Assn., USN League, Las Vegas Exch. Club. Achievements include patentee on automated electronic casino gaming system, progressive gaming systems, electronic funds transfer. Office: Crevelt Computer System Inc 5391 Aston Ave Las Vegas NV 89142-1818 E-mail: dwight@creveltcomputer.com.

CREW, ANDREW JACKSON, retired secondary school educator, band director; b. Whigham, Ga., Mar. 16, 1937; s. Andrew Jackson and Lucy Hull Crew; m. Shirley Wallace, Aug. 4, 1959; children: Sharon Metcalf, Sheryl Copeland, Shelly Jackson. MusB Edn., Fla. State U., Tallahassee, 1959, MusM Edn., 1972. Cert. tchr. Fla., 1959. Instrumental music tchr. Plant City (Fla.) Elem. Schools, 1960—64; dir. of bands Plant City H.S., 1964—68, Riverview H.S., Sarasota, Fla., 1968—83, Mosley H.S., Panama City, Fla., 1983—85, Lakeland (Fla.) H.S., 1985—94, Lincoln H.S., Tallahassee, 1994—2001; ret., 2002. Named Man of the Yr., VFW, Sarasota, FL, 1980, Mac Award to the Outstanding Bandmaster in Fla., A.R. McAllister Found., 1976, Outstanding Music Educator Sect. 3, Nat. Fedn. Interscholastic Music Assn., 1995; recipient Sudler Flag of Honor, John Philip Sousa Found., 1993, Legion of Honor award, 1990. Mem.: NEA, Music Educators Nat. Conf., Fla. Music Educators Assn. (Outstanding Music Educator 1991), Am. Bandmasters Assn. (bd. dirs. 1989—91), Nat. Band Assn., Fla. Bandmasters Assn. (pres. 1983—84), Phi Beta Mu (Outstanding Bandmaster 1986). Methodist. Avocation: tennis. Home: 3312 Clifden Dr Tallahassee FL 32309 Personal E-mail: acrew5@comcast.net.

CREW, SPENCER, museum administrator; b. Poughkeepsie, N.Y., Jan. 7, 1949; s. R. Spencer and Ada Lee (Scott) C.; m. Sandra Lorraine Prioleau, June 19, 1971; children: Alika, Adom. BA, Brown U., 1971; MA, Rutgers U., 1973, PhD, 1979. Asst. prof. U. Md. Baltimore County, Catonsville, 1978-81; historian Nat. Mus. Am. History, Smithsonian Instn., Washington, 1981-87, curator, 1987-89, chmn. dept. social and cultural history, 1989-91, dep. dir., acting dir., 1991-94, dir., 1994—2001; exec. dir., CEO Nat. Underground R.R. Freedom Ctr., 2001—. Commr. Md. Commn. on Afro-Am. History and Culture, Annapolis, 1990—; hist. cons. Nat. Civil Rights Mus., Memphis, 1987-91; cons. Civil Rights Inst., Birmingham, Ala., 1991-94; bd. dirs. Nat. History Day, 1994—. Exhbns. include Field to Factory: Afro-Am. Migration, 1915-40, 1987 (award 1988), Go Forth and Serve: Black Land Grant Colls., 1990. Bd. trustees Brown U., 1995—; adult leader Bapt. Youth Fellowship, St. John Ch., Columbia, Md., 1989-91; asst. coach Columbia Basketball Assn., 1990-92. Recipient Osceola award Delta Sigma Theta, 1988, Cert. award Smithsonian Instn., 1989, 90, 91, 92, Svc. award Assn. for Study of African Am. Life and History, 1994, Robert A. Brooks award Smithsonian Instn., 1994. Mem. African Am. Mus. Assn. (2d v.p. 1989-91), Orgn. Am. Historians (editl. bd. 1989-92), Am. Assn. Mus. (bd. dirs.), Nat. Coun. History Edn. (bd. trustees. 1995—), Am. Hist. Assn. (exhibit rev. co-editor 1990-95), Oral History in Mid Atlantic Region (exec. bd. 1987-90). Office: Nat Underground RR Freedom Ctr 312 Elm St Ste 1250 Cincinnati OH 45202

CREWDSON, JOHN MARK, journalist, author; b. San Francisco, Dec. 15, 1945; s. Mark Guy and Eva Rebecca (Doane) C.; m. Prudence Gray Tillotson, Sept. 11, 1969; children: Anders Gray, Oliver McDuff. AB in Econs. with gt. distinction, U. Calif., Berkeley, 1970; postgrad. studies in politics, Oxford (Eng.) U., 1971-72. Reporter N.Y. Times, Washington, 1973-77, nat. corr Houston, 1977-82; nat. news editor Chgo. Tribune, 1982-83, met. news editor, 1983-84, west coast corr., 1984-90, nat. corr. Washington, 1990-96, sr. writer, 1996—2002, sr. corr., 2002—. Author: The Tarnished Door, 1983, By Silence Betrayed, 1988, Science Fictions, 2002. Recipient Bronze medallion Sigma Delta Chi, 1974, Goldberg award N.Y. Deadline Club, 1977, Page One award N.Y. Newspaper Guild, 1977, Pulitzer prize for nat. reporting, 1981, Polk award for med. reporting L.I. U., 1990, William H. Jones award for investigative reporting, 1990, 95, 97, Peter Lisagor award Chgo. Headline Club, 1997. Office: Chgo Tribune 1325 G St NW Washington DC 20005-3104 E-mail: jcrewdson@tribune.com.

CREWE, ALBERT VICTOR, physicist, artist, business executive; b. Bradford, Yorkshire, Eng., Feb. 18, 1927; came to U.S., 1955, naturalized, 1961. s. Wilfred and Edith Fish (Lawrence) C.; m. Doreen Blunsdon, Apr. 9, 1949; children: Jennifer, Sarah, Elizabeth, David. BS in Physics, U. Liverpool, Eng., 1947, PhD, 1951; degree (hon.), Lake Forest Coll., 1972, U. Mo., 1972, Elmhurst Coll., 1972, U.Liverpool, 2001. Asst. lectr. U. Liverpool, Eng., 1950-52, lectr., 1952-55; rsch. assoc. U. Chgo., 1955-56, asst. prof., 1956-58, assoc. prof., 1958-63; prof. dept. physics Enrico Fermi Inst., 1963-71, dean phys. scis. divsn., 1971-81; also William Wrather Disting. Svc. prof. physics, 1958-61; emeritus, 1996—; dir. particle accelerator divsn. Argonne Nat. Lab., 1958-61, dir., 1961-66; pres. Orchid One Corp., 1987-90. Chmn. Chgo. Area R&D Coun. Recipient Outstanding Local Citizen in Field of Sci. award Chgo. Jr. Assn. Commerce and Industry, 1961; Outstanding New Citizen of Year award Citizenship Coun. Chgo., 1962; award for outstanding achievement in field of sci. Immigrant's Service League, 1962; Man of Year in Rsch. award Indsl. Rsch., Inc., 1970; Michelson medal Franklin Inst., 1977; Duddell medal Inst. of Physics, 1980. Fellow Am. Phys. Soc., Royal Microscopical Soc. (hon.), Chinese Electron Microscope Soc. (hon.); mem. NAS, Sci. Rsch. Soc. Am., Electron Microscopy Soc. Am. (Disting. Svc. award 1976), N.Y. Microscope Soc. (Abbe award 1979), Am. Acad. Arts and Scis., Palette and Chisel Acad. (artist mem.). Achievements include research on electron optics, design of electron microscopes, first images of single atoms. Home: 8 Summitt Dr Chesterton IN 46304-1024 E-mail: crewe@midway.uchicago.edu.

CREWE, NANCY MOE, psychologist and educator; b. Mpls., Aug. 27, 1939; d. Arnold O. and Ruby V. Moe; m. James C. Crewe (div.); 1 child, Laurel; m. John Pond. BA, U. Minn., 1961, MA, 1964, PhD, 1967. Lic. psychologist, Mich. Staff psychologist Am. Rehab. Found., Mpls., 1966-69, Robbinsdale (Minn.) Sch. Dist., 1969-71; asst. prof. psychology U. Minn., Mpls., 1971-78, assoc. prof. psychology, 1978-87; postdoctoral fellow New England Rehab. Hosp., Boston, 1985-86; prof. Mich. State U., East Lansing, 1987—. Co-author: Employment After Spinal Cord Injury, 1978; co-editor: Independent Living for Disabled People, 1983. Bd. dirs. Accessible Space, Mpls., 1980-82, Met. Ctr. for Ind. Living, Mpls., 1983-85; bd. dirs., chairperson Comprehensive Svcs. for Disabled Citizens, Mpls., 1980-87, Capital Area Ctr. for Ind. Living, 2000—. Recipient Disting. Faculty award Mich. State, 1997. Fellow APA (pres. div. 22, 1987-88, Disting. Contbns. to Rehab. Psychology award 1993); mem. ACA, Am. Congress Rehab. Medicine (Licht award 1981, Disting. Mem. award 1990), Am. Assn. Spinal Cord Injury Psychologists and Social Workers (Disting. Svc. award 1990, bd. dirs. 1995-98), Am. Rehab. Counseling Assn., Nat. Rehab. Assn., Nat. Coun. Rehab. Edn., Phi Beta Kappa. Office: Mich State U 237 Erickson Hall East Lansing MI 48824-1034

CREWS, FREDERICK CAMPBELL, humanities educator, writer; b. Phila., Feb. 20, 1933; s. Maurice Augustus and Robina (Gaudet) C.; m. Betty Claire Peterson, Sept. 9, 1959; children: Gretchen Detre, Ingrid Márquez. AB, Yale U., 1955; PhD, Princeton U., 1958. Faculty U. Calif., Berkeley, 1958—, instr. in English, 1958-60, asst. prof., 1960-62, assoc. prof., 1962-66, prof., 1966-94, vice-chair for grad. studies, 1988-92, chair dept., 1992-94; prof. emeritus, 1994—. Mem. study fellowship selection com. Am. Coun. Learned Socs., 1971-73; mem. selection com. summer seminars Nat. Endowment for Humanities, 1976-77; Ward-Phillips lectr. U. Notre Dame, 1974-75, Dorothy T. Burstein lectr. UCLA, 1984; Frederick Ives Carpenter vis. prof. U. Chgo., 1985; Lansdowne visitor U. Victoria, 1987-88; John Dewey lectr., 1988, Nina Mae Kellogg lectr. Portland (Oreg.) State U., 1989; mem. exec. com. bd. dirs. Mark Twain Project, 1984-94; faculty rsch. lectr. U. Calif., Berkeley, 1991-92; David L. Kubal Meml. lectr. Calif. State U., L.A., 1994; mem. sci. and profl. adv. bd. False Memory Syndrome Found., 1994—; mem. exec. coun. Com. for Sci. Investigation of Claims of the Paranormal, 2000—. Author: The Tragedy of Manners, 1957, E.M. Forster: The Perils of Humanism, 1962, The Pooh Perplex, 1963, The Sins of the Fathers, 1966, The Patch Commission, 1968, The Random House Handbook, 1974, 6th edit., 1992, Out of My System, 1975, Skeptical Engagements, 1986, 2000, The Critics Bear it Away, 1992, Postmodern Pooh, 2001; co-author: The Borzoi Handbook for Writers, 1985, 3d edit., 1993; prin. author: The Memory Wars, 1995; editor: The Red Badge of Courage (Crane), 1964, Great Short Works of Nathaniel Hawthorne, 1967, Starting Over, 1970, Psychoanalysis and Literary Process, 1970, The Random House Reader, 1981, Unauthorized Freud, 1998; mem. contbg. bd. editors The Common Review, 2000—. Recipient Essay prize Nat. Endowment Arts, 1968, Disting. Tchg. award U. Calif., Berkeley, 1985, Spielvogel Diamonstein PEN prize, 1992; named Fulbright lectr. Turin, Italy, 1961-62; fellow Am. Coun. Learned Socs., 1965-66, Ctr. for Advanced Study in Behavioral Scis., 1965-66, Guggenheim Found., 1970-71, Am. Acad. Arts and Scis., 1992. Fellow: Coun. for Sci. Medicine and Mental Health. Home: 636 Vincente Ave Berkeley CA 94707-1524 E-mail: fredc@socrates.berkeley.edu.

CREWS, FULTON TIMM, pharmacology educator; b. Raleigh, N.C., July 2, 1949; BS, Syracuse U., 1971; PhD in Pharmacology, U. Mich., 1978. Staff fellow sect. on pharmacology NIMH, Bethesda, Md., 1978-80; asst. prof. pharmacology Coll. Medicine U. Fla., Gainesville, 1980-85, assoc. prof., 1985-90, prof., 1990-94; prof., dir. pharmacology dept. U. N.C., Chapel Hill, 1995—. Dir. Ctr. for Neurobiology of Aging, 1989—, Ctr. for Alcohol Rsch., 1992—. Contbr. to books: Apomorphine and Other Dopaminomimetics, Vol. 2: Clinical Pharmacology, 1981, Phospholipids in the Nervous System, Vol. 1: Metabolism, 1982, Biochemistry of S-Adenosylmethionine and Related Compounds, 1982, Advances in Pharmacology and Therapeutics II, Vol. 2: Neurotransmitters receptors, 1982, Aging of the Brain, Vol. 22, 1983, Methods in Neurobiology: Vol. 1, Brain Neuro-transmitters and Neuromodulator Receptor Methodologies, 1984, Phospholipids in the Nervous System, Vol. 2. Physiological Roles, 1985, Phospholipids and Cellular Regulation, Vol. 1, Phospholipid Research and the Nervous System, Vol. 4, 1986, Treatment Development Strategies for Alzheimer's Disease, 1986, Alcohol and Alcoholism, 1987, Progress in Catacholamine Research, 1988, Psychoneuroendocrinology of Aging: Basic and Clinical Aspects, 1988, Biochemical and Molecular Pathology, 1989, Biomedical and Social Aspects of Alcohol and Alcoholism, 1988, Molecular Mechanisms of Alcohol, 1989, Neurochemical Aspects of Phospholipid Metabolism, 1989, Novel Approaches to the Treatment of Alzheimer's Disease, 1989, New Issues in Neurosciences: Basic and Clinical Approaches, 1990, Molecular Biology and Physiology of Insulin and Insulin-like Growth Factors, 1991, The Treatment of Dementias: A New Generation of Progress, 1991, Phospholipids and Signal Transduction, 1993; also articles. Recipient U. Fla. Merit Teaching award, 1990; NIH fellow U. Mich., 1973-78, NIMH fellow, 1978-80; grantee NSF, 1981-84, Nat. Inst. on Aging, 1982-83, Nat. Ins. on Alcohol Abuse and Alcoholism, 1982—, Am. Fedn. for Aging, 1983-84, GREC, 1984-85, NIH, 1984—; Grass traveling scientist, 1987. Mem. AAAS, Am. Coll. Neuropsychopharmacology, Am. Soc. for Pharmacology and Exptl. Therapeutics, Internat. Soc. for Neurochemistry, N.Y. Acad. Scis., Rsch. Soc. on Alcoholism, Soc. for Neuroscience. Office: U NC Skipper Bowles Ctr Alcohol Studies Cb 7178 Thurston Bowles Bldg Chapel Hill NC 27599-7178

CREWS, HARRY EUGENE, author; b. Alma, Ga., June 7, 1935; s. Ray and Myrtice (Haselden) C.; m. Sally Thornton Ellis, Jan. 22, 1960 (div.); children: Patrick Scott, Byron Jason. BA, U. Fla., 1960, MSEd., 1962. English tchr. Broward Jr. Coll., Ft. Lauderdale, Fla., 1962-68; assoc. prof. English U. Fla. at Gainesville, 1968-74, prof. English. Author: The Gospel Singer, 1968, reprint, 1995, Naked in Garden Hills, 1969, This Thing Don't Lead To Heaven, 1970, Karate is a Thing of the Spirit, 1971, Car, 1972, The Hawk is Dying, 1973, The Gypsy's Curse, 1974, A Feast of Snakes, 1976, A Childhood: The Biography of a Place, 1978, Blood and Grits, 1979, The Enthusiast, 1981, Florida Frenzy, 1982, A Grit's Triumph, 1983, Two, 1984, All We Need of Hell, 1987, The Knockout Artists, 1988, Body, 1990, Madonna at Ringside, 1991, Scar Lover, 1992, Classic Crews: A Harry Crews Reader, 1993, The Mulching of America, 1995, Where Does One Go When There's No Place Left To Go?, 1998, Celebration: A Novel, 1998; columnist Esquire mag. Served with USMC, 1953-56. Recipient Am. Acad. Arts and Scis. award, 1972; Nat. Endowment for the Arts grantee, 1974 Office: Simon & Schuster Inc Author Mail Ste C3-31 New York NY 10020*

CREWS, KRISTINE RADOMSKI, pharmacologist; b. Lansdale, Pa., Mar. 18, 1970; d. Edward F. and Joan M. Radomski; m. James Martin Crews, Aug. 12, 2000. BS in Pharmacology, PharmD, Rutgers U., 1994. Cert. pharmacotherapy specialist. Resident in pharmacy practice and pharmacokinetics Albert B. Chandler Med. Ctr. U. Ky., Lexington; rsch. fellow U. N.C. and Glaxo Wellcome, Inc., Chapel Hill, 1996—98; asst. mem. St. Jude Children's Rsch. Hosp., Memphis, 1998—. Recipient Clin. Pharmacy Rsch. award, Astra Zeneca, 2000. Office: St Jude Children's Research Hospital 332 N Lauderdale Memphis TN 38105

CREWS, MARA LYNNE, writer; b. Shreveport, La., Aug. 12, 1957; d. Marlin E. Crews and Velma L. Brannon. Prodn. technician City of Shreveport, 1977-91; job coach Job Boost-Bossier Parish C.C., Bossier City, La., 1992-94; direct svc. worker II Evergreen Presbyn. Ministry, Bossier City, 1994-96. Author (anthologies): A Break in the Clouds, 1993, American Poetry Anthology, 1995, Dimensions of Thought, 1997, Best Poems of the 90s, 1998. Capt. Givens St. Neighborhood Watch, Bossier City, 1993-95; mem. N.W. La. Brain Injury Support Group, Shreveport, 1989—.

CREWS, WILLIAM ODELL, JR., religious organization administrator; b. Houston, Feb. 8, 1936; s. William O. Sr. and Juanita (Pearson) C.; m. Wanda Jo Ann Cunningham; 1 child, Ronald Wayne. BA, Hardin Simmons U., 1957, HHD, 1987; BDiv, Southwestern Bapt. Theol. Sem., 1964; DD, Calif. Bapt. Coll., 1987; DMin, Golden Gate Bapt. Theol. Sem., 2000. Ordained to ministry Bapt. Ch., 1953. Pastor Grape Creek Bapt. Ch., San Angelo, Tex., 1952-54, Plainview Bapt. Ch., Stamford, Tex., 1955-57, 1st Bapt. Ch., Sterling City, Tex., 1957-60, 7th St. Bapt. Ch., Ballinger, Tex., 1960-65, Woodland Heights Bapt. Ch., Brownwood, Tex., 1965-67, Victory Bapt. Ch., Seattle, 1967-72, Met. Bapt. Ch., Portland, Oreg., 1972-77; dir. comm. N.W. Bapt. Conv., Portland, 1977-78; pastor Magnolia Ave Bapt. Ch., Riverside, Calif., 1978-86; pres. Golden Gate Bapt. Theol. Sem., Mill Valley, Calif., 1986—. Pres. N.W. Bapt. Conv., Portland, 1974-76, So. Bapt. Gen. Conv. Calif., Fresno, 1982-84. Trustee Fgn. Mission Bd., Richmond, Va., 1973-78, Golden Gate Bapt. Theol. Sem., 1980-85, Marin Cmty. Hosp. Found., 1992-95; bd. dirs. Midway Seatac Boys Club, Des Moines, 1969-72, Marin Gen. Hosp., 1998—, North Bay Coun., 1998—. Mem. Marin County C. of C. (bd. dirs. 1987-95), Midway C. of C. (bd. dirs. 1968-72), Rotary (bd. dirs. San Rafael chpt. 1992—, pres. Portland club 1975-76, pres.-elect Riverside club 1984-85). Baptist. Home: 157 Chapel Dr Mill Valley CA 94941-3168 Office: Golden Gate Bapt Theol Sem 201 Seminary Dr Mill Valley CA 94941-3197

CRIBBET, JOHN EDWARD, law educator, former university chancellor; b. Findlay, Ill., Feb. 21, 1918; s. Howard H. and Ruth (Wright) C.; m. Betty Jane Smith, Dec. 24, 1941; children: Carol Ann, Pamela Lee. BA, Ill. Wesleyan U., 1940, LLD, 1971; JD, U. Ill., 1947. Bar: Ill. 1947. Pvt. practice in law, Bloomington, Ill., 1947—; prof. law U. Ill., Urbana, 1947-67, dean. Coll. Law, 1967-79; chancellor Urbana-Champaign Campus, U. Ill., 1979-84, Corman prof. law, 1984-88, prof. emeritus, 1988—. Author: Cases and Materials on Judicial Remedies, 1954, Cases on Property, 8th edit., 2002; (with others) Principles of the Law of Property, 1975; (with Corwin Johnson), 3d edit., 1989; editor: U. Ill. Law Forum, 1947-55; contbr. articles to profl. jours. Chmn. com. on jud. ethics Il. Supreme Ct.; pres. United Fund Champaign County, (Ill.), 1962-63; trustee Ill. Wesleyan U.; mem. exec. com. Assn. Am. Law Schs., 1973-75, pres., 1979. Served to maj. AUS, 1941-45. Decorated Bronze Star; decorated Croix de Guerre Mem. ABA, Ill. State Bar Assn., Champaign County Bar Assn., Order of Coif Lodges: Rotary. Office: U Ill Coll of Law 504 E Pennsylvania Ave Champaign IL 61820-6909

CRIBBS, MAUREEN ANN, artist, educator; b. Marinette, Wis., Feb. 17, 1927; d. Roy Cecil Hubbard and Lillian Worner (Hubbard) Yeoman; m. James Milton Cribbs, Apr. 22, 1950; children: Cynthia, Valerie. BA, DePauw U., 1949; student, Sch. of Art Inst., Chgo., 1971-72, 79-81; MA, Govs. State U., 1973. Cert. secondary sch. tchr., Ill. Tchr. art Sch. Dist. 163, Park Forest, Ill., 1960-78; instr. humanities Sch. Dist. 227, Park Forest, Ill., 1978-79; artist, painter, printmaker Park Forest, 1979—; instr. painting Village Artists, Flossmoor, Ill., 1980-87. Lectr. Chgo. State U., 1980—81; chair study group Homewood-Flossmoor cmty. assocs. of woman's bd. Art Inst. Chgo., 1989—95, sec., 1995—96; adj. prof. Govs. State U., University Park, 1995; artist-in-residence Ox Bow Sch. of Art, 1993; outreach presenter Art Insights, Art Inst. of Chgo., 1995—; docent Nathan Manilow Sculpture Park, Govs. State U., 1996—; instr. art, art history Robert Morris Coll., Orland Park, Ill., 1996—2001; woodcut printing and presenter Sr. Celebrations, Art Inst. Chgo., 1998—2002; participant printmaking Santa Reparata Graphic Art Ctr., Florence, Italy, 1999; mem. faculty Tall Grass Arts Assn. Sch., Park Forest, Ill., 2000, Tall Grass Arts Assn., 2001—. Exhibitions include Union St. Gallery, Chicago Heights, 2001, Recent Work South Suburban C.C., Thornton, Ill., 2001, Farnsworth House Gallery, Plano, Ill., 2001—, Art de Chgo. Gallery, Highland Park, Ill., 2001, Union St. Gallery, Chicago Heights, 2002, Creative Experience Gallery, Frankfort, Ill., 2002—03, Mid Am. Print Coun., Denver (Colo.) Airport, 2002, Ox Bow Benefits, 2002, 2003, A Portrait of Music, Ill. Philharm. Orch., 2003, numerous others, one-woman shows include S. Suburban Coll., 2001, Moraine Valley Cmty. Coll., 2001, Tall Grass Arts Assn. Gallery, Park Forest, 2002, Prairie State Coll., 2002, No. Ind. Arts Assn., 2002, Denver Internat. Airport, 2002, Lessedra Gallery, Sofia, Bulgaria, 2003, World Art Print Ann., Palace of Culture, Sofia, Represented in permanent collections Amity Found., Woodbridge, Conn., Lessedra Gallery. Bd. dirs. Ill. Philharm. Orch., Park Forest, 1981-83, Grace Migrant Day Care, Park Forest, 1981-85, LWV, Park Forest chpt., 2003-; adminstrv. chair Grace United Protestant Ch., Park Forest, 1984-94, v.p. Women's Christian Assn., 1995—, lay mem. No. Ill. Ann. Conf. of United Meth. Ch., 1996—, mem. commn. on christian unity and interreligious concerns, 1996—. Monetary grantee to produce 15 works Freedom Hall, 1982, Ill. Arts Coun. and Park Forest Cmty. Arts Coun.; Artist-in-Residence Cmty. Arts Coun. Park Forest, 1983, Sch. of Art Inst. of Chgo. at Ox Bow, 1993; recipient Russia Peace ribbon, 1987—. Mem. LWV, Mid-Am. Print Coun., Am. Print Alliance, Chgo. Artists Coalition, Chgo. Southland Visual Arts Coalition. Methodist. Avocations: reiki master, studying herbs & wildflowers, reading, travel, swimming. Home: 74 Blackhawk Dr Park Forest IL 60466-2146 Studio: 266 Somonauk St Park Forest IL 60466-2241

CRICHTON, DOUGLAS BENTLEY, editor, writer; b. Petersburg, Va., Sept. 12, 1959; s. James Bentley and Marjorie Ulalier (Robertson) C.; m. Virginia Elizabeth Munsch, Sept. 5, 1981; children: Christopher Winfield, Alexander Douglas, William Perry, Susannah Elizabeth. BA in English, U. Va., 1981. Reporter Richmond (Va.) Times-Dispatch, 1982-84; reporter, editor AP, Dallas, 1984-88; mng. editor, then editor Am. Way Mag., Dallas, 1988-93; exec. editor, then editor, v.p. Cooking Light Mag., Birmingham, Ala., 1993-2001; v.p., editor Health Mag., Birmingham, Ala., 2001—. Judge Maggie awards Western Pub. Assn., L.A., 1989-93. Named Va. Young Journalist of Yr., UPI, 1983; recipient over 150 awards for edit. and artistic excellence ; scholar James Hay Found., 1980. Mem. Am. Soc. Mag. Editors, Assn. Food Journalists. Office: Health 2100 Lakeshore Dr Birmingham AL 35209

CRICHTON, JOHN HAYES, investment banker; b. Minden, La., July 21, 1920; s. Thomas and Bernard Moore (Hayes) C.; children by previous marriage: Kate, Bunnie, Lili, John Hayes; m. Flora Atherton, June 2, 1989. BS, Davidson Coll., 1942; JD, La. State U., 1949; exec. program, Stanford U., 1970. Bar: La. 1949. Assoc. Smitherman, Smitherman & Purcell, 1949-51; mng. dir. Better Hotels of La., Shreveport, 1951-61; exec. v.p., asst. to pres. Allied Properties, San Francisco, 1961-62; pres. Guaranteed Reservations Inc., Palm Beach, Fla., 1962—; also bd. dirs. Golden Rim Investment Corp., Palm Beach, Fla., 1989—. Pres., dir. Computer Controls Corp., 1967-70; chmn. bd. dirs. Commonwealth Group Inc.; bd. dirs. H & K Corp. Downtown Real Estate Inc., Lee Hardware Co., 1st Nat. Bank Sheveport. Maj., inf. AUS, 1942-46. Decorated Bronze star with oak leaf cluster. Mem. ABA, La. Bar Assn., Bath and Tennis Club (Palm Beach), Sigma Alpha Epsilon, Phi Delta Phi. Republican. Presbyterian. Home: 315 Westover Rd San Antonio TX 78209-5653 Office: Three Two Corp PO Box 6570 San Antonio TX 78209

CRICHTON, MICHAEL (JOHN CRICHTON), author, film director; b. Chgo., Oct. 23, 1942; AB summa cum laude, Harvard U., 1964, MD, 1969. Postdoctoral fellow Salk Inst., La Jolla, Calif., 1969-70. Vis. writer MIT, Cambridge, 1988; vis. lectr. Cambridge U., 1965; creator, co-exec. prodr. TV show ER, 1994. Creator, co-exec., prodr.: ER, 1994; author: (as Jeffrey Hudson) A Case of Need, 1968 (Edgar award Mystery Writers of America 1968); (as John Lange) Odds On, 1966, Scratch One, 1967, Easy Go, 1968, Zero Cool, 1969, The Venom Business, 1969, Drug of Choice, 1970, Grave Descend, 1970, Binary, 1972; The Andromeda Strain, 1969, Five Patients, 1970 (Writer of the Year award Assn. American Medical Writers 1970), (with Douglas Crichton) Dealing: Or, The Berkeley to Boston Forty-Brick Lost-Bag Blues, 1971, The Terminal Man, 1972, The Great Train Robbery, 1975 (Edgar award Mystery Writers of America 1979), Eaters of the Dead, 1976, Jasper Johns, 1977, rev. edit., 1994, Congo, 1980, Electronic Life, 1983, Sphere, 1987, Travels, 1988, Jurassic Park, 1990, Rising Sun, 1992, Disclosure, 1994, Lost World, 1995, Airframe, 1996, Timeline, 1999, Prey, 2002; screenwriter, dir. film Westworld, 1973, Coma, 1978, The Great Train Robbery, 1979, Looker, 1981, Runaway, 1984; dir. film Pursuit, 1972, Physical Evidence, 1989; co-screenwriter Jurassic Park, 1993, Rising Sun, 1993; co-screenwriter, co-writer Twister, 1996; co-prodr. (film) Disclosure, 1994, Sphere, 1998, 13th Warrior, 1999. Mem. bd. overseers Harvard U. Recipient George Foster Peabody award ER, 1995, Emmy Best Dramatic series ER, 1996, Best Long Form Television Script for ER, Writer's Guild Am., 1995, Acad. Motion Pictures Arts and Scis. Tech. Achievement award for pioneering computerized motion picture budgeting and scheduling, 1995; Henry Russell Shaw traveling fellow, 1964-65. New ankylosaur named in honor Bienosaurus crichtoni, 2000. Mem. Authors Guild (coun. 1995—), Writers Guild Am. West, Dirs. Guild Am., PEN Am. Ctr., Acad. Motion Picture Arts and Scis.; bd. dirs. Internat. Design Conf. at Aspen, 1985-91, Western Behavioral Scis. Inst., La Jolla, 1986-91; Phi Beta Kappa. Avocation: computer games. Office: Constant C Prodns Ste 433 2118 Wilshire Blvd Santa Monica CA 90403

CRICHTON, THOMAS, IV, lawyer; b. Shreveport, La., Dec. 2, 1947; Student, Vanderbilt U.; BS, La. State U., 1969, JD, 1972. Bar: Tex. 1972, La. 1972, D.C. 1988. Mem. Vinson & Elkins, LLP, Dallas. Adj. prof. sch. law U. Houston, 1978-86. Mem. Order of Coif, Beta Alpha Psi, Beta Gamma Sigma, Omicron Delta Kappa, Phi Kappa Phi. Office: Vinson & Elkins LLP 3700 Trammell Crow Ctr Dallas TX 75201-2975 also: Vinson & Elkins LLP 2500 First City Tower 1001 Fannin St Ste 3300 Houston TX 77002-6706 also: Vinson & Elkins LLP 1455 Pennsylvania Ave NW Fl 7 Washington DC 20004-1008

CRICK, FRANCIS HARRY COMPTON, science educator, researcher; b. June 8, 1916; s. Harry Crick, Mary Elizabeth (Wilkins) Crick; m. Ruth Doreen Dodd, 1940 (div. 1947); 1 child; m. Odile Speed, 1949; 2 children. BSc, Univ. Coll., London; PhD, Cambridge U., Eng. Scientist Brit. Admiralty, 1940-47, Strangeways Lab., Cambridge, Eng., 1947-49; with Med. Rsch. Coun. Lab. of Molecular Biology, Cambridge, 1949-77; Kieckhefer Disting. prof. Salk Inst. Biol. Studies, San Diego, 1977—, non-resident fellow, 1962-73, pres., 1994-95. Adj. prof. psychology U. Calif, San Diego; vis. lectr. Rockefeller Inst., N.Y.C., 1959; vis. prof. chemistry dept. Harvard U., 1959; adj. prof. psychology U. Calif., San Diego, 1959; fellow Churchill Coll., Cambridge, England, 1960—61; Korkes Meml. lectr. Duke U., 1960; vis. prof. biophysics Harvard U., 1962; Henry Sedgwick Meml. lectr. Cambridge U., 1963; Graham Young lect., Glasgow, 63; Robert Boyle lectr. Oxford U., 1963; Vanuxem lectr Princeton U., 1964; William T. Sedgwick Meml. lectr. MIT, 1965; Cherwell-Simon Meml. lectr. Oxford U., 1966; Shell lectr. Stanford U., 1969; Paul Lund

lectr. Northwestern U., 1977; DuPont lectr. Harvard U., 1979; numerous other invited meml. lectrs. Author: (books) Of Molecules and Men, 1966, Life Itself, 1981, What Mad Pursuit, 1988, The Astonishing Hypothesis: The Scientific Search for the Soul, 1994, 1994; contbr. scientific papers to sci. jours. Recipient Prix Charles Leopold Mayer award, French Acad. Scis., 1961, Rsch. Corp. award, (with J. D. Watson), 1961, Warren Triennial prize, 1959, Lasker award, (with J. D. Watson and Maurice Wilkins), 1960, Nobel Prize for Medicine, 1962, Gairdner Found. award, 1962, Royal medal, Royal Soc., 1972, Copley medal, 1975, Michelson-Moley award, 1981, Benjamin P. Cheney medal, 1986, Golden Plate award, 1987, Albert medal, Royal Soc. Arts, London, 1987, Friends of Libr., 1995, Liberty medal, 2000, Benjamin Franklin award Disting. Achievement in Scis., 2001, Trotter Prize, 2001, Disting. Svc. award, Miami Nature Biotechnology Winter Symposium, 2003, Life Scis. Achievement award, U. Calif. San Diego, 2003. Fellow: AAAS, Rochester Mus., Indian Nat. Sci. Acad., Univ. Coll., London, Inst. Biology London (hon.), Caius Coll. Cambridge (hon.), John Muir Coll. U. Calif. San Diego (hon.), Tata Inst. Fundamental Rsch., Bombay (hon.), Royal Soc., Royal Soc. Edinburgh (hon.), Indian Acad. Scis. (hon.), Churchill Coll., Cambridge (hon.); mem.: Acad. Europaea, Am. Soc. Biol. Chemists (hon.), Acad. Arts and Scis. fgn. (hon.), U.S. Nat. Acad. Scis. fgn. (assoc.), French Acad. Scis. fgn. (assoc.), Royal Irish Acad. (hon.), Am. Philos. Soc. fgn., Hellenic Biochem. and Biophys. Soc. (hon.), German Acad. Sci. Office: Salk Inst Biol Studies PO Box 85800 San Diego CA 92186-5800

CRIDER, ALLEN BILLY, English educator, novelist; b. Mexia, Tex., July 28, 1941; s. Billy and Frances Antoinette (Brodnax) C.; m. Judy Laverne Stutts, June 4, 1965; children: Angela Antoinette, Allen Blake. BA, U. Tex., Austin, 1963; MA, North Tex. State U., 1967; PhD, U. Tex., Austin, 1972. English tchr. Corsicana (Tex.) H.S., 1963—65; prof. English Howard Payne U., Brownwood, Tex., 1971—83; prof. English, chair dept. English Alvin (Tex.) C.C., 1983—, chmn. divsn. fine arts; ret., 2002. Author: (with Jack Davis) The Coyote Connection, 1981, Too Late to Die, 1986, 89, Shotgun Saturday Night, 1987, 89, Cursed to Death, 1988, 90, Keepers of the Beast, 1988, One Dead Dean, 1988, Ryan Rides Back, 1988, A Time for Hanging, 1989, Blood Dreams, 1989, Death on the Move, 1989, 90, Dying Voices, 1989, Galveston Gunman, 1989, Goodnight, Moom, 1989, Evil at the Root, 1990, 91, Just Before Dark, 1990, Medicine Show, 1990, Rest in Peace, 1990, Vampire Named Fred, 1990, Blood Marks, 1991, Dead on the Island, 1991, Booked for a Hanging, 1992, Gator Kill, 1992, The Texas Capitol Murders, 1992, When Old Men Die, 1994, Murder Most Fowl, 1994, A Dangerous Thing, 1994, Mike Gonzo and the Almost Invisible Man, 1996, Mike Gonzo and the Sewer Monster, 1996, The Prairie Chicken Kill, 1996, Winning Can Be Murder, 1996, Mike Gonzo and the UFO Terror, 1997, Murder Takes a Break, 1997, Death by Accident, 1998, 99, Outrage at Blanco, 1998, Murder Is an Art, 1999, Texas Vigilante, 1999, A Ghost of a Chance, 2000, 2001, A Romantic Way to Die, 2001, 2002, A Knife In the Back, 2003, (with Willard Scott) Murder Under Blue Skies, 1998, 1999, Murder in the Mist, 1999, 2000, (short story collection) The Nighttime Is the Right Time, 2001; contbr. short stories to publs. Recipient Anthony award for Best 1st Mystery Novel, Bouchercon, 1987. Mem. Tex. C.C. Tchrs.' Assn., Mystery Writers of Am., Pvt. Eye Writers of Am., Sisters in Crime, Western Writers of Am., Tex. Inst. Letters. Avocations: collecting old paperback books, running. Office: Alvin Cmty Coll 3110 Mustang Rd Alvin TX 77511-4807 E-mail: abc@wt.net.

CRIDER, ROBERT AGUSTINE, international financier, law enforcement official; b. Washington, Jan. 3, 1935; s. Rana Albert and Terasa Helen (Dampf) C.; m. Debbie Ann Lee, Feb. 1960. Student, U. Md., 1959-63. Police officer Met. Police Dept., Washington, 1957-67; substitute tchr., bldg. trades instr. Maries R-1 Sch., Vienna, Mo., 1968-70; vets. constrn. tng. officer VA Dept. Edn., Mo., 1968-70; constrn. mgr. Tectonnics Ltd., Vienna, 1970-79; owner, dir. R-A Crider & Assocs., St. Louis, 1979—. Bd. dirs. TI-CO Investment Corp., Langcaster Corp. With USAF, 1952-56. Mem. Assn. Ret. Policemen, Internat. Conf. Police, Internat. Assn. Chiefs of Police, Nat. Police Assn., World Future Soc., Internat. Platform Assn., Mo. Police Chiefs Asn., Mo. Sheriff's Assn., Am. Correctional Assn., Law Enforcement Intelligence Assn., Internat. Drug Enforcement Assn., Nat. Assn. Fin. Cons., Internat. Soc. Financiers, Am. Legion, St. Louis Honor Guard, Lions, K.C. (4th degree). Roman Catholic. Home: PO Box 109 Vienna MO 65582-0109 Office: R-A Crider & Assocs 2644 Roseland Ter Saint Louis MO 63143-2304 E-mail: p9468w@aol.com.

CRIDER, RUDYARD LEE, psychotherapist; b. Abilene, Kans., Oct. 16, 1942; s. Clarence A. and Myrtle (Cox) C.; m. Doris Elaine Heisey, Aug. 3, 1962; 1 child, Michele Renee. BA, Messiah Coll., 1971; MS, Shippensburg U., 1978. Cert. clin. mental health counselor; nat. cert. counselor; cert. diplomate in psychotherapy; lic. profl. counselor. Mental health worker King's View Hosp., Reedley, Calif., 1966-68; crisis intervention counselor Holy Spirit Hosp. Mental Health, Camp Hill, Pa., 1974-78, sr. psychotherapist, 1978—, asst. coord. outpatient svcs., 1989—2001, program supr. behavioral health svcs., 2001—; pvt. practice psychotherapy, 1992—. Sr. peer reviewer Holy Spirit Hosp. Mental Health, Camp Hill, 1990-96, quality assurance com., 1990—, clin. site supr., 1983—, mem. extended mgmt. team, 1994—. Recipient Recognition for Outstanding Svc. award Cumberland Perry County Mental Health-Mental Retardation Program, 1993. Mem. Acad. Clin. Mental Health Counselors, Am. Counseling Assn., Am. Mental Health Counselors Assn., Am. Psychotherapy Assn., Pa. Counselors Assn., Pa. Psychol. Assn. Lutheran. Avocations: photography, bicycling, hiking, drawing, backpacking. Home: 438 Parkside Rd Camp Hill PA 17011-2127 Office: Holy Spirit Hosp 21st St Camp Hill PA 17011 Fax: 717-972-4172. E-mail: RCrider@HSH.org.

CRIGGER, GARY BRANT, retired manufacturing executive; b. Marlinton, W.Va., July 20, 1946; s. Frank Beryl and Ethel Bernice (Compton) C.; m. Bonne Marie Bell, Nov. 29, 1969. BA in Econs., Harvard U., 1968; MBA in Mgmt., Golden Gate U., 1973; MS in Acctg., U. Akron, 1975. V.p. Firestone Tire & Rubber Co., Akron, Ohio, 1988-90; pres. Firestone Indsl. Products, Indpls., 1990-92, Firestone Bldg. Products, Indpls., 1992; sr. v.p. Bridgestone/Firestone, Inc., Nashville, 1992-98, exec. v.p., 1998-2000; ret. Chmn. bd. dirs. Credit First Nat. Assn., Brookpark, Ohio, 1993-2000; pres. Nashville Ballet, 1998-99; v.p. Rape and Sexual Abuse Ctr., Nashville, 2002-03. Mem. Sigma Alpha Epsilon.

CRIGLER, B. WAUGH, US magistrate judge; b. Charlottesville, Virginia, July 17, 1948; s. Bernard Weaver and Jayne (Waugh) C.; m. Anne (Kendall), June 20, 1970; children: C. Kendall, Jason C., and Anne Stuart. BA in history, Washington and Lee U., 1970; JD, U. Tenn., 1973. Bar: Tenn., 1973, U.S. Dist. Ct. (ea. dist.) Tenn., 1973, Va., 1974, D.C., 1974, U.S. Dist. Ct. (we. and ea. dist.) Va., 1975, U.S. Ct. Appeals (4th cir.) 1978, U.S. Supreme Ct., 1979. Law clk. to presiding judge U.S. Dist. Ct. Tenn., Knoxville, Tenn., 1973-74; ptnr. Lea and Crigler, Culpeper, Va., 1974-75, Lea, Davies, Crigler, and Barrell, Culpeper, Va., 1975-79, Davies, Crigler, Barrell, and Will, PC, Culpeper, Va., 1979-81; magistrate judge U.S. Dist. Ct., Charlottesville, Va., 1981—. Instr. Trial Practice Sch. Law, U. Va., 1986—; mem. criminal rules adv. com. Jud. Conf. U.S., 1992-97; mem. Fed. and State Jud. Coun., Va., 1992-2001. Mem.: ABA (criminal law com. young lawyers divsn. 1974—80), Tenn. Bar Assn., Va. Bar Assn. (chmn. criminal law corrections young lawyers divsn. 1979—80), Va. State Bar (standing com. on professionalism 1997—2003, chmn. and moderator VSB Professionalism for Law Students. 2000—03), Thomas Jefferson Inn of Ct. (pres. 1991—92), Order of Coif, Phi Kappa Phi. Avocations: landscaping, swimming, biblical studies. Home: 100 Peterson Pl Charlottesville VA 22901-3175 Office: US Magistrate Judge 255 W Main St Rm 328 Charlottesville VA 22902-5058

CRIKELAIR, GEORGE FRANCIS, retired plastic surgeon, educator, researcher; b. Green Bay, Wis., July 15, 1920; s. Frank L. and Alma Margaret (Stenger) C.; m. Eleanor Parkhurst Hoesli, July 30, 1944; children John, Dave, Tom, Amy, Carol, Paul, Mary. BA, U. Wis., 1942, MD, 1944; PhD (hon.), St. Norbert Coll., De Pere, Wis., 1979. Diplomate Am. Bd. Plastic Surgery (past chmn.). Prof. surgery emeritus Columbia U., N.Y.C.; former dir. divsn. plastic surgery Columbia-Presbyn. Med. Ctr., N.Y.C.; pvt. practice. Former cons. to Surgeon Gen. Initiator, past pres. Info. Coun. Fabric Flammability; former advisor to Sec. Commerce on children's flammable nightwear. Mem. Am. Acad. Pediatrics (hon.), Am. Soc. Plastic Surgeons (former pres.). Home: 2500 SE 21st St Fort Lauderdale FL 33316-3220

CRILLY, EUGENE RICHARD, engineering consultant; b. Phila., Oct. 30, 1923; s. Eugene John and Mary Virginia (Harvey) C.; m. Alice Royal Roth, Feb. 16, 1952. ME, Stevens Inst. Tech., 1944, MS, 1949, U. Penn., 1951; postgrad., UCLA, 1955-58. Sr. rsch. engr. N.Am. Aviation, L.A., 1954-57, Canoga Park and Downey, Calif., 1962-66; process engr. Northrop Aircraft Corp., Hawthorne, Calif., 1957-59; project engr., quality assurance mgr. HITCO, Gardena, Calif., 1959 62; sr. rsch. splist. Lockheed-Calif. Co., Burbank, Calif., 1966-74, engrng. splist. N.Am. aircraft ops. Rockwell Internat., El Segundo, Calif., 1974-89. Author tech. papers. Mem. nat. com. 125th Anniversary Founding of Stevens Inst. Tech. in 1870. Served with USNR, 1943-46; comdr. Res. ret. Mem. Soc. for Advancement Material and Process Engring. (chmn. L.A. chpt. 1978-79, gen. chmn. 1981 symposium exhbn., nat. dir. 1979-86, treas. 1982-85, Award of Merit 1986), Naval Inst., Naval Res. Assn., VFW, Mil. Order World Wars (adj. San Fernando Valley chpt. 1985, 2d vice comdr. 1986, comdr. 1987-89, vice comdr. West, Dept. Cen. Calif., 1988-89, comdr. Cajon Valley San Diego chpt. 1990-92, adj./ROTC chmn. region XIV 1990-91, comdr. Dept. So. Calif. 1991-93, vice comdr. region XIV, 1992-93, dept. comdr. Gen. Staff Officer region XIV 1993-94, comdr. region XIV, 1994-95, Disting. Chpt. Comdr. Region XIV 1990-91, treas. region XIV 1998-99, treas. San Diego chpt. 1999-2000), Former Intelligence Officers Assn. (treas. San Diego chpt. one 1990-94), Ret. Officers Assn. (treas. Silver Strand chpt. 1992-2000, asst. treas. San Diego natl. conv., 2000), Navy League U.S. (treas. Coronado coun. 1997-2001), Naval Order U.S., Naval Intelligence Profls. Assn., Brit. United Svc. Club L.A., Marines Meml. Club (San Francisco), Coronado Round Tab le, Hammer Club of San Diego, Sigma Xi, Sigma Nu. Republican. Roman Catholic. Home and Office: 276 J Ave Coronado CA 92118-1138 E-mail: genecrilly@aol.com.

CRIM, ELEANOR C. obstetrician, gynecologist; b. Bangalore, India, Apr. 13, 1935; MD, U. Wash., Seattle, 1961. Intern King Co. Hosp.-Harborview, Seattle, 1961-62; resident in ob-gyn. Swedish Hosp. Med. Ctr., Seattle, 1962-66; chief ob-gyn LBJ Med. Ctr., Pago Pago, Am. Samoa, 1969-75; med. exec. com. Castle Med. Ctr., Kailua, Hawaii, 1992-95, staff sec.-treas., 1995-97, chief-elect staff, 1997-99, chief of staff, trustee, mem. fin. com., 1999-2001, bd. trustees, mem. fin. com., 1999-2001, chair ob-gyn. and pediats., 2003—; ob-gyn. pvt. practice, Kailua, Hawaii, 1975—2001. Mem. med. exec. com. Castle Med. Ctr., 2001—, dir. new physician orientation, 2002—. Mem. ACOG, Alpha Omega Alpha.

CRIMANDO, THOMAS IGNATIUS, history educator; b. Batavia, N.Y. s. Gasper Joseph and Joan (Hilbert) C. BA in History cum laude, St. John Fisher Coll., 1976; MA in European History, U. Rochester, 1977, PhD in Early Modern European History, 1984. Lectr. history Nazareth Coll., Rochester, N.Y., 1985-88; adj. faculty history Rochester Inst. Tech., 1987-2001, SUNY, Brockport, 1988-2001, 2003. Vis. asst. prof. history SUNY, Brockport, 2001—03, adj. faculty history, 2002, Rochester Inst. Tech., 2002. Contbr. articles and revs. to profl. jours., articles to reference works. Named to Hall of Fame, Notre Dame H.S., Batavia, N.Y., 2001; recipient John A. Murray award, St. John Fisher Coll., 1976. Mem.: Nat. Geog. Soc., Eire Philatelic Soc., Vatican Philatelic Soc. (pres.), Western Front Assn., Am. Philatelic Assn., Phi Alpha Theta, Pi Gamma Mu. Roman Catholic. Avocation: philately. E-mail: tcrimand@brockport.edu.

CRIMINALE, WILLIAM OLIVER, JR., applied mathematics educator; b. Mobile, Ala., Nov. 29, 1933; s. William Oliver and Vivian Gertrude (Sketoe) C.; m. Ulrike Irmgard Wegner, June 7, 1962; children: Martin Oliver, Lucca. BS, U. Ala., 1955; PhD, Johns Hopkins U., 1960. Asst. prof. Princeton (N.J.) U., 1962-68; asso. prof. U. Wash., Seattle, 1968-73, prof. oceanography, geophysics, applied math., 1973—, chmn. dept. applied math., 1976-84. Cons. Aerospace Corp., 1963-65, Boeing Corp., 1968-72, AGARD, 1967-68, Lenox Hill Hosp., 1967-68, ICASE, NASA Langley, 1990—; guest prof., Can., 1965, 2001, France, 1967-68, Germany, 1973-74, Sweden, 1973-74, Scotland, 1985, 89, 91, Eng., 1990, 91, Stanford, 1990, Brazil, 1992, 2001, Italy, 1999; Nat. Acad. exch. scientist, USSR, 1969, 72. Author: Stability of Parallel Flows, 1967, Theory and Computation of Hydrodynamic Stability, 2003; contbr. articles to profl. jours. Served with U.S. Army, 1961-62. Boris A. Bakmeteff Meml. fellow, 1957-58, NATO postdoctoral fellow, 1960-61, Alexander von Humboldt Sr. fellow, 1973-74, Royal Soc. fellow, 1990-91. Fellow Am. Phys. Soc.; mem. Am. Acad. Mechanics, Am. Geophys. Union, Fedn. Am. Scientists. Home: 1635 Peach Ct E Seattle WA 98112-3428 Office: U Wash Dept Applied Math Box 352420 Seattle WA 98195-2420 E-mail: lascala@amath.washington.edu.

CRIMLISK, JANE THERESE, probation officer; b. Boston, Dec. 2, 1945; d. Herbert Leo and Grace Beatrice (McGilvray) C. AS, Aquinas Coll., Newton, Mass., 1968; BA in Sociology cum laude, Boston Coll., 1974; MS in Bus. Edn., Suffolk U., Boston, 1978; MEd in Rehab. Counseling, U. Mass., 1991, Cert. of Advanced Grad. Study, 1995. Tchr. religious edn., 1965-88, 93—; legal sec. Hale, Sanderson, Byrnes & Morton, Boston, 1968-69; sec. Boston Coll. Law Sch., Chestnut Hill, 1969-74, Life Resources, Inc., Boston, 1974-75; tchr. Archbishop Williams High Sch., Braintree, Mass., 1975-78; exec. sec. Cramer Electronics, Newton, Mass., 1978-79; jud. sec. Com. of Mass. Ct. Systems, Boston, 1979-95; probation officer Probate and Family Ct., Boston, 1995—; tchr. adult edn. Aquinas Coll., Milton, 1989—. Vol. counselor Pregnancy Help, Brighton, Mass., 1992, Arthur Clark for U.S. Congress campaign, Newton, 1980, Marian Walsh for State Senate campaign, 1992, 94, Mass. Citizens for Life. Mem. Boston Coll. Alumni Assn. (bd. dirs. 1982-84), Boston Coll. Evening Coll. Alumni Assn. (bd. dirs., past pres.), Aquinas Coll. Alumni Assn. Democrat. Roman Catholic. Avocations: swimming, ice skating, crewel, cross stitch, music. Home: 416 Belgrade Ave Apt 25 West Roxbury MA 02132-1540 Office: Probate and Family Ct Dept 24 New Chardon St Boston MA 02114-4703

CRIMLISK, JANET THERESE, pulmonary clinical nurse specialist, educator; b. Newton, Mass., June 25, 1945; d. Frank J. and Helen R. (Roman) C. BS, Boston Coll., 1967; MS, Boston U., 1971, geriatric nurse practitioner, 1978; adult nurse practitioner, Mass. Gen. Hosp. Inst. Health, Professions, 1995. RN, Mass.; cert. med.-surg. nurse, ANCC. Staff nurse Boston City Hosp., 1967-69, med. clin. nurse specialist, 1974-77, pulmonary clin. nurse specialist, 1977-96; pulmonary clin. nurse specialist, nurse educator Boston Med. Ctr., 1996—. Mem. faculty St. Elizabeth's Hosp. Sch. Nursing, Boston, 1971-73, Boston City Hosp. Sch. of Nursing, 1973-74, Boston State Coll., 1975. Contbr. numerous articles to profl. jours. H.E.W. fellow, Boston U., 1971; named Outstanding Nurse of Yr., City of Boston, 1985. Mem. ANA, Am. Acad. Nurse Practitioners (cert. nurse practitioner), Am. Heart Assn., Am. Thoracic Soc., Sigma Theta Tau.

CRIMM, RONALD E. state representative; b. West Lawn, Pa., Mar. 11, 1935; m. Phyllis Crimm; children: Cynthia, Scott. BS, Shippensburg Univ., 1957. State Rep. House of Rep., Dist. 33, Ky., 1996—; owner Ind. Ins. Agency, 1977—; sales/mgmt. Paul Revere Co., 1971—77; sales Conn. Gen. Life, 1961—71; tchr. Rose Tree Union, 1958—61. Bd. mem. West Shore Sch. Bd., Camp Hill, Pa., 1966—71; Vice Chair Local Gov.; mem. Banking and Ins., Occupations and Licensing. U.S. Army, 1957—63. caucuses. Mem. Alea-Telecommunications; mem. NCOIL. Republican. Methodist. Office: Capitol Capitol Annex, Rm 424F Frankfort KY 40601 also: Dist PO Box 43244 Louisville KY 40253*

CRIMMINS, PHILIP PATRICK, metallurgical engineer, lawyer; b. Poughkeepsie, N.Y., Aug. 1, 1930; s. Philip Patrick and Eva (Booth) C.; m. Janet E. Ballou, Feb. 14, 1953; children: Lisa Jane, Philip Patrick, Michael Mathew. BS, MIT, 1952; MS, Wayne State U., 1959; JD, U. Pacific, 1972. Registered profl. metall. engr. Metall. engr. Ford Motor Co., Livonia, Mich., 1954-58; dir. engring. Aerojet Space Boosters, Sacramento, 1958-95. Served with AUS, 1952-54. Recipient William Sparagen award Am. Welding Soc., 1968 Calif. Fellow Am. Inst. Chemists; mem. Am. Soc. Metals, Fed., Am., Calif. bar assns. Home: 9113 Rosewood Dr Sacramento CA 95826-4526

CRIMMINS, TIMOTHY JAMES, history educator; b. Pitts., July 20, 1943; s. John Michael Crimmins Sr. and Catherine Lucile O'Malley; children: Timothy James, Meghan Elizabeth. BA, LaSalle U., 1966; MA, George Washington U., 1970; PhD, Emory U., 1972. Tchr. O'Connell H.S., Fall Ch., Va., 1966-68, Fairmont Hill Jr.-Sr. H.S., Balt., 1968-70; from asst. prof. to assoc. prof. history Ga. State U., Atlanta, 1972-83, prof., 1988—, dir. heritage preservation program, 1983-98, chair dept. history, 1989-90, 91-98, assoc. provost acad. programs, 1998—2001. Dir. Nat. Coun. Preservation Edn., Washington, chmn.; chmn. Comm. Preservation Ga. Capitol, Atlanta. Co-author, co-host (TV series) The Making of Modern Atlanta, 1991-93; contbr. articles to profl. jours. Chmn. Atlanta Urban Design Commn., 1980-81, Easements Atlanta, 1983—; trustee Atlanta Hist. Soc., 1993—. Recipient Gov.'s Humanitics award, 2000, Jewett award, Ga. Trust for Hist. Preservation, 2002. Avocations: reading, jogging, birdwatching. Home: 852 Briarvista Way Atlanta GA 30329 Office: Ga State U Dept History Atlanta GA 30303 Fax: 404-651-1745.

CRINION, GREGORY PAUL, lawyer; b. Eau Claire, Wis., Feb. 19, 1959; s. Harlan D. and Shirley P. (Paff) C. BBA cum laude, U. Wis., Eau Claire, 1981; MBA, U. Minn., 1982; JD cum laude, U. Wis., 1985. Bar: Wis. 1985, Tex. 1985, U.S. Dist. Ct. (we. dist.) Wis. 1985, U.S. Dist. Ct. (so. dist.) Tex. 1985, U.S. Ct. Appeals (5th cir.) 1985, U.S. Dist. Ct. (ea. dist.) Tex. 1986, U.S. Ct. Appeals (7th cir.) 1986, D.C. 1987, Colo. 1994, U.S. Supreme Ct. 1989, U.S. Dist. Ct. (we. dist.) Tex. 1989, U.S. Dist. Ct. (no. dist.) Tex. 1990; cert. ski instr. Atty. Exxon Co., U.S.A., Houston, 1985-87, Exxon Corp., N.Y.C., 1987; from assoc. to ptnr. Jackson Walker, LLP (and predecessor firms), Houston, 1987-97; ptnr. Citti & Crinion, L.L.P., Houston, 1997-99, Ashby & Whitmire, LLP, Houston, 1999—. Bd. dirs., pres. Innovative Alternatives, Inc., 2000-02. Apptd. NORM (Naturally Occurring Radioactive Material) Adv. Com., 1996-99, sign ordinance rev. com. City of Friendswood, 1996-98, cmty. and econ. devel. com., 2000—, chair, 2002—; mem. Galveston County Mediation Svcs. Bd., 2000-02; mem. Leadership Friendswood Class I, 2001-02. Recipient Scroll of Appreciation U.S. Army, Europe, 1984. Mem. ABA, Houston Bar Assn., Tex. Petroleum Marketers and Convenience Store Assn. Office: Ashby & Whitmire LLP 1002 Gemini St Ste 116 Houston TX 77058-2746

CRINO, MARJANNE HELEN, anesthesiologist; b. Rochester, N.Y., Aug. 18, 1933; d. Michael Jay and Helen Barbara (Kennedy) C.; m. Michael Anthony La Iuppa, Nov. 12, 1960 (dec. Feb. 1996); children: James Michael, Barbara Helen, John Christopher. BS, Coll. St. Teresa, 1955; MD, Med. Coll. Wis., 1959; MA in Theology, St. Bernard's Inst., 1991. Diplomate Nat. Bd. Med. Examiners. House staff Genesee Hosp., Rochester, 1959-61; perinatal mortality rsch., resident in anesthesiology Jackson Meml Hosp.-U. Miami, 1962-65; attending staff in anesthesiology Genesee Hosp., Rochester, N.Y., 1969-2000; mem. exec. com., med. staff sec., 1980, 82; acting chmn. dept. anesthesiology Genesee Hosp., Rochester, N.Y., 1989, 91, chmn. pain control com., 1989-95; clin. instr. anesthesiology U. Rochester Sch. Medicine, 1983—. Cons. anesthesiology Rochester Psychiat. Ctr., 1975-85; instr. anesthesiology U. Miami Sch. medicine, 1966, 67; attending staff anesthesiology Jackson Meml. Hosp., Miami, 1966, 67. Mem. adv. bd. Isaiah House Hosp., 1994—, com. Pittsford (N.Y.) Rep. Party, 1970's-80's; vol. chaplain Genesee Hosp. Mem. N.Y. State Soc. Anesthesiologists (bd. dirs., vice spkr. 1983-86, del. 1971-82, 87-2002), Am. Soc. Anesthesiologists (del. 1979-86, 97), AMA, N.Y. State Med. Soc., Med. Soc. County of Monroe, Rochester Acad. Medicine, Cath. Physicians Guild Rochester (bd.dirs., pres. 1988-89), Margaret Roper Guild (pres. 1975-76), Cath. Women's Club (Diocese of Rochester). Roman Catholic. Avocations: reading, gardening, music. *Whether you are dealing with a large group, a small gathering or a single person, don't worry about the impression you are making or how uncomfortable you are. Try to find some way to make the others comfortable. You will never go wrong.*

CRIPPEN, BRUCE D. former state legislator, real estate manager; b. Billings, Mont., June 13, 1932; m. Mary Crippen; 4 children. BS, U. Mont., 1956, grad. Sch. Law, NYU. Mem. Mont. Ho. of Reps., Billings, 1981-99, minority whip, 1985-86, minority leader, 1991-92, 93-94; pres. pro tempore Mont. Senate, Billings, 1997-98, pres., 1999, mem. ethics com., jud. com., legis. administrn. com., rules com. Served USN, 1952-54. Lutheran.

CRIPPEN, GORDON MARVIN, chemist; b. Cheyenne, Wyo., Apr. 2, 1945; married. BS, U. Wash., 1967; PhD, Cornell U., 1971. Postdoctoral fellow U. Calif., San Francisco, 1972—73; instr. Gymnasium Klosterschule, Hamburg, Germany, 1973—75; adj. asst. prof. U. Calif., San Francisco, 1975—76, asst. prof. in residence, 1976—80; asst. prof. Tex. A&M U., College Station, 1980—82, assoc. prof., 1982—85, U. Mich., Ann Arbor, 1985—89, prof., 1989—. Author: Distance Geometry and Molecular Conformation, 1988; contbr. articles to profl. jours. Grantee, NIH, 1978—, NSF, 1978—. Office: University of Michigan College of Pharmacy Ann Arbor MI 48109 Fax: 734-763-2022. Business E-Mail: gcrippen@umich.edu.

CRIPPEN, JUANITA WITHERELL, elementary education educator; b. Burke, N.Y., Oct. 31, 1912; d. George and Nellie (Ennis) Witherell; m. Carter Martin Crippen, Sept. 22, 1944; children: Daniel F., Bonnie J. Crippen Trippany. Tchrs. permanent cert., Potsdam Normal Tchrs. Coll., 1936. Tchr. Local Rural One-Room Dist., Burke and Chateaugay, N.Y., 1931-33, 36-55; first grade tchr. Chateaugay Ctrl. Sch., 1955-77; migrant outreach tutor Migrant Tutorial Outreach, SUNY, Potsdam, N.Y., 1978—. Recipient Presdl. Recognition for 65 years of tchg. Pres. Clinton, 2000; named Oldest Tchr. in N.Y. Still Tchg., N.Y. State United Tchrs. Union, 2000. Democrat. Methodist. Avocations: reading, golf, walking. Home: PO Box 52 834 Depot St Burke NY 12917

CRIPPEN, TIMOTHY ALAN, sociology educator; b. Ft. Wayne, Ind., June 1, 1952; s. Raymond R. and Wilda E. Crippen; m. Pamela A. Crippen, Mar. 3, 1973. AB, Ind. U., 1974; MA, U. Tex., 1976, PhD, 1982. Asst. prof. sociology Mary Washington Coll., Fredericksburg, Va., 1982-88, assoc. prof. sociology, 1988-94, prof. sociology, 1994—. Author: Crisis in Sociology, 1999; contbr. articles to profl. jours. Mem. AAAS, Am. Sociol. Assn., Assn. for Politics and Life Scis., Human Behavior and Evolution Soc., So. Sociol. Soc., Phi Kappa Phi. Office: Mary Washington Coll Dept Sociology and Anthropology Fredericksburg VA 22401 E-mail: tcrippen@mwc.edu.

CRIPPS, DEREK J. dermatologist, educator; b. Sept. 17, 1928; s. Edmund James and Susan Ann (Mayell) C.; m. Eileen Wright, Dec. 21, 1963; children: Andrew, Alasdair, Annabelle, Amanda. MB BS, U. London, 1953, MD, 1965; MS, U. Mich., 1961. Diplomate Am. Bd. Dermatology. Resident in dermatology U. Mich., 1959-62; asst. prof. medicine U. Wis., Madison, 1965-68, assoc. prof. medicine, 1968-72, prof., head dermatology, 1972-2000, emeritus prof. medicine, 2001—. Cons. for sunscreens FDA, 1974-85. Conbr. over 100 articles to profl. jours. Mem. Great Brit. Nat. Swimming Team, 1950-51; surgeon lt. Royal Navy, 1954-58. Recipient Merit award AMA, 1968; grantee EPA, Porphyria in Turkey, 1979-84, NIH, 1965-84, Action spectra and Biochemistry of Photodermatoses. Fellow ACP; mem. Am. Acad. Dermatology (photobiology com., pres. 1976, Exhibit Gold award 1975), Brit. Dermatologic Assn., Ctrl. Soc. for Clin. Rsch., Soc. for Investigative Dermatology, Royal Soc. of Medicine, Wis. Dermatological Soc. (pres. 1976). Avocations: swimming, travel. Office: UW Health Dept Derm One South Park 7th Fl Madison WI 53715

CRIPPS, THOMAS ROBERT, history educator, writer; b. Balt., Sept. 17, 1932; s. Benjamin Franklin and Marian Norma C.; m. Alma Richardson Taliaferro, Dec. 26, 1954 (dec. Mar. 1994); children: Benjamin Taliaferro, Alma Richardson (dec.), Paul Hagan (dec.); m. Lynn Ann, June 24, 1995; stepchildren: Jason Ransdell, Brian Ransdell. BS in Edn., Towson State Tchrs. Coll., 1954; MA in History, U. Md., 1957, PhD in History and Lit., 1967. Cert. tchr., Md. Tchr. Milford Mill Jr. High Sch., Pikesville, Md., 1954-55; asst. prof. Pembroke (N.C.) State Coll., 1957-58, Harford Jr. Coll., Bel Air, Md., 1958-61; Univ. Disting. prof. emeritus Morgan State U., Balt., 1961-96; ret., 1996. Prodr., writer Westinghouse Broadcasting, Balt., 1968-71; vis. prof. Stanford U., Palo Alto, Calif., 1969-70, Harvard U., Cambridge, Mass., 1991-93; adj. prof., Johns Hopkins U., 2003. Author: Slow Fade to Black, 1977, Making Movies Black, 1993, Hollywood's High Noon, 1997; screenwriter: (motion picture) Black Shadows on a Silver Screen, 1976 (gold medals 1996); mem. editl. bd. Am. Quarterly, 1977-80, Jour. Film, Radio, TV, 1980's, Film and History, 1990's, Quarterly Jour. Film, 1999—. Mem. faculty So. Christian Leadership Conf., Atlanta, 1965; bd. mgrs. Black Rock YMCA, Timonium, Md., 1971; bd. chmn. Balt. Film Festival, 1974-75; mem. Md. Humanities Commn., Balt., 1976-81. Served with 101st Airborne, U.S. Army, 1955. Fellow Woodrow Wilson Ctr. Scholars, 1975-76, Nat. Humanities Ctr., 1980-81, J.S. Guggenheim Found., 1985-86, Dedalus Found., 1998-99, Rockefeller Fellow, Billa Serbeltoni, 1985.

Mem. AAUP, Am. Hist. Assn., Internat. Assn. Media and History, Orgn. Am. Historians, Soc. Cinema Studies, Edelweiss Soc. Democrat. Avocations: cooking, travel, tennis, shooting pool, sketching. Home: 126 W Lanvale St Baltimore MD 21217-4117

CRISCENTI, JOSEPH THOMAS, retired history educator; s. Salvatore Criscenti; m. Jacqueline L. Penez, Sept. 3, 1956; 1 child, Louise J. PhB, U. Detroit, 1942; MA, Harvard U., 1947, PhD, 1956. Asst. prof. Boston Coll., Chestnut Hill, Mass., 1955—62, assoc. prof., 1962—88, prof. emeritus, 1988—. Cons. CORE Collection, ALA, 1971-72; mem. case study Hispanic Divsn., Libr. of Congress, 1995-96. Author, editor: Sarmiento and His Argentina, 1993; contbg. editor: Handbook of Latin American Studies, 1984—96; contbr.: Latin America: A Guide to Historical Literature, 1971, Encyclopedia of Latin America, 1974, Encyclopedia of Latin American History and Culture, 1996; contbr. articles to profl. jours. Tech. sgt. U.S. Army Adjutant Gen. Corps, 1942-46, PTO. Mem. Am. Hist. Assn., Conf. of L.Am. History (chmn. Robertson prize com. 1962, 73, Robertson prize 1962), New Eng. Coun. of L.Am. Studies (sec.-treas. 1972-93, founder, sec.-treas. emeritus 1994—, Joseph T. Criscenti prize 1994). Home: 28 Richard Rd Needham MA 02492-4322

CRISCI, MATHEW G. marketing executive, writer; b. N.Y.C. s. Mathew Anthony and Frances (Coscia) C.; m. Mary Ann, Nov. 14, 1968; children: Mathew Joseph, Mark David, Mitchell Justin. BS, Iona Coll. Sr. v.p. Young & Rubicam, Inc., N.Y.C. and Sydney, Australia, 1968-82; exec. v.p., COO, bd. dirs. Integrated Barter Internat., N.Y.C., 1982-85; sr. v.p., gen. mgr., bd. dirs. Chiat/Day Advt. Inc., San Francisco, 1986-90; exec. v.p., mng. dir. Lowe Lintas Worldwide, N.Y.C., 1991-97; exec. v.p., chief mktg. officer Alton Entertainment Co., L.A., 1997—2001, also bd. dirs.; chief mktg. officer Asset Mktg. Sys., San Diego, 2001—. Author: Observations of a Kind, 1998, This Little Piggy, 2002. Office: Asset Mktg Sys 9715 Business Park Ave San Diego CA 92131 E-mail: mattcrisci@adelphia.net.

CRISCIMAGNA, NED HENRY, reliability engineer; b. Madison, Wis., Dec. 24, 1942; s. Frank Salvatore and Grace Mary Rose (Stancampiano) C.; m. Sandra Anne Kratina, June 19, 1965; children: Christine Marie Brent, Matthew Sean. BSME, U. Nebr., 1965; MS in Sys. Engring., Air Force Inst. Tech., 1970. Cert. reliability engr., profl. logistician. Apprentice engr. Henningson, Durham & Richardson, Omaha, 1965; commd. 2d lt. USAF, 1965, advanced through grades to lt. col., 1981, ret., 1985; staff prin. engr. ARINC Rsch. Corp., Annapolis, Md., 1985-93; sci. adv. IIT Rsch. Inst., Lanham, Md., 1993—2003, Alion Sci. & Tech., Lanham, Md., 2003—. Dep. tech. advisor US TAG to IEC TC56, 1995—, chair Z-1 dependability subcom., 1997—. Co-author: Product Reliability, Maintainability, and Supportability Handbook, 1995. Treas. Homeowners Assn., Annapolis, 1995-98; mem. Annapolis Chorale, 1990—, mem. bd. dirs.; mem., lector St. Anne's Episcopal Ch., Annapolis, 1987—. Mem. Internat. Soc. Logistics (sr., cert.), Am. Soc. Quality (cert. reliability engr.), Soc. Automotive Engrs., Order Sons of Italy in Am. (v.p. 1997-99). Avocations: college football, coin and stamp collecting, photography, music, computer simulation games. Home: 307 S Cherry Grove Ave Annapolis MD 21401-4234 Office: Alion Sci & Tech 8100 Corporate Dr Lanham MD 20785-2231 E-mail: ncriscimagne@alionscience.com.

CRISCOE, ARTHUR HUGH, religious organization administrator, educator; b. Union Grove, Ala., Feb. 21, 1939; BA, Samford U., 1964; MDiv, Southwestern Seminary, Ft. Worth, 1968, M in Religious Edn., 1969, PhD, 1975; MA in Edn., Cumberland U., 1993. Min. New Hope Bapt. Ch., Mansfield, Tex., 1965-71; prof. Columbia (S.C.) Bible Coll., 1972-76; dir. youth, children, presch. dept. Lifeway Christian Resources, Nashville, 1976—2001; prof. Cumberland U., Lebanon, Tenn., 2001—. Adj. prof. Cumberland U., Lebanon, Tenn., 1988—. Author: Original, Youth Becoming Leaders, 1984, The Doctrine of the Laity Teaching Workbook, 1985, The Doctrine of Prayer Teaching Workbook, 1986, The Doctrine of the Believers Teaching Workbook, 1987, (with others) A Biblical Model for Training Leaders, 1985. Mem. Nat. Assn. Profs. Christian Edn., Internat. Brotherhood Magicians, Am. Soc. Magicians. Baptist. Avocation: magic. Office: Cumberland University One Cumberland Square Lebanon TN 37087

CRISER, MARSHALL M. lawyer, retired university president; b. Rumson, N.J., Sept. 4, 1928; s. Marshall and Louise (Johnson) C.; m. Paula Porcher, Apr. 27, 1957; children: Marshall III, Edward, Mary, Glenn, Kimberly, Mark. BSBA, U. Fla., 1951, LLB, 1951 (replaced by J.D., 1967). Bar: Fla. 1951. Pvt. practice, Palm Beach, 1953-84; ptnr. Gunster, Yoakley, Criser & Stewart, 1955-84; atty. Palm Beach County Sch. Bd., 1958-64; pres. U. Fla., Gainesville, 1984-89, pres. emeritus, 1989—; shareholder Mahoney, Adams & Criser, Jacksonville, Fla., 1989-97; of counsel McGuire, Woods Battle, & Boothe, LLP, Jacksonville, 1998-2000, ret. ptnr., 2000—. Dep. chmn. Rinker Group Ltd., 2003—; chmn. bd. dirs. Rinker Materials, Corp., 1989-2002; mem. pres.'s coun. NCAA, 1986-87; chmn. Installment Land Sales Bd., 1963-64, chmn. Acad. Task Force rev. tort and ins. law, Fla., 1986-88, The Emerald Funds; chmn. bd. trustees Emerald Fund, 1997-98. Bd. dirs. Univ. Med. Ctr., Jacksonville, 1989-96, Shands at Jacksonville Hosp., 1999-2003, M.E. Rinker Found., 1998—; bd. dirs. Shands Tchg. Hosp., Gainesville, Fla., pres., 1984-89, bd. govs., 1996-2001; bd. govs. Good Samaritan Hosp., West Palm Beach, pres., 1979-84; mem. Fla. Bd. Regents, 1965, 71-81, chmn., 1974-77, Bus.-Higher Edn. Forum, 1987-89; trustee Collins Ctr., 1989-99; pres. Alliance for World Class Edn., Duval County, 1998-2001; chmn. Fed. Crt. Adv. Group Mid. Dist. of Fla., 1991-96; trustee U. Fla., 2001—, chmn., 2001-; mem. Fla. Fed. Jud. Nominating Com., 2001—; mem. Gov.'s Med. Malpractice Task Force, 2002—. With U.S. Army, 1951-53. Fellow Am. Bar Found.; mem. Fla. Coun. 100 (chmn. 1979-80), ABA (ho. dels. 1968-72), Fla. Bar (gov. 1960-68, pres. 1968-69), Fla. Blue Key, Phi Delta Phi, Sigma Nu. Office: McGuire Woods Et Al 100 NW 20th St Gainesville FL 32603

CRISHAM, THOMAS MICHAEL, lawyer; b. Chgo., June 7, 1939; s. John and Ellen (Moore) C.; m. Catherine Marie Schaab, Oct. 2, 1965; children: Catherine Marie, Megan, Maura. BBA, Loyola U., 1962, JD cum laude, 1965. Bar: Ill. 1965, U.S. Dist. Ct. (no. dist.) Ill. 1965, U.S. Supreme Ct. 1971, U.S. Ct. Appeals (7th cct.) 1978. Ptnr. Hinshaw & Culbertson, Chgo., 1965-95; sr. ptnr. Quinlan & Crisham, Ltd., Chgo., 1996—2001, Crisham & Kubes, Ltd., Chgo., 2001—. Mem. editl. bd. Ins. Outlook, Colorado Springs, Colo., 1990; pres. Def. Rsch. and Trial Lawyers Inst., Chgo., 1989, chmn. bd., 1990; mem. advisors Expert Evidence Reporter, Colorado Springs, 1990. Contbg. author: Abortion and Social Justice, 1973, Human Life: Our Legacy and Our Challenge, 1975, Architect and Engineer Liability: Claims Against Design Professional, 1987, Prosecuting and Defending Insurance Claims, 1989. Bd. dirs. Wendy Will Case Cancer Rsch. Found., Boys' Hope Scholars. With USMCR, 1959-60. Fellow Am. Coll. Trial Lawyers, Internat. Soc. Barristers; mem. ABA, Am. Bd. Trial Advs. (diplomate), Def. Rsch. Inst. (pres. 1989-90, chair 1990-91), Internat. Assn. Def. Counsel, Ill. Bar Assn., Trial Lawyers Club Chgo. (pres. 1975-76), Soc. Trial Lawyers Ill., Appellate Lawyers Assn., Assn. Def. Trial Lawyers, Am. Inns of Ct., Chgo. Bar Assn. Roman Catholic. Office: Crisham & Kubes Ltd 30 N Lasalle St Ste 2800 Chicago IL 60602-2511 E-mail: tcrisham@crishamlaw.com.

CRISMAN, MARY FRANCES BORDEN, librarian; b. Tacoma, Nov. 23, 1919; d. Lindon A. and Mary Cecelia (Donnelly) Borden; m. Fredric Lee Crisman, Apr. 12, 1975 (dec. Dec. 1975). BA in History, U. Wash., 1943, BA in Librarianship, 1944. Asst. br. libr. in charge work with children Mottet br. Tacoma Pub. Libr., 1944-45, br. libr., 1945-49, br. libr. Moore br., 1950-55, asst. dir., 1955-70, dir., 1970-74, dir. emeritus, 1975—; mgr. corp. libr. Frank Russell Co., 1985-96, ret., 1997. Chmn. Wash. Cmty. Libr. Coun., 1970-72. Hostess program Your Libr. and You, Sta. KTPS-TV, 1969-71. Mem. Highland Homeowners League, Tacoma, 1980—, incorporating dir. 1980, sec., registered agt., 1980-82; mem. Denham West Condominium Assn., Sun City, Ariz., 1995—, chair by laws com., 1999, sec., 2002, 2003. Mem. ALA (chmn. mem. com. Wash. 1957-60, mem. nat. libr. week com. 1965, chmn. libr. adminstrn. divsn. nominating com. 1971, mem. ins. for librs. com. 1970-74, vice chmn. libr. adminstrn. divsn. personnel adminstrn. sect. 1972-73, chmn. 1973-74, mem. com. policy implementation 1973-74, mem. libr. orgn. and mgmt. sect. budgeting acctg. and costs com. 1974-75), Am. Libr. Trustee Assn. (legis. com. 1975-78, conf. program com. 1978-80, action devel. com. 1978-80), Pacific N.W. (trustee divsn. nominating com 1976-77), Wash. Libr. Assn. (exec. bd. 1957-59, state exec., dir. Nat. Libr. Week 1965, treas., exec. bd. 1969-71, 71-73), Urban Librs. Coun. (editl. sec. Newsletter 1972-73, exec. com. 1974-75), Ladies Aux. to United Transp. Union (past pres. Tacoma), Friends Tacoma Pub. Libr. (registered agt. 1975-83, sec. 1975-78, pres. 1978-80, bd. dirs. 1980-83), Smithsonian Assocs., Nat. Railway Hist. Soc., U. Wash. Alumni Assn., U. Wash. Sch. Librarianship Alumni Assn. Clubs: Quota Internat. (sec. 1957-58, 1st v.p. 1960-61, pres. 1961-62, treas. 1975-76, pres. 1979-80) (Tacoma). Home: 6501 N Burning Tree Ln Tacoma WA 98406-2108 also: 9054 N 109th Ave Sun City AZ 85351-4676

CRISMAN COLLIER, RUTH MARIE, writer; b. Oak Park, Ill., June 16, 1914; d. John Henry and Ruth Ethel (Stiles) Thorup; m. James Lester Crisman July 7, 1941 (dec. 1992); children: Carol Ann, James Alan; m. Lennart Carlson, Feb. 6, 1993 (dec. 1998); m. Robert Collier, Jan. 8, 2000 (dec. Dec. 2002). BA in Elem. Edn., Calif. State Coll., L.A., 1966, MA in Elem. Edn., 1971, MA in Spl. Edn., 1976. Cert. tchr. reading, elem. edn. Dental asst. Dr. Bartram, L.A., 1931-41; dental clerk, typist, libr., 1954-65; tchr. L.A. City Schs., 1966-79. Author: The Mississippi Franklin Watts, 1984, Hot Off the Press, 1991, Thomas Jefferson, a Biography, 1992, Racing the Iditarod Trail, 1993; contbr. articles to newspapers, publs. Recipient PEN award. Mem. Soc. Children's Book Writers and Illustrators, Nat. League Am. PEN Women (pres. L.A. chpt. 1994-98), Calif. Fedn. Chaparral Poets, Calif. Writers Club, Pi Lambda Theta, Alpha Psi. Democrat. Methodist. Avocations: line dancing, gardening.

CRISMOND, LINDA FRY, public relations executive; b. Burbank, Calif., Mar. 1, 1943; d. Billy Chapin and Lois (Harding) Fry; m. Donald Burleigh Crismond, 1965 (dec.). BS, U. Calif.-Santa Barbara, 1964; M.L.S., U. Calif.-Berkeley, 1965. Cert. county libr., Calif., assn. exec. Reference libr., EDP coordinator San Francisco Pub. Library, 1965—72; head acquisition San Francisco Pub. Libr., 1972-74; asst. univ. libr. U. So. Calif., L.A., 1974-80; chief dep. county libr. L.A. County Pub. Libr., L.A., 1980-81, county libr. Downey, 1981-89; exec. dir ALA, Chgo., 1989-92; v.p. public rels. Profl. Media Svc. Corp., Chgo., 1992-98; v.p. pub. rels. Follett Media Distbn., Crystal Lake, Ill., 1999—2003; nat. media cons. BWI, Lexington, Ky., 2003—. Western rep. quality control council Ohio Coll. Libr. Ctr., Columbus, 1977-80; mem. Am. Nat. Standards Inst., N.Y.C., 1978-80; bd. councillors U. So. Calif. Sch. Libr. and Info. Mgmt., 1980-83, adv. bd. mem. UCLA Libr. Sch., 1981-89; chmn. bd. dirs. L.A. County Pub. Libr. Found., 1982-85; mem. OCLC Users Coun., 1988-89; mem. exec. com. L.A. County Mgmt. Coun., 1986-88, pres., 1988; cons. libr. Trinity Coll., 1995-99; prin. The Charleston Group, Inc., 1996—. Author: Directory of San Francisco Bay Area, 1968, Against All Odds, 1994; editor: Urban Librs. Coun. Exch., 1994—, The Charleston Report, 1996-99. Bd. dirs. So. Meth. U. Libr., 1992-98. Named Staff Mem. of Year San Francisco Pub. Libr., 1968 Mem. ALA, Calif. Libr. Assn. (council 1980-82), Calif. County Libr. Assn. (pres. 1984), L.A. County Mgmt. Assn. (pres. 1988). Home: 303 Mariner Dr Tarpon Springs FL 34689-5840

CRISP, FRED, retired publishing executive; m. Betty, Sept. 2, 1956; children: Michele Crisp Narron, Fred Durham III. Student, Mars Hill Coll., N.C.; BA, U. N.C. Advtsg. salesman Charlotte (N.C.) Observer, 1957-59, Virginian Pilot and Ledger Star, Norfolk, Va., 1959-68; advtsg. dir. The No. Va. Sun, Arlington, 1968-69; retail advtsg. mgr. The News and Observer Publ. Co., Raleigh, N.C., 1969-76, advtsg. dir., 1976-85, dir. sales, mktg., 1985-87, v.p. sales, mktg., 1987-90, v.p. gen. mgr., 1990-96, assoc. publ., 1996, pres., publ., 1997-2000. Mem. First Presbyn. Ch. Raleigh; bd. dirs. N.C. Citizens for Bus. and Industry, Vital Ctr. Alliance, Downtown Raleigh Alliance; past bd. dirs. Theatre in the Park, Wake County Boys' Club; past vice chmn. adv. bd. Salvation Army; mem. presdl. bd. advisors Mars Hill Coll.; bd. dirs. bd. vis. journalism and mass comm. U. N.C., v.p. Sch. Journalism and Mass Com. Found.; bd. trustees Peace Coll.; mem. Peace Coll. Found. Bd. Recipient Silver Medal awrd Am. Advtsg. Fedn., 1979; inducted to N.C. Advtsg. Hall of Fame, 1991. Mem. Am. Advtsg. Fedn. (past gov. N.C.), Internat. Newspaper Advtsg. and Mktg. Execs. (hon. life, past pres.), Mid-Atlantic Newspaper Advtsg. and Mktg. Execs. (hon. life), N.C. Retail Merchant Assn. (bd. advisors), N.C. Press Assn. (past pres.), Newspaper Assn. Am. (past mem. exec. bd.), Distributive Edn. Clubs Am. (hon. life), Mid-Atlantic Newspaper Advtsg. and Mktg. Execs. (past pres.), Triangle Advtsg. Fedn. (past pres.), Raleigh Sales and Mktg. Execs., Inc. (past bd. dirs.). Avocation: golf. Office: McClatchy Newspapers 215 S McDowell St PO Box 191 Raleigh NC 27602-9150

CRISP, SANDRA SUE, procurement analyst; b. Jefferson City, Sept. 13, 1941; d. William Frederick and Marguerite Walter (Wilson) Meyer; m. Samuel Henry White, Sept. 20, 1965 (div. Feb. 1982); 1 child, Janelle Lynn; m. Richard Leslie Crisp, Apr. 26, 1982. BSBA, Lincoln U., 1963; MS in Mgmt., Naval Postgrad. Sch., 1996. Missile components buyer McDonnell/Douglas Corp., St. Louis, 1977-78; contract specialist U.S. Army Aviation R&D Command, St. Louis, 1978-80; contracting officer U.S. Army Aviation Materiel Command, St. Louis, 1980-82; chief facilities and materials br. U.S. Army-Europe, Frankfort, Germany, 1982-83, chief host nations br., 1983-85; spl. tech. asst. to dir. comml. activities Asst. Sec. of Army for Installations, Logistics & Environ., Arlington, Va., 1985-87; spl. tech. asst. to U.S. Army Competition Adv. Gen. Asst. Sec. of Army for Rsch., Devel. and Acquisition, Arlington, 1987-92; dep. chief of staff for procurement, prin. asst. contracting U.S. Army Depot Sys. Command, Chambersberg, Pa., 1992-95; chief ammunition procurement divsn. U.S. Army Indsl. Ops. Command, Rock Island, Ill., 1995-98; chief acquisitions policy divsn. U.S. Army Ops. Support Command, Rock Island, Ill., 1999—2001, command ombudsman, competition advocate, 2002—. Mem. Nat. Contract Mgmt. Assn. (pres. Monterey chpt. 1995-96, edn. chair Quad City chpt. 1997-99), Nat. Def. Indsl. Assn. (bd. dirs. 1996—), U.S. Army Acquisition Corp. (sect. Army award for Professionalism in Contracting 1998), Women in Def. (founder, 1st pres. Ill.-Iowa chpt. 2001—). Avocations: volksmarching, needlework, gardening, reading. Home: 228 Longview Ct Geneseo IL 61254-9270 E-mail: crisps@osc.army.mil.

CRISPIN, ANDRE ARTHUR, international trading company executive; b. Brussels, Aug. 23, 1923; came to U.S., 1947; naturalized Am. citizen; m. Sylvia Clevenger; 5 children. Ed., U. Louvain, Belgium, 1943. V.p. Am. Supply and Equipment Co., Houston, 1947-48; chmn. Crispin Co., Houston, 1949—; hon. consul-gen. Belgium; ret. hon. consul-gen. Past chmn. bd. trustees so. region Inst. Internat. Edn.; mem. Citizens Environ. Coalition; past pres. Music Guild Houston; past chmn. bd. trustees Awty Internat. Sch., Houston; mem. internat. bd. Tex. A&M U., College Station. With Belgian Army, 1944-46. Decorated officier Ordre de Leopold II, Civic Cross 1st class, officier Ordre de Leopold ler (Belgium); chevalier Legion d'Honneur (France), Commdr.'s Cross Order of the Crown (Belgium), 1997; named one of 5 Outstanding Young Texans, 1953; recipient Houston Internat. Svc. award, 1986. Mem. Nat. Assn. Steel Pipe Distbrs. (past pres., bd. dirs.), Academie Internationale du Vin, Alliance Française de Houston (past pres., dir., exec. com.), Am. Inst. Imported Steel (past dir.), Commanderie de Bordeaux d'Amerique (grand maitre emeritus, gov.), Commanderie de Bordeaux du Texas à Houston (past maitre, commandeur), Commanderie du Bontemps, de Medoc et de Graves (France, commandeur d'honneur), German Wine Soc., Prodhomme, Jurade de St. Emilion Stylobate, Piliers Chablisiens, Compagnon de Loupiac, Echevin, Lussac Puisseguin St. Emilion, Lalande de Pomerol, Hospitaliers de Pomerol, Downtown Houston Assn., Belgian-Am. C. of C. (past bd. dirs.), French-Am. C. of C. (past pres. Houston chpt., dir.), Houston C. of C. (now named Greater Houston Partnership, bd. dirs. world trade divsn., internat. bus. com., past chmn.), Jr. C. of C. (internat. senator 2001), World Trade Assn. (past pres., dir.), Petroleum Club of Houston (past dir., past 1st v.p.). Home: One Crestwood Dr Houston TX 77007 Office: Crispin Co 2009 Lubbock St Houston TX 77007-7621

CRISPIN, PATRICIA LYNNETTE, social worker; b. Akron, Ohio, Apr. 29, 1969; d. Eddie Mae Robinson. BA, BA, Cleve. State U., Cleveland, OH, 1997; Masters Edn., Cleve. State Univeristy, Cleveland, OH, 2000. Intern East Cleve. Straight Talk, Cleveland, Ohio, 1996—96; instr. Urban League Cleve., Cleveland, Ohio, 1997—98, adminstrv. asst., 1997—98; spl. student asst. dean Cleve. State U. Dept. Student Life, Cleveland, Ohio, 1997—98; retention specialist Mt. Sinai Employment Moblzn., Cleveland, Ohio, 2000—01; program dir. Mt. Sinai Project Synergy, Cleveland, Ohio, 2001—01; staff asst. NASA, Cleveland, Ohio, 2001—01, SEMAA, Cleveland, Ohio, 2001—01, Tri-C, Cleveland, Ohio, 2001—01; americorp vista North East Ohio Coalition for the Homeless, Cleveland, Ohio, 2002—. Vol. coord. Cleve. State U. Black Studies Dept., Cleveland, Ohio, 1999—99, Rock N' Roll Hall of Fame, Cleveland, Ohio, 1999—99; event coord. Cleve. State U. Black Studies Dept., Cleveland, Ohio, 2000—01; notary pub. Nat. Assn. Notary Publics, Cleveland, Ohio, 2000—. Mem., sec., treas. Cleve. State U. NAACP Chpt., Cleveland, Ohio, 1989—97; advisor Cleve. State U. NAACP, Cleveland, Ohio, 1998—2001. Recipient Coloster B. Currant award, Nat. Hdqs. NAACP, 1993; scholar James Doodman scholarship, Cleve. State U., 1995, scholarship, Zeta Phi Beta Sorority Inc., 1999. Mem.: Cleve. State U. NAACP (advisor 1998—2001), Nat. Assn. Student Pers. Administrators, Order Ea. Star, Zeta Phi Beta Sorority Inc. (advisor 1998—2001, ednl. 2000). Christian. Avocations: writing, poetry, reading, entertainment business, planning events. Office: Ultimate Connexions PO Box 6792 Cleveland OH 44101 Personal E-mail: plcrispine@hotmail.com.

CRISS, CECIL M. chemistry educator; b. Wheeling, W.Va., Apr. 22, 1934; s. Cecil M. and Anna (Reece) C.; m. Laura Hopkins, Aug. 18, 1958; children: Cecil M. III, Laura Anna. AB, Kenyon Coll., 1956; PhD, Purdue U., 1961. Asst. prof. U. Vt., Burlington, 1961-65, U. Miami, Coral Gables, 1965-69, assoc. prof., 1970-75, prof., 1976—, chmn. dept., 1984—91, interim chmn. dept., 2002—. Vis. scientist U. Lund, Sweden, 1977-78; vis. prof. Calif. State Coll., San Diego, 1978; program officer NSF, Washington, 1982-83; vis. scholar U. Del., 1992. Recipient Fla. award Fla. Sect. Am. Chem. Soc. Mem. Am. Chem Soc., Sigma Xi, Phi Lambda Upsilon. Episcopalian. Home: 4910 San Amaro Dr Coral Gables FL 33146-1632 Office: Dept Chemistry U Miami Coral Gables FL 33124 E-mail: ccriss@umiami.ir.miami.edu.

CRISSEY, HARRINGTON E., JR., English as second language educator; b. Schenectady, N.Y., Feb. 21, 1945; s. Harrington Edgar and Ruth Evelyn (Stone) C.; m. Yelena Lvovna Sergeeva, June 19, 1992. BA, U. Rochester, 1966; MEd, Temple U., 1974. Instr. Temple U., Phila., 1974—79, Nationalities Svc. Ctr., Phila., 1980—84, Phila., 1984—86, 1989—91; instr. evening sch. New World Assn., Phila., 1985—; instr. Arcadia U., Glenside, Pa., 1986—87, Sch. Dist. Phila., 1987—89, English Lang. Svcs., St. Joseph's U., Phila., 1991—. V.p. Composer Svcs., Inc., Phila., 1990—; pub.'s liaison Penn TESOL-East, Phila., 1992—, pres., 2002—03. Author: (book) Teenagers, Graybeards, and 4-Fs, vol. 1, 1981, Teenagers, Graybeards, and 4-Fs, vol. 2, 1982, Athletes Away, 1984; contbr. articles to mags. and periodicals; presenter: concerts of solo and chamber music. Comdr. USNR, 1963—93. Recipient Sportsters award, Sportsters Club, 1984, Achievement award, Phila. chpt. Am. Composers Forum, 2000. Mem.: Internat. Horn Soc., Soc. for Am. Baseball Rsch. (pres. 1980—82). Presbyterian. Avocations: classical music, sports, history, geography, military and concert band research. Home: 7439 Elizabeth Rd Elkins Park PA 19027-3322 Office: English Lang Svcs 5414 Overbrook Ave Philadelphia PA 19131 Fax: 215-473-3220.

CRISSMAN, JOHN D. dean, physician; b. Detroit, Feb. 3, 1939; children: John, Allison. SBME, MIT, 1961; MD, Western Res. U., 1966. Physician U. Cin., 1974-81, Wayne State U., Detroit, 1981-87, Henry Ford Hosp., Detroit, 1987-90; prof., chmn. dept. pathology Wayne State U., Detroit, 1990—; interim dean Wayne St. Univ. Sch. of Med., 1999—2000, dean, 2000—. Chief pathologist Detroit Med. Ctr. Hosps., 1990—2000. Capt. USAF, 1968—70.

CRIST, BAINBRIDGE, volunteer; b. Boston, Dec. 19, 1916; s. Lucien Bainbridge and Florence Libbey Crist; m. Elizabeth Green, Ag. 26, 1944 (dec. Aug. 1963); children: Anne Whitaker, William Bainbridge; m. Madeleine Mercier, May 16, 1964 (dec. Jan. 1994). BS, Harvard Coll., 1939. Reporter Washington Star, 1939-45; assoc. editor Nat. Aeronautics, Washington, 1945-46; Washington corr. Tide, Washington, 1946-50; chief Trade Press, news divsn. Office Price Stabilization, Washington, 1951; mem. staff, then v.p. Newmyer Assocs., Washington, 1951-74. Bd. mem. Legal Aid Soc., Washington, 1960-62; pres. South Yarmouth (Mass.) Libr., 1981-94; mem. Yarmouth Hist. Commn., 1979-81. Mem. Bass River Yacht Club (chmn. membership com. 1997—2003), Hyannis Yacht Club (assoc.), Harvard Club (sec. Washington 1964-73), Hist. Soc. Old Yarmouth (pres. 1980-83), Cape Islands Hist. Assn. (pres. 1986-90), Harvard Alumni Assn. (regional dir. 1980-83). Democrat. Home: Apt 160 579 Buck Island Rd West Yarmouth MA 02673-3225

CRIST, CHARLES (CHARLIE CRIST), state attorney general; b. Altoona, Pa., July 24, 1956; Student, Wake Forest U., 1974-76; BS in Govt., minor in edn., Fla. State U., 1978; JD, Samford U., 1981. Mem. Fla. State Senate, Tallahassee, 1992—98; dep. sec. Fla. Dept. Bus. and Profl. Regulation, 1999—2000; atty. gen. State of Fla., 2003—. Mem. Subcom. D. Criminal Justice Ways and Means Com., 1996-98, Judiciary Com., 1996-98, Govtl. Reform and Oversight Com., 1996-98, Criminal Justice Com., 1996-98; chmn. Exec. Bus., Ethics and Elections Com., 1996-98; former state dir. U.S. Sen. Connie Mack; chmn. anti-trust adv. com. Sen. Connie Mack's Baseball Anti-Trust Adv. Com.; mem. Sen. Connie Mack's Fed. Jud. Adv. Com.; mem. ethics com. Fla. Bar. Mem. Pinellas County Rep. Exec. Com., Area Agy. on Bay Mgmt.; mem. adminstrv. bd. First United Meth. Ch.; mem. Booster Fla. State U.; bd. dirs. Found. for Fla.'s Future, Op. PAR, Police Athletic League; mem. adv. com. Tampa Bay MDA. Recipient Phil Piton award for svc. Major League Baseball, Leadership St. Petersburg, Roll Call award Fla. C. of C., 1993, PACE award, 1993, Legis. award Pinellas Sch. Adminstrs., 1993, Fla. Assn. Sch. Adminstrs., 1993, Fla. Sheriffs Assn., 1994, 96, Govt. award Urban League, 1995, Senatorial Leadership award Fla. Prosecuting Attys. Assn., 1995, Legis. Conservation award Fla. Conservation Assn., 1996, Disting. Legislator award Fla. Police Benevolent Assn., 1996; named Conservationist Legislator of Yr. Fla. Wildlife Fedn., 1995, Legislator of Yr. Police Benevolent Assn., 1995, Hon. Sheriff, 1995. Fellow Am. Swiss Assn.; mem. ABA, Am. Lung Assn. (mem. pres.'s coun. Pinellas County), Fla. Conservation Assn., St. Petersburg C. of C., Pinellas Pk. C. of C., Hillsborough Bar Assn., St. Petersburg Bar Assn., Rep. Nat. Lawyers Assn. (bd. govs.), Suncoasters Civic Club, Rotary, Suncoast Tiger Bay Club (bd. dirs., True Grit award). Republican. Methodist. Avocations: water skiing, reading, jogging. Office: Office of Atty Gen State of Fla The Capitol PL-01 Tallahassee FL 32399*

CRIST, CHRISTINE MYERS, consulting executive; b. Harrisburg, Pa., Feb. 5, 1924; d. John Eyster and Eunice Horton (Ingham) Myers; m. Robert Grant Crist, June 25, 1949; children: Catherine Ingham Crist Marcson, Jessica Rogers Crist, Robert Jeffrey Myers Crist. BA, Dickinson Coll., 1946. Reporter The Patriot, Harrisburg, Pa., 1946-49; editor West Shore Times, Lemoyne, Pa., 1964-65; adminstr. arts in edn. Pa. Dept. Edn., Harrisburg, 1974-77, dir. leadership in arts edn., 1977-79; press sec. gov.'s office Pa. Commn. for Women, Harrisburg, 1980-83, dir. Gov.'s Commn. for Women, 1983-87; exec. dir. com. for women Evang. Luth. Ch. in Am., Chgo., 1987-90; ptnr. Crist and Crist, Cons., Camp Hill, Pa., 1990—. Mem. State Employees Retirement Bd., 1986-88; state coord. We the People Edn. Program. Editor: Song As A Measure of Man, 1975 (excellent pub. 1975). Mem. Camp Hill (Pa.) Sch. Bd., 1967-73, Capital Area Intermediate Bd., Lemoyne, Pa., 1970-73; pres. Camp Hill (Pa.) Civic Club, 1970-72, women's orgn. Trinity Lutheran Ch., 1999; chair Ch. in Society, Lower Susquehanna Synod, Evang. Lutheran Ch. in Am.; mem. coun. Trinity Congregation, 1991-94; mem. Harrisburg Choral Soc., Dickinson Alumni Coun., 1992—; bd. dirs. Women's Polit. Network Pa., Camp Hill Cmty. Found., 1996—; mem. candidacy bd. Lutheran Ch., 1992—; Pa. bd. Common Cause, 1997—. Recipient Women in Comms. Freedom of Info. award, 1982, Great Commicators award, 1985, Pa. Women's History award, Pa. Com. for Women, 2003. Mem. Monday Club, Cumberland County Fedn. Women's Clubs (pres. 1996—). Lutheran. Home and Office: Crist and Crist 1915 Walnut St Camp Hill PA 17011-3854

CRIST, GERTRUDE H. civic worker; b. Barnard, S.D. d. Jacob H. and Lillian Belle (Freeman) Hartman; m. Howard Grafton Crist, Jr., Nov. 2, 1940; children: Howard Grafton III, Douglas Freeman. Student, S.D. State Coll., 1936-38. Owner, ptnr. Farm and Home Svc. Chmn. Westmoreland County chpt. ARC, 1946, sec., 1943-45, chmn. vol. spl. svcs., 1944-45; dist. chmn. Cancer drive Howard County; mem. Howard County Bd. Edn., 1953-70, pres., 1963-65; bd. dirs. Howard County Tb Assn.; adv. coun. Catonsville C.C., 1962-70; chmn. Emergency Civil Def. Hosp. Howard County, 1961-62; sec. Cmty. Action Coun. Howard County, 1965, dir., 1966; bd. dirs. Girl Scout Coun. Ctrl. Md., 1967-68; mem. Md. Coun. Higher Edn., 1968-76, State Bd. for C.Cs., 1968-77; trustee Howard C.C., 1966-71, v.p., 1969-70; bd. dirs. Howard County chpt. ARC, 1973-77, v.p., 1976-77; mem. Md. Bd. for Higher Edn., 1977-86, Howard County Comm. on Arts, 1975-77; v.p. Farm and Home Svc., Inc., 1968-78. Mem. LWV (county sec. 1957-59, dir. 1960-62, pres. 1959), Nat. Sch. Bds. Assn. (dir. 1968-71), Nat. Congress Parents and Tchrs. (hon. life mem.), Md.

Congress Parents and Tchrs. (life), Md. Assn. Bds. Edn. (pres. 1966, 67), W. Friendship PTA (sec. 1949-51), Delta Kappa Gamma (hon. Alpha Beta State and Lambda chpts.), Cattail River Garden Club. Episcopalian (vestryman, chmn. parish day sch. bd. 1970-73). Home: Fairhaven C-87 7200 Third Ave Sykesville MD 21784

CRIST, JUDITH, film and drama critic; b. N.Y.C., May 22, 1922; d. Solomon and Helen (Schoenberg) Klein; m. William B. Crist, July 3, 1947 (dec. Apr. 1993); 1 son, Steven Gordon. AB, Hunter Coll., 1941; tchg. fellow, State Coll. Wash., 1942-43; MSc in Journalism, Columbia, 1945; DHL (hon.), SUNY, New Paltz, 1994. Civilian instr. 3081st Army AFB Unit, 1943-44; reporter N.Y. Herald Tribune, 1945-60, editor arts, 1960-63, assoc. theater critic, 1957-63, film critic, 1963-66; film, theater critic NBC-TV Today Show, 1963-73; film critic World Jour. Tribune, 1966-67; critic-at-large Ladies Home Jour., 1966-67; contbg. editor and film critic TV Guide, 1966-88; founding film critic N.Y. mag., 1968-75; film critic The Washingtonian, 1970-72, Palm Springs Life, 1971-75; contbg. editor, film critic Saturday Rev., 1975-77, 80-84, N.Y. Post, 1977-78, MD/Mrs., 1977—, 50 Plus, 1978-83, L'Officiel/USA, 1979-80; arts critic Sta. WWOR-TV, 1981-87; critical columnist for Coming Attractions, 1985-93; cons. editor Hollywood Mag., 1985-93; contbg. editor Columbia Mag., 1993-95. Instr. journalism Hunter Coll., 1947, Sarah Lawrence Coll., 1958-59; assoc. journalism Columbia Grad. Sch. Journalism, 1958 62, lectr. journalism, 1962-64, adj. prof., 1964—. Author: The Private Eye, The Cowboy and the Very Naked Girl, 1968, Judith Crist's TV Guide to the Movies, 1974, Take 22: Moviemakers on Moviemaking, 1984, rev. edit., 1991; contbr. articles to nat. mags. Trustee Anne O'Hare McCormick Scholarship Fund. Named to 50th Anniversary Honors List, Columbia Grad. Sch. Journalism, 1963, Hunter Alumni Hall of Fame, Hunter Coll., 1973; recipient Page One award, N.Y. Newspaper Guild, 1955, George Polk award, 1950, Newswomen's Club of N.Y. award, 1955, 1959, 1963, 1965, 1967, Edn. Writers Assn. award, 1952, Alumni award, Columbia Grad. Sch. Journalism, 1961, Centennial Pres.'s medal, Hunter Coll., 1970, Hall of Fame award for outstanding profl. achievement, 2003, Grad. Sch. Journalism's Faculty and Alumni award, Columbia U., 1998, Univ. Alumni medal, Fedn. for Conspicuous Svc., 2003. Mem.: Soc. of the Silurians, Columbia Journalism Alumni Exec. Com. (pres. 1967—70), Sigma Tau Delta. Office: 180 Riverside Dr New York NY 10024-1048 *Care about people-not things.*

CRIST, PAUL GRANT, lawyer; b. Denver, Sept. 9, 1949; s. Max Warren and Marjorie Raymond (Catland) C.; m. Christine Faye Clements, June 4, 1972; children: Susan Christine, Benjamin Warren, John Willis. BA, U. Nebr., 1971; JD cum laude, NYU, 1974. Bar: Ohio 1974, U.S. Ct. Mil. Appeals 1975, Calif. 1976, U.S. Dist. Ct. (no. dist.) Ohio 1979, U.S. Ct. Appeals (6th cir.) 1982, U.S. Dist. Ct. (no., ea., so. and ctrl. dists.) Calif. 2003, U.S. Ct. Appeals (9th cir.) 2003. Assoc. Jones, Day, Reavis & Pogue, Cleve., 1974, 78-83, ptnr., 1984—. Rsch. editor NYU Law Rev., 1972-74. Capt. JAGC, USAF, 1974-78. Decorated Meritorious Svc. medal. Fellow Am. Coll. Trial Lawyers; mem. Ohio State Bar Assn., Cleve. Bar Assn., State Bar Calif., Order of Coif, Am. Inns of Ct. Democrat. Presbyterian. Home: 3003 Hillside Dr Burlingame CA 94010 Office: Jones Day 555 California St 26th Fl San Francisco CA 94104

CRIST, STEPHEN ALAN, music educator; b. Winston-Salem, N.C., Apr. 24, 1957; s. Donald Ralph and Eugenia Schultz Crist; m. Susan Ann Jesitus, Aug. 19, 1978; children: Caitlin Nicole Ruth, Hannah Rebecca. AB, Harvard U., 1978; MusM, U. South Fla., 1980; PhD, Brandeis U., 1988. Instr. musicology New Coll., Sarasota, Fla., 1983—86; asst. prof. music Geneva Coll., Beaver Falls, Pa., 1986—90; asst. prof. music history Emory U., Atlanta, 1990—96, assoc. prof. music history, 1996—, chair music, 2003—. Editor: (book) Bach in America, Historical Musicology: Sources, Methods, Interpretations; author: Enchiridion Geistliker Leder vnde Psalmen, Magdeburg 1536: Introductory Study and Facsimile Edition. Recipient Disting. Alumnus Award for Outstanding Svc. to the Arts, Coll. Fine Arts, U. South Fla., 2001; grantee, German Academic Exch. Svc., 1982—83; Univ. Tchrs. fellow, NEH, 1993—94. Mem.: Soc. for Seventeenth-Century Music, Riemenschneider Bach Inst., Neue Bachgesellschaft, Forum on Music and Christian Scholarship (chair steering com. 2002—), Coll. Music Soc., Bach Colloquium (mem. program com. 1999—), Am. Musicological Soc. (chair local arrangements com. 2001), Am. Bach Soc. (sec.-treas. 1996—2000, William H. Scheide Rsch. fellow 1998). Avocations: hiking, backpacking. Office: Dept Music Emory Univ Atlanta GA 30322 Office Fax: 404-727-0074.

CRIST, WILLIAM GARY, artist, retired educator; b. Pocatello, Idaho, Jan. 17, 1937; s. Margaret Alice (Zimmerman) C.; 1 child, Julie Anne. BA in Art Edn., U. Wash., 1966, postgrad., 1966-69; MFA in Sculpture, Cranbrook Acad. Art, Detroit, 1971; student, Staatliche Kunstakademie, Dusseldorf, West Germany, 1981, 83. Tchr. Mt. Si High Sch., Snoqualmie, Wash., 1966-69; instr. Bellevue (Wash.) C.C., 1967-69; asst. prof. Wesleyan Coll., Macon, Ga., 1971-72; instr. Cameron U., Lawton, Okla, 1972-74; asst. prof. art U. Mo., Kansas City, 1974-78, assoc. prof., 1978-88, prof., 1988-2000, prof. emeritus, 2000—. Vol. art tchr. St. Helens (Oreg.) Sch. Dist., 2003—; cons. Wayne (Nebr.) State Coll., 1987, Ctrl. Mo. State U., Warrensburg, 1985, Spelman Coll., Atlanta, 1984, U. Akron, Ohio, 1984; part-time art instr. Portland (Oreg.) C.C., 2003—. Creator computer art, exhibited in shows at Pleiades Gallery, N.Y.C., 1992, 3d Nat., Phoenix, 1992, 31st Nat., Ft. Collins, Colo., 1992, Images '92, Highland, Kans., 1992, Columbia Ctr., St. Helens, Oreg., 2000. Served as sgt. U.S. Army, 1959-62, Korea. Rockefeller/Nat. Endowment Arts interdisciplinary arts fellow, 1986; U. Mo. grantee, 1981, 82, 92, 99. Avocations: outdoor activities, boating, hiking. Office: U Mo Kansas City Dept Art 51st and Holmes Kansas City MO 64110

CRIST, WILLIAM MILES, dean, physician; b. Florence, S.C., July 21, 1943; s. Harry Brogan and Rosemary (Reid) C.; m. Helen Lucille Valle, June 5, 1971; 1 child, Brian. BA cum laude, Cen. Meth. Coll., 1965; MD, U. Mo., 1969. Intern in pediatrics Mott Children's Hosp., Ann Arbor, Mich., 1969-70; resident fellow in pediatrics and pediatric hematology St. Louis Children's Hosp., 1971-72; trainee Nat. Cancer Inst. Wash. U. Sch. Medicine, St. Louis, 1974-75; asst. prof. pediatrics U. Ala., Birmingham, 1975-78; assoc. scientist Comprehensive Cancer Ctr. U. Ala., Birmingham, 1975-78; acting dir., then dir. hematology/oncology Children's Hosp. U. Ala., Birmingham, 1976-85; prof. pediatrics, dir. pediatrics, hematology/oncology U. Tenn., Memphis, 1985—2000; chmn. dept. hematology/oncology St. Jude Children's Rsch. Hosp., Memphis, 1985—94, dep. dir., 1994—2000; dean U. of Missouri-Columbia Sch. of Med., 2000—; chair dept. pediats. and adolescent medicine Mayo Clinic, Rochester. Chair dept. pediats. and adolescent medicine Mayo Clinic, Rochester, Minn.; mem. Children's Oncology Group, 1976—. Maj. USAF, 1972-74. Mem. Am. Soc. Hematology, Sigma Epsilon Pi, Omicron Delta Kappa. Office: St Jude Children's Rsch Hosp 332 N Lauderdale St Memphis TN 38105-2729 also: U of Missouri Columbia Sch of Med One Hospital Dr Columbia MO 65212

CRISTE, VIRGINIA SPIEGEL, lawyer; b. Chgo., Feb. 7, 1944; d. Gerhard and Hilde (Fabian) S.; m. Michael A. Criste, Feb. 7, 1970 (div. Dec. 1995); m. Larry Allen, May 20, 2000; children: Michael J., Julia. BA, Mt. Holyoke Coll., 1966; JD, George Washington U., 1969. Bar: Calif. 1977, D.C. 1969, Md. 1971, Pa. 1976, U.S. Dist. Ct. (mid. dist.) Pa., U.S. Dist. Ct. Md., U.S. Dist. Ct. (ctrl. dist.) Calif., U.S. Ct. Appeals (D.C. and 9th cirs.). Atty. Neighborhood Legal Svcs., Washington, 1969—71; assoc. county atty. Prince George's County, Md., 1971-74; sr. atty. Ctrl. Pa. Legal Svcs., Lancaster, 1974-79, Inland Counties Legal Svcs., Indio, Calif., 1979-81; assoc. Robert Stewart Law Corp., Palm Desert, Calif., 1981-84; ptnr. Mack, Kahn, Criste, Palm Springs, Calif., 1984-86, Criste Criste & Pippin, Palm Desert, 1991-94; sole practitioner Palm Desert, 1982-84, Rancho Mirage, Calif., 1986-91, 94—. Mem. Parks and Recreation Commn., Palm Desert, 1994-97. Mem. ABA, Desert Bar Assn. (trustee to pres. 1990-97). Avocations: historical research, musical theater. Home: 44047 Erie Ct Indian Wells CA 92210-7200 Office: 45200 Club Dr # B Indian Wells CA 92210-8860 E-mail: vcriste@aol.com.

CRISTEA SALBERG, RICHARD LITZ, neurologist, health facility administrator; b. Valparaiso, Ind., July 3, 1962; s. Jo Ann Litz; m. Lauri L. Leviton, May 21, 1994; children: Lexi, Liza, Zachary. BA in Biology, Ind. U., 1984; MD, Chgo. Med. Sch., 1988. Intern, resident in internal medicine Rush-Presbyn.-St. Luke's Med. Ctr., Chgo., 1988-89; resident in neurology Cleve. Clinic Found., 1989-92, adj. staff dept. neurology, 1994; v.p. No. Ind. Neurol. Inst., Merriville, 1992—, dir. electromyography, 1992—; v.p., dir. environ. toxicology Hemisphere Corp., Cleve., 1994—. Mem. med. adv. bd. N.W. Ind. chpt. Lupus Found. Am., Inc., 1993—, mem. edn. com., 1995—; lectr. Contbr. articles to profl. jours. Traveling fellow Ronald and Patti Rosenfeld Internat., 1992. Fellow Stroke Coun. Am. Heart Assn., Am. Assn. Electrodiagnostic Medicine; mem. AMA, ACP, Am. Acad. Neurology, Am. Soc. Neurorehabilitation, Nat. Headache Found., Ind. State Med. Soc., Lake County Med. Soc. Avocations: golf, food, wine. Office: No Ind Neurol Inst 521 E 86th Ave Merrillville IN 46410-6173

CRISTESCU, NICOLAIE DAN, engineering educator; b. Chelmenti, Romania, Feb. 17, 1929; married; 1 child. Diplomat, Bucharest U., Romania, 1951, docent, 1967; PhD, Romanian Acad., 1955. Asst. prof. U. Bucharest, Romania, 1951-55, lectr., 1955-57, assoc. prof., 1957-66, prof., 1966-92, dept. chmn., 1982-90, pres., 1990-92; vis. grad. rsch. prof. U. Fla., 1970-76, grad. rsch. prof. dept. aerospace engring. mechanics and engring. sci., 1992—. Vis. prof. Johns Hopkins U., Balt., 1968-69, Drexel U., Phila., 1969; lectr. in field. Author: Dynamic Problems in Theory of Plasticity, 1958, The Mechanics of Extensible Strings, 1964, Dynamic Plasticity, 1967, 70 (in Japanese), Introduction to Rate-Dependent Plasticity (A Dynamic Approach), 1971, Rock Mechanics, 1983, 2d edit., 1984, supplemental 1988, Mechanics of Composite Materials, 1983, Rock Rheology, 1989, Rock Mechanics-Rheology Aspects, 1990, Rock Viscoplasticity, 1992, Viscoplasticity of Geomaterials, 1994, (with I. Suliciu) Viscoplasticity, 1976, 82, (with S. Cleja-Tigolu) Theory of Plasticity with Application to Metal Working, 1985, (with U. Hunsche) Time Effects in Rock Mechanics, 1998, (with E.M. Craciun and E. Soos) Mechanics of Elastic Composites, 2003; contbr. articles to profl. jours.; sr. editor: Internat. Jour. Plasticity; mem. editl. bd. Internat. Jour. Mechanical Sci., Mechanics Rsch. Comm., Mechanics of Cohesive-Frictional Materials and Structures, others. Fellow Romanian Acad., Acad. Europaea; mem. ASME (Arpad L. Nadai award 1995), Soc. Scholars, Internat. Soc. Interaction of Mechanics and Maths. (founder), Am. Rock Mechanics Assn. (founder), Am. Acad. Mechanics, Soc. Exptl. Stress Analysis, Group Français de Rheology, Internat. Assn. Computer Methods and Advances in Geomechanics, Internat. Soc. Rock Mechanics, Tau Beta Pi, Sigma Xi. Achievements include research in mechanics of solid deformable bodies, theory of plasticity, rheology, rock and soil mechanics, mechanics of powder-like materials. Office: U Fla 231 Aerospace Bldg PO Box 116250 Gainesville FL 32611-6250 Fax: 352-392-7303. E-mail: ndc@mae.ufl.edu.

CRISTIANO, MARILYN JEAN, speech communication educator; b. New Haven, Jan. 10, 1954; d. Michael William and Mary Rose (Porto) C. BA, Marquette U., 1975, MA, 1977; postgrad., Ariz. State U., 1977; EdD, Nova Southeastern U., 1991. Speech comm. instr. Phoenix Coll., 1977-87, Paradise Valley C.C., Phoenix, 1987—. Presenter at profl. confs., workshops and seminars, comm. and humanities divsn. chair, Paradise Valley Cmty. Coll. Author tng. manual on pub. speaking, 1991, 92, 95, 97, 99, 2002. Named Technology Tchr. of Yr. for Ariz. Cmty. Colls., CCS Presentation Systems and Proxima Corp., 2000. Mem. Nat. Comm. Assn., Western Speech Comm. Assn., Ariz. Comm. Assn. Avocation: digital photography. Office: Paradise Valley CC 18401 N 32nd St Phoenix AZ 85032-1210

CRISTOL, A. JAY, federal judge; b. Fountain Hill, Pa., Feb. 25, 1929; s. Samuel and Mae (Stein) C.; m. Eleanor Rubin; children: Stephen Michael, David Alan. BA, U. Miami, 1958, LLB, 1959, PhD, 1997. Bar: Fla. 1959. Spl. asst. to Atty. Gen. of Fla., Tallahassee, 1959-65; sr. ptnr. Cristol, Mishan, Sloto, Miami, 1959-85; judge U.S. Bankruptcy Ct., Miami, 1985-93, chief judge, 1994-99, trustee, 1982-84, chief judge emeritus, 1999—. Adj. prof. U. Miami Law Sch.; bd. govs. 11th cir. Nat. Conf. Bankruptcy Judges; bankruptcy rules adv. com. Jud. Conf. of U.S., 1995-2001; bankruptcy com. U.S. Ct. Appeals (11th cir.), 1996-2002; tchr. bankruptcy law to judges in Czech Republic, Slovenia, Thailand, Russia, India, Malaysia, Hong Kong, South Africa. Bd. trustees U. Miami, 1988-90, Coral Gables; bd. dirs. ARC, Miami, 1989—, Wings Over Miami Aviation Mus., 2001—. Capt. USNR, 1951-89. Fellow Am. Coll. Bankruptcy; mem. ABA, Am. Bankruptcy Inst., Nat. Conf. Bankruptcy Judges, Bankruptcy Bar Assn. (so. dist. of Fla.), Fla. Bar Assn., Dade County Bar Assn. Avocations: water skiing, windsurfing, flying, reading. Office: US Bankruptcy Ct 1412 Fed Bldg 51 SW 1st Ave Miami FL 33130-1669

CRISTOL, STANLEY JEROME, chemistry educator; b. Chgo., June 14, 1916; s. Myer J. and Lillian (Young) C.; m. Barbara Wright Swingle, June 1957; children: Marjorie Jo, Jeffrey Tod. BS, Northwestern U., 1937; MA, UCLA, 1939, PhD, 1943. Rsch. chemist Std. Oil Co., Calif., 1938-41; rsch. fellow U. Ill., 1943-44; rsch. chemist U.S. Dept. Agr., 1944-46; asst. prof., then assoc. prof. U. Colo., 1946-55, prof., 1955—, Joseph Sewall Disting. prof., 1979—, chmn. dept. chemistry, 1960-62, grad. dean, 1980-81. Vis. prof. Stanford U., summer 1961, U. Geneva, 1975, U. Lausanne, Switzerland, 1981; with OSRD, 1944-46; adv. panels NSF, 1957-63, 69-73, NIH, 1969-72 Author: (with L.O. Smith, Jr.) Organic Chemistry, 1966; editorial bd., Chem. Revs., 1957-59, Jour. Organic Chemistry, 1964-68; contbr. rsch. articles to sci. jours. Guggenheim fellow, 1955-56, 81, 82; recipient James Flack Norris award in phys.-organic chemistry, 1972, Alumni Merit award Northwestern U., 1987. Fellow AAAS (councilor 1986-92); mem. NAS, AAUP, Am. Chem. Soc. (chmn. organic chemistry div. 1961-62, adv. bd. petroleum rsch. fund 1963-66, coun. policy com. 1968-73), Colo.-Wyo. Acad. Sci., Royal Soc. Chemistry, Phi Beta Kappa, Sigma Xi, Phi Lambda Upsilon. Home: 2918 3d St Boulder CO 80304-3041 Office: U Colo Dept Chemistry-Biochemistry Cb 215 Boulder CO 80309-0215 E-mail: stanley.cristol@colorado.edu.

CRISWELL, ELEANOR CAMP, psychologist; b. Norfolk, Va., May 12, 1938; d. Norman Harold Camp and Eleanor (Talman) David; m. Thomas L. Hanna. BA, U. Ky., 1961, MA, 1962; EdD, U. Fla., 1969. Asst. prof. edn. Calif. State Coll., Hayward, 1969; prof. psychology, former chair Calif. State U., Sonoma, 1969—. Faculty adviser Humanistic Psychology Inst., San Francisco, 1970-77; dir. Novato Inst. Somatic Rsch. and Tng.; editor Somatics jour.; cons. Venturi, Inc., Autogenic Sys., Inc.; clin. dir. Biotherapeutics, Kentfield Med. Hosp., 1985-90; founder Humanistic Psychology Inst., 1970. Author: How Yoga Works, 1987, Biofeedback and Somatics, 1995; co-editor: Biofeedback and Family Practice Medicine, 1983; patentee optokinetic perceptual learning device. Mem. APA (past pres. divsn. 32), Biofeedback Soc. Calif. (past pres.), Assn. for Humanistic Psychology (past pres.), Somatic Soc. (pres.), Equine Hanna Somatics (founder). Office: Sonoma State U Psychology Dept 1801 E Cotati Ave Rohnert Park CA 94928-3609 E-mail: criswell@sonoma.edu.

CRISWELL, KIMBERLY ANN, executive coach, communications consultant, performing artist; b. L.A., Dec. 6, 1957; d. Robert Burton and Carolyn Joyce (Semko) C. BA with honors, U. Calif., Santa Cruz, 1980; postgrad., Stanford U., 1993-94, Coaches Tng. Inst., 2000. Cert. profl. co-active coach. Instr. English Lang. Svcs., Oakland, Calif., 1980-81; freelance writer Verbum mag., San Diego, 1986, Gambit mag., New Orleans, 1981; instr. Tulane U., New Orleans, 1981; instr., editor Haitian-English Lang. Program, New Orleans, 1981-82; instr. Delgado Coll., New Orleans, 1982-83; instr., program coord. Vietnamese Youth Ctr., San Francisco, 1984; dancer Khadra Internat. Folk Ballet, San Francisco, 1984-89; dir. mktg. comm. Centram Sys. West, Inc., Berkeley, Calif., 1984-87; comm. coord. Safeway Stores, Inc., Oakland, 1985; dir. corp. comm. TOPS divsn. Sun Microsystems, Inc., 1987-88; pres. Criswell Comm., 1988—. Dir. corp. comm. CyberGold, Inc., Berkeley, 1996-97; co-founder, v.p. Conferenza, Inc., 1998-99. Vol. coord. Friends of Haitians, 1981, editor, writer newsletter, 1981; dancer Komenka Ethnic Dance Ensemble, New Orleans, 1983; mem. Contemp. Art Ctr.'s Krewe of Clones, New Orleans, 1983, Americans for Nonsmokers Rights, Berkeley, 1985. Mem. Mem. Sci. Meets the Arts Soc. (founding). Democrat. Avocations: visual arts, travel, creative writing.

CRITCHFIELD, SCOTT A. investment broker; b. Defiance, Ohio, Dec. 20, 1962; s. HH and Hilary (Moore) C.; m. Kathryn Barker, May 30, 1992; children: Thomas, Sarah, Anne. BS in BA, Valparaiso (Ind.) U., 1986. CFP. Floor salesperson Bachrach, Decatur, Ill., 1986-87, auditor, 1987-88, catalog mgr., 1988; ins. salesperson United Trust, Springfield, Ill., 1988-90, tng. dir., 1990-96; assoc. v.p., new broker trainer A.G. Edwards, St. Louis, 1996—2002, FC bus. devel. coach, 2002—. V.p. Roosevelt Equity, Springfield, 1992-96, fin. prin., 1992-96, bd. dirs., 1993-96. Vocal soloist Nat. Ch., Washington, 1991, Powell Hall, St. Louis, 1982, Opera House, Chgo., 1982, Air Force Acad. Cathedral, Boulder, Colo., 1983. Mem. Inst. of Cert. Fin. Planners. Avocations: sailing, skiing, travel, tennis, singing. Home: 1229 Du Motier Dr Ballwin MO 63011-3612 Office: AG Edwards & Son 100 N Jefferson Ave Saint Louis MO 63103-2207

CRITCHLOW, CHARLES HOWARD, lawyer; b. Morristown, NJ, Nov. 23, 1950; s. George F. and Florence Critchlow; m. Mary Ellen Donnelly (dec.); children: Katharine F., Mary E.G. BA, Yale U., 1972; JD, Columbia U., 1975. Bar: N.Y. 1976, U.S. Dist. Ct. (so. and ea. dists.) N.Y. 1976, U.S. Ct. Appeals (2d cir.) 1982, U.S. Ct. Appeals (3d and 10th cirs.) 1991, U.S. Supreme Ct. 1993, U.S. Ct. Appeals (5th cir.) 1994, U.S. Ct. Appeals (4th cir.) 1995, U.S. Ct. Internat. Trade 1996, U.S. Ct. Appeals (Fed. Cir.) 1996. Assoc. Lord, Day & Lord, N.Y.C., 1975-85, ptnr., 1985-86, Coudert Bros. LLP, N.Y.C., 1986—. Contbr. to Antitrust Law Developments; contbr. articles to profl. jours. Active Yale Alumni Fund; mem. Yale Alumni Schs. Com. Mem.: ABA. Office: Coudert Bros LLP 1114 Avenue of the Americas New York NY 10036-7703 E-mail: critchlowc@coudert.com., ccbk91@aol.com.

CRITELLI, MICHAEL J. lawyer, manufacturing executive; b. 1948; BA, U. Wis., 1970; JD, Harvard U., 1974. Bar: Ill. 1974, N.Y. 1982. Assoc. Ross & Hardies, Chgo., 1974-76, Schwartz & Freeman, Chgo., 1976-79; counsel Pitney Bowes, Inc., 1979-83, sr. counsel, 1983-84, asst. gen. counsel, 1984-86, assoc. gen. counsel, 1986-88, v.p., sec., gen. counsel, 1988, chief pers. officer, 1990-94, vice chmn., 1994—, chmn., CEO, 1996—. Office: Pitney Bowes Inc 1 Elmcroft Rd Stamford CT 06926-0700

CRITES, CARL D. auditor; b. Cushing, Okla., Aug. 13, 1956; s. Paul W. and Anna F. Crites; m. Sue B. Britton, Dec. 20, 1986; 1 child, Courtney B. BS in Elec. Engring. Tech., Okla. State U., 1986; MS in Mgmt., So. Nazarene U., 1994; MBA, Okla. City U., 1998. Audio visual technician White Ho. Comm. Agy., Washington, 1975—78; sound technician Tele-Hifi, Tulsa, 1980—84; sr. assoc. systems engr. E-Sytems/ETAG, Fairfax, Va., 1987—89; systems engr./paws support team leader Eagle Tech., Fairfax, 1989—92; v.p. Okla. ops. Potomac Systems Engring., Oklahoma City, 1992—95; staff engr. BDM Internat., Oklahoma City, 1995—97; yr. 2000 project mgr. U. Okla., Norman, 1997—99; sr. assoc. PricewaterhouseCoopers, Oklahoma City, 1999—2001; info. systems audit supr. The Hertz Corp., Oklahoma City, 2001—. Bd. dirs. Mid. Earth Child Devel. Ctr., Norman, Okla., 1996—99, mem. fund raising com., 2000—03; info. systems audit cons., Oklahoma City, 2002—03. With U.S. Army, 1975—78. Decorated Presdl. Svc. Badge U.S. Army. Mem.: Inst. Internal Auditors (cert. internal auditor), Info. Systems Control and Audit Assn. (cert. info. sys. auditor). Democrat. Avocation: auto racing. Home: 1608 Old Farm Rd Norman OK 73072 Office: The Hertz Corp 14501 Hertz Quail Springs Blvd Oklahoma City OK 73134

CRITES, GAYLE, artist, educator; b. Denver, June 23, 1949; d. Melvin V. and Mary E. Crites; children: Mychael Moe, Travis Moe. BA, Colo. State U., 1971. Artist-image Dairy Ctr. for the Arts, Boulder, Colo., 1999. Exhibitions include Colo. Gov.'s Invitational Exhibit, 1993—99, Rocky Mtn. Nat. Pk., Estes Pk., Co., 2002—03, Represented in permanent collections Art in Embassies, U.S. Dept. State, commd., City of Boulder, 2002, Silver Canyon Coffee, Boulder C. of C. Home: 4280 Peach Way Boulder CO 80301-1737

CRITES, RICHARD DON, lawyer; b. Sept. 3, 1943; s. Ewell Barnett Crites and Frances Loretta (Prichard) Castro; m. Annabel Lee Sheilds, June 1964 (div. 1976); children: Amy Lee, Jonathon Peter; m. Judith Jean Gildig, May 30, 1976 (div. 1997); children: Kimberly Ann, Kevin John. BA, Ariz. State U., 1965; JD, U. Ariz., 1968. Bar: Ariz. Assoc. Knez & Glatz, Tucson, 1968—73; ptnr. Knez, Glatz & Crites, Tucson, 1973—78; chief counsel City Utilities, Sprinfield, Mo., 1978—79; pvt. practice Sprinfield, 1979—. Referee Pima County Juvenile Ct., Tucson, 1972—76. Contbr. articles to law revs. Recipient Excellence in Ins. Law award, Bancroft-Whitney Co., 1967, Excellence in Criminal Law award, 1968. Mem.: ABA, Greene County Bar Assn., Mo. Bar Assn., Royal Order of Jesters, Optomists, Shriners, Elks. Republican. Presbyterian. Home and Office: 2045 S Glenstone Ste 201 Springfield MO 65804 E-mail: rcrites1@mindspring.com.

CRITES, RICHARD RAY, financial planner, investment advisor, financial services company executive; b. Rapid City, S.D., Aug. 29, 1952; s. Charles Dayton and Marcia Ann (Heil) C.; m. Randel E. Golobic, Dec. 27, 1980 (div. May 1988); m. Ellen L. Edmondson, Mar. 13, 1998. B of Liberal Studies, U. Okla., 1975; MS, Stanford U., 1978; cert. sr. security checker, Advanced Orgn. L.A., 1987, cert. false purpose rundown auditor, 1988. Cert. staff status II, exec. status I, Am. St. Hill Orgn., exec. dir. full hat course Celebrity Ctr. Internat., 1992; cert. in ins.: series 7 securities lic., series 63, series 24 gen. securities principal lic., series 66 investment adv. rep. lic.; cert. life and disability ins., Fla.; lic. mortgage broker, Fla. From nat. sales trainer to regional sales mgr. Continental Mktg. Corp., Detroit, 1975—80; pres., CEO Retail Packaging Specialists, Inc., San Mateo, Calif., 1982-86; owner, CEO Miracle Method of San Mateo, Inc., 1985-87, Miracle Method of Beverly Hills, Inc., L.A., 1987-90, Miracle Method of So. Calif., Inc., L.A., 1986-92, Miracle Method of No. Calif., Inc., L.A., 1988-89; v.p., treas., chmn. bd. Miracle Method of the U.S., Inc., L.A., 1988-92; pres., chmn. bd. Internat. Miracle Method Appearance Ctrs. Pacific, Inc., L.A., 1988-92, Internat. Miracle Method Ctrs. Equip. & Supply, Inc., L.A., 1989-92; pres., chmn. bd. dirs. Miracle Method of the U.S., Inc., L.A., 1992-96; gen. mgr. Stellar Mgmt. Co., L.A., 1993-96; mng. mem. Stellar Mgmt. LLC, 1996—; securities prin. WMA Securities, Inc., Norcross, Ga., 1996—2002; mgr. br. office Graham Group Mortgage Corp., 2001—; registered rep., br. office supr., investment advisor rep. CapWest Securities, 2002; investment adv. rep., registered rep. SAL Fin. Svcs., Inc., Birmingham, Ala., 2002—. Trustee New Civilization Found., 1996—. Mem. Citizen's Commn. on Human Rights, Citizens for an Alternative Tax System. Mem. Internat. Assn. Scientologists (sponsor), Assn. for Better Living Through Edn. Republican. Scientologist. Avocations: skiing, jazz vocal music, tennis, camping, flying. Office: Stellar Mgmt LLC 600 Bypass Dr Ste 106 Clearwater FL 33764

CRITES, STEPHEN DECATUR, religion educator; b. Elida, Ohio, July 27, 1931; s. Beryl Anderson and Martha Crites; m. Gertrud Elizabeth Bremer, Sept. 11, 1955 (div. June 1990); children: Dorothea, Stephanie, Lilian, Hannah; m. Ann Lindberg, Dec. 26, 1990. BA, Ohio Wesleyan U., 1953; BD, Yale U., 1956, MA, 1959, PhD, 1961; student, U. Heidelberg, Germany, 1959-60. Ordained to ministry United Meth. Ch., 1956. Minister Grace Meth. Ch., Southington, Conn., 1956-58; instr. philosophy and religion Colgate U., 1960-61; asst. prof. religion Wesleyan U., Middletown, Conn., 1961-66, assoc. prof., 1966-69, prof., 1969-2001, prof. philosophy, 1991-2001, prof. emeritus, 2001—. Author: In the Twilight of Christendom: Hegel vs. Kierkegaard on Faith and History, 1972, Dialectic and Gospel in the Development of Hegel's Thinking, 1998; translator: Kierkegaard, Crisis in the Life of an Actress and Other Essays on Drama, 1967; editor: Studies in Religion, Am. Acad. Religion monograph series, 1971-79. Mem. Am. Acad. Religion, Soc. for Values in Higher Edn. Home: 281 Beaver Brook Rd Lyme CT 06371-3203 Office: Philosophy Dept Wesleyan U Middletown CT 06457 E-mail: critesann@aol.com.

CRITOPH, EUGENE, retired physicist, nuclear research company executive; b. Vancouver, B.C., Can., Mar. 29, 1929; s. Dennis Basil and Lilian Sarah Critoph; m. Mary Elizabeth Ivens, Feb. 9, 1952 (dec. Oct. 2000); children: Christopher Michael, Stephen Bard, Eugene Mark, Boyd. B in Applied Sci., U. B.C., 1951, M in Applied Sci., 1957. Physicist Chalk River (Ont., Can.) Nuc. Labs., Atomic Energy of Can. Ltd., 1953-67, br. head, reactor physics, 1967-75, dir. fuels and materials div., 1975-76, dir. advanced projects and reactor physics div., 1976-79, v.p., gen. mgr., 1979-86; v.p. strategic tech. mgmt. Atomic Energy of Can. Ltd. Rsch. Co., Ottawa, Ont., 1986-92. Mem., sec., chmn. European-Am. Com. on Reactor Physics, 1962-69. Co-author, coord. Canada Enters the Nuclear Age, 1997. Mem. Can. Nuclear Soc. (W.B. Lewis medal 1986). E-mail: ecritop@attglobal.net.

CRITTENDEN, EUGENE DWIGHT, JR., chemical company executive; b. Feb. 27, 1927; s. Eugene Dwight and Meltina Ester (Feldkamp) C.; m. Sarah Ann Rogers, June 23, 1951; children: Sarah Ann Crittenden D'Alonzo, Susan Gray Crittenden Chambers. BS, Purdue U., 1947; MS, U. Pa., 1949; PhD, 1951. With Hercules, Inc., 1951-92; sr. engr. Rsch. Ctr., Wilmington, Del., 1951-53;

asst. to dir. devel. Naval Stores Dept., 1953-55; sr. chem. engr. Brunswick, Ga., 1955-56, Wilmington, 1956-57; tech. asst. to devel. dir., 1957-60; sr. tech. rep., 1960-62; asst. dir. devel. synthetics dept. Wilmington, 1962-63; asst. to gen. mgr. internat. dept., 1963-64; dir. Hercules Europe, Brussels, 1965-66; dir. sales organic chem. divsn., synthetic dept. Wilmington, 1966-67; asst. gen. mgr. synthetics dept., 1967-68; gen. mgr. new enterprise dept., 1968-72; indsl. sys. dept., 1972-77; divsn. v.p. adminstrn. and pub. affairs, 1977-82; divsn. v.p. ops., corp. dir., mem. exec. and mgmt. com., 1982; corp. v.p. internat., 1983-87; pres., CEO Aqualon Group, 1987-89; sr. v.p., 1982-92; ret.; corp. dir. Hercules Inc., Wilmington, 1982-92. Bd. dirs. City of Wilmington and New Castle County YMCA, 1968-92, pres. 1977-82; trustee, c.p., pres. Eleutherian Mills-Hagley Found., 1981-2001; bd. dirs. World Affairs Coun., 1981-92; trustee, bd. dirs. Med. Ctr. of Del., 1978-92, vice chmn., 1990—, bd. dirs. Chritsiana Care Corp., 1992—, del. met. chmn. Nat. Alliance of Bus., 1981-82; mem. Gov.'s Internat. Trade Coun., 1984-92; mem. Del. and Ea. Pa. Dist. Export Coun., 1984-92; del. Econ. and Fin. Adv. Coun., 1977—2001. chmn. 1989-93. Mem.: AIChE, AAAS, Am. Chem. Soc., Sea Island Golf Club, Ocean Forest Golf Club, Bidermann Golf Club, Wilmington Country Club (bd. govs.), Wilmington Vicmead Hunt Club, Pine Valley Golf Club, Sigma Xi. Republican. Episcopalian. Avocations: piano, golf, tennis. Home: 908 N Dupont Rd Wilmington DE 19807-2963

CRITTENDEN, GARY LEWIS, diversified financial services company executive; b. Ogden, Utah, July 13, 1953; s. Charles Lee and Ruth Emily (Fowers) C.; m. Catherine Jean Cox, Dec. 19, 1975; children: KelliAnn, Stephanie, Spencer. BS, Brigham Young U., 1976; MBA, Harvard U., 1979. V.p. Bain & Co., Boston, 1979—90; exec. v.p. Filenés Basement, Wellesley, Mass., 1990—94; CFO Melville Corp., Rye, NY, 1994—95, Sears Roebuck & Co., 1996—98; sen. v.p., CFO Monsanto, 1998—2000; CFO Am. Express, N.Y.C., 2000—. Mem. Lds Ch. Avocation: running. Home: 183 Ferris Hill Rd New Canaan CT 06840-3826 Office: Am Express 3 World Fin Ctr 200 Vesey St Tower C New York NY 10285

CRITTENDEN, JAMES ARTHUR, physicist; b. Aurora, Colo., May 3, 1956; s. Ray Ryland and Kathryn Ellen (Harmison) C.; m. Micheline Zion, May 12, 1990. BA, Reed Coll., 1978; AM, Columbia U., 1980, MPhil, 1981, PhD, 1986. Vis. scientist Fermi Nat. Accelerator Lab., Batavia, Ill., 1984-86; collaborateur étranger temp. Ctr. d'Etudes Nucleaires de Saclay, Gif sur Yvette, France, 1986-88; Wissenschaftlicher Mitarbeiter Phys. Inst. U. Bonn, Germany, 1988-91, Wissenschaftlicher asst., 1991-97; pvt. dozent, 1997-2000; Wissenschaftlicher Mitarbeiter Deutsches Elektronen-Synchrotron, 2000-01; rsch. scientist Cornell U., Ithaca, N.Y., 2001—. Contbr. articles to profl. jours. Mem. Phi Beta Kappa. Home: 112 Larchmont Drive Trumansburg NY 14886 Office: Wilson Synchrotron Lab Cornell Univ Ithaca NY 14853-8001 E-mail: critten@mail.lns.cornell.edu.

CRITTENDEN, JOHN CHARLES, civil and environmental engineering educator; b. Nov. 12, 1949; BS in Chem. Engring., U. Mich., 1971, MS in Civil and Environ. Engring., 1972, PhD in Civil and Environ. Engring., 1976. Sr. v.p. Limno-Tech, Inc., Ann Arbor, Mich., 1975-77; asst. prof. civil and environ. engring. Wash. State U., Pullman, 1977-78; asst. prof. civil engring., environ. engring. sect. U. Ill., Urbana, 1978-79, Mich. Tech. U., Houghton, 1979-81, assoc. prof. civil engring., environ. engring. sect., 1981-84, adj. prof. chem. engring., 1981-84, prof. civil and environ. engring., 1984—. Dir. Ctr. for Clean Indsl. and Treatment Techs., Houghton, 1992—; presdl. prof. civil engring. CenCITT Mich. Tech. U., 1988—. Mem. AIChE, ASCE (Rudolph Hering award 1980, Walter L. Huber rsch. prize 1991), Am. Acad. Environ. Engrs., Water Pollution Control Fedn., Internat. Soc. Humic Substances, Assn. Environ. Engring. Profs., Am. Water Works Assn. (publs. award 1989), Am. Chem. Soc. Achievements include patents in field. Office: Mich Tech U Dept Civil & Environ Engr 1400 Townsend Dr Houghton MI 49931-1200

CRITTENDEN, MARTHA A. disability specialist; b. Georgiana, Ala., Nov. 2, 1957; d. Walter Ray and Martha Pugh C. AA, Lomax - Hannon Jr. Coll., Greenville, Ala., 1978; BS, Troy State U., 1987, MS, 1993. Cert. counselor Am. Counseling Assn./Ala. Alochol and Drug Abuse Assn.; cert. instr. HIV & AIDS, ARC; cert. criminal justice addiction profl., Ala. Patient care asst. Jackson Hosp., Montgomery, Ala., 1978-89, psychiat. tech., 1989-90; drug program specialist Bullock County Correctional, Union Spring, Ala., 1990-95; drug treatment counselor Montgomery Cmty. Based Facility, Mt. Meigs, Ala., 1995-99, Ala. Dept. Corrections, Birmingham, 1999-2000; disability specialist Ala. Dept. Edn. Birmingham Disability Determination Svcs., 2000—. Vol. Neighbors Who Care, 1999; tchr. Bethel Full Gospel Ch., Montgomery, 1986—, Faith Chapel Christian Ctr. Ch., 1986—. Recipient Supr. of Yr. award Ala. Dept. Corrections, 1994. Mem. Ala. Alcohol and Drug Abuse Assn., Ala. Dept. Corrections (supr. 1990-95, Supr. of Yr. 1994), Addiction and Offender Counselors, Gamma Beta Phi. Avocations: reading, church, friends, walking or jogging, school. Office: Birmingham Disability Determination Svcs PO Box 830300 Birmingham AL 35283 also: Faith Chapel Christian Ctr 800 Quebec St Birmingham AL 35224-1571

CRITTENDEN, SOPHIE MARIE, communications executive; b. Mansfield, Ohio, Apr. 14, 1926; d. Joseph S. and Mary Ellen (Hagerman) Wojcik; m. Robert Eugene Crittenden, Aug. 24, 1946 (dec. 1987); children: Robert J., Mark A., Christopher E., Laura Ann. Student, Coll. St. Francis, 1944-45, Ohio U., 1945-46, North Central Tech. Coll., 1976-78. Substitute tchr. Mansfield City Schs., 1956-62; lab. technician The Ohio Brass Co., Mansfield, 1962-68, draftsman, 1968, mgr. internal publs., 1969-78, mgr. advt., 1978-83, mgr. comm., 1983-88; cons. comm. EFE N.Am., Inc., Mansfield, 1989-90; account coord. D & S Creative Advt., Inc., Mansfield, 1990—2001; ret., 2001. Creator and shower of quilts. Com. chmn. United Way Campaign, Mansfield and Richland, Ohio, 1978; pub. relations chmn. Tribute to Women and Industry Project, Mansfield, 1986 (award 1985). Named Mrs. Mansfield/Mrs. Am. Contest, 1961. Mem. Altrusa (pres. 1976, internat. chmn. mktg. and pub. rels. 1991-93). Republican. Roman Catholic. Avocations: fiber arts, antiques, quilting. Home: 84 Briarwood Rd Mansfield OH 44907 E-mail: sophiec@att.net.

CRIVELLI, KENNETH JOHN, physical therapist, athletic trainer; b. Balt., July 18, 1953; s. Raymond John Sr. and Virginia Mae (Bender) C.; m. Carol Virginia Stitz, Aug. 23, 1975; children: Jennifer Ann, Steven James. BS, Towson State U., 1975; BS, cert. phys. therapy, U. Md. Sch. Medicine, 1978; MA, U. Md., 1984. Cert. athletic trainer, sports clin. specialist; lic. phys. therapist, Md. Athletic trainer, grad. asst. Towson State U., 1975-76; staff phys. therapist Dennis H. Buchman, P.A., Burnie, Md., 1978-81, Buchman and Ude, Annapolis, Md., 1979-81, Hepburn & Assocs., Balt., 1981-84, Howard County Gen. Hosp., Columbia, Md., 1983-85; chief phys. therapy Martin Z. Kanner, P.A., Reisterstown, Md., 1985; coord. sports medicine program Patuxent Med. Group, P.A., Columbia, 1985-95; sr. phys. therapist Ctrl. Md. Rehab. Ctr., Columbia, 1995—. Mem. Howard County Gen. Hosp. Speakers Bur., 1984—; coord. care and prevention of athletic injuries courses, scholastic coach certification several Md. pub. sch. systems and Howard C.C., 1986—; adj. faculty in health scis. Howard C.C., 2002—; mem. phys. therapy practice issues com. Md. State Bd. Phys. Therapy Examiners, 1987-88; mem. health svcs./phys. edn. com. Howard C.C., 1987—; qualified examiner Nat. Athletic Trainers Assn., 1986-89; cons. Md. State Commn. on Phys. Fitness, 1986-95, Howard County Bd. Edn., 1985-95; interim athletic trainer Howard C.C., 2003. Pres. Pine Orchard Meadows Improvement Assn., Ellicott City, Mo., 1985-88; mem. adminstrv. bd. Bethany United Meth. Ch., 1987-90; People to People Internat. sports amb. to Australia and New Zealand, Oct. 1998. Mem. Nat. Athletic Trainers Assn., Md. Athletic Trainers Assn., Phi Kappa Phi. Republican. Methodist. Avocations: fishing, cooking, boating. Office: Ctrl Md Rehab Ctr 6300 Woodside Ct Ste 5 Columbia MD 21046-3210 E-mail: tabow@prodigy.net.

CRIVELLI-KOVACH, ANDREA, public health and nutrition consultant, educator; b. Drexel Hill, Pa., Sept. 27, 1947; d. Albert Francis and Philomena Maria Crivelli; m. Gerald Charles Scullin, Apr. 24, 1971 (div. 1980); m. Edward Raphael Kovach, Aug. 6, 1982. BA in Biology, Immaculata Coll., 1969, MA in Nutrition Edn., 1988; MPH, PhD in Cmty. Health, Temple U., 1995. Cert. health edn. specialist. Info. specialist E.I. DuPont de Nemours & Co., Wilmington, 1969-83, contract info. specialist, 1987-91; nutrition cons. Health Choices Unltd., Media, Pa., 1988—; asst. prof., cmty. health coord. Phila. Coll. Osteopathic Medicine, 1994-96; rsch. evaluation cons. Crivelli Assocs., Media, Pa., 1996—; asst. prof., dir. cmty. health programs Arcadia U., Glenside, Pa., 1996—. Adj. prof. women's studies U. Pa., Phila., 1996—. Contbr. articles to profl. jours. including Jour. of Human Lactation, Birth, Jour. Korean Acad. Nursing, Jour. Osteo. Medicine. Chair Media Bd. of Health, 1997—; dep. health officer Media Borough, 1994—97; mem. nutrition adv. bd. Nursing Mothers Network, Springfield, Pa.; mem. profl. adv. bd. Breastfeeding Clinic of Montgomery County, Women's Health and Environ. Network. Mem. Am. Dietetic Assn., Am. Pub. Health Assn., Soc. of Pub. Health Educators, Soc. of Nutrition Edn. (Del. Valley chpt.), Kappa Omicron Nu. Democrat. Achievements include research in cross-cultural international breastfeeding; development of measurement instrument to evaluate hospital breastfeeding policies based on the UNICEF/WHO baby-friendly hospital initiative; research in role of community lay health advocates in empowering low income pregnant women. Avocations: biking, swimming, boating, gardening, hiking, cross country skiing. Office: Arcadia U 450 S Easton Rd Glenside PA 19038-3215

CRNKOVIC, DENIS, language educator; b. Lancaster, Pa., Dec. 14, 1953; s. Leo R. and Geraldine M. Crnkovich; m. Kathy Marie Olson, Mar. 19, 1954; children: Jenna Katherine Murphy, Damon Patrick Murphy, Michaella. AB, Franklin & Marshall Coll., 1974; MA, MPhil, PhD, Yale U., 1985. Lector Yale U., New Haven, 1977—79, instr. Summer Programs, 1977—83; instr. Trinity Coll., Hartford, Conn., 1983—84, Gustavus Adolphus Coll., Saint Peter, Minn., 1984—85, asst. prof., 1985—91, assoc. prof., 1991—. Fellow, Yale U., 1976—80; grantee, Ford Found., 1974, Internat. Rsch. and Exchanges Bd., 1984. Mem.: Calico (assoc.), Amer. Assn. of Tchrs. of Slavic and East European Langs. (assoc.), Phi Beta Kappa. Roman Catholic. Avocation: music. Office: Gustavus Adolphus College 800 West College Avenue Saint Peter MN 56082

CROAKE, PAUL ALLEN, lawyer; b. Janesville, Wis., Sept. 1, 1947; s. Willard m. and Dorothy R. Croake; m. Denise L. Croake; children: Katherine, John Paul, Patrick. BA, Lawrence U., 1969; JD, U. Wis., 1972. Bar: Wis. 1972, U.S. Dist. Ct. (we. dist.) Wis. 1972, U.S. Tax Ct. 1982. Lawyer DeWitt Ross & Stevens S.C., Madison, Wis., 1972-2001. Capt. U.S. Army, 1969-80. Mem. ABA, Madison Club. Roman Catholic. Avocations: tennis, golf. Office: 2 E Mifflin St Ste 600 Madison WI 53703-2890 E-mail: pac@dewittross.com.

CROAN, ROBERT JAMES, music critic, singer; b. N.Y.C., Apr. 30, 1937; s. Sydney Joseph and Sylvia (Zorn) C. BA, Columbia U. 1958, MA 1959; PhD, Boston U., 1968. Prof. voice Duquesne U. Sch. of Music, Pitts., 1962-2000, chmn., 1983-2000; ret. Pitts. Post-Gazette, 1999, music critic, 1964-99, sr. editor, 1999—. Mem. Music Critics Assn. N.Am. (chmn. ednl. activities 1978-90, pres. 1997-2001), Nat. Assn. Tchrs. of Singing. Democrat. Avocations: travel, culinary arts. E-mail: rcroan@lycos.com.

CROARKIN, DONALD J. librarian; b. Chgo., Feb. 12, 1933; s. Eugene Croarkin and Rose Valeria Staskiewicz. BA in Philosophy, St. Mary of the Lake, Mundelein, Ill., 1955; MEd, Loyola U., 1957; MLS, Dominican U., River Forest, Ill., 1975. Tchr. jr. high Pub. Sch. #143, Midlothian, Ill., 1959—64; libr. h.s. Sch. Dist. #206, Chicago Heights, Ill., 1964—2000; ret., 2000. With Bloom & Bloom Trail Alumni Assns. Sgt. U.S. Army, 1957—59. Roman Catholic. Avocation: Avocations: golf, stamp collecting. Home: 40 W 15th St Chicago Heights IL 60411-3421

CROAT, THOMAS BERNARD, botanical curator; b. May 23, 1938; s. Oliver Theodore and Irene Mary (Wilgenbush) C.; m. Patricia Swope, Sept. 4, 1965; children: Anne Irene, Thomas Kevin. BA, Simpson Coll., 1962; MA, U. Kans., 1966, PhD, 1967. Tchr. sci. pub. schs., Virgin Islands and Iowa, 1962-64; rsch. botainst Mo. Bot. Garden, St. Louis, 1967-71, P.A. Schulze curator of botany, 1977—. Vis. fellow Smithsonian Tropical Research Inst., Ancon, Canal Zone, 1968-71; adv. com. NSF Resources in Systematic Botany, 1972-74; faculty assoc. biology Washington U., St. Louis, 1970—; adj. faculty U. Mo., St. Louis, 1974—; adj. assoc. prof. St. Louis U., 1982—. Author: Flora of Barro Colorado Island, 1978; contbr. articles to profl. jours. With U.S. Army, 1956-58. Recipient Rsch. award Soc. Sigma Xi, 1975; grantee NSF, 1972-2000, Nat. Geog. Soc., 1973, 83, 86, 89, 95, 99, NEA, 1975, 79. Mem. Am. Soc. Plant Taxonomists, Assn. Tropical Biology, Internat. Soc. Plant Toxonomist, Internat. Aroid soc. (hon. bd. 1978-84), Bot. Soc. Am. Republican. Roman Catholic. Avocations: welding, electronics, auto repair, construction. Home: 5600 Hill View Dr Pacific MO 63069-3523 Office: Mo Bot Garden PO Box 299 Saint Louis MO 63166-0299

CROCE, ALAN J. government agency executive; m. Patricia Acampora; 4 children. BS in Criminal Justice, SUNY; grad., FBI Nat. Acad., Quantico, Va., Nat. Correctional Acad., Boulder, Colo. From dep. sheriff to sgt. dep. sheriff Suffolk County Sheriff's Dept., 1971-86, undersheriff, 1986-97; commr. and chmn. N.Y. State Commn. of Correction, 1997—. Mem. Suffolk County Police Assn. (past pres.). Office: State of NY Commn of Correction Four Tower Pl 2d Fl Albany NY 12203-3764

CROCE, ARLENE LOUISE, critic; b. Providence, May 5, 1934; d. Michael Daniel and Louise Natalie (Pensa) C. Student, Women's Coll., U. N.C., 1951-53; BA, Barnard Coll., 1955. Founder, editor Ballet Rev., 1965-78; dance critic New Yorker mag., 1973-98. Dance panelist Nat. Endowment for Arts, 1977-80. Author: The Fred Astaire & Ginger Rogers Book, 1972, Afterimages, 1977, Going to the Dance, 1982, Sight Lines, 1987, Writing in the Dark, Dancing in the New Yorker, 2000. Recipient AAAL award 1979, award of Honor for Arts and Culture Mayor N.Y.C., 1979, Janeway prize Barnard Coll., 1955; Hodder fellow Princeton U., 1971; Guggenheim fellow, 1972, 86, NEH fellow 1992, Nat. Arts Journalism Program sr. fellow, 1999. Office: New Yorker Mag 4 Times Sq New York NY 10036-6561

CROCE, PAT, author, fitness trainer, former sports team executive; m. Diane Croce; children: Kelly, Michael. Grad. cum laude, U. Pitts., 1977. Conditioning coach for Bobby Clarke Phila. Flyers, 1980; owner Sports Phys. Therapists, Inc., Broomall, Pa.; ptnr., pres. Phila. 76ers, 1996—2001. Motivational spkr.; internat. karate champion. Contbr. articles. Instrumental in bringing 1999 NBA All-Star Weekend to Phila.; vol. Sixers Slam Dunk Diabetes Family Festival, JDF Walk to Cure Diabetes; hon. chmn. Nat. Multiple Sclerosis Soc. Office: c/o Running Press 125 S 22nd St Philadelphia PA 19103

CROCE, ROBERT J. corporate government relations executive; b. Hartford, Conn., Oct. 31, 1953; s. John F. and Angela P. Croce; m. Donna J. Auner, Mar. 3, 1978; children: Catherine, Emily, Paige, Robert J. BA, U. Denver, 1975; MPA, U. Colo., 1977. Adminstrv. analyst City of Hartford, 1977-79; chief of staff State of Conn., Office of Sec. of State, 1979-82; dist. dir. Office of U.S. Rep. B. Kennelly, Hartford, 1982-98; dir. govt. rels. ADVO Inc., Windsor, Conn., 1998—.

CROCK, JONATHAN MARK, diplomat; b. Oct. 30, 1976; Student, Georgetown U., 1994—2000, Moscow State U., 1997, U. Kiev, Ukraine, 1997. Asst. to dir. of adminstrn. Dole/Kemp '96 Presdl. Campaign, Washington, 1995—96; publs. clk. U.S. Supreme Ct., Washington, 1995; Belarus desk officer USAID, Washington, 1995—97; state field rep. Dole/Kemp '96 Presdl. Campaign, Great Falls, Mont., 1996; comml. asst. U.S. Embassy to the Republic of Poland, Warsaw, 1998; congl. liaison Bush-Cheney 2000 Presdl. Campaign, Washington, 1999—2000; sanctions specialist U.S. Dept. of the Treasury, Office of Fgn. Assets Control, Washington, 1999—2000; asst. to the attache Embassy of France to the U.S., Attache for Sci. and Tech., Washington, 1999—2000; policy asst. Bush-Cheney Transition Team, Washington, 2000—01; spl. asst. to amb., apptd. by Pres. George W. Bush U.S. Dept. of State, Office of the Sec. of State, Amb.-at-Large for War Crimes Issues, Washington, 2001—. Pres., founder Sadowska Translations, Washington, 2000—03. Mem., sponsor Rep. Nat. Com., Washington, 2001—03, Ohio Rep. Party, Columbus, 2001—03. Senator Robert C. Byrd scholar, Georgetown U., 1994—2000. Mem.: World Affairs Coun. Avocation: foreign languages. Office: US Dept of State 2201 C St NW Washington DC 20520

CROCK, STANLEY MILES, journalist; b. New Bedford, Mass., Apr. 6, 1950; s. Max and Lillian Rose (Kivowitz) C.; m. Pamela J. Brown, Mar. 21, 1987; children: Russell, Meryl. BA, Columbia Coll., 1972; MS in Journalism, Northwestern U., 1973; JD, Columbia U., 1977. Reporter AP, Chgo., 1973, Palm Beach Post, West Palm Beach, Fla., 1973-74, Wall St. Jour., Washington, 1978-82; cons. Worldwide Info. Resources Ltd., Washington, 1982-83; editor McGraw-Hill World News, Washington, 1983-86; news editor Bus. Week, Washington, 1986-95, chief diplomatic corr., 1995—. Pres. Rollingwood Citizens Assn., Chevy Chase, Md., 1993-94; comptr. Temple Sinai, Washington, 2001—. Jewish. Avocation: golf. Home: 7016 Western Ave Chevy Chase MD 20815-3111 Office: Bus Week # 1100 1200 G St NW Ste 1100 Washington DC 20005-3844 E-mail: stan_crock@businessweek.com.

CROCKER, ALLEN CARROL, pediatrician; b. Boston, Dec. 25, 1925; Student, MIT, 1942-44; MD, Harvard U., 1948. Lab. house officer Children's Hosp., Boston, 1948-49, jr. asst. resident medicine, 1949-51, fellow pathology, 1953-56, from asst. to assoc. physician, 1956-62, rsch. assoc. pathology, 1956-60, assoc. medicine, 1962-66, sr. assoc., 1966—, dir. devel. evaluation ctr., 1967-93, program dir. Inst. for Cmty. Inclusion, 1993—. Rsch. assoc. pathology Med. Sch., Harvard U., 1956-60, rsch. assoc. pediatrics, 1960-66, tutor med. sci., 1964-70, asst. prof., 1966-69, assoc. prof., 1969—, assoc. prof. maternal and child health Sch. Pub. Health, 1989—. Mem. Am. Assn. Mental Retardation (v.p. medicine 1980-82), Am. Assn. Univ. Affiliated Programs for Persons with Devel. Disabilities (pres. 1982-83), Nat. Down Syndrome Congress (v.p. 1984-85), Soc. Behavioral Pediatrics (pres. 1987-88). Achievements include research in pediatric metabolic diseases, biochemistry of the lipids, mental retardation. Office: Inst for Cmty Inclusion Children's Hosp 300 Longwood Ave Boston MA 02115-5724

CROCKER, BARBARA JEAN, clinical nurse specialist; b. Worcester, Mass., Oct. 13, 1942; d. Roy A. and Mildred E. (Ewing) Benson; m. David L. Crocker, Aug. 29, 1964; children: Beth, Mark, Matthew. Diploma, Henry Heywood Meml. Hosp., Gardner, Mass., 1963; BS, Anna Maria Coll., Paxton, Mass., 1982, MS in Nursing, 1985. Cert. infection control nurse. Staff nurse Worcester Hahnemann Hosp., 1965-72, nursing supr., 1972-81, infection surveillance nurse, 1981-85; nurse epidemiologist The Med. Ctr.-Hahnemann, Worcester, 1985-92; infection control practitioner U. Mass. Meml. Health Care, Worcester, Mass., 1992—2002, clin. nurse specialist, 2002—. Mem. Assn. Profls. in Infection Control and Epidemiology, Inc., Henry Heywood Meml. Hosp. Alumnae Assn.

CROCKER, CHESTER ARTHUR, diplomat, scholar, federal agency administrator; b. N.Y.C., Oct. 29, 1941; s. Arthur M. and Clare V.; m. Saone Baron, Dec. 18, 1965; children: Bathsheba, Karena, Rebecca. BA, Ohio State U., 1963; MA in Internat. Studies, Johns Hopkins U., 1965, PhD, 1969. News editor Africa Report, 1968-69; lectr. Am. U., 1969-70; staff officer NSC, 1970-72; dir. M.S. in Fgn. Svc. program Georgetown U., Washington, 1972-78, dir. African studies Ctr. for Strategic-Internat. Studies, 1976-81, disting. prof. diplomacy Sch. Fgn. Svc., 1989-98, James R. Schlesinger prof. strategic studies, 1998—; asst. sec. state African affairs, 1981-89; chmn. bd. dirs. U.S. Inst. Peace, 1992—. Cons. in strategy and negotiation; chmn. Africa working group Reagan campaign, 1980; coord. for Africa Bush campaign; bd. dirs. A.S.A. Ltd., Ashanti Goldfields, Co., Ltd., Henry-Dunant Ctr. for Humanitarian Dialogue, Nat. Def. U., Modern Africa Growth Investment Co., LLC. Author: High Noon in Southern Africa, 1992, Managing Global Chaos, 1996, Herding Cats: Case Studies in International Mediation, 1999, Turbulent Peace: The Challenges of Managing International Conflict, 2001, also others; contbr. articles to profl. jours. Recipient Disting. Svc. award Sec. State, 1988, Presdl. Citizen's award, 1989 Mem. Coun. Fgn. Rels., Internat. Inst. Strategic Studies, Cosmos Club, Tahawus Club. Republican. Office: Georgetown U Sch Fgn Svc Intercultural Ctr Rm 813 Washington DC 20057-0001

CROCKER, EVELYNE MARIE, retired physical education educator; b. Hollis, Okla., Mar. 13, 1936; d. Horace Norton Crocker and Maezell Elizabeth Tarr; m. Kenneth D. Burgess-Bean, May 6, 1956 (div. 1980); children: R. N. Burgess-Bean, K.R. Burgess-Bean, W. R. Burgess-Bean. Student, Cisco Jr. Coll., N.Mex. State U. Cert. Medical Specialist 1956. Governess Brown Family, Snyder, Tx, 1954—55, The Burgess-Bean Family, Maryville, Tn, 1956—68; instr. phys. edn. Bishop Bryan Cath. H.S., Port Arthur, Tex., 1968—69; governess The Hitch Family, Albany, Tex., 1981—82; owner, operator Bean's Lawn and Landscape Co., 1982—; proprietor King Crocker Am. Boers, Abilene, Tex., 1997—2001, Crocker Scouting Svc., Abilene, Tex., 2000—01. Author (web sites): Texann Prairie Land Country, 1996. Vol. state coord., owner Tex. Am. Local History Net; webmaster, author A.M. Crocker -1720 rootsweb.com project; vol. county coord., webmaster TXGenWeb projects; den leader, coach Scouting, Maryville, Tenn., 1977—79. Pfc WAC, 1955—57. Recipient Cold War Cert., Sec. War, 2000. Mem.: Founding Families of the State of S.C. Before Statehood, Tex. Sheriff Assn. (assoc. Appreciation award 1999, 2000, 2001). Spiritualist. Avocations: historical re-enactment, genealogy, photography, preservation. Business E-Mail: ecrocoil@camalott.com.

CROCKER, JOY LAKSMI, concert pianist and organist, composer; b. San Antonio, June 12, 1928; d. Hugo Peoples and Anna Kathryn (Ball) Rush; m. Richard Lincoln Crocker, July 24, 1948 (div. July 1977); children: Nathaniel Homer, Martha Wells, David Laramie. MusB, Yale U., 1950; MS, Yale U., Berkeley, Calif., 1956; postgrad., Grad. Theol. Sem., 1978-81. Min. music First Congl. Ch., Branford, Conn., 1949-62; dir. music therapy West Haven (Conn.) VA Hosp.; min. music St. Stephen's Episcopal Ch./Sch., Orinda, Calif., 1963, First Bapt. Ch., Oakland, Calif., 1964-66, Greek Orthodox Cathedral, Oakland, 1969, San Quentin (Calif.) Protestant Chapel, 1976-78, Plymouth United Ch. of Christ, Oakland, 1977-84; pianist, assoc. dir. First Bapt. Ch., Managua, Nicaragua, 1984-94; organist, pianist Mills Grove Christian Ch., 1995—96; organist St. Andrews Presbyn. Ch., Pleasant Hill, Calif., 1996—2001; dir. music ministries Trinity Meth. Ch., Berkeley, 2001—. Prof. organ San Francisco Conservatory Music, 1962-69; chmn. piano dept. Nicaraguan Nat. Conservatory Music, 1984-93; founder-dir., prof. Bapt. Conservatory of Music, Managua, 1989—; instr. Yogalayam Yoga Ashram; creator, dir. diverse low-budget innovative music edn. programs, 1969—; mem. adjudicator Nat. Guild Piano Tchrs., Music Tchrs. Assn. Calif.; invited lectr. 3d Encuentro Iberoamericano de Profesores y Estudiantes de Musica, Cuba, 1999; piano concert and master class tours, Cen. and South Am., 1995. Pianist, Internat. Symposium of Universal Articulate Understanding of Sci., 1999; concert/presentation World Parliament of Religions South Africa, 1999; pianist Balboa Park Pause for Peace Millennial Concert, 1999-2000, World Bank Counter Summit, Prague, UN 55th Anniversary Global Peace Walk Vigil, 2000. Civic and legislation coord. Ch. Women United, Oakland unit and state unit, 1996—, chair for global concerns; bd. dirs. Quantum Leap 2000, 1999—; pianist, organist Ch. Women United State Unit; San Francisco Bay area coord. for Hague Appeal for Peace; commr. World Summit on Peace and Time, Costa Rica, 1999, del./concert pianist World Social Forum, Brazil, 2001; pianist World Coun. Ch. Ann. Conv., Oakland, Calif., 2002, Forgiveness First Internat. Conv., Kamloops B.C., 2002. Named Woman of Yr., Bus. and Profl. Women's Club, Inc., 1995; recipient prizes for compositions, San Francisco Concerto Orch., 1997, Music Tchrs. Assn. Calif., 1998, 2000, 2001. Mem. Am. Guild Organists, Am. Coll. Musicians, Music Tchrs. Assn. Mem. United Ch. of Christ. Avocations: traveling, political activism. Home: 3065 Monterey Blvd Oakland CA 94602-3559 E-mail: jcrocker@rcn.com.

CROCKER, KENNETH FRANKLIN, data processing consultant; b. Centralia, Wash., July 29, 1950; s. Earl Thomas and Mary Jane (Hamil) C.; m. Mary Louise Underwood, June 15, 1974 (div. Dec. 1987); children: Matthew A., Benjamin F., Jonathan C.; m. Sally Marlene Gammelgard, Dec. 21, 1987 (div. 1992). AS in Computer Programming and System Design, Control Data Inst., Long Beach, Calif., 1972. Programmer City of Greenville, S.C., 1973; computer operator Winn Dixie Stores, Greer, S.C., 1973-75; programmer Piedmont Industries, Greenville, S.C., 1975-78; systems engr. Micro-Systems, Greenville, 1978; sr. programmer Reeves Bros., Lyman, S.C., 1978-80; systems analyst Cryovac div. W.R. Grace Co., Duncan, S.C., 1980-84; sr. cons. Cap Gemini Am., San Francisco, 1984-85; prin. mem. tech. staff Citibank-FSB Calif., Oakland, 1985-91; sr. software engr. Lucky Stores Inc., Dublin, Calif., 1991-94; tech. cons. Lawrence Berkeley Labs., Berkeley, Calif., 1994-95, Delta-Net, San Francisco, 1995; plan architect, DBA technician Safeway, Walnut Creek, Calif., 1995-99; sr. software engr. Berkeley Labs., 1999—. Umpire Contra Costa Ofcls. Assn., 1990-96. Libertarian. Baptist. Avocation: motorcycles. Home and Office: 346 Kentucky St Vallejo CA 94590-5040 E-mail: kenn_crocker@yahoo.com.

CROCKER, MATTHEW HALLOWELL, historian, educator, writer, researcher; b. Providence, Ri, Aug. 25, 1962; s. John, Jr. and Elinor Winslow Crocker; m. Susan Duff Wilcox, July 16, 2000; 1 child, Samuel Winslow. Bachelor of the Arts, Macalester Coll., St. Paul, MN, 1980—84; MA, U. of Mass., Amherst, Amherst, MA, 1989—93, PhD, 1993—97. History tchr. Walnut Hill Sch., Natick, Mass., 1985—89; prof. of history Keene State Coll., Keene, NH, 2000—. Bd. of reviewers Hist. Jour. of Mass. History, Westfield, Mass., 1998—. Author: (historical monograph) The Magic of the Many: Josiah Quincy and the Rise of Mass Politics in Boston, 1800-1830, (scholarly article) Journal of the West, Massachusetts Politics: Selected Historical Essays; contbr. scholarly presentation. Mem.: New Eng. Hist. Assn., Orgn. of Am. Historians, Am. Hist. Assn. Democrat-Npl. Episcopalian. Avocations: sailing, squash, tennis. Office: Keene State College 229 Main St Morrison Hall Keene NH 03435 E-mail: mcrocker@keene.edu.

CROCKER, RAY DEAN, musician, musical director; b. Ft. Worth, Nov. 1, 1949; s. Ben Raglin and Nancy Mahota (Potts) C.; m. Emily Janice Holt. Student, Tex. Christian U., 1967-69; MusB, North Tex. State U., 1974, MusM, 1977. Pianist Casa Manana Musicals, Ft. Worth, 1979-83; mus. asst. Opera Theatre U. North Tex. (formerly North Tex. State U.), Denton, 1980-81, instr. music, 1983-84; staff accompanist Tex. Womans's U., Denton, 1982-85; mus. dir. Surflight Summer Theatre, Beach Haven, N.J., 1984-85; asst. condr. 42nd St., nat. tour, 1985-86; mus. dir. Dallas Repertory Theatre, 1986-89, Sacramento Music Circus, 1988-90, Oscar's Place Dinner Theatre, Milw., 1990, 42d St. European Tour Co., 1991-97, Great Lake Opera, Milw., 1992. Bd. dirs. Paint It Yellow Prodns., Inc., pres., 1999—. Composer: (mus.) Twas the Night Before Christmas, 1983, Frosty the Snowman, 1985, numerous instrumental, vocal, electronic chamber works; condr. mus. Dreamgirls, 1988. Mem. ASCAP, Am. Fedn. Musicians, Dramatists Guild, Phi Mu Alpha, Kappa Kappa Psi, Alpha Psi Omega. Home: 2764 N 90th St Milwaukee WI 53222-4609 E-mail: dcrocker@paintityellow.org., dcrocker@operamail.com.

CROCKER, RICHARD LINCOLN, retired music educator; b. Roxbury, Mass., Feb. 17, 1927; s. Richard Whitney Crocker and Constance Homer; m. Joy Rush, July 24, 1948; children: Nathaniel, David Laramie, Martha Wells; m. Gloria Andersen Pihl, Aug. 1, 1977. BA, Yale Coll., 1950; PhD in Music, Yale U., 1957. Asst. prof. dept. music Yale U., New Haven, 1957—63; prof. dept. music U. Calif., Berkeley, 1963—94; ret. Author: The Early Medieval Sequence, 1977, Introduction to Gregorian Chant, 2000. Fellow, Guggenheim Found., 1969. Mem.: Am. Musicol. Assn. (hon. Einstein award 1966, Kinkeldey award 1977). Avocations: yachting, woodworking, gardening. Home: 1643 Walnut St Berkeley CA 94709

CROCKER, SAMUEL SACKETT, lawyer; b. Washington, May 17, 1943; s. Reginald D. and Elizabeth (Sackett) C.; m. Dorothy Pamela Macdonald, Dec. 5, 1970; 1 child, Dorothy. BA, Williams Coll., 1965; LLB, U. Tex., 1968. Bar: Tex. 1968, Ohio 1969, Mich. 1973, N.Y. 1975. Atty., OEO/VISTA, Columbus, Ohio, 1968-69; atty. Schlumberger Ltd., Houston, 1969-73; gen. counsel Heath Co., Benton Harbor, Mich., 1973-75; corp. counsel, asst. sec. Schlumberger Ltd., N.Y.C., 1975-78; gen. counsel Schlumberger Well Services, Houston, 1978-80; v.p., sec., gen. counsel Moran Energy, Inc., Houston, 1980-84; v.p. legal affairs Baylor Coll. Medicine, 1984-97; ptnr. Gardere Wynne Sewell & Riggs, LLP, Houston, 1998-2000; v.p., gen. counsel Talent Tree, Inc., EESIS, Inc., 2000-. Mem. ABA, Forest Club. Republican. Episcopalian. Home: 3257 Huntingdon Pl Houston TX 77019-5925 Office: Talent Tree Inc 9703 Richmond Houston TX 77042 E-mail: samuel.crocker@talenttree.com.

CROCKER, SAONE BARON, lawyer; b. Bulawayo, Zimbabwe, Jan. 11, 1943; came to U.S., 1963; d. Benjamin and Rachel (Joffe) Baron; m. Chester Arthur Crocker, Dec. 18, 1965; children: Bathsheba Nell, Karena Wynne, Rebecca Masten. BA, U. Cape Town, 1961, BA with honors, 1962; MA, Johns Hopkins U., 1966; JD cum laude, Georgetown U., 1983. Bar: D.C. 1983, U.S. Ct. Appeals (D.C. cir.) 1985, U.S. Dist. Ct. D.C. 1990, U.S. Supreme Ct. 1990, U.S. Ct. Appeals (7th cir.) 1991, U.S. Ct. Appeals (4th cir.) 1998. Adminstr. Guinea program African Am. Inst., Washington, 1965-66, author Africa Report, 1966; writer fgn. affairs div. Am. U., Washington, 1967-68; freelance writer Washington, 1968-80; atty. firm Wilmer, Cutler & Pickering, Washington, 1983-84; clk. to judge U.S. Ct. Appeals for D.C. Circuit, 1984-85; atty. firm O'Melveny & Myers, Washington, 1985-90, Beveridge & Diamond, Washington, 1990-92, Wright & Talisman, P.C., Washington, 1992-2001; pvt. practice Washington, 2001—. Contbg. author: Zambia Handbook, 1967. AAUW fellow, 1963-65; Fulbright fellow, 1963; Johns Hopkins U. fellow, 1964-65; recipient Lawyers Coop. Pub. Co. awards, 1980. Mem. ABA, AAUW (state pres. 1992-94), Fulbright Assn. E-mail: saonec@aol.com.

CROCKER, STEPHEN L. federal magistrate judge; BA, Wesleyan U., 1980; JD, Northwestern U., 1983. Law clk. to Hon. Barbara Crabb U.S. Dist. Ct. (we. dist.) Wis., Madison, 1983-84; trial atty. D.O.J., 1984-86; asst. U.S. atty. No. Dist. Ill., 1986-90; assoc. Michael, Best & Friedrich, 1990-92; magistrate judge U.S. Dist. Ct. (we. dist.) Wis., Madison, 1992—. Office: US Courthouse 120 N Henry St Madison WI 53703-2559

CROCKER, THOMAS DUNSTAN, economics educator; b. Bangor, Maine, July 22, 1936; s. Floyd M. and Gloria F. (Thomas) C.; m. Sylvia Fleming, Dec. 31, 1961 (div. Sept. 1986); children: Sarah Lydia, Trena Elizabeth; m. Judith Powell, Sept. 9, 1989. AB, Bowdoin Coll., 1959; PhD, U. Mo., 1967. Asst. prof. econs. U. Wis., Milw., 1963-70; assoc. prof. U. Calif., Riverside, 1970-75; prof. U. Wyo., Laramie, 1975-2001, chairperson dept. econs. and fin., 1991-93, dir. Sch. Environment and Natural Resources, 1993-98, J.E. Warren disting. prof. of Energy and Environment, 1997—, disting. prof. emeritus, 2001—. Rsch. assoc. U. Calif., Berkeley, 1973, Pa. State U., 1974; cons. Asarco, Inc., 1985—89, Mathtech, Inc., Princeton, NJ, 1987—88, Princeton, 1999—2001, Indsl. Econs., Inc., Cambridge, Mass., 1998—99, Shea and Gardner, Washington, 1989, Arco, Inc., 1992, A. Coors Co., 1992, Eastern Rsch. Group, 1997; mem. sci. adv. bd. EPA, Washington, 1973—76; mem. panel on long range transport issues U.S. Congress, Washington, 1981; mem. Gov.'s Competition Rev. Com., State of Wyo.; mem. panel NSF, 2002—03. Co-author: Environmental Economics, 1971; author, editor: Economic Perspectives on Acid Deposition Control, 1984; editorial coun. Jour. Environ. Econs. and Mgmt., 1973-88, 95-99; contbr. articles to profl. jours. Mem. com. impacts pollution on agriculture Orgn. for Econ. Cooperation and Devel., Paris, 1987-88. Grantee, NSF, 1968, 1973, 1981, EPA, 1971, 1976—85, 1997—; scholar, Fulbright Found., 2001—. Mem.: European Assn. Environ. Resource Econs., Assn. Environ. Resource Econs. (contributed papers com. 1989, Rsch. of Enduring Quality award 2002), Am. Econ. Assn. (mem. awards structure com. 1981—83), The Nature Conservancy. Republican. Avocations: skiing, bicycling, travel, trekking, rafting. Office: Univ Wyo Dept Econs Laramie WY 82071-3985 E-mail: tcrocker@uwyo.edu.

CROCKER, VALERIE MARIAN, mechanical engineer; b. Annapolis, Md., July 21, 1962; d. Ernest O. and Virginia G. (Gleason) Crocker; m. Mark A. Young, May 18, 1991 (div. Apr. 1997); m. Christopher J. Day, Sept. 22, 2001. BS in Engring./Bioengring., U. Vt., 1984; MS in Biomed. Engring., Duke U., 1986; MBA, San Diego State U., 2002. Rehab. engr. Tufts U./New Eng. Med. Ctr., Boston, 1983; rsch. engr. Harvard Med. Sch., Southborough, Mass., 1987-88; project engr. surg. devices ETHICON Inc., Somerville, N.J., 1988-90; sr. mech. project engr. Abbott Labs., San Diego, 1990-92, supr. disposables mfg., 1992-94, mgr. mech. engring., R&D, 1994-2001; sr. program mgr. Gen-Probe, Inc., San Diego, 2001—. Contbr. articles to profl. jours. Avocations: triatholons, ocean swimming, marathons, bicycling, skiing. Home: 3624 Torrey View Ct San Diego CA 92130 Office: Gen-Probe Inc 10210 Genetic Ctr Dr San Diego CA 92121 E-mail: valerieday@gen-probe.com.

CROCKER, WILLIAM HENRY, ethnologist, researcher; b. San Francisco, Aug. 20, 1924; s. William Willard and Ruth (Hobart) C.; m. Roma Dillon Smyth, Apr. 11, 1969 (div. Nov. 1983); 1 child, Myles Hobart; m. Jean Galloway Thomas, Dec. 19, 1987. BA, Yale Coll., 1950, MA, Stanford U., 1953; PhD, U. Wis., 1962. Curator Smithsonian Inst., Washington, 1962-93, emeritus curator, 1993—. Author: The Canela: An Ethnographic Introduction, 1990; co-author: The Canela: Bonding through Kinship, Ritual and Sex, 1994. Trustee World Learning, Inc., Brattleboro, Vt., 1974-92. Cpl. U.S. Army, 1943-46. Mem. Bohemian Club, Cosmos Club. Democrat. Avocation: photography. Home: 4 Chalfont Ct Bethesda MD 20816-1805 Office: Smithsonian Inst Dept Anthropology MRC 112 Washington DC 20560-0112

CROCKETT, ANN HEMENWAY, psychotherapist; b. Springfield, Mass., Jan. 22, 1934; d. Howard Paul and Frances (Bennett) Becker; m. Jean Davis Bundy, Aug. 17, 1957 (div. 1981); children: Christopher, Alison, Lisa, Nicholas; m. Walter Franklin Crockett, Aug. 1, 1981. BA in English, French, Lawrence U., 1955; MS in Edn., U. Wis., 1957; PhD in Clin. Psychology, U. Maine, Orono, 1988. Lic. psychologist, Maine. Tchr. Oak Grove Coburn, Vassalboro, Maine, 1968-78, dir. of studies, 1973-78; psychologist Counseling Svcs. Inc., Saco, Maine, 1984-94; psychotherapist in pvt. practice Biddeford, Maine, 1994—. Dir. Com. Support Program, Saco, 1990-94; del. Dem. Party, Maine, 1978, 79, 88—. NIMH grantee, 1979-84. Mem. Soc. Of Friends. Avocations: reading, gardening, embroidery, singing. Home: 76 Maple Ave Scarborough ME 04074-9528 Office: 5 Washington St Biddeford ME 04005-2598

CROCKETT, CLYLL WEBB, lawyer; b. Preston, Idaho, Feb. 16, 1934; s. Frank Lee and Alta (Webb) C.; m. Nan Marie Mattice, June 27, 1958; children— Jeffrey Webb, Nicole, Karen, Cynthia. BS, Brigham Young U., 1958; MBA Northwestern U, 1959; LL.B., U. Ariz., 1962. Bar: Ariz. 1962, U.S. Supreme Ct. 1970. Clk. Ariz. Supreme Ct., 1962-63; ptnr. Fennemore Craig, Phoenix, 1968—. Instr. eve. div. Mesa (Ariz.) C.C.; bd. dirs. S.W. Airlines Co. Mem. editorial bd. Ariz. Law Rev, 1961. Mem. charter rev. com., Scottsdale, Ariz., 1966-67; mem. bd. adjustment, Scottsdale, 1968-73, chmn., 1971-73; bd. dirs. Maricopa Mental Health Assn., 1976-78, Phoenix Cmty. Alliance, Valley Forward Assn.; mem. Mesa Crime Commn., 1980-82; mem. social scis. adv. bd. LDS Ch.; mem. State of Ariz. Gov.'s Regulatory Rev. Coun; mem. bd. of adjustment City of Mesa, 1996—. Mem. ABA, State Bar Ariz., Maricopa County Bar Assn., Am. Judicature Soc., Phoenix C. of C., Ariz. Acad. Republican. Home: 1510 N Gentry Cir Mesa AZ 85213-4001 Office: Fennemore Craig Ste 2600 3003 North Central Ave Phoenix AZ 85012-2913

CROCKETT, DAVID ANTHONY, political science educator; b. Ft. Bragg, N.C., June 11, 1963; s. William Riley and Barbara Jean C.; m. Stacy Lyn Shaw, July 19, 1997; children: William, Alexander. BA, Georgetown U., 1985; MPA, U. Tex., Austin, 1993; PhD, 1999. Comms. officer U.S. Army, Wuerzburg, Germany, 1985-91; asst. prof. Trinity U., San Antonio, 1999—. Capt. U.S. Army, 1985-91. Mem. Am. Polit. Sci. Assn. Republican. Avocations: running, reading, writing, travel, music. Office: Trinity U 715 Stadium Dr San Antonio TX 78212 Fax: (210) 999-8320. E-mail: dcrocket@trinity.edu.

CROCKETT, DODEE FROST, brokerage firm executive; b. Oklahoma City, Oct. 19, 1956; d. Carl S. Frost and Mikki (Matheny) Marcus; m. Billy Crockett. M. in Theol. Studies, So. Meth. U., Perkins Sch. Theology, 2003. 1st v.p., wealth mgmt. advisor Merrill Lynch Pvt. Client, Dallas, 1980—. Author: (Book) Phthalocyanine Compounds, 1963, The Phthalocyanines, 1983; author: (with Frank H. Moser) Phthalocyanine Research and Applications, 1990. Bd. dirs. North Dallas Shared Ministries, 1988-91, Ronald McDonald House of Dallas, 1992—, Dallas Social Venture Ptnrs.; trustee Dallas Opera, 1991—; mem. investment com. Dallas Women's Found., 1991-94; mem. exec. bd. Perkins Sch. Theology, So. Meth. U., Dallas, Dallas Found.; pres. Cir. Shared Housing Ctr., Dallas. Mem. Nat. Assn. Securities Dealers (gen. securities prin., mcpl. securities rulemaking bd. prin., registered options prin., bd. arbitrators), NYSE (com. mem.), Merrill Lynch Dirs. Cir., Park Cities Exch. Club (charter). Office: Merrill Lynch Pierce Fenner and Smith 2000 Premier Pl 5910 N Central Expy Ste 2000 Dallas TX 75206-5152

CROCKETT, DONALD HAROLD, composer, university educator; b. Pasadena, Calif., Feb. 18, 1951; s. Harold Brown and Martha Amy C.; m. Karen Anne Gallagher Crockett, Nov. 11, 1972 (div. 1986); 1 child: Katherine Jane Crockett; m. Vicki Lyn Ray, June 6, 1988. MusB, U. So. Calif., 1974, MusM, 1976; PhD, U. Calif., Santa Barbara, 1981. Composer-in-residence Pasadena Chamber Orch., 1984-86, L.A. Chamber Orch., 1991-97. Asst. prof. U. So. Calif., L.A. 1981-84, assoc. prof., 1984-94, prof. 1994—; music dir., condr. U. So. Calif. Contemporary Music Ensemble, L.A., 1984—, Xtet, 1992-. Composer: Celestial Mechanics oboe and string quartet, 1990, Array string quartet number 1, 1987, Roethke Preludes for Orchestra, 1994, Concerto for Piano and Wind Ensemble, 1988, Scree for cello, piano and percussion, 1997, Island for concert band, 1998, The Falcon's Eye for solo guitar, 2000, Cascade for orchestra, 2001, Blue Earth for orchestra, 2002. Recipient Friedheim award Kennedy Ctr., Washington, 1991, Aaron Copland award Copland Heritage Assn., 1998; Goddard Lieberson Fellowship Am. Acad. of Arts and Letters, N.Y.C., 1994; Nat. Endowment for the Arts grantee, Washington, 1993; artists' fellow Calif. Arts Coun., 1999. Mem. BMI, Am. Music Ctr., Am. Composers Forum, Phi Kappa Phi. Avocations: reading, backpacking, skiing. Office: Univ Southern Calif Thornton School Of Music Los Angeles CA 90089-0851 E-mail: dcrocket@usc.edu.

CROCKETT, GEORGE EPHRIAM, secondary education educator; b. Chgo., July 5, 1940; s. Edmund and Ethel Teva (Cowan) C.; m. Ethelene Standifer, Nov. 25, 1968; children: Patricia Johnson, Ronald O'Neal, Michael O'Neal. BS, Ill. State U., 1964; MA in History, Northeastern Ill. U., 1981; postgrad., U. Ill., Champaign. Cert. tchr., Ill. History tchr. John Marshall Metro High Sch., Chgo., 1964—, chmn. social studies dept., 1992—. Tng. specialist John Marshall Metro Evening High Sch., 1966-69, counselor, 1980-83; cons. curriculum guide Chgo. Bd. Edn., 1970. Active Cen. Meml. Bapt. Ch., Chgo., 1957—; mem. com. explorer scouts Boy Scouts Am., 1977-79; mem. Citi-Educators Team Project, DePaul U., 1989. Recipient Tchr. of Yr. award Chgo. Bd. Edn., 1974, Black Educator award Push Found., 1977, Blum-Kovler Ednl. Found. award, 1984, merit award N. Eastern Ill. Alumni, 1985, Midwest Community award, 1990—. Mem. Ill. Coun. Social Studies, Chgo. Social Studies, Chgo. Afro-Am. Tchrs. Assn., Chgo. Area Alliance Black Sch. Educators, NAACP, Nat. Urban League, Midwest Community Coun., Operation Push, So. Christian Leadership Conf. Avocations: reading, sports, public speaking, gardening. Home: 3130 W Fulton St Chicago IL 60612-1728 Office: John Marshall Met High Sch 3250 W Adams St Chicago IL 60624-2901

CROFT, CANDACE ANN, psychology educator, academic administrator; b. Lancaster, Wis., Jan. 14, 1957; d. Wilford Stanley and Myrna Viola Croft. BA, St. Olaf Coll., 1979; MS, U. Ariz., 1980; PhD, Pa. State U., 1984. Psychotherapist Forrester Clinic, Chgo., 1984 86; dir. rsch. on child and adolescent health Am. Acad. Ped., Elk Grove Village, Ill., 1986-92; dir. rsch. and sci. affairs Am. Acad. Orthop. Surgeons, Rosemont, Ill., 1992-94; sr. program assoc. Aon Found., Chgo., 1994-95; dir. Strong Spirit Wellness Ctr., Chgo., 1995-96; adj. prof. DePaul U., Chgo., 1993-96; assoc. prof. psychology, chmn. dept. psychology Clarke Coll., Dubuque, Iowa, 1996—2003, chair instl. rev. bd., 2000—03; dean Health & Human Svc. Occupations, SW Tech. Coll., Fennimore, Wis., 2003—. Textbook reviewer McGraw-Hill, 1998-2003; media contact Nat. Coun. Family Rels., St. Paul, 1998—, Clarke Coll.-Fox-40, Dubuque, Iowa, KWWL Channel 7, Dubuque, Iowa; adv. Clarke Coll. Author: Annalia's Simply Splendid, 2003; contbr. articles to sci. and profl. jour.; exec. producer film Heart of the Matter, 1991 (bronze award Houston Internat. Film Festival 1991); contbr. column to on-line pub., Living With Heart, 2002—. Mem. liturg. ministry St. Mary's Ch., Platteville, Wis., 1999—2001. Mem. Nat. Coun. Family Rels. (cert. family life educator, sect. religion and the family, sect. on family and health), Assn. Humanistic Psychology, Inst. Noetic Scis., Assn. for Transpersonal Psychology, Phi Kappa Phi, Omicron Nu. Avocations: writing, music, aerobics, swimming, photography. Home: 119 North Monroe Lancaster WI 53813 Office: SW Tech Coll 1800 Bronson Blvd Fennimore WI 53809 E-mail: cacroft@pcii.net.

CROFT, DANIEL THOMAS, music educator; b. Pittsburgh, Pa., Oct. 15, 1951; s. Joseph Donald and Evelyn Marie Croft, m. Dawna LaRae Ainsworth, June 21, 1974; children: Daniel T., LaRae Marie. BS Music Ed., Clarion Univ., Clarion, PA, 1973. Band dir. North Star Area Sch. Dist., Boswell, Pa., 1973—. Founder/condr. Somerset County Cmty. Band, Somerset, Pa., 1988—; founder Somerset Alliance Ch. Band, Somerset, Pa.; faculty Clarion Univ. Summer Band Camp, Clarion, PA, 1975-1990. Tennis instr.; music ministry Chs.; referee Somerset Youth Basketball Assn., Somerset, Pa., 1982, pres., 1998. Recipient Grant B. Miller award-Man of the Yr., Somerset Chamber of Commerce, 1994. Mem.: Somerset County Music Educators Assn., PA State Educators Assn., PA Music Educators Assn., Music Educators Nat. Conf. (rep. to state music leadership conf.). R-Conservative. Christian. Avocation: raising cocker spaniels. Home: 262 Marker Dr Somerset PA 15501 Office: North Star Area School Dist 400 Ohio St Boswell PA 15531

CROFT, HARRY ALLEN, psychiatrist; b. Houston, July 2, 1943; s. Louis and Ida (Kaplan) C.; m. Benay Bleacher, Dec. 27, 1964; children— Jamie Sue, Bradley Lane, Chasen Ashley. BS, So. Meth. U., 1964; MD, U. Tex. at Galveston, 1968. Intern Brackenridge Hosp., Austin, 1968-69; resident in obstetrics and gynecology U. Tex. Med. Br., 1969-70, resident in psychiatry, 1970-73; dir. methadone program Galveston County, Tex.; dir. sex therapy program U. Tex., Galveston, 1972-73; commd. capt. U.S. Army, 1973, advanced through grades to maj., 1975; chief (Mental Hygiene Service, Brooke Army Med. Center), Houston, 1973-76; pvt. practice, 1976—. Clin. asst. prof. psychiatry and obstetrics and gynecology Med. Sch. San Antonio, 1973-75; columnist San Antonio Express-News, 1975-76; weekly contbr. Sta. KMOL-TV (NBC) newscast; dir. rsch. and edn. Covenant Behavioral Health. Contbr. articles to profl. jours. Recipient physician's recognition award AMA, 1974, awards for med. TV work Nat. Healthcare Assn., 1988, Women in Comm., 1988; Meritorious Svc. medal U.S. Army, 1976, Ware 1st place audio-visual award Dept. Army, 1976, Gov.'s award State of Tex., 1991, award City of San Antonio, award Acad. Radio and TV Health Comm., Jules Bergman award-Broadcaster of Yr. award, 1995, Best Radio Show In U.S., Nat. Mental Health Assn., 1996; named Honoree, Am. Heart Assn., 2003. Mem. Am. Psychiat. Assn. (award 1991), Tex. Med. Assn. (award 1988), Am. Soc. Sex Educators, Counselors and Therapists, Am. Soc. Addiction Medince (cert. addictionist). Home: 12738 Hunters Chase St San Antonio TX 78230-1930 Office: 8038 Wurzbach Rd Ste 570 San Antonio TX 78229-3815

CROFT, JANET BRENNAN, academic librarian; b. Pitts., May 5, 1961; d. Earl David and Marian (Maxwell) Brennan; m. Duane Shiffler, Aug. 11, 1984; 1 child, Sarah Gail. BA in English & Classical Civilization, Ind. U., 1982, MLS, 1983. Libr. Jenner and Block Law Firm, Chgo., 1983-84, Carnegie Libr. Pitts., 1985, Sewickley (Pa.) Pub. Libr., 1985-88, Moon Twp. Pub. Libr., Coraopolis, Pa., 1988-89, 90; libr. dir. Martin Meth. Coll., Pulaski, Tenn., 1993-2000, costume designer, 1997-2000; head access svcs. U. Okla. Libr., 2001—. Contbr. articles to profl. jours. Mem.: ALA, Popular Culture Assn., Mythopoeic Soc. Avocations: quilting, wearable art. Office: U Okla Bizzell 104NW 401 W Brooks St Norman OK 73019-6030 E-mail: jbcroft@ou.edu.

CROFT, KATHRYN DELAINE, business executive, consultant; b. Eastover, S.C., Jan. 13, 1944; d. Randolph and Ethel (Williams) Lloyd; m. Daniel Marranzini, June 26, 1987. BS, Wilberforce U., 1965; MS, Columbia U., 1982, New Sch. for Social Rsch., 1988. Cert. social worker, N.Y. Exec. dir. Family Dynamics, Inc., N.Y.C., 1987-92; asst. provost Columbia U., N.Y.C., 1992-94; commr. N.Y.C. Child Welfare Adminstrn., N.Y.C., 1994-96; dir. ops. Just One Break, Inc., N.Y.C., 1997-2000, exec. dir., 2000—02; chief program officer ARC Greater N.Y.C., 2002—. Cons. various nonprofit orgns., N.Y.C., 1996—. Bd. dirs. Artsgenesis, N.Y.C., 1993—, chmn., 1996-99; bd. dirs. Ackerman Inst., N.Y.C., 1997-2000. Recipient scholarships New Sch. for Social Rsch., 1985-88, Columbia U., 1978-82. Mem. NAFE, Assn. Black Women in Higher Edn. Avocations: travel, reading, photography.

CROFT, MICHELE IZZO, graphic designer, artist; b. Reading, Pa., Jan. 5, 1958; d. Nicholas Anthony and Virginia (Marsh) Izzo; m. Gene Alfred Croft, Sept. 10, 1983; children: Edward, Virginia. A in Visual Comm., Art Inst. Pitts., 1978. Graphic designer Lyons Studio, Wilmington, Del., 1978-80, Salisbury & Salisbury, N.Y.C., 1980-82, Jones Medinger Kindschi, North Salem, N.Y., 1982-91; freelance graphic designer, illustrator Cortlandt Manor, N.Y., 1991—. Deacon Scarborough (N.Y.) Presbyn. Ch., 1998-2003, mem. choir, 1980—. Mem. Am. Watercolor Soc. (signature; awards chmn. 1998—). Republican. Avocations: bicycling, painting, singing. Home: 80 Gallows Hill Rd Cortlandt Manor NY 10567

CROFT, TERRENCE LEE, lawyer; b. St. Louis, Apr. 13, 1940; s. Thomas L. and Anita Belle (Brown) C.; m. Merry Patton, July 9, 1977; children: Michael, Shannon, Kimberly, Kristin, BethAnn, Katherine. AB, Yale U., 1962; JD with distinction, U. Mich., 1965. Bar: Mo. 1965, U.S. Dist. Ct. (ea. dist.) Mo. 1965, Ga. 1970, Fla. 1970, U.S. Ct. Appeals (5th, 8th and 11th cirs.) 1970, U.S. Supreme Ct. Assoc. Coburn, Croft & Kohn, St. Louis, 1965-69, Hansell, Post, Brandon & Dorsey, Atlanta, 1969-73; ptnr. Huie, Sterne & Ide, Atlanta, 1973-78, Kutak, Rock & Huie, Atlanta, 1978-83; shareholder Griffin, Cochrane & Marshall, Atlanta, 1983-93; ptnr. King & Croft LLP, Atlanta, 1994—. Mem. ABA (ho. of dels. 1993-99), ATLA, State Bar Ga. (bd. govs. 2002, chair alt. dispute resolution sect.), Atlanta Bar Assn. (pres., sec., treas. bd. dirs. 1986-99, chmn., bd. dirs. litigation sect. 1982-86, pres. Alt. Dispute Resolution Lawyers sect. 1996-97), Am. Coll. Civil Trial Mediators, Atlanta Collegium of Arbitrators and Mediators (founder), Atlanta Bar Found. (pres. 1998—), Ga. Trial Lawyers Assn., Lawyers Club Atlanta, Old War Horse Lawyers Club. Episcopalian. Avocations: hiking, shooting, motorcycling, reading. Home: 2580 Westminster Heath NW Atlanta GA 30327-1449 Office: King & Croft LLP 707 The Candler Bldg 127 Peachtree St NE Atlanta GA 30303-1810 Fax: 404-577-8401. E-mail: tlc@king-croft.com.

CROFTS, ANTONY RICHARD, biochemistry and biophysics educator; b. Harrow, Eng., Jan. 26, 1940; came to U.S., 1978; s. Richard Basil Iliffe and Vera Rosetta (Bland) C.; m. Paula Anne Hinds-Johnson, June 7, 1969 (div. 1981); 1 child, Charlotte Victoria Patricia; 1 adopted child, Rupert Charles; m. Christine Thompson Yerkes, Dec. 23, 1982; children: Stephanie Boynton, Terence Spencer. BA, U. Cambridge, Eng., 1961, PhD, 1965. Asst. lectr. dept. biochemistry U. Bristol, Eng., 1964-65, lectr., 1966-72, reader, 1972-78; prof. biophysics U. Ill., Urbana-Champaign, 1978—, prof. microbiology, 1992-99, chmn. biophysics divsn., 1978-91, assoc. dean Coll. Liberal Arts & Scis., 1996-98, prof. biochemistry, 1998—. Mem. organizing com. 4th Internat. Congress Photosynthesis, Reading, Eng., 1977, 7th Internat. Congress Photosynthesis, Providence, 1986, Table Ronde, Rousel-UCLA Forum, Paris, 1985; vis. prof. Coll. de France, 1983; Melandri lectr. European BioEnergetics Conf., Lyon, France, 1982. Contbr. numerous articles, revs., etc., in area of biophysics, photosynthesis and bioenergetics; mem. editl. bd. Biochem. Jour., U.K., 1971-72, Biochimica Biophysica Acta, Holland, 1972-77, jour. Bacteriology, 1979-83, Archives Biochemistry and Biophysics, 1980-85. Major scholar nat. sci. U. Cambridge, 1958 61, U. Ill. scholar, 1989-92; grantee U.S. Dept. Energy, 1982-96, Guggenheim Found., 1985, NSF, NIH, U.S. Dept. Agr., 1979-2001. Fellow AAAS; mem. Biophys. Soc., Am. Soc. Biochemistry and Molecular Biology, Am. Soc. Plant Physiologists (Charles F. Kettering award 1992). Avocations: windsurfing, skiing, fishing, sailing. Office: U Ill Dept Biochemistry 419 Roger Adams Lab Box B4 600 S Mathews Ave Urbana IL 61801-3602 E-mail: a-crofts@life.uiuc.edu.

CROFTS, RICHARD A. academic administrator; PhD in Reformation History, Duke U. Mem. faculty U. Toledo; assoc. v.p. rsch., dean Grad. Sch. E. Tenn. State U.; dep. commr. acad. affairs Mo. Univ. Sys., Helena, 1994-96, commr. higher edn., 1996—. Office: Mont Univ Sys PO Box 203101 2500 E Broadway St Helena MT 59620-3101

CROGHAN, GARY ALAN, cancer research scientist, physician; b. Ft. Wayne, Ind., Oct. 2, 1954; s. Robert Thomas and Catherine Marie (Krantz) C.; m. Ivana Tallerico, July 3, 1982. BA, Wabash Coll., Crawfordsville, Ind., 1977; PhD, SUNY, Buffalo, 1982; MD summa cum laude, Buffalo Sch. Med., 1990. Rsch. asst. dept. diagnostic immunology rsch. and biochemistry Nat. Breast Cancer Project Lab., Roswell Park Meml. Inst., SUNY, Buffalo, 1980-82, rschr., 1982-84, rschr. cancer rsch. sci., 1984—, prin. investigator ovary and breast cancer lab, Diagnostic Immunology Rsch., 1985-90, asst. rsch. prof. pathology, 1986-87; intern gen. internal medicine Millard Fillmore Hosp., Buffalo, 1990-91; resident internal medicine Mayo Grad. Sch. Medicine, Rochester, Minn., 1991-94; clin. investigator Mayo Clinic, Rochester, 1994-97, cons., med. oncology and internal medicine, 1997—; physician investigator nicotine rsch. Mayo Found., 1997—; asst. prof. med. oncology and medicine Mayo Grad. Sch. of Medicine, Rochester, 1996—. Cons., lectr. in field. Contbr. articles in field. N.Y. State Cancer Predoctoral fellow, 1978-82, postdoctoral fellow, 1983-84, Cancer Immunology fellow Cancer Research Inst., 1984-86. Mem. AMA, Internat. Assn. Breast Cancer Rsch., Minn. Med. Assn., Am. Assn. Cancer Rsch., Am. Soc. Clin. Oncology, Am. Soc. Preventive Oncology, Soc. for Rsch. on Nicotine and Tobacco, Am. Soc. for Addiction Medicine, Sigma Xi, Alpha Omega Alpha. Democrat. Office: Mayo Grad Sch Medicine Dept Med Oncology Rochester MN 55905-0001

CROHN, MAX HENRY, JR., lawyer; b. Asheville, N.C., Feb. 4, 1934; s. Max Henry and Edith Pearl (Hoffman) C.; m. Barbara Jean Morris, Jan. 28, 1960; children: David Michael, Edith Ann, Randal Morris. BA in Polit. Sci, U. N.C., 1955; LL.B., Georgetown U., 1961. Bar: D.C. 1961, N.C. 1977, N.Y. 1986. Practiced in, D.C., 1961-68; trial atty. Bur. Restraint of Trade, 1963-65; atty. adviser to chmn. FTC, 1965-66; asso. mem. firm Arnold & Porter, Washington, 1966-68; asso. counsel R.J. Reynolds Industries, Inc., Winston-Salem, N.C., 1968-75, asst. gen. counsel, 1975-78; sec. R.J. Reynolds Tobacco Co., 1971-81, gen. counsel, 1978-81; ptnr. Jacob, Medinger and Finnegan, 1981-95. Former chmn. bd. dirs. Forsyth County Econ. Devel. Corp., 1975-78. Served to lt. (j.g.) USNR, 1955-58. Mem. ABA. Home: 517 Redbud Rd Chapel Hill NC 27514-1710

CROIS, JOHN HENRY, local government official; b. Chgo., Jan. 13, 1946; s. Henry F. and Dorothy M. (Priebe) C.; m. Mary E. Slattery. BA, Elmhurst Coll., 1969; MA, U. Notre Dame, 1972. Asst. village mgr. Village of Oak Lawn, Ill., 1975-85; village mgr. Village of Westchester, Ill., 1985; dir. West Cook County Solid Waste Agy., 1990—. Coord. Oak Lawn Swine Flu Immunization Program, 1976; bd. dirs. Ill. Met. Investment Fund. Mem. ASPA, West Ctrl. Mcpl. Conf. (chmn. intergovtl. com. 1991, exec. bd. 1991—), Ill. Met. Investment Fund (dir. 1996—), Chgo. Area Transp. Study Coun. Mayors (North Ctrl. region), Internat. City Mgmt. Assn. (credentialed mgr.), Ill. City Mgmt. Assn., Metro-Mgrs. Assn. (dir. 2003), Divinr Infant Golf League. Home: 331 Phillips Ave Glen Ellyn IL 60137 Office: 10300 W Roosevelt Rd Westchester IL 60154-2568

CROLAND, BARRY I. lawyer; b. Paterson, N.J., Jan. 11, 1938; s. Louis L. and Rae R. (Levine) C.; m. Joan Kohlreiter, Dec. 20, 1958; children: Richard, Heidi, Lizabeth, Jennifer. BA, Middlebury Coll., 1959; JD, Rutgers U., Newark, 1961. Bar: N.J. 1962, N.Y. 1983, U.S. Ct. Appeals (3d cir.) 1973. Law clk. to Hon. John Grimshaw N.J. Superior Ct., 1961, law clk. to Hon. Morris Pashman, 1961-62; assoc. Cole, Berman & Garth, Paterson, 1962-63, Shavick, Thevos, Stern, Schotz & Steiger, Paterson, 1963-68; ptnr. Shavick, Stern, Schotz, Steiger & Croland, Paterson, 1968-79, Stern, Steiger, Croland, Tanenbaum & Schielke, Paterson, 1979-95, Shapiro & Croland, Hackensack, N.J., 1995—. Asst. bar examiner State of N.J., 1965-68; mem. Fed. Ethics Com., Dist. of N.J., 1975; lectr. Inst. for Continuing Legal Edn., Trial Advocacy and Family Law, 1975—; sec. Dist. II Ethics Com. for Bergen County, 1980-81; mem. com. on civil practice N.J. Supreme Ct., 1965, matrimonial litig. com. 1980, family ct. com., 1982, family practice com., 1983-87, 2002—. Mem. bd. editors Rutgers Law Rev., 1959-61, case editor, 1960-61; sr. editor N.J. Family Lawyer, 1981-2002. Fellow Am. Bar Found., Am. Acad. Matrimonial Lawyers (N.J. bd. mgrs.); mem. ABA (family law sect.), ATLA (matrimonial trial lawyers sect. emeritus bd. 2002--), Am. Coll. Family Trial Lawyers (diplomate 1994—), Best Lawyers in U.S. (family law 1983—), Am. Inns of Ct. (master Morris Pashman 1990-95, pres.-master N.J. family law 1995-99), N.J. State Bar Assn. (mem. exec. com. family law sect. 1981-95), Bergen County Bar Assn. (chmn. jud. and prosecutorial appts. com. 1983-95, chmn. jud. performance com. 1999-2001). Home: 243 Myrtle St Haworth NJ 07641-1137 Office: Shapiro & Croland 411 Hackensack Ave Fl 6 Hackensack NJ 07601-6365

CROLL, JILLIAN KATHLEEN, dietician, researcher; b. Moorhead, Minn., Sept. 12, 1970; m. Walter Charles Croll, Dec. 31, 2000. BA, U. St. Thomas, St. Paul, Minn., 1992; MS, U. Vt., Burlington, Vt., 1994; MPH, U. Minn., Mpls., 1999, PhD, 2003. Clin. dietitian Rutland Regional Med. Ctr., Rutland, Vt., 1995—97; rsch. clin. practice dir. Eating Disorders Inst., St. Louis Park, Minn., 1999—, clin. dietitian St. Louis Park, Minn., 1999—. Fellow U. Minn., Mpls., 1998—2000. Grantee Residential Eating Disorder Treatment Outcome Study, Blue Cross Blue Shield Found. of Minn., 2003, Family Practice Physician Assessment: Eating Disorder Assessment and Treatment, Pk. Nicollet Found., 2002. Mem.: SCAN, Am. Dietetic Assn., Acad. for Eating Disorders. Office: Eating Disorders Inst 6490 Excelsior Blvd Ste 315E Saint Louis Park MN 55426 Office Fax: 952-993-5599. Personal E-mail: crollj@parknicollet.com. E-mail: crollj@parknicollet.com.

CROM, THOMAS LEROY, III, venture capitalist, accountant; b. Compton, Calif. m. Stacy Ann Crom; children: Lee, Desirae, Megan, Katerina, Stephen, Ariana. BSc, Santa Clara U., 1977; MS, Golden Gate U., 1983. CPA, Calif., cert. mgmt. accountant. Mgr. Ernst & Young, San Jose, Calif., 1977-80; v.p. Scott Enterprises, Santa Cruz, Calif., 1980-83; pres. North Lily Mining Co., San Bruno, Calif., 1983-91, Eureka Ventures, Inc., Payson, Ariz., 1991—. Dir. Timebeat.com Enterprises, Inc., N.Y.C., 1996—, Dragon Diamond, Vancouver, B.C., Canada, 1983—, Anthem, Inc., Vancouver, 1996—, Marbella, Inc. Southbroom, Natal, South Africa, 1996—, Minera Northern Resources Ltd., Santiago, Chile, 1989-93, Compania Minera Adamantine, Caracas, Venezuela, 1997—, Kansai Mining Corp., Vancouver, Can. Mem. AICPAs. Office: Eureka Ventures Inc PO Box 9 Payson AZ 85547-0009 Fax: 928-474-8354. E-mail: crom@theriver.com.

CROMARTIE, ERIC ROSS, lawyer; b. Washington, Jan. 14, 1955; s. William Adrian and Dorothy Jane (Cann) C.; m. Lynn Prendergast, Sept. 12, 1981; children: William Ross, Morgan Nicole. BA, Amherst (Mass.) Coll., 1977; JD, Harvard U., 1980. Bar: Tex. 1980, U.S. Dist. Ct. (no. and ea. dists.) Tex. 1980, U.S. Tax. Ct. 1983, U.S. Ct. Appeals (5th and 11th cirs.) 1980, U.S. Ct. Appeals (8th and 10th cirs.) 1984, U.S. Supreme Ct. 1985. Assoc. Hughes and Luce, Dallas, 1980-85, ptnr., 1985-97. Mem. ABA, Dallas Bar Assn., Am. Law Inst. Home: 4247 Brookview Dr Dallas TX 75220 3801

CROMARTIE, ROBERT SAMUEL, III, thoracic surgeon; b. Fayetteville, N.C., Dec. 25, 1943; s. Robert Samuel Jr. and May Hunter (Cook) C.; m. Mary Elaine Collier; children: Robert Samuel IV, David Alan, Kimberly Elaine. AB in Chemistry, U. N.C., 1965, MD, 1969. Diplomate Am. Bd. Surgery, Am. Bd. Thoracic Surgery, Am. Bd. Laser Surgery. Intern in surgery U. Miami, 1969-70, resident in gen. surgery, 1972-74, La. State U., New Orleans, 1974-76; resident in thoracic surgery Med. U. S.C., Charleston, 1976-78; asst. prof. surgery Ind. U. Med. Ctr., Indpls., 1978-80; thoracic and cardiovasc. surgeon Tampa (Fla.) Gen. Hosp., 1980-81, Meml. Hosp., Ormond Beach, Fla., 1981—, Columbia Med. Ctr., Daytona, Fla., 1981—, chief of surgery, 1996-97; thoracic and cardiovasc. surgeon, chief thoracic surgery Halifax Hosp., Daytona Beach, 1984—, Peninsula Med. Ctr., Ormond Beach, Fla., 1993—. Contbr. articles to profl. jours. Del. Fla. Med. Assn., 1992, 93, 94. Served to capt. U.S. Army, 1970-72. Decorated Bronze Star. Fellow ACS, Am. Coll. Cardiology, Am. Coll. Chest Physicians, Internat. Coll. Surgeons; mem. AMA, So. Thoracic Surg. Assn., Soc. Thoracic Surgeons, James D. Rives Surg. Soc., Am. Heart Assn., Soc. Critical Care Medicine. Avocations: snow skiing, racquetball, writing. Home: 236 John Anderson Dr Ormond Beach FL 32176-5706 Office: Coastal Cardiovasc & Thoracic Assocs 588 Sterthaus Ave Ormond Beach FL 32174-5128 E-mail: ccardio164@aol.com.

CROMARTIE, WILLIAM JAMES, medical educator, researcher; b. Garland, N.C., May 19, 1913; s. Robert Samuel and Mary Blanche (Jester) C.; m. Josephine Colter Rule, Nov. 19, 1945; children: William James, Robert Colter, Mary Blanche, John Benjamin, Martha Anne. Student, Presbyn. Jr. Coll., 1929-30, U. N.C., 1931, U. Ala., 1931-33; MD, Emory U., 1937. Diplomate Am. Bd. Internal Medicine. Intern Emory U. divsn. Grady Hosp., Atlanta, 1937-38; resident Vanderbilt U. Hosp., Nashville, 1938-40; instr. pathology Vanderbilt U., 1939-41; asst, prof. bacteriology and medicine U. Minn., Mpls., 1949-50, assoc. prof., 1950-51; assoc. prof. bacteriology and medicine U. N.C., Chapel Hill, 1951-59; chief divsn. infectious diseases, dept. medicine N.C. Meml. Hosp., Chapel Hill, 1952-65, chief of staff, 1967-72; prof. microbiology-immunology-medicine U. N.C., Chapel Hill, 1959-85, prof. emeritus, 1985—. Mem. adv. panel microbiology Office Naval Rsch., Washington, 1950-55; mem. Nat. Bd. Med. Examiners, Phila., 1966-68; mem. infectious disease adv. com. NIH, Bethesda, Md., 1971-75. Mem. bd. govs. Capital Health Planning Agy., Durham, N.C.; mem. exec. com. Regional Med. Program N.C., 1972-76; mem. intelligence mission investigating German rsch. on biol. warfare. Maj. U.S. Army, 1942-46, ETO. Decorated Legion of Merit; named Alumni Disting. Prof. U. N.C., 1980 Fellow ACP, Am. Acad. Microbiology (chmn. bd. govs. 1974-75); mem. Soc. Am. Microbiologists (mem. coun. 1974-75), Am. Assn. Pathologists, Infectious Disease Soc. Am., U. N.C. Med. Alumni Assn. (Disting. Faculty award 1983, Disting. Svc. award 1989). Democrat. Home: Glendale 204 Weaver Rd Chapel Hill NC 27514-5947 Office: U NC Sch Medicine Dept Microbiology and Immunology 804 FLOB 23L-H Chapel Hill NC 27514 E-mail: jrcrom@mindspring.com.

CROMARTY, G. GEOFFREY, academic administrator; b. Neptune, N.J., Feb. 22, 1962; s. George Alexander Cromarty and Patricia Leigh Cole; m. Loredana V. Pugliese, July 31, 1993; 1 child, William Geoffrey. BA, We. New Eng. Coll., 1984; MA, U. Pa., 1991. Dep. dir. Office of Gov., Trenton, NJ, 1984—87; adminstr. N.J. Dept. of Environ. Protection, Trenton, 1987—94; dep. chief staff Drew U., Madison, NJ, 1994—2000; dir./spl. asst. to pres. U. Pa., Phila., 2000—02; exec. asst./sec. to corp. Phila. U., Phila., 2002—. Fellow Leadership N.J.; trustee Ctr. for Analysis of Pub. Issues, Princeton, NJ, 1997—2000. Recipient Spirit of Excellence award, St. Barnabas Hosp., 1997. Mem.: Assn. Governing Bds. Univ. and Coll. (assoc.), Nat. Assn. Presdl. Assts. in Higher Edn. (assoc.). Home: 26 Jefferson St Lambertville NJ 08530 Office: Phila Univ School House Ln and Henry Ave Philadelphia PA 19144-5497 Office Fax: 215-951-2569. Personal E-mail: jeff_cromarty@excite.com. E-mail: cromartyg@philau.edu.

CROMBIE, DOUGLASS DARNILL, aerospace communications system engineer; b. Alexandra, N.Z., Sept. 14, 1924; came to U.S., 1962, naturalized, 1967. s. Colin Lindsay and Ruth (Darnill) C.; m. Pauline L.A. Morrison, Mar. 2, 1951. B.Sc., Otago U., Dunedin, N.Z., 1947, M.Sc., 1949. N.Z. nat. rsch. fellow Cavendish Lab., Cambridge, Eng., 1958-59; head radio physics divsn. N.Z. Dept. Sci. and Indsl. Rsch., 1961-62; chief spectrum utilization divsn., chief low frequency group Inst. Telecommunications Scis., Dept. Commerce, Boulder, Colo., 1962-71, dir. inst., 1971-76; dir. Inst. Telecommunication Scis., Nat. Telecommunications and Info. Adminstrn., Boulder, Colo., 1976-80; chief scientist Nat. Telecommunication and Info. Agy., 1980-85; sr. engring. specialist Aerospace Corp., Los Angeles, 1985—. Served with N.Z. Air Force, 1943-44. Recipient Gold medal Dept. Commerce, 1970, citation, 1972 Fellow IEEE; mem. NAE, Union Radio Sci. Internat. Home: 524 Standard St El Segundo CA 90245-3039 Office: The Aerospace Corp PO Box 92957 Los Angeles CA 90009-2957

CROMER, DONALD L. aerospace engineer; Commd. 2d lt. USAF, advanced through grades to lt. gen., 1980, mem. staff Project Gemini NASA; mem. staff Satellite Data Systems program office; directorate of space AF Hdqrs.; sec. AF Spl. Projects Office; responsible for paylods on space shuttle Dept. Def., 1984—86; comdr. Space and Missile Text Orgn., Vandenberg AFB, 1986; v.p. Hughes Electronics; chmn. policy bd. Hughes Space and Comms. Co., pres. Bd. dirs. Draper Labs. Recipient Schriever award. Mem.: AIAA (bd. dirs.), Am. Astron. Soc., Calif. Space and Tech. Alliance (bd. dirs.), Air Force Assn. (life). Office: ASEB Nat Acad Scis 2001 Wisconsin Ave NW Washington DC 20007

CROMLEY, ALLAN WRAY, journalist; b. Topeka, Apr. 11, 1922; s. Frank George and Elsie May (Leedom) C.; m. Marian Minor, Jan. 30, 1949; children: Kathleen, Janet, Carter. BS in Journalism (Summerfield scholar 1940-43, 46), U. Kans., 1948. Reporter Kansas City Kansan, 1948-49, Oklahoma City Times, 1949-53; Washington bur. chief Daily Oklahoman and Oklahoma City Times, 1953-87; sr. corr. Washington bur. Daily Oklahoman, 1987-95; ret., 1995. Sec. standing com. corrs. House and Senate Galleries, 1961. Bd. visitors U. Okla., 1970-72; trustee William Allen White Found. U. Kans., 1978-90; bd. dirs. Nat. Press Found., 1987-99. With AUS, 1943-45, ETO. Mem.: Nat. Gridiron Club (pres. 1978), Nat. Press Club (pres. 1968). Home: 3320 Stoneybrae Dr Falls Church VA 22044-1222 E-mail: alcromley@aol.com.

CROMLEY, BRENT REED, lawyer, state senator; b. Great Falls, Mont., June 12, 1941; s. Arthur and Louise Lilian (Hiebert) C.; m. Dorothea Mae Zamborini, Sept. 9, 1967; children: Brent Reed Jr., Giano Lorenzo, Taya Rose. AB in Math., Dartmouth Coll., 1963; JD with honors, U. Mont., 1968. Bar: Mont. 1968, U.S. Dist. Ct. Mont. 1968, U.S. Ct. Appeals (9th cir.) 1968, U.S. Supreme Ct. 1978, U.S. Ct. Claims 1988, U.S. Ct. Appeals (D.C. cir.) 1988. Law clk. to presiding justice U.S. Dist. Ct. Mont., Billings, 1968-69; assoc. Hutton & Sheehy and predecessor firms, Billings, 1969-77, ptnr., 1977-78, Moulton, Bellingham, Longo & Mather, P.C., Billings, 1979—, also bd. dirs.; mem. Mont. Ho. of Reps., 1991-92, Mont. Senate, 2003—; pres. State Bar Mont., 1998-99. Contbr. articles to profl. jours. Mem. Yellowstone Bd. Health, Billings, 1972—; chmn. Mont. Bd. Pers. Appeals, 1974-80. Mem. ABA (appellate practice com.), ACLU, Internat. Assn. Def. Counsel, State Bar Mont. (chmn. bd. trustees 1995-97, trustee 1991—, pres. 1998-99), Yellowstone County Bar Assn. (various offices), Internat. Assn. Def. Counsel, Christian Legal Soc., Internat. Brotherhood of Magicians, Kiwanis. Avocations: running, magic, pub. speaking. Home: 235 Parkhill Dr Billings MT 59101-0660 Office: Moulton Bellingham Longo & Mather PC 27 N 27th St Ste 1900 Billings MT 59101-2399 E-mail: Cromley@moultonlawfirm.com.

CROMLEY, JON LOWELL, lawyer; b. Riverton, Ill., May 23, 1934; s. John Donald and Naomi M. (Mathews) C. JD, John Marshall Law Sch., 1966. Bar: Ill. 1966. Real estate title examiner Chgo. Title & Trust Co., 1966-70; pvt. practice Genoa, Ill., 1970—; mem. firm O'Grady & Cromley, Genoa, 1970-96. Bd. dirs. Citizen's First Nat. Bank, 1984-92, Kingston Mut. Ins. Co., Genoa Main St., Inc. Mem.: ABA, DeKalb County Bar Assn., Chgo. Bar Assn., Ill. State Bar Assn. Home: 130 Homewood Dr Genoa IL 60135-1260 E-mail: jcromley@msn.com.

CROMLEY, RAYMOND AVOLON, syndicated columnist; b. Tulare, Calif., Aug. 23, 1910; s. William James and Grace Violet (Bailey) C.; m. Masuyo Marjorie Suto (dec. Apr. 1946); m. Helen Sue Holcomb (dec. July 1967); children: Donald Stowe, Helen Sue, Jessica Lynn, Linda Grace, William Holcomb, Mary Ann, John Austin. BS in Physics, Calif. Inst. Tech., 1933; student, Japanese Lang. Inst., Tokyo, 1936-39, Strategic Intelligence Sch., Washington, 1954. Reporter Pasadena (Calif.) Post, 1928-34, Honolulu Advertiser, 1934-35, Flintridge Sch., Pasadena, 1935-36; reporter, then financial editor Japan Advertiser, Tokyo, 1936-40; editor Trans Pacific (econ. and financial weekly), 1938-40; with Wall St. Jour., 1938-55; Far Ea. corr., 1938-47; Washington corr., 1947-55; sci. editor radio program Monitor, 1955-56; econ. and financial commentator NBC radio, 1956-57; asst. producer CBS Radio, 1957-58; mil. analyst Newspaper Enterprise Assn., 1958-64; pres. Cromley News-Features, 1976—; syndicated columnist, 1964—. Asst. logic, freshman English Calif. Inst. Tech., 1928-30; lectr. Air War Coll., 1952, 54, Dept. State Fgn. Service Inst., 1955, 65-67; cons. guerilla war, Asian politics, 1952—. Author: Veterans Benefits, 1966, 2d edit., 1970, 3d edit., 1973, rev. edit., 1975, Educational Benefits, 1968, Ariwara Narihira and Japanese Poetry of the Heian and Nara Periods. Chmn. dist. bds. charter rev. Boy Scouts Am., 1956-60; sec. bishop's com. pastoral benefits Va. Conf. Meth. Ch., 1967-68; organizer com. establishment Martha Washington Libr., Mt. Vernon, Va., 1954; chmn. Inter-ch. Coun. Teen Activities and Teen Clubs, Mt. Vernon, 1955-57, World Coun. Youth, 1932-35. Prisoner of war, 1941-42; col. AUS, 1943-46; comdg. officer U.S. Mil. and Dept. State mission to Mao-Tse-tung's hdqs., Yenan, Communist China. Decorated Legion of Merit, Bronze Star medal. Mem. Nat. Trust for Historic Preservation, Asiatic Soc. Japan, State Dept. Corrs. Assn. (pres. 1954-55), White House Corrs. Assn., Ret. Officers Assn., Smithsonian Assocs., Nat. Archives Assn., Nat. Press Found., Am. Fgn. Svc. Assn., Nat. Press Club Washington, Assn.Corcoran Gallery Art, Sigma Delta Chi, Pi Kappa Delta. Republican. Methodist (lay spkr., Sunday sch. tchr.). Clubs: Tokyo Correspondents (exec. com. 1947); Overseas Writers (Washington). Home and Office: Hollin Hills 1912 Marthas Rd Alexandria VA 22307-1952 *All great religions have one common theme -- Do unto others as you would have them do unto you. Some express it, do not do unto others what you would not want them to do unto you. I have seen the power of these beliefs first hand among ordinary men and women in Japan, Korea, China, Vietnam, Laos, Thailand, Bangladesh, India, Cuba, Mexico.*

CROMWELL, ADELAIDE M. sociology educator; b. Washington, Nov. 27, 1919; d. John Wesley, Jr. and Yetta Elizabeth (Mavritte) C.; 1 son, Anthony C. Hill. AB, Smith Coll., 1940; MA, U. Pa., 1941; cert. social work, Bryn Mawr Coll., 1943; PhD, Radcliffe Coll., 1952; LHD (hon.), U. Southwestern Mass., 1972, George Washington U., 1989, Boston U., 1995. Mem. faculty Hunter Coll., 1942-44, Smith Coll., 1945-46, Boston U., 1951-85, prof. sociology, 1971-85, dir. Afro-Am. studies, 1969-88, prof. emerita sociology, 1985—. Mem. adv. com. vol. fgn. aid AID, 1964-80; mem. NEH, 1968-70; adv. com. corrections Commonwealth Mass., 1955-68; mem. commn. instns. higher edn., 1973-74; adv. com. to dir. IRS, 1970-71, to dir. census, 1972-75. Bd. dirs. Wheelock Coll., 1971--74, Nat. Ctr. Afro-Am. Artists, 1971-80, African Am. Scholars Coun., 1971—, Nat. Fellowship Fund, 1974-75, Mass. Hist. Commn., 1993; bd. dirs. Sci. and Tech. for Internat. Devel., 1984-86; mem. exec. com. Am. Soc. African Culture, 1967; mem. Mass. Hist. Soc., 1997—. Mem. AAAS, African Studies Assn. (bd. dir. 1966-68), Am. Acad. of Arts and Scis., Am. Sociol. Assn., Coun. on Fgn. Affairs (bd. fgn. scholarships 1980-84), Mass. Hist. Soc., Phi Beta Kappa. Home: 51 Addington Rd Brookline MA 02445-4519

CROMWELL, FLORENCE STEVENS, occupational therapist; b. Lewistown, Pa., May 14, 1922; d. William Andrew and Florence (Stevens) Cromwell. BS in Edn., Miami U., Oxford, Ohio, 1943; BS in Occupl. Therapy, Washington U., St. Louis, 1949; MA, U. So. Calif., 1952; cert. in health facility adminstrn., UCLA, 1978. Mem. staff, then supervising therapist L.A. County Gen. Hosp., 1949—53; occupl. therapist Goodwill Industries, L.A., 1954—55; staff therapist Vis. Nurse Assn., Phila., 1955—56; rsch. therapist United Cerebral Palsy Assn., L.A., 1956—60; dir. occupl. therapy Orthopaedic Hosp., L.A., 1961—67; coord. occupl. therapy Rsch. and Tng. Ctr. U. So. Calif. Med. Sch., L.A., 1967—70; assoc. prof. U. So. Calif., L.A., 1970—76, acting chmn. dept. occupl. therapy, 1973—76, mem. adv. bd. project SEARCH, Sch. Medicine, 1969—72; founding editor Occupl. Therapy in Health Care jour., 1984—88, editor emerita, 1988—. Assoc. dir. L.A. Job Corps Ctr., 1977—78; cons. in edn. and program devel., 1976—95; freelance editor, 1986—. Author: Manual for Basic Skills Assessment, 1960; contbr. articles to profl. jours. Mem. scholarship com. L.A. March of Dimes, 1963—70; mentor U. Tex.-Galveston Class 1990 Occupl. Therapy; bd. dirs. Am. Occupl. Therapy Found., 1965—69, v.p., 1966—69; bd. dirs. Nat. Health Coun., 1975—78. Served to lt. (j.g.) WAVES USNR, 1943—46. Recipient Disting. Alumni award, Washington U., 1978, Disting. Lectr., Calif. Occupl. Therapy Found., 1986. Fellow: Am. Occupl. Therapy Assn. (pres. 1967—73, Pres.'s WLWest commendation AOTA-AOTF 1999); mem.: Assn. Schs. Allied Health Professions (dir. 1973—74), Coalition Ind. Health Professions (chmn. 1973—74), So. Calif. Occupl. Therapy Assn. (pres. 1950—51, 1975—76), Inst. Medicine NAS (emerita 2002), Cwen, Kappa Kappa Gamma, Kappa Delta Pi, Mortar Bd.

CROMWELL, JAMES, actor; b. L.A., Jan. 27, 1940; s. John Cromwell and Kay Johnson; m. Julie Cobb. Student, Carnegie Inst. Tech. Appeared in films including Murder by Death, 1976, The Cheap Detective, 1978, The Man with Two Brains, 1983, Tank, 1984, Revenge of the Nerds, 1984, Oh, God! You Devil, 1984, The House of God, 1984, Explorers, 1985, Revenge of the Nerds II: Nerds in Paradise, 1987, The Rescue, 1988, The Runnin' Kind, 1989, Pink Cadillac, 1989, The Babe, 1992, Romeo is Bleeding, 1993, Babe, 1995 (Oscar award nominee for best supporting actor), Star Trek: First Contact, 1996, Eraser, 1996, Owd Bob, 1997, The People vs. Larry Flynt, 1996, The Education of Little Tree, 1997, L.A. Confidential, 1997, Snow Falling on Cedars, 1998, Deep Impact, 1998, Species II, 1998, Babe: Pig in the City, 1998, Winter, 1998, The General's Daughter, 1999,The Green Mile, 1999, Space Cowboys, 2000, Spirit: Stallion of the cimarron (voice), 2002, Sum of All Fears, 2002, The Nazi, 2002, Blackball, 2003, Before the Devil Knows You're Dead, 2003; TV appearances include (TV series) All in the Family, 1971, Hot L. Baltimore, 1975, The Nancy Walker Show, 1976, The Last Precinct, 1986, Easy Street, 1986, Mama's Boy, 1988, (mini TV series) Once an Eagle, 1976, Dream West, 1986, Fail Safe, 2000, The Magnificent Ambersons, 2002, RFK, 2002, A Death in the Family, 2002, Angels in America, 2003, (TV movies) The Girl in the Empty Grave, 1977, Deadly Game, 1977, 1977, A Christmas without Snow, 1980, The Rainmaker, 1982, Spraggue, 1984, Alison's Demise, 1987, China Beach, 1988, Christine Cromwell: Things That Go Bump in the Night, 1989, Miracle Landing, 1990, In a Child's Name, 1991, Revenge of the Nerds III: The Next Generation, 1992, The Shaggy Dog, 1994, Revenge of the Nerds IV: Nerds in Love, 1994; guest TV appearances include Little House on the Prairie, 1974, Three's Company, 1978, Star Trek: the Next Generation, 1987, The Client, 1995, RKO 281, 1999

CROMWELL, JAMES JULIAN, lawyer; b. Washington, Feb. 19, 1935; s. Stephen Clusky Cromwell and Phyllis Elaine Spooner; m. Barbara Lawrence Betts, Dec. 8, 1962 (dec. Nov. 1995); children: Elisabeth, James Jr., David C.; m. Louise Mathews, Dec. 13, 1997. BA, U. Va., 1956, LLB, 1959. Bar: Va. 1959, Md. 1960, DC 1962, U.S. Supreme Ct. 1970. Of counsel Miles & Stockbridge, Rockville, Md., 1992—. Chmn. Potomac Valley Bank, Gaithersburg, Md. Chmn. Nat. Rehab. Hosp., Washington, 1995-97, St. Albans Sch., Washington, 1999-2001. Fellow Am. Coll. Trial Lawyers (state chair 1993-94), Am. Coll. Estate and Trust Coun. (chmn. commn. on future of Md. cts. 1995-97), Am. Law Inst. Avocation: golf. Home: 8301 Hectic Hill Ln Rockville MD 20854-2602 Office: Miles & Stockbridge PC 22 W Jefferson St Rockville MD 20850-4215

CROMWELL, OLIVER DEAN, investment banker; b. Cleve., Sept. 19, 1950; s. Oliver and Mildred Jeanette (Galko) C.; m. Sheila Lea Terry, May 19, 1984; children: Ashley Melissa, Oliver Spencer. AB, Brown U., 1972; MBA, Harvard U., 1976. CFA. Trust adminstr. Bankers Trust, N.Y.C., 1973-74; assoc. Donaldson, Lufkin & Jenrette, N.Y.C., 1976-79, v.p., 1980-84, sr. v.p., 1985-87, Oppenheimer & Co. Inc., N.Y.C., 1987-88; 1st v.p. Paine Webber, N.Y.C., 1988-90; founder, pres. Bentley Assocs. L.P., N.Y.C., 1990—; pres. Bentley Securities Corp., N.Y.C., 1991—. Co-author: Leading Investment Bankers: The Art & Science of Investment Banking, 2002. Exec. com., bd. dirs. Assoc. Alumni Brown U., 1985—87, bd. govs., 1997—98, co-head class agt. ann. fund, 1983—87, steering com. 5-yr. reunion fund, 1976—77, steering com. 10-yr. reunion fund, 1985—87, co-chmn. 20-yr. reunion fund, 1991—92, co-chmn. 25-yr. reunion fund, 1996—97, co-chmn. 30-yr. reunion fund, 2001—02, ann. fund exec. com., 1991—93; co-chmn. N.Y. met. area com. Brown Campaign, 1992—94; class '72 v.p. Brown U., 1997—; major gifts com. Harvard Bus. Sch. 20th Reunion, 1995—96; ann. fund exec. com. Riverdale County Sch., 2000—01, 2001—02, 2002—03. Recipient Alumni Svc. award Brown U., 1990. Mem. Assn. for Investment Mgmt. and Rsch., N.Y. Soc. Security Analysts, Securities Industry Assn. N.Y. (exec. com. 1987-90), Assn. Corp. Growth, Aston Martin Owners Club-East, Maserati Club Am., Rolls Royce Owners Club (bd. dirs. 1992-93), Bentley Drivers Club (U.K.), Brown U. Club N.Y.C. (bd. dirs. 1983-95, treas. 1984-89, v.p. 1989-91, pres. 1991-93), Harvard Bus. Sch. Club. N.Y. Home: 4 Eastway Bronxville NY 10708-4302 Office: Bentley Assocs LP 101 Park Ave 22d Fl New York NY 10178-0002 E-mail: odcromwell@bentleylp.com.

CROMWELL, WILLIAM C. health facility administrator, researcher; b. Lafayette, La., Oct. 9, 1961; s. Harvey and Virginia Cromwell; m. Jamie Darlene Oliver, June 25, 1983; children: Kayley, Jill, Andrew, Anna, Nathaniel. BA in Chemistry, U. Miss., Oxford, 1983; MD, La. State U., New Orleans, 1987. Diplomate Am. Acad. Family Physicians, 1990. Resident in family medicine Trover Clinic Found., 1987—90; head divsn. lipid disorders Trover Clinic, Madisonville, Ky., 1990—94; med. dir. Lipid Treatment Program, Lake Wales, Fla., 1994—97, Fla. Lipid Inst., Orlando, 1998—99; chief med. officer LipoScience, Inc., Raleigh, NC, 1999—. Adj. assoc. prof. Wake Forest U. Sch. Medicine, Winston Salem, NC, 2000—; nat. cons. - dyslipoproteinemia, 1990—. Author: (medical practice handbook) Establishing and Managing A Private Practice Lipid Clinic, 2000; contbr. articles to profl. jours. Capt. USAR, 1983—92. Decorated Bronze Star U.S. Army; Mead Johnson Grad. fellow, Am. Acad. Family Physicians, 1990. Mem.: Am. Heart Assn., Am. Diabetes Assn., S.E. Lipid Assn., Fla. Lipid Assocs. (bd. dirs. 1995—2002). Republican. Baptist. Achievements include research in clinical implications of lipoprotein quantification by nuclear magnetic resonance spectroscopy. Avocation: Tae Kwon Do. Office: LipoScience Inc 2500 Sumner Blvd Raleigh NC 27616 E-mail: wcromwell@liposcience.com.

CRON, THEODORE OSCAR, writer, editor, educator; b. Newton, Mass., June 20, 1930; s. Jacob and Anna Ruth (Siegel) C.; m. Rosalie Heilpern, Jan. 17, 1954 (dec. Dec. 1998); children: Elizabeth Daryl Koozmin, Adam David. AB, Harvard U., 1952, MAT, 1954. Asst. commr. FDA, Washington, 1965-68; cons., writer Cron Comm., Chevy Chase, Md., 1969-77, 91—; dir. info. FTC, Washington, 1977-79; speech writer Office of Surgeon Gen., Washington, 1979-89; dir. info. Nat. Assn. Elem. Sch. Prins., Alexandria, Va., 1989-91; editor Better Ways to Health, Chevy Chase, 1995-96. Adj. prof. journalism George Washington U., Washington, 1979-96; writer, editor NIH, Bethesda, Md., 1991—, Nat. Health Svc. Corps, Bethesda, 1992—, NSF, Washington, 1993—,

Cardiology Rsch. Found., Washington, 1995—, Nat. Acad. Scis., 1996—, Magnificent Pubs., 1998—. Author: Portrait of Carnegie Hall, 1966; contbr. articles to profl. jours. Chmn. bd. dirs. Edn. Study Ctr., Washington, 1968-73; trustee Intermet, Washington, 1971-75; bd. dirs. Nat. Coalition Consumer Edn., Madison, N.J., 1989-94. Recipient Spl. award Assn. Am. Indian Physicians, 1985, Freedom Found. at Valley Forge award 1989. Mem. Washington Ind. Writers, D.C. Sci. Writers Assn., N.Y. Acad. Sci. Avocation: watercolor painting. Home: 5517 Trent St Chevy Chase MD 20815-5511 E-mail: tedcron@aol.com.

CRONAN, JR. JOHN EMERSON, microbiologist; b. Long Beach, Calif., Dec. 2, 1942; s. John Emerson Cronan and Matilda Marceline; m. Elizabeth Ann Johnson; children: Mark Robert Cronan, Glen Emerson Cronan. BA, Calif. State U., Northridge, 1965; PhD, U. Calif., Irvine, 1968. Asst. prof. molecular biophysics and biochemistry Yale U, New Haven, 1970—74, assoc. prof. molecular biophysics, 1974—78; prof. microbiology U. Ill., Urbana, 1978—, prof. biochemistry, 1987—, head dept. microbiology Urbana. Cons. E. I. DuPont Demours, Wilmington, Del., 1984—88, BASF, Ludwigshaffen, Germany, 1994—96, Monsanto, St. Louis, 1994—98, Wacker Chemie, Munich, 2001—, LG Life Science, Taejon, 2000—, Dupont, Wilmington, 1983—87, Monsanto, St. Louis, 1993—98, Advanced Medicine, Inc., South San Francisco, 2001—, Kosan Biosciences, Hayward, 2000—, Surromed, Moutain View, 2001—. Recipient MERIT award, NIH, 1993—, Biogen Award in Bacterial Physiology, Biogen, SA, 1984; scholar Univ. scholar, U. Ill., 1992. Home: 305 W High St Urbana IL 61801 Office: University of Illinois 601 S Goodwin Ave Urbana IL 61801 Home Fax: 217-328-1153; Office Fax: 217-244-6697. Business E-Mail: j-cronan@life.uiuc.edu.

CRONE, EUGENE N. addictions counselor, retired educator; b. Newton Falls, Ohio., Apr. 17, 1929; s. Clarence Bennet and Violet Richards Crone. BM, Youngstown U., 1954; MA, Columbia U., 1958; PhD, Nat. U. Grad. Studies, Dallas, 1974. Cert. addiction profl., MAC-master addiction counselor, nat. cert. addiction counselor II, internat. cert. alcohol and drug counselor. Tchr., prof. various pub. schs. and colls., 1952—78; dir. addictions Horizon Psychiatric Hosp., Clearwater, Fla., 1978—95, Nat. Deaf Acad., Mt. Dora, Fla., 1995—, La Amistad Health Svcs., Maitland, Fla., 1999—2003; with Nat. Deaf Acad., Mt. Dora, Fla., 2003—. Presenter in field. Author: They Hear Through Their Eyes, 2003; contbr. articles to profl. jours. PFC U.S. Army, 1950—52. Recipient Profl. of Yr. Nat. award, NAADAC Nat. Conv., 1997, Profl. of Yr. award, Fla. NAADAC, 1996. Mem.: NAADAC, Addiction Profls. of Fla., Internat. Cert. Alcohol & Drug Counselors. Methodist. Home: 1001 Bristol Lake Rd #212 Mount Dora FL 32757 Office: Nat Deaf Acad 19650 US Hwy 441 Mount Dora FL 32757

CRONE, JAMES ALAN, sociologist, educator; b. Connersville, Ind., May 2, 1944; s. William Edward Crone and Alice Elizabeth McNaughton. PhD, U. of Kans., 1982. Sociology tchr. Danville (Ind.) HS, 1968—71; asst. prof. Ind. State U., Terre Haute, Ind., 1979—81. Pres. Habitat for Humanity. Named Outstanding Tchr. of the Yr., Order of Omega Greek Honors Soc. of Hanover Coll., 2002. Democrat. Home: PO Box 174 Hanover IN 47243 Office: Hanover College 210 Ball Street Hanover IN 47243 Home Fax: 812-866-2164. Personal E-mail: crone@hanover.edu.

CRONE, JOHN ROSSMAN, pharmacist; b. Franklin, Pa., Apr. 11, 1933; s. Wilmer Jennings and Lydia Juanita (Rossman) C.; m. Shirley Mae Parker, July 27, 1955; children: Michael John, David Jennings, Alan Parker. BS in Pharmacy, U. Pitts., 1955. Pharmacist King's Drug Store, Clarion, Pa., 1955-56; pharmacist, mgr. Cowdrick's Drug Stores, Inc., Philipsburg, Pa., 1956-57, pharmacist Warren, Pa., 1959-80, pharmacist, mgr., 1980-88; prin., pharmacist Crone's Drug Store, Warren, 1988—. Mem. adv. bd. Salvation Army, Warren, 1984—; bd. dirs. Warren County United Way, 1983-97, pres. bd. dirs., 1993-95; chmn. Warren Bus. Group, 1990-92, Warren Bus. Dist. Coalition, 1996—; bd. dirs. Pa. Lions Eye Rsch. Found., 1970-79, Warren Libr. Assn., 2002—; bd. dirs. Pa. Lions Hearing Rsch. Found., 1980—, chmn. bd., 1994—; pres. bd. dirs. Warren Bus. Dist. Coalition, 1998-2001. Recipient Warren Lions Club Melvin Jones Fellow award, 1990, C. of C. Cmty. Svcs. award, 1990. Mem. Am. Pharm. Assn., Pa. Pharm. Assn., Warren County Pharm. Assn., Nat. Cmty. Pharmacists Assn., Warren County C. of C. (bd. dirs. 1988-95, pres.-elect 1992-93, pres. 1993-94), Lions Club (dist. gov. 1969-70. Republican. Methodist. Avocation: photography. Home: 605 Madison Ave Warren PA 16365-2940 Office: Crones Drug Store 212-214 Liberty St Warren PA 16365-2347 E-mail: cronesdrugstore@cs.com.

CRONE, JOHN THOMAS, IV, portfolio manager, financial analyst; b. Nassau, Bahamas, May 8, 1969; came to U.S., 1971; s. John Thomas III and Kathryn (Abbott) C.; m. Tanya Melich Crone, May 3, 1997; children: Daisy Kathryn, Anne. BA, So. Meth. U., 1992. Rsch. asst. San Antonio Capital Mgmt., 1992-94; sales trader Bursa-Mex. Cast Bolsa, Mexico City, 1994-95; rsch. analyst Temp. Global Advisors, Nassau, 1995-2000; v.p., portfolio mgr. Templeton Global Advisors, Nassau, 2000—. Mem. Bahamas Soc. Fin. Analysts, Lyford Cay Club, Phi Delta Theta (v.p. 1990-91). Episcopalian. Office: Templeton Global Advisors PO Box 7759 Nassau The Bahamas E-mail: jcrone@templeton.com.

CRONE, RICHARD ALLAN, cardiologist, educator; b. Tacoma, Nov. 26, 1947; s. Richard Irving and Alla Marguerite (Ernst) C.; m. Becky Jo Zimmerlund, Dec. 11, 1993. BA in Chemistry, U. Wash., 1969, MD, 1973. Intern Madigan Army Med. Ctr., Tacoma, 1973-74, resident in medicine, 1974-76, fellow in cardiology, 1977-79; commd. med. officer U.S. Army, Tacoma, Denver, San Francisco, 1972, advanced through grades to lt. col., 1981; dir. coronary care unit Fitzsimons Army Med. Ctr., Denver, 1979-81; practice medicine specializing in cardiology Stevens Cardiology Group, Edmonds, Wash., 1981—, also dir. coronary care unit, cardiac catheter lab, 1982—. Clin. assoc. prof. medicine U. Wash., Seattle, 1983—. Mem. AMA, Am. Coll. Cardiology, Am. Heart Assn., Wash. State Med. Assn. Republican. Roman Catholic. Avocations: skiing, wine collecting. Home: 10325 66th Pl W Mukilteo WA 98275-4559 Office: 21701 76th Ave W Ste 100 Edmonds WA 98026-7536 E-mail: Rick.Crone@swedish.org.

CRONENWETT, JACK LEMOYNE, vascular surgeon educator; b. Ludington, Mich., Dec. 13, 1946; s. Jack L. and K. Marie (Grundmark) C.; m. Linda R. Houk, 1969 (div. 1980); children: Sara, Molly; m. Debra A. Cote, Sept. 26, 1981. BS, U. Mich., 1969; MD, Stanford U., 1973. Diplomate Am. Bd. Surgery. Resident in gen. surgery U. Mich., Ann Arbor, 1973-79; resident in vacsular surgery U. Tenn., Memphis, 1979-80; asst. prof. surgery U. Mich., Ann Arbor, 1980-84; assoc. prof. surgery Dartmouth Coll., Hanover, N.H., 1984-89, prof. surgery, 1989—. Editor Jour. Vascular Surgery, 2003—. Mem. Am. Surg. Assn., New Eng. Soc. Vascular Surgery (sec. 1991-96, pres. 1997-98), Soc. Vascular Surgery (recorder 1996-2001, pres. 2002-03), Soc. Univ. Surgeons, Am. Assn. Vascular Surgery, Ea. Vascular Soc., Midwestern Vascular Soc., New Eng. Surg. Soc., Assn. Program Dirs. in Vascular Surgery (sec.-treas. 1993-97, pres. 2000-02, surg. residency rev. com. 1996-2002). Office: Dartmouth-Hitchcock Med Ctr 1 Medical Center Dr Lebanon NH 03756-0002 E-mail: j.cronewett@hitchcock.org.

CRONENWETT, LINDA HOUK, dean; BSN, PhD in nursing, U. Mich.; MSN in maternal-child nursing, U. Washington. Dir. profl. nursing, dir. nursing rsch. and edn. Mary Hitchcock Meml. Hosp., Lebanon, N.H., Dartmouth-Hitchcock Med. Ctr., Lebanon; mem. faculty U. Mich., U. N.H., Dartmouth U.; with U. N.C., Chapel Hill, 1998—, dean Sch. Nursing, 1999—. Mem. editl. bd. Jour. Nursing Measurement. With USN. Recipient Disting. Profl. Svc. award Assn. Women's Health, Obstetric and Neonatal Nurses, 1993, Disting. Scholar Nursing award NYU, 1997. Fellow Am. Acad. Nursing. Office: U NC Sch Nursing CB 7640 Carrington Hl Chapel Hill NC 27599-0001

CRONIN, BONNIE KATHRYN LAMB, museum director; b. Mpls., Mar. 11, 1941; d. Edwin Rector and Maude Kathryn (MacPherson) Lamb; m. Barry Jay Cronin, Jan. 23, 1963 (div. Feb. 1972); 1 son, Philip Scott. BA, U. Mo., 1963, BS, 1964; MS, Ill. State U., 1970. Copywriter Neds & Wardlow Advt., Columbia, Mo., 1962-64; tchr. Columbia Sch. System, 1964-68, Normal (Ill.) Sch. Sys., 1968-69; asst. gen. mgr. Sta. WGLT, Normal, 1969-70; dir. devel. Radio Sta. WBUR, Boston, 1970-71, program dir., 1971-75, gen. mgr., 1975-78; dir. pub. rels. Joy of Movement Ctr., 1978-80; dep. scheduler Anderson for Pres., 1980; scheduler Spaulding for Gov., 1980-81; dir. scheduling John Kerry Campaign, 1982; dir. of scheduling Mass. Lt. Gov.'s Office, dir. ops., 1983-84; dep. campaign mgr. Kerry for Senate Com., 1984; dir. ops. Senator John Kerry, Washington, 1985-86, dir. constituency outreach Boston, 1986-92, exec. asst., 1992-95; chief staff to Senator John Kerry Boston, 1995-97; dir. devel. and pub. affairs Working Capital, 1997-2001; dir. found. and major donor rels. USS Constn. Mus., 2001—. Chair Mass. Micro Enterprise Coalition, 2000-01. Active Melrose Econ. Devel. Coun., 2000—. Mem.: Mass. Broadcasters Assn. (dir. 1973—78, chairperson scholarship com., pub. svc. com., advminstrv. oversight com.), Polymnia Choral Soc. (pres. 2002—), Nat. Pub. Radio (dir. 1974—77, chairperson devel. com.). Office: Box 1812 Boston MA 02129 E-mail: bonniemelrose@aol.com.

CRONIN, DAN, state legislator; b. Elmhurst, Ill., Nov. 7, 1959; BA, Northwestern U., 1981; JD, Loyola U., 1985. Campaign coord. Congressman John E. Porter, 1981; law clk. spl. prosecution divsn. Ill. Atty. Gen. Office, 1983; minority leader Ill. Ho. of Reps., 1985-87; with DuPage County State's Atty.'s Office, 1987-89; Ill. State sen. Dist. 39, 1993—. Mem. Elem. and Secondary Edn., Gen. Svcs. Appropriations and Health Care Coms.; atty. Kemp & Capanna, Ltd., Oak Brook, Ill. Mem. YMCA. Mem. ABA, ATLA,Ill. Bar Assn., DuPage County Bar Assn., Am. Cancer Soc., Lions, KC. Address: 105 E 1st St Elmhurst IL 60126-2801*

CRONIN, DANIEL ANTHONY, archbishop; b. Boston, Mass., Nov. 14, 1927; s. Daniel George and Emily Frances (Joyce) Cronin. STL, Gregorian U., 1953, STD summa cum laude, 1956; LLD, Suffolk U., Boston, 1969, Stonehill Coll., North Easton, 1971. Ordained priest Roman Catholic Ch., 1952. Attache Apostolic Internunciature, Addis Ababa, Ethiopia, 1957—61, Secretariat of State, Vatican City, 1961—68; named Monsignor by His Holiness Pope John XXIII, 1962; named titular bishop of Egnatia and aux. bishop of Boston, 1968—70; Episcopal ordination from Archbishop of Boston Richard Cardinal Cushing, 1968; pastor St. Raphael Ch., Medford, Mass., 1968—70; bishop Fall River, Mass., 1970—92; archbishop of Hartford Conn., 1992—. Mem.: KC (Father Michael J. McGivney award 1999). Office: 134 Farmington Ave Hartford CT 06105-3723*

CRONIN, JAMES WATSON, physicist, educator; b. Chgo., Sept. 29, 1931; s. James Farley and Dorothy (Watson) Cronin; m. Annette Martin, Sept. 11, 1954; children: Catheryn, Emily, Daniel Watson. AB, So. Methodist U. (1951); PhD, U. Chgo.; D (hon.), U. Paris, 1995, U. Leeds, 1996, Univ. Pierre & Marie Curie, 1994; DSc (hon.), U. Leeds, 1996. Asst. physicist Brookhaven Nat. Lab., 1955—58; asst. prof. Princeton, 1958—65, prof. physics, 1965—71; prof. physics and astronomy U. Chgo., 1971—, prof. emeritus physics and astronomy. Loeb lectr. physics Harvard U., 1967; participant early devel. spark chambers; co-discoverer CP-violation, 64; lectr. Nashima Found., 1993. Decorated chevalier Legion of Honor (France); recipient Rsch. Corp. Am. award, 1967, John Price Wetherill medal, Franklin Inst., 1976, E.O. Lawrence award, ERDA, 1977, Nobel prize for Physics, 1980, Nat. medal of Sci., 1999; fellow Guggenheim, 1982—83; Sloan fellow, 1964—66, Guggenheim fellow, 1970—71. Mem.: NAS (coun. mem.), Am. Phys. Soc., Am. Acad. Arts and Scis., Am. Philos. Soc. Office: U Chgo Enrico Fermi Inst 5630 S Ellis Ave Chicago IL 60637-1433

CRONIN, JEROME JOSEPH, JR., marketing educator, consultant; b. Springfield, Ohio, Apr. 27, 1952; s. Jerome Joseph Cronin and Edith E. Markley; m. Kern S. Westerberg, Oct. 9, 1976 (div. Aug. 1980). BS in Mktg., Wright State U., 1974; MBA, U. Dayton, 1976; PhD in Mktg., The Ohio State U., 1981. Vis. asst. prof. The Ohio State U., Columbus, 1981—82; asst. prof. U. Ky., Lexington, 1982—86; from asst. prof. to prof. Fla. State U., Tallahassee, 1986—94, prof., 1994—2002, Carl DeSantis Prof. Bus. Adminstrn., 2002—. Dir. edn. and tng. The Mktg. Inst. Fla. State U., 1997—; cons. Internat. Taxi & Literary Found., Raleigh, N.C., 1999-2001, Southwest Bell, San Antonio, Tex., 2000-01, Fla. Dept. Transportation, Tampa, 1997-2001, Ameritech, Chgo., 2000. Contbr. articles to profl. jours. Panel mem. Ctr. Clean Air Policy, Washington, 1999-2001, Transportation Rsch. Bd., Washington, 1999-2000, State of Ariz., Phoenix, 2000. Mem. Soc. Mktg. Advances, Am. Mktg. Assn., Acad. Mktg. Sci. Democrat. Roman Catholic. Avocations: baseball, travel, photography. Home: 3701 Sally Ln Tallahassee FL 32312 Office: Fla State Univ Coll of Business Tallahassee FL 32306 E-mail: jcronin@cob.fsu.edu.

CRONIN, KATHLEEN ANNE, executive search consultant; b. Oak Park, Ill., Sept. 17, 1933; d. Brendan C. and Rose J. (Mangini) Powell; m. Richard Cronin, May 29, 1954; children: Anne, Patrick, Richard, Edward, John, Michael, Eileen. BA, DePaul U., 1977. Cert. CPR instr. Sec., credit asst. Hills Bros. Coffee, 1951-53; estimator Alpha Portland Cement, 1953-54; v.p. adminstrn. and rsch. Hodge-Cronin & Assocs., Des Plaines, Ill., 1977—. Conflict resolution cons. Office Cath. Edn. Archdiocese. Mem. Human Rels. Com. City of Des Plaines, St. Mary Pastoral Coun., St. Mary Sch. Bd., Des Plaines; rsch. Ill. Ctr. Parapsychol. Rsch.; conciliator Archdiocese Chgo. Office Conciliation; mem. covenant com. St. Mary's/Trinity Luth. Ch.; mem. alumni bd. DePaul U. Sch. for New Learning, 1998-2000. Home: 1450 Harding Ave Des Plaines IL 60016-4379 Office: Hodge Cronin & Assocs PO Box 309 Des Plaines IL 60016-0309

CRONIN, KEVIN BRIAN, lawyer; b. Worcester, Mass., Sept. 2, 1943; s. Jeremiah Joseph and Julia Elizabeth (Alavosius) C.; m. Patti Adrienne Wright, May 1, 1971; 1 child, Kevin Brian. AB, U. Pa., 1965; JD, U. Wis., 1970, MA in Am. History, 1983, MA in Pub. Policy and Adminstrn., 1994. Bar: Wis. 1971, Hawaii 1979. Vol. U.S. Peace Corps, Turkey, 1965-67; asst. dist. atty. Rock County, Beloit, Wis., 1970-73; pvt. practice Janesville & Hartford, Wis., 1974-78; trust officer First Hawaiian Bank, Honolulu, 1978-79; pvt. practice Honolulu, 1980; legal counsel Beloit Coll., 1981-83, Wis. Elections Bd., Madison, 1983-87; chief counsel Wis. Dept. Employee Trust Funds, Madison, 1987-89; counsel Wis. Dept. Revenue, Madison, 1989-97; chief counsel elec. divsn. Pub. Svc. Commn. Wis., Madison, 1997-99, asst. gen counsel, 1999-2000, adminstr. nat gas divsn., 2000. Trustee in bankruptcy U.S. Dist. Ct., We. Dist., 1974-77; rsch. asst. U. Wis., Madison, 1980; mem. unemployment compensation adv. coun. Wis. Dept. Industry, Labor and Human Rels., Madison, 1992-94, utility tax, 1992-94, study group Wis. Dept. Revenue, Madison, 2000-01; cons. Uttar Pradesh Electricity Regulator commn., Lucknow, India, 2000-01, Philippines' Dept. of Energy, 2002--; counsel Wis. State Interagy. Land Use Coun. Report, Madison, 1996-97; selectee, tax policy advisor U.S. Treasury Dept. to Min. of Fin. Republic of Armenia, 1997. Mem. Mayor's Com. on Crime Prevention, Hartford, 1977; bd. dirs. Hartford Area Day Care Ctr., 1977. Recipient Cert. of Commendation, Hartford City Coun., 1977. Mem. State Bar of Wis. (interim bd. dirs. energy and telecom. sect. 1998-99, sect. bd. dirs. 1999-2001), Hawaii Bar Assn., Hartford Area C. of C. (bd. dirs. 1977). Home: 1215 Boundary Rd Middleton WI 53562-3862 Office: Pub Svc Commn Wis PO Box 7854 Madison WI 53707-7854

CRONIN, MICHAEL THOMAS IGNATIUS, pathologist, educator; b. Glasgow, Scotland, Feb. 1, 1924; came to U.S., 1952; naturalized, 1958; s. Thomas Mary and Susan Dorothea (O'Keeffe) C.; m. Carmel Sheridan, Nov. 21, 1950; children: Susan Mary Ingrid, Thomas Michael Sheridan, Agnes Wilhelmina Carmel, Geraldine Teresa Ruth, Charles Patrick Desmond, Arthur John Christopher, Carmel Marie Louise, Brenda Juliana Patricia, Michael Terence Richard. M.R.C.V.S., U. Dublin, 1945, M.Sc. in Bacteriology, 1946, PH.D. in Pathology and Bacteriology, 1948; cert. in mgmt., N.Y. U., 1959; MD, Georgetown U., 1965; postgrad., Yale U., 1965 68. Diplomate Am. Bd. Pathology. Research fellow Irish Racing Bd., 1947-50; research officer Equine Research Sta., Eng., 1950-52; dir. Regional Lab., Warrenton, Va., 1952-53; bacteriollogist dept. animal pathology U. Ky., 1953-55; assoc. pathologist Penrose Lab. Phila. Zoo; also asst. prof. vet. pathology U. Pa., 1955-57; head dept. pathology and toxicology Schering Corp., N.J., 1957-61; pathologist Woodard Research Corp., Herndon, Va., 1961-65, Vets. Meml. Med. Ctr., Meriden, 1990-93, dir. labs. east campus, 1990-93; intern, asst. resident, postdoctoral research fellow Yale-New Haven Hosp. and Yale U., 1965-67; resident VA Hosp., West Haven, Conn., 1967-68; pathologist, dir. labs. Meml. Hosp., Meriden, Conn., 1968-72, 74-90, chief of staff, 1981-83, cons. pathologist, 1972-74; pathologist, dir. labs. Masonic Hosp., Wallingford, Conn., 1968-70, 72-76; cons. pathologist Bradley Hosp., Southington, Conn., 1970-91; attending physician, assoc. pathologist Hosp. of St. Raphael, New Haven, 1972-76; asst. clin. prof. Yale U., 1972—. Cons. editor Am. Scientist, 1971-89. Med. Research Council Ireland fellow, 1948. Mem. Am. Soc. Investigative Pathology, Am. Coll. Vet. Pathologists (cert.), Conn. Med. Soc., U.S. and Can. Acad. Pathology, Meriden Med. Soc., New Haven County Med. Assn., Sigma Xi, Alpha Omega Alpha. Roman Catholic. Home: 71 Turtle Bay Dr Branford CT 06405-4977

CRONIN, PATRICK M. federal agency administrator; married; 2 children. Deputy dir., dir. rsch. Nat. Def. U.'s Inst. Nat. Strategic Studies; asst. adminstr. bur. policy and program coord. USAID, Washington, 2001—. Lectr. in field. Author: From Globalism to Regionalism: Ne wPerspectives on U.S. Foreign an dDefense Policies, 1993, Redefining the U.S.-Japan Alliance, 1994, 2015: Power and Progress, 1996, The U.S.-Japan Alliance: Past, Present and Future, 1999, Adapting to the New National Security Environment, 2000, Passing the Baton: Lessons of Statecradt for the New Administration, 2001, Effective Planning for Conflict Prevention and Management, 2001; contbr. articles to profl. jours.; mem. editl. adv. bd.: Internat. Studies in Perspectives, Jour. Korean Studies; editor: Strategic Rev. With USN, 1987—2000. Office: USAID RRB 1300 Pennsylvania Ave NW Washington DC 20523

CRONIN, PATTI ADRIENNE WRIGHT, state agency administrator; b. Chgo., May 25, 1943; d. Rodney Adrian and Dorothy Louise (Thiele) Wright; m. Kevin Brian Cronin, May 1, 1971; 1 child, Kevin. BA, Beloit (Wis.) Coll., 1965; JD with honors, U. Wis., 1983. Vol. Peace Corps, Turkey, 1965-67, recruiter, 1967-68; tchr. English Kamehameha III Sch., Lahaina, Hawaii, 1968-70, Evansville (Wis.) High Sch., 1972-77; tchr. math. and history Killian Sch., Hartford, Wis., 1977-78; tchr. English Kaiser High Sch., Honolulu, 1979-80; intern Wis. Ct. Appeals, Madison, 1983; exec. dir. Wis. Waste Facility Siting Bd., Madison, 1983—. Founder, v.p., bd. dirs. Justice Ctr. Honolulu, 1979-82; sec., treas. Cronin Constrn. Co., Inc., Madison, 1986—. Editor: Internat. Law Jour., 1982. Bd. dirs. Neighborhood Bd., Honolulu, 1979-82; chmn. United Way, 1989—; active Parent Citizens Adv. Coun. Recipient Mayor's award of outstanding achievement, City of Honolulu, 1980. Mem. Soc. Profls. in Dispute Resolution, ABA, State Bar Wis. Avocations: family, real estate, travel. Office: Waste Facility Siting Bd 201 W Washington Ave Madison WI 53703-2760 E-mail: patti.cronin@wfs.state.wi.us.

CRONIN, PHILIP MARK, lawyer; b. Boston, July 21, 1932; s. Herbert Joseph and Elizabeth Ann (Sullivan) C.; m. Paula Cook Budlong, June 8, 1957; children: Thomas B., Philip S. AB, Harvard U., 1953, LL.B., 1956. Bar: Mass. 1956. Sr. ptnr. firm Withington, Cross, Park & Groden, Boston, 1956 89, Peabody & Arnold, Boston, 1989—. Pres., pub. Harvard mag., 1971-78; city solicitor, Cambridge, Mass., 1968-72 Mng. editor: Mass. Law Rev. 1976-81; editor in chief, 1981-90; editor Mass. Legal History Jour., 1996—. Trustee Harvard Crimson, 1972—; pres. Cambridge Homes, 1991-94; overseer Mass. Supreme Jud. Ct. Hist. Soc., 1994—, editor jour., 1995—. Home: 3 Lincoln Ln Cambridge MA 02138-3351 Office: 50 Rowes Wharf Boston MA 02110-3339

CRONIN, ROBERT LAWRENCE, sculptor, painter; b. Lexington, Mass., Aug. 10, 1936; s. Daniel Augustus and Eileen Ursula (Keating) C.; m. Constance Marie Nelson, June 27, 1964 (div. 1974). BFA, R.I. Sch. Design, 1959; MFA, Cornell U., 1962. Tchr. Mich. State U., East Lansing, 1965-66, Bennington (Vt.) Coll., 1967-68, Brown U., Providence, 1969-71; tchrs. Sch. Worcester (Mass.) Art Mus., 1972-80. One-man shows Mus. Art Carnegie Inst., Pitts., 1981, Sculpture Ctr. Gallery, N.Y.C., 1981, Gimpel Fils Gallery, London, 1982, Gimpel & Weitzenhoffer Gallery, N.Y.C., 1982, 84, 87, 89, Watson de Nagy Gallery, Houston, 1983, 86, Gimpel-Hanover Galerien, Zurich, 1983, Clark Gallery, Lincoln, Mass., 1983, 85, 87, Janet Steinberg Gallery, San Francisco, 1985, Galerie Esperanza, Montreal, 1985, 87, Klonaridis Gallery, Toronto, 1984, 85, 87, 88, 89, Galerie Keeser-Bohbot, Hamburg, Germany, 1987, 89, Alice Simsar Gallery, Ann Arbor, Mich., 1988, Yoh Art Gallery, Osaka, 1989, Gallery Hiro, Tokyo, 1989, Helander, Gallery, Palm Beach, Fla., 1990, Fitchburg (Mass.) Art Mus., 1990, Munson Gallery, New Haven, 1991, Sound Shore Gallery, Stamford, Conn., 1992, Virginia Lynch Gallery, Tiverton, R.I., 1996, 98, Dillon Gallery, N.Y.C., 1996, 99, Tremaine Gallery, Hotchkiss Sch., Lakeville, Conn., 1999, Joseph Rickards Gallery, N.Y.C., 2001, Dillon Gallery, Oyster Bay, N.Y., 2002; represented in permanent collections Bklyn. Mus., Mus. Fine Arts, Boston, Mus. Art, U. Okla., Mus. Art, Carnegie Inst., Mus. Art, R.I. Sch. Design, Nat. Air and Space Mus., Mus. Fine Arts, Springfield, Worcester Art Mus., Worcester Polytech. Inst., De Cordova Mus., Nat. Acad. Design, N.Y.C. Recipient 1st prize for painting Boston Fine Arts Festival, 1963; recipient awards Mass. Artists Found., 1975, 79; individual support grantee Adolph and Esther Gottlieb Found., 1991. Mem. Nat. Acad. Design. Home: PO Box 74 Falls Village CT 06031-0074

CRONIN, THOMAS EDWARD, academic administrator; b. Milton, Mass., Mar. 18, 1940; s. Joseph M. and Mary Jane Cronin; m. Tania Zaroodny, Nov. 26, 1966; 1 child, Alexander. AB, Holy Cross Coll., 1961; MA, Stanford U., 1964, PhD, 1968; LLD (hon.), Marietta Coll., 1987, Franklin Coll., 1993. Tchg. fellow Stanford U., Calif., 1962—64; staff mem. The White House, Washington, 1966—67; faculty mem. U. N.C., 1967—70; staff fellow Brookings Instn., 1970—72; faculty mem. Brandeis U., Waltham, Mass., 1975—77, U. Del., Newark, 1977—79; McHugh prof. of Am. instns. The Colo. Coll., Colorado Springs, 1985—93, acting pres., 1991; pres. Whitman Coll., Walla Walla, Wash., 1993—. Bd. dirs. Cascade Natural Gas Co.; moderator Aspen Inst. Exec. Sems., 1975—; pres. CRC, Inc., 1980—, Presidency Rsch. Group, 1981—82; cons. in field; guest polit. analyst various tv programs; mem. Wash. Com. Humanities. Author: The State of the Presidency, 1980, Direct Democracy, 1989, Colorado Politics and Government, 1993, The Paradoxes of the American Presidency, 1998, 2004. Dir. IES Chgo., Jr. Statesmmman Found.; bd. dirs. Inst. Am. Univs.; trustee Jr. Statesman Am., 2002—. Mem.: Inst. Edn. Internat. Students, Western Polit. Sci. Assn. (pres. 1993—94), Am. Polit. Sci. Assn. (exec. com. 1990—92), C. of C., Pi Sigma Alpha. Avocations: tennis, hiking. Office: Whitman Coll Pres Ofc Memorial 303 345 Boyer Ave Walla Walla WA 99362-2067

CRONK, LEONARD, management consultant; b. Paterson, N.J., Apr. 19, 1943; s. Leonard and Ruth (Brewer) Cronk; m. Martha Fanning, Aug. 21, 1965 (div. 1998); children: Catherine Cronk Clifford, Martha Brewer; m. Hisayo Arikawa, Oct. 25, 1998. BS in Indsl. Engring., Cornell U., 1965, M in Indsl. Engring., 1966, MBA, 1967. Cert. mgmt. cons., mgmt. acctg., securities registrations. Mem. ops. rsch. staff Mobil Corp., N.Y.C., 1967-69; from cons. to sr. mgr. Price Waterhouse, N.Y.C., 1969-79; mgr. fin. systems Kennecott Corp., Stamford, Conn., 1979-82; v.p. Kidder, Peabody, N.Y.C., 1982-87, Merrill Lynch, N.Y.C., 1987-91; mgmt. cons. Rowayton, Conn., 1991—; v.p. Manley Mktg., Greenwich, Conn. Mem. adv. bd. Belle Haven Land Assn., Greenwich, Conn., 1983-85, bd. dirs., 1986-89; bd. dirs. Belle Haven Club, Greenwich, 1990-94. Republican. Episcopalian. Avocations: playing trumpet, tennis. Home: 110 Leroy Ave Darien CT 06820 E-mail: leonardcronk@sbcglobal.net.

CRONKITE, WALTER, radio and television news correspondent; b. St. Joseph, Mo., Nov. 4, 1916; s. Walter Leland and Helen Lena Cronkite; m. Mary Elizabeth Maxwell, Mar. 30, 1940; children: Nancy Elizabeth, Mary Kathleen, Walter Leland III. Student, U. Tex., 1933—35; LLD, Rollins Coll., 1966, Bucknell U., Syracuse U.; LHD, Ohio State U.; hon. degree, Am. Internat. Coll., Harvard U. News writer, editor Scripps-Howard, also UP, Houston, Kansas City, Dallas, Austin, El Paso; UP war corr., 1942—45; fgn. corr., reopening burs. in Amsterdam, Brussels, chief corr. Nuremberg war crimes trials, bur. mgr., Moscow, 1946—48; lectr., mag. contbr., 1948—49; CBS-News corr., 1950—81; spl. corr., 1981—; mng. editor CBS Evening News with Walter Cronkite, 1962—81. Chmn. The Cronkite Ward Co., 1993—; host spl. Universe, CBS, The Holocaust: In Memory of Millions, The Discovery Channel, 1993; anchor for TV news spls. Vietnam: A War That is Finished, 1975, In Celebration of US, 1976, Our Happiest Birthday, 1977, The President in China, 1975, Solzhenitsyn: 1984 Revisited. Author: The Challenges of Change, 1971, A Reporter's Life, 1996; co-author: South by Southeast, North by Northeast, Westwind; prodr.(host): The e Reports (12 episode series for Discovery Channel), 1994—96, Cronkite Remembers (8 part series for CBS and Discovery Channel, 1996. Recipient Cable Ace award for best program interviewer, 1993, Peabody award, 1962, 1981, Emmy awards, William A. White award for journalistic merit, 1969, George Polke Journalism award, 1971, Gold medal, Internat. Radio and TV Soc., 1974, Alfred I. DuPont-Columbia U. award in broadcast journalism, 1978, 1981, Presdl. medal of

Freedom, 1981. Mem.: Assn. Radio News Analysts, Acad. Arts and Scis. (pres. nat. acad. N.Y. chpt. 1959, Gov.'s award 1979), Bohemian Club, N.Y. Yacht Club, Nat. Press Club, Overseas Press Club, Explorers Club, Chi Phi. Office: CBS Inc 51 W 52nd St Ste 1934 New York NY 10019-6119

CRONON, WILLIAM, history educator; b. New Haven, Sept. 11, 1954; m. Nancy Elizabeth Fey. BA in History, English with honors, U. Wis., 1976; MA in Am. History, Yale U., 1979, M of Philosophy in Am. History, 1981, PhD in Am. History, 1990; DPhil in Brit. History, Oxford U., 1981. Asst. prof. history Yale U., New Haven, 1981-86, assoc. prof., 1986-91, prof., 1991-92, mem. studies in environment program creation com., 1983-84, co-chair studies environment program, 1989-92, dir. grad. studies, history dept., 1990-92; Frederick Jackson Turner chair of history, geography, and environ. studies U. Wis., Madison, 1992—, dir. honors program Coll. Letters and Sci., 1996-98, Vilas rsch. prof., 2003—; found. fac. dir. Chadbourne Residential Coll., 1997-2000. Asst. Am. sec. Rhodes Scholarship Trust, 1978-80, Wis. state sec., 1993-98; cons. in field; mem. adv. bd. The History Tchr., 1986-2000. Rhodes Dist. chmn., 2002-. Author: Changes in the Land: Indians, Colonists and the Ecology of New England, 1983 (Valley Forge honor cert. 1984, Soc. Colonial award citation of honor 1984, Francis Parkman prize 1984), Nature's Metropolis: Chicago and the Great West, 1991 (Chgo. Tribune Heartlaand prize 1991, Bancroft prize 1992, George Perkins Marsh prize 1993); editor: (with Miles and Gitlin) Under an Open Sky: Rethinking America's Western Past, 1992, Uncommon Ground: Rethinking the Human Place in Nature, 1995; mem. bd. editors Forest and Conservation History, 1986-91; also articles; gen. editor Weyerhaeuser Environ. Books, U. Wash. Press, 1993—. Bd. dirs. Conn. Fund for Environ., 1986-91, v.p., 1987-89; mem. adv. bd. TV series Am. Experience Sta. WGBH-TV; trustee Conn. Nature Conservancy, 1989-91; bd. dirs., mem. com. on problems and policy Social Sci. Rsch. Coun., 1991-96, chairperson com. on problems and policy, 1994-96. Rhodes scholar Oxford U., 1976-78; fellow Danforth Found., 1976-82, Newberry Libr., 1980, Mellon Found., 1982-83, Morse fellow Yale U., 1985-86, MacArthur Found., 1985-90, Whitney Humanities Ctr., 1987-89, fellow U. Calif. Humanities Rsch. Inst., 1994, Guggenheim fellow, 1995. Mem. AAAS, Am. Hist. Assn. (Robinson prize com. 1990), Am. Philos. Soc. (v.p. profl. divsn. 2002—), Orgn. Am. Historians (chmn. Curti prize com. 1987-88), Forest History Soc. (bd. dirs.), Econ. History Assn., Agrl. History Soc., Ecol. Soc. Am., Western Hist. Assn. (conv. program com. 1987, chmn. 1991-92), Assn. Am. Geographers, Am. Studies Assn., Am. Anthrop. Assn., Wilderness Soc. (gov. coun. 1995—), Am. Soc. for Ethnohistory, Chgo. Hist. Soc., Am. Antiquarian Soc., Soc. Am. Historians, Phi Beta Kappa (William C. DeVane award Yale chpt. 1988), Phi Kappa Phi, Phi Eta Sigma. Office: U Wis Dept History 3211 Humanities 455 N Park St Madison WI 53706-1405 Home: 2027 Chadbourne Ave Madison WI 53726-4046 E-mail: wcronon@wisc.edu.

CRONSON, ROBERT GRANVILLE, lawyer; b. Chgo., Dec. 23, 1924; s. Berthold A. and Ethel (Larson) C.; m. Agnes L. Diaz; children from previous marriage: Karen, Christopher, Keelyn, Morgan, Seth. AB in Econs., Dartmouth Coll., 1947; JD, U. Chgo., 1950. Bar: Ill. 1950. Atty. Daily, Dines, Ross & O'Keefe, Chgo., 1951-53; ptnr. DeBoice, Greening, Ackerman & Cronson, Springfield, Ill., 1957-60; asst. sec. of state of Ill. Springfield, 1958-64; sr. vp., sec. The Chgo. Corp., Chgo., 1965-73; assoc. prof. pub. adminstrn. Roosevelt U., 1973-74; adj. prof. adminstrn. Sangamon State U., 1983-87; auditor gen. State of Ill., 1974-92; retired, 1992. Mem. exec. com. post audit sect. Nat. Conf. State Legislatures, 1976-85, Nat. Assn. State Auditors, Comptrs. and Treasurers, 1979-81, and Nat. Intergovtl. Audit Forum, 1974-76; mem. Midwest Intergovtl. Audit Forum, 1974-92; adv. com. govt. acctg. standards Govt. Acctg. Stds. Bd. 1984-85. Chmn. Midwest Vehicle Proration Compact, 1959-61, Ill. Securities Adv. Com., 1964-73; chmn. William H. Chamberlain Scholarship Fund, Sangamon State U., 1972-85. Cpl. USMCR, 1942-46. Recipient Fin. Mgmt. Improvement (Scantlebury) award U.S. Govt., 1980 Mem. Midwest Securities Commrs. Assn. (chmn. 1959-64), Securities Industry Assn. Am. (chmn. state legislation com. 1970-72), Nat. State Auditors Assn. (pres. 1980-81), Pi Alpha Alpha (hon.), Phi Kappa Psi. E-mail: cronson@sbcglobal.net.

CROOG, ROSLYN ZEPORAH, chief systems engineer; b. New Haven, July 14, 1942; d. Herbert Bernard and Belle (Brown) Croog; children: Bradley Jordan Paul, Katie Miriam Paul. AS, Quinnipiac Coll., 1962; BS, Fla. Internat. U., 1982. Analyst, programmer DBA Systems, Inc., Melbourne, Fla., 1982-84, sys. mgr. Fairfax, Va., 1984-86; mem. tech. staff MRJ, Inc., Fairfax, Va., 1986-98; chief sys. engr. AverStar, Inc., Vienna, Va., 1998—2000. Avocations: photography, sailing, cross-country skiing.

CROOK, ALISON LAURA, academic administrator; b. Grafton, N.S.W., Australia, Oct. 7, 1947; d. Charles Robert and Nance Miriam (Mackney) Bunning; m. Alan Crook, Jan. 20, 1973. BA with honors, U. New Eng., N.S.W., 1969; Grad. Diploma Libr., U. S.A., 1976; Diploma in Edn., U. Adelaide, 1978; MBA, U. Queensland, 1983; D (hon.), U. South Australia, 1993; DLitt (hon.), U. Macquarie, 1995. Tutor in philosophy Flinders U., Australia, 1969-70; Australian vol. abroad, lectr. in art St. Pauls Tchrs. Coll., Vunakanau, Papua, New Guinea, 1971-72; cmty. liaison officer, accounts clk. Gunpowder Copper Ltd., Queensland, 1973-74; lectr. Resource Ctr. Tech. and Further Edn., South Australia, 1976-79; prin. libr. North Brisbane Coll. Advanced Edn., Queensland, 1980-82; dep. state libr. State Libr. of N.S.W., Sydney, 1982-87, state libr., CEO, 1987-94; dir.-gen. Dept. of State and Regional Devel., Sydney, NSW, 1995-97; exec. dir. ops. Serco, Asia-Pacific, 1997—2000; dep. vice-chancellor, v.p. resources Monash U., 2000—. Dir. IBM Australia, Lend Lease Corp. Fin. Svcs., 1992—96, Open Learning Agy. of Australia, 1993—94, Open Learning Tech. Corp., 1993—95, Open Net Pty. Ltd., 1994—95, Australian Tech. Park Ltd., 1995—97, Australian Chamber Orch., 1996—2000. Contbr. articles to profl. jours. Dir. St. James Ethics Ctr., 1992—, Overseas Svc. Bur., 1992—95; bd. govs. U. We. Sydney, 1993—94; mem. Small Bus. Devel. Corp., 1993—94, 1996—; pres. nat. coun. Australian Coun. of Libr. Info. Svcs., 1990—92; dir. Recruitment Solutions Party Ltd., 2001—02, Overseas Projects Corp. Victoria, 2002—. Decorated Officer in the Order of Australia Nat. Honor, Fed. Govt.; named Bus. Woman of the yr., Qantas/Bull., 1993, Bus. Leader of the Yr., Bus. Rev. Weekly/Alcatel, 1991, Univ. Qld. Alumnus of the Yr., 1995; recipient Award of Achievement, South Australian U. Grads. Assn., 1990. Fellow: Royal Inst. Pub. Adminstrn. of Australia (pres. NSW divsn. 1992—93), Australian Inst. Co. Dirs., Australian Inst. Mgmt., Australian Libr. and Info. Assn. (Libr. Mgr. of Yr. 1989); mem.: Chief Exec. Women, Sydney Rotary (Paul Harris fellow 1993). Avocations: theater, music, opera, canoeing, swimming.

CROOK, BETTY ROSS, lawyer; b. Shreveport, La., Aug. 16, 1927; d. John H. and Edna Allison (Wallette) Ross; m. Jack P.A. Crook, Sept. 25, 1966 (dec. 1976). BS, Centenary Coll., 1947; JD, Georgetown U. 1954. Bar: Tex. 1955. Claims examiner VA Regional Office, Waco, Tex., 1966-67; asst. fin. v.p. Baylor U., Waco, 1976-81, property mgmt. assoc. office bus. affairs, 1981-88, records rsch. coord., 1988—. Pres. Women's Guild St. Mary's Cath. Ch., Waco, 1982-84, 87-88, v.p., 1988-90, 95-96, chmn. liturgy commn., 1979-89, sec. parish bd., 1981-85, 88—, pres. parish bd., 1980-81, 87-88, mem. fin. com. 1987—; mem. legis. com. Regis-St. Elizabeth's Nursing Home, Waco, 1985; bd. trustees Reicher Cath. H.S., 1987-98, sec. bd., 1988-91, 94-96, pres. bd. trustees, 1991-93; parish historian St. Mary's Cath. Ch., 1991-95; bd. dirs. Holy Cross Cemetery Assn., 1991—. Mem. Tex. Bar Assn., Waco-McLennan County Bar Assn., Ctrl. Tex. Geneal. Soc. (bd. dirs. 1992—), Waco-McLennan County Libr. Commn. (chmn. 2001). Contbr. articles to numerous books. Avocations: reading, ch. choir singing. E-mail: Betty_Crook@baylor.edu. Home: 1810 Lyle Ave Waco TX 76708-2857 Office: Baylor U Bus Affairs Office PO Box 97086 Waco TX 76798-7086

CROOK, DONALD MARTIN, lawyer; b. Wichita, Kans., Dec. 18, 1947; s. Leroy R. and Audrey E. (Mattiason). BA in History/Polit. Sci. with honors, U. Kans., 1970; JD, U. Chgo., 1973. Bar: N.Y. 1974, Tex. 1982. Assoc. Kramer, Levin, Nessen, Kamin & Frankel, N.Y.C., 1973-75, Layton & Sherman, N.Y.C., 1975-80; counsel LTV Corp., Dallas, 1980-85; chief counsel corp. affairs Kimberly-Clark Corp., Dallas, 1985-99, v.p., sec., 1986-99. Mem. ABA, Tex. Bar Assn., Dallas Bar Assn. (chmn. corp. counsel sect. 1986-87), Am. Soc. Corp. Secs.

CROOK, ROBERT WAYNE, retired mutual funds executive; b. Hartford, Conn., Apr. 6, 1936; s. William Gregor and Laura Foster (Keenan) C.; m. Leslie C. Rischer, Oct. 22, 1988; children from previous marriage: Robert Wayne, Laura Sigrid. AB, Harvard U., 1959; postgrad., U. Va. Sch. Law, 1962. With White, Weld & Co., Inc., Boston, 1961—78, v.p., 1971—75, 1st v.p., 1975—78; pres., dir. White Weld Money Market Fund, Boston, 1974—78, White Weld Govt. Fund, Boston, 1977—78; with Merrill Lynch Asset Mgmt., Inc., Boston, 1978—2001, v.p., 1981—89, sr. v.p., 1989—2001; v.p. Merrill Lynch Funds Distbr., Inc., 1978—89, sr. v.p., 1989—2001; pres., trustee Merrill Lynch Funds for Instns. Series, Boston, 1978—2001, Merrill Lynch Tax-Exempt Fund, 1983—2001; mng. dir. Merrill Lynch Investment Mgrs., 1997—2001; ret., 2001. Served with U.S. Army, 1960.

CROOK, SEAN PAUL, aerospace systems division director; b. Pawtucket, R.I., July 6, 1953; s. Ralph Frederick and Rosemary Rita (Dolan) C.; m. Mary Wickman, June 10, 1978; children: Kimberly Anne, Kelly Dolan, Erin Webster, Mary Katherine. BSME, U.S. Naval Acad., 1975; MBA, U. So. Calif., 1991. Commd. ensign USN, 1975, advanced through grades to lt., 1979, resigned, 1981; sr. systems engr. space divsn. GE, Springfield, Va., 1982-84; sr. aerospace systems engr. Martin Marietta Aero. Def. Systems, Long Beach, Calif., 1984-87; sr. aerospace system engring. mgr. Martin Marietta Aero Def. Systems, Long Beach, Calif., 1987-93; chief engr. GDE Sys. Inc., A Tracer Co., San Diego, 1993-96, program mgr., 1996-99; program dir. BAE Sys., San Diego, 1999-2001; divsn. dir. BAE Sys.-Integrated Sys., Reston, Va., 2001—. Sec., bd. dirs. Guardian Minerals Inc. Comdr. USNR, 1992-97. Mem. Am. Mgmt. Assn., U. So. Calif. Exec. MBA Alumni Assn. (bd. dirs.), U.S. Naval Acad. Alumni Assn. Avocation: financial planning. Home: 23565 Via Calzada Mission Viejo CA 92691-3625 Office: BAE Sys PO Box 509008 San Diego CA 92150-9008 E-mail: scrook9344@aol.com., sean.crook@baesystems.com.

CROOK, STEPHEN RICHARD, sales and marketing management consultant; b. Madison, Wis., Apr. 20, 1963; s. Richard John and Marcia Jane (Monroe) C. AS in Computer Sci. with highest honors, BS in Indsl. Engring., Purdue U., 1985; MS in Ops. Rsch., Stanford U., 1986; MBA, Northwestern U., 1992. Systems engr. AT&T Bell Labs. Inc., Naperville, Ill., 1985-88; design engr. Smart House Venture, Upper Marlboro, Md., 1986-88; product mgr. new product devel. planning AT&T Network Systems Inc., Lisle, Ill., 1989-90, product mgr. intelligent network bus. planning Naperville, Ill., 1990-92; assoc. strategy discipline Gemini Consulting, Chgo., 1992-93; mgr. ZS Assocs., Evanston Ill. 1993-99; pres. Steve Crook Cons., Hoffman Estates Ill. 1999—. Inventor Smart House telephone gateway. Mem. Alpha Sigma Phi, Tau Beta Pi, Alpha Pi Mu. Office: Steve Crook Cons 1433 Diamond Drive Hoffman Estates IL 60195 E-mail: srcrook@attbi.com.

CROOKE, ROBERT ANDREW, media consultant, writer, educator; b. Bklyn., Apr. 17, 1947; s. Henry A. and Theresa E. (Dougherty) C.; m. Angela Keller Lynch, Sept. 13, 1969; 1 child, Sean Peter. BA in English, Providence Coll., 1969; MA in English, Fordham U., 1974. Sports reporter, columnist L.I. Press, Jamaica, N.Y., 1969-75; profl. radio, TV, ednl. film script writer N.Y.C., 1976-79; assoc. editor Mag. Age, N.Y.C., 1979-81; reporter, contbg. editor L.I. Bus. Newsweekly, Ronkonkoma, N.Y., 1981-86; sr. acct. exec. Howard J. Rubenstein, N.Y.C., 1986-87; dir. media rels. Reuters Am., Inc., N.Y.C., 1987-94; v.p. comm. Reuters New Media, N.Y.C., 1994-96; v.p. media rels. Reuters Am. Holdings, Inc., N.Y.C., 1996-2000; mng. dir. Broadgate Consultants Inc., N.Y.C., 2000-01; sr. v.p. Makinson Cowell (US) Ltd., 2001—. Adj. instr. English Suffolk County C.C., Selden, N.Y., 1972-76; lectr. Sch. Journalism, U. Nebr., 1998-99, Sch. Journalism, U. S.C., 2000—; adj. prof. pub. affairs NYU, 1998-2000. Author of poems and books; contbr. articles to profl. jours., newspapers and mags. Bd. dirs. Walt Whitmen Birth Place Assn., Huntington, N.Y., 1985-87; bd. corp. trustees The Vanderbilt Mus., Centerport, N.Y., 1984-87. Office: PO Box 392 334 Main St S Bridgewater CT 06752-1537

CROOKE, ROSANNE M. pharmacologist; b. Pittsfield, Mass., Oct. 30, 1955; d. Myron Michael and Marian Geneva (Russell) Muzyka; m. Stanley T. Crooke, Sept. 5, 1986. BA, Williams Coll., 1978; PhD, U. Pa., 1986. Rsch. asst. endocrine sec. dept. medicine U. Pa., Phila., 1978-81; fellow Wistar Inst. Anatomy and Biology, Phila., 1986-89; prog. leader cardiovasc. disease, dir. antisense drug discovery ISIS Pharms., Carlsbad, Calif., 1989—. Contbr. articles to profl. jours. Mem. AAAS, Soc. Toxicology. Avocations: hiking, gourmet cooking, bicycling. Home: 3211 Piragua St Carlsbad CA 92009-7840 Office: ISIS Pharms 2280 Faraday Ave Carlsbad CA 92008-7208

CROOKE, STANLEY THOMAS, pharmaceutical company executive; b. Indpls., Mar. 28, 1945; m. Nancy Alder (dec.); 1 child, Evan; m. Rosanne M. Snyder. BS in Pharmacy, Butler U., 1966; PhD, Baylor Coll., 1971, MD, 1974. Asst. dir. med. rsch. Bristol Labs., N.Y.C., 1975-76, assoc. dir. med. rsch., 1976-77, assoc. dir. R&D, 1977-79, v.p. R&D, 1979-80, Smith Kline & French Labs., Phila., 1980-82; pres. R&D Smith Kline French, Phila., 1982-88; chmn. bd., CEO ISIS Pharms., Inc., Carlsbad, Calif., 1989. Chmn. bd. dirs. GES Pharms., Inc., Houston, 1989-91; adj. prof. Baylor Coll. Medicine, Houston, 1982, U. Pa., Phila., 1982-98; chmn. bd. dirs. GeneMedicine, Houston, 1996-98; bd. dirs. Calif. Healthcare Inst., Indsl. Biotech. Assn., Washington, Idun Pharms., San Diego 1997-2002, Epix Med., Cambridge, Mass., 1996—, BIO, Washington; mem. sci. adv. bd. SIBIA, La Jolla, Calif. 1992-99; adj. prof. pharmacology UCLA, 1991, U. Calif. San Diego, 1994; bd. dirs. Synsorb Biotech Inc., Calgary, Can., 1999-2002; bd. dirs. Axon Instruments, Inc., Foster City, Calif. 1999—, Valentis, Inc., Burlingame, Calif., 1999-2002, Antisense Therapeutics Ltd., Toorak, Victoria, Australia, 2002—, Applied Molecular Evolutions, Inc., San Diego, Calif., 2001-02, Biocom/San Diego, Calif., 2003—; mem. arts and scis. adv. coun. No. Ariz. U., 2002-. Mem. editl. adv. bd. Molecular Pharmacology, 1986-91, Jour. Drug Targeting, 1992; editl. bd. Antisense Rsch. and Devel., 1994; sect. editl. bd. for biologicals and immunologicals Expert Opinion on Investigational Drugs, 1995. Trustee Franklin Inst., Phila., 1987-89; bd. dirs. Mann Music Ctr., Phila., 1987-89; children's com. Children's Svcs., Inc., Phila., 1983-84; adv. com. World Affairs Coun., Phila. Recipient Disting. Prof. award U. Ky., 1986, Julius Stermer award Phila. Coll. Pharmacy and Sci., 1981, Outstanding Lectr. award Baylor Coll. Medicine, 1984. Mem. AAAS, Am. Assn. for Cancer Rsch. (state legis. com.), Am. Soc. for Microbiology, Am. Soc. Pharmacology and Exptl. Therapeutics, Am. Soc. Clin. Pharmacology and Therapeutics, Am. Soc. Clin. Oncology, Indsl. Biotech. Assn. (bd. dirs. 1992-93). Achievements include numerous patents in field. Office: ISIS Pharms Inc 2292 Faraday Ave Carlsbad CA 92008-7208 E-mail: scrooke@isisph.com.

CROOKER, BARBARA ANN, writer, educator; b. Cold Spring, NY, Nov. 21, 1945; d. Emil Vincent and Isabelle Charlotte Poti; m. Michael James Gilmartin, 1967 (div. 1973); 1 child, Stacey Erin Gilmartin Krastek; m. Richard MacMaster Crooker, 1975; children: Rebecca Cameron Ceartas, David McKenzie. BA, Rutgers U., 1967; MSEd, Elmira Coll., 1975. Adj. instr. English Elmira (NY) Coll., 1975, Corning (NY) CC, 1974—76, Tompkins Cortland CC, Dryden, NY, 1975—76, County Coll. Morris, Randolph, NJ, 1978—79; instr. cmty. svcs. Leigh County CC, Schnecksville, Pa., 1980, 1993; adj. asst. prof. Northampton (Pa.) Area CC, 1980—82; instr. women's ctr. Cedar Crest Coll., Allentown, Pa., 1982—85, adj. prof., 1999—. Contbr. (poetry) lit. mags., anthologies, text-books, online mags.; author: Writing Home, 1983, Starting From Zero, 1987, Looking for the Comet Halley, 1987, Obbligato, 1992, The Lost Children, 1989, In the Late Summer Garden, 1998, The White Poems, 2001, Ordinary Life, 2002, Paris, 2002, Greatest Hits, 1980—2002. Nominee Pushcart prize, 1978, 1989, 1998, 1999, 2001; named winner, Passages North and NEA Emerging Writers Competition, 1987, Poet Laureate, Riverside Festival of Arts, Easton, Pa., 2000; recipient Phillips award, Stone Country, 1988, 1st prize, Karamu poetry contest, 1997, 3d pl., Kinloch Rivers Chapbook Competition, 1998, Internat. Merit award, Atlanta Review, 1999, 1st pl. Y2K writing prize, New Millenium Writings, 2000, Grand prize, Dancing Poetry Contest, 2000, 1st Pl., Byline Chapbook Competition, 2001, numerous others, Pushcart prize, 2002, Thomas Merton Poetry of the Sacred award, 2003, April is the Cruelest Month award; fellow lit., Pa. Coun. Arts, 1985, 1989, 1993, Va. Ctr. for Creative Arts, 1990, 1992, 1994, 1995, 1995, 1997, 1998, 2000, 2001, 2003. Mem.: Am. Acad. Poets. Avocations: gardening, cross country skiing. Home: 7928 Woodsbluff Run Fogelsville PA 18051 Personal E-mail: bcrooker@ix.netcom.com.

CROOKS, PATRICIA KAY, counselor; b. Dallas, Mar. 23, 1951; d. Robert Virgil and Billie Marie Jones; m. John O. Crooks, Sept. 25, 1970; children: Christopher, Chip. BA, U. Tex., Arlington, 1974; MEd, U. N. Tex., 1994. Lic. profl. counselor. Tchr. Christian Acad. Oakcliff, Dallas, 1988-89; reservations Am. Airlines, Ft. Worth, 1989-90; dir. guidance and counseling Dallas Christian Sch., Mesquite, Tex., 1990-00; crisis counselor Garland (Tex.) H.S., 2000—. Mem. Nat. Assn. Coll. Admissions Counselors, Am. Assn. Marriage/Family Therapist, Tex. Counseling Assn. Mem. Ch. of Christ. Avocations: sailing, scuba, golf, reading. Home: 105 France Ct Rockwall TX 75032-8400

CROOKSTON, R. KENT, agronomy educator; b. Magrath, Alta., Can., Mar. 8, 1943; s. Bryan Grant and Lisadore (Brown) C.; m. Gayle Loraine Jones, June 22, 1966; children: Rebecca, Casey, Polly, Daniel, Elizabeth, Emily, Sadie. BS, Brigham Young U., 1968; MS, U. Minn., 1970, PhD, 1972. Postdoctoral fellow Agr. Can., Lethbridge, Alta., 1972; rsch. assoc. Cornell U., Ithaca, N.Y., 1972-74; from asst. prof. to prof. U. Minn., St. Paul, 1974—82, dir. sustainable agr. program Coll. Agr., 1988-92, head dept. agronomy, 1990-98. Adj. prof. Inst. Agronomique Et Veterinaire Hassan II, Rabat, Morocco, 1984—; dean Coll. Biology and Agr., Brigham Young U., Provo, Utah, 1998—. Author rsch. manuscripts. With Can. armed forces, 1962. Fellow Am. Soc. Agronomy, Crop Sci. Soc. Am.; mem. Coun. Agrl. Sci. and Tech. Avocations: oil painting, woodworking, writing, photography. Home: 1055 N 1100 E Orem UT 84097-4390 Address: College of Biology and Agriculture 301 WIDB Brigham Young Univ Provo UT 84602-5250 E-mail: kent_crookston@byu.edu.

CROOM, FREDERICK HAILEY, academic administrator, mathematician, educator; b. Lumberton, N.C., Aug. 6, 1941; s. Robert DeVane and Anna Roslyn (Currie) Croom; m. Henrietta Brown, Aug. 17, 1963 (div. May 2000); children: Elizabeth Bonner, Frederick Hailey; m. Nancy Mishoe Brennecke, June 1, 2002. BS, U. N.C., 1963, PhD, 1967. Asst. prof. math. U. Ky., Lexington, 1967-71, U. of the South, Sewanee, Tenn., 1971-74, assoc. prof., 1974-81, prof., 1981—, dir. Summer Sch., 1980-88, assoc. dean, 1984-88, provost, 1989-2001. Author: (book) Basic Concepts of Algebraic Topology, 1978, Principles of Topology, 1989. Pres. Tenn. Coll. Assn., 1999—2000; bd. dirs. St. Andrews-Sewanee Sch., 1981—86, Tenn. Found. Ind. Colls., 1996—99; trustee U. of the South, 1983—85. Fellow Woodrow Wilson, 1963, NSF, 1963—67. Mem.: AAUP, Mat. Assn. Am., Am. Math. Soc., Sigma Xi. Episcopalian. Office: U South University Ave Sewanee TN 37383-0001 E-mail: fcroom@sewanee.edu.

CROOM, JOHN HENRY, III, utility company executive; b. Fayetteville, N.C., Dec. 12, 1932; s. John Henry and Mary Dance (Howard) C.; m. Verna Arlene Willetts, June 21, 1953; children: Mary, Karen, Elizabeth, John. BS in Mech. Engring., N.C. State Coll., 1954. Engr. United Fuel Gas Co., Charleston, W.Va., 1954-69; indsl. sales mgr. Charleston Group Cos., 1969-73; indsl. utilization mgr. Columbia Distbn. Cos., Columbus, Ohio, 1973-74, v.p. engring. and planning, 1974-79; sr. v.p. Columbia Gas Sys., Wilmington, Del., 1979-80, exec. v.p., dir., 1981-82, pres., 1982-84, chmn., pres., CEO, 1984-95; ret., 1995. Chmn. Gas Rsch. Inst., 1987-89. Past pres. Delmarva Coun., Boy Scouts Am. With AUS, 1954-56, Korea. Mem. NSPE, Del. Roundtable (bd. dirs., past chmn.), Nat. Eagle Scout Assn. (bd. regents). Home: 1160 Westover Terr Asheboro NC 27205-4157 E-mail: john@johncroom.com.

CROOP, JAMES MERRILL, pediatrician, educator; b. Jan. 25, 1953; BA, U. Pa., 1974, MD, PhD, 1980. Diplomate Am. Bd. Pediatrics. Asst. prof. Med. Sch. Harvard U., Boston, 1988-97; assoc. prof. Ind. U., Inpls., 1997—. Mem. gen therapy working group Ind. U., Indpls. Contbr. articles to profl. jours. Mem. Am. Soc. Hematologists, Am. Assn. Cancer Rsch., Am. Soc. Gene Therapy, Am. Soc. Pediatric Hematology/Oncology. Achievements include patents (with other) DNA Sequence that Encodes the Multidrug Resistance Gene, Antibodies for P-glycoprotein Encoded by the MDR1 Gene and Uses Thereof. Office: Ind U Riley Hosp Children 702 Barnhill Dr Rm 2720 Indianapolis IN 46202-5128

CROPP, LINDA W. city official; m. Dwight S. Cropp; children: Allison, Christopher. BA, MA, Howard U. Past pub. sch. tchr. and guidance counselor; city councilwoman at large, 1990-98; chmn. city councilwomen, 1999—. Past chair human svcs. com., past mem. regional authorities, pub. svc. and youth affairs, govt. ops. and self-determination coms. Rep. Ward 4 Bd. Edn., 1979, past v.p., pres.; past mem. Washington Met. Area Transit Authority; active Rock Creek Civic Assn., Travelers Aid Soc., Girl Scouts Nation's Capital, Jr. Achievement; mem. adv. bd. United Negro Coll. Fund. Office: Council DC 1350 Penn Ave NW Washington DC 20004*

CROPPER, SUSAN PEGGY, veterinarian; b. N.Y.C., Feb. 11, 1941; d. Eli and Ruth (Rader) Abrahams; divorced; 1 child, Tracy Lynn. BS, Kans. State U., 1962, DVM, 1964. Assoc. veterinarian Asbury Park (N.J.) Animal Hosp., 1964-65; instr. in Vet. Sci. Kans. State U., Manhattan, 1965-66; owner, veterinarian Markle (Ind.) Vet. Clinic, 1966-71, Meisels Animal Hosp. Clinic, Elmwood Park, N.J., 1971-73, Ridgewood (N.J.) Animal Hosp., 1973-75, Cropper House Call Practice, Wyckoff, N.J., 1975—. Editor Nat. Assn. Women Vets., 1966-68; mem. Audibon Soc. Mus. Natural History. Co-author: Loving and Losing a Pet; editor WJMA Jour., 1973; photographer: Best Diving Spots in Western Hemisphere, 1987. Leader Brownie troop Girl Scouts U.S., Glen Rock, N.J., 1976-77, Wyckoff, 1977-83; chairperson No. Jersey Tridents, Ridgefield, N.J., 1985-86. Mem. AVMA, Soc. Aquatic Vet. Medicine (treas.), No. N.J. Vet. Med. Assn. (pres. 1972-73), Met. Vet. Med. Assn., N.Y. Zool. Soc., Van Saun Zool. Soc., N.J.. Acad., Ski and Scuba Club of Westwood, North Jersey Tridents Club (Ridgefield, chair 1985-86, Millennial Cert. for philanthropic recognition). Avocations: scuba diving, underwater photography, travel, racquetball, markmanship practice. Office: 310 Newtown Rd Wyckoff NJ 07481-2608 E-mail: dvm2go@optonline.net.

CROPSEY, JOSEPH, political science educator; b. N.Y.C., Aug. 27, 1919; s. Gustave and Margaret (Dirnfeld) C.; m. Lilian Crystal Levy, Nov. 4, 1945; children— Seth, Rachel Cropsey Simons AB, Columbia U., 1939, A.M., 1940, PhD, 1952; DHL (hon.), Colo. Coll., 1989. Tutor, asst. prof. CCNY, 1946-57; instr. polit. sci. New Sch. Social Rsch., N.Y.C., 1949-54; asst. prof. U. Chgo., 1958-64, assoc. prof., 1964-70, prof., 1970-85, Disting. Svc. prof., 1985-89, prof. emeritus, 1989—. Author: Polity and Economy, 1957, Political Philosophy and the Issues of Politics, 1977, Plato's World, 1995; editor: Ancients and Moderns, 1964; co-editor, co-author: History of Political Philosophy, 1963. Served to 1st. lt. U.S. Army, 1941-46, PTO, ETO Office: U Chgo 5828 S University Ave Chicago IL 60637-1515

CRORY, ELIZABETH L. former state legislator; b. Gardner, Mass., Sept. 12, 1932; d. James Quaiel and Mary (Reilly) Lupien; m. Frederick E. Crory, Aug. 21, 1954; children: Thomas, David, Ellen, Ann, Edward, Stephen. AB, U. Mass., 1954; MALS, Dartmouth Coll., 1975. Tchr. Amherst (Mass.) Schs., 1954, Lyme (N.H.) Schs., 1972-76; mem. N.H. Ho. of Reps., 1977-87, 92-96, mem. commerce/consumer affairs com., 1977-87, 93-96, mem. spl. com. on med. malpractice, 1984; exec. dir. Children's Ctr. of Upper Valley, 1986-90. Bd. dirs. Mascoma Savs. Bank. Mem. character and fitness com. N.H. Supreme Ct., 1998-2002; chair N.H. Health Svcs. Planning and Rev. Bd., 1999—; bd. dirs. Kendal at Hanover, 2001—. Roman Catholic. Home: 40 Rip Rd Hanover NH 03755-1614 Fax: 603-643-4025.

CRORY, MARY, town official; b. Concord, Mass., Sept. 27, 1932; d. Lennart William and Mary Susan (Sullivan) Fougstedt; m. Arthur Donald Crory, Jan. 31, 1953; children: Michael, Patricia, Joanne, Paul, Mary Susan, Mark. Tax collector Town of Littleton, Mass., 1963-99, town clk., 1976—2003. Sec., St. Anne Sodality, 1960-76. Democrat. Roman Catholic. Avocations: golf, needlepoint. Home: 74 King St Littleton MA 01460-1518

CROSBIE, ALFRED LINDEN, mechanical engineering educator; b. Muskogee, Okla., Aug. 1, 1942; s. Alfred Henry and Jacquetta Hope (Stoneburner) C.; m. Ann Frances Cirou, July 18, 1963; children: Mark, Jacqueline. BSME, U. Okla., d1964; MSME, Purdue U., 1966, PhD, 1969. Asst. prof. U. Mo., Rolla, 1968-72, assoc. prof., 1972-75, prof., 1975-91, curators' prof., 1991—. Editor: Aerothermodynamics and Planetary Entry, 1981, Heat Transfer and Thermal Control, 1981; editor-in-chief Jour. Thermophysics and Heat Transfer, 1986—; assoc. editor Jour. Quantitative Spectroscopy and Radiative Transfer, 1979—; mem. editl. bd. Heat Transfer-Recent Contents, 1996-2000; mem. adv. bd. Internat. Jour. Thermal Scis., 2000—; contbr. over 80 articles on radiative heat transfer to profl. jours. Fellow AIAA (chmn. thermophysics com. 1984-86, tech. program chmn. 15th Thermophysics Conf. 1980, assoc. editor AIAA Jour. 1981-83, Thermophysics award 1987, Tech. Contbn. award, 1988), ASME (heat transfer com. on theory and fundamentals 1983—, heat transfer com. on

numerical heat transfer 1993—, Heat Transfer Meml. award 1990), AAAS; mem. Optical Soc. Am., Phi Eta Sigma, Sigma Pi Sigma, Tau Beta Pi, Pi Tau Sigma, Sigma Tau, Pi Mu Epsilon, Sigma Xi. Lutheran. Avocation: fishing. Home: 8 Mcfarland Dr Rolla MO 65401-3805 Office: U Mo 233 Mech Engring Rolla MO 65401 E-mail: crosbie@umr.edu.

CROSBIE, GARY MARK, research scientist, artist; b. Wilkinsburg, Pa., Dec. 20, 1951; s. Robert Harris and Grace Dill Crosbie; m. Patricia Ann Sorrells, May 29, 1978; children: Rebecca Ann, Stephen Alexander. BS in Metallurgy and Materials Sci., Carnegie Mellon U., 1973; MS in Materials Sci. and Engring., Northwestern U., 1975, PhD in Materials Sci. and Engring., 1977. Summer rsch. fellow Faculty of Metallurgy U. Sheffield, England, 1973; rsch. chemist Pfizer, Inc., MPM Divsn., Easton, Pa., 1977—79; sr. rsch. scientist Ford Motor Co., Dearborn, Mich., 1979—84, sr. tech. specialist, 1984—. Materials specialist, elec./electronics tech. team PNGV-FreedomCAR (US Automotive Materials Partnership), Southfield, Mich., 1996—. Patentee in field; Scarab Club juried show, 2003. Letter-writer, spkr. for bond issue Dearborn Pub. Schools; deacon Cherry Hill Presbyn. Ch., Dearborn, 1981—2003. Named J. E. Hilliard Symposium keynote lectr., Northwestern U., 1997; recipient R&D 100 award, R&D Mag., 1992; NSF Grad. fellow, 1973—76. Fellow: Am. Soc. Materials (Disting. Student Pitts. sect. 1973), Am. Ceramic Soc. (vice chair programs Lehigh Valley sect. 1978—79, symposium organizer 1996—, ACCE Track award (with Engring. Soc. Detroit) 1990); mem.: Soc. Automotive Engrs. (symposium organizer 2001—03), Electrochem. Soc. (F.M. Becket award 1973), German Lang. and Culture Club (pres. 2002—). Presbyterian. Achievements include development of silicon nitride synthesis process (vapor chloride-liquid ammonia); low-friction surface finishing of silicon nitride; potassium analog of the sodium-sulfur battery; ceramic forming methodologies; Corporate Reliability Database System (materials). Avocations: photography, aerobics, hiking, sketching. Home: 1430 Culver Ave Dearborn MI 48124-5018 Office: Ford Motor Company 2101 Village Rd MD 3083 Rm 2337 SRL Dearborn MI 48124-4356 E-mail: gcrosbie@ford.com.

CROSBIE, MICHAEL JAMES, architect, writer, educator; b. Denville, NJ, Aug. 10, 1956; s. Leo P. and Viola Marie (Nicolicchia) C.; m. Sharon Ann Maher, Oct. 5, 1985; children: Sean, Christopher, Brigit Rose. BS in Architecture, Cath. U., 1978, MArch, 1980, PhD, 1983. Lic. architect, Conn. Editor Architecture Mag., 1982-92; with Centerbrook Archs., 1987-92; editor Progressive Architecture Mag., 1993-96; sr. assoc. Steven Winter Assocs., Norwalk, Conn., 1996—. Architecture critic The Hartford Courant, 1990-96, bd. contbr., 2003—; adj. prof. architecture Roger Williams U., 1992—, U. Hartford, 1993-94; vis. lectr., critic Yale U., U. Pa., Columbia U., U. Calif., Berkeley, N.Y. Inst. Tech., U. Md., U. Utah, Moscow Archtl. Inst., others; spkr., panelist in field. Author: The Jersey Devil Design/Build Book, 1985, Centerbrook: Reinventing American Architecture, 1993, Architecture Counts, 1993, Architecture Colors, 1993, Architecture Shapes, 1993, Color and Context, 1995, Architecture Animals, 1995, Cesar Pelli: Recent Themes, 1998, Architecture for the Gods, 1999, Arches to Zigzags: An Architecture ABC, 2000, Home Rehab Handbook, 2002, Class Architecture, 2002, Architecture for the Gods Book II, 2003, Designing the World's Best Museums and Galleries, 2003, Multi-Family Housing: The Art of Sharing, 2003, others, introductions to several books; contbg. editor: Constrn. Specifier mag., 1996—2002; asst. editor: Faith & Form mag., 1998—2000, editor-in-chief:, 2001—; contbr. over 200 articles to profl. jours., Hist. Preservation, Landscape Architecture, New Shelter, Town and Country, Architecture Week.com, others; editl. advisor: Arch. Rsch. Quar. Bd. dirs. Yestermorrow Design/Build Sch., 1990-97. Recipient Neal award for editl. achievement, 1990, 94, William H. Donaldson award for editl. achievement, Henry Adams medal and cert. AIA, others. Mem.: Boston Soc. Archs., Sigma Psi, Tau Beta Pi. Episcopalian. Home: 47 Grandview Ter Essex CT 06426-1004 Office: 50 Washington St Norwalk CT 06854-2710 E-mail: paeditor@aol.com., mcrosbie@swinter.com.

CROSBY, DEBORAH BERRY, artist; b. Gulfport, Miss., Oct. 9, 1930; d. Thomas Davis and Deborah Bennett (Hewes) Berry; m. Charles E. McHale Jr., Nov. 23, 1950 (div. 1952); 1 child Deborah Bennett McHale; m. Hueston T. Fortner, Jr., Mar. 17, 1957 (div. 1963); 1 child, Hueston G. Fortner; m. Richard Louis Crosby, Dec. 27, 1981. BA, Sophie Newcomb Coll., 1951; MA, Ind. State U., 1968; postgrad., Utah State U., 1969, Tulane U., 1979; BA (hon.), U. New Orleans, 1984. Educator Wesleyan Coll., Rocky Mt., N.C., 1969-70; prof. Spanish, Bay de Noc Coll., Escanaba, Mich., 1970-72; instr. yoga, Spanish, U. So. Miss.-Gulf Park Campus, Long Beach, 1972-78, Miss. Gulf Coast Jr. Coll. Dist., Keesler AFB Ctr., 1972-78; instr. reading, English, Miss. Gulf Coast Jr. Coll. Dist.-Jefferson Davis Campus, Keesler AFB Ctr., 1972-78; freelance artist Metairie, La., 1988—. One-woman shows include Dixie Art Co., Jefferson, La., 1990, World Trade Ctr., New Orleans, 1993—2001, Reginelli's Eating Gallery, 1994, Marceline Bonorden Fine Arts Gallery, 1998, 1999, Agora Gallery, Soho, N.Y.C., 2000, Movie Pitchers, 2000—01, Ambassador Hotel, New Orleans, 2002—, exhibited in group shows at Artists Showroom Gallery, 1993—95, Rivertown Art Gallery, Kenner, La., Slidell Cultural Ctr., La. State Archives, Baton Rouge, La., Martin Hall, U. of Mobile, Ala., George E. Ohr Arts and Cultural Ctr., Biloxi, Miss., Stamford (Conn.) Mus., Havre de Grace (Mich.) Mus., West Wind Gallery, Casper, Wyo., Jefferson SQ, Klamath Falls, Oreg., Destrehan (La.) Plantation, Lexington (Ky.) Mus., Falls River Mills, Calif., Our Lady of the Rosary Gallery, NOLA Pitot Historic Ho., New Orleans, La., Marceline Bonorden Fine Arts Gallery, Agora Gallery, Soho, N.Y.C., The Purple Mullet Gallery, Ala., Serenity Gallery, The Artisan Mkt., Riverview Gallery, Zigler Art Mus., Jennings La., New Orleans Mus. Art, Amsterdam Whitney Internat. Fine Arts Gallery, Inc., N.Y.C., 2002—, New Orleans Art Assn. Fine Arts Festival (1st place), St. Charles Art Assn. Fall Show (1st place), Metairie Art Guild Summer Show, 1996 (1st place), Oil Met. Art Guild (1st place), Grumbacher Fall Show (1st, 2d and 3d place, 2002), Represented in permanent collections World Trade Ctr., commission, Juvenile Diabetes Assn., 2001, month long themed group Christmas exhibit, WTC, New Orleans, 1995—2001; designer, executor (cover chess book) The Art of Bisguier, 2003. Chmn. auction Heart Ambs., 1995; mem. Ladies Leukemia League, 1994-, program chmn., 1996; mem. Goodwill Industries VS, 1995-2002, BRAVO Ballet; fiesta hostess Napoleon's Home, Spring Fiesta Assn., 2002—; bd. dirs. Profl. Women's Adv. ABI, Inc., 2003; mem. Contemporary Arts Ctr. NOLA; mem. New Orleans Arts Coun., 2003—. Named Sweetheart, Local Br. Am. Heart Assn. Heart Ambs., 2001; recipient Spl. Painting award, Winsor-Newton, 1994, Great Lady award, New Orleans Met. area by East Jefferson Hosp. Aux., 2000. Mem. Nat. League Am. Pen Women (chaplain 1996—, v.p. 1998-2000), New Orleans Art Assn. (v.p. 1995-98), Le Petit Art Guild (program chair 1995-97, Le Grand chairperson, 1995—, officer 1995-97), St. Charles Art Assn. (pres. 1994-95, Artist of Yr. award 1991-92), Nat. Mus. Women in the Arts. Avocations: yoga, community activist, foreign languages study, travel, song-writing. Home: 5600 Kawanee Ave Metairie LA 70003-1414

CROSBY, FAYE JACQUELINE, psychology educator, author; b. Bethesda, Md., July 12, 1947; d. Robert A. and Andrée (Cohen) Newman; children: Matthew, Timothy. BA, Wheaton Coll., 1969; postgrad., London Sch. Econs., 1973-74; PhD, Boston U., 1976. Lectr. R.I. Coll., Providence, 1976-77; asst. prof. psychology Yale U., New Haven, 1977-82, assoc. prof., 1982-85; prof. psychology Smith Coll., Northampton, Mass., 1985-98, U. Calif., Santa Cruz, 1997—, vice provost acad. affairs, 2000. Prof. J.L. Kellogg Grad. Sch. Mgmt. Northwestern U., Evanston, Ill., 1992-93. Author: Relative Deprivation and Working Women, 1982, Juggling: The Unexpected Advantage of Balancing Careers and Home for Women and Their Families, 1991; co-author: Justice, Gender and Affirmative Action, 1992, Affirmative Action, Pros and Cons of Policy and Practice, 1996; editor: Spouse, Parent, Worker, 1987; co-editor: Affirmative Action in Perspective, 1989, Women's Ethnicities, 1996, Mentoring Dilemmas, 1999, Sex, Race and Merit, 2000; contbr. articles to profl. jours. Office: U Calif Santa Cruz Psych Dept Santa Cruz CA 95064 E-mail: fjcrosby@cats.ucsc.edu.

CROSBY, FRED MCCLELLAN, retail home and office furnishings executive; b. Cleve., May 17, 1928; s. Fred Douglas and Marion Grace (Naylor) C.; m. Phendalyne D. Tazewell, Dec. 23, 1958; children: Fred, James, Llionicia. Grad. H.S. V.p. Seaway Flooring & Paving Co., Cleve., 1959-63; chmn., CEO Crosby Furniture Co., Inc., Cleve., 1963—. Vice chmn. bd. First Bank Nat.; bd. dirs. Budget Rent-A-Car Systems, Greater Cleve. Growth Assn.; dir., chmn. First Intercity Banc Corp.; trustee Better Bus. Bur. Bd. dirs. Forest City Hosp. Found., Cleve. State U. Found., Greater Cleve. Growth Assn., 1971-90, 93—, Coun. Smaller Enterprise, 1973-80, Goodwill Industries, 1973-80, 97—, Woodruff Hosp., 1975-82, Cleve. Devel. Found., Pub. TV, Surveyors Telecom., Inc., Sta. WVIZ-TV, Cleve.-Cuyahoga Port Authority, 1986-90; dir. adv. coun. Ohio Bd. Workmen's Compensation, 1974-82; chmn. Minority Econ. Devel. Corp., 1972-83; chmn. bd. dirs. Glenville YMCA, 1973-76; trustee BBB, 1995—, Cleve. Play House, 1979-87, Eliza Bryant Health Care Ctr., 1984-86, Cleve. Small Bus. Incubator, 1986-90; bd. dirs., treas. Urban League Cleve., 1971-78; mem. adv. coun. Small Bus. Assn.; mem. adv. bd. Salvation Army, 1980; commr. Ohio State Boxing Commn., 1984-94, Pvt. Industry Coun., 1985, Nat. Small Bus. Adv. Coun., 1980; bd. advs. Antioch Coll.; county commrs. appointee to Cmty. Adv. Bd., 1987—; mem. Cleve. Opera Coun., 1987-89, Forest City Hosp. Found., 1985—; trustee Ohio Motorist, 1993—, Murtis H. Taylor Mental Health; Gov. Voinovich appointee to minority devel. fin. adv. bd., 1996—; bd. trustee Metro Hosp. Systems Found. With AUS, 1950-52. Recipient award bus. excellence Dept. Commerce, 1972; Presdl. award YMCA, 1974; Gov. Ohio award community action, 1973; First Class Leadership Cleve., 1977. named Family of Yr. Cleve. Urban League, 1971 Mem. Cleve. C. of C., NAACP (v.p. Cleve. 1969-78, exec. dir.), Ohio Coun. Retail Mchts. (chmn. 1991-93), Ohio Home Furnishings and Appliance Assn. (pres. 1981-87), Exec. Order Ohio Commodore, Am. Auto Assn. (corp. mem.), Mid-Day Club, Cleve. Play House, Harvard Bus. Sch. Club, Clevelander, Bratenahl Club, Univ. Club (Cleve.), Rotary. Clubs: Mid-Day, Cleve. Play House, Harvard Bus. Sch., Clevelander, Bratenahl, Univ. (Cleve.). Lodges: Rotary. Office: 12435 Saint Clair Ave Cleveland OH 44108-2013 E-mail: crosbyfurniture@msn.com.

CROSBY, GLENN ARTHUR, chemistry educator; b. nr. Youngwood, Pa., July 30, 1928; s. Edwin Glenn and Bertha May (Ritchey) C.; m. Jane Lichtenfels, May 29, 1950; children: Brian, Alan, Karen. BS, Waynesburg Coll., 1950; PhD, U. Wash., 1954. Rsch. assoc. Fla. State U., Tallahassee, 1955-57, vis. asst. prof. physics, 1957; asst. prof. chemistry U. N. Mex., Albuquerque, 1957-62, assoc. prof. chemistry, 1962-67; prof. chemistry and materials sci. Wash. State U., Pullman, 1967—2001, chmn. chem. physics program, 1977-84, prof. emeritus, 2001—. Mem. adv. com. Rsch. Corp., Tucson, 1981—88, 1990—92; vis. prof. phys. chemistry U. Tubingen, Germany, 1964; vis. prof. physics U. Canterbury, Christchurch, New Zealand, 1974; Humboldt sr. scientist, vis. prof. phys. chemistry U. Hohenheim, Germany, 1978—79; mem. commn. on life scis. NRC, 1991—96, com. on programs for advanced study math and sci. in U.S. h.s., 1999—2001. Author: Chemistry: Matter and Chemical change, 1962; also numerous sci. and sci.-related articles Recipient U.S. Sr. Scientist award Humboldt Found., Fed. Republic Germany, 1978-79, Catalyst award Chem. Mfrs. Assn., 1979, Disting. Alumnus award Waynesburg Coll., 1982, Wash. State U.Faculty Excellence award in instrn., 1984, Wash. State U. Faculty Excellence award for pub. svc., 1989, Disting. Prof. award Wash. State U. Mortar Bd., 1990, Pres.'s medallion Waynesburg Coll. for disting. lifetime sci. and ednl. achievement, 1998; named Prof. of Yr., U. N.Mex., 1967; NSF fellow U. Wash., Seattle, 1953-54; Rsch. Corp. Venture grantee, 1960; Fulbright fellow, 1964. Fellow: AAAS, Wash. Sci. Tchrs. Assn. (Outstanding Coll. Sci. Tchr. award 1975), Inter-Am. Photochem. Soc.; mem.: Nat. Sci. Tchrs. Assn., Am. Phys. Soc., Am. Chem. Soc. (numerous activities including chmn. divsn. chem. edn. 1982, chmn. com. on edn. 1990—91, bd. dirs. 1994—2002, We Conn. sect. Vis. Scientist award 1981, nat. award in chem. edn. 1985, Harry and Carol Mosher award Santa Clara Valley sect. 1998, Outstanding Svc. award 2003), Sigma Xi, Sigma Pi Sigma, Phi Kappa Phi. Home: 1208 E Excelsior Rd Spokane WA 99224-9257

CROSBY, IVAN KEITH, cardiologist, educator; b. Brisbane, Queensland, Australia, Mar. 11, 1938; s. Robert William James and Ivy Katherine Crosby; m. Roberta Brunfeldt, Oct. 30, 1971; children: Katherine Anne, Ivan Keith Michael, Kristen Anne. Asst. prof. to assoc. prof. to prof., surgery U. Va., Charlottesville, 1972—84; co-dir. heart transplantation Baylor U. Med. Ctr., Dallas, 1984—86; chief, cardiac surgery Forsyth Med. Ctr., Winston-Salem, NC, 1987—2000; prof., surgery U. Va., 2000—. Co-dir., heart ctr. U. Va., 2000—. Contbr. articles. Named Best Dr. in N.C., 1998, Best Dr. in Va., 2003; recipient, Am. Bd. of Surgery, 1971, Am. Bd. of Thoracic Surgery, 1972; James IV Travelling scholar, James IV Surg. Assn. of U.S., Gt. Britain and Ireland. Fellow: ACS; mem.: So. Surg. Assn., Soc. for Vascular Surgery, Internat. Soc. for Cardiovasc. Surgery, Am. Assoc. for Thoracic Surgery. Achievements include patents for Pericardioscope . Office: U Va Dept of Surgery Box 800679 Charlottesville VA 22908 Office Fax: 434-924-8068. E-mail: icrosby@virginia.edu.

CROSBY, JACQUELINE GARTON, newspaper editor, journalist; b. Jacksonville, Fla., May 13, 1961; d. James Ellis and Marianne (Garton) Crosby. ABJ, U. Ga., 1983; MBA, U. Cen. Fla., 1987. Staff writer Macon Telegraph & News, Ga., 1983-84; copy editor Orlando Sentinel, Fla., 1984-85; dir. spl. projects Ivanhoe Communications, Inc., Orlando, Fla., 1987-89; producer spl. projects Sta. KSTP-TV, Mpls., 1989-94; asst. news editor Star Tribune Online, Mpls., 1994—. Recipient award for best sports story Ga. Press Assn., 1982; award for best series of yr. AP, 1985, Pulitzer prize, 1985 Mem. Quill Avocations: competing in triathlons, playing electric bass, tutoring, reading. Home: 5348 Drew Ave S Minneapolis MN 55410-2006 Office: Star Tribune Online 425 Portland Ave Minneapolis MN 55488-0001

CROSBY, JANET HALLEY, retired secondary school educator; b. Tulsa, Okla., Nov. 19, 1930; d. Chester Carroll and Auretta Ida (Stephens) Carnahan; 1 child, Carol Anne Goodhue. Student, Coll. of Emporia, Kans., 1948-50; BS, Iona Coll., 1981, MS in Edn., 1986. Tchr. K-8 Lyon County Rural Sch., Olpe, Kans., 1950-51; home and substitute tchr. Union Free Sch. Dist., Lyndenhurst, N.Y., 1953-56; tchr., adminstr. Far Hills (N.J.) Country Day Sch., 1956-77; adminstr. K-8 Convent of the Sacred Heart, Greenwich, Conn., 1977-79, tchr. mid. sch., 1979—2002; ret., 2002. Mem. network faculty devel. com. Network of Sacred Heart Schs., Newton, Mass., 1992-94, mem. inst. planning com., 1990-91, 92-93, mem. editl. bd., 1996—. Life deacon, ch. coun. pres. United Ch. of Christ, 1999-2001. Mem. Nat. Coun. Tchrs. of English, Phi Delta Kappa. Avocations: reading, classical music, creative writing, walking, computers.

CROSBY, JOHN GRIFFITH, investment banker; b. Bayshore, N.Y., Feb. 10, 1943; s. Gordon Josiah and Ruth Louise (Plante) C.; m. Joan Louise Kelly, July 10, 1965; children: Bruce, Brian, David. BA with distinction, Lafayette Coll., 1965; MBA, Harvard U., 1969. V.p., stockholder, dir. Kidder, Peabody & Co. Inc., N.Y.C., 1969-80; mng. dir. Merrill Lynch & Co., N.Y.C., 1980-90; ptnr. The Lodestar Group, 1990-93; mng. dir. LSG Advisors, 1993-95; chmn., pres. Madison Ptnrs., Inc., 1995—. Author: Private Placement Market Review, 1975-81. Class fund mgr. Lafayette Coll., 1969-90, mem. leadership coun., 1997-2001, 1997-2001; bd. deacons Presbyn. Ch., Madison, N.J., 1972; campaign chmn. Madison YMCA, 1975; coach Little League, 1977-84; treas. troop 125 Boy Scouts Am., 1984-87; bd. dirs. asst. treas. Am. Coun. Arts, 1987-90; pres. PTO, 1979-80. 1st lt. U.S. Army, 1965-67, Vietnam. Decorated Bronze Star medal. Mem.: Orchid Island Golf and Beach Club. Address: 5972 Lake Shore Dr Bolton Landing NY 12814-4521 E-mail: nuinweh@aol.com.

CROSBY, JULIE LYNNE, theater industry executive, educator; b. Midland, Mich., Mar. 5, 1964; d. Wayne W. Crosby and Janet (Cuddie) Snyder. BA, Mich. State U., 1985; MA, Columbia U., 1994, MPhil, 1996, PhD, 2002. Company mgr. Black & Blue, N.Y.C., 1988-91; mgr. Lincoln Ctr. Theater, N.Y.C., 1992-97; preceptor Columbia U., N.Y.C., 1997-98, 00-01; co. mgr. On The Town, N.Y.C., 1998-99; gen. mgr. Laurie Anderson's Songs & Stories from Moby Dick--World Tour, 1999-2000. Assoc. gen. mgr. Carrie, N.Y.C., 1988; company mgr. Andre Heller's Wonderhouse, N.Y.C., 1991, Tango Pasión, N.Y.C., 1993, Black & Blue European Tour, 1996; fundraising cons. Joffrey Ballet Sch., N.Y.C., 1990-95; founder Midland-Joffrey Summer Dance Project, Midland, Mich., 1994. Assoc. prodr.: Black & Blue, 1991; dir.: Killing of the Children, 1995, Last Judgment, 1996, Mankind, 1997. Pres. fellow Columbia U., 1994-99, Judith D. Lipsey fellow Disting Studies in Humanities Columbia U. Alumni Assn. Bd., 1999; Milton Weintraub scholar Assn. Theatrical Press Agts., 1994-96. Mem. MLA, Assn. Theatrical Press Agts. and Mgrs, Medieval Acad. Am.

CROSBY, LYNN A. orthopaedic surgeon, educator; m. Sheila Crosby; children: Shanna, Allison, Ryan. MD, Ohio State U., 1983. Cert. Am. Bd. of Orthop. Surgeons, 1991, Re-Certified Am. Bd. of Orthop. Surgery, 2001, Fellow ACS, 1993. Transitional residency U. of N.D., Grand Forks, 1983—84; gen. surgery residency Creighton U., Omaha, 1984—85; orthop. surgery residency Creighton-Nebraska Health Found., Omaha, 1985—88, chief resident, 1988—89; instr. Creighton U. Sch. of Medicine, Divsn. of Orthop. Surgery, Omaha, 1989—91, asst. prof., 1991—94, chief shoulder svc., 1991—97, assoc. prof. surgery, 1995—97; chief shoulder svc. Omaha VA Hosp., 1989—97; traveling fellowship Mid-Am. Orthop. Assn., Fort Riley, Kans., 1990—91, Clin. Orthop. Soc., England, 1995—96; prof., chair U. of Tenn. Coll. of Medicine, Dept. of Orthop. Surgery, Chattanooga, 1997—99, chief shoulder divsn., 1997—2000, prof. dept. of orthop. surgery, 1997—2000; dir. shoulder surgery Wright State U. Sch. of Medicine, Dept. of Orthop. Surgery, Dayton, 2000—01, prof., 2000—01, interim chair, 2000—01; prof. biomedical scis. PhD program Wright State U. Sch. of Medicine, Dayton, 2001—; chief shoulder divsn. Wright State U. Sch. of Medicine, Dept. of Orthop. Surgery, Dayton, 2002—, prof., chair, 2002—; chief of shoulder svc. VA Med. Ctr., Dayton, 2000—. Mem., chmns. com. U. of Tenn. Coll. of Medicine, Chattanooga, 1997—99, bd. mem., u. of tenn. physicians, 1997—99, pres., CEO univ. orthop. assocs., 1997—99, mem. orthop. rsch. com., 1998—2000, founder, co-dir. biomechanical rsch. lab, 1998—2000; mem. instrument clin. evaluation group/capsular release forceps Smith & Nephew, 1999; total shoulder arthroplasty study group Zimmer Co., 1999—; state campaign coord. Orthop. Rsch. and Edn. Found., 2000—; resident ednl. curriculum coord., dept. orthop. surgery Wright State U. Sch. of Medicine, Dayton, 2000—01; mem. edn. com. Am. Orthop. Foot and Ankle Soc., 1997—98; faculty-shoulder arthroplasty seminar Hughston Sports Clinic, Columbus, Ga., 2000; mem. rsch. com. Wright State U. Sch. of Medicine, Dayton, 2000—, mem. exec. com., 2000—, chair orthopaedic rsch. com., 2000—; mem., grad. coun. Wright State U. Sch. of Grad. Studies, Dayton, Ohio, 2001—; mem. edn. com. Dayton Area Grad. Med. Edn. Consortium, Dayton, 2001—; mem. dirs. of edn. com. Miami Valley Hosp., Dayton, 2001—, mem. implant selection com., 2001—; mem. bd. trustees U. Med. Svcs. Assn., Inc., Dayton, 2001—, mem. fin. com., 2001—, mem. billing sys. com., 2001—, sec., mgmt. com., 2002—; participant, iliac crest bone biopsy/risedronate study Proctor & Gamble, 2002; cons. Coun. of Healthcare Advisors, 2002; mem. implant selection com. Erlanger Med. Ctr., Chattanooga, 1997—2000, mem. oper. rm. com., 1997—2000. Author: (book chptr.) Complications of Total Shoulder Arthroplasty, (textbook) Total Shoulder Arthroplasty. Maj. USAR, 1983—91. Decorated Commendation medal for Meritorious Svc. U.S. Army; recipient Meyerding Essay Contest Winner, Am. Fracture Assn., 1989, 1995, Outstanding Rev. Article of Yr., Orthop. Rev., 1991, Sci. Presentation award, Tenn. State Orthop. Soc., 1998, Physicians Tchg. award, Am. Acad. of Family, 1998, J. Albert Key Prize for Excellence in Med. Writing, 2001. Mem.: Am. Acad. of Orthop. Surgeons (mem. residency tng. com. 1999—2003, subcom. on shoulder and elbow evaluation 2001—03), Mid-Am. Orthop. Assn. (moderator shoulder session, 16th ann. meeting 1998, chmn. exhibit program com. 1998—2003, program site visitor 1998—2003, moderator 17th ann. meeting 1999, panel mem. shoulder symposium, 17th ann. meeting 1999, bd. dirs. 1999—, moderator shoulder session, 19th ann. meeting 2001, moderator, 3d plenary session, 20th ann. meeting 2002), AMA, Alpha Omega Alpha Med. Honor Soc. (mem. 1996—2003, mem. physical panel 1999—), Landacre Hon. Rsch. Soc. Achievements include research in Humeral head avascular necrosis after three or four part humerus fracture; Glenohumeral arthritis with irreparable rotator cuff tear. Office: WSU Department of Orthopaedic Surgery 30 E Apple Street Suite L200 Dayton OH 45409 Office Fax: 937-208-2920. E-mail: lynn.crosby@wright.edu.

CROSBY, MARENA LIENHARD, retired college administrator; b. Shreveport, La., Mar. 2, 1948; d. John Joseph and Clara Curtis (Lawton) L.; m. H.W. Patrick Obrien, Sept. 23, 1977; m. John L. Crosby, Nov. 23, 1997. MEd, U. New Orleans; JD, Loyola U., New Orleans. Bar: La. 1971; lic. profl. counselor, La.; diplomate Am. Coll. Profl. Mental Health Practitioners. Instr. Delgado C.C., New Orleans, 1973-80, counselor, 1980-86, coord. testing, 1986-88, dir. admissions, 1988-90, dir. counseling and mktg., 1990-93, dir. degree audit program, 1993-97, asst. to v.p. student affairs, 1997-98, ret., 1998. Mem. DAR, FBA, ACA, Internat. Assn. for New Sci., Assn. for Rsch. and Enlightenment, Am. Psychotherapy Assn., Inst. Noetic Scis., Theosophical Soc. Am., Family Mediation Coun., La. Bar Assn., La. Notary Assn., La. Assn. Spiritual and Religious Values in Counseling, New Orleans Bar Assn., New Orleans Womens Opera Guild, Colonial Dames, Magna Charta Dames. Republican. Avocations: reading, piano. E-mail: cmlc18@cox.net.

CROSBY, NORMAN LAWRENCE, comedian; b. Boston, Sept. 15, 1927; s. John and Ann (Lansky) C.; m. Joan Crane Foley, Nov. 1, 1966; children: Daniel Joseph, Andrew Crane. Student, Mass. Sch. Art, Boston. Ind. comedian, entertainer, 1947—. Nat. spokesman Anheuser-Busch Natural Light Beer. Began work as comedian in New England clubs, fraternity and polit. dinners, numerous civic and charity functions; N.Y.C. debut Latin Quarter; several appearances London Palladium, regular appearances at all major hotels in Las Vegas, numerous other night clubs, concert halls, theaters, TV variety and panel shows; host: (syndicated TV series) Norm Crosby's Comedy Shop; nat. co-host on Jerry Lewis Muscular Dystrophy Assn. Telethon. Nat. hon. chmn. better Hearing Inst., Washington; trustee Hope for Hearing Found., UCLA; sponsor Norm Crosby Ann. Celebrity Golf Tournament benefitting City of Hope. With USCG, 1945-46. Recipient Jack Benny Comedy award Authors and Celebrities, 1981, Star on Hollywood (Calif.) Walk of Fame, Hollywood C. of C., 1982, Lifetime Achievement award in Entertainment, Touchdown Club, Washington, 1988, Victory award, Kennedy Ctr. Pres. George Bush, 1991; honored by USO and given privilege of laying wreath at tomb of Unknown Soldiers, Washington, 2001; named Internat. Variety Clubs Man of Yr., 1986. Mem. Friars Club (N.Y.C., L.A.; 17th term Internat. Amb. of Good Will for City of Hope), Masons, Shriners. Jewish.

CROSBY, PETER ALAN, management consultant; b. Santa Barbara, Calif., Oct. 20, 1945; s. Harold Bartley and Margaret Maida (Peterson) C.; m. Stephanie Jay Ellis, Dec. 20, 1969; children: Kelly Michelle, Michael Ellis. BS in Engring., U. Calif., Berkeley, 1967; MS in Ops. Rsch., Stanford U., 1969; ED, Stanford Bus. Sch., 1971. Cert. mgmt. cons. Logistics inventory analyst Ford Motor Co., Palo Alto, Calif., 1967-71; corp. ops. planning analyst FMC Corp., San Jose, Calif., 1972; assoc. mgmt. cons. A.T. Kearney, Inc., San Francisco, 1972-75; mgr. materials mgmt. cons. svcs. Coopers & Lybrand, Los Angeles, 1976-78; ptnr. gen. cons. unit (Case & Co.) Towers Perrin Forster & Crosby, L.A., 1978-81; prin. Crosby, Gustin, Rice & Co. (CGR Mgmt. Cons.), 1981—. Dir. Carbide Products Internat. Co.; bd. dirs. Impact Cons. Group, Inc.; pres. Inst. of Mgmt. Cons. Mem. adv. bd. dirs. Stanton Chase. Mem. Coun. Logistic Mgmt., Inst. Mgmt. Cons., Phi Gamma Delta. Office: CGR Mgmt Consultants Ste 1900 1901 Avenue Of The Stars Los Angeles CA 90067-6020

CROSBY, RALPH WOLF, communications executive; b. Annapolis, Md., Dec. 16, 1933; s. Raymond Thomas and Lillian Sylvia (Wolf) C.; m. Carlotta Stafford, June 16, 1958; children: Laura Crosby Avallone, Raymond, Belinda Crosby Butler. BS in Journalism, U Md., 1956. Reporter, editor Balt. News-Am., 1956-60; bur. editor Iron Age Mag., Washington, 1960-65, Med. Econs. mag., Washington, 1966-67; assoc. editor Kiplinger's Changing Times, Washington, 1967-70; exec. v.p. Annapolis Harbour House, Inc., 1970-86; chmn., CEO Crosby Mktg. Comm., Annapolis, 1972—. Owner Severn Valley Racquet Club, Millersville, Md.; bd. dirs. Annapolis Bank and Trust Co. Editor (book) Person to Person Management, 1966; contbr. articles to numerous mags. including N.Y. Times Mag. Recipient Jesse H. Neal editorial award, 1966. Mem. Md. Direct Mktg. Assn., Advt. Assn. Balt., Greater Annapolis C. of C. (pres. 1975-76), Annapolis Bus. Coalition (pres. 1983-84), U. Md. Colonnade Soc. (nat. chair 1994-95), Nat. Press Club, Annapolis Touchdown Club (pres. 1976), U. Md. Dean's First Edit. Club (chmn. 1986—), Annapolitan Club. Democrat. Avocation: tennis. Home: 139 Wallace Manor Rd Edgewater MD 21037-1205 Office: Crosby Mktg Comms 705 Melvin Ave Ste 200 Annapolis MD 21401-1544

CROSBY, RICHARD ALLEN, music educator; b. Ashland, Ohio; s. Richard Byrd and Marilyn Elizabeth Crosby. MusB in Music Edn., U. Cin., 1979, MusM in Piano and Conducting, 1981, MusD in Piano, 1990. Prof. music Ea. Ky. U., Richmond, 1986—. Chmn. profl. orgns. coun. Am. Classical Music Hall of Fame, Cin., 1997—. Mem.: Ky. Music Tchrs. Assn. (sec. 1988—2000), Phi Mu Alpha Sinfonia (province gov. 1988—, pres. 1994—97, chmn. province gov.'s coun. 2000—03, nat. pres. 2003—). Office: Ea Ky U Dept Music 521 Lancaster Ave Richmond KY 40475

CROSBY, THOMAS ANTHONY, radio producer, broadcaster; b. New London, Conn., July 25, 1947; s. Franklin Clifton and Dorothy Rose (Perkins) C.; m. Sheryll Ann Bellotti, Jan. 4, 1970; children: Sunny Marie, Kevin Franklin, Michael Thomas, Matthew Stephen. BA, U. R.I., 1969; MA, Am. U., 1979. News anchor, reporter WSAV/TV/AM, Savannah, Ga., 1971-73; news dir., anchor WSPA/TV/AM/FM, Spartanburg, S.C., 1973-77, Assoc. Press Radio Network, Washington, 1979-80; bur. chief, corr. WLOS TV/FM, Asheville, N.C., 1977-78; grad. asst. Am. U. Sch. Communication, Washington, 1978-79; broadcaster, writer WAMU-FM, Washington, 1978-79; broadcaster, producer Voice of Am., Washington, 1979—. Narrator audio-visual presentations Wheeler Industries, Washington, 1978. Writer, producer, anchor documentary Vietnam Vets. Syndrome, 1979. 1st lt. U.S. Army, 1969-71, Vietnam. Decorated Bronze Star, Combat Infantry badge. Mem. North Springfield Racquet and Swim Club. Unitarian Universalist. Avocations: tennis, swimming, reading, horseback riding. Home: 5751 Heming Ave Springfield VA 22151-2714 Office: Voice of Am 330 Independence Ave SW Washington DC 20237-0001

CROSBY, THOMAS MANVILLE, JR., lawyer; b. Mpls., Oct. 9, 1938; s. Thomas M. and Ella (Pillsbury) C.; m. Eleanor Rauch, June 12, 1965; children: Stewart, Brewster, Grant, Brooke. BA, Yale U., 1960, LLB, 1965. Bar: Minn. 1965. Assoc. Faegre & Benson, Mpls., 1965-72, ptnr., 1965—. Served to lt. USNR, 1960—62. Office: Faegre & Benson 2200 Wells Fargo Ctr 90 S 7th St Ste 2200 Minneapolis MN 55402-3901

CROSBY, WILLIAM DUNCAN, JR., lawyer; b. Louisville, Ky., Sept. 1, 1943; s. William Duncan and Lucille (Edwards) C.; m. Constance Elaine Frederick, June 2, 1973; children: William Duncan III, Lelia Margaret. BA, Yale U., 1965; JD, Columbia U., 1968. Bar: Ky. 1968, U.S. Dist. Ct. D.C. 1971, U.S. Supreme Ct. 1977. Rep. chief counsel Com. on Rules U.S. Ho. of Reps., Washington, 1972-94, chief counsel Com. on Rules, 1995-99; v.p., COO The Solomon Group, Washington, 1999—2001; exec. dir. The Livingston Solomon Group, LLC, Washington, 2002—03, The Livingston Group, LLC, Washington, 2003—. Chmn. Dranesville Dist., Fairfax County (Va.) Rep. Party, 1987-89; mem. Fairfax County Rep. Com., 1981—, chmn. fin. com., 2003—. Lt. (j.g.) USNR, 1968-71. Mem. ABA, FBA, Ky. Bar Assn., D.C. Bar, Columbia Law Sch. Alumni Assn. of Washington (pres. 1987-89). Baptist. Avocation: swimming. Home: 920 Mackall Ave Mc Lean VA 22101-1618 Office: The Livingston Group 499 S Capitol St SW Ste 600 Washington DC 20003 E-mail: billcrosby1@aol.com., bcrosby@livingstongroupdc.com.

CROSKELL, MADELON BYRD, music educator, classical vocalist; b. Ardmore, Okla., Nov. 16, 1937; d. Lyndall Rae Byrd and Avis Madeline Bradshaw; m. Henry Croskell, July 24, 1955; children: Maralyn Lee and Mark Henry. Student, U. N.Mex., 1955, S.E. U. Okla., 1956-58; B of Music cum laude, U. Mo., St. Louis, 1979. Nat. cert. tchr. music - piano and theory. V.p. Ind. Piano Tchrs. Guild, Indpls., 1964-69, Okla. Music Tchrs. Assn., Bartlesville, 1969-72, St. Louis Area Music Tchrs. Assn., 1974-89; music tchr., choir dir. Parkway Ctrl. Jr. High, St. Louis, 1979-80. Founder Playathon, 1979—89, Music Masters, St. Louis Area Music Tchrs. Assn., 1984—99, Playathon Richardson Music Tchrs. Assn., 1995—2003. Performed 32 oratories with Indpls. Symphonic Choir, St. Louis Symphony; contbr. articles to Mo. Music Tchrs. Notes, 1980-89. Vol. sr. tour guide Mo. Bot. Garden, St. Louis, 1978-89. Mem. Nat. Fedn. Music Clubs (jr. counselor), Music Tchrs. Nat. Assn., Tex. Music Tchrs. Assn., Dallas Music Tchrs. Assn. (bd. dirs.), Richardson Music Tchrs. Assn. (bd. dirs., pres. 1989—), Sigma Alpha Iota (Sword of Honor award St. Louis chpt., pres. alumnae chpt. 1974-89). Republican. Presbyterian. Avocations: gardening, horseback riding, swimming, reading. Home and Office: 6817 Cliffbrook Dr Dallas TX 75254

CROSS, ALVIN MILLER (AL CROSS), political columnist, writer; b. Knoxville, Tenn, Apr. 24, 1954; s. Perry Martin and Winnie Cook (Miller) C.; m. Patricia Hodges, June 19, 1976. BA in Mass Comm., Western Ky. U., 1978; postgrad., Poynter Inst. Media Studies, 1999. Sports reporter Clinton County News, Albany, 1965—71; announcer WANY Radio, Albany, Ky., 1968-75; advt. mgr., reporter, editor College Heights Herald, Bowling Green, Ky., 1973-74; editor and gen. mgr. The Reporter, Monticello, Ky., 1974-75; asst. mng. editor Logan Leader & News-Democrat, Russellville, Ky., 1975-77; editor Leitchfield Gazette, Grayson County News Gazette, Ky., 1977-78; reporter Courier-Journal, Louisville, 1978-88, polit. writer, 1989—; polit. columnist, 1999—. Rep. acad. coun. Associated Student Govt. We. Ky. U., 1972-73. Recipient Founder's award Foothills Festival Inc., Albany, 1989, Outstanding Print Journalist in Ky. and Adjoining States award journalism dept. Western Ky. U., 1995, Deadline Reporting award Metro Louisville Journalism, 1989, 92, Column Writing award, 1989, Continuing Coverage award, 1992, 95. Mem. Soc. Profl. Journalists (regional dir. 1987-89, v.p. Louisville chpt. 1983-84, pres. 1984-85, chmn. nat. com. Project Watchdog 1995-99, nat. sec.-treas. 1999-2000, pres.-elect 2000-2001, pres. 2001-2002, Outstanding Newspaper in Region 5 award 1974), Ky. Hist. Soc., Western Ky. U. Alumni Assn. Baptist. Avocations: reading, gardening, boating, touring. Home: 123 W Todd St Frankfort KY 40601-2825 Office: Courier-Jour Bur 332 Capital Ave Frankfort KY 40601 E-mail: across@spj.org.

CROSS, AUREAL THEOPHILUS, geology and botany educator; b. Findlay, Ohio, June 4, 1916; s. Raymond Willard and Myra Jane (Coon) C.; m. Christina Aleen Teyssier, Mar. 11, 1945; children: Timothy Aureal, Christina Avonne Cross Collier, Jonathan Ariel, Cheryl Aleen (Mrs. Richard M. Bowman), Christopher Charles. BA, Coe Coll., 1939; MS in Botany, U. Cin., 1941, PhD in Botany and Paleontology, 1943. Instr. to asst. prof. U. Notre Dame, 1943-46; NRC fellow in geology, 1943-44; paleobotanist; Ctrl. Expt. Sta., U.S. Bur. Mines, Pitts., 1945; asst. prof. dept. geology U. Cin., 1946-49, asst. prof. dept. botany, 1948-49; part-time geologist Geol. Survey Ohio, 1946-51; coal geologist and paleobotanist W.Va. Geol. and Econ. Survey, 1949-57; assoc. prof. to prof. dept. geology U. W.Va., 1949-57; sr. rsch. engr. Pan Am. Petroleum Corp. Rsch. Center, Tulsa, 1957-61, supr. tech. group and rsch. group, 1959-61; prof. dept. geology Mich. State U., East Lansing, 1961-86, prof. dept. botany and plant pathology, 1961-86, prof. emeritus, 1987—. Prof. ecology U. Alaska, 1971; research palynologist U. So. Calif., 1972; Morton vis. prof. Ohio U., Athens Ohio, 1981; Nathaniel S. Shaler Disting. lectr. U. Ky., 1991; UNESCO adviser U. grants commn. India Coal Programs, 1983; Calcutta adviser geology dept. Jadavpur U., India, 1983. Editor: Palynology in Oil Exploration, 1964, Compte Rendu 9th Internat. Congress Carboniferous Stratigraphy and Geology, vol. 4, Econ. Geology: Coal, Oil and Gas, 1985; co-editor: Coal Resources and Research in Latin America, 1978, World Class Coal Deposits, Internat. Jour. Coal Geology, 1993; assoc. editor: Fossil Spores and Pollen, 41 vols, 1956-87; contbr. numerous articles, abstracts and revs. to profl. jours. Chmn. citywide rally Fellowship Christian Athletes, Tulsa, 1960; mem. nat. council U.P. Men, 1966-68, 74-84 ; active Boy Scouts Am., YMCA, others. Named Seward Meml. lectr. Sahni Inst. Palaeobotany, 1985, J. Sen Meml. lectr., 1985; named Disting. lectr. Am. Assn. Petroleum Geologists, 1964, Outstanding Educator Am. Assn. Petroleum Geologists Ea. Sect., 1987; recipient Gordon H. Wood Jr. Meml. award, 1993, John T. Galey medal, 1995. Mem. Am. Assn. Stratigraphic Palynologists (hon.; medal of Excellence in Edn. 1999), Bot. Soc. Am. (chmn. paleobotany sect. 1953, 77, grantee 1954, Disting. Svc. Paleobotany award 1985), Geol. Soc. Am. (Gilbert H. Cady Coal Geology award 1987, chmn. coal geology divsn. 1966, chmn. North Ctrl. sect. 1969-70, exec. sec. sect. 1971-80, grantee 1951), Soc. Econ. Paleontologists and Mineralogists (chmn. rsch. com. 1961-62, councillor in paleontology 1971-73, numerous other internat., nat. and regional profl. assns. Presbyterian. Home: 529 N Harrison Rd East Lansing MI 48823-3015 Office: Mich State Univ Dept Geol Scis East Lansing MI 48824 Fax: 517-353-8787. E-mail: cross1@msu.edu.

CROSS, BONHAM E(LWOOD), retired newspaper account executive; m. Marie Swanberg; children: Randi Lawrence, David. News photographer Star Tribune, Mpls., then with advt. dept.; ret. Chmn. Minn. Coun. for Hearing Impaired, interim exec. dir., 1991; mem. adv. com. Metro Regional Svc. Ctr. for Hearing Impaired; mem. Legis. Coalition for Hearing Impaired. Named Man of Yr., Minn. Assn. Deaf Citizens, 1987; recipient Virginia McKnight Binger award in human service, 2002, also various awards for news photography. Avocation: flying. Home: 3662 Shady Oak Rd Minnetonka MN 55305-4223 E-mail: bonhamc@worldnet.att.net.

CROSS, BRUCE MICHAEL, lawyer; b. Washington, Jan. 30, 1942; AB magna cum laude, Dartmouth Coll., 1964; JD magna cum laude, Harvard U., 1967. Bar: Wash. 1967. Law clk. to Hon. Frank P. Weaver Supreme Ct. Wash., 1967-68; mem. Perkins Coie LLP, Seattle. Office: Perkins Coie LLP 1201 3rd Ave Fl 40 Seattle WA 98101-3099 E-mail: crosb@perkinscoie.com.

CROSS, CHARLOTTE LORD, retired social worker, artist; b. Andalusia, Ala., Dec. 1, 1941; d. Roy Olice and Laura Emily (Smith) Lord; m. Jack Allen Cross, May 5, 1960; children: Jack Allen III, James Duane, Jeffrey Miles. BA in English, Auburn U., Montgomery, Ala., 1979, MS in Psychology, 1980, MS in Secondary Edn./English, 1993. Social worker dept. human resources State of Ala., Andalusia, 1980—2002, ret., 2002. Tchr. in English conversation to Nat. Cancer Inst. rsch. scientists, Tokyo, 1965-66; adj. instr. psychology Lurleen B. Wallace State Jr. Coll, 1988-98, Troy State U., Fort Rucker, 1991; owner Capriccio's Coffee Shop and Gifts; portrait artist. Recipient Dept. of Human Resources Commr.'s Merit award, 1989. Mem.: Am. Soc. Portrait Artists. Baptist. Home: PO Box 1364 Andalusia AL 36420-1364

CROSS, CHRISTOPHER T. education consultant; b. Lakewood, Ohio, May 30, 1940; s. Sterling Leonard and Virginia Mae (Taylor) C.; m. Constance Heatherly Woods, Aug. 26, 1961 (div. 1981); children: H. Allyson (dec.), Dana M., Charles M.B.; m. Diane Stricklan DeRoche, June 11, 1982; 1 child, Charles. BA in Polit. Sci., Whittier Coll., Calif., 1962; MA, Calif. State Coll., L.A., 1969. With Dept. HEW, Washington, 1969-70, dep. asst. sec. for legislation, 1970-73; sr. ednl. cons. US Ho. of Reps., Washington, 1973-77, Rep. staff dir., com. on edn. and labor, 1977-78; dir. Washington Office ops. Abt Assoc., Inc., 1978-80; mktg. mgr. fed. govt. Westinghouse Info. Svc., Washington, 1980-82, mgr. fed. svc., 1982-83; pres., chief operating officer Univ. Rsch. Corp., Chevy Chase, Md., 1983-89; asst. sec. for ednl. rsch. and improvement U.S. Dept. Edn., Washington, 1989-91; dir. Am. Inst. Rsch., 1993—. Exec. dir., edn. initiative The Bus. Roundtable, 1991-9 4; pres. Coun. for Basic Edn., 1994-2001; mem. Nat. Edn. Commn. on Time and Learning, 1992-94; mem. Md. State Bd. Edn., 1993-97, pres. 1994-97. Contbr. articles to profl. jour. Trustee Whitter Coll., 1999—; chair Nat. Coun. Edn. & Human Devel. George Washington U., 2000-2002. Mem. Profl. Svc. Coun. (exec. com. 1981-86, trustee), Coun. Enrollment in Govt. Congregationalist. Home: 109 Sunhaven Rd Danville CA 94506 E-mail: ctcross@sbcglobal.net.

CROSS, COY FRANKLIN, II, historian; b. Bourbville, Ky., Aug. 6, 1937; s. Coy Franklin Cross and Willie Alice Lentz; m. Carol Martha Cross, Feb. 14, 1988; children from previous marriage: Coy F. III, Elizabeth A., Mellissa R. BA, Fla. State U., 1971; MA, Calif. State U., Stanislaus, 1981; PhD, U. Calif., Santa Barbara, 1988. Enlisted USAF, 1956, attained rank of sr. master sgt., 1974; historian Mil. Airlift Command, Scott AFB, Ill., 1988-90, 30th Space Wing, Vandenberg AFB, Calif., 1990-92, 9th Reconnaissance Wing, Beale AFB, Calif., 1992—. Author: U-2 in Desert Storm, 1994, From the Stone Age to the Space Age, 1996, Go West, Young Man!, 1995, Justin S. Morrill, 2000. Mem. Am. Hist. Assn., Orgn. Am. Historians. Office: 9RW/HO 6000 C St Ste 113 Beale AFB CA 95903-1616 E-mail: coy.cross@beale.af.mil.

CROSS, DAVID RUSK, farmer, livestock raiser; b. Larned, Kans., July 25, 1952; s. Charles Rusk and Mary Helen (Gatterman) C.; m. Linda Rae Wheeler, Nov. 3, 1974; children: Aaron R., Carolyn R., Aimee E. BS in Agr., Fort Hays State U., 1974; AI Tech. Course, Kans. State U., 1988. Ptnr. Cross Bros., Lewis, Kans., 1974-94; bd. dirs. Home State Bank, Lewis, 1979-94, chmn. of the bd., 1991-94; bd. dirs. Star Alfalfa, Inc., Lewis, 1986—; pres. Cross Bros., 1994—; sec. Plaza Cattle Feeders, Inc., 1992—. Mem. adv. bd. Kennedy & Coe, LLC, Pratt, Kans., 1996—, class II grad. Wheat Industry Leaders of Tomorrow, St. Louis, 1998-99; panelist Kans. Farmer Mag., 1996—. Mem. sch. bd. United Sch. Dist. 503, Lewis, Kans., 1986-88; cub master Boy Scouts Am., Cub Pack 238, Lewis, Kans. 1987-89; mem. com. Troop 238 Boy Scouts Am., Lewis, 1989-96; trustee United Meth. Ch., 1994—; precinct com. Ctrl Com. Kans. Reps., Edwards County, Kans., 1984-91, chmn. 1996—; first dist. del. Kans. Rep. Party, Topeka, 2003; chmn. Edwards County Leadership, Kinsley, Kans., 1995-98. Recipient 20th N.Am. Big Game award, Boone and Crockett Club, 1987; owner Res. Champion Live, Heifer Beef Empire Days, Garden City, Kans., 1988. Mem. Nat. Cattleman's Beef Assn. (agr. policy com. 1995—), Kans. Livestock Assn. (bd. dirs. 1978-80, water com. 1994—, vice chmn. 1996-2002, policy and resolutions com., 1997—, cow, calf stocker coun. exec. com. 1999—), Kans. Assn. Wheat Growers (Edwards County chmn., 1994-95, bd. dirs. 1996—, state sec. 2002-03), Masons (master). Avocations: hunting, collecting western memorabalia. Home: RR 1 Box 22 Lewis KS 67552-9520 E-mail: crossbro@ruraltel.net.

CROSS, DENNIS WAYNE, academic administrator; b. Bristol, Va., Apr. 18, 1955; s. Brainard C. and Genevieve Cross; m. Susan Sydney Haire, Aug. 7, 1982; children: Walker Gray, Grier Gordon, Sydney Sullivan. BA, Vanderbilt U., 1976; MDiv, Harvard U., 1979, ThM, 1982; postgrad., Vanderbilt U., 1986, Williamsburg Devel. Inst., 1987. Banking officer 1st Am. Nat. Bank, Nashville, 1982-86; dir. alumni and devel. Coll. Arts and Sci. Vanderbilt U., Nashville, 1986-92; exec. dir. Arts and Scis. Found., Inc., assoc. dean for program devel. Coll. Arts and Scis. U. N.C., Chapel Hill, 1992-2000; v.p. for univ. devel. Coll. William and Mary, Williamsburg, Va., 2000—. Bd. dirs. mid. Tenn. chpt. ACLU, Nashville, 1991-92, Christopher Wren Assn., Williamsburg, Ash Lawn Music Festival, Charlottesville, Va.; exec. com. Friends of Music, Inc., Nashville, 1987-89; mem. membership com. U. Club of Nashville, 1991-92; former head edn. com. Chapel of the Cross, Chapel Hill, N.C., mem. campus ministry; mem. comm. commn. St. Martin's Episcopal Ch., Williamsburg, Va.; vol. bicentennial campaign Coll. of Arts and Scis. U. N.C., 1992-95; bd. dirs., sec.-treas. U. N.C.-Chapel Hill Arts and Scis. Found., Inc., 1992-2000; mem. Thomas Wolfe Centennial Com., 1997-99; advisor Ctr. for the Study of the Am. South, 1998-2000; bd. dirs., asst. sec. Endowment Assn. of Coll. William and Mary; mem. steering com. Campaign for William and Mary, 2000—; mem. exec. com. Arts and Scis. Advancement Profls., 1995-2000; bd. dirs. Chapel Hill-Carrboro Pub. Sch. Found., 1998-2000. Mem. Coun. for Advancement of Secondary Edn., Country Music Found., Coun. of Friends-Tryon Palace, N.C. Triangle Vanderbilt Club (organizer), Kingsmill Golf Club, Phi Beta Kappa (exec. com. U.N.C., chpt. officer 1997-2000), Delta Phi Alpha. Episcopalian. Avocations: reading, baseball, golf, studying southern folk art and material culture of the south. Home: 324 Yorkshire Dr Williamsburg VA 23185-3913 Office: Coll William and Mary Office of Univ Devel PO Box 8795 Williamsburg VA 23187-8795

CROSS, DEWITTE TALMADGE, III, physician, neuroradiologist; b. Birmingham, Ala., Feb. 28, 1953; s. DeWitte T. Jr. and Virginia G. Cross; m. Anne Haney, Apr. 19, 1980; children: Courtney Elizabeth, Kevin Andrew. BA, Vanderbilt U., 1975; MD, U. Ala., 1980. Diplomate Am. Bd. Radiology. Commd. ensign USN, 1976, advanced through grades to lt. commdr., 1987, intern, gen. med. officer, 1980-82; residency in radiology Nat. Navel Med. Ctr., Bethesda, Md., 1982-85; head radiology Naval Hosp., Memphis, 1985-87; fellow in neuroradiology N.Y. Med. Coll., N.Y.C., 1987-88, Columbia U., N.Y.C., 1988-89, asst. prof., 1989-91; dir. interventional neuroradiology Washington U., St. Louis, 1991—. Chmn. radiation safety oversight com. Barnes-Jewish Hosp., St. Louis, 1998—2002, chmn. prodecural sedation com., 2002—. Contbr. author: Abram's Angiography, 1996; contbr. articles to profl. jours. Mem. neighborhood coun. City of Clayton, Mo., 1998-2000. Named one of the Best Doctors in Am., Ctrl. Region, Woodward and White, 1996-97, 1998-99. Mem. AMA, Am. Soc. Interventional and Therapeutic Neuroradiology, Am. Soc. Neuroradiology, Am. Coll. Radiology, Radiol. Soc. N.Am. Presbyterian. Avocations: exercise, movies, cars. Office: Washington U Med Ctr Dept Radiology Campus Box 8131 510 S Kingshighway Saint Louis MO 63110 E-mail: CrossDe@mir.wustl.edu.

CROSS, DOROTHY ABIGAIL, retired librarian; b. Bangor, Mich., Sept. 9, 1924; d. John Laird and Alice Estelle (Wilcox) C. BA, Wayne State U., 1956; MA in Libr. Sci., U. Mich., 1957. Jr. libr. Detroit Pub. Libr., 1957-59; adminstrv. libr. U.S. Army, Braconne, France, 1959-61, Poitiers, France, 1961-63, area libr. supr., 1963, asst. commd. libr. Kaiserslautern, Germany, 1963-67, acquisitions libr. Aschaffenburg, Germany, 1967, Munich, Germany, 1967-69, sr. staff libr. specialist, 1969-72, commd. libr. Stuttgart, Germany, 1972-75, dep. staff libr. Heidelberg, Germany, 1975-77; chief libr. 18th Airborne Corps and Ft. Bragg, N.C., 1977-79; chief ADP sect. Pentagon Libr., Washington, 1979-80, chief readers svcs. br., 1980-83, dir., 1983-91. Mem. ALA, U. Mich. Alumni Assn., Delta Omicron. Methodist. Home: 6511 Delia Dr Alexandria VA 22310-2609 E-mail: dacross@starpower.net.

CROSS, EASON, JR., architect; b. Bisbee, Ariz., Nov. 14, 1925; s. Eason and Olive (Hardwick) C.; m. Diana Johnson, June 17, 1950; children: Ben, Becca, Amy, Susan. BA, Harvard U., 1949, MArch, 1951. Assoc. Charles M. Goodman, Washington, 1952-59, Keyes, Lethbridge & Condon, 1959-61; ptnr. Cross & Adreon, Arlington, Va., 1961-87; pres. Va. Architects Accord P.C., Alexandria, 1989—; prin. Cross Assocs., Alexandria, Va., 1987—. Patentee fastenings and furniture. Pres. Hollin Hills Cmty. Assn., 1978; chmn. Fairfax County Appeals Bd., 1970-80; pres. Old Dominion DESA, 1997-98, Purysburg Preservation Found., 1998—. With USNR, WWII. Recipient Ware prize, 1950, Washington Bd. Trade design award, 1965, Bethesda-Chevy Chase C. of C. design awards, 1966, 67; House and Home awards AIA, 1965-66; Mid-Atlantic Region design awards, 1967-, 69; Nat. Honor award, 1968; Nat. Honor award Am. inst. Steel Constrn., 1967; 4 awards HUD-Washington Ctr. Urban Studies furniture competition, 1971; Frameworks Home Desing Merit award, 1995; Fairfax County Exceptional Design award 1985, 87, N.V. CAA Design award 1999. Fellow AIA, Housing Competition ADPSR winner 1993; mem. Va. Soc. AIA (Energy award 1979, Design award 1986, Noland medal 1994), Harvard Club, Fox Club, Ga. Salzburger Soc. Purysburg Found., Ricochet Club. Episcopalian. Home: 2309 Glasgow Rd Alexandria VA 22307-1821 E-mail: ecross2@juno.com.

CROSS, FRANK MOORE, JR., foreign language educator; b. Ross, Calif, July 13, 1921; s. Frank Moore and Mary (Ellison) C.; m. Elizabeth A. Showalter, June 20, 1947; children: Susan E., Ellen M., Priscilla Rachel. AB, Maryville Coll., 1942; BD, McCormick Theol. Sem., 1946; PhD, Johns Hopkins, 1950; MA (hon.), Harvard U., 1957; LittD, Maryville Coll., 1968; PhD (hon.), Hebrew U. Jerusalem, 1984; DSc (hon.), Lethbridge U., 1990; DHL (hon.), Miami U., 1992; LHD (hon.), Albright Coll., 1994; D in Jewish Letters (hon.), Jewish Theol. Sem., 1997; DHL (hon.), U. Pa., 1998. Hancock prof. Hebrew and Oriental lang. Coll. Arts and Sci., Harvard U., Cambridge, Mass., 1957-92, Hancock prof. emeritus, 1992—; also curator Semitic Mus., 1958-61, dir., 1974-87, chmn. dept. neareastern langs., 1958-65; ann. prof. Am. Sch. Oriental Rsch., Jerusalem, 1953-54. Mem. internat. staff for editing Dead Sea Scrolls, 1953—; co-dir. archaeol. expdn. to Judaean Buqe'ah, 1955; prin. investigator Am. Schs. Oriental Rsch., Harvard U., U. Mich. expdn. to Carthage, 1975-80; archaeol. dir. Hebrew Union Coll., Jerusalem, 1963-64. Author: (with David N. Freedman) Early Hebrew Orthography, 1952, The Ancient Library of Qumran, 3rd ed. 1995; (with D.N. Freedman) Studies in Ancient Yahwistic Poetry, 2nd ed., 1997; Canaanite Myth and Hebrew Epic, 1973; From Epic to Canon, 1998; (with Eugene Ulrich) Qumran Cave 4:IX Deuteronomy, Joshua, Judges, Kings, 1995; (with Eugene Ulrich) Qumran Cave 4: X The Prophets, 1997, Qumran Cave 4: XI Psalms to Chronicles, 2000; Leaves from an Epigrapher's Notebook: Collected Papers in Hebrew and West Semitic Epigraphy, 2003; Epigraphy, 2003; editor: (with Michael Stone) Scrolls from the Wilderness of Judah, 1965 (with S. Talmon) Qumran and the History of the Biblical Text, 1975; (with P.D. Miller and W.E. Lemke) Magnalia Dei, 1976; editor: Harvard Semitic Studies, 1968-92, Harvard Semitic Monographs, 1968-92; assoc. editor: Harvard Theol. Rev, 1963-74, Bull. of Am. Schs. Oriental Rsch., 1969-91, contbg. editor, 1992—; contbr. articles for profl. jour. Trustee Am. Sch. Oriental Rsch., 1973-91, pres., 1974-76, hon. trustee, 1992—. Recipient Percia Schimmel award Israel Mus., 1980, Inst. for Advanced Studies fellow Hebrew U., Jerusalem, 1978-79, Medalla De Honor De La Universidad Complutense (Univ. Madrid), 1991; Am. Council Learned Socs. fellow, 1971-72 Fellow Am. Acad. Arts and Sci.; mem. Am. Philos. Soc., Am. Oriental Soc., Soc. Bibl. Lit. (pres. 1973-74, William Foxwell Albright award 1980), Bibl. Colloquium, Israel Exploration Soc. (hon.), British Soc. for Study Old Testament (hon.), Phi Beta Kappa. Home: 31 Woodland Rd Lexington MA 02420-2015 Office: Harvard Semitic Mus 6 Divinity Ave Cambridge MA 02420-2020 E-mail: fcross@fas.harvard.edu.

CROSS, FREDDIE LEE, research scientist; b. Arlington, Va., Oct. 17, 1959; d. William Raymond and Doris Louise Leighty; 1 child, Lance Allen. AS in Environ. and Sci. Tech., No. Va. C.C., 1980; BA in Gen. Studies, Mary Washington Coll., 1991; MA in Edn., Va. Poly. and State U., 1995, PhD in Ednl. Rsch. and Evaluation, 2003. Profl. tchr. lic. Va. Sci. mid. tchr. Fairfax County Sch., Va., 1991—93; math & sci. med. tchr. Spotsylvania County Sch., Va., 1993—98; rsch. assoc. Cons. Rsch. and Info. Svcs., Roston, Va., 1998—2000; rsch. analyst Coun. Advancement and Support Edn., Washington, 2000—. Rsch. assoc. Edn. Tech. Think Tank, McLean, Va., 2000. Mem.: Am. Statis. Assn., Kappa Delta Pi, Alpha Phi Sigma. Republican. Methodist. Avocations: hiking, photography, motorcycling, gardening, crafts. Office: Coun Advancement & Support Edn 1307 New York Ave Ste 1000 Washington DC 20005-4701 Fax: 202-387-4973. E-mail: cross@case.org.

CROSS, GEORGE ALAN MARTIN, biochemistry educator, researcher; b. Cheadle, Cheshire, Eng., Sept. 27, 1942; s. George Bernard and Beatrice Mary (Horton) C.; 1 child, Julia Elizabeth. BA, Cambridge (Eng.) U., 1964, PhD, 1968. Scientist Med. Rsch. Coun., Cambridge, 1970-77; dept. head Wellcome Found. Rsch. Labs., Kent, Eng., 1977-82; Andre and Bella Meyer prof. molecular parasitology Rockefeller U., N.Y.C., 1982—, dean grad. and postgrad. studies, 1995-99. Cons. Wellcome Found., Eng., 1982-87, World Health Orgns., Geneva, 1983-87, New Eng. Biolabs., Beverly Mass., 1985-99. Contbr. articles to profl. jours. Recipient Paul Ehrlich prize, 1984, Chalmers medal Royal Soc. of Tropical Medicine, 1983; named Fleming Lectr. Soc. for Gen. Microbiology, 1978. Fellow The Royal Soc. (Leeuwenhoek Lectr. 1998). Office: The Rockefeller Univ 1230 York Ave New York NY 10021-6399 E-mail: george.cross@rockefeller.edu.

CROSS, HAROLD DICK, physician; b. Wellington, Kans., Apr. 2, 1930; married, 1947; 4 children. BA, Colby Coll., 1953; MD, Yale Y., 1957. Intern Ea. Maine Med. Ctr., 1957—58, prof., physician, 1958—91; pvt. practice Elizabethtown, NC, 1995—95; emergency rm. physician Johnston Meml. Hosp., Smithfield, NC, 1996—98, Naval Hosp., Beaufort, SC, 1998—. Mem.: Inst. of Medicine of NAS. Office: 1 Pinckney Blvd Beaufort SC 29902-6122

CROSS, HAROLD ZANE, agronomist, educator; b. Portales, N.Mex., Dec. 25, 1941; s. Guy Edner and Hagabelle (Lawson) C.; m. Glenda Faye Wilhoit, Nov. 24, 1961; children: Carter Dale, Carson Lee, Curtis Don, Cathryn Faye. BS with honors, N.Mex. State U., 1965, MS, 1967; PhD, U. Mo., 1971. Rancher, Elida, N.Mex., 1965-67; grad. rsch. asst. N.Mex. State U., Las Cruces, 1965-67; NDEA fellow U. Mo., Columbia, 1967-71; asst. prof. N.D. State U., Fargo, 1971-77, assoc. prof., 1977-82, prof., 1982-98, prof. emeritus, 1998—. Cons. Agrl. Inst. Osijek, Yugoslavia, 1984, CIMMYT, Mexico City, 1984, Eli Lilly Co., Indpls., 1987, N.D. State U., Fargo, 1998—. Author: Descendents of Sir Robert Crosse, 2000; contbr. numerous articles to profl. jours. Crops judge N.D. Winter show, Valley City, 1973-98. Santa Fe Rwy. scholar, 1961-62; NDEA fellow, 1967-71; recipient Outstanding Sr. Rsch. award N.D. State U. Coll. Agr., 1992. Mem. Crop Sci. Soc. Am. (editor for maize germplasm 1989-92), Am. Soc. Agronomy, Sigma Xi, Phi Kappa Phi, Gamma Sigma Delta, Alpha Zeta. Achievements include development and release of 51 inbred parental lines of maize and 39 synthetic varieties of maize; 12 plant variety patents; development of maize breeding procedures to genetically improve grain drying rates, procedures to improve leaf growth rates, kernel growth. E-mail: hzcross@earthlink.net.

CROSS, J. BRUCE, lawyer; b. Sharon, Pa., Oct. 6, 1949; s. John Lantz and Agnes (Bruce) C.; children: Lantz Davis, Heather Lynn. BA, U. Notre Dame, 1971; JD, U. Ark., 1974. Bar: Ark. 1974, U.S. Ct. Appeals (8th cir.) 1979, U.S. Supreme Ct. 1980. Ptnr. House, Holmes and Jewell, Little Rock, 1974-90, Cross and Gunter, P.A., Little Rock, 1990, McGlinchey Stafford Lang, Little Rock, 1991-97, Cross, Gunter, Witherspoon & Galchus, P.C., Little Rock, 1997—. Chpt. atty. Ark. Subcontractors Assn., Little Rock, 1987-90; mem. young execs. coun. Associated Gen. Contractors, 1989. Contbr. to profl. pubs. Active Big Bros. Ark., Little Rock, 1976-87; pres., bd. dirs. Ark. divsn. Nat. Soc. to Prevent Blindness, 1987-90; bd. dirs. Urban League Ark., 1989; nat. bd. dirs. Associated Builders & Contractors Am., 1999-2001; bd. dirs. Ark. Constrn. Edn. Found., 1999; active Leadership Hot Springs; active Habitat for Humanity, Youth Home. Recipient Pres.'s award Nat. Soc. to Prevent Blindness. Mem. Ark.

Hospitality Assn. (bd. dirs. 1988-89), Ark. Subcontractors Assn., Assoc. Bldrs. and Contrs. (pres. 1999-2000), Ark. Bar Assn. (past chmn. labor sect.), Ark. Ready Mixed Concrete Assn., Little Rock C. of C. (ptnrs. in edn. com. 1989-90), ABA (sect. labor and employment law com. on labor arbitration and the law of collective bargaining agreements 1981-99, com. on devel. of the law under the NLRA 2000—), Greater Hot Springs C. of C., Notre Dame Club Ark. (pres.). Roman Catholic. Office: Cross, Gunter, Witherspoon & Galchus PC 500 President Clinton Ave Ste 200 Little Rock AR 72201-1747 E-mail: jbcross@cgwg.com.

CROSS, JAMES EDWARD, electrical engineering educator; b. Hampton, Va., May 29, 1937; s. Julia Ann-Cross Morgan; m. Velta Rose Jones, Dec. 1, 1965; children: Michael Levi, Andre Lene, Michelle Monique-Cross Brown. Diploma in radio, TV and electronics, DeVry Tech. Inst., 1956; B of Engring. Sci. in Elec. Engring., Johns Hopkins U., 1960; MSEE, La. State U., 1967; postgrad. in elec. engring., U. of Fla., 1972; student in Elec. Engring., La. State U., 1973; BTh, Christian Bible Coll., Baton Rouge, La., 1982, ThM, 1984, ThD, 1987. Asst. prof. in elec. engring. So. U., Baton Rouge, 1962—64, chmn. elec. engring. dept., 1964—91, assoc. prof. of elec. engring., 1991—2002. Reviewer, evaluator of proposals NSF, Washington, 1987—96; mem. tech. staff Western Electric Co., Allentown, Pa., 1970, GE Rsch. Ctr., Schenectady, NY, 1971, Westinghouse Corp., Youngwood, Pa., 1965, Western Electric Co., Atlanta, 1966, Autonetics divsn. N.Am. Rockwell, Anaheim, Calif., 1968, Radiation Inc., Melbourne, Fla., 1969; tchg. assoc. U. Fla., Gainesville, 1971—72; vis. lectr. La. State U., Baton Rouge, 1972—73, rsch. asst., 1973; NASA/ASEE summer faculty fellow Langley Rsch. Ctr., Hampton, Va., 1974; mem. tech. staff Bell Labs., Holmel, NJ, 1979, IBM, Charlotte, NC, 1981, Caterpillar, Inc., Peoria, Ill., 1990; rschr. Air Force Rsch. Lab., Wright-Patterson AFB, Ohio, 2002. Co-author tech. papers to confs. Mem. Baton Rouge Coun. on Human Rels., La., 1969—2003; mem., sec. Christian Bible Coll., La., 1964—2001; mem. deacon bd. Mt. Pilgrim Bapt. Ch., Baton Rouge, 1964—2003; mem. La. Coun. on Human Rels., Lafayette, La., 1990—2003. Capt. res. Army Corp of Engrs., 1960—62, Heidelberg, Germany. Grantee, Air Force Rsch. Lab., 1996—99, La. Bd. of Regents, 1989—90, Raytheon Co., 2000—02. Mem.: AAUP (pres. of local chpt. 1969—71), IEEE (life), Am. Soc. for Engring. Edn., Early Risers Kiwanis Club, Am. Legion, Masons (sec., Hon. Worshipful Master, Twilight Lodge # 166). Democrat. Baptist. Home: 13608 Alba Dr Baker LA 70714 Home Fax: 225-775-3710. Personal E-mail: cross4153@aol.com.

CROSS, JANIS ALEXANDER, lawyer; b. Plainview, Tex., Sept. 8, 1954; d. James Robert Alexander and Virginia May (Etter) Rech; m. Stephen Douglas Cross, Aug. 19, 1978; children: Beau Austin, Katherine Elizabeth. BA, Tex. Tech U., 1976, JD, 1979. Bar: Tex. 1979, U.S. Dist. Ct. (no. dist.) Tex. 1980. Pvt. practice, Amarillo, Tex., 1979-81; atty. Pioneer Corp., Amarillo, 1981-84, Cabot Corp., Amarillo, 1984-87; atty. (corp. counsel) Mason and Hanger, Silas Mason Co., Inc., Amarillo, 1987—. Instr. West Tex. State U., Canyon, 1983-87. Bd. dirs. March of Dimes, Amarillo, 1980-83, Campfire, Inc., Amarillo, 1980-83, women's programs Amarillo Coll., 1982-85, human relations com. Amarillo City Commn., 1984-86. Named one of Outstanding Young Women in Am., 1983. Mem. Tex. Bar Assn., Amarillo Bar Assn., Amarillo Area Young Lawyers Assn., Amarillo Women's Network (bd. dirs. 1980-83, pres.-elect 1987, pres. 1988). Delta Theta Phi, Gamma Phi Beta. Republican. Baptist. Avocations: bicycling, swimming, reading. Home: 5107 Emil Ave Amarillo TX 79106-4721 Office: Mason & Hanger Silas Mason Co Inc Pantex Plant PO Box 30020 Amarillo TX 79120-0020

CROSS, JOHN ROBERT, retired telecommunications industry executive, travel consultant; b. Richmond, Va., June 5, 1932; s. Everett Waverly and Annie Lamberth C.; m. Linda Gravatt Campbell, Dec. 13, 1931; children: John Robert Jr., Ann Campbell Ramage, Richard Hawes. BA, Wash. and Lee U., Lexington, Va., 1954. Contr. Bell Atlantic - Va., Richmond, Va., 1986—93; owner Bob Cross Travel Cons., Richmond, Va., 2001—. Pvt. 1st class U.S. Army, 1954—56, Ft. Jackson, SC. Mem.: Rotary Club (pres. We. Henrico 1987—2003). Episcopalian. Avocation: travel. Home: 9403 Midvale Rd Richmond VA 23229 Office: Bob Cross Travel Cons 9403 Midvale Rd Richmond VA 23229 Personal E-mail: bcross9403@aol.com. E-mail: bcross9403@aol.com.

CROSS, JOHN WILLIAM, foreign language educator; b. Franklin, Pa., June 1, 1943; s. William Robert and Madaline Ann (Maurin) C.; m. Beverly Jean Boor (div. 2000); 1 child, Catherine Elizabeth. BA, W.Va. U., 1965, MA, 1967; PhD, U. Conn., 1974. Instr. French U. N.C., Asheville, 1967-68; asst. Lycee Louis-Le-Grand, Paris, 1972-73; instr., asst. prof. French SUNY, Geneseo, N.Y., 1969-75; asst. prof. SUNY-Potsdam Coll., 1976-84, chair modern langs., 1985-86, 90-91, 93—, assoc. prof., 1984-91, prof. modern langs., 1991; dir. for lang. programs MLA of Am., N.Y.C., 1991-93. Advanced placement reader Ednl. Testing Svc., Princeton, N.J., 1983-87; cons. in field. Editor Assn. Depts. of Fgn. Langs. Bull.; contbr. articles and revs. to profl. jours. Recipient French Govt. scholarship, Svcs. Culturels Francais, 1990; grantee, NEH, 1977, 1985, 1988, 2001, Office des Universites, 1972—73. Mem. MLA of Am., Am. Assn. Tchrs. French, N.Y. State Assn. Fgn. Lang. Tchrs., Societe d'Analyse de la Topique du Roman, Internat. Courtly Lit. Soc. Avocations: music appreciation, performance, recreational sports, poetry translation. Home: 36 Pierrepont Ave Potsdam NY 13676-2111 Office: SUNY Dept Modern Langs Potsdam NY 13676 E-mail: crossjw@potsdam.edu.

CROSS, JOSEPH RUSSELL, JR., law librarian; b. Bennettsville, S.C., July 29, 1945; s. Joseph Russell and Julia Rogers C.; m. Inez Mary Robinson, May 12, 1973; children: David Sebastian, Sarah Harrington. BA, Wofford Coll., 1967; MLn, Emory U., 1972; JD, U. S.C., 1978. Bar: S.C. 1978. Tchr. Cross (S.C.) Schs., 1967-68, 70-71; reference librarian U. S.C., Columbia, 1972-75; head of pub. svcs. U. S.C. Law Library, Columbia, 1978—, assoc. dir., 1997—, acting dir., 1983-84, 97-98. Served as staff sgt. U.S. Army, 1968-70, Vietnam. Mem. ABA, S.C. Bar Assn., Am. Assn. Law Libraries, S.C. Library Assn. Democrat. United Methodist. Home: PO Box 305 Cross SC 29436-0305 Office: U SC Coleman Karesh Law Library Columbia SC 29208-0001

CROSS, JUNE CREWS, retired music educator; b. Creedmoor, N.C., Oct. 7, 1935; d. David Reid and Virginia Frances (Bullock) Crews; m. Joel Allen Cross, June 26, 1965; children: Dhedra Frances, Allen Reid. BS in Music, Reading, East Carolina U., 1957; MS in Recreation Adminstrn., U. N.C., Chapel Hill, 1964. Cert. tchr., N.C. Tchr. music Mecklenburg County Schs., Charlotte, N.C., 1957-58, Granville County Schs., Oxford, N.C., 1958-60, 65-66, tchr. reading, music, 1977-97, lead tchr., 1989-90; asst. dir. recreation John Elmstead Hosp., 1960—65. Pvt. tchr. piano, voice, Creedmoor, 1966-74. Choir dir. Creedmoor United Meth. Ch., 1988-2000; asst. dir. Sparkle, Granville County Show Choir, 1975-2003; accompanist The King and I prodn. Granville Little Theatre, Oxford, 1997; dir. Evening of Entertainment, Creedmoor United Meth. Ch., 2000—. Named Tchr. of Yr. Butner (N.C.) -Stem Elem. Sch., 1993-94. Mem. DAR (treas. John Penn chpt.), Delta Kappa Gamma, Sigma Alpha Iota. Methodist. Avocation: reading. Home: 701 Forest Ln Creedmoor NC 27522-8196

CROSS, KATHRYN PATRICIA, education educator; b. Normal, Ill., Mar. 17, 1926; d. Clarence L. and Katherine (Dague) C. BS, Ill. State U., 1948; MA, U. Ill., 1951, PhD, 1958; LLD (hon.), SUNY, 1988; DS (hon.), Loyola U., 1980, Northeastern U., 1975; DHL (hon.), De Paul U., 1986, Open U., The Netherlands, 1989. Math. tchr. Harvard (Ill.) Community High Sch., 1948-49; rsch. asst. dept. psychology U. Ill., Urbana, 1949-53, asst. dean of women, 1953-59; dean of women then dean of students Cornell U., Ithaca, N.Y., 1959-63; dir. coll. and univ. programs Ednl. Testing Svc., Princeton, N.J., 1963-66; rsch. educator Ctr. R&D in Higher Edn. U. Calif., Berkeley, 1966-77; rsch. scientist, sr. rsch. psychologist, dir. univ. programs Ednl. Testing Svc., Berkeley, 1966-80; prof. edn., chair dept. adminstrn., planning & social policy Harvard U., Cambridge, Mass., 1980-88; Elizabeth and Edward Conner prof. edn. U. Calif., Berkeley, 1988-94, David Pierpont Gardner prof. higher edn., 1994-96. Mem. sec. adv. com. on automated personal data sys. Dept. HEW, 1972-73; del. to Soviet Union, Seminar on Problems in Higher Edn., 1975; vis. prof. U. Nebr., 1975-76; vis. scholar Miami-Dade C.C., 1987; trustee Carnegie Found., 1999—, Berkeley Pub. Libr., 1998—; spkr., cons. in field; bd. dirs. Elderhostel. Author: Beyond the Open Door: New Students to Higher Education, 1971, (with S. B. Gould) Explorations in Non-Traditional Study, 1972, (with J. R. Valley and Assocs.) Planning Non-Traditional Programs: An Analysis of the Issues for Postsecondary Education, 1974, Accent on Learning, 1976, Adults as Learners, 1981, (with Thomas A. Angelo) Classroom Assessment Techniques, 1993, (with Mimi Harris Steadman) Classroom Research, 1996; contbr. articles, monographs to profl. publs., chpts. to books; mem. editl. bd. to several ednl. jours.; cons. editor ednl. mag. Change, 1980—. Active Nat. Acad. Edn., 1975—, Coun. for Advancement of Exptl. Learning, 1982-85; trustee Bradford Coll., Mass., 1986-88, Antioch Coll., Yellow Springs, Ohio, 1976-78; mem. nat. adv. bd. Nat. Ctr. of Study of Adult Learning, Empire State Coll.; mem. nat. adv. bd. Okla. Bd. Regents; mem. higher edn. rsch. program Pew Charitable Trusts; mem. vis. com. Harvard Grad. Sch. Edn., 1998—; bd. dirs. Elderhostel, 1999—; trustee Berkeley Pub. Libr., 1999—, Carnegie Found., 1999—. Mem. Am. Assn. Higher Edn. (bd. dirs. 1987—, pres. 1975, chair 1989-90), Am. Assn. Comty. and Jr. Colls. (vice chair commn. of future comty. colls.), Carnegie Found. Advancement of Tchg. (adv. com. on classification of colls. and univs.), Nat. Ctr. for Devel. Edn. (adv. bd.), New Eng. Assn. Schs. and Colls. (commn. on instns. higher edn. 1982-86), Am. Coun. Edn. (commn. on higher edn. and adult learner 1986-88). E-mail: patcross@socrates.berkeley.edu.

CROSS, MILTON H. lawyer; b. Phila., July 28, 1942; s. Sidney B. and Edythe Cross; m. Joyce Volchok, June 4, 1966; children: Brian, Jonathon. BS, U. San Francisco, 1965; JD, Villanova U., 1968. Bar: Pa. 1968. Corp. counsel AEL, Inc., Phila., 1968-75; assoc. Cohen, Verlin, Sherzer & Porter, Phila., 1975-78; pvt. practice Phila., 1978-79; ptnr. Monteverde & Hemphill, Phila., 1980-96, Spector, Gadon & Rosen, Phila., 1996—. Adj. prof. Phila. Coll. Textiles and Sci., 1970-73. Chmn. Cheltenham Twp. Sch. Bd. Authority. Mem. ABA (sect. corp., banking and bus. law), Pa. Bar Assn., Phila. Bar Assn. Home: 251 Ironwood Cir Elkins Park PA 19027-1315 Office: Spector Gadon & Rosen 7 Penn Ctr Fl 7 Philadelphia PA 19103-2200

CROSS, RICHARD B. bass, educator; s. Charles Willard Cross and Laura Phelps; m. Doris Yarick, June 21, 1963; children: Catherine Kalonia, Dylan Ma'is. BA, Cornell Coll., Mt. Vernon, Iowa, 1957. Prof. Juilliard Sch. Music, N.Y.C., 1994—2003; artist in residence SUNY, Stony Brook, 1994—2003; prof. voice Yale U., New Haven, 1997—, Mannes Coll. Music, N.Y.C., 2003. Judge Met. Opera Auditions, N.Y.C.; master class Juilliard Sch. Music Choral Seminar, N.Y.C., 2003, Opera Theater St. Louis, 2003. Soloist (Operas) Pitts. Symphony, San Francisco Symphony, bass Don Giovanni, Santa Fe Opera, Boris Gudonov, Spoleto Festival, Italy, Donato, Maria Golovin by Menotti, NBC-TV, 1959, Pimen, Boris Gudonov, Mussorgsky, Norma, Amahl and the Night Visitors, RCA, Dr. Schön, Festival dei due Mondi, Spoleto, Italy, Don Quichotte, Cervantes Festival, Guanajuato, Mex., N.Y.C. Opera, 1959—92, Stuttgart Opera, Dortmund Opera, Germany, Hungarian State Opera, Budapest, Forester Cunning Little Vixen, Live from Lincoln Center, N.Y.C., leading bass Sutherland Williamson Opera Co., Australia, 1965, Frankfurt Opera, Germany, 1966—85. Pvt. U.S. Army, 1959—61, Ft. Meade, Md. Avocation: cooking.

CROSS, RICHARD JOHN, banker; b. Denver, May 22, 1929; s. Arthur Chester and Gertrude Eva (Ryan) C.; m. Mildred Louise Mouton, Jan. 19, 1957; children: John Charles, Carolyn Louise, Paul Arthur. BS, U. Colo., 1950; M.B.A, Wharton Sch. Finance U. Pa., 1955. With Lloyds Bank Calif., 1962-81, exec. v.p., 1974-81; mng. ptnr. Cross Investment Co., 1971—. Dir. bus. program Woodbury U., L.A., 1985-87; adj. prof. fin. and mgmt., 1987-97; chmn. bd. Highland Fed. Bank; adv. bd. Archdiocese of L.A. Dept. Detention Ministries, 1991-97; bd. dirs. Atwater Park Ctr., treas. 2001—. Mem. bd. councilors U. So. Calif. Andrus Gerontology Ctr., 2001—, Am. Lung Assn. L.A. County, 2003—. Served with USN, 1950—53. Fellow Royal Soc. Arts; mem. Calif. Bankers Assn., So. Calif. Trust Officers Assn., Delta Tau Delta, Phi Epsilon Phi. Clubs: Sutter (Sacramento); Jonathan (Los Angeles); Oakmont Country (Glendale, Calif.). Democrat. Roman Catholic. Home: 1430 Greenbriar Rd Glendale CA 91207-1256

CROSS, RITA FAYE, librarian, early childhood educator, writer; b. Franklin, Va., Apr. 4, 1957; d. Alonza Riddick and Earleen (Smith) C.; m. Cameron Michael Moody. BS in Early Childhood Edn., Elizabeth City State U., 1979; MA in Libr. Sci., U. D.C., 1993. Tchr. kindergarten Great Mt. Zion Day Care, Washington, 1979-86, Woodridge Elem. Sch., Washington, 1986-92; libr. Ea. Sr. H.S., Washington, 1992—. Avocations: writing poetry, horseback riding, boating, concerts, theater. Home: 10207 Fort Hills Ct Fort Washington MD 20744-3913

CROSS, ROBERT CLARK, journalist; b. Cheboygan, Mich., May 12, 1939; s. Warren Clark and Meryle M. (Allaire) Cross; m. Juju Lien; children: Gabriel Francis, Amy Lien. BA in Journalism, Wayne State U., 1962. Writer, researcher Newsweek mag., 1962; reporter, editor Chgo. Tribune, 1962-66, 67-82, assoc. editor mag., 1973-82, writer, 1982—; reporter Newsday, 1966-67; travel writer, 1992—. Recipient Gold and Silver Lowell Thomas awards Soc. of Am. Travel Writers, 1995, 2000. Office: 435 N Michigan Ave Chicago IL 60611-4066 E-mail: bcross@tribune.com.

CROSS, ROBERT FRANCIS, commissioner; b. Port Jervis, N.Y., Dec. 17, 1950; s. Francis Stuart and Rita Clotilde (Beilman) C.; m. Sheila Lynne Cochrane, Sept. 24, 1983. AA, Orange County Coll., Middletown, N.Y., 1971; BS, SUNY, Albany, 1973; MA, SUNY, New Paltz, 1976. Reporter, photographer The Union-Gazette, Port Jervis, 1974-76; Albany (N.Y.) bur. chief Ottaway News Svc., 1976-78; Albany corr. The Wall St. Jour., 1976-78; sci. editor N.Y. State Dept. Environ. Conservation, Albany, 1978-83, spl. asst. to commr., 1983-85, exec. asst. to commr., 1985-87, asst. commr., 1987-95; commr. City of Albany Dept. of Water, 1996—. Author: Sailor in the White House: The Seafaring Life of FDR, 2003; contbr. articles to profl. jours. Mem. N.Y. State Gov.'s Task Force on the Del. Water Gap Nat. Recreation Area, 1973; chmn. People United to Restore the Environment, Orange County Coll., 1970-71, Mayor's Task Force on Water Resources; chmn. bd. Albany Port Dist. Commn.; bd. trustees U.S.S. Slater Mus.; mem. Albany City Planning Bd., 1995-96; mem. Minisink Valley Hist. Soc., Albany Inst. History and Art, N.Y. State Hist. Assn., Nantucket Hist. Assn., Dorflinger-Suydam Wildlife Sanctuary. Mem. Am. Philatelic Soc., Nantucket Wharf Rat Club, Pacific Club Nantucket. Democrat. Roman Catholic. Avocations: writing on historical topics, reading american history and presidential biographies. Home: 977 Washington Ave Albany NY 12206-1431 Office: City of Albany Dept Water Supply 35 Erie Blvd Albany NY 12204-2593

CROSS, ROBERT LOUIS, realtor, land use planner, writer, landscape architect, appraiser; b. Alton, Ill., Aug. 9, 1937; s. Louis William and Marion (Hanna) C.; m. Paula Sutton, June 8, 1958 (div. June 1970); children: Britomart, Christopher, Amoret; m. Carolee Sharko, May 5, 1990. BA, U. Kans., 1959, MA, 1961; grad., UCLA, 1969, Realtors Inst., L.A., 1980. Lectr. English lang. U. Kans., Lawrence, 1959-60, Washburn U., Topeka, Kans., 1960-61; editorial-mktg. rep. Prentice-Hall, Inc., Englewood Cliffs, N.J., 1962-64; dir. pub. info. Forest Lawn Meml. Pk., Glendale, Calif., 1964-68; account exec. pub. rels. J. Walter Thompson, L.A., 1968-70; sr. account exec. pub. rels. Botsford Ketchum, L.A., 1970-71, Harsh, Rotman & Druck, L.A., 1971-72; pres. Crossroads Combined Comm., L.A., 1973-80; real estate agt. Carmel (Calif.) Bd. Realtors, 1979—; gen. ptnr. Crossroads Design Ltd., Big Sur, Calif., 1990—; co-owner Big Sur Properties. Cons. Watts Mfg. Corp., L.A., 1970-73, U.S. Office Edn., Washington, 1971, U.S. Dept. Interior, Washington, 1972, Calif. State Coastal Commn., San Francisco, 1980-85. Author: Henry Miller: The Paris Years, 1991; assoc. editor Calif. Life Mag., 1976; contbr. IN Monterey Mag., 1977; real estate editor Monterey Life Mag., 1978. Pres., dir. Big Sur Hist. Soc., 1980-90, Coastlands Mut. Water Co., Big Sur, 1984—; co-founder Dialogue for Big Sur, 1984; dir. Big Sur Natural History Assn., 1984-86; founding docent Dept. Pks. and Recreation, Pt. Sur Historic State Park, Big Sur, 1987; active ARC Disaster Svcs.; founder Big Sur Cmty. Action Team. With U.S. Army, 1961-63. Mem. Agora Internat. Press Corps, Archeol. Inst. Am., Nat. Assn. Realtors, Am. Soc. Landscape Architects, Nat. Assn. Real Estate Appraisers (cert.), Calif. Assn. Realtors, Monterey County Assn. Realtors (Multiple Listing Svc. Sales award 1980), Carmel Multiple Listing Svc., Big Sur Grange, Coast Property Owners Assn., Environ. Assesment Assn. (cert.). Avocations: art, travel, automobiles, music, reading. Office: Big Sur Properties & Crossroads Design Ltd PO Box 244 Big Sur CA 93920-0244

CROSS, ROBERT WILLIAM, lawyer, venture capital executive; b. Balt., Oct. 9, 1937; s. Rosamond and Mildred (Fowler) C.; m. Deanna Louise Deerr, Feb. 7, 1965; children Ann Elizabeth, Robert William II. BSBA, Washington U., St. Louis, 1962; JD, Washington U., 1964. Bar: N.Y. 1964. Assoc. Winthrop, Stimson, Putnam & Roberts, N.Y.C., 1964-68; gen. counsel Electronic Data Systems Corp., Dallas, 1968-69; pres. R.W. Cross & Co., Dallas and N.Y.C., 1970-90; chmn., CEO Cross Tech. Inc., N.Y.C., also Solebury, Pa., 1990—; pres., CEO Nanophase Tech. Corp., Romeoville, Ill., 1993-98; pres., COO Vcapital Inc., Chgo., 1999—2002; pres., CEO Vcapital Securities, Chgo., 2000—02; chmn., CEO DigitalWork, Inc., Chgo., 2003—. With USMC, 1957—63. Mem.: Bus. Execs. for Nat. Security, Marine Corps Assn., Urban League Club, Univ. Club, Omicron Delta Kappa. Republican. Home: PO Box 200 Solebury PA 18963-0200 Office: Cross Tech Inc 6475 Upper York Rd Solebury PA 18963 E-mail: rcross@crosstechnologiesUS.com.

CROSS, RONALD, musicologist, educator; b. Fort Worth, Feb. 18, 1929; s. John Butler and Verna (Bailey) C. BA, Centenary Coll. La., 1950; MA, NYU, 1953, PhD, 1961; Fulbright scholar, U. Florence, U. Vienna, 1955—57. Mem. faculty Notre Dame Coll., S.I., 1958-68; assoc. prof. music Wagner Coll., S.I., 1968-75, prof., 1975—, chmn. music dept., 1981-84; dir. Collegium Musicum, S.I., 1968—; chair Kurt & Auguste Reimann, 1984—. Organist, choirmaster various chs.; recorded and directed Songs and Dances of the Renaissance (Lieder und Tänze der Renaissance) Collegium Pro Musica FSM Pantheon, 1984; author: Mathaeus Pipelare: Opera Omnia, 3 vols., 1966-67; reviewer Renaissance recs. for Music Quar., 1971-76; video: The Harpsichord Today: An Interview With Ronald Cross, 1991; contbr. articles to profl. jours. Recipient Founders Day award, NYU, 1962, Alumni Achievement award, 1988, Faculty award, Omicron Delta Kappa, 1996; grantee Am. Coun. Learned Socs. grantee, 1954, Performance grantee, S.I. Coun. on the Arts, 1986—92, grantee to present harpsichord recitals, N.Y. State Coun. on Arts, 1986—2003. Mem. Am. Guild Organists (asso.), Internat., Am. Musicol. Socs., Coll. Music Soc., Soc. for Ethnomusicology. Home: 221 Ward Ave Staten Island NY 10304-2140 E-mail: rcross@wagner.edu.

CROSS, STEVEN JASPER, finance educator; b. Hohenwald, Tenn., Apr. 19, 1954; s. Thomas Edward and Eula Mae Cross; m. Patricia Aldas, Jan. 6, 1995. BS, Mid. Tenn. State U., 1976, MAT, 1980, DA, 1984. Sales rep. U. Ford Inc., Murfreesboro, Tenn., 1976; ins. underwriter Continental Ins., Inc., Nashville, 1976—77; credit rep. SunAm, Inc., Murfreesboro, 1977—78; instr. mgmt. Dyersburg (Tenn.) State C.C., 1980—81; instr. econs. Motlow State C.C., Tullahoma, Tenn., 1981—83, asst. prof. econs., 1983—85; assoc. prof. fin. Delta State U., Cleveland, Miss., 1985—88, prof. fin., chmn. divsn. econs. and fin., 1988—91; dean Sch. Bus., prof. bus. Troy State U., Dothan, Ala., 1991—97, prof. fin., 1997—. Contbr. articles to profl. jours. Mem. AAUP, NEA, Am. Fin. Assn., Am. Econ. Assn., Delta Mu Delta. Home: 112 Wentworth Dr Dothan AL 36305-6906 Office: Troy State U Coll Bus Adminstrn PO Box 8368 Dothan AL 36304-0368

CROSS, THEODORE LAMONT, publisher, author; b. Newton, Mass., Feb. 12, 1924; s. Gorham Lamont and Margaret Moore (Warren) C.; m. Sheilah Burr Ross, Sept. 16, 1950 (div. 1972); children: Amanda Burr, Lisa Warren; m. Mary Warner, 1974. Grad., Deerfield Acad., 1942; AB, Amherst Coll., 1946; LLB, Harvard U., 1950. Bar: Mass. 1950, N.Y. 1953. With Hale and Dorr, Boston, 1950-52; chmn. bd., CEO Warren, Gorham & Lamont, Inc., 1980-83; chmn. Faulkner & Gray, Pubs., 1985-92, Hanover Pub., Inc., 1985—; editor in chief Bus. and Soc. Rev., 1971—; editor Jour. of Blacks in Higher Edn., 1993—. Cons. HEW, Fed. Office Econ. Opportunity, 1964-69; pub. gov. Am. Stock Exchange, 1972-77; bd. dirs. Inst. for Sci. Info., 1988—; lectr. on inner city econs. and minority econ. devel. Harvard, Cornell U., U. Va. Author: Black Capitalism: Strategy for Business in the Ghetto (McKinsey Found. book award 1969), (with Mary Cross) Behind the Great Wall, 1979, The Black Power Imperative, 1984, Birds of the Sea, Shore and Tundra, 1989; founder: Atomic Energy Law Jour., 1959; editor Harvard Law Rev., 1948-50. Trustee Amherst Coll., chmn. investment com., 1976-88; trustee Folger Shakespeare Libr., Princeton U. Press, Inst. Advanced Study, Nat. Humanities Ctr., John Simon Guggenheim Meml. Found.; mem. Coun. Fgn. Rels.; dir. Legal Def. Fund, NAACP, Century Assn., N.Y.C. With USNR, 1945-46. Mem. Coun. on Fgn. Rels. (treas.), Am. Philos. Soc. Home: 1 Campbelton Cir Princeton NJ 08540 Office: 200 W 57th St New York NY 10019-3211

CROSS, THOMAS H. former state legislator; b. Nashville, July 31, 1958; m. Eugenia Hovater; children: Eloise Reynolds, Thomas Hudson IV. BA, Ill. Wesleyan U., 1980; JD, Samford U., 1983. Asst. state's atty., Kendall County, Ill., 1983-92; Ill. state rep. Dist. 84. Mem. Judiciary I and II, Children & Youth and Elections-State Govt. Coms., 1993—, Ill. Ho. of Reps.; atty. Law Offices of Ingemunson, Yorkville, Ill., 1986-97, Hersbach, Tracy, Johnson, Berteni & Wilson, Oswego, 1997—. Recipient Humanitarian award Sr. Servants, 1990, 91. Mem. Yorkville C. of C. (bd. dirs. 1988—), Kendall County Found. (chmn. 1986-92), Oswego Lions (bd. dirs. 1990—), Navy League (judge adv. 1990—), Theta Chi. Office: 2701 Black Rd # 200 Joliet IL 60435-2926*

CROSS, THOMAS ROBERT, lawyer; b. Flint, Mich., Apr. 12, 1942; s. Robert Henry and Ora Leone (Adams) C.; m. Patricia Ann Witham, July 31, 1970; children: Scott, Stephanie, Timothy. BA, U. Mich., 1965, JD, 1968. Bar: Colo. 1971, U.S. Dist. Ct. Colo. 1971. Mgmt. trainee Met. Life, Colorado Springs, Colo., 1968-71; pvt. practice, Colorado Springs, 1971-76; ptnr. Cross, Gaddis, Kin & Quicksall, P.C., Colorado Springs, 1976-96; pvt. practice Colorado Springs, 1996—. Mem. Colo. Supreme Ct. Nominating Commn., Denver, 1982-88. Chmn. El Paso County Dem. Party, Colorado Springs, 1974-76; bd. dirs. NAACP, 1981-82; pres. Colorado Springs Philharm., 2003—. Fellow Am. Bar Found., Colo. Bar Found.; mem. ABA, Colo. Bar Assn. (sr. v.p. 1986-87, pres. 1991-92), El Paso County Bar Assn. (pres. 1982-83), Colo. Trial Lawyers Assn., Colorado Springs C. of C. (bd. dirs. 1977-78). Democrat. Roman Catholic. Office: 118 S Wahsatch Ave Colorado Springs CO 80903-3677

CROSS, W. THOMAS, investment company executive; b. Knoxville, Tenn., Sept. 1, 1949; s. Joseph Eugene and Wanda (Price) C.; children: Joseph, Victoria. BS, U. Tenn., 1971; CLU, Am. Coll., Bryn Mawr, Pa., 1983, ChFC, 1987. Sales rep. John Hancock Fin. Svcs., Knoxville, 1971-72, sales mgr., 1972-78, regional supr. Washington, 1978-79, agy. mgr. Appleton, Wis., 1979-84, Memphis, 1984-95; sr. v.p. product distbn. Securities Am., Inc., Omaha, 1995—; pres. Fin. Dynamics Am., Inc., Omaha, 1997—. Chair troop com., scoutmaster Boy Scouts Am., Germantown, Tenn., 1991-95. Mem. Am. Soc. CLU and ChFC (bd. dirs. 1992-95), Am. Health Ins. Assn., Gen. Agts. and Mgrs. Assn. (pres. Appleton chpt. 1977-78, pres. Memphis chpt. 1988-89, pres. 1993-94), Memphis Life Underwriters (bd. dirs. 1985-88). Avocations: golf, scouting. Office: Securities Am Inc 7100 W Center Rd Ste 500 Omaha NE 68106-2798 E-mail: tcross@saionline.com.

CROSS, WILLIAM DENNIS, lawyer; b. Tulsa, Nov. 7, 1940; s. John Howell and Virginia Grace (Ferrell) C.; m. Peggy Ruth Plapp, Jan. 30, 1982; children: William Dennis Jr., John Frederick. BS, U.S. Naval Acad., 1962; JD, NYU, 1969. Bar: N.Y. 1970, U.S. Dist. Ct. (so. and ea. dists.) N.Y. 1970, U.S. Ct. Appeals (2d cir.) 1970, U.S. Supreme Ct. 1974, Calif. 1977, U.S. Dist. Ct. (ctrl. dist.) Calif. 1977, U.S. Ct. Appeals (9th cir.) 1977, U.S. Ct. Appeals (5th, 10th and 11th cirs.) 1981, Mo. 1982, U.S. Dist. Ct. (we. dist.) Mo. 1982, U.S. Ct. Appeals (8th cir.) 1989, U.S. Ct. Appeals (fed. cir.) 1992, U.S. Dist. Ct. Ariz. 1997, U.S. Dist. Ct. Colo. 1997, U.S. Dist. Ct. Kans. 1998. Commd. ensign USN, 1962, advanced through ranks to lt., 1965, resigned, 1966; assoc. Cravath, Swaine & Moore, N.Y.C., 1969-76, Lillick, McHose & Charles, L.A., 1976-77; asst. gen. counsel FTC, Washington, 1977-82; of counsel Morrison & Hecker, Kansas City, Mo., 1982-83, ptnr., 1983—2002, Stinson Morrison Hecker, 2002—. Staff mem. NYU Law Rev., 1967-69, editor, 1968-69; assoc. editor Antitrust Mag. Mem. ABA, Calif. Bar Assn., Mo. Bar Assn., Assn. Bar City N.Y., Kansas City Bar Assn., Lawyers Assn. Kansas City. Home: 1223 Huntington Rd Kansas City MO 64113-1347 Office: Stinson Morrison Hecker LLP 1201 Walnut St STe 2800 Kansas City MO 64106-2150 E-mail: dcross@stinsonmoheck.com.

CROSSAN, JOHN ROBERT, lawyer; b. Buckhannon, W.Va., May 31, 1947; s. Thomas Benjamin Jr. and Margaret Windsor (Hicks) C.; m. Monique Margaretha Scheen, Dec. 22, 1973; children: Ashley Margaret, Aubry Kelly. BS with honors, U. Va., 1969; JD, U. Chgo., 1974. Bar: Ill. 1974, U.S. Dist. Ct. (no.

dist.) Ill. 1974, (ctrl. dist.) Ill. 1998, U.S. Ct. Appeals (4th and 10th cirs.) 1978, U.S. Ct. Appeals (7th cir.) 1979, U.S. Ct. Appeals (fed. cir.) 1983, U.S. Supreme Ct. 1985, U.S. Ct. Appeals (6th cir.) 1989. Staff atty. Ill. Task Force N.E. Ill. Pub. Transp., Chgo., 1972-73; assoc. Hill, Van Santen, Steadman, Chiara, Chgo., 1973-77; assoc., then ptnr. Cook, Wetzel and Egan, Ltd., Chgo., 1978-88; counsel Willian, Brinks, Hofer, Gilson and Lione, Chgo., 1989-90; ptnr. Brinks, Hofer, Gilson & Lione, Chgo., 1991-97, Chapman and Cutler, Chgo., 1998—. V.p. Va. Engring. Found., 1998—2000, pres., 2000—02. Author: Quick Guide to the Patent Law, 1994; contbr. articles to profl publs. Pres. aux. bd. Chgo. Architecture Found., 1983-85. Mem. ABA, Am. Intellectual Property Lawyers Assn., Chgo. Yacht Club. Home: 2825 N Cambridge Ave Chicago IL 60657-6018 Office: Chapman and Cutler 111 W Monroe St Ste 1700 Chicago IL 60603-4006 E-mail: crossan@chapman.com., jrcrossan@hotmail.com.

CROSSEN, REV. MR. JOHN F. writer, researcher; b. South Lafuna, Calif., Feb. 17, 1960; PhD, Ind. U., Bloomington, Indiana, 2003; MDiv, St. Thomas Seminary, Denver, Colorado, 1990; BA, Ariz. State U., Tempe, Arizona, 1982. Exec. dir. Force Internat., Inc., Scottsdale, Ariz., 1980—; chaplain Ft. Logan Mental Health Ctr., Denver, 1985—88; educator Yavapai Coll., Prescott, Ariz., 1991—92, Ind. U., Bloomington, Ind., 1992—97, Mansfield U., Mansfield, Pa., 1999—2001, Regis U., Denver, 2001—02. Contbr. articles to profl. jours. Fellow Mellon Fellowship, St. Louis U., 1998; scholar Sigma Delta Pi, Ariz. State U., 1982, Alpha Mu Gamma, 1982. Mem.: Ibero-American Soc. for 18th Century Studies, MLA. Avocations: music, autograph collecting. Office: Rev Mr John F Crossen PO Box 8513 Scottsdale AZ 85252 E-mail: clav2cavo@yahoo.com.

CROSSER, RICHARD H. real estate company executive; Pres., CEO Crossman Cmtys., Indpls., 1973—. Office: Crossman Communities Inc 9202 N Meridian St Ste 300 Indianapolis IN 46260-1833

CROSSFIELD, ALBERT SCOTT, aeronautical science consultant, pilot; b. Berkeley, Calif., Oct. 2, 1921; s. Albert Scott and Lucia (Dwyer) C.; m. Alice Virginia Knoph, Apr. 21, 1943; children: Becky Lee, Thomas Scott, Paul Stanley, Anthony Scott, Sally Virginia, Robert Scott. BS in Aero. Engring., U. Wash., 1949, MS in Aero. Sci., 1950; D.Sc. (hon.), Fla. Inst. Tech., 1982. Lic. pilot. Mem. U. Wash. staff charge wind tunnel operation, 1946-50; aerodynamicist, project engr., also pilot research airplanes X-1, X-4, X-5, D-558-I and II, X-F-92, F-102, F-100, F-86, NACA, 1950-55; participation proposal, design, 1st pilot X-15 research aircraft, design specialist, also chief engring. test pilot Los Angeles div. N.Am. Aviation, Inc., 1955-61, dir. test and quality assurance, space and info. systems div., 1961-66, tech. dir. research and engring., space and info. systems div., 1966-67; v.p. flight research and devel. div. Eastern Air Lines, Miami, Fla., 1967-71, staff v.p. transp. systems devel. Washington, 1971-74; sr. v.p. Hawker Siddeley Aviation Inc., Washington, 1974; tech. cons. House Com. on Sci. and Tech., Washington, 1977-93. Spl. work on the WS-131b, Apollo, Saturn S-II, Paraglider programs. Author: Always Another Dawn, 1960; also articles. Mem. aviation and space hist. preservation com. Calif. Mus. Found., mem. Aerospace Walk of Honor, City of Lancaster, 1990. Lt. USN, 1942-46, WWII, USNR. Recipient Aerospace Laureate for 1997, Aviation Week & Space Tech., Lawrence Sperry award Inst. Aero. Sci., 1954, Octave Chanute award, 1958, Flight Achievement award Am. Astronautics Soc., 1959, Astronautics award Am. Rocket Soc., 1960, Commendation award County L.A. Bd. Suprs., 1960, Internat. Clifford B. Harmon Trophy, 1961, Achievement award Nat. Aeronautics Assn., 1961, Collier Trophy, 1961, Charter award, 1963, Elder Statesman of Aviation award, 1983, Godfry Cabot award Aero Club New England, 1961, John J. Montgomery award Nat. Soc. Aerospace Profls., 1962, Kitty Hawk Meml. award City of L.A., 1969, Al J. Engel award We. Res. Hist. Soc., 1983, Meritorious Svc. to Aviation award Nat. Bus. Aircraft Assn., 1984, Disting. Alumnus award U. Wash., 1986, Crown Cir. award Nat. Congress Aviation and Space Edn., 1988, A. Scott Crossfield Elem. Sch. award Fairfax County Sch. Bd., 1988, Bernt Balchin Trophy, N.Y. State Air Force Assn., 1988, Glenn A. Gilbert Meml. award Air Traffic Control Assn., 1990, Aerospace Walk of Honor, City of Lancaster, Calif., 1990, Disting. Pub. Svc. medal NASA, 1993, Cert. of Appreciation, FAA, 1993, Ho. of Reps., 1993, Gold Air medal Fedn. Aeronautique Internat., Sun City, South Africa, 1995, Ray Lien award Internat. Sport Aviation Mus. and Sun 'N Fun, 1999, Ray Lien award for aviation edn. excellence, 2000, Glenn L. Martin medal, 2000, Lifetime Achievement award Nat. Air & Space Mus., 2000, Crystal Eagle award Aero Club No. Calif., 2002, Gathering of Eagles Recognition USAF, 2003; inducted into Nat. Aviation Hall of Fame, 1983, Internat. Aerospace Hall of Fame, 1963, Internat. Space Hall of Fame, 1988, Va. Aviation Hall of Fame, 1998. Fellow AIAA (hon., chmn. flight test tech. com. 1963-64, Disting. lectr. 1987, 88, 89, Pathfinder award 1999, hon. 1999), Soc. Exptl. Test Pilots (co-founder, chmn. East Coast sect. 1976-77, past exec. advisor, Ivan C. Kincheloe award 1960, Ray E. Tenhoff award 1978), Inst. Aerospace Scis., Aerospace Med. Assn. (hon.); mem. Am. Soc. Qualtiy Control (sect., chmn. L.A. 1964-66, Outstanding Contbn. to Quality Control award 1967), Flying Physicians Assn. (hon., Man of Yr. 1961), Exptl. Aircraft Assn. (hon., Svc. to Sport Aviation award 1979, cert. of appreciation 1982), First Flight Soc. (life), Sterman Alumnus Club, Mustang Pilot Soc. (charter), OX-5 Club, Nat. Aviation Club (pres. 1983, gov. emeritus, Achievement award 1960), Nat. Space Club (Dr. Wernher von Braun Space Flight trophy), Order of Daedalians (hon.), Sigma Xi, Tau Beta Pi. Republican. Episcopalian. Home: 12100 Thoroughbred Rd Herndon VA 20171-2009 E-mail: sxfield@cs.com.

CROSSLEY, FRANCIS RENDEL ERSKINE, former engineering educator; b. Quarndon Derby, Eng., July 21, 1915; came to U.S., 1937, naturalized, 1957; s. Erskine Alick and Edith Mary (Helme) C.; m. Mary Eleanore de Lacy Bernadotte Coyne, Aug. 23, 1941 (dec. May, 1, 1998); children: Phyllis de Lacy Mervine, Michael Francis Erskine Crossley; m. Virginia Morss Galpin, Aug. 31, 1999. BA in Mech. Scis., Cambridge (Eng.) U., 1937; MA, Cambridge U., Eng., 1941; D Engring., Yale U., 1949. Asst. prof. mech. engring. Yale U., New Haven, 1944-55, fellow Branford Coll., 1948-65, assoc. prof., 1955-65; vis. fellow U. Manchester (Eng.) Inst. Sci. and Tech., 1965; prof. mech. engring. Ga. Inst. of Tech., Atlanta, 1966-69, U. Mass., Amherst, 1970-78, prof. civil engring., 1978-80, prof. emeritus, 1980—. Adj. prof. mech. engring. Rensselaer Poly. Inst., 1978-79, U. Fla., 1988-91; Fulbright lectr. Technische Hochschule Munich, 1962-63, Tech. U. Bucharest, Romania, 1976; mem. U.S. del. forestry energy divsn. Internat. Energy Agy., Ottawa, Helsinki, Dublin, 1977-79; initiated talks with Soviet Acad. Scis. for U.S.-USSR exch. of info. on space flight, 1970; staff scientist Conn. State Legislature, Hartford, 1981-83. Author: Dynamics in Machines, 1954; editor-in-chief Mechanism and Machine Theory, 1971-73; founder, editor Jour. Mechanisms, 1966-71; designer mech. robot's 3-fingered hand for NASA Space Flight Ctr., 1973-74. Chmn. solid waste mgmt. commn. Town of Branford, Conn., 1985-86, bd. edn., 1987-92; chmn. land mgmt., 1995-96, trustee Branford Land Trust, 1996-99. Recipient sr. scientist award von Humboldt Found., Germany, 1975-76. Fellow ASME (life, chmn. mechanisms conf. Atlanta 1968, legis. fellow 1981-83, Centennial medal 1980, Machine Design award 1991); mem. Verein Deutscher Ingenieure (hon.), Internat. Fedn. for Theory Machines and Mechanisms (hon., founding com., author constn., 1st v.p. 1967-75). Episcopalian. Home: Evergreen Woods Apt 358 88 Notch Hill Rd North Branford CT 06471-1853

CROSSLEY, FRANK ALPHONSO, former metallurgical engineer; b. Chgo., Feb. 19, 1925; s. Joseph Buddie and Rosa Lee (Brefford) C.; m. Elaine J. Sherman, Nov. 23, 1950 (dec. 1996); 1 child, Desne Adrienne. *Elaine J. Sherman Crossley (1925-1996) was an artist. Her works, predominately abstract and characterized by strong design and bold use of color, were widely exhibited in the Bay Area of California. Frank Crossley's daughter, Desne Adrienne Crossley, Bachelor of Arts 1976, University of California at Santa Cruz, married, on July 31, 1999, Kenneth B. Hollman. Kenneth is a graphic design and animation specialist, Bachelor of Arts 1973 Dartmouth College. Desne is currently Individual Support Officer, Museum of Fine Arts, Boston.* BSChemE, Ill. Inst. Tech., 1945, MS in Metall. Engring, 1947, PhD in Metall. Engring, 1950. Instr. Ill. Inst. Tech., Chgo., 1948-49; prof. foundry engring., head dept. foundry engring. Tenn. Agrl. and Indsl. State U., 1950-52; sr. scientist Ill. Inst. Tech. Rsch. Inst., 1952-66; sr. mem. rsch. lab. Lockheed Missiles & Space Co., Palo Alto, Calif., 1966-74, mgr. dept. producibility and standards, 1974-78, mgr. dept. missile body mech. engring., 1978-79, cons. engr. missile systems div. Sunnyvale, Calif., 1979-86; dir. rsch. propulsion materials Aerojet Propulsion Rsch. Inst., 1986-87, rsch. dir. materials applications, 1987-90; tech. prin. Aerojet Propulsion div. GenCorp, Sacramento, 1990-91. Contbr. articles to metall. jours. and symposia. Served to ensign USNR, 1944-46, PTO. Recipient GenCorp Aerojet 1990 R.B. Young Tech. Innovation award. Fellow Am. Soc. for Metals Internat.; mem. AIAA (mem. materials tech. com. 1979-81), Minerals, Metals and Materials Soc. of AIME (chmn. titanium com. 1974-75), Sigma Xi. Congregationalist. Achievements include patent on Transage titanium alloys and grain refiner for titanium alloy castings; research in titanium alloys; diffusion bonding of metals and alloys. Home: 44 Goodnow Ln Framingham MA 01702-5505 *Choose well how your time is spent. Time spent doing one thing is time that cannot be spent doing something else.*

CROSSLEY, GARY EXLEY, organization executive; b. Charleston, S.C., Oct. 6, 1951; s. Gilbert Franklin and Elsie Neal (Exley) C.; m. Debra Ann Hulon, Aug. 8, 1976 (div. Nov. 1982); m. Sharon Louise Hiers, Nov. 9, 1985. BS in Mktg., U. S.C., 1973; postgrad., Coll. of Charleston. Labor market analyst S.C. Employment Security Commn., Columbia, 1973-85; labor market info. and rsch. dir. Interstate Conf. of Employment Security Agys., Inc., Washington, 1985-94; asst. dir. Charleston Naval Complex S.C. Employment Security Commn., Charleston, SC, 1994-96, field tax deputy, 1996—99, area dir. Charleston Workforce Ctr., 1999—. Cons. Army Transition Labor Market Info. Project, Washington, 1988-91. Editor, contbr. newsletter Labor Market Inform-the-Nation, 1985-94; co-editor Workforce, 1992-94; contbr. articles to profl. publs. Bd. dirs. Consortium Adolscent Pregnancy, Washington, 1987-90; asst. treas. St. Mark's Episcopal Ch., Washington, 1988-93; treas. Ashley River Creative Arts Elem. Sch. Governance Coun., 1997-2002, Edn. Found., 2001—; mem. Parents for Pub. Sch., 2000—, Greater Charleston Empowerment Corp., 1999—. Recipient Contbr.'s award Nat. Occupational Info. Coordinating Com., 1988, Vladimir Chavrid Meml. award Interstate Conf. of Employment Security Agys., 1995. Mem. Internat. Assn. Pers. in Employment Security (bd. dirs. S.C. chpt. 1980-81, nat. bd. dirs. 1987-94, S.C. Employee of Yr. award 1982, Individual Merit award S.C. 1989), Soc. Nat. Assn. Publs., Partnership for Employment and Tng. Careers, Assn. Pub. Data Users, Southeastern Employment and Tng. Assn. Avocations: sports, travel, coin collecting. Home: 314 Muirfield Pky Charleston SC 29414-6811 Office: SC Employment Security Commn 176 Lockwood Dr Charleston SC 29403

CROSSLEY, JOHN PARSHLEY, JR., religous studies educator, researcher, consultant; b. Oakland, Calif., Dec. 27, 1929; s. John Parshley and Ida Louise (Brown) C.; m. Judith Anne Webb, Mar. 14, 1958 (div. Feb. 1982); children: John P. III, Julianne Crossley Woronoff; m. De Anne Kenfield, Apr. 14, 1984. AB, Pepperdine U., 1951; BD, Princeton Theol. Sem., 1954; ThD, San Francisco Theol. Sem., 1962. Ordained to ministry Presbyn. Ch., 1954. Prof. Hastings (Nebr.) Coll., 1962-70, U. So. Calif., L.A., 1970—. Adult edn. tchr. Westwood Presbyn. Ch., L.A., 1982—. Contbr. articles to profl. jours. including Jour. Religious Ethics, New Athenaeum, Ann. Soc. Xian Ethics. Lt. USN, 1954-56. NEH fellow, 1969-70. Mem. ACLU (bd. dirs. 1982-90), Am. Acad. Religion (pres. Western region 1978-82), Soc. Christian Ethics (pres. Pacific sect. 1976-78), Pacific Coast Theol. Soc. Democrat. Presbyterian. Avocations: reading, hiking, theatre. Home: 618 Vallejo Villas Los Angeles CA 90042 Office: U So Calif Dept Religious Studies Los Angeles CA 90089-0355 E-mail: crossley@usc.edu.

CROSSMAN, WILLIAM WHITTARD, retired wire cable and communications executive; b. Mineola, N.Y., Aug. 10, 1927; s. Homer Danforth and Emily May (Whittard) C.; m. Mary DeJesu, Dec. 6, 1952; children: William Whittard Jr., Lindsay Maria, Michael DeJesu. BS in Engring. Sci., U. Miami, 1949. West coast mgr., gen. mgr. HiTemp Wires div. Simplex Wire & Cable Co., 1955-69; pres. surprenant divsn. ITT Corp., 1969-74, pres. royal electric divsn., 1974-77, group gen. mgr. N.Y.C., 1977-85, v.p., 1979-87, chmn. and group exec. comm. and info. svcs. Secaucus, N.J., 1985-88, sr. v.p., 1987-88, ret., 1988. With USNR, 1945-46, USAF, 1951. Mem.: Owls Head Harbor, San Remo, N.E. Wire and Cable. Republican. Episcopalian. Home (Winter): Apt M226 2871 N Ocean Blvd Boca Raton FL 33431-7065 Home (Summer): 563 Owl's Head Harbor Rd Vergennes VT 05491

CROSSON, FREDERICK JAMES, former university dean, humanities educator; b. Belmar, N.J., Apr. 27, 1926; s. George Leon and Emily (Bennett) C.; m. Mary Patricia Burns, Sept. 5, 1953; children: Jessica, Christopher, Veronica, Benedict, Jennifer. BA, Cath. U. Am., 1949, MA, 1950; postgrad., U. Paris, 1951-52; PhD, U. Notre Dame, 1956. Instr. U. Notre Dame, 1953-56, asst. prof., 1956-62, assoc. prof., 1962-66, prof., 1966—; dean Coll. Arts and Letters, 1968-76, O'Hara Disting. prof. philosophy, 1976-84, Cavanaugh Disting. prof. humanities, 1984—98. Author: The Modeling of Mind, 1963, Philosophy and Cybernetics, 1967, Science and Contemporary Society, 1967; Editor: Review of Politics, 1976-83. With USN, 1943-46. Mem.: North Ctrl. Assn. (exec. commr. 1984—89), Am. Cath. Philos. Assn. (pres. 1990—91), Am. Philos. Assn., Phi Beta Kappa (senator 1982—2000, v.p. 1994—97, pres. 1997—2000). Home: 51997 Heather Cv South Bend IN 46635-1074 Office: Coll Arts and Letters U of Notre Dame Notre Dame IN 46556

CROSTON, STEPHEN PAUL, writer, systems manager, social studies educator; b. Warrington, England, Jan. 16, 1954; arrived in USA, 1960; s. Louis Elliotte and Isebelle Anne Croston; m. Linda Marie Croston, Oct. 27, 1978 (div. Dec. 15, 1995); children: Emily Anne, Kate Marie, Michael Scott, David Scott. Archtl. drafting(hon.), Sch. of Drafting, Scranton, PA, 1985; MA (hon.), Sch. of Art, Scranton, PA, 1987; AAS, Shoreline Comm. Coll., Shoreline, WA, 1990—93; BA english lit., Seatle Pacific U, Seattle, WA, 1993—98; MA whole systems design, Antioch U, Seattle, WA, 2002—. Cert. civil engr. aid, Renton/ WA. Storeroom mgr. Swedish Hosp., Seattle, 1980—83; computer oper. Honeywell, Seattle, 1983—85, Gov. Svc. Admin., Seattle, 1985—87; asst. mgr. Indus Corp., Shoreline, Wash., 1987—89; asst. team mem. Seattle Sch. Dist., Seattle, 1989—2000; writer, creative artist New Work Shop, Seattle, 2000—. Poetry: various works Periodicals, 1995—; author: (novels) The Minister's Son, 2002. Mem. Amnesty Internat., Seattle, 1996. Recipient Design Ingenuity, James River Graphics/MA, 1980, Most Valuable Stud., Order of Elks/ WA, 1981. Mem.: Pact Partnership with God, Oral Roberts Blessing, Centurions - Seattle Pacific U. Achievements include Visual notes guide for visual thinkers; discovering the center of universe; concepts of living in chaos; seeing our divinity. Avocations: designing, challenger, dreamer, visionary. Home: 609 W Nickerson St #B Seattle WA 98119-1530 Office: New Work Shop 609 W Nickerson St #B Seattle WA 98119-1530

CROSWELL, KATRINA ANTOINETTE, writer; b. Chgo., Mar. 2, 1963; d. Bettye Jean Yeatman. Student, Columbia Coll., 2000—. Asst. Hillel Found., Washington, 1998—99; program asst. Met. Planning Coun., Chgo., 1998—. Co-author: (poems) American Poetry Anthology, 1989; author: LONG LIFE short stories, 1999, (novels) To Whom Much Is Given, 2002. Mem.: Acad. Am. Poets (assoc.). Baptist. Avocations: music, art, nature. Personal E-mail: Katant1@aol.com.

CROTEAU, JACK RANDALL, civil engineer; b. Ventura, Calif., Oct. 3, 1937; s. Lucian J. and Ola B. (Chambers) C.; m. Pamela S. Whitmore, May 20, 1961; children: Christopher L., Barry W. BA, BSCE, LeHigh U., 1964; MSCE, Drexel U., 1967; JD, Seton Hall U., 1981. Registered profl. engr., N.J.; bar: N.J., Pa. Rsch. mgr. N.J. Dept. of Transp., Trenton, 1964-93; project mgr. ASCE, Washington, 1993-95; cons. civil engring. Washington, 1995—. Contbr. articles to profl. jours. Fellowship Nat. Hwy Inst., 1981. Mem. ASCE, ASTM. Home: 4917 SW 26th Pl Cape Coral FL 33914-6631 E-mail: jrc1fla@aol.com.

CROTEAU, JAN HELLING, artist; b. Calif., Dec. 6, 1951; d. William Gray and Margaret Lynn Helling; m. Richard G. Croteau, Apr. 25, 1976; 2 children. BA in Theatre Arts Edn., Vt. Coll., 2002. Profl. juried artist League of N.H. Craftsmen, Concord, NH, 1985—2000; founder, co-dir. Young Women's Oral History Project, Tuftonboro, NH, 1996—98; founder, dir. Perform It! Stage Co., Wolfeboro, NH, 1994—. Cons. in field pub. schs., Wolfeboro, 1997—. Author: (book) Perform It! A Complete Guide to Theater, 2000. Pres. Friends of Libr., Tuftonboro, NH, 1997—98. Recipient Moss Hart theater award, New Eng. Theater Conf., Boston, 2000; grantee League of N.H. Craftsmen, Concord, 1989, Gov. Wentworth's Arts Coun., Wolfeboro, 1997. Mem.: League of N.H. Craftsmen, New Eng. Theater Conf. Avocation: hiking, reading, writing, painting, drawing. Office: Perform It! Young Peoples Stage Co PO Box 2093 Wolfeboro NH 03894

CROTTI, ROSE MARIE, special education educator; b. Scranton, Pa., Aug. 29, 1952; d. Frank Joseph and Cecelia Ann (Bossi) Leitza; m. John Anthony Crotti, Sept. 26, 1975; children: Annette Michelle, Joseph Francis, John Michael. BA, Marywood U., 1974, MS, 1984; student, U. Scranton, 1979-80. Cert. elem. and secondary prin., Pa.; cert. supt., Pa. Program dir. St. Joseph's Ctr., Dunmore, Pa., 1974-75; instr. Northeastern Ednl. Intermediate Unit #19, Scranton, 1976-80, 1980-83, tchr. Learning Disabilities Montdale, Pa., 1983-86, cons. Learning Disabilities Carbondale, Pa., 1988-89; cons., state validator Instrnl. Support Pa. Dept. Edn., Harrisburg, Pa., 1990—; instr. spl. edn. undergrad. and grad. dept. Marywood U., 1994—; asst. sec. prin. Lakeland Sch. Dist., Jermyn, Pa., 1998—2001, guidance dept. coord., 1999—, gifted coord., spl. edn. liaison, 1998—; secondary prin. Lakeland Jr./Sr. H.S., 2001—. Presenter Northeastern Ednl. Intermediate Unit #19, Scranton, 1988—; appeared on PBS, An Apple a Day, 1991, 92; coord., trainer peer tutors Carbondale Sch. Dist., 1992-93, peer mediators, 1993-94; mem. Oxford (England) Round Table, Lincoln Coll., U. Oxford. Co-author: Parent-to-Parent Handbook on Drugs and Alcohol Abuse Among Teenagers, 1993. Active Parent Tchrs. Guild, Clarks Summit, Pa.; chmn. Lackawanna County Handicapped Awareness Day, 1990; co-chmn. Children Without a Conscience Sch. Conf., 1990; coord. Students Against Driving Drunk, 1992-94; chair family festival Marywood Coll., 1993; chair reorgn. PTA Lakeland Elem. Sch., 1993; chairperson Bus. Cmty.-Non-Alcoholic Mix-Off, 1993; bd. govs. Scranton Prep. Sch., v.p., 1992; mem. lead tchr. governing bd., lead tchr. adv. coun., adv. bd. Bishop O'Hara H.S., 1994, pres. PTO, 1996—. Named N.E. Woman of Pa. Scranton Times Newspaper, 1989. Mem. CEC(local chpt. bd. dirs. 1989—), Platform Spkrs. Assn. Roman Catholic. Avocations: cooking, reading, crafts, Broadway shows, shopping. Home: 24 Grove Olyphant PA 18447 Office: Lakeland Sch Dist 1593 Lakeland Dr Jermyn PA 18433-3140 E-mail: rmlhsap@aol.com.

CROTTY, JEROME T. educator; b. Jacksonville, Fla., Oct. 3, 1957; s. John T. and June Dynan C.; m. Elizabeth Nettles, July 25, 1992; children: Kathleen Marie, Patrick Joseph. AA, U. So. Fla., 1976, BA, 1978; MEd, U. Mo., 1981. Resident dir. Ctr. Meth. Coll., Fayette, Mo., 1978-81; residence coord. U. N.C., Charlotte, 1981-83; dir. orientation and jud. affairs U. Ark., Fayetteville, 1983-85; asst. dean of students Fla. State U., Tallahassee, 1985-86; assoc. dean of student devel. U. S.C., Columbia, 1986-98; asst. dean of students Coll. of William and Mary, Williamsburg, Va., 1998—2001; dir. Savannah Ctr., St. Leo U., 2002—. Editor: (newsletter) ASJA Newsletter, 1988-90; panelist teleconf.; developer Carolinian Creed, Univ. Values Statement, 1990. Mem. Ctr. for Acad. Integrity, Assn. for Student Jud. Affairs. E-mail: jtcrot@aol.com.

CROTTY, LADONNA DEANE, librarian; b. Williamson, W.Va., July 22, 1939; d. Kenneth B. and M. Virginia (Parcell) Crockett; m. Robert E. Crotty, Nov. 25, 1959; 4 children. BA, Marshall U., 1960. English instr. Northwest HS, McDermott, Ohio, 1976—79; media specialist, libr. Valley Mid. Sch., Lucasville, Ohio, 1979—. Mem.: NEA, Valley Tchrs. Assn., Ohio Edn. Assn. Home: 228 Pleasant Dr Lucasville OH 45648-9008 Office: Valley Mid Sch 393 Indian Dr Lucasville OH 45648

CROTTY, M. MAGGIE, state senator; b. Chgo., Ill., Oct. 16, 1948; m. Larry Crotty; 1 child, Kevin;children: Keith, Mark. Dip., Mercy HS. State Senator US Senate, Dist. 19, 2002—; worker Spl. Ed. Rep. House of Rep., Ill., 1996—2002; mem. Exec. Appt., Health & Human Svc.; vice chair person Licensed Activities. Recipient Recognition Award, Women of Oak Forest Make a Dif., 1995, Outstanding Sch. Bd. Pres. of Ill., Nominee, Sch. Bd. of Ill., Theresa Roedl Meml. Award for Volunteerism, Theresa Roedl, 1988. Mem.: Oak Forest Civil Svc. Commn., Sch. Dist. #145 Bd. (pres.), Sch. Dist. #228 Ed. Found. (chmn.), Sch. Bd., 15 yr. (pres. 8 yr.), Kiwanis Club of Oak Forest (past pres.). Democrat. Office: Capitol 311 Capitol Bldg Springfield IL 62706 also: Dist 15028 So Cicero, Unit A Oak Forest IL 60452*

CROTTY, PATRICIA MCGEE, political science educator; b. Fall River, Mass., Mar. 25, 1939; d. Joseph James and Stella Helene McGee; m. David William Crotty, June 22, 1963; children: David William Jr., Kathleen Marie. BA, Coll. of New Rochelle, 1961; MA, Boston U., 1962; PhD, Binghamton U., 1985. Dir. Big Sisters, Wilkes-Barre, Pa., 1976-79, N.E. Pa. Environ. Coun., Wilkes-Barre, 1979-83; prof. polit. sci. East Stroudsburg (Pa.) U., 1984—. Author: Women and Family Law, 1997, Family Law in the U.S., 1999. Mem. citizen's adv. coun. Pa. Dept. Environ. Protection, Harrisburg, 1979-81; mem. adv. bd. Pa. Environ. Coun., 1983—. Recipient Gt. Tchr. award East Stroudsburg U. Alumni Assn., 1999; Fulbright-Hays fellow, 1988. Avocations: piano, voice. Home: 77 E Walnut St Kingston PA 18704 Office: East Stroudsburg U Normal St East Stroudsburg PA 18301 E-mail: pcrotty@po-box.esu.edu.

CROTTY, ROBERT BELL, lawyer; b. Dallas, Aug. 16, 1951; s. Willard and Betty (Bell) C.; m. Sarah (Smith), Mar. 8, 1980; children: Robert Edwin, Rebecca Bell. BA, Va. Mil. Inst., 1973; JD, U. Tex., 1976. Bar: Tex., 1976; US Dist. Ct. (no. dist.) Tex., 1977; US Ct. Appeals (5th cir.), 1978. Assoc. Akin, Gump, Strauss, Hauer, and Feld, Dallas, 1976-82, ptnr., 1983-92, hiring ptnr., 1988-91; prin. McKool and Smith, P.C., Dallas, 1992-94; ptnr. Crotty and Johansen, LLP, Dallas, 1995—. Vis. bd. Va. Mil. Inst., 1995-99. Mem. Leadership Dallas, 1981; dir. Salesmanship Club, 1989—90, 1994—95, 2001—02, Va. Mil. Inst. Alumni Assn., 1991—95, Highland Pk. Ind. Sch. Dist. Edn. Found., 1991—97, pres., 1997—2000; chmn. bd. dir. Salesmanship Club Youth & Family Ctr., Inc., 2001—02; chmn. G.T.E. Byron Nelson Classic, 1995; bd. dir. Goodwill Industries of Dallas, Inc., 2002—; pres. Dallas Bus. League, 1983, Big Bros. Big Sisters Met. Dallas, 1987—88. First lt. U.S. Army, 1976, first lt. USAR, 1973—81. Fellow Tex. Bar Found. (sustaining life); Dallas Bar Found., Fellows (pres. 1999-2000); mem. Dallas Bar Assn., Tex.; Law Rev. Assn. (life); State Bar Tex.; Northwood Club (pres. 2003). Avocations: golf, reading, hunting, hiking. Office: Crotty &Johansen LLP 2311 Cedar Springs Rd Ste 250 Dallas TX 75201-7810 E-mail: bcrotty@crojolaw.com.

CROTTY GUILE, JULIANNE MARIE, musician, educator, composer, writer; b. Omaha, Mar. 13, 1956; d. Richard and Beverly Ruth (Dillon) Crotty; m. Peter John Guile. BA, NYU, 1986; MA in English, U. Nebr., 1992; postgrad., 2001—. Singer Western Australian Opera, Perth, 1987-88; prof. English and Humanities U. Nebr., 1989-93, Metro C.C., Omaha, 1991-93, Coll. St. Mary's, Omaha, 1994; prof. English Buena Vista Coll., Iowa, 1996; prof. music Phoenix Acad., 1997; dir. Noteworthy Music, Omaha, 1992—. Composer "Children's Stories and Songs" to commemmorate Duchesne Choir reunion, 1974, Crest of Cedar, 1994 (music award 1996); poet, author: Love From The Inside Out, 1988 (poetry award 1989). Mem. Nat. Coun. Boys Town, Omaha, 1994; cantor, pianist St. Stephen the M., Nebr. Churches, 1974—. Recipient Stuart Creativity award Duchesne Acad., Omaha, 1974. Mem. Nat. Music Tchrs. Assn. (Omaha chpt.), Omaha Musicians Union. Avocations: sailing, walking, swimming. E-mail: jcrottyg@aol.com.

CROUCH, BETTY LOUISE, real estate broker; b. Lancaster, Ky., Aug. 8, 1930; d. Calvin Milton and Annie Lee (Hurt) Hulett; m. Manuel Russel Brackett, Dec. 26, 1947 (div. Jan. 1952); children: Shirley Katherine Brackett Woods, Donna Louise Brackett Brown; m. Edward Kenneth Crouch, Feb. 19, 1965; 1 child, Angela Betty Crouch Correll. Lic. real estate broker. From salesperson to mgr. Crouch Real Estate, Danville, Ky., 1975-81; broker Bill McAnly Better Homes & Gardens, Danville, 1981-88, Caudill & Assoc. Better Homes & Gardens, Danville, 1988—, Caudill & Assocs., Ind. Realtors, Danville, 1997—. Mem.: Danville Bd. Realtors (v.p. 1979, pres. 1980). Democrat. Baptist. Avocation: Avocations: crafts, self-taught artist. Office: Century 21 Wilson Realty 443 S 4th St Danville KY 40422 Home: 404 Coldstream Dr Danville KY 40422-1014

CROUCH, DIANNE KAY, secondary school guidance counselor; b. Campbellsville, Ky., Apr. 28, 1954; d. James Edgar and Imogene (Bailey) Gabbert; m. Thomas Frederick Crouch, June 6, 1987. BA, Campbellsville Coll., 1976; MS, U. Ky., 1984, EdS, 1991. Cert. tchr. English, psychology, counselor, secondary schs., Ky. Tchr. English Grayson County High Sch., Leitchfield, Ky., 1976-78, Jessamine County Jr. High Sch., Nicholasville, Ky., 1978-83, Jessamine County High Sch., Nicholasville, 1983-89, Tates Creek Jr. High Sch., Lexington, Ky., 1989-90; guidance counselor Tates Creek High Sch., Lexington, 1990—. Mem. pub. rels. com. Tates Creek H.S.; selected Inst. Women in Sch. Adminstrn. Ky. Active Calvary Bapt. Ch., Lexington, 1991—; bd. dirs. Lexington C.C. Nursing Program; mem. undergrad. adv. bd. U. Ky. Named Jessamine County Tchr. of

Yr., Jessamine County Bd. Edn., Nicholasville, Ky., 1986-87, Outstanding Tchr. 5th Dist., Campbellsville Coll., 1988; sponsor of Jr. High newspaper Tates Creek Clarion named 1 of top 5 in U.S Nat. Jr. Beta Club; recipient Ginny Rollins Leadership award, 2000-01. Mem. Ky. Assn. Secondary and Coll. Admission Counselors, Ky. Counseling Assn. (Ky. H.S. Counselor of Yr.), Ctrl. Ky. Counseling Assn. (past pres., named H.S. Counselor of Yr. 1999-2000, 01-02), Ky. Sch. Counselors Assn. (pres.), Kappa Delta Pi. Avocations: piano, dog training, walking, exercising, travel. Home: 1240 Litchfield Ln Lexington KY 40513 E-mail: dcrouch@fayette.k12.ky.us.

CROUCH, GARY CLINTON, financial management company executive, accountant; b. Wichita, Kans., Aug. 26, 1956; s. John Clinton and Patricia Roslyn (Reynolds) C.; m. Cindy Ranell Johnson, June 5, 1982; 1 child, Christina N. BA in Theology, Oral Roberts U., 1978, BS in Acctg., 1982. CPA, Okla; cert. Microsoft profl., info. tech. profl. Clk. Holloway Acctg., Tulsa, 1978-82; pvt. practice Tulsa, 1982—2001; pres. AlterComp Mgmt., Inc., Tulsa, 1986-96; sec.-treas. Smoke Foods, Ltd., Tulsa, 1991-94; pres. Crouch, Slavin & Co., PC, Tulsa, 1996—. Treas. Sertoma Handicapped Opportunity Program Found., Inc., Tulsa, 1986-88; bd. dirs. Evangelistic Temple, 1994— Mem. AICPA, Okla. Soc. CPAs (mgmt. adv. com. 1985-88, mgmt. of an acctg. practice com. 1992-98, tech. com. 2001—), Soc. for Human Resource Mgmt. (Okla. human resource conf. com. 2000, 02), Tulsa Area Human Resources Assn. (treas. 2003—), Sertoma (v.p. Tulsa chpt. 1986-87, treas. 1985-91). Republican. Office: 1799 E 71st St Tulsa OK 74136-5108 E-mail: gcrouch@crouchslavin.com.

CROUCH, JACK DYER, II, federal agency administrator; Advisor for U.S. Del. to Nuclear and Space Arms Talks U.S. Arms Control and Disarmament Agy., 1985—86; dep. asst. sec. def. for internat. security policy Dept. Def., Washington, 1990—92; assoc. prof. dept. def. and strategic studies S.W. Mo. State U.; asst. sec. for internat. security policy Dept. Def., Washington, 2001—. Office: Dept Def Internat Security Policy 2900 Defense Pentagon Washington DC 20301-2900

CROUCH, TONI L. principal; b. Roswell, N.Mex., Sept. 7, 1948; d. Harry Baker Jr. and Dorothy Jean (Hamme) C. BA, Vassar Coll., 1970; MEd, Salem State Coll., 1972. Cert. tchr. and prin., Mass.; cert. assn. exec. Tchr. Revere (Mass.) Pub. Schs., 1970-74; elem. and mid. sch. counselor Singapore Am. Sch., 1974-76; elem. and mid. sch. prin. Asociacion Escuelas Lincoln, Buenos Aires, 1979-83; Eastern European regional coord. Internat. Sch. Belgrade, Yugoslavia, 1983-85; asst. dir. edn. Am. Phys. Therapy Assn., Alexandria, Va., 1986-88; v.p. Found. for Phys. Therapy, Alexandria, Va., 1988-92; exec. dir. Counseling and Human Devel. Found., Alexandria, Va., 1992-94; regional rep. Johns Hopkins Inst. for Policy, Budapest, Hungary, 1994-95; assoc. exec. dir. Character Edn. Partnership, Washington, 1995-98; dir. edn. Am. Soc. Assn. Execs., Washington, 1998-2001; assn. dir. AAUW, 2001; dir. edn. tech. svcs. DelCor Tech. Solutions, Silver Spring, Md., 2001—03; head of sch. Merritt Acad., Fairfax, Va., 2003—. Exec. cons. Assn. for Specialized Accreditation, Alexandria, 1991-92. Youth leader Revere Cmty. Ctr., 1971-74; v.p. Lee Oaks Bd., Falls Church, Va., 1989—. Mem. Am. Soc. Assn. Execs. (Final Project award 1991). Avocations: gardening, photography, writing. Office: Merritt Acad 9211 Arlington Blvd Fairfax VA 22031

CROUSE, CAROL K. MAVROMATIS, elementary education educator; b. Phila., Nov. 27, 1950; d. George and Helen (Captis) Mavromatis; m. David Crouse (dec. 1998). BS in Edn., Temple U., 1972, MEd in Curriculum and Instrn., 1981. Elem. tchr. grades 1, 3, 4, 5, Upper Darby (Pa.) Sch. Dist., 1974—, mem. Sci. Curriculum Writing Comm., 1974—99. Mem. Excellence in Edn. Team, Hillcrest Elem. Sch., Pa., 1987; cert. NASA Lunar Rock and Meteorite Edn. Program, 1993—; tchr. adv. bd. Phila. Zoo, 1995—; mem. writing and evaluation team Schuylkill Valley Nature Ctr., 1993-94; coord. cmty. svc. Highland Park Elem. Sch. Learn and Serve com., Kids Care Club, 2000-2002, Safety Patrol Advisor, 2002—. Recipient Howard W. McComb award Temple U. Phi Delta Kappa, 1981. Mem.: NSTA, ASCD, Upper Darby Recreation Tennis Players (tournament co-dir. 1983—92).

CROUSE, FARRELL R. lawyer; b. Portsmouth, Va., Dec. 23, 1963; s. Farrell Rondall and Grace Alice (Kenworthy) C. BA in History and Sociology, Bucknell U., Lewisburg, Pa., 1986; JD, Widener U., Wilmington, Del., 1989, LLM in Taxation, 1992. Bar: N.J. 1989, Pa. 1989, U.S. Dist. Ct. N.J. 1989. Assoc. Law Offices John William Neef, Carneys Point, N.J., 1990-91; pvt. practice Woodstown, N.J., 1991—. Mem.: ABA, Pa. Bar Assn., NJ Bar Assn. Avocations: auto racing, travel, collecting auto racing books and memorabilia. Home and Office: 36 Crimson Ct East Sewell NJ 08080-2608

CROUSE, LINDSAY, actress; b. N.Y.C., May 12, 1948; d. Russel and Anna (Erskine) C. BA, Radcliffe Coll., 1970. Appearances include: (films) All the President's Men, 1976, Between the Lines, 1977, Slapshot, 1977, Prince of the City, 1981, The Verdict, 1982, Daniel, 1983, Iceman, 1984, Places in the Heart, 1984 (Acad. award nomination 1985), House of Games, 1987, Communion, 1989, Desperate Hours, 1990, Being Human, 1993, Bye Bye Love, 1995, Indian in the Cupboard, 1995, The Juror, 1996, The Arrival, 1996, Prefontaine, 1997, The Progeny, 1999, Man of the People, 1999, Stranger in My House, 1999, The Insider, 1999; (TV movies) Eleanor and Franklin, 1976, Eleanor and Franklin: The White House Years, 1977, Reunion, 1980, Paul's Case, 1980, Summer Solstice, 1981, Lemon Sky, 1987, Chantilly Lace, 1993, Final Appeal, 1993, Parallel Lives, 1994, Out of Darkness, 1994, Between Mother and Daughter, 1995 (Emmy award nomination), Norma Jean and Marilyn, 1996, If These Walls Could Talk, 1996, Beyond the Prairie: The True Story of Laura Ingalls Wilder, 1999; (TV series) Hill Street Blues, Murder She Wrote, Columbo, Law and Order, Lifestories, The Equalizer, Civil Wars, L.A. Law, Traps, ER, NYPD Blue, Millenium, Brimstone, Batman: The Animated Series, Buffy the Vampire Slayer, 1999-2000, Providence, The Division, Arliss, Fraiser, 2002. Recipient Obie award for Reunion, 1980, Theater World award for The Homecoming, 1992.

CROUSE, ROGER LESLIE, information technology executive; b. Medford, Mass., Mar. 24, 1944; s. Mahlon Dale and Doris Mabel (Butman) Crouse; m. Judy Avis Wiley, May 10, 1969; children: Alison, Erin. BS, U. Mass., 1966; MS, U. Vt., 1977. Programmer, analyst positions IBM, Essex Junction, Vt., 1966-77, adv. systems analyst, 1977-80, devel. mgr., 1980-82, adv. edn. analyst, 1982-83, adv. info. ctr. analyst, 1983-91, distributed computing cons., 1991-92, quality focus mgr., team facilitator, 1992-94, provisional ISO 9000 assessor, 1993-96; dir. info. tech. svcs. Trinity Coll. Vt., Burlington, 1996-2000; dir. info. tech. Vt. Tech. Coll., Randolph, 2000—01; program mgmt. svcs. mgr. IDX Corp., South Burlington, Vt., 2001—. Ptnr. in edn. Burlington Area Vocat. Ctr., 1986—88; pub. software specialist IBM, Burlington, 1988—89; adj. prof. U. Vt., 1990—. Contbr. articles to profl. jours. Nat. trainer Make-A-Wish Found. Am., 1992—, mem. nat. tng. com., 1995—97, mem. nat. nominating com., 1997—2001, mem. nat. corp. docs. com., 2001—; Treas. N.G. Assn. Vt., Burlington, 1980—86; 11-gallon blood donor ARC, Burlington, 1966—; pres. Make-A-Wish Found. of Vt., Burlington, 1994—97, bd. dirs., 1989—97, 1998—, Lake Iroquois Action Com., Hinesburg, Vt., 1980—. Col. Vt. Air N.G., 1967—95. Mem.: Ancient Accepted Scottish Rite (most wise master 1979—80, sovereign prince 1980—81, thrice potent master 1986—87), Masons (worshipful master local chpt. 1976—77). Avocations: jogging, swimming, cross-country skiing, music, acting. Office: IDX Systems Corp 40 IDX Dr South Burlington VT 05403 E-mail: roger_crouse@idx.com.

CROUSHORE, DEAN DARRELL, economist; b. Chateauroux, France, Dec. 3, 1956; (parents Am. citizens); s. John Z. and Sylvia J. (Engelbrite) C.; m. Claudette Kay Ishmael, June 17, 1978; children: David D., Monica E., Rachel J. AB, Ohio U., 1978; MA, Ohio State U., 1981, PhD, 1984. Asst. prof. dept. econs. Pa. State U., State College, 1984-89; staff economist Fed. Res. Bank Phila., 1989—2003; assoc. prof. dept. econs. U. Richmond, Va., 2003. Office: U Richmond 1 Gateway Rd Richmond VA 23173

CROUT, J(OHN) RICHARD, physician, pharmaceutical researcher; b. Portland, Oreg., Dec. 30, 1929; s. John Shaw and Georgia Crout; m. Carol Jean Keith, June 19, 1954; children: Linda Jane, Keith Richard, Andrew Richard. AB, Oberlin Coll., 1951; MD, Northwestern U., 1955, MS, 1956; DMed (hon.), U. Uppsala, Sweden, 1977. Intern Passavant Meml. Hosp., Chgo., 1955-56; asst. resident in internal medicine VA Rsch. Hosp., Chgo., 1956-57; clin. assoc. Nat. Heart Inst., Bethesda, Md., 1957-60; asst. resident in Medicine NYU-Bellevue Med. Ctr., N.Y.C., 1960-61; USPHS fellow, instr. pharmacology Harvard U., 1961-63; asst. prof. pharmacology and internal medicine U. Tex. Southwestern Med. Sch., Dallas, 1963-65, assoc. prof., 1965-70; prof. pharmacology and medicine Mich. State U., 1970-71; dep. dir. Bur. Drugs FDA, Rockville, Md., 1971-72, dir. office sci. evaluation Bur. Drugs, 1972-73, dir. Bur. Drugs, 1973-82; dir. Office of Med. Applications of Rsch. NIH, 1982-84; v.p. med. and sci. affairs Boehringer Mannheim Pharms., 1984-94; scholar in residence Inst. Medicine, 1994-95; pres. Crout Cons., Bethesda, 1994—. Mem. drug resch. bd. NAS-NRC; cons. WHO, 1974—84; trustee U.S. Pharmacopeia, 1985—95; mem. coms. Inst. Medicine, 1990, 1992—93, 1998, 2000; bd. dirs. Trimeris, Genelabs Techs., Biopure. Contbr. articles to profl jours. Served to sr asst surgeon USPHS, 1957—60, asst surgeon gen USPHS, 1976—84. Recipient Dist Serv Award, USPHS, 1977, Spec Citation, Comnr FDA, 1981, 1982, Distinguished Career Award, Drug Info Asn, 1994, Oscar B Hunter Award in Therapeutics, Am Soc Clin Pharmaceutical and Therapeutics, 1997; scholar Burroughs Wellcome, 1965—70. Fellow: ACP; mem.: Soc Clin Trials, Heart Asn, Am Soc Clin Pharmacology and Therapeutics, Am Soc Clin Investigation, Am Soc Pharmacology and Experimental Therapeutics, Am Fedn Clin Research, Phi Beta Kappa, Alpha Omega Alpha. Home and Office: 5300 Alta Vista Rd Bethesda MD 20814-1629 E-mail: jrcrout@aol.com.

CROUTER, RICHARD EARL, religion educator; b. Washington, Nov. 2, 1937; s. Earl Clinton and Neva J. (Crain) C.; m. Barbara Jean Williams, Jan. 30, 1960; children— Edward, Frances AB, Occidental Coll., 1960; B.D., Union Theol. U., N.Y.C., 1963, Th.D., 1968. Asst. prof. religion Carleton Coll., Northfield, Minn., 1967-73, assoc. prof., 1973-79, prof., 1979-92, Bryn-Jones disting. tchg. prof. humanities, 1993-96, Musser prof. religious studies, 1997—2003, Musser prof. religious studies emeritus, 2003—. Translator, editor: On Religion (F. Schleiermacher), 1988, 96; co-editor Jour. for the History of Modern Theology, 1993—. Chmn. parents adv. coun. Greenvale Sch. Northfield, 1977-78; resident dir. A Better Chance Program, Northfield, 1968-70. Fulbright scholar, 1976-77, 87, 91-92; Am. Council Learned Socs. fellow, 1976-77, Wallin fellow, 2001, DAAD fellow, 2001. Mem. Am. Acad. Religion (steering com. 19th century theol. group 1982-92, chmn. 1987-92), Hegel Soc. Am., Troeltsch Soc., German Studies Assn., Kierkegaard Soc., Schleiermacher Gesellschaft. Democrat. Avocations: hiking, travel, biking, piano. Home: 808 2d St E Northfield MN 55057-2307 Office: Carleton Coll Dept Religious Studies Northfield MN 55057 E-mail: rcrouter@carleton.edu., rcrouter@charter.net.

CROUTHAMEL, THOMAS GROVER, SR., editor, consultant; b. Berkeley, Calif., Sept. 10, 1930; s. Martin Luther and Elizabeth (Grover) C.; m. Madalene Donati, Sept. 6, 1954; children: Thomas Grover Jr., Annalise. BS, Thiel Coll., 1953. Sr. drug investigator FDA, L.A. and Edison, N.J., 1958-81; pres. Thomas G. Crouthamel, Inc., Bradenton, Fla., 1981—; ptnr. Crouthamel & Crouthamel, Bradenton, 1983-93; treas. Crouthamel Enterprises, Inc., Liberty Hill, Tex., 1986-92; sr. editor Keystone Press, Bradenton, 1982—. Author: Auditing EtO, 1982, It's OK, 1986, A History of Trailer Estates, 1987; When the Unthinkable Happens, 1995; contbr. articles to profl. jours. Cubmaster Boy Scouts Am., Pomona, Calif., 1963, committeeman, Spotswood, N.J., 1968-76, adult adviser Explorer Post, 1976-79; trustee Spotswood Libr. Bd., 1970-79; co-leader Compassionate Friends, Sarasota, Fla., 1984-90, chpt. advisor, facilitator, Englewood, Fla., 1989-91. With U.S. Army, 1953-55. Mem. Internat. Narcotics Officers Assn., The Authors Guild, Toastmasters (pres. 1969-71), Masons (high priest local chpt. 1967), FDA Alumni Assn., T.E. Masonic Square Club (pres. 2002, 2003). Avocations: travel, reading, fishing. Office: PO Box 6163 Bradenton FL 34281-6163

CROVETTI, ALDO JOSEPH, retired chemist, consultant; b. Lake Forest, Ill., Apr. 2, 1930; s. Aldo and Veneranda C.; m. Jean B. Crovetti, Aug. 1, 1959; children: Mary, Anna, Donna, Alan. BS, Lake Forest Coll., 1951; MS, U. Ill., 1952, PhD, 1955. With U.S. Army Chem. Corps, 1955-57; rsch. chemist Abbott Labs., North Chicago, Ill., 1957-65, group leader, 1965-67, sect. head, 1967-70; dept. mgr. Agrl. Products R&D, North Chicago, Ill., 1970-75, mgr. agrl. chems., 1975-78, mgr. field r&d, 1978-83, mgr. licensing and devel., 1983-92, ret., 1992. Mem. at large exec. com. Plant Growth Regulation Soc., 1988-92; cons. A.J. Crovetti & Assocs., Inc., Lake Forest, Ill., 1993—. Contbr. articles to profl. jours.; patentee in field. Mentor in career devel. Lake Forest Coll., 1994—; vol. Chgo., Naples, Botanical Garden, 1994-2002;Dir. Highwood Hist. Soc. 2000-. Mem. Am Chem. Soc. (mentor, tchr. 1994—), Am. Soc. Horticultural Sci., Am. Pathological Soc., Plant Growth Regulation Soc. Am., Am. Soc. Plant Physiologists, Licensing & Exec. Soc. Am., Assn. Univ. Tech. Mgrs. Avocations: gardening, golf, travel. Office: AJ Crovetti & Assocs Inc 735 Greenview Pl Lake Forest IL 60045-3222 E-mail: ajc.associates@worldnet.att.net.

CROW, BEN, sociologist, educator; b. Welwyn Garden City, Hertfordshire, England, June 18, 1947; s. Percy and Bobbie Crow; m. Deborah Gordon; children: Sam, Eleanor. PhD, Edinburgh (Scotland) U., 1980. Asst. prof. sociology U. Calif., Santa Cruz, 1996—2002, assoc. prof. sociology, 2002—. Author: Markets, Class and Social Change: Trading Networks and Poverty in Rural South Asia, 2001. Home: 365 Lakeview Way Redwood City CA 94062 Office: U Calif Sociology Dept Santa Cruz CA 95064 Personal E-mail: bencrow@ucsc.edu.

CROW, ELIZABETH SMITH, editor; b. N.Y.C. d. Harrison Venture and Marlis (deGreve) Smith; children: Samuel Harrison, Rachel Venture, Sarah Gibson. BA, Mills Coll.; postgrad., Brown U. Exec. editor New York mag., N.Y.C.; editor-in-chief Parents mag., N.Y.C., 1978—83; pres., editl. dir., CEO Gruner & Jahr USA Pub.; editor-in-chief Mademoiselle Mag., N.Y.C., 1993-99; free-lance book reviewer N.Y. Times Book Rev.; pres. N.Y. Women in Comm., 1999-2000; v.p., editl. dir. Rodale Pub., N.Y.C., 2001—02; exec. v.p., editl. dir. Primedia Consumer Mag. and Media Group, 2002—03. Judge Nat. Mag. awards; bd. trustees Alan Guttmacher Inst. Bd. trustees March of Dimes; pres. N.Y. Women Comm. Found., 1999—2000. Recipient Nat. Mag. award for gen. excellence, 1988. Mem.: Am. Soc. Mag Editors, Century Assn., Cosmopolitan Club. Democrat.

CROW, HAROLD EUGENE, physician, family medicine educator; b. Farber, Mo., Jan. 17, 1933; s. Leslie J. and Laura L. (Sparks) C.; m. Mary Kay Krenke, July 5, 1974; children: Janet L., Jason P. MD, U. Mo., 1963. Diplomate Am. Bd. Family Practice, Am. Bd. Med. Examiners. Intern E.W. Sparrow Hosp., Lansing, Mich., 1963-64; pvt. practice medicine specializing in family practice Lansing, 1964-70; dir. family practice residency E.W. Sparrow Hosp., Lansing, Mich., 1970-82; chmn. dept. family and community medicine Sch. Medicine, U. Nev., Reno, 1982-87, dir. office Rural Health Sch. Medicine, 1984-87; med. dir. S.W. Med. Assocs., Reno, 1987-88; dir. Lynchburg (Va.) Family Practice Resident Program, 1988-96; patient advocate Cons. for Caring, Sun City Center, Fla., 1996—98; dir. Outer Banks Edn. and Program Devel. Project, East Carolina U. Sch. Medicine, Nags Head, NC, 1999—. Dir. Outer Banks Edn. and Program Devel. Project. Developer non-rotational residency model for family practice tng., tng. model for rural med. practice; innovator computerized health info. systems for family physicians. Numerous civic activities. With U.S. Army, 1955-57. Mem. Am. Coll. Physician Exec., numerous profl. assns. Presbyterian. Home: 408 Stoneham Dr Sun City Center FL 33573-5841 *Not being hampered by Dogma, but being freed up by curiousity. Not being a heavy handed teacher, but a caring helper of learning; that's the essense of a successful innovator and educator.*

CROW, JAMES FRANKLIN, retired genetics educator; b. Phoenixville, Pa., Jan. 18, 1916; s. H. Ernest and Lena (Whitaker) C.; m. Ann Crockett, Aug. 9, 1941; children: Franklin, Laura, Catherine. AB, Friends U., 1937; PhD, U. Tex., 1941; DSc. (hon.), U. Chgo., 1991. Instr., then asst. prof. zoology Dartmouth U., 1941-48; faculty U. Wis., 1948—, prof. genetics, 1954-86, chmn. dept. med. genetics, 1958-63, 65-71, acting dean sch. medicine, 1963-65, prof. emeritus, 1986—. Chmn. genetics study sect. NIH, 1965-68 Author: Genetics Notes, 8th edit, 1983, Introduction to Population Genetics Theory, 1970, Basic Concepts in Population, Quantitative and Evolutionary Genetics, 1986, also articles. Chmn. mammalian genetics study sect. NIH, 1985-88. Mem. Nat. Acad. Scis. (chmn. com. genetic effects atomic radiation 1960-63, 70-72, chmn. com. chem. environ. mutagens 1980-83), Japan Acad. (fgn. mem.), Genetics Soc. Am. (pres. 1960), Am. Soc. Human Genetics (pres. 1963), Royal Soc. (fgn. mem.). Home: 24 Glenway St Madison WI 53705-5206 E-mail: jfcrow@facstaff.wisc.edu.

CROW, LAURA JEAN, design educator, costume designer; b. Hanover, N.H., Sept. 29, 1945; d. James Franklin and Rebecca Ann (Crockett) C.; m. Daniel Caine, Apr. 28, 1980 (div. Mar. 1987); children: Sarah Katherine, Matthew Jordan Caine. BFA, Boston U., 1967; MFA, U. Wis., 1969; postgrad., U. London, 1969-70, Courtauld Inst. Lectr. Brandeis U., Waltham, Mass., 1985; assoc. prof. U. Mass., Amherst, 1986-87, U. Mich., Ann Arbor, 1987-94; prof. U. Conn., Storrs, 1994—. Active NEA Theatre Comms. Group; U.S. rep., head costume working group OISTAT. Costume designer : (Broadway plays) Sweet Bird of Youth; The Water Engine; Fifth of July; Burn This; The Seagull; Redwood Curtain; Book of Days; Moby Dick; (off-Broadway prodns.) The Farm; (Broadway plays) Warp; (off-Broadway prodns.) An Immaculate Misconception; Winter Signs; Hamlet; A Tale Told; Orchards; Brilliant Traces; Cakewalk; Raft of Medusa; Moby Dick; Book of Days; Sympathetic Magic; (films) Fifth of July; Harry and the Hendersons; The Lathe of Heaven; Charlie Smith & the Fritter Tree; designer regional theaters including : Seattle Rep; ACT; Milw. Rep.; Goodman Theatre, Berkeley Rep., Mark Taper Forum, Arena Stage; Alley Theatre; Long Wharf Theatre; designer regional theaters including, designer regional theaters including: Hartford Stage; Old Globe Theatre; Asolo Theatre; Ctr. Stage. Recipient Drama Desk award, N.Y. Drama Critics, 1973, Joseph Jefferson award, Jeff Com., Chgo., 1975, 1976, 1977, 1978, 1988, Obie Award, Village Voice, 1980, Am. Theatre Wing award, 1980, 1997, Dramalogue award, L.A. Drama Critics, 1988, 1997, Backstage West Garland award, 1997, San Francisco Bay Area Critics award, 1998, Zoni award, Phoenix Drama Critics, 1998, 1999; Fulbright scholar, 2001—02. Mem. United Scenic Artists, U.S. Inst. Theatre Tech. Home: 88 Hillyndale Rd Storrs CT 06268-1802 Office: U of Conn Dept Dramatic Arts 802 Bolton Rd Storrs CT 06269-1127 Fax: 860-486-3110. E-mail: laura.crow.@uconn.edu.

CROW, LYNNE CAMPBELL SMITH, insurance company representative; b. Buffalo, Oct. 13, 1942; d. Stephen Smith and Jean Campbell (Ruggles) Hall; m. William David Crow II, Apr. 16, 1966 (div. Dec. 1989); children: William David III, Alexander Fairbairn, Margaret Campbell. BA, Sweet Briar (Va.) Coll., 1964; postgrad., Am. Coll., 1986. CLU; ChFC. Claims rep. Liberty Mut. Ins. Co., Bklyn. and N.Y.C., 1964-66; with McGraw-Hill Corp., N.Y.C., 1966-67; claims rep. Liberty Mut. Ins. Co., East Orange, N.J., 1967-68; sales assoc. Realty World/Allsopp Realtors, Millburn, N.J., 1981-82; field rep. Guardian Life Ins. Co., 1982—. Bd. dirs. Jr. League Oranges and Short Hills, Millburn, 1979-80, 95-96, Millburn LWV, 1979-80; campaign chair, bus. chair, bd. dirs. United Way Millburn/Short Hills, 1981-88, 90-96, sec., 1990-91; adult planning chair Cora Hartshorn Arboretum, 2000-03, bd. dirs., trustee, 2000—, sec., 2003. Named Life Underwriter of Yr., 1996. Mem. Nat. Assn. Ins. and Fin. Advisors (Nat. Quality award 1988, 91, 95, Nat. Health Achievement award 1988, 90), Nat. Assn. Health Underwriters, Am. Soc. Fin. Svc. Profls. (bd. dirs. 1994-99), N.J. Assn. Ins. and Fin. Advisors (dir. region II 1993-95, health chair 1995—, sec. 1998-99, 2d v.p. 1999-2000, 1st v.p. 2000-01, pres. 2001-2002, immediate past pres. 2002), Newark Assn. Life Underwriters (bd. dirs. 1986-94, sec. 1987-88, treas. 1988-89, 3d v.p. 1989-90,, 2d v.p. 1990, pres.-elect 1991-92, pres. 1992-93, health chair 1995-98, Life Underwriter of Yr. 1986), Women in Fin. Svcs., Million Dollar Round Table (qualifying and life, capt. focus session on non-core products & investments 1999-2000, chair spl. events 2000-2001), Million Dollar Round Table Found. (bd. trustees 2002, knight), Assn. Health Ins. Advisors, Nat. Assn. Security Dealers, Chatham (Mass.) Beach and Tennis Club. Republican. Episcopalian. Avocations: travel, sailing, reading, hiking, photography. Home: 22 Winding Way Short Hills NJ 07078-2530 Office: 1150 Raritan Rd Cranford NJ 07016-3369 E-mail: lscrow22ww@aol.com.

CROW, MARTI, state representative; b. Bryan, Tex., Dec. 7, 1944; m. Michael Crow; children: Jennifer, Emily, Bryan. BA, Baker U., 1966; JD, Washburn Law Sch., 1992. Tchr., 1966—68; law clerk Freilich & Leitner, 1991—92; atty. Kans. Dept. Revenue, 1992—93; cons. Kans. Dept. Health and Environ., 1993—95; atty., ptnr. Crow, Clothier, and Bates, 1995—; mem. Kans. Ho. of Reps., 1997—. Mem. City Planning Commn., Leavenworth, 1978—90, 1993—96, Bd. Zoning Appeals, Leavenworth, 1979—90, 1993—96; mem. bd. edn. VSD 453, Leavenworth, 1983—96. Democrat. Methodist. Office: 284-W State Capitol 300 SW 10th Ave Topeka KS 66612 Address: 1200 S Broadway Leavenworth KS 66048-3118*

CROW, MICHAEL, academic administrator; BA in polit. sci. & environ. studies, Iowa State U., 1977; doctorate in pub. adminstrn., Syracuse U. Pres. Ariz. State U., 2002—; exec. vice provost Columbia U., prof. sci., tech. policy; prof. tech. mgmt. Iowa State U., dir., inst. phys. rsch. & tech. Contbr. articles;, editor numerous books. Office: Az State U PO Box 872203 Tempe AZ 85287-2203

CROW, NANCY REBECCA, lawyer; b. Ridgecrest, Calif., Nov. 3, 1948; d. Edwin Louis and Eleanor Elizabeth (Gish) C.; 1 child, Rebecca Ann Carr; m. Mark A.A. Skrotzki, Apr. 4, 1987. BA, Antioch Coll., 1970; JD, U. Colo., 1974; LLM in Taxation, NYU, 1977. Bars: Colo. 1974, Calif. 1977. Atty., advisor IRS, N.Y.C., 1975-77; assoc. Brawerman & Kopple, Los Angeles, 1977-80; prof. Sch. Law, U. Denver, 1980-81; of counsel Krendl & Netzorg, Denver, 1981-84; shareholder Krendl & Krendl, Denver, 1984-92, Pendleton, Friedberg, Wilson & Hennessey, P.C., Denver, 1992—. Editor estate and trust forum Colorado Lawyer, 1992-93, bd. editors, 1993-2000; contbr. chpts. to books. Mem. alumni bd. Antioch Coll., 2000—; bd. dirs. Centennial Philharmonic Orch., 1998—2001; bd. trustees Centennial Philharmonic Found., 2001—. Fellow Am. Coll. Trust and Estate Counsel; mem. ABA (chmn. Welfare Benefits subcom. of personal svcs. orgns. com. com., tax sect. 1987-92), Colo. Bar Assn. (exec. coun. tax sect. 1990-93, sec. tax sect. 1993-94, chair-elect 1994-95, chair 1995-96, bd. govs. 1996-98), Colo. Women's Bar Assn. (chair pub. policy com. 1982-83), Denver Bar Assn., Denver Tax Assn., Denver Tax Inst. Planning Com., Alliance of Profl. Women, Women's Estate Planning Com. (bd. dirs. 1996-98), U.S.-Mex. C. of C. (bd. dirs. Rocky Mountain chpt., sec. 1998-2001), Sierra Club. Democrat. Unitarian Universalist. Avocations: skiing, backpacking, cello, running. Home: 1031 Marion St Denver CO 80218-3016 Office: Pendleton Friedberg Wilson & Hennessey PC 303 E 17th Ave Ste 1000 Denver CO 80203-1263 E-mail: nrc@penberg.com.

CROW, PAUL ABERNATHY, JR., clergyman, religious council executive, educator; b. Birmingham, Ala., Nov. 17, 1931; s. Paul Abernathy and Beulah Elizabeth (Parker) C.; m. Mary Evelyn Matthews, Sept. 11, 1955; children: Carol Ann, Stephen Paul, Susan Margaret. BS, U. Ala., 1954; BD, Lexington Theol. Sem., 1957; STM, Hartford Sem. Found., 1958, PhD, 1962; postdoctoral studies, Oxford U., 1967-68, U. Geneva, Ecumenical Inst. Bossey, 1981, 87; DD, Phillips U., 1983, Bethany Coll., 1983, Yale U., 1986, Va. Theological Sem., 1987; DHL, Lynchburg Coll., 1997. Ordained to ministry Disciples of Christ, 1957. Minister in various Disciples congregations, Ala., Ky., 1955-57; min. First Congl. Ch., Hadley, Mass., 1957-61; assoc. prof. ch. history Lexington Theol. Sem., 1961-66, prof., 1966-68; Am. Assn. Theol. Schs. vis. fellow Oxford U., 1967-68; gen. sec. Consultation on Ch. Union, Princeton, N.J., 1968-74; pres. Coun. on Christian Unity, Indpls., 1974-98; vis. lectr. Princeton Theol. Sem., 1969-78; affiliate prof. Christian Theol. Sem., 1974—. Vis. prof. Lexington Theol. Sem., 2001-; mem. ctr. com. World Coun. Chs., exec. com., faith and order plenary commn., 1975-98; vice moderator Faith and Order Commn., 1992-98; del. faith and order confs., St. Andrews, Scotland, 1960, Montreal, Que., Can., 1963, Bristol, Eng., 1967, Louvain, Belgium, 1971, Accra, Ghana, 1974, Bangalore, India, 1978, Lima, Peru, 1982, Stavanger, Norway, 1985, Budapest, Hungary, 1989, Santiago de Compostela, Spain, 1993, Moshi, Tanzania, 1996; del. World Coun. Chs. assembly Uppsala, Sweden, 1968, Nairobi, Kenya, 1975, Vancouver, Can., 1983, Canberra, Australia, 1991, Harare, Zimbabwe, 1998; del. ch. union confs., Limuru, Kenya, 1970, Toronto, Ont., Can., 1975, Colombo, Sri Lanka, 1981, Potsdam, German Democratic Republic, 1987, WCC World Missionary Conf., San Antonio, Tex., 1989, Ocho Rios, Jamaica, 1995; mem. exec. com. Consultation on Ch. Union; chmn. Disciples of Christ del., 1974-98, mem. exec. com., mem. gen. bd. Nat. Coun. Chs., 1974-98; co-chmn. Disciples of Christ-Roman Cath. Internat. Bilaterals, 1977-2002; co-chmn. Disciples-Russian Orthodox Internat. Bilateral, co-chmn. Disciples-Reformed Internat. Bilateral, Disciples-Finnish Luth.; gen. sec. Disciples Ecumenical Consultative Coun., 1975-98. Author: Where We Are in

Church Union, 1965, The Ecumenical Movement in Bibliographical Outline, 1965, No Greater Love: The Gospel and Its Imperatives, 1967, Church Union at Mid-Point, 1972, Christian Unity: Matrix for Mission, 1982, The Anatomy of a Nineteenth Century United Church, 1983, The Vision of Christian Unity: Essays in Honor of Paul A. Crow, Jr., 1997; author: (with James Duke) The Church for Disciples of Christ, 1998; contbr. over 300 articles to maj. scholarly jours. and ency.; editor: Mid-Stream: An Ecumenical Jour., 1974—99. Bd. dirs., moderator Ecumenical Inst., Bossey, 1974-83; trustee Disciples of Christ Hist. Soc. Jacobus fellow Hartford Sem. Found., 1958; Recipient Disting. Alumni award Hartford Sem. Found., 1986, Nat Ecumenical Svc. award, 1998, Focolare Internat. Luminos (Light) of Christian Unity award, 1998. Mem. Nat. Assn. Ecumenical Officers (pres. 1988-93), Am. Soc. Ch. History, North Am. Acad. Ecumenists, Societas Oecumenica, Fellowship of St. Alban and St. Sergius, Nassau Club (Princeton, N.J.), Indianapolis Athletic Club, Omicron Delta Kappa, Theta Phi, Pi Kappa Phi. Democrat. Home: 7215 Vauxhall Rd Indianapolis IN 46250-2737 Fax: 317-585-0015.

CROW, SAM ALFRED, judge; b. Topeka, May 5, 1926; s. Samuel Wheadon and Phyllis K. (Brown) Crow; m. Ruth M. Rush, Jan. 30, 1948; children: Sam A., Dan W. BA, U. Kans., 1949; JD, Washburn U., 1952. Ptnr. Rooney, Dickinson, Prager & Crow, Topeka, 1953—63, Dickinson, Crow, Skoog & Honeyman, Topeka, 1963—70; sr. ptnr. Crow & Skoog, Topeka, 1971—75; part-time U.S. magistrate, 1973—75; U.S. magistrate, 1975—81; judge U.S. Dist. Ct. Kans., Wichita, 1981—92, Topeka, 1992—96, sr. judge, 1996—. Bd. rev. Boy Scouts Am., 1960—70, cubmaster, 1957—60; chmn. Kans. March of Dimes, 1959, bd. dirs., 1960—65, Topeka Coun. Chs., 1960—70; mem. Kans. Hist. Soc., 1960—; pres., v.p. PTA; bd. govs. Washburn Law Sch. Alumni Assn., 1993—99; mem. vestry Grace Episcopal Ch., Topeka, 1960—65. Col. JAGC USAR, ret. Named to, Topeka H.S. Hall of Fame, 2000; recipient Washburn U. Sch. Law Disting. Svc. award, 2000. Fellow: Kans. Bar Found.; mem.: ABA (del. Nat. Conf. Spl. Ct. Judges 1978), Topeka Lawyers Club (sec. 1964—65, pres. 1965—66), Wichita Bar Assn., Topeka Bar Assn. (chmn. jud. reform com., chmn. bench and bar com., chmn. criminal law com., Disting. Svc. award 2000), Nat. Assn. U.S. Magistrates (com. discovery abuse), Kans. Trial Lawyers Assn. (sec. 1959—60, pres. 1960—61), Kans. Bar Assn. (chmn. mil. law sect. 1965, 1967, 1970, trustee 1970—76, chmn. mil. law sect. 1972, 1974, 1975), Shawnee Country Club, Shriners, Am. Legion, Sigma Alpha Epsilon, Delta Theta Phi. Office: US Dist Ct 444 SE Quincy St Topeka KS 66683

CROW, SHERYL, singer/songwriter, musician; b. Kennett, Mo., 1963; Degree in classical piano, U. Mo., 1984. Backup singer Bad tour Michael Jackson, 1987; backup singer The End of the Innocence tour Don Henley, 1989; also backup singer George Harrison, Joe Cocker, Stevie Wonder, Rod Stewart; singer, songwriter Tuesday Night Music Club, 1992—. Albums Tuesday Night Music Club, 1993, Sheryl Crow, 1996, The Globe Sessions, 1998, C'mon, C'mon, 2002 (Grammy award best female rock vocal performance, 2003), singles Leaving Las Vegas, All I Wanna Do (Grammy awards for Record of Year and Female Pop Vocal, 1995), Strong Enough, Flesh & Blood, 2002, participant Lilith Fair, 1998, 1999. Recipient Grammy award for Best New Artist, 1995. Address: A&M Records Inc 70 Universal City Plz Universal City CA 91608-1011*

CROW, TODD WILLIAM, pianist; b. Santa Barbara, Calif., July 25, 1945; s. Andrew and Grace (Platt) C.; m. Linda Goolsby; children: Evelyn, Daniel. BA, U. Calif., Santa Barbara, 1967; MS, Juilliard Sch., 1968. Prof. music, chmn. music dept. Vassar Coll., Poughkeepsie, N.Y., 1969—; music dir. Mt. Desert Festival of Chamber Music, Northeast Harbor, Maine, 1996—. Editor: Bartók Studies, 1976; contbr. articles to profl. jours. and The Compleat Brahms, 1999; performed with Composers String Quartet, Concord String Quartet, Brentano String Quartet, Miami String Quartet, Shanghai Quartet, Borromeo String Quartet, St. Luke's Chamber Ensemble and Aspen Wind Quintet; concert pianist appearances in N.Am., S.Am. and Europe, including Met. Mus., N.Y., Avery Fisher Hall, N.Y., Weill Recital Hall, N.Y., Nat. Gallery of Art, Washington, South Bank, London, Concertgebouw, Amsterdam, Bard Music Festival, Casals Festival, Maverick Concerts, Music Mountain; debuts: London, Wigmore Hall, 1975, London orchestral, Barbican Hall with London Phiharmonic, 1986, N.Y., Alice Tully Hall, 1982, New York orchestral Carnegie Hall with Am. Symphony, 1992; chamber music with Walter Trampler, Nathaniel Rosen, Eugene Drucker, David Krakauer, Mark Peskanov, and Benny Goodman; radio broadcasts include BBC, Sta. WQXR, Sta. WNCN, Sta. WNYC; rec. (compact disc) Schubert piano sonatas, Haydn piano sonatas, Berlioz/Liszt Symphonie fantastique, works of S. Taneyev, E. Toch Piano Concerto No. 1 (with NDR Symphony Orch., Hamburg) and (with M. Shuman) complete music for cello and piano by Mendelssohn. Scholarships S. D. Epstein Found., 1958-63, Pillsbury Found., 1967, 68; recipient Disting. Alumni award U. Calif., 1986; winner Young Artists Competition, Santa Barbara Symphony Orch., 1960. Mem. The Liszt Soc. (London).

CROWDER, BARBARA LYNN, judge; b. Mattoon, Ill., Feb. 3, 1956; d. Robert Dale and Martha Elizabeth (Harrison) C.; m. Lawrence Owen Taliana, Apr. 17, 1982; children: Paul Joseph, Robert Lawrence, Benjamin Owen. BA, U. Ill., 1978, JD, 1981. Bar: Ill. 1981. Assoc. Louis E. Olivero, Peru, Ill., 1981-82; asst. state's atty. Madison County, Edwardsville, Ill., 1982-84; ptnr. Robbins & Crowder, Edwardsville, Ill., 1985-87, Robbins, Crowder & Bader, Edwardsville, Ill., 1987-88, Crowder, Taliana, Rubin, and Buckley, Ill., 1988-98; assoc. judge 3d. Jud. Cir. Madison County, Ill., 1999—; presiding judge family divsn. 3d. Jud. Cir. Madison County, Ill., 2000—01, 2003—. Spkr. C.L.E. seminars Family Law Update, 1993—, 2003; co-chair 3d. Jud. Cir. Family Violence Coord. Coun., 1999—, chair ct. com., 1999—; spkr. edn. Conf. Adminstrn. Office Ill. Ct., 2002—03; mem. Spl. Supreme Ct. Com. on Child Custody Issues, Ill., 2002—03. Co-author chpts. in ISBA Family Law Handbook, 1995, Maintenance Chapter Ill. Family Law Ill. Inst. Continuing Legal Edn., 1998, supplement, 2001; contbr. articles to profl. jours. Chmn. City of Edwardsville Zoning Bd. Appeals, 1986-87; committee woman Edwardsville De, Precinct 15, 1986-98; mem. City of Edwardsville Planning Commn., 1985-87; bd. dirs. Madison-Bond County Workforce Devel. Bd., 1995-96, 96-97. Named Best Oral Advocate, Moot Ct. Bd., 1979, Outstanding Young Career Woman, Dist. XIV, Ill. Bus. and Profl. Women, 1986; recipient Alice Paul award Alton-Edwardsville NOW, 1987, Outstanding Working Woman of Ill. Ill. Fed. of Bus. and Profl. Women, 1988-89, Woman of Achievement YWCA, 1996; recipient Athena award Edwardsville/Glen Carbon C. of C., 1991. Fellow Am. Acad. Matrimonial Lawyers; mem. Ill. Bar Assn. (family law coun. sect. 1990-99, chair 1997-98, co-editor Family Law newsletter 1993, vice chair 1996-97, mem. Bench and Bar sect. coun. 2002-2003, 2003—), Ill. Judges' Assn. (bd. dirs. 2000—), Am. Judicature Soc., Ill. Fedn. Bus. and Profl. Women (parliamentaria dist. XIV 1991-92), Women Lawyers Assn. Met. East (pres. 1986), Edwardsville Bus. and Profl Women's Club (pres. 1988-89, 95-96, treas. 1989-90, Woman of Achievement award 1985, Jr. Svc. award 1987), U. Ill. Alumni Assn. (v.p. met.-east club 1994-95, bd. dirs. 1995-97). Democrat. Office: Madison County Cthse 155 N Main St Edwardsville IL 62025-1955

CROWDER, BONNIE WALTON, small business owner, composer; b. Lafayette, Tenn., Apr. 14, 1916; d. Edward Samuel Bailey and Nannie Elizabeth (Goad) Walton; m. Reggie Ray Crowder, Nov. 19, 1936; 1 child, Rita Faye. Grad., Nashville Beauty Coll. Owner, operator Bonnie's Beauty Salon, Tampa, Fla. Composer: A Man of Faith, 1988, This Miracle, 1988; (with Willard E. Walton) God Bless Our President, 1988, Awake, Arise America, 1989, Touching My Jesus, 1990, (with W.E. Walton) Muscle Jerky Boogie, 1992. Active ch. choir, Tampa; mem. Bus. and Profl. Women's Chorus, 1960-70's, U. South Fla. Cmty. Chorus, 1973-81. Mem. Beta Sigma Phi. Home: 266 Oak Knob Rd Lafayette TN 37083-4137

CROWDER, HENRY ALVIN, military officer; b. Panama City, Fla., Aug. 30, 1953; s. Henry Ford and Margaret Ann (Bland) Crowder; m. Beth Marie Burlingame, Apr. 16, 1977; children: Heather Elizabeth, Jeremy Allen. Grad. high sch., Beckley, W.Va.; student, various univs., 1975-94, various mil. edn. programs; grad., U. Md., 1995. Enlisted U.S. Army, 1974, advanced through grades to chief warrant officer 4, 1995; order of battle analyst 502d Army Security Agy. Group, Augsburg, Germany, 1974-75; combat intelligence analyst 856th ASA Co. 3d Armored Div., Frankfurt, Germany, 1975-77; intelligence analyst, hdqrs. U.S. Army Field Arty. Ctr. and Sch., Ft. Sill, Okla., 1977-79; non-commd. officer in charge intelligence ctr. 2d M.I. 2d Inf. Div., Republic of Korea, 1979-80; team non-commd. officer in charge intelligence prodn. 504th M.I. Group III Corps, Ft. Hood, Tex., 1980-81; order of battle technician 9th Inf. Div., Ft. Lewis, Wash., 1981-84, 1st Armored Div., Ansbach, Germany, 1984-87; all source intelligence technician 513th Mil. Intelligence Bridgade/3rd U.S. Army/U.S. Forces Cen. Command, Ft. Monmouth, NJ, 1987-90; sr. all source intelligence technician Ops. Desert Shield, Desert Storm U.S. Army ARCENT/U.S. Forces CENTCOM, Saudi Arabia, 1990-91; sr. all source intelligence technician 513th Intel Support Element/3d U.S. Army/U.S. Forces CENTCOM, Ft. McPherson, Ga., 1991-96; ops. officer Advanced Studies Br. U.S. Army Warrant Officer Career Ctr., Ft. Rucker, Ala., 1996-97; chief joint intel support element Spl. Ops. Commd. Ctrl., MacDill AFB, Fla., 1997-2000; ops. officer Desert Thunder, Desert Fox, Kuwait, 1998-99; chief current intel sect. ARCENT CFLCC Hdqs., Fort McPherson, 2000—01, spl. ops. Operation Enduring Freedom, 2001—02, spl. projects Operation Iraqi Freedom, 2002—03. Asst. pack leader, asst. scoutmaster, active Atlanta coun. Order of Arrow Boy Scouts Am. Decorated Bronze Star; named one of Outstanding Young Men of Am., U.S. Jaycees, 1982. Mem.: U.S. Army Warrant Officers Assn. (sec. Ansbach chpt. 1984—87, ways and means chmn. Jersey Shore-Ft. Monmouth chpt. 1989—91, greater Atlanta chpt. 1992—96, pres. Ft. Rucker chpt. 1996—97). Office: US Army Ctrl Command 3d Army HQ AFRD CW4 Crowder 1881 Hardee Ave SW Fort Mcpherson GA 30330

CROWDER, LENA BELLE, retired special education educator; b. Winston-Salem, N.C., Apr. 4, 1931; d. Henry Lee and Janie (Woods) Thomas; m. Raymond Crowder, June 12, 1954; 1 child, Rayonette Janease. BS in Edn., Winston Salem State U., 1952; MS in Edn., Agrl. and Tech. Coll., 1959. Cert. elem. edn. tchr., N.C. Tchr. 1st grade Early County Sch. Sys., Blakely, Ga., 1953-56; tchr. kindergarten Thomas-Anderson Kindergarten, Winston-Salem, 1956-57, 58-60, 61-62; tchr. 1st grade Beaufort (S.C.) County Schs., 1957-58; tchr. Chapel Hill (N.C.) City Sch. System, 1960-61, Forsyth County Sch. System, Winston-Salem, 1961-62, 1962-67, Winston-Salem/Forsyth County Schs., 1967-93, ret., 1993. Precinct election recorder Winston-Salem/Forsyth County Election Bd., 1961; fin. sec. Mt. Zion Bapt. Ch. Sunday Sch., Winston Salem, 1977—; supporter Crisis Control Ministry, Winston-Salem, 1982—; participant neighborhood watch system Winston-Salem Police Dept.; chair sch. involvement projects ARC, 1991-92. Mem. NEA, Nat. Assn. Univ. Women, Coun. Exceptional Children, Nat. Women of Achievement (rec. sec. S.E. region 2000, S.E. bd. dirs., Winston-Salem bd. dirs.), Assn. Classroom Tchrs. Democrat. Home: 1140 Rich Ave Winston Salem NC 27101-3432

CROWDER, MARJORIE BRIGGS, lawyer; b. Shreveport, La., Mar. 26, 1946; d. Rowland Edmund and Marjorie Ernestine (Biles) Crowder; m. Ronald J. Briggs, July 11, 1970 (div. Nov. 2000); children: Sarah Briggs, Andrew Briggs. BA, Carson-Newman Coll., 1968; MA, Ohio State U., 1969, JD, 1975. Bar: Ohio 1975, U.S. Ct. Appeals (6th cir.) 1983, U.S. Ct. Claims 1992, U.S. Supreme Ct. 2001. Asst. dean of women Albion Coll., Mich., 1969-70; dir. residence hall Ohio State U., Columbus, 1970-71, acad. counselor, 1971-72; assoc. Porter, Wright, Morris, Arthur, Columbus, 1975—83, ptnr., 1983-2000; AmeriCorps atty. Southeastern Ohio Legal Svs., Portsmouth, Ohio, 2000—02, staff atty., 2002—. Legal aide Cmty. Law Office, Columbus, 1973—74. Co-author: (book) Going to Trial, A Step-By-Step Guide to Trial Practice and Procedure, 1989. Trustee, pres. Epilepsy Assn. Ctrl. Ohio, Columbus, 1977—84; bd. dirs. Scioto County Domestic Violence Task Force, v.p., 2001—; bd. dirs. Action Ohio Coalition Battered Women, 2002—, Columbus Speech & Hearing, 1977—82. Fellow: Columbus Bar Found. (trustee 1993—95); mem.: Scioto County Bar Assn., Columbus Bar Assn. (com. chmn. 1979—83, docket control task force 1989—91, editor 1981—83), ABA (mem. gavel awards com. 1989—96, gen. practice sect. 1983—, chair litig. com. 1987—89, mem. exec. coun. 1989—93, dir. bus. com. group 1990—91, chair program com. 1991—93, torts and ins. practice sect. 1993—, vice chair health ins. law com. 1993—96), Ohio Bar Assn. (mem. joint task force gender fairness 1991—93), Scioto County Bar Assn. Home: 2106 Summit St Portsmouth OH 45662 Office: Southeastern Ohio Legal Svcs 800 Gallia St Ste 700 Portsmouth OH 45662-4035 E-mail: mcrowder@oslsa.org.

CROWDER, MARY THELMA, obstetrician/gynecologist; b. Durham, N.C., Feb. 28, 1960; d. Thomas Harold and Thelma Cole (Barclift) C.; m. William Reed Paden; children: step daughter: Sarah Elizabeth Paden; children: William Thomas Paden, ANdrew Reed Paden. AB, Duke U., Durham, N.C., 1982; MD, U. Va., Charlottesville, 1986. Cert. obstetrician/gynecologist, 1992-02. Intern Lenox Hill Hosp., N.Y.C., 1986-87; MD Presbyn. Hosp., Charlotte, N.C., 1990—. Mem. AMA, Am. Coll. Obstetricians/Gynecologists, N.C. Obstetricians/Gynecologists Soc., N.C. Med. Soc. Office: Bradford Clin 150 Providence Rd Charlotte NC 28207-1218 Fax: 704-384-1242.

CROWDER, REBECCA BYRUM, music educator, elementary school educator; b. Suffolk, Va., Apr. 27, 1951; d. Joseph Etheridge and Jane Carroll Byrum; m. Melvin Linnwood Crowder, July 19, 1997. BS in Music Edn., Radford U., 1973, MS in Music Edn., 1976. Cert. music tchr. grades K-12, tchr. grades 4-7. Profl. musician, 1973—; music tchr. East Salem Elem., Salem, Va., 1973—78; music dir. Colonial Ave. Bapt., Roanoke, Va., 1973—79; music tchr. Andrew Lewis Jr. High, Salem, 1979—83, Salem High and Glenvar High, Salem, 1983—84, Glenvar High, Salem, 1984—90, Oak Grove Elem., Roanoke, 1990—. Music tchr. Hollins U., Roanoke, 2000; pianist, accompanist Colonial Ave. Bapt., Roanoke, 1963—79, Shady Grove Bapt., Thaxton, 1979—92, First Bapt., Roanoke, 1992—97, Salem Ch. of Christ, 1997—. Mem.: Music Educators Nat. Conf., Va. Congress Parents and Tchrs., Phi Kappa Phi. Avocations: ballroom dancing, reading, playing piano, crossword puzzles, singing. Home: 1606 Mountain Hgts Dr Salem VA 24153

CROWDER, RICHARD MORGAN, pilot; b. Wurzburg, Bavaria, Germany, July 22, 1963; (parents Am. citizens); s. Richard Thomas and Margaret Taylor (Rainey) C. BS, U. Minn., 1986; postgrad., U. Colo., 1995-96. Capt., pilot Classic Aviation, Mpls., 1985-87; pilot Air South, Homestead, Fla., 1987, AVAir, Raleigh, N.C., 1987-88, Am. Eagle, Dallas, 1988-89, USAir, Arlington, Va., 1989-92, United Airlines, Chgo., 1992—. Republican. Methodist. Avocations: reading, running, bible study, trap shooting, foreign travel.

CROWDUS, GARY ALAN, film company executive; b. Lexington, Ky., Jan. 2, 1945; s. Charles Dallas and Bess May (Rice) C. BFA, NYU Inst. Film and TV, 1969. Founding editor Cineaste mag., N.Y.C., 1967—; assoc. editor Film Society Review, N.Y.C., 1968-72; v.p. Tricontinental Film Ctr., N.Y.C., 1972-79, Unifilm Inc., N.Y.C., 1979-80; gen. mgr. The Cinema Guild, Inc., N.Y.C., 1981—. Mem. U.S. Conf. on Alternative Cinema, N.Y.C., 1978-79; mem. internat. adv. com. Internat. Documentary Film Week, 1989. Co-author: (with others) Quinze de Cinema Mondial, 1975, The Documentary Tradition, 1979, The Cineaste Interviews, 1983, New Challenges for Documentary, 1988, Film and Politics in the Third World, 1988, Celluloid Power: Social Film Criticism from The Birth of a Nation to Judgement at Nuremberg, 1992, The Political Companion to American Film, 1994, The Cineaste Interviews, Vol. 2, 2002. Mem. Assn. Ind. Video and Filmmakers, Internat. Documentary Assn. Home: 116 Saint Marks Pl Apt 8 New York NY 10009-5856 Office: The Cinema Guild 130 Madison Ave Fl 2 New York NY 10016-7038 also: Cineaste Mag Art Politics Cinema 304 Hudson St New York NY 10013

CROWE, CAMERON, screenwriter, film director; b. Palm Springs, Calif., July 13, 1957; Student, Calif. State U., San Diego. Writer Rolling Stone mag., N.Y.C. Scripts include Fast Times at Ridgemont High, 1982, The Wild Life, 1984; screenwriter, dir.: Say Anything, 1989, Singles, 1992, Jerry Maguire, 1996; actor: American Hot Wax, 1978; creative cons.: (TV series) Fast Times, 1986. Office: care Columbia Tristar 10202 Washington Blvd Culver City CA 90232-3119

CROWE, CAMERON MACMILLAN, chemical engineering educator; b. Montreal, Que., Can., Oct. 6, 1931; s. Ernest Watson and Marianne (Macmillan) C.; m. Jean Margaret Gilbertson, Feb. 15, 1969. Student, Royal Mil. Coll., 1948-52; B.Eng., McGill U., 1953; PhD, Cambridge (Eng.) U., 1957. Sr. devel. engr. DuPont of Can., Maitland, Ont., 1957-59; mem. faculty dept. chem. engring. McMaster U., Hamilton, Ont., 1959—, assoc. prof., 1964-70, prof., 1970-96, prof. emeritus, 1996—, chmn. dept., 1971-74. Author: (with others) Chemical Plant Simulation, 1971; Assoc. editor: Canadian Jour. Chem. Engring, 1975-81. C.D. Howe Meml. fellow Rice U., Houston, 1967-68; Athlone fellow, 1953-55 Fellow Chem. Inst. Can.; mem. Am. Inst. Chem. Engrs., Can. Soc. Chem. Engring. (bd. dirs. 1984-87, v.p. 1990-91, pres. 1991-92). Home: 821 Glenwood Ave Burlington ON Canada L7T 2J8 Office: Chem Engring Dept McMaster U Hamilton ON Canada L8S 4L7

CROWE, DANIEL WALSTON, lawyer; b. Visalia, Calif., July 1, 1940; s. J. Thomas and Wanda (Walston) C.; m. Nancy V. Berard, May 10, 1969; children: Daniel W., Karyn Louise, Thomas Dwight. BA, U. Santa Clara, 1962; JD, U. Calif. Hastings Coll. Law, 1965. Bar: Calif. 1966, U.S. Dist. Ct. (ea. dist.) Calif. 1969, U.S. Dist. Ct. (cen. dist.) Calif. 1973, U.S. Ct. Appeals (9th cir.) 1973, U.S. Supreme Ct. 1973. Assoc. Crowe, Mitchell & Crowe, and predecessors, Visalia, Calif., 1968-74, ptnr., 1974-83; ptnr. Crowe, Williams, Jordan and Richey and predecessor firm Crowe & Williams, 1975-90, The Crowe Law Offices, 1991—; sec., treas., dir. The Exeter Devel. Co., 1969-84, Willson Ranch Co., 1983—2001. Founding mem., dir. Visalia Balloon Assn., Inc. Served to capt. U.S. Army, 1965-68. Decorated Bronze Star, Air medal, Purple Heart, Nat. Def. Svc. medal. Mem. ABA, Calif. Bar Assn., Tulare County Bar Assn., NRA, Rotary, Elks, Moose, Am. Radio Relay League, DAV. Address: PO Box 1110 Visalia CA 93279-1110

CROWE, DON RAYMOND, music educator, consultant; s. William Francis and Sue Carithers Crowe; m. Linda Delaine Callans, June 16, 1990; 1 child, Susanna Colleen. MusB in Music Edn., Furman U., 1972—76; MusM in Music Theory, Fla. State U., 1976—77; Mus D in Music Edn., Wind Conducting, U. of Ariz., 1987—89. Band dir. Woodmont H.S., Greenville, SC, 1977—80, Gainesville H.S., Ga., 1982—86; asst. prof. S.W. Bapt. U., 1989—93, Ball State U., 1994—95; assoc. prof. S.D. State U., 1995—. Mem.: S.D. Bandmasters Assn., S.D. Music Educators Assn. (bd. dirs. 1997—2000, pres. 2000—02), Nat. Assn. for Music Edn. (state pres. 2000—02), Rotary Internat., Phi Beta Kappa, Phi Mu Alpha, Pi Kappa Phi, Phi Beta Mu. Office: SD State U PO Box 2212 Brookings SD 57007 Office Fax: 605-688-4307. E-mail: don_crowe@sdstate.edu.

CROWE, EDITH LOUISE, librarian; b. Buffalo, N.Y., Nov. 12, 1947; d. Harold Peter and Edith Louise (Robinson) C. BA in Art History with honors, SUNY, Buffalo, 1970; MLS, SUNY, Geneseo, 1971; MA in Humanities, Calif. State U., Dominguez Hills, 1980. Libr. San Jose (Calif.) State U., 1971-75, 77—, Calif. State U., Hayward, 1976-77. Book reviewer Art Documentation, 1988—. Contbr. articles to profl. jours. Mem. ALA, Nat. Women's Studies Assn., Art Librs. Soc. (chair No. Calif. chpt. 1982-83, 93), Mythopoeic Soc. (exec. bd. 1998—), Phi Beta Kappa. Democrat. Avocations: illustration, creative writing. Office: San Jose State U King Libr 1 Washington Sq San Jose CA 95192-0028

CROWE, JAMES JOSEPH, lawyer; b. New Castle, Pennsylvania, June 9, 1935; s. William J. and Anna M. (Dickson) C.; m. Joan D. (Verba), Dec. 26, 1959. BA, Youngstown State U., 1958; JD, Georgetown U., 1963. Bar: Va. 1963, Ohio 1966. Atty. SEC, Washington, 1964-65, Gen. Tire and Rubber Co., Akron, Ohio, 1965-68; sr. atty. Eaton Corp., Cleve., 1968-72; sec. gen. counsel U.S. Shoe Corp., Cin., 1972-95, v.p., 1975-95; ptnr. Kepley, Gilligan, and Eyrich, Cin., 1996-2000; counsel Thompson Hine LLP, Cin., 2001—. Chmn. divsn. Fine Arts Fund, 1976; trustee Springer Ednl. Found., 1978-84, Cin. Music Festival Assn., 1980-86, 96—2003; group chmn. United Appeal, 1980; mem. pres. coun. Coll. Mt. St. Joseph, 1985-88; trustee Tennis for Charity Inc., 1986—, Playhouse in the Park, 1990-96, Greater Cin. Ctr. for Econ. Edn., 1992-96, Leadership Cin., Class XIV, 1990-91; trustee Cin. Nature Ctr., 1993-2000, chmn. 1996-98; bd. visitors U. Cin. Coll. Law, 1993-2002; trustee Invest in Neighborhoods, 1982-89, pres. 1984-86; trustee Cin. Hort. Soc., 1996-2002, Am. Music Scholarship Assn., 1999—. 2d lt. U.S. Army, 1958-59. Mem. Ohio Bar Assn., Cin. Bar Assn., Am. Soc. Corp. Secs., Cin. Country Club, Met. Club, Univ. Club. E-mail: jcrowe7246@aol.com.

CROWE, JAMES QUELL, communications executive; b. Camp Pendleton, Calif., July 2, 1949; s. Henry Pierson and Mona (Quell) C.; m. Pamela L. Powell, June 20, 1986; children: Sterling, Angela, James Michael. BS in Mech. Engring., Rensselaer Poly. Inst., 1972; MBA, Pepperdine U., 1982. Project engr. Cozzolino Constrn. Co., Port of Albany, N.Y., 1971-73; ind., cons. engr. Albany, 1973-74; engr. Morrison-Knudsen, Saratoga, N.Y., 1974-75, project engr. Washington, 1975-76, project mgr. various cities, 1976-80, v.p. ops. Boise, 1980-83, group v.p. power, 1983-86; pres. Kiewit Indsl. Co., Omaha, 1986—. Chmn., CEO MFS Comms. Co., Inc., Omaha, 1988-97; chmn. WorldCom, Inc., 1997; CEO, dir. Level 3 Comms., Inc., 1997—. Mem. Am. Nuclear Soc.

CROWE, JOHN ALBERT, JR., surgeon; b. Cartersville, Ga., June 21, 1939; s. John Albert Sr. and Laura (Sanford) C.; m. Gail Ellyn Drake, June 26, 1970. BS, Valdosta State Coll., 1963; MD, Med. Coll. Ga., 1967. Diplomate Am. Bd. Surgery. Intern U. Hosp., Augusta, Ga., 1967-68; resident surgery Med. Coll. Ga. Hosps., 1968-72; chief of surgery Little Rock AFB, Jacksonville, 1972-74; surgeon VA Med. Ctr., Salisbury, N.C. Fellow ACS, Southeastern Surg. Congress; mem. Soc. Am. Gastrointestinal Endoscopic Surgeons. Republican. Baptist. Office: VA Med Ctr 1601 Brenner Ave Salisbury NC 28144-2515

CROWE, JOHN T. lawyer; b. Cabin Cove, Calif., Aug. 14, 1938; s. J. Thomas and Wanda (Walston) C.; m. Marina Protopapa, Dec. 28, 1968; 1 child, Erin Aleka. BA, U. Santa Clara, 1960, JD, 1962. Bar: Calif. 1962, U.S. Dist. Ct. (ea. dist.) Calif. 1967. Lawyer, Visalia, Calif., 1964—; ptnr. Crowe, Mitchell & Crowe, 1971-85. Bd. dirs. Willson Ranch Co., pres. 1997—; referee State Bar Ct., 1976-82; gen. counsel Sierra Wine, 1986-96. Bd. dirs. Mt. Whitney Area coun. Boy Scouts Am., 1966-85, pres., 1971-72, bd. dirs. Sequoia coun., 2003—; bd. dirs. Visalia Associated In-Group Donors (now United Way Tulare County), 1973-81, pres., 1978-79; bd. dirs. Tulare County Libr. Found., 1997—; mem. Visalia Airport Commn., 1982-90; Army Res. Forces Policy Com., 1995-99, chmn., 1997-99. 1st lt. U.S. Army, 1962-64, maj. gen. Res., 1964-99. Decorated DSM with oak leaf cluster, Legion of Merit with oak leaf cluster, Meritorious Svc. medal with 3 oak leaf clusters, Army Commendation medal; named Young Man of Yr., Visalia, 1973; Senator Jr. Chamber Internat., 1970; recipient Silver Beaver award Boy Scouts Am., 1983, Rudder medal Assn. U.S. Army, 1999; named to Sr. Army Res. Comdrs. Assn. Hall of Fame, 2003. Mem. ABA, Tulare County Bar Assn., Nat. Assn. R.R. Trial Counsel, State Bar Calif., Assn. U.S. Army (bd. dirs. 2000—, No. Calif. state pres. 2001--), Visalia C. of C. (pres. 1979-80), Rotary (pres. 1980-81), Visalia Country Club. Republican. Roman Catholic. Home: 3939 W School Ave Visalia CA 93291-5514

CROWE, KENNETH CHARLES, writer; b. N.Y.C., Aug. 19, 1934; s. William F. and Loretta (Connolly) C.; m. Rae Lord, Sept. 8, 1956; children: Kenneth C. II, Roy, Daniel, Carol Crowe Hattler. B in English, Fordham U., 1956. Reporter Daily Bulletin, Endicott, N.Y., 1958-60, Herald Jour., Syracuse, N.Y., 1960-63; labor writer Newsday, Melville, N.Y., 1963-99. Author: America For Sale, 1978, Collision, 1993. Sgt. U.S. Army, 1956-58. Mem. reporting team at Newsday that won the 1970 Pulitzer prize; recipient John Commerford award N.Y. Labor History Assn., N.Y.C., 1994; Alicia Patterson fellow Alicia Patterson Found., Washington, 1974. Mem. Author's Guild, Silurians, W.B Yeats Soc. N.Y. Democrat. Roman Catholic. Home: 37 E Lyons St Melville NY 11747-1121 E-mail: kencrowe@optonline.net.

CROWE, LINDA K. speech pathology/audiology services professional, educator; d. George A. Smith and Anna L. Martin; m. James L. Crowe, Dec. 27, 1970; children: James Jeffry, Laurie Ann. AA, Trenton Jr. Coll., 1973; BS in Elem. Edn. magna cum laude, S.E. Mo. State U., 1978; MS in Speech Pathology, U. Nebr., 1986; PhD in Comm. Scis. and Disorders, La. State U., 1996. Cert. tchr. Mo. State Bd. Edn., 1978, lic. speech-lang. pathology Kans. Dept. Health and Environment, 1999. Elem. tchr. Nebr. Pub. Schs., Valparaiso and Wahoo, 1980—83, speech-language pathologist Seward and Milford, 1986—92; clin. instr., asst. lab. La. State U., Baton Rouge, 1992—93; instr. U. Nebr., Lincoln, 1993—97; asst. prof. St. Louis U., 1997—99, Kans. State U., Manhattan, 1999—. Adj. instr. Concordia U., Seward, Nebr., 1989—92; cons., project mgr. Cmty. Devel. Inst., Liberty, Mo., 2002—02; presenter in field. Author: (book) The Source for Early Literacy Development, (manual) Language Intervention Tool Kit; editl. cons.: Am. Jour. Speech-Lang. Pathology, Jour. Speech, Lang., Hearing Rsch.; contbr. articles to profl. jours. Grantee Rsch. Tng. Inst., Am. Speech-Lang. Hearing Assn. & Thomas Jefferson U. Ctr. for Collaborative Rsch., 1999, Kans. State U., 1999, 2000; Beaumont Faculty Devel. grantee, St. Louis U., 1998. Mem.: Nebr. Speech-Lang. Hearing Assn.

(co-chair nominations com. 1988—90, sec. 1995—97), Am. Speech-Lang. Hearing Assn. (cert. clin. competence 1987, adv. bd. mem. IDEA Part C 2000, award for continuing edn. 2000), Sertoma Internat. (exec. bd. mem. 2002—03), Phi Kappa Phi. Achievements include research in Factors Impacting Language and Literacy Development. Office: Kansas State Univ Sch FSHS 317 Justin Hall Manhattan KS 66506-1403 Office Fax: 785-532-5505. E-mail: lcrowe@ksu.edu.

CROWE, ROBERT ALAN, lawyer; b. N.Y.C., Feb. 20, 1950; s. John Thomas and Annette (Korall) C.; m. Carolyn Ann Kruse, Apr. 14, 1974; children: Emily, Andrew. AB, St. Louis U., 1971, JD, 1974. Bar: Mo. 1974, U.S. Dist. Ct. Mo. 1975, U.S. Ct. Appeals (8th cir.) 1976, U.S. Ct. Appeals (7th cir.) 1977, U.S. Supreme Ct. 1977. Assoc. Law Office of Harry J. Nichols, St. Louis, 1974-76; sole practice St. Louis, 1976-83; ptnr. Kell, Kell, Custer, Weller & Crowe, St. Louis, 1983-85, Crowe & Shanahan, St. Louis, 1985—. Mem. editl. adv. bd. West's Social Security Reporting Service, 1983—; pres. U.S. Arbitration and Mediation Midwest, St. Louis, 1985-. Mem. ABA, Mo. Bar Assn., Bar Assn. Met. St. Louis, Nat. Orgn. Social Security Claimants Reps. (exec. com. 1984-92, treas. 1986-87, sec. 1987-88, v.p. 1988-89, pres. 1989-90). Home: 1101 Hawken Pl Saint Louis MO 63119-3911 Office: Crowe & Shanahan 720 Olive St Ste 2020 Saint Louis MO 63101-2317 E-mail: racrowe@crowe-shanahan.com.

CROWE, ROBERT WILLIAM, lawyer, mediator; b. Chgo., Aug. 20, 1924; s. Harry James and Miriam (McCune) C.; m. Virginia C. Kelley, Mar. 25, 1955 (dec. Feb. 1976); children— Robert Kelley, William Park; m. Elizabeth F. Roenisch, Oct. 22, 1977. AB, U. Chgo., 1948, JD, 1949. Bar: Ill. 1949. Practice in, Chgo., 1949-57; with R.R. Donnelley & Sons Co., Chgo., 1957-83, sec., 1965-83, v.p., 1970-83; chmn. Resolve Dispute Mgmt. Inc., Chgo., 1983-92; pres. Dearborn Inst. for Conflict Resolution, Chgo., 1992-94. Dir. Peoria Jour. Star, Inc., 1972-95. Bd. dirs. Chgo. Child Care Soc., 1963—; trustee Christian Century Found., 1966— ; vis. com. U. Chgo. Divinity Sch. Served to 1st lt. USAAF, 1943-45. Decorated Air medal with 5 oak leaf clusters. Mem. ABA, Chgo. Bar Assn., Lawyers Club Chgo., Econ. Club (Chgo.), Univ. Club (Chgo.). Presbyterian. Home and Office: 1228 Westmoor Rd Winnetka IL 60093-1845 E-mail: RWCROWE@aol.com. *Cultivate a sense of gratitude as an approach to all of life, for the gift of life itself and for the potential for finding something joyful, empowering or at least instructive in every circumstance. These are the seeds for sharing the best of one's life with others.*

CROWE, RUSSELL, actor; b. Wellington, New Zealand, Apr. 7, 1964; m. Danielle Spencer, Apr. 7, 2003. Appeared in films The Crossing, 1993, The Quick and the Dead, 1995, Proof, 1995, Romper Stomper, 1995, Rough Magic, 1995, Virtuosity, 1995, Under the Gun, 1995, Heaven's Burning, 1997, Breaking Up, 1997, L.A. Confidential, 1997, Mystery Alaska, 1999, The Insider, 1999, Gladiator, 2000 (Acad. award for best actor), Proof of Life, 2000, A Beautiful Mind, 2001 (Golden Globe award for best actor, 2002, Screen Actors Guild award for best actor, 2001). Recipient Global Achievement award, Australian Film Inst., 2001. Office: ICM 8942 Wilshire Blvd Beverly Hills CA 90211 Address: c/o Shirley Pearce Bedford & Pearce Mgmt Party Ltd 2/263-269 Alfred St North Sydney 2060 Australia*

CROWE, SHELBY, educational specialist, consultant; b. Irvine, Ky., July 5, 1935; s. Claude and Lena (Clem) C.; m. Ina House, May 22, 1961 (div. 1977); children: Craig, Cara; m. Bonnie Wohlslagel, Aug. 6, 1977; children: Tyler, Trisha, Matthew. BA in Edn., Ea. Ky. U., 1958; MEd, Miami U., Oxford, Ohio, 1961; PhD in Ednl. Founds., Ohio State U., 1980. Cert. permanent spl. K-12 art edn. tchr., Ohio. Tchr. Cin. Pub. Schs., 1958-66; tchr. McGuffey Lab. Sch. Miami U., Oxford, Ohio, 1966-70; prof. edn. Wright State U., Dayton, Ohio, 1970-88, U. Dayton, 1988-90; ednl. specialist Dorothy Lane Markets, Dayton, 1990—. Cooperating tchr. U. Cin., 1960-66; instr. Ohio U., 1966; instr. Morehead (Ky.) State U., summers 1964-65; adj. prof. Union for Experimenting Colls. and Univs., Cin., 1982; condr. insvc. workshops, presenter in field local, regional, state and nat. level. Contbr. book revs. to various publs. Recipient Tchg. Excellence award Wright State U. Coll. Edn., 1981, 82, Wright State U. Alumni Assn., 1982, Faculty Mem. of Yr. award Wright State U. Student Govt., 1985, Mem. NEA, ASCD, AAUP, Nat. Coun. for Scoial Studies Edn., Ohio Confedn. Tchr. Edn. Orgns., Ohio Edn. Assn., Nat. Art Edn. Assn. (Students Best Educator award 1973), Ohio Art Edn. Assn., Phi Delta Kappa. Home: 412 Corona Ave Dayton OH 45419-2605

CROWE, THOMAS LEONARD, lawyer; b. Amsterdam, N.Y., Aug. 3, 1944; s. Leonard Hector and Grace Agnes (O'Malley) C.; m. Barbara Ann Hauck, Aug. 2, 1969; children: Patrick, Brendan. AB, Georgetown U., 1966, JD, 1969. Law clk. to chief judge U.S. Dist. Ct. (no. dist.), Elkins, W.Va., 1969-70; trial atty. U.S. Dept. Justice, Washington, 1970-72; asst. U.S. atty. Balt., 1973-78; chief of criminal divsn. U.S. Atty.'s Office, Balt., 1977-78; ptnr. Cable, McDaniel, Bowie & Bond, Balt., 1979-91, McGuire, Woods, Battle & Boothe, Balt., 1991-95; of counsel Monshower & Miller, LLP, Columbia, Md., 1996-98; pvt. practice Balt., 1998—. Mem. jud. conf. U.S. Ct. Appeals for 4th Cir. Fellow Md. Bar Found.; mem. Fed. Bar Assn. (pres. Balt. chpt. 1981-82), Md. Bar Assn., Barristers Club (pres. 1990-91),. Democrat. Roman Catholic. Home: 11 Osborne Ave Baltimore MD 21228-4935 Office: Law Offices of Thomas L Crowe 1622 The World Trade Ctr 401 E Pratt St Baltimore MD 21202-3117

CROWE, VIRGINIA MARY, retired librarian; b. Meadville, Pa., Mar. 8, 1933; d. Harold Augustus and Daisy Lee (Ervin) Shartle; m. Robert William Crowe, Mar. 22, 1951; children: Thomas Robert, David William, Steven Michael. BS in Edn., Edinboro U. of Pa., 1965; MLS, U. Pitts., 1967, PhD, 1973. Elem. sch. librarian Saegertown (Pa.) Area Schs., 1965, Gen. McLane Sch. System, Edinboro, 1965-67, sec. sch. librarian, 1967-68; asst. prof. libr. sci. Edinboro Univ. of Pa., 1968-72, dept. chair of libr. sci. and assoc. prof., 1972-82; asst. dir. outreach svcs. U. Libr. Svcs., Va. Commonwealth U., Richmond, 1982-83, assoc. dir. for pub. svcs., 1983-87; dean libr. and media svcs Shippensburg U. of Pa., 1987-95; ret., 1995. Adj. faculty Cath. U. Am., Washington, 1984-87; cons. Weston Woods Studios, Conn., 1980-85. Contbr. articles to profl. jours. Pres. Venango (Pa.) Borough Coun., 1973-79; dir. Cambridge Springs Joint Sch. Bd., 1958-69; trustee Venango Pub. Libr., 1975-80. U.S. Office of Edn. grantee, 1975, 77, 79. Mem. ALA, Pa. Libr. Assn., State System of Higher Edn. Librs. Coun. (chair 1989-91). Home: 499 Hartz Ave Meadville PA 16335-1326

CROWE, WILLIAM JAMES, JR., educator, international consultant; b. La Grange, Ky., Jan. 2, 1925; s. William James and Eula (Russell) C.; m. Shirley Mary Grennell, Feb. 14, 1954; children: William Blake, James Brent, Mary Russell. BS, U.S. Naval Acad., 1946; MA in Edn., Stanford U., 1956; PhD in Politics (Harold W. Dodds fellow), Princeton U., 1965. Commd. ensign U.S. Navy, 1946, advanced through grades to adm.; comdg. officer U.S.S. Trout, 1960-62; comdr. Submarine Div. 31 San Diego, 1966-67; sr. adviser Vietnamese Navy, 1970-71; dep. to Pres.'s Spl. Rep. for Micronesian Status Negotiations, 1971-73; dep. dir. strategic plans CNO Staff, 1973-75; dir. East Asia and Pacific region Office of Sec. of Def. Washington, until 1976; comdr. Middle East Force Bahrain, 1976-77; dep. chief naval ops. plans and policy Washington, 1977 80; comdr.-in-chief Allied Forces So. Europe, 1980-83; comdr.-in-chief Pacific, 1983-85; chmn. Joint Chiefs of Staff, 1985-89; prof. geopolitics U. Okla., Norman, 1989-94; chmn. Fgn. Intelligence Adv. Bd., Washington, 1993-94; U.S. amb. to U.K. London, 1994-97. Counselor Ctr. for Strategic and Internat. Studies, Washington, 1989-94; prof. U. Okla., 1989-94. Author: Line of Fire, 1993; co-author: Reducing Nuclear Danger: The Road Away from the Brink, 1993; author supr. ops. plan for repatriation of U.S.S. Pueblo crew. Trustee Princeton U., 1995-2000; dir. USNA Found., 1998—. Decorated Defense DSM with three oak leaf clusters (Dept. Def.), Navy DSM with two oak leaf clusters (USN), DSM (U.S. Army, USAF, USCG), Legion of Merit, Bronze Star with combat V, Air medal with six oak leaf clusters. Mem. U.S. Naval Inst., Am. Polit. Sci. Assn., Internat. Studies Assn., Coun. on Fgn. Rels., Washington Inst. Fgn. Affairs, Phi Gamma Delta, Phi Delta Phi. Office: Global Options 1615 L St NW Ste 300 Washington DC 20036-5655

CROWE, WILLIAM JOSEPH, librarian; b. Boston, Feb. 27, 1947; s. William J. and Mary (Dawley) C.; m. Nancy P. Sanders, June 10, 1978; children: Katherine. BA in European history with highest honors, Boston State Coll., 1968; MLS, Rutgers U., 1969; PhD in Adminstrn. Acad. Librs., Ind. U., 1986. Cataloger Boston Pub. Libr., 1969-70, asst. to acquisitions libr., 1970-71; coord. processing Ind. U. Librs., Bloomington, 1971-76, asst. to dean univ. librs., 1977-79; mgmt. intern U. Mich. Libr., Ann Arbor, 1976-77; asst. to dir. libr. Ohio State U., Columbus, 1979-83, asst. dir. librs. adminstrn. and tech. svcs., 1983-90; dean librs. U. Kans., Lawrence, 1990-96, vice chancellor, dean, 1996-99, libr. Spencer Rsch. Libr., 1999—. Trustee Online Computer Lit. Ctr., 1996—. Contbr. articles to profl. jours. Sr. fellow UCLA, 1991. Mem. ALA, Kans. Libr. Assn., Beta Phi Mu, Phi Alpha Theta. Home: 910 E 850th Rd Lawrence KS 66047-9578 Office: U Kans Spencer Rsch Libr Lawrence KS 66045-7616 E-mail: wcrowe@ku.edu. *We must work to expand the next generation's opportunity for education--to foster greater equality of intellectual privilege.*

CROWELL, ALLEN, music educator; b. Mobile, Ala., Apr. 5, 1937; s. Allen Cantey and Nan Jo Green Crowell; m. Phyllis Merry, Dec. 27, 1938; children: Venetia Coffey, Johanna Norry. MusB, Westminster Choir Coll., 1959; MusM, Cath. U. Am., 1964. Assoc. bandmaster U.S. Army Band, Fort Myer, Va., 1964—79; prof. conducting Westminster Choir Coll., Princeton, NJ, 1979—99, Westminster Choir Coll., Rider U., 1979—99; Heyward prof. choral music U. Ga., Athens, 1999—; dir. U.S. Army Chorus, Fort Myer, 1964—79. Musician conduct clinics, workshops, concerts. Maj. U.S. Army, 1959—79. Decorated Legion of Merit; recipient Marshall Bartholomew award, Intercollegiate Musical Coun., 1980, John Gaius Baumgartner award, Westminster Choir Coll., 1959, Alumni Merit award, 1972, Alumni Svc. award, 1994. Mem.: Am. Choral Dirs. Assn. (corr.), Intercollegiate Male Choruses (hon.), Pi Kappa Lambda (hon.), Phi Mu Alpha Sinfonia (hon.), Kappa Kappi Psi (hon.). Avocations: cooking, travel. Home: 215 Tanglewood Dr Athens GA 30606-3820 Office: The University of Georgia School / Music 250 River Rd Athens GA 30602 Home Fax: 706-549-6498; Office Fax: 706-542-2773. E-mail: acrowell@arches.uga.edu.

CROWELL, CRAVEN H., JR., retired federal agency administrator; b. Nashville, Aug. 27, 1943; s. Craven H. and Addie Ailene (Cooper) C.; m. Fredricka Friedli, Nov. 27, 1970; 1 child, Stephanie Kaye. BA, Lipscomb U., 1965. Reporter, city editor Nashville Tennessean, 1964-77; press sec. Senator Jim Sasser, 1977-80, chief of staff, 1989-93; dir. info. TVA, Knoxville, 1980-87, v.p. govtl. and pub. affairs Nashville, 1987-89, chmn. bd. dirs., 1993-2001; ret., 2001. Mem. exec. com. Nuclear Energy Inst.; past chmn. bd. dirs., exec. com., bd. adv. coun. Electric Power Rsch. Inst.; bd. dirs. EPRI Worldwide, eVionyx, Utility Automation Integration. Hon. pres. Hohai U., China, 1997. With USMC, USNR. Recipient Nat. Headliner award, 1969; named Alumnus of Yr. Lipscomb U., 1995. Mem. Econ. Club of N.Y., Pi Delta Epsilon. Mem. Ch. of Christ.

CROWELL, DAVID HARRISON, retired biomedical researcher, consultant; b. Trenton, Nj, July 19; m. Doris Collins; children: Michael David, Sandra Crowell Lupton, Shannon Kathleen Atkinson, Megan Crowell Sheridan. Ph. D., State U. of Iowa, Iowa City, Iowa, 1946—50. Internship-fellowship U. Iowa 49;Yale 66, Scientist Commd. Corps,USPHS, 1954. Rsch. cons. Straub Clinic and Hosp., Honolulu, Hawaii, 1983—; prin. investigator Kapiolani Med. Crnter, Honolulu, 1991—2002, rsch. cons. Nat'l Inst. Health, Washington, DC, 1973—89; prof. emeritus U. of Hawaii, Honolulu. Author: (scientific articles) Psychophysiology; dir.(researcher): (experimental studies) Scientific Articles (Continuing Grants, 1963). 1st lt. Ordnance Dept., U. Grantee Clin Home Infant, Clin. Study, Nichd, Nih, 1999-2000. Fellow: Amer Psychol. Assn., Amer Assn Adv Sci. (life); mem.: Amer. Acad. Sleep Medicine, Population Assoc Am. (assoc.), Hawn Acad Sci. (assoc.; pres. 1953—54), Soc Rsch Child Devel (assoc.), Amer Acad Sleep Med (assoc.), Amer Clin Neurophysiology Soc (assoc.), Sigma Xi (assoc.). Office: Department of Pediatrics University of Hawaii at Manoa Honolulu HI 96822 Office Fax: 808-956-4700.

CROWELL, DONALD W. diversified financial services company executive, financial consultant; BA, Stanford U., 1956, MBA, 1958. Mng. ptnr., CEO Crowell, Weedon & Co., L.A., 1967—. Office: Crowell Weedon & Co 1 Wilshire Blvd Los Angeles CA 90017

CROWELL, ELDON HUBBARD, lawyer; b. Middletown, Conn., May 15, 1924; s. Eldon Lewis and Alice (Hubbard) C. A.B., Princeton U., 1948; LL.B., U. Va., 1951. Bar: D.C. 1951, Conn. 1951, U.S. Dist. Ct. D.C. 1951, U.S. Ct. Appeals (D.C. cir.) 1951, U.S. Ct. Appeals (3d cir.) 1956, U.S. Supreme Ct. 1958. Assoc. Cummings, Stanley et al Washington, 1951-52, ptnr., 1952-53; ptnr. Sellers, Conner & Cuneo, Washington, 1953-70, Jones, Day, Reavis, Washington, 1970-79, Crowell & Moring, Washington, 1979— ; lectr. U. Va. Law Sch., Charlottesville, 1967-80, Judge Adv. Gen. Sch., Charlottesville, 1975—, George Washington Nat. Law Sch., 1975—, Fed. Publs. Inc., Washington, 1975— . Contbr. articles to legal jours. Trustee Williston-Northampton Sch., Easthampton, Mass., 1965-75, Madeira Sch., Greenway, Va., 1970-75, Expt. in Internat. Living, Putney, Vt., 1950-60; chmn. law firm div. United Way Campaign for Met. Washington, 1983-85; bd. dirs. City Lights Sch., Washington, Procurement Round Table, 1993—. Served with U.S. Army, 1942-45. Fellow Am. Bar Found., Nat. Contract Mgmt. Assn.; mem. ABA, Internat. and Comparative Law Ctr. (bd. advisors), D.C. Bar Assn., Nat. Security Indsl. Assn. Democrat. Episcopalian. Clubs: Metropolitan, Chevy Chase. Home: 2101 Connecticut Ave NW Washington DC 20008-1728 Office: Crowell & Moring 1001 Pennsylvania Ave NW Fl 10 Washington DC 20004-2595

CROWELL, JOHN B., JR., lawyer, former government official; b. Elizabeth, N.J., Mar. 18, 1930; s. John B. and Anna B. (Trull) C.; m. Rebecca Margaret McCue, Feb. 13, 1954; children— John P., Patrick E., Ann M. AB, Dartmouth Coll., 1952; LL.B., Harvard U., 1957. Bar: N.J. bar 1958, Oreg. bar 1959. Law clk. to Judge Gerald McLaughlin U.S. Ct. Appeals, Newark, 1957-59; atty. Ga.-Pacific Corp., Portland, Oreg., 1959-72; gen. counsel La.-Pacific Corp., Portland, 1972-81; asst. sec. for natural resources and environment Dept. Agr., Washington, 1981-85; ptnr. Lane Powell Spears Lubersky, Portland, 1986-98, of counsel, 1998—. Served with USN, 1952-54. Mem. Am. Ornithologists Union, Wilson Ornithol. Soc., Cooper Ornithol. Soc., Soc. Am. Foresters, Soil Conservation Soc. Am. Clubs: Univ. (Portland). Republican. Presbyterian. Home: 1185 Hallinan Cir Lake Oswego OR 97034-4970 Office: Lane Powell Spears Lubersky 601 SW 2nd Ave # Ste #2100 Portland OR 97204-3154

CROWELL, JOHN C(HAMBERS), geology educator, researcher; b. State College, Pa., May 12, 1917; s. James White and Helen Hunt (Chambers) C.; m. Betty Marie Bruner, Nov. 22, 1946; 1 child, Martha Lynn Crowell Bobroskie. BS in Geology, U. Tex., 1939; MA in Oceanographic meteorology, Scripps Inst. Oceanography UCLA, 1946; PhD in Geology, UCLA, 1947; DSc (hon.), U. Louvain, Belgium, 1966. Geologist Shell Oil Co., Inc., Ventura, Calif., 1941-42; from instr. to prof. geology UCLA, 1947-67, chmn. dept., 1957-60, 63-66; prof. geology U. Calif., Santa Barbara, 1967-87, prof. emeritus, 1987, rsch. geologist Inst. for Crustal Studies, 1987—. Chmn. Office of Earth Scis., NRC, Nat. Acad. Scis., 1979-82. Served to capt. U.S. Army USAAF, 1942-46. Fellow AAAS, Geol. Soc. Am. (Penrose medal 1995), Am. Acad. Arts and Scis.; mem. Am. Assn. Petroleum Geologists, Am. Geophys. Union, Nat. Acad. Scis. Achievements include special research in structural geology, tectonics, interpretation sedimentary rocks, studies Andreas fault system, California tectonics, ancient glaciation, continental drift. Home: 300 Hot Springs Rd Apt 99 Santa Barbara CA 93108 Office: U Calif Inst Crustal Studies Santa Barbara CA 93106 E-mail: crowell@geol.ucsb.edu.

CROWELL, RICHARD LANE, microbiologist, educator; b. Springfield, Mo., Sept. 27, 1930; s. Thomas Rolla and Addie Malinda (Lane) Crowell; m. Arlene Mildred Prell, June 27, 1953; children: Steven Richard, Kathleen Margaret Crowell Miller, Barbara Lane, Wendy Jane. BA, U. Buffalo, 1952; MS, U. Minn., 1954, PhD, 1958. Instr. microbiology U. Minn. Med. Sch., Mpls., 1958-60; asst. prof. Med. Coll. Pa./Hahnemann U. Sch. Med., Phila., 1960-64, assoc. prof., 1964-71; prof. Drexel U. Coll. Medicine (formerly Med. Coll. Pa./Hahnemann U. Sch. Med., Phila., 1971-95, chmn. microbiology and immunology, 1979-95, emeritus prof., 1995—. Rsch. cons. Smith Kline Corp., Phila., 1975—77, Lehn and Fink Co., Montvale, NJ, 1976—80; ad hoc reviewer NIH, Bethesda, Md., 1966—. Editor: (book) Tumor Virus Infections and Immunity, 1976, Virus Attachment and Entry into Cells, 1986, Innovations in Antiviral Development and the Detection of Virus Infections, 1992; assoc. editor: Jour. Microbial Pathogenesis, 1985—91, mem. editl. bd.:, 1991—95. Rsch. Career Devel. grantee, NIH, 1962—72. Fellow: Am. Acad. Microbiology; mem.: Am. Assn. Immunologists, Assn. Med. Sch. Microbiology Chmn. (pres. U.S. and Can. 1986), Found. Microbiology (lectr. 1994—96), Am. Soc. Microbiology (pres. 1991—92, pres. ea. Pa. br. 1974—76), Am. Soc. Virology, Pa. Geneal. Soc., Sigma Xi, Phi Beta Kappa. Democrat. Presbyterian. Home: 407 Hutchins Dr Ambler PA 19002-2822 E-mail: crowellrl@aol.com.

CROWELL, ROSEMARY ELAINE, criminal justice professional; b. Monroe, N.C., Sept. 14, 1942; d. Frederick Perry and Berthenia (Alexander) C. AA, Clinton Jr. Coll., 1961. Mem. staff Betty Bacharach Home Afflicted Children, Atlantic City, 1964-66, Murdoch Ctr., Butner, N.C., 1964-66; cottage parent N.C. Dept. Human Resources, Butner, 1966-68, cottage parent, then cottage mgr. C.A. Dillon Sch. div. youth svcs., 1968-82, asst. unit adminstr., 1982—98. Del. to Dem. Nat. Conv., Atlanta, 1988; Dem. precinct chmn., Butner, 1989; active Dem. presdl. candidate campaigns, 1988; mem. Dem. Leadership Coun., 1990; mem. Granville County Dem. Steering Com. for N.C. Gov., 1996; mem. Granville County Steering Com. for Sen. John Edwards, 1998; com. mem. Granville County 2015 Task Force Comprehensive Land Devel. Plan, 2002. Mem. Nat. Abortion Rights Action League, Elks. Episcopalian. Avocations: reading, travel, politics. Home: PO Box 334 Butner NC 27509-2144

CROWELL, SAMUEL MARVIN, JR., education educator; b. Lexington, N.C., May 8, 1949; s. Samuel Marvin and Margaret Louise (Riddle) C.; m. Deborah Jane Costolo, Jan. 1, 1987; 1 child, Chesley Carole. BA, Carson-Newman Coll., 1971; MS, Radford U., 1975; EdD, U. Va., 1992. Tchr. elem. edn. Carroll County Sch. Dist., Hillsville, Va., 1971-73; dir. career opportunities program Carroll County Schs., Hillsville, 1973-75, prin., 1975-78; dir. elem. edn., dir. ednl. adminstrn. U. Redlands, Calif., 1982-87; prof. Calif. State U., San Bernardino, 1987—. Coord. elem. edn. Calif. State U., San Bernardino, 1987-89, dir. Ctr. for Rsch. in Integrative Studies, 1989—; acting exec. dir. Idyllwild Charter H.S., 2000, co-coord. MA in Integrative Studies. Author: Mindshifts, 1994, Reenchantment of Learning, 1997; contbr. chpts. and articles to profl. publs. Mem. Idyllwild (Calif.) Environ. Group, 1993—, Idyllwild Poetry Readings, 1995—; co-founder Ctr. for Environment, Arts and Edn., 2001—; mem. exec. bd. Skillful Meditation Project, Spirituality and Edn. Network, Ctr. Scholarship in Spirituality. Mem. ASCD, Phi Beta Delta, Phi Delta Kappa. Avocations: poet, naturalist, tai chi. Home: PO Box 1511 Idyllwild CA 92549-1511 Office: 5500 University Pkwy San Bernardino CA 92407-2318 E-mail: sam@greencafe.com.

CROWFOOT, BETSY M. writer; b. Bayshore, N.Y., Oct. 16, 1958; d. Donald W. Haak, Barbara Dee Haak; m. James Addison Crowfoot, May 16, 1981 (div.); 1 child, Caroline Grace. AA in Mktg. Comm., F.I.T., 1982. Editl. asst. Vogue Patterns Mag., N.Y.C., 1978—81; acct. exec. various advt. and pub. rels. firms, N.Y.C., 1981—83; mgr. sales various furniture cos., N.Y.C. and L.A., 1983—95; journalist Log Newspapers, San Diego, 1995—97; screenwriter, assoc. prodr. CS TV, Newport Beach, Calif., 1997—99; sports writer Quokko Sports, San Francisco, 1999—2001; author, writer Carpinteria, Calif., 2001—. Author: The World's Toughest Yacht Race, 2001. Bd. dirs. Women of Vision, Orange City, Calif. Mem.: Transpacific Yacht Club (bd. dirs.). Episcopalian. Avocations: sailing, kayaking, photography. Office: 5662 Calle Real #310 Goleta CA 93117

CROWL, JOHN ALLEN, retired publishing company executive; b. Winchester, Va., Aug. 10, 1935; s. John Decatur and Cora Elizabeth (LLoyd) C.; m. Dana Jane Bernasek, Aug. 27, 1960 (div. 1986); 1 son, Patrick Joseph; m. Gaal Shepherd, Feb. 10, 1988. BA, U. Md., 1957, MA, 1961; LhD (hon.), Lebanon Valley Coll., 1993. Instr. Staunton (Va.) Mil. Acad., 1958-59; asst. dir. pub. rels. Johns Hopkins U., Balt., 1961-64; assoc. dir. Editl. Projects for Edn., Inc., Balt. and Washington, 1964-75, v.p., 1975-78; assoc. editor Chronicle of Higher Edn., Washington, 1966-72, mng. editor, 1972-79, pub., 1978-91, v.p., 1979-92. Founder Thistle Hill Publs., 2000—. Contbg. editor: Vt. Mag., 1995—2001; mem. editl. adv. bd. Vt. Life mag., 2002—. Trustee Vt. Folklife Ctr., 1994-99, Vt. Arts Coun., 1994-98; trustee Planned Parenthood of No. New Eng., 1994-2000, chair 1997-99. With U.S. Army, 1958. Recipient Edn. Writers award AAUP, 1971 Home: Thistle Hill North Pomfret VT 05053 E-mail: crowl1@earthlink.net.

CROWL, RODNEY KEITH, lawyer; b. Houston, July 23, 1948; s. Julian Charles and Joyce Hetty (Crump) C.; m. Linda Sue Wansbrough, May 17, 1974; children— Audrey, Blaire, Sarah, David. B.A. cum laude in Econs. and English, Rice U., 1970; J.D., U. Tex.-Austin, 1973. Bar: Tex. 1973, U.S. Dist. Ct. (so. dist.) Tex. 1974. Assoc. firm Woody & Rosen, Houston, 1973-74; atty. Pennzoil Co., Houston, 1974-77; oil and gas atty. Kaneb Services, Inc., Houston, 1977-80; sr. atty., asst. sec. Monsanto Oil Co., Houston, 1980-83; v.p. Instnl. Adv. U. Thomas, Houston, 1990-98; chief devel. officer St. Joseph Hosp. Found.; guest speaker U. S.C. Coll. Internat. Bus. Adminstrn., Columbia, 1974, 76. Class chmn. Rice U. Ann. Fund., Houston, 1979-80. Mem. Assn. Internat. Petroleum Negotiators. Episcopalian. Clubs: Rice Owl (pres. 1984-86), Rice Rebounders (pres. 1981) (Houston). Home: 6016 Fordham St Houston TX 77005-3126

CROWL, SAMUEL RENNINGER, former university dean, English language educator, author; b. Toledo, Oct. 9, 1940; s. Lester Samuel and Margaret Elizabeth (Renninger) C.; m. Susan Richardson, Dec. 29, 1963; children: Miranda Paine, Samuel Emerson. AB, Hamilton Coll., 1962; MA, Ind. U., 1969, PhD, 1970. Resident lectr. Ind. U., Indpls., 1967-69; asst. prof. English, Ohio U., Athens, 1970-75, assoc. prof., 1975-80, prof., 1980—, dean Univ. Coll., 1981-92, trustee prof. Eng., 1992—; cons. NEH, Washington, 1980—; observer Royal Shakespeare Co. Mem. Ohio Humanities Coun., 1985-91, Ohio Student Loan Commn., 1985-88. Author: Shakespeare Observed: Studies in Performance on Stage and Screen, 1992, Shakespeare at the Cineplex, 2003; co-author: Ohio University's Educational Plan, 1977-78; contbr. articles to profl. and Shakespearian jours. Recipient O'Bleness award for pub. broadcasting Ctr. Telecommunications, Ohio U., 1976, several awards disting. teaching. Fellow Royal Soc. Arts (London); mem. Nat. Assn. Univ. and Gen. Coll. Deans (pres. 1991—), Nat. Humanities Faculty, Ohio Shakespeare Assn. (founding mem.), Ohio U. Alumni Assn. (hon.), Univ. Club (Chgo.), Phi Kappa Phi. Avocations: Royal Shakespeare Co., Detroit Tigers. Office: Ohio U Eng Dept Ellis Hall Athens OH 45701

CROWLEY, DEAN TIMOTHY, occupational therapist; b. Gardner, Mass., Mar. 15, 1964; s. George John and Patricia (Salerno) C.; m. Jean M. Crowley, May 20, 1995; 1 child: Alexandra I. AHS, Mt. Wachusett C.C., Gardner, 1986; BS in Psychology, U. Mass., 1986; BS in Occupl. Therapy, Worcester State Coll., 1992. Cert. alcohol and drug abuse counselor, Middlesex Coll., 1999. Supr. Neighborhood Youth Corps, Gardner, summer 1986, counselor Fitchburg, Mass., summer 1987; staff occupl. therapist Heritage Health Sys., Somerville, Mass., 1993-94, dir. occupl. therapy, 1994; chief occupl. therapist, unit mgr. Cambridge (Mass.) Hosp., 1994—; owner Jean and Dean's Occupational Therapy Cons. and Supr. Svc., 2001—. Student coord. Heritage Health Systems, 1993-94; student coord. and supr. Cambridge Hosp., 1994—. Poet. Mem. ACLU, 1991—, Zero Population Growth, 1991—, So. Poverty Law Ctr., 1990—, Gardner Cmty Land Host, 1989-93. Commonwealth scholar U. Mass., 1988, Talented and Regents Student Senate scholar Mt. Wachusett C.C., 1985, Gardner's Retarded Citizens Assn. scholar. Mem. Am. Occupl. Therapy Assn., Mass. Occupl. Therapy Assn., Italian Am. Citizens Club, Phi Theta Kappa (Theta Epsilon). Avocations: biking, hiking, basketball, music, reading. Home: 33 Buckman St Woburn MA 01801-5558

CROWLEY, DIANE NITA, home health administrator; b. Pasadena, Calif., Sept. 23, 1941; d. Dorothy Inez Nelson and Warren J. Auld; m. Larry Olson Crowley; children: Dana Dietz, Larry, Gregory, Janelle Breen. RN, Victor Valley Jr. Coll., 1984; BA Psychology, U. Calif., San Bernardino, 1982; MSN, U. Phoenix, 1999. Cert. Fetal Monitoring 2002. Edn. coord. ARMC Home Health Care, Colton, Calif., 1996—2001; cmty. nurse/educator Arrowhead Regional Med. Ctr., Colton, 2001—02, adminstr., dir. patient svcs. for home health care. Educator labor/delivery (high risk) Arrowhead Regional Med. Ctr., 1987—96. Democrat. Avocation: writing, collecting antiques, handwriting analysis. Home: PO Box 402455 Hesperia CA 92340 Office: Arrowhead Regional Med Ctr 400 North Pepper Colton CA 92324 Personal E-mail: crowleydiane1@netscape.net. Business E-Mail: crowleyd@armc.co.san_bernardino.ca.us.

CROWLEY, JAMES FRANCIS, composer, educator; b. Chgo., Dec. 24, 1963; s. Bernard Francis and Mary Colleen Crowley; m. Eun-Joo Kwak, June 6, 1998. MusB, U. Ill., 1986; MusM, Northwestern U., 1987, MusD, 1993. Acctg. asst. Lyric Opera Chgo., 1987-90; lectr. Northwestern U., Evanston, Ill., 1990-94; asst. prof. music Drury U., Springfield, Mo., 1994-98; assoc. prof. music U. Wis., Parkside, 1998—. Tchg. fellow Aspen (Colo.) Music Festival, 1991; faculty cons. Ednl. Testing Svc., Princeton, N.J., 1997. Composer (orchestral work) 220 S. Michigan Ave., 1990, The Piezoelectric Effect, 1997, (wind ensemble) Serpentine, 1991, (chamber work) Cold Pastoral, 1996. Travel grantee Meet-the-Composer Inc., N.Y.C., 1995. Mem. Soc. Composers Inc., Broadcast Music Inc., Am. Music Ctr. (Jury award 2000), Wis. Alliance of Composers (bd. dirs. 1998—). Office: 900 Wood Rd Kenosha WI 53144-1133

CROWLEY, JAMES MICHAEL, lawyer; b. Phila., Feb. 16, 1942; s. Joseph M. and Mary V. (McCall) C.; m. Beverly Ann Crystal, Mar. 28, 1987; children: David M., Benjamin T., Lauren R. PhB magna cum laude, Lateran U., Rome, 1965; STB magna cum laude, Lateran U., 1967, STL, 1969, JCB magna cum laude, 1970, JCL magna cum laude, 1973; JD, Notre Dame U., 1972. Bar: N.Y. 1973, U.S. Dist. Ct. (so. dist.) N.Y. 1973, U.S. Supreme Ct. 1976. Assoc. Shearman & Sterling, N.Y.C., 1972-78; resident Algiers, Algeria, 1976-78; sole practice N.Y.C., 1978-80; sr. counsel CIGNA Corp., Phila., 1980-84; v.p. CIGNA Internat. Holdings Ltd., Wilmington, Del., 1982-97; sr. v.p., chief counsel CIGNA Worldwide, Inc., Phila., 1984-96; sr. v.p. govt. affairs CIGNA Internat., 1996-97; mng. cons. Aon Religious Instns. Alliance, 1999—. Dir. CIGNA Worldwide Ins. Co., Wilmington. Mem. Archdiocesan Fin. Coun., Phila., 1984-87; exec. bd. Phila. coun. Boy Scouts Am., 1983-86; pro bono publico litig. Matter of Karen Ann Quinlan, N.J., 1976; trustee Country Day Sch. of the Sacred Heart, Bryn Mawr, Pa., 1999—. Recipient Cardinal Dougherty medal St. Charles Coll., Phila., 1963; Silver medal Pope Paul VI, Rome, 1967. Mem. Am. Soc. Internat. Law, ABA, Assn. Bar City N.Y., N.Y. State Bar Assn., N.Y. County Bar Assn., University Club (N.Y.C.). Roman Catholic. Home: 3503 Tall Oaks Ln Newtown Square PA 19073-2767 E-mail: jmcrowley@msn.com.

CROWLEY, JAMES PATRICK, hematologist, medical educator, immunologist; b. Birmingham, Eng., Oct. 13, 1943; came to U.S., 1947; s. Francis Michael and Rose Ann (Donaghy) C.; m. Carol Ann Crowley, Dec. 6, 1943; children: Jason W.F., James M. AB, Providence Coll., 1965; MD, Georgetown U., 1969; MA, Brown U., 1981. Intern Boston City Hosp./Harvard Med. Sch., 1969, resident, 1970, Mass. Gen. Hosp., Boston, 1971, Peter Bent Brigham Hosp., Boston, 1974; instr. medicine Harvard Med. Sch., Boston, 1974; asst. prof. medicine Brown U., Providence, 1975-81, assoc. prof., 1981-92, prof., 1992—; dir. hematology R.I. Hosp./Brown U., Providence, 1992-2000; chief hematology/oncology Meml. Hosp. of R.I., Pawtucket, 2000—; dir. Cancer Ctr. Meml. Hosp. of R.I., 2003—. Bd. dirs. Providence Ambulatory Health Care Found., Inc.; cons. Naval Blood Rsch. Program, USN, 1977—; adj. prof. medicine Tufts U. Sch. Vet. Medicine, 1986—1996. Author: Principles of Transfusion Medicine, 2nd edit., 1995; contbr. articles to profl. jours. Mem. Retirement Bd. City of Providence, 1993—; physician Camp Yawgoog Boy Scouts Am., 1992—. Capt. USNR, 1971-95, ret. Recipient Transfusion Medicine Acad. award NIH, 1984-89, award R.I. Blood Banking Soc., 1986. Mem. Am. Soc. Hematology, R.I. Med. Soc. (pres. 1992-93), Providence Med. Assn., (pres. 1992-92), Mt. Tom Club (v.p. 1994). Democrat. Roman Catholic. Achievements include important contbns. to the devel. of successful system for freezing blood and deglycerolizing blood for transfusion on Navy hosp. ships, successful demonstration that erythropoeitin could enhance autologous predonation prior to orthopedic surgery and the immunosuppressive effects of passenger leukocytes during allogeneic transfusion. Office: Cancer Ctr Meml Hosp RI 111 Brewster St Pawtucket RI 02860 E-mail: james_crowley@mhri.org.

CROWLEY, JAMES WORTHINGTON, retired lawyer, business consultant, investor; b. Cookville, Tenn., Feb. 18, 1930; s. Worth and Jessie (Officer) C.; m. Laura June Bauserman, Jan. 27, 1951; children: James Kenneth, Laura Cynthia; m. Joyce A. Goode, Jan. 15, 1966; children: John Worthington, Noelle Virginia; m. Carol Golden, Sept. 4, 1981. BA, George Washington U., 1950, LLB, 1953. Bar: D.C. 1954. Underwriter, spl. agt. Am. Surety Co. of N.Y., Washington, 1953-56; adminstrv. asst., contract adminstr. Atlantic Rsch. Corp., Alexandria, Va., 1956-59, mgr. legal dept., asst. sec., counsel, 1959-65, sec., legal mgr., counsel, 1965-67, Susquehanna Corp. (merger with Atlantic Rsch. Corp.), 1967-70; pres., dir. Gen. Communication Co., Boston, 1962-70; v.p., gen. counsel E-Systems, Inc., 1970-95, sec., 1976-95; ret., 1995; ind. cons. bus. and fin., investor, 1995—. V.p., asst. sec., dir. Cemco, Inc.; v.p., dir. TAI, Inc., Serv-air, Inc., Greenville, Tex., Engrng. Rsch. Assocs., Inc., Vienna, Va., HRB Systems, Inc., State Coll., Pa.; mem. adv. bd. sec. Internat. and Comparative Law Ctr.; v.p., sec., dir. Advanced Video Products, 1992-95; v.p., sec., gen. counsel E-Systems Med. Electronics, Inc., 1992-95. Mem. Am. Soc. Corp. Secs. (pres. Dallas regional group 1988-89, nat. dir. 1989-92), Inf. Mus. Assn., Nat. Security Indsl. Assn., Mfrs.' Alliance for Productivity and Innovation (mem. law coun.), Omicron Delta Kappa, Alpha Chi Sigma, Phi Sigma Kappa. Republican. Baptist. Home and Office: 16203 Spring Creek Rd Dallas TX 75248-3116 E-mail: jwcrowle@ix.netcom.com.

CROWLEY, JEROME JOSEPH, JR., retired retail executive; b. South Bend, Ind., Sept. 18, 1939; s. Jerome J. and Rosaleen C.; m. Carol Ann Ellithorn, June 23, 1962; children: Michael, Karen, Brian, Colleen. BS, U. Notre Dame, 1961; MBA, U. Chgo., 1967. With O'Brien Corp., South Bend, Ind., 1965—2002, pres., 1975—2002. With USMC, 1961-65. Roman Catholic.

CROWLEY, JOHN CRANE, real estate developer; b. Detroit, June 29, 1919; s. Edward John and Leah Helen (Crane) C.; m. Barbara Wenzel Gilfillan, Jan. 12, 1945; children: F. Alexander, Leonard, Philip, Eliot, Louise, Sylvia. BA with honors, Swarthmore Coll., 1941; MS, U. Denver, 1943. Asst. dir. Mcpl. Fin. Officers Assn., Chgo., 1946-48; So. Calif. mgr. League Calif. Cities, Los Angeles, 1948-53; mgr. City of Monterey Park, Calif., 1953-56. Founder, exec. v.p. Nat. Med. Enterprises, L.A., 1968; pres. Ventura Towne House (Calif.), 1963-96; mem. faculty U. So. Calif. Sch. Pub. Adminstrn., 1950-53; bd. dirs. Regional Inst. of So. Calif., The L.A. Partnership 2000, Burbank-Glendale-Pasadena Airport Authority. Trustee Pacific Oaks Friends Sch. and Coll., Pasadena, 1954-57, 92-98, Swarthmore Coll., 1987—; bd. dirs. Pasadena Area Liberal Arts Ctr., 1962-72, pres., 1965-68; bd. dirs. Pacificulture Found. and Asia Mus., 1971-76, pres., 1972-74; bd. dirs. Nat. Mcpl. League, 1986-92, AAF Rose Bowl Aquatics Ctr., 1997—; chmn. Pasadena Cultural Heritage Commn., 1975-78; city dir. Pasadena, 1979-91; mayor City of Pasadena, 1986-88; bd. dirs. Western Justice Ctr., 1992—, v.p., 1995—, LA County Commn. on Efficiency and Economy, 1994—; mem. L.A. County Commn. on Local Govt., 2000—. Sloan Found. fellow, 1941-43; recipient Arthur Nobel award City of Pasadena. Mem. Am. Soc. Pub. Adminstrn. (local chpt., Winston Crouch award 1990), Internat. City Mgmt. Assn., Nat. Mcpl. League (nat. bd. 1980-92, Disting. Citizen award, 1984), Inst. Pub. Adminstrn. (sr. assoc.), Phi Delta Theta. Democrat. Unitarian Universalist. Home: 615 Linda Vista Ave Pasadena CA 91105-1122

CROWLEY, JOHN FRANCIS, III, university dean; b. New Haven, Jan. 29, 1945; s. John Francis Jr. and Anna Cecil (Elliott) C.; m. Alice Ann Kennedy, Dec. 26, 1970; children: John Francis IV, Sarah Ann. MA in Regional and City Planning, U. Okla., 1973, PhD in Urban Geography, 1977. Dir. planning City of Seminole, Okla., 1972—73; chief planner Okla. Divsn. State Parks, Oklahoma City, 1973—74; asst. prof. environ. design U. Ga., Athens, 1974—78, prof., dean Sch. Environ. Design, 1996—2001, dean Coll. Environ. and Design, 2001—; exec. dir. Tulsa Metro Area Planning Commn., 1978—80; v.p., devel. Williams Realty Corp., Tulsa, 1980—87; pres. Urbantech Inc., Tulsa, 1987—; dir. Okla. Dept. of Transp., Oklahoma City, 1993—95. Bd. dirs. Downtown Tulsa Unltd., 1983-89; chmn. Sales Tax Overview Com., Tulsa, 1988-90; sec. bd. trustees Tulsa County Pub. Facilities Authority, 1983-96. 1st lt. U.S. Army, 1965-69. Sara Moss faculty fellow U. Ga., 1976. Mem. Am. Soc. Landscape Architects, Am. Inst. Cert. Planners, Am. Planning Assn., Nature Conservancy, Urban Land Inst., Transp. Rsch. Bd. Democrat. Roman Catholic. Avocations: art, sports, travel. Home: 335 Crystal Ct Athens GA 30606-3245 E-mail: jcrowley@arches.uga.edu.

CROWLEY, JOHN W(ILLIAM), English language educator; b. New Haven, Dec. 27, 1945; s. John Adam and Mary T. (McKenna) C.; m. Sheila A. Myers, Mar. 17, 1967 (div. 1977); children: Matthew, Anne; m. Susan Wolstenholme, May 27, 1978 (div. 2001); children: Raphael, Mary; m. Emily T. Smith, Nov. 23, 2001. BA, Yale U., 1967; MA, Ind. U., 1969, PhD, 1970. Asst. prof. English Syracuse (N.Y.) U., 1970-74, assoc. prof., 1974-79, prof., 1979—2002, dir. humanities doctoral program, 1985—88, 1996—2002, dir. grad. studies, 1986-89, chair, 1989—92; prof. U. Ala., Tuscaloosa, 2002—, chair dept., 2002—03. Author: George Cabot Lodge, 1976, The Black Heart's Truth, 1985, The Mask of Fiction, 1989, The White Logic, 1994, The Dean of American Letters, 1999, Bill W. and Mr. Wilson, 2000; co-author: Drunkard's Refuge, 2003; editor: New Essays on Winesburg, Ohio, 1990, Genteel Pagan, 1991, The Sunnier Side, 1996, The Rise of Silas Lapham, 1996, Drunkard's Progress, 1999; co-editor: The Haunted Dusk, 1983. Hon. Woodrow Wilson fellow, 1967; NDEA fellow, 1967-70; Nat. Endowment for Humanities summer stipend, 1975 Mem. Phi Beta Kappa. Democrat. Office: Dept of English U Ala Tuscaloosa AL 35487-0244 Home: 2400 Yorktown Dr Tuscaloosa AL 35406

CROWLEY, JOSEPH, congressman; b. Queens County, N.Y., Mar. 16, 1962; BA, Queens Coll., 1985. Mem. N.Y. State Assembly, 1987-98, U.S. Congress from 7th N.Y. dist., Washington, 1999—; mem. internat rels. com., fin. svcs. com. Former mem. standing com. in banking N.Y. State Assembly, elec. law com., consumer affairs com., labor & housing com., ways and means com., chmn. racing & wagering com Mem. Cavan Men's Assn., VFW, K. of C. Democrat. Office: US Ho of Reps 312 Cannon Ho Office Bldg Washington DC 20515*

CROWLEY, JOSEPH NEIL, university president, political science educator; b. Oelwein, Iowa, July 9, 1933; . James Bernard and Nina Mary (Neil) C.; m. Johanna Lois Reitz, Sept. 9, 1961; children: Theresa, Neil, Margaret, Timothy. BA, U. Iowa, 1959; MA, Calif. State U., Fresno, 1963; PhD (Univ. fellow), U. Wash., 1967. Reporter Fresno Bee, 1961-62; asst. prof. polit. sci. U. Nev., Reno, 1966-71, asso. prof., 1971-79, prof., 1979—, chmn. dept. polit. sci., 1976-78, pres., 1978-2000, pres. emeriyus, regents prof., 2000—. Bd. dirs. Citibank Nev.; policy formulation officer EPA, Washington, 1973-74; dir. instl. studies Nat. Commn. on Water Quality, Washington, 1974-75. Author: Democrats, Delegates and Politics in Nevada: A Grassroots Chronicle of 1972, 1976, Notes From the President's Chair, 1988, No Equal in the World; An Interpretation of the Academic Presidency, 1994, The Constant Conversation: A Chronicle of Campus Life, 2000; editor: (with R. Roelofs and D. Hardesty) Environment and Society, 1973. Mem. coun. NCAA, 1987—92, mem. pres.' commn., 1991—92, pres., 1993—95; bd. dirs. Nat. Consortium for Acads. and Sports., 1992—; Honda Awards Program Adv. Bd., 1994—; bd. dirs. campaign chmn. No. Nev. United Way, 1985; bd. dirs. campaing chmn., 1997—2002; mem. Commn. on Colls., 1980—87; mem. adv. commn. on mining and minerals rsch. U.S. Dept. Interior, 1985—91. Recipient Thornton Peace Prize U. Nev., 1971, Humanitarian of Yr. award NCCJ, 1986, Alumnus of Yr. award Calif. State U., 1989, ADL Champion of Liberty award, 1993, Disting. Alumni award U. Iowa, 1994, Giant Step award Ctr. for Study of Sport in Soc., 1994, William Anderson award AAHPERD, 1998, Lifetime Achievement award Nat. Consortium for Acads. and Sports, 2001; Nat. Assn. Schs. Pub. Affairs and Adminstrn. fellow, 1973-74. Mem. Nat. Assn. State Univs. and Land Grant Colls. (bd. dirs. 1999-2000). Roman Catholic. Home: 1265 Muir Dr Reno NV 89503-2629 Office: U Nev Mail Stop 310 Reno NV 89557 E-mail: crowley@unr.edu.

CROWLEY, L. C. telecommunications company executive; b. Pitts., Feb. 21, 1949; d. David A. and Elsie M. (Stark) C.; m. Thomas G. Wilson, June 21, 1969 (div. Nov. 1972); m. James W. Wilson Jr., Mar. 20, 1987. Student, Lowell Inst., 1984-86, Loyola U., 1975, MIT, 1967-69, 72-74; MS in Mgmt., Purdue U., 1992. Prodn. mgr. High Performance Products Inc., Hingham, Mass., 1969-71; mfg. mgr. Quadex (Compugraphic), Cambridge, Mass., 1977-81; asst. gen. mgr. Commerce Handling Co., Boston, 1982-83; dir. EDP Inter Consult Inc., Cambridge, 1984-86; mgr. receivables systems Sprint, Dallas, 1987-97, mgr. billing, 1997—. Graphics editor: Corporate Electronic Publishing Systems, 1986. Head SMITF Garden Guild, Southlake, Tex., 1997—; mem. St. Martin-in-the-Fields Episcopal Choir, 1988—. Mem. Purdue Pres.' Coun. Republican. Avocations: genealogy, organic gardening, legends car racing, target shooting. Home: 410 Lakewood Dr Trophy Club TX 76262-5296 Office: Sprint 1510 Rochelle Blvd Irving TX 75039-4307

CROWLEY, MARY ELIZABETH (MARY ELIZABETH CROWLEY-FARRELL), editor, journalist; b. Hackensack, N.J., Nov. 7, 1956; d. Jeremiah Christopher and Charlotte Mary (Keith) C.; m. William Christopher Farrell, Sept. 1, 1979; children: Eliza Carolyn Farrell, Luke Jeremiah Farrell. BA in Polit. Sci. & Comm. magna cum laude, Rutgers U., 1978; MA, U. Pa., 1980; postgrad., Trinity Coll., Dublin, Ireland. Reporter various local newspapers, 1974-77; regional corr. Capitol Hill News Svc., Washington, 1977; Washington corr. Thomson Newspapers, 1978-83; dep. mng. editor Comm. Daily, Washington, 1983-92; Washington bur. chief Stevens Pub. Corp., 1992; exec. editor, v.p. editl. Bus. Pubs., Inc., Silver Spring, Md., 1992-94; group editl. dir. news and info. svcs. Phillips Bus. Info., Inc., Potomac, Md., 1995-99; prin. EditWrite, Silver Spring, Md., 1999—. Lectr., spkr. in field. Contbr. articles to profl. publs., chpts. to books. Active many profl. and local civic orgns. Annenberg fellow, 1978-80, Rotary Internat. fellow for profl. journalists, 1980-81, Found. Am. Comms. econs. fellow, 1996; recipient Outstanding Newswriting award N.J. Press Assn., 1976, N.Y. Bldg. and Trades Assn. award, 1976, Spot News/Exclusive Story award Newsletter Pubs. Found., 1999, Apex award Comm. Concepts, Inc., 1997, 99. Mem. Am. Soc. Bus. Editors, Soc. Profl. Journalists (past pres. Washington chpt., Outstanding Newswriting award (2), Outstanding Profl. Chpt./Large award), Investigative Reporters and Editors, Soc. Environ. Journalists, Quill Big Inch Club, Nat. Press Club (former v.p. spkrs. com., mem. awards com., Outstanding Newsletter Journalism 1st Place award 1987), Newsletter Pub. Assn., Reporters Com. for Freedom of the Press (former mem. steering com.), Pi Sigma Alpha, Sigma Delta Chi (past vice chmn.) Avocations: furniture refinishing, landscape gardening, performing on recorder. Fax: 301-593-5936.

CROWLEY, ROBERT KENAN, radio station executive; b. Dec. 22, 1955; Student, U. Houston, 1973, Trinity U., San Antonio, 1977. Radio announcer radio stations, Tex./La., 1973-78; radio prodr., radio mass Archdiocese of San Antonio, 1979-80; announcer Sta. KENS-TV, San Antonio, 1979-82; news dir. Sta. KSAQ, San Antonio, 1984-85, Sta. KRNN, San Antonio, 1985, Sta. KPEZ-FM, Austin, 1987-93; news reporter Sta. WOAI, San Antonio, 1985-87; news announcer Stas. KVET-AM-FM and KASE-FM, Austin, 1993-99; radio cons. Lower Colo. River Auth. KWTR, 1994; news dir. Stas. KVET-AM-FM and KASE-FM, Austin, 1998-99; exec. dir. TXN The news of Texas, Austin, 1999-2000; acct. exec. Radio Sta. KENS-AM, San Antonio, 2001—; reporter Sta. KRLD Radio, Arlington, Tex., 2001—. Bur. reporter Tex. State News Network, Austin, 2000. Bd. dirs. Teach the Children, Austin, 1988, Austin Cmty. TV, 1988-89. Bd. dirs. Any Baby Can, Austin, 1993-94.

CROWLEY, THOMAS B., JR., water transportation executive; b. 1966; BS in Fin., U. Wash. With Crowley Maritime Corp., Oakland, Calif., 1987—, chmn., CEO, 1994—. Office: Crowley Maritime 155 Grand Ave Oakland CA 94612-3758*

CROWLEY, THOMAS JAMES, psychiatry educator; b. Mpls., Aug. 10, 1937; s. Cornelius Thomas and Rose Crowley; m. Hildegard Heinrich, June 16, 1962 (dec. 2000); children: Christopher T., Devin P. BA, BS, U. Minn., 1960, MD, 1962. Lic. physician, Colo. Resident in psychiatry U. Minn. Sch. Medicine, Mpls., 1963-66; prof. psychiatry U. Colo. Sch. Medicine, Denver, 1968—; pres. T.J. Crowley Corp., Denver, 1996—. Inventor ski safety equipment; cons. U.S. Nat. Inst. on Drug Abuse, Rockville, Md., 1975-98; mem. panel Inst. Medicine/Nat. Acad. Sci., Washington, 1996-98. Contbr. chpts. to books, articles to profl. jours.; patentee avalanche-victims air-from-snow breathing device. Mem. adv. panel on drug dependence WHO, Geneva, 1995—. Capt. USAF, 1966-68. Recipient MERIT grant award Nat. Ins. on Drug Abuse, 1997—. Fellow: Coll. on Problems of Drug Dependence (pres. 1991—92), Am. Psychiat. Assn.; mem.: AAAS, Am. Assn. Psychiatrists in Addiction, Rsch. Soc. on Alcoholism, Am. Avalanche Assn. Avocations: skiing (alpine and nordic), windsurfing, cooking. Office: U Colo Sch Medicine Box C-268-35 4200 E 9th Ave Denver CO 80262 E-mail: Thomas.Crowley@uchsc.edu.

CROWLEY, WELDON SAMUEL, retired history educator; b. Kerens, Tex., July 1, 1935; s. William Samuel and Vera Jewel (Cook) C.; m. Patricia L. Bennett, Aug. 3, 1958; children: Lisa Lynette, Gregory Weldon. BA in English, McMurry U., 1957; MDiv, Drew U., 1961; MA, U. Iowa, 1963, PhD in History, 1966. Asst. prof. history U. Pacific, Stockton, Calif., 1965-70; dean acad. programs Ramapo Coll. N.J., Mahwah, 1970-71; assoc. prof. history Fla. So. Coll., Lakeland, 1971-76; prof. dept. history Southwestern U., Georgetown, Tex., 1976-97, prof. emeritus, 1997—, William Carrington Finch prof., 1983-85, Lucy King Brown chair in history, 1976-97. Contbr. articles to profl. jours. Folger Shakespeare Libr. fellow, 1965. Mem. AAUP, World History Assn. Democrat. Mem. United Meth. Ch. Avocations: boating, racquetball, tennis. Home: 4105 Val Verde Dr Georgetown TX 78628-1422

CROWN, DAVID ALLAN, criminologist, educator; b. Long Beach, N.Y., Sept. 13, 1928; s. John and Florence (Coe) C.; m. Maria Braml, Feb. 13, 1954; children: Ingrid, Eric. BS, Union Coll., 1948; M in Criminology, U. Calif., 1960, D in Criminology, 1969. Spl. agt. CIC, 1951-53; asst. dir. San Francisco Indentification Lab., U.S. Postal Inspection Service, 1957-67; dir. Questioned Document Lab., Records Analysis Group, Dept. Army, Washington, 1967-72, Questioned Documents Staff, INR/DDC, U.S. Dept. State, Washington, 1972-77; chief Questioned Documents Lab., Office of Tech. Services, 1977-82. Lectr. Chabot Coll., Hayward, Calif., 1966-67, Georgetown U., Washington, 1973; adj. prof. Am. U., Washington, 1971-80; professorial lectr. George Washington U., 1973-77, Antioch Sch. Law, 1977-1981; guest lectr. FBI Acad., Quantico, Va.; pres. Crown Forensic Labs., Inc.; chmn. recert. com. Am. Bd. Forensic Document Examiners. Author: The Forensic Examination of Paints and Pigments, 1968; co-author: Forensic Science, 1982, Legal Medicine, 1985, Forensic Handwriting Examination, 1993; contbr. articles to profl. publs.; mem. editl. bd.: Jour. Forensic Scis., 1971-73, Internat. Jour. Forensic Document Examiners; book rev. editor, 1973-74, assoc. editor, 1974-84. Pres. Temple Bat Yam, Sanibel, Fla., 1996-98. Mem. Am. Acad. Forensic Scis. (chmn. questioned document sect. 1969-70, exec. com. 1970-74, pres. 1974-75), Am. Soc. Questioned Document Examiners (chmn. accreditation com. 1969-70, sec.-treas. 1976-78, pres. 1980-82), ASTM (chmn. questioned document com. 1970-71, vice chmn. 1972), Forensic Sci. Found. (dir. 1971-72, trustee 1973-75). Home: 3344 Twin Lakes Ln Sanibel FL 33957-5528 E-mail: crowndа@aol.com.

CROWN, ERIC J. information systems executive; BSc in Bus. Computer Info. Sys., Ariz. State U., 1984. Chmn., CEO, founder Insight Enterprises, Tempe, Ariz., 1988—. Office: Insight Enterprises 6820 S Harl Ave Tempe AZ 85283-4318 E-mail: ecrown@insight.com.

CROWN, JAMES SCHINE, investment executive; b. Chgo., June 25, 1953; s. Lester and Renée (Schine) Crown; m. Paula Ann Hannaway, June 27, 1985; children: Victoria, Hayley, Andrew, Summer Olivia. BA, Hampshire Coll., 1976; JD, Stanford U., 1980. Bar: Ill. 1980. V.p. Salomon Bros. Inc., N.Y.C., 1980-85; gen. ptnr. Henry Crown and Co., Chgo., 1985—. Bd, durs, Gen. Dynamics Corp., Falls Church, Va., Bank One Corp., Sara Lee Corp. Trustee U. Chgo., Mus. Sci. and Industry, Chgo., Orchestral Assn., Chgo. Mem.: Ill. State Bar Assn. Office: Henry Crown and Co 222 N La Salle St Chicago IL 60601-1003

CROWN, JOHN S. military officer, statistician, consultant; s. George N. and Rosa L. Crown; m. Shannon E. Langham, Aug. 14, 1993; children: John V., James A. BS in Math., Midwestern State U., 1985; MS in Math., MS in Ops. Rsch., Air Force Inst. Tech., 1991; PhD in Stats., Tex. A&M U., 1997. Officer promotion analyst Air Force Pers. Ctr., Randolph AFB, San Antonio, Tex., 1987—89, chief analysis br., 2000—; munitions logistics analyst Air Force Operational Test & Evaluation Ctr., Kirtland AFB, Albuquerque, 1991—93; asst. prof. stats. Air Force Inst. Tech., Wright Patterson, AFB Dayton, Ohio, 1996—2000. Adj. prof. U. Dayton, 1998—2000. Pres. So. Plantation Homeowners Assn., College Station, Tex., 1995—96. Lt. col. USAF, 1998—2000. Mem.: Am. Statis. Assn., Air Force Assn. (life), Omega Rho, Tau Beta Pi. Avocations: softball, billiards.

CROWN, LESTER, manufacturing company executive; b. Chgo., June 7, 1925; s. Henry and Rebecca (Kranz) C.; m. Renee Schine, Dec. 28, 1950; children: Steven, James, Patricia, Daniel, Susan, Sara, Janet. BS in Chem. Engring., Northwestern U., 1946; MBA, Harvard U., 1949. Instr. math. Northwestern U., 1946-47; v.p., chem. engr. Marblehead Lime Co., 1950-56, pres., 1956-66, also bd. dirs.; v.p. Material Svc. Corp. subs. Gen. Dynamics Corp., Chgo., 1953-66, pres., 1970-83, chmn., 1983—, also bd. dirs.; chmn. exec. com. Gen. Dynamics Corp., 1982—2001, also bd. dirs.; pres. Henry Crown & Co., Chgo., 1969—2002, chmn., 2002—, also bd. dirs. Bd. dirs. Maytag Corp.; ptnr. N.Y. Yankees Partnership, from 1973. Trustee Aspen Inst. Humanistic Studies, Northwestern U., Michael Reese Found.; bd. dirs. Lyric Opera Corp., Children's Meml. Med. Ctr., Jewish Theol. Sem., Jerusalem Found.; mem. bd. govs. Weizmann Inst. of Sci./Tel Aviv U. Mem. Am. Acad. Arts and Scis., Lake Shore Country Club, Northmoor Country Club, Old Elm Club, Standard Club, Econ. Club (dir. 1972), Chgo. Club, Comml. Club, Mid-Am. Club (Chgo.), John Evans Club of Northwestern U., Tau Beta Pi, Pi My Epsilon, Phi Eta Sigma. Office: Material Svc Corp 222 N La Salle St Ste 1200 Chicago IL 60601-1087 also: Gen Dynamics Corp 3190 Fairview Park Dr Fl 1 Falls Church VA 22042-4510

CROWN, NANCY ELIZABETH, lawyer; b. Bronx, N.Y., Mar. 27, 1955; d. Paul and Joanne Barbara (Newman) C.; children: Rebecca, Adam. BA, Barnard Coll., 1977, MA, 1978; MEd, Columbia U., 1983; JD cum laude, Nova Law Sch., 1992. Cert. tchr.; Bar: Fla. 1992. Tchr. Sachem Sch. Dist., Holbrook, N.Y., 1978-82; v.p. mail order dept. Haber-Klein, Inc., Hicksville, N.Y., 1984-88; mgr. mdse., dir. ops. Sure Card Inc., Pompano Beach, Fla., 1988-89; legal intern Office U.S. Trustee/Dept. Justice, 1992; assoc. John T. Kinsey, P.A., Boca Raton, Fla., 1993-95; pvt. practice Nancy E. Crown, P.A., Boca Raton, Fla., 1995—; owner Crystal Title, Inc., 1999—. Recipient West Pub. award for acad. achievement, 1992. Mem. NOW, Fla. Bar Assn., South Palm Beach County Bar Assn., Bus. Partnership Coun., Phi Alpha Delta. Democrat. Jewish. Avocations: theatre, walking, reading, jazz. E-mail: necrownpa@aol.com.

CROWSON, HENRY LAWRENCE, mathematician, educator; b. Okeechobee, Fla., Apr. 16, 1927; s. Ernest Hubbard and Mary Elizabeth Crowson; m. Betty Mae George, June 16, 1951; children: Lawrence George, James Maxwell, Timothy David. BChemE, U. Fla., Gainesville, 1953, MS in Math., 1955, PhD in Math., 1959. Cert. engr. in tng., Fla. Asst. prof. U. Fla., Gainesville, 1958-60; advisory mathematician IBM Corp., Gaithersburg, Md., 1960-72; sr. mathematician CACI Corp., Arlington, Va., 1975-77; assoc. prof. U. P.M., Saudi Arabia, 1977-79, U. Houston, 1982-86, TIEC/MUCIA, Shah Alam, Malaysia, 1986-89, Tex. A&M Internat. U., Laredo, 1990-98. Cons. Bell Labs., CACI, Vitro Labs., Cornell U., others, 1955—. Reviewer books and math. texts, 1965-68. Mem. Am. Math. Soc., Sigma Xi, Pi Mu Epsilon. Republican. Avocations: reading, music, composing poetry. Home: 10127 Falls Rd Potomac MD 20854-4107

CROWSON, JAMES LAWRENCE, lawyer, financial company executive, academic administrator; b. Duncan, Okla., Aug. 3, 1938; s. George L. and Emry Elifair (McKee) C.; children from previous marriage: James Lawrence Jr., Jason Phillips, Kristan Fair Nickel; m. Linda Sue Crowson, Mar. 2, 1986; stepchildren: Chadwick Lanier Johnson, Kim Johnson Osborn. BA in English Lit., U. Okla., 1960; LLB, So. Meth. U., 1963. Bar: Tex. 1963. Legis. counsel Tex. Legis. Coun., Austin, 1966-67; dir. hearings Tex. Water Quality Bd., Austin, 1967-68, chief legal officer, 1967-68, dir. hearings and enforcement, 1969-70; adminstrv. asst. Office of Gov., Austin, 1968-69; univ. atty. U. Tex. System, Austin, 1970; asst. to pres. U. Tex., Austin, 1970-71, Dallas, 1971-74, v.p., 1974-77, exec. v.p., 1977-80; vice chancellor, gen. counsel U. Tex. System, Austin, 1980-87; sr. v.p., gen. counsel Lomas Fin. Group, Dallas, 1987-94, exec. v.p., 1994-95; pvt. investment practice Dallas, 1995-96; dep. chancellor adminstrn. Tex. Tech. Univ. System, Lubbock, 1996—2002. Sec. Tex. Higher Edn. Found., 1988-1996, Higher Edn. Legis. Polit. Action Com., 1987-1996; vice chmn. HCB Enterprises Inc., 1995—; bd. dirs. KOHM Pub. Radio Sta., 1997-99, Tex. Univs. Health Plan, 1998-2002; bd. dirs. Market Lubbock, Inc., 1997-99, v.p. 1999. Trustee Alliance for Higher Edn., 1991-96, Dallas Edn. Ctr., 1995-96. Capt. U.S. Army, 1963-66. Mem. Mortgage Bankers Assn. Am. (mem.

legal issues com., mem. legis. com.), U.S. C. of C. (mem. edn. employment and tng. com., mem. labor rels. com., mem. S.W. pub. affairs task force). Office: 5109 82d St Ste 7 # 258 Lubbock TX 79424 E-mail: crowsonj@swbell.net.

CROWSON, WATIE DEE, foundation administrator; b. Vian, Okla., Aug. 29, 1953; s. Harvey and Gussie B. Crowson; m. Sandra G. Brewster, Aug. 26, 1972 (div. June 1974); 1 child, Regina Lea; m. Sharon K. Moody, Mar. 27, 1979 (div. Aug. 1979); children: Joshua, Angel. Student, Carl Albert U. Former welder, iron worker, home builder, power plant operator, lakes and park ranger asst.; legis. chmn. DAV, Sallisaw, Okla., 1998—. Second vice comdr. Disabled Am. Vets. Chpt. 83, Post Comdr. Post 27; chmn. Marble City; mem. Marble City Bapt. Ch. With USN, 1974-75. Mem. Am. Legion (Honor Guard, legis. chmn.), USS Kitty Hawk Assn, Marble City Citizen Bank, Hist. Soc., VFW. Democrat. Avocations: guitar, gardening, cooking, reading, landscaping. Home: 210 #E N Walnut Sallisaw OK 74955

CROWSTON, WALLACE BRUCE STEWART, management educator; b. Toronto, Ont., Can., Jan. 28, 1934; s. Arthur William and Clara Helena (Donnelly) C.; m. Taka Ohkubo, Sept. 15, 1961; children: Kevin, Cathy, Clare. BA Sc, U. Toronto, 1956; SM, MIT, 1958; MSc, Carnegie Mellon U., 1965, PhD, 1968. Asst. prof. U. Alta., 1960-62, MIT, 1966, assoc. prof., 1969-72; prof., faculty adminstrv. studies York U., 1972-87, dean, 1976-84; dean faculty mgmt. McGill U., Montreal, Que., Can., 1987-2000, dir. Ctr. Internat. Mgmt. Studies, 1990—. Mem. Univ. Club (Montreal). Office: McGill U Faculty Mgmt 1001 Sherbrooke St W Montreal QC Canada H3A 1G5

CROWTHER, G. RODNEY, III, television production company executive, writer, photographer; b. Asheville, N.C., Jan. 11, 1927; s. G. Rodney Jr. and Martha Maria (Lewis) C. Grad., Boys' Latin Sch., Balt., 1944; student, Sch. Modern Photography, N.Y.C., 1949-50. Fashion photographer Amos Parrish & Co., N.Y.C., 1950-53; ind. comml. photographer Chevy Chase, Md., 1956-61; free-lance writer Washington, 1962—; pres. The Carrollian Age, Washington, 1987—. Author: Surname Index to Sixty-Five Volumes of Colonial and Revolutionary Pedigrees, 1964; contbr. articles to Nat. Geneal. Soc. Quar., 1962—; photograph Sputnik and the Big Dipper in Modern Mus. Art, N.Y.C., Echo I satellite in Smithsonian Inst., Where 'KONG' Stood, UN, N.Y.C., 1951. Served with USN, 1945-46, PTO. Episcopalian. Avocations: miniature gardening, audio-video editing. Office: PO Box 369 Ben Franklin Sta Washington DC 20044

CROWTHER, JAMES EARL, radio and television executive, lawyer; b. Cleve., Jan. 2, 1930; s. Byron Scott and Leota Belle (Frye) C.; m. Nancy Louise Swanner, Nov. 28, 1953; children: Richard Scott, Robert Phillip, Paul William. BA, Ohio Wesleyan U., 1956; JD, U. Mich., 1958. Bar: Tex. 1959. Assoc. Butler, Binion, Rice, Cook & Knapp, Houston, 1959-67; v.p. Channel Five TV Co., Nashville, 1975-86, Channel Two TV Co., Houston, 1970-86; v.p., gen. counsel Houston Post Co., 1967-76, exec. v.p., gen. counsel, 1976-83; v.p. Channel Four TV Co., Tucson, 1982-86, Channel Eleven TV Co., Meridian, Miss., 1981-84, KPRC Radio Co., Houston, 1983-86, WESH-TV, Inc., Daytona Beach, Fla., 1985-86, KCCI-TV, Inc., Des Moines, 1985-86; sec. H & C Comm., Inc., Houston, 1979-83, pres., 1983-94; gen. counsel U. Houston Sys., 1995-96, dep. chancellor, gen. counsel, 1996-97. Adj. prof. law South Tex. Law Sch., Houston, 1974-75. Pres. Briargrove Park Property Owners, Inc., 1969-70; bd. dirs. Uptown Houston, 1990-94, Post Oak YMCA, 1991-93. With USAF, 1951-55. Mem. Tex. Bar Assn., Houston Bar Assn., Galleria Area C. of C. (bd. dirs. 1988-92). Methodist.

CROWTHER, RICHARD LAYTON, architect, consultant, researcher, author, lecturer; b. Newark, Dec. 16, 1910; s. William George and Grace (Layton) C.; m. Emma Jane Hubbard, 1935 (div. 1949); children: Bethe Crowther Allison, Warren Winfield, Vivian Layton; m. 2d Pearl Marie Tesch, Sept. 16, 1950. Student, Newark Sch. Fine and Indsl. Arts, 1928-31, San Diego State Coll., 1933, U. Colo., 1956. Registered architect, Colo. Prin. Crowther & Marshall, San Diego, 1946-50, Richard L. Crowther, Denver, 1951-66, Crowther, Kruse, Landin, Denver, 1966-70, Crowther, Kruse, McWilliams, Denver, 1970-75, Crowther Solar Group, Denver, 1975-82, Richard L. Crowther FAIA, Denver, 1982—. Vis. critic, lectr. U. Nebr., 1981; holistic energy design process methodology energy cons. Holistic Health Ctr., 1982-83; adv. cons. interior and archtl. design class U. Colo., 1982-83, Cherry Creek, Denver redevel., 1984-88, Colo. smoking control legislation, 1985, interior solar concepts Colo. Inst. Art, 1986, Bio-Electro-Magnetics Inst., 1987-88; mentor U. Colo. Sch. Architecture, 1987-88. Author Sun/Earth, 1975 (Progressive Architecture award, 1975), rev. edit., 1983, reprint, 1995, Affordable Passive Solar Homes, 1983, reprint, 1996, Paradox of Smoking, 1983, Women/Nature/Destiny: Female/Male Equity for Global Survival, 1987, (monographs) Context in Art and Design, 1985, Existence, Design and Risk, 1986, Indoor Air: Risks and Remedies, 1986, Human Migration in Solar Homes for Seasonal Comfort and Energy Conservation, 1986, 88, Ecologic Architecture, 1992, Ecologic Digest, 1993, Ecologic Connections, 1996, Colorado Architect Monographs on Environmental Themes, 1998, Environmental Sustainability, 1999. NSF grantee, 1974-75; archtl. plans, drawings, photographs, ecol. and solar writings in archibes of western history dept. Denver Pub. Libr., 2002. Fellow AIA (commr. research, edn. and environ. Colo. Central chpt. 1972-75, bd. dirs. chpt. 1973-74 AIA Research Corp. Solar Monitoring Program contract award, spkr. and pub. Colo. Ecologic Connections open forum 1996). Achievements include ecologic bio-toxic and bio-electromagnetic research. *Inner awareness, relevancy, persistence and adaptiveness are all that we have in a world of vanity, variety and change.*

CROYLE, BARBARA ANN, health care management executive; b. Knoxville, Tenn., Oct. 22, 1949; d. Charles Evans and Myrtle Elizabeth (Kellam) C. BA cum laude in Sociology, Coll. William and Mary, 1971; cert. corp. tax and securities law, Inst. Paralegal Tng., 1971; JD, U. Colo., 1975; cert. program mgmt. devel., Colo. Women's Coll., 1980; MBA, U. Denver, 1983. Bar: Colo. 1976. Paralegal Holland & Hart, Denver, 1972-73; law clk. Colo. Ct. Appeals, Denver, summer 1976; assoc. firm Shaw Spangler & Roth, Denver, 1976-77; mgr. acquisitions/lands Petro-Lewis Corp., Denver, 1977-85; mgr. strategic planning Westinghouse, Transp. Divsn., Denver, 1985-87; mng. dir. Benefit Resource Mgmt. Group (subs. Blue Cross We. Pa.), 1987-92; COO, v.p. D.T. Watson Rehab. Hosp., 1992-93; v.p. ambulatory care svcs., compliance officer Franciscan Med. Ctr., Dayton campus, Ohio, 1994-2000; exec. dir. Swedish Am. Ctr. for Complementary Medicine, Rockford, Ill., 2000—02; legal advisor Peninsula United Meth. Homes, Inc., Hockessin, Del., 2003—. Tchr. oil and gas law Colo. Paralegal Inst., 1978, 79; arbitrator Am. Arbitration Assn.; mediator Dayton Mediation Ctr. Mem. ABA, Del. Bar Assn., Inst. Noetic Scis., Am. Coll. Healthcare Execs. Home: 150 Mercer Mill Rd Landenberg PA 19350 Office: Peninsula United Meth Home 726 Loveville Rd Hockessin DE 19807 E-mail: bcroyle@earthlink.net.

CROZIER, JANE E. educational consultant, researcher; d. Mervin Thomas and Marilyn June Crozier. BA in elem. edn., U. of Mich., Ann Arbor, 1981; EdM in instrnl. tech. and adminstrn., Harvard Grad. Sch. of Edn., Cambridge, Mass., 1991; EdS in instrnl. tech., U. Ga., Athens, 2001. Cert. tchr. k-8 Mich., 1981. Programmer-analyst Info. Systems Govt., 1983—89; cons. ednl. tech. Detroit Med. Ctr., 1992—94; sr. ednl. specialist Ga. Dept. of Edn., Atlanta, 1994—96; cons. instrnl. tech. Atlanta, 1997—2002; program assoc. North Central Regional Edn. Lab. Ctr. Tech., Naperville, Ill., 2002—. Mem. Innovative Tchr. selection com. Ga. Ctr. Advanced Telecom. Tech., Atlanta, 1994—98; Ga. dept. of edn. rep. Governor's Tech. Policy Coun., Atlanta, 1996; edn. tech. coop. rep. So. Regional Edn. Bd., Atlanta, 1995—96. Lead designer (web site) Virtual Folklore Mus., 1998 (Laureate award for innovation, Smithsonian Inst., 1998). Bd. dir. Boston Computer Soc., 1988—92; trustee, youth adv. Rochester Area Comm. Found., Rochester Hills, Mich., 1991—93; chmn. Ga. Net Day, Atlanta, 1996—97. Recipient Leadership award, Boston Computer Soc., 1989. Mem.: Assn. Ednl. Comm. and Tech., Am. Ednl. Rsch. Assn., Harvard Club. Avocations: travel, reading, writing, hiking, philanthropy, biking.

CROZIER, PRUDENCE SLITOR, economist; b. Boston, Oct. 27, 1940; d. Richard Eaton and Louise (Bean) S.; m. William Marshall, June 20, 1964; children: Matthew Eaton, Abigail Parsons, Patience Wells. BA with honors, Wellesley Coll., 1962; MA in Econs., Yale U., 1963; PhD in Econs., Harvard U., 1971. Rsch. asst. Fed. Res. Bank, Boston, 1963-64; tchg. fellow, tutor Harvard U., Cambridge, Mass., 1966-69; instr. Wellesley Coll., Mass., 1969-70; sr. economist Data Resources Inc., Lexington, Mass., 1973-74; bd. dirs. Omega Fund, 1984-87, Mass. Ednl. Facilities Authority, 1985-93, Boston Pub. Libr. Found., 1994—, vice chmn., 1996—. Vis. com. Harvard Sch. Pub. Health, 1993—2000, Coll. des Conseillers French Libr. and Cultural Ctr., Boston, 1995—, trustee, 1996—2002. Contbr. articles to profl. jours. Trustee Newton Wellesley Hosp., Mass., 1978—90; overseer Ctr. Rsch. of Women, Wellesley, 1982—83, Mus. Fine Arts, Boston, 1999— ; trustee Wellesley Coll., 1980—98, Nantucket Hist. Assn., 1997—2002, Nantucket Atheneum, 2001.

CROZIER, WILLIAM MARSHALL, JR., bank holding company executive; b. N.Y.C., Oct. 2, 1932; s. William Marshall and Alice (Parsons) C.; m. Prudence van Zandt Slitor, June 20, 1964; children: Matthew Eaton, Abigail Parsons, Patience Wells. BA in Econs., Yale U., 1954; MBA with distinction, Harvard U., 1963. With Hanover Bank, N.Y.C., 1954-61, asst. sec., 1959; with BayBanks, Inc., Boston, 1964—, asst. treas., 1965, asst. v.p., 1968, v.p., sec., 1969, sr. v.p., sec., 1973, chmn. bd., chief exec. officer, 1974-96, pres., 1977-96, dir., 1974-96; chmn. bd. dirs. BankBoston Corp., 1996-97, chmn. emeritus, 1997—. Served with U.S. Army, 1955-57. Mem.: Comml.-Mchts. (Boston), Union (Boston), Harvard (Boston); Yale (N.Y.C.). Episcopalian.

CRUDDEN, ADELE LOUISE, social work research educator; b. New Orleans, Sept. 25, 1957; d. Edwin Francis and Eunice Louise (Courtault) C.; m. Curtis Edward Alford; children: Abigail Louise Alford. BS, Miss. State U., Starkville, 1979; MEd, Miss. State U., 1980, PhD, 1997; MSW, La. State U., 1989. Lic. social worker, profl. counselor; cert. rehab. counselor, ins. rehab. specialist. Vocat. therapist Developmental Ctr., Decatur, Ala., 1981-82; supr. New Orleans Assn. Retarded Citizens, 1982-84; rehab. specialist Sullivan Rehab., New Orleans, 1984-90; social worker Nat. Med. Care, New Orleans, 1990-91; adminstr., dir. Vocat. Rehab. for Blind, Jackson, Miss., 1991-94; rsch. sci. Miss. State U., Starkville, 1994—, dir. social work program. Counselor Children's Hosp., New Orleans, 1988, social work cons., 1989; social work cons. La. State U. Human Devel. Ctr., 1989. Active NOW, PTA, Coalition for Citizens with Disabilities, Miss., Parents for Pub. Schs., Starkville. Grantee Miss. Dept. Human Svcs., 1995-96, Nat. Inst. for Disability on Rehab. Rsch. Mem. NASW, Nat. Assn. Rehab. Profls. in Pvt. Sector, Assn. Edn. and Rehab. Blind and Visually Impaired. Office: Miss State U RRTC PO Box 6189 Mississippi State MS 39762-6189

CRUDEN, JOHN CHARLES, lawyer; b. Topeka, Feb. 23, 1946; s. George Harry and Agnes (Telban) C.; m. Sharon Lynn Holland, June 15, 1968; children: Kristen, Heather. BS, U.S. Mil. Acad., 1968; JD, U. Santa Clara, 1974; MA, U. Va., 1975; grad., Gen. Staff Coll., 1982; fellow, Army War Coll., 1988. Bar: Calif. 1975, D.C. 1979, U.S. Supreme Ct. 1979. Commd. 2d lt. U.S. Army, 1968, advanced through grades to col., 1987, with airborne, ranger, spl. forces, 1968-71, clk. Calif. Supreme Ct., 1974, pros., 1975-76, chief litig. br. Hdqrs. Europe, 1976-78, sr. trial atty. comml. br. litig. divsn., 1978-79, gen. counsel Def. Nuclear Agy., 1979-80; prof., chief Adminstrv. and Civil Law divsn. Judge Adv. Gen.'s Sch., Charlottesville, Va., 1982-85; staff Judge Adv. Europe, 1985-87; spl. counsel to asst. atty. gen. civil divsn. U.S. Dept. Justice, 1987-88; chief legis. counsel Dept. Army, 1988-91; chief environ. enforcement sect. Environ. & Natural Resource divsn. U.S. Dept. Justice, Washington, 1991-95, dep. asst. atty. gen., 1995—2001, acting asst. atty. gen., 2001—02, dep. asst. atty. gen., 2002—. Contbr. articles to profl. jours. Mem. Fed. Bar Assn. (chpt. pres. 1984-85, Younger Fed. Lawyers award 1981), JAG Sch. Alumni Assn. (pres. 1982-85), D.C. Bar Assn. (bd. govs. 2001—), Calif. Bar Assn., ABA (mem. coun. sect. on environment, energy and resources 2002—, vice chmn. adminstrv. law and gen. practice sect. 1985-88, vice chmn. fed. legis. com. 1989-92, adv. com., standing com. on law and nat. security 1988-94). Office: US Dept Justice 950 Pennsylvania Ave NW Washington DC 20530-0001 E-mail: john.cruden@usdoj.gov.

CRUDEN, ROBERT WILLIAM, botany educator; b. Cleve., Mar. 18, 1936; m. Diana Benedict Loeb, Dec. 21, 1967; children: Nathalie Rebecca, Lyda Marie; m. Diana Ruth Gannett, July 1996. AB, Hiram (Ohio) Coll., 1958; MS, Ohio State U., Columbus, 1960; PhD, U. Calif., Berkeley, 1967. Asst. prof. U. Iowa, Iowa City, 1967-71, assoc. prof., 1971-78, prof., 1978-99, prof. emeritus, 1999—. Acting dir. Iowa Lakeside Lab., Wahepton, 1989-94, past asst. dir.; adj. prof. U. Mich, Ann Arbor, 2001- Editor Ecol. Soc. Am., 1983-86; editl. bd. Madrono; contbr. numerous articles to profl. jours. Mem. pres.'s coun. on sci. initiatives Hiram Coll., 1994—. Recipient J.J. Turner award Hiram Coll., 2001. Fellow Iowa Acad. Sci.; mem. AAAS, Am. Soc. Plant Taxonomists, Bot. Soc. Am., Ecol. Soc. Am., Iowa Acad. Sci., Soc. for the Study of Evolution, Assn. for Tropical Biology, New Eng. Bot. Soc. Office: U Iowa Dept Biol Scis Iowa City IA 52242 Home: 550 Woodhill Dr Saline MI 48176 E-mail: robert-cruden@uiowa.edu.

CRUESS, LEIGH SAUNDERS, financial executive; b. N.Y.C., Jan. 5, 1958; s. Richard Leigh and Sylvia (Robinson) C.; m. Susan Andrews, July 11, 1981. BA with honors, Queens U., Kingston, Ont., Can., 1979; MBA, Dartmouth Coll., 1981. Analyst Cargill, Inc., Mpls., 1981-84; account mgr. Cargill Leasing Corp., Chgo., 1984-86; asst. v.p. Citicorp N.Am., Leveraged Capital Group, Chgo., 1986-88; v.p. AT Comml. Corp. (subs. Ameritrust), Chgo., 1988-89; mng. dir. MASI Ltd., Chgo., 1990-95; v.p. corp. devel. Utilicorp United Inc., Kansas City, Mo., 1996-99, Enbridge Inc., Calgary, Canada, 1999—2003, v.p. fin. svcs., 2003—. Chmn. Hinsdale Village Caucus, 1994-95; bd. elders Union Ch. of Hinsdale, 1992-95, bd. worship Colonial Ch., 1997-2000. Avocations: tennis, skiing, cooking, music. Home: 8924 Baylor Cr SW Calgary AB Canada T2V 3N4 Office: Enbridge Inc 3000 425 1st St SW Calgary AB Canada T2P 3L8 E-mail: lscruess@shaw.ca., leigh.cruess@enbridge.com.

CRUESS, RICHARD LEIGH, surgeon, university dean; b. London, Ont., Can., Dec. 17, 1929; s. Leigh S. and Martha A. (Peever) C.; m. Sylvia Crane Robinson, May 30, 1953; children: Leigh S., Andrew C. BA, Princeton U., 1951; MD, Columbia U., 1955. Diplomate Am. Bd. Orthopedic Surgery. Intern Royal Victoria Hosp., Montreal, Que., 1955-56, resident surgery, 1956-57, N.Y. Orthopedic Hosp., 1959-60, asst. resident orthopedic surgery, 1960-61, resident orthopedic surgery, 1961-62, Annie C. Kane fellow orthopedic surgery, 1961-62; research asso. depts. orthopedic surgery and biochemistry Columbia U., N.Y.C., 1962-63; John Armour Travelling fellow, 1962-63; Am.-Brit.-Can. Travelling fellow, 1967; practice medicine specializing in orthopedic surgery, 1963-95; orthopedic surgeon Royal Victoria Hosp., orthopedic surgeon-in-charge, 1968-81, asst. surgeon-in-chief, 1970-81; chief surgeon Shriner's Hosp. for Crippled Children, Montreal, 1970-82; prof. surgery McGill U., Montreal, 1970—, chmn. div. orthopedic surgery, 1976-81, dean faculty medicine, 1981-95, prof. Ctr. for Med. Edn., 1995—. Hon. cons. orthopedic surgery Queen Elizabeth Hosp., 1972-95; mem. clin. grants com. Med. Rsch. Coun., 1972-75, mem. coun., 1980-86, mem. exec., 1983-86. Contbr. articles on surgery to profl. jours.; mem. editl. bd. Jour. Internat. Orthopedics, 1976-85, Jour. Bone and Joint Surgery, 1977-83, Current Problems in Orthopedics, 1977-83, Jour. Orthopaedic Rsch., 1986-88. Served to lt. M.C., USN, 1957-59. Decorated mem. and officer Order of Can. Fellow Royal Coll. Physicians and Surgeons Can. (chief examiner orthopedic surgery 1970-72), ACS, Am. Acad. Orthopedic Surgeons, Royal Soc. Can.; mem. Can. Orthopedic Assn. (sec. 1971-76, pres. 1977-78), Can. Orthopedic Rsch. Soc. (pres. 1971-72), Am. Orthopedic Rsch. Soc. (pres. 1975-76), Am. Orthopedic Assn., Am. Orthopedic Surgeons Province Que. (treas. 1971-72), Société Française de Chirurgie Orthopedique (hon.), McGill Osler Reporting Soc., Assn. can. Med. colls. (pres. 1987-89). Home: Apt 903 2333 Sherbrooke St W Montreal QC Canada H3H 2T6 Office: McGill U 1110 Pine Ave W Montreal QC Canada H3A 1A3 E-mail: Richard.Cruess@McGill.ca.

CRUIKSHANK, DAVID EARL, lawyer; b. Painesville, Ohio, Apr. 23, 1945; s. Earl W. and Kathryn (Schlender) C.; m. Nancy Kathryn Heine, June 9, 1984. B.A., DePauw U., 1967; J.D., Case West Res. U., 1973. Bar: Ohio 1973, U.S. Dist. Ct. (so. dist.) Ohio 1973, U.S. Supreme Ct. 1980. Assoc. Turner & Badger, Mount Vernon, Ohio, 1973-75, Baker, Byron & Hackenberg, Painesville, 1975-76; assoc., ins. mgr. E.W. Cruikshank, Painesville, 1976-84; assoc. Byron & Ryan, Willoughby, Ohio, 1984— ; mem. faculty Ohio Legal Ctr. Inst., 1985, 86, U. Toledo Sch. of Law, CLE div., 1985. 1st lt. USMC, 1968-71, Vietnam. Mem. ABA, Ohio Bar Assn. (chmn. ins. law com. 1984-87, vice chmn. 1981-84), Lake County Bar Assn., Def. Research Inst., Ohio Bar Found, Ohio Acad. Civil Trial Attys. (lectr. 1984, 86), Masons. Home: 30 Wintergreen Hill Dr Painesville OH 44077-5332 Office: Byron & Ryan 36100 Euclid Ave Willoughby OH 44094-4456

CRUIKSHANK, JOHN W., III, life insurance underwriter; b. Sharon, Pa., Aug. 22, 1933; s. John W. and Jeannette Sprague (Lane) C.; m. Myrna Jean Wright, Nov. 25, 1960; children— Nancy Lynn, David Wright BA, Princeton U., 1955. CLU. Group ins. sales rep. Conn. Gen. Life Ins. Co., Hartford, also Chgo., 1955-56; spl. agt. Northwestern Mut. Life Ins. Co., Chgo., 1959—, pres. Spl. Agts., Inc., 1983-84, faculty advanced planning sch. Northbrook, Ill., 1978-97; pres. Assn. of Agts. Northwestern Mut. Life, 1994-95. Pres. Million Dollar Round Table Found., 1988—89; divisional v.p. Million Dollar Round Table, 1976—77, 1986—87, 1992—93, exec. com., 1994—98, pres., 1996—97; trustee Life Underwriter Tng. Coun., 1997—2001. Bd. dirs. Life and Health Ins. Found. for Edn., 1997—, chmn., 2002; bd. dirs. North Shore Sr. Ctr., 2001—; trustee Pikeville (Ky.) Coll., 1969—75, The Am. Coll., 2001—02; pres. Nat. Coun. United Presbyn. Men, 1971—72; elder United Presbyn. Ch. in U.S.A., 1975—, mem. gen. assembly mission coun., 1972—78; chmn. mission divsn. Presbytery of Chgo., gen. coun., 1966—67, 1980—84; bd. dirs. Vocation Agy., Presbyn. Ch. in U.S.A., 1982—87. Recipient Circle of Life award Million Dollar Round Table Found., 1998, Huebner Scholar award Am. Soc. CLU and ChFC, Chgo., 1995, Distinguished Citizen award Ill. St. Andrew Soc., 1998, Grauer Disting. Svc. award Chgo. Chpt. Fin. Svc. Profls., 2000; named one of Most Outstanding Life Underwriters in the U.S. for decade of 1990s, Leaders Mag., 1999. Home: 1412 Ridge Rd Northbrook IL 60062-4628

CRUIKSHANK, THOMAS HENRY, energy services and engineering executive; b. Lake Charles, La., Nov. 3, 1931; s. Louis James and Helene L. (Little) Cruikshank; m. Ann Coe, Nov. 17, 1955; 1 child, Thomas Henry Jr.;children: Kate Martin, Stuart Coe. BA, Rice U., 1952; postgrad., U. Tex. Law Sch., 1952—53, U. Houston Law Sch., 1953—55. CPA Tex.; bar: Tex. Accountant Arthur Andersen & Co., Houston, 1953-55, 58-60; mem. firm Vinson & Elkins, Houston, 1961—69; v.p. Halliburton Co., Dallas, 1969—72, sr. v.p., 1972—80, exec. v.p., 1980, pres., CEO subs. Otis Engring. Corp., 1980—81, pres., 1981—83, pres., CEO, 1983-89, chmn., CEO, 1989—95, dir., 1977—95. Bd. dirs. Williams Cos., Inc., Lehman Bros. Holdings, Inc.; former dir. Goodyear Tire & Rubber Co.; former mem. Nat. Petroleum Coun.; policy com. Bus. Roundtable. Pres. Jr. Achievement, Dallas, 1974—76, chmn., 1976—78; trustee Calif. Inst. Tech., 1991—96; mem. nat. bd. dirs. Jr. Achievement, 1976—95, chmn., 1989—90; bd. dirs. Up With People, 1998—2000. Lt. (j.g.) USNR, 1955—58. Mem.: Am. Petroleum Inst., Tex. Bar Assn., ABA, Eldorado Country Club (Calif.), Grandfather Golf and Country Club (N.C.), River Oaks Country Club (Houston), Dallas Country Club. Home: 4201 Lomo Alto Dallas TX 75219 Office: 5949 Sherry Ln Dallas TX 75225-6532

CRUISE, TOM (TOM CRUISE MAPOTHER IV), actor; b. Syracuse, N.Y., July 3, 1962; s. Thomas C. III and Mary Lee Mapother; m. Mimi Rogers, May 9, 1987 (div. 1990); m. Nicole Kidman, Dec. 24, 1990 (div. 2001); adopted children: Isabella Jane Kidman, Connor Antony Kidman. Grad. H.S., Glen Ridge, N.J. Actor: stage prodn. Godspell; feature film appearances include Endless Love, Taps, 1981, Losin' It, 1981, The Outsiders, 1983, Risky Business, 1983, All the Right Moves, 1983, Top Gun, 1986, Legend, 1986, The Color of Money, 1986, Cocktail,1988, Rain Man, 1988, Born on the Fourth of July, 1989 (Acad. award nominee for best actor 1990, Golden Globe award Best Actor Drama, Chgo. Film Festival Critics award, Best Actor), Days of Thunder, 1990, Far and Away, 1992, A Few Good Men, 1992, The Firm, 1993, Interview with the Vampire, 1994, Mission Impossible, 1996, Jerry McGuire, 1996 (MTV Movie award Best Male Performance, Golden Globe award Best Performance Comedy/Musical, Blockbuster Entertainment award Favorite Actor-Comedy/Romance, nominated Oscar award Best Actor), Eyes Wide Shut, 1998, Magnolia, 1999 (Golden Globe 2000, nominee Best Supporting Actor Acad. award 1999, Favorite Supporting Actor in Drama Blockbuster Entertainmnet award 2000, Best Supporting Actor CFCA award, 2000), Mission Impossible 2, 2000 (Best Male Performance MTV Movie award 2001), Vanilla Sky, 2001 (Best Actor Saturn award 2002), (voice) Space Station, 2002, Minority Report, 2002; prodr. Without Limits, 1998; exec. prodr. The Others, 2001.*

CRUM, ALBERT BYRD, psychiatrist, consultant; b. Omaha, Nov. 17, 1931; s. J. Rufus and Alberta (McCreary) C.; m. Rosa Maria Hennessy y Sinclair; children: Rosa Maria Crum O'Brien, Elsie Crum McCabe, Alberta Crum Fousek. BS, U. Redlands, Calif., 1953; MD, Harvard U., 1957; MS, NYU, 1987; DSc (hon.), U. Redlands, 1974. Diplomate Am. Bd. Forensic Medicine, in Psychotherapy Am. Psychotherapy Assn., Am. Bd. Forensic Examiners. Med. intern Columbia U. div. Bellevue Med. Ctr., N.Y.C., 1957—58; rsch. fellow, psychiat. resident Creedmoor Inst. for Psychobiol. Studies, Queens Village, NY, 1958—59; chief, neuropsychiatric svcs. Continental Air Command Hdqtrs 2500 USAF Hosp., 1959-61; psychiat. resident Columbia U. Psychiat. Inst. of Columbia-Presbyn. Hosp., N.Y.C., 1961—63; pvt. practice Brooklyn Heights, NY, 1963—. Co-chmn. U.S. Coordinating Commn. for Nomination of His Holiness the Dalai Lama of Tibet for the Nobel Peace Prize, Brooklyn Heights, 1986; chmn. Human Behavior Found., Brooklyn Heights, 1968—; chmn. selection com. Human Behavior Found.'s Albert Schweitzer Humanitarian Award, Brooklyn Heights, 1986—; expert Nat. Forensic Ctr.; pres. Stress Watchers, Inc., The ProImmune Co., LLC., Y.F. One/N.Y., Ltd., 1991—; advisor Office of Tibet, N.Y.C., 1984—; clin. prof. mgmt. sci., adj. prof. anatomy and neuroanatomy NYU, 1987-2002. Author: The 10-Step Method of Stress Relief: Decoding the Meaning and Significance of Stress, CRC Press, 2000; contbr. articles to profl. jours. Bd. dirs. Albert Schweitzer Fellowship, N.Y.C., 1982—; bd. dirs. Burdick Internat. Ancestry Library, Sarasota, Fla., 1985—; mem., chn., bd. advisors NYU's Coll. of Dentistry, N.Y.C., 1988-96; mem. Bklyn. Heights Assn., 1970-96; class agent Harvard Med. Sch. Class of 1957; pres. Stress Watchers Inc. Capt. USAF, 1959-61. Recipient Disting. Svc. award Bklyn. Jr. C. of C., 1966, Bicentennial award Nat. Jogging Assn., 1976; Citizen of Yr. award, Achievements in Medicine and Human Understanding, Bklyn. Philharm., 1986; named Disting. Lectr., NYU Coll. Dentistry, Omicron Kappa Upsilon lectr., 1986. Fellow Royal Coll. Physicians and Surgeons in Psychiatry; mem. Am. Acad. of Forensic Scis. (assoc.), Nat. Bd. Med. Examiners, Med. Coun. of Can., Am. Acad. Clin. Psychiatrists, Am. Physicians Art Assn., Harvard Med. Soc., Harvard Club of N.Y., MENSA (life, nat. coord. 1980-84), Phi Beta Kappa (councillor 1981-84). Achievements include patents for immune/nutrional field. Avocations: jogging, studying world religions, history, leadership. Home and Office: StressWatchers Inc 77 Remsen St Brooklyn NY 11201-3401

CRUM, CLARENCE F. music educator, school system administrator; b. Lorain, Ohio, Feb. 21, 1956; s. Clarence and Dolores F. Crum; m. Jennifer L. Schering, Apr. 21, 2001; children: Allison K., Brent P., Ellie A. Schering. MusB, Youngstown (Ohio) State U., 1978; MEd, Ashland (Ohio) U., 2001. Cert. sch. administrator State of Ohio, 2001, tchr. State of Ohio, 1978. Band dir. Tri-Valley Local Sch. Dist., Dresden, Ohio, 1978—80; dir. of bands Fairless Local Sch. Dist., Navarre, Ohio, 1980—90; supr. of music Massillon (Ohio) City Schs., 1990—95, adminstrv. asst., 1995—96; dir. of fine and performing arts Lake Local Sch. Dist., Hartville, Ohio, 1996—99; sch. adminstr. Brown Local Sch. Dist., Malvern, Ohio, 1999—. Pres. Inter-Valley Conf., New Phila., Ohio, 2002. Contbr. articles to profl. jours. Ch. coun. mem. St. Paul's Luth., Massillon, 1986—90. Named to Music Hall of Fame, Avon Lake Sch. Dist., 1989; recipient Medal of Honor, Mid-West Internat. Band and Orch., 1989, Citation of Excellence, Nat. Band Assn., 1989, Sudler Silver Scroll, John Philips Sousa Assn., 1997. Mem.: OASSA, Music Educators Nat. Conf. Lutheran. Avocations: flying, golf, reading. Office: Brown Local Schools 401 West Main Street Malvern OH 44644 Personal E-mail: jccrum3@neo.rr.com. E-mail: c_crum@sparcc.org.

CRUM, DENNY (DENZEL EDWIN CRUM), retired collegiate basketball coach; b. San Fernando, Calif., Mar. 2, 1937; s. Alwin Denzel and June (Turner) C.; m. Susan H. Sweeney, June 9, 2001; children from previous marriage: Cynthia Lynne, Steven Scott, Robert Scott. BA, UCLA, 1959; secondary tchg. cert., San Fernando Valley State Coll., 1960. Asst., then head basketball coach Pierce Coll., Los Angeles, 1962-67; asst. coach UCLA, 1968-70; head basketball coach U. Louisville, 1971—2001; coach champion team NCAA Basketball Tournament, 1980, 86; ret., 2001. Coach U.S. basketball team Pan Am. Games, 1987. Author articles in field. Named Mo. Valley Conf. Coach of Year, 1973, 75,

Coll. Coach of Year, 1974, Metro Conf. Coach of Year, 1979, 83, Coach of Yr. Sporting News mag., 1983, 86, Playboy mag., 1986; named to UCLA Hall of Fame, 1990. Mem. Nat. Assn. Basketball Coaches (bd. dirs. 1989). Achievements include coaching U. Louisville team to 10 Metro Conf. titles and 8 Metro Conf. Tournament championships. Earned 400th career coaching victory, Feb. 3, 1988. Office: Univ of Louisville Belknap Campus 2301 S 3rd St Louisville KY 40292-0001

CRUM, JAMES FRANCIS, waste recycling company executive; b. Pitts., July 23, 1934; s. Frank J. and Martha (Huffman) C.; m. Madeleine Jones, July 3, 1957 (dec. Feb. 2001); children: Cynthia Anne, James Joseph. BMechE, U. Rochester, 1956. Trainee to supt. transp. U.S. Steel Corp., Braddock, Pa., 1959-74, supt. transp. South Chgo., Ill., 1974-75, supt. operating maintenance, 1975-76, asst. divsn. supt. iron Gary, Ind., 1976-83; divsn. mgr. iron. U.S. Steel div. USX, Gary, 1983-88; exec. v.p., COO McGraw Construction Co., Middletown, Ohio, 1988-92; from dir. bus. devel. to v.p. ops. Nat. Recovery Systems, East Chicago, Ind., 1992-99, pvt. practice Flossmoor, Ill., 1999—. Adv. coun. South Suburban Hosp., 1993—; cons. in field. Vol. U. Rochester Admissions Network, N.Y., 1987—; cons. Clean City Coalition, Gary, 1988-90; bd. dirs. South Suburban Hosp. Found. Mem. AIME, Eastern States Blast Furnace Assn., Western States Blast Furnace Assn. (bd. dirs. 1985-88), Assn. Iron & Steel Engrs. Republican. Roman Catholic. Avocations: golf, photography, foreign travel, stained glass. Home: 736 Central Park Ave Flossmoor IL 60422-2220 E-mail: jfcrum@aol.com.

CRUM, JOHN KISTLER, chemical society director; b. Brownsville, Tex., July 28, 1936; s. John Mears and Mary Louise (Kistler) C. BS, U. Tex., 1960, PhD, 1964; grad. Advanced Mgmt. Program, Harvard U., 1975. Research fellow Robert A. Welch Found., 1962-64; asst. editor Am. Chem. Soc., Washington, 1964-65, assoc. editor, 1966-68, mng. editor, 1969-70, group mgr. jours., 1970, dir. books and jours. div., 1971-75, treas., chief fin. officer, 1975-80, dep. exec. dir. and chief operating officer, 1981-82, exec. dir., 1983—. Chmn. bd. Centcom Ltd., chmn. governing bd. Chem. Abstracts Svc., 1991-1996; chmn. bd. Sci. Info. Internat., Ltd., 1995—; mem. U.S. nat. com. Internat. Union Pure and Applied Chemistry; sr. mem. Con. Bd.; mem. Bretton Woods Com., 2002—; chmn. gov. bd. ACS publs., 1997—; bd. dirs. Consumers Union of U.S., 1991-93. Mem. editorial adv. bd. Am. Men and Women of Sci.; contbr. articles to profl. jours. Fellow Washington Acad. Scis.; mem. Royal Chem. Soc. (London), Am. Chem. Soc., Am. Soc. Assn. Execs., Coun. Engrng. and Sci., Soc. Execs., Assn. Sci. Soc. Editors, N.Y. Acad. Scis., Chem. Soc. Washington, Cosmos Club, City Club, Univ. Club (Washington), Chemists Club (N.Y.), Sigma Xi, Phi Theta Kappa. Republican. Home: 1701 N Kent St Arlington VA 22209-2112 Office: Am Chem Soc 1155 16th St NW Washington DC 20036-4800

CRUM, JULIE WADE, literature educator; d. Harold and Beth Wade; m. Andrew Crum, Aug. 15, 1992. BA in English, Abilene (Tex.) Christian U., 1992; MEd, Tex. A&M U., 1998. Cert. provisional secondary English tchr. State Bd. for Educator Certification, Tex., 1992, profl. mid-mgmt. administr. State Bd. for Educator Certification, Tex., 1998. English tchr. Needville (Tex.) HS, 1992—93; english and reading tchr. Hempstead (Tex.) HS, 1993—94; english and lang. arts tchr. Brenham (Tex.) Mid. Sch., 1994—97; lectr. and lab. coord. Tex. A&M U., Coll. Sta., Tex., 1997—99; instr. Arapahoe C.C., Littleton, Colo., 2000—. Cons. charter sch. application Desert Hills of Tex., Coll. Sta., 1998—99. Editor: Washington County's Future Looks at the Past, 1997. Youth mentor Brenham (Tex.) Ch. of Christ, 1993—99; grant writer Women of God, Houston, 1998—2000; mentor Tex. A&M U. Mem.: AAUP. Republican. Avocations: travel, reading, writing, socializing. Office: Arapahoe Community College 5900 S Santa Fe Drive Littleton CO 80160-9002 E-mail: julie.crum@arapahoe.edu.

CRUM, LAWRENCE LEE, banking educator; b. Brownsville, Tex., July 25, 1933; s. John Mears and Mary Louise (Kistler) Crum. BBA with highest honors (Alpha Kappa Psi scholar 1954), U. Tex., Austin, 1954, MBA, 1956, PhD, 1961; postgrad., Carnegie-Mellon U., 1962, Harvard U., 1965. Ayres fellow Am. Bankers Assn., 1966; asst. prof., then assoc. prof. U. Fla., 1959-65; mem. faculty U. Tex., Austin, 1965—, prof. fin., 1969-82, Tex. Commerce Bancshares Centennial prof. comml. banking, 1982-94, Tex. Commerce Bancshares Centennial prof. emeritus, 1994—, chmn. dept. fin., 1969-76, fellow, Ben F. Love chair in bank mgmt., 1991-93, dir. banking program, 1980-92. Chmn. bd. dirs. San Antonio br. Fed. Res. Bank, Dallas, 1980-86; cons. in comml. banking field; loan com. Franklin Lindsay Student Aid Fund, 1980-94. Author: Time Deposits in Present Day Commercial Banking, 1964, Transition in the Texas Commercial Banking Industry, 1970; co-author: The Development of State-Chartered Banking in Texas, 1978, Competition for the Commercial Banking Industry in the Establishment and Operation of an Electronic Payments System, 1971; contbr. articles to profl. jours. Fellow, Ford Found., 1963—64. Mem. Am. Fin. Assn., Am. Econ. Assn., Fin. Mgmt. Assn., Beta Gamma Sigma, Phi Kappa Phi. Republican. Presbyterian. Home: 3920 Sierra Dr Austin TX 78731-3912 Office: U Tex CBA 6 222 Austin TX 78712

CRUMB, GEORGE HENRY, composer, educator; b. Charleston, W.Va., Oct. 24, 1929; s. George Henry and Vivian (Reed) C.; m. Elizabeth May Brown, May 21, 1949; children: Elizabeth Ann, David Reed, Peter Stanley. B.Mus., Mason Coll., 1950; M.Mus., U. Ill., 1952; postgrad. (Fulbright fellow), Hochschule für Musik, Berlin, Germany, 1955-56, Berkshire Music Center, Tanglewood, Mass., summer 1955; D.Mus. Arts, U. Mich., 1959. Instr. theory Hollins Coll., Va., 1958-59; asst. prof. composition and piano U. Colo., 1959-64; creative asso. composition State U. N.Y. at Buffalo, 1964-65; asst. prof. composition U. Pa., Phila., 1965-66, asso. prof., 1966-71, prof., 1971—, Annenberg prof., 1983—. Composer: String Quartet, 1954, Sonata; for solo violincello, 1955; Variazioni; for large orch., 1959; Five Pieces; for piano, 1962, Night Music I; for soprano, keyboard and percussion, 1963; Four Nocturnes Night Music II; for violin and piano, 1964; Madrigals, Books I and II; for solo voice and instruments, 1965; Eleven Echoes of Autumn; for violin, alto flute, clarinet and piano, 1966; Echoes of Time and the River, 1967 (Pulitzer prize 1968); for orch. Songs, Drones and Refrains of Death for baritone and electric instruments; U. Iowa commn., 1968, Madrigals, Books III and IV; for soprano and instruments, 1969; Night of the Four Moons; for alto and instruments, 1969; Black Angels (Thirteen Images from the Dark Land); for electric string quartet, U. Mich. commn., 1970; Ancient Voices of Children; for soprano and instruments, Coolidge Found. commn., 1970; Vox Balaenae; for electric flute, electric cello and electric piano, 1971; Lux Aeterna; for soprano, sitar, bass flute and two percussionists, 1971; for amplified piano Makrokosmos, Vol. I, 1972, Vol. II, 1973; Makrokosmos, Vol. I Music for a Summer Evening; for 2 amplified pianos and percussion, Fromm Found. commn., 1974; Dream Sequence; for violin, cello, piano, percussion and glass-harmonica, 1976; Star-Child: A Parable; for Solo Soprano, Antiphonal Children's Voices, Bell Ringers and Large Orch., Ford Found. Commn., 1977; Celestial Mechanics, Cosmic Dances; for Amplified Piano, 4-Hands, 1979; Apparition; elegiac songs and vocalises for soprano and amplified piano, 1979; A Little Suite for Christmas, A.D. 1979, 1980, Gnomic Variations for Piano, 1981, Pastoral Drone for Organ, 1982, Processional for piano, 1983, A Haunted Landscape for Orchestra, 1984, The Sleeper for Soprano and Piano, 1984, An Idyll for the Misbegotten for Flute and Drums, 1985; Federico's Little Songs for Children for Soprano, Flute and Harp, 1986, Zeitgeist for two amplified pianos, 1987, Easter Dawning for Carillon, 1991; also commns. Koussevitzky Found., 1964, Bowdoin Coll., 1965, U. Chgo., 1966; Quest, 1994 for guitar and chamber ensemble, Mundus Canis for Guitar and Percussion, 1997, for amplified piano, Eine Kleine Mitternachtmusik, 2002, Unto the Hills, 2002 for voice, percussion quartet and amplified piano, Otherworldly Resonances, 2002 for amplified pianos. Edward MacDowell Colony medal, Peterborough, 1995. Mem. B.M.I., Nat. Inst. Arts and Letters, German Acad. Arts (hon.), Bavarian Acad. Fine Arts, Am. Acad. Arts and Scis., Pi Kappa Lambda, Phi Mu Alpha. Office: U Pa Music Bldg Philadelphia PA 19104

CRUMBAUGH, JAMES CHARLES, psychologist; b. Terrell, Tex., Dec. 11, 1912; s. Charles Miller and Hallie Virginia (Dansby) C.; m. Edna Mae Bailey, 1938 (dec. 1946); 1 child, Charles; m. Teresa Amanda Croteau, June 14, 1975 (dec. Feb. 1989); m. Lois Dickson Hicks, Nov. 10, 1992. AB, Baylor U., 1935; AM, So. Meth. U., 1938; PhD, U. Tex., 1953. Lic. psychologist, Miss.; cert. logotherapist. Psychologist, tchr. Memphis State U., 1947-56; chmn. dept. Psychology MacMurray Coll., Jacksonville, Ill., 1957-59; rsch. dir. Bradley Ctr., Inc., Columbus, Ga., 1959-64; staff psychologist VA Med. Ctr., Augusta, Ga., 1964-65, Gulfport, Miss., 1965-80; so. regional dir. Inst. Logotheraphy, Berkeley, Calif., 1980—. Rsch. cons. Internat. Graphoanalysis Soc., Chgo., 1968—. Author: Counseling for Graphoanalysts, 1970, Everything to Gain, 1973; co-author: Logotherapy, 1980; sr. author (with M.T. Manolick) The Purpose-in-Life Test, 1967; co-editor: Primer of Projective Techniques, 1990. With U.S. Army air Corps, 1941-45. Rsch. fellow Duke U., 1954-55. Mem. APA, Miss. Psychol. Assn. (Kinlock Gill award 1989), Southeastern Psychol. Assn., So. Soc. Philosophy and Psychology, Psi Chi. Roman Catholic. Avocation: writing. Home: 140 Balmoral Ave Biloxi MS 39531-4701 Office: 140A Balmoral Ave Biloxi MS 39531-4701 E-mail: texasjim2@aol.com.

CRUMBLEY, DONALD LARRY, accounting educator, writer, consultant; b. Kannapolis, N.C., Jan. 18, 1941; s. Carl Donald and Velvia Luetta (Kelly) C.; m. Donna Darlene Loflin, Aug. 31, 1963; children: Stacey Lynn, Dana Lea, Heather Ann. BS cum laude, Pfeiffer U., 1963; MS, La. State U., 1965, PhD, 1967. CPA, N.C.; diplomate Am. Bd. Forensic Accts.; cert. fin. svcs. auditor, forensic acct. Grad rsch. asst. La. State U., Baton Rouge, 1963-65, tchg. asst., 1965-66; asst. prof. acctg. Pa. State U., State College, 1967-69; staff acct. Arthur Andersen & Co., N.Y.C., 1969-70; adj. asst. prof. NYU Grad. Sch. Bus., spring 1970; faculty resident Laventhol & Horwath, summer 1972; assoc. prof., dir. M. Bus. Taxation program U. So. Calif., Los Angeles, 1973-74, U. Fla., Gainesville, 1970-73, 74-75; prof. Tex. A&M U., College Station, 1975-97, Shelton prof. taxation, 1984-97; KPMG endowed prof. La. State U., Baton Rouge, 1997—. Newspaper and mag. columnist; creator Soc. for a Return to Acad. Stds., 1993—. Author: Financial Management of Your Coin-Stamp Estate, 1978, Practical Guide to Preparing a Federal Gift Tax Return, 1981, Readings in Selected Tax Problems of the Oil Industry, 1982, Handbook of Accounting for Natural Resources, 1986, Handbook of Estate Planning, 1988, Handbook of Governmental Accounting and Finance, 1988, 1992, Handbook of Financial Management for Banks, 1988, The Ultimate Rip-off: A Taxing Tale, 1999, Accosting the Golden Spire, 1989, Handbook on Financial Aspect of Divorce and Separation, 1989, Keys to Understanding the Financial News, 2000, Keys to Estate Planning and Trusts, 1989, Keys to Personal Financial Planning, 1991, Keys to Surviving a Tax Audit, 1991, Handbook of Natural Gas Accounting, 1991, Keys to Understanding Social Security Benefits, 1992; co-author: Donate Less to the IRS, 1981, Readings in Oil Industry Accounting, 1980, Estate Planning: A Guide for Advisers and Their Clients, West's Federal Taxation, 4 vols., Trap Doors and Trojan Horses, 1991, Financial Analysis, 1994, How To Manage Corporate Cash, 1994, Costly Reflections in a Midas Mirror, 1995, Barron's Guide to Tax Terms, 1995, Activity Based Costing, 1995, Deadly Art Puzzle: Accounting for Murder, 1996, The Bottom Line is Betrayal, 1995, Non-profit Sleuths: Follow the Money, 1997, Simon the Incredible: A Novel, 1998, Chemistry in Whispering Caves, 1998, Computer Encryptions in Whispering Caves, 1999, The Big R: An Internal Auditing Action Adventure, 2000, U.S. Master Auditing Guide, 2002, Forensic and Investigating Accounting, 2003; contbr. chpts. to books, articles to profl. publs.; editor Oil, Gas & Energy Quar., 1977—, Jour. Forensic Acctg., 1999—; co-editor Tex. Tax Services, 1983—; cons. editor Lawyers and Judges Pub. Co., Tucson; contbg. editor Hard Facts and Tax Angles; mem. editorial bd. Jour. Petroleum Acctg., Jour. Managerial Issues, Jour. East-West Bus., Forensic Examiner Acctg. Educators' Jour., Acctg. Rev.; mem. editl. adv. bd. Advances in Acctg. Named to Alumni Hall of Fame, A.L. Brown High Sch., 1972; recipient Contbn. to Community award Sta. WRUF, 1972; Coll. Bus. Adminstrn. Rsch. award Tex. A&M U., 1982; Ford Found. grantee, 1966-67; Disting. Alumni award Pfeiffer Coll., 1972; Arthur Young rsch. grantee, 1984-85. Mem. Am. Taxation Assn. (pres. 1974-75, trustee 1975-77, founder), Am. Inst. CPA's, Am. Acctg. Assn., Nat. Taxation Assn., Am. Tax Assn. (founding pres.), Govt. Fin. Officers' Assn., Tex. Soc. CPA's, La. Soc. CPA's, Numis. Lit. Guild, Order of Sundial, Phi Kappa Phi, Beta Gamma Sigma, Beta Alpha Psi. Methodist. Office: La State U Dept Acctg 3101 Ceba Bldg Baton Rouge LA 70803-0001

CRUMBLEY, ESTHER HELEN KENDRICK, realtor, former councilwoman, retired secondary education educator; b. Okeechobee, Fla., Oct. 3, 1928; d. James A. and Corrine (Burney) Kendrick; m. Chandler Jackson, Oct. 24, 1949 (dec.); children: Pamela E., Chandler A., William J. BS in Math. Edn., Ga. So. Coll., 1966; M in Math., Jacksonville (Fla.) U., 1979. Cert. secondary edn. tchr., Ga. Secondary edn. tchr. Camden County Bd. Edn., St. Mary's, Ga., 1958-92, ret.; realtor Watson Realty, St. Mary's, 1985-98, ret., 1998. Dept. chairperson Camden H.S., St. Mary's, 1966-72; pres., sec., treas. Camden GMA, St. Mary's, 1976-78. Reporter: for hometown newspaper. Councilwoman City of St. Mary's, 1979-86, mayor pro tem, 1981-86. Named Star Tchr., 1972, Camden GMA, 1979-88. Mem. Camden Ga. Assn. Educators (pres. 1976, sec.-treas. 1977-78, star tchr. 1972), PAGE (biog. com. rep. 1984-92, 1992 retired, named outstanding 8th dist. bldg. rep.), Camden Gen. Mcpl. Assn. (pres., sec.-treas. 1979-88), fin. and budget coms.), Math. Assn., Internat. Platform Assn. Internat. Dictionary Ctr., ABI. Republican. Baptist. Avocations: reading, art. Home: RR 3 Box 810 Folkston GA 31537-9729 *Hard work, perseverance and determination will get you to any goal in life. Put God first, country and family in that order. Can't should not be in your vocabulary.*

CRUMBLEY, R. ALEX, lawyer; b. McDonough, Ga., Jan. 31, 1942; s. Reuben Alexander and Lucy Margaret (Turner) C.; m. Claire Herd, Nov. 11, 1967; 1 child, Alexander Herd. BA in Journalism, U. Ga., 1964, JD, 1966; postgrad., Am. Acad. Jud. Adminstrn., 1980. Bar: Ga. 1965, U.S. Dist. Ct. (no. dist.) Ga. 1970, U.S. Supreme Ct. 1976. Asst. atty. gen. State of Ga., 1967-70; ptnr. Weltner, Kidd, Crumbley & Tate, Atlanta, 1970-76; pub. defender Flint Jud. Cir., 1976-77; judge Flin. Jud. Cir. Superior Ct., 1978-83; ptnr. Crumbley & Crumbley, McDonough, 1983—. Senator 17th dist. Ga. Senate, 1987-89; mem. bd. gov. state bar Ga., 1992-94; prof. Woodrow Wilson Coll. Law, Atlanta, 1971-75; counsel to com. on judiciary Ga. State Senate, 1970. Contbr. articles to profl. jours. With Ga. N.G., 1966-72. Mem. ABA, Henry County Bar Assn., State Bar Ga. (disciplinary bd. 1985-87), Lawyers Club Atlanta, Henry County Kiwanis (hon.). Episcopalian. Office: PO Box 2080 80 Macon St Mcdonough GA 30253-3221 E-mail: racrumb@bellsouth.net.

CRUMBLING, DEANA MARIE, environmental scientist; b. Moses Lake, Wash., Oct. 2, 1958; d. Dean Arthur and Fayalene Rae (Kunkel) C. AA in Life Scis., Harrisburg Area C.C., 1986; BA in Psychology, BS in Biochemistry, Lebanon Valley Coll., 1989; MS in Environ. Sci., Drexel U., 1997. Med. technologist several hosps., Pa., Va., 1977-87; rsch. technician Weiss Ctr. Rsch./Geisinger Clinic, Danville, Pa., 1988-89; chemist United Tech. Assn., Hershey (Pa.) Foods, 1989-90; environ. chemist Pa. Dept. Environ. Resources, Harrisburg, 1990-91; rsch. asst. Drexel U., Phila., 1991-93; med. technologist West Jersey Health System, Voorhees, N.J., 1991-97; asst. environ. scientist Woodward-Clyde Cons., Phila., 1995-96; lab. mgr., mem. adj. faculty Sch. Sci. and Health, Phila. Coll. Textiles and Sci., 1996-97; phys. scientist Tech. Innovation Office EPA, Washington, 1997—. Gay-rights activist, spokesperson Pa. Justice Campaign, Harrisburg, 1990, 91. Recipient Andrew Bender Meml. Chemistry award Lebanon Valley Coll., Annville, Pa., 1989, Jean O. Love Meml. award Psychology, 1989. Mem. AAAS, Am. Chem. Soc., Am. Inst. Biol. Sci., Soc. Environ. Toxicology and Chemistry, Environ. Def. Fund, Natural Resources Def. Coun., Sierra Club. Democrat. Avocations: canoeing, camping, needlework crafts, snorkeling. E-mail. Office: EPA (5102G) 1200 Pennsylvania Ave NW Washington DC 20460 E-mail: crumbling.deana@epa.gov.

CRUMLEY, DAVID OLIVER, publisher, author, foundation executive; b. New Orleans, May 18, 1949; s. David Shiffer III and Martha Ann (Carey) C. BA, Tulane U., 1974. Sec., editor The Social Dir. of Greater New Orleans, Inc., 1975-77, pres., pub., 1977-92. Pres. Laser Documentation Inc. Author, historian: Reflection of Life in New Orleans: Architecture & Interior Decoration as Historical, Social & Cultural Commentary, 1970; pub., author: Mardi Gras in New Orleans 1971, 1971; researcher Town & Country, 1979. Historian hist. marker Ashland Plantation, 1969, La Maison Blanche Plantation, 1974; co-founder Soc. Huguenot A Nouvelle, New Orleans, 1973, The Grand Priory of the South, The Mil. and Hospitaller Order of St. Lazarus of Jerusalem, New Orleans, 1976; vestry Mt. Olivet Episc. Ch., 1971-90, jr. warden of vestry, 1976-88, sr. warden of vestry, 1989. Internat. Rels. scholar Tulane U., 1974. Mem. Sons of the Revolution (genealogist La chpt. 1974-88), Societe Huguenot A Nouvelle Orleans (bd. dirs. 1973—), Soc. of the War of 1812 (vice-genealogist La. chpt. 1974-80), Royal Soc. of St. George (bd. dirs. New Orleans chpt. 1974-76), Soc. Colonial Wars (dep. genealogist La. chpt. 1974-77, 79-88, genealogist La. chpt. 1977-79), SAR (genealogist George Washington chpt. 1986-87), La. Hist. Soc., Masons. Avocation: reading. Office: Social Dir of Greater New Orleans Inc 4403 Maple Leaf Dr New Orleans LA 70131-7455

CRUMLEY, JAMES ROBERT, JR., retired clergyman; b. Bluff City, Tenn., Mar. 30, 1925; s. James Robert and Ida Frances (Fine) C.; m. Sara Annette Bodie, May 26, 1950; children: Frances Crumley Holman, James Robert, Jeanne Crumley Lindemann. BA, Roanoke Coll., 1948, DD (hon.), 1973; MDiv, Luth. Theol. So. Sem., Columbia, S.C., 1951; DD (hon.), Newberry (S.C.) Coll., 1971, Augustana Coll., 1982, Muhlenberg Coll., Allentown, Pa., 1983; LLD (hon.), Susquehanna U., Selinsgrove, Pa., 1977; LHD (hon.), Lenoir-Rhyne Coll., Hickory, N.C., 1979; LittD (hon.), Bethany Coll., 1981; LHD (hon.), Manhattan Coll., 1984, U. S.C., 1987. Ordained to ministry Luth. Ch., 1951. Pastor chs. in, Greenville and Oak Ridge, Tenn., Savannah, Ga., 1951-74; sec. Luth. Ch. in Am., N.Y.C., 1974-78, bishop, 1978-88. Vis. prof. ecumenism Luth. Theol. So. Sem., Columbia, S.C., 1988, ret., 1993. Lutheran. Home: 362 Little Creek Dr Leesville SC 29070-9379 E-mail: jcrum362@aol.com.

CRUMLEY, JOHN WALTER, lawyer; b. Ft. Worth, July 20, 1944; s. Frank E. and Mary Cecilia (Gaudin) C.; m. Paulette Gavin, July 25, 1970; children: John Gavin, Brian Christopher. BS, Springhill Coll., 1967; JD, So. Meth. U., 1970, M of Comparative Law, 1973. Bar: Tex. 1970, U.S. Dist. Ct. (no. dist.) Tex. 1976, U.S. Ct. Appeals (5th cir.) 1981, U.S. Tax Ct. 1988. Assoc. McBryde & Bogle, Ft. Worth, 1973-75; ptnr. Crumley, Murphy & Shrull, Inc., Ft. Worth, 1975-85, Tracy, Crumley & Holland, Ft. Worth, 1985-92; prin. John W. Crumley, P.C., Ft. Worth, 1992—. Mem. bd. dirs. Goodrich Ctr. for the Deaf, 1995—, pres., 1998-2002; vice chair Bingo Advisor Com., 1995-96. Mem. steering com. Tarrant County Vol. Guardianship, Ft. Worth, 1986-87; bd. dirs. Camp Fire, Ft. Worth, 1985-87, Cath. Social Svcs., Ft. Worth, 1985-86. Capt. U.S. Army, 1970-72. Mem. State Bar Tex., Tarrant County Bar Assn., Tex. Assn. Def. Counsel, Tex. Assn. Diocesan Attys., U.S. Conf. Diocesan Attys. Assn., Serra Club (pres. Ft. Worth club 1985-86), KC (state adv. 1986-91, 95-96). Office: 316 University Ctr 1300 S University Dr Fort Worth TX 76107-5737 E-mail: crumley1@airmail.net.

CRUMLEY, MARTHA ANN, company executive; b. New Orleans, Aug. 8, 1910; d. Mark Oliver and Mary Elizabeth (Schroder) Carey; m. David Shiffer Crumley III, May 7, 1947; 1 child, David Oliver. Grad., Tulane U., New Orleans, 1974. Pres., chief exec. officer Westbank Acad., Gretna, La., 1953-68; sr. v.p. The Social Directory Greater New Orleans, Inc., 1975-92, pres., 1992-94. Pres. Algiers Little Theatre, New Orleans, 1930; tchr. speech and drama YWCA, New Orleans, 1938-39, producer, dir. plays, 1938-39; prs. Krewe of Aparamest, New Orleans, 1938; chmn. fundraising New Orleans Philharmonic Symphony, New Orleans, 1967; mem. women's vol. com. New Orleans Mus. Art, 1967-68; dir. sr. and jr. choir Mt. Olivet Episcopal Ch., New Orleans, 1922-83, mem. altar guild, 1922-83; pres. Mt. Olivet's Women Aux., New Orleans, 1950; mem. women's guild New Orleans Philharmonic; pres. Social Directory of Greater Ne Orlenas, 1992-94. Mem. DAR, English Speaking Union, La. Landmark Soc., Friends of the Cabildo, Children of the Am. Revolution (sr. prs. 1969), Colonial Dames XVII Century (pres. La. chpt. 1977). Home: 4403 Maple Leaf Dr New Orleans LA 70131-7455

CRUMLEY, ROGER LEE, surgeon, educator; b. Perry, Iowa, Oct. 8, 1941; s. Dwight Moody and Helen Ethelwyn (Anderson) C.; m. Janet Lynn Conant, Nov. 13, 1987; children: Erin Kelly Helen, Danielle Nicole. BA, Simpson Coll., 1964; MS, U. Iowa, 1975, MD, 1967; MBA, U. Phoenix, 1999. Diplomate Am. Bd. Otolaryngology (dir. 1992—). Intern L.A. County Gen. Hosp., 1967-68; resident in surgery Highland-Alameda Hosp., Oakland, Calif., 1968-69; bn. surgeon 1st Marine Div., Vietnam, 1968-69; resident in otolaryngology U. Iowa, Iowa City, 1971-75; chief otolarygology San Francisco Gen. Hosp., 1975-81; assoc. prof., then prof. U. Calif., San Francisco, 1981-87, prof., chief otolaryngology-head and neck surgery Irvine, 1987—. Guest prof. Humboldt U., East Berlin, 1982, M.S. McLeod vis. prof. S. Australian Postgrad. Edn. Ctr., Adelaide, 1988; treas., pres. Am. Acad. Facial Plastic Surgeons, 1994-95, Triological Soc., 2002-03; McBride lectr. U. Edinburgh, 1998. Contbr. articles and book chpts. to profl. publs. With USN, 1969-71, Vietnam. Recipient Alumni Achievement award Simpson Coll., 1984. Fellow ACS, Am. Acad. Otolaryngology (bd. dirs. 1988—, award 1989); mem. Soc. Univ. Otolaryngologists, Triological Soc. (pres. 2002-), Bohemian Club (San Francisco), Center Club (Costa Mesa, Calif.). Republican. Methodist. Avocations: music, piano, jazz flügelhorn, running, skiing. Office: U Calif-Irvine Med Ctr Dept Otolaryngology Head & Neck 101 The City Dr S Orange CA 92868-3201

CRUMLISH, JOSEPH DOUGHERTY, lawyer; b. Phila., Aug. 19, 1922; s. James Charles and Ruth (Hardy) C.; m. Rebecca Kelley, Sept. 12, 1950 (div. 1979); 1 child, Rebecca Kelley. B.S.S., Georgetown U., 1946, PhD, 1954; MA, Cath. U. Am., 1948, JD, 1966. Bar: D.C. 1967, U.S. Ct. Appeals (D.C. cir.) 1968, U.S. Supreme Ct. 1975, U.S. Ct. Appeals (Fed. cir.) 1982, U.S. Claims Ct. 1980. Rsch. coord. Ford Motor Co., Dearborn, Mich., 1953-61; fund dir. Georgetown U. Alumni Assn., Washington, 1961-62; econ. devel. adminstr. U.S. Dept. Commerce, Washington, 1962-64; rsch. program mgr., cons. Nat. Bur. Standards, Washington, 1964-77; counsel Casey, Scott & Canfield, Washington, 1977-88; counsel Dahlgren and Close, 1994—; dir., co-founder, former pres. and chmn., bd. mem. Thomas More Soc. Am., Washington, 1980—; adj. faculty Georgetown U., U. Md., George Washington U., 1973-79. Author: A City Finds Itself, 1950; author monographs; contbr. articles to profl. jours. Co-founder, First Friday Club of Phila., 1959; bd. dirs. Georgetown U. Alumni Assn., 1961-62, Cath. U. Am. Alumni Assn., 1962-65; sec., co-founder Men of Mercy, 1983—. With USAAF, 1943-46. Recipient Outstanding Cmty. Svc. award Ford Motor Co., 1959, High Quality Performance, Nat. Bur. Standards, 1966, Commendation, Presdl. Clemency Bd., 1975. Mem. Found. for Rsch. in Human Behavior (bd. advisors 1959-60), Ctr. for Applied Rsch. in the Apostolate (lay bd. advisors 1978-83), Pastoral Coun. Ch. Annunciation, D.C. Bar Assn., Fed. Bar Assn., John Carroll Soc., Sharswood Law Club, Friendly Sons of St. Patrick, Am. Legion (elected judge adv. of Washington dept., 2d vice comdr., comdr. Dept. of Justice Post). Home: 3900 Watson Pl NW # G-1eb Washington DC 20016-5416 Office: 1000 Connecticut Ave NW Ste 204 Washington DC 20036-5337

CRUMP, DAVID LEE, lawyer; b. Miami, Fla., Jan. 7, 1959; s. Edward III and Eileen M. Crump; m. Kathy J. Smith, Nov. 11, 1964. BA, Wash. State U., Pullman, 1981; JD, Calif. Western U., 1984; grad., Gerry Spence's Trial Lawyers Coll., Wyo., 1996. Prin. Law Office of David L. Crump, Seattle, 1989—. Former protem judge Seattle Mcpl. Ct. and Seattle/Bellevue Dist. Cts. Big brother Big Bros. King County, Kirkland, Wash., 1987-94. Mem. ATLA, Plantiff's Attorneys Legal Soc., Wash. State Bar Assn. (chmn. editl. adv. bd. Bar News 1998-99), Wash. State Trial Lawyers Assn. (Downtown Seattle roundtable 1998-2000, chmn. demonstrative evidence sect. 2000-2003, mem. editl. bd. Trial News, 1999-2003), Rotary (Paul Harris fellow). Avocations: musician, painting, scuba diving. Office: 100 2nd Ave So Ste 210 Edmonds WA 98020 Office Fax: 425-673-1884. E-mail: david@davidcrump.com.

CRUMP, FRANCIS JEFFERSON, III, lawyer; b. Alexandria, Va., Dec. 4, 1942; s. Ross Gault and Pauline (DeVore) C.; m. Nancy Jo Burkle, Aug. 20, 1966; children: Tom, Laura, Elizabeth. BS in Math., Va. Mil. Inst., 1964; JD, Ind. U., 1967. Bar: Ind. 1967, U.S. Dist. Ct. (so. dist.) Ind. 1967. Gen. ptnr. Jewell, Crump & Angermeier, Columbus, Ind., 1971—. Pres. First Nat. Corp.; lectr. on estate planning and legal aspects of child abuse and neglect; bd. dirs., sec., treas. Hawpatch Corp. Past pres., bd. dirs. Columbus Boys' Club; past pres., bd. dirs., v.p., treas. Found. Youth, Inc., Babe Ruth Baseball, Inc., dir., sr. v.p. 1983-88; deacon First Presbyn. Ch. Columbus, 1972-75, elder 1977-79, 2000-03; bd. dirs. Ecumenical Assn. Barth County Chs., Inc., v.p., 2001, pres., 2002-03; dir. Presbyn. Found. Columbus, Ind., Inc., 2002—; dir. Hoosier Hills Estate Planning Coun., 2001—. Mem. Ind. State Bar Assn., Bartholomew County Bar Assn., Inc. (pres. 1983-84, treas., dir. 2001—), Rotary, Phi Alpha Delta. Republican. Home and Office: PO Box 1061 Columbus IN 47202-1061

CRUMP, GERALD FRANKLIN, retired lawyer; b. Sacramento, Feb. 16, 1935; s. John Laurin and Ida May (Banta) C.; m. Glenda Roberts Glass, Nov. 21, 1959; children: Sara Elizabeth, Juliane Kathryn, Joseph Stephen. AB, U. Calif., Berkeley, 1956; JD, U. Calif., 1959; MA, Baylor U., 1966. Bar: Calif. 1960. Dep. county counsel L.A. County, 1963-73, legis. rep., 1970-73, chief pub. works div., 1973-84, sr. asst. county counsel, 1984-85, chief asst. county

counsel, 1985-97; ret., 1997. Lectr. Pepperdine U., 1978, U. Calif., 1982. Former v.p. San Fernando Valley Girl Scout Coun. Served to capt. USAF, 1960-63; to maj. gen. USAFR, 1963-95, ret.; mobilization asst. to the JAG. Decorated DSM, Legion of Merit. Mem. ABA, State Bar Calif., L.A. County Bar Assn. (past chmn. trustee govtl. law sect., past mem.exec. com. litig. sect.), Air Force Assn., Res. Officers Assn., Phi Alpha Delta, Delta Sigma Phi. Home: 4020 Camino De La Cumbre Sherman Oaks CA 91423-4522

CRUMP, GWYN NORMAN, engineer; b. Granite Falls, N.C., Dec. 14, 1932; m. Frederick Andrew Sr. and Annie Mae (Bowman) C.; m. Amy Brown, June 11, 1960; children: Gwyn Norman Jr., James R., Melanie L. BSEE, N.C. State U., Raleigh, 1959; postgrad., U. Pitts., 1960-61. Sr. engr., mgr. Miller Electric Mfg. Co., Appleton, Wis., 1969-73; chief elec. engr. Tektran Div. Air Products & Chem., Allentown, Pa., 1973-76; sr. elec. engr. R & D Hobart Bros. Co., Troy, Ohio, 1976-83, mgr. govt. bus., 1983-87; pres. Crump Enterprises, Troy, 1987-88, Spencer, Ohio, 1993—96; ops. mgr. govt. bus. Controlled Systems Inc., Fairmont, W.Va., 1988; sr. corp. mgr. tech. rsch. project engr. Rohr Industries MP&T Dept., Chula Vista, Calif., 1989-92. Cons. Hobart Bros., Seoul, 1980. Inventor SCR arc weld power supply, arc weld robots, space shuttle automatic plasma arc weld sys., power transformer insulation and sound level reduction sys., titanium med. implant tooling, hip joint and heart pacemaker case computer controlled GTAW system for aerospace critical manned flight controls, space shuttle variable polarity automatic plasma arc weld system, first CNC adaptive control for US artillery shell copper rotation band wielded onto steel shells. Chmn. com. Boy Scouts Am., Newark and Troy, 1972-79; town councilman Sykesville (Md.) City Coun., 1967-69. With USAF, 1951-55. Mem. IEEE (life sr.), Am. Welding Soc. (silver mem., nat. safety com.), Nat. Elec. Mfrs. Assn. (com. on label and safe practices), Nat. Contract Mgrs. Assn., ANSI (nat. safety com.), Air Force Assn., Am. Def. Preparedness Assn., Nat. Mgmt. Assn. (bd. dirs., charter). Republican. Lutheran. Avocations: bridge, fishing, hunting, photography, Heritage tree orchards. Home: 3144 Mosteller Rd Boonville NC 27011 Personal E-mail: normcrump@yadtel.net.

CRUMP, JOHN, lawyer; Exec. dir. Nat. Bar Assn., Washington. Office: Nat Bar Assn 1225 11th St NW Washington DC 20001-4217

CRUMP, MICHAEL DAVID, electrical engineer; b. Birmingham, Ala., June 18, 1975; s. David E. Crump and Kathy G. Beavers, Jim Beavers (Stepfather) and Sandy Y. Crump(Stepmother). AAS in Electronic Engring. Tech., I.T.T. Tech. Inst., 1999; diploma in network tech., Herzing Coll., 2000, BS in Computer, Electronic, and Telecom. Tech., 2002; postgrad., U. Phoenix, 2002—. Adminstrv. intern City of Birmingham, Ala., 1998—99; electronic technician Bellsouth Telecom., Inc., Birmingham, 2000—. Bellsouth pioneer mem. Bellsouth Telecom., Inc., Birmingham, 2002—, bellsouth women's networking alliance, 2003—. Mem. Soc. Civil Anchranisms, Birmingham, 2002. Mem.: Soc. Women Engrs. (historian 1998—99). Avocations: computers, collecting memorbilia, music history, volunteering, travel. Home: 3904 Memory Brook Circle Birmingham AL 35213 Office: Bellsouth Telecommunications Inc 600 North 19th St Birmingham AL 35203 Home Fax: 205-871-7036. Personal E-mail: mdcrump@bellsouth.net. E-mail: michael.crump@bellsouth.com.

CRUMP, RONALD CORDELL, lawyer; b. Washington, Nov. 2, 1951; s. Robert Callwell and Marie Evangeline (Greene) C. BS, U. Ariz., 1974; JD, U. Notre Dame, 1979. Bar: D.C. 1980, U.S. Dist Ct. D.C. 1980, U.S. Ct. Appeals 1980, U.S. Ct. Claims 1980, U.S. Tax Ct. 1980, U.S. Ct. Mil. Appeals 1980, U.S. Ct. Appeals (4th cir.) 1981, U.S. Supreme Ct. 1984. Intern Law Revision Counsel U.S. Ho. of Reps., Washington, 1978; law clk. to assoc. judge D.C. Ct. Appeals, Washington, 1979—80; gen atty. VA, Washington, 1980—86; asst. atty. Office of U.S. Atty., Washington, 1986—90; atty. com. on stds. ofcl. conduct U.S. Ho. of Reps., Washington, 1990—93, atty. com. on internat. rels., 1995—2001; pvt. practice, 1993—95; chief inv. and counsel Senate Spl. Com. on Aging, 2001—. Mem. FBA (bd. dirs. 1984—), Washington Bar Assn. (pres. 1995-97), D.C. Bar Assn., Notre Dame Club, Sigma Delta Tau. Republican. Roman Catholic. Home: 3819 Kansas Ave NW Washington DC 20011-5709

CRUMPACKER, REX K. anesthesiologist; b. Lindsborg, Kans., Apr. 13, 1964; s. John Edward and Shirley Jane (Heidebrecht) Dornberger; m. Katherine J. Jones Crumpacker, Apr. 28, 1990; children: Kristen Jane, Michael Curtis, Matthew Kyle. BA in Life Sci., Kans. State U., 1986; MD, U. Kans., 1990. Diplomate Am. Bd. Anesthesiology. Intern U. Nebr., Omaha, 1990-92, resident, 1992-95; attending anesthesiologist Freeman Hosp., Joplin, Mo., 1995—, dir. gen. anesthesiology. Mem.: AMA, Soc. Cardiovascular Anesthesiologists, Internat. Anesthesia Rsch. Soc., Am. Soc. Regional Anesthesiologists. Republican. Presbyterian. Home: 602 Seville Cir Joplin MO 64804-4568 Office: 931 E 32d St Joplin MO 64804 E-mail: rex@ipa.net.

CRUMPLER, HUGH ALLAN, author; b. Rolla, Mo., Mar. 14, 1918; s. Hugh Dinsmore and Addye Adelle (Alexander) C.; m. Dorothy Carter, May 28, 1945; children: Hugh III, Shelley Ann Hexom, Joan Carter Gross. B of Journalism, U. Mo., 1941. Journalist NY Herald Tribune, 1941-43; field cashier Am. Field Svc. Motor Ambulance, India, 1943-44, 1943—44; war correspondent United Press, China, Burma, India, Philippines, Okinawa, Japan and Korea, 1944-45; coll. instr. Mo. Sch. of Mines and Metallurgy, Rolla, 1946-49; lectr. U. Minn., Mpls., 1949-50; asst. attache, press officer Am. Embassy, Karachi, Pakistan, 1950-52, attache, press officer Ankara, Turkey, 1952-54; counsul, pub. affairs officer Am. Consulate Gen., Istanbul, Turkey, 1955-56; country pub. affairs officer Am. Embassy, Amman, Jordan, 1957-58; attache, pub. analyst Office of Rsch. and Intelligence, U.S. Info. Agy., Washington, 1958-60; v.p., Washington rep. Dean Internat., Inc., Long Beach, Calif., 1960-65, Global Van Lines, Inc., Anaheim, Calif., 1965-67; v.p. advt., pub. rels. Four Winds Internat., Inc., Washington, 1967—, San Diego, 1967; lectr. Continuing Edn. Ctr. San Diego State U., Rancho Bernardo, Calif., 1992—. V.p., dean Indpls. Racing Team, 1963-65; columnist San Diego Union-Tribune, 1975—, How's Your CBI IQ, 1979—, Ex-CBI Roundup, 1979—; adv. bd. San Diego Union-Tribune, 1994—; comml. lectr. WWII, world deserts, desert wildflowers, classic poets, medieval crusades, Himalayan kingdoms. Spl. corr. NY Herald Tribune, India, Burma, 1943-44; author: On the Trail of the Desert Wildflower, 1994, The Last Patrol: A Correspondent's Journey to the War in Asia and the Pacific, 1997; author, co-editor: (with Theodore Wertheim) Communist Propaganda: A Fact Book, 1957-58; artist, oil paintings. Decorated Burma star (Great Britain), Medal of Freedom Fighters (China), U.S. Pacific campaign ribbons. Mem. Assn. Former Intelligence Officers, Sigma Nu, Gen. MacArthor Honor Guard Assoc. Home: 17205 Montero Rd San Diego CA 92128-2339 E-mail: warwriter@aol.com.

CRUMPTON, CHARLES WHITMARSH, lawyer; b. Shreveport, La., May 29, 1946; s. Charles W. and Frances M. (McInnis) C.; m. Thu-Huong T. Cong-Huyen, Sept. 17, 1971; children: Francesca, Ian. BA, Carleton Coll., 1968; MA, U. Hawaii, 1974, JD, 1978. Bar: Hawaii 1978, U.S. Dist. Ct. Hawaii 1978, U.S. Ct. Appeals (9th cir.) 1982. Tchr. dept. edn. State of Hawaii, Honolulu, 1972-73, 75-77; Fulbright prof. U. Can Tho, Vietnam, 1973-75; assoc. John S. Edmunds, Honolulu, 1978-80, Ashford & Wriston, Honolulu, 1980-85, David W. Hall, Honolulu, 1985-88; dir. Hall & Crumpton, Honolulu, 1988-93; dir., shareholder Stanton Clay Chapman Crumpton & Iwamura, Honolulu, 1993—. Pres./dir. Internat. Law Found., 1996—; fellow Am. Coll. Civil Trial Mediators, 2000—; barrister Am. Inn of Ct. IV, Honolulu, 1985-87; arbitrator Court-Annexed Arbitration program 1st Cir. Ct. State of Hawaii, 1987—; arbitrator, mediator Am. Arbitration Assn., 1988—, Arbitration Forums, 1990—, Mediation Specialists, 1994—, Dispute Prevention & Resolution, 1995—; mem. com. on lawyer professionalism Hawaii State Jud. Conf., 1988-89; arbitrator/mediator com. fee disputes Hawaii Bar Assn., 1990—, mem. com. jud. adminstrn., 1990—, mem. com. jud. performance, 1992-94, chair sect. on alternative dispute resolution, 1997—; prof. Hawaii Pacific U., 1995—; faculty/spkr. on ins. law, employment law, alternative dispute resolution, civil litigation, 1993—. Asst. dir. youth vols. Am. Cancer Soc., Honolulu, 1972-73. Fulbright grantee U.S. Dept. State, 1973-75. Fellow Am. Coll Civil Trial Mediators; mem. ATLA, ABA (practice sect., litigation sect., alt. dispute resolution sec.), Am. Coll. Civil Trial Mediators, Hawaii Bar Assn., Inter-Pacific Bar Assn. Avocations: sports, guitar. Home: 1521 Alexander St # 403 Honolulu HI 96822- Office: Stanton Clay Chapman Crumpton & Iwamura 700 Bishop St Ste 2100 Honolulu HI 96813-4120 E-mail: crumpton@paclawteam.com.

CRUNDWELL, DUNCAN JAMES, electronics executive; b. Maidstone, Kent, Eng., Mar. 18, 1957; s. James Stanley and June (Reid) C.; m. Bridgette Grieve, Dec. 24, 1983 (div. Jan. 1995); 1 child, Ben; m. Natasha Shankova, May 12, 1995. BS in Mech. Engring., Brunel U., London, 1979; MBA, Henley Mgmt. Coll., Eng., 1996. Chartered Engr. Student engr. Dowty Group, Cheltenham, Eng., 1975-79; chief engr. Yamco, London, 1979-80; tech. mgr. Bandive, London, 1980-84; custom projects mgr. Solid State Logic, Oxford, Eng., 1984-86, systems mgr., 1986-88, product group mgr., 1988-90; mng. dir. Solid State Logic Organ Systems, Brandon, Eng., 1990-95, CEO, pres. Detroit, 1995—2002, 1602 Group LLC, Alexandria, Va., 2002—. Tchr. Opening Windows on Engring., Oxford Schs., 1988-91. Prodr.: (radio program) Glad to Be Gay or Not?, 1977 (UK Local Radio award 1977); client/project mgr. new hdqs. bldg. Solid State Logic (Royal Inst. Brit. Architects award 1989); inventor in field. Recipient Dir. Gen.'s cert. Engring. Coun., London, 1990. Mem.: Instn. Mech. Engrs. (chmn. YM panel 1988—89, sec. 1987—88, Outstanding Project Work award 1979). Anglican. Avocations: photography, architecture, music, fine art. Home: 1501 N Highview Ln # 412 Alexandria VA 22311-2036 Office: 1602 Group LLC 4900 Seminary Rd Ste 560 Alexandria VA 22311-1009

CRUSE, ALLAN BAIRD, mathematician, computer scientist, educator; b. Aug. 28, 1941; s. J. Clyde and Irma R. Cruse. Postgrad. (Woodrow Wilson fellow), U. Calif., Berkeley, 1962-63; MA, 1965. Fellow Dartmouth Coll., 1963-64; instr. U. San Francisco, 1966-73; asst. prof. math., 1973-76; assoc. prof., 1976-79; prof., 1979—. Chmn. math. dept. 1988-91; vis. instr. Stilman Coll., summer 1967; vis. assoc. prof. Emory U., spring 1978; prof. computer sci. Sonoma State U., 1983-85; cons. math edn. NSF fellow, 1972-73. Author: (with Millianne Granberg) Lectures on Freshman Calculus, 1971; rsch. publs. in field. Mem. Am. Math. Soc., Math. Am. Math. Soc., Math. Assn. Am. (chmn. No. Calif. sedt. 1995-96), Assn. Computing Machinery, U. San Francisco Faculty Assn., Sigma Xi (dissertation award 1974). Office: U San Francisco Harney Sci Ctr San Francisco CA 94117

CRUSE, DENTON W. marketing and advertising executive, consultant; b. Washington, May 21, 1944; s. Denton W. Sr. and Frances Rankin (Moore) C.; m. Susan Costello, June 11, 1988; 1 child, Thomas Moore. BS, Va. Commonwealth U., 1966; MBA, So. Ill. U., 1977. Media supr. Procter & Gamble Co., Cin., 1967-73; assoc. media dir. Ralston Purina Co., St. Louis, 1973-78; dir. advt. Armour-Dial Co., Phoenix, 1978-81; mktg. dir. Valentine Greeting Inc., Phoenix, 1981-82; dir. mktg. svc. J. Walter Thompson/USA, LA, 1982-83; cons. LA, 1983-86; dir. advt. svcs. Mattel Inc., LA, 1986-88; cons. C and O Assoc., LA, 1988—. Instr. UCLA, 1986-99; spkr. internat. mktg. seminar Tech. Tng. Corp., 1993-98. Editor-in-chief: Cobblestone, 1965. Marathon monitor L.A. Olympic Organizing Com., 1984; bd. dirs. Old Hometown Fair. Mem. Mktg. Club L.A., Beta Gamma Sigma, Pi Sigma Epsilon. Republican. Presbyterian.

CRUSE, JULIUS MAJOR, JR., pathologist, educator; b. New Albany, Miss., Feb. 15, 1937; s. Julius Major and Effie (Davis) C. BA, BS with honors, U. Miss., 1958; DMS with honors, U. Graz, Austria, 1960; MD, U. Tenn., 1964, PhD in Pathology (USPHS fellow), 1966, USPHS postdoctoral fellow, 1964-67; DD (hon.), Gen. Theol. Sem., N.Y., 1999. Prof. immunology and biology Grad. Sch. U. Miss., 1967—74, prof. pathology, 1974—, assoc. prof. microbiology, 1974—, dir. grad. studies program in pathology, 1974—, dir. clin. immunopathology, 1978—, dir. immunopathology sect., 1978—, dir. tissue typing lab., 1980—, assoc. prof. medicine, 1989—, disting. prof. history medicine Med. Sch., 2003—. Lectr. pathology U. Tenn. Coll. Medicine, 1967-74; adj. prof. immunology Miss. Coll., 1977-1992; mem. NIH study section on transplantation immunology, 1992; mem. sci. adv. bd. Immuno Tech. Corp., L.A.; active FDA Expert Panel on Alternatives to Silicone Breast Implants, 1994—. Author: Immunology Examination Review Book, 1971, rev. edit., 1975, Introduction to Immunology, 1977, Principles of Immuno-pathology, 1979; editor-in-chief Immunologic Rsch., 1981—, Pathology and Immunopathology Rsch., 1982-90, Concepts in Immunopathology, 1985—, The Year in Immunology, 1984—, Pathobiology: Jour. Immunopathology, Molecular and Cellular Biology, 1990-98, Exptl. & Molecular Pathology, 1999—, Transgenics: Biological Analysis Through DNA Transfer, 1992-; author immunology cons.: Dorland's Illustrated Medical Dictionary, 1967-1994; contbns. to Microbiology and Immunology; editor Immunomodulation of Neoplasia, Antigenic Variation: Molecular and Genetic Mechanisms of Relapsing Disease, 1987, Autoimmunoregulation and Autoimmune Disease, 1987; The Year in Immunology, vol. 1, 1984-85, vol. 2, 1985-86, The Year in Immunology, vol. 3, 1987, The Year in Immunology, vols. 4, 5, 1988, vol. 6, 1989-90, Genetic Basis of Autoimmune Disease, 1988, Cellular Aspects of Autoimmunity, 1988, Therapy of Autoimmune Diseases, 1989, B Lymphocytes: Function and Regulation, Conjugate Vaccines, 1989, Molecules and Cells of Immunity, 1990, Immunoregulation and Autoimmunity, 1986, Organ-Based Autoimmune Diseases, 1985, Autoimmunity: Basic Concepts, Systemic and Selected Organ-Specific Diseases, 1985, Clinical and Molecular Aspects of Autoimmune Diseases, 1990, Immunoregulatory Cytokines and Cell Growth, 1989, Complement Profiles, 1992; co-editor: Self-Nonself Discrimination in the Immune System, 1992, Complement Profiles, vol. 1, 1992, Illustrated Dictionary of Immunology, 1995, 2d edit., 2002, Atlas of Immunology, 1998, 2d edit., 2003, Immunology Guidebook, 2003, T.S. Eliot Bibliography, 2003; contbr. chpts. to books and articles to profl. jours; editor-in-chief: Experimental and Molecular Pathology, 1999—. Recipient Pathologists award in continuing edn. Coll. Am. Pathologists-Am. Soc. Clin. Pathologists, 1976; Julius M. Cruse collection in immunology established in his honor Middleton Med. Libr., U. Wis., Madison, 1979, Julius M. Cruse collection of T.S. Eliot's works, St. Mark's Libr., Gen. Theol. Sem. (Episcopal), N.Y.C.; Wilson Found. grantee, 1990-95, 93-94, 95-98, 99-2003; B.S. Guyton lectr. on history of medicine, 1998; Fulbright scholar, Univ. Graz, Austria, 1958-60. Fellow AAAS, Royal Soc. Medicine, Royal Soc. Promotion Health, Am. Acad. Microbiology, Am. Soc. for Histocompatibility and Immunogenetics (chmn. publs. com. 1987-95, councillor 1997-99, historian 2000—), Intercontinental Biog. Assn.; mem. AMA (Physicians Recognition award 196-75), Clin. Immunology Soc., Am. Inst. Biol. Scis., Am. Soc. Clin. Pathologists, Can. Soc. Microbiologists, N.Y. Acad. Scis. Exptl. Biology and Medicine, Am. Diabetes Assn., Soc. Francaise d'Immunologie, Reticuloendothelial Soc., Transplantation Soc., Electron Microscopy Soc. Am., Am. Assn. History Medicine, The Paul Ehrlich Soc., Am. Soc. Investigative Pathology, Am. Assn. Pathologists, Am. Chem. Soc., Brit. Soc. Immunology, Can. Soc. Immunology, Am. Soc. Microbiology, Internat. Acad. Pathology, Am. Assn. Immunologists (historian 1990—), T.S. Eliot Soc., Sigma Xi, Phi Kappa Phi, Phi Eta Sigma, Alpha Epsilon Delta, Gamma Sigma Epsilon, Beta Beta Beta. Anglo-Catholic. Office: U Miss Med Ctr Dept Pathology 2500 N State St Jackson MS 39216-4500

CRUSE, ROBERT RIDGELY, retired research chemist; b. Tucson, Ariz., Aug. 20, 1920; s. Samuel Ridgely Cruse, Jr. and Hellen Gurganus Patrick; m. Pauline Julia McIntire, Mar. 1, 1947 (dec. Oct. 18, 1987). BS, Antioch Coll., 1942; postgrad., U. Ariz., 1951—52, Trinity U., 1956—58, Ohio State U., 1946, Tex. A & I U., U. Fla., 1969—79. Owner, developer Los Ranchitos, Tucson, 1947—53; chemist, metallurgist U.S. Bur. Mines, Tucson, 1953—55; assoc. indsl. chemist S.W. Rsch. Inst., San Antonio, 1955—61; instr. organic chemistry Trinity U., San Antonio, 1957—58; rsch. chemist Allied Chem. Corp., Hopewell, Va., 1961—68, USDA, ARS, Weslaco, Tex., 1968—82; cons. in field Weslaco, Tex. and Midlothian, Va., 1982—; ret., 1982. Cons. chemist S.W. Agrl. Inst., San Antonio, 1959—61; rsch. engr. Battelle Meml. Inst., Columbus, Ohio, 1942—47. Contbr. articles to profl. jours. Judge Bds. of Election, Ariz., Tex., Va., 1948—98. Mem.: Am. Chem. Soc. (emeritus, ret.). Achievements include patents in field. Avocations: philately, collecting, monitoring Alzheimer's disease, aromatherapy. Home: 144224 Foliage Ct Midlothian VA 23112-4129

CRUSEMANN, F(REDERICK) ROSS, advertising agency official; b. Ft. Worth, Nov. 9, 1953; s. Frederick Ross and Louise (Russell) C. BA, Austin Coll., 1975; MBA, Tex. Christian U., 1977. Supr. Ben E. Keith Co., Ft. Worth, 1977-78; project dir. Parmer Cos., Ft. Worth, 1978-80; mktg. mgr. Shoreline Products, Ft. Worth, 1980-85; mktg. cons. Dallas, 1986; mgr. programs visibility FW divsn. Gen. Dynamics, Ft. Worth, 1986-89; dir. mktg. Motel 6, Dallas, 1989-94; v.p. Peter A. Mayer Advt., Baton Rouge, 1994—. Sponsor Spl. Olympics Internat., Washington, 1992-94, Dallas Symphony Assn., 1992—, Sta. KERA-PBS Affiliation, Dallas, 1993—. Recipient Commendation award Radio Advt. Bur., N.Y.C., 1993; named Am. Advt. Assn. Ad Person of Yr., New Orleans Ad Club, 1998 Mem. Am. Mktg. Assn. (Tomy award 1989), Assn. Nat. Advertisers (com. chmn. 1989—), Travel Industry Assn. (com. mem. 1992—, nat. conf. planning com. 1992—, POW WOW internat. planning com. 1993—), Am. Hotel and Motel Assn. (comms. com. 1991—), Hotel Sales and Mktg. Assn. Internat. (Adrian award 1989—). Avocations: skiing, water-skiing, bicycling, cooking. Home: 6403 Ellsworth Ave Dallas TX 75214-2723 Office: Peter A Mayer Advt 5757 Corporate Blvd Ste 300 Baton Rouge LA 70808-2559

CRUSIE, JENNIFER, writer, literature educator; b. Wapakoneta, Ohio, Sept. 17, 1949; d. Jack Eldon and JoAnn Katherine Smith; m. Mollie Amanda Smith. BS in Art Edn., Bowling Green (Ohio) State U., 1973; MA in Feminist Criticism, Wright State U., 1986; MFA in Fiction, Ohio State U., 1996. From elem. art coord. to HS English tchr. Beavercreek (Ohio) Schs., 1977—87, HS English tchr., 1987—92; instr. Ohio State U., Columbus, Ohio, 1992—. Instr. Antioch Coll., Yellow Springs, Ohio, 1985; English tchg. asst. Wright State U., Fairborn, Ohio, 1985—87; instr. Ohio State U., 1987, Antioch Coll., 2001. Author: Manhunting, 1993, Getting Rid of Bradley, 1994, Strange Bedpersons, 1995, What the Lady Wants, 1996, Anyone But You, 1997, The Cinderella Deal, 1996, Trust Me On This, 1997, Tell Me Lies, 1998, Crazy For You, 1999, We Come To Temptation, 2000, Fast Women, 2001, Faking It, 2002; contbr. essays. Mem.: Author's Guild, Romance Writers of Am. (pub. author liason 1998, nat. bd. dirs. 1999—2000, Rita award 1995). Office: c/o Jane Rotrosen Agency 318 E 51st St New York NY 10022

CRUSTO, MITCHELL FERDINAND, lawyer, educator, consultant; b. New Orleans, Apr. 22, 1953; BA magna cum laude, Yale U., 1975; BA, Oxford U., Eng., 1980, MA, 1985; JD, Yale U., 1981. Bar: La. 1982, Mo. 1984, Ill. 1985. Law clk. to Hon. John M. Wisdom U.S. Ct. Appeals (5th cir.), New Orleans, 1981-82; assoc. Jones, Walker, Waechter, Pointevent, Carrere & Denegre, New Orleans, 1982-84; sr. v.p., gen. counsel, asst. corp. sec. Stifel, Nicolaus & Co., Inc., St. Louis, 1984-88; CEO Crusto Capital Resources, Inc., St. Louis, 1988-89; assoc. dep. adminstr. for fin., investment and procurement U.S. Small Bus. Adminstrn., Washington, 1989-91; dir. corp. environ. policy Monsanto Co., St. Louis, 1991-93; sr. mgr. Arthur Andersen Environ. Svcs., Chgo., 1993-95; prof. Loyola Sch. Law, New Orleans, 1995—. Vis. prof. Vt. Law Sch., summers 2000-2003, Washington U. Sch. Law, summer 1999; mem. faculty Washington U., St. Louis, 1985-89, St. Louis U. Law Sch., 1987-88, Webster U., St. Louis, 1986; securities advisor to sec. of state State of Mo., 1986-89; lectr. legal divsn. Securities Industry Assn., 1986-88; mem. Pres. Clinton transition team natural resource cluster EPA, 1992; owner Angelic Asset Mgmt., 1998—. Contbr. articles in newspapers, mags., jours. Mem. ABA, La. Bar Assn., Mo. Bar Assn., Ill. Bar Assn., Middle Temple (London). Home: PO Box 791719 New Orleans LA 70179-1719 Office: Loyola U Sch Law 7214 Saint Charles Ave # 901 New Orleans LA 70118-3538 Business E-Mail: mfcrusto@loyno.edu.

CRUTCHFIELD, ALEXANDER, investor, investment banker, venture capitalist; b. Tucson, Ariz., Dec. 12, 1958; s. Alec Randall and Virginia Cushing (Smith) C. BA, Claremont McKenna Coll., Calif., 1980; MBA, Columbia U., 1984. Assoc. RRY Ptnr., Buckingham, Pa., 1984-86; pres. First Del.-Colo. Corp., 1985—87; exec. v.p. 1st Colo. Corp., Denver, 1986-87, vice chmn., 1987-95, Am. Water Devel., 1987-95; pres. Crutchfield & Co., Denver, 1988-93; gen. ptnr., mng. dir. Oasis Ptnr. (Mex.), Phoenix, 1993—, also bd. dir. Mng. dir. Griffin Capital, London, 1998—; pres. Crutchfield & Co., 1984-94, Baca Minerals Inc., Denver, 1985-90; chmn. Western Internat. Holdings, Inc., 1991—; prin. RRY Ptnr., 1986-87, mng. dir., 1988; chmn. ATFAB Corp., Boca Raton, Fla., 1986—; vice chmn. The Water Exch., 1989-91; pres. Weis, 1988-90; founder, ptnr. Ironwood Advisors, 1999-; mem. adv. bd. Cisco Learning Inst., 2001—, Ariz. Biovest LLC, 2002—, Ariz. Cancer Ctr., 2002—; bd. dir. MEDAM SA, Buenos Aires, Firstwall Internat., NYC, Whitehead Inst. for Biomed. Rsch., 2001—; spl. ptnr. Raintree Capital, 2002—. Recipient City of Hope and Spirit of Life award; scholar Disting. Acctg. African Studies, Claremont McKenna Coll., 1980. Mem. Nat. Cattleman's Assn., Econs. Club NY, Denver Petroleum Club, Ariz. Club (bd. dir. 2001—).

CRUTCHFIELD, CAROLYN ANN, physical therapy educator; b. New Castle, Colo., Apr. 2, 1942; d. Leland Arnold and Josephine Kathyrn (Leppink) C. BA, Western State Coll., 1964; cert. phys. therapy, Duke U., 1965; MS in Anatomy, West Va. U., 1970, EdD, 1976. Lic. phys. therapist, Ga. Dir. Rockingham Crippled Children's Ctr., Harrisonburg, Va., 1967-68; staff therapist Woodrow Wilson Rehab. Ctr., Fisherville, Va., 1966-67, West Va. U. Hosp., Morgantown, Va., 1968-70; asst. prof., asst. dir. dept. phys. therapy W.Va. Sch. Medicine, Morgantown, 1970-75, assoc. prof., dir. dept. phys. therapy, 1975-78, prof., acting chair dept. phys. therapy, 1978-80; prof., dir. grad. studies dept. phys. therapy Ga. State U., Atlanta, 1980—, Disting. prof., 1984. Chair Am. Bd. Phys. Therapy Specialties, Alexandria, Va., 1978-90; sec. Soc. for Behavioral Kinesiology, 1977-79. Author: The Muscle Spindle, 1972, Reflexes in Motor Development, 1978, Patient at Home, 1970, 84, Reflex and Vestibular Aspects of Motor Control, Motor Learning, Motor Development, 1990, Peripheral Components of Motor Control, 1984, Motor Control and Motor Learning in Rehabilitation, 1993, others; contbr. numerous chpts. to book and articles to jours. Chair ushers North Decatur Presbyn. Ch., Decatur, Ga., 1990, co-treas., 1991—. Recipient Cert. of Merit award Am. Bd. Phys. Therapy Specialties, 1990, Innovation in Tchg. award Ga. State U., 1999, Spark award, 2002. Mem. Am. Phys. Therapy Assn. (chair neurology sect. 1983-85, treas. 1989-91, pres. West Va. chpt. 1978-79, Baethke-Carlin Teaching award 1984, Lucy Blair Svc. award 1991, Catherine Worthingtham fellow 1996, Svc. to Neurology Sect. award 1999), Assn. Clin. Electrophysiology. Avocations: poet, amateur archaeologist, model maker. Home: 133 Santolina Park Peachtree City GA 30269 E-mail: phtcac@langate.gsu.edu.

CRUTCHFIELD, GEORGE THOMAS, journalism educator; b. Sutton, W.Va., Sept. 11, 1933; s. Harry Lee and Grace Rae (Gibson) C.; m. Carmen Rhodes, Aug. 28, 1955 (dec. Oct. 30, 1966); children: Lisa Susan, Laurence Steven; m. Frances Bailey, May 6, 1995; 1 stepchild, Henry Ruffin Broaddus. BS, Fla. So. Coll., 1955, DHL (hon.), 1990; MS, Fla. State U., 1959; postgrad., Syracuse U., 1959—63. Writer, editor Braxton Dem., Sutton, 1953-55; dir. pub. rels. Athens (Ala.) Coll., 1955-57; writer AP, Tallahassee, 1957-59; copy editor Syracuse (N.Y.) Post-Std., 1959-63; dir. coll. rels. Emory (Va.) & Henry Coll., 1963-65; asst. prof. U. S.C., Columbia, 1965-70; prof., dir. Sch. Mass. Comms. Va. Commonwealth U., Richmond, 1970-99; disting. prof., endowed chair in mass comms. Fla. So. Coll., Lakeland, 1999—2001. Educator-in-residence Richmond Newspapers, Inc., 1989-90. Bd. dirs. Better Bus. Bur., Richmond, 1991-2001, Va. Inst. Pastoral Care, Richmond, 1997—; bd. dirs. Tuckahoe Little League, Richmond, 1972-92, pres., 1978-79; bd. govs. Va. Home for Boys, Richmond, 1998—; exec. dir. N.Y. State Soc. Newspaper Editors, Syracuse, 1960-63, S.C. Scholastic Press Assn., Columbia, 1965-68; mem. exec. bd. Robert E. Lee coun. Boy Scouts Am., 1989—, v.p., 1989—. Recipient Communicator of Achievement award Va. Press Women, 1992, Disting. Alumnus award Fla. So. Coll., 1992, Silver Antelope award Boy Scouts Am., 1999; named to Va. Comms. of Fame, 1990. Mem. Soc. Profl. Journalists (George Mason award 1982), Fine Creek Club, Kappa Tau Alpha (nat. pres. 1986-88). Episcopalian. Avocations: camping, backpacking. Home: 1196 Huguenot Tr Midlothian VA 23113 E-mail: oldscouts2@aol.com.

CRUTCHFIELD, JAMES N. publishing executive; b. McKeesport, Pa., Dec. 7, 1947; m. Cynthia L. Parish; 1 child. BA in Journalism, Duquesne U., 1992. Reporter Pitts (Pa.) Press, 1968-71; pub. info. officer Pitts. Model Cities Program., 1971; reporter Pitts. Post-Gazette, 1971-76, Detroit Free Press, 1976-79; press. sec. for U.S. Sen. Carl Levin of Mich., 1979-81; chief of bur. Free Press., Lansing, Mich., 1981-83; asst. city editor, dep. city editor, dept. mng. editor Free Press, Lansing, Mich., 1983-89; mng. editor Akron (Ohio) Beacon Jour., 1989—93; exec. editor Press-Telegram, Long Beach, Calif., 1993—98; gen. man. Akron (Ohio) Beacon Journal, 1999—2001, pres., 2001—, pub., 2001—. Mem.: Ohio Newspaper Assn., Asian Am. Journalists Assn., Nat. Assn. Minority Media Execs., Nat. Assn. Black Journalists, Am. Soc. Newspaper Editors.*

CRUTCHFIELD, WILLIAM RICHARD, artist, educator; b. Indpls., Jan. 21, 1932; s. William C. and Vera Eleanor (Wiggam) Neidlinger; m. Barbara Jean Seaman, June 14, 1964. B.F.A., Herron Sch. Art, Ind. U., 1956; M.F.A., Tulane U., 1960. Instr. Herron Sch. Art, Ind. U., Indpls., 1963-65; asst. prof. Mpls. Coll. Art and Design, 1966-67, chmn. found. studies, 1966-67. Author: Owl Feathers, 1975, (film) William Crutchfield, Sage of Machine Wit, 1973, Crutchfield, A Recollection of the Future, 1977; principal works include Alphabet Spire, Corbins Corner, Conn., 1974, Countdown, Short Hills, N.J., 1980, Punctuation

Spire, Herron Sch. Art, Ind. U., Indpls., 2002, Wish, Glen Burnie, Md., 1986, The Importance of Being A Bubble, Ft. Lauderdale/Hollywood Internat. Airport, Ft. Lauderdale, Fla., 1989, Fifty Years of Flight, SAS Hdqs., Stockholm, 1996. Served with U.S. Army, 1957-59. Recipient Mary Milliken award Herron Sch. Art, 1956, Mayor's award for outstanding achievement in arts, L.A., 1988; Fulbright scholar, 1961; named Disting. Artist of Los Angeles 100 Club, Music Center, 1982 Home: 2011 S Mesa St San Pedro CA 90731-5515

CRUTCHFIELD, WILLIAM WARD, lawyer, state legislator; b. Chattanooga, Dec. 6, 1928; married; two children. Student, U. Chattanooga; JD, U. Tenn., 1951. Lawyer; mem. Tenn. Ho. of Reps. 80th-82nd Gen. Assemblies, Tenn. Senate 83rd, 84th, 94th-103rd Gen. Assemblies; chmn. senate labor com. Tenn. Senate 83rd and 84th Gen. Assemblies, former senate Dem. caucus chmn. Atty. Hamilton County Bd. Edn.; former acting atty. Hamilton County; chmn. Hamilton County Legis. Del.; former chmn. Hamilton County Dem. Party, 1970-84; Met. Govt. Charter Commn. With U.S. Army. Mem. ATLA, Tenn. Trial Lawyers Assn., Tenn. Bar Assn., Am. Legion, Temple Lodge, Scottish Rite, Alhambra Shrine Temple, High Twelve, Phi Alpha Delta. Methodist. Office: 13 Legislative Plaza Nashville TN 37243 also: Ste 301 Flatiron Bldg 707 Georgia Ave Chattanooga TN 37402-2003 E-mail: sen.ward.crutchfield@legislature.state.tn.us.

CRUTE, JAMES JOHN, biochemist, researcher; s. George and Judith Crute; m. Marilyn Kehry, Apr. 6, 1990; children: Bergren Walter, Henry Clemens. BS in biochemistry, Binghamton U., 1976—80; MS in biochemistry, PhD in biochemistry, U. of Rochester, 1981—85. Postdoctoral fellow DNAX Rsch. Inst., Palo Alto, Calif., 1985—86, Dept. of Biochemistry, Stanford U., 1986—90; prin. scientist, sr. prin. scientist Boehringer Ingelheim Pharmaceuticals, Inc., Ridgefield, Conn., 1990—2000; group leader Aurora Bioscience and Vertex Pharmaceuticals (San Diego) LLC, San Diego. New Your State Regents scholarship, State of NY Dept. of Edn., 1976—80, Genetics and Regulation Tng. grant, Nat. Inst. of Health, 1983—85, Sr. Postdoctoral fellowship, Am. Cancer Soc., Calif. Divsn., 1988—90. Mem.: AAAS (assoc.). Achievements include first to DNA polymerase epsilon, one of the enzymes essential for replicating the chromosomes in all complex organisms; discovery of herpes simplex virus helicase-primase enzyme, critical for replication of all herpesvirus pathogens; inhibitors of the herpes simplex virus helicase primase, first class of antiviral agents that can target viral growth and replication in this way; patents for compounds that can be developed into new drugs that treat herpes simplex virus infections; assays that measure protein-protein interactions for to identify molecules that can disrupt singanling theough TNF receptors; patents pending for improved assays that can measure binding of glucocorticoids to the glucocorticoid receptor, a key regulator of inflammation in humans. Office: Vertex Pharmaceuticals LLC 11010 Torreyana Rd San Diego CA 92121

CRUTHIRD, ROBERT LEE, sociology educator; b. Dec. 10, 1944; s. Harvie and Mary Florence (Black) Cruthird; m. Julie Mae Boyd, Dec. 17, 1965 (div.); 1 child, Robert Lee; m. Jeanette M. Williams. BA, U. Ill., Chgo., 1976; PhD, Heed U., 1994. Correctional counselor Ill. Dept. Corrections, Joliet, 1977—78; instr. in sociology Kennedy-King Coll., Chgo., 1978—80, 1981—84, asst. prof., 1984—87, assoc. prof., 1987—, chmn. social sci. dept., 1996, dir. instnl. rsch., 1980—81. With Chgo. State U., 1982, U. Chgo., 1986. Author: Black Rural-Urban Migration 1915-50, 1984, Remedial/Developmental Instructions in Classroom, 1987. With U.S. Army, 1965—67. Named Most Disting. Advisor Ill., 1989; recipient Monarch award in edn., Alpha Kappa Alpha, 1999, crime and delinquency rsch. tng. fellowship, U. Ill.-Chgo., 1976—77, NEH fellowship, U. Wis., 1983. Mem.: Assn. Study of Afro-Am. Life and History, Nat. Assn. Devel. Edn., Assn. Instl. Rsch., Am. Sociol. Assn., U. Ill. Chgo. Alumni Assn. (life), Phi Theta Kappa (named to Ill. Hall of Honor 1984, 1986, 1988, hon. scholar 23d ann. inst., hon. scholar 24th ann. inst. 1991), Alpha Phi Alpha (life). Democrat. Baptist. Home: 259 E 107th St Chicago IL 60628-3668 Office: Kennedy-King Coll 6800 S Wentworth Ave Ste 350 Chicago IL 60621-3728

CRUTZEN, PAUL JOSEF, research meteorologist, chemist; b. Amsterdam, The Netherlands, 1933; PhD in Meteorology, Stockholm U., 1973; DSc (hon.), York U., Can., 1986, U. Catholique de Louvain, Belgium, 1992, U. East Anglia, Norwich, Eng., 1994, Aristotle U., Thessaloniki, Greece, 1996, U. Liège, Belgium, 1997, U. San José, Costa Rica, 1997, Tel Aviv U., 1997, Oreg. State U., 1997, U. Chile, Santiago, 1997, U. Bourgogne, Dijon, France, 1997, U. Athens, Greece, 1998, Democritus U. Thrace, Xanthi, 2001, Nova Gorica Polytech., Slovenia, 2002, U. Hull, 2002. Prof. Max-Planck-Inst. fur Chemie, Mainz, Germany, 1980—2000; exec. dir. Max-Planck-Inst. for Chemistry, Mainz, Germany, 1983—85; prof. dept. geophys. scis. U. Chgo., 1987—91; adj. prof. Scripps Instn. Oceanography, U. Calif., La Jolla, 1992—; prof. Utrecht U., Inst. Marine and Atmospheric Scis., Netherlands, 1997—2000, prof. emeritus, 2000—. Vis. fellow St. Cross Coll., Oxford, England, 1969—71; mem. Sci. and Tech. Adv. Panel UN Environment Programme, 1993—98; vice chmn., sci. com. Internat. Geosphere-Biosphere Project, 1998—; co-chief scientist, Indian Ocean Expt. Scripps Instn. Oceanography, 1999. Editor: Jour. Atmospheric Chemistry; mem. editl. bd. Jour. Atmospheric Chemistry. Named Commandeur in de Orde van de Nederlandse Leeuw, Queen of Netherlands, 1996; recipient Nobel prize in Chemistry, 1995. Mem.: Coun. Pontifical Acad. Scis., Acad. Nat. dei Lincei, Rome, The Vatican, Pontifical Academy, Academia Europea, Royal Swedish Acad. Engring., Royal Swedish Acad. Scis., Swedish Meteorol. Soc. (hon.), European Geophys. Soc. (hon.), Am. Meteorol. Soc. (hon.), Russian Acad. Scis. (assoc.), NAS (assoc.).

CRUVER, SUZANNE LEE, communications executive, writer; b. Indpls., Mar. 24, 1942; d. William Edward and Margaret Rosetta (McArtor) Ozzard; m. Donald Richard Cruver, June 9, 1963 (div. Feb. 1989); children: Donald Scott, Kimberly Sue, Brian Richard. BA in English, Rutgers U., 1964; postgrad., Rice U., 1990—. Asst. dir. pub. rels. dept. Upsala Coll., East Orange, N.J., 1964-65; asst. planner, pub. editor N.J. Divsn. State & Regional Planning, Trenton, 1967-68; realtor Vonnie Cobb Realtors, Houston, 1979-81; owner Sugar Land Comm., 1980-94; exec. v.p., mktg. mgr. Photoflight Aviation Corp., Sugar Land, Tex., 1982; exec. v.p., artist mgr. H. McMillan Orgn., Inc., Sugar Land, 1983-85; account exec. Mel Anderson Comm., Inc., Houston, 1986; exec. dir. Ft. Bend Arts Coun., Sugar Land, 1986-87; dir. resource devel., vol. svcs., pub. info. Richmond (Tex.) State Sch., Tex. Dept. Mental Health/Mental Retardation, 1987-93; dir. corp. and found. giving Meml. Found., Meml. Healthcare Sys., Houston, 1993-94; owner SLC Comms., Houston & Englewood, Fla., 1994-2000; mktg. coord., pub. info. officer Gulf Coast Workforce Bd. Houston-Galveston Area Coun., 2000—. Mem. adv. bd. Ft. Bend Regional Coun. on Alcoholism and Drug Abuse, Rosenburg, Tex., 1989—. Writer, editor: PATCH Handbook: A Parent to Parent Guide to Texas Children's Hospital, 1983, Ft. Bend mag., 1985-86; book editor, contbg. writer: Fort Bend County, Texas - A Pictorial History, 1996. Pres. Ft. Bend Arts Coun., Ft. Bend County, Tex., 1987-89; founding dir. PATCH, Tex. Children's Hosp., Houston, 1982; mem. adv. bd. Challenger Ctr. of Ft. Bend; committeeman Houston Livestock Show & Rodeo, 1996—; co-coord. 25th Anniversary of lunar landing celebration and internat. space expo, Houston, 1994; bd. dirs. United Way South Sarasota County. Mem. NAFE, Nat. Soc. Fundraising Execs., Women in Comm., Ft. Bend Profl. Women, Pub. Rels. Soc. Am., Houston World Trade Assn., Ft. Bend C. of C., Rosenberg/Rich C. of C., Leadership Tex. Alumni Assn., Exch. Club of Sugar Land, Ft. Bend Exch. Club (charter bd. mem.). Republican. Presbyterian. Avocations: travel, scuba diving, golf, dancing, photography. E-mail: sue.cruver@theworksource.org.

CRUZ, ABELARDO MER NILO, physician, geriatrician, internist, rheumatologist, medical educator; b. Manila, Philippines, Aug. 13, 1969; came to U.S., 1994; s. Carmelo Nilo and Teresita (Calalang) C.; m. Monina S. Cabrera, Jan. 11, 2003. BS in Basic Med. Scis., U. Philippines, 1988, MD, 1993. Cert. bd. cert. Philippine Bd. Medicine, 1993, diplomate Am. Bd. Internal Medicine, Am. Bd. Geriat. Medicine, Am. Bd. Rheumatology, cert. ACLS, BLS provider. Intern U. Philippines-Philippine Gen. Hosp. Med. Ctr., 1992—93; cmty. practice Cmty. Hosp. of San Pablo, The Philippines, 1993; intern SUNY-Health Scis. Ctr., Downstate Med. Ctr. and VA Med. Ctr., Bklyn., 1994—95; resident in internal medicine U. Medicine and Dentistry of N.J. - Robert Wood Johnson, New Brunswick, 1995-96, U. Hosp. - Med. Ctr. of Newark, 1996-97; fellow in geriatric medicine SUNY-Health Scis. Ctr. at Stonybrook/Northport VA Med. Ctr., L.I. State Vets. Home and Gurwin Geriatric Ctr., Stony Brook, 1997-99; fellow in rheumatology SUNY-Health Scis. Ctr. at Stony Brook and Northport VA Med. Ctr., Stony Brook, 1999-2001; med. dir. Brookestone Nursing Home, Omaha, 2003—. Founding mem. Pagsama, Manila, 1988-93. Eusebio Garcia scholar, Manila, 1986-93. Fellow: Am. Coll. Rheumatology; mem.: AMA, ACP, Met. Area Geriatrics Soc., Am. Geriatrics Soc. Roman Catholic. Achievements include research on falls in the elderly, osteoporosis, pressure ulcer management, arthritis. Office: Physicians Clinic Health West 16120 W Dodge Rd Omaha NE 68118 also: Meth Hosp Geriatric and Evaluation and Mgmt Clinic 8303 Dodge St Omaha NE 68114 Fax: 402-354-0555. E-mail: geriatricrheum@yahoo.com.

CRUZ, CELIA, vocalist; b. Havana, Cuba, Oct. 21, 1929; d. Simon and Catalina (Alfonso) C.; m. Pedro Knight, July 14, 1962. Salsa singer with various artists including: La Sonora Matancera, Ray Barretto, Willie Colón, and Tito Puente; appeared in film Affair in Havana 1957, Amorcito Corozon, 1961, The Mummy's Revenge 1973, Juegos de Sociedad, 1974, Salsa, 1988, Fires Within, 1991, The Mambo Kings, 1992, The Perez Family, 1995, Las Damas del Swing, 1997,, Yo Soy, del Son a la Salsa, 1997, (TV shows) Roque Santeiro, 1985, Valentina, 1993, El Alma no tiene color, 1997, RMM 10th Anniversery Collection VOL.I, 1997, The 22nd N.Y. Salsa Festival, 1997, Summer Video Jams, 1999, Celia Cruz and Friends: A Night of Salsa, 1999, Gloria Estefan's Caribbean Soul: The Atlantis Concert, 2000, VH1 Divas Live: The One and Only Aretha Franklin, 2001, Pavarotti and Friends for Afghanistan, 2001, 2nd Annual Latin Grammy Awards, 2001. Recipient Grammy award for Latin tropical performance (with Ray Barretto) 1989, Nat. Medal of Arts, 1994. Died July 16, 2003.

CRUZ, JOSE BEJAR, JR., engineering educator, educator; b. Bacolod City, The Philippines, Sept. 17, 1932; came to U.S., 1954, naturalized, 1969; s. Jose P. and Felicidad (Bejar) C.; m. Stella E. Rubia; children by previous marriage: Fe E. Cruz Langdon, Ricardo A., Rene L., Sylvia C. Cruz Loebach, Loretta C. Cruz Spray. BSEE summa cum laude, U. Philippines, 1953; MS, MIT, 1956; PhD, U. Ill., 1959. Lic. profl. engr., Ill., Ohio. Instr. elec. engring. U. Philippines, Quezon City, 1953-54; rsch. asst. MIT, Cambridge, 1954-56, vis. prof., 1973; from instr. to assoc. prof. U. Ill., Urbana-Champaign, 1956-65, prof. elec. engring., 1965-86, assoc. mem. Ctr. Advanced Study, 1967-68; rsch. prof. Coordinated Sci. Lab., 1965-86; prof. dept. elec. and computer engring. U. Calif., Irvine, 1986-92, chmn. dept., 1986-90; prof. elec. engring. Ohio State U., Columbus, 1992—, dean Coll. Engring., 1992-97, Howard D. Winbigler chair in engring., 1997—. Vis. assoc. prof. U. Calif., Berkeley, 1964-65; vis. prof. Harvard U., 1973; pres. Dynamic Sys.; mem. theory com. Am. Automatic Control Coun., 1967; gen. chmn. Conf. on Decision and Control, 1975; mem. profl. engring. exam. com. State of Ill., 1984-86; mem. Nat. Coun. Engring. Examiners, 1985-86; mem. project adv. group on engring. and sci. edn. project Dept. Sci. and Tech., Republic of The Philippines, 1993-98. Author: (with M.E. Van Valkenburg) Introductory Signals and Circuits, 1967, (with W.R. Perkins) Engineering of Dynamic Systems, 1969, Feedback Systems, 1972, translated into Chinese, 1976, Polish, 1977, System Sensitivity Analysis, 1973, (with M.E. Van Valkenburg) Signals in Linear Circuits, 1974, translated into Spanish, 1978; Assoc. editor: Jour. Franklin Inst, 1976-82, Jour. Optimization Theory and Applications, 1980—; series editor Advances in Large Scale Systems Theory and Applications; contbr. articles on network theory, automatic control systems, system theory, sensitivity theory of dynamical systems, large scale systems, dynamic games and dynamic scheduling in mfg. systems to sci., tech. jours. Recipient Purple Tower award Beta Epsilon U., Philippines, 1969, Diamond award, 1999, Curtis W. McGraw Rsch. award Am. Soc. for Engring. Edn., 1972, Halliburton Engring. Edn. Leadership award, 1981, Most Outstanding Alumnus award U. of the Philippines Alumni Assn. Am., 1989, Most Outstanding Overseas Alumnus Coll. Engring., U. of the Philippines Alumni Assn., 1990, Richard E. Bellman Control Heritage award Am. Automatic Control Coun., 1994, various alumni awards. Fellow AAAS (sect. com. for sect. on engring. 1991-94, sec. 1998-2003, chair-elect, 2003—), IEEE (chmn. linear sys. com., group on automatic control 1966-68, assoc. editor Trans. on Circuit Theory 1962-64); mem. Control Sys. Soc. (adminstrv. com. 1966-75, 78-80, v.p. fin. and adminstrv. activities 1976-77, pres. 1979, chmn. awards com. 1973-75, ednl. activities bd. 1973-75, editor Trans. on Automatic Control 1971-73, mem. tech. activities bd. 1979-83, chmn. 1982-83, v.p. tech. activities 1982-83, edn. med. com. 1977-79, dir. 1980-85, vice-chmn. publs. bd. 1981, chmn. 1984-85, chmn. panel of tech. editors 1981, chmn. TAB periodicals com. 1981, chmn. PUB. Soc. publs. com. 1981, v.p. publ. activities 1984-85, exec. com. 1982-85, Richard M. Emberson award 1989), Philippine Engrs. and Scientists Orgn., Am. Soc. Engring Edn. (awards policy com.), U.S. Nat. Acad. Engring. (mem. peer com. for electronics engring. 1982, 2000—, vice chair 2002-03, chair 2003-, com. on nat. agenda for career-long edn. for engrs. 1986-88, membership com. 1987-90, 2003—, acad. adv. bd. 1994-97, com. on diversity in engring. workforce 1999-2001), Philippine-Am. Acad. Sci. and Engring. (founding mem. 1980, pres. 1982, chmn. bd. dirs. 1998-2000, Founders Lecture award 2001), Internat. Fedn. Automatic Control (chmn. theory com. 1981-84, vice-chmn. tech. bd. 1984-87, policy com. 1987-93, vice-chmn. 1993, 99, chmn. 1996, congress internat. program com.), Philippine Engrs. and Scientists Orgn., Sigma Xi, Phi Kappa Phi, Eta Kappa Nu. Achievements include introduction of concept of comparison sensitivity in dynamical feedback systems, of leader-follower strategies in hierarchical engineering systems; development of synthesis methods for time-varying systems. Office: Ohio State U Dept Elec Engring Columbus OH 43210-1272 E-mail: jbcruz@ieee.org.

CRUZ, JOSÉ EDGARDO, political science educator; b. San Juan, P.R., Mar. 7, 1953; s. José Manuel and Gloria Esther (Figueroa) C.; m. Myrna Luz Rivera; 1 child, Victor; m. Elizabeth Kimberly Allen, Aug. 3, 1984; children: Gabriel, Elena. BS, N.H. Coll., 1981; MA, CUNY, 1984, PhD, 1994. Rsch. dir. Nat. Puerto Rican Coalition, Washington, 1988-92; prof. polit. sci. SUNY-Albany, 1994—. Adv. bd. Nat. Coun. of La Raza, Washington, 1995—, Nat. Com. Responsive Philanthropy, Washington, 1988—; adv. welfare reform The White House, 1994; advisor race rels. Gov.'s Office, Albany, N.Y., 1994. Author: Identity and Power, 1998; co-author: Adios Boringuen Querida: The Puerto Rican Diaspora, 2000; author chpts. in books; assoc. editor Latino Rsch. Rev., 1995-2001; mem. editl. bd. Conn. History, 1999-2003, Hog River Jour., 2002—. Spokesperson Census 2000 Initiative, Washington, 1999-2000; advisor Hartford (Conn.) Pub. Libr., 2000—; founding mem. Puerto Rican Socialist Party, San Juan, 1971. SUNY-Albany Faculty Rsch. grantee, 1994, 98, 2001; Grad. Minority fellow NSF, 1983, Congl. fellow Congl. Hispanic Caucus, 1984. Mem. Acad. of Polit. Sci., Am. Polit. Sci. Assn., L.Am. Studies Assn., Puerto Rican Studies Assn. Democrat. Avocation: percussionist. Office: SUNY-Albany 135 Western Ave Albany NY 12222 E-mail: conga@albany.edu.

CRUZ, NELSON XAVIER, healthcare executive; b. N.Y.C., June 30, 1950; s. Jaime and Angela (Vega) C.; m. Asuncion Rosado, July 10, 1971 (div. 1976); children: Celena, Jasmin; m. Lydia Cordero, 1987; 1 child, Lauren A. BA, Hunter Coll., 1974; MS, Herbert H. Lehman Coll., 1978; MBA, Manhattan Coll., 1985; JD, Rutgers U., 1998. CLU, ChFC. Recreation therapist Bronx (N.Y.) Children's Psychiat. Hosp., 1974-78; dir. rehab. svc. Rockland Children's Psychiat. Hosp., Orangeburg, N.Y., 1978-79; dir. mktg. Fordham-Tremont Community Mental Health Ctr., Bronx, 1979-83; adminstr. dept. emergency Woodhull Hosp., Bklyn., 1983-85, assoc. dir. quality assurance, 1985-86; dir., fin. CFO Promesa, Inc., Bronx, 1986-87; adminstr. ambulatory care network Bronx-Lebanon Hosp. Ctr., 1987-92; exec. dir. United Cmty. Health Plan/United Hosps. Med. Ctr., Newark, 1992-95; dir. network devel. PruCare HMO, Prudential Life Ins. Co. of Am., Iselin, N.J., 1995-97; v.p., COO Universal Inst., Inc., Livingston, N.J., 1997-98; mgr. St. Mary's Hosp. Family Health Ctr., 1998-2000; pres., CEO Henry J. Austin Health Ctr., Inc., Trenton, N.J., 2001—; dir. Hurtado Health Ctr., Rutgers U. Health Svcs., New Brunswick, N.J., 2000-01. Project coord., cons. Inst. Puerto Rican Hispanic Elderly, N.Y.C., 1983; account exec. Medi-Scan, Inc., Worcester, Mass., 1983; health-care mktg. cons. BSquared Comm., Inc., 1999-2000. Adv. bd. Bronx Legal Aid Soc.; bd. dirs. Community Planning Bd. 6, 1981-82; mem. Bronx-Boro-Wide Mental Health Svcs. Com., 1979-81. Leadership Mgmt. Urban Execs. Inst. fellow, Rutgers U., 1996; Leadership N.J. fellow, 1994—; Hispanic Leadership Opportunity Program fellow, 1993-94. Fellow Am. Managed Care and Rev. Assn. (cert.); mem. Am. Coll. Healthcare Execs. (diplomate, cert. health care exec.), Assn. Healthcare Execs. of N.J., Med. Group Mgmt. Assn., Am. Coll. Med. Practice Execs., Group Health Assn. Am., Am. Coll. CLUs and ChFCs, N.J. Med. Group Mgmt. Assn., Am. Coll. Healthcare Mktg., Hispanic Assn. Health Svcs. Execs. (mktg. cons. 1986-87), N.Y. Assn. Ambulatory Care, Health Adminstrs. Assn. N.Y., Acad. Health Svcs. Mktg., Nat. Assn. Health Svcs. Execs. Democrat. Roman Catholic. Avocations: running, squash, swimming, music. Office: Henry J Austin Health Ctr Inc 321 N Warren St Trenton NJ 08618 E-mail: Nelsonxc@henryjaustin.org.

CRUZ, NILO, playwright; MFA, Brown U. Playwright-in-residence New Theatre; tchr. Brown U., U. Iowa; participant Audrey Skirball-Kenis exch. program; guest artist Royal Ct. Theatre. Author: (plays) Night Train to Bolina (W. Alton Jones award), Dancing on her Knees, A Park in Our House, Two Sisters and a Piano (Kennedy Ctr. Fund for New Am. Plays award), A Bicycle Country, Hortensia and the Museum of Dreams, Lorca in a Green Dress, Beauty of the Father; translator Doña Rosita the Spinster (Lorca), The House of Bernarda Alba (Lorca); author Anna in the Tropics, 2002 (Pulitzer prize for drama, 2002). Recipient NEA/TCG Nat. Theatre Artist Residency grant (2), Rockefeller Found. grant, Pulitzer prize for drama, 2003. Office: Peregrine Whittlesey Agy 345 E 80th St New York NY 10021

CRUZ, PENELOPE, actress; b. Madrid, Apr. 26, 1974; d. Eduardo and Encarna Cruz. Studied classical ballet, Nat. Conservatory, Madrid. Actor: (films) El Laberinto griego, 1991; (TV films) Framed, 1992; (films) Belle époque, 1992, Jamón, jamón, 1992, La Ribelle, 1993, La Celestina, 1996, Más que amor, frenesí, 1996, Et Hjørne af paradis, 1997, Carne trémula, 1997, Abre los ojos, 1997, Don Juan, 1998, The Man with Rain in His Shoes, 1998, Talk of Angels, 1998, La Niña de tus ojos, 1998, The Hi-Lo Country, 1998, Todo sobre mi madre, 1999, Volavèrunt, 1999. Address: William Morris Agy 151 E Camino Dr Beverly Hills CA 90212*

CRUZ, ROBYN FLAUM, research scientist, clinician; b. Atlanta, July 13, 1954; d. Manning Herman and Jean Miller Flaum; m. Mario Cruz. BS, Vanderbilt U., 1975; MA, NYU, 1981; PhD, U. Ariz., 1995. Cert. nat. cert. counselor. Rsch. specialist Nat. Ctr. for Neurogenic Comm. Disorders, U. Ariz., Tucson, 1994—99; dir. rsch. COPE Behavioral Svcs., Inc., Tucson, 1999—2002; dir. creative and expressive art therapy Western Psychiat. Inst. & Clinic, Pitts., 2002—. Co-Editor American Journal of Dance Therapy, American Dance Therapy Association, Columbia, MD, 1997—2001; adj. asst. prof. dept. ednl. psychology U. Ariz., 1997—2000; adj. faculty mem. grad. creative arts therapy program Pratt Inst. of Arts, N.Y.C., 2000—. Contbr. , editor in chief. The Arts in Psychotherapy, 2002—. Mem.: APA, Am. Dance Therapy Assn. (cert., v.p. 2002—). Home: 5900 Jackson St Pittsburgh PA 15206 Office: Western Psychiat Inst & Clin Univ Pitts Med Ctr 3811 O'Hara St Pittsburgh PA 15213 E-mail: robyncruz@stargate.net., cruzrf@msx.upmc.edu.

CRUZ, TED, lawyer; s. Rafael Bienvenido and Eleanor Elizabeth (Darragh) Cruz; m. Heidi Suzanne Nelson, May 17, 2001. AB, Princeton U., Princeton, NJ., 1992; JD, Havard Law Sch., Cambridge, Mass., 1995. Bar: Tex. 1997, D.C. 1998. Law clk. U.S. Ct. Appeals 4th Cir., Washington, 1995—96, U.S. Supreme Ct., Washington, 1996—97; atty. Cooper, Carvin, and Rosenthal, Washington, 1997—99; domestic policy advisor Bush - Cheney 2000, Austin, Tex., 1999—2000; assoc. dep. atty. gen. U.S. Dept. of Justice, Washington, 2001; dir. of policy Fed. Trade Comm., Washington, 2001—03; solicitor gen. of Tex. Austin, Tex., 2003—. Editor: (primary) Harvard Law Rev., 1995, (exec.) Harvard Jour. of Law and Pub. Policy, 1995, (co founding) Harvard Latino Law Rev. Dept. of Justice Coord. Bush Cheney Transition Team, Washington, 2001; atty. Bush Cheney Presdl. Recount, Washington, 2000. Recipient U.S. Nat. Champion Debate Team, Am. Parliamentary Debate Assn., 1992, U.S. Nat. Champion Spkr., 1992, Ranked #1 Spkr. in No. Am., No. Am. Debate Championship, 1992. Mem.: steering com. Tex. Rev. of Law and Politics. Republican. Achievements include twice named 100 Most Influential Hispanics, Hispanic Business Mag; named to 20 young Hispanics to watch, 1999, Newsweek Mag; named to 50 Most Influential People in Poltics, 2001, George Mag. Office: Office of Atty Gen PO Box 12548 Austin TX 78711

CRUZ, WILHELMINA MANGAHAS, critical care physician, educator; b. Bulacan, Philippines, July 20, 1942; d. Rectorino Bernardo and Mercedes Correa (Mangahas) C.; m. Antonio I. Lee, May 28, 1977; children: Richard Anthony, Alexander Victor. AA, U. Santo Tomas, The Philippines, 1960, MD, 1965. Diplomate Am. Bd. Internal Medicine, Am. Bd. Nephrology (spl. qualifications in critical care medicine). Intern Meml. Hosp., Albany, N.Y., 1967-68; resident in internal medicine Coney Island Hosp., Bklyn., 1968-71; fellow in nephrology VA Hosp., Bronx, 1971-72, SUNY Downstate Med. Ctr., Bklyn., 1972-73; staff physician King's County Hosp. Ctr., Bklyn., 1973-76; coord. in medicine Kingsbrook Jewish Med. Ctr., Bklyn., 1976—; assoc. med. dir. ICU Doctors Cmty. Hosp., 1976—99, med. dir. CCU, 1999—. Assoc. med. dir. ICU Drs. Cmty. Hosp., Lanham, Md., 1977-99, med. dir. critical care svcs., 1999—; clin. asst. prof. SUNY Downstate Med. Ctr., 1977—. Mem. ACP, Med. and Chirurg. Soc. Md., Prince George's Med. Soc., Soc. Critical Care Medicine, Philippine Med. Assn. Washington. Roman Catholic. Office: 7700 Old Branch Ave Ste D205 Clinton MD 20735-1611

CRUZAN, CLARAH CATHERINE, dietitian; b. Cushing, Okla., Mar. 17, 1913; d. Ulysses Grant and Mamie Amanda (Montgomery) C. BS, Okla. State U., 1941; MS, U. Iowa, 1942. Lic. dietitian, Okla., 1984. Instr. household sci. Okla. State U., Stillwater, 1942-43, instr. home econs. edn., 1947-49; cons. dietitian Rest Haven Nursing Home, Cushing, Okla., 1967-91. Sec. Cushing Sr. Citizens Steering Coun., 1972-91; reporter Okla. Pioneer club, Cushing, 1973-85; precinct election judge, 1989-94. 1st lt. U.S. Army, 1943-46, ETO. Decorated Bronze Star. Mem. AAUW (life, treas. 1970-72, pres. 1974-75), Am. Dietetic Assn., Okla. Heritage Assn., Iris Garden Club (pres. 1971-73), Eastside Garden Club (reporter 1970-75), Omicron Nu, Phi Kappa Phi. Republican. Presbyterian. Home: 201 W Van Buren St Broken Arrow OK 74011-6639

CRUZE, KENNETH, retired surgeon; b. Takoma Park, Md., Oct. 10, 1927; s. Conrad Ellis and Claudia Eleanore (Carpenter) Cruze; m. Jean Anna Hansen, June 13, 1948; children: Wendy Jean, Lori Ann, Barbara Lee. BA, Columbia Union Coll., 1949; MD, Loma Linda U., 1955. Diplomate Am. Bd. Gen. Surgery, Am. Bd. Thoracic Surgery. Intern L.A. County Gen. Hosp., 1955—56; resident in surgery Wadsworth Gen. Med. and Surg. Hosp., West Los Angeles, Calif., 1956—60; resident in pediatric surgery Children's Hosp. Los Angeles, L.A., 1958—59; fellow in thoracic and cardiovasc. surgery U. Fla., Gainesville, 1960—62; practice medicine specializing in thoracic and cardiovasc. surgery Takoma Park, Md., 1962—89; mem. staff Washington Adventist Hosp., Takoma Park, Md., 1962—89, dir. open heart surgery program, 1970—89; ret. Editl. bd. Md. State Med. Jour., 1972—77. Contbr. articles to med. jours. Mem. exec. com., bd. trustees D.C. Blue Shield, Columbia Union Coll., Takoma Park. Served to capt. med. corps U.S. Army, 1956—63. Fellow: ACS, Am. Coll. Angiology, Am. Coll. Chest Physicians; mem.: Soc. Thoracic Surgeons, Md. Heart Assn., Med. and Chirurg. Faculty Md., Am. Trauma Soc., Am. Thoracic Soc., Civitan Club. Republican. Home: 919 Brick Manor Cir Silver Spring MD 20905-3818

CRUZ-KORCHIN, NORMA I. plastic surgeon; b. Habana, Cuba, Dec. 23, 1952; d. Carlos E. Cruz and Norma Del Pilar Mendieta; m. Leo Korchin, July 1, 1914. MD, U. of P.R., Rio Piedras, 1972—76; Gen. Surgery Residency, U. of PR, San Juan, P.R., 1977—81; Plastic Surgery Residency, Yale U., New Haven, CT, 1981—83. Diplomate U. of P.R., 1976, cert. Am. Board of Plastic Surgery Am. Bd. of Med. Specialties, 1984. Gen. surgery residency U.P.R., 1977—81; plastic surgery residency Yale U., 1981—83; assoc. prof., plastic surg. Sch. of Medicine, U.P.R., San Juan, 1900—99; prof., plastic surgery U.P.R., 1999—. Chief of plastic surgery Sch. of Medicine, U.P.R., 1990—. Mem.: Am. Soc. Plastic Surgeons (p.r. regional soc. pres. 1994—96). Avocation: tennis. Office: Div of Plastic Surgery Univ of PR PO Box 365067 San Juan PR 00936-5067 Home Fax: 787-758-1119; Office Fax: 787-758-1119.

CRUZ-ROMO, GILDA, soprano; b. Guadalajara, Jalisco, Mexico; came to U.S., 1967; d. Feliciano and Maria del Rosario (Diaz) C.; m. Robert B. Romo, June 10, 1967. Grad., Coll. Nueva Galicia, Guadalajara, 1958; student, Nat. Conservatory of Music of Mexico, Mexico City, 1962-64. Tchr. voice U. Tex., Austin, 1990—. Assoc. prof., coach, voice tchr. U. Tex., Austin, 1990—. With, Nat. and Internat. Opera, Mexico City, 1962-67, toured, Australia, N.Z., S.Am., with, Dallas Civic Opera, 1966-68, N.Y.C. Opera, 1969-72, Lyric Opera Chgo., 1975, Met. Opera debut as Madama Butterfly, 1970, leading soprano, 1970—, appeared in U.S. and abroad including Covent Garden, La Scala, Vienna State

Opera, Rome Opera, Paris Opera, Florence Opera, Torino Opera, Verona Opera, Portugal, Buenos Aires, others, concert appearances in U.S., Can., Mexico; U.S. rep. World-Wide Madama Butterfly Competition, Tokyo, 1970; La Scala rep. in: Aida, USSR, 1974; appeared on radio, TV; filmed and recorded: Aida, with Orange Festival, France, 1976; roles include Aida, Madama Butterfly, Suor Angelica, Tosca, Odabella in Attila; Manon Lescaut, Leonora in Il Trovatore; Norma; Maddelena in Andrea Chenier; Desdemona in Otello; Donna Anna in Don Giovanni; Santuzza in Cavalleria Rusticana; (title role) La Gioconda; Adriana Lecouvreur; Luisa Miller; Elisabetta in Don Carlo; Margherite in Faust; Venus in Tannhauser; Giorgetta in Il Tabarro; also roles in Macbeth, Turnadot, Norma, Medea; recipient Gold medal in Fine Arts, Mexico. Named Winner Met. Opera Nat. Auditions, 1970, Best Singer, 1976—77; recipient Critics award, Union Mexicana de Cronistas de Teatro y Musica, 1973, Minerva al Arte award, Mexico, 1991, Silver Bird award, Govt. of Jalisco, Mexico, 1998, season Cronistas de Santiago de Chile, 1976, Baccarat 2001 award, The Licia Albanese-Puccini Found., 2001, Lifetime Achievement award, Nat. Opera Assn., 2003.

CRYAN, JOSEPH P. assemblyman; b. East Orange, N.J., Sept. 1, 1961; children: John, Megan. BA in Bus. Adminstrn., Belmont Abbey Coll., 1983. Ethics rev. bd. Twp. of Union, 1993—94, mcpl. chmn., 1995 ; assemblyman N.J. Gen. Assembly, 2002—; vice chair N.J. Dem. Party, 2002—. Ops. mgr. ITT Avionics, 1983—93; mgr., owner Cryan's Restaurant, 1993—. Chmn. Union County St. Patrick's Day Parade, 1997; v.p. Brain Borough, 1999—; mem. std. br. Cryan Civic Assn., 2000—; vice chair regulatory oversight Appropriations Budget. Democrat. Roman Catholic. Office: 985 Stuyvesant Ave Union NJ 07083 E-mail: AsmCyran@njleg.org.*

CRYAN, RICHARD JAMES, JR., academic administrator; b. Buffalo, Nov. 28, 1955; s. Richard James Sr. and Geraldine C.; m. Lee Ann Cryan; children: Richard, Christine, Sean, Amy, Jonathan, Sharon. BS, Heritage Coll., 1983; M in Christian Edn., Freedom U., 1996, EdD in Higher Edn., 1994. Dir. N.Y. Inst. Theology, Buffalo, 1985-2001; lt. gen., pres., chancellor Kings Coll. War, Buffalo, 2001—. Author: The Art of Makahiya, God's Purpose and Plan, 2000, Heritage Preparatory Academy, 2000, New York Institute of Theology, 2000, The Professional Lies of Modern Educators and Pastors, 2000, Kings College of War, 2000, Renew Counseling Institute, 2002, United States of America Bible Society, 2003. Avocation: makahiya (black belt ninth degree). Home: 1911 Seneca St Buffalo NY 14210 Office: Kings Coll War 1911 Seneca St Buffalo NY 14210

CRYER, DENNIS ROBERT, pharmaceutical company executive, researcher; b. Dearborn, Mich., Mar. 30, 1944; s. Earl Wilton and Marguerite Gladys C.; children: Jonathan Eric, Catherine Grace, Laura Rose. BA in Biology, Johns Hopkins U., 1968; MD, Albert Einstein Coll. Medicine, 1977. Intern Children's Hosp. Phila., 1977-78, resident, 1978-79, 80-81; fellow in pathology and molecular biology U. Pa. Sch. Medicine, Phila., 1979-80; fellow in human genetics Sch. Medicine U. Pa., Phila., 1981-84, clin. asst. prof. pediatrics Sch. Medicine, 1983-84, asst. prof. pediatrics Sch. Medicine, 1984-87; assoc. clin. rsch. dir. E.R. Squibb and Sons, Princeton, N.J., 1987-89; assoc. med. devel. dir. Squibb U.S. Pharm. Group, Princeton, 1989-90, med. ops. dir., 1990-91, med. dir., 1991-94; sr. med. dir. cardiovascular/metabolism Women's Healthcare, 94-96, v.p. cardiovascular/metabolics, 1996; v.p. cardiovascular/metabolic advocacy programs Bristol Myers Squibb U.S. Pharm., Princeton, N.J., 1996—. Corp. rep., corp. affairs com. Am. Soc. Hypertension, 1991—, chair, 2001—; mem. internat. adv. bd. Internat. Symposium on Drugs Affecting Lipid Metabolism, 1993—95, 1999—; corp. rep. Am. Heart Assn., Pharm. Round Table, 1997—; mem. sci. and tech. com. Liberty Sci. Ctr., NJ, 1998—. Author: with others Cold Spring Harbor Symposium on Quantitative Biology, 1974, Methods in Cell Biology, 1975; contbr. articles Jour. of Molecular Biology, Jour. Lipid Rsch., Jour. Clin. Investigation. Grantee Nat. Heart, Lung, and Blood Inst., NIH, 1986, Am. Heart Assn., 1987; recipient Merck Faculty Devel. award Merck, Sharp, and Dohme, 1984. Fellow Am. Heart Assn. (arteriosclerosis coun., corp. rep. Pharm. Round Table, 1997—); mem. AAAS, Am. Diabetes Assn., Am. Fedn. Med. Rsch., Am. Soc. Human Genetics, Am. Soc. Hypertension (corp. rep., corp. affairs com., chmn. 2002—), Endocrine Soc., Fedn. Am. Socs. for Exptl. Biology, Internat. Soc. for Hypertension in Blacks, Internat. Atherosclerosis Soc., Molecular Medicine Soc., NY Acad. Scis., Soc. Women's Health Rsch., Alpha Epsilon Delta. Achievements include pioneering development of evidence that eukaryotic chromosomes contain a single, double-stranded DNA molecule; demonstration of a gene dosage effect for mitochondrial DNA (using mating strains of yeast); development of methods using stable isotopes and gas chromatography-mass spectrometry to study human lipoprotein metabolism; demonstration of accurate measurement of hepatic lipoprotein synthesis using these methods; demonstration of a powerful autosomal dominant human gene which lowers cholesterol in a family with coexistent familial hypercholesterolemia. Home: 530 Aspen Woods Dr Yardley PA 19067-6314 Office: Bristol-Myers Squibb Co PO Box 4500 Princeton NJ 08543-4500

CRYER, GRETCHEN, playwright, lyricist, actress; b. Indpls., Oct. 17, 1935; d. Earl William and Louise Gerladine (Niven) Kiger; m. Donald David Cryer, June 7, 1958 (div. June 1970); children: Robin, Jon, Shelly. BA, DePauw U., 1957; MAT, Harvard U., 1960; ArtsD (hon.), Ea. Mich. U., 1986. Cert. tchr. Writer and lyricist, N.Y.C., 1967—; founder, owner The Extended Family, N.Y.C., 1991—. Founder, pres. The Extended Family. Writer, lyricist (with Nancy Ford) Off-Broadway and Broadway musicals Now Is the Time for All the Good Men, 1967, The Last Sweet Days of Isaac, 1970 (Obie award 1970), Shelter, 1973, Booth Is Back in Town, 1981, I'm Getting My Act Together and Taking it on the Road, 1978, Hang on to the Good Times, 1984, The American Girls Revue, 1998; (with Doug Dyer and Peter Link) The Wedding of Iphigenia and Iphigenia in Concert, 1971; theater appearances in Little Me, 1962, 110 In The Shade, 1963, Now is the Time For All Good Men, 1967, I'm Getting My Act Together and Taking it on the Road, 1978, A Circle of Sounds, 1978, Blue Plate Special, 1983, To Whom It May Concern, 1985-86, Alterations, 1986, The Fabulous Party, 1996, The American Girls Review, 1999; film appearances include Hiding Out, 1987; author, singer: (albums) Cryer and Ford, 1976, You Know My Music, 1977; author: (musical) Booth is Back in Town, 1981, Eleanor, 1984; playwright: The House That Goes On Forever, 1988. Recipient Ind. Arts award Gov. of Ind., 1982. Mem. Dramatists Guild (council), Actors Equity Assn., Screen Actors Guild. Democrat. Avocation: playing the piano. Home and Office: 885 W End Ave Apt 1A New York NY 10025-3512

CRYER, JOHN, military officer, government agency administrator; Grad., Jacksonville U., 1976; Master, Naval War Coll., Salve Regina U., Nat. War Coll. Commd. ensign USN, 1976, advanced through grades to rear adm.; electronic countermeasures officer Tactical Electronic Warfare Squadron, VAQ-130; with USS Saratoga; exec. officer VAQ-129, USS Theodore Roosevelt; exec. officer, commdg. officer VAQ-141; comdr. Electronic Attack Wing U.S. Pacific Fleet; operational test dir. Air Test and Evaluation Squadron Five, Naval Air Systems Command, Washington; ops. officer Joint Chiefs of Staff; comdr. Naval Space Command. Achievements include logged over 3,200 flight hours; 750 carrier-arrested landing. Office: Naval Space Command Attn Pub Affairs 5280 Fourth St Dahlgren VA 22448-5300

CRYER, PHILIP EUGENE, medical educator, scientist, endocrinologist; b. El Paso, Ill., Jan. 5, 1940; s. Clifford Eugene and Carol Ruth (Cherry) C.; m. Susan Odette Shipman, Dec. 23, 1963 (div. May 1990); children: Philip Clifford, Justine Laurel; m. Carolyn Elizabeth Havlin, Sept. 16, 1994. BA, Northwestern U., 1962, MD, 1965; MD (hon.), U. Copenhagen, 2000. Diplomate Am. Bd. Internal Medicine, diplomate Am. Bd. Endocrinology and Metabolism. Intern Barnes Hosp., St. Louis, 1965-67; fellow in endocrinology Barnes Hosp./Washington U., 1967-68, resident in medicine, 1968-69, 71-72; investigator Naval Med. Rsch. Inst., Bethesda, Md., 1969-71; from instr. to assoc. prof. Washington U. Sch. Medicine, St. Louis, 1971-80, prof., 1981—, Irene E. and Michael M. Karl prof. endocrinology/metabolism, 1995—, dir. gen. clin. rsch. ctr., 1978—, dir. div. endocrinology, diabetes and metabolism, 1985—2002. Connaught-Novo lectr. Can. Diabetes Assn., 1987; Pimstone lectr. Soc. Endocrinology, Metabolism and Diabetes, South Africa, 1989; Kellion lectr. Australian Diabetes Soc., 1992; Plenary lectr. Japan Diabetes Soc., 1994, plenary lectr. Argentine Diabetes Assn., 1998, plenary lectr. Asean Fed. Endocrine Socs., 1999. Author: Diagnostic Endocrinology, 1976, Diagnostic Endocrinology, 2d edit., 1979, Hypoglycemia, 1997, also 74 book chpts.; editor: Diabetes; mem. editl. bd.: Jour. Clin. Investigation, Am. Jour. Physiology; contbr. over 300 articles to profl. jours. Recipient Rorer Clin. Investigator award Endocrine Soc., 1988, Rumbaugh Sci. award Juvenile Diabetes Found., 1989, Banting medal Am. Diabetes Assn., 1994, Excellence in Clin. Rsch. award NIH, 1994, Claude Bernard medal European Assn. Study Diabetes, 2001; Am. Diabetes Clin. Rsch. grantee, 1988-96, NIH Rsch. grantee, 1980—. Fellow ACP; mem. Am. Fedn. Clin. Rsch. (councilor 1979-80), Am. Soc. Clin. Investigation (v.p. 1985-86), Assn. Am. Physicians, Am. Diabetes Assn. (pres. 1996-97), Phi Beta Kappa, Alpha Omega Alpha. Office: Washington U Sch Medicine 660 South Euclid Ave PO Box 8127 Saint Louis MO 63156-8127 E-mail: pcryer@im.wustl.edu.

CRYER, RODGER EARL, educational administrator; b. Detroit, Apr. 2, 1940; AB in Fine Arts, San Diego State U., 1965; MA in Edn. Adminstrn., Stanford U., 1972; PhD in Psychol. Svcs. Counseling, Columbia-Pacific U., 1985; Cert. Credit Union Dir., London Sch. of Bus., U.K., 2000. Cert. tchr., N.J., Calif.; cert. gen. adminstrn., Calif. Spl. asst. to commr. N.J. State Dept. Edn., Trenton, 1967-68; cons. N.J. Urban Sch. Devel., Trenton, 1969-70; mgmt. cons. Rodger E. Cryer, Co., Pinole, Calif., 1970-73; adminstrv. asst. Franklin McKinley Sch. Dist., San Jose, Calif.; pres. Chief Exec. Tng. Corp., San Jose, 1981-82; prin. McKinley Sch., 1986-91, Hellyer Sch., 1991-96. Bd. instl. rev. Calif. State Dept. Edn. Accreditation Commn., 1996 ; adj. prof. Nat. U., San Jose, 1996—; ptnr. Guided Learning Enterprises, treas.; bd. dirs. Commonwealth Cen. Credit Union, Our City Forest, Inc., 1994-98. Contbr. articles to profl. jours. Bd. dirs., pres. Friends of San Jose Beautiful, Inc., 1994-95; adv. com. City of San Jose Bicycle, 1994-95; pres. Friends of Evergreen Libr., 2000-01. Mem.: Calif. Sch. Pub. Rels. Assn. (pres.), Nat. Sch. Pub. Rels. Assn. (sec. 1975—86), The Villages Golf and Country Club (rules com. 2002—). Home: 6328 Whaley Dr San Jose CA 95135-1447 E-mail: rodcryer@aol.com.

CRYER, THEODORE HUDSON, ophthalmologist, educator; b. Chgo., May 8, 1946; s. Arthur William and Maxine Ritter C.; children: Timothy Hudson, Jordan Tinley, Megan Elizabeth, Rebecca Jeanne. AB in Chemistry, Taylor U., 1968; MD, U. Md., 1972. Straight med. intern South Balt. Gen. Hosp., 1972-73, jr. asst. resident, 1973-74; asst. resident U. Md. Hosp., Balt., 1974-76, resident, 1976-77; pvt. practice Waynesboro, Pa., 1977—, Westminster, Md., 1977-85. Instr. U. Md. Sch. Medicine, 1979-91, clin. asst. prof. medicine, 1991—; chmn. com. on ethics Waynesboro Hosp., 1984, chmn. com. quality assurance, 1996-97, v.p.-03—, treas. med. staff, 2001-03, trustee, 1991-97. Clk. session Westminster Reformed Presbhn. Ch., 1980-83; trustee Christ United Meth. Ch., 1997—. Fellow ACS; mem. AMA, AAAS, Am. Acad. Ophthalmology, Pa. Med. Soc., Franklin County Med. Soc., Md. Eye Physicians and Surgeons, Pa. Acad. Otolaryngology and Ophthalmology, Nat. Soc. to Prevent Blindness (charter mem.), Ophthal. Assn. Rsch. to Prevent Blindness. Republican. Methodist. Office: 1647 E Main St Waynesboro PA 17268-1874 Fax: 717-762-8858. E-mail: thcryer@supernet.com.

CRYMES, MARY COOPER, secondary school educator; b. Abilene, Tex., Oct. 27, 1950; d. James Travis and Mary Francis (Chapple) Cooper; m. David Stuart Crymes, Dec. 25, 1970. BS, U. Tex., 1974. Tchr. govt. Midland (Tex.) Ind. Sch. Dist., 1974-80, Abilene (Tex.) Ind. Sch. Dist., 1980—. Author: (poem) Young America Sings, 1970; co-author: County Records Inventory, 1974. Mem. Big Country Tchr. Ctr. Recipient Tchg. Excellence in Free Enterprise 1st prize award West Tex. C. of C., 1980, Martha Washington medal SAR, 1990; named Taft Sr. fellow Taft Inst., 1993. Mem. NEA, Tex. State Tchrs. Assn., Abilene Educators Assn., Nat. Coun. for Social Studies, Tex. Coun. for Social Studies, Abilene Coun. for Social Studies (pres. 1984-86), Daus. of Republic of Tex. (treas. 1990-95, v.p. 1995-2000), West Tex. Geneal. Soc., Big Country Masters Gardeners Assn., Big Country Emmaus Cmty., Big Country Tchr. Ctr., Taylor County Dem. Club, Tex. Exes. Avocation: genealogical research. Office: Abilene High Sch 2800 N 6th St Abilene TX 79603-7190

CRYSTAL, J. SCOTT, publishing executive; BS, State Univ. of NY, Binghamton, NY. Pub./exec. v.p. Gemstar - TV Guide, Ave. of the Americas, NY, 2001—; pres., CEO Gruner & Jahr USA Bus. Innovator Group, 2001—02; exec. v.p., pub. dir. Consumer Mag. Group, Ziff Davis Media, Inc., 2000—01; v.p. & pub. dir. Nat. Geog. Soc., Inc., 1994—2000, western advt. dir., 1992—94; mktg., sales mgmt. The New York Times Co., USA Today, Hearst Corp., 1982—92. As pub. dir. of Nat. Geog. Mag. Mr. Crystal oversaw all publishing activities related to Nat. Geog. Matg., Nat. Geog. Internat. and Nat. Geog. Traveler and led his division through six consecutive years of record advt. revenue. He managed global advt. and fgn. lang. expansion of Nat. Geog. Mag. and was responsible for the successful launch of Nat. Geog. Advt., the first new mag. from the Nat. Geog. Soc. since 1984. Recipient Advt. Hall of Achievement, Am. Advt. Fed. In his new role, Mr. Crystal will be responsible for mng. the sales and mktg. teams for all of TV Guide's print publ. and online platform. Office: TV Guide 4th Floor 1211 Avenue of the Americas New York NY 10036-8701

CRYSTAL, JAMES WILLIAM, insurance company executive; b. N.Y.C., Oct. 9, 1937; s. I. Frank and Evelyn G. Crystal; m. Jean Crystal; children: James F., Sanford F., Jonathan F. BS, Trinity Coll., 1958. With Royal Globe Ins. Group, N.Y.C., 1956; underwriter Home Ins. Co., N.Y.C., 1957, spl. agt. San Francisco, 1958-59; chmn., CEO Frank Crystal & Co. Inc., N.Y.C., 1960—. Chmn. bd. F.F.H. Ins. Co., N.E. Inst. Co.; bd. dirs. Atlantic Internat. Ins. Co., Arrow Air Holdings, Inc., Auto Resources, Inc. Chmn. Internat. Space Brokers; vice chmn. Mt. Sinai Med. Ctr.; trustee Mt. Sinai NYU Health Orgn., N.Y.C., Mt. Sinai Med. Sch., Trinity Coll. Mem.: Nat. Assn. Casualty and Surety Agts., Wings Club N.Y., Century Country Club, India Ho. Club N.Y., N.Y. Stock Exch. Lunch Club, Harmonie Club. Republican. Home: 875 Park Ave New York NY 10021-0341 Office: Frank Crystal & Co 40 Broad St New York NY 10004-2315

CRYSTAL, JONATHAN ANDREW, executive recruiter; b. New Rochelle, N.Y., May 18, 1943; s. Robert Garrison and Luella (Peters) C.; m. Pamela Paterson, July 31, 1965; children: Alexandra, Laura, Elizabeth, Matthew. BSBA, Northwestern U., 1965; MBA in Fin., Columbia U., 1971. Mktg. rep. Texaco, Inc., 1965-66; trainee Chase Manhattan Bank, 1971; assoc. corp. fin. Drexel Burnham & Lambert, Inc., 1971-73; acct. officer Citicorp, N.Y.C., 1973-77, asst. v.p., 1975-77, v.p., regional treas. mgr. Houston, 1977-80; prin. Russell Reynolds & Assocs., Houston, 1980-88, SpencerStuart, Houston, 1988—, chmn. audit com., 1997-98. Guest lectr. bus. schs. of Rice U., U. Houston, U. St. Thomas; spkr. in field. Contbr. articles to profl. jours. Adv. bd. Ctr. for Bus. Ethics U. St. Thomas, 1998—. Lt. (j.g.) USN, 1966-69. Named one of Top 200 Recruiters in the U.S. The Career Makers, 1990. Mem. Houston Forum (bd. govs. 1992-2000, exec. com. 1995-2000), Spring Branch Edn. Found. (bd. dirs. 1993-2001, exec. com. 1994-2000, vice-chmn., 1999-2000), Univ. Club, Galveston (Tex.) Country Club. Home: 14419 Broadgreen Dr Houston TX 77079-6635 E-mail: jcrystal@spencerstuart.com.

CRYSTAL, NATHAN MAXWELL, law educator, consultant; b. Macon, Ga., Mar. 30, 1946; s. William Harrison Crystal and Gladys (Solomon) Sorentrue; m. Nancy Campbell McCormick, Aug. 5, 1973; children: Abe, Miriam. BA, U. Pa., Phila., 1968; JD with honors, Emory U., 1971; LLM, Harvard U., 1976. Bar: Ga. 1971, Mass. 1976, S.C. 1980, U.S. Ct. Appeals (4th cir.) 1995. Assoc. Nall, Miller & Cadenhead, Atlanta, 1971-74; dir. legal methods Harvard Law Sch., Cambridge, Mass., 1975-76; asst. prof. to prof. law Univ. S.C., Columbia, 1976-82, prof. law, 1982-92, assoc. dean, 1987-92, Roy Webster and Class of 1969 prof. law, 1991—. Dir. ctr. for legal prof. & pub. policy Univ. S.C., 1991-99; examiner U.S. Bankruptcy Ct., Columbia, S.C.; cons. on ethics and contract matters; pro bono S.C. Bar Assn., 1989; lectr. on profl. ethics. Author: Professional Responsiblity: Problems of Practice and the Profession, 1996, 2d edit., 2000; (with Charles Knapp and Harry G. Prince) Problems in Contract Law: Cases and Materials, 1993, 5th edit., 2003, Rules of Contract Law, 2003, An Introduction to Professional Responsibility, 1998; contbr. articles to profl. jours. Mem. and chair S.C. Ethics Adv. Com., Columbia. Mem. S.C. Bar Assn. (chair profl. responsibility com.). Order Coif. Democrat. Jewish. Avocation: golf. Home: 3000 Forest Dr Columbia SC 29204-4021 Office: Univ SC Law Sch Rm 305 Main & Greene Sts Columbia SC 29208 E-mail: nathan@law.sc.edu.

CRYSTAL, RAYMOND FREDERICK, former surgeon; b. N.Y.C., Mar. 15, 1939; s. Hyman Seelig and Cecile Francis (Nevins) C.; m. Laura May Barr, Mar. 26, 1961; children: James Barr, Catherine Robin Crystal Foster, Steven Louis. BA summa cum laude, Yale U., 1960; MD, Harvard U., 1964. Diplomate Am. Bd. Surgery, Am. Bd. Colon and Rectal Surgery. Surg. intern Med. Coll. Va. Hosps., Richmond, 1964-65, gen. surgery resident, 1965-69; preceptee colon and rectal surgery St. Barnabas Med. Ctr., Livingston, N.J., 1971-73, assoc. attending surgeon, 1973-2000; mem. staff (hon.), 2000—; attending surgeon Morristown (N.J.) Meml. Hosp., 1974-2000; mem. staff emeritus, 2000—; attending surgeon St. Clare's Hosp., Denville, N.J., 1974-2000; mem. staff (hon.), 2000—; pvt. practice, 1974-85, Colon Surgery and Proctology Assocs., P.A., Morris Plains, N.J., 1985-2000. Clin. asst. prof. surgeryU. Medicine and Dentistry N.J. Newark, 1982—; adj. asst. prof. dept. neurosci. and cell biology Robert Wood Johnson Med. Sch., Piscataway, NJ, 2001—. Contbr. articles to profl. jours. Maj. U.S. Army, 1969-71, ret. Fellow ACS, Am. Soc. Colon and Rectal Surgeons, Am. Soc. for Gastrointestinal Endoscopy; mem. AMA, Humera Soc., Yale Club of N.Y.C., Phi Beta Kappa. Avocations: music, sailing.

CSAR, MICHAEL F. lawyer; b. Chgo., May 26, 1950; s. Frank J. and Rosaria (Motto) C.; children: Cordelia, Christian. BA, Yale U., 1972, Kings Coll., Cambridge, 1974; JD, Yale U., 1977. Bar: Ill. 1977, U.S. Dist. Ct. (no. dist.) Ill. 1977. Assoc. Wilson & McIlvaine, Chgo., 1977-83; ptnr. Quarles & Brady (formerly Wilson & McIlvaine), Chgo., 1983-98, Gardner Carton & Douglas LLC, Chgo., 1998—. Office: Gardner Carton & Douglas LLC 191 N Wacker Dr Ste 3700 Chicago IL 60606-3700

CSASZAR, PETER, software engineer; b. Budapest, Hungary, 1967; arrived in U.S., 1992; BEE, Tech. U. Budapest, 1989; PhD in Computer Sci., U. Ill., Chgo., 1998. Software engr. MMG Automation Works, Budapest, 1991-92, Motorola, Inc., Schaumburg, Ill., 1998—2002, Lawrence Technol. U., Southfield, Mich., 2002—. Author: Object-Oriented Simulator Design for an Automated High-Speed Modular Placement Machine Family, 1999, Optimization of a High-Speed Placement Machine Using Tabu Search Algorithms, 2000, Tabu Search for Rugged Search Spaces with Multiple Symmetric Basins, 2001. Mem.: IEEE. Business E-Mail: csaszar@ltu.edu.

CSERE, CSABA, magazine editor; b. Cleve., June 16, 1951; s. Zoltan and Theresa (Balazs) Csere; m. Mary Patricia O'Brien, July 6, 1975; 1 child, Madeline Christine. SB, MIT, 1975. Design engr. Data Gen. Corp., Southboro, Mass., 1975—77, Ford Motor Co., 1978—80; tech. editor Car and Driver mag., 1980—87, tech. dir., 1987—93, editor-in-chief, 1993—. Mem.: Am. Soc. Mag. Editors, Soc. Automotive Engrs. Office: Car and Driver Hachette Filipacchi Mags Inc 2002 Hogback Rd Ann Arbor MI 48105-9795*

CSERR, ROBERT, psychiatrist, physician, hospital administrator; b. Perth Amboy, N.J., May 29, 1936; s. Frank Joseph and Helen (Bodzany) C.; m. Helen Fitzgerald, May 28, 1962; 1 dau., Ruth. AB magna cum laude, Harvard U., 1958, MD, 1962. Med. intern U. Va. Hosp., 1962-63; resident, fellow in psychiatry Mass. Gen. Hosp., Harvard Med. Sch., 1963-66; alcohol coordinator Mass. Gen. Hosp., 1967-68, clin. assoc. psychiatry, 1968—; asst. supt. Medfield State Hosp., Harding, Mass., 1968-70, supt., 1970-74, area program dir., 1970-74; dir. Outlook Psychiat. Facility, Hampstead, N.H., 1974-76; med. dir. Charles River Hosp., Wellesley, Mass., 1976-80, psychiatrist-in-chief, 1980-87, Hahnemann Hosp., Boston, 1982—; med. dir. Taunton Hosp. and Regional Svc. Ctr., 1990-92; assoc. med. dir. psychiatry PHCS, Lexington, Mass., 1991-93, v.p., med. dir. mental health svcs. Waltham, Mass., 1993-96. V.p. clin. affairs Cmty. Care Systems Inc., 1979-86, sr. cons., 1986—; asst. clin. prof. psychiatry Boston U. Sch. Medicine, 1968-74, assoc. clin. prof., 1979— ; assoc. psychiatrist Beth Israel Hosp., 1970— ; lectr. in psychiatry Harvard Med. Sch., 1972-89; cons. Med. Mgmt., Managed Care Programs, 1986—. Pres. Medfield Found.; bd. overseers Mt. Desert Island Biol. Lab. Served with AUS, 1966-68. Mem. Am. Coll. Mental Health Adminstrn., Mass. Med. Soc., BCN Med. Soc. Home: Green Acres North Dighton MA 02764 Office: Chase St North Dighton MA 02764

CSIKSZENTMIHALYI, MIHALY, psychology educator; b. Fiume, Italy, Sept. 29, 1934; came to U.S., 1956; s. Alfred and Edith (Jankovich) C.; m. Isabella Selega, Dec. 30, 1961; children: Mark, Christopher. BA, U. Chgo., 1960, PhD, 1965. Reporter European News Service, Rome, 1952-56; free-lance artist Rome, 1954-56; translator U.S.A. Pubs., Chgo., 1958-64; prof. sociology Lake Forest (Ill.) Coll., 1965-70; prof. psychology human devel., edn. U. Chgo., 1971—. Adv. bd. Ency. Britannica, Chgo., 1985—, J.P. Getty Mus., Malibu, Calif., 1985—. Author: Beyond Boredom and Anxiety, 1975, Flow: The Psychology of Optimal Experience, 1990, The Evolving Self, 1993, Creativity, 1996, Finding Flow in Everyday Life, 1997; (with others) The Creative Vision, 1976, The Meaning of Things, 1981, Being Adolescent, 1984, Optimal Experience, 1988, Television and the Quality of Life, 1990, The Art of Seeing, 1990, Talented Teenagers, 1993, Creating Worlds, 1994. Fulbright Sr. scholar, 1984, 1990, Fellow Ctr. for Advanced Studies in the Behavioral Sci., 1994-95. Fellow Am. Acad. Edn., Am. Acad. Leisure Scis. Clubs: Quadrangle (Chgo.). Avocations: mountain climbing, reading, art, chess. Home: 700 Alamosa Dr Claremont CA 91711 Office: 1021 N Dartmouth Ave Claremont CA 91711

CSONKA, PAUL L. theoretical physicist, educator; b. Budapest, Hungary, Aug. 10, 1938; came to U.S., 1957; s. Pal Csonka and Margit Warga; m. Martha E. C.; children: Emese C., Paul J., Livia M. PhD, Johns Hopkins U., 1963. Postdoctoral fellow Lawrence Livermore (Calif.) Nat. Lab., 1964-66; NSF postdoctoral fellow CERN Labs., Geneva, Switzerland, 1966-68; prof. physics U. Oreg., Eugene, 1968—, dir. Robert D. Clark Honors Coll., 1997-2000. NORDITA vis. prof. to Scandinavia, 1972-73; dir. Inst. of Theoretical Sci., U. Oreg., 1977-79. Alfred P. Sloan fellowship, 1970-72; recipient Fulbright Sr. Rsch. award Budapest, Hungary, 1993, 94. Office: U Oreg Dept Physics Eugene OR 97403 E-mail: pcsonka@oregon.uoregon.edu.

CSÖRGŐ, MIKLOS, mathematics and statistics educator; b. Egerfarmos, Hungary, Mar. 12, 1932; arrived in Can., 1957, naturalized, 1962; s. Miklos and Ilona (Veres) Csörgő; m. Anna Eszter Toth, Aug. 10, 1957; children: Adria, Lilla. BA, Karl Marx U. Econs., Budapest, Hungary, 1955; MA, McGill U., 1961, PhD, 1963. Instr., postdoctoral fellow Princeton U., NJ, 1963—65; asst. prof. McGill U., Montreal, Canada, 1965—68, assoc. prof., 1968—71; vis. prof. U. Vienna, 1969—70; assoc. prof. math. and stats. Carleton U., Ottawa, Canada, 1971—72, prof., 1972—, co-dir. Lab. for Rsch. in Stats. and Probability, 1983—. Vis. prof. U. Utah, 1991—92. Author (with P. Révész): Strong Approximations in Probability and Statistics, 1981; author: Quantile Processes with Statistical Applications, 1983; author: (with others) An Asymptotic Theory for Empirical Reliability and Concentration Processes, 1986; author: (with L. Horváth) Weighted Approximations in Probability and Statistics, 1993; author: (with L. Horvath) Limit Theorems in Change-Point Analysis, 1997; assoc. editor The Annals of Probability, 1979—81, mem. editl. bd. Stats. and Decisions, 1981—2002, Jour. Multivariate Analysis, 1986—87. Fellow, Can. Coun., 1969—70, 1976—77, Killam sr. rsch. fellow, 1978—79, 1979—80. Fellow: Inst. Math. Stats., Royal Soc. Can.; mem.: Hungarian Acad. Sci. (external mem.), Internat. Stats. Inst., Bernoulli Soc., Statis. Soc. Can., Can. Math. Soc., Am. Math. Soc. Office: Carleton U Lab Rsch in Stats 1125 Colonel By Dr Ottawa ON Canada K1S 5B6 E-mail: mcsorgo@math.carleton.ca.

CTVRTNICEK, SCARLETT JANE, physician assistant; b. Dayton, Sept. 18, 1969; d. Tom Eric and Anna Rochelle (Roškova) C. AS, Coll. Lake County, Grayslake, Ill., 1990; BS in Physician Assisting, Finch U. Health Scis., 1994, MS in Physician Asst. Practice, 1996. Cert. physician asst., Ohio. Skating coach Columbus (Ohio) Figure Skating Club, 1987-88; sports medicine trainer Kettering (Ohio) Fairmont H.S., 1985-87; transp. assoc. Kettering Meml. Hosp., 1985-87; physician asst. Valley Cardiovascular and Thoracic Surgeons Inc., Dayton, 1994-2000, Miami Valley Emergency Specialists, Inc., Dayton, 2000—; physician asst. in orthop. surgery VA Med. Ctr., 2002—. Med. student and physician asst. student mentor Valley Cardiovasc. and Thoracic Surgeons, 1995—2000, Dayton VA Med. Ctr., 2003—. Contbr. articles to Surg. Physician Asst. Jour. With U.S. Army, 1989-91. Mem. Am. Acad. Physician Assts., Assn. Physician Assts. in Cardiovascular Surgery. Office: Miami Valley Hosp Emergency Ctr 30 E Apple St Dayton OH 45409-2939

CUA, ANTONIO S. philosopher, educator; b. Manila, July 23, 1932; arrived in U.S., 1953, naturalized, 1971; s. Oh and Chio (So) Cua; m. Shoke-Hwee Khaw, June 11, 1956; 1 child, Athene K. BA, Far Eastern U., Manila, 1952; MA, U. Calif, Berkeley, 1954; PhD, U. Calif., Berkeley, 1958. Instr., asst. prof. Ohio U.,

1958-62; prof., chmn. dept. philosophy SUNY Coll. at Oswego, 1962-69; prof. philosophy Cath. U. Am., Washington, 1969-96, prof. emeritus, 1996—. Vis. prof. U. Mo., Columbia, 1974—75, U. Hawaii, 1976—77. Author: (book) Reason and Virtue: A Study in the Ethics of Richard Price, 1966, Dimensions of Moral Creativity: Paradigms, Principles, and Ideals, 1978, The Unity of Knowledge and Action: A Study in Wang Yang-ming's Moral Psychology, 1982, Ethical Argumentation: A Study in Hsün Tzu's Moral Epistemology, 1985, Moral Vision and Tradition: Essays in Chinese Ethics, 1998; editor: Encyclpedia of Chinese Philosophy, 2003; co-editor: Jour. Chinese Philosophy; assoc. editor: Internat. Jour. Philosophy Religion, mem. editl. bd.: Am. Philos. Quar., 1972—2002, Philosophy East and West, Dao: A Jour. Comparative Philosophy; contbr. articles to profl. jours. Mem.: Aristolelian Soc., Mind Assn., Soc. Asian and Comparative Philosophy (pres. 1978—79), Internat. Soc. Chinese Philosophy (pres. 1984—86), Am. Philos. Assn. Office: Cath U Am Sch Philosophy Washington DC 20064-0001 E-mail: cua@cua.edu.

CUA, CHRISTOPHER LEE, thoracic surgeon; b. Harrisburg, Pa., May 1, 1959; s. Cicero and Rosita Cua; m. Elizabeth Johnson, Apr. 25, 1987; children: Lily, Christopher. BA, Ind. U., 1978, MD, 1982. Diplomate Am. Bd. Surgery, Am. Bd. Thoracic Surgery, Am. Bd. Surgery Critical Care. Intern U. Ill., Chgo., 1982-84; resident U. Mass., Worcester, 1984-87; fellow Northwestern U., Chgo., 1987-89; thoracic surgeon pvt. practice, 1989—. Office: 1153 Centre St Ste 4990 Boston MA 02130-3446

CUADRA, CARLOS ALBERT, information scientist, management executive; b. San Francisco, Dec. 21, 1925; s. Gregorio and Amanda (Mendoza) C.; m. Gloria Nathalie Adams, May 3, 1947; children: Mary Susan Cuadra Nielsen, Neil Gregory, Dean Arthur. AB with highest honors in Psychology, U. Calif., Berkeley, 1949, PhD in Psychology, 1953. Staff psychologist VA, Downey, Ill., 1953-56; with Sys. Devel. Corp., Santa Monica, Calif., 1957-78, mgr. libr. and documentation sys. dept., 1968-70, mgr. edn. and libr. sys. dept., 1971-74; gen. mgr. SDC Search Svc., 1974-78; founder Cuadra Assocs., L.A., 1978—. Contbr. articles to profl. jours.; Editor: Ann. Rev. of Info. Sci. and Tech., 1964-75. Mem. Nat. Commn. Librs. and Info. Sci., 1971-84. Served with USN, 1944-46. Recipient Merit award Am. Soc. Info. Sci., 1968, Best Info. Sci. Book award, 1969, Miles Conrad award Nat. Fedn. Abstracting and Info. Svcs., 1980, hon. fellow, 1997, Roger Summit award Assn. Ind. Info. Profls., 2001, named Disting. Lectr. of Yr., 1970. Mem. Info. Industry Assn. (bd. dirs., Hall of Fame award 1980), Chem. Abstracts Soc. (governing bd. 1991-96), Am. Chem. Soc. (governing bd. pub. 1997-2000), Phi Beta Kappa. Home: 13213 Warren Ave Los Angeles CA 90066-1750 Office: Cuadra Associates 11835 W Olympic Blvd Ste 855 Los Angeles CA 90064-5033

CUALING, HERNANI DEL MUNDO, physician, researcher; s. Pablo Mateong and Flor Del Mundo Cualing; m. Rawia Salem Yassin, Dec. 20, 1989; children: Kareem Yassin Khozaim, Phillip, Andrew. BS, U. Philippines, Quezon City, 1974; MD, U. Philippines, Manila, 1978. Diplomate Am. Bd. of Pathology, 1991. Chief resident Nassau County U. Med. Ctr., East Meadow, NY, 1990—91; fellow dept. pathology Ind. U. Med. Ctr., Indianapolis, 1991—92; asst. prof. U. Cin. Med. Ctr., 1992—2002; assoc. prof. dept. pathology U. Cin., 2002—02; assoc. prof. U. South Fla./Moffitt Cancer Ctr., Tampa, 2002—. Consulting hematopathology staff VA Med. Ctr., Cin., 1993—2002; med. dir. U. Cin. Med. Ctr., 1993—96, Diagnostic Immunology and Flow Cytometry Interpretation of Leukemias and Lymphomas, Diagnostic Flow Cytometry by Health Alliance, 2000—02; med. dir. immunohistochemistry/histology Moffitt Cancer Ctr. and Rsch. Inst., Tampa, Fla., 2002—. Period furniture, Queen Anne Desk; contbr. articles to profl. jours. Mem. U. Philippines Med. Alumni Soc., Tampa, Fla., 2002—03. Grantee Biomedical Engring. of Leukemia/Lymphoma, Whitaker Found., 1997-2000; Pioneering grant, U. Cin. Biomed. Engring., 1994. Fellow: Coll. Am. Pathologists (assoc.); mem.: Soc. Applied Immunohistochemistry (assoc.), Internat. Soc. Optical Engring. (assoc.). R-Liberal. Catholic. Achievements include invention of Computerized Aided Counting of Immunostained cells; design of Software design of Hybrid Pathologist-Computer Interface for Cell analysis; discovery of Three dimensional method for thresholding colored objects. Avocations: woodworking, sailing. Home: 18804 Chaville Rd Lutz FL 33558

CUARON, ALFONSO, film director; b. Mex., 1961; Student, Cooperative Universataria Edigtrice Cagliaritana, Mex. 1st asst. dir. : (films) Gaby, A Love Story, 1987; Romero, 1989; dir.: Love in the Time of Hysteria, 1991, The Little Princess, 1995 (L.A. Film Critics New Generation award), Great Expectations, 1997, (and co-author) And Your Mother, Too, 2001 (Best Screenplay award Venice Film Festival, L.A. Film Critics award, Ind. Spirit award for Best Fgn. Film), : (TV episode) Fallen Angels, 1993 (CableACE award).*

CUATRECASAS, PEDRO MARTIN, research biochemist, pharmaceutical executive; b. Madrid, Sept. 27, 1936; came to U.S., 1947; s. Jose and Martha C.; m. Carol Zies, Aug. 15, 1959; children: Paul, Lisa, Diane, Julia. AB, Washington U., St. Louis, 1958, MD, 1962; DSc honoris causa, U. Barcelona, 1984, Mt. Sinai Sch. Medicine, 1985, U. Buenos Aires, 1990, U. Naples, Italy, 1990. Intern, then resident in internal medicine Osler Svc. Johns Hopkins Hosp., 1962-64, asst. physician, 1972-75; clin. asso., clin. endocrinology br. Nat. Inst. Arthritis and Metabolic Diseases, NIH, 1964-66; spl. USPHS postdoctoral fellow Lab. Chem. Biology, 1966-67, med. officer, 1967-70; professorial lectr. biochemistry George Washington U. Med. Sch., 1967-70; assoc. prof. pharmacology and exptl. therapeutics, assoc. prof. medicine, dir. div. clin. pharmacology, Burroughs Wellcome prof. clin. pharmacology Johns Hopkins U. Med. Sch., 1970-72, prof. pharmacology and exptl. therapeutics, assoc. prof. medicine, 1972-75; v.p. rsch., devel. and med. Wellcome Rsch. Labs.; dir. Burroughs Wellcome Co., Research Triangle Park, N.C., 1975-86; sr. v.p. R&D Glaxo Inc., 1986-89; also bd. dirs. Glaxo Inc., Glaxo Internat. Rsch., Ltd., London, 1986-89; pres. pharm. rsch. divsn., and co. v.p. Warner-Lambert Co., Ann Arbor, Mich., 1989-97; ind. pharm. rsch. cons. Rancho Santa Fe, Calif., 1997—; prof. dept. medicine & pharm. U. Calif., San Diego, 1997—. Adj. prof. Duke U. Med. Sch., 1975-89; adj. prof., mem. adv. com. cancer rsch. program U. N.C. Med. Sch., 1975-90; adj. prof. dept. pharm. and medicinal chemistry, U. Mich., 1990-97; bd. dirs. Alliance Pharms., Metabolex Inc.; mem. FDA sci. bd., 1994-98. Editor: Receptors and Recognition Series, 1975-98, Jour. Solid-Phase Biochemistry, 1975-80, Handbook of Experimental Pharmacology, 1984-99, Internat. Jour. Biochemistry, 1973, Molecular and Cellular Endocrinology, 1973-77, Biochimica Biophysica Acta, 1973-79, Life Scis., 1978-88, Neuropeptides, 1979—, Jour. Applied Biochemistry, 1978-91, Cancer Research, 1980-81, Jour. Applied Biochemistry and Biotech., 1980—98, Toxin Revs., 1981-90, Biochem. Biophys. Research Communications, 1981-94; contbr. articles to profl. jours. Active Am. Diabetes Assn., 1972—, PMA Commn. on Drugs and Rare Diseases, 1982-89; bd. dirs. Burroughs Wellcome Fund, 1975-86. Recipient John Jacob Abel prize, 1972, Laude prize Pharm. World, 1975, Beerman award Soc. Investigative Dermatology, 1981, Isco award U. Nebr., 1985, Dupont Splty. Diagnostics award Clin. Ligand Assay Soc., 1986, Alumni Achievement award Washington U. Sch. Medicine, 1987, Wolf Found. prize in medicine, 1987, N.C. Gov.'s medal award in sci., 1988, Achievement award Soc. for Biomolecular Screening, 1999, Johns Hopkins U. Disting. Alumnus award, 2000; FDA Commr.'s Spl. citation, 1997, City of Medicine award (disting. achievement in medicine), 1998; inducted into Johns Hopkins Soc. Scholar, 1990. Fellow Am. Acad. Arts. and Scis.; mem. Am. Soc. Biol. Chemists, Nat. Acad. Scis., Inst. Medicine of Nat. Acad. Scis. (governing council 1988-96), Am. Soc. Pharmacology and Exptl. Therapeutics (Goodman and Gilman award 1982), Am. Soc. Clin. Investigation, Am. Soc. Clin. Rsch., Spanish Biochem. Soc., Md. Acad. Scis. (Outstanding Young Scientist of Year 1970), Am. Cancer Soc., Endocrine Soc., Am. Chem. Soc., Am. Diabetes Assn. (Eli Lilly award 1975), Am. Diabetes Assn., Sigma Xi. E-mail: pedrocuatrecasas@znet.com.

CUBA, BENJAMIN JAMES, lawyer, mediator; b. Dec. 12, 1936; s. Ben and Patricia (Machalek) C.; m. Bernadette Theresa Haney, Sept. 4, 1964; children: Benjamin Courtney, Tristan Konrad. AA, Temple Coll., 1957; BBA, U. Tex., 1959; JD, Baylor U., 1963. Bar: Tex. 1964, U.S. Dist. Ct. (we. dist.) Tex. 1970, U.S. Ct. Appeals (5th and 11th cirs.) 1981, U.S. Supreme Ct. 1978. Assoc. Law Offices of Jarrard Secrest, Temple, Tex., 1964-66; ptnr. Secrest & Cuba, Temple, Tex., 1966-68; sr. ptnr. Cuba & Cuba and predecessor firms, Temple, Tex., 1968—. Dir. founding trustee, atty. Inst. for Humanities at Salado, Tex., 1980—, founding trustee, legal counsel First House, Inc., Temple, 1981-86; legal counsel, mem. cmty. adv. bd. Jr. League of Bell County, Inc. (and predecessor orgn. Svc. League of Temple, Inc.), 1976—; v.p. Temple Indsl. Devel. Corp., 1984-89; pres. Trailblazer Corp., 1973-. Fellow Tex. Bar Found. (life); mem. Bell-Lampasas-Mills Counties Bar Assn. (pres. 1973-74), State Bar Tex., U. Tex. Ex Student's Assn., Baylor Law Alumni Assn., Quarterback Club (dir. 1984, 85), Phi Delta Phi. Lutheran. Office: Cuba & Cuba PLC 18 S Main St Ste 802 Temple TX 76501-7608

CUBA, IVAN, artist; b. Notts, Eng., 1920; Student, U. Auckland, New Zealand; DLitt, Editorial Poets Acad. India. Editor: International Poets India. Hon. rep., pres. Temple of Arts Mus., U.S.A., Centro Studi E Scambi Internat., Italy. Served in WWII, POW. Recipient Poet Laureate gold Medal Rome, 1979, Greek gold medal, 1941; named poet laureate Internat. Acad., 1995, M. Madhusudan award India, 2000, silver medal Internat. Man of Yr., 1996. Fellow Acad. Leonardo da Vinci Rome (life). Achievements include development of Cuba-Lox theory on Stars and Tannin theory on Arteriosclerosis. Home: PO Box 5199 Auckland New Zealand

CUBA, NAN BRINDLEY, small business owner, writer; b. Temple, Tex., Aug. 25, 1947; d. Hanes Hanby and Julia Martha (Barton) Brindley; m. Donald Lynn Cuba, July 10, 1967; children: Donald Lynn, Jr., Julia Nan. AA, Sullins Coll., Bristol, Va., 1965-67; BS, U. Tex., 1967-69; MFA, Warren Wilson Coll., 1989. Cert. tchr., Tex. Elem. sch. tchr. pub. and parochial schs., Dallas, San Antonio, 1970-81; freelance mag. writer San Antonio, 1982-87; fiction writer and poet, 1986—; host TV interview show Rogers Cablevision, San Antonio, 1984-88; writer in the schs. Tex. Commn. on Arts, San Antonio, 1986-91; faculty English dept. U. Tex, San Antonio, 1989-92; vis. writer Grad. dept. St. Mary's U., San Antonio, Spring 1992; founder readers' theater and alternative sch. Gemini Ink, San Antonio, 1992—. Co-creator and cons. Writers' Inst. at Our Lady of the Lake U., San Antonio, 1986-2003; vis. writer grad. dept., summer 1996; mem. Lit. Peer Rev. Panel, Tex. Commn. on the Arts, Austin, 1990-92; adv. bd. Guadalupe Cultural Ctr. Lit., San Antonio, 1990-92; cons. Arts Teach Program San Antonio Arts and Cultural Affairs Dept., 1991; faculty advisor literary mag. U. Tex. at San Antonio, 1991-92. Author, poet: contbr. anthologies and literary revs., 1992— including poetry in Descant, Inheritance of Light, Poets of the Lake, Bloomsbury Rev. and others; works of fiction in Quar. West, Columbia, Crosscurrents, books revs. in Harvard Rev. and San Antonio Express-News; contbr. popular articles to regional magazines including San Antonio Mag., San Antonio Monthly, D. Magazine, Third Coast, cons. for Life, 1981; as editor (book) Writers at the Lake, 1997. Voting place official, Democrat, San Antonio, 1980's. Recipient 1st place fiction award San Antonio Writer's Guild, 1983, 1st place investigative article San Antonio chpt. Women in Comm., Inc., 1986; alt. Dobie Paisano fellowshp U. Tex. and Tex. Inst. Letters, 1989, 1st runner up Dobie Paisano, U. Tex., and Tex. Inst. Letters, 1991; honoree at Pen Party Friends of San Antonio Pub. Libr., 1984; Imagineer award Mind Sci. Found., 2000; Headliner in Edn. award Women in Comm., Inc., 2002. Episcopalian. Avocations: theater, opera, antiquing, roaming Tex. hill country.

CUBA, STANLEY L. government official; b. Denver, Apr. 30, 1948; s. Frank L. ((Czuba)) Cuba and Wanda Helen Kugaczewska; m. Ewa Zofia Galkowska, Sept. 18, 1998. BA in Polit. Sci., Europe-Columbia U., 1970; cert. in East European studies, Inst. on East Cen., 1972; MA in History, Columbia U., 1978. Assoc. conf. coord. Polish Inst. Arts and Scis., N.Y.C., 1970-72; asst. to pres. Kosciuszko Found., N.Y.C., 1972-79; assoc. dir. Andre Zarre Gallery, N.Y.C., 1980-82; transl. Denver, 1983-90; ct. clk. II Denver County Ct., 1986-90; cert. investigator Mayor's Office of Contract Compliance, Denver, 1990-2000; prevailing wage investigator auditor's office Denver Internat. Airport, 2000—. Mayor's Office of Contract Compliance liaison to Asian C. of C., Denver, 1993-2000; presenter in field. Author: (exhbn. catalogs) Stefan Mrozewski (1894-1975) Wood Engravings: A Posthumous Exhibition, 1976, Jozef Pankiewicz (1886-1940): A Loan Exhibition of Oils, Watercolors, Sketches and Graphics, 1978, Hussars and the Crescent: The Polish Relief of Vienna, 1983, The Art of Jozef Bakos: An Early Modernist, 1891-1977, 1988, Colorado Women Artists, 1859-1950: An Unprecedented Exhibition of Women Artists Living or Working in Colorado from 1859 to 1950, 1989, Jan Sawka: A Selected Retrospective, 1990, The Art of Jozef Bakos: Selections from the Estate of Jozef Gabryel Bakos, 1992, Olive Rush: A Hoosier Artist in New Mexico, 1992, John F. Carlson and Artists of the Broadmoor Art Academy, 1999; co-author: (book) Great Drawings of the 20th Century, 1981, The Colorado Book, 1993, The Art of Charles Partridge Adams, 1993, (exhbn. catalogs) George Luks: An American Artist, 1987, Pikes Peak Vision: The Broadmoor Art Academy, 1919-1945, 1989, Hayes Lyon: A Colorado Regionalist (1909-1987), 1991; contbr. to Allgemeines Kunstler Lexikon, 1998-99, also to exhbn. catalogs and mags. Mem. Denver Cath. Archdiocesan Adv. Coun., 1999-2002; mem. Denver Cath. Archdiocesan Due Process Panel, 2003-- mem. mus./gallery com. Arvada (Colo.) Ctr. for Arts and Humanities, 1990-2002. Recipient Bicentennial Recognition of Exhbn. Curated on History of Polish Cmty. in Colo., 1859-1876, Colo. Bicentennial Commn./Denver Mayoral Bicentennial Commn., 1976; Interpreter grantee Ford. Found./Citizens Exch. Corps, 1969, Polonian Rsch. Ctr. grant Jagiellonian U., Krakow, 1980. Mem. Polish Nat. Alliance (lodge 134, v.p. 1990-96, fin. sec. 1996-98), Polish Am. Hist. Assn. (mem., chmn. award com. 1979-83, Rev. Joseph Swastek prize 1984), Polish Inst. Arts & Scis., Kosciuszko Found. Democrat. Roman Catholic. Avocations: collecting art, travel, attending art exhibitions, concerts, and theater, films. Home: 2643 Utica St Denver CO 80212-3007

CUBAS, JOSE M(ANUEL), advertising agency executive; b. Matanzas, Cuba, Mar. 1, 1930; came to U.S., 1960; s. Jose M. and Luisa M. (Ruiz) C.; m. Edith Perez, Apr. 26, 1952; children: Mercedes, Alina. Student, U. Havana Law Sch. Pres. Publicidad Siboney, S.A., Havana, 1953-60, San Juan, P.R., 1962-84, Internat. Mktg. and Advt. Services Corp., Fla., 1979-84; pres., CEO Foote Cone & Belding-Latin Am., N.Y.C., 1985-86, pres., 1987-97; chmn., CEO Siboney USA, Miami, Fla., 1998—. Mem. Internat. Advt. Assn., U.S.-Hispanic C. of C. (recipient awards). Republican. Roman Catholic. Avocations: travel, swimming, tennis. Office: Siboney USA 1401 Brickell Ave Ste 1100 Miami FL 33131-3504

CUBBIN, CATHERINE, social epidemiologist; PhD, Johns Hopkins U., 1998. Postdoctoral fellow Stanford U., Palo Alto, Calif., 1998—2000; rsch. scientist UCSF, Family and Cmty. Medicine Dept., San Francisco, 2000—; rsch. assoc. Stanford U., Palo Alto, Calif., 2000—. Contbr. articles to profl. jours.

CUBEÑAS, JOSÉ ANTONIO, social worker, consultant; b. Manzanillo, Oriente, Cuba, Sept. 27, 1925; came to U.S., 1961; s. José Amador Cubeñas and Maximina Peluzzo; m. Elsie Mujica, Sept. 22, 1979. LLD, U. Havana, 1950; MA in Spanish, St. John's U., 1975. Practice law, Cuba, 1950-60; co-founder Fundación Cultura Hispánica, N.Y.C., 1980—. Author: Rubén Darío: Restaurador de la conciencia de armonía del mundo, 1975, Spanish and Hispanic Presence in Florida - The Oliveros House, 1979, Pandemocracia: La solución política de Iberoamérica?, 1991; contbr. articles to profl. and polit. jours. Cand. N.Y. State Assembly, 1994; mayor City of Manzanillo, Cuba 1959; co-founder Hispanic sect. of N.Y. State Rep. Party, 1980. Mem. Acad. Norteamericana de la Lengua Expañola, Círculo de Escritores y Poetas Iberoamericanos de N.Y. Republican. Roman Catholic. Avocations: soccer, history, literature. Office: Empress Travel 161 Dreiser Loop Bronx NY 10475

CUBILLOS, ROBERT HERNAN, church administrator, philosophy educator; b. Long Beach, Calif., Sept. 16, 1957; s. Roberto Hernan and Jacqueline Lee (Smith) C.; m. Deborah Sue Forbes, June 21, 1986; children: Robby, Kelli, Kami. BS, Calif. State U., Carson, 1983; cert. in human rights, Internat. Inst. Human Rights, Strasbourg, France, 1984; MA in Apologetics, Simon Greenleaf Sch. of Law, Orange, Calif., 1985; MA in Theology, Fuller Theol. Sem., Pasadena, Calif., 1986; postgrad. studies, Claremont (Calif.) Grad. Sch., 1987.; MA in Social Ethics and Religion, U. So. Calif., 1996, PhD in Social Ethics and Religion, 2002. Ch. bus. adminstr. The Harbor Ch., Lomita, Calif., 1983-87, Rolling Hills Covenant Ch., Rolling Hills Estates, Calif., 1987—; asst. prof., co-editor Law Review Simon Greenleaf Sch. of Law, Orange, Calif., 1987-95, thesis sec., dean of students, 1988-95. Contbr. articles to religious and philos. jours. Mem. Am. Acad. Religion, Christian Mgmt. Assn., Evangel. Theol. Soc., Soc. Bibl. Lit., Pi Delta Phi. Office: Rolling Hills Covenant Ch 2221 Palos Verdes Dr N Palos Verdes Peninsula CA 90274-4220

CUBIN, BARBARA LYNN, congresswoman; b. Salinas, Calif., Nov. 30, 1946; d. Russell G. and Barbara Lee (Howard) Sage; m. Frederick William Cubin, Aug. 1; children: William Russell, Frederick William III. BS in Chemistry, Creighton U., 1969. Chemist Wyo. Machinery Co., Casper, Wyo., 1973-75; social worker State of Wyo.; office mgr. Casper, Wyo.; mem. Wyo. Ho. Reps., 1987-92, Wyo. Senate, 1993-94; pres. Spectrum Promotions and Mgmt., Casper, 1993-94; at-large repr. U.S. Ho. Reps. from Wyo., Washington, 1995—; mem. resources com., energy and commerce com. Mem. steering com. Exptl. Program to Stimulate Competitive Rsch. (EPSCOR); mem. Coun. of State Govts.; active Gov.'s Com. on Preventive Medicine, 1992; vice chmn. Cleer Bd. Energy Coun., Irving, Tex., 1993—; chmn. Wyo. Senate Rep. Conf., Casper, 1993—; mem. Wyo. Rep. Party Exec. Com., 1993; pres. Southridge Elem. Sch. PTO, Casper, Wyo. Toll fellow Coun. State Govts., 1990, Wyo. Legislator of Yr. award for energy and environ. issues Edison Electric Inst., 1994. Mem. Am. Legis. Exch. Coun., Rep. Women. Republican. Avocations: duplicate bridge, golfing, singing, reading, hunting. Office: US Ho Reps 1114 Longworth Ho Office Bldg Washington DC 20515-5001*

CUBITTO, ROBERT J. lawyer; b. Globe, Ariz., Aug. 1, 1950; s. Claude A. and Arizona C. (DiMario) C. BA, U. Ariz., 1972, BSBA, 1974; JD, Harvard Law Sch., 1976. Bar: Mass. 1977, N.Y. 1979, U.S. Dist. Ct. (so. and ea. dists.) N.Y. 1979, U.S. Tax Ct. 1979. Cons. Boston Cons. Group, 1976-78; assoc. Debevoise & Plimpton, N.Y.C., 1978-84, ptnr., 1985—. Mem. ABA, N.Y. State Bar Assn. (exec. com. tax sect. 1987-88), Assn. of Bar of City of N.Y., Harvard Club N.Y.C. (asst. treas. 1985-89, bd. mgrs. 1990-93), The Club of Turtle Bay (treas. 1994-97, pres. 1998—). Office: Debevoise & Plimpton 919 3rd Ave New York NY 10022-3904

CUCCHIARA, ALFRED LOUIS, health physicist; b. Greenport, N.Y., Mar. 3, 1948; s. Mario Victor Cucchiara and Florence (Osinski) Lopez; children: Troy Adam Cucchiara, Daved Chane Cucchiara. BS, Coll. Emporia, 1970; MS in radiation biophysics, U. Kans., 1975; cert. nuclear medicine, Wesley Medical Ctr., 1971. Cert. radiol. technician for nuclear medicine, Am. Registry Radiol. Technicians; cert. Nat. Registry Radiol. Proctection Technicians. Asst. health physicist U. Kans., Lawrence, 1971-73; environ. engr. United Nuclear Industries, Hanford, Wash., 1974-78; health physicist Los Alamos (N.Mex.) Nat. Lab., 1978-89, section leader/team leader, 1989—. Mem., std. reviewer ASTM, 1994; cons., author Am. Nat. Stds. Inst., 1984—; session chmn., co-organizer Fine Particle Soc., 1984—; pres. Muscular Devel. and Rehab., LTD, Los Alamos, 1990—; profl. witness City of Santa Fe versus INS, 1996; speaker Rio Grande chpt. Health Physics Soc. ann. mtg., 1997, presenter Calif. Rad Safety Officer's mtg., 1998-2002; organizer, chair semi-ann. meeting RSO, Santa Fe, 2002; Internat. ALARA Symposium, 1999. Contbr. over 30 articles to profl. jours. Recipient 1st place YMCA, Los Alamos Bench Press Contest, 1997, 99, 5 km. race walking champion for 40-49 years, Am. Bus. Women's Annual Race, 1997. Mem. Coll. Emporia Student Body (v.p. 1969-70), Los Alamos Recreational Club 1663 (bd. dirs., vice chmn. 1982-84). Republican. Achievements include patents in sequentially dispensing syringe with multiple needle assembly, isolation leverage weight training cuff, long range detection of alpha particles. Home: 929 Estates Dr Los Alamos NM 87544-2785 Office: Los Alamos Nat Lab PO Box 1663 Los Alamos NM 87544-0600 E-mail: alcucchiara@lanl.gov.

CUCCHIARA, SANDRA CHIAVARAS, special education educator; b. Clinton, Mass., Apr. 8, 1949; 2 children. BS in Spl. Edn., Fitchburg State Coll., 1970, MEd in Reading, 1976; postgrad. (fellow), Clark U., 1981-83; postgrad., Merrimac Ednl. Ctr., Chelmsford, Mass. Cert. in elem. and spl. edn., reading, reading supervision, learning disabilities, secondary English Mass. Tchr. spl. class Webster Schs., Mass., 1970—73; asst. coord. program materials, resource rm. Webster Schs., 1974; tchr./coord. primary spl. needs program Webster Schs., 1975—78, tchr. jr. high English, 1978-79, reading tchr. jr. high, 1979—80; adminstrv. asst. intern Shepherd Hill Regional Sch., Dudley, Mass., 1980—81; dir., owner Teddy Bear Day Care Ctr., Dudley, 1983—85; devel. specialist Ft. Devens Post Learning Ctr., Shirley, 1985—86; resource rm. tchr. Murdock H.S., Winchendon, Mass., 1986; tchr. behavioral modification Mid. Sch., Winchendon, 1986—87; coord., tchr. gifted and talented Lancaster Pub. Schs., 1987—90; tchr. learning disabilities Leominster Pub. Schs., Mass., 1990—91, tchr. primary level behavior modification, 1991—97, learning disabilities specialist, 1997—99, tchr. fifth grade, 1999—2000, tchr. eighth grade, 2000—02; dean of students Samoset Sch., Leominster, 2002—. Tchr. assistance team/pre-referal process Samoset Sch., 1998—, profl. devel. program com., 2001—; mid. sch. dean of students Leominster Pub. Schs., 2001—; adminstr. preparation program Merrimack Edn. Ctr., 2002—; adv. coun. Samoset Mid. Sch., Leominster, 2002—, coord. spelling bee, 2003, student coun. advisor grades 5 and 6, 2003—. Sec. Samoset Sch. PTO, Leominister, 1995—97; mem. edn. reform change team Samoset Mid. Sch., 1998—. Mem.: NEA, Mass. Reading Assn. (North Worcester County coun. 1994—95), Internat. Reading Assn. (v.p. 1994—95, Chmn. Celebrate Literacy award 1994—95), Leonminster Tchrs. Assn. (bldg. rep. 1992—95, negotiating com. 1993—, sec. 1995—, welfare com. chair 1997—, sec./treas. 1999, negotiating team 2000—, pres. 2001—), Mass. Tchrs. Assn., Webster Emblem Club (pres. 1984—85, newsletter editor 2000—), Phi Delta Kappa (Horace Mann grantee 1989—90). Home: 29 Chapman Pl Leominster MA 01453-6149

CUCCO, JUDITH ELENE, international marketing professional; b. Summit, N.J., Aug. 09; d. Louis John and Patricia T. (Procaccini) C. BS in Internat. Rels. and Spanish, Am. U., 1973; MBA, U. Md., 1983. Prof. English Universidad Nacional Autonoma de Mex., Mexico City, 1971-72; tchr. Spanish, ESL Montgomery (Md.) County Pub. Schs., 1973-81; acct. exec., industry cons. AT&T Comms., Parsippany, N.J., 1983-87; mgr. internat. mktg. support ctr. AT&T, Morristown, N.J., 1987-89, dir. market devel. internat. ops. divsn. Caracas, Venezuela, 1989-91, mgr. global product line Sch. Bus. Somerset, N.J., 1991-93, regional mgr. market mgmt. Latin Am., Network Wireless Systems Bus. Unit Whippany, N.J., 1994-95; bus. devel. dir. Asia/Pacific and Caribbean/L.Am. AT&T Global Bus. Multimedia Svcs., 1995-96; Ams. regional mgr. AT&T Internat. Product Mgmt., 1996-97; market analysis and bus. planning AT&T Internat. Traffic Mgmt., Morristown, N.J., 1997-2000; dir. bandwidth ops. Concert, Global Svcs. Direct, Morristown, 2000—02; data channel mgmt. AT&T Wholesale, Morristown, 2002; dedicated transit and sub sea cable product mgmt. AT&T, 2003—. Sponsor Child Reach, Warwick, R.I., 1984—, Friends of India, 1995—; mem. Small Faith Cmty., Bridgewater, 1992-98; vol. Interfaith Hospitality Network, Bridgewater, 1993—; mem. Womyn Included, 1994-2000. Mem. U. Md. Alumni Assn., Am. U. Alumni Assn., Pandora's Cir. Avocations: scuba diving, sailing, reading, traveling. Home: 308 Greenfield Rd Bridgewater NJ 08807-3714 Office: AT&T Rm N473 412 Mount Kemble Ave Morristown NJ 07960-6617

CUCCO, ULISSE P. obstetrician, gynecologist; b. Bklyn., Aug. 19, 1929; s. Charles and Elvira (Garafalo) C.; m. Antoinette DeMarco, Aug. 31, 1952; children— Carl, Richard, Antoinette Marie, Michael, Frank, James BS cum laude, L.I. U., 1950; MD, Loyola U., Chgo., 1954. Diplomate Am. Bd. Ob-Gyn. Intern Nassau County Hosp., Hempstead, N.Y., 1954-55; resident in ob-gyn Lewis Meml. Mercy Hosp., Chgo., 1955-58; practice medicine specializing in ob-gyn Des Plaines, Ill., 1960—. Past pres. med. staff, chmn. dept. ob-gyn. Holy Family Hosp., Des Plaines, Ill.; clin. asst. prof. Stritch Sch. Medicine, Loyola U. Contbr. articles to med. jours. Mem. ACS, Am. Fertility Soc., Ctrl. Assn. Ob-Gyn., Ill. Med. Soc., Chgo. Med. Soc., Chgo. Gynecol. Soc. (past pres.), Chgo. Inst. Medicine, Sunset Ridge Country Club. Roman Catholic. Home: 665 Midfield Ln Northbrook IL 60062-5507

CUCIN, ROBERT LOUIS, plastic surgeon, lawyer; b. N.Y.C., Apr. 17, 1946; s. Robert and Julia C.. BA magna cum laude, Cornell U., 1967, MD, 1971; JD, Fordham U., 1985; MBA, Columbia U., 2003. Bar: N.Y. 1983, N.J. State Sureme Ct., Washington Ct. of Appeals; bd. cert. legal medicine; diplomate Am. Bd. Surgery, Am. Bd. Plastic Surgery; licensed physician, N.J., N.Y. State, Calif., Va. Intern Cornell-N.Y. Hosp., N.Y.C., 1971-72, resident in gen. surgery, 1972-76, resident in plastic surgery, 1977-79; fellow in surgery Meml.-Sloan Kettering Found., 1972-76, 77-79; practice medicine specializing in plastic surgery Columbia MBA, N.Y.C., 1979—; instr. surgery Cornell U. Med. Coll., 1980—; asst. attending plastic surgeon Beth Israel North, N.Y. Downtown Hosp., 1979—, N.Y. Hosp., 1980—, Drs. Hosp., 1987—. Pres. Esquire Cadillac Limousine Svc. Inc., 1977—93, Beaux Arts Holdings, 1979—, Rocin Labs., Inc., 1981—; pres., CEO Biosculpture Tech., Inc., 2001—. Author: The Kindest Cut, Keeping Face, Medical Malpractice: Handling Plastic Surgical Cases; contbr. articles to profl, jours. Mem. N.Y. County Health Svc. Rev. Orgn., 1976—; founder, dir Rocin Found. for Plastic Surg. Rsch., 1979—; Maj. M.C.,

USAF, 1976-77; Japan. Fellow: ACS, Am. Coll. Legal Medicine, Internat. Coll. Surgeons; mem.: ABA, ATLA, AMA (Physicians Recognition award 1978, 1981), N.Y. Acad. Scis., N.Y. County Med. Soc. (health systems, pub. rels., peer rev. coms.), N.Y. State Med. Soc., Royal Soc. Medicine, Am. Soc. Plastic and Reconstructive Surgery, Am. Mensa, Cornell Club, N.Y. Athletic Club, Le Club, Phi Beta Kappa. Republican. Office: 120 Central Park S New York NY 10019-1560

CUCINA, RUSSELL JOSEPH, medical researcher; b. Thousand Oaks, Calif., Apr. 10, 1972; s. Vincent and Rosemary Cucina. AB, U. Calif., Berkeley, 1994; MD, U. Calif., Davis, 1998. Diplomate Am. Bd. Internal Medicine. Resident internal medicine Stanford U., Palo Alto, Calif., 1998—2001, chief resident internal medicine, 2001—02, clin. instr. internal medicine, 2001—. Trustee Calif. Med. Assn., San Francisco, 1997—98; cons. rsch. assoc. Stanford Med. Informatics, Palo Alto, 1999—, fellow med. informatics, 2002—; cons. physician clin. info. sys. Stanford Hosp. and Clinics, Palo Alto, 2002—; presenter in field. Contbr. articles to profl. jours. Scholar Regents' and Chancellor's scholar, U. Calif., 1990—94, Regents' scholar in health scis., 1994—98, Alumni Leadership scholar, U. Calif., Berkeley, Alumni Assn., 1990—94. Mem.: ACP, Am. Med. INformatics Assn., Phi Beta Kappa, Alpha Omega Alpha (co-pres. 1997—98, Eta chpt.). Personal E-mail: rjcucina@stanford.edu.

CUCINA, VINCENT ROBERT, retired financial executive; b. Balt., Mar. 31, 1936; s. Anthony James and Josephine (Lazzaro) C.; m. Rosemary Warrington, Apr. 24, 1965; children: Victor, Gregory, Russell. BS in Acctg. magna cum laude, Loyola Coll., Balt., 1958; MS in Fin. Mgmt., George Washington U., 1967. CPA, Calif. Auditor Haskins & Sells, CPAs, Balt., 1958, 61-63; acctg. mgr. books and reports Chesapeake & Potomac Telephone Co. (AT&T), Cockeysville, Md., 1964-68; mgr. fin. controls ITT, N.Y.C., 1968; contr. ITT World Directories, N.Y.C., 1969-70; v.p. fin. analysis and planning Dart Industries, Inc., L.A., 1970-82; v.p. fin., CFO Epson Am., Inc., Torrance, Calif., 1984-87; cons. Westlake Village, Calif., 1988-95. Lectr. planning and fin. Calif. Luth. U., 1991-95. Capt. U.S. Army, 1959-60, USAR, 61-64. Mem. AICPA, Fin. Execs. Internat. Roman Catholic. Avocations: travel, reading, target shooting. Home: 32305 Blue Rock Rdg Westlake Village CA 91361 E-mail: vrcwlv@aol.com.

CUCKOVIC, ZELJKO, education educator; b. Zagreb, Croatia, Nov. 12, 1955; arrived in U.S., 1987; s. Bozidar Cuckovic and Mila Vojnovic. BA math., Univ. Zagreb, Croatia, 1979, MA math., 1985; PhD math., Mich. State Univ., E. Lansing, Mich., 1991. Tchg. asst. Univ. Zagreb, Zagreb, Croatia, 1980—87, Mich. State Univ., E. Lansing, Mich., 1987—91, instr., 1991—92; asst. prof. Univ. Wis., Waukeska, Wis., 1992—94, Univ. Toledo, Toledo, 1994—99, assoc. prof., 1999—. Contbr. articles to profl. jour. Mem.: Am. Math. Soc. Office: Univ Toledo Dept Math 2801 W Bancroft St Toledo OH 43606

CUCULO, JOHN A. chemist, educator; b. Providence, June 23, 1924; s. John Joseph Paul and Carolina Cuculo; m. Eve Katherine Cortese, July 13, 1946; children: Cheryl Alison, Patricia Carol, Lauren Maria. ScB in Chemistry, Brown U., 1946; PhD in Chemistry, Cuke U., 1950. Rsch. chemist E.I. DuPont de Nemours, Wilmington, Del., 1950—60, sr. rsch. chemist Kinston, NC, 1960—61, Richmond, Va., 1961—65, Wilmington, 1965—68; prof. dept. chemistry N.C. State U., Raleigh, NC, 1968—, Hoechst Celanese prof. emeritus, 1995—. Cons. in field. Contbr. Recipient The S.. Smith Meml. medal, Brit. Fiber Soc., London, 1993, Decoration for Merits, Tech. U. Lodz, Poland, 1993. Mem.: Am. Chem. Soc., Sigma Xi. Roman Catholic. Achievements include patents for for Stren fishing line; discovery of of two new reactions of cellulose; of new solvents for sellulose. Office: North Carolina State Univ Dept Chemistry Raleigh NC 27695

CUDAHY, RICHARD D. judge; b. Milwaukee, Feb. 2, 1926; s. Michael F. and Alice ((Dickson)) Cudahy; m. Ann (Featherston), July 14, 1956 (dec. 1974); m. Janet (Stuart), July 17, 1976; children: Richard D., Norma K., Theresa E., Daniel M., Michaela A., Marguerite L., Patrick G. BS, U.S. Mil. Acad., 1948; JD, Yale U., 1955; LLD, Ripon Coll., 1981, DePaul U., 1995, Wabash Coll., 1996, Stetson U., 1998. Bar: Conn. 1955, D.C. 1957, Ill. 1957, Wis. 1961. Commd., 2d. lt. U.S. Army, 1948, 1st. lt., 1950; law clk. to presiding judge U.S. Ct. Appeals (2d cir.), 1955—56; asst. to legal adv. Dept. State, 1956—57; assoc. Isham, Lincoln, and Beale, Chgo., 1957—60; pres. Patrick Cudahy, Inc., Wis., 1961—71, Patrick Cudahy Family Co., Wis., 1968—75; ptnr. firm Godfrey and Kahn, Milw., 1972; commr., chmn. Wis. Pub. Svc. Commn., 1972—75; ptnr. Isham, Lincoln, and Beale, Chgo. and Washington, 1976—79; judge U.S. Ct. Appeals (7th cir.), Chgo., 1979—94, sr. judge, 1994—. Lectr. law Marquette U. Law Sch., 1962; vis. prof. law U. Wis., 1966—67; prof. lectr. law George Washington U., Washington, 1978—79; adj. prof. DePaul U. Coll. Law, 1995—. Commr. Milw. Harbor, 1964—66; pres. Milw. Urban League, 1965—66; trustee Environ. Def. Fund, 1976—79; chmn. DePaul U., Human Rights Law Inst., 1990—98; mem. adv. com. Ctr. for Internat. Human Rights, Northwestern U., 2000—; chmn. Wis. Dem. Party, 1967—68; Dem. candidate for Wis. Atty. Gen., 1968. Mem.: ABA (spl. com. on Energy Law 1978—84, 1990—96, pub. utility sect. coun. group), Am. Inst. for Pub. Svc. (bd. selectors), Fed. Judges' Assn. (bd. dirs.), Chgo. Bar Assn., Milw. Bar Assn., Wis. Bar Assn., Am. Law Inst., Cath. Theol. Union (trustee emeritus 1997—2003), Lawyers Club, Chgo. (pres. 1992—93, spl. divsn. D.C. cir. for appt. ind. counsel 1998—2002). Office: US Ct Appeals 219 S Dearborn St Ste 2648 Chicago IL 60604-1874

CUDAK, GAIL LINDA, lawyer; b. Bellville, Ill., July 13, 1952; d. Robert Joseph and Margaret Lucille C.; m. Thomas Edward Young, Sept. 15, 1979. BA, Kenyon Coll., 1974; JD, Case Western Res. U., 1977, MBA, 1991. Bar: Ohio 1977, U.S. Dist. Ct. (no. dist.) Ohio 1977, U.S. Ct. Appeals (6th cir.) 1977, U.S. Ct. Appeals (fed. cir.) 1989. Assoc. Fuerst, Leidner, Dougherty & Kasdan, Cleve., 1977-79; staff atty. The B.F. Goodrich Co., Akron, Ohio, 1979-84, sr. corp. counsel Independence, Ohio, 1985-89, divsn. counsel Brecksville, Ohio, 1990-98, group counsel, 1998-99; sr. attorney Eaton Corp., Cleve., 1999—. Trustee Great Lakes Theater Festival, 1996—, mem. exec. com.; fundraiser Ohio Found. Ind. Colls., 1993—. Mem.: ABA, Cleve. Internat. Lawyers Group, Cleve. Bar Assn. (chair corp. sect.), Ohio State Bar Assn. Home: 12520 Edgewater Dr Apt 1405 Lakewood OH 44107-1639 Office: Eaton Corp 1111 Superior Ave E Cleveland OH 44114-2507

CUDDIHY, ROBERT VINCENT, JR., finance and marketing executive; b. Rochester, N.Y., July 15, 1959; s. Robert Vincent Sr. and June Marie (Tuck) C.; m. Michele Pittenger; children: Brendan, Shea, Tara. BA in Acctg., Franklin and Marshall Coll., Lancaster, Pa., 1981. CPA N.Y. Sr. mgr. KPMG Peat Marwick, N.Y.C., 1981-87; pres., CFO, COO, sec. HMG Worldwide Corp., N.Y.C., 1987-2001, bd. dirs., 1988—2001, chief oper. officer, 1989-2000, pres., 1990-93, chief info. officer, 2000-01; CFO, treas., sec. Nat Auto Credit, Inc., 2001—; pres. Shannon Hill Assocs., 2001—. Cons. in field. Bd. dirs., pres. Bridgewater Bears Hockey Assn. Mem. Am. Inst. CPAs, N.Y. State Soc. CPAs, Nat. Assn. Accts. Republican. Avocations: home improvements, hockey, reading. Office: Nat Auto Credit Inc 555 Madison Ave 29th Fl New York NY 10022

CUDDY, BRIAN GERARD, neurosurgeon; b. Syracuse, N.Y., July 13, 1959; s. Edward Michael and Mary Elizabeth (O'Brien) C. BS in Biology, SUNY, Albany, 1981; MS in Physiology, Albany Med. Coll., 1983, MD, 1987. Clin. asst. prof. neurosurgery Med. Coll. Wis., 1993-94; assoc. prof. neurosurgery Med. U. S.C., 1994—. Adj. assoc. prof. bioengring. Clemson U., 1996—. Contbr. articles to profl. jours. Fellow Am. Coll. Surgeons; mem. Am. Assn. Neurol. Surgeons, Sigma Xi. Roman Catholic.

CUDDY, DANIEL HON, bank executive; b. Valdez, Alaska, Feb. 8, 1921; s. Warren N. and Lucy C.; m. Betty Puckett, Oct. 6, 1947; children: Roxanna, David, Gretchen, Jane, Lucy, Laurel. BA, Stanford U., 1946; LLD (hon.), U. Alaska, 2000. Bar: Alaska 1948. Pvt. practice, Anchorage, 1948-53; pres. First Nat. Bank Anchorage, 1951—, chmn. bd.; consul for the Netherlands, 1975—85. With U.S. Army, World War II, ETO. Named Alaskan of Yr., 2002. Office: First Nat Bank 101 W 36th Ave Anchorage AK 99503-5904

CUDKOWICZ, LEON, medical educator; b. Lodz, Poland, Jan. 18, 1923; came to U.S., 1956; s. Mauryce and Masza (Malynski) C.;m. Margaret Chandler, Mar. 14, 1950 (div. July 1981); children: Alexander, Penelope; m. Teresa Cuiza de Alfaro, Jan. 18, 1986. BS, U. London, 1946, MD, 1951. James Hudson Brown fellow Yale U. Sch. Medicine, 1956-58; registrar St. Thomas Hosp., U. London, 1958-59; asst. prof. then assoc. prof. medicine Dalhousie U., Halifax, N.S., Can., 1960-69; prof. medicine Thomas Jefferson U., Phila., 1970-74; prof., chmn. Wright State U., Dayton, 1974-79, King Faisal U., Dammam, Saudi Arabia, 1979-81; prof. medicine U. Cin., 1981-95, prof. emeritus, 1995—. Author: Human Bronchial Circulation, 1970; contbr. 107 articles to profl. jours. Capt. RAMC, 1946-49. Fellow RCP, Nat. Pediat. Soc. Bolivia (hon.), NIH (sr.). Avocations: writing, mountaineering, gardening, travel. Home: Yonder Hill Farm Highland OH 45132 Office: U Cin Sch Medicine 253 Bethesda Ave Cincinnati OH 45229-2827

CUELLO, JOEL L. biosystems engineer, educator; b. San Pablo City, Philippines, Nov. 20, 1962; s. Vicente Reyes and Gertrudis B. (Lansigan) C. BSin Agrl. and Biol. Engring., U. Philippines, 1984; MS in Agrl. and Biol. Engring., Penn State U., 1990, PhD in Agrl. and Biol. Engring., 1994, MS in Plant Physiology, 1999. Instr. U. Philippines, Los Baños, 1984-88; grad. rsch. asst. Pa. State U., University Park, 1988-93; rsch. assoc. U.S. NRC, NASA Kennedy Space Ctr., Cape Canaveral, Fla., 1994; asst. prof. U. Ariz., Tucson, 1995-2000, assoc. prof., 2001—. Mem. editl. bd. Life Support and Biosphere Sci. Internat., Jour. for Earth and Space; contbr. articles to profl. jours. Rsch. grantee USDA, 1996-2002, NASA, 1997-2002, DOE, 2001-03; recipient Outstanding Alumnus award U. Philippines, 2000. Mem.: AAAS (rep. 2003—), Am. Soc. Engring. Edn., Inst. Biol. Engring. (councilor 1998—99, chmn. ann. mtg. program 2003), Am. Soc. Agrl. Engring. (plant biol. engring. com. 1995, advisor Ariz. student br. 1996—2000, pres. Ariz. chpt. 1997—98, chmn. biol. engring. exec. com. 1998—99, chmn. emerging areas divsn. 1999—2000, chmn. plant structures, environ. com. 2002—03, rep. to AAAS, chmn. biol. engring. divsn. 2003—, Best Paper award 1992, Pres. Citation award 2000, CIGR Outstanding Contbn. award 2000), Honor Soc. Agrl. and Biol. Engring. (pres. Pa. chpt. 1993), Nat. Honor Soc. Engring., Nat. Honor Soc. Agr. Avocations: reading, hiking. Office: U Ariz Dept Agrl and Biosystems Engring 507 Shantz Bldg Tucson AZ 85721-0001

CUETTER, ALBERT CAYETANO, neurologist; b. Cartagena, Colombia, Aug. 7, 1938; MD, Med. U. Cartagena, Colombia, 1963. Diplomate Am. Bd. Neurology. Internist Hosp. Santa Clara, Cartagena, Colombia, 1963-64; res. neur. Northwestern U., 1965-68, fellowship in electromyography, 1968 69. Prof. neurology Tex. Tech. U. Health Scis. Ctr., 1990.

CUEVAS, EDUARDO SAMANIEGO, internist; b. Manila, Oct. 7, 1958; came to U.S., 1985; s. Porfirio Carmona and Erlinda Samaniego Cuevas; m. Gigi Mariette Delos Reyes, Aug. 19, 1985; children: Elizabeth Grace, Edilene Gayle, Edward Gabriel, Emmanuel Gregory. BS in Psychology, U. of the Philippines, Quezon City, 1979; MD, Feu Inst. of Medicine, Manila, 1983. Diplomate Am. Bd. Internal Medicine. Intern San Juan de Dios Hosp., Pasay City, The Philippines, 1983-84, surg. resident, 1985; internal medicine resident Bklyn. Hosp. Ctr., 1989-92; pvt. practice Tacoma, 1992—. Dir., chair membership com. Southcare HMO, Tacoma, 1995—98; mem. policy bd. Doctors Health Plan, Auburn, Wash., 1996—98; mem. exec. com., chair pharmacy and therapeutics com. Puget Sound Hosp., Tacoma, 1996—97; mem. oper. bd., bd. mem. Physicians Health Network, Tacoma, 2001—03. Reviewer, contbr. Am. Bd. Internal Medicine, 1997—. With U.S. Army, 1986-88. Recipient Army Achievement award, 1988. Mem.: ACP-ASIM, AMA (Physicians Recognition award 1999—), Catholic Physicians Guild of Washington, Filipino Am. Physicians of Wash., Tacoma Acad. Internal Medicine, Pierce County Med. Soc., Wash. State Med. Assn., Beta Sigma (grand princep 2001—03). Avocations: piano, travel. Home: 6306 89th Ave W University Place WA 98467-1644 Office: 3611 S D St # 9 Tacoma WA 98418-6813 E-mail: edcuevas@aol.com.

CUEVAS-SANTIAGO, NELLY, collections and bad debt manager; b. San Juan, PR, Nov. 11, 1962; d. Luis Moises Cuevas and Emilia Antonia Santiago. MBA in Environ. Mgmt., Met. U., PR; cert. in purchasing mgmt., Sacred Heart U., PR, 1994. Purchasing mgr. Laboratorio Clinico Caparra, Inc., San Juan, PR, 1995 97, billing supr., 1999—2001, credit and collections agt., 1997—. Co-author (rsch.) Receptor Ontogeny in Rat Vas Deferens; contbr. rsch. Vol. orgns. for homeless, Bayamon, PR, 2002. Achievements include research in AChE activity of the vasa deferencia of normal and drug tolerant rats; effects of haloperidol on neurotransmitters activity on vas deferens; evidence that dopamine is acting at the adrenoreceptor of rat vas deferens. Home: #790 Habana St Urb Las Americas San Juan PR 00921 Office: Laboratorio Clinico Caparra Inc PO Box 11560 Caparra PR 00922 Home Fax: 787-783-7695; Office Fax: 787-793-7695. Personal E-mail: ncuevas@asem.net. E-mail: ncuevas@asem.net.

CUFFE, ROBIN JEAN, nursing educator; b. Frankfurt, Sept. 8, 1951; d. Russell Bates and Jean May (Clark) Preuit; m. Ronald Frederick Cuffe, Mar. 9, 1974; 1 child, Matthew David. Diploma, Richmond Meml. Hosp., 1973; BSN, Marymount U., 1982; MS in Edn., Va. Technol. and State U., 1990. RNC; cert. in cardiac rehab. nursing AACN; cert. health edn. specialist. Staff nurse Fairfax Hosp., Falls Church, Va., 1973-75; asst. head nurse, staff nurse, supr. ICU Arlington (Va.) Hosp., 1975-78, asst. coord. cardiac rehab., 1978-81, coord. cardiopulmonary rehab., 1981—. Bd. dirs. Am. Heart Assn., Northern, Va., 1982-91; jr. high youth group leader Ch. of the Holy Comforter, Vienna, Va., 1988-90, mem. adult edn. commn., 1990—. Fellow Am. Assn. Cardiovasc. and Pulmonary Rehab. (chmn. stds. and reimbursement com. 1991—, pres.-elect 1994-95, pres. 1995-96, treas. 1996-98), Va. Assn. Cardiovasc. and Pulmonary Rehab., Sigma Theta Tau (pres. chpt. 1984-86). Episcopalian. Home: 1804 Cloverlawn Ct Mc Lean VA 22101-4299 E-mail: rcuffe@mindspring.com.

CUFFE, STAFFORD SIGESMUND, engineering company executive, consultant; AAS, N.Y.C. Community Coll., 1975; BS in Engring. Tech., CCNY, 1977; MS in Adminstrn., Ctrl. Mich. U., 1993; PhD in Adminstrn./Mgmt., Walden U., 1995. Project engr. PPG Inds. Inc., Wichita Falls Tex., 1977-79; mfg. engr. Ford Motor Co., Tulsa, 1979-85, sr. mfg. engr. Lincoln Park, Mich., 1985-90, sr. mfg. engr. Glass Tech. Ctr. Dearborn, 1992-95, sr. mfg. engr. Rsch. & Engring. Ctr., 1996; pres. Cuffe & Assocs., Bloomfield Hills, Mich., 1996—. Mem. Dearborn (Mich.) plant modernization team (Japanese venture), 1990-92; adj. prof. Nova Southeastern U., Sch. Bus. and Entrepreneurship-MBA program, 1996—, Oakland U., Sch. Mgmt. and Mktg., Bus. Adminstrn.-MBA program, 1997—; adj. prof. MBA program U. Dallas, 2000—, Capella U., 2000—, Baker Coll., 2000—, Regis U., Colo., 2000. Bd. dirs. Tulsa Jaycees, 1981; tech. advisor Boy Scouts Am., Tulsa, 1982; exec advisor Jr. Achievement of S.W. Mich., 1986; fund raiser United Way Found. of Mich., 1988. Mem. IEEE (nat. chmn. glass industry com. 1990—), Am. Mgmt. Assn., Soc. Mfg. Engrs., Rotary (Southfield Mich. chpt.). Democrat. Roman Catholic. Avocations: golf, tennis, cross-country skiing. Office: Cuffe & Assocs Inc PO Box 7123 Bloomfield Hills MI 48302-7123 E-mail: caimmts@aol.com.

CUFFE, STEVEN PAUL, psychiatrist; b. Teaneck, N.J., Jan. 16, 1956; s. Frank Oliver and Lois Ann Cuffe; m. Barbara Ivey Kissam, Aug. 27, 1977; children: Edward Patel, Barbara Ivey. BA in History, Davidson Coll., 1978; MD, Wake Forest U., 1982. Lic. gen. psychiatry and child and adolescent psychiatry Am. Bd. Psychiatry and Neurology. Resident physician U. Calif., San Francisco, 1982—87; staff psychiatrist, med. dir. Orangeburg (S.C.) Area Mental Health, Orangeburg, 1987—91; outpatient dir. William S. Hall Psychiat. Inst. and U. S.C. Sch. Medicine dept. psychiatry, Columbia, SC, 1993—96, dir. divsn. child and adolescent psychiatry, 1996—. Office: U SC Dept Neuropsychiat and Behavioral Sci PO Box 202 Columbia SC 29202-0202

CUGELL, DAVID WOLF, medical educator; b. New Haven, Conn., Sept. 19, 1923; s. Abel George and Rose (Weiss) C.; m. Christina A.E. Enroth, Sept. 4, 1955. BS, Yale U., 1945; MD, SUNY, Bklyn., 1947. Diplomate Am. Bd. Internal Medicine, Am. Bd. Pulmonary Disease. From assoc. in medicine to Bazley prof. pulmonary diseases Northwestern U. Med. Sch., Chgo., 1955—. 1st lt. U.S. Army, 1953-55, Korea. Grantee Am. Lung Assn., NIH, 1955-85. Mem. Am. Lung Assn. Met. Chgo. (past pres.), Inst. Medicine of Chgo. Office: Rehab Inst Chgo 345 E Superior St Rm 354 Chicago IL 60611-4805 E-mail: mymble@northwestern.edu.

CUGGINO, MICHAEL JOSEPH, financial executive; b. Cambridge, Mass., Feb. 9, 1963; s. Joseph Anthony Jr. and Christine Adele (Dabrowski) C. Ed., Bentley Coll., 1985. CPA, Mass., Calif.; CISA. With Ernst & Young, LLP, 1985-91; pvt. practice acctg., 1991—2002; founder, pres., CEO, Pacific Heights Asset Mgmt., LLC, 2002—. Treas. Permanent Portfolio Family of Funds, Inc., 1993—, pres., 2003—, also bd. dirs.; treas. World Money Securities, Inc., 1993-96, Bullion Security Corp., 1993-2002, Passport Fin., Inc., 1993-2002. Mem. AICPA (pvt. cos. practice sect., mgmt. cons. practice sect., pers. fin. planning practice sect., tax practice sect.), Mass. Soc. CPAs, Calif. Soc. CPAs, EDP Auditors Assn. Home: 2201 Pacific Ave Apt 703 San Francisco CA 94115-1440 Office: Transam Ctr 600 Montgomery St 27th Fl San Francisco CA 94111-2702

CUGLER, CAROL MARIE MILLER, retired mental health services professional; b. Elizabeth, N.J., Dec. 25, 1942; d. Wilhelm Johannes Rudolph and Frances Caroline (Blank) Miller; m. Harry Clarke Cugler, Jan. 12, 1974; 2 stepchildren. Accredited records technician, Am. Med. Record Assn. Sec. Chris Craft Corporation, Salisbury, Md., 1960-64, Civil Def. Adminstrn., Salisbury, 1964-66; med. records libr. Pine Bluff State Hosp., Salisbury, 1966-74; dir. records/stats./quality assurance Holly Ctr., Salisbury, 1974-93, adminstrv. officer, 1993-95; ret., 1995. Vol. statistician Ea. Shore Hall of Fame, 1986; vol., sec. bd. Humane Soc. Wicomico County, Salisbury, 1988-95, capital campaign sec., 1990-95. Recipient numerous Appreciation awards United Charities Campaign, Appreciation award Ea. Shore Hall of Fame, 1986, Vol. of Yr. award Humane Soc. Wicomico County, 1992. Mem. Delmarva Peninsula Golf Assn. (sec. to adminstrv. asst. 1984-95). Democrat. Methodist. Avocation: travel. Home: 902 Rosalie Way Salisbury MD 21804-5266

CUIFFO, FRANK WAYNE, lawyer; b. Houston, Oct. 13, 1943; s. Richard and Helen (Giaco) C.; m. Barbara Joyce Streeter, Nov. 26, 1966; children: Karen, Deborah, Richard, Steven. BS, U. Notre Dame, 1964; JD, Fordham U., 1967. Bar: N.Y. 1967. Assoc. Pennie & Edmonds (formerly Pennie, Edmonds, Morton, Taylor & Adams), N.Y.C., 1967-69; sr. assoc. Emmet, Marvin, & Martin, N.Y.C., 1969-74, Golenbock & Barell, N.Y.C., 1974-78; mng. ptnr. Carro, Spanbock, Kaster & Cuiffo, N.Y.C., 1978-93; chmn. real estate dept., exec. com. Donovan, Leisure, Newton & Irvine, N.Y.C., 1993-98; ptnr. McDermott, Will & Emery, N.Y.C., 1998—. Mem. ABA, U.S. Patent Bar, N.Y. State Bar, Siwanoy Country Club, South Seas Club. Office: McDermott Will & Emery 50 Rockefeller Plz Fl 12 New York NY 10020-1600

CUKROWICZ, KEVIN FRANCIS, information technology manager, military officer; b. South Bend, Ind., Feb. 24, 1967; s. Brian Francis and Charlotte Anne (Shafer) C.; m. Denise Lynn Gilroy, Mar. 6, 1971; 1 child, Katherine Elizabeth. BS in Edn., Ohio State U., 1991; AS in Aircraft Sys., C.C. of the Air Force, Maxwell AFB, 1998; MBA, Ashland U., 2000; student, Comm. Officer Sch., Kessler AFB. Cert. project mgmt. profl. Sys. planner Sprint Network Sys., Mansfield, Ohio, 2000—; project mgr. Progressive Ins., Mayfield, Ohio, 2003—. Pres. N.E. Ohio chpt. Project Mgmt. Inst., Mansfield, 2000—. Pillar United Way of Richland County, Mansfield, 2000—; vol. instr. Jr. Achievement, Mansfield, 1996—. Project mgr., comm. flight commdr. USAF, 1985—, 179th Airlift Wing, Mansfield Lahm Airport. Mem. Res. Officers Assn., Air Force Assn., Nat. Guard Assn. U.S., Ohio Nat. Guard Assn., Nat. Geographic Soc., Ohio State U. Alumni Assn., Kappa Phi Kappa. Roman Catholic. Avocations: running, reading, skiing, travel. Home: 438 Marion Ave Mansfield OH 44903-2051 Office: 300 N Commons Blvd Mayfield OH 44143 E-mail: kevin_cukrowicz@hotmail.com.

CULBERSON, GARY MICHAEL, hotel manager; b. Jackson, Miss., Sept. 16, 1955; s. William James and Peggy Ann (Pickett) C.; m. Mary Lee Yadron, May 8, 1986; children: Ashley Victoria, Brent Michael. Student, Miss. State U., 1973-78. Cert. hotel adminstr. Resident mgr. Kingston Plantation, Myrtle Beach, S.C.; exec. asst., mgr. Brown Palace Hotel, Denver; mng. dir. Tremont Hotel, Chgo., 1991; gen. mgr. Embassy Suites Hotel, Denver, 1996-97; hotel mgr. Casino Magic Hotel, Biloxi, Miss., 1997—2002; v.p. Beau Rivage Resort, Biloxi, 2002—. Mem.: So. Innkeepers (v.p. 2001—), Miss. Hotel and Lodging Assn. (pres. 2002—, v.p. 2001—02, Gen. Mgr. of Yr. 2002), Miss. Gulf Coast Hotel and Motel Assn. (v.p. 1998—99, pres. 2000—02), Confrerie de la Chaine des Rotisseurs (Maitre of Table Restaurateur 1991—92), Mensa. Avocations: snow skiing, golf. Office: Beau Rivage Resort 875 Beach Blvd Biloxi MS 39530

CULBERSON, JOHN, congressman; b. Houston, June 24, 1956; m. Belinda Burney, Dec. 1989; 1 child: Caroline Virginia. BA in history, Southern Meth. U.; JD, South Tex. Coll. Law. Mem. Tex. House of Reps., 1986-2000, U.S. Congress 7th Tex. dist., 2001—, House Appropriations Com. Mem. Congressional com. Steering, Budget, Edn. and Workforce, Transportation and Infrastructure; served on House Environ. Regulation and Corrections com., House Public Edn. and Natural Resources com.; selected as House Rep. Whip. Mem. United Meth. Church. Office: 1728 Longworth House bldg Washington DC 20515-4307*

CULBERT, DAVID HOLBROOK, history educator, writer, editor; b. San Antonio, July 7, 1943; s. Robert William Culbert and Dorothy Fairfax Kift; m. Lubna Aranki, May 26, 1979. BA, Oberlin Coll., 1966; BMus, Oberlin Conservatory Music, 1966; PhD, Northwestern U., 1970; student, Mozarteum, Salzburg, Austria, 1963-64. Asst. prof. history Yale U., New Haven, Conn., 1970-71, La. State U., Baton Rouge, 1971-76, assoc. prof. history, 1976-84, prof. history, 1984—. Author: News for Everyman, 1976, Mission to Moscow, 1980; editor: (with Nicholas Cull and David Welch) Propaganda and Mass Persuasion: A Historical Encyclopedia (1500 to the Present), 2003; editor-in-chief: Film and Propaganda in America, 5 vols., 1990-93; co-editor: (with John Chambers) World War II Film and History, 1996, (with K.R.M. Short) Cambridge Studies in the History of Mass Comm., 1999—, (with David Welch) Studies in Propaganda, 1999—; editor Hist. Jour. of Film, Radio and TV, 1992—; contbr. numerous articles to profl. jours.; dir. hist. rsch., assoc. prodr. film Huey Long, 1985; hist. cons. film Die Macht der Bilder: Leni Riefenstahl, 1993; co-prodr. film essay Television's Vietnam: The Impact of Media, 1986; sr. cons. 6-part history of newsreel) Dawn of the Eye, 1998. Organist-choirmaster St. James Episcopal Ch., Baton Rouge, 1981—. Fellow Woodrow Wilson Ctr. for Scholars, Washington, 1976-77, Nat. Humanities Inst., Yale U., New Haven, 1977-78, vis. fellow Inst. for Advanced Study, Princeton, 1995. Mem. Orgn. Am. Historians (1st chmn. com. on radio-TV-film media, 1st chmn. Erik Barnouw Prize Com. 1981-84), Am. Hist. Assn. (chmn. John O'Connor Prize Com. 2000-01), Internat. Assn. Media and History (coun., pres. 1987-89), City Club of Baton Rouge, Phi Beta Kappa, Pi Kappa Lambda. Republican. Episcopalian. Home: 2933 Reymond Ave Baton Rouge LA 70808 Office: Dept History La State U 224 Himes Hall Baton Rouge LA 70803 E-mail: dhculbert@aol.com.

CULBERTSON, CHARLES RANDALL, historian, writer; b. Athens, Ga., May 10, 1952; s. Claude Harrison and Betty Juanita Culbertson; m. Janet Hamilton. BA, Mary Baldwin Col;/, Staunton, Va., 1986. Dir. pub. relations New Market Battlefield Mil. Mus., New Market, Va., 1989—99; writer Daily News Leader, Staunton, Va., 1993—; staff writer, photographer The News-Virginian, Waynesboro, 1986—93; assoc. dir. coll. rels. Mary Baldwin Coll., Staunton, 1997—98; writer James Madison U., Harrisonburg, Va., 1998—. Writer/rschr. New Market Battlefield Mil. Mus., New Market, 1989—99; polit. columnist The News-Virginian, Waynesboro, 2000—01. Author: (article) A World That is Dimly Lit, 2000 (CASE Award of Distinction, 2000), Why'd Johnny Go Marchin' Off to Civil War?, 1999 (CASE Award of Merit, 1999), (series of articles) Communities, 1997 (1st place Va. Press Assn., 1998). Mem.: Pub. Relations Coun. of the Shenandoah Valley. Republican. Avocations: Stage acting, public speaking, hiking, treasure hunting, writing. Office: James Madison University 1321 S Main St Ste 24 MSC 5714 Harrisonburg VA 22807 Business E-Mail: culbercr@jmu.edu.

CULBERTSON, FRANCES MITCHELL, psychology educator; b. Boston, Jan. 31, 1921; d. David and Goldie (Fishman) Mitchell; m. John Mathew Culbertson, Aug. 27, 1947; children: John David, Joanne, Lyndall, Amy. BS, U. Mich., 1947, MS, 1949, PhD, 1955. Diplomate Am. Bd. of Profl. Psychology; lic. psychologist, Wis. Clin. child psychologist Wis. Diagnostic Ctr., Madison, 1961-65; chief clin. psychologist dept. child psychiatry U. Wis., Madison, 1965-66; resident rsch. psychologist NIMH, Berkeley, Calif., 1966-67; psy-

chologist Madison Pub. Schs., 1967-68; prof. psychology U. Wis., Whitewater, 1968-88, prof. emeritus, 1988—; psychologist Mental Health Assocs., Madison, 1987—2003. Clin. psychologist Counseling and Psychotherapy Assn., Madison, 1982-87; clin. hypnotherapy cons. Family Achievement Ctr., Oconomowoc, Wis., 1984-89; cons. Wis Disability Determination Bur., 2001—. Author: Voices in International School Psychology, 1985; contbr. chpts. to books, articles to profl. jours. Mem. Dane County Mental Health Bd., Madison, 1980-82. Fellow: APA (bd. conv. affairs 1990—94, pres. sect. clin. psychology women 1991—92, coun. rep. liaison and bd. mem. internat. psychology divsn. 52 1997—97, chmn. membership com. 1998—99, coun. rep. psychol. hypnosis divsn. 1998—99, coun. rep. internat. psych. divsn. 1999—2003, mem. coun. 1999—, bd. dirs. 2003—, Contbn. award for internat. achievement 1994, Divsn. 1 Eminent Woman in Psychology award 1999, Divsn. 52 Career award for outstanding contbns. to internat. psychology 1999); mem.: Madison Hypnotherapy Soc. (pres. 1986—94), Brazilian Soc. Clin. Psychology (hon. pres. 1979), Wis. Psychol. Assn. (pres. divsn. psychol. hypnosis 1991—99), Internat. Coun. Psychologists (pres. 1979), Internat. Soc. Clin. Psychology (founding co-chair 1997—98, treas. 1997—), Internat. Assn. Applied Psychology Divsn. Applied Gerontology (pres.-elect 1994—98, exec. bd. mem. 1995—, pres. 1998—2003, past pres. 2003—), Phi Kappa Phi, Pi Lambda Theta, Sigma Xi. Avocations: skiing, walking, hiking, reading, gardening. Home: 8301 Old Sauk Rd Apt 323 Middleton WI 53562-4394 Office: Mental Health Assn 20 S Park St #408 Madison WI 53715 also: Mental Health Assocs 20 S Park St Ste 408 Madison WI 53715-1378

CULBERTSON, JACK ARTHUR, education educator; b. Nickelsville, Va., July 16, 1918; s. Otto Cecil and Lola Kate (Fuller) C.; m. Mary Virginia Pond, Aug. 12, 1952; children: Karen Anne Hasselo, Margaret Lynn. AB in Edn., Emory and Henry Coll., 1943; MA in German, Duke U., 1946; PhD in Edn. Adminstrn., U. Calif., Berkeley, 1955. Cert. tchr., sch. adminstr., Va., Calif. Tchg. prin. Scott County Sch. Sys., Gate City, Va., 1937—41, Jewell Ridge (Va.) Sch. Sys., 1941—42, Tazewell (Va.) County Sch. Sys., 1947—49; H.S. tchr. Mineral Springs (N.C.) Sch. Sys., 1943—44; tchr. jr. H.S. El Centro (Calif.) Sch. Sys., 1949—51; sch. supt. Ellwood Sch. Dist., Goleta, Calif., 1951—53; prof. U. Oreg., Eugene, 1955—59; exec. dir. Univ. Coun. for Ednl. Adminstrn., Columbus, 1959—81; prof. Ohio State U., Columbus, 1981—86, emeritus prof., 1986—. Cons. W.K. Kellogg Found., Battle Creek, Mich., 1968, Ford Found., N.Y.C., 1967, advisor Edn. Commn. States, Denver, 1967, Pan Am. Union, Washington, 1968; founder 1st Internat. Intervisitation Program in Ednl. Adminstrn., 1966; spkr. OAS, Brasilia, Brazil, 1968, Australian Coun. for Ednl. Rsch., Sydney, 1967, German Assn. for Tng. Sch. Adminstrs., 1975. Author: Building Bridges, 1995; co-author: Administrative Relationships, 1960, Preparing Educational Leaders for the Seventies, 1969. Recipient Commonwealth Fellow award Commonwealth Coun. for Ednl. Adminstrn., 1978, Roald F. Campbell Lifetime Achievement award Univ. Coun. for Ednl. Adminstrn., 1993. Mem. Am. Ednl. Rsch. Assn. (v.p. 1964-66), Am. Assn. Sch. Adminstrs. (adv. commn. 1974-76), Nat. Coun. for Profs. of Ednl. Adminstrn. (exec. com. 1957-60, Living Legends award 1999-2000), Nat. Soc. for Study of Edn. (co-editor yearbook 1986). Avocations: reading, television, card playing. Home: 145 Montrose Way Columbus OH 43214-3634

CULBERTSON, JAMES THOMAS, psychologist; b. Scranton, Pa., Dec. 25, 1911; s. Walter Edwards and Katharine (Evans) C.; m. Jean Herman, Nov. 1, 1941; children: Elizabeth, Hazel, Jamie, Samuel. BA, Yale U., 1934, PhD, 1940. Sterling Rsch. fellow Yale U., 1941; rsch. assoc. in math. and biology U. Chgo., 1946-49; prof. philosophy U. So. Calif., Los Angeles, 1949-51; math. rsch. assoc. Rand Corp., Santa Monica, Calif., 1951-53; prof. math. and computer sci. Calif. Poly. State U., San Luis Obispo, 1953-65, chmn. philosophy dept., 1968-78; rsch. prof. psychology UCLA, 1965-68; freelance theoretical brain rschr. San Luis Obispo, 1978—. Mem. nat. bd. advisers Inst. Advanced Philos. Research. Author: Consciousness and Behavior, 1950; Mathematics and Logic for Digital Devices, 1958; A Student's Survey of the Mind-Body Problem, 1960; The Minds of Robots, 1963; Sensations, Memories and the Flow of Time, 1976; Consciousness: Natural and Artificial, 1982; contbr. book chpts. and articles to profl. jours. Mem. IEEE, AAAS, Am. Math. Soc., Am. Philos. Assn., Philosophy of Sci. Assn., Soc. Philosophy and Psychology, Mind Assn. Achievements include contributions to early work on neural nets and designs for any input-output; helped develop RAND robots. Home: 115 Del Norte Way San Luis Obispo CA 93405-1507

CULBERTSON, JANET LYNN, artist; b. Greensburg, Pa., Mar. 15, 1932; d. Joseph F. and Helen C. (Moore) Culbertson; m. Douglas I. Kaften, Sept. 30, 1964. BFA, Carnegie Inst. Tech., 1953; MA, NYU, 1963. Instr. art Pace Coll., N.Y.C., 1964-68, Pratt Art Inst., Bklyn., 1973; assoc. prof. Southampton Coll., 1976; drawing instr. Parrish Art Mus., 1979. Exhibited one-woman shows 20th Century West Gallery, N.Y.C., 1967, Molly Barnes Gallery, L.A., 1970, Midtown Gallery, Atlanta, 1971, Lerner-Misrachi Gallery, N.Y.C., 1971, Lerner-Heller Gallery, N.Y.C., 1973, 75, 77, Tower Gallery, Southampton, N.Y., 1976, Benson Gallery, Bridgehampton, N.Y., 1978, 81, 89, Interart Gallery, N.Y.C., 1979, Harriman Coll., N.Y., 1980, Nardin Gallery, N.Y.C., 1981, Aronson Gallery, Atlanta, 1982, Harrisburg State Mus. Pa., 1988, Women Artists Series Rutgers U., N.J., 1988, Carnegie Mellon U., Pitts., 1991, Acme Art Co., Columbus, Ohio, 1992, Islip (N.Y.) Mus., 1992, Suffolk Coll., Riverhead, N.Y., 1996, Stone Quarry Art Park, Cazenovia, N.Y., 1996, Wave Hill, Bronx, N.Y., 1997, Atelier A/E Gallery, N.Y.C., 1997, U. Alaska, Anchorage, 1997, Nat. Acad. Scis., Washington, 1998, Hoyt Mus., New Castle, Pa., 1998, U. Nebr., Omaha, 2002, Huntington Arts Coun. Gallery, N.Y., 2002-03, Cambridge Multicultural Arts Ctr., 2003; two-women shows Women's Art Ctr., San Francisco, 1975; four-women show Heckscher Mus., Huntington, N.Y., 1980; group exhbns. include Carnegie Mus., Pitts., 1953, ann. drawing Bucknell U., 1966-68, Palos Verdes (Calif.) Mus., 1970, 16th ann. all Calif. purchase L.A. Art Assn., 1969-70, nat. drawing ann. San Francisco Mus., 1970, Princeton Gallery Fine Arts, 1972, drawing show Fleisher Meml., Phila., 1974, Am. Acad. Arts and Letters, N.Y.C., 1975, Kingpitcher Gallery, Pitts, 1976, West Broadway Galley, N.Y.C., 1976, Bronx Mus., 1976, Guild Hall, East Hampton, N.Y., 1976, 79, 82, 89, (invitational) 94 (Abstract award 1979, Mixed Media award 1992), Orgn. Ind. Artists, N.Y.C., 1978, Parrish Mus., Southampton, N.Y. Meml. Art Gallery, Rochester N.Y., 1979, Western Carolina U., Cullowhee, Phoenix Mus, Tucson Mus., 1980, The Arsenal, N.Y.C., 1981, 50 nat. women artists Edison Coll. Art Gallery, Ft. Myers, Fla., 1982, Norton Art Gallery, W. Palm Beach, Fla., 1985-86, Easthampton (N.Y.) Ctr. Contemporary Arts, 1988, Newport (R.I.) Art Mus., 1988, 91, Trabia Macafee Gallery, N.Y.C., 1988, Vered Galley, Easthampton, 1989, 90, 92, Hillwood Mus., Brookville, N.Y., 1990, Islip Art Mus., N.Y., 1990, Ucross Wyo. (invitational), 1990, Women's Caucus for Art, Dallas, 1990, Wash., 1991, Benton Gallery, Southampton, N.Y., 1991, 92, 93, Ark. Arts Ctr. (invitational), Little Rock, 1991, Arlene Bujese Gallery, East Hampton, N.Y., 1994, Hillwood Art Mus., L.I. U., Brookville, N.Y., 1994, Hamilton Coll., Clinton, N.Y., 1995, Staller Mus., SUNY, Stony Brook, 1995, N.J. Ctr. Visual Arts, 2000, Censorship, Woman Made Gallery, Chgo., 2002, others; Babcock Gallery traveling exhibit, 1993-94, Art and the Law traveling exhbn., 1995-97, Anita Shapolsky Gallery, N.Y.C., 1995, Gerald Peters Gallery, 1996-97, ("Women Realists") Ringling Sch. Art and Design, Sarasota Fla., Nabi Gallery, Sag Harbor, 1997, Baruch Coll., N.Y.C., Telfair Mus. Art, Savannah, Ga., Seton Hall U., South Orange, N.J., U. Wyo., Laramie, C.W. Post U., N.Y., Staller Art Mus., SUNY, Stony Brook, Benson Gallery, 2001, Bridgehampton, N.Y., 1999, Parrish Art Mus., Southampton, N.Y., 2000, N.J. Ctr. Visual Arts, Summit, 2000. Toxic Landscapes, Puffin Found. traveling exhib., Morning, Noon and Night, The Long Island Mus. of Stony Brook, N.Y., Earth 2002, U. of Miami Coral Gables, FL, Denise Bibro Fine Art, N.Y.C., 2002, Soho Photo, N.Y.C., 2002, Savannah Coll. Art and Design, Ga., 2002, Long Beach Found. for Arts, NJ, 2002; contbr. collage to Attica Book, 1972; contbr. articles to profl. jours., prodr. and contbr. Heresies #13 mag. Creative Artists Pub. Service grantee, 1979. Recipient Shirk Meml. award for oil painting Nat. Assn. Women Artists, Inc., 1993, first place award Notorious L.I. exhibit Hillwood Art Mus., Brookville, N.Y., 1994, Purchase award Hoyt Art Inst., 1995, Purchase award Nassau County Mus. Art, 1997, Print Ctr. Excellence award, Phil., Pa., 2001; fellow Ossabaw Found., 1981, Dorland, 1983, Ucross Found., 1989, 99, Blue Mt. Found., 1991, 94, 96, 2000, 02, VCCA Ctr. Found., Ragdale Found., 1984, 2001. Home: PO Box 455 Shelter Island Heights NY 11965

CULBERTSON, PHILIP EDGAR, SR., aerospace company executive, consultant; b. Colfax, Wash., Aug. 19, 1925; s. Julian L. and Lucia Culbertson; m. Shirley E. Coskey, Aug. 19, 1950; children: Camden E. Culbertson Gooch, Philip E. Jr. BS in Aero. Engring., Ga. Inst. Tech., 1946; MS, U. Mich., 1949. Mem. research staff U. Mich., 1948-52; aerodynamicist Convair divsn. Gen. Dynamics Corp., 1952-56, chief project engr. Atlas space launch vehicles, 1958-64, dir. manned space flight syss., 1964-65; head aerodynamics and propulsion Bendix Sys. Divsn., 1956-57; dir. advanced manned lunar syss. NASA, 1965-69; project mgr. Apollo Applications/Skylab, 1969-73; dir. payload integration and mission analysis Office Manned Space Flight, 1973-76, asst. adminstr. planning and program integration, 1976-78, dep. assoc. adminstr. space transp. systems, 1979-81; assoc. dep. adminstr. NASA, 1981-84, assoc. adminstr. space sta., 1984-85, gen. mgr., 1985-87, assoc. adminstr. policy and planning, 1987-88; exec. dir. President's Com. Sci. and Tech., 1976-77; pres. Lew Evans Found., Washington, 1988-96; sr. v.p., bd. dirs. Space Destinations Svcs., Inc., Boulder, 1995-98. Mem. v.p.'s space policy adv. bd., 1992-93; bd. dirs. Ctr. for Space and Advanced Tech., NASA Alumni League; bd. govs. Krafft A. Ehricke Inst. for Space Devel.; mem. bd. advisors Luna Corp.; lectr. in field. Served with USNR, World War II. Fellow AIAA, Am. Astron. Soc.; mem. Internat. Acad. Astronautics, NASA Alumni League. E-mail: philipculbertson@msn.com. *We grow and improve by seeking and accepting challenge. Whatever the job - give it the best you have in a way that you can take pride in it. Work with integrity and live with honesty. Never give up curiousity and the desire to learn.*

CULBERTSON, RICHARD ALLEN, healthcare educator, health system director; b. Fremont, Ohio, Aug. 13, 1946; s. Raymond Clark and Ruth Elizabeth Culbertson; m. Linnea VanDyne, July 11, 1970 (div. Dec. 1981); m. Susan Mary Leary, May 3, 1986. BA, Lawrence U., 1967; MDiv, Harvard U., 1970; M in Health Adminstrn., U. Minn., 1973; PhD, U. Calif., San Francisco, 1993. Cert. healthcare exec. Am. Coll. Health Execs. Asst. prof. U. Minn., Mpls., 1976—78; dep. dir., COO St. Paul-Ramsey Med. Ctr., 1978—84; hosp. dir., CEO Kaiser Found. Hosp., LA, 1984—87; dir. adminstrn. U. Calif. San Francisco Med. Group, 1987—92; assoc. dean, vice chancellor U. Wis., Madison, 1992—95; assoc. prof., dir. Ind. U., Indpls., 1995—97; assoc. prof. Tulane U., New Orleans, 1997—. Chmn. bd. dirs. Aurora HealthCare Inc., Milw.; mem. strategic planning subbd. Touro Infirmary, New Orleans, 2002—; cert. site reviewer NCAA, Indpls., 2001—; chair senate com. on intercollegiate athletics Tulane U., spl. asst. to pres. for NCAA cert., 1999—2002. Contbg. author The Nation's Health, 6th edit., 2001; contbr. articles to profl. jours. Mem. Mardi Gras Krewe of Mid-City; pres. Humane Soc. Ramsey County, St. Paul, 1981—84; bd. dirs. Wis. Profl. Rev., Madison, 1994—95, Eldercare Dane County, Madison, 1994—95. Named Emerging Leader in Healthcare, Healthcare Forum, San Francisco, 1986; recipient Spurgeon award for cmty. svc., Explorer Scouts, St. Paul, 1983; Nat. Leader fellow, W.K. Kellogg Found., 1985—88. Mem.: Harvard Club (La.), Delta Omega Soc. (Eta chpt.), Beta Theta Pi, Phi Beta Kappa (La. Alpha chpt.). Avocations: swimming, intercollegiate athletics, dance organizations patron. Office: Tulane U Sch Pub Health 1430 Tulane Ave SL-29 New Orleans LA 70112

CULEBRAS, ANTONIO, neurologist; b. Madrid, Apr. 3, 1940; s. Antonio Culebras-Souto and Manuela Fernandez-Notario; m. Susan Zara, June 14, 1969; children: Katerina, Andrea. Degree in medicine, U. Madrid, Spain, 1963; PhD in Medicine, U. Alicante, Spain, 1990. Asst. prof. neurology Boston U., 1971-74; assoc. prof. neurology SUNY, Syracuse, N.Y., 1977-83, prof. neurology, 1984—; chief neurology VA Med. Ctr., Syracuse, NY, 1977—2001. Author: Clinical Handbook of Sleep Disorders, 1996, Sleep Disorders and Neurological Disease, 2000. Mem. Am. Acad. Neurology (sec. 1997-99), Am. Bd. Sleep Medicine (dir. 1998—), Acad. Norteamerican de la Lengua Espanola (elected), Bolivian Soc. Neurology (hon.), Colombian Soc. Neurology (hon.), Ecuadorian Soc. Neurology (hon.). Office: VA Med Ctr 800 Irving Ave Syracuse NY 13210 E-mail: ancufe@hotmail.com.

CULHANE, HIND RASSAM, psychologist, educator, film historian; b. Mosul, Iraq, Feb. 20, 1939; came to U.S., 1955; d. Noel Michael and Sophie (Bakhazy) Rassam; m. John William Culhane, Aug. 27, 1960; children: Michael Noel, T.H. AA, Cazenovia (N.Y.) Jr. Coll., 1957; BA, Rockford Coll., 1959, MA, 1963; MEd, Columbia U., 1988, EdD, 1992; M Pedagogy (hon.), Mercy Coll., 1998. Edn. coord. Head Start, Chgo., 1965-69, Westchester County, NY, 1969-77; assoc. dean grad. program L.I. U., Dobbs Ferry, NY, 1976-82; asst. prof. Mercy Coll., Dobbs Ferry, 1982-92, assoc. prof., assoc. chair social scis. divsn., 1992—2002, co-chair, social scis. divsn., 2003—; sr. edn. adv. Revitalization of Iraqi Edn., U.S. State Dept., Baghdad, 2003—. Adj. prof. Mercy Coll., Dobbs Ferry, 1970-76; guest lectr. The U. Baghdad (Iraq), 1981-84; campus coord. Woodrow Wilson fellows program Mercy Coll., 1990-97; group dynamics leader NAIM Found. Workshop, Washington, 1992-93; guest psychologist Mental Health Hour Arabnet radio, Washington, 19945; psychologist, admissions com. U. Poznań (Poland) Med. Sch., 1994—; commentator on Arab film, CUNY TV, 1998, commentator on overthrow of Saddam Hussein, Phil Donahue TV show, 2003. Author (Arab film history) East/West, An Ambiguous State of Being, 1995; vocalist Arabic songs, U.S. State Dept. Rock and Roll Tour of Syria with U.S. Rock Band Circus Guy, 2003; contbr. article to Ency. Modern Mid. East, 1996. Mem. Arab-Am. Anti-Defamation League, Washington, 19875. Nat. Multicultural Faculty Devel. fellow, 1995-97; Nat. fellow Tchg. for a Change, C.C. of Aurora, Colo., 1995; Fulbright Scholar to Syria, 2000—. Mem. Psi Chi, Delta Pi. Avocations: collecting arab songs, world travel, environmental concerns. Office: Social Scis Bldg Mercy Coll 555 Broadway Dobbs Ferry NY 10522-1134

CULHANE, JOHN WILLIAM, journalist, author, film historian; b. Rockford, Ill., Feb. 7, 1934; s. John William and Isabel June (Fissinger) C.; m. Hind Noel Rassam, Aug. 27, 1960; children: Michael Noel, T.H. BS, St. Louis U., 1956; cert. in advanced internat. reporting, Columbia U., 1966. Reporter St. Louis (Mo.) Globe Dem., 1955; daily columnist, reporter Rockford Register-Republic, 1956-61; reporter, feature writer, fgn. corr. Chgo. Daily News, 1962-66; assoc. editor Newsweek mag., N.Y.C., 1966-71; freelance journalist N.Y. Times mag., others, N.Y.C., 1971-85; roving editor Reader's Digest, Pleasantville, N.Y., 1985-93; roving writer Johimith Robidoux Prodns., 1994—. Jury chmn. 2d N.Y. Internat. Animation Film Festival, 1974; lectr., Northwestern U., 1995, NYU, 1996; lectr. film festival, Mulhouse, France, 1990, Am. animation U.S. State Dept., Damascus, Syria, 2001, Art Inst. Pitts., 2001, spirituality in animation Marble Collegiate Ch., N.Y.C., 2002, Linc Svcs., Atlantis Resort, The Bahamas, 2003; moustro-of-ceremonies Mickey Mouse's 50th Birthday Retrospective and Whistle-Stop Train Tour Across the U.S., 1978; guest clown Ringling Bros., Barnum and Bailey Circus, 1974-84; instr. 1st course in history of animation for coll. credit Sch. Visual Arts, N.Y.C., 1972; sr. lectr. animation history U. Arts, Phila., 1997-98, NYU, 1997—, Fashion Inst. of Tech., N.Y.C., 2000—, Mercy Coll. Digital Arts Ctr., White Plains, N.Y., 2003—; vis. artist Disney Inst., Fla., 1999—; writer Richard Williams Animation, London, 1973; moderator, lectr. in field.. Author: (critical essays) Walt Disney, 1972, Special Effects in the Movies, 1981, Walt Disney's Fantasia, 1983, The American Circus: An Illustrated History, 1990 (Washington Irving Book Selection Westchester Libr. Assn. 1991), Disney's Aladdin: The Making of an Animated Film, 1992, Fantasia 2000: Visions of Hope, N.Y. Hyperion, 1999, (documentaries) The Making of Aladdin: A Whole New World, 1992, Backstage at Disney's 1983, The Making of The Jungle Book, 1997, Walt Disney: The Man Behind the Myth, 2001; co-author: The Art of the Muppets, 1980, (TV spls.) Noah's Animals, 1974, King of the Beasts, 1976, Last of the Red Hot Dragons, 1980; contbr. The 50 Greatest Cartoons, 1994; voice of cartoon dragon, moderator: (coll. tour) Disney on Film: A Forum on Animation and Fantasy Filmmaking, 1981; co-prodr. (documentary) Circus!, 1983; commentator (documentaries) Fantasia: The Making of a Masterpiece, 1991, Frank and Ollie, 1995, (TV spl.) The Flying Wallendas: Legends on the High Wire, 1998; writer (TV spl.) Illusionist David Copperfield Vanishes the Statue of Liberty, 1983, (feature films) Something Wicked This Way Comes, 1983, The Thief and the Cobbler, 1995; (CD-ROM essay) Walt Disney's Snow White and the Seven Dwarfs, 1998, (essays) The Disney Century, Fantasia Set for a New Millennium, 1998, "Charlie Brown: A Boy for all Seasons" N.Y. Mus. of Broadcasting, 1984, others; model for Mr. Snoops character Walt Disney's The Rescuers, 1977, model for 2nd Disney character, Flying John in "Rhapsody in Blue" in "Fantasia 2000". Master-of-ceremonies Winnebago County Sesquicentennial, Rockford, 1968; mem. Clearwater Assn. (author: PCBs: The Poison That Won't Go Away). Served with AUS, 1957-58. Recipient 4 1st Prize awards Ill. AP, 1960, 61, 63, 64, St. Louis U. Alumni Merit award as writer and film historian, 1982; Ford fellow Columbia U., 1965-66; Ill. Humanities Coun. grantee, 1991; Woodrow Wilson fellow in writing and film history, 1993. Mem. Writer's Guild Am., Clearwater Assn., Alpha Sigma Nu, Sigma Delta Chi (2 awards for pub. service journalism 1964, 69). Avocations: global travel, environment. Office: care Joelle Delbourgo Assocs 450 7th Ave Ste 3004 New York NY 10123-3004

CULICK, FRED ELLSWORTH CLOW, physics and engineering educator; b. Wolfeboro, N.H., Oct. 25, 1933; s. Joseph Frank and Mildred Beliss (Clow) C.; m. Frederica Mills, June 11, 1960; children: Liza Hall, Alexander Joseph, Mariette Huxham. Student, U. Glasgow, Scotland, 1957-58; SB, MIT, 1957, PhD, 1961. Rsch. fellow Calif. Inst. Tech., Pasadena, 1961-63, asst. prof., 1963-66, assoc. prof., 1966-70, prof. mech. engring. and jet propulsion, 1970-97, Richard L. and Dorothy M. Hayman prof. mech. engring., 1997—, prof. jet propulsion, 1997—. Cons. to govt. agys. and indsl. orgns. Fellow AIAA; mem. Internat. Acad. Astronautics, Internat. Fedn. Astronautics, Am. Phys. Soc. Home: 1375 Hull Ln Altadena CA 91001-2620 Office: Calif Inst Tech Caltech 205-45 207 Guggenheim Pasadena CA 91125

CULKIN, CHARLES WALKER, JR., retired trade association administrator; b. Aug. 22, 1947; s. Charles Walker and Helen Elizabeth (Wilson) C.; m. Carolyn DeWayne Franklin, Apr. 5, 1974; children: David Laurence Franklin, Kimberly Anne Franklin. Assoc. in Bus. Adminstrn., Benjamin Franklin U., 1968, BA in Comml. Sci., 1970. Asst. auditor United Va. Bank, Vienna, 1967-70; sr. asst. dir. U.S. GAO, Washington, 1970-97; exec. dir. Assn. Gov. Accts., Washington, 1997—2003; ret., 2003. Chmn. Pacific Emerging Issues Conf., Honolulu, 1982; spkr. confs. and seminars; founder, incorporator Reston Commuter Bus., Inc., 1971, treas., dir., 1971-78. Pub. The Jour. Govt. Fin. Mgmt.; contbr. articles to profl. jours. Recipient RCB Bd. Dirs. award 1978. Outstanding Achievement award Fairfax County (Va.) Bd. Suprs., 1978, Nat. Pres. award Am. Soc. of Mil. Comptrollers, 1999. Mem. Am. Assn. for Budget Program Analysis, Inst. Internal Auditors (sec. no. Va. chpt. 1984-86), Assn. Govt. Accts. (dir. Hawaii chpt. 1981-84, conf. mgr. fed. leadership conf. 1994, No. Va. chpt. 1991—, Nat. AGA Spl. Recognition award 1988, 90, 93, President's award 1992, 95-96, Outstanding Mem. award 1983, nat. treas.-elect, 1995-96, nat. treas. 1996-97, Edn. award 1994), Nat. Assn. Accts. (no. Va. Chpt. dir. 1977-78, v.p. 1979-80), Benjamin Franklin U. Alumni Assn. (pres. 1988-92, Outstanding Leadership award 1991, Bd. Govs. Svc. award 1992, Disting. Alumni award 1995), George Washington U. Gen. Alumni Assn. (dir. 1991-92, Vol. of Yr. award 1992). Roman Catholic. Office: AGA 2208 Mount Vernon Ave Alexandria VA 22301-1314 Home: 5351 Fox Run Rd Sarasota FL 34231-7348

CULL, JOHN JOSEPH, novelist, playwright; b. Ogdensburg, N.Y., Oct. 4, 1925; s. John Joseph and Adah Jane (Hyde) C.; m. Carol June Andrews (dec. Dec. 1992); stepchildren: Cathy Andrews Jordan, Michael R. Andrews. Cert., U. Buffalo, 1952. Office clk. N.Y. State Electric & Gas Corp., Lockport, 1956-76; creative writing instr. Genesee C.C., Batavia, N.Y., 1984-86; writer Lockport, 1986—. Facilitator Write Touch, Lockport, N.Y., 1997. Author: (novels) Windweir, 1999, Out of the Night, 1994, In Silent Hours, 1994, Of Gnarled Roots, 1997, The Miracle at Resthaven, 2003, (plays) The Late Mark Jordan, 1984, Of Gnarled Roots, 1997, (poetry) The Hedgerow Chapbook, 1988; poetry editor Lockport Union-Sun & Jour., 2000—02, author numerous short stories and poems. Recipient Non-Fiction Book award Am. Soc. Writers, 1977, Golden Poetry award World of Poetry, 1987, Genesee Arts Coun. award, 1985, 87, Editor's Choice award Nat. Libr. of Poetry, 1989. Avocations: symphony concerts, opera, live theatre, films, classic novels. Home: 546 Birchwood Dr Lockport NY 14094-9160

CULL, ROBERT ROBINETTE, electric products manufacturing company executive; b. Cleve., Sept. 24, 1912; s. Louis David and Wilma Penn (Robinette) C.; m. Gay Cornwell, Oct. 4, 1986. BS in Physics, M.I.T., 1934. Supr. Eastman Kodak Co., Rochester, N.Y., 1934-39; asst. to gen. mgr. Cleve. Chain & Mfg. Co., 1940-45; partner Tenna Mfg. Co., Cleve., 1945-56; pres. Tenatronics Ltd., Newmarket, Ont., Can., 1956—, Sterling Mfg. Co., Cleve., 1960—. Trustee Garden Center Greater Cleve., 1975-80, pres., 1979-80; trustee Musical Arts Assn. of Cleve. Orch., 1976—2003. Mem. IEEE, Cleve. Engring. Soc., Sigma Psi. Clubs: Hermit, Union.

CULLARI, SALVATORE SANTINO, clinical psychologist, educator, writer; b. Caroniti, Calabria, Italy, Apr. 1, 1952; came to U.S., 1955; s. Carmelo and Carmela (Cullari) C.; m. Kathryn Plesce, Apr. 26, 1985; children: Catherine, Dante. BA, Kean Coll., 1974; MA, Western Mich. U., 1976, PhD, 1981. Lic. psychologist, Pa., W.Va. Dir. psychology White Haven (Pa.) Ctr., 1982—83; psychologist Danville (Pa.) State Hosp., 1983—84; coord. of psychology Harrisburg (Pa.) State Hosp., 1984—86; prof., chair dept. psychology Lebanon Valley Coll., Annville, Pa., 1986—2003, prof. emeritus, 2003—. Cons. Bur. Disability Determination, Harrisburg, 1987—. Author questionaire acad. social evaluation scales, 1990, Treatment Resistance, 1996; editor Found. of Clin. Psychology, 1998, Counseling and Psychotherapy, 2001; contbr. numerous articles to profl. jours. Mem. APA, Assn. Advancement of Behavior Therapy, Pa. Psychol. Assn. (Psychology in the Media award 2003), Soc. for the Exploration of Psychotherapy Integration. Office: Lebanon Valley Coll Psychology Dept Annville PA 17003 E-mail: cullari@lvc.edu.

CULLEN, CHARLES THOMAS, historian, librarian; b. Gainesville, Fla., Oct. 11, 1940; s. Spencer L. and Blanche J. Cullen; m. Shirley Harrington, June 13, 1964; children: Leslie Lanier, Charles Spencer Harrington. BA, U. of South, 1962; MA, Fla. State U., 1963; PhD, U. Va., 1971; HHD (hon.), Lewis U., 1987; DLitt (hon.), U. South, 1994; LLD (hon.), John Marshall Law Sch., 1995; DHist (hon.), Lincoln Coll., 2000. Asst. prof. history Averett Coll., 1963-66; assoc. editor Papers of John Marshall Inst. Early Am. History and Culture, Williamsburg, Va., 1971-74, co-editor, 1974-77, editor, 1977-79; lectr. history Coll. William and Mary, 1971-79; sr. research historian, editor Papers of Thomas Jefferson Princeton (N.J.) U., 1979-86; pres., librarian Newberry Library, Chgo., 1986—. Mem. N.J. Hist. Commn., 1985-86, Nat. Hist. Publs. and Records Com., 1990—; mem. adv. bd. Abraham Lincoln Presdl. Libr. and Mus. Nat. Hist. Publs. and Records Commn. fellow, 1970-71. Mem. Assn. Documentary Editing (pres. 1982-83), Orgn. Am. Historians, Am. Hist. Assn., Am. Antiquarian Soc., Heartland Lit. Soc. (pres. 1994—), Modern Poetry Assn. (trustee 1987—, v.p. 1998—), Ind. Rsch. Librs. Assn. (pres. 2000—), Caxton Club, Grolier Club. Office: Newberry Libr 60 W Walton St Chicago IL 60610-3380

CULLEN, DANIEL EDWARD, management consultant; b. Oak Park, Ill., Feb. 16, 1942; s. Kenneth Arthur and Ruth (Voltz) C.; m. Paula Bramsen, Aug. 24, 1963; children: Sean Paul, Erik Svend Arthur. BS, Stanford U., 1963; MS, U. Ill., 1964; DSc, Washington U., St. Louis, 1967. Mem. tech. staff Bell Telephone Labs., Naperville, Ill., 1967-68; cons. Mathematica, Princeton, N.J., 1968-69, asst. dir., 1969-76; v.p. Mathtech subs. Mathematica, Princeton, 1976-94; sr. cons. Mathtech, Inc., 1994—; pres. Am. Renaissance Ventures, L.L.C., Princeton, 1994—, Design Cast Corp., 1994—2000; dir., chmn. audit com. Spraying Sys. Co., Wheaton, Ill., 1984—. Dir. Spraying Systems Co., 1984—. Trustee Chapin Sch., Princeton, 1981-87, pres., 1982-86. Mem. Inst. Ops. Rsch. and Mgmt. Sci., Am. Math. Soc., Soc. for Indsl. and Applied Math., The Opportunity Found. (treas. and trustee, 1994—). Office: Am Renaissance Ventures 202 Carnegie Ctr Ste 111 Princeton NJ 08540-6239

CULLEN, EDWARD PETER, bishop; b. Phila., Mar. 15, 1933; Student, St. Charles Borromeo Sem., Overbrook, Pa.; MSW, U. Pa., 1970; M in Edn., LaSalle U., 1971; MDiv, St. Charles Borromeo Sem., 1974. Ordained priest Roman Cath. Ch. 1962. Asst. pastor St. Maria Goretti Ch., Hatfield, St. Bartholomew Ch., Phila.; chaplain to Sisters of Mercy Merion Motherhouse; chaplain St. Edmond's Home for Children, See of Allentown; titular bishop Diocese of Paria, 1994—; aux. bishop Diocese of Phila., 1994—99; bishop Diocese of Allentown, Pa., 1998—. Mem. Cath. Social Svcs. Named Hon. Prelate to His Holiness Pope John Paul II, 1982. Office: Diocese of Allentown PO Box F Allentown PA 18105-1538*

CULLEN, JAMES D., lawyer; b. St. Louis, May 18, 1925; s. James and Frances C. Cullen; m. Joyce Marie Jackson, Aug. 19, 1950 (div.); children: Mary Lynn Cullen Walsh, James D., Michael Parnell, Carol Cullen Bernstein. LLD, St. Louis, 1948. Bar: Mo. 1948. Pvt. practice law, St. Louis. Bd. dirs. Gen.

Protestant Children's Home, Richard Greene Co. 1st lt. USAF, 1943—45. Mem.: ABA, Lawyers Assn. St. Louis, St. Louis Bar Assn., Mo. Bar Assn. Roman Catholic. Office: 15 Sussex Dr Saint Louis MO 63144-2767

CULLEN, JAMES DOUGLAS, banker, finance company executive; b. N.Y.C., Jan. 26, 1945; s. Eugene Richard and Anna Marie (Constantine) C.; m. Wendy Stephens, May 24, 1969; children: John W., Anne T. BSBA, U. Denver, 1968. Mgmt. trainee Wells Fargo Bank, San Francisco, 1968-69, credit officer, 1969-72, asst. v.p., 1972-77, v.p., 1977-82, Rainier Nat. Bank (now Bank of Am.), Seattle, 1982, sr. v.p., 1982-85, sr. v.p., mgr. internat. divsn., mem. mgmt. com., 1985, exec. v.p., mgr. internat. divsn., 1986, exec. v.p., mgr. corp. banking divsn., 1987; exec. v.p. Comml. Markets Group Bank of Am., 1992-93; mng. dir. J.D. Cullen and Co., Inc., Seattle, 1993-94; sr. v.p. and mgr. internat. divsn. U.S. Bancorp, Seattle, 1995-96, exec. v.p., 1996-98; sr. v.p., regional mgr. Nat. Bank Alaska, Seattle, 1998-2000; sr. v.p. Wells Fargo Bank, Internat. Banking Group, 2000—. Trustee Seattle Opera; dir. Found. for Russian Am. Econ. Coop. Mem.: Rainier, Seattle Yacht, Seattle Tennis, Tanglin, Cricket (Singapore); Royal Hong Kong Yacht, Ladies Recreation (Hong Kong), University Club San Francisco. Avocations: running, skiing, travel. Home: 1320 Lexington Way E Seattle WA 98112-3712 E-mail: jdcullenco@yahoo.com.

CULLEN, MARK KENNETH, lawyer; b. Springfield, Ill., Sept. 27, 1962; s. Richard W. and Ann (Orr) Carlson; m. Marica L. Heagy, Aug. 5, 1989; 1 child, Kristin Anne. BA with honors, Northwestern U., 1984; MBA/JD, U. Ill., Urbana-Champaign, 1988. Bar: Ill. 1988, U.S. Dist. Ct. (no. dist.) Ill. 1988, U.S. Dist. Ct. (ctrl. dist.) Ill. 1991. Rsch. analyst Fed. Res. Bank Chgo., Chgo., 1983-84; tchg. and rsch. asst. U. Ill., Urbana-Champaign, 1984-88; atty., asst. cashier The First Nat. Bank Chgo., Chgo., 1988-91; shareholder, dir. Sorling Northrup Hanna Cullen and Cochran Ltd., Springfield, Ill., 1991—. Vice-chmn., trustee First United Meth. Ch., Springfield, 1991-95; exec. bd. Boy Scouts Am., Springfield, 1994—, pres., 2002. Mem. Springfield Lions Club (pres. 1996-97). Avocations: golf, scouting, computers, basketball, collectibles. Office: Sorling Northrup Hanna Cullen & Cochran Ltd PO Box 5131 607 E Adams St Ste 800 Springfield IL 62701-1623

CULLEN, MARY LYNNE, artist; b. Camden, N.J., Nov. 2, 1962; d. Philip Anthony and Elizabeth (Townsend) Chiusano; m. James Francis Cullen; children: Lynne Marie, Taylor Lynne, Christyn Maureen. Student, Santa Reparata Arts Studio, Florence, Italy, 1990; Cert., Pa. Acad. Fine Arts, 1992; BFA magna cum laude, U. Pa., 1993; MFA, Pa. Acad. Fine Arts, 1995. Artistic cons., adminstr. Chiusano, Inc., Marlton, N.J., 1985-93; shop asst. graphics dept. Pa. Acad. Fine Arts, Phila., 1991-96; owner, ptnr. Cullen and Howard Decorative Interior Finishes, Marlton, N.J., 1995-98. Residency, drawing instr. Inst. for Arts and Humanities Edn./Summer Arts Inst., Rider U., Lawrenceville, N.J., 1995; adj. prof. printmaking Rowan U., Glassboro, N.J., 1997-99. Exhibited in group shows at the Meyerson Gallery U. of Pa., Phila., 1998, Westby Hall Art Gallery, Rowan U., Glassboro, N.J., 1998, Maitland (Fla.) Art Ctr., 1995, West Chester (Pa.) U., 1995, Artist House Gallery, Phila., 1994, 96, 2001, Marketplace Design Ctr., Phila., 1993, Episcopal Acad., Merion, Pa., 1993, William Penn Charter Upper Sch., Phila., 1992, Art Ctr. Gallery, Westtown, Pa., 1992, The Plastic Club, Phila., 1993, The Painted Bride, Phila., 1995, Lincoln Gallery, Historic Yellow Springs, Pa., 1998, Lincoln Gallery, Historic Yellow Springs, Pa., 1998, Pa. Acad. Fine Arts, Phila., Revsin Gallery, 2000. Recipient Edna Pennypacker Stauffer Meml. prize, 1991, spl. notice Traditional Media Print prize, 1990, John R. Conner Meml. prize in printmaking, 1991, Morris Blackburn Print prize Fellow Pa. Acad. Fine Arts (Trust purchase award); mem. Phila. Print Club (prize 1990), Plastic Club Phila. (award 1992). Avocations: hiking, running, water skiing, gardening, reading. Home and Office: 305 Blueberry Ct Marlton NJ 08053-1015 E-mail: thecullens@netzero.com.

CULLEN, PAULA BRAMSEN, writer; b. May 12, 1942; d. Svend and Elizabeth (Hastie) Bramsen; m. Daniel E. Cullen, Aug. 24, 1963; children: Sean Paul, Erik Svend Arthur. BS in English, Washington U., 1967. Freelance writer, Princeton, NJ, 1968—. Pres. Opportunity Found., Princeton, 1992—; co-owner Spraying Sys. Co., Wheaton, Ill., 1984—. Author: Journey of Storms, 1994; author of poetry; contbr. articles to publs.

CULLEN, ROBERT JOHN, financial planner, investment advisor; b. York, Pa., Feb. 14, 1949; s. John Joseph and Florence Susanne (Staab) C.; m. Elizabeth Maule, Oct. 20, 1984; 1 child, Michael Joseph. BA, Winona (Minn.) State U., 1972. CFP; registered investment advisor. Editor-in-chief Overseas Life, Leimen, Fed. Republic of Germany, 1978-80; feature editor L.A. Daily Commerce, 1980-83; pres. HighTech Editorial, L.A., 1983-99; fin. planner Cullen Fin. Svcs. Inc., Upland, Calif., 1989—; br. mgr. LPL Fin. Computer editor Plaza Communications, Irvine, Calif., 1984-91. With U.S. Army, 1974-78, ETO. Mem. Inst. of Cert. Fin. Planners, Calif. Advs. Nursing Home Reform. Avocations: creative writing, public speaking.

CULLEN, VALERIE ADELIA, secondary education educator; b. Northampton, Mass., May 28, 1948; d. Stanley Walter and Wanda Mary (Rup) Helstowski; m. Lawrence Joseph Cullen, June 26, 1982; 1 child, Shanna Valerie. BA, Westfield (Mass.) State Coll., 1970; MALS, SUNY, Stony Brook, 1975. Cert. secondary math. tchr., N.Y., Mass. Tchr. math. Brentwood (N.Y.) Pub. Schs., 1970-71, Center Moriches (N.Y.) Jr.-Sr. High Sch., 1971-88, BOCES I, Alternative High Sch. and Adolescent Pregnancy Program, Riverhead, N.Y., 1988-90, Ctr. Moriches (N.Y.) Jr.-Sr. High Sch., 1990—2002. Mem. Nat. Com. to Preserve Social Security and Medicare. Mem.: N.Y. State Ret. Tchrs., N.Y. Math. Tchrs. Assn., N.Y. State United Tchrs., Nat. Coun. Tchrs. Math., Smithsonian Assocs. Home: 4 Keswick Dr East Islip NY 11730-2808

CULLEN, WANDA JANE, writer, financial consultant; b. Ithaca, NY, Oct. 19, 1949; d. Howard Forrest Cullen, Irma Jean Griffith, Ernest Clairton Griffith (Stepfather); life ptnr. Ed Diettrich Jr.; children: Elizabeth Rothka, John Piccio. Assoc. in Specialized Bus., Sawyer Bus. Sch., Pitts., 1999. Nurse Hermann Hosp., Houston, 1983—95, Humbert Lane Nursing Home, Washington, Pa., 1985—86; nurse Woodville State Hosp., Heidelberg, Pa., 1986—96; psychiat. nurse Mayview State Hosp., Bridgeville, Pa., 1986—96; admissions psychiat. nurse Chrysler, McMurray, Pa., 1997—98; fin. svcs. cons. PNC Bank, Pitts., 2000—. Author: Tanner's Empire, 2001. Blood pressure screener ARC, Houston, 1983—84. Grantee, Good Samaritan Found., 1983—84. Avocations: travel, camping, hiking, writing. Home: 1228 Sunset Dr Bulger PA 15019 Office: Nat Fin Svcs Ctr 600 Grant St Pittsburgh PA 15219 Home Fax: 412-331-5185. Personal E-mail: wjcullen@adelphia.net.

CULLEN, WILLIAM ZACHARY, lawyer; b. Stamford, Conn., Feb. 15, 1955; s. John Cornelius and Ann D. (Woytowicz) C. BA, U. Conn., 1977; JD, New Eng. Sch. Law, 1980. Bar: Ala. 1989, U.S. Dist. Ct. (no. dist.) Ala. 1989, U.S. Ct. Appeals (11th cir.) 1989. Legal asst. Birmingham (Ala.) Legal Svcs., 1980-82, Cooper, Mitch, Crawford, Kuykendall & Whatley, Birmingham, 1983-89, atty., 1989-98, Sexton, Cullen & Jones P.C., Birmingham, 1998—. Office: 2116 10th Ave S Birmingham AL 35205-2712 Office Fax: 205-252-9557.

CULLER, ARTHUR DWIGHT, English language educator; b. McPherson, Kans., July 25, 1917; s. Arthur Jerome and Susanna (Stover) C.; m. Helen Lucile Simpson, Sept. 14, 1941; children: Jonathan Dwight, Helen Elizabeth. BA, Oberlin Coll., 1938; PhD, Yale U., 1941. Instr. English Cornell U., 1941-42; instr., then asst. Yale U., 1946-55; prof. English, 1958-85; chmn. English dept., 1971-75. Assoc. prof. English U. Ill., 1955-58 Author: The Imperial Intellect: A Study of Newman's Educational Ideal, 1955; Editor: (J.H. Newman) Apologia pro Vita Sua, 1956, (with G.P. Clark) Student and Society, 1959, Poetry and Criticism of Matthew Arnold, 1961, Imaginative Reason: The Poetry of Matthew Arnold, 1966, The Poetry of Tennyson, 1977, The Victorian Mirror of History, 1986 Fulbright fellow in Eng., 1950-51; Guggenheim fellow, 1961-62, 76; NEH fellow, 1979-80 Mem. Am. Acad. Arts and Scis., MLA, Phi Beta Kappa. Home: 200 Leeder Hill Dr Apt 518 Hamden CT 06517-2723

CULLER, GLEN, retired electrical engineer, electrical engineer, educator; Degree, U. Calif., Berkeley, UCLA. With Lawrence Radiation Lab., 1951—56; mem. math. faculty U. Calif., Santa Barbara, 1959—66, mem. elec. engring. dept., 1966—84, prof. emeritus, 1984—. Asst. dir. Computer Rsch. Lab. at Ramo-Woodridge (now TRW), 1961—64; founder Culler-Harrison, Inc. (now Culler Sci. Sys.), 1971. Recipient Nat. Medal of Tech., Pres. Clinton. Office: U Calif Office of Dean Engring I Rm 1038 Santa Barbara CA 93106

CULLER, JONATHAN DWIGHT, English language educator; b. Cleve., Oct. 1, 1944; s. Arthur Dwight and Helen Lucille (Simpson) Culler; m. Cynthia Chase, Dec. 27, 1976. BA, Harvard U., 1966; BPhil, St. John's Coll., Oxford, Eng., 1968, DPhil, 1972. Fellow Selwyn Coll. Cambridge (Eng.) U., 1969-74; fellow Brasenose Coll., lectr. French Oxford U., 1974-77; vis. prof. French and comparative lit. Yale U., New Haven, 1975; prof. English and comparative lit. Cornell U., Ithaca, NY, 1977—, chair dept. comparative lit., 1993-96, chmn. dept. English, 1996-99, sr. assoc. dean, Coll. Arts & Scis., 2000—. Dir. Soc. Humanities Cornell U., Ithaca, 1984—93. Author: (book) Flaubert: The Uses of Uncertainty, 1974, Structuralist Poetics: Strucutralism, Linguistics and the Study of Literature, 1975 (James Russell Lowell prize MLA, 1975), Ferdinand de Saussure, 1976, The Pursuit of Signs: Semiotics, Literature, Deconstruction, 1981, On Deconstruction: Theory and Criticism after Structuralism, 1982, Roland Barthes, 1983, Framing the Sign: Criticism and Its Institutions, 1988, Literary Theory: A Very Short Introduction, 1997; translator: Jacques Derrida's Memoires for Paul de Man, 1986; editor: The Harvard Advocate, Centennial Anthology, 1966; adv. editor: New Literary History, 1972—, PTL, 1976—79, mem. editl. bd.: Diacritics, 1974—; editor, 1994—. Fellow Guggenheim, 1979—80, NEH, 1987—88; scholar Rhodes, 1966—69. Mem.: MLA (mem. adv. bd. publs. 1978—81, exec. coun. 1985—88, 1990—91), Am. Comparative Lit. Assn. (v.p. 1997—99, pres. 1999—2001), Semiotic Soc. Am. (v.p. 1987, pres. 1988). Office: Cornell U Dept English Lit Ithaca NY 14853 E-mail: jdc9@cornell.edu.

CULLERTON, JOHN JAMES, state senator, lawyer; b. Chgo., Oct. 28, 1948; s. John James and Mary Patricia (Tyrrell) C.; m. Pamela J. Wilson, Sept. 8, 1979; children: Maggie, John, Garritt, Kyle, Josephine. BS, Loyola U., 1970, JD, 1974. Bar: Ill. 1974. Asst. pub. defender Cook County, Chgo., 1974-79; state rep. State of Ill., Springfield, 1979-91, state senator, 1991—; from assoc. to ptnr. Fagel & Haber, Chgo., 1987—. With U.S. Nat. Guard, 1970-76. Democrat. Roman Catholic. Office: Fagel & Haber 140 S Dearborn St Ste 1400 Chicago IL 60603-5293*

CULLETON, JAMES FREDERICK, neurologist; b. Sewickley, Pa., Apr. 6, 1918; s. James and Jessie (Scragg) C.; m. Flora McDonald Stuart Brown, Mar. 22, 1943; four children. BS, U. Pitts., 1940, MD, 1943. Diplomate Am. Bd. Psychiatry and Neurology. Intern, resident in pathology U. Pitts. Med. Ctr., 1943-44; fellow in neuropsychiatry Inst. Living, Hartford, Conn., 1947-49; resident in neurology Neurol. Inst. N.Y.C., 1949-51, attending neurologist, 1951-84; assoc. in neurology Columbia-Presbyn. Med. Ctr., N.Y.C., 1951-84; dir. EEG and Neurology, New Rochelle Hosp. Med. Ctr., 1954-82; cons. in neurology Miami VA, 1984-95. Maj. M.C. U.S. Army, 1944—47. Mem. AMA, Am. Acad. Neurology, N.Y. State Med. Soc., Westchester County Med. Soc., Westchester Acad. Medicine, Scottish Rite, Masons. Home: 87 Chase Point Rd Mirror Lake NH 03853-6152 E-mail: jimflo1@earthlink.net.

CULLEY, PETER WILLIAM, lawyer; b. Dover-Foxcroft, Maine, Oct. 17, 1943; s. William Redfern and Kathryn (Boyle) C.; children: Courtney Little, Jonathan Redfern. BA, U. Maine, 1965; JD, Boston U., 1968. Bar: Maine 1969, U.S. Dist. Ct. Maine 1969. Asst. atty. gen. Dept. of Atty. Gen. State of Maine, 1969-72, chief, criminal divsn., 1971-72; ptnr. Hewes, Culley and Beals, Portland, Maine, 1972-85, Pierce Atwood, Portland, 1985—. Chmn. Falmouth (Maine) Town Coun., 1986-87. Fellow Am. Coll. Trial Lawyers (state chmn. 1990-92), Am. Bar Found.; mem. ABA, Maine Bar Assn., Internat. Assn. Def. Counsel, Def. Rsch. Inst. (state chmn. 1978-87), No. New Eng. Def. Counsel (pres. 1985-86), Am. Bd. Trial Advocates. Home: 406 Chandlers Wharf Portland ME 04101-4653 Office: Pierce Atwood One Monument Sq Portland ME 04101 E-mail: pculley@pierceatwood.com.

CULLEY-FOSTER, ANTHONY ROBERT, international business consultant; b. Londonderry, No. Ireland, July 31, 1947; came to U.S., 1971; s. Allen Foster and Eileen Louisa Culley; children: Joshua, Daniel, Valentina. Diploma, Reading U., 1969, Coll. Preceptors, U.K., 1971; BA magna cum laude, Roosevelt U., Chgo., 1973, MA, 1981. Cert. tchr., U.K. High sch. tchr., London, 1969-71; dir. Boys & Girls Clubs of Chgo., 1971-77; personal asst. to chmn. Combined Internat. Corp., Chgo., 1977-81; founding dir., chief exec. officer The Congl. Award, Washington, 1981-85; pres. CFCO Internat., Washington, 1985—. Cons. W. Clement Stone Enterprises, Chgo., 1978-86, Brit., French, Irish and Am. Multinat. Corps., 1985—. Nat. organizer Run Across Am. program Am. Bicentennial Com., 1976, Run for Ireland program Olympic Coun., Ireland, 1980; co-founder Congl. Award U.S., 1979, Pres.'s Award for Youth, Ireland, 1983; founding chmn. No. Ireland Partnership U.S., 1990, No. Ireland-U.S. C. of C. Inc., 1993; mem. Nat. Boys Club U.K., 1966—; trustee Internat. Fedn. Keystone Youth orgns., Boys and Girls Clubs No. Ireland, Boys and Girls Clubs-Chgo. Alumni Assn.; dir. Solid Terrain Modeling, Inc., Calif. Recipient Duke of Edinburgh's Gold Award, 1966, Pub. Service commendations Office of Pres. of U.S., 1976, 79, 83, 91, 96, Congl. award U.S. Congress, 1981, Nat. Achievement award Pres.'s Coun. on Phys. Fitness and Sports, 1976, Nat. Achievement award Olympic Coun. Ireland, 1980. Mem.: Brit.-Am. Bus. Assn. Washington DC, French-Am. C. of C., U.S. C. of C., Irish Rowing Union (hon. life), Nat. Press Club. Office: CFCO Internat Ste 200 1919 Pa Ave NW Washington DC 20006

CULLIGAN, JOHN WILLIAM, retired corporate executive; b. Newark, Nov. 22, 1916; s. John J. and Elizabeth (Kearns) C.; children: Nancy, Mary Carol, Elizabeth, Sheila (dec.), Jack, Neil. With Wyeth (formerly Am. Home Products), 1937—; also bd. dirs. emeritus Am. Home Products Corp., N.Y.C., chmn. bd. dirs., CEO, 1981-86, chmn. exec. com., 1988-90. Chmn. bd. dirs. Scios Inc., 1987-93. Bd. dirs. pres. Valley Hosp. Found., Ridgewood, N.J.; mem. adv. bd. St. Benedict's Prep. Sch., Newark; chmn. Archbishop's Com. of Laity, Newark. Wtih AUS, 1942-46. Mem. Non-Prescription Drug Mfrs. Assn. (hon. v.p.), N.Y. Athletic Club, Sky Club, Union League Club (N.Y.C.), Hackensack Golf Club (pres.), Knights of Malta, Knights of St. Gregory, Knights of Holy Sepulchre, Friendly Sons of St. Patrick. Office: Wyeth 685 3rd Ave New York NY 10017-4024

CULLIGAN, PATRICK JOHN, obstetrician, gynecologist, surgeon, researcher; s. Thomas Michael and Lois Fern Culligan; m. Kimberly D Dovey, May 20, 1995; children: Brian Thomas, Clare Dovey. BS, Ga. Inst. of Tech., 1989; MD, Mercer U., 1993. Diplomate Am. Bd. of Obstetrics and Gynecology, 2001. Resident ob-gyn. Greenville (S.C.) Hosp. Sys., 1993—97; fellow urogynecology and reconstructive pelvic surgery Northwestern U. Med. Sch., Evanston, Ill., 1997—99; asst. prof. of ob-gyn. U. of Louisville (Ky.) Health Scis. Ctr., 1999—, assoc. prof. of ob-gyn., 2002—; v.p. U. OB-GYN Assocs., PSC, Louisville, 2002. Cons. Domain Assocs., LLC, Princeton, NJ, 1994—; bd. dirs. U. OB-GYN Found., Inc. Co-author: Urogynecology and Reconstructive Pelvic Surgery, 2002; contbr. articles to profl. jours. Bd. dir. Girls on the Run, Louisville, 2001. Recipient Thompson A Gailey award for academic achievement, Greenville Hosp. Sys. Dept. of OB-GYN, 1997, Faculty Devel. award, Berlex Found., 2002. Fellow: ACS (assoc.), Am. Coll. of Ob-Gyn. (assoc. grantee 1999); mem.: Am. Urogynecologic Soc. (assoc.; pub. rels. com. mem. 2001—02), Soc. of Gynecologic Surgeons (assoc.), Young President's Org. Republican. Roman Catholic. Avocations: tennis, skiing, bicycling, travel. Home Fax: same; Office Fax: 502-629-2444. E-mail: pculligan@louisville.edu.

CULLIGAN, THOMAS M. electronics executive; b. Aug. 1951; BS, MS, Fla. State U. Legis. dir. Fla. Congressman Earl Hutto, Fla.; chief of staff Fla. Sec. of State; exec. McDonnell Douglas; pres. govt. ops. Allied Signal, 1994—96, v.p. mktg., sales and svc., 1996—99; v.p., gen. mgr. def. and space Honeywell Internat., Inc., 1999—2001; CEO Raytheon Internat., Inc., 2001—; exec. v.p. Raytheon Co., Arlington, Va., 2001—. Office: Raytheon Co 1100 Wilson Blvd Arlington VA 22209-3978*

CULLINA, WILLIAM MICHAEL, lawyer; b. Hartford, Conn., July 22, 1921; s. Michael Stephen and Margaret (Carroll) C.; m. Gertrude Evelyn Blasig, Apr. 29, 1961; children: William Gregory, Kevin Michael, John Stephen, Susan Margaret. AB, Catholic U. Am., 1942; LLB, Yale U., 1948. Bar: Conn. bar 1948. Assoc. Murtha Cullina LLP, Hartford, 1948—, ptnr., 1952-91, of counsel, 1992—. Bd. dirs. St. Francis Hosp. and Med. Ctr., 1968-2002, hon. dir., 2002—; trustee St. Joseph Coll., 1986-98, trustee emeritus, 1998—; bd. govs. The Hartford Club, 1984-89, chair, 1987-88. Served with USNR, 1942-46. Fellow Am. Bar Found.; mem. ABA, Conn. Bar Assn., Hartford County Bar Assn., Hartford Tennis Club, Country Club of Farmington, Knight of St. Gregory, Phi Beta Kappa. Roman Catholic. Office: Murtha Cullina LLP City Pl 185 Asylum St Ste 29 Hartford CT 06103-3469

CULLINAN, BERNICE E(LLINGER), education educator; b. Hamilton, Ohio, Oct. 12, 1926; d. Lee Alexander and Hazel (Berry) Dees; m. George W. Ellinger, June 5, 1948 (div. 1966); children: Susan Jane, James Webb; m. Paul Anthony Cullinan, June 9, 1967 (div. 1994); m. Kenneth Seeman Giniger, Apr. 13, 2002.. BS, Ohio State U., 1948, MA, 1951, PhD, 1964. Cert. elem. educator, Ohio, N.Y. Tchr. Maple Pk. Elem. Sch., Middletown, Ohio, 1944-46, Trotwood (Ohio) Elem. Sch., 1946-47, Columbus (Ohio) Pub. Schs., 1948-50, Upper Arlington (Ohio) Pub. Schs., 1950-52; instr. Ohio State U., Columbus, 1959-64, asst. prof., 1964-67, Ohio State U./Charlotte Huck prof. children's lit., 1997; assoc. prof. NYU, N.Y.C., 1967-72, prof. reading, 1972-97, prof. emeritus, 1998—; editor-in-chief Wordsong Books, Honesdale, Pa., 1990—. Adv. bd. The Reading Rainbow, 1979—, WGBH-TV, 1989—; chair selection com. Ezra Jack Keats New Writer award, 1984-2000; exec. sec. English Standards Project, 1993-94. Author (Lee Galda): Literature and the Child, 1989, 5th edit., 2001; author: Children's Literature in the Classroom: Weaving Charlotte's Web, 1989, 2nd edit., 1994, Read to Me: Raising Kids Who Love to Read, 1992, 2d edit., 2000, Let's Read About: Finding Books They'll Love to Read, 1993; author: (with Brod Bagert) Helping Your Child Learn to Read, 1993; author: (with Diane G. Person) The Continuum Ency. of Children's Literature, 2002; author: (with Dorothy Strickland and Lee Galda) Language Arts: Learning and Teaching, 2003; author: (with L. Galda and D. Strickland) Language, Literacy and the Child, 1993; author:, 2002; author: (with Marilyn Scala and Virginia Schroder) Three Voices: Invitation to Poetry Across the Curriculum, 1995; author: 75 Authors and Illustrators Everyone Should Know, 1994; author: (with David Harrison) Poetry Lessons That Dazzle and Delight, 1999; editor: Children's Litature in the Reading Program, 1987, Invitation to Read: MOre Children's Literature in the Reading Program, 1992, Black Dialects and Reading, 1974, Fact and Fiction: Literature Across the Curriculum, 1993, Children's Vices, 1993, Pen in Hand, 1993, A Jar of Tiny Stars, 1996; editor: (with Diane Person) The Continuum Ency. of Children's Literature, 2001; mem. editl. bd. The New Advocate, 1987—99, mem. adv. bd. Ranger Rick Mag., 1992—; contbr. articles; author, editor, with M. Jerry Weiss: Books I Read When I Was Young, 1980, Literature and Young Children, 1977, Children's Literature in the Classroom: Extending Charlotte's Web, 1993; author (with Bonnie Kunzel): Encyclopedia of Children's Literature, 2003. Editorial bd. Nat. Coun. Tchrs. English, Champaign, Ill., 1973-76; selection com. Caldecott Award Am. Libr. Assn., Chgo., 1982-83; trustee Highlights for Children Found., 1993—. Named Outstanding Educator in Lang. Arts, Nat. Coun. Tchrs. English, 2003; named to Ohio State U. Coll. Edn. Hall of Fame, 1995; recipient Ind. U. Citation for outstanding contbn. to literacy, 1995. Mem.: Reading Hall of Fame (pres. 1998—99, inducted 1989), Internat. Reading Found. (trustee 1984—91, Jeremiah Ludington award 1992), Internat. Reading Assn. (bd. dirs. 1979—84, chair Tchrs. Choices 1988—91, Arbuthnot award for outstanding tchr. children's lit. 1989, Outstanding Educator of Lang. Arts 2003). Avocations: tennis, reading for pleasure, poetry. Home: 1045 Park Ave Apt 6A New York NY 10028 Office: 3 Tudor Ln Sands Point NY 11050-1104 E-mail: BerniceCullinan@Worldnet.att.net.

CULLINEY, JOHN JAMES, radiologist, educator; b. N.Y.C., Oct. 17, 1955; s. Michael and Marion (Dakowski) C.; m. Margaret Mary Steinhardt, Oct. 11, 1986. BS, Rutgers U., 1977, MS, 1981; MD, U Medicine and Dentistry N.J., 1984. Diplomate Am. Bd. Radiology, Nat. Bd. Med. Examiners. Intern physician Med. Coll. of Pa. Hosp., Phila., 1984-85; resident physician U. Medicine & Dentistry N.J., Newark, 1985-89; fellow body imaging, instr. diagnostic radiology Hahnemann U. Hosp., Phila., 1989-90, asst. prof. clin. diagnostic radiology, 1990-92; asst. prof. clin. diagnostic radiology, chief uroradiology U. Med. and Dentistry N.J., Newark, Pa., 1990-92; clin. instr. diagnostic radiology, chief cross-sect. imaging Mercy & Moses Taylor Hosps. affiliates Temple Med. Sch., Scranton, Pa., 1992-2001; pres. Radiol. Cons. Inc., 1999-2001; radiologist and radiation safety officer Kauai Med. Ctr, Hawaii, 2001—, vice-chmn. dept. radiology, 2003—, also bd. dirs. Chief uroradiology U. Med. and Dentistry N.J., Newark, 1990-92; bd. dirs. Radiol. Cons., Inc., Dunmore, Pa., 1994-2001; co-dir. Phoenix Vascular Lab.; dir. radiology Mercy Hosp. Scranton, Clin. Vascular Lab. Mem. AMA, AAUP, Am. Coll. Radiology, Am. Soc. Breast Imagers, Roentgen Soc. N.Am., KC. Roman Catholic. Avocations: amateur radio technician class, skiing. Home: 2940 Kanani St Lihue HI 96766 Office: Kauai Med Clinic 3-3420 Kuhio Hwy Ste B Lihue HI 96766 E-mail: culliney@aol.com.

CULLINS, MARGARET CARTER, customer service administrator, small business owner; b. Winston-Salem, N.C., May 27, 1961; d. Richard Andrew Carter, Eleanor Neal Carter; m. Larry Cullins. BS in Bus. Adminstrn., N.C. Agrl. and Tech. State U., 1984; postgrad., Piedmont Bible Coll., Winston-Salem, 1988—90. Author poetry. Mem.: Kernersville Craft Guild, Winston-Salem Craft Guild. Avocations: rubber stamping, Bible studies, poetry. Home: 1344 W Sedgefield Dr Winston Salem NC 27107 Personal E-mail: MCullins@juno.com.

CULLISON, ALEXANDER C. (DOC CULLISON), mediator, arbitrator; b. Balt., May 24, 1951; m. Diana Cullison; children: Alexander Paul, Holly. BS, USNY, 1987; BA in Labor Studies, Antioch U., 1983; MA in Labor and Policy Studies, SUNY, Empire, 1988; PhD in Labor Rels. and Conflict Resolution, Union Inst., 1997. Cert. mediator, Fla., Va. Union rep. dist. 1 Marine Engrs. Benficial Assn., 1978-93, nat. pres., 1992-93; founder, pres. Soc. for AIDS Prevention, Humanitarianism, and Edn., Fairfax, Va., 1993—. Panel mem. Am. Arbitration Assn., 1991. Mem. SAR; bd. advisers Dem. Leadership Coun.; mgn. trustee Dem. Nat. Com., del., 1992; del. Fla. Dem. Conv., 1991, Tex. Dem. Conv., 1988. With USAFR, 1969. Named Outstanding Labor Leader of Yr. Plantation (Fla.) Dem. Club, 1991, Outstanding Labor Leader of Yr. Dania (Fla.) Dem. Club, 1992. Mem. Am. Income Life Labor Adv. Bd., Soc. Naval Architects and Marine Engrs., Acad. Family Mediators. Home: 13232 Pleasantview Ln Fairfax VA 22033-3014 E-mail: AlexCullison@aol.com.

CULLMAN, HUGH, retired tobacco company executive; b. N.Y.C., Jan. 27, 1923; s. Howard S. and Elsie (Gottheil) C.; m. Nan Alva Ogburn, May 12, 1951; children: Katherine Victoria, Hugh Jr., Alexandra Miriam. BS, U.S. Naval Acad., 1945. With Benson & Hedges, 1949-54, mgr. research, 1952-54; with Philip Morris Inc., 1954—, treas., 1959-60, v.p., asst. chief ops., 1960-64, exec. v.p. ops., 1966—, also bd. dirs.; exec. v.p. Philip Morris Internat., 1965, pres., 1967-78, also bd. dirs.; group exec. v.p. Philip Morris Inc., 1978-84; chief exec. officer Philip Morris U.S.A., 1978-84; vice chmn. Philip Morris Cos. Inc., 1985-88. Sr. trustee U.S. Coun. for Internat. Bus.; mem. Tryon Palace Commn.; bd. dirs. N.C. Cmty. Found.; trustee The Kellenberger Hist. Found.; mem. adv. bd. Duke U. Marine Lab. Lt. USN, 1945—47, PTO, Lt. USN, 1951—52, Europe. Address: 821 Front St Beaufort NC 28516-2230

CULLMAN, JOAN, theatrical producer; Adv. bd. dirs. Musical Theatreworks; bd. dirs. Bay Street Theatre; vice chmn. Lincoln Ctr. Theatre, Inc. Co-prodr. plays Carmelina, One Night Stand, Oh, Brother!, The Rink, Mademoiselle Colombe, Eating Raoul, Orphans, Anything Goes, Cole, Art (Tony award best play 1998). Office: c/o Royale Theatre 242 W 45th St New York NY 10036-3901

CULLOM, JOSEPH WILLIAM, surgeon; b. Orangeburg, S.C., Aug. 13, 1947; MD, U. S.C., 1973. Cert. in surgery, recert. Intern Med. U. S.C. Hosps., Charleston, 1973-74, resident in surgery, 1974-78; with High Point (N.C.) Regional Hosp. Mem. Am. Coll. Surgeons. Office: 624 Quaker Ln Ste 1-00C High Point NC 27262-3832

CULLOM, WILLIAM OTIS, trade association executive; b. Huntsville, Ala., Mar. 20, 1932; s. Otis McKinley and Elna (Reese) C.; m. Caryl James, May 26, 1956; children: Cheryl Ann Cullom Stewart, Jennifer James Cullom Barksdale. BS, Fla. State U., 1958. Finger-print expert FBI, 1950-52; asst. bus. mgr. Fla. State U., 1954-64; with Ryder Truck Rental Inc., Miami, Fla., 1964-79, exec. v.p. mktg., to, 1979; pres., chief operating officer Jartran, Inc., Coral Gables,

Fla., 1979-81; pres. Greater Miami C. of C., 1981—. V.p. Orange Bowl Com., 1992—. Sec., bd. dirs. Miami-Dade Coll. Found.; mem. cabinet exec. com. Beacon Coun. United Way, Miami, 1974-80; trustee Bethune Cookman Coll., Daytona Beach, Fla., Barry U., St. Thomas U., Miami-Dade C.C. Found.; past chmn. bd. trustees Fla. State U; chmn. adminstrv. bd. Kendall Meth. Ch.; mem. pres.'s adv. com. Fla. Meml. Coll., Miami; bd. dirs. Bapt. Hosp. Found., Coconut Grove Playhouse, Goodwill Industries, Salvation Army; v.p. Orange Bowl Com.; chmn. bd. trustees Fla. State U. Found., 1994-95; chmn. Greater Miami Chamber Coalition. With U.S. Army, 1952-54. Recipient Miami Black Bus. Cmtys. Econ. Unity award, 1984, Anti Defamation League Human Rels. award, 1992, Disting. Cmty. Svc. award, 1998, Cedars Found. Concern award, 1994, NCCJ Humanitarian award, 1995, Silver Medallion award Greater Miami NCCJ, Citizen of Yr. award Greater Miami Rotary Club, Club at Dornal award, Life Achievement award Nat. PTA; named South Fla. Scout of Yr., Scouts Internat. in South Fla., 1997. Mem. Am. Trucking Assn., Truck Leasing and Renting Assn. (pres. Fla. chpt. 1972-73), Fla. State U. Nat. Alumni Assn. (pres.), Miami Hist. Assn., Brickell Club, Univ. Club, Riviera Country Club, City Club, Bankers Club, Ocean Reef Yacht Club, Gov.'s Club (Tallahassee), Dearing Bay Yacht Club, Biscayne Bay Yacht Club, Mountain Air Country Club (Burnsville, N.C.), Rotary, Doral Country Club (mem. of. bd. Doral Golf Championship). Democrat. Methodist. Home: 8445 SW 151st St Miami FL 33158-1961 Office: Greater Miami C of C 1601 Biscayne Blvd Miami FL 33132-1224

CULLUM, JAMES EDWARD, lawyer; b. Kingston, N.Y., Sept. 10, 1940; s. James Edward and Dorothy Ann (Donnelly) C.; m. Constance Mary Dyer, July 30, 1966; children— James Cullum, Kristin, Michael. B.S., Union U. Albany Coll. Pharmacy, 1962; LL.B., Albany Law Sch., 1967. Bar: N.Y. 1968, U.S. Dist. Ct. (no. dist.) N.Y. 1968, U.S. Ct. Apls. (2d cir.) 1971. Assoc. Wager, Taylor, Howd & Brearton, Troy, N.Y., 1967-69; adv. atty. N.Y. State Envron. Facilties Corp., Albany, 1969-71; asst. U.S. atty. U.S. Dept. Justice, Albany, 1971-76; ptnr. McPhillips, Fitzgerald, Meyer & McLenithan, Glens Falls, N.Y., 1976— . Lic. pharmacist, N.Y. Bd. dirs. United Cerebral Palsy Tri Counties, 1978—, chmn. bd., 1980-83; bd. dirs. Glens Falls YMCA, 1981-87, Tricounty United Way, 1988-94. Recipient Spl. Achievement award U.S. Atty. Gen., 1976. Mem. N.Y. State Bar Assn., Warren County Bar Assn. (bd. dirs. 1980-82, 94—, chmn. com. on ops. of ct. 1980-82, 84-85), Assn. Trial Lawyers Am. Republican. Roman Catholic. Home: 10 Cedarwood Dr Queensbury NY 12804-1313 Office: McPhillips Fitzgerald Meyer & McLenithan 288 Glen St Glens Falls NY 12801-3501

CULLUM, LEE BROOKS, journalist; b. Dallas, Mar. 18, 1939; d. Charles Gillespie and Garland Chapman Cullum; m. James Howard Clark Jr., June 29, 1962 (div. June 1976); 1 child, James Howard Cullum Clark. Student, Sweet Briar Coll.; BA, So. Meth. U., 1961; DHL (hon.), Monterey Inst. Inter. Studies, 1997, U. Puget Sound, 2002. Reporter, then exec. prodr. and on-air moderator Newsroom Sta. KERA-TV, Dallas, 1970-76, v.p. program devel., 1976-81; account exec. Hill & Knowlton, Dallas, 1981-82; editor D Mag., Dallas, 1982-85; dir. client svcs. Hill & Knowlton, Dallas, 1985-86; editor editl. page Dallas Times Herald, Dallas, 1986-91; commentator Newshour with Jim Lehrer (formerly Macneil-Lehrer Newshour), Washington, 1988—; contbg. columnist Dallas Morning News, Dallas, 1992—. Bd. dirs. Coun. Fgn. Rels., N.Y., Pacific Coun. Internat. Policy, L.A. Author: Genius Came Early: Creativity in the Twentieth Century, 1999. Bd. dirs. S.W. Legal Found., Dallas, 1995-99, The Hockaday Sch., Dallas, 1997-2003; bd. visitors Internat. Programs Ctr., Okla. U., 1997—; mem. Am. Coun. on Germany; mem. Nat. Com. on U.S.-China Rels. Dallas Inst. for Humanities and Culture fellow; recipient Matrix award Women in Comms., 1977, 85, J. B. Marryatt award Dallas Press Club, 1996. Mem.: InterAm. Dialogue, Nat. Conf. Editl. Writers. Episcopalian. Avocations: the arts, traveling, books.

CULMER, LEOME FRANCES, volunteer; b. Miami, Fla., July 19, 1925; d. Arthur Francis and Manette Aileen Scavella; m. John Edwin Culmer, July 3, 1947 (dec. June 18, 1963); children: Francena Culmer-Brooks, John E., Angela M., Lona Culmer-Schellbach, James A. BS, Bethune-Cookman Coll., 1949. Cert. tchr. Exhibit chair, 100-Yr History of St. Agnes' Episcopal Ch., 1998. Rschr., writer African Am. com. Dade Heritage Trust; program chmn. African Am. Com. Commemorative Svc.; script writer African Am. Com.; mem. City of Miami Cemetery Task Force, Dade Heritage Trust, Hist. Mus. So. Fla.; trustee, bd. dirs., chmn. spkrs.' bur. Black Archives Found., Inc.; former bd. dirs. Children's Home Soc. Fla.; co-parliamentarian St. Ceceilia chpt. Order of Daus. of the King; diocesan exec. bd. Orders of Daus. of the King; pres. St. Cecelia's chpt. Episcopal Ch. Women; parish historian, vacation bible sch. tchr., mem. exec. bd., parish coun. St. Agnes' Episcopal Ch.; mem. Union of Black Episcopalians; former mem. com. Fla. Coun. Chs.; former mem. archives and records com. Diocese of S.E. Fla. Named Citizen of the Day, Black Archives, Citizen of Yr., King of Clubs, 2000; recipient Congl. Nat. Parents' Day awrd, 1995, Woman of Distinction award, Miami-Dade Pub. Schs., 2000, Woman of Impact award, Miami-Dade Coalition Women's History, Black Archives Founder's award medallion, 2002, award of appreciation, BellSouth, 1997—98, cert. appreciation, Dade County Pub. Schs. Sch. Vol. Program, Spl. Black Woman cert. appreciation, Miami-Dade Pub. Libr. Sys., Outstanding Cmty. Svc. award, Women's C. of C., Patronal Appreciation award, St. Agnes' Episcopal Ch., 1983, Resolution, Chpt. of Trinity Episcopal Cathedral, Pres.' cert, AAUW, cert. appreciation, Booker T. Washington Sr. H.S., Black Archives, cmty. svc. award, Dade County Pub. Sch., award of excellence for cmty. svc., Collegians Club, Inc., rector's award, dedicated and devoted svc. award, cert. commendation, St. Agnes' Episcopal Ch., cert. honor, Fla. State Tchrs. Reunion Assn., Outstanding Cmty. Svc. award, Womenb's C. of C., Citizen of Day award, Miami-Dade County, Proclamation of Appreciation for Cmty. Svc., Miami-Dade County Office of Mayor, 2001, Enid C. Pinkney Humanitarian award, 2001, commendation, City of Miami, 2001, numerous others. Mem.: AAUW, Bethune-Cookman Coll. Alumni Assn., Soc. Episcopal Historians and Archivists. Episcopalian. Avocations: research, writing, preservation activism, history. Home: 1434 NW 55th Terr Miami FL 33142 E-mail: amculmer@aol.com.

CULMO, ELISABETH M. lawyer; b. Medford, Mass., Aug. 4, 1969; d. Robert Johnson and Kathleen Anne Francisca McCloskey; m. Thomas A. Culmo, Feb. 19, 2000. BA in Govt. and Law, Am. U., 1991; JD, U. Fla., Gainesville, 1994. Bar: Fla., U.S. Dist. Ct. (so. dist.) Fla. Assoc. Josephs, Jack & Gaebe, Miami, Fla., 1994—. Mem. AMA, Fla. Bar Assn., Dade County Bar Assn., Coral Gables Bar Assn., Acad. Fla. Trial Lawyers, Assn. Trial Lawyers Am. Democrat. Episcopalian. Avocations: running, cycling, guitar, piano, cooking. Office: Josephs Jack and Gaebe 2950 SW 27th Ave Ste 100 Miami FL 33133-3765

CULNON, SHARON DARLENE, reading specialist, special education educator; b. Balt., Apr. 20, 1947; d. Clayton Claude and Ann (McIntyre) Legg; m. Allen William Culnon, July 9, 1975. BA in Elem. Edn., U. Mich., 1972; MAT in Reading Edn., Oakland U., 1980; Learning Disabilities Cert., Ariz. State U., 1983. Cert. K-8 edn., K-12 reading specialist, K-12 learning disabilities specialist. Tchr. Mt. Morris (Mich.) Consolidated Schs., 1972-77; reading specialist Paradise Valley Schs., Phoenix, 1978-87, learning disabilities specialist, 1987-90, tchr., 1990-2000. Mem. Kachina Jr. Women's Club, Phoenix, 1980-83, sec., 1981-82. Recipient Learning Leader/dist. award Paradise Valley Bd. of Edn., Phoenix, 1986. Mem. Phi Delta Kappa (historian 1987-88). Presbyterian. Avocations: travel, wildlife viewing and study, reading, pets, photography. Home: 9035 N Concho Ln Phoenix AZ 85028-5318

CULP, CHARLES WILLIAM, lawyer; b. Louisville, Nov. 13, 1931; s. Charles Cantrell and Carolyn Marticia (O'Bannon) C.; m. Elisabeth Martha Stoker, Sept. 22, 1962; children: Charles Cantrell, Virginia Sheldon. BA, Yale U., 1953; JD, Harvard U., 1958. Bar: Ind. 1958. Ptnr. Cadick, Burns Duck & Peterson, Indpls., 1958-81, Shortridge & Culp, Indpls., 1981-88; pvt. practice Indpls., 1988—. Mem. Traders Point Hunt, Lawyers Club, Univ. Club, Dramatic Club. Home: 9251 Spring Forest Dr Indianapolis IN 46260-1267

CULP, GORDON LOUIS, consulting engineer; b. Topeka, Dec. 30, 1939; s. Russell Louis and Dorothy Marion (Wilson) C.; m. Rosemary Anne Smith, Apr. 7, 1990. BS in Civil Engring., U. Kans., 1961, MS in Environ. Health Engring., 1962; MA in Applied Psychology, U. Santa Monica, 1991. Registered; cert. Myers Briggs practitioner. San. engr. USPHS, Cin., 1962-64, CH2M/Hill Engrs., Corvallis, Oreg., 1964-66; rsch. engr. Neptune Microfloc, Corvallis, Oreg., 1966-70; rsch. mgr. Battelle N.W., Richland, Wash., 1970-71; regional mgr. CH2M/Hill Engrs., Reston, Va., 1971-73; pres. Culp, Wesner Culp (acquired by HDR Engring. 1986), Cameron Park, Calif., 1973-93, Smith Culp Consulting, Las Vegas, 1993—. Author: New Concepts in Water Purification, 1974, Handbook of Advanced Wastewater Treatment, 1978, 2d edit., 2001, Managing People (including Yourself) for Project Success, 1991, others; assoc. editor Jour. Engring. Mgmt. Mem. ASCE, Am. Water Works Assn., Water Pollution Control Fedn., Am. Acad. Environ. Engrs., Assn. Psychol. Type, Rotary (pres. 1977-78). Office: Smith Culp Consulting 653 Ravel Ct Las Vegas NV 89145-8628 E-mail: gordon@smithculp.com.

CULP, H. LAWRENCE, manufacturing executive; BA in Econs., Wash. Coll., 1985; MBA, Harvard U., 1990. Product mgr. Veeder-Root, 1990, v.p. mktg. and sales, pres., 1993—95; group exec., corp. officer Danaher Corp., 1995—99, exec. v.p., 1999—2000, COO, 2000—01, CEO, pres., 2001—. Office: 2099 Pennsylavania Ave NW Washington DC 20006-1813*

CULP, JAMES DAVID, lawyer, educator; b. Montgomery, Ala., June 12, 1951; s. Delos Poe and Martha Edwardine (Street) C.; m. Gretchen Ina Greene, Aug. 4, 1974; children: James Delos, Sarah Diana, Rebecca Caroline. BS, East Tenn. State U., 1973, MA, 1978; JD, U. Tenn., 1977. Bar: Tenn. 1978, U.S. Dist. Ct. (ea. dist.) Tenn. 1978. Pvt. practice, Johnson City, Tenn., 1978-79; pvt. practice Jonesborough, Tenn., 1983-86; ptnr. Culp and Fleming, Johnson City, 1979-81, Thornton, Culp and Fleming, Johnson City, 1981-83; city staff atty. Johnson City, 1987—2001; ptnr. Charles and Culp, 2001—. Instr. polit. sci. East Tenn. State U., 1980, Milligan Coll., 1994-98; instr. bus. law Draughons Jr. Coll., 1983-85 Active Johnson City Symphony Orch., 1969-74, Jr. Achievement, 1978-79; pres. Alcohol and Drug Counseling and Prevention Ctr., 1981-82; mem. East Tenn. State U. Wesley Found., 1979—, treas., 1981-82; mem. Upper East Tenn. Council on Alcoholism and Drug Dependence, 1981-83; mem. East Tenn. State U. Friends of Music, 1981-82, pres., 1982; mem. Johnson City Bd. Dwelling Standards and Rev., 1983-87, Washington County Election Commn., 1986-87. Served with USNR, 1971-73. Mem. Washington County Bar Assn., Tenn. Mcpl. Attys. Assn. (pres. 1992-93), Tenn. Trial Lawyers Assn., Mensa, Internat. Soc. for Philos. Enquiry, Am. Legion (judge adv. 1981-82), Johnson City Jaycees (state dir. 1979, named Spoke of Yr. 1978-79), Rotary. Democrat. Methodist. Home: 1634 Fairway Dr Johnson City TN 37601-2614 Office: 804 West Market St Johnson City TN 37604 E-mail: jcinjc@charter.net.

CULP, JOE C(ARL), electronics executive; b. Little Rock, July 23, 1933; s. Charles Carl and Doris Evelyn (Jackson) C.; m. Norma Carol Kennan, Jan. 26, 1954; 1 dau., Karen Gay Culp Ashorn. BSEE, U. Ark., 1955. Staff asst. to exec. v.p. Collins Radio, Dallas, 1967-68; with Rockwell Internat., Dallas, 1968-88, dir. data sys. mktg., 1968-71, dir. mktg. transmission sys. divsn., 1971-78, v.p. L.Am. divsn., 1978-80, v.p., gen. mgr. transmission sys. divsn., 1980-82, pres. telecom. group, 1982-88; pres., CEO Lightnet, Rockville, Md., 1988-89; exec. v.p. Comm. Transmission Inc., Austin, Tex., 1989—90. Pres. Culp Comm. Assocs., Austin, 1990—; chmn. Gen. Bandwidth Inc.; bd. dirs. March Telecom, Breconridge, Inc., Brecon Ridge Mfg. Sys. Chmn. engring. bd. U. Tex., Arlington, 1984; bd. advisors Coll. Engring. U. Ark., Fayetteville, 1982. Named Disting. Grad., Coll. Engring. U. Ark., 1981, Disting. Engr., U. Tex., Arlington, 1984. Mem. Electronic Industry Assn. (bd. govs. 1984-88), U.S. Tel. Suppliers Assn. (dir. 1984-88), Ind. Tel. Pioneers. Republican. Methodist. Office: Culp Comm Assocs Inc 5 Hedge Ln Austin TX 78746-4963

CULP, MICHAEL BRONSTON, investor, writer, publisher; b. N.Y.C., June 17, 1952; s. Robert Walter and Anna Lee (Filtzer) C.; m. Deborah T. Bronston. BA in Econs. cum laude, CUNY, 1973; CFA, U. Va., 1979. Securities analyst Standard & Poor's, N.Y.C., 1974—79; v.p., securities analyst E. F. Hutton & Co., Inc., N.Y.C., 1979—82; v.p., sr. securities analyst Prudential Securities Inc., N.Y.C., 1982-86, sr. v.p., mng. dir. rsch., 1986-94, sr. v.p., dir. global rsch., 1994-97, bd. dirs., 1986-91, oper. coun., 1991-97, chmn. stock selection com., 1989-97, chmn. equity devel. com., 1991-97, equity transactions bd., 1994-97, investment banking com., 1994-97; mem. investment com. Roman Arch Fund, 1996-97; mng. dir., dir. rsch., mem. oper. com. PaineWebber Inc., N.Y.C., 1997-2000, also bd. dirs., 1997-2000; pres. Michael Culp & Co., Inc., N.Y.C., 2000—01, Mecox Bay Press LLC, 2002—. Author: Conflicted, A Novel, 2003. Mem. Pubs.' Mktg. Assn., N.Y. Soc. Security Analysts, Fin. Analysts' Fedn., Inst. CFAs, Internat. Soc. Fin. Analysts, Assn. for Investment Mgmt. and Rsch., Mensa, Phi Beta Kappa, Omicron Delta Epsilon. Home: 11 Jule Pond Dr Southampton NY 11968

CULP, MILDRED LOUISE, corporate executive; b. Ft. Monroe, Va., Jan. 13, 1949; d. William W. and Winifred (Stilwell) C. BA in English, Knox Coll., 1971; AM in Religion and Literature, U. Chgo., 1974, PhD The Com. on History of Culture, 1976. Faculty, adminstr. Coll., 1976-81; dir. Exec. Résumés, Seattle, 1981—; pres. Exec. Directions Internat., Inc., Seattle, 1985—2000, Clive, Iowa, 2000—03. MBA mgmt. skills adv. com. U. Wash. Sch. Bus. Adminstrn., 1993; spkr. in field; contract rschr. U.S. Army Recruiting Command, 1997. Author: Be WorkWise: Retooling Your Work for the 21st Century, 1994; columnist Seattle Daily Jour. Commerce, 1982-88; writer Singer Media Corp., 1991-98, Worldwide Media, 1999-2002, Globalvision, Inc., 2002—, WorkWise syndicated column, 1994—, Universal Press Syndicate, 1997-2001, syndicated in U.S., in print and online svcs., WorkWise Registered, 1992 (radio), 96 (print), 2000 (Internet audio); WorkWise Internet audio program, 2000-03; WorkWise radio program, 2003-; featured on TV and radio; contbr. articles and book revs. to profl. jours.; presenter WorkWise Report, Sta. KIRO, 1991-96. Admissions counselor U. Chgo., 1981—; mem. Nat. Alliance Mentally Ill, 1984—, mem. adv. bd., 1988; mem. A.M.I. Hamilton County, 1984—; founding mem. People Against Telephone Terrorism and Harassment, 1990; co-sponsor WorkWise award, 1999-2000. Recipient Alumni Achievement award Knox Coll., 1990, 8 other awards; named Hon. Army Recruiter. Mem.: U. Chgo. Puget Sound Alumni Club (bd. dir. 1982—86), Knox Coll. Alumni Network.

CULP, WILLIAM COMBS, radiologist; b. McAlester, Okla., Sept. 7, 1942; s. Chesley Key and Irma (Combs) C.; m. Theresa Anthony, July 16, 1966; children: Jenniffer, William Jr., Laura, Thomas, Ben. MD, U. Okla., 1967. Diplomate Am. Bd. Radiology. Mixed intern U. Okla., Oklahoma City, 1967-68; resident in diagnostic radiology U. Tex. Med. Br., Galveston, 1970-74; fellow in vascular and interventional radiology U. Nebr. Med. Ctr., Omaha, 1994-95; radiologist St. Edwards Med. Ctr., Ft. Smith, Ark., 1974-92; interventional radiologist U. Fla., Gainesville, Fla., 1995-97, U. Nebr., Omaha, 1997-2001; assoc. prof. radiology U. Ark. for Med. Scis., 2001—. Dir. fellowships Vascular Interventional Radiology; assoc. prof. U. Ark., Little Rock, 1985-92; com. chair Ark. Coll. Radiology, Ft. Smith, 1988. Contbr. articles to profl. jours. Pres. Ft. Smith Symphony, 1979; bd. dirs. First Meth. Ch., Ft. Smith, 1980, Ft. Smith Chorale, Ft. Smith, 1992. Lt. Comdr. USPHS, 1968-70. Named Yachtsman of Yr. Galveston Yacht Club, 1972, Nat. Champion award Catalina 22 Sailing Assn., 1978. Mem. Inst. Nautical Archaeology (bd. dirs.), Am. Coll. Radiology, Inst. Nautical Archaeology, Soc. Cardiovascular/Interventional Radiology (rsch. com.), Radiol. Soc. N.Am., Ark. Coll. Radiology. Avocations: sailing, diving, archaeology. Office: UAMS Dept Radiology 4301 W Markham Slot 556 Little Rock AR 72205-7199

CULPAN, REFIK, finance educator; b. Adana, Turkey, May 5, 1944; arrived in U.S., 1980; s. Mustafa and Muzeyyen Culpan; m. Oya Culpan, Nov. 12, 1975; children: Burcu, Alpay. Law diploma, Istanbul U., Turkey, 1966; MPA, U. Pitts., 1970; PhD, NYU, 1977. Asst. prof. Hacettepe U., Ankara, Turkey, 1974—80; assoc. prof. U. Conn., Storrs, 1979—80; prof. Pa. State U., Middletown, 1980—. CEO, chmn. Etibank Bankacilik AO, Ankara, 1994—95. Editor: Multinational Strategic Alliances, 1993; co-editor: Transformation Management, 1995; author: Global Business Alliances, 2002. Bd. dirs. Turkish Am. Assn. Ctrl. Pa., Harrisburg, 2002, pres., 2001. Mem.: Acad. Mgmt., Acad. Internat. Bus. Avocations: golf, skiing. Office: Pa State U 777 W Harrisburg Pike Middletown PA 17057 Fax: 717-948-6456. Business E-Mail: rculpan@psu.edu.

CULPEPPER, DAUNTE, football player; b. Jan. 28, 1977; Football player Minn. Vikings, 1999—. Office: Minn Vikings 9520 Viking Dr Eden Prairie MN 55344

CULPEPPER, JO LONG, librarian; b. Franklin, Va., Mar. 10, 1945; d. Sidney Earl and Fannie Lou (Flythe) Long; m. Britton Barclay Culpepper, Jr., Aug. 19, 1967; children: Britton B. III, Edmond Scott, Lou Ann. BS, Radford (Va.) U., 1967; MS, Old Dominion U., 1983. Min. of activities Westmoreland Bapt. Ch., Huntington, W.Va., 1967-70; libr. Walter Cecil Rawls Libr. and Mus., Courtland, Va., 1971-79, Hunterdale Elem. Sch., Franklin, Va., 1979—. Dir. Sunday sch. Franklin Bapt. Ch., 1988-98, bd. deacons, 1994-97; trustee Walter Cecil Rawls Libr. and Mus., 1985-89; troop leader Boy Scouts Am. Mem. Va. Ednl. Media Assn., Franklin/Southampton Reading Coun., Va. Reading Coun. Avocations: scouting, reading, bowling, camping. Home: 401 Trail Rd Franklin VA 23851-2909 Office: Hunterdale Elem Sch 23190 Sedley Rd Franklin VA 23851-3848 E-mail: britt_jo_culpepper@hotmail.com.

CULPEPPER, MABEL CLAIRE, artist; b. St. Louis, Mo., June 20, 1936; d. John Raymond and Mabel Lorene (Hardy) Bondurant; m. James William Culpepper, Dec. 24, 1957; children: Julie Ann, James Jeffrey, John William. AA, Columbia Coll., 1956; BS in Edn., Mo. U., 1958, MEd, 1965. Represented by Artel Gallery, Emmitsburg, Md., 1987-88, Nob Hill Artisans, Albuquerque, 1993-94, Amapola Gallery, Albuquerque, 1995—. Art tchr. Twinbrook BApt., Rockville, Md., 1972-75. One-woman shows include Artel Gallery, 1987, exhibited in group shows at Rockville (Md.) Art League, 1987, N.Mex. Watercolor Soc., 1989—2002, Nat. Watercolor Soc. Nat. Exhbn., Brea, Calif. Host parent, officer Am. Field Svc., Damascus, Md., 1978-80; program chmn. Albuquerque Newcomers, 1989-91; docent Albuquerque Mus., 1990-94. Recipient First Prize Rockville Art League, 1987. Mem.: Frederick County Art Assn. (pres. 1988), N.Mex. Watercolor Soc. (pres. 1992—93, 1st prize 1990, Best of Show 1993, 1st prize 1998, Best of Show 1999, Peter Walker award 2001), Nat. Watercolor Soc. (signature mem.) (western fedn. show hospitality chair 2002, Collectors Guide Award 2002, Village Framers Award 2003, Collector's Guide award 2002, Village Framers award 2003), Nat. League Am. Penwomen (pres. Yucca br. 1998—2000, editor newsletter 2001), Nat. Mus. Women in the Arts (Peter Walker Award 2000), Mortar Board, Delta Gamma. Avocations: hiking, singing in church choir, crafts, bible study, travel. Home: 3208 Casa Bonita Dr NE Albuquerque NM 87111-5610

CULPEPPER, MARY KAY, publishing executive; With Weight Watchers; exec. dir. Coastal Living, 2000—01; v.p. Cooking Light Mag., 2002—, editor, 2001—. Office: Cooking Light Magazine P O Box 62376 Tampa FL 33602

CULPEPPER, MICHAEL IRVING, researcher, educator; b. Mobile, Ala., Sept. 28, 1951; s. Milton Irving and Betty Jean (Wimpee) C.; m. Cynthia Ann Langner, Mar. 11, 1972; children: Amber Joy, Amy Celeste, Amanda Kaye. Student Auburn U., 1969-71; BS, U. Ala.-Birmingham, 1973, MS, 1975, CASE, 1978; EdD, U. Ala., 1981. Cert. tchr., Ala. Asst. lab. technician div. orthopaedic surgery U. Ala.-Birmingham, 1971-72, lab. asst., 1972-73, research technician, 1973-74, research asst., 1974-75, research assoc., 1975-81, instr. stats., biomechanics/kinesiology, 1981-87, asst. prof., 1987; dir. research Kerner-Quarterback Sports Medicine Inst., Children's Hosp., Birmingham, 1982— ; lectr. to orgns. on sports medicine and health care. Tchr., coach Chelsea High Sch. (Ala.), 1987, Thompson (Ala.) H.S., 2000—; bd. dirs. Dixie Softball Inc., Central Shelby League; chmn. long-range planning com. Chelsea Youth Club. Recipient M. Ray Loree research award U. Ala., Tuscaloosa, 1981. Fellow Am. Coll. Sports Medicine; mem. Ala. Acad. Sci., Am. Alliance Health Phys. Edn., Recreation and Dance, Am. Coll. Sports Medicine (chpt. membership com.), Nat. Athletic Trainers Assn., Soc. for Biomaterials, U.S. Sports Acad. (nat. faculty)Sigma Xi, Kappa Delta Pi. Baptist. Contbr. articles to profl. jours.; developer U. Ala.-Birmingham sports injury/illness data storage and retrieval system. Home: 583 Hwy 335 Chelsea AL 35043

CULPEPPER, RICHARD GROOM, engineer; b. Norfolk, Va., Mar. 5, 1940; s. August Hume and Olive Gertrude (Birmingham) C.; m. Martha Louise Edwards, Nov. 5, 1966; children: Carolyn Ann, Richard Brian. B.S. in Aerospace Engring., Va. Poly. Inst., 1962; grad. Nat. Defense U., 1984. Asst. project engr. U.S. Army Aviation Material Lab., Newport News, Va., 1962-66; flight test engr. NASA-Langley Rsch. Ctr., Hampton, Va., 1966-70, sr. flight test engr., 1970-78, tech. mgr., 1978-80; NASA rep. Wright Patterson AFB, 1981-86, chief tech. transfer Nat. Aerospace Plane Joint Project, 1986-90; asst. to dir. Nat. Aerospace Plane Program, 1990-95; NASA prin. dep. program dir. Air Force Hypersonic Tech. Program, 1995-99; dir. aerospace programs Accurate Automation Corp., Chattanooga, Tenn., 1999-2001; aviation cons., 2001—. Contbr. papers to profl. publs. Com. mem. Pack 56, Tecumseh council Boy Scouts Am., 1981, chmn., 1982-83. Recipient Spl. Achievement award NASA, 1974, 76, 80, 88, 94, 95. Fellow AIAA (v.p. tech. activities 1999-2001). Avocations: stamp collecting, gardening. E-mail: rgculpepper@earthlink.net. Home and Office: 9256 Tower Pines Cv Ooltewah TN 37363-9348 E-mail: rgculpepper@earthlink.net.

CULTON, PAUL MELVIN, retired counselor, educator, interpreter; b. Council Bluffs, Iowa, Feb. 12, 1932; s. Paul Roland and Hallie Ethel Emma (Paschal) C. AB, Minn. Bible Coll., 1955; BS, U. Nebr., Omaha, 1965; MA, Calif. State U., Northridge, 1970; EdD, Brigham Young U., 1981. Cert. tchr., Iowa. Tchr. Iowa Sch. for Deaf, Council Bluffs, 1956-70; ednl. specialist Golden West Coll., Huntington Beach, Calif., 1970-71, dir. disabled students, 1971-82, instr., 1982-88; counselor El Camino Coll., Via Torrance, Calif., 1990-93, acting assoc. dean, 1993-94, counselor, 1994-97. Interpreter various state and fed. cts., Iowa, Calif., 1960-90; asst. prof. Calif. State U., Northridge, Fresno, Dominguez Hills, 1973, 76, 80, 87-91, L.A., 1999—; vis. prof. U. Guam, Agana, 1977; mem. allocations task force, task force on deafness, trainer handicapped students Calif. C.C.s, 1971-81. Editor: Region IX Conf. for Coordinating Rehab. and Edn. Svcs. for Deaf proceedings, 1970, Toward Rehab. Involvement by Parents of Deaf conf. proceedings, 1971; composer Carry the Light, 1986. Bd. dirs. Iowa NAACP, 1966-68, Gay and Lesbian Cmty. Svcs. Ctr., Orange County, Calif., 1975-77; founding sec. Dayle McIntosh Ctr. for Disabled, Anaheim and Garden Grove, Calif., 1974-80; active Dem. Cent. Com. Pottawattamie County, Council Bluffs, 1960-70; del. People to People N.Am. Educators Deaf Vis. Russian Schs. & Programs for Deaf, 1993. League for Innovation in Community Coll. fellow, 1974. Mem. Registry of Interpreters for Deaf, Am. Fedn. Tchrs., Am. Sign Lang. Tchrs. Assn., Nat. Assn. Deaf. Mem. Am. Humanist Assn. Avocations: vocal music, languages, community activism, travel, politics. Home: 3939 N Virginia Rd 110 Long Beach CA 90807

CULTRA, SHANE, state representative; married; 3 children. Grad. agr. tech. in Landscape & Nursery Mgmt., Mich. State Univ. Pres. Onarga Nursery, 1989—2001. Coach girls' basketball St. John's Luth. Sch., Buckley; elder, sec., and trustee local ch.; mem. Agr. and Conservation, Appropriations - Elem. Secondary, and Higher Ed. Comm., Judiciary I - Civil Law Comm., Labor Comm. Mem.: Iroquois County Bd. (chmn. 2001—03), Grand Prairie Seminary (chmn. of Bd. Trustees), Onarga Cmty. Ctr. (chmn.), Lions Club. Lutheran. Office: Capitol 230-N Stratton Office Bldg Springfield IL 62706 also: 608 N Oak St Onarga IL 60955*

CULVAHOUSE, ARTHUR BOGGESS, JR., lawyer; b. Athens, Tenn., July 4, 1948; s. Arthur Boggess and Ruth Webb (Wear) C.; m. Pamela Smith Comparato, Apr. 29, 2001; children: Sarah Abbott, Arthur Boggess (dec.), Elizabeth Louise, Anne Pierce. BS, U. Tenn., 1970; JD, NYU, 1973. Bar: Tenn. 1973, Calif. 1977, D.C. 1977. Chief legis. asst. to U.S. Sen. Howard Baker, Washington, 1973-76; assoc. O'Melveny & Myers, Washington, 1976-81, ptnr., 1982-84, 89—; chmn., 2000—; ptnr. Vinson & Elkins, Washington, 1984-87; counsel to the Pres. The White House, Washington, 1987-89. Recipient Presdl. Citizen's medal, 1989, Def. Dept. Disting. Svc. medal. 1992. Republican. Episcopalian. Office: O'Melveny & Myers 1625 Eye St NW Washington DC 20006

CULVER, CHESTER J. state official, educator; m. Mari Thinnes Culver. BA in Polit. Sci., Va. Polytechnic Inst. and State U., 1988; MA in Tchg., Drake U., 1994. Tchr. HS govt., history, coach Hoover HS, Des Moines; investigator Atty. Gen.'s Office; sec. of state State of Iowa, 1999—. Established Iowa Student Polit. Awareness Club; elder mem. Ctrl. Presbyn. Ch. Mem.: Iowa State Edn. Assn. (Fulbright Meml. Fund Tchrs. scholarship 1997), Coun. State Govts., Elections Task Force, New Millenium Youth Initiative, Presdl. Caucuses and Primaries Com., Elections and Voter Participation Com., Nat. Assn. Secs. State,

State Records Mgmt. Com., State Voter Registration Commn. (chmn.), Exec. Coun. (chmn.). Democrat. Office: Office of Secretary of State State House Des Moines IA 50319-0001 Business E-Mail: sos@sos.state.ia.us.*

CULVER, DAN LOUIS, federal agency administrator; b. Savannah, Ga., Dec. 7, 1957; s. Louis and Jean Culver. BS in Mktg., U. Tenn., 1981; postgrad., Air Force Acad., 1982, Cornell U., 1985; BS in Edn. and Tng., U. W. Fla., 1995, MEd in Orgnl. Devel. and Leadership, 1998. Cert. tchr. Fla. Logistics support officer USAF, Ft. Walton Beach, Fla., 1982-86; mgmt. assoc. Barnett Bank, Ft. Walton Beach, Fla., 1987-89; program adminstr. disaster relief SBA, Atlanta, 1989—. Diplomatic observer UN, N.Y.C.; promoter lectrs., entertainers and authors. Pioneered automation of airforce support ops., 1982—84. Vol. disaster relief for victims of Hurricane Hugo, Charleston, SC, 1989, Hurricane Andrew, Miami, Fla., 1992, Miss. River flood, 1993, L.A. earthquake, 1994, World Trade Ctr. destruction, N.Y.C., 2001; bd. dirs. non-profit orgns. Recipient Comdr.-in-Chief's Spl. Recognition for Excellence award, Pres. Ronald Reagan, 1986. Mem.: Asia Soc., Internat. Parliament Safety and Peace, Maison Internat. des Intellectuels, Internat. Platform Assn., Order of Knight Templars. Avocations: flying, skiing, sailing. Office: PO Box 145 Niceville FL 32588-0145

CULVERHOUSE, CECIL GRIFFITH, minister; b. Birmingham, Ala., June 16, 1924; s. Carl Reed and Alma Boyce Griffith Culverhouse; m. Patricia Ann Braswell, Feb. 22, 1957 (dec. Aug. 10, 1996); children: Ian Stewart, Robert Christopher. BA, Howard Coll., Birmingham, AL, 1944; MDiv, Union Theol. Sem., Richmond, VA, 1947, ThM, 1948; DD (hon.), Westminster Coll., Fulton, MO, 1970. Pastor Marion Presbyn. Ch., Marion, Ala., 1948—53, West Nashville Presbyn. Ch., Nashville, Tenn., 1955—60, First Presbyn. Ch., Fulton, Mo., 1960—87; parish assoc. First Presbyn., Jefferson City, Mo., 1991—. Trustee Montreat Conf. Ctr., Montreat, NC, 1972—80, Presbyterian Sch. for Christian Edn., Richmond, Va., 1977—80; chmn. nat. missions Presbyn. Ch. US, Atlanta, 1978—80. Author: (book) No Strings Attached, Do Not Be Afraid; contbr. articles to profl. jours. Recipient Sun-Gazette-Mcubbin Award, Kingdom Supper, 1980, Mo. Cmty. Betterment, Chamber of Commerce, 1968, 1969, Mo. Union Presbyn. Moderator's Svc. Award, Mo. Union Presbyn., 1996, 1998. Democrat. Presbyterian. Avocation: travel. Personal E-mail: culverhouse@midamerica.net.

CULVERN, JULIAN BREWER, retired chemist, educator; b. July 23, 1919; m. Shirley Bowman, 1946; children: Janine Amelia, David Bowman, Linda Hazel. BS, N.C. State U., 1942; MSc, Ohio State U., 1948; postgrad., U. Tenn., 1970-72. Assay chemist Haile Gold Mine, 1940-41; shift supr. Anhydrous Ammonia Plant TVA, Wilson Dam, Ala., 1942-44; asst. mgr. Chem. & Microscopical Lab., 1949-61; sr. process engr. Am. Enka Corp., Lowland, Tenn., 1961-69; instr. gen. chemistry, earth and space sci., environ. sci. Morristown (Tenn.) Coll., 1969-76, chmn. div. natural sci., 1969-73. Condr. libr. rsch. in field sci. and religion Sir John M. Templeton Found., 1970; chemist atomic bomb project Corps of Engrs., Manhattan Dist., Oak Ridge, Tenn., 1944-46. Columnist Daily Gazette-Mail, Morristown, 1960-74; contbr. articles to Sci. of Mind mag., others. Chmn. Cherokee dist. Boy Scouts Am., 1957-58, 91-92, exec. bd. Great Smoky Mountain coun., 1991-2003; ruling elder 1st Presbyn. Ch., Morristown, Tenn., Marshall, N.C.; sci. judge So. Appalachian Sci. and Engring. Fair, U. Tenn., Knoxville, 1995-2001. Recipient Silver Beaver award, Boy Scouts Am., 2003; James E. West fellow, 1995. Mem. AAUP, Am. Chem. Soc. (emeritus; 60-yr. mem.), Tenn. Acad. Scis., Gamma Sigma Epsilon, Phi Lambda Upsilon. Home: Birdsong Hill 2832 Indian Trl Morristown TN 37814-5824

CULVERWELL, ALBERT HENRY, historian; b. Portland, Oreg., Jan. 28, 1913; s. John Albert and Nettie L. (Kingery) C.; m. Ethel E. Klein, Aug. 17, 1941 (dec.); children: Cheryl Evelyn, John Albert; m. Eleanor M. Liere, May 6, 1986 (dec.). Scholarship student in stagecraft, color and design, Cornish Sch., Seattle, 1935-36; BA, U. Wash., Seattle, 1936, MA, 1941; postgrad., Am. U., Wash. State U. Mem. faculty Whitworth Coll., Spokane, Wash., 1941-42, 46-50; civilian U.S. Naval Air Sta., Seattle, 1942-45; safety engr., asst. dir. personnel Pacific Car & Foundry Co., Renton, Wash., 1945-46; instr. social sci. Wash. State U., Pullman, 1949-50; asst. prof. history Western Wash. State Coll., Bellingham, 1950-53; historian, supr. interpretation Wash. State Parks, Olympia, 1953-62; chief br. interpretive services Region 4, U.S. Forest Service, Ogden, Utah, 1962-68; dir. Eastern Wash. State Hist. Soc., Spokane, 1968-82; pres. Wash. Art Consortium, 1979-82. Mem. Wash. Archives Adv. Bd., 1977-82, Adv. Coun. Preservation of Hist. Sites and Bldgs., 1968-78, com. to develop Hist. Interpretive Ctr., Wash. State Capitol Bldg., 1983-84; mem. design com. Main St. Program, San Jacinto, Calif., 1988-91; vol. art assoc. in support and adminstrn. Fine Arts Gallery, Mt. San Jacinto Coll., 1988-98; vol. history assoc. in preservation and interpretation of Estudillo Mansion in San Jacinto, 1993-98, pres. Resident Coun. SunWest Village, Hemet, CA, 1998-99. Author articles in field, also, film and TV scripts. Elder United Presbyn. Ch. U.S.A., 1942—; adminstrv. adv. com. Sheldon Jackson Jr. Coll., Sitka, Alaska, 1961-63; bd. dirs. Westminster Found., 1961-62; mem. Woodway (Wash.) Planning Commn., 1961-63, Wash. Gov.'s Adv. Coun. on Observance Civil War Centennial, 1961; Gov. Wash. Coun. Boundary Survey Centennial, 1961. Recipient cert. of commendation Am. Assn. State and Local History, 1965 Mem. Am. Assn. Museums (pres. Western regional conf. 1969-71), Orgn. Am. Historians, Pacific N.W. Hist. Soc., Idaho Hist. Soc., Utah Hist. Soc., Westerners, Phi Sigma Kappa, Pi Sigma Alpha. Clubs: Rotary. Home: 973 Sunwest Dr Hemet CA 92545-1626 *In my life I have striven to achieve something positive in whatever I have done. Success depends on faith in myself as well as in someone greater than I, and, to an extent, with those with whom I have worked. This has brought a measure of patience to me which has made it possible to accept setbacks which make achievement slow. But when one has gained confidence and patience, success is often achieved.*

CULVERWELL, ROSEMARY JEAN, principal, elementary education educator; b. Chgo., Jan. 15, 1934; d. August John and Marie Josephine (Westermeyer) Flashing; m. Paul Jerome Culverwell, Apr. 26, 1958; children: Joanne, Mary Frances, Janet, Nancy, Amy. BEd, Chgo. State U., 1955, MEd in Libr. Sci., 1958; postgrad., DePaul U., 1973. Cert. supr., tchr. Tchr. Otis Sch., Chgo., 1955-59; tchr., libr. Yates Sch., Chgo., 1960-61, Nash Sch., Chgo., 1962-63, Boys Chgo. Parental, 1969-72, Edgebrook and Reilly Schs., Chgo., 1965-67; counselor, libr. Reilly Sch., Chgo., 1968, tchr., libr., asst. prin., 1973, prin., 1974—. Reviewer Ill. State Bd. Edn. Quality Review Team. Pres. Infant Jesus Guild, Park Ridge, Ill., 1969-70; troop leader Girl Scouts U.S., Park Ridge, 1967-69; sec. Home Sch. Assn., Park Ridge, 1969, v.p. spl. projects, 1970; mem. Ill. Svc. Ctr. Six Governing Bd., 1994; vol. Ctr. of Concern, Park Ridge, Ill., 1997; quality reviewer Ill. State Bd. Edn., 1998; mem. Ill. Quality Edn. Rev. Team, 1998; v.p. Renaissance Art Club, 1999—. Recipient Outstanding Prin. award Citizens Schs. Com., Chgo., 1987, For Character award, 1984-85, Whitman award for Excellence in Edn. Mgmt., 1990, Local Sch. Coun. award Ill. Bell Ameritech, 1991, Ill. Disting. Educator award Milken Family Found. Nat. Educators, 1991, Ill. Edn./Bus. Partnership award, 1994, 96. Mem. AAUW, LWV (chmn. speakers bur. 1969), Delta Kappa Gamma, Phi Delta Kappa. Avocations: acrylic painting, reading, swimming, making doll houses and furniture. Home: 1929 S Ashland Ave Park Ridge IL 60068-5460 Office: FW Reilly Sch 3650 W School St Chicago IL 60618-5358 E-mail: rosemary.culverwell@mciworldcom.net.

CULWELL, CHARLES LOUIS, retired manufacturing company executive; b. Putnam, Tex., Apr. 26, 1927; s. Willie and Ila Alberta (Crosby) C.; m. Virginia Green, June 10, 1949; children: Andrew Scott, Perry Neal, Curtis Austin, Travis Lee. BSEE, U.S. Naval Acad., 1949; MS in Mgmt., U.S. Naval Postgrad. Sch., 1969. Commd. ensign U.S. Navy, 1949, advanced through grades to capt., 1969; service in Korea and Vietnam; comdg. officer Naval Supply Center, Oakland, Calif., 1975-76; ret., 1976; asst. to pres., then v.p. Purex Corp., 1976-79; group v.p., gen. mgr. indsl., instl. and comml. products Purex Industries, Inc., Lakewood, Calif., 1979-84, v.p., asst. to CEO Carson, Calif., 1984-86, Purex Industries Liquidation, Carson, Calif., 1986-87, ret., 1987. Decorated Legion of Merit, Bronze Star with combat V, Meritorious Svc. medal. Mem. U.S. Naval Acad. Alumni Assn. Baptist.

CUMBERBATCH, ELLIS, education educator, researcher; life ptnr. Suzanna Stafford; children: Guy Lawrence, Evelyn, Louis Richard. BS, Manchester U., Eng., 1952—55, PhD, 1955—58. Author: (rsch. pub.) Jour. of Engring. Math. Mem.: SIAM. Office: Claremont Graduate U 121 E 10th St Claremont CA 91711 Office Fax: 909-607-8261.

CUMBOW, ROBERT CHARLES, lawyer, writer, educator; b. Columbus, Ohio, Oct. 22, 1946; s. Robert M. and Margaret Joan (O'Connor) C.; m. Grace Blond, Sept. 6, 1975; children: Rachel Elizabeth, Irena Alexis. BA in English, Seattle U., 1967, MA in English, 1969; JD, U. Puget Sound, 1991. News media rep. Puget Sound Power and Light, Bellevue, Wash., 1984-86, corp. communications coordinator, 1986-91; assoc. Perkins Coie, Seattle, 1991-99; shareholder Graham & Dunn, 1999—. Prof. law Seattle U. Law Sch., 1997—. Author: Pardon Me, Roy, 1983, Once Upon a Time: The Films of Sergio Leone, 1987, A Century of Service: The Puget Power Story, 1987, Order in the Universe: The Films of John Carpenter, 1990, 2d edit., 2000, West Pointers and Early Washington, 1992; contbr. articles on film to profl. jours. Bd. dirs. Wash. Lawyers for the Arts, 1994-2001, pres., 2000-01, Seattle Mime Theatre, 1996-99; vol. Bus. Vols. for the Arts, 1994-99. With U.S. Army, 1969-71. Recipient Copy Desk awards Dept. of Def., 1970-71, Army Commendation medal, 1971, George Boldt scholar, 1989, 90, 91, Wash. Superior Ct. Judges, 1989-90. Mem. Wash. State Bar Assn. (mem. editl. bd. 1993-97, internat. property sec., 1999-) Republican. Roman Catholic. Avocations: film, music, games, puzzles. Office: Graham & Dunn 2801 Alaskan Way Seattle WA 98121-1128 E-mail: rcumbow@grahamdunn.com.

CUMIFORD, WILLIAM LLOYD, historian, educator, curator; b. Ponca City, Okla., Jan. 23, 1942; s. Lloyd Leon and Thelma Louise Cumiford; divorced; 1 child, Senta Simone. AA, Harbor Coll., Wilmington, Calif., 1962; BA, Chapman Coll., Orange, Calif., 1963; MA, Calif. State U., Fullerton, 1969; PhD, Tex. Tech. U., Lubbock, 1977. Instr. Chapman Coll. World Campus, Orange, Calif., 1965—66, Tex. Tech. U., Lubbock, Tex., 1969—75, project dir., 1976—78; assoc. prof. of history Western Tex. Coll., Snyder, 1978—80; lectr, Calif. State U., Fullerton, 1981—84; curator LA County Mus. of Natural History, LA, 1984—91; assoc. prof. of history Chapman U., Orange, 1993—. Editor: (jour.) West Tex. Historian, 1972—73, (books) A Pictorial History of Lubbock, Tex., 1976, New Mex. Engring. Sites. With U.S. Army, 1966—68, Germany. Grantee fgn. study grant, Tex. Tech. U., 1974. Mem.: Assn. of Third World Studies, Am. Hist. Assn. Green Party. Disciples Of Christ. Avocations: hiking, tennis, bicycling, horseback riding. Home: #3 935 West 18th St San Pedro CA 90731 Office: Chapman Univ One University Dr Orange CA 92866 Office Fax: 714-532-6079. Business E-Mail: cumiford@chapman. edu.

CUMISKEY, GERALD JOHN, radio communications technician; b. Cleve., Aug. 25, 1928; BA in Physics, SUNY, Plattsburgh, 1987. Enlisted USAF, 1951, advanced through grades to master sgt., 1970, radio comm. mechanic, 1951-77; ret., 1977; electronic technician U.S. Postal Svc., Plattsburgh, N.Y., 1989—. Past scout master, Adirondack Coun., Boy Scouts Am. Recipient Vigil honor, 1976, Silver Beaver award, 1992, Boy Scouts Am., Plattsburgh. Mem. Am. Inst. Physics, Math. Assn. Am., Order of the Arrow (Boy Scouts Am.). Republican. Roman Catholic. Home: 41 Golden Rd West Chazy NY 12992-2204

CUMMING, DOUGLAS O. journalist, educator; b. Augusta, Ga., July 5, 1951; s. Joseph Bryan and Emily (Wright) Cumming; m. Elizabeth Waring, Nov. 20, 1982; children: Daniel, William, Sarah. Student, Fla. Presbyn. Coll., St. Petersburg, 1969—71; BA, Bennington Coll., Vt., 1974; MA, Brown U., Providence, 1980; PhD, U. N.C., 2002. Reporter The News & Observer, Raleigh, NC, 1974—76; staff reporter Providence Jour.-Bull., 1976—88, Sun. mag. editor, 1988—89; sr. editor features Southpoint Mag., Atlanta, 1989—90; staff writer, asst. metro editor Atlanta Jour.-Constn., 1990—2000; asst. prof. journalism Loyola U., New Orleans, 2002—03, Washington and Lee U., Lexington, Va., 2003—. Co-author: (book of poetry) The Family Secret, 1982 (Dixie Coun. of Authors and Journalists award, 1983). Recipient George Polk award, L.I. U., 1982; fellow Nieman fellow, Harvard U., 1986—87, Freedom Forum fellow, Freedom Found., U. NC, 2000—02. Episcopalian. Office: Washington and Lee Univ Dept Journalism Reid Hall W&L Lexington VA 24450-0303

CUMMING, MARILEE, apparel company executive; b. Columbus, Nebr. m. Andrew Cumming; 1 child, Melissa. BA in Psychology, Rosemont Coll., 1969. Buyer trainee children's divsn. J.C. Penney, Inc., N.Y.C., 1975, asst. and assoc. buyer positions in children's and women's, 1975-82, catalog dress buyer, 1982-84, sr. buyer misses blouses, 1984-86, merchandise mgr. men's accessories and furnishings, 1986-87, merchandise mgr. women's, misses and updated apparel, 1987-90, dir. women's merchandise dept., 1990, dir. merchandising women's divsn., 1990-93, pres. home and leisure divsn., 1993-96, pres. women's apparel divsn., 1996-99; pres. merchandising J.C. Penney Stores and Catalog, 1999—. Co-chmn. nat. campaign March of Dimes, 1999—2000; bus. ethics com. J.C. Penney, supplier diversity com. Campaign vice chmn. Met. Dallas United Way Campaign, 1996; mem. NWCA N.Y., Acad. Women Achievers; adv. bd. Women's Ctr. U. Tex., 1999—2000; steering com. Dallas Mother of Yr. Luncheon. Avocations: health and fitness, family activities. Office: JC Penney Co Inc 6501 Legacy Dr Plano TX 75024-3698

CUMMING, PATRICIA A. writer; b. N.Y.C., Sept. 7, 1932; d. Egmont Arens and Camille Davied Rose; m. Edward Chandler Cumming, July 6, 1954 (dec. Feb. 6, 1960); children: Julie Emelyn, Susanna Arens. BA magna cum laude, Radcliffe/Harvard, 1954; MA, Middlebury U., 1956. Editl. assoc. Deadalus, Cambridge, Mass., 1966—69; assoc. prof. MIT, Cambridge, 1969—79. Mem. adv. bd. Sojourner, Cambridge, 1976—79; guest faculty Sarah Lawrence Coll., Bronxville, NY, 1988; vis. asst. prof. Wheaton Coll., Norton, Mass., 1988—96. Author: Afterwards, 1974, Letter from an Out-lying Province, 1976. Recipient grant-in-aid, St. Botolph Club Found., Cambridge, 1996. Mem.: Phi Beta Kappa. Home: PO Box 251 Adamsville RI 02801

CUMMING, ROBERT EMIL, editor, writer; b. Lincoln, Nebr., June 2, 1933; s. Eugene Earl and Christiana (Jensen) C. Student, U. Nebr., 1955; Music Ed. (Presser Found. scholar), Nebr. Wesleyan U., 1956. With Music Jour. mag., N.Y.C., 1958-75, editor in chief, 1964-75; with Weekly Reader Corp. (formerly Xerox Edn. Publs. and Field Publs.), 1977-97; founder, pres. Conn. Singers Agy., 1997—. Theater editor Middlesex mag., 1995—, The Trumpeter, 1997—, critic Hometown News Pubs., 1999—; critic, condr., singer, stage dir. Village Light Opera Group, Hunter Coll., N.Y.C., Cmty. Opera, Little Orch. Soc.; founder-mem. Singing Editors, nationally concertized, 1974-76; toured U.S. and Can. as stage dir. Naughty Marietta, Little Orch. Concerts, 1976; compiler, editor: The Power of Music by Dmitri Shostakovich, 1968, They Talk About Music, 1971-72; editor Spl. Librs. Assn. Bull., Publ. Divsn., 1989—, Life is a Poem, 1999; composer children's operettas Rumplestiltskin, 1952, Song of Andorra, 1953; songs: God Is My Salvation, 1954, How Sly, 1954, Ya Gotta Have Love, 1955, The Hills of Sand, 1969; ann. music report for Living History of the World, 1967-68; contbr. articles to profl. jours. Mem. East Haddam Hist. Soc., 1977—, pres., 1998—; bd. dirs. East Lyme Arts Coun., 1990—93, U. Conn. Gilbert and Sullivan Summer Prodns., 1985—88. Mem. N.Y. Gilbert and Sullivan Soc. (pres. 1967-69), Conn. Gilbert and Sullivan Soc. (founder, dir. 1980—), Conn. Sinfonia Soc. (founder), So. Conn. Libr. Coun. (bd. dirs. 1986-89). Episcopalian. Home: PO Box 196 East Haddam CT 06423-0196 Office: PO Box 294 Moodus CT 06469-0294 *I have developed an awareness of the need for: enough strength to overcome loneliness; enough ego to communicate well; enough vision to perceive the need; enough ambition to overcome laziness; enough drive to complete what is begun; enough compassion to wish to help others; enough insight to grow humility; enough talent to be grateful; enough intelligence to remain practical; enough wisdom to be open; enough sensitivity to be myself; enough pain to keep in balance; enough pleasure to retain my humor; enough culture to be knowing; enough honesty to admit ignorance; enough love to appreciate symbols; enough religion to sense God.*

CUMMING, THOMAS ALEXANDER, stock exchange executive; b. Toronto, Ont., Can., Oct. 14, 1937; s. Alison A. and Anne B. (Berry) C.; m. E. Mary Stevens, Mar. 12, 1965; children: Jennifer, Allison, Katy. BAS, U. Toronto, 1960. Registered profl. engr., Can. With Bank of Nova Scotia, 1965-88; spl. rep. Toronto, 1965-68; br. mgr. Dublin, Ireland, 1969-71, London, 1971-75; v.p. Calgary, Alta., Can., 1975-80; sr. v.p. Calgery, Alta., Can., 1980-85, Toronto, 1986-88; pres., CEO Alta. Stock Exchange, Calgary, 1988-99. Mem. coun. Power Pool of Alta; bd. dirs. Calgary Techs Inc., Pengrowth Corp., E-Tronics Inc. Bd. dirs. YMCA of Calgary Found. Mem. Assn. Profl. Engrs., Calgary C. of C. (pres. 1991), Calgary Golf and Country Club, Calgary Petroleum Club. Home and Office: 2906 10th St SW Calgary AB Canada T2T 3H2

CUMMINGS, CAROLE EDWARDS, retired special education educator; b. Dover, Ohio, June 17, 1942; d. John T. and Dorothy M. (Plotts) Edwards; children: Kimberly Cummings Wood, Rebecca Cummings. BS, Kent State U., 1964; MA, Ohio State U., 1986. Cert. elem. tchr., learning disabilities tchr., spl. edn. supervision., Ohio. Elem. tchr. Dover Pub. Schs., 1965-66, 70-71; mid. sch. tchr. South-Western City Schs., Grove City, Ohio, 1971-74, tutor, 1974-76; elem. and high sch. tutor Hamilton Local Sch., Columbus, Ohio, 1976-77, elem. tchr. learning disabilities, 1978-85; high sch. tchr. learning disabilities Southwest Licking Local Schs., Kirkersville, Ohio, 1985-86; cons. Cen. Ohio Spl. Edn. Regional Resource Ctr., Columbus, 1987-91, Lincoln Way Spl. Edn. Regional Resource Ctr., Louisville, Ohio, 1991-93; supr. Stark County Sch. Dist., Canton, Ohio, 1993—2000; prof. Kent State U., 2001—. Mem. Coun. for Exceptional Children, Coun. for Adminstrs. Spl. Edn., DAR, Order Ea. Star, Phi Delta Kappa.

CUMMINGS, DAROLD BERNARD, aircraft engineer; b. Batavia, N.Y., June 27, 1944; s. Bernard Laverne and Doris Helen (Klotzbach) C.; children from a previous marrage: Carla, Bret; m. Karen Jean Cacciola, Dec. 19, 1992; children: Kyle, Scott. BS in Indsl. Design, Calif. State U., Long Beach, 1967. Engr. aircraft design Rockwell Internat., L.A., 1967-82; chief engr. Boeing, Long Beach, Calif., 1988—; chief designer advanced design Northrop Corp., Hawthorne, Calif., 1982-88. Lectr. Calif. State U., Long Beach, 1969-73; pres. Matrix Design, Hawthorne, 1967—; tech. fellow Boeing, 1997. Author: What Not to Name Your Baby, 1982; cons., actor (movie) Search for Solutions, 1979; multiple patents in field. Mem. AIAA, Air Force Assn. Republican. Avocations: motorcycle speed record racing, hunting. Home: 5320 W 124th Pl Hawthorne CA 90250-4154 Office: Boeing Long Beach CA 90807

CUMMINGS, DAVID WILLIAM, artist, educator; b. Okmulgee, Okla., July 15, 1937; s. Harold Raymond and Mildred Delores (Smith) C.; m. Marcia Mills Laging, June 20, 1964 (div. 1970); m. Beatrice M. Mady, Oct. 2, 1981. BFA, Kansas City Art Inst., 1963; MFA, U. Nebr., 1967. Prof. SUNY, New Paltz, 1964-70; adj. instr. Wagner Coll., S.I., N.Y., 1970-71; prof. CUNY, 1971-89; adj. prof. St. Peter's Coll., Jersey City, 1985—. Vis. prof. NYU, 1980-82, SUNY, Purchase, 1984, Rochester (N.Y.) Inst. Tech., 1983, U. N.D., Grand Forks, 1982, Colo. Mountain Coll., Vail, 1975-84. One-man shows include Katz Galleries, N.Y.C., 1970, Henri Gallery, Washington, 1969-70, Allan Stone Gallery, N.Y.C., 1974-77, Gallery Alexandra Monett, Brussels, 1975, 77, 78, Sebastian/Moore Gallery, Denver, 1978, Ericson Gallery, N.Y.C., 1981, U. N.D., Grand Forks, 1981, Shahin Requicha Gallery, Rochester, N.Y., 1983, La Petite Galeria, Bayonne, N.J., 1986, Gallery Jupiter, Little Silver, N.J., 1987, A.M.B. Galleries, Hoboken, N.J., Cabrillo Coll. Gallery, Aptos, Calif., 1991, Clin. Ctr. Galleries, NIH, Bethesda, Md., 1993, Rabbet Gallery, New Brunswick, N.J., 1996, St. John's U., Jamaica, N.Y., 1999, Johnson and Johnson Galleries, New Bruswick, N.J., 2001. Served with U.S. Army, 1957-59. Wood Found. fellow, 1966-67, N.J. State Coun. of Arts fellow, 1985, 91; Ford Found. grantee, 1963.

CUMMINGS, ELIJAH E. congressman; b. Balt., Jan. 18, 1951; BS, Howard U., 1973; JD, U. Md., 1976. Bar: Md. 1976. Atty. Md. Gen. Assembly, 1982; mem. Md. Ho. of Dels., Annapolis, 1983—96, vice chmn. constl. and adminstrv. law com., 1987—96, chmn. com. econ. devel., 1996, vice chmn. house econ. matters com., 1994—96, speaker pro tempore, 1995—96; mem. transp. subcom. for coast guard and maritime transp., mem. transp. subcom. for water resources and environ. 104th-108th Congress from 7th Md. dist., 1996—; mem. govt. reform com. and transp. infrastructure com. Chmn. Md. Legis. Black Caucus; chmn. Gov.'s Commn. on Black Males, 1990—; pres. Bancroft Lit. Soc., Congressional Black Caucus Found. (first vice chmn., bd. dirs., now chair) 1998, chmn., 2003-. Named Outstanding U.S. Student Govt. Leader Royal Arts Soc. of London. Mem. Md. Bar Assn. Democrat. Office: 1632 Longworth Ho Office Bldg Washington DC 20515-2007

CUMMINGS, ERIKA HELGA, business consultant; b. Offenbach, Germany; came to U.S., 1978; d. Erwin and Edith (Trunski) Maier; 1 child, Marisa Anne. BSBA, Calif. State U., Bakersfield; MBA in Internat. Mgmt., Am. Grad. Sch. Internat. Mgmt., Glendale, Ariz., 1983. Inflight supr. TWA, Paris; internat. ops. mgr. Cooper LaserSonics, Santa Clara, Calif., 1983-85; bus. cons. Suncoast Bus. Industries, Sarasota, Fla., 1985-89; cert. fin. planner Am. Express Fin. Advisors, Sarasota, 1989-94; Peace Corps. vol. City Adminstrn. of Vladimir, Russia, 1994-96; internat. cons. Solutions Internat., Sarasota, Fla., 1996—. Mem. Toastmasters, Beta Gamma Sigma. Avocations: travel, tennis, reading, langs. E-mail: ericum@aol.com.

CUMMINGS, ERWIN KARL, information technology executive; b. Toledo, June 19, 1954; s. Idell and Mae Sue (Jones) C. AS in Electronic Engring., U. Toledo, 1976, BS in Bus. Svcs., 1981; postgrad., Bowling Green State U., 1990-96. Computer ops. analyst Owens-Ill. Inc., Toledo, 1972-73, telecomms. analyst, 1975-78, ops. and planning analyst, 1978-81, software systems analyst, 1981-83, sr. data comms. analyst, 1983-86, lead data comms. analyst, 1986-89, mgr. voice and data comms., 1989-97, mgr. infrastructure and comms., 1997—. Pres. Christian Youth Fellowship, Phillips Temple, 1971-72, young adult tchr., 1971-79, supt. Sunday sch., 1979-81, steward, 1982-2000, asst. supt., 1983-87, sec. steward bd., 1983-93, head basketball coach, 1986-87, chmn. budget com., 1988-89; bd. dirs. Rosa Morgan Enrichment Ctr., 1988-92, chmn. fin. com., 1989-92, treas., 1990-92; mem. Christian Appalachian Project, 1989—. Mem. NAACP (life), DAV (Comdrs. Club 1985—), YMCA Century Club, Nat. Assn. Systems Programmers, Black Data Processing Assocs., Sacred Heart Automobile League, TV30/FM91, United Way Comdrs. Club, Handymen of Am. Club (life), Quiet Storm Skating Club. Democrat. Methodist. Avocations: personal computing, roller skating, basketball, bicycling, bowling. Home: 1180 Bernath Pky Toledo OH 43615-6742 Office: Owens-Ill Inc 1 Seagate Toledo OH 43604-1558

CUMMINGS, FRANK, lawyer; b. N.Y.C., Dec. 11, 1929; s. Louis and Florence (Levine) Cummings; m. Jill Schwartz, July 6, 1958; children: Peter Ian, Margaret Anne. BA, Hobart Coll., 1951; MA, Columbia U., 1955, LLB, 1958. Bar: N.Y. 1959, D.C. 1963. Adminstrv. asst. to U.S. Senator Jacob Javits, 1969-71; minority counsel com. labor and pub. welfare U.S. Senate, Washington, 1965-67, 71-72; assoc. Cravath, Swaine & Moore, N.Y.C., 1958-63, Gall, Lane & Powell, Washington, 1967-68, ptnr., 1972-75, Marshall, Bratter, Greene, Allison & Tucker, Washington, 1976-85, Nossaman, Keurger & Knox, 1982-83, Cummings & Cummings, P.C. and predecessor firm, 1983-86, LeBoeuf, Lamb, Greene & MacRae, LLP, Washington, 1986-2000, of counsel, 2000—. Lectr. law Columbia U. Law Sch., 1970-74, U. Va. Sch. Law, 2000—; adj. prof. Georgetown U. Law Sch., 1983-86; chmn. Am. Law Inst.-ABA Ann. Course Employee Benefits Litigation, 1989—, Employment and Labor Rels. Law for Corp. Coun. and Gen. Practitioner, 1978—; mem. pub. adv. coun. employee welfare and pension benefit plans Dept. Labor, 1972-74; mem. adv. bd. Pension Reporter Bur. Nat. Affairs. Author: Capitol Hill Manual, 1976, Capitol Hill Manual, 2d edit., 1984, Pension Plan Terminations-Single Employer Plans, 3rd edit., 2002, Multiemployer Plans, 2d edit., 1986; articles editor: Columbia U. Law Rev., 1957—58. Fellow Am. Coll. Employee Benefits Counsel; mem. ABA (chmn. com. pension, welfare and related plans 1976-79), Am. Law Inst. (advisor to restatement of employment law 2002—), Bar Assn. D.C. (chmn. com. labor rels. law 1972-73), Cosmos Club, Phi Beta Kappa. Office: LeBoeuf Lamb Greene & MacRae LLP 1875 Connecticut Ave NW Washington DC 20009-5728 Home: 800 25th St NW Washington DC 20037 E-mail: fcumming@llgm.com.

CUMMINGS, FREDERIC ALAN, lawyer; b. Mobile, Ala., Sept. 5, 1944; s. J. V. and Alice Cummings; children: Christian Gordon, Sara Elise, Alice Kate Griffith, James Cale, Camille Pichard. BS in Econs., Auburn U., 1967; JD, Fla. State U., 1975. Bar: Fla. 1976, U.S. Ct. Appeals (11th cir.), U.S. Dist. Ct. (mid. and no. dists.) Fla. Ptnr. Holland & Knight, Tallahassee, 1975-86, Cummings, Lawrence & Vezina PA, Tallahassee, 1986-97, Cummings & Snyder PA, Tallahassee, 1997-2000, Smith, Currie & Hancock LLP, Tallahassee, 2001—. Office: Smith Currie & Hancock LLP PO Box 589 Tallahassee FL 32302-0589

CUMMINGS, GERARDO TONATIUH, literature educator, researcher; b. Acapulco, Guerrero, Mexico, Mar. 6, 1970; s. James Edward Cummings and Yolanda Bertha Rendón. BA, Wayne State U., Detroit, 1995, MA, 1997, PhD, 2003. Grad. tchg. asst. Wayne State U., Detroit, 1995—2000, adj. faculty, 2000—01; vis. prof. Spanish peninsular lit. and film Cleve. State U., 2002—. Author numerous poems. Bd. dirs. Coll. Liberal Arts Alumni Assn. Wayne State U., Detroit, 2002. The King-Chavez-Parks Future Faculty Fellowship, The State of Mich., 2001—03, Grad. Tchg. Assistantship, The Grad. Sch. at Wayne State U., 1995—2000. Mem.: MLA (assoc.). Home: 1700 E 13th St Apt # 20XE Cleveland OH 44114 Office: Cleve State U 2121 Euclid Ave RT 1619 Cleveland OH 44115 Personal E-mail: gerardincummings@netscape.net. E-mail: g.t.cummings@csuohio.edu.

CUMMINGS, JAMES WILLIAM, poet; b. Bangor, Maine, Mar. 9, 1960; s. Donald Ernest and Marjorie May (Condon) C. Grad., Nokomis Regional H.S., Newport, Maine, 1978. With Cianbro Corp., Pittsfield, Maine, 1979, Stinson Seafood Co., Belfast, Maine, 1987—2001, Little River Apparel, 2001—. Contbg. author (book anthology) Treasured Poems of America, 1990—92, Memories of Tomorrow, 2000; contbr. Maine Genealogist; author: (song anthology) Stars and Stripes, 1991; songwriter See You that Manger, After the Storm, Lights of the City, creator audiotape (poetry) Caliburn, A Sidney Family, A Death in Loudon, 2000, A Respectable Man: Captain Abiel Lovejoy, 2001; author: For My Grandmother's Hundredth Birthday, 2002, Visions of the Maine Coast, 2002, The Brothers Maguire, 2003 (named Poet of Merit, 2003, Understanding Achievement in Poetry award, 2003); pub. poems Poetry.com; author: Ode to the Muses", 2003; included in: poetry anthologies. Mem.: Libr. of Congress (charter), Smithsonian Instn., Poetry Guild, Sparrowgrass Poetry Forum, Internat. Soc. of Poets (various anthologies 1993—), History Channel Club. Home: 56 Masonic Rd Dixmont ME 04932-3543 E-mail: jwc1870@aol.com.

CUMMINGS, JOHN PATRICK, lawyer; b. Westfield, Mass., June 28, 1933; s. Daniel Thoams and Nora (Brick) C.; m. Dorothy June D'Ingianni, Dec. 27, 1957 (div. May 1978); children: John Patrick, Mary Catherine, Michael Brick, Kevin Andrew, Colleen Elise, Erin Christine, Christopher Gerald; m. Marilyn Ann Welch, May 23, 1980. BS, St. Michael's Coll., 1955; PhD, U. Tex., 1969; JD, U. Toledo, 1973, MCE, 1977. Bar: Ohio 1973, U.S. Mil. Appeals 1974, U.S. Dist. Ct. (no. dist.) Ohio 1979. Mgr. Hamilton Mgmt., Inc., Austin, Tex., 1962-68; scientist Owens Ill., Toledo, 1968-73, risk mgr., 1974-76, staff atty., 1977-80, mgr. legis. affairs, 1981-84; pres. Hansa World Cargo Svc., Inc., Oakland, Calif., 1984-86; in-house counsel Brown Vence & Assocs., San Francisco, 1987-88; gen. counsel Pacific Mgmt. Co., Sacramento, 1986-88; pres. John P. Cummings & Assoc., Fremont, Calif., 1988—. Cons. Glass Packaging Inst., Washington, 1970-83, EPA, Washington, 1970-74. Contbr. articles to profl. jours.; patentee in field. With USAF, 1955-62, 68-69, 75-76, 84-85, col. ret. 1986. USPHS fellow, 1963-66. Fellow Royal Chem. Soc.; mem. ABA, VFW, ASTM (chmn. 1979), Am. Ceramic Soc. (chpt. chmn. 1973), Am. Indsl. Hygiene Assn., Am. Chem. Soc., Res. Officers Assn. (legis. chmn. 1979-85), Am. Legion, KC (4th degree), Amvets. Roman Catholic. Avocations: reading, travel, coin and stamp collecting. Home: 843 Barcelona Dr Fremont CA 94536-2607 Office: PO Box 2847 Fremont CA 94536-0847 E-mail: epigeneint@aol.com.

CUMMINGS, JOHN WILLIAM, JR., logistician, systems analyst; b. Washington, Apr. 5, 1942; s. John William Sr. and Helen Gerhold (Schanberger) C.; m. Carol Fron King, July 12, 1964; children: Kathleen Ellen Cummings Maloney, Eizabeth Nan Cummings MacBride, Abigail Helen Cummings Sidell, John William III. BA, Am. U., 1964; MA, U. N.Mex., 1971. Ordained elder, Sunday Sch. supt. Presbyn. Ch. Commd. 2d lt. USAF, 1964, advanced through grades to lt. col., 1980, dep. sys. program mgr., 1984-87; ret., 1987; sys. simulation mgr. Riverside Rsch. Inst., Arlington, Va., 1987-92; mem. tech. staff Analytic Scis. Corp., Arlington, 1992; missile def. program mgr. Dynamics Rsch. Corp., Arlington, 1992—. Asst. editor Logistics Spectrum, 1996-2000; contbr. articles to profl. jours. Mem. AIAA, Soc. Logistics Engrs. (sr.; chpt. vice chair, Pres.'s award 1996), Air Force Assn., VFW, Ret. Officers Assn. Republican. Avocations: sunday school teaching and administration, gardening. Home: 17006 Horn Point Dr Gaithersburg MD 20878-2086 Office: Dynamics Rsch Corp 1755 Jefferson Davis Hwy Arlington VA 22202-3509

CUMMINGS, JOSEPHINE ANNA, writer, consultant, advertising executive; b. Gainesville, Fla., July 12, 1949; d. Robert Jay and Marcella Dee (Mount) Cummings. ABJ./Design cum laude, U. Ga., Athens, 1971; MA, NYU, 1999. Copywriter William Cook, Jacksonville, Fla., 1971-73; creative dir. Leo Burnett, Chgo., 1973-76; sr. v.p., group creative dir. D. D. B. Needham, Chgo., 1976-84; sr. v.p., creative dir. Saatchi-Saatchi, N.Y.C., 1984; sr. v.p., sr. creative dir. Ted Bates, N.Y.C., 1984; exec. v.p., chief creative officer Tracy-Locke, Dallas, 1985-87; exec. v.p., exec. creative dir. Bozell, Chgo, 1989; exec. v.p., creative dir. Y&R, N.Y.C., 1990-92; pres. The Joey Co., N.Y.C., 1992—. Author: (play) Azaleas, 1988, (short story collection) Crimes of Passion, 1988, (childrens' book) The Hospital is a Funny Place, 1988, (short film) Night Magic, 1989. Named as creator One of Hundred Best TV Commls. Advt. Age, 1978-79, one of Advt. 100 Best Advt. Age, 1986, one of People to Watch Fortune mag., 1986, Ad Age one of Best and Brightest, N.Y. Mem. Amelia Earhard, Ninety Niners Club, N.Y. Women in Film. Avocations: reading, writing, juggling. Office: The Joey Co Ste 656S 55 Washington St Brooklyn NY 11201

CUMMINGS, K. MICHAEL, research scientist; b. Syracuse, N.Y., Sept. 25, 1953; s. C. Kenneth and Catherine Cummings; m. Susan J. Johnson, Aug. 23, 1975; children: Michael A, Timothy K, Nicholas S. PhD, U. Mich., 1980. Asst. prof. Wayne State U., Detroit, 1979—81; rsch. scientist Roswell Pk. Cancer Inst., Buffalo, 1981—. Dep. editor Tobacco Control, London, 1997—; expert witness Tobacco Litig., 1997—. Contbr. articles various profl. jours. Med. adv. com. Flight Attendant Med. Rsch. Found., Miami, Fla., 2000—02. Recipient Outstanding Rsch. Scientist award, Roswell Pk. Cancer Inst., 1999, Joseph Cullen Tobacco Scientist award, Am. Soc. of Preventive Oncology, 2003; grantee Rsch. grants, NIH, 1980-2002, Robert Wood Johnson Found., 1980—2000, Am. Legacy Found., 1980—2000. Achievements include research in studies on tobacco product marketing and consumer risk perceptions. Avocations: tennis, reading. Office: Roswell Park Cancer Inst Elm & Carlton Strs Buffalo NY 14263 Office Fax: 716-845-8487. E-mail: michael.cummings@roswellpark.org.

CUMMINGS, KENNETH ILA, coroner, medical examiner; b. Athens, La., Mar. 14, 1936; s. Otto L. and Idelle (James) C.; m. (div. 1981); children: Alison, Courtney, Kurt, Emily; m. Sandra Tipton Gamble, July 2000. BS in Liberal Arts, La. Tech. U., 1958; MD, La. State U., New Orleans, 1962; M in Dermatology, Tulane U., 1966. Diplomate Am. Acad. Dermatology. Intern Confederate Meml. Med. Ctr., Shreveport, La., 1962-63; resident Tulane U. Charity Hosp. of La., New Orleans, 1963-66; chief resident dermatology La. State U. Sch. Med., New Orleans, 1965-66; clin. prof. dermatology La. State U. Med. Sch., Shreveport, 1968-87; chief resident dermatology Tulane U. Med. Sch., New Orleans, 1965-66, Charity Hosp. La., New Orleans, 1965-66; instr. U.S. Naval Aerospace Med. Inst., Pensacola, Fla., 1966-68; pvt. practice Shreveport, La., 1968-87; coroner, med. examiner Bienville Parish, Arcadia, La., 1987-96. Fed. referee disability cases U.S. Govt., Shreveport, 1972—. Author: (novel) Poppies in the Field, 1998, Next to Nod, 2000; contbr. articles to profl. jours. Lt. comdr. USNR, 1966-68. Recipient Award for Surg. Treatment for Baldness Tex. Med. Assn., 1967, Peterkin prize La. Dermatol. Soc., 1966. Mem. SAG, Am. Acad. Dermatology, La. State Med. Soc., Shreveport Med. Soc., La. Coroners Assn., Screen Writers Guild. Democrat. Episcopalian. Avocations: nusmismatics, fiction writing, movie acting, freelance work. Home: 3072 Hazel St Arcadia LA 71001-4100 E-mail: cumm3399@bellsouth.net.

CUMMINGS, KEVIN BRYAN, minister; b. Lake Charles, La., Dec. 8, 1967; s. Kenneth Richard and Sharon Elaine (Kinchen) C.; m. Terri Lynn Pickering, June 11, 1988; children: Brent Andrew, Ashley Lynn. BS cum laude, Liberty U., 1989; M in Bibl. Sci., Phila. Coll. Bible, 1995. Ordained to ministry Bapt. Ch., 1989. Camp counselor Milldale Bapt. Teen Retreat, Zachary, La., 1985-86; youth pastor Tamuning (Guam) Bapt. Ch., 1986-87; dir. campus club Thomas Rd. Bapt. Ch., Lynchburg, Va., 1987-88; youth worker Temple Bapt. Ch., Madison Heights, Va., 1988-89; pastor youth and Christian edn. Ch. of the Open Door, Ft. Washington, Pa., 1989-93; asst. pastor Second Cape May Bapt. Ch., Marmora, N.J., 1993-97; sr. pastor Fincastle (Va.) Bapt. Ch., 1997—. Republican. Office: Fincastle Bapt Ch PO Box 707 Fincastle VA 24090-0707 *When all you can do is pray, you have done all you can do!.*

CUMMINGS, MARTIN MARC, medical educator, physician, scientific administrator; b. Camden, N.J., Sept. 7, 1920; s. Samuel and Cecelia (Silverman) C.; m. Arlene Sally Avrutine, Sept. 27, 1942; children: Marc Steven, Lee Bernard, Stuart Lewis. BS, Bucknell U., 1941, DS., 1969; MD, Duke U., 1944; DHL (hon.), Georgetown U., 1971; DS. (hon.), Duke U., 1985; DSc, U. Nebr., Emory U.; MD (hon.), Karolinska Inst., 1972; MD (hon.), U. Lvov, 1975; DHL, Georgetown U., 1976. Diplomate Am. Bd. Microbiology. Intern, resident Boston Marine Hosp., 1944—46; resident Tb Grasslands Hosp., Valhalla, NY, 1946—47; dir. Tb evaluation lab. Communicable Disease Ctr., USPHS, Atlanta, 1947—49; instr. medicine Emory U. Sch. Medicine, 1948—50, assoc. medicine, 1950—52, asst. prof., 1953; chief Tb sect., also dir. Tb rsch. lab. VA Hosp., Atlanta, 1949—53; dir. rsch. svcs. VA Cen. Office, Washington, 1953—59; prof. microbiology, chmn. dept. Okla. U. Sch. Medicine, 1959—61; chief Office Internat. Rsch., NIH, USPHS, 1961—63; dir. Nat. Libr. of Medicine, 1964—84, dir. emeritus, 1984—; cons. Coun. on Libr. Resources, 1984—, chmn., bd. dirs., 1994—96. Assoc. dir. for rsch. grants NIH, 1963-64; chmn. com. med. rsch. Nat. Tb Assn., 1958-59; chmn. panel Sarcoidosis NRC-Nat. Acad. Scis., 1958-60; dist. prof. cmty. medicine Georgetown U. Sch. Medicine, 1986-90. Author: (with Dr. H.S. Willis) Diagnostic and Experimental Methods in Tuberculosis, 1952, The Economics of Research Libraries, 1986; contbr. chpt. on Tubercle Bacilli, Diagnostic Procedures and Reagents, 1950; editor: Influencing Change in Research Libraries, 1989. Served with AUS, 1943-44. Served with AUS, 1943—44. Recipient Exceptional Svc. award VA, 1959; Disting. Svc. award HEW, 1968; Rockefeller Pub. Svc. award, 1973; Disting. Achievement award Modern Medicine, 1976; Disting. Svc. award Am. Coll. Cardiology, 1978; John C. Leonard award Assn. Hosp. Med. Edn., 1979. Fellow AAAS (dir.), Royal Soc. Medicine, Med. Libr. Assn., N.Y. Acad. Medicine (hon.), Phila. Coll. Physicians; mem. Am. Soc. Clin. Investigation (sr. mem.), Am. Fedn. Clin. Rsch., Inst. Medicine, Nat. Acad. Scis. Home: 700 John Ringling Blvd Apt 1407 Sarasota FL 34236-1555 E-mail: martincummings@comcast.net.

CUMMINGS, NICHOLAS ANDREW, psychologist; b. Salinas, Calif., July 25, 1924; s. Andrew and Urania (Sims) C.; m. Dorothy Mills, Feb. 5, 1948; children: Janet Lynn, Andrew Mark. AB, U. Calif., Berkeley, 1948; MA, Claremont Grad. Sch., 1954; PhD, Adelphi U., 1958. Chief psychologist Kaiser Permanente No. Calif., San Francisco, 1959-76; pres. Found Behavioral Health, San Francisco, 1976—; chmn., CEO Am. Biodyne, Inc., San Francisco, 1985-93, Kendron Internat., Ltd., Reno, Nev., 1992-95; chmn. Nicholas & Dorothy Cummings Found., Reno, 1994—; chmn., pres. U.K. Behavioural Health, Ltd., London, 1996-98; Disting. prof. U. Nev., 1997—; chmn., CEO DynaMed Integrated Care, Inc., 1998—. Co-dir. South San Francisco Health Ctr., 1959-75; pres. Calif. Sch. Profl. Psychology, L.A., San Francisco, San Diego, Fresno campuses, 1969-76; chmn. bd. Calif. Cmty. Mental Health Ctrs., Inc., L.A., San Diego, San Francisco, 1975-77; pres. Blue Psi, Inc., San Francisco, 1972-80, Inst. for Psychosocial Interaction, 1980-84; mem. mental health adv. bd. City and County San Francisco, 1968-75; bd. dirs. San Francisco Assn. Mental Health, 1965-75; pres., chmn. bd. Psycho-Social Inst., 1972-80; dir. Mental Rsch. Inst., Palo Alto, Calif., 1979-80; pres. Nat. Acads. of Practice, 1981-93. Served with U.S. Army, 1944-46. Fellow APA (dir. 1975-81, pres. 1979); mem. Calif. Psychol. Assn. (pres. 1968). Office: Nicholas & Dorothy Cummings Found 561 Keystone Ave PMB 212 Reno NV 89503-4331

CUMMINGS, RICHARD J. retired otologist; b. Topeka, Nov. 18, 1932; s. John Edward and Mary J. (Harrington) C.; m. Laura Roberta Herring, Dec. 21, 1956; children: Thomas, Anne, William, John. BA, U. Kans., 1954, MD, 1957; LLD, Newman U., 2000. Intern St. Benedict Hosp., Ogden, Utah, 1957-58; resident U. Okla. Med. Ctr., Oklahoma City, 1959-62; practice medicine specializing in ear, nose, throat Colorado Springs Med. Clinic, Colo., 1961-62; practice medicine specializing in otology Wichita (Kans.) Ear Clinic, 1962—2002. Clin. asst. prof. U. Kans. Sch. Medicine; pres. med. staff St. Francis Hosp., Wichita, 1974-75; mem. med. staff St. Joseph Hosp., Wichita, pres., 1990-91; host M.D. Radio program, Wichita, 1978-79. Contbr. articles to med. jours. Bd. dirs. Kans. State Bd. of Healing Arts, 1981-83, Kans. Commn. for Deaf and Hearing Impaired, 1988-91, Newman U., 1995—; mem. Kans. tissue transplantation com. ARC, 1990-94; chmn. St. Joseph Charity Classic Tournament, 1981; physician's group chmn. United Way Campaign, 1968, 69, 77, 84; mem. U. Kans. Athletic Bd., 1991-95. With USPHS, 1958-59. Fellow ACP, ACS, Am. Acad. Otolaryngology; mem. AMA, Am. Audiol. Soc., Kans. Med. Soc., Kans. Ear Nose Throat Soc. (pres. 1975), Wichita Surg. Soc. (pres. 1989), Sedgwick County Med. Soc. (pres. 1978), Otosclerosis Study Group, Hearing Conservation Assn., Pan Am. Soc. Otolaryngology, Wichita Cochlear Implant Program (bd. dirs.), Rotary (bd. dirs. Wichita chpt. 1978-79), U. Kans. Nat. Alumni Assn. (bd. dirs. 1979-84, vice chmn. 1994-95, chmn. 1995-96). Home: 1258 Burning Tree Dr Wichita KS 67230-1410

CUMMINGS, RICHARD M. law educator, consultant, writer; b. N.Y.C., Mar. 23, 1938; s. Albert Martin and Betty (Benjamin) Cohen; m. Mary Araminta Johnson, Aug. 3, 1965; children: Benjamin, Orson. AB, Princeton U., 1959; JD, Columbia U., 1962; MLitt, Cambridge (Eng.) U., 1964, PhD, 1989. Bar: N.Y. 1964, U.S. Dist. Ct. (so. dist.) N.Y. 1970. Assoc. Breed, Abbott & Morgan, N.Y., 1964-65; atty. adv. Agy. for Internat. Devel., 1965-66; asst. prof. U. Louisville Sch. Law, 1966-70; ptnr. Ross & Cummings, Southampton, N.Y., 1971-73; lectr. law U. W.I., Barbados, 1973-74; assoc. prof. SUNY, Stony Brook, 1974-77; legis. counsel N.Y. State Assembly, Albany, 1978-80; dir. natural resources Town of East Hampton, N.Y., 1981-82; ptnr. Richard Cummings, Sanford Katz, Ira Kornbluth, Attys.-at-Law, East Hampton, 1982—; of counsel Beatie & Osborn, N.Y.C. Vis. asst. prof. Haile Sellassie I U, Addis Ababa, Ethiopia, 1967-69; vis. assoc. prof. Southampton (N.Y.) Coll., 1970-71; adj. prof. Duke U., Durham, N.C., 1977—; polit. cons. Richard Cummings Comm., Bridgehampton, 1979—; prof. law Pace U., White Plains, N.Y., 1987-95. Author: Proposition 14, 1980; The Pied Piper, 1985, The Immortalists 2002. The Prince Must Dies (Gower Le Comfield pen name). 2003, Soccer Moms from Hell (play) 2003; editor: Nine Scorpions in a Bottle, 1995; contbr. articles to law jours.; polit. columnist East Hampton (N.Y.) Star, 1971-77. Committeeman Town Dem. Com., Southampton, 1971-73; del. Dem. Nat. Conv., Miami, Fla., 1972; chmn., N.Y. State campaign Terry Sanford for Pres., 1976; candidate for U.S. Congress, Suffolk County, N.Y., 1971, 1980. Recipient Buchanan Prize in politics Princeton U., 1959; grantee Albert and Bessie Warner Fund, Bridgehampton, 1974-82, N.Y. Coun. for Humanities, 1974-77; James Kent scholar Columbia U., 1962. Fellow Nat. Assn. Trial Lawyers (hon.); mem. Authors Guild, Am. Soc. Journalists and Authors,, PEN Am. Ctr. Home and Office: PO Box 349 Bridgehampton NY 11932-0349

CUMMINGS, RUSSELL MARK, aerospace engineer, educator; b. Santa Cruz, Calif., Oct. 3, 1955; s. Gilbert Warren and Anna Mae (Phillips) C. BS, Calif. Poly. State U., 1977, MS, 1985, BA, 1999; Engr. Aerospace Engring., 1982; PhD, U. So. Calif., 1988. Tech. staff Hughes Aircraft Co., Canoga Park, Calif., 1979-86; rsch. assoc. Nat. Rsch. Coun. at NASA Ames Rsch. Ctr., Moffett Field, Calif., 1988-90; prof. aerospace engring. Calif. Poly. State U., San Luis Obispo, Calif., 1986—. Dept. chmn. aero. engring. dept. Calif. Poly. State U., 1992-96; vis. acad. computing lab. Oxford U., 1995-97; Disting. vis. prof. aeronautics U.S. Air Force Acad., 2001-03; presenter in field. Assoc. editor: Jour. Spacecraft and Rockets, 1994—2003; contbr. chapters to books, over 25 articles to profl. jours. Hughes Engring. fellow 1980-84, Howard Hughes Doctoral fellow 1984-86, Boeing faculty summer fellow, 2000; NASA grantee, 1986-2000, Office Naval Rsch. grantee, 2002, NSF Panel Rev., 2002; recipient AIAA Nat. Faculty Advisor award, 1994, Northrop Grumman Excellence in Teaching and Applied Rsch. award, 1995, Undergraduate Faculty Advisor award BF Goodrich Nat. Collegiate Inventors Program, 1998, Excellence in Tchg. award TRW, 1999, Litton Excellence in Rsch. award, 2000, Sci. and Engring. award USAF, 2003. Fellow: AIAA (assoc.; missile sys. tech. com. 1988—91, student activities com. 1991—2002, chair 1999—2002); mem.: Aircraft Owners and Pilots Assn., Royal Aero Soc., Am. Soc. Engring. Educators, Sigma Gamma Tau, Sigma Xi. Republican. Mem. Evangelical Christian Ch. Avocations: piano, tennis, skiing, volleyball, baseball. Office: Calif Poly State U Dept Aero Engring San Luis Obispo CA 93407 E-mail: rcumming@calpoly.edu.

CUMMINGS, SEAN SPENCER, oil and gas industry executive; b. Oklahoma City, Okla., Feb. 20, 1959; s. Douglas Raymond and Peggy Jane C.; m. Terri Lynn Cummings, Apr. 8, 1989; 1 child, Sean Conor Spencer Cummings. BBA in Fin., Okla. U., 1982. Controller Kirkpatrick Supply, Oklahoma City, 1977-81; v.p. Cummings Oil Co., Oklahoma City, 1982-98, pres., 1999—; owner Seacon Energy LLC, Oklahoma City, 1982—; v.p. Seabrea Gas Systems, Inc., Oklahoma City, 1988—. Past pres. Big Bros./Big Sisters, Oklahoma City, 1985-94; Okla. Children's Health Found. (dir., pres. 1991—), Okla City YMCA (dir., vice chair 1996—); bd. dirs. Leadership OKC, Oklahoma City, 1992—. Mem. Okla. Ind. Petroleum Assn. (bd. dirs. 1996—), Petroleum Club of Oklahoma City (dir., pres. 1990-96). Avocation: golf. Office: Cummings Oil Company 4917 N Portland Ave Oklahoma City OK 73112-6113 E-mail: ssc@cummingsoil.com.

CUMMINGS, SHARON SUE, state extension service youth specialist; b. Trinidad, Colo., Aug. 26, 1945; d. James H. and Mima (McDonald) C. BS, Colo. State U., 1967, MEd, 1974; PhD, Ohio State U., 1991. Summer agt. Colo. State Coop. Extension, Canon City, 1966, extension home agt. Colo. Springs, 1967-68; county dir. Leadville, 1968-70; area extension home economist San Luis Valley, 1970-74; agt., home economist Castle Rock, 1974-80; specialist 4H youth Ft. Collins, 1980-89, '91—; grad. assoc. Ohio State U. Coop. Extension, Columbus, 1989-91. Co-author: National Ambassador Handbook, 1984; (curriculum for youth) over 20 pubs.; assoc. editor (newsletter) Youthoughts, 1990, '91. Com. mem. United Meth. Ch., Colo., 1975—. Recipient Agrl. Extension scholarship Ohio State U., 1991; spotlighted alumna Dept. Human Resources Colo. State U., 1985-86; 1 of 50 in U.S chosen for Exec. Devel. Inst. USDA Extension Svc., 1987-89. Mem. Nat. Assn. Extension 4-H Youth Agts. (pres. Colo. 1981-82), Colo. Home Econs. Assn. (treas. 1983-85), Colo. State U. Extension Specialist Assn. (pres. 1982-84), CERES (assoc., chpt. advisor 1983-85), Phi Kappa Phi, Gamma Sigma Delta (pres. 1999-2000), Epsilon Sigma Phi (pres. Colo. 1996-97). Avocations: reading, walking, working out, yard care S.W. history and lore. Office: Colo State U Coop Extension 127 Aylesworth NW Fort Collins CO 80523-0001

CUMMINGS, WILLIAM ROBERT, JR., business executive; b. Detroit, July 13, 1937; s. William Robert Sr. and Geraldine Alberta (Leffel) C.; children: William, Michael. B of Gen. Studies in Math., U. Nebr., 1970. Commd. 2nd lt. USAF, 1959, advanced through grades to lt. col., 1975, ret., 1978; owner Bill's Shell Svc., Ft. Wayne, Ind., 1980-97, Cummings Shell Svc., Ft. Wayne, 1980-96, Cummings Shell Svc. II, Ft. Wayne, 1993-97, ret., 1997. Bd. dirs., vice chmn. Northeastern Rural Electric Mgmt. Coop., Columbia City, 1986; bd. dirs. Wabash Valley Power Assn., Ind. State Assn. Electric Coop. Arbitrator Better Bus. Bur., Ft. Wayne; ward chmn. Rep. Party. Decorated Air medal with thirteen oak leaf clusters, Meritorious Svc. medal with oak leaf clusters, Cross of Gallantry with Palm. Mem. Air Force Assn. (life, state pres. Ind.), Order of Daedalians (life). Republican. Home: 12031 Mahogany Dr Fort Wayne IN 46814-4513 E-mail: jetbill37@cs.com.

CUMMINGS, WILLIAM ROGER, international tax consultant, property management executive; b. Apr. 30, 1946; BBA, U. Miami, 1968, LLM, 1973; JD, Suffolk U., 1968; MBA, Fla. Atlantic U., 1978. Pvt. practice internat. tax mgmt., Palm Beach, Fla., 1971—. Mem.: English Spkg. Union, Mensa, Palm Beach C. of C., Phi Delta Theta. Republican. Episcopalian. Office: PO Box 7 Palm Beach FL 33480-0007

CUMMINGS, WILLIAM STANLEY, real estate company executive; b. Somerville, Mass., Mar. 11, 1937; BS in Econs., Tufts U., 1958. With Vick Chem. Co., divsn. Richardson/Vicks Inc., Greensboro, N.C., 1958-61, Gortons of Gloucester, divsn. Pillsbury Co., Gloucester, Mass., 1961-64; founder, pres. Old Medford Foods, Inc., Medford, Mass., 1964—68; founder, chmn. bd. Cummings Properties LLC, Woburn, Mass., 1968—. Bd. dirs. Tanners Nat. Bank. Founder, former pub.: (comty. newspapers) The Woburn Advocate, Stoneham Sun, Winchester Town Crier, 1991-94; founder, pres. New Horizons Retirement Comtys., Woburn and Marlborough, Mass., 1990—; trustee emeritus Tufts U.; former overseer Tufts Med. Sch.; former mem., chair Winchester (Mass.) Planning Bd., 1986-89; dir. Winchester Hosp., 1979-82. Named Entrepreneur of Yr. for Real Estate in New Eng., Ernst & Young, LLP, 1998; recipient disting. svc. award Tufts U., 1998. Office: Cummings Properties LLC 200 W Cummings Park Woburn MA 01801-6396

CUMMINGS ROCKWELL, PATRICIA GUILBAULT, psychiatric nurse; b. Ludlow, Mass., June 22, 1939; d. Lee Allen and Mavis Isabella (White) Guilbault; m. Philip W. Cummings, Oct. 23, 1960 (dec. Jan. 1978); children: Sharon Ellen Timmons, Geoffrey Scott Cummings, Susan Mavis Lornitzo, Lee Millett Cummings, Mary Rockwell Thon; m. William Leonard Rockwell Jr., Aug. 18, 1990. ADN, Vt. Coll., 1982; BSN, Norwich U., 1987. RN, Vt. Staff nurse Ctrl. Vt. Hosp. Nursing Home, Berlin, 1982-84, 87—; staff psychiat. nurse Va. Hosp. Ground East, White River Junction, Vt., 1987-94; owner Globe Travel, Bradford, Vt., 1988-94; rschr. Norwich U., Northfield, Vt., 1988—. Nurse-entrepeneur Globe Travel, 1988—. Tchr. adult edn. ARC, Bradford, Vt., 1988, 89; dir. Vt. Lakes and Pond Assn.; v.p. Vale Hospice Internat.; dir. Fedn. Vt. Lakes and Ponds Inc. Mem. ANA (nat. and Vt. chpts.), AAUW, New Eng. Hist. Geneal. Soc. Avocations: writing, traveling, medical genealogy. Home: 307 Godfrey Rd East Thetford VT 05043-9517 E-mail: patsy@together.net., patsy@valehospice.org.

CUMMINS, CHARLES FITCH, JR., lawyer; b. Lansing, Mich., Aug. 19, 1939; s. Charles F. Sr. and Ruth M. Cummins; m. Anne Warner, Feb. 11, 1961; children: Michael, John, Mark. AB in Econs., U. Mich., 1961; LLB, U. Calif., Hastings, 1966. Bar: Calif. 1966, Mich. 1976. Assoc. Hall, Henry, Oliver & McReavy, San Francisco, 1966-70, ptnr., 1971-75, Cummins & Cummins, Lansing, Mich., 1976-82, Pitto & Ubhaus, San Jose, Calif., 1982-85; prin. Law Offices Charles F. Cummins Jr., San Jose, 1985-87; ptnr. Cummins & Chandler, San Jose, 1987-92; prin. Law Offices of Charles F. Cummins, Jr., San Jose, 1992—. Bd. dirs., officer various civic orgns., chs. and pvt. schs. Lt. (j.g.) USNR, 1961-63. Mem. Rotary. Office: 224 E Jackson St Ste B San Jose CA 95112 E-mail: cfclaw@ix.netcom.com.

CUMMINS, DAVID LOYAL, mission director; b. Detroit, Apr. 26, 1929; B Religious Edn., Tyndale Coll., 1955. Pastor Faith Baptist Ch., La Crosse, Wis., 1977—81, Warren, Mich., 1981—97; deputation dir. Baptist World Mission, Decatur, Ala., 1997—. Office: Baptist World Mission 811 Second Ave SE Decatur AL 35602

CUMMINS, DELMER DUANE, academic administrator, historian; b. Dawson, Nebr., June 4, 1935; s. Delmer H. and Ina Z. (Arnold) C.; m. Darla Sue Beard, Oct. 6, 1957; children: Stephen Duane, Cristi Sue, Caroline Renee. BS, Phillips U., Enid, Okla., 1957; MA, U. Denver, 1965; PhD, U. Okla., 1974; LLD, Williams Woods Coll., 1979; HHD (hon.), Phillips U., 1983; DLitt (hon.), Chapman U., 1996. Tchr., Jefferson County Pub. Schs., Denver, 1956-67; mem. faculty Oklahoma City U., 1967-77, Darbeth-Whitten prof. history, 1974-77, curator George Shirk Collection, 1977. Chmn. dept. history Oklahoma City U., 1969—72; dir. Robert A. Taft Inst. Govt., 1972—77; pres. Bethany (W.Va.) Coll., 1988—2002, pres. emeritus, 2002—; pres. Brite Div. Sch., 2002—03; vis. scholar in history Johns Hopkins U., 2002—. Author: The American Frontier, 1968, Origins of the Civil War, 1971; : 2d edit., 1978, The American Revolution, 1968, Contrasting Decades, 1920's and 1930's, 1972; : 2d edit., 1978, Consensus and Turmoil, 1972, William R. Leigh: Biography of a Western Artist, 1980, A Handbook for Today's Disciples, 1981, 3d edit., 2003; author: (with D. Hohweller) An Enlisted Soldier's View of the Civil War, 1981, 3d edit., 2003; author: (with others) Seeking God's Peace in a Nuclear Age, 1985; author: The Disciples Colleges: A History, 1987, The Search for Identity, Disciples of Christ-The Restructure Years, 1987, Dale Fiers: Twentieth Century Disciple, 2003; editor: The Disciples Theol. Digest, 1986—88; contbr. articles to profl. jours. Mem. Pitts. Opera Bd., 1996—2001; moderator, active multiple nat. bds. and task forces Christian Ch., 1993—95, pres. higher edn., 1978—88; trustee Culver-Stockton Coll., 1978—88, Tougaloo Coll., 1978—88, vice chmn., 1985—88; bd. dirs. Disciples of Christ Hist. Soc.; Danforth assoc., 1976—78. Mem. Okla. Coun. Humanities (grantee 1974), Phillips U. Alumni Assn. (pres. 1975-76), Nat. Assn. Ind. Colls. and Univs. (secretariat, policy

commn. 1990-94), chair pres.'s athletic conf. 1990-92), W.Va. Assn. Ind. Colls. (chair 1994-97, chair east ctrl. coll. consortium 1997-98), Co. of Ind. Colls. (bd. dirs. 1998-2001). Home: 255 Sears Ln Swanton MD 21561 E-mail: d.cummins@mail.bethanywv.edu.

CUMMINS, HERMAN ZACHARY, physicist; b. Rochester, N.Y., Apr. 23, 1933; s. Louis H. and Rhoda Edith (Kitay) Kominz C.; m. Marsha Z. Hirsch, Aug. 18, 1963. BS, MS, Ohio State U., 1956; Diplome d'Etudes Superieures (Fulbright fellow), U. Paris, 1957; PhD, Columbia U., 1963; D honoris causa, U. P. et M. Curie, 1999. Rsch. assoc. Columbia U., N.Y.C., 1963-64; asst. prof. physics Johns Hopkins U., Balt, 1964-67, assoc. prof., 1967-69, prof., 1969-71; prof. physics N.Y..U., 1971-73; disting. prof. physics City Coll., CUNY, 1973—. Guggenheim fellow, 1984-85; Sloan fellow, 1969-72; recipient von Humboldt Sr. Rsch. award, 1998. Fellow Am. Phys. Soc., N.Y. Acad. Scis.; mem. NAS, Am. Acad. Arts and Scis. Achievements include research in laser light scattering physics; phase transitions and critical phenomena; laser Doppler velocimetry; solid state and biophysics; liquid-glass transition; alloy solidification and pattern-forming instabilities. Office: City Coll CUNY Dept Physics New York NY 10031 E-mail: cummins@sci.ccny.cuny.edu., hzcummins@aol.com.

CUMMINS, HOWARD WALLACE, lawyer; b. Portland, Oreg., May 4, 1937; s. Robert Vinton and Lenore Ethel (Lindholm) C.; m. Susan Roberta Smith, Dec. 21, 1969 (div. Apr. 1982); children: Mark, Jason. BA, Stanford U., 1959; JD, Golden Gate U., 1964; MA, U. Oreg., 1968, PhD, 1972. Asst. prof. U. Alta., Edmonton, 1969-74, assoc. prof., 1974-78; legis. liaison Bd. Commrs., Lane County, Oreg., 1979; adminstrv. asst. Congressman Jim Weaver 4th Dist. Oreg., 1984-86; CEO, rsch. dir. Profiles Northwest, Portland, 1980-92; rsch. dir., adj. rsch. dir. Portland State U., 1987—; dir. Radlaw, Washington, 1992-95; mng. ptnr. Cummins & Brown, Washington, 1995-99; pres. Cummins & Assoc., Washington, 1999-2000; CEO, Environ. Svcs. Group Internat., Inc., Washington, 1999—. Host, commentator Radio Noon Show, CBC/Radio Can., Edmonton, 1972-76, freelance interviewer pub. affairs divsn., 1970-73; guest commentator CTV and ITV TV Networks, Edmonton, 1971-73; v.p. Garneau Cmty. League, 1974-75; jour. referee Sage Profl. Papers in Internat. Studies, 1974, Gonzaga Law Rev., 1995; mem. panel Can. Inst. Internat. Affairs, Edmonton, 1970; spkr. Christian Fellowship Conf., Edmonton, 1970, Hinton Citizens Conf., Edmonton, 1970, Can. Inst. Internat. Affairs, Calgary, 1972, U. Alta., Edmonton, 1972, Hinton Citzens Edn. Coun., 1971, U. Alta., 1972; dir. Western Regional Symposium on Instrnl. Simulations, Edmonton, 1971; mem. planning commn. Athabasca U., Edmonton, 1972, mem. seminar on human cmty. studies program, 1972; chmn. panel Western Polit. Sci. Assn., L.A., 1978; keynote spkr. Nat. Assn. Radiation Survival Nat. conf., Seattle, 1991, Nat. Assn. Atomic Vets. Nat. conf., Orlando, Fla., 1991, Hanford Concerns of Wash. conf., Spokane, 1992, Healing Global Wounds conf., Las Vegas, Nev., 1992; mem. univ. coll. health phsyics adv. bd. U. Md., 1992—; co-founder, mng. atty. Human Experiments Litigation Project, 1995-2000; bd. dirs. Mirus Visual Arts, Inc. Contbr. articles to profl. jours. Bd. dirs. Centennial Montessori Sch., 1973-76; treas. Oregonians for McCarthy, 1968-69. Capt. U.S. Army, 1962-66. Mem. Pa. Bar Assn. Avocations: travel, fitness, writing. Office: ESGI 5432 Connecticut Ave NW Washington DC 20015-2811 E-mail: hwcummins@earthlink.net., hwcummins@esqicorp.com.

CUMMINS, JAMES DONALD, retired electrical engineer; b. Lima, OH, Nov. 4, 1928; s. Charle Benjamin and Viola Ethel Cummins; m. Aina Wuanita Dsirlank, Dec. 29, 1965. AA, City Coll. of San Francisco, San Francisco, Calif., 1964; BSEE, Univ. of Calif., Berkeley, Calif., 1966; MSCS, Univ. of Santa Clara, Santa Clara, Calif., 1980. Marine Elect. PMA/MFOW, San Francisco, 1952—65; engr. various, No. Calif., 1966—96; writer self employed, Columbus, Ga., 1997—2003. Cons. self employed, Union City, Calif., 1995, Union City, 97. Inventor (invention) Patent #5,691,959, 1997, Patent #6,278,864, 2001; author: (novels) The Souse Am. Run, 2001. Avocations: travel, flying, skiing, water-skiing. Home: 924 Northridge Dr Columbus GA 31904

CUMMINS, JAMES DUANE, correspondent, media executive; b. Cedar Rapids, Iowa, Mar. 11, 1945; s. Dewey Homer and Dorothy Marie (Colgan) Cummins; m. Constance Marie Driscoll; children: Kimberly, Christine, Douglas, John, Molly, Bill. BS in journalism, Northwestern U., 1967, MS in journalism, 1968. News reporter Sta. KGLO-TV, Mason City, Iowa, 1969-70, Sta. WOOD-TV, Grand Rapids, Mich., 1970-73, Sta. WTMJ-TV, Milw., 1973-75, Sta. WMAQ-TV, Chgo., 1975-78; corr. NBC News, Chgo., 1978-89, corr./bur. chief Dallas, 1989—. Corr. (news reports) Civil War-El Salvador, 1981, Korean Airline Disaster, 1983, Hurricane Hugo, 1989, Waco Standoff, 1993, Calif. Earthquake, 1994, Okla. City Bombing, 1995, Oklahoma Tornadoes, 1999, Fla. Presdl. Recount, 2000, Shuttle Disaster, 2003. Nominee Emmy award, 1981; named to, Iowa H.S. Basketball Hall of Fame, 1982; recipient Nat. News Emmy award for "Floods", 1993, Emmy award, Chgo. TV Acad., 1976, 1st place award, Nat. Assn. Black Journalists, 2000, Nat. News Emmy award nomination for "Oklahoma Tornadoes", 2000, Nat. News Emmy award nomination for "Shuttle Disaster", 2003. Mem. Northwestern U. Sch. Journalism Alumni Assn., Northwestern U. N Men's Club, Elfun Soc., Sigma Delta Chi (journalism soc.). Roman Cath. Avocations: reading, swimming, golf, fishing. Home: 5815 Flintshire Ln Dallas TX 75252-5132 Office: NBC News 3100 Mckinnon St Dallas TX 75201-7003

CUMMINS, JOHN DAVID, economics educator, consultant; b. Falls City, Nebr., Oct. 22, 1946; s. Samuel James and Jeanne Ellen (Jenkins) C.; m. Tranda Ann Schultz, Dec. 23, 1965 (div. 1980); 1 child, Marnie Kay; m. Mary Alice Weiss, Aug. 21, 1981. BA with high distinction, U. Nebr., 1968; MA, U. Pa., 1971, PhD, 1972. Asst. prof. U. Pa., Phila., 1972-77, assoc. prof., 1977-81, prof., 1981-83, Harry J. Loman prof., 1983—. Exec. dir. S.S. Huebner Found., Phila., 1988—; cons. ABA, Washington, 1983-85, Johnson & Higgins, N.Y.C., 1985, Data Resources, Inc., N.Y.C., 1985, IBM, White Plains, N.Y., 1987-89, Automobile Insurers Bureau of Mass., 1987—, Mass. Rating Bur., 1987—, Nat. Coun. on Compensation Ins., 1989—, Liberty Mut., Boston, 1989—, Amerco Corp., 1990, Sears Roebuck & Co., 1990, Alliance Am. Insurers, 1992—, Federal Reserve Bank of New York, 2000-, Casualty Actuarial Soc., 2000-03; vis. prof. U. S.C., Columbia, 1984; editor Journal of Risk and Insurance, 1992—. Author: Consumer Attitudes Toward Auto and Homeowners Insurance, 1974, Econometric Model of Life Insurance Sector of the U.S. Economy, 1974, Impact of Consumer Services on Independent Insurance Agencies, 1977, Risk Classification in Life Insurance, 1985, Fair Rate of Return in Property-Liability Insurance, 1986, Classical Models of Insurance Solvency, 1988, Financial Models of Insurance Solvency, 1989, Managing the Insolvency Risk of Insurance Companies, 1991; co-editor: The Underwriting Cycle in Property-Liability Insurance, 1991, Financial Management Life Insurance Companies, 1993, Changes in the Life Insurance Industry: Efficiency, Technology and Risk Management, 1999; editor: Deregulating Property-Liability Insurance: Restoring Competition and Increasing Market Efficiency, 2002; contbr. articles to profl. jours. Recipient Jour. Risk and Ins., Spangler Award, Alpha Kappa Psi, Internat. Actuarial Assn. Prize, 1995, Robert I. Mehr Award, 1997, 1998, 2000, Brian Hey Prize (Inst. of Actuaries), 1998, Casualty Actuarial Soc. Award, 1999, 2000, Jour. Fin. Intermediation Award, 2000, Robert C. Witt Award, 2003. Mem. Am. Risk and Ins. Assn. (editorial bd. 1974-84, 88—, acad. bd. dirs. 1981-84, v.p. 1984-85, pres.-elect 1985, pres. 1986), ASTIN, Am. Econ. Assn., Am. Fin. Assn. (chmn. risk theory seminar 1980). Democrat. Office: Univ of Pa 3641 Locust Walk 314 CPC Philadelphia PA 19104-6218 E-mail: cummins@wharton.upenn.edu.

CUMMINS, KATHLEEN K. retired elementary school educator; b. Fountain County, Ind., June 20, 1919; d. Homer Elston Krout and Edith Zerilda Allen; m. Robert E. Cummins, Oct. 4, 1940 (dec. Mar. 1984); 1 child, Robert E. Jr. BS in Edn., Ind. State U., 1952. Elem. tchr. East Allen Cmty. Schs., New Haven and Ft. Wayne, Ind., 1940—76; ret., 1976. Deaconess Trinity English Luth. Ch., Ft. Wayne, 1982—. Recipient Ret. Tchr. of Yr. award, Instant Copy, Ft. Wayne, 1993. Mem.: AAUW (grantee 1984), Allen County Ret. Educators Assn. (pres. 1986—88), Ft. Wayne Hist. Mus. (past pres. Barr St. Irregulars), Ft. Wayne Women's Club (bd. dirs. 1988—, chmn. fine arts dept.), Fortnightly Club (pres. 1994—96), Delta Kappa Gamma (chpt. pres. 1964—66). Democrat. Lutheran. Avocations: painting, reading, bridge, knitting, gardening. Home: 3808 Oak Park Dr Fort Wayne IN 46815

CUMMINS, MARSHA Z. retired literature educator; b. Detroit, June 21, 1938; d. Ephraim and Bluma Hirsch; m. Herman Z. Cummins, Aug. 18, 1963. BA, Wayne State U., 1959; MA, U. Mich., 1963; PhD, U. Md., 1973. Instr. English Morgan State U., Balt., 1964—71; prof. CUNY, Bronx, 1971—2002, prof. emeritus, 2003—. Author: Writing the Research Paper, 1979. Mem.: MLA.

CUMMINS, MICHELLE MARIE, otolaryngologist, head and neck surgeon; b. Windsor, Ont., Can., July 14, 1959; came to U.S., 1994; d. James Thomas and Helen Mary (Weiler) C.; m. Jerry Dean Pilkington. BS, U. Waterloo, Can., 1982; MD, U. Toronto, 1987, MSc, 1994. Intern St. Joseph Health Ctr., Toronto, 1987-88; resident Santa Barbara (Calif.) Cottage Hosp., 1988-89, U. Toronto, 1989-92; otolaryngologist Dalhousie U., Nova Scotia, Can., 1992-94. Lectr. in field. Contbr. articles to profl. jours. Otolaryngology & Profl. Voice fellow Bowman Gray Sch. Medicine, Winston-Salem, N.C., 1994-96. Mem. AMA, Am. Acad. Sleep Disorders, Am. Acad. Otolaryngology Head & Neck Surgery, Am. Rhinological Soc., European Laryngological Soc., Can. Soc. Otolaryngology, Pan Am. Allergy Soc. Roman Catholic. Avocations: fitness walking, pottery, skiing, swimming, biking. Office: 1300 N Virginia St Ste 112 Port Lavaca TX 77979-2512

CUMMINS, NANCYELLEN HECKEROTH, electronics engineer; b. Long Beach, Calif., May 22, 1948; d. George and Ruth May (Anderson) Heckeroth; m. Weldon Jay Cummins, Sept. 15, 1987; children: Tracy Lynn, John Scott, Darren Elliott. Student, USMC, Memphis, 1966-67. From tech. publ. engr. to engrng. instr. Missile and Space divsn. Lockheed Corp., Sunnyvale, Calif., 1973-77; test engr. Gen. Dynamics, Pomona, Calif., 1980-83; quality assurance test engr. Interstate Electronics Co., Anaheim, Calif., 1983-84; quality engr., certification engr. Rockwell Internat., Anaheim, 1985-86; sr. quality assurance programmer Point 4 Data, Tustin, Calif., 1986-87; software quality assurance specialist Lawrence Livermore Nat. Lab., Yucca Mountain Project, Livermore, Calif., 1987-89, software quality mgr., 1989-90; from sr. constrn. insp. to sr. quality assurance engr. EG&G Rocky Flats, Inc., Golden, Colo., 1990-91, engr. IV software quality assurance, 1991-92, instr., developer environ. law and compliance, 1992-93; software, computer cons. CRI, Dabois, Wyo., 1993-97; contractor Dept. of Energy, Golden, Colo., 1997-98; test mgr. Keane Inc., Lakewood, Colo., 1998, project officer, 1998—. Customer engr. IBM Gen. Sys., Orange, Calif., 1979; electronics engr. Exhibits divsn. LDS Ch., Salt Lake City, 1978; electronics repair specialist Weber State Coll., 1977-78. Author: Package Area Test Set, 6 vols., 1975, Software Quality Assurance Plan, 1989. Vol., instr. San Fernando (Calif.) Search and Rescue Team, 1967-70; instr. emergency preparedness and survival, Claremont, Calif., 1982-84, Modesto, Calif., 1989; mem. Lawrence Livermore nat. Lab. Employees Emergency Vols., 1987-90, EG&G Rocky Flats Bldg. Emergency Support Team, 1990-93, Dubois Search and Rescue, 1995-97. Mem. NAFE, NRA, Nat. Muzzle Loading Rifle Assn., Am. Soc. Quality, Job's Daus. (majority mem.), Ea. Star. Republican. Avocations: history, weapons, camping, native American crafts. Fax: 406-882-4554. E-mail: whiltierna@Fortindsl.net.

CUMMINS, PAUL ZACH, II, insurance company executive; b. Fitchburg, Mass., May 1, 1936; s. Paul Z. and Camille M. (Hook) C.; children: Paul Zach III, Colleen Elizabeth. BS, U.S. Naval Acad., 1958, MS, 1964. Mgr., engrng. liaison Carrier Corp., Syracuse, N.Y., 1969-73; mgr. systems, mfg. group Republic Steel Corp., Youngstown, Ohio, 1973-74, mgr., bus. planning, 1974-76; dir. adminstrn. planning Republic Builders Products Corp., Atlanta, 1976-77; dir. corp. strategy and devel. Blue Cross/Blue Shield Md., 1978-89, cons. internal ops., 1989-92; ind. cons., 1992—. Instr. U.S. Naval Acad., Annapolis, 1964-65. Past chmn., mem. Md. Gov.'s Vietnam and Disabled Vets. Bus. Resource Coun., SBA Adv. Bd. Balt Dist. With USN, 1958-69. Decorated Joint Svc. Commendation medal. Mem. U.S. Naval Acad. Alumni Assn., Am. Legion, Kiwanis (past pres. Liverpool, N.Y., past pres. Camillus, N.Y.). Methodist. Home: 16933 Flickerwood Rd Parkton MD 21120-9767

CUMMINS, WILMA JEANNE, actress; b. Guthrie, Okla., Sept. 25, 1927; d. Chauncey Dewitt and Etta (Marshall) Anderson; m. Joseph Sylvester Cummins, May 24, 1952; children: Jeanetta Kay Arnold, Bunny Gail Cline, Mary Jo Stoops, Susan Dee. BA, Phillip's U., 1948; MA, U. Tulsa, 1980. Cert. tchr., lic. real estate broker. Ops. base payload control United Air Lines, Denver, 1948-50; lab. tech. Barnes Hosp., St. Louis, 1950; elem. tchr. Kans., Mo., 1951-53; actress Gaslight Dinner Theatre, Tulsa, 1984, Discoveryland's Okla., Prattville, 1985; tchr. Tulsa Pub. Schs., 1970-78; part time tchr. Tulsa Jr. Coll., 1987-89; freelancer in TV and radio SAG, AFTRA, Dallas, Tulsa, 1991—. Real estate broker, Tulsa, 1981—93. Actor: (films) The Ripper, 1985, UHF, 1988; (TV series) Rosie O'Donnell Show, 1997, America's Funniest People, 1991, Howie Mandel Show, 1999, Tonight Show with Jay Leno, 2001, 30 Seconds to Fame, 2002, Lawrence Welk Champagne Theatre, 1997, Spotlight Theatre, 1983—, (commercial) Tex. Transp. Inst., 2002; (films) Christmas Child, 2003. Vol. Gilcrease Mus., Tulsa, 1995—2002; pres. Internat. Club, Tulsa, 1996, Pan-Am. Round Table, Tulsa, 1990, Altrusa Club, Tulsa, 1985, Christian Women's Fellowship, 1983, Conversing Couples, 1986—, Pro-Am., 2001—02. Recipient 1st pl. monologue, Internat. Platform Assn., 1989, 2d pl., 1991, 1st pl., Srs. Take Ctr. Stage, Welk Resort, 2000. Republican. Methodist. Avocations: theater, commercials.

CUMMIS, CLIVE SANFORD, lawyer; b. Newark, Nov. 21, 1928; s. Joseph Jack and Lee (Berkie) C.; m. Ann Denburg, Mar. 24, 1956; children: Andrea, Deborah, Cynthia, Jessica. AB, Tulane U., 1949; JD, U. Pa., 1952; LL.M., N.Y. U., 1959. Bar: N.J. 1952. Law sec. Hon. Walter Freund, Appellate Div., Superior Ct., 1955-56; partner firm Cummis & Kroner, Newark, 1956-60; chief counsel County and Mcpl. Law Revision Commn., State of N.J., Newark, 1959-62; partner firm Schiff, Cummis & Kent, Newark, 1962-67, Cummis, Kent, Radin & Tischman, Newark, 1967-70; sr. v.p., dir. Cadence Industries, N.Y.C., 1967-70; dir. Plume & Atwood Industries, Stamford, Conn., 1969-71; chmn., chmn. emeritus Sills Cummis Radin Tischman Epstein & Gross, Newark, 1970—; exec. v.p. law and corp. affairs, sec. Park Place Entertainment corp., Las Vegas, Nev., 1999—2001, vice chmn. bd. dirs., 2000—. Dir. Essex County State Bank, Financial Resources Group; instr. Practising Law Inst. Chief counsel County and Mcpl. Revision Commn., 1959-62, N.J. Pub. Market Commn., 1961-63; counsel Bd. Edn. of South Orange and Maplewood, 1964-74, Town of Cedar Grove, 1966-70, Bd. Edn. of Dumont, 1968-72; mem. com. on rules and civil practice N.J. Supreme Ct., 1975-78. Assoc. editor NJ. Law Jour., 1961—. Trustee Newark Beth Israel Med. Ctr., 1965-75, Northfield YM-YWHA, 1968-70, U. Medicine and Dentistry N.J., 1980-84, Newark Mus., N.J. Performing Arts Ctr., Blue Cross and Blue Shield N.J., 1983-93; gen. coun. N.J. Turnpike Authority, 1990-94; mem. bd. overseers U. Pa. Law Sch., 1991-96; mem. bd. govs. Daus. of Israel Home for Aged, 1968-70; mem. N.J. Commn. on Statue of Liberty; mem. pres.'s coun. Tulane U., 1992—; pres. bd. dirs. Tulane Assocs., 1994-96; mem. Pres.'s commn. on White House Fellows, 1993-2001; dir. N.J. Regional Planning Assn. Recipient 1st Ann. Judge Learned Hand award Am. Jewish Com., 1994, First Ann. Disting. Citizen award N.J. Med. Sch., 2002. Fellow Am. Bar Found.; mem. ABA (life), Am. Law Inst., Am. Judicature Soc., U. Pa. Law Sch. Alumni Soc. (pres.), N.J. Bar Assn., Essex County Bar Assn., N.Y. Athletic Club (N.Y.C.), Greenbrook County Club (North Caldwell, N.J.), Stockbridge Golf Club (Mass.). Democrat. Jewish. Office: Sills Cummis Radin Tischman Epstein & Gross One Riverfront Pl Newark NJ 07102 E-mail: ccummis@sillscummis.com.

CUNDEY, PAUL EDWARD, JR., cardiologist; b. Phila., Sept. 9, 1936; s. Paul Edward and Ann Elizabeth (Morris) C.; m. Katharine Zerbey, Aug. 1, 1959; children: Richard David, Paul Edward III, Heath John, Elizabeth Ann. BA, LaSalle U., 1958; MD, Temple U., 1962. Intern Temple U. Med. Ctr., Phila., 1962-63; resident in cardiology Med. Coll. Ga., Augusta, 1965-69, assoc. prof. medicine, 1968-70, prof. medicine, 1978—; practice medicine specializing in cardiology Univ. Hosp., Augusta, 1970—. Bd. dirs. East Cen. Ga. Emergency Med. Systems, Augusta, 1989. Contbr. numerous articles and abstracts to profl. publs. Mem. exec. com. Richmond County div. Am. Heart Assn., 1972-84. Capt. U.S. Army, 1963-65. Rsch. fellow, Nat. Heart Inst., 1967-79, NIH, 1967-69. Fellow ACP, Am. Coll. Angiology, Am. Coll. Cardiology. Office: Cardiology Assocs 1348 Walton Way Ste 5100 Augusta GA 30901-5108

CUNDIFF, EDWARD WILLIAM, marketing educator; b. Long Beach, Calif., Sept. 28, 1919; s. Harry Thomas and Martha Magdalene (Koltes) C.; m. Margaret Wallace Stroud, Sept. 8, 1956; children: Richard Wallace, Gregory Edward, Geoffrey William. BA, Stanford, 1940, MBA, 1942; Ed.D., 1952; Ford Fellow, Harvard Sch. Bus. Adminstrn., 1956. Retailing exec., 1946-48; instr. mktg. San Jose State Coll., 1949-52; asst. prof., later asso. prof. mktg. Syracuse U., 1952-58, asst. dean, 1954-58; prof. mktg., chmn. dept. mktg. adminstrn. U. Tex., 1958-73, assoc. dean Grad. Sch. Bus., 1973-76; L.J. Buchan distinguished vis. prof. U. Tex. at San Antonio, 1976-77; Charles C. Kellstadt prof. mktg. Emory U., 1977-87; John A. Beck Centennial prof. comm. U. Tex., Austin, 1987-94, John A. Beck emeritus prof. comm. dept. advt., 1994-96, emeritus prof. mktg., 1996—. Vis. prof. mktg., Fontainebleau, France, Palermo, Sicily, 1960-61. Author: (with R.R. Still) Sales Management: Decisions, Policies and Cases, 5th edit, 1988, Basic Marketing: Concepts, Environment, and Decisions, 1964, rev. edit., 1970, Essentials of Marketing, 1966, 3d edit., 1986, (with R.R. Still and N.A.P. Govoni) Fundamentals of Modern Marketing, 3d edit, 1980, (with Marye Hilger) Marketing in the International Environment, 2d edit., 1988; editor: Jour. Mktg, 1973-76. Served to lt. (s.g.) USNR, World War II. Mem. Am. Mktg. Assn. (v.p. 1980—), So. Mktg. Assn. (pres. 1967-68), Beta Gamma Sigma, Delta Sigma Pi, Theta Chi. Home: # 1281 4100 Jackson Ave Apt 229 Austin TX 78731-6038 Office: U Tex Coll Communication Austin TX 78712 E-mail: ecundiff@uts.cc.utexas.edu.

CUNDIFF, GEOFFREY WILLIAM, physician; b. Austin, Tex., Mar. 2, 1962; s. Edward William and Margaret Wallace (Stroud) C.; m. Valerie Filippi, Oct. 22, 1994; children: Victoria, Thomas, Ian, Adrenna. BA, U. Tex., 1984; MD, U. Tex. Southwestern Med. Ctr., 1989. Diplomate Am. Bd. Ob-Gyn. Resident ob-gyn Parkland Meml. Hosp., Dallas, 1989-93; fellow in urogynecology/endoscopy Greater Balt. Med. Ctr., 1993-94; fellow in reconstructive pelvic surgery Duke U. Med. Ctr., Duham, N.C., 1994-95, asst. prof. gynecology, 1995-98; assoc. prof. gynecology, dir. divsn. gynecology Johns Hopkins U., 1999—2001, chmn. dept. ob-gyn., 2002—; vice chair ob-gyn. Johns Hopkins Med. Inst., 2002—. Dir. gynecol. endoscopy Duke U. Med. Ctr., 1996—. Author: (book) Endoscopy of Female Lower Urinary Tract, 1998, Osteogards Urogynecology; med. illustrator multiple books and jours.; contbr. articles to profl. jours. Recipient Nat. Faculty award Coun. for Residency Edn. Ob-Gyn, 1996. Fellow ACOG; mem. Am. Urogynecol. Soc. (edn. com. 1993-97, rsch. com. 1997—), Internat. Continence Soc., Soc. Gynecol. Surgeons (rsch. com. 2000-, program comn. 2001-, exec. com. 2001-), Soc. Gynecol. Investigators. Avocations: martial arts, med. illustration. Office: Johns Hopkins Medicine Dept Ob-Gyn 4940 Eastern Ave AIC Baltimore MD 21224-0001

CUNEO, DENNIS CLIFFORD, automotive company executive; b. Ridgway, Pa., Jan. 12, 1950; s. Clifford Francis and Erma Theresa (Nissel) C.; m. Bonnie Frances Mish, Aug. 18, 1972; children: Corinne, Kyle, James. BS, Gannon U., 1971; MBA, Kent State U., 1973; JD, Loyola U., New Orleans, 1976. Bar: D.C. 1977. Trial atty. U.S. Dept. Justice, Washington, 1976-80; assoc. Arent, Fox, Kintner, Plotkin & Kahn, Washington, 1980-84; gen. counsel New United Motor Mfg. Inc. joint venture GM-Toyota, Fremont, Calif., 1984-88, v.p. legal and govt. affairs, 1988-90, v.p. corp. planning and legal affairs, 1990-92, v.p. corp. planning and external affairs, corp. sec., 1992-96; sr. v.p. legal, environ., external affairs Toyota Motor Mfg. N.Am., 1996-2000, sr. v.p., 2000—. Chmn. Calif. Workside Rsch. Com., Sacramento, 1988—96; lectr. exec. program U. Calif., Davis, 1988—95; lectr. internat. motor vehicle program MIT, Berlin and Beijing, 1994; mem. Gov. Pete Wilson Trade Mission to Asia, 1993; bd. dirs. Toyota Motor Corp. Svcs., Inc., 1996—99; mem. Cin. Bus. Com.; mem. gov.'s econ. adv. com., Frankfort, Ky., 2001—. Campaign chmn. United Way, Alameda County, 1993-95, No. Ky. United Way, 2000; co-chmn. Blue Ribbon com. to Save the Oakland A's, 1994; vice chmn. Alameda County Econ. Devel. Bd., Oakland, 1990-96, Team Calif., Sacramento, 1994; bd. visitors Loyola Law Sch., 1987-95; mem. Calif. Select Com. on Jud. Retirement, 1993; mem. steering com. Bay Area Coun., San Francisco, 1990-95, Bay Area Dredging Coalition, San Francisco, 1991-96; mem. Statewide Pupil Assessment Rev. Panel, Sacramento, 1996-97; bd. dirs. Oakland-Alameda County Coliseum, 1995-97, Cin. United Way, 1997—, Bay Area Regional Tech. Alliance, Oakland, 94-96; mem. flood relief cabinet ARC, 1997; mem. Gov.'s Task Force on Child Devel., Frankfort, Ky., 1999— . Mem.: ABA, Calif. Mfrs. Assn. (vice chmn. 1994—99, pres. Calif. manufactures svcs. corp. 1996—97), Nat. Mfrs. Assn. (chmn. human resources policy group 1999—, bd. dirs., exec. com.), Oakland Football Mktg. Assn. (pres. 1995—96), Greater Cin. C. of C. (bd. dirs. 1998—), No. Ky. C. of C. (bd. dirs. 1997—98), Assoc. Industries Ky. (bd. dirs. 1999—), Cin. Club, Metro. Club (bd. dirs. 1999—). Avocations: skiing, model trains. Office: Toyota Motor Mfg NAm 25 Atlantic Ave Erlanger KY 41018-3188

CUNEO, DONALD LANE, lawyer, educator; b. Alameda, Calif., Apr. 19, 1944; s. Vernon Edmund and Dorothy (Lane) c.; m. Frances Susan Huze, Aug. 8, 1981; children: Kristen Marie, Lane Michael. BA, Lehigh U., 1966; JD, MBA, Columbia U., 1970. Bar: N.Y. 1971, D.C. 1992, U.S. Claims Ct. 1972, U.S. Tax Ct. 1972, U.S. Dist. Ct. (so. dist.) N.Y. 1973, U.S. Dist. Ct. (no. dist.) 1978, U.S. Dist. Ct. D.C. 1992, U.S. Ct. Appeals (2nd cir.) 1979, U.S. Ct. Appeals (D.C. cir.) 1992, U.S. Ct. Internat. Trade 1979, U.S. Ct. Appeals (fed. cir.) 1979, U.S. Supreme Ct. 1979. Assoc. Shearman & Sterling, N.Y.C., 1971-79, ptnr., 1979-93; pres., CEO Internat. House, 1993—. Sec./trustee Internat. House, N.Y.C., 1977-93; pres. Morningside Area Alliance, N.Y.C., 2000—. Author: (with others) Prevention and Prosecution of Computer and High Technology Crime, 1988; contbr. articles to profl. jours. Reginald Heber Smith Cmty. Lawyer fellow U.S. Govt., 1970-71. Mem. Coun. Fgn. Rels. Avocations: sports, travel. Home and Office: Internat House 500 Riverside Dr New York NY 10027-3916

CUNEO, JACK ALFRED, real estate investment executive; b. Bklyn., Dec. 7, 1947; s. Alfred Louis and Elvira Clementina (Landolphi) C.; m. Barbara Rose Kenig, May 9, 1970 (div. Nov. 1981); 1 child, Andrew; m. Renee Joan Savastano, May 26, 1984; children: Matthew, Christina. BA in Psychology, CCNY, 1969; postgrad., U. Mass., 1969-72. Rschr. Continental Rsch. Inst., N.Y.C., 1967-70; lectr. U. Mass., Amherst, Mass., 1970-72; ptnr. Skcra-Retail Craft, Northampton, Mass., 1972-77; broker Town and Country Realtors, Amherst, Mass., 1972-74; pres. New England Real Vest, Amherst, 1974-75; account exec. Merrill Lynch Pierce Fenner and Smith, Springfield, Mass., 1975-77; sr. dept. rep. Merrill Lynch Investment Banking, N.Y.C., 1977-78; v.p. real estate investment Merrill Lynch Hubbard, N.Y.C., 1978-86, sr. v.p., chief investment officer, 1986-97, chmn., CEO, 1997-2000; mng. dir. investment banking Merrill Lynch & Co., N.Y.C., 2000—02; mng. prin. Cuneo Capital Group, Princeton, NJ, 2002—. Investor Nat. Bank of Calif., L.A., 1984—. Fellowship Nat. Inst. Mental Health, 1969. Mem. Urban Land Inst., Ctr. for Real Estate and Urban Econs. U. Calif. (policy adv. bd.), MIT (real estate ctr.), 200 Club, Nat. Italian Am. Found. Avocations: golf, fishing, military aircraft, shooting. Office: Merrill Lynch Hubbard World Fin Ctr S Tower New York NY 10080-0001

CUNHA, BURKE A. physician; b. Hartford, Conn., Mar. 25, 1942; m. Marie A. Boyer; children: Zachary A., Cheston B. AB, U. Conn., 1965; MD, Pa. State U., 1972. Diplomate in internal medicine and infectious disease Am. Bd. Internal Medicine. Resident Hartford (Conn.) Hosp., 1973-75, fellow in infectious disease, 1975-77, asst. chief infectious disease divsn., 1977-79, chief med. svc., 1977-79; asst. prof. medicine U. Conn. Sch. Medicine, Farmington, 1977-80; chief infectious disease divsn., vice chmn. dept. medicine, epidemiologist Winthrop-Univ. Hosp., Mineola, N.Y., 1980—. Asst. prof. medicine SUNY, Sch. Medicine, Stony Brook, 1980-82, assoc. prof. medicine, 1982-91, prof. medicine, 1991—; dir. arts and humanities series Winthrop-Univ. Hosp., 1994—, history of medicine series, 1995—, multicultural aspects of medicine, 1996—. Editor-in-chief Infectious Disease Practice, 1991—, Antibiotics for Clinicians, 1996—; editor 10 books, 1984—; author 150 chpts. to books, 120 abstracts, and over 800 articles to profl. jours. Vol. Peace Corps, Chile, 1965-68. Recipient Disting. Alumni Fellow award Pa. State U. Coll. Medicine, 1997. Master: ACP; fellow: Am. Acad. Microbiology, Am. Coll. Clin. Pharmacology, Am. Coll. Chest Physicians, Infectious Disease Soc. Am.; mem.: Spanish Infectious Disease Soc., Italian Infectious Disease Soc., French Infectious Disease Soc. Avocations: classical studies, philosophy, history, art. Office: Winthrop-Univ Hosp Infectious Disease Divsn 259 1st St Mineola NY 11501-3987

CUNHA, CARLOS ALBERTO, political scientist, educator; b. Sao Martinho de Cortica, Portugal, Feb. 17, 1956; came to U.S., 1961; BA in French, U. Mass., 1978, PhD in Polit. Sci., 1987; MA in Polit. Sci., U. Conn., 1980. Asst. prof. Northeastern Ill. U., Chgo., 1987-88, SUNY, Geneseo, 1988-91; prof. Dowling Coll., Oakdale, NY, 1992—. Vis. asst. prof. Sarah Lawrence Coll., Bronxville, N.Y., 1991-92; Portuguese rep. to European Cooperation in Sci. and Tech. Rsch. com. European Commn., 1998-2003. Author: The Portuguese Communist Party Struggle for Power 1921-1987, 1991; contbr. articles to profl. jours.; mem. editl. bd. Portuguese Studies Rev., 2001—. Office: Dowling Coll Idle Hour Blvd Oakdale NY 11769

CUNHA, MARK GEOFFREY, lawyer; b. Lexington, Mass, Sept. 26, 1955; s. John Henry and Dolores (DeRosas) C.; children: Celine Yvonne, Nicholas Brian. AB magna cum laude, Cornell U., 1977; JD, Stanford U., 1980. Bar: N.Y. 1981, U.S. Dist. Ct. (so. and ea. dists.) N.Y. 1981, U.S. Ct. Appeals (2nd cir.) 1991, U.S. Tax Ct. 1992, U.S. Supreme Ct. 1996, U.S. Ct. Appeals (3d cir.) 2001. Intern The White House, Washington, 1979-80; assoc. Simpson Thacher & Bartlett, NYC, 1980-88, ptnr., 1989—. Mediator comml. divsn. NY State Supreme Ct., NY County, 1996—; bd. dir. legal svc. for NYC, 1997—. Bd. dir. NY Lawyers for Pub. Interest, 1989—; trustee Inst. for Ednl. Achievement, 1995—, Lycee Francais NY, 1998—. Recipient Outstanding Vol. Lawyers award Legal Aid Soc., 1990, Pro Bono award NY County Lawyers Assn., 1991. Mem.: Assn. Bar City NY (chmn. exec. com., chmn. com. on legal assistance, chmn. del. to NY State Bar Assn. Ho. of Dels., steering com. on legal assistance), NY State Bar Assn. (exec. com. on comml. and fed. litigation sect.), Internat. Bar Assn., ABA, Phi Beta Kappa. Democrat. Home: 1150 Fifth Ave Apt 3A New York NY 10128-0724 Office: Simpson Thacher & Bartlett 425 Lexington Ave New York NY 10017-3954 E-mail: mcunha@stblaw.com.

CUNNICK, GLORIA HELEN, artist; b. N.Y.C., Oct. 19, 1926; d. Charles and Sigrid (Andersen) Mason; m. William Rhoslyn Cunnick Jr., Oct. 21, 1978 (div.); children: William Rhoslyn III, Alice Louise, Joan Lenci. BFA summa cum laude, L.I. U., 1987. Represented by Graphic Eye. One-woman shows include L.I. U.-C.W. Post, 1987, Artist of the Month-Dime Savs. Bank, 1990, Seymour Berger Ctr. for the Arts, 1992, Plandome Gallery, 1993, Fine Art Mus. of L.I., 1994, Manhasset Libr., 1998, 99, South Huntington Libr., 1999, Am. Inst. Architects, Ft. Totten, 2000, Shelter Rock Gallery, 2000, Omni Art Gallery, 2000, Graphic Eye Gallery, 2000; exhibited in groups shows including Washington and Lee U., 1993, Hecksher Mus. Fine Art, 1993, Sea Cliff Gallery, 1993, Temple Emanuel of Great Neck, 1993, Fine Arts Mus. L.I., 1993, Islip Mus., 1993, Spazi Contemporary Art Gallery, 1993, Oceanside Libr., 1993, Shelter Rock Gallery, 1993, Manhasset Libr., 1993, Hillwood Art Mus., 1994, 97, Firehouse Art Gallery, 1994, Nassau County Mus. Art, 1994, 97, 395 West Broadway, 1994, Sea Cliff Gallery, 1994, Basil Leaf Gallery, 1994, Discovery Gallery, 1994, Ceres Gallery, 1995, 97, Lever House, 1995, Tex. Nat. 95 Art Exhbn., 1995, Authentic Gallery, 1995, Islip Art Mus., 1995, Art Ctr. of Municipality of Athens, Greece, 1996, Islip (N.Y.) Mus., 1996, 479 Gallery, N.Y.C., 1997, Nat. Assn. Women Artists, 2001, Small Works-Graphic Eye, 2001, also others; permanent collections include Pall Corp., Zimmerli Art Gallery, Rutgers U., Islip Art Mus., Fine Art Mus. L.I., Hillwood Art Mus., L.I. U. One Person, Manhaset Libr., 2003. Mills Pond House Art Gallery, 2002 (1st prize). Recipient grand prize North Shore YW-YMHA, 1992, Denis and Catherine Krusos award Hecksher Mus., 1992, Silver award Nassau County Mus. Fine Arts, 1992, award of Merit, Nassau County Mus. Fine Art, 1992, 2d prize works on canvas or other support Great Neck Libr., 1993, winner Fine Arts Mus. L.I., 1993, award Excellence, Art. League L.I., 1999, 1st prize Smithtown Arts Coun., 2003, many others. Mem. Nat. Assn. Women Artists (William Meyerowitz Meml. award 1992), Graphic Eye Gallery, Nat. Mus. Women in Arts (artist mem.). Home: 3 Orchard Farm Rd Port Washington NY 11050-3309

CUNNIFF, SUZANNE, surgical technician; b. Detroit, Dec. 3, 1960; d. Louis Thomas and Joyce Lenore (Barkell) C. AA in Surgical Tech., Marygrove Coll., 1986; BS Med. Tech., Mich. State U., 1984. Cert. surgical technologist. Surg. technologist Botsford Gen. Hosp, Farmington Hills, Mich., 1986-88, St. Joseph Mercy Hosp., Pontiac, Mich., 1988-91; cardiothoracic surg. asst. Cardiothoracic Surgeons, Pontiac, 1991-97, Lynchburg, Va., 1997—. Mem. Assn. Surg. Technologists. Avocations: figure skating, volleyball, bowling, wool spinning. Office: 2015 Tate Springs Rd Lynchburg VA 24501

CUNNIGEN, DONALD, sociologist, educator; b. Tuscaloosa, Ala., Feb. 16, 1952; s. Oliver Wendell and Corinne Griffin Cunnigen; m. Bernadine Grady, Aug. 3, 1985. BA, Tougaloo Coll., 1974; MA, U. N.H., 1976; AM, Harvard U., 1979, PhD, 1988. Lectr. U. Mass., Boston, 1982-83; vis. lectr. Tufts U., Medford, Mass., 1985-87; asst. prof. U. Pa., Phila., 1988-92, U. Mo., Columbia, 1992-93; assoc. prof. U. R.I., Kingston, 1993—. Pew postdoctoral fellow Wesleyan U., 1990-91; W.E.B. DuBois fellow Harvard U., Cambridge, Mass., 1994-95 Contbr. articles to profl. jours.; mem. editl. bd. Jour. Negro Edn., 1991-93. Chmn. minority scholarship com. Soc. for Study of Social Problems; bd. dirs. United Black & Brown Fund, Providence, 1993-98; bd. pres. LeCount Scholarship Fund, Providence, 1998-99; mem. Com. of 158, Providence. Mem.: St. George Tucker Soc., Assn. Social and Behavioral Scientists (past pres. 1998), Soc. for Study of Social Problems, Assn. for Black Sociologists (pres. 2001), So. Sociol. Assn., Am. Sociol. Assn., Alpha Phi Alpha (v.p. 1995—99, pres. 2000). Episcopalian. Home: # 115 500 Angell St Apt 115 Providence RI 02906-4485 Office: U RI Dept Sociology Kingston RI 02881 E-mail: dcunn@uriacc.uri.edu.

CUNNINGHAM, ALICE WELT, lawyer, legal educator; b. Washington, Aug. 18, 1949; d. Samuel Louis and Beatrice (Boxer) Welt; m. Daniel Paul Cunningham, Aug. 10, 1975; adopted children: Stephen Paul, Philip James 1 child, Samuel Paul (dec.). BA summa cum laude, Yale U., 1971; JD, Harvard U., 1974; MA in Math. Edn., Columbia U., 2001, postgrad., 2001—. Bar: N.Y. 1975, Calif. 1975, U.S. Dist. Ct. (no. dist.) Calif. 1975, U.S. Ct. Appeals (fed. cir.) 1980, U.S. Tax Ct. 1976. Assoc. Shearman & Sterling, N.Y.C., 1974-75, Heller Ehrman, White & McAuliffe, San Francisco, 1975-78, Debevoise & Plimpton, N.Y.C., 1978-83; assoc. prof. N.Y. Law Sch., N.Y.C., 1983-86. Contbr. articles to profl. jours. Mem.: ABA, Assn. Bar City N.Y., N.Y. State Bar Assn., Kappa Delta Pi, Phi Beta Kappa. E-mail: ACunnin167@aol.com.

CUNNINGHAM, ANTHONY WILLARD, lawyer; b. Lakeland, Fla., Nov. 10, 1931; s. Elmo and Anna Catherine Cunningham; m. Kathleen, 1960 (div. 1974); children: Matthew, Tracy, Melisse, Megan, Joshua, Alexandra; m. Robin Richards, Nov. 22, 1980. LLB, U. Fla., 1962. Bar: Fla. 1963, U.S. Dist. Ct. (mid. dist.) Fla. 1964, U.S. Ct. Appeals (5th cir.) 1964, U.S. Supreme Ct. 1975. Assoc. Fishback, Davis, Dominick & Troutman, Orlando, Fla., 1962-64, Nichols, Gaither, Beckham, Colson, Spence & Hicks, Miami, Fla., 1964-65, Orlando and Tampa, Fla., 1965-67; prin. Wagner, Cunningham, Vaughan & McLaughlin, P.A., Tampa, 1967-92, Cunningham Law Group, P.A., Tampa, 1992—. 1st lt. USAF, 1951-56. Mem. ATLA (bd. govs. 1979—, 90, 95), Trial Lawyers Pub. Justice (bd. dirs. 1986—, pres. elect 1990-91, pres. 1991-92), Acad. Fla. Trial Lawyers (bd. dirs., past pres. 1971—). Democrat. Avocations: boating, fishing, snow skiing. Office: Cunningham Law Group Ste 100 100 Ashley Dr S Tampa FL 33602-5348 E-mail: AWC8669@aol.com.

CUNNINGHAM, ATLEE MARION, JR., aeronautical engineer; b. Corpus Christi, Tex., Aug. 17, 1938; s. Atlee Marion and Carlos Dean (Shepherd) Cunningham; m. Diana Wahl Bonelli, July 17, 1976; children from previous marriage: Christopher Atlee Acie, Scott Patrick, Sean Michael. BSME, MSME, U. Tex., 1961, PhD, 1966. Rsch. scientist Def. Rsch. Lab., Austin, Tex., 1965; engring. staff specialist Gen. Dynamics Corp., Ft. Worth, 1965—93, Lockheed Corp., Ft. Worth, 1993—95, Lockheed Martin, 1995—, sr. prin. rsch. engr., sr. tech. fellow, 2002—. Vis. indsl. prof. So. Meth. U. Inst. Tech., Dallas, 1969—70; vis. assoc. prof. aero. engring. U. Tex., 1978—; lectr. in aeroelasticity Nat. Cheng Kung U., Taiwan, 1984, U. Tex., Arlington, 1990—; cons. NASA, USAF, USN, U. Tex.; cons. on aeroelastic and vibration issues for Lockheed Martin F-16, C-130J, F-22 and F-35 aircraft. Contbr. tech. articles to AGARD publs. V.p. Tex. Fine Arts Assn., Ft. Worth, 1972. Served with USN, 1962—64. Recipient NASA Cert. of Recognition for tech. publ., 1980, Achievement award, Gen. Dynamics, 1980, 1983, 1989; Welding Rsch. Assn. fellow, 1961—62. Fellow: AIAA (assoc.; tech. reviewer jours.); mem.: Sigma Xi. Achievements include innovations in subsonic, transonic and supersonic steady and oscillatory aerodynamics method; major contributions to aeroelastic developments and improvements for Gen. Dynamics F-16 and F-111 aircrafts; development of new methods for predicting high angle of attack aerodynamics in subsonic and supersonic flows; steady and unsteady force testig techniques for aerodynamic investigations using water tunnels, new concepts and methods for nonlinear aeroelasticity; pioneered new technology development for unsteady separated flows and buffeting on aircraft maneuvering at high angle of attack involving support of Air Force; first to Navy; NASA; Nat. Aerospace Lab. (Netherlands); Lockheed; U. Tex., Austin; patents in field. Home: 4932 Black Oak Ln Fort Worth TX 76114-2936

CUNNINGHAM, BRIAN C. lawyer, corporate executive; b. Sparta Ill., Oct. 17, 1943; s. Robert C. and Gail L. (McDill) C.; m. Martha Elizabeth Kerr; children: Laura, Scott, Colby. B.S. in Elec. Engring., Washington U., St. Louis, 1965, J.D., 1970. Bar: N.Y. 1971, Mo. 1980, Calif. 1983, U.S. Dist. Ct. (so. dist.) N.Y. 1974, U.S. Dist. Ct. (no. dist.) Calif. 1983. Vol., U.S. Peace Corps, Washington, 1965-67; assoc. Winthrop, Stimpson Putnam & Roberts, N.Y.C., 1970-79; assoc. corp. counsel Monsanto, St. Louis, 1979-82; v.p., sec., gen. counsel Genentech, South San Francisco, 1982—, also bd. dirs. Home: 525 Pepper Ave Burlingame CA 94010-6437 Office: Cooley Godward et al 5 Palo Alto Sq Ste 400 Palo Alto CA 94306-2122

CUNNINGHAM, BRUCE ARTHUR, biochemist, educator; b. Winnebago, Ill., Jan. 18, 1940; s. Wallace Calvin and Margaret Wright (Clinite) C.; m. Katrina Sue Susdorf, Feb. 27, 1965; children— Jennifer Ruth, Douglas James. BS, U. Dubuque, 1962; PhD, Yale U., 1966. NSF postdoctoral fellow Rockefeller U., N.Y.C., 1966-68, asst. prof. biochemistry, 1968-71, assoc. prof., 1971-77, prof. molecular and devel. biology, 1978-92; prof. dept. neurobiology The Scripps Rsch. Inst., San Diego, 1992—. Editl. bd.: Jour. Biol. Chemistry, 1978-82, Jour. Cell Biology, 1992-96. Camille and Henry Dreyfus Found. grantee, 1970-75; recipient Career Scientist award Irma T. Hirschl Trust, 1975-80. Mem. AAAS, Am. Soc. Biol. Chemists, Am. Soc. Cell Biology, Protein Soc., Am. Chem. Soc., Harvey Soc., Am. Gynecol. Obstet. Soc. (hon.), Sigma Xi. Achievements include research on structure and function of molecules on cell surfaces. Office: Scripps Rsch Inst 10550 N Torrey Pines Rd La Jolla CA 92037-1000 E-mail: bcunning@scripps.edu.

CUNNINGHAM, CAROL CLEM, biochemistry educator, researcher; b. Woodland, Calif., July 14, 1938; s. Cecil Clem Cunningham and Gertie Arvona Strong; m. Lelia Ouida Scott; children: Theodore, Cheryl Michalec, Craig. BS, Okla. State U., 1961, MS, 1963; PhD, U. Ill., 1968. Asst. prof. biochemistry Wake Forest U. Sch. Medicine, Winston-Salem, NC, 1970—76, assoc. prof. biochemistry, 1976—82, prof. biochemistry, 1982—. Cons. NIH, Bethesda, 1984—, NSF, Washington, 1987—, VA, 1990—, Pharmacia, Kalamazoo, 2001. Contbr. articles to profl. jours. Recipient Career Development award, Nat. Inst. on Alcohol Abuse and Alcoholism, 1978—84, MERIT Award, 1993—2003, Sr. Scientist award, 1999—2004; fellow NIH predoctoral fellow, 1965—68, NIH postdoctoral fellow, 1968—70. Mem.: AAAS, Rsch. Soc. on Alcoholism, Am. Soc. for Biochemistry and Molecular Biology. Avocations: birdwatching, fishing. Office: Wake Forest U Dept Biochemistry Sch Medicine Winston Salem NC 27157 Personal E-mail: cunn@wfubmc.edu. Business E-Mail: cunn@wfubmc.edu.

CUNNINGHAM, DAVID FRATT, lawyer; b. N.Y.C., May 23, 1944; s. David Fratt Cunningham and Burnley Chenery Wadsworth; m. Tracy Griswold, June 1966 (div. 1973); 1 child, David Fratt, Jr.; m. Helen C. Sturm, Feb. 1979 (div. 1988); children: Meghan, Cory; m. Janet Clow, 2989. BA, Stanford U., 1966; JD, U. Calif., Hastings, 1969. Bar: N.Y. 1970, N.Mex. 1983. Asst. dist. atty. Manhattan Dist. Attys. Office, N.Y.C., 1969—72; chief asst. and acting spl. prosecutor Office of Spl. Narcotics Prosecutor, N.Y.C., 1972—80; chief investigative divsn. Manhattan Dist. Attys. Office, N.Y.C., 1980—83; shareholder, chief litigation sect. White, Koch, Kelly & McCarthy, PA, Santa Fe, 1983—. Commr. N.Mex. Organized Crime Commn., 1983-87; gen. counsel Zuni Tribe, 1987—. Co-author: Trial of a Criminal Case, 1980. Mem. ABA, Inn of the Ct. (Oliver Seth br. counsel 1994—). Democrat. Avocations: fly fishing, running. Office: White Koch Kelly & McCarthy PA PO Box 787 433 Paseo De Peralta Santa Fe NM 87501-1958

CUNNINGHAM, DOUGLAS D. state legislator; b. Osmond, Nebr., Oct. 13, 1954; m. Deb Cunningham; 1 child, John. Owner, operator D&D Foodliner, Wausa, Nebr.; mem. Nebr. Legislature from 18th dist., 2001—. Bd. dirs. Osmond Gen. Hosp. Found., Knox County Block Grant; mem. com. Wausa Appreciation Day; mem. strategic planning com. Wausa Pub. Schs.; coun. treas., Sunday sch. prin. Thabor Luth. Ch.; mem. Vol. Fire Dept.; del. Rep. State Conv.; co-chairperson Knox County Hagel for Senate campaign; vice chmn. Knox County Reps., 1996. Mem. Nat. Grocers Assn. (mem. govt. rels. coun., mem. polit. edn. com., Spirit of Am. award 2000), Nat. Grocery Industry (bd. dirs.), Knox County Pork Prodrs. (assoc.), Knox County Cattle Feeders (assoc.), Wausa Cmty. Club. Home: Box 160 Wausa NE 68786 Office: Rm 1010 State Capitol Lincoln NE 68509

CUNNINGHAM, GARY ALLEN, lawyer; b. Seattle, July 4, 1940; s. Chester Martin and Elsie Annette (Peterson) C.; m. Marilyn Phyllis Thunman, June 13, 1964. B in Engring., Yale U., 1962; JD, U. Wash., 1965. Bar: Wash. 1965, U.S. Dist. Ct. (we. dist.) Wash. 196t, U.S. Ct. Appeals (9th cir.) 1967, U.S. Supreme Ct. 1993. Dep. prosecutor King County Pros. Atty., Seattle, 1965-67; ptnr. Bishop, Cunningham & Andrews, Inc., P.S., Bremerton, Wash., 1967—. Bd. dirs. Hood Canal Environ. Coun., Seabeck, Wash., 1970—, pres., 1974, 78; bd. dirs., sec. Olympic Peninsula Kidney Ctr., Bremerton, 1980—; bd. dirs. Kitsap Land Trust, Bremerton, 1989-2000, pres., 1993-2000; bd. dirs. Great Peninsula Conservancy, 2000—, pres., 2000-02. Mem. ABA, Wash. State Bar Assn., Kitsap County Bar Assn. (pres. 1975-76), Kitsap Golf and Country Club, Bremerton Rotary Club. Avocations: golf, hiking, skiing, foreign travel. Home: 8411 Sunset Ln NW Seabeck WA 98380-9529 Office: PO Box 5060 Bremerton WA 98312-0469 E-mail: bca@silverlink.net.

CUNNINGHAM, GARY H. lawyer; b. Grand Rapids, Mich., Jan. 11, 1953; s. Gordon H. and Marilyn J. (Lookabill) C.; children: Stephanie M., Gregory H. B.Gen. Studies, U. Mich., 1975, MA, 1977; JD, Detroit Coll. Law, 1980. Bar: Mich. 1980, U.S. Dist. Ct. Mich. 1983, U.S. Ct. Appeals (6th cir.) 1986, U.S. Ct. Appeals (Fed. cir.) 1990. Law clk. and estate adminstr. U.S. Bankruptcy Ct., Ea. Dist. Mich., Detroit, 1980-83; assoc./ptnr. Schlussel, Lifton, Simon, Rands, Galvin & Jackier, Southfield, Mich., 1983-90; ptnr./shareholder Kramer Mellen, P.C., Southfield, Mich., 1990-95; prin. shareholder Strobl Cunningham Caretti & Sharp, P.C., Bloomfield Hills, Mich., 1995—. Sr. staff mem. Detroit Coll. of Law Rev., 1978-80; contbr. articles to profl. jours. Mem. ABA (bus. law sect.), Fed. Bar Assn. (chmn. bankruptcy sect. 1989-91), Oakland County Bar Assn. (bus. law com.), State Bar of Mich. (mem. corp., fin. and bus. law sect.), Am. Bankruptcy Inst. (sponsor), Comml. Law League of Am., Detroit Econ. Club, Detroit Inst. Arts, Delta Theta Phi. Avocations: sailing, skiing, tennis. Home: 3399 Roxbury Dr Troy MI 48084-2613 Office: Strobl Cunningham & Sharp PC 300 E Long Lake Rd Ste 200 Bloomfield Hills MI 48304-2376 E-mail: gcunningham@stroblpc.com.

CUNNINGHAM, GLORIA SWORD, retired librarian; b. Bath, Pa., June 28, 1929; d. Roy and Hilda (Brown) S; children: Rebekah Ann (dec.), Timothy David. BS, Trenton (N.J.) State Coll., 1974, MEd, 1984. Cert. tchr., libr., reading specialist. 4th and 6th grade tchr., now libr. Mansfield Twp. Elem. Sch. Dist., Port Murray, N.J., 1974—, ret., 1999. Russian exch. tchr. Hands Across the Water, 1992. Mem. NEA, Internat. Reading Assn., Am. Libr. Assn., N.J. Edn. Assn., Kappa Delta Pi. Avocations: reading, gardening, music, art, travel. Home: 52 Kinter St Clinton NJ 08809-1215

CUNNINGHAM, GORDON ROSS, financial executive; b. Toronto, Nov. 15, 1944; s. Wendell Carson and Catherine Ann C.; m. Patricia Dorothy Westheuser, Dec. 22, 1966; children: Kristyn Catherine, Kaleigh Ann, James Gordon. BA, U. Toronto, 1966, LLB, 1969; LLD (hon.), U. Victoria, 1995. Bar: Ont. 1971. With Tory, Tory, DesLauriers & Binnington, Toronto, 1971-76; ptnr. Toronto, 1977-84; exec. v.p., COO Trilon Fin. Corp., Toronto, 1984-88, pres., COO, 1988-89, bd. dirs.; pres., CEO London Life Ins. Co. and London Ins. Group Inc., 1989-96; pres. Cumberland Asset Mgmt. Corp., 1997—. Pres., dir. Fairmoor Holdings Inc.; bd. dirs. Intertape Polymer, Inc., Allied Properties Real Estate Investment Trust. Former nat. corp. campaign chmn. Diabetes Can. Mem. Can. Bar Assn., Can. Life and Health Ins. Assn. (past chmn.), Bus. Coun. Nat. Isues, Upper Can. Law Soc., Rosedale Golf Club, Univ. Club, Devil's Glen Ski Club, Mad River Golf Club, Portmarnock Golf Club (Dublin), Ristigouche Salmon Club. Avocations: golf, squash, fishing, tennis, skiing. Office: Cumberland Asset Mgmt Corp M99 Yorkville Ave Toronto ON Canada M5R 3K5

CUNNINGHAM, GUNTHER, professional football coach; m. Rene Cunningham; children: Natalie, Adam. BS in Gen. Sci., U. Oreg., 1969. Football coach U. Oreg., 1969-71, U. Kar., 1972, Stanford (Calif.) U., 1973-76, U. Calif., 1977-80; coach defensive line, linebackers CFL's Hamilton Tiger Cats, 1981; defensive line coach Balt. Colts, 1982-84; mentor defensive line San Diego Charters, 1985-90; coach linebackers Oakland (Calif.) Raiders, 1991, defensive coord., 1992-93, defensive line, 1994; defensive coord. Kansas City (Mo.) Chief, 1995-98, head coach, 1999—2001; coach linebackers Tenn. Titans, Nashville, 2002—. Office: Tennessee Titans Baptist Sports Park Nashville TN 37228

CUNNINGHAM, GUY HENRY, III, lawyer; b. Teaneck, N.J., Sept. 28, 1941; s. Guy Henry and Leonor (Lavedan) Cunningham; m. Kathleen Schneider, June 11, 1966; children: Thomas, Douglas. BA, Alfred U., 1964; JD, Georgetown U., 1967; MBA, U. Pa., 1983. Bar: D.C. 1967, Wash. 1991, Ohio 1998, U.S. Ct. Appeals (D.C. cir.) : 1970, U.S. Supreme Ct.: 1972. Asst. U.S. atty. Dept. Justice, Washington, 1969—72; atty. AEC, Washington, 1969—72; asst. gen. counsel Dept. Energy, Washington, 1975—78; atty. supr. Nuclear Regulatory Commn., Washington, 1978—82, exec. legal dir., 1982—86; gen. counsel Pacific N.W. divsn. Battelle Meml. Inst., Richland, Wash., 1986—97, assoc. gen. counsel, 1997—. Capt. U.S. Army, 1967—69, Vietnam. Decorated Bronze Star medal. Republican. Roman Catholic. Home: 167 Green Springs Dr Columbus OH 43235-4644 Office: Battelle Meml Inst 505 King Ave Columbus OH 43201-2693

CUNNINGHAM, JAMES BLAIR, ambassador; b. Sept. 2, 1952; s. Blair Walter and Julia Katherine (Knowles) C.; m. Leslie Ann Genier, Aug. 9, 1975; children: Emma Julianne, Abigail Kathleen. B of Polit. Sci. & Psychology cum laude, Syracuse U., 1974. Staff asst. to the ambassador, polit. officer fgn. svc. U.S. Embassy, Stockholm, 1975-77; deputy Spanish affairs officer U.S. State Dept., Washington, 1977-79, sec. affairs, 1979-81; polit.-mil. affairs officer U.S. Embassy, Rome, 1981-85; U.S. mission NATO, 1985-88, dir. pvt. office of NATO sec. gen. Manfred Woerner U.S. Dept. State, Washington, 1988-90, deputy polit. counselor U.S. mission to UN, 1990-92, deputy dir. office of European security and polit. affairs, 1992-93, dir. office of European security and polit. affairs, 1993-95; dep. chief of mission U.S. Embassy, Rome, 1996—99; dep. U.S. ambassador U.S. Dept. State, Washington, 1999—. Office: US Mission UN 799 United Nations Plz New York NY 10017-3505

CUNNINGHAM, JAMES GERALD, JR., transportation company executive; b. Morristown, N.J., Aug. 5, 1930; s. James Gerald and Kathryn Virginia (Cannon) C.; m. Marilyn Swanson, Sept. 22, 1956; children: Kathleen, Jean Marie, Barbara, James Gerald, III, Carl. BS in Civil Engring, Newark Coll. Engring., 1952. Civil engr. Pa. R.R., 1952-54; trainmaster Erie-Lackawanna R.R., 1956-62; divsn. mgr., dir. transp. Consol. Freightways, Menlo Park, Calif., 1962-69; sr. v.p., dir. REA Express, Inc., N.Y.C., 1969-75; also dir. REA Holding Corp.; pres., dir. Gateway Transp. Co., La Crosse, Wis., 1976-78; gen. mgr. intermodal ops. Consol. Rail Corp., Phila., 1978-79; pres., CEO PTL Truck Line LLC, Phila., 1980—. Served with Transp. Corps AUS, 1953-55. Mem. Am. Trucking Assn. (chmn. met. planning orgn. task force, exec. com.), Equipment Interchange Assn. (exec. com., past pres.), Intermodal Transp. Assn. (exec. com., past pres.), N.Y. Athletic Club, Aronimink Country Club. Home: 3505 Saint Davids Rd Newtown Square PA 19073-1417 Office: PTL Truck Line LLC 1100 E Hector St Ste 222 Conshohocken PA 19428-2378

CUNNINGHAM, JAMES OWEN, lawyer; b. Janesville, Wis., Jan. 16, 1951; s. James A. and Mary E. (Owen) C.; m. Joyce Dickinson, Dec. 16, 1978; children: Emily, James A. BS, Fla. State U., 1973, JD, 1977; MS in Mgmt., Rollins Coll., Winter Park, Fla., 1975. Bar: Fla. 1977, U.S. Ct. Appeals (5th cir.); cert. civil trial adv. Nat. Bd. Trial Adv. Assoc. Fisher & Matthews, Altamonte Springs, Fla., 1970-77, Billings & Durie, Orlando, Fla., 1979, Billings & Durie & Morgan, Orlando, Fla., 1980; ptnr. Billings, Cunningham, Morgan & Boatwright, Orlando, Fla., 1981—. Bd. dirs. Fla. State U. Coll. Law. Bd. dirs. Orange County Bar Found., 1998—. Mem. Fla. Bar Assn., Am. Trial Lawyers Assn., Fla. Trial Lawyers Assn., Orange County Bar Assn., Orange County Legal Aid Soc. (bd. dirs. 1996-99, pres. 1999—), Seminole County Bar Assn. Republican. Presbyterian. Home: 251 Rippling Ln Winter Park FL 32789-2841 Office: Billings, Cunningham Morgan & Boatwright 330 E Central Blvd Orlando FL 32801-1998 E-mail: jim@bcmb.com.

CUNNINGHAM, JAMES PATRICK, lawyer; b. Chgo., Mar. 15, 1937; AA, Phoenix Coll., 1956; student, Ariz. State U., 1956-58; LLB, U. Ariz., 1961. Bar: Ariz 1961, U. S. Dist. Ct. Ariz. 1963, U.S. Ct. Appeals (9th cir.) 1969, U.S. Supreme Ct. 1974, U.S. Ct. Appeals (10th cir.) 1976; cert. specialist injury and wrongful death litigation Ariz. Bd. Legal Specialization, 1991. Dep. county atty. County Atty.'s Office, Phoenix, 1961-63, spl. dep. county atty. sch. affairs, 1965-69; ptnr. Cunningham, Goodson & Tiffany, Phoenix, 1969-78, Cunningham, Tiffany & Hoffman, Phoenix, 1978-86; prin. Cunningham Law Firm, Phoenix, 1987—. Bd. dirs. Am. Ireland Fund, 1994-2001. Mem. ABA, ATLA, Am. Bd. Trial Advocates, Ariz. Trial Lawyers Assn. (bd. dirs.), State Bar Ariz., Maricopa County Bar Assn. Democrat. Roman Catholic. Office: Cunningham Law Firm 330 N 2nd Ave Phoenix AZ 85003-1517

CUNNINGHAM, JAMES WILLIAM, literacy education educator, researcher; b. Chattanooga, Jan. 22, 1947; s. Ernest James and Ann Louise Katherine (Martin) C.; m. Patricia M. Cunningham, Aug. 24, 1974; 1 child, David Ernest. BA in English, U. Va., 1970; MA in Reading Edn., U. Ga., 1973, PhD in Reading Edn., 1975. Classroom tchr. South Pittsburg (Tenn.) Elem. Sch., 1970-72; project coord. Right-to-Read Project, Athens, Ga., 1972-74; asst. prof. edn. U. N.C., Chapel Hill, 1975-80, assoc. prof., 1980-93, prof., 1993—, dir. literacy studies, 1991—96, 2002—. Contbr. articles to profl. jours. and chpts. to books; co-author 11 textbooks, including: Developing Readers and Writers in the Content Areas: K-12, 4th edit., 2003, Reading and Writing in Elementary Classrooms, 4th edit., 2000, Guided Reading the Four-Blocks Way, 2000; mem. editl. bd. Reading Rsch. Quar., Reading Psychology, Literacy Tchg. and Learning: An Internat. Jour. Early Reading and Writing. Mem. Internat. Reading Assn., Nat. Reading Conf. (bd. dirs. 1997-99), Nat. Conf. on Rsch. in Lang. and Literacy (fellow). Home: 811 Leigh Dr Gibsonville NC 27249-2734 Office: U NC 018 Peabody Hall Cb 3500 Chapel Hill NC 27599-3500 E-mail: jwcunnin@email.unc.edu.

CUNNINGHAM, JESSIE JEROME, entrepreneur; b. Miami, Fla., Oct. 10, 1963; s. Jesse James and Racheal Mae Cunningham. Student, Morristown Coll., 1989—91, Knoxville Coll., 1992—93. CEO, founder Cunningham Family Enterprises, Phila. Author: (novels) The Flame of Silence Jones Book One/Ever Prevailing Enemy!, 2001, Insights for Our Days and Time, 2002, Trilogy of the Gods, 2002; editor: The Midnight Mail-Order Almanac, 2002; prodr.: (TV) The Last Resort, 2002. Avocations: running, travel, painting, sculpting, acting. Office: Cunningham Family Enterprises PO Box 26406 Philadelphia PA 19141 Personal E-mail: Explode10j@netscape.net. Business E-Mail: explode10j@netscape.net.

CUNNINGHAM, JOEL LUTHER, university president, vice-chancellor; b. Mooresville, N.C., Jan. 11, 1944; s. Elbert Claxton and Ruth Morton (Journey) Cunningham; m. Trudy Bender, June 12, 1965; children: Nancy Elizabeth, Susan Ruth. BA, U. Tenn., Chattanooga, 1965; MA, U. Oreg., 1967, PhD, 1969. Asst. prof. math. U. Ky., Lexington, 1969—74; dean continuing edn. U. Tenn., Chattanooga, 1974—79; acad. v.p. Susquehanna U., Selinsgrove, Pa., 1979—84, pres., 1984—2000; vice-chancellor, pres. U. South, Sewanee, Tenn., 2000—. Trustee Assn. of Episcopal Coll., 2000—, chair, 2002—; bd. dirs. Sunbury (Pa.) Hosp., 1984—2000, v.p., 1992—98, pres., 1998—2000; bd. dirs. Pa. Campus Compact, 1987—92, Coll. & U. Anglican Commn., 2001—; treas. Coll. & U. Angelican Commn., 2002—; mem. St. Mary's Conf. Ctr., 2000—. Fellow Woodrow Wilson fellow, 1965, Am. Coun. on Edn. fellow, 1976—77. Mem.: Soc. for Values in Higher Edn. (bd. dirs. 1992—99, v.p. 1994—95, pres. 1995—99), Am. Assn. for Higher Edn., Math. Assn. Am., Am. Math. Soc.,

Sigma Chi (chmn. bd. leadership tng. 1977—87, treas. 1987—89, v.p. 1989—91, pres. 1991—93, Internat. Balfour award 1965), Sigma Xi. Episcopalian. Home: PO Box 3326 Sewanee TN 37375 Office: U South Office VC & Pres 735 University Ave Sewanee TN 37383 E-mail: jcunning@sewanee.edu.

CUNNINGHAM, JOHN RANDOLPH, project manager; b. Alexandria, La., July 17, 1954; s. John Adolphus and Zelma Audrey (Cox) C.; m. Teresa Ellen Toms, Jan. 22, 1977. BS in Computer Sci., La. Tech. U., 1976; masters cert. in project mgmt., George Washington U., 1999. Cert. project mgmt. profl. Customer support specialist South Ctrl. Bell Tel. Co., New Orleans, 1977-81; data comm. designer Weyerhaeuser, Tacoma, 1981-87, acct. rep., 1987-89, planning mgr., 1989-92, EDI project leader, 1992-2000, capacity planning mgr., 2001—; project mgr. Vision Compass, Inc., Seattle, 2000, Network Commerce, Seattle, 2000-01. Adv. bd. U. Wash., Seattle, 1989-94; spkr. fin. EDI confs. Contbr. articles to profl. jours. Vol. Big Bros., Tacoma, 1989—99, Wash. State First Responder, 1989—2000; instr. CPR, 1999—2000; instr. neighborhood emergency tng., 1999—2000; instr. emergency first aid, 2001—. Mem. NRA, Computer and Automated Systems Assn. (treas. 1991-95, pres. 1995-99), Project Mgmt. Inst., Indsl. Computing Soc., Instrument Soc. Am., Toastmasters Internat., Upsilon Pi Epsilon. Republican. Baptist. Home: 319 SW 328th St Federal Way WA 98023 5615 E mail: randy.cunningham@weyerhaeuser.com.

CUNNINGHAM, JUDY MARIE, lawyer; b. Durant, Okla., Sept. 7, 1944; d. Rowe Edwin and Margaret (Arnott) C. BA, U. Tex., 1967, JD, 1971; postgrad., Schiller Coll., Heidelberg, Fed. Republic Germany, 1976. Bar: Tex. 1972. Quizmaster U. Tex. Law Sch., Austin, 1969-71; rschr. Tex. Law Rev., Washington, 1970; staff atty. Tex. Legis. Coun., Austin, 1972-75; adminstrv. law judge, dir. sales tax div., assoc. counsel Comptr. of Pub. Accounts, Austin, 1975-85; owner, editor J.C. Law Publs., Austin, 1986—; pvt. practice Austin, 1986—. Author: (with others) Texas Tax Service, 1985; pub., editor, contbr. (newsletter) Tex. State Tax Update, 1986—; contbr. articles to Revenue Adminstrn.; assoc. editor Tex. Law Rev., 1968-71. State del. Dem. Party, Ft. Worth, 1990, county del., Austin, 1972, 88, 90, 92; vol. numerous Dem. campaigns, Austin, 1972-90. Mem. Industry Practitioners Liaison Group (comptr. pub. accts.), State Bar Tex. (taxation sect.), Travis County Bar (bus. corp. and taxation sect.), Tex. Taxpayers and Rsch. Assn. Avocations: traveling, cooking, reading mysteries, photography, swimming. Office: 4905 W Park Dr Austin TX 78731-5535

CUNNINGHAM, JULIA WOOLFOLK, author; b. Spokane, Oct. 4, 1916; d. John George and Sue (Larabie) C. Grad., St. Anne's Sch., Charlottesville, Va., 1933. Author: (juveniles): The Vision of Francois the Fox, 1960, Dear Rat, 1961, Macaroon, 1962, Candle Tales, 1964, Dorp Dead, 1965 (Children's Spring Book Festival award), 2002, Violet, 1966, Onion Journey, 1967, Burnish Me Bright, 1970, Wings of the Morning, 1971, Far in the Day, 1972, The Treasure Is the Rose, 1973, Maybe, A Mole, 1974, Come to the Edge, 1977 (Christoper award 1978), Tuppenny, 1978, A Mouse called Junction, 1980, Flight of the Sparrow, 1980 (Commonwealth Club Calif. award, Honor Book award Boston Globe), The Silent Voice, 1981, Wolf Roland, 1983, Oaf, 1986, (poetry) Shadow Heart, 1999, The Stable Rat and Other Christmas Poems, 2001, Cicada, 2001. Mem. Authors Guild. Home: Rancho Santa Barbara 333 Old Mill Rd Space 88 Santa Barbara CA 93110-4429

CUNNINGHAM, JULIAN ANTONIA, retired protective services official; b. Mobile, Ala., Oct. 24, 1954; s. Booker Telefaro Cunningham Jr. and Julia Aldonia Cunningham; 1 child, Tüvora Chanel Cook. Grad. h.s., Mobile. Salesman Treadwell Ford, Mobile, 1976, Al Trovinger Ford, Mobile, 1977; lt. Ala. Security Police & K9, Mobile, 1978—80; clk. U.S. Census Bur., Mobile, 1980; merchant civilian USN, Bayonne, NJ, 1985; ret. Radio operator, basic obedience trainer Mobile Ala. Security Police, 1979; chief usher Rock of Faith Bapt. Ch., 1998, trustee, 2001. With USNR, 1972—78. Democrat. Baptist. Avocations: dog training, horses. Home: 1150 Freeman St Mobile AL 36605

CUNNINGHAM, KEITH ALLEN, II, computer services company executive; b. Belington, W.Va., Aug. 1, 1948; s. Keith A. and Jeanne Antionette (Viquesney) C.; m. Barbra Anne McCoy, 1991. Student, Oakland U., 1972; BA, Mich. State U., 1973. Asst. mgr. Joseph Lucas N.Am., Inc., Detroit, 1973; distbn. ctr. mgr. Lucas Industries, Inc., San Francisco, 1974-78; export mgr. Primark, Inc., San Mateo, Calif., Reno, Nev., 1978-79; operational planning mgr. United Nuc. Corp, Falls Church, Va., 1979-80; pres., CEO, dir. Unicore, Inc. subs. United Nuc. Corp., North Haven, Conn., 1980-82; dir. bus. devel. UNC Resources, 1982, pres., CEO, dir., 1982, UNC Teton Exploration Drilling Co., a UNC Resources Co., 1982-84; prin., dir. ATLIS Systems, Inc., Vienna, Va., v.p. fin. and adminstrn., CFO, 1985-87, pres., COO, 1987—; chmn., CEO Allegiance Staffing, Inc., Silver Spring, Md., 2001—. Mem. Mich. State U. Alumni Assn., Izaak Walton League Am., Inc., ATLIS/Allegiance 8455. Home: 6 Coral Gables Ct North Potomac MD 20878-3801 Office: Atlis Systems Inc 8455 Colesville Rd Ste 1050 Silver Spring MD 20910 E-mail: keithii@atlis.com.

CUNNINGHAM, KEITH ALLEN, corporate executive, accountant, lawyer, engineer; b. Weaver, W.Va., Aug. 21, 1922; s. James Arthur and Blanche (Proudfoot) C.; m. Jeanne Antoinette Viquesney, June 6, 1942; children: Keith Allen, Kathe Jan. BSBA, W.Va. U., 1948, JD, 1951. Bar: W.Va. 1951; CPA, Mich., Ohio, N.Y., Ind., La. Bldg. constrn. engr. Gibbs & Hills, Inc., N.Y.C., 1942-43; pvt. practice Belington, W.Va., 1952; assoc. Touche, Niven, Bailey & Smart, CPAs, Detroit, 1952-60; ptnr.-in-charge Dayton (Ohio) office Touche, Ross, Bailey & Smart, 1960-65, dir. adminstrn. and office ops., 1965-67, exec. adminstrv. ptnr., vice chmn. bd. dirs., 1967-70; pres. Energy Conversion Devices, Inc., Troy, Mich., 1969-72, dir., 1969-74; exec. v.p. United Nuclear Corp., Falls Church, Va., 1973-75, pres., CEO, 1975-84, chmn. bd., 1982-84, also dir. Chmn. bd., CEO Atlis Systems, Inc., Atlis Cons. Group, Atlis Fed. Svcs., Inc., Atlis Legal Info. Svcs., Inc., Atlis Micrographics Svcs., Inc., Atlis Pub. Svcs., Inc., 1984—; dir. Clevepak Corp.; chmn. bd. Atlis Corp.; lectr. W.Va. Tax Inst. Mem. Coun. for Reorgn. Ohio State Govt., 1963-64; treas. Mich. Employers Umployment Compensation Bur., 1957-60; mem. adv. com. Mich. Security Commn., 1958-60. Served with USAAF, 1943-46. Mem. AICPAs, Am. Acctg. Assn., Nat. Assn. Accts., Mich. Soc. CPAs, Ohio Soc. CPAs (dir.), N.Y. Soc. CPAs, N.J. Soc. CPAs, Mich. Bar Assn., W.Va. Bar Assn., Detroit Bar Assn., Mining Club (N.Y.C.), Detroit Athletic Club, Petroleum Club, Albuquerque Country Club, Congl. Country Club, Farmington Country Club (Charlottesville, Va.), Vero Beach Country Club, Phi Beta Kappa, Phi Delta Phi. Methodist. Home: 12208 Meadow Creek Ct Potomac MD 20854-1408 also: 653 Lake Dr Vero Beach FL 32963-2166 Office: 8728 Colesville Rd Silver Spring MD 20910-3918 E-mail: kac@atlis.com.

CUNNINGHAM, LAINE, editor, educator, writer, consultant; d. Richard Wayne and Edna Arlene Cunningham. BA, George Mason U., Fairfax, Va., 1990. Pres. Ink Imp Editl., Asheboro, NC, 1994—; creative writing instr. The Loft Lit. Ctr., Mpls., 2000—02; sr. editor This Side Up Newspaper, Sacramento, 1997—98; editl. cons. Fine Arts Festival, Fergus Falls, Minn., 2001—02. Arts juror Minn. State Arts Bd., St. Paul, 2002; regional rep. Nat. Writers Union, Sebeka, Minn., 2001; arts juror Lakes Region Arts Coun., Fergus Falls, Minn., 2001, N.Y. Mills Cultural Ctr., New York Mills, Minn., 1999; newsletter editor SGA, Sacramento, 1988—99; writing cons. Writing Assocs., Sacramento, 1996; lectr. in field. Author: (travel guide series) All Over Down Under; contbr. mural; author: (poetry) Amazing Instant Novelist contest (Hon. Mention, 1998); contbr. Recipient Arts Residency (alt.), Va. Ctr. for Creative Arts, 2002, Career Opportunity award, Lake Region Arts Coun., 2002, Minn. Writers Directory award, Blanden Found./Loft, 2001, Month-long Arts Residency, Cornucopia Arts Ctr., 2001, Arts Residency, NY Mills Cultural Ctr., 1999, fellow Jerome Found. fellow, 2001, 1999; scholar Va. Studio Ctr. full scholarship (alt.), 2001. Mem.: Sacramento Pub. Assn., Calif. Lawyers for the Arts, N.C. Writers Network, ZICA Creative Arts and Lit. Guild, Nat. Writers Union. Office: Ink Imp Editorial 501 Martin Luther King Jr Dr Asheboro NC 27203

CUNNINGHAM, LEON WILLIAM, biochemist, educator; b. Columbus, Ga., June 9, 1927; s. Leon W. and Annie (Bussey) C.; m. Jean Swingle, Aug. 21, 1948; children: Hugh, Pamela, Sue Ellen. BS, Auburn U., 1947; MS, U. Ill., 1949, PhD, 1951. Rsch. fellow protein chemistry U. Wash., Seattle, 1951-53; asst. prof. biochemistry Sch. Medicine, Vanderbilt U., Nashville, 1953-60, assoc. prof., 1960-65, prof., 1965-94, Branscomb Disting. prof., 1989-94, chmn. dept. biochemistry, 1973-88, assoc. dean Sch. Medicine, 1967-73; prof. emeritus Vanderbilt U., Nashville, 1994. Vis. staff Nat. Inst. for Med. Rsch., London, 1976; vis. prof. physiol. chemistry U. Utrecht, Netherlands, 1980, 85, 91. Served with USNR, 1945-46. USPHS spl. fellow Netherlands Nat. Def. Orgn., 1961-62 Mem. AAAS, Am. Soc. Biochemistry and Molecular Biology. Home: 105 Longwood Pl Nashville TN 37215-1926

CUNNINGHAM, MADELEINE WHITE, microbiologist, immunologist; b. Greenville, Miss., Feb. 24, 1946; d. L.C. and Josephine (Kersh) White; m. Curtis Phillip Cunningham, Dec. 19, 1969 (div. 1986); children: Catherine, Nicole, Luke; m. Michael Paul Lerner, Oct. 2, 1999. BS, Miss. U. for Women, 1968; MS, U. Tenn., 1971, PhD, 1973. Postdoctoral fellow Okla. Med. Rsch. Found., Oklahoma City, 1973-76; rsch. assoc. U. Okla. Health Sci. Ctr., Oklahoma City, 1980-81, asst. prof., 1981-86, assoc. prof. microbiology, 1986-93, prof., 1993—2000, dir. Flow Cytometry Core Ctr., 1990-92, George Lynn Cross prof., 2000—. Mem. bacteriology-mycology study sect. NIH, Washington, 1989-93, mem. myocarditis working group, 1985; mem. grant-in-aid rev. com. Am. Heart Assn., 1993-2000, co-chmn., 1996, chair, 1996-2000; bd. dirs. Presbyn. Health Fedn., Oklahoma City, 1995—; cons. com. on vaccines NAS, 1996; mem. nat. rsch. com. Am. Heart Assn., 1996-2001, mem. rsch program and evaluation com., 1997-2002; mem. merit rev. infectious disease subcom. VA, 2000—. Mem. editl. bd. Infection and Immunity, 1993-99; contbr. articles to sci. jours. Bd. dirs. Canterbury Choral Soc., Oklahoma City, 1988. Grantee Am. Heart Assn., 1984-86, Nat. Heart, Lung and Blood Inst., 1986-89, 89-94, 95—, others; recipient NIH Rsch. Career Devel. award, 1986-91, NIH Merit award, 1999—, Provost's Rsch. award U. Okla., 1986, Regent's award for outstanding rsch. and creative activity, 1994. Mem. AAAS, Am. Soc. Microbiology, Am. Assn. Immunologists, Lancefield Soc. for Streptococci and Strep Diseases (pres., v.p. 1991-93). Presbyterian. Office: U Okla Health Sci Ctr Dept Microbiology PO Box 26901 Oklahoma City OK 73126-0901

CUNNINGHAM, MARY ELIZABETH (MARY CUNNINGHAM-LUSBY), physician; b. Newark, N.J., Apr. 21, 1931; d. William Rutherford and Mary Agnes Veronica (Harvey) C.; m. Perry Minor Lusby, Nov. 30, 1996. AB, Mount Holyoke Coll., 1953; MS, U. Ill., 1957; PhD, U. Oregon, 1964; MD, U. Conn., 1982. Diplomate Am. Bd. Emergency Medicine. Sr. physicist Lawrence Livermore Nat. Lab., Livermore, Calif., 1964-78; residency in emergency medicine Mich. State U. Affiliated Hosp., 1982—85, sr. resident, 1984—85; sr. physician The Permanente Med. Group, Sacramento, 1985-96 (ret.), vol. physician, 1996—. Cons. emergency medicine King Faisal Specialist Hosp. and Rsch. Ctr., Jeddah, KSA, 2000-01. Contbr. articles to profl. jours. Physician Flying Samaritans-Mother Lode chpt., Sonoma, Calif., 1991—. Fellow Am. Coll. Emergency Physicians; mem. AMA (Calif. chpt.), Am. Physical Soc., N.Y. Acad. Scis., Phi Beta Kappa, Sigma Xi (grant-in-aid-of-rsch. award 1963-64). Roman Cath. Office: Kaiser Permanente Med Ctr 6600 Bruceville Rd Sacramento CA 95823-4671

CUNNINGHAM, MERCE, dancer; b. Centralia, Wash. Student, Cornish Sch.; PhD (hon.), U. Ill.; DFA (hon.), Wesleyan U., 1995. Own dance co., 1953—; tchr. Sch. Am. Ballet, 1948-51; propr. own dance sch. N.Y.C., 1959—. Dancer world tour, 1964, S.Am. tour, 1968, 1976, 1982, 1988, Mideast tour, 1972, 1976, Australia tour, 1976, Japan tour, 1964, 1976, 1987, 1994, 1998, Far East tour, 1984, India tour, 1964, 1984, 1990, numerous tours including U.S. and Europe, 1949, 1958, 1960, 1966, 1969—70, 1972, 1976—77, 1979—, choreographer The Seasons, 1947, Sixteen Dances for Soloist and Company of Three, 1951, Septet, 1953, Minutiae, 1954, Suite for Five, 1956, Nocturnes, 1956, Rune, 1959, Crises, 1960, Aeon, 1961, Story, 1963, Winterbranch, 1964, Variations V, 1965, How to Pass, Kick, Fall and Run, 1965, Place, 1966, Canbield, 1969, Tread, 1970, Second Hand, 1970, Signals, 1970, Landrover, 1972, Changing Steps, 1975, Solo, 1975, Un Jour on Deux, 1973, Sounddance, 1975, Rebus, 1975, Torse, 1976, Squaregame, 1976, Travelogue, 1977, Inlets, 1977, Fractions, 1977, Exchange, 1978, Locale, 1979, Duets, 1980, Channels/Inserts, 1981, Trails, 1982, Quartet, 1982, Coast Zone, 1983, Roaratorio, 1983, Pictures, 1984, Doubles, 1984, Phrases, 1984, Native Green, 1985, Arcade, 1985, Points in Space, 1986, Fabrications, 1987, Shards, 1987, Five Stone Wind, 1988, Cargo X, 1989, August Pace, 1989, Polarity, 1990, Neighbors, 1991, Trackers, 1991, Beach Birds, 1991, Loosestrife, 1991, Change of Address, 1992, Touchbase, 1992, Enter, 1992, Doubletoss, 1993, CRWDSPCR, 1993, Ocean, 1994, Ground Level Overlay, 1995, Windows, 1995, Rondo, 1996, Installations, 1996, Scenario, 1997, Pond Way, 1998, BIPED, 1999, Interscape, 2000, Way Station, 2001, Loose Time, 2002, Fluid Canvas, 2002. Decorated Comdr. Order of Arts and Letters Legion of Honor France; recipient Gold medal, Internat. Festival Dance, 1966, Grand prix, Belgrade Internat. Theatre Festival, 1972, Creative Arts award, Brandeis U., 1973, Capezio award, 1977, Samuel H. Scripps/Am. Dance Festival award, 1982, Mayor's award of honor for arts and culture, N.Y.C., 1983, Kennedy Ctr. honors, 1985, Laurence Olivier award, 1985, Meadows award for Excellence in Arts, So. Meth. U., 1987, Nat. Medal of Arts, 1990, Digital Dance Premier award, 1990, Wexner prize, Wexner Ctr. for Arts, Columbus, Ohio, 1993, Golden Lion award, Venice Biennale, 1995, Nellie Cornish Arts Achievement award, Cornish Coll. of Arts, Seattle, 1996, Medal of Distinction, Barnard Coll., 1997, Grand Prix, SACD, France, 1997, Belknap award in Humanities, Princeton U., 1998, Key to City, Montpellier, France, 1999, Established Artists award, Bagley Wright Fund, Seattle, 1998, Isadora Duncan award for Lifetime Achievement in Dance, Nat. Dance Week, San Francisco, 1999, Premio Tani, Rome, 1999, Handel Medallion, N.Y.C., 1999, Nijinsky Spl. prize, Monaco, 2000, Dorothy and Lillian Gish prize, 2000; MacArthur Found. fellow, 1985. Mem.: Am. Acad. and Inst. Arts and Letters (hon.). Office: Cunningham Dance Found 55 Bethune St New York NY 10014-2010

CUNNINGHAM, MICHAEL, author, educator; b. Cin., 1952; BA, Stanford U., 1975; MFA, U. Iowa, 1980. Adj. asst. prof. Creative Writing Ctr., Columbia U., N.Y.C. Author: Golden States, A Home at the End of the World, Flesh and Blood, The Hours (Pulitzer prize for fiction 1999, PEN/Faulkner award), Crowns: Portraits of Black Women in Church Hats, 2000, Land's End: A Walk through Provincetown, 2002, (short story) White Angel (Best Am. Short Stories, 1989); contbg. author: The Penguin Book of Gay Short Stories; contbr. to Atlantic Monthly, Redbook, Paris Rev., New Yorker, WigWag. Grantee Michener fellowship, 1982, Nat. Endowment for the Arts fellowship, 1988, Guggenheim fellowship, 1993. Office: Crown Pub Random House Inc 1540 Broadway New York NY 10036*

CUNNINGHAM, MICHAEL GERALD, composer, music educator; b. Warren, Mich., Aug. 5, 1937; s. Edmund John and Mary Ann (Etienne) C. MusB, Wayne State U., 1959; MusM, U. Mich., 1961; MusD, Ind. U., 1973. Accompanist, music dir. dance dept. Wayne State U., Detroit, 1961, 64-67, instr. music dept., 1967-69; teaching asst. Ind. U. Sch. Music, Bloomington, 1969-71; lectr. music theory U. Kans. Sch. Fine Arts, Lawrence, 1972; asst. prof. Conservatory Music, U. Pacific, Stockton, Calif., 1973; prof. music theory and composition U. Wis., Eau Claire, 1973—. Author: The Inner World of Traditional Theory, 1989, The Romantic Century, 2000, Progressive Bach, 2001; composer: numerous compositions. With U.S. Army, 1962-63. Mem. ASCAP (ann. stipend 1969—), Wis. Alliance Composers, Sigma Alpha Iota. E-mail: cunninmg@uwec.edu.

CUNNINGHAM, MILAMARI ANTOINELLA, anesthesiologist; b. Cody, Wyo., Oct. 4, 1949; d. Milo Leo and Mary Madeline (Haley) Olds; m. Michael Otis Webb, June 4, 1970 (div. Feb. 1971); m. James Kenneth Cunningham, June 14, 1975. BA with honors, U. Mo., 1971, MD, 1975. Diplomate Am. Bd. Anesthesiologists. Intern and resident U. Mo., Columbia, 1975-78; jr. ptnr. Anesthesiologist, Inc., 1979-82, ptnr., 1982-86; owner Cunningham Anesthesia, 1986—; dir. anesthesia dept. Ellis Fischel Cancer Ctr., 1991-92; acting chief anesthesia Harry S. Truman Meml. Vets. Hosp., 1994-95. Mem. med. staff Columbia Regional Hosp., U. Mo. Hosp. and Clinics, Columbia; mem. rev. com. Mo. Health Facilities, 2001—. Mem. editl. bd.: Mo. Medicine Jour., 2001. Active Mo. Med. Polit. Action Com., 1991-2000, Friends of Music, Friends of Libr., Boone County Fair, 1978-94, with ham breakfast divsn., 1978-85, with draft horse and mule show, 1986-88; bd. dirs. A Call to Serve Mo., 1996. Fellowship Am. Coll. Anesthesiologists, 1977. Mem.: AMA (Physicians Recognition award 1978, 1985, 1987, 1991, 1995), Vis. Nurses Assn. (bd. dirs. 1982—89, chair 1984—86, adv. bd. 1989—93), Am. Soc. Anesthesiologists (Mo. dist. dir. 2003—, alt. dir. dist. 17 2003), Mo. State Med. Assn. (commn. econs. third party payors 1986—89, chair 1989, Mo. health facilities rev. com. 2001—), Boone County Med. Soc. (membership chair 1982—84, alt. del. 1986, del. 1987—89, pres. 1988—98, sec.-treas, 1996, bd. dirs. 1996—99, del. 1997), Mo. Soc. Anesthesiologists (v.p. 1986—87, pres. elect 1987—88, pres. 1988—89, del. 1989—98, 2000, del 2000—02, alternate dist. 17 dir. 2003—, dist. dir. 2003—), Am. Med. Women's Assn., Phi Beta Kappa. Home: 8202 S Bennett Dr Columbia MO 65201 9178 Office: PO Box 1301 Columbia MO 65205-1301 E-mail: mila@tranquility.net.

CUNNINGHAM, MONICA DIXSON, lawyer, city administrator; b. Potsdam, N.Y., Aug. 19, 1948; d. William Clyde and Alice Condlin Dixson; m. Harry Halstead Cunningham, Dec. 8, 1973 (div. 1981); m. John Eugene Edmonson, Oct. 17, 1998. BA in History with honors, Russell Sage Coll., 1970; JD, Am. U., 1973. Bar: Tex. 1974. Pvt. practice law, El Paso, Tex., 1974-78; legal asst. to county judge County of El Paso, 1979-82; asst. city atty. City of El Paso, 1983-85, 87-95; v.p., legal counsel SYT Corp., El Paso, 1985-87; chief adminstrv. officer City of El Paso, 1995—2002; of counsel Kemp Smith Law Firm, El Paso, Tex., 2002—. Office: 6006 Balcones #16 El Paso TX 79912 E-mail: mcunnin1@elp.rr.com.

CUNNINGHAM, PATRICK COLM, research scientist, science administrator; b. Kilmacthomas, County Waterford, Ireland, May 24, 1933; s. Edmond and Marcella Mary (Power) C.; m. Anastasia Dolores Quigley, June 28, 1961; children: Eamon, Donal, Colm, Niamh, Niall, Orla, Dara, Ciara. B. Agr. Sci., U. Coll. Dublin, 1956; M. Agr. Sci., 1958, PhD, 1967; MS, Cornell U., 1964. Scientific officer Dept. Agr. and Food, Dublin, 1958-59; rsch. officer An Foras Taluntais, Dublin, 1959-64; sr. rsch. officer Carlow, Ireland, 1964-70; prin. rsch. officer, 1970-79; sr. prin. rsch. officer, 1979-87; head plant pathology dept., 1980-88; sr. prin. rsch. officer TEAGASC, Carlow, 1987-88; cons. fungicide efficacy, 1988—. Contbr. articles to profl. rsch. jours., chpts. to books. Bd. mgmt. Christian Bros. Sch., Carlow, 1988-91. Recipient Sir Edwin J. Butler award for plant pathology rsch., 1994. Mem. Am. Phytopathol. Soc., Soc. Irish Plant Pathologists (founder, pres. 1991-94), Brit. Soc. Plant Pathology (founder), Brit. Mycological Soc., Assn. Applied Biology, Carlow Golf Club (pres. 1994-95). Roman Catholic. Avocations: reading, golf, walking, ecology. Home: Mayfield Athy Rd Carlow Ireland Office: TEAGAS Oak Park Research Center Carlow Ireland Fax: 0503-42423. E-mail: dolorescun@eircom.net.

CUNNINGHAM, PAUL GEORGE, minister; b. Chgo., Aug. 27, 1937; s. Paul George Sr. and Naomi Pearl (Anderson) C.; m. Constance Ruth Seaman, May 27, 1960; children: Lori, Paul, Connie Jo. BA, Olivet Nazarene U., 1960; BDiv., Nazarene Theol. Sem., 1964; DD, Mid Am. Nazarene Coll., 1975. Sr. pastor Coll. Ch. of the Nazarene, Olathe, Kans., 1964-93; gen. supt. Internat. Ch. of the Nazarene, 1993—. Adv. bd. Kansas City Dist. Ch. of the Nazarene, Overland Park, Kans., 1971-93; trustee Mid Am. Nazarene Coll., Olathe, 1971—; chmn. book com. Nazarene Pub. House, Kansas City, Mo., 1974-90; pres. gen. bd. Internat. Ch. of the Nazarene, Kansas City, 1985-93. Police chaplain Olathe (Kans.) Police Dept., 1975-93; adv. bd. Good Samaritan Ctr., Olathe, 1990—. Recipient Disting. Svc. award Jaycees, Olathe, 1967, Paul Harris fellow Rotary Internat., Olathe, 1989. Mem. Nat. Assn. Evangs., Rotary. Mem. Ch. Of The Nazarene. Home: 12543 S Hagan Ln Olathe KS 66062-6075 Office: Ch of the Nazarene 6401 Paseo Blvd Kansas City MO 64131-1213 E-mail: pcunningham@nazarene.org.

CUNNINGHAM, RANDY, congressman; b. L.A., Dec. 8, 1941; m. Nancy Jones; 3 children. BA, MA, U. Mo., 1967; MBA, Nat. U. Lt. commander U.S. Navy, 1966—68; mem. U.S. Congress from 50th (formerly 44th) Calif. dist., 1991—; mem. intelligence com.; mem. appropriations com. Republican. Office: US Ho Reps 2350 Rayburn Ho Office Bldg Washington DC 20515-0551*

CUNNINGHAM, RAYMOND CAROL, JR., elementary school educator; b. Blackshear, Ga., Jan. 10, 1962; s. Raymond Carol Cunningham Sr. and Irma Lucille (Anderson) Cunningham; m. Elizabeth Laura Jones, July 11, 1998; children: Brett Christian, Reason Chandler, Emmaline Lois. AA in Psychology, Waycross Jr. Coll., Waycross, Ga., 1983; BSED in Health/Phys. Edn., U. Ga., 1984; postgrad., Valdosta State U. Cert. Tchg. cert. Ga. Tchr. Grady St. Elem. Sch., Blackshear, 1984—87, Patterson Elem. Sch., Ga., 1987—. Ch. pianist Patterson Bapt. Ch., 1985—. Named Tchr. of Yr., Pierce County Bd. Edn., 1990; recipient Cmty. Svc. award, Patterson Lions Club, 1996. Mem.: Ga. Assn. Educators, Profl. Assn. Ga. Educators. Office: Patterson Elem Sch 3444 Drawdy St Patterson GA 31557-2439 Home: PO Box 531 Patterson GA 31557

CUNNINGHAM, RAYMOND LEO, retired research chemist; b. Easton, Ill., Jan. 5, 1934; s. Raymond J. and Minnie G. (Vaughn) C. BA, St. Ambrose U., Davenport, Iowa, 1955. Phys. sci. aid in chemistry Nat. Ctr. Agrl. Utilization Rsch USDA Agrl. Rsch. Svc., Peoria, Ill., 1957-61, chemist Nat. Ctr. Agrl. Utilization Rsch., 1961-78, rsch. chemist Nat. Ctr. Agrl. Utilization Rsch., 1978-97; ret., 1997. Contbr. articles to profl. jours. With U.S. Army, 1958. Co-recipient R&D 100 award R&D mag., 1988. Fellow Am. Inst. Chemists; mem. AAAS, Am. Chem. Soc., Ill. State Acad. Sci. Home: 1108 W MacQueen Ave Peoria IL 61604-3310 E-mail: raymond.cunningham@att.net.

CUNNINGHAM, ROBERT JAMES, lawyer; b. Kearney, Nebr., June 27, 1942; m. Sara Jean Dickson, July 22, 1967. BA, U. Nebr., 1964; JD, NYU, 1967, LLM in Taxation, 1969. Bar: N.Y. 1967, Ill. 1969, U.S. Dist. Ct. (no. dist.) Ill. 1969, U.S. Ct. Claims 1970, U.S. Tax Ct. 1970, U.S. Ct. Appeals (D.C. cir.) 1972, U.S. Ct. Appeals (9th cir.) 1975, U.S. Ct. Appeals (7th cir.) 1979, U.S. Ct. Appeals (fed. cir.) 1982. Instr. law NYU, N.Y.C., 1967-69; assoc. Baker & McKenzie, Chgo., 1969-74, ptnr., 1974—. Spkr. in field. Contbr. articles to profl. jours. Mem. ABA, Ill. Bar Assn., Chgo. Bar Assn. Office: Baker & McKenzie One Prudential Plz 130 E Randolph Dr Ste 3700 Chicago IL 60601-6342 E-mail: robert.j.cunningham@bakernet.com.

CUNNINGHAM, RONNIE WALTER, venture capitalist; b. Creston, Iowa, Mar. 16, 1932; s. Walter Wilfred and Gladys (Backen) C.; m. Dorothy League, Dec. 27, 1997; children: Brian Keith, Kimberly Ann. BS in Physics, UCLA, 1960, MA, 1961; advanced mgmt. program, Harvard Grad. Sch. Bus., 1974. Rsch. asst. Planning Rsch. Corp., Westwood, Calif., 1959-60; physicist RAND Corp., Santa Monica, Calif., 1960-64; astronaut NASA, 1964-71; crew member of first manned Apollo spacecraft Apollo 7; chief, Skylab br., 1968-71; sr. v.p. Century Devel., 1971-74; pres. Hydrotech Devel. Co., Houston, 1974-76; sr. v.p. 3D/Internat., Houston, 1976-79; founder The Capital Group, Houston, 1979-86; mng. ptnr. Genesis Fund, 1986-98. Bd. dirs. numerous tech. based cos.; mem. adv. bd. Nat. Renewable Energy Lab.; lectr. in field. Author: The All American Boys, 1977; host radio talk show Lift-Off to Logic, 1998—. Judge Rolex awards for enterprise, 1984. With USNR, 1951-52, fighter pilot USMCR, 1952-74, col. ret. Recipient NASA Exceptional Service medal, also; Haley Astronautics award; Profl. Achievement award UCLA Alumni, 1969; Spl. Trustee award Nat. Acad. Television Arts and Scis., 1969; medal of valor Am. Legion, 1975; Outstanding Am. award Am. Conservative Union, 1975, George Haddaway award, 2000; named to Internat. Space Hall of Fame, Houston Hall of Fame, Astronaut Hall of Fame, 1997. Fellow Am. Astronautical Soc.; mem. Soc. Exptl. Test Pilots, Am. Inst. Aeros. and Astronautics, Assn. Space Explorers-U.S.A., Am. Geophys. Union, Sigma Pi Sigma. Office: 2425 West Loop S Ste 200 Houston TX 77027-4207

CUNNINGHAM, SHAWN PETRICE, TV anchor; b. Bronx, NY, June 27, 1973; d. Louis Howard and Catherine Elizabeth Cunningham. BA media studies, Fordham U, NY, NY, 1999; MA broadcast journalism, NYU, NY, NY, 2001. Cert. TV news production NYU/ NY. Reporter WZBN-TV, Trenton, NJ, 1999—2000; reporter, anchor WRNN-TV, New York, NY, 1999—2000; anchor WEVU-TV, Naples, Fla., 2000—01, WWAC-TV, Atlantic City, 2001; morning anchor WAGN-TV, Presque Isle, Maine, 2001—02; anchor, reporter WAGM-TV8, Presque Isle, Maine, 2001—02. Pres. N. Maine Media Women, Presque Isle, Maine, 2002, N. Maine Women in Comm., 2002. Pres. Nat. Coun. of Negro Women, Maine, 2002, Key Women of Am., Maine, Top Ladies of distinction, Maine, 2002, Polit. Congress of Black Women, Maine. Recipient Outstanding Young Careerist, Bus. and Prof. Women, 2002, Telly, The Telly Found., 2002, Outstanding Communicator, 2000—02. Mem.: RTNDA, Soc. of Prof. Jour. Achievements include spokesperson on breast cancer awareness; literary activist; philanthropist. Home: 201 Parkhurst Rd Presque Isle ME 04769

CUNNINGHAM, STANLEY LLOYD, lawyer; b. Durant, Okla., Feb. 7, 1938; s. Stanley Ryan and Hazel Dell (Dillingham) C.; m. Suzanne Yerger, Sept. 18, 1960; children: Stanley William, Ryan Yerger. BS in Geology, U. Okla., 1960, LLB, 1963. Bar: U.S. Dist. Ct. (we. dist.) Okla. 1963; U.S. Ct. Appeals (10th cir.) 1965; U.S. Supreme Ct. Okla. 1963. Atty. Phillips Petroleum Co., Oklahoma City, 1963-64, Bartlesville, Okla., 1964-71; counsel McAfee, Taft, et al., Oklahoma City, 1971—. Lectr. U. Okla. Coll. Law, Norman, 1977, 79, S.W. Legal Found., Dallas, 1986, 89. Contbr. articles to profl. jours. Layreader All Souls' Episcopal Ch., Oklahoma City, 1972-75. 1st lt. USAFR, 1963-72. Harry J. Brown scholar, U. Okla., 1960-63 Mem. ABA, Fed. Energy Bar Assn., Am. Soc. Internat. Law, Geological Soc. Am., Alumni Adv. Coun., U. Okla. Assoc., Oklahoma City Golf & Country Club, Order of Coif, Phi Alpha Delta, Sigma Gamma Epsilon. Republican. Episcopalian. Avocations: golf, reading. Office: McAfee & Taft 2 Leadership Sq Fl 10 Oklahoma City OK 73102

CUNNINGHAM, TERENCE THOMAS, III, hospital administrator; b. Bell, Calif. s. Terence Thomas and Leone (Downey), C.; m. Mary Katherine Kasarda; children: Wendy Victoria C., Terence Thomas IV. BS in Microbiology, Calif. State U., Long Beach, 1967; MA in Hosp. Adminstrn., George Washington U., Washington, 1974. Commd. 2d lt. USAF, 1967, advanced through grades to col., 1989; adminstrv. resident MacDill Hosp., Tampa, Fla., 1973-74; adminstr. Rhein-Main Clinic, Frankfurt, Germany, 1974-79; hosp. cons. Air Force Med. Inspection Ctr., San Bernardino, Calif., 1979-81; CFO David Grant Med. Ctr., Fairfield, Calif., 1981-82; adminstr. Torrejon Hosp., Madrid, 1982-85; chief fin. and materials officer Office Command Surgeon, Hdqrs. Mil. Airlift Command, Bellville, Ill., 1985-87; adminstr. Wright Patterson Med. Ctr., Dayton, Ohio, 1987-92, Wilford Hall Med. Ctr., San Antonio, 1992-94; v.p. adminstrn. Johns Hopkins Hosp., Balt., 1994-2000; pres. Ben Taub Gen. Hosp., Houston, 2000—. Instr. grad. program health care adminstrn. Chapman Coll., Calif., 1981-82; preceptor grad. students in hosp. and health care adminstrn. Xavier U., Cin., 1987—, Baylor U., San Antonio, 1988—, George Washington U., Washington, 1995—, Johns Hopkins U., Balt., 1995—; asst. clin. prof. Wright State U. Sch. Medicine, Dayton, Ohio, 1990—; assoc. prof. Dept. Health Policy and Mgmt. Johns Hopkins U. Sch. Pub. Health and Hygiene; clin. instr. Baylor Coll. Medicine, 2001; cons. Surgeon Gen. USAF, 1986—. Book reviewer Hosps. and Health Svcs. Adminstrn., Jour. Quality Assurance, Mil. Medicine; edtl. bd. Frontiers of Health Svcs. Mgmt. Active Am. Red Cross. Fellow Am. Coll. Healthcare Execs. (various coms., regent to U.S. Air Force); mem. Ohio Hosp. Assn. (chmn. accreditation com.), Greater Dayton Area Hosp. Assn. (bd. dirs.), Tex. Hosp. Assn. (mem. edn. com., Disaster Readiness Task Force), Assn. Mil. Surgeons U.S. (Young Fed. Healthcare Adminstr. of Yr. 1983, Fed. Healthcare Adminstr. of Yr. 1989, Sr. Fed. Healthcare Adminstr. of Yr. 1992), Interagy. Inst. Fed. Health Care Alumni Assn. Avocations: bicycling, photography, sailing, reading. Address: 1919 Spann St Houston TX 77019

CUNNINGHAM, THOMAS JUSTIN, lawyer; b. Hinsdale, Ill., Feb. 27, 1968; s. Thomas J. and Diane (Carlton) C.; m. Paula J. Friant, Sept. 9, 1989; children: Thomas Justin, Nicholas Joseph. BS, Ariz. State U., 1989; JD, DePaul U., 1993. Bar: Ill. 1993, U.S. Dist. Ct. (no. dist.) Ill. 1993, U.S. Ct. Appeals (7th cir.) 1993, U.S. Dist. Ct. (ctrl. dist.) Ill. 1996, U.S. Dist. Ct. (we. dist.) Mich. 2002, U.S. Supreme Ct. 1996, Tribal bar 1997. Dep. clk. U.S. Bankruptcy Ct., Chgo., 1989-90; law clk. Burke, Smith & Williams, Chgo., 1990-93; assoc. Smith, Lodge & Schneider, Chgo., 1993-98, Hopkins & Sutter, Chgo., 1998-2001; ptnr. Lord, Bissell & Brook, Chgo., 2001—. Contbr. articles to profl. jours. Pres. Ill. Dist. 58 Bd. Edn. Mem. Chgo. Bar Assn. (chair moot ct. com. 1995, co-editor in chief YLS jour.). Republican. Presbyterian. Avocations: hunting, fishing. Home: 5135 Fairview Ave Downers Grove IL 60515-5211 Office: Lord Bissell & Brook 115 S LaSalle 31st Fl Chicago IL 60603 E-mail: tcunningham@lordbissell.com.

CUNNINGHAM, TOM ALAN, lawyer; b. Houston, Nov. 5, 1946; s. Warren Peek and Ellen Ardelle (Benner) Cunningham; m. Jeanne Adrienne Moran, July 21, 1972; 1 child, Christopher Alan. BA, U. Tex., 1968, JD, 1974. Bar: Tex. 1974, U.S. Dist. Ct. (so. dist.) Tex. 1976, U.S. Dist. Ct. (no. dist.) Tex. 1982, U.S. Dist. Ct. (we. dist.) Tex. 1984, U.S. Ct. Appeals (5th and 11th cirs.) 1981, U.S. Ct. Appeals (8th cir.) 1919. Ptnr. Fulbright & Jaworski L.L.P., Houston, 1974—98; founding ptnr. Cunningham, Darlow, Zook & Chapoton, L.L.P., Houston, 1998—. Bd. trustee Children's Charity Fund, Houston, 1983—88; active South Tex. Ctr. Legal Responsibility; mem. exec. com., bd. dirs. Assn. for Cmty. TV. Lt. (j.g.) USNR, 1969—72. Fellow: Houston Bar Found., Tex. Trial Lawyers Assn., Am. Coll. Trial Lawyers, Am. Bd. Trial Advs., Tex. Bar Found. (life; chmn. bd. trustees, adv. bd., chair 1995—, chair Lola Wright com., chair bd. trustees 1995—, adv. bd., mem. new fellows com., mem. awards com., mem. pub. com., bd. dirs., ct. ruels com.), Am. Bar Found.; mem.: CPR Inst. for Dispute Resolution, Resolution Forum, Inc. (pres.), Tex. Empowerment Network (bd. dirs.), Tex. Ctr. Legal Ethics and Professionalism, Tex. Assn. Def. Counsel, Tex. Bd. Legal Specialization, State Bar Tex. (chmn. dist.4H grievance com. 1982—88, chmn. spl. com. on lawyer adt. and solicitation 1982, bd. dirs. 1989—92, chair bd. dirs. exec. com. 1991—92, chair com. for lawyer discipline 1992—94, chair gen. counsel adv. com., mem. exec. com., ct. rules com., Pres.'s award 1983, Pres.'s citation for meritorious svc. 1991, Pres.'s spl. recognition for meritorious svc. 1993, 1994, nominee Outstanding Young Lawyer 1981), Houston Bar Assn. (professionalism com., chmn. constn. bicentennial com., arbitration com., membership com., Pres.'s award 1988), Am. Arbitration Assn. (panel of arbitrators), ABA (litigation sect., discovery com., alternate dispute resolution com., forum com. constrn. industry, arbitration com. 1995—), Lakeside Country Club, Coronado Club, Houston Club, Phi Delta Phi. Home: 10811 Pine Bayou St Houston TX 77024-3018

CUNNINGHAM, WALTER JACK, electrical engineering educator; b. Comanche, Tex., Aug. 21, 1917; s. Walter Jack and Percy Adele (Moore) C.; m. Barbara Virginia Lynch, Feb. 26, 1944; children: Lawrence Bradford, John Hartwell. AB, U. Tex., 1937, AM, 1938; PhD, Harvard U., 1947. Instr. physics and communication engring. Harvard, 1939-46; part-time research OSRD, in acoustics and electric circuits, 1939-46; asst. prof. elec. engring. Yale U., 1946-50, assoc. prof., 1950-56, prof. engring. and applied sci., 1956-81, prof. elec. engring., 1981-88, assoc. chmn. dept. engring. and applied sci., 1969-72, prof. emeritus, 1988—. Author: Introduction to Nonlinear Analysis, 1958, Engineering at Yale, 1992; bd. editors Am. Scientist, 1955-81, 83-90, Jour. Franklin Inst., 1962-75; also articles. Mem. IEEE, Acoustical Soc. Am., Sigma Xi (bd. editors, chmn. com. on publs. 1983-87). Home: 200 Leeder Hill Dr Apt 326 Hamden CT 06517-2798

CUNNINGHAM, WILLIAM FRANCIS, lawyer; b. Chgo, Feb. 24, 1945; s. Michael and Catherine B. Cunningham; m. Rae C. Cunningham; children: Kellie Marie, Kiera Megan, Michael Grant. BA, DePaul U., 1967, JD, 1971. Bar: Ill. 1971, U.S. Dist. Ct. (no. dist.) Ill. 1971. Mem. firm Gates W. Clancy, Geneva, Ill., 1971-74, O'Reilly & Quetsch, Wheaton, Ill., 1974—75; ptnr. Law Offices of Roger K. O'Reilly, 1975—78, O'Reilly & Cunningham, 1978-95, Cunningham, Meyer & Vedrine, 1995—. Lectr. in field. Mem. ABA, Ill. Bar Assn., DuPage County Bar Assn., Kane County Bar Assn., Ill. Assn. Def. Trial Counsel, Soc. Trial Lawyers, Am. Coll. Trial Lawyers, Am. Bd. Trial Advocates. Roman Catholic. Home: ONO64 Forbes Dr Geneva IL 60134 Office: Cunningham Meyer & Vedrine Ste B 1050 PO Box 988 Wheaton IL 60189-0988 also: 111 W Washington Ste 937 Chicago IL 60602 Fax: (630) 260-8080.

CUNNINGHAM, WILLIAM FRANCIS, JR., English language educator, university administrator; b. Holyoke, Mass., Feb. 9, 1931; s. William Francis and Constance Emma (Cox) C.; m. Eleanor Mary Bissonette, Dec. 27, 1956; children— Margaret Ann, William John, Mary Elizabeth. AB, Holy Cross Coll., 1954; MA, Boston Coll., 1956; PhD, U. Pitts., 1961; DHL honoris causa, Le Moyne Coll., 1994. Asst. prof. English, Duquesne U., 1955-63; prof. Le Moyne Coll., 1963-78; prof. English Creighton U., 1978—, dean Coll. Arts and Scis., 1978-87, acting v.p. for acad. affairs, 1986-87, v.p. acad. affairs, 1987-93, spl. asst. to pres., 1993-96; dean emeritus, 1994—; ret., 1997. Danforth assoc., 1974—. Contbr. articles on 18th-century Brit. lit. to profl. jours. Mem. Coll. Bd. (coun. on coll.-level svcs., exec. com. Midwestern regional assembly 1980-84), Am. Soc. 18th-century Studies.

CUNNINGHAM, WILLIAM HENRY, retired food products executive; b. Oxnard, Calif., Dec. 2, 1930; s. William Henry and Carrie Edna (Wilson) C.; m. Carmen Nelson Alden, Jan. 19, 1957; children: Nelson, Clifford, Cynthia. BA, U. Calif., Santa Barbara, 1952; B of Foreign Trade, Am Grad. Sch. Internat. Mgmt., 1958. With Colgate-Palmolive Internat., N.Y. and Colombia, El Salvador, 1958-63; mktg. cons. Anderson, Clayton Co., Mexico City, Buenos Aires and Lima, 1963-66; mgr. consumer divsn. Cyanamid, Buenos Aires, 1966-69; dir. mktg. and sales Alimentos Kraft, Caracas, Venezuela, 1969-74; gen. mgr. Panama and Cen. Am. Panama and Ctrl. Am. Kraft Foods, Inc., 1974-80; pres. Alimentos Kraft Alimentos Kraft Foods, Inc., Venezuela, 1980-86; v.p., dir. Kraft Foods, Inc. Kraft Gen. Foods, Walt Disney World, Fla., 1986-92. V.p., dir. The Land, Epcot Ctr., Walt Disney World, Fla. Stewareship chmn. St. Lukes Meth. Ch., Windermere, Fla., 1991-92; vol. Inter Exec. Svc. Corp. for assignment in L.Am. to help local industry, 1993, assignment to Bogota Colombia, 1994, Ctrl. Russia, 1996; vol. Second Helping; Spanish transl. Free Clinic, Deep Well; pres. Hosp. Aux., Hilton Head, S.C.. 2002-03. Recipient Tribute Appreciation award U.S. State Dept., 1980, Order of Vasco Nunez de Balboa, Govt. Panama, 1980, First Class Work Merit award Govt. Venezuela, 1985, Jonas Mayer Disting. Alumni award Thunderbird Grad. Sch. for Internat. Mgmt., 1997, Citizen's Honor award Hilton Head. Mem. Am. C. of C. (pres., founder Panama City chpt. 1979, sec. Caracas 1986), Am. Soc. (pres. Panama City chpt. 1977), Walt Disney World Participant Assn. (pres. 1990-91), U. Calif. Alumni Assn. (bd. dirs. Santa Barbara 1992-98, chair awards), Bear Creek Golf Club, Hilton Head. Democrat. Methodist. Avocations: golf, tennis, skiing. Home: 11 Bear Creek Dr Hilton Head Island SC 29926-1904

CUNNINGHAM, WILLIAM HUGHES, former academic administrator, marketing educator; b. Detroit, Jan. 5, 1944; married; 1 child BA, Mich. State U., 1966, MBA, 1967, PhD, 1971, LLD (hon.), 1993. Mem. faculty U. Tex., Austin, 1971—, assoc. prof. mktg., 1973-79, prof., 1979—, assoc. dean grad. programs, 1976-82, Foley/Sanger Harris prof. retail merchandising, 1982-83, acting dean Coll. Bus. Adminstrn. and Grad. Sch. Bus., 1982-83, dean, 1983-85, pres., 1985-92, Centennial Chair Bus. Edn. Leadership, 1983-85, Regents Chair Higher Edn. Leadership, 1985-92, Lee Hage and Joseph D. Jamail Regents Chair Higher Edn. Leadership, 1992-2000, James L. Bayless Chair for Free Enterprise, 1988—; chancellor U. Tex. Sys., Austin, 1992-2000. Bd. dirs. Jefferson-Pilot Corp., John Hancock Funds, S.W. Airlines Co., Introgen Therapeutics, Hayes Lemmerz Internat., LIN TV; mem. corp. Conf. Bd. Author: (with W.J.E. Crissy and I.C.M. Cunningham) Selling: The Personal Force in Marketing, 1977, 2d edit. (with D.W. Jackson and Cunningham), 1988, Effective Selling, 1977, Spanish edit., 1980, (with S. Lopreato) Consumers' Energy Attitudes and Behavior, 1977, (with Cunningham) Marketing: A Managerial Approach, 1981, 2d edit. (with Cunningham and C. Swift), 1988, (with R. Aldag and C. Swift) Introduction to Business, 1984, 3d edit. (with R. Aldag and S. Block), 1992, 4th edit. (with R. Aldag and M. Stone), 1995, (with B. Verhage and Cunningham) Grondslagen van het Marketing Management, 1984, (with R. Aldag and S. Block) Business in a Changing World, 1992, also monographs and articles; editor Jour. Mktg., 1981-84. Bd. dirs. Houston Area Rsch. Coun., 1984; mem. Mental Health/Mental Retardation Legis. Oversight Com., 1984; mem. adv. bd. Found. for Cultural Exch./The Netherlands-U.S.A.; bd. dirs. Lyndon Baines Johnson Found. Recipient Tchg. Excellence award U. Tex. Coll. Bus. Adminstrn., 1972, Alpha Kappa Psi, 1975, Hank and Mary Harkins Found., 1978, Disting. Scholastic Contbn. award Coll. Bus. Adminstrn. Found. Adv. Council, 1982, Disting. Alumnus award Coll. and Grad. Sch. Bus., Mich. State U., 1983, 93, Tree of Life award Jewish Nat. Fund, 1992; named among top 20 profs. Utmost Mag., 1982; Rsch. grant Univ. Rsch. Inst., 1971-73, Latin Am. Inst., 1972, So. Union Gas Energy, 1975-76, ERDA, 1976 Mem. Am. Inst. for Decision Scis., Am. Mktg. Assn., Assn. Consumer Rsch., So. Mktg. Assn., S.W. Social Sci. Assn., Phi Kappa Phi, Omicron Delta Kappa Office: U Tex PO Box E Austin TX 78713 E-mail: wcunningham@mail.utexas.edu.

CUNNINGHAM-STEVENS, VANDETTA ANTOINETTE, practical nurse, poet; b. Newark, Apr. 21, 1965; d. Claude Stoddard and Rose Ethel Cunningham-Bemory, Joseph Thomas Bemory (Stepfather); m. Lovell Stevens; children: Aquil Cunningham, Natasha Cunningham, Khayri Cunningham, Whitney Troupe. Diploma, Jersey City Practical Nursing Program, 1991. Lic. practical nurse 1991. LPN Clara Maas Med. Ctr., Belleville, NJ, 1991—92; LPN St. Elizabeth Hosp., Elizabeth, NJ, 1992—94, Vis. Health Svc. NJ, Totowa, 1995—2002, NJ Vet. Meml. Home, Paramus, NJ, 2003. Author: (book) Flowing in the Spirit, 1999, His Words, 2000, After Midnight, 2001, If He Really Loved You, He'll Wait: How To Say No To Sexual Sin, 2001, A Woman's Survival Guide for True Lasting Intimacy, 2002. Youth counselor, minister-in-tng. Deliverance Jesus Is Coming Church, Inc., Irvington, NJ, 1999—. Recipient Cert. of Appreciation, Maranatha Bible Institute, 1999, Cert. of Outstanding Performance, Maranatha Bible Inst., 1999. Mem.: Nat. Fedn. of Lic. Practical Nurses, Nat. League for Nurse, Internat. Poets Soc. (Outstanding Poet 1998). Conservative. Avocation: literature, dramatic performances, bowling, scenic sites exploration, travel. Office: His Words Publishing PO Box 22125 Newark NJ 07101 Business E-Mail: hiswordspub@aol.com.

CUNO, KENNETH M. historian, educator; b. Syracuse, NY, Jan. 4, 1950; s. Ernest A. Cuno and Dortha D. Wade; m. Marilyn L. Booth, Dec. 11, 1986; children: Paul Cuno-Booth, Carrie Cuno-Booth. BA in History, Lewis and Clark Coll., 1972; MA in History, UCLA, 1977, PhD in History, 1985. Vis. asst. prof. of history Am. U., Cairo, 1985—90, dir. program in Mid. Eastern studies, 1986—88; asst. prof. history U. Ill., Urbana, 1990—96, assoc. prof. history, 1996—, dir. program in South Asian and Mid. Eastern studies, 2002—. Mem. editl. bd. Internat. Jour. of Mid. East Studies, 1999—, Annales Islamologiques, 2000—. Author: (book) The Pasha's Peasants: Land, Society and Economy in Lower Egypt 1740-1858, 1992 (Hon. Mention, Albert Hourani Book prize of Mid. East Studies Assn., 1993), Arabic translation of The Pasha's Peasants, 2000; contbr. articles to profl. jours. Recipient Templeton Nat. Merit scholarship, Lewis and Clark Coll., 1968—72, Spkr. and Specialist grant, U.S. Info. Agy., 1998; fellow, Ctr. for Arabic Studies Abroad, 1979—80, Fulbright-Hays, 1980—81, Social Sci. Rsch. Coun., 1981—82, Ctr. for Advanced Study, U. of Ill., 1994, Am. Rsch. Ctr. in Egypt, 1994; Fulbright scholar, 1998—99. Mem.: Turkish Studies Assn., Am. Hist. Assn., Am. Rsch. Ctr. in Egypt (mem. exec. com. 2002—), Mid. East Studies Assn. of N.Am. (mem. nominating com. 2002). Office: U Ill History Dept 309 Gregory Hall 810 S Wright Street Urbana IL 61801 Office Fax: 217-333-2297.

CUNSOLO, RONALD S. historian, educator; b. N.Y.C., May 3, 1923; s. Philip and Rose Barbagallo Cunsolo; m. Audrey Ann Cunsolo, May 19, 1951; children: Ronald Charles, Robert Harold. BA, NYU, 1950; MA in Humanities, U. Chgo., 1956; PhD in History, NYU, 1963. Instr. history CUNY, 1962—63; prof. history SUNY, N.Y.C., 1963—94; chmn. Columbia U., 1974—76; ret. Vis. assoc. prof. history NYU, 1978; vis. prof. history Adelphi U., 1984. Author: Italian Nationalism, 1990. With U.S. Army, 1942—45. Avocations: reading, crossword puzzles, travel, baseball, walking. Home: 8 Hunt Master Ct Ormond Beach FL 32174-2445

CUNTZ, MANFRED, astrophysicist, researcher, educator; b. Landau, Rheinland-Pfalz, Federal Republic of Germany, Apr. 21, 1958; arrived in U.S., 1988; s. Gerhard Hermann and Irene Emma (Messerschmitt) C.; m. Anne-Gret Vera Friedrich, Sept. 19, 1988; 1 child, Heiko Benjamin. Diplom in Physics, U. Heidelberg, Fed. Republic of Germany, 1985, PhD in Astronomy, 1988. Postdoctoral, rsch. assoc. Joint Inst. Lab. Astrophysics-U. Colo., Boulder, 1989-91; postdoc. rsch. assoc. High Altitude Obs. divsn. Nat. Ctr. Atmospheric Rsch., Boulder, 1992-94; habilitation in astronomy U. Heidelberg, Germany, 1995; sr. rsch. assoc., lectr. mech. engring. Ctr. Space Plasma, Aeronomy and Astrophysics Rsch., U. Ala., Huntsville, 1996-99, adj. assoc. prof. dept. mech. engring., 1999-2000. Vis. prof. dept. physics U. Tex., Arlington, 2000-01, asst. prof. dept. physics, 2001—; guest observer Internat. Ultraviolet Explorer, Hubble Space Telescope, ROSAT, Chandra Newton XMM. Contbr. articles to profl. jours. Grantee German Rsch. Found., NASA, NSF, Dutch Nat. Sci. Orgn. Mem.: AAAS, Astron. Soc. of the Pacific, N.Y. Acad. Scis., German Phys. Soc., German Astron. Soc., Am. Astron Soc., Internat. Astron. Union. Achievements include research in theoretical astrophysics, solar physics, extra-solar planets, astrobiology, magnetohydrodynamics, thermal bifurcation and physics of stellar atmospheres and winds. Office: Dept Physics U Tex Arlington Arlington TX 76019 E-mail: cuntz@uta.edu.

CUNY, HOWARD SAMUELS, writer; b. Woodside, NY, July 20, 1931; s. Horace Samuels Cuny and Hortense Livia Sununnu; m. Elaine Jackie Spooner, Oct. 8, 1952 (div. Sept. 5, 1979). BA in english lit., Harvard U., 1958; MA in psychology (hon.), Miskatonic U., 1976. Reporter Times-Pacayune, Providence, 1956—62; analyst Environ. Conservation Dept., Washington, 1962—63; freelance writer NYC, 1963—74; analyst EPA, Washington, 1974—76; freelance writer NYC, 1977—. Cons. IBM, NYC, 1983—84, Xerox, NYC, 1985—86, Compaq, NYC, 1996—97. Author: (novel) Silk Embrace (East Asian Narcissus award, 1965). Advisor for minority recruitment Dem. Socialists of Am., NYC, 1977—85, Working Families Party, NYC, 1986—2002. Cpl. U.S. Army, 1950—51, Korea. Decorated Purple Heart U S Congress. Zoroastrian. Avocations: sky diving, rock climbing, backgammon. Home: 1899 Irving St New York NY 10012 Office: Howard Samuels Ctr 365 Fifth Ave New York NY 10016 Home Fax: 212-817-1578; Office Fax: 212-817-1578. Personal E-mail: hscuny@yahoo.com. E-mail: hscuny@yahoo.com.

CUOCO, LORIN (JEAN), editor, writer; b. San Antonio, Nov. 4, 1954; d. Leonard Joseph and Mary Jean (Turner) C.; m. John Hutchings Fowler, May 25, 1982. BA, So. Ill. U., Edwardsville, 1978; MA, St. John's Coll., Santa Fe, N.Mex., 1997. Prodr. Sta. KWMU-FM, St. Louis, 1978-89; writer St. Louis Mag., 1989-90; assoc. dir. Internat. Writers Ctr., St. Louis, 1990-2001. Pres. River Styx, 1987-89; panelist Nat. Endowment for Arts, Washington, 1995, 98, Ky. Arts Coun., Louisville, 1998, 2000; judge Arts & Edn., St. Louis, 2000. Editor: The Writer in Politics, 1996, Dual Muse: Exhibition, 1997, The Writer and Religion, 2000; author, editor: Dual Muse: Symposium, 1999, Literary St. Louis, 2000. Home: 7024 Cornell Ave Saint Louis MO 63130-2304 E-mail: lorincuoco@sbcglobal.net.

CUOMO, ANDREW, former federal agency administrator; b. Dec. 6, 1957; m. Kerry Kennedy, 1990; 3 children. BA, Fordham U., 1979; JD, Albany Law Sch., 1982. Asst. dist. atty. Dist. Atty's Office, Manhattan; ptnr. Blutrich, Falcone and Miller, N.Y.C.; chmn. N.Y.C. Commn. on the Homeless, 1991-93; asst. sec. cmty. planning and devel. HUD, Washington, 1993-97, sec., 1997-2001. Pub. spkr. The Allen Agy.; vis. fellow Inst. of Politics, Harvard U. Author: Crossroads: The Future of Am. Politics, 2003. Campaign mgr. Mario M. Cuomo for Gov. N.Y., 1982; founder, pres. H.E.L.P., 1986, founder Genesis, 1992. Recipient Good Neighbor award ARC, Outstanding Comty. Svc. award Latin Soul, 1988, Man of the Yr. award Coalition of Italian Am. Orgns., 1988, Ed Sulzberger award Our Town newspaper, 1989, Pub. Svc. award Coun. of Jewish Orgns., 1989, Disting. Comty. Svc. award NYU, 1991, Bard award, 1992, Albert Einstein award, 1993, Encore Heart to Heart award, 1994, Innovation Am. Govt. award John F. Kennedy Sch. Govt. Harvard U., 1996. Office: Inst Politics 79 JFK St Cambridge MA 02138

CUOMO, ANDREW, information technology executive; BS Govt. Studies, JD magna cum laude, U. Notre Dame. Atty. Haynes & Boone, Dallas; sr. atty., mng. dir. airline mgmt. svcs., corp. devel. Am. Airlines; from dir. acct. mgmt. team to sr. v.p., chief staff Sabre Inc., Southlake, Tex. Office: Sabre Inc 3150 Sabre Dr Southlake TX 76092

CUOMO, JEROME JOHN, materials scientist; b. N.Y.C., Sept. 30, 1936; s. Gennaro and Rose Cuomo; m. Rita Cossa, June 20, 1959; children: Stephanie, Gennaro, Andrea. BS in Chemistry, Manhattan Coll., 1958; MS in Phys. Chemistry, St. Johns U., 1960; PhD in Physics, Odense U., Denmark, 1979. Chief chemist Secon Metal, 1960—63; staff mem. spl. techniques cen. sci. svcs. IBM, Yorktown Heights, NY, 1963—68, mgr. materials processing group cen. sci. svcs., 1968—75, sr. mgr. materials lab. cen. sci. svcs., 1975—93; Disting. rsch. prof. materials sci. & engring. N.C. State U., Raleigh, 1993—. Mem. adv. com. materials rsch. lab. Pa. State U., 1990; adj. prof. elec. engring. dept. Mich. State U., 1990; past adj. prof. Colo. State U.; affiliate prof. dept. materials sci. and engring. Cornell U., 1983—; elected mem. Japanese and U.S. Workshop on Diamon Tech.; mem. adv. bd. materials rsch. lab. on diamonds Case Western Res. U., Cleve., 1990; organizer-chmn. 1st tech. symposium on silicon nitride Electrochem. Soc., 1966; organizer, co-chmn. 1st Topical Symposium on Energetic Condensation, Am. Vacuum Soc., 1992; mem. Metro Atlanta Chamber Clean Water Initiative, 2000, chmn., 2002—. Co-editor (with S. Rossnagel, H. Kaufman): Handbook of Ion Beam Processing Technology, 1989; co-editor: (with S. Rossnagel, W. Westwood) Handbook of Plasma Processing Technology, 1989; contbr. more than 300 articles and papers to jours. Recipient Indsl. Rsch. IR-100 award, 1974, 1975, Outstanding Paper award, Am. Soc. Metals, 1985, Morris N. Liebman Field award, IEEE, 1992, Nat. Medal of Technology, 1995. Fellow: Am. Vacuum Soc. (organizer-chmn. sputtering topical symposium 1986, mem. program com. thin film divsn. 1983—84, program chmn. thin film divsn. 1977, 1982, bd. dirs. 1981—82, mem. steering com. 1973—79); mem.: Nat. Acad. Engring. Roman Catholic. Achievements include 110 patents in field. Office: NC State U Materials Sci & Engring PO Box 7907 Raleigh NC 27695-0001

CUOMO, MARIO MATTHEW, lawyer, former governor; b. Queens County, N.Y., June 15, 1932; s. Andrea and Immaculata (Giordano) Cuomo; m. Matilda Raffa, June 5, 1954; children: Margaret Cuomo Maier, Andrew, Maria Cuomo Cole, Madeline Cuomo O'Donoghue, Christopher. BA summa cum laude, St. John's Coll., 1953; LLB cum laude, St. John's U., 1956. Bar: NY 1956, U.S. Dist. Ct. (no. dist.) NY 1957, U.S. Dist. Ct. (so. dist.) NY 1998, U.S. Supreme Ct. 1960, U.S. Dist. Ct. (ea. dist.) NY 1962, U.S. Ct. Appeals (2d cir.) 1967. Confidential legal asst. to Hon. Adrian P. Burke, NY State Ct. Appeals, 1956—58; assoc. Corner, Weisbrod, Froeb and Charles, Bklyn., 1958—63; ptnr. Corner, Cuomo & Charles, 1963—75; sec. of state State of NY, 1975—79, lt. gov., 1979—83, gov., 1983—94; ptnr., now of counsel Wilkie Farr & Gallagher, N.Y.C., 1995—. Mem. faculty St. John's U. Sch. Law, 1963—73; counsel to cmty. groups, including Corona Homeowners, 1966—72; charter mem. First Ecumenical Commn. of Christians and Jews for Bklyn. and Queens, NY. Author: Forest Hills Diary: The Crisis of Low-Income Housing, 1974, Diaries of Mario M. Cuomo, Campaign for Governor, 1982; co-author: Lincoln on Democracy, 1990, More Than Words, 1993, The New York Idea: An Experiment in Democracy, 1994, Reason to Believe, 1995, The Blue Spruce, 1999; contbr. articles to legal publs. Spkr. keynote address Dem. Nat. Conv., San Francisco, 1984, nominating address Dem. Nat. Conv., N.Y.C., 1992. Recipient Rapallo award, Columbia Lawyers Assn., 1976, Dante medal, Italian Govt.-Am. Assn. Tchrs. Italian, 1976, Silver medallion, Columbia Coalition, 1976, Pub. Adminstr. award, C.W. Post Coll., 1977, Theodore Roosevelt award, Internat. Platform Assn., 1984. Mem.: ABA, Am. Judicature Soc., Assn. of Bar of City of NY, Queens County Bar Assn., Nassau Bar Assn., Bklyn. Bar Assn., NY State Bar Assn., Cath. Lawyers Guild of Queens County (pres. 1966—67), St. John's U. Alumni Fedn. (chmn. bd. 1970—72), Skull and Circle. Home: 50 Sutton Pl S New York NY 10022-4167 Address: Wilkie Farr & Gallagher 787 7th Ave Rm 203 New York NY 10019-6018*

CUOZZO, STEVEN DAVID, newspaper editor; b. N.Y.C., Jan. 17, 1950; s. Joseph and Lillian (Picini) C.; m. Jane Hershey, Nov. 29, 1980 BA in English, SUNY, Stony Brook, 1971. Arts and leisure editor N.Y. Post, N.Y.C., 1978-80, asst. mng. editor features, 1980-91, mng. editor, 1991-93, exec. editor, 1993—. Author: It's Alive: How America's Oldest Newspaper Cheated Death and Why It Matters, 1996. Office: NY Post 10th Fl 1211 Avenue Of The Americas New York NY 10036 E-mail: scuozzo@nypost.com.*

CUPKA, NANCY IRVINE, artist, educator; b. Indpls., Oct. 9, 1942; d. Don E. and Marie Irvine; m. W. Roger Cupka, Apr. 8, 1961; children: Gregory, Thomas. Group shows include Am. Artists Profl. League Nat. Exhbn., N.Y.C., 2001, Lafayette Art Assn.,1997, Hoosier Salon, 1970, 89, 92, 93, 97, 98, 2001, 2002, Ind. Heritage Arts Exhbn. Contemporary Ind. Artists, 1991, 92, 93, 94, 97, 98, 99, 2000, 01, Southside Art League, Inc., 1992, 93, 94, 95-97, Ind. Artist's Club, Indpls., 1995, 98, 2000, 01, Brown County Art Gallery, Nashville, 1988-97, Renditions Fine Art Gallery, Indpls., 1998-2002, Honeysuckle Gallery, Nashville, 1998-2002; permanent collections include St. Elizabeth's Hosp., Lafayette, Ind., Ind. State Mus., Indpls., Franklin (Ind.) Coll. Past bd. dirs. Brown County Art Gallery, Nashville, Southside Art League, Indpls.; founder Eastview Women's Support Group for Women with Chronic Pain, Martinvsville, Ind.; assoc. mem. So. Ind. Ctr. for the Arts, Brown County Art Gallery Hist. Assn. Recipient numerous awards. Mem. Am. Artists Profl. League (artist mem.), Allied Artists Am. (assoc.), Southside Art League, Hoosier Salon Patron's Assn., Ind. Heritage Arts (artist mem.), Brown County Art Guild (assoc.), Ind. Artists Club. Avocations: walking trails, photography. Home and Office: 272 Painted Hls Martinsville IN 46151-8677

CUPP, DAVID FOSTER, photographer, journalist; b. Derry Twp., Pa., Feb. 4, 1938; s. Foster Wilson and Elizabeth (Erhard) C.; m. Catherine Lucille Lum, Nov. 20, 1965; children: Mary Catherine, David Patterson, John. BA in Journalism, U. Miami (Fla.), 1960. Staff photographer Miami News, 1960-63, Charlotte (N.C.) Observer, 1963-66; photographer, writer Internat. Harvesters, Chgo., 1966-67; picture editor Nat. Geog. Mag., Washington, 1967, photographer, 1967-69; picture editor Detroit Free Press, 1969; writer, photographer Denver Post, 1969-77; freelance writer, photographer, 1977-88; dir. photography Press-Enterprise, Riverside, Calif., 1988-90; instr. photojournalism, dept. journalism U. Mo., Columbia, 1990; instr. Sch. Vis. Communication Ohio U., Athens, 1991-92; working book author Cupp Design, Inc., Atlanta, 1993; graphics editor Ft. Lauderdale (Fla.) Sun-Sentinel, 1993-94; freelance writer & photographer Hilliard, Ohio, 1994—; pres., creative dir. Photos Online, Inc., Hilliard, OH, 1995—; pres. Half Moon Pub. Tchr. jr. and sr. h.s.-adult classes, including Journalist-in-the-schs., pilot program, Aurora, Colo., 1974-76, Nat. Endowment Arts poet-in-residence 5 Colo. schs.; photography aboard Voyager Spacecraft Co-author Search and Rescue Dogs, 1988; contbg. author: Nat. Geog. books; co-author: Cindy, a Hearing Ear Dog, The Animal Shelter, All Wild Creatures Welcome; contbr. article, photographs to popular mags. Bd. dirs. Friends of Children of Vietnam, adoption agy., 1973. Mem. Nat. Press Photographers Assn. (recipient numerous awards, citations, including, named Nat. runner-up Photographer of Year 1965, 72, named Regional Photographer of Year 1974, recipient 2nd Place News Picture Story award 1974, 3rd Place Sports Picture Story award 1974, McWilliams award for picture story 1974, McWilliams award for single picture 1974, 75, 2d Home, Family Picture Story award 1972, co-chmn. nat. conv.), Colo. Press Photographers Assn. (v.p.), Am. Soc. Mag. Photographers. Home: 4508 Swenson St Hilliard OH 43026-3811 *I don't think it's possible to sum life up in a few sentences, life is too complex, but if I were to try, I would have to say that I try to live my life in such a way that my children have pride in me, what I do, and how I do it. I don't feel I can tell my children to be honest, then I be dishonest, or tell them to have compassion, while I have none. I cannot punish a child for doing something at night, that I do during the day. In short, I try to be the person that I would want my children to be.*

CUPP, HORACE BALLARD, surgeon, educator; b. Bristol, Va., Nov. 30, 1930; s. Horace Ballard and Laura Reece Cupp; m. Ann Miller, Dec. 3, 1958; children: Robert Ballard, Laura Cupp Oliva. BA, U. Tenn., 1951; MD, Duke U., 1955. Resident neurosurgery Duke U., Durham, N.C., 1958-64; pvt. practice Johnson City, Tenn., 1964-93; clin. prof. of surgery East Tenn. State U. Coll. of Medicine, Johnson City, 1980—. Bd. dirs. Johnson City Med. Ctr. Hosp., 1990-2000. Past comdr. Johnson City Power Squadron, 1965—. Lt. comdr. USNR, 1956-58. Fellow ACS; mem. AMA, Congress of Neurol. Surgeons, Assn. of Neurol. Surgeons, So. Neurol. Soc., Coral Lodge #142, Johnson City Rotary Club. Seventh-Day Adventist. Avocations: travel, photography, fly fishing. Home: 604 E Holston Ave Johnson City TN 37601-4014 Office: Appalachian Neurosurg Clinic 408 N State Of Franklin Rd Johnson City TN 37604-6089 E-mail: horacebcupp@earthlink.net.

CUPP, ROBERT ERHARD, land use planner, golf course architect; b. Lewistown, Pa., Dec. 27, 1939; s. Foster Wilson and Elizabeth (Erhard) C.; m. Glenda Dell, Aug. 26, 1962 (div. 1983); children: Robert E. II, Caren E., Laura G.; m. Pamela Patricia Amy, Dec. 27, 1986. BA, U. Miami, Coral Gables, Fla., 1962; MA, U.S. Army, Anchorage, 1966. Art dir. Jefferson, Inc., Miami, 1966-67; golf profl. Colonial Palms Country Club, Miami, 1967-68, Crooked Creek Country Club, Miami, 1968-69; pvt. practice golf course architect Miami, 1969-72; golf course architect Golden Bear Enterprises, North Palm Beach, Fla., 1972-86; pvt. practice golf course architect Atlanta, 1984—. Sr. designer Jack Nicklaus Design, North Palm Beach, 1972-86; pres. Cupp Design, Inc., Atlanta, 1984—. Designed East Sussex (Eng.) Nat. Golf Club, site of 1993-94 European Open Championship (Best New Golf Course, Golf Monthly), Pumpkin Ridge Golf Club, Portland, Oreg., Site of 1996 U.S. Amateur Championship, 1992 & 2003 U.S. Women's Open Championship, 2000 U.S. Boys and Girls Nat. Champtionship, Old Waverly Golf Club, West Point, Miss. (Top 100 Golf Course in U.S., Golf Digest, Site of U.S. Women's Open Championship), Settindown Creek Golf Club, Atlanta, site of U.S. Nike Tour Championship, 1995, 96, Pumpkin Ridge, Ghost Creek, 1992 (Best New Course, Golf Digest), Western Gales, Osceola, Mich., 1993, Indianwood, Lake Orion, Mich., 1988 (Runner up Best New Course, Golf Digest), Pumpkin Ridge, Witch Hollow, Portland, 1992, Old Waverly, West Point, 1989, Big Sky Country Club, Pemberton, B.C., Can., 1994, Crosswater Golf Club, Sunriver, Oreg., 1995 (Best New Course 1995), Hawks Ridge, Atlanta, 2000 (Best New Course runner up Golf Digest). Served to capt. U.S. Army, 1963-66. Named Golf World/Golf Digest Designer of Yr., 1992. Office: Cupp Design Inc 5457 Roswell Rd NE Ste 103 Atlanta GA 30342-1900 also: Bob Cupp Inc PO Box 191581 Atlanta GA 31119-1581 E-mail: cuppdsgn@aol.com.

CUPPO CSAKI, LUCIANA, foreign language educator, writer; b. Trieste, Italy, May 30, 1941; came to U.S., 1965; d. Bruno Cuppo and Nerina Dimini. BA in German, U. Heidelberg, Germany, 1962; MA in German, U. Kans., 1970; PhD in Latin, Fordham U., 1995. Adj. prof. Manhattanville Coll., Purchase, N.Y., 1989-92, CUNY, 1991-95, SUNY, Westchester, 1996—, Albany, 1997-98. Author: The Vivarium Monastery of Cassiodorus After the Year 575 A.D., 1998, The Year 680 as Caput Saeculi in Cas 641, 1998, De schematibus et tropis in Italian Garb, 2002. NEH scholar Summer Seminar, Anglo-Saxon Manuscripts and Texts, 2001. E-mail: dcsakio@yahoo.com.

CURBEAM, ROBERT L., JR., astronaut; b. Balt., Md., Mar. 5, 1962; m. Julie Dawn Lein; 2 children. BSc in Aerospace Engring., U.S. Naval Acad., 1984; MSc in Aero. Engring., Naval Postgraduate Sch., 1990, degree in Aero. & Astronautical Engring., 1991. Commd. 2d lt. USN, 1984, advanced through grades to comdr.; sta. on USS Forrestal, 1986—91; project officer Strike Aircraft Test Directorate, 1991—94; instr. U.S. Naval Acad., 1994—95; astronaut NASA, Houston, 1995—. Astronaut space mission, 1997, 2001. Mem.: U.S. Naval Acad. Alumni Assn., Assn. Old Crows. Avocations: weightlifting, bicycling, family activities. Office: Astronaut Office CB NASA Johnson Space Center Houston TX 77058

CURCIO, CHRISTOPHER FRANK, city official; b. Oakland, Calif., Feb. 3, 1950; s. Frank William and Virginie Theresa (Le Gris) C. BA in Speech/Drama, Calif. State U., Hayward, 1971; MBA in Arts Adminstrn., UCLA, 1974; MPA in Pub. Policy, Ariz. State U., 1982. Intern John F. Kennedy Ctr. for Arts, Washington, 1973; gen. mgr. Old Eagle Theatre, Sacramento, 1974-75; cultural arts supr. Fresno Parks and Recreation Dept., 1975-79; supr. cultural and spl. events Phoenix Parks & Recreation Dept., 1979-87, budget analyst, 1987, mgmt. svcs. adminstr., 1987-97, dep. dir., 1997—. Mgmt. and budget analyst City of Phoenix, 1985; grants panelist Phoenix Arts Commn., 1987, Ariz. Commn. on Arts, 1987-88; voter Zony Theatre Awards, 1991-92; freelance theater critic, 1987-89; theater critic Ariz. Republic, 1990-98, PHX Downtown, 1997-98, CityAZ, 1997-98, Ariz. Foothills Mag., 1998-2002, Sunday Showtunes Broadway's Biggest Hits, 1998-2000, In Theater Mag., 1999-2000, Variety, 1995—, KBAQ-FM Radio, 1999—, Broadway's Biggest Hits, 2000—, Ariz. Producton Assn., 2002—. Active Valley Leadership Program, Phoenix, 1987—, Valley Big Bros./Big Sisters, 1980-94; chair allocation panel United Way, 1990-92; sec. Los Olivos Townhome Assn., Phoenix, 1986-92. Mem. Am. Soc. Pub. Adminstrn., Nat. Recreation and Park Assn., Am. Theatre Critics Assn., Internat. Theater Critics Assn., Ariz. Park and Recreation Assn. Republican. Avocations: theater history, writing, reading, cooking, gardening. Office: Phoenix Parks & Recreation Dept 200 W Washington St Fl 16 Phoenix AZ 85003-1611

CURE, CAROL CAMPBELL, lawyer; b. Phoenix, Dec. 16, 1944; d. Richard Converse Nowell and Nancy (Newcomb) Olson; m. Robert Norman Campbell, Jan. 2, 1965 (div. 1968); 1 child, Kelly Christine; m. Harding Briggs Cure, June 28, 1984. BA with distinction, Ariz. State U.-Tempe, 1972, JD, 1978. Bar: Ariz. 1979, Calif. 1979, U.S. Dist. Ct. Ariz. 1979, U.S. Ct. Appeals (9th cir.) 1981, U.S. Dist. Ct. (cen. dist.) Calif. 1984, White Mountain Apache Tribal Ct.; cert. specialist in personal injury and wrongful death litigation. Ptnr. O'Connor, Cavanagh, Anderson, Westover, Killingsworth & Beshears, Phoenix, 1978—; faculty mem. Pacific regional chpt. Nat. Inst. Trial Advocacy, 1985-86; faculty mem. Ariz. Trial Coll., 1988-92. Bd. dirs. Ariz. Coun. of the Blind, Social Svcs. and Rehab. Inc., 1980-85, Community Forum, 1994-95, Phoenix Childrens Theatre, 1981-83, Ariz. Cen. Credit Union, 1985-87; judge pro tem Ariz. Ct. Appeals, 1985; judge pro tem Maricopa County Superior Ct., 1988-95; mem. steering com. Pro Bono Juvenile Project, 1989-90; mem. Camelback East Village Planning Com., 1987-90; mem. coun. of the future Nat. Judicial Coll.; candidate U.S. Ho. Reps., Ariz., 1994. Fellow Am. Bar Found., Am Bd. Trial Advs.; mem. ABA (chair civil procedure and evidence com. tort and ins. practice sect., chair professionalism com. 1989-92, chair litigation sect. use of expert witness subcom. of com. trial practice 1982-90, mem. standing com. on professionalism, 1992—, del. ho. dels. 1993—), State Bar Ariz. (bd. govs. 1990-93, com. on rules of civil practice and procedure, chair trial practice sect.), Maricopa County Bar Assn. (bd. dirs. 1983-88, chair med./legal liaison com., 1987-89), Maricopa County Bar Found. (trustee 1984-88), Nucleus (chair membership com. 1984-85, chair 1986-87, bd. dirs. 1988—), AAUW (parliamentarian, bd. dirs. Ariz. State div. 1980-82, pres. elect 1994), Internat. Ins. Law Soc. (mem. presdl. coun.), Ariz. Epilepsy Assn. (bd. dirs. cmty. arts coun.), Ariz. State U. Coll. Law, Law Soc. (bd. dirs. 1995—), Ariz. State U. Coll. Law (bd. visitors), Ariz. State U. Alumni Assn. (bd. dirs. 1980-83), Kappa Delta Pi, Assn. Trial Lawyers Am., Phoenix Assn. Def. Counsel, Ariz. Women Lawyers Assn., Def. Rsch. Inst. (practice and procedure com.), Fedn. Ins. and Corp. Counsel. Democrat. Episcopalian. Office: O'Connor Cavanagh 1 E Camelback Rd Ste 1100 Phoenix AZ 85012-1691

CURETON, CLAUDETTE HAZEL CHAPMAN, biology educator; b. Greenville, S.C., May 3, 1932; d. John H. and Beatrice (Washington) Chapman; m. Stewart Cleveland, Dec. 27, 1954; children: Ruthye, Stewart II, S. Charles, Samuel. AB, Spelman Coll., 1951; MA, Fisk U., 1966; DHum (hon.), Morris Coll., Sumter, S.C., 1996. Tchr. North Warren High Sch., Wise, N.C., 1952-60; tchr. Sterling High Sch., Greenville, 1960-66, Wade Hampton High Sch., Greenville, 1967-73; instr. Greenville Tech. Coll., 1973-95, ret., 1995. Bd. dirs. State Heritage Trust, 1978-91; commr. Basic Skills Adv. Program, Columbia, 1990—; mem. adv. bd. Am. Fed. Bank, NCNB Bank, Greenville, 1991—. Mem. Greenville Urban League, NAACP, S.C. Curriculum Congress; v.p. Woman's Bapt. E.& M. Conv. of S.C.; mem. S.C. Commn. on Higher Edn. Com. for Selection of the 1995 Gov.'s Prof. of the Yr.; mem. Gov.'s Task Force on Juvenile Crime, S.C., Gov.'s Juvenile Justice Task Force, 1997, S.C., Gov.'s Juvenile Justice Youth Coun., S.C., 1996—, Best Chance Network Task Force of Am. Cancer Soc., 1995—; bd. dirs. Sisters Saving Sisters, Roper Mountain Sci. Ctr., 2003—. Recipient Presdl. award Morris Coll., 1987, 91, Svc. award S.C. Wildlife and Marine Dept., 1986, Outstanding Jack and Jill of Am. citation, 1986, Excellence in Tchg. award Nat. Inst. for Staff and Orgnl. Devel., U. Tex., Austin, 1992-93, Educator of Yr. award Greenville chpt. Am. Cancer Soc., 1994, Outstanding Svc. award Best Chance Network/Am. Cancer Soc., 1994, Citation S.C. House of Reps., 1995; named Unsung Hero of the Cmty. for Outstanding Svc. to Humankind Greenville Tech. Coll., 1999. Mem. AAAS, AAUW, Nat. Assn. Biology Tchrs., S.C. Curriculum Congress, Nat. Coun. Negro Women, Inc., Higher Edn. S.C. Com. for Selection Prof. of Yr. 1995, Delta Sigma Theta (past v.p. Greenville chpt. alumnae). Home: 501 Mary Knob Greenville SC 29607-5242

CURFMAN, DAVID RALPH, neurological surgeon, civic leader, musician; b. Bucyrus, Ohio, Jan. 2, 1942; s. Ralph Oliver and Agnes Mozelle (Schreck) C.; m. Blanche Lee Anderson, June 6, 1970. Student, Capital U., 1960-62; AB, Columbia Union Coll., 1965; MS, George Washington U., 1967, MD, 1973. Diplomate Nat. Bd. Med. Examiners. Asst. organist, choirmaster Peace Luth. Ch., Galion, Ohio, 1956-62; bus. mgr. Mansfield/Galion Ambulance Svc., Galion, Ohio, 1962-66; with news divsn. Sta. WTOP-TV, Washington, 1965; choirmaster, assoc. organist Grace Luth. Ch., Washington, 1966-73, historian, curator, 1969—; tchg. fellow in anatomy George Washington U., Washington, 1966-67, gen. surgery intern, 1973-74, resident in neurol. surgery, 1974-78, clin. instr. neurol. surgery, 2000—; resident in neuropathology Armed Forces Inst. Pathology, Washington, 1975; resident in pediatric neurol. surgery Children's Hosp. Nat. Med. Ctr., Washington, 1976; teaching fellow in anatomy Georgetown U., Washington, 1967-69, clin. instr. neurol. surgery, nuerol. surgeon, 1978—; neurosurgery faculty George Washington U., Washington, 2001—. Chief divsn. neurol. surgery Jefferson Hosp., Alexandria, Va., 1989-93, Wash. Hosp. Ctr. Soc., 1992—, operating room com. 1998—; vice-chmn. bylaws com. Providence Hosp., 1987-95, chief of neorosurgery divsn.; panelist ann. meeting ethical issues in neurol. surgery Am. Assn. Neurol. Surgery; guest spkr. Nat. Youth Leadership Forum, 1996—. Chmn., chief author: Physician's Reference Guide for Medicolegal Matters, 1982, Nat. Capital Astronomers' Association, 1986-87. Elected mem. D.C. Rep. Com., 1988-94; bd. dirs., historian The Christmas Pageant of Peace, Inc., Washington, The Leo Sowerby Found.; pres., bd. govs. Nat. Columbus Celebration Assn. Hon. mem. Quiz Kid Show, 1953; recipient Found. award Cathedral Choral Soc., 1997. Mem.: SAR (bd., D.C. Soc. 1997—), AMA (Phys. Recognition award 1983—), D.C. Soc. (3d v.p.), Order of the Crown in Am., Assn. Mil. Surgeons U.S. (Continuing Edn. Neurosurgery award 1993—), Washington Acad. Neurosurgery (pres.-elect 2003—), Am. Coll. Legal Medicine, Congress Neurol. Surgeons (joint sect. neuro-trauma and critical care), Pan Am. Med. Soc. (mem. exec. bd. 1993—97, pres. 1997—), Med. Soc. D.C. (chmn. medicine and religion com. 1981—83, chmn. medico-legal com. 1986—88), Am. Soc. Law, Medicine and Ethics, Assn. Am. Med. Colls. (nat. student chmn. rules and regulations com. 1971—73), Nat. Gavel Soc., Soc. War 1812 (surgeon gen., Md. chpt., 1st v.p. D.C. chpt., dist. dep. pres. gen.), Pilgrim Soc. (Plymouth chpt.), Hymn Soc. Am., St. Andrew's Soc. (Washington D.C.), Mil. Order of the Crusades, Sovereign Mil. Order Temple of Jerusalem (grand chirurgeon emeritus, Order of Merit), The Baronial Order of Magna Carta, Mil. Hospitaller Order Saint Lazarus Jerusalem (knight), U.S. Capitol Hist. Soc. (founding supporting mem., trust mem.), Nat. Cathedral Assn., Cathedral Choral Soc. (repertoire chmn. 1981—82, v.p. bd. trustees 1981—83, pres. 1984—86, found. award 1977), Am. Guild Organists (dean D.C. chpt. 1974—76, publicity chmn. nat. conv. 1982, state chmn. 1984—91, nat. com. long-range devel. 1990—96), Internat. Congress Organists (Washington program chmn. 1977), Royal Sch. Ch. Music (Eng.), Order of the Crown of Charlemagne (surgeon gen.), Nat. Soc. Ams. Royal Descent (councillor), Order of Ams. of Armorial Ancestry (chaplain), Children Am. Revolution (pres. Ohio 1963—64, hon. sr. nat. v.p. 2001—, hon. Ohio pres.), Gen. Soc. Sons of the Revolution (chmn. bicentennial commemorative com. death of Gen. George Washington 1999, N.Y. and D.C. bd. 2002—), Hereditary Order Descendants of the Loyalists and Patriots of the Am. Revolution, Baronial Order of Magna Charta, Sons & Daughters of Colonial & Antebellum Bench & Bar, Samuel Victor Constant Soc., Order of Wash., Osler Soc., Galion Hist. Soc. (charter), Continental Soc. Sons Indian Wars, Ordo Sancti Constantini Magni, Colonial Order of the Acorn N.Y., Vet. Corps Artillery State N.Y., Am. Revolution Soc., Soc. of 1812, Nat. Soc. Children Am. Colonists (pres. gen. 2003—), Mil. Order Loyal Legion U.S. (Aide-de-Camp to comdr.-in-chief), Sons Am. Colonists (surgeon gen. 1997—), Soc. Colonial Wars (surgeon 1997—), Order of Indian Wars in the U.S. (historian 1999—), Am. Polit. Items Collectors Assn., Sons/Daus. of the Pilgrims (historian gen. 1999—2001, first dep. gov. gen. 2003—), Hospitaller Order of St. John (knight), Lincoln Birthday Nat. Commemorative Com (master of ceremonies 1995—99, vice chmn.), Sons of Union Vets. Civil War (chmn. historic Memorial Day observances), Order Three Crusades (1096-1192), Columbus Philatelic Soc., Crawford County Coin Club (charter mem.), George Washington U. Club, Sr. Nat. Officer's Club (hon. sr. nat. v.p. 2001—, historian 2003—), Elks (Galion Lodge No. 1191), Sigma Xi (pres. George Washington U. chpt. 1981—82), Phi Delta Epsilon (life). Home: 4201 Massachusetts Ave NW Washington DC 20016-4701 Office: 3301 New Mexico Ave NW Ste 210 Washington DC 20016-3622

CURFMAN, FLOYD EDWIN, engineering educator, retired; b. Gorin, Mo., Nov. 16, 1929; s. Charles Robert and Cleo Lucille (Sweeney) C.; m. Eleanor Elaine Fehl, Aug. 5, 1950; children: Gary Floyd, Karen Elaine. BSCE, U. Mo., 1958; BA in Math. Edn., Mt. Mary Coll., 1988. Registered profl. engr., Wis., Mo.; cert. tchr., Wis. Forest engr. U.S. Forest Svc., Rolla and Harrisburg, Mo., Ill., 1958-70, engring. dir. Milw., 1970-84, chief tech. engr. Washington, 1984-86; tchr. Wauwatosa (Wis.) High Sch., 1987-89, Our Lady of Rosary, Milw., 1989-96; retired, 1996. Author: (booklet) Forest Roads-R-9, 1973; co-author: (tng. manual) Transportation Roads, 1966. Co-leader Boy Scouts Am., Harrisburg, 1958-62; activities coord. Cmty. Action Com., Brookfield, 1970-76; bike and hiking trails com. City of Brookfield (Wis.), 1982-83; program chair Math Counts, 1982. With U.S. Army, 1952-54. Mem. ASCE (program chair, Letter Nat. award 1970), NSPE (coms. 1970-86), Nat. Coun. Tchrs. Math., Wis. Soc. Profl. Engrs. (pres. Milw. chpt. 1982-83, State Recognition award 1983). Avocations: travel, auto trips, reading. Home: 1755 N 166th St Brookfield WI 53005-5114

CURIE, CHARLES G. federal agency administrator; b. Ind. m. Candace Curie. Grad., Huntington Coll.; Masters Degree, U. Chgo. Cert. Acad. Cert. Social Workers. Dir. risk mgmt. svcs. Henry S. Lehr Inc., Bethlehem, Pa.; pres., CEO Helen H. Stevens Cmty. Mental Health Ctr., Carlisle; exec. dir., CEO Sandusy Valley Ctr., Tiffin, Ohio; dep. sec. for mental health and substance abuse svcs. Dept. Pub. Welfare, State of Pa.; adminstr. Substance Abuse and Mental Health Svcs. Adminstrn. Dept. HHS, Rockville, Md., 2001—. Chmn. Greater Carlisle United Way Annual Campaign; mem. adv. bd. Tiffin Mercy Hosp.; pres. Huntington Coll. Student Union; senate mem. Huntington Coll. Bd. Trustees; pres. Alpha Sigma Eta; past mem. bd. dirs. Greater Carlisle C. of C. Mem.: Rotary Internat. Office: Dept HHS Substance Abuse and Mental Health Svcs 5600 Fishers Ln Rockville MD 20857

CURINGTON, THOMAS FRANKLIN, III, photographer, writer; s. Thomas Franklin Curington Jr. and Kitty Sue Garrett. BS in psychology, Ga. Coll. and State U., 1993, MS in psychology, 1996. Mental health counselor Baldwin State Prison, Milledgeville, Ga., 1996—97. Democrat.

CURL, LAYTON SETH, psychologist, consultant, educator; b. Batesville, Ark., Apr. 3, 1976; s. Eric Lynn and Rita Kay Curl. Diploma in Asian Studies, Kansai Gaidai U., Japan, 1997; BA in Psychology, Lyon Coll., Batesville, AR, 1998; MA in Exptl. Psychology, U. Miss., Oxford, 2000, PhD in Social and Cross-Cultural Psychology, 2002. Instr. English Kansai Gaidai U., Kyoto, 1996—97; instr. psychology U. Miss., Oxford, 1998—2002; mng. editor Internat. Jour. of Intercultural Edn., Hilo, Hawaii, 2000—02; prof. cross-cultural psychology Hobart and William Smith Colleges, Geneva, NY, 2002—. Mem. Human Rights Campaign, New York City, 2000. Scholar, Dept. of Higher Edn. & Century Tube Corp., 1996. Fellow: Internat. Assn. Intercultural Rels. (assoc.); mem.: Asian Assn. Social Psychologists, Internat. Assn. Cross-Cultural Psychology. Democrat. Home: 554 S Main St Apt # 8 Geneva NY 14456 Office: Hobart and Wm Smith Colls 4147 Scandling Ctr Geneva NY 14456 Office Fax: 315-781-3458. E-mail: curl@hws.edu.

CURL, ROBERT FLOYD, JR., chemistry educator; b. Alice, Tex., Aug. 23, 1933; s. Robert Floyd and Lessie (Merritt) Curl; m. Jonel Whipple, Dec. 21, 1955; children: Michael, David. BA, Rice U., 1954; PhD, U. Calif., Berkeley, 1957; D (hon.), U. Buenos Aires, 1997, U. Littoral, 2002. Rsch. fellow Harvard U., Cambridge, Mass., 1957—58; from asst. prof. chemistry to prof. Rice U., Houston, 1958—2003, Kenneth S. Pitzer-Schlumberger prof. natural scis., 2003—; master Lovett Coll., 1968—72, prof., 2003—. Vis. rsch. officer NRC Can., 1972—73; vis. prof. Inst. Molecular Sci., Okazaki, Japan, 1977, U. Bonn, 1985; Erskine fellow U. Canterbury, 1999; hon. prof. USTC, 2002—. Contbr. articles to profl. jours. Co-recipient Nobel prize in Chemistry, 1996; named to, Tex. Sci. Hall Fame; recipient Clayton prize, Instn. Mech. Engrs., London, 1958, Internat. New Materials prize, Am. Phys. Soc., 1992, Alexander von Humboldt sr. U.S. scientist award, 1984, Order of Golden Plate, 1997, Achievement award, Am. Carbon Soc., 1997, Tex. Disting. Scientist award, 1997, Johannes Marcus Marci award in spectroscopy, 1998, Madison Marshall award, 1998, Space Act award, 1998, Centenary medal, Royal Soc. Chemistry, 1999; fellow NSF, Alfred P. Sloan, 1961—63, NATO postdoctoral, 1964. Fellow: Am. Acad. Arts and Scis., Am. Optical Soc., Royal Soc. of New Zealand (hon.); mem.: NAS, European Acad. Scis., Arts and Letters (titulaire mem.), Am. Chem. Soc., Sigma Xi, Phi Beta Kappa. Methodist. Home: 1824 Bolsover St Houston TX 77005-1728 Office: Rice University PO Box 1892 6100 Main St Houston TX 77005-1892 E-mail: rfcurl@rice.edu.

CURL, SAMUEL EVERETT, university dean, agricultural scientist; b. Ft. Worth, Dec. 26, 1937; s. Henry Clay and Mary Elva (Watson) C.; m. Betty Doris Savage, June 6, 1957 (div.); children: Jane Ellen, Julia Kathleen, Karen Elizabeth; m. Mary Behrends Reeves, Sept. 11, 1993; stepchildren: Ryan Andrew, Shelly Lyn. Student, Tarleton State Coll., 1955-57; BS, Sam Houston State U., 1959; MS, U. Mo., 1961; PhD, Tex. A&M U., 1963. Mem. faculty Tex. Tech U., Lubbock, 1961, 63-76, 79-97, tchr., rschr. animal physiology and genetics, 1963-76, asst., assoc. and interim dean Coll. Agrl. Sci., 1968-73, assoc. v.p. acad. affairs, prof., 1973-76, dean Coll. Agrl. Scis. and Natural Resources, prof., 1979-97; pres. Phillips U., Enid, Okla., 1976-79; agrl. cons., 1964-76; dean and dir. divsn. agrl. scis. and natural resources Okla. State U., Stillwater, 1997—; past pres. So. Assn. Agrl. Scientists. Bd. dirs. Am. Distance Edn. Consortium, Okla. Sci. and Tech. R&D Bd., Food and Agr. Ednl. Info. Sys., Oka. Youth Expo.; past chmn. So. Region Adminstrv. Heads, So. Region Adminstrv. Heads Liaison to Coun. on Agrl. Rsch., Ext. and Tchg.; mem. adminstrv. com. Okla. State U. Sch. Internat. Studies; former bd. dirs. Mid Am. Internat. Agrl. Consortium, 1997—2002, past chmn., 1998—99, 2001—02; mem. Gov.'s Task Force on Agrl. Devel. in Tex., 1982—83, 1988, Tex. Crop and Livestock Adv. Com., 1985—91, Tex. Agrl. Resources Protection Authority, 1989—97, Tex. Agribus. Rsch. Promotion Coun., 1995—97, Okla. State Com., Exptl. Program to Stimulate Competitive Rsch.; del. Eisenhower Consortium for Western Environ. Forestry Rsch., 1979—84; mgmt. com. S.W. Consortium on Plant Genetics and Water Resources, 1984—97, chmn., 1989—95; mem. USDA Nat. Planning Com. on Hispanic Minority Recruitment, 1988—93; trustee Consortium for Internat. Devel., 1979—97, mem. exec. com., 1981—84, 1986—87, 1989—90; former mem. High Plains Rsch. Coord. Bd., So. Regional Coun., U.S. Joint Coun. Food and Agrl. Scis.; former trustee Water Inc.; chmn. agrl. and natural resources program rev. task force Sam Houston State U., 1982—83; mem. adv. com. Sch. Agr. Angelo State U., 1989—95; mem. 1995 farm bill task force Tex. Dept. Agr., 1994—95; chair agrl. team Okal. Govs. EDGE project. Author: (with others) Progress and Change in the Agricultural Industry, 1974, Food and Fiber for a Changing World, 1976, 2d edit., 1982; contbr. 95 articles to profl. jours. Pres. Lubbock Econ. Coun., 1982; bd. dirs. Market Lubbock Econ. Devel. Corp., 1995-97; former mem. bd. overseers Ranching Heritage Assn.; mem. Goals for Lubbock: A Vision into the 21st Century Com., 1995-96; elder Westminster Presbyn. Ch., Lubbock, 1994-97; mem. First United Meth. Ch., Stillwater, 1997—. 2d lt. U.S. Army, 1959, capt. USAR. Danforth Assn. fellow, 1964-76, Am. Coun. Edn. fellow, 1972-73; recipient Disting. Alumnus award, Faculty-Alumni Gold medal U. Mo., 1975, Outstanding Agr. Alumnus award Sam Houston State U., 1986, Disting. Alumnus award, 1993, Tex. Citation for Outstanding Svc. award Tex. 4-H Found., 1987, Tex. 4-H Alumni award, 1993, Disting. Svc. award Vocational Agrl. Tchrs. Assn. Tex., 1987, Blue and Gold Meritorious Svc. award Tex. Future Farmers of Am., 1988, Tex. State degree Future Farmers Am., 1988, Area Disting. Svc. award Vocat. Agr. Tchrs., 1987, Okla. Hon. State degree Future Farmers Am., 2002. Mem.: Profl. Agrl. Workers Tex. (bd. dirs., Disting. Svc. to Tex. Agr. award 1984), Coun. Adminstrv. Heads of Agr., Nat. Assn. State Univs. and Land-Grant Colls. (exec. com. bd. agr. 1994—97, 1998—2001), Assn. U.S. Univ. Dirs. Internat. Agrl. Programs, Am. Assn. Univ. Agrl. Adminstrs., Am. Soc. Animal Sci. (program com. Biennial Symposium on Animal Reprodn. 1972—76, reviewer Jour. Animal Sci.), Lubbock C. of C. (chmn. agr. task force, chmn. rsch. com. 1981—86, bd. dirs. 1988—92, water com., legis. affairs com., agr. com., gubernatorial appointments task force), Century Club, Okla. State U. Alumni Assn., Centennial Rotary (hon.), West Tex. C. of C. (former bd. dirs., chmn. agrl. and ranching com.), Lubbock Club (bd. dirs., 1st v.p.), Sirloin Club Okla., Rotary, Gamma Sigma Delta, Phi Kappa Phi, Sigma Xi, Omicron Delta Kappa, Farmhouse Frat. (assoc.). Home: 32 Yellow Brick Dr Stillwater OK 74074-1726 Office: Office Dean & Dir Divsn Agrl Scis & Natural Resources Okla State U Stillwater OK 74078-0001 E-mail: securl@okstate.edu.

CURL, WADE, JR., (MACK CURL JR.), health facility administrator, consultant; b. Louisville, Feb. 15, 1950; s. Mack Wade Curl Sr. and Mary Elizabeth (Luckett) Shultz. Diploma in nursing, USAF Hosp., Wiesbaden, Germany, 1970; tchg. credential, techniques of tchg., UCLA, 1982; AA, L.A. Pierce Coll., Woodland Hills, Calif., 1987; B in Healthcare Adminstrn., Kennedy-Western U., Agoura, Calif., 1990; MBA, Kennedy-Western U., Boise, Idaho, 1992. RN, former CCRN; cert. tchr., Calif.; cert. profl. healthcare quality. Corp. dir. NSI Ednl. Systems, Beverly Hills, Calif., 1990—91; dir. edn. and tng. West Valley Hosp. & Health Ctr., Canoga Park, Calif., 1991—95; dir. edn. & performance improvement Westlake (Calif.) Med. Ctr., 1995—96; asst. adminstr. Kaiser Permanente, Sunset, L.A., 1996; mgr., quality mgmt. dept. Encino-Tarzana (Calif.) Regional Med. Ctr., 1996—98; dir. risk quality mgmt. North Hollywood (Calif.) Med. Ctr., 1998; cons. risk and quality mgmt. Steven Hirsch and Assocs., Fountain Valley, Calif., 1998—2002, sr. assoc., 2002—. Editor, co-author: Total Quality Management, 1995. Mem.: Orgn. Healthcare Educators (past pres.), Valley Nursing Edn. Coun. Granada Hills, Calif. (treas. 1994—95,

pres.-elect 1996, pres. 1997), Am. Soc. Healthcare Edn. & Tng. (treas. 1996—98, pres.-elect 1999, pres. 2000—01). Office: Steven Hirsch and Assocs 18837 Brookhurst St Ste 209 Fountain Valley CA 92708-7302

CURLANDER, PAUL JOSEPH, computer company executive; b. Balt., Dec. 15, 1952; s. John Carroll and Shirley Jean (Reiter) C.; m. Gretchen Lyn Vosseller, Feb. 7, 1986. BSEE, U. Colo., 1974; MSEE, MIT, 1977, PhD in Elec. Engring., 1979. Elec. engr. gen. products divsn. IBM, Boulder, 1974-76, staff printer tech. group office product divsn., 1979-85, product mgr. entry page printers, 1985-86, product mgr. letter quality printers info. products divsn., 1986-89, dir. printer products, 1989-91; gen. mgr. Lexmark Printer Bus., 1991-93; v.p. Lexmark, Lexington, Ky., 1993, gen. mgr. printing sys. bus., 1993-95, exec. v.p. ops., 1995-97, pres., COO, 1997-98, pres., CEO, 1998—, chmn., 1999—. Contbr. articles to profl. jours.; patentee in field. Office: Lexmark Internat Inc 1 Lexmark Center Dr Lexington KY 40550-0001*

CURLE, ROBIN LEA, computer software industry executive; b. Denver, Feb. 23, 1950; d. Fred Warren and Claudia Jean (Harding) C.; m. Lucien Ray Reed, Feb. 23, 1981 (div. Oct. 1984). BS in Bus. Comm., U. Ky., 1972. Systems analyst 1st Nat. Bank, Lexington, Ky., 1972-73, SW BancShares, Houston, 1973-77; sales rep. Software Internat., Houston, 1977-80; dist. mgr. UCCEL, Dallas, 1980-82; v.p. and gen. mgr. Southeastern region Info. Sci., Inc., Atlanta, 1982-83; v.p. sales and mktg. TesserAct, San Francisco, 1983-86, Foothill Rsch., San Francisco, 1986; pres., founder Curle Cons. Group, San Francisco, 1986-89; mgr. strategic mktg. MCC, Austin, Tex., 1989-90; founder, exec. v.p. Evolutionary Tech., Inc., Austin, 1991-99; pres., CEO Journée Software, Austin, Tex., 1999-2000; founder, mng. dir. CEO Partnerships, Austin, 2000—02; pres., CEO Zebra Imaging and the Gov. Bus. Council, 2002—. Bd. dirs. Evolutionary Techs. Internat., Austin Software Coun., Tex. Property and Casualty, Zebra Imaging, Govs. Bus. Coun.; adv. bd. 360 Summit; dir. adv. bd. U. Tex. Engring. Sch. Recipient Ma Ferguson award Exec. Women Internat. 1997, Grad of Yr. award Nat. Bus. Incubator Assn. 1996, Profiles in Power award, 1999, Entrepreneur of Yr. award 360 Summit Adv. Bd.; feature in Forbes Mag., 1996, Entrepreneur Mag., 1997; named top 50 most prestigious people Digital South; profile documentary Entrepreneurial Revolution, 1997, Inc 500 List, 1997, 98. Mem. U. Ky. Alumni Assn., Women in Tech., Women of Austin, Software Exec. Com., Inc. 500 Cos., Austin C. of C., Delta Gamma (pres. 1969). Republican. Avocations: scuba diving, running, skiing, cooking. Home: 7009 Quill Leaf Cv Austin TX 78750-8306 E-mail: rcurle@ceopartnerships.com.

CURLEY, AUGUSTINE JAMES FRANCIS, priest, educator; b. Orange, N.J., Jan. 9, 1956; s. Michael Joseph and Rose (McEnery) Curley. BA, Assumption Coll., 1977; MA, Seton Hall U., 1992; PhD, Boston Coll., 1992. Author: Augustine's Critique of Skepticism, 1996, New Jersey Catholicism: An Annotated Bibliography, 1999; contbr., articles to profl. jour. Publ. chmn. N.J. Cath. Historical Records Commn., South Orange, NJ. Roman Catholic. Home: 528 M L King Blvd Newark NJ 07102-1314 Office: St Benedict's Prep 520 M L King Blvd Newark NJ 07102-1314 Home Fax: 973-643-6922; Office Fax: 973-643-6922. Business E-Mail: acurley@sbp.org.

CURLEY, EDWIN MUNSON, philosophy educator; b. Albany, N.Y., May 1, 1937; s. Julius Edwin and Gertrude E.; m. Ruth Helen Snyder, Dec. 12, 1959; children: Julia Anne, Richard Edwin. BA, Lafayette Coll., 1959; PhD, Duke U., 1963. Asst. prof. philosophy San Jose State Coll., 1963-66; research fellow Australian Nat. U., Canberra, 1966-68, fellow, 1968-72, sr. fellow, 1972-77; prof. philosophy Northwestern U., 1977-83, U. Ill.-Chgo., 1983-93, U. Mich., 1993—. Author: Hellenistic Philosophy, 1965, Spinoza's Metaphysics, 1969, Descartes Against the Skeptics, 1978, The Collected Works of Spinoza, vol. 1, 1985, Behind the Geometrical Method, 1988, A Spinoza Reader, 1994, Hobbes' Leviathan, 1994; Am. co-editor Archiv für Geschichte der Philosophie, 1979-95; contbr. articles to profl. jours. Fellow AAAS; mem. Am. Philos. Assn. (v.p. ctr. divsn., 1989-90, pres. 1990-91). Home: 2645 Pin Oak Dr Ann Arbor MI 48103-2370 Office: U Mich Dept Philosophy 2215 Angell Hall Ann Arbor MI 48109

CURLEY, ELMER FRANK, librarian; b. Florence, Pa., Jan. 13, 1929; s. Augustus Wolfe and Bessie (Andrews) C. BA, U. Pitts., 1961; MLS, Carnegie Mellon U., Pitts., 1962; Adv. Cert., U. Pitts., 1964. Ref. libr. U. Pitts., 1962-64; head ref. dept. SUNY-Stony Brook, 1964-67; head pub. svcs. U. Nev.-Las Vegas, 1967-76, asst. dir. libr. svcs., 1976-81, ref. bibliographer, 1981-94, ret., 1994.

CURLEY, JOHN J. diversified media company executive; b. Dec. 31, 1938; m. Ann Conser; 2 children. BA, Dickinson Coll., 1960; MS, Columbia Univ., 1963. Reporter, editor AP, 1961—66; with Gannett Co., Inc., Arlington, Va., 1969—; pres. Mid-Atlantic newspaper group Gannett Co., Inc., Washington, 1980—82; sr. v.p. Gannett Co., Inc., Washington, 1983—84, pres., 1984—97, COO, 1984—86, CEO, 1986—2000, chmn., 1989—, also bd. dirs. Lt. U.S. Army, 1960—62. Home: 7402 Normandy Dr Richmond VA 23229-6714 E-mail: gcishare@info.gannett.com., tconnell@gci1.gannett.com.

CURLEY, JOHN FRANCIS, JR., mutual fund executive; b. Wollaston, Mass., July 24, 1939; s. John Francis and Ann (Omar) C.; m. Loretta Mae O'Keeffe, Oct. 20, 1962; children: William Laurance, Edward Reid, David Neil. Grad., Phillips Acad.; AB, Princeton U., 1960; MBA, Harvard U., 1962. With Paine, Webber, Jackson & Curtis, Inc., N.Y.C., 1964—, gen. ptnr., 1969-72, exec. v.p., 1972-77, pres., 1977-80, chmn. fin. com., 1980-82; vice-chmn. bd. Legg Mason, Inc., Balt., 1982-98, Legg Mason Wood Walker, Inc., Balt., 1982-98. Pres., bd. dirs. Legg Mason Value Trust, Inc., 1982—; chmn. bd. dirs. other Legg Mason Mutual Funds; bd. govs. Investment Co. Inst., ICI Mut. Ins. Co., 1994-98, Sellinger Sch. Bus., 1995-98. 1st lt. AUS, 1962-64. Mem. Securities Industry Assn. (dir., exec. com. 1978-80), Investment Assn. N.Y. (past pres.). Office: Legg Mason Wood Walker Inc 100 Light St Baltimore MD 21202-1099

CURLEY, JUANITA DALE, pilot, writer; b. Chgo., Aug. 11, 1939; d. James Frank Beran and Eleanor Levinia Dusek; m. Patrick Joseph Curley; children: Diane Curley (Angove), Debra Curley (McNulty), Denise Curley (Dangel). Assoc. degree, Washtenaw C.C., Ypsilanti, Mich., 1982. Author: The Genealogy and History of Robert Bradish in America, 2001. Active Girl Scouts of Am., Livonia, Mich., 1964—81, bd. dirs. No. Oakland County coun. Pontiac, Mich., 1980—81; charter/life mem. Mich. Aviation Hall of Fame, Lansing, 1993. Mem.: DAR, VFW (life; Ladies Aux. post 4012 1983), Geneal. Soc. of Washtenaw County, Nat. Geneal. Soc., The Ninety-Nines, Inc. (chpt. chair Mich. chpt. 1994—96, Greater Detroit Area chpt. 1996—), Aircraft Owners and Pilots Assn., Mich. Aviation Assn. (treas. 1988—93, dir. 1997—99). Roman Catholic. Avocations: private pilot, trout fishing, volunteer work, charitable projects. Office: Unicorn Press 7191 Angle Rd Northville MI 48167-9413

CURLEY, ROBERT AMBROSE, JR., lawyer; b. Boston, June 5, 1949; s. Robert Ambrose and Terese M. (O'Hara) C.; m. Kathleen M. Foley, June 10, 1972; children: Christine, Elizabeth, Margaret. AB cum laude, Harvard U., 1971; JD, Cornell U., 1974. Bar: Mass. 1974, U.S. Dist. Ct. Mass. 1975, U.S. Ct. Appeals (1st. cir.) 1976. Prin. Curley & Curley, P.C., Boston, 1974—, pres. Lectr. Mass. Continuing Legal Edn., Mass. Def. Attys., Mass. Acad. Trial Attys., Flaschner Judicial Inst., Nat. Bus. Inst.; dir. IADC Found., 2003—. Mem. ABA, ATLA (assoc.), Internat. Assn. Def. Counsel (dir. found. 2003—), Def. Trial Acad., Mass. Bar Assn. (lectr., chmn. civil trial practice sect., civil litig. com. 1990-91, mem. ho. of dels. 2001-2002), Mass. Def. Lawyers Assn. (co-chmn. products liability sects. 1994-96, bd. dirs., sec. 1998-99, treas., v.p. 1999-2000, pres. 2001-2002), Nat. Bus. Inst., Def. Rsch. Inst. (state rep. 2002—), Harvard Club (Hingham, treas. 1983-84, v.p. 1984-85, pres. 1985-86), Clover (Boston). Roman Catholic. Office: Curley & Curley PC 27 School St Ste 600 Boston MA 02108-4391 E-mail: rac@curleylaw.com.

CURLEY, THOMAS, newspaper executive; b. Easton, Pa., July 6, 1948; s. John Joseph and Emily Dixon (Sprague) Curley; m. Marsha Stanley, Sept. 14, 1974; children: Laura Stanley, Melinda Burke. BA in Polit. Sci., La Salle U., 1970; MBA, Rochester Inst. Tech., 1977. Reporter The News Tribune, Woodbridge, NJ, 1967, 1968, reporter, copy editor, 1970—72; night city/suburban editor The Times-Tribune, Rochester, NY, 1972—76; dir. info. Gannett Co., Inc., Rochester, 1976—80, dir. rsch., 1980—82; editor Norwich (Conn.) Bulletin, 1982—83; pub. The Courier-News, Bridgewater, NJ, 1983—85; exec. v.p. USA Today, Washington, 1985—86, pres., 1986—89, pres., COO, 1989—91, pres., pub., 1991—2003; sr. v.p. Gannett Co., Inc., 1998—; pres., CEO The Associated Press, 2003—. Trustee LaSalle U., Phila., 1987—, Rochester Inst. Tech., Ronald McDonald House Charities; former chmn. Am. Advertising Fed. Hall of Fame; mem. exec. bd. Ad Council. Pres. Ctrl. Jersey C. of C., Plainfield, NJ, 1984—85; exec. v.p. United Way Somerset Valley, Bridgewater, 1985; bd. dirs. Assn. for Retarded Citizens, Manville, NJ, 1983—85. Recipient Alumnus of Yr. award, Rochester Inst. Tech., 1986; Pub. Opinion Rsch. fellow, Northwestern U., 1976. Office: The Associated Press 50 Rockefeller Plz Flr 7 New York NY 10020-1605*

CURLEY, WALTER JOSEPH PATRICK, diplomat, investment banker; b. Pitts., Sept. 17, 1922; s. Walter Joseph and Marguerite Inez (Cowan) C.; m. Mary Walton, Dec. 18, 1948; children: Margaret Cowan, Walter Joseph, Patrick III, John Walton, James Mellon (dec. 1994). BA, Yale U., 1944; cert., U. Oslo, 1948; MBA, Harvard U., 1948; LLD (hon.), Trinity Coll., Dublin, Ireland, 1976. Mgr. Caltex Oil Co., India, 1948-52, 1952-55, 1955-57; v.p. San Jacinto Petroleum, 1957-60; ptnr. J.H. Whitney Co., 1961-75. Bd. dirs. France Growth Fund, N.Y.C.; commr. pub. events, chief protocol City of N.Y., 1973-74; amb. to Ireland, 1975-77, amb. to France, 1989-93; prin. W.J.P. Curley, 1978—; pres. Curley Land Co., Pitts., 1993—; chmn. adv. bd. Sotheby's Internat., 1999—. Author: Letters From The Pacific, 1965, Monarchs in Waiting, 1974. Trustee Buckley Sch., 1960-75, Miss Porter's Sch., Farmington, Mass., 1965-74, Barnard Coll., 1966-75, N.Y. Pub. Libr., 1972-75, The Frick Collection, 1993—; hon. chmn. French-Am. Found., N.Y., 1993—. Decorated Bronze Star; Cloud and Banner (Republic of China); comdr. French Legion of Honor. Mem. Coun. Fgn. Rels., Yale Club, Knickerbocker Club, Links Club, Racquet and Tennis Club, Rolling Rock Club (Ligonier, Pa.), Kildare St. Club (Dublin), Bedford Golf and Tennis Club, St. Stephen's Green Club (Dublin), Traveller's Club (Paris), Seminole Golf Club (Palm Beach, Fla.). Office: 625 Fifth Ave 18th Fl New York NY 10022 E-mail: curleywjp@aol.com.

CURLIN, JAY RUSSELL, English educator; b. El Paso, Tex., Oct. 3, 1960; s. James Howard Curlin and Mary Laverne Dodd; m. Bonnie Dale Kesner, Sept. 1, 1987; children: Christopher, Adam, Jason, Gideon, Charity, Gabriel. BA, Ouachita Bapt. U., 1983; MA, U. Ark., 1985; PhD, U. Mich., 1993. Asst. prof. English U. Ctrl. Ark., Conway, 1990-97, S.W. Bapt. U., Bolivar, Mo., 1997-98; assoc. prof. English Ouachita Bapt. U., Arkadelphia, Ark., 1998—, chmn. dept. English, 2000—. Book rev. editor Publs. Ark. Philol. Assn., Conway, 1994-97; bd. readers Slant, Conway, 1995—. Author: (essays) Arenas of Conflict, 1997 (Ireme Samuel award 1998), English Civil Wars in the Literary Imagination, 1999; contbr. articles to profl. jours. Mem. Milton Soc. Am. Baptist. Home: 207 N 5th St Arkadelphia AR 71923 Office: Ouachita Bapt U Box 3751 Arkadelphia AR 71998 E-mail: curlinj@obu.edu.

CURLIN, WILLIAM G. bishop; b. Portsmouth, Va., Aug. 30, 1927; Student, Georgetown U., St. Mary's Sem., Balt. Ordained priest Roman Catholic Ch., 1957. Titular bishop Rosemarkie and aux. bishop, Washington, 1988-93; bishop diocese of Charlotte Pastoral Ctr, Charlotte, N.C., 1994—. Roman Catholic. Office: Chancery Office PO Box 36776 Charlotte NC 28236-6776

CURLOOK, WALTER, management consultant; b. Coniston, Ont., Can., Mar. 14, 1929; s. William and Stephanie (Acker) C.; m. Jennifer Burak, May 28, 1955; children: Christine, William Paul, John Michael, Andrea. BA in Sci., U. Toronto, 1950, MA in Sci., 1951, PhD, 1953; D.Sc. (hon.), Laurentian U., 1983; D Engring. (hon.), U. Toronto, 2002. Postdoctoral fellow Imperial Coll. Sci. and Tech., London, 1954; rsch. metallurgist Inco, Sudbury, Ont., Can., 1954-59, supr. rsch. sta. Port Colborne, Ont., 1959-60, supr. rsch. Copper Cliff, Ont., 1960-64, asst. to gen. mgr., 1964-69; dir. tech. COFIMPAC, Paris, 1969-72; v.p. adminstrv. and engring. svcs. Inco, Copper Cliff, 1973-74, v.p. N.Y.C., 1974-77; sr. v.p. prodn. Inco Metals Co., Toronto, 1977-80, pres., chief exec. officer, 1980-82; exec. v.p. Inco Ltd., Toronto, 1982-91, vice chmn., 1991-94, dir., 1989-94; pres. Inco Gold Co., Toronto, 1987-89; pres. commr. P.T. Inco, Indonesia, 1990-93; pres., dir. gen. Goro Nickel, S.A., Noumea, New Caledonia, 1992-97. Disting. adj. prof. U. Toronto, 1999—; mem. Nat. Adv. Com. Mining Industry, 1980-94; mem. Premier's Coun. Econ. Renewal, 1991-94. Patentee in field. Bd. dirs. Foundation Cambrian Found., Sudbury, 1983; first chmn. bd. Cambrian Coll. Applied Arts and Tech., Sudbury, Ont., 1967. Named to Can. Mining Hall of Fame, 1997; recipient McCharles prize, U. Toronto, 1989, Charles F. Rand medal, AIME, 2002. Fellow Can. Acad. Engring.; mem. Assn. Profl. Engrs. of Ont., Metall. Soc. of Can. Inst. Mining and Metallurgy (Airey 1979, Platinum medal 1994), Mining Assn. Can. (bd. dir. and past chmn.), Sci. North (hon. life Sudbury chpt. 1988), Ont. Mining Assn. (past pres.), Order of Can. Home and Office: 25 Cluny Dr Toronto ON Canada M4W 2P9

CURNOW, KATHY, art historian, educator; BA in Art History magna cum laude, Pa. State U., 1974; MA in Art History, Ind. U., 1980, PhD in Art History, African Studies, 1983. Prin. lectr. dept. design Nigerian TV Coll., Jos Plateau State, 1983-85, head dept. gen. studies, sr. lectr., 1985-88; exec. asst. Am. Found. Negro Affairs, Nat. Edn. Rsch. Fund, Phila., 1988-89; vis. asst. prof. dept. art Cleve. State U., 1990-91, asst. prof., 1991-94, assoc. prof., 1995—. Grad. asst. Ind. U., Bloomington, 1978-80; adj. asst. prof. U. Pa., Phila., 1989-91; vis. asst. prof. dept. art Lincoln U., Pa., 1989-90, dept. humanities U. Arts, Phila., 1990; lectr. Met. Mus. Art, N.Y.C., 1990; vis. Fulbright assoc. prof. U. Benin, Benin City, Nigeria, 1997-98. Author: (chpt.) Communications Training and Practice in Nigeria, 1987, Kulte, Kunstler, Könige in Afrika, 1997; contbr. articles to profl. jours. Recipient Nigerian Learning Materials award, 1987, Nat. Merit award Nigerian Festival TV Programming, 1987; Westinghouse scholar, 1973; Ind. U. fellow, 1977-80; grantee Rsch. Challenge, 1992, Social Sci. Rsch. Coun., 1993, NEH, 1993-98, Fulbright award, 1997-98. Mem. African Studies Assn. (arts coun., textbook writing com. 1991-93, bd. dirs. 1993-97, chair book prize com. 1994-95, sec.-treas. 1995-97), African Studies Assn., Coll. Art Assn., Delta Studies Assn., Midwest Art Historians Assn., Sierra Leone Studies Assn. Avocation: writing fiction. Office: Cleve State U Art Dept 111 AB Cleveland OH 44115

CURNS, EILEEN BOHAN, counselor, author, speaker; b. Chgo., May 22, 1927; d. Alvin Joseph and Lorraine Bohan; m. John R. Curns, July 1, 1950 (div. 1975); children: James, Barbara. BA in Sociology, DePaul U., Chgo.; MEd in Psychology and Edn., Loyola U., Chgo.; postgrad. in health edn., U. Wis. Cert. Gestalt therapist, Gestalt Inst. Chgo.; Ill. lic. clin. profl. counselor; cert. energy healer Jaffe Inst. for Spiritual and Med. Healing, Anguin, Calif. Prin. ACCORD, Vernon Hills, Ill. Cons. in health care cost containment, stress rschr., inner healing; lectr. on the five stress signals leading to disease and how to reverse them. Author: First Aid for Stress charts, 5 workbooks. Recipient Golden Deeds award Exch. Club, 1965, commendation Queen Mary Vets. Hosp., Montreal, 1975. Mem. Am. Bd. Med. Psychotherapists (cert.). Achievements include author of the first aid for stress charts and workbooks. Home: 825 Waterview Cir Vernon Hills IL 60061-2550

CURNUTTE, MARK WILLIAM, lawyer; b. Vinita, Okla., May 28, 1954; s. William Elmer and Genevieve Gertrude (Fitzgerald) C.; m. Lou Ann Coffman, Aug. 4, 1979; children: Meredith Blake, Amelia Leigh. BBA in Accountancy, U. Okla., 1976, JD, 1979. Bar: Okla. 1979, U.S. Dist. Ct. (no. dist.) Okla. 1980, U.S. Dist. Ct. (ea. and we. dists.) Okla. 1984, U.S. Tax Ct. 1979, U.S. Ct. Appeals (10th and fed. cirs.) 1980, U.S. Supreme Ct. 1984. Tax staff acct. Arthur Andersen & Co., Tulsa, 1979-81; assoc. Jones, Givens, Gotcher, Doyle & Bogan, Tulsa, 1981-84, Logan & Lowry, LLP, Vinita, Okla., 1984-87, ptnr., 1987—. Bd. dirs. C&L Supply, Inc., Vinita. Trustee Craig County Law Libr., Vinita, 1984—; chmn. bd. trustees Vinita Pub. Libr., 1987-89, 91-92; treas. Vinita chpt. ARC, 1991—. Fellow: Okla. Bar Found. (trustee 2000—), Am. Coll. Trust and Estate Counsel; mem.: U. Okla. Coll. Law Assn. (bd. dirs. 1989—91), Craig County Bar Assn. (sec.-treas. 1984—91, v.p. 1995—96, pres. 1997), Okla. Bar Assn. (title stds. com. real property sect. 1988—89, clients' security fund com. 1989—91, probate code com. 1995—, legal ethics and unauthorized practice com. 1995—97), ABA (com. on estate and gift tax 1987—90, small bus. com. 1987—, com. on small law firms 1987—), Rotary (pres. Vinita 1988—89, Paul Harris fellow 1989), Shriners, Masons, Phi Delta Phi. Republican. Presbyterian. Avocations: hunting, fishing. Office: PO Box 558 Vinita OK 74301-0558

CURNUTTE, MARY E. artist, restorer of painting, educator; b. Valera, Tex., Dec. 15, 1920; d. Robert Franklin and Mary Elizabeth (Walker) Line; m. James Richard Curnutte, Oct. 14, 1950 (dec. Feb. 1972); 1 child, Sandra Elizabeth Curnutte Ziter; m. Robert Frederick Furman, Apr. 27, 1985 (dec. Apr. 2003). Grad. h.s., 1936. Bookkeeper, sec. drug stores, 1942-49, NCO Club, Goodfellow AFB, San Angelo, Tex., 1949-51; bookkeeper Boyce Hardware and Fuel Oil, Portsmouth, Va., 1953; artist/logs/filing Christian Broadcasting Network, Portsmouth, 1972-73; tchr. art Frederick Mil. Acad., Portsmouth, 1978-82, Alliance Christian Sch., Portsmouth, 1981-85; artist and pvt. tchr. art and music, restorer of art Portsmouth, 1959-89; artist Winter Haven, Fla., 1989—. Recipient Silver Cup award Alliance Christian Sch., 1984. Mem. Nat. Mus. Women in the Arts (charter mem.), Women of the Moose. Baptist. Avocations: photography, swimming, fishing, music, travel.

CURPHEY, THOMAS JOHN, chemist, researcher; b. N.Y.C., N.Y., Oct. 7, 1934; s. Theodore Joscelyn and Aies Curphey; m. Marilyn Gomulka, Aug. 2, 1959; children: Linda Lee, Alison. AB, Harvard U., 1956, PhD, 1960. Rsch. assoc. U. of Wis., Madison, Wis., 1960—62; instr. in chemistry Yale U., New Haven, 1962—64; asst. prof. of chemistry St. Louis U., St. Louis, 1964—68, assoc. prof. of chemistry, 1968—73, prof. of chemistry, 1973—74; adj. prof. of chemistry Dartmouth Coll., Hanover, NH, 1974—; sr. rsch. assoc. Dartmouth Med. Sch., Hanover, NH, 1974—80, rsch. assoc. prof. of pathology, 1980—85, rsch. prof. of pathology, 1985—. Cons. Crime Lab, St. Louis Met. Police, St. Louis. Contbr. articles to profl. jours. Grantee More than 30, NIH, NSF, 1962 - 2002. Mem.: Am. Chem. Soc. (treas. St. Louis sect. 1971—72, dir. 1974—75, chmn. organic tropical group 1966—67). Home: 12 Dresden Rd Hanover NH 03755 Office: Dartmouth Med Sch Hanover NH 03755 E-mail: tjc@dartmouth.edu.

CURRAN, AUDREY, psychologist, educator; b. Cleve., Dec. 12, 1943; d. Millard and Nora Maria Harwell; children: Robert Criste Jr., Michaelann, Aline, Audrey. BA magna cum laude, Seaton Hill Coll.; MA, Fielding Inst., 1984, PhD, 1986. Lic. clin. psychologist, Calif., Ohio, internat. forensic psychologist. H.S. tchr., counselor, Glendora, Calif.; pvt. practice clin. psychologist Beachwood, Ohio, 1986—; chair psychology dept. Notre Dame Coll., South Euclid, Ohio, 1989—. Adj. prof. psychology/grad. program John Carroll U., Ohio, 1994-98; cons. in field. Contbr. articles to newspapers and mags., wrici syndicated column, Curran Events, 1980-87, Headlines, 1980-87. Recipient Disting. Alumnae award Seton Hill Coll., 2000. Mem. APA, Am. Psychol. Assn., Ohio Psychol. Assn. Avocations: travel, snow and water skiing, snorkeling, horse riding, reading. Home: 27020 Cedar Rd alt109 Beachwood OH 44122-1163 E-mail: acurran@ndc.edu.

CURRAN, BARBARA SANSON, lawyer; b. Wiesbaden, Fed. Republic of Germany, Jan. 25, 1955; came to U.S., 1973; d. Allan David and Gertrude Maria (Trendl) S.; m. Stephen P. Curran, Sept. 15, 1990; 1 child, Catherine L. Student, U. London, 1975-76; AB, Bryn Mawr Coll., 1977; JD, Dickinson Sch. Law, 1980. Bar: Pa. 1980, U.S. Dist. Ct. (ea. dist.) Pa. 1981. Law clk. Lehigh County Ct., Allentown, Pa., 1980-82; assoc. Duane Morris & Heckscher, Phila., 1982-84; atty. ICI Americas Inc., Wilmington, Del., 1984-90, corp. sec., 1991-2000, ICI American Holdings Inc., Wilmington, 2000—. Mem. ABA, Pa. Bar Assn. Avocation: ice skating. Home: 105 Montana Dr Chadds Ford PA 19317-9284 Office: ICI Ams Inc 1000 Uniqema Blvd New Castle DE 19720

CURRAN, CHRISTOPHER, economics educator; b. Washington, Nov. 5, 1943; s. Charles Daniel and Virginia (Wray) C.; m. Nannette Carter, June 10, 1978; children: John Fredrick, Christianne Michelle. BA in History, Rice U., 1967; MS in Econs., Purdue U., 1969, PhD in Econs., 1972. Grad. instr. econs. Purdue U., 1967-70; asst. prof. econs. Emory U., Atlanta, 1970-77, sr. acad. assoc. Law and Econs. Ctr., 1983-86, sr. acad. assoc. law and econs., 1986—, assoc. prof. econs., 1977—, dir. undergrad. studies, 1994-96. Fulbright lectr., Peru, 1976; adj. assoc. prof. Fuqua Sch. Bus., Duke U., 2000. Contbr. articles and book revs. to profl. jours. Bd. mem. Lullwater Sch., Atlanta, 1975; v.p. Virginia Hill Condo Assn., Atlanta, 1993, pres. 1994, treas. 1995. Krannert rsch. grantee, 1969-70, grantee Emory U., 1972, 75, 79, Emory Bus. Sch., 1978-80, 82. Mem. Am. Econ. Assn., So. Econ. Assn., Am. Law and Econs. Assn., European Assn. Law and Econs. (assoc.), Therapy Dogs Internat., Inc. (assoc.), Belgian Sheepdog Club Am. Avocations: tennis, dog training. Home: 578 N Superior Ave Decatur GA 30033-5402 Office: Emory U Dept Econs Atlanta GA 30322-0001

CURRAN, DARRYL JOSEPH, photographer, educator; b. Santa Barbara, Calif., Oct. 19, 1935; s. Joseph Harold and Irma Marie (Schlagel) C.; m. Doris Jean Smith, July 12, 1968. AA, Ventura Coll., 1958; BA, UCLA, 1960, MA, 1964. Designer, installer UCLA Art Galleries, 1963-65; mem. faculty Los Angeles Harbor Coll., 1968-69, UCLA Ext., 1972-79, Sch. Art Inst. Chgo., 1975; prof. art Calif. State U., Fullerton, 1967-2001, chmn. art dept., 1989-99; curator various shows, 1971—. Bd. dirs. Los Angeles Center Photog. Studies, 1973-77, pres., 1980-83; juror Los Angeles Olympics Photog. Commns. Project, 1983 One-man shows include U. Chgo., 1975, U. R.I., 1975, Art Space, L.A., 1978, Photoworks Gallery, Richmond, Va., 1979, Alan Hancock Coll., Santa Maria, Calif., 1979, G. Ray Hawkins Gallery, L.A., 1981, Portland (Maine) Sch. Art, 1983, Grossmont Coll., San Diego, 1982, (retrospective) Chaffey Coll., Alta Loma, Calif., L. A. Ctr. for Photographic Studies, 1984, U. Calif. Ext. Ctr., San Francisco, 1986, Cuesta Coll., San Luis Obispo, Calif., 1992, Cypress Coll., 1993, Tex. Woman's U., Denton, 1997, Irvine Valley Coll., 1997, Ellen Kim Murphy Gallery, Santa Monica, 2000, William Marten Gallery, Rochester, N.Y., 2001; two-person show No. Ky. U., 1995; group exhbns. include Laguna Mus. Art, San Francisco, 1992, Friends of Photography, San Francisco, 1993, U.S. Info. Agy. Empowered Images, 1994—, USIA, Jan Abrams Gallery, L.A., 1995; group exhibns. include Mt. St. Mary's Coll., 1997, Ranch Santiago Coll., 1997; represented in permanent collections Mus. Modern Art, Royal Photog. Soc., London, Nat. Gallery Can., Ottawa, Mpls. Inst. Art, Oakland Mus., U. N.Mex., UCLA, Seagram's Collection, N.Y.C., Mus. Photog. Arts, San Diego, Phila. Mus. Art, J. Paul Getty Mus., Phila. Mus. Art, San Francisco Mus. Art. Bd. dirs. Cheviot Hills Home Owners Assn., 1973. Served with U.S. Army, 1954-56. Recipient Career Achievement award Calif. Mus. Photography, 1986; NEA Photographers fellow, 1980; Honored Educator award Soc. Photographic Edn., 1996. Mem. Soc. Photog. Edn. (dir. 1975-79, honored educator 1996). Home: 10537 Dunleer Dr Los Angeles CA 90064-4317 E-mail: localdj@mindspring.com. *I am an artist with abstract expressionist sympathies who chooses to use the photographic medium in its broadest definition.*

CURRAN, DENNIS PATRICK, chemist, educator; b. Easton, Pa., June 10, 1953; s. William Curran; m. Suzanne Curran; children: Molly, Kelly. BS, Boston Coll., 1975; PhD, U. Rochester, 1979. Postdoctoral fellow U. Wis., Madison, 1979—81; from asst. prof. to Bayer prof. and Disting. Svc. prof. U. Pitts., 1981—96, Disting. Svc. prof. dept. chemistry, 1996—. Vis. prof. U. Basel, 1990, 94, U. Ill., 1995, Kyushu U., 1996; founder Fluorous Tech., Inc., 2000—, chief sci. adv., 2000—; mem. adv. bd. Tetrahedron Internat., 1992—; mem. sci. adv. bd. CombiChem, Inc., LaJolla, Calif., 1997—99, NeoGenesis, Inc., Boston, 1997—; mem. internat. adv. bd. Euchem Mtg. on Free Radicals, 2002; cons. in field. Co-editor: Tetrahedron Symposium in Print on Fluorous Chemistry, 2002; mem. editl. adv. bd.: Chemical Soc. Perkin: Jours., 1992—2002, Jour. Combinatorial Chemistry, 1999—, Advanced Synthesis & Catalysis, 2001—, Progress in Heterocyclic Chemistry, 1999—, mem. bd. editors: Tetrahedron, 1998—; editor: Advances in Cycloaddition, 1987—93; editor: (assoc.) Organic Reactions, 1991—2001, Organic Synthesis, 1999—; contbr. articles to profl. jours. Fellow Sherman Clarke fellow, 1977—79, Elon Huntington Hooker fellow, 1977—79, NIH, 1979—80, Alfred P. Sloan Found., 1985—87, Japan Soc. Promotion of Sci., 1994; grantee Dreyfus grantee, 1981—86, Merck Faculty Devel., 1986—88, Rsch. Career Devel. grant, NIH, 1987—92, Sr. Rsch. grant, Humbolt Found., 1998—2000. Fellow: AAAS; mem.: ACS (exec. coun. mem. organic divsn. 1990—92, alternate councilor organic divsn. 1992—94, chmn. graduate fellowship program organic chemistry 1999—, chmn.organic divsn. 2000, Creativity in Organic Synthesis award 2000, Cope scholar 1988), Soc. Heterocyclic Chemistry (internat. adv. bd. 1998—99, internat. adv. com. 2002), Pitts. Cancer Ctr. Office: Univ Pittsburgh Dept Chemistry 219 Parkman Ave Pittsburgh PA 15260

CURRAN, DONALD JAMES, artist, illustrator; b. St. Louis, May 6, 1955; s. Donald James Curran and Marjorie Jean Wiseman; m. Sharon Lee Kenney, Apr. 12, 1986; children: Donald James III, Marjorie Kenney. Student, Kansas City (Mo.) Art Inst., 1973; A, Forest Park C.C., St. Louis, 1975. Artist Sverdrup Corp., St. Louis, 1975-80; freelance artist/illustrator St. Louis, 1980—. Exhibitions include Maritime Gallery at Mystic Seaport, Conn., 2001, Maritime Gallery at Mystic, 2003, Nat. Oil and Acrylic Painters Soc., 2001, Salon Internat., Greenhouse Gallery of Fine Art, 2002, 2003, Bosque Conservatory of Art Ann. Exhbn., 2003, Fla. Invitational 2002, 2003, Cin. Art Club Viewpoint, 2002, Hilton Head Art League Nat. Exhbn., 2003. Republican. Roman Catholic. Avocation: family history research. Home and Office: 215 Parkland Ave Saint Louis MO 63122

CURRAN, G. MICHAEL, lawyer; b. Tarrytown, N.J., Mar. 20, 1949; s. Geoffrey C. and Marjorie May (Barnes) C.; m. Rose Marie Strong, June 5, 1970 (div. Feb. 1981); children: Christopher, Sarah, Deborah; m. Karol Ann Chumchal, Feb. 9, 1985; 1 child, Brandon. BBA, U. Tex., 1971; JD, St. Mary's U., San Antonio, 1973. Bar: Tex. 1974, U.S. Dist. Ct. (so. dist.) Tex. 1975, U.S. Dist. Ct. (no. dist.) Tex. 1984, U.S Ct. of Appeals, (5th cir.) 1991, U.S. Dist. Ct. Ariz, 1992. Briefing atty. First Ct. of Appeals, Houston, 1974; lawyer Vinson & Elkins, Houston, 1975-82, Axelrod, Smith, Komiss & Kirshbaum, Houston, 1983, Sheinfeld, Maley & Kay, Dallas, 1984-87; ptnr. Akin, Gump, Strauss, Hauer & Feld, Dallas, 1988—2001, McManemin & Smith, 2002—. Contbr. articles to profl. jours. Office: McManemin & Smith Plz Ams So Tower 600 N Pearl Ste 1600 LV175 Dallas TX 75201-2890 Fax: 214-953-0695.

CURRAN, J. JOSEPH, JR., state attorney general; b. West Palm Beach, Fla., July 7, 1931; s. J. Joseph Sr. and Catherine (Clark) Curran; m. Barbara Marie Atkins, 1959; children: Mary Carole, Alice Ann, Catherine Marie, J. Joseph III, William A.(dec.). LLB, U. Balt., 1959. Bar: Md. 1959, U.S. Dist. Ct. Md., U.S. Supreme Ct. 1987. State senator from Md., 1963—82; lt. gov. State of Md., 1983—87, atty. gen., 1987—. Mem. Md. Regional Planning Coun., 1963—82. Mem.: Balt. Bar Assn., Md. Bar Assn. Democrat. Office: Office of Atty Gen 200 Saint Paul Pl Baltimore MD 21202-2002*

CURRAN, JAMES W. epidemiologist, educator, academic administrator; b. Monroe, Mich., Sept. 16, 1944; married; 2 children. BS, U. Notre Dame, 1966; MD, U. Mich., 1970; MPH, Harvard U., 1974. Rsch. instr. dept. preventive and cmty. medicine U. Tenn. Med. Sch., 1971—73; career devel. tng. Ctr. Disease Control, USPHS, 1973—75; asst. commr. health med. svc. Columbus (Ohio) City Health Dept., 1975—78; chief oper. rsch. br. Venereal Disease Control Ctr. Disease Control and Prevention, 1978—82; dir. Acquired Immune Deficiency Syndrome Activ. 1982—84; chief AIDS br. Divsn. Viral Diseases, Ctr. Infectious Diseases, 1984—85; dir. WHO Referal Ctr. AIDS & Retroviruses, 1985—92; assoc. dir. human immunodeficiency virus/AIDS Ctr. Disease Control and Prevention, 1992—95; dean Rollins Sch. Pub. Health Emory U., Atlanta, 1995—. L. Vernon Scott lectr. U. Okla. Health Sci. Ctr., 1985; Verna & Mars lectr. Baylor Coll. Medicine, 1988; Oliver Cope lectr. Mass. Gen. Hosp., 1988; clin. rsch. investigator Venereal Disease Br., Ctr. Disease Control, 1971—73; med. dir. Influenza Immunization Program, Franklin County, 1976—77; clin. rsch. investigator, coord. Oper. Rsch. Bd., Venereal Disease Control Divsn., Ctr. Disease Control, 1975—78; clin. asst. prof. dept. preventive ve and cmty. medicine Coll. Medicine, Ohio State U., 1976—79; John Forbes fellow infectious disease Fairfield Hosp., Melbourne, Australia, 1985; vis. prof. Coll. Medicine, U. Ill., 1988; asst. surgeon gen. USHPS, 1991. Recipient William C. Watson Jr. award, 1987. Fellow: Am. Epidemiol. Soc., Am. Coll. Preventive Medicine, Infectious Disease Soc. Am.; mem.: AAAS, Am. Venereal Disease Assn., Inst. Medicine-NAS, Sigma Xi. Office: Emory U Rollins Sch Pub Health 1518 Clifton Rd NE Rm 1820 Atlanta GA 30322-4201

CURRAN, JOHN MARK, military career officer; b. West Palm Beach, Fla., Jan. 27, 1952; m. Cindy Templon; children: Jennifer, Jessica, Julia. Grad., Fla. So. Coll.; M in Mil. Arts and Scis.; grad., Command & Gen. Staff Coll., Nat. War Coll. Commd. officer U.S. Army, advanced through grades to brig. gen., 1998, evaluation officer 1st ROTC region, armored cavalry platoon leader, trans sect. leader, officer Ft. Bliss, Tex., hdqrs. co. exec. officer, aeroscout platoon leader, bn. S1, flight comdr., ops. officer, br. comdr., dept. flight tng., tng. devel. officer dept. combined arms tactics, co. comdr., G3 air, attack bn. exec. officer Aviation Brigade S3 Ft. Campbell, Ky., dep. aviation brigade comdr. 101st Airborne Divsn.; dept. of the Army programs, priorities & requirements divsn. Office Dep. Chief Staff for Ops. and Plans, Force Devel.; comdr. aviation brigade 2nd Inf. Divsn. U.S. Army, Republic of Korea, dep. chief staff ops. USAREUR Forward, asst. divsn. comdr. for support 1st Inf. Divsn., asst. dep. chief of staff for tng. west, 1998—. Decorated Bronze Star, Legion of Merit with oak leaf cluster, Meritorious Svc. medal with three oak leaf clusters, Army Commendation medal, two Air medals, Army Achievement medal, Nat. Def. Svc. medal, NATO medal, Kuwait Liberation medal Govts. of Saudi Arabia and Kuwait.

CURRAN, JOSEPH PATRICK, lawyer; b. Providence, Apr. 25, 1951; s. Joseph Patrick and Susan (Donohue) C.; m. Sheila Jane McGowan, July 14, 1974; children: Christopher, Peter. BA, Holy Cross Coll., 1973; MA, London Sch. Econs., 1974; JD, U. Mich., 1978. Bar: R.I. 1978. Spl. asst. to gen. counsel Office of Sec. USN, Washington, 1978-81; assoc. Hinckley, Allen & Snyder, Providence, 1981-86; ptnr. Hinckley, Allen & Snyder, Providence, 1986—. Editor U. Mich. Law Rev., 1976-78. Pres. Improvise Inc., Providence, 1989—. Lt. USN, 1978-81. Mem. ABA, R.I. Bar Assn., Order of Coif. Home: 232 Taber Ave Providence RI 02906-3351 Office: Hinckley Allen Snyder 1500 Fleet Ctr Providence RI 02903-2319 E-mail: jcurran@haslaw.com.

CURRAN, MAURICE FRANCIS, lawyer; b. Yonkers, N.Y., Feb. 20, 1931; s. James F. and Mary (O'Brien) C.; m. Deborah M. Dee, May 7, 1960; children: James, Maurice, Amy, Bridget, Ceara, Sara. Student, Cathedral Coll., 1950; BA in Philosophy, St. Joseph Coll. and Sem., 1952; LLB, Fordham U., 1958. Bar: N.Y. 1958, U.S. Dist. Ct. (so. and ea. dists.) N.Y. 1960, U.S. Ct. Appeals (2d cir.) 1982, U.S. Supreme Ct. Assoc. Kelley, Drye, Newhall & Maginnes, N.Y.C., 1958-60, Wilson & Bave, Yonkers, 1960-65; divsn. counsel Merck & Co., Rahway, N.J., 1965-67; asst. gen. counsel E.R. Squibb & Sons, Inc., N.Y.C., 1967-70; corp. counsel, chief law dept. City of Yonkers, 1970-72; ptnr. Bleakley, Platt, Schmidt & Fritz, White Plains, N.Y., 1972-83, Banks, Curran & Schwam, LLP, Mt. Kisco, NY, 1983—. Past trustee, vice chmn. Westchester C.C. Capt. USMC, 1952-58. Mem. Fed. Bar Coun., N.Y. State Bar Assn., Assn. Bar City N.Y. Roman Catholic. Home: 388 Bronxville Rd Bronxville NY 10708-1233 Office: 61 Smith Ave Mount Kisco NY 10549-2813

CURRAN, MICHAEL WALTER, management scientist; b. St. Louis, Dec. 6, 1935; s. Clarence Maurice and Helen Gertrude (Parsons) Curran; m. Jeanette Lucille Rawizza, Sept. 24, 1955 (div. 1977); children: Kevin Michael, Karen Ann, Kathleen Marie(dec.), Kimberly Elizabeth; m. Mary Jane Lemanek, Aug. 18, 1981. BS, Washington U., St. Louis, 1964. With Monsanto Co., St. Louis, 1953-65, supervisory positions dept. adminstrv. services, 1956-64, rsch. technician inorganic chems. divsn., 1964-65; sr. ops. rsch. analyst Pet Inc., St. Louis, 1965-68; pres., CEO, dir. Decision Scis. Corp., St. Louis, 1968—. Former mem. adv. bd. Entrepreneurial Bus. Ctr., U. Mo., St. Louis; judge Tech. Excellence Awards, St. Louis, 2002, 03. Co-author: (book) Handbook of Budgeting, 1981, Handbook of Budgeting, 4th edit., 1999, Effective Project Management Through Applied Cost and Schedule Control, 1996; editor: Professional Practice Guide to Risk, Vols. 1-3, 1998; contbr. articles to profl. jours.; developer theories of bracket budgeting and range estimating. Adviser Jr. Achievement, St. Louis, 1958—59; active United Way, 1958—62. Mem.: Soc. Cost Estimating and Analysis, Project Mgmt. Inst., Assn. Advancement Cost Engring. (chmn. risk mgmt. com. 1991—, mem. editl. adv. com. 1997—, Tech. Excellence award 2000), Ops. Rsch. Soc. Am., Inst. Mgmt. Scis. (chmn. St. Louis chpt. 1971—72), Intertel, Mensa, Alpha Sigma Lambda, Sigma Xi. Office: Decision Scis Corp PO Box 28848 Saint Louis MO 63123-0048

CURRAN, PHYLLIS MARIE, counselor; b. Cleve., Jan. 22, 1933; d. Herbert Charles Eisele and Edna Marie Huesman; m. James Francis Curran, Dec. 27, 1955 (div. Dec. 30, 1985); children: Debbie, Sean, Terry, Holly. Cert. chem. dependency counselor Ohio, internat. Sec.-counselor Chisholm Ctr., Cleve., 1982—84; counselor, clin. dir. Stella Maris Detox Ctr., Cleve., 1984—90; clin. dir., counselor, co-founder Freedom House Inc., Cleve., 1991—98, Ed Keating Ctr. Inc., Cleve., 1998—. Mem.: Internat. Cert. Alcohol and Drug Counselor, Ohio Dept. Alcohol and Drug Addiction Svcs., Nat. Assn. Alcoholism and Drug Abuse Counselors. Democrat. Roman Catholic. Office: Ed Keating Ctr Inc PO Box 770108 Cleveland OH 44107

CURRAN, RAYMOND M. paper-based packaging company executive; b. 1948; CEO Smurfit Paribas Bank, 1981—91; with Jefferson Smurfit Group plc, 1981—, CFO, 1991—98; with Data Exch. Corp., sr. v.p. ops., 1991—96, pres., gen. mgr. U.S. ops. N.Am. divsn., 1996; exec. v.p., dep. chief exec. Smurfit-Stone Container Corp., Chgo., 1998—99, pres., CEO, 1999—. Office: Smurfit-Stone Container Corp 150 N Michigan Ave Chicago IL 60601-7553

CURRAN, RICHARD EMERY, JR., lawyer; b. Portland, Maine, Jan. 31, 1950; s. Richard Emery and Catherine Margaret (Bunker) C.; m. Nancy Bokron, Aug. 16, 1975 (div. May 1982); m. Margaret Cary, Sept. 17, 1988. AB, Dartmouth Coll., 1972, MBA, 1973; JD, Harvard U., 1977; LLM, Boston U., 1983. Bar: Maine 1977, U.S. Dist. Ct. Maine 1977, U.S. Tax Ct. 1984. Assoc. Pierce, Atwood, Scribner, Allen, Smith & Lancaster, Portland, Maine, 1977-82, ptnr., 1983—. Mem. ABA, Maine Bar Assn. Republican. Congregationalist. Clubs. Portland Country, Falmouth Country, Yale (N.Y.C.). Avocations: skiing, sailing, art, running, reading. Home: 1 Winn Farm Ln Falmouth ME 04105-1195

CURRAN, ROBERT BRUCE, lawyer; b. Charleston, W.Va., July 2, 1948; s. Bruce Frederick and Hazel Viola (Hoy) C.; children: Michael Robert, Laura Elizabeth, Emily Ann. BA, U. Del., 1971; JD, U. Md., 1974. Bar: Md. 1974. Ptnr. Frank, Bernstein, Conaway & Goldman, Balt., 1974-92, Whiteford Taylor & Preston, Balt., 1992—. Co-author: Tax Planning Forms for Businesses and Individuals, 1985. Mem. Md. Bar Assn. (sec. and treas. taxation sect. 1985-86, chmn. taxation sect. 1987-88). Office: Whiteford Taylor & Preston 7 Saint Paul St Baltimore MD 21202-1626 E-mail: rcurran@wtplaw.com.

CURRAN, ROBERT EMMETT, history educator; b. Balt., May 23, 1936; s. Joseph Francis and Marie Anna (Mahrenholz) C. AB, Coll. of Holy Cross, 1958; MA, Fordham U., 1965; PhD, Yale U., 1974. Lectr. Georgetown U., Washington, 1972-74, asst. prof., 1974-77, assoc. prof., 1977-97, prof., 1997—. Author: Michael Augustine Corrigan and the Shaping of a Conservative Catholicism in America, 1978, The Bicentennial History of Georgetown, 1993; editor: American Jesuit Spirituality, 1988. Bd. dirs. St. Joseph's U., Phila., 1979-85, Coll. of the Holy Cross, 1988-96, Worcester, Mass., Loyola Coll., Balt., 1991-97. Mem. Am. Hist. Assn., Orgn. Am. Historians, Am. Cath. Hist. Assn., Am. Soc. Ch. History, Immigration History Soc., So. Hist. Assn. Democrat. Roman Catholic. Avocation: running. Home: 1919 Youngblood St Mc Lean VA 22101-5532 Office: History Dept Georgetown U 37th And O Sts NW Washington DC 20057-0001 E-mail: currane@georgetown.edu.

CURRAN, WARD SCHENK, economist, educator; b. Springfield, Ill., June 26, 1935; s. Nathaniel Buckmaster and Clara Marguerite (Schenk) C.; m. Kathleen Marie Jannett, Nov. 25, 1963; children: Andrea Jannett, Colleen Thayer. AB, Trinity Coll., Hartford, Conn., 1957; MA, Columbia U., 1958, PhD, 1963. Mem. faculty Trinity Coll., Hartford, 1960—, prof. econs., 1971—, George M. Ferris prof. corp. fin. and investments, 1981—. Vis. prof. Yale U., Wesleyan U., Middletown, Conn.; mem. Gov. Conn. Commn. Higher Edn.; cons. adv. in field. Author: An Economic Approach to Regulation of the Corporate Securities Market, 1976, Principles of Financial Management, 1970, Principles of Corporate Finance, 1988; also articles, revs. Mem. Am. Econ. Assn., Am. Fin. Assn., Fin. Mgmt. Assn. Office: Trinity Coll Dept Econs 300 Summit St Hartford CT 06106-3100

CURRAN, WILLIAM P. lawyer; b. Mpls., Feb. 27, 1946; s. William P. and Margaret L. (Killoren) C.; m. Jean L. Stabenow, Jan. 1, 1978; children: Patrick, Lisa, John. BA, U. Minn., 1969; JD, U. Calif., Berkeley, 1972. Law clk. Nev. Supreme Ct., Carson City, 1973-74, state ct. adminstr., 1973-74; assoc. Wiener, Goldwater & Galatz, Las Vegas, Nev., 1974-75; chief dept. dist. atty. Clark County Dist. Atty.'s Office, Las Vegas, 1975-79; county counsel Clark County, Las Vegas, 1979-89; pvt. practice Las Vegas, 1989-94; ptnr. Curran & Parry, Las Vegas, 1994—. Co-author: Nevada Judicial Orientation Manual, 1974. Mem. Nev. Gaming Commn., 1989-99, chmn., 1991-99. Recipient Educator Yr. award UNLV Internat. Gaming Inst., 1998. Mem. ABA (state del. 1994—), Internat. Assn. Gaming Regulators (chmn. 1992-94), Nat. Assn. County Civil Attys. (pres. 1984-85), State Bar Nev. (pres. 1988-89). Democrat. Roman Catholic. Office: Curran & Parry 300 S Fourth St #1201 Las Vegas NV 89101 E-mail: curranparry@curranparry.com.

CURRAN-EVERETT, DOUGLAS C. scientist, educator, physiologist; b. Oct. 21, 1956; BA, Cornell U., 1978; MS in Phys. Therapy, Duke U., 1983; PhD in Physiology, SUNY, Buffalo, 1989. Instr. dept. pediat. U. Colo. Health Scis. Ctr., Denver, 1991-92, asst. prof. dept. pediat., 1992-99, clin. asst. prof. dept. preventive medicine biometrics and physiology biophysics, 2000—. Biostatistician Nat. Jewish Med. and Rsch. Ctr., 2000—. Author: (manual) Glencoe Health: Health Labs, 1998; author revs.; presenter in field. Judge, Colo. State Sci. Fair, 1990—. Office: Nat Jewish Med and Rsch Ctr Divsn Biostats M222 1400 Jackson St Denver CO 80206-0001 E-mail: everettd@njc.org.

CURRERI, PETER WILLIAM, health policy consultant; b. Milw., Sept. 2, 1936; s. Anthony Rudolph and Dorothea Christiana (Heubsch) C.; m. Patricia Ann Egry, Aug. 14, 1958 (div. 1975); children: Charles Anthony, James Bradley, Regina Dawn. BA, Swarthmore Coll., 1958; MD, U. Pa., 1962. Intern Hosp. of U. Pa., 1962-63, resident in surgery, 1963-68; asst. prof. surgery U. Tex., Southwestern MEd. Ctr., Dallas, 1971-74; assoc. prof. surgery U. Wash. Med. Sch., Seattle, 1974-77; prof. surgery Cornell U. Med. Ctr., N.Y.C., 1977-81; prof., chmn. surgery U. South Ala. Med. Sch., Mobile, 1981-88; pres. Strategem of Ala., Inc., Daphne, 1988—. Mem. surgery anesthesiology and trauma study sect. NIH, Washington, 1980-84, chmn., 1986-88; commr. Physician Payment Rev. Commn., Washington, 1988-97; mem. Medicare Payment Adv. Com., 1997-99. Contbr. articles to profl. jours. Lt. col. U.S. Army, 1968-71. Decorated Meritorious Svc. medal; recipient Rsch. Career Devel. award NIH, 1972, Curtis P. Artz award Am. Trauma Soc., 1989. Mem. Am. Assn. for Surgery of Trauma (pres. 1989-90), Am. Burn Assn. (pres. 1983-84), Am. Coll. Surgeons (sec. bd. govs. 1987-89), Halstead Surg. Soc. (pres. 1988-89), Soc. Univ. Surgeons (pres. 1980-81), Assn. Acad. Surgery (recorder 1972-74). Baptist. Avocations: golf, hunting, walking. Office: Strategem Inc 26064 Capital Dr Ste A Daphne AL 36526-6166

CURREY, CECIL BARR, history educator; b. Clarks, Nebr., Nov. 29, 1932; s. Cecil Chalmers Currey and Edith Estelle Barr; m. Laura Gene Hewett, Aug. 14, 1952; children: Samuel Bowman, Anne Estelle, Laura Alise. BA, Ft. Hays State U., 1958, MS, 1959; PhD, U. Kans., 1965. From asst. to assoc. prof. history Nebr. Wesleyan U., Lincoln, 1964-67; prof. mil. history U. So. Fla., Tampa, 1967—2001, prof. emeritus, 2001—. Vis. prof. U. Nebr., 1966-67; vis. prof. mil. history U. Hawaii, Honolulu, summers 1991, 92; edn1. cons., 1967-98; mil. analyst Desert Shield/Desert Storm, various T.V. stas., 1990-91; invited speaker Viet Nam Fgn. Ministry, Hanoi, 1988. Author: Road to Revolution: Benjamin Franklin in England, 1765-1775, 1968, Follow Me and Die: The Destruction of an American Division in World War II, 1984, Edward Lansdale: The Unquiet American, 1989, Victory at Any Cost: The Genius of Viet Nam's General Vo Nguyen Giap, 1996 (Pulitzer nomination 1997), Long Binh Jail: An Oral History of the U.S. Army's Notorious Prison in Viet Nam, others, (novel) Innocence Dies, 1999; contbr. to books, encys., and dictionaries, also over 25 articles to profl. publs. Col. USAR, 1953-92. Grantee U. So. Fla. Rsch. Found., 1988, 89; recipient Disting. Alumni award Ft. Hays State U., 1975. Mem. Assn. 3d World Studies (book prize 1997). Avocation: travel. Home: 3330 Lake Crenshaw Lutz FL 33548 Office: U South Fla Dept History 4202 E Fowler Ave Tampa FL 33620-8000 E-mail: cbcthor123@aol.com.

CURRIE, BARBARA FLYNN, state legislator; b. LaCrosse, Wis., May 3, 1940; d. Frank T. And Elsie R. (Gobel) Flynn; m. David P. Currie, Dec. 29, 1959; children: Stephen Francis, Margaret Rose. AB cum laude, U. Chgo., 1968, AM, 1973. Asst. study dir. Nat. Opinion Rsch. Ctr., Chgo., 1973-77; part time instr. polit. sci. DePaul U., Chgo., 1973-74; mem. Ill. Ho. of Reps., 1979—, chmn. House Dem. Study Group, 1980-83, asst. majority leader, 1993, asst. minority leader, 1995, majority leader, 1997. V.p. Chgo. LWV, 1965-69; mem. Hyde Park-Kenwood Cmty. Conf., Ind. Voters of Ill. Ind. Precinct Orgn., Hyde Park Coop. Soc., Ams. for Dem. Action. Named Best Legislator Ind. Voters of Ill., 1980, 82, 84, 86, 88, 90, 92, 94, 96, 98, Best Legislator Ill. Credit Union League, Outstanding Legislator Ill. Hosp. Assn., 1987; Legislator of Yr. Ill. Nurses Assn., 1984, Nat. Assn. Social Workers, 1984, Ill. Women's Substance Abuse Coalition, 1984; recipient Leon Despres award, 1991, Ill. Environ. Coun. award, Ill. Women's Polit. Caucus Lottie Holman O'Neill award, Susan B. Anthony award, honor award Nat. Trust Historic Preservation; awards Welfare Rights Coalition of Orgns., Ill. Pub. Action Coun., Chgo. Heart Assn., BEST BETS award Nat. Ctr. Policy Alternatives, 1988, Svc. award Nat. Ctr. for Freedom of Info. Studies, 1989, Beautiful Person award Chgo. Urban League, 1989, Friend of Labor award Ill. AFL-CIO, 1990, Ill. Maternal and Child Health Coalition award, 1990, Ill. Hunger Coalition award, 1991, Cert. of Appreciation SEIU Local 880, 1989, March of Dimes, 1988, Chgo. Tchrs. Union, Ill. Hosp. Assn., Ptnr. Vision award Families' and Children's AIDS Network, Woman of Vision award Womens' Bar Assn. Ill., 1997, Nat. Elected Pub. Offcl. award Nat. Assn. Social Workers, 1997, Outstanding Working Woman of Ill. award Ill. Fedn. Bus. and Profl. Women, Dist. Pub. Health Legislator award Am. Pub. Health Assn., 1999, others. Mem.: ACLU (bd. dirs. Ill.), Ill. Primary Health Care Assn. (Legls. Recognition award 2002), Ill. Conf. Women Legislators. Office: Ill Gen Assembly 300 State House Springfield IL 62706-0001

CURRIE, BRUCE, artist; b. Sac City, Iowa, Nov. 27, 1911; s. Malcolm and Clara Mabel (Austin) C.; m. Ethel Magafan, June 30, 1946; 1 dau., Jenne Magafan. Student, Northwestern U., 1930-32, U. Chgo., 1932-33. One-man shows include Am. embassy, Athens, Greece, 1952, Ganso Gallery, N.Y.C., 1953, 54, Roko Gallery, 1958, 60, Albany Inst. History and Art, 1958, Ulster County Cmty. Coll., Kingston, N.Y., 1967, Joseloff Gallery, U. Hartford, 1968, Schenectady Mus., 1970, Jacques Seligmann Galleries, N.Y.C., 1978, Midtown Galleries, N.Y.C., 1980, 83, retrospective exhbn. Woodstock (N.Y.) Artists Assn., 1993; represented in permanent collections SUNY-Albany, Dwight Art Meml., Mt. Holyoke Coll., Colorado Springs Fine Arts Ctr., Butler Inst. Am. Art, Kalamazoo Inst. Arts, N.A.D., Ulster County C.C., Kingston, Berkshire Cmty. Coll. Served with USAAF, 1942-45, ETO. Decorated European - African - Middle Ea. Theater ribbon with 1 Silver and 1 Bronze Battle Star; recipient Purchase award Henry Ward Ranger Fund, N.A.D., 1964, 75, Clarke prize, 1966, Benjamin Altman figure prize, 1979, Gold medal of honor Nat. Arts Club, 1964; Albany Inst. History and Art award, 1967, Berle award Berkshire Art Assn., 1967, purchase award, 1973, Soletsky award Nat. Soc. Painters in Casein and Acrylic, 1973, Grumbacher award, 1974, John J. Newman Meml. award, 1976, Wallach Meml. award, 1980, Wright Meml. prize Cooperstown Art Assn., 1978, grand prize, 1981, also others. Mem. NAD (acad.), Audubon Artists (Medal of Honor 1963, 82, 98, Joseph Raskin Meml. award 1987, Ralph Fabri Medal of Honor 1989, Emily Lowe award 1990, Richeson award 2000, Salmagundi award 2002), Am. Watercolor Soc. (Silver medal 1958, Emily Lowe award 1968, Whitney award 1975, Winsor-Newton award 1981, Mario Cooper award 1985, Elsie and David WU Ject-Key Meml. award 1997, Audubon Artists Silver Medal 1998), Adirondack Nat. Exhbn. of Am. Watercolors (Martin award 1988, Smith Packing Co. award 1990), Conn. Acad. Fine Arts (Conn. Acad. prize for Painting, 1965, The Charles Noel Flagg Meml. prize 1968). Home: 72 Boggs Hill Rd Woodstock NY 12498-2706

CURRIE, DONALD M, medical educator; b. Hamilton, Ohio; s. John M and Doris G Currie; m. Rhonda Fulton, July 18, 1994; children: Jared Ellis Blakely, Jonathan Andrew Blakely children: Rachel E Dixon, Andrew M. MS, U. Wash., 1977. Lic. MD U TX Southwestern Med Sch., 1972. Assoc prof UTHSC, San Antonio, Tex., 1977—. Editor: Rehabilitation Medicine: Principles and Practice. Mem. Woodlawn Lake Pk. Devel. Com., San Antonio, Tex., 1995—97. Recipient Outstanding Imagineer, Learning about Learning Ednl. Found., 1984. Mem.: Am. Bd. of Phys. Med and Rehab. (licentiate). Achievements include first to 1st Presidential Award in Clinical Excellence, UTHSCSA. Avocations: running, reading, teaching christian edn. hs boys, piano. Office: UTHSC MC 7798 Dept Rehab Med 7703 Floyd Curl Dr San Antonio TX 78229-3900 Office Fax: 210-567-5354. E-mail: currie611@pol.net.

CURRIE, EARL JAMES, transportation executive; b. Fergus Falls, Minn., May 14, 1939; s. Victor James and Calma (Hammer) Currie; m. Kathleen P. Phalen, June 3, 1972; children: Jane, Joseph. BA, St. Olaf Coll., 1961; cert. in transp., Yale U., 1963; PMD, Harvard U., 1974. With Burlington No. Inc., 1964-85, asst. v.p., 1977-78, Chgo., 1978-80, v.p., gen. mgr. Seattle, 1980-83, sr. v.p. Overland Park, Kans., 1983-85; pres. Camas Prairie R.R., Lewiston, Idaho, 1982-83, Longview Switching Co., Wash., 1982-83, Western Fruit Express Co., 1984-85; exec. v.p. ops. Soo Line R.R. Co. & Rail Units, 1986-89; v.p. engring. CSX Transp. Co., Jacksonville, Fla., 1989-92, v.p., chief transp. officer, 1992-95; v.p. planning, chief safety officer Wis. Ctrl. Ltd., 1996-99; sr. v.p. ops. Rail World, Inc., 1999—2001; mng. dir. Estonian Rlwy. Sys., Tallinn, 2001—02; cons. rlwy. ops. and maintenance, 2002—. Bd. dirs. Belt Ry. Co. Chgo., Terminal R.R. Assn., St. Louis, Norfolk and Portsmouth Ry. Co. Bd. dirs. United Way, King County, Wash., 1980—83, Corp. Coun. Arts, Seattle, 1980—83, Jr. Achievement, 1980—82, North Shore Scenic R.R., 1999—, Hist. Union Depot, 2003—, Lake Superior Mus. Transp., 1986—89, 1999—, pres., 2001—; mem. Mpls. Neighborhood Employment Network; trustee St. Martins Coll., Lacey, Wash., 1982—83. Mem.: Roadmasters Assn., Internat. Assn. R.R. Oper. Officers, Am. Assn. R.R. Supts. (bd. dirs. 1979—80), Am. Rlwy. Engring. and Maintenance Assn., Am. Rlwy. Engring. Assn. (bd. dirs. 1989—92), St. Olaf Coll. Alumni Assn. (bd. dirs. 1993—97), Seattle C. of C. (bd. dirs. 1980—83). Home: PO Box 2827 Warba MN 55793-2827

CURRIE, EDWARD JONES, JR., lawyer; b. Jackson, Miss., May 23, 1951; s. Edward J. and Nell (Branton) C.; m. Barbara Scott Miller, June 26, 1976; children: Morgan E., Scott E. BA, U. Miss., 1973, JD, 1976. Bar: Miss. 1976, U.S. Dist. Ct. (no. and so. dists.) Miss. 1976, U.S. Ct. Appeals (5th cir.) 1978, U.S. Supreme Ct. 1979. Assoc. Wise, Carter, Child, Steen & Caraway, Jackson, 1976—80; ptnr. Steen, Reynolds, Dalehite & Currie, Jackson, 1980—94, Currie Johnson Griffin Gaines & Myers, P.A., Jackson, 1994—. Adj. prof. Miss. Coll. Sch. Law, Jackson, 1977-81, 84-86. Bd. dirs. Miss. chpt. Am. Diabetes Assn., Jackson, 1980-82. Mem. Fed. Bar Assn. (pres. Miss. chpt. 1989), Internat. Assn. Def. Coun. (trial acad. faculty 1992), Nat. Inst. Trial Advocacy, Nat. Lawyers Assn. (chmn. ins. sect. 1998-99), Nat. Lawyers Assn. Found. (bd. dirs. 1998-00), Miss. Jud. Coll. (model civil jury instrn. com. 1991), Miss. Def. Lawyers Assn. (bd. dirs. 2000-2003, v.p.), Miss. Bar Assn. (bd. dirs. young lawyers sect. 1981-82, chmn. litigation/gen. practice sect. 1992, mem. MDP Task Force 2000), Miss. Bd. Bar Commrs., Jackson Young Lawyers (bd. dirs. 1980-81), Hinds County Bar Assn., Phi Delta Phi, Sigma Alpha Epsilon (pres. Ctrl. Miss. alumni 1981), Omicron Delta Kappa. Presbyterian. Home: 50 Moss Forest Cir Jackson MS 39211-2905 Office: Currie Johnson Griffin Gaines & Myers PA PO Box 750 Jackson MS 39205-0750

CURRIE, JANET M. economics educator; b. Kingston, Ont., Can., Mar. 29, 1960; came to U.S., 1983; d. Kenneth Lyell and Edrith Delores Currie; m. William Bentley MacLeod, May 18, 1996; children: Joana Marion, Daniel Bentley. BA, U. Toronto, 1982, MA, 1983; PhD in Econs., Princeton U., 1988. Asst. prof. econs. UCLA, 1988-91, MIT, Cambridge, Mass., 1992, assoc. prof. econs., 1993, UCLA, 1994-95, prof. econs., 1995—. Panel mem. NAS, Washington, 1998-99, 2000-01, NSF, Washington, 1998-2001; rsch. assoc. Nat. Bur. Econ. Rsch., 1995—; mem. Brookings Roundtable on Children and Families, 1998—; affiliate Joint Ctr. Poverty Rsch., 1998—; cons. RAND, 1993—. Author: Welfare and the Well Being of Children, 1994; contbr. chpts. to books, articles to profl. jours.; co-editor Jour. Labor Econs., 1994-2000; mem. edit. bd. Quar. Jour. Econs., 1995—; assoc. editor Jour. Health Econs., 2000—02. Alfred P. Sloan Found. fellow, 1993-95, Olin fellow Nat. Bur. Econ. Rsch., 1993, Can. Inst. Advanced Rsch. fellow, 1998-2000. Avocation: gardening. Office: UCLA Dept Econs 405 Hilgard Ave Los Angeles CA 90095-1477

CURRIE, JOHN THORNTON (JACK CURRIE), retired investment banker; b. Houston, Aug. 4, 1928; s. John Felix and Irma Lillian (Haxthausen) C.; m. Dorothy Lee Peek, May 30, 1959; children: Harriss Thornton, Laura Graef. BA, U. Tex., 1949, BBA, 1950. Salesman Harris, Upham & Co., N.Y.C. and Houston, 1950-52; ptnr. Moreland, Brandenberger & Currie, Galveston, Tex., 1955-60; pres., bd. dirs. Moroney, Beissner & Co., Inc., Houston, 1960-74; sr. v.p., bd. dirs. Rotan Mosle Inc., Houston, 1974-81, chmn., 1981-83; vice chmn. Rotan Mosle Fin. Corp., Houston, 1984; mng. dir. Mason Best Co.,

Houston, 1984-86. Bd. dirs. family mut. funds managed by Am. Nat. Ins. Co., Galveston; dir. Artspace Inc., Mpls., Minn., Internat. Exec. Svc. Corps rep. Muslim Comml. Bank, Karachi, Pakistan, 1992, Govt. of Lithuania, Vilnius, 1993, Capital Ptnrs., Bratislava, Slovakia, 1997. Trustee Holly Hall, Houston, 1968-73, Harris and Eliza Kempner Fund, Galveston, Tex., 1975—; mem. devel. bd. U. Tex. Health Sci. Ctr., Houston, 1978-89, U. Tex. Med. Br., Galveston, 1992—; mem. Chancellor's Coun. U. Tex. System; established Mary Tucker Currie Professorship, Tex. A&M U.; 1st lt. U.S. Army, 1952-54. Mem. Houston Country Club, Galveston Artillery Club, Krewe of Momus Galveston, The Yacht Club (Galveston). Republican. Episcopalian. Avocations: sailing, hunting, history. Home: 323 Longwoods Ln Houston TX 77024-5615 Office: 520 Post Oak Blvd Ste 125 Houston TX 77027-9495 *The acquisition of material goods makes life comfortable. Love received and given is the only real hallmark of a successful life.*

CURRIE, JOSEPH ALOYSIUS, campus ministry director, theology studies educator; b. Phila., Aug. 20, 1936; s. Charles Leonard Currie and Elizabeth Katherine Harper. BA in Philosophy, Fordham U., 1961, MA in History, 1963; MEd in Counseling, Loyola U., Chgo., 1970; MDiv, St. Mary's Coll., 1969. Dir. cmty. ctr. Jesuit Province Jamshedpur, Bihar, India, 1970—76; dir. pastoral edn. and supervised ministry Indian Jesuit Assistancy, Delhi, India, 1977—83, dir. tertianship Kodaikanal, India, 1983—85; campus min. Georgetown U., Washington, 1985—87; dir. Manresa Retreat Jesuit Province Md., Annapolis, 1987—90; dean Campus Ministry Loyola U., New Orleans, 1991—97; dir. Campus Ministry Fordham U., Bronx, NY, 1997—. Cons. and workshop dir. in supervisory appraisal Xavier Labor Rels. Inst and Tata Iron & Steel, Bombay, Delhi, Goa, Bihar, India, 1974—84; retreat presenter various renewal ctrs., 1985—. Author: Barefoot Counselor, 1988, Letting Go...Letting God, 1990, Shepherds After My Own Heart, 1993. Founding mem. Indsl. Areas Found.-Jeremiah Group, New Orleans, 1992—96; coun. mem. Pax Christi, New Orleans, 1992—95; bd. mem. Crispaz, U.S.-El Salvador, 2002—. Recipient Outstanding Achievement award, Black Student Union, Loyola U., New Orleans, 1995. Mem.: Cath. Campus Ministry Assn., Amnesty Internat., Alpha Sigma Nu. Democrat. Roman Catholic. Avocations: travel, writing, sports, reading. Home: 441 E Fordham Rd Bronx NY 10458 Office: Fordham Univ Office Campus Ministry McGinley Ctr 102 Bronx NY 10458 E-mail: currie@fordham.edu.

CURRIE, LARRY LAMAR, insurance agent; b. Rome, Ga., Dec. 30, 1946; s. Kaylor and Mary R. (Lee) C.; m. Linda Marie Warner, Nov. 9, 1968; children: Kristin Denise, Jeremy Scott, Matthew Lamar. Student, U. N.D., 1968-69, Gadsden State Coll., 1972-73; MS in Mgmt., Am. Coll., 1997. CLU, 1987; cert. facilitator Covey Leadership; registered rep. Agt. State Farm Ins., Millbrook, Ala., 1974-81, agy. mgr. Alexandria City, Ala., 1981-88, agy. dir. Birmingham, Ala., 1988-96, agy. field exec., 1996—. Mem. adv. bd. East Tallapoosa County Med. Ctr., Dadeville, Ala., 1987-88. Editor: Multiline Family Practice, 1995-98. Mem. adv. bd. U. Ala.-Birmingham, Golden 100 Club, 1993-94; high sch. econs. cons. Jr. Achievement, 1996-98; mem. adv. bd. Project Kids in Distress, 1997-98; bd. dirs. Kid One Transport, 1998-2001; bd. dirs. N.E. Ala. Boys and Girls Club; exec. com. mem. Shelby County Rep. Party, 1998-2001; mem. Pres. Bush's Bus. Com., 2002—. Mem. Nat. Assn. Life Underwriters, Autauga-Elmore County Life Underwriters (pres. 1978-79), Birmingham Assn. Life Underwriters (bd. dirs. 1996-97), Soc. Fin. Svc. Profls. (chair leadership and mgmt. sect.), N.E. Ala. Ins. and Fin. Assn. (bd. dirs. 2002—), Pres.'s Cir. Am. Coll., Porsche Club Am. Republican. Roman Catholic. Avocations: jogging, sailing. Home: 524 Marsh Ln Oxford AL 36203-3967 Office: 1130 Quintard Ave Anniston AL 36201

CURRIE, LEAH RAE, special education educator, retired; b. Chgo., Feb. 14, 1942; d. Raymond Carl and Esther Dorthea (Hansen) Strahl; m. William W. Currie, June 15, 1963; children: Raymond, Robert (dec.), Christopher. BS, Nat. Coll. Edn., 1979, MEd, 1989. Cert. elem., spl. edn. tchr., Ill. Learning disabilities tchr. Sch. Dist. 81, Schiller Park, Ill., 1979-80; resource tchr. Sch. Dist. 5, Fox River Grove, Ill., 1980-85; learning disabilities, behavior disorders tchr. Sch. Dist. 84, Franklin Park, Ill., 1985-2000, ret., 2000. Cons., interdistrict learning disabilities guide Leyden Area Spl. Edn. Coop., 1987. Mem. ASCD, Coun. for Exceptional Children, Ill. Divsn. for Learning Disabilities, Ill. Reading Coun., Learning Disabilities Assn. Ill. Avocation: fashion design. Home: 33632 N Christa Dr Ingleside IL 60041-9320 E-mail: leachc14@aol.com.

CURRIE, MALCOLM RODERICK, aerospace and automotive executive, scientist; b. Spokane, Wash., Mar. 13, 1927; s. Erwin Casper and Genevieve (Hauenstein) C.; m. Sunya Lofsky, June 24, 1951; children: Deborah, David, Diana; m. Barbara L. Dyer, Mar. 5, 1977. AB, U. Calif., Berkeley, 1949, MS, 1951, PhD, 1954. Rsch. engr. Microwave Lab., U. Calif. at Berkeley, 1949-52; elec. engrng. faculty microwave lab. U. Calif., Berkeley, 1953-54; lectr. UCLA, 1955-57; rsch. engr. Hughes Aircraft Co., 1954-57, v.p., 1965-66; head electron dynamics dept. Hughes Rsch. Labs., Culver City, Calif., 1957-60, dir. physics lab. Malibu, Calif., 1960-61, asso. dir., 1961-63, v.p., dir. rsch. labs., 1963-65, v.p., mgr. R & D divsn., 1965-69; v.p. R & D Beckman Instruments, Inc., 1969-73; undersec. rsch. and engrng. dept. Office Sec. Def., Washington, 1973-77; pres. missile sys. group Hughes Aircraft Co., Canoga Park, Calif., 1977-83, exec. v.p., 1983-88, CEO, chmn. bd. dirs., 1988—, also bd. dirs.; pres., CEO Delco Electronics Corp., 1986-88. Chmn., CEO Hughes Aircraft Co., 1988—92, chmn. emeritus, 1992—; CEO Currie Techs. Inc., 1997—, Med-Electvic, 2001—; bd. dirs. Innovative Micro Techs., LSI Logic Corp., Sion Power Corp., Inamed Corp., Regal One, Enova Sys. Corp.; mem. Def. Sci. Bd.; bd. overseers Keck Med. Sch., U. So. Calif.; trustee U. So. Calif., 1989—, chmn., 1995—2000. Contbr. articles to profl. jours.; patentee in field. Mem. adv. bd. U. Calif., Berkeley, UCLA, Galaxy Edn. Inst., Calif. Coun. Sci. and Tech.; former chmn. bd. trustees U. So. Calif., 1989; trustee Howard U., 1989-92, UCLA Found.; bd. dirs. western region United Way, 1987; coord., head U.S. Savs. Bond Dr., So. Calif., 1991. With USNR, 1944-47. Decorated comdr. Legion of Honor France; named Nation's Outstanding Young Elec. Engr. Eta Kappa Nu, 1958, one of 5 Outstanding Young Men of Calif. by Calif. Jr. C. of C., 1960; recipient Nat. Achievement medal Am. Elec. Assn. 1992, Goddard Astronautics award AIAA, Chester Nimitz award U.S. Navy League, 192, Thomas White award USAF, 1992. Fellow IEEE (Founders award 1995), AIAA (pres. 1994, Goddard Astronautics award), AAAS, Royal Aeroantuics Soc., Am. Acad. Arts and Scis.; mem. NAE, Am. Phys. Soc., Berkeley Fellow, Commn. on Competitiveness, Calif. Coun. on Sci. and Tech. (co-chair project Calif.), Cosmos Club, Phi Beta Kappa, Sigma Xi, Lambda Chi Alpha. Home: 28780 Wagon Rd Agoura Hills CA 91301-2732 E-mail: mrcurrie@sbcglobal.net.

CURRIE, NANCY JANE, astronaut; b. Wilmington, Del., Dec. 29, 1958; m. David W. Currie; 1 child. BA in Biol. Scis., Ohio State U., 1980; MS in Safety, U. So. Calif., 1985; D in Indsl. Engring., U. Houston, 1997. Neuropathology rsch. asst. Ohio State U. Coll. Medicine; commd. 2nd lt. U.S. Army, 1981, helicopter instr. pilot, sect. leader, platoon leader, brigade flight standardization officer, master army aviator; flight simulation engr. shuttle tng. aircraft NASA Johnson Space Ctr., Houston, 1987, astronaut, 1991, flight crew rep. for crew equipment, lead for remote manipulator sys., spacecraft communicator, flight engr. mission specialist on STS-57, 1993, flight engr. mission specialist on STS-70, 1995, flight engr. mission specialist on STS-88, 1998, flight engr. mission specialist on STS-109, 2002, chief asstronaut office robotics br. Mem. Army Aviation Assn. Am., Ohio State U. and ROTC Alumni Assns., Inst. Indsl. Engrs., Human Factors and Ergonomics Soc., Phi Kappa Phi. Avocations: weightlifting, running, swimming, scuba diving, skiing. Office: NASA Lyndon B Johnson Space Ctr Houston TX 77058

CURRIE, PHILIP JOHN, research paleontologist, museum curator; b. Toronto, Ont., Can., Mar. 13, 1949; children: Tarl, Devin, Brett. BSc, U. Toronto, 1972; MSc, McGill U., 1975, PhD in Biology, 1981. Curator paleontology Provincial Mus. Alta., Edmonton, 1976-81; mus. curator Palaeontology Mus. and Rsch. Inst., Drumheller, Alb., Can., 1981-82; asst. dir. rsch. Tyrrell Mus. Palaeontology, Drumheller, 1982-89, head dinosaur rsch., 1989—. Sec. Alta. Paleontology Adv. Com., 1977-89; treas. Palaeont Can., 1981-84. Author: Flying Dinosaurs, 1991, Dinosaur Renaissance, 1994; co-author: The Great Dinosaurs, 1994, 101 Questions About Dinosaurs, 1996, Troodon, 1997, Albertosaurus, 1998, Centrosaurus, 1998, Sinosauropteryx, 1999; co-editor: Dinosaur Systematics, 1990, Dinosaur Encyclopedia, 1997, Newest and Coolest Dinosaurs, 1998; contbr. articles to profl. publs.; featured in numerous articles and programs. Recipient Commendation medal 125th Anniversary of Govt. of Can., 1993, Sir Frederick Haultain award Govt. of Alta., 1988, Michel Halbouty award Am. Assn. Petroleum Geologists, 1999. Fellow Royal Soc. Can.; mem. Soc. Vertebrate Paleontology (program officer 1985-87, conf. chmn. 1988, conf. chmn. Mesozoic Terrestrial Ecosystems 1987), Paleontol. Soc., Can. Soc. Petroleum Geologists, Am. Soc. Zoologists, Sigma Xi. Achievements include research in fossil reptiles including Permian Sphenacodonts from Europe and United States; Permian eosuchians from Africa and Madagascar; Jurassic and Cretaceous dinosaurs from Canada, Argentina and Asia and their footprints. Office: Royal Tyrrell Mus Palaeontology Box 7500 Drumheller AB Canada T0J 0Y0

CURRIE, ROBERT, communications executive; b. Plainfield, N.J., July 30, 1959; s. Ashton Markoe and Evelyn Margaret (Gautreau) C.; m. Suzanne Jean Morris, Oct. 18, 1987; 1 child, Claire MacPherson Currie; 1 stepchild, Hilary Buchanan Boller. BS in Mktg. cum laude, Fairleigh Dickinson U., 1981, MA in Corp. and Orgnl. Comms., 1996. Journalist Foster Pubs., Scotch Plains, NJ, 1979-81; internat. specialist Hoechst Celanese Corp., Bridgewater, NJ, 1981-89, mktg. coord. Summit, NJ, 1989—96; dir. global comms. GAF Corp., Wayne, NJ, 1996—98; dir. corp. comms. J.M. Huber Corp., Edison, NJ, 1998—. V.p. HCC Sci. and Tech. Co., Inc., Bridgewater, 1989-92. Producer/dir. film: Trade Secrets and Technology, 1991 (Disting. Achievement award Am. Soc. Indsl. Security); editor (book): With Sword and Harp, 1992, (webiste) clancurrie.com; writer/dir. films: Winning Strategies, 1993 (Bronze medal N.Y. Festival, Bronze plaque Columbus Internat. TV Festival), The Pipes of Christmas, 2002, 2003 (Telly award); prodr. Tartan Day on Ellis Island, 2002, 2003. Comdr. The Clan Currie, 1991—; pres Clan Currie Soc. N.Am., Summit, N.J., 1990—; dir. Bonnie Brae Scottish Games, Millington, N.J., 1985-88, U.S. Equestrian Team - Horse Trials, Gladstone, N.J., 1990-91; chmn. Ethnic Adv. Coun. State N.J., 1993—; hon. plankowner USS John Paul Jones Am. Scottish Found., Scottish Heritage U.S.A.; chmn. NJ Nat. Tartan Day.; bd. dirs. Save Ellis Island! Found.; mem. N.J. Gov.'s Adv. Com. on Preservation and Use of Ellis Island, 1998-2000. Recipient James S. Cogswell Outstanding Indsl. Security Achievement award Dept. Def., 1992, World Pairs Driving Championship, Gladstone, N.J., 1993, 9 Telly awards for broadcast and non-broadcast TV programming, 1993-2002. Mem. St. Andrew's Soc. of N.Y., Coun. Comm. Mgmt. Pub. Rels. Soc. Am., Nat. Investor Rels. Inst., Am. Soc. Media Photographers, Finlaggan Trust. Avocations: golf, photography, genealogy, music. Home: PO Box 541 Summit NJ 07902-0541 Office: JM Huber Corp 333 Thornall St Edison NJ 08837-2220 E-mail: clancurrie@mail.com.

CURRIE, ROBERT EMIL, lawyer; b. Jackson, Tenn., Oct. 10, 1937; s. Forrest Edward Currie and Mary Elizabeth (Nuckolls) Empson; m. Brenda Ray Eddings, July 2, 1960; children: Cheryl Lynn, Forrest Clayton, Kristin Emil. BS with distinction, U.S. Naval Acad., 1959; LLB cum laude, Harvard U., 1967. Bar: Calif. 1967, U.S. Ct. Appeals (9th cir.) 1970, U.S. Supreme Ct. 1979. Assoc. Latham & Watkins, L.A., 1967-75, ptnr. Costa Mesa, Calif., 1975—, mng. ptnr., 1993—96. Dir. Constl. Rights Found., Orange County, Calif., 1986-91; lawyer rep. 9th Cir. Jud. Conf., 1991-93. Mem. exec. com. Orange County coun. Boy Scouts Am., Costa Mesa, 1982-95. Capt. USNR, 1955-83. Recipient Silver Beaver award Boy Scouts Am., Orange County coun., 1991. Fellow Am. Coll. Trial Lawyers; mem. Orange County Bar Assn. (dir. 1984-91), U.S. Supreme Ct. Hist. Soc. (chmn. So. Calif. 1992-93), Orange County Bar Found. (dir. 1999—). Home: 24 Pinehurst Ln Newport Beach CA 92660 Office: Latham & Watkins 650 Town Center Dr Ste 2000 Costa Mesa CA 92626-1925 E-mail: robert.currie@lw.com.

CURRIE, STEVEN RAY, artist; b. Flint, Mich., Sept. 1, 1954; s. Richard Lee and Gwen Laurie (Cummings) C.; m. Annette Marie Davidek, July 27, 1985. BFA, U. Mich., 1977; MFA, Yale U., 1984. One man shows include Borgenicht Gallery, N.Y.C., 1988, 90, 92, 93, Ctr. Contemporary Art, Chgo., 1989, 91, Weatherspoon Art Gallery, Greensboro, N.C., 1995, Revolution Gallery, Detroit, 1995, Littlejohn Contemporary, N.Y.C., 1997; group shows include Boise (Idaho) Art Mus., 1994, Faulconer Gallery, Grinnell (Iowa) Coll., 2001; represented in various mus. collections including Bklyn. Mus., Modern Art Mus. Ft. Worth, Walker Art Ctr., Mpls., Met. Mus. Art, N.Y.C., Albright-Knox Art Gallery, Buffalo, Orange County Mus. Art, Newport Beach, Calif. NEA fellow, 1988, N.Y. Found. Arts fellow, 1990, 97.

CURRIER, DOUGLAS GILFILLAN, II, urban planner; b. Chelsea, Mass., Jan. 11, 1960; s. Douglas G. and Anita Louise Currier; m. Susan Mary Golabek, Feb. 10, 2001; 1 child, Douglas G. III. BA, U. South Fla., 1987. Assoc. planner Tampa Bay Regional Planning Coun., St. Petersburg, Fla., 1985-90; resource planner West Coast Regional Water Supply Authority, Clearwater, Fla., 1990-96; city planner City of Dade City, Fla., 1996—. Mem. Temple Terrace Mcpl. Code Enforcement Bd., 1990-99, Temple Terrace Bd. Adjustment, 1999-2000. Mem. Am. Planning Assn., Hillsborough Literacy Coun. (sec. 1994-2001), 1000 Friends of Fla., U. South Fla. Alumni Assn., U. South Fla. Athletic Assn., Phi Kappa Phi (hon.). Avocations: adult literacy, environmental causes, traveling, reading. Office: City of Dade City 38020 Meridian Ave Dade City FL 33525-3836 E-mail: dcurrier@helios.acomp.usf.edu.

CURRIER, ROBERT DAVID, neurologist; b. Grand Rapids, Mich., Feb. 19, 1925; s. Frederick Plummer and Margaret (Hoedemaker) C.; m. Marilyn Jane Johnson, Sept. 1, 1951; children: Mary Margaret, Angela Maria. AB, U. Mich., 1948, MD, 1952, MS in Neurology, 1956; postgrad., Nat. Hosp., U. London, 1955; postgrad. Medico-Social Research Bd, Dublin, Ireland, 1972. Intern, then resident in neurology Univ. Hosp., Ann Arbor, 1952-56; from instr. to asso. prof. U. Mich. Med. Sch., 1956-61; mem. faculty U. Miss. Med. Ctr., Jackson, 1961—, prof. neurology, 1971—, chief div., 1961-77, chmn. dept., 1977-90, H.F. McCarty prof., 1987-94, prof. emeritus, 1994—. Mem. adv. bd. Nat. Ataxia Found., rsch. dir., 1985-93; mem. clin. adv. coun. Amyotrophic Lateral Sclerosis Soc. Am., 1979-85; mem. Ataxia com. World Fedn. Neurology, 1981-95, sec., 1985-93. Co-editor; Yearbook of Neurology and Neurosurgery, 1981-88, editor, 1989-92; co-editor (jour.) Key Quar. Neurology and Neurosurgery, 1986-92; asst. editor for history Archives of Neurology, 1983-97; assoc. editor Jour. Neurosci., 1990-95; contbr. articles to med. jours. Served with USAAF, 1943-45, ETO. Decorated Air medal with 2 oak leaf clusters; NIH grantee, 1961-74 Fellow Am. Acad. Neurology (chmn. history com. 1980-82, treas. 1991-95); mem. Am. Neurol. Assn., Ctrl. Soc. Neurol. Rsch. (pres. 1971), Sigma Xi, Alpha Omega Alpha. Home: 5529 Marblehead Dr Jackson MS 39211-4249 *It has been interesting.*

CURRIER, RUTH, dancer, choreographer and educator; b. Ashland, Ohio, Jan. 4, 1926; d. Elmer MacDonald and Zada (Holliman) Miller. Student, Black Mountain Coll., 1942-44, NYU, 1944-45. Soloist José Limón Dance Co., N.Y.C., 1949-63, artistic dir., 1973-77; asst. to Doris Humphrey, 1950-58; prin. Ruth Currier and Dance Co., N.Y.C., 1957-68; asso. prof. dance, dir. Am. Dance in Repertory, Ohio State U., Columbus, 1968-73; freelance choreographer N.Y.C., 1978-81; dir. Ruth Currier Dance Studio, N.Y.C., 1981-90. Adj. mem. faculty Bennington Coll., 1958-63; guest tchr., choreographer numerous colls., dance cos. Choreographer over 50 mus. prodns.

CURRIN, SAMUEL THOMAS, lawyer, former judge; b. Oxford, N.C., Dec. 13, 1948; s. Thomas Benjamin and Lois (Brady) C.; m. Margaret Person, June 24, 1973. BA cum laude, Wake Forest U., 1971; JD, U. N.C., 1974. Bar: N.C. 1974. Asst. U.S. atty. Eastern Dist. N.C., Raleigh, 1976-78; legis. asst. to Sen. Jesse Helms Washington, 1978-81; U.S. atty. Eastern Dist. N.C., Raleigh, from 1981; now judge Spl. Superior Ct., Raleigh; pvt. practice Raleigh, 1988—. Chmn. pub. affairs com. So. Bapt. Conv., 1983—; chmn. N.C. Rep. Com. Mem.: Lions (Raleigh). Republican. Home: PO Box 269 Raleigh NC 27602-0269 Office: Curran Law Bldg 20 Market Plz Raleigh NC 27601

CURRIVAN, JOHN DANIEL, lawyer; b. Paris; s. Gene and Rachel Currivan; m. Patrice Salley; children: Christopher, Melissa. BS with distinction, Cornell U.; MS, U Calif.-Berkeley; MS, U. West Fla.; JD summa cum laude, Cornell Law Sch., 1978. Bar: Ohio 1978. Mng. ptnr. S.W. Devel. Co., Kingsville, Tex., 1971-76; note editor Cornell Law Rev., Ithaca, N.Y., 1977-78; prosecutor Naval Legal Office, Norfolk, Va., 1978-79, chief prosecutor, 1979-81; sr. atty. USS Nimitz, 1981-83; trial judge Naval Base, Norfolk, 1983-84; tax atty. Jones, Day, Reavis & Pogue, Cleve., 1984-88, ptnr., 1989—. Adj. prof. law Case Western Res. U. Sch. Law, 1997—. Author: (with Rickert) Ohio Limited Liability Companies, 1999. Comdr. USN, 1969-84. Recipient Younger Fed. Lawyer award FBA, 1981. Mem. ABA, Nat. Assn. Bond Lawyers, Order of Coif, Tau Beta Pi, Eta Kappa Nu, Phi Kappa Phi. Home: 12700 Lake Ave Ste 2105 Lakewood OH 44107-1506 Office: Jones Day Reavis & Pogue 901 Lakeside Ave E Cleveland OH 44114-1190

CURRY, ALAN CHESTER, insurance company executive; b. Columbus, Ohio, Oct. 15, 1933; s. Harold E. and Martha (Dew) C.; children: Diane, Thomas, Timothy, Jeffrey. Student, U. Ill., 1951-52; EdB, Ill. State U., 1957. Various actuarial positions State Farm Mut. Automobile Ins. Co., Bloomington, Ill., 1952-70, v.p., actuary, 1970-97. Bd. dirs. State Farm Gen. Ins. Co. Fellow Casualty Actuarial Soc. (dir. 1970-73, 87-90); mem. Am. Acad. Actuaries (dir. 1977-80), Midwestern Actuarial Forum (pres. 1972-73), Shriners, Pi Gamma Mu, Pi Omega Pi, Kappa Delta Pi. Home: 7 Canterbury Ct Bloomington IL 61701-3401

CURRY, ALTON FRANK, lawyer; b. Dallas, Aug. 21, 1933; s. William Hadley and Myrtle Estelle (Posey) McKinney; m. Carole B. Piepgrass, Feb. 14, 1960 (div. Nov. 1979); children: Robyn, Mark, John; m. Ann O. Williams, Apr. 12, 1980. BA, Baylor U., 1958, LLB, 1960. Bar: Tex. 1960. Assoc. Fulbright & Jaworski, Houston, 1960-70, ptnr., 1970-98; spl. asst. to Atty. Gen. of Tex., 1964-65, 71-72. Trustee Found. for Bus., Politics and Econs., 1979-92, A.A. White Inst.; chmn. adminstrv. bd. Methodist Ch. Cpl. U.S. Army, 1953-55. Fellow Tex. Bar Found. (sustaining life); mem. ABA, Tex. Bar Assn., Houston Bar Assn., Baylor Law Alumni Assn. (dir. 1977-79, pres. 1979-80), Phi Alpha Delta, Houstonian Club (trustee 1980-83), Coronado Club, Masons. Home: 2707 Weslayan St Houston TX 77027-5123 Office: Fulbright & Jaworski 1301 Mckinney St Houston TX 77010-3031

CURRY, ANN, correspondent, anchor; b. Agana, Guam, Nov. 19, 1956; d. Robert Paul and Hiroe (Nagase) Curry; m. Brian Wilson Ross, Oct. 21, 1987; children: Anna McKenzie, William Walker. Student, U. Oreg., 1974—78. Reporter Sta. KTVL-TV, Medford, Oreg., 1978—81; reporter, weekend anchor Sta. KGW-TV, Portland, Oreg., 1981—84; reporter Sta. KCBS-TV, L.A., 1984—90; corr., anchor NBC News at Sunrise NBC News, N.Y.C., 1991—96; news anchor Today Show, 1997—. Nominee Emmy award, 1985, 1986, 1987, 1988; recipient Golden Mike award, RTNA, 1986, 1987, 1989, Cert. Excellence award, AP, 1987, 1988, Greater L.A. Press Club, 1987, Superior Reporting award, NAACP, 1989, Emmy award, Acad. TV Arts and Scis., 1987, 1989, Nat. award, AAJA, 2000, AmeriCares Humanitarian Medial award, 2002. Avocation: art history. Office: NBC News 30 Rockefeller Plz # 374E New York NY 10112-0002*

CURRY, BEATRICE CHESROWN, retired English educator; b. Lakefork, Ohio, Jan. 14, 1932; d. Tod Shields and Sadie Irene (Springer) C.; m. Elton Wheeler Curry, Sept. 9, 1967 (div. 1988); 1 child, James Christopher. BA, Ashland (Ohio) Coll., 1954; MA, Western Res. U., 1965. English tchr. Hamilton Jr. H.S., Houston, 1954-58, Oliver Hazard Perry Jr. H.S., Cleve., 1958-59, Glenville H.S., Cleve., 1959-60; tchr. English, head dept. Fonville Jr. H.S., Houston, 1960-66; prof. English, Columbia (Tenn.) State C.C., 1967-98; ret. Bd. dirs. Child Care Svc., Columbia, 1973-76; panel moderator So. Festival of Books and Authors, 1991. NEA grantee, 1979, Mellon grantee, 1981, 82; co-recipient Paragon award for Best Coll. Promotional Video, Nat. Coll. Coun. Mktg. and Advt., 1993. Mem. Maury County Creative Arts Guild (lit. chmn. 1984-86), Alpha Delta Kappa (Beta Alpha chpt. pres. 1990-92). Home: 810 Barrow Ct Columbia TN 38401-3115

CURRY, CARLTON E. corporate executive, city councilman; b. Lizton, Ind., Mar. 4, 1935; m. Ann Merritt, 1957. BS, Purdue U., 1958. Registered profl. engr., Ind., cert. profl. logistician. Program adminstr. Allison Gas Turbine divsn. GM, 1966-79, staff systems analyst, 1979-83, mgr. mktg. program, 1983-85, dir. logistics support, 1985-90; cons., 1990-93; pres. SaniServ, Inc., 1990-96, Curry Inc., 1997—. Chmn. Cable Franchise Bd., 1996-2002. City councilman, Indpls., 1983-99; bd. dirs. Dept. of Waterworks, 2002; dir. contracts & ops. Dept. of Waterworks, 2002—. With USN, 1958-66, USAR, 1956-63. Mem. AIAA, Am. Water Works Assn., Soc. Logistics Engrs., Lions, Kiwanis. Republican. Baptist. E-mail: accurry2@comcast.net.

CURRY, CATHERINE ANN, retired archivist; b. San Francisco, Feb. 10, 1927; d. John Francis Curry and Mary Agnes O'Donnell. BA in Math., U. Calif., Berkeley, 1948; MA in L.Am. History, Santa Clara U., Calif., 1965; MA in Theology, U. San Francisco, 1979; PhD, Grad. Theol. Union, Berkeley, 1987. Entered Sisters of the Presentation 1948. Elem. tchr. Archdiocese of San Francisco, 1950—53, 1955—57, Archdiocese of L.A., 1953—55, Montebello, Calif., 1958—59, Archdiocese of Santa Fe, Pecos, N.Mex., 1957—58; secondary sch. tchr. Archdiocese of L.A., 1959—65, 1968—78, Sisters of the Presentation, Berkeley, 1965—68; asst. archivist Archdiocese of San Francisco, Menlo Park, Calif., 1993—2002; ret., 2002. Dir., sec. Calif. Coun. Social Studies, Sacamento, 1971—78; dir. Inst. Hist. Study, San Francisco, 1994—98. Author: Statistical Survey of Religious Women in America in the Nineteenth Century, 1989, Life of Mother Teresa Comerford, 1980; contbr. articles to profl. jours., encys. Mem.: Am. Cath. Hist. Assn., Orgn. Am. Historians, Am. Hist. Assn., History of Women Religious Network, We. Assn. Women Historians, Inst. Hist. Study. Roman Catholic. Avocations: art and architecture, embroidery, photography. Home: 2340 Turk Blvd San Francisco CA 94118

CURRY, CLIFTON CONRAD, JR., lawyer; b. Tampa, Fla., July 8, 1957; s. Clifton C. and Louise (Owens) C.; m. Teresa D. Cox, Dec. 22, 1979; children: Mary Beth, Clifton C. III, Colton Cox. BS, Fla. State U., 1979; JD, Stetson U., 1981. Bar: Fla. 1982, U.S. Dist. Ct. (mid. dist.) Fla. 1982. Assoc. Mark R. Horwitz, P.A., Orlando, Fla., 1981-83; pres. Tittsworth and Curry, P.A., Brandon, Fla., 1984—, Curry and Assocs., P.A., Brandon, 1991—. Bd. dirs. Kiwanis Children's Clinic, 1988-90; vol. Missing Children's Help Ctr.; bd. dirs. Big Bros./Big Sisters, 1985-88, Rough Riders, 1987—, Brandon Outreach Clinic; chmn. Brandon Walk, March of Dimes Birth Defects Found., 1989; gen. coun. Grand Lodge of Fla. Masons, Egypt Temple Shrine, Tampa, Fla. 1996-97; active various polit. campaign coms. Recipient Alice Be. Thompkins Community Svc. award, 1991; named hon. mayor City of Brandon, 1985-86; recipient svc. award Brandon Lions Club, 1985. Mem. ABA, Assn. Trial Lawyers Am., Fla. Bar Assn., Hillsborough County Bar Assn., Brandon Bar Assn., Acad. Fla. Trial Lawyers, Brandon C. of C. (pres. 1989, bd. dirs. 1987-91, chmn. exec. bd. 1990-91, Small Bus. Leader of Yr. 1990), Kiwanis Club Brandon (past bd. dirs., pres. 1988-89), Krewe of Venus King's Guard (bd. dirs.), Fla. State Alumni Assn., Brandon Yacht Club, Ducks Unlimited, YMCA Century Club, Masons, Shriners, Scottish Rite, York Rite. Office: Curry and Assocs PA 750 W Lumsden Rd Brandon FL 33511-6217

CURRY, DALE BLAIR, journalist; b. Memphis, May 30, 1941; d. Hamilton Minter and Doris (Terry) Blair; m. Douglas Hester Curry, Dec. 21, 1963; children: Jennifer, Elizabeth. BA, U. Miss., 1963. Reporter The Commerical Appeal, Memphis, 1962-63, Atlanta Constn., 1963-65, The States-Item, New Orleans, 1969-72, The Morning Advocate, Baton Rouge, 1974-76, 82-84; food editor The Times-Picayune, New Orleans, 1984—. Elder St. Charles Avenue Presbyn. Ch., New Orleans, 1984-87, 91-94. Recipient award AP, UPI, New Orleans Press Club; named among Top 50 alumni 50th Anniversary U. Miss. Sch. Journalism, 1998. Mem. Assn. Food Journalists (pres. 1994-96), Theta Sigma Phi (Alumni of Yr. U. Miss. chpt.). Office: The Times-Picayune 3800 Howard Ave New Orleans LA 70125-1429 Business E-Mail: dale.curry@timespicayune.com.

CURRY, DANIEL ARTHUR, judge; b. Phoenix, Mar. 28, 1937; s. John Joseph and Eva May (Wills) C.; m. Joy M. Shallenberger, Sept. 5, 1959. BS, Loyola U., Los Angeles, 1957, LL.B., 1960. Bar: Calif. 1961, Hawaii 1972, N.Y. 1978. Pvt. practice, L.A. County, Calif., 1964—67; counsel Technicolor Inc., Hollywood, Calif., 1967-70; sr. v.p., gen. counsel Amfac, Inc., Honolulu and San Francisco, 1970—87; v.p., gen. counsel Times Mirror, L.A., 1987-92; judge Superior Ct. of State of Calif., 1992-98; assoc. justice Calif. Ct. Appeal 2d dist., L.A., 1998—. Served to capt. USAF, 1961-64. Office: Calif Ct Appeal 2d Dist 4th Fl North Tower 300 S Spring St Los Angeles CA 90013-1230

CURRY, DANIEL FRANCIS MYLES, filmmaker; b. N.Y.C., Sept. 22, 1946; s. John Joseph Curry Jr. and Florence Cecelia (Rattler) Curry; m. Ubolvan Chaiwatana, July 27, 1972; children: Devin, Daniel. BA, Middlebury Coll.

1968; MFA, Humboldt State U., 1979. Vol. cmty. devel. U.S. Peace Corps, Khon Kaen, Thailand, 1969—71; writer-dir. ednl. TV Ministry of Edn., Govt. of Thailand, Bangkok, 1971—72; freelance filmmaker/artist/designer various clients Bangkok, 1972—74; instr. fine arts Cape Cod Community Coll., West Barnstable, Mass., 1974—77; instr. film and theatre Humboldt State U., Arcata, Calif., 1977—79; visual effects artist Universal Studios Hartland Facility, North Hollywood, Calif., 1979—80; art dir. Modern Film Effects, Hollywood, Calif., 1980—85; v.p., dir. creative svcs. Cinema Rsch. Corp., Hollywood, 1985—88; visual effects producer-dir. Star Trek, the Next Generation, Paramount Pictures, Hollywood, 1987—; pres. O.M.R. Prodns., Manhattan Beach, Calif., 1989—. Supr., title designer : Star Trek IV; Top Gun; Flash Dance; Fatal Attraction; Cujo; The Blob; Rocky IV; Cobra; Staying Alive; Tootsie; Risky Business; Amadeus; The Right Stuff; Mommie Dearest; Uncommon Valor; Pure Luck; Back to School; Raging Bull; Class; Cool World; Captured; Christine; Body Double; Flashpoint; Tiger Town; Invasion U.S.A.; Fast Forward; Bolero; Wild Thing; Pray for Death; Days of Thunder; Indian Jones & The Temple of Doom; Star Trek, Generations; visual effects prodr. : 6th Season Star Trek, The Next Generation (best spl. visual effects Emmy award, 1992); Star Trek Deep Space Nine, 1993—; Star Trek Voyager, 1995— (Emmy award). Nominee Emmy award, 1989, 1990; recipient Emmy award for spl. visual effects, Acad. TV Arts and Scis., 1992, 1994, Internat. Monitor award, 1996. Mem.: Am. Soc. Cinematrographers, Am. Film Inst., Soc. Motion Picture and TV Engrs., Acad. TV Arts and Scis. Avocations: painting, sculpture, world travel.

CURRY, DAVID GORDON, engineer, consultant; b. Scott AFB, Ill., Nov. 17, 1959; s. Charles Gordon Curry and Geraldine Ann Barnes, Hubert Herald Barnes (Stepfather); m. Julie M. Poeppelmeier, Jan. 2, 2003; children: Cassandra Lee, James Robert. BS in Behavioral Sci., USAF Acad., 1982; MA in Exptl./Human Factors Psychology, U. Dayton, 1985; PhD in Psychology, MS in Idsl./Ops. Engr., U. Mich., 1991; MBA, Ind. U., 2000. Certified Human Factors Professional Bd. of Certification in Profl. Ergonomics, 1997. Crew sys. behavioral engr. USAF Wright Aero. Lab., Wright-Patterson AFB, Ohio, 1982—85; adj. faculty mem. Embry-Riddel Aero. U., Williams AFB, Ariz., 1985—87; prin. investigator/rsch. psychologist USAF Human Resources Lab., Williams AFB, 1985—87; behavioral sci. rsch. mgr. USAF Armstrong Lab., Wright-Patterson AFB, 1990—92; chief scientist, JCCD contractor team Sci. Applications Internat. Corp., Vicksburg, Miss., 1993—95; sr. human factors engr. Delphi Delco Electronics Syst., Kokomo, Ind., 1995—2000; NASA rsch. fellow U. Mich., Ann Arbor, 1997—2000; dir. human factors Packer Engring., Naperville, Ill., 2000—. Contbr. scientific papers,,, technical paper. Capt. USAF, 1982—92, lt. col. USAFR, 1992—. Fellow NASA Rsch. Fellowship, NASA Ctr. of Excellence, U. of Mich., 1997-2001; scholar Nat. Merit Scholarship, Nat. Merit Scholarship Corp., 1978, Appointment USAF Acad., USAF Acad., 1978-1982, US Air Force Res. Office Tng. Corps Scholarship, US Air Force, 1978. Mem.: Human Factors and Ergonomics Soc., Am. Psychol. Soc., Soc. of Automotive Engr. (safety and human factors com. mem. 1998—2003). Achievements include patents for U.S. Patent #4.658.931-Evacuated Plenum Hearing Protection; U.S. Patent #4, 671, 015-Rapid Dismount Medium Security Door; U.S. Patent #6, 493, 669-Speech Recognition Driven System With Selectable Speech Models; U.S. Patent #6, 470, 178-Vehicle Radio Having RDS Presets and Method Therefor. Avocations: motorcycling, corvettes. Home: 3140 Timber Valley Drive Kokomo IN 46902 Office: Packer Engineering 1950 N Washington Street Naperville IL 60563 Office Fax: 630-505-1986. E-mail: dgc@packereng.com.

CURRY, DONALD ROBERT, lawyer, oil company executive; b. Pampa, Tex., Aug. 7, 1943; s. Robert Ward and Alleith Elizabeth (Elliston) C.; m. Carolyn Sue Boland, Apr. 17, 1965; 1 son, James Ward. BS, West Tex. State U., 1965; JD, U. Tex., 1968. Bar: Tex. 1968, U.S. Dist. Ct. (no. dist.) Tex. 1970, U.S. Tax Ct. 1973. Assoc. Day & Gandy, Ft. Worth, 1968-69, ptnr., 1970-72; pvt. practice Ft. Worth, 1972—; mng. ptnr. Curry & Thornton Oil, 1981—. Lectr. in field. Mem. bd. regents West Tex. State U., Canyon, 1969-77, sec., mem. exec. com., 1972-75; mem. exec. bd. Longhorn coun. Boy Scouts Am., 1970—, dist. chmn., 1970-75; precinct chmn. Tarrant County (Tex.) Dem. Party, 1982-88, election judge, 1982-94; mem. aviation adv. bd. City of Ft. Worth, 1990-95, vice chmn. bd., chmn. bd. dirs., 1994-95. Recipient Silver Beaver award Boy Scouts Am., 1995; James E. West fellow, 1997. Fellow Tex. Bar Found.; mem. ABA, State Bar Tex., Ft. Worth-Tarrant County Bar ASsn., Ft. Worth Bus. and Estate Coun., Ft. Worth Club, Petroleum Club of Ft. Worth, Phi Alpha Delta, Phi Delta Theta. Methodist. Home: 3800 Tulsa Way Fort Worth TX 76107-3346 Office: 905 Ft Worth Club Bldg Fort Worth TX 76102-4911

CURRY, EMMA BEATRICE, secondary education and college educator; b. Commerce, Ga., July 7, 1927; d. John Henry and Annie Bell (Wilkins) Thomas; m. Harvey Curry, Aug. 4, 1946; children: Gloria Dawn, Harvey Nathaniel, Norbert. BA in Psychology, U. Hawaii, 1971; MEd, counseling degree, Boston U., 1973; postgrad., U. So. Calif., Heidelberg, 1981; postgrad. in fine arts, City Coll., Heidelberg, 1986; postgrad., U. Md., Woxton Coll., Eng., U. Calif., Berkeley. Cert. tchr. social studies, N.J., English, cosmetology, psychology, social studies, DOD. Substitute tchr. Waupahu (Hawaii) H.S. and Leilehua (Hawaii) H.S., 1961-67, DOD, Augsberg, Germany, 1967-69; tchr. Mannheim Am. H.S., Germany, 1971-73, 1977-99; substitute tchr. Pennsauken (N.J.) Ctrl. Elem. Sch., 2000—. Author: (poetry) Feelings: Contemporary Verse, 1999. Bd. dirs. PTA, Mannheim Am. H.S., 1985-86, multicultural chairperson, 1971-73, 77-99; choir condr., soloist Meth. Ch., Wahiwai, 1964, Augsberg, Germany, 1968-69; Sunday sch. tchr. arts and crafts ch., Dachau, Germany, 1955-59. Mem. Nick Virgilio Haiku Assn. Democrat. Methodist. Avocations: poet, artist, sculpturing, piano, guitar. Home: 2251 Merchantville Ave Pennsauken NJ 08110

CURRY, ESTELLA ROBERTA, education educator, consultant; d. John Henry and Grace Gannon; m. Carl Alton Curry, Apr. 7, 1950 (dec. Feb. 1986); children: John, Carl, Carla, David. BS, Ohio U., 1968, postgrad., 1973—2002; MA, Marshall U., 1969, postgrad., 1971—73. Cert. elem. tchr. Ohio, 1961, sch. counselor Ohio, 1969, sch. psychologist Ohio, 1973. Middle sch. tchr. South Point (Ohio) Local Schs., 1961—64, elem. sch. tchr., 1964—68, elem. guidance counselor, 1969—72; grad. asst. Marshall U., Huntington, W.Va., 1968—69; sch. guidance counselor Fairland Local Schs., Proctorville, Ohio, 1972—73; G.E.D. adminstr., coordinator of psychological svcs., sch. psychologist/counselor Lawrence County Ednl. Svc. Ctr., Ironton, Ohio, 1973—. Therapist, clin. supr. Prestera Mental Health Ctr., Huntington, 1991—96; instr. Ohio U., Ironton, 1999—; ednl. cons. Oakridge Treatment Ctr., Ironton, 1999—. Mem.: Sch. Psychology Assn. South Ea. Ohio, Ohio Sch. Psychologist Assn., Coun. for Exceptional Children. Avocations: reading, travel, cooking, art collecting, gardening. Home: 3964 County Rd 15 South Point OH 45680 Office: Lawrence County Ednl Svc Ctr 111 S 4th St Ironton OH 45638

CURRY, EVERETT WILLIAM, JR., college official, minister; b. Glendale, Calif., Mar. 7, 1942; s. Everett William and Sylvia Pauline (Burkholder) C.; m. Barbara Kay Orman, June 13, 1964; children: Kimberly Suzanne Curry McSwain, Kevin Everett. BA, Calif. State U., Northridge, 1964; MDiv, Am. Bapt. Sem., Berkeley, Calif., 1967; cert. pub. rels., UCLA, 1971; Doctor of Ministry, San Francisco Theol. Sem., San Anselmo, Calif., 1977. CFP; chartered mut. fund counselor. Min. to youth First Bapt. Ch., San Fernando, Calif., 1960-62; assoc. pastor Valley Park Bapt. Ch., Sepulveda, Calif., 1962-66; dir., media ministries Coachella Valley Bapt. Found., Thermal, Calif., 1966-68; pastor Lakeview Terrace Bapt. Ch., Lakeview Terrace, Calif., 1968-71; dir., media ministries L.A. Bapt. City Mission Soc., 1971-74; pastor Cmty. Bapt. Ch., Pearl Harbor, Hawaii, 1974-78, First Bapt. Ch., Coos Bay, Oreg., 1978-86; planned giving counselor Am. Bapt. Found., Valley Forge, Pa., 1986-98; assoc. exec. min. Am. Bapt. Chs. Oreg., Portland, 1998-2000; dir. planned giving Linfield Coll., McMinnville, Oreg., 2000—; pub. info. coord. Oreg. sect. ARRL, 2003—. Editor: Oscillator, Oreg. Tualatin Valley Amateur Radio Club, 1999—. Chmn., bd. dirs. Coos Bay Sch. Dist., Coos Bay, 1988-89; sec. Interchurch Ctr. Corp., 1990-2000; chief, chaplain corps, Coos Bay Police Dept., 1979-85; pres. Hawaiian Islands Pub. Radio, Honolulu, 1977-78; bd. dirs. Rose Villa Found., 1998—, Am. Bapt. Homes Found., 2002—. Named Alumnus of Yr., Am. Bapt. Sem. of the West, 1995. Mem. Am. Bapt. Ministers Coun. (sen. 1983-87, 92, 94-95), Western Commn. on Ministry (sec. 1988-91, chair 1992-94), Coos-Bay North Bend Rotary (Outstanding Citizen award 1985). Republican. Baptist. Avocations: amateur radio, backpacking, genealogy, travel. Home: 1546 NE Greensword Dr Hillsboro OR 97124-6139 E-mail: ecurry@linfield.edu. *The test of my generation is found in whether we pass along values in faith and democracy for adoption by the new generation—to be adapted by them for their world.*

CURRY, GREGORY WILLIAM, lawyer; b. Tulsa, June 1, 1961; s. William H. and Shirley Dean (England) C.; 1 child, Alanna England. BBA, U. Okla., 1983; JD magna cum laude, Tex. Tech. U., 1989. Bar: Tex., 1989, Okla., 1996, U.S. Dist. Ct. (all dists.) Tex., Tex. Supreme Ct., U.S. Ct. Appeals (5th 7th, 8th cirs.). Landman Getty Oil Co., Midland, Tex., 1983-84, Mitchell Energy Co., Midland, 1984-86, VIP Photos, Maui, Hawaii, 1986, Thompson & Knight, Dallas, 1989—. Bd. dirs. Sequia Inc. Exec. com. mem. Nat. Marrow Donor Softball Tournament, Dallas, 1993-95, Making Strides Against Cancer, Dallas, 1995-96; com. chmn. Am. Cancer Soc. Evergreen Gala Com., Dallas, 1996-97; vol. North Tex. Legal Svcs., Dallas, 1989-2001; vol. judge advocacy comps. So. Meth. Law Sch., Dallas, 1989-91. Recipient Svc. award North Tex. Legal Svcs., 1989-2001. Fellow Dallas Bar Assn. (chair numerous coms.), Tex. Bar Found., Dallas Bar Found., Dallas Young Lawyers Assn. Found. (trustee, founding fellow); mem. Tex. Assn. of Def. Counsel (bd. dirs., v.p.), Order of Coif, Phi Kappa Phi. Home: 2705 Brookside Mc Kinney TX 75070-4030 Office: Thompson & Knight 1700 Pacific Ave Ste 3300 Dallas TX 75201-4693 E-mail: curryg@tklaw.com.

CURRY, JANE LOUISE, writer; b. East Liverpool, Ohio, Sept. 24, 1932; d. William Jack and Helen Margaret (Willis) C. Student, Pa. State U., 1950-51; BS, Indiana U. of Pa., 1954; postgrad., UCLA, 1957-59; AM, Stanford U., 1962, PhD, 1969; student, U. London, 1961-62, 65-66. Tchr. art East Liverpool schs., 1955, L.A. schs., 1956-59; teaching asst. dept. English Stanford (Calif.) U., 1959-61, 64-65, acting instr., 1967-68, instr., 1983-84, lectr., 1987. Storyteller, 1962—. Author: Down from the Lonely Mountain, 1965, Beneath the Hill, 1967, The Sleepers, 1968, The Change-Child, 1969, The Daybreakers, 1970, Mindy's Mysterious Miniature, 1970, Over the Sea's Edge, 1971, The Ice Ghosts Mystery, 1972, The Lost Farm, 1974, Parsley Sage, Rosemary and Time, 1975, The Watchers, 1975, The Magical Cupboard, 1976, Poor Tom's Ghost, 1977, The Birdstones, 1977, The Bassumtyte Treasure, 1978, Ghost Lane, 1979, The Wolves of Aam, 1981, Shadow Dancers, 1983, The Great Flood Mystery, 1985, The Lotus Cup, 1986, Back in the Beforetime, 1987, Me, Myself and I, 1987, The Big Smith Snatch, 1989, Little Little Sister, 1989, What the Dickens?, 1991, The Great Smith House Hustle, 1993, The Christmas Knight, 1993, Robin Hood and his Merry Men, 1994, Robin Hood in the Greenwood, 1995, Moon Window, 1996, Dark Shade, 1998, Turtle Island, 1999, A Stolen Life, 1999, The Wonderful Sky Boat, 2001, The Egyptian Box, 2002, Hold Up the Sky, 2003. Office: Simon & Schuster Children's Publ Divsn 1230 Ave of Ams New York NY 10020

CURRY, JOHN JOSEPH, professional organization executive; b. Brooklyn, Feb. 6, 1936; s. John and Maude (Smith) C.; m. Claire Degnan (div. Apr. 1987); children: Claire, Julianne, Marie; m. Elizabeth Keiser, Dec. 9, 1989. BA, CCNY, 1958. Pers. mgr. Royal Globe Ins. Co., Phila., 1960-70; dept. adminstr. Thomas Jefferson U. Hosp., Phila., 1970-75; dir. Phila. office Am. Coll. Radiology, 1975-84, exec. dir., Reston, Va., 1984—2003; ret., 2003. Capt. inf. U.S. Army. Mem.: Am. Soc. Assn. Execs.

CURRY, JOHN MICHAEL, investment banker; b. Buffalo, N.Y., Dec. 30, 1942; s. John Vincent and June (Eisele) C.; m. Thea Adrian Kirk, July 12, 1969 (div. 1982); children: John Adrian, James Prescott; m. Margaretta Buckley, Mar. 17, 1990; 1 child, Michael Jeremiah. BA, U. San Francisco, 1968; MBA, Harvard U., 1970; postgrad., Suffolk U., 1971. Cert. property mgr.; registered rep. and gen. securities rep.; registered fiduciary and investment adviser, registered securities prin. Developer Devel. Corp. Am., Boston, 1970-73; founder, chmn. APT Fin. Svcs., Inc., Boston, 1977—, Am. Securities Team, Inc., Boston, 1992—, Am. Properties Team, APT Asset, Boston, 1987—; chmn. Am. Devel. Team, 1985-92, Am. Realty Team, Fla., 1994—, Infrastructure Repair Technologies, 1998—. Bd. dirs. six corps.; Boston rep. Taylor Woodrow PLC, London, 1983-85. Vol. various fed., state, local polit. orgns. and campaigns. Sgt. U.S. Army, 1961-64. Recipient Modernization award Building Mag., 1980-81, Outstanding Restoration award Lowell C. of C., 1981, Nat. Jewish Life award, 1987. Mem. Harvard Club (Boston), various securities firms orgns. Avocations: scuba diving, Karate, golf.

CURRY, JOHN PATRICK, insurance company executive, management consultant; b. Logan, W.Va., May 3, 1934; s. Albert Bruce and Mary Naomi (Shugert) C.; m. Patricia Jean Blessington, Oct. 26, 1956; children: Joseph Patrick, Mary Patricia, Kathleen Anne, Carmen Frances, John Gregory. Student, St. Charles Coll., Catonsville, Md., 1949-52; BA, U. Notre Dame, 1956; MS in Ops. Rsch., Western Mich. U., 1976. Lic. prof. cons., Mich. Agt. Conn. Mut. Life Ins. Co., 1959-65; gen. agt. Occidental Life Ins. Co., L.A., 1965-66; pres. Investment Assocs. Inc., L.A., 1966-69; gen. agt. Fed. Life Ins. Co., Peoples Home Life Ins. Co. and Home Assurance Cos., 1969-71; actuarial cons. Am.-Brit. Ins. & Annuity Co. Ltd. (Bermuda), Battle Creek, Mich., 1979-87, mgmt. cons., 1971-88; owner, mgr. Nat. Search Cons., exec. search firm, Kalamazoo; owner, operator Curry Supply Co., Portage, Mich., 1978-83; pres. The Consulting Group Inc. (Del.), Kalamazoo, 1985—. Pres. The Pilot Co., Turks and Caicos Islands, 1985-90; dir. Anglo-Am. Ins. Co., Ltd. (Bermuda), 1979-87. Served with U.S. Army, 1957-59. U. Notre Dame scholar, 192-55; Pat O'Brien scholar, 1956. Mem.: Pres.'s Round Table, Sertoma Club (charter dir. Kalamazoo club 1961—64, mem. Pres.' Round Table). Republican. Roman Catholic. Home: 7226 Rockford St Portage MI 49024-4122 Office: The Consulting Group Kalamazoo MI 49024 E-mail: jcurry@voyager.net.

CURRY, KATHLEEN BRIDGET, retired librarian; b. Parnell, Iowa, May 19, 1931; d. John Michael and Ellen Theresa (Clear) C. BS in Libr. Sci., Marycrest Coll., 1953. Head libr. Moline (Ill.) Sr. H.S., 1953-90. Part-time libr. Moline Pub. Hosp. Sch. Nursing, 1957-66; mem. sch. nursing libr. St. Anthony's Hosp., Rock Island, Ill., 1955; hist. libr. Rock Island Hist. Libr., Moline, 1956-59; libr. Black Hawk Coll., Moline, 1958-59. Exec. bd. Miss Iowa Pageant, Davenport, Iowa, 1987—; bd. dirs. Miss Black Hawk Valley Pageant, Moline, 1986—, Quad City Arts Coun., Davenport, 1990; guild mem. Quad City Symphony Orch., Davenport, 1972—. Recipient Disting. Svc. award Marycrest Coll., 1987, Disting. Svc. award Moline High Sch. PTA, 1983. Mem. Ill. Edn. Assn., NEA, Ill. Sch. Libr. Assn., AAUW, Moline Edn. Assn., Iowa Libr. Assn., Zonta Internat., Delta Kappa Gamma. Democrat. Roman Catholic. Avocations: playing the piano, cooking. Home: 3646 71st St Ct Moline IL 61265-1833 E-mail: gmedhus@aol.com.

CURRY, MARY EARLE LOWRY, poet; b. Seneca, S.C., May 13, 1917; d. Ullin Sidney and Mary Sloan (Earle) Lowry; m. Peden Gene Curry, Dec. 25, 1941; children: Eugene Lowry, Mary Earle (dec.). Student, Furman U., Greenville, S.C., 1944-45. Author: (poetry books) Looking Up, 1949, Looking Within, 1961, reprinted, 1980, Hymn, 1973; contbr. to Yearbook of Modern Poetry, Poets of Am., Poetic Voice of Am., We the People, Poetry Digest, Poetry Anthology of Verse, Internat. Anthology on World Brotherhood and Peace, Parnassas of World Poets, others; weekly poetry columns in Inman Times, Fountain Inn Times, Fort Mill Times, Laurens Advertiser, Ware Shoals Life, others. Recipient World award for culture Centro Studi E Ricerche Delle Naioni, Italy, 1985. Mem. Centro Studi Scambi Internat. Roma, United Meth. Women's Orgns., United Meth. Ministers' Wives Clubs, various cmty. clubs. Avocations: music, photography, reading. Home: 345 Curry Dr Seneca SC 29678-1907

CURRY, NANCY ELLEN, educator, psychoanalyst, psychologist; b. Brockway, Pa., Jan. 26, 1931; d. George R. and Mary F. (Covert) C. BA, Grove City Coll., 1952; MEd, U. Pitts., 1956, PhD, 1972; grad., Pitts. Psychoanalytic Inst., 1988, grad. child analytic program, 1992. Lic. psychologist, Pa. Tchr. public schs., East Brady and Oakmont, Pa., 1952-55; presch. demonstration tchr. Arsenal Family and Children's Center, U. Pitts., 1955-79, assoc. dir., 1971-79; from instr. in psychiatry to prof. child devel. Sch. Social Work, U. Pitts., 1957-93; prof. emeritus Sch. Social Work, U. Pitts.; also mem. faculty U. Pitts Sch. Medicine, Sch. Edn., Sch. Health Related Professions.; pvt. practice in psychanalysis and psychotherapy; ret., 2000. Supr., cons.; Fulbright exchange tchr. North Oxford Nursery Sch., Oxford, Eng., 1957-58; vis. prof. Oreg. State U., summer, 1964, Ariz. State U., summer, 1969; assoc. dir. early childhood project Edn. Professions Devel. Act, U.S. Office of Edn., 1970-74; cons. in field. Co-producer 12 films on children's play; co-author Beyond Self-esteem, 1990; editor The Feeling Child; author numerous articles on child devel. Mem. APA, Am. Psychoanalytic Assn., Assn. Child Psychoanalysis. Home: 149 Shadow Ridge Dr Pittsburgh PA 15238-2133

CURRY, PAUL RUSSELL, law enforcement official, lobbyist; b. Portland, Oreg.; s. Russell John and Elma Arlene Curry; m. Kathryn Gene, Nov. 3, 1972; children: Heather Marie Curry Sharpe, Emily Kathryn Ackerman Hodges. AA in Police Sci., San Bernardino (Calif.) Valley Coll., 1974; BS in Pub. Mgmt., Pepperdine U., 1975. Dep. sheriff San Bernardino County Sheriff, 1970—, from detective to lt., 1976-97. Chair legis. com. Calif. Peace Officers Assn., Sacramento, 1995-2002, chmn. legal svc. program, 1992—; author child pornography increased penalty legis., 1994-98, pub. records act modification, 1992-99, civil easement law, 1998-2002; bd. dir. Calif. State U. Athletic Assn., San Bernardino, 1996—; chmn. Citizens for Good Govt., Fontana, Calif., 1998—. With USN, 1965-69. Recipient Micky Rainey award Calif. Peace Officers Assn., 1997. Mem. Am. Soc. Indsl. Security (chpt. pres.), Calif. State Sheriff's Assn. (assoc.), 1st Amendment Coalition, Am. Legion, Footprinters, Derby Club. Republican. Roman Catholic. Avocations: woodworking, vintage automobiles. Office: San Bernardino County Sheriff's Dept 655 E 3d St San Bernardino CA 92415 E-mail: paulcurry@usa.net.

CURRY, RAYMOND HOWARD, physician; b. Lexington, Ky., June 5, 1956; s. Howard Jr. and Venita (Dawson) C. AB, U. Ky., 1977; MD, Washington U., St. Louis, 1982. Diplomate Am. Bd. Internal Medicine. Resident in internal medicine McGaw Med. Ctr. Northwestern U., Chgo., 1982-85; internist Northwestern Med. Faculty Found., Chgo., 1985—; instr. Northwestern U. Med. Sch., Chgo., 1985-89, asst. prof., 1989-96, assoc. prof., 1996—2002, prof., 2002—, dir. undergrad. edn. dept. medicine, 1992—98, exec. assoc. dean, 1998—; mem. staff Northwestern Meml. Hosp., Chgo., 1985—. Mem. ACP, Soc. Gen. Internal Medicine, Am. Acad. Physician and Patient, Phi Beta Kappa. Office: Northwestern U Feinberg Sch of Medicine 303 E Chicago Ave Chicago IL 60611

CURRY, ROBERT EMMET, JR., lawyer; b. N.Y.C., N.Y., Jan. 18, 1946; s. Robert Emmet and Rose Ann (Mooney) Curry; m. Margaret Courtney Kennedy, May 6, 1973; 1 child, Robert Emmet III. BA (hon.), Georgetown U., 1967; JD, Columbia U., 1970. Bar: N.Y. 1971, U.S. Supreme Ct. 1973. Assoc. Patterson, Belknap, Webb & Tyler, N.Y.C., 1971—73; sr. coun. Rouse Co., Columbia, Md., 1973—75; assoc. coun. Ogden Corp., N.Y.C., 1976—80, v.p., 1981—85, gen. coun., 1983—87, sr. v.p., 1985—87; ptnr. Dickstein, Shapiro & Morin, 1987—. Mem.: Am. Corp. Counsel Assn. (pres. Met. N.Y. chpt.), ABA, N.Y. State Bar Assn., Assn. Bar City N.Y. (energy com.), Washington (Conn.) Club. Roman Catholic. Office: Ogden Corp 277 Park Ave New York NY 10172-0003

CURRY, ROBERT LEE, lawyer; b. Lamont, Wis., May 10, 1923; s. Irving Gregg and Emma (Zimmerman) C.; m. Muriel Clapp, July 29, 1950; children—Robert Lee J., Laura Lynne, Melinda Ann. BS, Lawrence U., 1948; LL.B., U. Wis., 1953. Bar: Wis. bar 1953. Assoc. firm Boardman, Suhr, Curry & Field, Madison, Wis., 1953-56, sr. partner, 1956-73, of counsel, 1989-94. V.p., gen. counsel CUNA Mut. Ins. Group, Madison, 1964-73, pres., 1973-88, bd. dirs., 1972-88, dir. emeritus, 1988—; dir. CUNA Credit Union, 1965-70, pres., 1968-69; bd. dirs. Cumis Ins. Soc., 1972-88, pres., 1973-88; bd. dirs. Cumis Ins. Group Can., 1972-88; pres., dir. Cudis Ins. Soc., Inc., 1972-88, C.M.C.I. Corp. Chmn., United Way of Dane County, Wis., 1981. Served with USAAF, 1942-46. Mem. Am. Law Inst., U. Wis. Law Alumni Assn. (dir. 1967-70, pres. 1969-70), Order of Coif. Home: 4805 Fond Du Lac Trl Madison WI 53705-4814

CURRY, ROBERT LEE, III, lawyer; b. New Orleans, Sept. 29, 1931; s. Robert Lee Jr. and Lydia (Sporl) C.; m. Courtney Davis, June 11, 1955; children: Robert Lee IV, Cynthia Curry Alexander, Thomas Davis, Kevin Courtney. BS, JD, La. State U., 1954; LLM in Taxation, NYU, 1958. Bar: La. 1954, U.S. Ct. Appeals (5th cir.) 1961, U.S. Supreme Ct. 1958. Judge advocate USAF, Wichita, Kans., 1954-56; teaching fellow NYU Sch. of Law, 1956-57; atty. advisor U.S. Tax Ct., Washington, 1957-60; atty. Theus, Grisham, Davis & Leigh, Monroe, La., 1960—. Coun. mem. La. Law Inst. Coun., Baton Rouge, 1978—, pres., 1995-98. Fellow Am. Coll. Trust and Estate Counsel, Am. Coll. Tax Counsel; mem. Internat. Acad. Trust and Estate Law. Episcopalian. Office: Theus Grisham Davis & Leigh 1600 Lamy Ln Monroe LA 71201-3736 E-mail: rcurry@theuslaw.com.

CURRY, ROBERT RICHARD, health facility administrator; b. Pitts. s. Richard Lee and Mary Louise (Schnuth) Curry; life ptnr. Douglas D. Jasinske, Dec. 2, 1999. BA, U. Dayton, 1985, MSEd, 1989. Asst. exec. dir. Sigma Nu Found., Lexington, Va., 1985—87; asst. dean of students U. Dayton, Ohio, 1987—89; dean of students Rider U., Lawrenceville, NJ, 1989—94; program coord. NENY AIDS Coun., Albany, NY, 1994—95; dir. edn. and tng. Upper Hudson Planned Parenthood, Albany, 1995—. Cons. Cicatelli and Assocs., N.Y.C., 1998—; faculty mem. Albany Med. Coll., 2000—; prin. investigator Ctrs. Disease Control, Atlanta, 2000—01; corp. trainer, Albany, 2000—; mem. rev. com. best practices in reproductive health care and male med. svcs. NY State Dept. Health, 2002. Contbr. articles to profl. jours. Assoc. Planned Parenthood Fedn. Am. Leadership Inst., 2000, 2002—03; co-chmn. N.Y. State AIDS Prevention Planning Group, 2002—03; founder, pres. bd. dirs. Names Project AIDS Meml. Quilt, Albany, 1997; adv. bd. Albany Med. Coll. AIDS Program, 2001; Albany Cmty. Author; ward leader Dem. Com.; bd. dirs. Lark St. Bus. Improvement Dist., Albany, 2000—. Named one of Outstanding Young Man of Am., 1987, 1989; recipient Leadership award, N.Y. State AIDS Inst., 2002, Excellence in Edn. and Tng. award, Planned Parenthood Fedn. Am., 2002, Excellence in Tng. award, Hudson Valley CC Physician's Assts. Program, 2002; grantee, Ctrs. Disease Control; CDC scholar, U. S.C., Columbia, 2001. Mem.: APHA, U. Dayton Alumni Assn. (new student recruiter 2003). Democrat. Avocations: travel, gourmet cooking, wines, music, acting. Home: 75 Willett St Apt 4-F Albany NY 12210

CURRY, SUSAN MARGARET, not-for-profit administrator, writer; b. Washington, Nov. 5, 1945; d. Robert Aaron Gulick and Helen Knight Iredell; m. Andrew Eugene Curry (dec. Oct. 1988); m. Gail Mary Daniels, Oct. 25, 1997. BA, Pitzer Coll., 1968; MA, Norwich U., 2001. Project coord. Project SEED, Inc., 1969-89, dir., 1989-94, Phila., 1994-98; pres. Alliance for a Sustainable Future, Ambler, Pa., 2001—. Chair Ambler Environl. Adv. Coun., 2000—. Project coord. minimal lawn chems. campaign, founder Pennypack Farm CSA; organizer ann. Phila. Earth Charter Summits, 2001—. Avocations: gardening, community activism, animal rights, voluntary simplicity. Home and Office: 316 Edgewood Dr Ambler PA 19002-4305

CURRY, THOMAS FORTSON, electronics engineer, defense industry executive; b. Thomasville, Ga., Nov. 22, 1926; s. Bostick Underwood and Bertie Eugenia (Cook) C.; m. Mary Ann Kemper, July 2, 1949; children: Bostick U., Thomas Lee, Ruthann, David C.K., Laurie F., Clinton M. BEE, Ga. Inst. Tech., 1949; MSEE, Pa. State U., 1954; PhD, Carnegie-Mellon U., 1959. Registered profl. engr., Pa., Va. Rsch. fellow elec. engring. dept. Carnegie-Mellon U., Pitts., 1955-57; tech. staff Bell Telephone Labs., Murray Hill, N.J., 1957-58; lab. dir. Syracuse (N.Y.) U. Rsch. Corp., 1959-64; chmn. bd. dirs. Curry, McLaughlin & Len Inc., Syracuse, 1964-65; dept. mgr., chief engr. Melpar, Inc., Falls Church, Va., 1966-70; product line dir. LTV-Electrosystems, Inc., Garland, Tex., 1970-71; tech. advisor to pres. Melpar, Divsn., E-Systems, Inc., Falls Church, 1971-74; v.p., dir. Microwave Systems, Inc., Syracuse, 1974-76; asst. dir. Signals Intelligence, Office Sec. of Def., Washington, 1976-80; assoc. dep. asst. sec. of Navy, Office Sec. of Navy, Washington, 1980-83; pres., dir. C-Systems, Inc., Oakton, Va., 1983—; chief scientist E-Systems, Inc., Fairfax, Va., 1983-93; chief engr. C-Systems, Inc., Oakton, Va., 1993—. Mem., dir. Navy Intelligence Cons. Group, Office of Navy Ops., 1983-86; mem. tech. working group 9F Crit. Techs. Rev., Office Strategic Def., 1988-93. Contbr. articles to profl. jours. Pres. Kemper Park Civic Assn., Fairfax County, Va., 1972-73; treas. Centerville Coun. Civic Assn., Fairfax County, 1973-74; mem. trustees vis. com. elec. engring. dept. Carnegie-Mellon U., 1972-74. 1st lt. U.S. Army, 1944-47, 50-52. Named Fellow in Elec. Comm., Bell Telephone Labs., Murray Hill, N.J., 1956-57. Fellow IEEE (chmn. No. Va. sect. 1973, Centennial award 1984); mem. Assn. Old Crows (life; pres. Capitol Club 1972, nat. dir. 1976-85); mem.

Security Affairs Support Assn., Assn. Energy Engrs., Hunter Mill Swim and Racquet Club (bd. dirs. 1979-83), Sigma Xi, Tau Beta Pi, Eta Kappa Nu, Alpha Tau Omega. Office: C-Systems Inc PO Box 310 Oakton VA 22124-0310 E-mail: csys@earthlink.net., tcurry@ieee.org.

CURRY, THOMAS FRANCIS, lawyer; b. Brookline, Mass., Dec. 1, 1920; s. Thomas and Mary T. (Ward) C.; m. Mary Anita Finnegan, June 30, 1943; children— Kevin T., Maureen C., Kathleen A. Student Boston Coll., 1939-41; A.B., Catholic U. Am., 1944; LL.B., Georgetown U., 1950. Bar: D.C. 1951, U.S. Dist. Ct. D.C. 1951, Md. 1953, U.S. Dist. Ct. Md. 1956, U.S. Ct. Appeals (4th cir.) 1958, Mass. 1962, U.S. Dist. Ct. Mass. 1964, U.S. Ct. Appeals (3d cir.) 1975. Mem. FBI, 1946-52; exec. v.p. Balt. Transit Co., 1952-61; v.p. Eastern Mass. State Ry., 1961-64; pres. Eastern Mutual Ins. Co., 1961-64; gen. counsel Dennison Mfg. Co., 1964— . Served to lt. USNR, 1944-51. Mem. ABA, Mass. Bar Assn., Boston Bar Assn. Clubs: Wellesley Country (Mass.); Indian River Plantation (Fla.); National Lawyers (Washington). Office: Dennison Mfg Co 1 Clarks Hl Framingham MA 01702-8163

CURRY, THOMAS JAMES, retired manufacturers representative; b. New Brunswick, N.J., Sept. 8, 1921; s. Thomas Christopher and Leanore Margaret (Craven) C.; m. Mary Louise Bisaccio, Apr. 1, 1945. BA, Rutgers U., 1944. Export sales traffic mgr. Am. Cyanamid Corp., Bound Brook, N.J., 1945-47; sales coord. Interchemical Corp., Bound Brook, 1948-52; sales rep. Sun Chem. Corp., N.Y.C., 1953-67; pvt. practice mfrs. rep. Pa., 1968-2000; retired, 2001. Pres. coun. Rutgers U. Mem. Col. Henry Rutgers Soc. Avocations: golf, geneaology, photography, history. Home: 10 Crestline Rd Wayne PA 19087-2607

CURRY, WILLIAM SIMS, county official; b. Mt. Vernon, Washington, Feb. 6, 1938; s. Eli Herbert Curry and Winona Geraldine Davis; m. Kirsten Ingeborg Arms, May 20, 1971; children: William II, Kevin, Randal, Kim Cannova, Derek. BS in Bus. Mgmt., Fla. State U., 1967; MBA, Ohio State U., 1968. Cert. profl. contracts mgr. Asst. purchasing officer Stanford (Calif.) Linear Accelerator Ctr., 1977-80; subcontract adminstr. Lockheed Missiles & Space Co., Sunnyvale, Calif., 1980-81; materials mgr. Altus Corp., San Jose, Calif., 1981-86; purchasing mgr. Litton Electron Devices, San Carlos, Calif., 1986 95, Comms. & Power Industries, Palo Alto, Calif., 1995-97; contracts mgr. Landacorp, Chico, Calif., 1998; purchasing svcs. mgr. Butte County, Oroville, Calif., 1998-01, dep. adminstrv. officer, 2001—, gen. svcs. dir., 2001—. Bd. dirs. Industry Coun. for Small Bus. Devel., Sunnyvale, 1992-97, v.p. programs, 1992-93, exec. v.p., 1994-95, pres., 1995-97. Contbr. articles to profl. jours. Capt. USAF, 1955-77. Decorated Meritorious Svc. medal with one oak leaf cluster, USAF, 1977. Fellow Nat. Contract Mgmt. Assn.; mem. Calif. Assn. Pub. Purchasing Officers, Am. Mensa, Beta Gamma Sigma. Republican. Avocations: chess, writing, cycling. Home: 17 Northwood Commons Pl Chico CA 95973-7213 Office: Butte County 3-A County Center Dr Oroville CA 95965-3334 E-mail: bnkcurry@sbcglobal.net.

CURSCHMANN, MICHAEL JOHANN HENDRIK, German language and literature educator; b. Cologne, Germany, Jan. 11, 1936; came to U.S., 1963; s. Fritz Heinrich and Hanna Regine (Schinnerer) C.; m. Beryl G. Davies, Jan. 14, 1961; children: Jane, Paul (dec. 1982). Student, Munich U., 1954-56, 58-62, London U., 1957-58; Phd, Munich U., 1962. Asst. prof. Munich U., 1961-63; asst. prof. dept. Germanic langs. and lit. Princeton U., 1963-65, assoc. prof., 1965-69, prof., 1969—2002, chmn. dept., 1979-82, 86-89, dir. program in medieval studies, 1993-2001. Vis. prof. Munich U., 1985-86, Tübingen U., 1990, Fribourg U., 1996. Author works on German and European medieval literature, literature and other arts. Guggenheim fellow, 1970-71; fellow Inst. for Germanic Studies, U. London. Fellow: Medieval Acad. Am.; mem.: Bavarian Acad. Sci. (corr.). Home: 134 Sycamore Rd Princeton NJ 08540-5325 E-mail: micur@princeton.edu.

CURSIEFEN, CLAUS, ophthalmologist, researcher; arrived in U.S., 2002; s. Wilhelm and Gisela Cursiefen; m. Simone Gutmann; children: Christina Louise, Isabella Birgitta. MD, U. Würzburg, Germany, 1990—95. ECFMG certificate (USMLE I and II) Ednl. Com. Fgn. Med. Graduates, 1997, cert. European Bd. of Ophthalmology, 2001, Internat. Coun. of Ophthalmology, 2001, German Bd. of Ophthalmology 2001. Postdoctoral rsch. fellow Harvard Med. Sch., The Schepens Eye Rsch. Inst., Boston, Mass., 2002—; jr. faculty ophthalmologist U. of Erlangen-Nürnberg, Dept. of Ophthalmology, Erlangen, 1995—96. Author: (book) On the traces of Janusz Korczak in Israel (German UNESCO Commn. Study Travel Award, 1989), more than 40 scientific articles. Grantee Study grant, Konrad Adenauer Found., Bonn, Germany, 1988-1995, Rsch. Fellowship, German Rsch. Coun. DFG, 2001; scholar German Academic Exch. Svc. Fellowship, 1990. Mem.: Am. Acad. of Ophthalmology, Ocular Surface Tearfilm Soc., German Ophthalmic Pathologists Soc., German Ophthal. Soc., European Vision and Eye Rsch. Assn., Assn. for Rsch. in Vision and Ophthalmology. Office: Schepens Eye Rsch Inst 20 Staniford Street Boston MA 02114 Office Fax: 617-912-0101. E-mail: cursiefen@vision.eri.harvard.edu.

CURSON, THEODORE, musician; b. Phila., June 3, 1935; s. Leroy and Reava (Paige) C.; m. Marjorie N. Goltry, Apr. 1, 1967; children: Charlene, Theodore II. Student, Mastbaum Sch., Granoff Music Conservatory, Phila., 1952-53. Mem. Charles Mingus' Jazz Workshop, 1959-60. Guest instr. U. Vt. Festival of Contemporary Music, 1968; instr. music Warsaw U.; pres. Nosruc Pub. Co., Jersey City, from 1961 Trumpeter with Max Roach, Philly Joe Jones, Cecil Taylor, Eric Dolphy, 1960—63; musician: appeared on radio, TV, clubs, jazz festivals include Riga, Latvia, Tallinn, Estonia, Vienna, France, NorthSea, The Hague, Nice, Jazz Yatra, India, Antibes, Aix en Provence, Lugano, Bologna, Macerata, Prague, Bled, Warsaw, Molde, Kongberg, Ahus, Laren, Pori, Caracas, Amsterdam, 1964, U.S. festivals New Music Across America, Birdland, Newport/N.Y., Newport Rebels Festival, univ. concerts include Princeton U., U. Wis., Baton Rouge, Columbia U., N.Y.U., Hobart Coll., We. Wash. Coll., Grinnell Coll., U. Calif., Santa Monica and Berkeley, U. Vt., toured India, Middle East and N. Africa for State Dept., 1980, toured Siberia, 1996; guest soloist Norddeutscher Rundfunk TV, star PBS TV show Jazz Set, 1972, star, with NOS Dutch TV (jazz video) Last Date; composer: Nosruc Waltz, 1960, Flatted Fifth, 1960, The Leopard, 1964, Straight Ice, 1965, Typical Ted, 1970, Reava's Waltz, Airi's Tune, Searchin for the Blues, Lost Her, 1987; musician: (recording) Plenty of Horn, 1961, Fire Down Below, 1963, Tears for Dolphy, 1976, 1994, New Thing and Blue Thing, 1965, Urge, 1966, Ode to Booker Ervin, 1970, Pop Wine, 1972, Quicksand, 1975, Jubilant Power, 1976, Blue Piccolo, 1976, Flip Top, 1977, Typical Ted, 1977, The Trio, 1979, I Heard Mingus, 1980, Snake Johnson, 1981, Round Midnight, 1990, Cattin' Curson, 1993, Traveling On, 1997, Sugar'n Spice, 1999, Pori Jazz, 2001, Face to Face, 2002, (music for films) Teorema, 1968, Notes for a Film on Jazz, 1968, The Brown Bunny, 2003; dir.: Blue Note Open Jam, 1984—93. Named New Star Montery Jazz Festival 1962, winner Trumpet sect. Down Beat Internat. Critics Poll, 1966, Ted Curson & Co. winner Down Beat Reader's Poll, 1978, named New Jazz Artist Jazz Podium, Germany; recipient L.I. Musicians Soc. award 1970, Pori (Finland) City Standard 1978, Keys to City, 1998, Paul Robeson Community Arts award Jersey City Pub. Libr., 1994. Mem. Am. Fedn. Musicians.

CURT, DENISE MORRIS, artist, limner, photographer; b. New Haven, Nov. 15, 1936; d. Bertrand and Anna Geraldine (Fiak) Rocheleau; m. John Morris, Oct. 4, 1954 (dec.); children: Tyler John, Cynthia Leigh Morris Bell; m. Albert A. Curt, 1973 (div. 1981). Student of Louis Crescenti, Orange, Conn., 1950-52; student, Whitney Sch. Art, New Haven, 1950, Luchetti Sch. Art, 1951, Paier Sch. Art, Hamden, Conn., 1951. Dir. Meet The Artists and Artisans, Milford, Conn., 1962—; interior designer State of Conn., Hartford, 1972-75. One-woman shows Gull Gallery, Provincetown, Mass., Chapelle Jean Cocteau, Villefranche Sur Mer, France, Garfield Galleries, Orange, Conn., Yale U., Stratford Gallery, Stevenson (Md.) Galleries, also others; represented in numerous pvt. and pub. collections throughout world. Lectr. to numerous civic orgns.; mem. Vis. Artists in Schs., 1970—; commr. Conn. Commn. on Arts, 1974-79; photography chmn. Milford Fine Arts Coun., New Haven Arts Coun.; bd. dirs. Milford Hosp. Aux.; mem. Literacy Vols., Milford. Recipient award Mystic Art Festival, 1969, Sterling House Art Show, 1985, Glastonbury Art Guild, 1988. Mem. Guilford Art League (bd. dirs. 1975-80), Nat. League Am. Pen Women (category painting, bd. dirs. Fairfield chpt., art chair), Conn. Classic Arts, Milford Hist. Soc., Yale U. Gallery, Met. Mus. Art. Republican. Congregationalist. Avocations: renaissance and baroque music, antiques, foreign travel. Home: 41 Green St Milford CT 06460-4709 E-mail: ctlimner@snet.net.

CURTIN, BRIAN JOSEPH, ophthalmologist; b. N.Y.C., July 25, 1921; s. James Joseph and Julia Margaret (Smith) C.; m. Claire Margaret Flood, June 18, 1955; children: Edward Brian, James Martin, Thomas Hayes, Deirdre Claire. BS, Fordham U., 1942; MD, NYU, 1945. Intern St. Vincent's Hosp., N.Y.C., 1945-46; resident surgeon Manhattan Eye, Ear and Throat Hosp., 1950-53, asst. attending surgeon, asso. attending surgeon, 1953-74, surgeon dir., 1974-89, surgeon dir. emeritus, 1990—, pres. med. bd., 1977-79, vice chmn. dept. ophthalmology, 1983-89, med. dir., 1989-91; attending ophthalmologist, chief svc. Misericordia-Lincoln Affiliated Hosps., 1958-79; attending ophthalmologist N.Y. Hosp., 1969-84; assoc. attending ophthalmologist Columbia Presbyn. Med. Ctr., 1985-92; asst. prof. clin. ophthalmology NYU, 1954-70; assoc. prof. clin. ophthalmology Cornell Med. Coll., 1970-84, Columbia U. Coll. Physicians and Surgeons, 1985-98; pvt. practice N.Y.C. Med. adv. bd. Eye Bank for Sight Restoration, N.Y.C., 1978-90, chmn., 1988-90; attending ophthalmologist, chmn. dept. St. Clare's Hosp. and Health Ctr., 1978-81. Author: The Myopias: Basic Science and Clinical Management, 1985; mem. editorial bd. Cornea, 1981-85; contbr. chpts. to textbooks, articles to med. jours. With U.S. Navy, 1946-48. Recipient Achievement award Fordham U., 1976. Mem. ACS, AMA, AAAS, Am. Ophthalmol. Soc., N.Y. State Med. Soc., N.Y. County Med. Soc., N.Y. Acad. Medicine, N.Y. Acad. Scis., Am. Acad. Ophthalmology, N.Y. Ophthal. Soc. (v.p. 1981-82, pres. 1982-83), Am. Eye Study Club, Siwanoy Country Club. Home: 4402 Theall Rd Rye NY 10580-1480

CURTIN, DANIEL JOSEPH, JR., lawyer; b. San Francisco, Jan. 7, 1933; s. Daniel Joseph and Nell Helen (Lenihan) C.; m. Myrtle Rose Wanke, Feb. 7, 1959; children: Kathleen, Mary, Patricia, Thomas, Carol. AB in Polit. Sci., U. San Francisco, 1954, JD, 1957. Bar: Calif. 1958. Asst. sec. State Senate Calif., Sacramento, 1959; cons., counsel Assembly Com. on Local Govt., Sacramento, 1959-60; dep. city atty. Richmond, Calif., 1961-65; city atty. Walnut Creek, Calif., 1965-82; with Williams, Caploe, Robbins & Curtin, Benicia, Calif., 1983-84; ptnr. McCutchen, Doyle, Brown & Enersen, Walnut Creek, 1984—2001; counsel Bingham McCutchen, 2002—. Mem. bd. advisors environ. affairs Boston Coll. Sch. of Law, 1987—; mem. State Sen. Housing Adv. Task Force, 1983-84, State Sen. Subcom. on the Redevel. of Antiquated Subdivs., 1986; instr. continuing edn. of the bar, 1975, 82, 88, U. San Francisco Sch. of Law, 1988-92, Golden Gate U. Sch. of Law, 1979-82, U. Calif. Extension, 1973—, John F. Kennedy U. Sch. of Law, Walnut Creek, 1983-90; mem. adv. com. Alcohol and Drug Abuse Coun., Pleasant Hill, Calif. Contbr. articles to profl. jours. Lt. U.S. Army, 1958, 56-64. Recipient Disting. Leadership award, Nat. Planning award Am. Planning Assn., 1988; named City Atty. of Yr., 1971 and others. Mem. ABA (sect. on state and local govt. law, coun. chair 2001-02, chmn. land use, planning and zoning com. 1976-78, vice-chair 1999, Lifetime Achievement award 2003), Calif. State Bar Assn. (mem. exec. com., real property law sect. 1988-91, mem. com. on environ. 1977-80), Nat. Inst. Mcpl. Law Officer (chmn. zoning and planning com. 1969-79, regional v.p. 1979-82, Lifetime Achievement in Mcpl. Law Charles S. Rhyne award), Calif. Pk. and Recreation Soc., League of Calif. Cities (pres. city atty.'s dept. 1973-74), Lambda Alpha, others. Democrat. Roman Catholic. Avocations: pub. speaking, gardening. Office: Bingham McCutchen 1333 N Calif Blvd Ste 210 PO Box V Walnut Creek CA 94596-4534 Office Fax: 925-975-5390. E-mail: daniel.curtin@bingham.com.

CURTIN, DAVID, music educator; b. Newburgh, N.Y., Sept. 19, 1967; s. Robert Denis and Kathleen Anne Curtin; m. Hyun Ju Heo, Mar. 16, 1996; children: Brian, Benjamin. BA in English (magna cum laude), MusB (magna cum laude), SUNY, 1991; MusM (magna cum laude), U. of Louisville, Ky., 1993; DMA (magna cum laude), U. of Cin. College, 1996. Lectr. The U. of Wis., Platteville, 1996—98; asst. prof. UT State U., Logan, 1998—2000, Albion Coll., Mich., 2000—01, Angelo State U., San Angelo, 2001—. Author: (doctoral thesis) The Piano Works of Allen Sapp; a Performer's Guide to the Complete Miscellaneous Works. Recipient 1st prize, Ann. Piano Competition, Erie Pa. Music Tchrs. Assn., 1990. Office: Angelo State U Box 10906 ASU Station San Angelo TX 76904

CURTIN, GARY LEE, air force officer; b. Washington, Apr. 24, 1943; s. Thomas Francis and Lois Sarah (Hall) C.; m. Karen Marcella Reinmann, Nov. 26, 1966; children: Jennifer Lynne, Scott Marshall. BS in Aerospace Engring., U. Md., 1965; MS in Econs., S.D. State U., Ellsworth AFB, 1970. Commd. 2d lt. USAF, 1965, advanced through grades to maj. gen., 1992; launch officer 44th Strategic Missile Wing, Ellsworth AFB, 1965-70; intelligence officer Pacific Air Forces, Udorn, Thailand, Hickam AFB, Hawaii, 1971-75; internat. polit. affairs staff officer Hdqrs. USAF/Dep. Chief of Staff, Plans Pentagon, Washington, 1976-80; comdr. 400th Strategic Missile Squadron, Warren AFB, Wyo., 1980-82; dir. Intercontinental Ballistic Missile requirements Hdqrs. Strategic Air Command, Offutt AFB, Nebr., 1983-86; comdr. 90th Strategic Missile Wing, Warren AFB, Wyo., 1986-88; dir. comd. control Hdqrs. SAC, Offutt AFB, 1988-90; Joint Chiefs of Staff rep. to START negotiations Joint Staff, Geneva, 1990-91; dep. dir. for internat. negotiations Joint Staff/J-5/Pentagon, Washington, 1991-93; dir. of intelligence U. S. Strategic Command, Offutt AFB, Neb., 1993-95; dir. Def. Nuclear Agy./Def. Spl. Weapons Agy., Alexandria, Va., 1995-98; sr. v.p. for strategic devel. Def. Group Inc., 1998—. Mem. Air Force Assn., Tau Beta Pi, Omicron Delta Epsilon. Avocations: computers, travel, reading, model aircraft. Office: Defense Gp Inc 2034 Eisenhower Ave Ste 115 Alexandria VA 22314-4678 E-mail: curting@defensegp.com.

CURTIN, JEANNE B. lawyer; b. Bradford, Pa., Jan. 5, 1971; d. Roberta Elizabeth (Rusk) Clark. BS in Polit. Sci., Fla. State U., 1992, MBA cum laude, 1999, JD, 2002. Coord. Paint Your Heart Out, Tampa, 1993; publs. specialist Fla. Bankers Assn., Tallahassee, 1993; from legis. analyst to govt. affairs adminstr. Beer Industry Fla., Inc., Tallahassee, 1993—97; intern 1st Dist. Ct. Appeals, Tallahassee, 2001; sr. cabinet aide Sec. of State Katherine Harris, Tallahassee, 2001—02; assoc. Ard, Shirley & Hartman, P.A., 2002—. Mentor Wesson Elem. Sch., 2002—, Boys and Girls Clubs of Big Bend, 2003—. Adminstrv. editor: FSU Jour. Land Use and Environ. Law, 2001. Chair fundraising Tallahassee Fedn. Rep. Women, 1999, Meals on Wheels, 1999, 2002, Refuge House Capital Campaign, 1999; v.p. Women's Law Symposium, Fla. State U. Coll. Law, 1999-2000. Mem. Fla. State U. MBA Assn. (v.p. 1999), Golden Key Internat. Honor Soc., Beta Gamma Sigma, Phi Alpha Delta. Presbyterian. Avocations: fitness, current events, reading, travel.

CURTIN, LAWRENCE N. lawyer; b. Glen Ridge, N.J., Apr. 29, 1950; BS with honors, Fla. State U., 1972, JD with honors, 1976. Bar: Fla. 1976, U.S. Dist. Ct. (no. dist.) Fla., U.S. Ct. Appeals (4th, 5th, 11th and D.C. cirs.). Law clerk to Hon. William Stafford U.S. Dist. Ct. (no. dist.) Fla., 1976-78; mem. Holland & Knight, Tallahassee. Co-author: Surface Water Pollution Control, vol. 1, 1986-96. Mem. ABA, Fla. Bar (chmn. energy law com. 1983-84), Tallahassee Bar Assn., Beta Gamma Sigma, Sigma Iota Epsilon. Office: Holland & Knight LLP PO Drawer 810 315 S Calhoun St Ste 600 Tallahassee FL 32301-1897 E-mail: lcurtin@hklaw.com.

CURTIN, PHYLLIS, music educator, former dean, operatic singer; b. Clarksburg, W.Va. d. E. Vernon and Betty R. (Robinson) Smith; m. Eugene Cook, May 6, 1956 (dec.); 1 child, Claudia Madeleine. BA, Wellesley Coll., 1943. Prof. Yale Sch. Music, New Haven, 1974-83; master Branford Coll. Yale U., New Haven, 1979-83; dean Coll. Fine Arts, prof. music Boston U., 1983-91, prof. music, 1983—, dean emerita, prof. music, 1991—; artist-in-residence Tanglewood Music Ctr., Tanglewood, Lenox, Mass., 1965—. Former mem. Nat. Coun. on the Arts; named Amb. for the Arts; tchr. master classes U.S., Can., Beijing, Moscow. Made recital debut Town Hall, N.Y.C., 1950, opera debut, N.Y.C. Opera in U.S. premiere of The Trial, 1953, recitals throughout, U.S. and fgn. countries; soprano soloist leading symphony orchestras; performer, tchr., Aspen Mus. Festival, 1953-57, appeared as Cressida in, Walton's Troilus and Cressida in, N.Y. premiere, 1955; title role in Floyd's: Susannah, world premiere, Tallahassee, 1955; title role in: Darius Milhaud's Medea, U.S. premiere, Brandeis U., 1955; world premiere Floyd's opera Wuthering Heights, 1958, Floyd's Passion of Jonathan Wade, 1959, Flower and Hawk, 1971; U.S. Premier Peter Grimes, 1946, leading soprano: Vienna Staatsoper, 1960, 61; debut as Fiordiligi in Cosi Fan Tutte, Met. Opera Co., 1961; debut, La Scala Opera, Milan, 1962; U.S. premiere Benjamin Britten's War Requiem, with Boston Symphony, 1963; world premiere of Darius Milhaud's opera La Mére Coupable, Geneva, 1966; U.S. premiere Dimitri Shostakovitch's Symphony No. 14, with, Phila. Orch., 1971. Recipient Alumnae Achievement award Wellesley Coll., Nadia Boulanger Achievement award Longy Sch. Music, Letter of Distinction for Svc. to Am. Music, Am. Music Ctr. Home: 9 Seekonk Rd Great Barrington MA 01230-1558 E-mail: curtinphyllis@msn.com.

CURTIN, THOMAS LEE, ophthalmologist; b. Columbus, Ohio, Sept. 9, 1932; s. Leo Anthony and Mary Elizabeth (Burns) C.; m. Constance L. Sallman; children: Michael, Gregory, Thomas, Christopher. BS, Loyola U., L.A., 1954; MD, U. So. Calif., 1957; cert. navy flight surgeon, U.S. Naval Sch. Aerospace Med., 1959. Diplomate Am. Bd. Ophthalmology. Intern Ohio State U. Hosp., 1957-58; resident in ophthalmology U.S. Naval Hosp, San Diego, 1961-64; pvt. practice medicine specializing in ophthalmology Oceanside, Calif., 1967—. Mem. staff Tri City, Scripps Meml. hosps.; sci. adv. bd. So. Calif. Soc. Prevention Blindness, 1973-76; bd. dirs. North Coast Surgery Ctr., Oceanside, 1987-96; cons. in field. Trustee Carlsbad (Calif.) Unified Sch. Dist., 1975-83, pres., 1979, 82, 83; trustee Carlsbad Libr., 1990-99, pres., 1993, 98. Officer, MC, USN, 1958-67. Mem. AMA, Calif. Med. Assn., San Diego County Med. Soc., Am. Acad. Ophthalmology, Aerospace Med. Assn., San Diego Acad. Ophthalmology (pres. 1979), Calif. Assn. Ophthalmology (bd. dirs.), Carlsbad Rotary, El Camino Country Club. Repubican. Roman Catholic. Office: 3231 Waring Ct Ste S Oceanside CA 92056-4510

CURTIN, TIMOTHY JOHN, lawyer; b. Detroit, Sept. 21, 1942; s. James J. and Irma Alice (Sirotti) C.; m. B. Colleen Lindsey, July 11, 1964; children: Kathleen, Mary. BA, U. Mich., 1964, JD, 1967. Bar: Ohio 1968, Mich. 1970, U.S. Dist. Ct. (no. dist.) Ohio 1968, U.S. Dist. Ct. (we. dist.) Mich. 1970, U.S. Dist. Ct. (ea. dist.) Mich. 1980, U.S. Dist. Ct. Del. 1996, U.S. Dist. Ct. (no. dist.) Ill. 1999, U.S. Ct. Appeals (6th cir.) 1968. Assoc. Taft, Stettinius & Hollister, Cin., 1967-70, McCobb, Heaney & Van't Hof, Grand Rapids, Mich., 1970-72; ptnr. Schmidt, Howlett, Van't Hof, Snell & Vana, Grand Rapids, 1972-83, Varnum, Riddering, Schmidt & Howlett, Grand Rapids, 1983—. Contbr. articles to legal publs. Treas. Kent County Dem. Com., 1976-78, chmn. 3rd Dist. Dem. Com., 1993—. Mem. ABA, Mich. Bar Assn., Grand Rapids Bar Assn., Fed.. Bar Assn., Am. Bankruptcy Inst., Egypt Valley C.C. Roman Catholic. Avocations: travel, fishing. Office: Varnum Riddering Schmidt & Howlett Box 352 333 Bridge St SW Grand Rapids MI 49501-0352 E-mail: tjcurtin@varnumlaw.com.

CURTIS, ALBERT BRADLEY, II, financial planner, tax specialist; b. Oklahoma City, Dec. 17, 1957; s. William Clyde Jr. and Ava Rene (Sewell) C.; m. Patricia Rae Curtis; children: A. Bradley III, Patrick Troy, Michael Gabel, Lori Gabel. BS in Bus., Oklahoma City U., 1981. CPA, Okla. Cost acct. Macklangurg-Duncan Corp., Oklahoma City, 1976-81; sr. auditor, tax acct. Ephraim, Sureck & Miller, CPA's, Oklahoma City, 1981-83; tax mgr., mem. joint com. Ward Petroleum Corp. & Associated Entities, Enid, Okla., 1983-90, 93—; asst. treas. Dewey F. Bartlett Ctr., Inc., Oklahoma City, 1989—; prin. A. Bradley Curtis II, CPA, Oklahoma City, 1990—; asst. sec./treas. TNT Resources, Inc., 1990—. Mem. employee benefits adv. com. Ward Petroleum, 1997—. Fundraiser profl. div. United Way, Oklahoma City, 1981-83, 86-88; registrar Enid Voter Registration Campaign, 1986. Mem. AICPA, Ind. Petroleum Assn. Am. (tax com. 1995—), Okla. Soc. CPA's. Avocations: music, basketball, bowling, reading, family. Home: 7316 NW 118th St Oklahoma City OK 73162-1507 Office: 502 S Fillmore St Enid OK 73703-5703

CURTIS, ARNOLD BENNETT, retired lumber company executive; b. Astoria, Oreg., May 5, 1940; s. Arnold Bennett and Irja Virginia (Thompson) C.; m. Erica Katherine Mitchell, Dec. 23, 1985; children: Braden Thomas, Bryce Bennett. BS, Oreg. State U., 1962. Brewing chemist Gen. Brewing, San Francisco, 1962-67; v.p. N.W. Hardwoods, Inc., Portland, Oreg., 1967-71, pres., 1971-80, also bd. dirs.; pres. N.W. Hardwoods divsn. Weyerhauser Co., Federal Way, Wash., 1980-97, v.p. Hardwood Bus. Group, 1990-98; ret., 1998. Bd. dirs. Puyallup Internat. Inc., Weyerhaeuser New Zealand Ltd., Pine Solutions Australia; chmn. bd. dirs. Columbia Forest Products, 2001. Mem. adv. bd. Ctr. Retail and Bus. Market Strategy. Mem. Hardwood Mfrs. Assn. (dir., exec. com. 1985-95, pres. 1993). *When you commit yourself to an answer it's best to always tell the truth - then you never have to worry about remembering what you said.*

CURTIS, ARTHUR WILLIAM, otolaryngologist; b. Detroit, July 10, 1947; MD, Northwestern U., 1971. Diplomate Am. Bd. Otolaryngology. Intern Wesley Meml. Hosp., Chgo., 1971-72; resident in gen. surgery Northwestern Hosps., Chgo., 1972-73, resident in otolaryngology, 1973-76; attending staff Ill. Masonic Med. Ctr., Chgo., 1978—; asst. prof. clin. otolaryngology Northwestern U., Chgo., 1978-94. Mem. AMA, ARS, ACS, Am. Acad. Otolaryngology. Office: 104 S Michigan Ste 505 Chicago IL 60603-5957

CURTIS, CAROLINE A. S. community health and oncology nurse; b. Salem, Mass., June 7, 1941; d. Lawrence A. and Celestine L. (Wyman) Sager; m. John S. Curtis, July 31, 1981; children: Richard H. Smith, Craig A. Smith. Diploma, Lynn (Mass.) Hosp., 1962. Cert. oncology nurse. Head nurse, developer inpatient oncology unit Atlanticare Med. Ctr., Lynn, 1981-86; hospice nurse Greater Lynn Vis. Nurses Assn., Lynn, 1986-87; case manager Bon Secours Home Health, Englewood, Fla., 1988—; terminal care coord., oncology & pain cons., 1992—; terminal care coord. Bd. dirs., guest spkr. support group Am. Cancer Soc.; mem. pain mgmt. task force Bon Secours health Sys., 1996—. Clin. Jour. Oncology Nursing Soc.; editor: Oncology Home Health newsletter. Mem. Care of the Dying. Mem.: Hospice & Palliative Care Nurses Assn., Am. Soc. Pain Mgmt., Am. Pain Soc., Home Health Nursing Assn., Internat. Soc. Nurses in Cancer Care, Oncology Nursing Soc. Home: #201 6610 Gasparilla Pines Blvd Englewood FL 34224-7517 E-mail: chicknstu@ewol.com.

CURTIS, CAROLYN ANNE BERNARDETTE, nurse midwife; b. Balt., Oct. 21, 1954; d. Bernard and Annie Veronica (Butler) C. BSN, Cath. U., 1976, MSN, 1989. Cert. nurse midwife. Staff nurse George Washington Med. Ctr., Washington, 1976-78, Prince George's Med. Ctr., Cheverly, Md., 1985-86, 89; staff nurse midwife Booth Maternity Ctr., Phila., 1980-82; chief nurse midwife Cities in Schools, Washington, 1982-84; staff nurse midwife D.C. Gen. Hosp. Washington, 1989—94; dir. nurse midwifery svc. D.C. Health and Hosp. Pub Benefit Corp., 1998—2001; pub. health specialist U.S. agency for internat. devel., 2002—; instr. Howard Univ., 1998—. Nurse cons. Nursing Enterprises Washington, 1988, Am. Coll. of Nurse Midwives, 1997; guest lectr. Georgetown U., Washington, 1983-84, Howard U., 1989—; founder, pres. CARAB Corp., 1995—; faculty Frontier Sch. Midwifery and Family Nursing, 1995— Case Western Reserve U., Charles Drew U., U. Ala., 1995-96; childbirth educator D.C. Gen. Hosp., Washington, 1986—01; instr. Howard U., 1995— nurse midwifery subcom. Mayor's Adv. Bd. for Infant and Maternal Health Washington, 1982-83; adv. task force Licensure of Maternity Ctrs. in D.C. 1985. lect. Howard U., 1989-1994. Author: Early Postpartum Discharge, 1989 Adv. bd. Capitol Hill Crisis Pregnancy Ctr., Washington, 1985—; pulpit nominating com. New Life Presbyn. Ch., Waldorf, Md., 1991-92. Recipient Martha Comiskey award Cath. U., 1976. Mem. ANA, Assn. Women's Health Obstet. and Neonatal Nursing, D.C. Nurses Assn., Am. Coll. Nurse Midwives (chair nurse midwives of color com. 1991-94), v.p. 1998-2000, Sigma Theta Tau. Presbyterian. Avocations: singing, sewing, reading, dance, old movies Home: 3900 16th St NW Apt 439 Washington DC 20011-8310 Office: US Agency For International Development 1300 Pennsylvania Ave Washington DC 20003-2595

CURTIS, CHARLES EDWARD, Canadian government official; b. Winnipeg, Man., Can., July 28, 1931; s. Samuel and May (Goodison) C.; m. Hilda Marion Simpson, Oct. 30, 1954; 1 dau., Nancy Maude. C.A., U. Manitoba, 1955 Chartered acct. Dunwoody & Co., Winnipeg, 1949-54; chief assessor nat revenue, income tax bd. Province of N.B., Can., 1954-67; asst. dep. min. budget fin. and adminstrn. Province of Man., Winnipeg, 1967-75, dep. min., 1976-96 Past CEO Man. Energy Authority; acting CEO MTX subs. Man. Telephone Sys.; mem. Man. Hydro-Electric Bd.; bd.mem. Man. Commodity Exch.; mem investment coms. Superannuation Bd., WPG Found., Manitoba Mus. Man & Nature, Law Soc. Manitoba; fin. advisor Min. of Fin.; exec.-in-residence faculty of mgmt. U. Man.; bd. dirs. WPG Commodity Exch.; dir. Mizuao Corp. Bank (Can.). Fellow Can. Inst. Chartered Accts. (past chmn. pub. sector acctg. and audit standards com.); mem. Man. Inst. Chartered Accts. (pres. 1975-76), Law

Soc. of Man. (lay bencher), Rotary (hon. treas. 1974-2000), Man. Club. Home: 596 South Dr Winnipeg MB Canada R3T 0B1 Office: Provincial Govt Province MN 109-450 Broadway Ave Winnipeg MB Canada R3C 0V8

CURTIS, CHARLES W. mathematician, writer; b. Providence, Oct. 13, 1926; s. William W. and Ethel Whittlesey Curtis; m. Elizabeth Henn Curtis, June 17, 1950; children: Timothy, Daniel, Robert. BA, Bowdoin Coll., Brunswick, Maine, 1947; MA, Yale U., 1948, PhD, 1951. Instr. U. Wis., Madison, 1951—53, asst. prof. math, 1953—57, assoc. prof. math, 1957—61, prof. math, 1961—63, U. Oreg., Eugene, 1963—91, prof., head dept. math., 1970—73, prof. emeritus math, 1991—. Algebra editor Transactions of the Am. Math. Soc., Providence, 1998—. Co-author (with I. Reiner): Representation Theory of Finite Groups and Associative Algebras; author: Pioneers of Representation Theory: Frobenius, Burnside, Schur, and Brauer. With USNR, 1944—46. Mem.: London Math. Soc., Am. Math. Soc. (exec. com. 1975—77), Am. Math. Soc. (mem. of coun. 1974—77). Office: Dept Math U Oreg Eugene OR 97403 E-mail: cwc@darkwing.uoregon.edu.

CURTIS, DOLORES ROGERS, writer; b. Columbus, Ohio, Apr. 16, 1929; d. Charles William and Lillian Beatrice Rogers. Student, Ctrl. State U., Xenia, Ohio, 1956—57; B.Elem.Edn., Ohio State U., 1963; attended, John Carroll U., 1980. Bookkeeper Spiegel's, Chgo., Kronfeld's, Manhattan, NY; libr. U.S. Govt. Facility, Columbus; sec. to traveling entertainer, 1949—54; tchr. Columbus Pub. Schs., 1963—68, Cleve. Bd. Edn., 1968—93. Author: Rhyming Pretzels, 2002. Avocations: reading, art, playing piano and organ, writing.

CURTIS, DOUGLAS HOMER, small business owner; b. Jackson, Mich., July 19, 1934; s. Homer K. and Luella D. (Hall) C.; m. Jean A. Breaux; children: Rebecca, Linda, Colleen, Robert. BA, Park Coll., Parkville, Mo., 1956. With Gen. Electric Co., 1958-69, mgr. Boston region Gen. Electric Supply Co. div., 1967-69; v.p. fin. and adminstrn. internat. Data Corp., Boston, 1969; v.p. fin. Franklin Electric Co. Inc., Bluffton, Ind., 1969-80; pres. Curtis Assocs., Inc., Bluffton, 1980-82; pres., COO Satelco, Inc., San Antonio, 1983-84; v.p. adminstrn. Lyall Electric Co., Kendallville, Ind., 1984-86; pres., owner Flexible Personnel Group of Cos., Inc., Ft. Wayne, Ind., 1987-97, Nat. On-Site Pers., 1991-2001, HR America, 1992—, On-Site Med. Staffing, 2000—. Bd. dirs. Wabash Valley Mfg., Inc., Silver Lake, Ind.; pres. Wells County (Ind.) Hosp. Authority, 1974-75 Served to capt. USMCR, 1956-58. Mem. Nat. Assn. Securities Dealers (vicechmn. fin. 1980, chmn. fin. com. 1980), Fin. Execs. Inst. (chpt. dir. 1975) Home: 3206 Covington Lake Dr Fort Wayne IN 46804-2516 Office: 1833 Magnavox Way Fort Wayne IN 46804-1539

CURTIS, EDWARD JOSEPH, JR., gas industry executive, management consultant; b. Boston, May 26, 1942; s. Edward Joseph and Violet Ella (Upton) C.; m. Virginia Carolyn Fye, May 6, 1976; children: Jane Mercedes, Sherri Jean, Virginia Amy. BSChemE, Worcester Polytech., 1964, MSChemE, 1966. Engr. Cabot Corp., Boston, 1966-68; mgr. corp. devel. Distrigas Corp., Boston, 1968-72; pres. E.J. Curtis Assocs., Inc., York Harbor, Maine, 1972—. Pres. Pine Hill Assocs., Inc., Hollis, N.H., 1976-80; ptnr. ABC Mgmt. Systems, Bellingham, Wash., 1977-82; mng. ptnr. Essex Cons. Svcs., Boston, 1981-82; bd. dirs. SEMCO Energy Inc. Pres. York Harbor Neighborhood Assn., 1989-92. Mem. AIChE, Am. Gas Assn., New Eng. Gas Assn. (bd. dirs. 1988-91, 95-2001), Soc. Gas Lighting, Assn. Energy Engrs., Internat. Assn. Energy Economists,, Guild Gas Mgrs., York Golf and Tennis Club, Rosedale Golf and Country Club, Agamenticus Yacht Club, York Harbor Reading Rm., Theta Chi. Republican. Mem. Congl. Ch. Avocations: sailing, skiing, golf, computer science, music.

CURTIS, GEORGE WARREN, lawyer; b. Merrill, Wis., Sept. 24, 1936; s. George Gregory and Rose E. (Zimmerman) C.; m. Judith Olson, 1956 (div. 1966); m. Mary Pelman, 1967 (dec. 1973); children: George, Catherine Schmidt, Eric, Greg, Paul, David; m. Mary Ruth Kersztyn, Dec. 27, 1973 (div. 1999); children: Emily, Benjamin; m. Suzette Bigler Whyte, July 10, 1999; stepchildren: Erika, Evan. BA, U. Minn., 1959; JD, U. Wis., 1962. Bar: Wis. 1962, Fla. 1968. Assoc. Russell & Curtis, Merrill, 1962-68; ptnr. Nolan, Engler, Yakes & Curtis, Oshkosh, Wis., 1968-74, Curtis, MacKenzie, Haase & Brown, Oshkosh, 1974-83, Curtis, Wilde & Neal, Oshkosh, 1984-96, Curtis & Neal, Oshkosh, 1997-98; with Curtis Law Offices, 1999. Host TV program It's Your Environment. Host (TV show) It's Your Law. Mem. ATLA, Am. Coll. Trial Lawyers, Am. Bd. Trial Advocates (pres. Wis. chpt.), Wis. Acad. Trial Lawyers (bd. dirs. 1978-83, treas. 1984, sec. 1985, v.p. 1986, pres. 1987), Assn. Trial Lawyers Am. (bd. govs.), Internat. Soc. Barristers. Democrat. Avocations: conservationist, dog trainer. Home: 7361 Canary Rd Pickett WI 54964-9724 Office: Curtis Law Offices 2905 Universal St Oshkosh WI 54904-6341

CURTIS, JAMES RICHARD, flight engineer; b. Champaign, Ill., Feb. 2, 1930; s. John Wesley and Jessie May (Quackenbush) C.; m. Constance Ann Sticher, Jan. 10, 1954; children: Christie Lynn, James Richard Jr., Stephen Lawrence. Student, U. Ill., 1947-48. Profl. flight engr.; cert. airframe and power plant mechanic, comml. pilot. Plant mgr. Dean's Dairy, Champaign, 1947-50; aircraft mechanic USAF, 1950—55; draftsman C.S. Johnson Co., Champaign, 1955; aircraft mechanic Am. Airlines, Ft. Worth, 1955; flight engr. Chgo., 1956-95; trained flight crews Spantax Airlines, Madrid, 1966-69, Mid. East Airlines, Beirut, 1966-69; ret., 1995. Check airman, flight engring. instr. Am. Airlines, Chgo., 1964-86; examiner designee FAA, Chgo., 1966-67. Served as sgt. USAF, 1950-54. With USAF, 1950—54.

CURTIS, JAMES THEODORE, lawyer; b. Lowell, Mass., July 8, 1923; s. Theodore D. and Maria (Souliotis) Koutras; m. Kleanthe D. Dusopol, June 25, 1950; children: Madelon Mary, Theodore James, Stephanie Diane, Gregory Theodosius, James Theodore Jr. BA, U. Mich., 1948; JD, Harvard U., 1951; ScD (hon.), U. Mass., 1972. Bar: Mass. 1951. Assoc. Adams & Blinn, Boston, 1951-52; legal asst., asst. atty. gen. Mass., 1952-53; pvt. practice law, 1953-57; sr. ptnr. firm Goldman & Curtis, and predecessors, Lowell and Boston, 1957—. Elected mem. Lowell Charter Commn., 1969—71; del. Dem. Party State Convs., 1956—60; chmn. Greater Lowell Heart Fund, 1967—68; mem. adv. bd. Salvation Army, sec., 1956—58; mem. bd. Higher Edn. Msss., 1967—72; bd. dirs. U. Mass. Rsch. Found., Lowell, 1965—72, Merrimack Valley Health Planning Coun., 1969—72, trustee U. Mass., Lowell, 1965—72, chmn. bd., 1968—72. Spl. agt. 10th mt. divsn. U.S. Army, 1943—46. Decorated Knight Order Orthodox Crusade Holy Sepulcher. Mem.: ATLA, ABA, U. Mich. Alumni Assn., Harvard Law Sch. Alumni Assn., Am. Judicature Soc., Mass. Acad. Trial Lawyers, Middlesex Conty Bar Assn., Mass. Bar Assn., DAV, Lowell Hist. Soc., Harvard Club (Lowell, pres. 1969—71, bd. dirs.), Masons, Delta Epsilon Pi. Home: 111 Rivercliff Rd Lowell MA 01852-1471 Office: Goldman & Curtis PC 144 Merrimack St Ste 444 Lowell MA 01852-1789 E-mail: law@goldman-curtis.com.

CURTIS, JAMIE LEE, actress; b. L.A., Nov. 22, 1958; d. Tony Curtis and Janet Leigh; m. Christopher Guest; 1 child. Student, U. of the Pacific. Actress: (films) Halloween, 1978, The Fog, 1980, Prom Night, 1980, Terror Train, 1980, Halloween II, 1981, Road Games, 1981, Love Letters, 1983, Trading Places, 1983, Grandview USA, 1984, Adventures of Buckaroo Banzai, 1984, Perfect, 1985, Amazing Grace and Chuck, 1987, Un Homme Amoreux, 1987, Dominick and Eugene, 1988, A Fish Called Wanda, 1988, Blue Steel, 1990, Queens Logic, 1991, My Girl, 1991, Forever Young, 1992, Mother's Boys, 1994, My Girl 2, 1994, True Lies, 1994 (Golden Globe award Best Actress - Musical or Comedy), House Arrest, 1996, Ellen's Energy Adventure, 1996, Fierce Creatures, 1996, Halloween H2O, 1998, Homegrown, 1998, Virus, 1999, Drowning Mona, 2000, The Tailor of Panama, 2001, Daddy and Them, 2001, Rudolf the Red-Nosed Reindeer and the Island of Misfit Toys (voice), 2001, Halloween: Resurrection, 2002, Freaky Friday, 2003; (TV pilots) Callahan, She's in the Army Now, 1981, Tall Tales, (TV series) Operation Petticoat, 1977-78, Anything but Love, 1990-93, (TV movies) Death of a Centerfold: The Dorothy Stratten Story, 1981, Money on the Side, 1982, As Summers Die, 1982, The Heidi Chronicles, 1995, Nicolas' Gift, 1997; author: When I Was Little, 1993; dir.: Anything But Love, 1989. Office: Creative Artists Agy care Rick Kurtzman 9830 Wilshire Blvd Beverly Hills CA 90212-1804*

CURTIS, JESSE WILLIAM, JR., retired federal judge; b. San Bernardino, Calif., Dec. 26, 1905; s. Jesse William and Ida L. (Seymour) C.; m. Mildred F. Mort, Aug. 24, 1930; children: Suzanne, Jesse W., Clyde Hamilton, Christopher Cowles. AB, U. Redlands, 1928, LLD, 1973; JD, Harvard Law Sch., 1931. Bar: Calif. 1931. Pvt. practice, 1931-35; mem. firms Guthrie & Curtis, San Bernardino, 1935-40, Curtis & Curtis, 1946-50, Curtis, Knauf, Henry & Farrell, 1950-53; judge Superior Ct. of Calif., 1953-62, U.S. Dist. Ct. (cen. dist.) Calif., 1962-90, ret., 1990; with Jud. Arbitration and Mediations Svc., L.A., 1990-95. Rep. dist. ct. on Jud. Council U.S., 1972-74. Chmn. San Bernardino Sch. Bd., 1942-46, mem., 1946-49; mem. Del Rosa Bd. Edn., 1950-53; chmn. San Bernardino County Heart Fund; dir., past pres. YMCA; bd. dirs. GoodWill Industries, Crippled Children's Soc., Arrowhead United Fund; adv. bd. Cmty. Hosp. Mem. ABA, Calif. State Bar, Orange County Bar Assn., Am. Judicature Soc., Am. Law Inst., Newport Harbor Yacht Club, Phi Delta Phi. Democrat. Congregationalist. Home: Apt Sunridge 211 Regents Point Irvine CA 92612-8615 E-mail: judgecurtis@aol.com.

CURTIS, JOHN JOSEPH, lawyer; b. Fairmont, W.Va., Nov. 23, 1942; s. John Joseph and Marie Francis (Christopher) C.; m. Shirley Ann Slater, Oct. 15, 1971 (div. June 1993); children: Christopher, Kevin. AB, U. W.Va., 1964, JD, 1967. Bar: W.Va. 1967, Ill. 1972, Calif. 1979. Pvt. practice law, South Charleston, W.Va., 1967-68; chief counsel, asst. dir. W.Va. Tax Dept., Charleston, 1968-71; tax atty. Sears, Roebuck & Co., Chgo., 1971-73; chief tax counsel, dir. taxes Pacific Lighting, L.A., 1973-87; ptnr. Baker & Hostetler, L.A., 1987-93, Law Offices of John Curtis, L.A., 1994—. Com. mem. Pasadena Tournament Roses, 1978-93. Lt. comdr. USNR, 1968-80. Mem. ABA, L.A. County Bar Assn. (chmn. com. 1989), Calif. Bar Assn., Inst. Property Tax, So. Calif.Tax Found. (pres. 1990-96), L.A. Taxpayers Assn. (pres. 1990-95), Calif. Taxpayers Assn. (pres. 1987-88). Avocations: skiing, scuba, fishing. Office: 2 Arado Rancho Santa Margarita CA 92688-2749 E-mail: jcurtis@aol.com.

CURTIS, JOHN WALTER, investment banker; b. Cleveland, Tenn., July 7, 1948; s. Wesley James and Irene Helen (Kinnaird) C.; m. Margaret Ann Sarkela, Aug. 20, 1977; children: Sarah Esther, John Viljo. AB, Harvard U., 1970, JD, 1976; BA, MA, Oxford (Eng.) U., 1973. Assoc. atty. Sullivan & Crowwell, N.Y.C., 1976-82; assoc. gen. counsel Goldman, Sachs Co., N.Y.C., 1983-86, v.p. investment banking divsn., 1986-97, mng. dir. investment banking divsn., 1997-99, dir. global compliance, 1999—2002, mng. dir. legal, 2002—. 1st lt. U.S. Army, 1970-76. Episcopalian. Avocation: golf. Home: 21 Ridgebrook Rd Greenwich CT 06830-4747 Office: One New York Plaza New York NY 10004

CURTIS, JOYCELYN, social worker; b. Mobile, Ala., Nov. 2, 1956; d. Albert Earl and Barbara Faye (Maye) Autry; m. Wayne Curtis, June 19, 1982; 1 child, Imari Solomon Curtis. BA in Polit. Sci., U. South Ala., 1979; postgrad., Clark Atlanta U.; PhD, Clark Atlanta (Ga.) U., 2002. Credit investigator Sears, Mobile, 1978-80, catalog sales rep. Carlsbad, Calif., 1982-83; social worker Dept. Human Resources State of Ala., Mobile, 1980-82; counselor, facilitator, intern Ga. Coun. on Child Abuse, Atlanta, 1993; counselor First Steps, Atlanta, 1993—98; intern Families First, Atlanta, 1994—98; Rapha therapist, 1995—98; contract counselor AT&T, 1998—2000; with Keystone Counseling, 2003—; program developer Nextstep Directions, 2003—. Poll taker U. South Ala., 1977; nursing home ministry coord., Portsmouth, Va., 1989-91. Mem. NASW, Nat. Assn. Black Social Workers. Baptist. Avocations: writing children's stories, making flower arrangements, walking, bicycling, baking. Home: 2940 Forest Highlands Dr Marietta GA 30062-6675 Office: 275 Country Club Drive Stockbridge GA 30281 E-mail: u2day@yahoo.com.

CURTIS, KAREN HAYNES, lawyer; b. Laurel, Miss., Sept. 15, 1951; d. John Travis Haynes Jr. and Jeannine Burkett Tanner; children: Laurel Elizabeth Cornell, Jaime Rodriguez Cornell. BS in Biology, Tulane U., 1973; JD summa cum laude, Nova Law Ctr., 1978. Bar: Fla. 1978; U.S. Ct Appeals (5th cir.) Fla. 1980, U.S. Ct. Appeals (11th cir.) Fla. 1981; U.S. Dist Ct. (so. dist.) Fla. 1986, U.S. Dist Ct. (mid. dist.) Fla., 1986; U.S. Supreme Ct. 1994. Law clk. Steel, Hector & Davis, Miami, Fla., 1978; law clk. to Judge William M. Hoeveler U.S. Dist. Ct., Miami, Fla., 1978-80; assoc. Shutts & Bowen, Miami, Fla., 1980-84, ptnr., 1985-95; founding ptnr., pres. Gallwey Gillman Curtis & Vento, P.A., Miami, Fla., 1995—. Treas., dir. Ch. by the Sea, 1994—. Listed in Leading Fla. Attys. for Civil Appellate Law. Mem. ABA, Fla. Assn. Women Lawyers, Fed. Bar Assn., Dade County Bar Assn. (ins. law com. 1990-91, banking and corp. litigation com. 1992-93, appellate ct. com. 1991—) Fla. Bar (appellate ct. rules com. 1993-2002, grievance com. 1988-91), Fla. Bar Bd. of Legal Specialization and Edn.(cert. in appellate practice), Acad. Fla. Trial Lawyers, Assn. Trial Lawyers of Am., Supreme Ct. Historical Soc., Am. Judiciary Soc. United Ch. of Christ. Avocations: reading, piano, computer. Home: 18720 SW 33rd Court Miramar FL 33029 Office: Gallwey Gillman Curtis & Vento PA 200 SE 1st St Ste 1100 Miami FL 33131-1912

CURTIS, LEGRAND R., JR., lawyer; b. Ogden, Utah, Aug. 1, 1952; BA summa cum laude, Brigham Young U., 1975; JD cum laude, U. Mich., 1978. Bar: Utah 1978, U.S. Ct. Appeals (10th cir.) 1985, U.S. Ct. Claims 1986, U.S. Supreme Ct. 1987. Ptnr. Manning, Curtis Bradshaw & Bednar, LLC, Salt Lake City, 1997—. Mem. Utah State Bar, Salt Lake County Bar Assn. Office: Manning Curtis Bradshaw & Bednar LLC 10 Exchange Pl Ste 300 Salt Lake City UT 84111-5104

CURTIS, LINDA S, vocal instructor; b. Chgo., Ill. d. Arthur and Suzanne Sullivan; m. Samuel G Curtis, May 15, 1976; children: Patrick, Molly, William. BA, Wells Coll., 1970; MusM, Northwestern U., 1971. Music instr. Colo. Rocky Mountain Sch., Carbondale, 1972—75; voice instr. Colo. Mountain Coll., Glenwood Springs, 1974—75; pvt. voice instr. Music Arts Ctr., Bozeman, Mont., 1984—; adj. prof. of voice Mont. State U., Bozeman, Mont., 2000—02; artistic dir. Intermountain Opera, Bozeman, Mont., 2000—. Bd. of dirs., pres. of bd. Intermountain Opera, Bozeman, Mont., 1995—97. Mem.: Music Teachers Nat. Assn., Nat. Assn. of Teachers Singing.

CURTIS, MARK ALLEN, engineering educator, author, consultant; b. Battle Creek, Mich., Aug. 2, 1951; s. Lawrence Arthur and Marlene Fay (Furlott) C.; m. Margaret Elizabeth Hustwick, Aug. 14, 1971; children: Aaron, Leah. AAS, Kellogg C.C., 1971; BS, Western Mich. U., 1977, MA, 1982, EdD, 1992. Cert. vocat. tchr., Mich. Tool designer Eaton Corp., Marshall, Mich., 1971-75, prodn. supr., 1977-78, process engr., 1975-77, 78-80, design supr. Galesburg, Mich., 1980-81; asst. prof. Ferris State U., Big Rapids, Mich., 1981-85, assoc. prof., 1985-92, prof., 1992-96, interim dean Coll. Tech., 1996-98; v.p. engring. Millennium Plastics Technologies LLC, El Paso, Tex., 1998-99; dean Coll. Tech. and Applied Scis., asst. provost No. Mich. U., Marquette, 1999—. Author: Tool Design for Manufacturing, 1986, Process Planning, 1988, Handbook of Dimensional Measurement, 3d edit., 1994, Dimensional Management, 2002. Recipient Disting. Faculty award Mich. Assn. Governing Bd. of State Univs., 1993. Mem.: Soc. Mfg. Engrs. (sr.). Episcopalian. Avocations: stained glass, golf, fishing. Home: 1540 W Ridge #4 Marquette MI 49855 Office: No Mich U 101A Jacobetti Ctr 1401 Presque Isle Marquette MI 49855 E-mail: mcurtis@nmu.edu.

CURTIS, MARVIN VERNELL, music educator; b. Chgo., Feb. 12, 1951; s. John Wesley Jr. and Dorothy Marva Curtis. MusB, North Park Coll., 1972; MA, Presbyn. Sch. Christian Edn., 1974; EdD, U. of Pacific, 1990. Asst. prof. music Calif. State U.-Stanislaus, Turlock, 1988-91; assoc. prof. music Va. Union U., Richmond, 1991-94, Lane Coll., Jackson, Tenn., 1995-96, Fayetteville (N.C.) State U., 1996—2002, prof., chmn. dept. performing and fine arts, 2002—. Music advisor In Harmony series Richmond Symphony, 1996-99. Composer City on the Hill written for 1st Inauguration of Pres. Clinton, 1993; contbr. articles to profl. jours. Bd. dirs. Fayetteville Symphony, 1998—, 1st v.p., 2001; bd. dirs. Cmty. Concert Series, 1998-99. Recipient Key to City, Savannah, Ga., 1992, Medallion of City of Richmond, Mayor's Office, 1993, Outstanding Rsch. award Nat. Assn. for Equal Opportunity, 1992, Edn. and Cultural Devel. award Cumberland Regional Improvement Corp., 2000, Noah Ryder Composer award Norfolk State U. Alumni Assn., 2000. Mem. Music Educators Nat. Conf., Nat. Coun. for Black Studies, Am. Choral Dirs. Assn. Democrat. Home: 4911 Cooper Rd Fayetteville NC 28311-0823 E-mail: mcurtis@uncfsu.edu.

CURTIS, MARY CECELIA, journalist; b. Balt. d. Thomas Eugene and Evelyn Cecelia (Thomas) C.; m. Martin F. Olsen, Oct. 16, 1976; 1 child, Zane Anthony Curtis-Olsen. BA, Fordham U., N.Y.C. Copy editor, wire editor The Ariz. Daily Star, Tucson, 1981-83; asst. features editor, travel editor The Balt. Sun, 1983-84, features editor, arts and entertainment, 1984-85; copy editor, culture and style The N.Y. Times, N.Y.C., 1985-88, asst. editor The Living Arts, 1988-90, editor The Living Arts, 1990-92, editor The Home Sect., 1992-93, edn. life editor, 1993-94; features editor, columnist The Charlotte Observer, 1994—. Editor The Maynard Inst. Editing Program for Minority Journalists, U. Ariz., 1981; Cmty. Journalism Wkshp., Poynter Inst., St. Petersburg, 1996. Recipient Excellence award Internat. Assn. Bus. Comms., 1979, 1st place for columns N.C. Press Assn., 2000. Mem.: Soc. Profl. Journalists (Green Eyeshade award 2002), Am. Asn. Sunday and Feature Editors (2d Pl. Commentary award 1995, 3d Pl Commentary award 2001), Nat. Assn. Black Journalists. Avocations: reading, theater, music, fitness. Office: The Charlotte Observer 600 S Tryon St Charlotte NC 28202-1842 E-mail: mcurtis@charlotteobserver.com.

CURTIS, MARY E. (MARY CURTIS HOROWITZ), publishing company executive; d. Lloyd E. and Jean Curtis; m. Irving Louis Horowitz, Oct. 30, 1979 AB cum laude, Washington U., St. Louis, 1968. Editl. dir. Transaction Pubs., New Brunswick, N.J., 1968-74, exec. v.p., 1987-97, pres., 1997—, chmn. bd. dirs., 1994-97; editor in chief Praeger Pubs. subs. CBS Ednl. Pub., N.Y.C., 1974-79; v.p., pub. periodicals John Wiley and Sons, N.Y.C., 1979-87; v.p. Scripta Techica subs. John Wiley and Sons, Washington, 1984-87; mem. mgmt. bd. MIT Press, 1998—; vice chair, trustee Horowitz Found. for Social Policy, 1998—. Chair adv. com. Serials Industry Systems, 1985-88; dir. Transaction Pubs. (U.K.) Ltd.; mem. external adv. bd. MIT Press, 1998—; lectr. in field. Contbr. articles to profl. jours. Mem. Soc. Scholarly Pubs. (bd. dirs. 1984-88), Assn. Am. Pubs. (Freedom to Read com.). Jewish. E-mail: mcurtis@transactionpub.com.

CURTIS, PAUL JAMES, mime director; b. Boston, Aug. 29, 1927; s. Lawrence D. and Madeleine Maria (Schwager) C. Studied directing with Erwin Piscator, New Sch. for Social Rsch., 1947-49. Dir. Deal Conservatory Theatre, 1948; founder, dir. Am. Mime Theatre, N.Y.C., 1952—; founder Am. Mime, Inc., N.Y.C., 1970—, Internat. Mimes & Pantomimists, 1972-74; chmn. mime dept. Am. Acad. Dramatic Arts, N.Y.C., 1956-71; sr. lectr. Cornell U., Ithaca, N.Y., 1969-89. Instr. mime Bennington (Vt.) Coll., Jacob's Pillow Dance Festival, Mass., Ohio U., Austin Coll., Goodman Sch. Drama, Chgo., Pace U., N.Y.C., Hunter Coll., N.Y.C., Met. Opera Ballet Sch., N.Y.C., New Sch. Social Rsch., N.Y.C., Gene Frankel Theatre Workshop, N.Y.C., Guggenheim Mus., N.Y.C., Johns Hopkins U., Balt., Am. Conservatory Theatre, San Francisco, Circle in Sq. Theatre Sch., N.Y.C., Sarah Lawrence Coll., N.Y., D'Youville Coll., N.Y., Lincoln Sch., Calif., Fairleigh Dickinson U., N.J., Stockton State Coll. N.J., Rutgers U., New Brunswick, N.J., The Leonardo's, Paris; Am. mime course established at Salle Pleyel, Paris, 1998, 59 Centre d'Art, Paris workshops, 2000. TV appearances NBC Exploring the Performing Arts, 1963, NBC Profile on the Arts, 1966, Nippon TV Japan, 1970, NBC To Tell The Truth, 1973, NY Live Cable TV, 1974, NBC Today Show, 1975, WNYC-TV, 1975, 1978, ABC Kids Are People Too, 1978, WNEW Broadway Extra, 1978, ABC The Last Word, 1983, TV appearance Documentary Film on the American Mime Theatre, 2003; actor: (textbook) American Mime, the Medium, 1952; author: (plays) The Pinball Machine, 1953, Fate, 1953, The Tell Tale Heart, 1953, Escapade, 1953, The Demon Lover, 1953, Of Identity, 1953, Once Upon An Island, 1954, Monolotry, 1954, The Triple Goddess, 1954, The Western, 1954, Improvisation, 1955, Presentation, 1955, Eden, 1956, Abstraction, 1956, Commedia, 1956, Dreams I, 1958, The Scarecrow, 1962, Dreams II, 1962, The Godstuff, 1962, The Lovers, 1963, Birds, 1965, Female, 1967, Light, 1968, Hurly-Burly, 1969, Evolution, 1973, Sludge, 1974, Six, 1975, Work in Progress, 1976, Abstraction, 1977, The Unitaur, 1982, Peepshow, 1988, Pageant, 1989, Music Box, 1991, Couplings, 1999. With USN, 1944—46. Mem. AEA, AFTRA, Nat. Movement Theatre Assn. Avocation: antique collector. Office: Am Mime Theatre 61 4th Ave Fl 2 New York NY 10003-5204 E-mail: Mime@Americanmime.org.

CURTIS, PAULA ANNETTE, elementary and secondary education educator; b. Natrona Heights, Pa., Apr. 16, 1953; d. Stephen John and Josephine Kathleen (Killian) C. BS in Edn., Geneva Coll., 1974; postgrad., U. Vt., 1975, Pa. State U., New Kensington, 1978. Cert. religious edn. tchr., Pitts. Diocese. Tchr. Transfiguration Sch., Russellton, Pa., 1979—, dir. religious edn., 1995-98; tchr. continuing edn. C.C. of Allegheny County, Pitts., 1992—, Pa. State U., New Kensington, 1988—; tchr. O'Mara Driving Sch., Lower Burrell, Pa., 1976—, Lenape Votech., 1990—; CCD tchr. Transfiguration Sch., Russellton, 1995-97, head tchr., head fine arts dept., 1995-97. Chmn. vision and values in Pitts. Diocese, Transfiguration Sch., 1980-97; CCD tchr. St. Clement Parish, Tarentum, Pa., 1986-92, dir. religious edn., 1987-92; dir. religious edn. St. Joseph Parish, Natrona, Pa., 1992-93; product tester Nat. Family Opinion Poll, 1987—; model Van Enterprises, Cranberry, Pa., 1989-92; tchr. driver edn. Plum (Pa.) Sr. H.S., 1996-98; Act 48 presenter for Penn Hills Sch. Dist. and Pitts. Diocesan Schs., 2002—; freelance model, Fashion Bug, 1998—. Vol. Help Beautify the Cmty. with Art, Russellton. Mem. Nat. Cath. Educators Assn., Nat. English Tchrs. Assn. Democrat. Roman Catholic. Avocations: craft designs, needle work, collecting reptiles, collecting and breeding tropical birds, breeding shih-tzus. Home: 211 W 9th Ave Tarentum PA 15084-1241 Office: Transfiguration Sch CCD Office 100 Mckrell Rd Russellton PA 15076-1100

CURTIS, PETER ANDREW, music educator, musician; b. Montreal, Que., Can., Apr. 24, 1970; s. Gerald Morris and Susan Caren Curtis. MusB magna cum laude, Berklee Coll. Music, 1992; MusM, Yale U., 1995; postgrad., Ind. U., 1997—. Cert. tchr. Suzuki Teachers Assn. Music instr. Temple Beth Elohim, Wellesey, Mass., 1992—93; guitar instr. Suzuki Inst. of Boston, 1992—93; guitar/music instr. Appel Farm Arts and Music Ctr., Elmer, NJ, 1995; grad. asst./guitar U. S.C., Columbia, 1996—97; assoc. instr./guitar instr. Ind. U., Bloomington, 1997—2000; adj. prof. guitar Ind. State U., Terre Haute, 2000—01; guitar/music instr. Riverside (Calif.) C.C., 2001—. Performer Carnegie Hall, The Jazz Bakery; presenter confs. in field; leader Peter Curits Trio. Mem. (jazz group) The Din of Inequity, singer, songwriter, guitarist Stubborn Blood (CITR Shindig winner, 1987), guitarist, bassist (rock group) The Overeducated Jewish Rock Machine, performed with (klezmer group) Drei Kohp. Vol. feeding the homeless Yale U. Hillel, New Haven, 1994. Scholar Andres Segovia Meml. scholar, Banff Ctr. for the Arts, 1995, Jeanne and Peter Lougheed scholar, 1995. Mem.: Calif. Tchrs. Assn. Jewish. Avocations: reading, travel.

CURTIS, PHILIP KERRY, real estate developer, real estate company executive; b. Mineola, New York, Nov. 6, 1945; s. William Kerry and Cherry (Smith) C.; m. Janet (McDowell), Sept. 9, 1970; 1 child, Kerry Bowen. BA, Dartmouth Coll., 1968; JD, Harvard Law Sch., 1971; MBA, Harvard U., 1974. Bar: N.Y., 1971; Ga., 1976. Assoc. White and Case, N.Y.C., 1971-72, Hansell and Post, Atlanta, 1975-76; counsel, asst. to pres. Wiggins and Assoc., Atlanta, 1976-82; exec. v.p. Coers, Steinemann, and Co., Atlanta, 1982-84; exec. v.p., ptnr. Western Devel. South East, Atlanta, 1984-87; ptnr., sr. v.p. Charter Properties, Inc., Atlanta, 1987-93; exec. v.p. JDN Realty Corp., Atlanta, 1994-96; pres. Habersham Ptnr., Atlanta, 1996—; ptnr. Matteson Ptnr., Atlanta, 2002—. Vis. lectr. real estate, Kennesaw Coll., Grad. Bus. Sch., 1992-93. Elder Peachtree Presbyn. Ch., Atlanta, 1983-86; dir. Met. Arts Found., Atlanta, 1983-87; 1st lt., U.S. Army, 1971-78. Mem. German Club (pres. 1986); Harvard Club of Ga.; Cherokee Town and Country Club; Buckhead Rotary; Dartmouth Club of Ga. (pres. 1982-84), Club of the Yr. 1984; Harvard Bus. Sch. Club of Atlanta (pres. 1982-83); Atlanta Forum; The Ravinia Club; SAR; Sigma Chi Club Atlanta (bd. dir. 1985-86); Old Guard Republican. Home: 3111 Arden Rd N W Atlanta GA 30305-1916 Office: Two Ravinia Dr Ste 310 Atlanta GA 30346

CURTIS, R. CRAIG, political science educator; b. Meridian, Miss., July 8, 1960; s. D.L. and Jeanne Claire Curtis; m. Leah E. Adams, May 16, 1982; children: Anna Chimene, Galen Russell. BA, Millsaps Coll., 1982; JD, U. of Pacific, 1985; MA, Wash. State U., 1987, PhD, 1991. Rsch. asst. McGeorge Sch. Law, Sacramento, Calif., 1983-85; tchg. asst. Wash. State U., Pullman, 1986-90; local govt. specialist Wash. State Coop. Ext., Pullman, 1990-91; asst. prof. polit. sci. Bradley U., Peoria, Ill., 1991-97, dir. adminstrn. criminal justice program, 1996-99, assoc. prof. polit. sci., 1997—. Mem. ASPA (pres. chpt. 1995-96, 98-99), Am. Polit. Sci. Assn., Acad. Criminal Justice Scis., Midwest Polit. Sci. Assn. Avocations: folk music, tennis, home brewing. Office: Bradley Univ Dept Polit Sci 1501 W Bradley Ave Peoria IL 61625-0003 E-mail: rcc@bradley.edu.

CURTIS, RICHARD EARL, former naval officer, former company executive, business consultant; b. Beckley, W.Va., Nov. 17, 1930; s. Herbert Earl and Lizzie Belle (Ramsey) C.; m. Martha Rhodes Lancaster, June 6, 1953; children:

Steven Andrew, Richard Earl, Elizabeth Graham. BSEE, U.S. Naval Acad., 1953; MBA, Harvard U., 1961; grad., Indsl. Coll. Armed Forces, 1972. Commd. ensign U.S. Navy, 1953, advanced through grades to rear adm., 1980; logistics mgr. Strategic Systems Project Office, Washington, 1972-76; comdg. officer Naval Supply Center, Charleston, S.C., 1976-78; asst. for logistic project Naval Material Command, Washington, 1978-79; dep. dir. policy, programs, projects and systems Naval Supply System Command, Washington, 1979-81, vice comdr., 1981-82, ret., 1982; v.p. U.S. Elevator Co., Spring Valley, Calif., 1982-85; v.p. adminstrn. Cubic Corp., San Diego, 1985-86. Leader, dist. commr. Boy Scouts Am. Decorated Legion of Merit, Bronze Star with combat V, Navy-Marine Corps medal for heroism. Republican. Episcopalian. Home: 5130 Choc Cliff Dr Bonita CA 91902-2538

CURTIS, ROBERT KERN, lawyer, physics educator; b. N.Y.C., June 11, 1940; s. Sargent Jackson and Phyllis (Kern) C.; m. Beverley Meadows, Dec. 26, 1971; 1 child, Phyllis. AB in Physics, Fordham U., 1964, MS in Edn., 1970; Lic. in Philosophy, Woodstock Coll., 1965; JD, Seton Hall U., 1985. Tchr. Bklyn. Prep. Sch., 1965-67; dir. Jesuit Sem. and Mission Bur., N.Y.C., 1967; tchr. Xavier High Sch., N.Y.C., 1967-69, Hackensack (N.J.) High Sch., 1969—; sole practice Hackensack, 1985—. Tchr. law Hackensack Evening Sch., 1980, law for tchrs. Hackensack Pub. Schs., 1986. Mem. Am. Phys. Soc., Assn. Trial Lawyers Am., ACLU, N.Y. Acad. Scis., Am. Assn. Physics Tchrs., Math. Assn. Am., Hackensack Edn. Assn. (pres. 1979-81, 97—). Home and Office: 287 Hamilton Pl Hackensack NJ 07601-3614 E-mail: rkc@rcurtis.com.

CURTIS, SUSAN GRACE, lawyer; b. N.Y.C., Apr. 24, 1950; d. Henry G. and Helen Curtis; m. Robert Y. Pelgrift Jr., June 8, 1974; children: Robert III, Henry, Victoria. A.B., Yale Coll., 1971; J.D., Columbia U., 1974. Bar: N.Y. 1975, U.S. Ct. Appeals (2d cir.) 1975. With Lord, Day & Lord, N.Y.C., 1974-79, Shearman & Sterling, N.Y.C., 1979-84, Proskauer, Rose, 1984-87, 93-98; ptnr. Epstein, Becker & Green, N.Y.C., 1987-93; of counsel White & Case, N.Y.C., 1998—; adj. asst. prof. law NYU Sch. Law, 1995-98; mem. faculty Practising Law Inst., 1990—. Contbg. editor: Jour. Pension Planning and Compliance, 1991—; mem. editl. adv. bd. BNA Pension Reporter, 1993—, tax mgmt. adv. bd., 1993—; contbr. articles to profl. jours. Mem. ABA (com. employee benefits), N.Y. State Bar Assn. (com. employee benefits), Assn. Bar City N.Y. (sec. com. employee benefits 1987-90). Office: White & Case Bldg LL1155 Avenue Of The Americas New York NY 10036-2787

CURTIS, SUSAN VIRGINIA, social worker; b. N.Y.C., Apr. 19, 1943; m. Robert Maxwell Curtis, July 30, 1967; children: Benjamin William, Rebecca Elizabeth. BA in Lit., William Smith Coll., Geneva, N.Y., 1965; M of Social Scis. Adminstrn., Case Western Res. U., 1980; student Anglo-Irish Lit., Trinity Coll., Dublin, Ireland, 1964; grad. in Gestalt Therapy, Gestalt Inst. Cleve., 1983. Lic. social worker, Ohio; cert. social worker; diplomate Am. Bd. Social Work. Grant asst. Wenner Gren Found., N.Y.C., 1965-66; editorial asst. Edn. and World Affairs, N.Y.C., 1966-67; tchr. Birch Wathen Sch., N.Y.C., 1967-68; adminstrv. asst. Columbia U. Tchrs. Coll., N.Y.C., 1968-69; with VISTA, OEO, Dahlonega, Ga., 1969-70; tchr. Tng. in Lamaze Childbirth, Chesterland, Ohio, 1973-76; social worker Lake County Mental Health Ctr., Mentor, Ohio, 1980-88; pvt. practice Highland Counseling Svcs., Inc., Cleve., 1987—. Owner, ptnr. Highland Counseling Svcs. Inc. Bd. mem. Greater Cleve. Audubon Soc. Mem. NASW, Acad. Cert. Social Workers (diplomate), Stepfamily Assn. Am., Amnesty Internat., Nat. Wildlife Fedn. Avocation: walking. Office: Highland Counseling Svcs 5564 Wilson Mills Rd # 201 Cleveland OH 44143-3265 E-mail: scurtis@highlandcounseling.com., svcurtis@adelphia.net.

CURTIS, THOMAS H. physicist; b. Detroit, July 26, 1941; s. Henry Lambton Curtis and Alice Caren Hasbrook; m. Christine Cassaday Curtis (div.); children: Cathleen, Caren; m. Audrey Jane Kames, Apr. 8, 1979; children: Andrew, Steven. BA in Math., Kenyon Coll., 1963; MS in Physics, Yale U., 1965, PhD in Physics, 1968. Post doctoral fellow U. of Calif. Law. Rad. Lab., Livermore, 1968—70; mem. tech. staff Bell Labs, Holmdel, NJ, 1970—78, supr., 1978—84; dept. head A T & T Labs, Holmdel, 1984—96, devel. dir. Florham Pk., NJ, 1996—99; pres./CEO Ultra Fast Optical Sys., Princeton, 2000—03; pres. Kambrook Tech. Assoc., Holmdel, 2003—. Dir. Ultra Fast Optical Sys., Princeton, 2001—02; cons. Johns Hopkins U., Applied Physics Lab., 2002—03; vis. fellow Princeton U., 2003. Author: (rsch. papers) Phys. Rev., Bell Labs Tech. Jour., IEEE Jours., Jour. Acoustical Soc. of Am. Mem.: NY Acad. of Sci., Optical Soc., Am. Phys. Soc., IEEE, Atlantic Highlands Yacht Club. Avocations: sailing, skiing, bagpipes, chess, reading. Home: 5 Canyon Run Rd Holmdel NJ 07733

CURTIS, VERNA POLK, reading educator; b. Jackson, Miss., Mar. 20, 1940; d. William Grady Polk and Mary Ann Gray; m. Edward L. Curtis, Apr. 12, 1968; 1 child, Vera. BS cum laude, Jackson State U., 1962; MEd, Boston U., 1968; EdS, Jackson State U., 1987; postgrad., Cornell U.; EdD, Jackson State U., 1991. Reading specialist/reading facilitator Jackson Pub. Schs., tchr.; reading instr. Jackson State U. Instr., adj. prof. edn., advisor for second chance careers program Tougaloo Coll. Recipient fellowship. Mem. ASCD, Jackson Area Reading, IRA, MSCD, Miss. Reading Assn. Home: 114 Waylawn Ct Jackson MS 39206-2305

CURTIS, WILLIAM EDGAR, conductor, composer; b. Aberdeen, Scotland, Mar. 11, 1914; came to U.S., 1940; s. William Alexander and Florence (Malseed) C.; m. Doris Gray Schauffler, June 20, 1942; children: Michael Gray, Julie Malseed Curtis, Annie Curtis Chittenden. MusB magna cum laude, U. Edinburgh, 1935, MA magna cum laude, 1936; studies with Rudolph Serkin, Adolph and Fritz Busch, 1936-39; postgrad., Curtis Inst., 1940-42, Cleve. Orch. Condrs. Workshop, 1956. Condr., founder Curtis String Orch., Boston, 1942-44; mem. faculty Boston Conservatory and Boston U., 1946-48; music dir., condr. Albany (N.Y.) Symphony Orch., 1948-67; dir. music, chmn. dept art, music, drama Union Coll., Schenectady, N.Y., 1955-72; founder, condr. Northeastern N.Y. Student Orch., Schenectady, 1965—, Northeastern N.Y. Philharm., Schenectady, 1966—; guest condr., composer, 1979—. Guest condr. Boston Symphony Orch., 1944, BBC, Swiss Radio, Zürich, Switzerland, Oslo (Norway) Philharm., Brabant Orkest, Holland, others. Composer: Suite for contralto, viola and orch, 1966, Concerto for organ, 1967, Three Piano Pieces, 1968, Suite for solo flute, 1969, Double Exposure for String Quartet and Prerecorded Tape, 1969, music for film To Open Eyes, 1968, Music for Brass, 1973, Sonata for Two (flute and guitar), 1974, Brass Quintet, 1976, Music for Dance Perhaps, retitled Music in Search of a Choreographer (1 piano, 4 hands), 1976, Music for Chamber Orch., 1985, Sonata for Unaccompanied Violin, 1989-90, Music for Carillon, 1993; Essays: What Is Music About?, 1991—. Served with USN, 1944-46. Recipient Mark Twain award Mark Twain Soc., 1971; Title III U.S. Govt. grantee, 1967. Mem. Am. Fedn. Musicians (award 1952). Avocations: hiking, traveling. Home: PO Box 471 Brimfield MA 01010 *Two lifelong convictions remain clear: that music, and each of the arts, is directly accessible to any person whose early exposure was a happy one; and that a piece of music, a painting. . . approached as an art work, reveals itself to the mind; but approached as an experience to be shared, enters into the whole person. For these reasons, teaching and learning is, in any field, a shared artistic experience, no less than the composing, conducting or performing of music. We need, in Josef Albers' phrase, "To teach the young more search, less research."*

CURTISS, CAROL PERRY, health care consultant; b. Worcester, Mass., Dec. 9, 1946; d. Joseph Anthony and Marjorie Ruth (Riedle) Perry; m. Jack Daniel Curtiss, Feb. 8, 1970; children: Paul Daniel, Jennifer Perry. Diploma in nursing, Mass. Gen. Hosp. Sch. Nursing, Boston, 1967; BS, Am. Internat. Coll., Springfield, Mass., 1978; MSN, Yale U., 1981. RN Mass. Staff nurse Franklin Med. Ctr., Greenfield, Mass., 1970, Greenfield Ob-Gyn. Assocs., 1972-74, Greenfield Vis. Nurses, 1974-75; instr. Slim Living Program YMCA, Greenfield, 1977-78; instr. nursing Greenfield C.C., 1978; asst. prof. nursing Elms Coll., Chicopee, Mass., 1981-84; oncology program mgr. Franklin Med. Ctr, Greenfield, 1986-93; cancer care cons. Curtiss Cons., Greenfield, 1981—. Mem. faculty Greenfield C.C., 1985—87; vis. lectr., clin. instr. Fitchburg (Mass.) State Coll., 1985—86; vis. lectr. Elms Coll., Chicopee, Mass., 1984—85; mem. adj. faculty SUNY, 1987—90, U. Mass., Amherst, 1989—; peer reviewer Agy. for Health Care Policy and Rsch., Cancer Pain Gidelines, HHS, 1993; presenter in field, U.S. and abroad, 1981—. Co-author: Cancer Doesn't Have to Hurt, 1997; guest editor Oncology Nursing Forum, 1993; contbr. articles to profl. jours. Bd. dirs. Franklin County, Am. Cancer Soc., Greenfield, 1979-95, mem. nurse and social work scholarship com., 1988-96, nursing com. liaison, 1990-98; mem. steering com. Mass. Cancer Pain Initiative, 1988-90, 2002—, liaison, 1990-97; trustee Oncology Nursing Found., 1995-2000. Mem.: Internat. Union Against Cancer, Oncology Nursing Soc., Am. Soc. Pain Mgmt. Nurses, Am. Pain Soc., Internat. Union Against Cancer (U.S. com. 1992—2000), Oncology Nursing Soc. (mem. numerous sub coms. 1987—, mem. numerous subcoms. 1987—, pres.-elect 1991—92, 1991—92, corp. adv. bd. 1991—93, corp. adv. bd. 1991—93, bd. dirs. 1991—, 1991—, nat. pres. 1992—93, Oncology Nursing Press pres. 1992—94, pres. Oncology Nursing Press 1992—94, pres. 1993—94, co-chair conf. on pain 1994, Disting. Svc. award 1999), Am. Soc. Pain Mgmt. Nurses, Am. Pain Soc., Sigma Theta Tau. Avocations: biking, skiing, tennis, carpentry. Home: 73 James St Greenfield MA 01301-3607 E-mail: carol.curtiss@verizon.net.

CURTISS, CHARLES FRANCIS, chemist, educator; b. Chgo., Apr. 4, 1921; s. Ralph Charles and Camille (Guthormsen) C.; m. Lois Pauline Hruska, Mar. 23, 1946; children: Larry A., Glenn D., Ned S. BS, U. Wis., 1942, PhD, 1948. Faculty U. Wis., 1949—, prof. chemistry, 1960-89, emeritus, 1989—. Author: (with others) Molecular Theory of Gases and Liquids, 1954, Dynamics of Polymeric Liquids, 1977, 87; also research papers. Fellow Am. Phys. Soc., AAAS; mem. Am. Chem. Soc. Home: 6317 Keelson Dr Madison WI 53705-4368 E-mail: curtiss@chem.wisc.edu.

CURTISS, ELDEN F. bishop; b. Baker, Oreg., June 16, 1932; s. Elden F. and Mary (Neiger) C.. BA, St. Edward Sem., Seattle, MDiv, 1958; MA in Ednl. Adminstrn, U. Portland, 1965; postgrad., Fordham U., U. Notre Dame. Priest Roman Cath. Ch., 1958. Campus chaplain, 1959—64, 1965—68; supt. schs. Diocese of Baker, Oreg., 1962—70; pastor, 1968—70; pres., ector Mt. Angel Sem., Benedict, Oreg., 1972—76, mem. bd. regents, 1976—93; bishop Diocese of Helena, Mont., 1976—93; archbishop Diocese of Omaha, 1993—; mem. ecumenical ministries State of Oreg., 1972; mem. pastoral svcs. Oreg. State Hosp., Salem, 1975—76; bishop Diocese Helena, 1976—93, Archdiocese of Omaha, 1993. Chmn. bd. Boys Town USA, Cath. Mut. Relief Soc. Am.; mem. Pontifical Coun. for Family, Rome; Episcopal advisor Serra Internat. Mem.: Nat. Cath. Ednl. Assn. (bishops and pres's com. coll. dept., Outstanding Educator 1972). Office: Archdiocese of Omaha 100 N 62nd St Omaha NE 68132-2702*

CURTISS, HOWARD CROSBY, JR., mechanical engineer, educator; b. Chgo., Mar. 17, 1930; s. Howard Crosby and Susan (Stephenson) C.; m. Betty Ruth Cloke, Mar. 24, 1956 (dec. June 1985); children: Lisa Crosby, Jonathan Cloke; m. Elizabeth M. Fenton, May 22, 1988. B in Aero.Engring., Rensselaer Poly. Inst., 1952; PhD, Princeton U., 1965. Mem. rsch. staff dept. aerospace and mech. scis. Princeton U., 1956-65, mem. faculty, 1965—, prof., 1970-98; mem. Army. Sci. Bd., 1978-82; prof. emeritus Princeton U., 1998—; mem. Army Sci. Adv. Panel, 1972-77. Mem. Naval Rsch. Adv. Com., 1978-80; hon. prof. Nanjing Aero. Inst., Nanjing, China, 1985—. Author: (with others) A Modern Course in Aeroelasticity, 1978; Editor: (with others) Jour. of Am. Helicopter Soc, 1972-74. Served with USN, 1952-54. Mem. Am. Helicopter Soc. (dir. 1978-79), AIAA, Sigma Xi, Tau Beta Pi. Clubs: Metedeconk River Yacht, Princeton of N.Y. Home: 24 Chestnut St Princeton NJ 08542-3806 Office: Princeton Univ Dept Mech and Aerospace Engring Princeton NJ 08544-0001

CURTISS, RICHARD HOLDEN, magazine editor, writer; b. Grand Rapids, Mich., June 13, 1927; s. Fred Adelbert and Alma Clement (Holden) C.; m. Donna Jean Bourne, June 18, 1950; children: Diana Ruth Sreebny, Delinda Louise Hanley, Andrew Bourne, Raymond Holden. BA in Journalism, U. So. Calif., L.A., 1949. Reporter OMGUS Observer, Berlin, Germany, 1946-47; editor/reporter Whittier (Calif.) Star Reporter, 1949-50; newsman UP, L.A., 1950-51; pubs. officer U.S. Embassy, Djakarta, Indonesia, 1951-53, press attache Ankara, Turkey, 1957-59, Baghdad, 1963-66, pub. affairs officer Damascus, Syria, 1966-67, counselor for pub. affairs Beirut, 1973-76; info. officer Am. Consulate Gen., Stuttgart, Germany, 1954-56; newswriter USIA, Washington, 1959-62, program coord. Near East, South Asia, 1967-69, dep. asst. dir. Near East, North Africa, 1976-78, chief insp., 1979-80; dir. Voice of Am. Program Ctr., Rhodes, Greece, 1970-73; exec. dir. Am. Edn. Trust, Washington, 1981—. Exec. editor Washington Report on Mid. East Affairs, 1983—; founding dir. Mid.-East Policy Coun., Washington, 1981-82, Coun. for Nat. Interest, Washington, 1985-86. Author: A Changing Image: American Perceptions of the Arab-Israel Dispute, 1982, 2d edit., 1986, Stealth Pacs: Lobbying Congress for Control of U.S.-Mid. East Policy, 1990, 4th edit., 1996; co-editor: Seeing the Light: Personal Encounters with the Middle East and Islam, 1997; contbr. numerous articles to profl. jours. Recipient Edward R. Murrow award for excellence in pub. diplomacy Fletcher Sch. for Law and Diplomacy, 1976, Superior Honor award USIA, 1976, Lifetime Achievement award Am.-Arab Anti-Discrimination Com., 1992, Achievement award Ptnrs. for Peace, 1993, Dedicated Svc. award Islamic Assn. for Palestine in N.Am., 1994, Lifelong Dedication award United Muslims of Am., 1994, Cert. of Appreciation The Jerusalem Fund for Edn. and Cmty. Devel. and Ctr. for Policy Analysis on Palestine, 1995, They Dared to Speak Out award Coun. for Nat. Interest, 1995, Voice of Conscience of Am. Journalism award Am. Muslim Alliance, 1998, Cmty. award for journalism Coun. on Am. Islamic Rels., 1999, Constn. to World Awareness award Solidarity for Palestinian Human Rights Orgns. of McGill and Concordia Univs., Montreal, Liberty and Justice award Am. Muslim Coun., Muslim Am. Soc., and United Assn. for Studies and Rsch., 1999. Mem. Nat. Press Club. Avocations: archaeology, paleontology, environmental protection, human rights. Office: American Educational Trust 1902 18th St NW Washington DC 20009-1707 E-mail: wrmea@aol.com.

CURTISS, ROY, III, biology educator; b. May 27, 1934; m. Josephine Clark, Dec. 28, 1976; children: Brian, Wayne, Roy IV, Lynn, Gregory Clark, Eric Garth, Megan Kimberly. BS in Agr., Cornell U., 1956; PhD in Microbiology, U. Chgo., 1962. Instr., research asst. Cornell U., 1955-56; jr. tech. specialist Brookhaven Nat. Lab., 1956-58; fellow microbiology U. Chgo., 1958-60, USPHS fellow, 1960-62; biologist Oak Ridge Nat. Lab., 1963-72; lectr. microbiology U. Tenn., 1965-72, lectr. Grad. Sch. Biomed. Scis., 1967-69; prof. U. Tenn. (Grad. Sch. Biomed. Scis.), 1969-72, assoc. dir., 1970-71, interim dir., 1971-72; Charles H. McCauley prof. microbiology U. Ala., Birmingham, 1972-83; sr. scientist Inst. Dental Rsch., 1972-83, Comprehensive Cancer Ctr., 1972-83; dir. molecular cell biology grad. program, 1973-82; dir., sr. scientist Cystic Fibrosis Rsch. Ctr., 1981-83; prof. cellular and molecular biology Sch. Dental Medicine Washington U., St. Louis, 1983-91; George William and Irene Koechig Freiberg prof. biology Wash. U., St. Louis, 1984—, chmn. dept. biology, 1983-93, dir. Ctr. Plant Sci. and Biotech., 1991-94. Mem. Ctr. for Infectious Disease, Wash. U., St. Louis; vis. prof. Instituto Venezolana de Investigaciones Científicas, 1969, U. P.R., 1972, U. Católica de Chile, 1973, U. Okla., 1982; recombinant DNA molecule program adv. com. NIH, 1974-77, genetic basis disease rev. com., 1979-83, chmn., 1981-83, vaccine study panel, 2001—; genetic biology com. NSF, 1975-78. Editor: Jour. Bacteriology, 1970-76, Infection and Immunity, 1985-92, Escherichia coli and Salmonella: Cellular and Molecular Biology, 1993-96, exec. editor-in-chief, 2000—. Active Oak Ridge City Coun., 1969-72, Cystic Fibrosis Found. (rsch. devel. program rev. com. 1984-89), Conf. Rsch. Workers on Animal Diseases, Heiser Found. Scientific Adv. Bd., 1996—; bd. dirs. Am. Type Culture Collection, 1989-99, presdl. adv., 2003—; bd. dirs. Whitfield Sch., 1997—, exec. com., 2002—; founder, dir. and sci. adv. MEGAN Health, Inc., 1992-2000, v.p. rsch., 1998-99; mem. Mo. Seed Capital Investment Bd., 2000—. Named Mo. Inventor of Yr., 1997. Fellow: AAAS, Acad. Sci. St. Louis, Am. Acad. Microbiology; mem.: NAS, Internat. Soc. Vaccines, World Health Orgn. (steering com. immunology of TB 1982—85), Coun. Advancement Sci. Writing (dir. 1976—82, v.p. 1978—82), N.Y. Acad. Scis., Am. Soc. Microbiology (parliamentarian 1970—75, dir. 1977—80, editl. bd. ASM News 1987—99, dir. 1989—94, 1999—), Soc. Gen. Microbiology, Internat. Soc. Mucosal Immunology, Am. Assn. Avian Pathologists, Genetics Soc. Am. (chmn. genetics stock ctrs. com. 1987—89), Gateway Strikers Soccer Club (pres. 1995—2001, chmn. bd. dirs. 2001—, founder), Sigma Xi. Home: 6065 Lindell Blvd Saint Louis MO 63112-1009 Office: Washington U Dept Biology Saint Louis MO 63130

CURTRIGHT, TOBY ARTHUR, music educator; b. Elgin, Ill., June 11, 1973; s. Jerry Davis and Jackie Lee Curtright; m. Patricia Ann Welzen, Mar. 25, 1976. MA, Western Ill. U., 1998. Music tchr. East Peoria (Ill.) Sch. Dist. 86, 2000—. Bass instr. Bradley U., Peoria, Ill., 2001—. Nominee Grammy award, 1993. Mem.: Phi Mu Alpha Sinfonia (sec. 1993—94). Methodist. Avocations: music, athletics. Home: 324 Simon Dr East Peoria IL 61611 Office: East Peoria Sch Dist 86 601 Taylor St East Peoria IL 61611 Personal E-mail: tobycurtright@yahoo.com.

CURTS, HAROLD LAYNE, construction executive; b. Dallas, Oct. 30, 1957; s. Harold Franklin and Betty Ann (Moulton) C.; m. Trina Elizabeth Roach, Aug. 16, 1980; children: Steven Robert, Valerie Layne. AA in Design and Drafting, Mountain View Coll., 1978; AA in Civil Constrn., Tarrant County Coll., 1985; BS, Letourneau U., 1994. Project engr. Broyles & Broyles, Inc., Ft. Worth, 1978-80; project mgr. Precision Concrete and Constrn., Inc., Dallas, 1980-81; constrn. mgr. Methodist Hosps. of Dallas, 1981-83; v.p. constrn. Medco Constrn., Baylor Health Care System, Dallas, 1983-85; v.p. design and constrn. The Centra Group, Ft. Worth, 1985-91; pres. Tech. Interiors, Ft. Worth, 1991—. Mem. Tex. Assn. Hosp. Engrs., Nat. Eagle Scout Assn. Republican. Baptist. Avocations: travel, fishing. Office: Technical Interiors PO Box 14824 Fort Worth TX 76117-0824

CURTZ, CHAUNCEY S.R. lawyer, real estate company executive; b. Ann Arbor, Mich., July 14, 1954; s. Thaddeus Bankson and Rebecca Parkhill (Reeve) C.; m. Brenda Lee Kyriss, Sept. 2, 1976; children: Lydia Lorraine, Charles Edward. Student, Georgetown U., 1972-73; BS, McGill U., 1976; JD, U. Wis., 1981. Bar: Wis. 1981, Ky. 1981, U.S. Dist. Ct. (ea. dist.) Ky. 1981, U.S. Ct. Appeals (6th cir.) 1983, U.S. Supreme Ct. 1986, U.S. Dist. Ct. (we. dist.) Ky. 1993. Assoc. Wyatt, Tarrant & Combs, Lexington, Ky., 1981-87, ptnr., 1987-97; counsel Dinsmore & Shohl, Lexington, 1997—; sr. v.p. ops., gen. coun. Big Sandy Mgmt. Co., Inc., Lexington, 1997—2002; pres., CEO, chmn. bd. Beaver Dam Coal Co., Hartford, Ky., 2000—02; bd. dirs., pres. Coal Energy Investments & Mgmt., LLC, 2002—. Bd. dirs., sec. Curtz & Shine, Inc., Lexington, 1985—; bd. dirs., pres. CSR Curtz, Inc., Lexington, 1997—. Contbr. articles to profl. jours.; contbg. author: UK/CLE Practitioners Manual, 1989. Chmn. Lexington Arts & Cultural Coun., 1995-96, chmn., 2003—; bd. dirs. Lexington Philharmonic, 1996-97, Lexington Children's Theatre, 1997-99; mem. Pritchard Com. Acad. Excellence, Lexington, 1995-98; trustee Energy and Mineral Law Found., 2000—, mem. exec. com., 2001—, asst. sec., 2003—; mem. adv. com. Gov.'s Sch. for Arts, 2001-02. Mem. Lexington Coal Exchg. Avocations: travel, gardening, cooking, wine. Office: Dinsmore & Shohl 250 W Main St Ste 1400 Lexington KY 40507-1735 E-mail: curtz@dinslaw.com.

CURWEN, RANDALL WILLIAM, journalist, editor; b. Hazel Green, Wis., Apr. 18, 1946; s. Charles William and Theda (Hillary) C. BS, U. Wis., 1968. Reporter Rockford (Ill.) Morning Star, 1968-69, copy editor/asst. city editor, 1969-72; copy editor Chgo. Today, 1972-74; copy editor/asst. sect. editor Chgo. Tribune, 1974-80, assoc. features editor, 1980-91, co-editor evening edit., 1992, travel editor, 1992—. Recipient 1st place headline writing award Ill. UPI, 1977, Johnrae Earl award Chgo. Tribune, 1979, 96, Soc. Am. Travel Writers Ctrl. States award for best travel sect., 1994, 99, 2001, 02. Mem. Soc. Am. Travel Writers (Lowell Thomas award for best travel sect. 1995, 97), Nat. Lesbian and Gay Journalists Assn. Avocations: travel, baseball, video. Home: 930 W Roscoe Rear Coachhouse Chicago IL 60657 Office: Chgo Tribune Co 435 N Michigan Ave PO Box 25340 Chicago IL 60625-0340

CURY, BRUCE PAUL, lawyer, magistrate, law educator; b. Englewood, N.J., Mar. 19, 1942; s. Beddy Galib and Violet (Maloof) C.; m. Orahdella Elizabeth Green, Oct. 14, 1972; 1 child, Lauren Elaine. BS, U. Ky., 1965; JD, U. Louisville, 1972. Bar: Fla. 1972, U.S. Dist. Ct. (mid. dist.) Fla. 1974, U.S. Ct. Appeals (5th cir.) 1980, U.S. Ct. Appeals (11th cir.) 1982, U.S. Supreme Ct. 1976. Assoc. George McDowell P.A., Tampa, Fla., 1972-73; sole practice Tampa, 1973-76; adj. prof. bus. law U. Tampa, 1977-85; adj. prof. criminal law U. South Fla., 1984-85, lectr., 1981-87; chief asst. pub. defender Office of Pub. Defender, Tampa, 1974-85; sole practice Tampa, 1985-90; gen. counsel Fla. Dept. Transportation, Bartow, 1990—. Magistrate traffic ct. Jud. 13 cir., Tampa, 1993—; chmn. Hills County Zoning Bd. Tampa, 1989-97; pres., dir. Bay Area Legal Svcs., Inc., Tampa, 1980-92; chmn. Hills County Land Use Appeals Bd. Tampa, 1997—. Legal counsel Big Bros./Big Sisters Greater Tampa, Inc., 1983-95; pres, bd. dirs. Rape Crisis Ctr., Tampa, 1982-84; bd. dirs. Hillsborough Edn. Found., Tampa, 1999—; mem. Hillsborough County City-County Planning Commn., Tampa, 1999—. Served to 1st lt. U.S. Army, 1966-69. Recipient Indigent Accused award Fla. Pub. Defender, 1985, Dirs. award Sexual Abuse Treatment Ctr. Tampa, 1986, Pres. and Dirs. award Bay Area Legal Svcs. Tampa, 1992, Sec. of Transp. Leadership award Fla. Dept. Transp., 2000. Mem. Criminal Def. Lawyers Assn. Hillsborough County, Fla. Bar Assn. (mem. several sects., chmn. 13th Jud. Circuit grievance com.), Hillsborough County Bar Assn. (mem. several coms., exec. counsel trial lawyers sect.), Fla. Leadership 2000, Am. Inn of Cts. (master). Republican. Methodist. Home: 1301 Bayshore Blvd Tampa FL 33606 Office: Fla Dept Transportation 801 N Broadway Ave Bartow FL 33830-3809 E-mail: bruce.cury@dot.state.fl.us.

CURZON, SUSAN CAROL, university administrator; b. Poole, Eng., Dec. 11, 1947; came to U.S., 1952. d. Kenneth Nigel and Terry Marguerite (Morris) C. AB, U. Calif., Riverside, 1970; MLS, U. Wash., 1972; PhD, U. So. Calif., 1983. Spl. libr. Kennecott Exploration, San Diego, 1972-73; various positions L.A. County Pub. Libr., 1973-89; dir. libr. Glendale (Calif.) Pub. Libr., 1989-92; dean univ. libr. Calif. State U., Northridge, 1992—, 1992—. Cons. Grantsmanship Ctr., L.A., 1981-83; vis. lectr. Grad. Sch. Libr. and Info. Sci. UCLA, 1986-92. Author: Managing Change, Managing the Interview. Libr. of the Year, Libr. Jour., 1993. Mem. ALA, Calif. Libr. Assn. Democrat. Avocations: history, horseback riding. Office: Calif State U Libr Office of the Dean 18111 Nordhoff St Northridge CA 91330-8326

CURZON, THOMAS HENRY, lawyer; b. Ft. Leonard Wood, Mo., Apr. 11, 1954; s. James E. and Vera (Roush) C.; m. Anne M. Halverhout, July 29, 1977; children: Peter Thomas, Daniel Henry. BA with highest distinction, U. Kans., 1976; JD with high honors, U. Tex., 1979. Bar: Tex. 1979, Ariz. 1980. Law clk. to Hon. James K. Logan, U.S. Ct. Appeals for 10th Circuit, Olathe, Kans., 1979-80; ptnr. Meyer, Hendricks, Osborn & Maledon, Phoenix, 1986—96, Osborn Maledon, P.A., Phoenix, 1995—. Bd. dirs. Ariz. Tech. Incubator; bd. dirs. Enterprise Network, Phoenix, 1989-96, pres., 1995-96. Author: Ariz. Legal Forms: Business Organizations-Corporations, 2 vols., 1990, 2d edit., 2001. Mem. exec. com. Ariz. Strategic Planning for Econ. Devel., Phoenix, 1990-91; bd. dirs. Downtown YMCA, Phoenix, 1997; chmn. troop 644 com. Boy Scouts Am., Phoenix, 2000—. Mem. Ariz. Tech. Coun. (bd. dirs. 1997—). Avocations: figure skating, Tae Kwon Do, sailing, hunting, scouting, bicycling. Office: Osborn Maledon PA 2929 N Central Ave Phoenix AZ 85012-2727

CUSACK, JOHN THOMAS, lawyer; b. Oak Park, Ill., June 22, 1935; s. Thomas Jr. and Clare (Hock) C.; m. Mary Louise Coughlin, Nov. 1, 1969; children: John, James, Mary Helen, Cathleen. AB cum laude, U. Notre Dame, 1957; JD, U. Mich., 1960; postgrad., Harvard U., 1961-62. Bar: Ill. 1960, U.S. Dist. Ct. (no. dist.) Ill. 1961, U.S. Dist. Ct. (no. dist.) Ind. 1983, U.S. Tax Ct. 1984, U.S. Ct. Appeals (7th cir.) 1973, U.S. Ct. Appeals (5th and 9th cirs.) 1975, U.S. Ct. Appeals (3d cir.) 1986, U.S. Ct. Appeals (10th cir.) 1987, U.S. Ct. Appeals (11th cir.) 1988, U.S. Supreme Ct. 1966. Trial atty. antitrust div. U.S. Dept. Justice, 1962-70; assoc. Gardner, Carton & Douglas, Chgo., 1970-74, ptnr., 1974—, chmn. litigation dept., 1978-86, chmn. antitrust practice group, 1986—. Contbr. articles to legal jours. Trustee Fenwick H.S. 1st lt. JAGC, USAR, 1963-67. Mem. ABA (antitrust and litigation sect., health law com. 1960—), Chgo. Bar Assn., Law Club City Chgo. Roman Catholic. Home: 1030 Franklin Ave River Forest IL 60305-1340 Office: Gardner Carton & Douglas 191 N Wacker Dr Ste 3700 Chicago IL 60606-1698 E-mail: jcusack@gcd.com.

CUSACK, THOMAS JOSEPH, retired banker; b. N.Y.C., Aug. 12, 1938; s. Thomas Joseph and Josephine (Mingalone) C.; m. Elizabeth Mary McAuliffe, June 4, 1960; children: Thomas, Elizabeth, Bridget. BBA, St. Francis Coll., 1968; grad., Stonier Grad. Sch. Banking, New Brunswick, N.J. Asst. v.p. Irving Trust Co., N.Y.C., 1959-79; v.p., sr. ops. mgr. Mellon Bank Internat., N.Y.C., 1979-83, gen. mgr., 1983-85; v.p., sr. ops. mgr. Creditanstalt, Greenwich, Conn., 1985-90, v.p. planning and devel., 1990-93, v.p., COO, 1993-94, sr. v.p., COO, 1995-98; ret., 1998. U.S. rep. Swift Documentary Credit Working Group, Brussels, Belgium, 1983-85; mem. Payments and Settlement Systems Com., Bankers Assn. Fgn. Trade, 1983-85. Fin. com., trustee St. Vincent DePaul Roman Cath. Ch., Elmont, N.Y., 1988—. Mem.K.C.(4th deg.), U.S. Coun. on

Internat. Banking (chmn. 1987-88). Avocations: camping, touring. Home: 10 John Ave Elmont NY 11003-1916 E-mail: tjccat@optionline.net. *If we all would realize that the only lasting thing we leave in this world is our reputation, what a better world this would be.*

CUSANO, CRISTINO, mechanical engineer, educator; b. Sepino, Italy, Mar. 22, 1941; s. Crescenzo and Carmela (D'Anello) C.; m. Isabella Pera, Aug. 7, 1974 BS, Rochester Inst. Tech., 1965; MS, Cornell U., 1967, PhD, 1970. Asst. prof. mech. engring. U. Ill., Urbana, Ill., 1970—74, assoc. prof., 1974—83, prof., 1983—99, prof. emeritus, 1999—. Cons. Carrier Corp., Copeland Corp., Whirlpool Corp. Contbr. articles to profl. jours. NSF fellow, 1965-69, ASME fellow; recipient Capt. Alfred E. Hunt award, Al Sonntag award, Xerox award Mem. Soc. Tribologists and Lubrication Engrs., Am. Soc. Engring. Edn., Sigma Xi, Phi Kappa Phi, Pi Tau Sigma. Roman Catholic. Home: 110 E Stoughton St Champaign IL 61820-4103 Office: Univ Ill Dept Mech Engring 1206 W Green St Urbana IL 61801-2906

CUSH, JOHN PATRICK, priest, theology studies educator; b. Bklyn., Jan. 20, 1972; s. Edward Joseph Cush and Catherine Mary Flynn. BA in Philosophy and English, St. John's U., Jamaica, NY, 1994; STB in Theology, Gregorian U., Rome, 1997, STL in Theology, 1999. Parochial vicar Good Shepherd Roman Cath. Ch., Bklyn., 1998, St. Helen Roman Cath. Ch., Howard Beach, NY, 1999—; chaplain St. Edmund's H.S., Bkln., 1999—2000; instr. deacon program Diocese of Bklyn., 1999—2000, mem. Cath.-Luth. bilaterals, 2000—, censor of books, 2001—. Theology instr. Diocesan Pastoral Inst. for Formation of Lay Ecclesial Ministers, 2001—; presenter ministry workshops Diocesan Liturgical Commn., 2002—. Contbr. articles to Bklyn. Tablet. Mem.: Canon Law Soc. Am., Cath. Biblical Assn. Am. Home and Office: St Helen Roman Cath Ch 157-10 83d St Jamaica NY 11414 Fax: 718-835-5144.

CUSHEN, WALTER EDWARD, contractor, consultant; b. Hagerstown, Md., Mar. 21, 1925; s. Walter Frank Cushen and Edith Louella Sheeley; m. Helen Lingenfelter, Sept. 1, 1949; children: Donna Gail, Mark Edward. BA summa cum laude, Western Md. Coll., 1948; PhD, U. Edinburgh, Scotland, 1951; DSc, Western Md. Coll., 1966. Assoc. prof. ops. rsch. Case Inst. of Tech., 1961—63; ops. rsch. analyst Inst. for Def. Analyses, 1963—65; divsn. chief Nat. BUR Stds., Gaithersburg, Md., 1965—80; oper. rsch. analyst Ops. Rsch. Office, Bethesda, Md., 1952—61; v.p. MathTech, Inc., Bethesda, 1980—82; project leader Logistics Mgmt. Inst., Bethesda, 1982—84; ops. rschr. Def. Info. Sys., Falls Church, Va., 1984—93; sr. fellow war gaming and simulation Nat. Def. U., Washington, 1993—2001, contractor, 2001—. Mem. Govs. Sci. Adv. Bd. Md., 1965—68. With AUS, 1944—46. Fellow: AAAS; mem.: Ops. Rsch. Soc. Am. (pres. 1970—71, Kimball medal 1992). Methodist. Avocations: gardening, genealogy. Home and Office: 6910 Maple Ave Chevy Chase MD 20815-5114

CUSHING, STEVEN, linguist, educator, writer, researcher, consultant; b. Brookline, Mass., June 25, 1948; s. Alfred Edward and Evelyn Cushing. SB, MIT, 1970; MA, UCLA, 1972, PhD, 1976. Rsch. asst. MIT, 1967-70, UCLA, 1973-74; instr. U. Mass., Boston, 1974-75, Roxbury C.C., Boston, 1975-77; rsch. staff Higher Order Software Inc., Cambridge, Mass., 1976-82; rsch. assoc. Rockefeller U., N.Y.C., 1979; lectr. Northeastern U., Boston, 2003—; from master lectr. to assoc. prof. Boston U., 1986-94; rsch. fellow NASA-Ames Rsch. Ctr., Mountain View, Calif., 1987-88, Stanford U., Palo Alto, Calif., 1987-88, NASA-Langley Rsch. Ctr., Hampton, Va., 1989; asst. prof. St. Anselm Coll., Manchester, N.H., 1983-85, Stonehill Coll., North Easton, Mass., 1985-89; adj. prof. Union Inst. Grad. Sch., Cin., 1994—; lectr. Boston U., 2002—; instr. Mass. Sch. Law, 2002—. Mem. bd. editl. commentators The Behavioral and Brain Scis., 1978—; chmn. software design Internat. Conf. Sys. Scis., Honolulu, 1978; mem. 1st fgn. del. USSR Acad. of Scis., 1989; session chmn. session on internat. comm. Internat. Pragmatics Conf., Kobe, Japan, 1993; invited spkr. Internat. Conf. on Maritime Edn. and Tng., Rijeka, Croatia, 1999. Author: Quantifier Meanings: A Study in the Dimensions of Semantic Competence, 1982, Fatal Words: Communication Clashes and Aircraft Crashes, 1994, Japanese edit., 2001; assoc. editor Language, 1998-2000; contbr. articles to profl. jours. and mags. Mem. nat. exec. coun. Nat. Ethical Youth Orgn., 1965-66; fiddler Strathspey and Reel Soc. N.H. Recipient New Eng. Regional award Future Scientists of Am., 1965, 1st pl. award U.S. Nat. Scottish Fiddle Composition Competition, 1996; NSF grantee, 1965, 70-71, NIMH grantee, 1970-71, NDEA grantee, 1970-73; Woodrow Wilson Found. fellow, 1970-71, NASA Summer Faculty fellow, 1987-89; rsch. affiliate MIT, 1978-79, Boston U., 1986-88. Mem. Linguistic Soc. Am., Nat. Ctr. for Sci. Edn., Internat. Pragmatics Assn. Home: 20 Parks Dr Sherborn MA 01770 E-mail: stevencushing@alum.mit.edu.

CUSHMAN, HELEN MERLE BAKER, retired management consultant; b. Perth Amboy, N.J. d. Ivan F. and Lucile (Atkinson) Baker; m. Robert Arnold Cushman, June 2, 1945; children— Lucinda Ann, Robert Rorem. AB in History, Barnard Coll., 1942; postgrad., NYU, 1944. Route analyst intelligence divsn. Air Transport Command, Washington, 1943-44; personnel asst. Gen. Cable Corp., N.Y.C., 1944-45; sr. staff asst. to chmn. bd. Trans World Airlines, N.Y.C., 1945-50; pres. H.M. Baker Assocs., Westfield, N.J., 1958-93; ret., 1993. Past archivist-historian N.J. chpt. Am. Records Mgmt. Assn. Author: ARMA-New Jersey, The Founding Years, 1972, A History of Shreve, Crump and Low, 1974, Butterick and the Story of Sewing, 1975, The Anniversary Manual, 1976, Gears, Machines, Systems, 1978, Mountainside Chapel: Yesterday, Today, Tomorrow, 1981, Serving Westerly Since 1800, 1985, The Mill on the Third River, 1992, From Seed to Harvest, 1993, The Church at the Crossroads, 1999; editor, pub. Ministry Press, The Bus. History Letter; contbr. to Am. Archivist. Recipient Lit. award Am. Records Mgmt. Assn., 1972. Mem.: PEO Sisterhood (pres. chpt. AE,.Princeton N.J.), various hist. socs., Newcomen Soc., Barnard Coll. Club North Ctrl. NJ (past pres.). Address: 321 Sharon Way Monroe Township NJ 08831-1561

CUSHMAN, KAREN LIPSKI, writer; b. Chgo. married; 1 child, Leah. BA in English/Greek, Stanford U., 1963; MA in Human Behavior, USIU, 1977; MA in Mus. Studies, JFK U., 1987. Faculty mus. studies dept. John F. Kennedy U., San Francisco. Author: Catherine, Called Birdy, 1994, The Midwife's Apprentice, 1995 (John Newberry award 1996), The Ballad of Lucy Whipple, 1996, Matilda Bone, 2000, Rodzina, 2003. Office: Clarion Books 215 Park Ave S New York NY 10003-1603*

CUSHMAN, MARGARET JANE, home care executive, nurse; b. Pahokee, Fla., Nov. 17, 1948; d. Edmund Francis and Mary Margaret (Adams) C. Diploma in nursing, Johns Hopkins Hosp., 1969; BSN, U. Pa., 1972; MSN, Yale U., 1976; student, TAI Sophia Inst., 2002—. Asst. dir. nursing St. Joseph's Hosp., Phila., 1972-74; asst. dir. Regional Vis. Nurse Agy., North Haven, Conn., 1976-78; exec. dir. Waterbury (Conn.) Vis. Nurse Assn., 1978-82; exec. v.p. VNA Health Care, Inc., Plainville, Conn., 1982-86; pres. Vis. Nurse And Home Care, Inc. (name changed to VNA Health Care, Inc.), Plainville, Conn., 1986-98; CEO Home Care U. Nat. Assn. for Home Care, Washington, 1998—2002; v.p. Nat. Assn. Home Care, Washington, 1999—2002; exec. dir. Home Healthcare Nurses Assn., Nat. Assn. for Home Care, 1999—2002; editor-in-chief Caring Mag., Nat. Assn. for Home Care, 1999—2002; editl. cons. Caring Mag., 2003—. Asst. clin. prof. Yale U. Sch. Nursing, New Haven, 1978-99, assoc. clin. prof., 1999—; asst. clin. prof. U. Tex. Sch. Nursing, San Antonio, 1990-97; cons. U. S.C. Sch. Nursing, 1987-89, U. Tex. Sch. Nursing, San Antonio, 1989-90; corporator Am. Savs. Bank, 1993-98, Hartford Hosp., 1993—, Hosp. for Special Care, 1994-98. Contbg. author: Home Health Adminstration, 1988; mem. editl. adv. bd. Home Healthcare Nurse, 1988-95; co-editor Certification for Home Care/Hospice Execs. Study Guide; contbr. articles to profl. jours. Mem. Conn. Gov.'s Blue Ribbon Com. to Investigate Nursing Home Industry in Conn., Hartford, 1975-77; mem. nat. adv. com. Ctr. for Health Policy Rsch., Denver, 1989-94; mem. Conn. Award for Excellence Health Adv. Task Force, 1993-94; sec. Found. for Hospice and Home Care, 1989-95; mem. joint adv. coun. and pub. health adv. coun. Conn. Dept. Pub. Health and Addiction Svcs., 1994-95; bd. dirs. St. Mary's Hosp., Waterbury, Conn., 1996-98, Health Tech, 1997-98. Robert Wood Johnson/Nat. League for Nursing fellow, 1975, fellow Found. for Hospice and Home Care, 1992; recipient Andrew Veckerelli prize Yale U. Sch. Nursing, 1976, Disting. Alumni award, 1986, Creative Thinking Assn. Tribute, 1990, Leadership award Conn. Assn. for Home Care, 1995. Fellow Am. Acad. Nursing; mem. ANA, Am. Herbalists Guild, Inst. of Noetic Scis., Creative Thinking Assn., World Future Soc., Nat. League for Nursing (nat. adv. coun. home health outcome study 1989-93), Nat. Assn. Home Care (chmn. 1986-88, sec. 1984-86, 91-94, vice chair 1995-98, Mem. of Yr. award 1984, 97, Virginia Henderson award for excellence in nursing 1997), Conn. Assn. Home Care (sec. 1981-85), Greater Hartford C. of C. (women execs. com. 1990-98), Alumni Assn. Leadership Greater Hartford, Sigma Theta Tau. Avocation: herb gardening. Home: 560 N St SW N615 Washington DC 20024

CUSHMAN, ORIS MILDRED, retired nurse, hospital education director; b. Springfield, Mass., Nov. 22, 1931; d. Wesley Austin and Alice Mildred (Vaile) Stockwell; m. Laurence Arnold Cushman, Apr. 16, 1955; children: Lynn Ann Cushman Wronker, Laurence Arnold III. Diploma in nursing, Hartford Hosp. Sch. Nursing (Conn.), 1953; BS, Western Mich. U., 1978, MA, 1980. Staff nurse Wesson Maternal Hosp., Springfield, 1953—54, acting supr., 1954—55; staff nurse Hartford Hosp., 1955—56, head nurse, 1956, staff nurse, 1957—59; staff nurse, charge nurse Reed City Hosp. (Mich.), 1961—67; supr. Meml. Hosp. (Mich.), St. Joseph, 1967—75; clin. supr. maternal/child health Meml. Hosp., St. Joseph, 1975—77, dir. maternal/child health, 1977—80; dir. edn. Pawating Hosp. (Mich.), Niles, 1980—87; ret., 1987. Sec. Women's aux. Reed City Hosp., 1964—65, v.p., 1965—66, pres., 1966—67; program com. Venice (Fla.) Presbyn. Ch., 2000—02, mem. health ministries cabinet, 2002—; mem. adv. bd. on family life edn. St. Joseph Sch. Bd. (Mich.), 1979—80, Krasl Art Ctr., St. Joseph, 1987—94. Republican.

CUSHMAN, STEPHEN BIGELOW, English educator, writer; b. Norwalk, Conn., Dec. 17, 1956; s. Bigelow Paine and Anne Toffey C.; m. Sandra Bain Cushman, June 19, 1982; children: Samuel Bain, Simon Bain. BA, Cornell U., 1978; MA, Yale U., 1980, MPhil, 1981, PhD, 1982. Asst. prof. U. Va., Charlottesville, 1982-87, assoc. prof., 1987-94, prof. English, 1994—2001, Robert C. Taylor prof. English, 2001—. Author: William Carlos Williams and the Meanings of Measure, 1985, Fictions of Form in American Poetry, 1993, Blue Pajamas, 1998, Bloody Promenade: Reflections on a Civil War Battle, 1999, Cussing Lesson, 2002; adv. editor Va. Quar. Rev., 1999—. Fellowship Am. Coun. of Learned Socs., 1986-87, Va. Found. for the Humanities, 1997, tchg. fellowship Fulbright Found., 1993. Mem. Am. Studies Assoc., Modern Poetry Assoc., MLA, William Carlos Williams Soc., Phi Beta Kappa. Office: Dept English U Va 219 Bryan Hall PO Box 400121 Charlottesville VA 22904-4121

CUSIMANO, ADELINE MILETTI, educational administrator; b. Jamestown, N.Y., 1939; d. Joseph and Rose Miletti; m. John Cusimano, Sept. 24, 1960; children: Judith Cusimano Higgins, John. BS, Elmira Coll., 1961, MS, 1976. Cert. reading specialist, N.Y., Pa. Tchr. Horseheads (N.Y.) Sch. Dist., 1961-62; diagnostician, clinician Horseheads, 1962-76; reading specialist Elmira Heights Schs., N.Y., 1976-78; dir. Achievement Ctr., Horseheads, 1978-95. Presenter ednl. N.Y. St. Reading Conf., Kiamesha Lake, N.Y., 1982, Bd. Coop. Ednl. Svcs. Tchrs. Tng., Horseheads, 1978-80; researcher learning disabilities, Horseheads, 1962—. Author: Achieve Visual Memory Teaching Material, 4 vols., 1980, Learning Disabilities: There is a Cure, 2002, Achieve: A Visual Memory Program, Levels V and VI, 2003. Mem. pub. affairs edn. home life Chemung Valley Jr. Women's Club, 1968-78, 1st v.p., 1971-72; asst. treas. Horseheads Women's Club, 1983-85; fundraiser com. Lansdale Pub. Libr. Recipient Outstanding Jr. Women's Club award, 1975. Mem. Nat. Assn. Learning Disabilities, N.Y. State Head Injury Assn., Chemung Valley Reading Assn., Horseheads Women's Club (asst. treas. 1983, corr. sec. 1990-91), Welcome Wagon Club (2d v.p. North Pa. chpt. 1997-99, sec. 2000-02, 2d v.p. 2002—), Lansdale Women's Club (2d v.p. 2000-02). Republican. Roman Catholic. Avocations: reading, needlework, golf, swimming, bridge, genealogy.

CUSMANO, J. JOYCE, public relations executive; b. Mich. BA, Eastern Mich. U.; MA, U. Md., 1972. Asst. dir. Detroit Youtheatre Detroit Inst. Arts; spl. events dir. Detroit Renaissance, 1979—84; v.p. Franco Pub. Rels. Group, Detroit, 1985-90, sr. v.p., 1991—98, dir., consumer group, 1991—98; pres. Sojourn Comm. Grp., Grosse Point Woods, Mich., 1998—. Mem. Women's Econ. Club. Office: Sojourn Comm Grp 19776 E Ida Ln Grosse Pointe Woods MI 48236

CUSSLER, CLIVE ERIC, author; b. Aurora, Ill., July 15, 1931; s. Eric E. and Amy (Hunnewell) C.; m. Barbara Knight, Aug. 28, 1955; children: Teri, Dirk, Dana. Student, Pasadena City Coll., 1949-51; PhD in Maritime History, N.Y. State Maritime Coll., 1997. Owner Bestgen & Cussler Advt., Newport Beach, Calif., 1961-65; creative dir. Darcy Advt., Hollywood, Calif., 1965-67; chmn. Nat. Underwater and Marine Agy. Author: (novels) The Mediterranean Caper, 1973, Iceberg, 1975, Raise the Titanic!, 1976, Vixen 03, 1978, Night Probe, 1981, Pacific Vortex, 1982, Deep Six, 1984, Cyclops, 1986, Treasure, 1988, Dragon, 1990, Sahara, 1992, Inca Gold, 1994, Shock Wave, 1995, Sea Hunters, 1996, Flood Tide, 1997, Clive Cussler & Dirk Pitt Revealed, 1998, Atlantis Found, 1999, Valhalla Rising, 2001, (with Paul Kemprecos) Serpent, 1999, Blue Gold, 2000, Fire Ice, 2002, Sea Hunters II, 2002, White Death (with Paul Kemprecos), 2003, Golden Buddha, 2003, Trojan Odyssey, 2003. Served in USAF, 1950-54. Recipient Disting. Svc. award, Nat. Maritime Hist. Soc., Navy Meml. Heritage award, Nat. Trust for Hist. Preservation award, numerous advt. awards. Fellow Nat. Soc. Oceanographers, N.Y. Explorers Club (Lowell Thomas Underwater Explorers award), Royal Geog. Soc. London, Classic Car Club Am. Achievements include discovering over 60 historic shipwrecks.

CUSSLER, EDWARD LANSING, JR., chemical engineer, educator; s. Edward Lansing and Eleanor Christine (Lloyd-Jones) C.; m. Elizabeth Campbell Beidler. BS in Chem. Engring., Yale U., 1961; MS in Chem. Engring., U. Wis., 1963, PhD, 1965. Rsch. asst. U. Wis., Madison, 1961—65, postdoctoral fellow, 1961—65, U. Adelaide, Australia, 1965-66, Yale U., 1966-67; asst. prof. Carnegie-Mellon U., 1967-70, assoc. prof., 1970-73, prof., 1973-80, U. Minn., Mpls., 1980—. Mem. editl. bd. Jour. Membrane Sci., 1975—, AIChE, 1996—. Recipient William H. Frances S. Ryan award Carnegie-Mellon U., 1975, George Taylor Tchg. award U. Minn., 1987, Separations Sci. award ACS, 2002, Separations Sci. award NAE, 2002. Mem. NAE, AIChE (Alan P. Colburn award 1975, bd. dirs. 1989-92, v.p. 1993, pres. 1994, W.K. Lewis award 2001), Am. Assn. Engrs. Soc. (chair 1996). Office: U Minn Chem Engring Dept 421 Washington Ave SE Minneapolis MN 55455-0373 E-mail: cussler@cems.umn.edu.

CUSSON-CAIL, KATHLEEN, consulting company executive; b. Manchester, N.H., Mar. 17, 1971; m. Alan Cail, Feb. 26, 2000. AS in Archtl. Engring. Tech., N.H. Tech. Inst., 1994; BS in Mgmt., Franklin Pierce Coll., 1995, MBA, 2000. Lic. securities, life, property, casualty. Personal fin. analyst Primerica Fin. Svcs., Nashua, NH, 1996—2003; instructor Introduction to Windows and Word Processing, Adult Comm. Education program Merrimack Sch. District, 2000—02; prin., owner Aggregate Bus. & Comm. Cons., Inc., Manchester, NH, 2002—, Collabresource, Manchester, 2002—, Ideal Instr., Manchester, 2002—. Vol. Vt. Adaptive Ski and Sport, 1996—98, Jerry Lewis Labor Day Telethon, 1998—2002, Riverfest, 1999. Recipient Good Citizenship award DAR, 1985. Avocations: volleyball, horseshoes, motorcycling, winter hiking. Office: Aggregate Business & Communication Cons Inc 1361 Elm Street Ste 208 Manchester NH 03101

CUSTER, BARBARA ANN, lawyer; b. Mineola, N.Y., Mar. 2, 1945; d. Merton Davis and Virginia Mary (Estabrook) C. B.A., Trinity Coll., 1966; J.D., Southwestern U., 1977. Bar: Calif. 1977, U.S. Dist. Ct. (cen. dist.) Calif. 1978, U.S. Ct. Appeals (D.C. cir) 1979. Adminstrv. asst. United Calif. Bank, N.Y.C., 1968-70; asst. to exec. dir. Am. Council for the Arts in Edn., N.Y.C., 1971-74; asst. to reference librarian Southwestern U., Los Angeles, 1975-78; atty. network anti-trust project Columbia Pictures, Burbank, Calif., 1979; sole practice, Los Angeles, 1980; atty. Orion Pictures Corp., Los Angeles, 1981—, now v.p. bus. and legal affairs. Home: 803 N La Jolla Ave Los Angeles CA 90046-6809 Office: Orion Pictures Corp 2500 Broadway Santa Monica CA 90404-3065

CUSTER, CHARLES FRANCIS, lawyer; b. Hays, Kans., Aug. 19, 1928; s. Raymond Earl and Eva Marie (Walker) C.; m. Irene Louise Macarow, Jan. 2, 1950; children: Shannon Elaine, Charles Francis, Murray Maxwell, Kelly Sue. AB, U. Chgo., 1948, JD, 1958. Bar: Ill. 1958, U.S. Dist. Ct. (no dist.) Ill. 1971, U.S. Supreme Ct. 1991. Assoc. Meyers & Matthias, Chgo., 1958-72; pvt. practice Chgo., 1972-78; ptnr. Vedder, Price, Kaufman & Kammholz, Chgo., 1978-98, of counsel, 1998—. Arbitrator, mediator. Past dir. Family Care Svcs., Chgo. Mem. ABA (mem. fed. regulation of securities and devels. in investment svcs. coms., dispute resolution sect.), Chgo. Bar Assn. (mem. securities law com., mem. investment cos. subcom., alternative dispute resolution com.), Cliff Dwellers (past officer and dir.). Avocations: music, theater. Home: 5210 S Kenwood Ave Chicago IL 60615-4006 Office: Vedder Price Kaufman & Kammholz 222 N La Salle St Ste 2600 Chicago IL 60601-1100

CUSTER, GERALD STOCKTON, conductor; b. Balt., Sept. 18, 1953; s. Robert Stockton and Monica (Pellens) Custer; m. Mary Virginia Kramer, Nov. 26, 1977 (div. 1993); children: Nathanael, Robert, Michael, Monica, Joseph. BMus in Choral Conducting, Westminster Choir Coll., 1975; MusM in Conducting, George Washington U., 1980. Cert. tchr. music N.J., 1975. Adj. faculty Music George Washington U., Washington, 1975—79, St. John's Provincial Sem., Plymouth, Mich., 1980—82; dir. Choral Activities Schoolcraft Coll., Livonia, Mich., 2001—. Dir. Liturgy and Music St. Francis Assisi Ch., Ann Arbor, Mich., 1979—82; dir. music, condr. The Arbor Consort, Ann Arbor, 1996—; artistic dir., condr. Jefferson St. Chorale, Ann Arbor, 2000—; chorus master Mich. Chamber Symphony Orch., Dearborn, Mich., 2002—; panelist Choral Music Mich. Coun. Arts and Cultural Affairs, Lansing, 2002—; specialist Choral Music Mich. Coun. Humanities, Lansing, 2002—. Co-author: The Choral Experience, 1976; composer: numerous choral music pieces. Pres., bd. dirs. Serenity House, Ypsilanti, Mich., 1995—97. Recipient 1st prize Column Writing, Mich. Press Assn., 1992, 1st prize 75th Ann. Composition Competition, Westminster Choir Coll., 2000. Mem.: Hymn Soc. Am., Chorus Am., Am. Choral Dirs. Assn. Office: Schoolcraft Coll 18600 Haggerty Rd Livonia MI 48152-3932

CUSTER, JOHN CHARLES, investment broker; b. Chgo., Aug. 30, 1934; s. John Howard and Irene Lillian (McGovern) C.; m. Barbara Ann Welcher, Sept. 5, 1959 (dec. Sept. 1996); 1 child, John Thomas. AB, Ind. U., 1956; MHA, U. Minn., 1959; grad., Harvard U., 1975. Asst. adminstr. Johns Hopkins Hosp., Balt., 1966-67; clin. adminstr. Kaiser Permanente Med. Care Program, Oakland, Calif., 1967-69, dir. materials, 1969-70; mgr. health plan Cleve., 1970-74; v.p., health plan mgr., 1974-79; v.p. Kaiser Permanente Adv. Svcs., Oakland, 1979-84; pres., CEO Keystone Health Plan, Camp Hill, Pa., 1984—87, Custer & Assocs., Hummelstown, Pa., 1987—92; investment broker Legg Mason Wood Walker, Inc., 1992—. Lectr. U. Minn. Grad. Sch. of Pub. Health, Mpls., 1981-85, Harvard U. Grad. Sch. of Pub. Health, Boston, 1977-80. Chmn. Pa. Assn. HMO's, Harrisburg, 1984-86. 1st lt. U.S. Army, 1956-58, col. USAR. Mem. APHA, Am. Coll. Health Care Execs., Am. Hosp. Assn., Med. Group Mgmt. Assn., Internat. Fedn. of Employee Benefit Plans, Pa. State C. of C. (health care cost contain com.), Pa. State Dept. of Pub. Welfare (health care adv. subcom. 1984-85), Country Club Hershey, Delta Upsilon. Clubs: Cosmos (Washington), Army-Navy (Washington). Lodges: Elks. Episcopalian. Home: 589 Lovell Ct Hummelstown PA 17036-9156 Office: 214 Senate Ave Ste 700 Camp Hill PA 17011-2382 Fax: (717) 737-0800. E-mail: jccuster@leggmason.com.

CUSUMANO, JAMES ANTHONY, filmmaker, retired pharmaceutical company executive, former recording artist; b. Elizabeth, N.J., Apr. 14, 1942; s. Charles Anthony and Carmella Madeline (Catalano) Cusumano; m. Jane LaVerne Melvin, June 15, 1985 (dec. June 2001); children: Doreen Ann, Polly Jean. BA, Rutgers U., 1964, PhD, 1967; grad. Exec. Mktg. Program, Stanford U., 1981, Harvard U., 1988. Mgr. catalyst rsch. Exxon Rsch. and Engring. Co., Linden, N.J., 1967-74; pres., chief exec. officer, founder Catalytica Inc., Mountain View, Calif., 1974-85, chmn., 1985-2000, also bd. dirs.; pres., CEO, bd. dirs. Catalytica Fine Chems., Inc., Mountain View, Calif., 1993-97; chmn., CEO, bd. dirs. Catalytica Pharms., Inc., 1997-99, chmn., chief strategic officer, 1999-2000; pres., CEO, founder Chateau Wally Films LLC, Ojai, Calif., 2000—; exec. dir. Chateau Sapiens Found., 2002—. Dir. Ojai Film Festival, 2002—; lectr. chem. engring. Stanford U., 1978, Rutgers U., 1966-67, Charles D. Hurd lectr. Northwestern U., 1989-90, Jean Day hon. lectr. Rutgers U.; advisor Fulbright scholar progam Inst. Internat. Edn.; mem. dean's adv. bd. Rutgers U., 1997—; speaker in field; mem. com. on catalysts and environ. NSF; exec. briefings with Pres. George Bush and Cabinet mems., 1990, 92, plenary lectr. in field; bd. dirs. Catalytica Advanced Techs., Inc. Author: Catalysis in Coal Conversion, 1978, (with others) Critical Materials Problems in Energy Production, 1976, Advanced Materials in Catalysis, 1977, Liquid Fuels from Coal, 1977, Kirk-Othmer Encyclopedia of Chemical Technology, 1979, Chemistry for the 21st Century, Perspectives in Catalysis, 1992, Science and Technology in Catalysis 1994, 1995; contbr. articles to profl. jours., chpts. to books; founding editor Jour. of Applied Catalysis, 1980; exec. prodr. feature film: What Matters Most, 2001; exec. prodr. documentary film: One Tough Biscotti: A Woman, A Film and A Fight, 2001; rec. artist with Royal Teens and Dino Take Five for ABC Paramount, Capitol and Jubilee Records, 1957-67; single records include Short Shorts, Short Shorts Twist, My Way, Hey Jude, Rosemarie, Please Say You Want Me, Lovers Never Say Goodbye; albums include The Best of the Royal Teens, Newies But Oldies; appeared in PBS TV prodn. on molecular engring., Little by Little, 1989. Recipient Surface Chemistry award Continental Oil Co., 1964; Henry Rutgers scholar, 1963, Lever Bros. fellow, 1965, Churchill Coll. fellow Cambridge Univ., 1992. Mem.: ASCAP, AIChE, World Future Soc., Smithsonian Assocs., Pres.'s Assn., Am. Mus. Natural History, Soc. Organic Chems. MFrs. (bd. dirs. 1996), N.Y. Acad. Scis., Am. Phys. Soc., Am. Chem. Soc. (planetary lectr. to chem. educators nat. meeting 1994), Phi Lambda Upsilon, Sigma Psi. Republican. Roman Catholic. Achievements include 20 patents in catalysis and surface science. Home: 620 McNell Rd Ojai CA 93023-9315 Office: Chateau Wally Films LLC 323 E Matilija St #110 Ojai CA 93023 E-mail: jim@chateauwallyfilms.com.

CUTCHIN, JAMES MCKENNEY, IV, lawyer, engineer; b. Whitakers, N.C., Oct. 11, 1933; s. James McKenney III and Helen Christine (Perkins) C.; m. Nancy Lucille Elks, June 12, 1955; children: James McKenney V, John William. BS, U.S. Mil. Acad., 1955; MS in Mech. Engring., N.C. State U., 1962; JD, George Washington U., 1975. Bar: Va. 1975, D.C. 1976, U.S. Dist. Ct. (ea. dist.) Va. 1976, U.S. Dist. Ct. D.C. 1976, U.S. Ct. Appeals (4th and D.C. cirs.) 1976, U.S. Supreme Ct. 1978. Engr., sr. engr. Babcock & Wilcox Co., Lynchburg, Va., 1962-68; licensing supr., 1968-71; sr. project mgr. U.S. Nuclear Regulatory Commn., Washington, 1971-76, atty., 1976-78, sr. litigation atty., 1978-83, legal adviser to commr., 1983-90; special counsel office of the General Counsel, 1990-95. Pres. Lynchburg Young Rep. Club, 1967-69; v.p. Sandusky Jr. High Sch. PTA, 1970; chmn. Lynchburg City Rep. Com., 1970-71. Served to 1st lt. USAF, 1955-59. Mem. Va. Bar, D.C. Bar, ASME (bd. dirs. Va. sect. 1970), Am. Nuclear Soc. (pres. N.C.-Va. sect. 1968), Lynchburg Jaycees (v.p. 1967-68), Sigma Xi, Westwood Country Club, Tau Beta Pi. Home: 11000 Devenish Dr Oakton VA 22124-1804

CUTCHIN, JOHN FRANKS, lawyer; b. Roanoke Rapids, N.C., Dec. 19, 1949; s. Joseph Henry Jr. and Janie Priscilla (Franks) C.; m. Melissa Jane Ikerd, Dec. 22, 1979; children: Jennifer Erin, Joshua Ikerd. AB, Davidson Coll., 1972; JD, U. N.C., 1975. Bar: N.C. 1975, U.S. Dist. Ct. (we. dist.) N.C. 1975; cert. family fin. mediator. Assoc. Lefler, Gordon & Waddell, Newton, N.C., 1975-78; pvt. practice, Newton, 1978—. Mem. Catawba County Bar Assn. (pres. 1982-83), Lincoln County Bar Assn., Newton Mchts. Assn. (pres. 1978-80), Davidson Coll. Alumni Assn. (pres. Catawba County chpt. 1979-80). Episcopalian. Office: 16 S College Ave PO Box 173 Newton NC 28658-0173 E-mail: cutchlaw@bellsouth.net.

CUTCHINS, CLIFFORD ARMSTRONG, III, banker; b. Southampton County, Va., July 12, 1923; s. Clifford Armstrong Jr. and Sarah (Vaughan) C.; m. Ann Woods, June 21, 1947; children: Clifford Armstrong IV, William Witherspoon, Cecil Vaughan. BSBA, Va. Poly. Inst. and State U., 1947; grad., Stonier Grad. Sch. Banking, 1953. From asst. cashier to pres., dir. Vaughan & Co. Bankers, Franklin, Va., 1947-62; pres., cashier dir. Tidewater Bank & Trust Co., Franklin, 1962-63; sr. v.p., bd. dirs. Tidewater Bank & Trust Co. (merged with Va. Nat. Bank 1963), Norfolk, 1963-65; exec. v.p. Va. Nat. Bank, Norfolk, 1965-69, pres., 1969-80, chmn. bd., CEO, dir., 1980-83, Sovran Bank, N.A., Norfolk, 1983-86; CEO, dir. Sovran Fin. Corp., Norfolk, 1983-90, chmn. bd., 1983-89, ret. chmn. bd., 1989; rector Va. Poly. Inst. and State U., 1989-91. Bd. dirs. Franklin Equipment Co. Bd. dirs. Camp Found., Franklin, 1962—, Tidewater Scholarship Found.; bd. dirs. Va. Retirement Sys.; bd. visitors Va. Poly. Inst. and State U., 1965-70, 87-91; mem. Future of Hampton Rds., Inc.; bd. dirs. Greater Norfolk Corp., Olympia Devel. Corp., German Club Alumni

Found., Inc., Va. Tech. Found.; trustee Va. Hist. Soc.; mem. adv. coun. Va. Tech. Bus. Coun.; active Va. Inst. Marine Sci. Mem. Va. Tech. Alumni Assn. (hon. bd. dirs.). Presbyterian. Home: Virginia Beach, Va. Deceased.

CUTCHINS, CLIFFORD ARMSTRONG, IV, lawyer; b. Norfolk, Va., May 13, 1948; s. Clifford Armstrong III and Ann (Woods) C.; m. Jane McKenzie, Aug. 14, 1971; children: Sarah Helen, Ann Woods. BA, Princeton U., 1971; JD, MBA, U. Va., 1975. Bar: Va. 1975, U.S. Dist. Ct. (ea. dist.) Va. 1975, U.S. Ct. Appeals (4th cir.) 1975. Ptnr. McGuire, Woods, Battle & Boothe, Richmond, Va., 1975-90; sr. v.p., gen. counsel, sec. James River Corp. Va., Richmond, 1990-97, Ft. James Corp., Deerfield, Ill., 1997-2000; ptnr. McGuireWoods LLP, Richmond, 2001—. Bd. dirs. Arts Coun. Richmond, 1980-86, Richmond Heart Assn., 1980-83, St. Catherine's Sch., Richmond, 1983-86, Richmond Ballet, 1986-88, Richmond Children's Mus., 1986-94, Richmond on the James, 1986-88, Henrico Drs. Hosp., 1986—, Hist. Richmond Found., 1990-94, Richmond Met. Blood Svc., 1995-97, Kohl Children's Mus., Wilmette, Ill., 1998-2000; chmn. Fort James Found., 1997-2000, Richmond First Tee, 2001-, Nature Conservancy of Va., 2002-. Mem.: ABA, Va. Bar Assn., Commonwealth Club (bd. dirs. 1983—86, 1996—97), Kinloch Golf Club, Country Club Va. (bd. dirs. 1990—93, 2003—). Republican. Baptist. Avocations: golf, travel, reading. Home: 118 Tempsford Ln Richmond VA 23226-2319 Office: McGuireWoods LLP 901 E Cary St Richmond VA 23219 E-mail: ccutchins@mcguirewoods.com.

CUTERI, FRANK R., JR., automotive executive; married; 2 children. BA cum laude, Waynesburg Coll., 1975. Auto. sales rep. North Hills Chrysler-Plymouth, Inc., Pitts., 1974-75; dist. sales mgr. Chrysler Corp., 1975-77; gen. sales mgr. Dodge City Inc., Morgantown, W.Va., 1977-80, Ted McWilliams Volkswagen, Monroeville, W.Va., 1980-83; gen. mgr. Ted McWilliams Porsche-Audi-Toyota, Monroeville, W.Va., 1983-86, West Hills Motors, Inc. Pontiac-Nissan-Jeep Eagle, Coroapolis, W.Va., 1986-91; pres., gen. mgr. Brown's Volvo-Subaru-Hyundai, Alexandria, Va., 1991-92, Brown's Fairfax (Va.) Nissan, 1992; exec. v.p. sales ops. Mid-Atlantic Cars, 1992-95, pres., 1996-98, Dulles Internat. Autopark, Inc., Ashburn, Va., 1998—. Avocations: golf, basketball, rollerblading. Office: Dulles Auto Park 20245 Ordinary Pl Ashburn VA 20147-3314*

CUTHBERT, ROBERT LOWELL, retired product specialist; b. Bay City, Mich., June 28, 1939; s. Lowell Robert and Katherine Ann (Popp) C.; m. Carol Ann Barcia, Apr. 23, 1960; children: Steven Robert, Douglas Brian, Kristi Ann. Student, Bay City Jr. Coll., 1957-59; A in Liberal Arts, Saginaw Valley State U., 1990-94; AAS, Delta Coll., 1999. Lab. tech. coatings Dow Corning Corp., Midland, Mich., 1964-70, silicone acrylic rsch., 1970-72, electronic tech., 1972-78, solar cell rsch., 1978-81, electrical prodn. tech. rep., 1981-88, masonry products tech. rep., 1988-90, product specialist, 1990-99; ret., 2000. Contbr. articles to profl. jours. With USAF, 1959-63. Mem. NRA, Am. Radio Relay League. Independent. Methodist. Achievements include patents for masonry water repellent compositions and research in field.

CUTHBERTSON, GILBERT MORRIS, political science educator; b. Warrensburg, Mo., Nov. 20, 1937; s. Gilbert and Marion Darlington (Morris) C. BA, U. Kans., 1959; PhD, Harvard U., 1963. Asst. prof. Rice U., Houston, 1963-68, assoc. prof., 1968-77, prof., 1977—. Resident assoc. Will Rice Coll., Houston, 1964—. Author: (book) Political Myth and Epic, 1975, (monographs) Political Power, 1968, Myth, Power, Value, 1982; co-author: Teacher Immortal, 1984. Mem. curator's bd. Mus. of Printing History. Recipient George R. Brown lifetime award for excellence in teaching, 1993; Summerfield scholar U. Kans., 1955-59; Woodrow Wilson fellow Harvard U., 1959-63; Wilson C. Morris fellow. Mem. Am. Polit. Sci. Assn., Scottish Heritage Found. (bd. dirs. Great Scot award), River Oaks Rotary (bd. dirs., Paul Harris fellow), Knife and Fork Club, Phi Beta Kappa (past pres. chpt.), Pi Sigma Alpha, Sigma Tau Gamma, Delta Phi Alpha. Democrat. Presbyterian. Avocation: bridge. Office: Rice U Dept Polit Sci Houston TX 77251-1892 E-mail: poli@rice.edu.

CUTHRELL, CARL EDWARD, lawyer, educator, clergyman; b. Norfolk, Va., Aug. 13, 1934; s. Cecil Edward and Edna Catherine (Kirby) C.; m. Naomi Lorene Marshall, Dec. 23, 1960; children: Byron Eugene, Benjamin Dean. LLB, LaSalle U. Law Sch., Chgo., 1959; diploma Egyptian studies, Oriental Inst., U. Chgo., 1960; BD, Brantridge Forest Sch., Eng., 1970; MA in Med. History, Sussex (Eng.) Coll. Tech., 1972; MA in Classical Studies, Christ Ch. Coll., Oxford, Eng., 1973; diploma Germanic langs., Heidelberg (Fed. Republic Germany) U., 1975; BA, Upper Iowa U., 1979; MA, Covington Theol. Sem., 1982; BRE, Cen. Bapt. Bicle Coll., 1989. Pvt. practice, Hampton, 1962-75; ordained to ministry Evang. Friends Ch., 1972; pastor Rescue (Va.) Friends Ch., 1968-96. Mem. faculty dept. theology, Norfolk extension Washington Bible Coll., Lanham, Md., dept. spl. programs/history Coll. William and Mary, Williamsburg, Va., dept. secular studies Cen. Bapt. Bible Coll., Hampton, Va. Author: Ancient Mummies, 1967, Paul's Voyage, 1971; Contbr.: lit. criticisms to Times Herald Newspaper; also numerous short stories. Bd. dirs. Nat. Philatelic Inst.; trustee Quincy Coll., 1970, Nat. Coll. Surgeons Hall of Fame, 1972. Served with M.C. AUS, 1950-57, Korea. Decorated Silver Star; recipient Scouter's award medal Boy Scouts Am., 1956, Silver Beaver award, 1976, Nat. Tchrs. medal Freedoms Found., 1973, Peace medal UN, 1973, Good Citizenship medal SAR, 1976 Mem. U.S. Capital, Nat. hist. socs., S.R., Sons Confederate Vets., Christian Educators Assn., Va. Herpetological Soc., Mil. Order Stars and Bars. Republican. Home: 307 Agusta Dr Newport News VA 23601-1436 E-mail: carloreneva@aol.com.

CUTLER, ALEXANDER MACDONALD, manufacturing company executive; b. Milw., May 28, 1951; s. Richard Woolsey and Elizabeth (Fitzgerald) C.; m. Sarah Lynn Stark, Oct. 11, 1980; children: David Alexander, William MacDonald. BA, Yale U., 1973; MBA, Dartmouth Coll., 1975. Fin. analyst Cutler-Hammer, Milw., 1975-77, bus. group contr., 1977-79; contr. custom distbn. and control divsn. Eaton Corp., Atlanta, 1979-80, plant mgr. custom distbn. and control divsn., 1981-82, mgr. custom distbn. and control divsn., 1982-83, mgr. power distbn. divsn. Milw., 1984-85, gen. mgr. indsl. control and power distbn., 1985-86, pres. controls group Cleve., 1986-91, exec. v.p. ops., 1992-93, exec. v.p., COO controls, 1993-95, pres., COO, 1995-2000, chmn., CEO, 2000—, also bd. dirs. Bd. dirs. Axcelis Techs. Bd. dirs. United Way Svcs. Cleve., N.E. Ohio Coun. on Higher Edn., 1993-97, Mus. Arts Assn., 2000—, Greater Cleve. Growth Assn., 2001-, Cleve. Tomorrow, 2000-, Greater Cleve. Roundtable, 2000-; class agt. alumni fund Loomis Chaffee Sch., Windsor, Conn., 1969—; bd. dirs. alumni fund Yale U., New Haven, 1974-89; trustee The Cleve. Play House, 1987—, Gt. Lakes Mus., Inc., 1988-91, Mus. Natural History, Cleve., 1989-97; bd. overseers Amos Tuck Sch. Bus. Dartmouth Coll., 1996—; active Keycorp., 2000—, Bus. Roundtable, 2002-. Mem. Nat. Elec. Mfrs. Assn. (bd. govs. 1987-99, indsl. automation divsn. 1986-90, treas. 1993-95, bd. govs. 1996-99), Elec. Mfrs. Club (bd. dirs.), Yale U. Alumni Assn. (pres. Cleve. chpt. 1991-93, exec. com. of vis. com. Weatherhood Sch. Mgmt. 1993-2002, Yale devel. bd. 1998—), Chagrin Valley Hunt Club. Avocation: tennis. Office: Eaton Corp 1111 Superior Ave Eaton Ctr Cleveland OH 44114-2584

CUTLER, BERNARD JOSEPH, editor-in-chief, writer; b. N.Y.C., May 26, 1924; s. Joseph Louis and Sophie (Appel) C.; m. Carol Ann Rataic, Mar. 6, 1948. BSME, Pa. State Coll., 1945. Reporter Pitts. Press, 1945-51; reporter N.Y. Herald Tribune, 1951-56, Moscow corr., 1956-58, chief Paris bur., 1958-60, mng. editor European edition, 1960, editor European edition, 1961-66; European corr. Scripps-Howard Newspapers, Paris, 1966-69, fgn. editl. writer Washington, 1969-72, chief editl. writer, 1972-80, editor-in-chief, 1980-89, fgn. affairs columnist, 1989-95. Author: Reactionary! Sgt. Lloyd W. Pate's Story, 1956. Recipient Disting. Alumni award Pa. State U., 1972. Mem.: Gridiron, National Press. Office: 2735 P St NW Washington DC 20007-3065

CUTLER, CAROL ANN, food writer, consultant; b. Pitts. d. John Michael and Stella (Kope) Rataic; m. B.J. Cutler, Mar. 6, 1948. Student, U. Pitts., 1945-46, Hunter Coll., 1953, U. Paris-Sorbonne, 1959-60, Le Cordon Bleu, Paris, 1962-66; diploma, Ecole des 3 Gourmandes, Paris, 1967. Art critic Paris Herald Tribune, 1959-69; European corr. Art in Am., N.Y.C., 1963-71; cons. Nat. Gallery Art, Washington, 1970, Met. Mus. Art, N.Y.C., 1971; food columnist Washington Post, 1971-73; pub. affairs officer Nat. Portrait Gallery, Washington, 1974-78; chief food cons. Time-Life Books, Alexandria, Va., 1978-86; syndicated columnist Copley News Service, San Diego, 1986—. Restaurant critic, Dossier, Washington, 1988, Washington Bus. Forward, 1999—. Author 8 cookbooks including The Six-Minute Souffle and Other Culinary Delights, 1976 (Tastemaker award); freelance author and food cons. Mem. Am. Wine Soc., Am. Inst. Wine and Food, Les Dames d'Escoffier (pres. 1983-84), Les Cercle des Goumettes. Avocations: music, touring architectural sites. Home and Office: 2735 P St NW Washington DC 20007-3065 E-mail: cabjcutler@aol.com.

CUTLER, CHARLES EDWARD, lawyer; b. Des Moines, Apr. 2, 1956; BS, U. Iowa, 1978, JD, 1981. Bar: Iowa 1981, U.S. Dist. Ct. (no. and so. dists.) Iowa 1981, U.S. Ct. Appeals (8th cir.) 1981. Ptnr. Patterson, Lorentzen, Duffield, Timmons, Irish, Becker & Ordway, Des Moines, 1981—2002; shareholder Cutler Law Firm, P.C., W. Des Moines, 2002—. Mem. ABA, Iowa Bar Assn., Iowa Defense Counsel Assn., Defense Rsch. Inst., Iowa Assn. Workers Compensation Lawyers, Polk County Bar Assn. Office: Cutler Law Firm PC 4949 Pleasant St Ste 101 West Des Moines IA 50265 E-mail: CEC@cutlerfirm.com.

CUTLER, DAVID HORTON, editor, publisher; b. Boston, May 26, 1934; s. Fred Abbott and Elizabeth Horton (Carnahan) C.; m. Martha Marie Emery, Dec. 6, 1959; children: Geoffrey, Gregory. BA in Journalism, U. Nev., 1959. Editor, publ. The Merchant mag., Newport Beach, Calif., 1962—; publ., founder Bldg. Products Digest, Newport Beach, 1982—, ret. With U.S. Army, 1953-55. Mem. Masonic Lodge, Scottish Rite, Shriners.

CUTLER, EVERETTE WAYNE, history educator; b. Beaumont, Tex., Nov. 29, 1938; s. Homer Everette and Mary Abbie (Osborne) C.; m. Leta Harriet Rush; 1 child, Lori Catherine. BA, Lamar U., 1959; BD, So. Meth. U., 1964; MA, U. Tex., 1967, PhD, 1971. Rsch. assoc. U. Tex., Austin, 1965-67, U. Ky., Lexington, 1970-75; assoc. prof. history Vanderbilt U., Nashville, 1975-87; rsch. prof. history U. Tenn., Knoxville, 1987—. Dir. Polk Project, Vanderbilt U., Nashville, 1975-87, Polk Project, U. Tenn., 1987—. Asst. editor Southwestern Hist. Quar., 1965-67; asst. editor: Papers of Henry Clay, vols. 4 and 5, 1970-75; editor: Correspondence of James K. Polk, vols. 5-10, 1975—, North for Union, 1986. Pres. Nashville Symphony Chorus, 1982-83; vestry St. George's Episc. Ch., Nashville, 1984-87; dir. Tenn. Pres. Trust, 1991—; commodore Concord Yacht Club, 2000-02. Grantee NEH, 1984, 88-96, 2002-03, Nat. Hist. Publs. and Records Commn., 1975—, Tenn. Hist. Commn., 1975—. Mem. Am. Hist. Assn., Orgn. Am. Historians, So. Hist. Assn., Assn. for Documentary Editing, Phi Kappa Phi, Alpha Tau Omega. Democrat. Episcopalian. Avocations: choral music, sailing, fiction writing. Home: 7901 High Heath Knoxville TN 37919-4410 Office: U Tenn Hoskins Libr 216 Knoxville TN 37996-0001 E-mail: wcutler@utk.edu.

CUTLER, GORDON BUTLER, JR., endocrinologist, researcher; b. Cin., Oct. 16, 1947; s. Gordon Butler and Elizabeth Turner (Healy) C.; m. Hazel Jane Park, Feb. 5, 1977; children: Elizabeth Park, Joseph Clark. AB in Biochemistry, Harvard Coll., 1969; MD, Harvard U., 1973. Diplomate Am. Bd Internal Medicine. Intern Barnes Hosp., Washington U. Sch. Medicine, St. Louis, 1973-74, jr. asst. resident, 1974-75; fellow in endocrinology Nat. Inst. of Child Health & Human Devel., NIH, Bethesda, Md., 1975-78, sr. investigator, 1978-83, sect. chief-Developmental Endocrinology, 1983—97; dir. growth rsch. and clin. investigation Eli Lilly & Co., 1997—. Editor: Sexual Precocity, Etiology, Diagnosis, and Management, 1993; contbr. articles to profl. jours. Capt. USPHS, 1975-97. Thompson prize Texas A & M Univ., 1991. Fellow ACP; mem. AAAS, Soc. for Pediat. Rsch., Am. Soc. for Clin. Investigation, Endocrine Soc., Lawson Wilkins Pediat. Endocrine Soc. Methodist. Avocation: sailboat racing.

CUTLER, IRWIN HERBERT, lawyer; b. Mar. 28, 1943; s. Irwin Herbert Cutler and Eva Gloe (Thomas) Benedict; m. Carol Jean Smith, Dec. 28, 1965; children: Rachel, Alice. BA, Yale U., 1965; JD, Cornell U., 1968. Bar: Ky. 1968, U.S. Dist. Ct. (ea. dist.) Ky. 1969, U.S. Dist. Ct. (we. dist.) Ky. 1969, U.S. Ct. Appeals (6th cir.) 1970, U.S. Ct. Appeals (7th cir.) 1975. Mem.: Louisville Bar Assn. (co-chmn. labor law sect. 1984, 1992), Ky. Bar Assn. Democrat. Presbyterian. Home: 2249 Woodford Pl Louisville KY 40205-1651 Office: 1400 B Waterfront Plz 325 W Main St Louisville KY 40202-4251

CUTLER, JOHN CHARLES, physician, educator; b. Cleve., June 29, 1915; s. Glenn Allen and Grace Amanda (Allen) C.; m. Eliese Helene Strahl, Nov. 21, 1942. BA, Western Res. U., 1937, MD, 1941; M.P.H., Sch. Hygiene and Pub. Health, Johns Hopkins U., 1951. Diplomate: Am. Bd. Preventive Medicine and Pub. Health. Commd. asst. surgeon (lt. j.g.) USPHS, 1941, advanced through grades to asst. surgeon gen. (rear adm.), 1958; intern USPHS Hosp., Staten Island, N.Y., 1941; venereal disease investigations Pub. Health Svc. Venereal Disease Rsch. Lab., Stapleton, N.Y., 1943-46; venereal disease rsch. and demonstration Guatemala, 1946-48; assigned WHO, 1949-50; with venereal disease divsn. USPHS, 1951-54; program office Bur. State Svcs., 1954-57; asst. dir. Nat. Inst. Allergy and Infectious Diseases, 1958; asst. surgeon gen. for program, 1958-59; health officer Central dist. Allegheny County Health Dept., 1959-61; dep. dir. Pan Am. San. Bur., regional office for Americas WHO, 1961-68; prof. internat. health, dir. population program Grad. Sch. Public Health, U. Pitts., 1968-79, chmn. dept. health svcs. adminstrn., 1979-80, assoc. dept. chmn., prof. internat. health, 1980-85, prof. emeritus, 1985—. Pres. Family Planning Coun. Southwestern Pa., 1971-72; sec. Am. Social Health Assn., 1972-76; pres. Internat. Health Soc., 1972-73, Am. Assn. World Health, 1973-75, Assn. Voluntary Sterilization, 1977-83; sec.-treas. World Fedn. Health Agys. for Advancement Vol. Surg. Contraception, 1975-81, pres.-elect., 1981-85, pres. 1985-87. Contbr. articles to med. publs. Pres. UN Assn., Pitts., 1988-90. Fellow APHA; mem. Phi Beta Kappa. Home: Pittsburgh, Pa. Died Feb. 8, 2003.

CUTLER, JOHN EARL, landscape architect; b. Houston, Nov. 21, 1943; s. John Cecil and Dorothy Evelyn (Hewett) C.; m. Paula Helene Murdy, Dec. 27, 1969; children: Christian Hewett, Leigh Helene. BS in Landscape Architecture, Tex. A&M U., 1967. Registered landscape arch., Tex. Landscape arch. Caudill Rowlett Scott, Houston, 1968-69, Marmon Mok Green, Houston, 1969-70; campus landscape arch. U. Houston, 1970-74; ptnr., landscape arch. Office of George Porcher, Houston, 1974-79; prin., landscape arch. The SWA Group, Houston, 1979—. Bd. dirs. Trees for Houston, 1984—. Fellow Am. Soc. Landscape Archs. Avocations: sailing, checker automobiles, ice cream scoops. Home: 2235 Bartlett St Houston TX 77098-5201 Office: The SWA Group 1245 W 18th St Houston TX 77008-3392 E-mail: jpcutler@earthlink.net.

CUTLER, KENNETH BURNETT, lawyer, investment company executive; b. Muskegon Heights, Mich., June 19, 1932; s. Stanley and Lucile (Miles) C.; m. Cecelia Bilsly, Mar. 9, 1967; children: Kenneth Burnett, Randall Miles, Cynthia Bilsly, Robert Appleby, Jeffrey Lamont Derrick. BBA, U. Mich., 1954, JD, 1957. Bar: Mich. 1957, N.Y. 1960. Assoc. Dewey Ballantine, Bushby, Palmer & Wood, N.Y.C., 1957-66; v.p., sec. The Lord Abbett Managed Funds, N.Y.C., 1966-97; gen. counsel Lord, Abbett & Co., N.Y.C., 1966-97, ptnr., 1972-97. Past pres. Bronxville Scout Com., Inc. Mem.: NASD (arbitration bd.), Bronxville Field Club, Winged Foot Golf Club, Met. Club (N.Y.C.), Phi Delta Phi, Delta Tau Delta. Avocations: golf, tennis, skiing. Home: 10 Westway Bronxville NY 10708-4311

CUTLER, LAURENCE STEPHAN, architect, urban designer, museum founder, advertising executive, educator; b. New Haven, Conn., Aug. 27, 1940; s. Hermann Shepard and Doris Winifred Cutler; m. Sherrie Stephens, Jan. 24, 1967 (div. 1992); children: A. Maximilian S., Zachary Wolf S.; m. Judy Goffman, Feb. 7, 1995; stepchildren: Jennifer Paige Greenawalt, Andrew Douglas Goffman. BA, U. Pa., 1962; MArch, Harvard U., 1966, MArch in Urban Design, 1967. Nationally cert. architect. Founder, co-prin. ECODESIGN, Cambridge, 1966; with ECODESIGN subs. Combustion Engring., Inc., 1972—79; founder C-E Tec Internat., Inc., 1972-79, ECODESIGN/SPC Internat., 1979—82; with Architects Collaborative, Eero Saarinen & Assocs.; group dir. Lodigiani U.S.A. Ltd., 1985-87, also bd. dirs. Prof. MIT, 1967-72, Harvard U., 1965-73, R.I. Sch. Design, 1965-68; group dir. N.Am. Gold Greenless Trott (USA) Holdings, Inc., London, 1988-91. Prin. archtl. works include Chase Manhattan Bank Hdqrs. for Caribbean, St. Thomas, Ballys Park Pl. Casino Hotel, Sugarloaf/USA Ski Area, Maine, fire and police complex, Westford Mass., Lockhart Gardens Shopping Ctr., U.S. Virgin Islands, Am. Embassy housing, Lagos, Nigeria; author: (with Albert G.H. Dietz) Industrialized Building Systems for Housing, 1971, (with Sherrie Stephens Cutler) Recycling Cities for People: The Urban Design Process, 1976, 3d edit., 1983, Handbook of Housing Systems for Designers and Developers, 1974, (with Judy Cutler) Parrish & Poetry, 1995, 99, Maxfield Parrish: A Retrospective, 1996, 99,(with Judy Cutler) Maxfield Parrish, 2000. Incorporator Cambridge Sch. Weston; founder, trustee The Woodbridge Found.; adv. dir. Am. Illustrators Gallery, N.Y.C., 1984—, founder, chair ARTShows and Products, Corp., 1993—, Maxfield Parrish Orgn.; officer The Cezanne Family Orgn., Inc.; founder, chair Nat. Mus. Am. Illustration, Newport, R.I., 1998—; chair Am. Civilization Found., 1998. Recipient Alpha-Rho Chi Gold medal Harvard U., 1966, Engring. Excellence award Colo. Cons. Engrs. Coun., 1973, Design and Environment award, 1975, Design Arts Program award NEA, 1980; Milton Fund grantee, Harvard U., 1966, Fulbright-Hays grantee, India, 1968. Mem. AIA (Regional Honors award 1974, 75), Royal Inst. Brit. Architects, Am. Soc. Planning Ofcls., Nat. Coun. Archtl. Registration Bds., Harvard Club N.Y., Nat. Arts Club, Carnegie Club, Skibo Castle Scotland, Carnegie-Abbey (Portsmouth, R.I.). Address: 18 E 77th St Apt 2A New York NY 10021-1700 also: Vernon Ct Bellevue Ave Newport RI 02840 E-mail: lcutler@americanillustration.org.

CUTLER, LEONARD SAMUEL, physicist; b. Los Angeles, Jan. 10, 1928; s. Morris and Ethel (Kalech) C.; m. Dorothy Alice Pett, Feb. 13, 1954; children: Jeffrey Alan, Gregory Michael, Steven Russell, Scott Darren. BS in Physics, Stanford U., 1958, MS, 1960, PhD, 1966. Chief engr. Gertsch Products Co., Los Angeles, 1948-56, v.p. R&D, 1956-57; with Hewlett-Packard Co., Palo Alto, Calif., 1957-69, dir. physics rsch., 1969-85, dir. instruments and photonics lab., 1985-87, dir. superconductivity lab., 1987-89, disting. contbr., 1989-99; disting. contbr. tech. staff Agilent Techs., 2000—. Mem. adv. panels Nat. Bur. Standards; cons. Kernco, Inc., Danvers, Mass., 1982—, others. Patentee in field. Served with USNR, 1945-46. Recipient Achievement award Indsl. Rsch. Inst., 1990, Industrial Applications prize Am. Inst. of Physics, 1993 Fellow IEEE (Morris Leeds award 1984, Rabi award 1989), Am. Phys. Soc.; mem. AAAS, NAE, Sigma Xi. Home: 26944 Almaden Ct Los Altos CA 94022-4349 Office: Agilent Techs PO Box 10350 Palo Alto CA 94303-0867 E-mail: len_cutler@agilent.com.

CUTLER, LESLIE STUART, academic administrator and medical educator; b. New Brunswick, N.J., Jan. 20, 1943; s. Norman Jack and Marian (Lazerowitz) C.; m. Terry Ruth Grubman, July 30, 1966; children: Adam, Matthew. Student, UCLA, 1960-62, Los Angeles Valley Coll., Van Nuys, Calif., 1962, Calif. State U., Northridge, 1962-64; DDS, Washington U., St. Louis, 1968; PhD, SUNY, Buffalo, 1973; M in Mgmt., Hartford Grad. Ctr., 1984. Asst. prof. dept. oral biology U. Conn. Health Ctr., Farmington, 1973-77, assoc. prof. depts. oral diagnosis and pathology, 1977-83, prof., chmn. dept. oral diagnosis, 1977-87, assoc. v.p. adminstrn. and rsch., 1987-91, assoc. v.p., assoc. provost heath affairs, 1991-92, interim v.p., provost for health affairs, exec. dir., 1992-93, v.p., provost for health affairs, exec. dir., 1993—; pres. U. Conn. Health Ctr. Fin. Corp., Farmington, 1994—, U. Conn. Health Sys., Farmington, 1994—, v.p., provost for health affairs, exec. dir., 1993-95, pres., 1994-2000, chancellor, provost for health affairs, 1995-2000; chief sci. and tech. bus. U. Conn., 1999—2001; mng. dir. Lambert's Cove Ptnrs., 2001—. Pres. U. Conn. Health Ctr. Fin. Corp., 1992-2000; speaker Am. Dental Assn., 1988-89; co-chair biotech. implementation team Gov.'s Econ. Competitiveness Package, Dept. Econ. and Cmty. Devel., 1997-99, co-chair health svcs. implementation team, 1997-99; bd. dirs. Conn. Tech. Coun. Editor, contbr. chpts. to books, articles to profl. jours. Bd. dirs. Avon (Conn.) Old Farms Sch., 1991—, U. of Conn. Found., 1992-99, Conn. Capital Region Growth Coun., Inc., 1994-97; bd. dirs. corp. adv. coun. Am. Cancer Soc., 1995-99; chair Juvenile Diabetes Found.'s Walk for the Cure, Hartford County, 1999. Recipient Tech. Bus. Leader of Yr. award Greater Hartford C. of C., 1997. Fellow Am. Coll. Dentists; mem. Internat. Assn. Dental Rsch. (pres. salivary rsch. group 1985-86), Histochem. Soc. (councilor 1990—), Assn. Acad. Health Ctrs. (task force on sci. policy 1990—, bd. dirs. 1998-2000), Omicron Kappa Upsilon. Office: U Conn Health Ctr 263 Farmington Ave # 3800 Farmington CT 06030-0002

CUTLER, LLOYD NORTON, lawyer; b. N.Y.C., Nov. 10, 1917; s. Aaron Smith and Dorothy (Glaser) C.; m. Louise W. Howe, 1941 (dec. July 1988); children: Deborah Norton (Mrs. James Notman Jr.), Beverly Winslow (Mrs. Mark Troutman), Lloyd Norton Jr., Louisiana Winslow (Mrs. Lamar Johnson); m. Rhoda Winton Kraft, 1989. AB cum laude, Yale U., 1936, LLB magna cum laude, 1939, LLD (hon.), 1983, Princeton U., 1994; LLD (hon.), Trinity Coll., 2000. Bar: N.Y. 1940, D.C. 1946. Pvt. practice, N.Y.C., 1940-42, Washington, 1946—; ptnr. Wilmer, Cutler & Pickering, 1962-79, 81-90, sr. counsel, 1990—; counsel to Pres. of U.S., 1979-81, 94; sec. Lawyers Com. Civil Rights Under Law, 1963-65, co-chmn., 1971-73; chmn. D.C. Com. on Adminstrn. Justice under Emergency Conditions, 1968; exec. dir. Nat. Commn. on the Causes and Prevention of Violence, 1968-69; President's spl. rep. for maritime boundary and resource negotiations with Can., 1977-79; President's spl. rep. for revision Pacific Salmon Treaty, 1999. Sr. cons. Pres.'s Commn. on Strategic Forces, 1983; vis. lectr. Yale U. Law Sch., 1973-76, Yale U. Sch. Orgn. and Mgmt., 1977-79, All Souls Coll., Oxford (Eng.) U., 1983, Nuffield Coll., Oxford, 1986; mem. U.S. Group to Permanent Ct. Arbitration, The Hague, 1984-93; mem. Quadrennial Commn. on Legis., Exec. and Jud. Salaries, 1984, chmn., 1989; mem. Pres.'s Commn. on Fed. Ethics Law Reform, 1989; co-chair Dept. Energy Task Force on Non-Proliferation Programs in Russia, 2000-01, Nat. Commn. on Fed. Election Reform, 2001—; mem. internat. adv. coun. World Bank, 2001—. Hon. trustee Brookings Instn.; chmn., mem. coun. Yale U., 1966-71, 89-94, chmn. devel. bd., 1972-77, chmn. campaign for Yale U., 1978-79; exec. bd. dirs. Met. Opera Assn., 1974-79; chmn. Salzburg Seminar, 1984-94. Recipient Jefferson medal in law U. Va., 1995, Marshall-Wythe Sch. Law medal Coll. William and Mary, 1998. Mem. Am. Law Inst. (coun.), ABA, Coun. on Fgn. Rels. (bd. dirs. 1977-79), Am. Acad. Arts and Scis., Mid. Temple of London (Hon., Bencher). Clubs: Metropolitan, Chevy Chase (Washington), Century Assn. (N.Y.C.). Home: 3115 O St NW Washington DC 20007-3117 Office: Wilmer Cutler & Pickering 2445 M St NW Washington DC 20037-1435

CUTLER, NORMAN BARRY, funeral service executive; b. Chgo., Mar. 5, 1942; s. Jerome and Hannah (Feinberg) C.; m. Gail Weinstein, June 30, 1965; children: Brett, Rebecca. BSBA, Northwestern U., 1964, MBA, 1965. Mgmt. trainee First Nat. Bank Chgo., 1965-66; ptnr. Chgo. Jewish Funerals, Buffalo Grove, Ill., 1966-98; pres., CEO Weinstein Family Svcs., Inc. (formerly Weinstein Bros. Inc.), Wilmette, Ill., 1966-99; pres. Levitt-Weinstein, Inc., North Miami Beach, Fla., 1979-97; exec. v.p. Beth David Meml. Gardens, Hollywood, Fla., 1985-97, Mt. Nebo Meml. Gardens, Miami, Fla. Gen. ptnr. Wilmette Computer Assocs., Dixie Ptnrs., N.M.B. Assocs.; faculty Worsham Coll., Skokie, Ill., 1981-82. Gen. co-chmn. Channel 11 Pub. TV Auction, 1974-75; bd. govs Congregation Am Ahalom, Glencoe, Ill., v.p., pres., 1986-88; bd. dirs. North Suburban Jewish Cmty. Ctr., 1975-85, also past pres.; pres. ctrl. bd. dirs. Jewish Cmty. Ctrs., Chgo.; pres. Bernard Horwich Jewish Cmty. Ctr., 1993—; bd. govs. Nat. Found. Funeral Svc., Des Plaines, Ill., 1991-93; bd. dirs. Writers Theatre of Ill., 1999—. Mem. Jewish Funeral Dirs. Am. (pres. 1985-86, bd. govs.), Acad. Profl. Funeral Svc. Practice (pres. 1988-89), B'nai B'rith (v.p.).

CUTLER, PHILIP EDGERTON, lawyer; b. Evanston, Ill., Mar. 18, 1948; s. John A. and Catherine (Hedman) C.; m. Barbara Anne Phippen, Oct. 27, 1948; children: David, Nathanael, Andrew. AB in History, Georgetown U., 1970; JD with honors, Northwestern U., 1973. Assoc. Perkins Coie, Seattle, 1973-79; ptnr. Sax and MacIver, Seattle, 1979-85; ptnr., shareholder Sax and MacIver merged Karr Tuttle Campbell, Seattle, 1986-89; shareholder, pres. Cutler, Nylander & Hayton PS (formerly Cutler & Nylander), Seattle, 1990—, also bd. dirs. Ct.-approved arbitrator King County Superior Ct., 1982—, U.S. Dist. Ct. (we. dist.) Wash., 1992—; mediator U.S. Dist. Ct. (we. dist.) Wash., 1982—; judge pro tem King County Superior Ct., 1993—; mem. comml. arbitration panel Am. Arbitration Assn., 1992—, mediator, 1997—; lectr., program chmn. numerous continuing legal edn. programs; mem. arbitration panel Nat. Assn. Securities Dealers, 1996—. Co-founder Country Dr. Cmty. Legal Clinic, Seattle, 1974—; co-pres. parents club St. Joseph Sch., Seattle, 1984-86, mem. sch. adv. bd., 1985-88; dir. St. Joseph Endowment Fund, 1986-2002, St. Joseph Parish Sch. Fund, 1990-2002, St. Joseph Sch. Endowment Found., Seattle, 1994-2002, sec., 1996-2002; mem. sch. adv. bd. Blanchet H.S., Seattle, 1991-2000, mem. devel. com., 1992-2000; chair Georgetown Alumni Admissions Interviewing Program, 1975-2000; active St. Patrick Parish, Seattle, 1974-82, St. Joseph Parish, Seattle, 1982—, Cursillo Movement, 1975-85, Cath.

Archdiocese of Seattle, 1979-82, YMCA Indian Guides/Indian Princesses program, 1980-84, chief of Husky Nation, 1982-84. Mem. ABA (antitrust, dispute resolution, and litigation sects., civil practice and procedure com. antitrust sect. 1980-90), FBA (chair ct. congestion/alt. dispute resolution com. 1985-99, mem. spl. alt. dispute resolution task force 1994 western dist. Wash.), Wash. State Bar Assn. (consumer protection, antitrust and unfair bus. practices sect., litigation sect., dispute resolution sect.), St. Thomas More Soc. Seattle (pres. 1993-95), Georgetown Alumni Assn. (bd. dirs. 1977-80, alumni sen. 1980—), King County Bar Assn. (numerous coms.), Rainier Club, Wash. Athletic Club, Col. Club Seattle, Georgetown Club Wash. (pres. 1980-86, mem. exec. com. 1986—). Roman Catholic. Avocations: swimming, downhill skiing, gourmet cooking, reading, furniture-making and woodworking. Office: Cutler Nylander & Hayton PS 505 Madison St Ste 220 Seattle WA 98104-1111

CUTLER, RICHARD W. lawyer; b. New Rochelle, N.Y., Mar. 9, 1917; s. Charles Evelyn and Amelia (MacDonald) C.; m. Elizabeth Fitzgerald, Oct. 18, 1947; children: Marguerite Blackburn, Alexander MacDonald, Judith Elizabeth. BA, Yale U., 1938, LLB, 1941. Bar: Conn. 1941, N.Y. 1942, Wis. 1950, D.C. 1975, U.S. Supreme Ct. 1980. Practiced in NYC, 1941—49, Milw., 1949—87; assoc. Donovan, Leisure, Newton & Lumbard, 1941—42; atty. Legal Aid Soc., 1946—47, RCA Comm., Inc., 1947—49; ptnr. Quarles & Brady, and predecessors, 1954—87; gen. ptnr. Sunset Investment Co., Milw. Author: Zoning Law and Practice in Wisconsin, 1967, Greater Milwaukee's Growing Pains, 1950-2000: An Insider's View, 2001. Chmn. Milw. br. Fgn. Policy Assn., 1951-53; pres. Childrens Service Soc. Wis., 1961-63, Neighborhood House, 1971-74; sec. Southeastern Wis. Regional Planning Commn., 1960-84, Yale Devel. Bd., 1973-79; bd. dirs. Wis. Dept. Resource Devel., 1967-68; Met. Milw. Study Commn., 1957-61; bd. dirs. Milw. Innovation Ctr., 1985-89, pres., 1984-85, exec. v.p., 1985-89; bd. dirs. Greater Milw. Com., 1982-89. Capt. USAAF, 1943-46 and OSS, 1944-46. Recipient Disting. Leadership award Am. Planning Assn., 1992. Mem. ABA, Wis. Bar Assn., Milw. Club, Milw. Country Club, Town Club, Phi Beta Kappa. Presbyterian. Home: 938 W Shaker Cir Mequon WI 53092-6032 Office: 411 E Wisconsin Ave Milwaukee WI 53202-4461 E-mail: rwc@quarles.com.

CUTLER, ROBERT BRIAN, medical educator, researcher; b. Myrtle Point, Oreg., Dec. 31, 1947; s. Kenneth Wayne and Frances Joella C. BA, U. Ala., 1970; MS, U. Miami, 1980, PhD, 1987. Instr. U. Miami, Coral Gables, 1989-90, rsch. assoc. in neurol. surgery, 1990-94, vol. faculty psychiatry and behavioral scis., 1994-95, asst. prof., 1995—. Home: 2565 SW 27th St Apt 4 Miami FL 33133-2247 Office: U Miami Med Sch D-79 Dept Psychiatry Dominion Towers Miami FL 33136

CUTLER, ROBERT SUMNER, engineering educator; b. Springfield, Mass., June 27, 1933; s. Samuel L. and Sara (Damask) C.; m. Natalie Meyers, Aug. 22, 1954 (div. July 1979); children: Mark, Debra, Beth; m. Sarah Taylor, Aug. 31, 1986. BSME, U. Mass., 1955; MS in Mgmt., Sci., Stevens Inst. Tech., 1966. Test engr. Bell Tel. Labs., Whippany, N.J., 1960-62; engrng. mgmt. cons. Ford, Bacon & Davis, Inc., N.Y.C., 1962-67; staff analyst R&D U.S. Dept. Transp., Washington, 1967-68; ops. rsch. analyst Nat. Bur. Stds., Gaithersburg, Md., 1968-73; sr. staff assoc. NSF, Washington, 1973-90; adj. prof. Georgetown U., Washington, 1991, George Washington U., Washington, 1997—. Exptl. test engr. Aerojet-Gen. Corp., Sacramento, 1954-60, Pratt & Whitney Aircraft, E. Hartford, Conn., 1955-56; cons. Bakers Creek Meml. Assn., Mackay, Australia, 1990—. Hitachi, Ltd., Tokyo, 1993-94, Nat. Tech. U., Ft. Collins, Colo., 1993, Kushi Inst., Becket, Mass., 1996—. Author: MacKay's Flying Fortress, 2003; editor: Science in Japan, 1989, Engineering in Japan, 1991, Technology in Japan, 1993. Horace A. Smith Found. scholar, 1951; Fulbright Japan fellow Internat. Exch. Scholars, 1986-87. Fellow AAAS. Jewish. Avocations: aviation, photography, computer technology, travel. Office: 12306 Captain Smith Ct Potomac MD 20854-6211

CUTLER, ROBERT W. biologist, educator; b. Toronto, Ontario, Can., May 27, 1972; s. Robert W. Cutler and Marcia W. Weis. PhD, Vanderbilt U., 1998. Prof. of biology Bard Coll., Annadale, NY, 1999—. Vol. Childlife, MaeSai, Thailand, 2002—03. Recipient Gold Congl. award, U.S. Congress, 1997; fellow, Fulbright Found., 2002—. Achievements include patents for statistical method to recognize gene regions in microbial genomes. Home: Bard College Annandale NY 12504 Office: Bard College 302 Hegeman Annandale NY 12504 E-mail: cutler@bard.edu.

CUTLER, SARAH TAYLOR, educator, enamelist; b. NYC, July 18, 1940; d. James Karr and Nedra Mary (Evans) Taylor; m. George Aylwin Otto, Aug. 31, 1963; (div. Aug., 1977) children: Sarah Perin Otto, Richard Talbot Otto; m. Robert Sumner Cutler, Aug. 31, 1986. BA, Duchesne Coll., 1962; MA, U. Nebr., 1982. Cert. prin. elem., secondary, Eng., Spanish. Tchr. pub. and pvt. sch., NYC, 1961—65, Omaha, 1961-65; tchr. Am. Sch., Lima, Peru, 1971-72, Buffalo County Sch., Nebr., 1977-79, Cen. Tech. C.C., Grand Is., Nebr., 1977-79; asst. Ctr. for Leadership Devel. Am. Coun. on Edn., Wash., DC, 1980-82; asst. to dep. dir. Coun. for Internat. Exch. of Scholars, Wash., 1982-85; adminstr. sci. and tech. courses AAAS and Confed. Ctr. Am. Nat. U., Washington, 1986-90. Cons. Pacific War Project, NHK-TV, Japan, 1991-92; Interciencia observer AAAS, Bogota, Columbia, 1993, Trinidad, 1994. Group exhbns. include Enamelist Soc., Newsport, Ky., 1989, Kennedy Ctr. Artist Gallery, 1991—, Fort Myers Women's Exhibit, Arlington, Va., 1994. Citizen lobbyist for War Clause of Constitution, 1990—; assoc. Women Strike for Peace, 1992, chair 23d precinct, 1994-99; mem. Sedona Intensive Clearing for Millenium, 1999; vol. Montgomery County Hospice, Nat. Mus. Women in Arts; garden docent Hillwood Marjorie Merriweather Post Mus. Grantee Nebr. Art Coun., 1978-80, Reading is Fundamental, Nebr., 1979-81; recipient 1st and 2d pl. medals US Army Rec. Svc. Nat. Craft Contest, 1994. Mem. Washington-Tokyo Women's Club, Past Parents Assn. Washington Internat. Sch., DAR (regent Great Falls chpt. 1998-99, vol. genealogist, mus. docent), DAR Mex. Soc. (assoc.), Colonial Dames C17. Spiritualist. Avocations: textile arts, theatre arts. E-mail: SarahTCutler@hotmail.com.

CUTLER, STEPHEN JOEL, sociologist, educator; b. Lawrence, Mass., Jan. 1, 1943; s. Lewis J. and Minnie C.; m. Karan Elizabeth Davis, Apr. 25, 1968; children: Ellen Min, Timothy Spence. BA, Dartmouth Coll., 1964; MA, U. Mich., 1965, PhD, 1969. Faculty Oberlin Coll., Ohio, 1969-84, prof. sociology-anthropology, 1979-84, chmn. dept., 1979-82; prof. sociology, Bishop Robert F. Joyce Disting. Prof. gerontology U. Vt., Burlington, 1984—, dir. Ctr. Study of Aging, 1993-96. Sr. fellow Ctr. Study Aging and Human Devel., Duke U., 1975-76; adv. bd. nat. data program social scis. Nat. Opinion Rsch. Ctr., 1980-85; mem. human devel. and aging study sect. NIH, 1979-84, 88-92, chmn., 1990-92; vis. scholar Oreg. State U., 2002; Fulbright scholar, 2003—. Co-author: Middle Start: An Experiment in the Educational Enrichment of Young Adolescents, 1978; co-editor: Major Social Problems: A Multidisciplinary View, 1979, Promoting Successful and Productive Aging, 1995; assoc. editor Gerontol. Monographs, 1976-82; mem. editl. bd. Internat. Jour. Aging and Human Devel., 1980—, Jour. Gerontology, 1981-86, Rsch. on Aging, 1987—, Am. Jour. Alzheimer's Disease, 2002—; editor Jour. Gerontology: Social Scis., 1990-93. Grantee, NIMH, NSF, NIH, Alzheimer's Assn.; Woodrow Wilson fellow, 1965, Univ. scholar, 2000—01, Fulbright scholar, 2003—. Fellow Gerontol. Soc. Am. (exec. com. behavioral and social scis. sect. 1979-81, chmn. 1987, coun. mem. 1986-88, pres.-elect 1997, pres. 1998); mem. Am. Sociol. Assn. (coun. sect. on aging 1982-84, chmn.-elect 1993-94, chmn. 1994-95), Assn. for Gerontology in Higher Edn. (bd. dirs., exec. com. 1985-87, 95-97, Clark Tibbitts award 2001). Home: 54 Sleepy Hollow Rd Essex Junction VT 05452-2722 Office: U Vt Dept Sociology Burlington VT 05405-0001

CUTLER, VERNE CLIFTON, engineering educator, consultant; b. Brookings, S.D., Jan. 2, 1926; s. Jesse C. and Mabel Cutler; m. Norma K. Cutler, Feb. 18, 1948; children: Susan, Janice, Diane, Robert, David. BS, Kans. State U., 1950, MS, 1951; PhD, U. Wis., 1960. Registered engr., Wis. Design engr. Boeing Airplane Co., Wichita, 1951—61; instr. U. Wis., Madison, 1951-60, asst. prof., 1960-63; assoc. prof. U. Wis., Milw., 1963-67, prof., 1967—, dept. chair, 1963-73. Cons., expert witness, Milw., 1963—; cons. Allis-Chalmers, Milw., 1984. Author: Encyclopedia Britannica-Compton's, 1988. Asst. scout leader Boy Scouts Am., Milw., 1964. Recipient ATT Tchg. Excellence award, 1990; U. Wis.-Milw. Alumni Assn. Tchg. Excellence award, 1988. Mem. Am. Soc. Engrng. Edn. (Outstanding Campus Rep. 1990, Centennial cert. 1993), Sigma Xi. Republican. Methodist. Avocations: woodworking, gardening, hunting, fishing, tennis. Home: 8630 N Spruce Rd Milwaukee WI 53217-2126

CUTLER, WALTER LEON, diplomat, foundation executive; b. Boston, Nov. 25, 1931; s. Walter Leon and Esther Dewey (Bradley) C.; m. Sarah G. Beeson, Mar. 16, 1957 (div. 1981); children: Allen Bradley, Thomas Gerard.; m. Isabel K. Brookfield, Nov. 28, 1981. BA, Wesleyan U., Middletown, Conn., 1953; MA, Fletcher Sch. of Law & Diplomacy, 1954. Joined U.S. Fgn. Service, 1956; vice consul Am. consulate Yaounde, Cameroon, 1957-59; fgn. affairs officer Dept. State, Washington, 1959-60, staff asst. to sec. of state, 1960-62; 2d sec. Am. Embassy Algiers, Algeria, 1962-65; prin. officer Am. Consulate Tabriz, Iran, 1965-67; polit. officer, 1st sec. Am. Embassy Seoul, Korea, 1967-69, Saigon, Vietnam, 1969-71; spl. asst. for Vietnam Peace Negotiations U.S. Dept. State, 1971-73; mem. Sr. Seminar in Fgn. Policy, 1973-74; dir. Office Ctrl. African Affairs, 1974-75; amb. to Zaire, 1975-79; amb.-designate to Iran, 1979; prin. dep. asst. sec. for congl. rels. Dept. State, Washington, 1979-81; amb. to Tunisia, 1982-84, Saudi Arabia, 1984-87, 1988-89; rsch. prof. diplomacy Georgetown U., Washington, 1987-88; pres. Meridian Internat. Ctr., Washington, 1989—; spl. emissary for sec. gen. UN, N.Y.C., 1994. Served with U.S. Army, 1954-56. Recipient Disting. Alumnus award Wesleyan U., 1983, King Abdul Aziz award Saudi Arabia, 1986, Presdl. Performance award, 1986, 87, Wilbur J. Carr award U.S. Dept. State, 1989, Dir. Gen.'s Cup award, 1993; decorated Order of the Leopard, Zaire, 1979. Mem. Coun. Fgn. Rels., Am. Fgn. Svc. Assn., Am. Acad. Diplomacy (bd. dirs.), Washington Inst. Fgn. Affairs (bd. dirs.), Mid. East Inst., Am. Tunisian Assn. (hon. com. The Am. Coms. on Foreign Rels.), Met. Club, Am. Iranian Coun. (bd. dirs.). Office: Meridian Internat Ctr 1630 Crescent Pl NW Washington DC 20009-4004

CUTLIP, RANDALL BROWER, retired psychologist, university president emeritus; b. Clarksburg, W.Va., Oct. 1, 1916; s. M.N. and Mildred (Brower) C.; m. Virginia White, Apr. 21, 1951; children: Raymond Bennett, Catherine Baumgarten. AB, Bethany Coll., 1940; cert. indsl. pers. mgmt., So. Meth. U., 1944; MA, East Tex. U., 1949; EdD, U. Houston, 1953; LLD, Bethany Coll., 1965, Columbia Coll., 1980; LHD, Drury Coll., 1975; ScD, S.W. Bapt. U., 1978; LittD, William Woods U., 1981. Tchr. adminstr. Tex. pub. sch., 1947-50; dir. tchr. placement U. Houston, 1950-51, supr. counselling, 1951-53; dean students Atlantic Christian Coll., Wilson, NC, 1953-56, dean, 1956-58; dean personnel, dir. grad. divsn. Chapman U., Orange, Calif., 1958-60; pres. William Woods Coll., Fulton, Mo., 1960-81, pres. emeritus, 1981—; trustee William Woods U., Fulton, Mo., 1981-85, 92—. Chmn. bd. dirs. Mo. Colls. Fund, 1973-75; chmn. Mid-Mo. Assn. Coll., 1972-76; bd. dir. Marina del Sol, bd. pres., 1985-90, 92-95. Mem. visitors' bd. Mo. Mil. Acad., 1966-70, chmn., 1968-72; trustee Schreiner Coll., Kerrville, Tex., 1983-92, Amy Shelton McNutt Charitable Trust, 1983—, Permanent Endowment Fund, 1987-96, Scholarship Found. and Res. Fund of Christian Ch., 1992-96, Christian Found., 1990—; bd. dir. Univ. of the Americas, 1984-96, exec. v.p., 1985-96; bd. dirs. Tex. State Aquarium, 1994, exec. com., 1994—, pres. 1998; elder emeritus Christian Ch., bd. dir., exec. com. Recipient McCubbin award, 1968, Delta Beta Xi award, 1959 Mem. Am. Pers. and Guidance Assn., Alpha Sigma Phi, Phi Delta Kappa, Kappa Delta Pi, Alpha Chi. Address: 1400 Ocean Dr Corpus Christi TX 78404-2109

CUTLIP, SUSIE SAUNDERS, librarian; b. Kimball, W.Va., Dec. 30, 1946; d. Charles Harry and Pauline (Farris) S.; m. Gary Lee Cutlip, June 21, 1969 (div. Aug. 1988); children: Carri Elizabeth, Charles Edward. BS in Secondary Edn., W.Va. U., 1967; MS in Ednl. Media, Radford U., 1976. Tchr. Baileysville (W.Va.) High Sch., 1968; asst. libr. Washtenaw C.C., Ypsilanti, Mich., 1968-70; libr. asst. New River C.C., Dublin, Va., 1972, 75-77; reference libr. Radford (Va.) U., 1977-78; libr. Dublin Mid. Sch., 1978-87; audio visual libr. Pulaski County High Sch., Dublin, 1987-96, head libr., 1996—. Mem. ALA, Va. Ednl. Media Assn. Methodist. Office: Pulaski County High Sch 5414 Cougar Trail Rd Dublin VA 24084-3841

CUTNAW, MARY-FRANCES, emeritus communications educator, writer, editor, publisher; b. Dickinson, N.D., June 15, 1931; d. Delbert A. and Edith (Calhoun-Pritchard) C. BS, U. Wis., 1953, MS, 1957, postgrad., to 1968. Life tchg. license in speech, English and French, Wis. Vol. tchr. Vocat. Sch. for World War II Displaced Persons, Stevens Point, Wis., 1951-52; speech tchr. Pulaski H.S., Milw., 1953-55; tchg. asst. dept. speech U. Wis., Madison, 1956-57, spl. asst. Sch. Edn., summer 1957; instr. speech U. Wis.-Stout, Menomonie, 1957-58, dean of women, 1958-59, asst. prof. speech, 1959-64, assoc. prof. speech, 1964-74, prof. emeritus, 1974—. Comm. and pers. cons., St. Paul, 1974—; writer, editor, pub. New Legal Press, 1995—. Author: How to Settle a Living Trust, 1996, 4th edit., 2003. Organizer, past advisor Young Dems., Menomonie, 1959—; founder Edith and Kent Cutnaw Scholarship, U. Wis., Stevens Point, 1960—; bd. dirs. Blaisdell Place, Mpls., 1980-85. Hon. scholar U. Wis., Madison, 1959-60, 67-68. Mem. ACLU, NOW, Internat. Platform Assn., Wis. Acad. Arts and Scis., Wis. Women's Network, Progressive Roundtable (Mpls.), Calhoun Beach Club (Mpls.), Amnesty Internat., World Jewish Congress (charter), U. Club St. Paul, Greenpeace, Dunn County Humane Soc., Sierra Club, Soc. for Prevention of Cruelty to Animals, Humane Soc. U.S., Gamma Phi Beta, Phi Beta, Sigma Tau Delta, Pi Lambda Theta. Roman Catholic. Avocations: ecology, civil rights, animal rights, consumer protection, health and wellness. Office: New Legal Press PO Box 282 Menomonie WI 54751-0282 E-mail: cutnawm@uwstout.edu.

CUTNER, ROLANDE REGAT, lawyer; b. Paris, Sept. 6, 1934; came to U.S., 1963, naturalized, 1970; d. Luis Felipe and Marguerite (Thibault) Ibarra; m. Charles Yves Regat, Feb. 4, 1960 (dec. 1971); m. David Alan Cutner, June 25, 1977 (div. 1985). Diploma in Polit. Sci., U. Paris, 1959; Lic. in Law, Paris Faculty of Law, 1971; grad. Inst. Jud. Studies, 1972. Bar: Paris 1976, N.Y. 1978, U.S. Dist. Ct. (so. dist.) N.Y. 1978. Atty. Compagnie General d'Electricite, Paris, 1972-76, Usinor Steel Corp., N.Y.C., 1976-77; mem. firm Griggs, Baldwin & Baldwin, 1978-79, Regat-Cutner, 1980— . Mem. Internat. Bar Assn., ABA, Am. Fgn. Law Assn., Fed. Bar Council, Ordre des Avocats a la Cour de Paris, N.Y. County Lawyer Assn. (com. on immigration, nationality, and naturalization), Asia-Pacific Lawyers Assn. (com. on Customs and Internat. Trade Law). Office: 67 Park Ave Ste 12D New York NY 10016-2557

CUTSHAW, KENNETH ANDREW, lawyer; b. Knoxville, Tenn., Sept. 2, 1953; s. Harvey Audley and Frankie Janelle (Temple) C.; m. Diane Dracos. BA, U. Tenn., 1975, JD, 1978; LLM, Am. U., 1987. Bar: Tenn. 1978, D.C. 1987, U.S. Dist. Ct. (mid. dist.) 1978, Tenn., (ea. dist.) 1978, Tenn. Supreme Ct. 1978, U.S. Supreme Ct. 1987, U.S. Fed. cir., 1991. Sr. atty. State of Tenn. Legis., Nashville, 1979-80, The 1982 World's Affair, Knoxville, 1980-83, cons., 1984; campaign mgr. for candidate U.S. Senate, 1983-84; asst. dep., asst. sec. import adminstrn. Dept. Commerce, Washington, 1985-87, chief of staff export adminstrn., 1987-89, dep. asst. sec. export enforcement, 1989-91; ptnr. Miller & Steuart, Washington, 1991-93; pres. Global Trading Ptnrs., Inc., Washington, 1991-93; of counsel Troutman Sanders, LLP, Atlanta, 1993-95, Smith Gambrell & Russell, LLP, 1995-99; ptnr. Holland & Knight, LLP, Atlanta, 1999—. Mem. U.S. Govt. Industry Adv. Com. on Customs and Trade, 1994-96; adj. fellow Hudson Inst.; adj. prof. Ga. State U., 1997—, Emory U., 2002—; hon. counsul, India. Author: Tennessee Criminal Law Statutes, 1980; co-author: Doing Business in China, 1995, Doing Business in Russia, 1999, Doing Business in India, 2001; contbr. articles to profl. jours. Vice chmn., exec. com. Tenn. Rep. Party, 1982-85; internat. chmn. Boy Scouts Am., Atlanta; mem. Bretton Woods Com.; co-chmn. Awakening Weekend. Roddy Acad. scholar U. Tenn., 1971-72. Mem. ABA, Internat. Bar Assn., Ga. Bar Assn., Atlanta Bar Assn., Tenn. Bar Assn. (com. chmn. 1983-84), D.C. Bar Assn., Am. Coun. Young Polit. Leaders (bd. dirs., co-chmn.), Coun. on Fgn. Rels., Atlanta Round Table (chmn.), World Trade Ctr. (bd. dirs.), Elks, Sigma Chi. Baptist. Avocations: flying, skiing, hiking, cultural events, golfing. Home: 4417 Dunmore Rd Marietta GA 30068-4224 Office: Holland & Knight LLP One Atlantic Center 1201 W Peachtree St NW Ste 2000 Atlanta GA 30309-3453 E-mail: kcutshaw@hklaw.com.

CUTSUMPAS, LLOYD, judge; b. Danbury, Conn., Oct. 14, 1933; s. John and Pauline (Dalacas) C.; m. Nicolletta Kakavas, July 31, 1960; children: John, Theodore. BBA, U. Conn., 1955; JD, Georgetown U., 1960. Bar: Conn. 1962, U.S. Dist. Ct. Conn. 1963. Pvt. practice, Conn., 1962-97; ptnr. Cutsumpas, Collins, Hannafin, Garamella, Jaber and Tuozzolo, P.C., Danbury, 1962-97; judge Superior Ct., Conn., 1998—. Lectr. family and bus. law Western Conn. State U., Danbury, 1980-97. Contbr. articles on family law to profl. jours. Pres. regional YMCA; pres. Parish Coun. Assumption Greek Orthodox Ch.; vice-chmn. Richter Park Authority. Served with U.S. Army, 1955-57. Named one of Outstanding Men of Am., Danbury Jaycees, 1967. Fellow Am. Acad. Matrimonial Lawyers (pres. Conn. chpt.), mem. ABA (family law div.), Conn. Bar Assn. (family law divsn., jud. com.), Danbury Bar Assn. (pres.). Democrat. Greek Orthodox. Home: 12 Maplecrest Dr Danbury CT 06811-4262

CUTTER, CHARLES ROSS, historian, educator; b. Berkeley, Calif., Sept. 22, 1950; s. Donald Colgett and Charlotte Leona (Lazear) C.; m. Maryann Williams, Aug. 8, 1976 (div. Aug. 1989); children: Francisco, Casandra; m. Susan Curtis, Jan. 11, 1992. BA, U. N.Mex., 1976, MA, 1984, PhD, 1989. Vis. asst. prof. Lewis & Clark Coll., Portland, Oreg., 1987-88; vis. asst. prof. Purdue U., West Lafayette, Ind., 1988-91, asst. prof., 1991-95, assoc. prof., 1995—, asst. head, dir. grad. studies Dept. of History, 1998—2001. Author: The Legal Culture of Northern New Spain, 1700-1810, 1995 (Presidio La Bahia award 1996, Fray Francisco Atanasio Dominguez award 1996), The Protector de Indios in Colonial New Mexico, 1659-1821, 1986; editor and introduction: Libro de los Principales Rudimentos Tocante a Todos Juicios, Criminal, Civil y Executivo, 1764, 1994. Recipient Fulbright Sr. Scholar award, 1993-94, Fulbright-Hays/Spanish Govt. Rsch. grant, 1985-86, Purdue Rsch. Found. Summer Faculty grant, 1992, 96, Dorothy Woodward Meml. fellowship U. N.Mex., 1985; Ctr. for Humanistic Studies fellow Purdue U., 2002. Mem. Instituto Internacional de Historia del Derecho Indiano (elected 1992); Am. Hist. Assn., Conf. on Latin Am. History, Western History Assn., Am. Soc. for Legal History, Phi Alpha Theta (treas. Sigma chpt. 1982-83, pres. 1983-84). Avocations: basketball, gardening, woodworking, guitar playing. Home: 492 Littleton St West Lafayette IN 47906-3013 Office: Dept History Purdue U West Lafayette IN 47907-1358 E-mail: ccutter@sla.purdue.edu.

CUTTER, CURTIS CARLY, consulting company executive; b. Sacramento, Oct. 27, 1928; s. Curtis Harold and Leita (Carly) C.; m. Christiane Kühne, Jan. 29, 1965; children: Colette, Curtis Brooks, Lucho Antonio, Kai Kirsten, Sasha Christiana, Knut Carly. AB, U. Calif., Berkeley, 1951; cert., U. Geneva, 1955; MA, Stanford U., 1969. Consular officer Am. Embasssy, Phnom Penh, Cambodia, 1957-59; U.S. del. to UN and Trusteeship Coun., 1959-62; polit. officer Am. Embassy, Lima, Peru, 1962-65; chief Office Peruvian Affairs, State Dept., Washington, 1965-67; U.S. del. OAS, 1967-68; prin. officer Am. Consulate, Porto Alegre, Brazil, 1969-70; polit. officer Am. Embassy, Madrid, 1970-72; prin. officer, consul gen. Am. Consulate Gen., Seville, Spain, 1972-75; dep. dir. Office UN Polit. Affairs, 1975-77; acting dep. asst. sec. for congl. rels., 1977-78; pres. Interworld Cons., 1978-93, chmn., 1994—. Pres. ChinaMetrik, 1988-98; mng. dir. IMS ChinaMetrik Ltd., 1998-2003; sr. cons. Nat. Dem. Inst. Bd. dirs. China Med. Tribune; dir. AMS Found. Capt. AUS, 1951-53. Recipient State Dept. award for heroism, 1970, State Dept. Meritorious Honor award, 1971; Woodrow Wilson fellow, 1983-94. Mem. Am. Fgn. Svc. Assn., Union League (N.Y.C.), Nat. Press Club (Washington), Alpha Delta Phi. Address: 175 Commonwealth Ave Boston MA 02116-2215 E-mail: curtcutter@aol.com.

CUTTER, DAVID LEE, pharmaceutical company executive; b. Oakland, Calif., Jan. 3, 1929; s. Robert Kennedy and Virginia (White) C.; m. Nancy Lee Baugh, Sept. 14, 1950; children: David Lee, Jr., Thomas White, William Baugh, Steven Kennedy, Michael Lee. Student, U. Calif.-Berkeley, 1947; AB, Stanford U., 1950, MBA, 1952. C.P.A., Calif. Staff accountant Webb & Webb, C.P.A.'s, San Francisco, 1952-54; with Cutter Labs., Inc., 1954-84, pres., 1967-74, chmn., 1974-80, vice-chmn., 1980-82; sr. cons., 1982-84. Bd. dirs. Chad Therapeutics, Inc., Chatsworth, Calif., Civic Bancorp. Active various community drives; mem. Citizens Com. to Study Discrimination in Housing, Berkeley, 1961-62; troop committeeman Boy Scouts Am., 1964-74; v.p. Mt. Diablo Coun., 1975-77, pres., 1978-80, bd. dirs., 1975—; bd. dirs. Golden Gate Scouting, 1978-90, pres. 1980-84; bd. dirs. Park Hills Homes Assn., 1961-63, HEALS, Emeryville, Calif., 1980-87, Alameda County (Calif.) Taxpayers Assn., 1967-69, Insts. Med. Scis., San Francisco, 1974-76, San Francisco Bay Area Coun., 1968-84, pres. Cutter Found., 1967-86; trustee United Way of Bay Area, 1981-86, Miles Found., 1986-92; mem. adv. bd. Herrick Hosp., 1968-76, trustee, 1976-84, pres. bd. trustees, 1978-84; mem. Accrediting Commn. on Edn. in Health Svcs. Adminstrn., 1982-88, adv. coun. Sch. Bus., San Francisco State Coll., 1966-70; bd. dirs. Alta Bates Health Sys., 1984-95, Alta Bates Med. Ctr., 1988-95, chmn., 1991-95, East Bay Community Found., 1984-89, Hosp. Coun. No. Calif., 1983-89, Pathology Inst., 1986-90; bd. dirs. Acute Care Affiliates, 1987-89, chmn. 1988-89, Calif. Healthcare System, 1992-95; bd. govs. Vol. Trustees Not-for-Profit Hosps., 1989-95, vice chmn. 1990-92, treas. 1993-95; dir. Rossmoor Med. Ctr., 2000—, chmn., 2000—. Recipient Silver Beaver award Boy Scouts Am., 1982. Mem. AICPA, Stanford Alumni Assn., Berkeley C. of C. (dir. 1977-83, v.p. 1978-83), Rotary (Paul Harris fellow 1990), Delta Upsilon. E-mail: Davcutter@aol.com.

CUTTER, JEFFREY S. secondary education educator, music educator; b. Royal Oak, Mich., July 20, 1956; s. George E. and Joy G. (Dolby) C. MusB with distinction, Wayne State U., 1978, MEd, M in Ednl. Leadership/Adminstrn., 1994. Cert. tchr., Mich. Performing arts facilitator Warren (Mich.) Consol. Cmty. Edn., 1980—; curriculum cons. Warren Consol. Schs., 2000—. Dir. entertainment The Detroit Lions, Inc. Chmn. Warren Cultural Commn., Warren-Ctr.-Line Thanksgiving Parade Com., Inc. Mem. Am. Sch. Band Dirs. Assn. (chmn. Mich. chpt., nat. treas.), Mich. Sch. Band and Orch. Assn., Optimist (pres., treas. Warren chpt.). Home: 32774 McConnell Ct Warren MI 48092-3111 Office: Frost Curriculum Ctr 14301 Parkside Warren MI 48088 E-mail: cutter@attglobal.net.

CUTTER, JOHN MICHAEL, dentist; b. Columbus, Ohio, May 28, 1952; s. John Raymond and Betty Mae (Paripovich) C.; m. Alice May Mcquitty, Aug. 6, 1977 (div. May 1984); 1 child, John David Benjamin; m. Linda Ann Hovis-Smith, Oct. 20, 1990 (div. Jan. 1997). BA, Ohio State U., 1974, DDS, 1976. Pvt. practice family dentistry and laser-assisted care, Fairfield, Ohio, 1976—, Loveland, Ohio, 1993-96. Assoc. staff dental outpatient dept. Jewish Hosp. Cin., 1977-80, courtesy staff mem. 1980-84; also dental outpatient rep. to med. records and ambulatory care com.; instr. radiology div. dental hygiene U. Cin., 1977, supervising dentist clin. affairs; clin. dentist Rockdale Elem. and Condon Schs. for Handicapped, 1977-79; founding mem., trustee DenCare, 1986-89. Contbr. articles to profl. jour. Sr. clin. dentist Cin. Bd. Edn.; mem. programming com. Southwestern Ohio chpt. Am. Heart Assn., 1983; co-chmn. fin. com., ch. bd. Lindenwald United Meth. Ch., 1982 Mem. ADA, Ohio Dental Assn., Acad. Gen. Dentistry (nat. spokesdentist in laser-assisted dentistry), Am. Endodontic Soc., Internat. Acad. Laser Dentistry, Cin. Dental Soc. (assoc.), Keely Dental Soc. (co-chmn. programming com. 1980, chmn. continuing edn. 1979-82, editor Keely Bull. 1982-85, mem.-at-large coun. 1982), Psi Omega. Republican. Avocations: cross-country bicycling, collecting antique banks and toys, skiing. Office: 1251 Nilles Rd Fairfield OH 45014-7206 E-mail: xerxes9@cinci.rr.com.

CUTTING, COURT BALDWIN, plastic surgeon, computer graphics researcher; b. N.J., June 26, 1949; s. Richard Park and Holly Cutting; m. Sherry Cutting. BS, Pa. State U., 1971; MD, U. Chgo., 1975. Diplomate Am. Bd. Plastic Surgery, Am. Bd. Otolaryngology. Intern in surgery Yale U. Hosp., New Haven, Conn., 1975; head and neck surgery resident U. Iowa, Iowa City, 1976-80; craniofacial rsch. fellow N.Y. Med. Ctr., N.Y.C., 1980, plastic surgery resident, 1981-83, craniofacial surgery fellow, 1984, assoc. prof. surgery, 1984—. Dir. cleft lip and palate program NYU Med. Ctr., 1984—. Office: Court Cutting MD PC 333 E 34th St # Ik New York NY 10016-4977

CUTTING, LAURIE E. psychology educator, researcher; b. Washington, Oct. 2, 1970; d. James Hulbert Barnes and Mary Dorthea Little Cutting; m. Pete Finis Long, Feb. 26, 2000. BA, Am. U., 1993; MA, Northwestern U., 1995, PhD, 1997. Clinic supr. Northwestern U., Evanston, Ill., 1994-97; postdoctoral fellow Johns Hopkins Sch. Medicine, Balt., 1997-99; ednl. and learning disabilities specialist Washington, 1997—; instr. Kennedy Krieger Inst./Johns Hopkins Sch. Medicine, Balt., 1997-99, asst. prof., 2000—. Mem. Gen. Clin. Rsch. Ctrs. Adv. Com., Balt., 2000—. Contbr. chpt. to book, articles to profl. jours. Grantee Dept. Def., 2000—. Mem. APA, Coun. for Exceptional Children (Dissertation of Yr. award 1998), Internat. Dyslexia Assn., Soc. for Sci. Study of Reading, Soc. for Rsch. in Child Devel., Jr. League. Episcopalian. Avocations: biking, running, skiing, reading. E-mail: cutting_l@yahoo.com., cutting@kennedykrieger.org.

CUTTING, MARY DOROTHEA, audio and audio-visual communications company executive; b. N.Y.C., Feb. 20, 1943; d. Elliotte Robinson and Mary Dorothea (Clarke) Little; m. James H. B. Cutting, July 18, 1964; children—Gwendolyn Louise, Laura Elizabeth. Student Whitman Coll., 1960-62; B.A. in English Lit., U. Wash., 1964. Tchr. English, Severna Park High Sch., Md., 1965-66; remedial reading substitute tchr. St. Patrick's Day Sch., Washington, 1976-77; v.p. mktg. The Cutting Corp., Washington, 1978—; bd. dirs. Potomac Talking Book Svcs, Inc., 1990—; Editor children's cassettes: Fisher-Price Toys Spellbinder Series, 1983 (Consumer Com. of Ams. for Democratic Action award for being one of nation's 6 best toys for under $5 1983). Vol. chmn., bd. dirs. Washington Assn. for TV and Children, 1977. Mem. Internat. Assn. Bus. Communicators, Jr. League Washington (bd. dirs. 1977). Republican. Episcopalian. Office: 4940 Hampden Ln Ste 300 Bethesda MD 20814-2945

CUTTNER, JANET, hematologist, educator; b. N.Y.C. d. William Robert and Ida Edith C. BA, NYU, 1953; MD, Med. Coll. of Pa., 1957. Diplomate Am. Bd. Internal Medicine, Am. Bd. Hematology. Intern, resident King's County Hosp., Bklyn., 1957-61; hematology fellow Mt. Sinai Med. Ctr., N.Y.C., 1961-63, rsch. assoc. hematology, 1963-65, asst. prof. medicine, 1965-72, assoc. prof. medicine, 1972-86, prof. medicine, 1986—. Recipient Jacobi Medallion Alumni Mt. Sinai Med. Ctr., 1999. Fellow N.Y. Acad. Scis.; mem. Am. Soc. Hematology, Am. Soc. Clin. Oncology, Am. Assn. for Cancer Rsch. Office: 1735 York Ave Ste P2 New York NY 10128

CUTTS, CHARLES EUGENE, civil engineering educator; b. Sioux Falls, S.D., May 15, 1914; s. Charles Clifford and Ethel May (Gardner) C.; m. Jane Bebensee, Mar. 16, 1946; children: George Gardner, Elizabeth Anne. B.C.E., U. Minn., 1936, MS in Civil Engring, 1939, PhD, 1949. Registered profl. engr., Minn., Fla., Mich. Instrumentman Milw. R.R., 1936- 38; teaching asst. dept. civil engring. U. Minn., 1938-39, instr., asst. prof., 1946-50; engr. C.F. Haglin & Sons, summer 1939; asst. prof. dept. civil engring. Robert Coll., Istanbul, Turkey, 1939-42; engr. Braithwaite Co., Ltd., Iskenderun, Turkey, summer 1942, 43; assoc. prof., assoc. rsch. engr. U. Fla., 1950-53; engr. Engring. Scis. Program NSF, Washington, 1953-56; profl. lectr. civil engring. George Washington U., 1955-56; prof., chmn. dept. civil engring. Mich. State U., 1956-69, prof., 1969-84, prof. emeritus, 1984—. Cons. U. Minn. Morocco Project, 1986. Author: Structural Design in Reinforced Concrete, 1951, other tech. publs. Served to maj. C.E. AUS, 1943-46; lt. col. Res. ret. Mem. Nat. Acad. Scis. (fellowship com. 1961-63), ASCE (chmn. com. on mech. properties of materials 1965, pres. Mich. sect. 1967, chmn. com. on engring. edn. 1969-70), Am. Concrete Inst., Am. Soc. Engring. Edn. (chmn. civil engr. div. 1965-66, v.p. 1970—, chmn. constn. and bylaws com. 1981-83), Engrs. Coun. Profl. Devel. (chmn. region 5 1972-73), Nat. Soc. Profl. Engrs., Column Rsch. Coun., Tau Beta Pi, Chi Epsilon. Home: 4599 Ottawa Dr Okemos MI 48864-2028 Office: Civil Engring Mich State Univ East Lansing MI 48824

CUTTS, STEPHEN PAUL, civil engineer, linguistics researcher; b. Detroit, Dec. 5, 1965; s. John Peter and Sonja Edla (Bealing) C.; m. Rebecca Angela Cotter, Oct. 24, 1998; 1 child, Christopher Anthony. BS, Oakland U., 1985; MS, Calif. Inst. Tech., 1988; MA in Linguistics, Calif. State U., Fullerton, 1993. Registered profl. engr., Calif. Engr. and project mgr. Calif. EPA, Glendale, Calif., 2000—; hazardous substances engr. Dept. Toxic Substances, State of Calif., Glendale, 2000—. Contbr. articles to profl. jours., including Gen. Linguistics, Solid Waste Assn. N.Am. Ann. Landfill Gas Symposia. Earle C. Anthony fellow Calif. Inst. Tech., 1986-87. Avocation: numismatics. Home: 585 Palo Verde Ave Pasadena CA 91107-2327 Office: Dept Toxic Substances Control 1011 N Grandview Ave Glendale CA 91201 E-mail: cuttssp@aol.com.

CUYPERS, CHARLES JAMES, lawyer; b. Dec. 11, 1949; s. Donald Charles and Hazel Charlotte (Hollingsworth) Cuypers; m. Judy Arlene Stutzman, Dec. 18, 1971; children: Christina Jean, Julie Anne. BS, Kearney State Coll., 1974; JD, Creighton U., 1976. Bar: Nebr. 1976, U.S. Dist. Ct. Nebr. 1976. Ptnr. Sherwood & Cuypers, Oxford, Cambridge, Nebr., 1976—86; pres. Oxford Devel. Corp., Oxford, Cambridge, 1979—86; asst. city atty. Grand Island, Nebr., 1986—89, city atty., 1995—; v.p., gen. mgr. 3-D Investment, Inc., Doniphan, Nebr., 1989—95. Cons. Butler Meml. Libr. Found., Cambridge, Nebr., 1983—86; cons., lawyer Cambridge Mus. Found., Inc., 1983—86, Fairview Cemetary Found., 1983—86; village atty., Orleans, Nebr., 1976—81, Oxford, Nebr., 1976—86; city atty., Cambridge, 1982—86. Author (and narrator): (radio) Oxford Centennial Radio Series, 1980. Bd. dir. Oxford Pub. Libr., 1978—86; mem. Hall County Regional Planning Commn.; county chmn. Gov. Thone Reelection Com., Oxford, Nebr., 1982. Mem.: Grand Island Indsl. Found. (trustee 1987—88, mem. Grand Island Civic Ctr. com. 1987—90), Young Lawyers Study Group, 14th Jud. Dist. Bar Assn. (pres. 1980—81), Nebr. Bar Assn., Oxford C. of C. Republican. Lutheran. Home: 1508 Spruce Pl Grand Island NE 68801-7048 Office: City Hall 100 E 1st St Grand Island NE 68801-6023

CVANCARA, ALAN MILTON, geologist, educator; b. Ross, N.D., Mar. 7, 1933; s. Charles Cvancara, Lillian Amelia Cvancara; m. Ella Jane Wangerud, June 7, 1959; children: Mark Alan, Julie Ann Leatherman. BS in Geology, U. N.D., 1955, MS in Geology, 1957; PhD in Geology, U. Mich., 1965. From asst. prof. to prof. U. N.D., Grand Forks, 1963—91, prof. emeritus, 1992—. Author: A Field Manual for the Amateur Geologist, 1995, At the Water's Edge, 1989, Sleuthing Fossils, 1990, Exploring Nature in Winter, 1992, Edible Wild Plants and Herbs, 2001, Back Trip, 2002, Windows Into Legacy, 2003; editor: N.D. Acad. Sci., 1969—72, 1974—76; contbr. 1st lt. USAF, 1957—60. Fulbright scholar, U.S. Govt., 1956—57. Achievements include discovery and naming of several species of fossils. Avocations: photography, writing, playing acoustic stringed instruments. Home: 4920 S Oak St Casper WY 82601

CVENGROS, JOSEPH MICHAEL, manufacturing company executive; b. Pana, Ill., Oct. 8, 1931; s. Joseph John and Mary Bernice (Sturgeon) C.; m. Mary Elizabeth Ainsworth, Feb. 11, 1956; children: Joseph J., Mary E., Andrew T., Katherine A., J. Michael, Robert A., David L., Susan M. BABS, Washington U., St. Louis, 1955; MBA, Northwestern U., 1960. Pers. mgr. Continental Baking Co., Chgo., 1956-57; asst. to chmn. bd. dirs. Automatic Canteen Co. divsn. ITT, Chgo., 1957-65; cons. Spencer Stuart and Assoc., Chgo., 1965-68; investor High Tech., Inc., Chgo., 1968—; chmn. bd. dirs., CEO Anaconda Metal Hose divsn. Anamet, Inc., Glen Ellyn, Ill., 1984—. Fellow Econ. Club Chgo. Office: Anamet Inc 739 Roosevelt Rd Ste 204 Glen Ellyn IL 60137-5873

CVETANOVICH, DAN L. lawyer; b. Wheeling, W.Va., Oct. 2, 1952; s. Louis J. and Nila J. (Hall) C.; m. Sharon M. Smith, Sept. 8, 1979; children; Gregory L., Steven W. BA, West Liberty State Coll., 1974; JD, Harvard U., 1977. Bar: Ohio 1977, U.S. Dist. Ct. (so. dist.) Ohio 1978, U.S. Ct. Appeals (6th cir.) 1980, U.S. Dist. Ct. (no. dist.) Ohio 1984, W.Va. 1985, U.S. Dist. Ct. (so. dist.) W.Va. 1985, U.S. Ct. Appeals (4th cir.) 1986, U.S. Dist. Ct. (we. dist.) Tex. 1998, U.S. Dist. Ct. (no. dist.) W.Va. 2001. Assoc. Bricker & Eckler, Columbus, Ohio, 1977-82, ptnr., 1983-87, Arter & Hadden LLP, Columbus, 1987—2003; mem. Bailey Cavalieri LLC, Columbus, 2003—. Mem.: ABA, Columbus Bar Assn., W.Va. State Bar, Ohio State Bar Assn. Republican. Avocations: hunting, fishing, golf. Office: Bailey Cavalieri LLC One Columbus 10 W Broad St Columbus OH 43215-3422 Office Fax: 614-221-3155. Business E-Mail: Dan.Cvetanovich@baileycavalieri.com.

CWIK, LAWRENCE JOHN, artist, lawyer; b. Wheeling, W.Va., Jan. 16, 1959; s. Henry John and Grace Madeline (Justus) Cwlk. BS, Pa. State U., 1980; Cert., U. Hawaii, 1981, MA, 1982; Assoc. (hon.), Macquarie U., Sydney, Australia, 1982; JD, Lewis and Clark Coll., 1987. V.p. Impulse Pub. Corp., Honolulu, 1981—82; artist Portland, Oreg., 1983—; environ. law specialist Oreg. Dept. Environ. Quality, Portland, 1985—; filmmaker Portland, 1996—; photographer Bidwell & Co., Portland, 2001. Photographer The Visitor, Photographs of Mexico, 1982—; author: (films) Fair, 1999—, Totems, 1999—, (book) Earth Trauma, Earth Hope, 1992; one-man shows include Blue Sky Gallery, Portland, 1987, Stonington Gallery, Seattle, 1992, Galeria H20, Barcelona, 1992, 2003, Galeria 57, Madrid, 2001, Omni Gallery, Portland, 1999, 2000, Portland Open Studios, 2002, 2003, exhibited in group shows at Rena Bransten Gallery, San Francisco, 1990, Portland Art Mus., 1987, 2001, Seattle, 2003, Contemporary Art Gallery, Tucson, 2003, Represented in permanent collections Bibliotheque Nationale de France, Paris, Levi Strauss and Co., San Francisco, Bank of Am., Seattle, Std. Ins. Co., Portland; author: (films) Gold Beach, 2003. Del. Multnomah County Citizens Conv., Portland, 1992. Recipient Purchase award, Lewis and Clark Coll., 1983, Hon. Mention award, Biennial, Tacoma Art Mus., 1999; grantee, Portland Photographers Forum, 1988, East-West Ctr., 1980—82. Office: PO Box 5912 Portland OR 97228

CYGANOWSKI, MELANIE L. bankruptcy judge; b. Chgo., June 8, 1952; d. Daniel F. and Sophia A. C.; married, 1989. AB in anthropology, Grinnell Coll., 1974; postgrad. in urban devel., Cornell U., 1975; JD magna cum laude, SUNY, Buffalo, 1981. Bar: N.Y. 1982, U.S. Supreme Ct., U.S. Ct. Appeals (2d cir.), U.S. Dist. Ct. (so., ea. and we. dists.) N.Y. Coord. program planning, planner, cons. dept. community devel. and human resources City of Buffalo, N.Y., 1974-78; dir. individual referral program Broadway-Filmore Area Coun., Inc., Buffalo, 1978-79; summer assoc. Hodgson, Russ, Andrews, Wood & Goodyear, Buffalo, 1980; law clk. to Hon. Charles L. Brieant U.S. Dist. Ct. (so. dist.) N.Y., 1981-82; litigation assoc. Sullivan & Cromwell, N.Y.C., 1982-89; sr. atty. Milbank, Tweed, Hadley & McCloy, 1989-93; judge U.S. Bankruptcy Ct. (ea. dist.) N.Y., Ctrl. Islip, 1993—. Adj. prof. law bankruptcy program St. John's U. Sch. Law. Contbr. articles to legal jours. Mem. ABA, N.Y. State Bar Assn., N.Y.C. Bar Assn. Roman Catholic. Avocations: bicycling, gardening, fishing. Office: US Bankruptcy Ct The Long Island Fed Ct 290 Federal Plz Central Islip NY 11722

CYLKE, FRANK KURT, librarian; b. New Haven, Conn., Feb. 13, 1932; s. Frank Anton and Helen Mary (Callahan) C.; m. Mary Elizabeth Newhouse, Dec. 28, 1962; children: Frank Kurt, Mary Amanda, Virginia Ann. BA, U. Conn., 1954; M.L.S., Pratt Inst., 1957; postgrad., Fairfield U., Am. U., Georgetown U. Libr. Graham-Eckes Sch., Palm Beach, Fla., 1957-58; reference libr. Bridgeport (Conn.) Pub. Libr., 1958-62; head pub. svc. New Haven Pub. Libr., 1962-65; asst. libr. Providence Pub. Libr., 1965-68; chief libr. rsch. U.S. Office Edn., 1968-69; exec. dir. fed. libr. com. Libr. of Congress, 1970-73; dir. nat. libr. svc. for blind, physically handicapped Library of Congress, 1973—. Instr. Grad. Libr. Sch. U. R.I., 1967-68; instr. Grad. Libr. Sch. Cath. U. Am., 1974—, bd. visitors, 1980—; exec. sec. panel edn. & tng. Com. Sci. and Tech. Inst.; chmn. librs. tech. com. Met. Washington Coun. Govts., 1970-71; sec. U.S. Book Exch., 1972-74; sec.-treas. Joint Venture Pub. Activity, 1970-74; mem. E. Greenwich (R.I.) Free Libr. Corp., 1967—; adv. bd. Ednl. Resources Info. Ctr./Clearinghouse Libr. and Info. Sci., 1970-72; bd. visitors Grad. Sch. Libr./Info. Sci., Pratt Inst., 1980—. Editor: Captains Shelf, 1964-66, PLC Newsletter, 1970-73, Library Service for the Blind and Physically Handicapped: An International Approach, 1979, Recipient Va. Cultural Laureate, 1992, Dayton M. Forman Meml. award, 1996 (Can. Nat. Inst. for the Blind); grantee U.S. Office Edn., 1972 Mem.: KC, ALA (Joseph W. Lippincott award 1992, F.J. Campbell medal 1975—76), Friends of Librs. for Blind in N.Am. (founder, ex-officio bd. dirs.), Internat. Fedn. Libr. Assns. (founder, chmn. sect. for blind), World Blind Union, Am. Soc. Info. Sci. (sec. 1874—1975), Spl. Librs. Assn. (chpt. pres. 1975—76), Dinghy Cruising Assn., Mystic Seaport (pilot), Crow's Nest (st. John's, Nfld.), Shenandoah Nat. Park Assn., Ancient Order of Hibernians, Knights of Columbus. Roman Catholic. Avocations: sailing, birding. Home: PO Box 192 Great Falls VA 22066-0192 Office: Libr of Congress Nat Libr Svc for the Blind 1291 Taylor St NW Washington DC 20542-0002 Personal E-mail: kurt.cylke@verizon.net. Business E-Mail: fcyl@loc.gov.

CYMBLER, MURRAY JOEL, corporate professional; b. Germany, July 20, 1948; came to U.S., 1949; s. Harry and Adele C.; m. Carol Horowitz, Nov. 23, 1972; children: Adam, Robyn. BA, Hunter Coll., 1970. Tchr. N.Y. Bd. Edn., Bronx, 1970-71; contract analyst The Equitable Life Assurance Soc., N.Y.C., 1972-86; chmn., CEO Astro-Stream Corp., Levittown, N.Y., 1986-91; mgr. fin. Landmark Plaza Properties Corp., Sayville, N.Y., 1991-99; fin. sales Met Life, 2001, Nat. Life, 2002. Inventor Orbi Sport-toy, 1985. Supr. Intown Theatres, Sayville, N.Y., 1998-2000. Office: Orbico Inc 133 Ronni Dr East Meadow NY 11554-1330

CYMROT, MARK ALAN, lawyer; b. Queens, N.Y., Oct. 8, 1947; s. Irwin Morris and Anne (Kipnis) C.; m. Janinne Dall' Orto; children: Isaac, Erin, Isabella. BA, George Washington U., 1969; JD, Columbia U., 1972. Bar: D.C. 1973, N.Y. 2000. Trial lawyer civil divsn. U.S. Dept. of Justice, Washington, 1972-77; sr. litigator Consumers Union of U.S. Inc., Washington, 1977-79; spl. litigation counsel civil divsn. U.S. Dept. of Justice, Washington, 1979-83; ptnr. Cole Corette & Abrutyn, Washington, 1983-91, Baker & Hostetler LLP, Washington, 1991—. Contbr. articles to profl. jours. Named one of 50 Best Lawyers in Washington by Washingtonian Mag., 1992. Avocations: photography, writing, golf, tennis. Office: Baker & Hostetler LLP 1050 Connecticut Ave NW Washington DC 20036-5304

CYNADER, MAX SIGMUND, psychology, physiology, brain research educator, researcher; b. Berlin, Feb. 24, 1947; arrived in Can., 1951; s. Samuel and Maria (Kraushar) C.; m. Moira Elizabeth Langton, May 30, 1985; children: Madeleine Maria, Rebecca Kay, Alexandra Josephine. BSc, Mc Gill U., Montreal, Que., Can., 1967; PhD, MIT, 1972. Fellow neuroanatomy Max-Planck Inst. Psychiatry, Munich, 1972-73; asst. prof. psychology Dalhousie U., 1973-77, assoc. prof., 1977-81, assoc. prof. physiology, 1979-84, prof. psychology, 1981-84, Killam rsch. prof., 1984-88, prof. physiology, 1984-88; prof. psychology U. B.C., 1988—, prof. physiology, 1988—, prof. dept. ophthalmology, 1988—, dir., 1988-99; dir. Brain Rsch. Ctr., U. B.C. and Vancouver Hosp. and Health Scis. Ctr., 1997. Mem. pres.'s workshop on five yr. plan strengthening sci. support in Can. Natural Scis. and Engring. Rsch. Coun. Can., 1984, workshop for Steacie fellows, 1988; mem. task force on curriculum devel. in Can. neurosci., 1984; mem. spl. adv. panel on rsch. preparedness USAF, 1985; rep. Internat. Human Frontiers Sci. program Med. Rsch. Coun. Can., 1988; mem. grants com. behavioural scis. Med. Rsch. Coun. Can., 1988; program grants com. 1989—; referee senate rev. grad. program in neurosci. U. Western Ont., 1989; mem. math., computational and theoretical spl. rev. com. NIMH, 1989—; external reviewer Med. Rsch. Coun. Can., Alta. Heritage Fund Med. Rsch., NIH, NSF, USAF Office Sci. Rsch., Multiple Sclerosis Soc. Can., Vancouver Found., March of Dimes, Fight for Sight; CRC chair in brain devel., 2001-06. Mem. editorial bd. jours. Behavioral Brain Rsch., Clin. Vision Scis., Concepts in Neurosci., Devel. Brain Rsch., Exptl. Brain Rsch., Neural Networks, Visual Neurosci.; mem. adv. bd. series Rsch. Notes in Neural Computing; contbr. articles to profl. jours. Recipient Killam Rsch. prize U. B.C., 1989—; E.W.R. Steacie fellow Natural Sci. and Engring. Rsch. Coun. Can., 1979, Can. Inst. Advanced Rsch. fellow, 1986—. Bank of Montreal fellow Can. Inst. for Advanced Rsch., 1998; grantee Med. Rsch. Coun. Can., 1973—, Natural Sci. and Engring. Rsch. Coun. Can., 1975—, NIH, 1978-81. Fellow Can. Inst. Advanced Rsch., Royal Soc. Can.; mem. Soc. Neurosci. (Halifax chpt., pres. 1985, edn. com. 1986-89), Can. Assn. Neurosci. (pres. 1986), Assn. Rsch. Otolaryngology, Assn. Rsch. in Vision and Opthalmology, Can. Physiol. Soc., Internat. Brain Rsch. Orgn., Internat. Soc. Devel. Neurosci., Internat. Strabismol. Assn., World Fedn. Neuroscientists. Achievements include being named semifinalist Can. Astronaut program, 1983. Office: U BC Vancouver Hosp Brain Rsch Ctr 2211 Wesbrook Mall Vancouver BC Canada V6T 2B5 E-mail: cynader@brain.ubc.ca.

CYPESS, RAYMOND HAROLD, bioscience organization executive; BS, Bklyn. Coll., 1961; DVM, U. Ill., 1967; PhD, U. N.C., 1970. From asst. to assoc. prof. microbiology and epidemiology U. Pitts. Sch. Pub. Health, 1970-76; chmn., dir. diagnostic lab. N.Y. State Coll. Vet. Medicine, 1977-87, chmn. dept. preventive medicine, 1978—84; prof. microbiology and immunology U. Tenn., Memphis, 1988-93, vice-provost for rsch. and rsch. tng., dean, 1988-93; pres., CEO Am. Type Culture Collection, Manassas, Va., 1993—. Adj. prof. U. Pitts. Sch. Pub. Health, 1977; bd. dirs. MD-IPA Corp. Mem. editl. bd. Jour. Parasitology, 1979-82, Exptl. Parasitology, 1983-89; contbr. over 70 revs. and articles to profl. jours., chpts. to books. Gov.'s appointee Va. Biotech. Authority, 1995—2001. Fellow Fogarty Internat., Mexico, 1975; recipient Career Devel. award NIH, 1975-79. Mem. Am. Soc. for Microbiology (com. on internat. affairs pub. and sci. affairs bd. 1995-2001). Office: Am Type Culture Collection 10801 University Blvd Manassas VA 20110-2204 Fax: 703-365-2725.

CYPHERS, CHRISTOPHER JOHN, academic administrator; b. New London, Conn., Sept. 24, 1965; s. Walter Glenn and Patricia Lundy Cyphers. BA, Hampden-Sydney Coll., 1988; MA, Wesleyan U., 1992; PhD, SUNY, Albany, 1998. Instr. Berkshire C.C., Pittsfield, Mass., 1992-98, SUNY, Albany, 1996-98; assoc. dean Devry Inst. Tech., N.Y.C., 1998-2000; provost Sch. Visual Arts, N.Y.C., 2000—. Bd. dirs. Projectile Arts, N.Y.C. Author: National Civic Federation and the Making of a New Liberalism, 1900-1915, 2002. Active N.Y. Progressive Network, N.Y.C., 1998. Mem. Assn. for Instnl. Rsch., Am. Hist. Assn., Orgn. Am. Historians, Social Sci. History Assn., Nat. Arts Club (N.Y.C.), Mus. of Modern Art, (N.Y.C., exec. mem.) Democrat.

CYPHERT, MICHAEL A. lawyer; b. Cleve., Jan. 15, 1948; BA, Case Western Reserve U., 1970, JD, 1973. Bar: Ohio 1973, U.S. Supreme Ct. 1985. Mem. Thompson Hine LLP, Cleve. Adj. mem. faculty Case Western Reserve U. Sch. of Law, 1976-90. Mem. Def. Rsch. Inst. Office: Thompson Hine 127 Public Square #3900 Cleveland OH 44114

CYPHERT, STACEY TODD, health facilities administrator; b. Torrance, Calif., Mar. 14, 1959; s. Frederick Ralph and Lois Florence Cyphert; m. Rosemary Wilmoth, July 25, 1992. BS, Ohio State U., 1981, MHA, 1983; PhD, U. Iowa, 1990. Fellow Duke U. Med. Ctr., Durham, N.C., 1983-84; coord. prospective payment U. Cin. Hosp., 1984-86; rsch. and tchg. asst. U. Iowa, Iowa City, 1986-89, program assoc., 1989-92, adminstrv. assoc. statewide health, 1993-95, asst. to v.p. for statewide health, 1995-97, asst. v.p. for statewide health, 1997—2002, asst. v.p. for health affairs Iowa, 2002—, asst. dir. hosps. and clinics, 1997—2001, sr. asst. dir. hosps. and clinics, 2001—; asst. dir. Iowa Hosp. Quality Assessment and Enhancement Inst., Iowa City, 1992-93. Reviewer Hosp. and Health Svc. Adminstrn., 1988-92; adj. lectr. U. Iowa, 1990—. Contbr. articles to jours. in field. Vol. Iowa Spl. Olympics, Iowa City, 1995—; mem. Iowa Med. Assistance Adv. Coun., 1991—, vice chair, 1995, chair, 1996, 97; mem. Iowa Welfare Reform Adv. Group, 1996-98; mem. adv. com. Iowa Plan, 1998—. Mem. Assn. Health Svcs. Rsch. and Health Policy, Nat. Speleological Soc., Am. Coll. Healthcare Execs., Am. Hosp. Assn., Iowa Hosp. Assn. (coun. on representation and advocacy 1997—), Iowa City C. of C. (health and human svcs. subcom. 1994—), Optimists (bd. dirs. 1996-2000). Avocations: photography, volleyball, caving, tennis. Home: 316 Monroe St Iowa City IA 52246-1614 Office: U Iowa Hosps and Clinics 200 Hawkins Dr Iowa City IA 52242-1009

CYPSER, DARLENE ANN, lawyer, movie producer; b. Tulsa, Jan. 3, 1958; d. Donald A. and Evelyn D. (Carrigan) Chappell, 1 child, Christopher A. BA U. Okla., 1980, JD, 1986. Bar: N.Y. 1987, Colo. 1988. Pvt. practice, Boulder, Colo., 1988-99. Pres. The Midgard Corp., 1999—, Inferno Film Prodns., 1999—. Contbr. articles to profl. jours. Vol. Boulder County Legal Svcs., 1987-99, Legal Aid Soc. Westchester County, White Plains, N.Y., 1986-87; bd. dirs. Nyx Net, 1997--. Mem. Am. Geophys. Union, Colo. Film and Video Assn. Avocations: macrame, hiking, photography, cooking. Office: 3410 W Bowles Ave Littleton CO 80123-6666 E-mail: darlene@milehigh.net.

CYR, ARTHUR I. political science and economics educator; b. L.A., Mar. 1, 1945; s. Irving Arthur and Frances Mary Cyr; m. Betty Totten (div.); children: David Arthur, Thomas Harold, James Price. BA, UCLA, 1966, MA, 1967; AM, Harvard U., 1969, PhD, 1971. Teaching fellow Harvard U., 1970-71; program officer internat. and edn.-rsch. divs. Ford Found., 1971-74; asst. prof., adminstr. UCLA, 1974-76; program dir. Chgo. Coun. Fgn. Rels., 1976-81, v.p., 1981-96; pres., CEO, World Trade Ctr. Assn., Chgo., 1996-98; Clausen disting. prof. polit. econ. and world bus. Carthage Coll., Kenosha, Wis., 1998—; dir. Clausen Ctr. World Bus., 2000—. Author: Liberal Politics in Britain, 1977, rev. edit., 1988, British Foreign Policy and the Atlantic Area, 1979, U.S. Foreign Policy and European Security, 1987, After the Cold War—American Foreign Policy, Europe and Asia, 1997, rev. edit., 2000; contbr. articles to profl. jours. Capt. USAR, 1966—73. Mem. Internat. Inst. Strategic Studies, Royal Inst. Internat. Affairs, Am. Polit. Sci. Assn., Coun. Fgn. Rels., Century, Econ. Club Chgo., Phi Beta Kappa. Office: Carthage Coll Kenosha WI 53140-1994 E-mail: acyr@carthage.edu.

CYR, CONRAD KEEFE, federal judge; b. Limestone, Maine, Dec. 9, 1931; s. Louis Emery and Kathleen Mary (Keefe) Cyr; m. Judith Ann Pirie, June 23, 1962 (dec. Mar. 1985); children: Keefe Clark, Jeffrey Louis Frederick; m. Diana Kathleen Sanborn, Sept. 25, 1987. BS cum laude, Holy Cross Coll., 1953; JD, Yale U., 1956; LLD (hon.), Husson Coll., 1991. Bar: Maine 1956. Pvt. practice, Limestone, 1956—59; asst. U.S. atty., Bangor, Maine, 1959—61; pvt. practice Winchell & Cyr, Bangor, Maine, 1961—62; judge U.S. Bankruptcy Ct., Bangor, 1961—81, U.S. Dist. Ct., Bangor, 1981—83, chief judge, 1983—89; judge U.S. Fgn. Intelligence Surveillance Ct., 1987—89, U.S. Ct. Appeals (1st cir.), Boston, 1989—97, sr. judge, 1997—. Standing spl. master U.S. Dist. Ct., Maine, 1974—76; chief judge Bankruptcy Appellate Panel Dist., Mass., 1980—81; mem. Jud. Council (1st cir.), 1987—; com. on adminstrn. of bankruptcy sys. Jud. Conf. U.S., 1987—. Founder, editor-in-chief: Am. Bankruptcy Law Jour., 1970—81, contbg. author, editor: Collier on Bankruptcy, vol. 10. Steering com. U.S. AID Project for Assisting Bankruptcy and Reorgn. Procedures in Ctr. and Ea. Europe; treas. Limestone Rep. Com., 1958; chmn. budget com. Town of Limestone, 1959. Named one of Outstanding Young Men of Maine, 1963; recipient cert. of appreciation, Kans. Bar Assn., 1979, U. Maine, 1983, Nat. Judge's Recognition award, Nat. Conf. Bankruptcy Judges, 1979, Key to Town Limestone, 1983. Fellow: Am. Coll. Bankruptcy, Maine Bar Found. (charter); mem.: Aroostook Bar Assn., Am. Judicature Soc., Nat. Bankruptcy Conf. (exec. bd. 1974—77), Nat. Conf. Bankruptcy Judges (pres. 1976—77), Penobscot Bar Assn., Maine Bar Assn., Limestone C. of C. (pres.). Roman Catholic.*

CYR, J. V. RAYMOND, telecommunications industry executive; b. Montreal, Que., Can., Feb. 11, 1934; s. Armand and Yvonne (Lagace) Cyr; m. Marie Bourdon, Sept. 1, 1956; children: Helene, Paul Andre. Student, Ecole Poly.; BASc, U. Montreal, 1958; postgrad., Bell Labs., NJ, Nat. Def. Coll., 1972—73; LLD (hon.), Concordia U., Montreal, 1988. With Bell Can., 1992-96, engr., 1958-65, staff engr., 1965-70, from v.p. ops. staff region to v.p., 1973-75, pres., 1983-85, chmn., pres., CEO, 1985-87, chmn. bd. dirs., 1987-89, pres., 1983-85, chmn., pres., CEO, 1985-87, chmn. bd., 1987-89, chief engr. Quebec City, 1970-73, from exec. v.p. to v.p. adminstrn., 1975-83, chmn., 1992-96; with BCE Inc. (formerly Bell Can. Enterprises), 1987-93, pres., 1987-88; pres., CEO BCE, Inc. (formerly Bell Can. Enterprises), Montreal, 1988-89, also bd. dirs., chmn., pres., CEO, 1989-90, chmn., CEO, 1990-92, chmn., 1992-93, dir., sr. advisor to chmn.'s office, 1993-97; chmn. Montreal Trust, 1989-90. Bd. dirs. Can. Nat., Air Can., SR Telecom., ART Advanced Rsch. & Techs. Inc., Polyvalor Inc., G.T.C. Transcontinental Ltd., Cable Satisfaction Internat. Inc., Isac Techs. Inc., Univalor Inc., Fonds de Solidarite des Travailleurs du Que., Cogni-Sci. Inc., Triton Electronik Inc., Old Port of Montreal Corp. Inc., Transp. Can. Pipelines, chmn. bd., 1989—92. Past chmn. Jr. Achievement Can., Montreal Mus. Contemporary Art, Opera de Montreal; assoc. gov. U. Montreal. Named chair in mgmt. in his honor, Ecole Polytechnique, Laureate Personnalite, 125th Anniversaire de l"Ecole Polytechnique, 1998; recipient Gold Medal award, Can. Egnrs., 1987, Ordre du Mérite des Diplies, U. Montreal, 1988, Laureate of Prix des comm. du Que., 1990, Mgmt. Achievement award, McGill U., 1991, Gt. Montrealer award, 1991, Commemorative medal, 125th Ann. Confederation Can., 1992. Mem.: Can. Acad. Engring. (founding), Islemere Club, St. James Club, St. Denis Club. Roman Catholic. Avocations: golf, swimming. Office: 1050 Beaver Hall Hill 19th Montreal QC Canada H2Z 1S4 Fax: 514-870-4136.

CYRIL, TODD ALEXANDER, military officer; b. Miami, Fla., July 12, 1965; s. Ronald Alexander Cyril and Judi M. Green; m. Laila Bensouda, Dec. 23, 1998; children: Mouda Iken, Ashley. BS in Gen. Engring./French, U.S. Mil. Acad., 1987; MPA, Harvard U., 1997. Commd. 2d lt. U.S. Army, 1987, advanced through grades to maj., 1998; tank platoon leader CO XO B Co./2-77 AR 4th ID, Ft. Carson, Colo., 1987-91; tank CO comdr. HHC CDR, BDE A/S3, 2-37 AR 3d Bde, 3 ID, Vilseck, Germany, 1992-95; joint staff crisis intelligence ops. officer J-2, Joint Staff, U.S. Dept. Def., Washington, 1998-2001; UN mil. observer, Iraq, 2001, 2001-02; assistance and policy officer U.S. Ctrl. Command Security, 2002—. Decorated Order of St. George, U.S. Armor Assn., 1994. Mem. Am. Legion, Assn. of U.S. Army (life), Phi Kappa Phi (life). Republican. Avocations: military history, travel, literature. Home: 13021 Prestwick Dr Riverview FL 33569

CYS, RICHARD L. lawyer; b. Boulder, Colo., Oct. 9, 1944; BS with honors, U. Colo., 1966; JD, Georgetown U., 1969. Bar: D.C. 1969. Law clk. to Hon. John Pratt D.C., 1969-70; asst. U.S. atty. D.C., 1970-77; mem. Davis Wright Tremaine LLP, Washington. Mem. ABA, D.C. Bar, Bar Assn. D.C. Office: Davis Wright Tremaine LLP 1500 K St NW Ste 450 Washington DC 20005-1272

CYTOWIC, RICHARD EDMUND, neurologist; b. Trenton, N.J., Dec. 16, 1952; s. Edmund R. and Margaret A. (Ganyo) C. BA, Duke U., 1973; MD, Bowman Gray Sch. Medicine, 1977; postgrad., Nat. Hosp. Nervous Diseases, London, 1976. Diplomate Nat. Bd. Med. Examiners. Intern N.C. Bapt. Hosp./Bowman Gray Sch., Winston-Salem, N.C., 1977-78, resident in neurology, 1978-79, fellow in neurology, neuropsychology, cerebral blood flow, 1979-80; resident in neurology George Washington U., Washington, 1980-81; attending physician dept. neurology Washington Hosp. Ctr., 1981—; pres. Capitol Neurology, Washington, 1981—; med. advisor Med-Scene Teleconfs., Alexandria, Va., 1984—; resident fellow Hambridge Ctr. for Creative Arts and Scis., Rabum Gap, Ga., 1988, 89, 90, Va. Ctr. for Creative Arts, 1992; lectr. resident assocs. program Smithsonian Instn. Author: Studies in Nonfocal Brain Injury, 1987, Synesthesia: A Union of the Senses, 1989, 2d edit., 2002, Nerve Block for Common Pains, 1989, The Neurological Side of Neuropsychology, 1996, The Man Who Tasted Shapes, 1993, rev., 2003, Synasthesie: Interferenz, Transfer, Synthese der Sinne, 2002; contbr. articles to profl. jours., various newspapers; mem. editorial bd. Brain and Language, Brain and Cognition, 1987—. Pulitzer prize nominee, 1982 Fellow Royal Soc. Medicine; mem. AAAS, AMA, Internat. Neuropsychol. Soc., Med. Soc. D.C. (publs. com. 1984—, pub. info. and edn. bd. 1987—), Am. Acad. Neurology, Am. Assn. for History of Medicine, N.Y. Acad. Scis., Sigma Xi. Mem. Log Cabin Republicans. Roman Catholic. Home: 4720 Blagden Ter NW Washington DC 20011-3720 E-mail: R@Cytowic.net.

CYWAR, ADAM WALTER, management engineer; b. Kearny, N.J., Mar. 14, 1937; s. Adam Benjamin and Sophie Julia (Kurak) C.; m. Gloria Ella Beresford, Mar. 29, 1956 (div. May 1973); children: Victoria Cywar, Douglas A., Sophia; m. Rose Barter Tubb, May 11, 1973. BSME, N.J. Inst. Tech., Newark, 1960, MSMgtE, 1965. Design engr. Colgate-Palmolive, Jersey City, N.J., 1956-60; indsl. engr. Lionel Corp., Hillside, N.J., 1960-63; sr. engr. IBM Corp., Boca Raton, Fla., 1963-93; pres. Adam Cywar Indsl. Engr., Austin, Tex., 1993—. V.p. info. sys. RPM Assocs., Georgetown, Tex., 1993-97; founder IBM Worldwide Activity Based Mgmt. Competency Ctr. Author: Handbook of Industrial Engineering, 1982 (IBM Achievement award 1983). Chmn. Town of Poughkeepsie Rep. Com. to Elect Jim Buckley, 1968. Mem. ASME (sr. mem.), Inst. Indsl. Engrs. (sr., treas. 1975-90, dir. honors and awards 1970-75, Disting. Svc. award 1977). Avocations: writing, industrial engineering research. Home and Office: Adam Cywar Indsl Engr 4307 Las Palmas Dr Austin TX 78759-5062 E-mail: acywar@yahoo.com.

CZAJA, ALBERT JOSEPH, physician, educator; b. Phila., Feb. 17, 1943; s. Albert Joseph and Lillian Teresa Czaja; m. Herschel Carpenter, Jan. 13, 1969; children: Christopher Albert, Jonathan Joseph. AB, Dartmouth Coll., 1965, BMS, 1966; MD, Harvard U., 1968. Diplomate Am. Bd. Internal Medicine, Am. Bd. Gastroenterology. Intern Phila. Gen. Hosp., 1968-69, resident in medicine, 1969-72; staff gastroenterologist Burn Unit USA Insts., San Antonio, 1972-75; NIH rsch. fellow Mayo Clin., Rochester, Minn., 1975-77, gastroenterology cons., 1977—; prof. medicine Mayo Med. Sch., Rochester, Minn., 1986—. Editor: Chronic Active Hepatitis, 1986, Autoimmune Hepatitis, 2002. Maj. USMC, 1972-75. Recipient Meritorius Svc. medal USA Med. Corps, 1975. Fellow ACP, Am. Coll. Gastroenterology; mem. Am. Gastroenterol. Assn. (Disting. Achievement award 1997), Am. Assn. Study Liver Diseases, Internat. Assn. Study Liver Diseases, Am. Soc. Gastrointestinal Endoscopy. Avocations: sailing, opera. Office: Mayo Clin 200 1st St SW Rochester MN 55905-0001

CZAJKA, JAMES VINCENT, architect; b. Lackawanna, N.Y., Dec. 6, 1950; s. Joseph Martin and Livia Maria (Jengo) C. BS in Art and Design, MIT, 1972, MArch, 1975. Registered architect, N.Y. Asst. prof. architecture SUNY, Buffalo, 1975-79; architect Ehrenkrantz Group Architects and Planners, N.Y.C., 1979-84, Beyer, Blinder, Belle Architects and Planners, N.Y.C., 1984-91, assoc., 1987-91, studio dir., 1988-91; pvt. practice N.Y.C., 1991-92; prin. Allanbrook Benic Czajka Architects & Planners, N.Y.C., 1993-2001, James Vincent Czajka Architects, N.Y.C., 2001—. Prin. works include Baird Point Amphitheater, SUNY, Buffalo, 1978, Social Security Adminstrn. Bldg., Queens, N.Y., 1982, Paul Klapper Hall, Queens Coll., 1986, N.Y. Hall Sci. Master Plan, Queens, N.Y., 1992, Am. Acad. Arts and Letters Master Plan, 1994, St. Joseph Parish Master Plan, Queens, 1994, World Monuments Fund Hdqrs., Manhattan, 1995, Loyola Sch. Sci. Ctr. renovation, Manhattan, 1996, Rutgers Ch. renovation, Manhattan, 1997, Bklyn. Conservatory of Music renovation, 1998, Blue Heron Arts Ctr., Manhattan, 1999, Preissner House, East Hampton, N.Y., 2000, Conard House, Manhattan, 2000, The Rockwell Mus. of Western Art, Corning, N.Y., 2001, N.Y. Soc. Libr. Master Plan, 2002, Lefferts Homestead Children's Mus., Bklyn., 2002, Elephant House Renovation, Bronx Zoo, 2003. Mem. AIA, Nat. Coun. Archtl. Registration Bds. (cert.). Avocation: piano. Home: 303 E 84th St Apt 2F New York NY 10028-4435 Office: 611 Broadway Rm 817 New York NY 10012-2608 E-mail: jvc@jvcarchitects.com.

CZAJKO, JAKUB, computer scientist, researcher, mathematician, physics researcher; Contbr. papers to sci. jours. Achievements include discovery of spatial decomposition of time flow, equipotential effects of gravity; multispatial structure of the physical reality we live in -- with nine already identified physical dimensions -- which implies existence of an abstract 27-dimensional hyperspace. Personal E-mail: sunswing77@yahoo.com.

CZAJKOWSKI, EVA ANNA, aerospace engineer, educator; b. New Britain, Conn., Sept. 4, 1961; Student, Yale U., 1978; BS in Aero. Engring. cum laude, M in Aero. Engring., Rensselaer Poly. Inst., 1983; SM in Aeronautics and Astronautics, MIT, 1985; PhD in Aerospace Engring., Va. Poly. Inst. and State U., 1988. Registered profl engr, NY. Student trainee U.S. Govt., Washington, 1981-82; intern N.Y. State Assembly, Albany, 1983; teaching asst. Rensselaer Poly. Inst., Troy, N.Y., 1983, rsch. asst. U.S. Army Rsch. Office Ctr. Excellence, 1982-83; engring. analyst Pratt & Whitney Aircraft, West Palm Beach, Fla., 1984; rsch. asst. Gas Turbine and Plasma Dynamics Lab., Cambridge, 1984-85; rsch. asst., tchg. asst. dept. aerospace & ocean engring. Va. Poly. Inst. and State U., Blacksburg, 1985-88, aerospace engr., 1988-91, sr. aerospace engr., 1991-94, prin. aerospace engr., 1994-2001, aerospace engring. and tech. mgr., 2001—. Participant U.S. dels. to nine European nations, 1991—2003. Author: (book) Russian Aeronautical Test Facilities, 1994; contbr. scientific papers confs, articles profl jours and ency. Assoc mem Nat Air and Space Mus, Am Mus Natural History; vol. New Britain Gen Hosp, 1977—79. Recipient Medal Hon. Sci. Award, Bausch & Lomb, 1978, Joseph B. Platt Award, 1997, Int. Sci. Medal, 2001, Internat. Woman of Yr., 1991—92, 1996—97, Scientist of Yr., 2001; fellow Amelia Earhart, Zonta Int., 1983—85, Prat Presdl. Eng. Program, 1985—88; scholar, Unico Nat., 1979—80, Am. Helicopter Soc. Vertical Flight Found., 1983. Mem.: NAFE, AIAA, London Diplomatic Acad, NY Acad Scis, Confederation Chivalry (Dame) (dame, named Dame), Nat Space Soc, World Found Successful Women, Int Platform Asn, Planetary Soc, Polish Rotorcraft Asn, Am Helicopter Soc, Am Astronaut Soc, World Order Sci.-Edn.-Culture (Dame) (dame, named Dame), Gamma Beta Phi, Phi Kappa Phi, Tau Beta Pi, Sigma Gamma Tau, Sigma Xi. Avocations: art, horseback riding, piano, flying private plane, sailing. Home: 170 Carlton St New Britain CT 06053-3106

CZAJKOWSKI, FRANK HENRY, lawyer; b. Bklyn., Jan. 7, 1936; m. Cecilia J. Artowicz, Sept. 3, 1955. BA, St. John's U., Bklyn., 1957; JD, St. John's U., 1959; LLM, George Washington U., 1966. Bar: N.Y. 1960, Pa. 1970, Conn. 1974, U.S. Supreme Ct. 1964. Claims adjustor Hartford Accident & Indemnity Ins. Co., N.Y.C., 1959-60; agt. Equitable Life Assurance Soc., N.Y.C., 1960; atty. Corp. Counsel's Office, N.Y.C., 1960-62, Fgn. Claims Settlement Commn., Washington, 1962-68, Atlantic-Richfield Co., N.Y.C., 1968-70, Phila., 1970-72; assoc. gen. counsel Unilever U.S.A. Co., Greenwich, Conn., 1972-98; pvt. practice, 1998—. Instr. Fairfield U. Ctr. Lifetime Learning, 1976, Sacred Heart U., 1983; arbitrator Am. Arbitration Assn. Mem. ABA, Conn. Bar Assn., Westchester-Fairfield Corp. Counsel Assn. Office: 7 Lafayette Dr Trumbull CT 06611-2751

CZAJKOWSKI-BARRETT, KAREN ANGELA, human resources management executive; b. Bklyn., Sept. 13, 1957; d. Frank Henry and Cecilia (Artowicz) Czajkowski; div. Mar. 1992; children: Jennifer Marie, Michael Joseph. BSBA, Fairfield U., 1979; MBA, Sacred Heart U., 1984. Office systems analyst Union Trust Co., Stamford, Conn., 1979-80, sr. office systems analyst, 1980-81; ops. analyst Homequity, Inc., Wilton, 1981-82, project leader human rels. dept., 1982-85, organization devel. cons., 1985-87; tng. and devel. cons. People's Bank, Bridgeport, Conn., 1987-90; mgr. human resource planning and devel. Pitney Bowes Mgmt. Svcs., Stamford, 1990-93, dir. human resources planning and devel., 1993-98; regional learning mgr. Hewitt Assocs. LLC, Rowayton, Conn., 1998—. Adj. instr. Sacred Heart U., Bridgeport, 1987. Sec. Cub Scouts Adv. Com., 1991-92; mem. regional bd. Conn. Fedn. Cath. Sch. Parents, 1993-94; treas. St. Theresa Sch.-Home Sch. Assn., 1994-96. Recipient award Nash Engring., 1979; named Bus. Advisor of Yr., INROADS/Fairfield-Westchester Counties, Inc., 1993. Mem. ASTD, Am. Mgmt. Assn., Human Resource Planning Soc.. Exec. Women's Golf Assn. Home: 28 Wendover Rd Trumbull CT 06611-1530 Office: Hewitt Assocs LLC 45 Glover Ave Norwalk CT 06850

CZARKOWSKI, DARIUSZ, electrical engineer; PhD, U. of Fla., Gainesville, FL, 1994—96. Assoc. prof. Poly. U., Brooklyn, NY, 2002—. Mem.: Inst. of Elec. and Electronic Engineers. Office: Polytechnic University Six Metrotech Center Brooklyn NY 11201

CZARNECKI, ANTHONY J. correction administrator, educator; b. Mt. Vernon, N.Y., Aug. 28, 1948; s. Stanley and Lucy (Calabrese) C.; m. Lorraine Portman, Oct. 9, 1971; children: David, Pamela. BA, Iona Coll., 1970; MA, John Jay Coll., 1975; MPA, Pace U., 1990. Probation officer, sr. probation officer, tng. dir. Westchester County Probation Dept., White Plains, N.Y., 1970-83; spl. asst. to commr. Westchester County Correction Dept., Valhalla, N.Y., 1983—. Adj. prof. criminal justice Westchester C.C., Valhalla, 1976—, Iona Coll., New Rochelle, N.Y., 1981—. Editor-in-chief Jour. Probation and Parole, 1980-82; contbr. articles to profl. jours. Recipient Disting. Alumnus award, John Jay Coll. Criminal Justice, 2003. Mem. Am. Correctional Assn., Am. Probation and Parole Assn. (Probation officer Yr. award 1981), Am. Soc. Pub. Adminstrn., Middle Atlantic States Correctional Assn. (pres. 1997-99, trustee 1979—, Achievement award 1989, Leadership award 1997, Founders award 2000), N.Y. State Probation Officers Assn. (pres. 1978-80). Roman Catholic. Office: Westchester County Correction Dept PO Box 389 Hdq Bldg Valhalla NY 10595-0389

CZARNECKI, GERALD MILTON, investment banker, venture capitalist; b. Phila., Mar. 22, 1940; s. Casimir M. and Rose-Mary (Grajek) C.; m. Lois Rae DiJoseph, July 9, 1965; 1 dau., Robyn Alexandra. BS, Temple U., 1965; MA, Mich. State U., 1967; LHD (hon.), Nat. U., 1994. C.P.A., Ill., Tex. With Continental Bank, Chgo., 1968-79, v.p., operating gen. mgr. trust ops. and gen. mgr. corp. svcs., 1971-78; pres. Fla. Computing Svcs., 1979; exec. v.p. Houston Nat. Bank, 1979-82; sr. v.p. fin. Republic Bank Corp., 1982-83, exec. v.p., 1983-84; pres., CEO Altus Bank, 1984-87; chmn., chief exec. officer Bank of Am. Hawaii, Honolulu, 1987-93; sr. v.p. human resources and adminstrn. IBM Corp., Armonk, N.Y., 1993-94; pres. UNC Inc., Annapolis, Md., 1994-95; chmn., CEO Deltennium Group, Inc., Bethesda, Md., 1995—, Renaissance, Inc., 1999—2001, also bd. dirs. Mem. faculty DePaul U., Chgo., 1975-78; adj. prof. econs. Houston Bapt. U., 1980-82; mem. faculty Bank Adminstrn. Inst., 1978-85, Grad. Sch. Banking, U. Wis., 1979-86; chmn. bd. dirs. Inroads, Inc./Chgo., 1977-79, Inroads, Inc./Houston, 1981 vis. prof. Jones Sch. Bus., Rice U., 1980; adj. prof. policy and strategy So. Methodist U., 1983-84; mem. adv. com. Banking Center, Tex. So. U., 1980-82; chmn. securities processing sub-com. Am. Nat. Standards Inst., 1974-79, mem. Tuskegee Inst. State Adv. Council, 1984-87; treas., mem. exec. com., bd. dirs. Nat. Council Savs. Instns., 1984-90; pres. thrift adv. council Fed. Res. Bd., 1986-90; bd. dirs. State Farm Ins. Cos.; chmn. bd. dirs. Great Clips Mid-Atlantic, Inc., 1997—, Deltennium Corp., 1996—; bd. dirs. State Farm Ins. Co., 2000-, State Farm Banks, 2000-, ATM Nat., Inc.; chmn. bd. Renaissance, Inc., 1999- Contbr. articles to profl. publs. Bd. dirs., treas. Hawaii Theatre Ctr., 1988-93; bd. dirs. Honolulu Econ. Devel. Corp., 1988-93, Nature Conservancy Hawaii, 1988-93, U. Hawaii Pres.' Coun., 1988-93, Aloha United Way, 1988-93; mem. Bus. Roundtable of Hawaii, 1989-93; chmn. Mil. Affairs Coun., 1992-93; mem. exec. and policy coms. Bus. Coun. N.Y. State, 1993-94; mem. adv. bd. Corp. Leadership Coun., 1993-94; nat. bd. dirs. Jr. Achievement, 1993—; bd. trustees Nat. U., 1994—. Mem. AICPA, Am. Bankers Assn. (chmn. securities processing com. 1974-77, trust ops. com. 1978, mem. exec. com. ops. and automation div. 1980-83, rsch. com.), Am. Econ. Assn., Nat. Assn. Corp. Dirs. (bd. dirs. D.C. chpt. 1999), Tex. Soc. CPAs, Fin. Execs. Inst., Consumer Bankers Assn. (bd. dirs. 1986-89), N. Am. Soc. Corp. Planners (bd. dirs. Dallas Chpt. 1982-83), Assn. for Corp. Growth, Orgn. Resource Counselors, Inc., Hawaii C. of C. (bd. dirs. 1988-89, chmn. bd. 1990-92), Omicron Delta Epsilon, Alpha Delta Phi. E-mail: gmczar@deltennium.com.

CZARNECKI, KRISTIN E. humanities educator; b. South Bend, Ind., Sept. 22, 1969; d. Donald Paul and Nancy Ann Kommers; m. Paul Edward Czarnecki, June 17, 1995. BA in English and German, U. Notre Dame, 1991; MA in English, Northwestern U., 1997; postgrad., U. Cin., 1999—. Program asst. Northwestern U., Evanston, Ill., 1994—98; editor Duff & Phelps, LLC, Chgo., 1998—99; tchg. asst. U. Cin., 1999—. Contbr. articles to profl. publs. Tchg. assistantship, Fulbright Found., 1991—92, practicum grantee, Woodrow Wilson Found., 2000, Charles P. Taft grad. fellow, U. Cin., 2002—03. Mem.: MLA, Soc. for Study of Multi-Ethnic Literatures of the U.S. (rep. grad. student devel. com. 2000—). Democrat. Roman Catholic. Office: U Cin Dept English Cincinnati OH

CZARNY, PH.D. FRANK SILVEY, social problems specialist, human and organizational systems consultant; b. Cincinnati, OH, Nov. 28, 1951; s. Doris Majura Harris, Frank Henry Harris. Bachelors of Arts in Psychology, Miami University, Oxford, Ohio, 1969—73, Masters of Arts in Teaching, 1973—75; Master of Arts in Organizational Development, Fielding Graduate Institute, Santa Barbara, CA., PhD in Human and Organizational Systems, 1998—2000. Social Problems Specialist Rockbridge Communications, Seattle, 1994—2002; Faculty, Undergraduate and Graduate Business Administration University of Phoenix, Seattle. President, Diversity Committee US West Communications, Carrier and Information Provider Division, Denver, 1993—94; Public Relations Correspondent US West Communications, 102+ Committee, Denver, 1989—90; Urban League Corporate Representative US West Communications, Carrier and Information Provider Division, Denver, 1993—94. Author: (Children's Paleontology Workshop) "Cookie Monsters", 1987 (Denver Natural History Museum Honorarium, 1987); performer: Cin. Youth Sumphony, 1968—69, Cin. All-City Youth Symphony, 1969. Workshop Presenter: "Communities of Faith and Public Education" Washington Education Association, Seattle; Member West Seattle Chamber of Commerce, Seattle, 2001—02. Recipient President's Club award, US West Communications Carrier and Information Provider Division, 1990; scholar Kenneth Kinnard scholarship, Kenneth Kinnard Found., 1969—73, Hebrew U. Summer Studies scholarship, Cin. Colored Woman's Assn., 1968. Mem.: NAACP, Urban League, American Black Anthropologists, American Anthropological Association. Avocation: RV, Snow Shoe, Ski, Hike. Office: Rockbridge Communications 11404 Marine View Dr SW Seattle WA 98146-1822 Office Fax: (206) 246-3066. Business E-Mail: fczarny@worldnet.att.net.

CZARRA, EDGAR F., JR., lawyer; b. Langhorne, Pa., Oct. 4, 1928; s. Edgar F. and Mary Agnes (Copeland) C.; m. Doris Catharine Lane, June 14, 1952; children: Penelope L., Edgar F. III, Jonathan C., Melanie A. BS, Yale U., 1949, LLB, 1952. Bar: U.S. Dist. Ct. D.C. 1954, U.S. Ct. Appeals (D.C. cir.) 1954, U.S. Supreme Ct. 1959. Assoc. Covington & Burling, Washington, 1952, 55-63, ptnr., 1963-97, ret., 1997. Served to lt. (j.g.) USN, 1952-55. Mem.: DC Bar Assn. Office: Covington & Burling 1201 Pennsylvania Ave NW Washington DC 20004-2401

CZECH, BRIAN MARTIN, biologist, economist; b. Green Bay, Wis., Mar. 25, 1960; s. Alex Roman Czech, Shirley Ann Czech. BS, U. Wis., 1982; MS, U. Wash., 1988; PhD, U. Ariz., 1997. Recreation and wildlife dir. San Carlos (Ariz.) Apache Tribe, 1991—93; conservation biologist U.S. Fish and Wildlife Svc., Arlington, Va., 1999—. Adj. prof. Va. Polytechnical Inst. and State U., Falls Ch., Va. Author: Shoveling Fuel for a Runaway Train: Errant Economists, Shameful Spenders, and a Plan to Stop Them All, 2000, The Endangered Species Act: History, Conservation Biology, and Public Policy, 2001. Mem.: Ecol. Soc. Am., U.S. Soc. for Ecol. Econs., Internat. Soc. for Ecol. Econs., Soc. for Conservation Biology, The Wildlife Soc. (chmn. local governance working group for state economy 1997—2002, cert.). Avocations: hiking, hunting, fishing. Home: 5101 S 11th St Arlington VA 22204 Office: US Fish and Wildlife Svc 4401 N Fairfax Dr - MS670 Arlington VA 22203 Business E-Mail: brian_czech@fws.gov.

CZECH, PAUL ANDREW, lawyer; b. Queens, N.Y., Aug. 4, 1961; s. Michael and Marie Czech. BA, JD, Temple U. Bar: Pa., N.J. Assoc. Anapol Schwartz Weiss & Cohen, Phila., 1992-94; pvt. practice Phila., 1994—; CEO YB Entertainment Group Inc., 2000—, YB420 Records, Inc., 2001—. Mem. Phila. Bar Assn. (arbitration com.). Avocation: band management. Office: 1735 Market St Ste A-428 Philadelphia PA 19103 E-mail: law@ybentertainment.com.

CZEKANSKI, JAMES P. military officer; BS in History, U. Mass., 1968; postgrad., Squadron Officer Sch., 1974, Air War Coll., 1981; MS in Counseling and Human Devel., Troy State U., 1978. Commd. 2d lt. USAF, 1968, advanced through grades to maj. gen., 2001; tactical airlift pilot Pope AFB, NC, 1969—72; gunship aircraft comdr. Ubon Royal Thai AFB, Thailand, 1972—74; instr., evaluator AC-103A Gunship Sch., Hurlburt Field, Fla., 1974—75; instr. pilot, scheduling officer, tactics officer, chief standardization 919th Spl. Sop. Group, Eglin Aux. Field, Fla., 1975—79; dir. ops. 756th Tactical Airlift Squadron, Andrews AFB, Md., 1979—81; chief safety, dir. ops. 910th Tactical Fighter Group, Youngstown Mcpl. Airport, Ohio, 1981—84; chief tactical airlift ops. Hdqrs. 14th AF, Dobbins AFB, Ga., 1984—86; comdr. 301st Aerospace Rescue and Recovery Squadron, Homestead AFB, Fla., 1986—87, 913th Tactical Airlift Group, Willow Grove Air Res. Facility, Pa., 1987—89; vice comdr., sr. air res. tech. 315th Mil. Airlift Wing, Charleston AFB, SC, 1989—91, comdr., 1991—92, 439th Airlift Wing, Westover Air Res. Base, Mass., 1992—97; inspector gen. Hdqrs. AF Res. Command, Robins AFB, Ga., 1998—2000, 4th Air Force, Air Force Res. Command, March Air Res. Base, Calif., 2000—. Decorated Kuwait Liberation medal Govt. of Saudi Arabia, Govt. of Kuwait, Legion of Merit with 2 oak leaf clusters, Air medal with two oak leaf clusters. Mem.: Airlift and Tanker Assn., Res. Officer Assn., Air Force Assn., Order of Daedalians. Office: March AFB Air Force Res Command Riverside CA 92518

CZEPIEL, LORI ANNE, lawyer; b. Chicago, Ill., Aug. 23, 1963; BA in economics, Northwestern U., 1981—84; JD cum laude, Boston U. Sch. of Law, 1984—87. Counsel, assoc. Skadden, Arps, Slate, Meagher & Flom LLP, Los Angeles, 1987—97; ptnr. Sidley Austin Brown & Wood LLP, New York, NY, 1997—. Current dir. and v.p., etc. prior roles Northwestern Alumni Assn., Evanston, Ill., 1998—2003; exec. bd. mem. and pac fundraising chair Young Executives of Am., Los Angeles, 1996—97; mem. Northwestern U. Coun. of 100, Evanston, Ill., 1998—2003. Mem.: Assn. of the Bar of the City of NY, ABA. Office: Sidley Austin Brown & Wood LLP 787 Seventh Ave New York NY 10019

CZERWIEC, IRENE THERESA, gifted education educator; b. Holyoke, Mass., Dec. 1, 1948; d. Stanley John and Pauline Martha (Zerek) Matuszek; m. Stanley Joseph Czerwiec, Jan. 24, 1970; children: Keith John, Daniel Paul. BS, U. Mass., 1969, MEd, 1987, EdD, 1992. Cert. secondary math. tchr., Mass. Math., physics tchr. Holyoke Cath. High Sch., 1969-71; substitute tchr. Chicopee (Mass.) Pub. Schs., 1979-85; gifted tchr. Bellamy Mid. Sch., Chicopee, 1985-90, math., gifted tchr., 1990-92, tchr. computer, gifted, 1992—. Coach Future Problem Solving Program, Chicopee, 1985—; evaluator State of Mass., 1986—, cons., 1988—; presenter World Future Soc. Conf., Cambridge, 1994, Mass. Future Problem Solving Conf., Harvard, 1994, Worcester, 1996, NSTA conv., Boston, 1992, 2d Ann. Conf. on Gifted and Talented Edn., Worcester, Mass., 1996, New Eng. Future Problem Solving Fall Tng. Conf., Sturbridge, Mass., 1998-99; presenter New Eng. League of Middle Schs.-Unified Arts Conf., Sturbridge, Mass., 1997; participant current students, future scientists, and engrs. workshop, Smith Coll., 1993; bd. dirs. Mass. Future Problem Solving Program. Co-author. Coord. looking forward program Chicopee Centennial, 1990. Recipient Merit award Chicopee Coun. Parents and Tchrs., 1990, cert. of recognition for excellence in coaching a team Internat. Future Problem Solving Conf., Ann Arbor, Mich., 1987, 88, Ednl. Leaders in Math., 1987, 88, Cert. of Merit Mass. Bar Assn., 1988, 89; SpaceMet fellow NSF, 1990-91. Mem. NEA, AAUW, ASCD, World Future Soc., Coun. Exceptional Children, Mass. Tchrs. Assn., Nat. Space Soc., Hampden County Tchrs. Assn., Chicopee Edn. Assn. Roman Catholic. Avocations: reading, gardening. Home: 4 Plainville Cir South Hadley MA 01075-2664 Office: Bellamy Mid Sch 314 Pendleton Ave Chicopee MA 01020-2135

CZESTOCHOWSKI, JOSEPH STEPHEN, museum administrator; b. Bklyn., Aug. 6, 1950; s. Joseph Stephen and Julia (Skowron) C.; m. Debra J. Nicholson, Nov. 18, 1972; 1 child, J. F. Stefan Parker. Diploma, Jagiellonian U., Poland, 1971; BA, U. Ill., 1971, MA, 1973. Curator of collections Brooks Mus. Art, Memphis, 1973-75; dir. Decker Gallery, Md. Inst., Balt., 1975-78; exec. dir. Cedar Rapids (Iowa) Mus. Art, 1978-94; dir. The Dixon Gallery and Gardens, Memphis, 1994—. Sr. examiner Accreditation Commn. of the AAM; field reviewer Inst. Mus. Svcs.; govt. and art com. Assn. Art Mus. Dirs. Monographs include The Pioneers, 1977, Polish Posters, 1979, The Combined Works of Arthur B. Davies, 1980, Prints by Childe Hassam, 1980, John S. Curry and Grant Wood - A Portrait of Rural America, 1981, The American Landscape Tradition 1738-1965, 1982, Marvin D. Cone - An American Tradition, 1985, Arthur B. Davies - Catalogue Raisonne of Prints, 1988, Degas Complete Sculptures, 2002, Georgia O'Keeffe and the Sublime, 2003. Mem. adv. bd. Krannert Art Mus. Fellow Vatican Mus. and Smithsonian Inst., 1976, Smithsonian Instn., 1977-79; recipient first Nancy Hanks Meml. award for profl. excellence Am. Assn. Mus., 1985. Mem. Am. Assn. Mus. Dirs., Internat. Coun. Mus., The Kosciuszko Found. (trustee 1988-96), The Polish Inst. Arts and Scis. in Am., Inc. (trustee 1986—), Ctr. for the Study of the Presidency (trustee), Coll. Liberal Arts and Scis. U. Ill. Alumni Assn. (trustee 1994—), Rotary Internat. Office: Internat Arts 319 Goodwyn St Memphis TN 38111-3311 E-mail: interarts@parkers.com.

CZIFRA, LISA TAKACS, piano educator; b. Buffalo, Oct. 17, 1934; d. Nicholas J. and Mary (Bene) Takacs; m. Louis J. Czifra, Aug. 26, 1961; children: Louis, William, David, Mark, Mary Beth. BMus, Youngstown U., 1956; MMus, Mich. State U., 1958. Piano instr. Cornell Coll. Conservatory of Music, Mount Vernon, Iowa, 1958-61, Youngstown (Ohio) U., 1961-64, asst. prof., 1964-67; pvt. piano instr. Mineral Ridge, 1967—. Recipient Winner Symphony competition YMTA, 1954, St. Cecelia Soc. competition, 1958. Mem. Music Tchrs. Nat. Assn. (profl. cert.), Ohio Music Tchrs. Assn. (profl. cert.), Ohio Fedn. of Music Clubs (program chair 1990—), Nat. Guild of Piano Tchrs. (adjudicator 1969, mem. faculty), Youngstown Music Tchrs. Assn. (past pres.), Sigma Alpha Iota (life; Sword of Honor). Republican. Roman Catholic. Avocations: house plants, church choir. Home and Office: 1802 Warner Ave Mineral Ridge OH 44440-9564

CZIKOWSKY, LEON LAWTON, legislative aide; b. N.Y.C., Oct. 23, 1956; s. Leon Lincoln and Dorothy (Dwyer) Czikowsky. BS in Economics, U. Pa., 1977, M of City and Regional Planning, 1980; MS in Urban Studies, So. Conn. State Coll., 1978. Investigator Com. of 70, Phila., 1975-76; environ. impact statement reviewer U.S. Environ. Protection Agy., Phila., 1980; real estate bail clerk City Contr., Phila., 1984-85, rsch. analyst House Labor Rels. Com., Harrisburg, Pa., 1985-91; legis. asst. Rep. Kevin Blaum, Harrisburg, Pa., 1991-93; specialized rsch. cons. Legis. Devel. Unit, Harrisburg, Pa., 1991-93; sr. rsch. analyst House Majority Whip, Harrisburg, Pa., 1993-95, House Dem. Caucus Chmn., Harrisburg, Pa., 1995-2001, rsch. specialist, 2001—. Mem. econ. devel. com. Assembly on the Legis., 1987-89, mem. labor com., 1989-90, mem. families and health com., 1996-2001, staff chmn., 2001-02, budget and fin. com., 2002—. Mem. Dem. Nat. Com. Target Group, 1976; constable, Lyme, Conn., 1977-78, Steelton, Pa., 1991-92, 96-98; mem. Dem. State Com., 1984-86; chmn. 27th Ward Dem. Exec. Com., 1986-88; treas. Future Reagan Deficit Payors for Dukakis, 1988; pres. Young Dems. of Pa., 1988-91, exec. v.p. Young Dems. of U.S., 1989-90; mem. Dauphin County Dem. Com., 1990—2002; mem., nat. del. Dem. Leadership Coun., 1991-93, 95-97, Ams. for Dem. Action, 1992-2000; planning commr., Harrisburg, 1999—; co-chmn., Spl.

Com. Motor Voter, U.S. Congress. Recipient Key to Erie, Pa., Mayor Louis Tulio, 1989, Ark. Traveler award Gov. Bill Clinton, 1989, Key to Allentown, Pa., Mayor Joseph Daddonna, 1990; named to Legion of Honor, Chapel of Four Chaplains, War Coll., Carlisle, Pa., 1991, Ky. Col., Honorable Order of Ky. Cols., 1991. Congregationalist. Home: 660 Boas St Apt 903 Harrisburg PA 17102-1321 Office: House of Reps 417 Main Capitol Building Harrisburg PA 17120-0022

CZIN, FELICIA TEDESCHI, Italian language and literature educator, small business owner; b. Vallata, Avellino, Italy, Jan. 20, 1950; came to U.S., 1958; d. Pasquale Aurelio and Maria (Branca) Tedeschi; m. Peter Czin, Oct. 19, 1972; children: Jonathan, Michael. BA, Douglass Coll., Rutgers U., 1972; MA, NYU, 1978, ABD, 1981, postgrad. Prodr. RAI Corp. Italian TV, N.Y.C., 1973-84; tchg. asst. dept. Italian NYU, 1977-79, adj. instr. dept. English, 1979-81; asst. prof. Vassar Coll., Poughkeepsie, N.Y., 1981-84; co-owner Czin Opticians, Teaneck, N.J., 1984—. Coord. Symposium on Italian Poetry, N.Y.C., 1978; adj. prof. SUNY at the Fashion Inst. Tech., N.Y.C., 2000—. Editor Out of London Press, N.Y.C., 1977-82, dir. pub. rels., 1977-82; editor jour. Yale Italian Studies, 1979-82; translator for jours. Avocations: hiking, swimming, knitting, cooking, sewing. Home and Office: 489 Cedar Ln Teaneck NJ 07666-1710

CZINKOTA, MICHAEL RUDOLF, business educator; b. Augsburg, Bavaria, Germany, Oct. 5, 1951; came to U.S., 1975; s. Michael and Ursula (Magerl) C.; m. Ilona Rosa Vigh, Aug. 10, 1984; 1 child, Margaret Victoria. Vordiplom, U. Erlangen-Nuremberg, Fed. Rep. Germany, 1974; MBA, Ohio State U., 1976, PhD, 1979. Ptnr., owner Fellwa GmbH, Ingolstadt, Germany, 1972-75; lectr. Ohio State U., Columbus, 1977-79; prof. Georgetown U., Washington, 1980—. Sr. trade advisor U.S. Dept. Commerce, Washington, 1986; dep. asst. sec. Internat. Trade Adminstrn., U.S. Dept. Commerce, Washington, 1987-89; head U.S. delegation OECD Industry Com., Paris, 1987-89; chmn. Found. for Internat. Bus. Edn. and Rsch., Washington, 2000-01. Co-author: Unlocking Japan's Market, 1991, The Global Marketing Imperative, 1995, International Marketing, 7th edit., 2003, International Business, 6th edit., 2002, Mastering Global Markets, 2003. Recipient Dr. Wernher v. Braun award Soc. Logistics Engrs., 1979; Fulbright grantee, 1975, 76; Acad. Mktg. Sci. disting. fellow, 1991. Mem. Am. Mktg. Assn. (bd. dirs.), Acad. Mktg. Sci. (bd. govs.), Cosmos Club. Avocation: skeet. Home: 2811 US Highway 211 E Luray VA 22835-4770 Office: Georgetown U 37th And O St NW Washington DC 20057-0001 E-mail: czinkotm@georgetown.edu.

CZNADEL, JOHN PAUL, music educator; b. NYC, Apr. 2, 1950; s. Paul Peter and Frances A. Cznadel; m. Debora Madsen, July 28, 1979; 1 child, Rebecca. MusB in Edn., Yankton Coll., 1972; MA, Western Ill. U., 1974. Dir. bands Aldrich H.S., Beloit, Wis., 1974—79; band dir. Woodbridge (Va.) Mid. Sch., 1979—81; dir. bands Saunders Mid. Sch., Manassas, Va., 1981—. Vice pres., asst. dir. Prince William (Va.) Cmty. Band, 1996—2002. Office: Saunders Middle School Bands 13557 Spriggs Road Manassas VA 20112 Personal E-mail: im4band@aol.com. E-mail: im4band@aol.com.

CZUJ, CHESTER FRANCIS, JR., food service professional; b. Greenfield, Mass., Apr. 28, 1955; s. Chester Francis and Mary Theresa (O'Sullivan) Matthews; m. Joanne M. Divece, Nov. 25, 1989; children: Chester Francis III, Matthew Joseph, Elizabeth Marie. B in Math., Worcester State Coll., 1978. Cert. dietary mgr. Dietary Mgrs. Assn., food mgmt. profl. Nat. Restaurant Assn. Food svc. mgr. Dining and Kitchen Adminstrn. Inc., Wakefield, Mass., 1973-81; asst. food svc. adminstr. Quincy (Mass.) City Hosp., 1981-84; owner, operator Parkar Bros. Inc., Weymouth, Mass., 1984-86; food svc. mgr. Seiler Corp., Waltham, Mass., 1986-88, resident dist. mgr. Phila., 1988-90; dist. mgr. All Seasons Svcs., Inc., Mid-Atlantic, 1990-94, Chester F. Czuj, Jr., food svc. mgmt. cons., Broomall, Pa., 1994—; food svc. dir. Brock & Co., Malvern, Pa., 1995-97, dist. mgr., 1997-98, Wood Dining Svcs., Allentown, Pa., 1998-2000; regional ops. mgr., v.p. ops. Acorn Food Svcs., Newton Square, Pa., 2000—. Instr. Quincy (Mass.) Jr. Coll., 1985-86. Democrat. Roman Catholic. Avocations: soccer, stained glass. Home and Office: 2168 St Peters Rd Pottstown PA 19465 E-mail: chernet@sysmattix.com.

DAAB-KRZYKOWSKI, ANDRE, pharmaceutical and nutritional manufacturing company administrator; b. Warsaw, May 16, 1949; came to U.S., 1973, naturalized, 1981; s. Aleksy Czeslaw crest Polkozic and Zofia (Dyszkiewicz crest Kudrys) Krzykowski; m. Susan Elizabeth Read, June 26, 1987; 1 child, Cecylia. MSChemE, Tech. U., Warsaw, 1973; MBA, Memphis State U., 1979. Rsch. chemist Schering-Plough, Memphis, 1974-77; process control mgr. Ralston Purina Co., Memphis, 1977-80; dir. pharm. projects Bristol-Myers Squibb Co., Mayaguez, P.R., 1980-90; process devel. group mgr. R&D Ross Labs. divsn. Abbott Labs., 1990—. Patentee in field. Served to 2d lt. Polish Army Res. Mem. Am. Mgmt. Assn., Am. Chem. Soc., Toastmasters (pres. local chpt. 1986). Republican. Lutheran. Avocations: sailing, scuba diving, Karate. Office: Ross Labs 625 Cleveland Ave Columbus OH 43215-1724

DAADI, MARCEL M. neuroscientist, researcher; s. Jilali and Zahra Daadi; m. Sarah E. Hoernig, June 18, 1994; children: Elyas S., Etienne W. BS, U. Mohammed V, Rabat, Morocco, 1987; Advanced Grad. Studies, U. Aix-Marseille, Marseille, France, 1988, PhD, 1992. Postdoctoral fellow U. Calgary, Canada, 1993—95; sr. rsch. scientist NeuroSpheres Ltd., Calgary, 1995—98; asst. prof. neurosurgery U. South Fla., Tampa, 1999—2000; R&D program mgr. Layton Biosci. Inc., Tampa, 1999—2000, sr. rsch. scientist stem cell program Sunnyvale, Calif., 2000—03; assoc. scientist dept. neurosurgery U. Calif., San Francisco, 2003—. Contbr. chapters to books, articles to profl. jours. Grantee, NRC Can., 1996—98, NIH, 2000—01. Mem.: AAAS, Am. Soc. Cell Biology, Am. Soc. Neuroal Transplantation and Brain Repair, Am. Soc. Neurosci. Achievements include research in generation of dopaminergic neurons from stem cells to treat Parkinson's Disease; isolation and development of stem cell lines for therapeutic use; patents pending for method of treating Alzheimer's disease with cell therapy; invention of endogenous mobilization of neural stem cells in the brain; discovery of gene involved in inducing and stabilizing neuronal lineage. Avocations: soccer (play, coach youth), jogging, swimming, surfing, skiing. Office: U Calif Dept Neurosurgery 1855 Folsom St MCB230 San Francisco CA 94103-0555 Office Fax: 415-514-2864. E-mail: mdaadi@itsa.ucsf.edu.

DAALEMAN, TIMOTHY PAUL, physician, researcher; b. Elizabeth, NJ, Feb. 16, 1960; s. Henry James and Elizabeth Ann Daaleman; m. Elizabeth Ann Denton, July 2, 1988; children: Peter Timothy, Claire Elizabeth, Brian James. BA, Yale U., 1978—82; DO, U. of Health Sciences, 1987—91. Fellow Am. Acad. of Family Physicians, 1996, Diplomate Am. Bd. of Family Practice, 2000. Assoc. prof. U. of Kans. Med. Ctr., 2000—02, U. of NC, Chapel Hill, 2002—. Office: Dept of Family Medicine UNC-CH CB#7595 Manning Dr Chapel Hill NC 27599-7595

DAANE, JAMES DEWEY, banker; b. Grand Rapids, Mich., July 6, 1918; s. Gilbert L. and Mamie (Blocksma) D.; m. Blanche M. Tichenor, Apr. 28, 1941 (div. 1952); 1 dau., Elizabeth Marie Daane Mallek; m. Onnie B. Selby, Jan. 23, 1953 (dec. Dec. 1961); m. Barbara W. McMann, Feb. 16, 1963; children: Elizabeth Whitney, Olivia Quartel. AB magna cum laude, Duke U., 1939; MPA, Harvard U., 1946, D in Pub. Adminstrn. (Littauer fellow), 1949. With Fed. Res. Bank, Richmond, Va., 1939-60, asst. v.p., 1953-57, v.p., 1957-60, also cons. to pres. bank, adviser to pres. Mpls., 1960; asst. to sec. treasury, 1960-61; dep. undersec. treasury for monetary affairs, 1961-63; mem. bd. govs. Fed. Reserve System, Washington, 1963-74; vice chmn. bd. dirs. Commerce Union Bank, Sovran Bank/Cen. South, Nashville, 1974-78; chmn. internat. policy com. Commerce Union Corp., 1978-87; dir. Nat. Futures Assn., Ill., 1983—2002; chmn. internat. policy com Sovran Fin. Corp., Nashville, 1988; chmn. money market com. Commerce Union Bank, 1974-87; chmn. money market com. cen. S. Sovran Bank, 1988-90; dir. Nat. Futures Assn. Assoc. economist Fed. Open Market Com., 1955-56, 58-59; chief IMF Fiscal Mission to Paraquay, 1950-51; vice chmn. Tennessee Valley Bancorp. Inc., 1975-78; Frank K. Houston prof. banking and fin. Owen Grad. Sch. Mgmt., Vanderbilt U., 1974-85, Valere Blair Potter prof. banking and fin., 1985-89, Frank K. Houston prof. emeritus, 1989—, Alan R. Holmes prof. econs. Middlebury Coll., 1991-93; bd. dirs. Chgo. Bd. of Trade, 1979-82; prof. fin. Vanderbilt U. Editor: (with David C. Colander) The Art of Monetary Policy. Bd. advisers Patterson Sch. Diplomacy and Internat. Commerce, U. Ky. Mem. J.F. Kennedy Sch. Govt. Assn. of Harvard U., Am. Econ. Assn., Am. Finance Assn. Home: 102 Westhampton Pl Nashville TN 37205-3439 Office: Vanderbilt U Owen Grad Sch Mgmt 401 21st Ave N Nashville TN 37203 E-mail: dewey.daane@owen.vanderbilt.edu.

DABABNEH, AWWAD J. human factors specialist, ergonomist, consultant; b. Amman, Jordan, July 1, 1964; arrived in U.S., 1991, permanent resident; s. Jamil A and Fadwa B Dababneh. PhD, U. of Cin., Ohio, 1997. Cert. Profl. Ergonomist 1999. Vis. rschr. Nat. Inst. for Occupl. Safety & Health, Cin., 1994—2000; cons. Tex. Instruments, Inc, Dallas, 2000—, ErgoConsultant, Co., Dallas, 2002—. Inventor (invention) Ergonomic design of wheeled luggage, 2000. Personal E-mail: awwadd@hotmail.com.

DABBAGH, KARIM, research scientist; b. Ankara, Turkey, Feb. 16, 1970; arrived in U.S.A., 1996; s. Mohammad and Stephane Grassioulet Dabbagh; m. Marie Blandine Praud, Oct. 12, 2000; 1 child, Zoe. BSc(hon.), Imperial Coll., London, Eng., 1993; PhD biochemistry, Univ. Coll., London, Eng., 1997. Post doctoral fellow U. Calif., San Francisco, 1997—99, Stanford Univ., Palo Alto, Calif., 1999—2001; rsch. scientist Roche- Palo Alto, Calif., 2001—. Reviewer Respiratory Rsch., London, 2001—, Internat. Journal - cell biology and biochemistry, London, 2001—. Author rsch. articles in scholorly journals. Mem.: Am. Anogialian of Immunotogist, Am. Thoraic Soc. Achievements include pioneering work on novel findings relevant to pulmonary diseases such as asthma and chronic bronchitis. Avocations: drama, triathlon. Office: Roche Palo Alto 3401 Hillview Ave S3-1 Palo Alto CA 94304-1320 Fax: 650-855-6111.

DABBS, HENRY ERVEN, television and film producer, educator; b. Clover, Va., Oct. 15, 1932; s. Charles E. and Gertrude (Hudson) D.; m. Loretta D. Young, Jan. 9, 1957. B.F.A., Pratt Inst., 1955. Book designer Berton Wink, Inc., N.Y.C., 1958-62; pres., owner Henry Dabbs Prodns. (A Total Comm. Complex), 1978—; partner Henry Dabbs Prodns. (DAK Comm. divsn.), 1980—; instr. cinema Jersey City State Coll., 1977—. Art dir.-prodr.: Dancer, Fitzgerald Sample, N.Y.C., 1963—; editor, prodr., dir.: motion picture Joshua, 1975-76; prodr., dir.: documentary film The Movers, 1978; original paintings depicting famous Afro-Americans in Am. history in permanent collection Smithsonian Instn., Washington; creator: Afro-American History Fact Pack, 1968; author: Afro-American History Highlights, 1968, Black Brass, 1983, 2d edit. 1990 (NAACP Humanitarian award 1995), Black Generals and Admirals in the Armed Forces of the United States; audio video series The ABC's of Black History, 1983; prodr., dir., writer: comprehensive black history video program, 1990, Afro-Centric Black Videos including: African Homeland, Black American Women, The World's Great Black Men and Women and the Great Ones, 1991, Served with AUS, 1955-58. Mem. NAACP.

DABBS, JOHN MORRIS, II, health facility administrator, director; b. Bristol, TN, Apr. 23, 1966; s. John Morris and Phyllis Ann Dabbs; m. Elizabeth Ellen Harbin; children: John, Robert. Emergency Med. Tech., Tri-Cities State Tech.Inst., Blountville, Tenn., 1985—87; AS, Am. Coll. Prehosp. Medicine, New Orleans, 1992, BS, 1998. Cert. EMT-Paramedic Tenn., 1987; Forestry & Wildlife Conservation Profl. Career Devel. Inst., Atlanta, 1996, Home Inspector Profl. Career Devel. Inst., Atlanta, 1998, Electrician Profl. Career Devel. Inst., Atlanta, 2002. Crew Chief Bluff City (Tenn.) Rescue Squad, 1985—87, pres., 1994—95; EMT-paramedic Sullivan County EMS, Blountville, Tenn., 1987—99, pub. rels. officer, 1990—99; team leader High County Rescue Team, Bristol, Tenn., 1994—99; regional dir. Tenn. Dept. of Health - Divsn. of Emergency Med. Svcs., Johnson City, 1999—; pres. Dabbs and Assocs. Consulting Group, 1998—. Cons. The RHP Group, Washington, 1984—, Water Fitness, Bristol, Tenn., 1997—; aide de camp Gov.'s Staff, Tenn., 1998. Member Teen Age Republicans, Bluff City, 1979—83. Named Hon. Mem., Tenn. Nat. Guard, 1985, Outstanding Instr., ARC, 1985; recipient Appreciation award, Dir. Pub. Edn. and Outreach, 1998. Mem.: Tenn. Emergency Med. Svcs. Educators Assn., Earthsavers, Inc. (assoc.). Presbyterian. Avocations: camping, scuba diving, reading, skiing, mountaineering. Home: 168 Wampler Road Bristol TN 37620-0770 Office: Tenn Dept Health - EMS Divsn 1233 Southwest Avenue Extension Johnson City TN 37604-6519 Office Fax: 423-979-3267. Business E-Mail: John.Dabbs@state.tn.us.

DABBS RILEY, JEANNE KERNODLE, retired public relations executive; b. Corsicana, Tex., 1922; d. Robert and Anne (Forrest) McCluer; m. John David Kernodle, June 27, 1942 (div. 1968); 1 child, Elizabeth Kernodle Cabell; m. Jack Autrey Dabbs, Feb. 14, 1981 (dec. 1992); m. James J. Riley, Jr., June 28, 1997 (dec. 1999). BS in Sociology, Tex. Woman's U., 1970. Supr., writer pub. rels. St. Paul's Hosp., Dallas, 1974-76; dir., v.p. mktg. svcs. Fidelity Union Life Ins. Co., Dallas, 1976-81, ret., 1981. Pres. aux. Seton Med. Ctr., Austin, 1985—86; mem. Dallas Civic Chorus, Austin Choral Union. Recipient Editl. medal Freedoms Found. Valley Forge, 1973, Eddy award Internat. Assn. Bus. Communicators, 1974, 76, 79, Matrix award Women in Comm., Inc., 1975, Best of Show award Life Ins. Advts. Assn., 1980, Sr. Vol. award Retirees Coordinating Bd., 1989. Mem. Tex. Women's U. Alumnae Assn. (pres. Capital Area chpt. 1987-89), Tuesday Book Club Austin (pres. 1986), Austin Poetry Soc. Methodist. Avocations: book reviewer, singing. Home: 2211 W North Loop # 126 Austin TX 78756

DABERKO, DAVID A. banker; b. Hudson, Ohio, 1945; BA, Denison U., 1967; MBA, Case Western Res. U., 1970. Mgmt. trainee Nat. City Bank, Cleve., 1968-72, asst. v.p., 1972-73, v.p. bank investment divsn., dept. head mtt. lending divsn., 1973-80, sr. v.p. corp. banking, 1980-82, pres., 1987-93; exec. v.p. corp. banking Nat. City Corp., Nat. City Bank, Cleve., 1982-85; pres., bd. dirs. Nat. City Bank (formerly BancOhio Nat. Bank), Columbus, 1985-87; dep. chmn. Nat. City Corp., Cleve., 1987-93, pres., CEO, 1993-95, chmn., CEO, 1995—. Dir. Fed. Res. Bank, Cleve. Trustee Cleve. Tomorrow, Greater Cleve. Growth Assn., Case Western Res. U., Hawken Sch., Neighborhood Progress, Univ. Cir. Inc., Univ. Hosp. Health Sys.; co-chair Harvest for Hunger Campaign, 1992, 93. Mem. Bankers Roundtable. Office: Nat City Corp National City Center 1900 E 9th St Cleveland OH 44114-3401

DABICH, ELI, JR., insurance company executive; b. Chgo., June 7, 1939; s. Eli and Helen (Radakovich) D.; m. Eileen Dabich, June 8, 1963; children: Michael, Charles, Mary, Kathleen BS, U.S. Naval Acad., 1963; MS, George Washington U., 1970. Mktg. rep. IBM, Balt., 1970-74; sr. v.p. adminstrn. Sun Life, Atlanta, 1974-82; sr. exec. v.p. adminstrn. and fin. Md. Casualty Co., Balt., 1982-88; nat. dir. ins. cons. Coopers & Lybrand, N.Y.C., 1988-90; sr. v.p. Nationale Nederlanden, Washington, 1990-93; sr. v.p., chief adminstrv. officer TIG Ins. Co., 1993-95; pres. Synergy 2000 Inc., 1995—. Bd. dirs. Ivans. Pres. Oak Hill Elem. Sch., PTA, Severna Park, Md., 1970; sec. U.S. Naval Acad., Annapolis, Md., 1963-70; bd. dirs. Ins. Tech., Securities Software & Cons. Capt. USN, 1963-85. Home: 2815 Cox Neck Rd Chester MD 21619-2345

DABINETT, DIANA FRANCES, visual artist; b. Bulawayo, Zimbabwe, Apr. 20, 1943; d. Leslie Frank and Ivy Annie (Eastwood) May; m. Patrick Dabinett, Aug. 1969; children: Emily Thomas. BA in fine arts, U. Cape Town, 1963. H.S. art tchr., Zimbabwe, 1965-66; H.S. English tchr., 1967-69; asst. curator London (Ont.) Art Gallery, 1969-73. Visual arts advisor, adv. panel Fed.-Prov. Cultural Agreement, Newfoundland, Can., 1992-00; Can. artists rep. Newfoundland and Labrador, 1980-97; artist in residence Hopedale, Labrador, 1998-99, Gros Morne Park Newfoundland. One-woman shows include St. John's, 1989-92, Lunenberg, N.S., 1992, Christina Parker Fine Art St. John's, 1994, 98, 2000, 02; two-person exhbn. Pathways, 1997-99; exhibited in group shows at Discovery Travelling Maritimes, 1997; commd. works at Birthing Ctr. and Cancer Ctr., Cmty. Hosp. of the Monterey Peninsula, St. Lawrence Hosp. and Labrador Health Ctr., Newfoundland, N.S. Health and Welfare Dept. Halifax; illustrator: Iceburgs—Castles in the Sea, 2000; collection HRH Queen Elizabeth II. Mem.: Canadian Soc. Water Colour Painters. Avocations: reading, nordic skiing, hiking. Address: Box 1005 Torbay NF Canada A1K 1K9 E-mail: dabinett@avint.net.

DABKOWSKI, JOHN, electrical engineering executive; b. Chgo., Feb. 15, 1933; s. John and Harriet (Sierakowski) D.; m. Mary A. Walkosz, Aug. 15, 1959 (dec. Apr. 1973); 1 child, Colette A.; m. Cecilia Klonowski, June 26, 1976; 1 child, Katherine A. BSEE, Ill. Inst. Tech., 1955, MSEE, 1960, PhD in Elec. Engring., 1969. Sr. rsch. engr. Ill. Inst. Tech. Rsch. Inst., Chgo., 1957-79; ops. mgr. Sci. Applications Internat. Corp., Hoffman Estates, Ill., 1979-85, dir. EM effects rsch., 1985-87, divsn. mgr., 1987-88; pres. Electro Scis., Inc., Crystal Lake, Ill., 1988—. Instr. Grad. Sch., Ill. Inst. Tech., Chgo., 1962-79. Contbr. articles to profl. jours. With U.S. Army, 1955-57. Mem. IEEE (sr.), Nat. Assn. Corrosion Engrs. Republican. Roman Catholic. Home: 7021 Foxfire Dr Crystal Lake IL 60012-1641 Office: Electro Scis Inc PO Box 1438 Crystal Lake IL 60039-1438 E-mail: electrosci@electrosciences.com.

DABNEY, H. SLAYTON, JR., lawyer; b. Charlottesville, Va., Sept. 14, 1949; s. Hovey S. and Patricia S (Schmidt) D.; m. Donna C. Warns, Jan. 14, 1983; children: Slayton, Kate, Andrew. BA, U. Va., 1971, JD, 1974. Bar: Va. 1974, U.S. Dist. Ct. (ea. and we. dists.) Va., U.S. Bankruptcy Ct. (ea. and we. dists.) Va., U.S. Ct. Appeals (4th cir.), U.S. Dist. Ct. D.C. Ptnr. McGuire Woods, LLP, Richmond, Va. Mem. ABA, Am. Bankruptcy Inst., Va. Bar Assn., Richmond Bar Assn. (chmn. bankruptcy sect. 1990-91). Office: McGuire Woods LLP One James Ctr 901 E Cary St Richmond VA 23219-3229

DABROWSKA, DOROTA MARIA, statistician, educator; b. Warsaw, Dec. 10, 1954; arrived in U.S., 1981, naturalized, 1992; d. Emma Katalin Juhasz-Dabrowska and Cyryl Alfons Dabrowski. MA in Math., Warsaw U., 1978; PhD in Stats., U. Calif., Berkeley, 1984. Rsch. assoc. Polish Acad. Sci., Warsaw, 1978—81; asst. prof. Carnegie-Mellon U., Pitts., 1984—88, U. Calif., L.A., 1988—91, assoc. prof., 1991—96, prof., 1996—. Assoc. editor: Jour. Multivariate Analysis, 1999—, Lifetime Data Analysis, 2002—; contbr. articles. Recipient Evelyn Fix Meml. medal, U. Calif., 1984; fellow Earl C. Anthony fellowship, 1981—82, Regents fellowship, 1982—83, Presdl. fellowship, 1986—88; grantee, NSF, 1989—91, 1991—2003, NIH, 1995—2003. Fellow: Inst. Math. Stats.; mem.: Biometric Soc., Bernoulli Soc., Am. Statis. Assn. Roman Catholic. Avocations: music, travel, art. Office: Univ Calif LA Sch Pub Health/Biostatistics Los Angeles CA 90095-1772

DABROWSKI, DORIS JANE, lawyer; b. Paterson, N.J., May 20, 1950; BA, Rutgers U., 1972, JD, 1975. Bar: Pa. 1975, U.S. Dist. Ct. (ea. dist.) Pa. 1976, U.S. Ct. Appeals (3d cir.) 1977, N.J. 1979, U.S. Dist. Ct. N.J. 1979, U.S. Ct. Appeals (fed. cir.) 1985. Staff atty. Delaware County Legal Assistance, Chester, Pa., 1975-77; assoc. Tabas, Horwitz & Furlong (later Tabas, Furlong & Roser), Phila., 1977-83; pvt. practice Phila. and Cherry Hill, N.J., 1983—. Arbitrator Nat. Assn. Securities Dealers; participant Nat. Pension Assistance Project, Patient Advocate Network; mem. adv. coun. 18th Police Dist., 1997—. Mem. editorial bd. Women's Rights Law Reporter, 1974-75. Dir. Well Woman, Phila., 1983-87, Pa. Pro Musica, Phila., 1983-84; mem. adv. bd. Clara Bell Duvall Edn. Fund, Phila.; mem. gov. bd. Health Systems Agy., S.E. Pa., 1980-86. Recipient Cert. of Achievement Bus. Women's Network, Phila., 1984. Mem. Nat. Employment Lawyers' Assn. (pres. Ea. Pa. chpt. 1992-98), Nat. Assn. Women Lawyers (amicus com., bd. dirs. 1994-95), Phila. Bar Assn. (mem. evidence code task force 1992-93, chair support subcom. of small firm and sole practice com. 1992, exec. com. pub. interest sect., co-chair women's rights com. 2000-01), Assn. for Union Democracy, Am. Guild Organists (exec. com.). Office: 1500 Walnut St Ste 900 Philadelphia PA 19102 also: 1930 E Marlton Pike Ste I48 Cherry Hill NJ 08003-4105 E-mail: dabrowskidoris@hotmail.com.

DABROWSKI, THADDEUS E. art educator, art consultant, painter; b. Bronx, N.Y., July 17, 1945; s. Theodore J. and Wanda K. (Curylo) D.; m. Althea M. Smith, May 17, 1970; children: Veronika D. Bulkin, Sibyl T. Jayne. BBA, U. Mass., 1968, MFA, 1970, MEd, 1972. Tech. specialist U. Mass., Amherst, 1972-78, adminstrv. asst., 1978-95, textbook adminstr., 1995—2001, adj. lectr. art, 1981—; art edn. cons., 2001—. Pres., v.p., treas. Leverette (Mass.) Artists and Craftsmen, 1982—; mem. Pub. Arts Commn., Amherst, 1990-94; cons. Nat. Edn. Systems, Amherst, 2001—. Solo exhbns. include Campus Cinema, Hadley, Mass., 1968, U. Mass. Student Union Gallery, Amherst, 1970, Leverett (Mass.) Crafts and Art Ctr., 1990, Burnett Gallery, Jones Libr., Amherst, 1995; showcase artist New Eng. Arts Festival, U. Mass., 1983. Loaned exec., mem. cabinet United Way of Hampshire, Amherst, 1987-2002; mem. Commonwealth of Mass. Employees Charitable Campaign Com., 1987—, Region 4 Charity Application Rev. Com., 1987-2003; elected town meeting mem. Town of Amherst, 2001—. Recipient Milton Bradley award Springfield (Mass.) Art League, 1976. Mem. NEA, Nat. Art Edn. Assn., Mass. Tchrs. Assn., Mass. Assn. for Ednl. Tech. (charter), Univ. Staff Assn. (steward, chief steward 1995-02), Rotary (sec. Amherst 1989-91, v.p. 1991-92, pres. 1992-93, Paul Harris fellow 1984—). Avocations: classic automobile preservation, piano, computer systems. Home: 9 Squire Ln Amherst MA 01002-3232 Office: U Mass Dept Art Amherst MA 01003 E-mail: thaddeus@art.umass.edu.

DACBERT-FRIESE, SHARYN VARHELY, social worker, evangelist; b. Utica, N.Y., Dec. 10, 1947; d. Henry Alexander Varhely and Elouise Fulmore; m. Thomas Jewett Mitchell III, Oct. 20, 1968 (div. Dec. 1982); children: Sharyn Mitchell Wallace, James Bailey Mitchell, Jaclyn Ashley Mitchell; m. Guenther Roland Friese, Dec. 16, 1998. BA, U. Ala., 1968; MSW, Our Lady of the Lake U., San Antonio, Tex., 1991. Lic. master social worker Advanced Clin. Practitioner, 1991, cert. clin. supr. 1998, LCSW 2003. Entrepreneur, Laredo, Tex., 1972—85; founder, owner Jacob's Well, Laredo, Tex., 1980—87; corp. v.p. Dacbert Music Co., San Antonio, 1992—94; individual and family psychotherapist Fuller & Assocs., San Antonio, 1991—94; pvt. practice San Antonio, 1994—97; sr. pastor, founder, pres., chmn. Sheepgate Fellowship, San Antonio, 1997—; dir., founder, pres., chmn. Christian Family Counseling Ctr., San Antonio, 1997—. Radio personality, counselor Sta. KSLR-AM, San Antonio, 1997—2001; individual and family psychotherapist Adult Parent Child, San Antonio, 1991—92. Contbr. articles to profl. jours. Mem.: NASW, Nat. Assn. Bus. and Profl. Women, Am. Assn. Christian Counselors, Play Therapy Assn., Tuesday Musical Club. Avocations: oil painting, camping, drawing, cooking, fishing. Office: Christian Family Counseling Ctr PO Box 460686 San Antonio TX 78246 Office Fax: 210-493-2169. E-mail: sdacbert1@aol.com.

D'ACCONE, FRANK ANTHONY, music educator; b. Somerville, Mass., June 13, 1931; s. Salvatore and Maria (DiChiappari) D'A. Mus. B., Boston U., 1952, Mus.M., 1953; A.M., Harvard U., 1955, PhD, 1960. Asst. prof. music SUNY at Buffalo, 1960-63, assoc. prof., 1964-68; prof. music UCLA, 1968-94, chmn. dept., 1973-76; chmn. faculty UCLA (Coll. Fine Arts), 1976-79; chmn. dept. musicology UCLA, 1989-93. Vis. prof. music Yale U., 1972-73 Author: The History of a Baroque Opera, 1985, The Civic Muse, 1997; editor: Music of the Florentine Renaissance, vols. 1-12, 1967-94; gen. editor Corpus Mensurabilis Musicae, 1986-2001; co-editor Musica Disciplina, 1990-2001; contbr. articles to profl. jours. Fellow Am. Acad. Rome, 1963-64, Fulbright Found., 1963-64, NEH, 1975; recipient G.K. Delmas Venetian Studies award, 1977, J.S. Guggenheim Found. award, 1980, Internat. Galilei prize, Pisa, 1997. Fellow Am. Acad. of Arts and Scis.; mem. Am. Musicol. Soc. (dir. 1973-74), Internat. Musicol. Soc. Home: 725 Fontana Way Laguna Beach CA 92651-4010 Office: U Calif Dept Music Los Angeles CA 90024

DACEY, EILEEN M. lawyer; b. NYC, Dec. 15, 1948; d. Gabriel A. and Mary (Breen) D.; m. Kinchen C. Bizzell, Jan. 1, 1984. BA in Sociology, SUNY, Stony Brook, 1970; JD, St. John's U., 1975. Assoc. Mendes & Mount, NYC, 1976-80, jr. ptnr., 1980-88; ptnr. Adams, Duque & Hazeltine, NYC, 1988-94, Morrison Mahoney & Miller, NYC, 1994-96, Querrey & Harrow, NYC, 1996-98. Mem. mediation program U.S. Dist. Ct. (so. dist.) N.Y. Vol. Lawyers for the Arts, Jewish Braille Inst.; mem. elderly project Vols. of Legal Svc. Recipient Candle of Understanding award, Jewish Braille Inst., 2001. Mem. ABA (tort and ins. practice sect.), N.Y. State Bar Assn., Assn. Bar City N.Y., Practicing Law Inst. (mem. ins. law adv. bd.), Assn. Profl. Ins. Women. Home: New York, NY. Died Oct. 7, 2002.

DACEY, GEORGE CLEMENT, retired laboratory administrator, consultant; b. Chgo., Jan. 23, 1921; s. Clement Anthony Dacey and Helyn MacLachlan; m. Anne Zeamer, June 20, 1954; children: Donna Lynn, John Clement, Sarah Anne. BSEE, U. Ill., 1942; PhD in Physics, Calif. Inst. Tech., 1951. Rsch. engr. Westinghouse Rsch. Labs, East Pittsburgh, 1942-45; mem. tech. staff transistor rsch. Bell Telephone Labs, 1952-55, head transistor devel., 1955-58, dir. solid state electronics rsch., 1958-61, exec. dir. telephones div., 1963-68, v.p. customer equipment devel., 1968-70, v.p. transmission systems, 1970-79, v.p. ops. systems, 1979-81; pres. Sandia Nat. Labs., 1981-86. V.p. rsch. Sandia Corp., Albuquerque, 1961-63. Contbr. articles on transistor physics, lasers to tech. jours; patentee transistors. Mem. exec. bd. Monmouth coun. Boy Scouts Am., 1970-75; bd. dirs. Monmouth Mus., 1972-81. Recipient distinguished

alumnus award U. Ill. Elec. Engring. Alumni Assn., 1970 Fellow IEEE, Am. Phys. Soc.; mem. Nat. Acad. Engring., Sigma Xi, Phi Kappa Phi, Tau Beta Pi, Eta Kappa Nu. Home: 2612 Golfside Ct Naples FL 34110-8675

DACEY, KATHLEEN RYAN, judge; b. Boston; m. William A. Dacey (dec. Aug. 1986); 1 child, Mary Dacey White AB with honors, Emmanuel Coll., 1941; MS in L.S., Simmons Coll., 1942; JD, Northeastern U., 1945; postgrad., Boston U. Law Sch., 1945-46; LLD (hon.), Suffolk Law Sch., 1990, Emmanuel Coll., 1992. Bar: Mass. 1945, U.S. Supreme Ct. 1957. Law clk. to justices Mass. Supreme Jud. Ct., 1945-47; Practiced in Boston, 1947-75; asst. dist. atty. Suffolk County, Mass., 1971-72, 1971-72; auditor, master Commonwealth of Mass., Boston, 1972-75, Suffolk and Norfolk Counties, Mass., 1972-75; asst. atty. gen., chief civil bur. Mass. Dept. Atty. Gen., Boston, 1975-77; U.S. adminstrv. law judge Commonwealth of Mass., Boston, 1977-99; of counsel Cushing & Dolan P.C., Mass., 1999—; asst. dist. atty. Suffolk County, Mass., 1971-72. Mem. panel def. counsel for indigent persons U.S. Dist. Ct. Dist. Mass.; lectr., speaker in field Contbr. articles to profl. jours. Bd. dirs. Mission United Neighborhood Improvement Team, Boston; mem. Boston Sch. Com., 1945-46, chmn., 1946-47 Recipient Silver Shingle award Boston U. Sch. Law, 1980; named Alumnae Woman of Yr., Northeastern U. Law Sch. Assn., 1976 Mem. ABA (ho. of dels. 1982—, exec. com. conf. of adminstrv. law judges jud. adminstrn. divsn. 1987—), Internat. Bar Assn., Mass. Bar Assn., Boston Bar Assn., Norfolk Bar Lawyers Assn., Nat. Assn. Women Lawyers (pres.), Mass. Assn. Women Lawyers, Internat. Fedn. Women Lawyers, Boston U. Law Sch. Alumni Assn. (corr. sec. 1974-76), Boston U. Nat. Alumni Coun.

DACEY, PAUL, artist; b. Toledo, July 16, 1960; s. Eleanor Dacey. BFA in Painting, Cleve. Inst. Art, 1984. Commns., Nokia U.S. Hdqrs., Dallas, 1999, Credit Suisse First Boston, London, 1999—2000, U.S. Embassy, Ottawa, Can., 1999, Kampala, Uganda, 2000. Ellen Battell Stoeckel fellow, Yale U., 1983. Home and Office: Apt 23 35-21 80th St Jackson Heights NY 11372

DACH, LESLIE ALAN, public relations company executive; b. N.Y.C., Apr. 17, 1954; s. Joseph and Edith (Lipsyzc) D.; m. Mary Ann Dickie, Nov. 19, 1983; children: Jonathan Alexander, Eliza May. BS in Biology, Yale U., 1975; MPA, Harvard U., 1981. Staff scientist Environ. Def. Fund., Washington, 1977-79; assoc. dir. Nat. Audubon Soc., Washington, 1981-84, legis. dir., 1984-87; dir. scheduling Mondale-Ferraro campaign, Washington, 1984; spl. asst. to chmn. U.S. Senate Agr. Com., Washington, 1987; dir. comm. Dukakis for Pres., Boston, 1987-88; sr. v.p. Edelman Pub. Rels., Washington, 1989-90, exec. v.p., 1990-96, vice chmn., 1996—. Office: Edelman Pub Rels 1875 Eye St NW Ste 900 Washington DC 20006-5422

DACHOWSKI, PETER RICHARD, manufacturing executive; b. Hillingdon, Middlesex, Eng., June 2, 1948; came to U.S., 1969; s. Teodor and Mary (Stracey) D.; m. Victoria Kaplan Ortiz, May 1, 1977. MA in Econs. with first class honors, Queens' Coll., Cambridge, Eng., 1969; MBA, U. Chgo., 1971. Fin. analyst Exxon Corp., 1971-73; mgr. Boston Cons. Group, 1973-76; asst. treas. CertainTeed Corp., Valley Forge, Pa., 1976-78, asst. to chief exec. officer, 1979-80; v.p. planning and devel. CertainTeed Co., Valley Forge, Pa., 1980-81, v.p., treas., 1981-83, v.p., compt., 1983-85; v.p., pres. Roofing Products Group, 1985-90, Vinyl Bldg. Products Group, Valley Forge, 1987-90; sr. v.p., pres. Exterior Products Group, 1990-93; exec. v.p., 1994—. Mem. corp. devel. staff Saint Gobain, Paris, 1978—79; chmn. Saint-Gobain Isover, 1996—, Saint-Gobain Isover AB, British Gypsum Isover, Saint-Gobain Ecophon AB; pres. Worldwide Insulation Saint-Gobain, 1996—; bd. dirs. C&D Techs., SG Isover G&H AG; adv. coun. U. Chgo. Grad. Sch. Bus., 2001—. Trustee Internat. House of Phila., 1994-96; bd. dirs. Philadelphia Orch. Assn., 2002—. Recipient Wall St. Jour. award Dow Jones-Chgo., 1971. Mem.: Union League Phila., Alliance Francaise Phila. (trustee 1994—96), Brit.-Am. C. of C., World Pres. Orgn., Beta Gamma Sigma. Avocations: travel, listening to live music, sailing, diving. Home: 321 Woodmont Cir Berwyn PA 19312-1431 Office: CertainTeed Corp PO Box 860 Valley Forge PA 19482-0860

DACHS, ALAN MARK, investment company executive; b. N.Y.C., Dec. 7, 1947; s. Sidney and Martha (Selz) D.; m. Lauren B. Dachs, June 23, 1973. BA, Wesleyan U., Middletown, Conn., 1970; MBA, NYU, 1978. Account officer Chem. Bank, N.Y.C., 1971-74; various positions Bechtel Group, Inc., San Francisco, 1974-81; v.p., CFO Dual Drilling Co., Wichita Falls, Tex., 1981-82; sr. v.p., mng. dir. Bechtel Investments, Inc., San Francisco, 1982-89; pres., dir., mem. exec. com. and CEO Fremont Group, L.L.C., San Francisco, 1989—. Bd. dirs. Bechtel Group, Bechtel Enterprises, Inc. Charter trustee, chair bd. trustees Wesleyan U.; trustee The Brooking Instn., The Conf. Bd. Office: Fremont Group LLC 199 Fremont St Ste 2500 San Francisco CA 94105-2230

DACKAWICH, S. JOHN, sociology educator; b. Loch Gelley, W.Va., Jan. 31, 1926; s. Samuel and Estelle (Jablonski) D.; m. Shirley Jean McVay, May 20, 1950; children: Robert John, Nancy Joan. BA, U. Md., 1955; PhD, U. Colo., 1958. Instr. U. Colo., 1955-57; instr. Colo. State U., 1957-59; prof., chmn. sociology Calif. State U., Long Beach, 1959-70, prof. sociology Fresno, 1970-94, chmn. dept., 1970-75, prof. sociology emeritus, 1994—. Pvt. practice survey rsch., 1962— Author: Sociology, 1970, The Fiery Furnace Effect, 2000; contbr. articles and rsch. papers to profl. publs. Mem. Calif. Dem. Ctrl. Com., 1960-62; co-dir. Long Beach Ctrl. Area Study, 1962-64, Citizen Participation Study, Fresno. With USMCR, 1943-46, U.S. Army, 1950-53. Mem. Am., Pacific sociol. assns. Home: 5841 W Judy Ct Visalia CA 93277-8601 Office: Calif State U Dept Sociology 5340 N Campus Dr Fresno CA 93740-8019

DACORTE, ALLAN FRANCIS, priest, financial consultant and advisor; b. Evergreen Park, Ill., June 30, 1946; s. Cyrus (Pat) DaCorte and Helen Regina Nachman. BA, Maryknoll Coll., 1969; MDiv, Cath. Theol. Union, Chgo., 1971. Ordained priest Roman Cath. Ch., 1971. Dir. candidate formation Franciscan Friars, Joliet, Ill., 1989—96, dir. fin. St. Louis, 1996—2002. Cons. Order of Friars Minor, Rome, 1989—91. Contbr. Ratio Formationis, 1992. Trustee Quincy (Ill.) U., 1988—93, 1999—2002, Padua HS, Parma, Ohio, 1997—99. Mem.: Franciscan English Spking Conf. Treas., Nat. Assn. Treas. Religious Insts. (exec. com. 2000—02, pres. 2002—, bd. dirs. 1999—2002). Roman Catholic. Avocations: music, travel, sports. Home: 3140 Meramec St Saint Louis MO 63118 Office: Franciscan Friars Office Fin 3140 Meramec St Saint Louis MO 63118

DADABHOY, ZERIN P. anesthesiologist; b. Poona, India, 1945; came to U.S., 1973; MD, BJ Med. Coll.-Poona U., Maharashtra, India, 1968. Diplomate Am. Bd. Anesthesiology. Intern Grant Hosp., Chgo., 1976-78; resident in anesthesiology U. Ill., Chgo., 1978-80, fellow, 1980-81, anesthesiologist, 1981—, clin. asst. prof. anesthesiology, 1981—, dir. obstet. anesthesia, 1981-92; acting chmn. obstet. anesthesiology Cook County Hosp., Chgo., 1992-98, chmn. obstet. anesthesiology, 1998—. Asst. clin. prof. Rush U., 1995. Mem.: Soc. of Obstet. Anesthesia and Perinatology, Chgo. Soc. Anesthesiology, Ill. Soc. Anesthesiology, Internat. Anesthesiology Rsch. Soc., Am. Soc. Anesthesiology.

D'ADDARIO, ALICE MARIE, school administrator; b. N.Y.C., Feb. 9, 1942; d. Ralph and Rose Marie (Ventigmiglia) DeMartino; m. Joseph L. D'Addario, June 27, 1964; children: Joseph R., Paul T. BS in Social Studies, St. John's U., 1962, MS in Secondary Edn., 1963; MA in Liberal Studies, NYU, 1981. Cert. sch. adminstr., secondary educator of English and Social Studies, N.Y. Tchr. social studies So. Huntington Schs., Huntington Station, N.Y., 1963-83; dept. chair Walt Whitman H.S., Huntington Station, 1983—. Adj. prof. Adelphi U., Garden City, N.Y., 1989-02, inservice instr. S. Hungington Tchr. Ctr., 2002—; tchg. adv. panelist, program reviewer America, Pathways to the Present, Prentice Hall, 1998, program reviewer, tchr. adv. panel World History, Connections to Today, 1999; counselor Ind. Coll., 1988—. Author: Writing Across the Curriculum, 1988, Participationin Government-A Guide for Teachers I, 1989, II, 1991, Asian Studies Elective Curriculum. PTA pres. P.S. 144 Queens, 1981-83, Russell Sage Jr. High Sch. 190, Queens, 1983-85, Parents Assn. Hillcrest H.S., Queens, 1986-88, Queen's Confederation of Parents, 1987-88. Recipient Parent Svc. award Hillcrest H.S., Queens, 1986-88, Profl. Recognition award Bd. Edn. South Huntington Schs., 1983, Tchr. of Yr. award Walt Whitman H.S. Parent Assn., 1984, Spl. Tchrs. Are Recognized award Cornell U., 1992, Dartmouth Coll. Freshman Tchr. Recognition award, 1994, Outstanding Social Studies Supr. award L.I. Coun. for the Social Studies, 1997. Mem. L.I. Council for the Social Studies, Assn. Sch. Adminstrs., So. Huntington Chairperson Assn. (v.p. 1985-87, pres. 1987—). Democrat. Roman Catholic. Avocations: reading, theater, art museums, cycling, jogging. Home: 68-47 Harrow St Flushing NY 11375-5157 Office: Walt Whitman High Sch West Hills Rd Huntington NY 11746 E-mail: aljog29@aol.com.

D'ADDARIO, EDITH, performing company executive; Dir. Joffrey Ballet Sch., N.Y.C., 1961—. Office: Joffrey Ballet Sch Am Ballet Ctr 434 Ave of the Ams New York NY 10011 Office Fax: 212-614-8148.

DADDARIO, EMILIO QUINCY, retired lawyer; b. Newton Centre, Mass., Sept. 24, 1918; s. Attilio Dante and Julia (Ciovacco) D.; m. Berenice Mary Carbo, Oct. 20, 1940; children: Edward, Stephen, Richard. BA, Wesleyan U., 1939; LLB, U. Conn, 1942; DSc, Wesleyan U., 1967; LLD, Rensselaer Polytech. Inst., Troy, N.Y., 1967, Phila. Coll. Osteo. Medicine, 1976. Bar: Conn., Mass., D.C., 86th-91st Congresses from 1st Conn. dist. Judge Mcpl. Ct., Middletown, Conn., 1948-50; mem. 86th, 87th, 88th, 89th, 90th and 91st Congresses, from 1st Conn. dist., 1958-71; dir. Office Tech. Assessment, Washington, 1973-77; mem. Wilkes, Artis, Hedrick & Lane, Washington, 1977-87. Vis. prof. MIT, Cambridge, 1970-71; co-chmn. ABA-AAAS Conf. of Lawyers and Scientists, Washington, 1976-88. Contbr. articles on sci. policy to profl. publs. Mayor, City of Middletown, Conn., 1946-48; mem. Commn. on Sci., Engring. and Pub. Policy, Nat. Acad. Scis., Washington, 1981—; trustee Wesleyan U., 1962—; adv. bd. Georgetown U. Sch. of Nursing. Served to maj., inf. U.S. Army, 1942-45, 50-52, ETO, PTO, Korea. Decorated Legion of Merit; Medaglia D'Argento (Italy). Mem. Silver Anniversary All-Am. Football Team, 1964; recipient Ralph Coats Roe award ASME, 1974; honor award and medal Stevens Inst. Tech., 1975; Pub. Welfare award Nat. Acad. Scis., 1976; Disting. Svc. award Nat. Sci. Found., 1990, W.R. Grace award Am. Cham. Soc., 1992. Mem. ABA, AAAS (pres. 1977, chmn. 1978, chmn. governance com. 1989-90), Inst. Medicine (bd. health sci. policy 1991-97), D.C. Bar Assn., Oak Ridge Associated Univs. (bd. dirs. 1991-97), Nat. Acad. Sci. (com. nat. forum on sci. and tech. goals 1995), Vets of OSS (v.p. 1990—). Clubs: Cosmos (Washington). Democrat. Roman Catholic. Home: #1027 3133 Connceticut Ave NW Washington DC 20008-5112

DADE, JOANN, critical care nurse, small business owner; b. Dewitt, Ark., June 27, 1948; d. Roosevelt and Ersylene (Ledbetter) Shorter; m. Paul Dade; children: Marvin, Marcus. ADN, U. Ark., 1980; BSN, Clayton State U., 1998; MS, St. Francis U., 1995. RN, Ga.; cert. critical care nurse; cert. BLS instr./trainer, ACLS provider. Staff nurse Bapt. Med. Ctr., Little Rock, 1968-78; plant nurse Timex Corp., Little Rock, 1978-80; staff nurse Cen. Ark. Home Health Agy., Little Rock, 1980-86, VA Med. Ctr., Atlanta, 1986—, mgr. nurse, cardiology adminstr., 1999—; pres. Dade Enterprise, Decatur, Ga., 1994—. Mem. There is Hope-Ministries, Decatur, Ga., 1992, Arthritis Found., Atlanta, 1992, Dekalb County Concerned Citizens, Decatur, 1991—. Recipient Outstanding Nurse award Ga. Hosp. Assn., 1993. Mem. ANA (cert. med.-surg.), ACA, Ga. Nursing Assn. Pentecostal. Avocations: sewing, reading, jogging, voluntary works. Home: 2621 Rainwater Ct Decatur GA 30034-2249 E-mail: joann.dade@med.va.gov.

DADE, LENNELL R. humanities educator; PhD, Howard U., 1993. Asst. prof. U. Wis., Milw., 1992—95; assoc. prof. Lincoln (Pa.) U., 1995—. Office: Lincoln U PO Box 179 Lincoln PA 19352-0999

DADISMAN, JOSEPH CARROL, newspaper executive; b. Statesboro, Ga., May 24, 1934; s. Howard Dean and Mary Lou (Moore) D.; m. Mildred Jean Sparks, Aug. 19, 1956; children: David Carrol, Ellen Clarice. AB, U. Ga., 1956. Reporter, editorial writer, mng. editor Augusta (Ga.) Chronicle, 1956-66; editor Marietta (Ga.) Daily Jour., 1966-72; mng. editor Macon (Ga.) News, 1972-74; exec. editor, v.p. Columbus (Ga.) Ledger-Enquirer, 1974-80; gen. mgr. Tallahassee Dem., 1980-81, pub., pres., 1981-97; Knight Internat. Press fellow to Russia, 1998. Pres. adv. bd. U. Ga. Sch. Journalism, 1979-81, Fla. A&M U. Sch. Journalism, 1988-90; pres. Jr. Achievement of Columbus-Phenix City, 1977-78, United Way of Leon County, 1985-86, Ga. AP Assn., 1976-77; pres. Cmty. Found. of North Fla., 1997-2001. Served with AUS, 1957-59. Recipient Pub. Svc. award Cobb County C. of C., 1968, Fearless Editl. award Ga. Press Assn., 1963, Outstanding Alumnus award U. Ga. Sch. Journalism, 1994, Disting. Leader award Tallahassee Area C. of C., 1995, meritorious achievement award Fla. A&M U., 1996, Knight-Ridder excellence award in cmty. svc., 1997; named Young Man of Yr., Augusta Jaycees, 1962. Mem. Am. Soc. Newspaper Editors, Fla. Press Assn. (bd. dirs. 1984-86, v.p. 1986-87, pres. 1987-88), So. Newspaper Pubs. Assn. (bd. dirs. 1989-92), Econ. Club Fla. (pres. 1993-94, chmn. 1995-97), Orange Bowl Com., Governors Club (bd. dirs. 2000-02, pres. 2002), Killearn Country Club, Capital Tiger Bay Club, Rotary. Methodist. Home: 1235 Live Oak Plantation Rd Tallahassee FL 32312-2509 Home Fax: 850-386-8254. E-mail: jedadisman@aol.com.

DADLEY, ARLENE JEANNE, sleep techologist; b. Cleve., Sept. 13, 1941; d. Bernard and Bernice Anne (Selleck) Davis; m. Charles Dadley, Sept. 15, 1967 (div. Oct. 1977); children: Anitra, Charles. BA in Bus., Ursuline Coll., 1980; postgrad., Case Western Res. U., 1983-85, Stanford U., 1988. Registered polysomnographic technologist. Jr. fund acct. Am. U., Washington, 1967-70; htn and cancer rsch. asst. Case Western Res. U., Cleve., 1976-87, gastroent. rsch. assoc., 1984, sleep rsch. assoc., 1985-87; sr. clin. sleep technologist Metrohealth Med. Ctr., Cleve., 1987—2003, sleep diagnostics tchr., trainer, 1987—. Judge regional and state sci. fairs. Exhibited in group shows at Cleve. Mus. Art, Butler Inst. Art, Corcoran Gallery Art, Washington, Internat. Traveling Am. Artists Exhibit (Jury 1st award); contbr. articles to profl. jours. Recipient Presdl. Lit. Achievement citation, League Am. Pen Women, 1974, citation, ARC, 1991; scholar, Case Western Res. U., 1976—80, Yale U., 1982, Respironics, Inc., 1988; Pell grantee, 1976—80, Ohio Instl. grantee, 1976—80. Mem.: Assn. Polysomnographic Technologists, Internat. Platform Assn. Avocations: oil painting, sleep education, thoroughbred horses, photography. Home: PO Box 894 Columbia Station OH 44028-0894 Office: Metrohealth Med Ctr 2500 Metrohealth Dr Cleveland OH 44109-1900 *Waking or sleeping be alert to the surprises and dreams which produce insight to unveil discoveries. Be creative, make things happen. Have the courage of your convictions, fear neither success or failure. You may not change the whole world. You can change your world.*

DADMARZ, KEWMARS EBRAHIM, physician, educator; b. Tehran, Iran, Mar. 13, 1928; s. Ebrahim and Nosrat (Hooshyar) D.; m. Lili Azmoudeh; children: Mitra, Ali. MD, U. Tehran, 1955. Diplomate Am. Bd. Surgery, Am. Bd. Disability Analysts. Intern Nashville Gen. Hosp., 1955—56, resident in surgery, 1956—57, Meharry Med. Coll., Nashville, 1957—62; resident in cancer surgery Meml. Ctr. Cancer and Allied Diseases, N.Y.C., 1960-61; resident in thoracic and cardiovascular surgery U. Alta., Edmonton, Canada, 1962-64, fellow in surg. pathology, 1964-65; staff surgeon Wilmington (Del.) VA Med. Ctr.; rct.; assoc. prof. surgery, former chief dept. thoracic surgery U. Tehran; instr. surgery Thomas Jefferson U. Fellow ACS; mem. Assn. Iranian Surgeons, Matthew Walker Surg. Soc. Office: 300 Benham Ct Newark DE 19711-6009 E-mail: kewdadmarz@hotmail.com., kewmars@comcast.net.

DADO, DIANE VALENTINA, pediatric plastic and reconstructive surgeon; b. Chgo., Feb. 14, 1952; d. Ralph N. and Violet M. Dado; 1 child, Joseph. BA, St. Xavier Coll., Chgo., 1973; MD, Loyola U., Maywood, Ill., 1976. Cert. Am. Bd. Plastic and Reconstructive Surgeery. Intern in surgery Loyola U. Med. Ctr., Maywood, 1976-77, resident in surgery, 1977-79, resident plastic surgery, 1979-82; fellow plastic surgery Children's Meml. Hosp., Chgo., 1982-83; instr. surgery Stritch Sch. Medicine Loyola U., Maywood, 1983, asst. prof. surgery, 1983-89, assoc. prof. surgery, pediatrics, 1989—. Mem. plastic surgery rsch. coun. Loyola U. Cleft Palate/Craniofacial Team, 1983—; attending physician Loyola U. Med. Ctr. div. Plastic Surgery, 1983—. children's Meml. Hosp. div. plastic surgery, 1983—. Contbr. articles to profl. jours. Mem. Am. Soc. Plastic and Reconstructive Surgeons, Am. Acad. Pediatrics, Am. Burn Assn., ACS, Am. Cleft Palate Assn., Ill. Assn. Craniofacial Teams, Chgo. Soc. Plastic Surgery, Can. Soc. Plastic Surgeons, Desmond A. Kernahan Soc. (founding). Avocations: martial arts, scuba diving, sailing, skiing. Office: Loyola U Med Ctr 2160 S 1st Ave Maywood IL 60153-3304

DADRIAN, VAHAKN NORAIR, sociology educator; b. Istanbul, Turkey, May 26, 1926; came to U.S., 1947, naturalized, 1961; s. Hagop and Mayreni (Der Garabedian) D. Ed. (Alexander von Humboldt fellow), U. Berlin, Germany, U. Vienna, Austria; ed. (scholar), U. Zurich, Switzerland; MA, Wayne State U., 1950; PhD (Reynolds fellow), U. Chgo., 1954. Asst. prof. sociology Washington Coll., Chestertown, Md., 1955-56, Boston U., 1957-59; rsch. fellow Harvard Ctr. for Middle Eastern Studies, 1961-62; sr. analyst dept. strategic studies div. missiles and space Raytheon, 1962-63; lectr. Boston Coll., 1963-65; asso. prof. Wis. State U., Superior, 1965-67, Fla. Atlantic U., 1967-68, prof., 1968-70, SUNY, Geneseo, 1970-91; dir. genocide study project H.F. Guggenhiem Found., Conesus, N.Y., 1991—. Vis. scholar Mass. Inst. Tech. Ctr. Internat. Studies, 1960-61; guest rschr. Inst. for Rsch. on Soviet Union, Munich, Germany, summer 1962; participant, Am. Sociol. Assn. grantee 6th World Congress of Sociology, Evian, France, fall 1966; vis. prof. Duke, summer 1971; dir. genocide study project NSF, 1977— ; lectr. at univs., confs. and on TV in, U.S., Europe, Soviet Union, S.Am. Contbg. author: World Book Ency., 1972— ; Cons. editor: Internat. Jour. Contemporary Soc; translator, editor: United and Independent Turania (Zarevand), 1971; Contbr. articles to profl. jours., newspapers. Harvard Lab. Social Relations grantee, 1959; Am. Philos. Soc. grantee, 1961; Am. Com. Travel grantee-in-aid, 1962; Wenner-Gren Found. Anthropol. Rsch. grantee, 1963, 65; Am. Coun. Learned Socs. grantee, summer 1966; recipient Wis. U. Bd. Regents award, 1966, St. Vardan medal for scholarship in field of Soviet nationalities Cardinal Aghadjanian, Rome, 1968; NSF grantee, 1968, 73, 76; State U. N.Y. grantee-in-aid, 1974; H.F. Guggenheim Found. grantee, 1990-91. Mem. Delta Tau Kappa (hon.) Home: PO Box 99 Conesus NY 14435-0099 Office: Genocide Rsch Zoryan Inst PO Box 99 Conesus NY 14435-0099

DADY, ROBERT EDWARD, lawyer; b. N.Y.C., Nov. 11, 1936; s. Edward Joseph and Florence (Scheidt) D.; m. Mollie D. Richman; children: Michael, Andrew, Rachel. BA, Queens Coll., 1958; LLB, Fordham U., 1961. Bar: N.Y. 1962, Fla. 1974. Asst. gen. counsel The Equity Corp., N.Y.C., 1962-66; gen. atty. ITT_Levitt and Sons, Inc., Washington, Lake Success, N.Y., 1966-70; sr. v.p.-legal First Realty Investment Corp., Miami Beach, Fla., 1970-71; v.p.-legal, sec. Cavanagh Cmtys. Corp., Miami, Fla., 1971-75; ptnr. Mann & Dady, P.A., Miami, 1975-80, Mann, Dady, Corrigan & Zelman, P.A., Miami, 1980-83, Dady, Siegfried & Kipnis, P.A., Miami, 1984-85; pvt. practice Miami, 1985-87; ptnr. Kimbrell and Hamann, P.A., 1987-89; shareholder Popham, Haik, Schnobrich & Kaufman, Ltd., 1990-96; of counsel Fieldstone, Lester, Shear & Denberg, Coral Gables, Fla., 1996—. Past adj. prof. law U. Miami Sch. Law.; bd. dirs. Spectrum Programs, Inc., pres., 1984-86, Spectrum Found., Inc., pres. 1988—. Author: Land Acquistion and Development, 1975. Bd. dirs., exec. comm. Miami Coalition for a Safe and Drug Free Cmty., 1992-99; vice-chmn. Childrens Home Soc. Found. Miami, 1993-96, bd. dirs., 1993—; appointed to (by gov.) Fla. Jud. Nom. Com., 1995-98; bd. dirs. Wellness Cmty., Miami, 2001—. Mem. Nat. Land Coun. (pres. 1974-81, vice chmn. bd. dirs. 1973—), Builders Assn. So. Fla. (life dir., gen. counsel 1982-2001), ABA (environ. law com., timesharing and recreation law com., vice chmn.), Fla. Bar Assn. Republican. Home: 8440 SW 143rd St Miami FL 33158-1457 Office: Fieldstone Lester Shear & Denberg Sun Trust Plaza 201 Alhambra Cir Ste 601 Coral Gables FL 33134-5107 E-mail: bd@flsdlaw.com.

DAEHN, GLENN STEVEN, materials scientist; b. Chgo., July 4, 1961; s. Ralph Charles and Beverly S. (Shanske) D.; m. Margaret A. Burkhart, Oct. 25, 1987; children: Andrew Joseph, Katrin Ellen, Matthew Charles. BS, Northwestern U., 1983; MS, Stanford U., 1985, PhD, 1988. Rsch. asst. Stanford U., Palo Alto, Calif., 1983-87; asst. prof. dept. materials sci. and engring. Ohio State U., Columbus, 1987-92, assoc. prof. dept. materials sci. and engring., 1992-96, Fontana prof. dept. materials sci. and engring., 1996—. Co-founder, v.p. technology Excera Materials Group, 1992—. Co-editor: Modeling the Deformation of Crystalline Solids, 1991. Named Nat. Young Investigator, NSF, 1992; recipient Young Investigator award Army Rsch. Office, 1992, R.L. Hardy Gold medal TMS, 1992, Marcus Grossman award ASM Internat., 1990. Mem. ASM Internat., Am. Ceramic Soc., Materials Rsch. Soc., Minerals, Metals and Materials Soc. Achievements include description and practical applications of how temperature changes accelerate the deformation of composite materials; co-development of new class of ceramic-metal composites; development of hyperplasticity --practical application of extended metal ductility observed at high velocity. Home: 2076 Fairfax Rd Upper Arlington OH 43221-4319 Office: Ohio State U Materials Sci Dept 2041 N College Rd Columbus OH 43210-1124 E-mail: Daehn.1@osu.edu.

DAENZER, BERNARD JOHN, insurance company executive, legal consultant; b. N.Y.C., Jan. 15, 1916; s. Bernard Cornelius and Amelia Catherine (Heinze) D.; m. Valerie Antoinette Lee, June 8, 1941; children— Peter, Jean Daenzer Aiken, John, Richard (dec.). AB, Fordham Coll., 1937, LL.D., 1942, Coll. Ins. N.Y.C., 1981. Spl. agt. Loyalty Group, Westchester, N.Y., 1937-43; with Security-Conn. Group, 1943-57, exec. v.p., 1955-57; pres. Wohlreich & Anderson Ltd., Cranford, N.J., 1957-81. Bd. dirs. RLI Ins. Co. Ltd., Hamilton, Bermuda; dir. Alexander Howden Group Ltd., London, 1968-81; underwriter Lloyds of London, 1968—; dir. RLI Corp., Peoria, Ill., 1972—. Columnist: Weekly Underwriter, 1964-86; Author publs. in field. Trustee Ocean Reef Chapel, Loman Found., Malvern, Pa. Served with USNR, 1944-46. Mem.: Soc. Chartered Property and Casualty Underwriters, Coll. Ins. N.Y.C., Racquet Club, Card Sound Country Club, Ocean Reef Club. Republican. Roman Catholic. Office: Ocean Reef 29 Angelfish Cay Dr Key Largo FL 33037-5271 Fax: (305) 367-3354. E-mail: bjdlondon@aol.com.

DAESCU, DACIAN N. mathematics educator; m. Ya-Chun Huang. BS in Math, U. Craiova, Romania, 1994, MS in Math, 1995; PhD in Applied Math., U. Iowa, 2001, MS in Computer Sci., 2001—01. Tchg. asst. U. Craiova, 1995—96, U. Iowa, 1996—2001; postdoc. assoc. U. of Minn., Mpls., 2001—03; asst. prof. dept. math. and stats. Portland (Oreg.) State U., 2003—. Fellow Grad. Student Summer Program fellow, USRA/NASA Goddard Space Flight Ctr., 2000; scholar Tempus scholar, U. Complutense, 1993—94, Rsch. scholar, Supercomputing Inst., U. Minn., 2002—03. Mem.: Soc. Indsl. Applied Math, Am. Math. Soc. Office: Dept Math and Stats Portland State U Neuberger Hall M314 PO Box 751 Portland OR 97207 Office Fax: 503-725-3661. E-mail: daescu@mth.pdx.edu.

DAFERMOS, CONSTANTINE MICHAEL, applied mathematics educator; b. Athens, Greece, May 26, 1941; came to U.S., 1964; s. Michael Constantine and Sophia (Raptarchis) D.; m. Stella Theodoracopoulos, Sept. 6, 1964; children: Thalia, Michael. Diploma, Athens Nat. Tech. U., 1964; PhD, Johns Hopkins U., 1967. Fellow Johns Hopkins U., 1967-68; asst. prof. Cornell U., 1968-71; assoc. prof. Brown U., 1971-76, prof. applied math., 1976—, Univ. prof., 1988—, dir. Lefschetz Ctr. for Dynamical Systems, 1988-94. Author: Hyperbolic Conservation Laws in Continuum Physics, 2000; mem. editl. bd. Archive for Rational Mechanics and Analysis, 1972—, Jour. of Thermal Stresses, 1978-2000, Quar. Applied Math., 1985—, Math. Modeling and Numerical Analysis, 1986-96, Proc. Royal Soc. Edinburgh, 1987—, Advances Math. Applied Sci., 1989—, Math. Models and Methods, 1990-97, Comm. on Applied Nonlinear Analysis, 1995—, Ricerche di Matematica, 1997—, Jour. Am. Math. Soc., 1999—, Revista Matematica Complutense, 2000, Jour. Dynamics and Differential Equations, 2002—; contbr. articles to profl. jours. NSF grantee, 1970—, Office Naval Rsch. grantee, 1972-80, 92—, USAF grantee, 1972-73, U.S. Army grantee, 1973-96. Mem. Soc. Natural Philosophy (treas. 1975-76, chmn. 1977-78), Am. Math. Soc., Acad. of Athens, Am. Acad. Arts and Scis. Office: Brown U Lefschetz Ctr Dynamical Sys 182 George St Providence RI 02912-9056 E-mail: dafermos@cfm.brown.edu.

DAFFORN, GEOFFREY ALAN, biochemist; b. Cunningham, Kans., Feb. 4, 1944; s. Francis Elston and Anna Elizabeth Dafforn; m. Gail McLaughlin, July 14, 1973; 1 child, Christine Elizabeth. BA cum laude, Harvard U., 1966; PhD, U. Calif., Berkeley, 1970. Postdoctoral fellow U. Calif., Berkeley, 1973; asst. prof. U. Tex., Austin, 1974; from asst. prof. to assoc. prof. Bowling Green (Ohio) State U., 1974-81; sr. chemist Syva Co., Palo Alto, Calif., 1982-87, rsch. fellow, 1987—, group mgr., 1999—2000; prin. scientist Nugen Techs., San Carlos, Calif., 2001—. Author articles and abstracts; patentee in field. Grantee Army Rsch. Office, 1979-82, Am. Chem. Soc., 1975-80. Mem. AAAS, Am. Chem. Soc., Sierra Club. Office: Nugen Techs 821 Indsl Rd Unit A San Carlos CA 94070 E-mail: alandafforn@aol.com.

DAFFRON, MARYELLEN, librarian; b. Richmond, Va., Nov. 12, 1946; d. William Charles and Ellen (Ahern) D. BA, Coll. Mt. St. Joseph on Ohio, Cin., 1968; MLS, Drexel U., 1970. Libr. Richmond Pub. Libr., 1969-73, FMC, Washington, 1973-93; with U.S. Immigration and Naturalization Svc. Office of Gen. Counsel, Washington, 1993—. Vol. No. Va. Hotline, Arlington, 1974-79. City of Richmond fellow, 1968. Mem. Law Libr. Soc. Washington, Beta Phi Mu. Roman Catholic. Office: Dept Homeland Security Bur Immigration and Customs Enforcement 425 I St NW Rm 6100 Washington DC 20536-0001

DAFOE, BYRON JAROMIR, professional hockey player; b. Sussex, Eng., Feb. 25, 1971; Goaltender L.A. Hockey Team, Washington Capitals, Boston Bruins, 1997—. Winner Am. Hockey League Calder Cup championship, 1993-94. Avocations: tennis, golf. Office: Boston Bruins Fleet Center one Fleet Ctr Ste 250 Boston MA 02114-1303

DAFOE, WILLEM, actor; b. Appleton, Wis., July 22, 1955; s. William Dafoe; 1 child. Student, U. Wis. Mem. Theatre X theatrical co., 1975, co-founder, The Wooster Group theatrical co., N.Y.C., 1977—. Actor (feature films) The Loveless, 1983, The Hunger, 1983, New York Nights, 1984, Roadhouse 66, 1984, Streets of Fire, 1984, To Live and Die in L.A., 1985, Platoon, 1986 (Acad. award nomination 1987), The Last Temptation of Christ, 1988, Off Limits, 1988, Mississippi Burning, 1988, Triumph of the Spirit, 1989, Born on the Fourth of July, 1989, Cry-Baby, Flight of the Intruder, Wild at Heart, 1990, White Sands, 1992, Light Sleeper, 1992, Body of Evidence, 1992, Far Away So Close!, 1993, The Night and the Moment, 1994, Clear and Present Danger, 1994, Tom and Viv, 1995, Victory, 1995, The English Patient, 1996, Basquiat, 1996, Speed 2: Cruise Control, 1997, Affliction, 1997, New Rose Hotel(also co-prod.), 1998, Lulu on the Bridge, 1998, eXisten Z, 1998, American Psycho, 1999, The Boondock Saints, 1999, Bullfighter, 2000, The Animal Factory, 2000, Shadow of the Vampire, 2000, The Gangs of New York, 2000, Pavillion of Women, 2001, Edges of the Lord, 2001, Spider-Man, 2002, Auto-Focus, 2002, Finding Nemo (voice only), 2003, Once Upon A Time in Mexico, 2003, Camel Cricket City (voice only), 2003; TV appearances: The Hitchhiker, 1985, The Simpsons (voice only), 1997.*

DA FONSECA, AUGUSTO J. social worker; b. Elizabeth, N.J., May 18, 1952; s. Abilio and Emilia De Fonseca; m. Maryann Tokasz, Aug. 7, 1976; children: Amanda Marie, Andrea Augusta. BA, U. Miami, 1975; MSW, Barry U., 1977. Diplomate Am. Bd. Examiners in Clin. Social Work; lic. clin. social worker, N.J.; notary public, N.J. Clin. social worker Mt. Carmel Guild Cmty. Mental Health Ctr., Newark, 1977-78; psychiat. clinician dept. psychiatry Elizabeth Gen. Med. Ctr., 1978-81; psychiat. social worker U. Medicine and Dentistry of N.J.-N.J. Med. Sch., Newark, 1982-86; social svc. adminstr. Ironbound Ednl. and Cultural Ctr., Newark, 1986-87; renal social worker Alexian Bros. Hosp., 1988-90, Elizabeth Gen. Med. Ctr., 1990-98; med. social worker Runnells Spec. Hosp. Union County, 1998—2000; clin. social worker Dialysis Clinic Inc.-North Brunswick Dialysis Ctr., 2000—03; social worker U. Medicine and Dentistry N.J.- Cancer Inst. N.J., 2003—. Active coun. of nephrology social workers Nat. Kidney Found., legis. chairperson, 1993-94; Dem. committeeman, Elizabeth, 1977-82. Mem. NASW, Acad. Cert. Social Workers, Assn. Pediatric Oncology Social Workers, Soc. for Clin. and Exptl. Hypnosis (assoc.), The Internat. Soc. Hypnosis, Internat. Assn. Lions, Inc. (dist. 16E regional chmn., treas.), KC, Elizabeth Portuguese Lions (sec. 1983-84, 2002-03, pres. 1984-85, 88-89, dist. 16E region chmn. 1988-89, zone chmn. 1986-87, treas. 1996-97), Portuguese Instructive Social Club, Portuguese Am. Congress N.J. (bd. dirs. 1986-90).

DAFT, DOUGLAS N. food products executive; With Coca-Cola Co., 1969—, pres. ctrl. pacific divsn., 1984, pres. north pacific divsn., 1988, pres. pacific group, 1991, head mid., far east and Africa groups, Schweppes divsn., 1999, pres., COO, 1999—2000, chmn., CEO, 2000—. Office: 1 Coca Cola Pl SE Atlanta GA 30303-3008

DAFTER, ROGER E. psychologist; BA, NYU, 1976; PhD in Behavioral Medicine, PhD in Clin. Psychology, U. North Tex., 1982. Counselor Oakview Vocat. Rehab., Wilmington, Del., 1976-78; clinician psychology U. North Tex., Denton, 1978-81; intern in psychology Sepulveda VA Med. Ctr., L.A., 1981-82; psychologist Heart Inst. St. Jude Med. Ctr., Fullerton, Calif., 1982-86; staff psychologist Ctr. Rehab. Med. Northridge (Calif.) Hosp. Med. Ctr., 1986-88; clin. psychologist Calif. Health Psychology Group, Westwood, Calif., 1985—; assoc. dir. Mind-Body Medicine Svc. UCLA Sch. Medicine divsn. Head & Neck Surgery, 1994—. Mem. APA, Calif. Psychol. Assn., L.A. County Psychol. Assn. Office: 11911 San Vicente Blvd Ste 270 Los Angeles CA 90049-6634 E-mail: rdafter@ucla.edu.

DAGAVARIAN-BONAR, DEBRA AGHAVNI, college administrator, consultant; b. N.Y.C., Oct. 26, 1952; d. Harry O. Dagavarian and Norma Siran (Cazanjian) Hansen; m. James B. Bonar, Dec. 26, 1988. BA, SUNY, New Paltz, 1973; MA, SUNY, Albany, 1975; EdD, Rutgers U., 1986. Transfer admissions counselor Mercy Coll., Dobbs Ferry, NY, 1976—79, asst. dir. spl. sessions, 1979—81, dir. evening programs, 1981—86, dir. acad. advising, 1986—87; asst. dean for assessment Empire State Coll., Hartsdale, NY, 1987—88; dir. testing assessment Thomas Edison State Coll., Trenton, NJ, 1988—96, dep. vice provost, 1996—2002; asst. v.p. acad. affairs Richard Stockton Coll. NJ, Pomona, 2002—. Adj. prof. Empire State Coll., Mercy Coll., 1979-95; cons. various instns. and corps., 1987—. Author: Saying It Ain't So: American Values as Revealed in Children's Baseball Stories, 1987; author, editor: A Century of Children's Baseball Stories, 1990, (jour.) Jour. of the Nat. Inst. on Assessment of Experiential Learning, 1989-2002; contbr. articles to profl. jours., periodicals, books. Mem. NAFE, Am. Sociol. Assn., Soc. for Am. Baseball Rsch., Coun. for Adult and Experiential Learning, Assn. for Continuing Higher Edn. Democrat. Avocations: baseball research, singing, jewelry making. Office: Richard Stockton Coll of NJ PO Box 195 Jim Leeds Rd Pomona NJ 08240

DAG-ELLAMS, IDRIS, neurosurgeon; b. Agenebode, Edo, Nigeria, Oct. 2, 1949; s. Alhassan Garba and Rekyia (Aigbona) E.; m. Ugonwa Okpara; children: aisha, Nkechi, Naema, Ayman. Grad., Christiana Albertina U., Kiel, Germany, 1979, MD, 1982. Resident, rsch. fellow Justus Liebig U. Hosp., Giessen, Germany, 1979-85; cons., sr. lectr. Ahmadu Bello U. Hosp., Zaria, Nigeria, 1985-89; neurosurgeon King Khalid Hosp., Najran, Saudi Arabia, 1989-90; cons. Kign Abdul Aziz Hosp., Jeddah, Saudi Arabia, 1990-91; locum sr. cons. King Fahd Hosp., Hofuf, Saudi Arabia, 1991-92; sr. cons. Al-Noor Specialist Hosp., Makkah, Saudi Arabia, 1993—, head dept. neurosurgery, 1993—, chmn. surg. divsn., 1993-99, dep. chief med. dir., 1993-99. Chmn., exec. dir. Nanfield Inc., Mississauga, Can., 1999. Contbr. articles to profl. jours. Fellow West African Coll. Surgeons; mem. AAAS, N.Y. Acad. Scis., Nigeria Med. Assn. Germany (pres. 1982-85), Rotary. Avocation: reading. Fax: 905-816-0281. E-mail: idris_dr@yahoo.com., iyaghumeh@hotmail.com., nanfield1@rogers.com.

DAGENAIS, MARCEL GILLES, economist, educator; b. Montreal, Que., Can., Feb. 22, 1935; s. Emilien and Antoinette (Girard) D.; m. Denyse Laberge, July 5, 1958; children— Danielle, Michel, Jean-Francois BA, Coll. Jean de Brébeuf, 1952; MA, U. Montreal, 1958, Yale U., 1960, PhD, 1964. Asst. prof. U. Montreal, 1961-66; vis. prof. Ecole de Hautes Etudes Commerciales de Montreal, 1966-67, assoc. prof., 1967-70, prof., 1970-72; vis. prof. U. Montreal, 1972-73, prof., 1973-97, rsch. fellow ctrl. R&D econs., from 1987; rsch. dir. Ctr. for Interuniversity Rsch. and Analysis on Orgns., from 1994; prof. emeritus U. Montreal, from 1997; cons. econometrician Amstec Inc., from 1998. Spl. prof. Sir George Williams U., 1969-73; assoc. dir. Internat. Inst. Quantitative Econs., 1969-74; dir. Centre d'econometrie, 1968-72; tech. mgr. econ. rsch., dir. Automatec Inc., Montreal, 1965-67; pres. Rotec Inc., 1967-69; invited prof. McGill U., 1998-99, U. Bourgogne, 1998, U. d'Auvergue, 1999-2000. Book rev. editor Canadian Jour. Econs., 1969-74; assoc. editor Jour. of Econometrics, 1980-2000, Revue Canadienne de Statistique, 1980-84; mem. editl. bd. Advanced Studies in Theoretical and Applied Econometrics, 1982—; adv. com. on systems of nat. accounts Statistics Can., 1984—. Mem. steering com. on audit of nat. accts. Inst. Nat. de la Statistique et des etudes economiques, France. Woodrow Wilson hon. fellow, 1958, Can. Coun. fellow, 1958-60, Imperial Oil Grad. Rsch. fellow, 1958-61, Killam Rsch. fellow, 1987-89, Prix du statisticien d'expression française, Soc. Statistique de Paris, 1990, Prix Marcel-Vincent Assn. Can. Française pour L'Avancement des Sci., 1991, Bourse de chercheur de haut niveau du Ministère de l'education nationale de France, 1995-96, Prix Leon Gerin, Govt. du Que., 1999. Fellow Royal Soc. Can., Jour. Econometrics; mem. Can. Econ. Assn. (v.p. 1980-82), Econometric Soc., Societè canadienne de science economique (pres. 1980-81, award 1982), Cons. on Rsch. in Income and Wealth, Assn. de Comptabilité nationale, Assn. d'econométrie appliquée. Home: Ile des Soeurs, Canada. Died Feb. 2001.

DAGENHART, BETTY JANE MAHAFFEY, nursing educator, administrator; b. Welch, W.Va. d. Charley F. and Edith L. (Lucas) Mahaffey; divorced; 1 child, Cynthia Leigh. BA in Health Care Adminstrn., Mary Baldwin, Staunton, Va., 1991; postgrad., St. Joseph's Coll. RN, Va.; cert. nursing adminstr., ANA. Nurse mgr. ortho. and emergency svcs. Cmty. Hosp. of Roanoke (Va.) Valley, Va., 1967-77; asst. dir. nursing svc. Cmty. Hosp. of Roanoke Valley, Va., 1977-83, coord. quality mgmt., dir. occupl. health svcs., dir. emergency svc., 1983-92, dir. med./surg. nursing, 1992-94; dir. nursing edn. City of Salem Sch. Sys., Va., 1994—; dir. med. office asst. program Dominion Coll., Roanoke, 1997. Mem. disaster planning coun. City of Roanoke, 1980-90, pre-hosp. care providers, 1982-88, chmn. pers. com.; organized free standing clinic Cmty. Hosp. Roanoke, 1986. Bd. dirs. Emergency Med. Svcs. Western Va., 1979-92; mem. pers. com. Cave Spring Bapt. Ch., Roanoke, 1991-92. Mem. ANA, Va. Orgn. Nurse Execs., Exec. Females, Health Occupation Educators, Accrediting Coun. Ind. Colls. and Univs. (accreditation team). Avocations: golf, walking, cooking. Home: 139 Ferrum Drive Salem VA 24153 Office: ecpi Technical Coll Dean of Allied Health Sciences 5234 Airport Rd Roanoke VA 24012

DAGENHART, LARRY JONES, lawyer; b. Taylorsville, N.C., July 20, 1932; s. Luther Jones and Louise (Icenhour) D.; m. Sarah Katheryne Petty, June 23, 1956; children: Katie Dagenhart Satterwhite, Mary Louise Dagenhart Culpepper, Larry Jones Jr. BS, Davidson (N.C.) Coll., 1953; LL.B., NYU, 1958, LLD, 2003. Bar: N.C. 1958. Pvt. practice, Charlotte, 1958—; ptnr. Helms, Mulliss & Wicker, Charlotte. Bd. dirs. So. Webbing. Trustee Davidson Coll., 1970-2002, chmn., 1998-2000; trustee U. N.C., Wilmington, 1997—, chmn., 2001—, chmn., chancellor search com., 2002—; trustee Kate B. Reynolds Trust, 1990-96; chmn. Ben Craig Incubator Ctr., 1998—; bd. dirs. N.C. Citizens for Bus. and Industry, 1995-2001; past chmn. Charlotte C. of C., 1983, Charlotte Arts and Scis. Coun., 1976-77, Mecklenburg County Bar Assn., 1974-75, Charlotte United Way, 1978, Found. for the Carolinas, 1987-89, Charlotte Country Day Sch., 1985-87, Charlotte City Club, 1979, Charlotte World Affairs Coun., 1996-98. Named George F. Baker scholar, 1949-53, Root-Tilden scholar, 1953-58; fellow Am. Bar Found., 1970—; recipient Harold Josephson award, Ben Craig Incubator Ctr., 2002. Mem. ABA, Am. Law Inst. Democrat. Lutheran. Home: 1601 Biltmore Dr Charlotte NC 28207-2611 Office: Helms Mulliss & Wicker PO Box 31247 Charlotte NC 28231-1247 E-mail: larry.dagenhart@hmw.com.

DAGER, WILLIAM ERLING, pharmacist specialist, educator; b. Long Beach, Calif., Oct. 20, 1958; s. William Elwood and Olivia G. Dager; m. Karen Renee Helmle, Aug. 31, 1985; children: William Randall, Jessica Lynn, Laura Michelle. PharmD, U. Calif., San Francisco, 1985. Cert. Residency Cert. U. Calif. Davis Med. Ctr., 1986, Nephrology Preseptorship U. Calif. of Pitts., 1995. Pharmacist specialist U. Calif. Davis Med. Ctr., Sacramento, 1986—. Fellow Calif. Soc. of Hosp. Pharmacists, Calif., 1992—; clin. prof. of pharmacy UCSF Sch. of Pharmacy, San Francisco, 2000; assoc. clin. prof. of medicine U. Calif. Davis Sch. of Medicine, 2000; affiliate acls facility Am. Heart Assn., Calif. Edit. bd. pannel chairperson (annals of pharmacotherapy reviews and editorials); author numerous papers, medical/pharmacy jours. Founding mem. Shingle Springs (Calif.) Adv. Com., 2000—02. Mem.: ISTH, ACCP, ASHP, CSHP. Achievements include research in Clinical Pharmacokinetic observations; Anticoagulation approaches. Avocations: skiing, house restoration, trumpet music. Office: U Calif Davis Medl Ctr 2315 Stockton Blvd Sacramento CA 95817 Personal E-mail: william.dager@ucdmc.ucdavis.edu.

DAGGER, RICHARD KEITH, political science and philosphy educator; b. Cape Girardeau, Mo., Oct. 23, 1948; s. Richard Ball Dagger and Julia Bea Verhines; m. Barbara Ann Duepner, Oct. 17, 1946; children: Emily Abbott, Elizabeth Bennett. BA, U. of Missouri-St. Louis, 1966—70; PhD, U. of Minn., 1970—76. Prof., polit. sci. and philosophy Ariz. State U., 1976—. Dir., program in philosophy, politics, and law Barrett Honors Coll., Ariz. State U., 2001—. Author: (book) Civic Virtues: Rights, Citizenship, and Rep. Liberalism (Elaine and David Spitz Award, Conf. for the Study of Polit. Thought, 1999); co-author: Polit. Ideologies and the Dem. Ideal; co-editor: Ideals and Ideologies: A Reader. Hubert H. Humphrey Fellow, U. of Minn., 1972—73. Mem.: Conf. for the Study of Polit. Thought, Am. Soc. for Polit. and Legal Philosophy, Am. Polit. Sci. Assn. (program com. 1993—94, 2000—01). Roman Catholic. Office: Arizona State U Dept of Polit Sci Tempe AZ 85287-3902 Office Fax: 480-965-3929. E-mail: rdagger@asu.edu.

DAGGER, WILLIAM CARSON, lawyer; b. Lancaster, Ohio, May 5, 1949; s. William Carson Sr. and Thelma (Downing) D.; m. Barbara Schaeffer, Sept. 6, 1981; children: Alison Golden; Jaclyn Hedi. AB, Kenyon Coll., 1971; postgrad., Vanderbilt U., 1971-72; JD cum laude, Suffolk U., 1978. Bar: Mass. 1979, Vt. 1981, U.S. Dist. Ct. (ea. dist.) Mass. 1979, U.S. Dist. Ct. Vt. 1981, U.S. Ct. Appeals (1st cir.) 1980, U.S. Ct. Appeals (2nd cir.) 1990. Legal asst. Bernkopf, Goodman & Baseman, Boston, 1976-78; assoc. Rodick & Flavell, Weymouth, Mass., 1978-80, Dick, Hackel & Hull, Rutland, Vt., 1980-88; ptnr. Hull, Webber, Reis & Canney, Rutland, 1989-90; pvt. practice Dagger Law Offices, Woodstock, Vt., 1990—. Legal counsel The Howard Bank, Burlington, Vt., 1981-89, Vt. Indsl. Devel. Authority, Montpelier, 1982-84, Vt. Nat. Bank, 1990—, Woodstock Nat. Bank, 1993—, Vt. Housing Fin. Agy., 1990—, Ames Dept. Stores, 1990—, New London Trust Co., 1997—; trustee, treas. The Homestead, Inc., Woodstock, 1991-96. Bd. dirs. Woodstock Area Coun. Aging, 2000—, Woodstock Ctrl. Supervisory Union Cmty. Coun., 1991—; com. mem. Boy Scouts Am., 1990—. Master Sterry R. Waterman Am. Inn of Ct. (founding); mem. ABA, Vt. Bar Assn. (jud. evaluation com. 1981), Vt. Trial Lawyers Assn., Rotary Internat., Woodstock Rotary (pres. 1999-2000), Sierra Club (state rep. 1973-75). Home: 4702 Riverside Rd Woodstock VT 05091-9630 Office: The French Block 2 Central St PO Box 539 Woodstock VT 05091-1007 E-mail: daggrlaw@sover.net.

DAGGETT, BEVERLY CLARK, state legislator; b. Florence, S.C., Sept. 9, 1945; d. John and Beth Clark; m. Thomas A. Daggett, May 8, 1971; children: John, Page, Paul. BS in Biology, Hillsdale Coll., 1967. Mem. Maine Ho. of Reps., Augusta, 1987-96; chair commn. to study biotech. and genetic engring., 1995—; house chair joint standing com. on state and local govt., 1995-96; mem. Dist. 15 Maine Senate, Augusta, 1996—, Dem. leader, 2001—, majority leader, 2002—, pres., 2002—. Chair joint standing com. on legal and vets. affairs Maine State Senate, mem. taxation com.; mem. Substance Abuse Svcs. Commn. Bd. dirs. Dem. Legis. Campaign Com., 2000—. Coun. State Govts. Toll fellow, 1990; Flemming fellow, 1997. Democrat. Home: 16 Pine St Augusta ME 04330-5340 Personal E-mail: senatorbdaggett@aol.com. E-mail: senbeverly.daggett@legis.maine.gov.

DAGHLIAN, JOHN EDWARD, advertising agency executive; b. Hoboken, N.J., Jan. 23, 1946; s. John and Mildred (Gross) D.; m. Linda Parker, Aug. 14, 1976. BS, Fairleigh Dickinson U., 1970; MBA, Fordham U., 1974. Market research mgr. McGraw-Hill Publs., N.Y.C., 1964-71; mortgage cons. J.I. Kislak Mortgage Corp., Newark, 1972; v.p. account supr. Compton Adv., Inc., N.Y.C., 1973-80; group brand dir. Lorillard, Inc., N.Y.C., 1980-90; v.p. strategic mktg. Campbell-Mithun-Esty Advt., N.Y.C., 1991-93; sr. v.p. Direct Mktg. Group, N.Y.C., 1993-95; pres. Strategic Mktg. Group, Wayne, N.J., 1995-98; exec. v.p. Richantz Fliss Clark & Pope, Denville, N.J., 1998—. Exec. dir. R&D Coun. of NJ, 1998—. Mem. Packanack Lake Golf Club (pres. 1989-90).

DAGI, LINDA RABINOWITZ, pediatric ophthalmologist; b. N.Y.C., Apr. 25, 1957; d. Abraham and Florence (Wasserman) Rabinowitz; m. Teodoro Forcht Dagi; children: Lora, Ariella, Alexander. BA, Harvard Coll., 1978; MD, Harvard Med. Sch., 1983. Intern Georgetown U. Hosp., Washington, 1983-84, resident, 1985-88; fellowship neuroophthalmology NIH, Bethesda, Md., 1984-85; fellowship pediatric ophthalmology Boston Childrens Hosp., Boston, 1988-89; clin. asst. prof. Emory U. Hosp., Atlanta, 1990—; pvt. practice Atlanta, 1990—; academic practice Boston Children's Hosp., 2003—. Contbr. articles to profl. jours. Bd. dirs. Harvard Pub. Interest Health Found., Boston, 1981-82. Recipient Von L. Meyer Traveling award Boston Children's Hosp. Fellow Am. Assn. of Pediatric Ophthalmology and Strabismus; mem. Ga. Soc. Ophthalmology (bd. dirs., mem. ethics com.). Avocations: skiing, photography. Home: 423 Commonwealth Ave Newton Centre MA 02459- E-mail: ldagi@post.harvard.edu.

DAGIT, CHARLES EDWARD, JR., b. Phila., July 1, 1943; s. Charles E. and Janet (Donnelly) D.; m. Alice M. Murdoch, June 3, 1967; children: Charles Edward, J. Murdoch. BA, U. Pa., 1965, B.Arch., 1967, M.Arch., 1968. Registered architect, Pa., N.Y., N.J., Conn., Va., Md., Vt. Designer Henry D. Dagit & Sons, Phila., 1965-68, Mitchell, Giurgola Assocs., Phila., 1968-69; project designer Henry D. Dagit & Sons, Phila., 1969-70; ptnr. Dagit Saylor Architects, Phila., 1970—. Adj. asst. prof. Sch. Arch. and Engring., Temple U., 1973-80; adj. prof. dept. arch. Phila. Coll. Art, 1979-80; vis. prof. U. Pa., 1980; prof. dept. arch. Drexel U. Prin. works include Peale House of Pa. Acad. Fine Arts (Design award Phila. chpt. AIA 1983, Merit award Pa. Mus. and Hist. Com.), Agrl. Arena at Pa. State U. (Silver medal Pa. State U. 1985, Design award Phila. chpt. AIA 1985), Spring Garden Health Ctr. (runner-up for Rudi Brunner award), Phoenix City Ctr. for Arts (NEA grant), 1983, Cumberland Union Bldg. Shippensburg U. (Phila. chpt. AIA Design award 1992, Design award PSA 1992), Bartram's Garden (Pa. Mus. and Hist. Commn. Preservation award 1993), Campus Ctr. Bldg. Haverford Coll. (Phila. chpt. AIA Design award 1994, Design award PSA 1994, F.W. Olin Bldg. (Phila. chpt. AIA Design award 1992, Design award PSA 1992), Pa. Ballet (Design award PSA 1989), Gwynedd Mercy Coll. Lourdes Libr. Addition (Phila. chpt. AIA Design award 1986), Magee Rehab. Hosp. (Phila. chpt. Design award 1984), Logan Mus. Anthropology, Beloit Coll. (Phila. chpt. AIA Design award 1995, Internat. Illumination Design award, Preservation award WI Preservation Trust 1995), Grove Hall, Coll. Bus. Bldg., Shippensburg U. (Design award Phila. chpt. AIA 1999). Pres. Gladwyne Civic Assn., 1981-82; pres. Friends of St. Christopher's Hosp., Phila., 1977-78; trustee Bryn Mawr. (Pa.) Country Day Sch., 1975-79; bd. dirs. Phila. Zool. Soc., 1979-87; pres. bd. trustees Gladwyne Libr. Bd., 1990-91; trustee Acad. Cmty. Music, 1997—. Recipient Design award Progressive Architecture, 1974, 40 Under 40 award A&U Mag., Japan, 1977, View of World Contemporary Architecture award Japan Architect, 1977; winner nat. design competition Cultural Arts Pavillion, Newport News, Va., 1985. Fellow AIA (Silver medal Phila. chpt. 1976, Gold medal 1978, pres.-elect Phila. chpt. 1989, pres. Phila. chpt. 1990, chair Nat. Design Conf. commn. on architecture for arts and recreation, Cin. 1976, chair Nat. Design Conf. commn. on design, Louis I. Kahn & Phila. Sch. 1991, chmn. designate commn. on design 1992, vice chmn. commn. design, 1993, chmn. commn. design 1994); mem. Pa. Soc. AIA (Silver medal 1985), Soc. Coll.and U. Planners, Facilities Planning Acad., Downtown Club Phila. (bd. dirs. 1986-89), Merion Golf Club (Ardmore, Pa.), Mask and Wig Club, U. Pa. Spinx Sr. Soc. (bd. dirs. 1973-76), The Carpenter's Co. Republican. Roman Catholic. Home: 381 Williamson Rd Gladwyne PA 19035-1618 Office: Dagit Saylor Architects 100 S Broad St Ste 1100 Philadelphia PA 19110-1003 Business E-Mail: cdagit@dagitsaylor.com.

DAGLEY, JOHN C. psychologist; b. Newton, Ill., Oct. 3, 1942; s. Howard M. and Mary L. (Langston) Dagley; m. Peggy Anne Leamer, June 5, 1968; children: Ryan, Ross, Reghan. BA, Culver-Stockton Coll., 1964; MEd, Ind. U., 1965; PhD, U. Mo., 1972. Lic. psychologist. Admission counselor, instr. psychology Culver-Stockton Coll., Canton, Mo., 1965-68; assoc. project dir. U. Mo., Columbia, 1971-72; from asst. prof. to assoc. prof. U. Ga., Athens, 1972—, grad. coord., 1996—, dept. head, 2000—03; assoc. prof., program dir. Auburn U., 2003—. Vis. assoc. prof. Boston U., 1988-89. Co-author: Intentionally Structured Groups, 1989; contbr. articles to profl. jours. Mem. APA, ACA, NCDA. Methodist. Avocations: sports, travel. Home: 100 Featherwood Holw Athens GA 30601-1050 E-mail: jdagley@coe.uga.edu.

DAGLI, CIHAN HAYREDDIN, engineering educator; b. Ankara, Turkey, Oct. 18, 1949; came to U.S., 1985; s. Kenan and Zuhre (Kavlakoglu) D.; m. Refia Oner, Nov. 3, 1975; children: Cagri, Ediz. BS in Indsl. Engring., Middle East Tech. U., Ankara, 1971, MS in Indsl. Engring., 1972; PhD in Engring. Prodn., U. Birmingham, Eng., 1979. Cert. engr., Turkey. From tchg. asst. to instr. Middle East Tech. U., Ankara, 1972-76, from asst. to assoc. prof., 1979-85; Brit. coun. rsch. fellow U. Birmingham, 1976-79; assoc. prof. U. Mo., Rolla, 1988-95, prof., 1995—. Vis. assoc. prof. Wichita (Kans.) State U., 1985-88; indsl. and engring. dept. chmn. Middle East Tech. U., Ankara, 1979-82; cons. UN Indsl. Devel., Ankara, 1980, AT&T Bell Labs., N.J., 1989. Editor: Artificial Neural Networks for Intelligent Manufacturing; co-editor: Intelligent Engineering Systems Through Artificial Neural Networks, Vols. 1-12, 1991-2002, Intelligent Systems in Design and Manufacturing, 1994; editor-in-chief Internat. Jour. Smart Engring. System Design; contbr. articles to profl. jours. Aspirant lt. Turkish Army, 1975. Brit. Coun. Rsch. fellow, 1976-79; Ed Smith Rsch. grantee U. Mo., Rolla, 1989, 90. Mem. Internat. Neural Network Soc., Internat. Found. for Prodn. Rsch. (bd. dirs. 1987—), Inst. Indsl. Engring. (chmn. Wichita chpt. 1987-88). Home: 401 Greenbriar Dr Rolla MO 65401-3694 Office: Univ Missouri 229 Engineering Management Rolla MO 65409-0370 E-mail: dagli@umr.edu.

D'AGNESE, JOHN JOSEPH, sanitation, public health and pest management consultant; b. N.Y.C., Apr. 2, 1920; s. Michele and Liberata (Cucolo) D'A.; m. Helen DeSantis, Oct. 29, 1942; children: John Jr., Linda, Diane, Michele, Helen, Gina, Paul. BS, CCNY, 1946; student, U. San Francisco, 1953-54. Lic. pest mgmt., Fla., Ga.; cert. food safety mgr.; lic. chief purser USCG. Chief purser U.S. Merchant Marine, 1942-46; quarantine officer USPHS, Staten Island, N.Y., 1946-53, supervisory quarantine officer San Francisco, 1953-62, Mexican border supervisory quarantine officer El Paso, Tex., 1962-68, chief program ops. quarantine div. Ctr. Disease Control Atlanta, 1968-80, dir. quarantine div., 1980-81, ret., 1981; dir. Cruise Ship Consultation Svc., Fernandina Beach, Fla., 1981—. Dir. D'Agnese Studio Fine Art Gallery; adminstr., trainer Chartered Inst. Environ. Health/Nat. Registry of Food Svc. Profls. Contbr. sci. and health-related articles to nat. mags. and jours. including Pest Control Tech., Jour. Environ. Health, Jour. Milk Food Tech., Pest Control Jour. Mag. Bd. dirs. Nat. Coun. Aging, 1986-90. Recipient United Fund Leadership award El Paso Tex., 1966-67. Fellow Nat. Sanitation Found.; mem. APHA, Fla. Pest Control Assn., Ga. Pest Control Assn., Nat. Assn. Fed. Ret. Employees. Democrat. Roman Catholic. Avocations: music, tennis, fencing, chess, fishing, cooking. Home: 3240 S Fletcher Ave Fernandina Beach FL 32034-4378 Fax: 904-321-1518. E-mail: jjdcscs@yahoo.com.

D'AGNILLO, FELICE, biomedical researcher, physiologist; PhD in Physiology, McGill U., Montreal, 1997. Vis. scientist Cber. Fda, Bethesda, Md., 2002—. Contbr. articles. Fellow NIH Fogarty Vis. Fellowship, Fogarty Ctr., NIH, 1997—2002. Mem.: Internat. Soc. for Blood Subsitutes. Achievements include patents for Novel Hemoglobin-Based Oxygen Carrier No# 5, 606, 25; research in Mechanisms of Vascular injury Induced by Heme Proteins. Avocations: football, swimming, biking, hiking, baseball. Office: CBER Food and Drug Adminstrn 8800 Rockville Pike Bldg 29 Rm B16 Bethesda MD 20892

DAGNON, JAMES BERNARD, human resources executive; b. St. Paul, Jan. 31, 1940; s. James Lavern and Margaret Elizabeth (Coughlin) D.; m. Sandra Ann McGinley, June 4, 1960; children: Sheri T. Dagnon Tice, Terry J., Laurie M., Diana L. BS in Bus. with distinction, U. Minn., St. Paul, 1979, cert. in indsl. rels., 1978. Various clerical positions No. Pacific Ry. Co., St. Paul, 1957-70; supr., then mgr. pers. rsch. and stats. Burlington No. R.R. Co., St. Paul, 1970, mgr. manpower planning, 1970-78, dir. compensation and orgnl. planning, 1978-81; asst. v.p. compensation and benefits Burlington No. Inc., Seattle, 1981-84, from v.p. labor rels. to exec. v.p. employee rels. Ft. Worth, 1984-95; sr. v.p. employee rels. Burlington No. Santa Fe Ry Co., Ft. Worth, 1995-97; sr. v.p. people The Boeing Co., Seattle, 1997—2002. Bd. trustees Bellvue Cmty. Coll., 2000—; bd. dirs. Inroads Inc., Seattle Inroads, Inc., Washington Early Learning Found. Pres. Cath. Evang. Outreach, Seattle, 1981-84; chmn. Corp. Champions, Ft. Worth, 1994-96; bd. trustees Cook-Ft. Worth Children's Med. Ctr., 1995-97; bd. dirs. United Way Met. Tarrant County, 1995-97, Wash. State Gov.'s Commn. on Higher Edn. in 2020; trustee Bellvue C.C., 1999-, Washington Early Learning Found., 1999-. Capt. USAR, 1957-70. Mem. Beta Gamma Sigma; fellow Nat. Acad. Human Resources. Republican. Avocations: flying, scuba diving, photography. Home: PO Box 605 Medina WA 98039-0605

DAGOGO-JACK, SAMUEL E. medical educator, physician scientist, endocrinologist; b. Abonnema, Rivers, Nigeria, Mar. 17, 1954; came to U.S., 1990; s. Karibi Jim and Titty (Biribota) D.-J.; m. Agbani Ibinabo Iyalla, May 28, 1983;

children: Karibi, Ibi, Alali, Tari. MBBS, U. Ibadan (Nigeria), 1978, MD, 1994; MSc, U. Newcastle Upon Tyne (U.K.), 1988. Diplomate Am. Bd. Internal Medicine, Am. Bd. Endocrinology, Am. Bd. Diabetes and Metabolism. Rsch. assoc. U. Newcastle Upon Tyne (U.K.), 1983—85; cons. physician U. Port Harcourt (Nigeria), 1985—89; chief resident endocrinologist King Faisal Specialist Hosp., Riyadh, Saudi Arabia, 1989—90; from rsch. fellow to assoc. prof. medicine Washington U. Sch. Medicine, St. Louis, 1990—2000; assoc. chief internal medicine svc. Barnes-Jewish Hosp., St. Louis, 1996—2000; prof. medicine, endocrinology, diabetes and metabolism, prof. physiology and biophysics, dir. diabetes programs U. Miss. Med. Ctr., Jackson, 2000—01; dir. minority health rsch. Montgomery VAMC, Jackson, 2000—01; prof. medicine, endocrinology, diabetes and metabolism U. Tenn. Coll. Medicine, Memphis, 2001—; assoc. dir. Gen. Clin. Rsch. Ctr., 2001—; prin. investigator DCCT/EDIC NIH Diabetes Rsch. Study, 2001—. Endocrinology and diabetes grant rev. study sect. NIH, 2000—; Todd Brown Disting. Heritage lectr. Meharry Med. Sch., Nashville, Tenn., 2003; Charles Drew vis. prof. Charles Drew U. Sci. and Medicine, 2000; extra-mural rschr. diabetes drugs devel. programs for pharm. cos.; chair Excellence Diabetes Mgmt. Symposium, 1998-99; dir. sophomore endocrine pathophysiology course U. Tenn., 2002—; ad-hoc reviewer in field; lectr. in field. Author: The Diabetes Guide, 1992; (with others) The Washington Manual, 2002, The Uncomplicated Guide to Diabetes Complications, 1999; mem. editl. bd. Kuwait Med. Jour., 1995-98, Current Drug Targets, Cardiology, Cardiology Spl. Edit., 2001—; contbr. over 100 articles to profl. jours. Diabetes Rsch. & Tng. Ctr. grantee, 1999—; recipient Young Investigator Travel award Internat. Soc. Endocrinology, 1987. Fellow ACP (co-dir. workshop urban health 1998), Royal Coll. Physicians (London), Am. Coll. Endocrinology; mem. AAAS, Am. Diabetes Assn. (sec. St. Louis chpt. 1997-98, pres. 1998-00, sci. and med. adv. group, rsch. fellow 1990-91, Clin. Rsch. award 1997-2000), Endocrine Soc., Am. Fedn. for Med. Rsch., Ctrl. Soc. for Clin. Rsch. (chmn. endocrinology sect. 2000-02), Am. Assn. Clin. Endocrinologists. Achievements include rsch. in diabetes edn. and rsch. programs. Office: U Tenn Coll Medicine Dept Med Endocrinology 951 Court Ave Memphis TN 38163 Business E-Mail: sdagogojack@utmem.edu.

D'AGOSTINO, JAMES SAMUEL, JR., financial executive; b. Balt., July 4, 1946; s. James Samuel and Betty Ann (List) D'A.; m. Diane Martin Greener, Sept. 25, 1971; children: James Martin, Ann Diestel. BS in Econs., Villanova U., 1968; JD, Seton Hall Sch. Law, Newark, 1974; postgrad., Harvard U., 1993. Bar: N.J. 1974, Tex. 1979. Trust officer Fidelity Union Trust Co., Newark, 1968-73; asst. treas. The Chase Manhattan Bank, N.A., N.Y.C., 1973-76; v.p. Citibank/Citicorp, Houston, 1976-86; v.p., treas. Am. Gen. Corp., Houston, 1986-90, sr. v.p. investor rels., 1990-91, sr. v.p. adminstrn., 1991-93, exec. v.p. adminstrn., 1993; pres., CEO Am. Gen. Life and Accident Ins. Co., Nashville, 1993-95, chmn., CEO, 1995-97; pres. Am. Gen. Corp., Houston, 1997-98; vice-chmn., group exec. Consumer Fin. Am. Gen. Corp., Houston, 1998-99; chmn., pres., CEO Encore Bank, 1999—. Republican. Presbyterian. Office: Encore Bank 1220 Augusta Dr Houston TX 77057-2212

D'AGOSTINO, MATTHEW PAUL, bakery executive; b. Yonkers, N.Y., Apr. 15, 1948; s. Paul Francis and Mary Cristina D'A.; m. Kathleen Marie Karpinski, July 18, 1951; children: Carolyn, Paul. BA in English, Polit. Sci., Nathaniel Hawthorne Coll., Antrim, N.H., 1970. Cert. master baker, 1992. Bakery mgr. Pathmark Supermarkets, Woodbridge, N.J., 1971; gen. mgr. La Bonbonniere Bake Shoppes, Edison, N.J., 1972-83, CEO, 1983—2001, pres., 2001—. Master baker cert. judge, 1998-2002, mem. cert. bd., 2001—; adv., judge N.J. Family Career and Cmty. Assn., 1997-03. Judge and mem. tech. sports com., Skills USA Olympics, 1993-2003, NJ skills coord., 2001-2002. Mem. Am. Soc. Bakery Engrs., Tri-County Bakers Assn. (pres. 1986-88), N.J. Bakers Bd. Trade (pres. 1988-90), Retail Bakers Am. (dir.-at-large 1988, mem. exec. com. 1990-97, v.p. 1992-95, N.J. dir. 1990-94, pres. 1995-96, mem. cert. bd. 2000-2003). Roman Catholic. Avocations: fitness, fishing, computer programming. Home: 16 Huntington Rd Edison NJ 08820-3109 Office: La Bonbonniere Bake Shoppes PO Box 981 Edison NJ 08818-0981 E-mail: matt@labon.com.

D'AGOSTINO, RALPH BENEDICT, mathematician, statistician, educator, consultant; b. Somerville, Mass., Aug. 16, 1940; s. Bennedetto and Carmela (Piemonte) D'A.; m. Lei Lanie Carta, Aug. 28, 1965; children: Ralph Benedict, Lei Lanie Maria. AB, Boston U., 1962, MA, 1964; PhD, Harvard U., 1968. Lectr. math. Boston U., 1964-68, asst. prof., 1968-71, assoc. prof., 1971-76, lectr. law, 1975-91, assoc. dean Grad. Sch., 1976-78, prof. math. and stats., 1976—, prof. pub. health, 1982—, dir. data analysis and stats. Framingham Heart Study, 1985—, chmn. dept. math., 1986-91, dir. stats. cons. unit, 1986—, dir. Biostats MA/PhD Program, 1988—, prof. law, 1991—. Exec. dir. data mgmt. and biostats. Harvard Clin. Rsch. Inst., 2002—; vis. lectr. Am. Statis. Assn., 1975-86, 88-92; vis. prof. biostats. clin. epidiology unit Univ. Hosp., Geneva, 1993; Rankin vis. prof. U. Wis., 1995; spl. lectr. clin. trials symposium U. Fla., 1995; vis. scientist NHLBI, 1993; Lowell Reed lectr. APHA, 1996; spl. scientist Boston City Hosp., 1981-95, Boston Med. Ctr., 1996—, New Eng. Med. Ctr., 1990—; mem. Health Inst. New Eng. Med. Ctr., 1990—; cons. stats. United Brands, 1968-76, Diabetes and Arthritis Control Unit, Boston, 1971-75, City of Somerville, Mass., 1972, ednl. Harvard U. Dental Sch., 1969, Lahey Clinic Found., 1973-85, Walden Rsch., 1974-79, FDA Biometrics Divsn. and Over-the-Counter Divsn., 1975—, Cardio and Renal Divsn. FDA, 1987—, Gastrointestinal Drug Divsn., FDA, 1994-96, Medical Devine Divsn., Arnold & Porter, 1980, Bedford Rsch. Assn., 1976-81, Corneal Scis., 1976, Biotek, 1979-88, GCA, 1979-87, Lever Bros., 1982-87, Conrail, 1981, FBI, 1984, Ctr. Psychiat. Rehab., Boston U., 1985—, NIMH, 1985, Dade Clin. Assays, 1986-90, Millipore, 1983-92, VLI Corp., 1985-90, New Eng. Coll. Optometry, 1985-93, Dupont Corp., 1985, Bristol Myers, 1986, 93, Cheeseborough Ponds, 1987-96, med. decision making divsn. and health svcs. rsch. unit Tufts New Eng. Med. Ctr., 1986—, Am. Inst. Rsch. in Social Scis., 1983-88, New Eng. Rsch. Insts., 1987-92, Thompson Med., 1987-96, Merck, Sharpe and Dohme, 1988-94, Carter Ctr., Emory U., 1969-75, Unilever, 1991-96, Miles, 1991-95, Ultra Fem., 1991-93, Health Effects Inst., 1992—, Forsyth Dental Clinic, 1992-93, 95—, Bard Vascular, 1990-95, Ultra Slim Fast, 1990-95, Block Med., 1993-95, Bayer Pharm., 1993-98, Astra Pharm., 1993-97, Cytyc, 1993-97, Regua, 1994-96, SmithKline Beechman, 1994-95, Proctor and Gamble, 1994-96, 2000—, Sandoz, 1994-96, R W Johnson Pharms., 1997, Mass. Med. Assistance, 1995-97, Cambridge Heart, 1996—, Merck/ Johnson & Johnson, 1999—, Aventis, 2000—, Ajinomoto, 2000, Discovery Lab, 2000—; mem. various FDA coms. including fertility and maternal health drugs adv. com, 1978-81, life support subcom., 1979-81, drug abuse adv. com., 1987-90, gastrointestinal drugs adv. com., 1990-94, nonprescriptive drug adv. com., 1995—, chair, 1996-98; mem. task force on design and analysis of dental and oral rsch., 1979—, Harvard U. health tech. com., 1986-90; mem. Honolulu Heart Study Adv. Com., NIH, 1989-96, Balt. Longitudinal Study of Aging Adv. Com., 1990, NIH Consensus Panel on Liver Transplantation, 1983, Consensus Panel on Fresh Frozen Plasma, 1984, Consensus Panel on Geriatric Assessment Methods for Clin. Decision Making, 1987; mem. task force Office Tech. Assessment, 1980; mem. consensus panel on intraoral techniques ADA, 1990; mem. study sect. Agy. for Health Care Policy and Rsch., 1990-94; mem. Bethesda Conf. on Matching Intensity of Risk Factor Mgmt. With the Hazard for Coronary Disease Events, 1996; prin., co-prin. investigator or sr. statistician on grants Nat. Ctr. Health Svcs. Rsch., 1976-82, NHLBI, 1982—, USAF, 1980-85, Nat. Cancer Inst., 1985—, Nat. Inst. Criminal Justice, 1982-85, Nat. Ctr. Child Abuse and Neglect, 1982-85, Robert Wood Johnson Found., 1981-85, Social Security Adminstrn., 1982-86, 90-93, Motor Vehicles Mem. Assn., 1987, NIOSH, 1985, Nat. Insts. Aging, 1986—, Agency for Health Care Policy and Rsch., 1989—; grant and contract reviewer NAS, 1979—, Nat. Ctr. Health Svcs. Rsch., 1976, 89, NIH, 1983, NSF, 1987-95, AHCPR, 1990; co-prin. investigator Framingham Heart Study, 1993-; chair spl. emphasis panel reviewing small bus. grant proposal Nat. Inst. Dental Rsch., 1996. Author: (with E.E. Cureton) Factor Analysis, An Applied Approach, 1983, (with Shuman and Wolf) Mathematical Modeling, Applications in Emergency Health Services, 1984, (with Stephens) Goodness of Fit Techniques, 1986, (with D. Schiff) Practical Engineering Statistics, 1996; assoc. editor Am. Statistician, 1972-76, Jour. Am. Statis. Assn., 1993-96; editor Emergency Health Svc. Rev., 1981-88, Stats. in Medicine (biostat. tutorials), 1993—, Stats. in Medicine, 1997—; mem. editl. bd. Biostatistica, 1990-99; book reviewer Houghton-Mifflin, Holden, Day, Duxbury Press, Prentice Hall, 1969; contbr. articles to profl. jours.; co-developer instrument for predicting acute ischemic health disease, stroke health risk appraisal function and coronary heart disease risk assessment function. Recipient Spl. citation FDA Commr., 1981, 95, Metcalf awrd for excellence in teaching Boston U., 1985; Am. Heart Assn. fellow, 1991; pre-doctoral fellow NIH, 1962-68. Fellow Am. Statis. Assn. (pres. Boston chpt. 1972, v.p. 1971, mem. nat. coun. 1973-75, vis. lectr. 1976-78, 80—, Statistician of Yr. Boston chpt. 1993, chmn. sect. Health Policy Stats. 1996chmn. sect. 2003); mem. APHA (Lowell Reed lectr. 1996, chmn. sect. emergency health svcs. 1982-83, governing coun. 1983-85), Am. Heart Assn. (mem. cardiovasc. epidemiology coun.), Inst. Math. Stats., Am. Soc. Quality Control, Biometrics Soc. (mem. regional adv. com. 1989 94), Phi Beta Kappa, Sigma Xi. Home: 5 Everett Ave Winchester MA 01890-3523 Office: Boston U Statistics & Cons Unit 111 Cummington St Boston MA 02215-2411 E-mail: ralph@bu.edu.

D'AGOSTINO, STEPHEN IGNATIUS, bottling company executive; b. N.Y.C., Oct. 23, 1933; s. Nicholas J. and Josephine D'Agostino; m. Mary Egan, July 2, 1955; children: Mary Jo D'Agostino Razook, Joseph, Christopher, Gregory, Elizabeth Anne Ross, Sarah D'Agostino Christensen, Constance. BA, Holy Cross Coll., 1955. With D'Agostino Supermarkets, New Rochelle, N.Y., 1955-82, controller, 1960-78, chmn., CEO, 1978-82; pres., COO, JTL Corp., Chattanooga, 1982—; pres., chief operating officer Gt. Western Coca-Cola Bottling Co., Chattanooga, 1982-87; mng. ptnr. CSD Investments, 1987-88; chmn. Lord Capital Corp., N.Y.C., 1988-92; pres., CEO D'Agostino Enterprises Inc., Hobe Sound, 1992—.

DAGUM, CAMILO, economist, educator; b. Argentina, Aug. 11, 1925; arrived in Can., 1972, naturalized, 1978; s. Alexander and Nazira (Hakim) D.; m. Estela Bee, Dec. 22, 1958; children: Alexander, Paul, Leonardo. PhD (gold medal summa cum laude), Nat. U. Cordoba, 1949, degree (hon.), 1988, U. Bologna, 1988, U. Montpelier, France, 1995. Mem. faculty Nat. U. Cordoba, 1950-66, prof. econs., 1956-66, dean Faculty Econ. Scis., 1962-66; sr. rsch. economist Princeton U., 1966-68; prof. Nat. U. Mex., 1968-70; vis. prof. Inst. d'Etudes du Devel. Econ. and Social U. Paris, 1967-69, U. Iowa, 1970-72; prof. econs. U. Ottawa, Ont., Can., 1972-91, chmn. dept., 1973-75, mem. acad. senate, 1981-84, bd. govs., 1983-84, prof. emeritus, 1992—. Prof. stats. and econs. U. Milan, 1990-94, chmn. Inst. Quantitative Methods, 1993-94; prof. econs. and stats. U. Bologna, Italy, 1994-02; pres. Cordoba Inst. Social Security, 1962-63; cons. to govt. and industry, 1956—; rsch. prof. U. Rome, 1956-57, London Sch. Econs., 1960-62, Inst. Sci. Econmique Appliquèe, Coll. France, 1965; vis. fellow Birkbeck Coll., U. London, 1960-61, Australian Nat. U., 1985; guest scholar Brookings Instn., 1978-79; vis. prof. U. Siena, Italy, 1987, 88, U. Rome, 1989; spkr. in field. Author books on eocn. theory; editor econ. and statis. jours.; contbr. articles to profl. jours. Mem. Acad. Coun. Rsch. Ctr. on Income Distbn., U. Siena, 1986—, Sci. Com. on Econ. Rsch. and Analysis Program, U. Montreal, 1992-96, Sci. Adv. Com. U. Bologna, Buenos Aires. Res. officer Argentina Army, 1948. Decorated Pro-Patria Gold medal, 1948; hon. prof. Inst. Advanced Studies, Salta, Argentina, 1972; extraordinary prof. Cath. U. Salta, 1981; elected mem. Accademia di Scienze e Lettere, Istituto Lombardo, 1992—. Mem. Internat. Inst. Sociology, Internat. Statis. Inst., Statis. Soc., Econ. Soc., Econ. History Soc. Argentina, U.S. Eastern Econ. Assn., Econometric Soc., Am. Statis. Assn., Am. Econ. Assn., Can. Econ. Assn., Can. Statis. Soc., Assn. Social Econs., N.Y. Acad. Scis., Acad. Scis. of Bologna. Roman Catholic. Home: PO Box 74080 5 Beechwood Ave Ottawa ON Canada Office: U Ottawa Faculty Social Scis Dept Econs 550 Cumberland St POB 450 Station A Ottawa ON Canada K1N 6N5 also: U Bologna Dept Statis Scis Via delle Belle Arti 41 40126 Bologna Italy E-mail: dagum@stat.unibo.it.

DAHBANY, AVIVAH, psychologist, educator; BA, CCNY, 1974, MS, 1978; PhD, Temple U., 1996. Fellow in clin. psychology Albert Einstein Coll. Medicine, 1976-77; psychologist Adams Sch., N.Y.C., 1977-78; dir. spl. edn., psychologist Dov Revel Yeshiva, Forest Hills, N.Y., 1978-79; psychologist Franklin Twp. Pub. Schs., Somerset, N.J., 1979—; adj. lectr. CCNY, 1977—78; adj. instr. Raritan Valley C.C., 1987—88, Monmouth U., 1981, 1988—92, 1995—2001, Montclair State U., 2001—02; psychol. cons. Robert Wood Johnson Meml. Hosp., Laurie Devel. Inst. Child Evaluation Ctr., 1985—89. Mem.: APA, NEA, N.J. Assn. Sch. Psychologists, Nat. Assn. Sch. Psychologists. Office: Pupil Pers Svcs 1755 Amwell Rd Somerset NJ 08873-2746 E-mail: adahbany@aol.com.

DAHIYA, RAJBIR SINGH, mathematics educator, researcher; b. Rattangarh, Haryana, India, Dec. 3, 1940; came to U.S., 1968; s. Ram S. and Kesar (Devi) D.; m. Krishna Tavathia, Dec. 11, 1966; children: Madhu, Ranjan. PhD, Birla Inst. Sci. and Tech., Pilani, India, 1967. Lectr. Birla Inst. Sci. and Tech., 1967-68; asst. prof. math. Iowa State U., Ames, 1968-72, assoc. prof., 1972-78, prof., 1978—. Reviewer math. revs. Zentrallblat; referee applied math. jours. Contbr. over 150 rsch. papers on delay and advanced differential equations, transform theory and spl. functions to U.S., European and Australian profl. jours. Mem. Am. Math. Soc., Soc. Indsl. and Applied Math. Democrat. Hindu. Home: 3144 Sycamore Rd Ames IA 50014-4510 Office: Iowa State U Dept Math Ames IA 50011-0001

DAHL, ARLENE, actress, writer, designer, cosmetic executive; b. Mpls., Aug. 11, 1928; d. Rudolph and Idelle (Swan) D.; m. Marc A. Rosen; children: Lorenzo Lamas, Carole Christine Holmes, Stephen Andreas Schaum. Student, U. Minn., 1943-44, Mpls. Inst. Art, 1945, Minn. Coll. Music, 1944, Minn. Bus. Coll., 1944. Pres. Arlene Dahl Enterprises, 1952-67; v.p. Kenyon & Eckhart, 1967-72; pres. Woman's World divsn. Kenyon & Eckhart Advt. Agy., 1967-72; nat. beauty and health advisor Sears Roebuck Co., 1970-75; internat. dir. Sales and Mktg. Execs. Internat., 1972-75; fashion dir. O.M.A., 1975-78; pres. Dahlia Parfums, Inc., 1975-80, Dahlia Prodns., Inc., 1978-81, Dahlmark Prodns., 1981—, Scandia Cosmetics, Ltd., 1978-80; pres., chmn. Lasting Beauty Ltd., 1986—. Author: Always Ask a Man, 1965, 12 Beautyscope books, 1968, rev. edit., 1978, Arlene Dahl's Secrets of Hair Care, 1969, Arlene Dahl's Secrets of Skin Care, 1972, Beyond Beauty, 1980, Arlene Dahl's Lovescopes, 1983, Arlene Dahl's Weekly Astro Forecast, 1991, 92, 93, 94, 95, 96, 97, 98, 99, 2000, 01, 02, Arlene Dahl's Hollywood Horoscope internat. syndicated weekly column, 1990—; actress: (Broadway plays) including Mr. Strauss Goes to Boston, Questionable Ladies, Cyrano de Bergerac, Applause (Tony award musical), (films) including (debut) My Wild Irish Rose, The Bride Goes Wild, Reign of Terror, A Southern Yankee, Ambush, The Outriders, Three Little Words, Watch the Birdie, Scene of the Crime, Inside Straight, No Questions Asked, Desert Legion, Slightly Scarlet, Sangaree, Caribbean Gold, Jamaica Run, Diamond Queen, Here Come the Girls, Bengal Brigade, Kisses for My President, Woman's World, Journey to the Center of the Earth, Wicked as They Come, She Played with Fire, Les Poneyettes, Du Blé Enliases, The Land Raiders, The Way to Kathmandu, Fortune Is a Woman, The Big Bank Roll, Who Killed Maxwell Thorn?, Midnight Warrior, 1991, (TV shows) Lux Video Theatre, 1952-53, guest starring appearances on The Love Boat, Fantasy Island, Love American Style, One Life to Live, 1981-84, Night of 100 Stars, 1983, Happy Birthday Hollywood, 1987, All My Children, 1995, Renegade, 1995, 96, 97, Air America, 1999; hostess (TV series): Pepsi-Cola Theatre, 1954, Opening Night, 1958, Arlene Dahl's Beauty Spot, 1966, Arlene Dahl's Starscope, 1979-80, Arlene Dahl's Lovescope, 1980-82; played throughout U.S. in One Touch of Venus, The Camel Bell, Blithe Spirit, Liliom, The King and I, Roman Candle, I Married an Angel, Bell, Book and Candle, Applause, Marriage Go Round, Pal Joey, A Little Night Music, Forty Carats, Life with Father, Murder Among Friends, Dear Liar; nightclub acts Flamingo Hotel, Las Vegas, Latin Quarter, N.Y.C., musical stage appearances: Carnegie Hall, 1997, London Paladium, 1992, 1998, Salute to MGM Musicals; internat. syndicated beauty columnist Chgo. Tribune/ N.Y. News Syndicate, 1950-70, Arlene Dahl's Lucky Stars Column, Globe Communications, 1988-90, Arlene Dahl's Starscope Weekly Column, 1991, 92, 93, 94, 95, 96, 97, 98, 99, 2000, 01, 02, Horoscope Yearly Forecast 1991-2002; designer sleepwear for A.N. Saab & Co., 1952-57, In Vogue with Arlene Dahl (Vogue Patterns), 1980-85, Arlene Dahl Pvt. Collection Jewelry, 1989-94, Arlene Dahl's Jewels of Fortune Home Shopping Network, 1996. Hon. life mem. Father Flannagan's Boys Town; internat. amb. Pearl Buck Found.; founder, pres. Broadway Walk of Stars Found., Inc.; bd. dirs. Hollywood Mus. Recipient 10 Box Office Laurel awards, Hollywood Walk of Fame Star, 1961, Coup de Chapeau Deaville Film Festival award, 1982, 92; named Best Coiffed, Heads of Fame awards, 1967-72, 80, award Scandinavian Hall of Fame, 1997; named Woman of the Yr., Advt. Club of N.Y.C., 1969, Mother of the Yr., 1982, Lifetime Achievement award WorldFest, 1994, Leadership in the Arts, 1997; named to Scandinavian Hall of Fame, 1997. Fellow: Vesterheim Norwegian/Am. Found. (life); mem.: UNIFEM, NATAS (trustee), Film Soc., Edward Grieg Soc., Authors Guild, Acad. Motion Picture Arts and Scis. (vice chair N.Y. spl. events), Acad. TV Arts and Scis. (bd. govs., v.p.), Smithsonian Assocs., Nat. Trust for Hist. Preservation, Commanderie de Bordeaux (N.Y.), Commanderie de Bontemps du Medoc et Graves, France. Office: Dahlmark Prodns PO Box 116 Sparkill NY 10976-0116

DAHL, COREY SHANE, physical therapist; b. Fort Riley, Kans., Sept. 27, 1971; s. Richard Jameson and Jennifer Ann Dahl; m. Brandi Ann Brumfield, Apr. 7, 2001. BA in Biology, Concordia Coll., 1994; M in Phys. Therapy, U.S. Army-Baylor U., 1997. Cert. orthopedic specialist Am. Bd. of Phys. Therapy Splty. Practitioners. Staff phys. therapist Bur. of Prisons, Fed. Med. Ctr., Fort Worth, Tex., 1997—99, sr. phys. therapist Rochester, Minn., 1999—2003. Contbr. case report and rsch. articles to profl. jours. Lt. USPHS. Conservative. Lutheran.

DAHL, CURTIS, English literature educator; b. New Haven, July 6, 1920; s. George and Elizabeth Eudora (Curtis) D.; m. Mary Huntington Kellogg, Nov. 15, 1952; children: Julia Curtis (dec.), Winthrop Huntington Kellogg. BA, Yale U., 1941, MA, 1942, PhD, 1945. Dir. fellowships, asst. to editor Dodd, Mead & Co., 1944-46; instr. English, U. Tenn., 1946-48; mem. faculty Wheaton Coll., Norton, Mass., 1948—, prof., 1958-91, Samuel Valentine Cole prof. English lit., 1966 91, Samuel Valentine Cole prof. emeritus, 1991—. Vis. prof. So. Ill. U., 1964, 66, 70, U. Wash., 1967, Brown U., 1970; vis. lectr. in English Bridgewater State Coll., 1992-98. Author: Robert Montgomery Bird, 1963; editor: There She Blows: A Narrative of a Whaling Voyage, 1971, Around the World in 500 Days, 1999; contbr. articles to profl. jours. Fence-viewer Town of Norton, 1964-77, 1989—, selectman, 1970-73; chmn. Norton Historic Dist. Commn., 1975-87, 1990-99, Norton Hist. Commn., 1976-80. Carnegie fellow Harvard U., 1954-55; Guggenheim fellow, 1957-58; Fulbright prof. U. Oslo, 1965-66 Mem. MLA, Nat. Assn. of Scholars, Melville Soc., Boston Browning Soc., Presbyn. Hist. Soc. Republican. Home: 189 N Washington St Norton MA 02766-1801 E-mail: morgan132@juno.com. *Too few people today know the difference between "uninterested" and "disinterested.".*

DAHL, CURTIS RAY, photographer; b. Valparaiso, Ind., Sept. 1, 1954; s. Ray Gustav and Vera Mae (Guse) D.; m. Bren Bennington, Mar. 18, 1990; children: Austin, Darren. BA, Principia Coll., 1976. Tennis instr. Westlake Tennis & Swim, 1976-80; co-owner, photographer Kaish Dahl Photography, Inc., 1980-99; owner, pres. Curtis Dahl Photography, Inc., 2000—. Bd. dirs. So. Calif. chpt. Tourette Syndrome Assn., L.A., 1995-98, mem. Kodak Pro Team, 1996. Mem. Profl. Photographers of Am., Wedding and Portrait Photographers Internat. (spkr. 1997—), Ohr Hatorah Synagogue. Republican. Jewish. Avocations: tennis, philanthropies, floral arranging. Home: 31962 Doverwood Ct Westlake Village CA 91361 E-mail: curtis@curtisdahl.com.

DAHL, DONALD L. state representative; b. Hillsboro, Kans., Mar. 19, 1945; BS, Tabor Coll., 1968. Commdr. USN, 1968—90; ret., 1990; mem. Kans. Ho. of Reps., 1997—. Mem.: Ret. Officers Assn., Nat. Assn. Realtors, Lions. Republican. Office: 156-E State Capitol Topeka KS 66612 Address: 205 S Wilson Hillsboro KS 67063-1823*

DAHL, EVERETT E. lawyer; b. Sandy, Utah, June 21, 1923; m. Ann Kosovich, June 21, 1947; children: Annette, EvAnn. BS, U. Utah, 1947, JD, 1949. Bar: Utah 1949, U.S. Dist. Ct. Utah 1959, U.S. Ct. Mil. Appeals 1959, U.S. Supreme Ct., U.S. Ct. Appeals (10th cir.). Commd. 2d lt. U.S. Army, 1943, advanced through grades to col., ret., 1975; pvt. practice Midvale, Utah, 1949—. Mayor City of Midvale, 1986-94; exec. sec. Midvale C. of C., 1950-60; bd. dirs. Rsch. Inst., 1955—; pres. Palo Verde Park, Inc., Safford, Ariz., 1970's; chmn. Salt Lake County Coun. Govts., South Valley Emergency Ctr.; bd. dirs. Trans Jordan Landfill. Mem. Res. Officers Assn. (life, dept. comdr. nat. exec. com.), Amvets (dept. pres. nat. exec. com. 1993—), VFW, Phi Kappa Phi. Avocations: fishing, golf. Office: 49 W Center St Midvale UT 84047-7451

DAHL, GERALD LUVERN, psychotherapist, educator; b. Nov. 10, 1938; s. Lloyd F. and Leola J. (Painter) Dahl; m. Judith Lee Brown, June 24, 1960; children: Peter, Stephen, Leah. BA, Wheaton Coll., 1960; MSW, U. Nebr., 1962; PhD in Psychotherapy (hon.), Internat. U. Found., 1987. Diplomate Am. Psychotherapy Assn. Juvenile probation officer Hennepin County Ct. Svcs., 1962—65; cons. Citizens Coun. on Delinquency and Crime, Mpls., 1965—67; dir. patient svcs. Mt. Sinai Hosp., Mpls., 1967—69; clin. social worker Mpls. Clinic of Psychiatry, 1969—82, G.L. Dahl & Assocs., Inc., Mpls., 1983—. Assoc. prof. social work Bethel Coll., St. Paul, 1964—83; spl. instr. sociology Golden Valley Luth. Coll., 1974—83; pres. Strategic Team-Makers, Inc., 1985—; adj. prof. U. Wis., River Falls, 1988—90. Author: Why Christian Marriages Are Breaking Up, 1979, Everybody Needs Somebody Sometime, 1980, How Can We Keep Christian Marriages from Falling Apart, 1988, The Sandwich Generation, 1995; contbr. articles to profl. jours. Founder, bd. stewards Family Counseling Svc., Minn. Bapt. Conf., 1994—; bd. dirs. Edgewater Bapt. Ch., 1972—75, chmn., 1974—75; vice chmn. bd. stewards Minnetonka Bapt. Ch., 1995. Mem.: AAUP, Am. Assn. Behavioral Therapists, Pi Gamma Mu. Office: 4825 Highway 55 Ste 140 Minneapolis MN 55422-5155 E-mail: jerryd@stmi.biz., stmi@stmi.biz.

DAHL, JOHN, film director; b. Billings, Mont., 1956; Student, Mont. State U., Am. Film Inst. Dir., writer: Kill Me Again, 1989, Red Rock West, 1992 (nominated Ind. Spirit awards for best dir., best screenplay, 1995); dir.: (TV movie) The Last Seduction, 1994, Unforgettable, 1996, Rounders, 1998 (nominated Golden Lion award Venice Film Festival, 1998), (videos) Kool & The Gang, Joe Santriani, others; dir., prodr.: Striking Back: A Jewish Commando's War Against the Nazis, 1998; writer: Meltdown, 1999, Joy Ride, 2001. Recipient New Generation award L.A. Film Critics Assn., 1994. Office: c/o Josh Donen Creative Artists Agy 9830 Wilshire Blvd Beverly Hills CA 90212*

DAHL, LAUREL JEAN, human services administrator; b. Chgo. d. James Edward and Gladys Uarda (Boquist) Findlay; m. Philip Nels Dahl, Aug. 29, 1970; children: Eric Nels, John Philip. BA, Trinity Coll., 1970; MS in Human Svcs., Nat. Louis U., 1992. Cert. sr. alcohol and other drug preventionist. Tchr. Grove Sch., Lake Forest, Ill., 1971, Little Bear Child Care Ctr., Waukegan, Ill., 1975-77; sec. to dir. Strang Funeral Home, Antioch, Ill., 1981-87, comptroller, office mgr. Village of Antioch, 1987-92; prevention specialist Lake County Dept. of Health: Mental Health Div., 1992; cmty. coord. Fighting Back Project of Lake County, Round Lake, Ill., 1992-94; dir. prevention svcs. Nicasa, Lake, 1994—. Adj. faculty Nat. Louis U., 1994—; adv. bd. U. Ill. Extension, 1999; dir. Lake County Gang Prevention Alliance, 2000—03; mem. Character Matters in Lake County Found., 1999—, treas., 2001—03, pres., 2003—. Mem. editl. adv. bd. Family Times. Mem. Antioch Cmty. H.S. Bd. Edn., 1987—95, pres., 1991—95, sec., 1989—91; mem. Antioch Cmty. H.S. Drug Task Force, MADD; past pres. PTO; vice chair Human Svc. Coun., 1994—96, chmn., 1996—98, 1999—2003; mem. peer rev. com. Ill. Alcohol and Other Drug Abuse Profl. Cert. Assn., 1996—; mem. women's bd. No. Ill. Coun. on Alcoholism and Substance Abuse, 1996—2003, v.p. for programs, 1997—2003; mem. Cmty. Partnership Bd., 2003—. Recipient commendation for Gt. Lakes Naval Tng. Ctr. for Drug Edn. for Youth, 1994-95, Disting. Svc. award Ill. chpt. Nat. Sch. Pub. Rels. Assn., Enrique Camarena "One Person Can" award, 1995, State Prevention Leadership award Ill. Alcoholism and Drug Dependence Assn., 1996, Individuals in the Forefront for Lake County award, 1998; Paul Harris fellow. Mem.: Ill. Assn. for Prevention, Ill. Student Assistance Profls., Alliance Against Intoxicated Motorists, Round Lake Exch. Club (charter mem. 1999). Home: PO Box 613 Antioch IL 60002-0613

DAHL, MARILYN GAIL, psychotherapist, nurse; b. Louisville, Dec. 6, 1946; d. James Blair and Dorothy Emma (McDermott) Swartzwelder; m. Charles Dalton Weaver, Dec. 30, 1967 (div. Apr. 1969); m. Donald Allan Dahl, Sept. 18, 1985. BSN, U. Ky., 1968; MEd in Clin. Counseling, The Citadel, 1987. Lic. profl. counselor, Ill. Instr. med.-surg. nursing Sch. Nursing Ky. Bapt. Hosp., Louisville, 1973-79; child psychiat. nurse Norton's Children's Hosp., Louisville, 1980-81; asst. prof., psychiat. nurse Sch. Nursing, U. Louisville, 1981-82; primary therapist/child psychiat. nurse Children's Treatment Svc., Louisville, 1982-83; instr. psychiat. nursing Sch. Nursing Bellarmine Coll., Louisville, 1983-84; adult and geriat. therapist Seven Counties Svcs., Louisville, 1984; psychiat. nurse So. Pines Hosp., Charleston, S.C., 1985-86; rev. specialist S.C. Peer Rev. Orgn., Charleston, 1986-87; psychotherapist Ctr. for Change, Charleston, 1987-88; pvt. practice North Charleston, 1988-94; hospice nurse Condell Home Health Agy., Libertyville, Ill., 1994-95; home health nurse

Manpower Temporary Agy., Waukegan, Ill., 1996-97; staff nurse Hospice of Highland Park (Ill.) Hosp., 1996-99; pvt. practice psychotherapy Goshen, Ky., 1999—; home health nurse Manpower Temp. Agy., Waukegan, 1996-97. Hospice nurse Hospice of Charleston, Inc., 1991-92; pub. health nurse Trident Home Halth Svcs., 1992; mental health profl. Charleston/Dorchester Mental Health Ctr., 1993. Vol. Hospice of Louisville, Inc., 1978-85, ARC State and Nat. Response Team, 1996—, Hospice and Palliative Care Louisville, Inc., 1999—; mem. steering com. Highlands Adult Day Ctr., Louisville, 1984-85; bd. dirs. Ashley River Fire Dept., Charleston, 1986-90, chair, 1989-90, mem. ladies aux., 1985-94; mem. test rose panel Jackson & Perkins, 1989-91. Named to Honorable Order Ky. Cols., Commonwealth of Ky., 1977. Mem. ACA, Am. Assn. for Mental Health Counselors. Avocations: cross stitching, raising roses, wildflower gardening, singing, making stained glass projects. Home and Office: 1120 Cliffwood Dr Goshen KY 40026-9558

DAHL, MARK VICTOR, dermatologist, educator; b. Mpls., Aug. 24, 1942; s. Victor E. and Edith M. D.; m. Arlene C., July 1, 1966; children: Kristian Mark, Jonathan Mark. BA, Wesleyan U., 1964; MD, U. Minn., 1968. Diplomate Am. Bd. Dermatology. Intern U. Ore. Med. Sci. Ctr., Portland, 1968-69; fellow in dermatology U. Copenhagen, 1969-70; rsch. assoc. Walter Reed Army Med. Ctr., Washington, 1970-72; from assoc. prof. to prof. dermatology U. Minn. Med. Sch., Mpls., 1974—2000, chmn. dept. dermatology, 1995—2000; prof., chmn. Dept. Dermatology, Mayo Clinc, Scottsdale, 2000—. Pres. Mark Dahl & Assocs., Inc., 1994—. Author: Clinical Immunodermatology, 1981, 3d edit., 1996, Common Office Dermatology, 1983, Clinical Dermatology, 1990, 2d edit., 3d edit., 2003, 1995, Dermatology, 1991; mem. editl. bd. jours. in field; contbr. articles to profl. jours. Founder Camp Discovery for children with severe skin diseases. Maj. U.S. Army, 1970-72. Mem. ACP, Am. Soc. Allergy and Immunology (pres. 1981-82), Am. Acad. Dermatology (pres. 1993-94, Henry Stelwagen award 1972, Gold Triangle award 1998, Gold medal 2002), Am. Dermatology Assn., Assn. Profs. Dermatology, Internat. Soc. Dermatology, Soc. Investigative Dermatology (v.p. 1994-95), Br. Dermatol. Assn., Mex. Acad. Dermatology, Can. Dermatol. Assn., Minn. Dermatol. Assn., Phoenix Dermatol. Soc. Office: Mayo Clinic Scottsdale 13400 Shea Blvd Scottsdale AZ 85259

DAHL, REYNOLD PAUL, applied economics educator; b. Willmar, Minn., Feb. 10, 1924; s. Paul Efraim and Margaret Elizabeth (Peterson) D.; m. Alyce Rosalind Druskis, Sept. 11, 1948; children— John, Ann Student, North Park Coll., Chgo., 1942-43; BS, U. Minn., 1949, MS, 1950, PhD, 1954. Instr. agrl. econs. U. Minn., St. Paul, 1950-54, asst. prof., 1954-58, assoc. prof., 1958-63, prof., 1963-94, prof. emeritus, 1994—, chief of party, economist Tunis, Tunisia, 1967-70. Agrl. economist Soybean Coun. of Am., Brussels, 1962-63; dir. Mpls. Grain Exchange, 1972-80; agrl. economist U.S. AID, Port-au-Prince, Haiti, 1972, 74 Contbr. articles to profl. jours., chpts. to books. Served with USAAF, 1943-46; PTO Mem. Am. Agrl. Econs. Assn., Am. Inst. Coop. (trustee 1981-84), Xi Sigma Pi, Alpha Zeta Roman Catholic. Avocations: gardening, fishing, outdoor activities. Home: 1666 Coffman St Apt 326 Saint Paul MN 55108-1344 Office: U Minn Dept Applied Econs 1994 Buford Ave Saint Paul MN 55108-6038 E-mail: dahlx008@umn.edu.

DAHL, ROBERT ALAN, political science educator; b. Inwood, Iowa, Dec. 17, 1915; s. Peter Ivor and Vera (Lewis) D.; m. Mary Louise Bartlett, 1940 (dec. 1970); children: Ellen Kirsten, Peter Bartlett (dec.), Eric Lewis, Christopher Robert; m. Ann Goodrich Sale, 1973. AB, U. Wash., 1936; PhD, Yale U., 1940; LLD (hon.), U. Mich., 1985, U. Alaska, 1987; D of Philosophy (hon.), U. Oslo, 1994; LLD (hon.), Law Sch. for Social Rsch., 1996, Harvard U., 1998; D honoris causa, U. Macrid Complutense, 2001; LLD, Grinnell Coll., 2001. Mgmt. analyst USDA, 1940; economist Office Prodn. Mgmt., Office Price Adminstrn. and Civilian Supply, War Prodn. Bd., 1940-42; faculty Yale U., 1946—, Eugene M3yer prof. polit. sci., 1955-64, Sterling prof. polit sci., from 1964, Ford Rsch. prof., 1957-58, chmn. dept. polit. sci., 1957-62. Lectr. polit. sci., Flacso, Santiago, Chile, 1967; pres. Am. Polit. Sci. Assn., 1967. Author: Congress and Foreign Policy, 1950, (with E. Browne) Domestic Control of Atomic Energy, 1951, (with C.E. Lindblom) Politics, Economics and Welfare, 1952, A Preface to Democratic Theory, 1956, (with Haire and Lazarsfeld) Social Science Research on Business, 1959, Who Governs?, 1961, Modern Political Analysis, 1963, Political Oppositions in Western Democracies, 1966, After the Revolution?, 1970, Polyarchy: Participation and Opposition, 1971, Regimes and Oppositions, 1972, Democracy in the United States, 1972, (with E.R. Tufte) Size and Democracy, 1973, Dilemmas of Pluralist Democracy, 1982, A Preface to Economic Democracy, 1985, Controlling Nuclear Weapons, 1985, Democracy, Liberty and Equality, 1986, Democracy and the Critics, 1989, The New American Political (Dis) Order, 1994, Toward Democracy: A Journey Reflections: 1940-1997, 1997, On Democracy, 1999, Politica e virtu, 2001, How Democratic Is the American Constitution?, 2002, Intervista sul Pluralismo, 2002. With U.S. Army, 1943-45. Decorated Bronze Star with cluster; Cavaliere of Republic of Italy, 1988; recipient Woodrow Wilson prize, 1963, 90, Talcott Parsons prize, 1977, Wilbur Lucius Cross medal, 1986, Elaine and David Spitz award, 1991; Guggenheim fellow, 1950, 78, fellow Ctr. for Advanced Study in Behavioral Scis., 1955-56, 67. Fellow Am. Acad. Arts and Scis. (Talcott Parsons prize 1977); mem. NAS, Am. Philos. Soc., Am. Polit. Sci. Assn. (pres. 1966-67, Woodrow Wilson prize 1963, James Madison prize 1978, Gladys Kammerer award 1983, Benjamin Lippincott award 1989, Johan Skytte prize 1995), New Eng. Polit. Assn. (pres. 1951), ACLU, Brit. Acad., Phi Beta Kappa. Home: 17 Cooper Rd North Haven CT 06473-3001 E-mail: robert.dahl@yale.edu.

DAHL, TYRUS VANCE, JR., lawyer; b. Elizabeth City, N.C., July 23, 1949; s. Tyrus Vance and Emerald (Taylor) D.; m. Susan Morrow Fitzgerald, Aug. 7, 1976 (div. Apr. 1992); children: Katherine Fitzgerald, Elizabeth Sommers; m. Angela Wheelock, Aug. 8, 1998. AB, Duke U., 1971; JD, U. Tulsa, 1979. Bar: Tenn. 1979, U.S. Dist. Ct. (mid. dist.) Tenn. 1979, Okla. 1981, U.S. Dist. Ct. (no. and we dists.) Okla. 1982, U.S. Ct. Appeals (10th cir.) 1982, N.C. 1985, U.S. Dist. Ct. (ea., mid., and we. dists.) N.C. 1985, U.S. Ct. Appeals (4th cir.) 1985, U.S. Supreme Ct. 1985, U.S. Ct. Appeals (6th cir.) 1987. Law clk. to chief fed. judge, Nashville, 1979-81; assoc. Hall, Estill, Tulsa, 1981-84; ptnr. Womble Carlyle Sandridge & Rice, Winston-Salem, N.C., 1984—. Adj. prof. clin. program, adj. prof. trail practice and advanced trial practice Sch. Law, Wake Forest U. Editor and contbr. articles to law rev. Mem. ATLA, N.C. Bar Assn., Forsyth County Bar Assn. Democrat. Methodist. Avocations: photography, music. Office: Womble Carlyle Sandridge & Rice 1 W 4th St Winston Salem NC 27101-4019 E-mail: tdahl@wcsr.com.

DAHLBEN, SALIN ABRAHAM, neuropsychiatrist; b. Rio de Janeiro, Nov. 2, 1945; came to U.S., 1973; s. Abraham and Emilia D.; m. Sonia Sapolnik, July 8, 1971 (div. 1975); m. Jean Annette Leupold, Nov. 7, 1982 (div. 1996); children: Deborah, Rachael Emily, Lindsay Johanna, Joshua Robert, Brian Andre. BS, Hebrew Coll., Rio de Janeiro, 1963; MD, Fed. U., Rio de Janeiro, 1969. Cert. Bd. Med. Quality Assurance, Calif.; diplomate Am. Bd. Psychiatry and Neurology in gen. psychiatry with added cert. in geriatric psychiatry. Mem. med. staff Naval Hosp., Rio de Janeiro, 1970-71; intern Mt. Sinai Hosp. Svcs., N.Y.C., 1973-74; resident Boston City Hosp., 1974-75; fellow in neurosurgery Lahey Clinic, Boston, 1975-76; resident in neurosurgery U. Iowa Hosps., Iowa City, 1976-78, resident in psychiatry, 1979-80; chief resident Mt. Sinai Hosp. Med. Ctr., Chgo., 1981; med. unit dir. Bridgewater State Hosp., 1983-85; med. dir. Dorchester Mental Health Ctr., Mass., 1985-87; asst. psychiatrist McLean Hosp., Belmont, Mass., 1983—. Clin. instr. psychiatry Harvard Med. Sch., Boston, 1983—; clin. assoc. Mass. Gen. Hosp., 1988—98, Mass. Mental Health Ctr., 1999—; assoc. Cambridge Hosp., 1990—; unit med. dir. psychiatry Metro Boston Lemuel Shattuck Hosp., Boston, 2001—. 1st lt. M.D. Brazilian Navy, 1970-71. Recipient prize Assn. Med. Students, Rio de Janeiro, 1968, 69, Abbey Norman Prince award Mt. Sinai Hosp. Med. Ctr., Chgo., 1981; named one of Am.'s Top Psychiatrists in Neuropsychiatry, Consumers Rsch. Coun. Am., 2003; scholar Nat. Coun. for Rsch., 1969-70. Mem. Mass. Med. Soc., N.Y. Acad. Scis., Am. Mensa, Harvard Faculty Club, Sigma Xi (MIT chpt.). Office: 25 Mount Alvernia Rd Chestnut Hill MA 02467-1057 E-mail: sdahlben@hms.harvard.edu.

DAHLBERG, ALBERT EDWARD, biochemistry educator; b. Chgo., Sept. 19, 1938; s. Albert Archer and Thelma Elizabeth (Ham) D.; m. Pamela Kathy Voth, June 29, 1963; children: Albert Andrew, Krista Katherine, Paul Eric BS, Haverford Coll., 1960; MD, U. Chgo., 1965, PhD in Biochemistry, 1968. Rsch. assoc. Nat. Cancer Inst.-NIH, Bethesda, Md., 1967-70; European Molecular Biology Orgn. fellow Molecular Biol. Inst., U. Aarhus, Denmark, 1970-72; prof. biochemistry Brown U., Providence, 1972—, chmn. dept. biochemistry, 1985, 87. Vis. prof. U. Wis., Madison, 1978-79; v.p. rsch. Mora Pharms., Inc., Miami, Fla., 1983—; founder, bd. dirs. Milkhaus Lab. Inc., Delanson, N.Y., 1993—; mem. bd. sci. counselors divsn. cancer biology diagnosis and ctrs. Nat. Cancer Inst., 1992-95; mem. Corp. of Haverford Coll., 1995—. Contbr. articles to profl. jours., chpts. to books NIH grantee, 1972— ; recipient USPHS Rsch. Career Devel. award NIH, 1975-80 Fellow AAAS, Am. Soc. Microbiology; mem. Am. Soc. Biochemistry and Molecular Biology (sec. 2001—), The Monroe Inst. Mem. Society Of Friends. Home: 554 Wayland Ave Providence RI 02906-4723 Office: Brown U Dept Molecular and Cell Biology and Biochemistry Dept Biochemistry Box G Providence RI 02912 E-mail: Albert_Dahlberg@Brown.edu.

DAHLBERG, ALFRED WILLIAM, electric company executive; b. Atlanta, 1940; Grad., Ga. State U., 1970. Chmn., pres., CEO Southern Co., Atlanta, 1999—; pres., chmn. bd. dirs., CEO So. Co., Atlanta, 1999—. Bd. dirs. So. Co., So. Co. Svcs., Inc., So. Electric Generating Co., Protective Life Corp., Electric Power Rsch. Inst., Trust Co. Ga., Trust Co. Bank; pres., dir. Piedmont-Forrest Corp.; mem. Southeastern Electric Exch., Edison Electric Inst. Office: Southern Co 270 Peachtree St NW Ste 2200 Atlanta GA 30303-1247

DAHLBERG, BURTON FRANCIS, real estate corporation executive; b. Ashland, Wis., Dec. 14, 1932; s. Oscar A. and Estelle (Bratton) D.; m. Gloria Dahlberg, Aug. 23, 1957 (div. Nov. 1982); children: Michael, Andrea, David; m. Sandy Sieverson, Jan. 22, 1985 BA, U. Minn., 1960. Cert. property mgr. Property mgr., leasing Oneida Realty, Duluth, Minn.; real estate analyst Control Data Corp., Bloomington, Minn., 1965-68; v.p., real estate mgr. Kraus-Anderson Realty Co., Bloomington, 1968-84, pres., 1984—; ret., 2002. Bd. dirs. Am. State Bank, Bloomington, 1985-94. Bd. dirs. Minn. Taxpayers Assn., 1984—. Mem. Minn. C. of C. (bd. dirs. 1994—), Blomington C. of C. (bd. dirs. 1983-80), Nat. Assn. Office and Indsl. Parks (bd. dirs.), Mpls. Bldg. Onwers and Mgrs. Assn. (past pres.), Internat. Council Shopping Ctrs. (bd. dirs.), Inst. Real Estate Mgmt. Clubs: Decathlon Athletic (Bloomington, bd. dirs. 1983-86). Avocations: racquetball, hunting, cooking, race horses.

DAHLBERG, CARL FREDRICK, JR., entrepreneur; b. New Orleans, Aug. 20, 1936; s. Carl Fredrick and Nancey Erwin (Jones) D.; m. Constance Weston, Dec. 30, 1961; children: Kirsten Erwin Dahlberg Turner, Catherine Morgan Dahlberg Stokes. BSCE, Tulane U., 1958; MBA, Harvard U., 1964. Regional mgr. bond dept. E.F. Hutton & Co., Inc., New Orleans, 1965-67; chmn. exec. com. Dahlberg, Kelly & Wisdom, Inc., New Orleans, 1967-71; pres. St. Mary Galvanizing Co., Inc., New Orleans, 1971-2000, chmn., 2000—. Co-organizer, dir. Charter Med. Corp., 1969-72; adv. dir. Rathborne Cos., 1985-91; with Internat. Trade Mart, 1974-89, mem. exec. com., 1981-84, treas., 1983-84; consul gen. of Monaco, New Orleans, 1981-98; treas. Consul Corps of New Orleans, 1990-94. Co-author: Hydrochloric Acid Pickling, 1979. Trustee Metairie Park Country Day Sch., New Orleans, 1976-85, treas., 1980-82, chmn., 1982-84; trustee Eye, Ear, Nose and Throat Hosp., New Orleans, 1980-96, mem. exec. com., 1980-83; trustee Eye, Ear, Nose and Throat Found., 1980-83, U. South, Sewanee, Tenn., 1984-90; bd. dirs. New Orleans Tech. Coun., 1993-98, Mus. Arts Soc. New Orleans, 2000—; vis. com. Monroe libr. Loyola U., New Orleans, La., 2002-; vestryman Christ Ch. Cathedral, New Orleans, 1981-85. With U.S. Army, 1958-59. Mem. ASCE, Nat. Assn. Mfrs. (bd. dirs. 1997—), Venerable Order Hosp. of St. John of Jerusalem, Mil. and Hospitaller Order St. Lazarus, Order of Merit of Italian Republic, Order of Grimaldi (Monaco), New Orleans Country Club, Pickwick Club, Army and Navy Club (Washington), The Brook Club (N.Y.C.). Republican. Episcopalian. Home: 199 Audubon Blvd New Orleans LA 70118-5538 Office: 201 Saint Charles Ave Ste 2531 New Orleans LA 70170-1000

DAHLBERG, ERIC ROSS, music educator; b. Mpls., Nov. 7, 1962; s. Jerome E. and Marilyn D. Dahlberg; m. Suzanne Marie Parenteau, May 22, 1993; children: Madeline Rae, Heather Marie. MusB, U. Minn., 1985, MEd, 1999. Lic. tchr. State Minn., 2002. Pvt. instrumental music instr., Woodbury, Minn., 1985—; instr. longterm band, strings, classroom music Hopkins Pub. Schools #270, Golden Valley, Minn., 1985—86; dir. orch. Oskaloosa Cmty. Schools, Oskaloosa, Iowa, 1987—90; tchr. instrumental music St. Paul Pub. Schools #625, St. Paul, 1993—. Mem. cello sect. Bloomington Symphony Orch., Minn., 1990—2000; condr. Rondo Cmty. Orch. (formerly 'Capitol Hill Symphony'), St. Paul, 1995—2000, Woodbury Youth Orch., 2001—. Writer (article) Gopher Music Notes, photographer (photograph/color print) Voyage Through Time, Lasting Illusions. Mem.: Minn. Music Educators Assn. (Minn. All State Orch. award 1979—81), Minn. Band Dirs. Assn., Music Educators Nat. Conf. (no. state coord. - student chpt. 1984—85). Achievements include Have held the position of 'Principal Cello' for the following orchestras:Armstrong Sr. H. School; University of Minnesota, Duluth, Symphony Orchestra & Chamber Orchestra; Oskaloosa Community Orchestra; Currently hold a 'Brown Belt' in karate. Have won 1st, 2nd, and/or 3rd place trophies at 'Green, Blue and Red' belt levels at local karate tournaments. Avocations: photography, Karate, fishing, alpine skiing, travel. Office: Linwood A+ Elem School 1023 Osceola Ave Saint Paul MN 55105

DAHLBERG, THOMAS ROBERT, writer, lawyer, educator, software company executive; b. Pitts., Nov. 28, 1961; s. J. Robert (dec.) and Patricia Ann (McSweeney) D.; m. Teresa Marie Dorr, Aug. 21, 1981 (div. 1989); 1 child, Mary Katherine (dec. 2000); m. Jeanne Marie Henderson, July 19, 1992 (dec. 1994). BS, Pa. State U., 1984, postgrad, 1982-84; AM, Georgetown U., 1986; JD, U. Notre Dame, 1987; PhD, Stanford U., 1994. Legis. asst. U.S. Senate, Washington, 1985; fin. dir. Ctr. Judical Studies, Washington, 1986; fgn. svc. officer U.S. Dept. State, Reston, Va., 1987-88; assoc. various firms, 1988 90; columnist, screenwriter, author Sacramento, 1991—; instr. U. Calif. at Berkeley, 1996—2002; adj. prof. U. Notre Dame Law Sch., 1997—; CIO Precept Software Inc., Palo Alto, Calif., 1997-98, Virtuosi, Inc., 1998—. Author: Drug Crazy, 1993, Literary Transaction Guide, 1993, (screenplay) Sequential Monogamy, 1992, (screenplay) Spooks and Loggers, 1992, (screenplay) Whippers and Slippers, 1992, (screenplay) Trauma Drama, 1993; editor Benchmark, Washington, 1986-87; Notre Dame Law Sch. editorial group, Harvard Jour. Law & Public Policy, editor, 1985-86, sr. editor, 1986-87; contbr. articles to profl. jours. and mags. Bd. dirs., chair strategic planning com. Boulder Vol. Connection, 1994-95, Rocky Mountain Wolf Sanctuary, 1994-96, Frontier Airlines, 1995-96; spkr. Sacramento AIDS Found., 1991-92; caticical min. 1998-00. Maj. gen. USAR, 1979—. Decorated Knight of the Gallant Cross of the Most Hon. Order of Bath; nominee Pulitzer prize for Disting. Commentary, 1993, Nobel prize in Physics, 2003; recipient Exceptional Svc. medallion, CIA, 1987. Mem. Federalist Soc. for Law and Pub. Policy Studies (past pres. Notre Dame chpt. 1985-87), Assn. Trial Lawyers Am., Nat. Assn. Criminal Defense Lawyers (com. on prosecutorial misconduct, com. to free the innocent imprisoned, death penalty project), Writers Guild Am. (west), Amnesty Internat. (lawyers' com.). Avocations: travel, reading. Office: 15466 Los Gatos Blvd # 109-324 Los Gatos CA 95032-2542 E-mail: tom@virtuosi.com.

DAHLBURG, JOHN-THOR THEODORE, newspaper correspondent; b. Orange, N.J., Apr. 30, 1953; s. Donald Russell and Madeline (Blackadore) D.; m. Yvonne Michelle Bastien, Nov. 18, 1980; children: Cecile, Charlotte. BA summa cum laude, Washington and Lee U., 1975; LLD with highest honors, U. Toulouse, France, 1980. Reporter, pub. affairs dir. Sta. WLUR-FM, Lexington, Va., 1971-75; stringer Lynchburg (Va.) News, 1974-75; news clk., intern Time Mag., Paris, 1974; reporter, editor Boca Raton (Fla.) News, 1980-81; newsman AP, Miami, Paris, 1981-83, editor, fgn. desk N.Y.C., 1984-86, corr. Moscow, 1986-90, L.A. Times, Moscow, 1990-93, bur. chief New Delhi, 1993-96, Paris, 1996-2001, Miami, 2001—. Journalistes en Europe fellow, 1983-84; recipient George Polk award L.I. U., 1993, Excellence citation Overseas Press Club Am., 1993, Hal Boyle award, 1996, Cert. of Merit AP News Execs. Coun., 1993, Robert F. Kennedy Journalism award, 1996, Soc. Profl. Journalists award for internat. reporting, 1997; named finalist Pulitzer Prize in internat. reporting, 1992, 93. Avocations: Model T Ford restoration, rowing. Office: LA Times 3050 Biscayne Blvd Ste 500 Miami FL 33137

DAHLE, JOHANNES UPTON, retired academic administrator; b. Ada, Minn., Nov. 28, 1933; s. Upton Emmanuel and Marte (Goli) D.; m. Arlene Isabel Powell, Dec. 27, 1956; children: Randall Douglas, Lisa Johanna. BS, U. Minn., 1956, MA, 1966. Choral dir. U. Minn., Mpls., 1960-62-63-66; dir. choirs Macalester Coll., St. Paul, 1962-63; dir. student activities and univ. programs U. Wis., Eau Claire, 1966-71, dir. univ. ctrs., 1971-84, dir. devel., 1984-95, ret., 1995. Pres., dir. Eau Claire Conv. Tourism Bur., 1979-84; v.p., dir. Eau Claire Regional Arts Coun., 1982-84; bd. dirs. United Way of Eau Claire; mem. Plymouth Congrl. Ch., Mpls. Capt. USAF, 1956-60. Mem. Internat. Assn. Coll. Unions, Coun. for Advancement and Support Edn., Kiwanis (pres. Eau Claire chpt. 1975-76), Phi Kappa Phi (sec. 1982-84), Omicron Delta Kappa (sec. 1981-84), Phi Mu Alpha Sinfonia. Home: 1929 Hunter Hill Rd Hudson WI 54016-5818

DAHLGREN, CARL HERMAN PER, educator, arts administrator; b. N.Y.C., July 2, 1929; s. Harry W.A. and Ester Florence (Carlson) D.; m. Ella Kate Bowes, Oct. 8, 1960; children: Robert C., John L., Per M., Eva B. MusB, Westminster Choir Coll., Princeton, N.J., 1954. Project dir. Benson & Benson, Princeton, 1954-55; asst. head spl. research and analysis Gallup & Robinson, Princeton, 1956-57; v.p., artist mgr. Columbia Artists Mgmt., Inc., N.Y.C., 1958-68, dir., 1962-68; v.p. Hurok Concerts, Inc., N.Y.C., 1968-70, assoc., 1970-74; pres. Dahlgren Arts Mgmt., Inc., Denver, 1970-78; sr. ptnr. Dahlgren, Schiffmann & Assocs., N.Y.C., 1978-80; assoc. prof. arts adminstrn. U. Cin., 1978—, acting head broadcasting divsn., 1979-80. Dir. masters program in arts adminstrn. Coll. Conservatory of Music, 1978—, prof., 1989—, prof. emeritus, 1992; prin. Dahlgren & Yaffe, Arts Cons., 1992; acting exec. dir. Assn. for Advancement of Arts Edn., Cin., 1995-96; mem. faculty senate U. Cin., 1988-90. *At Columbia Artist Management, Dahlgren managed artist and attractions in the Judson, O'Neal and Jud Division, later re-named Jud, Reis and Dahlgren. These included: Rudolf Serkin, Eileen Farrell, Richard Tucker, Jaschac Heietz, George London, Anna Moffo, Micheal Robin, Mildred Miller, Claude Frank, Jamie Laredo, Malcom Frager, the young Robert Joffery Co., David Lloyd, Tom Krause, Brian Sullivan, Betty Allen, Lilian Kalliar, Phyllis Curtain, Andre Watts, Eleanor Steber, Beverly Wolf. He also toured various group attractions including the New York Philharmonic, the Boston Symphony and Sarah Caldwell's Boston Opera Co. Later with Hurok: Cellist YO-YO Ma, the conductor Erich Leinsdorf, tenor Nicoli Gedda and the French National Orchestra.* Co-founder, exec. dir. Westminster Choir Coll. Alumni Fund Assn., 1954-59; mgr. Princeton Symphony Orch., 1957-59; gen. mgr., dir. Central City (Colo.) Opera House, 1970-72; bd. dirs. Gilpin County Arts Assn., 1970-76; bd. dirs., sec. Colo. Celebration of Arts, 1974-76; pres. Classic Choral, 1975-78, Cin. Chamber Orch., 1982-91, trustee Westminster Choir Coll., 1967-74. With AUS, 1947-49. Decorated knight 1st Class Order of Lion, Finland; recipient Merit award Westminster Choir Coll. Mem. AAUP (v.p. U. Cin. chpt. 1990-92), Assn. Arts Adminstrn. Educators (trustee 1988, pres. 1990), Am. Assn. Mus., Faculty Club U. Cin. Episcopalian.

DAHLGREN, DOROTHY, museum director; b. Coeur d'Alene, Idaho; m. Robert Eagan, 1985; 1 child, Ivan. BS in Museology and History, U. Idaho, 1982; M in Orgnl. Leadership, Gonzaga U., 1998. Dir. Mus. N. Idaho, Coeur d'Alene, 1982—. Mem. Kootenai County Hist. Preservation Commn. Author: (with Simone Carbonneau Kincaid) In All the West No Place Like This; A Pictorial HIstory of the Coeur d'Alene Region, 1996. Mem. Idaho Heritage Trust com. N. region. Office: Mus N Idaho PO Box 812 Coeur D Alene ID 83816 E-mail: museumni@nidlink.com.

DAHLIN, DENNIS JOHN, landscape architect, environmental consultant; b. Ft. Dodge, Iowa, June 12, 1947; s. Fred E. and Arlene (Olson) D.; m. Jeanne M. Larson, Mar. 2, 1969 (div. 1990); 1 child, Lisa. BA, Iowa State U., 1970; M in Landscape Architecture, U. Calif., Berkeley, 1975. Lic. landscape arch., Calif. Assoc. planner San Luis Obispo County, Calif., 1971-73; prin. Dennis Dahlin Assoc., Modesto, Calif., 1975-90; pres. WPM Planning Team, Inc., Sacramento, 1991—. Contbg. author: The Energy Primer, 1976; author: Restoring Our River, 1997, Earth-Friendly Inns Northeast, 2000. Bd. dirs. Ecology Action Ednl. Inst., Modesto, 1984-85, Econ. Conversion Coun., San Diego, 1988-89, El Porvenir Found., Sacramento; pres. San Joaquin Habitat for Humanity, Stockton, Calif., 1986-87. Ferrand fellow U. Calif., 1974, Kearney fellow Harvard U., 1975. Mem. Am. Soc. Landscape Architects (bd. dirs. Sierra chpt. 1993-95). Methodist. Avocations: canoeing, travel, folk music. Office: PO Box 261 Sacramento CA 95812-0261 E-mail: arbornet@aol.com.

DAHLIN, DONALD C(LIFFORD), academic administrator; b. Ironwood, Mich., June 18, 1941; married; 2 children. BA magna cum laude in history, Carroll Coll., 1963; PhD in Govt. (Univ. Departmental fellow), Claremont Grad. Sch., 1969; fellow in ct. mgmt., Inst. Ct. Mgmt., 1980. Asst. prof. govt. U. S.D., Vermillion, 1966-70, assoc. prof., 1970-75, prof., 1975—, dir. criminal justice studies program, 1972-75, 78-89, chmn. dept. polit. sci., 1978-89, 95-98, fellow Pres.'s office, 1984-85, interim v.p. acad. affairs, 1988-90, acting dean continuing edn., 1995, v.p. acad. affairs, 1997—, acting pres., 2002. Mgmt. analyst Law Enforcement Assistance Adminstrn., Dept. Justice, Washington, 1970-71; sec. S.D. Dept. Public Safety, Pierre, 1975-78; lectr., cons. in field; mem. S.D. Human Resource Cabinet Sub-Group, 1975-78, chmn., 1977-78; mem. S.D. Planning Commn., 1975-78; adv. bd. Criminal Justice Statis. Analysis Center, 1975-78; chmn. S.D. Criminal Justice Commn., 1976-78; mem. U. So. Calif. Criminal Justice Tng. Center Planning Com., 1977-79, U. S.D. Research Inst. Adv. Panel, 1978-80, Gov.'s Corrections Task Force, 1987; mem. acad. resource council S.D. Planning Agy., 1978-79; chmn. S.D. County Commr.'s Juvenile Justice Com., 1986-89; chmn. S.D. Youth Advocacy Project; mem. Commn. on Advancement of Fed. Law Enforcement, 1997-99. Author: Models of Court Management, 1986; contbr. articles to profl. publs. Recipient Sustained High Performance award Law Enforcement Assistance Adminstrn., 1971, Disting. Safety Svcs. award S.D. Auto Club, 1978, Disting. Faculty award U. S.D., 1980, Friend of Law Enforcement award S.D. Peace Officers, 1983; Haynes Found. rsch. fellow, 1965-66; ASPA fellow, 1970-71; Bush Leadership fellow, summer 1975; Law Enforcement Edn. Program grantee, 1972-75; S.D. Criminal Justice Commn. grantee, 1972-74, 72-75; Criminal Justice Standards and Goals for S.D. grantee, 1974-75; Criminal Justice Data Collection grantee, 1974-75. Mem. ASPA (pres. Siouxland chpt. 1980-81, exec. bd. dirs. and sec./treas. criminal justice adminstrn. sect.), Am. Polit. Sci. Assn., Am. Judicature Soc. Home: 608 Poplar St Vermillion SD 57069-3529 Office: U SD Acad Affairs Vermillion SD 57069 E-mail: ddahlin@usd.edu.

DAHLING, GERALD VERNON, lawyer; b. Red Wing, Minn., Jan. 11, 1947; s. Vernon and Lucille Alfrieda (Reuter) D.; m. Edell Marie Villella, July 26, 1969; children: David (dec.), Christopher, Elizabeth, Mary. BS, Winona (Minn.) State Coll., 1968; MS, U. Minn., 1970; PhD, Harvard U., 1974; JD, William Mitchell Coll. of Law, 1980. Bar: U.S. Patent Office 1979, Minn. 1980, Ind. 1980, Pa. 1997, U.S. Dist. Ct. (so. dist.) Ind. 1980. Patent atty. Eli Lilly and Co., Indpls., 1980-84, mgr. biotech. patents, 1984-86, asst. patent counsel biotech., 1986-89, asst. patent counsel biotech. and fermentation products, 1990, asst. gen. patent counsel, 1991-95; dir. intellectual property Pasteur Mérieux Connaught, Lyon, France and Swiftwater, Pa., 1995-97, corp. v.p., dir. intellectual property, 1997-98, sr. v.p. intellectual property, 1998-99, Rhone Poulenc Rorer, Collegeville, Pa., 1998-99; sr. v.p. global patents Aventis Pharms., Bridgewater, N.J., 2000—. Mem. ABA, Ind. Bar Assn., Pa. Bar Assn., Am. Intellectual Property Law Assn., Intellectual Property Owners Assn. (bd. dirs.), INTERPAT. Democrat. Roman Catholic. Home: 501 Waterford Ct New Hope PA 18938 Office: Rt 202-206 PO Box 6800 Bridgewater NJ 08807-0800 also: Aventis Pasteur 13 Pont Pasteur 69348 Lyon France

DAHLQUIST, JOHN PAUL, economics educator; b. Oakland, Calif., Jan. 1, 1939; s. Paul Theodore and Margaret Ann (Ekroot) D. BS in Bus., San Jose State U., 1965, MA in Econs., 1974. Systems analyst Gen. Electric, San Jose, 1965-69; instr. econs. Peralta Community Coll. Dist., Oakland and Alameda, Calif., 1971—. Author, narrator: (films) A Demand Schedule for Wumpets, 1980, A Supply Schedule for Wumpets, 1981. Bd. dirs. San Jose Community Concerts Assn., 1967-70. Mem. Balalaika and Domra Assn. Am. (contbr. revs. to newsletter 1979-82), Joaquin Miller Heights Homeowners Assn. (bd. dirs. 1985-86). Democrat. Avocations: music, hiking, catamaran sailing, wine collecting. Office: Coll Alameda 555 Atlantic Ave Alameda CA 94501-2109

DAHLSTROM, BECKY JOANNE, journalist; b. Olympia, Wash., Sept. 24, 1957; d. Timothy Craddick and Shirleen (Stout) Roan; m. Kenneth W. Dahlstrom, Mar. 17, 1978 (div. Aug. 1984); children: Levi, Olivia; m. Robert Salley, Sr., Feb. 21, 1986 (div. Sept. 1994); 1 child, Robert, Jr. Student, Am. Coll., 1985-86. Writer Hospital, 1988-89; admitting clerk County Ventura

(Calif.) Healthcare Agy., 1989—. Writer, editor West Fork (Ark.) Elem. Sch., 1970-73. Author: (poem) My Authority, 1980 (Hon. mention 1980). Mem. Future Bus. Leaders Am. Republican. Baptist. Avocations: drawing, writing, horseback riding, ceramics.

DAHN, JEFF RAYMOND, physics educator; b. Bridgeport, Conn., Jan. 9, 1957; arrived in Can., 1970; s. Raymond Charles and Margery (Halsted) D.; m. Katherine Mary Lillian Macdonald, July 1, 1987 (div.); children: Hannah, Tara, Jackson. BSc in Physics with honors, Dalhousie U., Halifax, N.S., Can., 1978; MSc in Physics, U. B.C., Vancouver, Can., 1980, PhD in Physics, 1982. Rsch. assoc. Nat. Rsch. Coun. Can., Ottawa, Ont., 1982-83, mem. continuing staff, 1983-85; project leader materials sci. Moli Energy Ltd., Vancouver, 1985-87, rsch. dir., 1987-90; assoc. prof. physics Simon Fraser U., Burnaby, B.C., 1990-94, prof. physics, 1994-96; prof. physics and chemistry Dalhousie U., Halifax, N.S., Can., 1996—. Cons. Moli Energy (1990) Ltd., 1990-96, 3M Co., 1996—. Contbr. more than 240 sci. papers to profl. jours.; patentee in field. Recipient Medal for Innovation in Physics from Can. Assn. Physicists, 1987, Herzberg medal Can. Assn. Physicists, 1996, Gold medal B.C. Sci. Coun., 1996. Fellow Royal Soc. Can.; mem. Am. Phys. Soc., Electrochem. Soc. (Lash Miller award Can. sect. 1993, Battery divsn. Rsch. award 1996), Internat. Battery Materials Assn. (Rsch. award 1995). Avocations: woodworking, basketball, hiking in mountains. Office: Dalhousie U Dept Physics Halifax NS Canada B3H 3J5 E-mail: jeff.dahn@dal.ca.

DAHOTRE, NARENDRA BAPURAO, materials scientist, researcher, educator; b. Poona, India, Dec. 2, 1956; came to U.S., 1981; s. Bapurao B. and Latika B. Dahotre; m. Anita Thangan, Dec. 6, 1984; children: Shreyas, Shruti, Sanket. BS in Metall. Engring., U. Poona, 1980; MS in Metallurgy, Mich. State U., 1983, PhD in Materials Sci., 1987. Instr. metallurgy and materials sci. Mich. State U., East Lansing, Mich., 1985-86; postdoctoral fellow, instr. materials sci. U. Wis., Milw., 1987-88; rsch. metallurgist U. Tenn. Space Inst., Tullahoma, 1988-91, adj. asst. prof. engring. sci. and mechanics, 1991-95, adj. asst. prof. materials sci. and engring., 1995-96, assoc. prof. of materials sci. and engring., 1997-99, prof. materials sci. & engring., 1999—, chmn. Ctr. for Laser Applications, 2001—02; UT-ORNL prof., 2003. Vis. rsch. fellow electrotech. lab. Agy. Indsl. Sci. and Tech., Ministry Internat. Trade and Industry, Tsukuba, 1995; hon. tech. cons. Ascan Tribology Ctr., Manila, 1996—; tech. advisor Ctr. for Laser Processing of Materials, NFTDC, Hyderabad, India, 1996—; chmn. Ctr. Excellence for Laser Applications, 2001—. Prin. editor: Elevated Temperature Coatings: Science and Technology-I, 1995, Elevated Temperature Coatings: Science and Technology-II, 1996, Elevated Temperature Coatings: Science and Technology-III, 1998, Elevated Temperature Coatings: Science and Technology-IV, 2001; mem. internat. editl. bd. Indsl. Laser Handbook, 1992-94; editor: Lasers in Surface Engineering, 1998, Intermetallic and Ceramic Coatings, 1999; reviewer Jour. Meall. Transactions, 1991—, Jour. Materials and Mfg. Processes, 1991—; editor: Surface Engineering in Materials Science I; contbr. articles to profl. jours. Grantee rsch. grantee, Internat. Lead Zinc Rsch. Orgn., 1990—91, NASA Marshal Flight Ctr., 1990—91, Energy Conversion Program, U. Tenn. Space Inst., 1992—, Dept. Energy, 1993—, NASA Godard, 1994—, Dept. Def., 1994—, Ford Motor Co. Found., 2000—02, Alumninum Co. of Am. Found., 1997—2002, R & D grant, Honda, 1998, 2000. Mem. Am. Soc. for Metals, The Metall. Soc. of AIME, Laser Inst. Am. Materials Rsch. Soc., Am. Ceramic Soc., Soc. Mfg. Engrs., Sigma Xi. Achievements include rsch. on laser processign of composites, ceramics and intermetallic compounds, phase transformations, characterization of materials using analytical techniques; patentee in field. E-mail address. Office: U Tenn Dept Materials Sci and Engring 326 Dougherty Engring Bldg Knoxville TN 37996 E-mail: ndahotre@utsi.edu.

DAHRENDORF, LORD RALF GUSTAV, social scientist, educator; b. Hamburg, Germany, May 1, 1929; s. Gustav and Lina (Witt) D.; m. Ellen de Kadt. PhD, U. Hamburg, 1952, London Sch. Econs., 1954; 26 hon. degrees from various univs. Privatdozent sociology U. Saar, Fed. Republic Germany, 1957; fellow Ctr. for Advanced Studies in Behavioral Scis., Palo Alto, Calif., 1957-58; prof. sociology U. Hamburg, 1958-60, U. Tubingen, 1960-66; prof. U. Constance, 1966-69, dean faculty social scis., 1966-67; mem. Fed. Parliament Govt. of Fed. Republic Germany, 1969-70; parliamentary sec. of state in German Fgn. Office, 1969-70; mem. Commn. of the European Cmtys., 1970-74; dir. London Sch. Econs., 1974-84; warden St. Antony's Coll., Oxford, 1987-97; mem. House of Lords, London, 1993—, chmn. delegated powers select com., 2002—. Trustee Ford Found., 1976-87; mem. Coun. of Brit. Acad., 1980-83, House of Lords, 1993—; chmn. bd. Friedrich-Naumann Stiftung, 1982-87, Delegated Powers Select com., 2002—. Author: Marx in Perspective, 1953, Industrie-und Betriebssoziologie, 1956, Class and Class Conflict, 1959, Die angewandte Aufklä rung, 1963, Gesellschaft und Demokratie in Deutschland, 1965, Pfade aus Utopia, 1967, Essays in Theory of Society, 1968, Konflikt und Freiheit, 1972, Plä doyer für die Europä ische Union, 1973, The New Liberty, 1975, Life Chances, 1980, On Britain, 1982, Die Chancen der Krise, 1983, The Modern Social Conflict, 1988 (all transl. into many langs.), Reflections on the Revolution in Europe, 1991, LSE: A History of the London School of Economics 1895-1995, 1995, Morals, Revolution and Civil Society, 1997, After 1989, 1997, Liberal und unabhängig, Gerd Bucerius und seine Zeit, 2000, Universities after Communism, 2000, Über Grenzen, 2002, Auf der Suche nach einer neuen Ordnung, 2003. Mem. Hansard Soc. of Electoral Reform, 1975-76; mem. Royal Commn. on Legal Svcs., 1976-79; mem. Com. to Rev. the Functioning of Fin. Instns., 1977-80; mem. German PEN Ctr., 1971—. Decorated Knight Comdr., Order Brit. Empire, also by govts. of Senegal, Luxembourg, Fed. Republic Germany, Austria, Belgium. Fellow Anglo German Soc. (presidium), British Acad., Royal Soc. Arts, Royal Coll. Surgeons (hon.); mem. AAAS (hon.), NAS (fgn. assoc.), Am. Philos. Soc., Royal Irish Acad. (hon.), others. Office: House of Lords London SW1A 0PW England

DAI, LIANG, electrical engineer; b. Beijing, Nov. 30, 1971; s. Zuoyi Dai and Mengli Zhang; m. Rong Wu, Oct. 17, 1971. PhD, U. Minn., 2002. Rsch. asst. U. Minn., Mpls., 1995—2000; mem. tech. staff Lucent Technologies, Inc., Allentown, Pa., 1998, 1999; staff design engr. Prominent Comm., Inc., San Diego, 2001—. Recipient IEEE Pre-doctoral Fellowship award, 2000—01. Mem.: IEEE (assoc.). Achievements include research in high-performance CMOS VCOs for communications. Home: 5591 Foxtail Loop Carlsbad CA 92008 Office: Prominent Communications Inc 10675 Sorrento Valley Rd San Diego CA 92121 Personal E-mail: dailiang2000@yahoo.com.

DAI, SHENG, chemist, materials scientist; b. Wenzhou, Zhejiang Province, China, Aug. 24, 1963; s. Xiuqiu Dai and Cuihua Chen; m. Huimin Luo, Sept. 1, 1986; children: David, Thomas, Ashley. PhD, U. Tenn., 1990. Postdoctoral fellow Oak Ridge (Tenn.) Nat. Lab., 1990—93, staff scientist, 1994—. Adj. prof. U. of Tenn., Knoxville, 1997—. Patentee in field. Mem.: Am. Chem. Soc. Office: Oak Ridge National Lab Bethel Valley Rd Oak Ridge TN 37831

DAI, WEIZHONG, applied mathematician, educator; b. Fujian Province, China, Nov. 14, 1962; s. Zili Dai and Xiurong Chu; m. Chuhan Li; 1 child, Sijie. PhD, U. Iowa, 1994. Lectr. Xiamen U., 1986—89; assoc. prof. La. Tech. U., Ruston, 1994—. Co author: Modelling of Microfabrication Systems, 2003; contbr. articles to profl. jours. Grantee, LEQSF, La., 1996—98. Home: 1511 Bonaparte Dr Ruston LA 71270 Office: La Tech U PO Box 10348 Ruston LA 71272 Office Fax: 318-257-2562. Business E-Mail: dai@coes.latech.edu.

DAI, XINGDE, mathematics educator; b. Shanghai, Nov. 28, 1946; s. Hongming Dai and Yuqing Zhang; m. Lianfen He; 1 child, Pingping. PhD, Texas A&M U., 1990. Prof. math. U. N.C., Charlotte, 2002—. Mem.: Am. Math. Soc. Office: U NC Charlotte 9201 University City Blvd Charlotte NC 28223 Office Fax: 704-687-6415. Business E-Mail: xdai@uncc.edu.

DAIE, JALEH, investment company executive; PhD(hon.), Dominican U. Calif. Mng. ptnr. Aurora Equity LLC; dir. sci. The David and Lucile Packard Found.; prof. Rutgers U., dir. plant biology grad. program, dept. chmn., founder, dir. Interdisciplinary Studies Turfgrass Scis.; sr. sci. advisor U. Wis. System, Madison; prof. U. Wis., Madison. Sci. liaison to pres.'s nat. sci. and tech. coun.; spl. asst. office of chief scientist NOAA, U.S. Dept. Commerce, Commn. Biotech. and Global Food Security, Ctr. Internat. Strat. Studies; dir. Leadership Found., Internat. Women's Forum; trustee World Affairs Coun. No. Calif.; treas. U.S. Space Found.; spkr. in field. Inducted into Hall of Fame Women in Tech. Internat.; named to 25 Smartest, Madison mag., Internat. Women Forum; featured Leaders of Sci., The Scientist, 1994; Henry Rutgers Rsch. fellow, Tchg. Acad. fellow U. Wis. Fellow AAAS, Assn. for Women in Sci.; mem. Coun. of Sci. Soc. Presidents (chmn. 1998), Band of Angels, Sigma Xi (bd. dirs. 1998—), Phi Kappa Phi.

DAIL, JOSEPH GARNER, JR., judge; b. Elloree, S.C., June 15, 1932; s. Joseph Garner and Esther Vernette (Harbort) D.; m. Martha E. MacReynolds; children: Edward Benjamin, Mary Holyoke. BS, U. N.C., 1953, JD with honors, 1955. Bar: N.C. 1955, Va. 1976. Pvt. practice, Washington, 1959-76; ptnr. Croft, Dail & Vance (and predecessor), 1966-76; sole practitioner McLean, Va., 1976—83; counsel Gabeler, Ward & Griggs, 1983-87; judge U.S. adminstrv. law Fresno, Calif., 1987-94, San Francisco, 1994-97, Tampa, 1997-99; sr. U.S. adminstrv. law judge, 1999—. Assoc. editor: N.C. Law Rev, 1954-55. Lt. USNR, 1955-59; capt. Res. (ret.). Mem. Fed. Bar Assn., N.C. Bar Assn., Va. Bar Assn., Transp. Lawyers Assn. (Disting. Svc. award 1976), Order of Coif, Phi Beta Kappa. Republican. Home: 103 Masters Ln Safety Harbor FL 34695-3722 Office: Times Bldg 1000 N Ashley Dr Ste 200 Tampa FL 33602-3719 E-mail: macdail@aol.com.

DAILEY, COLEEN HALL, magistrate, lawyer; b. East Liverpool, Ohio, Aug. 10, 1955; d. David Lawrence and Deloris Mae (Rosensteel) Hall; m. Donald W. Dailey Jr., Aug. 16, 1980 (div. May 2001); children: Erin Elizabeth, Daniel Lester. Student, Wittenberg U., 1973-75; BA, Youngstown State U., 1977; JD, U. Cin., 1980. Bar: Ohio 1981, U.S. Dist. Ct. (no. dist.) Ohio 1981. Sr. libr. assoc. Marx Law Libr., Cin., 1979-80; law clk. Kapp Law Office, East Liverpool, 1979, 1980-81, assoc., 1981-85; pvt. practice East Liverpool, 1985-95; magistrate Columbiana County, Ohio, 1995—. Spl. counsel Atty. Gen. Ohio, 1985-92. Pres. Columbiana County Young Dems., 1985-87; bd. dirs. Big Bros./Big Sisters Columbiana County, Inc., Lisbon, Ohio, 1984-87, Planned Parenthood Mahoning Valley, Inc., 1993-97; trustee Ohio Women Inc., 1991-95; mem. Columbiana County Progress Coun., Inc. Mem. ABA, Ohio Bar Assn. (Ohio Supreme Ct. Joint Task Force on Gender Fairness, family law specialization bd.), Ohio Assn. Magistrates (chmn. domestic rels. sect. 1998-2000, 02-03), Columbiana County Bar Assn., East Liverpool Bus. and Profl. Women's Assn., Ohio Women's Bar Assn. (trustee 1997-99). Democrat. Lutheran. Office: Columbia County Common Pleas Court 105 S Market St Lisbon OH 44432-1255 E-mail: cdailey@ccclerk.org.

DAILEY, DANIEL OWEN, artist, educator, designer; b. Phila., Feb. 4, 1947; s. David Bireley and Barbara Tarleton (Tricebock) D.; m. Linda MacNeil, Aug. 19, 1977; children: Allison MacNeil, Owen MacNeil. B.F.A., Phila. Coll. Art, 1969; M.F.A., R.I. Sch. Design, Providence, 1972. Tchr., fellow MIT Ctr. for Advanced Visual Studies, Cambridge, 1975-80; founder, prof. glass program Mass. Coll. Art, Boston, 1973-89; mem. faculty Pilchuck Glass Sch., Stanwood, Wash., 1974—; designer, artist Cristallerie Daum, Paris and Nancy, France, 1975—; designer Steuben Glass, Corning, N.Y., 1982—. Tchr. glass R.I. Sch. Design, 1970-72, Haystack Mountain Sch. Crafts, Deer Isle, Maine, 1976—; owner Dan Dailey Inc., Kensington, N.H., 1977—; mem. faculty Mass. Coll. Art, 1989—; bd. govs. Mus. Arts and Design, N.Y.C., 2000—. One-man shows throughout U.S. and Europe, 1970—, numerous nat. and internat. group shows, 1970—; represented in permanent collections Renwick Gallery, Smithsonian Inst., Washington, Toledo Mus. Art, J.B. Speed Mus., Louisville, Creative Glass Ctr. Am., Millville, N.J., Morris Mus., Morristown, N.J., Royal Ont. (Can.) Mus., Met. Mus. Art, N.Y.C., Smithsonian Inst., Washington, Corning (N.Y.) Mus. Glass, Huntington (W.Va.) Mus., New Indian Mus., Flagstaff, Ariz., Les Archives Daum, Nancy, France, U. Ill. Art Gallery, Normal, Brockton (Mass.) Art Mus., Nat. Gallery Victoria, Melbourne, Australia, Nat. Mus. Modern Art, Kyoto, Japan, St. Louis Mus. Art, High Mus. Art, Atlanta, Phila. Mus. Art, Kestner Mus., Hannover, Fed. Republic Germany, Mus. Art, Darmstatt, Fed. Republic Germany, Indpls. Mus. Art, Mus. Arts & Design, N.Y.C., L.A. County Mus. Art, Musée des Arts Decoratifs, Paris, Boston Mus. Fine Arts, Detroit Inst. Art, Yokohama Mus. Art, Japan, Musée de Design et Dárts Appliques Contemporairs, Lausanne, Switzerland, Wheaton Mus., Millville, N.J., Milw. Mus. Art, Boca Raton (Fla.) Mus. Art, Carnagie Mus. Art, Pitts., Racine Art Mus., Wis., Currier Gallery of Art, Manchester, N.H., Darmstatt Mus., Germany, Dayton Art Inst., Ohio, Greatest Bar on Earth, Windows on the World Corp., One World Trade Ctr. Towers, N.Y.C., Hunter Mus. of Am. Art, Chattanooga, Tenn., The Pilchuck Glass Collection at City Centre and U.S. Bank Centre, Seattle, WA, Pacific First Ctr., Seattle, Rockefeller Ctr. Corp., N.Y.C., The Chase Manhattan Bank Collection, N.Y.C., Town of Vail, Colo., Toyama Inst. of Glass, Toyama City, Japan, Visions, N.Y.C., Mus. of Art Royal Ontario Mus., Toronto, Can., Renwick Gallery, Smithsonian Inst., Washington; major exhibitions of 53 works, 1972-87, Renwick Gallery, 1987, Smithsonian Inst., 1987, Mus. Am. Art, 1987; numerous arcthl. commns. include sculptural installation: 5 abstract vases, Jasper's Restaurant, Boston, 3 cast glass murals for Dreyfus Corp. Hdgrs., Met Life Bldg., N.Y.C., 3 cast glass murals, The Children's Hosp., Boston, cast glass mural for No. Essex County Courthouse, Newburyport, Mass., illuminated (cast) glass mural, Rockefeller Ctr., Rainbow Room, N.Y.C., 9 cast glass murals Commonwealth Energy Svcs. Corp. Hdqrs., Cambridge, Mass., cast glass mural and street lamps for the Town of Vail, Colo., 1992—, cast glass mural, L.A. County Mus., 1993, cast and fabricated bronze 3-story stair railing, pvt. residence, Zurich, Switzerland, bronze and glass vestibule and corridor, gates, pvt. residence, N.Y.C., 26 vases, Boca Raton (Fla.) Mus. Art, 1 cast glass mural 92d St. Y, N.Y.C., 1998, 4 large sconces, Restaurant Daniel, N.Y.C.; 15 yr. retrospective Renwick Gallery, Smithsonian Inst., 1987; represented in pvt. collections. Trustee Haystack Mountain Sch., Deer Isle, Maine, 1983-92, Urban Glass; mem. nat. adv. bd. U. Arts, Phila., 1989—, Renwick Gallery, Smithsonian Instn., Washington. Fulbright Hayes fellow Venice, Italy, 1972, 73; NEA glass fellow, 1979, Masters fellow Creative Glass Ctr. Am., 1989, Mass. Coun. for Arts, 1980, 85-87, MIT Ctr. Advanced Visual Studies fellow, 1975-79, grad. tchg. fellow RISD, 1970-72, fellow award Am. Craft Coun., 1998; recipient Hon. Lifetime Mem. award Glass Arts Soc., 1998, Libensky award Chateau St. Michelle Vineyards and Winery, 2000, Masters of the Medium award Renwick Smithsonian, 2001, The President's Disting. Artist award, U. of the Arts, Philadelphia, 2001, Art of Liberty award, Nat. Liberty Mus. Fellow Am. Craft Coun.; mem. Glass Art Soc. (pres., chmn. bd. dirs. 1980-82, hon life).

DAILEY, DIANNE K. lawyer; b. Great Falls, Mont., Oct. 10, 1950; d. Gilmore and Patricia Marie (Linnane) Halverson. BS, Portland State U., 1977; JD, Lewis & Clark Coll., 1982. Assoc. Bullivant, Houser, Bailey, et. al., Portland, Oreg., 1982-88, ptnr., 1988—, pres., 2002—. Contbr. articles to profl. jours. Mem.: ABA (chair task force on involvement of women 1990—93, governing coun. 1992—99, liaison to commn. on women 1993—97, vice chair tort and ins. practice sect. 1995—96, chair-elect tort and ins. practice sect. 1996—97, standing com. environ. law 1996—99, chair tort and ins. practice sect. 1997—98, chair sect. officers conf. 1998—2001, governing coun. 2003, del. 2003, property ins. law com., ins. coverage litigation com., chair task force CERCLA reauthorization, law practice mgmt. sect., comm. com.), Fedn. Ins. and Corp. Counsel, Def. Rsch. Inst., Internat. Assn. Def. Counsel, Multnomah Bar Assn. (bd. dirs. 1994—95), Oreg. State Bar, Wash. Bar Assn. Office: Bullivant Houser Bailey 300 Pioneer Tower 888 SW 5th Ave Ste 300 Portland OR 97204-2089

DAILEY, DONALD HARRY, adult education educator, volunteer; b. Sommerville, Mass., Mar. 26, 1949; s. Walter Merle Dailey and Shirley Esma (Clarke) Davidson; m. Janet Lynn Johnson, May 25, 1974; children: Catherine Shirley, Amanda Margaret. AS in Behavioral Scis., SUNY, Albany, 1978, BS in Liberal Arts, 1987; MPA, Ball State U., 1991, M in Adult Edn., 1995. Substitute Tchrs.' Cert., Ind. Career non-commissioned U.S. Army, 1968-88; field ennumerator U.S. CENSUS Dept., Indpls., 1990, 2000; course developer Veteran's Upward Bound, Indpls., 1994. Demographic cons. DataSource, Indpls., 1985—; com. mem. at large INCONJUCTION; spokesman Parents Adv. Coun. Author, critical reviews: Sherlock Holmes Review, 1990—; author, editor: Media Newsletter INTERCOM: 1705, 1983-88 (Best in Orgn. 1983-85). Polit. cons. Ind. State Senate, Indpls., 1994-95; mem. sci.-fiction rsch. group First Fandom. With U.S. Army, 1968-88. Recipient Appreciation Plaque INCONJUNCTION, Indpls., 1991, 94, Cert. of Appreciation Salvation Army, Indpls., 1990-94. Mem. VFW, Mensa, Mutual Unidentified Flying Object Network, First Fandom. Republican. Lutheran. Avocations: newsletter editing/publishing, media fan organizations, literary history. Home: 8003 Maple Grove Dr Georgetown IN 47122-9047 E-mail: fadmdon@otherside.com.

DAILEY, FRANKLYN EDWARD, JR., electronic image technology company executive, analyst, consultant; b. Rochester, N.Y., Feb. 5, 1921; s. Franklyn Edward and Isabel Louise (Lasher) D.; m. Marguerite Virginia Parker, Apr. 1, 1944; children: Franklyn III, Michael, Philip, Elizabeth, John, Paul, Thomas, Vincent. BS, U.S. Naval Acad., 1942; BSEE, U.S. Naval Postgrad. Sch., 1950; MS in Applied Physics, UCLA, 1951. Commd. ensign USN, 1942, advanced through ranks to capt.; mgr. planning and engring. ops. Stromberg-Carlson Co., Rochester, N.Y, San Diego, 1956-61; treas. Stati-Systems Inc., Springfield, Mass., 1962-65; dir. mfg. Tecnifax Corp., Holyoke, Mass., 1965-66; asst. dir. rsch. The Plastic Coating Corp., South Hadley, Mass., 1966-67; asst. v.p. mktg. Scott Graphics Inc., South Hadley, 1967-68, v.p. new bus. devel., 1968-70, v.p. rsch., 1970-76; cons. Image Tech. & Application, Wilbraham, Mass., 1977—; prin. Dailey Internat. Pub., 1996—. Pres. Photon Chroma Inc., Westfield, Mass., 1982, 84; image cons. McGraw-Hill, N.Y.C., 1978, Isomet Corp., Springfield, Va., 1980; v.p. mfg. Coulter System Corp., Bedford, Mass., 1981; chmn. Electronic Imaging Conf., Boston, Anaheim, 1985-90; speaker in field. Author: Joining the War at Sea, 1939-45, 1998, 2nd edit., 1999, My Times with the Sisters and Other Events, 1st edit., 2000. Pres. Pioneer Valley chpt. Am. Diabetes Assn., 1986-88. Roman Catholic. Avocations: tennis, biking. Home and Office: 19 Brookside Cir Wilbraham MA 01095-2102 E-mail: franklyn@daileyint.com.

DAILEY, FRED L. state agency administrator; m. Rita Dailey; children: Dawn, Shawn, Calley. BA in Polit. Sci. and History, Anderson U., Ind.; MPA, Ball State U. Formerly rodeo cowboy and amateur mountaineer; with Ind. Dept. Corrections; later with U.S. Treasury; dir. Ind. Divsn. Agr., 1975-82; exec. v.p. Ohio Beef Coun., 1982-91; exec. sec. Ohio Cattlemen's Assn., 1982-91; dir. Ohio Dept. Agr., 1991—. Served with U.S. Army, Vietnam. Recipient numerous awards include Agri-Marketer of Yr., Industry svc. awards, Golden Boot award, Nat. Outstanding State Agrl. Exec. award, 1998; named Man of Yr. Progressive Farmer mag., 1999, FFA Hon. State Farmer degree, Ohio, Ind. Mem. Nat. Assn. State Depts. Agr. (pres. 1999—2001), Midwest Assn. State Depts. Agr. (past pres.), Mid-Am. Internat. Agri-Trade Coun. Office: Ohio Dept Agr Divsn Adminstrn 8995 E Main St Reynoldsburg OH 43068-3399 E-mail: agri@odant.agri.state.oh.us.

DAILEY, GARRETT CLARK, publisher, lawyer; b. Bethesda, Md., Mar. 22, 1947; s. Garrett Hobart Valentine and Margaret (Clark) Dailey; m. Carolynn Farrar, June 21, 1969; children: Patrick, Steven. AB, UCLA, 1969; MA, Ariz. State U., 1974; JD, U. Calif., Davis, 1977. Bar: Calif. 1977, U.S. Dist. Ct. (no. dist.) Calif. 1969. Assoc. Stark, Stewart, Simon & Sparrowe, Oakland, Calif., 1977-80; ptnr. Davies & Dailey, Oakland, 1980-85, owner, 1986-90; ptnr. Blum, Davies & Dailey, Oakland, 1985-86; pres., pub. Attys. Briefcase, Inc., Oakland, 1989—, pres., CEO, 1989—. Lectr. U. Calif. Davis Sch. Law, 1988-90, Golden Gate U. Grad. Sch. Taxation, San Francisco, 1986—. Author: SupporTax, 2001; co-author: Attorney's Briefcase, Calif. Family Law, 1990—, Calif. Evidence, 1993—, Children and the Law, 1992—, Calif. Lawgic Marital Termination Agreements, 1996—, Calif. Divorce Guide, 1997—, Lawgic Premarital Agreements, 1997—. Bd. dirs. Amigos de las Americas, San Ramon Valley, Calif., 1980-85, Rotary 517 Found., Oakland, 1985, Kid's Turn, 1993. Recipient Hall of Fame award Calif. Assn. Cert. Family Law Specialists, 1995, Spencer Brandeis award LA County Bar Assn., 2003. Fellow Am. Acad. Matrimonial Lawyers; mem. Assn. Cert. Family Law Specialists (Hall of Fame award 1995). Democrat. Congregationalist. Home: 1651 W Livorna Rd Alamo CA 94507-1018 Office: Attys Briefcase Inc 2915 McClure St Oakland CA 94609 E-mail: briefcase@aol.com.

DAILEY, IRENE, actress, educator; b. New York, Sept. 12, 1920; d. Daniel James and Helen Therese (Ryan) D. Student attended, Uta Hagen, N.Y.C., 1951-61, Herbert Berghof, 1951-61. Cons. Am. Nat. Theatre and Acad., 1965-68; cons., coach for various theatre groups and individual artists., 1956—. Guest artist and tchr. various univ. in U.S., 1965—; founder Sch. of the Actors Co., N.Y.C., 1961, artistic dir., 1961-72, mem. faculty, 1961-72. Appeared in: (films) Daring Game, 1967, No Way to Treat A Lady, 1968, Five Easy Pieces, 1970, The Grissom Gang, 1970, The Last Two Weeks, 1977, The Amityville Horror, 1978, Stacking, 1986; Broadway plays Andorra, 1962, The Subject Was Roses, 1964-65 (Drama Critics Cir. award), Rooms, 1966-67, (Drama Desk Award), You Know I Can't Hear You When the Water's Running, 1968, (off-Broadway) The Loves of Cass Maguire, 1982; appeared as Jasmin Adair in Tomorrow With Pictures (London Mag. Critics Award), Duke of York's, London, 1960; appeared in The Effect of Gamma Rays on Man-In-the-Moon Marigolds, Chgo., 1970 (Sarah Siddons Award), The House of Blue Leaves, Chgo., 1972 (Joseph Jefferson nomination), Lost in Yonkers, 1993, If We Are Women, Syracuse, 1993, (off-Broadway) Edith Stein, 1993-94, The Last Adam, Syracuse, 1994-95, (Broadway) The Father, 1995-96; appeared in Another World, NBC-TV, 1973-92 (Emmy Award 1980); appeared in (plays) Desire Under the Elms, Princeton, N.J., 1961; The Sea Gull, 1973; author: (play) Waiting for Mickey and Ava, 1978. Mem. Actors Equity Assn., Screen Actors Guild, Nat. Acad. TV Arts and Sci., Am. Ednl. Theatre Assn., AFTRA. Unitarian Universalist.

DAILEY, JANET, writer; b. Storm Lake, Iowa, May 21, 1944; d. Boyd and Louise Haradon; m. William Dailey; 2 stepchildren. Student pub. schs., Independence, Iowa. Sec., Nebr., Iowa, 1963-74. Author: No Quarter Asked, 1976, After the Storm, 1976, Boss Man From Ogallala, 1976, Savage Land, 1976, Land of Enchantment, 1976, Fire and Ice, 1976, The Homeplace, 1976, Dangerous Masquerade, 1977, Night of the Cotillion, 1977, Valley of the Vapors, 1977, Fiesta San Antonio, 1977, Show Me, 1977, Bluegrass King, 1977, A Lyon's Share, 1977, The Widow and the Wastrel, 1977, Giant of Mesabi, 1978, The Ivory Cane, 1978, The Indy Man, 1978, Darling Jenny, 1978, Reilly's Woman, 1978, To Tell the Truth, 1978, Sonora Sundown, 1978, Big Sky Country, 1978, Something Extra, 1978, Master Fiddler, 1978, Beware of the Stranger, 1978, The Matchmakers, 1978, For Bitter or Worse, 1979, Green Mountain Man, 1979, Six White Horses, 1979, Summer Mahogany, 1979, Touch the Wind, 1979, Strange Bedfellow, 1979, Low Country Liars, 1979, Sweet Promise, 1979, For Mike's Sake, 1979, Sentimental Journey, 1979, A Land Called Deseret, 1979, The Bride of the Delta Queen, 1979, Tidewater Lover, 1979, Lord of the High Lonesome, 1980, Kona Winds, 1980, The Boston Man, 1980, The Rogue, 1980, Bed of Grass, 1980, The Thawing of Mara, 1980, The Mating Season, 1980, Southern Nights, 1980, Ride the Thunder, 1980, Enemy in Camp, 1980, Difficult Decision, 1980, Heart of Stone, 1980, One of the Boys, 1980, Wild and Wonderful, 1981, A Tradition of Pride, 1981, The Traveling Kind, 1981, The Hostage Bride, 1981, Dakota Dreamin', 1981, For the Love of God, 1981, Night Way, 1981, This Calder Sky, 1981, Lancaster Men, 1981, Terms of Surrender, 1982, With a Little Luck, 1982, Wildcatter's Woman, 1982, Northern Magic, 1982, That Carolina Summer, 1982, This Calder Range, 1982, Foxfire Light, 1982, The Second Time, 1982, Mistletoe and Holly, 1982, Stands a Calder Man, 1983, Separate Cabins, 1983, Western Man, 1983, Calder Born, Calder Bred, 1983, Best Way to Lose, 1983, Leftover Love, 1984, Silver Wings, Santiago Blue, 1984, The Pride of Hannah Wade, 1985, The Glory Game, 1985, The Great Alone, 1986, Heiress, 1987, Rivals, 1989, Masquerade, 1990, Aspen Gold, 1991, Tangled Vines, 1992, Riding High, 1994, The Proud and The Free, 1994, Touch the Wind, 1994, Summer Mahogany, 1995, Legacies, 1996, Homecoming, 1997, Illusions: A Novel, 1997, The Prodigal Daughter, 1998, This Calder Sky, 1999, Calder Pride, 1999, A Capital Holiday, 2001, Green Calder Grass, 2002. Recipient Golden Heart award Romance Writers Am., 1981, Romantic Times Contemporary award, 1983.*

DAILEY, JOHN REVELL, museum administrator, former career officer; b. Quantico, Va., Feb. 17, 1934; s. Frank Galvin and Flora (Revell) D.; m. Mimi Leni Rodian, July 11, 1964; children: Lisa Charlotte, Patrick Dailey. BS, U. Calif., L.A., 1956. Commd. 2d lt. USMC, 1956, advanced through grades to gen.; retired, 1992; assoc. dep. adminstr. NASA, 1992-1999; dir. National Air and Space Museum, Washington, 2000—. Contbr. articles to Marine Corps Gazette. Mem. Marine Corps Assn. (pres. 1991—). Avocation: golf. Home: Quarters 1 Marine Barracks Washington DC 20390-0001 Office: Nat Air and Space Museum 7th & Independence Ave SW Washington DC 20560-0001

DAILEY, MACEO CRENSHAW, JR., humanities educator; b. Norfolk, Va., July 4, 1943; s. Maceo Crenshaw Dailey, Sr. and Marguerite Britton; m. Sandra Prettyman, Feb. 13, 1967 (div. Apr. 1, 1998); children: Michael, Christopher, Crenshaw, Cameron, Cranston; m. Sondra Elise Banfield, June 7, 2003. BS,

Towson State U., 1967; MA, Morgan State U., 1971; PhD, Howard U., 1983. Instr. African Am. studies Smith Coll., Northampton, Mass., 1976—80; lectr. dept. history Howard U., Washington, 1981—82; assoc. prof. dept. history Boston Coll., 1982—87, Spelman Coll., Atlanta, 1988—93, Morehouse Coll., Atlanta, 1993—96; dir. African Am. studies U. Tex., El Paso, 1996—. Sr. editor Marcus Garvey and UNIA Editl. Project UCLA, 1980—81; vis. lectr. Black studies Brown U., Providence, 1986—87; cons. Atlanta History Ctr., Smithsonian Mus.; spkr. in field. Co-editor (with K. Navarro): Wheresoever My People Chance to Dwell: Oral Interviews with African American Women of El Paso, 2000; asst. editor: Jour. Negro History; co-editor (with R. Winegarten): Tuneful Tales, 2002; contbr. chapters to books, articles to profl. jours. Bd. dirs. El Paso Symphony Orch., 2000—; commr. Tex. Juneteenth Commn., Austin, 2000—; chair bd. dirs. Tex. Coun. for Humanities, Austin, 2003—. Recipient Alex W. Bealer prize, Atlanta Hist. Soc. Mem.: Nat. Coun. for Black Studies, Inc., Assn. for the Study of Afro Am. Life and History, Am. Hist. Assn. Avocations: reading, travel, music, drama. Home: 508 Tawny Oak Pl El Paso TX 79912 Office: Univ Tex El Paso 500 University Ave El Paso TX 79968

DAILEY, MICHAEL DENNIS, painter, educator; b. Des Moines, Aug. 2, 1938; s. Malcolm Nelson and Lois Marjorie (Rider) D.; children: John, Susanne. BA, U. Iowa, 1960, MFA, 1963. Prof. Sch. of Art U. Wash., Seattle, 1963-98, prof. emeritus, 1998—. Mem. Phi Beta Kappa. Office: Francine Seders Gallery 6701 Greenwood Ave N Seattle WA 98103-5294

DAILEY, MICHAEL PATRICK, music educator; b. Miller, S.D., Oct. 21, 1957; s. Warren Elmo and Magdalen Theresa (Kluthe) D.; m. Suzanne Marie Dickes, June 7, 1986; children: Michael Francis, John Warren. MusB, Concordia Coll., Moorhead, Minn., 1979; MusM, U. S.D., 1985. Music educator Spencer (S.D.) Pub. Sch., 1980-81, Jefferson (S.D.) Pub. Schs., 1981-83; tchg. asst. U. S.D., Vermillion, 1983-85; music educator Auburn (Nebr.) Pub. Schs., 1985-86, St. Paul (Minn.) Acad., 1987-88, Robbinsdale Pub. Schs., New Hope, Minn., 1988-91, Farmington (Minn.) Pub. Schs., 1991-92, South Sioux City (Nebr.) City Cmty. Schs., 1993—. Faculty advisor Music Educator Nat. Conf., U. S.D., Vermillion, 1984-85; curriculum writing com. Robbinsdale Pub. Schs., New Hope, 1988-91; comprehensive arts planning program Farmington (Minn.) Pub. Schs., 1991-92; Nebr. K-12 visual and performing arts curriculum framework South Sioux City Schs./State Nebr., 1992. Campaign vol. George McGovern Senate Campaign, Miller, S.D., 1974; contbr. Toy for Tots, South Sioux City, 1994. Alliss Found. scholar Concordia Coll., Moorhead, 1978. Mem. NEA, Am. Choral Dirs. Assn., Music Educators Nat. Conf. (faculty advisor 1984-85), Voice Care Network. Avocations: reading, listening to classical music, golfing. Home: 501 E 32nd St South Sioux City NE 68776-3351 Office: South Sioux City Cmty Schs 820 E 29th St South Sioux City NE 68776-3344

DAILEY, THOMAS F. religious studies educator, director; b. Phila., May 7, 1959; s. Mary Elizabeth Dailey. STD, Pontifical Gregorian U., Rome, Italy, 1993. Prof. De Sales U., Center Valley, Pa., 1986—. Dir. Salesian Ctr. for Faith & Culture, Center Valley, 2000—. Author: The Repentant Job: A Ricoeurian Icon for Biblical Theology, 1994, Praying with Francis de Sales, 1997; translator: St. Francis de Sales as Preacher: A Study, 1992; editor: (festschrift) With Mind and Heart Renewed, 2001; contbr. articles to profl. jours. Past pres. Fellowship of Cath. Scholars, Washington, 2001—02; dir. The Salesianum Sch., Wilmington, Del., 1998—2003; u. liaison Collegium, Worcester, Mass., 2001—03. Grantee, Metanexus Inst., 2003—. Mem.: Collegiate Mission Consortium, Fellowship Cath. Scholars (sec., pres. 1997—2002), KC (life; chaplain 1989—98). Office: De Sales University 2755 Station Ave Center Valley PA 18034-9568 Home Fax: 610-282-2254; Office Fax: 610-282-2254. Personal E-mail: thomas.dailey@desales.edu. E-mail: thomas.dailey@desales.edu.

DAILEY, THOMAS HAMMOND, retired surgeon; b. Orange, N.J. s. Louis Bird and Evelyn (Hammond) D.; m. Denise Benzacar Dailey, Aug. 22, 1959; children: Andrea, Erika, Seth. AB, Princeton U., 1957; MD, Cornell U. Med. Coll., 1961. Assoc. prof. clin. surgery Columbia U. Coll. Phys. and Surg., N.Y.C., 1991; sr. attending dept. surgery St. Luke's-Roosevelt Hosp. Ctr., N.Y.C., 1982, dir. divsn. colon and rectal surgery, 1990-96, chief med. officer, 1996-99; clin. prof. surgery Columbia U. Coll. Phys. and Surg., N.Y.C., 1997-99; ret., 1999. Pres. med. bd. St. Luke's-Roosevelt Hosp., N.Y.C., 1989-91; v.p. Rsch. Found. of Am. Soc. Colon and Rectal Surgeons, pres., 1995-98. Pres. Am. Soc. Colon and Rectal Surgeons Rsch. Found., 1995—; bd. dirs. Riverside Symphony Orch., N.Y.C., 1998-2003. Capt. M.C., U.S. Army, 1966-68, Vietnam. Mem. Med. Strollers, Physician's Sci. Soc., N.Y. Soc. of Colon and Rectal Surgeons (pres. 1979-81).

DAILEY, VICTORIA ANN, economist, policy analyst; b. San Antonio, Aug. 30, 1945; d. John Thomas and Helen (Bass) D. BA, Swarthmore Coll., 1967; PhD, U. Va., 1973. Economist FTC, Washington, 1972-79, U.S. Dept. Transp., Washington, 1979-95, ret., 1995. Econ. rsch. fellow Brookings Instn., 1971-72.

DAILY, ELLEN WILMOTH MATTHEWS, technical publications specialist; b. Marfa, Tex., Aug. 13, 1949; d. Lynn Henry Sr. and Wilmoth Hamilton (Cox) Matthews; m. John Scott Daily Sr., Mar. 21, 1970; children: John Scott Jr., Kristen Michelle. BS in Physics, U. Tex., El Paso, 1971; postgrad., George Mason U., Fairfax, Va., 1980; continuing edn., North Lake Coll., Irving, Tex., 1996; MS in Computer Ednl. Cognitive Scis., U. North Tex., 1998, postgrad., 1998—. House dir., activity counselor Southwestern Children's Home, El Paso, Tex., 1965-68; analyst Schellenger Rsch. Found. Labs, El Paso, 1968-70; computer operator, supr. keypunch El Paso Nat. Bank, 1970-73; supr., progam analyst El Paso Sand Products, 1973-74; tech. rep. Xerox Corp., Jackson, Miss., 1975-77, product tech. specialist, 1977-79, tech. trainer Leesburg, Va., 1979-82, sr. tech. writer, tng. analyst Lewisville, Tex., 1982-95; tech. publs. specialist RFMonolithics, Inc., Dallas, 1995-96. Group rep. Xerox Corp., various cities, 1975-90; owner Daily Delight Cattery, Chantilly, Va. and Carrollton, Tex., 1979-89; co-owner J & M Answering Svc., Dallas, 1983-84, Triple "D" Enterprises, 1994—; tchg. fellow U. North Tex., Denton, 1997-98, 2000—, tchg. asst., 1998-99. Co-author: (electronic Bible verse) Verse of the Day, 1987-92. Team and divsn. mgr. Chantilly Youth Assn., 1980-82; bd. dirs., swim team dir. Brookfield Swim Club, Chantilly, 1980-82; vol. Metrocrest Svc. Ctr., Carrollton, 1986-89; elder Nor'Kirk Presbyn. Ch., Carrollton, 1989-91; founding mem. United We Stand Am., 1993-97; vol. Catherine the Great, 1992, Tex. Storytelling Festival, 1999-2000. Recipient Toulouse doctoral fellowship, 1998—. Mem. Internat. Platform Assn. (red carpet com. 1994—, newsletter editor 1999—), U. Tex. El Paso Cannoneers Club (sec.-treas. 1967-71), Nat. League Am. Pen Women (Dallas br. publ. chair 2001-02, Dallas br. pres. 2002-03), Xerox Bowling League (pres. 1988-89), Sigma Pi Sigma, Kappa Delta (social svc. dir. 1969-70), Kappa Delta Phi, Phi Kappa Phi. Avocations: web site development, computers, internet. Home: 3701 Grassmere Dr Carrollton TX 75007-2616 E-mail: edaily@comcast.net.

DAILY, FRANK J(EROME), lawyer; b. Chgo., Mar. 22, 1942; s. Francis Jerome and Eileen Veronica (O'Toole) D.; m. Julianna Ebert, June 23, 1996; children: Catherine, Eileen, Frank, William, Michael. BA in Journalism, Marquette U., 1964, JD, 1968. Bar: Wis. 1968, U.S. Dist. Ct. (ea. dist.) Wis. 1968, U.S. Dist. Ct. (we. dist.) Wis. 1971, U.S. Dist. Ct. (ctrl. dist.) Ill. 1990, U.S. Dist. Ct. (ea. dist.) Mich. 1994, U.S. Ct. Appeals (7th cir.) 1977, U.S. Ct. Appeals (3d and 5th cirs.) 1985, U.S. Ct. Appeals (4th, 6th, 8th, 9th, 10th, 11th cirs.) 1990, U.S. Supreme Ct. 1998, U.S. Dist. Ct. (no. dist.) Ill. 1999. Assoc. Quarles & Brady, Milw., 1968-75, ptnr., 1975—. Lectr. in product liability law and trial techniques Marquette U. Law Sch., U. Wis., Harvard U.; lectr. seminars sponsored by ABA, State Bar Wis., State Bar S.D., State Bar S.C., Product Liability Adv. Coun., Chem. Mfrs. Assn., Wis. Acad. Trial Lawyers, Trial Attys. Am., Marquette U., Southeastern Corp. Law Inst., Risk Ins. Mgmt. Soc., Inc.; life mem. pres.'s coun. Wake Forest U., U. Dayton, Boston Coll. Author: Your Product's Life Is in the Balance: Litigation Survival-Increasing the Odds for Success, 1986, Product Liability Litigation in the 80s: A Trial Lawyer's View from the Trenches, 1986, Discovery Available to the Litigator and Its Effective Use, 1986, The Future of Tort Litigation: The Continuing Validity of Jury Trials, 1991, How to Make an Impact in Opening Statements for the Defense in Automobile Product Liability Cases, 1992, How Much Reform Does Civil Jury System Need, 1992, Do Protective Orders Compromise Public's Right to Know, 1993, Developments in Chemical Exposure Cases: Challenging Expert Testimony, 1993, The Spoliation Doctrine: The Sword, The Shield and The Shadow, 1997, Trial Tested Techniques for Winning Opening Statements, 1997, Litigation in the Next Millennium -- A Trial Lawyer's Crystal Ball Report, 1998, What's Hot and What's Not in Non-Daubert Products Liability In the Seventh Circuit, 1998. Ct. commr. Milwaukee County, Wis., 2001; bd. visitors Wake Forest U. Law Sch. Named Marquette U. Law Alumnus of Yr., 2000. Fellow Internat. Acad. Trial Lawyers; mem. ABA (past co-chair discovery com. litigation sect., vice chmn. products, gen. liability and consumer law com. of sect. tort and ins. practice, litigation sect. and mfrs. liability subcom.), ATLA, AAAS, Trial Atty. of Am., Wis. Bar Assn., Chgo. Bar Assn., Milw. Bar Assn., 7th Cir. Bar Assn., Am. Judicature Soc., Def. Rsch. Inst., Supreme Ct. Hist. Soc., Indsl. Truck Assn. (lawyers com.), Am. Law Inst., Product Liability Adv. Coun., Am. Agrl. Law Assn., Wis. Acad. Trial Lawyers, Assn. for Advancement of Automotive Medicine (life), Nat. I-Club U. Iowa, U. Ala. Nat. Alumni Assn., Circle of Champions. Roman Catholic. Office: Quarles & Brady 411 E Wisconsin Ave Ste 2040 Milwaukee WI 53202-4497 E-mail: fjd@quarles.com.

DAILY, JAMES WILLIAM, III, manufacturing executive; b. Chattanooga, July 10, 1948; s. James William Daily Jr. and Mary Jo Daily; m. Ruth Elizabeth Gust, Sept. 21, 1975; children: Anne Marie, Jackquelie Shane, James William IV. BA, So. Adventist U., 1970; MS, U. Tenn., 1994, PhD, 1996. Prodn. mgr. Daily Mfg., Rockwell, NC, 1970—76, v.p. r&d, 1996—; asst. mgr. Economy Health Foods, Knoxville, Tenn., 1976—78; assoc. realtor AAAIM Realty, Knoxville, 1978—80; owner Eden Way Natural Foods, Knoxville, 1980—91; rsch. assoc., tech. asst. U. Tenn., Knoxville, 1991—96. Internat. editor: Nutraceuticals & Foods Jours., 2002—03; contbr. articles. Mem.: Am. Coll. Nutrition, Am. Soc. Clin. Nutrition, Am. Soc. Nurtition Sci. Jehovah'S Witness. Office: Daily Mfg Inc 4820 Pless Rd Rockwell NC 28138 Office Fax: 704-784-8400.

DAILY, JEAN A. marketing executive, spokesperson; b. Bloomington, Ill., Nov. 20, 1949; d. William H. and Niola N. (Thompson) D.; m. Ronald R. Willis, June 14, 1968 (div. 1972); m. Rodger D. Melick, Aug. 15, 1981. BS, Ill. State U., 1975. Sr. acctg. clk. Country Cos., Bloomington, 1976-78; owner, mgr. Danvers (Ill.) Motor Co., 1979-85; office mgr., ops. mgr. Goods Carpet, Bloomington, 1986-87, dir. mktg. Westminster Village Inc., Bloomington, 1987—. Chair Com. to Elect Judge Prall, Bloomington, 1996; publ. chair Danvers Days, 1982—85; bd. dirs., publ. rels. & devel. advisor Twin Cities Ballet, Bloomington, 1994—96; bd. dirs. ARC, 1991—94; pres. Chestnut Health Sys. Aux., 1995—98, 1999, treas., 1997—2001; vol. Arthritis Telethon, St. Jude Golf Tournament, 1997—2003; publicity chair Gardenwalk 97; mem. adv. bd. Arthritis Found., 1997—2001; apptd. cabinet bd. Ill. Life Svcs. Network Assisted Living, 1997—2003, sec., 1997—99, sec. housing cabinet, 2003. Mem. Women in Comms., Nat. Soc. Fund Raising Execs. (co-editor chpt. newsletter 1989-91). Avocations: reading, crafts, golf, photography, country dance. Office: Westminster Village 2025 E Lincoln St Bloomington IL 61701-5995

DAILY, JOHN G. retired protective services official; b. Lafayette, Ind., June 27, 1950; s. Jewell T. and Barbara (Gunnels) D.; m. Carolyn Jean Schorr, May 31, 1975; children: Jeremy Scott, Jennifer Lynn. BSME, Purdue U., 1972; postgrad., U. Wyo., 1973, 75. Owner Jackson (Wyo.) Hole Engring., 1977-93, Jackson Hole Sci. Investigations, 1993—; dep. sheriff Teton County Sheriff's Office, Jackson, 1977-89, sgt., 1989—2002; ret., 2002. Mem. adj. teaching faculty U. North Fla., Jacksonville, 1982—, course devel. cons., 1982—; cons. traffic accident reconstruction Jackson Hole Sci. Investigations. Inventor new type of discarding sabot; author: Fundamentals of Traffic Accident Reconstruction, 1988; co-author: Fundamentals of Applied Physics for Traffic Accident Investigators, 1996. Chmn. J.H. chpt. ARC, Jackson, 1976—. Named Peace Officer of Yr., Teton County Peace Officer Assn., 1981, Outstanding Instr. award IPTM 1996, 98, 2001, 02. Mem. SAE, ASME, Ill. Assn. Tech. Accident Investigators, J.H. Rotary Club (dir. 2002—), Elks, 4-H (ch. coun. 1980-94). Republican. Lutheran. Avocations: hiking, fishing, hunting, back-packing, golf. Home: PO Box 2206 Jackson WY 83001-2206

DAILY, JOSEPH IGNATIUS, JR., civil and structural engineer, consultant; b. Phila., Aug. 14, 1923; s. Joseph Ignatius and Margaret Josephine (Platt). BS in Civil Engring., U. Pa., 1949. Registered profl. engr., Pa., Mass., Conn., W.Va., La., Ga., Md., Mo., Wash. Resident engr. Pa. Turnpike Commn., Harrisburg, 1949-51; constrn. engr. U.S. Steel Corp., Fairless Hills, Pa., 1951-55; project engr. Howard, Needles, Tammen & Bergendorf, N.Y.C., 1955-59; supervising civil and structural engr. United Engrs. & Constructors, Inc., Phila., 1960-88; pvt. practice Malvern, Pa., 1989—. Bd. dirs. West Town Travel, West Chester, Pa. Lt. U.S. Army, 1941-46, col. USAR, 1946-76. Mem. ASCE, Nat. Soc. Profl. Engrs., Soc. Am. Mil. Engrs., Res. Officer's Assn. U.S. (nat. v.p. 1976-77), Engr. Club, Army & Navy Club. Repubican. Roman Catholic.

DAILY, LARRY Z. psychology educator; b. Fort Campbell, Ky., June 6, 1958; s. Larry Z. and Ruth E. Daily; m. Ingrid Plant, Oct. 10, 1992; children: Jonathan, Benjamin. PhD, George Mason U., Fairfax, Va., 1998. Vis. lectr. George Mason U., Fairfax, 1996-97; post doctoral rsch. assoc. Carnegie Mellon U., Pitts., 1997-2000; asst. prof. psychology Shepherd Coll., Shepherdstown, W.Va., 2000—. Mem. APA, Am. Psychol. Soc. Avocations: model railroading, railroad history. Office: Shepherd Coll White Hall Rm 213 Shepherdstown WV 25443 Office Fax: (304) 876-5193. E-mail: ldaily@shepherd.edu.

DAILY, RICHARD W. lawyer; b. Boulder, Colo., Nov. 10, 1945; s. L. Donald and Lois W.; m. Patricia A. Cronin, June 30, 1986; 1 child, Samuel. BA, Antioch Coll., 1968; JD, Harvard U., 1971. Bar: Colo. 1971, U.S. Dist. Ct. Colo. 1971, U.S. Ct. Appeals (10th cir.) 1973, Fed. Cir. 1983, U.S. Supreme Ct., 2002. Assoc. Hodges, Kerwin, Otten & Weeks, Denver, 1972-73, Davis, Graham & Stubbs, Denver, 1973-79, ptnr., 1979-91; spl. counsel Burns, Wall, Smith & Mueller, P.C., Denver, 1991-93; interim staff Gt. Outdoors Colo. Trust Fund, 1993-94; shareholder Powers Phillips, P.C., 1994-99; ptnr. Hale Hackstaff Tymkovich, LLP, Denver, 1999—. Gen. counsel Colo. Dem. Party, Denver, 1987-93; bd. dirs. Goodwill Industries Denver, 1981-87; mem. Colo. Coun. on Arts and Humanities, 1983-89, Colo. Pub. Radio, 1994-2000. Capt. USAR, 1971-77. Mem. ABA, Colo. Bar Assn., Denver Bar Assn. Office: Hale Hackstaff Friesen 1430 Wynkoop St Ste 300 Denver CO 80202 E-mail: rdaily@halehackstaff.com.

DAILY-WASHINGTON, JOYCE MARIE (JOYCE MARIE JACKSON), utilization management nurse; b. Topeka, Oct. 27, 1942; d. William L., Jr. and Juanita R. (Frazier) Jackson; m. William L. Daily, July 19, 1969 (dec.); children: Tobin L. Daily, Tracey L. Daily; m. Earl J. Washington, Aug. 23, 1986 (dec.). Student, Washburn U., 1961; diploma, William Newton Meml. Hosp. Sch. Nursing, Winfield, Kans., 1964; BS, U. St. Francis, 1999. RN Ariz. Head nurse Wesley Med. Ctr., Wichita, Kans., 1965-69; clinic head nurse Maricopa Med. Ctr., Phoenix, 1971-75, staff nurse III, clinic nurse, 1976-89; community health nurse V, Maricopa County Health Dept., Glendale, Ariz., 1989-94. Utilization mgmt. coord. Maricopa Mananged Care Sys., 1994—. Mem.: Links Inc., Consortium of Blacks for the Arts (bd. dir.). Home: 4537 W Frier Dr Glendale AZ 85301-1629 Office: Maricopa Managed Care Sys 2502 E University Dr Phoenix AZ 85034

DAIM, TUGRUL UNSAL, technology management specialist, educator; b. Istanbul, May 22, 1967; s. Turhan Hasan and Tulay Ayse D.; m. Yonca Tarman. BS, Bogazici U., Istanbul, 1989; MSc, PhD, Portland State U., 1998. Program mgr. Intel Corp., Hillsboro, Oreg., 1995—. Adj. prof. Portland State U., 1997—, Oreg. Grad. Inst. Sci. and Tech., Beaverton, 1999—; cons. KOC Corp., Istanbul, 1992-93, Turkpetrol Corp., Istanbul, 1993-96. Contbr. articles to profl. jours., chpts. to books. Pres. Turkish Am. Students Cultural Assn., Portland, 1993-95, Suadiye LEO Club, Istanbul, 1989. Mem. IEEE, Am. Soc. Engring. Mgmt., Nat. Geographic Soc., Internat. Assn. MGmt. Tech., Product Devel. Mgmt. Assn., Inst. Ops. Rsch. and Mgmt. Sci., Portland Downtown Lions Club (dir. 1995-96), Omega Rho (pres. Portland State U. chpt. 1995-97), Sigma Xi, Tau Beta Pi. Avocations: european comics, soccer, tennis, gourmet cooking. Office: Intel Corp JF1-231 25th Ave Hillsboro OR 97124 Home: 16125 SW Kessler Tigard OR 97224 Fax: 503-725-4667. E-mail: tugrul@emp.pdx.edu., tugrul.u.daim@intel.com.

DAIN, PHYLLIS, retired library educator, historian; b. N.Y.C., Nov. 29, 1929; d. Jacob Louis and Bessie Segal; m. Norman Dain, Mar. 10, 1950; 1 child, Bruce Russell. BA, Bklyn. Coll., 1950; MS, Columbia U., 1953, MA, 1957, DLS, 1966. From cataloger to chief med. cataloging Columbia U., N.Y.C., 1953-60; from lectr. to prof. libr. svc. Columbia U. Sch. Libr. Svc., N.Y.C., 1961-95, prof. emerita, 1995—. Author: The New York Public Library: A History of Its Founding and Early Years, 1972; The New York Public Library: A Universe of Knowledge, 2000; co-author: Civic Space/Cyberspace: The American Public Library in the Information Age, 1999; co-editor: Libraries and Scholarly Communication in the United States, 1990; co-editor issues Biblion, Library Trends; mem. editl. bd. Libr. & Culture, 1976—; contbr. articles to profl. jours. Officer, bd. trustees Leonia (N.J.) Pub. Libr., 1976—, Flat Rock Brook Nature Assn., 1997—. Rsch. grantee NEH, 1973-75; Coun. Libr. Resources fellow, 1973-74; named Outstanding Vol. of Yr., Bergen County, N.J., 1998. Mem. ALA, Phi Beta Kappa, Beta Phi Mu. Jewish. E-mail: ndain@andromeda.rutgers.edu.

DAINES, RICHARD, health services executive; b. 1950; MD, Cornell U. Sch. Medicine. Cert. Am. Bd. Internal Medicine, Am. Bd. Internal Medicine, Critical Care. Various positions St. Barnabas Med. Ctr., Bronx, NY; med. dir. and sr. v.p. med. affairs St. Luke's-Roosevelt Hosp. Ctr., N.Y.C., 2000—02, pres. and CEO, 2002—. Office: Roosevelt Hosp 1000 Tenth Ave Ste 1a-15 New York NY 10019 Address: St Lukes Hosp 1111 Amsterdam Ave New York NY 10025

DAISLEY, WILLIAM PRESCOTT, lawyer; b. Washington, Aug. 11, 1935; s. Gordon Walford and Augusta Greenleaf (Prescott) D.; m. Linda L. Thelin, Nov. 3, 1962; children: William Prescott Jr., Susan DeLeon. BA, Randolph Macon Coll., 1959; LL.B., George Washington U., 1962. Bar: D.C. 1962, Md. 1968, U.S. Supreme Ct. 1978. Law clk. firm King & Nordlinger, Washington, 1960-62, assoc., 1963-69, ptnr., 1969-90; prin. McChesney, Duncan & Dale, Washington, 1991-93; pres., chief exec. officer, chmn. of bd. William P. Daisley, Esq., P.C., Bethesda, Md., 1993—2003; chief exec. officer, chmn. of bd. Daisley Fin. Svc., 2003. Mem. Montgomery County (Md.) Juvenile Ct. Com., 1970-73; guest lectr. law George Washington U., 1972-76, 79; bd. dir., trustee McLeod, Strasbaugh Scholarship Fund, 1984-99; bd. dir. Citizens Bank Washington (formerly McLachlen Nat. Bank), 1982-97, chmn. audit com., 1992-94; mem. audit com. Citizens Bank of Md., 1994-97. Trustee St. Andrew's Episc. Sch., Bethesda, Md., 1985-87. Mem. Md., Am., Montgomery County, DC bar assn., 1962-2003; Phi Delta Theta, Phi Delta Phi. Clubs: Columbia Country (bd. gov. 1983-86). Republican. Episcopalian. Home and Office: 18304 Brewer House Rd Rockville MD 20852 *Success, though rarely achieved with utter perfection, is a goal not to be eschewed, but rather one sought with diligent preparation. Those who achieve a fair modicum of success are often called "lucky". The lucky people I have known have one quality in common— they are invariably the best prepared.*

DAITZ, RONALD FREDERICK, lawyer; b. N.Y.C., Sept. 1, 1940; s. Abraham and Anne (Birnbaum) D.; m. Linda Fay Rosenberg, Aug. 2, 1964; children: Paul Bennett, Carlie Spencer. AB, Amherst Coll., 1961; LLB, Harvard U., 1964. Bar: N.Y. 1966, Colo. 1964, U.S. Dist. Ct. Colo. 1964, U.S. Ct. Appeals (10th cir.) 1964, U.S. Dist. Ct. (so. dist.) N.Y. 1979. Assoc. Henry & Adams, Denver, 1964-65; from assoc. to ptnr. Weil, Gotshal & Manges LLP, N.Y.C., 1965—. Mem. ABA (fed. regulation of securities com., bus. law sect. 1979—), Am. Coll. Comml. Fin. Lawers, N.Y. State Bar Assn. (mem. com. securities regulation, bus. law sect. 1984—, chmn. 1990-93, sec. bus. law sect. 1994-95, 2d vice-chair and fiscal officer 1995-96, mem. exec. com. 1991-2001, 1st vice chair 1996-97, chair 1997-98), Assn. Bar City N.Y. (com. corp. law 1975-77, 87-88, 95-97). Office: Weil Gotshal & Manges LLP 767 5th Ave Fl Concl New York NY 10153-0119

DAJANI, ESAM ZAPHER, pharmacologist; b. Jaffa, Palestine, May 30, 1940; arrived in U.S., 1958; s. Zapher Rageb and Mamdouha Dajani; m. Najwa Said Beidas, July 16, 1964; children: Mona, Zapher, Noura. BS in Pharmacy, U. Mo., 1963; MS in Pharmacology and Med. Chemistry, Auburn U., 1966; PhD in Pharmacology, Purdue U., 1969. Sr. pharmacologist Rohm and Hass Co., Spring House, Pa., 1968-72; sr. rsch. investigator G.D. Searle and Co., Chgo., 1972-74, group leader, 1974-80, chmn. G.I. diseases, 1974-80, sect. head, 1980, asst. dir., 1980-82, assoc. dir., 1982-85, dir. Cytotec sci. and med. affairs, 1985-87, dir. clin. rsch., 1987-93; founder, pres. Internat. Drug Devel. Cons. Corp.-IDDC, Long Grove, Ill., 1993—. Editl. adv. bd. Drug Devel. Rsch., Dallas, 1983—93, Jour. Assn. Acad. Minority Physicians, Bklyn., 1992—, Jour. Physiology and Pharmacology, Krakow, Poland, 1993—; adj. prof. medicine UCLA, 1984—95, Loyola U., Chgo., 1995—; adj. prof. pharmacology Chgo. Med. Sch., 1983—90; sci. adv. bd. Atlantic Pharm., Inc., C. V. Therapeutics, Inc.; presenter in field. Author (with others): Prostaglandins and GI Mucosa, 1987, Pharmacology of Misoprostol, 1989, Prostaglandins and Esophagus, 1991, Pharmaceutical Industry Perspective, 1991, Prevention and Treatment of Ulcers induced by NSAIDS, 1995, EGF Prevents Esophogeal Ulcers Induced by Sclerotherapy, 1995, Drug Induced Ulcers, 1998, Gastrointestinal Toxicity of Over the Counter Analgesics, 1998, Idiopathic Esophageal Ulceration in HIV Patients, 1998, Gastroesophageal Reflux Disease: Pathophysiology and Pharmacology, 2000; editor: Gastrointestinal Cytoprotection, 1987; contbr. articles to profl. jours.; assoc. editor: Med. Sci. Monitor, 2003. Mem. Arab-Am. Anti-Discrimination Com., Washington, 1972. Named Disting. Alumnus, Purdue U., 1991; recipient Edward M. Queeny award, Monsanto Corp., 1991. Fellow: Am. Coll. Gastroenterology; mem.: Chgo. Biotech Network (founder, bd. dirs.), N.Y. Acad. Scis., Assn. Acad. Minority Physicians (councillor), European Soc. Gastroenterology and Endoscopy, Am. Pharm. Assn., Drug Info. Assn., Soc. Exptl. Biology and Medicine, Gastroenterology Rsch. Group, Am. Gastroent. Assn., Am. Soc. Pharmacology and Exptl. Therapeutics, Arab-Am. Univ. Grads., Phi Kappa Phi, Rho Chi. Achievements include patents in field; co-discovery and development of Cytotec, the first commercial prostaglandin anti-ulcer drug; directed pre-clinical and clinical research at multinational pharmaceutical companies; considerable expertise in worldwide drug development and pharmacological consulting services. Office: IDDC Corp 1549 RFD Long Grove IL 60047-9532 E-mail: esamd@aol.com.

DAJANI, JARIR SUBHI, civil engineer, consultant; b. Jerusalem, Apr. 5, 1940; s. Subhi T. and Lisa (Stori) D.; m. Rihab Dajani, Aug. 23, 1965; children: Jumana, Subhi, Dina. B in Civil Engring., Am. U. Beirut, 1961; MS, Stanford U., 1966; PhD, Northwestern U., 1971. Project engr. Assoc. Consulting Engrs., Lebanon, Saudi Arabia, 1961-65; assoc. prof. Civil Engring. and Policy Scis. Duke U., Durham, NC, 1971—76; assoc. prof. Civil Engring. Stanford (Calif.) U., Calif., 1976-82; cons. Amman, Jordan, 1980-82; adv. Abu Dhabi Fund For Devel., 1982—. Cons. U.S. Agy. for Int. Devel., 1976-82, World Bank, Washington, 1979. Office: Abu Dhabi Fund For Devel PO Box 814 Abu Dhabi United Arab Emirates

DAJANI, VIRGINIA, arts association administrator; Exec. dir. Am. Acad. Arts and Letters, N.Y.C., 1990—. Office: Am Acad Arts and Letters 633 W 155th St New York NY 10032-7501

DAJNOWICZ, JAN, software and hardware designer, researcher; BSc in Electronics and Telecomm., Silesian Tech. U., Gliwice, Poland, 1995. Engr. Welding Inst., Gliwice, 1982-92, group leader, 1992-95, head computer sci. dept., 1995-98; programmer JLA, Park Ridge, N.J., 1998-2001; I/T specialist IBM-Corp., Armonk, N.Y., 2001—. Cons./programmer AVREX, Gliwice, 1990-93, Technologia, Gliwice, 1993-95, Gambit, Gliwice, 1995-98, IBM-Armonk, 1998—. Inventor in field; contbr. chpt. to book, articles to profl. jours. Recipient Silver medals, Eureka, Brussels, 1995, 96, 97, award of gt. invention competition Ministry Environ. Protection Natural and Forest, Warsaw, 1997. Mem.: N.Y. Acad. Scis., NY Acad. Scis., Am. Assn. Artificial Intelligence. Avocations: Karate, japanese and chinese cultures. Home: 256 Davey St Apt C Bloomfield NJ 07003-6176 Office: IBM North Castle Dr Armonk NY 10504 E-mail: jdajnowi@sdf.lonestar.org., jandajn@us.ibm.com.

DAKAI, STEVEN HENRY, alcohol/drug abuse services professional; b. Wausau, Wis., Aug. 19, 1952; s. Henry George and Carol Ruth Dakai; m. Brenda Joyce Dakai, June 2, 1984; children: Amanda J., Julia E., Rebecca R. BS in Sociology, Ashington U., 2000; doctorate in addictive disorders, Brening Inst., 2003. Cert. chem. dependency counselor, relapse counselor, bd. cert. interventionist, grief recovery specialist. Contractor, Phoenix, 1970—85; adult trainer State of Ariz., Phoenix, 1985—96; behavioral tech. Devereaux, Phoenix,

1996—98; practicum Salvation Army, Phoenix, 1997—98; counselor Maniilaq Assoc., Kotzebue, Alaska, 1998—. Author: (book) Sand Paintings, 2001, Looking Out My Backdoor, 2001. Scoutmaster Boy Scouts Am., Phoenix, 1970—82; pres. PTA, Phoenix, 1985—86; trustee Christ Ch., Phoenix, 1984—86, facilitator 12 steps, 1987—89. Named Wildlife Educator of the Yr., Wildlife Fedn., 1992. Mem.: Alaska Chem. Dependency Counselors Assn., Am. Coun. Ethics, Grief Recovery Inst., Nat. Assn. Drug Abuse Counselors. Republican. Lutheran. Home: PO Box 836 Kotzebue AK 99752 Office: Maniilaq Assoc PO Box 256 Kotzebue AK 99752

DAKE, MARCIA ALLENE, retired nursing educator, university dean; b. Bemus Point, N.Y., May 22, 1923; d. Earl B. and Bernice DeLeo (Haskin) D. Diploma, Crouse Irving Hosp., 1944; BS, Syracuse U., 1951; MA, Columbia U., 1955, EdD, 1958. RN. Sch. nurse tchr. various locations, 1946-48; chmn. health dept. SUNY, Oneonta, 1982-56; dean coll. nursing U. Ky., Lexington, 1958-72; dir. dept. nursing edn. Am. Nurses Assn., Kansas City, 1972-74; project dir. program devel. nursing ARC, Washington, 1975-79; dir. nursing edn. James Madison U. Coll. Nursing, 1981-88; prof. dean Coll. Nursing, 1981-88; ret., 1988. Mem. Ky. Bd. Nursing Edn. Nurse Registration, 1969-72, pres., 1970-72; pres. Va. Coun. Deans of Baccalaureate Nursing Programs, 1981-84, nurse officer Civil Def. Otsego County, N.Y., 1953-56; mem. Def. Adv. Com. on Women in Svcs., 1963-65; mem. Ky. Comprehensive Health Planning Coun., 1968-71; pres. Ky. League for Nursing, 1961-65; bd. dirs. Cmty. Ch. Coll., Sun City Ctr., Fla., 1989-92, Sun City Ctr. Guardianship Found., 1990-98; trustee United Cmty. Ch., Sun City Ctr., 1993-96, chmn. personnel com., 1994-96, fin. com., 1994-95, vice chmn. bd. trustees, 1995-96, stewardship com., 1996, mem. pastoral rels. com., 1996—, mem. ling range planning com., 1996-97, chmn. pastoral rels. com., 1998—; sec. Caloosa Women's Golf Assn., Sun City Ctr., 1991-92; treas. Greater Sun City Ctr. Disaster Coun., 1992-94; mem., vice chmn. resident adv. com. Greenspring Village, Springfield, Va., 1999-2000, corr. sec. resident adv. com., 2001. 1st lt. U.S. Army Nurse Corps, 1945-46. Fellow Nat. League Nursing; mem. ANA, Va. Nurses Assn. (pres. dist. 9 1983-85), Va. Soc. Profl. Nurses (treas. 1983-88), Va. Assn. Colls. of Nursing (sec. 1980-82, pres. 1982-85), Alliance of Nursing Orgns. (chmn. Va. 1985-88), LWV, Delta Kappa Gamma, Kappa Delta Pi, Pu Lambda Theta. Address: PV 222 7442 Spring Village Dr Springfield VA 22150-4444

DAKIN, KARL JONATHAN, new product developer; b. Sugar Creek Twp., Kans., June 2, 1954; s. John R. and Vera (Stockabrand) D.; m. Darla Anne Click, Nov. 29, 1986; children: Tara Nicole, Emma Ariel. BBA, Washburn U., 1976, JD, 1979. Bar: Colo. 1980; cert. new product devel. profl. Legal counsel Educo Corp., Arvada, Colo., 1979-81; jr. ptnr. Corporon & Keene, Englewood, Colo., 1981-83; sr. assoc. Berkowitz, Berkowitz & Brady, Denver, 1985-86; pres. Karl J. Dakin & Assocs., P.C., Englewood, 1983-84, Karl J. Dakin, P.C., Englewood, 1986-95, Dakin LawTek LLC, Centennial, Colo., 1995—; exec. dir. Tekquity Ventures LLC, 1998—, Wave Dance Audio, 1998. Adj. prof. U. Denver, 1983-85, 93, 95, Met. State Coll., Denver, 1989, 90, U. Colo., 1994. Author: (seminars) Trade Secrets, 1985, Seminar Information Technology Conflict Avoidance, 2003; co-author: Computer Law, 1990, Technology Transfer, 1991; editor: IEEE Jour. on Software, 1995-97. Mem.: Nat. Assn. Comm. Sys. Engrs. (bd. dirs.), Product Devel. Mgmt. Assn. (treas. Colo. chpt.), Licensing Execs. Soc., Tech. Transfer Soc. (pres. Colo. chpt. 1992—93, nat. bd. dirs. 1994—97, v.p. fin. 1995—97, pres.-elect 1997—98).

DAKOFSKY, LADONNA JUNG, radiation oncologist, educator; b. N.Y.C., Oct. 30, 1960; d. George S. and Kay (Han) Chung. BA magna cum laude, Columbia U., N.Y.C., 1982; MD, NYU, 1987. Bd. cert. radiation oncologist. Rsch. asst. dept. neurology UCLA, 1980-81, Harvard U., Boston, 1982; tchr. chemistry St. Ann's Sch., Brooklyn Heights, N.Y., 1982-83; resident in internal medicine Lenox Hill Hosp., N.Y.C., 1987-88; resident in radiation oncology Hosp. of U. Pa., Phila., 1988-91; instr. in radiation oncology New Eng. Med. Ctr., Boston, 1991-92; attending physician Norwalk (Conn.) Hosp., 1992—. Clin. asst. prof. radiation oncology Yale U., 1994—; prin. investigator RTOG cancer rsch. Norwalk Hosp., exec. com. hosp. staff, IPA chair of quality improvement subcom.; physician adminstr. Norwalk Radiology Cons. Mem. jr. com. Boys Club N.Y.; sponsor Mus. City of N.Y.; mem. com. Vocat. Found., N.Y.C.; mem. Jr. League of Stamford-Norwalk. Marine Biol. Lab. scholar, 1981. Mem. AMA, Assn. Therapeutic Radiology and Oncology, Fairfield County Med. Assn. (Melville Magida award 1998, Best Younger Physician in Fairfield County 1998), New Eng. Cancer Soc., Met. Breast Cancer Group. Presbyterian. Avocations: writing, sailing, voice. Home: 14 Lamplight Ln Westport CT 06880-6106

DALAMBAKIS, CHRISTOPHER A. sales executive; b. Dayton, Ohio, Mar. 11, 1960; s. Angelo George and Irene D.; m. Judy Ann Schneider, July 28, 1984. BS in Biology, U. Cin., 1983. Asst. mgr. Brendamour's, Dayton, 1976-79; asst. to dir. U. Cin. Alumni Assn., 1982-83; service rep. United Technologies Otis, Chgo., Cin., 1983-84, new equipment rep. Cin., 1984-86; dist. mgr. Steelcase, Inc., Cin., 1986-97, nat. sales mgr., 1997—. Co-author: Fast Fieldbook, 1995. Mem. exec. com. bd. govs. U. Cin. McMicken Coll., 1987-93; trustee U. Cin., 1981-82; bd. dirs., chmn. com. Cin. Art Mus. Friends Assn., 1989-94; trustee Cin. Fire Mus., 1994—, mem. exec. com., 1998-2001; trustee Nat. Hemophilia Found., 1995—, Leukemia Soc., 1999—; active Nat. Trust for Hist. Preservation. 1990-94. Named One of Outstanding Young Man of Am., 1982. Mem. NRA, Metro Men's Spirit (hon. 1980—), Am. Student Assn. (nat.dir. 1981-83), Cincinnatus (hon. 1980-83), U.S. Senatorial Club, Sigma Sigma (pres. 1982-83, social chmn. 1990—). Republican. Greek Orthodox. Avocations: gardening, british cars, antique swords, skeet shooting. Home and Office: 3759 Old Heritage Ct Loveland OH 45140-5506 E-mail: cdalamba@steelcase.com.

DALAVERIS, LOUIS, ophthalmologist; b. Myteline, Greece, Sept. 15, 1953;, U.S.1955; s. James and Helen Dalaveris. BA, Columbia U., 1975; MD, Johns Hopkins U., 1979. Pvt. practice, N.Y.C., NY, 1985—. Avocations: piano, classical music. Home: 160 W 66th St New York NY 10023 Office: 30 W 60th St New York NY 10023

DALBECK, RICHARD BRUCE, insurance executive; b. Cambridge, Mass., May 17, 1929; s. Harold Lewis and Elizabeth (Kessell) D.; m. Shirley Carolyn Wells, Apr. 7, 1956; children: Barbara Jane, Elizabeth Ann, Bruce Wells. AB, Dartmouth Coll., 1952, MBA, 1953. With GE, Lynn, Mass., Lynchburg, Va., 1956-62, A.T. Kearney & Co., Inc., Chgo. and N.Y.C., 1962-69; from v.p. to first sr. v.p. Union Mut. Life Ins. Co., Portland, Maine, 1969-84; first sr. v.p. Unionmutual Life Ins. Co., Portland, 1984-86; exec. v.p. Unum Corp., Portland, Maine, 1987-91. Bd. dirs, 1st Unum Life Ins. Co., N.Y.C., 1972-91, Unuim Life Ins. Co. of Am., Portland, Maine, 1988-91; commr. Maine Health Care Fin. Commn., 1991-96; co-chmn. Maine Blue Ribbon Commn. on Workers Compensation, 1992; councilor Town of Cape Elizabeth, Maine, 1992-95; trustee Maine Mcpl. Assn. Property and Casualty Pool, 1995-98. Trustee Camp Bishopswood, 1975-96, Masterton Found. for Tech. Edn., 1988-93, Maine Maritime Mus., 1991—, Camp O-At-Ka, 1996-2002, Sweetser, 1996—, treas., 1997—; trustee Park Danforth Home for Aged, Portland, 1981-91, pres., 1988-90; bd. dirs. United Way Greater Portland, 1980-83, campaign chmn., 1985; former warden St. Albans Episc. Ch.; formerly active Episcopal Diocese of Maine, lic. chalice bearer. Lt. Supply Corps, USNR, 1953-56. Mem. Greater Portland C. of C. (bd. dirs., exec. com., 1985-92, vice chmn. 1988-90, chmn. 1990-92), Phi Beta Kappa. Episcopalian (lic. lay reader). Home: 17 Spoondrift Ln Cape Elizabeth ME 04107-2934 Office: 17 Spoondrift Ln Cape Elizabeth ME 04107-2934

DALBERG, ANABELLE HANSON, church organist, piano and organ teacher; b. Oshkosh, Wis., June 15, 1927; d. Clarence Julius and Anna (Nelson) Hanson; m. Leonard Edwin Dalberg, Sept. 9, 1950; children: Denise, Lana, Ben, Janelle. Grad., Luth. Bible Inst., Mpls., 1947; student, Augsburg Coll., Mpls., 1948-50; BS in Elem. Edn., U. Minn., 1951; organ studies with, Gordon Keddington; studies with, Jay Colyar; pvt. organ studies with, James Welch. Lic. tchr., Minn. Children's camp tchr. Zion Soc., St. Paul, 1947-48; grade 2 tchr. Oakwood Pub. Sch., Columbia Heights, Minn., 1951-53; asst. dir. Montessori Sch., Concord, Calif., 1972-76; tchr. Released Time Christian Edn., Orange, 1976-84; organist, choir dir. Reformation Luth. Ch., Westminster, Calif., 1977-84; organist various chs., Solvang, Calif., 1985—, Santa Ynez Valley Presbyn. Ch., Solvang, Calif., 1989—. Developer children's choir schs. in Ogden, Concord and Solvang, including basic music tng., hymn study, crafts, devotional material, and original curriculum; instr. piano and organ, 1984—. Numerous performances, as soloist and accompanist, at various organ recitals, choir concerts, weddings, funerals, style shows, Solvang, 1984—. Vol. pianist, organist, children's choir dir. Faith Luth. Ch., Caldwell, Idaho, Elim Luth. Ch., Ogden, Utah, and Good Shepherd Luth Ch., Concord, 1958-75; peace activist various orgns., 1979—; activist supporting people of El Salvador, 1987—; participant in polio immunization in India, Rotary, 2000. Mem. Am. Guild Organists, Women of the Evang. Luth. Ch. in Am. (local and synod bd. mem., chmn. 1980-87, local pres. 1995-2002), Santa Ynez Valley Women's Club (club pianist). Democrat. Lutheran. Avocations: world travel, national parks.

DALBO, JOANNE, social worker, writing teacher, secondary educator, poet; b. Poughkeepsie, N.Y., Aug. 23, 1952; d. Joseph and Salina (Francese) Nardone: m. Timothy J. Dalbo, Aug. 29, 1970 (div.); children: Rosanne, Amie. AA, Dutchess C.C., Poughkeepsie, 1987; BA, SUNY, New Paltz, 1990, MA, 1997. Teaching asst. Poughkeepsie Mid. Sch., 1982-86; edn. coord. YWCA Battered Women's Svcs., Dutchess County, N.Y., 1986-88; dir. YMCA Battered Women's Svcs., Dutchess County, N.Y., 1988-91; rsch. asst. Dutchess County Dept. Mental Hygiene, Poughkeepsie, 1991; family specialist Mental Health Assn., Kingston, NY, 1991—2001; tchr. English Arlington H.S., Lagrangeville, NY, 2001—03; family support coord. Mental Health Assn., Kingston, 2003—. Tchr. writing SUNY, New Paltz. Contbr. poetry to mags. Treas., bd. dirs. Dutchess County Coalition Against Domestic Violence, Poughkeepsie, 1988-91; com. mem. Children at Risk, Poughkeepsie, 1986-88; mem. citizen's adv. com. domestic violence Dutchess County Legislature, Poughkeepsie, 1989-91. Avocations: writing, reading, competitive running, weight lifting. Office: Mental Health Assn Tuytenbridge Rd Kingston NY E-mail: jdalbo@aol.com.

DAL COL, RICHARD HERBERT, cardiothoracic surgeon; b. Amityville, N.Y., May 18, 1956; s. Rino Angelo and Joan Dal Col; m. Kathleen Ciancetta Dal Col, Aug. 24, 1985; children: Devan, Alexis, Brendan. BS, Le Moyne Coll., 1978; MD, Albany (N.Y.) Med. Coll., 1982. Diplomate Am. Bd. Surgery, 1990, cert. Am. Bd. Thoracic Surgery, 1992. Internship Albany Med. Ctr. Hosp., 1982—83, residency, 1983—87, fellowship in cardiothoracic surgery, 1987—90; cardiothoracic surgeon Albany (N.Y.) Cardiothoracic Surgeons, 1990—. Fellow: ACS; mem.: Soc. Thoracic Surgeons. Avocations: fishing, skiing. Home: 28 East Ridge Rd Loudonville NY 12211 Office: Albany Cardiothoracic Surgeons 319 S Manning Blvd Ste 301 Albany NY 12208

DALE, BEVERLY A. biochemist, researcher; b. Detroit, Oct. 19, 1942; d. Paul H. and Elsie May Goodell; m. Philip S. Dale (div.); children: Jonathan, Jessica; m. Fred W. Crunk. BS, U. Mich., 1964, PhD, 1968. Rschr. U. Wash., Seattle, 1968—70, rsch. asst. prof., 1971—78, rsch. assoc. prof., 1978—85, rsch. prof., 1985—89, prof. oral biology, 1989—, sci. dir. Comprehensive Ctr. Oral Health Rsch., 1999—. Sci. adv. bd. Thetagen Inc., Seattle, 1998—2000, Iris Genomic Tech., 2001—. Mem. editl. bd.: Jour. Biol. Chemistry, 1999—2001, Jour. Dental Rsch., 1999—2003. Recipient Merit award, NIH, 1988—98; fellow, NSF, 1968—70. Mem.: AAAS, Am. Soc. Cell Biology, Am. Assn. Dental Rsch. Avocations: music, horseback riding, gardening. Office: Univ Wash Dept Oral Biology Box 357132 Seattle WA 98195

DALE, DAVID C. physician, medical educator; b. Knoxville, Tenn., Sept. 19, 1940; s. John Irvin and Cecil (Chandler) D.; m. Rose Marie Wilson, June 22, 1963 BS magna cum laude, Carson-Newman Coll., 1962; MD cum laude, Harvard U., 1966. Intern and resident Mass. Gen. Hosp., 1966-68; resident U. Wash. Hosp., Seattle, 1971-72; clin. assoc. NIH, 1968-71; prof., assoc. chmn. dept. medicine U. Wash., Seattle, 1976-82, dean Sch. of Medicine, 1982-86. Contbr. numerous articles to profl. jours. Served to comdr. USPHS, 1968-70, 72-74 Mem. Am. Soc. Hematology, Assn. Am. Physicians, Am. Soc. for Clin. Investigation, ACP Avocations: woodworking, gardening, backpacking, sports. Office: U Wash Sch Medicine RG-22 PO Box 356422 Seattle WA 98195-6422 E-mail: dcdale@u.washington.edu.

DALE, DEBORAH ANN, library technician, poet; b. Puyallup, Wash., Apr. 2, 1962; d. Gleason Ripley and Elizabeth Ann Dale. M in LIbr. Info. Sci., U. Wash., 2001. William E. Henry scholar, U. Wash., 2000. Achievements include research in poetry research in public libraries; digital reference. Home: 5151 E Lakeside Dr Langley WA 98260 Office: Everett Curriculum Resource Ctr City Univ Libr 1000 SE Everett Mall Way Ste 101 Everett WA 98208 Personal E-mail: ddale@cityu.edu. E-mail: daleda@u.washington.edu.

DALE, ERWIN RANDOLPH, lawyer, author; b. Herrin, Ill., July 30, 1915; s. Henry and Lena Bell (Campbell) D.; m. Charline Vincent, Aug. 27, 1955; children: Allyson Ann (Mrs. Earl A. Samson III), Kristan Charline (Mrs. Victor L. Zimmermann). BA, U. Tex., El Paso, 1937; JD, U. Tex., 1943. Bar: Tex. 1943, D.C. 1953, Mich. 1956, N.Y. 1960. Atty. IRS, 1943-56, chief reorgn. and dividend br., 1954-56; legal staff Gen. Motors Corp., 1956-57; ptnr. firm Chapman, Walsh & O'Connell, N.Y.C. and Washington, 1957-59, Hawkins, Delafield & Wood, N.Y.C., 1959-84; of counsel Hutchison, Price, Boyle & Brooks, Dallas, 1985-86, Jenkens, Hutchison & Gilchrist, Dallas, 1986, Hutchison, Boyle, Brooks & Dansfield, Dallas, 1986-87. Lectr. tax matters; dir. Md. Electronics Mfg. Corp., 1948-58; dir., treas. The Renaissance Corp., 1968-72; dir., asst. treas. Shancom Reconstrn. Corp., 1968-72, Newhaven Corp., 1968-72 Author numerous articles on fed. tax matters; bd. editors: Tex. Law Rev., 1941-42, 42-43. Mem. ABA (chmn. com. consol. returns sect. taxation 1959-60), Tex. Bar Assn., Mich. Bar Assn., N.Y. State Bar Assn. (chmn. corp. tax com. tax sect. 1967-68, mem. exec. com. 1968-70), Tax Inst. Am. (bd. dirs. 1967-69, treas. 1966), Assn. of Bar of City of N.Y., Nat. Tax Assn., Nat. Assn. Bond Lawyers, Am. Coll. Tax Counsel, Ex-Students Assn. U. Tex., Ex-Students Assn. U. Tex., El Paso, Bronxville Field Club (N.Y.), Masons. Home: 10 Holly Ln Darien CT 06820-3303 Fax: 203-662-9386. E-mail: erdale@aol.com.

DALE, JOHN SORENSEN, investment company executive, portfolio manager; b. Mpls., Sept. 30, 1945; s. John Sorensen and Ruth Elaine (Bergstrom) D.; m. Cheryl Lee Woolley, June 19, 1965; children: John, Christopher. BA in Mktg. and Humanities, U. Minn., 1968. CFA. Securities analyst, portfolio mgr. Norwest Corp., Mpls., 1968-78, v.p., sr. trust investment strategist, 1978-84, sr. v.p., mgr. equity advisors, 1984-87; sr. v.p., sr. portfolio mgr. Peregrine Capital Mgmt., Mpls., 1987—. Fellow Inst. Chartered Fin. Analysts; mem. Assn. Investment Mgmt. and Rsch., Twin Cities Soc., Security Analysts, Internat. Soc. Fin. Analysts. Avocations: travel, fishing, hunting. Office: Peregrine Capital Mgmt LaSalle Plz Ste 1850 8th and LaSalle Minneapolis MN 55402-2018

DALE, JUDY RIES, religious organization administrator, consultant; b. Memphis, Dec. 13, 1944; d. James Lorigan and Julia Marie (Schwinn) Ries; m. Eddie Melvin Ashmore, July 12, 1969 (div. Dec. 1983). BA, Rhodes Coll., 1966; M in Religious Edn., Grad. Specialist in Religious Edn., So. Bapt. Theol. Sem., 1969. Cert. tchr. educable mentally handicapped, secondary English, adminstrn. and supervision in spl. edn. EMH tchr., curriculum writer, tchr. trainer Jefferson County Bd. Edn., Louisville, 1969-88, cdnl. cons., 1988-90; dist. coord. Gt. Lakes dist. Universal Fellowship Met. Cmty. Chs., Louisville, 1990—2002. Lectr. Jefferson C.C., Louisville, 1987-93, U. Louisville, 1976-77, 87-90; mem. faculty Samaritan Inst. for Religious Studies, 1992-98; mem. program adv. com. Internat. Conf. Spl. Edn., Beijing, 1987-88. Editor, writer: (handbook) Handbook for Beginning Teachers, 1989, A Manual of Instructional Strategies, 1985; author: (kit) Math Activities Cards, 1978. Bd. sec. Com. of Ten, Inc., Louisville, 1987-91; v.p. GLUE, 1988-92, pres., 1992-94; mem. Universal Fellowship of Met. Cmty. Chs., programs and budget divsn., 1990-97, mem. gen. coun., 1990-2002, mem. core team, 1993-2000, chair, 1997-2000, active Women's Secretariat steering com., 1991-95, fin. team, 2000—, bd. adminstrn., 2003—, chmn. risk mgmt. team, 2003—; dist. coord. Gt. Lakes Dist. (parliamentarian 1987-89); mem. membership com. Cmty. Health Trust, 1991-94; trustee Samaritan Inst. Religious Studies, 1992-98, chair acad. affairs com., 1996-97. Recipient Honorable Order of Ky. Cols., 1976, MCC Disting. Lay Leadership award, 1999; named Outstanding Elem. Tchr. Am., 1975. Mem. AAUW, NOW, ACLU, Nat. Gay & Lesbian Task Force, Parents, Family & Friends of Lesbians & Gays, Nat. Ctr. for Lesbian Rights, Lambda Legal Def. & Edn. Fund, Gay & Lesbian Assn. Anti-Defamation, Coun. Exceptional Children (keynote speaker 1984-88, internat. pres. 1986-87, exec. com. 1984-88, bd. govs. 1981-88), Ky. Coun. Exceptional Children (bd. dirs. 1976-90, Mem. of Yr. 1987), Internat. Platform Assn., Women's Alliance, Phi Delta Kappa. Democrat. Avocations: people, church work, reading, handwork. Home and Office: 1300 Ambridge Dr Louisville KY 40207-2410

DALE, KENNETH RAY, computer executive; b. Garnett, Kans., Aug. 22, 1948; s. Earnest Kenneth and Dorothy Mae (Root) D.; m. Sheila Rae Talbott, June 23, 1979; children: Anne Marie Camp, Carolee Talbott. BA, Washburn U., 1978. Programmer trainee Kans. Power and Light Co., Topeka, 1978-79, programmer, 1979-80, sr. programmer, 1980-81, programmer, analyst, 1981-82, sr. programmer, analyst, 1982-83, systems analyst, 1983-85; programmer, analyst Vol. Shoe Corp., Topeka, 1985-86, sr. programmer, analyst, 1986-87, computer ops. shift mgr., 1987-88, lead programmer, analyst, 1988-91; pvt. practice cons. Overbrook, Kans., 1991-92; staff analyst Profl. Resources Inc., Shawnee Mission, Kans., 1992; tech. svcs. cons. CAP Gemini Am, Overland Park, Kans., 1992-97; cons. Maximgroup Info. Systems Cons., Overland Park, Kans., 1997-2001; applications analyst Hallmark Cards Inc., Kansas City, 2001—. With USN, 1967-70. Mem. Am. Mgmt. Assn., Data Processing Mgmt. Assn., Masons. Democrat. Home: 605 Walnut Overbrook KS 66524-9598 Personal E-mail: kdale@sftnet.org. Business E-Mail: kdale2@hallmark.com.

DALE, LEON ANDREW, economist, educator; b. Paris; m. Arlene R. Dale, Mar. 18, 1975; children: Melinda Jennifer, David Benjamin. BA, Tulane U., 1946; MA, U. Wis., 1947, PhD, 1949. Grad. asst. in econs. U. Wis., 1946-48; Asst. prof. labor econs. U. Fla., 1949-50; internat. economist AFL, Paris, 1950-53; AFL rep. at nat. labor convs. Greece, 1951, 1951, 1950-53; cons. U.S. Govt., 1954-56; internat. economist U.S. Dept. Labor, Washington, 1956-59; prof., chmn. dept. mgmt. and indsl. rels., dir. internat. ctr., coord. courses for fgn. students U. Bridgeport, Conn., 1960-69; chief union task force Coll. Bus. Admstrn. Calif. State Poly. U., Pomona, 1980, coord. internat. activities Sch. Bus. Adminstrn., 1969-77, prof. mgmt. and human resources, 1969-91, prof. emeritus, 1991—, also, acting chmn. bus. mgmt. dept., summer 1973; chief Coll. Bus. Adminstrn. Calif. State U., Pomona, 1981. Lectr. Internat. Conf. Tree Trade Unions Summer Sch., Wörgl, Austria, 1951; lectr. on Am. labor UN, Stockholm, 1952; lectr. U. Wis., Milw., 1960; asst. rschr., asst. moderator Labor Mgmt. Roundtable, 1961; participant televised ednl. programs Sta. WNHC-TV, New Haven, Conn., 1963; seminar leader Mgmt. Ctr, Cambridge, 1962-63, Rey area Police Dept.; Columbia U., 1966, 67, Bernard Baruch Sch. Bus. and Pub. Adminstrn., 1966-69; corrd. adminstrv. ops. and pub. rels. Rey Area Police Pers., 1966; instr. Perkins-Elmer Corp., Wilton, Conn., 1966; cons., arbitrator, fact-finder State of Conn., 1964-69; Am. del., speaker 3d Internat. Symposium on Small Bus., Washington, 1976, 4th Internat. Symposium on Small Bus., Seoul, Korea, 1977, 5th Internat. Symposium on Small Bus., Anaheim, Calif., 1978, 6th Internat. Symposium on Small Bus., Berlin, 1979; also mem. U.S. steering com. Internat. Symposium on Small Bus.; chief union task force Coll. Bus. Adminstrn. Calif. State Poly. U., Pomona, 1980; sr. cons. Am. Grad. U., Covina, Calif., 1981-82; adj. prof. econs. Nat. U., San Diego, 1981-90, Pepperdine U., 1986; discussion leader Calif. Inst. Tech. Internat. Conf. on Combining Best of Japanese and U.S. Mgmt., Anaheim, 1981; lectr. on indsl. rels. to execs. Miller Brewing Co., Irwindale, Calif., 1983; cons. Agy. Internat. Devel., N'Djamena, Republic of Chad, 1987; cons. to Minister for Planning, Republic of Chad; cons., instr. behavior courses U. Chad.; instr. mgmt. French-speaking African Students internat. ctr. Calif. State Poly. U., 1988; participant Ea. Europe and the West: Implication for Africa, So. Calif. Consortium on Internat. Studies conf., Pomona, 1990; lectr. confs. on leadership in French, Dakar, Senegal, 1990; seminar tchr. on leadership and mgmt. Citibank of N.Y., Dakar, Senegal, 1991; presenter, speaker numerous seminars in field; adj. prof. mgmt. Chapman U., Orange, Calif., 1994; adj. prof. econs. Saddleback Coll., Mission Viejo, Calif., 1996, Irvine (Calif.) Valley Coll., 1997, prof. French and econs., 2001. Author: Marxism and French Labor, 1956, A Bibliography of French Labor, 1969; (video tape) Industrial Relations and Human Resources, 1982, Labor Relations in Crisis, 1989; originator Liberté (first French newspaper published in liberated France, 1944); French news announcer to occupied France, BBC London; contbr. articles to profl. jours. Served with U.S. Army, 1942-45. Recipient U. Bridgeport Faculty rsch. grantee, 1962; U. Wis. fellow, 1949; named one of Outstanding Educators of Am., 1972, 73. Mem. Am. Arbitration Assn. (nat. labor panel 1967—), N.Y. Acad. Scis. Avocations: tennis, swimming, ancient and modern art, horticulture, numismatics, philately. Home and Office: 30 S La Senda Dr Laguna Beach CA 92651-6733

DALE, MADELINE HOUSTON MCWHINNEY, banker; b. Denver, Mar. 11, 1922; d. Leroy and Alice Barse (Houston) McWhinney; m. John Denny Dale, June 23, 1961; 1 son, Thomas Denny. BA, Smith Coll., 1943; MBA in Fin, NYU, 1947. With Fed. Res. Bank N.Y., 1943-73; pres. First Women's Bank, N.Y.C., 1974-76. Vis. lectr. NYU Grad. Sch. Bus., 1976-77; pres. Dale, Elliott & Co., Inc., N.Y.C., 1977-97; dir. Carnegie Corp. N.Y., 1974-82, vice chmn. bd., 1980-82; asst. dir. Whitney Mus. Am. Art, 1983-86; mem. adv. bd. NYU Grad. Sch. Bus. Adminstrn., 1974-85, U. Denver Grad. Sch. Bus. and Pub. Adminstrn., 1974-86; dir. Atlantic Energy Inc., 1983-93. Adv. bd. Banking Law Jour., 1973-83. Bd. dirs. Investor Responsibility Rsch. Ctr., 1975—80, Charles F. Kettering Found., 1975—93, chmn., 1987—91; mem. Pres.'s Commn. White House Fellows, 1975—77; mem. adv. com. profl. ethics N.J. Supreme Ct., 1983—98; mem. N.J. Com. on Humanities, 1988—93; trustee Retirement Sys. Fed. Res. Banks, 1955—58, Mgrs. Funds, 1983—, Inst. Internat. Edn., 1976—, treas., 1979—85, 1988—96; bd. govs. Am. Stock Exch., Inc., 1977—81; commr. N.J. Casino Control. Commn., 1980—82; trustee Monmouth Mus., 1995—, Ctrl. Jersey Vis. Nurses Assn., 1995—, Monmouth Conservatory of Music, 2001, Planned Parenthood Ctrl. Jersey, 1995—. Recipient medal Smith Coll., 1971, Alumni Achievement award N.Y. U., 1971 Mem. Am. Fin. Assn. (dir. 1955-57), Alumni Assn. NYU Grads. Bus. Adminstrn. (pres. 1957-59), Money Marketeers (pres. 1960-61), Women's Bond Club, Soc. Meml. Ctr., Phi Beta Kappa. Home: PO Box 458 Red Bank NJ 07701-0458

DALE, ROBERT GORDON, business executive; b. Toronto, Ont., Can., Nov. 1, 1920; s. Gordon McIntyre and Helen Marjorie (Cartwright) D.; m. Mary Austin Babcock, Apr. 3, 1948; children: Robert Austin, John Gordon. Ed., U. Toronto Schs., 1930-39, Trinity Coll.; student, U. Toronto, 1939 40. Cert. in bus. adminstrn., 1946. With Maple Leaf Mills, Ltd., Toronto, 1947—, plant mgr., 1957-61, gen. product mgr., 1961-65, asst. to pres., 1965-67, exec. v.p., 1967-68, chmn., pres., chief exec. officer, 1968-86, dir.; chmn. Upper Lakes Group Inc., Toronto, 1993—95; dep. chmn. Upper Lakes Group, Inc., Toronto, 1996—; pres. Pinedale Investments Inc., Toronto, 1994—. Hon. pres. Air Cadet League Can.; past chmn. Ont. Provincial Com.; trustee United Comty. Fund Greater Toronto; past chmn. bd. govs. Can. Corps Commissionaires; bd. dirs. Sunnybrook Med. Ctr.; past pres. Branch 165 Royal Can. Legion. With RCAF, 1940-45. Decorated D.F.C., Can. Forces Decoration, Disting. Service Order. Mem. Phi Kappa Pi. Clubs: Rosedale Golf, Nat, Royal Can. Mil. Inst., Empire. Conservative. Anglican. Office: Upper Lakes Group Inc 49 Jackes Ave Toronto ON Canada M4T 1E2 E-mail: daleroberg@hotmail.com.

DALE, SCOTT, Spanish educator; b. Bellflower, Calif., Nov. 2, 1969; s. Douglas and Penny D.; m. Gemma Dale, Dec. 20, 1997. BA, U. Calif., Irvine, 1991; MA, NYU, 1993; PhD, U. Pa., 1997. Asst. prof. Spanish U. N.D., Grand Forks, 1997-99, Marquette U., Milw., 1999—, resident dir. Madrid, 2003—. Dir. U. N.D., 1998-99; com. mem. Mellon Found., Milw., 2000—. Author: Novela innovadora en las "Cartas marruecas" de Cadalso, 1998; book reviewer Hispanic Rev., 1997—, Revista Canadiense de Estudios Hispanicos, 1997—, Dieciocho, 1997—. Rsch. grant Program for Cultural Cooperation, 2000; conf. fellowship Internat. Soc. for 18th Century Studies, 1998, Andrew Mellon Found., 1996-97. Mem. MLA, Soc. for Spanish and Portuguese Hist. Studies, Am. Soc. for 18th Century Studies, Mediterranean Studies Assn. Avocations: tennis, travel, foreign film, travel novels. Office: Marquette U Dept Fgn Langs Lalumiere Lang Hall 254 Milwaukee WI 53201-1881

DALE, SHIRLEY MARIE, protective services official; b. Camden, Ala., Aug. 22, 1959; children: Velda Venessa, Teresa Almeta. Diploma, William J. Jones, 1971—77; BA, U. of Detroit Mercy, 1990—94. Clk. typist, data entry, sec. Designers, Detroit, 1981; switchboard operator Western Temp. Svc., Detroit, 1984—86; police cpl. Wayne County Sheriff's, Detroit, 1986—; studio/porta pak workshop assoc. prodr. Barden Cablevision, 1989. Office: Wayne County Sheriff Dept 1441 St Antoine Detroit MI 48226 Home: 15467 Heyden Detroit MI 48226

DALE, WESLEY JOHN, chemistry educator; b. Milw., Aug. 8, 1921; s. Colin B. and Irma P. (Pohl) D.; m. Pattie Surine, Aug. 20, 1949; 1 dau., Claudia. BS in Chemistry with highest honors, U. Ill., 1943; PhD, U. Minn., 1949. Teaching asst. U. Minn., 1943; rsch. chemist Govt. Synthetic Rubber Rsch. Program, 1943-46; mem. faculty U. Mo. at Columbia, 1949-66, prof. chemistry, 1958-66, chmn. dept., 1961-64; asst. to dean U. Mo. at Columbia (Coll. Arts and Scis.), 1954-55; staff assoc. sci. facilities evaluation group, divsn. instl. programs NSF, 1964, sr. staff assoc. sci. devel. evaluation group, divsn. instl. programs, 1964-66; dean Sch. Grad. Studies, U. Mo. at Kansas City, 1966-72, prof. chemistry, 1966-85, univ. rsch. adminstr., 1969-72, acting provost and dean faculties, 1971, provost, 1972-79, acting chancellor, 1976-77; prof. chemistry and chmn. dept. Principia Coll., Elsah, Ill., 1985-89. Cons. long range academic planning; chmn. Midwest Conf. Grad. Study and Rsch., 1970-71 Contbr. articles to profl. jours. Bd. dirs. Sci. Pioneers, Kansas City, Mo., 1967-78, Inst. Community Studies, 1970-73; trustee Mid-Continent Regional Ednl. Lab., Kansas City, 1972-73; mem. adv. com. U.S. Army Command and Gen. Staff Coll., Fort Leavenworth, Kans., 1973; bd. dirs. Harry S. Truman Library Inst., 1977, Kansas City Mus., 1976-77, The Principle Found., 1993-99. Fellow Am. Inst. Chemists; mem. AAAS, Am. Chem. Soc., Sigma Xi, Phi Kappa Phi, Phi Eta Sigma, Phi Lambda Upsilon, Pi Mu Epsilon, Gamma Alpha, Alpha Chi Sigma.

D'ALEMBERTE, TALBOT (SANDY D'ALEMBERTE), academic administrator, lawyer; b. Tallahassee, June 1, 1933; m. Patsy Palmer; children: Gabrielle Lynn, Joshua Talbot. BA in Polit. Sci. with honors, U. South, 1955; postgrad., London Sch. Econs. and Polit. Sci., U. London, 1958-59; JD with honors, U. Fla., 1962. Bar: Fla. 1962, U.S. Ct. Appeals (5th cir.) 1962, U.S. Supreme Ct. 1970. Assoc. Steel Hector & Davis, Miami, Fla., 1962-65, ptnr., 1965-84, 89-93; prof. Fla. State U., 1984—, dean Coll. Law, 1984-89, pres., 1994—2003. Lectr. U. Miami Coll. Law, 1969-71, adj. prof., 1974-76; reader Fla. Bd. Bar Examiners, 1965-67; mem. jud. nominating commn. Fla. Supreme Ct., 1975-78; chief counsel Ho. Select Com. for Impeachment of Certain Justices, 1975; mem. Fla. Law Revision Coun., 1968-74; chmn. Fla. Constl. Revision Commn., 1977-78. Articles editor U. Fla. Law Rev. Mem. Fla. Ho. Reps., 1966-72, chmn. com. on ad valorem taxation, 1968-70, chmn. judiciary com., 1970-72, mem. various coms.; chmn. Fla. Commn. on Ethics, 1974-75; trustee Miami Dade Community Coll., 1976-84. Served with USN, 1955-58; to lt. USNR. Recipient award Fla. Acad. Trial Lawyers, 1972, 93, Fla. Patriots award Fla. Bicentennial Commn., 1976, Disting. Alumnus award U. Fla., 1977, Nelson Poynter award Fla. Civil Liberties Union, 1984, Gov.'s Emmy award Nat. Acad. TV Arts and Scis., 1985, 1st Amendment award Nat. Sigma Delta Chi/Soc. Profl. Journalists, 1986, Medal of Honor award Fla. Bar Found., 1987, Juris prudence award Anti-Defamation League of S. Fla., 1990, Fla. Acad. of Criminal Def. Lawyers Annual Justice award, 1993, Acad. of Fla. Trial Lawyers Perry Nichols award, 1993, Nat. Coun. of Jewish Women's Hannah G. Soloman award, 1996, Am. Judicature Soc. Justice award, 1996; named Outstanding First Term House Mem., 1967, Most Outstanding Mem. of House, Capital Press Corps; Rotary Found. fellowship, London Sch. Economics, 1958-59. Mem. ABA (pres. 1991-92, chmn. spl. com. on election reform 1973-76, chmn. spl. com. on resolution of minor disputes 1976-79, chmn. spl. com. on med. malpractice 1985-86, state del. from Fla. 1980-89, commn. on governance 1983-84, rules and calender com. ho. of dels. 1982-84, commn. on women in profession 1987, co-founder Ctrl. and East European Law Initiative, World Order Under Law award 1998, Robert J. Kutak award sect. legal edn. 1998), Fla. Bar Assn. (bd. govs. 1974-82), Dade County Bar Assn. (pres. young lawyers sect. 1965-66, bd. dirs.), Am. Judicature Soc. (pres. 1982-84), U. Fla. Law Ctr. Assn. (trustee 1967—), Order of Coif, Omicron Delta Kappa, Phi Beta Kappa. Office: Fla State U Coll Law 425 W Jefferson St Tallahassee FL 32306-1601 E-mail: dalember@mailer.fsu.edu.

DALEN, JAMES EUGENE, cardiologist, educator; b. Seattle, Apr. 1, 1932; s. Charles A. and Muriel E. (Joanise) Robinson. BS, Wash. State U., 1955; MA, U. Mich., 1956; MD, U. Wash., 1961; MPH, Harvard U., 1972. Intern and asst. med. resident Boston City Hosp., 1961—63; sr. resident New Eng. Med. Ctr., Boston, 1963—64; rsch. fellow in cardiology Peter Bent Brigham Hosp., Boston, 1964—67, assoc. dir. cardiovascular lab., 1967—75; instr., asst. prof., asso. prof. medicine Harvard Med. Sch., 1967—75; chmn. dept. cardiovascular medicine U. Mass. Med. Sch., 1975—77, prof., chmn. dept. medicine, 1977—88; physician-in-chief U. Mass. Hosp., 1977—88; acting chancellor U. Mass., Worcester, 1986—87; editor Archives Internal Medicine, 1987—; dean, vice provost med. affairs U. Ariz. Coll. Medicine, Tucson, 1988—95, dean, v.p. health scis., 1995—2001. Contbr. articles to profl. jours. With USN, 1951—53. Mem.: ACP, Am. Coll. Chest Physicians (pres. 1985—86), Am. Coll. Cardiology, Assn. U. Cardiologists. Home: 5305 N Via Velazquez Tucson AZ 85750-5989 Office: 1840 E River Rd Ste 207 Tucson AZ 85718 E-mail: jamesdalen@yahoo.com.

DALES, SAMUEL, microbiologist, virologist, educator; b. Warsaw, Aug. 31, 1927; emigrated to Can., 1948, naturalized, 1953; s. James and Helen (Ochs) D.; m. Laura L.R.J. Fischer, Dec. 28, 1952 (dec.); children: Adam Charles, Pamela Ann. BA with honors, U. B.C., 1951, MA, 1953; PhD, U. Toronto, 1956. Postdoctoral fellow Nat. Cancer Inst. Can., 1957-60; rsch. assoc., asst. prof. Rockefeller U., N.Y.C., 1960-66; assoc. mem., mem., chief cytobiology Pub. Health Rsch. Inst. City of N.Y., Inc., 1966-76; prof. U. Western Ont., Can., 1975-93, prof. emeritus, 1993—, chmn. microbiology and immunology, 1975-80. Research prof. NYU Med. Sch., 1969-75; mem. adv. bd. spl. virus cancer program Nat. Cancer Inst., NIH, 1969-73; mem. virology study sect. NIH, 1971-75, ad hoc, 1977, 79; mem. sci. adv. bd. Banting Rsch. Found., 1978-80; mem. rev. panels virology and cancer USPHS, Med. Rsch. Coun. Can.; adj. prof. Rockefeller U., 1996—. Author: Biology of Poxviruses, 1981; mem. editl. bd. Virology, 1963—, Jour. Cell Biology, 1973-76, Intervirology, 1973-91, Virus Rsch., 1983-92, Microbial Pathogenesis, 1985—, Jour. Virology, 1989-97, Ency. Virology, 1990-95; contbr. sci. articles and revs. to profl. publs. Fellow Royal Soc. Can.; Macy Found. scholar, 1981-82; rsch. grantee USPHS; rsch. grantee Med. Rsch. Coun. Can.; rsch. grantee Multiple Sclerosis Soc. Fellow AAAS; mem. Fedn. Am. Socs. for Exptl. Biology, Harvey Soc., Am. Soc. Cell Biology, N.Y. Soc. Electron Microscopy (coun. 1968-70), Amyotrophic Lateral Sclerosis Soc. An. (sci. adv. bd.) Home: 262 Central Park W Apt 4C New York NY 10024-3512 E-mail: drssdfr@aol.com.

D'ALESANDRO, PHILIP ANTHONY, parasitologist, immunologist, retired educator; b. Bound Brook, N.J., Apr. 2, 1927; s. Philip and Antoinette Ann (Vaccaro) D'A.; m. Rosemary Natale Falzarine, Nov. 25, 1961. BSc, Rutgers U., 1952, MSc, 1954; PhD, U. Chgo., 1958. Rsch. assoc. U. Chgo., 1958-59; assoc. prof. Rockefeller U., N.Y.C., 1959-75; assoc. prof., acting head divsn. tropical medicine Columbia U., N.Y.C., 1975-92, emeritus prof., 1992—. Chmn. tropical medicine and parasitology study sect. NIH, Bethesda, Md., 1976-80. Author: (with others) Immunity to Parasitic Animals, 1970, Pathogenicity of Trypanosomes, 1979, Parasitic Protoza, Vol. 1, 1991; editor Jour. Protozoology, 1980-88; contbr. articles to profl. jours. Sgt. U.S. Army Air Corps, 1945-46. Grantee NIH, 1972-90, 79-82. Fellow AAAS; mem. Phi Beta Kappa. Avocations: antique cars, model railroading, photography.

D'ALESSANDRI, ROBERT M. dean; b. N.Y.C., June 26, 1945; m. Elaine D'Alessandri; 2 children. BA, Fordham U., 1967; MD, N.Y. Med. Coll., 1971. Diplomate Am. Bd. Internal Medicine, Am. Bd. Infectious Diseases. Intern dept. medicine Met. Hosp., N.Y.C., 1971—72; fellowship divsn. infectious diseases U. Fla., Gainesville, 1974—76, resident dept. medicine, 1976—77; instr., chief resident dept. medicine W.Va. U. Sch. Medicine, 1977—78, asst. prof. dept. medicine, 1978—81, assoc. prof. dept. medicine, 1981—84, prof. dept. medicine, 1985—, chief sect. of comprehensive medicine dept. medicine, 1979—87, assoc. dean ambulatory svcs. dept. medicine, 1987—90, dean Sch. of Medicine dept. medicine, 1989—; v.p. for health scis. W.Va. U., 1992—. Bd. dirs. Nat. Bank of W.Va., Morgantown, MountainView Regional Rehab. Hosp., W.Va. U. Rsch. Corp., Chestnut Ridge Psychiat. Hosp., W.Va. U. Hosps., W.Va. U. Med. Corp., Morgantown HealthRight Clinic, Morgantown Hospice; commentator Sta. WNPB, W.Va. Pub. Radio; host weekly Doctors on Call; weekly med. corr. Sta. WCHS-TV, Charleston, Sta. WDTV, Clarksbur, Sta. WTRF, Wheeling; elected shc. medicine rep. Univ. Faculty Senate, 1980-84; chair credentials com. W.Va. Hosps., 1984-85, med. exec. bd. chair 1985-86, chair infection control com., 1985-86, exec. com. chair 1986-87, mem. 1983-87, chair hosp. med. records com., 1986-87, chair hosps. patient care rev. com., 1986-87, chair ambulatory care bldg. com., 1987-89, chair dean's com. VA Med. Ctr., Martinsburg, 1991—, Clarksburg, 1989—; chair sch. of medicine ednl. adv. coun. W.Va. U. Health Scis. Ctr., 1989—, chair sch. of medicine exec. faculty, 1989—, chair health scis. ctr. exec. com., 1992—; coord. intro. clin. medicine dental studies, 1979-84, coord. intro. to clin. medicine, phys. diagnosis course, 1979-84; spl. lectr. Guiyang (China) Med. Coll., 1988, Hangzhou (China) Red Cross Hosp., 1988. Contbr. numerous articles to profl. jours. Bd. dirs. Monongalia Arts Ctr., Morgantown, 1989—. Mem. AMA, Am. Coll. of Physicians, Infectious Diseases Soc., Soc. for Gen. Internal Medicine, Nat. Rural Health Assn., W.Va. State Med. Assn., Monongalia County Med. Soc. Office: RC Byrd Health Scis Ctr 1150 Health Scis N PO Box 9000 Morgantown WV 26506-9000*

D'ALESSANDRO, DANIEL ANTHONY, lawyer, educator; b. Jersey City, Oct. 10, 1949; s. Donato Marino D'Alessandro and Rose Teresa (Casamassimo) Drennan; m. Beth Anne Lill, Sept. 2, 1978; children: Daniel Patrick, Eric Charles. BA, St. Peter's Coll., 1971; JD, Seton Hall U., 1974; LLM in Criminal Justice, NYU, 1981. Bar: N.J. 1975, U.S. Dist. Ct. N.J. 1975, N.Y. 1982, U.S. Supreme Ct. 1985, U.S. Dist. Ct. (so. dist.) N.Y. 1989, cert.: (ct. approved family law mediator). Law clk. to presiding judge Juvenile and Domestic Relations Ct., Hudson County, N.J., 1974-75; pub. defender City of Jersey City, 1975-76; prosecutor Town of Secaucus, NJ, 1976-77; prin. D'Alessandro & Assocs., Jersey City, 1977-82; ptnr. D'Alessandro & Tutak, Jersey City, 1982-90; pres. D'Alessandro, Tutak & Aschoff, P.C., Jersey City, 1990-92; ptnr. D'Alessandro & Aschoff, P.C., Jersey City, 1992—93; pvt. practice Jersey City, 1994—2003; ptnr. D'Alessandro & Cieckiewicz, P.C., Jersey City, 2003—. Adj. prof. Middlesex County Coll., Edison, NJ, 1981—83, St. Peter's Prep., 1981—83; arbitrator automobile arbitration program N.J. Supreme Ct., mem. ethics com. dist. VI, vice-chair fee arbitration com.; counsel Employees Retirement Sys. Jersey City, 1985—89. Vol. probation officer Hudson County Probation Dept., 1977; pro bono counsel Anthony R. Cucci Civic Assn., Jersey City, 1981—89, Battered Women's Shelter, Jersey City, 1982, Mayor's Task force for Handicapped, Jersey City, 1985—89; v.p. Jersey City Boys Club, 1991, pres., 1993—98, also trustee; baseball coach Jersey Shore Thunderbirds, N.J. AAU, 1993—2001, Mater Dei HS, 2000—02, Monmouth Monarchs Atlantic Baseball Coll. League, 2003. Named Prof. of the Yr., Secaucus Patrolmen's Benevolent Assn., 1980; recipient Disting. Svc. award, Jersey City Police Dept., 1988, cert. of Merit, N.J. Supreme Ct., Meritorious Pub. Svc. award, 1990, Outstanding Bd. Mem. award, N.J. Boys and Girls Clubs Hudson County, 1998, Cmty. Svc. award, Boys & Girls Clubs, 2003. Mem.: ABA, Hudson County Bar Assn. (treas. 1991, sec. 1992, v.p. 1994, 1995, pres.-elect 1996, pres. 1997—98, past chmn., mem. various coms., trustee, Outstanding Bd. Mem. award 1998, Cmty. Svc. award 2001, 2002), N.J. State Bar Assn. Democrat. Roman Catholic. Avocations: renovating old homes, sports, renovating scholastic athletic fields. Office: 3279 John F Kennedy Blvd Jersey City NJ 07306-3418 E-mail: dadpclaw@aol.com.

D'ALESSANDRO, DAVID FRANCIS, insurance company executive; b. Utica, N.Y., Jan. 6, 1951; s. Dominick Vincent and Rosemary (Pallaria) D'A.; children: Michael, Andrew. BA, Utica Coll. of Syracuse U., 1972. Account supr. Daniel J. Edelman Inc. Pub. Rels., 1972-74; info. programs mgr. svc. bur. Control Data Corp., 1974-77, comm. mgr. data svcs., 1977-79, gen. mgr. comml. credit, 1980-84; asst. v.p. Citibank Comm. Svcs., 1979-80; v.p. John Hancock Fin. Svcs., Boston, 1984-85, sr. v.p., 1985-88, pres. corp. sector, mem. mgt. com., 1988-91, sr. exec. v.p. retail sector, 1991—, pres., CEO, 1996, also bd. dirs. Trustee, mem. exec. com. Wang Ctr. for Performing Arts, Boston, 1989—; chmn. Harvard U. Kennedy Sch. Govt., 1990—; bd. trustees Syracuse U., 1990—, Utica (N.Y.) Coll., 1988—. Office: John Hancock Fin Svcs John Hancock Pl Boston MA 02117

D'ALESSANDRO, DIANNE MARIE, public defender; b. NYC, Apr. 20, 1952; d. Frank and Marie A. D'A.; m. John P. Foley, July 24, 1977; children: Maria, James. BA in Psychology, Upsala Coll., East Orange, NJ, 1974; JD, NY Law Sch., 1981. Bar: NJ 1981, US Dist. Ct. NJ 1981. Staff atty. Bergen City Legal Svc., Hackensack, N.J., 1981-83; sr. trial atty. Office Pub. Defender, Hackensack, 1983—. Dist. II B ethics com., Office of Atty. Ethics of the Supreme Ct. of NJ, 1992-95; bd. dir. Bergen County Legal Svc. Recipient citation from Susan Reisner, pub. advocate, for work done on State vs. Harris. Mem.: Friends of Ringwood Manor, Nat. Trust for Hist. Preservation, Nat. Assoc. Criminal Def. Lawyers. Avocations: reading, hiking, historic preservation. Office: Office of Pub Advocate/Pub Defender 60 State St Hackensack NJ 07601-5451 E-mail: dalessandro_d@opd.state.nj.us.

D'ALESSANDRO, DOMINIC, financial executive; b. Italy, Jan. 18, 1947; arrived in Can., 1954; 3 children. BSc., Loyola Coll., 1967; postgrad., McGill U., 1971. Acct. Coopers & Lybrand, 1968-75, dep. mgr. Paris office, 1970-71; asst. contr. GenStar, Ltd., 1975; from dir. fin. to gen. mgr. GenStar, Saudi Arabia, 1976-79; v.p. Materials and Constrn. Group, San Francisco, 1979-81; dep. contr. Royal Bank of Can., Toronto, 1981, v.p. and contr., 1982, sr. v.p., 1983-87, exec. v.p. fin., 1987; pres., CEO Laurentian Bank of Can., 1988, Manulife Fin., Toronto, 1994—; also bd. dirs. ManuLife Fin., Toronto. Adv. bd. Lazard Can., Ltd., Willis Inc.; past chmn. Canadian Life and Health Ins. Assn.; bd. dirs. Hudsons' Bay Co., Am. Coun. of Life Ins., Washington, TransCan. Pipe Lines. Mem. Bus. Coun. on Nat. Issues; chmn. United Way of Greater Toronto, 1998. Fellow Inst. Chartered Accts. (chartered). Office: Manulife Financial 200 Bloor St E Toronto ON Canada M4W 1E5

D'ALESSIO, DAVID WESLEY, communications educator; b. Glen Head, N.Y., May 7, 1956; s. John Joseph and Helen (Munn) D'A. BS in Comm., Rensselaer Poly. Inst., 1978, MS in Comm., 1980; PhD in Comm., Mich. State U., 1997. Chemist Schenectady Chems., Nyskayuna, N.Y., 1978-80; grad. asst. Mich. State U., East Lansing, 1980-85; instr. Albion (Mich.) Coll., 1985-86, Grand Valley State U., Allendale, Mich., 1986-88; ops. mgr. GRTV, Grand Rapids, Mich., 1989-91; adj. prof. Lansing (Mich.) C.C., 1991-93; asst. prof. comm. Richard Stockton Coll., Pomona, N.J., 1993-97, U. Conn., Stamford, 1997—. Animator (film) The Three Penny Operation, 1990 (Philo award 1991); contbr. articles to profl. jours. Ops. dir. Galloway (N.J.) TV, 1995-97. Named Bd. Mem. of Yr. Jaycees, Grand Rapids, 1990; recipient Innovation in Tchg. award AAUP, 2000. Mem. Internat. Comm. Assn. (reviewer 1995—), Nat. Comm. Assn. Avocations: reading, golf, model trains. E-mail: ddalessio@stamford.stam.econn.edu.

DALESSIO, DONALD JOHN, internist, neurologist, educator; b. Jersey City, Mar. 2, 1931; s. John Andrea and Susan Dorothy (Minotta) Dalessio; m. Jane Catherine Schneider, Sept. 4, 1954 (dec. Mar. 1998); children: Catherine Leah, James John, Susan Jane. BA, Wesleyan U., 1952; MD, Yale U., 1956. Diplomate Am. Bd. Internal Medicine. Intern N.Y.C. Hosp., 1956-57, asst. resident in medicine and neurology, 1959-61; resident in medicine Yale Med. Ctr., 1961-62; pres. med. staff Scripps Clinic, La Jolla, Calif., 1974-78; chmn. dept. medicine Scripps Clin., La Jolla, Calif., 1974-89, chmn. emeritus, 1989—, cons., 1982—, pres. med. group, 1980-81; clin. prof. neurology U. Calif., San Diego, 1973—. Physician in chief Green Hosp., La Jolla, 1974—89; pres. Am. Assn. Study Headache, Chgo., 1974—76; chmn. Fedn. Western Soc. Neurology, Santa Barbar, Calif., 1976—77; Musser-Burch lectr. Tulane U., 1979; Kash lectr. U. Ky., 1979. Author: (book) Wolff's Headache, 7th edit., 2001, Approach to Headache, 1973, Approach to Headache, 6th edit., 1999; editor: Headache jour., 1965—75, 1979—84, Scripps Clinic Personal Health Letter; mem. editl. bd. Jour. AMA, 1977—87; columnist: San Diego Tribune. Pres. Nat. Migraine Found., Chgo., 1977—79. Capt. U.S. Army, 1957—59. Recipient Disting. Alumnus award, Wesleyan U., 1982. Fellow: ACP; mem.: World Fedn. Neurology (Am. sec. 1980—90, mem. rsch. group migraine), Am. Acad. Neurology (assoc.), La Jolla Beach/Tennis Club, La Jolla Country Club. Avocations: tennis, squash, piano. Home: 8891 Nottingham Pl La Jolla CA 92037-2131 Office: Scripps Clinic & Rsch Found 10666 N Torrey Pines Rd La Jolla CA 92037-1092

D'ALESSIO, GINA MARIA, music educator; b. Bklyn. d. Gennaro D'Alessio and Josephine Ann D'Anna-D'Alessio. MusB, Wayne State U., Detroit, 1985; MusM, Wayne State U., 1991. Prof. music Henry Ford C.C., Dearborn, Mich., 1993—. Piano accompanist European concert tour Roosevelt H.S. Choir, 2002. Singer (soprano soloist): (CD) Paul Paray - The Oratorios, 2002; performer: The Paray Mass, 1998. Recipient Great Lakes Province Achievement award, Mu Phi Epsilon, 1985; Josephine Li Puma Vocal scholar, 1987. Office: Henry Ford Cmty Coll 5101 Evergreen Rd Dearborn MI 48128-2407

D'ALESSIO, JACQUELINE ANN, English educator; b. Morristown, N.J., Jan. 26, 1943; d. Clifford Corbet and Helen Ann (Chrenko) Compton; m. Harold F. D'Alessio, Oct. 28, 1967. BA in English, Coll. New Rochelle, 1964; MA in English, Seton Hall U., 1969. Tchr. Bridgewater (N.J.)-Raritan Regional Sch. Dist., 1964—. Advisor dramatics Bridgewater-Raritan Mid. Sch., Bridgewater, N.J., 1983—. Chmn. pub. rels. Mt. St. Mary Devel. Office, 1985-2000; bd. dirs. N.J. Legis Agenda for Women, Inc., 1993-94. Recipient Gov. Tchr. Recognition, N.J. Dept. Edn., Trenton, 1989, Disting. Svc. award Bridgewater-Raritan Regional Sch. Dist., 2001; named Outstanding Elem. Tchr. in U.S., 1971. Mem. AAUW (N.J. pres. 1990-94, program v.p. 1988-90, rep. Women's Agenda 1989-94, dir. pub. policy 1997-99, treas. 1999—, mid-Atlantic region dir. 2001—). Roman Catholic. Avocations: travel, golf, biking, gardening. Home: 30 Putnam St Somerville NJ 08876-2737

D'ALESSIO, VALAIDA CORRINE, artist, consultant; b. Dwight, Ill., Jan. 7, 1938; d. Roy Selmer and Agnes Irene (Seversen) Christiansen; m. Terald Ramon Stevens, July 5, 1958 (div. Dec. 1974); children: Christian Stevens, Curt Stevens, Kirsten Stevens, Karlin Stevens; m. Paul D'Alessio, July 16, 1976. Student, Joliet (Ill.) Jr. Coll., 1957, Aurora (Ill.) Coll., 1964, Am. Acad. Art, Chgo., 1969. Expereicned-based master endl. resources Joliet Twp. High Schs. Adult art educator Joliet Jr. Coll., 1980-88; art workshop leader various art leagues, Chgo. area, 1980-96, State of Ill. Gallery, Lockport, 1994. Art cons. Lockport St. Gallery, Plainfield, Ill., 1994—96, Prairie View Gallery, Lockport, 1999—. Contbr. paintings and mixed media collages, book, . Vol. Crisis Line Will County, 1990—96. Mem.: North Coast Collage Soc., Soc. Exptl. Artists, Soc. Layerists in Multi-Media.

DALEY, ARTHUR JAMES, retired magazine publisher; b. St. Paul, Aug. 15, 1916; s. John and Mary (Mayer) D.; m. Lorayne Mary Mongan, June 7, 1941; children: Michael, Kay. Student pub. schs., Fond du Lac, Wis. Advt. salesman Fond du Lac Commonwealth Reporter, 1936, sports editor, 1937-40; sports writer Green Bay (Wis.) Press-Gazette, 1941-43, sports editor, 1946-68, telegraph, picture editor, 1968-78; pub. Green Bay Packer Yearbook, 1960-83, assoc. pub., 1984-88, ret., 1988; columnist Green Bay Packer Report, 1974—. Mem. Wis. Hall of Fame Com. Served with AUS, 1943-46, ETO. Inducted into Green Bay Packer Hall of Fame, 1993. Mem. Pro Football Writers Am., Nat. Football League Alumni Assn., Oneida Golf and Country Club. Home: 1146 Highview Ln Green Bay WI 54304-2222

DALEY, ARTHUR STUART, retired humanities educator; b. Osceola, N.Y., Sept. 16, 1908; s. Kieran A. and Mary (Adams) D.; m. Jean Abendroth, Aug. 29, 1942; 1 child, Arthur Stuart. AB with honors in English, Syracuse U., 1932; postgrad., Harvard U., 1932-33; PhD, Yale U., 1942. Instr. English Syracuse (N.Y.) U., 1935-37, Ind. U., 1946-47, UCLA, 1947-49; asst. prof. English U. Nev., 1949-54; prof., chmn. dept. Coe Coll., 1954-59; prof. Drake U., Des Moines, 1959-76, chmn. dept., 1959-67, coord. humanities div., 1967-75, prof. emeritus, 1976—. Co-author: Private Charity in England, 1747-57, 1938; contbr. articles, especially on Shakespeare, to profl. jours.; contbr. articles to rev. Norton crit. edit. Wuthering Heights (Emily Bronte), Shakespeare Studies XXI, The Upstart Crow XIV. Served to lt. col. AUS, 1941-46, 51-53; lt. col. AUS ret. Decorated Bronze Star; hon. grant of English armorial bearings, 1978; mem. by right Ancient and Hon. Arty. Co. Mass. Mem. MLA, Soc. Mayflower Descs., Shakespeare Assn., The Mediaeval Acad. Am., Am. Bronte Soc., Theta Alpha Phi, Sigma Nu. Home: 2705 Barnson Pl San Diego CA 92103-6103

DALEY, CHARLES MIKE, consumer products company executive; b. Boston, June 7, 1936; s. Francis Daniel and Kathleen (Gillin) Daley; m. Janet Marie Richards, Aug. 24, 1957; children: Stephen M., Kevin F., Thomas P., Mary E. BS, Boston Coll., 1958. With S. S. Kresge Co., Boston and Burlington, Vt., 1958-59; sales staff Libby McNeill & Libby, Chgo., 1960-63; account exec. J. Daren & Sons, Norwich, Conn., 1963-66; CEO, pres., treas. Daley Care Mgmt. Co., Boston, 1966-88; CEO, chmn., treas. Lojack Corp., Dedham, Mass., 1986—2001. Bd. dirs., v.p., pres., chmn. Mass. Fedn. Nursing Homes, Boston; v.p., pres. Mass Health Coun., Boston; bd. advisors Bit Group. Pres. Norwich (Conn.) Jaycees, 1964—65; v.p. Conn. Jaycees, state chmn., 1964—66; v.p., nat. dir., pres., chmn. Mass. Jaycees, 1966—72; co-chair 150th anniversary com. YMCA, 2001—02, vice chmn., 2002; bd. dirs., mem. exec. com. Greater Boston YMCA, 1998—; mem. exec. com. Inner City Scholarship Fund, 1998—; trustee, vice chmn., chmn. Emmanuel Coll., Boston, 1993—; mem. nat. devel. bd. Boston Coll., nat. campaign com.; chmn. patrons com. Boston Coll. McMullen Mus. Art. Named Man of the Yr., Norwich C. of C., 1965, Disting. Nursing Home Adminstr., Boston chpt. Am. Coll. Nursing Home Adminstrs. Mem.: Boston Coll. Alumni Assn., Bonita Country Club, Oyster Harbors Club (bd. govs. 2003), Boston Coll. Club (founder, trustee 1998—). Roman Catholic. Avocations: music, walking, art and antique collecting. Home: 60 Elm St Canton MA 02021-1230 Office: Lojack Corp Ste 1000 200 Lowder Brook Dr Westwood MA 02090-1190

DALEY, MARGARETMARY, language educator, literature educator; b. Washington, July 27, 1961; d. Joseph C. and Edwina A. Daley; children: Blake, Devin Ann Ford. Student, Freie U., Berlin, 1980—81; AB, Stanford U., 1983; MA, PhD, Yale U., 1994. Tchg. asst. Yale U., New Haven, 1985—86; under-asst. libr. Beinecke Libr. and Rare Book Mus., New Haven, 1986; lectr. Lawrence U., Appleton, Wis., 1989—92; vis. asst. prof. Brigham Young U., Provo, Utah, 1993—94; asst. prof. Case Western Res. U., Cleve., 1994—2000, assoc. prof., 2000—, dept. chair modern langs. and lits., 2000—. Chair faculty senate com. on women Case Western Res. U., Cleve., 1997 2000, mem. steering com. women's studies, Judaic studies, German studies. Author: Women of Letters: A Study of Self and Genre, 1998; contbr. articles to profl. jours. Hon. fellow, St. Hilda's Coll., Oxford, Eng., 2000. Roman Catholic. Home: 2948 Brighton Rd Shaker Heights OH 44120 Office: Case Western Res Univ 10900 Euclid Ave Cleveland OH 44106-7118

DALEY, MICHAEL EDWARD, financial consultant; b. Fall River, Mass., Aug. 19, 1952; s. James and Mary Elizabeth (Roberts) D.; m. June MacDonald Froehlich, Dec. 27, 1978. A in Bus. Adminstrn., Quinsigamond C.C., Worcester, Mass., 1972; BBA, U. Mass., 1979; MBA, U. Mass., Dartmouth, 1984. Gen. mgr. Capt. Bill's Fish, Inc., Hyannis, Mass., 1975-82; controller, asst. treas. Olde Cape Cod Ins., Inc., Hyannis, 1982-86; acct. Town of Falmouth, Mass., 1986-88, Town of Plymouth, Mass., 1988-91, dir. fin., 1991-97; pres. Fin. Adv. Assocs., Inc., Buzzards Bay, Mass., 1994—. Instr. mktg. Fisher Jr. Coll., Bourne, Mass., 1984; instr. econs. Cape Cod C.C., West Barnstable, Mass., 1985. Contbr. articles to profl. jours. Chmn. fin. com. Town of Barnstable, 1985, chmn. charter commn., 1988; treas., bd. dirs. Mid Cape Congregate Care, Inc., Hyannis, 1991-92. Recipient Mktg. Idea of Yr. award Redshaw Computer System User Group, 1985. Mem. Govt. Fin. Officers Assn. U.S. and Can., New Eng. States Govt. Fin. Officers Assn. (bd. dirs.), Mass. Mcpl. Auditors and Accts. Assn. (pres. 1993-94), Marstons Mills Village Assn. (treas. 1986-88), Barnstable Conservation Found. (treas. 1987-88). Democrat. Roman Catholic. Avocations: golf, travel, hiking. Home: 11 Little Pond Cir Marstons Mills MA 02648-1102 Office: Fin Adv Assocs Inc 258 Main St Ste A-2 Buzzards Bay MA 02532 E-mail: mdaley@FAA-Inc.com.

DALEY, PAUL PATRICK, lawyer; b. Boston, July 10, 1941; s. Patrick Joseph and Catherine Josephine (Ford) D.; m. Barbara Sabin, May 24, 1980; 1 child, Patrick. AB, Boston Coll., 1963; MBA, JD, Harvard U., 1973. Bar: Mass. 1973, U.S. Ct. Appeals (1st cir.) 1974, U.S. Dist. Ct. (Mass.) 1974, U.S. Ct. Appeals (5th cir.) 1980, U.S. Supreme Ct. 1980, N.Y. 1983, U.S. Ct. Appeals (2d cir.) 1998. Assoc. Hale and Dorr LLP, Boston, 1973-78; jr. ptnr. Hale and Dorr, Boston, 1978-82, sr. ptnr., 1982—. Lectr. CLE programs. Assoc. editor Mass. Law Rev., 1998—; contbr. articles to profl. jours. Trustee Mass. Sch. Profl. Psychology, Boston, 1985-2003, chair, 1994-2003; trustee St. Sebastians Sch., Needham, Mass. 1981, Naval War Coll. Found., 1996—, pres., 2000-02, chmn., 2002—; bd. dirs. Am. Sail Train Assn., Newport, R.I., 1982-86. Capt. USNR, 1963-94, Vietnam 1965-67. Decorated DFC, Air Medals (16), Vietnamese Air Gallantry Cross. Fellow Am. Coll. Bankruptcy; mem. ABA, Mass. Bar Assn. (past chmn. bus. bank com., bus. law sect., fee arbitation bd.), Boston Bar Assn. (coun.), Am. Bankruptcy Inst., Nat. Def. U. Found., Tailhook Assn., U.S. Naval Inst., Naval Res. Assn., Assn. Naval Aviation, Comml. Law League, Navy League, Windsor Club (Waban, Mass.), Brae Burn Country Club, Wardroom

Club. Democrat. Roman Catholic. Avocations: flying, scuba diving, biking, reading, theater. Home: 9 Crofton Rd Waban MA 02468-1931 Office: Hale and Dorr LLP 60 State St Boston MA 02109-1816 Fax: (617) 526-5000. E-mail: paul.daley@haledorr.com.

DALEY, PETER EDMUND, business and human resources company executive; b. Washington, Mar. 28, 1943; s. Edmund Frances and Marie (Herbert) D.; m. Alexandra Stanish, June 27, 1970; children: Peter, Gina, Melissa, Angela, Thomas, Paul, Alexis, Kara, Nikos. BS, Wheeling Coll., 1966; MBA, U. MD., 1968; JD, U. Balt., 1975. With Westinghouse Electric Co., Balt., 1970-75, Pitts., 1975-77; corp. mgr. compensation benefits PHH Group, Hunt Valley, Md., 1977-78, corp. mgr. human resources, 1978-79, dir. human resources, 1979-81; dir. employee rels. Fairchild Industries, 1981-83; v.p. human resources and adminstrv. svcs. Fairchild Space and Fairchild Comms. and Electronics Cos., 1983-84; pres., CEO P.M.A. Inc., 1985-90; dir. Washington Hosp. Ctr., Washington, 1991-95; pres. Harbor Consulting Group, 1995-97; v.p. human resources and adminstrn. Digex, Inc., 1997-98, Clarity Integrated, 1999—. Bd. dirs. Girl Scouts U.S. Ctrl. Md., 1978-81; mem. exec. bd. com. indsl. rels. and labor studies U. Md., mem. Naval Indsl. Facilities Adv. Panel. Mem. ABA, Am. Mgmt. Assn., Am. Assn. Pers. Adminstrs., Md. Bar Assn., Greater Balt. Pers. Assocs., Am. Compensation Assn. Home: 411 Deacon Brook Cir Reisterstown MD 21136-2228

DALEY, RICHARD HALBERT, museum director; b. Centralia, Ill., Oct. 8, 1948; s. Richard Glen D.; m. Lucy W. Costen, Nov. 27, 1976. Student, Lake Forest (Ill.) Coll., 1966-67; BS, Colo. State U., 1970, MS, 1972. Instr. Colo. State U., Ft. Collins, 1972; from dir. biol. svcs. to dir. programs Mo. Bot. Garden, St. Louis, 1973-84; exec. dir. Mass. Hort. Soc., Boston, 1984-91, Denver Botanic Gardens, 1991-94; instr. Environ. Ethics Denver U., 1992-94; exec. dir. Sonara Desert Museum, Tucson, Ariz., 1994—. Mem. editorial com. Am. Mus. Natural History, N.Y.C., 1983-92. Bd. trustees Ctr. for Plant Conservation, 1994—. Mem. Am. Assn. Bot. Gardens (bd. trustees), Hort. Club Boston, Rotary Club Denver. Office: Ariz Sonara Desert Museum 2021 N Kinney Rd Tucson AZ 85743-9719

DALEY, RICHARD MICHAEL, mayor; b. Chgo., Apr. 24, 1942; s. Richard J. and Eleanor (Guilfoyle) D.; m. Margaret Corbett, Mar. 25, 1972; children: Nora, Patrick, Elizabeth. BA, DePaul U., Chgo., 1964, JD, 1968. Bar: Ill. 1969. Ptnr. Simon and Daley, Chgo., 1970-72, Daley, Riley & Daley, Chgo., 1972-80; mem. Ill. State Senate, 1973-80, chmn. Judiciary I Com., 1975, 77; state's atty. Cook County, Ill., 1980-89; mayor Chgo., 1989—; pres. U.S. Conf. Mayors, 1996. Bd. dirs. Little City Home; mem. Citizens Bd. U. Chgo.; mem. adv. bd. Mercy Hosp., Chgo.; bd. mgrs. Valentine Boys Club; active Nativity of Our Lord Parish, Chgo. Recipient Golden Rule plaque Chgo. Boys Club Am.; named Outstanding Legislator of Yr., Lt. Gov's. Sr. Legis. Forum, 1979, Outstanding Leader in Revision of Ill. Mental Health Code, Ill. Assn. Retarded Citizens, 1979, Outstanding Leader, Ill. Assn. Social workers, 1978. Mem. Chgo. Bar Assn., Ill. State Bar Assn., ABA, Cath. Lawyers Guild. Democrat. Roman Catholic. Office: Office of the Mayor City Hall Rm 507 121 N La Salle St Chicago IL 60602-1202*

DALEY, ROBERT EMMETT, retired foundation executive; b. Cleve., Mar. 13, 1933; s. Emmett Wilfred and Anne Gertrude (O'Donnell) D.; m. Mary Berneta Fredericks, June 7, 1958; children: Marianne Fredericks, John Gerard. BA in English, U. Dayton, 1955; MA in Polit. Sci., Ohio State U., 1968, MA in Pub. Adminstrn., 1976. Local govt. reporter, Washington corr., fin. editor Jour. Herald, Dayton, Ohio, 1957-65, pub. affairs reporter, 1967; staff writer Congressional Quar., Inc., Washington, 1966; pub. affairs reporter Dayton Daily News, Dayton, 1969; dir. pub. affairs & comm. Charles F. Kettering Found., Dayton, 1977-94, ret., now assoc., 1994—. Part-time copy boy, sports reporter Jour. Herald, Dayton, 1953-55. Past pres., bd. trustees St. Joseph Home for Children; former mem. adv. bd. Ctr. for Religious Telecomms., U. Dayton; traveling press sec. sen. candidate John J. Gilligan, 1968, for gubernatorial candidate, 1970-71, asst. to Gov. Gilligan, 1971-75; media rels. dir. Nat. League of Cities, Washington, 1976-77; mem. Montgomery County Hist. Soc.; past mem. Ind. Sector Pub. Info. & Edn. Com. With U.S. Army, 1955 57. Mem. Pub. Rels. Soc. Am., Soc. Profl. Journalists, Nat. Press Club, KC, Ancient Order Hibernians. Roman Catholic. Home: 888 Cranbrook Ct Dayton OH 45459-1525 Office: Charles F Kettering Found 200 Commons Rd Dayton OH 45459-2788 E-mail: daley@kettering.org.

DALEY, RON (RONALD EUGENE DALEY), playwright, poet, director, producer; b. Washington, Sept. 24, 1945; s. Russell Eugene and Dorothy Sybil (Krouse) D.; m. Virginia Ann Bean, Nov. 7, 1986; children: Jackson Phillip Wesley, Bryan Augustin, Geoffrey Eugene. BA in Philosophy, North Park Coll., 1967; MA in English with honors, Roosevelt U., 1968; MA in Drama, Syracuse U., 1975. founder ACT-Argyle, 1999—. Instr. English/Philosophy Malcolm X C.C., Chgo., 1968-70, Orange County C.C., Middletown, N.Y., 1970-73; English N.Y.C. C.C., Bklyn., 1975-78; dir., designer various theatre companies, 1978-80; producer Jerron Prodns., N.Y.C., 1980-81; assoc. artistic dir. New World Theatre, N.Y.C., 1981-82; artistic dir. Nat. Shakespeare Co., N.Y.C., 1982-85; resident dir., producer Riverside Shakespeare Co., N.Y.C., 1986; exec. dir. RED Prodns., Argyle, Wis., 1985—. Guest dir. Broom St. Theatre, Madison, 1987-94, Classic Theatre, N.Y.C., 1979-84, AMDA Studio One, N.Y.C., 1977-78, Camden (Maine) Shakespeare Festival, 1979, Mercury Players, Madison, 1994—. Author of plays off Broadway including Beyond the Veil, Damphools and Wowsers, Argyle Wisconsin 53504, In the Matter of John David Hutchins, It's Gotta Be the Shoes, Nobody Dies, 5:45, Badger Orpheus, The Third Blackhawk War, Journeys with Nanabozo, The Abrazo, The Knight of the Burning Pestle, The Red Palace; editor Amphibious Maneuvers. Prodr. Free Shakespeare in the Parks, N.Y.C., 1986. Mem Soc. of Stage Dirs. and Choreographers, Dramatists Guild, Chgo. Area Playwrights, U.S. Holocaust Meml. Mus., ACLU. Avocations: fishing, gardening, carpentry. Home: 17740 River Rd Argyle WI 53504-9726

DALEY, SANDRA, retired artist, filmmaker, photographer; b. Fargo, ND, Feb. 28, 1940; d. Cecil Raymond and Margaret (Anderson) D. AB cum laude, Oberlin Coll., 1961; MFA with high distinction, Calif. Coll. Arts and Crafts, 1965. Show (with Andy Warhol and Roy Lichtenstein), Dwan Gallery, L.A., 1964, show (with Nicholas Quennell), 1965, Experiments in Art and Tech., Osaka Pavilion, World's Fair, 1970; prodr., dir. : (film (with Sally Potter) London Mysteries, 1964; (film (with Robert Mapplethorpe and Patti Smith) Robert Having His Nipple Pierced, 1970; (film (Patti Smith, Sam Shepard and Vali) Patti Having Her Knee Tattooed, 1971. Avocations: writing, drawing.

DALEY, SUSAN JEAN, lawyer; b. New Britain, Conn., May 27, 1959; d. George Joseph and Norma (Woods) D. BA, U. Conn., 1978; JD, Harvard U., 1981. Bar: Ill. 1981. Assoc. Altheimer & Gray, Chgo., 1981-86, ptnr., 1986—. Mem. ABA (real property, probate and trust law sect. 1983—, chmn. welfare plans com. real property, probate and trust law sect. 1989-95, employee benefits com. taxation sect. 1984—, chmn. EEOC issues subcom. employee benefits com. taxation sect. 1990-2001, chmn. fed. securities law subcom. employee benefits com. taxation sect. 2001--), Nat. Assn. Stock Plan Profls. (pres. Chgo. chpt. 1995—), Ill. Bar Assn. (chmn. employee benefits divsn. fed. taxation sect. 1984-86, chmn. employee benefits sect., 1995-96, mem. employee benefits sect. 1990-97), Chgo. Bar Assn. (chmn. employee benefits divsn. fed. taxation com. 1985-86, chmn. employee benefits com. 1990-91, chmn. fed. taxation com. 1992-93), Chgo. Coun. on Fgn. Rels. Avocation: marathons. Home: 1636 N Wells St Apt 415 Chicago IL 60614-6009 Office: Altheimer & Gray 10 S Wacker Dr Ste 4000 Chicago IL 60606-7407 E-mail: daleys@altheimer.com.

DALEY, TODD MAURICE, mathematician, educator; b. Jersey City, July 12, 1944; s. Thomas Francis (Healy) Daley and Claire Hanson; children: Kimberly, Lauren. BS in Math., CCNY, 1966; MAT, Johns Hopkins U., 1967; PhD, NYU, 1981. Physics tchr. Curtis H.S., Staten Island, NY, 1967—82; math prof. Union County Coll., Cranford, NJ, 1982—. Adj. math. prof. Coll. S.I., NY, 1982—. Author: Apples & Oranges, 1995, Math Concepts: An Interdisciplinary Approach, 1998. Home: 200 W Hazelwood Ave Rahway NJ 07065 Office: Union County Coll 12 W Jersey St Elizabeth NJ 07202

DALEY, VINCENT RAYMOND, JR., real estate company executive, consultant; b. Evanston, Ill., June 21, 1940; s. Vincent R. and Carole V. (Johnson) D.; m. Viola Elizabeth Bursiek, May 6, 1967; children: Kathleen Marie, Colleen Patricia. AA, Lincoln Coll., 1961; BS, Loyola U., Chgo., 1963; student in real estate, Roosevelt U., 1964. From salesman to store mgr. Sears Roebuck & Co., Chgo., 1962-73; v.p., cons. Kencoe Corp., Des Plaines, Ill., 1973-74; pres. Daley & Assocs., Chgo., 1974—; chmn. Wacker Real Estate Svcs., Chgo., 1997—. Chmn. Wacker Mgmt. Corp., Chgo. State legis. asst. 8th Legis. Dist., Chgo., 1985—93; mem. econ. devel. com. State of Ill., Springfield, 1985—88; bd. trustees Lincoln Col. Chartered Lincoln U., 2001—. Men. Chgo. Bd. Realtors (life) (bd. dirs.), Nat. Assn. Realtors (bd. regents), Ill. Assn. Realtors (bd. dirs.), Realtors Land Inst. (bd. govs.), Realtors Nat. Mktg. Inst. (CCIM), Internat. Real Estate Fed. (sr. cert. valuerer, registered internat. mem., cert. investment financier). Democrat. Roman Catholic. Avocation: traveling. Home: 1807 N Orleans St Chicago IL 60614-5325 Office: Wacker Real Estate Svcs 400 N Michigan Ave Ste 820 Chicago IL 60611-4129

DALEY, WILLIAM M. former federal government official; m. Loretta Daley; 3 children. BA, Loyola U.; LLB, LLD (hon.), John Marshall Law Sch., Chgo. Bar: Ill. 1975. With Daley and George, Chgo.; ptnr. Mayer, Brown & Platt; vice chmn. Amalgamated Bank, Chgo., 1989, pres., COO, 1990-93; sec. Dept. Commerce, Washington, 1997-2000. Bd. dirs. Electronic Data Sys. Corp., Plano, Tex., 2001—; spl. counsel to Pres. for NAFTA. Recipient St. Ignatius award fro Excellence in the Practice of Law, 2995, World Trade award World Trade Ctr., Chgo., 1994. Office: EDS 5400 Legacy Dr Plano TX 75024-3199

DALGARNO, ALEXANDER, astronomy educator; b. London, Jan. 5, 1928; s. William and Margaret (Murray) D.; m. Barbara W.F. Kane, Oct. 31, 1957 (div.); children: Penelope, Rebecca, Piers, Fergus; m. Emily K. Izsak, June 23, 1972 (div.). BSc, U. London, 1947, PhD, 1951; MA (hon.), Harvard U., 1967; DSc (hon.), Queen's U. Belfast, 1980, York U., Can., 2000. Lectr. Queen's U., Belfast, Northern Ireland, 1951-56, reader, 1956-61, prof. math. physics, 1961-67, dir. computation lab., 1961-66; prof. astronomy Harvard U., Cambridge, Mass., 1967—, Phillips prof., 1977—, chmn. dept., 1971-76; dir. Inst. for Theoretical Atomic and Molecular Physics, 1989-93. Assoc. dir. Ctr. for Astrophysics Harvard U., 1973-80; acting dir. Harvard Coll. Obs., 1971-73; rsch. scientist Smithsonian Astrophys. Obs., Cambridge, Mass., 1967—; Vikram A. Sarabhai prof. Phys. Rsch. Lab., Ahmedebad, 2002; Jan Hendrik Oort prof. U. Leiden, 2003; Charles M. and Martha Hitchcock prof. U. Calif., Berkeley, 2003. Editor: Astrophys. Jour. Letters, 1973—2002; contbr. articles to profl. jours. Recipient Hodgkins medal Smithsonian Instn., 1977, Spiers Medal, Royal Soc. Chemistry, 1992; fellow UMIST, 1992, Univ. Coll. London, 1976. Fellow: Internat. Acad. Quantum Molecular Sci. (ann. prize 1967), Internat. Acad. Astronautics, Royal Astron. Soc. (Gold medal 1986), Am. Acad. Arts and Scis., Am. Geophys. Union (Fleming medal 1995), Optical Soc. Am. (Meggers award 1986), Am. Phys. Soc. (Davisson-Germer award 1980), Phys. Soc. (London), Royal Soc. (Hughes medal 2002), Royal Irish Acad. (hon.); mem.: NAS. Home: 27 Robinson St Cambridge MA 02138-1403 Office: Harvard-Smithsonian Ctr Astrophysics 60 Garden St Cambridge MA 02138 E-mail: adalgarno@cfa.harvard.edu.

DALGLISH, ARTHUR RAY, journalist; b. Springfield, Ohio, Oct. 23, 1950; s. Arthur Clark and Jane Ellen (Marble) D.; m. Lorraine Margaret Johnson, July 31, 1982; children: Sarah Lorraine, Evan Clark. BA in Journalism, Ohio State U., 1973, MA in Journalism, 1976. Reporter The Review Times, Fostoria, Ohio, 1973; copy editor The Palm Beach Post, West Palm Beach, Fla., 1973-75, The Corpus Christi (Tex.) Caller, 1976; layout editor The Chgo. Daily News, 1977-78; telegraph editor Chgo. Sun-Times, 1978-82; news editor Internat. Herald Tribune, Paris, 1982-87; assignment editor Atlanta Jour. and Constn., 1987-89; news editor Cox Newspapers, Washington, 1990-2000, enterprise editor, 2000—. Home: 13909 Dowlais Dr Rockville MD 20853-2639 Office: Cox Newspapers 400 N Capitol St NW Ste 750 Washington DC 20001-1536 E-mail: artd@coxnews.com.

DALGLISH, LUCY ANN, lawyer, organization executive; b. Mpls., Mar. 24, 1959; d. James Mark and Joanne Elizabeth (Speikers) D. BA, U. N.D., 1980; MSL, Yale U., 1988; JD, Vanderbilt U., 1995. Bar: Minn. 1995, D.C. 2001. Reporter Grand Forks (N.D.) Herald, 1978-80, St. Paul Dispatch, 1979, 80-81, St. Paul Pioneer Press., 1981-89; night city editor St. Paul Pioneer Press, 1989-90, nat./fgn. editor, 1991-93; rsch. asst. Freedom Forum, Nashville, 1993-95; assoc. Dorsey & Whitney, Mpls., 1995-2000; exec. dir. Reporters Com. for Freedom of Press, Arlington, Va., 2000—. Instr. Hamline U., St. Paul, 1989, 90. Nat. chair Project Watchdog, Greencastle, Ind., 1990-92. Inducted into Nat. Freedom of Info. Act Hall of Fame, Washington, 1996; Yale Law Sch. fellow, 1987-88. Mem. Soc. Profl. Journalists (bd. dirs. 1987-91, nat. chairwoman, freedom of info. com. 1991-95; recipient Wells Meml. Key 1995), First Amendment Congress (nat. bd. mem. 1991-97), Minn. AP Assn. (v.p. 1991-93), Sigma Delta Chi Found. (bd. dirs. 1990-91), Minn. Bar Assn. (bar/media com. 1992-93, 95-97, bar-media chairwoman 1997-2000). Roman Catholic. Avocations: downhill and water skiing, golf, reading, antiques, gardening. Office: Reporters Com for Freedom of Press 1815 N Ft Myer Dr Arlington VA 22209

DALIA, THOMAS A. architectural firm executive; B in Architecture, Tulane U. Sch. of Architecture, 1978. Lic. NCARB, La., 1987, Mich., 1988, N.C., 1992, Fla., 1997, S.C., 1997. With Audubon Constrn. Corp., New Orleans, 1978—80, T. Byron Smith Assocs., Ltd., New Orleans, 1980—82, E. Eean McNaughton & Assocs., New Orleans, 1982—86, Edge Group Archs., West Palm Beach, Fla., 1986—87, Smith Dalia Archs., Atlanta, 1987—. Office: Smith Dalia Archs Ste C-140 621 N Ave NE Atlanta GA 30308 Fax: 404-892-2470.*

DALIA, VESTA MAYO, artist; b. Atlanta, Aug. 14, 1932; d. Frank and Winnifred (Layton) Mayo; m. William Barber Macke, May 30, 1952 (div. 1971); children: William Barber Jr., Michael Mayo, Vesta Melissa, Mary Sue Macke Mullen; m. Joseph William Dalia, Aug. 31, 1973 (dec. 1990); stepchildren: Joseph W. Jr., Jeffrey Meade, Denise Marie Dalia Cooper, Nancy Dalia Cook. Student, U. Ga. Tchr. art Cen. Piedmont Coll., Charlotte, N.C. Exhibited art in shows in Charlotte and Atlanta. Bd. dirs., officer Caribbean Condo; poll worker Fla. elections. Mem. Nat. Tole and Decorative Painters (past pres. Dogwood chpt., recipient Golden Palet award 1990), Missle Tole Decorative Painters, Seaside Decorative Painters (Daytona Beach chpt.), Team Network S.E. Painters, Weinman Mineral Mus., West Fulton Owls Club, Frog Club, Zoo Atlanta, Friendship Force, Native Atlantans Club, The Etowah Found. NATAS (Atlanta chpt.), NRA, Ga. Ensemble Theatre. Republican. Episcopalian. Home: 2425 S Atlantic Ave Apt 1603 Daytona Beach Shores FL 32118-5431 E-mail: vdalia@bellsouth.net.

DALINKA, MURRAY KENNETH, radiologist, educator; b. Bklyn., May 13, 1938; s. Joseph and Gertrude (Cohen) D.; m. Janice L. Kolber, Feb. 28, 1982; 1 son, Bradford Gordon; children by previous marriage: Ilene, Ian Scott. BS, U. Mich., 1960, MD, 1964. Diplomate Am. Bd. Radiology. Intern Pa. Hosp., Phila., 1964-65; resident in radiology Montefiore Hosp., N.Y.C., 1965-68; instr. radiology Harvard Med. Sch., 1970-71; from asst. prof. to assoc. prof. radiology Thomas Jefferson U. Hosp., Phila., 1971-76, prof., 1976—; chief orthop. radiology Hosp. U. Pa., 1976—. Chief diagnostic radiology Thomas Jefferson U. Hosp., Phila., 1974-76; . cons.hila. Naval Hosp., 1974-79, Walson Hosp., Ft. Dix Army Base, 1972-77. Author: Arthography, 1980, Symposium on Orthopedic Radiology, 1983; mem. editorial bd. Bone Syllabus IV, 1982—, Skeletal Radiology, 1982—, Conversations in Radiology, 1977-79; guest editor Emergency Medicine Clinics of North America, Vol. 3, 1985; editor: (with J.J. Kaye) Radiology in Emergency Medicine Clinics in Emergency, Vol. 3, 1984, (with J. Edeiken and D. Karasick) Edeiken's Roentgen Diagnosis of Diseases of Bone, 4th edit. Served to capt. USAF, 1968-70. James Picker research fellow, 1972-73 Mem. Internat. Skeletal Soc. (past pres.), Radiol. Soc. N.Am., Am. Coll. Radiology (chmn. panel on musculoskeletal imaging, mem. task force on appropriateness criteria/diagnostic patient care guidelines), Phila. Roentgen Ray Soc. (past pres.). Home: 318 S 21st St Philadelphia PA 19103-6531 Office: U Pa Hosp Dept Radiology 3400 Spruce St Philadelphia PA 19104-4206 E-mail: dalinka@oasis.rad.upenn.edu.

DALIS, IRENE, mezzo-soprano, opera company administrator, music educator; b. San Jose, Calif., Oct. 8, 1925; d. Peter Nicholas and Mamie Rose (Boitano) D.; m. George Loinaz, July 16, 1957; 1 child, Alida Mercedes. AB, San Jose State Coll., 1946; MA in Teaching, Columbia U., 1947; MMus (hon.), San Jose State U., 1957; studied voice with, Edyth Walker, N.Y.C., 1947-50, Paul Althouse, 1950-51, Dr. Otto Mueller, Milan, Italy, 1952-72; MusD (hon.), Santa Clara U., 1987; DFA (hon.), Calif. State U., 1999. Prin. artist Berlin Opera, 1955-65, Met. Opera, N.Y.C., 1957-77, San Francisco Opera, 1958-73, Hamburg (Fed. Republic Germany) Staatsoper, 1966-71; prof. music San Jose State U., Calif., 1977—; founder, gen. dir. Opera San Jose, 1984—. Dir. Met. Opera Nat. Auditions, San Jose dist., 1980-88. Operatic debut as dramatic mezzo-soprano Oldenburgisches Staatstheater, 1953, Berlin Staedtische Opera, 1955; debut Met. Opera, N.Y.C., 1957, 1st Am.-born singer, Kundry Bayreuth Festival, 1961, opened, Bayreuth Festival, Parsifal, 1963; commemorative Wagner 150th Birth Anniversary; opened 1963 Met. Opera Season in Aida; premiered: Dello Joio's Blood Moon, 1961, Henderson's Medea, 1972; rec. artist Parsifal, 1964 (Grand Prix du Disque award); contbg. editor Opera Quar., 1983. Recipient Fulbright award for study in Italy, 1951, Woman of Achievement award Commn. on Status of Women, 1983, Pres.'s award Nat. Italian Am. Found., 1985, award of merit People of San Francisco, 1985, San Jose Renaissance award for sustained and outstanding artistic contbn., 1987, Medal of Achievement Acad. Vocal Arts, 1988; named Honored Citizen City of San Jose, 1986; inducted into Calif. Pub. Edn. Hall of Fame, 1985, others. Mem. Beethoven Soc. (mem. adv. bd. 1985—), San Jose Arts Round Table, San Jose Opera Guild, Am. Soc. Univ. Women, Arts Edn. Week Consortium, Phi Kappa Phi, Mu Phi Epsilon. Office: Opera San Jose 2049 Paragon Dr San Jose CA 95131 E-mail: dalis@operasj.org.

DALITSCH, WALTER WILLIAM, aerospace medicine specialist; s. Walter William Dalitsch, II and Carol Jeanne Dalitsch. BS in Philosophy/Biology, U. Ill., 1988; MD, U. Ill., Chgo., 1993; MPH, U. Kans., 2001. Cert. aerospace medicine Bd. Preventive Medicine. Fellow: Aerospace Med. Assn. (assoc.); mem.: Aircraft Owners and Pilots Assn., U.S. Naval Inst. Avocations: flying, music, canoeing, skiing.

DALLAGER, JOHN R. career officer; BS in Mech. Engring., USAF Acad., 1969; disting. grad. pilot tng., Craig AFB, Ala., 1970; student F-4 replacement tng., Davis-Monthan AFB, Ariz., 1970-71; MBA, Troy State U., 1978; student, Air Command and Staff Coll., 1983, Nat. Def. U., 1983, U.S. Army War Coll., 1988. Commd. 2d lt. USAF, 1969, lt. gen., 2000, various pilot assignments, 1971-74; air staff tng. officer, legis. liaison Pentagon, Washington, 1974-75; flight comdr., chief wing aircrew tng. 347th Tactical Fighter Wing, Moody AFB, Ga., 1975-76; air liaison officer 601st Tactical Air Support Group, Gelnhausen, W. Germany, 1976-77; instr. Air and Ground Ops. Sch. USAF Europe, Sembach Air Base, W. Germany, 1977-79; A-10 weapons and tactics instr. then exec. officer 355th Tactical Tng. Squadron/Wing, Davis-Monthan AFB, 1979-82; mgr. tactical flying hour programs, other positions Hdqs. USAF, Pentagon, Washington, 1983-85; stationed at Davis-Monthan AFB, 1985-87; various comdr. positions USAF, 1988-92, 94-98; dep. dir. logistics and security asst. then dep. chief staff Hdqs. U.S. Ctrl. Command, MacDill AFB, Fla., 1992-94; asst. chief staff ops. and logistics Supreme Hdqs. Allied Powers Europe, 1998-2000; dir. ops. Joint Guard Bosnia, Joint Guarantor Bosnia, Mons, Belgium, 1998-2000; commd. lt. gen., supt. USAF Acad., 2000—. Decorated D.S.M., Legion of Merit with oak leaf cluster, D.F.C. with two oak leaf clusters, Air medal with 15 oak leaf clusters, Rep. Vietnam Gallantry Cross with Palm, Rep. Vietnam Campaign Medal. Office: Lt Gen Supt Ste 342 2304 Cadet Dr U S A F Academy CO 80840 E-mail: john.dallager@usafa.af.mil.

DALLAS, JOSEPH ANTHONY, JR., music educator; s. Joseph Anthony and Elizabeth Jo Dallas; m. Donna Ann Sporny, July 1, 1994. MusB in Edn., Youngstown (Ohio) State U., 1989. Cert. tchr. Ohio, 1994, Fla., 1996. Music educator Ripley (Ohio) Union Lewis Huntington Sch. Dist., 1994—96, Monroe County Sch. Dist., Key West, Fla., 1996—. Pres. Paradise Big Band, Inc., Cudjoe Key, Fla., 1999—. Recipient First Class Tchrs. award, Sallie Mae. Mem.: Fla. Bandmaster's Assn. (Enrollment award 1997), Fla. Music Educator's Assn. Avocations: jet skiing, music, travel, star wars. Home: 22931 Blackbeard Lane Cudjoe Key FL 33042 Office: Sugarloaf School 255 Crane Boulevard Summerland Key FL 33042 Office Fax: 305-745-2019. Personal E-mail: bassforce@webtv.net. E-mail: dallasj@monroe.k12.fl.us.

DALLAS, NOELLE MARIE, financial analyst; b. Louisville, Sept. 24, 1959; d. Glenn Hoyle and Micheline Alice (Boudrias) Madison; m. Stephen Stavros Dallas Jr., Nov. 4, 1989; children: Dominique Marie, Stephen Stavros III. Student, Benjamin Franklin U., 1978-80; BS in Biology, George Mason U., 1984, postgrad, 1988. Montgomery Coll., 1986-88. Mgr. Holly Enterprises, Alexandria, Va., 1975-81; gov. rels. intern TRW, Rosslyn, Va., 1984-85; med. asst. Cardiology and Internal Medicine, P.A., Chevy Chase, Md., 1985-86; sr. cons. Ernst & Young, Washington, 1986-90; sr. fin. analyst Community Energy Alternatives, Ridgewood, N.J., 1990-92; pvt. practice Chester Springs, Pa., 1993—. Treas. Vincent PTA, Spring City, Pa., 2000—02; mem. food svc. task force Owen J. Roberts Sch. Dist., Spring City, 2002—03; treas. Mid. Sch. PTA, Spring City, 2003—. Roman Catholic. Avocations: travel, sports, scuba diving, fencing, reading. Home and Office: 32 Barrington Ln Chester Springs PA 19425-3404

DALLAS, SANDRA, writer; b. Washington, June 11, 1939; d. Forrest Everett and Harriett (Mavity) Dallas; m. Robert Thomas Atchison, Apr. 20, 1963; children: Dana Dallas, Povy Kendal Dallas. BA, U. Denver, 1960. Asst. editor U. Denver Mag., 1965-66; editl. asst. Bus. Week, Denver, 1961-63, 67-69, bur. chief, 1969-85, 90-91, sr. corr., 1985-90; freelance editor, 1990—. Book reviewer Denver Post, 1961—, regional book columnist, 1980—. Author: Gaslights and Gingerbread, 1965, rev. edit., 1984, Gold and Gothic, 1967, No More Than 5 in a Bed, 1967, Vail, 1969, Cherry Creek Gothic, 1971, Yesterday's Denver, 1974, Sacred Paint, 1980, Colorado Ghost Towns and Mining Camps, 1985, Colorado Homes, 1986, Buster Midnight's Cafe, 1990, reissued 1998, The Persian Pickle Club, 1995, The Diary of Mattie Spenser, 1997, Alice's Tulips, 2000, The Chili Queen, 2002; editor: The Colorado Book, 1993; contbr. articles to various mags. Bd. dirs. Vis. Nurse Assn., Denver, 1983-85, Hist. Denver, Inc., 1979-82, 84-87, Rocky Mountain Quilt Mus., 2001—, Historic Georgetown, Inc., 2002—. Recipient Wrangler award Nat. Cowboy Hall of Fame, 1980, Lifetime Achievement award Denver Posse of Westerners, 1996, disting. svc. award U. Colo., 1997; named Colo. Exceptional Chronicler of Western History by Women's Library Assn. and Denver Pub. Library Friends Found., 1986; finalist Spur award We. Writers of Am., 1998, recipient, 2003, Willa award Women Writing the West, 2000, Colo. Book awards, 2000. Mem. Women's Forum Colo., Denver Woman's Press Club, Western Writers Am. (Spur award 2003), Women Writing the West. Democrat. Presbyterian. Home and Office: 750 Marion St Denver CO 80218-3434

DALLAS, SATERIOS (SAM DALLAS), aerospace engineer, researcher, consultant; b. Detroit, May 9, 1938; s. Peter and Pauline (Alex) D.; m. Athena Ethel Spartos, July 12, 1964; children: Gregory Dean, Paula Marie. BS in Aero. Engring., U. Mich., 1959, BS in Engring. Math., 1960; MS in Astrodynamics, UCLA, 1963, PhD in Engring., 1968. Rsch. engr. astrodynamics dept. Jet Propulsion Lab., Pasadena, Calif., 1965-78, supr. tech. group mission design, 1978-82, flight engring. office mgr. Voyager Project, 1982-84, sci. and mission design mgr. Magellan Project, 1984-89, tech. mgr. spacecraft analysis, 1989-90, mission mgr. Mars Observer Project, 1990-93, mission mgr. Mars Global Surveyor Project, 1994-97, mission mgr. space interferometry mission, 1997-99, flight project mentor, 2002—. Instr. Pepperdine U., Malibu, Calif., 1973-75; lectr. on space missions Kennedy Space Ctr., Cape Canaveral, Fla., 1988, Australian Dept. Industry, Tech. and Commerce, Canberra, 1988, USAF-CAP-PLR Ctr. Aerospace Edn., Las Vegas, Neb., 1991. Author: Progress in Astronautics and Aeronautics, 1964, Natural and Artificial Satellite Motion, 1979; contbr. articles to sci. jours. Coach Glendale (Calif.) Little League, 1979-82; com. mem. troop 125 Boy Scouts Am., Glendale, 1980. Recipient Apollo achievement award NASA, 1969, cert. of recognition, 1974, Laurels award Aviation Week, 1989, 94, Exceptional Achievement award NASA, 1998. Mem. AIAA, Am. Astron. Soc. (astrodynamics tech. com. 1970-80). Republican. Greek Orthodox. Avocations: snow skiing, hiking, woodworking, tennis, computer applications development. Home: 3860 Karen Lynn Dr Glendale CA 91206-1218 Office: Jet Propulsion Lab 4800 Oak Grove Dr Pasadena CA 91109-8001 E-mail: ssd1938@hotmail.com.

DALLAS, WILLIAM MOFFIT, JR., lawyer; b. Cedar Rapids, Iowa, May 7, 1949; s. William Moffit and Winifred Mae (Lillie) D.; m. Lynne Louise Russo, July 30, 1977 (div. July 1984); m. Janet Neustaetter, Apr. 19, 1985; children: Sarah Anne, Steven Kurt. AB, Oberlin Coll., 1971; JD, Harvard U., 1974. Bar: N.Y. 1975, U.S. Dist. Ct. (so. and ea. dists.) N.Y. 1975, U.S. Ct. Appeals (2d cir.) 1976, U.S. Ct. Appeals (3d cir.) 1983, U.S. Ct. Appeals (8th cir.) 1984. Assoc. Sullivan & Cromwell, N.Y.C., 1974-82, ptnr., 1982—. Fed. mediator U.S. Dist. Ct., 1995—. Contbr. articles on antitrust issues to law revs., 1978—, chpt. to book. Served to lt. USN, 1971-77. Mem. ABA, Assn. of Bar of City of N.Y. (chmn. com. on judicial admin., 1999—, sec. judiciary com. 1977-80, chmn. com. jud. adminstrn. 1999-2002), N.Y. County Lawyers' Assn. (chmn. com. on trade regulation 1978-81), India House Club (N.Y.C.). Office: Sullivan & Cromwell 125 Broad St Fl 28 New York NY 10004-2489

DALLA-VICENZA, MARIO JOSEPH, steel company executive; b. Sudbury, Ont., Can., Oct. 30, 1938; s. Mario Valentino and Cecilia (Bonaldo) D.-V.; m. Deanna Karen Leblanc, July 15, 1961; children: Janice, Peter, Mark. Grad. in acctg., Queens U., Kingston, Can., 1962, McMaster U., Can., 1969; MBA, Lake Superior State U., 1983. Chartered acct., Can.; cert. mgmt. acct., Can. Acct. Tessier, Massicotte & Co., Sault Ste Marie, Ont., 1957-63; with Algoma Steel Corp., Sault Ste Marie, 1963-83, gen. mgr. corp. acctg. svcs., 1981-83; treas. IPSCO Inc., Regina, Sask., Can., 1983-87, v.p., CFO, 1987-88, sr. v.p., CFO, 1988-96, sr. v.p. corp. affairs, 1996-97; pres. Demar Enterprises, Sault Ste Marie, Ont., Can., 1998—. Pres., bd. dirs. Sault Ste Marie C. of C., 1974-79; chmn. econ. devel. coun. City of Sault Ste Marie, 1981-83. Fellow Inst. Chartered Accts. (nat. coun., nat. exec. com. 1994-95, provincial coun. 1990-96, pres. 1996); mem. Soc. Mgmt. Accts. (pres., provincial coun. 1984-88, fellow 1993, nat. bd. 1989-90), Fin. Execs. Inst. (bd. dirs. Regina chpt. 1985-90, chpt. pres. 1989-90), Ranch Ehrlo Soc. (bd. dirs. 1992-99, chmn. 1997-99). Office: Algoma Steel PO Box 1400 Sault Sainte Marie ON Canada P6A 5P2

DALLEK, ROBERT, history educator; b. Bklyn., May 16, 1934; s. Rubin and Esther (Fisher) Dallek; m. Ilse F. Shatzkin, Nov. 20, 1959 (dec. Oct. 1962); m. Geraldine R. Kronmal, Aug. 22, 1965; children: Matthew J., Rebecca R. BA, U. Ill., 1955; MA, Columbia U., 1957, PhD, 1964. Lectr. history CCNY, 1959-60; instr. history Columbia U., N.Y.C., 1960-64; from asst. prof. to prof. UCLA 1964—, vice-chmn. dept. history, 1972-74; prof. history Boston U., 1996—. Rsch. assoc. So. Calif. Psychoanalytic Inst., L.A., 1981—85; Commonwealth Fund lectr. Univ. Coll., London, 1984; Thompson lectr. U. Wyo., Laramie, 1986; Charles Griffin lectr. Vassar Coll., Poughkeepsie, NY, 1987; George W. Littlefield lectr. U. Tex., Austin, 1990; vis. Harmsworth prof. Oxford U., England, 1994—95; cons. ABC, N.Y.C., 1981—82, Ednl. Film Ctr., Annandale, Va., 1988, Sta. KCET-TV, L.A., 1988, KERA-TV, Dallas, 1989—91. Author: Democrat and Diplomat: the Life of William E. Dodd, 1968, Franklin D. Roosevelt and American Foreign Policy, 1932-1945, 1979, The American Style of Foreign Policy: Cultural Politics and Foreign Affairs, 1983, Ronald Reagan: The Politics of Symbolism, 1984, Lone Star Rising: Lyndon Johnson and His Times, 1908-1960, 1991, Hail to the Chief: The Making and Unmaking of American Presidents, 1996, Flawed Giant: Lyndon Johnson and His Times 1961-1973, 1998, An Unfinished Life: John F. Kennedy, 1917-1963, 2003; editor: 3 books; contbr. Mem. adv. com. on diplomatic documents Dept. State, Washington, 1985—88; mem. adv. com. Mayor Tom Bradley, L.A., 1986; mem. adv. com. on ethics L.A. City Coun., 1989—90; bd. dirs. FDR and Eleanor Roosevelt Inst., 2003—, Nat. Portrait Gallery, 2003—. John Simon Guggenheim fellow, 1973—74, sr. fellow, NEH, 1976—77, Humanities fellow, Rockefeller Found., 1981—82, Am. Coun. Learned Socs. fellow, 1984—85, Rsch. grant, Eleanor Roosevelt Inst., 1976—77, Lyndon B. Johnson Found., 1984—85, 1988—89. Fellow: Am. Acad. Arts and Scis., Soc. Am. Historians; mem.: Com. on History Second World War, Soc. for Historians of Am. Fgn. Rels. Home: 2138 Cathedral Ave NW Washington DC 20008-1502 Office: Boston U Dept History Boston MA 02215

DALLEMAGNE-COOKSON, ELISE CAMILLE, writer; b. Tarrytown, N.Y., Mar. 31, 1933; d. Edmund Leo and Irene (Poisson) Cookson; m. Jeremy Gaige, June 6, 1951 (div. June 1955); m. Pierre Georges Dallemagne (dec. May 1979); children: Pierre E. (dec. May 1994), Paul C. AB, Katherine Gibbs Bus. Sch., 1951; student, NYU, 1951-52, Syracuse U., 1952-54, Fla. Inst. Tech., 1973-75. Publicist, prodn. asst. United Artists, 20th Century Fox, Columbia Pictures, Robert Rossen Prodns., N.Y., Hollywood, Calif., 1955—59; ptnr. Katzka, Farrell, Gaige Films; pub. affairs officer U.S. Fgn. Svc., 1959—60; farmer Congo and Argentina, 1959-68; internat. hi-tech sales rep. Harris Computers Fla., 1975-78; registered rep. Wall Street various internat. banks, N.Y.C., 1980-89; fgn. lang. tchr. Cherry Valley (N.Y.) Schs., 1989-93. Author: Simplified Swahili, 1970, The Bearded Lion Who Roars, 1995, The Ombu Tree, 1998, The Filmmaker, 2000, The Red-Eye Fever, 2002, Marie Grandin-Sent by the King, 2003; contbr. articles to mags. and features to newspapers. Avocations: farming, teaching. Home and Office: 311 County Highway 34A Cherry Valley NY 13320-2404 E-mail: Elise@Dallemagne-Cookson.com

DALLEN, RUSSELL MORRIS, JR., investment company executive, lawyer, publishing company executive; b. Biloxi, Mississippi, Jan. 20, 1963; s. Russell Morris and Faye Annette (Werner) D.; m. Claire Lucia (Hodgson), May 27, 1995; children: Allegra Julia Faye, Arabella Sarah Emma. BA in econ. and polit. sci., U. Miss., 1985; M in internat. affairs, Columbia U., 1987; diploma in internat. law, Nottingham U., Eng., 1988; BA in jurisprudence, Oxford U., Eng., 1990, MA in law, 1994. Fgn. corr. Newsweek, London, 1990-91; sr. fellow, dir. UN Assn., USA, N.Y.C., 1991-93; assoc. Morgan Stanley and Co., Inc., N.Y.C., 1994-96; ptnr. Stires, O'Donnell and Co., Inc., 1996-99, Brisbane, Mendez de Leon and Co., Fahnestock and Co.,Inc., Oppenheimer and Co., Inc., 2000—; pres., editor in chief The Daily Jour., 2003—. Author with others: Revitalizing The United Nations, 1993; Issues Before the United Nations, 1989, A Global Agenda, 1992; contbg. articles to profl. jour. Bd. gov. Harold W. Rosenthal Fellowship, Washington, 1985—; exec. com. Manhattan coun. Boy Scouts Am., N.Y.C., 1992—; vol. Big Bros. and Big Sisters, N.Y.C., 1992—. Recipient Ner Tamid Leadership Award; Nat. Jewish Com. on Scouting, 1979; Kluwer Internat. Law Award, 1990; Article of Yr. Award Common Market Law Rev.; named Century III Leader, 1981; Harry S. Truman scholar, 1983; U.K. Fgn. and Commonwealth Office scholar, 1987; Harold Rosenthal Fellow, 1985; Am. Fellow European Communities, 1986; Ctr. Fellow Ctr. for Study of Presdy., 1985. Mem. N.Y. State Bar Assn.; N.Y. County Lawyers Assn. (chmn. sub-com. 1992—); Oxford and Cambridge Club; Squadron A Club; Cornell Club; Landsdowne Club. Avocations: sailing, flying, riding. Home: M 365 PO Box 3340 New York NY 10185-3340

DALLENBACH, WALLY, JR., professional race car driver; b. May 23, 1963; s. Wally Dallenbach Sr.; m. Robin Dallenbach; children: Jacob, Wyatt, Katie. Driver Team Sabco, 1998, Hendrick Motorsports, 1999—. Named SCCA Trans-Am. Rookie of Yr., 1984, SCCA Trans-Am. champion, 1985, Roush Racing champion, 1985, SCCA Trans-Am. champion, 1986, Roush Racing champion, 1986, IMSA GTO Series runner-up, 1988—89, NASCAR Winston Cup series debut, 1991; recipient 2d place, 1993 Bud at the Glen, 1995 MBNA Pontiac, divsn. title, IMSA Rolex 24 Hours of Daytona, 1985, 1991, 1992, 1993. Avocation: hunting.

DALLER, JOHN ALFONS, transplant surgeon; b. N.,Y.C., Mar. 8, 1960; s. John A. and Therese Daller; m. Debra Gail DelPeschio, Nov. 10, 1995; children: Bethany Morgan, John James, Kelsey Suzanne, Christopher Michael, Matthew Alfons, Nathan J. Thomas. BS, St. John's U., Jamaica, N.Y., 1981, MS, 1983; MD, SUNY, Bklyn., 1987; PhD, U. Ariz., 1994. Diplomate gen. surgery Am. Bd. Surgery, 2000, surg. critical care Am. Bd. Surgery Phila., 2000. Asst. prof. surgery U. Tex. Med. Br., Galveston, 1999—2003, U. Rochester, NY, 2003—. Cons. Daller Consulting, Rochester, 1996—; med. dir. Fingerlake Organ Procurement Orgn., Rochester, 2003—; dir.renal and pancreas transplantation U. Rochester, 2003—. Career Devel. fellow, Soc. U. Surgeons, 2002—03. Fellow: ACS; mem.: Soc. Critical Care Medicine, Am. Soc. Transplantation, Am. Soc. Transplant Surgeons, Assn. for Academic Surgery (program com. 2002—). Achievements include research in transplant immunology. Home: 2514 Gerol Cir Galveston TX 77551-1582 Office: Univ Tex Med Br 301 University Blvd Galveston TX 77555-0533 Home Fax: 409-747-7364; Office Fax: 409-747-7364. Personal E-mail: jadaller@utmb.edu. E-mail: jadaller@utmb.edu.

DALLER, WALTER E., JR., banking executive; b. Parkesburg, Pa., Mar. 31, 1939; s. Walter E. and Edna (Miller) D.; m. Ruth Ann Daller (Bridgie); children: Walter III, Gregory, Susan. BBA, Lafayette Coll., 1961. With Harleysville Nat. Bank and Trust Co., Pa., 1962—, pres., CEO, chmn., 1981-98, also bd. dir., chmn., CEO, 1999—; dir. Fed. Res. Bank of Phila., Pa., 2003—; op. Citizens Nat. Bank, Lansford, Pa. Bd. dirs. Harleysville Nat. Corp., Citizens Nat. Bank, Lansford, Pa., Security Nat. Bank, Pottstown, Pa.; rep. 3rd dist. adv. coun. Fed. Res. Bank, 1996, 97, 98; Visa nat. bd. Merchant Bank Svcs., 1993—; founding bd. dirs. TCM Bank; op. twenty-three offices Harleysville Nat. Bank and Trust Co., Montgomery and Bucks Counties. Named Paul Harris Fellow, The North Penn Rotary (chpt. of The Rotary Found.), 1999; recipient the coveted Muhlenberg Leadership award, Hist. Soc. of Trappe and the Muhlenberg House, 1999. Mem.: Montgomery County Lands Trust (bd. dir.), Fed. Adv. Coun. (rep. Pa., NJ, Del., the Third Fed. Reserve Dist. 1993—96), TCM Bd. Dir., Ind. Cmty. Bankers of Am. Assn. (ICBA) (mem. bd. dir., mem. Nominating Com., mem. Fed. Ligis. Com., mem. Payments and Tech. Com., mem. Nat. Task Force for Electronic Funds Transfer, two terms treas., mem. exec. com.), Cmty. Bankers Pa. (past pres. 1988, bd. dir. 1988—93), Pa. Bankers Assn. (governing coun. 1989—91), Ind. Commercial Bankers Assn. (exec. com. 1990—, mem. nominating com.), St. Luke's United Ch. of Christ Coun. (past pres.), Perkiomen Valley Watershed (bd. dir.), The Muhlenberg House (bd. dir.), the Lower Salford Hist. Soc. (bd. dir.), North Penn United Way (bd. dir.), Lions (past pres. Limerick, Pa. club), Masons. Republican. Avocations: hunting, golf. Office: Harleysville Nat Bank/Trust PO Box 195 483 Main St Harleysville PA 19438-2311

DALLES, JOHN ALLAN, minister; b. Pitts., Sept. 13, 1954; s. John Samuel and Patricia (Yolton) D.; m. Judith Ann Taylor; children: John Taylor, Anne Elizabeth. MDiv, Lancaster Theol. Sem., 1982; D Ministry, Pitts. Theol. Sem., 1994. Ordained minister Donegal Presbytery, 1982. Assoc. pastor First Presbyn. Ch., South Bend, Ind., 1982-86, Fox Chapel Presbyn. Ch., Pitts., 1986-97; sr. pastor Wekiva Presbyn. Ch., Longwood, Fla., 1997—. Author over 250 hymn texts, appearing in the Presbyn. Hymnal, New Century Hymnal, Worship Together, Come, O Spirit, Moravian Book of Worship; author, editor: (book) In Life and in Death We Belong to God, Covenant Hymnal, Book of Praise (Canadian), Australian Book of Praise, (anthology of hymns) Swift Currents and Still Waters, 2000, also others: contbr. articles to profl. jours. Mem. area coun. of various religions orgns.; bd. dirs., awards chmn. St. Joseph County Scholarship Found.; mem. worship task force, mem. com. on discipleship and ch. life Wabash Valley Presbytery; chmn. theology and worship com. Ctrl. Fla. Presbytery, Ctrl. Fla. Presbyn. Ch. Alt. commr. to 215th and 216th Gen. Assemblies, Presbyn. Coun. U.S.A.; founding mem. Notre Dame Civitan, South Bend Habitat for Humanity. Paul Harris fellow Rotary Internat., 1998. Mem. Hymn Soc. Presbyterian. Office: 211 Wekiva Springs Ln Longwood FL 32779-3601

D'ALLESANDRO, DAVID F. insurance company executive; b. Utica, N.Y., Feb. 6, 1951; children: Michael, Andrew. BS in Pub. Rels. and Journalism, Syracuse U., 1972. Reporter Gannett Newspaper, Utica, 1969; account supr. Daniel J. Edelman, Inc., N.Y., 1972; gen. mgr. Comml. Credit Co., N.Y., 1974-84; v.p. corp. comms. John Hancock Mut. Life Ins., Boston, 1984-86, sr. v.p. corp. comms., 1986-87, pres. corp. sector, 1988-91, sr. exec. v.p. retail sector, 1991—, mem. mgmt. com., 1989—, now pres., COO, also bd. dirs. Dir. John Hancock Freedom Securities, Boston, 1988—, John Hancock Subs., Inc., Boston, 1988—. Bd. advisors Red Auerbach Fund for Youth, Boston; chair Fenway Fantasy Day, Jimmy Fund, Boston; bd. dirs. Mass. Sports Partnership, The Kennedy Sch., Harvard U.; bd. trustees Syracuse U., Boston U.; chmn. bd. The Wang Ctr. Named one of 100 Most Powerful People in Sports, Sporting News, 1996, Marketer of Yr., ADWEEK Mag., 1986. Office: John Hancock Fin Svcs John Hancock Place Boston MA 02117-0111

DALLEY, GEORGE ALBERT, lawyer, consultant; b. Havana, Cuba, Aug. 25, 1941; s. Cleveland Ernest and Constance Joyce (Powell) D.; m. Pearl Elizabeth Love, Aug. 1, 1970; children: Jason Christopher, Benjamin Christian. AB, Columbia U., 1963, JD, MBA, Columbia U., 1966. Bar: N.Y. 1966, D.C. 1971, U.S. Supreme Ct. 1972. Asst. to pres. Met. Applied Rsch. Ctr., N.Y.C., 1967-69; counsel The Children's Found., Washington, 1970-71; assoc. counsel Stroock and Stroock and Lavan, Washington, 1970-71, Com. on Judiciary, U.S. Ho. of Reps., Washington, 1971-72; adminstrv. asst. to Rep. Charles B. Rangel, N.Y.C., Washington, 1973-77, counsel, staff dir., 1985-89; dep. asst. sec. for human rights and social affairs Bur. Internat. Orgns. Affairs Dept. State, Washington, 1977-80; mem. CAB, 1980-82; dep. dir. Mondale for Pres. Com., Washington, 1983-84; counsel, staff dir. Congressman Charles B. Rangel, U.S. Ho. of Reps., Washington, 1985-89; sr. v.p. Neill and Co., Washington, 1989-93; ptnr. Neill, Dalley, Carroll, Nealer and Assevero, Washington, 1992-93; sr. ptnr. Holland and Knight, Washington, 1993—. Adj. prof. Am. U. Sch. Law. Mem. legal adv. com. Dem. Nat. Com., 1975-76; bd. dirs. Africare, TransAfrica; Joint Ctr. for Polit. and Econ. Studies Internat. Inst., Jamaica Nats. Devel. Found. Mem. ABA, Nat. Bar Assn., Fed. Bar Assn., Nat. Conf. Black Lawyers, Cosmos Club, Coun. Fgn. Rels., Coun. Ams. Presbyterian. Home: 1328 Vermont Ave NW Washington DC 20005-3607 Office: Rm 2354 US House Rep Washington DC 20515

DALLMAN, MARY F. physiologist, science educator; BA in Chemistry, Smith Coll., 1956; PhD in Physiology, Stanford U., 1967; postgrad., Swedish Royal Vet. Sch., 1968, U. Calif., San Francisco, 1969—70. Lectr. U. Calif. Dept. Physiology, San Francisco, 1970—72, aast., 1972—76, assoc. prof., 1976—81, prof., 1981—, vice-chair, 1987—. Assoc. editor Am. Jour. Physiol.: Endocrnology and Metabolism, 1979—85, Steroids, 1919—87, Am. Jour. Physiol.: Regulatory, Integrative and Comparative Physiology, 1990—92; contbr. articles to profl. jours. Recipient Am. Diabetes Rsch. award, 1996. Mem.: NIH (mem. endocrine study sect. 1977—81, mem. diabetes, digestive, kidney grants rev. subcom. 1988—92, chair 1992—93), Internat. Soc. Neuroendocrinology (pres. 1996), Women in Endocrinology (pres. 1993—95). Office: U Calif Dept Physiology Box 0444 HSW 747 513 Parnassus Ave San Francisco CA 94143

DALLMAN, PAUL JERALD, engineer, writer; b. Washington, July 7, 1939; s. Paul Frederick and Helen Anna (Roloff) D. BS in Civil Engring., U. Md., 1963, Mus.M., 1972. Registered profl. engr., Md., Va. Engr. Washington Surburban San. Commn., Hyattsville, Md., 1963-72; pvt. cons. engr., 1972—; engr. Joyce Engring. Corp., Beltsville, Md., 1987-88, Greenman-Pedersen, Inc., Laurel, Md., 1989, MK Enterprises, Silver Spring, Md., 1989-90, Clark, Finefrock and Sackett, Columbia, Md., 1993-94; customer rels. assoc. Sky Alland Rsch., Laurel, Md., 1994—; interview specialist Mathematica Policy Rsch., Inc., Columbia, Md., 1997—, Arbitron, Columbia, 1997—. Dir. Nat. Assn. Ind. Record Distbrs. and Mfrs., Washington, 1975; also editor NAIRD News; lectr., demonstrator early music machines and phonographs Smithsonian Instn., 1977—; jazz dir. Sta. WMUC-FM, 1980-87; host, producer, engr. Sta. WDCU-FM, 1982, Sta. WAMU-FM, 1982-85; programmer Studioline Nat. Cable Stereo Svc., 1985-86; music editor films and TV USIA, Washington, 1967-68. Profl. singer St. Paul's Ch., Alexandria, Va., 1967-71, Washington Camerata Chorus, 1968, St. John's Ch., Chevy Chase, Md., 1974-83; composer, performer (film) Hairspray, 1988; actor: (extra) The Pelican Brief, 1993; TV appearances include Good Morning America, CBS Morning News, The Buddy Deane Show, The Milt Grant Show, Krazy Greg's Platter Party; author: Guitar Teaching in the United States (The Life and Work of Sophocles Papas), 1978; critic Washington Star newspaper, 1970-73; contbg. writer Washington Times newspaper, 1991-92; contbr. articles to profl. jours.; writer, producer narrator Nat. Pub. Radio-program Hist. Am. Patriotic Recs., 1976. Music Critics Assn. fellow Round Top, Tex., 1977; Nat. Endowment Arts grantee, 1976 Mem. BMI. Home: 125 Irving St Laurel MD 20707-4503

DALLMAN, ROBERT EDWARD, lawyer; b. Shawano, Wis., Apr. 16, 1947; BA, Valparaiso U., 1970; JD, U. Kans., 1973; LLM, Georgetown U., 1977. Bar: Kans. 1973, U.S. Tax Ct. 1973, U.S. Supreme Ct. 1978, Wis. 1980. Chief counsel IRS, Washington, 1973-77, Milw., 1977-80; shareholder Reinhart, Boerner, Van Deuren, Norris & Rieselbach S.C., Milw. Instr. corp. tax. planning and advanced real estate tax planning U. Wis., Milw., 1981—; cons. to chief counsel IRS, Washington, 1980. Co-author: Tax Planning for Real Estate Transactions, 1983; contbr. articles to profl. jours. Mem. ABA, State Bar Wis., Milw. Bar Assn. Office: Reinhart Boerner Van Deuren PO Box 92900 1000 N Water St Ste 2100 Milwaukee WI 53202-3197 E-mail: rdallman@reinhartlaw.com.

DALLMANN, WILLIAM CHARLES, speech educator, writer; b. Detroit, Nov. 16, 1929; s. Bertram and Lillian Dallmann; m. Constance Joan Covington; children: Shane, Alan, Lara. AB in Speech and Drama, San Francisco State U., 1954, MA in Drama, 1963; PhD in Speech Pathology, Purdue U., 1973. Cert. Am. Speech Hearing and Lang. Assn. Prof. communicative disorders Valparaiso (Ind.) U., 1964—84; Ju-Jutsu sensei Pacific Acad. Life Arts, Monterey, Calif., 1984—89; freelance writer Monterey, 2001—. Pvt. investigator Wittlinger Agy., Indpls., 1982—84; speech pathologist, clin. hypnotist Counseling Assocs., Valparaiso, 1976—81, exec. dir., 1976—81; dir. Speech Lang. Clinic, Valparaiso, 1964—84. Author: The Children of Prometheus, 1999, 2 Kill or Not to Kill, 2001. 1st lt. U.S. Army, 1951—53, Korea. Mem.: ACLU, Internat. Soc. Gen. Semantics, Vets. for Peace, Amnesty Internat., 25th Infantry Divsn. Assn. (life). Lutheran. Avocations: reading, languages, quantum physics, theology, semantics. Home: 4080 Los Altos Drive Pebble Beach CA 93953 E-mail: raven@redshift.com.

DALLMEYER, ROBERT FREDERICK, exhibitions executive; b. Pittsfield, Mass., Jan. 1, 1938; s. Frederick Charles and Madeline Rita (Morrissey) D.; children: Kimberly Ann Kapelson, Kristen Elizabeth Nimr. BA in Sociology and English, U. Mass., 1959. Dir. tech. presentations United Tech., Hartford, Conn., 1960-82; v.p. Elec. Convention Mgmt., L.A., 1982-83; pres. Event Exhbn. Enterprises, L.A., 1983; v.p. Brussels Exhbn. Ctr.; owner, founder Robert Dallmeyer Internat., L.A., 1984—. Pres. Sterling Gavin Assocs., Conn., 1975—77; cons. Monterrey (Mex.) Conv. and Visitors, Bastizan Data Systems, Calif. Restaurant Assn., 2000; pres. adv. bd. Project Return, L.A., 1994—; instr. event mgmt. George Washington U., Washington, 1999—. Author: International Exhibition Handbook, 1980, Snapshots, 1984, (booklet) Successful Logistics, 1999; columnist (mag.) Ideas mag., 1982—. Bd. dirs., v.p. U. Mass. Alumni, Amherst, 1965-72, U. Mass. Found., Amherst, 1972-78; bd. dirs. Hill Ctr., Hartford, 1976-79. Recipient Disting. Svc. award U. Mass., 1981. Mem.: Ctr. Exhbn. Industry Rsch. (bd. dirs. 1976—), Trade Show Exhibitors Assn. (chmn., Pres. award 1979, 1979, Disting. Svc. award 1983, Life Mem. award 2001), Internat. Assn. Exhbn. Mgrs. (chmn.). Avocations: theater, music, bicycling, teaching. Home: 357 S Curson Ave Ste 5D Los Angeles CA 90036 E-mail: dallmeyer@cs.com.

DALLOS, JOSEPH, general contractor, remodeler; b. Cleve., July 13, 1937; s. Joseph Zoltan and Elizabeth Dallos; m. Dianne L. Dallos, Sept. 14, 1957 (div. July 1989); children: Carol, Nora Dallos-Stephan, Brad, Gordon; m. Nancy J. Montgomery, Mar. 20, 1992; 1 child, Ray Montgomery. Student, Case Inst. Tech., 1955—56, Fenn Coll., 1956—58. Mem. fin. com., safety com., city growth and devel. com., wastewater sys. com., chmn. city city svcs. and improvements Euclid City Coun., 1989-99, mem. coun., 1975-77, 89-99, mem. litter control bd., 1983, mem. charter rev. commn., 1982. Recipient regional award NARI, 1984, 86, 90, 91, Contractor of Yr. award NARI, 1990, 91, 93, 99. Mem. Am. Arbitration Assn. (constrn. area arbitrator), Bldg. Industry Assn., Downtown Euclid Assn., Euclid C. of C., Nat. Assn. Remodeling Industry, Euclid Jaycees (life, Presdl. award of honor 1961, 63, Key Man in Chpt. 1961, Outstanding Young Men 1962, 1st v.p. 1953, state dir. 1965, Outstanding Chmn. Com. 1967, Businessperson of Yr. 1983). Address: 22660 Shore Center Dr Euclid OH 44123-1699

DALLOS, PETER JOHN, neurobiologist, educator; b. Budapest, Hungary, Nov. 26, 1934; came to U.S., 1956, naturalized, 1962; s. Ernest and Maria Dallos; m. Joan Usis, Aug. 18, 1977; 1 child by previous marriage, Christopher. Student, Tech. U. Budapest, 1953-56; BS, Ill. Inst. Tech., 1958; MS, Northwestern U., 1959, PhD, 1962. Rsch. engr. Am. Machine and Foundry Co., 1959; cons. engr., 1959-60; mem. faculty Northwestern U., 1962—, prof. audiology and elec. engring., 1969—, prof. neurobiology and physiology, 1981—, chmn., 1981-84, 86-87, assoc. dean Coll. Arts and Scis., 1984-85, John Evans prof. neurosci., 1986—, Hugh Knowles prof. audiology, 1994—. Vis. scientist Karolinska Inst., Stockholm, 1977-78; chmn. behavioral and neurosci. rev. panel No. 5 Nat. Inst. Neurol., Communicative Disorders and Stroke, NIH, 1982-85, mem. nat. adv. council, 1984-87 Author: The Auditory Periphery: Biophysics and Physiology, 1973; editor: The Cochlea, 1996; contbr. articles to profl. jours. Recipient 12th ann. award Beltone Inst. Hearing Rsch., 1977, Internat. prize Amplifon Rsch. and Study Ctr., 1984, Senator Jacob Javits Neurosci. Investigator award, 1984, Honors of Assn. award Am. Speech-Lang.-Hearing Assn., 1994, Bekesy medal of Acoustical Soc. Am., 1995, Sigma Xi Disting. Nat. lectr., 1997-98, Acta Otolaryngologica Internat. prize, 1997, Kresge-Mirmelstein prize La. State U., 2000; Guggenheim fellow, 1977-78; McKnight sr. fellow, 1997-2000. Fellow IEEE (life), AAAS, Acoustical Soc. Am., Am. Acad. Arts and Scis.; mem. Soc. for Neurosci., Assn. for Rsch. in Otolaryngology (pres. 1992-93, award of merit 1994), Collegium Otolaryngologicum Amicitae Sacrum, Sigma Xi, Tau Beta Pi, Eta Kappa Nu. Office: Northwestern U 2299 N Campus Dr Evanston IL 60208-0837 E-mail: p-dallos@northwestern.edu.

DALLURA, SAL ANTHONY, physician; b. Flushing, N.Y., Nov. 7, 1960; s. Russ and Mayann (Taranto) D.; m. Donna Ann Baldassare, Aug. 6, 1983 (div. Mar. 1993); children: Christopher Anthony, Corinne Elizabeth; m. Stacy Elizabeth Carberry, July 1, 1995 (div. Jan. 1999); 1 child, Matthew Anthony; m. Tammy L. Chance, Dec. 27, 1999. BS, U. Notre Dame, 1982; DO, N.Y. Coll. Osteo. Medicine, 1986. Diplomate Am. Acad. Family Physicians. Mng. ptnr. Flashner Med. Ptnrship., Babylon, N.Y., 1989-91; assoc. physician Moriches Med. Care, Center Moriches, N.Y., 1989-91, Digiovanna, Massepequa Park, N.Y., 1991-92, Tippecanoe Family Physicians, Tipp City, Ohio, 1992-98, Milton Union Med. Ctr., West Milton, Ohio, 1998-2000; physician mng. ptnr. After Hours Family Care, Tipp City, 1994-98; physician Upper Valley Profl. Corp., 1994-2000, Kenbrook Med. Ctr., 2000—02, St. Marys (Ohio) Family Practice, St. Marys, Ohio, 2002—. Mem. sci. adv. bd. nutrition Superstores Am., Radiation Ctrs. Am.; mem. med. adv. bd. HAWA Corp. Med. Divsn.; expert witness malpractice def., case revs., depositions, testimony for family practice. Mem. Am. Osteo. Assn., Am. Acad. Family Practice, Ohio Osteo. Assn., Ohio State Med. Assn. Republican. Roman Catholic. Avocations: model railroading, coin and stamp collecting, reading, music, computer research. Office: 1300 Greenville Rd Saint Marys OH 45885-2427 E-mail: sdallura@bright.net.

DALLY, JAMES WILLIAM, mechanical engineering educator, consultant; b. Sardis, Ohio, Aug. 2, 1929; s. William Hiram and Martha (Siebert) D.; m. Anne Evangeline Tziritas, Dec. 22, 1955; children: Lisa, William, Michelle. BSME, Carnegie Mellon U., 1951, MSME, 1953; PhD, Ill. Inst. Tech., 1958. Registered profl. engr., Md. Asst. dir. rsch. Armour Research Found., Chgo., 1961-64; prof. Ill. Inst. Tech., Chgo., 1964-71; prof., chmn. dept. U. Md., College Park, 1971-79; dean Coll. Engring. U. R.I., Kingston, 1979-82; mgr. mech. devel. IBM, Manassas, Va., 1982-84; prof. mech. engring. U. Md., College Park, 1984-97. Disting. vis. prof. USAF Acad., 1995-96; mem. tech. assessment bd. Army Rsch. Lab., 1997-2000. Author: Experimental Stress Analysis, 1965, 3rd edit., 1991, Photoelastic Coatings, 1977, Engineering Measurements, 1984, 2nd edit., 1993, Packaging Electronic Systems, 1990, Introduction to Engineering Design, 1997, Product Engineering and Manufacturing, 1998, Design Analysis of Structural Elements, 3rd edit., 2003; contbr. articles. Recipient Boeing Outstanding Educator award, 1996. Fellow ASME, Am. Acad. Mechanics (bd. dirs. 1984-88, pres. 1990-91), Soc. Exptl. Mechanics (hon., pres. 1970-71, Murray lectureship 1979, Past Pres. award 1971, M.M. Frocht award 1976, Hetenyi award 1995, F.G. Tatnall award 2001, Charles E. Taylor award 2002); mem. Nat. Acad. Engring., U.S. Nat. Com. Theoretical and Applied Mechanics (chmn. 1982-84, vice-chmn., 1984-86). Achievements include patents in field. E-mail: jdally0829@comcast.net.

DALMAN, GISLI CONRAD, electrical engineering educator; b. Winnipeg, Man., Can., Apr. 7, 1917; s. Conrad Fred and Valgerdur (Thorsteinsdottir) D.; m. Catherine Stewart, Dec. 24, 1941; children: Diana Dalman Dotson, Kristine, Karen, Conrad. B.E.E., Coll. City N.Y., 1940; M.E.E., Polytechnic U., Bklyn., 1947, D.E.E., 1949. Mfg. engr. RCA, 1940-45; mem. tech. staff Bell Telephone Labs., 1945-47; engring. sect. head Sperry Gyroscope Co., Great Neck, N.Y., 1949-56; mem. faculty Cornell U., Ithaca, N.Y., 1956—, prof. elec. engring., 1956-87, prof. emeritus, 1987—; acting dir. Sch. Elec. Engring., 1972-73, dir., 1975-80. Adj. prof. Polytechnic U., Bklyn., 1954-56; cons. to industry, 1956—; cons. on millimeter wave amplifiers to TRW, Redondo Beach, Calif., 1980-81 Author articles on microwave solid state devices; co-author two textbooks;

holder 5 U.S. patents. Project mgr. UN Spl. Fund China Project, Chiao Tung U., Hsinchu, Taiwan, 1962-63. Fellow IEEE, AAAS; mem. Sigma Xi, Tau Beta Pi, Eta Kappa Nu. Home: 5 Dandyview Hts Lansing NY 14882-8852 E-mail: gdalman@twcny.rr.com.

DALMAS-BROWN, CARMELLA JEAN, special education educator; b. Dec. 31, 1959; d. Bruno L. and Mary S. (Pashinski) Dalmas; m. Charles T. Brown; 1 child, Kathlina. AS in Edn., Luzerne County C.C., 1979; BS in Spl. and Elem. Edn., Coll. of Misericordia, 1981; MS in Elem. Edn., Wilkes Coll., 1989. Cert. mentally/physically handicapped tchr., Pa. Substitute tchr. Luzerne Intermediate Unit 18, Kingston, Pa., 1983-84, Pope John Paul II Sch., Nanticoke, Pa., 1983-84, Genesis Sch./First Hosp. Wyo. Valley, Wilkes-Barr, Pa., 1983-84, tchr., 1984-88, head tchr., 1988-94; dir. edn. Genesis Sch., 1995—2000; tchr. spl. edn. Greater Nanticoke Area Sch. Dist., 2000—. Presenter in field; spl. edn. advisor Best Buddies chpt., cheerleader advisor Greater Nanticoke HS. Tchr. Diocese of Scranton, St. Mary's Parish, Nanticoke; former leader brownie troop Girl Scouts USA, now junior leader. Mem. Coun. of Exceptional Children. Democrat. Roman Catholic. Avocations: reading, sports, arts and crafts, photography. Home: 124 W Broad St Nanticoke PA 18634-2205 Office: Greater Nanticoke Area Sch Dist Nanticoke PA 18634-

D'ALOIA, G(IAMBATTISTA) PETER, corporate executive; b. Sao Paulo, Brazil, Jan. 10, 1945; s. John and Rosali (Picarelli) D'A.; m. Marguerite Ann Fuccello, Aug. 3, 1946; children: Jonelle, Tara. BS, NYU, 1966, LLM, 1976; JD, St. John's U., 1969. Bar: N.Y. 1969. Tax atty. Arthur Young and Co., N.Y.C., 1969-72, Allied Chem. Co., Morristown, N.J., 1972-79; chief tax counsel Allied Corp., Morristown, 1979-81, dir. taxes, 1981-83; v.p. taxes Allied-Signal Inc., Morristown, 1983-88, v.p., treas., 1988-92, v.p., contr., 1992-95, v.p., CFO, 1995-2000; sr. v.p., CFO Am. Standard Cos., Piscataway, 2000—. Mem. Bd. Edn., Mendham, N.J., 1977-80. Mem. ABA, Assn. of Bar City of N.Y., N.Y. State Bar Assn. Roman Catholic. Avocations: jogging, sailing, gardening. Office: Amer Standard Cos One Centennial Ave PO Box 6820 Piscataway NJ 08855-6820

D'ALOISE, LAWRENCE T., JR., lawyer; b. Port Chester, NY, Dec. 3, 1944; s. Lawrence Thomas and Lillian Teresa D'Aloise; children: Scott, Sean, Kimberly. BS, Holy Cross Coll., 1966; JD, Villanova U., 1969. Bar: NY 1970, US Dist. Ct. (so., ea. and no. dists.) NY, US Ct. Appeals (2d cir.), US Ct. Appeals (5th cir.), US Supreme Ct. Ptnr. Clark, Gagliardi & Miller PC, White Plains, N.Y., 1970—. Contbr. Mem.: ABA, White Plains Bar Assn., Westchester County Bar Assn., NY State Bar Assn. Avocation: auto restoration. Home: 130 Old Mamaroneck Rd White Plains NY 10605-2413 Office: Clark Gagliardi & Miller 99 Court St White Plains NY 10601-4265 E-mail: ldaloise@cgmlaw.com.

DALPINO, IDA JANE, retired secondary education educator; b. Newhall, Calif., Oct. 20, 1936; d. Bernhardt Arthur and Wahneta May (Blyler) Melby; m. Gilbert Augustus, June 14, 1963 (div. 1976); 1 child, Nicolette Jane. BA, Calif. State U., Chico, 1960; postgrad., Sacramento State, 1961-65, Sonoma State, 1970-71; MA, U. San Francisco, 1978. Cert. cmty. counselor, learning handicapped, c.c. instr., exceptional children, pupil pers. specialist, secondary tchr., resource specialist. Tchr. Chico High Sch., 1959-60; counselor Mira Loma High Sch., Sacramento, 1960-66; tchr. ESL Phoenix Ind. High Sch., 1968-69; resource specialist Yuba City (Calif.) High Sch., 1971-2000; ret., 2000. English tchr. Rough Rock Demonstration Sch., summers, 1975, 76. Office sec. Job's Daus., North Bend, Oreg., 1953—; active Environ. Def. Fund, Centerville Hist. Assn., Chico, 1991—. Mem. NEA, Calif. Tchrs. Assn., Chico State Alumni Assn., Sierra Club, Nature Conservancy, Audubon, Greenpeace, Sigma Kappa Alumni. Democrat. Mem. Science of the Mind Church. Avocations: reading, ecology, genealogy. Home: 6 Navajo Ln Corte Madera CA 94925 E-mail: idajane@comcast.net.

DAL PORTO, MARK DANIEL, music educator; b. Sacramento, Calif., July 29, 1955; s. Dante and Shirley Louise Dal Porto. BA, Calif. State U., Sacramento, 1978, MA, 1981; DMA, U. Tex., 1985. Asst. prof. music Ea. N.Mex U., Portales, 2001—; from asst. prof. to assoc. prof. music Tex. Woman's U., Denton, 1994—2001, No. State U., Aberdeen, SD, 1989—94; vis. asst. prof. music S.W. Tex. State U., San Marcos, 1987—89. Presenter at confs. and meetings. Author: (music composition) Three Nocturnes for Oboe, Voice, and Piano, 2003, Domestic Suite: Scenes and Memories from Childhood for Piano Solo, 2001, Spring, the Sweet Spring for Choir with Piano Accompaniment (Winner of Denton Cmty. Chorus Composition Contest, 2001), Dream for Piano Solo (Pub. by Choral Web Pub., Inc., 1999), Galactica for Symphonic Wind Ensemble (Pub. by So. Music Co., 2001). Mem.: ASCAP (Royalties 1986 - present), Soc. Music Theory, Coll. Music Soc. Home: 1116 Gemini Drive Portales NM 88130-6134 Office: Eastern New Mexico University Department of Music Station 16 Portales NM 88130 Office Fax: 505-562-4480. Personal E-mail: mark.dalporto@enmu.edu.

DAL POZZO, MARK BRIAN, music educator, director; b. Staunton, Ill., Sept. 18, 1953; s. Elmer Michael and Shirley Marie Dal Pozzo; m. Mary Margaret (McGann) Robb, Dec. 26, 2000; children: Margaret LaVigne, Christopher Robb. MusB Edn., Ill. State U., Normal, 1975, MusM Edn., 1983—83. Elem. band dir. Olympia Sch. Dist., Stanford, Ill., 1976—77; unit band dir. Ford Ctrl. Sch. Dist., Piper City, Ill., 1977—81, Minonk-Dana-Rutland Sch. Dist., Minonk, Ill., 1981—83, Pikeland Sch. Dist., Pittsfield, Ill., 1983—87; dir. of bands/music dept. chair Hillsboro (Ill.) Sch. Dist., 1987—. Music contest adjudicator Ill. Grade Sch./H.S. Assns., Ill., 1990—; performer Capital Area Concert Band, Springfield, Ill., 1999—; student Ill. State U.-European band study, Normal, Ill., 1977—84; mem. music content adv. com. for tchr. cert. test Ill. State Bd. Edn. Arranger/performer (European Band march music) various works, 2002. Performer Carlinville (Ill.) Mcpl. Band, 1993—2002. Mem.: Music Educator's Nat. Conf. (Nat. registered Music Educator 1998), Internat. Mil. Music Soc., Ill. Music Educators Assn., Soc. of Magna Carta Barons, Windjammers Unltd. Circus Band Orgn., Internat. Trombone Assn., Frantisek Kmoch Czech Band Soc., Kappa Kappa Psi, Phi Beta Mu, Phi Mu Alpha Sinfonia (historian 1974—75). Democrat. Avocations: art, camping, travel, trombone, gardening. Home: 710 St Louis St Hillsboro IL 62049 Office: Hillsboro HS 522 E Tremont St Hillsboro IL 62049

DALRYMPLE, CHRISTOPHER GUY, chiropractor; b. Beaumont, Tex., Sept. 2, 1958; s. Guy H. and Betty Jane (Williams) D.; m. Angela Hackley, Dec. 15, 1979; children: Sarah E., William C., Clayton G. Student, Baylor U., 1976-78; D in Chiropractic Medicine, Tex. Chiropractic Coll., 1982. Diplomate Nat. Bd. Chiropractic Examiners, Tex. Bd. Chiropractic Examiners; ordained Baptist Deacon, 1988. Chiropractor Brassard Chiropractic Clinic, Beaumont, 1982-85; chiropractic physician, adminstr. Brenham (Tex.) Chiropractic Clinic, 1985—. Host Back Talk, 1987-88; chair Tex. Chiropractic PAC; cons., lectr. in field. Author: Brenham & Masonry...150 Years Together, 1995; contbr. articles to profl. jours. Team chiropractor track team Blinn Coll., Brenham, 1987-94, Tex. track and field participants Olympics, 1992; Sunday sch. dir. First Bapt., 1986-87, 90-93, Sunday sch. tchr., 1987-89, bd. trustees Calvary Bapt. Ch., Brenham, 1992-94, Sunday sch. tchr. youth, 1993-94, actor, playwright ch. pageants, 1993-94, 96, 98, 99, deacon, chmn., 1994-98, chmn. pers. com., 1995-98, chmn. long range planning com., 1995-98, adult Sunday sch. tchr., 1995-99; treas. Brenham Ind. Sch. Devel.-PAC, 1994; participant Health Occupation Students of Am. Program, Brenham H.S., 1992—. Recipient State Sweepstakes Winner "Jake", Tex. Jaycees, 1984, Outstanding Officer, 1984. Mem.: Christian Chiropractic Assn., Tex. Chiropractic Assn. (labor rels. 1983, dist. 9 sec. 1983—84, chmn. publ. com. 1987—99, editor-in-chief 1987—99, membership com. 1994—95, dist. 8 state dir. 1996—99, state sec. 1999, pres.-elect 2000, pres. 2001, internal affairs coord. 2002—03, state com., Young Chiropractor award 1997, Pres.'s award 1999), Am. Chiropractic Assn., Gideons Internat. (bible chmn. 1994—), Tex. Chiropractic Coll. Alumni Assn., Baylor Alumni Assn. (life), K.T., Graham Masonic Lodge (various offices), Delta Sigma Chi (sec. 1981, bd. dirs. 1982). Republican. Baptist. Avocation: kendo. Office: Brenham Chiropractic Clinic PO Box 2350 Brenham TX 77834-2350

DALRYMPLE, GARY BRENT, research geologist; b. Alhambra, Calif., May 9, 1937; s. Donald Inlow and Wynona Edith (Pierce) D.; m. Sharon Ann Tramel, June 28, 1959; children: Stacie Ann, Robynne Ann Sisco, Melinda Ann Dalrymple McGurer. AB in Geology, Occidental Coll., 1959; PhD in Geology, U. Calif., Berkeley, 1963; DSc (hon.), Occidental Coll., Los Angeles, 1993. Rsch. geologist U.S. Geol. Survey, Menlo Park, Calif., 1963-81, 84-94, asst. chief geologist we. region, 1981-84; dean, prof. Coll. Oceanic and Atmospheric Sci., Oreg. State U., Corvallis, 1994-2001, dean and prof. emeritus, 2001—. Vis. prof. sch. earth scis. Stanford U., 1969-72, cons. prof., 1983-85, 90-94; disting. alumni centennial spkr. Occidental Coll., 1986-87. Author: Potassium-Argon Dating, 1969, Age of Earth, 1991; contbr. chpts. to books and articles to profl. jours. Fellow NSF, 1961-63; recipient Meritorius Svc. award U.S. Dept. Interior, 1984. Fellow Am. Geophys. Union (pres.-elect 1988-90, pres. 1990-92), Am. Acad. Arts and Scis.; mem. NAS (chair geology sect. 1997-2000), Am. Inst. Physics (bd. govs. 1991-97), Consortium for Oceanographic Rsch. and Edn. (bd. govs. 1994-2001), Joint Oceanographic Inst. (bd. govs. 1994-2001, chair 1996-98). Achievements include discovery that the earth's magnetic field reverses polarity and determination of time scale of these reversals for the past 3.5 million years; development of ultra-fast high-sensitivity thermoluminescence analyzer for studying lunar surface processes; development and refinement of K-Ar and 40 Ar/39 Ar dating methods and instrumentation, continuous laser probe for determining ages of microgram-sized mineral samples; research on volcanoes in the Hawaiian-Emperor volcanic chain, chronology of lunar basin formation, development and improvement of isotopic dating techniques and instrumentation, geomagnetic field behavior, plate tectonics of the Pacific Ocean basin, evolution of volcanoes, various aspects of Pleistocene history of the western U.S. Home: 1847 NW Hillcrest Dr Corvallis OR 97330-1859 E-mail: bdalrymple@attglobal.net.

DALRYMPLE, JACK, lieutenant governor; m. Betsy Dalrymple; 4 children. BA, Yale U., 1970. Farmer, 1970—; state rep. dist. 22, 1985—2001; lt. gov. State of N.D., 2001—. Chmn. appropriations com. N.D. Ho. Reps.; bd. dirs. Prairie Pub. TV, N.D. State U. Devel. Found., Golden Growers Coop.; mem. Edn. Broadcasting Coun.; co-founder Share House Inc. Recipient Outstanding Young Farmer award, 1983. Mem. Cass Coounty Rural Water Users Assn. (past bd. dirs.), Casselton Econ. Devel. Found., Univ. Pres. Agr. Club (pres.), Durum Growers Assn. (bd. dirs.), Jaycees. Republican. Address: PO Box 220 Casselton ND 58012-0220 Office: 600 E Boulevard Ave Bismarck ND 58505*

DALRYMPLE, MARILYN ANITA, small business owner, photographer; b. Vancouver, B.C., Can., Apr. 2, 1945; d. Herbert Walter and Eudora Ethelyn (Walters) Hortin; m. Randall William Duffey (div. Jan. 1971); m. Ronald Vern Dalrymple, Sept. 27, 1972; children: Valerie Ann, Leslie Thomas, Kelly Walter Duffey. AA, Antelope Valley Coll., 1987. Cert. fine art photography, Calif. Pvt. practice writer, photographer, Lancaster, Calif., 1987-89; owner Images by Marilyn, Lancaster, 1989—, Red Rose Fine Photography, Lancaster, 1998—. Author: My Lives as an Editor, 1993, To Catch a Butterfly, 1993, Have You Tried Everything, 1996, Bartholomew's Buttons, 1997. Dir., pres. Antelope Valley Com. Aging, Lancaster, 1994—; v.p. Antelope Valley Calif. Rep. League; mem. Calif. Coalition Juvenile Justice, Lancaster citizens and govt., Lancaster City Planning Commn.; founder Respect for Parents Day-Aug. 1st. Recipient Excellence award, Photographer Forum's Mag., 1993, L.A. County New Photography Silver award, 1994, 1995, Merit award, World Poetry, 1997, Profl. Photographers of Am., 2001. Mem. Photographic Soc. Am., Profl. Photographers Am. (Merit award), Profl. Photographers Calif., Photo Mktg. Assn., Assn. Photo Educators, Royal Photographic Soc. (licentiateship distinction: Images by Marilyn/Red Rose Fine Photography PO Box 1563 Lancaster CA 93539-1563 Office: Images by Marilyn/Red Rose Fine Photography PO Box 1563 Lancaster CA 93539-1563 E-mail: mailyn@rglobal.net.

DALRYMPLE, THOMAS LAWRENCE, retired lawyer; b. Wellsburg, W. Va., May 20, 1921; s. Lawrence Chester and Ethel May (Taylor) D.; m. Marjorie May Keeler; children: Bruce Lawrence, Dale Brian. AB, U. Mich., 1943, JD, 1947. Bar: Ohio 1947, U.S. Supreme Ct. Practiced in, Toledo, 1947-96; assoc. Williams, Eversman & Morgan and successor firms, 1947-50, Welles, Kelsey, Fuller, Harrington & Seney and successor firms, 1950-52; ptnr. Fuller & Henry and predecessor firms, 1953-96. Mem. Trout Unltd., Toledo Mus. Art. Served to capt. inf. AUS, 1943-46. Decorated Combat Inf. badge, Silver Star medal, Purple Heart. Fellow Am. Coll. Trial Lawyers, Am. Bar Found., Ohio Bar Found.; mem. Order of Coif, Phi Beta Kappa. Home: 4307 Stannard Dr Toledo OH 43613-3636

DAL SANTO, DIANE, writer, retired judge; b. East Chicago, Ind., Sept. 20, 1949; d. John Quentin Dal Santo and Helen (Koval) D.; m. Fred O'Cheskey, June 29, 1985. BA, U. N.Mex., 1971; cert., Inst. Internat. and Comparative Law, Guadalajara, Mex., 1978; JD, U. San Diego, 1980. Bar: N.Mex. 1980, U.S. Dist. Ct. N.Mex. 1980. Ct. planner Met. Criminal Justice Coordinating Coun., Albuquerque, 1973-75; planning coord. Dist. Atty.'s Office, Albuquerque, 1975-76, exec. asst. to dist. atty., 1976-77, asst. dir. atty. for violent crimes, 1980-82; chief dep. city atty. City of Albuquerque, 1983; assoc. firm T.B. Keleher & Assocs., 1983-84; judge Met. Ct., 1985-89, chief judge, 1988-89; judge Dist. Ct., 1989-2000. Mem. faculty Nat. Jud. Coll., 1990-95, 97-, trustee, 1995-96; adj. faculty Internat. Law Enforcement Acad., Roswell, N.Mex., 2002-. Columnist Albuquerque Jour., 1996-98. Bd. dirs. Nat. Coun. Alcoholism, 1984, S.W. Ballet Co., Albuquerque, 1982-83; mem. Mayor's Task Force on Alcoholism and Crime, 1987-88, N.Mex. Coun. Crime and Delinquency, 1987-97, bd. dirs., 1992-94, Task Force Domestic Violence, 1987-94; pres. bench, bar, media com., 1987, pres. 1992, rules of evidence com. Supreme Ct., 1993-96, chair com. access to pub. records Supreme Ct., 1988; steering com. N.Mex. Buddy Awards, 1995—; mem. metro. Criminal Justice Coordinating Coun., 1998—. U. San Diego scholar, 1978-79; recipient Women on the Move award YWCA, 1989, Disting. Woman award U. N.Mex. Alumni Assn., 1994, Outstanding Alumnus Dept. Sociology U. N.Mex., 1995; named Woman of Yr. award Duke City Bus. and Profl. Women, 1985. Mem. ABA (Nat. Conf. State Trial Judges Jud. Excellence award 1996), LWV, AAUW, Am. Judicature Soc., N.Mex. Women's Found., N.Mex. State Bar Assn. (silver gavel award 1997), N.Mex. Women's Bar Assn. (bd. dirs. 1991-92, Power and Caring award 2000), Albuquerque Bar Assn., Nat. Assn. Women Judges (bd. dist. dirs. 1999-00), Greater Albuquerque C. of C. (steering com. 1989), N.Mex. Magistrate Judges Assn. (v.p. 1985-89), Dist. Judges Assn. (pres. 1994-95), Pennies for Homeless. Office: Dist Ct 415 Tijeras Ave NW Albuquerque NM 87102-3252 E-mail: dianedalsanto@aol.com.

DALSIMER, ANTHONY STEARNS, retired foreign service officer, educator; b. N.Y.C., July 30, 1935; s. Allan Furth Dalsimer and Helen Stearns; m. Isabel Ann Price (div.); m. Marilyn Nowak (div.); children: Allyn Ann, Melanie, Heather. BA, Grinnell Coll., 1957; MA, Fletcher Sch. Law & Diplomacy, 1958; postgrad., Stanford U., 1971-72, Howard U., 1973-75; MS, U. D.C., 1991. Staff econ. office Dept. of State, Washington, 1960, officer in charge Guinea and Dahomey, 1971-73, divsn. chief Exch. North and West Africa, 1973-75, divsn. chief Cultural Exch. So. and East Africa, 1975-77, dir. rsch. for Africa, 1985-88, dir. Office Ctrl. African Affairs, 1988-91, dir. Office Hist. Document Rev., 1994-97; vice consul/econ. officer Am. Embassy, Ouagadougou, Upper Volta, 1961-63, vice consul Bamako, Mali, 1965, comml. attache Kinshasa, Zaire, 1967-69, dep. chief of mission Ndjamena, Chad, 1977-79, counselor polit. affairs Kinshasa, Zaire, 1979-81, dep. chief of mission Ouagadougou, Burkina Faso, 1981-84, counselor for labor affairs Paris, 1991-94; gen. mgr. Dalsimer Florist, Cedarhurst, N.Y., 1963-64; vice consul Am. Consulate, Hargeisa, Somalia, 1966-67, consul Bukavu, Congo, 1969-70; adj. faculty African history, internat. rels., govt. and politics U. South Fla., Sarasota, 1997—. Lectr. Elder Hostels Eckerd Coll., 2001—. Vol. ARC, Helen Payne Sch. Mem.: Fgn. Svc. Ret. Assn. Fla. (bd. dirs.), Diplomats and Consular Officers, Am. Fgn. Svc. Assn., Greencroft Condo Assn. (pres. 2001—). Democrat. Unitarian Universalist.

DALTAS, ARTHUR JOHN, management consultant, software services manager; b. Mpls., Aug. 5, 1945; s. John Howard Locken and Adella Marie (DeChaney) D.; stepfather, John Paul Daltas; m. Ellen Causey Peckham, Feb. 23, 2001; children: Alexander, Andrew, Elizabeth; stepchildren: Samuel Peckham, Anne Peckham. BA, Coll. St. Thomas, 1968; MBA with high honors, Boston U., 1973. Tchr. U.S. Dept. Def., Frankfurt, Germany, 1970-71; treas., mgr. Cambridge (Mass.) Comm. Group, Inc., 1973-78; v.p. The MAC Group/Gemini Inc., Cambridge, 1978-84; founder, pres. The Mgrs. Group, Concord, Mass., 1984-87; prin., chmn. Concord Cons. Group, 1987-2000. Pres. Exec. Advisors Corp., 1997, Global Svcs. Offerings Mgmt., Progress Software Corp., 2000. Contbg. author: Implementing Strategy, 1982, Marketing Management, 1991; contbr. articles to various publs. Bd. dirs. Make a Wish Boston, 1991-96; asst. scoutmaster Boy Scouts Am., 1999-2002; deacon, standing com. Hancock Ch., 2000—. With U.S. Army, 1968-70. Mem. Nat. Alumni Coun. Boston U., SMG Alumni Bd. Dirs. Boston U., Beta Gamma Sigma. Avocations: skiing, hiking, golf. Office: Progress Software Corp 14 Oak Park Bedford MA 01730

DALTON, ANNE, lawyer; b. Pitts., Dec. 6, 1951; d. Thomas John and Mary Olive (Paul) D.; m. Oliver E. Martin, Dec. 26, 1987. BA in Polit. Sci., NYU, 1973; JD, Fordham U., 1977. Bar: N.Y. 1978, U.S. Dist. Ct. (so. and ea. dists.) N.Y. 1979, Pa. 1987, Fla. 1990. Assoc. Mendes & Mount, N.Y.C., 1979-80; atty. news divsn. ABC, N.Y.C., 1980-85; TV news prodr. ABC Network, N.Y.C., 1985-86; sr. atty. Radio City Music Hall Prodns., Inc., N.Y.C., 1986-87; pvt. practice Stroudsburg, Pa., 1987-91; asst. county att., asst. port authority atty. Lee County, Ft. Myers, Fla., 1991-94; pvt. practice Ft. Myers, 1994—. Spl. hearing master 20th Jud. Cir., Fla., 1991—, ct. Commr., gen. master family civil and probate divsn., 1995—; adj. prof. Edison C.C., Ft. Myers, Barry U., Ft. Myers; Fla. family, cir. civil, dependency, county, fed. mediator, 1995; arbitrator, state ct., 1998. Recipient Clio award Internat. Clio Award Com., 1978. Mem. Pa. Bar Assn., Fla. Bar Assn., N.Y. Bar Assn., Lee County Bar Assn. Roman Catholic. Avocations: reading, gardening, swimming. Office: 2044 Bayside Pkwy Fort Myers FL 33901-3102

DALTON, CLAUDETTE ELLIS HARLOE, anesthesiologist, educator, university official; b. Roanoke, Va., Jan. 18, 1947; d. John Pinckney and Dorothy Anne (Ellis) Harloe; m. Henry Tucker Dalton, May 17, 1973 (div. 1979); 1 child, Gordon Tucker; m. H. Christopher Alexander, III, April 29, 2000. BA, Sweet Briar Coll., 1969; MD, U. Va., 1974. Resident in anesthesiology U. N.C., Chapel Hill, 1974—77; med. edn. Lenoir County Meml Hosp./East Carolina U., Kinston, 1978—80; med. edn. in intensive care Presbyn Hosp., Charlotte, NC, 1981—82; practice anesthesiology Charlotte Eye, Ear, Nose and Throat Hosp., 1982—85, Medivision of Charlotte and Orthopedic Hosp. of Charlotte, 1985—89; asst. prof. U. Va. Health Scis. Ctr., Charlottesville, Va., 1992—; dir. Office of Cmty. Based Med. Edn., Charlottesville, 1994—; asst. dean for cmty. based med. edn. U. Va., Charlottesville, 1996—, med. dir. Pre-Anesthesia Clinic, 1996—, asst. prof. anesthesiology and med. edn., 1996—. Author developer patient edn. materials for illiterate patients, 1979—, emergency med. svc. tng. program, 1981. Bd. dirs. Charlottesville Family Svcs., Family Svcs. Albemarle County, 1992-93, U. Va. Women's Ctr., 1996—, Coun. on Aging, Lenoir County C.C., Am. Cancer Soc.; exec. dir. Cmty. Involvement Coun. Lenoir County, Kinston, 1979; county coord. Internat. Yr. of Child, Kinston, 1979; mem. sch. medicine com. on women U. Va. Med. Sch.; also others. Named Commencement spkr., U. Va. Sch. Medicine Graduation, 1993; recipient Gov.'s award, State of N.C., 1980, cert. of merit for svc. to children, N.C. Dept. Human Resources, Outstanding Tchg. award, U. Va. Sch. Medicine, 1993, Sharon L. Hostler U. Va. Outstanding Woman in Medicine award, 2002. Mem.: Va. Soc. Anesthesiology, Albemarle County Med. Soc., Va. Med. Soc. (bd. dirs. Va. Health Quality Coun. 1995—97, chair ad hoc com. on telemedicine 1996—99, 2d v.p. 1998—99, chair scope of practice com. 1999—2002, dist. dir. 1999—, Med. Sch. Va. alt. del. 2001—, coun. on med. edn. AMA 2003, editor med. news Va. Med. Quar., mem. legis. com., mem. health access com., del. to ann. meeting, reference com., mem. strategic planning and implementation com., mem. women's com., mem. med. affairs com., mem. bd. medicine adv. com., U. Va. del. to AMA, alt. del. for Med. Sch. Va. to AMA), Alpha Omega Alpha, U. Va. Med. Alumni Assn. (assoc. bd. dirs. 1989—92, chair women in medicine leadership conf. 1998—99). Avocations: natural history, environment, dancing, writing, gardening. Office: U Va Med Sch PO Box 800325 Charlottesville VA 22908-0325 E-mail: ced2t@virginia.edu.

DALTON, DAVID ROBERT, chemistry educator; b. Chgo., Nov. 16, 1936; s. William Edward and Ethel (Shaykin) D.; m. Cecile Kaplan, Aug. 31, 1958; children: Nathaniel, Rachel, Aaron. BA, Northwestern U., 1957; PhD, UCLA, 1962. Chemist G. D. Searle & Co., Skokie, Ill., 1958-63, Monsanto Rsch. Corp., Dayton, Ohio, 1963-64; postdoctoral instr. Ohio State U., Columbus, 1964-65; asst. prof. chemistry Temple U., Phila., 1965-68, assoc. prof. chemistry, 1968-73, prof. chemistry, 1973—, assoc. dean rsch. and grad. studies, 1993-95, chmn. dept. chemistry, 2000—. Cons. Noramco, Wilmington, Del., 1987—, Auxillium Pharm. Co., 99—, McNeil Pahrm. Co., 99—, Inkine Pharm. Co., 99—. Author: The Alkaloids, 1979, Organic Chemistry in the Lab, 1979. Recipient Scroll award Am. Inst. Chemists, 1982, Section award undergrad. edn. Am. Chem. Soc., 2003. Mem.: AAAS, Am. Chem. Soc. (Undergrad. Edn. award 2003). Home: 143 Gulph Hills Rd Radnor PA 19087-4615 Office: Temple U 13th And Norris St Philadelphia PA 19122 E-mail: david.dalton@temple.edu.

DALTON, DENNIS GILMORE, political science educator; b. Morristown, N.J., Mar. 12, 1938; s. Andrew John and Emily Snow (Smith) D.; m. Sharron Louise Scheline, May 22, 1961; children: Kevin Andrew, Shaun Michael. BA, Rutgers U., 1960; MA, U. Chgo., 1962; PhD, U. London, 1965. Lectr. politics U. London, 1965-69; Ann Whitney Olin prof. polit. sci. Barnard Coll., Columbia U., N.Y.C., 1969—. Condr. series of e-seminars Nonviolent Power, M.K. Gandhi, M.L. King, Jr. and Nonviolent Resistance Around the World, Columbia U. Digital Knowledge, 2002. Author: Indian Idea of Freedom, 1982, Mahatma Gandhi: Nonviolent Power in Action, 1993; editor: States of South Asia, 1983, Mahatma Gandhi: Selected Political Writings, 1996. Mem. War Resisters League, N.Y.C., 1969— . Recipient Emily Gregory Disting. Teaching award, 1978; Am. Coun. Learned Socs. grantee, 1975, Am. Philos. Soc. grantee, 1975; Am. Inst. Indian Studies fellow, 1974; Fulbright scholar to Nepal, 1994-95. Home: 390 Riverside Dr Apt 3e-1 New York NY 10025-1867 Office: Columbia Univ Barnard Coll 606 W 120th St New York NY 10027-5706 E-mail: ddalton@barnard.columbia.edu. *My research for the last four decades on the life and thought of Mahatma Gandhi has convinced me that his example carries universal implications for the study of conflict resolution. The theory and practice of nonviolence offer us today a system of values and a hope for the future that should serve to inspire humanity.*

DALTON, HARRY JIROU, JR., (JERRY DALTON), public relations executive; b. San Antonio, Feb. 7, 1927; s. Harry Jirou and Dorothy Bess (Black) D.; m. Marion Packard Hume Dalton, Aug. 21, 1954; children: Cynthia Kay, Robert Hume, Steven Jirou. BBA in Advt., U. Tex., 1949, postgrad., 1949-50, Boston U., 1958, U. Nebr., Omaha, 1958-60. Commd. 2d lt. USAF, 1950, advanced through grades to brig. gen., 1975; from assoc. to dir. corp. com. EDS Corp., Dallas, 1980-84; mgr. corp. comm. The LTV Corp., Dallas, 1984-92, Vought Aircraft Co., Dallas, 1992-93; pvt. practice as pub. rels. counsel Dallas, 1994—. Named Outstanding Govt. Pub. Info. Officer Aviation/Space Writers Assn., Washington, 1974. Fellow Pub. Rels. Soc. Am. (pres. 1990); mem. Tex. Pub. Rels. Assn. (Outstanding Pub. Rels. Practitioner in Tex. award 1989, Silver Spur award 1991). Presbyterian. Home and Office: 6411 Laurel Valley Rd Dallas TX 75248-3904 Fax: 972-404-1278. E-mail: jerrydaltn@aol.com.

DALTON, JAMES EDGAR, JR., health facility administrator; b. Gretna, Va., Sept. 17, 1942; married. Bachelors degree, Randolph-Macon Coll., 1964; Masters degree, Va. Commonwealth U., 1966. Adminstrv. resident Lynchburg (Va.) Gen. Hosp., 1965-66, adminstrv. asst., 1966-69, asst. adminstr., 1969-70; adminstr. Princeton (W.Va.) Cmty. Hosp., 1970-72; regional adminstr. Humana Inc., Dallas, 1972-73, regional v.p. Tampa, Fla., 1973-76; dir. hosp. svcs. Am. Medicorp Inc., Atlanta, 1976-77, Dallas, 1977-78; v.p. Hosp. Corp. Am., Nashville, 1978-79, Arlington, Tex., 1979-87, HealthTrust, Inc., Arlington, 1987-89, Nashville, 1989-90; pres., CEO Quorum Health Group, Inc., Brentwood, Tenn., 1990-2001; pres. Edinburgh Assocs., Inc., 2001—. Home and Office: 6305 Edinburgh Dr Nashville TN 37221-3707

DALTON, JENNIFER FAYE, accountant; b. Maryville, Tenn., May 1, 1959; d. James Theodore Teffeteller and Melody (Potts) Allison; m. Robert Byron Dalton, Dec. 15, 1979. Student, U. Tenn., 1977-79, Coastal Carolina Community Coll., 1980-81, 84-86; BS in Mgmt., Golden Gate U., Camp Lejeune, N.C., 1982. Bookkeeper, with accounts payable dept. McMar Too, Inc., Jacksonville, N.C., 1980-83; acctg. technician City of Jacksonville, 1983-89; acctg. mgr., corp. sec. treas. Bankers Mortgage Corp., Louisville, 1990-92; sr. acct., payroll officer City of Louisville, 1992-96; sr. acct. Louisville Zoo, 1996—. Alcoa Found. scholar, 1977. Mem. Amateur Radio Transmitting Soc., Inst. Mgmt. Accts., Gamma Beta Phi. Republican. Baptist. Avocations: amateur radio, pistol shooting, sailing, water skiing, swimming. Home: 827 Markham Ln Louisville KY 40207-4444

DALTON, JOHN HOWARD, former secretary of the navy, financial consultant; b. New Orleans, Dec. 13, 1941; s. William Carl and Jaunice Dalton (Davenport) Winterrowd Dalton; m. Margaret; children: John Jr., Chris. BS cum laude, U.S. Naval Acad., 1964; MBA, U. Pa., 1971. Commd. ensign USN, 1964, advanced through grades to lt., resigned, 1969; investment bank trainee Goldman, Sachs & Co., N.Y.C., 1971-72, with security sales sect. Dallas, 1972-77; pres. Govt. Nat. Mortgage Assn., Washington, 1977-79; nat. treas. Carter/Mondale Presdl. Campaign, Washington, 1979; chmn., mem. Fed. Home Loan Bank Bd., Washington, 1979-81; pres. real estate divsn. Gill Cos., San Antonio, 1981-84; chmn., pres. Seguin Savs. Assn., San Antonio, 1984-88; chmn., chief exec. officer Freedom Capital Corp., San Antonio, 1984-88; former pres. Stephens, Inc., San Antonio; former managing dir. Best Assocs. & Mason Best Co., Houston/Dallas; sec. USN, 1993-98. Chmn. fin. inst. adv. com. Fed. Res. Bank Dallas; bd. dirs. Capstead Mortgage (formerly Lomas Mortgage Corp.). Trustee Ecumenical Ctr. Religion and Health, San Antonio, 1983—, Mental Health Assn. Tex., Austin, 1986-88, YMCA, San Antonio, 1984-89; chmn. World Affairs Coun., San Antonio, 1987-89. Lt. comdr. USN Res. Mem.: Elks. Democrat. Episcopalian. Achievements include being a finalist for the Rhodes Scholarship Competition.

DALTON, LARRY RAYMOND, chemistry educator, researcher, consultant; b. Belpre, Ohio, Apr. 25, 1945; s. Leonard William Henry and Virginia (Maylee) D.; m. Nicole A. Boand. BS with honors, Mich. State U., 1965, MS, 1966; AM, PhD, Harvard U., 1971. Asst. prof. chemistry Vanderbilt U., Nashville, 1971-73, assoc. prof., 1973-77, research prof. biochemistry, 1977-98; assoc. prof. SUNY-Stony Brook, 1976-81, prof., 1981-82, U. So. Calif., Los Angeles, 1982-94, Harold Moulton prof. chemistry, 1994-98, sci. co-dir. Loker hydrocarbon rsch. inst., 1994-98, prof. materials sci. and engring., 1994-98; prof. chemistry U. Wash., 1998—. Dir. NSF Sci. and Tech. Ctr. for Info. Tech. Rsch., 2002—; cons., IBM Corp., Yorktown, N.Y., IBM Instruments Co., Danbury, Conn., 1977-85, Celanese Rsch. Corp., 1987-90, Lockheed Missiles and Space Co., 1988-90, Maxdem Inc., 1990; cons. rev. of NIH sickle cell ctrs. USPHS, 1981-82; mem. parent com. for rev. of comprehensive sickle cell ctrs. Nat. Heart, Lung, Blood Inst.-NIH, 1987, 92; panelist for presdl. young investigator awards NSF, Washington, 1983, 89, panelist for presdl. faculty fellow awards, 1986, mem. materials rsch. adv. com., 1984-90, mem. high magnetic field panel, 1987, info. tech. rsch. panel, 2000; bd. dirs. Key Mgmt., Inc., Bomans, Inc.; mem. NAS-NRC panel for selection of NSF predoctoral fellows, 1989—; mem. panel for selection DOD predoctoral fellows. Editor-author: EPR and Advanced EPR Studies of Biological Systems, 1985 Recipient Burlington No. Found. Faculty Achievement award, 1986, U. So. Calif. Assocs. award, 1990, Profl. Achievement award Spring Arbor Coll., 1993, Disting. Alumni award Mich. State U., 2000; Camille and Henry Dreyfus tchr./scholar, 1975-77; rsch. career devel. grantee NIH, 1976-81; Alfred P. Sloan Found. fellow, 1974-77. Mem. Am. Chem. Soc. (Richard C. Tolman medal 1996, Chemistry of Materials award 2003), Sigma Xi. Avocations: skiing, hiking. Office: U Wash Dept Chemistry PO Box 351700 Seattle WA 98195-1700 E-mail: dalton@chem.washington.edu.

DALTON, MARGARET STIEG, library and information sciences educator; b. Utica, N.Y., May 20, 1942; d. Lewis Francis and Mildred Graf Stieg; m. Jack Dalton (dec. July 7, 2000). AB cum laude, Harvard U., 1963; MSLS with honors, Columbia U., N.Y.C., 1964; MA, U. Calif., Berkeley, 1966, PhD, 1970. Reference libr. Harvard Coll. Libr., Harvard U., Cambridge, Mass., 1968—71; asst. prof. Sch. Libr. Svc., U. Ala., Tuscaloosa, Ala., 1972—75, Sch. Libr. Svc., Columbia U., N.Y.C., 1975—83; assoc. prof. Sch of Libr. and Info. Studies, U. Ala., Tuscaloosa, 1983—87; prof. Sch. Libr. and Info. Studies, U. Ala., Tuscaloosa, 1987—96, Bristol/Ebsco prof., 1996—. Author: (book) Laud's Laboratory: The Diocese of Bath and Wells in the Early Seventeenth Century, 1982, The Origin and Development of Scholarly Historical Periodicals, 1986, Public Libraries in Nazi Germany, 1992 (Fraenkel prize Wiener Libr., London, 1989), Change and Challenge in Library and Information Science Education, 1992; contbr. Grantee Fulbright German Studies Seminar, Fulbright Assn., 1997, research grantee, various orgns. Mem.: ALA (life Juston Winsor prize Library History Round Table 1991), Am. Cath. Hist. Assn., Am. Hist. Assn., Assn. for Libr. and Info. Sci. Edn. (Profl. Contbn. to Libr. and Info. Sci. award. 1995). Episcopalian. Avocations: dogs, travel, quilting. Office: U Ala Sch of Libr and Info Studies Box 870252 Tuscaloosa AL 35487 Office Fax: 205-348-3746. Business E-Mail: mdalton@slis.ua.edu.

DALTON, MATT, retired foundry executive; b. Chgo., June 27, 1922; s. Donald J. and Jessie (Shrimplim) D.; children: D. J., J. B., Katherine A.; m. Frances Walter, Jan. 1, 1994. Student, Pomona Coll., Claremont, Calif., Butler U.; grad. advanced mgmt. program, Harvard U., 1956. Pres. Dalton Foundries, Inc., Warsaw, Ind., 1959-68, chmn. bd., 1968-91, chmn. emeritus, 1992-94. Founder Warsaw Jr. Achievement, 1953; charter mem. bd. dirs. Warsaw Devel. Corp., 1973; mem. Warsaw Cmty. Sch. Bd., 1962-68, Kosciusko County Coun., 1981-84—; trustee Ind. Vocat. Tech. Coll., 1964-70; chmn. Gov. of Ind. Com. on Youth Employment, 1979-82; pres. Lake Tippecanoe Property Owners Assn., 1979-82; founder, chmn. Kosciusko Econ. Devel. Corp., 1984, Kosciusko Leadership Acad., 1981; mem. Ind. Econ. Devel. Coun., 1984-88, Ind. Commn. on Vocat. and Tech. Edn., 1988-89; del. Ind. Gov.'s Far East Tour, 1987. With AUS, 1943-45. Mem. Ind. State C. of C. (chmn. 1982-84), Warsaw C. of C. (chmn., found. Indsl. Div. 1959). Office: PO Box 181099 Coronado CA 92178-1099

DALTON, MAURICE FRANK, mechanical engineer; b. San Salvador, El Salvador, Nov. 30, 1956; s. Francis Edward and Maria (Del'pech) D.; m. Colomba Maria Vignolo, July 28, 1978; children: Martha, Maurice, Alexandra. BSME, La. State U., 1981, MSME, 1984. Edison engr. GE, Erie, Pa., 1984-85, diesel engine structural engr., 1985-86, propulsion structural engr., 1986-88, gears, bearings and lubrication engr., 1988-93, 93—; motor devel. engr. Franklin Electric, Bluffton, Ind., 1993. Cons. GE, Erie, 1993. Mem. ASME, Am. Gear Mfg. Assn., KC. Republican. Roman Catholic. Achievements include design of transmission for 320 ton off highway truck, transmission for 500 KW wind turbine, 1000 HP AC motor/transmission mechanical design for the new GE 6000 HP locomotive; patent AC Motorized Wheel Arrangement. E-mail: mfdalton@yahoo.com.

DALTON, PHYLLIS IRENE, library consultant; b. Marietta, KS, Sept. 25, 1909; d. Benjamin Reuben and Pearl (Travelute) Bull; m. Jack Mason Dalton, Feb. 13, 1950. BS, U. Nebr., 1931, MA, 1941, U. Denver, 1942. Tchr. City Schs., Marysville, Kans., 1931-40; reference libr. Lincoln (Nebr.) Pub. Libr., 1941-48; libr., asst. state libr. Calif. State Libr., Sacramento, 1948-72; pvt. libr. cons. Scottsdale, Ariz., 1972—. Libr. U. Nebr., Lincoln, 1941-48. Author: Library Services to the Deaf and Hearing Impaired Individuals, 1985, 91 (Pres.' Com. Employment of Handicapped award 1985), also poems; contbr. chpt., articles, reports in books and publs. in field. Mem. exec. bd. So. Nev. Hist. Soc., Las Vegas, 1983-84; mem. So. Nev. Com. on Employment of Handicapped, 1980-89, chairperson, 1988-89; mem. adv. com. Nat. Orgn. on Disability, 1982-94; mem., sec. resident coun. Forum Pueblo Norte Retirement Village, 1990-91, pres. resident coun., 1991-94; bd. dirs. Friends of So. Nev. Libraries; trustee Univ. Libr. Soc., U. Nev.-Las Vegas; mem. Allied Arts Coun., Pres.' Com. on Employment of People with Disabilities, emeritus, 1989—, Ariz. Gov.'s Com. on Employment of People with Disabilities, 1990—, Scottsdale Mayor's Com. on Employment of People with Disabilities, 1990—, chmn., 1996—; mem. Scottsdale Publ Libr. Ams. With Disabilities Com., 1994—. Recipient Libraria Sodalitas, U. So. Calif., 1972, Alumni Achievement award U. Denver, 1977, U. Nebr., Lincoln, 1983, Outstanding Sr. Citizen Vol. award City of Scottsdale, 1997, citation for svc. to people with disabilities Mayor of Scottsdale, 1999; named Mover and Shaker Scottsdale Mag., 1994. Mem. LWV, ALA (councilor 1963-64, Exceptional Svc. award 1981, award com. O.C.L.C. Humphreys Forest Press award 1994), AAUW, Assn. State Librs. (pres. 1964-65), Calif. Libr. Assn. (pres. 1969), Nev. Libr. Assn. (hon.), Internat. Fedn. Libr. Assns. and Instns. (chair working group on libr. svc. to prisons, standing com. Sect. Librs. Serving Disadvantaged Persons 1981-95), Nat. League Am. Pen Women (Las Vegas chpt. 1988-94, com. on qualifications for Letters membership 1994—, parlimentarian Scottsdale chpt. 1989-94, v.p. 1992-94, 96-98, v.p. state chpt. 1996-98, sec. 1998-2001), Am. Correctional Assn. (libr. svcs. instns. com. 1994—), Internat. Soc. Poets (disting.), Pilot Internat. (at-large). Home: 7090 E Mescal St Apt 261 Scottsdale AZ 85254-6125

DALTON, ROBERT EDGAR, mathematician, computer scientist; b. Boston, May 2, 1938; s. Robert Evelyn and Mildred Louise (Zoellick) D.; m. Sally Turner, Sept. 12, 1961 (div. 1977); children: Stephen Howard, Alena Lynn; m. Judith Eyges, July 17, 1993. BS in Math., U. Chgo., 1959; MS in Applied Math., N.C. State U., 1961, PhD in Applied Math., 1964; MS in Computer Sci., Fla. State U., 1982. Systems analyst RCA Svc. Co., Cocoa Beach, Fla., 1964-65; mem. tech. staff TRW Systems Group, Cocoa Beach, 1965-71; ops. rsch. analyst Naval Underwater Systems Ctr., West Palm Beach, Fla., 1971-79; grad. teaching asst. Fla. State U., Tallahassee, 1980-81; asst. prof. Am. U., Washington, 1981-83; mem. tech. staff Mitre Corp., Greenbelt, Md., 1983-85; prin. investigator Vitro Corp., Silver Spring, Md., 1985-93; sr. software devel. engr. Raytheon Co., Bedford, Mass., 1995—. Adj. prof. Fla. Inst. Tech., 1964-68, Fla. Atlantic U., 1979. Contbr. chpts. to books, articles to jours. Sec. U.S. Jaycees, Boynton Beach, Fla., 1974; chmn. U. Chgo. Alumni Fund, Palm Beach County, Fla., 1975-79. Recipient Spl. Achievement award Naval Underwater Sys. Ctr., 1974, 76. Mem. IEEE Computer Soc., Am. Assn. Artificial Intelligence. Achievements include research in underwater acostics, knowledge acquisition and learning, computer games, pattern recognition, knowledge-based system development, and decision support with fuzzy logic. Home: 26 Crescent Rd Winchester MA 01890-2814

DALTON, STEVEN PAUL, physician assistant; b. New Milford, Conn., Aug. 3, 1955; s. John Edgar and Callie Nettie (Wheeler) D.; m. Claudia Tinnin, Aug. 15, 1981; children: Rebecca, Matthew. Diploma in Nursing, Harlem Valley Sch. Nursing, Wingdale, N.Y., 1976; BS, Western Conn. State Coll., 1980; Physician Asst., Pa. State U., 1983. Cert. physician asst. Physician asst. Commerce St. Med. Ctr., Clinton, Conn., 1983-85, Rural Internists of Maine, P.A., Skowhegan, 1985-93, Cmty. Health Plan, North Adams, Mass., 1993-94, Shaftsbury (Vt.) Med. Assocs., Inc., 1994—, Vt. Vets. Home, Bennington, 1994—. Lectr. health occupations Southwestern Vt. Sch. Union, Bennington, 1995. Bd. trustees Old First Ch. of Bennington, 1995-98. Fellow Am. Acad. Physician Assts. Avocations: violin, guitar, outdoor sports, fly fishing, baseball. Office: Shaftsbury Med Assocs Inc PO Box 379 Shaftsbury VT 05262-0379

DALTON, THOMAS GEORGE, paralegal, social worker, legal consultant; b. Hoonah, Alaska, Mar. 13, 1940; s. George and Jessie K. (Starr) D.; m. Hazel Hope, Nov. 1960 (div. Sept. 1965); children: Roderick O., Rhoeda J. Garcia, Pamela Y. Masterman; m. Kathy Pelan, Sept. 1972 (div. Feb. 1980); children: Deirdra J. (dec.), Thomas L., Michael G. AAS, Shoreline Community Coll., Seattle, 1981; BA, Seattle Pacific U., 1984. Paralegal, social worker Law Office of Defender's Assn., Seattle, 1983—; client adv. criminal justice sys. Seattle, 1984—. Legal cons., Seattle; tchr. Tlingit Culture and Lang., Northwest Indian Coll., Bellingham, Wash. Elder United Presbyn. Ch., Hoonah, 1973—; pres. Alaska Native Brotherhood, Seattle, 1984—, Nat. Am. Community Coun., Seattle, 1990—; del. Seattle chpt. Tlinget and Haida Indians Alaska, auditor; bd. dirs. LANCE (Leading Am. Native for Excellence), 1996—. Recipient Founder's award Alaska Native Brotherhood, 1989. Democrat. Home: 7009 10th Ave NW Seattle WA 98117-5242 Office: Ctrl Bldg 8th Fl 810 3rd Ave Seattle WA 98104-1655

DA'LUZ VIEIRA, LORRAINE CHRISTINE C. acupuncturist, researcher; b. London, Apr. 30, 1955; arrived in U.S., 1999; d. Archibald Carlysle and Christine Heather (Ward) Da'Luz V.; m. Schuyler Mead Jones; children: Jesse Christopher, Cassandra Laurie. Licentiate in Acupuncture, C.T.C.M., Leamington Spa, Eng., 1983, B in Acupuncture, 1986, M in Acupuncture, 1989; M in Anthropology, Oxford U., 1994; MPh in Med. Anthropology, Oxford (Eng.) U., 1995, PhD, 1999. Lectr. Coll. Traditional Chinese Medicine, U.K., 1985-96; cons. Drug and Alcohol Rehab. Centre, London, 1994-97; acupuncturist privately owned clinic, London, 1982—. Cons. to various clinics, U.K., 1987—, Can., U.S. and Europe, 1983—; lectr. and cons. 10 hosps., China, 1993; lectr. hosps. throughout U.K., 1984—. Bd. dirs. O.A.C.M., Oxford, 1981, W.I.S.E., Netherlands/Denmark, 1979-82. Oxford U. grantee, 1997. Mem. Brit. Acupuncture Coun. Avocations: travel, reading, cooking, tapestry, music. Office: Linacre Coll/Oxford U St Cross Rd Oxford OX1 3JA England

DALY, CHARLES ARTHUR, health services administrator; b. Hartford, Conn., Aug. 22, 1945; s. Robert William and Josephine Frances (Gustafson) D.; m. Leslie Jane Lane, Nov. 5, 1967; children: Cheryl, Christopher. BA, Yale U., 1967; MHA, U. Mich., 1974. Mgr. Blue Cross and Blue Shield of Mich., Detroit, 1974-83; v.p. Del. Valley Hosp. Coun., Phila., 1984-96, Health Visions, Inc., Pennsauken, N.J., 1996-97, South Ctrl. Health Planning Coun., Brick, N.J., 1997-98, Health Resources and Svcs. Adminstrn., Bethesda, Md., 1999. Bd. dirs. Health Strategy Network, Phila., Phila. AIDS Consortium, Phila. Health Mmgt. Corp.; mem. Phila. Emergency Med. Svcs. Coun., 1984-96. Lt. USN, 1967-72. Fellow Am. Coll. Healthcare Execs., Coun. Excellence in Govt. Avocations: swimming, golf, baseball. Home: 501 Kegworth Ct Severna Park MD 21146-1720 E-mail: cdaly2@hrsa.gov.

DALY, CHARLES ULICK, foundation executive; b. Dublin, May 29, 1927; came to U.S., 1934, naturalized, 1940; s. Ulick deBurgh and Violet (Sealy-King) D.; m. Mary Larmonth, June 11, 1949 (dec.); children: Michael, Douglas; m. Christine Sullivan, Nov. 5, 1988; children: Charles, Kevin. BA Internat. Relations, Yale U., 1949; MS Journalism, Columbia U., 1959. Mgr. then v.p. Mexican subs. Pacific Molases Co., San Francisco, 1949-50, 52-58; congl. fellow Am. Polit. Sci. Assn., 1959-60; editor Stanford U., Calif., 1961; staff asst. Pres. Kennedy and Pres. Johnson, 1962-64; v.p. U. Chgo., 1964-71; v.p. govt. and cmty. affairs Harvard U., Cambridge, Mass., 1971-76; editor Media and the Cities, The Quality of Inequality, Urban Violence; pres. Joyce Found., Chgo., 1978-86; dir. John F. Kennedy Found., Boston, 1988-2001, dir. emeritus, 2001—. Mem. Lloyd's of London, 1976—; freelance writer, 1958—. Mem. Commn. on Adminstrv. Rev., U.S. Ho. of Reps.; chmn. Donor's Forum, Chgo., 1980; bd. dirs. Am. Ireland Fund, Joint Ctr. for Polit. Studies, Ind. News and Media, and Chorus Comms., Ireland. With USNR, 1945-46; USMCR, 1950-52. Decorated Silver Star, Purple Heart. Mem. Bantry Golf Club (Ireland), Bantry Sailing Club (Ireland), Boca Grande Club (Fla.), Wightman Tennis Club. Home: 32 Forest Ridge Rd Weston MA 02493

DALY, CHERYL, broadcast executive; b. Providence, Apr. 20, 1947; d. Francis Patrick and Mary Ann (Wallis) D.; m. Arthur James Generas, July 18, 1970; 1 child, Caroline. BA, Rutgers U., 1969; postgrad., New Sch. for Social Rsch., 1975-78. Account exec. Phil Dean Assocs., N.Y.C., 1969—72; dir. pub. rels. Kirkland Coll., Clinton, 1972—75; mgr. press svcs. CBS Radio, N.Y.C., 1976—80; assoc. dir. internal comm. CBS, Inc., 1980—81, dir. corp. info., 1981—83; v.p. pub. rels. Group W Satellite Comm., 1984—95, sr. v.p. pub. rels., 1995—97, CBS Cable, 1997—2000; sr. v.p. comm. TNN, MTV Networks, 2000—01; v.p. media relations MSNBC, 2002; pub. rels. cons. N.Y.C., 2003—. Examiner Westinghouse Quality Awards, Pitts., 1990. Recipient Best Co. Comm. award Cable TV Bus., 1986, Mktg. award Westinghouse Broadcasting Co., 1991. Mem. Cable TV Pub. Affairs Assn. (bd. dirs. 1985-87), Media Mommies (co-founder 1987). Democrat. Roman Catholic. Home: 1 W 67th St New York NY 10023-6200 Office: One West 67 st New York NY 10023-6200

DALY, CHRISTOPHER BURKE, journalist, educator; b. Boston, July 7, 1954; s. John Edward and Mary Gertrude (Duggan) D.; m. Anne K. Fishel, Sept. 9, 1955; children: Gabriel, Joseph. BA magna cum laude, Harvard U., 1976; MA, U. N.C., 1982. Statehouse bur. chief AP, Boston, 1986-89; contbg. editor New England Monthly, Haydenville, Mass., 1987-90; instr. Harvard U., Cambridge, Mass., 1994-97; lectr. Brandeis U., Waltham, Mass., 1995; New England corr. Washington Post, Boston, 1989-97; contbg. writer Commonwealth Mag., Boston, 1995—; vis. assoc. prof. journalism Boston U., 1997-98, now assoc. prof. journalism, 1998—. Cons. Trellix Corp., Waltham, 1996-97. Co-author: Like a Family, 1987 (Taft & Beveridge award 1988); contbr. articles to various mags. Waddell fellow U. N.C., Chapel Hill, 1980-82. Mem. Nat. Writers Union, Soc. Profl. Journalists. Avocations: gardening, birding. Office: Boston Univ Dept Journalism 640 Commonwealth Ave Boston MA 02215-2422 E-mail: cdaly@bu.edu.

DALY, DANIEL ANTHONY, artist, illustrator; b. Albany, NY, Feb. 17, 1947; s. Daniel A. Daly and Mary Kathleen Rivers; m. Cheryl A. Oliveri, Sept. 16, 1996. BFA, Mass. Coll. of Art, 1981. Illustrator courtroom drawing Sta. WBZ TV News, Boston, 1976-78. Artist various books, mags. and orgns.; commd. by Mills Corp. to do various murals, 1998-2002. Recipient Mus. Purchase award Springfield Art Mus., 1994. Mem. Trout Unltd. (pres. local chpt. 1997-98). Avocations: fly fishing, hunting, cross country skiing. Home and Office: 23 Limerock St Camden ME 04843-2116

DALY, DAVID MICHAEL, information technology executive; b. Mpls. s. David and Harriett Daly; m. Ellen Boozer; 1 child, David. BA, Stanford U.; PhD, U. Tex. Chief tech. officer Hugin, Inc., Dallas, 2000—. Contbr. articles to profl. jours.; author: books. Co-dir. Stanford Undergrad. Admit Initiative, N. Tex. Mem.: AAAS, Soc. Neurosci., Acoustical Soc. Am., Stanford Assocs. (Cntennial medallion), Sigma Xi. Office: Box 210855 Dallas TX 75211

DALY, DONALD F. retired engineering company executive; b. Morristown, N.J., Jan. 10, 1933; s. John F. and Sophie E. (Podeski) D.; m. Bennie L. London, Nov. 2, 1963; children: Stephen, David, Eric. ME, Stevens Inst. Tech., 1955. Equipment engr. Corning (N.Y.) Glass Works, 1955-56; sales engr. Mundet Cork, 1958-60; process engr. Thiokol Chem. Corp., 1961-65; dir. engring. Syntex Corp., 1966-78; v.p., project mgr. Indsl. Design Corp., 1978-2000; dir. Tech. Design & Constrn. Co., Portland, Oreg., 1992-94; ret., 2000. Republican. Avocations: golf, skiing, horse ranching.

DALY, DONALD FRANCIS, consultant, retired investment counsel; b. Bridgeport, Conn., Aug. 6, 1928; s. Christopher M. and Anne F. (Kelleher) D.; m. Magdalene Johnston, July 10, 1953 (div. 1975); children: Candace, Jacqueline, Elizabeth, Patrick; m. Susan S. Coyle, Mar. 21, 1976 (div. 1984); 1 child, Jennifer (dec.); m. Sandra R. Godfrey, Apr. 19, 1985; 1 child, Samuel. AB, Yale U., 1950. Account exec. Hemphill Noyes, N.Y.C., 1957-63; v.p. Scudder Stevens & Clark, N.Y.C., 1963-78; ptnr. Brundage Story & Rose, N.Y.C., 1978-95; sr. v.p. Mellon Bank Pvt. Asset Mgmt., Phila., 1995-96; dir. acquisitions Mellon Pvt. Asset Mgmt., 1996-98; cons. Mellow Pvt. Asset Mgmt., 1998-2000. Pres. Brundage Story & Rose Mut. Funds, 1990-95; adv. bd. Charles Schwab & Co., 1993-94; cons. in field. Mem. Korean Meml. Commn., 1989-91; pres. Diocesan Trust, Episc. Diocese of NY, 1990-94; trustee PLAN of Penn. Capt. U.S. Army, 1950-57. Decorated Disting. Svc. Cross, Bronze Star medals (2), Purple Heart (2), Gold Medal of Valor, Greece, Chung Mu Disting. Svc. Cross, Korea; Fellow Phila. Soc. Security Analysts; mem. Am. Inst. Investment Mgrs., Investment Counsel Assn. (former gov.), Phila. Estate Planning Coun., Order of St. John of Jerusalem, Yale Club N.Y., Church Club Phila., Point O'Woods Club, The Pilgrims. Republican. Home and Office: 321 S Roberts Rd Bryn Mawr PA 19010-2103 E-mail: chorwon@aol.com.

DALY, GEORGE GARMAN, college dean, educator; b. Painesville, Ohio, Oct. 5, 1940; s. George Ferdinand and Helen May (Garman) D.; m. Barbara Leigh Anthony, Mar. 13, 1977. AB, Miami U., Oxford, Ohio, 1962; MA, Northwestern U., 1965, PhD, 1967. Asst. then assoc. prof. Miami U., Oxford, 1965-69; asst. prof. U. Tex., Austin, 1969-70; asst. prof., then prof. U. Houston, 1971-77, dean Coll. Social Sci., 1979-83; dean Coll. Bus. U. Iowa, Iowa City, 1983-93; dean Stern Sch. Bus. NYU, N.Y.C., 1993—. Sr. economist Exec. Officer Pres., Washington, 1974; economist Fed. Energy Agy., Washington, 1975-76; adv. bd. Ctr. Pub. Policy, Houston Mem. Am. Econs. Assn., Public Choice Soc., Phi Beta Kappa, Beta Gamma Sigma Home: 29 Washington Sq W Apt 10A New York NY 10011-9128 Office: Mgmt Ctr NYU 44 W 4th St New York NY 10012-1106 E-mail: gdaly@stern.nyu.edu.

DALY, GERALD, accountant; b. Montreal, Que., Can., Apr. 1, 1948; s. Paul and Rejane (De RePentigny) D.; m. Danielle Raymond, Dec. 20, 1969 (div. 1978); m. Nicole Huot, June 17, 1994. BA, U. Mont., 1969; MS in Comm., U. Sherbrooke, 1973. CA, cert. info. systems auditor, cert. mgmt. cons., fraud examiner. Mgr. Coopers & Lybrand, Montreal, 1973-80; ptnr. Raymond, Chabot, Grant, Thornton, Montreal, 1980—. Mem. Inst. Internal Auditors (gov. 1989-92), EDP Auditors Assn. (v.p., sec. 1983-86). Office: Raymond Chabot Grant Et Al 600 Rue de la Gauchetiere O Montreal QC Canada H3B 4L8

DALY, JENNIFER, physician; d. John Arthur Daly; m. Mark William Cohen; children: Andrew Paul Cohen, Natalie Louise Cohen. BA, Sarah Lawrence Coll., N.Y., 1973; MD, Columbia U. Coll. of Physicians and Surgeons, 1978. Cert. infectious diseases and internal medicine Am. Bd. Internal Medicine. Asst. prof. medicine Tufts U. Sch. Medicine, Boston, 1984—90; staff physician St. Elizabeth's Hosp., Boston, 1984—90; physician Univ. Mass. Meml. Hosp., Worcester, 1990—; assoc. prof. medicine Univ. Mass. Sch. Med., 1994—, clin. chief infectious diseases, 2001—. Author (editor): Jour. Clin. Microbiology, numerous chapts. in textbooks, numerous jour. articles. Achievements include discovery of described new species of bacteria, Bartonella elizabethae; described new class of antibiotics- oxazolidinones. Avocation: dancing. Office: Univ Mass Meml Health Care 55 Lake Ave N Worcester MA 01655

DALY, JOE ANN GODOWN, publishing company executive; b. Galveston, Tex., Aug. 7, 1924; d. Elmer and Jessie Fee (Beck) Godown; m. William Jerome Daly, Jr., Jan. 25, 1958 (dec.). BA in Journalism, U. Okla., 1945, BA in Piano, 1952. Asst. editor house organ Southwestern Bell Telephone, St. Louis, 1945-47; sec. to city mgr. Okla. Daily News, Oklahoma City, 1947-49; pvt. piano tchr. Alva, Okla., 1952-54; sec. to editor Prentice-Hall, Inc., N.Y.C., 1954-55, asst. to children's book editor, 1955-58; asst. editor children's books Dodd, Mead & Co., N.Y.C., 1963, dir. children's books, 1965-88, asst. v.p., assoc. pub. children's books, 1986-88; editl. dir. Cobblehill Books affiliate Dutton Children's Books, N.Y.C., 1988-97, ret., 1997. Mem. Children's Book Council, N.Y.C., 1963, treas., 1969; mem. CBC/LA Com., N.Y.C., 1980, CBC/Prelude Com., N.Y.C., 1983 Active Bklyn. Heights Assn., 1976— ; friend Carnegie Hall, N.Y. Philharm.; mem. Met. Opera Guild, Mus. Modern Art, Mus. Natural History. Mem. Phi Beta Kappa, Sigma Delta Chi, Theta Sigma Phi, Mu Phi Epsilon Democrat. Methodist. Home: 80 Cranberry St Brooklyn NY 11201-1726

DALY, JOHN NEAL, investment company executive; b. Washington, Nov. 14, 1937; s. John Charles, Jr. and Margaret Criswell (Neal) D.; m. Barbara Claire Krueger, Apr. 2, 1966; children: John Gorman, Cristina Reed. BA, Yale U., 1959, postgrad. Law Sch., 1959-60; AMP, Harvard Bus. Sch., 1979. With E.F. Hutton & Co., Inc., N.Y.C., 1960-83, exec. v.p., dir., to 1983; v.p. Salomon Bros. Inc., N.Y.C., 1983-87, 89, Salomon Bros Internat. Ltd., London, 1987-89; pres. RS&A Cons. Inc., 1990-93; mng. dir. Spears Benzak Salomon & Farrell, N.Y.C., 1993-98, Trainer, Wortham & Co., Inc., 1999—. Exch. ofcl. Am. Stock Exch., 1979; trustee Culinary Inst. Am., 1992—, treas., 1993—; dir. Hist. Soc. of the Town of Greenwich, 1991-97. Mem. Bond Club N.Y. (sec. 1973-74, gov. 1975-78), Securities Industry Assn. (chmn. nat. syndicate com. 1978-78), Comex Clearing Assn. (dir. 1981-87), Burning Tree Club, Yale Club N.Y., Mark's Club, Knickerbocker Club, Round Hill Club, The Sky Club. Home: 338 Stanwich Rd Greenwich CT 06830-3530 Office: Trainer Wortham & Co Inc 845 3rd Ave Rm 600 New York NY 10022-6677 E-mail: jdaly@trainerwortham.com.

DALY, JOSEPH LEO, law educator; b. Phila., July 31, 1942; s. Leo Vincent and Genevieve Delores (McGinnis) D.; m. Kathleen Ann Dolan, July 24, 1965; children: Michael, Colleen. BA, U. Minn., 1964; JD, William Mitchell Coll. Law, 1969. Bar: Minn. 1969, U.S. Dist. Ct. Minn. 1970, U.S. Supreme Ct. 1972, U.S. Ct. Appeals (8th cir.) 1973, U.S. Ct. Appeals (D.C. cir.) 1974; cert. mediator and arbitrator alternative dispute rev. bd. Minn. Supreme Ct. Ptnr. Franke & Daly, Mpls., 1969-74; prof. law Hamline U. Sch. Law, St. Paul, 1974—. Arbitrator Am. Arbitration Assn., N.Y.C., 1980—, U.S. Fed. Mediation and Conciliation Svc., Washington, 1988—, for the states of Minn., Hawaii, Idaho, Ind., Mass., Mich., N.D., Pa., Oreg., Wisc., V.I and City of L.A.; arbitrator Bur. Mediation Svcs., St. Paul, 1978—; vis. scholar Ctr. for Dispute Resolution, Willamette U., Salem, Oreg., 1985; facilitator Minn. Internat. Health Vols., Kenya, 1985; observer Philippine Constl. Conv., Manila, 1986; participant European Arab Arbitration Congress, Bahrain, 1987; human rights investigator in the Philippines, 1989; vis. scholar U. Oslo, 1990, 91, 92, 96, 97; lectr. on trial skills for human rights lawyers, The Philippines, 1989; lectr. to leaders at Site 2 Cambodian Refugee Camp, Thai/Cambodian border, 1989; lectr. U. Cluj-NAPACA, Romania, 1991; vis. lectr. for developing countries Internat. Bar Assn., 1991-92; lectr. U. Tirana, Albania, 1992, London, 1993, Nat. Econs. U., Hanoi, Vietnam, 1993, 94, Danang (Vietnam) Poly. U., 1993, Ho Chi Minh Econs. U., Saigon, Vietnam, 1993, U. Hanoi Law Sch., 1994, U. Modena, Italy, 1994, Hanoi, Danang and Saigon, 1995, Phnom Penh, Cambo-

dia, 1995, Hong Kong, 1996, Shenzhen, China, 1996, Oslo, Norway, 1996, Karolinska Inst., Stockholm, 1997; vis. prof. So. Cross U., Lismore, Australia, 1998, 99, U. Bergen, Norway, 1999, Tongji U., Shanghai, China, 1999, U. Saigon, Vietnam, 1999, 2000; cons. Chua U., Tokyo, 2001; team leader UN Devel. Programme mid-term evaluation of UN project, Vietnam, Hanoi, 2001; vis. prof. U. Queensland, Brisbane, Australia, 2001, 02; Fulbright scholar U. Montevideo, Uruguay, 2002, 03. Co-author: The Law, the Student and the Catholic School, 1981; co-author, editor: The Student Lawyer: A High School Handbook of Minnesota Law, 1981, rev. edit., 1986, Strategies and Exercises in Law Related Education, 1981, International Law, 1993, The American Trial System, 1994; contbr. more than 50 articles to profl. jours. Mem. Minn. Legislature Task Force on Sexual Exploitation by Counselors and Therapists, St. Paul, 1984-85, Nat. Adv. Com. on Citizen Edn. in Law, 1982-85; bd. dirs. Scenic Am., Washington, 1989-92. Recipient Spurgeon award Mayor and Citizens of St. Paul and Indianhead Scouting, 1983; named a Leading Am. Atty. in Alternative Dispute Resolution: Employment Law; fellow U. Miss. Law Sch. Mem. ABA (contbg. editor Preview of U.S. Supreme Ct. Cases mag. 1984—), Internat. Bar Assn. (London, vis. lectr. for devel. countries 1991—), Minn. State Bar Assn., Minn. Lawyers Internat. (human rights com., rep. to Philippine Constl. Conv. 1986), St. Paul Athletic Club, Phi Alpha Delta. Avocations: jogging, sailing. Office: Hamline U Sch Law 1536 Hewitt Ave Saint Paul MN 55104-1205 E-mail: jdaly@gw.hamline.edu.

DALY, JOSEPH PATRICK, management educator, researcher; b. N.Y.C., Jan. 17, 1958; s. William Joseph Daly and Margaret Daly Clarc; m. Mary Anne Daly, July 5, 1987; children: Justin, Christina, Nicholas. BA magna cum laude, Columbia U., 1980; M in Profl. Studies, Cornell U., 1983; PhD, Northwestern U., 1991. Asst. prof. Appalachian State U., Boone, NC, 1989-95, assoc. prof., 1995—2003, prof., 2003—. Contbr. articles to profl. jours. including Adminstrv. Sci. Quar., Jour. Applied Behavioral Sci., Jour. Orgnl. Behavior. Recipient Outstanding Rschr. award Coll. Bus., Appalachian State U., 1998; Northwestern U. fellow, 1984; NSF grantee, 2000. Mem. Acad. Mgmt., So. Mgmt. Assn., Orgn. Behavior Tchg. Soc., Sigma Iota Epsilon (faculty advisor Epsilon Mu chpt.), Phi Beta Kappa (N.Y. Delta chpt. 1980). Avocations: walking, guitar, real estate investments. Home: 176 Rhododendron Ln Boone NC 28607-4342 Office: Appalachian State U Mgmt Dept Coll Bus Boone NC 28608-0001

DALY, KAY R. public relations professional; b. Santa Monica, Calif., Oct. 31, 1966; d. Walter Francis and Joy Ray Ryon; m. Jack Williams Daly, Dec. 14, 1996; 1 child, Patrick Bryan. BA in Comms., U. Calif., San Diego, 1989; postgrad., George Washington U. Prodn. intern TV show Dukes of Hazzard, fall 1982, Hill Street Blues, spring 1984; lab. asst. George C. Page Mus., summer 1983; salesperson Saks Fifth Ave., Beverly Hills, summer 1985; intern Phillips-Ramsey Advt. & Pub. Rels., fall 1987; press intern U.S. Sen. Pete Wilson Washington, summer 1988; press intern Senate campaign Californians for Pete Wilson, fall 1988; press asst. to campaign mgr. Sen. Pete Wilson's Campaign for Gov., 1989; state projects asst. U.S. Sen. Phil Gramm, 1989-91; dir. polit. analysis Booz-Allen & Hamilton, Inc., 1991-92; chief of staff Office of Tex Lezar, 1992-94; press sec., dep. campaign mgr. Tex Lezar for Lt. Gov., 1994; press sec., projects dir. U.S. Rep. Fred Heineman, 1995-96; rsch. cons. U.S. Rep. Robin Hayes' Campaign for Gov., 1996; comms. cons. N.C. Rep. Party, 1996, dir. comm., 1996-97; v.p., Wash. ops & publ. rels. dir. Signature Agy., 1997—. Various positions Mitsui Mfrs. Bank, summer 1984, 86, 87; rsch. dir. radio/TV talk show The Tom Joyner Show, N.C., mng. editor newsletter The Amen Corner, 1996; dir. Am. for Ashcroft Comm., 2001; spokesperson Coalixan for A Fair Judiuicay. Asst. editor: (book) Making Government Work, 1992; newsletter editor: N.C. Fed. Rep. Women. Mem. exec. com. Wake County GOP, 4th Congl. Dist. GOP.; bd. dirs. state coord. Ronald Reagan Legacy Project. Recipient speech and debate awards Nat. Forensics League, commendation letter U. So. Calif. Reading Ctr. for Tapes for the Blind, Top Honors in Crisis Comm., Infogroup, 2000, Ronald Reagan award Am. Conservative Union, 2003. Mem. Internat. Rep. Inst. (trainer issue advocacy/campaign comms. seminar in Ukraine), Internat. Assn. Bus. Communicators, Rep. Comms. Assn., Ind. Women's Forum, Mil. Order of World Wars (hereditary mem.), Delta Delta Delta. Republican. Avocations: gourmet cooking, politics, traveling. Home: 6035 Woodlake Ln Alexandria VA 22315 Office: The Signature Agy 4515 Falls of Neuse Rd Ste 450 Raleigh NC 27609-6290 E-mail: krdaly@ad.com.

DALY, PATRICK F. real estate executive, architect; b. Chgo., Jan. 25, 1949; s. John F. and Margaret M. (Gleason) D.; m. Shirley J. Kumis, June 25, 1971; children: Sean P., James P. BArch with honors and distinction, BA in Archtl. History with honors and distinction, U. Ill., Chgo., 1972. Cert. architect. Chmn. bd. Dalan Realty Corp., Chgo., 1980—, Dalan Devel. Corp., Chgo., 1986—; pres. Dalan/ Jupiter, Inc., Chgo., 1987—; mng. ptnr. Rising Sun Riverboat Casino and Resort, LLC, Chgo., 1995—; chmn. The Daly Group LLC, 1995—. Bd. dirs. Internat. Marine & Gaming, Inc. (chmn. bd.) Empire Cruise Lines, Inc. Contbr. articles to profl. jours. Chmn. Ill. Ambs., Chgo., 1990-98; vice chmn. Met. Pier & Expn. Authority, Chgo., 1985-2002; commr. Nat. Adv. Commn. U.S. Dept. Labor, Washington, 1991-93; trustee Fund Am. Studies, 1993—, Univ. Ill. Found., 1993—, dir. emeritus 1999; trustee Inst. Cmty. Empowerment, 1991-98; trustee Chgo. Acad. Scis., 2001—, chmn., 2002—; chmn. Chancellor's Corp. adv. com. U. Ill., Chgo., 1995—; adv. bd. mem. Ind. Univ. Ctr. Real Estate Studies, 1994—, Roosevelt U. Sch. Real Estate, 2000—; dir. U.S. Com. for UNICEF/Chgo., 1996—, U.S.O., Chgo.; chmn. U. Ill. Alumni Assn., 1997-99; mem. leadership com. United Way, 1998; mem. coun. Brookings Instn.; co-chmn. Chgo. Am. Heartwalk, Am. Heart Assn., 2002; mem. commissioning com. U.S.S. Ronald Reagan, 2002—. Recipient Alumni Achievement award U. Ill., 1993; inducted into Chgo. Area Entrepreneurship Hall of Fame, 2002. Mem. Alpha Rho Chi. Office: The Daly Group 20 N Wacker Dr Ste 1500 Chicago IL 60606-2903 E-mail: pdaly@thedalygroup.com.

DALY, PAUL SYLVESTER, mayor, retired academic administrator, management consultant; b. Belmont, Mass., Jan. 8, 1934; s. Matthew Joseph and Alice Mary (Hall) D.; m. Maureen Teresa Kenny, May 25, 1957; children: Judith Mary, Paul S. Jr., Susan Marie, John Joseph, Maureen Hall. BS in Engring. Sci., Naval Postgrad. Sch., 1968; MBA, U. W. Fla., 1971. Commd. ensign USN, 1955; advanced through grades to capt., 1979; coll. dean Embry-Riddle Aero. U., Daytona Beach, Fla., 1979-81, chancellor, 1981-95; mayor City of Prescott, Ariz., 1996-99; mgmt. cons., 1999—; legis. affairs cons. Lectr. seminars, 1979-85; cons. British Aerospace, 1979-84, McDonnell Douglas, 1979-84, IBM, 1983-84; sr. faculty U. Phoenix, 1983-86. Bd. dirs. Yavapai Regional Med. Ctr., Prescott, Ariz., 1983-86, Prescott C. of C., 1982-84; chmn. Ariz. State Bd. Pvt. Postsecondary Edn.; pres. Ind. Coll. and Univs. of Ariz., Phoenix, 1982—; pres., founder West Yavapai County Am. Heart Assn. Chpt., chmn. affiliate of Am. Heart Assn./Ariz. Decorated Legion of Merit. Mem. Ret. Officers Assn. Republican. Roman Catholic. Avocation: sports. E-mail: daly@myway.com.

DALY, ROBERT W. psychiatrist, medical educator; b. Watertown, N.Y., Oct. 1, 1932; s. Robert Joseph and Margaret Florence (Ward) D.; m. Elizabeth Mary McCarthy, July 4, 1958; children: Kendra, Lauren, Robert, John, Erik. BS, St. Lawrence U., 1957; MD, SUNY, Syracuse, 1957. Diplomate Am. Bd. Psychiatry and Neurology, Nat. Bd. Med. Examiners. Resident in psychiatry SUNY, Syracuse, 1958-60, chief resident in psychiatry, 1960-61; chief Dept. Psychiatry & Neurology, Barksdale AFB, Bossier City, La., 1961-63; asst. prof. psychiatry SUNY Upstate Med. Ctr., Syracuse, 1963-69, assoc. prof. psychiatry, 1969-75; visiting scholar U. Cambridge, England, 1969-70; sr. fellow Nat. Endowment for the Humanities, 1974-75; prof. psychiatry SUNY Upstate Med. Ctr., Syracuse, 1975—; adj. prof. philosophy Syracuse U., 1980—; prof. med. humanities, dir. program in med. humanities SUNY Health Sci. Ctr., Syracuse, 1984-2000; prof. bioethics and humanities SUNY Umpstate Med. U., 2000—. Exec. dir. Syracuse Consortium for the Cultural Found. of Medicine, 1978-2001; chmn. bd., pres. Inst. for Ethics in Health Care, Inc., 1995—; examiner Am. Bd. Psychiatry and Neurology, 1980-90; pvt. practice psychiatry, Syracuse, 1963—2001 cons. to hosps., govt. agencies, religious orgns., law firms, 1964—. Contbr. articles to profl. jours.; co-editor: The Cultures of Medicine, Vol. 8 of Literature and Medicine. Mem. mental health adv. bd., County Onondaga, N.Y., 1976-77. Capt. USAF, 1961-63. Rsch. fellow N.Y. State Dept. Mental Hygiene, 1969-70; recipient award in recognition of svcs. Ctrl. N.Y. Eye Bank & Rsch. Corp., 1985. Fellow Am. Psychiat. Assn. (life; pres. Onondaga dist. bd. 1968-69), Onondaga County Med. Soc. (life, Disting. Svc. award 2002); mem. N.Y. State Med. Soc., Internat. Soc. for Comparative Study Civilization (coun. 1977-80), Soc. Health and Human Values, Assn. Faculty in Med. Humanities (program chmn. 1986-87, pres., program dir. sect. 1995-96), Assn. for Advancement of Philosophy and Psychiatry, Soc. for Bioethics and Humanities. Democrat. Roman Catholic. Avocations: fishing, tennis, gardening, furniture design and building. Home: 101 Revere Rd Syracuse NY 13214-1938 Office: SUNY Upstate Med U 750 E Adams St Syracuse NY 13210-1834 E-mail: dalyr@upstate.edu.

DALY, SARALYN R. retired humanities educator, writer; b. Huntington, W.Va., May 11, 1924; d. John Ross and Ruth (Kaufman) Daly. BA with honors, Ohio State U., 1944, MA, 1945; postgrad., Yale U., 1945—46; PhD, Ohio State U., 1950. Instr. Ohio State U., Columbus, 1947—49; prof., dept. chair Coll. Emporia, Kans., 1949—50; prof. Midwestern U., Wichita Falls, Tex., 1950—61; assoc. prof. Tex. Christian U., Ft. Worth, 1961—62; prof. Calif. State U., L.A., 1962—88; ret., 1988. Exch. prof. Université de Aix-en Provence, France, 1986, Universität Tübingen, Germany, 1986—87, U. Ottawa, Canada, 1987—88. Author: Katherine Mansfield, 1964, rev., 1994, In the Web, 1978, Love's Joy, Love's Pain, 1983; translator: (poetry) Book of True Love, 1978 (Harold Morton Landon prize Acad. Am. Poets, 1978). Grantee Fulbright, Am. U. Beirut, 1964—65, Tokyo Gakugei & Tsuda Coll., 1967—68, U. Bujumbura, 1970 71. Mem.: MLA (life), Acad. Am. Poets, Medieval Acad. Am. (life). Home: 6211 Gyral Dr Tujunga CA 91042

DALY, SIMEON, retired librarian; b. Detroit, May 9, 1922; s. Philip T. and Marguerite I. (Ginzel) D. BA, St. Meinrad Coll., 1945; Licentiate in Sacred Theol., Cath. U., 1949, MLS, 1951; MDiv, St. Meinrad Sch. Theol., 1985. Joined Benedictines, 1943, ordained priest Roman Cath. Ch., 1948. Libr. dir. St. Meinrad (Ind.) Coll. and St. Meinrad Sch. Theol., 1951-2000; pres. Four Rivers Area Libr. Svcs. Authority, Ind., 1974-75, Am. Theol. Libr. Assn., St. Meinrad, 1979-81, exec. sec., 1985-90. Mem. ALA, Ind. Libr. Assn., Am. Theol. Libr. Assn. (bd. dirs., pres., exec. sec.), Am. Benedictine Acad. Home: St Meinrad Archabbey 100 Hill Dr Saint Meinrad IN 47577-1010 E-mail: fsimeon@saintmeinrad.edu.

DALY, TOM, county official, mayor; m. Debra Daly; children: Anna, Ryan. BA, Harvard U., 1976. Elected mem. City Coun. of Anaheim, 1988, elected mayor, 1992—2001; clk. recorder Orange County, Santa Ana, Calif., 2002—. Mem. bd. trustees Anaheim Union Hish Sch. Dist., 1985—; active Anaheim Library Bd., 1985—; mem. adv. bd. Anaheim Boys and Girls Club; mem. bd. dirs. cmty. support group Anaheim Meml. Hosp.; mem. bd. dirs. Orange County Transp. Authority, Urban Water Inst.; mem. El Toro Citizens Adv. Commn.; chair regional adv. planning coun. Orange County, 1992—. Office: 12 Civic Ctr PO Box 238 Santa Ana CA 92702 E-mail: tom.daly@ocgov.com.*

DALY, TYNE, actress; b. Madison, Wis., Feb. 21, 1946; d. James Daly and Hope Newell; m. Georg Stanford Brown (div.); children: Alyxandra, Kathryne, Alisabeth. Student, Brandeis U., Am. Music and Dramatic Acad. Performed at Am. Shakespeare Festival, Stratford, Conn.; appeared on Broadway in Gypsy, 1990, 91 revivals, The Seagull, 1992; films include Angel Unchained, 1970, The Enforcer, 1976, The Entertainer, 1976, Speed Trap, 1977, Telefon, 1977, Zoot Suit, 1982, The Aviator, 1985, Movers and Shakers, 1985; made TV debut in series The Virginian; guest appearances in various TV series including Veronica's Closet, 1996, appearances in TV series include Cagney & Lacey, 1982-88 (Emmy awards 1983, 84, 85, 88), Christy, 1994, (Emmy award 1996), Judging Amy, 1999-, (Emmy award best sup. actress, 2003); TV films include In Search of America, 1971, A Howling in the Woods, 1971, Heat of Anger, 1972, The Man Who Could Talk to Kids, 1973, Larry, 1974, Intimate Strangers, 1977, Better Late Than Never, 1979, The Women's Room, 1980, A Matter of Life and Death, 1981, The Great Gilly Hopkins, 1981, Your Place or Mine, 1983, Kids Like These, 1987, Stuck With Each Other, 1989, The Last to Go, 1990, Face of a Stranger, 1991, On the Town, 1993, Scattered Dreams, 1994, Colombo: Bird in the Hand, 1994, Bye Bye Birdie, 1994, Columbo: Undercover, 1994, The Forget-Me-Not Murders, 1994, Cagney and Lacey: The Return, 1994, Cagney and Lacey: Together Again, 1995, A Perfect Mother, 1996, Autumn Heart, The Simian Line, Shades of Gray, Three Secrets, Tricks, 1997, The Perfect Mother, 1997, Vig, 1998, Execution of Justice, 1999, The Wedding Dress, 2001; appearance one-woman show Mystery School. Recipient Tony award for Mama Rose role in Gypsy, 1990. Address: 272 S Lasky Dr Unit 402 Beverly Hills CA 90212-3671*

DALY, WALTER JOSEPH, physician, educator; b. Michigan City, Ind., Jan. 12, 1930; s. Walter Hayes D.; m. Joan Brown, June 12, 1953; children: Lois Kay, Alice Louise. AB, Ind. U., 1951, MD, 1955, ScD, 1998. Diplomate Am. Bd. Internal Medicine. Intern Ind. U., 1955-56, resident, 1956-57, 59-62, instr. medicine, 1962-63, asst. prof., 1963-65, assoc. prof., 1965-68, prof., 1968-77, John B. Hickam prof., 1977-80, J.O. Ritchey prof., 1980-95, J.O. Ritchey prof. emeritus, 1995—; chmn. dept. medicine, 1970-83; dean Sch. Medicine, 1983-95; dean emeritus Ind. U., 1995—. Dir. Regenstrief Inst. Health Rsch., 1976-83. Capt. M.C., U.S. Army, 1957-59. Master ACP (gov. 1980-84), Am. Physiol. Soc., Ctr. Soc. Clin. Rsch. (pres. 1980-81), Am. Soc. Clin. Investigation, Am. Clin. and Climatol. Assn., Assn. Am. Physicians. Office: Ind U Sch Medicine 1120 South Dr Indianapolis IN 46202-5135

DALY, WILLIAM JOSEPH, lawyer; b. Bklyn., Mar. 19, 1928; s. William Bernard and Charlotte Marie (Saunders) D.; m. Barbara A. Longenecker, Nov. 19, 1955; children: Sharon, Nancy, Carol. BA, St. John's U., 1951, JD, 1953. Bar: N.Y. 1954, U.S. Dist. Ct. (so. and ea. dists.) N.Y. 1958, U.S. Ct. Mil. Appeals 1969, U.S. Ct. Claims 1969, U.S. Tax Ct. 1969, U.S. Supreme Ct. 1973. Assoc. Garvey & Conway, Esquires, N.Y.C., 1954-55, Wing & Wing, Esquires, N.Y.C., 1955-58; ptnr. Daly Lavery & Hall, Esquires and predecessors, Ossining, N.Y., 1958—. Adj. prof. law Mercy Coll., Dobbs Ferry, N.Y. V.p. Legal Aid Soc., Westchester County, N.Y., 1983—; mem. 9th Jud. Dist. Grievance Com., 1981-89, chmn. 1988-89; spl. referee in disciplinary procs.; trustee Supreme Ct. Libr. at White Plains, 1985—. With U.S. Army, 1946-48; ret. col. JA-AUS, 1978; mem. Hall of Fame U.S. Army Officer Cand. Sch., Ft. Benning, Ga. Fellow Am. Bar Found., N.Y. Bar Found.; mem. ABA, N.Y. State Bar Assn. (ho. of dels. 1977-89, 90-96, exec. com. 1983-89, 90-96, v.p. 1985-89, 90-96), Westchester County Bar Assn. (pres. 1979-81, dirs. coun. 1981—), Westchester County Bar Inst. (bd. dirs. 1982-98), Ossining Bar Assn. (pres. 1966-67), ATLA, N.Y. State Trial Lawyers Assn., Res. Officers Assn. U.S., Skull and Circle, Phi Delta Phi. Roman Catholic. Home: 232 Hunter Ave Sleepy Hollow NY 10591-1317 Office: 73 Croton Ave Ste 209 Ossining NY 10562-4971

DALY-GAWENDA, DEBRA, health facility administrator, nursing educator; b. Chgo., Aug. 30, 1956; m. Tom Gawenda; children: Christopher, Haley, Zachary. Diploma, Michael Reese Hosp. Sch. Nsg., 1978; AA in Liberal Arts, Richard J. Daley Coll., 1982; BSN, Rush U., 1983; MS, U. Ill., Chgo., 1984. RN, Ill. Staff nurse emergency room Rush Med. Ctr., Chgo., Mercy Hosp. and Med. Ctr., Chgo.; asst. prof. Rush U., Chgo.; dir. employee & corp. health svcs. Rush-Presbyn.-St. Luke's Med. Ctr., Chgo. Lectr. in field. Author 2 books; contbr. articles to profl. publs. Mem. NAFE, Nat. Wellness Inst., Am. Assn. Occupl. Health Nurses, Internat. Platform Assn., Ill. Hosp. Assn. Occupl. Health Nurses (pres.), Ill. Coun. Nurse Mgrs., Worksite Wellness Coun. Ill. (bd. dirs.), Sigma Theta Tau (mem. nominating com.).

DALZELL, KIMBERLY KAY, nutritionist; b. Bismark, N.D., Oct. 27, 1961; d. Raymond Cliffert Voegele and Rose Ruth Kroh-Voegele; m. Mark Allan Dalzell, Dec. 22, 1985; children: David Mark, Kathryn Allison. BS in Human Nutrition, Ariz. State U., 1986—89; MS in Clin. Nutrition, Tex. Tech U., 1992—94; PhD in Holistic Nutrition, Clayton Coll. of Natural Health, Birmingham, Alabama, 1997—99. Ap-4 ADA, N.C., 1990, registered Dietitian ADA, 1991, Cert. Nutrition Support Dietitian ASPEN, 1992. Clin. dietitian HCA - Highsmith-Rainey Hosp., Fayetteville, NC, 1990—93, Aramark - U. Med. Ctr., Lubbock, Tex., 1993—94, asst. dir., food and nutrition services, 1994—95; dir., holistic nutrition services Cancer Treatment Centers of Am., Arlington Heights, Ill., 1996—; nutrition educator Ctr. for Complementary Medicine, Pk. Ridge, Ill., 2003—. Pres. NutriQuest Press, Round Lake, Ill., 2001—. Author: (book) Challenge Cancer and Win!; contbr. mag. article; editor: (cookbook) Cancer Fighter's Cookbook; author: (doctoral dissertation) Perceptions and Practices of Complementary Nutritional Therapies by Registered Dietitians in the U.S.; contbr. mag. article. Recipient Featured Author, Ill. Authors Book Fair, 2002. Mem.: Nat. Writer's Union, Oncology Dietetic Practice Group, Nutrition in Complementary Care Dietary Practice Group, Ill. State Dietetic Assn., Am. Dietetic Assn. Mem.Christian Ch. Avocations: travel, cooking, jogging, tennis, biking, sewing, reading. Office: PO Box 874 Round Lake IL 60073 Personal E-mail: nutriquest@att.net.

DALZELL, ROBERT FENTON, JR., historian, educator; b. Cleve., Apr. 28, 1937; s. Robert Fenton and Lucile (Cain) D.; m. Lee Baldwin, June 18, 1960; children: Frederick, Jeffery, Victoria, Alex. BA, Amherst Coll., 1959; MA, Yale U., 1962, PhD, 1966. Instr. history Yale U., New Haven, 1962-66, asst. prof., 1966-70; assoc. prof. history Williams Coll., Williamstown, Mass., 1970-75, prof., 1975-77, Ephraim Williams prof. Am. history, 1977—, chmn. Am. civilization program, 1981—91, dep. coll. marshal, 1984—87, coll. marshal, 1987—95. Vis. prof. U. Va., 1985-86; mem. mass. Found. Humantities and Pub. Policy, 1982-89, v.p. 1987-88; trustee Hist. Deerfield, 1983--, Bennington Mus., 2000-2002. Author: American Participation in the Great Exhibition of 1851, 1960, Daniel Webster and the Trial of American Nationalism, 1973, Enterprising Elite: The Boston Associates and the World They Made, 1987, (with Lee B. Dalzell) George Washington's Mount Vernon: At Home in Revolutionary America, 1998. Morse fellow, 1968-69, Guggenheim fellow, 1973-74, Charles Warren fellow, 1973-74, Williams Coll. Ctr. for Humanities and Social Scis. fellow, 1990; Mass. Soc. of the Cin. George Washington Disting. Prof., 1998-2003. Fellow Mass. Hist. Soc.; mem. Orgn. Am. Historians, Colonial Soc. Mass., Am. Studies Assn., Berkshire County Hist. Soc. Home: 148 South St Williamstown MA 01267-2822 Office: Williams Coll Stetson Hall Williamstown MA 01267 E-mail: rdalzell@williams.edu.

DALZELL, STEWART, federal judge; b. Hackensack, N.J., Sept. 18, 1943; s. Stewart V. and Jeannette (Johnson) D.; m. Kathleen Regan, Mar. 28, 1981; children: Rebecca, Andrew. BS in Economics, U. Pa., 1965, JD, 1969. Bar: Pa. 1970, U.S. Dist. Ct. (ea. dist.) Pa. 1970, U.S. Ct. Appeals (11th cir.) 1979, U.S. Ct. Appeals (9th cir.) 1977, U.S. Ct. Appeals (Fed. cir.) 1983, U.S. Ct. Appeals (5th cir.) 1984, U.S. Ct. Appeals (2d cir.) 1986, U.S. Ct. Appeals (3d cir.) 1991, U.S. Supreme Ct. 1975. Fin. analyst NBC, N.Y.C., 1965-66; assoc. Drinker, Biddle & Reath, Phila., 1970-76, ptnr., 1976-91; judge U.S. Dist. Ct. (ea. dist.) Pa., 1991—. Vis. lectr. law Wharton Sch. U. Pa., 1969-70. Contbr. articles to law revs. and profl. jours. Recipient Speiser award. Mem. Beta Gamma Sigma. Episcopalian. Avocations: movies, music. Office: US Dist Cts US Courthouse Rm 10613 601 Market St Philadelphia PA 19106-1713

DALZIEL, SEAN MARK, pharmaceuticals researcher; m. Gena Dalziel. BS, U. Sydney, 1991—94; B in applied sci. with honours, U. Western Sydney Hawkesbury, 1995—96; PhD in chem. engring., U.Queensland, 1996—2000. Exptl. scientist Commonwealth Sci. and Indsl. Rsch. Org., Sydney, 1994—96; sr. rsch. engr. DuPont Ctrl. Rsch. & Devel., Wilmington, Del., 2000—. Engring. cons. Mem.: Am. Inst. Chem. Engrs., Am. Assn. Pharm. Scientists. Achievements include patents pending for drug delivery technologies; novel pharma and food excipients; protein purification systems. Office: E I du Pont de Nemours & Co Experimental Station Rt 141 Wilmington DE 19880-0304

DAM, KENNETH W. lawyer, law educator, federal agency administrator; b. Marysville, Kans., Aug. 10, 1932; s. Oliver W. and Ida L. (Hueppelsheuser) D.; m. Marcia Wachs, June 9, 1962; children: Eliot, Charlotte. BS, U. Kans., 1954; JD, U. Chgo., 1957; LLD (hon.), New Sch. Social Rsch., 1983. Bar: N.Y. State 1959. Law clk. to justice U.S. Supreme Ct., 1957-58; assoc. Cravath, Swaine & Moore, N.Y.C., 1958-60; faculty U. Chgo. Law Sch., 1960-82, prof., 1964-71, 74-82, Harold J. and Marion F. Green prof., 1976-82, provost, 1980-82; dep. sec. of state Dept. State, 1982-85; v.p. law and external rels. IBM Corp., 1985-92; pres., CEO United Way Am., 1992; Max Pam prof. of Am. and fgn. law U. Chgo. Law Sch., 1992—2001; dep. sec. Dept. Treasury, Washington, 2001—. Asst. dir. nat. security and internat. affairs Office Mgmt. and Budget, 1971-73; exec. dir. Coun. Econ. Policy, 1973; vis. prof. U. Freiburg, Germany, 1964; adv. bd. BMW of N.Am., 1990-95. Author: The GATT: Law and International Economic Organization, 1970, Oil Resources: Who Gets What How?, 1976, The Rules of the Game: Reform and Evolution in the International Monetary System, 1982, The Rules of the Global Game: A New Look at U.S. International Economic Policymaking, 2001; co-author: Federal Tax Treatment of Foreign Income, 1964, Economic Policy Beyond the Headlines, 1977, 2d edit., 1998; co-editor: Crytography's Role in Securing the Information Society, 1996; chair bd. advisors Fgn. Affairs jour., 1997-2001. Bd. dirs. Am. Coun. on Germany, 1986-95, Am.-China Soc., 1989-99, Coun. on Fgn. Rels., 1992-2001, Chgo. Coun. on Fgn. Rels., 1992-2001; trustee Brookings Inst., 1989-2001; co-chmn. Aspen Strategy Group, 1991-2001. Mem. Am. Acad. Arts and Scis., Am. Acad. Diplomacy, Am. Law Inst., Met. Club (Washington), Quadrangle Club. Office: Dept Treasury Office of the Secy 1500 Pennsylvania Ave NW Washington DC 20220

DAMADIAN, RAYMOND VAHAN, biophysicist; b. N.Y.C., Mar. 16, 1936; s. Vahan and Odette (Yazedjian) Damadian; m. Elizabeth Donna Terry, June 4, 1960; children: Timothy, Jevan, Kiera. BS in Math., U. Wis., 1956; MD, Albert Einstein Coll. Medicine, 1960. Univ. rsch. fellow in biophysics Harvard U., Cambridge, Mass., 1963—65; sr. investigator Sch. Aerospace Medicine, USAF, 1965—67; asst. prof. SUNY, Bklyn., 1967—71, assoc. prof., 1971—80; pres., chmn. Fonar Corp., Melville, NY, 1978—. Career investigator Health Rsch. Coun., N.Y.C., 1967—72. Capt. USAF, 1963—65. Recipient Lawrence Sperry award, 1984, Nat. medal of Tech., 1988. Mem.: AAAS, Biophys. Soc., Am. Chem. Soc., Sigma Xi. Office: Fonar Corp 110 Marcus Dr Melville NY 11747-4292

DAMAN, ERNEST LUDWIG, mechanical engineer; b. Hannover, Germany, Mar. 14, 1923; came to U.S., 1940, naturalized, 1944; s. Fritz and Ruth Edith (Meyer) Dammann; m. Jan. 20, 1945 (div.); children: Diane Cathrine, Cynthia Ruth, Bruce Hershey; m. Dorothy Russo, June 21, 1980; stepchildren: Christopher Walsweer, Jonathan Walsweer. BS in Mech. Engring, Poly. Inst. Bklyn., 1943. With Foster Wheeler Corp., Livingston, N.J., 1947—; dir. rsch. Foster Wheeler Energy Corp., Livingston, N.J., 1960-73, v.p., 1973-81, sr. v.p., 1981-88; chmn. Foster Wheeler Devel. Corp., Livingston, N.J., 1977-88, chmn. emeritus, 1988—; chmn., chief exec. officer HDS Fibers Inc., 1986-89; tech. exec. Exec. Office of Pres., The White House, Washington, 1995-97. Chmn. Nat. Materials Property Data Network, Inc., 1986-94; mem. sci. and tech. info. bd. NRC, 1989-91; lectr. in field. Patentee in field. Chmn. Westfield (N.J.) Democratic Com., 1956-60, Westfield Area Com. for Human Rights, 1962-68; mem. Westfield Charter Study Commn., 1964. Served with U.S. Army, 1944-46. Decorated Bronze Star. Fellow: ASME (pres.-elect 1987, pres. 1988—89), AAAS; mem.: NAE, United Engring. Trustees (bd. dirs. 1989—92, trustee 1989—2000, chmn. 1993), Am. Assn. Engring. Socs. (chmn. engring. roundtable 1993, bd. dirs.), Welding Rsch. Coun. (chmn. 1985), Westfield Tennis Club, Pi Tau Sigma. Achievements include development of advanced naval propulsion machinery, fluidized bed combustion, fast breeder reactor steam generators and intermediate heat exchangers; 19 patents in energy conversion processes and heat system. Office: Foster Wheeler Corp 12 Peach Tree Hill Rd Livingston NJ 07039-5701 Home: 307 Elm St Westfield NJ 07090 E-mail: damande@worldnet.att.net. *As a naturalized citizen my life has been influenced by my strong admiration for American Democracy and all that it implies.*

DAMAN, HARLAN RICHARD, allergist, educator; b. N.Y.C., Nov. 1, 1941; s. D. Leon and Frances (Weissler) D. AB cum laude, Harvard U., 1963; MD, Albert Einstein Coll. Medicine, 1967. Diplomate Am. Bd. Pediat., Am. Bd. Allergy and Immunology. Intern, then resident Yale-New Haven Hosp. and Med. Ctr., 1967-69; fellow in allergy and clin. immunology Nat. Jewish Hosp. Rsch., Ctr., U. Colo. Med. Ctr., Denver, 1971-73; pvt. practice, Yonkers, NY, 1974—. Instr. Albert Einstein Coll. Medicine, 1974-81; clin. asst. prof. pediat. Albert Einstein Coll. Medicine, N.Y.C., 1981—; dir. pediatric allergy clinic Bronx Mcpl. Hosp. Ctr., 1982-92; mem. Mt. Sinai Med. Ctr. and Sch. Medicine, 1976-90. Co-editor: Psychobiologic Aspects of Allergic Disorders, 1986; contbg. author: Outpatient Medicine, 1980; contbr. articles on pulmonary function testing in asthmatic disorders. Maj. M.C., USAF, 1969-71. Fellow Am. Acad. Pediat., Am. Coll. Allergy, Asthma and Immunology, Am. Coll. Chest Physicians, Am. Acad. Asthma, Allergy and Immunology; mem. N.Y. Allergy Soc., Westchester Allergy Soc. (dir. edni. program 1978-79, treas. 1980-81, pres. 1982-83), Westchester Acad. Medicine. Office: 769 Kimball Ave Yonkers NY 10704-1534

DAMASHEK, PHILIP MICHAEL, lawyer; b. N.Y.C., May 18, 1940; s. Jacob and Esther (Sassower) D.; m. Judith Ellen Gold, Dec. 3, 1967; children: Alan S., Jonathan S., Harris R. BBA, U. Miami, 1964. Bar: N.Y. 1969, U.S. Dist. Ct. (so. and ea. dists.) N.Y. 1977. Lawyer Cosmopolitan Mut. Ins. Co., N.Y.C., 1969-70, Schneider, Kleinick, Weitz & Damashek, 1971-73; sr. ptnr. Philip M. Damashek, P.C., N.Y.C., 1974-89; ptnr. Damashek, Godosky & Gentile, 1989-94; mng. ptnr. Schneider, Kleinick, Weitz, Damashek & Shoot, 1994—2000, The Cochran Firm Schneider, Kleinick, Weitz, Damashek & Shoot, 2000—02, Schneider, Kleinick Weitz & Damashek, 2002—. Chmn. Combined Bar Assns. Jud.Screening Panel, N.Y.C., 1983—88; co-chair NYSTLA Law Pac, 1997—, trustee, 1989—91; legis. appointment mem. Com. to Rev. Audio-Visual Coverage of Ct. Procs., 1993—94; exec. apptd. to govs. N.Y. Jud. Screening Com., 1997—; adv. bd. N.Y. Israel Econ. Devel. Partnership, 1997—; apptd. Com. on Case Mgmt. Office of Ct. Adminstrn., Cts. of State of N.Y., 1993—, Task Force on Reducing Litigation Cost and Delay, 1st Jud. Dist., 1996—, Differentiated Case Mgmt. Project, Kings County, 1996—, Alt. Dispute Resolution Adv. Com. N.Y. State Unified Ct. Sys., 1999—, N.Y. State Jud. Salary Commn., 1997—, N.Y. State CLE Bd., 1997—, charter bd. mem., 1997—2000; trustee N.Y. Law Sch., 1996—; malpractice panel Supreme Ct. of the State of N.Y., County of N.Y., 1990—91; dir. and v.p. for govt. rels. Respect for Law Alliance, Inc., 1995—; adv. com. on the jud. N.Y.C. Mayor, 2002—; mem. bus. devel. bd. First Nat. Bank of L.I., 2003. Named Lawyer of Yr., Inst. Jewish Humanities, 1990, Lawyer of the Yr., UJA Fedn., 1993, N.Y. Law Schs. Lifetime Achievement award, 2000, Philip M. Damashek Lifetime Achievement award, NY State Trial Lawyers Assn., 2003. Mem. ABA, Am. Bd. Trial Advs. (advocate), Am. Judicature Soc., Am. Bar Found., Assn. Trial Lawyers Am. (life, Wiedemann Wysocki citation of excellence 1990, bd. govs. 1990-92, state rels. com. 1990-92, no-fault coordinating com. 1990-92), N.Y. State Bar Assn. (ct. adminstrn. com., com. jud. adminstrn. 1990-94), Assn. of Bar of City of N.Y., N.Y. State Trial Lawyers Assn. (pres. 1990-91, bd. dirs., trustee, Ann. Philip M. Damashek Lifetime Achievement award 2003), Assn. Trial Lawyers City N.Y. (bd. dirs.), N.Y. County Lawyers Assn., Jewish Lawyers Guild (bd. govs.). Office: Schneider Kleinick Weitz & Damashek 233 Broadway Fl 5 New York NY 10279-0599

DAMAST, STAN, assisted living design consultant; b. Bronx, N.Y., Apr. 17, 1947; s. Joseph H. and Mary (Kutchinsky) D.; 1 child, Robyn; m. Livia Mallon, Dec. 25, 1990. BS in Edn., City Coll., N.Y.C., 1969, MS in Edn., 1971. Cert. tech. edn. tchr. N.Y. Tchr. John Bowne H.S., Queens, N.Y., 1969-71, Jamaica H.S., Queens, N.Y., 1971-74, City Coll. N.Y., N.Y.C., 1974-94, South Shore H.S., Bklyn., 1974-94, Thomas A. Edison Vocat. Tech. H.S., Queens, 1994—2002; pvt. practice cons. Westbury, NY, 2002—. Instr., adj. lectr. City Coll. N.Y., N.Y.C., 1971-81; asst. prof. N.Y.C. Tech. Coll., 1996—; instr., guest speaker Project Superteach N.Y. State Edn. Dept., Queens, 1981; curriculum writer, cons. Bur. Tech. Edn. N.Y.C. Bd. Edn., Bklyn., 1976-93. Author: V.T.R.-A Curriculum Guide for Teachers for Junior High School and Senior High School, 1972; contbr. articles to profl. jours. Pres. Parent Assn. Temple Isaiah, Forest Hills, N.Y., 1990-92. Recipient Ind. Arts Tchr. of Yr. award N.Y. State Tech. Edn. Assn., 1982, Regional Tchr., 1980, 81. Mem. United Fedn. Tchrs., In-Plant Printing Mgmt. Assn., Tchrs. Printing Guild of N.Y., N.Y.C. Tech. Edn. Assn. (pres., v.p. pub., editor, mug of yr. 1980, tchr. of yr. 1981, ind. arts tchr. of yr. 1980, 81, ind. arts regional tchr. 1980), Assn. Graphic Arts/L.I. Econ. Devel. Assn. (mem. ednl. com. 1996—), Epsilon Pi Tau. Democrat. Avocations: graphic design, electronics, photography, woodworking, computer technology. E-mail: sdamast@usa.net.

D'AMATO, ALFONSE M. lawyer, former senator; b. Bklyn., Aug. 1, 1937; m. Penelope Ann Collenburg, 1960 (div. 1995); children: Lisa, Lorraine, Daniel, Christopher. BS, Syracuse U., 1959, JD, 1961. Bar: N.Y. 1962. Adminstr., Nassau County, N.Y., 1965-68; receiver of taxes Town of Hempstead, L.I., N.Y., 1971-77, presiding supr., vice chmn. county bd. suprs., 1977-80; U.S. senator from N.Y., 1981-98; lawyer, comm. Fox News, 1999—; mng. dir. Park Strategies LLC, 1999—. Chmn. banking, housing and urban affairs com., mem. fin. com., caucus on internat. narcotics control; co-chmn. U.S. Commn. on Security and Coperation in Europe. Mem. Island Park Vol. Fire Dept. Mem. Lions, Sons of Italy, KC. Roman Catholic. Avocations: reading, piano. Office: Park Strategies LLC 101 Park Ave, Ste 2506 New York NY 10178

D'AMATO, ANTHONY ROGER, recording company executive; b. N.Y.C., Jan. 21, 1931; s. Agostino and Luisa (Galiani) D'A.; m. Gabrielle Hilton, June 26, 1958; children— Luisa, Jennie, Tania, Joanna, Antonia. BA in Music and English Lit. cum laude (Founders Day award 1956), N.Y. U., 1956; Ml.A. (teaching fellow), Brandeis U., 1957. Artist and repertoire dir. stereophonic div. Decca Record Co., Ltd., Eng., 1958-78; pres. TDA Prodns. Ltd., N.Y.C., 1978—; exec. dir. Winnipeg (Man., Can.) Symphony Orch., 1979-80; v.p. artist and repertoire AudioFidelity Enterprises, N.Y.C., 1980-81; mng. dir. Mantovani Prodns., Mantovani Orch., N.Y.C., 1982—. Mng. cons. Leopold Stokowski, 1964-72 Served with USMCR, 1951-53. Recipient Grand Prix du Disque, Charles Cros award rec., 1969 Mem. Assn. Cultural Execs. Can., Winnipeg C. of C., Phi Beta Kappa.

DAMAZ, PAUL F. architect; b. Portugal, Nov. 8, 1917; came to U.S., 1947, naturalized, 1953; s. Pierre L. and Maria A. (Leite) D.; m. Solange Guillon, Dec. 26, 1981. BA in Architecture, Ecole Speciale d'Architecture, 1941; M. Town Planning, U. Paris, Sorbonne, 1946. Archtl. designer UN Hdqrs., N.Y.C., 1948-51, Harrison & Abramowitz, N.Y.C., 1951-53; chief designer Cajetan Baumann, N.Y.C., 1953-61; ptnr. Damaz & Weigel, N.Y.C., 1962-76; pres. Adasco Tech Internat., N.Y.C., 1976-81; prin. Paul Damaz Assos., East Hampton, N.Y., 1981—. Design critic Columbia, 1953; writer, critic, lectr. maj. univs. and TV. Dir. N.Y. Fine Arts Fedn.; Mem. nat. panel arbitrators Am. Arbitration Assn. Author: Art in European Architecture, 1956, Art in Latin American Architecture, 1962. Capt. French Army, 1939—45, POW in Germany. Fellow AIA; mem. French Ordre des Architectes, Archtl. League N.Y. (past v.p., Arnold W. Brunner award 1958), Mcpl. Arts Soc., French-Am. Soc., Am. Inst. Planners. Office: 218 Old Stone Hwy East Hampton NY 11937-1621

D'AMBOISE, JACQUES JOSEPH, former dancer, choreographer, educator, director; b. Dedham, Mass., July 28, 1934; s. Andrew Ahearn and Georgette d'Amboise; m. Carolyn George, Jan. 1, 1956; children: George Jacques, Christopher R., Charlotte Lorraine, Catherine Liza. DHL, DFA, Coll. New Rochelle, 1976, Bates Coll., 1978; DHL (hon.), St. Peters Coll., 1978; DFA (hon.), Monmouth U., 1984; DHL, DFA, Conn. Coll., 1991, The Juilliard Sch., 2000; DHL (hon.), Franklin Pierce Coll., 2000; DFA (hon.), U. of the South, 2001; DHL (hon.), St. Joseph Coll., 2003. With N.Y.C. Ballet Co., 1949-84; prin. Dancer, 1953-84; instr. Sch. Am. Ballet; prof., dean SUNY Sch. Dance, Purchase, 1977-80. Dancer (films) Seven Brides for Seven Brothers, 1954, The Best Things in Life Are Free, 1956, Carousel, 1956, Off Beat, 1986, He Makes Me Feel Like Dancin', 1983; co-author: Teaching the Magic of Dance, 1983; choreographer Scherzo Opus 42, Valse-Scherzo Concert Fantasy, Celebration, The Chase, Tschaikovsky Suite No. 2, Sarabande and Danse II, Quatouor, Prologue and Saltarelli. Recipient Paul Robeson award, 1988, Capezio award, 1990, Disting. Svc. to Arts award, Am. Acad. Arts and Letters, 1993, Kennedy Ctr. Honors, 1995, St. Elizabeth Ann Seton award, NCEA, 1996, Nat. Medal of Arts award, U.S. Pres., 1998, Dance Mag. award, 1999, Arison award, Nat. Assn. for Advancement of Arts, 2002, James Keller award, The Christophers, 2002, Town Hall Friend of Arts award, 2000, Heinz award for Arts and Humanities, 2001, others; MacArthur fellow, 1990. Office: Nat Dance Inst Inc 594 Broadway Rm 805 New York NY 10012-3257

D'AMBROSIO, VINNI MARIE, writer; b. N.Y.C. d. Melvin Mix and Lucille DeMarco Aguanno; (div. 1962): 1 child, Cynthia Johnson. BA, Smith Coll., Northhampton, Mass.; PhD, NYU, 1981. Prof. CUNY, 1972-94. V.p. T.S. Eliot Soc., 1990-93, pres., 1993-96; assoc. prof. San Diego State U., 1981. Author: Life of Touching Mouths, 1971, Eliot Possessed, 1989, Mexican Gothic, 1995, (Pen and Brush, Inc. award 1998). Bd. dirs. Jefferson Market Garden com., mem. Caring Cmty. Adv. Com. Fellow Va. Ctr. for Creative Arts, Sweet Briar, 1994, 96. Mem. AAUW (bd. dirs.), Pen and Brush Inc. (pres. 1994-98, v.p. 1998—), PEN-Am. Ctr., Poetry Soc. Am.; mem. Salmaqundi Club; Itlian Am. Writers Assn., Ralph Waldo Emerson Soc. E-mail: vinnimarie@aol.com.

DAME, CATHERINE ELAINE, acupuncturist; b. Holyoke, Mass., Oct. 1, 1951; d. Josaphat Charles and Lillian Geneva (Archer) Boulanger; m. William Henry Dame, Jan. 9, 1970 (div. May 1999); 1 child, Cristinna Lian. Acupuncture Diplomate, N.E. Sch. Acupuncture, Watertown, Mass., 1992; student, Ind. U., 1988-93; MEd, Cambridge Coll., 1994. Lic. acupuncturist, Mass.; nat. bd. cert. in acupuncture. Dept. mgr. Zayre Dept. Store, Chicopee, Mass., 1969; retail sales clk. Woodward & Lothrop Store, Alexandria, Va., 1971-72; dept. mgr. Steiger Dept. Store, Enfield, Conn., 1972-73; retail sales clk. Point Dept. Store, Ft. Walton Beach, Fla., 1973-74; assembly, repair mfg. Texas Instruments, Ft. Walton Beach, 1974-75; tller Third Nat. Bank, Springfield, Mass., 1975-81, customer svc. rep., 1981-82; teller Bank of N.E./Fleet Bank, Springfield, 1990-93; owner, mgr. Acupuncture Svcs., Chicopee, 1994—. Cons. Cambridge Coll., Springfield, Mass., 1994-95; bus. office liaison Cambridge Coll., 1995-98; Traditional Chinese Med. tour, China, 2001. Mem. People to People Internat. Mem.: Acupuncture Soc. Mass., Bus. and Profl. Trade Exch., Nat. Commn. for Cert. of Acupuncturists Directory, Am. Assn. Oriental Medicine, Chicopee C. of C., Kings Bridge Equine Rescue, Inc., Granby Regional Horse Coun. Office: Acupuncture Svcs Chicopee 665 Prospect St Chicopee MA 01020-3064

DAME, LAUREEN EVA, nursing administrator, educator; b. Framingham, Mass., Mar. 15, 1947; d. Irving Lawrence Jr. and Cora Justina (Wells) Dame; children: Daryl Lawrence, Jeffrey Lee. Diploma, Dartmouth-Hickock Med. Ctr., Hanover N.H., 1968; BSN, Clayton State Coll., Morrow, Ga., 1996; MSN, Emory U., 1997. RN, Ga., Fla.; cert. profl. in healthcare quality. Staff nurse, charge nurse, team leader maternity and surgical nursing various hosps., N.H., Boston, St. Louis, 1968-69, 80-83; sch. nurse practitioner Dept. Pub. Health, Bedford, Mass., 1983-85; perioperative nurse, 1st asst. South Fulton Hosp., East Point, Ga., 1985-86; nurse, first asst., plastic surgery John Munna M.D., Atlanta, 1986-90; resource nurse, intake coord. Shallowford Hosp., Atlanta, 1989-91, staff educator, quality assurance coord. dept. surg. svcs., 1991-92; quality improvement coord., nursing South Fulton Med. Ctr., East Point, Ga., 1992; nurse coord. quality assurance Kaiser Permanente, Atlanta, 1992-93, dir. quality assurance, 1993-95; mgr. coord. care Egleston Children's Hosp., Emory U., Atlanta, 1995-96; mgr. quality mgmt. Egleston Pediat. Group, Decatur, Ga., 1996-97; dir. dept. surgery Emory U. Hosp., Atlanta, 1997-98; dir. regulatory and quality mgmt. MATRIA Healthcare, Inc., 1998—99; clin. instr. Ga. State U., Atlanta, 2000; adminstr. Midtown Urology Surg. Ctr., 2000—. Mem. NAACOG (charter; chmn. steering com. 1972), AORN (chmn. hospitality com. 1992, mem. workshop and publicity coms. 1983), NAFE, Am. Soc. Plastic and Reconstructive Surg. Nurses, Nat. Assn. Quality Profls., Ga. Assn. Quality Profls., Ga. North Ctrl. Dist. Quality Profls., Am. Acad. Disting. Students, Am. Needlepoint Guild (life), Embroiderers Guild Am. (life), Sigma Theta Tau. Lutheran. Avocations: needlepoint, embroidery, fiber artist (nat. cert. judge). Home: 8726 Twin Oaks Dr Jonesboro GA 30236-5152 Fax: 404-881-6398. E-mail: nedlptprincess@msn.com.

DAME, THOMAS MICHAEL, radio astronomer; b. Winthrop, Mass., Oct. 16, 1954; s. Chester Thomas and Claire J. (White) D.; m. Geraldine Ann Healey, Aug. 23, 1985. BA, Boston U., 1976; PhD, Columbia U., 1983. Rsch. assoc. Goddard Inst. for Space Studies NASA, N.Y.C., 1983-84; rsch. assoc. Columbia U., N.Y.C., 1985-86; radio astronomer Smithsonian Astrophys. Obs., Cambridge, Mass., 1986—. Lectr. astronomy Harvard U., Cambridge, 1989—. Contbr. articles to Astrophys. Jour., Sky and Telescope Mag., NASA Publ. NAS fellow, 1983-84. Mem. Am. Astron. Soc. Achievements include publication of first and only complete maps of molecular gas in the Milky Way and Andromeda galaxies; catalogued largest molecular clouds in Milky Way; calibrated conversion from CO intensity to molecular mass. Home: 40 Magoun St Cambridge MA 02140-1617 Office: Ctr for Astrophysics 60 Garden St Cambridge MA 02138-1516 E-mail: tdame@cfa.harvard.edu.

DAME, WILLIAM PAGE, III, bank executive, educational administrator; b. Balt., July 6, 1940; s. William Page and Harriet Carrington (Brent) D.; m. Laura Jacqueline Cordier, June 28, 1968 (div. 1975); children: William Page IV, Laura Alexandra; m. Beverly Ann Reece, July 4, 1998. BA, U. Va., 1963. Ofcl. asst., asst. treas. Bankers Trust Co., N.Y.C., 1963-68, dep. rep. Tokyo, 1968-70, asst. treas. N.Y.C., 1970-71; asst. v.p. Franklin Nat. Bank, N.Y.C., 1971-72, regional rep. Singapore, 1972—74; v.p. Riggs Nat. Bank, Washington, 1974-76, Security Pacific Nat. Bank, L.A., 1976-77, San Francisco, 1977-79, Sydney, Australia, 1979-80, J. Henry Schroder Bank and Trust Co., N.Y.C., 1981-82; sr. v.p. Palmer Nat. Bank, Washington, 1982-84; v.p. Sovran Bank, Arlington, Va., 1985-86; chief fin. officer DITT, Inc. subs. Electricité de France, Washington, 1986-88; v.p. Am. Security Bank, Washington, 1988-91; internat. fin. cons. Washington, 1991-93; adminstr. Grace Episc. Day Sch., Silver Spring, Md., 1993-95, Evergreen Sch., Kensington, Md., 1995-98, Alexandria Country Day Sch., Alexandria, Va., 1998—2002; asst. headmaster Lyndon Inst., Lyndon Ctr., Vt., 2002—. Sr. warden St. Paul's Episc. Ch., Washington, 1995-96; dir. The Woodley Ensemble, Washington, 1997-2002, The Piggery Theater, North Hatley, Que., 2003—. Mem. Soc. Colonial Wars, Am. Bus. Coun.-Singapore (founding mem.), World Affairs Coun., Asia Soc., Old Asian Hands Soc., BT Alumni Assn., The Soc. of the Cin., North Hatley Club, Tanglin Club, Singapore Cricket Club. Democrat. Episcopalian. Home: 235 Skyline Dr Lyndonville VT 05851 Office: College Rd Box 127 Lyndon Center VT 05850 Fax: 802-626-6138. E-mail: chantman@mindspring.com., pdame@lyndon.k12.vt.us.

DAMELIN, HAROLD, federal official; m. Harriet Damelin; 2 children. Grad. magna cum laude(hon.), Boston Coll., 1969, Boston Coll. Law Sch., 1972. Fed. prosecutor Criminal Div. of the Dept. of Justice, Wash., DC, 1974—86; asst. US Atty. Dist. of Columbia, Wash., DC, 1974—86; ptnr. Powers, Pyles, Sutter & Verville, Wash., DC, 1986—95; staff dir. US Senate Permanent Subcomm. on Invest., Wash., DC, 1995—97; sr. counsel US Senate Comm. on Govtl. Affairs, Wash., DC, 1997—98; atty. Pyles, Sutter & Verville, Wash., DC, 1999—2003; Insp. Gen. US Small Bus. Admin., Wash., DC, 2003—. Office: 409 Third St, SW, Rm 7150 Washington DC 20416*

D'AMELIO, FRANK ANTHONY, communications company executive; b. Jersey City, Dec. 9, 1957; s. Joseph and Rose (Giordano) D'A.; m. Carmel Rachel Zampaglione, Mar. 31, 1984. BS, St. Peter's Coll., 1979; MBA, St. John's U., 1983. Asst. fin. analyst AT&T Bell Labs., Short Hills, N.J., 1979-80, sr. asst. fin. analyst, 1980-81, supr. payroll dept., 1981-82, fin. analyst, 1982-83, supr. fin. services, 1983-84, property mgr., 1984, mgr., services and personnel div., 1984-85, mgr. engring., adminstrn., 1985-86, mgr. facility ops. Murray Hill, N.J., 1986-88, mgr. govt. systems fin. and corp. customer relations Short Hills, NJ, 1988—94; controller AT&T Network Systems, 1994—96, CFO, 1996—98, Lucent Technologies, Murray Hill, NJ, 2001—. Mem. Bldg. Owner's Mgmt. Assn. Republican. Roman Catholic. Avocations: weightlifting, football, basketball, real estate, water sports. Office: Lucent Technologies 600 Mountain Ave Murray Hill NJ 07974

DAMER, LINDA K. music educator; b. Springfield, Ill., Dec. 5, 1938; d. J. Fred and Mary Jane (Thurmond) Welsh; children: Diana, Cynthia, John. BA, William Jewell Coll., 1959; MA, Boston U., 1967; EdD, U. N.C., Greensboro, 1979. Tchr. Kearney (Mo.) Pub. Schs., 1959-60, Consol. Sch. Dist. 1, Kansas City, Mo., 1960-63, Wellesley (Mass.) Pub. Schs., 1963-64, Newton (Mass.) Pub. Schs., 1966-67, Smyth County (Va.) Pub. Schs., 1969-72, Washington County (Va.) Pub. Schs., 1973-76, Burlington (N.C.) Pub. Schs., 1978-79; assoc. prof. music Ind. State U., Terre Haute, 1979-88, prof. music, 1988—, coord. music edn. divsn., coord. grad. studies music. Grad. tchg. asst. U. N.C., Greensboro, 1977-78. Fellow U. N.C., 1976-77. Mem. Music Educators Nat. Conf., Ind. Music Educators Assn., Am. Orff Schulwerk Assn., Univ. Club, Pi Kappa Lambda, Sigma Alpha Iota. Home: 525 S 21st St Terre Haute IN 47803 Office: Ind State U Dept Music Terre Haute IN 47809-0001 E-mail: midamer@isugw.indstate.edu.

DAMERST, WILLIAM, English and humanities educator; b. Pelham, Mass., Aug. 21, 1923; s. Steven M. and Clara (Peterson) Damerst; m. Dorothy Blackburn, Feb. 16, 1946 (dec. 2001); children: Jeffrey W., Laura Barron, Gail Pashek. Student, Amherst Coll., 1941—43, student, 1945—46, Mich. State U., 1943; BS, U. Ill., 1946; MA, U. Mass., 1955. Officer family bus., 1946—55; instr. English Pa. State U., University Park, 1955—60, asst. prof., 1960—65, assoc. prof., 1965—72, prof., 1972—85, prof. emeritus, 1985—. Cons. Gulf Oil Corp., Phila., Gulf R&D Co., Phila., GE Co., Erie, Pa., St. Joseph Lead Co., Monaca, Pa. *A new literary genre appeared when William A. Damerst's "Joey, Joe, and Joseph" was published. Each of his book's three stories reveals a different development of the way a nightmare-haunted, bitter World War II combat flyer might think, act, and behave after he comes home believing he was betrayed. His just-widowed mother had married a man he despised, his fiancée had married his best friend, and her twin sister, his confidante in college, had married a man twice her age! All three stories take place at the same time, and all three contribute to the book's climactic ending.* Author: (text) Good Gulf Letters and Reports, 1959, Resourceful Business Communication, 1965, Clear Tech. Reports, 1972, Clear Tech. Comm. 3d edit., 1990, (novel) Joey, Joe, and Joseph, 2001. 1st lt. USAF, 1943—45. Decorated Air medal with 5 oak leaf clusters; grantee, Gulf Aid to Edn., 1959, 1960. Address: 705 Jerdon Cir North Myrtle Beach SC 29582

DAMESHEK, H(AROLD) LEE, physician; b. Balt., Mar. 16, 1937; s. Samuel and Rose (Rudick) D.; m. Michelle Zubasic, Sept. 12, 1965; children: Lynne R. Shine, Amy D. Brumbaugh, David, Deborah. BS in Chemistry, Franklin and Marshall Coll., 1959; MD, Tufts U., 1963. Diplomate Am. Bd. Internal Medicine. Intern Presbyn.-Univ. Hosp., Pitts., 1963-64, resident in internal medicine, 1966-68; hematology fellow Ohio State U. Hosp., Columbus, 1968-69; practice medicine specializing in hematology and oncology Pitts., 1969—. Clin. instr. medicine U. Pitts., 1969-74, clin. asst. prof., 1974-81, clin. assoc. prof., 1981—; instr. West Penn Hosp., Pitts., 1969-77; chmn. cancer com. Presbyn.-Univ. Hsop., 1980—; cons. various hosps.; bd. dirs. Physicians' Healthg Plan Pa., 1986—. Contbr. articles to med. jours. Bd. dirs. Leukemia Soc. West Pa., 1971—, v.p., 1977-79, Am. Cancer Soc.; treas. Presbyn.-Univ. Hosp., 1984-86, v.p., 1986-88, pres. med. staff, 1988-90, mem. med. quality improvement com., 1991—; mem. med. adv. com. Cancer Support Ctr., 1987—; vol. faculty promotions com. U. Pitts. Med. Ctr., 1994—. Capt. U.S. Army, 1964-66. Fellow ACP; mem. AMA, Am. Soc. Hematology, Allegheny County Med. Soc. (treas. 1980-81, v.p. 1982, pres. 1984, bd. dirs., 1996-99, peer rev. bd. 1991-94, Frederick Jacob award 1988), Pa. Med. Soc., Pitts. Acad. Medicine (treas. 1981—), Westmoreland Country Club (sec., bd. dirs.), Univ. Club Pitts. Home: 421 Radcliff Dr Pittsburgh PA 15235-5326

DAMGARD, JOHN MICHAEL, trade association executive; b. Ottawa, Ill., Dec. 7, 1939; s. Theodor Miller and Dorothy (Oughton) D.; m. Darcy Mead, Oct. 23, 1965 (div.); children: Michael Theodor, Julie Mead. BA, Knox Coll., Galesburg, Ill., 1964; student, U. Munich, Ger., 1962, U. Va., 1960. Chair, CEO Ill. Valley Investment Co., Dwight, Ill., 1966-70, dir., pres., 1976—; asst. to Vice Pres. U.S. White House, 1971-74; dep. asst. sec. U.S. Dept. Agr., Washington, 1974-77; v.p. ACLI Internat., Washington, 1977-82; pres., dir., exec. com. Futures Industry Assn., Washington, 1982—, president, present. Adv. Republican Heritage Group, 1976; mem. Rep. Nat. Com. Policy Group; bd. dirs. Washington Internat. Horse Show, 1975-81. Mem. Futures Industry Inst. (trustee), Am. Soc. Assn. Execs., Met. Club (Washington), Racquet Club (Chgo.), Meadow Club (Southampton, N.Y.), Farmington Country Club (Charlottesville, Va.). Home: 2439 Tracy Pl NW Washington DC 20008-1628 Office: Futures Industry Assn 2001 Pennsylvania Ave NW Washington DC 20006-1850

DAMIANAKOS, PHAEDRA VASILIKI, secondary school educator; b. Manhattan, N.Y., Mar. 23, 1943; d. Chris Paplakis and Mary Dandini-Paplakis; children: Anastasia, Maria. BA, CUNY, 1964, MS in Edn., 1972. Tchr. N.Y.C. Bd. Edn., Manhattan, 1964—93; tutor Pub. Sch. 6 Manhattan, 1995—96; tutor New Student Ctr. Hunter Coll., CUNY, Manhattan, 1997—99; singer Glek Club United Fedn. Tchrs., Manhattan, 1999—. Author: Single Mother: A New York Story, 1999. Active numerous animal rights orgns. Mem.: United Fedn. Tchrs., Hunter Coll. Alumni Assn. Greek Orthodox. Avocations: reading, writing, piano, embroidery. Home: Apt 2L 525 E 89th St New York NY 10128

D'AMICO, ANDREW J. lawyer; b. Phila., Feb. 18, 1953; s. Joseph J. and Alice H. (Falotica) D'A.; m. Georgiana R. Etheridge, Feb. 25, 1978; children: Andrew J. Jr., Joseph W., Jennifer T., Theresa J. BA, St. Joseph's U., Phila., 1975; JD, Villanova U., 1978. Bar: Pa. Supreme Ct. 1978, U.S. Dist. Ct. (ea. dist.) Pa. 1979, U.S Ct. Appeals (3d Cir.) 1981, U.S Supreme Ct. 1982. Sole practitioner Law Offices Andrew J. D'Amico, Media, Pa., 1979—. Coach Llanerch Hills Little League, Drexel Hill, Pa., 1986-96, St. Bernadette CYO Basketball, 1996-2000. Mem.: ATLA, Guy G. deFuria Am. Inn of Ct., Delaware County Bar Assn. (bd. dirs. 1991—92, chmn. ADR com. 1996—, bd. dirs. 1997—98, chmn. civil trial practice com. 2001), Pa. Trial Lawyers Assn., Alpha Sigma Nu. Roman Catholic. Avocations: music, coaching sports, reading. Office: PO Box 605 115 N Monroe St Media PA 19063-3037

D'AMICO, CAROL, federal agency administrator; MS in Adult Edn., EdD in Leadership and Policy Studies, Ind. U. Sr. program analyst Ind. Gen. Assembly; policy and planning specialist Ind. Dept. Edn.; dean workforce devel. Ivy Tech. C.C. Ind.; asst. sec. vocat. and adult edn. Dept. Edn., Washington, 2001—. Expert workforce devel. and edn. issues; testified before Congress and several state legislatures; sr. fellow Hudson Inst.; spkr. in field. Co-author: (book) Workforce 2020: Work and Workers in the 21st Century; contbr. articles to newspapers and profl. jours. Office: Dept Edn Vocat and Adult Edn 400 Maryland Ave SW Washington DC 20202-7100

D'AMICO, FRANCINE J. political scientist, educator; b. Geneva, N.Y., July 29, 1958; d. Francis J. and L. Bernadette (Roesch) D'Amico; m. Douglas J. Roll, July 17, 1982; children: James F. D'Amico Roll, Patrick C. D'Amico Roll. BA in English and Polit. Sci., William Smith Coll., 1980; MA in Govt., Cornell U., 1985, PhD in Govt., 1989. Asst. prof. Ithaca (N.Y.) Coll., 1987—93, Hobart & William Smith Colls., Geneva, NY, 1994—97; lectr. SUNY, Cortland, 1998—2001; asst. prof. polit. sci. Syracuse (N.Y.) U., 2000—. Vis. rsch. fellow peace studies program Cornell U., Ithaca, 1993—96, vis. asst. prof. dept. govt., 1996—97; vis. asst. prof. LeMoyne Coll., Syracuse, 1999, Syracuse, 2000; presenter/lectr. in field. Co-editor: Women, Gender & World Politics, 1994, Women in World Politics, 1995, Gender Camouflage: Women and the U.S. Military, 1999; contbr. articles to profl. jours. Chair Town of Geneva Dem. Com., 2000—02; candidate N.Y. State Assembly 129th Dist., 2002. Mem.: Women in Internat. Security, Am. Polit. Sci. Assn., Internat. Studies Assn. (rep. at large, exec. coun. 2002—). Democrat. Roman Catholic. Home: 4625 Whites Point Geneva NY 14456-9708

D'AMICO, JOHN, JR., judge; b. Long Branch, N.J., Jan. 24, 1941; s. John and Elvira (Caravello) D'A.; m. Sandra V. Vaccarelli, Nov. 25, 1967; 1 child, Kimberly Jean. AB cum laude, Harvard U., 1963, JD, 1966. Bar: N.J. 1966. Law clk. to presiding justice Monmouth County Ct., Freehold, N.J., 1966-67; assoc. Drazin, Warshaw, Auerbach & Rudnick, Red Bank, N.J., 1967-70; atty. Mut. Benefit Life Ins. Co., Newark, 1970-72, asst. counsel, 1972-74, assoc. counsel, 1974-77, counsel, 1978-81, 2d v.p., counsel, 1981-91; of counsel Shea & Gould, 1991; judge Superior Ct. of N.J., 1992—2002; chmn. N.Y. State Parole Bd., 2003—. Counsel Nat. Soc. to Prevent Blindness, New Brunswick, 1978-91, Partnership for N.J., New Brunswick, 1984-91; 1st vice chmn. N.J. Transp. Coordinating Coun.ää, Newark, 1984-89; mem. Monmouth County Bd. Social Services, Freehold, 1986; councilman Borough of Oceanport, N.J., 1979-84; freeholder Monmouth County, N.J., 1983-89; senator State of N.J., 1988-89; bd. dirs. Shore Commuter Coalition, Eatontown, N.J., 1982-91. Recipient Disting. Svc. award Nat. Soc. to Prevent Blindness, 1983. Mem. ABA, N.J. Bar Assn., Monmouth County Bar Assn., Assn. Life Ins. Counsel, Harvard U. Law Sch. Assn. Democrat. Avocations: reading, golf, tennis. Home: 53 Wittenberg Ct Oceanport NJ 07757-1027 E-mail: jdamic@juno.com.

DAMICO, JOSEPH F. medical company executive; BA, James Madison U., 1976, MBA in Mgmt. and Mktg., 1977. Sales rep. to various mgmt. positions Am. Hosp. Supply Corp. (now merged with Baxter), 1979-87; former group v.p. to pres. divsns. Baxter Internat., Inc., 1987-93; former pres., COO Allegiance Corp., 1996—98; group pres. Cardinal Health, Dublin, Ohio, 1996—; founding partner, operating principal Roundtable Healthcare Partners, Lake Forest, Ill.; chair. Vanguard Med. Concepts. Bd. dirs. Xillix Technologies Corp., Richmond, B.C., Lake Forest Hosp., Ill., Health Industry Mfrs. Assn., Washington, The Baxter Allegiance Found., Deerfield, Ill., Coll. of Lake County, Grayslake, Ill. Office: Roundtable Healthcare Partners 272 E Deerpath Rd, Ste 350 Lake Forest IL 60045

D'AMICO, MICHAEL, architect, urban planner; b. Bklyn., Sept. 11, 1936; s. Michael and Rosalie (Vinciguerra) D.; BArch, U. Okla., 1961; postgrad. So. Meth. U. Sch. Law, 1962-63, Coll. Marin, 1988-89;, San Francisco Law Sch., 1994—; m. Joan Hand, Nov. 26, 1955; children: Michael III, Dion Charles.

Supr. advanced planning sect. Dallas Dept. City Planning, 1961-63; designer, planner in charge Leo A. Daly Co., San Francisco, 1963-66; project planner Whisler, Patri Assos., San Francisco, 1966-67; architect, urban planner D'Amico & Assocs., San Francisco, N.Y., Guam, 1967-73, pres. D'Amico & Assocs., Inc., Mill Valley and San Francisco, Calif., and Guam, 1973—; pres. Jericho Alpha Inc., 1979-82, pres. Alpha Internet Syss., Inc., 1996—; cons. arch., planner City of Seaside (Calif.), 1967-72, 79-81, 89—; cons. urban redevel. Eureka (Calif.), 1967-82; cons. planner, Lakewood, Calif.; redevel. cons. to Daly City (Calif.), 1975-77; redevel. adviser to Tamalpais Valley Bus. Assn., 1975-77; archtl. and hist. analyst to Calif. Dept. Transp., 1975-77; agt. for Eureka, Calif. Coastal Commn., 1977-79; devel. cons. City of Scotts Valley, 1988-95, City of Suisun, 1988-89, City of Union City, 1989-91. Mem. steering com. San Francisco Joint Com. Urban Design, 1967-72. Recipient Cmty. Design award AIA, 1970; First prize award Port Aransas (Tex.) Master Plan Competition, 1964; Design award Karachi Mcpl. Authority, 1987, Merit award St. Vincent's/Silveira. Mem. AIA (inactive), Am. Inst. Cons. Planners, Am. Planning Assn., Calif. Assn. Planning Cons. (sec., treas. 1970-72), World Future Soc., Solar Energy Soc. Am. Office: 525 Midvale Way Mill Valley CA 94941-3705

DAMICO, NICHOLAS PETER, lawyer; b. Chester, Pa., June 29, 1937; s. Ralph A. and Mary C. (Ametrane) D.; m. Patricia Ann Swatek, Aug. 26, 1967; children: Christine, Gregory. BS in Acctg., St. Joseph's U., 1960; LLB, U. Pa., 1963; LLM, Georgetown U., 1967. Bar: Pa. 1963, D.C. 1967, Md. 1986. Tax law specialist IRS, Washington, 1963-66; assoc. Silverstein & Mullens, Washington, 1966-72, ptnr., 1972-76; prin. Damico & Assocs., Washington, 1976—2003; sole practice Bethesda, Md., 2003 . Adj. prof. Georgetown U. Law Ctr., Washington, 1973-75. Mem. ABA. Office: 7700 Old Georgetown Rd Ste 540 Bethesda MD 20814

DAMICO, PAUL ANTHONY, lawyer, educator; b. Rockville Centre, N.Y., July 3, 1960; s. Anthony and Connie Ida Damico; m. Jennifer Lynn Damico, Sept. 26, 1992; children: Alec Anthony, Kyle James. BS, Fla. State U., 1983, JD, 1986. Bar: Fla. 1983, U.S. Ct. Appeals (11th cir.), U.S. Ct. Appeals (D.C. cir.), U.S. Dist. Ct. (so., mid. and no. dists.) Fla., U.S. Supreme Ct.; bd. cert. in criminal trial. Atty. Palm Beach County State Atty.'s Office, West Palm Beach, Fla., 1986—2001; chief asst. Palm Beach County Pub. Defender's Office, 1996—2001; cty. criminal ct. judge, 2001—. Adj. prof. legal studies Barry U., 1991—; bd. dirs. Weed/Seed Orgn., West Palm Beach, Cmty. Ct. Task Force, West Palm Beach, Anti-Drug Grant Com. Mem. Lake Worth Criminal Justice Acad., 1998—. Mem. Kiwanis (pres.-elect Ctrl. Palm Beach County 1998, pres. 1999, Pres. award 1991), Masons. Christian. Avocations: scuba diving, golf. Office: WPB Courthouse 205 N Dixie Hwy West Palm Beach FL 33401

DAMJANOV, IVAN, pathologist, educator; b. Subotica, Yugoslavia, Mar. 31, 1941; came to U.S., 1967; s. Milenko and Ana (Pavkovic) D.; m. Andrea Zivanovic, Jan. 18, 1964; children: Nevena, Ivana, Milena. MD, U. Zagreb (Croatia), 1964, PhD, 1971. Lic. physician, Croatia; diplomate Am. Bd. Pathology. Intern Gen. Hosp., Zagreb, 1964-65; resident in pathology U. Zagreb, 1966-67; intern in pathology Cleve. Met. Gen. Hosp., 1967-68; resident in pathology Mt. Sinai Hosp., N.Y.C., 1968-69; asst. in pathology U. Zagreb, 1969-71; postdoctoral fellow Fels Rsch. Inst., Temple U., Phila., 1971-72; asst. prof. pathology U. Zagreb, 1972-73; from asst. prof. to assoc. prof. U. Conn., Farmington, 1973-77; from assoc. prof. to prof. Hahnemann Med. Coll. and Hosp., Phila., 1977-86; prof. pathology Jefferson Med. Coll. of Thomas Jefferson U., Phila., 1986-94; prof. pathology, chmn. U. Kans. Sch. Med., Kansas City, 1994-98, prof. pathology, 1998—. Cons. pathologist VA Hosp., Newington, Conn., 1975-77, Cancer Info. Dissemination and Analysis Ctr. for Virology, Immunology and Cancer-Related Biology, Franklin Inst., Phila., 1977-82, VAMC, Kansas City, Mo., 1995—, Pathology Stedman's Med. Dictionary, Phila., Pa., 2001—; mem. group for rsch. in pathology edn. U. Iowa, 1977-82; ad hoc reviewer, mem. site vis. teams and study sects. NIH, Bethesda, Md., 1978—; mem. basic sci. merit award bd. VA, 1989-92; mem. Croatian Acad. Arts and Scis., 1992; mem. coun. U.S.-Can. Acad. Pathology, 1996-99. Mem. editl. bd. Ultrastructural Pathology, 1985-96, Virchows Archiv, 1986—2003, In Vivo, 1988—, Modern Pathology, 1989—, Hosp. Physician, 1990-96, Human Pathology, 1991—, Lab. Investigation, 1994—, Jour. Urologic Pathology, 1991-2000, editor-in-chief, 2000-2002; mem. editl. adv. bd. Am. Registry of Pathology, Washington, D.C., 2000—; assoc. editor Lab. Investigation, 1982-94; regional editor N.Am. Differentiation, 1985-96, Pathology Rsch. Practice, 1998-2002; co-editor Anderson's Pathology, 10th edit., 1996; mem. editl. rev. group chairperson for pathology/surg. pathology Doody's Health Sciences Book Rev. Jour., 1998—. Recipient Christian R. and Mary F. Lindback award for disting. teaching Jefferson Med. Coll., Phila., 1988. Mem. Am. Soc. Investigative Pathology, Internat. Acad. Pathology, European Soc. Pathology, Am. Soc. Clin. Pathologists. Office: U Kansas Sch of Med Dept Pathol & Lab Med 3901 Rainbow Blvd Kansas City KS 66160-0001 E-mail: idamjano@kumc.edu., idamjanov@kc.rr.com.

DAMKEN, JOHN AUGUST, computer systems engineer; b. Hackensack, N.J., June 13, 1950; s. John August and Margaret Ann (Kearney) D.; m. Sheryl Elizabeth Lancaster, Sept. 8, 1979; children: Shanna Elizabeth, Stacey Michelle. BS in Elec. Engring., U. Mich., 1972, MS in Indsl. Engring., 1973; MBA in Fin., Ga. State U., 1983. Computer programmer E.I. duPont, Martinsville, Va., 1974-78; project mgr. Am. Express, Atlanta, 1978-90; dir. Glasrock Home Health Care, Atlanta, 1990-91; computer systems engr. EDS at Verizon Wireless Account, Roswell, Ga., 1992—2002, EDS at Bellsouth, Atlanta, 2002—. Capt. USAF, 1972-80. Mem. Digital Equipment Users Soc. Home: 235 Chiswick Close Alpharetta GA 30022-6675 Office: EDS/Bellsouth 675 W Peachtree Atlanta GA 30308

DAMMEL, RALPH RAINER, chemist, researcher; b. Mainz, Germany, Apr. 29, 1954; came to U.S., 1991; s. Kurt and Hildegard (Schreiber) D.; m. Barbara Krause, June 28, 1979; children: Anne-Kathrin, Christian. Grad., U. Sussex, Eng., 1976; Master, U. Mainz, Germany, 1981; PhD, J.W. Goethe U., Frankfurt, Germany, 1985. Rsch. chemist Hoechst AG, Frankfurt, 1986-89; project mgr. Hoechst Ag, Frankfurt, 1989-90, exec., 1990-91; staff chemist Hoechst Celanese Corp., Coventry, R.I., 1991-93, product devel. mgr. Somerville, N.J., 1993-97; with Clariant Corp., Somerville, N.J., 1997—, technology dir., 2000—. Cons. Industrieverband Pflanzenschutz, Frankfurt, 1982-83. Assoc. editor Jour. Microlithography, Microfabrication and Microsystems, 2000--; contbr. numerous articles to profl. jours.; patentee in field. Mem. Tonisstein Cir., Cologne, Germany, 1981—. Recipient scholarship German Scholarship Found., 1982, Hermann Schlosser Found., 1984, Silver Innovation Prize of German Industry, German Minister of Sci., 1987. Mem. AAAS, Gesellschaft Deutsch Chemiker, Am. Chem. Soc., Internat. Soc. Optical Engring., Verband Angestel Akademiker. Home: 8 Quimby Ln Flemington NJ 08822-7068 Office: Clariant Corp 70 Meister Ave Somerville NJ 08876-3440 E-mail: ralph.dammel@clariant.com.

DAMON, EDMUND HOLCOMBE, retired plastics company executive; b. St. Louis, Aug. 5, 1929; s. Ralph Shepard Damon and Harriet (Dudley) Holcombe; m. Florence Elizabeth Drake, Apr. 14, 1956; children: Elizabeth, Leslie. BA, Amherst Coll., 1951; MA, U. Bridgeport, 1991. Contr., treas. Strategic Materials Corp., N.Y.C., 1955-63; ops. analyst Norton Co., Troy, N.Y., 1964-65; v.p. corp. devel. Singer Co., Stamford, Conn., 1965-82; pres., chief exec. officer Pantasote Inc., Greenwich, Conn., 1983-89. Elder First Presbyn. Ch., Greenwich, 1970-88; bd. dirs. Child Guidance Ctr., Stamford, 1983-84, Fairfield County Cmty. Found., exec. com., 1991-97; pres. Greenwich United Way, 1986-92, Greenwich Cmty. Fund, 1992-97; bd. dirs., vice chmn. Greenwich chpt. ARC, 1989-92; mem. ARC N.E. regional commn., 1992-93; chmn. adminstrv. coun. First Ch. of Round Hill, Greenwich, 1989-97; bd. dirs. United Way, York County, Maine, 1998—, Brick Store Mus., Kennebunk, Maine, 1998-2000; adminstrv. coun. Ch. on Cape, Cape Porpoise, Maine, 1997-98. Mem. Webhannet Golf Club (Kennebunk, Maine). Home: 5 Annies Way Kennebunk ME 04043-7533

DAMON, EDWARD GEORGE, retired biologist; b. Richland, N.Mex., Feb. 21, 1927; s. Frank Damon; m. Bettye Jean Wood; children: Georgia Jean Carrion, Ernest Edward, Alan Benge. BS, Ea. N.mex U., 1950; MS, Okla. Agrl. & Mech. Coll., 1957; PhD, U. N.Mex., 1965. Coord. Lovelace Inhalation Toxicology Rsch. Inst., Albuquerque, 1984—89; physiologist Radiobiology Group, Lovelace Inhalation Toxicology Rsch. Inst., Albuquerque, 1974—89; assoc. scientist Dept. Of Comparative Environ. Biology, Lovelace Found. For Med. Edn. And Rsch., Albuquerque, 1962—65; head of sci. dept. & biology tchr. Manzano H.s., Albuquerque, 1961—62; instr. of sci. Jimma Agrl. Tech. Sch., Jimma, Ethiopia, 1958—60; instr. (full-time rsch., cytomorphogenetic studies in sorghum) Dept. Of Botany & Plant Pathology, Okla. State U., Stillwater, Okla., 1957—58; rsch. biologist & author Imperial Ethiopian Coll. Of Agr. & Mech. Arts, Jimma, Ethiopia, 1958—62. Pvt AUS, 1946.

DAMON, MATTHEW PAIGE, actor; b. Cambridge, Mass., Oct. 8, 1970; Actor: (films) Mystic Pizza, 1988, School Ties, 1992, Geronimo: An American Legend, 1993, Courage Under Fire, 1996, Glory Daze, 1996, Chasing Amy, 1997, The Rainmaker, 1997 (nominee Blockbuster Entertainment award Favorite Actor-Drama), Rounders, 1998, Saving Private Ryan, 1998 (nominee SAG award Outstanding Performance by a Cast), The Talented Mr. Ripley, 1999 (nominee Best Performance by Actor in Motion Picture Drama Golden Globe award, 2000), Dogma, 1999, All the Pretty Horses, 1999, Titan A.E. (voice), 2000, The Legend of Bagger Vance, 2000, Jay and Silent Bob Strike Back, 2001, The Majestic (voice), 2001, Oceans Eleven, 2001, Gerry, 2002, The Bourne Identity, 2002, Spirit: Stallion of the Cimarron (voice), 2002; actor, writer (film) Good Will Hunting, 1997 (nominee SAG award Outstanding Performance by a Male Actor in a Leading Role, MTV Movie awards Best Kiss, Best Male Performance, Best On-Screen Duo, ALFS award London Critics Cir. Actor of Yr., Screenwriter of Yr., Writers Guild Am. Screen award Best Screenplay written directly for screen, Golden Satellite award Best Action in Motion Picture, Golden Globe award Best Performance by an Actor in a Motion Picture-Drama, 3d pl. Boston Soc. Film Critics award Best Screenplay, Blockbuster Entertainment award Favorite Actor-Video, Oscar award Best Actor, Golden Satellite award Best Motion Picture Screenplay, Golden Globe award Best Screenplay-Motion Picture, Fla. Film Critics Cir. award Newcomer of Yr., Chgo. Film Critics Assn. award Most Promising Actor, BFCA award Breakthrough Artist, Berlin Internat. Film Festival Silver Berlin Bear award Outstanding Single Achievement, Oscar award Best Writing, Screenplay Written Directly for Screen), actor, exec. prodr. The Third Wheel, 2002; prodr.: Stolen Summer, 2002. Office: Creative Artists Agy 9830 Wilshire Blvd Beverly Hills CA 90212-1825

DAMON, SHIRLEY STOCKTON, art gallery owner; b. San Francisco, Apr. 29, 1931; d. Andrew Benton and Melva Laverta (Harbin) Stockton; m. Terry Allen Damon, Oct. 20, 1956 (div. 1980); children: Benton Allen (dec.), Diana Clare, Denise Yvonne, Andrew Allen. BA, U. Calif., Santa Barbara, 1953; MA, Stanford U., 1956, postgrad., 1958. Tchr. Santa Barbara City Sch., 1953-54; demonstration tchr. U. Calif., Santa Barbara, 1954; dir. CIT program, asst. camp dir. Montecito Camp for Girls, Calif., 1955-57; tchr. Santa Clara County Sch., 1957; instr. Stanford U., 1958; tchr. Escambia County Sch., Pensacola, Fla., 1959; pres. Damon Galleries, Ltd., Vienna, Va., 1973—. Chair archtl. rev. bd. Town of Vienna, 1994—, mem., 1991—; mem. Police Chiefs Adv. Bd., Vienna, 1993-96; pres. Vienna Commons Assn., 1990-96; adult leader Girl Scouts USA Mem.: Am. Soc. Philat. Exhibitors, Internat. Soc. Japanest Philately, Ryukyu Philat. Soc. (charter), Profl. Picture Framers Assn. (chmn. cert. com. 1993—98, pres. 1990—93, assoc. regional dir. 1984—90, judge framing competitions 1990—, nat. instr. in tng. courses, award for svc. 1994), Am. Philat. Soc. (life). Republican. Episcopalian. Office: Damon Galleries Ltd 220 Maple Ave W Vienna VA 22180-5605

DAMON, STEVEN WILLIAM, music educator; b. Greenfield, Mass., Nov. 12, 1969; s. William Herbert and Martha Janice Damon; m. Joyana Jill Dean, July 14, 2002. MusM, U. Conn., 1997; MusB, U. Mass. Lowell, 1992; Fine Arts Dir. Cert., Fitchburg State Coll., 1999. Tchr. music Greenfield Pub. Schs., 1997—, Athol (Mass.)/Royalston Regional Sch. Dist., 1994—97, Belchertown (Mass.) Pub. Schs., 1993—94; oboe studio dir. Northfield Mt. Herman Sch., 2002—. Fine arts organizer Learning Ctr. at Oak Courts, Greenfield, 1999—; editl. bd. mem. Mass. Music News, West Springfield, Mass., 2001—. Composer: Jupiter's Joy -a wedding march, 2002. Condr. Shelburne Falls (Mass.) Mil. Band, 2000; big brother Big Bros./Big Sisters of Franklin County, Greenfield, 2002; founder, coord. TubaChristmas, Shelburne Falls, 1996; guest condr. Brattleboro Summer Pk. Band, Brattleboro, Vt., 2001; bd. dirs. Shelburne Falls Art Bank. Grantee Grants, various Mass. Arts Couns., 1998 - 2002. Mem.: Music Educators Nat. Conf., Nat. Assn. Music Edn., Mass. Music Educators Assn. (mgr. All-State Jazz Ensemble 2001—02, K-9 rep. 2001—, instrumental coord. western dist. 2001—, chair western dist. 2003—), Internat. Assn. for Jazz Edn. Baptist. Avocation: maple sugaring, dairy farming, red sox fan. Home: 475 Main Rd Gill MA 01376 Office: Greenfield Public Schools 141 Davis St Greenfield MA 01301 Office Fax: 413-774-7940. Personal E-mail: steve_damon@nmhschool.org.

DAMON, WILLIAM VAN BUREN, developmental psychologist, educator, writer; b. Brockton, Mass., Nov. 10, 1944; s. Philip Arthur and Helen (Meyers) D.; m. Wendy Obernauer (div. 1982); children: Jesse Louis, Maria; m. Anne Colby, Sept. 24, 1983, 1 child, Caroline. BA, Harvard U., 1967; PhD, U. Calif., Berkeley, 1973. Social worker N.Y.C. Dept. Social Svcs., 1968-70; prof. psychology Clark U., Worcester, Mass., 1973-89, dean Grad Sch., 1983-87, chmn. dept. edn., 1988-89; Disting. vis. prof. U. P.R., 1988; prof., chair edn. dept. Brown U., Providence, 1989-92, prof., Mittlemann Family dir. Ctr. for Study of Human Devel., 1993-98; univ. prof., 1997-98; fellow Ctr. for Advanced Study in the Behavioral Scis., 1994-95; prof., dir. Ctr. on Adolescence Stanford (Calif.) U., 1997—. Sr. fellow Hoover Instn., 1999—; mem. study sect. NIMH, Bethesda, Md., 1981-84; cons. State of Mass., 1976, State of Calif., 1978, Allegheny County, Pa., 1979, Pinellas County, Fla., 1990, Com. of Va., 1993, Hawaii, 1995, Children's TV Workshop, 1991-09, Annenberg Adv. Coun. on Excellence in Children's TV, 1996-99, Project for Excellence in Journalism, 2000—; mem. nat. adv. bd. Fox Family TV Network, 1998-2001. Author: Social World of the Child, 1977, Social and Personality Development, 1983, Self-Understanding in Childhood and Adolescence, 1988, The Moral Child, 1988, Child Development Today and Tomorrow, 1989, Some Do Care, 1992, Greater Expectations, 1995 (Parent's Choice Book award, 1995), The Youth Charter, 1997, Handbook of Child Psychology, 1998; : Good Work, 2001, Bringing in a New Era in Character Education, 2002, Noble Purpose, 2003; editor: New Directions for Child Devel., 1978—. Trustee Bancroft Sch., Worcester, Mass., 1982-84; mem. adv. bd. Ednl. Alliance, 1991—. Grantee Carnegie Corp., N.Y.C., 1975-79, 97—, Spencer Found., 1980, 92-96, 98-2001, N.Y. comty. Trust, 1984-88, Inst. Noetic Scis., 1988-90, MacArthur Found., 1990-95, Pew Charitable Trusts, 1990-95, 98-2000, Ross Inst., 1996—, Hewlett Found., 1997—, The Templeton Found., 1998—, Atlantic Philanthropies, 2003—. Mem. APA, Jean Piaget Soc. (bd. dirs. 1983-87), Am. Ednl. Rsch. Assn., Soc. for Rsch. in Child Devel., Nat. Acad. Edn. Republican. Episcopalian. Office: Stanford U Ctr on Adolescence Cypress Bldg C Stanford CA 94305-4145 E-mail: wdamon@stanford.edu. *Learn to thrive on the risks and challenges themselves rather than merely on the prospects of winning; expect that every right and privilege must be vigorously defended; and through it all never give up the principle of common decency.*

DAMOOSE, GEORGE LYNN, lawyer; b. Grand Rapids, Mich., Feb. 2, 1938; s. George G. and Geneva J. (Joseph) D.; m. Carol Sweeney, Dec. 7, 1968, children: Alison Dana, George Christopher. AB cum laude, Harvard U., 1959, JD cum laude, 1965. Bar: Calif. 1966, U.S. Tax Ct., 1973. Assoc. O'Melveny and Myers, L.A., 1965-72; ptnr. Jennings, Engstrand, Henrikson, P.C., San Diego, 1972-76, Procopio, Cory, Hargreaves, and Savitch, San Diego, 1976—. Bd. dirs. San Diego Civic Light Opera Assn., 1984-90, 92; trustee The Bishops Sch., LaJolla, 1987-90, La Jolla Chamber Music Soc., 1988-89; commr. San Diego Crime Commn., 1987-90. Served to lt. (j.g.) USN, 1959-62. Mem. Am. Bar Found., San Diego County Bar Assn. (chmn. tax sect. 1974-75, 86-87), Calif. Bar Assn. (ind. inquiry and rev. panel, program for certifying legal specialists 1986-87), State Bar Calif. (exec. com., taxation sect. 1990-95, chair 1994-95, chair CEB joint adv. com. taxation 1996-98), San Diego C. of C. (bd. dirs. 1994-96), La Jolla Country Club, La Jolla Beach and Tennis Club. Republican. Episcopalian. Avocations: tennis, music, reading, golf. Home: 208 Avenida Cortez La Jolla CA 92037-6502 Office: Procopio Cory et al 530 B St Ste 2100 San Diego CA 92101-4496

D'AMORE, VICTOR, director, choreographer, dance educator; b. Bronx, N.Y., May 31, 1943; s. Victor and Angela (Cavolina) D'Amore; m. Donna Marie Apple, Oct. 12, 1968 (div. Oct. 2001). BA, Adelphi U., 1976. Pres. and artistic dir. Vic D'Amore Studio Dance, Deer Park, NY, 1976—, pres. Coram, N.Y., 1976-89, Patchogue, N.Y., 1990-2000, Am. Studio of Performing Arts, Deer Park, 1976—. Pres. Am. Studio of Performing Arts, Deer Park, N.Y., 19782; ind. cons. Nikken Wellness. Dir./choreographer 5 ballets, 300 short works, CLUBJAM, (TV show) Zebby's Zoo TV and Stage Show, 60 com./mus. prodns. Served to sgt. U.S. Army, 1964-68. Mem. Soc. Stage Dirs. and Choreographers, Dance Masters Am. (bd. dirs.), Dance Educators Am. (bd. dirs., treas.), Brookhaven Theatre Dance Guild (v.p.). Roman Catholic. Home: 122 Woodbury Rd Hauppauge NY 11788-4728 Office: Vic D'Amore Studio of Dance 721 Acorn St Deer Park NY 11729-3202 E-mail: vicdamor@optonline.net.

D'AMOUR, DONALD H. supermarket chain executive; b. Holyoke, Mass., Feb. 15, 1943; Diploma, Assumption Coll., 1964, Univ. Notre Dame, 1971. Sr. v.p., CEO Big Y Foods, Springfield, Mass., chmn., CEO, 1998—. Office: Big Y Foods 2145 Roosevelt Ave Springfield MA 01104-1650

DAMPEER, JOHN LYELL, retired lawyer; b. Cleve., June 3, 1916; s. James W. and Felicia (Gressitt) D.; m. Lucie Augustin Kennerdell, June 30, 1950 (dec. July 1990); children: Lyell B., David K., G. Geoffrey. S.B., Harvard U., 1938, LL.B., 1942; student, New Coll., Oxford (Eng.) U., 1938-39. Bar: Ohio 1946. Practiced in, Cleve.; ptnr. Thompson Hine LLP, Cleve., 1955—97; ret., 1997. Trustee Family Svc. Assn. Cleve., 1951-70; trustee, chmn. bd. trustees Kelvin and Eleanor Smith Found., 1984-96; trustee, treas. Sea Rsch. Found., 1984-96. Henry fellow, 1938-39 Mem. ABA, Ohio Bar Assn. (chmn. corp. law com. 1960-62), Greater Cleve. Bar Assn. (exec. com. 1958-61), Phi Beta Kappa. Clubs: Union (Cleve.), Kirtland Country (Cleve.). Home: 44 Laurel Lake Dr Hudson OH 44236-2159 Office: Thompson Hine LLP 3900 Key Ctr 127 Public Sq Cleveland OH 44114-1216

DAMPIER, CARYN, self-defense instructor; b. San Angelo, Tex., June 9, 1956; d. Clyde Hampton and Betty Jean Harville; m. David Anthony Dampier, Feb. 4, 1983; children: David, Michael, Nicholas. BA, U. Tex., El Paso, 1978. Teen psychiat. counselor St. Joseph Hosp., El Paso, 1978-82; vol., counselor Ft. Stewart (Ga.) Drug Abuse Program, 1984-87; vol. Ft. Stewart Children's Camp, 1984-87; adminstrv. asst. Naval Rsch. Lab., Monterey, Calif., 1988-2000; claims asst. William Beaumont Army Med. Ctr., El Paso, Tex., 1988-2000; transp. specialist The Mil. Traffic Command, Washington, 1988-2000; rape/aggression/def. instr. Fairfax (Va.) County Police, 1999-2000, Miss. State U., 2000—, com. specialist Social Sci. Rsch. Ctr., 2000—02; program dir. First United Meth. Ch., 2002—. Chief instr., regional dir. Naval Postgrad. Sch. Tae Kwondo Assn., 1997—, master instr., 1999—. Vol. First United Meth. Ch. TV Ministry Missions Team. Recipient Presdl. Sports award Pres. Coun. on Phys. Fitness, 1998, 2000, 01, 02. Mem. Am. Legion Aux. Republican. Methodist. Home: 801 Cathys Pond Starkville MS 39759-7008 E-mail: caryn@fumc.org.

DAMRON, ROBERT R. state representative; b. Danville, Ky, June 20, 1954; m. Paula Damron; 1 child, Robert. MBA, Univ. of Ky, 1984, BS, 1976. State Rep. House of Rep., Dist. 39, Ky., 1992—; fin. adv., 1997—; regis. securities agt., 1997—; invest. banker Ross, Sinclaire & Assoc., 1997—; Independent Ins. agt. self-employed, 1992—; loan officer/credit mgr. Ctrl. Ky. Ag Credit, 1976—92. Vice chair Appropriations and Rev.; mem. Banking and Ins., Capital Projects & Bond Oversight, Health & Welfare. Caucuses: Tobacco Task Force, 1994-2000; Veterans Affairs Subcommittee, 1994-2000. Democrat. Disciple Of Christ. Office: Capitol State Capitol Annex, Rm 351A Frankfort KY 40601 also: Dist 231 Fairway West Nicholasville KY 40356*

DAMRON, TIMOTHY ARTHUR, orthopedic surgeon, researcher; s. Marvin Arthur and Patricia Ann Damron; m. Leatha Ann Roesner, July 16, 1963; 1 child, Neil Kurt. BS, U. of Ill., 1983; MD, U. of Ill., Chgo., 1988. Lic. orthopedic oncology Mayo Clinic Sch. of Medicine. Orthop. resident U. of Wis. Orthopedics, Madison, Wis., 1988—93; orthop. oncology fellow Mayo Clinic Sch. of Medicine, Rochester, Minn., 1993—94; asst. prof. SUNY Upstate Med. U., Syracuse, NY, 1994—97, assoc. prof., 1997—2002, prof., 2002—, David G. Murry Endowed prof., 2003—. Adj. assoc. prof. Syracuse U., Syracuse, NY, 2000—; reviewer Jour. of Bone and Mineral Rsch., 2000—, Cancer: Interdisciplinary Internat. Jour. of the Am. Cancer Soc., 2000—, Melanoma Rsch., 2000—, Jour. of Surg. Oncology, 1996—, Mayo Clinic Procs., 1997—; adj. assoc. prof. SUNY Neurosci. and Physiology, Syracuse, 2000—; editl. bd. Jour. of Surg. Oncology, 2000—, eMedicine Orthop. Surgery Text, 2000—; cons. reviewer Orthopaedic Care.net Online Text, 2001—; reviewer Jour. of Bone and Joint Surgery-Am., 2002—03, Jour. of Orthopaedic Rsch., 2002—, Jour. of Musculoskeletal Medicine, 2002—, Jour. of Kidney Diseases, 2002—. Recipient SUNY Pres.'s award for clin. rsch. by young investigator, 2003; grantee, Nat. Cancer Inst. Fellow: Am. Acad. of Orthop. Surgeons; mem.: Internat. Soc. for Limb Salvage, Musculoskeletal Tumor Soc., Orthopaedic Rsch. Soc. Office: SUNY Upstate Dept of Orthopedics Ste 130 550 Harrison Center Syracuse NY 13224 E-mail: damront@upstate.edu.

DAMSBO, ANN MARIE, psychologist; b. Cortland, N.Y., July 7, 1931; d. Jorgen Einer and Agatha Irene (Schenck) D. BS, San Diego State Coll., 1952; MA, U.S. Internat. U., 1974, PhD, 1975. Diplomate Am. Acad. Pain Mgmt., Am. Coll. Forensic Examiners, Am. Bd. Psychol. Spltys. Commd. 2d lt. U.S. Army, 1952, advanced through grades to capt., 1957; staff therapist Letterman Army Hosp., San Francisco, 1953-54, 56-58, 61-62, Ft. Devens, Mass., 1955-56, Walter Reed Army Hosp., Washington, 1958-59, Tripler Army Hosp., Hawaii, 1959-61, Ft. Benning, Ga., 1962-64; chief therapist U.S. Army Hosp., Ft. McPherson, Ga., 1964-67; ret. U.S. Army, 1967; med. missionary So. Presbyterian Ch., Taiwan, 1968-70; psychology intern So. Naval Hosp., San Diego, 1975; pre-doctoral intern Naval Regional Med. Ctr., San Diego, 1975-76, postdoctoral intern, 1975-76, chief, founder pain clinic, 1977-86. Chief pain clinic, 1977-86; adj. tchr. U. Calif. Med. Sch., San Diego; lectr., U.S., Can., Eng., France, Australia; cons. forensic hypnosis to law enforcement agys.; approved cons. in hypnosis. Contbr. articles to profl. publs., chpt. to books. Tchr. Sunday sch. United Meth. Ch., 1945—; Rep. Nat. Candidate Trust Presdl. adv. com., platform planning commn. at-large-del.; ARC psychology vol. Naval Hosp., San Diego. Fellow Am. Soc. Clin. Hypnosis (psychology mem.-at-large, exec. bd. 1989-90), San Diego Soc. Clin. Hypnosis (pres. 1980); mem. AAUW, Am. Phys. Therapy Assn., Calif. Soc. Clin. and Hypnosis (bd. govs.), Am. Soc. Clin. Hypnosis Edn. Rsch. Found. (trustee 1992-94), Internat. Platform Assn., Am. Soc. Clin. Hypnosis (exec. bd.), Ret. Officers Am., Ret. Officers Assn. (bd. dirs. Hidden Valley chpt., rep. presdl. task force, pres. adv. com.), Toastmasters (local pres.), Job's Daus. Republican. Home and Office: 1062 W Fifth Ave Escondido CA 92025-3802 *A purpose in life is essential to happiness. Success is a matter of making the most of the talents we are given, not receiving greater talents. Time is the most important gift. We can ill afford to waste it or wish it away. All accomplishment is meaningless unless one walks in harmony and fellowship with her maker and her fellow human beings. I am grateful to my parents and teachers for their examples and for providing me the opportunity for self-actualization.*

DAMSGAARD, KELL MARSH, lawyer; b. Darby, Pa., May 16, 1949; s. Kjeld and Dorothy (Fanck) D.; m. Katherine Elizabeth Stark, June 17, 1972; children: Peter Kjeld, Christopher William, David Zentner. BA cum laude, Yale U., 1971; JD, U. Pa., 1974. Bar: Pa. 1974, U.S. Dist. Ct. (ea. dist.) Pa. 1975, U.S. Ct. Appeals (3d cir.) 1984, U.S. Ct. Appeals (D.C. cir.) 1989, U.S. Ct. Appeals (8th cir.) 1990, U.S. Ct. Appeals (10th cir.), 1991, U.S. Ct. Appeals (9th cir.), 2003, U.S. Supreme Ct. 1991. Law clk. to judge Superior Ct. of Pa., Phila., 1974-75; assoc. Morgan, Lewis & Bockius LLP, Phila., 1975-81; ptnr. Morgan, Lewis & Bockius, Phila., 1981—, firm adminstrv. ptnr., 1996—. Fellow Am. Coll. Trial Lawyers; mem. ABA, Phila. Bar Assn. Avocations: skiing, jogging, tennis, antiques. Home: PO Box 141 Birchrunville PA 19421-0141 Office: Morgan Lewis & Bockius LLP 1701 Market St Philadelphia PA 19103-2903 E-mail: kdamsgaard@morganlewis.com.

DAMSON, BARRIE MORTON, oil and gas exploration company executive; b. N.Y.C., Jan. 29, 1936; s. Harry and Ethel (Brody) Damson; m. Joan Selig, Feb. 29, 1972; children: Blair, Laura, Bethany. AB, Harvard U., 1956; LLB, NYU, 1959. Bar: N.Y. 1959. Pres. Damson Petroleum Corp., N.Y.C., 1963-69, Bronco Oil Corp., Midland, Tex., 1965-69, Delta Minerals Inc., Lake Charles, La., 1967-69; pres., chmn. bd. Damson Oil Corp., N.Y.C., 1969-91. Pres., chmn. bd. First Crescent Corp.; chmn. Crescent Natural Resources, Inc.; bd. dirs., chmn., nominating com. Am. Stock Exch., 1981—91, bd. govs., chmn. audit com.; chmn. Damson Natural Resources, Inc., 1991, Damson Investment

Group, Inc., European Am. Oil Co., Inc., 1991—94, Stagebill, 1993; bd. dirs. United Gas Holding Corp., 1993—97. Chmn. bd. mem. N.Y.C. Econ. Devel. Corp., 1992—96; dir. Robert Steel Found. for Pediat. Cancer Rsch., 1995; bd. trustees Hosp. Spl. Surgery, 2002; mem. am. Am. Bus. Conf., 1980—94; mem. Dean's Coun. Harvard Sch. Pub. Health. Mem.: Bar. Assn. N.Y., Harvard Club. Address: 1095 Pequot Ave Southport CT 06490-1421

DAMTOFT, WALTER ATKINSON, editor, publishing executive, consultant; b. Asheville, N.C., June 1, 1922; s. Walter Julius and Dorothy (Atkinson) Damtoft; m. Janet Russell, Mar. 31, 1951; children: Russell Walter, Lisa. Student, Yale U., 1940-41; BS in Commerce, U. N.C., Chapel Hill, 1947. Salesman Sta. WKIX, Columbia, SC, 1947; reporter Ark. Gazette, Little Rock, 1947-50; reporter, city editor Asheville Citizen, 1950-55; city editor Charlotte (N.C.) Observer, 1956-58, N.C. editor, 1958-60, Carolinas editor, 1960-62; writer Nat. Observer, Silver Spring, Md., 1962-69, news editor, 1969-72, sr. editor, 1972-77; editor, pub. Am. Way mag., Ft. Worth, 1977-85, AA Mag. Publs., 1985-86, editor-in-chief, 1986-87; mag. cons., 1987—. Seminar leader Am. Press Inst., 1957. Editor: (book) The Consumer's Handbook II, 1971, Here's Help, 1974. Pres. Garrett Park (Md.) Citizen's Assn., 1969—70; mem. Garrett Park Town Coun., 1972—76. With USNR, 1943—46. Mem.: Soc. Profl. Journalists, Country Club Asheville, Men's Garden Club Asheville, Phi Delta Theta. Democrat. Home and Office: 65 Edgemont Rd Asheville NC 28801-1543

DAMUSH, TERESA MARIE, research scientist; b. Fort Dix, N.J. PhD, U. Calif., Riverside, 1996. Rschr. Ind. U. Sch. of Medicine, Indpls., 1997—; rsch. scientist Regenstrief Inst., Indpls., 1998—; ctr. scientist Ind. U. Ctr. on Aging Rsch., Indpls., 1998—. Cons. RAND Corp., Santa Monica, Calif., 1991—94; postdoctoral fellowship U. Calif, Inst. for Health Policy, San Francisco, 1996—97. Author: (article) The Gerontologist, Preventive Medicine, Arthritis Care and Research. Grantee New Investigator Behavioral Rschr., Arthritis Found., 2000-2002; Pilot Study Scholar award, Mary Margaret Walther Cancer Found., 2001. Mem.: APHA, Am. Coll. Sports Medicine, Assn. for Health Svcs. Rsch., Gerontol. Soc. Am., Soc. of Behavioral Medicine. Office: Regenstrief Inst RG6 1050 Wishard Blvd Indianapolis IN 46202-2872 E-mail: tdamush@regenstrief.org.

DAMUTH, JOHN ERWIN, marine geologist; b. Dayton, Ohio, Nov. 22, 1942; s. Jason Donald and Sarah Maxine (Simpson) D.; m. Patricia Jane Keenan, Oct. 8, 1971 (div. July 1990). BS in Geology, Ohio State U., 1965; MA in Geology, Columbia U., 1968, PhD in Geology, 1973. Grad. rsch. asst. Lamont-Doherty Geol. Obs., Columbia U., 1965-73, rsch. scientist, 1973-74, rsch. assoc., 1974-82, sr. rsch. assoc., 1982-83; rsch. geologist Dallas Rsch. Lab. Mobil R & D Corp., 1983-84, sr. rsch. geologist, 1984-92; sr. rsch. scientist Earth Rsch. and Environ. Ctr., U. Tex., Arlington, 1992—. Adj. sr. rsch. scientist Lamont-Doherty Earth Obs., Columbia U., 1996-2000; adj. prof. dept. geology U. Tex., Arlington, 1996—; adj. rsch. scientist Lamont-Doherty Geol. Obs., Columbia U., 1983-91; instr. ecology adult edn. N.J. H.S., 1977-83; mem. Nat. Site Assessment Com. Subseabed Disposal High-Level Nuc. Waste, 1978-83; lectr. in field. Assoc. editor Jour. Sedimentary Rsch., 1996-99; contbr. articles to profl. jours. Texaco scholar, 1964-65; Eugene Higgins fellow, 1965-66, Pan Am. Oil Co. fellow, 1967, Pres.'s fellow, 1968-69, Nat. Lord Britton fellow, 1967-68. Fellow Geol. Soc. Am.; mem. Am. Assn. Petroleum Geologists, Soc. Econ. Paleontologists and Mineralogists, Am. Geohphys. Union, Sigma Xi. Avocations: fishing, skiing, travel, exercise. Office: Univ Tex Dept Geology PO Box 19049 Arlington TX 76019-0001 E-mail: damuth@uta.edu.

DAN, ASIT, computer scientist, research scientist; arrived in US, 1982; s. Joy Krishna and A. L. Dan; m. Karen Frazier, Aug. 31, 1996; children: Indra Neil, Ariana Kajolee. BTech, Indian Inst. Tech., Kharagpur, India, 1982; MS, U. Mass., 1985, PhD, 1990. Rsch. staff mem. IBM Rsch., Hawthorne, NY, 1990—. Author: (book) Multimedia Servers Applications, Environments and Design, 2000, Performance Analysis of Data Sharing Environments (ACM Disting. Dissertation Hon. Mention, 1992); contbr. book chpt., articles to profl. jours. Mem.: IEEE, ACM. Achievements include patents for in the areas of multimedia servers, transaction processing architectures and B2B integrations. Home: 6 Heritage Dr Pleasantville NY 10570 Office: IBM T J Watson Rsch Ctr 19 Skyline Dr Hawthorne NY 10532

DAN, BERNARD W. trade association administrator; b. Chgo. BS in Acctg., St. John's U., Collegeville, Minn. With Nat. Futures Assn., 1983—85; adminstrv. mgr. oper. activities Cargill Investor Svcs., Ltd., London, 1986—89, adminstrv. mgr. N.Y.C., 1989—91, asst. v.p., 1991—93, v.p., 1993—94; dir. Cargill Investors Svcs. (Singapore) Pty. Ltd., 1994—97; v.p., Global Head of Execution Cargill Investors Svcs., Chgo., 1997—98; pres., CEO Cargill Investor Svcs., Chgo., 1998—2001; exec. v.p. Chgo. Bd. of Trade, 2001—02, pres., CEO, 2002—. Gov. Bd. of Trade Clearing Corp.; mem. bd. govs., 1st vice chmn. Office: Chicago Bd of Trade 141 W Jackson Blvd Chicago IL 60604-2994*

DAN, JOHNSON, state representative; b. Hays, Kans., Aug. 18, 1936; m. Gwen Dan; 2 children. BS, MS in Indsl. Arts, Ft. Hays State U. Tchr. Ft. Hays State U., 1961—69; mem. Kans. Ho. of Reps., 1997—. Mem. Econ. Devel. Corp., Ellis County. Lt. col. USAR, 1954—77, ret., 1977. Mem.: Kans. Livestock Assn., Ellis County Farm Bur., Ellis County Hist. Soc., Rotary, Epsilon Pi Tau, Phi Kappa Phi. Republican. Episcopalian. Office: 426-S State Capitol 300 SW 10th Ave Topeka KS 66612 Address: PO Box 247 Hays KS 67601*

DANA, F(RANK) MITCHELL, theatrical lighting designer; b. Washington, Nov. 14, 1942; s. John Daskum Mitchell and Elizabeth Francis (Woods) D.; m. Wendy Karen Bensinger, Dec. 31, 1967; children: Scott Cameron, Ian Michael. BFA, Utah State U., 1964; MFA, Yale Drama Sch., 1967. Asst. to Jo Mielziner, N.Y.C., 1968-69; tech. dir. Yale Drama Sch., New Haven, Conn., 1970-71; assoc. lighting dir. Ferd Manning, N.Y.C., 1978-88. Guest lectr. U. Wash., So. Meth. U., San Francisco State U.; lectr. Rutgers U., 1982-97, asst. prof., 1997-99, assoc. prof., 2000—. Prodn. mgr.: Stratford Festival, Pitts. Civic Light Opera; prodn. supr. Yale Repertory Theatre; lighting designer: Broadway Plays include The Freedom of the City, 1974, Once in a Lifetime, 1978, Inspector General, 1978, Man and Superman, 1978, The Suicide, 1980 (Drama Logue award), Mass Appeal, 1981, Monday After the Miracle, 1982, The Babe, 1984, Oh Coward, 1986; off-Broadway Plays include Three Acts of Recognition, 1982, A Coupla White Chicks, 1980, Mass Appeal, 1980, Oh Coward, 1981, Calling in Crazy, 1969, Songs My Mother Never Sang Me, 1982, Husbandry, 1984, A Hell of a Town, 1984, The Ninth Step, 1984, Daughters, 1986, Cold Sweat, 1988, Other People's Money, 1989, King Fish, 1991, Lust 1995, PaPa 1996, Pete 'n' Keely, 2000; operas World Premier of Harriet: The Woman Called Moses, Orphee, Patricia II, Tempest 94, Turandot, Royal Opera, Covent Garden, 1984, Olympic Arts Festival, 1984, L.A. Rondine, N.Y.C. Opera, 1984, Magic Flute, 1985, Merry Widow, 1986, Cleve. Symphony, Un Ballo in Maschera Va. Opera, 1985, Opera Festival of N.J., 1989-2001 Turandot, Royal Opera/Covent Garden at Wembly Arena, 1991, Carmen for L.A. Opera and Seville Expo92, La Traviata for Barcelona's Gran Licieu, 1992; Makropolous Case, Traviata, Midsummer Night's Dream, 1992, Elgato Montez, Madama Butterfly, Faust, Electra, Don Giovanni, L.A. Opera, 1994, other opera cos.; also Pitts. Civic Light Opera, 1973-74, 79, 84-87; tours Hello Dolly, 1981, Mass Appeal, 1982, Guys and Dolls, 1984, George M., Jesus Christ Superstar, 1985, Stop the World, 1986, Other People's Money, Okla., 1990; regional theaters Am. Conservatory Theatre, 1972-80, BAM Theatre Co., 1977, 78, 80, 81, Goodman Theatre, 1973-82, McCarter Theatre, 1969-71, 82, 86-90, Nat. Arts Ctr., Ottawa, 1982-84, others including Mark Taper Forum, Paper Mill Playhouse, Phila. Drama Guild, Va. Mus. Theatre, Crossroads Theatre Co., Geva Theater, Folger Theater, Hartford Stage Co., Interact Theatre, Ala. Shakespeare Co., Cin. Playhouse, St. Louis MUNY, Syracuse Stage, 1984, 87, 96, Seattle Repertory, Stratford Shakespeare Festival, Studio Arena Theatre, Stratford Festival Theatre, Roundabout Theatre, 1987, 88, George Street Playhouse, Interact Theatre Co., Derby Playhouse (U.K.). Mem. Internat. Alliance Theatrical Stage Employees, United Scenic Artists USA 829 (lighting trustee 1970-72, 96–, nat. v.p. 2002--). Republican. Office: 221 W 82d St New York NY 10024-5406 E-mail: fmdld@earthlink.net.

DANA, HOWARD H., JR., state supreme court justice; Grad., Bowdoin Coll., 1962; J.D., M.A., Cornell, 1966. Assoc. justice Supreme Jud. Ct. of Maine, Portland, 1993—. Office: Maine Judicial Center 65 Stone St Augusta ME 04330*

DANA, LAUREN ELIZABETH, lawyer; b. Hollywood, Calif., Sept. 30, 1950; d. Franklin Eugene and Margaret Elizabeth (Nixon) D.; m. Andrew Russell Willing, May 25, 1986; 1 child, Matthew Barkan Willing. BA cum laude, Calif. State U., Northridge, 1973; JD cum laude, Southwestern U., 1982. Bar: Calif. 1982, U.S. Dist. Ct. (cen. dist.) Calif. 1983, U.S. Ct. Appeals (9th cir.) 1983, U.S. Supreme Ct. 1987. Assoc. Law Office Andrew R. Willing, L.A., 1982-84; dep. atty. gen. Calif. Dept. Justice-Atty. Gen., L.A., 1984—. Temporary judge L.A. Mcpl. Ct. Assoc. editor legal update Police Officer Law Report, 1986-87. Recipient Am. Jurisprudence Book award Lawyers Coop. Pub. Co., 1980, Am. Jurisprudence Book award in Evidence, 1980. Mem.: ABA, Los Angeles County Bar Assn. (conf. of dels. 1998—), L.A. World Affairs Coun., Women Lawyers Assn. L.A., U.S. Supreme Ct. Hist. Soc., Selden Soc., Constnl. Rights Found., Am. Judicature Soc., Alliance for Children's Rights, Women of Pasadena, The Da Camera Soc., Town Hall, Phi Alpha Delta. Avocations: reading, music, collecting books on english history, travel, french. Office: Calif Dept Justice 300 S Spring St Los Angeles CA 90013-1230

DANAHAR, DAVID C. academic administrator, historian, educator; b. Dobbs Ferry, N.Y., Sept. 29, 1941; s. Walter Vincent and Catherine Marie (Charles) Danahar; m. Cecelia Upritchard, Aug. 24, 1985; children: Deirdre, Rebecca, Michael. BA, Manhattan Coll., Bronx, N.Y., 1963; MA, U. Mass., 1965, PhD, 1970. Instr. U. Mass., Amherst, 1969-70; asst. prof. SUNY, Oswego, 1970-73, assoc. prof., 1973-84, prof., 1984-85; dean Coll. Arts and Scis., prof. history Fairfield (Conn.) U., 1985-92; provost, acad. v.p. Loyola U., New Orleans, 1992-2001; pres. S.W. Minn. State U., 2001—. Vis. prof. U. Pisa, Italy, 1971—72. Contbr. articles to profl. jours. Mem. Fairfield 2000, 1983—88; bd. dirs. New Orleans Mus. Art, 1993—95. Grantee, SUNY Rsch. Found., 1971—73, NEH, 1983—88, others, 1985—; Univ. fellow, U. Mass., 1966—69, Rsch. fellow, Am. Coun. Learned Socs., 1975—76. Mem.: Am. Assn. Higher Edn., Conf. Ctrl. European History, Coun. Colls. Arts and Scis., Am. Conf. Acad. Deans, Am. Hist. Assn. Avocations: travel, sailing. Office: Southwest State U 1501 State St Marshall MN 56258

DANAHER, FRANK ERWIN, transportation technologist; b. Montclair, N.J., Mar. 5, 1936; s. Frank E. and Mildred (Acquino) D.; m. Joan Marie Donovan, Apr. 12, 1986; children: Maria (dec.), Frank, Heather (dec.). BA in Math., Rutgers U., 1961; MBA, Fairleigh Dickinson, 1982. Supr. programming ITT, Paramus, N.J., 1961-66; mgr. systems Lummus, Bloomfield, N.J., 1966-83; rsch. specialist Dun & Bradstreet, Basking Ridge, N.J., 1983-87; technologist Met. Transp. Auth., N.Y.C., 1987—. Cons. in field. Contbr. articles to profl. publs. Area gov. Toastmasters, N.Y.C., 1984-85, chpt. pres., 1993; pres. Fairleigh Early Birds, 1982, 94; spkr. in field. With U.S. Army, 1959. Urban Mass Transit Authority grantee, 1988, 90. Mem.: Info. Tech. Mgrs. Soc., Radio User Group Met. Transp. Authority, Tech. Mgrs. N.Y., User Group Met. Transp. Authority (chmn. 1990—2003), Computer Aided Design and Drafting, Geog. Info. Sys. Users (chmn. 1990—2003), Assn. Sys. Mgmt., Rock Spring Country Club, Delta Mu Delta. Republican. Roman Catholic. Home: 454-147 Prospect Ave West Orange NJ 07052-4103 Office: Met Transit Auth 341 Madison Ave New York NY 10017-3705 E-mail: fdanaher@mtahq.org.

DANAHER, JAMES P. philosopher, educator; b. Jersey City, N.J., Dec. 24, 1947; s. James P. and Caroline (von Atzinger) D.; m. Kathleen Cullere, Aug. 1, 1981; children: Kathleen Marie Cardenas, Kerry Gwen Nicholson. MA, Montclair State U., 1976, New Sch. for Social Rsch., 1983; MPhil, CUNY, 1989, PhD, 1990. Head dept. arts and scis. Berkeley Coll., White Plains, N.Y., 1980—; head philosophy dept. Nyack (N.Y.) Coll., 1990—. Philosopher in residence Whitehall, Newport, R.I., 1993. Author: Postmodern Christianity and the Reconstruction of the Christian Mind, 2001; Contbr. articles to profl. jours. Elder New Covenant Ch., Wyckoff, NJ, 1988—98. Mem. Am. Philos. Assn. Home: 42 Winding Rdg Oakland NJ 07436-2328 Office: Nyack Coll 1 S Boulevard Nyack NY 10960-3604 E-mail: danaherj@nyack.edu.

DANAHER, JAMES WILLIAM, retired federal government executive; b. St. Marys, Ohio, Feb. 20, 1929; s. William Louis and Cora Caroline (Hausfeld) D.; m. Ellen Serena Martin, Feb. 5, 1972; children— Patrick Brendan, Kathryn Annette BS in Econs., Villanova U., 1952; MA in Psychology, Ohio State U., 1958; grad., Fed. Execs. Inst., 1978; Indsl. fellow, Linacre Coll./Oxford U., 2000. Lic. comml. pilot. Rsch. assoc. Courtney & Co., Phila., 1958-62; v.p., rsch. scientist Matrix Rsch. Corp., Arlington, Va., 1962-70; chief human factors divsn. Nat. Transp. Safety Bd., Washington, 1970-76, from chief operational factors divsn. to dir. bur. techn., 1976-85, chief operational factors and human performance divsn., 1985-98; ret., 1998. Aviation safety cons., 1998—; mem. four study coms. for Nat. Rsch. Coun., Nat. Acad. of Scis., 1994—. Contbr. articles to profl. jours. Bd. dirs. Alexandria Soccer Assn., Va., 1983-86; v.p. Charles Barrett Sch. PTA, Alexandria, 1983-84. Capt. USNR, 1952-76. Mem. Human Factors and Ergonomics Soc., Internat. Soc. Air Safety Investigators, Assn. Aviation Psychologists, Naval Res. Assn. (life). Lodges: K.C. Roman Catholic. Avocations: long distance running; skiing; golf. Home: 717 S Overlook Dr Alexandria VA 22305-1215 E-mail: jwdanaher@aol.com.

DANAHER, MALLORY MILLETT (MALLORY JONES), actress, photographer, film producer, theater producer; b. St. Paul, 1939; d. James Albert and Helen Rose (Feely) Millett m. Thomas C. Danaher, Mar. 1985; 1 child by previous marriage, Kristen Vigard. BA, U. Minn. CFO Sheets & Co., N.Y.C., Happy Camper, N.Y.C., Everwarm, Inc., Mallory Inc. Active : N.Y. Theatre, 1971—; mem. : original co. of Annie; The Best Little Whorehouse in Texas; stage roles : Dodsworth, Berkshire Theatre Festival; Hedda Gabler; Kennedy's Children (dir. Olympia Dukakis); Edward Albee's Everything in the Garden (dir. Shelley Winters); House of Blue Leaves; Lincoln Ctr. Libr. Theatre; Stella; Cocteau's one-character play The Human Voice at Deutsches-Haus, NYU; Full Moon and High Tide (dir. Shelley Winters); (off-Broadway prodn.) Loose Connections, Judith Anderson Theatre; actor: (TV series) Love of Life, Another World, Hunter, Thirtysomething, Superior Court, Divorce Court, The Judge, Eischied: Only the Pretty Girls Die (NBC Movie of the Week); (films) Tootsie, Hell Hath No Fury with Barbara Eden, Alone in the Dark; exhibitions include Third Eye Gallery, NYC, Modernage Discovery Gallery, Gallery of St. Clement's; author: Fatherless Child, numerous poems; co-prodr., subject : (TV films) Three Lives; (broadway prodn.) Epic Proportions; exec. prodr., lead actress : Best Served Cold. Mem. Creative Coalition. Mem.: Ctr. for Study of Popular Culture (bd. dirs.), Claremont Inst., Am. Women's Econ. Devel., Nat. Assn. for Self-Employed, Women in Theatre, Legatus, The Actors Studio (chmn. auditions), The Friars Club.

DANAS, ANDREW MICHAEL, lawyer; b. Redwood City, Calif, Apr. 25, 1955; s. Michael George and Marjorie Jean (Bailey) D.; m. Barbara C. Matthews. BA in Polit. Sci. and History, U. Conn., 1977; JD, George Washington U., 1982. Bar: DC 1982, US Dist. Ct. (DC cir.) 1985, US Dist. Ct. Md. 1987, US Ct. Appeals (Fed. cir. 1984), US Ct. Appeals (11th cir. 1987), US Ct. Appeals (3d and 4th cirs.) 1988, US Ct. Appeals (6th cir.) 1990, US Ct. Appeals (2d cir.) 1998, US Ct. of Claims 1984, US Supreme Ct. 1994, US Couty Internat., nat., 2003. Atty. Assn. Am. R.R., Washington, 1983-84; assoc. Grove Jaskiewicz & Cobert, Washington, 1984-90, Ptnr., 1991—. Contbg. author: Freewheeling; author legal column Intermodal Reporter, 1986-94; contbr. articles to profl. jour. Exec. com. Friends Assisting the Nat. Symphony, Washington, 1996-97. Mem.: ABA, Transp. Lawyers Assn. (chmn. legis. com. 1995—98, co-chmn. 1999—2001, Disting. Svc. award 1996), Transp. Law Inst. (chair 1993—94), Euro-Am. Lawyers Group (mgmt. com. 2000—, sec. 2002—), Internat. Bar Assn., Mensa, Univ. Club (Washington), Phi Alpha Theta. Avocations: skiing, music, travel. Home: 621 Tivoli Psge Alexandria VA 22314-1932 Office: Grove Jaskiewicz and Cobert 1730 M St NW Ste 400 Washington DC 20036-4579

DANBOM, DAVID BYERS, history educator; b. Denver, Mar. 29, 1947; s. Raymond Carl and Rowene Caroline (Byers) D.; m. Karen Renee Poor, June 19, 1971; children: Elizabeth Poor, Mark Raymond. BA, Colo. State U., 1969; MA, Stanford U., 1970, PhD, 1974. Prof. history N.D. State U., Fargo, 1974—, faculty lectr., 1998. Editor N.D. Inst. for Regional Studies, Fargo, 1981-92. Author: The Resisted Revolution, 1979, The World of Hope, 1987, Our Purpose is to Serve, 1990, Born in the Country, 1995; editor: Publicly Sponsored Agricultural Research, 1988. Sec. bd. dirs. Red River Valley Heritage Soc., Moorhead, Minn., 1987-92; mem. Fargo Hist. Preservation Commn., 1990-99. Named N.D. Prof. of Yr., Coun. Advancement and Support of Edn., 1990, Disting. Prof., Fargo C. of C., 1990; recipient Faculty Achievement award Burlington No., 1990. Mem. Agrl. History Soc. (bd. dirs. 1990-94, pres. 1990-91), Orgn. Am. Historians (membership com. 1990-95), Soc. Historians of the Gilded Age and Progressive Period. Office: ND State U Dept History Fargo ND 58105 E-mail: DavidDanbom@msn.com.

DANBURG, JEROME SAMUEL, oil company executive; b. Houston, Dec. 21, 1940; s. August and Rosalie (Bornstein) D.; m. Gudrun Ella Ernestine Scholz, Sept. 8, 1965; children: Aron Ralf, Andrea Leda, Sylvia Freia, Sonja Rebecca. BS in Physics, MIT, 1962; Diplom in Physics, Freie Universität Berlin, 1964; PhD in Physics, U. Calif., Berkeley, 1969. Assoc. physicist Brookhaven Nat. Lab., Upton, N.Y., 1969-72; sr. rsch. geophysicist Shell Devel. Co., Houston, 1973-81, rsch. mgr., 1981-86, rsch. dir., 1992-93; mgr. Shell Oil Co., Houston, 1986-92, 93-94, Shell EP Tech Co, Houston, 1994-99, Shell Internat. EP Inc., Houston, 1999—. Physics dept. vis. com. mem. U. Tex., Austin, 1990-2001. Contbr. articles to profl. jours. Fulbright scholar, Freie Universität Berlin. Mem. Am. Phys. Soc., Fulbright Alumni Assn. Home: 5315 Huisache St Bellaire TX 77401-4933 Office: Shell Internat E&P Inc PO Box 481 Houston TX 77001-0481

DANCE, FRANCIS ESBURN XAVIER, communication educator; b. Bklyn., Nov. 9, 1929; s. Clifton Louis and Catherine (Tester) D.; m. Nora Alice Rush, May 1, 1954 (div. 1974); children: Clifton Louis III, Charles Daniel, Alison Catherine, Andrea Frances, Frances Sue, Brendan Rush; m. Carol Camille Zak, July 4, 1974; children: Zachary Esburn, Gabriel Joseph, Caleb Michael, Catherine Emily BS, Fordham U., 1951; MS, Northwestern U., 1953, PhD, 1959. Instr. speech Bklyn. Adult Labor Schs., 1951; instr. humanities, coord. radio and TV U. Ill. at Chgo., 1953—54; instr. Univ. Coll. U. Chgo., 1958; asst. prof. St. Joseph's (Ind.) Coll., Ind., 1958—60; asst. prof., then assoc. prof. U. Kans., 1960—63; mem. faculty U. Wis., Milw., 1963—71, prof. comm., 1965—71, dir. Speech Comm. Ctr., 1963—70; prof. U. Denver, 1971—, John Evans prof., 1995—; prof. homiletics St. John Vianney Theol. Sem., 2002—. Content expert and mem. faculty adv. bd. to Internat. U. on Knowledge Channel, 1993-95; cons. in field. Author: The Citizen Speaks, 1962, (with Harold P. Zelko) Business and Professional Speech Communication, 1965, 2d edit., 1978, Human Communication Theory, 1967, (with Carl E. Larson) Perspectives on Communication, 1970, Speech Communication: Concepts and Behavior, 1972, The Functions of Speech Communication: A Theoretical Approach, 1976, Human Communication Theory, 1982, (with Carol C. Zak-Dance) Public Speaking, 1986, Speaking Your Mind, 1994, 2d edit., 1996; editor Jour. Comm., 1962-64, Speech Tchr., 1970-72; adv. bd. Jour. Black Studies; editl. bd. Jour. Psycholinguistic Rsch; contbr. articles to profl. jours. Bd. dirs. Milw. Mental Health Assn., 1966-67. 2d lt. AUS, 1954-56. Knapp Univ. scholar in comm., 1967-68; recipient Outstanding Prof. award Std. Oil Found., 1967; Master Tchr. award U. Denver, 1985, Univ. Lectr. award U. Denver, 1986. Fellow Internat. Comm. Assn. (pres. 1967); mem. Nat. Comm. Assn. (pres. 1982), Psi Upsilon. Office: U Denver Dept Human Comm Studies Denver CO 80208-0001 E-mail: fdance@du.edu. *Life should include a personal commitment to excellence with a corresponding humane tolerance for failure in self or in others. A belief in the progressive acquisition of autonomy can help guide both personal and professional decisions.*

DANCER, RONALD S. assemblyman; b. May 31, 1949; Mayor Plumstead Twp., 1990—; assemblyman N.J. Gen. Assembly, 2002—. Chmn. Ocean County Bd. of Social Svcs., 1985—; bd. mem. Ocean County Natural Lands Preservation, 1998—; mem. N.J. Horse Racing Commn., 1999—2002, Ocean County Sr. Citizen Adv. Bd., 2001—. With U.S. Army, 1969—71. Republican. Office: 2110 W Country Line Rd Jackson NJ 08527*

DANCEWICZ, JOHN EDWARD, investment banker; b. Boston, Mass., Feb. 12, 1949; s. John Felix and Teresa Sophia (Lewandowski) D.; m. Barbaragail Jarrett, Jan. 23, 1971; children: John Lawrence, Jill Elizabeth, Jenna Gail. BA in Econs., Yale U., 1971; MBA, Harvard U., 1973. Project adminstr., cons. Nat. Shawmut Bank Boston, 1972-73; v.p., founder, mgr. U.S. investment banking Continental Ill. Nat. Bank Chgo., 1973-82; sr. mng. dir., mgr. corp. fin. Bear Stearns & Co. Inc., Chgo., 1982-96; founder, mng. ptnr. DN Ptnrs. LLP and DN Ptnrs. LP, 1996—. Chmn. bd. dirs. Ctrl. Can Co., Inc., Aztec Outdoor Advt. Co.; adv. dir. PPI, Inc., Crysteel, Inc. Contbr. articles to profl. jours. Active Yale U. Schs. Com., Spl. Gifts Com. (chmn. 25th Reunion Fundraising, sec. Yale class 1971); sec. Harvard Bus. Sch. sect.; mem. spl. gifts com. Harvard Bus. Sch. Fund. Mem. Scholarship and Guidance Assn. (bd. dirs., v.p. 1982—), Lake Forest H.S. Hockey Assn. (pres.), Harvard Bus. Sch. Club Chgo., Econ. Club, Univ. Club, East Bank Club, Mid-Am. Club. Home: 969 Spring Ln Lake Forest IL 60045-2302 Office: 77 W Wacker Dr Ste 4550 Chicago IL 60601 Business E-Mail: info@dupartners.com.

DANCEY, CHARLES LOHMAN, newspaper executive; b. Pekin, Ill., Nov. 28, 1916; s. Albert Duane and Bertha (Lohman) D.; m. Nina Evelyn Manker, Dec. 10, 1944; children: Richard, Burt Lee, Clinton Dancey. BS, U. Ill., 1938. Reporter Peoria (Ill.) Star, 1938-40, Peoria Jour., 1946-50; editor Peoria Jour. Star, 1958-80, asst. pub., 1980-87, cons., 1987-96, dir., 1993-96; dir., exec. bd. Dirksen Congrl. Rsch. Ctr., 1994-99. Owner rep., mgmt. bd. WTVH-TV, Peoria, 1956-58 Ill. state comdt. Marine Corps League, 1947; City councilman, commr. fire and plice, Pekin, 1946-50. Col. USMCR, 1941-46, 50-51. Recipient Peoria chpt. B'nai B'rith Citizenship award, 1964 Mem. Inter-Am. Press Assn. (dir., exec. bd.), Am. Soc. Newspaper Editors. Clubs: Mason. Home: 419 Haines Ave Pekin IL 61554-4229 E-mail: china@dpc.net.

DANCO, LÉON ANTOINE, management consultant, educator; b. N.Y.C., May 30, 1923; s. Leon A. and Alvira T. (Gomez) D.; m. Katharine Elizabeth Leck, Aug. 25, 1951; children: Suzanne, Walter Ten Eyck. AB, Harvard, 1943, MBA, 1947; PhD, Case Western Res. U., 1963. Asst. to divsn. pres. Interchem. Corp., N.Y.C., 1947-50; sales promotion mgr. Risdon Mfg. Co., Waterbury, Conn., 1950-55; mgmt. cons. Cheshire, Conn., 1955-57; prof., assoc. dir. mgmt. program Case Inst. Tech., Cleve., 1957-58, lectr., 1959—; mgmt. cons. L.A. Danco & Co., 1957—; lectr. John Carroll U., Cleve., 1959-66, prof., dir. mgmt. confs., 1966—. Vis. prof. econs. Cleve. Inst. Art, 1966-69, Kent State U., 1966-67; exec. dir. Univ. Svcs. Inst., Cleve., 1967-69, pres., 1969—, chmn., 1989—; pub. The Family in Business (newsletter), 1978—; pres. Center for Family Bus., 1978—, chmn. Ctr.for Family Bus., 1991. Author: Beyond Survival-A Business Owners Guide for Success, 1975, Inside the Successful Family Business, 1979, Outside Directors in the Family Owned Business, 1981, Someday It'll All Be...Whose?, 1990; (in French) L'Entreprise Familiale, 1998; (in Spanish) La Empresa Familiare, 1998; syndicated columnist: It's Your Business, 1973—. Lt. (j.g.) USCG, 1942-46, PTO. Mem. Am. Econ. Assn. Home: 28230 Cedar Rd Pepper Pike Cleveland OH 44124 Office: Ctr for Family Bus PO Box 24219 Cleveland OH 44124-0219 E-mail: grummi@aol.com. *Whatever success we may achieve in this life will come from the purpose to which we put God's priceless gift of time.*

DANDASHI, S. ALEXANDER, operations research scientist, consultant, corporate & government advisor; b. July 20, 1959; came to U.S., 1982; naturalized, 1989; m. Mami Dandashi, Apr. 12, 1989; 1 child, Leonard Levi. BSCE, George Washington U., 1987, Applied Scientist in Gen. Ops. Rsch., 1992; MSME in Aeronautics, Astronautics and Rocket Propulsion, George Washington U. & NASA, 1989; MSc in Math., Oxford (Eng.) U., 1994. Designer-analyst, design dir. George Washington U., Washington, 1985-89, head design div., 1989-91, doctoral fellow, 1992-93, applied scientist, sci. rsch. assoc., 1992-93; vice chmn. FANEX Australia Pty. Ltd., Brisbane, Australia, 1995-96, 1996-97, 1997-98, dir., 1994-98; pres., CEO Lynk Internat. Group, N.Y.C., Beverly Hills, Paris, 2000—. Co-founder, dir. ICQA Pty. Ltd., Brisbane, Australia, 1995-98, pres., CEO, 1995-96, dir. mktg. and client rels. in Japan, 1996-97; vis. scientist Kyoto (Japan) U., 1996-97; advisor external, polit. rels. Establishment Le Jour. du Parlement, France, 1999-2002, bus. devel., pub. rels. BDA Comm., France, 2000—, advisor for Le Comité de Miss France, Paris, 2000-2002; mem. bd. dirs. FANEX Party Ltd., ICQA Party Ltd., FANEX USA Inc., 1994-2000. Mem. AAAS, AIAA (sr.), Ops. Rsch. Soc. Am., Inst. Mgmt. Sci., Fedn. Am. Scientists, Am. Jewish Hist. Soc., Oxford Soc., N.Y. Acd. Sci., Sigma Xi, Omega Rho (v.p. 1993-94), Sigma Gamma Tau. Achievements

include studies in stochastic and mathematical modeling, mathematical programming and optimization, numerical analysis, nonlinear dynamics and complexity, design and analysis of aerospace, air-breathing single stage earth-to-orbit vehicles and rockets with APS/RAMJET/SCRAMJET/LACE propulsion systems using slush hydrogen and slush oxygen propellant, advanced aerospace technologies, science & technology policy, mathematical/statistical marketing models, mathematical and statistical theory of probability, co-founder and dir. Australian private college and its network worldwide. Office: Ste 4-A 48 W 68th St New York NY 10023-6015 Fax: (212) 787-4359.

DANDO, A. JEFFREY, lawyer, consultant; b. Phila., Dec. 19, 1938; s. William Albert and Margaret (Ellis) Dando; m. Margery Parris Luening, Aug. 10, 1985; children: Holly Heyward, Evan Griffith. Grad., Mercersburg Acad., 1956; BS civil engring., Cornell U., 1961; LLB, 1964. Bar: Mass. 1964. Ptnr. Goodwin, Procter & Hoar, Boston, 1972, hiring ptnr., 1976—83; exec. com., 1980—83, 1986—89, 1991—; mgmt. com., 1991—; chmn. mgmt. and exec. com., 1993—; gen., local counsel New Eng. real estate develop. co. Urban Investiment and Develop. Co.(Copley Pl.), Immobiliare New Eng., Charlestown Navy Yard, Congress Group, John M. Corcoran Co., Corcoran, Mullins, Jennison, Inc., Harbor Point, O'Connell Develop. (World Trade Ctr., Marina Bay), real estate counsel, real estate investment adv. Aldrich, Eastman & Waltch; lectr. New Eng. Law Inst., Mass. Copntinuing Legal Ed. Mem.: Boston Bar Assn., ABA. Office: Goodwin Procter & Hoar Exch Pl Boston MA 02109

DANDOY, MAXIMA ANTONIO, education educator emeritus; b. Santa Maria, Ilocos, Sur., Philippines; came to U.S., 1949, naturalized, 1951; d. Manuel and Isidra (Mendoza) Antonio. Tchg. cert., Philippine Normal Coll., 1938; AB, Nat. Tchrs. Coll., Manila, 1947; MA, Arellano U., Manila, 1949; Ed.D. (John M. Switzer scholar, Newhouse Found. scholar), Stanford U., 1951, postgrad. (Calif. Fedn. Bus. and Profl. Women's Club scholar), 1952. Tchr. elem. sch., Philippines, 1927-37; lab. sch. tchr. Philippine Normal Coll., Manila, 1938-49; instr. Arellano U., Manila, 1947-49; lab. sch. prin. U. of East, Manila, 1953-54, assoc. prof., 1952-55; prof. edn. Calif. State U., Fresno, 1956-82, prof. edn. emeritus, 1982—. Curriculum writer, gen. office supr. Manila Dept. Edn., 1944-45; Mem. com. for the selection social studies textbooks for state adoption Calif., 1970-71; vis. prof. UCLA, 1956; Floro Crisologo Meml. lectr. U. No. Philippines, 1977 Author: Teaching Competencies, A Workbook and Log, 1985. Mem. Friends of the Stanford (Calif.) U. Sch. Edn., 1993, Sch. of Edn. and Human Devel. Alumni and Friends, Calif. State U., Fresno, 1992-93; mem. Calif. Gov.'s Conf. on Traffic Safety, 1962, Calif. Gov.'s Conf. Delinquency Prevention, 1963. Named Disting. Woman of Year, Fresno Bus. and Profl. Women's Club, 1957, Woman of Achievement, 1973, Outstanding Filipino, 1982, 98; recipient Higher Edn. and Internat. Understanding award Philippine Normal Coll. Alumni Assn., 1986, One Moment in Time award Calif. Fedn. Bus. and Profl. Women, 1997-98. Mem. AAUW (liaison Calif. State U. Fresno 1970-71, bridge gen. coord. 1995--), Nat. Coun. Social Studies (chmn. sec. internat. understanding, nat. conv. 1966), Calif. Fedn. Bus. and Profl. Women's Clubs (state chmn. scholarships 1961-63, treas. Fresno), Calif. Tchrs. Assn., Orgn. Filipino-Am. Educators Fresno (pres. 1977-95, Outstanding Svc.), Filipino-Am. Women's Club (adv. 1969-74), Internat. Platform Assn., Phi Delta Kappa, Pi Lambda Theta, Kappa Delta Pi (counselor 1972-79, nat. com. attendance and credentials 1975, nat. com. regional confs. 1966). Home: 1419 W Bullard Ave Fresno CA 93711-2324

D'ANDREA, DEBORAH DAWN, nursing consultant, critical care nurse; b. Chgo. ADN, Prairie State Coll., Chgo. Heights, Ill., 1970; BA in psychology, Lewis U., 1980, BSN, 1984. RN, Ill., Fla. Staff nurse post anesthesia recovery-surg. ICU Cook County Hosp., Chgo., 1970-72; staff nurse surg. ICU U. Chgo. Hosp. and Clinic, 1972-75, dir. utilization review dept., 1975-79; cons. profl. review orgn. utilization review Chgo. Found. Med. Care, 1979-81; staff nurse psychiat. adolescent Chgo. Lake Shore Hosp., 1981-82; staff nurse psychiat. adolescent and adult Charter Barclay Hosp., 1982-84; utilization review quality assurance nurse Grant Hosp., Chgo., 1982-84, educator staff devel., 1983-84; staff nurse trauma ctr. Cook County Hosp., 1984-86; staff nurse emergency trauma Louis A. Weiss Hosp., Chgo., 1986-88; utilization review coord. Charter Barclay Hosp., 1986-90; prin. Deborah D. D'Andrea & Assoc., 1989—; legal nurse cons. Jeffrey M. Goldberg & Assoc., Chgo., 1991; owner D'Andrea Consulting Ltd. & Med. Legal Cons. Assoc., Chgo., 1992—. Recipient Internat. Woman of Yr., 1992-93. Mem. Am. Assn. Legal Nurse Cons., ATLA, Am. Assn. Legal Nurse Cons. (bd. dirs. 1994), Nat. Nurses Bus. Assn., Am. Coll. Legal Medicine. Avocations: reading, bicycling, sailing, swimming. Office: D'Andrea Cons Ltd and Med Legal Cons Assocs 716 W Briar Pl Ste 3 Chicago IL 60657-4515 E-mail: mlcarn@ameritech.net.

D'ANDREA, FRANCES MARY, special education educator; b. Southampton, N.Y., Nov. 17, 1960; d. John and Margaret (Faye) D'A.; m. Stephen F. Cox, June 23, 1985. BS, George Peabody Coll. Tchrs., Nashville, 1982; MEd, Ga. State U., 1996. Tchr. of visually impaired Utah Sch. for the Blind, Ogden, 1982-87, Salt Lake City, 1982-87, Fulton County Schs., Atlanta, 1987-94; with Am. Found. for the Blind, Atlanta, 1995—, rep. to Braille Authority of N.Am., dir. S.E. office, 1998-2000, dir. Nat. Literacy Ctr., 2000—. Mem. adv. com. Ga. Deafblind Project, Atlanta, 1995—. Co-author, editor Instructional Strategies for Braille Literacy, 1997 (Best Title in Category award Assn. Am. Pubs. 1997, C. Warren Bledsoe award 2000), Looking to Learn: Promoting Literacy for Students with Low Vision, 2000; cons. editor: Seeing Eye to Eye, 2000; editor: DOTS for Braille Reading, 1996—; contbr. articles to profl. publs. Mem. Assn. for Edn. and Rehab. of Blind and Visually Impaired (pres. Ga. chpt. 1991-93, 97-99, divsn. 16 chair 2000-2002, editor 1990-94, Bennett Baxley award for Outstanding Svc. 1991), Internat. Reading Assn., Coun. Exceptional Children (divsn. visual impairments), Nat. Coun. Tchrs. of English, Nat. Braille Assn., Calif. Transcribers and Educators of the Visually Handicapped, Omicron Delta Kappa. Office: Am Found for the Blind Nat Literacy Ctr 100 Peachtree St NW Ste 620 Atlanta GA 30303-1909

D'ANDREA, VINCENT CHARLES, postal clerk; b. Newport, R.I., Apr. 9, 1958; s. John Raymond and Ruth Rosabel D'Andrea. A, Cameron U., 1981; B, Salve Regina U., 1990. With mil. police U.S. Army, 1977—86, R.I. N.G., 1986—94; with U.S. Post Office, Providence, 1995—. Sgt. U.S. Army, 1977—86. Recipient S.W. Asian Campaign medal, U.S. Army, 1991, Kuwait Liberation medal, 1991. Mem.: NRA, TREA, VFW, Planetary Soc., AmVets, Am. Legion. Republican. Roman Catholic. Avocations: coin collecting, sports memorabilia, autograph collecting. Home: 2 Elliott Pl Newport RI 02840-1804 Office: US Post Office 24 Corliss St Providence RI 02904

DANDRIDGE, LENOR, paralegal; d. LeRoy and Lucille Dandridge; 1 child, LaMont Warren. Student, Malcolm X Coll., 1976—79, Roosevelt U., 1979—83, Harold Washington Coll., 2002—. Owner Dandridge Tutoring and Mentoring, Chgo., 1998—. Author: (children's coloring book) Color N History, 1992, poetry. Cons., vol. Home-Along-With Home, Chgo., 1987—; tutor, mentor YMCA, Chgo., 1998, Hull House, Chgo., 2002; vol., asst. Play and Learn Daycare, Burham, Ill., 1999—; respite worker Ada S. McKinley, Chgo., 2002; vol. Lincoln Park Zoo, Chgo., 2003. Avocations: writing, bowling, modern jazz dancing, exercising.

DANDY, ROSCOE GREER, clinical psychotherapist, educator, public health analyst; b. L.A., Dec. 20, 1946; s. Roscoe Conkling and Doris L. (Edwards) D.; m. Evelyn Wendy Dandy. BA, Calif. State U., 1970; MSW, U. So. Calif., 1973; MPH, U. Pitts., 1974, MPA, 1975, DPH, 1981; cert., Harvard U., 1981. Lic. clin. social worker. Youth counselor Calif. State Youth Authority, Ontario, Calif., 1971; pub. health intern Colo. State Dept. Health, Denver, 1974; health planning intern Green Engring Corp., Pitts., 1975; adminstrv. health intern Kane Hosp., Pitts., 1979; assoc. dir. U.S. Pub. Health Clinic, Washington, 1980-81; asst. chief trainee VA Hosp., Washington, 1981-83, asst. chief med. adminstrn. svc. Ft. Howard, Md., 1983-85, clinical social worker, 1985-93; psychotherapist Columbia Inst. of Psychotherapy, Inc., 1989-91, D.A. Wynne & Assocs. Inc., 1991-94; pub. health analyst USPHS, 1993—. Instr. U. Pitts., 1977-80, Grad. Sch. Washington ext. campus Cen. Mich. U., 1980—, Columbia Pacific U., San Rafael, Calif., 1990—, Nova U., Ft. Lauderdale, Fla., 1991—; vis. instr. Andrews AFB, Washington, Walter Reed Army Med. Ctr. Hosp., Washington, Aberdeen Proving Ground, Md., Ft. Meade, Md., Ft. Hamilton, N.Y.; mem. Nat. Review Panel for Substance Abuse Contracts, 1991-93. Author: (book) Board and Care Homes in Los Angeles County, 1976. Police cmty. liaison Howard County Police Dept., 1989-93. Named Project Officer of Yr., Inst. Coll. Rsch. Devel. and Support, 1999. Mem. APHA, NASW. Avocations: reading, poetry, music, track. Home: PO Box 871 Clinton MD 20735-0871

DANE, MAXWELL, former advertising executive; b. Cin., June 7, 1906; s. Abraham and Sophie (Sall) D.; m. Belle Sloan, Apr. 4, 1933 (dec. 1985), 1 child, Henry; m. Esther Levine, 1986. Advt. dept. Stern Bros., N.Y.C., 1928-32; retail promotion mgr. Evening Jour., 1933-36; account exec. Dorland Internat., 1937-39; advt. promotion mgr. Look mag., 1939-41; sales promotion mgr., radio sta. WMCA, 1941-44; pres. Maxwell Dane, Inc. (advt.), N.Y.C., 1944-49; founder, exec. v.p., sec.-treas. Doyle Dane Bernbach, Inc., N.Y.C., 1949-71, dir., 1971-86. Chmn. advt. and pub. div. UJA/Fedn., 1976-81, chmn. exec. com. Jewish Week, N.Y.C., 1976-81, pres., 1982-92; trustee Ctrl. Synagogue, N.Y., 1995—, Haverford Coll., 1967-80, emeritus, 1981—; exec. com. Nat. Com. for Effective Congress, 1979. Recipient Karl Menninger award Fortune Soc., 1983 Fellow Met. Mus. Art (life), N.Y. Civil Liberties Union (vice chmn. 1960-66, treas. 1966-89), Anti-Defamation League (chmn. nat. program com. 1969-76, hon. vice-chmn. 1976—), Fedn. Jewish Philanthropies (trustee, chmn. pub. rels. com. 1971-76), Am. Arbitration Assn. (arbitrator 1972-85), Am. Assn. Advt. Agys. (chmn. EEO com. 1970-72), Old Oaks Club (Purchase, N.Y.). Home: 650 Park Ave New York NY 10021-6115 Office: 437 Madison Ave New York NY 10022-7001

DANE, STEPHEN MARK, lawyer; b. Chillicothe, Ohio, Mar. 27, 1956; s. Clyde and Rita M. (Murray) D.; m. Kim P. Piatt, July 7, 1979; children: Tara, Adam, Shannon, Alexandra, Courtney. BS with honors, U. Notre Dame, 1978; JD magna cum laude, U. Toledo, 1981. Bar: Ohio 1981, U.S. Ct. Appeals (6th and 10th cirs.) 1982, U.S. Dist. Ct. (no. dist.) Ohio 1983, U.S. Dist. Ct. (no. dist.) Tex. 1983, U.S. Ct. Appeals (5th cir.) 1984, U.S. Supreme Ct. 1985, U.S. Ct. Appeals (7th cir.) 1993. Law clk. U.S. Ct. Appeals (6th cir.), Cin., 1981-82; ptnr. Cooper & Walinski, Toledo, 1986—. Judge pro tempore Perrysburg Mcpl. Ct., 1990—. Recipient Fair Housing award HUD, 1996, Spirit of Wood County award, 1988, Pub. Interest Law award Equal Access to Justice Com., 2000, Fair Housing award Oho Civil Rights Commn. 2001; named Lawyer of Yr. Lawyers Weekly, 1998; named to St. John's Jesuit H.S. Hall of Fame, 1991. Mem. ABA, Ohio State Bar Assn., Toledo Bar Assn. (chmn. fed. ct. com. 1987-89, trustee 2001--), Wood County Bar Assn.. Roman Catholic. Home: 501 Hickory St Perrysburg OH 43551-2206 Office: Cooper & Walinski 900 Adams St Toledo OH 43624-1505

DANES, CLAIRE, actress; b. N.Y.C., Apr. 12, 1979; d. Chris and Carla Danes. TV role as Angela Chase in series My So-Called Life, ABC, 1994-95 (nominee Emmy award for Best Lead in Drama Series 1995, Golden Globe award for Best Actress ina Drama 1995); appeared in HBO spl. More Than Friends: The Coming Out of Heidi Leiter, 1994, also guest appearances on TV series Law and Order, 1990; film appearances include: Dreams of Love, 1992, 30, 1993, Little Women, 1994, Dead Man's Jack, 1994, How to Make an American Quilt, 1995, Home for the Holidays, 1995, THe Pesky Suitor, 1995, I Love You, I love You Not 1996, To Gillian on Her 37th Birthday, 1996, as Juliet in William Shakespeare's Romeo and Juliet, 1996, Mononoke-hime (voive only), 1997, U-Turn, 1997, The Rainmaker, 1997, Les Misérables, 1998, Polish Wedding, 1998, The Mod Squad, 1998, Brokedown Palace, 1999, Hercules (voice only), 1998, Igby Goes Down, 2002, The Hours, 2002, It's All About Love, 2003, Terminator 3: Rise of the Machines, 2003, The Rage in Placid Lake, 2003.

DANES, ZDENKO FRANKENBERGER, physicist, consultant; b. Prague, Czechoslovakia, Aug. 25, 1920; came to U.S., 1952; s. Zdenko and Eleonora (Rebensteiger von Blankenfeld) F.; m. Marie V. Hankova, Jan. 20, 1945; children: Peter, Ellen. PhD in Math. and Physics, Charles U., Prague, 1949. Designer Vilnes Electronics, Prague, 1942-45; rsch. asst. Geophys. Survey, Prague, 1945-48; asst. prof. Charles U., Pilsen, Czechoslovakia, 1948-50; geophysicist Gulf Oil Corp., Pitts., 1952-59, Boeing Co., Seattle, 1959-62; prof. physics U. Puget Sound, 1962-84; ret., 1984.

DANESCU, RADU IOAN, engineering educator; b. Ramnicu Valcea, Valcea, Romania, Jan. 4, 1960; arrived in U.S., 1994; s. Gheorghe and Rodica Otilia Danescu; m. Mariana Laslau, Aug. 27, 1988; 1 child, Irina Elena. PhD, Clemson U., 1998. Asst. prof. N.D. State U., Fargo, 2000—. Vis. prof. Clemson (S.C.) U., 1998—99. Mem.: ASME. Office: ND State U Dept of Mech Engring Fargo ND 58105 Office Fax: 701-231-8913. E-mail: radu.danescu@ndsu.nodak.edu.

DANEY, BERNARD JOSEPH, accountant, consultant; b. Wilmington, Del., Feb. 19, 1925; s. Hugh J. and Margaret (Harkins) D.; m. Arlene R. Gudehus, Mar. 2, 1957; children: B. Christopher, Gregory K., Duane M., Michael H.A. BS, Temple U., 1948. CPA, Del., Pa., D.C. Ptnr. Daney, Truitt & Co., Wilmington, 1953-95, McBride Shopa & Co., Greenville, Del., 1995—; co-founder, v.p. Brandywine Coll., Wilmington, 1965-85. Trustee Lawyers Fund Client Protection, Wilmington, 1992-97; bd. dirs. Assn. Racing Commrs., Blue Cross Blue Shield, Care First, Inc.; treas. Nat. License Compact. Chmn. Del. Thoroughbred Racing Com., Wilmington, 1993—; active Del. Higher Edn. Com., Wilmington, 1993—; bd. dirs. Fair Hill Races, Elkton, Md., 1992—; trustee Christiana Care, Hosp. With US Army, 1943-45. Mem. Am. Inst CPAs, Pa. Horse Breeders Assn. (treas. 1985-2002), Univ. Club (pres. 1965-67). Avocation: thoroughbred horse breeding. Home: 121 Ponds Ln Greenville DE 19807-2129 Office: McBride Shopa & Co 270 Presidential Dr Greenville DE 19807-3353 E-mail: threecherubs@aol.com., bdaney@mcbridgeshopa.com.

DANFORTH, ARTHUR EDWARDS, finance executive; b. Cleve., Jan. 23, 1925; s. Arthur Edwards and Jane (Hillyard) D.; m. Elizabeth Wagley, Mar. 17, 1956; children: Hillyard Raible, Nicholas Edwards (dec.), Jonathan Ingersoll, Elizabeth Wagley, Michael Stowe. BA, Yale U., 1948. With Hayden Miller Co., Cleve., 1949-54, First Nat. City Bank (predecessor to Citibank N.A.), N.Y.C., 1954-63, asst. mgr. Buenos Aires office, 1959-61; treas. Bunge Corp., N.Y.C., 1963-65; sr. v.p., treas. Colonial Bank & Trust Co., Waterbury, Conn., 1965-70; chmn., CEO Farmers Bank of Del., Wilmington, 1970-76; prin. Danforthgroup, New Canaan, Conn., 1976-98; ret., 1998. Past bd. dirs. United Way of Del., Boys Club of Wilmington, Grand Opera House Inc. of Del., NCCJ, Audubon Soc. Conn., Greater Wilmington Devel. Coun. Ensign USNR, 1943-46. Mem.: Quail Valley Golf Club (Vero Beach, Fla.), Yale Club (N.Y.C.), Nantucket Yacht Club, Sankaty Head Golf Club. Home: 230 Bermuda Bay Ln Vero Beach FL 32963-3421

DANFORTH, CLARENCE EDWARD, priest, retired consultant; b. Winchendon, Mass., Apr. 27, 1921; s. Clarence Danforth and Eva Jane Morlock. SB, Boston U., Boston, MA, 1939—43; STB, Angelicum, Rome, Italy, 1978—81, STL, 1985—87. Ordained Catholic Priest 1981. Computations asst. GE, Lynn, Mass., 1943—47, supr. advanced mechanics Cincinnati, Ohio, 1953—60, mgr. advanced mechanics, 1960—75, cons., 1977—95. Ordained cath. priest Diocese of Gary, Gary, Ind., 1981—2002. Recipient Named to, Propulsion Hall of Fame, 1984. Fellow: AIAA (assoc.). Roman Catholic. Achievements include design of First Jet Engine All-Flexible System Vibration Analysis in 1955; founded Jet Aermechanical Technology and Life Design Aircooled Turbines. Avocations: languages, philosophy. Home: 1501 Hoffman Street Hammond IN 46327 Home Fax: 219-937-0575.

DANFORTH, DAVID NEWTON, JR., physician, scientist; b. N.Y.C., June 25, 1942; s. David Newton and Gladys Margaret (Blaine) D.; m. Anne Walker Nickson, Apr. 13, 1985. BA, Northwestern U., Evanston, Ill., 1965; MD, Northwestern U., Chgo., 1971; MS, U. N.Mex., Albuquerque, 1967. Diplomate Am. Bd. Surgery. Intern, then resident Cornell Med. Ctr., N.Y.C., 1971-74, 77-79; clin. assoc. NIH, Bethesda, Md., 1974-77; surg. fellow M.D. Anderson Hosp., Houston, 1979-80; sr. staff fellow NIH, Bethesda, 1980-82; sr. investigator Nat. Cancer Inst., NIH, Bethesda, 1982—. Editor: Diagnosis and Management of Breast Cancer, 1988; contbr. articles to profl. jours. Served to lt. comdr. USPHS, 1974-76. Fellow Am. Cancer Soc., 1979-80. Fellow ACS, Soc. Surg. Oncology, Am. Soc. Clin. Oncology, Am. Assn. Cancer Rsch., Endocrine Soc. Republican. Episcopalian. Avocations: travel, sports, reading. Home: 7301 Meadow Ln Chevy Chase MD 20815-5009 Office: Nat Cancer Inst Surgery Br Bldg 10 Rm 2B38 Bethesda MD 20892

DANFORTH, ELLIOT, JR., medical educator; b. Bainbridge, N.Y., Oct. 21, 1933; s. Elliot and Ellen (Roberts) D.; m. Joan C. Garrett, Dec. 26, 1959; children: Kimberly H., Noel, Peter E. AB, Dartmouth Coll., 1956; MS, Ohio State U., 1958; MD, Albany (N.Y.) Med. Coll., 1962. Resident Dartmouth Affliated Hosps., Hanover, N.H., 1962-65; instr. Dartmouth Med. Sch., Hanover, 1965-66; rsch. internist Walter Reed Army Inst. Rsch., Washington, 1966-70; asst. prof. U. Vt. Coll. Medicine, Burlington, 1970-74, assoc. prof., 1974-79, prof., 1979-94, prof. emeritus, 1993—, dir. clin. rsch. ctr., 1980-93, chief divsn. endocrinology, metabolism and nutrition, 1990-93; dir. Sims Obesity/Nutrition Rsch. Ctr., 1992-93; exec. dir. cardiovasc. metabolic rsch. Lederle Labs., Am. Cyanamid Co., 1993-95; med. cons. to pharm. industry, 1996—; pres., CEO Beartown Pharma, Underhill, Vt., 1998—. Cons. Walter Reed Gen. Hosp. Mem. editl. bd. J. Clin. Endocrinology and Metabolism, Jour. Gerontology, Obesity Rsch., Jour. Gerontology: Biol. Scis.; contbr. articles to profl. jours. Served to cpt. U.S. Army, 1966-68. NIH grantee, Washington, 1970-94. Mem. AAAS, Endocrine Soc., Am. Diabetes Assn., Am. Thyroid Assn., Am. Fedn. Clin. Rsch., Soc. Exptl. Biology and Medicine (mem. editl. bd. procs., coun. mem.), Internat. Assn. for Study of Obesity, N.Y. Acad. Scis., N.Am. Assn. Study Obesity. Avocations: travel, farming, fishing. Home and Office: 84 Beartown Rd Underhill VT 05489-9365 E-mail: edanforth@att.net.

DANFORTH, JEFFREY SCOTT, psychologist, educator; b. Providence, R.I., July 10, 1957; s. Guy Sage and Helen Mott Danforth; m. Julie Ann Polaski, Aug. 21, 1982; children: Nathaniel, Christopher, Nicholas. BA in English and Psychology, Marietta Coll., 1979; MA in Clin. Psychology, We. Mich. U., 1982; PhD in Clin. Psychology, W.Va. U., 1987. Lic. child psychologist 1992. Psychology intern U. Miss. Med. Sch., Jackson, 1986—87; assoc. dir. child inpatient mental health unit U. Mass. Med. Sch., Worcester, 1987—89; clin. dir. The Learning Clinic, Brooklyn, Conn., 1989—92; prof., chmn. dept. psychology Ea. Conn. State U., Willimantic, 1992—. Cons. in field. Co-author: The Treatment of Severe Behavior Disorders: Behavior Analysis Approaches, 1989, Handbook of Behavior Modification with the Mentally Retarded, 1990, Dialogues on Verbal Behavior, 1991, Handbook of Child and Adolescent Outpatient, Day Treatment and Community Psychiatry, 1998; mem. editl. bd.: The Analysis of Verbal Behavior, 2001—03, Clin. Psychology Rev., 2002—03; contbr. articles to profl. jours. Soccer coach Neconn Soccer Club, Woodstock, Conn., 1991—. Grantee, U. Mass., 1989, Conn. State U., 1993, 1998. Mem.: Assn. Advancement Behavior Therapy, Assn. Behavior Analysis. Office: Dept Psych Eastern Conn State Univ 83 Windham St Willimantic CT 06226 Fax: 860-465-4541. E-mail: danforthj@easternct.edu.

DANFORTH, WILLIAM HENRY, retired academic administrator, physician; b. St. Louis, Apr. 10, 1926; s. Donald and Dorothy (Claggett) D.; m. Elizabeth Anne Gray, Sept. 1, 1950; children: Cynthia Danforth Prather, David Gray, Maebelle Reed, Elizabeth D. Sankey. AB, Princeton U., 1947; MD, Harvard U., 1951. Intern Barnes Hosp., St. Louis, 1951—52, resident, 1954—57; now mem. staff; asst. prof. medicine Washington U., St. Louis, 1960—65, assoc. prof., 1965—67, prof., 1967—, vice chancellor for med. affairs, 1965—71, chancellor, 1971—95, chmn., bd. trustees, 1995—99, vice-chmn. bd. trustees, chancellor emeritus, 1999—. Pres. Washington U. Med. Sch. and Assoc. Hosps., 1965-71; program coord. Bi-State Regional Med. Program, 1967-68; dir. Energizing Holdings; chmn. bd. dirs. Donald Danforth Plant Sci. Ctr. Trustee Danforth Found.; trustee Am. Youth Found., 1963—, Princeton U., 1970-74; pres. St. Louis Christmas Carols Assn., 1958-74, chmn., 1975—; co-chair Barnes/Jewish Hosp., 1996-2002; bd. dirs. BJC Health Systems, 1996-2002. Named Man of Yr., St. Louis Gloe-Democrat, 1978. Fellow: AAAS, Am. Acad. Arts and Scis.; mem.: Inst. Medicine. Home: 10 Glenview Rd Saint Louis MO 63124-1308 Office: Washington U West Campus Campus Box 1044 7425 Forsyth Blvd Ste 262 Saint Louis MO 63105-2161

DANG, CHI VAN, hematology and oncology educator; b. Saigon, Vietnam, Nov. 2, 1954; came to U.S., 1967; s. Chieu Van and Nga Ngoc (Nguyen) D.; m. Mary Doreen Seeley, May 18, 1985; children: Eric Van, Vanessa Marie. BS in Chemistry, U. Mich., 1975; PhD in Chemistry, Georgetown U., 1978; MD, Johns Hopkins U., 1982. Diplomate Am. Bd. Internal Medicine, Am. Bd. Med. Oncology. Resident in internal medicine Johns Hopkins Hosp., Balt., 1982-85; fellow in hematology and oncology U. Calif., San Francisco, 1985-87; asst. prof. medicine Johns Hopkins U., 1987-91, assoc. prof., 1991-97, assoc. prof. oncol., pathology, molecular biology & genetics, 1995-97, dir. hematology, 1993—2003, prof. medicine, oncology, and pathology, 1997—, prof. cell biology, 2001—, dep. dir. basic rsch., dept. medicine, 1996-99, co-dir. immunology and hematopoiesis, oncology, 1998-2000; vice dean rsch. Johns Hopkins Sch. Medicine, 2000—. Mem. oncological scis. path B NIH, Bethesda, Md., 1993-97; cons. Abbott Lab., 2002, Novartis, East Hanover, N.J., 1993-98, Genentech, South San Francisco, Calif., 1995; sci. adv. bd. Lion Pharm. Corp., Balt. Contbr. articles to Nature, Molecular and Cellular Biology, Genes and Devel.; mem. editl. bd. Jour. Clin. Invest., 1998—, Neoplasia, 1999—; mem. editl. bd. Cancer Rsch., 2000—, sr. editor, 2003—. Scholar Leukemia Soc. Am., 1992-97, Stohlman scholar award Leukemia Soc. Am., 1996, Merit award NIH/NCI, 1999. Mem. Assn. Am. Physicians, Am. Soc. for Clin. Investigation (pres. 2002), Phi Beta Kappa, Alpha Omega Alpha, Phi Lambda Upsilon. Avocations: india ink sketching, poetry. Home: 217 Upnor Rd Baltimore MD 21212-3425 Office: Johns Hopkins U Sch Med Ross 1025 720 Rutland Ave Baltimore MD 21205-2109 E-mail: cvdang@jhmi.edu.

DANG, MARVIN S. C. lawyer; b. Honolulu, 1954; s. Brian K.T. and Flora Dang. BA with distinction, U. Hawaii, 1974; JD, George Washington U., 1978. Bar: Hawaii 1978, U.S. Dist. Ct. Hawaii 1978, U.S. Ct. Appeals (9th cir.) 1979. Atty. Gerson, Steiner & Anderson and predecessor firms, Honolulu, 1978-81; owner, atty. Law Offices of Marvin S.C. Dang, Honolulu, 1981—. Sr. v.p., bd. dirs. Rainbow Fin. Corp., Honolulu, 1984-95; bd. dirs. Foster Equipment Co. Ltd., Honolulu, 1986—, Hawaii Cmty. Reinvestment Corp., 1994-96; vice chmn. Hawaii Consumer Fin. Polit. Action Com., 1988-95, sec./treas., 1999—; hearings officer (per diem) Adminstrv. Drivers License Revocation Office, Honolulu, 1991-95. State rep., asst. minority floor leader Hawaii State Legislature, Honolulu, 1982-84; chmn., vice chmn., mem. Manoa Neighborhood Bd., Honolulu, 1979-82, 84-87; pres., v.p., mem. Hawaii Coun. on Legal Edn. for Youth, Honolulu, 1979-86, mem. Hawaii Bicentennial Commn. of U.S. Constn., Honolulu, 1986-88. Recipient Cert. of Appreciation award Hawaii Speech-Lang.-Hearing Assn., Honolulu, 1984; named one of Ten Outstanding Young Persons of Hawaii, Hawaii State Jaycees, 1983. Mem. ABA (standing com. on group and prepaid legal svcs. 2000—, coun. of fund for justice and edn. 1993-99, standing com. on law and electoral process 1985-89, spl. com. on youth edn. for citizenship 1979-85, 89-92, Hawaii membership chmn. 1981-93, exec. coun. young lawyers divsn. 1986-88), Hawaii State Bar Assn. (chair collection law sec. 1999—, bd. dirs. young lawyers divsn. 1990), Am. Prepaid Legal Svcs. Inst. (bd. dirs. 2000—), Hawaii Fin. Svcs. Assn. (sec. 1991, 2002—, treas. 1992, v.p. 1993, prs. 1994, lobbyist 1996—). Avocations: family, law, politics. Office: PO Box 4109 Honolulu HI 96812-4109 E-mail: dangm@aloha.net.

DANG, NAM HOANG, medical educator; b. Saigon, Vietnam, June 1, 1963; came to U.S., 1975; s. Dinh Van and Triem Nguyen Dang; m. Ann Truong Tong, May 10, 1992. BA, Harvard U., 1985, PhD, 1991, MD, 1992. Bd. cert. diplomate in internal medicine and med. oncology. Resident in internal medicine Mass. Gen. Hosp., Boston, 1992-94; fellow in med. oncology Dana Farber Cancer Inst., Boston, 1994-98; fellow in medicine Harvard Med. Sch., Boston, 1992-98; asst. prof. medicine M.D. Anderson Cancer Ctr., Houston, 1998—; assoc. dir. ed. program. Contbr. articles to sci. and med. jours. Named Outstanding Med. Student, Am. Coll. Rheumatology, 1990, M.D. Anderson Physician-Scientist award, 1999; Physician Rsch. fellow Howard Hughes Med. Inst., 1996, V Found. fellow, 1999. Mem. ACP, Mass. Med. Soc., Mensa, Am. Soc. Clin. Oncologists, Am. Soc. Hematologists, Am. Assn. Immunologists, Am. Assn. Cancer Rsch. Avocations: travel, sports. Office: M D Anderson Cancer Ctr Dept Lymphoma Box 429 1515 Holcombe Blvd Houston TX 77030 E-mail: nhdang@notes.mdacc.tmc.edu.

DANGELANTONIO, SARAH TERESA, academic administrator, educator; b. St. Albans, N.Y., Sept. 22, 1961; d. Victor Joseph and Mary Elizabeth Bearinger; m. Anthony Joseph, May 10, 1961; children: Matthew, Elizabeth, Peter. BA in English, Spring Hill Coll., Mobile, Ala., 1983; MA in English, Saint Louis U., 1985; PhD in English, U. Ga., 1996. Adj. faculty dept. Truett-McConnell Coll., Athens, Ga., 1987-90; instr. composition U. Ga.,

1988-99, asst. coord. Regents Remediation Office, 1989-90; prof. English, coord. individual and comty. integrated curriculum Franklin Pierce Coll., Rindge, NH, 1990—. Dir. writing ctr. Franklin Pierce Coll., Rindge, N.H., 1992-, coord. coll. writing, 1994-, individual and comty. first-yr. seminar coord., 1999-. Editor: The Riverside Guide to Writing Instructors Resource Manual, 1995. Assoc. New England Ctr. Civic Life, Rindge, 1999-. Recipient Tchg. Excellence and Leadership award Franklin Pierce Coll., 1992-93, Faculty of Yr. award Franklin Pierce Coll. Student Senate, 1996-97, Outstanding Tchg. Asst. award U. Ga., 1998. Mem.: Modern Language Assn., Internat. Thomas Hardy Soc., Assn. Integrative Studies, Coun. Writing Program Adminstrs., Nat. Coun. Tchrs. English, New Eng. Writing Ctr. Assn., Assn. Gen. and Liberal Studies, Am. Assn. colls. and Us., Nat. Writing Ctr. Assn., Iota Omega, Sigma Tau Delta (chpt. advisor 1993—2004). Conservative. Roman Catholic. Avocations: reading, gardening, regional cooking. Office: Franklin Pierce Coll College Rd Rindge NH 03461 Fax: 603-899-1052. E-mail: dangelst@fpc.edu.

D'ANGELO, ANDREW WILLIAM, retired civil engineer; b. Bklyn., Jan. 23, 1924; s. William and Filomena (Soviero) D'A.; m. Filomena Margaret Loiero, June 26, 1949; children: Carol Lorraine Mauch, William Andrew. BSCE, Bklyn. Poly. Inst., 1952, MCE, 1956. Lic. engr., Fla. Project engr. D.B. Steinman, N.Y.C., 1952-56, Merritt Chapman & Scott Corp., N.Y.C., 1956-67; v.p. engring. Murphy Pacific Marine Salvage Co., N.Y.C., 1967-74; chief engr. Internat. Underwater Contractors, City Island, N.Y., 1974-76; cons. self-employed N.Y.C., 1976-77; pres. D'Angelo, Schoenewaldt Assoc. Inc., Floral Pk., N.Y., 1977-85; project mgr. North Star Contracting, New Rochelle, N.Y., 1985-88; project engr. Yonkers Contracting Co. Inc., Yonkers, N.Y., 1988-97; cons. marine salvage, 1998—. Cons. in field, to 2000. Author: Salvage of Coastwise #1, 1975. Sgt. U.S. Army, 1943-45. Recipient Bronze star U.S. Army, 1945, Commendation USN, 1965. Mem. ASCE, NSPE, Soc. Naval Architects and Marine Engrs., The Moles. Republican. Roman Catholic. Achievements include patent for Mooring Apparatus. Home: 7751 Olympia Dr West Palm Beach FL 33411-5786

D'ANGELO, ERNEST EUSTACHIO, brokerage house executive; b. Jersey City, Jan. 21, 1944; s. Eustachio and Catherine (Valentino) D'A.; m. Carol Abramowitz, Apr. 23, 1966; 1 child, Ernest E. Jr. BS in Acctg., Rutgers U., 1972. Contract officer N.Y. State Urban Devel. Corp., N.Y.C., 1972-75; fin. dir. Ctr. Essex Health Plan, Orange, N.J., 1975-79, New Cmty. Corp., Newark, 1979-81; first v.p. corp. svcs. Prudential Securities, Inc., N.Y.C., 1981-95; v.p. adminstrv. svcs. Prudential Ins. Co., Newark, 1995—. Active Worldwide Marriage Encounter, Montclair, N.J., 1975-81; bd. dirs. United Scleroderma Found., Watsonville, Calif., 1987. Mem. Nat. Assn. Accts., Nat. Purchasing Mgrs. Assn., Assn. Corp. Travel Execs. (bd. govs.). Roman Catholic. Home: 57 Eastern Dr Kendall Park NJ 08824-1321 Office: Prudential Securities One New York Pla New York NY 10292-0804 E-mail: ernest.dangelo@prudential.com.

D'ANGELO, GONDA, retired social worker; b. Munich, Mar. 8, 1934; came to U.S., 1948; d. Karl and Caroline (Pauk) Süssheim; m. S. Michael D'Angelo; children: Carolyn, Lisa, Cynthia. BA, Queens Coll., 1955; MSW, Fordham U., 1984. Cert. social worker, N.Y. Med. social worker No. Westchester Hosp. Ctr., Mt. Kisco, N.Y., 1974-86, coord. sr. svcs., 1986-95; ret., 1995. Social work cons. Friends in Svc. Helping (FISH), Mt. Kisco, 1989—. Mem. adv. coun. N.Y. State Electric and Gas, Putnam, 1991—, Vol. Svc. Bur. of Westchester, N.Y., 1990-94; chair, co-chair No. Westchester Geriatric Com., 1990—; chair Geriatric Cmty. Care Network, Westchester, 1990-94; program asst. Am. Cancer Soc., Westchester County, 1992-94; vol. Bedford (N.Y.) Free Libr., 1995—; North Westchester rep. County Office for Aging, White Plains, N.Y., 1984-94. Mem. Queens Coll. Alumni Assn., Fordham U. Alumni Assn., Zeta Tau Alpha. Avocations: golf, tennis, reading, travel. Home: 101 Appleby Dr Bedford NY 10506-1341

D'ANGELO, JOSEPH FRANCIS, publishing company executive; b. Astoria, N.Y., July 4, 1930; s. Frank and Matilda (Oliveri) D'A.; m. Marcia Elaine Mackie, Mar. 4, 1965; children: Elena, Joseph Francis. BBA, St. John's U., 1952; PhD (hon.), St. John's U., William Penn Coll. Mem. Haskins & Sells CPAs, N.Y.C., 1952-61; treas., contr. internat. ops. Borden Co., Panama and P.R., 1961-65; from v.p. to pres. King Features Syndicate divsn. Hearst Corp., N.Y.C., 1973-96, chmn., 1997—; resident contr., 1965-73; bus. mgr., 1968-73; gen. mgr., 1973-75; pres., dir. King Features Syndicate, Inc., 1973-97. Pres., bd. dirs. Cowles Syndicate Inc., 1986-97, NAS, Inc., 1987-97; chmn. King Features Syndicate, Inc., Cowles, Inc., NAS, Inc., 1997—. Mem. Com. of 300 Archdiocese of N.Y.; bd. dirs. Alcoholism Coun. Greater N.Y.; trustee Emerson Coll., Boston, North Shore Univ. Hosp., pres. Mus. Cartoon Art and Hall of Fame, Boca Raton, Fla., Bd. of Trade. Mem. Artists and Writers Assn., Nat. Cartoonists Soc., Newspaper Features Coun., N.Y. Newspaper Pubs. Assn., N.Y. State Soc. Newspaper Editors, So. Newspaper Pubs. Assn., Sigma Delta Chi, Dutch Treat Club, Friars Club, N.Y. Athletic Club, Overseas Press Club, Wheatley Hills Golf Club, Knights of Malta. Republican. Roman Catholic. Office: King Features Syndicate Inc 959 Eighth Ave New York NY 10019

D'ANGELO, ROBERT WILLIAM, lawyer; b. Buffalo, Nov. 10, 1932; s. Samuel and Margaret Theresa Guercio D'A.; m. Ellen Frances Neary, Sept. 17, 1959; children: Christopher Robert, Gregory Andrew. BBA, Loyola U. Los Angeles, 1954; JD, UCLA, 1960. Bar: Calif. 1960; cert. specialist taxation law. Practiced in L.A., 1960-89; mem. firm. Myers & D'Angelo, Pasadena, Calif., 1967—. Adj. prof. law, taxation Whittier Coll. Sch. of Law., 1981 Served to capt. USAF, 1954-57. Mem. ABA, AICPA, State Bar Calif., L.A. County Bar Assn., Wilshire Bar Assn., Pasadena Bar Assn., Calif. Soc. CPAs, Am. Assn. Atty. CPAs, Calif. Assn. Atty. CPAs (pres. 1980), Phi Delta Phi, Alpha Sigma Nu. Home: 1706 Highland Ave Glendale CA 91202-1265 Office: 301 N Lake Ave Ste 800 Pasadena CA 91101-4108 E-mail: m-dlaw@pacbell.net.

D'ANGELO, THOMAS J. not-for-profit developer, financial consultant; b. Paterson, N.J., July 31, 1941; s. Stephen and Ann D'Angelo; m. Patricia LaGatutta, Nov. 15, 1998; m. Ruth D'Angelo (div.); children: Christine, Thomas. BA in econ., Fairleigh Dickinson U., Teaneck, N.J., 1968. Credit supr. Irving Trust Co., N.Y.C., 1965—68; sr. regional mgr. Summit Bank, Princeton, NJ, 1968—99; pres., CEO Charitable Emporium.Com, Inc., Newark, 1999—. Adv. coun. Independence Cmty. Bank, Newark, 2001—. Exec. com., bd. dirs. New Cmty. Found.; bd. trustees Essex County Work Force Investment Bd., Essex County Econ. Devel. Corp. Meadowlink; bd. dirs. Althea Gibson Found., chmn. fund raising gala, 1999—2000; bd. dirs. Hispanic Am. C. of C. Found., chmn. fund raising gala, 2002; first v.p., bd. dirs. Meadowlands C. of C. Nat. guard, 1960—66, Lodi, N.J. Recipient Bus. & Cmty. Leadership commendation, Meadowlands Regional C. of C., 1996, Outstanding Achievement award, Girl Scout Coun. Bergen County, Paramus, N.J., 1999. Avocations: golf, music. Home: 3 Diamond Ct Glen Rock NJ 07452 Business E-Mail: tj@cecharity.com.

D'ANGELO-MAYER, IDA, lawyer; b. Long Island City, N.Y., Aug. 22, 1967; d. Fileno Domenico and Nicoletta D'Angelo; m. Robert Michael Mayer, May 6, 1995; children: Robert Mayer, Ariana Nicole Mayer. BS, Fordham U. at Lincoln Ctr, 1988; JD, St. John's U., Jamaica, N.Y., 1992. Bar: N.Y. 1992, N.J. 1993, U.S. Dist. Ct. (ea. and so. dists.) N.Y. 1993. Assoc. atty. Law Offices of Peter T. Roach, Westbury, N.Y., 1992-94, Ida D'Angelo & Assocs., P.C., Melville, NY, 1994—. Mem. ABA, N.Y. State Bar Assn., Suffolk County Bar Assn. Office: 555 Broadhollow Rd Melville NY 11747-5078

D'ANGIO, GIULIO JOHN, radiologist, educator; b. N.Y.C., May 2, 1922; s. Carlo and Rosa (Calderazzo) D'A.; m. Jean Chittenden Terhune, Aug. 27, 1955; children: Carl, Peter. AB, Columbia U., 1943; MD, Harvard U., 1945; D. Medicine and Surgery (hon.), U. Bologna, 1983. Diplomate: Am. Bd. Radiology, Am. Bd. Therapeutic Radiology. Surg. intern Children's Hosp., Boston, 1945-46, tng. in pathology, 1948-49; resident in radiology Boston City Hosp., 1949-53; also mem. staff; radiation therapist Children's Hosp., Boston, 1956-62; researcher Donner Lab., also Lawrence Radiation Lab., U. Calif., Berkeley, 1962-63; dir. divsn. radiation therapy U. Minn. Med. Sch., 1964-68; chmn. dept. radiation therapy Meml. Hosp., N.Y.C., 1968-76; dir. children's cancer rsch. ctr. Children's Hosp., Phila., 1976-89; prof. radiation oncology Hosp. of U. Pa., Phila., 1976-92, vice chmn., clin. dir. dept. radiation oncology, 1989-92, prof. emeritus, 1992—; prof. pediatric oncology U. Pa. Med. Sch., Phila., 1976-92. Chmn. Nat. Wilms Tumor Study Com., 1968-91; past chmn. cancer clin. investigation rev. com. Nat. Cancer Inst. Editor-in-chief Med. and Pediat. Oncology, 1996-2003; contbr. numerous articles to med. jours. Capt. M.C. AUS, 1946-48. Decorated Commendation medal; recipient ann. award Am. Cancer Soc., 1978, Heath Meml. award M.D. Anderson Tumor and Cancer Inst., 1979, Gold medal Am. Soc. Therapeutic Radiation Oncologists, 1999, Gold medal Charles U., Prague, cert. merit Pres. Italian Republic, 2003, Charles U., 2003. Fellow Royal Coll. Radiology, Am. Acad. Pediatrics; mem. Am. Acad. Pediat. (past chmn. sect. oncology-hematology), AAAS, Am. Assn. Cancer Rsch., Am. Coll. Radiology, Am. Soc. Therapeutic Radiologists, Mass. Med. Soc., Pa. Med. Soc., Royal Soc. Medicine, Internat. Soc. Pediat. Oncology (pres. 1987), Radiol. Soc. N.Am., Am. Radium Soc., Soc. Pediat. Radiology, Phi Beta Kappa. Episcopalian. Home: 518 Cedar Ln Swarthmore PA 19081-1105 Office: U Pa Hosp Dept Radiation Oncology 3400 Spruce St Philadelphia PA 19104-4206

DANGOOR, DAVID EZRA RAMSI, consumer goods company executive; b. Teheran, Iran, Aug. 3, 1949; arrived in sweden, 1950, came to U.S., 1987; s. Selim Eliaho and Ruth (Lehr) D.; m. Ida (Ide) Weitzen, May 24, 1992; children: Rebecca Frances, Diana Katherine, Louisa Faye, Selim Edward. Civilekonom (MBA), Stockholm Sch. Econs., Sweden, 1973. Asst. dir. Scandinavian Supplies AB, Stockholm, 1970-74; asst. corp. treas. AGA Group AB, Stockholm, 1974-76; asst. to v.p. Philip Morris Europe, Middle East & Africa, Lausanne, Switzerland, 1976; dept. mktg. dir. Philip Morris Co. Germany, Munich, Fed. Republic Germany, 1977-80; area dir. No. Europe Seven Up Internat., London, 1980-84; pres. Benson & Hedges Can. Inc., Philip Morris Internat., Montreal, Que., Can., 1984-86; sr. v.p. mktg. Philip Morris USA, N.Y.C., 1987-92; exec. v.p. Philip Morris Internat., Rye Brook, N.Y., 1992—. Bd. dirs. Rothmans, Benson & Hedges, Inc., Toronto, 1987—; mem. bd. dirs. and exec. com. Swedish Am. C. of C., N.Y., 1996-2001, chmn., 1998-2001; bd. dirs. Fgn. Policy Assn. N.Y., 1997—. Exec. v.p. Student Assn. Palmgrenska Samskolan, Stockholm, 1966-68; bd. dirs. Student Assn. Stockholm Sch. Bus. Adminstrn. and Econs., 1969-72, Am. Scandinavian Found., 1999—; officer Royal Swedish Coast Art; exec. bd. dirs. Raoul Wallenberg Com. of U.S., 1990-93; trustee Arthur F. Burns Fellowships, 1997—; mem. internat. devel. com. Internat. Fedn. Multiple Sclerosis Socs., 1993-95. Fellow Amaranten, Sweden, 1971. Mem. Swedish Am. C. of C. (bd. dirs. exec. com. 1996—), Sallskapet Club (Stockholm), Hurlingham Club (London), Hillside Tennis Club (Montreal), Southampton (N.Y.) Bath and Tennis Club, The Tuxedo Park (N.Y.) Club. Avocations: squash, tennis, sailing, bridge.

DANGREMOND, DALE JOAN, executive director, chief operating officer, consultant; b. Seneca Falls, N.Y., Dec. 31, 1957; d. James Leroy and Joan Ottellie (Kross) Dangremond; m. William P. Tedesco, July 19, 1997; children: Zachary James, William Lucas. B of Social Work, Rochester Inst. Tech., 1979; cert., Nat. Tech. Inst. for the Deaf, Rochester, N.Y., 1980; MBA, U. Phoenix, 1990. Ind. interpreter, Rochester, 1980-81; social worker Rochester Rehab. Ctr., 1981-82; coord. deaf svcs. The Workshop, Inc., Albany, N.Y., 1982-84; instr., interpreter tng./human svcs. Cen. Piedmont Community Coll., Charlotte, N.C., 1984-85; exec. dir. Ctr. on Deafness, Denver, 1985-88; asst. exec. dir. Seneca ARC, Waterloo, N.Y., 1988-90; cons. Labor Rels. Alternatives, Albany, N.Y., 1990-98; COO Nat. Chldrns. Ctr., Wash., DC, 1998-2000; chief program ops. Dept. Human Svcs. Mental Retardation/Devel. Disabilities Adminstrn., Washington, 2000; ind. cons. Washington, 2000—. Adj. instr. interpreter tng. SUNY, Albany, 1982-84; dir. adv. com. on deafness State of Colo., Denver, 1985-88. Sec. Colo. Ind. Living Network, Denver, 1985-88. Democrat. Unitarian Universalist. Avocations: tennis, gourmet cooking. Home: 8413 River Rock Terrace Bethesda MD 20817 E-mail: ddangremon@aol.com.

DANGREMOND, DAVID W. fine arts educator; b. Norristown, Pa., June 8, 1952; s. James L. and Joan O. (Kross) D.; m. Mary Plant Spivy, Oct. 18, 1980; children: Saumel Plant Chapin, Augustus Welles Ewing. BA cum laude, Amherst Coll., 1974; MA, U. Del., 1976, Yale U., 1987, MPhil, 1990. Dir. Webb-Deane-Stevens Mus., Wethersfield, Conn., 1976-80, Bennington Mus., Vt., 1980-96; adj. prof. fine arts Trinity Coll., Hartford, Conn., 1996—. Adj. prof. art history U. Hartford, Conn., 1977-80; tutor Historic Deerfield, Mass., 1975; trustee Williamstown (Mass.) Regional Art Conservation Lab., 1981-86, Florence Griswold Mus., Old Lyme, Conn., 1987—, v.p., 1992—; trustee Conn. Humanities Coun., 1997—; mem. adv. bd. Gunston Hall Plantation, Lorton, Va., 1985—, Nat. Trust Hist. Preservation; dir. Attingham Summer Sch., Shropshire, Eng., 1980—; profl. adv. bd. Victoria Mus., Portland, Maine, 1985—; bd. overseers Strawberry Banke Mus., Portsmouth, N.H., 1987—, v.p., 1988-90; mem. exec. com. Yale U. Art Gallery Assocs., 1987-93; mus. cons. various mus., 1995. Foreword author: Heritage Houses: the American Tradition in Connecticut 1660-1900, 1979; contbr. articles to jours. Bd. dirs. Hartford Architecture Conservancy, 1978-80; mem. adv. bd. Deacon John Grave Found.; mem. art and antiques coun. Conn. Pub. TV, Hartford, 1977-80; mem. concert com. Vt. Symphony Orch., 1980-86; trustee Musical Masterworks, 1992—, v.p. 1998—; div. head United Way Bennington County, 1982-84; del. Gov.'s Conf. on Future of Vt.'s Heritage, Montpelier, 1982; sr. warden St. Peter's Episcopal Ch., 1985—; bd. govs. Hill-Stead Mus., Farmington, 1990—; trustee Wadsworth Atheneum, Hartford, 1991—, exec. com., 1995—, chmn. curatorial com., 1995—, chmn. ethics com. 1996—, v.p. 1998—; trustee Conn. Hist. Soc., 1989—. Fellow Historic Deerfield, 1973; Winterthur fellow H.F. duPont Winterthur Mus., 1974-76; Sir George Trevelyan scholar Attingham summer sch., Shropshire, Eng., 1976 Mem. Am. Assn. for State and Local History (state awards chmn.), New Eng. Mus. Assn. (exec. com. 1985-86), Am. Assn. Mus. (accreditation vis. com., mus. assessment program cons.), Vt. Mus. and Gallery Alliance (pres. 1983-86), Greater Hartford Assn. of Historic Houses (bd. dirs.), Decorative Arts Soc., Am. Ceramics Circle, Coll. Art Assn., Soc. Archtl. Historians, Century Assn. (N.Y.C.), Knickerbocker Club (N.Y.C.), Grolier Club (N.Y.C.), Hartford Club, Old Lyme Country, Yale Club N.Y.C., Lawn Club (New Haven), Dauntless Club (Essex), Newport Reading Rm. Episcopalian.

DANGUE REWAKA, DENIS, diplomat; Permanent rep. of Gabonese Republic UN, N.Y.C. Office: UN Permanent Mission Gabon 18 E 41st St Fl 9 New York NY 10017-6222

DANIEL, ARLIE VERL, speech education educator; b. Spencer, Iowa, May 15, 1943; s. Arlie Verl and Eleanor Marie (Grover) D. AA, Iowa Lakes C.C., 1963; BA, Morningside Coll., 1965; MA, U. Iowa, 1978; PhD, U. Nebr., 1981. High sch. tchr. Missouri Valley (Iowa) Pub. Schs., 1965-68, Clinton (Iowa) Pub. Schs., 1971-78; dir. speech edn. East Cen. U., Ada, Okla., 1981—. Co-author: Project Text for Public Speaking, 6th edit., 1991; co-author chpt. in Basic Communication Course Annual, 1994; editor: Activities Integrating Oral Communication Skills for Students in Grades K-8, 1992; contbr. chpt. to Teaching and Directing the Basic Communication Course, 1993; contbg. author Creating Competent Communicators: Activities for Teaching, Speaking, Listening and Media Literacy in the K-12 Classroom, 2003. 1st lt. U.S. Army, 1968-71. Mem. AAUP, Assn. Tchr. Educators, Internat. Comm. Assn., Okla. Speech Theatre Comm. Assn. (pres. 1986-87, exec. sec. 1989-92, Outstanding Comm. Educator award 1985, Josh Lee Svc. award 1992, Spl. award for contbns. to profession 1994), Ctrl. States Comm. Assn. (life, exec. dir. 1994-97, v.p., 1997-98, pres. elect, 1998-99, pres. 1999-2000, past pres. 2000-2001, Outstanding Young Speech Tchr. award 1985), Nat. Comm. Assn. (life), Rotary Internat. (chair youth com. Ada chpt. 1994—, pres. elect 2002-03, pres. Ada 2003-04, dist. 5770 Interact chair 1995-2003, Rotaract chair, 2003—), Pi Kappa Delta. Democrat. Methodist. Avocations: golf, bowling, wine making. Home: 1206 Tower Rd Ada OK 74820-6106 Office: East Cen U Communication Dept Ada OK 74820-6899 E-mail: adaniel@csca.ecok.edu.

DANIEL, BARBARA ANN, retired elementary school educator; b. LaCrosse, Wis., Mar. 22, 1938; d. Rudolph J. and Dorothy M. (Farnham) Beranek; m. David Daniel; children: Raychelle, Clarence, Bernadette, Brenda. BS in Edn. cum laude, Midwestern U., Wichita Falls, Tex., 1967; postgrad., U. Alaska, Fairbanks, Anchorage, Juneau, U. Alaska, Bethel. Cert. tchr., Alaska. Primary tchr. Bur. Indian Affairs, Nunapitchuk and Tuntutuliak, Alaska, 1967-70; tchr., generalist, English, English Lang. Devel., ESL, U.S. Govt. journalism and health Lower Kuskokwim Sch. Dist., Tuntutuliak, 1981—2003, English lang. leader grades k-12, 1995—2002, ret., 2003. Mem. lang. arts curriculum revision task force Lower Kuskokwim Sch. Dist., 1990; past mem. state bd. Academic Pentathlon, Alaska; past acad. decathlon, pentathlon coach, 1980's. Rsch. video rec. of elders in Alaskan village. Mem.: NEA, Alaska Coun. Tchrs. English. Home: 25 West Circle PO Box Wtl-8048 Tuntutuliak AK 99680

DANIEL, BARBARA ANN, realtor, advertising executive; b. Pineville, Ky., May 28, 1954; d. Charles Edward and Emma Walters; m. Michael Daniel, Dec. 23, 1973; children: Michael Alan, Charles Edward. A, S.E. C.C., Cumberland, Ky., 1992. Lic. real estate Tenn. Real Estate Commn., 2000. Receptionist Daniel Boone Clinic, Harlan, Ky., 1973—81; instrnl. tchr.'s aide Loyall (Ky.) Elem., 1986—89; tchr.'s aide, bus driver Ky. Cmty. Econ. Opportunity Coun./Head Start, Harlan, 1989—90; spl. edn. instrnl. aide Harlan (Ky.) Elem., 1991—92; 4-H asst. U. Ky. Coop. Ext. Svc., Harlan, 1992—93; advt. sales rep. Middlesboro (Ky.) Daily News, 1994—95, The Bargain Banner, Harlan, 1995—96, Powell Valley News, Pennington Gap, Va., 1996—. Affiliate broker The Realty Group, Tazewell, Tenn., 2000—01; realtor Rosenbalm Real Estate, 2001—. Author: (children picture book) Kara and the Butterfly. Writer/dir. plays Liggett (Ky.) Bapt. Ch., 1982—88, youth dir., 1982—88; vol. instrnl. tchr.'s aide Holy Trinity Sch., Harlan. Recipient Ready award (real estate advt. of distinction), Nat. Newspaper Am., 2001. Baptist. Avocations: painting, hiking, travel, bicycling. Home: 457 Boone Dr Harrogate TN 37752 Personal E-mail: daniel2@netcommander.com.

DANIEL, BETH, professional golfer; b. Charleston, S.C., Oct. 14, 1956; d. Robert and Lucia D. Grad., Furman U., 1978. Profl. golfer Ladies Profl. Golf Assn. tour, 1979—. Winner U.S. Amateur Title, 1975, 77; youngest mem. S.C. Hall of Fame, 1979. Winner 32 LPGA events including Patty Berg Classic, 1979, World Ladies, Japan, 1979, World Series Women's Golf, 1980, 81, Columbia Savs. Classic, 1980, 82, Patty Berg Classic, 1980, Golden Lights, 1980, J.C. Penney Classic, 1981, 90 (with Davis Love III), Lady Citurs, 1981, Bent Tree Classic, 1982, Sun City Classic, 1982, Birmingham Classic, 1982, J & B Putting Championship, 1982, 85, WUI Classic, 1982, McDonald's Kids Classic, 1983, Kyocera Inamori Classic, 1985, Rail Charity Classic, 1989, 90, Konica San Jose Classic, 1989, Greater Washington Open, 1989, Safeco Classic, 1989, LPGA Championship, 1990, Orix Hawaiian Open, 1990, Kemper Open, 1990, Centel Classic, 1990, Northgate Classic, McDonald's Championship, Phar Mor Classic, 1990, 91, Corning Classic, 1994, Oldsmobile Classic, 1994, Big Apple Classic, 1994, Ping Welch's Championship, 1995; Mazda Series winner, 1982; named Rookie of Yr., Ladies Profl. Golf Assn., 1979, Player of Yr., 1980, 90, 94, Golfer of Yr., Seagrams Seven Crown Royal, 1981, A.P. Female Athlete of Yr., 1990; inducted into L.P.G.A. Hall of Fame, 1999, World Golf Hall of Fame, 2000. Achievements include being the leading money winner in LPGA, 1980, 81, 90.

DANIEL, CATHY BROOKS, tutor, educational consultant; b. Nashville, Sept. 1, 1946; d. Conway William and Alliene Marie (Gilliam) B.; m. James Newton Daniel Jr., Dec. 29, 1967 (div. July 1988; children: Laura Marie, James Newton III. Student, Memphis State U., 1964-66; BS, George Peabody Coll., 1968, MA, 1971. Cert. elem. tchr., special edn. tchr., learning disabilities and behavior disorders. Tchr. Fairview (Tenn.) Elem. Sch., 1968-69; special edn. tchr. Ross Elem. Sch., Nashville, 1969-70, Rosebank Elem. Sch., Nashville, 1970-71, Graymar Elem. Sch., Nashville, 1971-73, Norman Binkley Elem. Sch., Nashville, 1973-74; cons. ednl. and family counseling, ednl. testing Franklin, Tenn., 1976—. Methodist. Avocation: tennis. Home and Office: 2203 Springdale Dr Franklin TN 37064-4962

DANIEL, CHARLES DWELLE, JR., consultant, retired army officer; b. San Antonio, Oct. 30, 1925; s. Charles Dwelle and Jean Elizabeth (Stormont) D.; m. Ann Meredith Carter, June 7, 1946; children: Charles Dwelle III, Peter C. BS, U.S. Mil. Acad., 1946; MS, Tulane U., 1961, PhD, 1968; BA in Studio Art, Am. U., 1987. Joined U.S. Army; advanced through grades to maj. gen.; F.A. battery comdr. U.S. Army (3d inf. div.), Korean War, 1950-52; adviser Ky. N.G., Louisville, 1953-55; F.A. missile officer 7th U.S. Army Europe, 1956-59; physicist Def. Atomic Support Agy., 1963-66; F.A. bn. and divsn. artillery comdr. 1st inf. divsn., 1966-67; divsn. chief, dir. Office of Chief of U.S. Army R&D, 1968-71; comdg. gen. I Corps, Arty., Korea, 1971; dep. comdg. gen. Korean Support Command, 1971-72; dir. army rsch. Dept. Army, Washington, 1972-74, dir. combat support systems, 1974; dep. comdt. Nat. War Coll., Ft. McNair, Washington, 1974-75; spl. asst. to comdg. gen. U.S. Army Materiel Command, Alexandria, Va., 1975-77; comdg. gen. U.S. Army Electronics R&D Command, Adelphi, Md., 1977-79; ret., 1979. Dir. target acquisition BDM Corp., McLean, Va., 1979-80; cons. Burdeshaw Assocs., 1981—; bd. dirs. Microwave Semicondr. Corp. 1983-89. Decorated D.S.M., Silver Star, Legion of Merit with oak leaf cluster, D.F.C., Bronze Star with 4 oak leaf clusters, Air medal with 16 oak leaf clusters, Joint Svc. Commendation medal, Army Commendation medal U.S., Vietnamese Cross of Gallantry with silver star; named Hon. Col. 33d Regiment, U.S. Field Artillery, 2003. Mem. SAR, Assn. U.S. Army, Assn. Grads. U.S. Mil. Acad. Home: 4904 Baltan Rd Bethesda MD 20816-2404 Office: Burdeshaw Assocs Ltd 4701 Sangamore Rd Bethesda MD 20816-2508

DANIEL, CHARLES TIMOTHY, transportation engineer, consultant; b. N.Y.C., Aug. 3, 1958; s. John Carl and Eleanor (Sauer) D.; m. Melissa J. Sanft, Mar. 4, 1995. BA in Engring., Lafayette Coll., 1980; MS in Transp., MIT, 1982; MBA, NYU, 1991. Staff engr. George Beetle Co., Phila., 1983-84; project engr. Transamerica Leasing, Purchase, N.Y., 1984-87, mgr. tech. svcs. White Plains, N.Y., 1987-89, engring. cons., 1989—. Treas. Midtown Daniel Corp., 1990—, pres., 1995—; mem. domestic freight container stds. subcom. Internat. Standardization Orgn. Tech. Com. on Freight Containers, 1986-88. Mem. alumni bd. Rutgers Preparatory Sch., Somerset, N.J., 1985—; county committeeman Middlesex County (N.J.) Dem. Orgn., 1992—. Mem. ASCE, Sigma Xi, Beta Gamma Sigma. Lutheran. Achievements include development of code structure for electronic data interchange of freight container chassis repair data. Home: 33 North Dr East Brunswick NJ 08816-1124 Office: Midtown Daniel Corp 645 Madison Ave Fl 20 New York NY 10022-1010

DANIEL, COLDWELL, III, economist, educator; b. New Orleans; s. Coldwell Jr. and Josephine Agnes (Weick) D.; children: Anne Alexis, Coldwell IV. BBA, Tulane U., 1949; MBA, Ind. U., 1950; PhD, U. Va., 1959; postdoctoral, U. Chgo., 1964-65. Instr. stats. U. Va., 1955-56; instr. econs. Pomona Coll., 1956-57; prof. econs., dept. chmn. U. So. Miss., 1958-65; prof. econs. U. Houston, 1965-70, U. Memphis, 1970—. Rsch. coord. So. Calif. Rsch. Coun., 1956-57; vis. prof. La. State U., 1959; sr. Fulbright prof. econs. Dacca U., Bangladesh, 1961-62; Disting. Fulbright lectr. Shanghai Jiao Tong U., 2001; project dir. Miss. Test Facility Econ. Impact Study NASA, 1963; prin. The Anwell Co., Memphis, 1974—; disting. Fulbright lectr. Shanghai Jiao Tong U., 2001; candidate Fulbright Sr. Specialist Roster, 2002-2005. Author: Mathematical Models in Microeconomics, 1970; reader Jour. Econ. and Bus., 1991—, Social Sci. Jour., 1988—, Am. Jour. Econs. and Sociology, 1990—, Jour. Econ. Edn., 1997—, Internat. Econ. Jour., 1999—, Am. Econ. Rev., 2000; founder, chmn. bd. editors, The So. Quar., 1962-64; co-founder and manuscript rev. editor Jour. Econs. and Fin., 1977-91; mem. editl. bd. Jour. Econs. and Fin., 1991-94, Jour. Econs. and Fin. Edn., 2002—; assoc. editor for econs. Social Sci. Quar., 1968-70, mem. editl. bd., 1972-84; contbr. articles to profl. jours. Trustee Christ United Meth. Ch. With USAF, 1945-46; 1st lt. U.S. Army, 1951-53. Decorated Bronze Star; NSF Sci. Faculty fellow, 1964-66. Fellow Acad. Econs. and Fin.; mem. Am. Econ. Assn., Pakistan Econ. Assn. (life), Southwestern Econs. Assn., Acad. Econs. and Fin. (co-founder, pres. 1977-78, area coord. Indsl. Orgn. and pub. Policy, 1990-94, Disting. Svc. award 1979, Cert. Appreciation 1981), Mo. Valley Econs. Assn. (pres. 1984-85, Meritorious Svc. award 1986), So. Econ. Assn., Atlantic Econ. Soc. (exec. com. 1991-94, area coord. Indsl. Orgn. and Pub. Policy 1989-94), The Raven Soc., Sigma Xi, Beta Gamma Sigma, Omicron Delta Kappa, Pi Kappa Pi, Omicron Delta Epsilon, Pi Gamma Mu, Delta Tau Kappa, Pi Sigma Epsilon, Delta Sigma Pi. Office: U Memphis Dept Econs Memphis TN 38152-0001

DANIEL, DANIELE MALLISON, elementary school educator; b. Portsmouth, Va., Aug. 16, 1962; d. Howard Danford and Norma Mae (Gibbs) Mallison; m. Edward W. Daniel; 1 child, Benjamin W. BFA in Art Edn., Va. Commonwealth U., 1984. Cert. tchr. K-12, Va.; cert. therapeutic recreation asst. Activity dir. Eldercare Gardens Nursing Home, Charlotteville, Va., 1985-86; itinerant art tchr. Henry County Pub. Schs., Collinsville, Va., 1986-87; contract substitute Louisa County (Va.) Pub. Schs., 1988; middle/h.s. art tchr. Grayson County Pub. Schs., Independence, Va., 1988-90; elem. art resource tchr. Orange County (Va.) Pub. Schs., 1990-99, elem. gifted edn. tchr., 1999—. Upward Bound art tchr. Wytheville (Va.) C.C., summer 1990; tchr./cons. Henry County Pub. Schs. in conjunction with Va. Dept. Edn., Collinsville, 1987. Lifetime mem. Va. 4-H All Stars; chmn. young adults Gordonsville United Meth. Ch.,

1994-2000, choir, 1994—. Folk Artist grantee Va. Commn. for the Arts, 1992-93, 93-94, Video Arts grantee, 1995-96. Mem. NEA, Va. Edn. Assn., Nat. Art Edn. Assn., Va. Art Edn. Assn., Nat. Therapeutic Recreation Assn., Gordonsville Jaycees (sec. 1992, 94, state dir. 1993). Avocations: arts and crafts, reading, travel, horses, researching native american heritage. Home: 11445 Knolls Rd Orange VA 22960-4554 Office: Orange County Pub Schs PO Waugh Rd Orange VA 22960-0204 E-mail: searchclass@yahoo.com.

DANIEL, DAVID EDWIN, civil engineer, educator; b. Newport News, Va., Dec. 20, 1949; s. David Edwin and Betty Ruth (Aschenback) D.; m. Frances Louise Locker, June 12, 1971 (div.); children: Katherine Ruth, William Monroe; m. Susan Nielsen Brady, May 12, 1989; 1 child, Alexander David. BS, U. Tex., 1972, MS, 1974, PhD, 1980. Staff engr. Woodward-Clyde, San Francisco, 1974-77; asst. prof. U. Tex., Austin, 1981-85, assoc. prof., 1985-91, prof., 1991-96; prof., head dept. civil engring. U. Ill., Urbana, 1996-2001, dean, engring., 2001—. Recipient Richard R. Torrens award Am. Soc. of Civil Engineers, 1995 Mem. ASCE (Norman medal 1975, Cross medal 1984, 2000, Middlebrooks award 1995), NAE. Office: U Ill Coll Engring Urbana IL 61801

DANIEL, DAVID RONALD, management consultant; b. Hartford, Conn., Feb. 26, 1930; s. David Richard and Marion (Ingalls) D.; m. Lise C. Scott; children: David, Peter, Stephen. AB, Wesleyan U., Middletown, Conn., 1952; MBA, Harvard U., 1954; LHD (hon.), Wesleyan U. Assoc. McKinsey & Co. Inc., NYC, 1957-63, prin., 1963-68, dir., 1968—, mng. dir. NY office, 1970-76, mng. dir. firm, 1976-88. Contbr. articles to profl. jours. Chmn. emeritus Wesleyan U.; mem. corp. and bd. overseers, treas. Harvard U.; chmn. Harvard Mgmt. Co.; chmn. bd. fellows Harvard Med. Sch.; trustee Rockefeller U., Thirteen/WNET, NY Mem. Coun. on Fgn. Rels. Home: 580 Park Ave New York NY 10021-7313 Office: McKinsey & Co Inc 55 E 52nd St Fl 21 New York NY 10055-0183

DANIEL, GARY WAYNE, motivation and behavior consultant; b. Wendall, Idaho, June 22, 1948; s. Milan Chauncey Daniel and Ila Fay (Cox) Harkins. AA, Boise Bus. Coll., 1969; PhD in Psychology, Westbrook U., 1994. Cert. master practitioner Neuro Linguistic Programming. Pres., chief exec. officer Victory Media Group, Santa Rosa, Calif., 1985—. Gen. mgr. Victory Record Label, 1986—; also bd. dirs.; bd. dirs. Bay City Records, San Francisco; pres. Lightforce Music Pub., Santa Rosa, 1987—; mktg. cons. Fienze Records, San Francisco, 1987—, Capital Bus. Sys., Napa, Calif., 1986-91. Author: Concert Operations Manual, 1987; devel. of the Neuro Achievement System. Named Top Radio Personality Idaho State Broadcasters Assn., 1971. Mem. ASCAP, NARAS, Ind. Record Mfrs. and Distbrs., Am. Coun. Hypnotist Examiners, Hypnotist Examiners Coun. Calif., Am. Assn. Behavioral Therapists, Internat. Assn. Neuro Linguistic Programming. Office: Allura du Jour 1606 4th St Santa Rosa CA 95404

DANIEL, JAMES, curator, business executive, writer, former editor; b. Davidson County, N.C., June 6, 1916; s. James Manly and Bert (Fletcher) Daniel; m. Ramona Teijeiro, Apr. 15, 1939 (dec. May 2000); children: Jane Clare, Ramona Nina. AB, U. N.C., 1937; Nieman fellow, Harvard, 1942-43. Reporter Raleigh (N.C.) News & Observer, 1937-40, Washington Daily News, 1941, city editor, 1946-47; with Office War Info., CBI, 1943-45; Washington corr. Scripps-Howard Papers, 1948-56; contbg. editor Time mag., 1957-60; roving editor Reader's Digest, 1961-81; pres. Healing Springs Properties, Inc.; curator Weston (Conn.) Town Hall Art Collection, 1992—. Author: (with J. G. Hubbell) Strike in the West, The Complete Story of the Cuban Crisis, 1963; editor: Private Investment, The Key to International Development, 1958. Mem.: Harvard (N.Y.C.). Home: 183 Good Hill Rd Weston CT 06883-2312

DANIEL, JAMES RICHARD, accountant, computer company financial executive; b. Chgo., June 26, 1947; s. Elmer Alexander and June B. (Bush) D.; m. Marsha Ruth Stone, Nov. 8, 1969; children: Jennifer Rae, Michael James. BS in Acctg., U. Ill., 1970; MBA, Loyola U., 1974. CPA, Ill., La. Dir. fin. Baxter Travenol Labs., Chgo., 1974-79; corp. contr. Bio-Rad Labs. Inc., Richmond, Calif., 1979-81; v.p., treas., contr. Lykes Bros. Steamship Co. Inc., New Orleans, 1981-84; CFO SCI Systems Inc., Huntsville, Ala., 1984-91; sr. v.p., CFO Dell Computer Corp., Austin, Tex., 1991-93; exec. v.p., CFO, pres. hdqrs. support, treas. MicroAge, Inc., Tempe, 1993-2000; cons., 2000-01; sr. v.p., CFO PetsMart Inc., Phoenix, 2001. Mem. issuer affairs com. NASDAQ, 1995-2001. With U.S. Army, 1970-73. Recipient Outstanding Alumnus award Loyola U. Grad. Sch. Bus., 1995. Mem. AICPA. Republican. Home: 3858 E Cholla Ln Phoenix AZ 85028-5023 E-mail: jdanieletal@aol.com.

DANIEL, JOHN GRIFFITH, physician; b. Richmond, Va., Apr. 27, 1955; s. Griffith Boyd and Evelyn Virginia (Patton) D.; m. Lisa Louise Newsome, Feb. 24, 1996; 1 child, Rebecca Lynn; 1 stepchild, Emma Katherine Harrison. BS, Va. Tech., 1977; MD, Med. Coll. Va., 1981. Diplomate Am. Bd. Family Practice. Intern Med. Coll. Va., Richmond; resident Blackstone (Va.) Family Practice, 1982-84; physician Reedville (Va.) Med. Clinic, 1984-85, Bay Harbor Med. Ctr., Burgess, Va., 1986-95, RCH Family Practice, Heathsville, Va., 1995—. Mem. AMA, Am. Acad. Family Practice, No. Neck Med. Assn. Home: 4 Surry St Heathsville VA 22473-2521 Office: CMG Family Medicine Heathsville VA 22473

DANIEL, KENNETH RULE, former iron and steel manufacturing company executive; b. Milford, Conn., Oct. 13, 1913; s. Cullen Coleman and Margaret Estelle (Elliott) D.; m. Virginia Moody Simpson, June 11, 1938; children: Kenneth Rule, Cullen Coleman, Robert Tennent Simpson, William Francis McKemie. BS, U. Ala., 1936, Profl. Degree in Mech. Engring., 1957, D.Sc., 1980. Registered profl. engr. Ala. With Am. Cast Iron Pipe Co., Birmingham, Ala., 1936-78, chief engr., 1948-55, v.p. engring., 1955-59, v.p. engring. and purchases, 1959-61, exec. v.p., 1961-63, pres., 1963-78, also dir., dir. various subsidiaries, 1963-78. Vice chmn. bd. 1st Ala. Bank of Birmingham, 1977-86; Sesquicentennial hon. prof. U. Ala., 1981; bd. dirs. L&N R.R., Seaboard Coast Line R.R., CSX R.R. Mem. Ala. Bd. of Registration for Profl. Engrs. and Land Surveyors, 1967-87; mem. regional adv. council Conf. Bd., 1967-78, Ala. Export Council, 1966-69; bd. dirs. Community Chest, 1965-78, Jr. Achievement, 1964-78, Birmingham Centennial Corp., 1968-73, Warrior Tombigbee Devel. Assn., 1963-78, L and N RR-Seaboard Coast Line RR-CSX RR, 1969-78; gen. co-chmn. United Appeal, 1964, chmn. indsl. div., 1958; chmn. Radio Free Europe, Birmingham, 1966; mem. Jefferson County Judicial Commn., 1967-72; chmn. adv. bd. Salvation Army, 1968-69, mem. adv. council home and hosp., mem. nat. adv. council, 1976— ; trustee Foundry Ednl. Found. (pres. 1964-65); trustee, mem. exec. com. So. Research Inst.; chmn. bd. trustees Jefferson County Cooper Green Hosp.; bd. visitors Berry Coll., Mt. Berry, Ga., 1968-78. Served to lt. col. AUS, 1941-46, ETO. Decorated Bronze Star, Legion of Merit; Croix de Guerre France; recipient Gold Knight of Mgmt. award Nat. Mgmt. Assn., 1965, William Booth award Salvation Army, 1967, Henry Laurence Gantt medal Am. Mgmt. Assn. and ASME, 1977, Exec. of the Yr. award Nat. Mgmt. Assn., 1978; named Engr. of the Yr., Birmingham Engring. Coun., 1967, Paladium medal Am. Engring. Soc. and Nat. Audubon Soc., 1986; elected to Ala. Acad. Honor, 1982, Nat. Mgmt. Assn. Hall of Fame, 1987, Ala. Engring. Hall of Fame, 1989. Fellow ASME (chmn. Birmingham sect. 1950-51, hon. mem. 1984); mem. NAM (dir. 1967-70), Am. Iron and Steel Inst. (bd. dirs. 1968-78), Assn. Industries Ala. (bd. dirs. 1963-78), Birmingham Area C. of C. (pres. 1969), Assn. Iron and Steel Engrs. (chmn. Birmingham Sect. 1954, nat. dir. 1955), Am. Ordnance Assn. (pres. Birmingham post 1964), Am. Foundrymen's Soc. (Thomas W. Pangborn Gold Medal award 1974), Am. Soc. for Engring. Edn., Engring. Soc. Birmingham, Newcomen Soc. N. Am., Birmingham Country Club, The Club, Mountain Brook Club, Masons (knight comdr. Ct. of Honor), Kiwanis, Sigma Alpha Epsilon, Theta Tau, Tau Beta Pi. Methodist. Office: PO Box 2727 Birmingham AL 35202-2727

DANIEL, LEON, journalist, newspaper columnist, editor; b. Etowah, Tenn., Aug. 8, 1931; s. Oscar Leon and Mary Nancy (Cook) D.; m. Carobel Heidt Calhoun, Oct. 26, 1963 (div.); 1 child, Lillian Fant. Student, U. Tenn., 1949-56. Reporter UP, Nashville, 1956-58; bur. mgr. UPI, Knoxville, Tenn., 1958-61, reporter Atlanta, 1961-66, corr. Saigon, 1966-67, Tokyo, 1967-70, mgr. for Thailand Bangkok, 1970-72, chief corr. for South Asia New Delhi, 1972-74, chief corr. for East Asia Manila, 1974, editor for Asia Hong Kong, 1974-77, editor for Europe London, 1977-80, nat. reporter Washington, 1980-87, mng. editor, internat., 1987-88, sr. editor, columnist, 1989-93; cons., columnist The Ind., Dhaka, Bangladesh, 1995. With USMC, 1950-53, Korea. Decorated Purple Heart. Mem. Phi Gamma Delta, Sigma Delta Chi. Democrat. Episcopalian. Home: 120 Turtle Creek Rd Charlottesville VA 22901-6763

DANIEL, MARIAN PHILLIPS, language educator, secondary school educator; b. Tulsa, Okla. d. Richard Tevier Daniel Jr. and Aena E. Martin. AA, Stephens Coll., Columbia, Missouri; BA in Romance Langs., U. Ark., 1964, MA, 1967. Cert. secondary edn. Tex. Edn. Agy. Editor, translator El Ganadero Internacional, San Antonio, 1967—82; secondary edn. educator South San Antonio Ind. Sch. Dist., 1993—2002; mem. faculty St. Philip's Coll., San Antonio, 2001—; secondary edn. educator N.E. Ind. Sch. Dist., San Antonio, 2002—. Mem. Cherokee Nation (western), Osage Tribe Indians. Mem.: Tex. Fgn. Lang. Assn. Roman Catholic. Avocations: swimming, scuba diving, travel, sailing. Office: St Philip's Coll 1801 Martin Luther King San Antonio TX 78203 E-mail: mdaniel16@mail.accd.edu.

DANIEL, MICHAEL EDWIN, insurance agency executive; b. Indpls., Sept. 8, 1948; s. Richard E. and Margret A. (Phillips) D.; m. Jeanne L. Nobbe, Sept. 29, 1979; children: Whitney Marie, Lindsay Michelle, Tyler Edwin. BA, Principia Coll., Elsah, Ill., 1970; German lang. degree, Dept. Def., Monterey, Calif., 1971. Sales mgr. Mr. Ins. of Ind., Indpls., 1973-77; pres. Ind. Ins. Svcs., Inc., Greenwood, 1977—, Ins. Svc., Inc., 5, 1990—. V.p. Brown County Water Utility, Helmsburg, Ind., 1982-85. Leader Johnson County 4-H, 1993-97; den leader pack 218 Cub Scout Am., 1999-2001, asst. scoutmaster, 2001—. With U.S. Army, 1970-73. Mem. Ind. Ins. Agts. Assn., Profl. Ins. Agt. Assn. (treas. Indpls. region 1990), Ind. Trail Riders Assn., BMW Motorcycle Owners Am. Christian Scientist. Avocations: appaloosa and quarter horses, camping. Office: Ind Ins Svcs 3115 Meridian Parke Dr Ste P Greenwood IN 46142-9414 E-mail: mdaniel@principia.edu., insure@indymall.com.

DANIEL, RAYMOND, economist; b. Tutor Key, Ky., July 29, 1940; s. Charlie J. and Alka D.; m. Gloria June Preston, Dec. 23, 1961; children— Shauna Lee, Darren Ray. BS, U. Ky., 1964; MS, Purdue U., 1968, PhD, 1970. Asst. prof. U. Tenn., Knoxville, 1970-73, assoc. prof., 1973-75; dir. agrl. econs. Chase Econometrics, Bala Cynwyd, Pa., 1975-78, v.p. for agr., 1978-81, mng. dir. for industry, 1981-91, v.p. industry analysis, 1991-95, sr. dir. Merck Ag. Vet. 1996—; cons., lectr. in field. Contbr. articles to profl. jours. Mem. Am. Agrl. Econs. Assn., Masons, Sigma Xi, Gamma Sigma Delta, Alpha Zeta. Avocations: fishing; coin collecting; travel. Home: 1588 Mulberry Lake Dr Dacula GA 30019-6691

DANIEL, ROBERT MICHAEL, lawyer; b. Rocky Mount, NC, Aug. 21, 1947; s. Harvey Derby and Edna Lois (McCullen) D.; m. Kaye Ruth Coates, Aug. 31, 1968; children: Robert M. Jr., John Matthew. AB in Econs., U. N.C., 1968, JD, 1971. Bar: N.C. 1971, Pa. 1976; U.S. Dist. Ct. (we. dist.) Pa. 1976; U.S. Tax Ct. 1979. Judge adv. U.S. Marine Corps., 1971-74; ptnr. Smith & Daniel, Pittsboro, N.C., 1974-75; trust officer Mellon Bank, N.A., Pitts., 1975-78; assoc. Buchanan Ingersoll, Pitts., 1978-82, ptnr., 1982—2001; dir. Cohen & Grigsby PC, Pitts., 2002—. Bd. dirs. Cohen & Grigsby, Pitts., 2002. Pres. Greater Pitts. coun. Boy Scouts Am., 1996-99, bd. dirs. N.E. region. Col. USMCR, 1966 98, ret. Fellow Am. Coll. Trust and Estate Coun.; mem. Pa. Bar Assn. (past chmn. real property, probate and trust law sect. 1998-99), Duquesne Club. Presbyterian. Avocations: travel, reading military history. Home: 1491 Redfern Dr Pittsburgh PA 15241-2956 Office: Cohen & Grigsby PC 11 Stanwix St 15th Flr Pittsburgh PA 15222-1319

DANIEL, ROSS PRESTON, III, economist, educator; b. Berkeley, W.Va., July 6, 1951; s. Ross Preston and Ruth Irene (Roby) Daniel. BA, Marshall U., 1973, MBA, 1975; MA, W.Va. U., 1979. Lectr. W.Va. U., Morgantown, 1981—82; asst. mktg. mgr. Mountaineer Mall, 1979—81; asst. prof. Nicholls State U., Thibodaux, La., 1982—85, U. Southwestern La., Lafayette, 1985—86; dir. Ctr. Econ. Edn. La. State U., Baton Rouge, 1986—. Instr. So. U., Baton Rouge, 1996—2001; asst. prof. Baton Rouge C.C., 2002—; pres. J.B. Enterprises Photography, 1986—93, Buff Daniel Photography, 1986—; v.p. R.D. Software, Inc., Thibodaux, 1983—. Fellow, W.Va. U., 1976—77, 1977—81, Benedum rsch. fellow, 1976. Mem.: Am. Econ. Assn., Tau Kappa Epsilon. Episcopalian. Home: 5115 Highland Rd Apt 135 Baton Rouge LA 70808-6529 E-mail: buffland@excite.com.

DANIEL, ROYAL THOMAS, III, lawyer, engineer, accountant; b. Portsmouth, Va., July 30, 1956; s. Royal Thomas Daniel, Jr. and Lillian Martha (Ellis) Daniel; m. Holly Ann Walsh, Oct. 30, 1993; children: Andrew Joseph, Royal Thomas IV, James David. BS in Nuclear Engring., N.C. State U., 1978, MS in Indsl. Mgmt., 1980; MS in Acctg., Bentley Coll., 1985, MS in Computer Info. Systems, 1986; JD, Suffolk U., 1990. Bar: N.C. 1991, Mass. 1991, D.C. 1992, N.Y. 2003, N.J. 2003, U.S. Tax Ct. 1993, N.Y. 2003, N.J., 2003; registered profl. mech. and indsl. engr., Mass., N.C.; CPA, Md., N.C.; cogeneration profl. Assn. Energy Engrs. Sr. proposal engr. Combustion Engring. Power Systems, Inc., Windsor, Conn., 1979-80; coordinating specialist Boston Edison Co., 1980-85, power supply coord., 1985-92; prin. Daniel Law Offices, P.A., Raleigh, N.C., 1992-94; v.p. PSEG Asia, Ltd., Hong Kong, 1994—2000; bd. dirs., v.p. Meiya Power Co. Ltd., Hong Kong, 1995-98, 2002—; pres., bd. dirs. Energy Infrastructure Devel., Bangkok, 1998-2000; vice chmn. ops. and fin. Sri U-Thong, Bangkok, 1998-2000; corp. devel. PSEG Global Inc., NJ, 2000—01, U.S. bus. mgr., 2001—. Contbr. chapters to books. Mem. NSPE, ABA, Am. Inst. Certification of Computer Profls., Am. Arbitration Assn. (panel arbitrators), Nat. Assn. Accts. (cert. Inst. Cert. Mgmt. Accts.), N.C. Assn. CPA's, N.C. Bar Assn., D.C. Bar Assn., Inst. Cert. Computer Profls. (cert. data processor, systems profl.), Rotary, Order St. Patrick, Phi Delta Phi, Tau Beta Pi. Baptist. Home: 333 Boulevard Mountain Lakes NJ 07046-1517 E-mail: royal_daniel@hotmail.com.

DANIEL, SAMUEL J. hospital administrator, medical educator; b. Leeward Islands, Sept. 13, 1950; MD, Columbia U., 1978. Diplomate Am. Bd. Internal Medicine, Am. Bd. Gastroenterology. Intern Roosevelt Hosp., N.Y.C., 1978—79, resident in internal medicine, 1979—80, St. Lukes-Roosevelt Hosp., N.Y.C., 1980—81, resident in gastroenterology, 1981—83; dir. medicine N. Gen. Hosp., N.Y.C., 1995—2001, CEO, 2001—. Asst. clin. prof. Columbia U.; assoc. clin. prof. Mt. Sinai Sch. Medicine, 2001—. Office: 425 W 59th St Fl 9B New York NY 10019-1128 Address: 1824 Madison Ave New York NY 10035-3832 Office Fax: 212-523-8123.*

DANIEL, SAMUEL MICHAEL, social worker, psychotherapist; b. Badarpur, Assam, India, Mar. 9, 1929; came to U.S., 1955; s. Michael and Yerushabai (Penkar) D.; m. Gussie Silberstein, Dec. 5, 1959 (div. Apr. 1963); m. Erna Weber, Jan. 15, 1975. BSc, Bombay U., 1951; MSW, Howard U., 1957. Social worker N.Y.C. Bd. of Edn., 1965—. Hon. pres. Congregation Bina, N.Y.C., 1981—. Mem.: NASW. Home: 600 W End Ave Apt 1C New York NY 10024-1643 E-mail: Shumeldivekar@aol.com.

DANIEL, SEAN, voice educator, baritone, artist; s. Eugene A. Walsh and Marion E. McCarthy; 1 child, Daniel Stovall Walsh. MusB in Voice, Syracuse U., 1961; MusM in Edn., Ind. U., 1963. Asst. prof. Syracuse (N.Y.) U., 1963—69; tchr. of voice Ind. U., Bloomington, 1966—67; assoc. prof. U. N.Mex, Albuquerque, 1973—82; artistic dir./mgr. Albuquerque Opera Theatre, 1974—76; prof. U. Okla., Norman, 1982—. Singer: 25 operatic roles; 3 one-man shows. Recipient Career award, Nat. Soc. Arts and Letters, 1963; Fulbright fellow, 1965. Home: 6502 Crooked Oak Cr Norman OK 73026 Office: Sch of Music U Okla Catlett Music Ctr Norman OK 73019

DANIEL-BERHE, SEQUARE, electrical engineering executive, researcher; b. Addis Ababa, Showa, Ethiopia, Oct. 22, 1963; s. Berhe Sequare-Kiflet Kinfaye and Welete-Kidan Welde-Selassie Welde-Gebreale. BSEE, Addis Ababa U., 1985, MSEE with honors, 1991; PhD in Elec. Engring. with honors, Ruhr U., Bochum, Germany, 1999. Registered engr., cert. elec. installation design., supr., Bldg. and Transport Constrn. Design Authority, Addis Ababa; postdoctroral in mech. engring. & aerospace engring., UCLA, 2001. Elec. engr. Water Resources Commn., Addis Ababa, 1985—88; design engr. Ministry Mines and Energy, Addis Ababa, 1988-89; office engr. Gilgel Gibe & Dembie Hydro Electric Project, Addis Ababa, 1989-92; lectr. I Addis Ababa U., 1989-92, lectr. II, 1992-94; sci. co-worker, instr. control engring. dept. Ruhr U., Bochum, 1994—99; assoc. rsch. engr. in mech. and aerospace engring. UCLA, 2000—, postdoctoral fellow in mech. and aerospace engring., 2001. Elec. engr. Indsl. Projects Svc., Addis Ababa, 1984, 85-86, Coop. Muratori & Cementisti di Ravenna & Aster Internat., Addis Ababa, 1992-93; cons., designer Pvt. Consultation Svc., Addis Ababa, 1986-94; computer softwares lectr. City Bus. Ctr., Addis Ababa, 1991-94; technologist Joint Air Force Component Comdr./Def. Advanced Rsch. Projects Agy., 2000--; lectr. in field. Contbr. articles and tech. reports to profl. publs.; inventor in field. Recipient cert. Pyongyang (Korea) Electro Project, 1988; MSc scholar Gilgel Gibe & Dembie Hydroelectric Project, Addis Ababa, 1989; PhD Rsch. fellow German Acad. Exch. Svc., Bonn, 1994. Fellow World Sci. and Engring. Socs.; mem. IEEE, Control Sys. Soc. of IEEE, Edn. Soc. of IEEE. Orthodox Christian. Avocations: table tennis, football, swimming, jogging, chess.

DANIEL-DREYFUS, SUSAN B. RUSSE, civic worker; b. St. Louis, May 30, 1940; d. Frederick William and Suzanne (Mackay) Russe; m. Don B. Faerber, Nov. 27, 1962 (div. Nov. 1968); 1 child, Suzanne Mackay; m. Marc Andre Daniel-Dreyfus, Aug. 9, 1969; 1 child, Cable Dunster. Student, Smith Coll., 1958-60, Corcoran Sch. Fine Arts, 1960-61, Washington U., St. Louis, 1961-62; MEd, Cambridge Coll., 1991. Mng. ptnr. Comm., Inc., 1980-82; asst. dir. Harvard Bus. Sch. Fund, Cambridge, 1982-86; pres. SCR Assocs. Corp., Cambridge, 1986—. Mem. bd. advisors Odysseum, Inc.; bd. dirs. Future Mgmt. Systems. Mem. St. Louis-St. Louis County White House Conf. on Edn., 1966-68; mem. Mo. 1st Gov.'s Conf. on Edn., 1966, 2d Conf., 1968; bd. dirs. Tunbridge Sch., 1973-78, St. Louis Smith Coll.; hon. bd. dirs. New Music Circle; mem. woman's bd. dirs. Washington U., New Music Circle, 1963-67; mem. woman's bd. Mo. Hist. Soc.; bd. dirs. Non-Partisan Ct. Plan for Mo., Young Audiences Inc., 1967-69; bd. dirs. Childrens Art Bazaar, 1968-70; founder St. Louis Opera Theater; chmn. Art. Mus. Bond Issue election St. Louis, 1966; jr. bd. dirs. St. Louis Symphony, 1966-68, Opportunities Indsl. Center, Boston; legis. chmn. bd. dirs. Boston LWV, 1969-72; mem. coun., bd. dirs. Jr. League Boston, 1970-72, 74-76, v.p. Bd. of Family Counseling Services-Region West, Boston, 1979—; pres. Family Counseling Bd., Brookline, Mass.; trustee Chestnut Hill Sch., Boston, Brookline Friendly Soc.; mem. steering com. ann. fund Boston Children's Hosp. Med. Center, 1980-84; v.p. Nat. Friends Bd., Joslin Diabetes Found., 1980-83; mem. corp. bd. Joslin Diabetes Ctr.; v.p. bd. dirs. Boston Ctr. Internat. Visitors, 1979-82; Boston bd. dirs. Mass. Soc. Prevention of Cruelty to Children, 1980-84; exec. v.p. Ctr. for Middle East Bus., 1978-82; pres. bd. Brookline Community Fund, 1984—; overseer Old Sturbridge Village, 1987—. Mem. Colonial Dames, Soc. Art Historians. Clubs: Women's City (dir., Boston); Vincent (dir.). Home: PO Box 638 Altona 3018 Australia

DANIELL, HERMAN BURCH, pharmacologist; b. Cadwell, Ga., May 25, 1929; s. Walter and Ruby Florence (Burch) Daniell; m. Mickey Marucheau, May 24, 1952 (dec.); m. Lorraine Smith, June 30, 1957 (dec.); children: Kimberley Ann, Anthony Burch, Walter Herman. BS in Pharmacy, U. Ga., 1951, MS in Pharmacology, 1964, PhD in Pharmacology. Owner-operator retail pharmacies, Savannah, Ga., 1953-62; instr. U. Ga., 1962-64; USPHS trainee Med. Coll. S.C., Charleston, 1964—66; mem. faculty Med. U. S.C., 1966-92, prof. pharmacology, 1978-92, prof. emeritus, 1992—. Contbr. articles to profl. jours. Served to capt. M.C. U.S. Army, 1951—53. Grantee, USPHS, 1966—85, S.C. Heart Assn., 1966—73. Mem.: Am. Soc. Pharmacology and Exptl. Therapeutics, Sigma Xi, Kappa Sigma, Rho Chi. Episcopalian. Home: 1549 Burningtree Rd Charleston SC 29412-2630

DANIELL, JERE ROGERS, II, retired history educator, consultant, public lecturer; b. Millinocket, Maine, Nov. 28, 1932; s. Warren Fisher and Mary (Holway) D.; m. Sally Ann Wellborn, Dec. 1955 (div. 1969); children: Douglas, Alexander, Matthew; m. 2d Elena Lillie, July 19, 1969; stepchildren: Breena Daniell, Clifford Brodsky. AB, Dartmouth Coll., 1955; MA, Harvard U., 1962, PhD, 1964. Asst. prof. history Dartmouth Coll., 1964-69, assoc. prof., 1969-74, prof., 1974—2003, chmn. dept., 1979-83; class of 1925 prof., 1984—; head tutor Heritage Found., Old Deerfield, Mass., 1960-64; ret., 2003. Author: Experiment in Republicanism: N.H. Politics and the American Revolution, 1970, Colonial N.H.: A History, 1981; bd. editors: Univ. Press of New England, 1978-86. Served to lt (j.g.) USN, 1955-58. Mem. Colonial Soc. Mass., N.H. Hist. Soc. (bd. trustee 1979-86, 1999—), Vt. Hist. Soc., Maine Hist. Soc., Mass. Hist. Soc. Home: 11 Barrymore Rd Hanover NH 03755-2401 Office: Dartmouth Coll Dept History Hanover NH 03755 E-mail: jere.r.daniell@dartmouth.edu.

DANIELOVITCH, ISSUR See DOUGLAS, KIRK

DANIELS, ANTONIO, professional basketball player; b. Mar. 19, 1975; Profl. basketball player Vancouver Grizzlies, 1997, San Antonio Spurs, Portland Trailblazers, 2002—. Named Mid-Am. Conf. Player of Yr., 1996—97. Office: Rose Quarter 1 Center Ct Ste 200 Portland OR 97227

DANIELS, ARLENE KAPLAN, sociology educator; b. N.Y.C., Dec. 10, 1930; d. Jacob and Elizabeth (Rathstein) Kaplan; m. Richard Rene Daniels, June 9, 1956. BA with honors in English, U. Calif., Berkeley, 1952; MA in Sociology, 1954, PhD in Sociology, 1960. Instr. dept. speech U. Calif., Berkeley, 1959-61; rsch. assoc. Mental Rsch. Inst., Palo Alto, Calif., 1961-66; assoc. prof. sociology San Francisco State Coll., 1966-70; chief Center for Study Women in Soc., Inst. Sci. Analysis, San Francisco, 1970-80; mem. faculty Northwestern U., Evanston, Ill., 1975-95, prof. dept. sociology, 1975-95, dir. Women's Studies, 1992-94, prof. emerita. Vis. prof. dept. sociology U. Calif., Berkeley, 1997—; cons. NIMH, 1971-73, NEH, 1975-80, Nat. Inst. Edn., 1978-82 Editor: (with Rachel Kahn-Hut) Academics on the Line, 1970; co-editor: (with Gaye Tuchman and James Benét) Hearth and Home: Images of Women in the Mass Media, 1978, (with James Benét) Education: Straightjacket or Opportunity?, 1979, (with Rachel Kahn-Hut and Richard Colvard) Women and Work, 1982, (with Alice Cook and Val Lorwin) Women and Trade Unions in Eleven Industrialized Countries, (with Teresa Odendahl and Elizabeth Boris) Working in Foundations, 1985, Invisible Careers, 1988, (with Alice Cook and Val Lorwin) The Most Difficult Revolution: Women in the Trade Union Movement, 1992; editor: Jour. Social Problems, 1974-78; assoc. editor: Contemporary Sociology, 1980-82, Symbolic Interaction, 1979-84, Am. Sociol. Rev., 1987-90. Trustee Bus. and Profl. Women's Rsch. Found. Bd., 1980-85, Women's Equity Action League Legal and Ednl. Def. Fund, 1979-81; mem. Chgo. Rsch. Assoc. Bd., 1981-87. Recipient Social Sci. Rsch. Council Faculty Rsch. award, 1970-71; Ford Found. Faculty fellow, 1975-76; grantee Nat. Inst. Edn., 1978-79, 1979-80, NSF, 1974-75, NIMH, 1973-74 Mem. Inst. Medicine NAS, Sociologists Women in Soc. (pres. 1975-76), Am. Sociology Assn. (coun. 1979-81, chmn. occupations and orgns. 1987, chmn. pubs. com. 1985-87, sec. 1992-95, Jessie Bernard award 1995), Soc. Study Social Problems (v.p. 1981-82, pres. 1987 Lee Founders award 1988), Soc. Study Symbolic Interaction. E-mail: akdaniels@aol.com.

DANIELS, ASTAR, artist; b. Fostoria, Ohio, Nov. 27, 1920; d. Alfred Henry and Edna Mae (Roush) Shultz; m. Bert Franklin Daniels, May 17, 1942 (div. Sept. 1976); children: Larry Bert, Cheri Hogue-Daniels, N. Dana Rahbar-Daniels. Honor grad., Art Instrn., Inc., Mpls., 1952; student, Toledo Mus. Sch. Design, 1950-52; studied with Emerson C. Burkhart, 1952-54; student, Thomas Moore Coll., 1971-73; grad. summa cum laude, U. Cin., 1977; student, Ohio U., 1984-85. Tchr. art pvt. adult and youth art classes, Forest and Cin., Ohio, 1950-57; portrait demonstrator numerous galleries, colls., mus., TV nationwide, 1951-79; dir. art, tchr. Defiance (Ohio) Coll., 1956-57; tchr. art and drama Meth. Ch. Camp, Sabina, Ohio, 1960-64; lectr. on liturgical art Hyde Park Comty. Ch., Cin., 1960-79; tchr. art and drama Fairview Arts Ctr., Cin., 1977-78; tchr. art Losantiville Summer Sch. Disadvantages Youth, 1996. Judge, mem. jury art shows, 1956—70; gallery guide Contemporary Art Ctr., Cin., 1972—73; costume designer Girl Scouts Symphony Music Hall, Cin., 1960, Cin., 62, Cin., 66; dir. art Ohio State Fair, Columbus, 1955—57; nat. art dir. Sr. Girl Scout Round-up, Button Bay, Vt., 1962; founder, chairperson Fine Arts Com. Ecclesia, Cin., 1960—79. One-woman shows include mus., colls., galleries, 1954—72, exhibitions include glass sculpture Schaff Gallery, Cin., 1996, commns., include Richard Nixon, Dr. A. B. Graham, James Arnes; author, illustrator: book Aiming in His Direction, 1971; illustrator (book) Woman Spirit Bonding, 1983. Art therapist Christ Hosp. Psychiat. Ward, Cin., 1959—61; citizen diplomat Soc. Positive Future, 1986; youth liturgical dance dir. Hyde Park Cmty. Ch., Cin., 1959—66. Recipient Scouters award for tng. leadership, Boy Scouts Am., Forest, 1957, Cert. of Achievement, Charlotte R. Schmidlapp Found., Cin., 1977, Exptl. Inst. Human Devel. award, Hyde Park Cmty. Ch.,

1976. Mem.: Nat. Mus. Women in Arts, Soc. Universal Human (founding mem. 1996). Avocations: world travel, exploring Incan and Mayan sites, mentoring young women, reading, metaphysical phenomena. Home and Office: 101 Solway Ct Cary NC 27511

DANIELS, BRUCE JOEL, lawyer; b. Denver, Apr. 16, 1935; s. Daniel Lester and Lillian Daniels; children: Julia K., Marya L., Jade A., Gregory R.S., Brenna J. AB, Ohio State U., 1957; JD, U. Mich., 1961. Bar: Fla. 1961, U.S. Dist. Ct. (middle dist.) Fla. 1962, U.S. Dist. Ct. (so. dist.) Fla. 1988. Pvt. practice, Fla., 1961—, 1987—. Co-author: (book) Eminent Domain, 1971. Mem.: AARP (regional advocacy team leader). Home: 336 Golfview Rd Apt 1018 North Palm Beach FL 33408-3513 Office: PO Box 14806 North Palm Beach FL 33408-0806 E-mail: brucedan@juno.com.

DANIELS, CAROLINE, publishing company executive; b. San Francisco, Dec. 11, 1948; d. William L. and Gladys Daniels; m. Jack Wernick, Nov. 30, 1985 (div.); children: Martin, Katherine. Student, U. Dijon, France, 1965; BA in Psychology, U. Colo., 1970; postgrad. mgmt. program, Harvard U., 1983-85. Export agt. Air Oceanic Shippers, San Francisco, 1972-73; library supr. Aircraft Tech. Pubs., San Francisco, 1973-75, ops. mgr., 1975-80, v.p., 1980-82, exec. v.p. Brisbane, Calif., 1982-84, pres., CEO, chmn. bd. dirs., 1984—. Pres. adv. bd. Embry Riddle Aero. U.; bd. dirs. Acad. Art Coll., San Francisco. Past mem. bd. dirs. Jr. Achievement of The Bay Area. Mem. Gen. Aviation Mfg. Assn. (bd. dirs., mem. exec. com., former chmn. pub. affairs com., chmn. safety affairs com.). Office: Aircraft Tech Pubs 101 S Hill Dr Brisbane CA 94005-1251

DANIELS, CHARLES JOSEPH, III, retired electrical engineer; b. L.A., July 1, 1941; s. Charles Joseph and Madeline Anna (Baldassare) D.; m. Joan Reichhold, Oct. 10, 1965; 1 child, Charles Joseph. BSEE, U. Md., 1971, MS in Physics, 1976. Draftsman Hazen & Sawyer Engrs., N.Y.C., 1960-62; technician EMR Corp., Greenbelt, Md., 1966-68; rsch. engr. Naval Rsch. Lab., Washington, 1971-73; sanitary engr. FDA, Rockville, Md., 1973-77; head of prodn. testing Digital Comm. Corp., Germantown, Md., 1977-78; mem. tech. staff Watkins-Johnson, Gaithersburg, Md., 1978-79; sr. engr. Digital Comm. Corp., Germantown, 1979-80; sr. staff engr. Frederick (Md.) Electronics, 1980-81; disting. mem. tech. staff AT&T Bell Labs, Allentown, Pa., 1981-2000, also tech. mgr. transmission integrated circuits appl. group; mgr. product validation PMC-Sierra inc., Allentown, Pa., 2000—01; mgr. hardware engring. Opticalis, Inc., Center Valley, Pa., 2001—02. Patentee in field; contbr. over 20 articles to profl. jours. Cpl. USMC, 1962-66. Mem. Am. Phys. Soc., Tau Beta Pi (pres. 1970-71), Sigma Xi, Phi Kappa Phi, Omicron Delta Kappa (sec. 1970-71), Sigma Pi Sigma. E-mail: cdaniels@epix.net.

DANIELS, CHARLIE, musician, songwriter; b. Wilmington, N.C., Oct. 28, 1936; Mem. (band) Jaguar band, 1958—67, session man (in Nashville with Flatt and Scruggs) Marty Robbins, Claude King, Pete Seeger, Bob Dylan, others, founder, mem. (band) Charlie Daniels Band, 1971—, recorded for (record cos.) Kama Sutra and Sony/Epic Records, —, records include (albums) Te John, Charlie Daniels, 1971, Grease and the Wolfman, 1972, Uneasy Rider, 1973, Whiskey, 1974, Fire on the Mountain, 1974, Nightrider, 1975, Saddle Tramp, 1976, Volunteer Jam Capricorn, 1976, Volunteer Jam III and IV, 1978, Volunteer Jam VI, 1980, Volunteer Jam VII, 1981, High Lonesome, 1976, Whiskey, 1977, Midnight Wind, 1977 (Grammy award best single of yr. Devil Went Down to Georgia), Million Mile Reflections, 1979, Full Moon, 1980, Windows, 1982, Decade of Hits, 1983, Me and the Boys, 1985, Powder Keg, 1987, Homesick Heroes, 1988, Simple Man, 1989, Christmas Time Down South, 1990, Renegade, 1991, America, I Believe in You, 1993, All Time Greatest Hits, 1993, The Door, 1994, Same Ole Me, 1995, 1st Christian Album The Door, 1994, Super Hits, 1994, 2d Christian album Steel Witness, 1996, SONY Legacy releases 1st CDB box set, The Roots Remain, 1996, By the Light of the Moon, 1997, Road Dogs, 2000, founder (record label) Blue Hat debut for label, 1998, Fiddle Fire, 1998, Tailgate Party, 1999; songwriter: ; songs recorded by (songs) Elvis Presley, Gary Stewart, Tammy Wynette, others; actor(appeared in): (TV films) PBS TV film The Lone Star Kid, 1986; also composed score; author: (short stories) The Devil Went Down to Georgia; songs This Ain't No Rag It's a Flag, 2001 (Biggest Single for CDB in 10 yrs.); Gospel album (albums) How Sweet The Sound: 25 Favorite Hymns and Gospel Greats. Recipient 3 Country Music Assn. awards, 1979, Grammy award for best performance by a country group, 1980, Toys for Tots Man of Yr. award, 1992, Humanitarian award Country Radio Broadcasters Seminar, 1992; named Instrumentalist of Yr., Instrumental Group of Yr., Winner Acad. Country Music's Pioneer award, 1998, Winner TNN Music City News Living Legend award, 1999. Office: The Charlie Daniels Band CDB Inc 17060 Central Pike Lebanon TN 37090-8019 Fax: 615-443-3140. E-mail: paulacdb@aol.com.

DANIELS, CHERYL LYNN, pediatrics nurse, case manager; b. Paterson, N.J., June 15, 1951; d. Nathan and Frances Avonna (Bradshaw) D. RN, Martland Hosp. Sch. Nursing, Newark, 1971; AAS in Health and Community Svc., NYU, 1984, BA in Journalism, 1987. Cert. pediat. nurse, ANCC. Evening charge nurse Martland Hosp. Unit, Newark, 1971-73; staff nurse Heal Econs. Advancement League, Paterson, N.J., 1972-74; neonatal intensive care nurse St. Joseph's Hosp. & Med. Ctr., Paterson, N.J., 1973-77, 1977-79, charge nurse, staff nurse ICN, 1979-89, intensive care nurse, pediatric HIV outpatient nurse, 1989-90; rsch. outpatient HIV/SJH case mgmt. nurse Aids Clin. Trial Group, 1990-2001; case mgr. outpatient pediat. HIV Clinic, 1989—; pediat. sedation nurse for CT scan procedures, 2001—02. Mentor Career Beginning Program, Paterson, 1988-90. Recipient Gobetz award, NYU, 1984. Mem. ARC, ANA, AACN (cert. pediat. nursing), Alpha Sigma Lambda. Baptist. Avocations: clarinet, swimming, reading, writing, oil painting. Home: 721 14th Ave Paterson NJ 07504-1531 Office: Saint Joseph Hosp 703 Main St Paterson NJ 07503-2691

DANIELS, CINDY LOU, space agency executive; b. Moline, Ill., Sept. 24, 1959; d. Ronald McCrae and Mary Lou (McLaughlin) Guthrie; m. Charles Burton Daniels, June 19, 1982. Student, Augustana Coll., Rock Island, Ill., 1977-78; BS cum laude, No. Mich. U., 1981; MS in Info. Sys., George Washington U., 1999, M Engring Mgmt., 2000. Field engr. Ford Aerospace, Houston, 1982-83; engr. flight ops. McDonnell Douglas Corp., Houston, 1983-85; electronics engr. Johnson Space Ctr. NASA, Houston, 1985-89, project mgr. multiple program control ctr., 1989-90, project mgr., 1989-91, mission control ctr. upgrade project mgr., 1990-91, mgr. program control office, 1991-93; mgr. ground facilities Space Sta. Program Office NASA, Houston, 1993-94; engring. and ops. mgmt., space sta. program NASA Hdqrs., Washington, 1994-96; spl. assessments and acquisition mgr. NASA Langley Rsch. Ctr., Hampton, Va., 1996—. Dynamics contr. NASA Johnson Space Ctr., 1982-83; payload data engr. NASA, 1983-84, earth radiation budget satellite joint ops. integration plan mgr., 1984; mem. payload assist module team NASA-McDonnell Douglas Corp., 1984-85. Home: 200 Barrington Ln Yorktown VA 23693 Office: NASA Langley Rsch Ctr 12 W Taylor Ave Hampton VA 23663-2206

DANIELS, DANIEL LLOYD, lawyer; b. New Milford, Conn., Nov. 17, 1962; s. C. Ross Jr. and Fayne M. (McGrath) D.; m. Jennifer A. Matteis, Aug. 27, 1988; children: Benjamin T., Elizabeth S. AB summa cum laude, Dartmouth Coll., 1984; JD cum laude, Harvard U., 1987. Bar: N.Y. 1988, Conn. 1991. Law clk. Mass. Supreme Ct., Boston, 1987-88; assoc. Sullivan & Cromwell, N.Y.C., 1988-89; prin. Settle Agy., Inc., Danbury, Conn., 1989-91; assoc. Cummings & Lockwood, Stamford, Conn., 1991-96, ptnr., 1997—. Contbg. author: The 401 (K) Plan Handbook, 1997. Mem. Danbury Econ. Devel. Commn., 1991; bd. dirs. Cmty. Ctrs., Inc., Grenwich, Conn., 1994-96, Cmty. Answers at Greenwich Libr., 1996—. Fellow Am Coll. Trust and Estate Counsel; mem. ABA, Conn. Bar Assn. (presenter 1996, mem. estates and probate exec. com. 1999—), N.Y. State Bar Assn., Stamford-Norwalk Regional Bar Assn., Harvard Law Sch. Assn. Conn. (trustee Stamford 1995—). Avocations: a capella singing, gilbert and sullivan, musical theater. Office: Cummings & Lockwood 4 Stamford Plz Stamford CT 06902-3834 E-mail: ddaniels@cl-law.com.

DANIELS, DEBORAH JEAN, federal agency administrator; BA, De Pauw U., 1973; JD, Ind. U. Bar: Ind., U.S. Dist. Ct. (so. dist.) Ind., U.S. Ct. Appeals (7th cir.), U.S. Supreme Ct. 1987. U.S. attorney U.S. Dist. Ct. So. Dist. Ind., 1988—; asst. atty. gen. justice programs U.S. Dept. Justice, DC, 2001—. Office: US Dept Justice Off Justice Programs 810 7th St NW Washington DC 20531

DANIELS, DIANA M. lawyer; b. Dillon, Mont. BA, Cornell U., 1971; JD, Harvard U., 1974; M of City Planning, MIT, 1974; diploma, U. Edinburgh, Scotland, 1976. Bar: N.Y. 1975, U.S. Dist. Ct. (ea. and so. dists.) N.Y. 1975, U.S. Ct. Appeals (2d cir.) 1975, D.C. 1978, U.S. Supreme Ct. 1988. Assoc. Cravath, Swaine & Moore, N.Y.C., 1975-78; asst. counsel Washington Post newspaper, 1978-79; gen. counsel Washington Post Co., 1988-89, v.p., gen. counsel, 1989-91, v.p., gen. counsel, sec., 1991—; v.p., counsel Newsweek, N.Y.C., 1979-85, v.p., gen. counsel, 1985-88. Trustee Cornell U., 1995-; trustee ABA Mus. of Law, 1997—, Appleseed Found., 1998—, Ctr. for Study of Presidency, 1997-2001, Com. Corp. Gen. Counsel, 2000—. Office: Washington Post Co 1150 15th St NW Washington DC 20071-0002

DANIELS, ELIZABETH ADAMS, English language educator; b. Westport, Conn., May 8, 1920; d. Thomas Davies and Minnie Mae (Sherwood) Adams; m. John L. Daniels, Mar. 21, 1942; children: John L., Eleanor B. (dec.), Sherwood A., Ann S. AB, Vassar Coll., 1941; A.M., U. Mich., 1942; PhD, N.Y. U., 1954. From instr. to prof. English Vassar Coll., Poughkeepsie, N.Y., 1948-85, dean freshmen, 1955-58, dean studies, 1965-73, chmn. dept. English, 1974-76, 81-84, acting dean faculty, 1976-78, chmn. self-study, 1978-80, Vassar historian, 1985—. Author: Jessie White Mario, Risorgimento Revolutionary, 1972, Main to Mudd, Bridges to the World, 1994, Main to Mudd, and More, 1996; co-author (with Clyde Griffen): Full Steam Ahead in Poughkeepsie, The Story of Coeducation at Vassar 1966-74, 2000, (with Maryann Bruno) Vassar College 1861-2000, 2000, also articles. Bd. dirs. Alzheimer's Assn. Mid-Hudson Valley. Recipient Grad. award Alumnae Assn. N.Y. U., 1954; Vassar fellow, 1941; Nat. Endowment Humanities summer stipend, 1981 Mem. MLA, AAUP, Poughkeepsie Tennis Club, Phi Beta Kappa. Democrat. Home: 56 Muirfield Ct Poughkeepsie NY 12603 Office: Vassar Coll PO Box 74 Poughkeepsie NY 12602-0074 *Growing up with intellectual ambitions, I was able to work out a very satisfactory career combining teaching, college administration, scholarship, family life, and a good marriage slightly forerunning the feminist movement of the late nineteen-sixties. I owe much of this to Vassar College, the first endowed woman's college in the U.S.*

DANIELS, FRANK ARTHUR, JR., newspaper publisher; b. Raleigh, N.C., 1931; s. Frank Arthur and Ruth (Aunspaugh) D.; m. Julia Bryan Jones, 1954; children: Frank Arthur III, Julia Graham Nowell. AB, U. N.C., 1953. With News and Observer Pub. Co., Raleigh, 1953-97, pres., pub., 1971-97; trustee Commonwealth Fund, N.Y.C., 1994—2002; chmn. Associated Press, 1992-97. Bd. dirs. Landmark Comm.; chmn. So. Pines Pilot newspaper. Bd. dirs., mem. exec. com., campaign chmn. Raleigh United Way, 1964, pres., 1974-75; bd. dirs. Greater Triangle Community Found.; former trustee Peace Coll., St. Mary's Coll.; former chmn. Rex. Hosp.; chmn., former pres. Am. Newspaper Pub. Assn. Found.; former mem. Raleigh-Durham Airport Authority; past trustee Woodberry Forest Sch.; past bd. visitors U. N.C.; chmn. nat. bd. Smithsonian Inst., 2001-2003, bd. dirs., 1996—; campaign chmn. Triangle United Way, 1996; trustee U. N.C. Health Care Sys., 1997-99. With USAF, 1954-55. Named Outstanding Young Man of Yr. Raleigh Jaycees, 1963 Mem. So. Newspaper Pubs. Assn. (chmn. bd. 1973-74, pres. 1972-73, dir.), Am. Newspaper Pubs. Assn. (past bd. dirs., treas.), N.C. Press Assn. (past pres.), Greater Raleigh C. of C. (bd. dirs.), Carolina Motor Club (dir.), Country Club of N.C., Capital City Club, Carolina Country Club, Sphinx Club, Univ. Club (N.Y.C.), Coral Beach Club (Bermuda), Delta Kappa Epsilon. Democrat. Presbyterian. Office: PO Box 671 Raleigh NC 27602-0671

DANIELS, FRANK EMMETT, mathematician, educator; b. Miami, Fla., Sept. 28, 1963; s. Dan and Jewell Rae (Morgan) D. BS, U. Fla., Gainesville, 1985, MS, 1987, PhD, 1994. Grad. teaching asst. math. dept. U. Fla., Gainesville, 1985-92; teaching asst. math. dept. Santa Fe Community Coll., 1992-94; prof. sys. adminstr. Great Basin Coll., Ely, Nev., dept. chair, 1999—2003. Co-designer Zdary Edn. program, 2003; faculty senate chmn. Great Basin Coll., 2003—. Mem. Campus Advance (pres. 1988-91), Campus Christian Fellowship (pres. 1991-92), Phi Beta Kappa. Republican. Avocations: comic book collecting, collecting Beatles items, Bibl. studies, role-playing games. Office: Great Basin Coll 2115 Bobcat Dr Ely NV 89301-3107

DANIELS, J. YOLANDE, architectural firm executive, educator; BS in Architecture, CUNY, 1987; M in Architecture, Columbia U., 1990. With Office of Thierry Despont, NY, 1990—91, Gaetano Pesce Ltd., NY, 1991, Smith-Miller and Hawkinson Archs., NY, 1991—93, Selldorf Archs., NY, 1993—95, Ralph Appelbaum Assocs., NY, 1996—98; ptnr. SUMO, 1995—. Adj. prof. CUNY, 1992—95; adj. asst. prof. Columbia U., 1997, Pratt Inst., 1997—98; asst. prof. U. of Mich., 1998—2000; women's studies seminar lectr. Josai Internat. U., Chiba, 2000, Chiba, 01, Chiba, 03; asst. prof. Columbia U., 2000—. Contbr. Finalist Young Archs. Program, Mus. of Modern Art, 2001; recipient Young Archs. award, Archtl. League of N.Y., 1999, Nat. Design award, Am. Collegiate Schs. of Architecture, 1999, Rome prize, Am. Acad. in Rome, 2003—; grantee, N.Y. Found. for Arts, 2002. Office: Studio Sumo 101 W End Ave #75 New York NY 10023 also: Sch of Architecture Planning & Preservation Columbia U 400 Avery 2960 Broadway New York NY 10027-6902 E-mail: studiosumo@rcn.com.*

DANIELS, JAMES DOUGLAS, retired academic administrator; b. Harmony, N.C., Nov. 14, 1935; m. Marie Brown, Oct. 6, 1957; children: Christopher James, Gregory John, Susan Marie. AB, Davidson Coll., 1957; MA, U. N.C., 1962, PhD, 1968. Exec. tng. program Deering-Milliken Textile Corp., Gainesville, Ga., 1957-58; history instr. Hargrave Military Acad., Chatham, Va., 1961-62, chmn., divsn. social sci., 1962-65, dean students, summer sch., 1964-65; asst. prof. history Valdosta (Ga.) State Coll., 1968-71, assoc. prof. history, 1971-78, history prof., 1978, dean, sch. arts, sci., 1970-80; pres., prof. history Coker Coll., Hartsville, SC, 1981—2002; ret., 2002. Bd. dirs. Byerly Hosp., 1981-85; Sunday sch. tchr. First Presbyn. Ch. Hartsville, 1981—. Com. on ministry Pee Dee Presbytery of S.C., 1985—, moderator, 1985; adv. bd. Bank of Am., 1988—, Pee Dee Heritage, 1982—, Darlington County Mental Health Citizens, 1987—. With U.S. Army, 1958—60. NDEA fellow, U. N.C., 1966-68; recipient Man and Boy award Valdosta Boys' Club Bd. Dirs., 1970. Mem. Greater Hartsville C. of C. (bd. dirs. 1982-88, v.p. 1986, pres. 1987, chmn. bd. 1988), Hartsville H.S. Acad. Boosters Club and Band Boosters, Rotary (bd. dirs. 1982-99, Citizen of Yr. award 1989), Order of Palmetto, Omicron Delta Kappa. Presbyterian. Avocations: reading, fishing. Home: 206 Persimmon Fork Rd Blythewood SC 29016

DANIELS, JAMES MAURICE, retired physicist; b. Leeds, Eng., Aug. 26, 1924; emigrated to Can., 1953, naturalized, 1971; came to U.S., 1984, naturalized, 1992. s. Bernard and Mary Mahala (Proctor) D.; married; children: Ian Nicolas James, Maurice Edward Bruce. BA, Oxford (Eng.) U., 1945, MA, 1949, D.Phil., 1952. Exptl. asst. Radar R & D Establishment, Malvern, Eng., 1944-46; tech. officer explosives div. Imperial Chem. Industries, Ardeer, Scotland, 1946-47; rsch. fellow Clarendon Lab., Oxford (Eng.) U., 1952-53; asst. prof. physics U. B.C., Vancouver, Can., 1953-56, assoc. prof., 1956-60; UNESCO expert U. Buenos Aires, Argentina, 1958-59; prof. U. Toronto, Ont., Can., 1961-87, prof. emeritus, 1987—, chmn. dept. physics, 1968-73, chmn. dept. stats., 1983-84. Vis. prof. Instituto de Fisica, S.C. de Bariloche Argentina, 1960-61, Helsinki U. Tech., 1974, Columbia U., 1978-79, Princeton U., 1984-85, Ecole Normale Superieure Paris, 1985-86, Nat. Tsing Hua U., Hsinchu, Republic of China, 1990, 91-92; vis. disting. prof. Oakland U., Rochester, Mich., 1994-95; pres. U. Toronto Faculty Assn., 1976-77; v.p. Can. Assn. Univ. Tchrs., Ottawa, 1979-80; sec., treas. Can. Inst. Particle Physics, Ottawa, 1970-73. Author: Oriented Nuclei, Polarized Targets and Beams, 1965; contbr. numerous articles to profl. jours. Alfred P. Sloan fellow, 1962-65, Guggenheim fellow, 1978-79 Fellow London Phys. Soc., London Inst. Physics (chartered physicist), London Royal Soc. Arts, Royal Soc. Can.; mem. Can. Assn. Physicists, Am. Phys. Soc., N.Y. Acad. Scis., Can. Inst. Particle Physics (sec-treas. 1971-73), Can. Assn. Univ. Tchrs. (v.p. 1977-78). Achievements include patent for Doppler Radar; first successful production of spatially oriented atomic nuclei, of compressed spin-polarized 3 He; application of the Mossbauer effect for determining spin arrangements in magnetic materials. E-mail: daniels@pupgg.princeton.edu.

DANIELS, JAMES R. poet, English language educator; b. Detroit, June 6, 1956; s. Raymond J. and Mary T. Daniels; m. Kristin M. Kovacic, Sept. 28, 1985; children: Ramsey, Rosalie. BA, Alma Coll., 1978; MFA, Bowling Green State U., 1980. Prof. English Carnegie Mellon U., Pitts., 1981—. Author: M-80, 1993, Blessing the House, 1997, No Pets, 1999, Blue Jesus, 2000, Night with Drive-By Shooting Stars, 2002, Detroit Tales, 2003, Show and Tell: New and Selected Poems, 2003. Office: Carnegie Mellon U Baker Hall Pittsburgh PA 15213 E-mail: jd6s@andrew.cmu.edu.

DANIELS, JAMES WALTER, lawyer; b. Chgo., Oct. 13, 1945; s. Ben George and Delores L. (Wolanin) D.; m. Gail Anne Rihacek, June 14, 1969; children: Morgan, Abigail, Rachel. AB, Brown U., 1967; JD, U. Chgo., 1970. Bar: Calif. 1970, U.S. Dist. Ct. (ctrl. dist.) Calif. 1970, U.S. Tax Ct., 1972, U.S. Supreme Ct. 1979. Assoc. firm Latham & Watkins, L.A. and Newport Beach, Calif., 1970-77, ptnr., 1977—2003. Arbitrator Orange County Superior Ct., Santa Ana, Calif., 1978-88, judge pro tem, 1979-87. Fin. dir. St. Elizabeth Ann Seton Parish, Irvine, Calif., 1975-82; sec. Turtlerock Tennis Com., Irvine, 1981-83, 86—, pres., 1985-86; bd. dirs. Turtlerock Terr. Homeowners Assn., 1983-85, 87-89. Mem. ABA, Internat. Coun. Shopping Ctrs., Center club, Irvine Racquet Club, Palm Valley Country Club. Democrat. Roman Catholic. Home: 19241 Beckwith Ter Irvine CA 92612-3503 Office: Latham & Watkins 650 Town Center Dr Ste 2000 Costa Mesa CA 92626-7135

DANIELS, JERRY CLAUDE, rheumatologist, educator; b. Ft. Worth, Feb. 7, 1943; s. Claude Ewell and Sarah Ruth D.; m. Mary Louise, Jan. 30, 1981; 1 child, Robyn Louise Buschmann Coburn. BS in Biology, U. Tex., Arlington, 1965; MD, U. Tex., Galveston, 1970, PhD, 1973. Intern U. Tex. Med. Br., 1970-71, resident in internal medicine, 1971-73; fellow in rheumatology Harvard Med. Sch., 1973-75; from asst. prof. to prof. medicine U. Tex., Galveston, 1975-85, prof., 1985—, vice chair medicine, 1986-91, assoc. chair, 1991—, asst. dir. medicine, 2002—. Author: (textbook) Serum Protein Abnormalities, 1975; contbr. articles to profl. jours. Fellow ACP (sec.-treas. 1996-99, Laureate 1999), Am. Coll. Rheumatology; mem. Am. Coll. Physician Execs., Tex. Soc. Internal Medicine(pres. 1996-97, 99-2000). Avocations: philately, computer programming, chess. Office: U Tex Med Br 301 University Blvd Galveston TX 77555-5302 E-mail: jdaniels@utmb.edu., jcdan@msn.com.

DANIELS, JOAN FRANCES, private school educator; b. Milw., Wis., Dec. 26, 1959; d. Lee Wilson and Jeanette Fairchild; m. Steven John Daniels, July 17, 1982; children: Timothy, David, Stevi, Evelyn. BS, U. Wis., 1982; grad. cert. Bible, Multnomah Sch. of the Bible, Portland, Oreg., 1981; MA in Edn. Fresno Pacific U., 2002. Cert. tchr. phys. edn./adaptive phys. edn. Wash., profl. clear tchg. cert. phys. edn., biology, introductory sci. Calif. Tchr. phys. edn. Contra Costa Christian Sch., Walnut Creek, Calif., 1982—83; tutor, vol. Accademia Los Pinares, Tegucigalpa, Honduras, 1987—91; tchr. K-8 phys. edn. Central Valley Christian Sch., Visalia, Calif., 1993—, tchr. grades 7-8 Bible, Spanish, sci., 1993—. Owner, instr. Aquatics Unltd., Visalia, 1993—. Food pantry adminstr. LOVE, Inc. (Covenant Ch.), Visalia, 1997—99; soccer coach Am. Youth Soccer Orgn., Visalia, 1998, 2000. Recipient Helen Pfuderer Smith scholarship, U. Wis., 1980, Assn. for Integrating Math. and Sci. scholarship, Fresno Pacific U., 2000. Mem.: Calif. Sci. Tchrs. Assn., Nature Conservancy. Avocations: running triathlons, cross country skiing, travel, gardening, reading. Home: 1507 S Bollinger Ct Visalia CA 93277-3910

DANIELS, JOHN DRAPER, lawyer; b. Bklyn., Feb. 11, 1939; s. Draper L. and Louise Parker-Lux (Cort) D.; m. Sara Josephine Sears, Dec. 27, 1962; children: Stephen Draper, Elizabeth Marie, Rebecca Cort. AB, Princeton U., 1961; JD, U. Chgo., 1964. Bar: Ill. 1964, U.S. Dist. Ct. (no. dist.) Ill. 1967. Assoc. Jacobs & McKenna, Chgo., 1964-70, Law Offices Dale L. Schlafer, Chgo., 1970-73; assoc. then ptnr. Jacobs, Williams & Montgomery, Chgo., 1973-87; ptnr. Sanchez & Daniels, Chgo., 1987—. Arbitrator Cir. Ct. of Cook County. Mem. admissions screening panel Princeton Alumni Coun. Capt. U.S. Army, 1964-66. Mem. ABA, Ill. Bar Assn. (chmn. ins. sect. coun. 1985), Chgo. Bar Assn., Am. Arbitration Assn. (arbitrator 1977—), Internat. Assn. Def. Counsel, Soc. Trial Lawyers (bd. dirs. 1990, '92), Am. Bd. Trial Advs., Ill. Assn. Defense Trial Counsel, Trial Lawyers Club of Chgo., Tower of Chgo. Club (bd. trustees. 1985-87), East Bank Club. Roman Catholic. Avocations: guitar, musical composition, tennis, fishing, golf. Home: 1611 Wilmette Ave Wilmette IL 60091-2424 Office: Sanchez & Daniels 333 W Wacker Dr Chicago IL 60606-1220 E-mail: jdaniels@sanchezdaniels.com.

DANIELS, JOHN HANCOCK, agricultural products company executive; b. St. Paul, Oct. 28, 1921; s. Thomas L. and Frances (Hancock) D.; m. Martha H. Williams, Dec. 23, 1942; children: Martha M., John Hancock, Jane P. Daniels Moffett, Christopher W. Student, St. Paul Acad., 1932-37; grad., Phillips Exeter Acad., 1939; BA, Yale, 1943; grad., Advanced Mgmt. Program, Harvard, 1957. With Archer-Daniels-Midland Co., Mpls., 1946-96, successively mem. staff linseed oil div., prodn. mgr. alfalfa divsn., mgr. feed divsn., v.p., dir., 1946-53, pres., dir., 1958-67, chmn., 1967-72, dir., mem. exec. com., 1972-96. With Mulberry Resources Inc. Author: Nothing Could Be Finer, 1996, Affectionately H, 1999. With Bus. Coun.; trustee Com. Econ. Devel.; chmn. 1972 Decatur United Way Campaign; bd. dirs. Nat. Sporting Libr. Served from 2d lt. to capt. F.A., AUS, 1943-46. Decorated Bronze Star medal. Mem. Masters of Foxhounds Assn. Am., Yale Libr. Assocs. (trustee), Grolier Club, Elizabethan Club, Nat. Sporting Libr. (dir.). Clubs: Links (N.Y.C.); Minneapolis; Woodhill (Minn.); Sprindale Hall (Camden, S.C.); Grolier. Republican. Episcopalian. Home: Mulberry Plantation PO Box 549 Camden SC 29020-0549 E-mail: CDE322@aol.com.

DANIELS, JOHN HILL, lawyer; b. Albany, N.Y., Oct. 17, 1928; s. David Samuel and Sadie (Davidson) D.; m. Helen R. Marcus, May 24, 1952; children: Marc, Scott, Seth. Grad., L.I. U., 1949; LLB, Bklyn. Law Sch., 1952; LLM, NYU, 1958. Bar: N.Y. 1954, U.S. Dist. Ct. (ea. and so. dists.) N.Y. 1954, U.S. Supreme Ct. 1958. Assoc. Friedman & Friedman, Bklyn., 1954, Finkelstein, Benton & Soll, N.Y.C., 1955-58, Levy & Kornblum, Bklyn., 1959; ptnr. Kamen & Daniels, Bklyn., 1959-61; sr. ptnr. Different people & Different Firm, Law offices of John H. Daniels & Marc A. Daniels, Mineola, N.Y., 1983—; sole practice Roosevelt, N.Y., 1960-88, Mineola, 1975—. Lectr. in field. Candidate for judge Nassau County Dist. Ct., Mineola, 1960-63; bd. dirs. Mental Health and Alcohol, Roosevelt, 1980-92; past pres. Civic Assn. of Woodbury. Sgt. U.S. Army, 1952-54. Mem. N.Y. State Bar Assn., Nassau County Bar Assn., Nassau Lawyers Assn. L.I. (dir. 1970—, pres. 1984), Jewish Lawyers Assn. Nassau County (bd. dirs. 1964—, pres. 1985-86), Yankee Sports and Gun Club (Roosevelt) (past pres.), Lions (dir. 1960-84), Kiwanis (dir. 1978-84), epsilon Phi Alpha, Iota Theta. Home: 29 Kodiak Dr Woodbury NY 11797-2706 Office: 114 Old Country Rd Mineola NY 11501-4400

DANIELS, JOHN PETER, lawyer; b. N.Y.C., Feb. 5, 1937; s. Jack Brainard and Isabelle (McConachie) D.; m. Lynn Eldridge, Aug. 28, 1978 (div. Jan. 1980); m. Susan Gurley, Apr. 1, 1983. AB, Dartmouth Coll., 1959; JD, U. So. Calif., 1963. Bar: Calif. 1964; diplomate Am. Bd. Trial Advocates. Assoc. Bolton, Groff and Dunne, L.A., 1964-67, Jones and Daniels, L.A., 1967-70, Acret and Perrochet, L.A., 1971-81; ptnr. Daniels, Baratta and Fine, L.A.Angeles, 1982-99, Daniels, Fine, Israel & Schonbuch, L.A.Angeles, 1999—. Mem. Assn. So. Calif. Def. Counsel (bd. dirs. 1975-80), Fedn. Ins and Corp. Counsel. Clubs: Wilshire Country (Los Angeles). Avocations: scuba diving, golf, hunting. Office: Daniels Fine Israel & Schonbuch 1801 Century Park E Fl 9 Los Angeles CA 90067-2302

DANIELS, JOSEPH, neuropsychiatrist; b. Linden, N.J., Mar. 18, 1931; s. Bennie and Dora (Chese) D.; m. Shirley Perkins, July 20, 1996; children: Joan Marie, Jean Dorene. BA cum laude, Lincoln U., Oxford, Pa., 1953; MD, Howard U., 1957. Rotating intern Med. Ctr. Jersey City, 1957-58; resident in internal medicine Worcester (Mass.) City Hosp., 1958-59; resident in psychiatry Ancora (N.J.) Hisp., 1962-65; dir. outpatient clinic Christian Health Care Ctr., Wyckoff, N.J., 1966-70; dir. outpatient dept. Cmty. Mental Health Ctr., N.J. Coll. Medicine, Newark, 1970-79; med. dir., pres. Ctr. for Growth and Reconciliation, East Orange, N.J., 1979-87; sr. staff psychiatrist Pine Rest Christian Hosp., Grand Rapids, Mich., 1987-96; cons. Kent County Cmty. Mental Health Ctr., Grand Rapids, 1996—. Mem. Healthy Kent 2000 Health Com., 1993-94; cons. psychiatrist Newark Bd. Edn., 1976-84, East Orange Bd. Edn., Victory House, Newark, 1976-82, Project Rehab, Grand Rapids, 1990-91. Author: The Urban Mission, 1974. Founder, pres., chmn. bd. Ministry Reconciliation Fellowship, 1980-87; bd. dirs. Grand Rapids Reach Inc., pres., 1991-93; selected mem. Leadership Grand Rapids, 1993-94. Capt. M.C., U.S. Army, 1959-62. Fulbright Sr. scholarship fellow U. Zimbabwe Sch. of Medi-

cine, 1998-99; decorated Am. Medal of Honor, 2001. Mem. Beta Kappa Chi. Baptist. Avocations: sports, writing, reading, volunteering. Office: 901 Eastern Ave NE Grand Rapids MI 49503-1201 E-mail: drsdsapd@juno.com.

DANIELS, KATHLEEN ANGELA, educational administrator; b. Detroit, Jan. 21, 1945; d. Leondro Cardinez and Lillian Mary (Murray) Castro; m. Donald W. Daniels, Jan. 30, 1971 (div. May 1983), 1 child, Donald. BA in Environ. Design, Wayne State U., 1967; student, U. Calif., L.A., 1969. Photographic artist Jana Taylor & Co., Venice, Calif., 1985-88; rep., founder Am. Child Found., Venice, 1986-88; exec. dir. Cmty. Assns. Inst., L.A., 1989—2000. Mem. NOW, Nat. Woman's Polit. Caucus, Nat. Assn. Female Execs., Am. Soc. Assn. Execs., Sierra Club, Nat. Dem. Club. Avocations: gardening, ceramic animal collector, reading, walking. Home and Office: 1903 W 9th St San Pedro CA 90732-3303

DANIELS, KURT R. speech and language pathologist; b. Chgo., Oct. 22, 1954; s. Donald R. and Phyllis D. (Lenz) D.; m. Renee Perry, July 5, 1980. BS, Ea. Ill. U., 1976, MS, 1977. Cert. clin. competence speech/lang. pathology; lic. speech/lang. pathologist, nursing home adminstr; tchr's. cert. spl. K-12th grades. Hearing and speech specialist Shapiro Devel. Ctr., Kankakee, Ill., 1977-80; dysphagia specialist lead prof. W.A. Howe Ctr., Tinley Pk., Ill., 1980—. Mem. adv. bd. program in comm. disorders Govs. State U., clin. adj. prof.; cons. in field; presenter in field of dysphagia and developmental disabilities. Recipient Editor's Choice award Nat. Libr. Poetry, 1994, 95. Mem. Am. Speech, Lang. and Hearing Assn., Ill. Speech, Lang. and Hearing Assn., Ill. Network for Augmentative and Alternative Commn., Internat. Soc. Poets, Chicagoland Dysphagia Forum (sec.), So. Cook County Speech, Hearing, and Lang. Assn., Chgo. Audiology-Speech-Lang. Assn. Office: Howe Clinic Howe Ctr 7600 W 183d St Tinley Park IL 60477

DANIELS, LEE ALBERT, state legislator; b. Lansing, Mich., Apr. 15, 1942; s. Albert Lee and Evelyn (Bousfield) D.; m. Pamela Mesha; children: Laurie Lynn, Rachael Lee, Julie, Thomas, Christina. BA, U. Iowa, 1965; JD, John Marshall Law Sch., 1967. Rep. precinct committeeman, 1965-74; mem. bd. auditors York Twp., Ill., 1966-73; vice chmn. York Twp. Rep. Comty. Orgn., 1973-74; former minority spokesman judiciary com. Ill. Ho. of Reps.; spl. asst. atty. gen., 1973-75; Ill. state rep. 46th Dist., 1975—, majority whip, 1981-82, minority leader, 1983-94; speaker of the House, 1995—. Full ptnr. Katten, Muchin & Zavis, 1984-91; ptnr. Bell, Boyd & Lloyd, Chgo., 1992— Trustee Elmhurst Hosp.; chmn. Ill. Rep. Party, 2001-2002. Recipient Everett McKinley Dirksen award, 1995; named one of Outstanding Legislators in Country, Nat. Rep. Legis. Assn., 1991, Legislator of Yr., Ill. Hosp. Assn., 1986, DuPage Mayors and Mgrs. Conf., 1995. Mem. ABA, Ill. Bar Assn., DuPage County Bar Assn., Shriners, Masons, Moose. Republican. Home: 611 N York Rd Elmhurst IL 60126-1903 Office: 316 State House Springfield IL 62706-0001*

DANIELS, MADELINE MARIE, forensic psychologist, educator, author; b. Newark, Oct. 14, 1948; d. William and Dorothy Barlow; m. Peter W. Daniels, Oct. 18, 1976 (div. July 27, 1988); children: Jonathan, Jedediah, Jeremiah. BA cum laude, CCNY, 1971; PhD, Union Grad. Sch., Yellow Springs, Ohio, 1975, Union Grad. Sch., Cin., 1988. Diplomate Am. Bd. Forensic Examiners; diplomate in forensic psychology Am. Bd. Psycol. Spltys; lic. psychologist, Calif. Lectr. Westchester C.C., 1973-74, Bronx (N.Y.) C.C., Purchase, 1973-74; mem. adj. faculty SUNY, Purchase, 1974-76; data processing coord. GTE Internat., 1976-78; lectr. divsn. continuing edn. U. N.H., 1979-87; exec. dir. Crossroads Ctr. Human Integration, East Kingston, N.H., 1979-88; adminstr. Spectrum Cross-Cultural Inst. Youth Inc., East Kingston, 1988-93; rsch./comm. cons. Metis Assocs., No. Calif., 1994-96; registered psychol. asst. Eureka, Calif., 1996-2000; lectr. Humboldt State U., 1998—2001; staff psychologist region III Parole Outpatient Clinic, Calif. Dept. Corrections, Eureka Station, 1998—99; pvt. practice, 2000—. Lectr., cons. in field. Author: Realistic Leadership, 1983, Living Your Religion in the Real World, 1985, A Culturally Different Perspective on Psychology, 1989, (video) The Rainbow Classroom, 1991. Mem. APA, Am. Coll. Forensic Examiners, Internat. Coun. Psychologists (area chair 1988), Biofeedback Soc. Am., Soc. Psychol. Anthropology, N.H. Psychol. Orgn., Phi Beta Kappa. Office: 1101 E Douglas Visalia CA 93292- E-mail: cawitchdoctor@comcast.net.

DANIELS, MARTHA K. artist; b. Bklyn., Sept. 21, 1943; d. Clifford William and Martha Katherine (Kreiss) Kirmss; m. Willem-Hendryk Daniels (div. 1973). Studied, Cooper Union, N.Y.C., 1961—64; BFA in Ceramics and Art History, Metrop. State Coll., Denver, 1975. Represented in permanent collections Kaiser Permanente, Taco Bell Corp., Native Am. Rights Found., Boulder, Colo., Amoco Oil Corp., Vance Kirkland Mus., exhibitions include Ivan Spence Gallery, Ibiza, Spain, 1965, Spectrum Gallery, Estes Park, Colo., 1970, Lodestone Gallery, Boulder, Colo., 1970—72, Boulder Designer Craftsman, 1970—72, Sebastian-Moore Gallery, 1978—81, Wash. Art, Wash., D.C., 1978, Ludlow-Hyland Gallery, N.Y.C., 1982—83, Spark Gallery, Denver, 1983, 1986, Pirate Gallery, Denver, 1984—92, Cafe Noir, Brussels, Belguim, 1988—90, David Rago Gallery, Lambertville, N.J., 1988, Mino, Japan, 1989—90, Boulder Pub. Libr., 1992, Denver Art Mus., 1978, 1990, 1994, one-man shows include, 2000, exhibitions include Foothills Art Ctr., Golden, Colo., 1992, 1998, Savageau Gallery, Denver, 1993—98, Saks Galleries, 1994—95, Rocky Mountain Women's Inst., 1995, Sage Gallery, Santa Fe, 1996, Elizabeth Schlosser Gallery, Denver, 1996, William Havu Gallery, 1999, 2000, 2001, 2003, Internat. Mus. Ceramics, Faenza, Italy, 2003, Robert Nichols Gallery, Santa Fe, 2003, Vance Kirkland Mus., Denver, Colo., 2003, Denver Mus. Contemporary Art, 1997, 2002, 2003. Recipient Mayor's Award, Rocky Mountain Women's Inst., 1995; fellow, 1995, Colo. Coun. on the Arts, 2001; grantee, Denver Art Mus., 1999. Home and Studio: 2138 Marion St Denver CO 80205

DANIELS, MICHAEL ALAN, lawyer; b. Cape Girardeau, Mo., Mar. 6, 1946; BS in Speech, Northwestern U., 1968, MA in Polit. Sci., 1969; JD, U. Mo., 1973. Bar: Fla. 1974, U. S. Supreme Ct. 1983. Spl. asst. for polit. sci. research Office Naval Research, Washington, 1969-71; legal aid Edwards, Seigfried, Runge and Hodge, Mexico, Mo., 1972-73; corp. atty. CACI, Inc., Washington, 1974-77; exec. v.p. gen. counsel Datex, Inc., Washington, 1977-78; chmn. bd., pres. Internat. Pub. Policy Research Corp., Falls Church, Va., 1978-86; sect. v.p. Sci. Applications Internat. Corp., Mc Lean, Va., 1986—; pres. U.S. Global Strategy Council, Washington, 1986-94; chmn. bd. Network Solutions, Inc., 1995—. Chmn. No. Va. Tech. Coun., 1996-97. Mem. Republican Nat. Com., Internat. Affairs Council, Nat. Security Adv. Council; mem. investment policy adv. com. Office U.S. Trade Rep., 1982-87. Recipient Outstanding Fed. Securities Law Student award U. Mo., 1973. Mem. ABA (chmn. working group on law, nat. security and tech., standing com. law and nat. security 1984-92), Fla. Bar Assn., Fed. Bar Assn. (chmn. internat. law com. 1979-86), Internat. Studies Assn. Office: SAIC 1710 Goodridge Dr # Ms1-125 Mc Lean VA 22102-3701

DANIELS, MICHAEL PAUL, retired lawyer; b. Maplewood, N.J., Apr. 22, 1930; s. Samuel and Lena E. (Oxman) D.; m. Lora Lee, June 23, 1949 (div. Aug. 1964); children: Lisa J., Rachel L., Aaron N.; m. Elaine Makris, Sept. 1, 1964; children: Anthony P., Maria. Alexander P. BA, U. Chgo., 1949, JD, 1952; student, U. Tokyo Sch. Law, 1958-59. Bar: U.S. Ct. Appeals (D.C. cir.) 1955, U.S. Supreme Ct., U.S. Ct. Internat. Trade; U.S. Ct. Appeals (fed. cir.). Atty. U.S. Congl. Reference Service, Washington, 1955-56; assoc. Becker & Maguire, Washington, 1956-57, Stitt & Hemendinger, Washington, 1958-63; ptnr. Stitt, Hemindinger & Daniels, Washington, 1963-67, Daniels, Houlihan & Palmeter, Washington, 1968-84; ptnr., internat. dept. head Mudge, Rose, Guthrie, Alexander & Ferdon, Washington, 1984-95; ptnr. Graham & James, Washington, 1995-97, Powell Goldstein Frazer & Murphy, Washington, 1997—2000; ret., 2000. Cons. Fasturn Inc., 2000—03. Served with U.S. Army, 1952-54, Korea. Decorated Meritorious Bronze Star; fellow Fulbright fellow. Mem. ABA, D.C. Bar Assn. Home: 5615 Bent Branch Rd Bethesda MD 20816-1049 E-mail: mpemd@erols.com.

DANIELS, MITCHELL ELIAS, JR., federal agency administrator; b. Monongahela, Pa., Apr. 7, 1949; s. Mitchell Elias and Dorothy Mae (Wilkes) D.; m. Cheri Lynn Herman, May 20, 1978; children— Meagan, Melissa, Meredith, Margaret. AB, Princeton U., 1971; JD, Georgetown U., 1979. Bar: Ind. 1979. Exec. v.p. Campaign Communicators, Inc., Indpls., 1971-74; dep. to mayor City of Indpls., 1974-75; campaign mgr. Lugar for U.S. Senate, Indpls., 1976; adminstrv. asst. U.S. Senator Lugar, Washington, 1977-83; exec. dir. Nat. Rep. Sen. Com., Washington, 1983-85; asst. to the Pres. White House, Washington, 1985—87; pres. corp. strategy, policy Eli Lilly and Co., 1997—2001; dir. Off. Mgt. and Budget, Washington, 2001—03. Vice pres., trustee Am. Council Young Polit. Leaders, Washington, 1983— ; mem. adv. com. Responsible Govt. for Am. Found., Washington, 1983— ; bd. dirs. Fund for Hoosier Excellence, 1984— Recipient Graham award Ind. Am. Legion, 1966; Presdl. scholar, 1967 Mem. Ind. Bar Assn. Clubs: Columbia (Indpls.). Republican. Presbyterian.*

DANIELS, NORMAN, philosopher, educator; b. N.Y.C., June 30, 1942; s. Manus and Evelyn (Auerbach) D.; m. Anne L. Hooker; 1 child, Noah. AB summa cum laude, Wesleyan U., 1964; BA, MA, Balliol Coll., Oxford, Eng., 1966; PhD, Harvard U., 1970. Asst. prof. philosophy Tufts U., Medford, Mass., 1970-76, assoc. prof. philosophy, 1976-81, prof. philosophy, 1981—2002, chmn. philosophy dept., 1983—2002; prof., sch. of public health Harvard U., Boston, 2002—. Faculty Harvard extension, Cambridge, Mass., 1976—; vis. assoc. prof. bioethics Brown U., Providence, 1979; reviewer NEH, NSF, 1982-85; panel mem. NSF-NEH Ethics and Values in Sci. and Tech., 1982. Author: (book) Thomas Reid's Inquiry: The Geometry of Visibles and the Case for Realism, 1974, Reading Rawls: Critical Studies of John Rawls' A Theory of Justice, 1975, In Search of Equity: Health Needs and the Health Care System, 1983, Just Health Care, 1985, Am I My Parent's Keeper? An Essay on Justice Between the Young and the Old, 1988; editorial bd. Australasian Jour. Philosophy, Ethics, Jour. Medicine and Philosophy; editor (with Keith Lehrer) series of philosophy textbooks; referee Isis, Nous, Philos. Forum, Philos. Studies, Social Theory and Practice, Jour. Medicine and Philosophy, Bus. and Profl. Ethics Jour., Milbank Meml. Fund Quar., Philosophy and Econs., Philosophy and Phenomenology Research; reviewer Wadsworth Pub. Co., Dickenson, Prentice-Hall, Oxford, Princeton, Garland Pub. Co., Cornell U. Press, Rowman and Littlefield, Cambridge U. Press. Recipient George Plimpton Adams prize, 1970, Woodrow Wilson Career Devel. award, 1980, Mass. Found. Humanities and Pub. Policy and Matchette Found. award, 1980; Harvard Grad. Nat. fellow, 1966-69, NEH Individual fellow, 1977-78; grantee Marsden Found., 1966, Nat. Ctr. Health Svcs. rsch. grantee, 1978-79, 79-80, 80-81, 81-82, NEH, 1983-85, 89—, Retirement Rsch. Found., 1983-86, NSF, 1987, USPHS, 1989—. Mem.: Nat. Institute of Health, 1999-, AAAS, AAUP, Am. Philos. Assn., Philosophy of Sci. Assn., Phi Beta Kappa. Office: Harvard Sch of Public Hlth 665 Huntington Ave Rm 1104C Boston MA 02115

DANIELS, RANDY A. secretary of state; married; 2 children. BA in Govt. and Journalism, So. Ill. U. Prof. adj. journalism CCNY, Columbia U.'s Grad. Sch. Journalism; reporter WVON Radio, Chgo., 1970—72; corr. CBS News, Chgo., 1972—77; fgn. corr. CBS News, Kenya, 1977—80, nat. corr., 1980—82; mng. editor Jacaranda Nigeria Ltd., 1982—84; dir. Comm. N.Y.C. Coun. Pres.'s Office, 1986—88; Press Sec. Prime Min. of Bahamas, 1988—92; v.p. Hirshfeld realty, N.Y.C., 1993—95; sr. v.p., dep. commr. econ. revitalization Empire State Corp. (ESDC), 1995—99; sr. v.p. Canyon Johnson Urban Fund, L.L.P., 1999—2001; Sec. of State State of N.Y., 2001—. Mem.: Exec. and Fin. Coms., SUNY Bd. Trustees (vice chmn., chmn. invetsment com., co-chmn. coms. on gen. edn. and charter schs.). Office: 41 State St 9th Fl Albany NY 12231-0001 Business E-Mail: info@dos.state.ny.us.*

DANIELS, RICHARD MARTIN, public relations executive; b. Delano, Calif., Feb. 24, 1942; s. Edward Martin and Philida Rose (Peterson) D.; m. Kathryn Ellen Knight, Feb. 28, 1976; children: Robert Martin, Michael Edward. AA, Foothill Coll., 1965; BA, San Jose State U., 1967; MA, U. Mo., 1971. News reporter Imperial Valley Press, El Centro, Calif., summers 1963-66, San Diego Evening Tribune, 1967-68, Columbia (Mo.) Daily Tribune, 1969-70; nat. news copy editor Los Angeles Times, 1966-67; staff writer San Diego Union, 1971-74, real estate editor, 1974-77; v.p. pub. rels. Hubbert Advt. & Pub. Rels., Costa Mesa, Calif., 1977-78; ptnr. Berkman & Daniels, San Diego, 1979-91; prin. Nuffer, Smith, Tucker, Inc., 1991-94, RMD Comms., 1994-97, 99—; exec. dir. comms. San Diego City Schs., 1997-99; prin. RMD Comms., 1999—. Lectr. various bus. groups and colls. Chmn. bd. dirs. March of Dimes San Diego County, 1984-87; bd. dirs. Nat. Coun. Vols., 1983-91; v.p. Escondido Rotary Club, 1995—, chair-elect Escondido C. of C., 2003—. Served with USN, 1959-62. Mem. Pub. Rels. Soc. Am. (accredited), Counselors Acad. Republican. Office: 2261 Ritter Pl Escondido CA 92029-5608 E-mail: dick@rmdcomm.com.

DANIELS, ROBERT SANFORD, psychiatrist, administrator; b. Indpls., Aug. 12, 1927; s. Harry H. and Mary (Bassett) D.; m. Vikki Ashley; children: Stephen, Allen, Lynn, Judith. BS, U. Cin., 1948, MD, 1951. Intern Cin. Gen. Hosp., 1951; resident U. Cin. Hosp., 1954-57; mem. faculty U. Chgo., 1957-71, dir. psychiat. cons. svc., 1961-63, asso. prof. psychiatry, acting chmn. dept., 1963-66, clin. dir., 1966-68, assoc. dean cmty. and social medicine, 1968-71, prof. psychiatry and social medicine, 1970-71; dir. Ctr. Health Adminstrn. Studies, Grad. Sch. Bus., 1970-71; dir. dept. psychiatry U. Cin., 1971-75; interim dean U. Cin. (Coll. Medicine), 1972-75; dean Coll. Medicine U. Cin., 1975-86, also sr. v.p., 1982-86; dean La. State U. Sch. Medicine, New Orleans, 1986-95, exec. asst. to chancellor, 1995-2000, dean, emeritus, 2000. Chief staff Cin. Gen. Hosp., 1972-86, Holmes Hosp., 1972-86; vis. prof. social medicine and clin. epidemiology St. Thomas' Hosp. Med. Coll., London, Eng.; sci. exchange visitor Ministry Health, Moscow, USSR; vis. scholar King Edward VII Hosp. Fund, London, 1977; cons. Cook County Hosp., Ill. State Psychiat. Inst.; spl. rsch. cmty. and group psychiatry, health planning, cmty. health, 1967-69; Chmn. Ill. Mental Health Planning Bd.; mem., chmn. rev. com., psychiatry edn. br. Health Services and Mental Health Adminstrn., 1971-75; mem. nat. mental health adv. bd. NIMH, 1975-79; bd. dirs. Hamilton County Bd. Mental Health and Retardation, 1974-78. Assoc. editor: Social Psychiatry. Bd. dirs. Central Ohio River Valley Planning Authority, 1979— . Served with AUS, 1946-47; Served with USAF, 1952-54. Recipient Stella Feis Hoffheimer award U. Cin., 1951 Mem. AMA, Am. Psychiat. Assn., Am. Group Psychotherapy Assn., Assn. Am. Med. Colls. (exec. coun. 1982-87, psychiatry residency rev. coun. 1990—, Daniel Drake medal 1988), Ill. Group Psychotherapy Soc. (pres. 1965-66), Ill. Psychiat. Soc. (pres. 1967), Phi Beta Kappa, Alpha Omega Alpha. Office: La State U Sch Medicine Office of the Chancellor 433 Bolivar St Rm 820 New Orleans LA 70112-2223

DANIELS, ROBERT VINCENT, history educator, former state senator; b. Boston, Jan. 4, 1926; s. Robert Whiting and Helen Underwood (Hoyt) D.; m. Alice May Wendell, July 2, 1945; children: Robert H., Helen L. Turcotte, Irene L., Thomas L. AB, Harvard U., 1945, MA, 1947, PhD, 1951; LLD (hon.), U. Vt., 1994. Rsch. assoc. MIT, 1951-52; social sci. faculty Bennington Coll., 1952-53, 57-58; asst. prof. Slavic studies Ind. U., 1953-55; rsch. assoc. Columbia U., 1955-56; from asst. prof. history to prof. U. Vt., Burlington, 1956-88, prof. emeritus, 1988—, chmn. dept., 1964-69, dir. exptl. program, 1969-71; mem. Vt. Senate, 1973-82, asst. minority leader, 1977-80, minority leader, 1981-82. Chmn. Vt. Gov.'s Commn. Med. Care, 1974-75; mem. Vt. Health Policy Corp., 1977-80; mem. adv. com. on East Europe and USSR, Coun. on Internat. Exch. of Scholars, 1983-85; adv. coun. Ctr. for Internat. Polit. Studies, Rome, 1989—; mem. sister state com. Vt.-Karelia, 1991—, co-dir. self-govt. tng. program, 1993-94; dir. U. Vt. Petrozavodsk U. partnership program, 1994-95; mem. supervisory bd. Internat. Coop. Ctr. Karelian br. St. Petersburg Acad. Pub. Adminstrn. Author: The Conscience of the Revolution, 1960, Documentary History of Communism, 1960, rev. edit., 1993, The Nature of Communism, 1962, Studying History, 1966, Red October, 1967, The Russian Revolution, 1972, Fodor's Europe Talking, 1975, Russia-The Roots of Confrontation, 1985, Is Russia Reformable?, 1988, Year of the Heroic Guerrilla, 1989, Trotsky, Stalin and Socialism, 1992, The End of the Communist Revolution, 1993, Soviet Communism from Reform to Collapse, 1994, Russia's Transformation, 1997; editor: The University of Vermont: The First Two Hundred Years, 1991. Mem. Chittenden County (Vt.) Dem. Com., 1959—; mem. Burlington City Dem. Com., 1965—; chmn. policy and planning platform com. Vt. Dem. Party, 1962-66, 69-73, 76-80, mem. exec. com., 1981-85; alt. Dem. Nat. Conv., 1968; mem. Dem. Platform Com., 1980; bd. visitors USAF Acad., 1965-67. Ensign USNR, 1944-46. U.S.-Soviet Cultural Exchange scholar U. Moscow, 1966, USSR Acad. Scis. scholar, 1976, 84, 88; NEH fellow, 1971-72, Guggenheim fellow, 1980-81, Kennan Inst. fellow, 1985. Fellow Vt. Acad. Arts and Scis.; mem. Am. Hist. Assn. (pres. conf. Slavic and East European history 1976-77), Am. Assn. Advancement Slavic Studies (bd. dirs. 1968-71, v.p. 1991, pres. 1992, chmn. com. on govt. affairs 1993-94, Disting. Contbns. award 2001), Can. Assn. Slavists, Authors' Guild, Vt. Hist. Soc. (trustee 1968-71), Vt. Coun. World Affairs, Norwich Ctr./Bridges for Peace (bd. dirs. 1988-94), Harvard Club Vt. (pres. 1974-75). Home: 195 S Prospect St Burlington VT 05401-3519 Office: University of Vermont Dept Of History Burlington VT 05405-0001

DANIELS, RONALD GEORGE, theater director; b. Niteroi, Rio de Janiero, Brazil, Oct. 15, 1942; arrived in U.S., 1991; s. Percy and Nellie (Chalmers) D.; m. Anjula Harman; children: Alexis, Eliena. Student, Fundacão Brasileira de Teatro, Rio de Janiero. Assoc. artistic dir. Am. Reperatory Theatre, Cambridge, Mass., 1991—96; head acting and directing programs Inst. for Advanced Theatre Tng. Harvard U., 1991—96. Hon. assoc. dir. Royal Shakespeare Co., Stratford-upon-Avon, London; lectr. Shakespeare Inst., U. Birmingham, Friends Royal Shakespeare Co., others. Dir.: (stage) Coriolanus, Major Barbara, Who's Afraid of Virginia Wolf, Sweeney Todd, Ghosts, Hamlet, Drums in the Night, The Samaritan, Time Travelers, The Long and Short and the Tall, The Word, Measure for Measure, Fear and Miseries of the Third Reich, The Insect Play, Twelfth Night, A Midsummer Night's Dream, Pillars of the Community, Man is Man, The Children's Crusade, Female Transport, Sgt. Musgrave's Dance, Into the Mouth of Crabs, By Common Consent, The Motor Show, Made in Britain, Bang, Afore Night Come, Bingo, Puntila and His Servant Matti, Ivanov, Destiny, T'is Pity She's a Whore, The Lorenzaccio Story, The Sons of Light, Pericles, The Suicide, Timon of Athens, Hippolytus, Camille, Hansel and Gretel, Peer Gynt, Romeo and Juliet, Ashes, The Beastly Beatitudes of Balthazar B, Across from the Garden of Allah, Playing with Trains, The Tempest, Julius Cesar, Maydays, Breaking the Silence, The Danton Affair, The Women Pirates, Real Dreams, They Shoot Horses, Much Ado About Nothing, The Plain Dealer, The Clockwork Orange, Earwig, Richard II, The Seagull, As You Like It, The Dream of The Red Spider, Silence, Cunning, Exile, Cakewalk, Henry IV parts I and II, The Cherry Orchard, Henry V, The Threepenny Opera, The Tempest, Slaughter City, Long Day's Journey into Night, Blinded by the Sun, Anthony and Cleopatra, The Shepherd King, One Flea Spare, Madama Butterfly, Henry V and Richard II, Richard III, Macbeth, Remember This, King Lear, Carmen, Hedda Gabler, The Feast of Snails, The Turn of the Screw, Sana que Sana, Havana is Waiting, Tosca; exec. prodr. Lawn Dogs. Mem. Soc. Stage Dirs. and Choreographers, Dir.'s Guild Gt. Britain.

DANIELS, RUSSELL HOWARD, lawyer; b. Dallas, Apr. 25, 1967; s. Charles Judd and Barbara Ann (Smith) D.; m. Pamela Beth Rhodes, June 24, 1989. BA in Criminal Justice, BA in Sociology, So. Meth. U., 1989; JD with honors, U. Tulsa, 1994. Bar: Tex. 1994, U.S. Dist. Ct. (no., we. and ea. dist.) Tex. 1995, U.S. Ct. Appeals (5th cir.) 1995, U.S. Ct. Appeals (10th cir.) 2001. Law clk. Law Offices of Doug Larson, Mesquite, Tex., 1991-93, assoc., 1994-96; sole practitioner Dallas, 1996—2001; assoc. Craddock, Reneker and Davis, LP, Dallas, 2001—. Articles editor Tulsa Law Jour., 1993-94. Master Mason Grand Lodge of Tex. A.F. & A.M., Mesquite, 1995—. Recipient Am. Jurisprudence award Lawyers Coop., 1991, 92. Mem.: ABA, Okla. Bar Assn., Bar Assn. Fifth Fed. Cir., State Bar of Tex., Dallas Bar Assn., Phi Delta Phi. Avocations: outdoors, travel, reading. Office: Craddock Reneker and Davis LP 3100 Monticello #550 Dallas TX 75205 Home: 5906 Prospect Ave Dallas TX 75206 E-mail: rdaniels@bcrlaw.com.

DANIELS, STEPHEN M. government official; b. Boston, Mar. 28, 1947; s. Everett Jerome and Helen Dorothy (Ettinger) Daniels; m. Maygene Louise Frost, June 25, 1972; children: Edward Frost, Leah Lillian. BA, Yale U., 1968, JD, 1972. Bar: Calif. 1972, D.C. 1973, U.S. Supreme Ct. 1980. Asst. to asst. sec. for legislation HEW, Washington, 1969-70; legislative analyst U.S. Office of Mgmt. and Budget, Washington, 1971; legislative asst. to Congressman U.S. Ho. Reps., Washington, 1972-73, with Com. on Govt. Ops., 1973-87, minority counsel Com. on Govt. Ops., 1980-87, minority staff dir. Com. on Govt. Ops., 1984-87; bd. contract appeals GSA, Washington, 1987—, chmn., 1992—. Treas. Capitol Hill Cmty. Found., Washington, 1999—. Commr. Congl. Softball League, Washington, 1977—81; pres. Capitol East Children's Ctr., Washington, 1982—83; trustee Capitol Hill Day Sch., Washington, 1988—92. Capt. USAR, 1970—71. Mem.: ABA, Calif. Bar Assn., D.C. Bar Assn., Fed. Bar Assn. Avocations: baseball, home restoration, camping, bicycling. Home: 816 Massachusetts Ave NE Washington DC 20002-6016 Office: 1800 F St NW Washington DC 20405-0001 E-mail: stephen.daniels@gsa.gov.

DANIELS, SUSANNE, broadcast executive; m. Greg Daniels. Grad., Harvard U. Asst. mgr. devel. Broadway Video Entertainment, mgr. devel.; dir. variety, reality and specials ABC TV Network; dir. comedy devel. The Fox Broadcasting Co.; pres. entertainment The WB Network, Burbank, Calif. Spkr. in field; developer (for Lorne Michaels) Saturday Night Live, Kids in the Hall, Am. Detective, America's Funniest People, Living Single, Martin, Buffy the Vampire Slayer, Dawson's Creek, Felicity, Roswell, Angel, Gilmore Girls, 7th Heaven; responsible for overseeing (ABCs spls.) Academy Awards, Muhammad Ali's 50th Birthday Spl., Am. Comedy Awards. Bd. dirs. The Nat. Campaign to Prevent Teenage Pregnancy. Named in the Power Issue Entertainment Weekly, 1997, one of most powerful women in entertainment, The Hollywood Reporter, 1998, 1999, 2000. Mem.: Acad. TV Arts and Sci. Office: WB Network 4000 Warner Blvd Bldg 34-r Burbank CA 91522-0001

DANIELS, SYDNEY ROBERT, theater director, educator; b. Sept. 16, 1941; s. James Monroe and Marie P. Daniels. BS in Edn., Ill. State U., Normal, 1963, MS in Edn., 1967. Art tchr. Wendell Phillips H.S., Chgo., 1965—67; instr. Harold Washington Coll., Chgo., 1967—70, asst. prof., 1971—89, assoc. prof., 1989—92, prof., 1992—. Tech. dir. theatre Harold Washington Coll., 1968—69, assoc. dir. theatre, 1969—74, dir. theatre, 1974—. Mem. Joseph Jefferson Theatre Awards Com., Chgo., 1970—. Recipient Excellence award, Nat. Inst. for Staff Devel., 1996, Alumni Achievement award, Ill State U. Alumni Assn., 1998. Roman Catholic. Avocations: painting, attending theatrical presentations, gardening, singing.

DANIELS, WILLIAM ALBERT, food products executive; b. Westboro, Mass., Dec. 7, 1937; s. Roy Oliver and Florine (Francesco) D.; m. Anne Farrell Richardson, Apr. 15, 1967; children: Paul, Kimberly, David. Student, Boston U., 1959-61. Lic. real estate broker. Pres. W.A. Daniels Real Estate Co., Peabody, Mass., 1959-64; with sales Sears, Roebuck and Co., Saugus, Mass., 1964-67; pres. Antech Chem. Co., Middleton, Mass., 1968-78; treas., co-owner Richardson Farms Inc., Middleton, 1978—. Corporator Danvers (Mass.) Sav. Bank, 1984—. Mem. New Eng. Ice Cream Retailers Assn., Nat. Trust for Hist. Preservation, Middleton Hist. Soc. Republican. Roman Catholic. Home: 105 Flint Farm Rd Middleton MA 01949-2491 Office: Richardson Farm Inc 156 S Main St Middleton MA 01949-2452

DANIELS, WILLIAM BURTON, retired physicist, educator; b. Buffalo, Dec. 21, 1930; s. William C. and Sophia (Penner) D.; m. Adriana A. Braakman, Sept. 2, 1958; children: Charlotte Mary, William Fredrik, Donald Christopher. BS in Physics, U. Buffalo, 1952; MS, Case Inst. Tech., 1955, PhD, 1957. Instr. to asst. prof. Case Inst. Tech., 1957-59; rsch. scientist Union Carbide Corp., 1959-61; mem. faculty Princeton U., 1961-72, prof. solid state scis., 1967-72; Unidel prof. physics U. Del., Newark, 1972-2000, Unidel prof. emeritus, 2001—. Rsch. collaborator Brookhaven nat. Lab.; cons. U.S. Army Rsch. Lb.; guest scientist rsch. facility, Denmark, 1976; invité Coll. France, 1977; exch. prof. U. Paris, 1977; guest scientist IBM Zurich Lab., 1977; guest scientist Max Planck Inst. for Festkörperforschung; vis. faculty Geophys. Lab., Carnegie Inst. of Washington, 2000. Recipient Alexander von Humboldt Sr. Scientist award, 1981, 92; John S. Guggenheim Meml. fellow, 1976-77. Fellow Am. Phys. Soc. Achievements include research in properties materials at high pressure, equation of state of solids, experimentation on solidified permanent gases, electronic structure of compressed solids, instrumentation high pressure research, non-linear optics. E-mail: Family_Daniels@yahoo.com.

DANIELSEN, ALBERT LEROY, economics educator, educational consultant; b. Council Bluffs, Iowa, May 26, 1934; s. Moroni Lloyd and Geneva Gale (Williford) D.; m. Eleanor Jean Gibson, June 7, 1958; children: Bartley Roland, Lea Anne, Albert William. B.S., Clemson U., 1960; Ph.D., Duke U., 1966. Dir. Office Internat. Market Analysis, U.S. Dept. Energy, Washington, 1977-78; from asst. prof. to prof. econs. U. Ga., Athens, 1963-97; prof. emeritus, 1997-; pres. Nat. Bus. and Econ. Edn. Assocs. Inc., 1988—; dir. James C. Bonbright Utilities Ctr., U. Ga., 1991—. Author: Evolution of OPEC, 1982, Principles of Public Utility Rates, 1988, Reliability of Electric Supply in Georgia, 2001, OPEC, Encyclopedia Britannica, 2002; contbr. articles to profl. jours. Social

Sci. Research Council grantee, 1982. Mem. Internat. Assn. Energy Economists (rep. Atlanta chpt., exec. com. 1981-99), Am. Econs. Assn., So. Econs. Assn. Baptist. Avocations: swimming, golf. Business E-Mail: bonbright@terry.uga.edu.

DANIELSON, GARY R. lawyer; b. Detroit, June 8, 1953; s. Ronald Gregory and Catherine (Gibson) D. BA in Psychology, Oakland U., Rochester, Mich., 1976; JD cum laude, Wayne State U., 1983. Bar: Mich. 1983, U.S. Dist. Ct. (ea. dist.) Mich., 1985, U.S. Supreme Ct. 1987. Sr. job placement counselor Ferndale (Mich.) Sch. Dist., 1976-79; employment and tng. adminstr. Oakland County Govt., Pontiac, Mich., 1979-82; sr. corp. labor rels. rep. Harper-Grace Hosps., Detroit, 1982-83; corp. labor rels. mgr. Vis. Nurse Assn., Detroit, 1983-85; atty., v.p., cons. Indsl. Rels., Inc., Detroit, 1985-90; pres. The Danielson Group, P.C., St. Clair Shores, 1989—. Bd. dirs. Henry Ford Village, Dearborn, Mich., 2002—. Mem. ABA, Mich. Bar Assn., Indsl. Rels. Rsch. Assn. Republican. Avocation: sailing. Office: Danielson Group PC 27735 Jefferson Ave Saint Clair Shores MI 48081-1309

DANIELSON, GILBERT LAWRENCE, consumer products company executive; b. Monmouth, Ill., Aug. 22, 1946; BS, Drake U., 1968. With Arthur Andersen & Co., Chgo.; various sr. fin. positions; v.p. fin., CFO Aaron Rents, Inc., Atlanta, 1990-98, exec. v.p., CFO, 1998, also bd. dirs. Bd. dirs. Abrams Industries, Inc. 1st lt. U.S. Army, Vietnam. Office: Aaron Rents Inc 309 E Paces Ferry Rd NE Atlanta GA 30305-2377 E-mail: Gil.Danielson@aaronrents.com.

DANIELSON, GORDON KENNETH, JR., cardiovascular surgeon, educator; b. Burlington, Iowa, Dec. 5, 1931; s. Gordon Kenneth and Helen H. (Hill) D.; m. Sondra Jean Bolich, Jan. 21, 1961; children: Gordon Kenneth III, Laura, Karen, Keith, Bruce, Susan, Jennifer. BA in Chemistry, U. Pa., 1953, MD (Pfizer, Senatorial, Clark scholar, Albert Einstein award 1956, Roche award 1956, Spencer Morris prize 1956), 1956, postgrad., 1960. Diplomate Am. Bd. Surgery, Am. Bd. Thoracic Surgery. Intern U. Mich. Hosp., Ann Arbor, 1956-57; asst. resident in surgery Hosp. of U. Pa., 1957-61, chief resident in surgery, 1961-62, gen. and thoracic surgeon, 1962-65, asst. chief surg. div. I, 1962-65; vis. fellow in thoracic surgery Thorax Kliniken, Stockholm, 1963-64; practice medicine specializing in thoracic and cardiovascular surgery Phila., 1963-65, Lexington, Ky., 1965-67, Rochester, Minn., 1967—. Assoc. prof. surgery U. Ky. Med. Sch.; also chief cardiac surgery Univ. Hosp., 1965-67; mem. faculty Mayo Grad. Sch. Medicine, Rochester, Minn., 1967—, prof. surgery, 1975—, Joe M. and Ruth Roberts prof. surgery, 1987—; past chmn. divsn. thoracic and cardiovascular surgery, cons. cardiovascular and thoracic surgery Mayo Clinic/Mayo Found., 1967-2003, St. Mary's Hosp., Meth. Hosp., Rochester, 1967-2003; Am. Heart Assn. vis. tchr., Singapore, 1975, Amman, Jordan, 1981, W.W.L. Glenn lectr., 1999. Editor Cardiovascular Surgery, 1972-78; contbr. numerous articles to med. jours. Markle scholar in acad. medicine, 1962-67 Fellow ACS, Am. Coll. Cardiology; mem. Am. Assn. Thoracic Surgery, Am. Surg. Assn., Am. Heart Assn. (fellow coun. cardiovascular surgery), Soc. Thoracic Surgeons (a founder), Soc. Univ. Surgeons, Soc. Vascular Surgery, Mexican Soc. Cardiology (hon.), Assn. Thoracic and Cardiovascular Surgeons of Asia (hon.), India (hon.), Chile Soc. Cardiology and Cardiovascular Surgery (hon.), Colombian Soc. of Cardiology (hon.), Congenital Heart Surgeons Soc., Peruvian Soc. of Cardiology (hon.), Phi Beta Kappa, Alpha Omega Alpha. Achievements include being the 1st fellow in congenital heart disease U.S.-USSR Health Exchange Program, 1973. Home: 6000 16th Ave NW Rochester MN 55901-2107 Office: Mayo Med Ctr 200 1st St SW Rochester MN 55905-0001

DANIELSON, LUKE JEFFRIES, lawyer; b. Boulder, Colo., Aug. 8, 1948; s. Philip A. and Mildred S. (Page) D.; m. Rosa Venezia, Aug. 9, 1975. BA in Econ., Antioch Coll., 1971; JD, U. Calif.-Berkeley, 1975. Bar: Colo. 1975, U.S. Dist. Ct. Colo. 1975, U.S. Ct. Appeals (10th cir.) 1975, U.S. Dist. Ct. Nebr. 1984. Assoc. Holland & Hart, Denver, 1975-78; editor-in-chief Solar Law Reporter, Golden, Colo., 1978-79; counsel Nat. Wildlife Fedn., Boulder, Colo., 1979-81; ptnr. Danielson & Euser, Denver, 1982-85; Gersh & Danielson, Denver, 1985—; adj. asst. prof. U. Denver Coll. of Law, 1978, 85, 87, U. Denver, 1994, U. Colo. Sch. Law, Boulder, 1979-81, 82, 84, 94; arbitrator Am. Arbitration Assn., other orgns. Author articles on solar energy and law, energy policy, mediation and mediation of environ. disputes. Chmn. bd. dirs. Eco-Cycle, Inc., Boulder, 1985-86, bd. dirs., mem. 1983-86; bd. dirs. Colo. Conservation Found., Denver, 1985-94, Global Response, 1991—; vice chmn., mem. Nat. Wildlif Fedn. Action, Inc., 1992—; mem. Mined Land Reclamation Bd., 1987—, chair 1989, 91, 94; counsel Univ. Corp. Atmospheric Rsch. Found., 1987-89. Mem. ABA (sect. natural resources, energy and environ. law, vice chair internat. resources com. 1994—), Colo. Bar Assn. (bd. govs. 1992-94), Denver Bar Assn., Boulder Bar Assn., Wyo. Wildlife Fedn. (life), Colo. Wildlife Fedn., AAAS, Am. Solar Energy Soc. Office: Gersh & Danielson 4747 Table Mesa Dr Boulder CO 80305-5573

DANIELSON, URSEL REHDING, psychiatrist; b. Hamburg, Germany, Aug. 15, 1935; came to U.S., 1954; d. Martin George and Gerda Maria (Muller) Rehding; 1 child, Richard. BS, U. Vt., 1964, MD, 1967. Diplomate Am. Bd. Psychiatry and Neurology. Intern Robert Packer Hosp., Sayre, Pa., 1967-68; resident in psychiatry U. Vt., Burlington, 1968-71; chief resident McGill U. and Children's Hosp., Montreal, Quebec, Can., 1971-72; pvt. practice Burlington, 1972-86; med. dir. Vt. State Hosp., Waterbury, 1986-90; child psychiatrist Dept. Psychiatry U. Vt., Burlington, 1990-94, pvt. practice, Burlington, 1994—. Cons. Franklin Grand Isle Mental Health Ctr., St. Albans, Vt., 1982-86, Essex Junction Sch. Sys., 1982-86, Chittenden Ctrl. Sch. Dist., 1972-86, Weeks Sch., Vergennes, 1972-80, Ogdensburg (N.Y.) State Hosp. Children's Svcs., 1980-84; asst. prof. dept. psychiatry U. Vt., Burlington, 1972-86, assoc. prof., 1986—, supr. psychiat. residents, 1972-98. Treas., dir. Providence Island Assocs., South Hero, Vt., 1988—; mem. Bd. Mental Health of State of Vt., 1992-98. Fellow APA; mem. Vt. Psychiat. Assn. (chair nominating com. 1984, 85, 88—, pres. 1985-86, rep. to APA assembly and area coun. 1978-84, 89-90). Avocations: boating, skiing, gardening, hiking, movies. Home: 120 Hailey's Way Colchester VT 05446

DANIELSON, WALTER GEORGE, lawyer; b. Anaconda, Mont., July 3, 1903; s. John and Tekla Christina (Jonsson) D.; m. Beryl Marie Pearce, Aug. 17, 1935; children— Karin Lynn Godfrey, John Howard. LL.B., U. Mont., 1929, J.D. (hon.), 1970; diploma of honor Pepperdine U., 1980. Bar: Calif. 1929, pvt. practice, Los Angeles; vice consul for Sweden, Los Angeles, 1937-55, consul, 1955-69, consul gen., 1969-76, emeritus, 1976; sec. Los Angeles Consular Corps, 1976— . Trustee Luth. Hosp. Soc. So. Calif., Los Angeles; bd. dirs. Calif. Hosp. Decorated Knight Royal Order Vasa, comdr. Royal Order Vasa, comdr. Royal Order North Star (Sweden); officers cross (Hungary); Knight Royal Order St. Olav (Norway); Knight's cross 1st class Royal Order Dannebrog (Denmark). Mem. Calif. State Bar, Los Angeles Bar Assn. Clubs: California, Vasa Order Am., Swedish (Los Angeles). Home: 68 Fremont Pl Los Angeles CA 90005-3858 Office: Danielson & St Clair 68 Fremont Pl Los Angeles CA 90005-3858

DANIELSON, WAYNE ALLEN, journalism and computer science educator; b. Burlington, Iowa, Dec. 6, 1929; s. Arthur Leroy and Bessie Ann (Bonar) D.; m. Beverly Grace Kinsell, Mar. 19, 1955 (dec. Oct. 1988); children: Matthew Henry, Benjamin Wayne, Grace Frances, Paul Arthur; m. LaVonne Walker Caffey, July 10, 1993; stepchildren: Kristin Marie, Bradley Neal. BA, State U. Iowa, 1952; MA, Stanford U., 1953, PhD, 1957. Reporter, research mgr. San Jose (Calif.) Mercury-News, 1953-54; acting asst. prof. Stanford U., 1956-57; asst. prof. journalism U. Wis., 1957-59; mem. faculty U. N.C., 1959-69, prof. journalism, 1963-69; research prof. Inst. Research Social Sci., 1963-69; dean Sch. Journalism, 1964-69, Sch. Communication, U. Tex. at Austin, 1969-79, prof. journalism and computer sci., 1969—, Jesse H. Jones prof. journalism, 1982-89; Dewitt C. Reddick chair, 1989; chmn. dept. journalism U. Tex. at Austin, 1991-93. Mem. steering com. News Rsch. Ctr., Am. Newspaper Pubs. Assn., 1964-73; mem. rsch. com. AP Mng. Editors Assn., 1963-69. Author: (with G. C. Wilhoit, Jr.) A Computerized Bibliography of Mass Communication Research, 1944-64, (with Blanche Prejean) Programed News Style, 1977, 2d edit., 1988; contbr. articles to profl. jours.; founding editor: Journalism Abstracts, 1963-68, 71; mem. editl. bd. Journalism Quar, 1964-72; author, editor instrnl. computer program series. Mem. pub. rels. com. N.C. Heart Assn., 1963-67; chmn. faculty senate U. Tex., 1989-90. Recipient Civitatis award, U. Tex., 2000. Mem. Assn. Edn. Journalism and Mass Comm. (chmn. publs. com. 1968-72, rsch. com. 1980-83, pres. 1970-71, Paul J. Deutschmann award 1993), Am. Assn. Schs. and Depts. Journalism (v.p. 1966-67, pres. 1967-68), Tex. Journalism Edn. Coun. (chmn. 1970-71), Phi Beta Kappa, Kappa Tau Alpha, Phi Kappa Phi. Office: U Tex Sch Journalism Austin TX 78712 E-mail: wayne@mail.utexas.edu.

DANIELYAN, ARTHUR A. mathematician, researcher; s. Arshaluys A. and Sirush A. Danielyan. PhD, Inst. Math. Armenian Acad. Scis., 1987. Sci. rschr. Inst. Math. Armenian Acad. Scis., Yerevan, Armenia, 1989—94; sr. sci. rschr. Moscow (Russia) Aviation Inst., 1994—98; vis. rsch. scholar U. of South Fla., Tampa, 1998—2000; vis. instr. and rschr. U. of Ctrl. Fla., Orlando, 2000—. Grantee, German Academic Exch. Svc., 1996. Office: U Ctrl Fla Dept Math PO Box 161364 Orlando FL 32816-1364 E-mail: adaniely@pegasus.cc.ucf.edu.

DANIKAS, DIMITRIOS, plastic surgeon; s. Charalambos and Anna D.. MD, U. Patras Med. Sch., Patras-Rion, Greece, 1991. Resident dept. gen. surgery St. Andrews' Gen. Regional Hosp., Patras, Greece, 1992—94; intern N.Y. Hosp. Med. Ctr. Queens, Flushing, 1994—95; resident dept. surgery Monmouth Med. Ctr., Long Branch, NJ, 1995—2001; rschr. dept. plastic surgery, hand surgery/microsurgery So. Ill. U., Springfield, 2001—02; plastic surgeon dept. plastic surgery SUNY, Bklyn., 2002—03; plastic surgeon divsn. plastic surgery N.Y. Presbyn. Hosp., 2003—. Chief resident gen. surgery Beth Israel Med. Ctr., Newark, 2000—01, Monmouth Med. Ctr., Long Branch, NJ, 2000—01. Contbr. articles, chapters to books. Mem.: Med. Soc. Patras, N.Y. Med. Soc., Sangamon Med. Soc., Hellenic Med. Soc. N.Y., Am. Soc. Gen. Surgeons, Soc.Laparoendoscopic Surgeons (hon. Outstanding Laparoendoscopy award 2000), Soc. Am. Coll. Surgeons (assoc.; candidate). Avocations: history, philosophy. E-mail: ddanikas@yahoo.com.

DANILEK, DONALD J. lawyer; b. N.Y.C., Mar. 25, 1937; s. Joseph A. and Mary (Dedina) D.; m. Jane Till, Mar. 26, 1958; children: Christopher, Mary Jane, Gregory, Thomas. A.B., Princeton U., 1958; J.D., U. Va., 1961. Bar: Va. 1961, N.Y. 1961, U.S. Tax Ct. 1983. Asst. prof. law U.S. Mil. Acad., West Point, N.Y., 1961-65; assoc. firm Kirlin, Campbell & Keating, N.Y.C., 1965-70, ptnr., 1970-71, 75-88; mng. dir. Bank In Liechstein Trust Co., N.Y.C., 1988-90; sr. v.p. pvt. banking, sec. and gen. counsel trust div., Bank of Bermuda (N.Y.) Ltd., 1990—, ptnr. Gasser & Hayes, N.Y.C., 1971-74. Named Yachtsman of Yr. Port Washington Yacht Club, 1974, 77. Mem. Va. State Bar. Republican. Roman Catholic. Clubs: N.Y. Yacht (N.Y.C.); Manhasset Bay Yacht (Port Washington). Office: Bank of Bermuda (NY) Ltd Pvt Banking Trust Div 350 Park Ave New York NY 10022-6022

DANILKOVITCH, ALLA, research scientist; d. Victor Suchkov and Ludmila Suchkova; m. Alexei V. Miagkov, Sept. 24, 1999; 1 child, Anton A. MS, Moscow State U., 1988, PhD, 1991. Cert. Nurse, Nursing Sch., Podolsk, Russia, 1981. Rschr. Moscow State U., 1991—95; vis. scientist Max-Planck Inst. of Biochemistry, Munchen, Germany, 1995—97; rsch. postdoctoral fellow Nat. Cancer Inst., Frederick, Md., 1997—2002; rsch. scientist PPD Devel., Richmond, 2002—. Author over 30 rsch. papers and reviews. Recipient Bursary for young scientists award, 22d FEBS Organizing Com., 1993, Rsch. Exellence award, Fare NIH, 2000, Exceptional Stipendium, Dir. Bd., NIH, 2001, 5th Spring Rsch. Festival award, NCI, 2001; fellow Short-Term Fellowship, FEBS, 1994, Max-Planck Stipendium, Max-Planck Soc., Germany, 1995, Personal Stipendium, Fogarty Found., NIH, 1997; grantee Individual Grant from Internat. Sci. Found., George Soros Fund, 1993, Travel Grant, ISICR Organizing Com., 1994. Mem.: Soc. Leukocyte Biology. Office: PPD Devel 2244 Dabney Rd Richmond VA 23230

DANILOV, VICTOR JOSEPH, museum management program director, consultant, author, educator; b. Farrell, Pa., Dec. 30, 1924; s. Joseph M. and Ella (Tominovich) D.; m. Toni Dewey, Sept. 6, 1980; children: Thomas J., Duane P., Denise S. BA in Journalism, Pa. State U., 1945; MS in Journalism, Northwestern U., 1946; EdD in Higher Edn., U. Colo., 1964. With Sharon Herald, Pa., 1942, Youngstown Vindicator, 1945, Pitts. Sun-Telegraph, 1946-47, Chgo. Daily News, 1947-50; instr. journalism U. Colo., 1950-51; asst. prof. journalism U. Kans., 1951-53; with Kansas City Star, 1953; mgr. pub. rels. Ill. Inst. Tech. and IIT Rsch. Inst., 1953-57; dir. univ. rels. and pub. info. U. Colo., 1957-60; pres. Profile Co., Boulder, Colo., 1960-62; exec. editor, exec. v.p. Indsl. Rsch. Inc., Beverly Shores, Ind., 1962-69, pub., exec. v.p., 1969-71; dir., v.p. Mus. Sci. and Industry, Chgo., 1971-77, pres., dir., 1978-87, pres. emeritus, 1987—; dir. mus. mgmt. program, adj. prof. U. Colo., 1987—. Mem. rural industrialization adv. group Dept. Agr., 1967; mem. panel internat. transfer tech. Dept. Commerce, 1968; mem. sci. info. coun. NSF, 1969-72; chmn. Conf. on Implications Metric Change, 1972, Nat. Conf. Indsl. Rsch., 1966-70; chmn. observance Nat. Indsl. Rsch. Week, 1967-70; chmn. Midwest White House Conf. on Indsl. World Ahead, 1972, Internat. Conf. Sci. and Tech. Museums, 1976, 82; mem. task force on fin. acctg. and reporting by non bus. orgns., others. Author: Public Affairs Reporting, 1955, Starting a Science Center, 1977, Science and Technology Centers, 1982, Science Center Planning Guide, 1985, Chicago's Museums, 1987, rev. edit., 1991, America's Science Museums, 1990, Corporate Museums, Galleries, and Visitor Centers: A Directory, 1991, A Planning Guide for Corporate Museums, Galleries, and Visitors Centers, 1992, Museum Careers and Training: A Professional Guide, 1994, University and College Museums, Galleries, and Related Facilities, 1996, Hall of Fame Museums: A Reference Guide, 1997, Colorado Museums and Historical Sites, 2000, Museums and Historic Sites of the American West, 2002; also articles; editor: Crucial Issues in Public Relations, 1960, Corporate Research and Profitability, 1966, Innovation and Profitability, 1967, Research Decision-Making in New Product Development, 1968, New Products--and Profits, 1969, Applying Emerging Technologies, 1970, Nuclear Power in the South, 1970, The Future of Science and Technology, 1975, Museum Accounting Guidelines, 1976, Traveling Exhibitions, 1978, Towards the Year 2000, 1981; editor profl. procs. Trustee Women of the West Mus., 1991-99, v.p., 1991-99; trustee La Rabida Childrens Hosp. and Rsch. Ctr., 1973-83; mem. U. Chgo. Citizens Bd., 1978-87. Mem. Am. Assn. Mus. (exec. com. 1976-77, bd. dirs. 1985-88, chmn. mus. studies task force 1988-89), AAAS, Assn. Sci.-Tech. Ctrs. (bd. dirs. 1973-84, sec.-treas. 1973-74, pres. 1975-76), Internat. Coun. Mus. (com. on sci. and tech. mus. 1972—, vice chmn. 1977-87, chmn. 1982-83, bd. dirs. 1985-88), Chgo. Coun. on Fine Arts (chmn. 1976-84), Ill. Arts Alliance (bd. dirs. 1983-86), Sci. Mus. Exhibit Collaborative (pres. 1983-86), Mus. Film Network (pres. 1984-86). Home: 250 Bristlecone Way Boulder CO 80304-0413 Office: Univ Colo Mus Mus Mgmt Program Campus Box 218 Boulder CO 80309-0218

DANILOVICH, JOHN J. ambassador; b. Calif., June 1950; m. Irene Forte, Mar. 19, 1977; children: John Charles, Alice, Alexander. HS, The Choate School, 1968; BA in Polit. Sci., Stanford U., 1972; MA in Internat. Rels., U. So. Calif. (London), 1980. U.S. amb. to Costa Rica Dept. State, 2001—. Bd. dirs. Panama Canal Commn., chmn. transition com.; former trustee Am. Mus. in Britain; former chmn. Republicans Abroad, Knight of Malta; former dir. Stanford Trust, U.S.-U.K. Fulbright Commn. Mem.: White's (London), Pacific Union Club (San Francisco). Office: US Embassy San Jose Unit 2501 Apo AA 34020

DANILOW, DEBORAH MARIE, singer, songwriter, musician, rancher, realtor; b. Mineral Wells, Tex., Dec. 9, 1947; d. Stanton Byron and Irval Leona (Vanhoosier) D.; m. William Paul Cook Jr., June 1965 (div. Oct. 1967); m. Chance Gentry, Oct. 1971 (div. May 1974); m. Ellis Elmer Aldridge, Dec. 3, 1977 (div. Nov. 1984); children: Chandra Desiree, Anthony Ellis; m. Carl Graham Quisenberry, Feb. 7, 1992 (div. May 1997). Student, Brantley Draughon Bus. Coll., Ft. Worth, 1965-66, Tex. Christian U., 1965-67, U. Ariz., 1967-69. Asst. to pres. Hollywood Video Ctr., L.A., 1969-72; producer Western Inst. TV, L.A., 1972-77; owner Chanelde Ranch, Weatherford, Tex., 1977-84; band musician Bonnie Raitt, Jerry Williams, Malibu, Calif., 1984, Mick Fleetwood, Malibu, 1984; lead musician Jazz Talk, Ft. Worth, 1985-96; owner Brazos Valley Ranch Inc., 1987—97, AAA Bail Bonds, Seymour, 1990-96; mgr., team leader Keller Williams Realty, Arlington, Tex., 2002—03, Manfield, Tex., 2002—03, realtor assoc. Ft. Worth, 2003—. Composer numerous pub. songs, 1969—; lead musician Debbie Danilow and Soul Full o' Jazz, 1996—; debut solo CD Primordial Heart, 1999. Active Sheriffs Assn. Tex., Seymour, 1991-97, North Tex. Taxpayers League, Wichita Falls, Tex., 1991-96, Tex. State Notary Bd., Austin, 1990-99. Mem. NRA, Nat. Assn. Realtors, Tex. Realtors Assn., Greater Ft. Worth Bd. Realtors, Greater Lewisville Bd. Realtors, Arlington Bd. Realtors, Tex. Limousin Assn., Tex. Southwestern Cattle Raisers Assn., Tex. Cattlewomen's Assn., Am. Quarter Horse Assn. (life), Nat. Found. Quarter Horse Assn., Dallas-Ft. Worth Profl. Musicians Assn., Ft. Worth Jazz Soc. (sec. 1987-89), N.Am. Limousin Found. (life), Australian Shepherd Club Am., Marchigiana Cattle Assn. (life). Avocations: music, investments, writing, performing. Home and Office: Debbie Danilow Inc 524 Pineview Ln Fort Worth TX 76140 E-mail: debbie@debbiedanilow.com.

DANITZ, MARILYNN PATRICIA, choreographer, videographer; b. Buffalo; BS in Chemistry, Le Moyne Coll.; MS in Chem. Engring., Columbia U. Artistic dir. High Frequency Wavelengths/Danitz Dances, 1976—. Assoc. prof. Tainan Cheng Chuan Coll., Taiwan, 1984; profl. dancer Ballet Mcpl. Strasbourg, France, Ballet Mcpl. Geneva, Switzerland; choreography commns. performances include The 11th Internat. Ballet Comp. Varna, Bulgaria, 1983, Tbilisi Ballet co., USSR, Nat. Ballet of Colombia, Nat. Inst. Arts, Taiwan, Nanatsudera Theatre, Nagoya, Japan, Shanghai Ballet and Shanghai Jiao Tung U., People's Republic of China, Nat. Cheng Kung Dance Group, Taiwan, Jacob's Pillow Dance Festival, Mass., 6th Internat. Dance Theatre Festival, Poland, 5th Anniversary Celebration Kannon Ctr., St. Petersburg, Russia, 15th Internat. Festival of Modern Choreography, Belarus, others; master choreography workshops include Ctrl. Ballet, Beijing, Chinese Cultural U., Taipei, Taiwan, Okuda Studio, Nagoya, Ballet Philippines, Manila, NSW Coll. Dance, Sydney, The Ballet Sch., Bogota, Colombia, Lublin, Lodz, Poznan and Bytom, Poland, Vitebsk, Belarus, others; video prodn. Real Art Ways Nat. Residency, funded by NEA, 1990; video art collaboration with Allen Ginsberg. Presentations include Internat. Conf. on Dance and Tech., 1993, Naropa Inst. 20th Anniversary Celebration, 1994; video work presented at Lincoln Ctr., N.Y.C., 1995, Hanyang U., Seoul, Korea, 1997, others; video work in permanent collection Lincoln Ctr. Dance Collection; TV prodns. of works include Nat. Broadcasting, Venezuela, Colombia, Bulgaria, Poland, Russia, Belarus, Pub. Broadcasting, Albany, N.Y.C., Mpls.; works performed by Nat. Ballet with the Nat. Philharm. Orch. of Colombia Gala Performance, 1984; co. tours include China, Japan, Taiwan, Europe, Hawaii; co-editor Branching Out, Oral Histories of the Founders of Six National Dance Orgns.; juror competitions. Recipient Outstanding Dance-Theater Work of 1986 award Dance Brew-ATV Cable Manhattan, award for disting. choreography Nat. Assn. Regional Ballet, 1982; Bessie Schoenberg Lab. for Experienced Choreographers Dance Theater Workshop; NIH fellow; Gold Medal scholar Conservatoire Geneve, N.Y. State Regents scholar, Le Moyne Coll. Chemistry scholar, others. Mem. Dance Theater Workshop, Am. Dance Guild (pres., editor Am. Dance, bd. dirs., nat. conf. planning com.), Soc. Dance History Scholars, Dance Films Assn. Address: 560 Riverside Dr Apt 16E New York NY 10027-3208 also: PO Box 216 Sand Lake NY 12153-0216 also: 3200 Holly Rd Apt 2 Virginia Beach VA 23451-2926 E-mail: HFW2000@aol.com.

DANJCZEK, DAVID WILLIAM, manufacturing company executive; b. Phillipsburg, N.J., Sept. 29, 1951; s. William Emil and Erna (Lob) D. BSFS, Georgetown U., 1973; postgrad., Waseda U., 1973-74, Loyola U., L.A., 1977-78. Contract adminstr. Aero Products, Woodland Hills, Calif., 1974-76, sr. contract adminstr., 1976-78; dir. internat. ops. Litton Industries, Washington, 1978-90, v.p. internat. bus., 1990-93; v.p. govt. and internat. affairs Western Atlas Inc., 1993-97; corp. v.p. Unova, Inc., Arlington, Va., 1997—; v.p. adminstrn. Mfrs. Alliance/MAPI, 2002—. Adj. prof. Georgetown U.; chmn. industry sector adv. com. U.S. Dept. Commerce; bd. dirs., past chair Exec. Coun. Diplomacy. Mem. Am. Countertrade Assn., Univ. Club., Washington Ind. Roundtable (sec., treas.). Roman Catholic. Avocations: squash, bridge. Home: 1300 Crystal Dr Arlington VA 22202-3200 Office: 1525 Wilson Blvd Arlington VA 22209

DANJCZEK, MICHAEL HARVEY, social service administrator; b. Phillipsburg, N.J., May 9, 1949; s. William Emil and Erna (Lob) D.; m. Cynthia Ann Johanson, June 9, 1973; children: William Emil II, Liesel J., Rachel L., Peter L. BA in Urban Studies, Lehigh U., Bethlehem, Pa., 1972, MEd in Social Restoration, 1974, EdD in Ednl. Adminstrn., 1985; PhD (hon.), Lafayette Coll., 2000. Exec. dir. Lehigh Valley Opportunity Ctr., Bethlehem, Pa., 1972-74; pres., exec. dir. Children's Home, Easton, Pa., 1974—. Adj. prof. Lehigh County C.C., 1987-91, Grad. Sch., Jersey City State Tchrs. Coll., 1989-92; treas. Pa. Coun. Children's Svcs., 1982-84; mem. Commn. on Accreditation, Nat. Assn. Homes for Children, 1982-87, chmn. bd. dirs., 1997-98; mem. authority bd. Northampton C.C., 1983-95; v.p. Pa. Coun. Children's Svcs., 1985-87, bd. dirs., 1987-89; bd. dirs. Lehigh Valley Drug Treatment Program, 1986-88; mem. Ea. U.S. Svc. Coun. of Coun. on Accreditation Svcs. for Families and children, 1987-92; treas. Nat. Assn. Homes and Svcs. for Children, 1988-93, chmn. bd. dirs., 1997-98; bd. dirs. Twin Rivers Cmty. Bank, 1991-98, Coun. on Accreditation Svcs. for Family and Children, 1993-98, Vista Bank, 1998-2002. Asst. wrestling coach Lafayette Coll., 1974-76; mem. exec. com. Rep. party of Northampton County, 1975-76; bd. advisors Jr. League Lehigh Valley, 1975-77; chmn. profl. adv. com. Family and Child Welfare of Lehigh Valley Cmty. Coun., 1976; mem. adv. bd. Cath. Social Svcs., Diocese of Allentown, 1976-81; mem. Wilson Boro Sch. Bd., 1980-83; bd. dirs. Pa. Coun. Vol. Child Care Agys., 1980-84; bd. dirs. Helen Beebe Speech and Hearing Ctr., 1980-89, pres. bd. dirs., 1987-89; bd. dirs. Parents Anonymous Pa., 1981-90, pres. bd., 1981-85; gen. campaign chmn. United Way of Northampton and Warren Counties, 1982-83; bd. dirs. Great Valley Girl Scout Coun., 1983-89; chmn. Minsi Trail Drug Abuse Prevention Rally for Forks of Del., Boy Scouts Am., 1987; mem. St. Bernard's Ch. Parish Coun., 1991-93; chmn. elect, v.p. econ. devel. Two Rivers Area Commerce Coun., 1991-92; chmn. Northampton County Sports and Spl. Events Com., 1994-97; mem. governing bd., CEO, chmn. BallYard, Inc., 1994; mem. governing bd. St. Vincent's Home for Children, 1995-99; bd. chair Children's Coalition of the Lehigh Valley, 1998-99, Pa. Coun. Children's Svcs., 1998-2000; bd. dirs. Families Internat., 1998—, Alliance for Children and Families, 1998—; co-founder Pro Kids Alliance, 1994—, CEO Alliance for Children and Families of the Lehigh Valley, 1999—. Recipient Disting. Cmty. Svc. award Easton Area Jaycees, 1975, Disting. Svc. award Pa. Com. on Internat. Yr. of Child, 1979, Coll. Edn., Lehigh U., 1983, Disting. Alumni award Lehigh U., 1987, Gafney award Lehigh U. Assn. Ednl. Adminstrs., 1988, Pres. award for cmty. svc. Easton Area Sales and Mktg. Execs., 1990, Svc. to Mankind award Sertoma Club, 1991; inducted to Notre Dame H.S. Athletic Hall of Fame, 1990. Mem. Lehigh U. Alumni Assn. Home Club (bd. dirs. 1990—), Lehigh U. Alumni Assn. (bd. dirs. 1987-90), Northampton Country Club (bd. govs. 1985-94), Nat. Fellowship Child Care Execs. (exec. sec. 1993-98, pres. 1992-93), Two Rivers Area C. of C. (chmn. 1993-95), Rotary (past pres. Easton). Republican. Roman Catholic. Avocations: private pilot, golf, skiing, travel. Home and Office: Childrens Home Easton 2000 S 25th St Easton PA 18042

DANK, LEONARD DEWEY, medical illustrator, audio-visual consultant; b. Birmingham, Ala., Dec. 21, 1929; s. George and Ellen (Balsam) D.; B.A. in Zoology, Cornell U., 1952; grad. Sch. Med. Illustration, Mass. Gen. Hosp., 1955; m. Beryl Eileen Jealous, Sept. 30, 1961; 1 dau., Amelia Theresa. Staff med. artist, plastic surgery clinic Manhattan Eye, Ear & Throat Hosp., 1955-57, Eye Bank for Sight Restoration, 1957-59; owner Leonard D. Dank Med. Illustration Studio, 1959-79; pres. Med. Illustrations Co., 1979— (all N.Y.C.); cons. med. illustrator St. Luke's Hosp., 1961-83, trans-vision div. Milprint, Inc., 1965—, Woman's Hosp., 1963-83, H.S. Struttman, Inc., 1964—, Home Library Press, 1960-70 (all N.Y.C.), Synapse Communications, Inc. (Conn.), 1973-75, Contemporary Orthopaedics and Contemporary Surgery, 1981-85, P.W. Communications, Inc., 1982-89, Esquire Mags. Health and Fitness Clinic, 1985-88, Whittle Communications, 1988—. Recipient 1st prize certificate merit A.M.A., 1959, 1st prize citation of merit in motion picture program A.C.S., 1959, 62; Better Teller award Assn. Indsl. Advertisers, 1973, Outstanding Sci. Book award for Children Nat. Sci. Tchrs. Assn., 1982, Cert. of Merit Soc. of Illustrators, 1986. Mem. Assn. Med. Illustrators, Guild Natural Sci. Illustrators. Roman Catholic. Co-author: Gynecologic Operations, 1978; med. illustrator for numerous med. books, jours., elementary textbooks, juvenile books, encys. Fax: 631-734-5496. Home and Office: 800 Cox Ln Cutchogue NY 11935

DANKANYIN, ROBERT JOHN, international business executive; b. Sharon, Pa., Sept. 4, 1934; s. John and Anna (Kohlesar) D.; m. Dorothy Jean Kuchel, Aug. 9, 1958 (div. June 1975); children: Douglas John, David Jay, Dana Jean; m. Georgia C. Oleson, Apr. 2, 1988 (dec. Sept. 1990); m. Charlene Marcella Bassett, May 16, 1998. BSCE, Pa. State U., 1956; MBA, U. So. Calif., 1961; MSEE, UCLA, 1963. Cert. level 2 Profl. Ski Instrs. Am. From mgr. mobile ICBM systems engring. dept. to mgr. space system lab. Hughes Aircraft Co.,

Culver City, Calif., 1956-68; program mgr. Litton Industries, Beverly Hills, Calif., 1968-70; v.p. program mgmt. Litton Ship Systems, Culver City, 1970-71, Litton Ship Sys., Pascagola, Miss., 1971-73; asst. mgr. for U.S. Roland program, Canoga Pk., Calif. Hughes Aircraft Co., Culver City, Calif., 1975-77, asst. divsn. mgr. missile devel. div. Canoga Pk., Calif., 1977-84, mgr. land combat systems divsn. Culver City, Calif., 1984-86, group v.p. missile systems group, 1986-87; v.p., asst. group exec. missle systems group Canoga Park, Calif., 1987-88; v.p., asst. group exec. space and communication group, El Segundo, Calif. Hughes Aircraft Co., Culver City, Calif., 1988-89, corp. sr. v.p. diversification L.A., 1989-92, sr. v.p. bus. devel., 1992-93; sr. v.p., pres. Hughes Indsl. Electronics Co., L.A., 1993-95; group exec. Whittaker Corp., Westwood Village, Calif., 1973-75; pres., chmn. bd. Whittaker Cmty. Devel. Corp., Englewood, Colo., Knoxville, Tenn., Westwood Village, San Juan, P.R., 1973-75; internat. bus. and mgmt. cons., pres., CEO ITI, Big Bear Lake, Calif., 1995—. Chmn. Hughes Program Mgr. Devel. Course, L.A., 1976-88; chmn., bd. dirs. Light Valve Products, Inc., 1988-92, Hughes/Japan Victor Tech. Inc., 1992-95, Hughes Micro Electronics Ltd., Glenrothes, Scotland, Hughes Europa Ltd., Brussels, Belgium, 1993-95; bd. dirs. Hughes Environ. Sys., Inc., Long Beach, Calif.; Hughes España, Madrid, Spain, Aero Sys., Inc., Paris; mem. adv. bd. Pulse Link Inc., San Diego, 2002—; dir. several wholly owned subs. including Direct TV, Spectrolab, Hughes Network Sys., RF Identification Sys.; lectr., guest spkr., author on tech. mgmt.; bus. ventures, fgn. mktg., def. conversion, diversification and entrepreneurship. Editor Inter Fraternity/Sorority Newsletter Pa. State U., 1955-56. Chmn. indsl. and profl. adv. coun. Coll. Engring, Pa. State U.; ski instr. Bear Mountain Ski Resort, Big Bear Lake, Calif., 1990—; chmn. several indsl. task forces reporting to U.S. congl. coms. Voted Ordo Honorium by Kappa Delta Rho Fraternity, 1991, outstanding Engr. of the Yr. by Pa. State U., 1991; honored as outstanding engineering alumnus, 1992. Mem. Am. Def. Preparedness Assn. (bd. dirs. 1986-94, chmn. fin. com. 1990-94), Hughes Mgmt. Club, Aero Club So. Calif., Marina City Club, Riviera Country Club (bd. govs. 1999—), Calif. Yacht Club. Republican. Roman Catholic. Avocations: skiing, scuba diving, sailing, hiking, fishing, golf. Home: 20700 Rockpoint Rd Malibu CA 90265 E-mail: rdankanyin@aol.com.

DANKE, VIRGINIA, educator, travel consultant; b. Spokane, Wash., Mar. 9, 1925; d. William Ernest and Daisy May (Norton) Danke. BS, Wash. State U., 1947; MEd, Whitworth Coll., 1950; postgrad., LaSalle U., 1973. Cert. tchr. Counselor Clarkston (Wash.) Sch. Dist., 1948—48; head phys. edn. dept. LCHS Spokane Sch. Dist., 1948—77; travel cons. Viking Travel, Spokane, 1982—, Empire Tours, Spokane, 1982—. Co-author (editor): Marching Together, 1955. Treas. Fedn. Western Outdoor Clubs, 1980 ; com. mem. Future Spokane, 1981—, bd. dirs., Pacific Crest Trail Conf., Santa Ana, Calif., 1984; mem. Friends Centennial Trial, 1992—, bd. dirs., 1994—96; mem. Am. Red Cross Disaster Unit. Named to Wash. State Officials Hall of Fame, 2003; recipient Scroll of Honor-Hall of Fame, Spokane C. of C., 1983, Greater Spokane Sports Assn., 1973, Wash. Interscholastic Activites Assn., 1990, State Officiating, 1992. Mem.: Spokane Ret. Tchrs. Assn. (pres. 1981—82), Wash. State Officials Assn. (Meritorious Svc. award 2002, Hall of Fame 2003), Wash. State Ret. Tchrs. Assn. (bd. dirs. 1987—), Nat. Ret. Tchrs. Assn., Wash. Edn. Assn., Spokane Edn. Assn. (com. chmn. 1960—70), Soroptimist (pres. 1970), Hangman Golf Club (Spokane pres. 1997), Hobnailers Club (pres. 1966—67, 1986—87). Home: 1103 E 14th Ave Spokane WA 99202-2541

DANKIN, PETER ALFRED, lawyer; b. Winsted, Conn., Oct. 23, 1942; s. Alexander Harry and Dorothy Barbara (Erfer) D. BA, Yale U., 1964; JD cum laude, U. Mich., 1967. Bar: N.Y. 1968, D.C. 1982, U.S. Dist. Ct. (so. and ea. dists.) N.Y. 1971, U.S. Ct. Appeals (2d cir.) 1972, U.S. Ct. Appeals (3d cir.) 1980, U.S. Ct. Appeals (D.C. cir.) 1980, U.S. Ct. Appeals (7th cir.) 1984, U.S. Supreme Ct. 1974, U.S. Ct. Appeals (5th cir.) 1985, U.S. Ct. Internat. Trade, 1987. Assoc. Chadbourne, Parke, Whiteside & Wolff, N.Y.C., 1968-71; assoc. Wender, Murase & White, N.Y.C., 1971-73, ptnr., 1973-86; ptnr. Shanely & Fisher, 1987-88; sole practitioner, 1988-93; prin. McPheters & Dankin, P.C., 1993—. Assoc. editor U. Mich. Law Rev., 1966-67. Served to 1st lt. U.S. Army, 1967-73. Mem. Am. Jurisprudence Soc. (book award 1965), N.Y.C. Bar Assn., Order of Coif. Office: McPheters & Dankin 757 3rd Ave New York NY 10017-2013 E-mail: pdankin@aol.com.

DANKNER, JAY WARREN, lawyer; b. Bklyn., June 15, 1949; s. Morris and Frances Dankner; m. Iris Rose Terens, May 15, 1983; children: Danielle Renee, Nicole Beth. BA cum laude, Bklyn. Coll., 1970, JD cum laude, 1973. Bar: N.Y. 1974, Fla. 1974, U.S. Dist. Ct. (ea. and so. dists.) N.Y. 1974, U.S. Ct. Appeals (2d cir.) 1974, U.S. Supreme Ct. 1977, U.S. Dist. Ct. (no. dist.) N.Y. 1986. From assoc. to ptnr. Sullivan & Liapakis P.C., N.Y.C., 1974-94; ptnr. Dankner & Milstein, P.C., N.Y.C., 1994—. Lectr. Practicing Law Inst., N.Y.C., 1983-87, N.Y. State Trial Lawyers Inst., 1985—, continuing legal edn. program Bklyn. Law Sch., 1986—, N.Y. State Bar Assn. CLE Programs, Nassau County Bar Assn., Queens Bar Assn.; mem. Bklyn. Law Rev., 1972-73; bd. dirs. Atty's Info. Exchange Group, Inc., 1981—. Author: Products Liability Practice Guide, 1988, Masters of Trial Practice, 1988, Deposing Corporate Defendants in Products Liability Actions, 1988, Trial Strategy - Plaintiffs View, 1988; contbr. articles to profl. jours. Named one of Best Trial Lawyers in the U.S., Town & Country, 1985. Mem. ABA, N.Y. State Bar Assn. (spl. com. on procedures for jud. discipline 1987-90), Assn. of Bar of City of N.Y. (mem. products liability com. 1993-94), Fla. Bar Assn., Assn. Trial Lawyers Am., N.Y. State Trial Lawyers Assn. (chair products liability com. 1991, 93-94), N.Y. County Lawyers Assn. Home: 524 E 72nd St New York NY 10021-9801 Office: Dankner & Milstein PC 41 E 57th St New York NY 10022-1908

DANKO, GENE ANDREW, materials scientist; b. McKeesport, Pa., Mar. 10, 1958; s. Andrew John and Margaret Mary (Mosher) Danko; m. April Jane Ludwig, Nov. 6, 1993 (div. Aug. 1996). BA in Biophysics, Johns Hopkins U., 1980, PhD in Materials Sci. and Engring., 1992; MBA, Rensselaer Polytech Inst., 2003. Rsch. staff Nat. Inst. Standards and Tech., Gaithersburg, Md., 1980-92; rsch. scientist Tech. Assessment & Transfer, Annapolis, Md., 1992-93; chief scientist Advanced Ceramics Rsch., Tucson, 1993-97; sr. materials scientist FM Techs., Fairfax, Va., 1997-99; pres. Exius Corp., Wilmington, Del., 1998—; sr. systems integration technologist Pratt & Whitney, East Hartford, Conn., 1999-2000, program mgr. ceramic materials, 2001, customer coord./tech. mgmt. and program office, 2002—. Assoc. TEIN, Vienna, 1998—2002. Mem.: AIAA, U.S. Power Squadrons, Nat. Inst. Ceramic Engrs., Am. Ceramic Soc., Electrochem. Soc., Sigma Xi. Republican. Roman Catholic. Avocations: sailing, photography. Home: 125 South St #283 Vernon Rockville CT 06066-4439 Office: Pratt & Whitney 400 Main St M/S 114-45 East Hartford CT 06108-0968

DANKO, GEORGE, engineering educator; b. Budapest, Hungary, Apr. 3, 1944; came to U.S., 1986; s. Gyorgy and Ilona (Mihaly) D.; m. Eva Arvay, Dec. 14, 1976; 1 child, Reka. BSME, Tech. U. Budapest, 1968, PhD, 1976; MS in Applied Math., Eotovs U. of Scis., Budapest, 1975; PhD, Hungarian Acad. Scis., Budapest, 1985. Cert. Profl. Ski Instrs. Am. Assn. Asst. prof. Tech. U. Budapest, 1968-75, assoc. prof., 1979-86; fellow Hungarian Acad. Scis., Budapest, 1975-79; rsch. assoc. U. Nev., Reno, 1986-90, assoc. prof., 1990-95, prof. mining engring., 1995—. Cons. Sierra Sci., Reno, 1990—; chmn. High-Level Radioactive Waste Mgmt. Conf., 1991, 92; portrait artist, Reno, 1987-92. Co-author: Methods for the Calculation of Pipeline Transients, 1976, Warming-up and Cooling of Electrical Machinery, 1982; contbr. articles to profl. jours. Com. rep. Truckee River Steering Com., Reno, 1993-94. Grantee U.S. Bur. Mines, 1986-97, U.S. Dept. Energy, 1991—, Clarkson Co., 1992-98. Mem. ASME, ISES (internat. organizing com. 1993-94), IFAC (internat. program com. 1995—), Soc. Mining Engrs., Am. Nuclear Soc. Achievements include patents for methods and apparatus for the determination of the heat transfer coefficient, process and apparatus for the determination of thermophysical properties, underground cooling enhancement for nuclear waste repository, method and apparatus for underground nuclear waste repository, others. Office: U Nev Reno Mining Engring Dept 173 Reno NV 89557-0001

DANKWORTH, CLEMENTINA DINAH See LAINE, CLEO

DANLEY, J. MARK, biologist, educator, actor; s. William Thomas and Frances Danley; life ptnr. Damien L.J. Shay. BS, Pa. State U., 1978; MS, W.Va. U., 2000. Rsch. asst. Fox Chase Cancer Ctr., Phila., 1980—81; group leader edn. and tng. BioSciences Info. Svc., Phila., 1981—84; rsch. specialist U. Pa., Phila., 1984—91; rsch. coord. Mt. Sinai Med. Ctr., N.Y.C., 1992—96; vis. instr. U. New Eng./Westbrook Coll. Campus, Portland, Maine, 1996—2002; instr. biology Albuquerque TVI C.C., 2003—. Actor: (plays) The Ugly Man, 2001, 12 Angry Men, 2002, Love! Valour! Compassion!, 2002; (films) The Lemon Sisters, 1990. Mem.: AFTRA, SAG, NSTA, Nat. Assn. Biology Tchrs. Democrat. Avocations: web page development, bodybuilding, exercise. Office: Albuquerque TVI Cmty Coll 525 Buena Vista SE Albuquerque NM 87106

DANN, EMILY, mathematics educator; b. Albany, Ga., July 26, 1932; d. Jesse Lyman and Evelyn (Calhoun) Dann; m. Christian A. Hansen, June 7, 1977; children: Leslie Montgomery Eagan, Ann Montgomery Brief, Robin Hansen, Randall Hansen, Rhonda Hansen McAleaivey, Rheta Hansen. BA, Huntingdon Coll., 1954; MS in Math., U. Houston, 1964; EdD, Rutgers U., 1976. Instr. Lee Coll., Baytown, Tex., 1965-67; prof. Middlesex County Coll., Edison, N.J., 1967-81; dir. human resources Hanlin Group (formerly LCP Chem. & Plastics Co.), Edison, N.J., 1981-84, systems analyst, 1986-89; v.p. Assoc. Svcs., Edison, N.J., 1989-91; sr. math. edn. assoc. Rutgers U. Sch. Edn., New Brunswick, N.J., 1991-95, 99—, sr. math. edn. specialist, 1995-99; asst. prof. edn. CCNY, N.Y.C., 1995-99; sr. math. edn. specialist Rutgers U. Grad. Sch. Edn., 1999—. Vis. assoc. prof. math. Drew U., 1984-86; cons. Title I math. program Bedminster (N.J.) Pub. Sch., 1976-77, mem. co-adj. faculty Grad. Sch. Edn., Rutgers U., 1976-81, Kean Coll., 1980-81. Contbr. articles to profl. jours. Mem. ASTD, Acad. Mgmt., Orgn. Devel. Network, Am. Math. Assn., Jean Piaget Soc. Home: 1 Scenic Dr Highlands NJ 07732-1329

DANN, JOHN CHRISTIE, historian, library director; b. Wilmington, Del., May 3, 1944; s. C. Marshall and Catharine (Christie) D.; m. Orelia Sparrow, Jan. 24, 1970; children: Catharine Christie, Orelia Eliabeth. BA, Dickinson Coll., 1966; MA, Coll. William and Mary, 1970, PhD, 1975. Prof. history U. Mich., Ann Arbor, 1975—, curator of manuscripts William C. Clements Libr., 1971-77, dir. William C. Clements Libr., 1977—. Author: 101 Treasures, 1998; editor: The Revolution Remenbered, 1980, The Nagle Journal, 1989; editor Am. Mag.; mem. various hist. and editl. bds. Mem. Dexter (Mich.) Village Coun., 1982-86. Mem. Cosmos Club (Washington), Azazels. Congregationalist. Avocations: fishing, golf. Home: 7580 4th St Dexter MI 48130-1424 Office: Clements Libr 909 S University Ave Ann Arbor MI 48109-1190

DANN, OLIVER TOWNSEND, psychoanalyst, psychiatrist, educator; b. Mansfield, Ohio, Aug. 10, 1935; s. Edward William and Mary Virginia (Townsend) D.; m. Linda Marie Schweers, July 15, 1961; children: Sara Katharine, Jonathan William Jenner, Luke Nathan Townsend, Jesse Charles. AB, Columbia U., 1958; MD, Yale U., 1962. Diplomate Am. Bd. Psychiatry and Neurology. Resident in psychiatry Yale U. Sch. Medicine, New Haven, 1963-67, asst., assoc. prof. psychiatry, 1967-79; clin. prof. psychiatry U. Miami (Fla.) Sch. Medicine, 1980—; dir. Fla. Psychoanalytic Inst., 1997—2001, chair edn. com., 2003—. Pvt. practice, Miami, 1979—. Contbr. articles to profl. jours. Mem. Mayflower Soc., Jamestowne Soc., Huguenot Soc. Fellow (life) APA, Ctr. for Advanced Psychoanalytic Studies; mem. SAR, Am. Psychoanalytic Assn., Internat. Psychoanalytic Assn., Western New England Inst. Soc. Psychoanalysis, Balt.-Washington Inst. Soc. Psychoanalysis, Fla. Psychoanalytic Inst. Soc. Found., Phi Beta Kappa, others. Avocations: sailing, canoeing, hiking. Home and Office: 4550 SW 74th St Miami FL 33143-6271 E-mail: lindadann@hotmail.com.

DANNEL, JAMES MICHEAL, voice educator; b. Athens, Tenn., May 16, 1956; s. J.W. and Eleanor Rose Dannel; m. Michelle Sue Hay, Dec. 16, 1983; children: James Matthew, Megan. BS in bus. adminstrn., Tenn. Wesleyan Coll., 1974—78. Min. of music/youth First Bapt. Ch., Riceville, Tenn., 1977—79; salesman Lansford Piano and Organ Co., Chattanooga, 1978—79; min. of music/youth Stuart Pk. Bapt. Ch., Cleve., Tenn., 1979—80; ins. agt. Nat. Life and Accident Ins Co., Cleve., Tenn., 1980—81; min. of music/youth East Athens Bapt. Ch., Athens, Tenn., 1980—; pvt. voice instr. self-employed, Athens, Tenn., 1983—. Tenor soloist Athens Area Cmty. Chorus, Tenn., 1983—; bd. mem. McMinn Co. Youth Affairs Bd., Athens, Tenn., 1988—; alumni rep. to bd. of trustees Tenn. Wesleyan Coll., Athens, 2003—. Bd. mem. Athens Parks and Recreation, Tenn., 1990—95, adv. bd., 1990—95; commr. Athens Housing Authority, Tenn., 2002—; mem. Coordinated Charities, Athens, 1996—2000, bd. mem., 1996—2000. Recipient William P. Miller award, Tenn. Wesleyan Coll. Choir, 1976-1977, Outstanding Young Man of Am., 1985. Mem.: Nat. Music Teachers Assn., Athens Area Music Tchr. Assn. (treas. 1988), Tenn. Bapt. Chorale (treas. 1996—99), Optimist Club of Athens (life; pres. 1992—93). R-Consevative. Southern Bapt. Avocations: barbershop quartets, running, mountain biking. Home: 1837 Timbercrest Dr Athens TN 37303 Office: East Athens Baptist Church 301 Central Ave Athens TN 37303 E-mail: mdannel@usit.net.

DANNELLY, WILLIAM DAVID, lawyer; b. Andalusia, Ala., 1951; SB, MIT, 1973; JD, U. N.C., 1977. Bar: N.C. 1977. Law clerk we. dist. U.S. Dist. Ct., N.C., 1977-78; ptnr. Hunton & Williams, Raleigh, N.C. Mem. N.C. Law Review, 1975-77; contbg. author: Toxic Tort and Hazardous Substance Litigation, 1995. Mem. Order of Coif. Office: Hunton & Williams One Hannover Square 14th Fl PO Box 109 Raleigh NC 27602-0109

DANNENBERG, ARTHUR MILTON, JR., experimental pathologist, immunologist, educator; b. Phila., Oct. 17, 1923; s. Arthur Mansbach and Marion (Loeb) D.; m. Aileen Rose Hart, Mar. 30, 1948; children: Arlene Dannenberg Bowes, Andrew Loeb, Audrey Ann. AB, Swarthmore Coll., 1944; MD, Harvard U., 1947; MA, U. Pa., 1951, PhD, 1952. Diplomate: Nat. Bd. Med. Examiners. Intern Albert Einstein Med. Ctr., Phila., 1947-48; rsch. resident Children's Hosp., Phila., 1948-49; fellow Henry Phipps Inst. U. Pa., Phila., 1950-52, asst. prof., 1956-64; fellow U. Utah, 1952-54; assoc. prof. environ. health scis. Johns Hopkins U. Bloomberg Sch. Pub. Health, Balt., 1964-73, prof., 1973—, prof. joint faculty sch. medicine dept. pathology, 1976—. Mem. editl. bd. Am. Rev. Respiratory Diseases, 1973-75, 79-84, Infection and Immunity jour., 1976-78; contbr. articles to profl. jours. and chpts. to books. Lt. comdr. Med. Rsch. Unit 1, USN, 1954-56. Mem. Am. Soc. Investigative Pathology, Histochem. Soc., Am. Soc. Microbiology, Soc. for Leukocyte Biology (sec. 1975-76), Am. Assn. Immunologists, Am. Thoracic Soc., Soc. Investigative Dermatology. Office: Johns Hopkins U Bloomberg Sch of Pub Health 615 N Wolfe St Baltimore MD 21205-2103 E-mail: artdann@jhsph.edu.

DANNENBERG, KONRAD K. aeronautical engineer; b. Weissenfels, Germany, Aug. 5, 1912; came to U.S. 1945. s. Hermann and Klara (Kittler) D.; m. Ingeborg M. Kamke, Apr. 8, 1944 (dec.); 1 child, Klaus Dieter; m. Jacquelyn E. Staiger, Mar. 31, 1990. MS Engring., Techn. U., Hannover, Ger., 1938. Asst. Tech. U., Hannover, 1938, engr. Frankfurt, Ger., 1939; rsch. HAP-Peenemuende, Germany, 1940-45; mgr. U.S. Army Ordnance, Ft. Bliss, Tex., 1945-50, ABMA, Huntsville, Ala., 1950-60, NASA/MSFC, Huntsville, 1960-73; assoc. prof. UTSI-U. Tenn., Tullahoma, 1973-78; cons. The Space & Rocket Ctr., Huntsville, 1978—. Author: In Memory of H. Oberth, 1990, Vahrenwald to Dresden, 1990; (with E. Stuhlinger) Rocket Center Peenemünde, 1993, Albert Püllenberg and the Gesellschaft für Raketenforschung, 1995, (with Donald Tarter) Mitchell R. Sharpe-Aerospace Historian, 1997. Lt. German Army, 1939-40. Recipient Meritorious Svc. award, U.S. Army, 1960, Exceptional Svc. award, NASA, 1969, Konrad K. Dannenberg scholarship, 1992. Fellow AIAA (chpt. chmn. 1967, Durand lectr. pub. svc. 1990), Holger N. Toftoy award, Hermann Oberth award 1996); mem. Hermann Oberth Soc. (hon., Golden Hermann Oberth medal 1994), Nat. Space Soc. (charter), Am. Rocket Soc. (chmn. 1962). Lutheran. Achievements include patents in rocket engine design. Home and Office: 233 Cheswick Dr Madison AL 35757-8712 E-mail: konrad2@aol.com.

DANNENBERG, ROGER BERRY, computer scientist; b. Houston, Mar. 9, 1955; s. Richard Martin and Isabel Drury (Holt) D.; m. Frances Lynn Krouse; 1 child, Richard Pierce. BSEE, Rice U., 1977; MSCE, Case Western Res. U., 1979; PhD, Carnegie Mellon U., 1982. Rsch. scientist Carnegie Mellon U., Pitts., 1982-89, sr. rsch. scientist, 1989-99, sr. rsch. scientist, artist, 1999—. Artist-in-residence Am. Ctr., Paris, 1983; fellow Next, Inc., Palo Alto, Calif., 1988; ptnr. ESL at the Movies, LLC, Iowa City, 1998. Editor: Multimedia Design, 1994; patentee computer accompaniment, 1984; composer: In Transit, 1997. NSF grad. fellow, 1977-81. Mem. IEEE, Internat. Computer Music Assn. (bd. dirs. 1992-97), Assn. for Computing Machinery. Office: Carnegie Mellon U Sch Computer Sci Pittsburgh PA 15213 E-mail: rbd@cs.cmu.edu.

DANNER, BRYANT CRAIG, lawyer; b. Boston, Nov. 18, 1937; s. Nevin Earle and Marjorie (Harms) D.; m. Judith I. Baker, Aug. 23, 1958; 1 child Debra Irene. BA, Harvard U., 1960, LLB, 1963. Bar: Calif. 1963, U.S. Dist. Ct. (cen. dist.) Calif. 1963. Assoc. Latham & Watkins, L.A., 1963-70, ptnr., 1970-92; sr. v.p., gen. counsel So. Calif. Edison Co., Rosemead, Calif., 1992-95, exec. v.p., gen. counsel, 1995-2000, Edison Internat., Rosemead, 2000—. Mem. L.A. County Bar Assn. (chmn. environ. sect. 1988-89). Avocations: fly fishing, astronomy. Office: Edison International 2244 Walnut Grove Ave Rosemead CA 91770-3714

DANNER, DAVID BIGELOW, pathologist; b. Boston, Mar. 29, 1953; s. Douglas Carl and Mary Stoddard (Bigelow) D.; m. Frances Gail Forster, Sept. 8, 1984; children: Katherine Mary, Alexander Hardwick. BA/Biochemistry/Biology summa cum laude, Harvard U., 1975; MD and PhD in Molecular Biology/Genetics, Johns Hopkins U., 1983. Helen Hay Whitney Found. postdoctoral fellow Harvard Med. Sch., Cambridge, Mass., 1983-86; asst. prof. Nat. Inst. Aging, Balt., 1986-90, sr. rsch. investigator, 1990-92; commd. lt. comdr. USPHS, 1990-92; resident and clinical fellow dept. pathology Johns Hopkins Med. Sch., 1992-96; pathologist Meml. Hosp., Easton, Md., 1996—; ptnr. Chesapeake Pathology Assocs., 1998—. Lectr. pathology Johns Hopkins U., 1996—. Author: (with others) Transformation, 1980, Ann. Rev. Biochemistry, 1981, Handbook of the Biology of Aging, 1990; assoc. editor: Johns Hopkins Atlas of Surgical Pathology; contbr. articles to Procs. Nat. Acad. Sci. USA, Nature, Sci., Molecular Cell Biology, others. Fellow Coll. Am. Pathologists; mem. Phi Beta Kappa. Achievements include patent for prohibition, an antiproliferative protein; determination of the DNA recognition site for Hemophilus transformation; showed that membrane-bound antibody mediates allelic exclusion. Office: Meml Hosp care labs 219 S Washington St Easton MD 21601-2913

DANNER, DEAN JAY, geneticist; b. Milw., Sept. 26, 1941; s. Julius Alexis and Evalyn Anna (Pautz) D.; m. Susan Melissa Reddin, Aug. 25, 1968; children: Mark Jay, Kirstin Melissa. BS in Chemistry/Biology, Lakeland Coll., 1963; PhD in Biochemistry, U. N.D., 1968. Postdoctoral fellow St. Jude Children's Rsch. Hosp., Memphis, 1968-70; asst. prof. Northwestern State U., Natchitoches, La., 1970-73, Emory U., Atlanta, 1973-78, assoc. prof., 1978-89, prof., 1989-97, chmn. dept. genetics, 1997—2001, vice chair Human Genetics, 2001—, acting chair Biochemistry, 2001—. Mem. NIH Study Sect. Med. Biochemistry, Bethesda, Md., 1989-93. Presbyterian. Home: 266 Winnona Dr Decatur GA 30030-3854 Office: Univ Emory Dept Human Genetics Sch Medicine 615 Michael St Atlanta GA 30322-1000

DANNER, PATSY ANN (MRS. C. M. MEYER), former congresswoman; b. Louisville, Ky., Jan. 13, 1934; d. Henry J. and Catherine M. (Shaheen) Berrer; children: Stephen, Stephanie, Shane, Shavonne.; m. C.M. Meyer, Dec. 30, 1982. Student, Hannibal-LaGrange Coll., 1952; BA in Polit. Sci. cum laude, N.E. Mo. State U., 1972. Dist. asst. to Congressman Jerry Litton, Kansas City, Mo., 1973-76; fed. co-chmn. Ozarks Regional Commn., Washington, 1977-81; mem. Mo. State Senate, 1983-1992, 103rd-106th Congress from 6th Mo. dist., 1993-2001. Mem. internat. rels. com., transp. and infrastructure com. Democrat. Roman Catholic.

DANNER, PAUL KRUGER, III, financial services executive; b. Cin. BS, Colo. State U., 1979; MBA, Old Dominion U., 1986. Mktg. rep. Control Data Corp., Denver, 1985-86; dist. mgr. NEC Home Electronics (U.S.A.), Inc., Denver, 1987-88; regional mgr. NEC Home Electronics, Inc. subs. NEC Corp. (Tokyo), L.A., 1988-89, v.p. NEC Techs., Inc. subs., 1989-91; v.p. Command Communications, Aurora, Colo., 1991-96; pres. Tech. Ventures, Inc., Denver, 1996-97; v.p. ops. Zekko Corp., Ponte Vedra Bch., Fla., 1997-98; CEO MyTurn.com., Alameda, Calif., 1999—2000; chmn. Paragon Fin. Corp., Inc., 2001—. Lt. USN, 1979-85; capt. USNR, 1985—.

DANNER, RONALD PAUL, chemical engineering educator; b. New Holland, Pa., Aug. 29, 1939; s. Alvin Charles and Arvilla Mae (Parker) D.; m. Faye Rosene Harnish, Sept. 3, 1960; children: Jeffrey Blaine, Wendy Sue Danner Flick. BS, Lehigh U., 1962, MS, 1963, PhD, 1966. Sr. rsch. scientist Eastman Kodak Co., Rochester, N.Y., 1965 67; asst. prof. Pa. State U., University Park, 1967-73, assoc. prof., 1973-78, prof., 1978—; faculty fellow U.S. Gen. Acctg. Office, Washington, 1974-75; co-dir. Ctr. for the Study of Polymer-Solvent Systems, 1990—. Vis. scientist Tech. U. Denmark, Lyngby, 1991-92. Author: (with others) API Technical Data Book - Petroleum Refining, 4th edit., 1982, Manual for Predicting Chemical Process Design Data, 1987, Physical and Thermodynamic Properties of Pure Compounds, Data Compilation, 1989, Handbook of Polymer Solution Thermodynamics, 1993, Thermodynamic Analysis of Vapor-Liquid Equilibria: Recommended Models and a Standard Data Base, 1991; contbr. over 100 articles to profl. jours. Fellow AIChE; mem. Sigma Xi. Avocations: scuba diving, rag-time piano. Home: 3301-922 Shellers Bnd State College PA 16801-3068 Office: Pa State U 163 Fenske Lab University Park PA 16802-4400

DANNER, WILLIAM BEKURS, lawyer; b. Mobile, Ala., Aug. 18, 1944; s. John J. and Helen B. (Bekurs) D.; m. Eleanor E. Uehlinger; children: William B., Christina T. BS, Spring Hill Coll., 1967; JD, U. Louisville, 1978. Bar: Ky. 1979. Commd. ensign USN, 1967, advanced through grades to lt., 1972, ret., 1977; atty. U.S. Ecology Inc., Louisville, 1979-80, assoc. gen. counsel, 1980-81; staff atty. McDermott Internat., New Orleans, 1981-83, counsel Europe and Africa area Brussels, 1983-86, mgr. legal office for domestic, S.A., West Africa ops. New Orleans, 1987-91, sr. counsel corp. staff, 1991-97, corp. compliance atty., 1997—. Vice chmn. parish council, New Albany, Ind., 1980-81; bd. dirs. parish council, Brussels, 1984—. Mem. ABA (internat. law and practice sect.), Ky. Bar Assn., Phi Kappa Phi. Republican. Roman Catholic. Avocations: furniture refinishing, reading. Home: 207 Driftwood Cir Slidell LA 70458-1437 Office: McDermott Legal Dept 1450 Poydras St New Orleans LA 70112-2401 E-mail: wdanner@bellsouth.net., wbdanner@mcdermott.com.

DANNHAUSER, STEPHEN J. lawyer; b. N.Y.C., May 23, 1950; s. Frank A. and Irene (Tinney) Dannhauser; m. Mary Elizabeth Robinson, July 1, 1973, children: Benjamin, Todd, Jess. BA with honors, SUNY, Stonybrook, 1972; JD with honors, Bklyn. Law Sch., 1975. Bar: NY 1976. Atty. Weil Gotshal & Manges LLP, N.Y.C., 1975—, exec. ptnr., 1989—2001, chmn., 2002—. Decisions editor: Bklyn. Law Rev., 1974—75. Pres. N.Y. Police and Fire Widows' and Children's Benefit Fund, N.Y.C., 1985—; chair, mem. various coms. Nat. Minority Bus. Coun., N.Y.C., 1993; chmn., bd. dirs. Boys and Girls Harbor, Inc., East Harlem, NY. Mem.: ABA. Avocations: running. Office: Weil Gotshal & Manges LLP c/o Grace F Lopez 767 5th Ave 10th Flr New York NY 10153-0119

DANNI, F. ROBERT, town official; b. Pitts., Oct. 26, 1939; s. Anthony Joseph and Lucille Marie (Kromer) D.; m. Patricia Arlene Maslona, Aug. 14, 1965 (div. Dec. 1980); children: Mark, Traci, Scott, Todd; m. Kathleen Anne Zimpfer, Jan. 13, 1990; 1 child, Adam. BS, U.S. Mcht. Marine Acad., 1961. Lic. chief stationary engr., City of Buffalo; lic. profl. engr., N.Y.; lic. officer U.S. Merchant Marine. Third asst. engr. Am. Export Lines, Hoboken, N.J., 1961-63; project engr. GM, Tonawanda, N.Y., 1964-69; asst. commr. of bldg. Town of Amherst, N.Y., 1969—. Chmn. Western Region Bd. Rev., 1984—. Instr. Baker Victory Rifle Drill Team, Lackawanna, N.Y., 1969-75; gen. chmn. Armed Forces Week Western N.Y., Buffalo, 1988, 93, 98, 2003; asst. scoutmaster Troop 440, Boy Scouts Am., Williamsville, N.Y. Capt. USNR, 1961-91; rear admiral N.Y. Naval Militia, 1991—, Region III comdr., 1984-98. Mem. N.Y. State Soc. Profl. Engrs. (pres. Erie-Niagara chpt. 1990-91, Basinski-Wohler distinguished svc. award 2000), N.Y. State Bldg. Ofcls. Conf. (tech. chmn. 1985-91), Naval Res. Assn. (life), Mil. Officers Assn. (life), Rotary Club Williamsville N.Y. (youth chmn. 1982-97, Rotarian of Yr. award 1997). Avocations: music, health club. Office: Town of Amherst Bldg Dept 5583 Main St Williamsville NY 14221-5499 E-mail: frdanni@amherst.ny.us.

D'ANNIBALLE-HOLDREN, PRISCILLA LUCILLE, contracting company executive; b. Martins Ferry, Ohio, Oct. 28, 1950; d. James Louis and Smyrna Isabell (Prieto) D'A; m. Terrence E. Holdren. BE, U. Toledo, 1973. Credit mgr. Kabat Distbg. Co., Toledo, 1973-80; comml. ops. officer Ohio Citizens Bank, Toledo, 1980-81, credit officer, 1981-82, mktg. officer, 1982-83, mortgage banking officer, 1983-85; owner, pres. D'Ann Enterprises, Inc. dba Paul Davis

Restoration, Holland, Ohio, 1985—; pres. district V Paul Davis Systems, Toledo, 1992-95, mem. nat. exec. com., 1992-95, treas. nat. exec. com., 1994-95. Chmn. arbitration com. Paul Davis Systems, 1991; dist. 3 acting pres. Paul Davis Restoration, 2002, dist. 3 v.p., 2001—. Mem. fund drive United Way, Toledo, 1982, Jr. Achievement, Toledo, 1983; bd. dirs. Voluntary Action Ctr., Toledo, 1981-82, Better Bus. Bur., 2002-03. Mem. Nat. Assn. Credit Mgmt. (bd. dirs. 1981-87, bd. dirs. Ednl. Forum 1976-82, pres. 1980, Credit Person of Yr. award 1982, Credit Exec. of Yr. award 1987), Holland-Springfield C. of C. (exec. bd. dirs. 1990-95, v.p. 1991-92, pres. 1993), Paul Davis Systems Franchisee Assn. (pres. 1991). Roman Catholic. Avocations: golf, swimming, gardening, antiques, traveling. Home: 704 Oak Park Dr Toledo OH 43617-2024 Office: D'Ann Enterprises Inc 1049 S Mccord Rd Holland OH 43528-9596

D'ANNOLFO, SUZANNE CORDIER, educational administrator, educator; b. Akron, Ohio, Oct. 20, 1946; d. Albert Tennyson and Luella Dorothy Cordier; m. Frank Joseph D'Annolfo, Feb. 12, 1982; children: Casey Cordier, Matthew Scott. BS, Boston U., 1970; student, Slippery Rock (Pa.) State U., 1964-67; MS, Cen. Conn. State U., 1973; EdD, Boston U., 1980. Tchr. West Hartford (Conn.) Pub. Schs., 1970-78, adminstr. health and phys. edn., dir. athletics, 1979-87; asst. prin. Farmington High Sch., 1988—93; prin. Litchfield (Conn.) High Sch., 1993-98, Nat. Sch. of Excellence; dir. curriculum and instrn. grades 9-12 Newington (Conn.) Pub. Schs., 1998-01; CREC prin. Met. Learning Ctr. Nat. Sch. Distinction, A Magnet Sch. for Global & Internat. Studies, 2001—. Coach U.S. Olympic Track and Field Team Learn-by-Doing Clinics, 1977—80; mem. Conn. Gov.'s Coun. on Phys. Fitness and Sport, 1978—87; drug. cons. Nutmeg State Games; mem. edn. coun. U.S. Olympic Com.; dean U.S. Olympic Acad., First World-Scholar Athlete Games, Newport, RI; Ethics Fellow Internat. Inst. of Sport, 1993; adj. prof. Ctrl. Conn. State U. Author: Secondary Physical Education, Stress Management, Ideas II, Drugs and AIDS Education for Elementary Students. Bd. dirs. Spl. Olympics, West Hartford, 1979-87; co-founder Pvt. Victories health newsletter for high sch. students, 1991-98. Named to N.E. Women's Hall of Fame, 1994; recipient Nat. Educator award Milken Found., 1995. Mem. ASCD, NASSP, AAHPERD (com., spkr. nat. conv.), NEA, Conn. Assn. Health, Phys. Edn., Recreation and Dance (pres. 1981-82, Profl. Honor award 1986), Ctrl. Conn. Conf. (life, treas. 1984-87, Leadership award 1987), Nat. H.S. Coaches Assn. (track v.p. 1978-80, Conn. Cross Country Coach of Yr. award 1976, Track Coach of Yr. award), Conn. Prins. Acad., Blue Ribbon Human Resource Bank, Phi Delta Kappa. Avocations: family, writing, swimming, biking, walking. Home: 30 Shadow Ln West Hartford CT 06110-1640 Office: Met Learning Ctr 1551 Blue Hills Ave Bloomfield CT 06002

DANOFF, DUDLEY SETH, surgeon, urologist; b. N.Y.C., June 10, 1937; s. Alfred and Ruth (Kauffman) D.; m. Hevda Amrani, July 1, 1971; children: Aurele, Doran. BA summa cum laude, Princeton U., 1959; MD, Yale U., 1963. Diplomate Am. Bd. Urology. Surg. intern Columbia-Presbyn. Med. Ctr., N.Y.C., 1963-64; resident in surgery Yale New Haven Med. Ctr., 1964-65; resident in urologic surgery Squier Urologic Clinic, Columbia-Presbyn. Med. Ctr., 1965-69; NIH trainee Francis Delafield Hosp., N.Y.C., 1969; asst. in urology Columbia U.-Columbia-Presbyn. Hosp., N.Y.C., 1969; cons., surgeon New Orleans VA Hosp., 1970; asst. surgeon Tulane U., New Orleans, 1970; pvt. practice urologic surgery L.A., 1971—. Attending urologic surgeon Cedars-Sinai Med. Ctr., L.A., Midway Hosp., L.A., Century City Hosp., L.A. VA Hosp., L.A.; attending urologic surgeon, clin. faculty UCLA. Author: Superpotency, 1993, Research: Laparoscopic Urologic Procedures; contbr. articles to profl. jours. Bd. dirs. Tel-Hashomer Hosp., Israel, Christian Children's Fund, Beverly Hills Edn. Found.; trustee Anti-Defamation League; mem. prof. adv. bd. The Wellness Comty.; mem. nat. exec. bd. Gesher Found.; mem. adv. com., past pres. Med. divsn. L.A. Jewish Fedn. Coun.; mem. nat. leadership cabinet United Jewish Appeal; chmn. Am. Friends of Assaf Harofeh Med. Ctr., Israel; pres. western states region and internat. bd. govs. Am. Friends Hebrew U. Jerusalem; pres. western region Am. Commn. for Shaare Zedek Med. Ctr. Jerusalem. Recipient Excellence in Medicine award Israel Cancer Rsch. Found., 1998. Fellow ACS; mem. AMA, Internat. Coll. Surgeons, Israeli Med. Assn., Am. Fertility Soc., Soc. Air Force Clin. Surgeons, Am. Urologic Assn., Societe International d'Urologie, Transplant Soc. So. Calif., Los Angeles County Med. Assn., Soc. for Laparoendoscopic Surgeons, Am. Technion Soc., Profl. Men's Club of L.A. (past pres.), Princeton Club So. Calif., Yale Club So. Calif., Hillcrest Country Club, Phi Beta Kappa, Sigma Xi, Alpha Omega Alpha, Phi Delta Epsilon (past pres., exec. com.). Jewish. Avocations: golf, swimming, reading, writing. Office: Cedars-Sinai Med Ctr Towers 8631 W 3d St Ste 915E Los Angeles CA 90048-5912 Fax: (310) 854-0267. E-mail: danoff@aol.com.

DANOFF-KRAUS, PAMELA SUE, real estate developer; b. Gallup, N.Mex., Aug. 29, 1946; d. Isadore Harry and Armida Catherine (Ceccardi) Danoff; m. Robert Warren Kraus, Nov. 30, 1985; 1 child, Jillian Amaris. BA, U. N.Mex., 1968. Lic. in real estate, Calif. Real estate rep. Kaiser Aetna, Newport Beach, Calif., 1975-76; leasing agt. Alexander Haagen Co., Rolling Hills, Calif., 1976-77; dir. leasing Warren Kellogg & Assocs., Newport Beach, 1977-81, Ctr. Devel. Co., Newport Beach, 1981-84; exec. v.p., ptnr. The Von Der Ahe Co., Newport Beach, 1984-86; ptnr., shopping center development executive Marketplace Properties, Tustin, Calif., 1986-92; owner Danoff Kraus Enterprises, Santa Ana, 1992—. Lectr. in field; panelist various convs., univs.; condr. seminars in field. Contbr. articles to profl. jours. Sponsor Californians Working Together to End Hunger and Homelessness, L.A., 1988; mem. Orange County Performing Arts Ctr., 1983-85. Mem. Internat. Coun. Shopping Ctrs. (program chmn. 1987-89, small ctr. devel. com., state dir. pub. rels. and cmty. affairs for Calif., 1989-92, chair pub. rels. and cmty. svc. Western divsn. 1992-95), Calif. Bus. Properties Assn., Calif. Redevel. Assn., Assistance League of Santa Ana, Women in Retail Real Estate, Chi Omega. Republican. Roman Catholic. Avocations: skiing, sailing, wine tasting, needlepoint, gardening. Home and Office: Danoff Kraus Enterprises 10182 Brier Ln Santa Ana CA 92705-1531 E-mail: danoffkraus@cox.net.

DANON, LAURENCE MIRIEL, business executive; b. Bordeaux, France, June 11, 1956; s. Yves N. and Arlette F. Arnaud; m. Pierre Danon; children: David, Felix. PhD, Ecole Normale Superieure, Paris, 1981; MBA, Ecole Mines, Paris, 1984. Econ. devel. mgr. Region of Picardy, France, 1984-87; head hydrocarbons dept. French Ministry of Industry, 1987-89; sales mgr. comodity plastics Elf-Atochem, France, 1989-91, gen. mgr. specialities, 1991-94, pres. functional polymers divsn., 1994-96; CEO Total Fina Elf group Bostik Findley, France, 1996—2001; chmn., CEO France Printemps, Paris, 2001—. Chmn. Ecole Mines de Nantes, 2000. Decorated chevalier Order duMerite (France), Ordre Legion d'Honneur (France). Avocations: travel, golf, yoga. Home: 30 bd Victor Hugo 92200 Neuilly Seine France Office: France Printemps 102 rue de Provence 75451 Paris France Fax: 33 1 42 82 59 82. E-mail: ldanon@printemps.fr.

DANOS, HARRY JOHN, architect, educator, artist; b. Enfield, Conn., May 5, 1924; s. John Christopher and Alice (Panagiota) D.; m. Catherine Magiopoulos, Sept. 5, 1948; 1 child, Michael (dec.). Apprentice program, GE Co., 1943; USAF tng., Amherst Coll., Yale U., 1943-44; student, Springfield Jr. Coll., 1946-47; BArch, Syracuse U., 1952; MArch, Rice U., 1953; studied watercolors with, Carlton Plummer, Barbara Nechis, Irving Shapiro and others. Registered arch., Conn., Vt., R.I., Mass. Arch., designer C.P. Kantianis, AIA, Springfield, Mass., 1952-55, Robert Carroll May (apprentice Frank Lloyd Wright), Hartford, 1955-57, Moore and Salsbury, U. Hartford, 1957-62, Charles DuBose Constn. Plz., 1952-55; prin., archtl. firm Harry Danos, AIA, Avon, 1955-80, Danos and Assocs., Archs., Hartford, 1962-80; staff arch., constrn. mgr. Associated Constrn. Co., Hartford, 1980-82; asst. dir. Bur. Pub. Works State of Conn., Hartford, 1982-84; profl. arch., devel. cons., 1984—. Instr. art and arch. Syracuse U., Rice U., U. Hartford, Boston Archtl. Ctr., Guilford Handcrafts and Art Ctr, 1984—, Mystic Art Assn., Mystic, Conn. Exhbns. include Peel Gallery, Danby, Vt., Leverett Gallery, Amherst, Mass., Hartford Nat. Bank, Waterford, Conn., E. Lyme Cmty. Ctr. Libr., Nat. Greek Am. Artists, Springfield, Mass.; represented in pvt. collections. Past chmn. E. Lyme Art League; exec. mem. E. Lyme Arts Coun.; mem. zoning and planning commn. Town of Avon, Conn., 1959-65; rep. Capitol Region Planning Agy., Avon, 1962-65. Commd. officer SAC, USAF, 1944-46, WWII, PTO. Recipient Archtl. Award of Merit, Am. Assn. Sch. Adminstrs., 1965, Carl E. Shawyer award of merit Archtl. Precast Assn., 1975, Facilities Excellence award World Wide Volkswagen Corp.-Porsche-Audi Ea. Div., 1981, various achievement awards; named Winner, Chgo. Tribune Better Rooms Competition, 1950; fellowship grantee Rice U., 1952-53. Mem. AIA (corp., Medal 1952), Am. Arbitration Assn. (arbitrator), Conn. Watercolor Soc., Mystic Art Assn., Salmagundi Club, Avon Lions Club (past treas.). Avocation: watercolorist teacher. Home and Office: 148 Old Black Point Rd Niantic CT 06357-3303

DANOS, PAUL, dean, finance educator; Chmn. acctg. dept. U. Mich., 1984-91, Arthur Andersen & Co. prof. acctg., 1985-95, dir. Paton Acctg. Ctr., 1988-91, sr. assoc. dean Sch. Bus. Adminstrn., 1992; dean, Laurence F. Whittemore prof. bus. adminstrn. Dartmouth Coll., Amos Tuck Sch. Bus. Adminstrn., Hanover, N.H., 1995—. Chmn. MBA rev. team, chmn. comprehensive studies program exec. com., dir. acctg. PhD com., mem. exec. com., sch. bus. adminstrn., mem. doctoral studies com. Sch. Bus. Adminstrn., U. Mich. Author two text books; ah hoc editor The Acctg. Rev.; mem. editl. bd. Advances in Acctg.; consulting editor Rev. of Bus. and Econ. Rsch.; contbr. articles to profl. jours. Mem. audit com. City of Ann Arbor. Mem. Am. Acctg. Assn. (chair doctoral fellowship com., bd. govs. adminstrs. of acctg. programs exec. com. and database com.). Office: Amos Tuck Sch Bus 100 Tuck Hall Hanover NH 03755-9027

DANOS, ROBERT MCCLURE, retired oil company executive; b. New Orleans, Dec. 9, 1929; s. Joseph A. and Muriel R. (McClure) D.; m. Barbara Umbach, Apr. 30, 1955; children: Robert M., Sally C., Susan M., Julie A., Richard F., Renee R. BS in Geology, Tulane U., 1950; MS, La. State U., 1952. Geologist Texaco, Inc., New Orleans, 1955-67, staff geologist Houston, 1967, divsn. geologist Tulsa, 1968-70, exploration mgr. Denver, 1970-80; sr. v.p. K N Energy, Inc., Lakewood, Colo., 1980-83; pres., CEO Midlands Energy Co., Lakewood, 1983-84; pres. McMoRan-Midlands Oil Co., New Orleans, 1984-86; pres., chief ops. officer McMoRan Oil & Gas Co., New Orleans, 1986-89; pres. Plains Petroleum Oper. Co., Lakewood, Colo., 1989-95; dir. Am. Exploration Co., Houston, 1996-97. 1st lt. U.S. Army, 1954. Mem. Am. Assn. Petroleum Geologists (del.), New Orleans Geolog. Soc. (v.p. 1965-67), Rocky Mountain Geolog. Assn., Bienville Club, Cherry Hills Country Club, Pickwick Club, Arlberg Club. Home: 124 High St Denver CO 80218-4018

DANS, PETER EMANUEL, medical educator; b. N.Y.C., June 17, 1937; s. Emanuel and Filomena (Lisanti) D.; m. Colette Lumina Lizotte, May 28, 1966; children: Maria Cristina, Paul Edouard, Thomas Emanuel, Suzanne Elise. BS in Chemistry, Manhattan Coll., 1957; MD, Columbia U., 1961. Intern, resident medicine Johns Hopkins Hosp., Balt., 1961-63; resident medicine Presbyn. Hosp., N.Y.C., 1963-64; fellow rsch. NIH, Bethesda, Md., 1964-67; infectious diseases fellow Harvard U., Boston, 1967-69; asst. prof. medicine U. Colo., Denver, 1969-74, assoc. prof., 1974-78; Robert Wood Johnson health policy fellow Inst. Medicine, Washington, 1976-77, sr. prof. assoc., 1977-78; assoc. prof. medicine Johns Hopkins U. Sch. Medicine and Health Policy and Mgmt., Balt., 1978—, Johns Hopkins U. Sch. Hygiene and Pub. Health, Balt., 1978—; clin. prof. Marshall U. Sch. Medicine, 1995—. Mem. Md. Physician Bd. Quality Assurance, sec. 1988-92; ind. cons. disease mgmt., outcomes, ethics, 1996—; med. cons. Advance PCS, 1996—. Author: Doctors in the Movies: Boil the Water & Just Say Aah!, 2000, Perry's Baltimore Adventure: A Bird's Eye View of Charm City, 2003; co-author: New Medical Market Place: A Physician's Guide to the Health Care Revolution, 1988; dep. editor: Annals of Internal Medicine, 1991—94, assoc. med. dir.: GMIS, Inc., 1994—95, mem. editl. bd.: Pharos, 1988—; contbr. articles; film reviewer Physician at the Movies, Pharos, 1990—. Pres. Falls Rd. Cmty. Assn., 1980—84, 1987—90; mem. adv. com. on gifted talented program Baltimore County, 1981—90, mem. zoning adv. com., 1985—86, mem. commn. on aging, 1996—98; pres. parish coun. Shrine of Sacred Heart, Balt., 1981—83; lector St. Francis Xavier, Balt., 1997—; bd. dirs. Ctr. Profl. Ethics U. Balt., 1999—2001. Fellow ACP; mem. Epsilon Sigma Pi, Alpha Omega Alpha. Roman Catholic. Avocations: film, birdwatching. Home and Office: 11 Hickory Hill Rd Cockeysville Hunt Valley MD 21030-1624

DANSBY, JOHN WALTER, retired oil company executive; b. Logan, W.Va., Dec. 29, 1944; s. Charles Eugene and Lillian (Maggard) D.; m. Karen Navarin, June 20, 1970; children: Andrew, David. BS in Econs, U. Pa., 1966; MBA, Emory U., 1967; PhD in Econs, U. Ky., 1976. Fin. analyst Ashland (Ky.) Oil, Inc., 1970-71, staff economist, 1975-77, mgr. fed. energy programs, 1977-81, exec. asst., 1981, v.p. strategic planning, 1981-84, v.p. planning, 1984-92, adminstrv. v.p. and treas., 1992-98. Part-time instr. No. Ariz. U., 2000—. Mem. U. Ky. Devel. Coun., U. Ky. Fellows; dir. Sedona Cultural Pk., Sedona Chamber Music Soc., treas., 2000—. Home: 75 Rim Shadows Cir Sedona AZ 86336-2196

DANSBY, RONNIE, transportation executive; b. Washington, Oct. 14, 1961; s. William Dansby and Helen Beatrice Bruce; life ptnr. Alma Floyd; 1 child, Brian. Student, No. Va. C.C., Annandale, Virginia, 1987—89. Cert. comml. driving instr. Bus operator Transit Mgmt. of Alexandria, Va., 1984—88, rd. supr., 1988—99, safety and loss control coord., 1999—2002, safety mgr., 2002—; CEO and owner Key Destination Directory, Inc., 2002—. Chmn. safety and accident rev. com. Transit Mgmt. of Alexandria, 1999—. Inventor detailed info. database mgmt. sys., 1995 (US Patent, 2000). Baptist. Avocations: racquetball, weightlifting, travel, jogging, martial arts.

DANSE, ILENE HOMNICK RAISFELD, physician, educator, toxicologist; b. Bklyn. d. Jack and Henrietta Homnick; m. James Atherton Danse, Aug. 10, 1982; children: Arthur Raisfeld, Robin Raisfeld. BS, CUNY, 1960; MD, NYU, 1964; student, Pratt Inst., Art Students League, Bklyn. Mus. Art Sch. Diplomate Nat. Bd. Med. Examiners, Am. Bd. Internal Medicine, Am. Bd. Toxicology. Assoc. prof. internal medicine SUNY, Stony Brook, 1975-83, assoc. prof. pharmacology, 1977-83, dir. clin. pharmacology and toxicology Sch. Medicine, 1978-83; acting chairperson clin. pharmacology Northport VA Hosp., L.I., N.Y., 1978-83; sr. advisor Chevron Environ. Health Ctr., San Pablo, Calif., 1982-84; prin. ENVIROMED Health Svcs., Inc., Novato, Calif., 1984-99; ind. med. examiner toxicology and internal medicine Dept. Indsl. Rels., State of Calif., 1985—; assoc. clin. prof. dept. medicine div. occupl. and environ. medicine U. Calif., San Francisco, 1986—, assoc. clin. prof. dept. epidemiol. and preventive medicine Davis, 1991—. Cons. in fields of toxicology, pharmacology, environ., occupl. and internal medicine, 1984—; mem. bd. sci. advisors Am. Coun. Sci. and Health; mem. sci. rev. panel Hazardous Substances Data Base, Nat. Libr. Medicine. Author: Common Sense Toxics In the Workplace, 1991; contbr. articles to sci. publs. Mem. bd. sci. advisors Am. Coun. on Sci. and Health; mem. sci. rev. panel Hazardous Substances Data Base, Nat. Libr. of Medicine. Fellow ACP, Am. Coll. Clin. Pharmacology; mem. AAAS, Am. Acad. Clin. Toxicology, Am. Chem. Soc. (environ. health and safety sect.), Am. Coll. Occupl. Medicine, Am. Indsl. Hygiene Assn. (occupational medicine sect.), Am. Coll. Toxicology, Am. Soc. Pharmacology and Therapeutics, Soc. Toxicology, Western Occupational Med. Assn. Achievements include patent for epithelial cell growth-regulating composition containing polyamines, and method of its use.

DANSER, BONITA KAY, legal administrator, consultant; b. Altadena, Calif., Mar. 26, 1949; d. Earl Peters and Sara Grace (Myer) Nissley; m. Robin Danser, Aug. 28, 1971 (div. Feb. 1978); m. John Hullett, June 3, 1989. AA, Pasadena City Coll., 1969; student, San Diego State U., 1970-76; BSBA, U. Redlands, 1988. Legal adminstr. Rhodes, Kendall & Harrington, Newport Beach, Calif., 1978-86, Gardner and Martin, Newport Beach, 1986, Martin and Wilson, Santa Ana, Calif., 1987-89; freelance contract legal adminstr. Irvine, Calif., 1986-88; legal administrator, cons. Parilla, Militzok & Shedden, Irvine, 1989—97; dir. adminstrn. Stevens & Kramer, Irvine and L.A., 1997—2000, Phillips, Lerner & Lauzon, Century City, Calif., 2001—02, cons., adminstr. Irvine, 2003; legal administrator, cons. Parilla, Militzok & Shedden, 2000. Citizen ambassador to China, People-to-People Internat., 1988. Mem. Assn. Legal Adminstrs. (treas. 1983, 85, sec. 1984, 2d v.p. 1990, 1st v.p. 1991, pres. 1992, region 6 comm. officer 1993, 94, 95), Theta Chi Epsilon (nat. bd. dirs. 1984-94, 95, Achievement award 1979, 94). Avocations: travel, writing.

DANSEREAU, PIERRE, retired ecologist; b. Montreal, Can., Oct. 5, 1911; s. J.-Lucien and Marie (Archambault) D.; m. Françoise Masson, Aug. 29, 1935. BA, U. Montréal, 1932, BS Agr., 1936; DSc, U. Geneva, Switzerland, 1939; DSc (hon.), U. Sask., 1959, U. N.B., 1959, U. Strasbourg, France, 1970, U. Sherbrooke, 1971, Concordia U., 1971, U. Waterloo, 1972, U. Guelph, 1973, U. Western Ont., 1973, Meml. U. Nfld., 1974, McGill U., 1976, U. Ottawa, 1978, Royal Mil. Coll., 1990, Laurentian U, 1993, U. Laval, 1994, U. Montreal, 1999, U. du Québec á Rimouski, 2002. Mem. faculty U. Montréal, 1940-42, 45, 55-61, 68-71; with Service de Biogéographie, 1943-50; prof. botany U. Mich., 1950-55; asst. dir., prof. ecology N.Y. Bot. Garden, 1961-68; adj. prof. Columbia U., 1962-68; mem. staff U. Qué., Centre de Recherches Écologiques de Montréal, 1971-72; prof. ecology U. Qué., Montréal, 1972-76, hon. prof., 1976—, emeritus prof., 1989—. Vice chmn. Can. Environ. Adv. Coun., 1972-76, Can. Fed. Task Force Housing and Urban Devel., 1968, Natural Scis. and Engring. Rsch. Coun., 1978-80; mem. Sci. Coun. Can., 1968-72, Can. Radio-TV Coun., 1968; v.p. Can. Commn. Internat. Biol. Programme, 1968; chmn. program urban devel. Sci. Coun. Can., 1970; pres. 1st Internat. Film Festival on Human Environ., 1973; sec. gen. Mich. Acad. Sci., Arts and Letters, 1953; 1st v.p. 9th Internat. Bot. Congress, 1959; chmn. bd. Gamma Inst., 1983-86; hon. chmn. Fondation de l'ACFAS, 1984; pres. Environment 2000, 1990, Festival Internat. du Film Scientifique de Qué., 1990; mem. internat. adv. com. rev. Ecodecision, 1992-94; bd. dirs. Biodome, Montréal, 1993-95. Author: Biogeography: An Ecological Perspective, 1957, Phytogeographia laurentiana II, 1959, Contradictions & Biculture, 1964, Dimensions of Environmental Quality, 1971, Inscape and Landscape, 1973, An Ecological Grading of Human Settlements, 1978, Essai de classification et de cartographie écologique des espaces, 1985, Les dimensions écologiques de l'espace urbain, 1987, Interdisciplinary perspective on production-investment-control processes in the environment, 1990, Harmonie et désordre dans l'environnement canadien, 1990, L'envers et l'endroit: le désir, le besoin et la capacité, 1991, L'envers et l'endroit: le désir, le besoin et la capacité, 2d edit., 1994, Biodiversity, Ecodiversity, Sociodiversity-three aspects of diversity. Global biodiversity, 1997, Ecologia humana, ética e educação: a mensagem de Pierre Dansereau, 1999; co-author: Studies on the Vegetation of Puerto Rico I and II, 1966, A Universal System for Recording Vegetation II, 1966; editor: Challenge for Survival, 1970; co-author: La terre des hommes et le paysage intérieur, 1973, Harmony and Disorder in the Canadian Environment, 1975, Ezaim: Écologie de la Zone de l'Aéroport International de Montréal, Le cadre d'une recherche écologique interdisciplinaire, 1976, Ecological Grading and Classification of Land-occupation and Land-use Mosaics, 1977. Decorated Companion Order Can., 1969, Grand officer Ordre Nat. du Qué., 1992; recipient Pierre Fermat medal, 1960, Léo Pariseau medal, 1965, Pfizer prize, 1965, Prix David, Qué., 1959, Disting. Svc. award N.Y. Bot. Garden, 1969, Massey medal, 1973, Molson prize, 1974, Esdras-Minville prize, 1983, Marie-Victorin prize, 1983, Izaak Walton Killam prize, 1985, Knight of Ordre Nat. du Qué., 1985, Can. Bot. Assn. Lawson medal, 1986, Lifetime Achievement award Environ. Can., 1989, Premier's medal, Qué., 1989, Prix Interamerica, 1990, Qué. Youth Edn. Excellence prize, 1990, Grand Prix du Mérite forestier, 1990, Dawson medal, 1995, Frederick Todd prize, 1998; named Gt. Montrealer in Sci., 1978, Personality of the Yr. in Sci., La Presse, Montreal, 1999; named to Can. Scis. and Engring. Hall of Fame, 2001; Guggenheim fellow, 1949, Commonwealth Pres. fellow, 1961. Fellow Royal Soc. Can., Royal Soc. New Zealand (hon.); mem. Can. Mental Health Assn. (pres. Qué. 1972-74), Am. Teilhard de Chardin Assn. (pres. 1967), Ecol. Soc. Am. (v.p. 1968), Assn. Canadienne-Française pour l'Avancement des Scis. (sec. gen. 1945-46), Geog. Soc. Montreal (pres. 1957), Argentina Acad. Environ. Scis. (fgn. corr. mem. 1984), Acad. Scis. Lisbon (fgn. corr. mem. 1985), Ordre nat. du Qué. (pres. 1987-89), PEN Club Internat. (hon.). Office: U du Qué à Montréal Case Postale 8888 Sta Ctr-ville Montreal QC Canada H3C 3P8 E-mail: dansereau.pierre@uqam.ca. *Teaching and research are parallel but complementary exercises. Contemplation and distillation in the ivory tower have to be fed by experience and exchange. My own experience has been mostly in the field: the sensorial witnessing of stones, plants, and animals, and men and cities, must be renewed all the time, in an endless addition to a personal treasury. But the translation into word-and-picture form needs interlocutors to test both the validity of perception and the communicability of rendering. This pulsation has varied in rhythm and content and has yielded both anxiety and happiness.*

DANTO, ARTHUR COLEMAN, author, philosopher, art critic; b. Ann Arbor, Mich., Jan. 1, 1924; s. Samuel Budd and Sylvia (Gittleman) D.; m. Shirley Rovetch, Aug. 9, 1946 (dec. July 1978); children: Elizabeth, Jane; m. Barbara Westman, Feb. 15, 1980. BA, Wayne State U., 1948; MA, Columbia U., 1949, PhD, 1952; postgrad., U. Paris, 1949-50. Instr. U. Colo., Colo., 1950-51; mem. faculty Columbia U., 1952—, Johnsonian prof. philosophy, 1975-92, chmn. dept., 1979-87, co-dir. Ctr. for Study of Human Rights, 1978-92; prof. emeritus, 1992. Andrew W. Mellon Fine Arts lectr., 1995. Author: Analytical Philosophy of Knowledge, 1968, What Philosophy Is, 1968, Analytical Philosophy of Hist., 1965, Nietzsche as Philosopher, 1965, Analytical Philosophy of Action, 1973, Mysticism and Morality, 1972, Jean-Paul Sartre, 1975, The Transfiguration of the Commonplace, 1981 (Lionel Trilling Book prize 1982), Narration and Knowledge, 1985, The Philosophical Disenfranchisement of Art, 1986, The State of the Art, 1987, Connections to the World, 1989, Encounters and Reflections: Art in the Hist. Present, 1990, Beyond the Brillo Box: Art in the Post Hist. Period, 1992, Mark Tansey: Visions and Revisions, 1992, Robert Mapplethorpe, 1992, Embodied Meanings: Critical Essays and Aesthetic Meditations, 1994, Playing with the Edge: The Photographic Achievement of Robert Mapplethorpe, After the End of Art: Contemporary Art and the Pale of Hist., 1997 (Eugene Kayden prize 1997), The Body/Body Problem, 1999, Philosophizing Art, 1999, The Madonna of the Future, 2000, The Abuse of Beauty: Aesthetics and the Concept of Art, 2003; editor Jour. Philosophy, 1965—, pres., 1987—; art critic The Nation, 1984—; contbg. editor ARTFORUM. Bd. dirs. Amnesty Internat., 1970-75, gen. sec., 1973. Served with AUS, 1942-45. Recipient prize for disting. criticism Mfr.-Hanover/Art World, 1985, George S. Polk award for criticism, 1985, Nat. Book Critics Circle prize for criticism, 1990, ICP Infinity prize for writing in photography, 1993; fellow Fulbright Found., 1949, Guggenheim Found., 1969, 82, Am. Coun. Learned Socs., 1961, 70; Fulbright disting. prof. Yugoslavia, 1976; Phi Beta Kappa prof. Arts and Scis.; mem. Am. Philos. Assn. (v.p. 1969, pres. 1983), Am. Soc. Aesthetics (v.p. 1987, pres. 1989). Fellow AAAS; mem. Am. Philos. Assn. (v.p. 1969, pres. 1983), Am. Soc. Aesthetics (v.p. 1987, pres. 1989), Coll. Art Assn. (Frank Jewett Mather prize for criticism). Office: 420 Riverside Dr New York NY 10025-7773 E-mail: acdi@columbia.edu.

DANTO, ELIZABETH ANN, social worker, educator; b. Detroit, May 31, 1952; m. Paul Werner. BA, Sarah Lawrence Coll., 1973; MS, Columbia U., 1984; PhD, NYU, 1996. ACSW, CSW, N.Y. Coord. social svcs. United Storeworkers Union, N.Y.C., 1983-86; EAP dir. N.Y.C. Office of Mayor, 1986-91; founding dir. Stillpoint, N.Y.C., 1996; assoc. prof. Hunter Coll. Sch. Social Work, CUNY, N.Y.C., 1997—. Contbr. articles to profl. jours. Mem. NASW (commr. 1989-92). E-mail: edanto@hunter.cuny.edu.

D'ANTONI, PHILIP, producer; b. Bronx, N.Y., Feb. 19, 1929; s. Peter and Josephine (Elici) D'Antoni; m. Ruth Ann Wiederecht, Sept. 12, 1953; children: Christopher, Jeanne, Carol, James, Robert. Student, Fordham U., 1948-50. Prodn. asst., assoc. producer CBS-TV, 1949-53; v.p., dir. Mut. Broadcasting Sys., 1955-61; pres. D'Antoni/Weitz TV Prodns. Prodr.: (TV series) Movin' On, 1961—73; (films) Bullitt, 1968, The French Connection, 1971 (Acad. award, 1971), (spls.) Elizabeth Taylor in London, 1964, Sophia Loren in Rome, 1965, Melina Mercouri in Greece, 1966, (dir): (films) The Seven Ups, 1974; (TV films) Strike Force, The Connection, Cabo, Inside-Outside, In Tandem, Rubber Gun Squad, 1974—77. Served with U.S. Army, 1946—48. Mem.: Motion Picture Acad., Screenwriters Guild, Dirs. Guild Am. Home: care of St Andrews G C 10 Old Jackson Ave Hastings On Hudson NY 10706

D'ANTONIO, CYNTHIA MARIA, sales and marketing executive; b. Chgo., Sept. 12, 1956; d. Michael Patrick and Joan Marie (Funk) D'A. BS in Natural Resource Devel., Mich. State U., 1979. Chemist Aqualab, Streamwood, Ill., 1980-83; R&D specialist Seaquist Closures, Crystal Lake, Ill., 1983-87; internat. sales & mktg. exec. Seaquist-Valois Australia, Sydney, 1987-93; internat. v.p. sales and mktg. cosmetics Pfeiffer Inc., Princeton, N.J., 1993—. Spkr. in field. Contbr. articles and photos to profl. jours. Mem. NAFE, Plastic Inst. Australia. Republican. Roman Catholic. Avocations: foreign current events, photography, golf, bike tours. Home: 5 Bradway Ave Ewing NJ 08618-2607

D'ANTONIO, JAMES JOSEPH, lawyer; b. Tucson, Jan. 13, 1959; s. Lawrence Patrick and Rosemary Catherine (Kane) D'A. Student, Tufts U., 1978-79; BA, U. Ariz., 1981, JD, 1984. Bar: Ariz. 1984, U.S. Dist. Ct. Ariz. 1984, U.S. Ct. Appeals (9th cir.) 1993. Assoc. Law Office of D'Antonio and D'Antonio, Tucson, 1984-93; pvt. practice law Law Offices of James J. D'Antonio, Tucson, 1993—. Chmn. bd. govs. U. Ariz. Coll. Law, 1983-84;

mem. Pima County Teen Ct. Adv. Bd; mem. Health South Rehab. Inst., Tucson Cmty. Adv. Bd.; bd. dirs. Coyote Task Force. Named Outstanding Pro Bono Lawyer Pima County Vol. Lawyers Program, 1993. Fellow Ariz. Bar Found.; mem. ABA, Assn. Trial Lawyers Am., Ariz. Bar Assn., Ariz. Trial Lawyers Assn., Pima County Bar Assn. Office: 751 N Country Club Rd Tucson AZ 85716

DANTZIC, CYNTHIA MARIS, artist, educator; b. NYC, Jan. 4, 1933; d. Howard Arthur and Sylvia Hazel (Wiener) Gross; m. Jerry Dantzic, June 15, 1958; 1 son, Grayson Ross. Student, Brooklyn Mus. Art Sch., Bklyn., 1947—50, Bard Coll., 1950—52; BFA, Yale U., 1955; MFA, Pratt Inst., 1963. Tchr. art Baldwin Sch., Bryn Mawr, Pa., 1955-58; head art dept. Bentley Sch., N.Y.C., 1958-62; coord. art prog., instr. North Shore Cmty. Arts Ctr., Roslyn, NY, 1962-64; instr. art CUNY-Bronx, N.Y.C., 1963-64; faculty L.I. U., Bklyn., 1964—, prof., 1975—, chair art dept., 1980-86. Adj. assoc. prof. art Cooper Union, 1992—99, adj. prof. art, 1999—2002; lectr., presenter in field. One-woman shows include Resnick Gallery, L.I. U., Bklyn., 1983, 89, 95, 2000, East Hampton Gallery, N.Y.C., 1965-66, St. John's U. Gallery, 1995; exhibited in group shows at Blue Mountain Gallery, N.Y.C., 1984-85, 94-98, 2001, 2002, Hillwood Gallery, Greenvale, N.Y., 1985; commd. artist edit. of photo collages Bklyn. Arts and Culture Assn., 1983; represented in permanent collections Bklyn. Mus., N.Y., Rose Art Mus., Mass., Bard Coll., N.Y.; author, illustrator: Stop Dropping BreAdcrumBs on my YaChts, 1974, Sounds of Silents, 1976, Design Dimensions: An Introduction to the Visual Surface, 1990, Drawing Dimensions: A Comprehensive Introduction, 1999, Antique Pocket Mirrors: Pictorial & Advertising Minatures, 2002; contbr. articles to profl. jours. Trustee Park Slope Civic Coun., 1991—. Mellon grantee, 1984, L.I. Univ. faculty rsch. grantee, 1985—; recipient Newton Teaching Excellence award, 1988, Trustees award single work, 1990, Trustees lifetime award for Scholarly Achievement in art and art edn. L.I. Univ., 1999. Mem. AAUP, Internat. Soc. Copier Artists, L.I. U. Faculty Fedn. (exec. com. 1975—), Coll. Art Assn., Soc. Scribes (bd. govs. 2003—). Avocations: piano, travel, collecting americana and tribal and folk art. Home: 910 President St Brooklyn NY 11215-1604 Office: LI U Art Dept University Pla Brooklyn NY 11201

DANTZIG, GEORGE BERNARD, applied mathematics educator; b. Portland, Oreg., Nov. 8, 1914; s. Tobias and Anja (Ourisson) Dantzig; m. Anne Shmuner, Aug. 23, 1936; children: David Franklin, Jessica Rose, Paul Michael. AB in Math. and Physics, U. Md., 1936; MA in Math., U. Mich., 1937; PhD in Math., U. Calif.-Berkeley, 1946; degree (hon.), Technion, Israel, Linkoping U., Sweden, U. Md., Yale U., Louvain U., Belgium, Columbia U., U. Zurich, Switzerland, Carnegie-Mellon U., U. Mich. Chief combat analysis br. Statis. Control Hdqrs. USAF, 1941—46, math. advisor, 1946—52; rsch. mathematician Rand Corp., Santa Monica, Calif., 1952—60; prof., chmn. Ops. Rsch. Ctr. U. Calif.-Berkeley, 1960—66; prof. ops. rsch. and computer sci. Stanford (Calif.) U., Calif., 1966—97, prof. emeritus, 1997—. Cons. to industry, 1960—97; chief methodology Internat. Inst. Applied Sys. Analysis, Austria, 1973—74. Author: Linear Programming and Extensions, 1963; co-author: Compact City, 1973, Linear Programming I Introduction, 1997; contbr. articles to profl. jours., assoc. editor Math. Programming, Math. of Ops. Rsch., others. Recipient Exceptional Civilian Svc. medal, War Dept., 1944, NAS award, 1971, NAS award in applied math. and numerical analysis, 1977, Nat. medal of Sci. for inventing linear programming and simplex algorithm, 1975, Von Neumann theory prize in ops. rsch., 1975, Harvey prize, Technion, 1985, Silver medal, Operational Rsch. Soc. Gt. Britain, 1986, Coors Am. Ingenuity award, 1989, Pender award, U. Pa., 1995. Fellow: Inst. Math. Stats., Econometric Soc., Am. Acad. Arts and Scis.; mem.: NAS, IEEE, AAAS, Inst. Mgmt. Sci. (pres. 1966), Math. Programming Soc. (chmn. 1973—74), Am. Math. Soc., Ops. Rsch. Soc., Nat. Acad. Engring., Assn. Computing Machinery, Phi Beta Kappa, Sigma Xi (hon.), Omega Rho Soc., Pi Mu Epsilon, Phi Kappa Phi. Home: 821 Tolman Dr Stanford CA 94305-1025 Office: Stanford Univ Dept Mgmt Sci and Engring Stanford CA 94305-4023 E-mail: goerge-dantzig@worldnet.att.net.

DANTZKER, DAVID ROY, venture capitalist; MD, SUNY, Buffalo, 1967. Diplomate Am. Bd. Internal Medicine, Am. Bd. Pulmonary Medicine, Am. Bd. CCM. Intern Buffalo Gen. Hosp., 1967-68; resident in medicine SUNY Affiliated Hosp., Buffalo, 1968-70; fellow in pulmonary medicine U. Calif., San Diego, 1972-75; mem. med. staff L.I. Jewish Med. Ctr., New Hyde Park, 1990—2002, CEO, 1994—97; pres. North Shore L.I. Jewish Health Sys., Great Neck, 1997-2000; mem. med. staff North Shore Univ. Hosp., Manhasset, N.Y., 1999-2000; pharm. co. CEO, chmn., gen. ptnr. BioTech Venture Capital Partnership, 2000—. Prof. medicine Albert Einstein Coll. Medicine, 1990—. Author 7 books; contbr. 130 articles to profl. jours. Fellow ACP, Am. Coll. Chest Physicians. Office: Wheatley Ptnrs 825 3d Ave New York NY 10022 E-mail: davidd@wheatleypartners.com.

DANTZLER, ANDREW ALAN, science administrator; b. Bethesda, Md., Mar. 25, 1962; s. Taft Earnest and Barbara Mae Dantzler; m. Wendy Lynne Bratzel, Aug. 24, 1985 (div. Sept. 1992); m. Erin E. O'Connor, June 26, 1994; children: Melanie Meade Celano, Nicholas Andrew, Wesley Stephen BS in Astronomy, U. Md., 1984. Optical engr. NASA Goddard Space Flight Ctr., Greenbelt, Md., 1984-88, earth observing sys. instrument mgr., 1988-94, Landsat 7 instrument mgr., 1994-98, asst. chief lab. high energy astrophysics, 1998—2001, asst. dir. Space Scis. Directorate, 2001—. Avocations: Judo, chess, astronomy. Office: NASA Goddard Space Flight Ctr Code 600 Greenbelt MD 20771-0001 Fax: 301-286-1772. E-mail: Andrew.A.Dantzler@nasa.gov.

DANVERS, DAVID BELL, equity broker; b. Poughkeepsie, N.Y., Jan. 15, 1968; s. William David and Rachel (Bell) Rosenberg; m. Karen Minor, Sept. 24, 1994; children: Andrew Bennett, Erik Payson, Alison Perry. BA in Econs, French, Union Coll., 1990. Cert. series 7 Nat. Assn. Securities Dealers. V.p. Salomon Smith Barney, Calif., 1992—. Ptnr. in Edn., Bd. Edn., N.Y.C., 1995-2001; house capt. (repairs) Americares, New Canaan, Conn., 1996-99; mem. mentor program steering com. Salomon Smith Barney. Mem. Nat. Assn. Securities Dealers, Securities Analyst of San Francisco, Assn. for Investment Mgmt. and Rsch. Democrat. Methodist. Avocations: ice hockey, skiing, running. Home: 12 Darnby Ct Orinda CA 94563 E-mail: dbdanvers@aol.com.

D'ANZA, LAWRENCE MARTIN, management consultant; b. Hindsdale, Ill., June 20, 1953; s. Joseph James and Evelyn (Martinek) D'Anza; m. Teresa D'Anza, June 14, 1980 (div. Sept. 2003). BBEd, Ea. N.Mex. U., 1975; MA, U. N.Mex., 1984. Instr. cashiering Albuquerque Tech. Vocat. Inst., 1975-85; mktg. edn. tchr. coord. Eldorado HS, 1975-2000; enrollment program coord. Del Norte HS, 1983-93; tchr. bus. mktg. Albuquerque Pub. Schs., 1984-85; cons., acct. mgr., ops./sales mgr. N.Mex. ops. DeLaPorte & Assoc., 2000—. Conf. cons. N.Mex DECA, 1978—, chmn., 1983—84, 1989—91, bd. govs., 1988—90, 1996—97; secondary adv. coun. Nat. DECA, 1992—93, 1997—99, chairperson, 1998—99, nat. bd. dirs., 1993—96, conf. coord. western region, 1992, 96, 98, 2000, 02, western region bd. dirs., 1993—98. Mem. N.Mex Gov.'s Workforce Devel. Bd., 1996—99; trustee Youth Opportunities in Retailing, 1996—2001. Recipient Nat. Educator award, Milken Family Found., 1995. Mem.: N.Mex Vocat. Assn. (pres. 1995—96, N.Mex Mktg. Tchr. of the Yr. 1981—82, 1987—88, 1992—93, 1993—94), Am. Vocat. Assn. (Region Iv Mktg. Edn. Tchr. of the Yr. 1994—95, Vocat. Tchr. of the Yr. 1994—95), N.Mex Mktg. Edn. Assn. Avocations: golf, sports, travel. Home: 11005 Costa Del Sol NE Albuquerque NM 87111-1891 E-mail: ldanzadeca@aol.com.

DANZBERGER, ALEXANDER HARRIS, chemical engineer, consultant; b. N.Y.C., Mar. 23, 1932; s. George Harris and Ruth P. (Alexander) D.; m. Jacqueline P. Pilcher, Mar. 12, 1954; children: Alison, Alexander, Diana, Robert; m. Anne Griggs Pierson, Apr. 23, 1977; stepchildren: Jennifer Pierson, Priscilla Pierson, Stephanie Pierson BSChemE, MIT, 1953. Registered profl. engr., Mass., Colo. Mem. staff Arthur D. Little Inc., Cambridge, Mass., 1953-60; engring. mgr. Linde div. Union Carbide Corp., Tonawanda, N.Y., N.Y.C., 1961-70; chief engr. Booz, Allen & Hamilton, Florham Park, N.J., 1971-72, Marcom Cons., N.Y.C., 1973-75; v.p. Hydrotechnic Corp., N.Y.C., 1976-81; mgr. pollution control group Dames & Moore, Golden, Colo., 1982-83; pres. Danzberger and Assocs., Inc., Lakewood, Colo., 1983—. Adj. prof. dept. arts and scis. Johnson and Wales U., Providence, 2001—. Served to 1st lt. U.S. Army, 1956-58. Recipient Kenneth B. Allen award N.Y. Water Pollution Control Assn., 1983. Fellow AIChE; mem. ASME, Am. Acad. Environ. Engrs. (diplomate), Water Pollution Control Fedn., Colo. Mountain Club, Masons, Bristol Yacht Club. Republican. Presbyterian. Home and Office: 273 N Farm Dr Bristol RI 02809-1560

DANZIG, FREDERICK PAUL, newspaper editor; b. Springfield, Mass., Sept. 17, 1925; s. Phillip and Sylvia (Levin) D.; m. Edith Goret, Mar. 16, 1952; children: Steven, Ellen Kay. BA, Washington Sq. Coll., NYU, 1949. Copy boy AP, N.Y.C., 1943; reporter Herkimer (N.Y.) Evening Telegram, 1949, Port Chester (N.Y.) Daily Item, 1950-51; reporter, columnist UPI, N.Y.C., 1951-62; sr. editor Advt. Age, N.Y.C., 1962-68, exec. editor, 1969-84, editor, 1984-94; contbg. editor, 1995—. Advt. newscaster Sta. wQXR, 1979-81, Sta. WMCA, 1982-86; adj. instr. New Sch. Social Rsch., N.Y.C.; pub. radio commentator, 1989-90; media cons. Comprehensive Cmty. Revitalization Program, N.Y.C, 1994-98; mem. adv. bd. Youth Law Ctr., Washington; dir. Greenshoe Inc., Southampton, N.Y. Author: (with Ted Klein) How to be Heard, 1974, Publicity, 1985. Served with inf. AUS, 1943-46. Decorated Bronze Star, Purple Heart; recipient Alumni Achievement award NYU, 1983. Mem. 29th Inf. Divsn. Assn., Amagansett Hist. Assn., The Battle of Normandy Found., U.S. Holocaust Meml. Mus., Internat. Mus. Cartoon Art (adv. bd.). E-mail: fredpep@aol.com.

DANZIG, RICHARD JEFFREY, former government official, lawyer; b. N.Y.C., Sept. 8, 1944; s. Aaron and Elinor (Moskowitz) D.; m. Andrea Auster, June 26, 1966; children: David, Lisa. BA, Reed Coll., 1965; B.Phil., Magdalen Coll., Oxford U., 1967, D.Phil., 1968; JD, Yale U., 1971. Bar: Calif. 1973, D.C. 1983. Asst. to pres. Rand Inst., N.Y.C., 1971; law clk. Justice White, U.S. Supreme Ct., Washington, 1971-72; fellow Harvard Soc. Fellows, 1975-77; asst. prof. Stanford Law Sch., 1972-75, assoc. prof., 1975-77; mem. faculty Harvard Program in the Law and Humanities, 1976; dep. asst. sec. of Def. for program devel. Dept. Def., Washington, 1977-79, acting prin. dep. asst. sec. of Def. for manpower, res. affairs and logistics, 1979, prin. dep. asst. sec., 1979-81; ptnr. Latham & Watkins, Washington, 1981-93; mem. Clinton presidl. transition team PNT, Washington, 1992-93; under sec. of the navy USN, Washington, 1993-97, sec of the navy DC, 1999—2001; chmn. Cntr. for Strategic & Budget Assesments, 2001—. Vis. prof. Georgetown U. Sch. Law, 1980-82; cons. Urban Affairs N.Y. Rand Inst., 1969-74; mem. NRC Com. Mil. Pers., 1983-91; cons. UN Ctr. Transnat. Corp.; dir. Nat. Semiconductor Corp., 1987-93; dir. Internat. Human Rights Law Group, 1991-93, vice chmn., 1992-93; fellow Nat. Acad. Pub. Adminstrn., 1994—; adj. prof. Syracuse U. Maxwell Sch. Citizenship; Travelling Fellow Ctr. for Internat. Polit. Economy, 1997-98. Author: The Capability Problem in Contract Law, 1978; co-author: National Service: What Would It Mean?, 1986; contbr. articles to profl. jours. Trustee Reed Coll., 1984-88. Rockefeller Found. fellow, 1976-77; Rhodes scholar, 1965-68; recipient Herbert prize U. Oxford, 1967, Harlan Fiske Stone prize Yale Law Sch., 1970, Tony Friedrich Meml. award Internat. Human Rights Law Group, 1991. Mem. Calif. Bar Assn., Phi Beta Kappa. Home: 3670 Upton St NW Washington DC 20008-3125 Office: 1730 Rhode Island Ave NW Ste 912 Washington DC 20036 E-mail: danzig.richard@hq.navy.mil.

DANZIGER, GERTRUDE SEELIG, metal fabricating executive; b. Chgo., Oct. 24, 1919; d. Isidor and Clara (Fuchs) Seelig; widowed; children: Robert, James. With Homak Mfg. Co., Inc., Chgo., 1966-79, pres., 1979—. Patentee in field.

DANZIGER, GLENN NORMAN, former chemical sales company executive; b. N.Y.C., Apr. 7, 1930; s. Victor and Freda (Lazar) D.; m. Florence Spielvogel, June 7, 1953; children: Jill Marla Danziger Hetson, Amy L. Tenenbaum, Beth J. Keyes (dec.). AB, Columbia U., 1952, BSCE, 1953. Chemist Breinig Bros., Hoboken, N.J., 1955-61; v.p., tech. dir. Flood and Conklin, Newark, 1961-65; tech. sales rep. Seabord Chem. Corp., Lodi, N.J., 1965-75; pres. Seaboard Sales Corp., Paterson, NJ, 1975—2002. Author: Formulation of Organic Coatings, 1967. Lt. (j.g.) USNR, 1953-55. Mem. N.Y. Met. Soc. Coatings Technology, Nat. Paint and Coatings Assn. Democrat. Jewish. Avocations: travel, golf, skiing, reading.

DANZIGER, JAMES NORRIS, political science educator; b. L.A., May 28, 1945; s. Edward and Beverly Jane Danziger; m. Lesley Robson, June 12, 1971; children: Nicholas James, Vanessa Margaret. BA, Occidental Coll., L.A., 1966; MA, Sussex U., Brighton, Eng., 1968; MA, PhD, Stanford U., 1974. Prof. polit. sci. U. Calif., Irvine, 1972—, chmn. dept. polit. sci., 1974-76, 81-83, 88-92, assoc. dean Sch. Social Scis., 1978-81, chmn. acad. senate, 1994-95, dean of undergrad. edn., 1995-99; rsch. assoc. Ctr. Rsch. Info. Tech. and Orgns., Irvine, 1974—, dir., 2000-01; scholar-in-residence LaVerne (Calif.) U., 1983-84. Vis. prof. Univ. Pitts., 1996; vis. prof. Aarhus (Denmark) U., 1985. Author: Making Budgets, 1978, Understanding the Political World, 1991, 6th edit., 2003; co-author: Computers and Politics, 1982, People and Computers, 1986; mem. editl. bd. local govt. studies, 1981—; assoc. editor Social Sci. Computer Rev. Bd. dirs. South Laguna Civic Assn., 1983-86, chair South Laguna Annexation Task Force, 1986, bd. dirs. Irvine Campus Housing Authority, 1996—. Recipient Disting. Teaching award U. Calif., 1979, Daniel Aldrich disting. svc. award, 1997; Marshall scholar Govt. of U.K., 1966-68; named Disting. Faculty Lectr. U. Calif. Acad. Senate, 1987, IBM Faculty fellow, 2003—; NSF grantee, 1973-79, 80-83, 1996-98, 99—. Mem. Am. Polit. Sci. Assn. (Leonard White award 1974), ASPA (Marshall Dimock award 1977), Phi Beta Kappa (pres. local chpt. 1988-89, sec.-treas. local chpt. 1996-99, Pi Sigma Alpha (pres. local chpt. 1987—). Avocations: travel, basketball, cycling, literature. Office: U Calif Sch Social Scis Irvine CA 92697-5100 E-mail: danziger@uci.edu.

DANZIGER, JERRY, broadcasting executive; b. N.Y.C., Jan. 23, 1924; s. Harry and Lillie (Lacher) D.; m. Zelda Bloom, Dec. 26, 1948; children: Sydney, Alan, Lee. Grad. high sch. With Sta. WTTV, Bloomington, Ind., 1950-53, ops. mgr. Indpls., 1953-57; program mgr. Sta. WTSK-TV, Knoxville, Tenn., 1953; pres. Sta. KOB-TV, Albuquerque, 1957-88, v.p., 1983-88, pres., 1988-93, vice-chmn., 1993—. Mem. Gov. N.Mex. Commn. for Film Entertainment, 1970-71 Bd. dirs. KIPC All Indian Pueblo Coun., 1975-88, Albuquerque Little Theatre, Albuquerque Pub. Broadcast, Albuquerque Jewish Welfare Fund, Albuquerque Econ. Devel. 1989-97, Albuquerque Conv. and Visitors Bur., 1990-93, Great Southwest Coun. Boy Scouts Am., 1994—; v.p. for TV AP Broadcasting, 1980-88, Goodwill Industries N.Mex., 1980, bd. dirs., 1991-2003; mem. Albuquerque Econ. Forum, 1997; adv. bd. AAA, 1995-2002. Recipient Compadre award Am. Women in Radio and TV, 1978, 80, Silver Medal award N.Mex. Advt. Fedn., 1990; named to N.Mex. Broadcasters Hall of Fame, 2001. Mem. N.Mex. Broadcasters Assn. (pres. 1972-73, Broadcaster of Yr. award, 1976, 78), Press Club, Advt. Club, Albuquerque Country Club. Office: Sta KOB-TV PO Box 1351 Albuquerque NM 87103-1351 E-mail: jdanziger@kobtv.com.

DANZIGER, JOEL BERNARD, lawyer; b. N.Y.C., Oct. 17, 1932; AB, Columbia Coll., 1953; LLB, Yale U., 1956. Bar: N.Y. 1958, Conn. 1958, U.S. Dist. Ct. (so. and ea. dists.) N.Y. 1963, U.S. Ct. Appeals (2d cir.) 1958, U.S. Supreme Ct. 1964. Ptnr. Danziger & Markhoff, White Plains, N.Y., 1958—. Adj. prof. law Bridgeport (N.Y.) Law Sch., 1982-85. Mem. ABA, N.Y. Bar Assn., Westchester County Bar Assn., Yale Club. Office: Danziger & Markhoff 123 Main St White Plains NY 10601-3104

DANZIGER, LOUIS, graphic designer, educator; b. N.Y.C., 1923; m. Dorothy Patricia Smith, 1954. Student, Art Ctr. Sch., Los Angeles, 1946-47, New Sch., N.Y.C., 1947-48. Asst. art dir. War Assets Adminstrn., Los Angeles, 1946-47; designer Esquire mag., N.Y.C., 1948; freelance designer, cons. Los Angeles, 1949—; instr. graphic design Art Ctr. Coll. Design, Los Angeles, 1952-60, 86—, Chouinard Art Inst., Los Angeles, 1960-72; instr. Calif. Inst. Arts, 1972-88, head graphic design program, 1972-82; vis. prof. Harvard U., Cambridge, Mass., summers 1978-80, 83, 84, 86-88; instr. Art Ctr. Coll. Design. Mem. graphic evaluation panel Fed. Design Program, Nat. Endowment Arts, 1975— ; design cons. Los Angeles County Mus. Art, 1957— Served with cav. U.S. Army, 1943-45; PTO Recipient Disting. Achievement award Contemporary Art Coun., L.A. County Mus. Art, 1982, Disting. Designer award NEA, 1985, "Stars of Design" Lifetime Achievement award Pacific Design Ctr., 1997, numerous awards and medals in art design. Mem. Alliance Graphique Internationale, Am. Inst. Graphic Arts (medal 1998), Am. Ctr. for Design (hon.). Home: PO Box 660189 Arcadia CA 91066-0189

DANZIGER, RAPHAEL, political scientist, researcher; b. Haifa, Israel, June 26, 1944; came to U.S., 1968; s. Norbert and Hanna Danziger; m. Carla Danziger, June 12, 1970; children: Elon, Tamar. BA in Polit. Sci. and History Islamic Countries, Hebrew U., Jerusalem, 1965; MA in Near Ea. Studies, U. Wash., 1970; MA in European and Near Ea. History, Princeton U., 1972, PhD in Near Ea. Studies, 1974. Rschr. Shiloah Ctr. for Mid. Ea. Studies Tel Aviv U., 1975-76; dep. dir. Inst. Mid. Ea. Studies U. Haifa, 1976-77; policy analyst commn. on internat. affairs Am. Jewish Congress, N.Y.C., 1981-86, asst. dir. commn. on internat. affairs, 1986-90; dir. rsch. and info. Am. Israel Pub. Affairs Com., Washington, 1990—. Cons. Hudson Inst., Croton-on-Hudson, N.Y., 1974-75; vis. rsch. fellow dept. history U. Bergen, Norway, 1980; vis. fellow dept. Near Ea. studies Princeton (N.J.) U., 1981; lectr. dept. Mid. East history U. Haifa, 1975-81; vis. asst. prof. dept. history U. Wash., Seattle, 1980-81; lectr. in field. Author: Abd al-Qadir and the Algerians: Resistance to the French and Internal Consolidation, 1977; editor Near East Report, 1992—; contbr. articles to profl. jours. Lt. Israeli Army, 1965-68. Mem. Mid. East Studies Assn., Mid. East Inst. Office: Am Israel Pub Affairs Com 440 1st St NW Ste 600 Washington DC 20001-2017 E-mail: rdanziger@aipac.org.

DANZIS, COLIN MICHAEL, lawyer; b. Newark, May 3, 1938; s. Sidney and Selma (Colin) D.; m. Jo-Ann Fine, Nov. 16, 1963; children: Mitchell, Nicholas. BA, Wesleyan U., 1960; LLB, NYU, 1962, LLM in Taxation, 1963. Bar: N.J. 1962. Mem., dir. Lum, Danzis, Drasco & Positan LLC, Roseland, NJ, 1970—. Dir. Pottermeter Corp. Pres. bd. govs. Newark Acad., 1971-75, trustee, 1973-96, vice chair, 1991-96. Mem. ABA, N.J. Bar Assn., Essex County Bar Assn., West Orange Tennis Club, Beta Theta Pi. Office: 103 Eisenhower Pky Roseland NJ 07068-1029 E-mail: cdanzis@lumlaw.com.

DANZL, DANIEL FRANK, emergency physician; b. Cin., Apr. 2, 1950; s. Frank Bernard and Mary Ellen (Doerger) D.; m. Joanna Colosimo Danzl, Nov. 25, 1978; children: Maggie, Julia. BS magna cum laude, U. Cin., 1972; MD, Ohio State U., 1976. Diplomate Am. Bd. Emergency Medicine. Intern St. Francis Med. Ctr., Peoria, Ill., 1976-77; resident in emergency medicine U. Louisville, 1977-79, asst. prof. emergency medicine, 1979-83, assoc. prof. emergency medicine, 1983-89, prof. emergency medicine, 1989-91, prof., chair, 1991—. Bd. dirs., councilman-at-large Univ. Assn. for Emergency Medicine, 1988-89, indsl./govtl. rels. com., 1984-85, nominating com., 1987-88; bd. dirs. Soc. for Acad. Emergency Medicine, 1989, mem. annals of emergency meidcine task force, 1989; bd. dirs. Am. Bd. Emergency Medicine, sec.-treas., 1995-96, pres.-elect, 1996-97, pres. 1997—, mem. ad hoc com., oral examiner, 1982—; mem. Com. to Advise the Nat. ARC, 1984-87; reviewer for various med. jours. Author book chpts., monographs and textbooks including Airway Management in the Trauma Patient in the Clinical Practice of Emergency Medicine, 1991; editl. bd. Jour. Emergency Medicine, 1983—, Poisindex-Emergindex, 1982—, Jour. Wilderness Medicine, 1991—; contbr. more than 70 articles to Jour. Wilderness Medicine, Jpur. Emergency Medicine, Annals of Emergency Medicine, Am. Jour. Emergency Medicine, others. Mem. Water Safety Com. Nat. Safety Coun.-Pub. Safety Div., 1981-84; alternate med. dir. Jefferson Vocat. Edn.-Louisville EMS Paramedic Tng. Program, 1989-90, 90-91. Recipient Silver Tongue Orator award Soc. Tchrs. of Emergency Medicine, 1986, 88; grantee Office of Naval Resources, 1983-85, Key Pharmaceuticals, 1985, Hoffman-LaRoche, Inc., 1988, 89. Fellow Am. Coll. Emergency Physicians (nat. coun. mem. 1981-93, reference com. mem. 1981, 85, 89, rsch. com. mem. 1982-83, 83-84); mem. AMA (Physician's Recognition awards), NAS, Am. Soc. Circumpolar Health, Soc. for Acad. Emergency Medicine (bd. dirs. 1989, task force 1989), Nat. Rsch. Coun., Undersea and Hyperbaric Oxygen Med. Soc., Ky. Chpt. Am. Coll. Emergency Physicians (councillor 1981-93, sec.-treas. 1983-84, pres.-elect 1984-85, pres. 1985-86), Wilderness Med. Soc., Phi Beta Kappa, Beta Theta Pi, Alpha Omega Alpha, Phi Eta Sigma. Roman Catholic. Achievements include research on hypothermia. Home: 4804 Smith Rd Floyds Knobs IN 47119-9238 Office: U Louisville Dept Emergency Med 530 S Jackson St Louisville KY 40202-1675

DAO, THUY DINH, nail salon manager; b. Bac Ninh, Vietnam, Apr. 12, 1942; arrived in U.S., 1991, naturalized, 1997; s. Tan Dinh Dao, Thu Thi Pham, Hoi Thi Nguyen (Stepmother); m. Dung Ngoc Tran, Mar. 30, 1968; children: Thuy-Van, Khai, Tri. *Grandparents Van-Dinh-Dao and Ba-Bac, living in poor village of Bac-Ninh Province, had the courage to send his father Tan-Dinh-Dao during the 1920's, to "Enfant De Troops" School in Ha-Noi, Viet-Nam, resulting later: Stepsister My-Tuong T. Dao, PhD in computer science, 2003, living and working in Canberra, Australia. Brother Phon-Xuan-Dao, son of uncle and aunt Chu-Tung, Ph. D. in printing industry, living and working in Berlin, Germany. Grandmother BA-Dinh, Caoutchouc Plantations owner, in Thanh-Hoa, Viet Nam in the 1920's. But mother Maria Thu-Thi- Pham (1921-1954) also graduated from French school has the most influenced on every corner of his life.* Diploma, Lycee Yersin Sch., Da-Lat, Vietnam, 1958; Baccalaureat 1st Degree, TRI-DUC Cath. Sch., Da-Lat, VIETNAM, 1961; cert. Radio/TV Technician, CAN-THO U., Can-Tho, Vietnam, 1987; cert. Computer/Elec. Cable Tech., AMTEK Inst., 1992; A+ cert., Nova C.C., 2001. Cert. nail tech. 1999. Interpreter, transplator U.S. Adv. Teams, Vietnam, 1965—70; tinsmith Vietnam, 1976—81; owner coffee shop, 1983—90; with The Ritz Carlton Hotel Pentagon City, Arlington, Va., 1991—96; owner Elegant Nails, New Castle, Del., 1999—2000, mgr. nail salon Alexandria, Va., 2001—02, Hollywood Image Inc., Wilmington, Del., 2003—. Trader Fgn. Currency Agy., (IMEX Can Tho) Can Tho, Vietnam, 1981—82. *He raised three concepts: The Berlin Wall was fallen apart because of one psychological equation, because it was built by military genius, and not by genius in psychology, nor by religious genius. The root cause is the most activated element of a right equation in a specific field. The root cause of the 1996 blizzard and its secondary consequence: The Flood. It's just a slim crystal of snow or just a supple drop of water of the romantic blue danuble. Are we ready for the unpredictable consequences of the new coming century, The Blooming Population with it's complex psychological consequences, which finally guide people into errant actions; The Unnamed War, The Economic War, The Real War (1995), with different scales of disasters and in a new dimension. The equal equation is this true that all the present status quo, of a material substance, mental substance, including in a explode status quo, or the blossom in mass of a certain kind of flower. Are they only the instant balancing process of one magic equation (1998)?* Author: The Nymph, 1980, (Poem) Pricess Diana, 1997, Rhymes for Mom, 1997, To shake hand with the subconcious, 1997, Farewell to Da Lat, 1998, The old battle on the Xich Bich river, 2000, Viet Nam the mother's land, 2001; contbr. With Army South Vietnam, 1970—75. Avocations: music, movies, travel, reading, sports. Office: Hollywood Image Inc 4403 A Kirkwood Hwy Wilmington DE 19808

DAOUD, GEORGE JAMIL, hotel and motel consultant; b. Beirut, Oct. 20, 1948; came to U.S., 1958, naturalized, 1970; s. Jamil G. and Shafika E. Daoud; divorced; 5 children. BS, NYU, 1967; MPS, Cornell U., 1969; PhD in Bus. Adminstrn., U. Palmer Green, 1986. Gen. mgr. Holiday Inn, New London and Groton, Conn., 1974-75, Gentle Winds Beach Resort, St. Croix, V.I., 1975-78; pres., cons. Motor Inn Mgmt., Inc., Dayton, Ohio, 1973—. Pres. Cen. Svcs. Group, Inc., First Group, Inc., Host Mgmt., Inc., Inn Group, Inc., 1981—, Metro Markets, Inc., Dayton, Triac Ventures, Inc., 1980-86. Mem Am. Hotel and Motel Assn. (cert. hotel adminstr., mem. Ednl. Inst.), Ohio Hotel and Motel Assn., Nat. Assn. Rev. Appraisers, Cert. Real Estate Rev. Appraisers, Masons. Republican. Roman Catholic. Office: Hotelvest Inc PO Box 730 Dayton OH 45402-0730

DAOUST, DONALD ROGER, pharmaceutical and toiletries company executive, microbiologist; b. Worcester, Mass., Aug. 13, 1935; s. G. Arthur and Alice Anne (Lavalee) D.; m. Johanna K. Kalinoski, May 30, 1959; children: Donna Jean, Stephen Michael, Sandra Marie. BA, U. Conn., 1957; MS, U. Mass., 1959, PhD, 1962. Sr. rsch. microbiologist Merck Sharp & Dohme, Rahway, N.J., 1962-70, rsch. fellow, 1970-72, mgr. biol. quality control West Point, Pa., 1972-75; dir. quality control Armour Pharm. Co., Kankakee, Ill., 1975-76, v.p. quality assurance and regulatory compliance Phoenix, 1976-78; v.p., quality control Carter-Wallace, Inc., Cranbury, NJ, 1978—2001. Contbr. articles to profl. jours., chpts. to books; patentee in field. Mem. Borough Coun., South Plainfield, N.J., 1970-72; treas. George Washington coun. Boy Scouts Am., 1981-84, pres., 1984-87, area v.p., bd.dirs. NE region U.S., 1987—. Recipient Disting. Svc. award South Plainfield Jaycees, 1969, silver Beaver award Boy Scouts Am., 1988, Silver Antelope award N.E. region, 1992; named Outstanding Young Man, N.J. Jaycees, 1970. Mem.: AAAS, Pharm. Mfrs. Assn. (quality

control adminstrn. 1979—82, adv. bd. 1982—94, vice chmn 1988—90, chmn. 1990—92), Am. Soc. for Quality Control, Am. Soc. Microbiology, Laurel Oak Country Club (Sarasota, Fla.), Bedens Brook Club (Stillman, NJ). Avocations: golf, jogging, reading, gardening. Home: 12212 Creekside Ct Lawrenceville NJ 08648 E-mail: don_daoust@msn.com.

DAPHNIS, NASSOS, artist; b. Krokeai, Greece, July 23, 1914; s. Panagiotes A. and Stamatico (Georgoulis) D.; m. Helen Avlonitis, Mar. 24, 1956 (div. 1987); children: Artemis, Demetrios. Student, Art Students League, N.Y.C., 1946-49, Acad. Frochot, Paris, 1950-51, Inst. Statale D'Arte, Florence, Italy, 1951-52. One-man shows Contemporary Arts Gallery, N.Y.C., 1938-47, Mint Mus., Charlotte, N.C., 1949, Collette Allendy Gallery, Paris, 1950, Leo Castelli Gallery, N.Y.C., 1959-61, 63, 65, 68, 71, 73, 75, 80, 83, 85, 86, 88, 90, 95, Toninelli Arte Moderna, Milan, Italy, 1961, Galerie Iris Clert, Paris, 1962, Franklin Siden Gallery, Detroit, 1967, Albright-Knox Mus., Buffalo, 1969, Everson Mus., Syracuse, N.Y., 1969, Brockton (Mass.) Art Center, 1970, Andre Zarre Gallery, N.Y.C., 1974, 76, 83, 85, 95, Printers Gallery, Ithaca, N.Y., 1975, Kingpitcher Gallery, Pitts., 1975, Phillips Gallery, Salt Lake City, 1980, Frank Fedele Fine Arts, N.Y.C., Eaton/Shoen Gallery, San Francisco, 1980, 85, Omega Gallery, Athens, 1983, Kouros Gallery, N.Y.C., 1985, Raynolds Gallery, Pitts., 1990, Iliana Tounta Contemporary Art Ctr, Athens, Greece, 1990, Berta Walker Gallery, Provincetown, Mass., 1992; retrospective Boca Raton (Fla.) Mus., Butler Inst. Am. Art, 1993; exhibited in group shows, Pitts. Internat., 1958, 61, 70, Whitney Mus. Am. Art, N.Y.C., 1959, 61, 62, 64, 65, 67, Corcoran Gallery, Washington, 1959, 63, 69, Columbus (Ohio) Gallery Fine Art, 1960, Osaka (Japan) Mus. Fine Art, 1960, Guggenheim Mus., N.Y.C., 1961, Lever House, N.Y.C., 1961, Walker Art Center, Mpls., 1961, 62, Brandeis U., 1962, Washington Gallery Modern Art, 1963, Washington Sq. Galleries, N.Y.C., 1964, de Cordova Mus., Lincoln, Mass., 1965, Aldrich Mus., Ridgefield, Conn., 1969, Westbeth Ct. Gallery, N.Y.C., 1970, Tirca Karlis Gallery, Provincetown, Mass., 1972, Leo Castelli Gallery, N.Y.C., 1974, Birmingham (Ala.) Mus. Art, 1976, Albright Coll., Reading, Pa., 1976, Leo Castelli Gallery, N.Y., 1997, United Nations, N.Y., 1999, Queens Mus., N.Y., 1999, Salonica Greece Mus. Art, 2000, numerous others; represented permanent collections at, Mus. Modern Art, N.Y.C., Whitney Mus. Am. Art, N.Y.C., Albright-Knox Gallery, Buffalo, Albany (N.Y.) Mall, Guggenheim Mus., N.Y.C., Balt. Mus., Providence Mus., Chrysler Mus., Norfolk, Va., Tel Aviv Mus., Israel, Munson-Williams-Proctor Mus., Utica, N.Y., Akron (Ohio) Art Inst., Reading (Pa.) Mus., Ann Arbor (Mich.) Art Mus., Balt. Mus., Pitts. Mus. Art, Hirshhorn Mus., Washington, Aldrich Mus., Ridgefield, Conn., Everson Mus., Syracuse, N.Y., Utah Mus. Fine Art, Salt Lake City., Provincetown Art Assn. and Mus., Vorres Mus., Athens, Goulandris Mus., Andros, Greece, Butler Inst. of Am. Art, Youngstown, Ohio, Queens (N.Y.) Mus. Art, Grinnell (Iowa) Coll., The Lowe Mus. at U. Miami, Jewish Mus. of Miami, Corcoran Gallery, Washington, DC, The Bass Mus. Miami. Recipient Ford Found. award, 1972, Pitts. award, 1966, Nat. Found. Arts and Humanities award, 1966, Nat. Endowment on Arts/Boca Raton Mus. award, 1971, A.P. Saunders medal, 1973, Francis J. Greenburger Found. award, 1987, The Richard A. Florsheim Art Fund award, 1993, Arts Achievement award Queens Mus. Art N.Y., 1999; Guggenheim fellow, 1977; Pollock-Krasner Found. grant, 1987. Office: 362 W Broadway New York NY 10013-5303

DA PONTE, JOHN JOSEPH, JR., lawyer; b. Bristol, R.I., May 12, 1933; s. John J. and Mary Elizabeth (Ferris) DaP.; m. Gunilla Karen Tornhagen, Apr. 18, 1971; children— Karen, Karsten. B.A., Providence Coll., 1955; J.D., Boston U., 1962; LL.M., Georgetown U., 1966; cert. U. Muenster, W.Ger., 1967. Bar: Mass. 1962, D.C. 1964, U.S. Supreme Ct. 1976. Atty. U.S. Dept. Def., Washington, 1962, U.S. Treasury, Washington, 1962-67; atty. U.S. Dept. Commerce, Washington, 1968—, exec. sec. Fgn. Trade Zones Bd. Contbr. articles on law and internat. trade to profl. jours. Bd. dirs. Friendship Neighborhood Assn. Coalition, Washington, 1974-78; mem. Sumner Citizens Assn., Bethesda, Md., 1978— . Served to 1st. lt. U.S. Army, 1956-59. Recipient Am. Jurisprudence award Lawyers Coop Pub. Co., Rochester, N.Y., 1966, Bronze award U.S. Dept. Commerce, 1975, Silver medal, 1984. Mem. Am. Soc. Internat. Law, Fed. Bar Assn., Mass. Bar Assn., D.C. Bar Assn. Home: 5804 Madawaska Rd Bethesda MD 20816-2342 Office: Fgn Trade Zones Bd US Dept Commerce 14th and Pennsylvania Washington DC 20230

DAPPLES, EDWARD CHARLES, retired geologist, educator; b. Chgo., Dec. 13, 1906; s. Edward C. and Victoria (Gazzolo) D.; m. Marion Virginia Sprague, Sept. 2, 1931; children: Marianne Helena, Charles Christian. BS, Northwestern U., 1928, MS, 1934; MA, Harvard, 1935; PhD, U. Wis., 1938. Geologist Ziegler Coal Co., 1928; geologist Truax-Traer Coal Co., 1928-32, mine supt., 1932; instr. Northwestern U., 1936-41, asst. prof., 1941, assoc. prof., 1942-50, prof. geol. scis., 1950-73, ret., 1973, prof. emeritus, 1973—. Geologist Ill. Geol. Survey, 1939, Sinclair Oil Co., 1945-50, Pure Oil Co., 1950; dir. Evanston Exploration Corp., 1954-84; sr. vis. scientist U. Lausanne, Switzerland, 1960-61; vis. prof. U. Geneva, Switzerland, 1970. Author: Basic Geology for Science and Engineering, 1959, Atlas of Lithofacies Maps, 1960. Fellow Geol. Soc. Am., Soc. Econ. Geologist; mem. Am. Inst. Mining Engrs. (Legion of Honor), Assn. Petroleum Geologists, Internat. Assn. Sedimentologists, Soc. Econ. Paleontologists and Mineralogists (pres. 1970, hon. mem. 1974), Am. Inst. Profl. Geologists (pres. Ill.-Ind. sect. 1979, pres. Ariz. 1982, hon. mem. 1986), Assn. Engring. Geologists. Home: The Montecito 17271 N 87th Ave Apt 2069 Peoria AZ 85382

DAPRON, ELMER JOSEPH, JR., communications executive; b. Clayton, Mo., Jan. 14, 1925; s. Elmer Joseph and Susanna (Kruse) D.; m. Sharon Kay Neuling, Feb. 22, 1977 (dec. Apr. 1987). Employed in constrn., Fairbanks, Alaska, 1947-48; tech. writer-editor McDonnell-Douglas Corp., St. Louis, 1948-57; freelance writer Paris, 1957; with Gardner Advt. Co., St. Louis, 1960-78, v.p., 1969-78; sr. v.p. Kenrick Advt. Inc., 1978-83; pres. Cornucopia Communications, Inc., 1979—. Producer syndicated radio and TV show Elmer Dapron's Grocery List; advt. and mktg. cons. to govt. and industry; commentator The Grocery List Armed Forces Radio Network (worldwide); contbr. articles to publs. Mem. Nat. Dem. Com., candidate for Gov. of Mo., 1992; nat. pres. Iwo Jima Task Force Two, 1994—; nat. chmn. Korea Task Force 2000, 1997—. With USMCR, 1943-45, PTO, 50-51, Korea. Recipient advt. awards including New Filming Techniques award Internat.-Film Festival; hon. fellow Harry Truman Libr. Inst. Mem. Nat. Agrl. Mktg. Assn., Miss. Valley Farm Mktg. (Man of Yr. 1974), Assn. R.R. Advt. and Mktg. (nat. membership chmn.), Marine Corps League (nat. vice comdt. 1967-69, nat. press officer 4th Marine Div. Assn. 1989—, publicity chmn.), Media Club, St. Louis Track Club. Democrat. Office: 119 Lakeview Estates Dr Warrenton MO 63383-5258

D'AQUILA, BARBARA JEAN, lawyer; b. Virginia, Minn., Aug. 2, 1955; d. Carl Mario and Dolores (Mae) Cassagrande) D'A. BBA, U. Notre Dame (Ind.), 1977; JD, U. Minn., 1979. Bar: Minn. 1980, U.S. Dist. Ct. Minn. 1980, U.S. Ct. Appeals (8th cir.) 1981, U.S. Ct. Appeals (11th cir.) 2003, U.S. Tax Ct. 1982, U.S. Supreme Ct. 1995; CPA, Minn. Audit acct. Arthur Andersen & Co., Mpls., summer 1977; tax acct. Peat, Marwick, Mitchell & Co., Mpls., 1979-80; law clk. Minn. Supreme Ct., St. Paul, 1980-81; assoc. Briggs & Morgan, St. Paul, 1981-83; shareholder/ptnr. Hart, Bruner & O'Brien, P.A., Mpls., 1983-91; assoc. Moss & Barnett, A Profl. Assn., Mpls., 1991-93; ptnr. Flynn, Gaskins & Bennett, L.L.P., Mpls., 1993—. Mem. U.S. Dist. Ct. Minn. fed. practice com., 1985-90; mem. Lawyers Trust Acct. Bd. Supreme Ct. Minn., 1993-2000, chair 1995-2000, Bar Admissions Adv. Coun. for Bd. Law Examiners, 1995—; mem. adv. com. on rules of civil procedure Minn. Supreme Ct., 1998—; co-chair MSBA com. on legal edn. and bar admissions, 1999—. Great Plains reg. rep. Am. Heart Assn., Dallas, 1989-91, chmn. bd., Mpls., 1987-88., first vice chmn., 1986-87, treas., 1984-86; sec. chmn. United Way of Mpls., 1989-91; bd. dirs. U. Minn. Law Sch., 1991-98. Recipient Disting. Svc. award Am. Heart Assn., 1988. Fellow Coll. Labor and Employment Lawyers; mem. ABA (EEO com., labor and employment sect., 1992—), Minn. Bar Assn. (labor and employment law sect. 1989—, tort and ins. sect. 2001—), AICPA, Minn. Soc. CPAs, Beta Gamma Sigma, Beta Alpha Psi. Avocations: golf, swimming, travel, reading, arts. Office: Flynn Gaskins & Bennett LLP 2900 Met Circle 333 S 7th St Ste 2900 Minneapolis MN 55402-2440 E-mail: bdaquila@flynngaskins.com.

D'AQUINO, THOMAS, lawyer, entrepreneur, educator, strategist, council chief executive; b. Trail, B.C., Can., Nov. 3, 1940; m. Susan Marion Peterson, 1965 BA, U. B.C., 1962, LLB, 1965; LLB, LLM, U. London, 1967; LLD (hon.), Queen's U., 1996, Wilfred Laurier U. Adj. prof. law U. Ottawa, Canada; chmn. Intercounsel Ltd.; pres., chief exec. Can. Coun. Chief Execs. (CCCE), Ottawa, 1981—. Former exec. asst. to Fed. Min., spl. asst. to Prime Min., Can., 1969-72; internat. cons. firm in London and Paris, 1972-75; frequent guest lectr.; mem. Chmn's Internat. Adv. Coun. of the Am.'s Soc.; founding mem. Pacific Coun. on Internat. Policy; adv. bd. Lazard Can.; chmn. Nat. Gallery of Can. Found., N.Am. security and prosperity initiative, Can. Coun. Chief Execs. (CCCE) Corp., co-chmn. govt. initiative. Co-author: Northern Edge: How Canadians Can Triumph in the Global Economy, 2001; contbr. articles to profl. jours. Mem. World Econ. Forum Geneva, Inst. for Strategic Studies, London. Mem. Can. Bar Assn., Internat. Bar Assn., B.C. Law Soc. Office: Can Coun Chief Execs 90 Sparks St Ste 806 Ottawa ON Canada K1P 5B4

DAR, HUMA BASHIR, computer scientist, researcher, educator, South Asianist; b. Murree, Punjab, Pakistan, Oct. 22, 1963; came to the U.S., 1990; d. Bashir Uddin and Khalida Bashir Ahmad; children: Natasha Dar, Zavain Dar. BA in Math. and Computer Sci., U. Calif., Berkeley, 1995, MS in Computer Sci., 2000; MA in South Asian Studies, U. Calif., 2002; postgrad., U. Calif., Berkeley, 2002—. Reader, tutor U. Calif., Berkeley, 1993-95, grad. student rschr., 1995—, grad. student instr., 1999, 2001—03. Rschr. Institut Nat. Polytechnique de Grenoble, France, 1997; organizer Boundaries in Question conf. on Women and War, U. Calif., Berkeley, 2002; presenter in field. Author of essays and poems. Pres. bd. dirs. Narika, San Francisco. Mem. Women in Computer Sci. and Engring. (treas. 1995-96, v.p. 1996-97), Mensa Internat. (devel. officer 1980-81), Phi Beta Kappa. Avocations: writing, volunteering in schools, painting, reading, traveling.

DARABONT, FRANK, screenwriter, director; b. Montebeliard, France, Jan. 28, 1959; Screenwriter: (films) (with Wes Craven, Chuck Russell, and Bruce Wagner) A Nightmare on Elm Street 3: Dream Warriors, 1987, (with Russell) The Blob, 1988, (with Mick Garris, Jim Wheat, and Ken Wheat) The Fly II, 1989, (with Steph Lady) Mary Shelley's Frankenstein, 1994; dir.: (TV movies) Till Death Do Us Part, 1990, Buried Alive, 1990, (TV series) The Young Indiana Jones Chronicles, 1992-; screenwriter, dir.: (films) The Shawshank Redemption, 1994 (Academy award nomination best adapted screenplay 1994, Humanitas prize for best screenplay), The Green Mile, 1999, The Majestic (also prodr.), 2001, exec. prodr., writer: (TV movies) Black Cat Run Office: William Morris Agency care Robert Stein 151 S El Camino Dr Beverly Hills CA 90212-2775*

DARAIO, ROBERT REID, technical director; b. Bronx, N.Y., July 20, 1955; s. Vincent and Patricia (O'Neill) D.; m. Gayle Marie Palmieri, Nov. 26, 1983. BFA, SUNY, Purchase, 1977. Freelance video engr., 1978-98; staff master control tech. dir. WPIX Channel 11, 1998—. Clients include ABC, CBS, NBC, WNYW, WWOR, WPIX, WNET, CNN, TBS, AOB, MTV, VH-1, Fox Sports, ESPN, Universal Pictures, CTW, HBO, Showtime, USA Network. Recipient Emmy award for WB11 News at 10, 2002. Mem. NATAS, Internat. Alliance Theatrical Stage Employees, Nat. Assn. Broadcast Engrs. and Technicians, Soc. Motion Picture and TV Engrs., Internat. Brotherhood Elec. Workers. Home: 45 Hunter St Ossining NY 10562 Office: WPIX 220 E 42d St New York NY

DARBELNET, ROBERT LOUIS, automobile association executive; b. Portland, Maine, Dec. 14, 1951; s. Jean Louis and Elizabeth (Matheson) D.; m. Mary Ann McCaughey, Aug. 27, 1977; children: John Kevin, Mary Jennifer. LLB, Laval U., Quebec City, 1978. Dir. consumer protection dept. Que. (Can.) Automobile Club, Quebec City, 1973-76, dir. road and tech. svcs., 1976-78, dir. gen. ins. dept., 1978-79, asst. gen. mgr., 1980-83, dir. gen., 1983-90, pres., 1990-94. Tchr. bus. Coll. Sainte Foy (Que.), 1978—84, v.p., 1981—82, pres., 1982—86; bd. dirs. Ont. Corp., Muncie, Ind., ITS Am., vice chair, 2002; mem. Nat. Petroleum Coun.; pres. Alliance Internat. Tourisme, 2001—, chair mgmt. com., 2001—; chair world bd. Alliance Internat. Tourisme/Fedn. Internat. de'lAutomobile, 2002; mem. Fedn. Internat. del'Automobile Senate, 1997—. Mem. Fedn. Internat. de l'Automobile, Paris, 1990—, dep. pres., 2001—; bd. dirs. Corp. de la Salle Albert Rousseau, 1990—94, Enfant Jesus Hosp., 1993—94, Union Canadienne Ins., 1993—94; bd. govs. Coll. Sainte-Foy, 1980—88, bd. govs. alumni fund, 1980—88, v.p., 1982—88; trustee AAA Found. for Traffic Safety, 1990—, sec., 1993—94; v.p. Internat. Tourism Commn., 1995—, world tng. coun., 1995—, mem. mgmt. com., 1995—. Mem.: Am. Automobile Assn. (pres., CEO 1994—). Office: 1000 Aaa Dr Heathrow FL 32746-5063

DARBY, EDWIN WHEELER, retired newspaper financial columnist; b. Oakland, Md., Jan. 7, 1922; s. John Dade and Nell (Bosley) D.; children— Ann Wheeler, John Dade; m. Susan E. Kroening, Mar. 14, 1970; 1 son, George Kroening. BS in Journalism, Ohio U. White House corr. Time mag., 1948-55; midwest corr. Time and Fortune mags., 1956-58; financial editor, columnist Chgo. Sun-Times, 1958-95; ret., 1995. Author: The Fortune Builders, 1987. Recipient Marshall Field award, 1974, Loeb award, 1975 Mem. Tavern Club. Home: 2703 W Logan Blvd Chicago IL 60647-1831

DARBY, G(EORGE) HARRISON, lawyer; b. N.Y.C., Jan. 24, 1942; s. Stephen John and Madge B. (Leh) D. BA, Muhlenberg Coll., 1963; LLB, Bklyn. Law Sch., 1967. Bar: N.Y. 1967. Ptnr. Jackson Lewis LLP, L.A. and other offices, 1967—. Mem. child adv. group Internat. Inst. of L.A., 1989-96. Office: Jackson Lewis LLP 725 South Figueroa St Los Angeles CA 90017-5408

DARBY, H. DARREL, podiatric surgeon; b. Jan. 8, 1928; m. Laura Darby. Student, Anderson (Ind.) Coll.; degree, Marshall Univ.; DPM, Ohio Coll., 1956. Diplomate Am. Bd. Podiatric Surgeons. Pvt. practice, Huntington, 1956—. Surg. staff Cabell Huntington Hosp., St. Mary's Hosp., Huntington Surgery Ctr.; cons. VA Hosp., Huntington, Mashall U. Athletic Dept.; clin. prof. surgery Marshall U. Sch. Medicine; adj. prof. podiatric surgery Ohio Coll. of Podiatric Medicine; chmn. bd. Podiatry Ins. Co. of Am.; chmn. bd. Laurel Lodge Enterprises, Inc.; pres. Darco Internat., Inc., Darco Europe, pres. Darco Internat. (Shanghai) Trading Ltd. Mem. W.Va. State Senate, 1972-76, chmn. health com., 1972-76; adult Sunday sch. tchr. Trinity Ch. of God; pres. Nat. Dems. for Life, 1976-78; mem. W.Va. State Dem. Exec. Com., 1978; co-chmn. Bush-Quayle campaign, W.Va., 1988. With USCG, 1945-47. Recipient Disting. Alumni award Ohio Coll. of Podiatric Medicine. Fellow Am. Coll. Foot Surgeons; mem. Am. Podiatric Med. Assn. (pres. 1976-77, del. nat. conv. 1957-69, bd. trustees 1969-76, chmn. com. on constitution and bylaws protocol officer), W.Va. Podiatric Med. Assn. (Disting. Svc. award), Nat. Academies of Practice (exec. com., chmn. podiatric med. divsn., Disting. Practitioner), Mid-Atlantic Podiatric Med. Assn. (pres.). Home: 655 Whitaker Blvd W Apt 502 Huntington WV 25701-4664 Office: 1038 6th Ave Huntington WV 25701-2308 E-mail: hddarby@darcointernational.com.

DARBY, JAY RODNEY, business and numismatic investment consultant; b. Valley City, N.D., Mar. 13, 1953; s. William Vincent and LaDonna Maurine (Nielson) D.; m. Mae Rose Francis Meyer, July 12, 1975; children: Kelly Katrina, Heather Christina, Ryan Christopher. Vice pres. SPG Cos., Inc., St. Cloud, Minn., 1979-80, pres., chief operating officer, 1980-81, chief exec. officer, 1981-83; pres. Jay R. Darby, Inc., St. Cloud, 1983-85, pres., ceo Flagstaff, Ariz., 1985-92; pres. AzTec, Ltd., Flagstaff, 1987-92; pres., ceo D.I.C., 1990—. Author: Coin Dealer Rating Guide, 1982-90; pubr.: A Consumers Guide to Coin Dealers, 1988, A Simplified Accounting System for Small Retail Businesses, 1992; contbr. articles to profl. jours. Past treas Minn. Senate Dist. 17, St. Cloud; candidate for St. Cloud City Coun., 1983, 85. Mem. Am. Numis. Assn., Numis. Guaranty Corp. Am. (assoc.), Rochester C. of C., Kiwanis. Democrat. Roman Catholic. E-mail: Darb1001@aol.com.

DARBY, JOANNE TYNDALE (JAYE DARBY), arts and humanities educator; b. Tucson, Sept. 22, 1948; d. Robert Porter Smith and Joanne Inloes Snow-Smith; stepchildren: Margaret Loutrel, David Michael. BA, U. Ariz., 1972; MEd, U. Calif., L.A., 1986, PhD, 1996. Cert. secondary tchr., gifted and talented tchr., Calif. Tchr. English, chmn. dept. Las Virgenes Unified Sch. Dist., Calabasas, Calif., 1979-82; tchr. English and gifted and talented edn. Las Virgenes Unified Sch.Dist., Calabasas, Calif., 1983-84; sch. improvement coord./lang. arts/social studies/drama tchr Las Virgenes Unified Sch. Dist., Calabasas, Calif., 1991-92; tchr. English and gifted and talented edn. Beverly Hills (Calif.) Unified Sch. Dist., 1982-83, 84-89, English and drama tchr., 1994; tchr., cons. Calif. Lit. Project, San Diego, 1985-87; cons., free lance editor L.A., 1977—; dir. Shakespeare edn. and festivals project Folger Libr., Washington, 1990-91; field work supr. tchr. edn. program Ctr. X, Grad. Sch. Edn. and Info. Studies, UCLA, 1992-96, Ctr. X postdoctoral scholar, tchr. edn. program, 1996-97; asst. rschr., founding co-dir. Project HOOP, Am. Indian Studies Ctr., UCLA, 1997—2000; asst. prof. Coll. Edn. San Diego State U., 2000—. Cons. arts and edn., L.A., 1991—. Co-editor (with Hanay Geiogamah) Stories of Our Way: An Anthology of American Indian Plays, 1999, American Indian Theater in Performance: A Reader, 2000, (with Stephanie Fitzgerald) Keepers of the Morning Star: An Anthology of Native Women's Theater, 2003; contbr. articles to profl. publs. Mem.: MLA, Assn. for Theatre in Higher Edn., Nat. Coun. Tchrs. English, Am. Ednl. Rsch. Assn., Phi Beta Kappa, Phi Lambda Delta, Phi Beta Phi. Home: 7350 Golfcrest Pl Apt 2001 San Diego CA 92119-2486

DARBY, JOSEPH BRANCH, JR., retired metallurgist, government official; b. Petersburg, Va., Dec. 12, 1925; s. Joseph Branch and Jessie Catherine (Frazier) D.; m. Eleanor Lee Daley, Mar. 25, 1951; children— Joseph III, John, Leslie, Peter. BS, Coll. William and Mary, 1948, Va. Poly. Inst., 1951; MS, U. Ill., 1955, PhD, 1958. Chemist Allied Chem. Corp., Hopewell, Va., 1948-49; devel. engr. Union Carbide Corp., Niagara Falls, N.Y., 1951-53; rsch. scientist Argonne (Ill.) Nat. Lab., 1958-86, assoc. dir. Fusion Energy Program, 1974-78, assoc. dir. ocean thermal energy conversion, 1978-84; program mgr. basic energy scis. Office Energy Rsch., Dept. Energy, Washington, 1986-94; adj. prof. U. Va. Sch. of Engring., Charlottesville, 1995-97; ret., 1997. Vis. sr. rsch. fellow U. Birmingham, Eng., 1970-71. Co-editor: The Electronic Structure of the Actinides and Related Properties, 2 vols., 1974; mem. adv. bd. Jour. Less-Common Metals, 1971-82, Materials Letters, 1988-92; co-editor Jour. Nuclear Materials, 1971-84, chmn. bd. editors, 1984-90, mem. adv. bd., 1990-94; contbr. articles to profl. jours. Mem. Nominating Com. for Sch. Bd., Wheaton, Ill., 1961-63, for Coll. of DuPage Bd. Trustees, 1963-65. Served with A.C. USMC, 1944-46. Sci. Rsch. Coun. sr. fellow, 1970-71; recipient Loyalty award U. Ill., Disting. Editor award The Materials Soc., 1994. Fellow Am. Soc. for Metals (mem. energy council div., mem. nuclear metallurgy com.); mem. Metall. Soc. Am. Inst. Mining, Metall. and Petroleum Engrs., ASTM, AAAS, Fedn. Materials Socs. (bd. dirs. 1988-94), Cape Cod Geneal. Soc. (co-pres. 1996-98), Sigma Xi, Tau Beta Pi, Alpha Sigma Mu, Sigma Gamma Epsilon. Presbyterian (elder). Home: PO Box 655 25 Pine St Yarmouth Port MA 02675-1838

DARBY, KAREN SUE, legal education administrator; b. Columbus, Ohio, Sept. 15, 1947; d. Emerson Curtis and Kathryn Elizabeth (Bowers) Dum; m. R. Russell Darby, Dec. 21, 1974; children: David Randolph, Michael Emerson. BA magna cum laude, Capital U., Columbus, 1969; JD, Ohio State U., 1980. Bar: Ohio 1980, Pa. 1998, U.S. Dist. Ct. (so. dist.) Ohio 1981. High sch. English tchr. Columbus Pub. Schs., 1969-72; employee rels. specialist GE, Circleville, Ohio, 1972-74, mgr. EEO and manpower programs chem. met. div. Worthington, Ohio, 1974-77; atty. Ohio Legal Rights Svc., Columbus, 1980-81; pvt. practice Columbus, 1981-90; assoc. dir. Ohio Continuing Legal Edn. Inst., Columbus, 1989-95; dir. Phila. Bar Edn. Ctr., 1995-97; assoc. dir. Pa. Bar Inst., Phila., 1997—2002; exec. dir. Ill. Inst. for Continuing Legal Edn., 2002—. Mem. rules adv. com. Supreme Ct. Ohio, Columbus, 1989-94. Author, editor: Civil Commitment in Ohio - A Manual for Respondents' Attorneys, 1980. Mem. divorce mediation panel Ohio State U. Commn. on Interprofl. Edn., Columbus, 1988-91; vol. Boy Scouts Am., Columbus, 1988-92, Columbus Pub. Schs., 1984-95. Mem.: ABA, Assn. Continuing Legal Edn., Ill. State Bar Assn., Univ. Club of Chgo. Democrat. Lutheran. Avocations: organ, piano, gardening. Office: IICLE 2395 W Jefferson St Springfield IL 62702

DARBY, MARIANNE TALLEY, elementary school educator; b. Adel, Ga., Nov. 8, 1937; d. William Giles and Mary (McGlamry) Talley; m. Roy Copeland Darby, Apr. 2, 1958; children: Susan, Leslie Darby Galifianakis, Allison Darby Davis. Student, Emory U., 1955-57; BS in Early Childhood Edn., Valdosta (Ga.) State Coll., 1973. Cert. early childhood and elem. edn. tchr., Ga. Tchr. 2d grade Adel Elem. Sch., spring 1973, tchr. 1st grade, 1973-98, ret., 1998. Pres. Cook County Jaycettes, Adel, 1962. Teacher of Year, Cook Elem. Sch., 1998—. Mem. Internat. Reading Assn. (South Cen. Ga. coun.), Profl. Assn. Ga. Educators, Adel Garden Club, Alpha Epsilon Upsilon, Alpha Delta Kappa (sec. 1980-82), Sigma Alpha Chi, Alpha Chi, Kappa Alpha Theta. Republican. Methodist. Avocations: sewing, piano, reading, african violets. Home: 710 S Forrest Ave Adel GA 31620-3523

DARBY, MICHAEL RUCKER, economist, educator; b. Dallas, Nov. 24, 1945; s. Joseph Jasper and Frances Adah (Rucker) D.; children: Margaret Loutrel, David Michael; Lynne Ann Zucker-Darby, 1992; stepchildren: Joshua R. Zucker, Danielle T. Zucker. AB summa cum laude, Dartmouth Coll., 1967; MA, U. Chgo., 1968, PhD, 1970. Asst. prof. econ. Ohio State U., 1970-73; vis. asst. prof. econ. UCLA, 1972-73, assoc. prof., 1973-78, prof., 1978-87, 96—, prof. Anderson Grad. Sch. Mgmt., 1987-94, Warren C. Cordner prof. money and fin. mkts., 1995—, vice-chmn., 1992-93; dir. John M. Olin Ctr. for Policy, 1993—; assoc. dir. orgnl. rsch. program UCLA Inst. for Social Sci. Rsch., 1995—; assoc. dir. Ctr. for Internat. Sci., Tech., Cultural Policy Sch. Pub. Policy and Social Rsch., UCLA, 1996—; rsch. assoc. Nat. Bur. Econ. Rsch., 1976-86, 92—; asst. sec. for econ. policy U.S. Dept. Treasury, Washington, 1986-89; mem. Nat. Commn. on Superconductivity, 1988-89; under sec. for econ. affairs U.S. Dept. Commerce, Washington, 1989-92; adminstr. Econs. and Stats. Adminstrn., 1990-92. V.p., dir. Paragon Industries, Inc., Dallas, 1964—83; mem. exec. com. Western Econ. Assn., 1987—90, v.p., 1998—99, pres.-elect, 1999—2000, pres., 2000—01; chmn. The Dumbarton Group, 1992—; adj. scholar Am. Ent. Inst. for Pub. Policy Rsch., 1992—; economist stats. income divsn. IRS, 1992—94; mem. regulatory coord. adv. com. Commodity Futures Trading Commn., 1992—96. Author: Macroeconomics, 1976, Have Controls Ever Worked: The Post-War Record, 1976, Intermediate Macroeconomics, 1979, 2d edit., 1986, The Effects of Social Security on Income and the Capital Stock, 1979, The International Transmission of Inflation, 1981, Labor Force, Employment, and Productivity in Historical Perspective, 1984, Reducing Poverty in America: Views and Approaches, 1996; editor Jour. Internat. Money and Fin., 1981-86, mem. editl. bd., 1986—; mem. editl. bd. Am. Econ. Rev., 1983-86, Contemporary Policy Issues, 1990-93, Contemporary Econ. Policy, 1994—, Internat. Reports, 1992—. Bd. dirs. The Opera Assoc., 1992—; mem. acad. adv. bd. Ctr. Regulation and Econ. Growth of the Alexis de Tocqueville Instn., 1993-96. Recipient Alexander Hamilton award U.S. Treasury Dept., 1989; sr. fellow Dartmouth Coll., 1966-67, Woodrow Wilson fellow, 1967-68, NSF grad. fellow, 1967-69, FDIC grad. fellow, 1969-70, Harry Scherman rsch. fellow Nat. Bur. Econ. Rsch., 1974-75, vis. fellow Hoover Instn., Stanford U., 1977-78. Mem. AAAS, Am. Econ. Assn., Am. Fin. Assn., Am. Statis. Assn., Am. Law & Econs. Assn., Nat. Assn. Bus. Economists, Royal Econ. Soc., So. Econ. Assn., Western Econ. Assn., N.Y. Acad. Scis., Capitol Hill Club (D.C.), Nat. Econ. Club. Episcopalian. Home: 18108 Meandering Way Dallas TX 75252-2763 Office: UCLA Anderson Grad Sch Mgmt Los Angeles CA 90095-0001

D'ARCANGELO, MARCIA DIANE, educational media producer; b. Meadville, Pa., May 16, 1945; d. Terrence Benjamin and Eileene Marie (Judy) Darcangelo; m. thomas Brown Andrews V, Sept. 16, 1989. BS in Chemistry, Grove City Coll., 1967. Info. specialist Eastman Kodak Co., Rochester, N.Y., 1967-68; singer/dancer Kids Next Door-Young Ams. Orgn. (Katand Prodns.), L.A., 1968-69, Stand Up and Cheer TV Show, The Johnny Mann Singers, L.A., 1970-74; singer, dancer, actor John Brown's Body AEA Nat. Tour, Fitzgerald Prodns., L.A., 1975-76; singer, dancer The Perry Como Show-Roncom Prodns., 1977-82; med. news journalist Physicians Radio Network, N.Y.C., 1983-84; prodn. asst., prodn. coord. ASCD, Alexandria, Va., 1985-86, producer, sr. producer, 1987-88, mgr. media prodns., 1989—. Cons. Holbrook & Kellogg, Falls Church, Va., 1990, Developmental Studies Ctr., San Ramon, Calif., 1991, Soc. for Preservation of Social Security and Medicare, Washington, 1991. Composer 4 mus. pieces (words and music); co-author 20 tng. manuals; author/co-author 46 video-based tchr. tng. programs, articles. Recipient award of merit VFW, 1971, Jack Kennedy Alumni Achievement award Grove City Coll. Alumni Assn., 1984, Clarion award Women in Comm., 1991, 6 Cine Golden Eagle awards Coun. on Internat. Nontheatrical Events, 1991, 92, 93, 94, Silver Apple award Nat. Ednl. Film and Video Festival, 1991, 93, 95, Bronze Apple award, 1993, 94, 99, Silver Screen award and Cert. for Creative Excellence U.S. Internat. Film and Video Festival, 1993, 94, 95, 96, Disting. Achievement award and Best of Category Ednl. Press Assn. Am., 1994, 95, 96, Telly Awards-Silver and Bronze, 1996, 98; award of excellence Nat. Sch. Pub. Rels. Assn., 1995, 96, Bronze award Columbus Internat. Film & Video, 1995.

Mem. SAG, AFTRA, NAFE, ASCD, Am. Guild Variety Artists, Actors Equity Assn., Nat. Staff Devel. Coun., Internat. TV Assn., Internat. Interactive Comm. Soc., Women in Film and Video Internat. Avocation: singing. E-mail: mdarcang@ascd.org.

DARCHUN, LINO AUKSUTIS, real estate professional; b. Chgo., Mar. 4, 1942; s. Joseph and Ursula (Shimkus) D.; m. Mary Lynn Burchette, Nov. 11, 1983; 1 child, Matthew. Student, So. Ill. U., 1960-62, 65, U. Ill., Chgo., 1966; grad., Realtor Inst., 1991. Cert. residential specialist, residential broker, internat. property specialist. Agt. Ea. Airlines, Chgo., 1967-68; sta. mgr. World Airways, Oakland, Calif., 1968-71; mgr. The Bulls Restaurant-Nightclub, Chgo., 1971-73, pres., 1977-88; v.p. Leber-Darchun, Inc., Chgo., 1973-74; adminstr. dept. aviation City of Chgo., 1974-77; assoc. realtor Palormo Realty, Chgo., 1987-88, realtor, 1988-93, v.p., 1990-93; realtor Rubloff, Inc., Chgo., 1988-90; asst. br. mgr. Coldwell Banker Residential Lincoln Park, Chgo., 1993-95, br. mgr., 1995-97; broker assoc. Coldwell Banker Residential Real Estate, Chgo., 1997—. Chmn. com. Old Wicker Park, Chgo., 1972-73; vol. Grant Hosp., Chgo.; v.p. Lincoln Park Inter-Agy. Coun., 1988; mem. adv. bd., bd. dirs. Friends of Lincoln Park/Lakeview Schs.; mem. Chgo.-Vilnius (Lithuania) Sister City Com.; mem. adv. bd. Acapulco (Mex.) Children's Home. Sgt. U.S. Army, 1962-65. Fellow Internat. Real Estate Fedn.; mem. Nat. Assn. Realtors, Chgo. Assn. Realtors (mem. multiple listing svcs. com.), Grievance Com., Internat. Real Estate Fedn., Internat. Cmty. Affairs, Lincoln Park C. of C. (v.p. 1991—, chmn. human svcs. com. 1987—, bd. dirs.), Lincoln Park Zool. Soc., Lincoln Park Conservation Assn. (1st v.p. 1988, bd. dirs., v.p. 1998-2000), Chgo. Pub. Schs. Alumni Assn. Democrat. Unitarian Universalist. Avocations: travel, music, epicure, arts. Home: 2731 N Wilton Ave Chicago IL 60614-1423 Office: Coldwell Banker Residential Lincoln Park 1840 N Clark St Chicago IL 60614-5881

D'ARCY, GERALD PAUL, engineering executive, consultant; b. Jackson, Mich., June 6, 1933; s. Merlin Wellington and Jessie Elizabeth (Sober) D.; m. Dorothy Lee Cordell, Nov. 27, 1953; children: Sherry, Janet, Nancy, Deborah, Helen. BSMechE, U. Tex., 1956; MSMechE, U. Colo., 1962; PhD, U. Tex., 1973. Registered profl. engr., Tex. Commd. 2d lt. USAF, 1956, advanced through grades to col., ret., 1986; asst. chief soil & rock mechanics group Air Force Weapons Lab., Kirtland AFB, N.Mex., 1962-67; rsch. assoc. Lawrence Radiation Lab., Livermore, Calif., 1967-70; chief phys. & engring. scis. divsn. Air Force Systems Command, Andrews AFB, Md., 1973-74; chief guns, rockets & explosives divsn. Air Force Armament Lab., Eglin AFB, Fla., 1975-79; comdr. Air Force Geophysics, Hanscom AFB, Mass., 1979-84, Air Force Office of Sci. Rsch., Bolling AFB, Washington, 1984-86; v.p. Applied Rsch. Assocs. Inc., Albuquerque, 1986-94; ret., 1994. Mech. engring. vis. com. U. Tex., Austin, 1976-79. Inventor soil stress gage; contbr. over 20 articles to profl. jours. Decorated Legion of Merit; recipient Meritorious Svc. award for nuclear weapons devel. U. Calif., Livermore, 1970; named Disting. Engring. Grad. U. Tex., Austin, 1985. Mem. Phi Kappa Phi. Democrat. Methodist. Avocation: woodworking. Home: 808 Plantation Way Panama City FL 32404-8603 E-mail: utdeg@aol.com.

D'ARCY, JAN THERESE, communications executive; b. Oneida, N.Y., June 18, 1939; d. George Thomas and Sarah Agnes (Sheehan) Baltusnik; m. Peter Eckel, Apr. 27, 1963 (div. Mar. 1985); children: Lisa, Paul, Colleen, Shane, Tyler. BA, Cath. U. Am., 1960; MA, UCLA, 1961. Instr. U. Wash., Seattle, 1983-88, Nat. Technol. U., Denver, 1990; actress ABC, CBS, NBC, 1970—; pres. Jan D'Arcy & Assocs., Bellevue, Wash., 1981—. Cons. NASA, Cleve., 1988-98, Immunex, Seattle, 1997-99, Battelle, Richmond, Wash., 1991-92. Author: (book) Technically Speaking, 1998, Dr. Jack's Adventure, 1990; contbr. articles to profl. jours.; film credits include: Ring, Convictions, Survival on the Mountain, High Stakes, Countdown, She Woke Up Pregnant, The Commish, The Other Mother, No Child of Mine, Better Off Dead, Alive, Posing Pictures, Hope Island, Sweet Revenge; television appearances include: Outer Limits, MANTIS, The X-Files, The Highlander, L.A. Law, Twin Peaks, 21 Jump Street, Wiseguy, others. Cons. N.W. Internat. Women's Conf., Seattle, 1995. Recipient Literary Lion award King County Libr., Seattle, 1994, 99, 2000, residency/writer Hedgebrook Cottages, Langley, Wash., 1988, Ralph Kaltenborn award Kaltenborn Found., Palm Beach, Fla., 1990. Mem. IEEE, Screen Actors Guild (bd. dirs. 1997-98), Am. Fedn. of TV Artists, Actor's Equity Union. Avocations: ballroom dancing, yoga. E-mail: jan@jdarcy.com.

D'ARCY, JOHN P. investment company executive; s. Raymond G. and Marguerite K. D'Arcy; m. Katherine M. McKenzie, Nov. 19, 1983. BA in History, Harvard U., 1961—65. V.p. Smith Barney, Providence, 1984—. Vice chmn. Dorcas Pl., Providence, 2000—03, Travelers Aide, Providence, 2002—03; investment com. John Hope Settlement Ho., RI, 2002—03. Lt. j.g., udt 12/seal team one NAVY, 1965—68, Coronado, CA. Mem.: Landfall Country Club, Squantum Assn., Agawum Hunt.

DARCY, KEITH THOMAS, finance company executive, educator; b. N.Y.C., June 18, 1948; s. Donald and Geraldine (Kindermann) D.; m. Lynne Alison Cumming, June 17, 1972; children: Erin Lyn, Timothy James. BS in Econs., Fordham U., 1970; MBA, Iona Coll., New Rochelle, N.Y., 1974; postgrad., N.Y. Theol. Sem., 1988-89. With Bankers Trust Co., N.Y.C., 1970—77; v.p. Marine Midland Bank N.A., N.Y.C., 1977—82; CEO, IGM divsn. Gen. Reins. Corp., Stamford, Conn., 1982—83; dir. human resource divsn. Marine Midland Bank, N.Y.C., 1984—89; pres., CEO, The Leadership Group, Inc., N.Y.C., 1989—94; v.p., assoc. ethics officer Prudential Securities Inc., N.Y.C., 1994—96, sr. ethics advisor, 1996—97; assoc. dean, disting. prof. bus. Georgetown U., Washington, 1995—96; exec. v.p. office of the pres. IBJ Whitehall Bank and Trust Co., N.Y.C., 1997—2002; pres., CEO Ctr. Integrity, Pound Ridge, NY, 2002—. Mem. adj. faculty Marymount Coll., 1978-96, Mercy Coll., 1975-96; mem. faculty advanced exec. edn. at Wharton, U. Pa., 1994—; mem. faculty grad. mgmt. program Antioch U., Seattle, 1989-96; exec.-in-residence grad. program in human resources and orgnl. devel. and grad. program in orgnl. leadership Manhattanville Coll., Purchase, N.Y., mem. corp. adv. bd., 1989—; exec. fellow Ctr. for Bus. Ethics, Bentley Coll., Waltham, Mass., 1993—, mem. exec. com.; tchg. fellow Smith Sch. Bus., U. Md., College Park, 2002—; bd. dirs. Barat House, Purchase, N.Y., 1989—; dir. emeritus Ethics Officer Assn., mem. steering com. Caux (Switzerland) Round Table, 1996—; nat. adv. bd. Worktalk, 1999—; vice chmn. Ctr. for Values-Based Leadership, 1999—, chmn., bd. trustees BBB Found., 2001—. Co-author: Change Management, 1993, The Ethics Companion, 1999; mem. editl. bd., contbr.: At Work: Stories of Tomorrow's Workplace, 1992—; featured in The Ethical Edge, The Portable Executive, Merchants of Vision, Career Crossroads, Winning the People Wars, Survival Skills in the Fin. Svcs. Industry. Treas. Westchester County Rep. Com., White Plains, N.Y., 1979-89; asst. treas. N.Y. State Friends for Jim Buckley, 1976; dir. NCCJ, 1977-85; trustee Bedford Presbyn. Ch., N.Y., 1982-87, Better Bus. Bur. Found., N.Y., 2001—; mem. Westchester Blue Ribbon Commn. to Formulate County Housing Policy, 1979; trustee March of Dimes, Westchester, 1978-84, chmn. Exec. Walkathon, 1978-81. Mem. Ethics Officers Assn. (dir. emeritus), Caux (Switzerland) Round Table (affil.). Clubs: Soc. Friendly Sons of St. Patrick (pres. 1985). Home: Horseshoe Hl W Pound Ridge NY 10576 Office: 27 Horseshoe Hill W Pound Ridge NY 10576 E-mail: keith.darcy@ethicsinleadership.com.

DARCY, ROBERT EMMETT, political scientist, educator, statistician; b. Elizabeth, N.J., Feb. 25, 1942; s. John William and Jane (Alton) D.; m. Lynne C. Murnane, Aug. 30, 1975; children: Mary Frances, Catherine Rose. BA, U. Wis., 1965; MA, U. Ky., 1970, PhD, 1971. Asst. prof. George Washington U., Washington, 1971-77, Okla. State U., Stillwater, 1977-80, assoc. prof. polit. sci., 1980-85, prof., 1985-90, Regents prof., 1991—. Expert witness on ballot and election procedures Atty. Gen., State of Okla., Oklahoma City, 1984-86, 91-95, 98, 2002, Ohio, 1991, N.H., 1995, N.C., 1998, N.Y., 1999; vis. guest prof. U. Conn., 1984; European lectr. USIA, Sweden, Germany, 1983, African lectr., Uganda, Swaziland, Kenya, Sierra Leone, 1988, Mozambique, South Africa, 1993; vis. prof. U. New Orleans, 1985, Nat. U. Ireland, U. Coll. Galway, 1988, Queen's U., Belfast, 1987, U. NSW, Australia, 1991, Trinity Coll., Dublin, 1993; mem. Okla. Commn. on Status Women, 1997—, co-chmn. summit 1997, 99; mem. Okla. Jud. Evaluation Commn., 1997-2001, Legis. Task Force on Jud. Selection, 1999-00. Author: Women, Elections and Representation, 1987, 90, 94, Guide to Quantitative History, 1995; editor Jour. Okla. Politics, 1991-99, Social Sci. Jour., 1983-85; contbr. articles to profl. jours. Recipient Liberty Bell award Okla. Bar Assn., 1999, Commendation, Okla. Ho. of Reps., 2000; Bruce fellow Keele U., Eng., 1998; vis. rsch. scholar Acad. Korean Studies, Seoul, 1983. Mem. AAUP (chpt. pres. 1984, 88), Polit. Studies Assn. Ireland, Am. Polit. Sci. Assn., Am. Assn. Pub. Opinion Rsch., Western Social Sci. Assn., Okla. Polit. Sci. Assn. (pres. 1992, Outstanding Okla. Polit. Scientist award 1993), So. Polit. Sci. Assn., Midwestern Polit. Sci. Assn. Republican. Home: 2215 W 5th Ave Stillwater OK 74074-2818 Office: Okla State U Dept Polit Sci Stillwater OK 74078-0001 E-mail: bdarcy@okstate.edu.

DARDAI, SHAHID MOINUDDIN, computer science educator; b. India, May 11, 1940; Prof. computer sci. dept. Richard J. Daley Coll., Chgo., 1993—, data processing coord. Chairperson computer sci. dept. Richard J. Daley Coll., 1993—; adj. faculty math. and computer sci. dept. Chgo. State U., 1993—. Recipient Disting. Prof. award, City Coll. Chgo., 2000—01. Mem. Data Processing Mgmt. Assn., Phi Theta Kappa. Office: Richard J Daley Coll 7500 S Pulaski Rd Chicago IL 60652-1242 Fax: (312) 838-7524. E-mail: sdardai@hotmail.com., sdardai@ccc.edu.

DARDANO, ANTHONY NICHOLAS, obstetrician and gynecologist; b. Utica, N.Y., May 27, 1942; s. Nicholas Salvatore and Catherine (Matt) D.; m. Marjorie Gamello, Aug. 8, 1963; children: Anthony, Kathryn. BS, Niagara U., 1963; MD, Bologna (Italy) U., 1968. Diplomate Am. Bd. Ob-Gyn. Intern Ellis Hosp., Schenectady, 1969-70; resident St. Mary's Hosp., Rochester, N.Y., 1970-73; pvt. practice Utica, 1973—; pvt. practice, St. Elizabeth Hosp., New Hartford, N.Y., 1980-81, chief dept. ob-gyn. Utica, 1980-90, chmn. laser com., 1986—. Fellow ACS, ACOG, Internat. Coll. Surgeons; mem. AMA, N.Y. Med. Soc. Republican. Roman Catholic. Office: 1 Paris Rd New Hartford NY 13413-2350

DARDECK, STEPHEN A. lawyer; b. N.Y.C., Aug. 13, 1945; s. Philip A. and Shirley R. (Hahn) D.; m. Judith K. Simpson, July 19, 1970; chi ldren: Adam, Aaron. BA, U. Pa., 1967; M in Journalism, U. Calif., Berkeley, 1968; JD, Boston U. Law Sch., 1973. Bar: Vt. 1973, U.S. Dist. Ct. Vt. 1973, U.S. Ct. Appeals (2d cir.) 1990. Dep. state's atty. Rutland County State's Atty.'s Office, Vt., 1973-78; ptnr. Tepper, Dardeck & Levins, LLP, Rutland, 1978—. Office: Tepper Dardeck & Levins LLP 73 Center St Rutland VT 05701-4046 E-mail: sdardeck@tepperdardeck.com.

DARDEN, BARBARA S. library director; b. Cleve., Apr. 6, 1947; d. Curley and Cora (Chambliss) Brown; m. Joseph S. Darden; children: Michelle, Crystal. BS, Ohio State U., 1967; MS in Ednl. Media, MLS, Kent State U., 1971; PhD, Rutgers U., 2002. Adminstrv. supr. Cleve. Pub. Schs., 1968-70; libr. Cuyahoga C.C., 1972-75, coord., 1975-77, interim dir., 1977-78, asst. dean, 1978-80, dir., 1980-84; dir. libr. Kean Coll., Union, N.J., 1984—. Cons. Dembsy Assocs., Boston, 1967-81; editl. cons. Max Pub. Co., N.Y.C., 1967-81; cons. reader U.S. Office Edn., Washington, 1979-80; editl. cons. Jossey-Bass Pub. Co., 1979. Cons. editor Probe, 1976, Sch. Media Ctr., 1968, Booklist, 1969; contbr. articles to profl. jours. Bd. dirs. N.J. Adv. Bd. on Status of Women, 1988, Africana Studies, 1988; mem. N.J. State Libr. Adv. Bd.; bd. dirs. N.J. Ednl. Activities Task Force Libr. Com. Recipient Phillips award Kent State U., 1970. Mem. ALA (chmn. pay equity com. 1996, chair LAMA-COLA 1999), Higher Edn. Reps., N.J. Acad. Libr. Network (chmn. 1987, bd. dirs. 1995—), Coun. N.J. Librs. (prs. 1987—), N.J. Libr. Assn., Oral History Soc., N.J. Hist. Soc., Libr. Adminstrn. Mgmt. Assn. (chair 1997-99, bd. dirs. 1999), Coun. N.J. Coll. and Univ. Libr. Dirs. (pres. 1999—), Jr. League (Cleve. vice chmn. 1981, 83), Concerned Parents Club (pres. 1984), Women's City Club (adv. bd. 1997—). Avocations: music, reading. Office: Kean Univ Libr Morris Ave Union NJ 07083

DARDEN, CLAIBOURNE HENRY, JR., marketing research professional; b. Greensboro, N.C., June 26, 1943; s. Claibourne Henry and Gerry (Bonkemeyer); m. Anita McMurry; children: Claibourne III, Prentiss. BS, Washington & Lee U., 1966; MBA, Emory U., 1968. Pres. Darden Rsch. Corp., Atlanta, 1968—. TV commentator, spkr. in field. Bd. dirs. Nat. Wild Turkey Fedn., Edgefield, SC, 1985—2000, Quality Deer Mgmt. Assn., Watkinsville, Ga., 2001—, Ga. Conservancy, 1985—91, Washington & Lee Alumni Assn., Atlanta, 1986—87. Mem. Am. Mktg. Assn. (bd. dirs. Atlanta chpt. 1970-75, Mktg. Profl. of Yr. 1976), N.Y. Yacht Club, Druid Hills Golf Club. Presbyterian. Avocations: hunting, sailing, fishing. Office: Darden Rsch Corporation 1534 N Decatur Rd NE Atlanta GA 30307-1022

DARDEN, DONNA BERNICE, special education educator; b. Portsmouth, Va., Sept. 15, 1956; d. Howard John and Joyce Bernice Jackson; m. John Holland Darden, June 20, 1975; children: Christopher John, Jamison Marie. AA, Piedmont Va. C.C., Charlottesville, Va., 1987; BA, M of Teaching, U. Va., 1990. Cert. tchr. spl. edn., learning disabilities, emotionally disturbed. Customer svc. rep. Landmark Comm., Inc., Norfolk, Va., 1976-79; computer operator Curtis Mathes Corp., Houston, 1979-80; chief fin. officer Darden, Inc./(div. ColorTyme TV), Charlottesville, 1980-87; learning disabilities tchr. Oakland Sch., Boyd Tavern, Va., 1990—; clin. instr. Curry Sch. of Edn. U. Va., 1995—. Mem. Albermarle County Rep. Com., Va., 1982—; area capt. Key West-Cedar Hills Community Assn., Albermarle County, 1985, 86, mem. chmn., 1987, 2000—; swim meet assoc., Key West Swim Team, 1986-93; co-chmn. Rivanna Scenic River Adv. Bd., 1997—; active Cornerstone Cmty. Ch.; sec. Cornerstone Wesleyan Women, 1998-99, asst. dir. 1999, dir, 2001-2003. Mem. Coun. Exceptional Children, Golden Key, Kappa Delta Pi. Avocations: music, tennis, gardening, nature. Home: 344 Key West Dr Charlottesville VA 22911-8426 Office: Oakland Sch Boyd Tavern VA 22947

DARDEN, EDWIN SPEIGHT, SR., architect; b. Stantonsburg, N.C., Oct. 14, 1920; s. Edwin Speight and Sallie (Jordan) D.; m. s. Pauline K. Bartlett, Feb. 26, 1944; children: Edwin Speight III, Judith Ann, Diane Russell. BS in Archtl. Engring., Kans. State U., 1947. Registered architect, Calif. Assoc., Fred L. Swartz and William G. Hyberg, Fresno, Calif., 1949-59; ptnr. Nargis and Darden (Architects), Fresno, 1959-69; pres. Edwin S. Darden Assocs., Inc., Fresno, 1969-85, cons., 1985—. Bd. dirs. Murphy Bank; mem. state adv. bd. Office of Architecture and Constrn., 1970-78; cons. ednl. facilities, 1975—. Prin. works include Clovis (Calif.) High Sch., 1969, Clovis W. High Sch., 1976, Ahwahnee Jr. High Sch., Fresno, 1966, Tehipite Jr. High Sch., Fresno, 1973, Fresno County Dept. Health, 1978, Floyd B. Buchanan Edn. Ctr., Clovis, 1990. Served to 1st lt. C.E., AUS, 1942-46. Fellow AIA; mem. Sigma Phi Epsilon, Alpha Kappa Psi. Clubs: Fresno Rotary. Presbyterian. Office: Edwin S Darden Assocs Inc 1177 W Shaw Ave Fresno CA 93711-3704 E-mail: esda@pacbell.net.

DARDEN, JOSEPH SAMUEL, JR., health educator; b. Pleasantville, N.J., July 25, 1925; s. Joseph Samuel and Blanche Catherine (Paige) D.; m. Barbara Cassandra Sellers, Dec. 30, 1955 (div. July 1979); 1 child, Michele Irene. AB, Lincoln U., 1948; MA, NYU, 1952, EdD (Danforth Found. fellow), 1963. Instr. biol. scis. Clark Coll., Atlanta, 1952-55; asst. prof. Albany (Ga.) State Coll., 1955-58, prof., 1959-64; asst. prof. Kean U. of N.J., Union, 1964-67, prof. health edn., 1970—, coord. health, 1977-79, chmn. dept. health and recreation, 1979-84, coord. health, 1984—2002, dir. minority enrollment, 1988-94, prof. emeritus, 2002—. Adj. prof. health Wagner Coll., S.I., N.Y., 1965-88; cons. N.J. Dept. Edn., 1968-73, 76-88. Author: (with others) Growth Pattern and Sex Education, 1967, Updated Supplement to Growth Pattern and Sex Education, 1972, Toward a Healthier Sexuality: A Book of Readings, 1997; editor, co-author: Critical Health Issues Reader, 2002. Bd. advisors Marylawn of Oranges, 1971-73; bd. dirs. N.J. Coun. Family Relations, 1981-83; trustee Planned Parenthood of Essex County, N.J., 1985—; trustee Planned Parenthood of Met. N.J, 1985—. With AUS, 1944-46. Recipient Alumni Achievement award, Lincoln U., 1993, Presdl. Excellence award, Kean U., 2002. Fellow Am. Assn. Health Edn. (charter); mem. AAHPERD (Eastern dist. v.p. for health edn. 1971-72, dist. pres. 1974-75, Eastern dist. rep. 1979-82, honor award Eastern dist. 1976, nat. honor award 1985, Outstanding Tchr. award Eastern dist. 1983, Charles D. Henry award 1988, Edwin B. Henderson award 1991), Am. Sch. Health Assn. (governing coun. 1970-73, Disting. Svc. award 1971), Assn. Advancement Health Edn. (dir. 1975-78, Profl. Svc. award 1990, presdl. citation 1996), N.J. Health Edn. Coun. (founder 1967, honor award 1975), N.J. Assn. Health, Phys. Edn. and Recreation (v.p. health edn. 1967-68, Honor fellow award 1972, Disting. Leadership award 1975), Alpha Phi Alpha. Home: 1416 Thelma Dr Union NJ 07083-6220 Office: Kean U NJ Union NJ 07083 E-mail: jdarden@kean.edu.

DARDEN, MARSHALL TAYLOR, lawyer; b. Porstmouth, Va., Dec. 6, 1952; s. Arthur Dandridge and Marian (Mann) D.; m. Claudia Kay Golay, Feb. 11, 1978; 1 child, Brandon Taylor. BA, La. State U., 1974, JD, 1977. Bar: La. 1977. Assoc. Milling, Benson, Woodward, Hillyer, Pierson & Miller, New Orleans, 1977-82, ptnr., 1983—; speaker 31st Ann. Mineral Law Inst., Baton Rouge, Mar. 1984, 34th Ann. Mineral Law Inst., 1987; mem. adv. coun. La. Mineral Law Inst., 1988-92, chmn. adv. coun., 1990-92; mem. coun. La. Law Inst., 1991-92. Mem. ABA, La. State Bar Assn., Lambda Chi Alpha. Republican. Episcopalian. Home: 3517 Pin Oak Ave New Orleans LA 70131-8441 Office: Milling Benson Woodward Hillyer Pierson & Miller 909 Poydras St Ste 2300 New Orleans LA 70112-1010

DAREN, SYLVIA, poet; b. N.Y.C., N.Y., Apr. 2, 1920; d. Louis Millman and Rose Beresnoger; m. Joseph Daren, Dec. 24, 1939; children: Edythe Hepner, Marsha. Student, grad. H.S., 1937. Lectr. Singles Group, N.Y.C.; poet laureat Temple Emeth; bd. mem. & by-law co-chair Temple Emeth Sisterhood; Instalation Chmn. Gold Coast Cancer Rsch. of Palm Greens, Women's Club of Palm Green; fund raising chair Delray B'nai B'rith; Poet and Mistress of Ceremonies Palm Greens Entertainers; actor, poet, story teller Yiddish Club of Palm Greens. Author (childrens poetry): Moses, The Hebrew Giant; author: (poetry book) How I Earned My Bachelor of Life Degree --You Can COunt Your Credits Too !!!; author: (plays and poetry) various including Temple Emeth of Delray Beach (Poet Laureat); co-dir.: Oakland Sr. Citizens -Oakland Jewish Ctr., 1962—80; editor (newspaper): Palms West O.R.T.; actor(co-author): (plays) My Unfair Lady. Leader Girl Scouts of Am., Queens, NY, 1953—54; vol. Creedmore Hosp., Queens; v.p. and trustee, adv. girls, fund raising, cmty. svc., jewish edn., Aid to Israel for Queens, vol. B'nai B'rith, Bayside, NY, 1953—2003, various, 1953—2003; founder Marsha Daren Fund Long Island Jewish Med. Ctr., Long Island, 1975—89. Recipient Honorary Mem. of Am. Legion, Am. Legion, 1933, Honoree- This is Your Life, Oakland B'nai B'rith, 1959, Honoree, Org. of people Undaunted by Stroke, 1976, United Jewish Appeal & Federation of Jewish Philanthropies, 1976, Jewish Nat. Fund Temple Emeth, 0955—2003, Mem. Award, B'nai B'rith Distrit 5. Mem.: Bowling League, B'nai B'rith. Jewish. Avocations: writing poetry, acting, bowling, golf, volunteering.

DARGAN, JOHN HENRY, business executive; b. Dublin, Dec. 16, 1965; s. Peter Anthony and Cecilia (Blake) D.; m. Janet Tsai Dargan, Aug. 31, 1997. B Engring., Trinity Coll., Dublin, 1987; MBA, U. Pa., 1993. Bus. analyst McKinsey & Co., London, 1987—89; assoc. GE Capital Corp., London, 1989—91; cons. Oliver, Wyman & Co., London, 1993—95; head of strategy London Stock Exch., 1995—97; dir. spl. projects Warner Bros., L.A., 1997—2000; pres., CEO Broadercast, L.A., 2000—. Adviser Russian Privatization Inst., Moscow, 1992. Fulbright scholar, 1991, Palmer scholar, 1993. Roman Catholic. Home: 952 10th St Manhattan Beach CA 90266-5902 Office: 1158 26th St Ste 548 Santa Monica CA 90403 E-mail: john.dargan@verizon.net.

DARGAN, PAMELA ANN, principal systems and software engineer; b. Norfolk, Va. d. Thomas J. and Stana E. (Verich) Piazza; m. W. Scott Dargan, Dec., 1990. BS in Math., Va. Poly. and State U., 1979; MS in Computer Sci., George Mason U., 1993. Programmer Control Data Corp., Rockville, Md., 1979-80; tech. staff BDM Corp., McLean, Va., 1980-81, TRW Fed. Sys. Group, McLean, 1981-87; dep. program mgr. Mystech, Inc., Alexandria, Va., 1987-89; lead engr. MITRE Corp., McLean, 1989-98, prin., 2001—02, Litton Tasc, Inc., Chantilly, Va., 1998—2001; sr. cons. Scitor Corp., 2002—03; prin. sys. engr. SAIC, 2003—. Program chair East Coast Artificial Intelligence Work Sta. Users Group, 1984-85; author on open sys. for internat. confs. and publs. Contbr. chpts. to books and articles to profl. jours. Mem. IEEE, Assn. Computing Machinery, Internat. Coun. on Sys. Engring. E-mail: pdargan@erols.com.

DARIANO, JOSEPH, publishing company executive; Pres. Reed Tech. & Info. Svcs., Horsham, Pa. Office: Reed Tech & Info Svcs 275 Gibraltar Rd Horsham PA 19044-2305 E-mail: jdariano@rtis-g.com.

DARIEN, STEVEN MARTIN, management consulting company executive; b. N.Y.C., Oct. 29, 1942; s. Leo and Laura Darien; m. Susan Ruth Kinsley, Nov. 29, 1942; children: Jodi Ellen, Andrew Todd. AB, Rutgers Coll., 1963; MBA, Columbia U., 1966. Claims settler Equitable Life, N.Y.C., 1963-64; mgmt. trainee Merck & Co., Inc., Rahway, N.J., 1966-69, mgr. coll. rels., 1969-74, exec. dir. pers. resources, 1974-79, exec. dir. U.S. Pers., 1979-85, v.p. employee rels., 1985-89, v.p. worldwide pres., 1989-90, v.p. human resources, 1990-96; pres. Darien Assocs., 1996-98; chmn., CEO The Cabot Adv. Group, Washington, 1998—. Bd. dirs. Somerset Hosp. Chmn. Olin Inst. for Employment Practice and Policy; chmn. Olin Found. for Employment Policy and Practice. Mem. Columbia U. Bus. Sch. Alumni Assn. (v.p.).

DARKE, CHARLES BRUCE, academic administrator, dentist; b. Chgo., Sept. 22, 1937; s. Paul Olden and Annie Waulene (Tennin) D.; m. Annetta McRae-Darke, Aug. 15, 1965 (div. 1982); 1 child, Charles B. II; m. Judith Anne Chew, Dec. 15, 1990. AA, Wilson Jr. Coll., Chgo., 1960; DDS, Meharry Med. Coll., 1964; MPH, U. Calif., Berkeley, 1972. Staff dentist Children's Hosp., Oakland, Calif., 1967-68, Mt. Zion Hosp., San Francisco, 1967-71; pvt. practice in dentistry San Francisco, 1967—; dir. dental svcs. San Francisco Gen. Hosp., 1973-88; asst. adminstr. outpatient svcs. San Francisco Med. Ctr., 1980-88; ops. officer primary care network San Francisco Dept. Health, 1988-89; exec. dir. Student Health and Counseling Ctr. Calif. State U., Fullerton, 1989-99; sr. cons. Kaiser Found. Hosps., 1999—. Dental cons. Dept. Labor Job Corps, Washington, 1973-88; chief examiner state dental bd. Calif. State Bd. Dental Examiners, Sacramento, 1976-89; surveyor ambulatory care and network Joint Commn. on Accreditation of Health, Oakbrook, Ill., 1986—; bd. dirs. Yorba Hills Med. Ctr., Yorba Linda, Calif., 1993-96. Found Tooth Trip-Free Dental Care, San Francisco, 1969. Capt. USAF, 1965-67. Mem. ADA, Am. Endodontic Soc., Nat. Dental Assn., Am. Coll. Health Assn., Pacific Coast Coll. Health Assn. (bd. dirs. 1993), Nat. Dental Soc. Bay Area (past pres.). Avocations: scuba diving, photography, magic.

DARKE, RICHARD FRANCIS, lawyer; b. Detroit, June 17, 1943; s. Francis Joseph and Irene Anne (Potts) D.; m. Alice Mary Renger, Feb. 14, 1968; children: Kimberly, Richard, Kelly, Sean, Colin. BBA, U. Notre Dame, 1965; JD, Detroit Coll. Law, 1969. Bar: Mich. 1969. Atty. AAA, Detroit, 1969-72; assoc. Oster & Mollett P.C., Mt. Clemens, Mich., 1972-73; ptnr. Small, Darke, Oakes P.C., Southfield, Mich., 1973-77; v.p., gen. counsel, sec. Fruehauf Corp., Detroit, 1977-92; ptnr. Darke & Wilson, Grosse Pointe Woods, Mich., 1993—. Mem. ABA, Mich. Bar Assn., Detroit Bar Assn., Machinery and Allied Products Inst. (counsel), Mich. Gen. Counsel Group, Essex Country Club, Lockmoor Club. Roman Catholic. Avocation: golfing. Home: 5700 N Pinnacle West Bloomfield MI 48322-1353

DARKO, DENIS F. research scientist, educator, physician; b. Indpls., July 13, 1947; s. Charles O. and Agnes Mary (Lauck) Darko; m. Ann Marie Barker, Oct. 15, 1983; children: Emily Marie, Roseann Michelle. BS in Physics, U. Notre Dame, 1969; MD, Ind. U., 1975. Diplomate Am. Bd. Psychiatry and Neurology. Staff rsch. assoc. biols. divsn. Eli Lilly Co., Indpls., 1970, U. Co. Sch. Medicine, 1971; resident physician family practice Maricopa County Hosp., 1975, Scottsdale (Ariz.) Meml. Hosp., 1975—76; resident physician psychiatry Good Samaritan Med. Ctr., Phoenix, 1977—80, chief resident in psychiatry, 1978—80; pvt. practice psychiatry Scottsdale, 1980—83; cons. psychiatrist Phoenix Indian Med. Ctr., 1980—81; supr. psychiatry residency program Maricopa County Med. Ctr., 1980—83; instr. pre-med. program Ariz. State U., 1980—83, instr. family practice residency program, 1980—83; fellow in consultation/liaison psychiatry U. Calif.-San Diego Med. Ctr., 1983—84, fellow in psychopharmacology and psychobiology Clin. Rsch. Ctr., 1984—85; asst. prof. psychiatry U. Calif., San Diego Sch. Medicine, 1985—92, assoc. adj. prof., 1992—, chmn. diagnostic com. NIMH mental health clin. rsch. ctr., 1984—89, rsch. fellow in immunology and allergy divsn. immunology and allergy Dept. Pediats., 1985—87, chmn. resident rsch. com. dept. psychiatry, 1989—92; attending physician Univ. Hosp., 1985—94; ward chief San Diego VA Med. Ctr., 1985—87, staff psychiatrist, 1985—93, med. dir. mental health clinic, 1987—92, chief psychiat. emergency svc., 1988—92; dir. Mood Disorders Rsch. Clinic U. Calif. San Diego Sch. Medicine and San Diego VA Med. Ctr., 1987—90; med. dir. NIMH Mental Health Clin. Rsch. Ctr., 1987—88; vis. scientist Scripps Clinic and Rsch. Found. Dept. Neuropharmacology, 1990;

assoc. adj. prof. Scripps Rsch. Inst. Dept. Neuropharmacology, 1991—92, assoc. prof., 1993—2002; attending physician Scripps Clin. Dept. Medicine, Divsn. Psychiatry, 1991—2002, head divsn. psychiatry and behavioral medicine, 1997—2002; head neuroimmunology lab., dept. neuropharmacology Scripps Rsch. Inst., 1993—2002; med. dir., v.p. Calif. Clin. Trials, LLC, 2002—03. Chmn. grant application rev. com., dept. acad. affairs Scripps Clinic Found., 1995—2002; cons. Hybritech, 1991—94. Editl. reviewer: Am. Jour. of Psychiatry in Medicine, 1987—2002, Internat. Jour. of Psychiatry in Medicine, 1987—97, Jour. of Neuropsychiatry and Clin. Neuroscis., 1988—2002, Biol. Psychiatry, 1988, Behavioral Science, 1990—92. Recipient review article award, Am. Coll. Allergists, 1986; fellow, USPHS, 1972, ACP, 1988. Fellow: ACP, Am. Psychiat. Assn.; mem.: AAAS, Am. Acad. Sleep Medicine, West Coast Coll. Biol. Psychiatry, Psychoneuroimmunology Rsch. Soc. (founding), Soc. Biol. Psychiatry, Endocrine Soc., San Diego Soc. Psychiat. Physicians (chmn. membership com. 1991—94, treas. 1993—94), Calif. Psychiat. Assn. Office: Calif Clin Trials 8501 Wilshire Blvd Ste 100 Beverly Hills CA 90211-1092

DARKOVICH, SHARON MARIE, nurse administrator; b. Ft. Wayne, Ind., Dec. 10, 1949; d. Gerald Antone LaCanne and Ida Eileen (Bowman) LaCanne Cutler; m. Robert Eliot Ness, July 17, 1971 (dec. Aug. 1976); m. Paul Darkovich, Jan. 23, 1981 (div. May 1994); 1 child, Amy Elizabeth. BSN, Case Western Res. U., 1973, BA in Psychology, 1978; cert. in advanced bioethics, Cleve. State U., 1990, MA in Philosophy and Bioethics, 1994. RN, Ohio. Staff nurse Univ. Hosps., Cleve., 1973, asst. head nurse, 1973-76; quality improvement coord. St. Luke's Med. Ctr., Cleve., 1976-83, 84-97, dir. nursing, 1983-84, quality improvement dir., 1997-98; dir. quality svcs. Lake Hosp. Sys., Inc., Painesville, Ohio, 1998-2000, corp. quality and compliance officer, 2000—. Cons. to long-term care facilities, 1986-92, pressure ulcer dressing devel. B.F. Goodrich Co., 1988-92; cons. to ambulatory facility for Joint Commn. for Accreditation of Health Care Orgns., Oakbrook, Ill., 1994, cons. to cmty. hosp. med. staff, bylaws, 1996; lectr. U. Akron, 1992-93, Northeast Ohio U. Coll. Medicine, 1993-95. Mem. ANA, Am. Soc. for Healthcare Bioethics, Am. Soc. for Quality, Greater Cleve. Nurses Assn. (mem. dist. coun. on practice, 1982-84), Sigma Theta Tau. Avocations: reading, needlework, sewing, camping. E-mail: sharondarkovich@lhs.net.

DARLING, GEORGE CURTIS, minister, administrator; b. Xenia, Ohio, Nov. 23, 1928; s. Russell M. and Mary Elizabeth (Young) D.; m. Edna Pearlen Phillips, May 1, 1960; (div. Apr. 1973) 1 child, Curtis; m. Mary Elizabeth Miller, Oct. 24, 1952 (div. Aug. 1956), 1 child, Kirk; m. Evelyn Cornelia Woodfork, Apr. 10, 1976 (dec. Nov. 1998; m. Anna Jean Parks, Aug. 30, 2002. Adrloma in Theology, Am. Bapt. Theol. Sem., Dayton, Ohio, 1970. Ordained to ministry Bapt. Ch., 1963. Pastor 2nd Bapt. Ch., Del., Ohio, 1966-71; supply pastor Tabernacle Bapt. Ch., Columbus, Ohio, 1974; pastor Flintridge Bapt. Ch., Columbus, 1980-91; asst. pastor Peace Bapt. Ch., Columbus, 1993—. V.p. Springfield (Ohio) Dist. Sunday Sch. and Bapt. Tng. Union. Author: How to Find God, 1969. Bd. dirs., pres. Liberty Ctr., Delaware, Ohio, 1968-70; mem. Delaware County Community Action Orgn., 1967; vol. motivational spkr. to stroke patients, 1996—. With U.S. Army, 1950-52, Korea.; ret. USAF, 1988. Recipient Hon. Sci. award, Bausch & Lomb, 1946. Mem. Eastern Union Missionary Bapt. Assn. (statis. clk. Ohio 1981-85, 3d vice moderator 1985-87, 2d vice moderator, 1987-91), Columbus Bapt. Ministers and Laity Bible League (instr. 1987-96, parliamentarian 1999—). Home: 884 E Weber Rd Columbus OH 43211-1174 *On cloudy days when the sun is hidden from view, flying above the clouds enables one to see the brightness of the sun. When things go wrong in my life, I take a spiritual trip beyond the darkness of the moment into the sunlight of hope.*

DARLING, JOHN ROTHBURN, JR., business educator; b. Holton, Kans., Mar. 30, 1937; s. John Rothburn and Beatrice Noel (Deaver) D.; m. Melva Jean Fears, Aug. 20, 1958; children: Stephen, Cynthia, Gregory. BS, U. Ala., 1959, MS, 1960; PhD, U. Ill., 1967; PhD (hon.), Chung Yuan Christian U., Taiwan, 1998. Divisional mgr. J.C. Penney Co., 1960-63; grad. teaching asst. U. Ill., Urbana, 1965-66; asst. prof. mktg. U. Ala., Tuscaloosa, 1966-68; assoc. prof. mktg. U. Mo., Columbia, 1968-71; prof. adminstrn., coord. mktg. Wichita State U., 1971-76; dean, prof. mktg. Coll. Bus. Adminstrn. So. Ill. U., Carbondale, 1976-81; v.p. acad. affairs and rsch., prof. internat. bus. Tex. Tech U., Lubbock, 1981-86; provost, v.p. acad. affairs, prof. mktg. and internat. bus. Miss. State U., Mississippi State, 1986-90; chancellor, disting. prof. internat. bus. La. State U., Shreveport, 1990-95; pres. Pittsburg (Kans.) State U., 1995-99, prof. mktg. and internat. bus., 1995-2000; vis. disting. prof. mktg. Rockhurst U., 2000—. Mktg. rsch. cons. Southwestern Bell, 1970; sr. v.p. Boothe Advt. Wichita, 1972; pres. Bus. Rsch. Assocs., 1972-76; cons. Bus. Rsch. Assocs., 1976-82; spl. cons. FTC, Washington, 1972-75, U.S. Dept. Justice, 1973-74, Atty. Gen., State of Kans., 1972-76, Dist. Atty. 18th Jud. Dist., Wichita, 1972-76, Maya Internat. Inc., Houston, 1995—, Morrison and Assocs., Inc., Shreveport, 1995-97; vis. disting. prof. internat. mktg. Helsinki Sch. Econs. and Bus. Adminstrn., 1993—. Author: (with Harry A. Lipson) Marketing Fundamentals, Text and Cases, 1980, (with Raimo Nurmi) International Management Leadership: The Primary Competitive Advantage, 1997; mem. bd. cons. editors Jour. Advt., 1984—; mem. editl. rev. bd. Jour. Internat. Bus. Studies, 1991—, Jour. Entrepreneurship, 1997—; contbr. articles to profl. jours. Bd. dirs. Outreach Found., 1973-79, v.p., 1975-77; trustee Graceland Coll., Lamoni, Iowa, 1976-82; mem. mgmt. com. Park Coll., Kansas City, 1976-79. Dist. Eagle Scout Awd., Boy Scouts Amer., 1998. Mem. Internat. Coun. Small Bus., Am. Mktg. Assn., Am. Mgmt. Assn., Acad. Internat. Bus., Am. Econs. Assn., Am. Arbitration Assn., (mem. nat. panel arbitrators and mediators 1993—), Nat. Assn. Intercollegiate Athletics (mem. governing bd. 1994-95), So. Bus. Adminstrn. Assn., So. Mktg. Assn., So. Econs. Assn., So. Assn. Colls. and Schs. (chair reaccreditation com. 1982-95, chair faculty qualifications criteria com. 1989-90, com. to rev. criteria for accreditation 1990-92, commr. 1992-95, Nat. Assn. State Univs. and Land-Grant Colls. (chair regional accreditation rev. com. 1989-90), Sales and Mktg. Execs. Internat., Beta Gamma Sigma, Phi Kappa Phi, Omicorn Delta Kappa, Phi Delta Kappa, Kappa Delta Phi, Mu Kappa Tau, Pi Sigma Epsilon, Alpha Kappa Psi, Chi Alpha Phi, Alpha Phi Omega, Phi Eta Sigma, Delta Mu Delta, Alpha Mu Gamma. Home: 12705 E 37th Terr Ct Independence MO 64055-3179 Office: Office of the President Pittsburg State Univ 1701 S Broadway St Pittsburg KS 66762-5856

DARLING, PAMELA ANN WOOD, writer, editor, speaker, religious consultant; b. Lake Forest, Ill., Aug. 31, 1943; d. Charles Edwards Jr. and Ann (Rayner) Wood. BA, Northwestern U., 1965; MS, Columbia U., 1971; MA, Gen. Theol. Sem., 1987, ThD, 1991. Cons. Episcopal Ch. Women's Program, 1985-96; adminstr. Episcopal Women's History Project, N.Y.C., 1985-91; fellow Gen. Theol. Sem., N.Y.C., 1987-91; spl. asst. to pres. House of Deps. Episcopal Ch. U.S.A., 1992-2000; mem. standing com. Episcopal Diocese of Pa., 2001—. Adj. prof. ch. history Gen. Theol. Sem., 1991-93; mem. steering com. Nat. Network of Lay Profls., 1987-90, mem. Gen. Bd. Examining Chaplains, 1991-97; bd. dirs. Episcopal Ch. Pub. Co., 1991-95; libr., cons. Preservation of Libr. Materials, 1971-90. Author: Preservation Planning Program, 1982, New Wine: The Story of Women Transforming Leadership and Power in the Episcopal Church, 1994, Stop Violence Against Women, 1994, Equally Applicable, 1994, Decently and in Order, 2000. Bd. dirs. Kirkridge, 1998-2003; mem. adv. bd. Archives of Women in Theol. Scholarship Union Theol. Sem., 1998—; mem. bd. Hist. Soc. Episcopal Ch., 2001—. Recipient Esther J. Piercy award ALA, 1979, Adelaide Teague Case award, 2000. Mem. Episcopal Women's History Project (asst. treas. 1987-91), Episcopal Women's Caucus, Episcopal Communicators. Democrat. Home and Office: 501 Somerton Ave Philadelphia PA 19116-2026 E-mail: pam.darling@ecunet.org.

DARLING, ROBERT EDWARD, designer, stage director; b. Oakland, Calif., Oct. 1, 1937; s. Irving Jackson and Helen Ellen (Hebel) D.; m. Ann Farris, Aug. 22, 1970. BA, San Francisco State U., 1959; M.F.A., Yale U. Sch. Drama, 1963; student, Bayreuth Festspiel Meisterclasse, 1965. Creative problem solving, idea design/graphic facilatation and transition mgr. MG Taylor Corp., 1984—; with Robert Darling & Assoc., Darling Assoc. Garden Design, 1991—, DTE Energy Learing Zone, 2000—01. Former mem. opera-musical theatre policy panel Nat. Endowment for Arts; panelist Nat. Opera Inst., Nat. Inst. for Music Theater, OPERA Am., 1997—. Designer, dir. numerous opera, theatre and ballet prodns. throughout U.S. and Can., 1960—; N.Y.C. debut with Another Evening with Harry Stoones, 1962; San Francisco Opera debut with L'Elisir d'Amore, 1967; Santa Fe Opera debut with Anna Bolena, 1970, Chgo. Lyric Opera debut with Don Carlo, 1972; N.Y.C. Opera debut with Der Fliegende Hollander, 1976, Hidden Valley Opera Don Giovanni, 1975, Seattle Opera Tannhaüser, 1984; dir. and designer world premiers of Medea, 1972, Colonel Johnathan the Saint, 1972, The Infanta, 1975, The Last of the Mohicans, 1976, The Face on the Barroom Floor, 1978, Soyazhe, 1979, Freddy the Leaf, 1987, 90-91, Recollections RLS, 1993, Williamstown Theatre Festival debut season J.B., 1963, Williamstown Theatre Festival: Marat/Sade, 1990, Speed The Plow, 1991, Miami City Ballet, Pan Nuit Suite, Jewels, 1993, debut Utah Festival Opera (Pagliacci, Gianni Schicchi), 1998; dramaturg-Coyote Tales Score, Kansas City Lyric Opera, 1998, Hidden Valley Opera La Boheme, 2002; artistic coord. Spring Opera Theatre, San Francisco, 1972, artistic adv. Kans. City (Mo.) Lyric Theatre, 1973; co-founder, prin. dir. Hidden Valley Opera Ensemble, Carmel, Calif., 1974-77; artistic dir. Central City Opera House Assn., Denver, 1977-82, Hidden Valley Opera, 1985-89, 2002—; illustrations, E.C. Schirmer, 2000; artistic prodr. Acorn Theatre, Washington, 1988—; site coord., founding mem. Alliance for New Music-Theater, 1994—; designs represented in collection Am. design Smithsonian Mus., Mus. of the City of N.Y., Prague Quadrennial Scenographic Design, 1987; contbr. articles to profl. jours. Mem. United Scenic Artists, Am. Guild Mus. Artists, Actors Equity-Can., OPERA Am., Logan Circle Assn., Washington Daffodil Soc. (past pres.). Democrat. Lutheran. E-mail: darlingr@aol.com.

DARLING, SCOTT EDWARD, lawyer; b. Los Angeles, Dec. 31, 1949; s. Dick R. and Marjorie Helen (Otto) D.; m. Cynthia Diane Harrah, June 1970 (div.); 1 child, Smokie; m. Deborah Lee Cochran, Aug. 22, 1981; children: Ryan, Jacob, Guinevere. BA, U. Redlands, 1972; JD, U.S.C., 1975. Bar: Calif. 1976, U.S. Dist. Ct. (cen. dist.) Calif. 1976. Assoc. atty. Elver, Falsetti, Boone & Crafts, Riverside, 1976-78; ptnr. Falsetti, Crafts, Pritchard & Darling, Riverside, 1978-84; pres. Scott Edward Darling, A Profl. Corp., Riverside, 1984—. Grant reviewer HHS, Washington, 1982-88; judge pro tem Riverside County Mcpl. Ct., 1980, Riverside County Superior Ct., 1987-88; bd. dirs. Tel Law Nat. Legal Pub. Info. System, Riverside, 1978-80. Author, editor: Small Law Office Computer Legal System, 1984. Bd. dirs. Youth Adv. Com. to Selective Svc., 1968-70, Am. Heart Assn. Riverside County, 1978-82, Survival Ministries, 1986-89; atty. panel Calif. Assn. Realtors, L.A., 1980—; pres. Calif. Young Reps., 1978-80; mem. GI Forum, Riverside, 1970-88; presdl. del. Nat. Rep. Party, 1980-84; asst. treas. Calif. Rep. Party, 1981-83, Rep. Congl. candidate, Riverside, 1982; treas. Riverside Sickle Cell Found., 1980-82, recipient Eddie D. Smith award; pres. Calif. Rep. Youth Caucus, 1980-82; v.p. Riverside County Red Cross, 1982-84; mem. Citizen's Univ. Com., Riverside, 1978-84, World Affairs Council, 1978-82, Urban League, Riverside, 1980-82. Calif. Scholarship Fedn. (life). Named one of Outstanding Young Men in Am., U.S. Jaycees, 1979-86. Mem. ABA, Riverside County Bar Assn., Speaker's Bur. Riverside County Bar Assn., Riverside Jaycees, Riverside C. of C. Lodges: Native Sons of Golden West. Avocations: skiing, swimming, reading. Office: 3697 Arlington Ave Riverside CA 92506-3938

DARLINGTON, DAVID ALAN, government relations professional; b. Providence, Sept. 4, 1962; s. Fred Jr. and Joan Catherine (Greene) D.; m. Erin P. Carroll. BA in Polit. Sci., Marquette U., 1984. Office mgr. Olde Discount Stockbroker, Madison, Wis., 1984-85; fin. cons. Merryl Lynch, Madison, 1985-86; owner, dir. of sales Am. Securities and Rsch., Providence, 1986-87; collections supr. AT&T, Providence, 1987-88; svc. rep. Nynex Corp., Marlboro, Mass., 1988-94; dir. scheduling, programs Gov. State of R.I., Providence, 1994-2000; dir. govt. rels. 3M New England, 2000—01; campaign mgr. Bennett for Gov. 2002, 2001—02; pres. MITKEM Corp., 2002—. Sec. R.I. Small Bus. Adv. Coun., Providence, 1996-99, sec. N.E. Alternative Vehicle Corp., Boston, 1997—; pres. bd. dirs. New Eng. Trade Adjustment, Boston, 1996—. Mem. R.I. Tpk. and Bridge Authority, Quonsett Point Davisville Mgmt. Bd.; vice chair R.I. State Planning Coun., 1995—98, R.I. Cmty. Devel. Block Grant Bd., 1995—; mem. R.I. Aviation Edn. Corp.; mem. exec. com. R.I. Rep. Party, Providence, 1990—; chmn. candidate selection com. R.I. Grand Old Party, Providence, 1990—96, Cumberland (R.I.) Rep. Com., 1992—94. Mem. Am. Mgmt. Assn., U.S. Ombudsman Assn., East Greenwich Yacht Club, PRovince Art Club, Capitol Hill Club, Quidresset Country Club. Roman Catholic. Avocations: yachting, politics. Office: 175 Metro Ctr Blvd Warwick RI 02886 E-mail: ddarlington@mitkem.com.

DARLINGTON, HENRY, JR., investment broker; b. N.Y.C., Jan. 8, 1925; s. Henry and Dorothy (Stone-Smith) D.; m. Frances Elizabeth Richardson, June 5, 1948 (div. Feb. 1965); children: Henry Darlington III, Elizabeth Aldrich, Victoria Wilde Darlington Yoder; m. Dorothea Fiske Page, July 1965 (div. Dec. 1973); m. Carla P. Barratt-Brown, June 1990. BA, Columbia U., 1949; LHD (hon.), St. Paul's Coll., Lawrenceville, Va., 1987. Salesman IBM, 1949-52; security salesman Cosgrave, Miller & Whitehead, 1952-55; gen. ptnr. Hill, Darlington & Co., 1955-62; v.p. B.J. Van Ingen & Co., Inc., 1956-59; registered rep. Cruttenden, Podesta and Miller, 1962; with syndicate dept. Loeb, Rhoades & Co., 1962-64, br. office adminstr., 1964-67, v.p., 1967-71, registered rep., 1972-79; investment exec. Shearson Loeb Rhoades, Inc. (now Salomon, Smith Barney), 1979-92. Trustee Hoosac Sch., Hoosick, N.Y., 1968-75, Ch. Heavenly Rest Day Sch., N.Y.C., 1968-74, Search and Care, N.Y.C., 1972-87, vestryman Ch. Heavenly Rest, 1969-75; bd. dirs. Fedn. Protestant Welfare Agys., 1962-89, asst. treas., 1971-79; bd. dirs. Episcopal Mission Soc., 1979-89, St. Paul's Ch., Rome, 1975-99, St. James' Ch., Florence, Italy; trustee Bd. Fgn. Parishes, 1975-97; warden Eglise Francaise du Saint Esprit, 1984-88. With USNR, 1943-46, lt. Res., 1946-65. Named to Order Ky. Cols. Mem. SAR, St. Nicholas Soc. (pres. 1976-78), S.R., St. Andrews Soc., St. George's Soc., The Soc. of the Cin., The Huguenot Soc. (pres. 1986-89), Soc. Colonial Wars in the State of N.Y. (gov. 1991-93), Mil. Order of World Wars (N.Y. chpt.), N.Y. Soc. Mil. and Naval Officers World War, Navy League U.S. (past sec., treas. We. Conn. Coun.), Naval Order, Pilgrim Soc., The Soc. of the Cin., St. George's Soc., Most Venerable Order of Hosp. of St. John of Jerusalem, Army and Navy Club, Union Club, Univ. Club, Everglades Club, Piping Rock Club, Delta Psi (trustee Alpha chpt. 1953-58). Home: 1115 5th Ave New York NY 10128-0100

DARLINGTON, RICHARD BENJAMIN, psychology educator; b. Woodbury, N.J., Nov. 16, 1937; s. Charles Joseph and Eleanor (Collins) D.; m. Elizabeth Day, June 13, 1959; children: Jean Susan, Lois Heather. BA, Swarthmore Coll., 1959; PhD, U. Minn., 1963. Asst. prof. psychology Cornell U., Ithaca, N.Y., 1963-68, assoc. prof., 1968-80, prof., 1980—. Author: Radicals and Squares, 1975, (with others) Lasting Effects of Early Education, 1982, (with Patricia M. Carlson) Behavioral Statistics: Logic and Methods, 1987, Regression and Linear Models, 1990; contbr. articles to profl. jours.; contbr. chpts. to books. Project dir. Am. Friends Service Com., 1960, 61. Fellow NSF, 1959-60; fellow Woodrow Wilson Found., 1959-60; grantee HEW, 1977-81, Office of Edn., 1966-67, 70-71, Dept. of Labor, 1980-81 Fellow AAAS; mem. Phi Beta Kappa Mem. Soc. Of Friends. Home: 204 Fairmount Ave Ithaca NY 14850-4804 Office: Cornell Univ Dept Psychology Uris H Ithaca NY 14853

DARLOW, GEORGE ANTHONY GRATTON, investor; b. Rochester, N.Y., June 16, 1938; s. Alfred Miltenberger and Lillian (Gratton) D.; m. Helen Julia Donovan, Mar. 2, 1971 (div.); 1 child, Gillian Darlow Jones; m. Christiana Sewall Alden (div.). BA, Yale U., 1961; JD, Columbia U., 1971; LLD, Yale U., 1979, Columbia U., 1979, U. Rochester, 1979, Sweet Briar Coll., 1979. Trustee Am. Indian Archeol. Inst., Washington, Conn., 1973-93; chmn., trustee Inst. Am. Indian Studies, Washington, Conn., 1993—. With USN, 1961-64; lic. capt. USCG. Mem. Colony Found. (trustee 1995—), Ancient Free Accepted Masons (32nd Degree), Rotary Internat., Berzelius Soc., Beta Theta Pi, Lions Club, Yale Club (N.Y.C.), Royal Palm Yacht Club, Mory's (New Haven). Republican. Episcopalian. Home: 18925 S River Rd Alva FL 33920

DARLOW, JULIA DONOVAN, lawyer; b. Detroit, Sept. 18, 1941; d. Frank William Donovan and Helen Adele Turner; m. George Anthony Gratton Darlow (div.); 1 child, Gillian; m. John Corbett O'Meara. AB, Vassar Coll., 1963; postgrad., Columbia U. Law Sch., 1964-65; JD cum laude, Wayne State U., 1971. Bar: Mich. 1971, U.S. Dist. Ct. (ea. dist.) Mich. 1971. Assoc. Dickinson, Wright, McKean, Cudlip & Moon, Detroit, 1971-78; ptnr. Dickinson, Wright, Moon, Van Dusen & Freeman and predecessor, Detroit, 1978—2001; sr. v.p. Detroit Med. Ctr., 2001—01; cons. mem. Dickinson, Wright PLLC, Detroit, 2002—. Adj. prof. Wayne State U. Law Sch., 1974-75, 96; commr. State Bar Mich., 1977-87, mem. exec. com., 1979-83, 84-87, sec. 1980-81, v.p., 1984-85, pres.-elect 1985-86, pres. 1986-87, coun. corp. fin. and bus. law sect. 1980-86, coun. computer law sect. 1985-88; mem. State Officers Compensation Commn., 1994-96; chair Mich. Supreme Ct. Task Force on Gender Issues in the Cts., 1987-89. Bd. dirs. Hutzel Hosp., 1984—2003, chair, 2002—03; bd. dirs. Mich. Opera Theatre, 1985—, Mich. Women's Found., 1986—91, Detroit Med. Ctr., 1990—2003, Marygrove Coll., 1996—; trustee Internat. Inst. Met. Detroit, 1986—92; trustee Mich. Met. coun. Girl Scouts USA, 1988—91; trustee Detroit coun. Boy Scouts Am., 1988—; mem. exec. com. Mich. Coun. Humnanities, 1988—92; mem. Blue Cross-Blue Shield Prospective Reimbursement Com., Detroit, 1979—81; v.p., mem. exec. com. United Found., 1988—95; mem. Mich. Gov.'s Bilateral Trade Team for Germany, 1992—98. Fellow Am. Bar Found. (Mich. State chairperson 1990-96; mem. state officers compensation commn., 1994-96); mem. Detroit Bar Assn. Found. (treas. 1984-85, trustee 1982-85), Mich. Bar Found. (trustee 1987-94), Am. Judicature Soc. (bd. dirs. 1985-88), Internat. Women's Forum (global affairs com. 1994—), Women Lawyers Assn. (pres. 1977-78), Mich. Women's Campaign Fund (charter), Detroit Athletic Club. Democrat. Office: Dickinson Wright PLLC 500 Woodward Ave Ste 4000 Detroit MI 48226-3416

DARMAN, RICHARD, investor, educator; b. Charlotte, N.C., May 10, 1943; m. Kathleen Emmet, Sept. 1, 1967; children: William Temple Emmet, Jonathan Warren Emmet, Christopher Temple Emmet. BA cum laude, Harvard U., 1964, MBA, 1967, DSc (hon.); DLaw (hon.). Dep. asst. sec. HEW, Washington, 1971-72; asst. to sec. Dept. Def., Washington, 1973; spl. asst. to atty. gen. Washington, 1973; fellow Woodrow Wilson Internat. Center for Scholars, Washington, 1974; prin., dir. ICF, Inc., Washington, 1975, 77-80; asst. sec. Dept. Commerce, 1976-77; lectr. public policy and mgmt. Harvard U., 1977-80; asst. to Pres. Reagan, The White House, Washington, 1981-85; dep. sec. Dept. Treasury, 1985-87; mng. dir. Shearson Lehman Hutton Inc., N.Y.C., 1987-88; dir. office mgmt. and budget, mem. Pres. Cabinet The White House, Washington, 1989-93; prof. JFK Sch. Govt. Harvard U., 1998—2002; ptnr. The Carlyle Group, 1993—. Bd. dirs. Frontier Ventures Corp., 1993—, AES Corp., 2002—, vice chmn., 2002, chmn., 2003—. Editor: Harvard Ednl. Rev, 1970; contbg. editor U.S. News & World Report, 1987-88; author: Who's in Control?, 1996; contbr. articles to profl. jours. Trustee Bennington Coll., Vt., 1974—75, The Brookings Inst., 1987—88; bd. dirs. Smithsonian Nat. Mus. Am. History, 2000—, vice chmn. bd., 2003—; trustee Coun. for Excellence in Govt., 1995—2002, CDC Nvest Funds, 1996—, Loomis Sayles Funds, 2003—; mem. overseers com. to visit Kennedy Sch. Govt. Harvard U., 1988—98, Harvard Med. Sch., 1994—99, to visit Kennedy Sch. Govt. Harvard U., 2003—. Office: The Carlyle Group 1001 Pennsylvania Ave NW Washington DC 20004-2505

DARMSTAETTER, JAY EUGENE, secondary education educator; b. Altadena, Calif., Nov. 30, 1937; s. Eugene Jamison and Virginia (Fagans) D. AA, L.A. City Coll., 1958; BA, L.A. State Coll., 1960, MA, 1962; postgrad., U. So. Calif., 1962-65. Cert. secondary edn. tchr., secondary adminstr. Tchr. L.A. Unified Schs., 1960-98, athletic dir., 1965-83; tng. tchr. UCLA, Calif. State U., Whittier Coll., L.A., 1966—; master tchr. L.A. Unified Schs., 1983-84. Announcer L.A. Unified Schs., 1970—, CIF/So. Section, Artesia, Calif., 1964-85, State CIF, Fullerton, Calif., 1970-85. Soloist Christian Sci. Chs., L.A., 1958—; mem. Citizens Community Planning Coun., L.A. County, 1989-96. Recipient Nat. Def. Edn. Assn. award Dept. of Edn., L.A., 1968. Mem. NEA, Calif. Tchrs. Assn., United Tchrs. L.A., Temple City Rep. Club, Meth. Hosp. of So. Calif. Friends Soc., Rose Soc. (charter), Phi Mu Alpha Sinfonia Soc. Republican. Avocations: music, reading. Office: Wilson High/LA Schools 4500 Multnomah St Los Angeles CA 90032-3703

DARMSTANDLER, HARRY MAX, real estate executive, retired air force officer; b. Indpls., Aug. 9, 1922; s. Max M. and Nonna (Holden) D.; m. Donna L. Bender, Mar. 10, 1957; children: Paul William, Thomas Alan. BS, U. Omaha, 1964; MS, George Washington U., 1965; grad., Nat. War Coll., 1965. Commd. 2d lt. USAAF, 1943; advanced through grades to maj. gen. USAF, 1973; served with (15th Air Force), Europe, 1943, (5th Air Force), Korea, 1952; comdr.-in-chief Pacific, 1960-63; served with joint chiefs of staff, 1965-68; supreme comdr. (Allied Powers Europe), 1969-71; comdr. 12th Air Div. SAC, 1972, dep. chief of staff for plans, 1973; spl. asst. to chief of staff USAF, 1974-75; chmn. bd. and chief exec. officer Rancho Bernardo Savs. Bank, San Diego, 1983-90; ptnr. Allied Assocs., Colorado Springs, Colo., 1968—, D & H Inc., Woodland Park, Colo., 1979—; founding ptnr. Assocs. Group, San Diego, 1995—. Cons. Mid East matters and bd. dirs. Palomar Pomerado Health Found, San Diego; bd. dirs. Clean Found., San Diego. Author numerous articles on nat. def. requirements. Elder, Rancho Bernardo Community Presbyn. Ch., San Diego. Decorated D.S.M. with oak leaf cluster, Legion of Merit with oak leaf cluster, D.F.C., Air medal with 3 oak leaf clusters; research fellow UCLA, 1969. Mem. AIAA, Order Daedalians, Soc. Strategic Air Command, Eagle Scout Alumni Assn., Bernardo Heights Country Club (San Diego, past pres.), Phi Tau Alpha. Home: La Jolla Village Towers 8515 Costa Verde Blvd #1707 San Diego CA 92122

DARNALL, ROBERTA MORROW, association executive; b. Kemmerer, Wyo., May 18, 1949; d. C. Dale and Eugenia Stayner (Christmas) Morrow; m. Leslie A. Darnall, Sept. 3, 1977; children: Kimberly Gene, Leslie Nicole. BS, U. Wyo., Laramie, 1972. Tariff sec., ins. adminstr. Wyo Trucking Assn., Casper, 1973-75; asst. clerical supr. Wyo. Legislature, Cheyenne, 1972-77, congrl. campaign press aide, 1974; pub. rels. dir. Casper, Wyo., Wyo. Rep. Ctr. Com., 1976-77; asst. dir. alumni rels. U. Wyo., 1977-81; exec. dir. Alumni Assn., 1981—. Bd. dir. Ivison Meml. Hosp. Found. Mem. St. Matthews Altar Guild (lector, usher, former acolyte, coord., mem. recognition and golf coms.), Higher Edn. Assn. Rockies, Am. Soc. Assn. Execs., Laramie C. of C. (past edn. com.), U. Wyo. Alumni Assn., Cowboy Joe Club, PEO (former courtesy com., officer). Republican. Episcopalian. Home: 15 Snowy View Ct Laramie WY 82070-5358 Office: PO Box 3137 Laramie WY 82071-3137 E-mail: robbie@uwyo.edu.

DARNELL, ALAN MARK, lawyer; b. N.Y.C., Dec. 6, 1946; s. Sidney and Serene (Rackow) D.; m. Joan Silverman, Sept. 5, 1971. B.A., U. Rochester, 1968; J.D., U. Pa., 1971. Bar: N.J. 1971. Assoc. Wilentz, Goldman & Spitzer, Woodbridge, N.J., 1971-79, ptnr., 1980— . Named Trial Lawyer of the Yr., Trial Lawyers for Pub. Justice, 1983. Mem. Assn. Trial Lawyers Am., Def. Research Assn., Middlesex County Bar Assn., N.J. Bar Assn. Democrat. Jewish. Home: 8 Old Weathersfield Rd Asbury Park NJ 07712-3325

DARNELL, DORIS HASTINGS, performance artist; b. Chgo., Sept. 14, 1916; d. Willard Seth and Faith Emily (Olmstead) Hastings; m. Howard Clayton Darnell, Aug. 27, 1938; children: Elizabeth Loyd, John Hastings, Eric Allen. BA in Latin, Bryn Mawr Coll., 1939. Head resident, asst. to dir. Pendle Hill Grad. Sch. Religious and Social Concerns, Wallingford, Pa., 1939-40; libr. Res. Rm. and sci. Bryn Mawr (Pa.) Coll., 1950-52; acting head libr. Westtown (Pa.) Friends Sch., 1952-53; head libr. Westtown Sch., 1954-55; libr. Res. Rm. Haverford (Pa.) Coll., 1953-54; exec. dir., editor Westtown Alumni Assn., 1955-64; from coord. recruitment to assoc. exec. sec. pers. Am. Friends Svc. Com., Phila., 1964-78; creator, owner A Century of Elegance in Costume and Story, State College, Pa., 1980—. Gov. com. Pendle Hill, Westtown Sch., Friends Select Sch., Pa., 1948—78; mem. Rufus Jones Assocs., Haverford Coll.; founding trustee Allen Hilles Fund, 1982—91, trustee emerita, 1991—; lectr., exhibitor 19th and 20th century fashions, 1980—. Mem.: Women's Nat. History Mus., Women in the Arts, Internat., Palmer Art Mus., Costume Soc. Am. Mem. Soc. Of Friends. Home and Office: #C 36 500 Marylyn Ave State College PA 16801 E-mail: eleganztoo@aol.com.

DARNELL, JAMES ORAL, lawyer; b. Oklahoma City, May 3, 1955; s. Victor Lee and Eileen (Bliss) D.; m. Susan Marie Cheslousky, Aug. 5, 1978; children: James Oral Jr., Jake Morris. AB cum laude, Dartmouth Coll.; JD cum laude, So. Meth. U. Bar: Tex. 1980, U.S. Dist. Ct. (we. dist.) Tex. 1982, U.S. Ct. Appeals (5th cir.) 1986, U.S. Dist. Ct. (no. dist.) Tex. 1987, U.S. Ct. Claims 1994, U.S. Supreme Ct. 1997. Ptnr. Grambling & Mounce, El Paso, Tex., 1980-90; pvt. practice El Paso, 1990-91; pntr. Grambling/Darnell, El Paso, 1991-95; sole practitioner Jim Darnell P.C., El Paso, 1995—. Mem. dist. 17 grievance com. State Bar Tex., 1986—92. Worker Sun Bowl Assn., 1981-82; chmn. com. Southwestern Internat. Livestock Show and Rodeo, Inc., 1982-97, bd. dirs., 1987-97, asst. v.p., 1989-90, exec. v.p., 1990-91, vice chmn., 1991-94, CEO, 1994-97; bd. dirs. El Paso Svcs. for Children, 1982, pres., 1984-85; bd. dirs. YMCA, 1984-90; participant Leadership El Paso, 1985; mem. exec. com. Yucca coun. Boy Scouts Am., 1990-2000. Mem. ABA, Am. Bd. Trial Advocates (pres. El Paso chpt. 1998), Tex. Bar Assn., Tex. Young Lawyers Assn., Tex. Criminal Def. Lawyers Assn., (assoc. dir. 1992-94, exec. com. 1995-97), El Paso Criminal Def. Lawyers Assn. (bd. dirs. 1988, v.p. 1989-90), El Paso Young

Lawyers Assn. (bd. dirs. 1983-85, treas. 1985-86), El Paso Legal Assistance Soc. (bd. dirs. 1982—, chmn. 1986-88), Tex. Trial Lawyers Assn., Tex. Bar Found., Nat. Assn. Criminal Def. Lawyers, El Paso Bar Assn. (bd. dirs. 1997-98). Democrat. Baptist. Avocations: basketball, baseball, horses, cattle, football. Home: 5 Paseo De Paz El Paso TX 79932-3501 Office: 310 N Mesa St Ste 212 El Paso TX 79901-1301 E-mail: jdarnell@jdarnell.com

DARNELL, RILEY CARLISLE, state government official, lawyer; b. Clarksville, Tenn., May 13, 1940; s. Elliott Sinclair and Mary Anita (Whitefield) D.; m. Mary Penelope Crockarell, June 2, 1963; children: Neil Whitefield, Duncan Edward, Mary Eve, Penelope Joy, Dawson Riley. BS, Austin Peay State U., 1962; JD, Vanderbilt U., 1965. Bar: Tenn. 1965. Gen. practice, Clarksville, 1965-66, 69—. Mem. Tenn. Ho. of Reps. from 67th Dist., 1971-80, treas. house-senate caucus, 1971-86, sec. house com. ways and means, chmn. joint house-senate fiscal rev. com., 1975-80; mem. Tenn. State Senate, 1980-92, chmn. transp. com., 1982-86, chmn. joint com. children and youth, 1987-89; senate majority leader, 1988-92; sec. of state State of Tenn., Nashville, 1993—. Served to Capt. JAGC, USAF, 1966-69. Fellow Tenn. Bar Found.; mem. ABA, Montgomery County Bar Assn., Tenn. Trial Lawyers, Tenn. Bar Assn., Nat. Conf. State Legislators (jud. task force), So. Legis. Conf. (mem. fiscal affairs com.), Clarksville C. of C., Moose, Clarksville Downtown Civitan Club. Democrat. Mem. Ch. Of Christ. Office: William A Snodgrass Tower 6th Fl 312 8th Ave N Nashville TN 37243 E-mail: riley.darnell@state.tn.us.

DARNELL, WILLIAM HEADEN, chemical engineer, medical/surgical nurse, nursing educator; b. Roanoke, Va., May 14, 1925; s. William Lee and Edythe Headen (Scott) Darnell; m. Kathryn Jane McManaway, June 3, 1950; 1 child, William Jamison. BS, Va. Poly. Inst. and State U., 1950; MS, U. Wis., 1951, PhD, 1953; ASN, Tri-County Tech. Coll., 1989. RN S.C., 1989. Prodn. asst. Merck Pharm. Co., Elkton, Va., 1946; rsch. engr., supr. E.I. du Pont de Nemours Co., Wilmington, Del., 1953—60, nylon tech. supt. Victoria, Tex., 1960—63, R&D mgr. Wilmington, Del., 1963—72, lab. adminstr., environmental mgr., 1972—85; RN staff Oconee Meml. Hosp. Inc., Seneca, SC, 1989—2001; pvt. practice RN educator Salem, SC, 2001—. Contbr. engring. handbook, articles to profl. jours. Chpt. pres. Rotary Internat., Wilmington, 1970—71, dist. sec., NJ, Del., 1971—72; elected judge of elections Kennett Twp., Kennett Square, Pa., 1976—78; mem. state bd. dirs. Am. Cancer Soc., Wilmington, 1968—70; bd. dirs., pres. Advanced Life Support, Inc., West Grove, Pa., 1982—87, Hospice of the Foothills, Inc., Seneca, SC, 1987—. 2d lt. U.S. Army, 1943—53, ETO, PTO. Recipient Best Tech. Paper award, AIChE, 1959; fellow, NSF, Washington, 1952. Mem.: SAR (chpt. pres. 1985—, Patriot award 1994), Nat. Soc. SAR (trustee 1996—97), S.C. Soc. SAR (state pres. 1994—96). Republican. Presbyterian. Avocations: music, furniture reproductions, swimming. Home: 7 Gybe Ho Ct Salem SC 29676

DARNELL, YOLANDA (YOLANDA DARNELL), videomaker, filmmaker, writer; b. L.A., May 23, 1960; d. Charles and Hortense (Decatur) Washington. Student, U. So. Calif., L.A., 1978-83, 85-86, UCLA, 1984-86. Pres. First Choice Entertainment, Lynwood, Calif., 1989—. Author: After the Dance, 1976, Heresay, 1995, Ten Weeks, 1997; prodr., writer, choreographer: young adult soap Almost There, 1988—93, prodr., writer, dir.: films Until Tomorrow Comes, 1992; author: Terror in the Darkness, 2003; prodr., writer, dir.: films, 2003; prodr.: (soundtrack) Terror in the Darkness, 2003; actor:, 2003. Democrat. Avocations: martial arts, cooking, phys. fitness, modern dance. Office: First Choice Entertainment/NVP PO Box 54502 Phoenix AZ 85078-4502

DARNELL, YOLANDA *See* **DARNELL, YOLANDA**

DARNTON, ROBERT CHOATE, history educator; b. N.Y.C., May 10, 1939; s. Byron and Eleanor (Choate) D.; m. Susan Lee Glover, June 29, 1963; children: Nicholas Campbell, Catherine Choate, Margaret Townsend. BA, Harvard U., 1960; BPhil, Oxford U., Eng., 1962, DPhil, 1964. Reporter N.Y. Times, N.Y.C., 1964; jr. fellow Harvard U., 1964-68; asst. prof. history Princeton U., N.J., 1968-71, assoc. prof., 1971-72, prof., 1972—. Author: Mesmerism and the End of the Enlightenment in France, 1968, The Business of Enlightenment: A Publishing History of the Encyclopédie, 1775-1800, 1979 (Am. Hist. Assn. Leo Gershoy prize 1979), The Literary Underground of the Old Regime, 1982, The Great Cat Massacre and Other Episodes in French Cultural History, 1984 (L.A. Times book prize), The Kiss of Lamourette: Reflections in Cultural History, 1989, Edition et Sédition, L'univers de la littérature clandestine au XVIII e siècle, 1991 (Prix Chateaubriand), Berlin Journal, 1989-90, 1991, Gens de lettres, gens du livre, 1992, The Forbidden Best-Sellers of Pre-Revolutionary France, 1995 (Nat. Book Critics Circle award 1996), The Corpus of Clandestine Literature in France, 1995, Jacques-Pierre Brissot, His Career and Correspondence, 1779-1787, 2001, George Washington's False Teeth. An Unconventional Guide to the Eighteenth Century, 2003. Decorated officer Ordre des Arts et des Lettres, chevalier Légion d'Honneur, 1999; recipient Koren prize Soc. French Hist. Studies, 1973, MacArthur Found. prize, 1982. Fellow Am. Acad. Arts and Scis., Am. Philos. Soc., Brit. Acad. (corr. 2001); mem. Am. Hist. Assn. (pres.-elect 1998, pres. 1999-2000), Am. Soc. 18th-Century Studies (Clifford prize 1971, 73), Internat. Soc. 18th-Century Studies (pres. 1987-1992), Academia Europaea, Belgian Royal Acad. French Lang. and Lit. Office: Princeton U Dept History Princeton NJ 08540

DAROFF, ROBERT BARRY, neurologist, educator; b. NYC, Aug. 3, 1936; s. Charles and May (Wolin) D.; m. Jane L. Abrahams, Dec. 4, 1959; children: Charles II, Robert Barry, Jr., William Clayton BA, U. Pa., 1957, MD, 1961. Intern Phila. Gen. Hosp., 1961-62; resident in neurology Yale-New Haven Med. Center, 1962-65; fellow in neuro-ophthalmology U. Calif. Med. Center, San Francisco, 1967-68; prof. neurology, assoc. prof. ophthalmology U. Miami (Fla.) Med. Sch.; also dir. ocular motor neurophysiology lab. Miami VA Med. Center, 1968-80; Gilbert W. Humphrey prof., chmn. dept. neurology Case Western Res. U. Med. Sch.; also dir. dept. neurology Univ. Hosps., Cleve., 1980-93; prof. neurology Case Western U., 1980—, assoc. dean, 1994—2003; staff neurologist Cleve. VA Med. Ctr., 1980-93; chief of staff, sr. v.p. acad. affairs U. Hosp., Cleve., 1994—2003. Med. sci. adv. bd., chmn. sci. program com. Myasthenia Gravis Found., 1984—87, exec. com., 1992—2003, sec., 1995—96, vice chair, 1997—99, chair, 1999—2001, chair nominating com., 2002—03; adv. bd. Nat. Multiple Sclerosis Found., 1988—90, Soc. Progressive Supranuclear Palsy, 1991—94; nat. adv. eye coun. sensory and motor disorders vision panel NIH, 1980—83; steering com. neurological disorders in comml. drivers U.S. Dept. Transp., chmn. task force, 1987; lectr. T.S. Srinivasan Endowment, Madras, India, 1994; Cumings lectr. Migraine Trust, London, 1994; lectr. Am. Coun. Headache Edn., 1996, vice chair, 2000—02; Soriano lectr., Israel, 2001; prof. (hon.) Astana-State Med. Acad., Kazakhstan, 1999; bd. advisors Capnia, Inc., 2000—. Book rev. editor: Neuro-ophthalmology, 1981-86, mem. editl. bd., 1987-2003; assoc. editor Jour. Biomed. Sys., 1970-72; editor Neurol. Progress, Anns. Neurology, 1981-84; editor-in-chief Neurology, 1987-96; co-editor World Neurology, 1991-98, editl. adv. bd. 1998—; mem. editl. bd. Archives of Neurology, 1976, Annals of Neurology, 1977-86, Neurology and Neurosurgery Update Series, 1978-93, Headache, 1980-86, Contemporary Neurology Series, 1989-93, Neurosci., 2003, Practical Neurology, 2003—; mem. editl. coun. Neurologia Croatica, 1991—; mem. editl. commn. Valeology, 2002-; contbr. articles to profl. jours. Chmn. Young Tae Kwon Do Acad., North Miami, 1977-80; bd. dirs. Benign Essential Blepharospasm Rsch. Found., 1983—; trustee Fairhill Ctr. for Aging, 1988—, The Learning Corp., 1992-2000, Edison Bio Tech. Ctr., 1994-2001, Great Lakes Sci. Ctr., 1994-2001, Myasthenia Gravis Found. Am., 1999-2001; mem. tech. adv. coun. BIOMEC, Inc., 1999—; bd. trustees Greater Cleve. chpt. ARC, 1999--, mem. exec. com., 2000-. Served with M.C. USAR, 1965-67. Recipient Ernst Jung-Medaille Für Medizin in Gold, 1993, Silver Jubilee Oration award Med. Coll. Trivandrum, India, 1994, John H. Budd Disting. Mem. award Cleve. Acad. Med., 2002, Disting. Grad. award U. Pa., 2003. Fellow: Am. Headache Soc. (pres. 2002, bd. dirs., sec.); mem.: AMA, Internat. Headache Soc., Neuromuscular Disease Assn. Romania (internat. sci. com. 1991—93), Acad. Med. Scis. Kazakhstan, Alliance Brain Initiatives (founding mem.), Dana Found., Coun. Sci. Editors, Asociación Colombiana Neurologia (hon.), Am. Neurol. Assn. (hon.; program adv. com. 1977—78, chmn. 1978, councillor 1980—82, membership adv. com. 1980—83, chmn. 1981—83, nominating com. 1984, chmn. Annals of Neurology oversight com. 1984—86, sec. 1985—89, pres.-elect 1989—90, pres. 1990—91, past pres. 1991—92), Am. Acad. Neurology (hon.; chmn. sci. program com. 1973—75, exec. bd. 1987—96, Netter lectr. 1989, pub. com. 1993—2001), World Fedn. Neurology (fin. com. 1985—, exec. com. Rsch. group on Neuro-Ophthalmology 1987—95, publs. com. 1987—, chmn. 1990—2001), Clin. Eye Movement Soc. (founder), Barany Soc., Internat. Neuro-Ophthalmology Soc. (organizing com. 1986), N.Am. Neuro-Ophthalmology Soc. (bd. dirs. 1986—94, chair cert. and accreditation com. 1997—98, publs. com. 1999—2001), Rocky Mountain Neuro-Ophthalmology Soc. (bd. dirs. 1980—86), Vietnam Vets Inst. (bd. scholars 1998—), Alpha Omega Alpha. Office: U Hosps Cleve 11100 Euclid Ave Cleveland OH 44106-1736 Business E-Mail: rbd2@cwru.edu.

DAROFF, WILLIAM CLAYTON, political organization executive, lawyer; b. Miami Beach, Fla., Nov. 30, 1968; s. Robert Barry and Jane Linda (Abrahams) D.; m. Heidi Ilyse Krizer, Aug. 31, 1997; children: Lillian Ahava Krizer Daroff, Arianna Reagan Krizer Daroff. BA summa cum laude, Case Western Reserve U., 1995, JD, MA in Polit. Sci., Case Western Reserve U., 1999. Bar: Ohio 1999, D.C. 2001. Lead advanceman Kemp for Pres., Washington, 1986-88, Bush-Quayle '88, Washington, 1988; spl. asst. U.S. Dept. Energy, Washington, 1989-90; campaign mgr. Brachman for State Treas., Columbus, Ohio, 1990; spl. asst. to gov. State of Ohio, Columbus, 1990-92; dep. dir. Ohio Dept. Liquor Control, Columbus, 1992-93; lead advanceman Dole-Kemp '96, Washington, 1996; assoc. Calfee, Halter & Griswold, LLP, Cleve., 1999-2000; dir. congl. affairs Rep. Jewish Coalition, Washington, 2000—01, dep. exec. dir., 2001—. Summer assoc. Calfee, Halter & Griswold, LLP, Cleve., 1998. Sports editor East Side News, 1984-86; mem. editl. bd. Pub. Pers. Mgmt., 1991-92. Rep. nominee for Ohio State Rep., 11th Dist., 1994; mem. exec. com. Cuyahoga County Rep. Party, Cleve., 1987-88, 91-2000, mem. ctrl. com., 1987-88, 94-2000, exec. vice chmn. 1997-2000; alt. del. Rep. Nat. Conv., 1996; co-chmn. candidate endorsement com. Cuyahoga County Rep. Party, 1997-2000; mem. edn. com., bd. dirs. Young Leadership Divsn., Cleve. Jewish Cmty. Fedn., 1997-2000, mem. cmty. rels. com., 1999-2000; bd. dirs. Cleve. chpt. Am. Jewish Com., 1999-2000, exec. com., 2000; mem. leadership cabinet Cleve. Israel Bonds com., 2000; bd. dirs. Ohio Jewish Communities, Inc., 1999-2000, Bellfaire Jewish Children's Bur., 2000. Named to Honorable Order of Ky. Cols., 1992; recipient Meritorious Svc. award Cleve. 4th Ward Rep. Club, 1989, 91, 93, Robert E. Hughes award Outstanding Svc., Cuyahoga County Rep. Party, 2000. Mem. NRA (life), Monday Thing Club (membership director 1989—), Case Western Res. U. Alumni Assn. (program com. 1998-2000). Republican. Jewish. Office: Rep Jewish Coalition 50 F St NW Ste 100 Washington DC 20001 E-mail: wdaroff@rjchq.org.

DA ROZA, VICTORIA CECILIA, human resources administrator; b. East Orange, N.J., Aug. 30, 1945; d. Victor and Cynthia Helen (Krupa) Hawkins; m. Thomas Howard Kaminski, Aug. 28, 1971 (div. 1977); 1 child, Sarah Hawkins; m. Robert Anthony da Roza, Nov. 25, 1983. BA, U. Mich., 1967; MA, U. Mo., 1968. Contract compliance mgr. City of San Diego, 1972-75; v.p. personnel Bank of Calif., San Francisco, 1975-77; with human resources Lawrence Livermore (Calif.) Nat. Lab., 1978-86; pvt. cons. Victoria Kaminski-da Roza & Assocs., 1986—. Lectr. in field; videotape workshop program on mid-career planning used by IEEE. Contbr. numerous articles to profl. jours. Mem. ASTD, Gerontol. Soc. Am., San Ramon Valley Genealogy Soc. (pres. 1999-01), P.E.O. (officer chpt. RV 1989-01). Home and Office: 888 Castle Rock Rd Walnut Creek CA 94598 E-mail: daRozal@go.com.

DARR, ALAN PHIPPS, curator, historian; b. Kankakee, Ill., Sept. 30, 1948; s. Milton Freeman, Jr. and Margaret (Phipps) D.; m. Mollie Hayden Fletcher, June 28, 1980; children: Owen, Alexander. BA, Northwestern U., 1970; MA, Inst. Fine Arts, NYU, 1975, PhD in Art History, 1980; Cert., Mus. Tng., Met. Mus. Art, 1976, Mus. Mgmt. Inst., U. Calif. Berkeley, 1980. Grad. intern Met. Mus. Art, N.Y.C., 1976; instr. NYU, 1976; asst. curator Detroit Inst. Arts, 1978-80, assoc. curator, 1980-81, curator in charge European sculpture and decorative arts, 1981—, Walter B. Ford II Family curator European sculpture and decorative arts, 1997—; postdoctoral fellow Harvard U. Ctr. for Italian Renaissance Studies at Villa I Tatti, Florence, 1988-89; adj. prof. Wayne State U., Detroit, 1982—; Paul Mellon vis. sr. scholar Ctr. Advanced Study in Visual Arts, Nat. Gallery, Washington, 1994. Co-editor/co-author: Italian Renaissance Sculpture in the Time of Donatello, 1985-86, Donatello Studien, 1989, Verrocchio and Late Quattrocentro Italian Sculpture, 1992, The Dodge Collection of Eighteenth Century French and English Art in the Detroit Institute of Arts, 1996, Woven Splendor: Five Centuries of European Tapestry in the Detroit Institute of Arts, 1996, Catalogue of Italian Sculpture in the Detroit Inst. of Art, 2 vols., 2002, The Medici, Michelangelo and the Art of Late Renaissance Florence, 2002, others; contbr. articles to profl. jours. Nat. Endowment Arts Mus. Profls. Fellow, 1983; John J. McCloy fellow, 1980-81, Ford Found. fellow, 1975-78, Met. Mus. Art fellow, 1975. Office: Detroit Inst Arts 5200 Woodward Ave Detroit MI 48202-4094

DARR, ANN RUSSELL, poet, educator; b. Bagley, Iowa, Mar. 13, 1920; d. Henry Horton and Lessie Rebecca (Hooper) Russell; m. George Campbell Darr, Nov. 7, 1941 (dic. Mar. 1981); children: Elizabeth Russell, Deborah Horton, Shannon Campbell. BA magna cum laude, State U. Iowa, 1941; postgrad., Harvard Coll., 1980, Am. U., 1981. Writer/actor NBC Radio, N.Y.C., 1941-43, 45-46; tape recs. for blind Libr. of Congress, Washington, 1950-60; instr. creative writing Poets in the Schs., Md., Va. and D.C., 1970-80, 92-93; co-dir. workshop Nethers (Va.) Arts Colony, 1979; poet/dir. Georgetown U., Washington, summer 1977-78; poet The Writers Ctr., Bethesda, Md., 1981—; adj. prof. dept. lit. Am. U., Washington, 1982—. Fine arts seminar poet Montgomery (Ala.) Seminars, summer 1975; poet-in-residence Columbia (S.C.) Coll., spring 1975, 76, Am. Wind Symphony aboard Point Counterpoint II, U.S., 1976, 86, Jamaica, 1981, Europe, 1989, Eckard Coll., St. Petersburg, Fla., spring 1977; workshop poet St. Mary's (Md.) Coll., spring 1981, 82, 94, 95, 98, 99; judge for poetry Eckerd Coll., St. Petersburg, Fla., 1977, Nat. Endowment for Arts, Washington, 1979, Radcliff Coll., Cambridge, Mass., 1980, New Eng. Poetry Soc., Boston, 1981; mem. lit. panel Nat. Endowment for Arts, 1979-80; mem. adv. com. Folger Libr. Poetry Series, Washington, 1974-96. Author: St. Ann's Gut, 1971, The Myth of a Woman's Fist, 1973, Cleared for Landing, 1978, Riding with the Fireworks, 1981, Do You Take This Woman..., 1986 (Pub. award 1986), The Twelve Pound Cigarette, 1991, Confessions of a Skewed Romantic, 1993, Flying the Zuni Mountains, 1994, Gussie, Mad Hannah & Me, 1999, Love In the Past Tense, 2000; editor: Hungry As We Are, 1995; author numerous poems, 1961-99; translator (with others) Reading the Ashes, 1978, (with others) After the First Rain, 1997; featured poet Nat. Mus. Radio and TV, 1997. Mem. election com. Somerset (Md.) Town Bd., 1975-79; vol. Arena Stage, Washington, 1949-52. With U.S. Army Airforce (Women's Airforce Svc. pilot), 1943-44, WWII. Recipient Bunting fellowship Radcliffe Coll., 1979-80, Discovery 70 award Poetry Ctr., N.Y.C., 1970, Yaddo fellowship Yaddo, 1979, 86, MacDowell fellowship MacDowell Found., 1979. Mem. White House Conf. for Poets, Poetry Soc. Am., Acad. Am. Poets, Phi Beta Kappa, Zeta Phi Eta. Avocations: flying, traveling, acting, reading, collecting birds. Home: Apt 101 3122 Gracefield Rd Silver Spring MD 20904 Office: Am Univ 4400 Massachusetts Ave NW Washington DC 20016-8001

DARR, MILTON FREEMAN, JR., banker; b. Oak Park, Ill., Oct. 30, 1921; s. Milton Freeman and Frances Anna (Kaiser) D.; m. Margaret Claire Phipps, Jan. 27, 1945; children: Alan Phipps, Bruce Milton. BS, U. Ill., 1942. With LaSalle Nat. Bank, Chgo., 1946-80, asst. cashier, 1950-53, asst. v.p., 1953, v.p., 1954-62, exec. v.p., dir., 1962-64, pres., 1964-68, chmn. bd., chief exec. officer, 1968-73, pres., 1974-77, vice chmn. bd., 1977-80. Organizer, founding dir. Buffalo Grove (Ill.) Nat. Bank, 1975; pres. Park Shore Tower Assn., Naples, Fla. Mem. Bd. Edn. Dist. 88 Community High Sch., 1963-68, Nat. Bd. YMCA's, 1973-77; past chmn., mem. Ill. Gov.'s Adv. Bd. on Cancer Control; chmn. commerce and industry com., treas. Chgo. Com. for Project Hope; state crusade chmn. Ill. div. Am. Cancer Soc., 1967, 68, chmn. bd., 1973-75, nat. bd. dirs., 1975-78; chmn. bd. mgrs., v.p. bd. trustees YMCA Met. Chgo., 1970-72; chmn. bd. trustees Elmhurst Coll., 1982-87, hon. life trustee, 1998—; chmn. YMCA Retirement Fund, 1986-92, trustee emeritus, 1994; trustee Ill. Cancer Council, Better Govt. Assn.; life trustee Union League Boys and Girls Clubs; chmn. Armed Forces Week, 1987; bd. dirs. Chgo. Crime Commn., United Charities of Chgo., Mid-Am. chpt. ARC; pres. Park Shore Tower Assn., Naples, Fla., 2001. Served to maj. USAAF, 1942-46. Recipient Distinguished Service award Am. Cancer Soc., 1976, Founders medal Elmhurst Coll., 1987; Citizen fellow Inst. Medicine of Chgo. Mem. Am. Inst. Banking (pres. Chgo. chpt. 1955-56, mem. exec. council 1956-59, nat. v.p. 1959-60, nat. pres. 1960-61), Am. Bankers Assn. (mem. adminstrv. com., exec. council 1960-61), Assn. Res. City Bankers (treas. 1969-72), Robert Morris Assos. (pres. Chgo. chpt. 1965-66), Chgo. Clearing House Assn. (past chmn.), Theta Chi. Clubs: Rotarian (pres. 1973-74, Paul Harris fellow, Ches Perry fellow), Chicago, Bankers (pres. 1973), Economic, Executives, Union League (pres. 1968-69), Commerical (life, treas.) (Chgo.); Glen Oak Country; Moorings Country Club of Naples, Fla. Presbyterian. Home: Residence N206 5 Oakbrook Club Dr Oak Brook IL 60523-6860 Office: 135 S La Salle St Chicago IL 60603-4159

DARR, WALTER ROBERT, financial analyst; b. Phila., June 19, 1956; s. John Fluke, Sr. and Lois Marilyn (Fry) Darr. BS in Commerce, Rider U., Lawrenceville, N.J., 1978, MBA, 1991. Collateral analyst First Nat. Bank & Trust Co., Beverly, NJ, 1978-84, First Peoples Bank N.J., Westmont, 1984-88, loan rev. analyst, 1988-92; loan acctg. tech. N.J. Nat. Bank, Trenton, 1992-93; sr. credit analyst Carnegie Bank, N.A., Princeton, NJ, 1993-94, asst. cashier, sr. credit analyst, 1994-97; credit officer, credit dept. supr. Broad Nat./Independence Cmty. Bank, Newark, 1997-99; asst. sec., bus. banking divsn. Ind. Cmty. Bank, Newark, 1999-2000, asst. v.p. SBA lending, 2001—; sr. underwriter, bus. banking div. Summit Bank, Dayton, NJ, 2000-2001. Treas. Cinnaminson (N.J.) Bapt. Ch., 1983—87, deacon, 1988—89, 1993—94; chmn.-treas. Mercer County chpt. Child Evangelism Fellowship N.J., 1996—99; mem. Lewis Shearer Chorale/Garden State Chorale, NJ, 1982—94. Recipient Sch. award, Am. Legion Post, Medford, N.J., 1974. Mem.: Rider U. Alumni Assn. (bd. dirs. 2002—, sec. 2003—), Gideons (camp pres. Mercer West, N.J. 2002—). Republican. Baptist. Avocations: classic cars, bicycling, classical music, Victorian architecture. Home: 107 Manlove Ave Apt E-B Hightstown NJ 08520-3234 Office: Independence Community Bank 909 Broad St Newark NJ 07102 E-mail: wdarr@icbny.com.

DARRABY, JESSICA L. lawyer, educator, writer; b. June 17; BA, UCLA, 1974; MA, U. Calif., 1976, JD, 1979. Bar: Calif. 1979. Gallery dir., owner Jessica Darraby Gallery, L.A., 1984-88; cons., expert witness, 1988—; adj. prof. Pepperdine Sch. Law, Malibu, Calif., 1988—. Treas. So. Calif. exec. com., Art Table, Inc., N.Y.C., 1992-93, lawyer, 1993—2001. Author: Art, Artifact and Architecture Law, 1995—. Fellow Can. Council Fellowship Canadian Govt., 1975. Mem. Contemporary Arts Coun., Mus. Modern Art (N.Y.C.), Rancho Pk. Women's Golf Club. Office: Pepperdine Sch Law Malibu CA 90263

DARRELL, CHARLES G. engineer; b. Middletown, Ohio, Nov. 3, 1929; s. George Durousseaux and Mary (Hines) Darrell; m. Lillian Christine Larson, June 19, 1954 (dec. Jan. 2003); children: Marcia, Robert, Susan. BS, U.S. Naval Acad., 1952. Commd. ensign USN, 1948, advanced through grades to capt., 1975, ret., 1982; prin. engr. Gen. Physics Corp., Columbia, Md., 1982—98; sr. staff Johns Hopkins U., Laurel, 1999—2003. Pres. parish coun. St. Louis Ch., 1977—78. Decorated (2) Meritorious Svc. medal, Navy Commendation medal. Mem.: Navy League, Naval Supreme League. Independent. Roman Catholic. Avocations: sailing, skiing, photography. Office: Johns Hopkins U Applied Physics Lab 11100 Johns Hopkins Rd Laurel MD 20723

DARRELL, NORRIS, JR., lawyer; b. Berlin, May 10, 1929; s. Norris and Doris Clare (Williams) D. (parents Am. citizens); m. Henriette Maria Haid, July 31, 1962; 1 child, Andrew. AB, Harvard U., 1951, LL.B. cum laude, 1954. Bar: N.Y. 1955, U.S. Supreme Ct. 1965. Assoc. Sullivan & Cromwell, N.Y.C., 1956-65, ptnr., 1965-92, sr. ptnr. European office Paris, 1968-71, sr. counsel, 1993—. Bd. dirs. Lumina Found. for Edn., Inc., Indpls., Ind. Trustee Cold Spring Harbor Lab., Inc., 1974-81, United Student Aid Funds, Inc., Fishers, Ind., 1974-94, USA Group Inc., Fishers, Ind., 1993-2000, East Woods Sch., Oyster Bay, N.Y., 1974-79; hon. trustee Heckscher Mus., Huntington, N.Y. With U.S. Army, 1954-56. Fellow Am. Bar Found.; mem. Am. Law Inst., ABA, Assn. Bar City N.Y., Harvard Club N.Y., Pilgrims Club, River Club (bd. govs. 1978-98), Cold Spring Harbor Beach Club, Edgartown Yacht Club. Home: 44 Walnut Tree Ln Cold Spring Harbor New York NY 11724 E-mail: norrisd482@aol.com.

D'ARRIGO, STEPHEN, JR., agricultural company executive; b. Stockton, Calif., Mar. 8, 1922; s. Stephen and Constance (Picciotto) D;A.; m. Rosemary Anne Murphy, Aug. 20, 1949; children: Stephen III, Kathleen Anne, Joanne Marie, Michael Anderw, Dennis Patrick, Patrick Shane. BS, U. Santa Clara, 1947. Sec.-treas. D'Arrigo Bros. Co. Calif., San Jose, 1946-62, Salinas, 1962-83; ret., 1983; sec.-treas. Santa Cruz Farms (co. merged with D'Arrigo Bros. 1970), Eloy, Ariz., 1947-52, pres., gen. mgr., 1952-70, bd. dirs., 1947-70. Mem. Nat. Def. Exec. Res. 2d lt. AUS, 1943-46. Decorated Bronze Star, Belgian Fouragere; recipient Disting. Svc. award Santa Clara Heart Assn. Mem. NRA (life), Springfield Armory Mus. (life), Smithsonian Assocs. (nat. chrter), Mil. Order World Wars, Assn. U.S. Army, Co. Mil. Historians, Am. Soc. Arms Collectors, Tex. Gun Collectors Assn. Home: 2241 Dry Creek Rd San Jose CA 95124-1216

DARRIN, KAREN IRENE, medical/surgical nurse, nursing administrator; Diploma of Nursing, Good Samaritan Sch. of Nursing, Portland, 1971. Cert. case mgr., Wash., geriatric case mgr., Good Samaritan Sch. Nursing. Critical care staff nurse Valley Med. Ctr., Renton, Wash., 1976—96; RN care mgr. Sound Options, Inc., Tacoma, 1996—2000, Pacific Med. Clinics, Seattle, 2000—. Rn consultant:case mgmt. and care coord. CareSolutions LLC, Renton, 2000—. Mem.: NAPGCM, CMSA. Home: 1523 Morris Ave South Renton WA 98055 Office: CareSolutions LLC 1523 Morris Ave South Renton WA 98055 Home Fax: 425-277-4660; Office Fax: 425-277-4660.

DARROW, EMILY M. public relations executive, writer; b. Kingston, NY, Sept. 21, 1964; d. H. Van Wyck and Marianne Darrow; m. Brendon Paul McCrane, Oct. 5, 2002. Student, Vassar Coll., 1983—84; BA, Hunter Coll., 1989; postgrad. in Fine Arts, NYU, 1992. Mus. mgr., edn. mgr. Hist. Hudson Valley-Montgomery Pl., Annandale-on-Hudson, NY, 1995; dir. pub. rels. and promotions Mohonk Mountain Ho., New Paltz, NY, 1997—98; pub. rels. assoc. Bard Coll., Annandale-on-Hudson, 1998—; asst. dir. Inst. Advanced Theology Bard Coll., Annandale on Hudson, 2001 . Rschr. Salander O'Reilly Gallery Stuart Davis Catalogue Raisonne Project, N.Y.C., 1989—90; writer, rschr. Art Commn. City of N.Y., 1989—90; internship in pub. rels. Opera Garnier de Paris-Paris Opera Ballet, Paris, 1990—91, N.Y.C. Ballet, 1982—84; cons., writer Vikarmasila Found., N.Y.C., 1999—. Recipient Zabar grad. scholarship, Hunter Coll., 1989; fellow Leon Levy and Shelby White, Inst. of Fine Arts/NYU, 1990. Mem.: Jr. League of Kingston (rec. sec. 1991—96, pub. rels. dir. 1991—96). Home: 250 Morton Rd Rhinebeck NY 12572 Office: Bard Coll Annandale Hotel Annandale On Hudson NY 12504 Personal E-mail: EMDarrow87@alum.vassar.edu. Business E-Mail: darrow@bard.edu.

DARROW, JANE, artist; b. Hollywood, Calif., Apr. 9, 1936; d. Reginald Ivan and Dorothy Gertrude Bauder; m. Henry Frank Smith, Oct. 1954 (div. June 1967); children: Michael Henry, Linda Lee, Nancy Ann; m. Lee Hunter Darrow, Nov. 21, 1981. Student, U. So. Calif., 1953-55, U. Oreg., 1960-61. Art tchr. and exhibiter Los Abrigados, Sedona, Ariz., 2002—. Art instr. Sedona (Ariz.) Art Ctr., 1995. One-woman shows include Miramar, San Juan, P.R., El Dorado Gallery, San Juan, Excelsior Hotel, San Juan, Conservation Soc., P.R., Galeria Isabella, Vieques, P.R., 1992-94, Inst. Culture, San Juan, 1995, Ch. of the Red Rocks, Sedona, 1996, Creekside Gallery, Sedona, 1997; exhibited in group shows at P.R. and Fla. Watercolo Assn. Shows, 1989, 90, Phila. Watercolor, 1992, Catherine Lorillard Wolfe Art Club, 1992-95, Rocky Mountain Nat., 1992, 97, San Diego Watercolor, 1993, Ariz. Aqueous, 1993, 94, 97, La. Watercolor, 1994, Salmagundi Non-members, 1994, Ariz. Watercolor Assn., 1994-97, N.W. Watercolor, 1994-98, No. Ariz. Watercolor Assn., 1995, 97, Allied Artists, N.Y., 1995, 96, Phippen Mus., Prescott, Ariz., 1999; commd. artist Mariott Hotel, San Juan, 1994; represented in permanent collections Condado Plaza Hotel, San Juan, Law Offices Guzman Esquilin and Assocs., San Juan, Crow's Nest Hotel, Vieques, Danmar Corp., San Juan; represented by Ratliff Gallery, Sedona, 1996-97, Raku Gallery, Jerome, Ariz., 1997—, Marcus Gallery, Santa Fe, 1997—, Golden Gecko Gallery, Sedona, 1999-2003. Mem. N.W. Watercolor Soc. (Miva/Walter Welt award 1997, No. Ariz. Watercolor Soc. (v.p. 1995-97, pres. 1997—, award of excellence 1996, best in show award 1997-99), Ariz. Watercolor Assn. (award of excellence 1995), Catherine Lorillard Wolfe Art Club. Home: 45 Ridge Rd Sedona AZ 86336-4035 E-mail: Janedarrow@aol.com.

DARROW, JILL E(LLEN), lawyer; b. N.Y.C., Jan. 6, 1954; d. Milton and Elaine (Sklarin) D.; m. Michael V.P. Marks, May 14, 1987. AB in English, Barnard Coll., 1975; JD, U. Pa., 1978; LLM in Tax Law, NYU, 1983. Bar: Pa. 1978, N.Y. 1979, U.S. Tax Ct. 1982. Assoc. Shearman & Sterling, N.Y.C., 1978-79, Rosenman & Colin, N.Y.C., 1979-86, ptnr., 1987—2002, Katten Muchin Zavis Rosenman, N.Y.C., 2002—. Mem. ABA, N.Y. State Bar Assn., Pa. Bar Assn., Phi Beta Kappa. Home: 860 5th Ave New York NY 10021-5856 Office: Katten Muchin Zavis Rosenman 575 Madison Ave Fl 12 New York NY 10022-2511 E-mail: jill.darrow@kmzr.com.

DARROW, MARY J. federal lawyer; b. Malone, N.Y. d. James William and Geraldine (Cosgrove) D.; m. Michael Ray Goebel, Dec. 30, 1982 (div. June 1990); 1 child, Jeanne Marie Darrow. BS, Clarkson U., 1979; JD, Loyola of New Orleans, 1985. CPA, 1984; Bar: La., 1985. Asst. controller Union Carbide Corp., Hahnville, La., 1979—82; tax. atty. Touche Ross, New Orleans, 1985; asst. dist. atty. Dept. Justice, New Orleans, 1990—99, asst. U.S. atty. Raleigh, NC, 1990—; adj. prof. Tulane U. Sch. Law, New Orleans, 1994—99. Mem. United Cerebral Palsy of New Orleans, 1985-99, pres., 1989-90; mem. United Way New Orleans, 1987-99. Recipient Vol. Yr., United Cerebral Palsy N.O., 1985, Outstanding Vol. United Way, 1991. Mem. La. State Bar Assn. Office: US Attorney 301 New Bern Ave Fl 8 Raleigh NC 27601-1417

DARROW, STEVE, state legislator; BS, U. Vt. State rep. Vt. Ho. of Reps., 1993—, mem. com. electric restructuring, 1997. Task force Vt. Yankee. Supr. Nat. Resources Conservation Dist. Address: PO Box 880-e Putney VT 05346-0880

DARROW, WILLIAM RICHARD, retired pharmaceutical company executive, consultant; b. Middletown, Ohio, Sept. 7, 1939; s. Richard William and Nelda Virginia (Darling) D.; m. Janet Elizabeth Swan, June 20, 1964; children: James William, Susan Elizabeth, Margaret Ellen. BA, Ohio Wesleyan U., 1960; MD, Western Res. U., 1964; PhD in Pharmacology, Case-Western Res. U., 1969. Intern Univ. Hosps., Cleve., 1964; sr. clin. rsch. assoc. CIBA Pharm. Co., 1969, asst. dir. clin. pharmacology, 1969-70; dir. clin. pharmacology CIBA-GEIGY Corp., 1970-75, exec. dir. clin. rsch., 1975-76; sr. v.p. rsch., med. dir. Wallace Labs. div. Carter Wallace, Inc., Cranbury, N.J., 1976-80; med. dir. Schering Labs. div. Schering-Plough Corp., Kenilworth, N.J., 1980, v.p. med. and regulatory affairs, 1981-82, sr. v.p. med. ops., 1982-94, sr. med. advisor, 1994—. Bd. dirs. AltaRex Corp., 2001-02; chmn. rsch. com. N.J. Health Scis. Group, 1973-76, mem. exec. com., 1973-74, 76-86, treas., 1977-80, v.p., 1980-86, Bernards Twp. Bd. Health, 1979-93, v.p., 1980, pres., 1981-85, 86-93; chmn. Bernards Twp. Deer Study Task Force/ Deer Mgmt. Adv. Com., 1999—; bd. dirs. N.J. chpt. Arthritis Found., 1990—, exec. com., 1991—, vice chmn., 1995-97, chmn. bd. dirs., 1997-2001, past chmn., 2001—; bd. dirs. Pharm. Ednl. and Rsch. Inst., 1993-2000, chmn. curriculum com., 1993-95; bd. dirs. Junior Achievement No. N.J., 1996; mem. sci. adv. bd. Clin. Rsch. Ctr. Robert Wood Johnson Med. Ctr., 1990-2000; mem. U.S. del. Internat. Conf. on Harmonization, 1991-99; mem. N.J. State Arthritis Adv. Coun., 2000—. Recipient Roche award, 1962, Humanitarian of Yr. award Arthritis Found. N.J., 1994; USPHS postdoctoral fellow, 1965-69. Fellow: Royal Soc. Medicine, Am. Acad. Pharm. Physicians (life); mem.: AMA, Pharm. Rsch. Mfrs. Am. Found. (sci. adv. bd. 1990—, chmn. 1994—, chief sci. advisor 1997—), Pharm. Rsch. Mfrs. Am. (steering com. med. sect. 1984—96, program chmn. 1988—89, vice-chmn. 1989—90, chmn. 1990—92, past chmn. 1992—96), Drug Info. Assn., Lakeside Country Club (Penn Yan, N.Y.), Basking Ridge (N.J.) Country Club, Pi Delta Epsilon, Omicron Delta Kappa, Phi Rho Sigma, Phi Gamma Delta. Republican. Presbyterian. Home: 42 Palmerston Pl Basking Ridge NJ 07920-2524 also: 521 E Lake Rd Penn Yan NY 14527-9422

DARSCH, NANCY, former professional basketball coach; b. Plymouth, Mass., 1951; BS, Springfield (Mass.) Coll., 1973. Coach Longmeadow (Mass.) H.S.; asst. coach U. Tenn., 1978-85; coach Ohio State U., 1985-97; head coach N.Y. Liberty, WNBA, 1997-98, Washington Mystics, WNBA, 1998—2000. Coach U.S.A. Olympic trials, 1980, 88, U.S.A. Pan Am. Games trials, 1979, 83; head coach U.S.A. Jr. Nat. basketball team, 1990; asst. coach U.S. Olympic team, 1984, 96.

DARSEY, JAMES FRANCIS, communication educator, author; b. Sarasota, Fla., Jan. 11, 1953; s. Francis Grover Darsey and Sharon Merritt. BA, Fla. State U., 1975; MA, Purdue U., 1978; PhD, U. Wis., Madison, 1985. Asst. prof. dept. English and comm. DePaul U., Chgo., 1983-88; vis. asst. prof. dept. comm. arts U. Iowa, Iowa City, 1986-88; asst. prof. dept. comm. Ohio State U., Columbus, 1988-95, No. Ill. U., DeKalb, 1995-98, assoc. prof., 1998-99; assoc. prof. dept. comm. Ga. State U., Atlanta, 1999—. Author: The Prophetic Tradition and Radical Rhetoric in America, 1997; assoc. editor Quar. Jour. of Speech, 2001—, Women's Studies in Comm., 2001—, Controversia, 2002--, Comm Theory, 2002--; contbr. articles to profl. jours. Legis. coun. Nat. Comm. Assn., Washington, 1997-99; chmn. pub. address divsn. Nat. Comm. Assn., Washington, 2002-03; active Georgia Stonewall Dems., 2000—; guest Sta. WBEZ Radio, 1998-2000. Recipient Outstanding Acad. Book Choice award, 1999, Aubrey Fisher award Western Comm. Assn., 2003; fellow NEH, 2000-01. Mem. MLA, Nat. Comm. Assn. (James A. Winans/Herbert A. Wichelns Meml. award 1998, Marie Hochmuth Nichols award 1998, Randy Majors Meml. award 1998), So. Comm. Assn., Am. Soc. for the Study of the History of Rhetoric, Am. Studies Assn. Avocations: photography, swimming, recorder, traveling. Office: Ga State U Dept Comm Atlanta GA 30303 Personal E-mail: jdarsey@mac.com. E-mail: jdarsey@gsu.edu.

DARSEY, JEROME ANTHONY (JERRY DARSEY), chemistry educator, consultant; b. Houma, La., Aug. 26, 1946; s. Elmer Joseph and Arline (Houghton) D.; m. Patricia Ann Bukowski, June 10, 1989; children: Brittany Angèle, Joseph Anthony, Mary Catherine. BS in Physics, La. State U., 1970, PhD in Chemistry, 1982. Asst. prof. chemistry and physics Gordon Coll. U. Ga. System, Barnsville, 1983-84; asst. prof. Tarleton State U./Tex. A&M U., Stephenville, Tex., 1984-88, assoc. prof., 1988-90; asst. prof. U. Ark., Little Rock, 1990-93, assoc. prof., 1993-96, prof., 1996—. Univ. scholar natural scis. Tarleton State U., Tex. A&M U., 1989-90; cons. Oak Ridge (Tenn.) Nat. Lab., 1990-95; co-chmn. 1st workshop neural network applications to material scis. Dept. Energy, 1994; chmn. 1st APS Symposium on Applications of Artificial Neural Networks to Chemical Systems; invited lectr. 21st Australian Polymer Symposium, 1996. Sci. book reviewer Jour. Am. Chem. Soc.; contbr. articles to profl. jours. Named Outstanding Univ. Rschr., U. Ark., Little Rock, 1995, Outstanding Rschr. Coll. Sci. and Math., 1995, 2000; grantee Am. Chem. Soc., 1986, 90, NSF, 1992, 96, NASA, 1994-2001. Fellow AAAS; mem. Am. Chem. Soc. (chmn. Ark. sect. 1993), Am. Phys. Soc., Ark. Acad. Sci., S.W. Theoretical Chemistry Conf. (chmn. 1986-87), Tex. Acad. Sci. (vice chmn. chemistry divsn. 1986-87, chmn. 1987-88). Home: 1514 Alberta Dr Little Rock AR 72227-5803 Office: U Ark Dept Chemistry 2801 S University Ave Dept Little Rock AR 72204-1099 E-mail: jadarsey@ualr.edu.

DARST, BETTY JANE, historian, educator; b. Columbus Grove, Ohio, Nov. 11, 1939; d. Edward and Mary Naomi Foulkes; m. John F. Darst, Dec. 17, 1993; children: Janet Moore, Diana Veid, Glenn Geiger. BS in Edn., Ohio No. U., 1960; cert. specialist media, Ohio U., 1979; MEd, U. Dayton, 1985. Cert. tchr., Ohio; cert. h.s. prin., supr., libr. media specialist, Ohio. Social studies tchr. North Plainfield (N.J.) H.S., Greenhills-Forest Park City Schs.; media specialist West Muskingum Mid. Sch.; coord. media svcs. Franklin City Schs., 1980-89; supr. ednl. media Springfield (Ohio) City Sch. Dists., 1989—2002; pvt. practice Dayton, Ohio, 2003—. Adj. faculty Wright State U., 2003—; leader nat. workshop in children's lit.; presenter in field. Co-author: Speaking of Flying, 2000; dramatist, creator: (video) Tour of Home: Wright Brothers. Mem. Lima City Bd. Edn., 1976; pres. Grtr. Miami Valley Ednl. Tech., 1992-94; mem. adv. bd. Aviation Trail; mem. Wright Rsch. Com. Mem. ALA, AASL, Phi Delta Kappa. Methodist. Achievements include listed as leading aviation performer. Avocation: living history presentations. Home: 2423 Brown Bark Dr Dayton OH 45431 E-mail: thedarsts@donet.com.

DARST, DAVID MARTIN, investment company executive, educator, writer; b. Knoxville, Tenn. s. Guy Bewley and Susan Mary (McGinnis) D.; m. Diane Wassman; children: Elizabeth Mathews, David Martin, Jr. BA, Yale U., 1969; MBA, Harvard U., 1971. Assoc. Goldman, Sachs & Co., N.Y.C., 1971-75, v.p., mgr., 1981—, v.p., resident mgr. Zurich, Switzerland, 1975-81, CFO global equities divsn., 1991—96; mng. dir. Morgan Stanley, N.Y.C., 1996—; founding pres. Morgan Stanley Investment Group, 1998—; dir. Morgan Stanley Trust Co., 1999—. Vis. lectr. Coll. and Sch. Mgmt., Yale U., New Haven, 1981—, Bus. Sch., Harvard U., Boston, 1987—. Author: The Complete Bond Book, 1975, The Handbook of the Bond and Money Markets, 1981, The Art of Asset Allocation, 2003; contbr. articles to profl. jours. Bd. dirs. Deer Park Assn., 1985—, pres., 1989—; bd. dirs. Can.-U.S. Found. for Ednl. Exch., 1996—, student sponsor partnership, 2002—; bd. profl. advisors N.Y.C. Ballet, 1997—; corp. adv. bd. Sch. Am. Ballet, N.Y.C., 2002—. William H. Donaldson Disting. Faculty fellow Sch. Mgmt. Yale U., 1986-87. Mem. The Money Marketeers, The Phelps Assn. (v.p., gov. 1974—), Assn. Internat. Bond Dealers (edn. com.), Yale Alumni Assn. of Greenwich (bd. dirs. 1996—), Yale Club of N.Y.C. (coun. 1987—, chmn. fin. com. 1987—). Office: Morgan Stanley 4th Fl 1221 Ave of the Americas New York NY 10020-1001

DARST, MARY LOU, secondary school educator; b. Houston, Aug. 12, 1943; d. Carl Kennedy and Sara Catharine (Emmott) Hughes; m. William Maury Darst, Apr. 20, 1963 (dec. May 1990); children: Robert Maury, Catharine Fontaine Darst Knight. Student, Stephen F. Austin State Coll., 1961—63, Galveston Coll., 1970-72, 76-77, U. Tex. Med. Br., 1983—84; BA, U. Houston, Clear Lake, 1989, MS, 1993, BA, 2001; postgrad., U. St. Thomas, 1999—2002, Rice U., 2003. Cert. tchr. elem. edn., secondary English, ESL, gifted and talented, Advanced placement. Sec. William Temple Found., Galveston, 1979-80; new accounts Tex. First Bank, Galveston, 1981-84; med. sec. U. Tex. Med. Br., Galveston, 1984-87; tchr. Galveston (Tex.) Ind. Sch. Dist., 1990—2002, Galveston Coll., 1995-96; ESL tchr. Clear Lake H.S., 2002—. Mem. Jr. League of Galveston, 1966-69; bd. dirs. YWCA, 1972-73. Recipient Title VII grantee, U. Houston at Clear Lake, Houston, 1991—93. Mem.: Galveston Art League, Rock Art, Tex. Neurofibromatosis Found. (sec. 1987—89, pres. 1989—91), Assn. Tex. Profl. Educators, Mus. Fine Arts Houston, Scenic Galveston, U. Houston Alumni Assn., Sierra Club, Theta Zeta, Alpha Chi Omega, Delta Kappa Gamma (v.p. Omicron chpt. 1995—96). Democrat. Episcopalian. Avocations: travel, music, swimming, walking, writing, artist. Home: 1431 San Sebastian Ln Houston TX 77058-3451 E-mail: mldarst@juno.com.

DART, JOHN SEWARD, journalist, author; b. Peekskill, N.Y., Aug. 1, 1936; s. Seward Homer and Vella Marion (Haverstock) D.; m. Gloria Joan Walker, Aug. 21, 1957; children: Kim, John W., Randall, Christopher. BA, U. Colo., 1958. Staff writer UPI, Indpls. and L.A., 1961-65; sci. writer Calif. Inst. Tech., Pasadena, 1966-67; religion writer L.A. Times, 1967-98; news editor Christian Century mag., 2000—. Author: The Laughing Savior, 1976, The Jesus of Heresy and History, rev., expanded edit., 1988, Decoding Mark, 2003; co-author: Unearthing the Lost Words of Jesus, 1998; contbr. reports for Freedom Forum First Amendment Ctr., Vanderbilt U. Served with U.S. Army, 1958-61 Recipient Supple Meml. award Religion Newswriters Assn., 1980, Merrell Meml. award Jim Merrell Religion Liberty Found., 1980, William F. Leidt award Episcopal Ch., 1980, Angel award Religion in Media, 1985; NEH fellow Stanford U., 1973-74, First Amendment Ctr. fellow Vanderbilt U., 1992-93. Mem. Soc. Profl. Journalists (chpt. pres. 1976), Religion Newswriters Assn. (pres. 1990-92), Soc. Bibl. Lit. (mem.-at-large exec. com. Pacific Coast region 1990-95). Democrat. Home and Office: 12122 Bowmore Ave Northridge CA 91326-1002

DART, KENNETH, food container manufacturing executive; Pres., CEO Dart Container Corp., Mason, Mich. Office: Dart Container Corp 500 Hogsback Rd Mason MI 48854-9547*

DARTER, JEFFREY ALLEN, data processing professional; b. Wichita, Kans., Jan. 31, 1958; s. Richard J. Darter and Elizabeth (Cannady) Baumgartner; m. Karen Darlene Dees; 1 child, Stephanie Elizabeth. Student, Palm Beach Atlantic Coll., 1976-79. Installer Teleprompter Cable TV, West Palm Beach, Fla., 1979-80, technician, 1980-83; prodn. coord. Group W Cable, West Palm Beach, 1983-84; coord. Palm-Comm Cable, Lake Worth, Fla., 1984-85; dir. engring. Palm Comm Cable, Lake Worth, Fla., 1985-87; branch mgr. Telesat Cablevision, Lake Worth, 1987-88; systems analyst RMS, 1988-91; info. tech. mgr. Palm Beach County Supr. Elections Office, 1991—. Assoc. info. tech. mgr. Broadcast Profls. Forum of Compuserve Computer Svc., Columbus, Ohio, 1986—87; cons. Palm Beach County Pub. Access, West Palm Beach, 1987—, West Palm Beach Pvt. Sch., 1987—91; mem. voter registration tech. adv. group, 2001—; chmn. Sequoia Customer Devel. Com., 2003—. Mem. com. Palm Beach Jr. Coll., West Palm Beach, 1986-87. Recipient Outstanding Citizen award Town of Palm Beach, Fla., 1984, Oracle Master certification Oracle Corp., 1993. Mem. Soc. Cable TV Engrs. Avocations: semi-profl. musician, computer programming, photography. Office: Palm Beach County Elections 240 S Military Trl West Palm Beach FL 33415 E-mail: jdarter@hotmail.com.

DARTER, THOMAS EUGENE, JR., composer, musician, writer; b. Livermore, Calif., Feb. 13, 1949; s. Thomas Eugene and Vivian Lorene Darter; m. Sibyl Heishman, Dec. 3, 1977 (div. Feb. 1992); children: Erika Borges, Lisa, Allana; m. Karen Lucille Hogan, Sept. 21, 1996. BA summa cum laude, Cornell U., 1969, MFA, 1972, D in Musical Arts, 1979. Instr. music theory and composition Roosevelt U., Chgo., 1972-75; editor Keyboard Mag., Cupertino, Calif., 1975-85, mng. editor, 1991-94, editor San Mateo, Calif., 1994-97, pub., 1997-98; editor AfterTouch Mag., Buena Park, Calif., 1986-89; engring. publs. mgr. Coactive Networks, Sausalito, Calif., 2000-01; freelance musician, writer, 1998—. Dir. contemporary music ensemble Roosevelt U., Chgo., 1972-75; lectr. music/film dept. U. So. Calif., L.A., 1984-88; consulting editor Keyboard Mag., Cupertino, 1990-91. Composer, pianist Scatter: Manring Kassin Darter Live in San Francisco, 2002; arranger Monk Suite (Kronos Quartet), 1985, Music of Bill Evans (Kronos Quartet), 1986. 1st prize Nat. Fedn. Music Clubs, 1969, 71. Mem. Am. Fedn. Musicians, Phi Beta Kappa, Phi Kappa Phi. Home: 750 South L St Livermore CA 94550

DARTON, ERIC, writer; b. N.Y.C., May 30, 1950; s. John Howard Darton and Beatrice Maria Kroll; m. Katie Kehrig, Nov. 21, 1980; 1 child, Gwendolyn Helena. BA with honors, Empire State Coll., 1990; MA, Hunter Coll., 1994. Art, dance and performance editor East Village Eye, N.Y.C., 1981-83; pres. Yomoma Arts, Inc., N.Y.C., 1985—; assoc. editor Conjunctions, N.Y.C., 1991-93; cons. Poets & Writers, Inc., N.Y.C., 1992-97; fiction editor Am. Letters and Commentary, N.Y.C., 1999—. Lectr. Hunter Coll., N.Y.C., 1991—95, Fordham U., N.Y.C., 1992—97, NYU, 1996—98; mem. faculty MFA writing program Goddard Coll. Author: Free City, 1996, Divided We Stand, 1999. Franklin Furnance fellowship N.Y. State Council on the Arts, 1987, N.Y. Found. for the Arts fellowship N.Y. Found. for the Arts, 1991, fellowship in fiction Breadloaf Writers Conf., 1998. Mem. Pen Am. Ctr.

DARVODELSKY, ALEXANDER, structural engineer; b. Marcevo, Bulgaria, Mar. 1, 1927; came to U.S., 1957; s. Nikola K. and Slavka N. Darvodelsky; m. Jenny Radeva. Diploma in engring., Tech. U., Graz, Austria, 1954. Registered profl. engr., Ill. Structural engr. Graham, Anderson, Probst & White, Chgo., 1957-76; cons. Park Ridge, Ill., 1976—. Editor mag. Borba, 1986—. Nat. chmn. Bulgarians for Goldwater, 1964. Mem. Bulgarian Nat. Front, Inc., (mem. presidium 1988—, merit award 1969). Eastern Orthodox. Avocations: travel, politics, reading. Office: PO Box 46250 Chicago IL 60646

DARWIN, DAVID, civil engineering educator, researcher, consultant; b. NYC, Apr. 17, 1946; s. Samuel David and Earle (Rives) D.; m. Diane Marie Mayer, June 29, 1968; children: Samuel David, Lorraine Marie. BS, Cornell U., 1967, MS, 1968; PhD, U. Ill., 1974. Registered profl. engr., Kans. Asst. prof. civil engring. U. Kans., Lawrence, 1974-77, assoc. prof., 1977-82, prof., 1982—, Deane E. Ackers disting. prof. civil engring., 1990—, dir. Structural Engring. and Materials Lab., 1982—; dir. Infrastructure Rsch. Inst., 1998-2001. Cons. David Darwin, Lawrence, 1976—. Author: Steel and Composite Beams with Web Openings, 1990; co-author: Concrete, 2d edit., 2003; contbr. articles to profl. jours. Mem. Uniform Bldg. Code Bd. Appeals, Lawrence, 1978-84. Capt. U.S. Army, 1967-72, Vietnam. Grantee NSF, 1976—, Kans. Dept. Transp., 1980-82, 90—, Air Force Office Sci. Rsch., 1985-92, Civil Engring. Rsch. Found., 1991-95, Fed. Hwy. Adminstrn., 1994-98, 2001—, SD Dept. Transp., 2001—, Nat. Coop. Hwy. Rsch. Program, 1994-95; Bellows scholar U. Kans., 2001-02; recipient Miller award U. Kans., 1986, Irvin Youngberg Rsch. Achievement award, 1992, Civil and Environ. Engring. Alumni Assn.'s Disting. Alumnus award U. Ill., 2003. Fellow ASCE (editor Jour. Structural Engring. 1994-2000, bd. govs. Structural Engring. Inst. 2000—, Kans. sect. v.p., pres.-elect 2001-02, pres. 2002-03, Huber Rsch. prize 1985, Moisseiff award 1991, state-of-the-art of civil engring. award 1996, 2000, Richard R. Torrens award 1997), Am. Concrete Inst. (pres. Kans. chpt. 1975, bd. dirs. 1988-91, Bloem Disting. Svc. award 1986, Arthur R. Anderson award for disting. rsch. 1992, Structural Rsch. award 1996); mem. AAAS, ASTM (award of appreciation 2003), Am. Soc. Engring. Edn., Am. Inst. Steel Constrn. (profl.), Prestressed Concrete Inst. (profl.), Post-Tensioning Inst. (profl.), Concrete Rsch. Coun. (chmn. 1990-96), Structural Engring. Inst. (bd. govs. 2000—), Phi Kappa Phi (pres. U. Kans. chpt. 1976-78). Democrat. Unitarian Universalist. Avocations: swimming, walking. Office: U Kans Civil Environ and Archtl Engring Dept 2142 Learned Hall 1530 W 15th St Lawrence KS 66045-7609 E-mail: daved@ku.edu.

DARWIN, JOHN SCOTT, language educator; b. Conway, Ark., Aug. 30, 1945; s. William Garland and Daphne Elise Darwin. PhD, U of AR, Fayetteville, AR, 1974—84. Prof. of German AR State U, Ark., 1969—2003. Pres. AR Assoc. Tchr. of German, Ark., 1988—90. Chair Regional AIDS Network, Jonesboro, Ark., 1994—2001. Recipient Outstanding Tchr. of the Yr., Burlington N Found., 1985, Pres. Fellow, AR State U, 1985—86, Tchr. Exch. with Berchtesgaden, Germany, Fulbright Tchr. Exch. Prog., 1986—87. Mem.: Am. Assoc. of Tchr. of German, AR Assoc. of Tchr. of German (pres. 1988—90). Democrat. Episcopal. Avocations: swimming, travel, canoeing, hiking, scuba diving. Office: Ark State U Dept of Languages PO Box 2400 State University AR 72467 Home: PO Box 146 State Univ. AR 72467

DARWOOD, JOHN JOSEPH, physician; b. Van Wert, Ohio, Feb. 6, 1956; s. Arthur Joseph and Marilyn Ruth Darwood. BS, U. Toledo (Ohio), 1978; MD, Wright State U., 1983, MS, 1989. Diplomate Am. Bd. Family Practice, Am. Bd. Preventive Medicine, Am. Bd. Occupl. Medicine, Am. Bd. Aerospace Medicine. Resident in family practice Good Samaritan Hosp., Dayton, Ohio, 1983-86; occupl. medicine physician Indsl. Med. Ctr., Dayton, 1986-90; physician Comprehensive Health Svcs. Kennedy Space Ctr. NASA, Fla., 1990—. Fellow Am. Acad. Family Physicians, Am. Coll. Occupl. and Environ. Medicine; mem. Nat. Mgmt. Assn. (chpt. pres. 1995-96, 2000-01, chpt. chmn. bd. dirs. 1997-99). Office: Chs 005 Kennedy Space Center FL 32899-0001 E-mail: john.darwood-1@kmail.ksc.nasa.gov.

DARY, DAVID ARCHIE, journalism educator, author; b. Manhattan, Kans., Aug. 21, 1934; s. Milton Russell and Ruth Engel (Long) D.; m. Carolyn Sue Russum, June 2, 1956; children: Catherine Lee, Carol Ann, Cynthia Kay, Cristina Sue. BS in Humanities, Kans. State U., 1956; MS in Journalism, Kans. U., 1970. Reporter, editor CBS News, Washington, 1960-63; mgr. local news NBC News, Washington, 1963-67; dir. pub. affairs Kans. Rep. State Com., Topeka, 1968; mem. faculty U. Kans., Lawrence, 1969-89, prof. journalism, 1970-89; dir. H.H. Herbert Sch. Journalism, U. Okla., Norman, 1989-2000; ret., 2000. Cons. broadcast journalism, 1967— Author: Radio News Handbook, 1967, Manual De Noticias Radiofonicas, 1970, Television News Handbook, 1970, How to Write News for Broadcast and Print, 1973, The Buffalo Book, 1974, Comanche, 1976, True Tales of the Old-Time Plains, 1979, Cowboy Culture, 1981, Lawrence, Douglas County Kansas: An Informal History, 1982, True Tales of Old-Time Kansas, 1984, Entrepreneurs of the Old West, 1986, Kanzana 1854-1900: A Selected Bibliography, 1986, More True Tales of Old-Time Kansas, 1987, Picturial History of Lawrence, Douglas County, Kansas, 1993, Seeking Pleasure in the Old West, 1995, Red Blood & Black Ink: Journalism in the Old West, 1998, The Santa Fe Trail: Its History, Legends, and Lore, 2000; contbr. numerous articles to various mags. and newspapers. Mem. Okla. Hist. Soc. (bd. dirs. 1990-93), Kans. State Hist. Soc. (bd. dirs. 1972-91), Western History Assn., Westerners Internat. (pres. 1986-89), Western Writers Am. (pres. 1988-92), Masons, Kappa Tau Alpha. Home: 1113 Robin Hood Ln Norman OK 73072-7503

DARZYNKIEWICZ, ZBIGNIEW D. research scientist; b. Dzisna, Poland, May 12, 1936; came to U.S., 1969; s. Boleslaw and Waclawa (Tarnowska) D.; m. Elizabeth, June 20, 1966; children: Richard, Robert. MD, Sch. Medicine, Warsaw, 1960, PhD, 1966. Resident 4th City Hosp., Warsaw, 1960-62; assoc. prof. Cornell U. Grad. Sch. Medicine Sci., N.Y.C., 1978-88, prof. cell biology & genetics, 1988-90; prof. pathology & medicine N.Y. Med. Coll., Valhalla, 1990—, dir. cancer rsch. inst., 1990—. Vis. scientist Nobel Med. Inst., Karolinska U., Stockholm, 1968-70; assoc. mem. Sloan Kettering Cancer Ctr., N.Y.C., 1978-88, mem., 1988-90; cons. NASA, Houston, 1987-92. Editor/co-author 10 books; contbr. over 450 articles to profl. jours., chpts. to books; patentee in field. Recipient NIH/NCI Merit award, Bethesda, Md., 1987. Mem. Polish Acadm Scis. Office: NY Med Coll Brander Cancer Rsch Inst 19 Bradhurst Ave Hawthorne NY 10532-2140

DAS, ASHOKE KUMAR, internist, consultant; b. Calcutta, W. Bengal, India, Nov. 1, 1934; came to U.S., 1974; s. Srikrishna and Durgeshnandini (Bose) D.; m. Geeta Mukhopadhyay, Aug. 15, 1961 (died 1993); 1 child, Arnab. MBBS, Calcutta U., 1957, MD, 1962, PhD, 1971. Diplomate Royal Coll. Physicians London, Am. Bd. Internal Medicine. Rotating intern NRS Med. Coll. Hosp., Calcutta, 1956, resident, 1957-58; chief resident Stafford Gen. Infrimary U.K., 1970; chief resident internal medicine and cardiology Rush Green Hosp. U.K., 1971-74; attending physician Our Lady Mercy Med. Ctr., Bronx, 1976—; chief sect. internal medicine Morrisania Clin., Bronx, 1980-83; pvt. practice Bronx, 1983—; attending physician St. Barnabas Hosp., Bronx, 1983—, Bronx Lebanon Hosp. Ctr., 1983—. Clin. asst. prof. medicine N.Y. Med. Coll.; cons. in field. Indian Coun. Med. Rsch. grantee, 1958-59. Fellow ACP, Royal Coll. Physicians. (Eng.), Royal Soc. London; mem. AMA, N.Y. State Med. Soc., Bronx Med. Soc., U. Calcutta Med. Assn. Am., Assn. Physicians India (U.S.), Lions Club (mem. fundraising campaign 1995—, v.p. 1999, pres. 2001). Avocations: walking, travel. Office: 2940 Grand Course Bronx NY 10458

DAS, DILIP KUMAR, chemical engineer; b. Khulna, India, Aug. 23, 1941; came to U.S., 1969; s. Murari Mohan and Sudha Rani (Roy) D.; m. Mala Mazumder, June 20, 1972; children: Shamik, Alina. BSc with honors, Rajshahi U., Bangladesh, 1961; BChE with honors, Jadavpur U., Calcutta, 1966; MSChemE, U. Wash., 1971. Profl. engr., La., Mo. Chem. engr. Kuljian Corp., Calcutta, 1966-67, A.P.V. Engrng. Co. Ltd., Calcutta, 1967-69; sr. chem. engr. C.F. Braun & Co., Alhambra, Calif., 1973-75; sr. process engr. Stauffer Chem. Co., Dobbs Ferry, NY, 1975-80; sr. project engr. Rhône-Poulenc, Inc., Princeton, NJ, 1980-84; prin. process engr. Ciba-Geigy Corp., St. Gabriel, La., 1984-96; prin. engr. Bayer Cropscience, Kansas City, Mo., 1997—. Co-author: Chemical Engineering for Professional Engineers Examination, 1984, Chemical Engineering License Review, EIT Chemical Review, Chemical Engineering Problems and Solutions; contbr. articles to profl. jours. Mem. AIChE Hindu. Achievements include patent for fail-safe diazotization dip tube. Home: 4701 NE Shady Lane Dr Kansas City MO 64119-5345 Office: Bayer Corp PO Box 4913 Kansas City MO 64120-0013 E-mail: dilip.das@bayer.cropscience.com.

DAS, KALYAN, lawyer; b. Calcutta, India, June 23, 1956; s. Amulyaratan and Chaitaly (Mitra) D.; m. Pia Mukherjee, Feb. 18, 1986; children: Sabrina, Rahul. Barrister-at-Law, The Lincoln's Inn, London, 1979; diploma, Assoc. of the Chartered Inst. of Arbitrators, London, 1980; LLM, NYU, 1989. Bar: Eng. 1979, Wales 1979, N.Y. 1983; advocate Supreme Ct. India, 1981; barrister and solicitor Melbourne, Australia, 1984. Barrister-at-law Fountain Ct. Temple, London, 1980-81; assoc. Malcolm A. Hoffmann, N.Y.C., 1981-82, White & Case, LLP, N.Y.C., 1983-88, Milbank, Tweed, Hadley & McCloy, LLP, N.Y.C., 1988-90, Seward & Kissel LLP, N.Y.C., 1990-93, ptnr., head global banking and instl. fin. restructuring/workout group, 1993—. Editor: Company Law, 1980. Internat. life v.p. Internat. Students' Trust, London, 1987—. Fellow Am. Coll. Investment Counsel (co-chair ann. meeting 1998); mem. ABA, N.Y. State Bar Assn., Assn. Bar City of N.Y., Am. Arbitration Assn. (panel mem.), Hon. Soc. Lincoln's Inn, Wine Soc. London, Met. Club (N.Y.C.). Avocation: travel. Home: Penthouse A and B 107 W 89th St New York NY 10024-1944 Office: Seward & Kissel LLP 1 Battery Park Plz Fl 23 New York NY 10004-1485 E-mail: das@sewkis.com.

DAS, LAMA SURYA, theology studies educator; b. Bklyn., Dec. 26, 1950; s. Harold Joseph and Joyce Rothouse Miller; m. Kathleen Joy Peterson, May 12, 2000. BA summa cum laude, SUNY, Buffalo, 1972. Lama Kagyu-Nyingma Sect, 88. Asst. prof. Kyoto (Japan) Seika Coll., 1974—76; founder, dir. Creative Edn. Ctr., Woodstock, NY, 1978—80; translator Padmakara Translation Group, Dordogne, France, 1988—90; lama, monk Shechen Monastery, Dordogne, 1980—88; spiritual dir. Dzogchen Found., Cambridge, Mass., 1990—. Author:

The Snow Lion's Turquoise Mane, 1992, Natural Great Perfection, 1994, Awakening the Buddha Within, 1995, Awakening to the Sacred, 1998, Awakening the Buddhist Heart, 2000, Letting Go of the Person You Used to Be, 2003; contbr. poetry to lit. publs. Founder Network of Western Buddhist Tchrs., Marin County, Calif., 1993—; bd. dirs. Seva Found., Kalamazoo, 1978—80. Recipient award, Libr. of Congress, 1994, award for Awakening book series, New Age Spiritual Book Pubs., Spiritual Svc. Broadcast award, Inner Dimensions Pubs., 1999, Best Buddhist Webset award, 1995. Buddhist. Avocations: poetry, sports, dogs, travel. Office: Dzogchen Found PO Box 400734 Cambridge MA 02140 Fax: 781-316-0115. E-mail: surya@surya.org.

DAS, NARESH CHANDRA, research scientist; PhD, CEERI, PIlani, Rajsthan, 1981—84. Chief scientist NASA/GSFC, Greenbelt, Md., 1994—2000; scientist Army Rsch. Lab., Adelphi, 2001—. Sr. scientist Air Force Weapons Lab, Albuquerque, 1990—94. Author: (research) Semiconductor Devices (Merit Award, 1986). Mem.: IEEE (sr.). Home: 9535 Ridgeview Dr Columbia MD 21046 Personal E-mail: nareshdas@yahoo.com.

DAS, NIROD K. engineering educator; b. Puri, Orissa, India, Feb. 27, 1963; came to U.S., 1985; s. Binayak and Sailabala Das; m. Nibedita Mohanty, Jan. 16, 1993. B in Tech., Indian Inst. Tech., Kharagpur, 1985; MSEE, U. Mass., 1987, PhD in Elec. Engring., 1989. Rschr. Indian Space Rsch. Orgn., Bangalore, summer 1984; rsch. asst. antenna lab. U. Mass., Amherst, 1985-89, postdoctoral rsch. assoc., 1989-90; asst. prof. dept. elec. enging. Poly. U., Bklyn., 1990-97, assoc. prof., 1997—. Contbr. articles to profl. jours.; co-editor: Directions for the Next Generation of MMIC Devices and Systems, 1997. Mem. IEEE (editl. bd. IEEE Microwave Theory and Techniques Transactions 1991—, tech. program com. Microwave Theory and Techniques Symposia 1996—, RWP King Best Paper award Antennas and Propagation Soc. 1993), N.Y. Acad. Scis. Avocations: astronomy, photography, camping. Office: Poly U 6 Metrotech Ctr Brooklyn NY 11201 E-mail: ndas@photon.poly.edu.

DAS, SUJIT, policy analyst; b. Calcutta, West Bengal, India, May 11, 1958; came to U.S. 1980; s. Hari Mohan and Sandhya Rani Das; m. Suchita De, June 16, 1987; 1 child, Sreetham. BTech, Indian Inst. Tech., 1979; MS, U. Tenn., 1982, MBA, 1984. Rsch. staff Oak Ridge (Tenn.) Nat. Lab., 1984—; vis. fellow Tata Energy Rsch. Inst., New Delhi, India, 1992-93. Contbr. articles to profl. jours. Mem. Soc. Automotive Engrs., Soc. for Internat. Devel. Achievements include research in plastics recycling, oil vulnerability, flood damage estimation, energy and environmental analysis, uranium assessment, assessment of advanced materials technologies and vehicle designs. Office: Oak Ridge Nat Lab PO Box 2008 Oak Ridge TN 37831-6073

DAS, SUMAN KUMAR, plastic surgeon, researcher; b. Calcutta, India, May 6, 1944; came to U.S., 1980; s. Bisweswar and Devi Rani (Ghosh) D.; m. Carole Ellen Simmons, July 10, 1976 (div. Apr. 1984); children: Louise Angelique, Natalie Krishna; m. Rosyln Tanner, Mar. 22, 1991. B of Medicine and Surgery, Calcutta (India) U., 1967; MD, Ednl. Commn. Fgn. Med. Grad., 1981. Diplomate Am. Bd. Plastic Surgery. Intern R.G. Kar Med. Coll. and Hosp., Calcatta, 1966-67, resident in gen. surgery, house officer, 1967-68; sr. house officer in accident and emergency, orthopaedics Royal Infirmary, Bolton, Lancs, Eng., 1968-69, house surgeon in gen. surgery, 1969-70; sr. house officer in gen. surgery Royal United Hosp., St. Martin's Hosp., Bath, Eng., 1970-72; house officer in medicine Whiston Hosp., Prescot, Liverpool, Eng., 1970; registrar in gen. surgery Frenchay Hosp., Bristol, Eng., 1972-73, sr. house officer in plastic surgery, 1973-74; registrar in plastic surgery Frenchay Hosp., Bristol, Eng., 1974, Royal Victoria Infirmary, Fleming Meml. Children's Hosp., Newcastle-Upon-Tyne, Eng., 1974-77; fellow in plastic and reconstructive surgery Hosp. for Sick Children, Toronto, Ont., Can., 1978; fellow in micro and hand surgery St. Vincent's Hosp., Melbourne, Australia, 1979-80, asst. plastic surgeon, 1979-80; rsch. assoc. in plastic surgery UCLA Med. Ctr., 1980-82; co-dir. microsurgery tng. program Harbor/UCLA Med. Ctr., 1980-82; dir. plastic surgery rsch. VA Wadsworth Med. Ctr., L.A., 1980-82; resident in plastic surgery U. Miss. Med. Ctr., Jackson, 1982-83, sr. and chief resident in plastic surgery, 1983-84; pvt. practice Jackson, 1984-86; chief and asst. prof. div. plastic surgery U. Miss. Med. Ctr., Jackson, 1986-87, chief and assoc. prof. div. plastic surgery, 1987-90, prof. plastic surgery, chief div. plastic surgery, chief, 1990-95, clin. prof. plastic surgery, 1995—. Cons. plastic surgery Miss. Bapt. Med. Ctr., River Oaks Hosp.; attending Meth. Rehab. Ctr., U. Miss. Med. Ctr., River Oaks East Hosp., St. Dominiso Hosp.; vis. prof. dept. surgery divsn. plastic surgery U. Calif., San Francisco, 1981, U. Ala., 1992; mem. patient care com. U. Miss., Jackson, 1990—92; pres. internet co. Nxmed.com. Inc., 1999—; dir. St. Dominic Ambulatory Surgery Ctr., 1999—; dir. outreach program St. Dominic Hosp.; presenter and exhibitor in field at numerous profl. meetings. Author: (with others) Manual of Operative Plastic and Reconstructive Surgery, 1980, Textbook of Surgery, 2nd edit., 1988, Ency. of Flaps, 1990; mem. editorial bd. So. Med. Jour., 1993—; contbr. articles to Brit. Jour. Surgery, Brit. Jour. Plastic Surgery, Indian Jour. Dermatology, Hand, Plastic Surgery Forum, Jour. Singapore Acad. Sci., Jour. Oral Surgery, Plastic Reconstrn. Surgery, Acta Anatomica, Jour. Clin. Pathology, others; inventor turmeric on wound healing. Pres. NxMed.com Internet Distant Edn., 2000—. Recipient prize North Eng. Surg. Soc., 1977, Plastic Surgery Ednl. Found. Rsch. grant 1983-84, other grants Eli Lilly 1989, Tyra, 1989, Collagen Corp. 1989, 90-91, NIH, 1989, Am. Soc. Aesthetic Plastic Surgery, 1990, 91. Fellow ACS, Royal Coll. Surgeons London, Royal Coll. Surgeons Edinburgh (traveling scholarship 1976); mem. AMA, AAAS, Am. Fedn. for Clin. Rsch., Am. Assn. Hand Surgery (rsch. grant com. 1990-91, chmn. rsch. grant com. 1992), Am. Assn. Acad. Plastic Surgeons (fellowship com. 1990), Am. Soc. Plastic and Reconstructive Surgeons, Am. Assn. Plastic Surgeons, Internat. Soc. Burn Injuries, Internat. Soc. Reconstructive Microsurgery, Internat. Soc. Surgery, Internat. Soc. Emergency Medicine and Critical Care (charter), Brit. Assn. Plastic Surgeons (best prize and cert. 1967), Brit. Soc. Surgery of Hands (European traveling scholarship 1977), Soc. N.Am. Skull Base Surgery (founding), Miss. State Med. Assn., Plastic Surgery Rsch. Coun., N.Y. Acad. Sci., S.E. Soc. Plastic and Reconstructive Surgeons (program com. 1990—, trustee 1997 2000, historian 2000-01, chmn. CME com. 1999-, asst. sec. 2001--), Miss. Acad. Scis. (chmn. 1992), Acad. Surg. Rsch., Assn. for Acad. Surgery, Southeastern Surg. Congress, Internat. Fedn. Surg. Colls., So. Med. Assn. (chmn. elect 1991, chmn. 1992), Lion's Club (Flora), Sigma Xi. Achievements include discovery that silicone does not elicit any change in T cell population; that capsular contracture with silicone implant is not an immunological effect; rsch. on best treatment for finger tip amputation in children, size and lengthening of human omentum, muscle transplantation by microvascular technique fatigue like normal muscle. Home: 242 Highland Hills Ln Flora MS 39071-9613 Office: 764 Lakeland Dr Ste 306 Jackson MS 39216-4616 Fax: 601-362-0192. E-mail: Sushrata@aol.com.

DAS, T. K. management educator, consultant; b. Calcutta, India, July 8, 1938; BS with honors, U. Calcutta, 1957; MS, Jadavpur U., Calcutta, 1959; M in Mgmt., Asian Inst. Mgmt., Manila, 1977; PhD, UCLA, 1984. Cert. Assoc. of the Indian Inst. of Bankers. Various exec. positions State Bank of India, 1960-76; part-time asst. prof. mgmt. Calif. State U., L.A., 1980-83; asst. prof. strategic mgmt. Tex. Tech U., Lubbock, 1984-86; mem. doctoral faculty CUNY, 1987—; asst. prof. strategic mgmt. Baruch Coll., CUNY, 1987-89, assoc. prof., 1990-96, prof., 1997—; area coord. Strategic Mgmt. and Bus. & Soc., 1997—. Author: Human Resource Management and Productivity: State of the Art and Future Prospects, Vol. I: Focus on the United States, 1984, Vol. II: International Perspectives, 1985, The Subjective Side of Strategy Making: Future Orientations and Perceptions of Executives, 1986, The Time Dimension: An Interdisciplinary Guide, 1990; assoc. editor Rev. of Business Studies, 1992-94, Internat. Jour. Orgnl. Analysis, 1993-96; mem. editorial bd. Jour. Managerial Issues, 1991-94, Internat. Jour. Commerce & Mgmt., 1997—, Jour. of Internat. Mgmt., 2000—; contbr. more than 120 articles to scholarly and profl. jours. Recipient 1st prize Indian Inst. Bankers Prize Essay Competition, 1964, Charat Ram Found. award All India Mgmt. Assn., 1968; grantee CUNY Rsch. Found., 1993-94, 97-98, 98-99, 99-2000, 2001-02. Mem. Strategic Mgmt. Soc., Acad. of Mgmt., Inst. for Ops. Rsch. and the Mgmt. Scis., Soc. for Bus. Ethics, World Future Soc., Internat. Soc. for the Study of Time, Indian Inst. Bankers (life), Beta Gamma Sigma. Office: CUNY Baruch Coll Zicklin Sch Bus Dept Mgmt One Bernard Baruch Way Box B9-240 New York NY 10010-5585 E-mail: TK_Das@baruch.cuny.edu.

DAS, TAPAS KUMAR, chemical and environmental engineer; b. Calcutta, India, Aug. 16, 1951; came to the U.S., 1984; s. Pramatha Nath and Minu (Sircar) D.; m. Deepali Das, July 15, 1985; children: Shiva Nath, Nikhil Chandra. BS in Chem. Engring. with honors, Jadavpur U., Calcutta, 1973; diploma in chem. engring., U. Newcastle Upon Tyne, Eng., 1975; PhD in Chem. Engring., U. Bradford, Eng., 1980. Registered profl. engr., Oreg., Wash., diplomate environ. engr., Am. Acad. Environ. Engrs. Chem. engr. Advanced Materials Engring., Newcastle Upon Tyne, 1975-76; rsch. and tchg. asst. Bradford U., 1977-80; postdoctoral rsch. assoc. Imperial Coll., London, 1981-83; postdoctorl rsch. fellow Princeton (N.J.) U., 1984-86; process engr. R&D Weyerhaeuser Co., Tacoma, 1987-89; sr. process engr. Rabanco Recycling Co., Seattle, 1989-90; environ. engr. Wash. Dept. Ecology, Olympia, 1991—; collaborating R&D with scientists Nat. Environ. Engring. Rsch. Inst., Nagpur, India; cons. Solutia Inc., Springfield, Mass. Tech. adv. bd. mem., Ctr. for Multiphase Environ. Rsch. Washington State U., Pullman; mem. adv. com. Internat. Ctr. Ecol. Engring., Kalyani U., India; mem. adv. com. rsch project Tex. A&M U., Dept. Chem. Engring.; rsch. project co-inventor U. Surray, Dept. Process and Info. Sys. Engring., England; cons. Solutia Inc., Springfield, Mass.; mem. adv. bd. pollution prevention, mass and energy conservation, molecular and product design, chem. engring. dept. Tex. A&M U. Editl. reviewer Clean Technologies and Environ. Policy, Atomization & Sprays, Environ. Progress, Jour. Indsl. Ecology, Ency. Chem. Tech., Jour. Hazardous Materials, 1988—; contbr. articles to profl. jours. Mem. AIChE (chair/co-chair conf. sessions 1997—, chair/co-chair best session 1998, dir. environ. divsn., chair water sect. environ. divsn., past chmn., vice chair, past sec. and treas., chair Puget Sound sect., liason between AIChE and Water Environ. Fedn. Bioenergy Tech. Subcom., mem. Inst. for Sustainability, chmn. tropical conf. on sustainability and life cycle assessment 2003), Air & Waste Mgmt., Internat. Inst. Liquid Atomization and Spray Sys., Inst. Chem. Engrs. Hindu. Avocations: cricket, soccer, fishing, walking, music. Home: 125 Mandy Pl NE Olympia WA 98516-1731 Office: Wash Dept Ecology 300 Desmond Dr SE Olympia WA 98504-0001 E-mail: tdas461@ecy.wa.gov., shivaniki@comcast.net.

DASBACH, OLIVER T. mathematician, educator; b. Cologne, Germany, Feb. 23, 1967; Dr. rer. nat, Heinrich-Heine U., Düsseldorf, 1997. Vis. scholar Columbia U., N.Y.C., 1997—98; vis. faculty mem. U. Calif., Riverside, 1999—2001, Okla. State U., Stillwater, 2001—02; asst. prof. La. State U., Baton Rouge, 2002—. Author: (book) On Subspaces of the Space of Vassiliev Invariants, 1997; contbr. articles. Rsch. fellow, Deutsche Forschungsgemeinschaft, 1997—99. Office: La State Univ Dept Math Baton Rouge LA 70803 Business E-Mail: kasten@math.lsu.edu.

DASBURG, JOHN HAROLD, restaurant executive; b. N.Y.C., Jan. 7, 1943; s. Jean Henry and Alice Etta Dasburg; m. Mary Lois Diaz, July 6, 1968; children: John Peter, Kathryn. AA, U. Miami, 1963; BS in Indsl. Engring., U. Fla., 1966, MBA, 1971, JD, 1973. Bar: Fla. 1974; CPA, Fla., Md. Staff Peat Marwick Mitchell & Co., Jacksonville, Fla., 1973-78, tax ptnr. in charge, 1978-80; v.p. tax Marriott Corp., Washington, 1980-82, v.p. fin., 1982-84, sr. v.p., 1984-85, exec. v.p., CFO, chief real estate officer, 1985-88, pres. lodging group, 1988-89; pres., CEO Northwest Airlines, 1990-2001; chmn. Burger King Corp., Miami, Fla., 2001—, pres., CEO, 2001—02. Bd. dirs. St. Paul Cos., Genuity. Contbr. articles to profl. jours. Lt. (j.g.) USN, 1966-69, Vietnam. Republican. Roman Catholic.

DASCENZI, HAZEL MARIE, real estate broker; b. Palestine, Tex., Sept. 6, 1920; d. Calvin Coolidge and Sarah Ethel (Evans) Click; divorced; children: Sharron Marie Beamer, Phillip Chris. Cert. paralegal, So. Calif. Coll. Law, 1990. Lic. real estate broker. Broker, owner Hazel's Realty, Buena Park, Calif., 1959-78, Sunnymead, Calif., 1980-82, San Juan Capistrano, Calif., 1982—; v.p. Harbor View Fin. Svcs., Newport Beach, Calif., 1989—92. Chmn. Silverado Days, Buena Park Gala. Recipient Plaque of Appreciation, Buena Park, Cypress, La Palma Bd. Realtors, 1963, Cert. and Plaque, Women's div. C. of C., Buena Park, 1966-69, Disting. Svc. award Buena Park Jr. C. of C., 1967, Outstanding Chairmanship award and Realtor of Yr. award Calif. Real Estate Assn. Mem. Am. Soc. Disting. Citizens (life). Republican. Mem. Sci. of Mind. Avocations: dancing, hiking, reading, cooking. Home and Office: 151 Gauguin Cir Aliso Viejo CA 92656-3878

DASCHER, PAUL EDWARD, university dean, accounting educator; b. Oct. 1, 1942; s. Albert Jacob abd Ruth (Mountney) D.; m. Nancy Patricia Byrne; children: Mitchell Paul, Heidi Beth. BS, Pa. State U., 1964, MS, 1966, PhD, 1969. Instr. acctg. Pa. State U., 1968-69; asst. prof. acctg. Va. Poly. Inst., Blacksburg, 1969-71, assoc. prof. acctg., 1971-73; prof. acctg. Drexel U., Phila., 1973-93, dept. head, 1974-77, dean Coll. of Bus. and Adminstrn., 1977-93; dean Sch. Bus. Adminstrn. Stetson U., Deland, Fla., 1993—, prof. acctg., 1993—. Vis. prof. Northeastern U., Boston, 1976; cons. Price Waterhouse and Co., N.Y.C., 1974-75; lectr. in field. Co-author: Financial Accounting, 1980, 4th edit., 1995, Accounting Readings, 1982, Managerial Accounting, 1985, 11th edit., 2002; contbr. numerous articles to profl. jours. Fellow Price Waterhouse & Co., Armstrong Cork Co.; recipient Nat. Assn. Accts. Socio-Econ. Disting. Service award, 1973, 75, 81, Drexel U. Faculty Appreciation award, 1977, Commendation Phila. chpt. Pa. Inst CPA's, 1977, Community Accts. Meritorious Service award, 1981; named one of Outstanding Young Men of Am., 1979. Mem. Am. Acctg. Assn., Fin. Execs. Inst., Inst. Mgmt. Accts. (nat. v.p. 1989-90), Accts. for Pub. Interest (pres. 1986-89), Alpha Kappa Psi, Beta Alpha Psi, Beta Gamma Sigma. Republican. Lutheran. Avocations: tennis, reading. Office: Stetson U Sch Bus Adm Deland FL 32723

DASCHLE, THOMAS ANDREW, senator; b. Aberdeen, S.D., Dec. 9, 1947; m. Linda Hall Daschle; children: Kelly, Nathan, Lindsay. BA, S.D. State U., 1969. Fin. investment rep.; chief legis. aide, field coordinator Sen. James Abourzek, 1973-77; mem. 96th-97th Congresses from 1st S.D. Dist., U.S. Ho. of Reps., 1978—86, 98th-99th Congresses at large, 1983-87; U.S. senator from S.D., 1986—; senate minority leader 104th, 105th, 106th, 107th Congress, 1996—2001; majority leader, 2001. Mem. agrl. nutrition and forestry com., mem. fin. com., rules com., co-chmn. Sen. Dem. steering and coord. com., co-chair Sen. Dem. tech. and comm. com., chmn. Sen. Dem. conf. com., co-chmn. Sen. Dem. policy com.; leader bipartisan effort ; author, enforcer Agent Orange Act, 1991; authored, reformulated gasoline provisions of Clean Air Act Amendment 1990. Founder Am. Grown Found., 1987. Served to 1st lt. USAF, 1969-72. Recipient Nat. Commdr.'s award Disabled Am. Vets., 1980, Disting. Alumni award S.D. State U., 1997, VFW Congl. award VFW, 1997, Legislator of Yr. award Vietnam Vets. Am., 1997, Cert. Appreciation, Nat. Assn. Federally Impacted Sch., 1997, Congl. Leadership award Cmty. Anti-Drug Coalitions Am., 1997, Golden Triangle award Nat. Farmer's Union, 1997-98, Outstanding Vets. Adv. of Yr. award Disabled Am. Vets. Dept. S.D., 1998, Pres. Recognition award Nat. Indian Impacted Schs. Assn., 1998, Cert. Appreciation, Nat. Assn. Alcoholism and Drug Abuse Counselors, 1998, Diplomat award Rapid City C. of C., 1998, Disting. Svc. award Nat. Rural Electric Coop. Assn., 2000; named Outstanding Young Man of Yr., U.S. Jaycees, 1981, Friend of Edn., S.D. Edn. Assn., 1997, Person of the Yr., Nat. Assn. Concerned Vets., 1997, Legislator of Yr., Renewable Fuels Assn., 1998, Maj. Gen. Williamson's S.D. Nat. Guard Militia Man of 1998, S.D. Nat. Guard. Democrat. Roman Catholic. Office: US Senate 509 Hart Senate Bldg Washington DC 20510-0001*

DASCOMB, AUDREY LYNN, dance educator; b. Chelmsford, Mass., Dec. 22, 1968; d. Edmund E. Jr. and Audrey Jane (Cooper) W. BFA, Lake Erie Coll., 1990. Cert. tchr. Ohio; registered dance educator. Dance educator Ashtabula (Ohio) Arts Ctr., 1990-92, Ashtabula City Schs., 1991-92, Phillips-Osborne Sch., Painesville, Ohio, 1990-96, Kirtland/Mentor (Ohio) Dances, 1991-96; dir. Dance Expressions Unltd., Mass., 1996—. Choreographer numerous dance concerts and musicals; appeared in Chorus Line, 1990, Tapestry, 1999, Nutcracker, 1999-2000, Impulse Dance Co., 1999, Sleeping Beauty, 2000. Active World Wildlife Fund, Sponsor the Whales, United Cerebral Palsy Found., Am. Cancer Soc., Epilepsy Found, Sponsor the Wolves. Dance Tchrs.' Club of Boston scholar, 1983-85. Mem. AAHPERD, Nat. Dance Edn. Assn., Nat. Dance Assn., Nat. Registry of Dance Educators, Internat. Tap Assn., Pythian Sisters, Arts Coun. Coop, Dance Tchr.'s Club Boston, Greater Lowell C. of C. Avocations: reading, sports, crafts, sewing. Office: 73 Progress Ave #1 Tyngsboro MA 01879-2725 E-mail: danceexpressionsunlimited@attbi.com.

DASENBROCK, REED WAY, literature educator; b. Sept. 18, 1953; Degree, McGill U., Oxford U.; PhD, Johns Hopkins U., 1982. Asst. prof. N.Mex. State U., Las Cruces, 1982—86, assoc. prof., 1986—91, prof. Eng., 1991, dept. head, 1994. Jerome S. Cardin vis. chair humanities Loyola Coll., Md., 1992—93. Office: NMex State Univ Dept Eng Dept 3E Las Cruces NM 88003 E-mail: rdasenbr@nmsu.edu.

DASGUPTA, INDRANIL, physician, educator; b. Barielly, India, May 24, 1960; came to the U.S., 1961; s. Sunil Pryia and Krishna Dasgupta. BA in Philosophy, Duke U., 1982; MPH in Internat. Health, Loma Linda U., 1987; cert. epidemiology, Johns Hopkins U., 1987; MBA in Fin., George Washington U., 1989; MD, St. George's (Grenada) U., 1994. Diplomate Am. Bd. Internal Medicine. Congl. intern U.S. Ho. of Reps., Washington, 1983; rsch. asst. Harvard Med. Sch., Boston, 1983-84, Dartmouth U. Med. Sch., Hanover, N.H., 1985-86; rsch. assoc. Loma Linda (Calif.) Sch. Pub. Health, 1986-87; congl. intern U.S. Senator Ed Kennedy, Washington, 1988-89; med. resident Med. Coll. Pa.-Hahnemann U. Hosps., Phila., 1995-98, rsch. assoc., 1998-99, geriatric fellow, 1998-99; cardiology fellow Robert Wood Johnson Med. Sch. U. Medicine and Dentistry N.J., Camden, 1999—2002, rsch. assoc., 1999—2002; clin. asst. prof. divsn. cardiology Jefferson Med. Coll., Phila., 2002—, attending cardiologist Thomas Jefferson U. Hosp., Phila., 2002—. Contbr.: U.S. House Select Committee on Aging, 1983. Vol. Muscular Dystrophy Assn., Winston-Salem, N.C., 1981, U.S. Spl. Olympics, Wilmington, Del., 1985, Dem. Fund Raising, Washington, 1988. Mem.: ACP, NY Acad. Scis., NJ Acad. Sci., Nat. Assn. for Advancement of Sci., Am. Heart Assn., Am. Coll. Cardiology, Delta Omega, Sigma Alpha Epsilon. Democrat. Avocations: traveling, sailing, snorkling, soccer. Home: 2528 Tigani Dr Wilmington DE 19808 Office: Thomas Jefferson U Hosp Jefferson Heart Inst 925 Chestnut St Mezzanine Level Philadelphia PA 19107 E-mail: indranildasgupta@aol.com.

DASGUPTA, RATHINDRA, metallurgical engineer; b. Calcutta, India, Nov. 12, 1948; s. Saral and Manjuli Dasgupta; m. Jean Marie Loritz, June 30, 1977; children: Steven Kumar, Ryan K. MS in Materials Sci., U. Wis., 1974, PhD in Metall. Engring., 1978. Lectr. dept. metall. engring. U. Wis., Madison, 1978—79; prof. dept. mech. engring. Milw. Sch. Engring., 1979—90; tech. dir. Meta Mold Divsn. AMCAST Indsl. Corp., Cedarburg, Wis., 1990—91; tech. and applications mgr. SPX Corp. CONTECH Divsn., Portage, Mich., 1991—96, chief scientist, 1997—. Vis. rsch. prof. China Steel Corp., Kaohsiung, Taiwan, 1985; program dir. dept. mech. engring. Milw. Sch. Engring., 1989—90; adj. prof. dept. materials sci. U. Wis., Milw., 1984—86. Co-author: Science and Technology of Semi-Solid Metal Processing. Recipient Ryerson Outstanding Undergraduate Tchr. award, Inland Steel, 1985. Mem.: N.Am. Dic Casting Assn. (R & D com. 1997, Doehler award 2000), Am. Soc. Metals, Am. Foundrymen's Soc. Achievements include patents pending for aluminum alloy, casting process and product. Home: 7109 Hickory Point Dr Portage MI 49024 Office: SPX Corp CONTECH Divsn 8001 Angling Rd Portage MI 49024 E-mail: babu.dasgupta@contech.spx.com.

DAS GUPTA, SUBAL, physics educator, researcher; b. Calcutta, India, Aug. 11, 1939; emigrated to Can., 1960; s. Subodh Chandra and Pritilata (Sen) Das G.; m. Sanjukta Sen Gupta, Aug. 12, 1965; children: Monidipa, Nandini. MSc, Calcutta U., 1959; PhD, McMaster U., 1963. Nat. Scis. and Engring. Rsch. Coun. Can. post-doctoral fellow AECL, Chalk River, Ont., Can., 1963-64; rsch. sci. Tata Inst. for Fundamental Rsch., Bombay, India, 1964-65; postdoctoral fellow in physics McGill U., Montreal, Que., Can., 1965-66, asst. prof. physics, 1967-71, assoc. prof., 1972-77, prof., 1978—, chair dept. physics, 1993-97, prof. physics, 1997—. Contbr. articles to profl. jours. Oper. grantee Nat. Sci. and Engring. Rsch. Coun. Can., 1966—. Office: McGill U Dept Physics ERP 319 3600 University St Montreal QC Canada H3A 2T8 E-mail: dasgupta@physics.mcgill.ca.

DASGUPTA, UDAYAN, electrical engineer, researcher; b. Calcutta, West Bengal, India, Nov. 22, 1970; arrived in U.S., 1996,arrived in U.S., 1996; s. Maniklal and Kabita Dasgupta; m. Sujayanti Bose, Aug. 4, 1997. BTech., Indian Inst.Tech, Bombay, India, 1993; PhD, Tex. A&M U., College Station,. 2000. Mgmt. trainee Philips India, Bombay, 1993—94; software engr. Fujitsu ICIM, Bombay, 1995; sr. rsch. assoc. CSRE, Indian Inst. of Tech., Bombay, 1995—96; rsch. asst. Tex. A&M U., College Station, Tex., 1996—2000; mem. of tech. staff DSP R&D Ctr., Tex. Instruments, Dallas, 2000—. Contbr. articles to profl. jours.; reviewer: Internat. Conf. on Comm., 2003. Mem.: IEEE Info. Theory Soc., IEEE Signal Processing Soc., IEEE Comm. Soc. (reviewer, vol. Vehicular Tech. Conf. 1999, reviewer comms. letters 2000—02). Achievements include patents pending for. Avocations: reading, travel. Office: Texas Instruments 12500 TI Blvd MS 8653 Dallas TX 75243 Business E-Mail: udayan@ti.com.

DASH, BARRY HAROLD, pharmaceutical company executive; b. N.Y.C., June 9, 1931; s. Joseph and Anna (Levine) D.; m. Selma Magid, Dec. 19, 1953; children: Faith, Neil, Jeffrey. BS, Columbia U., 1952, MS, 1954; PhD, U. Fla., 1956. Diplomate Am. Bd. Forensic Examiners. Asst. prof. Columbia U., N.Y.C., 1956-60; dir. rsch. and devel. Whitehall Labs., N.Y.C., 1960-70, v.p. sci. affairs, 1970-76; v.p., dir. labs. Am. Can Co., Greenwich, Conn., 1976-78; v.p. rsch. and devel. J.B. Williams Co., Div. Nabisco, N.Y.C., 1978-82; v.p. sci. affairs Whitehall div. Am. Home Products, N.Y.C., 1983-91, sr. v.p. sci. affairs, 1991-94, sr. v.p. adv. tech., 1994-95; pres. Dash Assocs. LLC, N.J., 1995—; indsl. cons., 1956-60; vis. staff Pfizer & Co., Bklyn., 1958; clin. prof. Coll. Podiatry, L.I. U., 1958-60; nat. seminar chmn. Soc. Cosmetic Chemists, N.Y.C., 1962. Contbg. editor: Remington's Practice of Pharmacy, 12th edit. 1960. Patentee in field. Mem. N.J. Fed. Bds. of Edn., Englewood Cliffs, 1965-68, v.p., 1965-68. Fellow Am. Found. Pharm. Edn., 1954-56; recipient Lascoff award, Columbia U., 1950, Merck award, 1952. Mem. AAAS, Am. Pharm. Assn., N.Y. Acad. Sci., Soc. Cosmetic Chemists, Phi Kappa Phi, Rho Chi. Avocations: boating, tennis. Home: 168 Wood Rd Englewood Cliffs NJ 07632-1625 Office: Dash Assoc LLC 168 Wood Rd Englewood Cliffs NJ 07632-1625

DASH, LEON DECOSTA, JR., journalist; b. New Bedford, Mass., Mar. 16, 1944; s. Leon DeCosta and Ruth Elizabeth (Kydd). BA, Howard U., 1968; DHD, Lincoln U., 1996. Reporter Washington Post, 1966—68, 1971—79, African bur. chief, 1979—83, with investigations desk, 1984—98; prof. journalism & afro-Am. studies U. Ill., Champaign, 1998—99, Swanlund chair prof. journalism and Afro-Am. studies, 2000—01, Swanlund prof. journalism, 2001—; prof. journalism Ctr. Advances Studies, 2003—. Vis. prof. U. Calif.-San Diego, 1978. Author (with Ben H. Bagdikian): (book) The Shame of the Prisons, 1972; author: When Children Want Children: The Urban Crisis of Teenage Childbearing, 1989, Rosa Lee: A Mother and Her Family in Urban America, 1996 (Polit. Book award Washington Monthly Mag., 1997, 1st prize Harry Chapin Best Book award World Hunger Yr. Orgn., 1997). Vol. Peace Corps, Kenya, 1969—70. Co-recipient Editl. award for news series, Chesapeake AP, 1987, Editl. award, 1989; named one of Best 100 Works in 20th Century Am. Journalism for 8-part series Rosa Lee's Story for Washington Post, 1999; recipient George Polk Meml. award, Overseas Press Club, 1974, award for internat. news reporting, Washington Balt. Newspaper Guild, 1974, hon. mention, 1975, Internat. Reporting award, Africare, 1984, Capitol Press Club, 1984, 1st Place Journalism award for gen. news, Nat. Assn. Black Journalists, 1986, Investigative Reporters and Editors award, 1987, 1st Prize award, Washington-Balt. Newspaper Guild, 1987, Pres.'s award, Washington Ind. Writers Assn., 1989, Martha Albrand Spl. Citation for Nonfiction, PEN, 1990, Pulitzer Prize for explanatory journalism, 1995, 1st Prize Robert F. Kennedy award for print journalism, 1995, Emmy award for pub. affairs, NATAS, 1996, Polit. Book award, The Washington Monthly mag., 1997, Prevention for a Safer Soc. award, Nat. Coun. on Crime and Delinquency for Rosa Lee book, 1997; Henry J. Kaiser Family Found. fellow, 1995—96. Office: U Ill Dept Journalism 119 Gregory Hall 810 S Wright St Urbana IL 61801-3644 E-mail: leondash@uiuc.edu.

DASH, SANFORD MARK, aerospace scientist; b. N.Y.C., May 26, 1943; s. Jack and Rachael (Calamar) D.; m. Barbara Gaile Held; children: David, Kenneth, Jonathan, Naomi. BSME, CCNY, 1964; MS in Aeronautics and Astronautics, NYU, 1966, PhD in Aeronautics and Astronautics, 1969. Rsch. scientist Gen. Applied Sci. Labs., Westbury, N.Y., 1969-77; cons. Aero. Rsch. Assocs. Princeton, N.J., 1977-80; v.p., mgr. propulsive scis. divsn. Sci. Applications Internat. Corp., Princeton, N.J., 1980-94; pres., chief scientist Combustion Rsch. and Flow Tech., Inc., Pipersville, Pa., 1994—. Cons. in field. Contbr. over 250 articles to profl. pubs., chpts. to books. Recipient Cert. of

Recognition, NASA, 1975, USAF, 1985. Fellow: AIAA (assoc.; chmn. aero-acoustics tech. com. 1997—99, Aerospace Profl. of Yr. 2002); mem.: NATO and Joint Army, Navy, NASA, Air Force Coms. Achievements include development of U.S. standard plume flowfield models for aircraft and missiles; rsch. on Nat. Aerospace Plane Program. E-mail: dash@craft-tech.com.

DASHER, BONITA ANN, accountant; b. Jacksonville, Fla., Nov. 22, 1955; d. Joseph Mitchel and Martha Ann (Petree) Davenport; m. Curtis W. Dasher, July 27, 1974; children: Jennifer Ann, Amy Kristina. BBA in Acctg. cum laude, U. North Fla., 1992. CPA, Fla. Staff acct. Robert Bradley, CPA, Green Cove Springs, Fla., 1994; in-charge sr. DuVal, Horne & Co., CPAs, PA, Orange Park, Fla., 1995—. Vol. J.P. Hall Children's Charities Bass Tournament, Green Cove Springs, 1992-94. Mem. Fla. Inst. CPA, Phi Kappa Phi, Beta Gamma Sigma. Republican. Baptist. Avocation: needlework. Home: 3969 Susan Dr Green Cove Springs FL 32043-9359 Office: 401 Walnut St Green Cove Springs FL 32043 E-mail: BDasher@aol.com., SJDuVal@aol.com.

DASHIELL, FRANK STEPHEN, IV, writer; b. Atlanta, Feb. 20, 1951; s. Stephen Frank Dashiell and Billie Carol Putman Dashiell; m. Matilon McKee, Nov. 4, 1974 (div. Nov. 1977). Degree in Environ. Econ., West Ga. Coll., 1974; postgrad., Harvard U. Author: Hoof, Roof, Woof, 1996, Compost Pile, 1996, Sledge & Wedge, 1997. Green Party. Methodist. Avocations: breeding rabbits, sports. Home and Office: Dashiell Cottages Inc PO Box 82483 Athens GA 30608

DA SILVA, DELIO P. investment advisor; b. Macau, Portugal, Aug. 20, 1948; came to U.S., 1978; s. João Santos and Maria Dionizia Eusebio Pereira Da Silva; m. Rosalie R. P. Da Silva, June 1980 (div. Aug. 1986); children: Alexia C. P., Simone P. BS, U. London, 1977; MBA, U. Calif., Berkeley, 1983. Registered investment advisor. Negotiator Bank of Tokyo, San Francisco; fgn. trade advisor Bank of Brasil, San Francisco; fin. advisor bus. devel. Coast Savs. Bank, San Francisco; specialist fin. advisor Roberts & Ryan, San Francisco; investment fin. advisor Am. Express, San Francisco; investment and fin. advisor Associated Securities, San Francisco; registered investment advisor D.P. Da Silva (R.I.A.) & Co., San Francisco. V.p. Marin Cultural Ctr. and Mus., Ross, Calif., 1988; mem. adv. bd. Portuguese C. of C., San Jose, 1995. With M.P., 1970-72, Portugal. Mem. San Francisco Fine Arts Mus., Commonwealth Club, World Trade Club, Portuguese Athletic Club, Marin Cricket Club. Republican. Roman Catholic. Home: 1100 Gough St 8th Fl San Francisco CA 94109-6648 Office: D P Da Silva (RIA) & Co Ste 200 Two Embarcadero Ctr San Francisco CA 94111

DA SILVA, ERCIO MARIO, physician; b. Catajuczes, Minas, Brazil; s. Mario and Rosa (Pinto) da S.; m. Doris Hale da Silva, Aug. 22, 1953; children: Robert, Suzanne. MD, U. Mines, Brazil, 1949. Diplomate Am. Bd. Colon Rectal Surgery. Physician U.S. Mil. Base, Columbia, S.C., 1988—. Mem. Am. Soc. Colon Rectal Surgery, Columbia Med. Soc. Home: 413 Brookshire Dr Columbia SC 29210-4203

DASILVA, WILLARD H. lawyer, educator; b. Freeport, N.Y., Oct. 17, 1923; BA, NYU, 1946; LLB, Columbia U., 1949. Bar: N.Y. 1949, U.S. Tax Ct. 1969, U.S. Supreme Ct. 1969. Pvt. practice, N.Y.C., 1969-70, Carle Place, N.Y., 1973-76, Garden City, NY, 1978—91; ptnr. Goodman & DaSilva, N.Y.C., 1970-73, DaSilva & Samuelson, Garden City, 1977, DaSilva & Keidel, Garden City, 1992—97, DaSilva, Garson & Hilowitz LLP, Garden City, 1998-99, DaSilva, Hilowitz & McEvily LLP, Garden City, 1999—. V.p. Marcus Bros. Textile Corp., N.Y.C., 1961-63; pres. Cortley Fabrics subs. Cone Mills Corp., N.Y.C., 1964-65; lectr. Columbia U. Law Sch., Bklyn. Law Sch., St. John's Law Sch., Cardozo Law Sch., Hofstra U. Law Sch., Touro Law Sch.; mem. faculty Practising Law Inst., N.Y.C., 1972—; mem. nat. panel arbitrators Am. Arbitration Assn., 1965-2001. Author: N.Y. Matrimonial Practice, 1980—; editor Matrimonial Law Jour., 1977-85, Fair Share mag., 1985-99, N.Y. Matrimonial Case Law, 1985—; editor-author Family Law Practice Systems Manual, 1982—; editor-in-chief N.Y. Domestic Rels. Reporter, 1992—; editor NY Bar Jour., 1999—; contbr. articles to law jours. Trustee NAFA Found., 1977-85; trustee North Shore U. Hosp., 1988=95, chmn. adv. bd. family in transition program, 1991—; atty. Edn. and Assistance Corp., 1992-97. 2d lt. USAAF, 1942-46. Fellow ABA (coun. family law sect. 1992—, editor-in-chief Family Adv. 1981—), N.Y. State Bar Found. (former mem.); mem. Am. Coll. Family Trial Lawyers (diplomate), Am. Acad. Matrimonial Lawyers (pres. 1982-84, bd. mgrs. 1977—), N.Y. State Trial Lawyers Assn., Am. Bar Found., N.Y. State Bar Assn. (CLE com. 1980-90, program chmn. family law sect. 1978-82, sec. gen. practice sect. 1994-95, chmn. matrimonial com. 1989—, coun. 1992—, chmn.-elect 1995-96, chmn. 1996-97, editor Jour. 2000—), Nassau County Bar Assn., Suffolk County Bar Assn. (chmn. family law sect. 1982-84), N.Y. Family Law Am. Inn of Ct. (master 1995—, sec. 1999-2000, counsel 2001-02, pres. 2003—), Internat. Soc. on Family Law, Am. Soc. Writers on Legal Subjects, Phi Beta Kappa. Office: 585 Stewart Ave Garden City NY 11530-4783

DASKIN, MARK STEPHEN, civil engineering educator; b. Balt., Dec. 3, 1952; s. Walter and Betty Jane (Fax) D.; m. Babette Reva Levy, July 2, 1978; children: Tamar, Keren. BSCE, MIT, 1974; postgrad. study in Engring., Cambridge, England, 1975; PhD in Civil Engring., MIT, 1978. Tchg. asst. trans. sys. divsn. civil engring. MIT, Cambridge, 1976-77; asst. prof. civil engring. Univ. Tex., Austin, 1978-79, Northwestern U., Evanston, Ill., 1980-83, assoc. prof. civil engring., 1983-89, prof., 1989—, chair dept. indsl. engring. and mgmt. scis., 1995—2001. Author: Network and Discrete Location: Models, Algorithms and Applications, 1995; editor-in-chief Transp. Sci., 1991-94; assoc. editor Location Sci., 1991-2000; contbr. articles to profl. jours. Bd. dirs. North Suburban Synagogue Beth El, Highland Park, Ill., 1991-94. Univ. Tex. Bur. Engring. Rsch. grant, 1978-79, Northwestern Univ. Transp. Ctr. grant, 1980, 81, NSF grant, 1980-82, 84-90, 93-97, 96-99, 1998-. Urban Mass Transp. Adminstr. grant, 1982-84, 84-85, United Parcel Svc. grant, 1983-86, 91-92, Thermo-King Corp. grant, 1990-91, 92-94, Heartland Blood Ctr. grant, 1992, 96; recipient Fulbright Rsch. award, 1989-90, Burlington Northern Found. Faculty Achievement award, 1985, NSF Presdl. Young Investigator award, 1984, Scott Paper Leadership award, 1973-75, IIE Tech. Innovation award in indusl. engring. Mem. ASCE, Inst. Indsl. Engrs. (editor-in-chief IEE Transactions 2001—), INFORMS (v.p. publs. 1996-99), Ops. Rsch. Soc. Am. (jour. editor 1991-94), Inst. Mgmt. Sci., Sigma Xi, Tau Beta Pi, Chi Epsilon. Avocations: swimming, photography. Office: Northwestern U Dept Indsl Engring Mgmt Sci Evanston IL 60208-0001 E-mail: daskin@iems.nwu.edu.

DASSANOWSKY, ROBERT VON, educator, producer, writer, editor; b. N.Y., Jan. 28, 1960; s. Elfi von Dassanowsky. Grad., Am. Acad. Dramatic Arts; BA with honors, UCLA, 1985, MA, 1988, PhD, 1992. Actor, 1975—; asst. prof. German, UCLA, 1992-93; asst. prof. German U. Colo., Colorado Springs, 1993-99, head German studies, 1993—, assoc. prof. German and film, dir. film studies, 1999—, interim chair dept. visual and performing arts, 2000-01, chair dept. langs. and cultures, 2001—. Author: (plays) The Birthday of Margot Beck, 1980, Briefly Noted, 1981, Vespers, 1982 (Beverly Hills Theatre Guild award 1984), Tristan in Winter, 1986, Songs of a Wayfarer, 1986, Coda, 1991, (criticism) Phantom Empires: The Novels of A. Lernet-Holenia and the Question of Postimperial Austrian Identity, 1996, Verses of a Marriage, Translation of Poetry Collection by Hans Raimund, 1996, Telegrams from the Metropole: Selected Poetry, 1999, Gale Encyclopedia of Multicultural America, 2nd edit., 2000; contbg. editl. advisor: International Dictionary of Films and Filmmakers, 4th edit., 2001, Mars in Aries, trans. of novel by A. Lernet-Holenia, 2003, Austrian Cinema: A History 1895-2003, 2003; founding editor Rohwedder: Internat. Jour. Lit. and Art, 1986-93; editor Pen Center mag., 1992-98; contbg. editor Osiris, Rampike, Adirondack Rev., Poetry Salzburg Rev.; exec. prodr. The Nightmare Stumbles Past, 2002, Semmelweis, 2001, Wilson Chance, 2003; co-prodr. Epicure, 2002, Believe, 2003. Mem. Accademia Culturale d'Europa, Italy; bd. dirs. L.A. Flickapalooza Film Festival, The Internt. Exptl. Film Exposition, Denver Brit. Film Festival. Decorated Knight, Constantinian Order St. George; City of L.A. cultural grantee, 1990, 91, 92, U. Colo. Pres. Fund for Humanities grantee, 1996, 2001; recipient Residency award Karolyi Found., France, 1979, Accademico Honoris Causa Diploma, Accademia Culturale d'Europa, Italy, 1989, Letters, Arts and Scis. Rsch. and Creative Work award U. Colo., 2002. Mem. MLA, PEN (West bd. dirs. L.A. 1992-99, founder and pres. Colo. chpt. 1994-99 2002-03), PEN Austria, Internat. Lernet-Holenia Soc. (v.p. 1998—), Austrian Am. Film Assn. (v.p. 1997—), Austria Mundi (U.S. rep. 2002—), Soc. Cinema Studies, Poets and Writers, L.A. Poetry Festival, SAG, Concordia Assn. Journalists and Writers (Austria), Am. Coll. Heraldry (bd. govs. 2000—), Am. Fedn. Film Prodrs., European Acad. Arts and Scis., U.S. Fencing Assn. Office: U Colo Dept Langs and Cultures Colorado Springs CO 80933 E-mail: belvederefilm@yahoo.com.

DASSO, JEROME JOSEPH, real estate educator; b. Neillsville, Wis., Jan. 12, 1929; s. Henry J. and Frances (Schweickert) D.; m. Patricia Mary Conger, June 13, 1959 (div. 1978); children: James Daniel, Mary Cecilia, Nancy Ann, Wendy Jo. BS, Purdue U., 1951; MBA, U. Mich., 1952; MS, U. Wis., 1960, PhD, 1964. Ptnr. Dasso Constrn. Co., Dubuque, Iowa, 1956-58; planner Franklin County, Columbus, Ohio, 1960-61; asst. prof. U. Ill., Urbana, 1964-66; vis. chairholder U. Hawaii, Honolulu, 1982-83; mem. faculty U. Oreg., Eugene, 1966-95, H.T. Miner chair in real estate, 1978-95, H.T. Miner chair emeritus, 1995—. Vis. prof. U. Wis., Madison, 1984; cons. Internat. Assn. Assessing Officers, Chgo., 1972-75; edl. cons. Hawaii Real Estate Commn., Honolulu, 1982-83. Co-author: (S. Kahn, R. Nesslinger et a)l Principle of Right of Way Acquisition, 1972, (with G. Kuhn) Real Estate Finance, 1983, (with A.A. Ring) Real Estate Principles and Practices, 8th edit., 1977, 9th edit., 1981, 10th edit., 1985, 11th edit., 1989, (with Jim Shilling) 12th edit., 1995, Computerized Assessment Adminstration, 1973; contbr. numerous articles to various publs. Lt. USNR, 1952—60. Vivian Stewart vis. fellow Cambridge U., spring, 1987. Fellow Am. Inst. Corp. Asset Mgmt. (bd. govs. 1988-91), Homer Hoyt Inst. Adv. Studies Real Estate & Urban Land Econs.; mem. Real Estate Educators Assn. (pres. 1980-81, Outstanding Svc. award 1981, Disting. Career award 1989), Am. Real Estate and Urban Econs. Assn. (bd. dirs. 1974-77, 80-83), Real Estate Ctr. Dirs. Chairholders Assn. (pres. 1987-88), Am. Real Estate Soc. (life, bd. dirs. 1985-86, v.p. 1988-89, pres. elect 1989-90, pres. 1990-91), Am. Fin. Assn. (life), Nat. Assn. Realtors (edn. com. 1970-76), Internat. Real Estate Soc. (pres. 1994-95), VFW. Roman Catholic. Avocations: golf, skiing, hiking, photography.

DASTIN, SAMUEL J. aerospace engineer, consultant; b. N.Y.C., Oct. 18, 1930; s. Murray Dastin and Gertrude Gold; m. Elaine Ruth Cohen, Jan. 24, 1953; children: Barry, Mona, Richard. BChE, CCNY, 1954. Chief materials and processes engr. Republic Aviation Corp., Farmingdale, NY, 1954—64; dir. advanced materials Northrop-Grumman Corp., Bethpage, NY, 1964—95; v.p., chief engr. Dastin Assocs. Co., Inc., Las Vegas, Nev., 1995—. Mem. tech. steering com. NASA, Langley, Va., 1985, mem. adv. bd. 1990—95; bd. dirs. Am. Def. Preparedness Assn., Washington, 1992; dir. Materials Property Coun., N.Y.C., 1992—; cons. Wright Patterson AFB, Dayton, Ohio, 1985—90. Author: Tooling for Aircraft Manufacture, 1964; contbr. articles to profl. jours. Recipient award of excellence, Soc. Plastics Inst., 1979, Merit award, NASA, 1983, cert. of appreciation, NSF, 1991. Fellow: Soc. Mfg. Engrs. (Jud Hall award 1989), Soc. for Advancement of Material and Process Engring. Achievements include development of advanced composite structures for both military and commercial aircraft; invention of hybrid composite structure. Avocations: restoring old autos, tennis, bridge, aircraft modeling. Home: 10713 Button Willow Dr Las Vegas NV 89134 Fax: 702-256-9335 ext. 5**. E-mail: samdastin@aol.com.

D'ASTOLFO, FRANK JOSEPH, graphic designer, educator; b. Charleroi, Pa., July 19, 1943; s. Galderino Joseph and Gustina Evlyn (Petaccia) D'A. BA, Pa. State U., 1966; MA, U. Pitts., 1973. Graphic designer The United Fund, Pitts., 1968-69, Fisher Sci. Co., Pitts., 1969-73; instr. U. Pitts., 1972-76; graphic designer Pitt Studios, Pitts., 1973-74; design cons. Frank D'Astolfo Design, Pitts., 1974-77; instr. Tyler Sch. Art, Phila., 1977-80; design cons. Infield & D'Astolfo, N.Y.C., 1980-88; prof. Rutgers U., Newark, 1980—; design cons. Frank D'Astolfo Design, N.Y.C., 1988—. Cons. in field; chmn. dept. art and design Rutgers U., Newark, 1989-92, dep. chmn. dept. visual and performing arts, 1992-00; bd. dirs. Ringside Inc., N.Y.C., 198 7—; mem. Newark Arts Coun., 1993-96. Graphic designer Print Mag., 1992, 93 (Fifty Best Ann. Reports 1984, 86, Best Logos and Symbols vol. II, III and IV), Graphis Diagram I, 1988, Am. Corporate Identity 5-12, 15, 1989-96, 99 (awards of excellence), Metropolis The Architecture and Design Mag., New York, 1985. Design cons. Architects, Designers and Planners for Social Responsibility, N.Y.C., 1985, ICIS Internat. Ctr. for Integrating Studies, N.Y.C., 1983; dir. Com. for Cultural Awareness and Discussion, Pitts., 1977; cons. Shelly Friedman for Judge Com., Pitts., 1977. Recipient Gold award Art Dir. Club Phila., 1981, Distinctive award Merit Soc. Pub. Designers NY, 1983, Cert. of Distinction Creativity, 19, 22, 29, 1989, Silver award Case Coun. for Advancement and Support of Edn., 1985, Desi award Graphic Design USA, 1982, 83, 85, 87, 88, 92, 94 (Am. Graphic Design award, 1994, 96), Typography 3, 4, 21, TDC, 28, TOC, 28, 29, 46, Cert. of Typo Excellence, Print mag. Regional Design Ann., 1982, 84, 89, 92, 96, 98, 2000; Cert. of Merit Art Dir. Club NY, 1978, 81, 85, 93, Cert. of Excellence Art Dirs. Club NJ, 1981, 82, 83, 85, 98, 2000, Inter Type Design 2 Award of Excellence, 1994, Graphis Letterhead 2 Award of Excellence, 1993, Cert. of Excellence Inter Logos and Trademarks II, V, 1992, 2000, Univ. and Coll. Designers Assn. award of Excellence, 1995, 99), Charles Pine Outstanding Tchr. of Yr. award and Warren I. Susman award for Excellence in Tchg., 1995, Faculty Scholar Tchr. award, 1999, Am. Corp. Identity 2000 and 2001 award, 1998, Cert. of Recognition for Logo Design, Graphis Logo Design 4 award of excellence, 1998., How Mag. Merit award, 2000. Mem. Am. Inst. Graphic Arts (Cert. Excellence 1977, 83), Coll. Art Assn., Graphic Design Edn. Assn., Woodstock Artist Assn., Woodstock Guild. Democrat. Roman Catholic. Home: PO Box 62 Willow NY 12495 Office: Rutgers U Dept Visual and Performing Arts Newark NJ 07102

DASTOOR, MINOO, biochemist; b. Bombay, Aug. 21, 1939; arrived in U.S., 1962; s. Norshir R. and Khorshed N. Dastoor; m. Marguerite J. van Gils, June 1965 (dec. Dec. 1997); children: Shiraz, Khorshed. BSc in Chemistry, U. Bombay, 1960; MS in Polymer Chemistry, U. Akron, 1965; PhD in Microbiology and Immunology, UCLA, 1976. Scientist Jet Propulsion Lab., Pasadena, Calif., 1976—96, program mgr., 1997—2000; chief technologist human exploration Office Space Flight NASA, 2000—01, sr. advisor Office Aerospace Tech., 2001—. Sci. adv. bd. Nicholas Piramal India Ltd., Bombay, 1999—2002; lectr. in field. Contbr. articles to profl. jours. Recipient Life Excellence award, Zoroastrian Assn., Toronto, Can., 1988. Achievements include first to early efforts at building non-biological method for detecting virus particles using UV fluorescence spectroscopy. Avocations: music, cosmology. Home: 801 15th St South #1601 Arlington VA 22202 Office: NASA 301 E St SW Washington DC 20546

DAT, MANABENDRA NATH, civil engineer, consultant; b. Agra, India, July 1, 1933; arrived in US, 1972; s. Manindra Lal and Prativa Moyee Dutt; m. Kalpana Dat, May 5, 1981. BSc, Agra U., 1951; B of Tech. with honors, Indian Inst. Tech., Kharagpur, 1955; MSCE, Okla. State U., 1972; PhD, Ohio State U., 1975, MBA, 1977. Registered profl. engr., NJ. Asst. engr. DVC, Maithon, India, 1955—57; sr. field engr. Kaiser Engrs., Tatanagar, India, 1957—59; sr. soils/pavement engr. Ammann & Whitney, Iran, 1959—67; project mgr. Frederic R. Harris, Inc., Vietnam, 1967—72, URS Co., Inc., NYC, 1979—81, Woodward Clyde Cons., Pa., 1981—84; sr. project mgr. Deleuw, Cather Internat., Indonesia, 1984—89, Upham Internat. Corp., Thailand, 1990—93, Sheladia, Inc., Bangladesh, 1994—. Cons. in field. Fellow: ASCE, Inst. Engrs. Home: 810 W Airy St Norristown PA 19401-5514

DATAR, RAM HEMANT, pathologist, educator; b. Nasik, India, Mar. 26, 1959; arrived in U.S., 1996; s. Hemant Madhusudan and Mrinalini Hemant Datar; m. Bharati Gajanan Deshpande, June 15, 1982; 1 child, Nakul R. BSc, Pune (India) U., 1979, MSc, 1981, MPhil, 1984; PhD, Bombay U., 1996. Jr. rsch. fellow Pune U., 1981—82, sr. rsch. fellow, 1983—84; sci. asst. Cancer Rsch. Inst., Bombay, 1983—84, sci. officer, 1991—96; vis. rsch. scholar U. So. Calif., L.A., 1996—98, asst. prof. clin. pathology, 1998—. Cons. spl. emphasis panel NIH, 2001—. Editor: Current Issues in Molecular Biology, 2000—; reviewer: Lancet, 2000—02, Internat. Jour. Cancer, 2000—02, Cancer Rsch., 2000—02. Grantee, NIH, 2000—01, 2001—02, Dept. Def., 2001. Mem.: Am. Assn. Cancer Rsch. (assoc.), Indian Assn. Cell Biology (life). Achievements include patent pending for protein display protocol. Avocations: reading, poetry, travel, writing. Office: U So Calif 2011 Zonal Ave #312C Los Angeles CA 90033

DATARS, WILLIAM ROSS, physicist, educator; b. Desboro., Ont., Can., June 14, 1932; s. Albert John and Leona Alberta (Fries) D.; m. Eleanor Wismer, Oct. 10, 2002; children— Timothy, Andrew, David. B.Sc., McMaster U., Hamilton, Ont., 1955; M.Sc., 1956; PhD, U. Wis., 1959. Physicist Def. Research Bd., 1959-62; mem. faculty McMaster U., 1962—, prof. physics, 1969-96, prof. emeritus, 1996—. E.W.R. Steacie fellow, 1968-70 Fellow Royal Soc. Can., Am. Phys. Soc.; mem. Can. Assn. Physics Lutheran. Home: RR 2 Lynden ON Canada L0R 1T0 Office: McMaster U Dept Physics & Astronomy Hamilton ON Canada L8S 4M1 E-mail: datars@mcmaster.ca.

DATCU, IOANA, visual artist; b. Bucharest, Romania, Apr. 22, 1944; arrived in U.S., 1981; d. Marin and Niculina Datcu; m. Vasile Porcisanu, Aug. 5, 1967 (div. 1983); 1 child, Isabelle Ioana. BA, Pedagogical Inst., Bucharest, 1967; BFA summa cum laude, U. Minn., 1987, MFA, 1991. Tchr. biology high sch., Argova, Preasna, Romania, 1967-74; photography asst. U. Minn., St. Paul, 1985-86; photographer civil rights dept. City Hall, St. Paul, 1986-87; darkroom supervisor Film in the Cities, St. Paul, 1987-88; gallery asst., curator Paul Whitney Gallery, St. Paul, 1987-91; art instr. Minn. Mus. Am. Art, St. Paul, 1993-94; instr. drawing & painting U. Minn., Mpls., 1996-97. One-woman shows include Flanders Contemporary Art, Mpls., 1994, Winona (Minn.) State U, 1995, Mont. State U., Billings, 1996, Ea. Wash. U., Cheney, 1996, Indpls. Art Ctr., 1996, Kansas City (Mo.) Artists Coalition, 1997, Grants Pass (Oreg.) Mus. Art, 1997, Trinity Presbyn. Ch., Denton, Tex., 1998, South Bend (Ind.) Mus. Art, 1998, U. Dayton, Ohio, 2000, exhibitions include North Park Coll., Chgo., 1991, Hist. Trinity, Detroit, 1993, 1995, 1996, Coll. St. Catherine, St. Paul, 1995, Barrett House Galleries, Poughkeepsie, N.Y., 1994, 1996, Coll. St. Catherine, St. Paul, 1995, Minot State U., N.D., 1995, St. John's U., N.Y., 1995, Katherine E. Nash Gallery, Mpls., 1992, 1995, 1996, Focal Point Gallery, N.Y.C., 1996, SoHo Photo Gallery, 1997, Greater Lafayette Mus. Art, 1997, Greater Lafayette Mus. Art., 1997, Truman State U., Mo., 1998, McNeese State U., La., 1998, Attleboro (Mass.) Mus. Art, 1998, 1999, New World Art Ctr., N.Y.C., 1999, Ctrl. Mo. State U., 1999, Am. Bible Soc. Gallery, N.Y.C., 2000, Internat. Print Triennial, Cracow, Poland, 2000, Internat. Print Triennial Krakow Nürnberg, Messezentrum Mus., Germany, 2000, Jewish Cmty. Ctr. Greater New Haven, Woodbridge, Conn., 2001, Korean Cultural Ctr., L.A., 2001, New Am. Paintings Exhibit in Print, Open Studio Press, 1995, Images of the Spirit Traveling Exhibit, 1995—97, CIVA CODEX III traveling exhibit, 1997—2001, represented in, CD-Rom collections of Art Comms. Internat., 1995, Artmax Internat., 1995, Ency. Internat. Women Artists, Alliance Women Artists, 1997, New Art Internat., Book Art Press, 1997, Christianity and the Arts Jour., 1999, Bridge to the Future, 2000. Grantee Pollock-Krasner Found., 1992, Minn. State Arts Bd., 1994; Jerome Found. Residency fellow, 1994; McKnight Photography fellow, 1992, fellow Arts Midwest NEA, 1994-95, Clowes Fund regional residency fellow, Indpls., 1997; Vt. Studio Ctr. Residency award, Johnson, Vt., 1997. Mem. Christians in the Visual Arts, Nat. Assn. Women Artists, Inc. Mem. Eastern Orthodox Ch. Avocations: classical music, movies, yoga, books, animals. Home: 1028 E Justin St Sunsites AZ 85625 E-mail: idatcu@vtc.net.

DATEMA, JESSICA VENNING, humanities educator; b. Raleigh, N.C., Dec. 18, 1970; d. Charles and Judy Venning; m. Jay Philip Datema. BA in Philosophy and Interdisciplinary Studies cum laude, Wheaton (Ill.) Coll., 1993; postgrad., No. Ill. U.; MA in Philosophy, SUNY, Binghamton, 2002, PhD in Comparative Lit., 2003. Grad. tchg. asst. No. Ill. U., DeKalb, 1995—98; instr. SUNY, Binghamton, 1998—2002. Presenter in field. Scholar, German Acad. Exch. Program, 2000. Mem.: MLA. Home: 620 W 138th St New York NY 10031

DATILES, J. MICHELLE, legal researcher; b. Manil, Philippines, Dec. 14, 1976; arrived in U.S., 1979; d. Manuel Bernaldes and Jacqueline Romero Datiles. BA in Philosophy, Cath. U. Am., 1998; postgrad., NY.Law Sch., 2001—. Intern UN, N.Y.C., 2003; rsch. asst. S.J. Ellmann N.Y. Law Sch., N.Y.C., 2002—. Student presenter Murray Hill Inst.: Women Transforming Culture, N.Y.C., 2001; asst. coord. Internat. Univ. Congress, N.Y.C., 2001—. Asst. dir. Program for Acad. and Leadership Skills, Washington, 1994—98; asst. dir. summer program Rosedale Achievement Ctr., N.Y.C., 2000. Fellow NYLS Pub. Interest, 2003. Mem.: ABA, Fellowship of Cath. Scholars, N.Y. State Bar Assn. Roman Catholic. Avocations: watercolor, writing verse and prose, piano, singing, reading.

DATILES, MANUEL BERNALDES, III, ophthalmologist, researcher; b. Manila, Feb. 26, 1951; arrived in U.S., 1979; s. Roberto Aguiling and Loretta (Bernaldes) Datiles; m. Jacqueline Romero, Mar. 13, 1976; children: Michelle, Margaret, Jennifer, Manuel IV, Michael, Joyce. BS cum laude, U. Santo Tomas, Manila, 1970; MD cum laude, U. Santo Tomas, 1974. Intern Jose Reyes Meml. Hosp. (North Gen. Hosp.); rsch. fellow Philippine Eye Rsch. Inst.-U. Philippines, Manila, 1975-76; resident in ophthalmology U. Philippines-Philippine Gen. Hosp., Manila, 1976-79; rsch. scholar, vis. scientist Lab. Vision Rsch. Nat. Eye Inst.-NIH, Bethesda, Md., 1979-82; clin. fellow corneal and cataract surgery Wilmer Eye Inst.-Johns Hopkins U. Hosp., Balt., 1982-83; sr. staff ophthalmologist Nat. Eye Inst.-NIH, Bethesda, 1983-88, acting chief cornea and cataract sect., clin. svc. br., 1989-92, chief cornea and cataract sect., clin. svcs. br., 1992—; chmn. surg. adminstrv. com. NIH Clin. Ctr. Hosp., 1994-95. Vis. lectr. Wilmer Eye Inst.-Johns Hopkins U., Balt., 1984, Osaka (Japan) U., 1986, U. Munich, 1988, Harkness Eye Inst., Columbia U., N.Y.C., 1994—97; presenter in field. Editor: cataract sect. Duane's Clinical Ophthalmology Textbook series, 1989—; guest editor: Jour. Investigative Ophthalmology and Visual Sci., 1999, 2000; contbr. chapters to books, articles to profl. jours.; reviewer jours. in field:. Recipient Most Outstanding Silver Jubilarian in Med. Rsch. award, U. Santo Tomas Alumni Assn. Am., 1999, Cert. Appreciation For Work With Indigents, James Cardinal Hickey and Archidiocese of Washington, Ophthalmology Rsch. award, Assn. Philippine Ophthalmologists in Am., 2001. Mem.: Contact Lens Assn. Ophthalmologists, Wilmer Eye Inst. Residents' Assn., Md. Soc. Eye Physicians and Surgeons, Washington Acad. Ophthalmology, Internat. Assn. Ocular Surgeons, Johns Hopkins Med. Surg. Assn., Castroviejo Soc. Corneal Surgeons, Am. Acad. Ophthalmology, Assn. Rsch. in Vision and Opthalmology, Johns Hopkins Alumni Assn. Roman Catholic. Achievements include research in medical treatment, surgical treatment, causes and methods of tracking and studying cataracts. Avocations: sketching, soap carving, target shooting, guitar, chess. Office: NIH Nat Eye Inst Rm 10n226 Bethesda MD 20892-0001 E-mail: datilesm@nei.nih.gov.

DATTA, SUKDEB, anesthesiologist, pain management specialist; b. Jamshedpur, India, June 6, 1967; s. Kartik Chandra and Bela Datta; m. Koel Chatterjee, Sept. 27, 1997. MBBS, NRS Med. Coll., Calcutta, India, 1989. Diplomate Am. Bd. Anesthesiology, Am. Bd. Pain Medicine, subspecialty cert. pain mgmt. Postgrad. trainee in surgery Calcutta (India) U., 1992-94; resident in surgery Nassau County Med. Ctr., East Meadow, N.Y., 1994-95; resident in anesthesiology New Eng. Med. Ctr., Boston, 1995-96, Cook County Hosp., Chgo., 1996-98, chief resident, clin. scientist, 1998-99, fellow pain mgmt. program, 1999-2000; asst. prof. U. Cin., 2000—. Author: Essentials of Practical Physiology and Viva in Physiology, 1987; contbr. articles to profl. jours. Recipient Midwest Anesthesiology Residents Conf. award Ohio State U., Columbus, 1999, Sigma Xi award, 1999. Mem. Am. Soc. Anesthesiologists, Internat. Anesthesia Rsch. Soc. (Best of Meeting award for sci. abstracts 74th Clin. and Sci. Congress 2000), Am. Soc. Regional Anesthesia, Ill. Soc. Anesthesiologists, Greater Cin. Pain Soc. (sec. 2002--), Internat. Spinal Injection Soc., Am. Soc. Interventional Pain Physicians, Am. Neuromodulation Soc., Am. Acad. Pain Mgmt. Avocations: music, software. Home: 8131 Village Dr Cincinnati OH 45242 Office: U Cin Hosps PO Box 670531 Cincinnati OH 45267-0531 Fax: 513-469-0476. E-mail: sukdeb@hotmail.com., sukdeb.datta@uc.edu.

DATTILO, NICHOLAS C. bishop; b. Mahoningtown, Pa., Mar. 8, 1932; Educated, St. Vincent Sem., Latrobe, Pa., St. Charles Borromeo Sem., Phila. Apptd. Eighth Bishop of Harrisburg 1989, ordained Bishop of Harrisburg 1990; cert. ordained priest Roman Cath. Ch., 1958. Bishop Diocese of Harrisburg, Pa., 1990. Home and Office: PO Box 2153 4800 Union Deposit Rd Harrisburg PA 17105*

DATTILO, THOMAS A. diversified corporation executive; BA, OH State U.; LLB, U. Toledo. Mem., corporate legal staff Dana Corp., 1977-82, with ins. operations dvsn., 1982-85, v.p. then gen. mgr., Precision Control Divsn., 1985—; pres. and CEO Hayes-Dana Inc., St. Cahtarines, Ont., Can.; pres. Victor Reinz Products, N. Am., Lisle, Ill., 1997-; pres., sealing products group Dana Corp., Toledo; pres. and COO Cooper Tire and Rubber Co., Findlay, Ohio, 1999—2000, chmn., pres., CEO, 2000—. Mem. Young President's Orgn., Automotive Parts Manufacturer's Assoc. Office: Cooper Tire & Rubber Co 701 Lima Ave Findlay OH 45840-2388

DATTNER, BENJAMIN, management consultant; BA, Harvard Coll., 1992; Ph.D., NYU, 1999. Prin. Dattner Cons., LLC, N.Y.C., 2001—. Alumni interviewer Harvard Coll., N.Y.C., 1994—2003. Mem.: Soc. for Indsl. and Orgnl. Psychology. Office Fax: 509-691-7851. Personal E-mail: bdattner@dattnerconsulting.com.

DATTNER, RICHARD, architect, educator; b. Bielsko, Poland, Sept. 12, 1937; came to U.S., 1946; s. David and Ella Dattner Student, Archtl. Assn., London, 1957-58; BArch, MIT, 1960. Registered architect, N.Y., N.J., Fla., Pa., Conn., S.C.; cert. Nat. Coun. Archtl. Registration Bds. Pres., prin., architect Richard Dattner Archs. P.C., N.Y.C., 1964—. Adj. prof. architecture Cooper Union, N.Y.C., 1962-69, CCNY, N.Y.C., 1970-80; disting. vis. prof. architecture U. Wis.-Milw., 1982; vis. design critic Columbia U., N.Y.C., Princeton (N.J.) U., Cornell U., Ithaca, N.Y., 1970-80. Author: Design for Play, 1969, Civil Architecture, 1994; inventor Streetscape modular shelters, 1972 (design award 1972), modular house constrn., Playcubes modular playground, Shelterscape modular canopies, 1996 (Design award 1996); prin. works include: Riverbank State Park, Estee Lauder Labs., 1992 Dem. Nat. Conv., Columbia U. Stadium, Asphalt Green, Aqua Ctr., N.Y.C. Prototype Intermediate Sch. Mem. adv. bd. Am. Revolution Bicentennial Commn., 1976; forum mem. White House Conf. on Children, 1970; mem. Bd. on Infrastructure and the Constructed Environment. Served with U.S. Army, 1960. Recipient Design award N.Y. State Assn. Architects, 1975, 87, 89, 93, Parks Coun. award, 1968, 72, 89, Design award Progressive Architecture Mag., 1975, Design award N.Y.C. Arts Commn., 1984, 86, 89. Fellow AIA (honor award 1971, Thomas Jefferson award 1994, Medal of Honor N.Y. chpt. 1992); mem. City Club of N.Y. (Bard award 1984, 89), Century Assn. Office: Richard Dattner Archs PC 130 W 57th St New York NY 10019-3321

DATTOLO, ALPHONSE A. language educator; s. Rocco Anthony and Rosetta Marie Dattolo. MA in Spanish Lit., Montclair State Univ., NJ, 1979. Instr. Montclair State Univ., 1971—72; tchr. Manchester Regional High Sch., Haledon, NJ, 1972—87, Glen Rock High Sch., NJ, 1987—; instr. William Paterson Univ., Wayne, NJ, 1986—, Bergen Cmty. Coll., Paramus, NJ, 1990—. Mem.: Cervantes Soc. Am., Abraham Lincoln Assoc., Nat. Spanish & French Hon. Soc. Achievements include He has achieved 31 years of perfect attendance in his teaching career. Avocations: 19th century Baseball History, reading.

DATZ, KIMBERLY MALAIKA, health facility administrator, consultant; b. Latrobe, Pa., Nov. 7, 1974; d. Charles E. and Noreen M. Datz. BA in Comms. and Rhetoric, U. Pitts., 1998. Fundraising intern Gore 2000 for Pres., Pitts., 1999; fundraising cons. Tom Foley for U.S. Senate, Phila., 1999, Sam Neill for Congress, Hendersonville, NC, 2000, major gift officer Gov. Bob Holden, St. Louis, 2000—01; dir. major gifts Planned Parenthood, Atlanta, 2001—. Mem.: Planned Parenthood, Assn. Fundraising Profls., The High Mus. Democrat. Office: Planned Parenthood 100 Edgewood Ave NE Ste 1604 Atlanta GA 30303 E-mail: kimdatz@aol.com.

DAUB, HAL, former mayor, former congressman; b. Fayetteville, N.C., Apr. 23, 1941; s. Harold John and Eleanor M. (Hickman) D.; m. Mary Mernin; children: Natalie Ann, John Clifford, Tammy Renee. BSBA, Washington U., St. Louis, 1963; JD, U. Nebr., 1966. Bar: Nebr. 1966, U.S. Ct. Appeals (8th cir.), U.S. Ct. Customs and Patent Appeals, U.S. Supreme Ct. Assoc. Fitzgerald, Brown, Leahy, McGill & Strom, 1968-71; v.p., gen. counsel Standard Chem. Mfg. Co., 1971-80; mem. 97th-100th Congresses from 2nd Nebr. dist., 1981-1989, mem. ways and means com., subcoms. on health and social security; prin., nat. dir. fed. govt. affairs Deloitte & Touche Acctg. and Cons. Firm, 1981-94; mayor City of Omaha, 1995—2000; ptnr. Blackwell Sanders Peper Martin, LLP, 2001—. Presdl. appointee Nat. Adv. Coun. on Pub. Svc., 1991—92; presdl. appointee chmn. Social Security Adv. Bd., 2001—, chmn., 2001—; prin. Coun. for Excellence in Govt.; staff intern to U.S. Senator Roman Hruska from Nebr., 1966; pres. Republican Mayors and Local Elected Ofcls., 1995—2001; adv. bd. U.S. Conf. Mayors, 1998—2001; chmn. pub. safety and crime prevention com. Nat. League of Cities, 1996—97. Mem. Congl. Regulatory Reform Task Force, 1981-83, Congl. Rep. Agrl. Task Force, 1981-88; co-founder Liability Ins. and Tort Reform Task Force, 1986; mem. exec. com. Rep. Nat. Congl. Com., 1981-88; co-founder, co-chmn. Budget Reform Task Force, 1981-84; jr. pres. Nebr. Founders' Day, 1971; jr. pres. Nebr. Founders' Day, 1971; mem. exec. com., bd. dirs. Combined Health Agys. Drive, 1976; nat. bd. dirs. Combined Health Agys. of Am., 2003—; pres. Douglas-Sarpy unit Nebr. Heart Assn.; bd. dirs. Metro Arts Coun., 1989-93; treas. Douglas County (Nebr.) Rep. Party, 1970-73, chmn., 1974-77; elder Presbyn. Ch. Capt. U.S. Army, 1963-68. Decorated Army Commendation medal with oak leaf cluster, Expeditionary medal; named Outstanding Nebraskan, 1966, Outstanding Vol. of Yr. award Douglas-Sarpy unit Nebr. Heart Assn., 1976, Disting. Eagle Scout; recipient Svc. award SAC, 1976, Leadership awards (4) Coalition for Peace Through Strength, Guardian of Small Bus. awards (4), 1981-88, Omaha C. of C. award, Watchdog of Treasury awards (5), 1981-88. Mem. Omaha Bar Assn., Nebr. Bar Assn., Nat. Assn. Credit Mgmt. (1st v.p. 1977), Res. Officers Assn., Am. Legion, 40 and 8, VFW, Urban League Nebr., Optimists, Masons (33d degree), Shriners, SAR, Kappa Sigma, Alpha Kappa Psi, Omicron Delta Kappa, Delta Theta Phi. Republican. Office: 13710 FNB Pkwy Ste 200 Omaha NE 68154 Fax: 402-397-1194. Personal E-mail: haldaub@cox.net. Business E-Mail: hdaub@blackwellsanders.com.

DAUB, PEGGY ELLEN, library administrator; b. Bluffton, Ohio, Oct. 15, 1949; d. Perry J. and Olive L. (Hoover) D.; m. Jeffrey H. Cooper, Dec. 13, 1975; 1 child, William P. Cooper-Daub. MusB summa cum laude, Miami U., 1972; MA, Cornell U., 1975; MSLS, U. Ill., 1980; PhD, Cornell U., 1985. Acting asst. music libr. Yale U., 1980-81, head of music tech. svcs., rare books libr. Music Libr., 1981-82; head Music Libr. U. Mich., Ann Arbor, 1982-89, head Spl. Collections & Arts Librs., 1989-99, head Spl. Collections Libr., 2000—. Presenter Rare Books and Manuscript Sect. Pre-Conf., New Orleans, 1993, Bloomington, 1995 and others. Contbr. articles to profl. jours. Co-clk. Ann Arbor Friends Meeting, 1997-2001. Travel grantee Ctr. for Internat. Studies, Cornell U., 1977. Mem. ALA (Assn. Coll. and Rsch. Librs. rare books and manuscripts sect., mem. task force on interlibr. loan 1991-93, mem. preconf. program planning com. 1992-94), Music Libr. Assn. (bd. dirs. 1985-87, mem. resource sharing and collection devel. com. 1982-91), Rsch. Librs. Group (chairperson music program com. 1985-87, mem. steering com. 1982-87), Am. Musicol. Soc. (mem. coun. 1988-91, mem. coun. com. on minorities/diversity 1988-91), Phi Beta Kappa. Mem. Soc. Of Friends. Office: U of Mich Spl Collections Libr 711 Graduate Libr Ann Arbor MI 48109-1205 E-mail: pdaub@umich.edu.

DAUB, S. SPENCER, b. N.Y.C., Feb. 12, 1927; s. Jerome Augustus and Susan (Schneider) D.; m. Annette Denise Teller, Feb. 1, 1946 (dec. Mar. 1951); children: (twins) Doron Allen (dec.) and Karen Andrea (dec.) BA in Math., U. Miami, 1961. Various positions, prior to 1971; v.p. engring. Terrarobotics Co., Miami, Fla., 1971-82; pres. Androtec, Miami, 1982—2002; dir. emeritus Androtec Mentaxis, Miami, 2003—. Contbr. articles to profl. jours. Mem. IEEE, Computer Soc. of IEEE, Assn. for Computing Machinery, Am. Math. Soc., Armed Forces Comm. and Electronics Assn., Soc. Mfg. Engrs., N.Y. Acad. Scis., Mensa. Republican. Roman Catholic. Avocations: sailboating, fencing, amateur radio, falconry, breeding clydesdales. Office: PO Box 694216 Miami FL 33269-1216

DAUBE, LORRIE O. sales executive; b. Toledo, Ohio, Feb. 3, 1951; d. Stanley and Marian Oberlin; m. Jeffrey Daube, Aug. 31, 1975; children: Ryan Oberlin, Danielle Elyse. BS in Comm., U. Ill., 1973. Media sales WDAI-ABC-FM, Chgo., 1973—74; media sales rep. Jack Masla, Chgo., 1974—75; media sales WMET Metromedia, Chgo., 1976—79, WIND-Westinghouse, Chgo., 1980—82; copywriter Burgess, Heynssen and Oberlin, Deerfield, Ill., 1983—85; sales cons. Coldwell Banker, Deerfield, 1990—. Charity fundraiser Med. Rsch. Inst., 1985—90, Jewish United Fund, Chgo., 1995—; active guest svcs. 2002 Winter Olympics, Deer Valley, Utah, 2002. Mem.: NSWTL (pres. 1986—88). Republican. Avocations: skiing, tennis, golf, platform tennis, swimming. Home: 8 Dunsinane Ln Bannockburn IL 60015

DAUBER, LEONARD GENE, oncologist, medical educator; b. Krakow, Poland, Mar. 12, 1938; came to U.S., 1940; s. Isidore and Beatrice (Young) D.; m. Lorraine Silverstein, Aug. 4, 1960; children: Paul, Jane, Daniel. AB, Columbia Coll., 1958; MD, Columbia Coll., NYC, 1962. Diplomate Am. Bd. Internal Medicine, Am. Bd. Hematology, Am. Bd. Medical Oncology. From instr. to assoc. clin. prof. medicine Albert Einstein, Bronx, NY, 1968—2000; attending physician and oncologist NY Med. Group, Bronx, NY, 1988—2000; assoc. prof. NY Med. Coll.; attend. physician Comprehensive Cancer Ctr., Our Lady of Mercy Med. Ctr., 2000—. Capt. USAR, 1966-68. Office: 600 E 233d St Bronx NY 10466-Our E-mail: LGD.LSD@worldnet.att.net.

DAUBERT, ERIK JOSEPH, organization administrator; b. Goshen, N.Y., June 21, 1966; s. Robert Louis and Madeline J.; m. Andrea Miele, Oct. 4, 1997. BA, U. N.C., Chapel Hill, 1989; postgrad. in non-profit mgmt., Duke U., 1992; MBA, Campbell U., 2002. Cert. fund raising exec. Exec. dir. Eco-Logical, Durham, NC, 1991-95; v.p. devel. YMCA of Triangle Area, Raleigh, NC, 1996—; cons. ptnr. We Improve It. Cons. in field, Research Triangle Park, N.C., 1995—. N.Am. YMCA Devel. Officers. Vice Chair Sierra Club, Durham, 1991-93; pres. bd. dirs. Child Advocacy Commn., Durham, 1995-97. Named Outstanding Vol. award, N.C. Pub. Allies, 1994, Cmty. Hero-Torchbearer, 1996 Olympic Games, 1996; recipient cert. merit The Nat. Arbor Day Found., 1993, 94. Mem. Triangle United Way, Carolina Prospect Rsch. Assn., Eno River Assn. (resource devel. com.). Avocations: canoeing, camping, cycling, reading, people. Home: 2917 Beech Grove Dr Durham NC 27705 Office: YMCA of the Triangle Area 1601 Hillsborough St Raleigh NC 27605 Home Fax: 919-383-3092.

DAUBERT, MADELINE J. accountant, educator; b. Norwich, N.Y., Aug. 22, 1941; d. Clifford T. and Marian A. Jones; m. Robert Louis Daubert, 1959; children: David, Lisa, Erik. BS, SUNY, Cortland, 1962; MLS, SUNY, Albany, 1969. CPA, N.C.; cert. libr., sch. media specialist, N.Y. Libr. various pub. schs., N.Y., 1966-78; mgr. mgmt. acctg. Peoples Security Life Ins., Durham, N.C., 1983-84; sys. acct. N.C. Ctrl. U., Durham, 1985-90; owner Madeline J. Daubert, CPA, Durham and Hendersonville, N.C., 1987—. Adj. faculty Tex. Woman's U., Denton, 1990-91, U. South Fla., Tampa, 1993, U. N.C., Chapel Hill, 1995, 98; cons., workshop leader Libr. Congress, Washington, 1999; continuing edn. instr. Spl. Librs. Assn., Washington, 1995-2000; software cons. various univs., Tex., Tenn., Colo., N.C., 1990-91, U. N.C.-Asheville, 1987-89. Author: Financial Management for Small and Medium-Sized Libraries, 1993, Money Talk: Accounting Fundamentals for Special Librarians, 1995, Control of Administrative and Financial Operations in Special Libraries, 1996, Analyzing Library Costs, 1997. Trustee Keller (Tex.) Libr. Bd., 1991—92; mem. Village of Flat Rock Bd. of Adjustment, 2000—, vice chmn., 2000—03; treas. Hendersonville Little Theater, 2002—03; dir. Cmty. Found. Henderson County, 2000—. Office: 42 Oak Gate Dr Hendersonville NC 28739-9342

DAUCH, RICHARD E. automobile manufacturing company executive; b. 1942; BS, Purdue U., 1964. With Gen. Motors Corp., 1964-75; group v.p. mfg. Volkswagen of Am., 1976-80; v.p. Chrysler Corp., 1980, exec. v.p. diversified ops., 1980-81, exec. v.p. stamping assembly diversified ops., 1981-84, exec. v.p. mfg., 1984-1994; co-founder, CEO Am. Axle & Mfg., 1994—, pres., 1994—2001, chmn., 2001—. Recipient Eli Whitney Meml. award Soc. Mfg. Engrs., 1987, Ellis Island medal of honor, 1997; named Industry Leader of Yr., Automotive Hall of Fame, 1997, Mfr. of Yr., Mich. Mfg. Assn., 1997, Newsmaker of Yr., Crain's Detroit Bus., 1998, World Trader of Yr.,Detroit Regional Chamber, 2002, Mich. Exec. of Yr., Wayne State U. Coll. Bus. Adminstrn., 2002. Office: American Axle & Mfg 1840 Holbrook St Detroit MI 48212-3442*

DAUCHER, LYNN M. state official; b. Washington, D.C., Feb. 20, 1946; m. Don Daucher; children: Kelly, Carl, Jill, Brian. BS in Edn., U. Rochester, 1968. Tchr., Williamsville, NY, 1968—69; mem. Brea Olinda Sch. Bd., 1981—94, Brea City Coun., 1994—2000; state assembly mem. Dist. 72 Calif. State Assembly, 2000—. Mem. budget com.; mem. local govt. com. Mem.: State League Fiscal Funding (reform task force), State League of Cities (revenue and taxation com.), Rep. Women of Brea, League of Calif. Cities, Placentia C. of C., La Habra C. of C., Fullerton C. of C., Brea C. of C., Kiwanis Club of Brea. Republican. Lutheran. Mailing: Rm 2158 PO Box 942849 Sacramento CA 94249 Office: Ste 202 210 W Birch St Brea CA 92821

D'AUDIFFRET, ALEXANDRE CHRISTOPHE, surgeon, researcher, medical educator; b. Paris, Nov. 14, 1964; arrived in U.S., 1991; s. Hugues Marie d'Audiffret; m. Joan Marie Huhta, Oct. 29, 1996; children: Griffin Georges, Maximillien Christophe. MD, U. Man., Winnipeg, Can., 1991. Diplomate Am. Bd. Surgery, 1997. Intern U. Min., 1991—92, resident in surgery, 1992—94; sr. and chief resident Grad. Hosp., of U. Pa., Phila., 1994—96; vascular surgery fellow SUNY, Buffalo, 1996—98; endovascular fellow U. Paris XII, 1998—2000; asst. prof. surgery U. Minn., Mpls., 2000—. Dir., prodr. : (films) The Forgotten Children. Mem.: Am. Assn. Vascular Surgery, Midwestern Vascular Soc. Achievements include patents pending for endovascular graft. Home: 4048 Elliot Ave Minneapolis MN 55407 Office: Univ Minn Dept Surgery 516 Delaware St SE Mail Code 195 Minneapolis MN 55455 Office Fax: 612-624-7168. Personal E-mail: daudi001@umn.edu. E-mail: daudi001@umn.edu.

DAUER, DONALD DEAN, investment executive; b. Fresno, Calif., June 1, 1936; s. Andrew and Erma Mae (Zigenman) D.; m. LaVerne DiBuduo, Jan. 23, 1971; children: Gina, Sarah. BS in Bus. Administrn., Calif. State U. Fresno; postgrad., U. Wash., 1964. Loan officer First Savs. and Loan, Fresno, 1961-66, v.p., 1966-71, sr. v.p., 1971-81, exec. v.p., 1978-81; pres. Uniservice Corp., Fresno, 1976-81, Don Dauer Investments, Fresno, 1981—; pres., chief oper. officer Riverbend Internat. Corp., Sanger, Calif., 1985-89. Chmn. bd. dirs. Univ. Savs. and Loan, 1991-92, acting pres., CEO, 1992; loan officer Norwest Mortgage, 1993-95; mgr. CMB Fin., 1995-96. Chmn. bd. dirs. City of Fresno Gen. Svcs. Retirement Bd., 1973-83, West Fresno Econ. and Bus. Devel. Program Bd., 1980-83; pres. bd. dirs. Cen. Calif. United Cerebral Palsy Assn., 1979-82; bd. dirs. Valley Children's Hosp. Found., Fresno, 1984-93; trustee, chmn. Valley Children's Hosp., 1987-93; bd. dirs. Youth for Christ USA, 1988-94, Twilight Haven Inc., 2000—; vice chmn. Riverbend Internat., 1985-91. Mem. Soc. Real Estate Appraisers (past pres.). Office: 2733 W Palo Alto Ave Fresno CA 93711-1110

DAUER, EDWARD ARNOLD, law educator; b. Providence, Sept. 28, 1944; s. Marshall and Shirley (Moverman) Dauer; m. Carol Jean Egglestone, June 16, 1966; children: E. Craig, Rachel P. AB, Brown U., 1966; LLB cum laude, Yale U., 1969; MPH, Harvard U., 2001. Bar: Conn. 1978, Colo. 1986. Asst. prof. law sch. U. Toledo, 1969-72; assoc. prof. law U. So. Calif., L.A., 1972-74; assoc. prof. Yale U., New Haven, 1975-85, assoc. dean, 1978-83, dep. dean Law Sch., 1983-85; dean, prof. U. Denver, 1985-90, dean emeritus, prof., 1991—. Of counsel Popham, Haik, Schnobrich and Kaufman, 1990—97; vis. scholar Harvard U. Sch. Pub. Health, 1996—2003; pres. CAEJAD Aviation Corp.; assoc. Health Care Negotiations Assocs., Inc. Author: (book) Materials on a Nonadversarial Legal Process, 1978, Conflict Resolution Strategies in Health Care, 1993, Manual of Dispute Resolution: ADR Law and Practice, 1994 (CPR Book award, 1994), Health Care Dispute Resolution, 2000; contbr. articles to profl. jours. Founder, pres. Nat. Ctr. Preventive Law; bd. dirs. New Haven Cmty. Action Agy., 1978—81; mem. Colo. Commn. Higher Edn., 1987—91; bd. dirs. Cerebral Palsy Found., Denver, 1989—, pres., 1992—95; commr. Colo. Advanced Tech. Inst., 1989—91. Recipient W. Quinn Jordan award, Nat. Blood Found., 1994, Paelia award, Harvard Sch. Pub. Health, 1996, Sanbar award, Am. Coll. Legal Medicine, 1999. Mem.: Am. Law Inst. (life), Met. Club, Cherry Creek Athletic Club, Order of Coif. Republican. Home: 127 S Garfield St Denver CO 80209 Office: U Denver Coll Law 1900 Olive St Denver CO 80220 E-mail: edauer@du.edu., edauer@hcna.net.

DAUER, SHEILA A. human rights program director; b. Phila., Pa., Oct. 17, 1943; d. Max G. and Sheila A. Dauer. BA in English, Temple U.; PhD in Anthropology, U. Pa. Asst. prof. anthropology Queens Coll. CUNY, 1971—73; asst. prof. anthropology Hunter coll. CUNY, 1973—74; exec. asst. to exec. dir. Amnesty Internat., N.Y.C, 1976—77, dir. country specialist program, 1977—81, acting nat. campaign dir., 1982—93, dir. women's human rights program, 1994—. Vis. lectr. Dartmouth Coll., Hanover, NH, 1975—76; vis. lectr. New Sch. for Social Rsch., N.Y.C., 1976—77; advisor Women Changing the World Series, the Feminist Press, 1999—; mem. adv. bd. Ctr. for Gender and Refugee Studies, Hastings Coll. Law, U. Calif., San Francisco, 2000—; participant in numerous internat. confs. on human rights in various roles including chair, 1991—. Contbr. articles to various publs. Recipient Aston scholarship, U. Pa., 1965—66; fellow for field rsch., NIMH, 1968—70, Dissertaion fellowship, Ford Found., 1974—75, Rsch. fellowship, NIMH, 1967—70. Fellow: Am. Anthrop. Assn. (mem. human rights com. 2000—02); mem.: Assn. for Feminist Anthropology. Office: Amnesty Internat USA 322 8th Ave 10th Fl New York NY 10001

DAUGAARD, DENNIS M. lieutenant governor; b. Garretson, S.D., June 11, 1953; m. Linda Kay Schmidt; 3 children. BS, U. S.D., 1975; JD, Northwestern U., 1978. Bar: S.D. Atty. Supena & Nyman, 1978-79, Shand Morahan & Co., 1979-81; bank trust officer 1st Bank S.d., 1981-90; devel. dir. Children's Home Soc., 1990—; mem. S.D. Senate from 9th dist., Pierre, 1996—. Mem. Nat. Soc. Fund Raising Execs., S.D. Bar Assn., S.D. Planned Giving Coun., Siox Falls (S.D.) Estate Planning Coun., Rotary. Republican. Lutheran. Office: State Capitol Bldg 500 E Capitol Ave Pierre SD 57501-5070

DAUGHADAY, DOUGLAS ROBERT, computer engineer; b. Highland Park, N.J., 1954; s. Robert Owings and Mary D.; m. Ilene D. Eichel, Feb. 14, 1987; 1 child, Brian Douglas. BSEE cum laude, W.Va. Inst. Tech., 1976; MSEE, U. So. Calif., 1979. Mem. tech. staff Hughes Aircraft Co., Culver City, Calif., 1977-79, sr. engr. Litton G&CS, Woodland Hills, Calif., 1979-80; lab. engr. Garrett Airesearch, Torrance, Calif., 1980-84; mem. tech. staff The Aerospace Corp., El Segundo, Calif., 1984-87, mgr., 1987-93; project engr., 1993-96; engring. specialist, 1996—. Mem. IEEE, ACM, Soc. Am. Magicians (pres. assembly #22), Nat. Assn. Underwater Instrs. (instr.), U. S.C. Alumni Assn. (life), Eta Kappa Nu (life). Republican. Avocations: magic, photography, scuba diving. Office: The Aerospace Corp 2350 E El Segundo Blvd El Segundo CA 90245-4691

DAUGHDRILL, JAMES HAROLD, JR., academic administrator; b. LaGrange, Ga., Apr. 25, 1934; s. James Harold and Louisa Coffee (Dozier) D.; m. Elizabeth Anne Gay, June 26, 1954; children: James Harold III, Louisa Rish Daughdrill Hoover, Elizabeth Gay Daughdrill Boyd. Student, Davidson Coll., 1952-54, D.D., 1974; AB, Emory U., 1956; B.D., Columbia Theol. Sem., 1967, M.Div., 1969. Ordained to ministry Presbyn. Ch., 1967. Pres. Kingston Mills, Inc., Cartersville, Ga., 1956-64; minister St. Andrews Presbyn. Ch., Little Rock, 1967-70; sec. of stewardship Presbyn. Ch. in U.S., Atlanta, 1970-73; pres. Rhodes Coll., 1973-99. Past chmn. Nat. Adv. Com. on Instl. Quality and Interity, Dept. Edn.; past chair Assn. Am. Colls.; past dir. Am. Coun. on Edn.; mem. Blue Ribbon adv. com. Memphis Pub. Schs.; dir. So. Univ. Conf., pres., 1998—; bd. dirs. Bulab Holdings, Inc., Union Planters Nat. Bank, Buckman Labs. Author: Man Talk, 1972; co-author: New Directions for Higher Education Source Book. Past chmn. Tenn. Coun. Pvt. Colls.; past pres. Coll. Athletic Conf.; past chmn. bd. So. Coll. Univ. Union; past trustee Memphis-Brooks Art Gallery, Hutchinson Sch.; past bd dirs. Tenn. Ind. Colls., Liberty Bowl, Chickasaw coun. Boy Scouts Am., Memphis U. Sch., Memphis Ptnrs.; mem. exec. bd. Dixon Gallery and Gardens; trustee The Frank E. Seidman Award in Polit. Economy; mem. blue ribbon adv. com. to the supt. Memphis Pub. Schs. Named Educator of Yr. Greater Memphis State, Memphis Planner of Yr., Pillar of Memphis Jewish Nat. Fund; recipient Spirit of Life award City of Hope, Svc. award Rotary Club Memphis Community, 1987, McCallie Sch. Alumnus of Yr. award 1978, Disting. Nat. Eagle Scout award, 1991; honored by Tenn. Legislature for disting. svc. to higher edn. and to State of Tenn., 1998. Mem. NCJJ (nat. trustee), Assn. Presbyn. Colls. and Univs. (bd. dirs.), World Bus. Coun. (young pres.' orgn., Young Man of Yr. 1961), Chief Execs. Orgn. (past), Memphis C. of C. (past bd. dir.), Univ. Club (N.Y.C.), Phi Delta Theta, Omicron Delta Kappa, Kappa Delta Epsilon (nat. hon.). Home: 4035 Dumaine Way Memphis TN 38117-2909 Office: Rhodes Coll 2000 N Parkway Office Pres Memphis TN 38112-1690

DAUGHENBAUGH, TERRY LEE, steel industry executive; b. Latrobe, Pa., July 20, 1939; s. Gladys Idella Hollobaugh; m. Cristine Zubaty, May 1, 1999; children: Thomas, Todd, Tracey; stepchildren: Leslie, Neil. BS, U. Pitts., 1968; postgrad., Columbia U., 1985. With Kennemetal Corp., Latrobe, Pa., 1957-58, Latrobe (Pa.) Steel Co., 1958-92, project engr., 1968-70, melt shop supt., 1970-73, mgr. primary ops., 1973-85, gen. mgr. mfg., 1985-88, gen. mgr. primary ops. and engring., 1988-92; pres. Innovative Water Tech., Inc. divsn. Innovative Group, Latrobe, 1992; pres., owner Spl. D Co., Latrobe, 1992-96; pres., chmn. bd. dirs. Baker Pyromet, Inc., Greenville, Pa., 1994-2000; gen. mgr. LWB Refractories, Greenville, 2000—. Cons. to steel industry, 1992-96. Chmn. bd. Ea. Westmoreland Devel. Corp., Latrobe, 1995-98, chmn. transp. com., 1989-99; mem. home rule commn. Borough of Latrobe, 1994-96; bd. dirs. Latrobe Area C. of C., 1995-98, Latrobe Area Devel. Coun., 1995—, Valley Players of Ligonier, 1997, Laurel Ballet, 1990-94, Westmoreland Blind Assn., 1987-89, Econ. Growth Connection, chmn. infrastructure com., 2000—; coach, mgr., commr. Latrobe-Derry Area Teener League, 1974-84. Mem. Am. Iron and Steel Engrs., Iron & Steel Soc., Assn. Iron and Steel Engrs., Loyalhanna Watershed Assn., Latrobe Area Devel. Coun., Alumni Elec. Metal Makers Guild, Ingot Metallurgy Forum, SPRPC Citizens Adv. Panel, Touchdown Club, Teutonia Mannechor. Republican. Lutheran. Avocations: skiing, golf. Home: 1129 Lauralynn Dr Latrobe PA 15650-4718

DAUGHERITY, BRIAN JAMES, historian, educator, historian, writer; b. Fort Belvoir, Va., Mar. 18, 1972; s. Richard David and Kathleen Ahearn Daugherity. Bachelors, Coll. William and Mary, 1994; postgrad., Coll. William & Mary, 1999—2002; MA, U. Mont., 1996, U. Miss., Oxford, 1998. Cert. secondary sch. tchr. Va., Miss. Instr. history Richard Bland Coll., Petersburg, Va., 1998—, U. Richmond, Va., 2001—. Dir. Appomattox Leadership Acad., Petersburg, 1999—. Andrew W. Mellon Rsch. fellow, Va. Hist. Soc., 2001, Richard C. Macquire scholar, Rock Island Arsenal Hist. Soc., 2002, Summer Reseach grantee, Coll. William & Mary, 2001—02, Spl. Collections Rsch. grantee, John Hope Franklin Ctr., Duke U., 2001, African-American History grantee, Va. Found. for the Humanities, 2002. Mem.: Assn. for the Study African-American Life and History (assoc.), Am. Hist. Assn. (assoc.), Orgn. Am. Historians (assoc.), Phi Alpha Theta (life), Nat. Honors Soc. (life). Avocations: travel, hiking, backpacking, skiing.

DAUGHERTY, FREDERICK ALVIN, federal judge; b. Oklahoma City, Aug. 18, 1914; s. Charles Lemuel and Felicia (Mitchell) D.; m. Marjorie E. Green, Mar. 15, 1947 (dec. Feb. 1964); m. Betsy F. Amis, Dec. 15, 1965. LL.B., Cumberland U., 1933; postgrad., Oklahoma City U., 1934-35, LL.B. (hon.), 1974; postgrad., Okla. U., 1936-37; HHD (hon.), Okla. Christian Coll., 1976. Bar: Okla. 1937. Practiced, Oklahoma City, 1937-40; mem. firm Ames, Ames & Daugherty, Oklahoma City, 1946-50, Ames, Daugherty, Bynum & Black, Oklahoma City, 1952-55; judge 7th Jud. Dist. Ct., Oklahoma City, 1955-61; U.S. dist. judge Western, Eastern and No. Dists. Okla., Oklahoma City, 1961—; chief judge Western Dist. Okla., Oklahoma City, 1972-82. Mem. Fgn. Intelligence Surveillance Ct., 1981-88, Temporary Emergency Ct. Appeals, 1983-93, Multi dist. Litigation panel, 1980-90; mem. codes of conduct com. U.S. Jud. Conf., 1980-87. Active local ARC, 1956—, chmn., 1958-60, nat. bd. govs., 1963-69, 3d nat. vice chmn., 1968-69; active United Fund Greater Oklahoma City, 1957—, pres., 1961, trustee, 1963—; pres. Community Coun. Oklahoma City and County, 1967-69; exec. com. Okla. Med. Rsch. Found., 1966-69. With AUS, 1940-45, 50-52. Decorated Legion of Merit with 2 oak leaf clusters, Bronze Star with oak leaf cluster, Combat Infantrymans badge; recipient award to mankind Okla. City Sertoma Club, 1962, Outstanding Citizen award Okla. City Jr. C. ofC., 1965, Disting. Alumni citation Samford U., 1974, Disting. Svc. citation Okla. U., 1973, Constn. award Rogers State Coll., 1988, Pathmakers award Oklahoma County Hist. Soc., 1991; named to Okla. Hall of Fame, 1969, Okla. Mil. Hall of Fame, 2000. Mem. Fed. Bar Assn., Okla. Bar Assn., Am. Bar Found., Sigma Alpha Epsilon, Phi Delta Phi, Men's Dinner Club (Oklahoma City) (pres. 1966-69), Kiwanis (pres. 1957, lt. gov. 1959), Masons (33 degree, sovereign grand insp. gen. in Okla. 1982-86), Shriners, Jesters, Order of Coif (hon. mem. Okla. chpt.). Episcopalian (sr. warden 1957).

DAUGHERTY, JAMES FRANKLIN, music educator; s. James Edward and Charlene Armentrout Daugherty; m. Florence Anne Millard, June 27, 1992; children: Ryan Edward, Eric Michaels. Cert., Staatliche Hochschule fuer Musik, Berlin, Germany, 1969; BA, Maryville (Tenn.) Coll., 1970; MEd, U. of Va., 1973; MDiv, Union Theol. Sem., N.Y., 1976; MA, Columbia U., 1978; PhD, Fla. State U., 1996. Tchr. Buford Jr. HS, Charlottesville, Va., 1970—73; assoc. pastor Second Presbyn. Ch., Newport News, Va., 1978—80; pastor First Presbyn. Ch., Big Stone Gap, Va., 1980—92; tchr. Powell Valley HS, Big Stone Gap, Va., 1980—94; dir. of choral & vocal music studies N.C. Gov.'s Sch.,

1993—98; prof. Radford (Va.) U., 1996—98, U. of Kans., Lawrence, Kans., 1998—. Contbr. articles profl. jours.; editor: Internat. Journ. Rsch. Choral Singing; mem. editl. bd.: Jour. Rsch. Music Edn., Rsch. Issues Music Edn. Moderator Abingdon (Va.) Presbytery, 1991—91; mem. governing assembly Va. Coun. of Chs., 1981—84; bd. dirs. Appalachia (Va.) Preschool, 1982—90; pres. Lawrence (Kans.) Children's Choir, 2001—03. Named Citizen of the Yr., Big Stone Gap VA Chamber of Commerce, 1988; recipient Julian Thomas Hansen award, Union Theol. Sem., 1976, Gov.'s award for the Arts, Commonwealth of Va., 1985; fellow, Roothbert Fund, 1976—77. Mem.: Coll. Music Soc., Am. Choral Directors Assn. (pres. Va. chpt. 1992—94, mem. exec. bd. Kans. chpt.), Nat. Assn. for Music Edn., Phi Kappa Lamda. Home: 1201 Jana Drive Lawrence KS 66049 Office: University of Kansas 1530 Naismith Drive Lawrence KS 66045 E-mail: jdaugher@ku.edu.

DAUGHERTY, KENNETH EARL, research company executive, educator; b. Pitts., Dec. 27, 1938; s. Thomas Hill and Laura Elizabeth (Schuda) D.; m. Joan Kay Ogrosky, Dec. 22, 1961; children: Brian Earl, Kirsten Kay. BS in Chemistry, Carnegie-Mellon U., 1960; PhD in Analytical Chemistry, U. Wash., 1964; M. Bus. Econs., Claremont Grad. Sch., 1971. Chemist Marbon Chem.-Borg Warner, Washington, W.Va., 1960; research chemist Rohm and Haas Corp., Bristol, Pa., 1964; group leader, sr. staff Amcord, Riverside, Calif., 1966-71; assoc. prof. chemistry U. Pitts., 1971-73; dir. research and devel. Gen. Portland Inc., Dallas, 1973-77; dir. energy and materials sci. Inst. Applied Scis. North Tex. State U., Denton, 1977-79, prof. chemistry, 1979—2000, chmn. analytical divsn., 1980—95. Pres., CEO, KEDS Inc., KD Cons., 1977—; owner TRAC Labs., Denton, 1981—; adj. prof. chemistry U. Pitts., 1973-2000, N. Tex. State U., Denton, 1974-2000; adj. faculty Army Command and Gen. Staff Coll., 1983—; cons. in field. Author numerous publs. in field. Patentee in field. Served to col. AUS, 1964-66, Res., 1966-95. Fellow DuPont, Shell Oil, Standard Oil, NSF, 1964. Decorated Army Commendation medal, Army Achievement medal, Army Meritorious Svc. medal. Fellow Am. Inst. Chemists; mem. Research Soc. Am., ASTM, Rilem, Nat. (transp. research bd.), N.Y. Acad. Scis., Am. Ceramic Soc. (program chmn. 1986), Am. Chem. Soc. (chpt. pres. 1960, chmn. Dallas-Ft. Worth 1986), Applied Spectroscopy Soc., Soc. Petroleum Engrs., Soc. Plastics Engrs., Sr. Army Comdrs. Assn., Sigma Xi, Pi Kappa Alpha, Omicron Delta Epsilon, Phi Lambda Upsilon, Alpha Chi Sigma, Masons (32 deg.), Shriners, Rotary. Republican. Methodist. Home: 1912 Hunsaker Rd Oak Harbor WA 98277-8666

DAUGHERTY, LINDA HAGAMAN, private school executive; b. Denver, Jan. 25, 1940; d. Charles B. and Agnes May (Wall) Hagaman; m. Thomas Daniel Daugherty, Nov. 20, 1965; children: Patrick, Christina Marie. BS in Bus., U. Colo., 1961; postgrad., Tulane U., 1963-64, U. St. Thomas, 1990-91. Sr. systems analyst Lockheed Electronics NASA, Houston, 1966-73; sr. systems cons. TRW Systems Internat., Caracas, Venezuela, 1973-74; sy. systems cons. TRW Systems, L.A., 1974-75; sr. systems analyst Intercomp, Houston, 1979-80; cons. Daugherty Fin. Svcs., Inc., Katy, Tex., 1980-82, pres., 1979-91; mng. ptnr. Motivated Child Learning Ctrs., Katy, 1976—; pres. Williamsburg Country Day Sch., Katy, 1983—, Nottingham Country Day Sch., Katy, 1977—. Pres. Mason Creek Women Reps. Club, Katy, 1980; treas. Nottingham Country Civic Club, Katy, 1979; mem. adv. bd. Nottingham Country Club, 1982-85; co-founder Friends of Archaeology U. St. Thomas, pres., 1991-93; mem. Epiphany Ch. Social Works Commn.; asst. curator Archaeology Gallery, U. St. Thomas; mem., pres. Friends of Boerne Pub. Libr., 1997—; San Antonio World Affair Coun. Mem. Houston Archeology Soc., Tex. Archeology Soc., Archaeology Inst. of Am., Boerne Women's Club. Roman Catholic. Avocations: archaeology, bridge. Office: Nottingham Country Day Sch PO Box 489 Boerne TX 78006-0489

DAUGHERTY, PHYLLIS LYN, secondary school educator; d. E. Sexton and Myra Catherine Daugherty; m. Kendell C. McMillan, 1973 (div. 1993); children: Erin, Rachel; m. G. James Jackson Jr., 2003. BA in English and Secondary Edn., Harding U., 1973; MA in Pub. History, U. Ill., Springfield, Ill., 1997, MA in Edn. Leadership (Adminstrn.), 2003. Cert. secondary edn. (6-12) Ill., 1973, adminstrv. Ill., 2002. Educator Granite City (Ill.) Sch. Dist., 1973—79; permanent substitute Lafayette (La.) Parish Sch. Dist., 1984—87, Dept. Def., Wiesbaden, Germany, 1990—93; tchr. Springfield (Ill.) Sch. Dist., 1993—97, Dept. Def., Taegu, Republic of Korea, 1997—98, Springfield (Ill.) Sch. Dist., 1998—. Transcriber: Lincoln's Legal Papers, 1996. Bd. dir. Sangamon County Hist. Soc., Springfield, 1997—98, Ill. Humanities Coun., Springfield, 1999—. Recipient Gulf War Commemorative medal, Dept. of Def. and Am. Red Cross, 1991; grantee LEAD grant, Readers Digest, 2002. Mem.: Ill. Principals Assn., Org. of Am. Historians, Phi Alpha Theta. Avocations: travel, cooking, gardening. Office: Springfield SE HS 2350 E Ash Springfield IL 62703 Fax: 217-525-3139.

DAUGHERTY, ROBERT MELVIN, JR., dean, medical educator; b. Kansas City, Mo., May 2, 1934; s. Robert Melvin and Mildred Josephine (Johnson) D.; m. Sandra Allison Keller, Aug. 10, 1957; children— Robert Melvin III, Allison, Christopher. BS, Kans. U., 1956; MD, U. Kans., 1960; MS, U. Okla. Med. Ctr., 1964; PhD, U. Okla., 1965. Intern Jefferson Davis Hosp., Houston, 1960-61; resident U. Okla. Med. Ctr., Oklahoma City, 1961-63, asst. prof. physiology and medicine, 1965-66; assoc. prof. physiology and medicine Mich. State U. Coll. Human Medicine, East Lansing, 1969-71; prof., dir. Office Curriculum Implementation, 1969-76; prof. physiology and medicine U. Wyo. Coll. Human Medicine, Laramie, 1976-78, dean, 1976-78; prof. physiology and medicine Ind. U. Sch. Medicine, Indpls., 1978-81, assoc. dean, 1978-81, dir. continuing med. edn., 1978-81; dean Sch. Medicine, U. Nev., 1981-99, dean emeritus, 1999—; dir. health care polity R&D, U. Nev. Sch. Medicine, Reno, 1999—2000; dean, v.p. for health sciences U. of South Florida Coll. of Med., Tampa, Fla., 2000—. Tchg. scholar Am. Heart Assn., 1970-75. Mem. AMA (coun. med. edn. 1991—), LCME (chair 1999—), Am. Physiol. Soc., Am. Heart Assn., Ctrl. Soc. for Clin. Investigation. Presbyterian. Office: U of S Florida Sch of Med 12901 Bruce B Downs Blvd, Box 3 Tampa FL 33612

DAUGHERTY, TONDA LOU, special education educator; b. Aurora, Mo., Aug. 17, 1954; d. Wilbur E. McCuller and Gynith P. (Murphy) Frederick. BS in Edn., S.W. Mo. State U., Springfield, 1982; MA in Spl. Edn., U. Mo., Kansas City, 1986, EdS in Reading, 1988. Tchr. learning disabilities and behavior disorders Consolidated Sch. Dist. 4, Grandview, Mo., 1982—. Ednl. cons. Perfection Form Pub. Co., Kansas City, 1990. Active PTA. Mem. Mo. State Tchrs. Assn., Phi Kappa Phi. Democrat. Roman Catholic. Avocations: swimming, reading, needlework. Home: 9705 Oakley Ave Kansas City MO 64137-1349 Office: Conn-West Elem Sch 1100 High Grove Rd Grandview MO 64030-2473

DAUGHTREY, MARGERY L. plant pathologist; b. Charlottesville, Va., Oct. 17, 1953; d. Edward Dixon and Carrie Baylor Daughtrey. BS, Coll. William and Mary, 1975; MS, U. Mass., 1978. Sr. ext. assoc. Cornell U., Riverhead, N.Y., 1978—. Plant pathology team leader Am. Floral Endowment, Edwardsville, Ill., 1996-99. Co-author: Ball Field Guide to Diseases of Greenhouse Ornamentals, 1992, Diseases of Annuals and Perennials, 1995, Compendium of Flowering Potted Plant Diseases, 1995; editor Phytopathology News, 2003—. Recipient Publ. award Profl. Plant Growers Assn., 1989, 92. Mem. Internat. Soc. Arboriculture, Am. Phytopathol. Soc. (pres. N.E. divsn. 2001-02, Disting. Svc. award 2002, editor, Phytopathology News, 2003), Soc. Am. Florists (chmn. rsch. com. 1992-94, Alex Laurie award 1998), Bedding Plants Internat. (Futura award 2000). Avocations: reading, photography, mycology. Office: Cornell U 3059 Sound Ave Riverhead NY 11901

DAUGHTREY, MARTHA CRAIG, federal judge; b. Covington, Ky., July 21, 1942; d. Spence E. Kerkow and Martha E. (Craig) Piatt; m. Larry G. Daughtrey, Dec. 28, 1962; 1 child, Carran. BA, Vanderbilt U., 1964, JD, 1968. Bar: Tenn. 1968. Pvt. practice, Nashville, 1968; asst. U.S. atty., 1968—69; asst. dist. atty., 1969—72; asst. prof. law Vanderbilt U., Nashville, 1972—75; judge Tenn. Ct. Appeals, Nashville, 1975—90; assoc. justice Tenn. Supreme Ct., Nashville, 1990—93; circuit judge U.S. Ct. Appeals (6th cir.), Nashville, 1993—. Lectr. law Vanderbilt Law Sch., Nashville, 1975—82, adj. prof., 1988—90; mem. faculty NYU Appellate Judges Seminar, N.Y.C., 1977—90, N.Y.C., 1994—. Contbr. articles to profl. jours. Pres. Women Judges Fund for Justice, 1984—85, 1986—87; active various civic orgns. Recipient Athena award, Nat. Athena Program, 1991. Mem.: ABA (chmn. appellate judges conf. 1985—86, ho. of dels. 1988—91, chmn. jud. divsn. 1989—90, standing com. on continuing edn. of bar 1992—94, commn. on women in the profession 1994—97, bd. editors ABA Jour. 1995—2001), Lawyers Assn. for Women (pres. Nashville 1986—87), Nat. Assn. Women Judges (pres. 1985—86), Am. Judicature Soc. (bd. dirs. 1988—92), Nashville Bar Assn. (bd. dirs. 1988—90), Tenn. Bar Assn. Office: US Ct Appeals 300 Customs House 701 Broadway Nashville TN 37203-3944*

D'AUGUSTINE, ROBERT, university administrator, lawyer; b. Tacoma, Wash., Apr. 22, 1947; s. Anthony Patrick and Marie Colette; m. Marcia Morgan, June 6, 1970; children: Matthew, Allie. BA, U. Pa., 1968, MA, 1971; MBA, Rutgers U., 1982, JD, 1996. Exec. asst. to dean U. Medicine and Dentistry N.J., Newark, 1977-83, asst. v.p. acad. affairs, 1983-87, assoc. v.p. acad. adminstrn., 1987-98, assoc. v.p. faculty adminstrn. New Brunswick, 1998-2000; exec. dir. budget and planning Rowan U., Glassboro, N.J., 2000—. Contbr. articles to scholarly and profl. jours. Co-founder, pres. Citizens for Quality Edn., Metuchen, N.J., 1988-93. With U.S. Army, 1968-70. Mem. Beta Gamma Sigma. Home: 110 Woodlane Ct Glassboro NJ 08028 E-mail: augustbob@aol.com.

DAUKANTAS, GEORGE VYTAUTAS, counseling practitioner, educator; b. Stolzenau, Germany, Dec. 20, 1946; arrived in US, 1949; s. Chester and Alexandra Daukantas. AA magna cum laude, Wesley U., 1973; BA in Psychology, U. Mass., 1976; cert. computer programming/ops., Control Data Inst., 1980; MA in Counseling Psychology, U. No. Colo., 1982; MEd in Psychol. Studies, Cambridge Coll., 2000; postgrad., 2001—. Cert. Coun. for Accreditation for Counseling and Related Ednl. Programs. Asst. tchr. severely challenged boys and girls Boston Pub. Sch., 1997—; tchr.'s asst. spl. needs Richard J. Murphy Elem. Sch., 2000—. Mem. Nat. Campaign for Tolerance, So. Poverty Law Program. Sgt. E-5 U.S. Army, 1964—67 USNG, 1975—82. Recipient Cold War Recognition Cert., US Army, 1999. Mem.: ACLU, ACA, VFW, Assn. Counselor Edn. and Supervision, Mass. Mental Health Counselors Assn., Sierra Club, Amnesty Internat., Am. Legion. Democrat. Roman Catholic. Avocations: yoga, chess, ocean swimming. Home: # 3 135 Eutaw St Boston MA 02128-2546 E-mail: daukantas@hotmail.com.

DAUKSHUS, A. JOSEPH, systems engineer; b. Tamaqua, Pa., Oct. 17, 1948; s. Anna N. Daukshus. BS in Aerospace Engring., Pa. State U., 1975. Devel. engr. Carl Zeiss Inc., Thornwood, N.Y., 1984-88; cons. Panasonic, Secaucus, N.J., 1988, Pratt & Whitney, E. Hartford, Conn., 1989, AT&T, Largo, Fla., 1990, Somerset, N.J., 1990-91, Torrington (Conn.) Co., 1990, Trecom Bus. Systems, Edison, N.J., 1990-91; systems engr. Canberra Industries, Meriden, Conn., 1991-93; sales assoc. Sears Roebuck and Co., Danbury, Conn., 1993-94; engr. EIS Internat., Stamford, Conn., 1995-96, Oxford Health Plans, Norwalk, Conn., 1996-98, Reuters, Stamford, 1998-2000; quality analyst Oxford Health Plans, Trumbull, Conn., 2000—. Cons. Executone, Darien, Conn., 1994-95, NASDAQ Stock Market Inc., Trumbull, Conn., 1994-95. Mem. N.Y. Acad. Sci. Home: PO Box 8916 New Fairfield CT 06812-8916 E-mail: jdaukshus@snet.net.

DAUM, JULIE HEMBROCK, executive recruiter; b. Cin., Aug. 5, 1954; d. Vincent and Mary Hembrock; m. Robert Charles Daum; children: Alexandra, Schuyler, Bailey. BS, Pa. State U., 1976; MBA, Wharton Grad. Sch., 1979. Assoc. McKinsey & Co., L.A., 1979-81; v.p. Chase Manhattan Bank, London, N.Y.C., 1981-85, Citibank, N.Y.C., 1985-87; cons. Nordeman Grimm, N.Y.C., 1988-90; mng. dir. corp. bd. resources Catalyst, N.Y.C., 1991-93; mng. dir. U.S. bd. svcs. practice leader Spencer Stuart, N.Y.C., 1993—. Bd. dirs. City Harvest, 1997—, Student Sponsor Partnership, 1998—, Women's Forum, 2000—. Mem.: Tuxedo Club, River Club, Colony Club. Episcopalian. Home: 120 E End Ave New York NY 10028-7552 Office: Spencer Stuart 277 Park Ave Fl 29 New York NY 10172-2998

DAUNS, JOHN, mathematician, educator; b. Riga, Latvia, June 11, 1937; BS, MIT, 1960; PhD, Harvard U., 1964. Asst. prof. Tulane U., New Orleans, 1964—68, assoc. prof., 1968—81, prof., 1981—. Vis. prof. U. Natal, Durban, South Africa, 1984. Author: A Concrete Approach to Division Rings, 1982, Modules and Rings, 1994; co-author (with K.H. Hofmann): Representations of Rings by Sections, 1968; contbr. over 57 articles to profl. jours. Fellow Woodrow Wilson, Harvard U., 1960, Humboldt Rsch. fellow, Tübingen U., 1972—73. Mem.: Am. Math. Soc. Avocation: swimming. Office: Dept Math Tulane U 6823 St Charles Ave New Orleans LA 70118

DAUPHINAIS, RICHARD MURRAY, pathologist; b. New Rochelle, N.Y., Sept. 4, 1935; s. Louis O. and Arline M. (Murray) D.; m. Linda Bigelow, June 17, 1961 (div. Jan. 1971); children: Leslie, Karen; m. Jane Saviteer, May 19, 1979; children: Matthew, David. BS in Biology, Holy Cross Coll., 1957; MD, St. Louis U., 1961. Cert. anatomic/clin. pathology, radioisotopic pathology. Resident pathology Hartford (Conn.) Hosp., 1962-66; pathologist U.S. Naval Hosp., Jacksonville, Fla., 1966-68; asst. pathologist St. Francis Hosp. and Med. Ctr., Hartford, 1968-75, assoc. pathologist, 1975-87, sr. attending pathologist, 1987-91; dir. pathology Westerly (R.I.) Hosp., 1991—. Asst. prof. U. Conn. Health Ctr., Farmington, 1969-74, 86-91, asst. clin. prof. pathology, 1974-86; clin. assoc. prof. biology and health scis. U. Hartford, West Hartford, Conn., 1981-87, clin. prof. biology and health scis., 1987-91. Guest editor: Am. Jour. Med. Tech., 1978; contbr. chpts. to books and articles to profl. jours. Judge Conn. Jr. Miss Pageant, Farmington, 1976. Lt. comdr. USN, 1966-68. Fellow Coll. Am. Pathologists; mem. Am. Assn. for Clin. Chemistry, Am. Soc. Clin. Pathology, Clin. Ligand Assay Soc. (pres. 1983-84, Best Abstract award 1985), R.I. Soc. Pathologists (sec./treas. 1997-98, pres. 1998-99), New Eng. Soc. Pathologists. Avocations: sports, piano, reading, travel. Office: Westerly Hosp 25 Wells St Westerly RI 02891-2934

D'AURORA, JACK, lawyer; b. Steubenville, Ohio, Oct. 22, 1955; s. Anthony C. and Ann Marie D'Aurora; children: Allison, John Joseph. BA, U. Notre Dame, 1977; JD, Georgetown U., 1987. Bar: Calif. 1987, Ohio 1991, Pa. 1991. Assoc. Baker & McKenzie, San Diego, 1987-89, Procopio Hargreaves Cory & Savitch, San Diego, 1989-91, Carlile Patchen & Murphy, Columbus, Ohio, 1991-93; of counsel Rishel & Kopech, Columbus, 1993-95, Rinehart Howarth Rishel & Kopech, Columbus, 1996-99, Luper, Neidenthal & Logan, Columbus, 2000—. Pres. cons. bd. Downtown YMCA, Columbus, 2000; pres. N.D. Club Columbus, pres. Salvation Army West Mound St. Corp. cons. bd. Lt. USN, 1977-85. Mem. C. of C. of Upper Arlington (pres. 1996). Democrat. Office: Luper, Neidenthal & Logan 12th Fl 50 W Broad St Columbus OH 43215 E-mail: jdaurora@lnlattorneys.com.

D'AURORA, JAMES JOSEPH, psychologist, consultant; b. Canton, Ohio, Feb. 10, 1949; s. James Joseph Sr. and Arsilia (Lombardi) D'A.; m. Denise Marie Linkenhoker, Dec. 28, 1974; children: Andrew David, Elizabeth Clare. BA, U. Notre Dame, 1971; MEd, Kent State U., 1974; PhD, U. Minn., 1984. Lic. psychologist Minn., cert. profl. qualification in psychology. Pre-major adv. Coll. of Liberal Arts U. Minn., Mpls., 1974-75; intern Bach Inst., Mpls., 1975-77, staff psychologist, 1977-79; psychologist Loring Family Clinic, Mpls., 1979-81; pvt. practice Mpls., 1981-86; cons. psychologist Solstice: A Ctr. for Psychotherapy and Learning, St. Paul, 1986-89; pvt. practice St. Paul, 1989—. Cons. in field; researcher Family Renewal Ctr., Mpls., 1982-85, Golden Valley Health Ctr. Psychology Subsect., 1988-92. Lectr., lay homilist, choir Christ the King Ch., parish pastoral coun., 1991—96; interim sch. bd. Christ the King-St. Thomas the Apostle Sch., 1992; bd. dirs. Twin Cities Marathon, 2001—, sec., 2001—03. Mem.: APA, Assn. State and Provincial Psychology Bds., Minn. Psychol. Assn. (chmn. ins. com. 1988—94), Minn. Soc. Clin. Hypnosis, Notre Dame Alumni Assn. (candidate regional dir.), N.W. Athletic Club (adv. bd. club run 1997—2000, chair 1999—2000), Notre Dame Club Minn. (bd. dirs. 1986—91, sec. 1987—88, v.p. 1988—89, pres. 1989—90). Mem. Democratic Farm Labor Party. Roman Catholic. Achievements include qualifier, finisher 100th Boston marathon, 1996; 104th Boston marathon, 2000. Avocations: running, rock climbing, snorkeling, singing. Home: 5536 Merritt Cir Edina MN 55436-2026 Office: 91 Snelling Ave N Ste 200 Saint Paul MN 55104-6753

DAUS, ARTHUR STEVEN, neurological surgeon; b. Louisville, Feb. 6, 1957; s. Arthur Theodore Daus Jr. and Marilyn Ann (McCord) Hanish; m. Victoria Lynn Schilla, July 10, 1982; children: Arthur S. Jr., Haley N. BS in Physics magna cum laude, Vanderbilt U., 1977; MD, St. Louis U., 1981. Diplomate Nat. Bd. Med. Examiners, Am. Bd. Neurol. Surgery, Fedn. State Licensing Examiners; lic. physician, Ky., N.Mex., Ariz., Mo., Calif. Rotating intern in surgery U. Ky. Med. Ctr., Lexington, 1981-82, resident neurosurgeon, 1982-88; pvt. practice Midwest Neurosurgery Ctr., Joplin, Mo., 1988—. Instr. cervical spine instrumentation A.M.E. Med. Co., Kansas City, Mo., 1992. Mem. Nat. Coalition of Physicians Against Family Violence, Chgo., 1994—. Recipient Ky. State Residents award Am. Coll. Surgeons com. on trauma, 1985; named Ky. Col. State of Ky., 1985—. Mem. AMA (2 Physician's Recognition awards 1990-94, 2003—, 3 Physician's Recognition awards with spl. commendation 1993-96, 96-2000, 2000-03), So. Med. Assn., Jasper-Newton County Med. Soc., So. Neurosurg. Soc. (first honorable mention residents competition 1984), Congress Neurol. Surgeons, Am. Assn. Neurol. Surgeons (4 continuing edn. awards 1990-92, 93-95, 96-98, 99-2001), Nat. Audubon Soc., Phi Beta Kappa, Phi Eta Sigma. Republican. Roman Catholic. Avocations: chess, swimming, archery, riflery, horseback riding. Home: 5 Teal Dr Joplin MO 64804-5816 Office: Midwest Neurosurgery Ctr 1111 McIntosh Cir Ste 305 Joplin MO 64804-3693

DAUS, JONATHAN MICHAEL, secondary education educator; b. Dover, N.J., Nov. 1, 1963; s. Jerome Martin and Ruth (Cohen) D.; m. Dori Helfgott, Apr. 12, 1997; children: Adam Samuel, Sara Miriam, Jacob Benjamin. BA, Rutgers U., 1986. Cert. sci. tchr., N.J.; cert. radiotelephone operator. Sci. tchr. East Brunswick (N.J.) Pub. Schs., 1987—. News dir., webmaster Israel Hour News Online, 1997-99; dir., webmaster Israel News Online, 1999—. Sr. host, prodr. The Israel Hour, Sta. WRSU-FM, New Brunswick, 1983-98. Sec.-treas., co-founder Project OPEN Inc., New Brunswick, 1984-97. Mem. N.J. Edn. Assn., N.J. Sci. Tchrs. Assn. Jewish. Avocations: astronomy, writing, shortwave listening, politics, reading.

DAUS, VICTORIA LYNN, nurse midwife; b. Cleve. m. Arthur Steven Daus; 2 children. RN, Luth. Med. Ctr., Cleve., 1975; BSN, St. Louis U., 1982; MSN, U. Ky., 1987; D of Nursing, Case Western Res. U., 1996; postgrad. in nursing, Francis Payne Bolton Sch. Nursing. RN, Mo., Ohio, Ky., NSW, Australia. Nurse newborn nursery, neonatal intensive care nurse, pediatrics nurse Fairview Gen. Hosp., Cleve., 1975-78; neonatal intensive care nurse, neonatal transport nurse Royal Alexandria Hosp. for Children, Sydney, NSW, Australia, 1978-79; midwife Crown Street Women's Hosp., Sydney, 1979-80; labor and delivery nurse, postpartum nurse Deaconess Hosp., Cleve., 1980; neonatal intensive care nurse Cardinal Glennon Meml. Hosp. for Children, St. Louis, 1981-82; labor and delivery nurse Chandler Med. Ctr. U. Ky., Lexington, 1982-83; labor and delivery nurse, tchr. childbirth edn., labor and delivery charge nurse Humana Hosp., Lexington, 1983-85; coord. quality assurance Prince of Wales Hosp. for Children, Sydney, 1986; hosp. floater for coronary care, neurosurg., orthopedics and med., surg. nurse Good Samaritan Hosp., Lexington, 1985-87; clin. instr. obstetrics and pediatrics Lexington C.C., 1988; clin. instr. pediat. nursing Pitts. State U., 2000—02. Mem. Am. Assn. Neurosci. Nurses, Am. Coll. Nurse-Midwives (cert.), Nat. Assn. Nurse Practitioners in Reproductive Health, N.Am. Nursing Diagnosis Assn., Assn. Reproductive Health Profls., Assn. Women's Health, Obstet. and Neonatal Nurses, Sigma Theta Tau. Republican. Roman Catholic.

DAUSCHER, RAYMOND G. lawyer. Corp. gen. counsel White Consolidated Industries, Inc., Cleve. Office: White Consol Industries Inc 11770 Berea Rd Cleveland OH 44111-1601

DAUSER, KIMBERLY ANN, physician assistant; b. Detroit, Nov. 20, 1947; d. George Leonard and Jeanne (Austin) Wilkie; 1 child, Aaron Thomas. AA, Pensacola Jr. Coll., 1971; BS in Medicine, physician's asst. cert. in medicine, U. Ala., Birmingham, 1976; cert. in mgmt., Am. Mgmt. Assn., 1989; postgrad., U. West Fla., 1995—. Cert. physician's asst. Asst. mgr. Christo's, Gulf Breeze, Fla., 1966-67; teller, bookkeeper loan dept. Bank Gulf Breeze, 1967-72; med. tech. aide USN Hosp., Pensacola, 1972, physician's asst., 1972-73, John Kingsley, MD, Pensacola, 1976, Mountain Comprehensive Health Corp., Whitesburg, Ky., 1976-78, N.W. Fla. Nephrology, Pensacola, 1978-87, med. adminstr., 1987-95, Nephrology Ctr. of Pensacola, Fla., 1987-95; COO Nephrology Ctr., Inc., Crestview, Pensacola, 1995—, Nephrology Ctr., Inc., Crestview, Pensacola, 1995-96, Nephrology Ctr. Assocs., Pensacola, 1995-96; regional COO, Renal Care Group Inc., Pensacola, Fla., 1996-98; COO Nephrology Ctr. Assoc. PA, 1998-99; area adminstr. Renal Care Group Inc., Houston, 1999—2002, clin. ops. cons., 2002, dir. clin. ops., 2002—. Fellow Am. Acad. Physician's Assts. (del. nat. meeting 1978—), Nat. Commn. on Cert. Physician's Assts., Fla. Acad. Physician's Assts. (mem. jud. com. 1979-80), Natural Wildlife Assn. Republican. Roman Catholic. Avocations: photography, antiques, reading, wildlife preservation. Office: Renal Care Group Ste 600 2525 W End Ave Nashville TN 37203 Home: 600 Enterprise Ave # 1028 League City TX 77573

DAUSSET, JEAN, immunologist; b. Toulouse, France, Oct. 19, 1916; s. Henri and Elizabeth Dausset; m. Rose Mayoral, Mar. 17, 1962. AB, Lycee Michelet, 1939; MD, U. Paris, 1945. Intern, then resident in internal medicine and hematology Paris Mcpl. Hosps., 1946—50; dir. lab. Nat. Transfusion Ctr., 1950—63; prof. immunohematology U. Paris, 1963—77; prof. exptl. medicine Coll. de France, Paris, 1977—87; dir. research unit on immunogenetics Hopital Saint-Louis, Paris, 1969—84; dir. Human Polymorphism Study Ctr., 1984—. Rschr. in field of man's histocompatibility system and human genome. Served to capt., WWII. Recipient Nobel Prize in physiology or medicine, 1980, Honda prize, Honda Found. Japan, 1987. Mem.: NAS (Washington), Am. Acad. Arts and Sci., Acadenue des Sciences de l'Institut de France. Home: 44 Rue des Ecoles 75005 Paris France Office: 27 Rue Juliette Dodu 75010 Paris France E-mail: dausset@aol.com.

DAUSSMAN, GROVER FREDERICK, electrical engineer, consultant; b. Warrick County, Ind., May 6, 1919; s. Grover Cleveland and Madeline (Springer) D.; m. Elli Margrite Kilian, Dec. 27. 1941; children: Cynthia Louise Daussman Quinn, Judith Ann, Margaret Elizabeth Daussman Davidson Cooper. Student, U. Cin., 1936-38, Carnegie Inst. Tech., 1944-45, George Washington U., 1948-56; BSEE, U. Ala., 1963, postgrad., 1963-64, 77, Indsl. Coll. Armed Forces, 1955, 63; PhD (hon.), Hamilton State U., 1973. Registered profl. engr., Ala., Va., D.C.; cert. fallout shelter analyst. Coop. engr. Sunbeam Elec. Mfg. Co., Evansville, Ind., 1936-38; engr., draftsman Phila. Navy Yard, 1941-42; resident engr., supr. shipbldg. USN, Neville Island, Pa., 1942-45; engr. Pearl Harbor Navy Yard, 1945-48; sect. head Bur. Ships USN, Washington, 1948-56; head guidance and control tech. liaison Army Ballistic Missile Agy., Huntsville, Ala., 1956-58, chief program coordination Guidance and Control Lab., 1958-60; chief program coordination Astrionics Lab., Marshall Space Flight Ctr., Huntsville, 1960-63, dir's staff asst. for advanced rsch. and tech., 1963-70, engring. cons., 1970—. Project dir. fallout shelter surveys Mil Dept. Tenn., 1971-73; head drafting dept. Alverson-Draughon Coll., Huntsville, 1974-77; instr. Ala. Christian Coll., 1977-79; engring. draftsman Reisz Engring., 1979; chief engr. Sheraton Motor Inn, 1979; sr. engr. Sperry Support Services, 1980; assoc. Techni-Core Profls., Huntsville, 1980-81; elec. engr. Reisz Engring., Huntsville, 1981-86; tutor in mathematics, scis. and engring. North Ala. Ctr. for Ednl. Excellence, Huntsville, 1986-2000, and U.S. Dept. Vet. Affairs, 2000—. Chmn. community spl. gifts com. Madison County Heart Assn., 1965; mem. Population Action Coun., Huntsville Track Club, Mended Hearts, Inc., Prayer Power Club, Nat. Assn. of Sr. Friends, Sierra Club. Recipient cert. of recognition, 1945, cert. of service USN, 1946; performance award cert. U.S. Army, 1960; certs. of appreciation AIEE, 1960, 61, 62; IEEE Centennial Medal, 1984, IEEE Honor Role of Outstanding Vols., 1986, IEEE Ednl. Activities Award, 1987, award for disting. services Huntsville sect. IEEE, 1964, Engr. of Yr. award, 1969; award for contbn. to successful launch of 1st Saturn V, George C. Marshall Space Flight Center, 1967, also award for contbn. to 1st manned lunar landing, 1969; Apollo achievement award NASA, 1969; cert. of Appreciation North Ala. Ednl. Opportunity Ctr., Inc., 1987, 88, 89, 90, 91, U.S. Space Walk of Fame. Fellow: Explorers Club; mem.: IEEE (sr. sect. chmn. NO. Ala. sect. 1961—62, founder, chmn. engring. mgmt. chpt. 1964—65, mem. inst. rsch. com. 1965—67, mem. adminstrv. com. engring. mgmt. soc. 1966—86, sec. soc. 1968—85, mem. Region 3 exec. com. 1969—79, mem. inst. bd. dirs. 1972—73, regional del.-dir. S.E. region), AARP, AAAS, AIAA, Jr. Engring. Tech. Soc. (organizer local high sch. chpts.), U.S. Naval Inst., Am. Soc. Naval Engrs., Huntsville Assn. Tech. Socs. (sec. 1969—70, v.p. 1970—71, founder), Nat. Assn. Retarded Children, Internat. Platform Assn., Am. Def. Preparedness Assn. (post dir. Tenn. Valley 1963—66), Am. Inst. Urban and Regional Affairs, Ala. Soc. Profl. Engrs., Nat. Socs. Profl. Engrs., Planetary Soc. (charter), Hellenic Profl. Assn. Am. (hon.), NASA Retirees Assn. (v.p. 1973—74, pres. 1974—75), Nat. Assn. Ret. Fed. Employees, Assn. U.S. Army, Missile, Space

and Range Pioneers (life), Cousteau Soc., U. Ala. Alumni Assn. (state dir. 1962—65, chpt. pres. 1966—67, state dir. 1968—71, 1985—91), Redstone Arsenal Officers Club. Democrat. Mem. United Ch. of Christ (treas. 1959-61, ch. council 1964-66; sec. ch. council, program com. chmn. ch. council 1965-66; vice moderator Ala.-Tenn. assn. 1965-68; bd. dirs. Southeast conf. 1965-66, mem. budget and finance com. 1965-66). Office: 200 Westside Sq Ste 205 Huntsville AL 35801

DAUSTER, WILLIAM GARY, lawyer, economist; b. Sacramento, Nov. 25, 1957; s. William Joe and Marianne Dauster; m. Ellen Lisa Weintraub, May 10, 1986; children: Matthew Isaac, Natanya Miriam, Emma Sophia. BA in Econs., Polit. Sci. and Internat. Rels., U. So. Calif., 1978, MA in Econs., 1981; JD, Columbia U., 1984. Bar: N.Y. 1985, U.S. Dist. Ct. (so. and ea. dists.) N.Y. 1985, D.C. 1986, U.S. Supreme Ct. 1997. Assoc. Cravath, Swaine & Moore, N.Y.C., 1984-86; chief counsel com. on budget U.S. Senate, Washington, 1986-94, acting staff dir., chief counsel, 1994, Dem. chief of staff, chief counsel, 1995-97, Dem. dep. staff dir., gen. coun. com. labor/human resources, 1997, Dem. chief of staff, chief counsel, 1997-98; counselor Wellstone Pres. Exploratory Com., Washington, 1998-99; dep. asst. to the Pres. for econ. policy, dep. dir. Nat. Econ. Coun., The White House, Washington, 1999-2000; sr. counselor to Senator Russ Feingold U.S. Senate, Washington, 2000—01, legis. dir., 2001—03, Dem. gen. counsel com. on fin., 2003—. Author: Congressional Budget Act Annotated, 1990, Budget Process Law Annotated, 1991, 1993; contbr. articles to profl. jours. Bd. visitors Columbia Law Sch., 1992—2000. Recipient Order of Palm, 1978, trustee scholarship, U. So. Calif., 1974, Harlan Fiske Stone scholar, 1982—84. Mem.: N.Y. Bar Assn., D.C. Bar Assn. Democrat. Jewish. Home: 9713 Connecticut Ave Kensington MD 20895-3528 E-mail: bill_dauster@finance-dem.senate.gov., bill_dauster@yahoo.com.

DAUTEL, CHARLES SHREVE, retired mining company executive; b. Cleve., Apr. 5, 1923; s. Robert Poe and Frances (Shreve) D.; m. Isabell Francis Brown, June 11, 1947; children: Charles Warren, Louis Craig. BSC, Ohio U., 1948; JD, U. Cin., 1952. Bar: Ohio 1952. With Nichols, Wood, Marx & Ginter, Cin., 1952-55, Eagle-Picher Industries, Inc., Cin., 1955-88, asst. sec., asst. gen. counsel, 1958-70, sec., 1970-87, v.p., 1980-87. With AUS, 1942-46. Mem. Phi Delta Theta, Phi Delta Phi. Clubs: Hidden Valley Lake Country. Home: 1448 Brookridge Circle Dr Lawrenceburg IN 47025-9332

DAVANI, BAHMAN FAGHAIE, telecommunications engineer; b. Abadan, Iran, Mar. 21, 1953; came to U.S., 1976; s. Mohammed and Bomanjan D.; B.Sc. in Applied Math., U. Tehran, Iran, 1975; M.Sc. in Applied Math., Fla. Inst. Tech., 1977, M.Sc. in Computer Sci., 1978; Ph.D. (A.B.D.) in Computer Sci., So. Meth. U., 1982. Instr. U. Tehran, 1975-76; research asst. So. Meth. U., Dallas, 1978-81; mem. tech. staff mem. Rockwell Internat., Richardson, Tex., 1979—91; sr. mgr. sys. engring. Alcatel USA, Plano, Tex., 1991—. Free U. Iran scholar, 1976-79. Mem. IEEE, Assn. Computing Machinery, Math. Assn. Am., Nat. Mgmt. Assn. (cert. in mgmt. 1985, cert. mgr. 1991). Home: 4417 Denver Dr Plano TX 75093-5442

DAVANT, JAMES WARING, investment banker; b. McComb, Miss., Dec. 1, 1917; s. Guy Hamilton and Em Reid (Waring) D.; m. Mary Ellis Westlake, Apr. 4, 1942; children: Mary Diane, John Hamilton, Patricia Jean (Mrs. Coleman Dupont Donaldson). Student, U. Va., 1939. With Paine, Webber, Jackson & Curtis, 1945—81, gen. ptnr., 1956—81, mem. policy com., 1963—81, mng. ptnr., 1964—81, pres., CEO, 1970—71, chmn. bd., CEO, 1971—80; chmn. Paine Webber Inc., 1974—81, ret., 1981. Chmn. Assn. Stock Exchange Firms, 1966-68; bd. dirs. N.Y. Stock Exchange, 1972-77, past chmn. cen. market com. Chmn. nat. adv. council Nat. Cystic Fibrosis Research Found.; bd. dirs. Securities Industry Assn., 1973-78, Manhattan Eye, Ear and Throat Hosp., Darden Sch., U. Va., 1978-1987; chmn. ctrl. market com. Stock Exchange. From aviation cadet to lt. comdr. USNR, 1940-46. Mem. Council Fgn. Relations, Econ. Club (chmn. 1976-77, trustee), Pilgrims of U.S., Bond Club (N.Y.C., gov. 1965—, pres. 1972—). Episcopalian. Office: 4600 N Ocean Blvd Boynton Beach FL 33435-7365

DAVATZES, NICKOLAS, broadcast executive; married; 2 children. BA, M, St. John's U. Various exec. positions Xerox Corp., 1965—75, v.p. sales and mktg., 1975—77; pres. Intext Comm. Sys., 1978—80; pres., CEO A&E TV Networks, N.Y.C., 1983—. Mem. adv. bd. Colls. Bus. Adminstrn. St. John's U.; bd. govs. Banff TV Festival. Founder Conn. Found. Childhood Leukemia; trustee St. John's U. Formerly with USMC. Co-recipient Salute to Freedom award, USS Intrepid Found., 1995; named to Broadcasting and Cable Hall of Fame, 1999; recipient Hist. Found. Heritage award, USMC, Chevalier des Arts et Lettres, French Govt., 1989, Pres.'s award, Cable TV Pub. Affairs Assn., 1996, Vanguard award, Nat. Cable TV Assn., 1994, Hellenic Heritage Achievement award, Am. Hellenic Inst., 2000. Mem.: NATAS (dir. internat. coun.), Brit. Acad. Film and TV Arts (east coast, trustee).

DAVATZIKOS, PH.D. CHRISTOS, research scientist, educator; Doctorate, Johns Hopkins U., 1989-1994;, B.S., Nat. Tech. U. of Athens, 1985-1989, Athens, Greece. Assoc. prof. of radiology and bioengineering U. of Pa, Philadelphia, Pa., 2002—; assoc. prof. of radiology and computer sci. Johns Hopkins U., Baltimore, Md., 2001—02, asst. prof. of computer sci., 1999—2001; asst. prof. of radiology Johns Hopkins U. Sch. of Medicine, Baltimore, Md. Chief Sect. of Biomedical Image Analysis, U. of Pa, Philadelphia, Pa., 2002—; dir. Ctr. for Biomedical Image Computing, Johns Hopkins U., Baltimore, Md. Author (scientific reviewer) scientific review and publications, scientific manuscript. Lead rschr. U. of Pa, Philadelphia, Pa. Na NA. Fellow Recipient, Fulbright Scholarship, 1989-1994, Johns Hopkins Fellowship, 1989-1994. Mem.: Orgn. for Human Brain Mapping, Computer Assisted Surg. Soc., Engring. in Medicine and Biology Soc. Achievements include first to World Leader In Computer-Assisted Research In Radiology. Office: University of Pennsylvania 3600 Market St Suite 380 Philadelphia PA 19104

DAVE, HARISH PRANLAL, hematologist; b. Kisumu, Kenya, July 28, 1957; came to U.S., 1985; s. Pranlal Girdharlal and Yasumati Pranlal (Vyas) D.; m. Jagruti Pathak, June 26, 1982; children: Devangi Harish, Raj Harish. BSc, U. Sheffield, Eng., 1979, MD, ChB, 1982. Diplomate Am. Bd. Internal Medicine, Am. Bd. Med. Oncology, Am. Bd. Hematology. Intern in internal medicine and surgery U. Sheffield, 1982-83; resident in internal medicine Royal Postgrad. Med. Sch., London, 1983-85; vis. postdoctoral fellow NIH, Bethesda, Md., 1985-90, vis. assoc., 1990-92; fellow hematology and oncology George Washington U., Washington, 1988-91, assoc. prof., 1993—; attending hematologist VA Med. Ctr., Washington, 1991—, asst. chief, hematology, 1992—, chief, lab of molecular hematology, 1992—. Grants reviewer U.S. Naval Rsch. Command, 1992—, NIH, 2000--; cons. Exon-Intron, Columbia, Md., 1992—. Contbr. articles to profl. jours. Michael Harrison scholarship U. Glasgow, Scotland, 1980. Mem. Royal Soc. of Health, Royal Inst. of Pub. Health and Hygiene, Inst. of Biomed. Scis., Am. Fedn. for Clin. Rsch., Am. Assn. for Cancer Rsch., Am. Soc. for Biochemistry and Molecular Biology, Am. Soc. Hematology, Am. Soc. Clin. Oncology, Washington Blood Club (chmn. 1992—). Home: 21304 Appenine Ct Germantown MD 20876-5907 Office: VA Med Ctr 50 Irving St NW Washington DC 20422-0001 E-mail: harish.dave@med.va.gov.

DAVE, ROMEEL, astronomer, educator, researcher; b. Palo Alto, Calif., May 20, 1969; s. Suresh B. Dave and Ronda D. Tycer; m. Jarita Charmian Holbrook; 1 child, Mirabai. PhD, U. Calif., Santa Cruz, 1998. Lyman J. Spitzer fellow Princeton (N.J.) U. Obs., 1998—2000; Hubble fellow Steward Obs., Tucson, 2000—03; asst. prof. dept. astronomy U. Ariz., 2003—. Avocations: acting, directing, travel, river rafting, kayaking. Office: Steward Obs 933 N Cherry Ave Tucson AZ Personal E-mail: rad@as.arizona.edu. Business E-Mail: rad@as.arizona.edu.

D'AVELLA, BERNARD JOHNSON, JR., publishing company executive, lawyer; b. Orange, N.J., Jan. 6, 1945; s. Bernard Johnson and Aida Santa (Magliacane) D'A.; m. Elaine Anne Benucci, Aug. 11, 1973; children: Bernard J. III, Anthony N. Student, Princeton U., 1962-66; AB, Rutgers U., 1970; JD, U. Penn., 1973. Bar: N.J. 1973, U.S. Dist. Ct. N.J. 1973. Assoc. atty. Hannoch Weisman, Newark, 1973-78, ptnr., dir. Newark, Roseland, Trenton, N.J., 1978-98, mng. ptnr., dir., 1980-91; pres., COO Prudent Pub. Co. and The Gallery Collection, Ridgefield Park, N.J., 1998—. Former class pres. Princeton U., mem. exec. com., 25th, 30th and 35th reunion coms., former chmn. Maclean fellow sel. com.; former treas., trustee The Joint Connection; chmn. emeritus bd. dirs. N.J. State Opera; former chmn. ethics commn. Borough of Roseland, N.J.; chmn. Juvenile Conf. Com. Twp. of Essex Fells, N.J. Sgt. U.S. Army, 1967-69. Decorated Bronze Star, Bronze Star with oak leaf cluster, Air medal, Army Commendation medal. Mem. ABA, N.J. State Bar Assn., Assn. Fed. Bar, Essex County Bar Assn., Princeton Alumni Assn. Essex County (exec. com., alumni schs. com., past pres.), Essex Fells Country Club, Fellsbrook Paddle and Tennis Club, Mantoloking Yacht Club (bd. govs.). Avocations: opera, house restoration and design, antiques and classic automobiles, tennis, golf. Home: 105 Rensselaer Rd Essex Fells NJ 07021-1400 Office: Prudent Pub Co Inc 65 Challenger Rd Ste 2 Ridgefield Park NJ 07660-2111

DAVENPORT, ALAN GARNETT, civil engineer, educator; b. Madras, India, Sept. 19, 1932; came to Can., naturalized; s. Tom and May Davenport; m. Sheila Rand Smith, Apr. 13, 1957; children: Thomas Sidney, Anna Margaret, Andrew Hope, Clare Rand BA, Cambridge U., Eng., 1954, MA, 1958; MASc, U. Toronto, Ont., Can., 1957, DEng (hon.), 1989; PhD, U. Bristol, Eng., 1960; D. in Applied Sci. (hon.), U. Louvain, Belgium, 1979; D. in Tech. (hon.), Tech. U. Denmark, 1982; DSc (hon.), McGill U., Montreal, Que., Can., 1983, U. Toronto, Ont., 1989; DEng (hon.), Waterloo (Ont., Can.) U., 1986; DSc (hon.), U. Guelph, Ont., 1993, U. La Plata, Argentina, 1993; DEng, Carlton U., 1996, U. Bristol, 1998; DSc (hon.), U. Western Ontario, London, Canada, 2002. Lectr. U. Toronto, Ont., Can., 1955-57; research officer Nat. Research Council, Ottawa, Ont., Can., 1957-58; asst. prof., then prof. U. Western Ont., London, Can., 1960—, dir. Boundary Layer Wind Tunnel Lab., 1960—, rsch. dir. Inst. for Catastrophic Loss Reduction, 1999; dir. Ctr. for Studies in Constrn., 1990—. Cons. on numerous bldgs., bridges and towers, including World Trade Ctr., N.Y.C., CN Tower, Toronto, Sears Bldg., Chgo., Sunshine Skyway Bridge, Fla., Hong Kong and Shanghai Bank Bldg., Hong Kong, Bank of China Bldg., Hong Kong, Great Belt Bridge, Denmark, Normandy Bridge, France. Editor: Can Jour. Civil Engring., 1974-79, mem. editorial bd., 1979-81 Chmn. Can. nat. com. UN-Internat. Decade for Natural Disaster Reduction, 1993—. Decorated Order of Canada; named to Engring. Hall of Distinction, U. Toronto, 1999; recipient Nobel prize, 1963, Cancam medal, Cancam 83, Saskatoon, Sask., Can., 1983, Queen Elizabeth medal, 1952—77, Gold medal, Inst. Structural Engrs., 1987, Oleg A. Kerensky medal, 1988, Ernest C. Manning award of distinction, Can. Confedn. medal, 1967—92, Killam prize, 1993, Can. Gold medal for sci. and engring., Natural Sci. and Engring. Rsch. Coun. Can., 1994, Gold ribbon d'Or award, French Autoroute Authority, Hellmuth prize for rsch., U. Western Ont., Otto H.G Flaschbard medal, Wind Engring. Soc. Germany, Austria and Switzerland, 2000, John F. Kennedy medal, Engring. Inst. Can., 2000, Albert Caquot prize, French Assn. Civil Engrs., 2001. Fellow Can. Soc. Civil Engring. (A.B. Sanderson award 1985), Engring. Inst. Can. (Duggan medal 1960, Gzowski medal 1963, 78, Julian C. Smith medal), Royal Soc. Can. (Rutherford lectr. 1988); mem. Am. Meteorol. Soc., Can. Meteorol. Soc. (prize in Applied Meterology 1965), ASCE (State of Art Civil Engring. award 1973, Can-Am Civil Engring. award 1977, Jack Cermak medal), Assn. Profl. Engrs. Ont. (Silver medal 1977, Bell Canada Forum award, 1992), Internat. Assn. Bridge and Structural Engring. (Award of Merit), Internat. Assn. Shell Structures (Tsubai prize 1997), Nat. Acad. Engring. (fgn. assoc.), Can. Acad. Engring. (founding mem., pres.), Royal Acad. Engring. (fgn. mem.). Avocations: sailing, squash, tennis. Home: 412 Lawson Rd London ON Canada N6G 1X8 Office: U Western Ont Boundary Layer Wind Tunnel Lab Engring Sci London ON Canada N6A 5B9 E-mail: agd@blwtl.uwo.ca.

DAVENPORT, ANN ADELE MAYFIELD, retired home care agency administrator; b. New Orleans, Nov. 12, 1941; d. Henry Louis and Myrtie Iola (Cason) Mayfield; m. John Wayne Davenport, June 18, 1966; children: Steven Lyle, Daniel Ryan, Elaine Adele. BA, Southeastern La. Coll., 1963; MA in Edn., George Peabody C., 1965; MA in Sociology, Tex. Tech. U., 1971. Tchr. various schs., 1963-70; instr. of sociology Tex. Tech. U., Lubbock, 1970-74, James Madison U., Harrisonburg, Va., 1981-82, Ga. So. Coll., Statesboro, 1982-84; 5th grade tchr. Bulloch county Schs., Statesboro, Ga., 1985-87; gerontology project coord. Dept. of Nursing Ga. So. Coll., 1987-88; project dir. Sr. Companion Program Ctr. for Rural Health and Rsch., Ga. So. U., Statesboro, 1988-93; instr. dept. health sci. edn. Ga. So. Coll., Statesboro, 1993-95; exec. dir. Ogeechee Home Health Agy., Statesboro, 1995-96, Homebound Svcs., Statesboro, 1996—2002; ret., 2002. Editor various newsletters, 1987-2002. Bd. dirs. Citizens Against Violence, Statesboro, 1987-88, Habitat for Humanity, 1990-2002; pres. Coun. on Children and Parents, Statesboro, 1988-89, 93-94; mem. steering com. Bulloch County Commn. on Human Svcs., 1989-2002; mem. adminstrv. bd. dirs., coun. on ministries, nominating com. Pittman Park United Meth. Ch.; pres. Ogeechee Wellness Coun., 1992-2002; bd. dirs. Ogeechee Home Health Agy., 1989-93. Mem. Ga. Rural Health Assn. (sec. 1988-89, editor state newsletter 1989-96), So. Sociol. Soc., Ga. Gerontol. Assn., Ga. Sociol. Assn., AAUW (newsletter editor Statesboro 1987-89), Am. Soc. on Aging, Nat. Coun. on the Aging, Am. Rural Health Assn. Avocations: tennis, reading. Home: 1920 Hampton Way Ada OK 74820

DAVENPORT, BILL, sculptor; b. Greenfield, Mass., 1962; BFA in Sculpture, R.I. Sch. Design, 1986; MFA in Sculpture, U. Mass., 1990. One-man shows include Student Uniion Gallery, U. Mass., Amherst, 1990, Wierzbowski Gallery, Houston, 1993, Inman Gallery Viewing Room, Houston, 1994, 95, 99, Christinerose Gallery, N.Y.C., 1997, Good/Bad Art Collective, Denton, Tex., 1997, Sala Diaz, San Antonio, 1998, Angstrom Gallery, Dallas, 1999; group shows include Wheeler Gallery, Providence, R.I., 1984, Helme House Gallery, Kingston, R.I., 1985, Bristol (R.I.) Art Mus., 1986, Hampden Gallery, U. Mass., Amherst, 1988, 89, Art league Houston, 1991, Robinson Gallery, Houston, 1991, Cullen Ctr. Gallery, Houston, 1992, 94, Graham Gallery, Albuquerque, 1992, Allen Ctr. Gallery, Houston, 1992, Hillwood Art Mus., L.I. Univ., 1993, Inman Gallery, Houston, 1993, 94, 96, 98, Whitney Mus. Am. Art, 1993, Conduit Gallery, Dallas, 1994, Lambert Hall, Houston, 1994, Ctr. Gallery, Bucknell U., Lewisburg, Pa., 1995, Lawndale Art Performance Ctr., Houston, 1995, U. Tex., San Antonio, 1995, San Antonio Mus. Art, 1995, Spanish Kitchen Gallery, L.A., 1996, Barry Whistler Gallery, Dallas, 1996, Cristinerose Gallery, N.Y.C., 1997, Arlington (Tex.) Mus. Art, 1997, Angstrom Gallery, Dallas, 1997, Austin (Tex.) Mus. Art, 1998, Smart Mus. Art, U. Chgo., 1998, City Gallery Chastain, Atlanta, 1998, Galveston (Tex.) Arts Ctr., 1998, Kohler Arts Ctr., 1999, Weatherspoon Art Gallery, U. N.C., 1999, Contemporary Art Collective, Las Vegas, 1999. Core fellow Mus. Fine Arts, Houston, 1990-92; Individual Artist grantee Cultural Arts Coun. Houston Harris County, 1996, Louis Comfort Tiffany grantee, 1997. Office: c/o Inman Gallery 1114 Barkdull St Houston TX 77006-6402

DAVENPORT, DEBORAH MORGAN, obstetrician, gynecologist; b. Phila., May 21, 1948; d. Michel Kerop and Gloria Anita (Kremens) Morgan; m. James Whitman Davenport, Jan. 27, 1968; children: Jesse, Christopher, Michael, Andrew. BA, Douglass Coll., 1971; MD, U. Pa., 1975. Diplomate Am. Bd. Obs.-Gyn. Resident SUNY Sch. Medicine, Stony Brook, N.Y., 1980-83, asst. prof. obs-gyn., 1983-86; physician Three Village Women's Hlth., Setauket, N.Y., 1986—. Clin. asst. prof. SUNY Sch. Medicine, 1986—, credentials com. dept. ob-gyn., 1990--; mem. med. bd. Univ. Hosp., 1997—. Bd. dirs. Suffolk Network Adolescent Pregnancy, 1982-85, Planned Parenthood Suffolk County, 1989—, chairperson medicinal affiliate com. Recipient NY Magazine Best Doctor award, NY Metro Area, 2003, Castle Connoly Best Drs. award, N.Y. Metro Area, 1995—2003. Fellow: ACOG; mem.: NOW, N.Am. Menopause Soc. (charter mem., nat. cert. menopause practionioner 2002—), Am. Women's Med. Assn. (br. pres. 1995—, adviser student chpt. SUNY-Stony Brook), Am. Orchid Soc., Alpha Omega Alpha, Phi Beta Kappa. Democrat. Unitarian Universalist. Avocations: gardening orchids, cooking, boating, reading. Office: Three Village Womens Hlth 100 S Jersey Ave Setauket NY 11733-2034

DAVENPORT, DENNIS LYNN, protective services official; b. Charleroi, Pa., July 12, 1947; s. Elmer Webb and Maude Elsie Davenport; m. Patricia Susan Davenport, May 10, 1980; children: Brian, Marc, Joshua. AA, Florissant (Mo.) Valley C.C., 1971; BA in Criminal Justice, U. Mo., St. Louis, 1976, MA in Criminology, 1993; grad., FBI Nat. Acad. Rsch. technician McDonnell Douglas, St. Louis, 1969-71; adminstrn. asst. to chief Clayton (Mo.) Police Dept., 1971—, accreditation mgr., 1997—. Sec. ops. planner Washington U. Presdl. Debate, St. Louis, 1992, 2000, safety com. chmn. St. Louis Art Fair, Clayton, 1993-2002, St. Louis Jazz Festival, Clayton, 2002. Contbr. articles to profl. jours. Booster Francis Howell Soccer, St. Charles, Mo., 1997-2001. Sgt. USAF, 1965-69, Vietnam. Recipient Fiction Writing award Springfield Writer's Conf., 1998. Mem. NRA, United Svcs. Orgn., Law Enforcement Orgn., FBI Nat. Acad. Assocs., Mo. Accreditation Coalition (sec., treas. 1999—), MidAm. Contingency Planning Forum, Civil War Preservation Trust, Friends of Nat. Parks at Gettysburg. Avocations: U.S. Civil War, hunting, police memorabilia. Office: Clayton Police Dept 227 S Central Ave Clayton MO 63105

DAVENPORT, GERALD BRUCE, lawyer; b. Adrian, Mich., May 17, 1949; s. Bruce Nelson and Mildred Louise (Avis) D.; m. RoxAnn Ferguson, Dec. 27, 1975; children: Jonathan Gerald, Christopher Bruce, Timothy Charles. AB, U. Mich., 1971; JD, U. Tex., 1975. Bar: Tex. 1975, Okla. 1993. Pvt. practice Law Office of Gerald B. Davenport, Cedar Park, Tex., 1975-77; atty. Milchem Inc., Houston, 1977-81, Baker Hughes Prodn. Tools Inc., Houston, 1981-87; sr. atty. Baker Hughes Inc., Houston, 1987-88; gen. atty. environ. law Tex. Ea. Corp., Houston, 1988; atty. Browning-Ferris Industries, Houston, 1988-89, mgr. environ. law sect., 1989-92; asst. gen. counsel environ. law Mapco Inc., Tulsa, 1992-94; of counsel McKinney, Stringer & Webster, P.C., Tulsa, 1994-95; dir. Davenport & Williams, P.C., Tulsa, 1995-96; shareholder Hall, Estill, Hardwick, Gable, Golden & Nelson, P.C., Tulsa, 1996-99; of counsel Shipley, Jennings & Champlin, P.C., Oklahoma City, 1999—2002, Elias, Books, & Brown, PC, Oklahoma City, 2002—. Contbr. articles to profl. jours. Mem. ABA, State Bar Tex. (environ. law sect.), Okla. Bar Assn. (environ. law sect.). Republican. Office: Elias Books & Brown Two Leadership Sq 211 N Robinson 1300 Oklahoma City OK 73102-7114 Business E-Mail: GBDavenport@EliasBooksBrown.com.

DAVENPORT, HORACE WILLARD, physiologist, science educator; b. Phila., Oct. 20, 1912; s. Horace Willard and Elizabeth Langendorf Davenport; m. Virginia Dickerson, Feb. 1, 1945 (dec. Mar. 1968); 2 children; m. Ingeborg L. Epstein, Aug. 15, 1969. BS, Calif. Inst. Tech., 1935, PhD, 1939; BA, U. Oxford, Eng.; BA (Rhodes scholar 1935-38), 1937, B.Sc., 1938, D.Sc., 1961. Instr. physiology U. Pa. Med. Sch., Phila., 1941—43; instr. physiology Harvard Med. Sch., 1943—45; prof., head dept. physiology U. Utah Med. Sch., 1945—56; prof. dept. physiology U. Mich., Ann Arbor, 1956—, chmn. dept., 1956—78, William Beaumont prof., 1978—83, prof. emeritus, 1983—. Vis. prof. Mayo Found., 1962—63. Contbr. articles on med. history. Recipient Friedenwald medal, Am. Gastroent. Assn., 1980. Mem.: NAS, Am. Physiol. Soc. (pres. 1961—62), Brit. Soc. Gastroenterology (hon.). Home: 3850 Galleria Woods Dr Birmingham AL 35244-1098

DAVENPORT, JAMES ROBERT, retired city official, retired utility executive; b. Roanoke, Va., Jan. 8, 1930; s. Henry Ashby and Mary Bruce (Doss) D.; m. Catherine Lee Wright, July 14, 1956; children: James Robert Jr., Catherine D. BA in Econs., Roanoke Coll., Salem, Va., 1952; MBA, U. N.C., 1955. Adminstrv. asst. Appalachian Power Co. (now Am. Elec. Power), Roanoke, 1955-63, area devel. cons., 1963-69, area mgr. Martinsville, Va., 1969-77, divsn. mgr. Lynchburg, Va., 1977-91; ret. Mem. City Coun., Lynchburg, 1993-98, vice mayor, 1995-98, chmn. fin. and planning com., 1995-98; bd. dirs. Region 2000, Lynchburg, 1994-98; dir. CentraHealth, Inc., Lynchburg, 1987—2003, chmn. bd. trustees 1990-93; dir. Va. Bapt. Hosp., Lynchburg, 1982-87, treas., 1985-86; mem. Indsl. Devel. Authority, City of Lynchburg, 1982-93, 98—, chmn., 1985-93; dir. Lynchburg Area Devel. Corp., 1977—, Ctrl. Va. Industries, Lynchburg, 1979-83, chmn. bd., 1980; dir. Presbyn. Home, Inc., Lynchburg, 1980-83, vice chmn. bd., 1983; mem. Lynchburg Rep. City Com., 1993—; bd. dirs. United Way of Ctrl. Va., Lynchburg, 1980-83, Daily Bread, Lynchburg, 1988-92, Ctrl. Lynchburg, Inc., 1980-82, Jr. Achievement, Lynchburg, 1980-83; mem. econ. and tech. devel. adv. com. Ctrl. Va. C.C., Lynchburg, 1988; chmn. Downtown Action Commn., Lynchburg, 1979-82; pres. Southeastern Cmty. Devel. Assn., Roanoke, 1976; chmn. United Way of Martinsville and Henry County, Va., 1976; mem. Va. Gov.'s Commn. on Transp. Policy, 1999-2000; elder Rivermont Presbyn. Ch. 1st Lt. U.S. Army, 1952-55. Recipient Outstanding Citizen award NCCJ, 1990. Mem. Greater Lynchburg C. of C. (pres. 1980-81, econ. devel. dept. head 1979-80, exec. adv. coun. 1982-86, Team 2000 1985-88, named Pro-Opera Civica 1988), Rotary Club of Lynchburg (v.p. 1983-84), Boonsboro Country Club. Avocations: tennis, church activities, travel. Home: 2131 Burnt Bridge Rd Lynchburg VA 24503-2215 E-mail: davenbob@adelphia.net.

DAVENPORT, JANET LEE, real estate agent, small business owner; b. Napa, Calif., Dec. 10, 1938; d. George Perry and Stella Dolores (Ramalho) Gomez; m. Bingo George Wesner, Aug. 4, 1957 (July 1978); children: Bing George, Diane Estelle; m. Marvin Eugene Davenport, Jan. 13, 1979. Student, U. Calif., Davis, 1956-57, Nat. Jud. Coll., 1975-79. Co-owner, operator Bar JB Ranch, Benicia, Calif., 1960-71, Lovelock, Nev., 1971-78; owner, mgr. Wesner Bookkeeping Svc., Lovelock, 1973-78; chief tribal judge Ct. Indian Offenses, Lovelock, 1975-79; justice of peace, coroner County of Pershing, Lovelock, 1975-79; paralegal, legal sec. Samuel S. Wardle, Carson City, Nev., 1979; dep. ct. adminstr. Reno Mcpl. Ct., Reno, 1979-81; co-owner horse farm Reno, 1979—; freelance real estate investor, 1979—; real estate saleswoman Merrill Lynch Realtors, Sparks, Nev., 1981-82; realtor, farm and ranch div. mgr. Copple and Assocs., Realtors, Sparks, 1982-91; real estate saleswoman Vail and Assocs. Realty, Reno, Nev., 1991—. Co-owner, operator Lovelock (Nev.) Merc. Co., 1988—; sec. Nev. Judges Assn., 1977-78. Dir. Pershing County Drug and Alcohol Abuse Council, Lovelock, 1976-78. Mem. Reno/Sparks Bd. Realtors, Nat. Assn. Realtors, Nev. Assn. Realtors, Am. Quarter Horse Assn. Republican. Roman Catholic. Office: Vail and Assocs Realty 2470 Wrondel Way # 105 Reno NV 89502-3701

DAVENPORT, LAWRENCE FRANKLIN, school system administrator; b. Lansing, Mich., Oct. 13, 1944; s. Theodore and Bernice (Alexander) D.; m. Cecelia Jackson, Sept. 24, 1966; children— Laurence, Anita, Anthony BA, Mich. State U., 1966, MA, 1968; Ed.D., Fairleigh Dickinson U., 1975; MS, Leicester Univ., Eng. V.p. devel. Tuskegee Inst., Ala., 1972-74; pres. ednl. complex San Diego C.C., 1974-79, provost, 1979-81; assoc. dir. ACTION, Washington, 1981-82; asst. sec. U.S. Dept. Edn., Washington, 1982-87; asst. sec. mgmt. and adminstrn. U.S. Dept. Energy, Washington, 1987-89; assoc. vice chancellor U. Calif., San Francisco, 1989-92; pres. Lawrence Davenport & Assocs., Mercer Island, Wash., 1989—; CFO, Seattle Pub. Schs., 1992-94; v.p. fin. and ops., CFO Milton Hershey (Pa.) Sch., 1994-2000; sr. v.p. Antin Neher Assocs., Hershey, 2000—01; dep. chief adminstrv. officer U.S. Ho. of Reps., 2001—; exec. dir. Hale House Ctr. Inc., N.Y.C., 2002—. Co-author (with Petty): Career Education and Minorities, 1973 Presbyterian. E-mail: lfdavenport@att.net.

DAVENPORT, LINDSAY, professional tennis player; b. Palos Verdes, Calif., June 8, 1976; Profl. tennis player, 1993—. Ranked 3d Doubles (with Chanda Rubin), 1993; recipient 3 career pro singles titles (1) Lucerne, 1993, (2) Brisbane, Lucerne, 1994, 95; winner singles & doubles (with Jana Novotna) Bausch & Lomb Champioships, 1997; named to Olympic Team 1996; gold medalist singles, 1996; ranked #1 1998, 99; winner Bank of the West, 1998, Toshiba Classic, 1998, Acura Invitational, 1998, U.S. Open, 1998, European Championships, 1998, Toray Pan Pacific (doubles) 1999, Sydney Internat., 1999; Wimbledon, 1999, Chase Championships, 1999, Madrid Internat., 1999, Stanford, 1999, Tokyo (Princess Cup), 1999, Phila., 1999; finalist New Haven, 1999; semifinalist Australian Open, 1999, U.S. Open, 1999, Grand Slam Cup, L.A., 1999; winner Australian Open, 2000. Office: US Tennis Assn 70 W Red Oak Ln White Plains NY 10604-3602

DAVENPORT, MARK, music educator, musician; b. N.Y.C., Feb. 9, 1956; s. LaNoue Davenport and Patricia Wood; children: Miles Joshua, Zachary Daniel. Student, Sarah Lawrence Coll., 1975—78; BA in Music History and Lit., SUNY, New Paltz, 1992; MusM in Musicology, U. Colo., 1994, PhD in Musicology, 2001. Instr. SUNY, New Paltz, 1991—92; grad. instr. U. Colo., Boulder, 1992—98, instr. music, 1998—2000; vis. asst. prof. music Met. State Coll. of Denver, 2000—03; asst. prof. music Regis U., Denver, 2002—. Pres. Landmark Press, Boulder, 1997—. Contbr. articles to profl. jours.; book rev. editor Am. Recorder, Littleton, Colo., 1993—97. Bd. dirs. Early Music Colo., Boulder, 1994—97. Mem.: Am. Recorder Soc., Soc. 17th Century Music, Am. Musicol. Soc. Office: Regis U Dept Fine Arts Mail Code C-4 3333 Regis Blvd Denver CO 80221 Business E-Mail: mdavenpo@regis.edu.

DAVENPORT, PAMELA BEAVER, rancher; b. Big Spring, Tex., Nov. 18, 1948; d. Frank Jones and Doris Glynn (Wills) Beaver; m. Robert Sampson Davenport, Feb. 2, 1982; 1 child, Danielle. BS in Mktg. and Textiles, Tex. Tech U., 1969, MS, 1970; cert. in spinal orthotics, Northwestern U., 1976. Adminstrv. asst. Tex-Togs, Inc., El Paso, Tex., 1971-75; dir. edn. Camp Internat., Jackson, Mich., 1975-79; realtor Tom Carpenter, Realtor, San Angelo, Tex., 1979-83; retailer Davenport Barber & Beauty, San Angelo, 1985-95; owner, mgr. The Little Gym, San Antonio, 1995-97; rancher Gail, Tex., 1968—. Contbr. articles to profl. jours. Vice-chmn. adv. bd. San Angelo Recreation Dept., 1987-88; chmn. adv. bd. Recreation Dept., River Stage, 1990; chmn. Tom Green County Adult Literacy Coun., 1989-90; publicity chmn. San Angelo Cultural Affairs Coun., 1986; treas. San Angelo Commun. Hosp. Aux., 1980-82; publicity chmn. Christmas at Old Fort Concho, 1986; mem. Leadership San Angelo; 1st v.p. Band and Spurs Assn., Alamo Heights H.S., San Antonio, 2000-01; v.p. audience devel. San Antonio Symphony League, 2001-03, v.p. svc., 2003—. Mem. AAUW (cultural chmn. Tex. bd. 1988-89, pres. 1986-88, chmn. conv. 1984-86). Methodist. Avocations: reading, painting, traveling, quilting. Home and Office: 107 Longsford San Antonio TX 78209-1822 E-mail: leaetta14@aol.com.

DAVENPORT, PAUL, academic administrator, economics educator; BA in Econs. with gt. distinction/honors, Stanford U., 1969; MA, U. Toronto, 1970, PhD, 1976, LLD (hon.), 2000, U. Alta., 1994; PhD (hon.), Internat. U. Moscow, 2002. Prof. econs. McGill U., Montreal, Que., Can., 1972-89, assoc. dean grad. studies, 1982-86, vice prin. planning and computer svcs., 1986-89; pres., vice chancellor U. Alta., Edmonton, Alta., Can., 1989-94, U. Western Ont., London, Can., 1994—. Chair Assn. Univs. and Colls. Can., 1997-99, Coun. Ont. Univs., 1999-2001. Editor: (with Richard H. Leach) Reshaping Confederation: The 1982 Reform of the Canadian Constitution, 1984. Mem. policy program adv. com. on econ. growth Can. Inst. for Advanced Rsch.; mem. bd. govs. London Health Scis. Ctr., Loncon Econ. Devel. Corp.; bd. dirs. Nat. Ballet Sch. Decorated chevalier Legion of Honor (France); officer Order of Can. Mem.: Am. Econ. Assn., Can. Assn. Economists, Phi Beta Kappa. Office: U Western Ont-Off of President Stevenson-Lawson Bldg London ON Canada N6A 5B8 E-mail: pdavenpo@uwo.ca.

DAVENPORT, PAUL, golfer; b. New Zealand, Mar. 16, 1966; Student, S.W. La. U. Named winner, Am. Express/Shell Cup, 1998, TELUS Edmonton Open, 2000, Shell Payless Open, 2001, TELUS Open, 2001. Mem.: Gorge Vale Club. Avocations: magic, music. Office: c/o Canadian Tour 212 King St W Ste 203 Toronto ON Canada M5H 1K5

DAVENPORT, ROGER LEE, research engineer; b. Sacramento, Oct. 27, 1955; s. Lee Edwin and Ada Fern (Henderson) D.; m. Cynthia Ann Carle, June 20, 1998. AB Physics, U. Calif., Berkeley, 1977; MSME, U. Ariz., 1979. Assoc. engr. Solar Energy Rsch. Inst., Golden, Colo., 1979-82; cons. Darmstadt, Fed. Republic Germany, 1982-84; missionary Eastern European Sem., Vienna, Austria, 1984-87; staff researcher Sci. Applications Internat. Corp., San Diego, 1987—. Mem. Am. Solar Energy Soc., Sierra Club, Phi Beta Kappa. Home: 706 Poinsettia Park N Encinitas CA 92024 Office: SAIC 9455 Towne Centre Dr M/S W-2 San Diego CA 92121 E-mail: solarguy@cal.berkeley.edu.

DAVENPORT, RONALD ROSS, JR., lawyer; b. New Haven, May 23, 1963; BA, Yale U., 1985; JD, Harvard U., 1988. Bar: Pa., D.C. Atty. Bd. Gov. Fed. Res., Washington, 1988-93; gen. counsel Sheridan Broadcasting Corp., Pitts., 1993—, also bd. dirs. Bd. dirs. Urban league of Pitts., Inc., The Pitts. Cultural Trust, Ecologic Development Fund, St. Edmund's Acad. Office: 960 Penn Ave Ste 200 Pittsburgh PA 15222-3811

DAVENPORT, THOMAS HERBERT, small business owner; b. Sandusky, Ohio, Mar. 15, 1933; s. Orme and Elva Mae (Bragg) D.; m. Annetta Henman, June 22, 1963; children: Deborah Ann, Mark Thomas, Brenda Kay. Grad., Coyne Electronic Sch., 1954-55. Lic. FCC gen. radio telephone. Clk. Nickel Plate R.R., Bellevue, Ohio, 1951, 1954; electronic technician various firms, Sandusky, 1955-56; prin. Bellevue Radio and TV, 1955—. Numerous inventions in field. Cpl. U.S. Army, 1952-53, 2d. lt USAF Aux., 1980-84. Mem. Am. Legion. Republican. Avocations: inventing, cartooning, gardening, poetry, reflexology. Home: 111 Seneca Dr Bellevue OH 44811-1635 Office: Bellevue Radio & TV 109 W Center St Bellevue OH 44811-1351

DAVERNE, STEVEN RICHARD, advertising director, artist, illustrator, behavior analyst; b. Patuxant, Md., July 10, 1955; s. Ronald Richard and Joan Beverly DaVerne. BA, U. South Fla., Sarasota, 1980; AS, Tampa Tech. Inst., 1990. Cert. Supervision and Employee Management Fla. Mental Health Inst., 1985, U. So. Fla., 1985. Therapist, behavior analyst Tampa Heights Hosp., 1980—84; behavior analyst, rschr. Fla. Mental Health Inst., Tampa, 1984—88; graphic gesigner, art dir. and illustrator numerous advt. and mktg. cos., 1988—98; creative dir. US West Comms., Denver, 1998—2000; owner, operator DaVerne Creative Group, Denver, 2000—. Cons. Young Authors Conf., Tampa, Fla., 1991, Communique Group Advt., Denver, 2000—01; judge, creative cons. Henry Wurst Press Inc., Denver, 2000—01. Exhibitions include American 76th Nat. Exhbn., Nat. Arts Club, Patrons Internat. Exhbn., others, Represented in permanent collections Carter Presdl. Ctr., Atlanta. Nat. children's cancer soc. nat., 1988—2002; presenter behavioral tng. seminars Fla. Mental Health Inst., Tampa, Fla., 1984—88. Recipient Am. Graphic Design award, Bus. Mktg. Awards, 1999, Internat. Summit Creative award, Summit Awards, 1999, 2000. Mem.: Assn. Behavior Analysis, Art Dirs. Club. Achievements include supr. in the establishment of the first pilot research program for mainstreaming severely emotionally disturbed (SED) children in the education system; created acclaimed series of paintinfs called the Learning Series which intrepreted and documented the social rsch. experience of (SED) children. Avocations: composing and performing music, snow skiing, water skiing, sailing.

DAVES, DON MICHAEL, minister; b. Wichita Falls, Tex., Mar. 4, 1938; s. Floyd Lee and Johnnie Majorie (Dunn) D.; m. Patricia N. McLean, Aug. 29, 1958; children: Paul Lee, Donna Michelle. BA, Midwestern U., 1959; ThM, So. Meth. U., 1963; D. Humanities (hon.), Southwestern Coll., 1971. Ordained to ministry Meth. Ch., 1963. Pastor 1st Meth. Ch., Holliday, Tex., 1963-66, Prarie Heights Meth. Ch., Grand Prairie, Tex., 1966-72; minister to soc. North Tex. Conf. United Meth. Ch., 1972-77; pastor Meml. United Meth. Ch., Dallas, 1977-78; assoc. pastor Preston Hollow United Meth. Ch., Dallas, 1978-81, 1st United Meth. Ch., Duncanville, Tex., 1981-85, pastor Cedar Hill, Tex., 1985-91; assoc. pastor Walnut Hill United Meth. Ch., Dallas, 1992-95; pastor First United Meth. Ch., VanAlstyne, Tex., 1995-99; ret., 1999. Ret. mem. North Tex. Conf.; mem. United Meth. Ch.; trustee Charlton Meth. Hosp., Dallas, 1986-95; mentor pastor Perkins Sch. Theology Intern Program, 1996-97; registrar Sherman-McKinney Bd. Ministry, 1996-99. Author: Devotional Talks for Children, 1961, Famous Hymns & Their Writers, 1962, Sermon Outlines on Romans, 1962, Meditations on Early Christian Symbols, 1963, Come with Faith, 1964, Young Readers Book of Christian Symbolism, 1967, Advent: A Calendar of Devotions, 1971, Joy is Now, 1988. Named for Best Children's Book by a Tex. Author, Tex. Inst. Letters, 1968. Mem. Am. Assn. Pastoral Counselors, Dallas (Tex.) Hall Soc., Order of St. Luke, Disciplined Order Christ. Home: Ste 231 5200 Keller Springs Rd Dallas TX 75248-2739

DAVES, DONALD RAE, entertainment industry executive; b. L.A., Dec. 6, 1930; s. Lester Brent and Edwina (Tothill) D.; m. Eleana Farrell, Jan. 26, 1957; children: Victoria Daves Bennett, Antoinette Daves Johnson. BA, U. So. Calif., 1955. Asst. dir. Dirs. Guild Am., L.A., 1957-65; asst. gen. mgr. Samuel Goldwyn Studios, L.A., 1973-80; v.p. Warner Bros. Hollywood Studios, West Hollywood, Calif., 1980-96; pres. Hill-Daves Prodns., 1996—. Dir., prodn. mgr. (TV) Bonanza, 1965-70; assoc. producer (film) Key West, 1972. V.p. West Hollywood Community Alliance, 1988-90; bd. dirs. Warner Bros. Hollywood Studio Fed. Credit Union, 1995—. Sgt. USAF, 1951-52. Mem. Phi Delta Theta. Republican. Episcopalian. Avocations: collecting paper weights, sports, antique smoking pipes.

DAVES, GLENN DOYLE, JR., science educator, chemist, researcher; b. Clayton, N.Mex., Feb. 12, 1936; s. Glenn Doyle and Billye (Parker) D.; m. Pamela Gannarelli, Sept. 5, 1959; children: Laura Lee Daves Schantz, Anne Kathryn, Glenn Graham. BS, Ariz. State U., 1959; PhD, MIT, 1964; PharmD (hon.), U. Uppsala, Sweden, 1987. Rsch. chemist Midwest Rsch. Inst., Kansas City, Mo., 1959-61, Stanford Rsch. Inst., Palo Alto, Calif., 1964-67; asst. prof. chemistry Oreg. Grad. Ctr., Beaverton, 1967-72, assoc. prof., 1972-74, prof., 1974-81, chmn. dept., 1972-79; prof., chmn. dept. chemistry Lehigh U., Bethlehem, Pa., 1981-88; dean provost Rensselaer Poly. Inst., Troy, 1989—2000, dean Project Kaleidoscope, Summer Insts., 2000—, dean provost, 2002—03. Vis. scientist NIH, Bethesda, Md., 1988. Co-editor: Advances in Polyamine Research, Vols. 1-2, 1978, Biologically Active Principals of Natural Products, 1984; contbr. numerous articles to profl. jours. Recipient numerous grants NIH, Am. Cancer Soc., U.S. Forest Svc., 1971—. Mem. Am. Chem. Soc., Internat. Soc. Heterocyclic Chemistry, Coun. for Chem. Rsch. (governing bd. 1985-86, chair manpower and resource com. 1984-87, mem. membership com. 1991). Democrat. E-mail: davesgs@yahoo.com.

DAVES, SANDRA LYNN, poet, lyricist; b. Sacramento, Mar. 14, 1950; d. Willard Glen and Rachel Lucille Humbert; m. Tommy Wilburn DAves, Nov. 16, 1971; children: Todd Eric, Brice Aaron. Grad., Roseville (Calif.) H.S., 1968; student, Internat. Libr. Poetry, 2003. Sec. McClellan AFB, Sacramento, 1969, Fish and Game Dept., Sacramento, 1970—71; poet, 1994—. Lyricist: songs Songs of Praise, Star of Bethlehem, America At War!, Gospel Millennium Celebration, Home For Christmas; author: (poem) An Hour At Sunrise, The Shining Light; contbr. poem. Mem.: Internat. Soc. Poetry (Editor's Choice award Md. chpt. 2000, 2001, 2002, Poet of Merit Hollywood chpt. 2002, Poet of Merit Fla. chpt. 2003, Poet of Yr. Fla. chpt. 2003, Poem Noble House Pub. 2003). Avocations: reading, writing, walking, crossword puzzles. Home: 6825 Susanna Ct Citrus Heights CA 95621

DAVEY, CLARK WILLIAM, newspaper publisher; b. Chatham, Ont., Can., Mar. 3, 1928; s. William and Marguerite (Clark) D.; m. Joyce Gordon, Sept. 13, 1952; children: Richard Gordon, Kevin William, Clark Michael. BA in Journalism, U. Western Ont., 1948, LLD (hon.), 1986. With Chatham Daily News, 1948-51; mng. editor No. Daily News, Kirkland Lake, Can., 1951; hydro. seaway corr. Globe and Mail., 1951-55; mem. Parliamentary Press Gallery, Ottawa, 1956-60; fgn. editor Globe and Mail, 1960-63, mng. editor, 1963-78; pub. Vancouver (B.C., Can.) Sun, 1978-83, Montreal Gazette, 1983-89; pres., chmn. The Canadian Press, 1981-83; pub. Ottawa Citizen, 1989-92; v.p. Southam Inc., 1983-92; dir. Am. Press Inst., 1988-94; commr. Ottawa Hydro, 1999-2000. Pres. Michener Awards Found., 1993-98. Named to Can. News Hall of Fame, 1992. Office: 29 Madawaska Dr Ottawa ON Canada K1S 3G5 E-mail: waldosplace@home.com.

DAVEY, DIANE DAVIS, pathologist, educator; b. Sioux Falls, S.D., June 23, 1956; d. Donald L. Cara Lee Davis; m. William Patrick Davey, May 30, 1981; children: James, Steven. BS with honors, CornellU., 1978; MD, Wash. U., 1981. Diplomate Am. Bd. Pathology, Hematology, Cytopathology, Anatomic and Clin. Pathology. Resident in pathology Ind. U., Indpls., 1981—84; resident U. Iowa, Iowa City, 1984—85, fellow, 1985—86, assoc. pathology, 1986—88; asst. prof. pathology U. Ky., Lexington, 1988—94, assoc. prof. pathology, 1994—2000, prof. pathology, 2000—, dir. Cytopathology Lab., 1988—. Mem. panel, cons. FDA, Rockville, Md., 1995—; moderator Bethesda 2001 Workship Nat. Cancer Inst., 2000—; mem. data safety and monitoring bd. Nat. Cancer Inst., 2000—; mem. test com. Am. Bd. Pathology, Tampa. Author: (with others) Clinical Cytopathology and Aspiration Biology, 2001; mem. editl. bd. Diagnostic Cytopathology, 1996—, Cancer Cytopathology, 1996—; contbr. articles to profl. jours. Mem.: Papanicoloau Soc. Cytopathology (com. chair 1993), Coll. Am. Pathologists (com. chair 1998—2001, William Kuehn Outstanding Communicator award 2001), Am. Soc. Cytopathology (exec. bd. dirs. 1995—, v.p. 1999—2000, pres.-elect 2000—01, pres. 2001—02). Office: U Ky Med Ctr MS 117 Pathology 800 Rose St Lexington KY 40536 E-mail: ddavey@uky.edu.

DAVEY, KENNETH GEORGE, biologist, university official; b. Chatham, Ont., Can., Apr. 20, 1932; s. William and Marguerite (Clark) D.; m. Jeannette Isabel Evans, Nov. 28, 1959 (separated); children: Christopher Graham, Megan Jeannette, Katherine Alison. BSc, U. Western Ont., 1954, MSc, 1955, DSc (hon.), 2002; PhD, Cambridge (Eng.) U., 1958. NRC Can. fellow U. Toronto, Ont., 1958-59; Drosier fellow Gonville and Caius Coll., Cambridge U., 1959-63; asso. prof. parasitology McGill U., Montreal, Que., Can., 1963-67, prof. parasitology and biology, 1967-74, dir. Inst. Parasitology, 1964-74; prof., chmn. dept. biology York U., Downsview, Ont., 1974-81, dean of sci., 1982-85, disting. research prof., 1984-2000, disting. rsch. prof. emeritus, 2001—, v.p. acad. affairs, 1986-91. Past pres. Huntsman Marine Lab.; pres. Biol. Coun. Can., 1979-81; mem. animal biology grant selection com. Natural Scis. and Engring. Rsch. Coun. Can., 1980-83, group chmn. life scis., 1983-86, mem. com. grants and scholarships, 1983-86; mem. panel on tropical health NIH, 1978-82; pres. World Exec. Coun., Inst. de la Vie; coun. Royal Can. Inst., 1996—, v.p., 1998-2000, pres. 2000-02; mem. Nat. Coun. on Ethics in Human Rsch., 1998—, pres., 2002—. Author: Reproduction in the Insects, 1965; editor Internat. Jour. Invertebrate Reprodn., 1978-86; mem. editl. bd. Internat. Jour. Parasitology, 1973-80, Exptl. Parasilology, 1970-76, Can. Jour. Zoology, 1966-76, editor, 1994—; assoc. editor Ency. Reprodn.; contbr. articles to profl. jours. Decorated officer Order of Can., 1997; recipient Queen's Jubilee medal Govt. Can., 1977, 2002, Hitschfeld award, Can. Assn. Rsch. Adminstrs., 1997. Fellow Royal Soc. Can. (sec. Acad. Sci. 1979-85), Entomol. Soc. Can. (Gold medal 1985); mem. Soc. Exptl. Biology, Internat. Union Biol. Scis. (Can. nat. com. 1977-82), Can. Soc. Zoologists (pres. 1981-82, Fry medal 1987), Can. Com. Univ. Biology Chmn. (chmn. 1975-77, Disting. Biologist medal 1992), Biol. Coun. Can. (Gold medal 1987). Office: York Univ Dept Biology North York ON Canada M3J 1P3 E-mail: davey@yorku.ca.

DAVEY, LYCURGUS MICHAEL, neurosurgeon; b. N.Y.C., Feb. 20, 1918; s. Michael Marco and Elizabeth (Delaveris) D.; m. Artemis Diana Pappas, June 7, 1942; children: Michael Dean, Elaine Anne, Elizabeth. BA, Yale U., 1939, MD, 1943. Diplomate Am. Bd. Neurol. Surgery, 1954. Surg. intern New Haven Hosp., 1943-44, asst. resident in surgery, 1946-50, William Harvey Cushing fellow, 1947-48, resident neurosurgeon, 1951-52; asst. resident in neurosurgery Hartford Hosp., 1950-51; clin. clk. Nat. Hosp., London, summer 1954; clin. instr. neurosurgery Yale U., 1952-60, asst. clin. prof., 1960-68, asso. clin. prof., 1968-77, clin. prof., 1977—. Assoc. fellow Trumbull Coll. Yale U., 1959—; cons. practice in neurosurgery New Haven, 1952-2002; emeritus staff Mid State Med. Ctr. (formerly Vets Meml. Med. Ctr.); emeritus Hosp. St. Raphael; attending staff mem., staff Yale-New Haven Med. Ctr., 1952-01, pres. med. staff, 1971-72, assoc. sect. chief emeritus, 1991-2001, hon. staff mem., 2002-; bd. dirs. Tex. Citrus Found. Editl. bd. historian Neurosurgery. Class sec. Yale U. Class of 1939, 1999—. Served to comdr. USNR, 1942-46, 52-54; capt. Res. ret. 1973. Fellow ACS, Internat. Coll. Surgeons; mem. AMA, Naval War Coll. Found., Inc. (life), U.S. Naval Inst. (life), Naval Res. Assn. (life), Navy League of U.S. (life), Conn. Med. Soc. (chmn. sect. on neurosurgery 1971-72), Conn. Soc. Neurol. Surgeons (hon. spkr. 2000), New Haven County Med. Soc. (pres. 1987), New Haven Med. Assn. (pres. 1972), Am. Assn. Neurol. Surgeons, New Eng. Neurosurg. Soc., Congress Neurol. Surgeons (mem. editl. bd., historian Neurosurgery Jour. 2001—, Disting. Svc. award 1966), Assn. Rsch. in Nervous and Mental Diseases, Soc. Med. Cons. to Armed Forces, Assn. Yale Alumni in Medicine (pres. 1995-97, Disting. Alumni Svc. award 1997, Peter Parker, M.D. Dean's medal 2003). Home: 1010 Hartford Tpke North Haven CT 06473-3038 Office: 2 Church St S Ste 304 New Haven CT 06519-1717 E-mail: lycurgus.davey@yale.edu. *My life has been enriched by treating tasks as a challenge to my resourcefulness, knowledge, originality, inventiveness and faith. The task becomes a game rather than a chore.*

DAVEY, MARK ELLIS, secondary school educator, band director; b. McMinville, Oreg., Sept. 23, 1961; s. Richard Keith and Patricia Louise Davey; m. Paula Louise Knapp-Davey, June 20, 1998; 1 child, Allyson Ping. MusB, U. of North Tex., Denton, 1984; MA in Tchg., U. Portland, Oreg., 1992. Cert. tchr. Wash. Tchr., band dir. Evergreen Sch. Dist., Vancouver, Wash., 1990—. Profl. saxophonist:. Mem.: NEA, Wash. Music Educators Assn., Music Educators Nat. Conf. Avocations: skiing, bicycling, swimming, running.

DAVID, CHRISTOPHER MARK, lawyer; b. Buffalo, Nov. 19, 1965; s. Thomas Leonard and Anne (Nickodemus) D.; m. Elizabeth Martina Wilson, Aug. 31, 1991; 1 child, Taylor Dawn. AA, Miami Dade C.C., 1989; BA, U. Fla., 1990; JD, U. Miami, 1993. Bar: Fla. 1993, U.S. Dist. Ct. (so. dist.) Fla. 1995. Ptnr. Hall, David and Joseph, P.A., Miami, Fla., 1993—, Hall, David and Joseph, PA, Miami, Fla., 1999—. Sgt. U.S. Army, 1983-87. Mem. ATLA, ABA, Acad. Fla. Trial Lawyers, Dade County Bar Assn. Office: Hall David and Joseph P A 1428 Brickell Ave Fl 8 Miami FL 33131-3438 E-mail: cdavid@hdjlaw.com.

DAVID, CLIVE, event planning executive; b. Manchester, Eng., June 6, 1934; came to U.S., 1957, naturalized, 1962; s. Marcus Wiener and Claire Rose (Levy) Wiener Kattenburg. Student, Blackpool Tech. Coll., 1951-52, Royal Coll. Art, 1955-57. Designer Chippendale's, London, 1955-57; asst. to pres. pub. relations Maybruck Assocs., N.Y.C., 1959; Ea. regional dir. City of Hope, Phila., 1960-62; pres. Clive David Assocs., N.Y.C., Clive David Enterprises div. Party Enterprises Ltd., Beverly Hills, Calif., Party Enterprises, Ltd., Beverly Hills, 1962—. Lectr. Party Planning par excellence, 1966—. Arranger major parties including Miss Universe Coronation Ball, Miami Beach, 1965, State visit of Queen Elizabeth and Prince Philip, Duke of Edinburgh, Bahamas, 1966, An Evening at the Ritz-Carlton, Boston, 1967, 69, Un Ballo in Maschera, Venice, 1967, An Evening over Boston, 1968, M.G.M. Cavalcade of Style, L.A., 1970, Symposium on Fund Raising through Parties, L.A., 1970, Great Midwest Limestone Cave Party, Kansas City, 1972, Une Soiree de Gala, Phila., 1972, 11th Anniv. of the Mike Douglas Show, Phila., 1972, The Mayor's Salue to Volunteers, Los Angeles, 1972, Twenty Fifth Anniv. Salute to Israel, Jerusalem, 1973, The Bicentenary, 1976, The World Affairs Council Silver Ball, Boston, 1977, The Ohio Theatre Jubilee, Columbus, 1978, Mayor's Salute to Vols., 1978, Dedication and Gala Performance, Northwestern U. Performing Arts Ctr., 1980, Memorabilia Gala, Los Angeles Bicentennial, 1981, The Albemarle Weekend, Charlottesville, 1985, The La Costa Weekend, Carlsbad, 1987, The Embassy Ball, N.Y.C., 1987, The Lagoon Cycle Premiere, Los Angeles, 1987, State Visit Gala for Her Majesty Queen Elizabeth, Miami, 1991, The Grand Brazilian Clambake, Southampton, 1995, The Democratic Senatorial Campaign Committee Gala, Charlottesville, 1996, DSCC reception for Hillary Rodham Clinton, 1996, Rep. Nat. Conv. Team 100 Reception, San Diego, 1996; mem. Pres.' Summit for Am.'s Future Leadership Roundtable, Phila., 1997, Rep. Govs. Conf. Opening Banquet, 1999; contbr. articles to profl. jours. Served with Royal Arty. Brit. Army, 1953-55. Recipient Freedom Found. award Valley Forge, Pa., 1961, City of Hope award Phila., 1962, Mayor's medal for vol. services Los Angeles, 1972, Shalom award State of Israel, 1974, Mayor's medal City of Columbus; named hon. citizen City of Columbus. Mem. AFTRA Jewish. Office: 282 S Reeves Dr Beverly Hills CA 90212-4005 *I consider myself so fortunate to participate in events that bring joy, employment and funds to diversified causes, and maybe leave a miniscule contribution to history.*

DAVID, DONALD J. chemist, researcher; b. St. Louis, Mo, June 25, 1930; s. Alfred A. David and Marie; m. Honore Joan Salmi, June 5, 1952; children: Michelle, David. BS in Chemistry, St. Mary's U., 1952; MS in Mgmt. Sci., U. Dayton, 1977, MS in Materials Sci., 1979, PhD in Materials Engring., 1981. Chief chemist Mobay Chem. Co., Pitts., 1959—67; program mgr. Tracor, Austin, Tex., 1967—72; contract mgr. Monsanto Rsch. Corp., Dayton, Ohio, 1972—79; R&D mgr. Monsanto Plastics & Resins, Springfield, Mass., 1979—88; mgr. exploratory rsch. Monsanto Co., Springfield, 1988—93, corp. sr. sci. fellow, 1988—93; adj. prof. U. Minn., Mpls., 1988—. Rsch. prof. U. Mass., Amherst, Mass., 1995—2002; pres. S.F. Technologies, Amherst, 1996—. Author: Analytical Chemistry of Polyurethanes, 1964, Gas Chromatographic Detectors, Relating Matierials Properties To Structure: Handbook and Software for Polymer Calculations and Material Properties. 1st lt. U.S. Army, 1952—54, Korea. Recipient Outstanding Profl. award, Engring. & Sci. Found. Dayton, 1977. Roman Catholic. Achievements include patents for twenty two. Avocations: photography, travel, computer science. Home and Office: 11 Indian Pipe Lane Amherst MA 01002-3457 Fax: 413-253-0847. E-mail: djdavid@polysci.umass.edu.

DAVID, EDWARD EMIL, JR., electrical engineer, business executive; b. Wilmington, N.C., Jan. 25, 1925; s. Edward Emil and Beatrice (Liebman) D.; m. Ann Hirshberg, Dec. 23, 1950; 1 dau., Nancy. BS, Ga. Inst. Tech., 1945; MS, MIT, 1947, Sc.D., 1950; D.Engring. (hon.), Stevens Inst. Tech., 1971, Poly. Inst. Bklyn., 1971, U. Mich., 1971, Carnegie-Mellon, 1972, Lehigh U., 1973, U. Ill.-Chgo., 1973, Rose-Hulman Inst. Tech., 1978, U. Fla., 1982, Rensselaer Poly. Inst., 1982, Rutgers U., 1984, N.J. Inst. Tech., 1985, U. Pa., 1985. Exec. dir. research Bell Telephone Labs., Murray Hill, N.J., 1950-70; sci. adviser to Pres. Nixon; dir. Office Sci. and Tech., Washington, 1970-73; exec. v.p. Gould, Inc., 1973-77; ind. cons., 1977, 86—; v.p. Exxon Corp., N.Y.C., 1978-80; pres. Exxon Research and Engring. Co., Florham Park, N.J., 1977-86, EED, Inc., Bedminster, N.J., 1986—; v.p., prin. Washington Adv. Group, Washington, 1997—. Bd. dirs. Spacehab, Inc., Washington, Medjet Inc., Edison, NJ, DeCorp, Nashville; bd. govs AGTA, Dallas; cons. NSC, 1974—77; mem. def. sci. bd. U.S. Dept. Def., 1974—75; mem. tech. adv. bd. Chrysler Corp., 1985—93; chmn. Nat. Task Force on Tech. and Soc.; U.S. rep. to NATO Sci. Com., 1979—95; mem. adv. bd. AMP, Inc., Harrisburg, Pa., Bellcore, Livingston, NJ, Electric Power Rsch. Inst., Palo Alto, Calif., Inst. Def. Analyses, Alexandria, Va., 1993—95, Poly Ventures, Farmingdale, NY, Rowan Coll. N.J., Glassboro; active White House Sci. Coun., 1980—88, N.J. Commn. on Sci. and Tech. Patentee in field. Mem. Bicentennial adv. com. Chgo. Mus. Sci. and Industry, 1974-75; mem. adv. bd. Office of Phys. Scis., NRC, 1976-81; mem. Pres.'s Commn. on Nat. Medal of Sci., 1975-78; mem. vis. com. to div. phys. sci. U. Chgo., 1976—; mem. adv. coun. Humanities Inst., 1976—; trustee Aerospace Corp., 1974-81, chmn. bd. trustees, 1975-81; life mem. corp. MIT, 1974—, also mem. exec. com., energy adv. bd.; bd. dirs. Summit (N.J.) Speech Sch., 1967-70; mem. Marshall Scholarships Adv. Coun.; mem. adv. and resource coun. Princeton U.; mem. cons. sci. com. Chateaubriand Scholarships; trustee Carnegie Instn. of Washington, 20th Century Fund, John Simon Guggenheim Mcml. Found. Served with USNR, 1943-46. Recipient Outstanding Young Engr. award Eta Kappa Nu, 1954, George W. McCarty award Ga. Inst. Tech., 1958, award Summit Jr. C. of C., 1959, award of merit ASME, 1971, Harold Pender award Moore Sch., U. Pa., 1972, N.C. award, 1972, award for disting. contbn. Soc. Rsch. Adminstrs., 1980, N.J. Sci. and Tech. medal, 1982, medal Indsl. Rsch. Inst., 1983, Scientist of Yr. award R & D mag., 1984, Fahrney medal Franklin Inst., 1985, Pub. Svc. award Conf. Bd. Math. Csic., 1985, Silver Stein award MIT, 1991; named to Hall of Fame, Ga. Inst. Tech., 1994. Fellow IEEE, AAAS (bd. dirs. 1974-75, 77-82, pres. 1977-78, chmn. bd. dirs. 1979-80), Acoustical Soc. Am., Am. Acad. Arts and Scis., Audio Engring. Soc.; mem. NAS (coun. 1995), NAE (Bueche award 1984), Am. Philos. Soc., Assn. Computing Machinery, Am. Soc. for Engring. Edn. (Hall of Fame 1993), Engring. Soc. Detroit, Nat. Acad. Pub. Adminstrn. Office: EED Inc PO Box 435 Bedminster NJ 07921-0435

DAVID, GEORGE, psychiatrist, economic theory lecturer; b. N.Y.C., Feb. 19, 1940; s. Norman and Jennie (Danziger) D. BA, Yale U., 1961; MD, NYU, 1965. Intern Children's Hosp., San Francisco, 1965; resident in psychiatry Colo. Psychiat. Hosp., Denver, 1965-66; practice medicine specializing in psychiatry San Francisco; staff Calif. Pacific Med. Ctr., San Francisco, 1966-67, San Mateo County (Calif.) Mental Health Svcs., 1968-71; lectr. on application of econ. theory to personal decision making. Mem. San Francisco Clin. Hypnosis (v.p. 1973-74). Libertarian. Office: 399 Laurel St San Francisco CA 94118-1951

DAVID, GEORGE A. lawyer; b. Miami, Sept. 27, 1961; s. Alexander E. and Patricia Anne D. BA, U. Fla., 1985, JD, 1989. Bar: Fla. 1991, U.S. Dist. Ct. (so. dist.) Fla. 1993. Lawyer Charlip Delgado & Befeler, Miami, 1990-91, Parrillo Weiss & O'Halloran, Miami, 1991-96, Thornton, Mastrucci & Sinclair, Miami, 1996-98, Ligman, Martin & Evans, Miami, 1998—2001; ptnr. Gordon J. Evans, P.A., 2001—. Mem. ABA, Dade County Bar Assn. Office: Gordon J Evans PA Ste 200 1570 Madruga Ave Coral Gables FL 33146

DAVID, GEORGE ALFRED LAWRENCE, aerospace transportation executive; b. Bryn Mawr, Pa., Apr. 7, 1942; s. Charles Wendell and Margaret (Simpson) David; m. Barbara Osborn, Sept. 4, 1965; children: Eliza Pell, Hannah Lawrence, Henry Gibb. BA, Harvard U., 1965; MBA, U. Va., 1967. Asst. prof. fin. and acctg. U. Va., Charlottesville, 1967—68; v.p. The Boston Cons. Group, 1968—75; sr. v.p. corp. planning and devel. Otis Elevator Co., N.Y.C., 1975—77, sr. v.p., gen. mgr. Latin Am. ops. West Palm Beach, Fla., 1977—81, pres. N.Am. ops. Farmington, Conn., 1981—85, pres., CEO, 1985—89, chmn., 1989—97; sr. v.p. (parent co.) United Techs. Corp., 1988—89, exec. v.p., pres. comml./indsl., 1989—92, pres., COO, 1992—, CEO, 1994—, chmn., 1997—. Chmn. Greater Hartford chpt. ARC, 1985—87; former chmn. US-ASEAN Coun. Bus. and Tech., Nat. Minority Supplier Devel.

Coun.; trustee Wadsworth Atheneum, Hartford, 1984—; bd. dirs. Inst. Internat. Econs., Washington. Republican. Episcopalian. Office: 1 Financial Plz # Ms526 Hartford CT 06103-2608 also: Otis Elevator Co 10 Farm Springs Rd Farmington CT 06032-2526

DAVID, GUY ALBERT, electrical engineer; b. Thiais, Paris, Mar. 29, 1932; arrived in US, 1985, naturalized, 1997; s. Emile and Suzanne (Laine) D.; m. Nicole Marguerite Cossin, Apr. 16, 1955 (div. Oct. 1985); children: Gilles, Bernard, Anne, Odile; m. Evelyne Lyliane Brenner, Jan. 5, 1986. Degree in engring., U. Caen, France, 1953; MA, U. Paris, 1963, PhD, 1967. Engr. Telecomms. Radio Electriques et Telephoniques, Paris, 1955—66, head advanced studies, 1967—75, dir. mil. comm., 1975—85, Global Positioning Sys. specialist, 1978—85, Sci. Application Internat. Corp., Torrance, Calif., 1980—; dep. mgr., Global Positions Sys. specialist Magnavox, Torrance, Calif., 1985—88; dir. engring. Amcomp, Torrance, Calif., 1988—93, Global Positioning Sys. specialist, 1988—2001, sr. engr., 1993—2001; sr. systems engr., Global Positioning specialist Sci. Application Internat. Corp., Torrance, Calif., 2001—. Advisor French Civil Aviation del. Internat. Civil Aviation Orgn., Montreal, Canada, 1972; cons. European Space Agy., 1974—76; mem. NATO Indsl. Adv. Group Subgroup 5, 1976—85; corr. Internat. Radio Consultative Com., 1976—85; mem. Internat. Schiffs-Studien Orgn., 1984—85; lectr. in field. Author: (book) Radio Communications; co-author: (book) Space Communications; contbr. articles to trade and tech. jours., mags., and procs.; holder 20 patents. Decorated Chevalier de l'Ordre du Mérite; recipient Grand Prix de l'Electronique Gen. Ferrié. Mem. IEEE, Inst. Navigation, Soc. des Electriciens et des Electroniciens, Anciens de la Radio et de l'Electronique. Avocations: music, golf, bicycling. Home: 108 Sweetbriar Walk Stockbridge GA 30281 Office: Sci Application Internat Corp 21151 Western Ave Torrance CA 90501

DAVID, HAL, lyricist; m. Eunice Forester, Sept. 2, 1988; children: Jim, Craig. MusD (hon.), Lincoln Coll., 1991; DHL (hon.), Claremont Grad. U., 2000. Books: What the World Needs Now and Other Love Lyrics, Bacharach and David Songbook; Songs include Raindrops Keep Fallin' On My Head (Acad. award), The Look of Love (Acad. award nomination), What's New Pussycat? (Acad. award nomination), Alfie (Acad. award nomination), Wives and Lovers, Casino Royale, It Was Almost Like a Song (all Grammy award nomination), What the World Needs Now is Love, To Love a Child (written for Foster Grandparents' Program), To All the Girls I've Loved Before (recorded by Julio Iglesias and Willie Nelson), America Is (official song of Liberty Centennial campaign for restoration of Statue of Liberty and Ellis Island); chief collaborator: Burt Bacharach; other collaborators include Henry Mancini, Joe Raposo; Broadway show Promises, Promises (Grammy award, Tony award nomination); films include April Fools; record producer for Dionne Warwick. Elected Songwriters Hall Fame, Nashville Songwriters Hall Fame Internat.; recipient Presdl. award National Association Recording Merchandisers, Creative Achievement award B'nai B'rith, Entertainer of Yr. award Cue Mag. Mem. ASCAP (pres. 1980—), Songwriters Guild Am., Lyricists Guild Am., Dramatist Guild, Authors League. Address: 15 W 53rd St New York NY 10019-5401 *How do you create a hit? I don't know. When I sit down to work, I write what I feel. What happens afterwards is out of my hands. The only thing I'm sure of is you can't write a hit if you don't write a song. Of course, the act of creation, itself, is only one part of being a professional songwriter. To succeed and sustain, you have to have a knowledge of the other parts of the music business. You have to recognize that you are in business for yourself, and as president of your own company, you must be on top of all its aspects.*

DAVID, HERBERT ARON, statistician, educator; b. Berlin, Dec. 19, 1925; arrived in U.S., 1957, naturalized, 1964; s. Max and Betty (Goldmann) David; m. Vera Reiss, May 13, 1950 (dec.); 1 child, Alexander John; m. Ruth Finch, Dec. 1, 1992. BSc, Sydney (Australia) U., 1947; PhD, London U., 1953. Rsch. officer Commonwealth Sci. and Indsl. Rsch. Orgn., Sydney, 1953-55; sr. lectr. dept. stats. U. Melbourne, Melbourne, Australia, 1955-57; prof. stats. Va. Poly. Inst., 1957-64; prof. U. N.C., Chapel Hill, 1964-72, Iowa State U., Ames, 1972-96, Disting. prof. liberal arts and scis., 1980-96, disting. prof. emeritus, 1996—, dir. stat. lab., head dept. stats., 1972-84. Author: (book) The Method of Paired Comparisons, 1963, 2d edit., 1988, Order Statistics, 1970; co-author: 3d edit., 2003, Annotated Readings in the History of Statistics, 2001; co-editor: Advanced in Biometry, 1996. Recipient J. Shelton Horsley award, Va. Acad. Scis., 1963, Wilks award, Army Rsch., 1983. Fellow: AAAS, Inst. Math. Stats., Am. Statis. Assn.; mem.: Internat. Statis. Inst., Biometric Soc. (editor Biometrics 1967—72, pres. 1982—83). Jewish. Home: 2334 Hamilton Dr Ames IA 50014-8201 E-mail: hadavid@iastate.edu.

DAVID, IVO, artist, poet, real estate broker; b. St. Leucio Sannio, Italy, Nov. 22, 1934; came to U.S., 1961; s. Arduino and Clarice-Olga (Lepore) D.; m. Nancy Pugliese, Sept. 26, 1962 (dec. Nov. 1997). Grad., Lyceum of Sci., Italy; MFA, Acad. Fine Arts, Naples, Italy, 1958; grad., Acad. Fine Arts Paestum Acad., Italy, 1975, Internat. Acad. Micenei, Reggio, Italy, 1976. Lic. real estate broker, N.J. Planning designer Candeub/Fleissig Assoc., Newark, 1963-66; chief architect Design Fed. Warehouses, Newark, 1966-74; archtl. designer Raritan Ctr., Edison, N.J., 1970-75; pres., broker, developer Union (N.J.) Ctr. Realty Corp., 1972—, art advt. cons., 1975—. Illustrator: Divine Comedy, 1970 (Gold medal Acad. Art/Micenei Reggio Cal 1997); exhibited in numerous one man shows in U.S. and Europe, 1960-99; author: Manifesto of Fusionism, 1956, Memories of an Artist, 1981; founder new art style Fusinism '56. Mem. Greater Union County Assn. Realtors. Avocation: tennis. Home: 1950 Haines Ave Fl 1 Union NJ 07083-3711 Office: Union Ctr Realty Corp 1950 Haines Ave Union NJ 07083-3711 E-mail: ivodavid@aol.com.

DAVID, JOHN DEWOOD, biology educator; b. Alton, Ill., Dec. 1, 1942; s. Wade Dewood and Mary (Kemper) David; m. Nancy M. Rock, Feb. 6, 1972; children: Henry Wade, Katherine Leslie. BA in Chemistry and Biology, Wabash Coll., 1964; PhD in Molecular Biology, Vanderbilt U., 1969. Postdoctoral fellow U. Calif., San Francisco, 1969-72; asst. prof. U. Mo., Columbia, 1972-78, assoc. prof., 1978—, chair divsn. biol. scis., 1989—. Mem. task force on tchg. of sci. and math. in secondary schs. U. Mo. Columbia, 1983—85; mem. sci., math. engring. and tech. task force U. Mo. Columbia, Mo. State Dept. Edn., 1997—99; chair Chancellor's Strategic Planning and Resource Allocation Coun. U. Mo. Columbia, 2002—, mem. task force on restructuring tchg. preparation, 1994—97. Contbr. Bd. dirs. Columbia Soccer Club, 1989—92. Recipient Recognition award for Integration of Rsch. and Edn., NSF, 1997—2002; grantee, Howard Hughes Med. Inst., 1989—99; Med. rsch. fellow, Giannini Found., 1970—72. Mem.: AAAS, Am. Soc. for Cell Biology, Soc. for Devel. Biology, Beta Beta Beta (hon.). Democrat. Presbyterian. Avocations: soccer refereeing, gardening. Office: U Mo 105 Tucker Hall Columbia MO 65211-7400 E-mail: davidj@missouri.edu.

DAVID, JOHN R. internist, educator; b. Eng., Feb. 15, 1930; married; 2 children. BA, U. Chgo., 1951, BS, MD, U. Chgo., 1955; D (hon.), U. F. Ceara, 1991. Diplomate Am. Bd. Internal Medicine. From intern to asst. resident Mass. Gen. Hosp., 1955—57; clin. assoc. Nat. Inst. Arthritis and Metab Dis., 1957—59; trainee Rheumatism Rsch. Unit, England, 1959—60; resident med. Mass. Gen. Hosp., 1960—61; fellow NYU, 1961—64, asst. prof. medicine, 1964—66; asst. physician-in-chief Robert B. Brigham Hosp., 1966—82; Richard Pearson prof., chair dept. tropical pub. health Harvard Sch. Pub. Health, Boston, 1981—97, prof. immunology and infectious diseases, 1997—. Prof. medicine NYU, 1973—; sr. assoc. med. Brigham & Women's Hosp., 1980—82, asst. chief dept. rheumatol.-immunol., 1982—, sr. physician dept. medicine, 1982—, sci. adv. bd. Internal Lab. Rsch. Animal Disease, 1980—; Burroughs Wellcome vis. prof. Johns Hopkins U., Balt., 1983, Royal Soc. Medicine, England, 1984; cons. sci. working group Dir. Cmty. Disease, 1981—; mem. steering com. Cmty. Immunology Tuberclosis, 1984—; mem. sci. adv. com. New Eng. Biolabs., 1982—; ad hoc cons. Bd. Sci. Coun. Rev. Lab. Parasitic Diseases, NIH, 1984—. Mem.: AAAS, Am. Acad. Arts and Sci. Rsch., Am. Assn. Physicians, Soc. Exptl. Biology and Medicine, Infectious Disease Soc. Am., Am. Rheumatism Assn., Am. Fedn. Clin. Rsch., Am. Assn. Immunologists, Am. Soc. Clin. Investigation, Am. Soc. Tropical Medicine and Hygiene (pres. 1989), Inst. Medicine NAS. Office: Harvard Sch Pub Health Dept Immunology/Inf Disease 665 Huntington Ave Boston MA 02115-6021

DAVID, JOSEPH RAYMOND, JR., writer, periodical editor; b. Chgo., July 9, 1936; s. Joseph R. Sr. and Elsie (Sarakhan) D. BA, Lake Forest Coll., 1957. Freelance writer various pubs., 1970—; editor Education in Focus, Alexandria, Va., 1990. Cons. Annenberg CPB Math & Sci. Project, 1993. Author: The Fire Within, 1981, Glad You Asked!, 1986, Teacher of the Year, 1996, As Best We Can, 2000. Mem. Nat. Press Club Washington (moderator forum com. 2001—). Home: PO Box 202 Warrenton VA 20188

DAVID, LYNN ALLEN, banking executive; b. Greeneville, Tenn., Nov. 14, 1948; s. Clayton Cunningham and Lenora Mildred (Scott) D. BS in Bus. Adminstrn., U. Ark., 1970; MS in Commerce, St. Louis U., 1973; cert., Stonier Grad. Sch. Banking, 1981, Nat. Comml. Lending Sch., 1984. Asst. v.p. Fed. Res. Bank St. Louis, 1970-84; v.p., dir. corr. banking Gen. Bank, St. Louis, 1984-86; sr. cons., supr. Deloitte Haskins & Sells, St. Louis, 1987; dir. KPMG Peat Marwick, St. Louis, 1987-95; pres. CBCS Cmty. Bank Cons. Svcs., Inc., St. Louis, 1995—. CBCS Corp. Behavior Cons. Svcs., Inc., St. Louis, 1995—. Sec. Pres. Conf., First V.P. Conf., Fed. Res. System, 1982. Recipient Status Cymbal award Mo. Bankers Assn., Jefferson City, 1985. Mem. Mo. Bankers Assn., Iowa Bankers Assn., Ill. Bankers Assn., Clayton C. of C. Republican. Methodist. Avocations: skiing, scuba diving. Home: 12704 St Lazare Ln Saint Louis MO 63127-1522 Office: 225 S Meramec Ave Ste 1232 Saint Louis MO 63105-3511

DAVID, MARTHA LENA HUFFAKER, educator; b. Susie, Ky., Feb. 7, 1925; d. Andrew Michael and Nora Marie (Cook) Huffaker; m. William Edward David, June 24, 1952 (div. Jan. 1986); children: Edward Garry, William Andrew, Carolyn Ann, Robert Cook. AB in Music magna cum laude, Georgetown (Ky.) Coll., 1947; postgrad., Vanderbilt U., 1957-58; Spanish cert., Lang. Sch., Costa Rica, 1959; MEd, U. Ga., 1972. Elem. tchr. Wayne County Bd. Edn., Spann, Ky., 1944-45; music tchr. Mason County, Mayslick, Ky., 1947-49, Hikes Grade Sch., Buechel, Ky., 1949-53; English and Spanish tchr. Jefferson (Ga.) High Sch., 1961-63; music and English tchr. Athens (Ga.) Acad., 1967-71; music tchr. Barrow County Bd. Edn., Winder, Ga., 1971-88; real estate agt. South Best Realty, Athens, 1986-90; ret., 1988. Data collector Regional Ednl. Svcs. Agy., Athens and Winder, 19176-78; tchr. music Union Theol. Sem., Buenos Aires, 1957-60. Author: (poems) Parcels of Love, Book I, 1984, Book II, 1999, Poems and Reflections; composer (music plays) The B.B.'s, The Missing Tune, A Dream Come True, The Stars Who Creep Out of Orbit, 1976-86. Active cultural affairs orgns., Athens, 1962—, Athens Area Porcelain Artists, YWCO; entertainer nursing homes and civic orgns., Athens, 1962; chmn. cancer drives, heart fund drive United Way, March of Dimes, Athens, 1962—; historian, elder, pianist Christian Ch. Winner regional piano competition Ky. Philharm. Orch., 1946; nominated Tchrs. Hall of Fame, Barrow County, 1981. Mem. Ret. Tchrs. Assn., Writer's Group, Ga. Music Tchrs., Nat. Music Tchrs. Assn., Athens Music Tchrs. Assn. (pres. recital chmn.), Ga. World Orgn. China Painters, Athens Area Porcelain Artists, Women's Mus. Arts (assoc.), Women's Mus. Art (Washington), Touchdown Club, Band Boosters, Alpha Delta Kappa (Fidelis Nu chpt., historian), Delta Omicron (life, scholar 1944). Democrat. Mem. Christian Ch. Avocations: porcelain art, oil and acrylic painting, swimming, square dancing, round dancing. Home: 105 Nassau Ln Athens GA 30607-1456

DAVID, MILES, association and marketing executive; b. Newark, Mar. 29, 1926; s. Samuel Harry and Estelle Rachel (Sklower) Ginsberg; m. Florence Cotton, Dec. 7, 1952; children: Steven, Amelia, Heidi. BA, NYU, 1946; postgrad., Columbia U., 1946. Assoc. editor Sci. Illustrated mag. McGraw-Hill Co., N.Y.C., 1946-48; editor Sponsor mag., N.Y.C., 1948-58; with Radio Advt. Bur., N.Y.C., 1958-86, formerly v.p. and dir. promotion, exec. v.p., pres., vice chmn., chief exec. officer, bd. dir., adv. bd. dirs.; pres. Am. Values: The Community Action Network; pres. nat. mktg. strategy nat. advertisers Mkt. Soundings subs. TradeOne Mktg. Inc., New York, 1986-88; vice chmn. TradeOne Mktg. Inc., New York, 1988-99; pres. Miles David Assocs., Inc., New York, 1999—. Lectr. Tobe-Coburn Sch. for Fashion Careers; speaker in field to nat., internat. groups.; formerly bd. dirs. Brand Names Found.; bd. dirs. Advt. Coun., Nat. Assn. Promotional and Advt. Allowances; bd. dirs. Nat. Assn. Promotional and Advertising Allowances, 1998—. Editor: Sponsor mag. (George W. Polk award). Former chmn. Scarsdale Adv. Coun. on Cable TV; mem. nominating com. Scarsdale Village Trustees; mem. procedure com. Non-Partisan Elections, Scarsdale; pres. Am. Values Cmty. Action Network. With AUS, 1943-45, ETO. Recipient Morris Meister award; named Outstanding Alumnus Bronx High Sch., Sci. Man of Yr. Radio Trade Assn., 1975, 76; named to Hall of Fame of Co-op Advt., 1997. Mem. Internat. Radio, TV Soc., Broadcast Pioneers, Perstare et Praestare, Scarsdale Club (N.Y.), Town Club (com. pub. rels. 1970-74). Jewish. Achievements include adminstr. Higbee Study, use of radio for dept. stores, and All-Radio Methodology Study, how to measure radio. Home and Office: 35 Jared Dr White Plains NY 10605-3411 E-mail: mdavid3442@aol.com.

DAVID, REUBEN, lawyer; b. Baghdad, Iraq, June 12, 1928; came to U.S., 1951; s. Isaac Solomon David and Tefaha (Nisan) Solomon D.; m. Nesta Paley David; 1 child, Aram. License in Law, Iraq Law Coll., Baghdad, 1951; BA, NYU, 1958; JD, N.Y. Law Sch., 1962. Bar: Iraq 1951, N.Y. 1969. Asst. corp. counsel City of N.Y., 1970-76, chief legal unit dept. personnel, 1976-78; dep. dir. for legal affairs N.Y.C. Employees' Retirement System, 1978—2002; pvt. practice law, 2002—. Mem. ABA, N.Y. State Bar Assn. Home: 30 Fifth Ave New York NY 10011-8812

DAVID, ROBERT JEFFERSON, lawyer; b. New Roads, La., Aug. 10, 1943; s. Joseph Jefferson and Doris Marie (Olinde) D.; m. Stella Marie Scott, Jan. 21, 1967; children: Robert J. Jr., Richard M. BA, Southeastern La. U., 1966; JD, Loyola U., New Orleans, 1969. Bar: U.S. Dist. Ct. (ea. dist.) La. 1969, U.S. Dist. Ct. (mid. dist.) La. 1969, U.S. Dist. Ct. (we. dist.) La. 1975. Assoc. Gainsburgh, Benjamin, Fallon, David, New Orleans, 1969-74; ptnr. Gainsburgh, Benjamin, David, New Orleans, 1974—. Adj. faculty mem. Tulane U. Sch. Law, New Orleans, 1982-84, law sch. Loyola U., New Orleans, 1996; mem. hearing com. La. Atty. Disciplinary Bd.; mem. Gov.'s Commn. on Med. Profl. Liability; lectr., spkr. continuing legal edn. seminars. Staff mem. Loyola U. Law Rev., 1967-69; bd. dir Loyola Law Sch. Alumni Assn., 2001-02, vis. com. Loyola Law Sch., 2002—. Reader, recorder for La. Blind and Handicapped, 1986-91; charter mem. Lawyers for Alliance for Nuclear Arms Control, New Orleans, 1986-1990, pres. Arden Hill Acad. Parent Tchr. League, 1979-80. Fellow: Am. Coll. Trial Lawyers; mem.: ATLA, ABA, La. Trial Lawyers Assn. (bd. govs. 1981—83, 1995—96, exec. com. 1996—97, coun. of dirs. 1997—, contbg. editor Civil Trial Tactics manual 1981, chmn. sect. med. malpractice 1992—94, legis. com.), La. Bar Found., La. State Bar Assn. (asst. examiner commn. on bar admissions 1974—93, spl. inst. commn. 1974—82, med. legal interprofl. com. 1987—, co-chmn. 1991—94, contbr. La. Bar Assn. Jour. column on Profl. Liability 1989—, disciplinary com.), Am. Bd. Profl. Liability Attys., Nat. Bd. Trial Advocacy, Phi Alpha Delta, Kappa Sigma. Avocation: sports. Home: 21 Cypress Point Ln New Orleans LA 70131-3351 Office: Gainsburgh Benjamin David 2800 Energy Ctr New Orleans LA 70163

DAVID, RONALD BRIAN, child neurologist; b. Richmond, Va., Aug. 3, 1937; m. Candace M. Heiderich; children: Ronald Bryan, Susan D. Staub, Elizabeth D. Kurtz, Thomas Edwin, Whitney Sears, Jennifer Pund. BS, Ea. Mennonite Coll., 1960; MD, Med. Coll. Va., 1964. Diplomate Am. Bd. Psychiatry and Neurology, Am. Bd. Pediatrics, Nat. Bd. Med. Examiners, Am. Bd. Child Neurology. Fellow in pediat. Mayo Grad. Sch. Medicine, Rochester, Minn., 1965-67, fellow in child neurology, 1967-70; from asst. prof. to assoc. prof. Med. Coll. Va., Richmond, 1970—. Vis. prof. Coll. William and Mary; bd. dirs. The Autism Program of Va. Found. for the Exceptional Individual. Editor: Pediatric Neurology for the Clinician, 1992; series editor: Mosby Neurology-Psychiatry Access Series, 1996, Blackwell Neurology Psychiatry Access Series, 2003—; editor: Blackwell Child and Adolescent Neurology, 2003—; contbr. articles to profl. jours., chpts. to books. Fellow Am. Acad. Neurology, Am. Acad. Cerebral Palsy and Child Devel., Am. Acad. Pediatrics; mem. Am. Neurol. Assn., Child Neurology Soc., Internat. Neuropsychol. Soc., Learning Disabilities Coun., Am. Epilepsy Found., Va. Neurol. Soc., Va. Pediat. Soc., Orton Soc. Office: Children's Neurol Svcs 5875 Bremo Rd Richmond VA 23226

DAVID, RONALD BRYAN, county official; b. Lewisburg, Pa., Dec. 27, 1958; s. Ronald Brian and Rhoda (Dillon) D.; m. Jamie Louise Barnicle, Jan. 6, 1990; children: Anne Claire, Mary Paige, Lane Elizabeth. BA, Hampden-Sydney Coll., Va., 1982; M in Urban and Regional Planning, Va. Commonwealth U., Richmond, 1990. Cert. Nat. Ctr. Paralegal Tng., Am. Inst. Cert. Planners. Environ. planner Isle of Wight County, Isle of Wight, Va., 1990-91, county planner, 1991-94, dir. planning and zoning, 1995-97; county adminstr. Brunswick County, Lawrenceville, Va., 1997-99, Amherst County, Amherst, Va., 2000—. Sec./treas. Brunswick Co. Indsl. Devel. Authority, Lawrenceville, Va., 1997-99, Amherst County Svc. Authority, 2000—; dir. Roanoke River Svc. Authority, South Hill, Va., 1998-99; treas. Region 2000 Regional Commn., Lynchgurg, Va., 2002-03, Regioal Econ. Devel. Partnership, 2003-. Mem. Good Shepard Parrish Coun., 1998-2000, Holy Cross Parish Coun., 2002— Mem. Am. Planning Assn. (Va. chpt., dir. legis. and policy), Internat. City/County Mgmt. Assn., Va. Local Govt. Mgmt. Assn. (mem. bd. dirs. 2002—, profl. devel. com.), Va. Economic Developers Assn., Va. Assn. Counties (vice chair cmty. devel. steering com.). Roman Catholic. Avocations: golf, sailing, skiing, hiking. Fax: 804-946-9370.

DAVID, THEOHARIS LAMBROS, architect, educator; b. Farmingdale, N.Y., June 9, 1938; s. Lambros L. and Thalia (Joaniddes) D.; m. Margarita T. Leptos, July 29, 1967; children: Melissa T., Alexis L. BArch, Pratt Inst., 1961; MArch, Yale U., 1964; studied with Serge Chermayeff and Paul Rudolph. Registered arch., N.Y., N.J., Republic of Cyprus; cert. Nat. Coun. Archtl. Registration Bd. Designer Whitlesy & Conklin Archs./Planners, N.Y.C., 1964-65, William F. Pedersen Assocs., N.Y.C., 1965-66, K. Vafeades, Arch., Nicosia, Cyprus, 1965-66; asst. arch. J & A Philippou, Archs., Nicosia, 1966-67, 72; sr. designer Max O. Urbahn Assocs., N.Y.C., 1968-72; ptnr. David & Dikaios Assocs., Architecture/Planning, Nicosia, N.Y.C., Bahrain, 1973-87; prin. Theo David & Assocs., N.Y.C., 1987—, Theo David Cons. Arch./Planner, Nicosia, 1992—. Founding dir. CAEC Architecture/Engring. Cons., Ltd., Cyprus, 1975; mem. faculty Pratt Inst., Bklyn., 1968-69, asst. prof. arch., 1969-79, assoc. prof., 1979-83, prof. arch., 1983—; nominator Aga Khan Award for Arch., 1984—; disting. juror 1st Presdl. Arch. Awards, Cyprus, 1992; guest lectr. U. Thessaloniki, Greece, 1972, Hellenic Conf. on Tall Bldgs., Athens, Greece, 1975, U. So. Calif., L.A., Archtl. Assn., London, 1982, Cyprus Archs. Assn. and Am. Ctr., Nicosia, 1982, 92, Tex. A&M U., 1984, Cyprus Popular Bank Cultural Ctr., Nicosia, 1987, 91, Hellenic Bank Cultural Ctr., Limassol, Cyprus, 1993, many others; guest critic CCNY, N.Y.C., Archtl. Assn., London, Temple U., Phila., Columbia U., N.Y.C., Yale U., New Haven, U. So. Calif., L.A., others. Author: Housing of a Culture/Cyprus, 1982; exhbns. include Pratt Manhattan Ctr., N.Y.C., 1971, 83, Pratt Inst. Gallery, Bklyn., 1978, Urban Ctr., N.Y.C., 1981, Cyprus House, N.Y.C., 1984, 92, Shafler Gallery Pratt Inst., Bklyn., 1987, Mcpl. Arts Soc., N.Y.C., 1987, Disting. Drawing Gallery, N.Y.C./AIA, 1988, Parson Sch. Design, N.Y.C., 1991, Higgins Hall Gallery, Pratt Inst., 1994; contbr. articles to profl. jours. Mem. design adv. com. Pub. Devel. Corp., N.Y.C., 1986; 1st v.p. Am. Cyprus Congress, N.Y.C., 1990-94; appointed mem. adv. com. for New Cultural Ctr., Cyprus Govt., 1992. Served U.S. Army, 1962-63. Grantee N.Y. State Coun. on Arts, 1982, Pratt Rsch. Coun., 1983; recipient Design award Nat. Inst. Archtl. Edn., 1961, Bard Honor award City Club, N.Y., 1992, 1st prize G.S.P. Stadium Competition, Cyprus, 1993. Fellow AIA (N.Y. chpt., mem. overseas practice com. 1980-82, chmn. design awards program 1989-90, honors com. N.Y.C. chpt. 2003, Interior Design award AIA Jour. 1988, Design Excellence citation 1993, Design citation 1993, Archs. Designers & Planners for Social Responsibility Project award 1994, Cyprus State Architecture award 2001), Am. Planning Assn. (chmn. com. on N.Y. Waterfront 1984-86), Inst. Urban Design. Greek Orthodox. Office: Theo David Architects 170 Duane St New York NY 10013 also: PO Box 20319 Nicosia Cyprus also: Pratt Inst Sch Arch Brooklyn NY 11205 E-mail: tdanyc@aol.com.

DAVID, WARD S. bank officer, retired federal agency executive; b. Bertrand, Nebr., Nov. 29, 1934; s. Stanton S. and Helen M. (Gifford) D.; married Aug. 12, 1956; children: Kim, Teri, Mick, Stan, Rod. BS in Agriculture, U. Nebr., 1956. Conservationist USDA, North Platte, Nebr., 1957-59, work unit conservationist Holdrege, Nebr., 1959-68, dist. conservationist Alma, Nebr., 1968-75, area conservationist Tucumcari, N.Mex., 1975-83, Escondido, Calif., 1983-86, divsn. ops. mgr. Washington, 1986-93, ret., 1993; ops. mgr., v.p. Bank of Am., Fallbrook, Calif., 1994—. Author: Ask Not for Victory, 1991; contbr. articles to various publs. Mem. sch. bd. Alma, 1971-75. With USAFR, 1956-57. Mem. Soc. Conservation Soc. Am. (charter, pres. 1967-69), Am. Assn. Ret. Persons (officer). Republican. Methodist. Avocations: sports, writing, reading, jogging, movies. Home: 4505 108th Street Lubbock TX 79424 Office: Morgan Stanley-Dean Witter 1615 S Mission Rd Fallbrook CA 92028-4155

DAVIDEK, ANNETTE MARIE, artist; b. Flint, Mich., Apr. 27, 1957; d. Edward John and Georgina Elizabeth (Crawford) D.; m. Steven Ray Currie, July 27, 1985. BFA, U. Mich., 1979; MFA, Hunter Coll., 1990. Exhbns. include Hunter Coll. Galleries, N.Y.C., 1991, 80 Washington Sq. East Galleries, N.Y.C., 1992, 95, Littlejohn Contemporary, 1996, 99, 2000, 02, Flint Inst. Arts, 1994, O'Hara Gallery, N.Y.C., 1995, 96, Richard Anderson Fine Art, N.Y.C., 1996, 2000, 01, Art Mus. Fla. Internat. U., Miami, 1997, others; represented in permanent collections Weil, Gotshal &Manges, N.Y.C., Viacom, N.Y.C., Trump Internat. Hotel, N.Y.C., The Prudential, Pan Pacific Yokohama, Japan, Mulia Hotel Senayan, Jakarta, IKON Ltd., L.A., MTA Arts for Transit Subway Installation, N.Y.C., N.Y. Home: 106 Franklin St Brooklyn NY 11222-2009

DAVIDEK, STEFAN, artist; b. Flint, Mich., May 15, 1924; s. Stephen Paul and Anna Davidek; m. Angelina Ann Davidek, June 19, 1948; children: Mark, Denise, Debra, Dennis. Home: 5391 W Coldwater Rd Flint MI 48504

DAVIDGE, K. GENEVIEVE, clinical social worker; b. Mason, Mich., Apr. 19, 1949; d. John and Margery (Lynk) Lippincott; children: Rebecca, Andrew. *Father John Lippincott was a minister in the Fona Methodist Conference from 1954-1982. Sister Rev. Anne Lippincott has also been a minister in the Fona Conference for more than ten years. Daughter, Rebecca lives in Brooklyn, NY where she is pursuing a career teaching theatre. Son, Andrew, attends the University of New Mexico in Albuquerque.* BA, U. Iowa, 1970, MSW, 1973. Therapist, program dir. Raintree Svcs., New Orleans, 1974-77, Family & Children's Svc., Tulsa, 1978-84; dir., social worker St. Francis Hosp., Tulsa, 1984-87; program coord., case mgr. Rebound, Inc., Lancaster, S.C., 1987-90; pvt. practice Albuquerque, 1990—. Mem. NASW. Methodist. Avocation: singing. Office: 3150 Carlisle Blvd NE Ste 22 Albuquerque NM 87110-1678 Fax: 505-830-6031.

DAVIDOFF, RICHARD SAYLES, lawyer; b. N.Y.C., Nov. 3, 1932; s. Eli and Minnie Phyllis (Selesko) D.; children: Andrew M., Jennifer A. BA, Dartmouth Coll., 1954; JD, Harvard U., 1959. BAr: N.Y. 1960. Ptnr. Davidoff, Levinson & Davidoff, N.Y.C., 1960-74, Kantor, Davidoff, Wolfe, Mandelker & Kass, P.C., N.Y.C., 1974—. Class officer Class of 1954, Dartmouth Coll., 1964-68, 79-84; bd. dirs. Parents Assn. Trinity Coll., Hartford, Conn., 1982-86. Served to lt. (j.g.) USNR, 1954-56. Mem.: N.Y. State Bar Assn. Home: 305 E 83d St New York NY 10028 Office: Kantor Davidoff Wolfe Mandelker & Kass PC 51 E 42nd St New York NY 10017-5404

DAVIDOVSKY, MARIO, composer; b. Medanos, Buenos Aires, Argentina, Mar. 4, 1934; came to U.S., 1960; s. Natalio and Perla (Bulanska) D.; m. Elaine Blaustein, Nov. 19, 1961; children: Matias Gabriel, Adriana. Dir. Electronic Music Center, Princeton and Columbia univs., 1964-94; vis. lectr. Sch. Music, U. Mich., 1964; guest prof. Inst. di Tella, Buenos Aires, 1965; prof. music CCNY, 1968-80, Columbia U., 1981-94, McDowell prof. music, 1989-94; Fanny Peabody Mason prof. music Harvard U., 1994—. Dir. Composer's Conf. Wellesley (Mass.) Coll. Composer chamber music, orchestral works, also works for electronic music.; recs. on, Columbia, Sonnova, C.I.R. Nonesuch, Turnabout, New World, Wergo, Bridge records. Bd. dirs. The Koussevitsky Music Found. in Libr. Congress, Fromm Found., Harvard U.; founder, bd. dirs. Robert Miller Fund for Music. Recipient award Koussevitzky Found., 1964, award Libr. of Congress, 1964, Nat. Inst. Arts and Letters, 1965, Creative Arts award Brandeis U., 1965, Aaron Copeland award Tanglewood, 1966, Naumburg award, 1971, Pulitzer prize in music, 1971, Seamus Nat. award, 1994, Cristoph & Stephan Kaske music prize, Munich, 1997; Guggenheim fellow, 1961-62, 62-63; Rockefeller fellow, 1964, 65. Mem. Am. Acad. Arts and Letters. Home: 490 West End Ave New York NY 10024 E-mail: davidovs@fas.harvard.edu.

DAVIDOW, JENNY JEAN, counselor, writer; b. Santa Monica, Calif., Mar. 25, 1953; d. Ray M. Davidow and Caroline D. (Kos) Lackmann. BA, UCLA, 1974; MA, Internat. Coll., Santa Monica, 1981; D Clin. Hypnotherapy, Am. Inst. Hypnotherapy, Irvine, Calif., 1994. Cert. clin. hypnotherapist. Pvt. practice, L.A., 1981-92, Santa Cruz, Calif., 1992—. Seminar leader, L.A.,

1981-92, Santa Cruz, 1992—; bd. dirs. Tidal Wave Press, Santa Cruz; featured guest various TV and radio shows, L.A., 1983-88; spkr. Whole Life Expo, L.A., 1983-87; mem. Am. Bd. Hypnotherapy, 1989—. Author: Dream Therapy Workbook, 1983, Embracing Your Subconscious, 1996, Corners of the Soul, 1998; contbg. author: anthology Dreamscaping, 1999; Love Games, 2000, The Spirit of Writing, 2001; contbr. articles to various pubs.; creator, presenter (audiotape collection) Comfortable and Capable, 1994. Mem.: Resource Ctr. for Nonviolence, World Wilflife Fund (ptnr. in conservation 1995, Mono Lake com., Treepeople), Focusing Inst., Found. for Shamanic Studies, Assn. for Humanistic Psychology, Sierra Club (life). Democrat. Avocations: photography, gardening.

DAVIDOW, JOEL, lawyer; b. N.J., July 24, 1938; s. Isadore Davidow; m. Katherine Davidow-Lucas (div.); m. Debra Lynn Miller (div.); children: Abigail, Molly. AB, Princeton U., 1960; LLB, Columbia U., 1963; postdoctoral, U. London, Stanford U. Bar: D.C. 1965, N.Y. 1981. Legal asst. to commr. U.S. Fed. Trade Commn., Washington, 1964-65; assoc. Freeman & Hanley, Chgo., 1969-70; trial atty. Antitrust divsn. U.S. Dept. Justice, Washington, 1966-69, evaluation atty. Antitrust divsn., 1970-73, chief fgn. commerce sect. Antitrust divsn., 1973-77, dir. policy planning antitrust div., 1978-81; ptnr. Mudge, Rose, Guthrie, Alexander & Ferdon, N.Y.C., 1981-87; ptnr., head internat. sect. Dickstein, Shapiro & Morin, Washington, 1987-93; ptnr., vice chmn. Ablondi, Foster, Sobin & Davidow, Washington, 1993-2001; ptnr. Miller & Chevalier, Washington, 2001—. Del. UN Conf. Restrictive Practice, Geneva, 1974—80; adj. prof. law Columbia U., N.Y.C., 1982—87, Am. U., 1987—91, George Mason U., 1992—2003, Georgetown Law Sch., 2003; arbitrator U.S.-Can. Free Trade Agreement, Washington and Ottowa, 1991—94. Author: Antitrust Rules for International Business (Bur. Nat. Affairs 1995); fgn. antitrust editor Antitrust Bulletin, 1981; adv. bd. Bur. Nat. Affairs Antitrust Bulletin, 1981; ocntbr. articles to profl. jours. Mem. ABA. Democrat. Avocation: tennis. Home: 3721 39th St NW Apt B194 Washington DC 20016 Office: Miller & Chevalier 655 15th St NW Washington DC 20005

DAVIDS, NORMAN, engineering science and mechanics educator, researcher; b. N.Y.C., Mar. 17, 1918; s. Max and Sarah (Flint) Davidowitz; m. Frances White, Mar. 17, 1945; children: Gerald, Laura, Stuart. BS, CCNY, 1937; MS, NYU, 1938, PhD, 1940. Instr. CCNY, 1941; physicist C.E., Cin., 1942; mathematician Carnegie Inst. Tech., Washington, 1943-45; instr. Johns Hopkins U., Balt., 1945-47; assoc. prof. engring. mechanics Pa. State U., University Park, 1947-53, prof., 1953-78, prof. emeritus, 1978—. Mem. Inst. Advanced Study, Princeton, N.Y., 1941-42; project dir. NIH, Bethesda, Md., 1968-78, Ballistics Research Labs., Aberdeen, Md., 1961-66; sr. sci. adviser Army Research Office, Durham, N.C., 1961 Editor: International Symposium on Stress Waves, 1960; contbr. articles to profl. jours. Recipient Naval Ordnance Devel. award Carnegie Inst., 1945; Fulbright scholar Israel Inst. Tech., 1959 Fellow Am. Acad. Mechanics (past treas., dir.); mem. ASME, Soc. Engring. Sci., Phi Beta Kappa, Sigma Xi Democrat. Jewish. Home: 236 E Irvin Ave State College PA 16801-6103 Office: Pa State U Engring Sci and Mechs Dept University Park PA 16802 E-mail: nxd2@psu.edu.

DAVIDSON, ABRAHAM ABA, art historian, educator, photographer; b. Dorchester, Mass., June 27, 1935; s. Isaac and Ruth (Feinsilver) D. AB in Archtl. Scis. cum laude, Harvard U., 1957; postgrad., Hebrew U., Jerusalem, 1957-58; AM in Art History, Boston U., 1960; B in Jewish Edn., Hebrew Tchrs. Coll., Boston, 1960; PhD in Art History, Columbia U., 1965. Vis. lectr. art history U. Iowa, 1963-64; instr. Wayne State U., Detroit, 1964-65; asst. prof. Oakland U., Rochester, Mich., 1965-68; mem. faculty Tyler Sch. Art, Temple U., Phila., 1968—, prof. art history, 1975—. Vis. asst. prof. U. Mass., Amherst, summers 1965-67, U. Colo., summer 1968; Thomas P. Johnson disting. vis. scholar Rollins Coll., Winter Park, Fla., 1997; cons. Burlington County C.C., Pemberton, N.J., 1976-77. Author: The Story of American Painting, 1974, 79, Japanese transl., 1976, The Eccentrics and Other American Visionary Painters, 1978, Early American Modernist Painting, 1910-1935, 1981, 3d edit., 1990, Ben Solowey, 1988, Ralph Albert Blakelock, 1996, The Paintings of E.M. Saniga, 2001; also articles; one-man exhbns. of photographs Temple U., 1972, 82, Painted Bride Gallery, Phila., 1974, Burlington County C.C., 1978, Gloucester County (N.J.) Coll., 1979, 92, Villanova U., 1982, Pavilion Galleries Burlington County Hosp., Mt. Holly, N.J., 1987, 1521 Café Gallery, 1997, Phila. C.C., 2001; represented in permanent collections Bank Leumi, Cigna Corp., Lehigh U., Sch. Pharmacy, Temple U., Villanova U., Sheldon Meml. Art Gallery, U. Nebr., Free Libr. Phila., Newark Pub. Libr., Hudson-United Bank, Jefferson divsn.; numerous TV appearances. Recipient Group 17 prize photography Detroit Inst. Arts, 1969, NEH grantee, 1985 Office: Tyler Sch Art Beech and Penrose Aves Elkins Park PA 19126 E-mail: adavidso@astro.ocis.temple.edu.

DAVIDSON, ANTHONY R. education educator, consultant; PhD, City U. of London. Electronic Document Profl. EDSA, 2002. Asst. prof. Adelphi U., Garden City, NY, 1990—2000; prof., dir. grad. programs in mgmt. and sys. NYU, N.Y.C., 2000—. Pres. Perfect Impressions Consultants, N.Y.C., 1992—. Author: (article) TQM Mag. (Literati Club award for Excellence: Outstanding Paper of the Yr., 2002). Advisor JCSE Ctr. for Spl. Edn., Bklyn., 1993; exec. adv. bd. of e-learn AACE, Norfolk, Va., 2000; advisor RCCS Cancer Soc., Bklyn., 2002; bd. trustees Med-Smart, Ann Arbor, Mich., 2002; chmn. QTL Free Lending Libr., Queens, 1990—97. Avocations: skiing, soccer, football, chess. Office: NYU 11 W 42nd St - Ste 429 New York NY 10036 Office Fax: 212-790-1676. E-mail: anthony.davidson@nyu.edu.

DAVIDSON, ARDETH ANDERSON, nurse, poet, writer; b. Princeton, Minn., May 21, 1940; d. Roy L. Anderson and Hazel Evangeline Dawson; m. Rodney William Davidson, Aug. 7, 1971 (div. Aug. 1981); children: Michael William, Rick William, Sheryl Lynn McDonald, Pamela Jean Gassman, Nicole Louise Cicerone. BS in Psychology (equivalency testing), Evergreen State Coll., 1980; diploma, Tech. C.C. Nursing, Olympia, Wash., 1981; student, Normandale C.C., Bloomington, Minn., 1992, North Oaks Coll. Exec. sec. CDC GSD, Bloomington, Minn., 1963-66, Comserv Corp., Bloomington, Minn., 1970-71; nurse numerous facilities in Wash. and Minn., 1981-98. Author: (poetry) Embrace the Morning, 1998, Above the Clouds, 1998, Shadows in the Mist; (children's lit.) Roberto and the Christmas Doll, 1977, 2d edit., 2000, Stormy, 1999, Jamie and the Mystery of the Mansion, 1999, Children of the Birds, 1999. Recipient scholarship March of Dimes, 1981. Achievements include discovery of cure for proetus in paraplegics. Avocations: music, playing the piano and organ, art, volunteering for women and children's abuse issues, writing children's stories.

DAVIDSON, BARRY RODNEY, lawyer; b. Boston, Aug. 12, 1943; s. Robert Bruce and Grace (Barry) D.; m. Paula Frances Miller, Sept. 2, 1967; children: Brent, Clay. BA, Vanderbilt U., 1964; postgrad., NYU, 1966; JD, U. Fla., 1967. Bar: Fla. 1968, U.S. Dist. Ct. (so. dist.) Fla. 1969, U.S. Ct. Appeals (5th cir.) 1971, (11th cir.) 1981, U.S. Supreme Ct. 1983, U.S. Dist. Ct. (mid. and no. dists.) Fla. 1989. Legis. aide Fla. State Senate, Tallahassee, 1968; law clk. to judge U.S. Dist. Ct. (so. dist.) Fla., Miami, 1968-70; assoc. Steel Hector & Davis, Miami, 1970-74, ptnr., 1974-87, Coll, Davidson, Carter, Smith, Salter & Barkett, P.A., Miami, 1987-2000, Hunton & Williams, Miami, 2000—. Chmn. mediation com. So. Dist. Fla., 1992-94; so. dist. rep. 11th cir. jud. conf., 1992-94; mem. Civil Justice Adv. Group So. Dist., 1992-95, Fed. Jud. Bar and Cmty. Liason Com., 1995—. Mem. Fla. Gov.'s Eminent Domain Study Com., Tallahassee, 1984-85; pres. Greater Miami Pop Warner League, Inc., 1987-89. Fellow Am. Bar Found. (life); mem. ABA, Fla. Bar Assn. (bd. govs. 1982-86. chmn. advt. com. 1977-80), Miami Vanderbilt Club (pres. 1977-80), Coral Reef Yacht Club, Ocean Reef Club, Ekwrnok Country Club. Democrat. Roman Catholic. Avocations: boating, skiing, golf. E-mail: bdavidson@hunton.com., bdbrd@aol.com.

DAVIDSON, BARRY SHELDON, academic administrator, education educator; b. Bklyn., Sept. 18, 1949; s. Jack and Iva Irene Davidson. BS, Pittsburg State U., Pittsburg, KS, 1971, MS, 1973; EDS, Vanderbilt U., Nashville, TN, 1974; EDD, U. Ark., Fayetteville, AR, 1977. Lifetime Teaching Credential NY State, 1973. Vis. prof. East Carolina U., Greenville, NC, 1977—80; assoc. dir. admissions U. Nevada-Reno, Reno, Nev., 1980—90; dir. admissions Pittsburg State U., Pittsburg, Kans., 1990—91; acad. historian Am. Cmty. Sch., Athens, Greece, 1991—2000; asst. prof. edn. Lander U., Greenwood, SC, 2000—01, McNeese State U., Lake Charles, La., 2001—02, Troy State U., Troy, Ala., 2002—. Guest scholar European Humanities U., Minsk, Belarus, 1998, Internat. Solomon U., Kiev, Ukraine, 1999, Ind. U. Tbilisi, Georgia, 1999. Contbr. articles to profl. jours. Chmn. No. Nev. Soccer League Disciplinary Com., Reno, 1980—84; vol. Probation and Parole, Reno, 1987—90; campaign vol. United Way, Pittsburg, Kans., 1990—91; cross country and track coach ACS Varsity Boys and Girls, Greece, 1991—96. Recipient Part-Time Tchg. Five-Year award, Truckee Meadows CC, 1984. Mem.: Am. Assn. U. Prof. Avocations: travel, gardening, coin and stamp collecting. Home: 1122 Brundidge Boulevard Troy AL 36081 Office: Troy State University 10 McCartha Hall Troy AL 36082 Office Fax: 334-670-3291.

DAVIDSON, BONNIE JEAN, gymnastics educator, sports management consultant; b. Rockford, Ill., Nov. 19, 1941; d. Edward V. and Pauline Mae (Dubbs) Welliver; m. Glenn Duane Davidson, June 4, 1960 (dec. Oct. 1993); children: Lori Davidson Aamodt, Wendy Davidson Seerup; m. James A. Johnson, Sept. 15, 2001. Student, Rockford Coll., 1965, Rock Valley Coll., Rockford, 1969-77. Founder, owner, dir. Gymnastic Acad. Rockford, 1977-95; pres., dir., owner Springbrook, Ltd., swim and tennis club, Rockford, 1986-95. Rep. trampoline and tumbling com. AAU, 1989-99—; coach nat. and world champion athetes; mgr., judge, head del. U.S.A. gynmastics teams, 1980—; speaker, lectr., clinician in field.; mem. organizing coms. world championships, also others, 1982-99 Contbr. World Book Ency. Bd. dirs. U.S. Olympic Com., 1995—, U.S.A. Gymnastics, 1991—; instr. ARC. Named one of Most Interesting People, Rockford mag., 1987; named to USA Gymnastics Hall of Fame, 2003; recipient YWCA Janet Lynn Sports award, 1996. Mem. Internat. Fedn. Trampoline and Tumbling (internat. judge, mem. tech. com. 1986-99—, del. to congress 1976-86, hon. lifetime mem. 1998), Internat. Fedn. Sport Acrobats (internat. judge), U.S.A. Trampoline and Tumbling Assn. (hon. life; nat. tumbling chairperson 1980-88, advisor 1988-99—, Coach of Yr. award 1980, Outsanding Contbn. to the Sport award 1987, 96, Master of Sport award 1989), U.S. Sports Acrobatics Fedn. (hon. life; v.p. 1984-95), Nat. Judges Assn. (exec. dir.). Republican. Avocations: skiing, boating, bicycling, birdwatching. E-mail: davidsonbj@aol.com., davidsonbj@insightbb.com.

DAVIDSON, CHANDLER, sociologist, educator; b. May 13, 1936; m. Sharon Lavonne Plummer, Nov. 1, 1986. BA, U. Tex., 1961; PhD, Princeton U., 1969. Assoc. prof. sociology Rice U., Houston, 1966—, prof. polit. sci., 1997—2003, prof. emeritus, 2003—, Radoslav Tsanoff prof. pub. affairs, 2000—03, chair dept. sociology, 1979-83, 86-89, 1995—2003, prof. emeritus, 2003—. Co-prin. investigator NSF, 1988-92, Rockefeller Found., 1990. Author: Biracial Politics, 1972, Race and Class in Texas Politics, 1990; editor: Minority Vote Dilution, 1984, (with Bernard Grofman) Controversies in Minority Voting, 1992, (with Grofman) Quiet Revolution in the South, 1994. Fulbright scholar, 1961-62; Woodrow Wilson fellow, 1963-64, rsch. fellow Nat. Endowment for Humanities, 1976-77; recipient Gustavus Myers Ctr. Human Rights award for outstanding book on human rights, 1993, Ally award Ctr. for the Healing of Racism, 1996, Brown award for superior tchg., Rice U., 1997, 99, 2000, 2002, Brown award for excellence in tchg. Rice U., 1998. Mem. Am. Sociol. Assn., Am. Polit. Sci. Assn. (Fenno prize 1995), Philos. Soc. Tex., Phi Beta Kappa. Office: Rice U Dept Sociology 6100 S Main St Houston TX 77005-1892 E-mail: fcd@rice.edu.

DAVIDSON, CLAYTON LESLIE, chemical engineer; b. Kingsford, Mich., July 21, 1930; s. James William and Fern Una (Shambeau) D.; m. Alice Mae Mitchell, Mar. 15, 1952; children: Richard L., Sonya M., Jeff A. BSChemE, Mich. Tech. U., 1951; postgrad., Ind. U., 1976. Registered profl. engr., Mich. Chem. engr. Dow Corning, Midland, Mich., 1953-58, bldg. supt., 1958-63, prodn. supt. Elizabethtown, Ky., 1963-69; plant mgr. Dow Corning Europe, Seneffe, Belgium, 1969-73, Dow Corning, Carrollton, Ky., 1973-75, tech. mgr. Midland, 1975-80, plant mgr. Campinas, Brazil, 1980-83; mfg. mgr. Dow Corning Interam., Midland, 1983-86; dir. supt. Silinor (Dow Corning JV), Salvador, Brazil, 1986-89; internat. cons. Lucky DC, Seoul, 1989-92. Mfg. cons. Dow Corning, Munich, Chiba, Japan, 1968-73. Cubmaster, scoutmaster Boy Scouts Am., Midland, Brussels, 1955-73; pres. PTA, Midland, 1958-63; vol. Internat. Exec. Svc. Corp., 1992—; bd. dirs. Hendersonville Little Theater, 1995-99; treas. Flat Rock Supporting Players, 2000—. 1st lt. U.S. Army, 1951-53. Decorated Bronze Star, Purple Heart; recipient Citoyan do Honor (Seneffe), Belgium, 1972, Native Son award Iron Mountain Rotary, 1991. Mem. AIChe, Dow Corning Retirees Club (v.p. 1991-93), Kiwanis (pres. 1981-82,bd. dirs. 2000—). Republican. Methodist. Avocations: ancient cultures, theatre, wine. Home: 111 Continental Dr Flat Rock NC 28731-8521

DAVIDSON, COLIN HENRY, architect, educator; b. Exeter, Eng., Mar. 4, 1928; emigrated to Can., 1968, naturalized, 1975. s. Douglas Nangle and Dulcie Rose (Winter) D.; m. Lucienne Fiant, Jan. 18, 1956; children: Dominique, Philip. Diploma architecture, Brussels Royal Acad., 1951; M.Arch., M.I.T., 1955. Archtl. asst. Luccichenti/Monaco, Rome, 1951-54; asst. architect Architects' Collaborative, Cambridge, Mass., 1954-55, London County Council, 1956-60; pres. C.H. Davidson Cons., London, 1960-68; prof. architecture U. Montreal, 1968—; dean Faculty Environ. Design, 1976-85, ACSA disting. prof., 1997—. Founder Indsl. Forum Rsch. Group, 1969; founder, pres. IF Rsch. Corp.; exec. dir. Cibat-Montreal Internat. Bldg. Ctr.; pres., Organisation Canadienne pour la jeunesse ev le développement. Prin. works include Cosmos and SB2 industrialized bldg. sys.; author numerous works in field of info. sci. in bldg. including 4 thesauri in bldg. sci. and tech., bldg. procurement, tech. transfer, and post-disaster reconstruction. Mem. Internat. Coun. Rsch. and Innovation in Bldg. and Constrn.-CIB, Order of Archs. Que. Office: U Montreal PO Box 6128 Montreal QC Canada H3C 3J7 E-mail: dav0528@allstream.net. *I have constantly been torn by the dilemma of the Architect: man-of-the-arts or man-of-science. Having opted for the latter (perhaps out of fear of the former), I find I must work in a scientific near-vacuum. For this reason, I dedicate my life to problems of research and its application, to the transfer of information in the building process.*

DAVIDSON, CYNTHIA ANN, writer, English language educator; b. San Diego, June 13, 1960; d. Donald Alan and Rosemary Lorraine (Drehobl) Poe. BA in English, Northeastern Ill. U., 1983, MA in Lit., 1989; PhD in English, U. Ill., Chgo., 1997. Libr. tech. asst. Northeastern Ill. U., Chgo., 1983-87, univ. tchg. asst., 1987-89; adj. English faculty Triton Coll., River Forest, Ill., 1989-90; coll. prep. instr. Harold Washington Coll., Chgo., 1990-91; univ. tchg. asst. U. Ill., Chgo., 1991-97, lectr. English, 1997-98; lectr. writing program SUNY, Stony Brook, 1998—, electronic classroom dir. of writing program, 2001—. Mem. young scholars' com. Ill. Humanities Coun., Chgo., 1994; participant poetry readings Café Voltaire Emerging Artists Project, Chgo., 1995, Caffé Trevi for Voices of Italian Am., Chgo., 1995. Author: (book) Athena's Mother; contbr. essays and articles to sci. fiction and poetry collections; editor, pub.: (electronic jour.) Rio: A Jour. of the Arts, 1997—; contbr. Contemporary Women Poets, 1998, Dictionary of Literary Biography. Talent scholar in creative writing Northeastern U., 1979-81; Presdl. grantee for innovative tchg., 1999-2000 Mem.: ACW, NCTE, MLA, Associated Writing Programs. Home: 104 Hoyt Ln Port Jefferson NY 11777-1319 E-mail: cdavidson@ms.cc.sunyb.edu.

DAVIDSON, DAN EUGENE, Russian language and area scholar, academic administrator; b. Wichita, Kans., Sept. 18, 1944; s. Clerin D. and Fay E. (Scott) D.; m. Maria D. Lekic, Apr. 20, 1976; children: Michael Scott, Paul Eugene. BA, U. Kans., 1966; MA, Harvard U., 1971, PhD, 1972; DSc (hon.), Russian Acad. Scis., 1995, Almaty State U., Kazakhstan, 1996, U. World Langs., Uzbekistan, 1997. Asst. prof., then assoc. prof. Amherst (Mass.) Coll., 1971-76; from assoc. prof. to prof. Russian Bryn Mawr (Pa.) Coll., 1976—; exec. dir. Am. Coun. Tchrs. of Russian, Washington, 1980—; pres. Am. Couns. for Internat. Edn. ACTR/ACCELS, 1998—. Adj. faculty U. Pa., Columbia U., Harvard U., 1975; cons. UN, N.Y.C., 1987, 88, 91, U.S. Dept. Edn., NEH, Washington; co-chair Internat. Task Force on Ednl. Reform in Russia, Ukraine, Belarus, Kyrgyzstan, Kazakhstan, 1992-94 (Soros Founds.); chmn. Alliance for Internat. Ednl. and Cultural Exch., 1997-99; chmn. U.S.-Uzbekistan Coun., 1997-99; pres. Am. Couns. Internat. Edn., 1998—. Series editor: Soviet-American Textbook Series of Russian, 1974—; author, co-author, editor univ. and high sch.-level textbooks on English and Russian; editor, co-editor scholarly collections, jours.; contbr. articles to scholarly publs. Bd. dirs. numerous non-profit ednl. orgns.; mem. leadership com. co-chmn. ann. fund and major gifts, Barrie Sch., 1995-96, trustee, 1997-2000; mem. Fair Share Campaign Sidwell Friends Sch., 1992-97. Recipient Pushkin medal, 1982, Order Internat. Friendship, USSR, 1990; inducted into Russian Acad. Edn., 1995; recipient Disting. Svc. to Profession award, Am. Assn. Tchrs. Slavic Langs., 1995, Disting. Svc. award Assn. Depts. Fgn. Langs./MLA, 1997; hon. fellow Woodrow Wilson Found., 1966. Mem. MLA, Am. Assn. Advancement Slavic Studies, Am. Coun. Tchrs. of Russian (pres. 1975-79), Internat. Assn. Tchrs. Russian Lang. and Lit. (v.p. 1975-80, 91—), Harvard Club, Phi Beta Kappa, Delta Phi Alpha. Democrat. Episcopalian. Avocations: travel, music, swimming. Office: Am Couns Ste 700 1776 Massachusetts Ave NW Washington DC 20036-1904 E-mail: ceo@americancouncils.org.

DAVIDSON, DANIEL IRA, lawyer; b. Bklyn., Sept. 19, 1936; s. Mitchell and Minnie (Needleman) D.; m. Susan Bettina Thomas, Mar. 13, 1966; 1 child, Jill. AB, Columbia Coll., 1957; JD, Columbia U., 1959. Bar: N.Y. 1959, U.S. Ct.Appeals (2d cir.), 1960, U.S. Ct. Appeals (D.C. cir.), 1970, D.C., 1972, U.S. Ct. Appeals (9th cir.), 1975, U.S. Ct. Appeals (5th cir.), 1980, U.S. Ct. Appeals (10th and 11th cirs.), 1981, U.S. Supreme Ct., 1982. Editor Columbia Law Rev., 1958-59; law clk. to Judges Harold R. Medina and Learned Hand U.S. Ct. Appeals 2d Cir., 1960; assoc. Cravath, Swaine & Moore, N.Y.C., 1961-65; spl. asst. to asst. sec. state East Asia and Pacific Affairs, Washington, 1965-67; spl. asst. to ambassador U.S. Dept. State, Washington, 1967-68; U.S. del. to Paris Peace Talks on Vietnam Paris, 1968-69; mem. staff Nat. Security Coun., Washington, 1969; assoc. Wilmer, Cutler & Pickering, Washington, 1969-70; exec. asst. to W. Averell Harriman Washington, 1971-72; assoc. Prather, Levenberg, Seeger, Doolittle, Farmer & Ewing, Washington, 1972-73, Spiegel & McDiarmid, Washington, 1973-74, ptnr., 1974—. Mem. Com. on Internat. Affairs Dem. Policy Coun., Washington, 1971-72; cons. U.S. Dept. State, Washington, 1978-79, pub. mem. fgn. svc. selection bd., 1995; mem. Coun. on Fgn. Rels.; lectr. in polit. sci. CUNY, 1960. Editor: Columbia Law Review; Contbr. articles and book revs to The Economist, NY Times, LA Times, Wash. Post, London Fin. Times, The Atlantic, others. 1st lt. USAR, 1960-66. Fellow Salzburg Seminar in Am. Studies, 1959. Mem. Cosmos Club, Phi Beta Kappa. Jewish. Home: 2900 Brandywine St NW Washington DC 20008-2138 Office: Spiegel & McDiarmid 1333 New Hampshire Ave NW Washington DC 20036 E-mail: daniel.davidson@spiegelmcd.com.

DAVIDSON, DANIEL MORTON, lawyer; b. Lynbrook, N.Y., July 9, 1950; BA summa cum laude, Williams Coll., 1972; JD magna cum laude, Harvard U., 1975. Bar: D.C. 1975, Calif. 1977, U.S. Tax Ct. 1979, U.S. Supreme Ct. 1992. Law clk. Mass. Supreme Ct., 1975-76; ptnr. Sidley & Austin, Washington, 1985-98, Hogan & Hartson, L.L.P., Washington, 1998—. Contbr. articles to profl. jours. Mem. ABA, D.C. Bar Assn., State Bar Calif., Phi Beta Kappa. Office: Hogan & Hartson LLP 555 13th St NW Ste 900W Washington DC 20004-1109 E-mail: dmdavidson@hhlaw.com.

DAVIDSON, DAVID EDGAR, lawyer; b. Louisville, Aug. 24, 1954; s. William R and Bernice Cline (Ashton) D.; m. Sally Anne Marguet, Dec. 27, 1975; children: Katherine Esther, Joseph William. BA, U. Louisville, 1976; JD, U. Cin., 1980. Bar: Ky. 1980, Ohio 1981, U.S. Dist. Ct. (ea. dist.) Ky. 1981, U.S. Dist. Ct. (so. dist.) Ohio 1985, U.S. Ct. Appeals (6th cir.) 1981, U.S. Supreme Ct. 1985. Assoc. Cobb and Oldfield, Covington, Ky., 1980-85, ptnr., 1986—2003, Oldfield Davidson Rieger PLLC, Covington, Ky., 2003—. Mem. adv. bd. Welcome House No. Ky., 1995—2002, exec. com., 1995—, chmn. bd. dirs., 2000—01; reader Radio Reading Svcs., Cin., 1982—99; trustee Covington Ladies Home, 1994—97; vestry mem. Trinity Episcopal Ch., Covington, 1988—95, 1997—99, 2003—, sr. warden, 1985—87, 1990—91, 1993—95; vice-chancellor Episcopal Diocese Lexington, 1988—2001, chancellor, 2001—; dep. Episcopal Ch. Gen. Convention; bd. dirs. St. Paul's Child Care Ctr., Newport, Ky., 2000—. Mem. Ky. Bar Assn., Ohio Bar Assn., No. Ky. Bar Assn. (CLE com. 1986—, bd. dirs. 1998-2000, pres. 2001-03), Ky. Assn. Criminal Def. Lawyers (bd. dirs.), Potter Stewart Inns of Ct. (so. dist. Ohio), Cin. Bar Assn. Democrat. Episcopalian. Home: 2446 Sheffiled Ct Covington KY 41017-4200 Office: PO Box 1078 213 E 4th St Covington KY 41011-1733 E-mail: ddavidson@cobbandoldfield.com.

DAVIDSON, DAVID SCOTT, architect; b. Great Falls, Mont., Dec. 17, 1925; s. David Adams and Florence Mae (Scott) D.; m. Marjorie Luella Huffman, Sept. 10, 1949; children: Carol M., Marilyn S., Scott L., Bruce F., Craig S. Student, U. Utah, 1943, Pasadena City Coll., 1944; BS in Architecture, Mont. State U., 1950. Registered architect, Mont. Architect in tng. Shanley & Shanley Architects, Great Falls, 1950-52; architect van Teylingen, Knight, van Teylingen, Great Falls, 1952-54; prin. David S. Davidson, Architect, Great Falls, 1954-56; ptnr. Davidson & Kuhr Architects, Great Falls, 1956-75; pres. Davidson & Kuhr Architects, P.C., Great Falls, 1975—. Dir., pres. Great Falls Arts Assn., 1980-83; dir., pres. Mont. Arts Inst., 1981—; mem. state constrn. adv. council State of Mont., 1983-84; dir., v.p. Paris Gibson Square, Great Falls, 1982—. Mem. Great Falls Zoning Bd., 1972-75; mem. rehab. com. Great Falls Housing Task Force, 1975-78; chmn. architecture div. United Way, 1975-78; dir. Great Falls Symphony Assn., 1992-93. Served with U.S. Army, 1943-46. Recipient 1st honor Mont. chpt. AIA, 1973, 75; recipient honor award in architecture Mont. chpt. AIA, 1973, 74, 78, 83, merit in architecture Mont. chpt. AIA, 1965, 2 awards U.S. Dept. Energy, 1986, Interior Design award Arch. Record, 1976, Internat. Union Bricklayers and Allied Crafts award, 1986, 87, 92. Fellow AIA (chpt. pres. 1965-66, dir. 1962-66), Great Falls Soc. Architects (pres. 1958-59), Jr. C. of C. (dir. 1956-60) Home: 1212 Buena Dr Great Falls MT 59404-3750 Office: Davidson and Kuhr Archs PC 401 Division Rd Great Falls MT 59404-1409

DAVIDSON, DENISE ZARA, historian, educator; b. N.Y.C., Jan. 9, 1967; d. Richard Charles and Marguerite Marie Davidson; m. Georges Alameddine, Nov. 17, 2000. BA, Rutgers U., 1989; MA, U. Md., 1992; PhD, U. Pa., 1997. Lectr. U. Pa., Phila., 1997-98; vis. asst. prof. St. Lawrence U., Canton, N.Y., 1998-99; asst. prof. Ga. State U., Atlanta, 1999—. Mem. Am. Hist. Assn., French Hist. Studies, Soc. 18th Century Studies, We. Soc. French History, Consortium on Revolutionary Europe (bd. dirs.). Office: Ga State Univ History Dept Atlanta GA 30303

DAVIDSON, DENNIS MICHAEL, preventive cardiologist; b. Detroit, May 30, 1939; s. Ralph Cornell and Amy Ernstine (Ray) D. BS, U.S. Naval Acad., 1960; MD, U. Mich., 1971; MA, U. Calif., Irvine, 1987, PhD in Health Psychology, 1995; MDiv, Grad. Theol. Union, 1992. Ordained to ministry Unitarian Universalist Ch., 1992. Commd. ensign USN, 1960, advanced through grades to capt., 1991; asst. prof. naval sci. U. So. Calif., L.A., 1964-66; exec. officer Naval Support Activity, Quinhon, Vietnam, 1966; med. resident USN Hosp., San Diego, 1971-74; med. dir., refugee camp Marine Corps Base, Camp Pendleton, Calif., 1975; staff internist USN, Camp Pendleton, 1974-77; cardiology fellow Stanford (Calif.) U., 1977-79, asst. prof. medicine, 1979-81; dir. preventive cardiology UCLA, 1981-83, U. Calif., Irvine, 1983-92, assoc. prof. medicine San Francisco, 1992-95; dir. cardiology clinic San Francisco Gen. Hosp., 1992-95; vis. scholar Harvard U. Divinity Sch., 1995-97; clin. prof. medicine U. Calif., Irvine, 1998—. Author: Preventive Cardiology, 1991. Pres. Unitarian Universalist Peace Fellowship, 1995—. Recipient Preventive Cardiology Acad. award NIH, 1984, Clin. Cardiology Teaching award Am. Heart Assn., 1986. Fellow Am. Heart Assn. Epidemiology Coun.; mem. Soc. for Preventive Cardiology (pres. 1989-90).

DAVIDSON, DONALD WILLIAM, advertising executive; b. Toronto, May 18, 1938; s. John Harvie and Harriet Gertrude Davidson; m. Olive Margaret Somerville, July 28, 1962; children: Scott, Susan. Student, U. Toronto, York U. Account exec. E.L. Ruddy, Toronto, 1957-68, Foster & Kleiser, Detroit, 1968-70; v.p. Outdoor Advt. Sales, 1971-72, 1972-73, v.p. mktg. group, 1973-75; v.p. nat. sales Claude Neon Ltd., Toronto, 1975-77, exec. v.p., 1977-79; pres. Mediacom Inc., Toronto, 1979-80, chmn., pres., 1980-84; exec. v.p., COO, Gannett Outdoor, N.Y.C., 1984-86, pres., CEO, 1986-96; pres. Trading Bay Media, 1996—; ptnr., pres. DCR Media Inc.; chmn. 3 Media Inc. Past vice chmn. Traffic Audit Bur. Trustee Madison Sq. Boys and Girls Club. Mem. The Advt. Coun. (bd. dirs.), Lambton Golf and Country Club, Bigwin Golf Club. Home: 40 Las Brisas Way Naples FL 34108 Office: 237 Park Ave Fl 21 New York NY 10017-3140

DAVIDSON, DONETTA, state official; County clk. and recorder Bent County, Colo., 1978-86; dir. of elections State of Colo., 1986-94; county clerk and recorder Arapahoe County, Colo., 1994-99; sec. of state State of Colo., 1999—. Republican. Office: Office of Sec of State Denver Post Bldg 1560 Broadway Ste 200 Denver CO 80202-5169 Fax: 303-869-4864. E-mail: sos.admin1@sos.state.co.us.

DAVIDSON, ERIC HARRIS, molecular and developmental biologist, educator; b. NYC, Apr. 13, 1937; s. Morris and Anne D. BA, U. Pa., 1958; PhD, Rockefeller U., 1963. Research asso. Rockefeller U., 1963-65, asst. prof., 1965-71; asso. prof. devel. molecular biology Calif. Inst. Tech., Pasadena, Calif., 1971-74, prof., 1974—, Norman Chandler prof. cell biology, 1981—. Author: Gene Activity in Early Development, 3d edit, 1986, Genomic Regulatory Systems, 2001. NIH grantee, 1965— ; NSF grantee, 1972— Mem. Nat. Acad. Scis. Achievements include research, numerous publs. on DNA sequence orgn., gene expression during embryonic devel., gene regulation, evolutionary mechanisms, gene networks. Office: Calif Inst Tech Div Biology Mail Code 156 29 Pasadena CA 91125-0001

DAVIDSON, ERNEST ROY, chemist, educator; b. Terre Haute, Ind., Oct. 12, 1936; s. Roy Emmette and Opal Ruth (Hugunin) D.; m. Reba Faye Minnich, Jan. 27, 1956; children: Michael Collins, John Philip, Mark Ernest, Martha Ruth. BSc, Rose-Hulman Inst. Tech., 1958, DEng (hon.), 1998; PhD, Ind. U., 1961; PhD (hon.), Uppsala U., 2000. NSF Postdoctoral fellow U. Wis.-Madison, 1961-62; asst. prof. chemistry U. Wash., 1962-65, assoc. prof., 1965-68, prof., 1968-84, Ind. U., Bloomington, 1984-86, disting. prof., 1986—2002, chmn. chem. dept., 1999—. Disting. vis. prof. Ohio State U., 1974-75; vis. prof. IMS, Japan, 1984, Technion, Israel, 1985; Boys-Rahman lectr. Royal Soc. Chemistry, 2002. Editor: Jour. Computational Physics, 1975-98, Internat. Jour. Quantum Chemistry, 1975—, Jour. Chem. Physics, 1976-78, 98—, Chem. Physics Letters, 1977-84, Jour. Am. Chem. Soc., 1978-83, Jour. Phys. Chemistry, 1982-90, Accounts of Chem. Rsch., 1984-92, Theoretica Chimica Acta, 1985-98, Chem. Revs., 1986—; contbr. numerous articles on density matrices and quantum theory of molecular structure to profl. jours. Union Carbide fellow Rose-Hulman Inst. Tech., 1958; NSF fellow Ind. U., 1961; recipient Hirschfelder prize in theoretical chemistry, 1997-98, Schrodinger medal, 2001, Nat. medal of sci., 2002; Sloan fellow, 1967-68; Guggenheim fellow, 1974-75; laureate l'Academie Internationale des Sciences Moleculaires Quantiques, 1971. Fellow Am. Phys. Soc., Sigma Xi; mem. NAS, Am. Chem. Soc. (Computers in Chemistry award 1992, Theoretical Chemistry award 2000), Am. Acad. Arts and Scis., Ind. Acad. Sci. (Chemist of Yr. award 1999), Phi Lambda Upsilon, Tau Beta Pi. Home: 1013 Woodbine Ct Bloomington IN 47401-5445 Office: Ind U Chemistry Dept 800 E Kirkwood Ave Bloomington IN 47405-7102

DAVIDSON, EUGENE ABRAHAM, biochemist, university administrator; b. N.Y.C., May 27, 1930; s. Jack and Sophie Miriam (Deutsch) D. BS, UCLA, 1950; PhD, Columbia U., 1955. Postdoctoral fellow, instr. U. Mich., 1955-58; asst. prof. biochemistry Duke U., 1958-62, assoc. prof., 1962-65, prof., 1965-67; prof., chmn. dept. biol. chemistry M.S. Hershey Med. Center, Pa. State U., 1967-87, assoc. dean for edn., 1975-87; prof., chmn. dept. biochemistry and molecular biology Georgetown U., Washington, 1988—. Mem. Nat. Bd. Med. Examiners, Part I; cons. in field. Author: Carbohydrate Chemistry, 1967; contbr. numerous articles to profl. publs.; Editorial reviewer for numerous jours. Guggenheim fellow, 1965-66; NIH grantee, 1958— Mem. AAAS, Am. Soc. Biol. Chemists, Assn. Med. Sch. Depts. Biochemistry, Biochem. Soc., Am. Assn. Cancer Research, Soc. Complex Carbohydrates, Glycoconjugate Soc. (pres. 1985-87), Sigma Xi. Home: 5506 Nebraska Ave NW Washington DC 20015-1256 Office: Georgetown U Dept Biochem/Molecular Biology Washington DC 20007

DAVIDSON, EZRA C., JR., physician, educator; b. Water Valley, Miss., Oct. 21, 1933; s. Ezra Cap and Theresa Hattie (Woods) Davidson; children: Pamela, Gwendolyn, Marc, Ezra K. BS cum laude, Morehouse Coll., 1954; MD, Meharry Med. Coll., 1958. Diplomate Am. Bd. Ob-Gyn. (examiner 1973-). Intern San Diego County Gen. Hosp., 1958—59; resident in ob-gyn. Harlem Hosp., N.Y.C., 1963—66, asst. attending ob-gyn, obstet. coordinator maternal and infant care clinics, 1967—68; dir. departmental research, assoc. attending, acting chmn. ob-gyn, co-dir. coagulation research lab. Roosevelt Hosp., N.Y.C., 1968—70; fellow blood coagulation, asst. ob-gyn Columbia U. Coll. Physicians and Surgeons, N.Y.C., 1966—67, instr. dept. ob-gyn, 1967—69, asst. clin. prof., 1970; cons. ob-gyn Office Health Affairs, OEO, Washington, 1970—72; prof. Charles R. Drew U. of Medicine and Sci., L.A., 1971—, acad. v.p., 1982—87, chmn. dept. ob.-gyn., 1971—96, assoc. dean primary care, 1997—; prof. U. So. Calif., Los Angeles, 1971—80, UCLA, 1980—. Chief svc. dept. ob-gyn. King/Drew Med. Ctr., L.A., 1971—96; attending physician dept. ob-gyn. L.A. County-U. So. Calif. Med. Ctr., 1971—80; mem. nat. med. adv. com. nat. found. March of Dimes, 1972—76; bd. cons. Internat. Childbirth Edn. Assn., 1973—81; mem. sec.'s adv. com. population affairs HEW, 1974—77, chmn. svcs. task force, 1975—77; chmn. bd. dirs. L.A. Regional Family Planning Coun., 1975—77; bd. dirs. Nat. Alliance Sch. Age Parents, 1975—79; mem. corp. bd. Blue Shield, Calif., 1989—; chair DHHS Sec.'s Adv. Com. on Infant Mortality, 1990—93; active FDA, 1990—96, chmn. fertility and maternal health drugs adv. com., 1992—96; mem. adv. com. to the dir. NIH, 1995—98, mem. dirs. adv. panel on clin. rsch., 1995—98; mem. roundtable on health care quality Inst. on Medicine, 1995—98; mem. coun. grad. med. edn. HHS, 1997—2000; bd. dirs., chair med. policy com. Blue Shield of Calif., 1998—. Bd. dirs. The Calif. Wellness Found., 1995—, chmn., 1996—98; bd. dirs. Children's Bur. So. Calif., 1999—, v.p., 1995—99, pres., 1999—2002; bd. dirs. Jacobs Inst. of Womens Health, 1999—. Served with USAF, 1959—63. Fellow Johnson Found. Health Policy, Inst. Medicine, NAS, 1979—80. Fellow: L.A. Ob-Gyn. Soc. (pres. 1982—83), Royal Coll. Ob-Gyn., Am. Coll. Ob-Gyn. (nat. sec. 1983—89, pres.-elect 1989—90, pres. 1990—91), ACS; mem.: Assn. of Acad. Minority Physicians (pres. 2002—03), Golden State Med. Assn. (pres. 1989—90), Assn. Profs. Ob-Gyn. (pres. 1989—90), Nat. Med. Assn. (chmn. nat. sect. ob-gyn. 1975—77, mem. sci. coun. 1979—88, bd. trustee 1989—95, chmn. bd. trustees 1992—95), Ob-Gyn. Assembly So. Calif. (chmn. 1989—90), Pacific Coast Ob-Gyn. Soc., N.Am. Soc. Pediatric and Adolescent Gynecology (pres.-elect 1993—94, pres. 1994—95), Am. Ob Gyn. Soc. Office: 12021 Wilmington Ave Los Angeles CA 90059-3019

DAVIDSON, FRANK GASSAWAY, III, lawyer; b. Lynchburg, Va., Feb. 25, 1945; s. Frank Gassaway and Katherine (Graves) G.; children: Christian O., Frank G. BA, Hampden-Sydney Coll., 1969; JD, Washington and Lee U., 1971; LLM, NYU, 1975. Bar: Va. 1975. With trust dept. Morgan Guaranty Trust Co., N.Y.C., 1971-72; trust officer The Fiduciary Trust Co., N.Y.C., 1973-75; pres. Davidson, Sakolosky & Moseley PC, Lynchburg, 1975—. Bd. dirs. Schewel Furniture Co., Inc.; past pres. Central Va. Speech, Hearing Ctr., Inc. Bd. dirs. Greater Lynchburg Habitat for Humaity, Inc.; past chmn. Lynchburg Fine Arts Ctr.; chmn. United Way Annual Fund, 1997. With USMC, 1968-74. Mem. ABA, Va. Bar Assn., Lynchburg Bar Assn., Oakwood Country Club (Lynchburg). Episcopalian. Home: 8340 Wards Rd Rustburg VA 24588-4283 Office: Davidson Sakolosky Moseley PO Box 798 Lynchburg VA 24505-0798 E-mail: davidsonlll@aol.com.

DAVIDSON, FRANK PAUL, macroengineer, lawyer; b. N.Y.C., May 20, 1918; s. Maurice Philip and Blanche (Reinheimer) D.; m. Izaline Marguerite Doll, May 19, 1951; children: Roger Conrad, Nicholas Henry, Charles Geoffrey. *Frank Davidson's father, Maurice P. Davidson, was founder and chairman of the City Fusion Party, which elected, with the support of the Republican Party, Fiorello H. LaGuardia as the reform Mayor of New York in the 1930's. As the Mayor's appointed Commissioner of Water Supply, Gas, and Electricity, Maurice P. Davidson signed the papers authorizing what remains the longest bored tunnel in the world. It carries fresh water to Manhattan from the Delaware Water Gap.* BS, Harvard U., 1939, JD, 1948; DHL (hon.), Hawthorne Coll., 1987; D in Engrng. and Diplomacy (hon.), Roger Williams U., 2003. Bar: NY 1953, U.S. Dist. Ct. (so. dist.) NY 1953. Dir. mil. affairs, gen. counsel Houston C. of C., 1948-50; contract analyst Am. Embassy, Paris, 1950-53; assoc. Carb, Luria, Glassner & Cook, N.Y.C., 1953-54; pvt. practice law N.Y.C., 1955-70; founding pres., counsel, bd. dirs. The Inst. for the Future, 1967-70; rsch. assoc. MIT, Cambridge, Mass., 1970-96, also chmn. system dynamics steering com. Sloan Sch. Mgmt., coord. macro-engring. Sch. Engring. Pres., gen. counsel Tech. Studies Inc., N.Y.C., 1957-96, vice chmn. Inst. for Ednl. Svcs., Bedford, Mass., 1980-84, spl. lectr. Société des Ingénieurs et Scientifiques de France, 1991, NAS del. to Renewable Resources Workshop, Katmandu, Nepal, 1981, governing bd. Channel Tunnel Study Group, 1957-85, co-founder Channel Tunnel Study Group, London, Paris, 1957, apptd. to NASA Exploration Task Force, Washington, 1989, mem. internat. sci. and tech. com. Ocean Cities Symposium, Monaco, 1995. *Frank Davidson was awarded the Bronze Star Medal by SHAEF Headquarters. A full account of Frank Davidson's role in the successful 1957 re-launching of the project for construction of a railway tunnel between the United Kingdom and France was published in "The Chunnel" by Drew Fetherston, in 1997. On May 20, 1998, on the occasion of Davidson's 80th birthday, a volume of "Essays in Honor of Frank Davidson" entitled MACRO-ENGINEERING and the EARTH was published in 1998 and edited by Professor Ernst G. Frankel of MIT Ocean Engineering Department and by Uwe Kitzinger, C.B.E., former President of Templeton College, Oxford U.* Author: Macro: A Clear Vision of How Science and Technology Will Shape Our Future, 1983, Macro: Big is Beautiful, 1986; editor: series of AAAS books on macroengring., Tunneling and Underground Transport, 1987; co-editor: Macro-Engineering, Global Infrastructure Solutions, 1992, Solar Power Satellites, 1993, 2nd edit., 1998, A Festschrift, Essays in Honor of Frank Davidson, Macro-Engineering and The Earth: World Projects for the Year 2000 and Beyond, 1998; mem. editl. bd. Interdisciplinary Sci. Revs., 1985—; mem. adv. bd. Tech. in Soc., 1979—, Mountain R&D, 1981-2000, Project Appraisal, 1986-98. Bd. dirs. Internat. Mountain Soc., Boulder, Colo., 1981-2000, Assn. Prospective 2100, Paris, 1997; trustee Norwich (Vt.) Ctr., 1980-83, mem. steering com. Am. Trails Network, 1986-88, bd. dirs. Am. Trails Washington, 1988-90. RCAC, 1941-46, ETO; Troop Leader 10th Cdn., Armoured Rgt. (Fort Garry Horse), Intelligence Officer and Squadron Leader, GSO III (Intelligence) Second Armoured Brigade Group, maj. Tex. State Guard; apptd. to Senate Ft. Garry Horse, 1995. Decorated chevalier Legion of Honor (France), 1999, Bronze Star medal; recipient Key to City Osaka, Japan, 1987, Twice the Citizen award Royal Mil. Inst., Manitoba, Can., 1999, William James award Rensselaerville Inst., 2001; elected Mem. Honoraire, Pres. d'Honneur Assn. Louis Armand, Paris, 1996-99; Lewis Mumford Fellow Rensselaerville Inst., 1982. Mem. ABA, Internat. Assn. Macro-Engring. Socs. (bd. dirs. 1987—, hon.chmn. 1997-2000), Am. Soc. Macro-Engring. (bd. dirs. 1982—, vice chancellor 1983-97, pres. 1997-98, chmn. 1998), Assn. Bar of City of N.Y. (internat. law com. 1959-62), Major Projects Assn. (mem. overseas adv. com. U.K. 1995—), Knickerbocker (N.Y.C.) Club, St. Botolph (Boston) Club, MIT Quarter Century Club. Home: 151 Main St Concord MA 01742-2436

DAVIDSON, GEORGE A., JR., retired utility company executive; b. Pitts., July 28, 1938; BS, U. of Pitts., 1960. Chmn., chief exec. officer, dir. Dominion Resources, Pitts., to 2000. Office: Dominion Resources CNG Tower 625 Liberty Ave Ste 22 Pittsburgh PA 15222-3111

DAVIDSON, GEORGE ALLAN, lawyer; b. N.Y.C., Apr. 6, 1942; s. George Roger and Jean Allan (McKaig) D.; m. Annette L. Richter, Sept. 4, 1965; children: Emily, Charlotte. AB, Brown U., 1964; LLB, Columbia U., 1967. Bar: N.Y. 1967, U.S. Dist. Ct. (so. and ea. dists.) N.Y. 1969, U.S. Ct. Appeals (2d cir.) 1970, U.S. Supreme Ct. 1974, U.S. Tax Ct. 1974, U.S. Ct. Appeals (D.C. cir.) 1976, U.S. Dist. Ct. (no. dist.) Calif. 1980, U.S. Ct. Appeals (9th cir.) 1981, U.S. Ct. Appeals (5th cir.) 1982, U.S. Dist. Ct. (no. dist.) N.Y. 1982, U.S. Ct. Appeals (11th cir.) 1983, U.S. Ct. Appeals (1st cir.) 1986, U.S. Ct. Appeals (7th cir.) 1992. Law clk., 1967-68; assoc. Hughes Hubbard & Reed, N.Y.C., 1968-74, ptnr., 1974—; dir. P.R. Legal Def. and Edn. Fund, Inc., 1980-84. Dir. Legal Aid Soc., 1979-92, pres. 1987-89, N.Y. Lawyers for Pub. Interest, Inc., 1984-86, Columbia Law Sch. Alumni Assn., 1987-91, Practicing Attys. for Law Students, 1989—, VIP Cmty. Svcs., 1994—, Greenwich House, Inc., 2002—. Contbr. writings to legal publs. Fellow Am. Coll. Trial Lawyers; mem. ABA, Internat. Bar Assn., Fed. Bar Coun., Am. Law Inst., N.Y. Sci. Policy Assn., N.Y. State Bar Assn., Assn. Bar City N.Y., Nat. Assn. Coll. and Univ. Attys., Union Internationale des Avocats, Century Assn. Office: Hughes Hubbard & Reed LLP 1 Battery Park Plz Fl 12 New York NY 10004-1482 E-mail: davidson@hugheshubbard.com.

DAVIDSON, GLEN HARRIS, federal judge; b. Pontotoc, Miss., Nov. 20, 1941; s. M. Glen and Lora (Harris) D.; m. Bonnie Payne, Apr. 25, 1973; children: Glen III, Gregory P. BA, U. Miss, 1962, JD, 1965. Bar: Miss. 1965, U.S. Ct. Appeals (5th cir.) 1965, U.S. Supreme Ct. 1971. Asst. dist. atty. First Jud. Dist., Tupelo, Miss., 1969-74, dist. atty., 1975; U.S. atty. U.S. Dist. Ct. (no. dist.) Miss., Oxford, 1981-85; U.S. district judge U.S. Ct. House, Aberdeen, Miss., 1985—; chief judge U.S. Dist. Ct. (no. dist.) Miss., 2000—. Atty. Lee County Sch. Bd., Miss., 1974-81. Bd. dirs. Community Devel. Found., Tupelo, 1976-81; exec. bd. Yocona Council Boy Scouts Am., 1972—. Maj. USAF, 1966-69. Mem. Fed. Bar Assn. (v.p. 1984), Miss. Bar Found., Lee County Bar Assn. (pres. 1974), Assn. Trial Lawyers Am., Miss. Prosecutors Assn., Kiwanis (pres. Tupelo 1978). Presbyterian. Office: US Dist Ct PO Box 767 Aberdeen MS 39730-0767 E-mail: Davidson@msnd.uscourts.gov.

DAVIDSON, GORDON BYRON, lawyer; b. Louisville, June 24, 1926; s. Paul Byron and Elizabeth (Franz) D.; m. Geraldine B. Geiger, Dec. 21, 1948; children: Sally Burgess, Stuart Gordon. AB, Centre Coll., 1949; JD, U. Louisville, 1951; LL.M., Yale U., 1952. Law clk. Supreme Ct. U.S., 1954; of counsel Wyatt, Tarrant & Combs, Louisville, 1955-92, mng. ptnr., 1978-92. Bd. dirs. DNP Select Income, Inc., Warner L. Jones Farm, Inc., Norton Healthcare, Inc., Warben, Inc. Pres. Louisville Ctrl. Area, Inc., 1971-73; chmn. River City Mall Com., 1973-74, Louisville Devel. Com., Ky. Ctr. for Arts, 1980-95, Louisville Area C. of C., 1986, trustee; bd. dirs., chmn. Norton Childrens Hosps., 1973-75, Louisville Fund for Arts, 1987-93; trustee emeritus Centre Coll. Recipient Louisville Citizen of Yr. award, 1973-74, Mayor's Fleur de Lis award, 1974, Louisville Man of Yr. award, 1981, Outstanding Lawyer of Ky. award, 1984, Disting. Alumnus award U. Louisville Law Sch., 1982, Disting. Citizen award City of Louisville, 1987, Man of Vision award, 1991, Ky. Commonwealth award, 1995, Caritas Found. award, 1998; named to Louisville Male High Sch. Hall of Fame, 1989. Mem. Harmony Club, Landing Country Club, Jefferson Louisville Country Club, Dennbarr Club, Lawyers Club, Gulf Stream Bath and Tennis Club (Fla.), Gulf Stream Golf Club (Fla.). Democrat. Presbyterian. Home: 435 Lightfoot Rd Louisville KY 40207-1853 also: 1102 Vista Del Mar Dr N Delray Beach FL 33483-7146 Office: Wyatt Tarrant & Combs Citizens Plz Louisville KY 40202-2823

DAVIDSON, HERBERT ALAN, Near Eastern languages and cultures educator; b. Boston, May 25, 1932; s. Louis Nathan and Ettabelle (Baker) D.; m. Kinneret Bernstein; children: Rachel and Jessica. BA, Harvard U., 1953, MA, 1955, PhD, 1959. Lectr. Harvard U., Cambridge, Mass., 1960-61; asst. prof. UCLA, 1961-66, assoc. prof., 1966-72, prof., 1972-94, prof. emeritus, 1994—, chmn. dept. near eastern langs. and cultures, 1984-91. Author: The Philosophy of Abraham Shalom, 1964, medieval Hebrew transls. of Averroes' Middle Commentary on the Isagoge and Categories, 1969, English transl., 1969, Proofs for Eternity, Creation, and the Existence of God in Medieval Islamic and Jewish Philosophy, 1987, Alfarabi, Avicenna, and Averroes on Intellect, 1992; contbr. articles and book revs. to profl. jours. Office: UCLA Dept Near Ea Langs and Cultures 405 Hilgard Ave Los Angeles CA 90095-9000

DAVIDSON, HERBERT M., JR., (TIPPEN DAVIDSON), newspaper owner; b. Chgo., Aug. 10, 1925; s. Herbert Marc and Liliane (Refregier) D.; m. Josephine Field, Dec. 27, 1947 (dec. July 1995); children: Marc, Julia. Student, Juilliard Sch., 1942-43, 45-46; Mus.D. (hon.), Stetson U., 1975. Reporter Chgo. Daily News, 1949-50, city editor Daytona Beach (Fla.) News-Jour., 1951-53, mng. editor, 1953-56, gen. mgr., 1957-85, pub., 1985-98, co-editor, 1985—, pres., CEO, 1998—. Pres. Ctrl. Fla. Cultural Endeavors, Inc., Daytona Beach, 1963—; chmn. Fine Arts Coun. of Fla., 1970-75, 81-82; mem. Fla. Alliance for Arts, 1998—; mem. Fla. Arts Coun., 1998-2000; prodr., artistic dir. Seaside Music Theater, Daytona Beach, 1976—. Cpl. U.S. Army, 1942-44, PTO. Named Ambassador of the Arts, State of Fla., Tallahassee, 1982, Hon. mem. London Symphony Orch., 1989, honoree Daytona Beach Community Coll.'s Tippen and Josephine Field Davidson Endowment for the Arts, 1992; hon. officer Civil divsn. Order of the Brit. Empire, 1998. Mem. Am. Soc. Newspaper Editors Avocations: music, theater, handicraft, philately. Home: 1608 N Oleander Ave Daytona Beach FL 32118-3415 Office: Daytona Beach News-Jour 901 6th St Daytona Beach FL 32117-3352 E-mail: tippen@news-jrnl.com.

DAVIDSON, JACK LEROY, academic administrator; b. Indpls., July 14, 1927; s. Lawrence L. and Emma (Jones) D.; m. Ina Stanfill, June 20, 1948; children: William (dec.), Nancy, Evan. BA, Franklin Coll., 1949; MA, Ind. U., 1955, Ed. Adminstrn., 1961, PhD, 1967. Tchr., guidance counselor, coach Mitchell (Ind.) Pub. Schs., 1949-57; elem. prin., supervising prin. Vincennes (Ind.) Pub. Schs., 1957-59; supt. Worthington (Ind.) Pub. Schs., 1959-61, Salem (Ind.) Pub. Schs., 1961-65, Oak Ridge (Tenn.) Pub. Schs., 1965-68, Manatee County (Fla.) Pub. Schs., 1968-70, Austin (Tex.) Pub. Schs., 1970-80, Tyler (Tex.) Public Schs., 1980-91; spl. asst. to pres. U. Tex., Tyler, 1991-96. Vis. prof. U. Tex.; chmn. Tex. Adv. Com. on Ednl. Improvement. Schs.; cons. Tex. Edn. Agy. Author: Effective School Board Meetings, 1970, The Superintendency & Leadership for Effective Schools, 1987; Contbr. articles to ednl. jours. Bd. dirs., pres. Southwest Ednl. Devel. Lab.; charter mem. Tex. Commn. on Inter-Govtl. Rels.; bd. dirs. Austin Jr. Achievement; pres. bd. dirs. Salvation Army. With USNR, 1945-47. Recipient Super Supt. award Tex. PTA, 1982, award of honor Nat. Sch. Pub. Rels. Assn., 1990, Disting. Svc. award AASA, 1992; named one of 100 Top Exec. Educators Exec. Educator mag., 1984, 89. Mem. Am. Assn. Suprs. Curriculum Devel., Am. Assn. Sch. Adminstrs., Tex. Assn. Sch. Adminstrs., Rotary (pres. Tyler club), Phi Delta kappa (outstanding educator award 1992). Methodist (deacon, dir.). Home: 1807 Picadilly Pl Tyler TX 75703-2409 E-mail: davidsonji@cox-internet.com. *The only real profit in life comes from the satisfaction gained in service to others.*

DAVIDSON, JAMES JOSEPH, III, lawyer; b. Lafayette, La., July 27, 1940; s. James Joseph and Virginia Lee (Dunham) D.; m. Kay Cecile Holloway, Aug. 7, 1962; children: Kimberly Kay, James Joseph IV, Lynda Leigh, Virginia Holland. BA, U. SW La., 1963; JD, Tulane U., 1964. Bar: La. 1964, U.S. Dist. Ct. (we. dist.) La. 1965, U.S. Dist. Ct. (ea. dist.) La. 1979, U.S. Dist. Ct. (mid. dist.) La. 1986, U.S. Ct. Appeals (5th cir.) 1972 U.S. Supreme Ct. 1975, U.S. Ct. Appeals (11th cir.) 1981. Ptnr. Davidson, Meaux, Sonnier & McElligott, Lafayette, La., 1964—. Mem. exec. bd. Evangeline Area coun. Boy Scouts Am., 1969-80; trustee U. La. Lafayette Found., 1980—, pres., 1988-91. Fellow Am. Bar Found. (life); mem. ABA (ho. of dels. 2002--), La. State Bar Assn. (del. 1970-96), La. Bar Found., La. State Law Inst. (coun. 2002--), La. Assn. Def. Counsel (dir. 1975-77), Nat. Assn. R.R. Trial Counsel, Am. Bd. Trial Advocates (adv. bd.), Am. Counsel Assn., Internat. Assn. Def. Counsel, Assn. Def. Trial Attys., Assn. Transp. Practitioners. Republican. Baptist. Home: 539 Girard Park Dr Lafayette LA 70503-2601 Office: PO Box 2908 Lafayette LA 70502-2908

DAVIDSON, JAMES MADISON, III, retired engineer, technical manager; b. San Antonio, Feb. 24, 1930; s. James Madison Jr. and Ella Louise (Wehmeyer) D.; m. Geneva Upchurch, Aug. 28, 1949; children: Robert John, William Allen, James Brian. BS, S.W. Tex. State U., 1951. Registered profl. engr., Wash. Engr., sr. engr. GE Co., Richland, Wash., 1951-65; mgr. fast flux test facility, materials and tech. dept. Battelle-Pacific N.W. Lab., Richland, 1965-67, sr. adviser to lab. dir., 1967-72, mgr. office nat. security tech., 1972-89; staff mem. Los Alamos (N.Mex.) Nat. Lab., 1989-90, acting group leader, 1990-91, group leader, 1992-94; sr. advisor nonproliferation and internat. tech., 1994—; ret. Tech. adviser Coordinating Com. on Munitions, Paris, 1987—. Exec. bd. Boy Scouts Am., 1970-75. Recipient Silver Beaver award Boy Scouts Am., 1972. Home: 44 W Wildflower Dr Santa Fe NM 87506-0126

DAVIDSON, JEANNIE, costume designer; b. San Francisco, Mar. 21, 1938; d. Willis H. and Dorothy J. (Starks) Rich; children from previous marriage: David L. Schultz (dec. Jan. 1996), Mark P. Schultz, Seana Davidson, Michael Davidson; m. Bryan N. St. Germain, June 14, 1980. BA, Stanford (Calif.) U., 1961, postgrad., 1965-68. Resident costume designer Oreg. Shakespearean Festival, Ashland, 1969-91; owner, designer Ravenna Fabric Studio, Inc., Medford, Oreg., from 1994. Mfr. custom ch. vestments and hand-dyed wearable art. Designer over 150 prodns. including all 37 of Shakespeare's plays. Recipient numerous awards for excellence in costume design. Mem. U.S. Inst. for Theatre Tech., Phi Beta Kappa. Avocations: fabric design, painting, writing. Deceased.

DAVIDSON, JEFFREY H. lawyer; b. Brookline, Mass., Apr. 7, 1952; s. Jacob and Bernice (Beckerman) D.; m. Cynthia J. Cohen, June 11, 1972; 1 child, Clifford. BA cum laude, Harvard U., 1973, JD cum laude, 1976. Bar: Calif. 1977, U.S. Dist. Ct. (cen. dist.) Calif. 1977, U.S. Dist. Ct. (so. dist.) Calif. 1981, U.S. Ct. Appeals (9th cir.) 1983, U.S. Dist. Ct. (no. dist.) Calif. 1986. Shareholder Stutman, Treister & Glatt, P.C., L.A., 1976—. Fellow Am. Coll. Bankruptcy; mem. ABA (sect. bus. law, bus. bankruptcy com., UCC com.), FBA (bankruptcy sect.), Fin. Lawyers Conf. (bd. govs. 1988-91, 2001—, exec. com. 1990-91), State Bar Calif. (exec. com. bus. law sect. 1987-90, treas. bus. law sect. 1989-90, chmn. UCC com. 1986-87), L.A. County Bar Assn. (chmn. comml. law and bankruptcy sect. 1987-88, exec. com. 1985—, chmn. bankruptcy com. 1984-86, mem. nominating com. for trustees and officers 1988), Phi Beta Kappa. Office: Stutman Treister & Glatt PC 1901 Ave of the Stars 12th Fl Los Angeles CA 90067 E-mail: jdavidson@stutman.com.

DAVIDSON, JO ANN, former state legislator; children: Julie, Jenifer. Mem. Ohio Ho. of Reps., Columbus, 1981—2001, minority whip, speaker, 1995—2001; Interim Dir. Ohio Dept. of Jobs and Family Services, 2001; owner JAD & Assoc. Government Cons. Firm, 2001. Mem. fin., ethics and stds. and rules coms., house speaker, minority leader, mem. joint com. on mental retardation and devel. disabilities. Mem. Reynoldsburg (Ohio) City Coun., 1968-77; former vice chmn. Ohio Turnpike Commn.; trustee Franklin U., U. Findlay, Ohio; mem. Columbus Area Women's Polit. Caucus. Named Legislator of Yr., Nat. Rep. Legislators Assn., 1991; named to Ohio Women's Hall of Fame, 1991. Mem. Oho C. of C. (v.p. spl. programs), Rotary. Republican. Home: 6639 Forrester Way Reynoldsburg OH 43068-4315 Office: 37 W Broad St Ste 970 Columbus OH 43215-0001

DAVIDSON, JOELINE DILLARD, laboratory services administrator; b. Bessemer, Ala., Oct. 4, 1942; d. Joel Alfred Sr. and Laura Christine Smith Dillard; m. John Pratt Davidson. BS in Chemistry, U. Ala., 1963, BMu, 1967; MBA, Ga. State U., 1984. Adminstrv. dir. Lab. Svcs. West Ga. Health Sys., LaGrange, Ga., 1974—. Mem. curriculum devel. com. for med. lab. technicians State of Ga.; adv. com. West Ga. Tech. Inst., 1996—, Ga. State U. Sch. of Med. Tech.; chair adv. com. Columbus State U. Sch. of Allied Health, 1996; mem. tech. adv. com. Auburn U. Sch. of Med. Tech., Montgomery; chmn. clin. lab., blood bank, tissue bank, adv. com. Ga. Dept. Human Resources, 1986—. Negotiated Rulemaking with HCFA Lab. Reimbursement, 1998-99. Advisor work study program Troup County H.S.; advisor Med. Explorer Scouts; tech. adv. com. ARC, 1984; bd. dir. Troup County Valley ARC, 2003—. Mem.: Ga. Hosp. Assn. (manpower task force 2002—03), Am. Soc. Clin. Chemistry, Clin. Lab. Mgmt. Assn., Ga. Soc. Clin. Lab. Sci. (pres. 1987—88), Nat. Accrediting Agy. for Clin. Lab. Scis. (bd. dirs. 1994—2002, pres. 1998—2001, chair masters level feasibility task force), Am. Soc. Clin. Lab. Sci. (bd. dirs. 1988—94, pres. 1992—93). Home: PO Box 1786 Lagrange GA 30241-0038 Office: West Ga Health System 1514 Vernon Rd Lagrange GA 30240-4131 Fax: 706-845-3349. E-mail: davidsonj@mindspring.com.

DAVIDSON, JOHN HENRY, legal educator; b. Washington, Pa., Dec. 9, 1942; s. John H. and Estous (Lee) D.; m. Cathy F. Beard, Oct. 14, 1967; children: Benjamin, Felix. BA, Wake Forest Coll., 1964; JD, U. Pitts., 1967; LLM, George Washington U., 1971. Bar: Pa. 1967, U.S. Dist. Ct. (we. dist.) Pa. 1967, S.D. 1974, U.S. Dist. Ct. S.D., 1972, U.S. Ct. Appeals (8th cir.) 1974. Sole practice, Pitts., 1967-69; staff atty. Neighborhood Legal Services, Pitts., 1969-71; lectr. in law George Washington U., Washington, 1971-72; prof. of law U. S.D., Vermillion, 1972—. Author: (with Delogu) Federal Environmental Regulations, 1989—; co-author, editor: Agricultural Law Treatise, 1981; Agricultural Law Cases, 1984. Mem. ABA (adv. com. forum on rural lawyers), Western Water Policy Rev. Com., Am. Trial Lawyers Assn., Am. Law Inst., Internat. Coun. Environ. Law, Am. Agrl. Law Assn. (bd. dirs. 1979-82), Dakota Plains Legal Services (bd. dirs. 1977—), Rocky Mountain Mineral Law Found. (trustee 1980-90). Democrat. Home: 31275 Saginaw Ave Vermillion SD 57069-6803 Office: U SD 414 E Clark St Vermillion SD 57069-2307 E-mail: jdavidso@usd.edu.

DAVIDSON, JOHN HUNTER, agriculturist; b. Wilmette, Ill., May 16, 1914; s. Joseph and Ruth Louise (Moody) D.; m. Elizabeth Marie Boynton, June 16, 1943; children: Joanne Davidson Hildebrand, Kathryn Davidson Bouwens, Patricia. BS in Horticulture, Mich. State U., 1937, MS in Plant Biochemistry,

1940. Field rschr. agrl. chems. Dow Chem. Co., Midland, Mich., 1936-42, with R&D dept. agrl. products, 1946-72, tech. adviser R&D agrl. products, 1972-80, tech. adviser govt. rels., 1980—86, cons., 1984—. Contbr. articles on plant pathology, horticulture and weed control to profl. jours. Lt. USNR, 1945. Mem. Am. Chem. Soc., Am. Soc. Hort. Sci., Weed Sci. Soc., Am. Pathol. Soc., Exch. Club of Midland, Phi Kappa Phi, Alpha Zeta. Republican. Home: 4319 Andre St Midland MI 48642-3779

DAVIDSON, JOHN KENNETH, SR., sociologist, educator, researcher, writer, consultant; b. Augusta, Ga., Oct. 25, 1939; s. Larcie Charles and Betty (Corley) D.; m. Josephine Frazier, Apr. 11, 1964; children: John Kenneth Jr., Stephen Wood. Student, Augusta Coll., 1956-58; BS in Edn., U. Ga., 1961, MA, 1963; PhD, U. Fla., 1974. Asst. prof. dept. psychology and sociology Armstrong State Coll., Savannah, Ga., 1963-67; asst. prof. sociology Augusta Coll., 1967-74; acting chmn., asst. prof. dept. sociology Ind. U., South Bend, 1974-76; assoc. prof. sociology U. Wis., Eau Claire, Wis., 1976-78, prof., 1978—, chmn. dept. sociology, 1976-80, asst. spl. projects to dean grad. studies and univ. rsch., 1987-91, coord. family studies, 1990—. Cons. family life edn.; rsch. cons. dept. ob-gyn. Med. Coll. Ga., Augusta, 1969-74, pediatrics, 1972-73, assoc. dir. health care project, 1971-73, rsch. instr., 1971, rsch. assoc., 1972-73, rsch. cons. dept. community dentistry, 1974-79; program coord. Community Devel. in Process Phase II and III, Title I Higher Edn. Act of, 1965, 1970; sociology and anthropology com. Univ. System Ga., 1970-74, chmn. curriculum sub-com., 1970-72; dir. Sex Edn., The Pub. Schs. and You project Ind. Com. on Humanities, 1975 Author: Marriage and Family, 1992, Speaking of Sexuality: Interdisciplinary Readings, 2001; co-author: Cultural Diversity and Families, 1992; editor: Marriage and Family: Change and Continuity, 1996, Speaking of Sexuality, 2001; editor: (assoc.) Jour. Marriage and the Family, 1975—85, Sociol. Inquiry, 1986—92, Sociol. Imagination, 1993—; editor: (cons.) Jour. Sex Rsch., 1991—95; editor: (cons) Sociol. Inquiry, 2001—; reviewer: Jour. Deviant Behavior, 1979—90, Sociol. Spectrum, 1985—, Jour. Family Issues, 1995—, Jour. Sex Rsch., 1996—; contbr. articles to profl. jours. Past state chmn. pub. affairs Ind. Assn. Planned Parenthood Affiliates, 1975-76; past bd. dirs. Planned Parenthood North Cen. Ind., chmn. pub. affairs com., 1975-76; past bd. dirs., 1st v.p., resources allocation com. Wis. Family Planning Coordinating Council; past bd. dirs., exec., info., internat. and edn. coms., chmn. social sci. rsch. com. Assn. for Vol. Sterilization, past pres. citizens adv. bd. Eau Claire and Chippewa Falls Planned Parenthood Clinics; past mem. dirs. Planned Parenthood of Wis., Inc.; past mem. Eau Claire Coord. Coun., Eau Claire County Adv. Health Forum, Eau Claire County Task Force on Family Planning, Eau Claire Task Force on Teen Pregnancy. Mem. Am. Sociol. Assn., Wis. Sociol. Assn., So. Sociol. Soc., Mid-South Sociol. Assn. (pres.-elect 1998-99, pres. 1999-2000, past pres. 2000-01, hotel negotiator, 2003—), Midwest Sociol. Soc., Groves Conf., Nat. Coun. Family Rels. (past chmn. com. stds. and criteria for cert., former mem. devel. com. and cert. com.), Wis. Coun. Family Rels. (bd. dirs., exec. com., past pres.), Soc. Sci. Study Sex., Tex. Coun. Family Rels., Augusta Coll. Alumni Soc., U. Fla. Alumni Soc., U. Ga. Alumni Soc., Pres. Club. U. Wis.-Eau Claire, Kappa Delta Pi, Phi Kappa Phi (chpt. pres. 1991-92, Nat. Forum editl. com. 1992-99), Phi Theta Kappa, Alpha Kappa Delta (editor nat. newsletter 1979-83, nat. v,p. 1992-94, nat. pres.-elect 1994-96, nat. pres. 1996-98, nat. past pres. 1998-2000, exec. coun. 1992-2000). Episcopalian. Home: 1305 Nixon Ave Eau Claire WI 54701-6574 Office: U Wis Dept Sociology Eau Claire WI 54702

DAVIDSON, JOHN ROBERT, dentist; b. Peru, Ind., Apr. 28, 1947; s. John Howard and Kathryn (Loughran) Davidson; m. Jean-Marie Dobler, Jan. 23, 1965 (div. Oct. 1972); children: James Michael, Jennifer Renee; m. Linda Mary Seasock, Oct. 22, 1977 (dec. Aug. 1997); children: Kathryn Cherise, John Richard. BS, Purdue U., 1969; DDS, UCLA, 1972. Diplomate Am. Bd. Forensic Dentistry, Am. Bd. Forensic Examiners. Gen. practice dentistry, Granada Hills, Calif., 1972-74; prof. clin. and community dentistry, dir. of clinics Ferris State Coll., Big Rapids, Mich., 1974-75; pvt. practice dentistry specializing in oral implantology Peru, Ind., 1975—. Chief dental staff Dukes Meml. Hosp., Peru, 1975—96; dep. coroner Miami County, 1987—. Recipient Citizen of the Yr. award, Peru, 1978, Pride award, Grissom AFB Cmty. Coun., Peru, 1980. Fellow: Internat. Congress of Oral Implantologists, Am. Coll. Oral Implantaologists (assoc.); mem.: ADA, Ind. Soc. Froensic Odontology (charter), Peru Area C. of C. (bd. dirs. 1976—83, Oustanding Svc. award 1979), Wabash Valley Dental Soc., Ind. Dental Assn., Am. Coll. Forensic Examiners, Mensa, Rotary (chmn. scholarship com. Peru 1975—95), Elks, Masons. Home and Office: 27 N Park Ave Peru IN 46970-1799 Fax: 765-473-5804. E-mail: drjrd@netusa1.net.

DAVIDSON, JOHN ROBERT (JAY), banking executive; b. LA, Mar. 30, 1950; s. John Robert Davidson and Carolyn Rose Monson; m. Kristina Maria Jonsson, Dec. 29, 1978; children: Joshua Kingseley, Michelle Maria. BSME, U. N.D., 1972; postgrad., AMP Corp. Leadership Coll., 1990. Engr. Dow Chem. Co., Pauls Valley, Okla., 1972-74; real estate investor Mpls., 1974-77; account exec. AMP Inc., Boulder, Colo., 1977-83, mkt. mgr. Harrisburg, Pa., 1983-86, dist. mgr. Denver, 1986-90, nat. mgr., 1990—95; chmn. bd., CEO, pres. 1st Am. State Bank of Colo., 1995—; dir. funds mgmt. com. Am. State Bank, Williston, ND, 1994—, dir. exec. com., 1996—, also bd. dirs.; founder, CEO, chmn. bd. dirs. First Am. State Bank, Denver, 1995—; CEO, chmn. bd. First Am. Bancorp, 1998—. Chmn., bd. dirs. Co. Housing Fin. Authority, 1999—; bd. dirs. Step 13. Supporter Denver Ctr. Performing Arts, F.A.C.E.S., Vols. of Am., Boy Scouts Am, Children's Hosp., Arthritis Found., Cherry Creek Sch. Found. and Cmty. Asset Program; bd. dirs. Kempe Children's Found., 1997—, treas., exec. com., chmn. fin. com., chair allocations com., 1998—2002; past bd. dirs., sec., chmn. devel. bd. Am. Heart Assn.; past. bd. dirs. Easter Seals Colo., event co-chmn.; co-chmn. Denver Ctr. Performing Arts New Years Gala, 2000; bd. dirs., event co-chmn. Arapahoe House; bd. dirs., sec. Denver Metro Area, 2000—; co-chair First Am. State Bank Fitness Festival, 2001—, Saturday Night Alive Gala; bd. dirs. Kenneth King Found. Honored as Pillar of the Cmty., Arapahoe House, 2000. Mem.: NRA (life), Glenmoore Country Club, Met. Club (bd. dirs. 2002—), Masons (Presdl. Legion of Merit). Avocations: snow skiing, mountain biking, photography, computers, music. Home: 5780 S Goldsmith Pl Greenwood Village CO 80111-3522 Office: 1st Am State Bank 8390 E Crescent Pkwy Greenwood Village CO 80111-2811 Business E-Mail: jdavidson@fasbank.com. E-mail: fasb32@earthlink.net.

DAVIDSON, JOY ELAINE, mezzo-soprano; b. Ft. Collins, Colo., Aug. 18, 1940; d. Clarence Wayne and Jessie Ellen (Bogue) Ferguson; m. Robert Scott Davidson, Aug. 9, 1959; children: Lisa Beth, Robert Scott II, Jeremy Fergus, Bonnie Kathleen, Jordan Christian. BA, Occidental Coll., Los Angeles, 1959; postgrad., Fla. State U., 1961-64. Robert A. Carrie Mastronardi endowed prof., 1995—. Dir. vocal/opera dept. New World Sch. of Arts Coll./Conservatory Divsn., Miami, Fla. 1992-2002. Debut 1965 with Miami Opera; has performed with Met. Opera, opera cos. throughout U.S. and Can., La Scala, Vienna State Opera, Bayerische State Opera, Lyons (France) Opera, Welsh Opera, Florence (Italy) Opera, Torino (Italy) Opera. (recipient Gold medal Internat. Competition Young Opera Singers, Sofia, Bulgaria 1969), Rio de Janeiro; performed with numerous orchs. including N.Y. Philharm., Los Angeles Philharm., Boston Orch., Pitts. Orch., Columbus (Ohio) Orch.; rec. artist. Named Outstanding Miami Artist at Orange Bowl; recipient Mastronardi endowed chair, 1995, NISOD award for tchg. excellence, 1996, Roberta Rymer Balfe award Fla. Grand Opera. Mem. PEO, United Meth. Women, Sigma Alpha Iota, Zeta Tau Zeta. Methodist. Avocations: swimming, camping, cycling, church activities. Home: 413 Walnut St #5032 Green Cove Springs FL 32043 E-mail: davidsons123@hotmail.com. *Success awaits those who dare to dream big enough. The success achiever is the possibility thinker.*

DAVIDSON, JUSTIN, music critic; b. Rome; m. Ariella Budick; 1 child, Milo. BMus, Harvard U.; D of Music, Columbia U. Dir. editl. Sony Classical, N.Y.C., 1995—96; music critic Newsday, Melville, NY, 1996—. Adj. prof. music Columbia U. Contbr. Recipient Pulitzer prize, 1999, award, Press Club of L.I., Deems Taylor award, ASCAP. Office: Newsday 235 Pinelawn Rd Melville NY 11747-4250

DAVIDSON, KENNETH LAWRENCE, lawyer, educator; b. Tulsa, Feb. 4, 1945; s. Joe and Elsie (Hutchens) D.; m. Anne Devine; children: Rebecca Marie, Deborah Shannon. BSBA, U. Tulsa, 1968, JD, 1970; LLM, Georgetown U., 1975. Bar: Okla. 1970, U.S. Dist. Ct. (no. dist.) Okla. 1970, U.S. Ct. Mil. Appeals 1971, U.S. Supreme Ct. 1976, U.S. Dist. Ct. (no. dist.) Ill. 2003, D.C. Ct. Appeals 1978, Ill. 1990. Assoc. CEO, assoc. legal counsel Bd. Regents Okla. State U. and A&M Colls., Stillwater, 1976-90; gen. counsel Regency Univs. System Ill. Bd. Regents, Springfield, 1990-96; parliamentarian, counsel to bd. trustees No. Ill. U., DeKalb, 1995-97, parliamentarian counsel for governance, risk mgmt., equity svcs., 1997-2000, corp. counsel, bd. parliamentarian, 2000—02, assoc. v.p. and gen. counsel, parliamentarian, 2002—. Adj. assoc. prof. Coll. Edn. Okla. State U., 1986-90; adminstrv. law judge Okla. Dept. Edn., Oklahoma City, 1978-90. Bd. dirs. YMCA Aquatic Club, Stillwater, 1985-86, Judith Karman Hospice, Stillwater, 1987. Capt. JAGC, USAF, 1970-76. Decorated Meritorious Svc. medal, Commendation medal. Mem. AAUP, Ill. Bar Assn., DeKalb County Bar Assn., Okla. Bar Assn., D.C. Bar Assn., Nat. Assn. Coll. and Univ. Attys., Am. Soc. Parliamentarians, Univ. Risk Mgmt. Assn., Univ. Club (Chgo.), Kappa Sigma. Democrat. Office: No Ill U 302 Lowden Hall DeKalb IL 60115-3080 E-mail: kdavidso@niu.edu.

DAVIDSON, LEE DAVID, insurance executive; b. Worcester, Mass., Sept. 1, 1959; s. Charles and Edith (Dwyer) D.; m. Tracy Eileen Stephenson; children: Adam, Ashley, Amanda. Student, Wachusett C. C., Gardner, Mass., 1991. Mgr. Black and White Restaurant, Spencer, Mass., 1982-84; asst. mgr. Valle's Steak House, Worcester, Mass., 1984; with Worcester Police Dept., 1985; facilities profl. State Mut. Ins., Worcester, 1985-86, self acctg., 1986-88, compliance analyst, 1988-92, mgr. compliance, 1992-94, asst. v.p., 1994—; dir. Allmerica Benefit Agy. Inc., 1996—; v.p. Sterling Risk Mgmt., Inc., 1996—; asst. v.p. Allmerica Fin. Life and Annuity Co., 1996—; chief compliance officer risk mgmt. Allmerica Fin. Corp., 1999. Treas. Fellowship Club, Worcester, 1994-95; v.p., bd. dirs. Allmerica Benefits, Inc., 1997—. Trustee South Athol United Meth. Ch., 1994—, treas., 1999—. With USN, 1977-81. Mem. Elks, Am. Legion. Republican. Avocations: woodworking, golf, swimming, private pilot. Home: 420 Templeton Rd Athol MA 01331-9769 Office: First Allmerica Fin Life Ins Co 440 Lincoln St Worcester MA 01653-0002 E-mail: ldavidson@allmerica.com.

DAVIDSON, LEE HOWARD, reporter; b. Murray, Utah, July 10, 1958; s. Howard LeRoy Davidson and Jennie May Atkinson; m. Deborah Christine Giunta, Aug. 27, 1981; children: Rachel, Jacob Aaron, Joshua Caleb, Sarah. BA in Journalism, Brigham Young U., 1981; MA in Journalism, Ohio State U., 1987. Reporter Brigham Young U. Daily Universe, Provo, Utah, 1977—81, editor, 1981; summer intern UPI, N.Y.C., 1981; reporter Deseret News, Salt Lake City, 1982—; editor Kiplinger Program Report, Columbus, Ohio, 1986-87. Recipient Robin Goldstein Regional Reporting award Nat. Press Club, 1989, 90, Washington Correspondence award, 1991. Mem. Lds Ch. Avocation: genealogy. Office: Deseret News 1061 National Press Building Washington DC 20045-2070

DAVIDSON, MARILYN, artist; b. NYC, Dec. 1, 1944; d. Sydney Irving and Miriam (Einhorn) D.; 1 child, Lisa Brayman Opel. BFA, Syracuse U., 1973, MFA, 1978. Owner Design in Silver and Gold, Syracuse, NY, 1973-84; faculty mem. Syracuse U. Sch. of Art, 1983-84; decorative arts designer various corps., 1984-89; owner Entre Nous Designs, 1989-93; decorative arts designer Hold-It Accessories, N.Y.C., 1994-95; sr. designer Liz Claiborne, Inc., N.Y.C., 1995-96; mktg.,design & product devel. Donna Karan, Williams-Sonoma Am. Mus. Natural History, Whitney Mus., 1996—; v.p. Hampton Forge; dir. licensing & product devel. The Jewish Mus., N.Y.C., 1998—. Cons. Pulos Design Assocs., Syracuse, 1978; adj. faculty Syracuse U. Sch. Art, 1981-83, Chautauqua Instn., Sch. Art, Penland Sch. Art; guest artist Loughborough Coll. Art and Design, Leicestershire, Brighton Poly. Coll. Art and Design, City of London Poly., Sir John Cass Sch. Art, London, Leeds Poly., Sch. Art, Camberwell Sch. Art, London; corr. Metalsmith Mag., London, Davidson Design & Devel. Exhibitions include Everson Mus. Art, 1979, Robert Elkon Gallery, N.Y.C., 1983, Alex Rosenberg Gallery, N.Y., 1984, Paula Allen Gallery, N.Y.C., 1986, Hudson Gallery, N.Y.C., 1986-87, Katzen-Brown Gallery, N.Y., 1986-89, Städische Galerie Regensburg, Deutsch-Amerikanisches Inst., West Germany, 1989, Sandy Carson Gallery, 1995; represented in pub. collections Met. Mus. of Art, Twentieth Century Dept., Victoria and Albert Mus, Everson Mu., Herbert F. Johnson Mus. Art, Munson-Williams-Proctor Inst.; featured mags., jours. in field. Fellowship Va. Ctr. for the Creative Arts, Ford Found., Ucross Found., N.Y. State Coun. on the Arts. Office: 74 W 68th St 9A New York NY 10023

DAVIDSON, MARK, writer, educator; b. N.Y.C., Sept. 25, 1928; BA in Polit. Sci., UCLA, 1948; MS in Journalism, Columbia U., 1950. Sci. writer U. So. Calif., L.A., 1980-90; prof. comm. Calif. State U., Dominguez Hills, Carson, 1985-99; freelance mag. writer. Faculty adviser Soc. Profl. Journalists, 1993-96; writer for Steve Allen Show, 1964, Dinah Shore Show, 1978, CBS Mag. Series with Connie Chung, 1980; sci. conf. spkr. Vienna Tech., 2001, U. Maribor, Slovenia, 2002. Author: Uncommon Sense (About Systems Science), 1984, Japanese transl., 2000, Invisible Chains of Thought Control, 1999, Watchwords: A Dictionary of American English Usage, 2001. Sackett scholar Columbia U.; recipient Nat. Emmy for writing hist. satires NATAS, 1978, Best Paper rating Conf. on Info. Sci., Pori, Finland, 2003. Mem.: PEN, Soc. Advancement of Edn. (assoc. mass media editor 1997—2001), Calif. Faculty Assn. (v.p. Dominguez Hills chpt. 1992—96), Nat. Writers Union (L.A. steering com. 2002—03), Writers Guild Am., Authors Guild, Am. Med. Writers Assn., Nat. Assn. Sci. Writers, Am. Soc. Journalists and Authors. E-mail: wordwatcher@earthlink.net.

DAVIDSON, MAYER B. medical educator, researcher; b. Balt., Apr. 11, 1935; s. David and Esther (Crockin) D.; m. Naomi Berger, Nov. 25, 1961 (div. 1977); children: Elke W., Seth J.; m. Roseann Herman, Aug. 31, 1980. AB, Swarthmore Coll., 1957; MD, Harvard U., 1961. Diplomate Am. Bd. Internal Medicine, Am. Bd. Endocrinology and Metabolism. Intern Bellevue Hosp., N.Y.C., 1961-62, jr. asst. resident, 1962-63; sr. asst. resident U. Wash. Affiliated Hosps., Seattle, 1963-64; rsch. fellow dept. endocrinology and metabolism King County Hosp., U. Wash., Seattle, 1964-66; asst. prof. medicine UCLA Sch. Medicine, 1969-74, from assoc. prof. to prof., 1974-95, clin. prof., 1996—, acting chief div. endocrinology and metabolism, 1973-74. Dir. diabetes program Cedars-Sinai Med. Ctr., L.A., 1979-95; assoc. dir. clin. diabetes City of Hope Nat. Med. Ctr., 1995-98; dir. clin. trials unit Charles R. Drew U.; nat. advisor Diabetes Ctr. Humana Hosp., Phoenix, 1985-91; attending physician diabetic clinic Boston City Hosp., 1966-68; clin. asst. Harvard Med. Sch., 1968-69; cons. AMA Dept. Drugs. Author: Diabetus Mellitus: Diagnosis and Treatment, 4th edit., 1998; contbr. more than 30 chpts. to books; founding editor: Current Diabetes Reports, 2000—02, editor-in-chief: Diabetes Care, 2002—. Co-founder, bd. dirs. free med. facility Venice (Calif.) Family Clinic, 1970. Maj. Med. Svc. Corps U.S . Army, 1966-69. USPHS rsch. fellow Nat. Inst. Arthritis and Metabolic Diseases, 1965-66; recipient Upjohn award for Outstanding Diabetes Educator, 1990, Robert H. Williams/Rachmiel Levine award for sci. contbns. and humanism in tng. young rschrs., 1995, Banting medal for Disting. Svc., 1998; named to Best Doctors in Am., 1992-93, 95-96, 96-97. Fellow ACP; mem. AAAS, Am. Diabetes Assn. (rsch. prizes 1965, 66, R&D award 1974-75, rsch. 1978-81, bd. dirs. 1986-89, 93-99, v.p. 1995-96, pres.-elect 1996-97, pres. 1997-98), Am. Fedn. Clin. Rsch., Western Soc. Clin. Rsch., Endocrine Soc., Am. Soc. Clin. Investigation, Western Assn. Physicians, Am. Assn. Diabetes Educators (editl. bd. jour. 1980-83), Boylston Med. Soc., Am. Diabetes Assn. (pres. 1997-98), Sigma Xi. Democrat. Jewish. E-mail: madavids@cdrewu.edu.

DAVIDSON, NANCY BRACHMAN, artist, educator; b. Chgo., Nov. 3, 1943; d. Philip and Jane (Blanch) Brachman; m. Donald Davidson, July 15, 1961 (div. 1977); 1 child, Lance A.; m. Greg Drasler, June 15, 1985. BEd, Northeastern Ill. U., 1965; BA, U. Ill., Chgo., 1972; MFA, Sch. Art Inst., Chgo., 1975. Vis. asst. prof. U. Ill., Champaign, 1977-79, Williams Coll., Williamstown, Mass., 1980-84; vis. artist, assoc. prof. SUNY, Purchase, 1984—. One-woman shows include Berkshire Mus., Pittsfield, Mass., 1982, Marianne Deson Gallery, Chgo., 1978, 1981, 1983, 1988, Richard Anderson Gallery, N.Y.C., 1991, 1993, 1995, Shoshana Wayne Gallery, Santa Monica, Calif., 1997, Nova Sin Gallery, Prague, Czech Republic, 1998, Neuberger Mus., Purchase, N.Y., 1998, Dorsky Gallery, N.Y.C., Inst. Contemporary Art, U. Pa., Phila., 1999, Vedanta Gallery, Chgo., 2000, The Contemporary Arts Ctr., Cin., 2001, Robert Miller Gallery, N.Y.C., 2001, Regina Gouger Miller Gallery, Carnegie Mellon U., Pitts., 2002, exhibited in group shows at Albright-Knox Gallery, Buffalo, 1980, Mus. Contemporary Art Chgo., 1984, Art Inst. Chgo., 1974, 1978, 1979, Bad Girls West-UCLA, 1994, Corcoran Biennial, 2002. Fellow NEA, 1978, Mass. Coun. Arts, 1981, Ford Found., 1978; Mass. Coun. Arts grantee, 1984, Anonymous Was a Woman grantee, 1997, Pollock-Krasner grantee, 2001. Home: 137 Duane St Apt 4W New York NY 10013-3892

DAVIDSON, NANCY ELLEN, oncologist; b. Denver, 1954; MD, Harvard U., 1979. Diplomate Am. Bd. Internal Medicine, Am. Bd. Med. Oncology. Intern Hosp. U. Pa., Phila., 1979-80; resident in internal medicine Johns Hopkins Hosp., Balt., 1980-82; fellow in med. oncology Nat. Cancer Inst., Bethesda, Md., 1982-86; mem. staff Johns Hopkins Hosp., 1986—; from asst. prof. to prof. oncology Johns Hopkins U., 1986—. Mem. Am. Assn. Cancer Rsch., Am. Soc. Clin. Oncology. Office: Johns Hopkins Oncology Ctr 1650 Orleans St Baltimore MD 21231-1000

DAVIDSON, RHONDA ELIZABETH, preschool educator; b. Phila., Nov. 26, 1954; d. Charles and Thelma Viola (Porter) Ash.; m. John Carl Davidson, June 10, 1975 (div. Aug. 1977). AAS, C.C. Phila., 1984; student, Chestnut Hill Coll., 1990—. Market rsch. intern WUSL Radio, Phila., 1983-84; telemarketing rschr. Sears Roebuck Inc., Phila., 1984-86; presch. tchr. Sch. Dist. of Phila., 1986—. Bus. cons. M & G Enterprises, Phila., 1984—. Active Girl Scouts U.S., Phila., 1994; majority inspector Dem. Party, Phila., 1993. Mem. ASCD, Assn. for Childhood Edn. Internat. Lutheran. Home: 5934 N Franklin Philadelphia PA 19120-1313 Office: M & G Enterprises 4534 N Smedley St Philadelphia PA 19140-1145

DAVIDSON, RICHARD ALAN, data communications company executive; b. Chgo., June 25, 1946; s. Jacob Aaron and Belle Rina (Feldman) D.; m. Sharyn Gail Ellman, Aug. 19, 1973; children: Kevin Scott, Caryl Elise. BSEE, U. Mich., 1970; MBA, Northwestern U., 1975. Project engr. Motorola, Inc., Schaumburg, Ill., 1967-74; ptnr. Feature Film Svcs., Skokie, Ill., 1974-77; mgr. planning Motorola, Inc., Schaumburg, Ill., 1977-78, mgr. mktg., 1978-79; tech. dir. Voice & Data Systems, Chgo., 1979-82; engring. mgr. Infolink Corp., Northbrook, Ill., 1982-84; pres. Davidson Data Communications, Lake Forest, Ill., 1984—. V.p. engring. Feature Film Svcs., Skokie, 1976—. Inventor pay TV system; contbr. articles to profl. jours. Unit commr. Boy Scouts Am., Lake County, Ill., 1989—; comms. officer USAF Aux. CAP, 1991—. Recipient Cert. of Appreciation Boy Scouts Am., 1990. MEm. IEEE, Assn. for Computing Machinery, Assn. for MBA Execs., North Shore Radio Club (tech. dir.), Tau Delta Phi. Republican. Jewish. Avocations: amateur radio, electronics, photography. Home and Office: 1900 S Millburne Rd Lake Forest IL 60045-4112

DAVIDSON, RICHARD DODGE, lawyer; b. Biloxi, Miss., June 1, 1945; s. Frank William and Elaine (Dodge) D.; m. Judith C. Carey, Aug. 16, 1969; children: Christopher, Scott, Julie. BS in Engring., Princeton U., 1967; JD, Cornell U., 1970. Bar: N.Y. 1971, Fla. 1978, U.S. Dist. Ct. (middle dist.) Fla., U.S. Ct. Appeals (2nd cir.) 1971, U.S. Ct. Appeals (5th cir.) 1978, U.S. Tax Ct. 1977, U.S. Supreme Ct. 1975. Assoc. Hiscock & Barclay, Syracuse, N.Y., 1970-78, ptnr., 1978-83, resident ptnr. Orlando, Fla., 1983-92, ptnr. Albany, N.Y., 1992-97; of counsel Lowndes, Drosdick, Doster, Kantor & Reed, P.A., Orlando, Fla., 1997, ptnr., 1999—. Pres. Ecology Compliance Ltd., Syracuse, 1983; asst. town atty. Town of Manilus, N.Y., 1974-83; bd. dirs. Boys Club Cen. Fla., Orlando, 1986—. Seminole Childrens' Village, Longwood, Fla., 1987-88. Mem. ABA, Fla. Bar Assn., N.Y. State Bar Assn., Orange County Bar Assn., Rotary, Princeton Club Cen. Fla. Avocations: amateur radio, youth sports, sailing. Office: Lowndes Drosdick Doster Kantor & Reed PA 215 N Eda Dr Orlando FL 32801 E-mail: rdavidson3@cfl.rr.com., richard.davidson@lowndes-law.com.

DAVIDSON, RICHARD J. medical association administrator; Pres. Am. Hosp. Assn., Washington, 1991—. Office: Am Hosp Assn 325 7th St NW Ste 700 Washington DC 20004-2801

DAVIDSON, RICHARD K. railroad company executive; b. Allen, Kans., Jan. 9, 1942; s. Richard B. and Thelma (Rees) D.; m. Lynne P. Durham, July 11, 1998; children: Richard Byron, Elizabeth Ann. BA in History, Washburn U., 1965, D of Commerce (hon.), 1984. Brakeman, conductor Mo. Pacific R.R., St. Louis, 1960-66, transp. tng. program, 1966, asst. trainmaster, trainmaster, 1966-75, asst. supt. to asst. v.p. ops., 1975-76; v.p. ops. Mo. Pacific Railroad, St. Louis, 1976-85, Union Pacific R.R., Omaha, 1985-89, exec. v.p. ops., 1989-91, chmn., CEO, 1991—; pres. Union Pacific Corp., Omaha, 1994—, COO, 1995-97, chmn., pres., CEO, 1997—. Mem. Happy Hollow Club. Office: Union Pacific RR 1416 Dodge St Omaha NE 68179-0002

DAVIDSON, ROBERT BRUCE, lawyer; b. N.Y.C., May 6, 1945; BS in Econs. cum laude, U. Pa., 1967; JD, Columbia U., 1972. Bar: NY 1973, US Dist Ct (so and ea dists) NY 1973, US Ct Appeals (2d cir) 1975, US Ct Appeals (DC cir) 1981, US Supreme Ct 1979, US Tax Ct 1984, US Ct Appeals (fed cir) 1989, US Ct Appeals (3d cir) 1990. Assoc. Baker & McKenzie, N.Y.C., 1972-79, ptnr., 1979—. Mem adv bd World Arbit Inst, New York, NY, 1984—. Author (with others): (book) Voting Laws and Procedures, 1973; contbr. articles to profl jours. Vol US Peace Corps, The Philippines, 1968—70. Mem.: ABA, Am. Arbitration Assn. (panels for large complex cases and for internat. cases 1997—), Fed. Bar Coun., Maritime Law Assn. U.S., Am. Fgn. Law Assn. (v.p.), Assn. Bar City N.Y. (chair com. arbitration 1982—85, com. internat. law 1986—89, com. arbitration 1999, chair com. arbitration 2003—, 2003—). Office: Baker & McKenzie 805 3d Ave New York NY 10022-7513 E-mail: rdavidsonlse@optonline.com.

DAVIDSON, ROBERT G. writer, English language educator; b. Duluth, Minn., Apr. 16, 1967; s. Donald M. Jr. and Mary F. Davidson; m. Linda I. Rogers, Mar. 4, 1989; 1 child, Sophia I. Rogers-Davidson. BA, Beloit Coll., 1989; MFA, Purdue U., 1997, PhD, 2002. Instr. English Purdue U., West Lafayette, Ind., 1994—2002; asst. prof. English Calif. State U., Chico, 2002—. Author: (fiction) Field Observations, 2001; editor-in-chief: Sycamore Rev., Purdue U., 1995-97. Vol. U.S. Peace Corps, Grenada, W.I., 1990-92 Dissertation rsch. grantee Purdue Rsch. Found., Purdue U., 2000-2001. Mem. MLA, Associated Writing Programs (Intro Jours. prize for fiction 1997). Office: Dept English Calif State U-Chico Chico CA 95929

DAVIDSON, ROBERT WILLIAM, not-for-profit executive; b. Colfax, Wash., Sept. 18, 1949; s. William Martin and Lena (Soli) D.; m. Molly Evoy, Apr. 16, 1977; children: Ford Patrick, Matthew Harpur, Marshall Andrew. AB, Harvard U., 1971; MBA, U. Wash., 2000. Exec. dir. Sabre Found., Cambridge, Mass., 1971-72; adminstrv. asst. Congressman Joel Pritchard, Washington, 1973-79; asst. sec. state State of Wash., Olympia, 1979-80; pres. Frayn Fin. Printing, Seattle, 1982-87, Frayn Printing Co., Seattle, 1985-87; exec. dir. Woodland Park Zool. Soc., Seattle, 1987-93, pres., 1993-94; prin. Alistar Capital Group, Bellevue, Wash., 1994—2001; CEO Seattle Aquarium Soc., Seattle, 2002—. Mem. adv. com. Wash. State Software Ind. Devel. Bd., 1984-85. Chmn. pub. funding com. Mayor's Zoo Commn., Seattle, 1984-85; dir. Discovery Inst., 1992—, Internat. Snow Leopard Trust, 1994-96; mem. sch. bd. Cath. Archdiocese of Seattle, 1995-98; mem. Seattle U. Exec. Masters in Not-for-Profit Mgmt. vis. com., 1995-96; mem. King County Bond Oversight Com., 1986-93. Mem. N.W. Devel. Officers Assn. (pres. 1994), Downtown Rotary Club (v.p. found. 1997-98), Wash. Athletic Club. Republican. Roman Catholic. Avocations: tennis, photography. Office: SEAS 1402 3d Ave # 1000 Seattle WA 98101 E-mail: rwd@aquariumsociety.org.

DAVIDSON, ROGER H(ARRY), political scientist, educator; b. Washington, July 31, 1936; s. Ross Wallace and Mildred (Younger) D.; m. Nancy Elizabeth Dixon, Sept. 29, 1961; children: Douglas Ross, Christopher Reed. AB magna cum laude, U. Colo., 1958; PhD, Columbia U., 1963. Asst. prof. govt. Dartmouth Coll., Hanover, N.H., 1962-68; assoc. prof. polit. sci. U. Calif., Santa Barbara, 1968-71, prof., 1971-83, assoc. dean letters and sci., 1978-80, vis. prof., 1994, 1999—; sr. specialist Congl. Rsch. Svc., Washington, 1980-88; prof. govt., politics U. Md., College Pk., 1981-99. Profl. staff mem. U.S. Ho. of Reps., Washington, 1973—74; rsch. dir. U.S. Senate, Washington, 1976—77; cons. White House, 1970—71, U.S. Com. on Violence, Washington, 1968—69, Ctr. for Civic Edn., 2002—; Leon Sachs vis. scholar Johns Hopkins U., Balt., 1997; John Marshall Disting. Fulbright prof. Debrecen U., Hungary, 2002. Author: The Role of the Congressman, 1969; co-author: A More Perfect Union, 4th edit., 1989, Congress and Its Members, 9th edit., 2003; editor: The Postreform Congress, 1992; co-editor: Remaking Congress, 1995, Masters of the House, 1998; contbr. articles to profl. jours. Co-chmn. Upper Valley Human Rights Coun., Hanover, N.H., 1966-68; chmn. Goleta Valley Citizens Planning Group, Santa Barbara, 1974-76; rsch. com. of legis. specialists Internat. Polit. Sci. Assn.; adv. commn. on records of Congress Nat. Archives and Records

Adminstrn., 1995-99; bd. dirs. Governance Inst., Archtl. Found. of Santa Barbara, 2003—. Woodrow Wilson Nat. Found. fellow, 1958, Gilder fellow Columbia U., 1960, Faculty fellow Dartmouth Coll., 1965-66. Fellow Nat. Acad. Pub. Adminstrn.; mem. Nat. Capital Area Polit. Sci. Assn. (pres. 1985-86), Legis. Studies Group (charter, nat. chmn. 1980-81), Am. Polit. Sci. Assn. (joint com. Project 87-Am. Hist. Assn./Am. Polit. Sci. Assn., chmn. congl. fellowship com. 1990, 93, endowed programs com. 1994-95, chmn. 1995-96, co-chmn. exec. com. Centennial Campaign 1997—), Western Polit. Sci. Assn. (bd. editors 1977-78). Baptist. Avocations: music, history. Home: Villa L 400 E Pedregosa St Santa Barbara CA 93103-1970 Office: Dept Polit Sci U Calif Santa Barbara CA 93106

DAVIDSON, RONALD CROSBY, physicist, educator; b. Norwich, Ont., Can., July 3, 1941; s. William Crosby and Annie Beatrice (Caley) D.; m. Jean Farncombe, May 18, 1963; children: Cynthia Christine, Ronald Crosby Jr. BSc, McMaster U., 1963; PhD, Princeton U., 1966. Faculty dept. physics U. Md., 1968-78; prof. physics MIT, 1978-91; prof. astrophys. scis. Princeton U., 1991—. Vis. scientist Los Alamos Sci. Lab., 1974-75; asst. dir. for applied plasma physics Office of Fusion Energy Dept. Energy, Washington, 1976-78; dir. Plasma Fusion Center MIT, Cambridge, Mass., 1978-88; chmn. magnetic fusion adv. com., 1982-86; dir. Princeton Plasma Physics Lab., 1991-96. Author: Methods in Nonlinear Plasma Theory, 1972, Theory of Nonneutral Plasmas, 1974, 2d edit., 89, Physics of Nonneutral Plasmas, 1990. Recipient Disting. Assoc. award Dept. Energy, 1986, Leadership award Fusion Power Assocs., 1986, Kaul Found. Excellence award, 1993; Ford Found. fellow, 1963-64, Imperial Oil fellow, 1963-66, Sloan Rsch. Found. fellow, 1970-72. Fellow AAAS, Am. Phys. Soc. (chmn. div. plasma physics, 1983-84). Office: Princeton U Plasma Physics Lab PO Box 451 Princeton NJ 08543-0451

DAVIDSON, SHAE RONALD, historian, researcher; b. Buckhannon, W.Va., Dec. 2, 1973; s. Ronald Davidson and Nancy Waugh. BA in History/Sociology, Marshall U., 1996, MA in History, 1998. Dir. Jenkins Plantation Mus., Lesage, W.Va., 1997—2000; fellow Ohio U. Contemporary History Inst., Athens, 2000—. Rschr. Ohio U. Contemporary History Inst., Athens, 2001—. Exhibit writer (civil war and folk art exhibitions) W.Va. State Mus.; contbr. reviews; author: (political commentaries) Portsmouth Free Press. Fellow, Ohio U. Contemporary History Inst.; John Marshall scholar, Marshall U. Ctr. for Academic Excellence, 1992—96. Mem.: Nat. Coun. on Pub. History, Am. Hist. Assn., Orgn. Am. Historians, Amnesty Internat., Sierra Club. Independent. Achievements include research in in devel. of fed. child nutrition programs, role of lobbyists in edn. Avocations: reading, birdwatching. Office: Ohio U Contemporary History Institute 2 University Terr Athens OH 45701

DAVIDSON, SHEILA KEARNEY, lawyer; b. Paterson, N.J., Dec. 16, 1961; d. John James and Rita Barbara (Burke) Kearney; m. Anthony H. Davidson, Oct. 5, 1996; children: Andrew John, Patrick Kearney. BA cum laude, Fairfield U., 1983; JD, George Washington U., 1986. Bar: N.Y. 1987, U.S. Dist. Ct. (so. dist.) N.Y. 1987, D.C. 1989. Assoc. Shearson Lehman Bros., Inc., N.Y.C., 1986-87; staff atty. Nat. Assn. Securities Dealers, N.Y.C., 1987-89, regional atty., 1989-90, sr. regional atty., 1990-91; regional counsel N.Y. Life Ins. Co., N.Y.C., 1991-93, assoc. counsel, 1993-94, asst. gen. counsel, 1994-95, v.p., assoc. gen. counsel, 1995-97, sr. v.p. in charge of corp. compliance dept., 1998-00, sr. v.p./gen. counsel, 2000—. Trustee Fairfield U., 2003—. Mem.: D.C. Bar Assn., Phi Delta Phi. Republican. Roman Catholic. Office: NY Life Ins Co 51 Madison Ave New York NY 10010-1603

DAVIDSON, SHIRLEY JEAN, elementary and secondary educator; b. DuQuoin, Ill., June 2, 1946; d. Richard Haley and Doris Jean Gaddis; m. Philip H. Davidson, Aug. 30, 1969; children: Susan Elizabeth, Matthew Philip. BS in Elem. Edn., So. Ill. U., Carbondale, 1969; MAT in Learning Disabilities and Reading, Rockford Coll., 1982; MA in Sch. Adminstrn., Concordia U., River Forest, Ill., 1997. Cert. in sch. adminstrn., learning disabilities, social emotion disorders, educable mentally handicapped, elem. edn., reading, Ill. Thcr. 4th grade Coulterville (Ill.) Elem. Sch., 1968-70; tchr. 2d grade Gifford (Ill.) Grade Sch., 1970-73, Rockton (Ill.) Grade Sch., 1973-85; reading and english/learning disabilities specialist Rockford (Ill.) Area Literacy Coun., 1988-93; spl. edn. tchr. Byron (Ill.) Sch. Dist., 1995-96, Dist. 47, Crystal Lake, Ill., 1993-95, 96—. Ind. reading cons. Elco Industries, Rockford, 1991-92; mem. peacemaking com. Indian Prairie Sch., Crystal Lake, 1998—, mem. tech. com., 1997—, mem. social com., 1996-97, mem. sch. improvement com., 1999—. Active First Presbyn. Ch., Rockford, 1975—. Mem. Crystal Lake Elem. Tchrs. Assn., Pi Lambda Theta, Phi Kappa Phi. Avocations: tennis, reading, cross stitch. Office: Indian Prairie Sch 651 Village Rd Crystal Lake IL 60014-2005

DAVIDSON, STEVEN J. emergency physician; b. Phila, Pa, Mar. 9, 1950; s. Jay Howard and Claire Beverly (Silverman) D.; m. Simone F. Mogul, June 21, 1987; children: Zoey Samuel, Masha Kalinkina. AB in Chemistry, Temple U., 1971, MD, 1975; MBA, U. Pa., 1989. Diplomate Am. Bd. Emergency Medicine. Intern in acute care Med. Coll. Pa., 1975-76, resident in emergency medicine, 1976-78, instr., asst. prof., assoc. prof. surgery, 1978-84, assoc. prof. emergency medicine, 1984-89, prof. emergency medicine, 1989-97, vis. prof., 1997—, head divsn. emergency med. svc., 1988-96; chmn. emergency medicine Maimonides Med. Ctr., Bklyn., 1995—. Med. dir. Phila. Emergency Med. Svc., 1983-94; oral examiner Am. Bd. Emergency Medicine, 1980—, bd. dirs., 1986-95. Assoc. editor Yearbook of Emergency Medicine, 1981-99; guest reviewer Annals of Emergency Medicine, 1983-99, Prehosp. and Disaster Medicine, 1992-97, Acad. Emergency Medicine, 1993-99; mem. editl. bd. Preshosp. Emergency Care, 1997-99. Recipient Modern Physician 2001 Phys. Exec. award of Excellence, 2001. Fellow Am. Coll. Emergency Physicians (bd. dirs. Pa. chpt. 1979-85, Emergency Svc. award 1992), Soc. Acad. Emergency Medicine (pres. 1985-86), Nat. Assn. Emergency Med. Svc. Physicians. Office: Maimonides Med Ctr Dept Emergency Medicine 4802 10th Ave Brooklyn NY 11219-2844

DAVIDSON, STUART WEST, lawyer; b. Natick, Mass., June 21, 1957; s. Edward William and Sonya (Westelman) D.; m. Ann Cohen, Oct. 8, 1988; 1 child, Anita Rose. BA in Polit. Sci., Johns Hopkins U., 1979; JD cum laude, Harvard U., 1982. Bar: Pa. 1982, D.C. 1983. Ptnr. Willig, Williams & Davidson, Phila., 1982—. Trustee Johns Hopkins U., 1979-84; adv. coun. environ. and occupl. health Johns Hopkins U. Sch. Hygiene and Pub. Health, 1983-93; adv. coun. labor studies Pa. State U., 1985-2002; nat. labor adv. bd. State of Israel Bonds, 1996—; mem. lawyers coord. com. AFL-CIO, 1984—; bd. dirs. Devel. Corp. of Israel, exec. com., 2000—. Contbr. articles to profl. jours.; speaker at various nat. conf. Mem. Attys. Com. Internat. Found. of Employee Benefit Plans; mem. Golden Slipper Found., 1999—. Mem. ABA, Pa. Bar Assn., Phila. Bar, Am. Arbitration Assn., Indsl. Rels. Rsch. Assn., Internat. Found. Employee Benefit Plans, Omicron Delta Kappa, Phi Beta Kappa. Home: 7501 Fowler St Philadelphia PA 19128-4149 Office: Willig Williams Davidson 1845 Walnut St 24th Fl Philadelphia PA 19103 4708 E-mail: sdavidson@wwdlaw.com.

DAVIDSON, SUSAN BETTINA, editor, writer; b. Wolverhampton, Eng., June 6, 1942; came to U.S., 1957; d. Basil Thomas and Hedi (Liebermann) Goldfarb; m. Daniel Ira Davidson, Mar. 13, 1966; 1 child, Jill. Student, Nat. U. Mex., Mexico City, 1962; BA in Langs., Ohio State U., 1963; postgrad., New Sch. for Social Rsch., 1963, Columbia U., 1963—65, Alliance Française, Paris, 1968, George Washington U., 1995—97. Editl. asst. Harcourt, Brace & Co., N.Y.C., 1963-64; asst. to prodr. ABC-News, N.Y.C., 1964-65; prodn. asst. UPI, N.Y.C., 1965-66; news prodr. Ind. TV News, Washington, 1966-69, freelance prodr. London Weekend TV, Washington, 1969-75; arts editor Washingtonian mag., Washington, 1977—. Contbg. editor Women's Work, 1972—75; Washington editor Changing Homes, 1985—87; nominator Helen Hayes Awards, Washington, 1983—99, Ortho 21st Century Women Awards; judge Washington Craft Show, 1996; reader Fund for New Am. Plays, Washington, 1997, Washington, 98, Washington, 99, Washington, 2000, Washington, 01; reviewer, rschr., editor books and plays. Contbr. articles to newspapers and various publs., including N.Y. Times, Washington Post, L.A. Times, Stagebill, Nat. Geographic Traveler, Savory Traveler, Art & Antiques. Panelist Prince George's County Arts Awards, Washington, 1992, Mayor's Arts Awards, Washington, 1993, Mayor's Arts Edn. Awards, Washington, 1996, USIA Selection Bd., Washington, 1997; vol. Women's Health Initiative. Democrat. Jewish. Avocations: going to the theatre, reading, listening to music, dancing, travel. Home: 2900 Brandywine St NW Washington DC 20008-2138 Office: Washingtonian Mag 1828 L St NW Ste 200 Washington DC 20036-5169 E-mail: sdavidson@washingtonian.com., s.davidson@starpower.net.

DAVIDSON, SUZANNE MOURON, lawyer; b. Oxford, Miss., Aug. 5, 1963; d. Bertrand D. Jr. and Barbara Jean (Baca) Mouron; m. Garrison H. Davidson III, Dec. 12, 1987; children: Jane Harrington, Catherine Stender. AB in English Lit., U. Calif., 1985, JD, 1988. Assoc. Peterson, Ross, L.A., 1988-89; asst. litigation counsel Ticor Title Ins., Rosemead, Calif., 1989-91; corp. counsel Forest Lawn, Glendale, Calif., 1991—. Deacon San Marino Cmty. Ch., 1995-98, elder, 2000—; bd. dirs. San Marino Cmty. Ch. Nursery Sch., 1995-2000; mem. Jr. League, Pasadena, Calif., 1989—, Nat. Charity League Jrs. (San Marino), 2002—, bd. dirs, 2003—. Mem. Calif. State Bar Assn., L.A. County Bar Assn., Pasadena Athletic Club, Salt Air Club, Chi Omega (chmn. nat. area rush info. 1988-95). Presbyterian. Office: Forest Lawn Co Legal Dept 1712 S Glendale Ave Glendale CA 91205-3320

DAVIDSON, THOMAS FERGUSON, chemical engineer; b. N.Y.C., N.Y., Jan. 5, 1930; s. Lorimer Arthur and Elizabeth (Valentine) D.; m. Nancy Lee Selecman, Nov. 10, 1951; children: Thomas Ferguson, Richard Alan, Gwyn Ann. BS in Engring., U. Md., 1951; HHD (hon.), Weber State U., 1998. Sr. project engr. Wright Air Devel. Ctr., Dayton, Ohio, 1951-58; dep. dir. Solid Sys. Divsn., Edwards, Calif., 1959-60; mgr. govt. ops. Thiokol Chem. Corp., Ogden, Utah, 1960-64, dir. aerospace mktg. Bristol, Pa., 1965-67, dir. tech. mgmt. Ogden, 1968-82; v.p. tech. Morton Thiokol Inc., Chgo., 1983-88, Thiokol Corp., Ogden, 1989-90; cons. Ogden, 1990-99. Subcom. lubrications and wear NACA, Washington, 1955-57; chmn. Joint Army, Navy, NASA, Air Force exec. com., 1959-60. Editor: National Rocket Strategic Plan, 1990; contbr. articles to profl. jours. Trustee Family Counseling Svc., Ogden, 1991—98, Weber State U. Found., 2001—, Ogden Dinosaur Park, 2000—03; mem. Utah State Bd. Edn., 1992—94; bd. dirs. Habitat for Humanity Internat., 1991—93; chmn. bd. dirs. Wesley Acad., Ogden, 1994—98; bd. dirs. Utah Musical Theatre, 1997—, ARC No. Utah, 1999—2001, Ogden Weber Applied Tech. Coll. Found., 2001—03; trustee Weber State U., 2000—. Fellow AIAA (assoc., sect. chmn. 1979-80, chmn. rocket propulsion com. 1987-90; mem. aerospace tech. com. 1987-90, Wyld Propulsion award 1991, WSU Crystal Crest award 2001); mem. Am. Newcomen Soc., Smithsonian Instn., Exch. Club (Book of Golden Deeds award 2001), Ogden Golf and Country Club, Weber State Wildcat Club (bd. dirs. 1996-2000). Republican. Methodist. Home: 4755 Banbury Ln Ogden UT 84403-4484

DAVIDSON, THOMAS MAXWELL, international management company executive; b. N.Y.C., Dec. 14, 1937; s. Alfred Edward and Claire Helen (Dreyfus) D.; m. Ruth Elizabeth Bovenkerk, Dec. 8, 1962; children: Douglas Edward, Anne Elizabeth. BA, Vanderbilt U., 1959; MBA, Columbia U., 1961. Mgr. Ford Motor Co., Dearborn, Mich., 1963-72; dir. credit ops. White Motor Corp., Eastlake, Ohio, 1972-73, v.p., treas., 1976-77; sr. v.p., chief ops. officer White Motor Credit Corp., Cleve., 1973-75, pres., chief exec. officer, 1975-77, also bd. dirs.; sr. v.p. fin., chief fin. officer, dir. Tex. Gas Transmission Corp., Owensboro, Ky., 1977-81; exec. v.p., chief fin. officer Arrow Electronics, Inc., N.Y.C., 1981-87; exec. v.p. Greenwich, Conn., 1987-89; also bd. dirs., 1981-94; pres., CEO Global TeleSystems Group, 1989-93, also bd. dirs., 1990-93; pres., CEO Internat. Techs., Inc., Greenwich, Conn., 1993—. Med. Info. Internat., 1995-98. Bd. dirs. SOVAM Teleport Russia, Sovintel, Russia, Baltic Comms., Ltd., Russia; bd. dirs., chair CEO XXI Century Hotel Network Ltd., 1998—2000; co-founder, sr. v.p. Vytek Wireless, Inc., 2000—01; mng. dir. Southporter Mgmt. Group, 2002—. Served with U.S. Army, 1959. Mem.: N.Y. Athletic Club. Home: 131 Doubling Rd Greenwich CT 06830-4040 Office: Internat Techs Inc 35 Mason St Greenwich CT 06830-5433 E-mail: tmd@pipeline.com.

DAVIDSON, THOMAS NOEL, business executive; b. Evansville, Ind., Oct. 4, 1939; s. Harry R. and Helen E. Davidson; m. Sally Anne Fries, 1958; children: Thomas N. Jr., John C., James R., Jennifer J. BSc with honors, Mich. State U., 1961. Chmn. bd. dirs. Quarry Hill Group, Nutech Precision Metals Inc., Quarry Hill Ptnrs. Past prin. owner and dir. Am. Brass Co., Ansonia Brass, Atco Controls, Inc., Buffalo Brass Co., Carborundum Abrasives, Inc., Cramco, Inc., Hanson Inc., Jensen Fitting Mfg., Ltd., Jensen Fittings Corp., PCL Industries Ltd., Sandbright & Co., Sklar-Peppler Furniture Inc., Stephenson's Rent-all Inc., Union Drawn Steel Ltd., Volstatic, Inc.; bd. dirs. TLC Laser Eye Ctrs., HMI, Inc., MDC Corp., Nutech Precision Metals, TLC Eye Ctr. Azure Dynamics, L.P., Am. Mus. Flyfishing; bd. Nat. Marine Sanctuary, Clemmer Industries, Ocean Reef Hist. Soc., Ocean Reef Culture Ctr., Ocean Reef Found.; past chmn. Gen. Trust Corp. Past chmn. Hugh MacMillan Children's Found., Ocean Reef Cmty. Assn., Ocean Reef Club, Inc., Can. CPGA Golf Championship, Metro Toronto Conv. Ctr.; past bd. dirs. Con. Smythe Rsch. Found., Westhem Corp., USF&G (Can.), Nat. Club, Can. Club, Silcorp Ltd., others; past chmn. and mem. bd. dirs. Ocean Reef Cmty. Found.; chmn. Ocean Reef Cultural Ctr. Recipient Fin. Post Can. award 1979; named Entrepreneur of Yr. by Fin. Post. Mem. Soc. Plastics Engrs. (past dir.), Soc. Plastics Industry (past chmn., Man of Yr. award 1985), Variety Ability Systems Inc. (past dir.), Variety Village (past dir.), Young Pres. Orgn. (internat. pres. 1988-89), World Pres. Orgn. (bd. dirs., internat. pres. 1997), Can. Club (past bd. dirs., N.Y. and Toronto), Nat. Club Toronto (past bd. dir.), Rosedale Golf Club (Toronto), Card Sound Golf Club (bd. dirs.), English Turn Golf & Country lub (New Orleans), Griffith Island Club (Wiarton, Ont., past chmn.), Ocean Reef Club (past chmn.), The Caledon Mountain Trout Club (Inglewood, Ont.), Tau Beta Pi, Pi Tau Sigma. Home: 7 Sunrise Cay Rd Key Largo FL 33037-5301 Office: Quarry Hill Group PO Box 83 Key Largo FL 33037-0083

DAVIDSON, TOM WILLIAM, lawyer; b. Madison, Wis., Oct. 10, 1952; s. Alvin William and Louise Elizabeth (Zeratsky) D.; m. Linda Mary Greiber, July 27, 1974; children: Jessica, Heather, Thomas. BA, U. Wis., 1977, JD, 1974. Bar: Wis. 1977, U.S. Dist. Ct. (we. dist.) Wis. 1977, U.S. Ct. Appeals (D.C. cir.) 1986, U.S. Supreme Ct. 1986, Va. 2001. Gen. atty. FCC, Washington, 1977-79, trial atty., 1979; assoc. Sidley & Austin, Washington, 1980-84, ptnr., 1985-91, Akin, Gump, Struass, Hauer & Feld, LLP, Washington, 1992—. Active Burke (Va.) Ctr. Cmty. Assn., 1977-79; chmn. Bass Pond Cluster Bd., 1977-78. Mem. ABA, FBA, Fed. Comm. Bar Assn., Lowe's Island Club, Tournament Players Club at Avenal, Phi Beta Kappa, Phi Eta Sigma, Phi Kappa Phi. Avocations: golf, softball, soccer, basketball, racquetball. Office: Akin Gump Strauss Hauer & Feld Ste 400 1333 New Hampshire Ave NW Washington DC 20036-1564

DAVIDSON, WILLIAM M. diversified company executive, professional basketball executive; b. Dec. 5, 1922; divorced. LL.B., Wayne State U.; BBA, U. Mich.; JD, Wayne State U. Pres. CEO Guardian Glass Co., Northville, Mich., 1957-68; pres., CEO, dir. Guardian Industries Corp., Northville, Mich., 1968—; majority owner Detroit Pistons, NBA, 1974—, mng. ptnr. Served with USN. Office: Guardian Industries Corp 2300 Harmon Rd Auburn Hills MI 48326 also: care Detroit Pistons 2 Championship Dr Auburn Hills MI 48326-1753*

DAVIDSON-KENNEDY, DORIS ANN, information technology executive, real estate broker; b. Philadelphia, Pa., Aug. 8, 1946; d. Ernest and Geneva Davidson; m. Edward Aaron Kennedy, Jr., Aug. 8, 1998; m. John B. Dunham, Apr. 18, 1964 (div. Jan. 28, 1978); 1 child, Reginald Bernard Dunham. BS Info. Mgmt., Rutgers U., Newark, New Jersey, 1980; AA Data Processing, Ctrl. Piedmont CC, Charlotte, North Carolina, 1971, AS Liberal Arts, 1976. Lic. Real Estate Brokers NC Real Estate Comm. Keypunch operator First Union Nat. Bank, Charlotte, NC, 1966—67; info. tech. scheduler Celanese Corp., Charlotte, NC, 1968—70; computer programmer City of Charlotte, Charlotte, NC, 1970—77; project mgr. Sea-Land Services, Inc., Elizabeth, NJ, 1977—92; computer cons. Various Companies, NJ, 1992—. Mem.: Delta Sigma Theta, Inc. Baptist. Avocations: golf, skiing, travel, writing, drawing.

DAVIDSON-SHEPARD, GAY, secondary education educator; b. Long Beach, Calif., Dec. 15, 1951; d. Leyton Paul and Ruth Leona (Gritzmaker) Davidson; m. Daniel A. Shepard, June 24, 1983. BA, U. Calif., Irvine, 1972; MA, Columbia Pacific U., 1986. Cert. elem. and secondary edn. tchr. Tchr. mid. sch. Ocean View Sch. Dist., Huntington Beach, Calif., 1973—; team mem. Calif. learning assessment system State Dept. of Edn., Sacramento, 1987—; chief reader Orange County pentathlon and decathlon Orange County Dept. Edn., Costa Mesa, Calif., 1980—; sr. reader new standards State Dept. Edn., Sacramento, 1995—. Lang. arts cons. various sch. dists., Calif., 1976—; chief reader Calif. Learning Assessment System, Sacramento, 1993—; sr. reader New Stds., 1995—; chief reader, asst. chief reader, table leader Golden State Exams, 1997—; item writer Calif. H.S. Exit Exam, 2000—. Author/cons.: Teacher's Guide for Direct Assessment Writing, 1990; test writer Acad. Pentathlon Test, 1984—, Dist. Lang. Art Proficiency Test, 1980—. Mem. NEA, AAUS, AAUW, Nat. Assn. Tchrs. of English, Calif. Reading Assn., Mensa, Calif. Tchrs. Assn., Ocean View Tchrs. Assn. Democrat. Avocations: reading, camping, travel, cooking. Home: 6782 Rook Dr Huntington Beach CA 92647-5641 Office: Mesa View Sch 17601 Avilla Ln Huntington Beach CA 92647-6612

DAVIDSSON, ROBERT IVER, librarian; b. Virginia, Minn., Dec. 10, 1953; s. Robert R. and Kathryn B. Johnson. BS in Journalism, U. Fla., 1976; MS in Info. Studies, Fla. State U., 1988. Asst. news editor Boca Raton (Fla.) News, 1981—86; govt. rsch. svc. mgr. Palm Beach County Libr. Dept., West Palm Beach, Fla., 1989—. Author: (book) Indian River: A History of the Ais Indians in Spanish Florida (Fla. Hist. Confederation - 2001 Best Fla. History Monograph, 2001); contbr. articles to profl. jours. Named to Transformers Honor Roll, Fla. Libr. Assn., 1996; recipient News Divsn. Outstanding Student Stipend award, Spl. Librs. Assn., 1988, County Adminstrs. Golden Palm award, Palm Beach County Govt., 1997. Mem.: Gold Coast Info. Specialists, Palm Beach County Libr. Assn. Office: Palm Beach County Library System - GRS 3650 Summit Blvd West Palm Beach FL 33406 E-mail: davidssonb@pbclibrary.org.

DAVID-WEILL, MICHEL ALEXANDRE, investment banker; b. France, Nov. 23, 1932; came to US, 1977; s. Pierre Sylvain and Berthe Marie (Haardt) David-W.; m. Helene Lehideux, July 20, 1956; children: Beatrice David-Weill Stern, Cecile David-Weill, Natalie Merveilleux du Vignaud, Agathe. Ed., Inst. Scis. Politiques, 1953. Ptnr. Lazard Freres & Co., 1961-65; ptnr. Lazard Freres & Cie, 1965—, sr. ptnr., 1975—, Lazard Freres & Co., NYC, 1977-95; chmn. Lazard Freres & Co. LLC, NYC, 1995—. Dir. Eurazeo, 1972—; pres. Eurazeo, 2003; vice chmn. Groupe Danone, 1970; dir. Publicis Groupe S.A., 1990. Bd. gov. Soc. of NY Hosp.; trustee Met. Mus. Art, 1985— . Mem. Academie des Beaux-Arts (mem. inst.). Clubs: Brook (NYC), Knickerbocker (NYC). Office: Lazard Freres & Co LLC 30 Rockefeller Plz Fl 59 New York NY 10112-5900

DAVIE, JOSEPH MYRTEN, physician, pathology and immunology educator, science administrator; b. La Porte, Ind., Oct. 14, 1939; s. John James and Dorothy Elizabeth (Hash) Davie; m. Janet Sue Whorwell, Dec. 17, 1960; children: Shelley, Jennifer, Melissa. AB, Ind. U., 1962, MA, 1964, PhD, 1966; MD, Washington U., St. Louis, 1968. Intern Washington U., 1968—69; staff assoc. NIH, 1969—71; resident Nat. Cancer Inst., 1971—72; assoc. prof. pathology Washington U. Sch. Medicine, 1972—75, asst. prof. microbiology, 1972—73, assoc. prof. microbiology, 1973—75, prof., head microbiology and immunology, prof. pathology, 1975—87; sr. v.p. research G.D. Searle and Co., Skokie, Ill., 1987, pres. research and devel., 1987—92, corp. sr. v.p. sci. and tech., 1993; v.p. rsch. Biogen, Inc., Cambridge, Mass., 1993—98, sr. v.p. rsch., 1999—2000; ret., 2000. Assoc. editor Jour. of Immunology, 1975—78, sect. editor, 1978—82. Served with USPHS, 1969—71. Mem.: Inst. Medicine. Home: 4992 Joewood Dr Sanibel FL 33957-7509

DAVIE, MALCOLM HENDERSON, city official; b. North Bay, Ont., Canada, Oct. 11, 1918; s. William Malcolm and Vera (Henderson) D.; m. Helen Marjorie Marsh, July 1948 (div. Oct. 1954). BA, U. Western Ont., 1945; MA, U. Toronto, 1947; BD, Andover-Newton Theol. Sch., 1950; MA in Psychology, Boston U., 1959. Ordained to ministry Congl. Ch., 1951. Salesman Davie Cheese Co., Idlerton, Ont., 1932-41; with London (Ont.) Provincial Hosp., 1942-44; psychol. counsellor, bus. agt. Gould Farm, Great Barrington, Mass., 1948-51; attendant Hall-Brooke San., Westport, Conn., 1951, Fernald State Sch., Waverly, Mass., 1954-56, acting night supr., 1959-61; minister Congl. chs., Monroe, Conn., 1951-53, Chaplin, Conn., 1953-54, Boston, 1955-58. Appeared as actor with Wellesley (Mass.) Players, Westport (Conn.) Parks and Recreation Commn., 1984-92, one-man show with kilt and bagpipe; sometime lectr. on history of bagpiping in Scotland and Ireland. Mem. Masons (life). Home and Office: PO Box 634 Ridgefield CT 06877-0634

DAVIES, ALMA (ALMA ROSITA), producer, playwright, lyricist, composer, designer, sculptor; b. Bloemfontein, South Africa; d. Walter David Davies and Elizabeth (Van der Kar); m. Lee Kaye, Dec. 9, 1956 (dec. Jan. 1967); children: Walter Ian Kaye, Elena-Beth Kaye; m. Edwin William Williams, June 22, 1985 (dec. Mar. 1997). Tchr., choreographer Spanish dance, ballet Sch. Dance Arts, Carnegie Hall, N.Y.C. Toured as solo dancer, actress with Manhattan Opera Co. in Desert Song, with Ana Maria Spanish Dance co.; soloist Dances of Spain, Am. Mus. Natural History, N.Y.C., featured soloist Jose Greco Dance Co., Washington; soloist, choreographer Jacobs Pillow Dance Festival, Mass., Radio City Music Hall; soloist Am. Youth Ballet, N.Y.C.; guest artist, soloist, choreographer Syracuse (N.Y.) Philharm. Orch.; soloist, dancer, actress Voice of Firestone NBC-TV, N.Y.C.; guest artist Simmons Cruise Concert-S.S. Olympia, Caribbean Seas; exhbns. for sculpted 3-D pictures include Schumacher Fabrics, N.Y.C., Warner Bros., Hollywood others; puppeteer Rose Rivero Charity Showcase, N.Y.C.; jewelry designer, manufacturer; author, composer, dir., prodr. musicals: Princesa, Moon Holiday, Little Lord, Dorinmore, Lord Fauntleroy, (TV film) Clash of Wills; author: I Blow Myself Away, Memoirs of a Remarkable Diva; composer, United In Spirit, We'll Never Forget. Recipient First prize for costume design Beaux Arts Ball, N.Y., Internat. Beaux Arts Ball, N.Y.. Mem. ASCAP, Dramatists Guild, The Drama League, Comml. Theatre Inst., Internat. Platform Assn. Avocations: sculpture, scenic design, costume design. Home: 2857 S Paradise Rd #1001 Las Vegas NV 89109

DAVIES, BRIAN EWART, environmental sciences educator; b. Newport, Wales, Aug. 7, 1937; s. Arthur Ewart and Charlotte (Bennett) D.; m. Gillian Jones, Dec. 29, 1964; children: Ffion C.W., Melissa G.W. BSc, Wales U., Bangor, 1959, PhD, 1963. Head lab. W.J. Chafer Ltd., Doncaster, Eng., 1962-64; lectr. Univ. Coll. Wales, 1965-76; sr. lectr. Dyfed-Wales, 1976-85; prof. dept. environ. sci. Bradford (Eng.) U., Yorkshire, 1985-96, also pro-vice-chancellor; adj. prof. earth sci. Clemson (S.C.) U., 1993-96, prof. geol. scis., 1996—2002, emeritus prof., 2002—. Author more than 140 published works. Home: Boscobel Country Club 107 Teeside Dr Anderson SC 29625-6937 Office: Clemson U Dept Geol Scis 340 Brackett Hl Dept Geolscis Clemson SC 29634-0001 E-mail: bdavies@clemson.edu.

DAVIES, CALEB, IV, lawyer; b. Hammond, Ind., Jan. 29, 1954; s. Caleb and Margaret Davies; m. Cheryl Davies, Oct. 9, 1982; children: Evan, Patrick, Ethan. BS, Ind. U., 1977; JD, Emory U., 1980. Bar: Ga. 1982, U.S. Dist. Ct. (no. dist.) Ga. 1982. Cir. mediator U.S. Ct. Appeals (11th cir.), Atlanta, 1997—. Mediator, arbitrator Am. Arbitration Assn., Atlanta, 1988—, Justice Ctr. Atlanta, 1989—, U.S. Arbitration and Mediation, Atlanta, 1991, Adminstrv. Conf. of U.S., Atlanta, 1990; arbitrator Nat. Assn. Securities Dealers, Atlanta, 1992—, Ga. Dept. Community Affairs, 1992—. Organizer Soc. of Profls. in Dispute Resolution, Atlanta, 1990-92. Recognized for Pro Bono Svc. State of Ga., 1988. Mem. ABA, State Bar Ga., Atlanta Bar Assn. (chair alternative dispute resolution sect., bd. dirs.), Fed. Bar Assn. Avocations: sailing, hiking, coaching, tennis. Office: US Ct Appeals Eleventh Jud Cir/Kinnard Mediation Ctr 56 Forsyth St NW Atlanta GA 30303-2289 E-mail: caleb_davies@call.uscourts.gov.

DAVIES, CHARLES R. lawyer; BS, Duquesne U., 1964; JD, Georgetown U., 1967. Bar: D.C. 1968. Asst. v.p., asst. gen. counsel Geico Corp., Washington, 1978, v.p., gen. counsel, 1992—, group v.p., gen. counsel, 1999, sr. v.p., gen. counsel, 2000—. Office: Geico Corp Geico Plz Washington DC 20076-0001

DAVIES, CHRIS THOMAS, plastic and reconstructive surgeon; b. Rantoul, Ill., 1954; s. Robert C. and Jan Davies. BS in Biology cum laude, U. Calif., Irvine, 1976, BA in Psychology cum laude, 1977; MD, Tulane U., 1982. Diplomate Am. Bd. Plastic Surgery; qualified med. examiner in plastic surgery, Calif. Resident gen. surgery U. Calif.-Irvine Med. Ctr., Orange, 1982-85; resident plastic surgery St. Francis Meml. Hosp., San Francisco, 1985-88; resident/fellow in microvascular surgery Davies Med. Ctr., San Francisco, 1988; pvt. practice Encinitas, Calif., 1988-95; plastic surgeon, mem. active staff Scripps Hosps., La Jolla, Calif., 1992-95, Encinitas, Calif., 1988-95, Tri-City Med. Ctr., 1988-95; assoc. plastic and reconstructive surgery Guthrie Clinic, Ltd., Sayre, Pa., 1995-98, chief plastic and reconstructive surgery, 1998—.

Chief divsn. subspecialty surgery Tri City Med. Ctr., Oceanside, Calif., 1991-92. Recipient Physicians Recognition award AMA, 1989-96. Fellow Internat. Coll. Surgeons; mem. Am. Soc. Plastic Surgeons, Inc., Pa. Med. Soc., Calif. Soc. Plastic Surgeons, Inc., Alpha Omega Alpha. Avocations: surfing, skiing, design. Office: Guthrie Clinic Dept Plastic Surgery Guthrie Sq Sayre PA 18840 also: The Cosmetic Ctr 31 Arnot Rd Horseheads NY 14845-8533

DAVIES, DAVID GEORGE, lawyer, educator; b. Waukesha, Wis., July 19, 1928; s. David Evan and Ella Hilda (Degler) D.; m. Elaine Kowalchik, May 12, 1962; children: Thea Kay, Bryn Ann, Degler Evan. BS, U. Wis., 1950, JD, 1953. Bar: Wis. 1953, Ariz. 1959. Trust rep. First Nat. Bank of Ariz., Phoenix, 1957-58, asst. trust officer, 1958-62, trust officer, head bus. devel. in trust dept., 1962-66, v.p., trust officer, 1966; practice in Phoenix, 1967—; assoc. Wales & Collins, 1967-68; ptnr. Wales, Collins & Davies, 1968-75, Collins, Davies & Cronkhite, Ltd., 1975-85, David G. Davies, Ltd., 1986—. Instr. bus. law local chpt. C.L.U.s, 1965; instr. estate and gift taxation, 1973— ; instr. estate planning Phoenix Coll., 1968— ; past instr. Maricopa County Jr. Coll. Pres. Central Ariz. Estate Planning Council; pres., bd. dirs. Vis. Nurse Service, United Fund Agy.; chmn. bd. Beatitudes Campus of Care; bd. dirs. Phoenix chpt. Nat. Hemophilia Found.; bd. dirs., treas. trusteeship St. Luke's Hosp. Med. Ctr., Phoenix, 1982—; mem. adv. bd. planned giving com. Salvation Army, 1997—. Served to capt. JAGC, AUS, 1953-57. Mem. Central Assn. Life Underwriters (asso.), ABA, Wis. Bar Assn., State Bar Ariz., Am. Assn. Homes for Aged (legal affairs com., future com.) Congregationalist (chmn. bd. trustees, moderator). Office: 5110 N 40th St Ste 236 Phoenix AZ 85018-2151

DAVIES, DON, education educator; b. Mpls., Dec. 28, 1926; s. Clifford Goetz and Gladys (Herr) D.; m. Mary Joyce Davies; children: Druanne, Donna. BA in Journalism, Stanford U., 1948, MA in Ednl. Adminstrn., 1949; EdD in Curriculum and Tchr. Edn., Columbia U., 1956. Tchr. Beverly Hills (Calif.) H.S., 1949-53; edn. instr. Adelphi Coll., 1953-56; asst. prof. edn. San Francisco State Coll., 1956-57; asst. prof. edn., dir. student teaching U. Minn., 1957-61; exec. sec. Nat. Commn. on Tchr. Edn. and Profl. Stds. NEA, 1961-67; assoc. commr. Dept. Edn., 1968-73; fellow in social sci. Yale U., 1973-74; founder Inst. for Responsive Edn., 1973-94; prof. edn. Boston U., 1974-96, prof. emeritus, 1996—, co-dir. Nat. Rsch. and Devel. Ctr. on Families, Communities, 1990-96; Vis. prof. Northeastern U.; preceptor in field; bd. dirs. Inst. for Responsive Edn.; vis. lectr. U. Liverpool, U. Cordoba, Argentina, U. Oviedo, Spain, U. Man., U. Lisbon, Portugal. Author: Low Income Parents and the Schools, 1989, Resource Guide on Parent and Citizen Parcipation in Education, 1988, Parents Make a Difference: An Evaluation of New York City's 1987-88 Parent Involvement Program, 1988, Portrait of Schools Reaching Out, 1992, Communities and Their Schools, 1981, Leading the Way, 1980, Schools Where Parents Make a Difference, 1976, Partnerships for Student Success, 1996, Crossing Boundaries: Report on a Multi-National Action Research Study, 1996; editor Jour. of Tchr. Edn., 1961-67; contbr. articles to profl. jours. Trustee Cambridge Coll.; v.p. Gores' planning com. Ann. Family Reunion Conf., 1999, Parents for Pub. Schs. With USN, 1945-46. Recipient Disting. Svc. medal Dept. Edn., 1971, Internat. Achievement award Nat. Coalition for Parent Involvement in Edn., 1994; grantee John D. and Catherine T. MacArthur Found., Pew Charitable Trusts, Leon Lowenstein Found., Aaron Diamond Found., Charles Stewart Mott Found., J.M. Found., Boston Globe Found., Nat. Inst., Edn., 1976-79. Mem. Phi Delta Kappa. Democrat. Avocations: travel, reading. Office: Northeastern Univ Inst for Responsive Edn Boston MA 02115 E-mail: dondav@bu.edu.

DAVIES, GARRY, biology educator; b. Blackpool, Eng., Jan. 12, 1943; came to U.S., 1954; s. John Verdon and Nellie (Rowley) D.; m. Rebecca Sue Truesdell, May 13, 1973. B of Forestry, Stephen F. Austin State Coll., 1967; MSc in Forestry, Stephen F. Austin State U., 1973; PhD in Forestry, Tex. A&M U., 1981. Seasonal naturalist Nat. Pk. Svc., Yellowstone Nat. Pk., Wyo., summers 1972-85, curator of collections Anchorage, 1987-90; assoc. prof. biology U. Alaska, Anchorage, 1990—. Vol. sci. tchr. Anchorage Elem. Schs., 1990—; comty. advisor Toshiba-Nat. Sci. Tchrs. Assn. Explora Vision Awards, 1996. With USN, 1967-71. Named Tchr. of Yr., 1999; Herbarium grantee Alaska Native Plant Soc., 1996. Avocations: cross country skiing, canoeing, rafting. Home: 8800 Tempest Cir Anchorage AK 99507-3969 Office: U Alaska 3211 Providence Dr Anchorage AK 99508-4614 E-mail: afgd@uaa.alaska.edu.

DAVIES, GEORGE PATRICK, city official; b. Newark, Aug. 2, 1966; s. George Patrick and Frances M. (Kaminski) D.; m. Virginia Annette Cutchins, Apr. 1, 1995. Cert. in Internat. Bus. Studies, Copenhagen U., 1987; BS in Mgmt. Sci., Kean Coll. of N.J., 1989; M.Urban and Reg. Planning, Va. Commonwealth U., 1991. Planning intern Richmond (Va.) Reg. Planning Dist. Commn., 1990; tchg. asst. Va. Commonwealth U., Richmond, 1991; cmty. planner Va. Dept. Housing & Cmty. Devel., Richmond, 1991-92; coord. housing and grant devel. Cmty. Alternatives Mgmt. Group, Virginia Beach, 1992-96, dir. housing, 1999—; housing specialist City of Portsmouth, Va., 1996-98; real estate devel. specialist Norfolk (Va.) Redevel. and Housing Authority, 1998-99; dir. housing Cmty. Alternatives Mgmt. Group, Virginia Beach, Va., 1999—. Mem. Hampton Roads Reg. Consortium, Chesapeake, 1997—. Mem. Am. Planning Assn., Nat. Assn. Housing and Redevel. Ofcls., Nat. Trust for Hist. Preservation, Phi Kappa Phi. Office: Cmty Alternatives Mgmt Group 3133 Magic Hollow Blvd Ste 120 Virginia Beach VA 23456-3094 E-mail: gdavies@comalt.org.

DAVIES, GRACE LUCILLE, real estate broker, educator; b. Providence, Apr. 6, 1926; d. Leonard Cerulle and Eleanor De Prete; m. David John Davies, Feb. 8, 1948; children: Mary Ellen, David L., Pamela, Amy. AA, Long Beach City Coll., 1946; BA, U. Calif., Berkeley, 1948; MA, Calif. State U., Long Beach, 1965. Gen. elem. credential Calif., life elem. credential Calif., elem. sch. adminstr. credential Calif., life elem. sch. adminstr. Calif. Elem. educator ABC Unified Sch. Dist., Artesia, Calif., 1956—85, MGM coord., 1960—70, bilingual coord., 1960—70, asst. prin., 1970—80; real estate, bus., investment D. Davies & Assoc., Long Beach, Calif., 1985—. Clk. Long Beach (Calif.) Election Bd., 1990—; mem., vol. Long Beach City Campaign, 1998. Mem.: Calif. Ret. Tchrs. Assn. (legis. chair 1985—, pres. 2000—), Apt. Mgmt. Assn., Delta Kappa Gamma (v.p., pres., Golden Rose award 1996), Pi Lambda Theta (treas., v.p., pres., Outstanding Contbn. Edn. award 1996). Avocations: travel, reading, theater, camping, music. Home: 6215 Parima St Long Beach CA 90803

DAVIES, HUGH MARLAIS, museum director; b. Grahamstown, South Africa, Feb. 12, 1948; came to U.S., 1956; s. Horton Marlais and Brenda M. (Deakin) D.; children: Alexandra, Dorian; m. Lynda Forsha; 1 stepdaughter, Mackenzie Forsha Fuller. AB summa cum laude, Princeton U., 1970, MFA, 1972, PhD, 1976. Dir. Univ. Gallery, U. Mass., Amherst, 1975-83, Mus. Contemporary Art (formerly La Jolla Mus. Contemporary Art), San Diego, 1983—. Vis. prof. fine arts Amherst Coll., 1980-83; mem. adv. coun. dept. art and archeology Princeton U., 1989—, panel mem. fed. adv. com. internat. exhbns., 1990-94; co-curator Whitney Mus. Am. Art Biennial, 2000. Author: (book) Francis Bacon: The Papal Portraits of 1953, 2001, Francis Bacon: The Early and Middle Years, 1928-1958; co-author: Sacred Art in a Secular Century: 20th Century Religious Art, 1978, Francis Bacon (Abbeville), 1986. Nat. Endowment Arts fellow, 1982, 95. Mem. Am. Assn. Mus., Coll. Art Assn., Assn. Art Mus. Dirs. (trustee 1994-2001, pres. 1997-98), Am. Fedn. Arts. Office: Mus Contemporary Art San Diego 700 Prospect St La Jolla CA 92037-4228

DAVIES, J. CLARENCE (TERRY DAVIES), government agency administrator; b. N.Y.C., Nov. 16, 1937; BA cum laude, Dartmouth Coll., 1959; PhD in Am. Govt., Columbia U., 1965. Instr. govt., dir. Bureau Rsch. in Mcpl. Govt. Bowdoin Coll., Brunswick, Maine, 1963-65; chief examiner environ. and consumer protection Bureau of Budget Exec. Office of Pres., Washington, 1965-67, sr. staff mem. Coun. Environ. Quality, 1970-73; asst. prof. politics and pub. affairs Princeton (N.J.) U., 1967-70; fellow, asst. dir. instns. and pub. decisions divsn. Resources for Future, Inc., Washington, 1973-76; exec. v.p. Conservation Found., Washington, 1976-89; asst. adminstr. policy, planning and evaluation U.S. EPA, Washington, 1989-91; exec. dir. Nat. Commn. on Environment, Washington, 1991-92; dir. Ctr. for Risk Mgmt. Resources for Future, Washington, 1992-2000, sr. fellow, 2000—. Cons. U.S. Bureau of Budget, 1967-68, U.S. Dept. Health, Edn. and Welfare, 1968-69, Pres.'s Adv. Coun. on Exec. Orgn., 1969-70, NSF, 1976-79; mem.-at-large exec. com. sci. adv. bd. EPA, 1976-81, chmn. adminstr.'s adv. com. toxic substances, 1977-78, co-chmn. com. on econs. sci. adv. bd., 1979-80, mem. subcom. environ. statis. Nat. Adv. Coun. for Environ. Policy and Tech., 1991-95; mem. sr. steering com. Ctr. Tech. and Adminstrn., Am. U., 1976-79; mem. sci. adv. bd. Internat. Joint Commn. U.S.-Can., 1984-87; mem. adv. bd. Ctr. for Chem. Process Safety, 1985-89; mem. bd. govs. Environ. Health and Safety Inst., Nat. Safety Coun., 1986-89; mem. adv. panel on systems at risk from climate change U.S. Office Tech. Assessment, 1991-92; bd. dirs. Inst. Coop. Environ. Mgmt., 1991-93; chmn. bd. dirs. Resolve, Inc., 1993-2001. Author: Neighborhood Groups and Urban Renewal, 1966, The Politics of Pollution, 2d edit., 1975, Pollution Control in the United States, 1998, (monographs) Risk Assessment and Risk Control, 1985, The Environmental Protection Act: An Integrated Pollution Control Law, 1988; co-author: Training for Environmental Groups, 1984, Determining Unreasonable Risk, 1979, Significant New Use Rules for Existing Chemicals, 1983, Controlling Cross-Media Pollutants, 1984; author: (with others) Growing Against Ourselves: The Energy-Environment Tangle, 1974, Federal Environmental Law, 1974, Environmental Management in the Colorado River Basin, 1974, The Governance of Common Property Resources, 1974, Social Research and Public Policies, 1975, Air Pollution and Administrative Control, 1977, Mechanisms of Toxicity and Hazard Evaluation, 1980, Strategies for Public Health, 1981, TSCA's Impact on Society and the Chemical Industry, 1983, Environmental Policy in the 1980s, 1984, Pollutants in a Multimedia Environment, 1986, Integrated Pollution Control in Europe and North America, 1990, Keeping Pace with Science and Engineering: Case Studies in Environmental Regulation, 1993, Encyclopedia of the Environment, 1994, Pollution Control in the United States, 1998, Reforming Permitting, 2001; co-editor: Business and Environment: Toward Common Ground, 1977, Risk Communication, 1987; mem. editorial bd. Toxic Substances Jour., 1979-89. Mem. bd. dirs. Wildlife Habitat Enhancement Coun., 1987-89. Ford Found. Met. Region fellow. Fellow AAAS; mem. NAS (com. environ. indices 1973-74, com. on environ. decision making 1975-77, com. on prevention significant deterioration under Clean Air Act 1979-81, com. on instl. means for assessment risks to pub. health 1982-83, environ. studies bd. 1983-85, com. on multimedia pollutants 1986-88, chmn. com. on prins. decision making for regulating chemicals in environment 1974-75), Nat. Inst. for Chem. Studies (nat. adv. bd. 1986-89), Nat. Acad. Engring. (steering com. symposium on environ. regulation 1992-93), Nat. Acad. Pub. Adminstrn. (panel on econ. incentives 1992-93, mem. panel on EPA priorities 1993-95), Phi Beta Kappa. Office: 1616 P St NW Washington DC 20036-1434 E-mail: davies@rff.org.

DAVIES, JOHN ARTHUR, physics and engineering educator, scientist; b. Prestatyn, North Wales, Mar. 28, 1927; emigrated to Can., 1940; s. Francis James and Doris Annie (Edkins) D.; m. Florence Smithson, July 29, 1950; children: Susan, Chris, Cathy, Paul, Jim, Anne. BA with honors in Chemistry, St. Michael's Coll., Toronto, 1947; MA in Phys. Chemistry, U. Toronto, 1948, PhD in Phys. Chemistry, 1950; D.Sc. (hon.), Royal Roads Mil. Coll., 1984, Salford U., Eng., 1993. With Atomic Energy of Canada, Chalk River, Ont., 1950-85; prof. engring. and physics McMaster U., Hamilton, 1969-92, prof. emeritus, 1992—. Vis. prof. physics U. Aarhus, Denmark, 1964-65, 69-70; vis. physicist Nobel Inst. Physics, Stockholm, Sweden, 1962, Calif. Inst. Tech., 1969, Osaka U., Japan, 1972. Author: (with J.W. Mayer, L. Eriksson) Ion Implantation, 1970; contbr. over 200 articles to prof. jours. Can. Ramsay Meml. fellow, 1954-56; recipient Noranda medal Chem. Inst. Can., 1965, Callinan award Am. Electrochem. Soc., 1968, W.B. Lewis medal Can. Nuclear Soc., 1998. Fellow Royal Soc. Can., Bohmische Phys. Soc.; mem. Chem. Inst. Can., Can. Assn. Physics, Danish Royal Soc. Roman Catholic. Home and Office: Box 224 7 Wolfe Ave Deep River ON Canada K0J 1P0

DAVIES, KELVIN JAMES ANTHONY, research scientist, educator, consultant, author; b. London, Oct. 15, 1951; came to U.S., 1975, dual citizenship, 1993; s. Alfred B. and Phyllis (Garcia) D.; m. Joanna Davies, Sept. 14, 1980; children: Sebastian, Alexander. BEd, Liverpool/Lancaster (Eng.) U., 1974; BS summa cum laude, MS, U. Wis., 1976, 77; CPhil, U. Calif., Berkeley, 1979, PhD, 1981; DSc (hon.), U. Moscow, Russia, 1993; MD (hon.), U. Gdansk, Poland, 1995; D of Univ. (hon.), U. Buenos Aires, 1998. Instr. Beal Sch. for Boys, London, 1974-75; rsch. asst. U. Wis., Madison, 1975-77, U. Calif., Berkeley, 1977-80, lectr. physiology dept. physiology and anatomy, 1980-81; rsch. assoc. dept. biochemistry, inst. toxicology U. So. Calif., L.A., 1981-82, asst. prof. biochemistry, toxicology, 1983-86, assoc. prof. biochemistry, toxicology, 1986-90, prof. biochemistry, toxicology, 1990; instr., sr. rsch. assoc. dept. physiology and biophysics med. sch. Harvard U., 1982-83; prof. biochemistry and molecular biology Albany (N.Y.) Med. Coll., 1991-96, John A. Muntz Univ. prof., 1991-96, chmn. dept. biochemistry and molecular biology, 1991-96, prof. molecular medicine dept. medicine, 1993-96; prof., assoc. dean rsch. Andrus Gerontology Ctr. U. So. Calif., L.A., 1996—; James E. Birren chair gerontology, dir. Andrus Rsch. Inst., 1996—2002. Dir. Nat. Parkinson's Found. Lab., 1996—; founder, dir. STAR program U. So. Calif./L.A. County Schs. Dist., 1984-90; dir. grad. studies inst. toxicology U. So. Calif., 1985-90, mem. cell biology program, 1986-91, fellow inst. molecular medicine, 1988-91; hon. dist. prof. Russian State Med. U., Moscow, 1989; coun. mem. Gordon Rsch. Confs. Frontiers of Sci., 1995-96. Author: Oxidative Damage and Repair: Chemical, Biological and Medical Aspects, 1992, Oxygen '93, 1994, The Oxygen Paradox, 1995; editor in chief: (jour.) Free Radical Biology and Medicine, 1981—, Biochemistry and Molecular Biology Internat., 1999; editor-in-chief IUBMB-LIFE, 1999-2000, mem. editl. bd., 2000—; assoc. editor: Mitochondrion; mem. editl. bd. Advances in Free Radical Biology and Medicine, 1985-87, The Biochem. Jour., 1989-95, Amino Acids, 1991—, Methods in Enzymology, 1991—, Molecular Aspects of Medicine, 1993—; assoc. editor: Jours. Gerontology, 1996—, Cell and Molecular Life Scis., 1999-; contbr. over 200 articles to profl. jours. and books. Active Arts Coun., Pasadena, Calif., 1988-90; pres. Calif. Philharm. Orch. Found., 1996—; bd. govs. The Albany Acad. for Boys, 1994-96. Recipient Chancellors award for Rsch., U. Calif., Berkeley, 1981, Young Investigator award NIH, 1984, 50th Anniversary medal U. Gdansk, 1995; rsch., program project grantee NIH, 1983—; fellow Hoffman-La Roche, 1981, Arco, 1981, Am. Heart Assn., 1982, NIH, 1983. Fellow AAAS, CNR (Italy), Russian Acad. Scis., Gerontol. Soc. Am.; mem. Am. Coll. Sports Medicine, Am. Physiol. Soc. (Harwood S. Belding award 1982), Am. Soc. for Biochemistry and Molecular Biology, Internat. Union Biochemistry and Molecular Biology (coun. mem. 1995—), Biochem. Soc., Biophys. Soc., European Soc. Free Radical Rsch., Internat. Soc. Free Radical Rsch. (coun. 1988—, pres. 2001—), Internat. Cell Rsch. Orgn., N.Y. Acad. Sci., Rsch. Coun. New Zealand, The Oxygen Soc. (fellow, sec. gen. 1987-90, pres. 1992-95, Disting. Achievement award 1997), Osyben Club of Calif. (pres. 2002-), Sigma Xi, Phi Beta Kappa, Kappa Delta Pi. Avocations: opera, symphony, cricket, soccer, food and wines. Office: Univ So Calif Andrus Gerontology Ctr 3715 Mcclintock Ave Rm 306 Los Angeles CA 90089-0001 E-mail: kelvin@usc.edu.

DAVIES, PAUL LEWIS, JR., retired lawyer; b. San Jose, Calif., July 21, 1930; s. Paul Lewis and Faith (Crummey) D.; m. Barbara Bechtel, Dec. 22, 1955 (dec. June 2001); children: Laura (Mrs. Segundo Mateo), Paul Lewis III. AB, Stanford U., 1952; JD, Harvard U., 1957. Bar: Calif. 1957. Assoc. Pillsbury, Madison & Sutro, San Francisco, 1957-63, ptnr., 1963-89; gen. counsel Chevron Corp., 1984-89. Hon. trustee Calif. Acad. Scis., trustee, 1970-83, chmn., 1973-80; pres. Herbert Hoover Found.; bd. overseers Hoover Instn., chmn., 1976-82, 91-93; hon. regent U. of Pacific, regent, 1959-90. Lt. U.S. Army, 1952-54. Mem. Bohemian Club, Pacific-Union Club, Villa Taverna, World Trade Club (San Francisco), Claremont Country Club, Cypress Point (Pebble Beach, Calif.), Sainte Claire (San Jose, Calif.), Collectors, Explorers, Links (N.Y.C.), Met. Club (Washington), Chgo. Club, Phi Beta Kappa, Pi Sigma Alpha. Republican. Office: 3470 Mt Diablo Blvd Ste A210 Lafayette CA 94549-3985 E-mail: pauldaviesjr@yahoo.com.

DAVIES, PAUL LEWIS, III, venture capitalist; b. Oakland, Calif., June 29, 1961; s. Paul Lewis Jr. and Barbara Bechtel Davies; m. Pilar Hanigan, Feb. 14, 1963; children: Robert H., Natalie L., Tyler S. BS in Indsl. Engring., Stanford U., 1983, MBA, 1987. With Bechtel Group, Inc., San Francisco, 1987-93; prin. Brentwood Assocs., Menlo Park, Calif., 1993-94, Fremont Group, San Francisco, 1995; mng. prin. Cambria Group, Menlo Park, 1996—. Bd. dirs. Crossbow Tech., Inc., San Jose, Calif., Lakeside Corp., Lafayette, Calif.; chmn. bd. dirs. DSA/Phototech, Inc., L.A. Nat. trustee Boys and Girls Clubs Am., Atlanta; bd. overseers Hoover Instn., Stanford, Calif.; pres., bd. dirs. Llagas Found., Lafayette; bd. dirs. Lakeside Found., Lafayette, Hoover Fedn., Ohio; bd. trustees Menlo Sch., Atherton, Calif.. Mem. Inst. Indsl. Engrs., Lincoln Club. Republican. Office: The Cambria Group 160 El Camino Real Ste 155 Menlo Park CA 94025 Fax: (650) 329-8601. E-mail: davies@cambriagroup.com.

DAVIES, PERCY (PETE) CHARLES, mechanical engineer; b. Pontrilas, Sask., Can., Sept. 18, 1920; s. George Davies, Alice Fanny Wall; m. Nancy Naidee Clark, June 28, 1941 (div. Feb. 1959); children: Denise Diane, Leslie Ann, Joyce Natalie; m. Betty Jean Martin; 1 child, Michael Lane. BSME, U. Wash., 1953. Cert. comml. balloon pilot FAA. Machinist inspector Continental Can Corp., Seattle, 1949—53; gen. mgr. Cert. Mfg., Seattle, 1953—58, Smith-Williston Co., Seattle, 1958—59, Dependable Bldg. Maint., Seattle, 1960—65; owner, gen. mgr. Dictamatic Corp., Portland, 1965—77; owner, chief pilot Rainbow Balloon Flights, Sun City, Ariz., 1983—87; owner Adna Press, Sun City, 1987—. Chmn. bd. Dictamatic Corp., Portland, 1965—77. Author: The Spartan Rebel, 2003, Big Man on Campus, 2003. With US Merchant Marines, 1945. Mem.: Nat. Assn. Bldg. Svc. Contrs. (nat. bd. dirs. 1965), Tau Beta Pi. Republican. Church Of The Nazarene. Avocations: writing, woodworking, travel, photography, portrait painting. Home and Office: 9206 W Glen Oaks Cir N Sun City AZ 85351

DAVIES, PETER JOHN, plant physiology educator, researcher; b. Sudbury, Middlesex, Eng., Mar. 7, 1940; came to U.S., 1966; s. William Bertram and Ivy Doreen (Parmentier) D.; m. Linda Kay DeNoyer, Aug. 2, 1976; children: Kenneth DeNoyer, Caryn Parmentier. BSc with honors, U. Reading, Eng., 1962; MS, U. Calif., Davis, 1964; PhD, U. Reading, 1966. Instr. Yale U., New Haven, 1966-69; asst. prof. plant physiology Cornell U., Ithaca, N.Y., 1969-75, assoc. prof., 1975-83, prof., 1983—, chmn. sect. plant biology, 1992-96. Vis. prof. Cambridge (Eng.) U., 1976-77, Univ. Coll. of Wales, Aberystwyth, 1983-84, U. Minn., 1984, U. Tasmania, Australia, 1996-97. Author: (with others) The Life of the Green Plant, 1980, Control Mechanisms in Plant Development, 1970; editor: Plant Hormones and Their Role in Plant Growth and Redevelopment, 1987, Plant Hormones: Physiology, Biochemistry and Molecular Biology, 1995; editor-in-chief Plant Growth Regulation, 1987-92. Mem. Am. Soc. Plant Physiology, Internat. Plant Growth Substance Assn. (coun. 1991-98). Office: Cornell U Plant Biology Ithaca NY 14853 E-mail: pjd2@cornell.edu.

DAVIES, ROBERT ABEL, III, consumer products company executive; b. Englewood, N.J., Sept. 10, 1935; s. Robert Abel Jr. and Lillian Louise (Vila) D.; m. Marilyn Jean Doering, June 16, 1957 (div.); children: Bruce Gregory, Mark Richard, Eric Doering, Nancy Louise; m. Diane M. Church, Sept. 2, 1995, children; Alexander Church, Sophia Catherine. AB, Colgate U., 1957; MBA, Columbia U., 1963. Salesman Proctor & Gamble Co., Cin., 1960-61; product mgr. Colgate Palmolive Co., N.Y.C., 1963-66; group product mgr. Boyle-Midway div. Am. Home Products, N.Y.C., 1966-69; v.p. mktg. Church & Dwight Co. Inc., Princeton, N.J., 1969-76, v.p., gen. mgr., 1976-81, pres., chief oper. officer, 1981-84, also dir., 1981-84; pres., chief exec. officer Calif. Home Brands Inc., Terminal Island, Calif., 1985-89; prin. Gold Coast Calamari Inc., Oxnard, Calif., 1990-94; pres., CEO Church & Dwight Co., Inc., Princeton, NJ, 1995-2001, chmn., CEO, 2001—, bd. dirs., 1995—. Served to lt. (j.g.) USNR, 1957-60. Office: 469 N Harrison St Princeton NJ 08540-3510

DAVIES, RUSS, quality assurance professional; b. London, Dec. 14, 1960; arrived in U.S., 2000; s. Edward George and Rita (Pyle) Davies; 1 child, Holly Amanda. MBA, Open Bus. Sch., Milton Keynes, 1993. Prodn. engr. Boc Medishield, England, 1980-86; product specialist Boc Medshield, England, 1986-90; quality assurance mgr. Boc Ohmeda, England, 1990-94; quality assurance and regulatory affairs mgr. SIMS Wallace, Colchester, England, 1994-95, SIMS Simcare, Colchester, 1995-96, SIMS Portex Ltd., Colchester, 1996-98, v.p. regulatory affairs and quality systems, 2000—; quality dir. SIMS Graseby Ltd., Watford, England, 1998-2000; v.p. Deltec, Inc., St. Paul, 2000—02. Avocations: guitar, music, medical device engineering, mba mentoring. Office: Deltec Inc 1265 Grey Fox Rd Saint Paul MN 55112

DAVIES, THOMAS MOCKETT, JR., history educator; b. Lincoln, Nebr., May 25, 1940; s. Thomas Mockett and Faith Elizabeth (Arnold) D.; m. Eloisa Carmela Monzón Abate, June 10, 1968 (dec. Jan. 1994); 1 dau., Jennifer Elena; m. Rosemarie Adele Lindsay, Jan. 7, 1995. BA, U. Nebr., 1962, MA, 1964; student, Universidad Nacional Autonóma de México, 1961; PhD, U. N.Mex., 1970; postdoctoral fellow, U. Tex., Austin, 1969-70. Lectr. U. N.Mex. Peace Corps Tng. Center, 1964-66; asst. prof. Latin Am. history San Diego State U., 1968-72, asso. prof., 1972-75, prof., 1975—, chmn. Latin Am. studies, 1979—; dir. Center Latin Am. Studies, Henry L. and Grace Doherty Charitable Found. fellow, 1966-68. Author: (with others) Historia, problema y promesa. Homenaje a Jorge Basadre, 1978, Research Guide to Andean History: Bolivia, Chile, Ecuador and Peru, 1981, The Spanish Civil War: American Hemisphere Perspectives, 1982, EL APRA de la Ideología a la Praxis, 1989, Latin American Military History: An Annotated Bibliography, 1992; author: Indian Integration in Peru: A Half Century of Experience, 1900-48, 1974 (co-winner Hubert Herring Meml. award Pacific Coast Coun. on Latin Am. Studies 1973), (with Victor Villanueva) 300 Documentos Para la Historia del APRA; Conspiraciones Apristas de 1935 a 1939, 1979, Secretos Electorales del APRA: Correspondencia y Documentos de 1939, 1982; (with Brian Loveman) The Politics of Anti-Politics: The Military in Latin America, 1978, 3d rev. edit., 1997, Che Guevara: Guerrilla Warfare, 1985 (Hubert Herring Meml. award 1985, 3d rev. edit., 1997); mem. editorial bd. Hispanic Am. Hist. Rev., 1985-1990; Contbr. (with Brian Loveman) articles to profl. jours. Recipient Outstanding Faculty award San Diego State U. Alumni Assn., 1981, 97, 1st ann. Internat. Scholar award Phi Beta Delta, 1992, Wiley W. Manuel award Calif. State Bar Assn., 1995, 98; grantee Dept. Edn. for Nat. Resource Ctr. for L.Am. Studies, 1979—; summer rsch. grantee San Diego State U. Found., 1971-73, 75, 76, 79, 80, faculty rsch. devel. grantee San Diego State U., 1988, 89, 90, grantee William and Flora Hewlett Found., 1997-2001. Mem. Latin Am. Studies Assn., Conf. Latin Am. History (exec. sec. 1979-84), Pacific Coast Council Latin Am. (bd. govs. 1989-91, pres. 1996-97), Rocky Mountain Council on Latin Am. Studies (exec. com. 1980—, pres. 1996-97), Am. Hist. Assn., Consortium L.Am. Studies Programs (exec. sec.-treas. 1994—). Home: 4617 Edenvale Ave La Mesa CA 91941-5508 Office: San Diego State U Dept History San Diego CA 92182

DAVIES, THOMAS YOUNG, III, lawyer, law educator; b. Taylor, Pa., Mar. 10, 1946; s. Thomas Young, Jr. and Elizabeth (Robling) D.; m. Susan McCall, Mar. 8, 1969. B.A., U. Del., 1969; J.D., M.A., Northwestern U., 1975, Ph.D. in Polit. Sci., 1980. Bar: Ill. 1975, U.S. Dist. Ct. (no. dist.) Ill. 1976, U.S. Supreme Ct. 1983. Assoc. Kirkland & Ellis, Chgo., 1976-81; research atty. Am. Bar Found., Chgo., 1981-86, editor research jour., 1983-85; assoc. prof. U. Tenn. Coll. Law, Knoxville, 1986—. Contbr. articles to profl. jours.; articles editor Northwestern U. Law Rev., 1974. Russell Sage resident in law and social sci. U. Calif.-Berkeley, 1975-76. Served with U.S. Army, 1968-71. Mem. ABA, Law and Soc. Assn., Am. Judicature Soc., Am. Polit. Sci. Assn., Order Coif, Phi Beta Kappa. Democrat. Office: Univ of Tenn Coll of Law 1505 Cumberland Ave Knoxville TN 37916-3199

DAVIES, WILLIAM RALPH, service executive; b. Santa Barbara, Calif., Aug. 17, 1955; s. Ralph Emmett and Georgann Marie (Cordingly) D.; m. Karen L. Blake, May 12, 1984 (div. 1999). AA in Real Estate, Am. River Coll., 1978; BS in Fin., Ins. and Real Estate, Calif. State U., Sacramento, 1980; postgrad. in Internat. Bus., Golden Gate U., 1982-84. Real estate assoc. Kiernan Realtors, Sacramento, 1975-77; co-owner real estate firm Sacramento, 1977; pvt. practice real estate cons., property mgr., 1978-80; broker assoc. MBA Bus. Svcs., Sacramento, 1980-85, pres., 1985—, El Dorado Hills, 1984—2002. Bd. dirs. WRD, Inc., El Dorado Hills, Vista Sr. Living, Inc., El Dorado Hills, v.p., 1999—2001. Republican. Avocations: history, bridge, golf. Office: 895 Embarcadero Dr Ste 203 El Dorado Hills CA 95762 E-mail: wdavies@mbabiz.com.

DAVIES-JONES, ROBERT PETER, meteorologist; b. Leicester, Eng., Feb. 15, 1943; arrived in U.S., 1964; s. Cyril and Gladys Marjorie Jesse Davies-Jones. BSc with honors, Birmingham (Eng.) U., 1964; PhD, U. Colo., 1969. Postdoctoral fellow Nat. Ctr. for Atmospheric Rsch., Boulder, Colo., 1969—70; meteorologist Nat. Severe Storms Lab., NOAA, Norman, Okla., 1970—. Adj. prof. U. Okla., Norman, 1976—; cons. on tornadoes Nuclear Regulatory Commn., 1973—79; leader tornado intercept project Nat. Severe Storms Lab., Norman, 1975—87. Co-editor: (book) The Tornado: Its Structure, Dynamics,

Prediction and Hazards, 1993 (Best New Book in Category, 1994). Recipient Bronze medal, Dept. Commerce, 1985, Outstanding Scientific Paper awards, Nat. Oceanic and Atmospheric Adminstrn., 1983, 1986, 1995—96, 1999, 2002; grantee, NSF, 1994—95, 2000—03. Fellow: Am. Meteorol. Soc. (co-chief editor Jour. Atmospheric Scis. 1993—95, Editor's award 1986). Anglican. Achievements include research in dynamics and origins of rotation in tornadoes and their parent supercell thunderstorms. Avocation: soccer. Office: Nat Severe Storms Lab 1313 Halley Cir Norman OK 73069 Fax: 405-366-0472.

DAVIES-MCNAIR, JANE, retired educational consultant; b. Topeka, May 21, 1922; m. K. Robert Davies, Aug. 27, 1949; m. John D. McNair June 4, 1989. BE, Nat. Louis U. (formerly Nat. Coll. Edn.), Evanston, Ill., 1944, ME, 1958; postgrad., Columbia U., Ill. State U., Nat. Coll. Edn. Tchr. various schs., Oak Park, Ill., Hillside, N.J., Elmont, N.Y., 1944-58, Sch. Dist., Dwight, Ill., 1959-67, Streater, Ill., 1968; asst. county supt. Livingston County, Pontiac, Ill., 1969-72; project cons., supr., trainer early prevention of sch. failure K W Curriculum Svc. Office, Peotone, Ill., 1972-77; freelance cons., speaker early childhood edn. Ill., 1977-80; ret., 1980. Author: Resource Guide for Developing Pre-Academic, Learning Skills and Other guides for the Early Prevention of School Failure, The Gifted and the Biligual and Migrant Programs. Mem.: DAR, ASCD, AAUW, Childhood Edn. Internat., Internat. Platform Assn., Ill. Edn. Assn. (life and ret. life com.), Ill. Ret. Tchrs. Assn. (dir. region II), Assn. Childhood Edn. (early childhood), Nat. Assn. Edn. Young Children, State Evaluation Team, U.S. Holocause Meml. Mus. Circle of Life (charter supporting mem.), Nat. Mus. Am. Indian (charter), Smithsonian Mus. Am. India, Nat. Soc. Sons and Daus. of Pilgrims, Am. Assn. Ret. Persons, Gen. Fedn. Women's Club, Delta Kappa Gamma, Order Eastern Star.

DAVIES SILCOTT, LOMA GEYER, freelance writer, English educator; b. Chgo., July 14, 1934; d. Fred Harry and May Belle Geyer; m. Robert Eugene Davies, Sept. 5, 1954; (dec. Nov., 1982); children: Kathleen, Daniel, Joel, John; m. Ralph R. Silcott, Jan. 8, 1994. BS, Valparaiso U., 1970; MS, Purdue U., 1975. Legal sec. Gavit and Richardson, Gary, Ind., 1954-58; tchr. Hobart (Ind.) H.S., 1970-87; freelance writer, 1975—; assoc. prof. Oglala Lakota Indian Coll., Rapid City & Kyle, S.D., 1995—. Author: (books) The Nuts and Bolts Writer's Manual, 1991, 201 Happy Hints, 1991, Cook's Corner Recipe Collection, 1991, Senior Sense, 1995. Mem. Nat. Writers Assn., Writers Info. Network, Rapid Valley Faith Bapt. Ch. Republican. Avocations: sewing, knitting, quilting, reading, piano and organ. Home: 1777 Zinnia St Rapid City SD 57703-6280 Office: Oglala Lakota Indian College PO Box 490 Kyle SD 57752-0490 E mail: lomasilcott@cs.com.

DAVIES-VENN, CHRISTIAN, environmental engineer; b. Freetown, Sierra Leone, Apr. 24, 1952; came to U.S., 1982; s. Reynold Jonathan and Mary Arabella (Davies) Venn; m. Rebecca Princess Thomas, Apr. 26, 1980; children: Esther, Cynthia. B of Engring., U. Sierra Leone, 1976; MS, U. Cin., 1984; PhD, U. Ark., 1989. Registered profl. engr., Va., Md., D.C.; diplomate Am. Acad. Environ. Engrs. Project engr. Techsult & Co. Engrs., Freetown, 1976-78, office mgr., 1978-82; rsch. assoc. U. Cin., 1984-87, U. Ark., Fayetteville, 1987 90; mgr. process devel. Parsons Engring. Sci., Inc., Fairfax, Va., 1990-94; sr. project mgr., process engring. program mgr. PEER Cons., P.C., Rockville, Md., 1994—. Ptnr. Techsult & Co., Freetown, 1978-83; mem. nutrient removal com. Parsons Engring.-Sci., Inc., Pasadena, Calif., 1992-94. Contbr. articles to profl. jours. Chmn. stewardship com. Oakton (Va.) United Meth. Ch., 1992-94; mem. Gideons Internat.; chmn., bd. trustees Fairhaven United Meth. Ch.; active Gideons Internat. Nat. scholar Govt. Sierra Leone, 1972, merit scholar, Govt. Republic of Germany, 1972; African grad. fellow African-Am. Inst., N.Y.C., 1982-89; recipient 1st pl. student presentation Ark. Water Works & Poll Control, 1988. Mem. ASCE, NSPE, Water Environment Fedn., Fed. Water Quality Assn., Chesapeake Water Environment Assn. (biosolids and residuals mgmt. com.), Am. Water Works Assn., Am. Water Resources Assn. (water policy and mgmt., water law working group), Am. Acad. Environ. Engrs., Internat. Assn. Water Quality, Gideons Internat., Chi Epsilon, Phi Kappa Phi. Avocations: creative writing, classical music, computer programming, volleyball, soccer. Office: PEER Consultants PC 12300 Twinbrook Pkwy Ste 410 Rockville MD 20852-1650 E-mail: daviesvenn@att.net., daviesc@peercpc.com.

D'AVIGNON, ROY JOSEPH, lawyer; b. Dallas, July 20, 1942; s. Roy J. and Ann (Ham) D'A.; m. Tania M. Mychajlyshyn, Nov. 29, 1969; children: Larissa A., Markian W. BSS, Loyola U., New Orleans, 1964; LLB, Harvard U., 1967. Bar: Tex. 1967, Mass. 1969. Assoc. Hutchins & Wheeler, Boston, 1969-77; counsel Raytheon Co., Lexington, Mass., 1977-86, div. counsel, 1986-90, asst. gen. counsel, 1990-99; v.p., sect. and gen. counsel Simplex Time Recorder Co., Gardner, Mass., 1999—2001; sole practitioner, 2001—. Capt. M.I., U.S. Army, 1967-69. Mem. ABA, Mass. Bar Assn., Tex. Bar Assn., Boston Bar Assn.

DAVILA, GREGORY DAVID, lawyer; b. Key West, Fla., May 17, 1967; s. Helio J. and Margarita E. Davila. BA in Polit. Sci., Fla. Internat. U., 1987; JD, Stetson U., 1990. Bar: Fla. 1991. Atty. Pub. Defender's Office, Key West, 1992-94; pvt. practice Key West, 1994—. Mem.: ABA, Monroe County Bar Assn., Dade Lodge No. 14. Office: 2505 Flagler Ave Key West FL 33040-3934 E-mail: davilaesq@aol.com.

DAVILA, RAFAEL ANGEL, III, college counselor, educator; b. Rio Piedras, P.R., Nov. 24, 1967; s. Rafael Angel Jr. and Maria Dávila; m. Krista Rae (Schneiderwind) Dávila, July 17, 1993; children: Alexia Irene, Rafael Angel IV. BS, U. Ctrl. Fla., 1990, MA, 1995, postgrad., 1997—. Cert. sch. guidance gounselor, correctional probation officer, Fla.; nat. cert. counselor. Behavior tng. specialist Threshold Inc., Winter Park, Fla., 1990-91, 92-93; probation and parole officer Dept. Corrections, Orlando, Fla., 1991-92; children's svcs. counselor Great Oaks Village, Orlando, 1993-95; sch. counselor Seminole County Pub. Schs., Sanford, Fla., 1995-99; counselor Seminole C.C., Sanford, 1999—, instr. Mem. sch. adv. coun. Winter Springs (Fla.) H.S., 1997-99. With USN, 1985-88. Tchr. edn. Am.'s minorities scholar U. Ctrl. Fla., 1994, scholar Universal Studios, 1999. Democrat. Roman Catholic. Avocations: playing softball and golf, attending sporting events and broadway shows, dancing.

DAVILA, SUSAN, guidance counselor; b. Bayaman, P.R., Aug. 11, 1961; came to U.S., 1962; d. Manuel Ramon Valcárcel and Maria Elena Garcia-Meitin; m. Daniel Ricardo Dávila, Dec. 12, 1982; children: Elena Susana, Daniel Antonio, Andrés Daniel. BA in Elem. Edn., St. Thomas U., 1986, MS in Guidance Counseling. Cert. elem. tchr., guidance counselor. Tchr. Sts. Peter and Paul Sch., Miami, Fla., 1986-98; guidance counselor St. Agatha Cath. Sch., Sts. Peter and Paul Cath. Sch., Miami, 1998—. Youth group coord. Sts. Peter and Paul Sch., 1994—, peer tchr., 1994—. Vocations com. Sts. Peter and Paul Ch., Miami, 1997—, festival com., 1990—. Mem. Fla. Counseling Assn., FASERVIC, Nat. Cath. Edn. Assn. Roman Catholic. Avocations: reading, walking.

DAVILLA, DONNA ELAINE, school system administrator; b. Galesburg, Ill., Aug. 14, 1948; d. Robert Harold and Melba Anne (Richmond) D. BFA, Drake U., 1970, MFA, 1972. Cert. art administr., Iowa. Grad. asst. Drake U., Des Moines, 1971, substitute tchr., 1971 78; secondary art tchr. Des Moines Pub. Schs., 1972-93, curriculum specialist for arts, 1988-93, art facilitator, 1992-99, art cons., 1999—, dir. gifted and talented program, K-12, 2002—. Facilitator Heartland AEA II, Johnston, Iowa, 1991-93, 2000; bd. dirs. Iowa Designer Crafts, Des Moines, 1978-79; chair art adv. coun. Des Moines Pub. Schs., 1990—, chair textbook selection, 1991—; Middle East Arts Edn. del. People to People, 1994; mem. art adv. bd. Grand View Coll., 1996—. Asst. to campaign mgr. Dole for Pres., Des Moines, 1990; active Greater Des Moines Leadership Inst., 1994, mem.'s coun. Des Moines Art Ctr., 1989—, Print Club, Des Moines Art Ctr. Bd., 1997-99, 2000-01; active Mayor's Task Force for Beautification Des Moines, 2000-01, Alliance Francaise Bd., 2002—. Recipient Take Pride in Des Moines Tchr. award Des Moines City Coun., 1993; Connie Belin fellow U. Iowa, 1985, 92, Fallingwater Conservancy fellow, 1992; named Iowa Disting. Tchr., U. Iowa, 1993, Outstanding Art Supr. of Iowa, Art Educators of Iowa, 1995; recipient Metro Arts Contbn. to Cultural Cmty. award, 1998. Mem. Nat. Art Edn. Assn (presenter 1988, 90-93, 2003), Art Educators Iowa (conf. com. 1994, 95), Nat. Assn. Gifted Children (conf. presenter 2002), Alliance for Arts (co-chair 1992—). Avocations: art collecting, watercolor painting, photography, travel. Home: 1441 Beaver Ave Des Moines IA 50311-2640 Office: Des Moines Pub Schs 1800 Grand Ave Des Moines IA 50309-3382 E-mail: donna.davilla@dmsp.k12.ia.us.

DAVIN, JAMES MANSON, investment banker; b. Allentown, Pa., Dec. 24, 1945; s. James Thomas and Louise (Manson) D.; m. Christine Sims, Feb. 27, 1971; children: James Christian, Alexander Manson, James Nicholas. BSBA, Georgetown U., 1967; grad., Bondurant Sch. Perf. Driving, Sonoma, Calif., 1978. Various positions to syndicate nat. mktg. mgr. First Boston Corp., N.Y.C., 1969-87, mng. dir. internat. equity dept., 1987-88; sr. v.p., mgr. internal equity sales and trading Drexel Burnham Lambert, N.Y.C., 1988—, exec. v.p., sr. trading ofcl., 1989-90; exec. v.p., mng. dir. worldwide sales Lehman Bros., 1990-93; vice chmn. Craig Drill Capital, N.Y.C., 1993-94; pres. Davin Capital Corp., N.Y.C., 1994; gen. ptnr. Davin Capital L.P., N.Y.C., 1994—. Gen. ptnr. New Tripoli Pa, L.P., 2000—; mem. hearing panel N.Y. Stock Exch., 1984-87; bd. dirs. Greg Manning Auction, Inc. With U.S. Army, 1967—69. Mem. N.Y. Investment Assn., Securities Industry Assn., Bond Club NY, Nat. Assn. Securities Dealers (chmn. NY dist. bus. conuct com., chmn. NY dist. com., bd. govs., vice-chmn. fin., chmn. nat. bus. conduct com., chmn. bd. govs., chmn. planning, internat. and corp. fin. coms.), Kappa Beta Phi. Roman Catholic. Home: 1120 Park Ave New York NY 10128-1242

DAVION, ETHEL JOHNSON, school system administrator, curriculum specialist; b. Raleigh, N.C., July 21, 1948; d. John Arthur and Ethel Mae (Morgan) Johnson; 1 child, Laura Christal. BA, Livingstone Coll., 1971; MA, Glassboro (N.J.) State U., 1983. Cert. tchr., prin., supr., N.J. Sr. English tchr. Camden (N.J.) Bd. Edn., 1977-81; tchr. of English Westfield (N.J.) Bd. Edn., 1982-85, Union County Regional Dist. 1, Berkeley Heights, N.J., 1981-82, Hillside (N.J.) Bd. Edn., 1985-87; supr. English, lang. arts Irvington (N.J.) Bd. Edn., 1987-92; vice prin. Frank H. Morrell H.S., Irvington, N.J., 1992-95, prin., 1996—; asst. supt. Acad. Affairs, 2001—. Writer, researcher Collegiate Rsch. Systems, Camden, 1976-77; participant profl. devel. programs Harvard U., 1989, Notre Dame U., 1990; participate Oxford Univ. Roundtable, Oxford, Eng., 2002. Author: A Tutorial Approach to Teaching English, 1983, Teachers' Resource Manual, 1987; contbr. articles to jours. Bd. dirs., sec. Emmanuel Tabernacle, Linden, N.J., 1988. Recipient Resolution Town Coun. Irvington, 1992. Fellow N.J. Edn. Assn., Nat. Coun. Tchrs. English; mem. Linden Scholarship Guild (sec. 1985—), Assn. for Supervision and Curriculum Devel., Prin. and Suprs. Assn., Irvington Adminstrs. Assn. (treas.), Internat. Platform Assn., Good Samaritans Club, Obsidian Civic Club (Westfield, historian 1985—), Diversity 2000 Coun. (sec. 1997—). Democrat. Pentecostal.

DAVIS, A. DANO, grocery store chain executive; b. 1945; Student, Stetson U. With Winn-Dixie Stores Inc., Jacksonville, Fla., 1968—, corp. v.p., mgr. Jacksonville div., 1978-80, sr. v.p. and regional dir. Jacksonville and Orlando (Fla.) and Atlanta divs., 1980-82, pres., 1982-88, chmn., CEO, also bd. dirs., 1988-2000, chmn., 2000—. Office: Winn-Dixie Stores Inc 5050 Edgewood Ct Jacksonville FL 32254-3699

DAVIS, ADA ROMAINE, nursing educator; b. Cumberland, Md., June 7, 1929; d. Louis Berge and Ethel Lucy (Johnson) Romaine; m. John Francis Davis, Aug. 1, 1953; children: Kevin Murray, Karen Evans-Romaine, William Romaine. Diploma in nursing, Kings County Hosp., Bklyn., 1949; BSN, U. Md., Balt., 1973, MS, 1974; PhD, U. Md., College Park, 1979, postdoctoral student, 1985-89. Cert. editor in life scis. Asst. prof. grad. program U. Md., Balt., 1974-79; chmn. dept. nursing Coll. of Notre Dame, Balt., 1979-82; assoc. dean grad. program Georgetown U. Sch. Nursing, Washington, 1982-87; nurse cons. Health Resources and Svcs. Adminstrn., Rockville, Md., 1987-93, HHS, USPHS, Bur. Health Profls., Rockville, 1987-93; assoc. prof. and dir. undergrad. program Johns Hopkins U. Sch. of Nursing, Balt., 1993-98, prof. emeritus, 1998—. Reviewer Choice, ALA; evaluator methodology and findings for rsch. studies; hist./med. biographer. Author: John Gibbon and His Heart-Lung Machine, 1992, Advanced Practice Nurses: Education, Roles and Trends, 1997; editor: Ency. of Home Care for the Elderly, 1995; contbr. articles to nursing jours.; assoc. editor Hopkins InteliHealth, Johns Hopkins Family Health Guide, 1999, Johns Hopkins Insider, 1998; sr. editor Am. Nurses Credentialing Ctr., Washington, 2001—. Recipient excellent performance award HRSA; rsch. grantee U. Md. Grad. Sch. Mem. AAAS, ANA (cert. adult nurse practitioner), Soc. for Neoplatonic Studies, Nat. Orgn. Nurse Practitioner Faculties, Am. Acad. Nurse Practitioners, Am. Pub. Health Assn., Gerontol. Soc. Am., Nat. Trust for Hist. Preservation, Am. Geriat. Soc., Md. History of Medicine Soc., Soc. for the Social History of Medicine (Oxford U.), N.Y. Acad. Scis., Coun. Sci. Editors, Sigma Theta Tau. E-mail: adarom@earthlink.net.

DAVIS, ADAM BROOKE, English educator; b. St. Louis, Apr. 14, 1961; s. Paul Douglas-Bozzell and Joan (Wollbrinck) D.; m. Andrea Wiedermann, Aug. 26, 1983; children: Naomi, Clement, Paul, August. BA in English, U. Mich., 1983, MA in English, 1984; PhD in English, U. Mo., 1991. Asst. prof. Truman State U., Kirksville, Mo., 1991-97, assoc. prof., 1997—. Guest prof. Albert-Ludwigs U., Freiburg, Germany, 1991-92. Contbr. articles, essays, poetry, fiction to profl. jours. Huggins fellow U. Mo., 1984-87, Cowden fellow U. Mich., 1984. Fellow Alexander von Humboldt Found.; mem. AAUP, Mo. Folklore Soc. (bd. govs. 1996—), Mo. Arch. Soc. (bd. dirs. 2001—), Nat. Coun. Tchrs. English, Conf. Coll. Composition and Comm., Internat. Soc. Anglo Saxonists, Medieval Acad. Am., KC. Home: 804 E Illinois St Kirksville MO 63501-5206 E-mail: adavis@truman.edu.

DAVIS, ALAN JAY, lawyer; b. Phila., Feb. 4, 1937; s. Rudolph Alan and Adele (Saver) Davis; m. Roslyn Kutcher; children: Jennifer C., Michael R. BA, U. Pa., 1957; JSD, Harvard U., 1960. Bar: Pa. 1961, U.S. Dist. Ct. (ea. dist.) Pa. 1961, U.S. Ct. Appeals (3d cir.) 1961, U.S. Supreme CT. 1979. Law clk. to chief judge U.S. Ct. Appeals (3d cir.), Phila., 1960-61; assoc. Wolf, Block, Schorr & Solis-Cohen, Phila., 1961-66, ptnr., 1968-91, chmn. litig. dept., 1987-91; chief asst. dist. atty. Office Dist. Atty., Phila., 1966-68; sr. litig. ptnr. Ballard Spahr Andrews & Ingersoll, Phila., 1991—. Spl. master to investigate prison sys. and sheriff's dept. Ct. Common Pleas, Phila., 1968—70; lectr. law U. Pa. Sch. Law, Phila., 1973—77; city solicitor City of Phila., 1980—82, chief labor negotiator, 1991—93, Southeastern Pa. Transp. Authority, Phila., 1982, Sch. Dist. Phila., 1984, 96. Chmn. met. adv. bd. Anti-Defamation League B'nai B'rith, Phila., 1986—88; mem. sch. com. Germantown Friends Sch., Phila., 1986—88; trustee Free Libr. Phila., 1995—98; pres. U. Pa. Law Sch. Am. Inns of Ct., 1998—2000. Fellow: Internat. Acad. Trial Lawyers, Am. Coll. Trial Lawyers; mem.: ABA, Am. Law Inst., Phila. Bar Assn., Pa. Bar Assn., Jr. Legal Club, Legal Club. Democrat. Jewish. Office: Ballard Spahr Andrews & Ingersoll 1735 Market St Fl 51 Philadelphia PA 19103-7599 E-mail: davisa@ballardspahr.com.

DAVIS, ALAN TUCKER, foundation administrator, philanthropist, minister; b. Lubbock, Tex., June 13, 1952; s. Ken W. Davis Jr.; m. Jilynn Elyce Spiers, Jan. 3, 1976; children: Alan, Jeniece. BA in Geology, Tex. Christian U., 1974; BA and M in Speculative Theol.-Philos., U. Metaphysics Internat., 2001, DDiv, 2001; diploma in forensic sci., 2002, diploma in criminal justice, 2003; BS in Psychology, Canyon Coll., 2003. Pres. Mastercraft Printing Co., 1977-79, Unit Rig and Equipment Co., Tulsa, 1982-85, Gt. Western Drilling Co., Midland, Tex., 0985—1995. Author: Texas Mussel Watch, 2000, Advanced Fishwatching, 2001, Reef Coral Identification, 2001, Reef Creature Identification, 2001. Chmn. bd. Riding Unltd., Justin, Tex., 1996-97; master instr. Am. Dragons Tae Kwon Do, N. Richland Hills, Tex., 1989—; SCUBA instr. We B Divin', Hurst, Tex., 1995—; vol. Multiple Sclerosis Soc., Ft. Worth, 1995—, Tarrant County Correctional Facility, Ft. Worth, 1995-96. Named Amateur Biologist of Yr., Tex. Parks and Wildlife Dept., 2000, Herman Smith Man of Yr., Ft. Worth Star Telegram Newspaper, 1995-96. Mem.: Am. Inst. Applied Sci., Coll. Profl. Studies. Avocations: painting, classical guitar, drawing. Office: Gt Western Drilling Co 309 W 7th St Ste 800 Fort Worth TX 76102 Fax: 817-332-4095. E-mail: Tuck52@aol.com.

DAVIS, ALBERT JOSEPH, languages and literature educator, novelist, poet; b. Houma, La., June 23, 1947; s. Albert Joseph and Belle Rita (Bellisle) D.; m. Carol Ann Campbell, Feb. 24, 1969 (div. June 1992); 1 child, Benjamin Campbell; m. Mary Archer Freet, Dec. 31, 1994; 1 child, Mary Martha. BA, Nicholls State U., Thibodaux, La., 1969; MA, Colo. State U., 1974; PhD, U. La., Lafayette, 2002. From instr. to assoc. prof. Nicholls State U., 1983—95, disting. svc. prof. langs. and lit., 1995—, novelist in residence, 1993—, assoc. dean arts and scis., 1999—2001, dir. dept. gen. studies, 2001—, Alcee Fortier disting. prof., 2003—. Author: (under penname Albert Belisle) (novels) Leechtime, 1989, Marquis at Bay, 1992, (poetry) What They Wrote on the Bathhouse Walls, 1989, Virginia Patout's Parish, 1999. Recipient Ione Burden award for the novel, 1983, John Z. Bennet award for poetry, 1984; creative writing fellow La. Divsn. Arts, 1989. Mem. NEA, PEN Am. Ctr., Am. Poetry Soc., Assoc. Writing Programs, La. Assn. Educators, Phi Kappa Phi. Office: Nicholls State U PO Box 2106 Thibodaux LA 70310 E-mail: engl-adj@nicholls.edu.

DAVIS, ALBERT RAYMOND, secondary education educator; b. Kansas City, Aug. 30, 1943; s. John Henry and Marsoleat E. (Minuette) D.; m. Rachel E., Feb. 14, 1971; children: Angelique Marie, Aaron Lee. BA in English/German, U. Mo., 1970; MA in Edn., Pacific Luth. U., 1972. Tchr. English, Tacoma Pub. Schs., 1970—. Tchr. curriculum devel. Evergreen Coll., Tacoma, 1994-98; tchr., mentor Mesa, Tacoma, 1982-83; television instr. Tacoma Pub. Schs., 1984-91. Co-author: (test accreditation manual) Helping Students Achieve, 1986. With U.S. Army, 1962-65. Recipient Mesa Instr. award, 1984. Avocations: gardening, exercising, reading, volunteering. Office: Wilson HS 1202 N Orchard St Tacoma WA 98406-3228

DAVIS, ALLEN, professional football team executive; b. Brockton, Mass., July 4, 1929; s. Louis and Rose Davis; m. Carol Segall, July 11, 1954; 1 child, Mark. Student, Wittenberg Coll., 1947; AB, Syracuse U., 1950. Asst. football coach Adelphi Coll., 1950—51; head football coach Ft. Belvoir, Va., 1952—53; player-personnel scout Baltimore Colts, 1954; line coach The Citadel, 1955—56, U. So. Calif., 1957—59; asst. coach San Diego Chargers, 1960—62; gen. mgr., head coach Oakland Raiders (now Los Angeles Raiders), 1963—66, owner, mng. gen. ptnr., 1966—, now pres., gen. ptnr. Former mem. mgmt. council and competition com. NFL. With AUS, 1952—53. Named Profl. Coach of Year, AP, UPI, Sporting News, Pro-Football Illustrated, 1963, Young Man of Yr., Oakland, 1963, only individual in history to be an asst. coach, head coach, gen. mgr., league commr. and owner. Mem.: Am. Football Coaches Assn. Office: Oakland Raiders 1220 Harbor Bay Pkwy Alameda CA 94502-6570

DAVIS, ALLEN FREEMAN, history educator, author; b. Hardwick, Vt., Jan. 9, 1931; s. Harold Freeman and Bernice Susan (Allen) D.; m. Roberta Hazel Green, June 16, 1956 (div.); children: Gregory Freeman, Paul Studley. AB, Dartmouth Coll., 1953; MA, U. Rochester, 1954; PhD, U. Wis., 1959. Instr. history Wayne State U., Detroit, 1959-60; asst. prof. history U. Mo., Columbia, 1960-63, assoc. prof., 1963-68; prof. Temple U., Phila., 1968-99, prof. emeritus, 1999—. Vis. prof. U. Tex., Austin, 1983, U. Amsterdam, 1986-87, John Adams chair. Co-author: March of American Democracy, Vol. V, 1966, Spearheads for Reform, 1967, 84, American Heroine, 1973, 2000, Postcards From Vermont, 2002; (with others) The American People, 1986, 6th edit., 2003; (with Jim Watts) Generations, 1974, 3d edit., 1983; (with Fredric Miller and Morris Vogel) Still Philadelphia, 1983, Philadelphia Stories, 1988; editor: (with Harold D. Woodman) Conflict and Consensus in American History, 1966, 9th edit., 1997; (with Mary Lynn McCree) Eighty Years at Hull House, 1969; (with Mark Haller) The Peoples of Philadelphia, 1973, 2d edit., 1998, Jane Addams on Peace, War and International Understanding, 1974, For Better or Worse, 1980; (with Mary Lynn Bryan) 100 Years at Hull House, 1990, Series in American Civilization, 1978-2000; contbr. articles to profl. jours. Served with AUS, 1954-56. Recipient Friends of Lit. award, 1970, Christopher award, 1974; Danforth Grad. fellow, 1953-59, Am. Council Learned Socs. sr. fellow, 1971-72, NEH fellow, 1975-76, Fulbright fellow, 1986-87; Am. Philos. Soc. grantee, 1962, 65. Mem. Am. Hist. Assn., Orgn. Am. Historians, Am. Studies Assn. (treas. 1971-72, exec. sec. 1972-77, pres. 1989-90, Bode-Pearson award 1996), Soc. Am. Historians. Home: 2032 Waverly St Philadelphia PA 19146-1343 E-mail: davisafd@aol.com.

DAVIS, ALLEN JEFFREY, academic administrator; b. N.Y.C., Dec. 20, 1946; s. Matthew Maurice and Bernice Davis. AB, U. Mass., 1968, EdD, 1973. Dir. grad. rels. Hampshire Coll., Amherst, Mass., 1973-74; asst. dean, prof. Western Coll. of Miami U., Oxford, Ohio, 1974-78; dir. sr. programs Pitkin County, Aspen, Colo., 1979-80; assoc. dean for student affairs Sarah Lawrence Coll., Bronxville, NY, 1981-82; dean Northfield (Mass.) Mount Herman Sch., 1982-87; exec. dir. United Way, Greenfield, Mass., 1987-91, 20/20 Vision, Amherst, 1991-93; dir. devel. Cooley Dickinson Hosp., Northampton, 1993-96; exec. dir. Greenfield (Mass.) Cmty. Coll. Found., 1996—. V.p. The Literacy Project, 1998-2000; mem. local dist. atty. Civil Rights Adv. Bd., 1998—. Mem. Coun. for Resource Devel., Nat. Soc. for Fundraising Execs., Assn. Healthcare Philanthropists. Democrat. Jewish. Email: davis@gcc.mass.edu. Office: Greenfield Cmty Coll Found 270 Main St Greenfield MA 01301

DAVIS, ALVIN G. company executive; b. Post, Tex., Nov. 12, 1927; m. Barbara Ann Hext, July 28, 1955; children: Glen Robert Davis, Debra Ann Garland, Jay Todd Davis. Student, Tex. A&M, 1944; BS in Agr., Tex. Tech. Coll., 1951; postgrad., South Plains Coll., 1980; grad., Tex. Tech. U., 1983-84. Agrl. advisor, asst. cashier, asst. v.p. Brownfield (Tex.) State Bank and Trust Co., 1952-64; owner, mgr. Hub Specialty Co., Post and Brownfield, 1952-59, The Cowboy Stores, Tex., 1959-79; exec. v.p., dir. First Nat. Bank, Clovis and Melrose, N.Mex., 1964-65; exec. v.p., gen. mgr. Ranching Heritage Assn. and Endowment Fund Nat. Ranching Heritage Ctr., Tex. Tech. U., Lubbock, Tex., 1981-93; ret., 1994. Owner, operator livestock farm; responsible for breeding, raising, showing, mktg. Quarter, Paint and Appaloosa horses, 1956-81; spkr. in field. Pub., writer numerous poems. Active Monterey Ch. of Christ, Lubbock, 1981—, elder, 1988-90; mem. Lubbock Heritage Soc., W. Tex. Hist. Assn., Tex. Mus. Assn.; mem. numerous 4-H Clubs; participant numerous livestock shows. With U.S. Army, 1946-47. Recipient Appreciation award San Juan Spring Roundup, 1995, Peter McCue award Petersburg, Ill., 1998, Lifetime Achievement award Am. Cowboy Culture Awards, 1999, numerous outstanding svc. awards. Mem. Am. Cowboy Culture Assn., Inc. (pres., founder), Am. Jr. Rodeo Assn. (adminstr., founder), Nat. Intercollegiate Rodeo Assn. (adminstr., life mem.), Nat. We. Artists Assn. (adminstr., founder), Former Tex. Ranger Assn. (life mem.), Old Trl. Drivers Assn. Tex. (hon. lifetime pres.), Ranching Heritage Assn. (chmn., adminstr., life mem.), Tex. Cowboy Reunion Old Timer's Assn. (life mem.), Tex. Tech. Animal Sci. Alumni Assn. (pres.), We./English Retailers Am. (chmn., founder, life mem.), We. Music Assn. (pres., Bill Wiley award 1995), Tex. Cowboy Poets Assn. (chmn., founder), Youth Rodeo Found. Am. (chmn., founder), Post C. of C. (mgr.), Brownfield C. of C. (pres.), Levelland C. of C. (pres.), Nat. Cowboy Symposium & Celebration (pres., chmn.), Am. Chuckwagon Assn. (pres.), Am. Legion. Home: 4124-62d Dr Lubbock TX 79413 Fax: 806-795-4749. E-mail: adavis@cowboy.org.

DAVIS, ANDRE MAURICE, judge, educator; b. Balt., Feb. 11, 1949; m. Chanda B. Hudson, May 1, 1971 (div. Oct. 1974); 1 child, Ahmed Jamal; m. Margaret Olevia Roberts, Aug. 15, 1987. BA, U. Pa., 1971; JD, U. Md., 1978. Asst. housing mgr. Housing Authority Balt., 1972-74, equal employment opportunity specialist, 1974-75; law clk. Hon. Frank A. Kaufman U.S. Dist. Ct., Balt., 1978-79; law clk. to Hon. Francis D. Murnaghan, Jr., U.S. Ct. Appeals for 4th Cir., Balt., 1979-80; appellate atty. Civil Rights Divsn. Dept. Justice, Washington, 1980-81; asst. U.S. atty. Office of U.S. Atty., Balt., 1981-83; assoc. atty., litigation Frank, Bernstein, Conaway and Goldman, Balt., 1983-84; from instr. to asst. prof. Sch. Law U. Md., Balt., 1984—; assoc. judge Dist. Ct. Md. for Balt. City, 1987-90, Cir. Ct. for Balt. City, Balt., 1990-95; judge U.S. Dist. Ct., Balt., 1995—. Bd. dirs., instr. Jud. Inst. Md.; mem. Dist. Ct. Commr. Edn.; pres., bd. dirs. Legal Aid Bur., Inc.; v.p., bd. dirs. Big Bros. and Big Sisters of Ctrl. Md., Ind.; trustee Goucher Coll., Park Heights Acad., Balt. Urban League, Inc.; mem. Gov.'s Task Force on Black and Minority Mental Health. Mem. ABA (exec. com., conf. fed. trial judges, jud. divsn.), Md. Bar Assn., Balt. City Bar Assn., Monumental City Bar Assn., U. Md. Sch. Law Alumni Assn., Lawyers Round Table, Rule Day Law Club, Wranglers Law Club, Phi Alpha Delta. Office: US Courthouse 101 W Lombard St Baltimore MD 21201-2605 E-mail: Judge_Andre_Davis@mdd.uscourts.gov.

DAVIS, ANDREW NEIL, lawyer, educator; b. Boston, Nov. 7, 1959; s. Gerald Stanley and Sarah Lee D.; m. Suzanne Frances DiBenedetto, Oct. 11, 1992; children: David R. Bray, Hannah M., Zachary G. BS in Biology, Trinity Coll., 1981; MS in Botany, U. Mass., 1983, PhD in Botany, 1987; JD, George Washington U., 1990. Bar: Conn. 1990, U.S. Dist. Ct. Conn. 1991, Mass. 1998. Atty. Pepe & Hazard, Hartford, Conn., 1990-93, Brown, Rudnick, Freed & Gesmer, Hartford, 1993-94; ptnr. LeBoeuf, Lamb, Greene & MacRae LLP, Hartford, 1994—. Adj. prof. environ. studies Conn. Coll., 1994—. Sr. author/co-author: The Home Environmental Sourcebook, 1996, ISO 14001: Meeting Business Goals Through An Effective Environmental Management System, 1998; contbr. articles to profl. jours. Mem. Leadership Greater Hartford, 1997; chmn. lake adv. commn. Town Marlborough, 1992—, zoning

commn., 1993-95. Recipient Hon. Sci. award Bausch & Lomb, 1977; Albert L. Deslisle Botany fellow, 1982. Mem. Am. Arbitration Assn. (environ. adv. com. 1993-95), Conn. Bar Assn. (exec. com. environ. law sect. 1996-2000), Conn. Bus. and Industry Assn. (environ. policies coun. 1991—), Internat. Coun. Shopping Ctrs. Avocations: photography, sailing, scuba diving, arctic travel, reading. Office: LeBoeuf Lamb Greene & MacRae LLP 225 Asylum St Fl 13 Hartford CT 06103-1529 E-mail: adavis@llgm.com.

DAVIS, ANITA YVONNE, small business owner, writer; b. Macon, Ga., Aug. 26, 1948; d. Clarence and Essie Davis. BS in English, Savannah State Coll., 1970; cert. in small bus. devel., Clayton State Coll., 1991; cert. in computer use, Concepts in Automation Tng. Sch., 1992; cert. in reading, Ga. State U., 1998; cert. in working with exceptional children, Ga. Coll. and Univ., 1998. Pres., owner Fashion Era Modeling Assn., Macon, 1970—72; English tchr. Ctrl. High Complex, Macon, 1970—72; monitor Learning Found., Macon, 1971—72; flight attendant Delta Airlines, Inc., Atlanta, 1972—78, acct., 1978—2000; pub. rels. mgr. Concepts in Automation, Atlanta, 1992—95; pres., owner A.Y. Davis Enterprises, Inc., Atlanta and Macon. Cmty. in schs. tutor, substitute tchr. Bibb County Bd. Edn., Macon, 2002—03; prodr. ednl. videos and movies A.Y. Davis Reading and Drama Club, Macon, 1998—; singer JOI, Atlanta, 1985—; exec. v.p., COO, exec. mgr. New Sys. Enterprises, Inc.; agt. Illuminations Band, New Sys. Apollo, 2003. Author: Cindé Reader in the Town of Reading Land, 2001; contbr. articles to profl. jours. Pres. Goals 2000 Read Am. Chellenge, Macon, 1998—2003. Recipient Goals 2000: Read Am. Challenge award, Pres. Clinton, 1998. Avocations: writing, reading, drawing, singing, dancing. Office: AY Davis Enterprises Inc PO Box 5573 Macon GA 31208 E-mail: Davisaydavis@aol.com.

DAVIS, ANN CALDWELL, history educator; b. Alliance, Ohio, June 3, 1925; d. Arthur Trescott and Jane Caldwell D. BA, Western Reserve U., 1947; MA, Columbia U., 1955; PhD, Columbia Pacific U., 1987. Cert. tchr., Ill., Ohio. Pres. The Clio Found. Inc., Gulfport, Fla., 1955—; tchr. Supr. Child Enterprise, Evanston, Ill., 1956-60; human rels. coun. U. Chgo., 1957-58, asst., 1961; tchr., dept. chair Evanston Pub. Schs., 1961-85; project English Northwestern U., Evanston, 1962-64, Cons. Dist. #65 Sch., Evanston, 1985-90, Presenter, author: (speech) Do-it-Yourself Help For The Top 10%, 1964, The Non-Graded School, 1976, Social Studies Reading & Reference Skills, 1979; author: (video) U.S. & Ill. Constn., 1986. Vol. Meals ON Wheels, Treasure Island, Fla., 1990-94, Pinellas County Schs., Fla., 1991, steering com. St. Petersburg, Fla., 1995, health care chair Older Women's League, St. Petersburg, 1995. Mem. Am. Assn. of U. Women, Orgn. of Am. Historians, Ill. & Nat. Edn. Assn. Office: The Clio Found Inc PO Box 5110 Gulfport FL 33737-5110 E-mail: cliofdn@aol.com.

DAVIS, ANN RICHARDSON, artist, sculptor, book dealer, writer; b. Savannah, Ga., Nov. 27, 1942; d. Charles Clifford and Nancy Lee (Powell) Richardson; m. Charles Hamilton Davis, July 13, 1962; children: Rhett, Christy Lee Davis Heatherly. Grad. high sch., Savannah. Represented by Sea Griffin Gallery & Books, Darien, Ga., 1997—. Author: (juvenile) The Tale of the Altamaha "Monster," 1997, Richardson and Allied Lines of the Southeast, 2000, McIntosh County Georgia Marriage and Deeds Reference Books, fiction) Heaven In A Hole In The Ground and Other Earthy Stories, 2003; one-woman shows include Parthenon Galleries, Nashville, 1984, Tenn. Art League Galleries, Nashville, 1983; represented in permanent collections First Am. Bank, Nashville, Blue Grass Reg. Libr., Columbia, Tenn. Mem. arts com. Ashantilly Ctr., Darien, 1997. Recipient 2d place for sculpture Exhbn. South, Tuscumbia, Ala., 1981, Tallix Foundry award Pen and Brush Club, N.Y.C., 1982, hon. mention for painting and sculpture Tenn. All-State Exhbn., Nashville, 1982, 83, award Chautauqua, N.Y., 1986. Mem. Acad. Artists Assn. (coun. Am. Artists award 1984). Avocation: genealogical and historical research. Office: Sea Griffin Gallery & Books 206 Ft King George Dr Darien GA 31305

DAVIS, ANNA JANE RIPLEY, elementary education educator; b. Uhrichsville, Ohio, Sept. 7, 1931; d. Emmet Frank and Lillie Hazel (Kinsey) Ripley; m. H. Joe Davis, Mar. 16, 1951; children: Alan Joe, Kendal Jay. Assoc., Asbury Coll., 1953; BS with honors, Kent State U., 1962, MEd with honors, 1978, postgrad., 1980—94; student, Richmond Coll., London U., St. Andrews U., Dundee U., Cambridge U., U. Paris, U. Rome, Ohio U. Cert. elem. tchr., Ohio. Tchr. Kenston Schs., Chagrin Falls, Ohio, 1953-55, 58-62, Firestone Rubber Plantation, Harbel, Liberia, West Africa, 1962-64, Newbury (Ohio) Schs., 1964-65, Orange Schs., Pepper Pike, Ohio, 1965-99. Chaperone, counselor Am. Inst. for Fgn. Study, British Isles and Europe, summers 1968-81. Author children's books. Active Kenston PTA, Chagrin Falls and Pepper Pike PTA, Am. Field Svc., Chagrin Falls; bd. dirs. Friends Geauga County Pub. Libr.; book project vol. traveling libr. Geauga County Pub. Libr. for Amish Schs., traveling libr., 1994—; vol. ARC, 1955—; elem. sch. tutor, 1998—; vol. Food Pantry and Clothing for Needy, Kiwanis; mem. Care Bears com., Prayer Chain, mem. Sunday sch. com., Sunday sch. membership com., prayer chain Pepper Pike Garfield Meml. United Meth. Ch. Mem. NEA (life), ASCD, Ohio Edn. Assn., N.E. Ohio Tchrs. Assn., Orange Tchrs. Assn. Avocations: family, travel, cycling, hiking, reading, writing.

DAVIS, ANNALEE RUTH CONYERS, clinical social worker; b. Bentonville, Ark., July 8, 1944; d. Lloyd Milton and Jessie Alberta (Robe) Conyers; m. Rushton Eric Davis, Aug. 26, 1967 (div. Apr. 1980); children: Michelle Leigh, Rushton Kendrick. BA, Hendrix Coll., 1966; MSW, U. Okla., 1982. Internat. cert. alcohol and drug counselor; diplomate Internat. Acad. Behavioral Medicine, Counseling and Psychotherapy; lic. marriage and family therapist, Okla.; lic. clin. social worker, Okla.; diplomate in clin. social work; cert. critical incident debriefer; bd. cert. expert in traumatic stress. Psychiat. intern Tulsa Psychiat. Ctr., 1980-82, postgrad. intern, 1982-83; clin. social worker New Choice, Inc., Tulsa, 1983-85; pvt. practice Tulsa, 1985—; EAP counselor Cmty. Care, Tulsa, 2001—. Bd. dirs. Associated Ctrs. for Therapy, 1994-2002, chair quality assurance and program devel. coms. Head edn. com. Sunbelt Alliance, Tulsa, 1978-80; mem. Fgn. Policy Study Group, Tulsa, 1980-88, 1999-2002; mem., tchr. Meth. Ch., Tulsa, 1967-90; bd. dirs. Ctr. Christian Counseling, 1978-88; mem. Singles Available for Cmty. Svc., 1999—. Mem. NASW (diplomate, clin. mem., bd. dirs. 2002-02), Am. Acad. Experts in Traumatic Stress (diplomate, clin. mem.), Acad. Cert. Social Workers, Okla. Assn. Social Workers, Okla. Assn. Profl. Alcohol/Drug Counselors, Okla. Assn. Alcohol and Drug Abuse, Acad. Behavioral Medicine, Counseling and Psychotherapy, Singles Available for Cmty. Svc., Rotary Internat. (Tulsa After Hours chpt. bd. dirs., pres.-elect), Amnesty Internat. Democrat. Methodist. Home: 6714 E 76th St Tulsa OK 74133-3422

DAVIS, ARTUR, congressman; b. Montgomery, Ala., Apr. 9, 1967; BA summa cum laude, Harvard U., 1990, JD cum laude, 1993. Intern So. Poverty Law Ctr.; law clk. U.S. Dist. Ct. Judge; asst. U.S. atty., 1994—98; pvt. practice, 1998—2002; congressman 7th Dist. Ala. U.S. Ho. Reps., 2003—. Scholar, Harvard U. Democrat. Office: 208 Cannon House Office Bldg Washington DC 20515-0107*

DAVIS, BARBARA JUDY, counselor, mental health educator; b. Lewisburg, W.Va., Apr. 27, 1955; d. Harris Wilson and Dorthea Pearl (Baker) Judy; m. Robin John Otis, May 10, 1980 (div. Nov. 1987); 1 child, Tamara; m. Ancel Barbour Davis Jr., Mar. 4, 1989; 1 child, Shannon. BA, U. Va., 1980, MEd, 1993. Lic. profl. counselor; cert. counselor. Benefits specialist Charlottesville (Va.) Dept. of Social Svc., 1988-91, social worker, 1991—96, Cumberland County (N.C.) Mental Health, 1996-97; coord. Thomas S program Edgecombe-Nash (N.C.) Mental Health Ctr., 1997-99; dir. mental health edn. Area L Area Health Edn. Ctr., Rocky Mount, N.C., 1999—. Adj. asst. prof. dept. psychiatry Sch. Medicine U. N.C., Chapel Hill, 2002—. Mem. adv. bd. Region X Cmty. Svc. Mental Retardation Divsn., Charlottesville, 1989-96; founding mem. planning com. Disability Awareness Day, Charlottesville, 1992-95, chair fund raising, 1993; mem. Thomas S. Provider/Area Program Work Group, 1998-99; bd. dirs., deacon, youth group sponsor First Christian Ch., Rocky Mount.; mem. exec. bd. S.W.I.M. Network, Inc., affiliate Christian Women's Job Corp., 2000—. Mem.: ACA, Counselors for Social Justice, Nat. Bd. Cert. Counselors, Chi Sigma Iota. Avocations: alpine skiing, hiking, church choir. Office: Area L Area Health Edn Ctr 1631 S Wesleyan Blvd Rocky Mount NC 27803-5627 E-mail: Barbara.Davis@ncmail.net.

DAVIS, BARBARA M(AE), librarian; b. Cranston, R.I., Dec. 23, 1926; d. Harrie S. and Marguerite M. (Cameron) D. BS in Chemistry, Brown U., 1948; MS in Libr. Sci., Simmons Coll., 1956. Asst. rsch. libr. R&D Dept. Cabot Corp., Cambridge, Mass., 1948-57, rsch. libr., 1957-61, Billerica (Mass.) Rsch. Ctr., Cambridge, Mass., 1961-68, head tech. info. svcs., 1968-81, mgr. tech. info. ctr., 1981-87. Dir. Cabot Boston Credit Union, 1956-59, 61-64, 72-78, clk., 1961-64, 72-77, v.p., 1977-78. Vol. Lexington Coun. Aging, 1990-2000, Lexington Hist. Soc., 1991-2003; chmn. rsch. com. Greater Boston Young Rep. Club, 1959-61; treas. Women's Rep. Club Lexington, 1988-2001; mem. Lexington Rep. Town Com., 1993-98; del. Mass. Rep. Conv., 1994, 98. Mem. Am. Chem. Soc. (sec. div. chem. lit. 1961-65), Simmons Coll. Libr. Sch. Alumni (v.p. 1965-66). Home: 37 Drummer Boy Way Lexington MA 02420-1222

DAVIS, BARBARA SNELL, college educator; b. Painesville, Ohio, Feb. 21, 1929; d. Roy Addison and Mabelle Irene (Denning) Snell; children: Beth Ann Davis Schnorf, James L., Polly Denning Davis Spaeth. BS, Kent State U., 1951; MA, Lake Erie Coll., 1981; postgrad., Cleve. State U., 1982-83. Cert. reading speicalist, elem. prin., Ohio. Dir. publicity Lake Erie Coll., Painesville, 1954-59; tchr. Mentor (Ohio) Exempted Village Sch. Dist., 1972-86, prin., 1986-97; prof. Lake Erie Coll., 1997—. Contbr. articles to profl. jours. Former trustee Mentor United Meth. Ch. Mem. Delta Kappa Gamma (pres. 1982-84), Phi Delta Kappa (pres. 1992-93), Theta Sigma Phi (charter). Home: 7293 Beechwood Dr Mentor OH 44060-6305 Office: 326 College Hall Lake Erie Coll Painesville OH 44077 E-mail: beachbumbarb@aol.com.

DAVIS, BENJAMIN GEORGE, theologian, educator; b. Honesdale, Pa., July 6, 1941; s. Benjamin George and Laura Teneyck (Swingle) D.; m. Janet Marie Gorden, June 21, 1980; children: Leslie Anne, John Nathan. AB, U. Mich., 1967, AM, 1969; M.Th., U. Nottingham, England, 1982; D. Min., St. Mary's Sem. & Univ., Balt., 1985. Draftsman, designer Munson Mill Machinery Co., Utica, N.Y., 1961-62; design engr. Gen. Motors Corp., Warren, Mich., 1963-66; devel. coord. City of Ann Arbor, Mich., 1967; research economist Exec. Office of the Pres., Washington, 1970; sr. assoc. RMC Research Corp., Bethesda, Md., 1971-75; dir. Research Svcs., Inc., Clinton, Md., 1975-80; regional dir. World Relief, Landover, Md., 1981-86; dir. Evangelicals for Social Action, Washington, 1987-89; pastor St. John United Ch., Columbia, Md., 1989-90; prof. St. Mary's Sem. and U., Balt., 1986—, assoc. dean Balt. Internat. Coll., 1988-95, Exec. dir. The Religious Coalition, Frederick, Md., 1995-98; dean, campus dir. Potomac Coll., Washington, 1998-2003; dir. acad. affairs U. Phoenix, Columbia, Md., 2003—. Author: A Modern Interpretation of Revelation, 1982, Understanding World Cultures: The United States and Canada, 1990, 2nd edit., 2000, Economics: An Integrated Approach, 1997; editor: The Dictionary of Essential English, 1987. Pres. Fgn.-born Info. and Referral Network, Columbia, 1986-92; chmn. Coalition fo r Refugee Resettlement, Washington, 1985-86; chairperson Md. Refugee Adv. Coun., Balt., 1985-86. Recipient Gov.'s Citation State of Md., 1985, 86; NDEA fellow in economics U. Md., 1969-71, Rickard's fellow in theology U. Nottingham, 1980-81. Mem. Assn. for Psychol. Type, Assn. Overseas Educators, Mensa, Omicron Delta Epsilon. Avocations: jazz, photography, motorcycling. Home: 6580 Madrigal Ter Columbia MD 21045-4628 E-mail: bdavis@potomac.edu. *The search for certainty in life leads only up blind alleys. Accepting the ambiguity and moving forward in faith is all.*

DAVIS, BERTRAM HYLTON, retired English educator; b. Ozone Park, N.Y., Nov. 30, 1918; s. Hubert Edwin and Gladys (Greenidge) D.; m. Ruth Austin Benedict, Jan. 11, 1946; children: Ralph Paul, Kathryn Davis Kohler, Richard Austin. Grad., Phillips Acad., Andover, Mass., 1933-37; student, Hamilton Coll., Clinton, N.Y., 1937-39; AB, Columbia, 1941, MA, 1948, PhD, 1956; LL.D., Dickinson Coll., 1974. Lectr. English Hunter Coll., 1947-48; instr., then asst. prof. English Dickinson Coll., 1948-57; staff assoc. AAUP, 1957-63, dep. gen. sec., 1963-67, gen. sec., 1967-74; prof. English Fla. State U., Tallahassee, 1974-85, svc. prof., 1985-90, prof. emeritus, 1991—. Author: Johnson Before Boswell, 1960, A Proof of Eminence, 1973, Thomas Percy, 1981, Thomas Percy: A Scholar-Cleric in the Age of Johnson, 1989; editor (Sir John Hawkins): Life of Samuel Johnson LL.D, 1961; editor bull., AAUP, 1960-65; field editor Twayne's English Authors Series, 1977-93; mem. editorial com. Yale Edition of Works of Samuel Johnson, 1979— . Served to capt. AUS, 1941-46. Guggenheim fellow, 1974 Mem. ACLU, MLA, Johnsonians, South Atlantic Modern Lang. Assn., Cosmos Club, Am. Soc. for 18th Century Studies. Home: 2309 Domingo Dr Tallahassee FL 32304-1310

DAVIS, BETTY BOURBONIA, real estate investment executive; b. Ft. Bayard, N.Mex., Mar. 12, 1931; d. John Alexander and Ora M. (Caudill) Bourbonia; children: Janice Cox Anderson, Elizabeth Ora Cox. BS in Elem. Edn., U. N.Mex., 1954. Gen. ptnr. BJD Realty Co., Albuquerque, 1977—. Bd. dirs. Albuquerque Opera Build, 1977-79, 81-83, 85-87, membership co-chair, 1977-78; mem. Friends of Art, 1978-85, Friends of Little Theatre, 1973-85, Mus. N.Mex. Found.; mem. grand exec. com. N.Mex. Internat. Order of Rainbow for Girls; mem. Hodgin Hall Preservation com. U. N.Mex.; sustainer Albuquerque Jr. League. Recipient Matrix award for journalism Jr. League. Mem. Albuquerque Mus. Assn., N.Mex. His. Soc., N.Mex. Symphonyy Guild, Jr. League Albuquerque (sustaining mem.), Alumni Assn. N.Mex., Mus. N.Mex. Found., Albuquerque Petroleum Club, Albuquerque Knife and Fork Club, Internat. Platform Assn., Order Eastern Star, Order Rainbow for Girls (past grand worth adv. N.Mex., past mother adv. Friendship Assembly 50, state exec. com. N.Mex. Order 1986-2002, chair pub. rels. com., co-chair gen. arrangements com. 1990-97), Tanoan Country Club, Las Amapolis Club, Mt. Vernon Ladies Assn., Albuquerque Mus. Found., Albuquerque Guild Santa Fe Opera, Alpha Chi Omega (chpt. advisor, bldg. corp. 1962-77). Republican. Methodist. Home: 9505 Augusta Ave NE Albuquerque NM 87111-5820

DAVIS, BILLIE JOHNSTON, school counselor; b. Charleston, W.Va., Sept. 24, 1933; d. William Andrew Jr. and Garnet Macil (Johnston) D. BS, Morris Harvey Coll., 1954; MA, W.Va. U., 1959. Nat. bd. cert. counselor; W.Va. lic. profl. counselor. Tchr. math. Kanawha County Schs., Charleston, 1954-59, counselor, 1959-98. Mem. pub. edn. study commn. W.Va. Legislature, 1980. Mem. W.Va. Commn. on Juvenile Law, 1982-97; bd. dirs. W.Va. Com. for Prevention Child Abuse, W.Va. Sch. Health Adv. Com.; apptd. W.Va. rep. at Tchr.'s Inaugural Experience for Inauguration of Pres. George Bush by Gov. of W.Va., 1989; mem. subcom. W.Va. Health Care Task Force, 1992; trustee W.Va. Youth Advocate Program, 1993-95, Nat. Youth Adv. Program, 1994-95; mem. oversite com. W.Va. Juvenile Predisposition Plan, 1993-97. Mem. adv. bd. W.Va. Divsn. Juvenile Svcs., 2001—. Recipient Anne Maynard award W.Va. Sch. Counselor Assn., 1986; named Am. mid./jr. high Sch. Counselor of Yr. Am. Sch. Counselors Assn., 1987, Citizen of Yr., Dunbar Lions Club, 1987. Mem. Am. Assn. Counseling and Devel. (Spl. Recognition award 1991), W.Va. Assn. Counseling and Devel. (pres. 1964-66, legis. chmn. 1974-98, spl. award legis. svcs. 1981), W.Va. Edn. Assn. (past legis. chmn.), Kanawha County Sch. Counselors Assn. (pres., legis. chmn. 1974-98), W.Va. Sch. Counselors Assn. (chmn. gov. rels., parliamentarian), Alpha Delta Kappa (past chpt. pres.), Phi Delta Kappa. Democrat. Baptist. Home: 12 Warren Pl Charleston WV 25302-3613 E-mail: bjdavis222@aol.com.

DAVIS, BLONDELL GILLIAM, business manager, evangelist, artist, author, poet; b. Ft. Pierce, Fla., Dec. 21, 1942; d. Fred Douglas and Mary Louise Gilliam; m. Levoid Davis, July 15, 1962; 1 child, Sherry Yvonne. AA, Lincoln Jr. Coll. Ordained to ministry Apostolic (Holiness) House of Prayer. State evangelist House of Prayer, Tampa, Fla., 1980—, mgr. bakery, 1987—. Author: Miracles on the Mind, 1993, Miracles Never Cease; editor Ho. of Prayer Gospel Press. Avocations: writing, cooking, drawing, painting, sewing. Home: 3210 E Lambright St Tampa FL 33610-3609 Office: The House of Prayer 3006 E Ellicott St Tampa FL 33610-2136

DAVIS, BOBBY J. pastor, family therapist; b. Cade, S.C., Feb. 28, 1942; s. Joseph Daniel and Ethel Martha (Gaskin) D.; m. Christine Virginia Booker, June 22, 1963; children: Melissa, Mark A., David, D., Tanya M., Katrina, Timothy. D in Theol. Studies, Vision Christian Coll., Ramona, Calif., 1992. Cert. marriage and family therapist. Sr. pastor Miracle Faith World Outreach, Monroe, Conn., 1969—. Office: Miracle Faith World Outreach 754 Main St Monroe CT 06468-2838 E-mail: mfwo@aol.com.

DAVIS, BONNIE CHRISTELL, judge; b. Petersburg, Va., July 13, 1949; d. Robert Madison and Margaret Elizabeth (Collier) D. BA, Longwood Coll., 1971; JD, U. Richmond, 1980. Bar: Va. 1980, U.S. Dist. Ct. (ea. dist.) Va. 1980, U.S. Ct. Appeals (4th cir.) 1982. Tchr. Chesterfield County Schs., Chesterfield, Va., 1971-77; pvt. practice, Chesterfield, 1980-83; asst. commonwealth atty. Chesterfield County, 1983-93; judge Juvenile and Domestic Rels. Ct. for 12th Jud. Dist. Va., 1993—. Adviser Youth Svcs. Commn., Chesterfield, 1983-93; cons. Task Force on Child Abuse, 1983-93, Met. Richmond Multi-Discipline Team on Spouse Abuse, 1983-93, Va. Dept. of Children for handbook "Step by Step Through the Juvenile Justice System in Virginia, 1988; mem. nat. adv. com. for prodn. on missing and runaway children Theatre IV; mem. adv. group to set stds. and tng. for Guardians Ad Litem, Supreme Ct. Va., 1994; chmn. jud. adminstrn. com. Jud. Conf. Va. for Dist. Cts., 1995-97; mem. state adv. com. for CASA and children's Justice Act, 1998-2002. Co-author: Juvenile Law and Practice in Virginia, 1994. Mem. Chesterfield County Pub. Schs. Task Force on Core Values, 1999. Mem.: Chesterfield-Colonial Heights Bar Assn., Met. Richmond Women's Bar Assn., Va. Trial Lawyers Assn., Va. Bar Assn., Va. State Bar (bd. govs. family law sect. 1997—2001), State-Fed. Jud. Coun. Va. Home: 415 Lyons Ave Colonial Heights VA 23834-3154 Office: Chesterfield Juvenile and Domestic Rels Dist Ct 7000 Lucy Corr Blvd Chesterfield VA 23832-6717

DAVIS, BRIAN ADAM, physician; b. Chgo., Jan. 21, 1966; s. Paul Michael and Arlene Carol Davis; m. Edith Carpio Bautista, May 23, 1992. BS magna cum laude, Northwestern U., 1986; MD, Meharry Med. Coll., 1992. Intern Hosp. of U. Pa./Presbyn. Med. Ctr., Phila., 1992-93; resident U. Medicine and Dentistry N.J., Newark, 1993-96; assoc. attending Runnells Specialized Hosp., Berkeley Heights, N.J., 1994-97; clin. asst. prof. dept. phys. medicine and rehab. U. Utah, Salt Lake City, 1997-99; staff physiatrist dept. phys. medicine and rehab. Salt Lake Regional Med. Ctr., Salt Lake City, 1997-99; cons. dept. phys. medicine and rehab. Primary Children's Med. Ctr., Salt Lake City, 1997-99; clin. asst. prof. dept. phys. medicine and rehab. U. Calif. Davis Med. Ctr., Sacramento, 1999—, clin. asst. prof. dept. anesthesiology and pain mgmt., 2001—. Cons. dept. phys. medicine and rehab. svcs. Vets. Affairs/N.J. Health System, Lyons, 1996-97; instr. dept. phys. medicine and rehab. U. Medicine and Dentistry N.J., Newark, 1997; med. edn. com. Am. Coll. Sports Medicine, 2000-03; med. advisor Utah State Boxing Commn., 1998-99; mem. Salt Lake organizing com. Paralympics Med. Svcs. Com., 1998-2000, aux. faculty divsn. phys. therapy, U. Utah, 1999. Contbr. articles to profl. jours. Student asst. I Have a Future, Nashville, 1991; med. dir. Paralympic Polyclinic U. Utah 2002 Paralympics, 1997-98, med. adv. paralympic br. Salt Lake Orgn. Com. Mem. AMA (AMA/Glaxo Leadership award), Am. Coll. Sports Medicine, Am. Acad. Phys. Med. & Rehab., Assn. Acad. Physiatrists, Utah Med. Assn., Salt Lake County Med. Assn., U.S. Amateur Boxing Assn., KC (participant, fundraiser 1985-86), Phi Kappa Delta (participant health screening 1990-92), Sigma Alpha Mu (participant, fundraiser 1985-86), Alpha Omega Alpha. Independent. Avocations: singing, collecting rare record albums, martial arts. Office: U Calif Davis Med Ctr Dept Phys Med and Rehab Ellison ACC Bldg 4860 Y St Ste 3850 Sacramento CA 95817-2307 E-mail: brian.davis@ucdmc.ucdavis.com.

DAVIS, BRITTON ANTHONY, retired lawyer; b. Highland Park, Ill., Jan. 2, 1936; s. James Archie and Anita (Blanke) D.; m. Lynn Marriott Wegner, 1958 (dec. 1975); children: Hilary, Shepard; m. Peggy M. Swint, 1986; children: Stephen Swint, Thomas Swint. Student, Denison U., 1954-57; BS in Law, Northwestern U., 1959, LLB, 1960. Bar: Ill. 1960. Assoc. Haight & Hofeldt, Chgo., 1959-89; pvt. practice Winnetka, Ill., 1989-96. Vol. Children's Spl. Edn. Programs, Winnetka. Mem.: ABA, Patent Law Assn. Chgo., Bar Assn. 7th Fed. Cir., Chgo. Curling Club, Indian Hill Club (Winnetka). Home: 285 Linden St Winnetka IL 60093-3826

DAVIS, BRUCE GORDON, retired principal; b. Fulton, Tex., Sept. 2, 1922; s. Arthur Lee and Clara Katherine (Rouquette) D.; B.A., U. Tex., 1950; M.Ed., U. Houston, 1965; m. Mary Virginia Jackson, Aug. 31, 1946; children— Ford Rouquette, Barton Bolling, Katherine Norvell Davis McLendon. Tchr., Edison Jr. High Sch., Houston, 1951; tchr. Sidney Lanier Jr. High Sch., Houston, 1957-60, asst. prin., 1966-74, prin., 1974-83; tchr. Johnston Jr. High Sch., Houston, 1960-66; prin. Sidney Lanier Vanguard Sch., Houston, 1974-82; ret., 1983. Served with USMC, 1942-45; with U.S. Army, 1951-57. Mem. Nat. Assn. Secondary Sch. Prins., Tex. Assn. Secondary Sch. Prins., Houston Profl. Adminstrs., U.S. Army Officers Res. Assn., Tex. Retired Tchrs. Assn., Am. Legion. Republican. Presbyterian. Club: Masons. Home: 6614 Sharpview Dr Houston TX 77074-6338

DAVIS, BUTCH, professional football coach; Former asst. coach Dallas Cowboys, 1989—94; head coach U. Miami Hurricanes, 1995—2001, Cleveland Browns, 2001—. Office: Cleve Browns 76 Lou Groza Blvd Berea OH 44017

DAVIS, C. VANLEER, III, lawyer; b. Camden, N.J., 1942; AB summa cum laude, Princeton U., 1964; LLB magna cum laude, Harvard U., 1967. Bar: Pa. 1969. Law clk. to Hon. Abraham L. Freedman U.S. Ct. Appeals (3d cir.), 1967-68; ptnr. Dechert, LLP, Phila. Lectr. Pa. State U. Tax Conf., 1980, mem. planning com., 1986—, chair, 1991-92; lectr. grad. tax program Temple U., 1988-89. Author: (with Jay Zagoren) Pennsylvania Limited Liability Company Forms and Practice Manual, 1996; co-editor (with Patrick Dolan) Securitization Handbook, 2000. Mem. Phi Beta Kappa. Office: Dechert LLP 4000 Bell Atlantic Tower 1717 Arch St Philadelphia PA 19103-2713

DAVIS, CALVIN DE ARMOND, historian, educator; b. Westport, Ind., Dec. 3, 1927; s. Harry Russell and Abbie Jane (Moncrief) Davis. AB, Franklin Coll., Ind., 1949; MA, Ind. U., 1956, PhD, 1961. Tchr. Wilson Sch., Columbus, Ind., 1949-51, 53-54; asst. prof. history Ind. Central Coll., Indpls., 1956-57; teaching assoc. Ind. U., 1958-59; asst. prof. history U. Denver, 1959-62, Duke U., Durham, N.C., 1962-64, assoc. prof., 1964-76, prof., 1976-96, prof. emeritus, 1996—. Cons. NEH, 1974. Contbr. articles to profl. jours.; author: (essays) Ency. U.S. Fgn. Rels., 1997, Oxford Companion to American Military History, 1999, Scribner's Ency. Am. Fgn. Policy, 2002, The United States and the First Hague Peace Conference, 1962 (Albert J. Beveridge award, 1961), The United States and the Second Hague Peace Conference, 1976. With U.S. Army, 1951—53. Mem.: Soc. Historians Am. Fgn. Rels., Orgn. Am. Historians, Am. Hist. Assn. Home: 511 E Nightingale Dr Greensburg IN 47240-8589 Office: Duke U Dept History Durham NC 27708

DAVIS, CARLA MIA, music educator; d. Philip A and Evelyn R Davis. MusB, U. of Miami, Coral Gables, Fla., 1998; MusM, U. of Miami, 2000. Lecturer-keyboard pedagogy dept. U. of Miami, Coral Gables, Fla., 2001—02; tchg. asst. music edn./keyboard depts. U. of Tex., Austin, 2002—. Classical pianist (performances) Solo and collaborative. U. Tex.-Austin scholar, 2002—, U. Miami scholar, 1998—2000. Mem.: Music Tchrs. Nat. Assn. (chpt. v.p. 2002—).

DAVIS, CAROL LYN, administrative assistant; b. West Palm Beach, Fla., Oct. 22, 1953; d. Robert Lee and Barbara Jean (Collett) D. BFA in Studio Arts, Tex. Christian U., Ft. Worth, 1975; MA in Am. Studies, Tex. Christian U., 1977. R&D product line designer Am. Handicrafts/Merribee Needlearts, Ft. Worth, 1977-81; ceramics/china sales cons. Dillard's, Ft. Worth, 1981-82; dept. mgr. Stripling-Cox, Ft. Worth, 1982-83; freelance ceramic and string art designer, 1982-83; rschr. with phase III, IV, V hist. sites inventory Tarrant County (Tex.) for Hist Preservation Coun., 1983-86, Page, Anderson & Turnbull, Inc., San Francisco, 1983-86; rschr. Tarrant County Greater Ft. Worth Housing Starts Tex. Update, Inc., 1987-94; rschr. M/PF Rsch., Inc., Dallas, 1989-94; sales adminstrv. asst. Trail Ridge, Bellaire Park, Summer Creek, Hulen Bend subdiv., Ft. Worth, 1994-2001, Summer Creek Ranch subdiv. Perry Homes, A Joint Venture, Ft. Worth, 2001—. Author pamphlets in field. Mem. mgmt. adv. panel Chem. Week, 1981; alternative precinct election judge Dem. Party, 1994—; mem. Tarrant County Dem. Party; mem. Arts Coun. Ft. Worth and Tarrant County. Mem. Royal Over-Seas League (London). Democrat. Episcopalian. Home: 7800 Garza Ave Fort Worth TX 76116-7717

DAVIS, CAROLE CARRERA, watercolor artist; b. Washington, July 18, 1942; d. Felix Lawrence and Martha Caroline (Schnautz) C.; m. Charles Young Davis, June 30, 1962; children: Sylvia D. Barnard Cynthia D. May. Student in art and art history, Mary Washington Coll., 1960-62; BA in Art, Va. Poly. Inst. and State U., 1978. Instr. watercolor painting Reynolds Homestead, Critz, Va., 1985, 86; instr. watercolor painting Degas program Montgomery County Schs., Christiansburg, Va., 1990-91; instr. watercolor painting Visual and Performing

Arts Inst., Blacksburg, Va., 1993; instr. watercolor I and II Va. Poly. Inst. and State U., Blacksburg, 1996; artist-in-residence for watercolor Margaret Beeks Elem. Sch., Blacksburg, 1997. Watercolor instr. Summer Arts Inst. for Talented and Gifted, Radford, Va., 1986. One- and 2-person exhbns. include Block Prints Gallery, Blacksburg, Va., 1982, Nat. Bank Blacksburg, 1983, 91, Exec. Offices V.P.I. and S.U., 1985, Reynolds Homestead, 1986, Miller and Main St. Galleries, Blacksburg, 1986, William King Art Ctr., Abingdon, Va., 1989, Fine Arts Ctr. New River Valley, Pulaski, Va., 1989, Montgomery Mus., Christiansburg, Va., 1991, Shenandoah Valley Arts Ctr., Waynesboro, Va., 1991, YMCA, Roanoke, Va., 1992, Mill Mountain Coffee and Tea, Blacksburg, 1992, Perspective Gallery, Va. Tech. and Living Gallery, North Cross Sch., Roanoke, 1993, Piedmont Art Assn., Martinsville, Va., 1992, U. Va. Health Scis. Ctr., Charlottesville, 1993, Wallace Hall Gallery, Va. Tech., 1993, Ctr. Behavioral Medicine, Radford, Va., 1994, Dean Witter, Blacksburg, 1994, Waste Policy Inst., Blacksburg, 1996, 2000, IMPAXX, Ltd., Blacksburg, 1996, 1st Nat. Bank, Christiansburg, 1997, The Arts Depot Gallery, Abingdon, 1998, Alleghany Highlands Arts Crafts Ctr., Clifton Forge, Va., 1998, Southwest Va. C.C., Studio 11, Lexington, 1999, The Nat. Bank, Blacksburg, 2000, The Shenandoah Club, 2000, Northcross Sch. Living Gallery, Roanoke, Va., 2001, First Nat. Bank, Christiansburg; numerous group exhbns., 1982—; represented in pub. and corp. permanent collections Carilion New River Valley Med. Ctr., Radford, Va., Cmty. Hosp., Roanoke, Shenandoah Club, Roanoke, Roanoke County Courthouse, Salem, Va., Bank of Va., Roanoke, Dominion Bank, Roanoke, First Nat. Bank, Christiansburg, Va., Nat. Bank Blacksburg, Blacksburg, Va., Neurology Clinic Blacksburg, Surg. Assocs., Blacksburg, Snyder and Assocs., Blacksburg, Northside Presbyn. Ch., Blacksburg, United Meth. Ch., Blacksburg, Urology Assocs. New River Valley, Blacksburg, others; contbr.: The Best of Watercolor: Painting Composition, 1997, The Best of Watercolor: Painting Color, 1997, Artimis XII, 1989. Bd. dirs. Newport (Va.) Village Studio, treas., 1996—; bd. mem. Arbor Day com., Blacksburg, 1995-97; mem. art benefit com. Free Clinic for New River Valley, 1995-97. Recipient Bowles award Bath County Ann. Art Show, 1996, Intertape Systems, Inc. Purchase award, 1994, New River Art '91 Original Frameworks award, 1991, Highlands Art Festival award of merit, 1988, 89, 91, VWS XII Nancy & Carson Moore award 1991, Highlands Art Festival award of distinction, 1990, Best Bot. Painting award Showcase of the Arts, 1990, Blacksburg Juried Art Show awards 1989, 90, 97, AAUW award 1989, Franklin Square Gallery 9th Ann. Exhbn. Best-in-Show Purchase award, 1989, Adirondacks (N.Y.) Nat. Exhbn. Am. Watercolors N.Y. Watercolor Soc. award 1989, Lynchburg Arts Festival C & P Telephone Co. award, 1989, Showcase of the Arts Best-in-Show award 1989, Roanoke Festival in the Park award for body of work, 1988, Bath County Ann. Art Show Best-in-Show award, 1988, Judge's Choice award, 1988, Showcase of Arts award of merit, 1988, Nat. Works on Paper Competition award of excellence, 1988. Mem. Va. Watercolor Soc. (artist mem.; sec. 1986-87, hospitality chmn. 1993-94), Blacksburg Regional Art Assn. exhbns. co-chair 1994-98, v.p. 1995-97, sch. art liaison, 1982-94), Phi Kappa Phi. Avocations: gardening (master gardener), tennis, skiing, bicycling. Home: 567 Hickory Hill Cir Blacksburg VA 24060-9239 E-mail: ccarrerad@aol.com.

DAVIS, CAROLE JOAN, psychologist, consultant; b. Norristown, Pa., Aug. 15, 1942; d. John Morgan and Eva (Pierson) D.; children: Kevin Jae, Kara Megan. AB in English Lit., U. Pa., 1964; MA in Psychology, Temple U., 1967; PhD in Child Devel. and Clin. Evaluation, Bryn Mawr (Pa.) Coll., 1973. Lic. psychologist Pa. Sr. clin. psychologist Camden County Psychiat. Hosp., Lakeland, N.J., 1967-76; psychologist counselling ctr. staff Chestnut Hill Coll., Phila., 1976-89; psychologist hearing impaired programs Phila. (Pa.) Sch. Dist., 1984-85; pvt. practice Phila., 1974-89, New Britain, Pa., 1989-98. Cons. psychologist Pa. Sch. for Deaf, Phila., 1970-84, Luth. Children & Family Svc., Phila., 1974-80, Willis & Elizabeth Martin Sch., Phila., 1975-84, Overbrook Sch. for Blind, 1978-94; psychologist Colonial Sch. Dist. 1994-95; adj. prof. psychology Chestnut Hill Coll. Grad. Divsn., Phila., 1980-98; psychologist APOGEE MHM, 1995-98; adj. faculty Coll. Notre Dame, Balt., 1999—, C.C. Balt. County, 2001—. Mem. Am. Psychol. Assn., Pa. Psychol. Assn., Phila. Soc. Clin. Psychologists (exec. bd. 1981-83), Nat. Register of Health Svc. Providers in Psychology, Psychologists for the Ethical Treatment Animals. Home: 28 Heavrin Ct Baltimore MD 21236-2981

DAVIS, CAROLYNE KAHLE, health care consultant; b. Penn Yan, N.Y., Jan. 31, 1932; d. Paul Frederick Kahle and Alice Edgerton (Kahle) Cargill; m. Ott Howard Davis, June 28, 1953; 1 son, Richard Ott. BS in Nursing, Johns Hopkins U., 1954; MS in Nursing, Syracuse U., 1965, PhD in Higher Edn. Adminstrn., 1972; LittD (hon.), Georgetown U., 1982; DSc (hon.), U. Evansville, 1982, U. Medicine & Dentistry N.J., 1984; LLD (hon.), Adelphi U., 1985; LHD (hon.), Med. U. S.C., 1986; DSc (hon.), Eastern Mich. U., 1989; DHL (hon.), Med. Coll. of N.Y., 1992. Chmn. baccalaureate nursing program Syracuse U., 1969-73; dean sch. nursing U. Mich., Ann Arbor, 1973-75, prof. nursing and edn., 1973-81, assoc. v.p. acad. affairs, 1975-81; adminstr. Health Care Fin. Adminstrn. HHS, Washington, 1981-85; cons. Ernst & Whinney, Washington, 1985-89, Ernst & Young, Washington, 1989-97. Bd. dirs. Cornell U., 1997-99, Prudential Ins. Co. of Am., Newark. Mem. editl. bd. Nursing Economics, Pitman, N.J., 1983-98; contbr. more than 100 articles to profl. jours. Bd. dirs. ARC, 1988-94; trustee U. Pa. Med. Ctr., Phila., 1987—; vice chmn. bd. trustees Nat. Rehab. Hosp., 1993-97; mem. health adv. com. GAO, 1990-97; vis. com. Med. U. S.C., 1985-99, U. Mich. Med. Ctr., 1986-96. Recipient Disting. Alumnus award Johns Hopkins U., 1981, Alumni award Syracuse U. Sch. Edn., 1983, Alumni award U. Mich., 1984, Spl. Recognition award Assn. Am. Med. Colls., 1986; named one of the Top Young Leaders in Am. Acad. Mag., 1978. Mem. NAS Inst. Medicine, Nat. League for Nursing (bd. dirs. 1979-81, chmn. Cmty. Health Accreditation Program 1987-92, Presdl. award 1993). Sigma Theta Tau, Phi Delta Kappa. Republican. Avocation: gardening.

DAVIS, CATHERINE LUCY, psychologist, medical researcher; b. Stamford, Conn., Oct. 28, 1968; d. Flavius Eugene Davis IV and Constance Anne Russell; m. Francisco Ignacio Robles, Nov. 9, 2002. AB in Psychology magna cum laude, Dartmouth Coll., 1990; MS in Clin. Health Psychology, U. Miami, 1995, PhD in Clin. Health Psychology, 1997. Lic. psychologist. Psychology resident Geisinger Med. Ctr., Danville, Pa., 1996—97; postdoctoral fellow U. Miami, Coral Gables, Fla., 1997—2000; asst. prof. pediat. Med. Coll. Ga., Augusta, 2000—. Mem. dean's student rsch. com. Med. Coll. Ga., Augusta, 2000—, mem. acad. coun., 2002—; investigator Ga. Ctr. for Prevention of Obesity and Related Disorders, Athens/Augusta, 2001—; ad hoc reviewer Jour. Pediat. Psychology, 2001—, Obesity Rsch., 2001—, Internat. Jour. Obesity, 2002—; faculty presenter. Motion Explosion exhibit Nat. Sci. Ctrs. Ft. Discovery, Augusta, 2002—02. Contbr. articles to profl. jours. Mem., vol. Cat Network, Miami, 1998—2000. Named Rufus Choate scholar, Dartmouth Coll., 1990; fellow Benjamin J. Benner '69 Rsch. Support fellow, 1989, Summer Diabetes Student Rsch. Program fellow, Juvenile Diabetes Found., 1992, Maytag fellow, U. Miami, 1992—95, T32 Rsch. fellow, NIH, Nat. Heart, Lung & Blood Inst., 1997—2000; grantee Diabetes rsch. grant, Fraternal Order of Eagles in Augusta, 1999, Summer Inst. on Behavioral Medicine Interventions stipend, NIH, 2001, Summer Inst. on Behavioral Randomized Clin. Trials stipend, NIH, Office Behavioral and Social Sci. Rsch., 2002, rsch. grant, NIH Nat. Inst. Diabetes and Digestive and Kidney Diseases, 2003—. Mem.: APA (divsn. 38 health psychology, divsn. 54 Soc. Pediat. Psychology), Soc. Pediat. Rsch., Soc. Behavioral Medicine, Am. Psychosomatic Soc., Am. Heart Assn., Am. Diabetes Assn. (profl. sect. coun. on behavioral medicine and psychology), Vol. Assn. Cultural Hispanoamericana, Phi Beta Kappa, Alpha Theta (pres. 1988—89). Democrat. Unitarian Universalist. Achievements include research in NIH R01 research grant from National Institute of Diabetes, Digestive & Kidney Diseases. Avocation: electronic music. Office: Med Coll Georgia Ga Prevention Inst 1499 Walton Way HS 1640 Augusta GA 30912

DAVIS, CHARLES CARROLL, aquatic biologist, educator; b. Azusa, Calif., Nov. 24, 1911; s. William Allen and Maude (Snyder) D.; m. Sally May Jacobsen, June 11, 1936; children: Peter Thomas, Betsy Ann. AB, Oberlin Coll., 1933; MS, U. Wash., 1935, PhD, 1940. Biologist II State of Md., 1942-43; instr. sci. Jacksonville Jr. Coll., 1944-46; asst. prof. zoology U. Miami, Coral Gables, Fla., 1946-48; asst. prof. biology Western Res. U., Cleve., 1948-52; assoc. prof. Case Western Res U., 1953-63, prof., 1964-68; prof. biology Meml. U. Nfld., St. John's, Can., 1968-78, ret., 1978, prof. emeritus, 1984—, prof. (part-time), 1978-84. Guest prof. aquatic biology U. Tromsø, Norway, 1975-76, Addis Ababa U., Ethiopia, 1986-87; adj. prof. biology U. Waterloo, Ont., Can., 1986-87; cons. for zoology terms New World Dictionary, 1965-69, 82-88. Author: The Pelagic Copepoda of the Northeastern Pacific Ocean, 1949, The Marine and Fresh-water Plankton, 1955, The Snouters Revisited: a Sequel, 1995; adv. editor Internat. Revue der gesamten Hydrobiologie, 1974-92; contbr. numerous articles on plankton, eutrophication of Lake Erie, hatching mechanisms of invertebrate eggs, biol. prodn. to profl. jours. Fellow AAAS, Ohio Acad. Sci.; mem. Ecol. Soc. Am., Am. Soc. Limnology and Oceanography, Plankton Soc. Japan, Internat. Soc. Limnology, Freshwater Biol. Assn. U.K., Can. Soc. Zoologists. Home: 310-12 Blackmarsh Rd Saint John's NF Canada A1E 1S3 Office: Meml Univ of Nfld Dept Biology Saint John's NF Canada A1B 3X9 E-mail: charlesd@mun.ca. *In all things, within the limits of my capabilities, to do what seems directly or indirectly of greatest value to humanity, regardless of its current popularity or unpopularity, and without aiming particularly at financial gain, honors or recognition, or especially at excelling over others. To trust all humans until they prove themselves untrustworthy, and to work towards a society in which no one will have occasion to be untrustworthy.*

DAVIS, CHARLES ELLIOT, accounting educator; b. Greenville, N.C., Sept. 18, 1959; s. Charles Cedric and Shirley (Newton) D.; m. Elizabeth Boozer, July 22, 1989; children: Charles Andrew, Claire Elizabeth. BBA, Coll. of William and Mary, 1981; MBA, U. Richmond, 1989; PhD, U. N.C., 1991. CPA, Va. Acctg. trainee Reynolds Metals Co., Richmond, Va., 1981-83, asst. cost acct., 1983, fin. sys. analyst, 1982-84; staff cons. Coopers & Lybrand, Richmond, 1985-86; fin. sys. acct. Investors Savs. Bank, Richmond, 1987; asst. prof. acctg. Baylor U., Waco, Tex., 1991-97, assoc. prof., 1997—, dir. grad. acctg. programs, 1998—2001, dept. chair, 2002—. Author: OMAR: Online, Multimedia Accounting Review, 2000; contbr. articles to profl. jours. Chmn. parent adv. bd. Baylor Piper Ctr. for Child Devel., Waco, 1998; coach H.O.T. Soccer Assn., Waco, 1998—. Ernst & Young tchg. fellow, 2001—. Mem.: AICPA (group of 100 1999—2000, chmn. acctg. careers subcom. 1998—99, chmn. acct. educator award task force 2000—02, grantee 1990), Am. Acctg. Assn. (webmaster chair ABO sect.). Baptist. Office: Baylor U Box 98002 Waco TX 76798-8002 Fax: 254-710-1067. E-mail: charles_davis@baylor.edu.

DAVIS, CHARLES HARVEY, neurosurgeon, consultant; b. London, Apr. 6, 1949; s. Albert and R. (L.) D.; m. Dec. 18, 1973; 2 children. MBBS, St Bartholumels, London, 1972; FRCS, London U., 1978. Trainee, London, 1981-87; cons. neurosurgeon, 1997—. Vis. fellow U. Ctr. Lawcashire, England, 1992. Contbr. chpt. to book Diseases of Spinal Cord. Fellow Royal Coll. Surgeons.; mem. Soc. British Neurosurgical Surgeons. Avocation: gardening. Office: Royal Preston Hosp Sharoe Green Ln PR2 4HT Preston England

DAVIS, CHARLES RAYMOND, political scientist, educator; b. Hampton, Va., Jan. 16, 1945; s. Cecil Raymond and Fronda Gail (Bradshaw) D.; m. Terry Lorraine Barr, Oct. 1, 1963 (div. July 1979); children: Kimberly Dawn Ingram, Charles Robert; m. Raymonda Carolyn Mays, Feb. 12, 1982. BA in Polit. Sci., U. Louisville, 1974; MA in Polit. Sci., U. Ky., 1975, PhD of Polit. Sci., 1985. Instr. Jefferson Community Coll., Louisville, 1976; claims rep. Aetna Casualty, Madisonville, Ky., 1977-78; rsch. asst. U. Louisville, 1979-80; rsch. analyst Ky. Health Svcs., Frankfort, 1981-85; asst. prof., masters degree program coord. U. So. Miss., Long Beach, 1986-89, asst. prof. Hattiesburg, 1989, assoc. prof., 1991-99, prof., 1999—. Policy analyst Ky. Gov's. Coalition on Health Costs, Frankfort, 1982; acting dir. grad. studies, U. So. Miss., Hattiesburg, 1990. Author: Organization Theories and Public Administration, 1996; editl. bd. Internat. Jour. Orgn. Theory & Behavior, 1997; contbr. numerous articles to profl. jours. Mem. AAUP, ASPA, Am. Polit. Sci. Assn., So. Polit. Sci. Assn., Miss. Polit. Sci. Assn., Miss. chpt. ASPA. Mem. Ch. of Christ. Avocations: photography, travel, reading, music, history of old west. Home: 417 Browns Bridge Rd Hattiesburg MS 39401-8703 Office: U So Miss Dept Polit Sci Southern Sta # 5108 Hattiesburg MS 39406 E-mail: raymond@usm.edu.

DAVIS, CHARLES WILLIAM, certified public accountant; b. Lexington, Ky., Dec. 7, 1948; s. Ordie Ulysses and Carolyn Marie (Massey) D.; m. Diana Lynn Arnold, June 22, 1971 (div. 1980); m. Mary Sue Joyner, June 10, 1989. BS, U. Ky., 1977, MBA, 1980. CPA, N.C. Controller Cor-Lite Constrn. Co., Inc., Lexington, 1976-77, Tucker & Assocs., Inc., Lexington, 1977-78; data analyst Ea. Ky. Health Systems Agy., Winchester, 1978-80; acct. Canteen Corp., Chgo., 1980-82; controller Continental Inn, Lexington, 1983-85, Ramada Hotel Miami, 1985-86, Radisson Hotel Columbia (S.C.), 1986 89; contr. The Park Hotel, Charlotte, N.C., 1989-90; pvt. practice Matthews, N.C., 1991-98. Instr. Midlands Tech. Coll., Columbia, 1987-89, Ctrl. Piedmont C.C., 1991-95; corp. contr. Cornerstone Mgmt. and Devel., Matthews, 1991-92; owner Bus. Success Seminars; assoc. Morris, Anderson & Assocs., Atlanta, Chgo. Author: How to Compete and Win in a Small Business, 1994, Insider Secrets to Profitable Futures Trading, 1998. Mem. Internat. Assn. Hospitality Accts. (co-chmn. organizing com. Charlotte chpt. 1990), Nat. Assn. Accts. (dir. acad. rels. 1988-89), NC Assn. CPAs, Turnaround Mgmt. Assn., Beta Alpha Psi, Beta Gamma Sigma. Avocations: software development, song writing, woodworking. E-mail: crisismg@bellsouth.net.

DAVIS, CHRISTOPHER, writer, retired writing educator; b. Phila., Oct. 23, 1928; s. Edward and Josephine Blitzstein Davis; (div.); children: Kirby, Katherine, Emily, Sarah; m. Sally Warner. BA, U. Pa., 1955. Writing tchr. U. Pa., Phila., 1958-69, Bryn Mawr (Pa.) Coll., 1977-95. Author: Lost Summer, 1958, First Family, 1959, A Kind of Darkness, 1962, Belmarch, 1964, The Shamir of Dachau, 1966, Sad Adam-Glad Adam, 1966, Ishmael, 1967, A Peep Into the 20th Century, 1971 (Nat. Book Award nominee), The Producer, 1972, The Sun in Mid-Career, 1975, Suicide Note, 1977, Waiting For It, 1980, Dog Horse Rat, 1990, (play) A Peep Into The 20th Century, 1988. Recipient Career award Am. Acad. and Inst. Arts and Letters, N.Y.C., 1991; grantee, NEA, 1967, 74, Guggenheim, 1972. Mem. Authors Guild, PEN West, Pasadena Soc. Artists, Phi Beta Kappa. Avocation: sculpture. Home: 2284 Norwic Pl Altadena CA 91001-2565 E-mail: kitdavis@earthlink.net.

DAVIS, CHRISTOPHER KEVIN, sales executive; b. Ogden, Utah, Apr. 8, 1959; s. James LaVerne and Margaret Mary (Brewer) D.; m. Christine Marie Davis, Oct. 27, 1984; children: Jennifer Lee, Christopher Kevin, Kelly Anne. A in Liberal Arts, Meremac Coll., St. Louis, 1979; B of Gen. Studies, U. Mo., St. Louis, 1988. Lic. in real estate sales. Prodn. supr. Survival Tech., St. Louis, 1982-84; salesman Cardinal Properties Real Estate Co., St. Louis, 1981-84; packaging supr. Sigma Aldrich Chem., St. Louis, 1984-85; sales mgr. Gen. Turf and Grounds Equipment Co., St. Louis, 1985-86, TNT Golf Car & Equipment Co., St. Peters, Mo., 1986-91, gen. mgr., 1991-93; pres., CEO Gateway Power Equipment, St. Louis, 1993-2001; pres. Eco-Green Techs., Inc., St. Louis, 1996-2000; pres., CEO Gateway Power Comm., Inc., St. Louis, St. Charles, Springfield, 1999—2002, pres. Lake Ozark, Mo., 2000—02; v.p. Magic Melt, LLC, Silex, Mo., 2000-01; PLC divsn. mgr. Outdoor Equipment Co., 2001—02; boat sales Bass Pro Shops, Sportsman Warehouse, 2002—; sales staff Precision Office Installers, St. Louis, 2002—03, Premier Wireless Sales, Destin, Fla., 2003—; health and life ins. sales agt. UGA Assn. Field Svcs., 2003—. Mem.: Gateway Bassmasters. Roman Catholic. Avocations: hunting, fishing, golf. Office: Premiere Wireless PO Box 833 Destin FL 32540

DAVIS, CHRISTOPHER PATRICK, lawyer; b. Allentown, Pa., July 12, 1954; s. Richard Arthur and Patricia Anne (Henry) D.; m. Carol Hecker, Aug. 19, 1978; children: Gregory Carl, Colin Stuart. AB summa cum laude, Dartmouth Coll., 1976; JD magna cum laude, Harvard U., 1980. Bar: Mass. 1981, U.S. Dist. Ct. Mass. 1981, U.S. Ct. Appeals (1st cir.) 1985, U.S. Dist. Ct. N.H. 1986. Law clk. to judge U.S. Dist. Ct., Boston, 1980-81; assoc. Goodwin Procter LLP, Boston, 1981-88, ptnr., 1988—, chair environ. dept., 1996-00. Editor Harvard Law Rev., 1978-80. Pres. Hamilton-Wenham Land Trust. Mem. ABA, Boston Bar Assn., Phi Beta Kappa. Clubs: Dartmouth Lawyers Assn. (Hanover, N.H.). Avocations: skiing, tennis, bicycling, backpacking, gardening. Office: Goodwin Procter LLP Exchange Pl Boston MA 02109-2803

DAVIS, CLARENCE CLINTON, JR., lawyer; b. Alexandria, La., Sept. 24, 1956; s. Clarence Clinton Sr. and Julia Isabel (Pace) D.; m. Lisa Cheryl Russell, Aug. 6, 1977 (div. Aug. 1978). BS with hons., Northwestern State U., 1977; JD cum laude, So. Meth. U., 1980. Bar: Fla. 1980, U.S. Tax Ct. 1981, U.S. Ct. Appeals (5th cir.) 1981, Tex. 1982; cert. tax law Tex. Bd. Legal Specialization; CPA, Tex. Assoc. Trenam, Simmons, Kemker, Scharf, Barkin, Frye & O'Neill, Tampa, Fla., 1980-81, Moore & Peterson, Dallas, 1981-85, mem., 1986-89; ptnr. Krage & Jarvey, LLP, Dallas, 1989—. Author: Partnership Taxation in Theory and Practice, 1991-95, Special Problems in Partnership Taxation, 1992—, Fundamentals of LLC and Partnership Taxation, 1996—, LLC and Partnership Allocations and Basis, 1996—, Real Estate and Tax Deferred Exchanges, 1996-99. Mem. ABA (taxation sect.), Tex. Bar Assn. (tax exempt orgn. subcom. taxation sect. 1986-87), Fla. Bar Assn., Dallas Bar Assn., Coll. State Bar Tex., Tex. Soc. CPAs, Order of Coif, Phi Kappa Phi. Republican. Episcopalian.

DAVIS, CLAUDE-LEONARD, lawyer, university official; s. James and Mary Davis; m. Margaret Earle Crowley, 1965; 1 child, Margaret Michelle. BA in Journalism, U. Ga., 1966, JD, 1974. Bar: Ga. 1974. Broadcaster Sta. WKLE Radio, Washington, Ga., 1958-62; realtor Assocs. Realty, Athens, Ga., 1963-66; bus. cons. Palm Beach, Fla., 1970-71; asst. to dir. Ga. Coop. Extension Svc., Athens, 1974-81; atty. Office of Pres. U. Ga., Athens, 1981—; mem. faculty, regent Ga. Athletics Inst., 1988-98; broadcaster Leonard's Losers.com, Athens, Ga., 2000—. Cons. numerous agrl. chem. industry groups nationwide, 1977—, Congl. Office Tech. Assessment, Washington, 1978-79, USDA, Washington, 1979-80; del. Kellogg Nat. Leadership Conf., Pullman, Wash., 1980. Editor and contbr. Ga. Jour. of Internat. and Comparative Law, 1972-74; contbr. articles on agr. and fin. planning to profl. jours.; author and editor: DAWGFOOD: The Bulldog Cookbook, 1981, Touchdown Tailgates, 1986. Del. So. Leader Forum, Rock Eagle Ctr., Ga., 1976-99; trainer Ga. 4-H Vol. Leader Assn., 1979—; coordinator U. Ga. Equestrian Team, Athens, 1985-87; mem. Clarke County Sheriff's Posse, 1985-2000. Capt. U.S. Army, 1966-70. Chi Psi Scholar, 1965; Recipient Outstanding Alumnus award Chi Psi, 1972, Service to World Community award Chi Psi, 1975. Mem. Nat. Assn. Coll. and Univ. Attys., DAV, Poets Soc., Am. Legion, Rotary, The President's Club (Athens), Gridiron Secret Soc., Chi Psi (advisor 1974). Baptist. Avocations: martial arts, creative writing, music. Home: 365 Westview Dr Athens GA 30606-4635 Office: U Ga Peabody Hall Ste 3 Athens GA 30602

DAVIS, CLAYTON, writer, pilot, photographer; b. Portersville, Ala., Feb. 27, 1931; s. Horace Milton Davis and Agnes Zama Meadows; m. Irene Alice Brink, Apr. 8, 1952; children: Lynne, Keith Harold. AA in Math. and History, San Antonio Coll., 1966; BA in Russian and Russian Studies, Syracuse U., 1967; postgrad., U. Md., 1971-75. Cert. comml. pilot and airline transport pilot, Md. Enlisted USAF, 1947, advanced through grades to master sgt., 1966, ret., 1970; math. tchr. Anne Arundel County Schs., Annapolis, Md., 1970-77; pilot Met. Air Charter, Balt., 1977-89, dir. ops., 1981-87; freelance writer rep. by West Coast Lit. Assocs., Severna Park, Md., 1989—. Flight instr., Md. Author: Flying Secrets, 1992, Flying Stories, 1992, So, You Want to Be a Pilot, 1999, Kindness: A Little Drop of Water Cures Everything, 2002, Where Pheasants Sing: Life in South Dakota 1900-2000, 2002; contbr. to Redfield (S.D.) Press, Golden Times, S.D., Severna Park Voice, Md., aviation mags., others. Founding mem. Md. Aviation Hist. Task Force. Recipient St. Ignatius Gold medal, Azov Acad., Russia, 2003. Mem. Nat. Writers Assn. (founder, pres. Balt.-Washington chpt. 1993). Republican. Lutheran. Avocations: photography, flying, gardening. Home: 2 Brenda Ct Severna Park MD 21146-3604 E-mail: cd19@erols.com.

DAVIS, CLIFTON DUNCAN, actor, composer; b. Chgo., Oct. 4, 1945; s. Toussaint L'Overture Davis and Thelma (Van Putten) Davis-Goring; m. Ann L. DeShae, Nov. 24, 1981 (div. May 1994); children: Christian Noel, Holly Danielle; m. Monica D. Durant, May 27, 2000. BA in Theology, Oakwood Coll., 1984; MDiv, Andrews U., 1987; LLD (hon.), Lincoln U., 1989. Composer Motown, L.A., 1971-76; co-star "Amen" NBC-TV, L.A., 1986-91; star of "Two Gentlemen of Verona" N.Y. Shakespeare Festival, N.Y.C., 1971-73; star of "That's My Mama" ABC-TV, N.Y.C., 1974-76; actor, singer, composer, lectr., 1971—; v.p. internat. bus. devel. Oasis Nuclear, 1993-94; interim vice chancellor devel. and planning Elizabeth City (N.C.) State U., 1995-96; pres., CEO Clifton Davis Enterprises, Inc., 1986-92, Clifton Davis Internat., Inc., 1996—. Hon. membership chmn. Nat. PTA, 1989-91; mem. adv. coun. The Children's Def. Fund. Author (short story) A Mason Dixon Memory, 1993; starred in The Melba Moore, Clifton Davis Show; guest appearances on (TV) The Jamie Foxx Show, Living Single, Sparks, Malcolm & Eddie, Grace Under Fire, Party of Five, The Sentinel, The Gregory Hines Show, The John Larroquette Show, The Love Boat, Police Story, (made-for-TV movies) Dream Date, Little Ladies of the Night, Cindy, Murder at the Superdome, Scott Joplin, Don't Look Back, The Night the City Screamed, (talk shows) The Tonight Show, Live! With Regis and Kathie Lee, Oprah, The Arsenio Hall Show; appeared on Broadway in Hello Dolly!, Jimmy Shine, The Engagement Baby, Hapgood, (Off-Broadway) How to Steal an Election, To Be Young, Gifted, and Black, No Place to be Somebody and others; toured with Guys and Dolls, Daddy Goodness; co-star (with Lena Horne) Pal Joey, And Still I Rise; composer Never Can Say Goodbye; films include Any Given Sunday, 1999, Kingdom Come, 2001, The Painting, 2001, The Climb, 2001, Max Keeble's Big Move, 2001. Recipient Tony award nomination (best actor in a mus.), 1972, Grammy award nomination (best R&B composition), 1972, Theater World award, 1971, Disting. Svc. citation UnCF, 1981, Oakwood Coll. Disting. Svc. citation UNCF, 1984, Disting. Leadership award UNCF, 1987, Disting. Svc. award UNCF, 1990, Svc. award UNDF, 1991, 92, Legacy of the Dreamer award SCLC, 1989, Heart and Torch award Am. Heart Assn., 1975, Dedicated Svc. award Nat. Black Child Devel. Inst., 1987 and others. Avocations: golf, pilot (lic.), scuba diver (cert.). Office: Clifton Davis Internat 4790 Irvine Blvd # 401 Irvine CA 92620-1973

DAVIS, CLIVE JAY, record company executive; b. Bklyn., Apr. 4, 1933; s. Herman and Florence (Brooks) Davis; children: Fred, Lauren, Mitchell, Douglas. BA magna cum laude, NYU, 1953; LLB cum laude, Harvard U., 1956. Bar: N.Y. 1957. Assoc. firm Rosenman Colin Freund Lewis & Cohen, N.Y.C., 1958—60; gen. atty. Columbia Records, 1960—65, pres., 1966—73, Arista Records, Inc., N.Y.C., 1974—2000, pres., CEO, 1974—2000; co-founder J Records, 2000—; chmn. RCA Records, NY, 2003—. Author: Clive: Inside the Record Business, 1975. Named Man of Yr., Am. Parkinson Disease, 1972, Record Co. Exec. of Yr., Nat. Assn. TV and Radio Announcers, 1973, Nat. Pop Music Survey, 1974, 1978, 1980, 1984, 1987, 1990—93, Pres. of Yr., Man of Yr., City of Hope, 1978, Man of Yr., Martell Found. for Cancer, Leukemia and AIDS Rsch., 1980, 1985, Humanitarian of Yr., Am. Cancer Soc., 1985; named to, Rock and Roll Hall of Fame, 2000; recipient Humanitarian award, Anti-Defamation League, 1970, Martin Luther King Humanitarian of Yr. award, Congress Racial Equality, 1991, Man of Yr. award, Friars Club Orgn., 1992, Amfar, 1998, Grammy Lifetime Achievement award, 2000. Mem.: Record Industry Assn. Am. (pres., chmn. bd. 1972—73, now dir.). Office: J Records Inc 745 Fifth Ave New York NY 10151 also: RCA Records 1540 Broadway 10036 *Experience has taught me to speak out again and again and, with right on one's side, the voice is eventually heard. Cheers for the reasoned vigilantes in society who prevent those in power from overwhelming the rights of the individual who otherwise cannot surface.*

DAVIS, CONCELOR DOMINGUEZ, marriage and family therapist; b. July 17, 1957; s. Lafayette Will and Stella Pearl (Dunning) D.; m. Rasute Jankeviciute. BBA in Mktg., St. Mary's U., San Antonio, 1991; MA in Counseling, Ministerial Tng. Inst., L.A., 1996; PhD in Counseling, Friends Internat. Christian U., 1999. Cert. Internat. Assn. Clin. Counselors, marriage and family therapist. Owner Davis Industries, San Antonio, 1985-91, Eva's Crystal Place, San Antonio, 1988-91; counselor Borgess Hosp., Kalamazoo, 1991-93; fiscal officer Passages Alternative Living, Chgo., 1994; resident coord. Hallmark, Chgo., 1995—96; mental health counselor Columbia Woodland Hosp., Hoffman Estates, Ill., 1996-97; clin. therapist Columbia Osteo. Family Health Ctr., Chgo., 1997-98, dir. child and adolescent counseling, 1998—, dir. family roots child and adolescent counseling, dir. mental health program. Counselor Kalamazoo Probation Enchancement Program; cons. Taylor Crawford Group, Chgo.; founder, pres. CD Davis World Ministries; owner DaJan Corp. Author: (booklets) Live for Christ, 1995, First Love Then Marriage, It's Time to Wake Up, 1995; prodr. TV show Ch. of God, Kalamazoo, editor PBS program; developer Eyroy method for cognitive-behavioral approach to psychotherapy, 1997, With USMC, 1976-79. Recipient cert. of achievement Cable Access Ctr., Kalamqzoo. Mem. Am. Assn. Christian Counselors, Am. Assn. Christian Counseling, Ill. Counseling Assn., Charles Menninger Soc., Am. Soc. Christian Therapists, Delta Sigma Phi. Avocations: sailing, travel, rafting. Home: 915 W Carmen Ave # 503 Chicago IL 60640 E-mail: Eyroy@aol.com.

DAVIS, CONNIE WATERS, public relations and marketing executive; b. Gainesville, Ga., July 3, 1948; d. Starling Randolph and Evelyn Jeanette (Bonds) Waters; m. John W. Davis Jr., Sept. 24, 1971; 1 child, John Christopher. AA, Gainesville Jr. Coll., 1968; BA in Human Resources Mgmt., Brenau U.,

1988; postgrad., Student Evaluation Inst. of Washington, 1988, U. Ga., 1972-73, 85—. Project evaluator Model Cities Program, Gainesville, 1970-74; pers. dir. Lanier Pk. Hosp., Gainesville, 1977-79; asst. dir. Ga. Mountains Ctr., Gainesville, 1979-83; owner, CEO Models by Davis and Davis, Gainesville, 1979—; dir. pub. rels. and sales Ramada Hotel, Gainesville, 1985—; dir. corp. devel. Chestatee Regional Hosp. Dir. Fashion Works, Gainesville; pres. Davis Consulting; owner & pres. Tastefully & Properly Growing Up, 1998—; cons. pub. rels. and mktg; dir. of pub. rels. UP Corp. Deve. Wakkins Chiropractic. Prodr., writer, implementor Gracefully and Properly Growing Up; contbr. articles to mags. and newsletters; writer nat. poulty industry publ., 1990, 95. Publicity chmn. Cancer Soc., 1982, 83, 85; mem. Theatre Wings and Arts Coun.; bd. dirs., mem. mktg. com. Gainesville Jr. Coll., 1985—, trustee, 1995—; bd. dirs. ARC, 1978-79; co-chmn. Flag Com. for Olympics; bd. dirs. Greater-Hall C. of C., 2003—. Recipient Peach award Lions Club, 1979, Vol. award ARC, 1978, various modeling awards So. Models Assn., 1983, 2 Silver Shovel award 1993, 94, state vol. award, 1995; named Best Dressed Woman, Fashion Tour Group, 1984. Mem. Am. Heart Assn. (pres. 1995-96), Am. Lung Assn. (state bd. dirs., Vol. of Yr.), Greater Hall C. of C. (bd. dirs.), Gainesville C. of C., Gainesville Coll. Exec. Coun., Tourism and Conv. Bur. (chmn. 1983-84), N.E. Ga. Advt. Club, Pers. Adminstrs. Group, Ga. Hospitality and Travel Assn., Phoenix Soc., Rotary (cotillion dir. 1998—), Fashion Club (bd. dirs.). Avocations: exercising, skiing, boating, jogging, writing, music, arts. Home: 1214 Chestatee Rd Gainesville GA 30501-2816

DAVIS, COURTNEY A. artist, educator; b. Chambersburg, Pa., June 18, 1977; d. Timothy J. and Nancy G. Redding; m. Mark E. Davis, May 23, 2000. BA, Shippensburg U., 1998; MFA, Marywood U., 2000. Computer art asst. Shippensburg (Pa.) U., 1996—97, gallery intern, 1996—98, gallery asst., 1997—98, instr. computer design II, 2001—; pvt. art tutor Shippensburg and Chambersburg, Pa., 1996—97; computer art intern Golden Apple Computer Lab., Shippensburg, 1996—97; ceramic instr. Harrisburg (Pa.) Arts Assn., 1998; drawing instr. Wilson Coll., 2002; ceramic instr. Shippensburg U., 2003—04. Demonstrator Chambersburg Coun. for Arts, 1998—2000; ceramic demonstrator Marywood U., Scranton, Pa., 1999. To various publs., exhibited in group shows, Gettysburg, Pa., Paris, Ein Vered, Israel, Shippnsburg, Pa. Vol. arts demonstrator Day with the Arts, Chambersburg, 1998. Recipient 1st, 2d and Hon. Mention awards, Chambersburg Coun. for Arts, 1999, 1st, 2d, 3d and Hon. Mention awards, 2000. Mem.: Franklin County Art Alliance, Ctrl. Pa. Guild of Craftsmen, Pa. Guild of Craftsmen, Nat. Mus. Women in the Arts. Avocations: art, ceramics, museums, piano. E-mail: cookieclaygirl@hotmail.com.

DAVIS, CRAIG ALPHIN, lawyer, manufacturing company executive; b. Oakland, Calif., July 28, 1940; s. Alphin Craig and Joyce Ida (Nevers) D.; m. Betty Rankin, July 13, 1963; children: Chelsea Alyson, Channing MacLaren. AB in Polit. Sci, U. Calif., Berkeley, 1964, JD, 1967. Bar: Calif. 1968. Assoc. Heller, Ehrman, White & McAuliffe, San Francisco, 1968-71; counsel Aluminum div. AMAX Inc., San Mateo, Calif., 1971-74; dir. law Alumax Inc., San Mateo, 1974, gen. counsel, sec., 1974-84, v.p., 1978-82, group v.p., gen. counsel, 1982-84, sr. v.p., 1984-86, exec. v.p., 1986-89; internat. bus. transaction advisor, of counsel Hughes, Hubbard & Reed, N.Y.C., 1990—; chmn. Ravenswood Aluminum Corp., N.Y.C., 1992—; chmn. & CEO Century Aluminum Co., Monteray, Calif. Mem. editorial bd., research editor: Hastings Law Jour, 1966-67. Mem. ABA, State Bar Calif. Office: Century Aluminum Co 2511 Garden Rd Monterey CA 93940

DAVIS, CRISPIN, publishing company executive; b. Mar. 19, 1949; Asst. brand mgr. Procter & Gamble, 1970—78, mktg. dir. U.K. ops., v.p. U.S. food ops., 1978—90; mng. dir. European ops. United Distillers, 1990—92, group mng. dir., bd. mem. Guinness (parent co.), 1992—94; CEO Aegis Group plc, London, 1994—99; exec. chmn. Reed Elsevier NV, Amsterdam, 1999—2000; co-chmn. Reed Elsevier plc, London, 1999—2000; CEO Reed Elsevier plc, Reed Elsevier NV, Reed Elsevier PLC, 1999—. Office: Reed Elsevier NV 25 Victoria St London SW1H 0EX England E-mail: crispin.davis@reedelsevier.co.uk.

DAVIS, CYNTHIA D'ASCENZO, lawyer; b. Galveston, Tex., Dec. 6, 1953; d. Austin Christofer and Leah (Ellis) D'Ascenzo; 1 child, Field. BA, Sam Houston State U., 1975; JD cum laude, South Tex. Coll. Law., 1985. Bar: Miss. 1987, U.S. Dist. Ct. (no. dist., so. dist.) Miss. 1987, U.S. Ct. Appeals (5th cir.). Actuarial policy analyst Am. Nat. Ins. Co., Galveston, 1975-76; tchr. ESL Texas City (Tex.) Indep. Sch. Dist., 1976-83; legal asst. Law Offices of Darrel D. Ryland, Marksville, La., 1985; pvt. practice Gloster, Miss., 1987—; municipal judge Town of Crosby, 1993—; prosecutor and municipal atty. Town of Gloster, 1993—. Atty. Town of Crosby, Miss., 1993-2000, mcpl. judge, Town of Gloster, 1994-2000; prosecutor Amite County Youth Ct., 1994—; atty. Amite County Sch. Bd., 1995—; mem. Jud. Coll. Juvenile Justice curriculum com. Treas. Amite County Hist. Soc., 1988—; mem. Miss. Animal Rescue League, Jackson, 1987—, Am. Cancer Soc., 1980—, past bd. dirs., past pub. relations chmn. Mem. ABA, Miss. Trial Lawyers Assn., S.W. Miss. Bar Assn., Miss. Bar Assn. (child advocacy com. 1990—, alternative dispute resolution com. 1991—, Pres.'s award 1990, 91, assoc. pro bono project), Miss. Women Lawyers Assn., Assn. Trial Lawyers Am., Miss. Mcpl. Judges Assn. (v.p. and pres.-elect, pres. 1999-2001, past pres. 2001—, bd. dirs. curriculum com. Miss. Judicial Coll. 1998—), Miss. Capital Def. Resource Ctr. (sec., exec. com. bd. dirs.), Gloster C. of C. (sec.), Jr. League. Avocations: antiques, water skiing. Home: PO Box 940 Gloster MS 39638-0940 Office: 349 E North St Gloster MS 39638-9795

DAVIS, DAISY SIDNEY, history educator; b. Matagorda County, Tex., Nov. 7, 1944; d. Alex C. and Alice M. (Edison) Sidney; m. John Dee Davis, Apr. 17, 1968; children: Anaca Michelle, Lowell Kent. BS, Bishop Coll., 1966; MS, East Tex. State U., 1971; MEd, Prairie View A&M, 1980; postgrad., U. Tex., Tex. A&M U. Cert. profl. lifetime secondary tchr., Tex.; mid-mgmt. adminstr. Tchr. Dallas pub. schs., 1966—, history dept chairperson, 1998—. Instr. Am. History El Centro Coll., 1991-98; adv. Am. history telecourse Dallas Country C.C. dist. Coord. Get Out the Vote campaign, Dallas, 1972, 80, 84, 88, 92, 94, 96, 98, 2000, 02; sec., bd. trustees St. John Bapt. Ch., 1995-98; pres. The Amazons. Recipient Outstanding Tchr. award Dallas pub. schs., 1980, Jack Lowe award for ednl. excellence, 1982; Free Enterprise scholar So. Meth. U., 1987; Constl. fellow U. Dallas, 1988; named to Hall of Fame, Holmes Acad., 1979. Mem. NEA, Tex. State Tchrs. Assn., Classroom Tchrs. Dallas (faculty rep. 1971-77, 95—), Dallas County History Tchrs., Afro-Am. Daus. Republic of Tex. (founder), Top Ladies of Distinction, Zeta Phi Beta. Clubs: Jack & Jill Assocs., (Dallas) (rec. sec., v.p., chair Beautillion Ball, pres., Disting. Mother award, Nat. Committment award 1997). Democrat. Baptist. Home: 1302 Mill Stream Dr Dallas TX 75232-4604 Office: 3000 Martin Luther King Jr Blv Dallas TX 75215-2470

DAVIS, DANNY K. congressman; b. Parkdale, Ark., Sept. 6, 1941; m. Vera Davis; children: Jonathon, Stacey BA, Ark. A. M. & N. Coll., 1961; MA, Chgo. State U., 1968; PhD, Union Inst., 1977. Mem. U.S. Congress from 7th Ill. dist., 1997—; mem. com. on govt. reform and oversight, com. on small bus.; mem. subcom. of census; mem. Com. on Education & Workforce. Chgo. alderman, 1979-90; commr. Cook. County, 1990-96; candidate Chgo. mayor, 1991; founder, pres. Westside Assn. for Community Action; pres. Nat. Assn. Community Health Ctrs.; co-chmn. Clinton/Gore/Moseley-Braun Ill. campaigns, 1992; bd. dirs. Nat. Housing Partnership. Democrat. Office: 3333 W Arthington St Ste 130 Chicago IL 60624-4102 also: 1222 Longworth Bldg Washington DC 20515-1307*

DAVIS, DARRELL L. automotive executive; b. Sharon, Pa., Aug. 8, 1939; s. Paul Darrell and Dorothy Jane (Snyder) D.; m. Jacqueline Donna Pain, July 18, 1986; children: Paul Darrell II, Robert Tod. BS, Youngstown State U., 1963; cert. Stanford Exec. Program, Stanford U., 1987; cert. Global Leadership Program, U. Mich., 1993. Svc. rep., warranty mgr., dist. mgr., asst. zone mgr. Chrysler Motors Corp., Orlando, Fla., 1966-77, zone mgr. Omaha, 1977-78, Troy, Mich., 1978-79, nat. distbn. mgr., regional mgr., gen. mgr. import export ops., gen. sales mgr. Detroit, 1979-88; pres., chief exec. officer Alfa Romeo Distbrs. N. Am., Orlando, 1988-91; gen. sales mgr. Chrysler Corp., Orange, Calif., 1991-93; v.p. Chrysler Internat. Corp., Detroit, 1993-95; gen. mgr. Europe Chrysler Corp., Detroit, 1993-95; pres., COO Chrysler Fin. Corp., Southfield, Mich., 1995-97, chmn., CEO, 1997-98; v.p. Chrysler Corp., 1997—98; sr. v.p. Daimler Chrysler Corp., 1998—2001; bd. mgmt. Daimler Chrysler Svcs. AG, 1999—2000; CEO Daimler Chrysler Fin. Svcs. N.Am., LLC, 1999-2000; sr. v.p., gen. mgr. global svc. and parts divsn. Daimler Chrysler Corp., 2000—01, ret., 2001. Hon. judge Pebble Beach Concours d'Elegance, Meadowbrook Concours d'Elegance; bd. dirs. Boys and Girls Clubs of S.E. Mich., 1998—2001, Walter P. Chrysler Mus., 2001—. Lt. U.S. Army, 1963—65. Mem.: Classic Car Club Am. (treas. Fla. region 2001—). Republican. Avocations: auto collecting, American history.

DAVIS, DARWIN JACOB, finance educator; m. Paula Huber. BA, Utah State U., 1989; MBA, U. Del., 1991; PhD, Ind. U., 1996. Vis. asst. prof. Syracuse (N.Y.) U., 1995—96; asst. prof. U. Del., Newark, 1996—2003, assoc. prof., 2003—. Contbr. articles to profl. jours. Cub scout den leader Boy Scouts Am., Newark, 2002—03, troop com. chmn., 1996—99, explorer post advisor Bloomington, Ind., 1992—94. Mem.: Am. Prodn. and Inventory Control Soc., Am. Soc. for Quality, Inst. for Ops. Rsch. and the Mgmt. Scis., Decision Scis. Inst. Mem. Lds Ch. Office: U Del Alfred Lerner Hall Newark DE 19716

DAVIS, DAVID BRION, historian, educator; b. Denver, Feb. 16, 1927; s. Clyde Brion and Martha (Wirt) D.; m. Toni Lisa Hahn, Sept. 9, 1971; children: Adam Jeffrey, Noah Benjamin; children by previous marriage: Jeremiah Jonathan, Martha Elizabeth, Sarah Brion. AB summa cum laude, Dartmouth Coll., 1950, LittD, 1977; AM, Harvard, 1953, PhD, 1956; MA, Oxford U., 1969; LHD, U. New Haven, 1986; LittD, Columbia U., 1999. Scheduler Cessna Aircraft Co., Wichita, Kan., 1950-51; instr. history Dartmouth, 1953-54; mem. faculty Cornell U., 1955-69, prof. history, 1963-69, Ernest I. White prof. history, 1964-69; prof. history Yale U., 1969—2001, Farnam prof. history, 1972-78, assoc. dir. Nat. Humanities Inst., 1975, Sterling prof. history, 1978—2002, Sterling prof. emeritus, 2001—, dir. Gilder Lehrman Ctr. Study Slavery Resistance Abolition, 1998—. Fulbright lectr., Hyderabad, India, 1967, univs. Guyana and W.I., 1974; Walter Lynwood Fleming lectr. So. history La. State U., 1969; Harmsworth prof. Oxford (Eng.) U., 1969-70; fellow Ctr. Advanced Study Behavioral Scis., 1972-73, Henry E. Huntington Libr., 1976, Whitney Humanities Ctr. Yale U., 2000-01 (sr. fellow); Benjamin Rush lectr. Am. Psychiat. Assn., 1976; French-Am. Found. chair in Am. civilization Ecole des Hautes Etudes en Sciences Sociales, Paris, 1980-81; Fulbright lectr., Israel, Holland, Italy, 1981; Patten lectr. Ind. U., 1981; Hanes lectr. U. N.C., 1982; Thompson lectr. Vassar Coll., 1983; Robert Fortenbaugh Meml. lectr. Gettysburg Coll., 1983; disting. scholar in residence Ky. State U., 1984; mem. Internat. Conf. on Capitalism and Slavery, Bellagio, Italy, 1984; Phi Beta Kappa vis. lectr., 1984-85; disting. resident Westminster Coll., Salt Lake City, 1985; project dir. rsch. grants NEH, 1980, 81; Gilbert Osofsky lectr. U. Ill., Chgo., 1986; Arnold Shankman lectr. Winthrop Coll., Rock Hill, S.C., 1987, William W. Cook lectr. U. Mich. Sch. Law, 1988; Elijah Lovejoy lectr. Colby Coll., 1989; James Neal Primm lectr. U. Mo.-St. Louis, 1989; Goltz lectr. Bowdoin Coll., 1989; William E. Massey Sr. lectr. Harvard U., 1989; Athearn lectr. U. Colo., 1990; Scofield lectr. U. Mo., Kansas City, 1991; lectr. Soc. Fellows NYU, 1991, U. Houston, 1991; participant conf. Hamilton Coll., 1992; tchr. summer course Gilder-Lehrman Inst., 1994-2000; John Hope Franklin lectr. Adelphi Coll., 1995; Paley lectr. Hebrew U., Jerusalem, 1995, Taft lectr. U. Cin., 1996, Byrn lectr. Vanderbilt U., 1996, Keynote lectr. U. Chgo., 1997, Wachova lectr. Coll. of Charleston, 1997, Keynote lectr. Rutgers U., 1997, Maisel lectr. Cornell U., 1998, Popkin lectr. UCLA, 1999; Conferences with Distinguished histoirans U. Houston, 2000, 2001; lectr. Black History Month Coll. Charleston, Commentator on Muslim-Christian mutual enslavement, American Historical Assn., 2001, Tercentennial Symposium Yale U., 2001, Hart lectr. Pomona Coll., 2001, Nathan I. Huggins lectr. Harvard U., 2002, After dinner lectr., Libr. Congress Civil War Sypusium, 2002; keynote lectr. conf. on global slavery Emory U., 2003, N.Y. Pub. Libr., 2003. Author: Homicide in American Fiction, 1790-1860, A Study in Social Values, 1957, The Problem of Slavery in Western Culture, 1966, rev. edit., 1988, Italian/Spanish trans., Portuguese trans., 2001, The Slave Power Conspiracy and the Paranoid Style, 1969, The Problem of Slavery in the Age of Revolution, 1770-1823, 1975, rev. edit. 1999, Slavery and Human Progress, 1984, From Homicide to Slavery: Studies in American Culture, 1986, Revolutions: Reflections on American Equality and Foreign Liberations, 1990 (German trans.), In the Image of God: Religion, Moral Values, and Our Heritage of Slavery, 2001, Challenging the Boundaries of Slavery, 2003; co-author: The Great Republic, 1977, 4th edit., 1992, The Antislavery Debate, 1992; editor: Ante-Bellum Reform, 1967, The Fear of Conspiracy, 1971, Ante-Bellum American Culture: An Interpretive Anthology, 1979, 97; contbg. author: The Stature of Theodore Dreiser, edit. Kazin, 1955, The Province of Pose, edit. Keast and Streeter, 1956, Why Man Takes Chances, edit. Klausner, 1968, Surveillance and Espionage in a Free Society, edit. Blum, 1972, Perspectives and Irony in America Slavery, edit. Owens, 1976, The American Family: Dying or Developing, edit. Reiss and Huffman, 1979, Slavery and Freedom in the Age of the American Revolution, edit. Berlin and Hoffman, 1983, British Caplitism and Carribean Slavery, edit. Solow and Eagerman, 1987, Lincoln, the War President, edit. Boritt, 1992; co-editor: The Boisterous Sea of Liberty: A Documentary History of America From Discovery Through the Civil War, 1998; contbg. author Essays in Slavery, Secession, and Southern History, ed., Paquette and Ferlinger, 2000, American Places: Encounters with History: America's Leading Historians Talk about the Sites Where the Past Comes Alive for Them, ed. Leuchtenberg, 2000; contbr. N.Y. Review of Books; co-curator nat. libr. exhibit Free at Last: A History of the Abolition of Slavery in America. Mem. Subcom. internal security Dem. Nat. Policy Coun., Pulitzer Prize Com., 1968, Bancroft Prize Com., 1989; co-chair adv. bd. Gilder-Lehrman Inst. Am. History, 1995—, tchr. summer sem., 1994-2002. With AUS, 1945-46. Recipient Anisfield Wolf award in race relations, 1967, Pulitzer prize for nonfiction, 1967, Mass Media award NCCJ, 1967, Bancroft prize, 1976, Nat. Book award for history and biography, 1976, Presdl. medal Dartmouth Coll., 1991; Guggenheim fellow, 1958-59; Fulbright grantee, 1980; NEH fellow, 1983-84, Gilder-Lehrman Inaugural fellow, 1996-97. Fellow Am. Acad. Arts and Scis., Brit. Acad. (corr.); mem. Am. Philos. Soc. (adminstrv. bd. Benjamin Franklin papers), Mass. Hist Soc., Am. Hist. Assn. (Albert J. Beveridge award 1975), Inst. Early Am. History and Culture (coun. 1976-79), Am. Antiquarian Soc., Soc. Am. Historians, Orgn. Am. Historians (pres. 1988-89, chair Frederick Jackson Turner award com. 1989, Lincoln prize com. 1992), Milan Group in Early U.S. Hist. Home: 733 Lambert Rd Orange CT 06477-1806 E-mail: david.b.davis@yale.edu.

DAVIS, DAVID EARL, lawyer; b. Barberton, Ohio, Feb. 14, 1960; s. Richard D. and Darlene F. Davis; m. Deborah L. Hammond, Jan. 21, 1995. BS, Ohio State U., 1982; JD, U. Miss., 1990. Bar: Fla. 1990. Paralegal Lyle & Skipper, PA, Tampa, Fla., 1985-86; clk. U.S. Bankruptcy Ct., Tampa, 1986-87; law clk. U.S. Dept. Justice, Tampa, 1989, Pub. Defenders Office, Pascagoula, Miss., 1990; lawyer Bidwell & Assocs., Tampa, 1991-93; pvt. prac., 1993—2002; in-house counsel CNA Ins., Rialto, Calif., 2002—. Vol. Bay Area Legal Svcs., Tampa, 1993-01, IRS income tax asst. program, Tampa, 1988-01, United Way Tampa, 1992-01. Vol. IRS Vol. Income Tax Asst. Program, Tampa, 1988—, United Way Agys., Tampa, 1992—. Mem. Fla. Bar, Hillsborough County Bar Assn., Ohio State U. Alumni, U. Miss. Alumni. Avocations: travel, skiing, horseback riding, hiking. Office: 822 W Cromwell St Rialto CA 92376

DAVIS, DAVID OLIVER, radiologist, educator; b. Danville, Ill., June 25, 1933; s. Oliver and Anna Marie (Collignon) D.; m. Agnes Layden, Dec. 26, 1955; children: Karen, Kathy, Diane, Janet, Nancy. BS, U. Ill., 1954; MD, St. Louis U., 1958. Diplomate Am. Bd. Radiology. Intern Starkloff Meml. Hosp., St. Louis, 1958-59; resident USPHS Hosp., S.I., N.Y., 1959-61, Columbia Presbyn. Med. Ctr., N.Y.C., 1962-63; asst. prof. radiology Washington U., St. Louis, 1966-68, assoc. prof., 1968-70; prof. U. Utah, 1970-72, George Washington U., 1972—, prof. neurology, 1977—, chmn. dept. radiology, 1978-82, 91-96, prof. neurosurgery, 1985—. Vis. prof. U. Calif., San Francisco, 1985; cons. UCLA, 1995-96, UNS; sec.-gen. 12th Internat. Symposium on Neuroradiology. Editor: Principles of Diagnostic Radiology, 1971, Reconstruction Tomography in Diagnostic Radiology and Nuclear Medicine, 1977; mem. editl. bd. Jour. Computer Assisted Tomography, 1977-88, Am. Jour. Neuroradiology, 1979-90, Neuroradiology, 1971-80; mem. editl. exec com. Jour. Investigative Radiology, 1971-80. With USPHS, 1959-64. NIH spl. fellow, 1964-66 Fellow Am. Coll. Radiology (mem. coun. steering com. 1992-94, mem. bd. chancellors 1994-99), Am. Heart Assn. (stroke coun.); mem. AMA, Am. Soc. Neuroradiology (sec. 1971-74, pres. 1979-80, chmn. publs. com. 1988-92, counselor 1992-94, Gold medal 2002), D.C. Med. Soc., D.C. Radiol. Soc. (pres. 1983-84, counselor 1985-91), Assn. Univ. Radiologists, 1973-1990, Soc. Chmn. Acad. Radiology Depts. (sec.-treas. 1981-83), Acad. Radiology Rsch. (bd. dirs. 1994-99), Internat. Microcirculation Soc., Blue Grass Radiology Soc. (hon.), Radiol. Soc. N.Am., Am. Roentgen Ray Soc. (mem. exec. coun. 1992-95, alt. del. to AMA 1995-99, del. 1999-2000), North Pacific Soc. Neurology and Psychiatry (hon.), Am. Head and Neck Radiology, Phila. Roentgen Soc. (hon.), Western Neuroradiology Soc., Am. Soc. Spine Radiology Splty. and Svcs. Soc., Alpha Omega Alpha. Office: George Washington U Med Ctr Dept Radiology 900 23rd St NW Washington DC 20037 E-mail: daveandagnes@yahoo.com.

DAVIS, DEBORAH, education educator, actor; d. Albert C. and Nonie (Goldwater, Bartfeld) Davis. BA, Calif. State U., Los Angeles, 1972; MA, San Francisco State U., 1974—77; PhD, U. of Oreg., 1978—82. Cmty. Coll. Instr. Calif. Instr. Cmty. Coll. Inst., Calif., Oreg. Poly. Inst., Portland, 1988—96, Western Bus. Coll., Portland, 1996—99, Hillsborough C.C., Tampa, Fla., 1999—2000; instr./chair gen. edn. Fla. Met. U., Tampa, 1999—. Adv. bd. mem. Shakespeare-in-the-Park, Portland, 1986—92; founding mem. Portland Area Theatre Alliance, 1987—99; adv. bd. mem. Columbia Theater Co., Portland, 1987—90; vol. Cascade Aids, Portland, Oreg., 1990—99; mentor Big Sisters of Am., Portland, Oreg., 1997—98. Actor: (performer) Tony 'n Tina's Wedding (interactive theatre performance), 1997—99; author: (novels) (book) Student Success: A Concise Guide for the Adult Learner; actor: (films) In The Little Mansion; (plays) Who's Afraid of Virginia Woolf? (Best Actress, 1992), Storefront Theatre, 1988—89. Mentor Big Sisters of Am., Portland, Oreg., 1997—98; vol. Cascade Aids, Portland, 1990—99. Recipient Best Actress "Angry Housewives", Storefront Theatre/Portland, Oreg., 1988—89, Best Actress "In the Little Mansion", Pan Productions/Tampa, Fla., 2001. Mem.: Northshore Animal League (life). Democrat. Avocations: directing, radio voice, cross channel (Oxford, 1980).

DAVIS, DEBORAH LYNN, lawyer; b. N.Y.C., Apr. 23, 1948; d. Melvin Jerome and Beatrice (Greenapple) D. BS, Case Western Res. U., 1970, JD, 1973. Bar: N.Y. 1974, U.S. Dist. Ct. (ea. and so. dists.) N.Y. 1974. Staff atty., dir. litigation Community Action for Legal Svcs., Inc., Bklyn., 1974-77, 78-81; atty. BLS Legal Svcs., N.Y.C., 1977-78; assoc. Gallet & Dreyer, N.Y.C., 1981-86; ptnr. Wagner, Davis & Gold, P.C., N.Y.C., 1986-99, of counsel, 1999—; ptnr. El-Baz Gallery N.Y. Ltd., N.Y.C., 1999-2000; pres., owner Deborah Davis Fine Art Inc., Hudson, N.Y., 2000—. Contbg. author chpts. in book. Incorporator, officer, bd. dirs. N.Y. Svc. Program for Older People, Inc., 1978-91; mem. Family Ct. Panel Screening and Oversight com. 1st Jud. Dept., 1985-88, vice-chair screening applicants, 1985-87. Mem. N.Y. State Bar Assn., N.Y. County Lawyers Assn., N.Y. Women's Bar Assn. Office: Deborah Davis Fine Art Inc 345 Warren St Hudson NY 12534 E-mail: deborahdavisfineart@earthlink.net.

DAVIS, DEMPSIE AUGUSTUS, former air force officer, educator, financial advisor; b. Roebuck, S.C., Oct. 11, 1929; s. Dempsie Augustus and Hontas (Frey) D.; m. Sally Frey, Mar. 5, 1956; children: Elizabeth, Peggy, Dempsie. Student, Primary Armament Sch. Air Tng. Command, Lowry AFB, Colo., 1948; BS, U.S. Mil. Acad., 1955; Edn. with Industry, A.F. Inst. Tech., 1961; MS in Bus. Econ., Clairmont Coll., 1969; diploma in nat. security mgmt., Indsl. Coll., 1973. Small arms tng. instr. USAF, 1946, N.C.O. in charge skeet range and tng., 1946—48, chief fire control sys. sect. 3525th Aircraft Gunnery Squadron Nellis AFB, Nev., 1948—51, commd. 2d lt., 1955, advanced through grades to col., 1978; served as maintenance officer and test support pilot USAF Spl. Weapons Detachment, Nev., 1967-69; project officer Sci. Advisors Office, Mil. Assistance Command Vietnam, Saigon, Vietnam, 1969-70; systems mgr. USAF Air Logistics Ctr., Warner Robins AFB, Ga., 1970-72; chief F-15 logistics evaluation USAF, Edwards AFB, Calif., 1972-75, dir. flight test evaluation, 1975-77; dir. Joint Acquisition Logistics, Eglin AFB, Fla., 1977-79; ret. USAF, 1979; sr. engrng. mgr. Westinghouse, Balt., 1981-82; fin. cons., prof. U. S.C., Spartanburg, S.C., 1982-90; sports shooting, gun safety and exhbn. shooting instr. Spartanburg, 1999—; tchr., video prodr., 1990-99. Decorated Legion of Merit, Bronze Star, Meritorious Service medal, Air medal, Joint Svcs. Commendation medal, Air Force Commendation medal; recipient Leading Skeet award Nat. Skeet Shooting Assn., San Antonio, 1958. Mem. Nat. Sporting Clays Assn. (life), NRA (life, Disting. Expert 1964), Quail Unltd. (charter), Ducks Unltd., Masons (32 degree). Avocations: upland hunting, clay shooting, reading, handball, travel.

DAVIS, DIANE J. director, educator; b. Philipsburg, Pa., Nov. 18, 1946; d. Richard August and Leah Margaret Srock; m. Dennis Lynn Davis, May 7, 1965 (dec. Nov. 1968); 1 child, Denise Lyn. BA in Psychology, Youngstown State U., 1972; PhD in Curriculum and Supervision, U. Pitts., 1979. Med. edn. specialist Mercy Hosp., Pitts., 1984—86; dir. external studies program U. Pitts., 1986—95, dir. Ctr. Instl. Develop., 1995—. Ednl. cons. Pa. Med. Soc., Harrisburg, 1988—96. Scholar, Nat. Inst. Edn., 1972—73. Mem.: Learning Tech. Consortium (pres. 1999—2001), Am. Ednl. Rsch. Assn. Avocations: reading, puzzles, theater. Office: Univ Pitts 4227 5th Ave Rm 820 Pittsburgh PA 15213 Fax: 412-624-7213. E-mail: djdavis@pitt.edu.

DAVIS, DIANN HOLMES, educator; b. N.Y.C., July 5, 1949; d. Henry F. and Pearl B. Holmes; m. Milton Davis, July 24, 1973; children: Milton, Keith, Madelyn. AA, N.Y. Tech. Coll., 1971; BS cum laude, Medgar Evers Coll., 1981; MA, Columbia U., 1994. Lic. reading and early childhood. Sci. tchr. JHS 166, IS 302 Future Day Care, Bklyn.; tchr. N.Y. Bd. Edn., Bklyn. Dance tchr. Faith Hope and Charity Day Care Ctrs.; parent rep. Start Smart; mem. Bklyn. (N.Y.) Reading Coun. Common Brs. Mem. Hall of Sci., Bklyn. Children's Museum, Assn. for Study of Curriculum Devel. Avocations: bicicycle riding, ice skating, roller skating, dancing, sewing.

DAVIS, DON H., JR., multi-industry high-technology company executive; Engrng. sales trainee Allen-Bradley (aquired by Rockwell 1985), 1963-66, dist. mgr., 1966-79, gen. mgr. programmable contr. divsn., 1979-80, v.p., gen. mgr. programmable contr. divsn., 1980-82, v.p., gen. mgr. indsl. control divsn., 1982-85, sr. v.p., 1985-86, head indsl. control group, 1986-87, sr. v.p., gen. mgr. indsl. computer and comm. group, 1987-89, pres., 1989-93, corp. sr. v.p., pres. automation, 1993-95, pres., COO, 1995-97, pres., CEO, 1997-98; chmn., CEO Rockwell Internat. Corp., 1998—. Bd. dirs. Sybron Internat., Ingram Micro, Inc. Nat. trustee Boys and Girls Clubs Am.; chmn. bd. L.A. Mfg. Learning Ctr.; regent Milw. Sch. Engrng. Mem. Internat. Soc. for Measurement and Control (hon. chmn.), Nat. Elec. Mfrs. Assn. (past chmn. bd. govs.), Bus. Roundtable, The Conf. Bd. (sr.). Office: Rockwell Internat Corp 777 E Wisconsin Ave Ste 1400 Milwaukee WI 53202-5302*

DAVIS, DONALD ALAN, news correspondent, writer, lecturer; b. Savannah, Ga., Oct. 5, 1939; s. Oden Harry and Irma Artice (Gay) D.; m. Robin Murphy, Mar. 17, 1983; children by previous marriage— Russell Glenn, Randall Scott. BA in Journalism, U. Ga., 1962. Reporter Athens (Ga.) Banner-Herald, 1961-62, Savannah Morning News, 1962; with UPI, 1963-65; reporter, editor St. Petersburg (Fla.) Times, 1965-66; with UPI, 1967-83, Vietnam corr., 1971-73, New Eng. editor, 1977-80, White House corr., 1981-83; polit. reporter, columnist San Diego Union, 1983-91; pub. Pacific Rim Report newsletter, 1985-88. Instr. journalism Boston U., 1979; instr. writing U. Colo., 1998-99; lectr. U.S. Naval War Coll., 1983, Queen Elizabeth 2, 1991; bd. dirs. Fgn. Corr. Club, Hong Kong, 1974 Author: The Milwaukee Murders, 1991, The Nanny Murder Trial, 1992, Bad Blood, 1994, Death of an Angel, 1994, Fallen Hero, 1994, Appointment with the Squire, 1995, Death Cruise, 1996, A Father's Rage, 1996, The Gris-Gris Man, 1997, Hush, Little Babies, 1997, The Last Man on the Moon, 1999, JonBenet, 2000, Dark Waters, 2002. Fellow Keizai Koho Ctr., Tokyo, 1985, Overseas Press Club, 2000. Mem. Overseas Press Club. Unitarian. Home: 2201 S County Rd 23E Berthoud CO 80513 E-mail: tedsalad@msn.com.

DAVIS, DONALD GLENN, lawyer; b. San Gabriel, Calif., Sept. 15, 1954; BS in Acctg., Calif. State U., Pomona; JD, U. So. Calif. Assoc. O'Melveny & Meyers, L.A.; prof. of law Southwestern U. Law Sch., L.A., 1972-80; gen. counsel Republic Corp., L.A., 1973; ptnr. Danielson, St. Clair & Davis, L.A., 1974-77; mng. ptnr. Davis & Assocs., L.A., 1980—, DGD Enterprises P.V., L.A., 1980—, DGD Investment Banking, L.A., 1980—. Exec. editor Law Rev. jour., U. So. Calif., 1968-69. Vice-pres. student body, Calif. State U., Pomona, 1964-65; candidate 42nd Congl. Dist., Calif., 1988. Mem. ABA, L.A. Bar Assn. (chmn. securities cooperative seminar 1988, chmn. bus. lawyers sect. 1986-87), Order of Coif, Calif. Club, Balboa Bay Club.

DAVIS, DONALD GORDON, JR., librarian, educator, historian; b. San Marcos, Tex., Aug. 15, 1939; s. Donald Gordon and Ethel Dorothy (Henning) D.; m. Avis Jane Higdon, Dec. 6, 1969; children: Lucinda Ellen, Samuel Higdon, Caroline Louise. BA, UCLA, 1961; MA, U. Calif., Berkeley, 1963, MLS, 1964; PhD, U. Ill., 1972; MA in Theological Studies, Austin Presbyn. Theol. Sem., 1996. Adminstrv. asst. Biola Coll. Libr., La Mirada, Calif., 1961-62; sr. libr. asst. U. Calif., Berkeley, 1961-64; sr. reference libr. Fresno State Coll. Libr., 1964-68, head dept. spl. collections, 1966-68; asst. prof. libr. sci. U. Tex., Austin, 1971-77, assoc. prof., 1977-86, prof., 1986—98, assoc. dean Grad. Sch. Libr. and Info. Sci., 2000—02, prof. dept. history, 1998—. Bd. dirs., v.p. Logos Bookstore, Austin, 1974-80; vis. prin. lectr. Birmingham (Eng.) Poly., 1980-81; coord. Libr. History Seminars VI, Austin, 1980, VII, Chapel Hill, N.C., 1985, VIII, Bloomington, Ind., 1990; coord. Ann. Tex. Libr. History Colloquium, 1982-97, Tex. Group for the Study of Books and Print Culture, 1995—; mem. planning com. Libr. History Seminar IX, 1995, Libr. History Seminar X, 2000. Author: The Association of American Library Schools, 1915-68, 1974, Reference Books in the Social Sciences and Humanities, 1977, American Library History: A Bibliography, 1978, ARBA Guide to Library Science Literature, 1970-83, 1987, American Library History: A Comprehensive Guide to the Literature, 1989, Encyclopedia of Library History, 1994, Librarianship and Library Science in India: An Outline of Historical Perspectives, 1994, Library History Research in America, 2000; editor: Libraraties and Culture: Proc. of Library History Seminar VI, 1981, Libraries, Books and Culture: Proc. of Library History Seminar VII, 1986, History of Library and Information Science Education: Library Trends, 1986, Reading and Libraries, proc. of Library History Seminar VIII, 1991, Libraries and Philanthropy, Proc. of Libr. History Seminar IX, 1996, Libraries and Culture jour., 1976—, Handbooks of Texas Libraries, 2000, Winsor, Dewey and Putnam: The Boston Experience, 2002, A Bibliography of Texas Library History, 1695-2000, 2002, A Chronology of Texas Library History, 1685-2000, 2002, Dictionary of American Library Biography, 2d edit., 2003; mem. editl. bd. America: History and Life, 1979—, Annual Bibliography of the History of the Printed Book and Libraries, 1994—, Library History (UK), 1998—; contbr. articles to profl. jours. Pres. PTA Robert E. Lee Sch., Austin, 1979-80; mem. adv. bd. Am. History and Life, 1979—, Heritage Soc. Austin, 1987-92; v.p. Hyde Park Neighborhood Assn., 1983-84; asst. scoutmaster local troop Boy Scouts Am., 1987-91; active USA-USSR Citizens Dialogue, Austin, 1985-93. Recipient Tex. Excellence Tchg. award, 1991-92; Am. Inst. Indian Studies fellow, 1988, Newberry Libr. fellow, 1974, John P. Commons Tchg. fellow, 1986-87, 95, 1998-2000, Alumni Tchg. fellow GSLIS, 2002-03. Mem. Am. Hist. Assn., ALA (chmn. libr. history round table 1978-79, internat. rels. com. 1988-92, exec. com. internat. rels. roundtable 1990-92, Lifetime Achievement award 2003), Internat. Fedn. Libr. Assns., Roundtable of Editors of Libr. Jours. (exec. com. 1987—), Round Table on Library History (exec. com. 1978—), Am. Printing History Assn., Assn. Libr. Info. and Sci. Edn., Assn. Bibliography History (exec. bd. 1982-85), Fellowship Christian Librs. and Info. Specialists (exec. com. 1978-87, 97-2001), Tex. Ctr. for Book (adv. coun. 1987—), Am. Antiquarian Soc. (adv. bd. program in history of book 1987-93), Conf. Faith and History, Hymn Soc. (U.S. and Can.), Libr. Assn. U.K., Tex. Libr. Assn. (program com. archives and local history round table 1997—), Orgn. Am. Historians, InterVarsity Christian Fellowship (nat. faculty and grad. student adv. bds. 1990—), Librarians Christian Fellowship (U.K., v.p. 1990—), Book Club Tex., Soc. Promoting Christian Knowledge/USA (bd. trustees 1999—), Presbyn. Hist. Soc., Presbyn. Hist. Soc. S.W., Tex. State Hist. Assn. (program com. for 1992), World History Assn., Beta Phi Mu (Golden Ann. Disting. award 1999), Phi Kappa Phi. Presbyterian. Home: 706 Harris Ave Austin TX 78705-2518 Office: U Tex Sch of Info 1 University Station D7000 Austin TX 78712-0390 E-mail: dgdavis@ischool.utexas.edu.

DAVIS, DONALD RAY, entomologist; b. Oklahoma City, Mar. 28, 1934; s. Esker Arnold and Mildred Louise (Fortson) D.; m. Mignon Marie Bush, Sept. 29, 1972; children: Marisa Marie, Steven Ray. BA, U. Kans., 1956; PhD, Cornell U., 1962. With Smithsonian Instn., Washington, 1961—, assoc. curator, then curator entomology, 1961-76, chmn. dept., 1976-81, curator entomology, 1981—. Contbr. articles to profl. jours. Recipient Smithsonian Instn. Rsch. Found. award, 1966-67, 73-74, Scholarly Studies grantee, 1990-92, Am. Philos. Soc. grantee, 1963; Rsch. Opportunity awardee, various yrs. Mem. Biol. Soc. Washington (pres. 1984-85), Lepidopterists Soc. (Jordan medal 1977, pres. 1985), Assn. Tropical Biology, Entomol. Soc. Am., Hennig Soc., Nat. Speleological Soc., Soc. Systematic Zoology, Entomol. Soc. Washington (pres. 1979), Washington Biologists Field Club. Office: Smithsonian Instn Stop 127 Washington DC 20560-0001 E-mail: davis.don@nmnh.si.edu. *I believe that life's major goal should be to contribute something of lasting value to earth's diverse heritage. Perhaps the most permanent heritage anyone can bequeath lies in the discovery of new knowledge. By thus enriching our common heritage, I feel that I can partially repay, in my own humble way, for the enormous privilege of having once lived on this fascinating planet.*

DAVIS, DONALD ROBERT, nutritionist, researcher, consultant; b. La Jara, Colo., Mar. 19, 1941; s. Robert Cristopher and Ida Mary (Blissard) D.; m. Vera Elaine Wilson, June 27, 1980 (div. Aug. 15, 1989). Grad., Calif. Inst. Tech., 1962; PhD, UCLA, 1965; post-doctoral fellow, Calif. Inst. Tech., 1965-67. Instr. Calif. Inst. Tech., Pasadena, 1965-67; asst. prof. U. Calif., Irvine, 1967-74; rsch. scientist assoc. U. Tex., Austin, 1974-86, rsch. assoc., 1986—. Mem. bd. trustees Internat. Acad. Nutrition and Preventive Medicine, 1983-85, The Wacker Found., 1987—; dir. Roger J. Williams Nutrition Inst., 1987-90; sr. rsch. cons. Ctr. for Improvement of Human Functioning, Wichita, Kans., 1989—. Editor-in-chief Jour. Applied Nutrition, 1986-91; mem. edtl. bds. Jour. Applied Nutrition, 1978—, Jour. Internat. Acad. Preventive Medicine, 1983-85, Jour. Advancement in Medicine, 1997—; contbr. over 45 articles to profl. jours; co-developer nutrient content software, Nutricircles, 1985—. Instr. Lifetime Learning, Austin, 1978—. Recipient Rsch. fellowship NSF, Washington, 1965-67; grantee Found. for Nutritional Advancement, Washington, 1986. Mem.: AAAS, Acad. Orthomolecular Medicine, Am. Coll. Nutrition. Office: Univ Tex Biochem Inst Austin TX 78712 E-mail: d.r.davis@mail.utexas.edu.*

DAVIS, DORIS ROSENBAUM (DEE DAVIS), artist, writer; b. N.Y.C., Nov. 7, 1919; d. Lewis Newman and Bella (Wretnikow) Rosenbaum; m. Lewis F. Davis, Aug. 13, 1940 (div. Dec. 1989); children: Laurie, Peter. BA, Sarah Lawrence Coll., 1941. Crafts instructor Cooper Hewitt Mus., N.Y.C., 1977-87, Pratt Inst., N.Y.C., 1988-92, Am. Craft Mus., N.Y.C., 1996—2003, Adventures in Crafts, N.Y.C., 1971—. Represented in permanent collections Cooper-Hewitt Mus., Am. Craft Mus., Mus. City of N.Y., Gracie Mansion, Sarah Lawrence Coll.; author: Découpage, 1995, Decoupage, A Practical Guide, 2000; co-author: Step by Step Découpage, 1976, The Découpage Gallery, 2001, The Victorian Scrap Gallery, 2003; contbr. articles; appeared in (TV series) Our Home, 1997—98, HGTV, 2001. Democrat. Jewish. Avocations: traveling abroad, visiting museums, galleries, reading, classical music. Office: Adventures in Crafts PO Box 6058 New York NY 10128-0001 E-mail: deecoupage@webtv.net.

DAVIS, DOROTHY SALISBURY, writer; b. Chgo., Apr. 26, 1916; d. Alfred Joseph and Margaret Jane (Greer) Salisbury; m. Harry Davis, Apr. 25, 1946 (dec.). AB, Barat Coll., Lake Forest, Ill., 1938. Mystery and hist. novelist, short story writer. Author: A Gentle Murderer, 1951, A Town of Masks, 1952, Men of No Property, 1956, Death of an Old Sinner, 1957, A Gentleman Called, 1958, The Evening of the Good Samaritan, 1961, Black Sheep, White Lamb, 1963, The Pale Betrayer, 1965, Enemy and Brother, 1967, God Speed The Night, 1968, Where the Dark Streets Go, 1969, Shock Wave, 1972, The Little Brothers, 1973, A Death in the Life, 1976, Scarlet Night, 1980, A Lullaby of Murder, 1984, Tales for a Stormy Night, 1985, The Habit of Fear, 1987, In the Still of the Night, 2000. Recipient Life Achievement award Bouchereon, 1989. Mem. Authors Guild, Mystery Writers of Am. (former pres., recipient Grand Master award 1985), Adams Roundtable. Home: PO Box 595 Palisades NY 10964-0595

DAVIS, DOUGLAS DONALD, physical education educator, coach; b. Brookings, S.D., May 24, 1967; s. Donald Ervin and Donna Alyce Davis; m. Stephanie M. Heiss, Nov. 24, 1995; 1 child, Mara Judith. BS in Mktg., Mankato State U., 1990, BA in Phys. Edn., 1994. Pool mgr. Tourtellotte Swimming Pool, Mankato, Minn., 1989—94; phys. edn. tchr. Detroit Lakes (Minn.) Sch. Dist., 1994—96, Chaska (Minn.) Sch. Dist., 1996—97, Northfield (Minn.) Sch. Dist., 1997—. Water safety instr. Tourtellotte Pool, Mankato, 1989—94; mem. parent adv. com. Northfield Sch., 1999—2001. Eucharistic min. All-Saints Cath. Ch., Lakeville, Minn., 2001—, parish sponsor, 1999—. Recipient Marie Bruce Leadership award, Mankato State U., 1991—92. Mem.: Nat. Interscholastic Swimming Coaches Assn., Minn. Girls Swimming Coaches Assn. (v.p. 1997—99, pres. 1999—2002, Coach of Yr. award 1998—99). Roman Catholic. Avocations: reading, competing in triathlons. Home: 7284 165th St W Rosemount MN 55068 Office: Northfield High School 1400 S Division St Northfield MN 55057 E-mail: doug.davis@nfld.k12.mn.us.

DAVIS, DUANE LEE, marketing educator; b. Aurora, Ill., July 10, 1950; s. Loren Gene and Gladys Lillian (Vandeveer) D. BS cum laude, No. Ill. U., 1972; MBA, So. Ill. U., 1975; D. Bus. Adminstrn., U. Ky., 1978. Nat. accounts mgr. Century Drill & Tool, Chgo., 1972-74; asst. prof. No. Ill. U., DeKalb, 1977-78; assoc. prof. U. Cen. Fla., Orlando, 1978-91, prof., 1991—; lectr. U. Md., Heidelberg, Fed. Republic Germany, 1984-85; acting chair U. Cen. Fla., Orlando, 1989-91; Fulbright scholar Univ. do Algarve, Faro, Portugal, 1991-92, Univ. do Porto, Portugal, 1991-92. Vis. prof. Pepperdine U., Malibu, Calif., 1987, Univ. do Porto, Portugal, 1999; cons. numerous clients, 1985—. Author: Business Research for Decision Making, 1985, rev. edit., 1996, 2000; contbr. articles to profl. jours. Named one of Outstanding Young Men in Am., U.S. Jaycees, 1980; Fulbright scholar, 1999. Mem. Am. Mktg. Assn. (Hugh G. Wales Faculty Advisor 1981-82), So. Mktg. Assn., Am. Assn. for Advances in Health Care Rsch. Avocations: offshore fishing, reading, traveling. Office: U Cen Fla Cocoa FL 32922-6598

DAVIS, DWIGHT, cardiologist, educator; b. Winston-Salem, N.C., Apr. 11, 1948; s. James C. Davis; m. Lorna Jean Enck, July 30, 1988; 1 child, Nathan James. BS, N.C. A&T State U., 1970; MD, U. Rochester, 1975. Rsch. asst. U. Rochester, N.Y., 1970-71; intern in medicine Boston U. Hosp., 1975-76, resident in medicine, 1976-78; cardiology fellow Duke U. Med. Ctr., Durham, N.C., 1978-81; asst. prof. medicine, cardiology divsn. Pa. State U., Hershey, 1981-87, assoc. prof., 1987-92, disting. lectr., 1986, prof. medicine, 1992—, cardiology dir. heart transplantation, artificial organs and preclinical tchg. program, dir. cardiology preclinical tng. program, 1984—, dir., cardiology fellow tng. program, 1984-87, dir. cardiac catheterization lab., 1987—, med. dir. cardiac rehab. program, 1988—, dir. clin. cardiology program, 1991—, asst. dean for admissions, 1994-99, assoc. dean admissions and student affairs, 1999—. Vice chmn. faculty affairs faculty senate Pa. State U., University Park, 1988—; mem. med. alumni coun. U. Rochester Sch. Medicine and Dentistry, 1992—; various disting. lectureships. Contbr. numerous articles to profl. jours.; editorial reviewer Annals Internal Medicine, 1983—; editorial adv. bd. Primary Cardiology, 1985—. Mem. Pa. Coun. on Aging, Harrisburg, 1989—. Recipient Outstanding Physician award Pa. State U. Sch. Medicine, 1984, Disting. Tchg. awards, 1988-89, Tchr. of Yr. award, 1991, Disting. Prof. award for tchg., 1991, Outstanding Tchr. of Yr. award med. sch. class of 1995, 93, Outstanding Tchr. of Yr. award med. sch. class of 1997, 1995, Alumni Excellence award N.C. A&T State U., 1986, Disting. Alumni award Nat. Assn. Equal Opportunity in Higher Edn., 1987. Fellow Am. Coll. Cardiology, Am. Coll. Angiology; mem. AAAS, Am. Heart Assn. (fellow coun. on clin. cardiology, rsch. com. Pa. affiliate 1992—, pres. elect Pa. affiliate 1997, pres. elect Pa./Del affiliate 1998, Disting. Svc. award Pa. Del. affiliate 2000), Am. Fedn. Clin. Rsch., Am. Assn. Med. Colls. (pres. elect North East group on student affairs 1998), Am. Assn. Cardiovasc. and Pulmonary Rehab. (expert panel cardiac rehab. guidelines project 1992—, chair cardiac rehab. criteria devel. panel 1995—), N.Y. Acad. Scis., Alpha Omega Alpha. Mem. United Ch. of Christ. Achievements include discovery that abnormalities of the sympathetic nervous system in patients with heart failure is due to an increase in norepinephrine spillover and a decrease in norepinephrine clearance from the circulation. Office: Pa State U Coll Medicine Divsn Cardiology PO Box 850 Hershey PA 17033-0850

DAVIS, EARL JAMES, chemical engineering educator; b. St. Paul, July 22, 1934; s. Leo Ernest and Mary (Steiner) D.; children: Molly Kathleen, David Leo. BS cum laude, Gonzaga U., 1956; PhD, U. Wash., 1960. Design engr. Union Carbide Chems. Co., South Charleston, W.Va., 1956; from asst. prof. chem. engring. to assoc. prof. Gonzaga U., Spokane, Wash., 1960-68, dir. computing ctr., 1967-68; rsch. fellow Imperial Coll., London U., 1964-65; assoc. prof. chem. engring. Clarkson U., 1968-73, head socio-environ. program, 1972-74, prof., 1973-78, chmn. chem. engring. dept., 1973-74, assoc. dir. Inst. Colloid and Surface Sci., 1974-78; prof., chmn. chem. and nuclear engring. dept. U. N.Mex., 1978-80; dir. engring. divsn., prof. Inst. Paper Chemistry, Appleton, Wis., 1980-83; rsch. fellow in chem. engring. U. Wash., Seattle, 1957-60, prof. chem. engring., 1983—, assoc. vice provost for rsch., 2001—03. Guest prof. Tech. U. of Vienna, Austria, 2000; sr. scientist, cons. Unilever Rsch. Lab., Port Sunlight, Eng., 1974-75; vis. scholar NAS/Chinese Acad. Scis., China, 1989; adj. prof. Sichuan U., Chengdu, China, 2001-03. Assoc. editor Aerosol Sci. and Tech., 1993-97; mem. editl. bd. Jour. Colloid and Interface Sci., 1984-86; mem. editl. bd. Jour. Aerosol Sci., 1992-98, editor-in-chief, 1999—; mem. adv. bd. Surface and Colloid Sci., 2000—; regional editor (N.Am. and S.Am.) Colloid and Polymer Sci., 1994-99; contbr. articles to sci. publs. NSF fellow, 1964-65, grantee, 1963-89, 92—; recipient Burlington No. award for rsch., 1988; Leeds and Northrup fellow U. Wash., 1960. Fellow AAAS, mem. AIChE (adminstr. Design Inst. Multiphase Processing 1979-87), Am. Chem. Soc., Am. Assn. Aerosol Rsch. (treas. 1990-92, David Sinclair award 1991, v.p. 1996-97, pres. 1997-98), Soc. Applied Spectroscopy, Gesellschaft für Aerosolforschung, Sigma Xi, Phi Lambda Upsilon. Achievements include research on air pollution control, aerosol physical chemistry and colloid science. Office: U Wash Dept Chem Engring PO Box 351750 Seattle WA 98195-1750 E-mail: davis@cheme.washington.edu.

DAVIS, EARON SCOTT, environmental health law consultant, lawyer; b. Chgo., Sept. 7, 1950; s. Milton and Grayce D.; m. Gilla Prizant, May 29, 1977; children: Jeremy Adam, Jonathan Michael, Daniel Benjamin. BA, U. Ill., 1972; JD, Washington U., St. Louis, 1975; MPH, UCLA, 1978. Bar: Ill. Asst. to chmn. Ill. Pollution Control Bd., Chgo., 1975-77; environ. cons. Fred C. Hart Assos., Washington, 1979-80; atty. coord. Migrant Legal Action Program, Washington, 1980-81; environ cons. Evanston, Ill., 1981—. Editor, pub. Ecol. Illness Law Report, Evanston, 1982-89; author: Toxic Chemicals: Law and Science, 1982; contbr. articles and book chpts. to various publs. Exec. dir. Human Ecology Action League, Evanston, 1983-84; mem. nat. adv. bd. Environ. Task Force, Washington, 1984-88, Nat. Ctr. for Environ. Health Strategies (Recognition of Excellence 1991); mem. adv. com. D.C. Lung Assn. (spl. commendation 1981), Washington, 1980-82, Clean Air Coalition, Phila, 1983-85, U.S. EPA's Indoor Air Quality clearinghouse Planning Team, 1990-92. Recipient Presdl. award Am. Acad. Environ. Medicine, 1983, Carlton Lee award Am. Acad. Environ. Medicine, 1988, Gargoyle award Coun. for Disability Rights, 1992. Mem. Soc. Environ. Journalists. E-mail: earondavis@aol.com.

DAVIS, EDGAR GLENN, science and health policy executive; b. Indpls., May 12, 1931; s. Thomas Carroll and Florence Isabelle (Watson) Davis; m. Margaret Louise Alandt, June 20, 1953; children: Anne-Elizabeth Davis Polestra, Amy Alandt, Edgar Glenn Davis Jr. AB, Kenyon Coll., 1953; MBA, Harvard U., 1955. With Eli Lilly & Co., Indpls., 1958—63, mgr. budgeting and profit planning, 1963—66, mgr. econ. studies, 1966—67, mgr. Atlanta sales dist., 1967—68, dir. market rsch. and sales manpower planning, 1968—69, dir. mktg. plans, 1969—74, exec. dir. pharm. mktg. planning, 1974—75, exec. dir. corp. affairs, 1975—76, v.p. corp. affairs, 1976—90, v.p. health care policy, 1990; pres., chmn. bd. dirs. Centre for Health Sci. Info., Boston, 1990—; fellow Ctr. for Bus. and Govt. Kennedy Sch. of Govt. Harvard U., 1991—; adj. prof. Butler U., Indpls. Exec. in residence Butler U. Coll. Bus.; mem. Inst. Ednl. Mgmt., Harvard U. Grad. Sch. Edn., 1987; chmn. staff Bus. Roundtable Task Force on Health, 1981—85; U.S. rep. UN Indsl. Devel. Orgn. Conf., Lisbon, 1980, Casablanca, 81, Budapest, 83, Madrid, 87; participant meeting of experts on pharms UNIDO, 1981; rep. to UN Commn. on Narcotic Drugs, Vienna, 1981, UN Econ. and Social Coun., N.Y.C., 1981, UN Indsl. Devel. Orgn. Conf. ; Ctr. for Bus. and Govt. fellow Kennedy Sch. Govt., Harvard U.; co-chmn. Harvard Conf. on Govt. Role in Civilian Tech., 1992, Harvard Conf. Pharmaceutical Rsch., Innovation and Pub. Policy, 1993, Harvard Biotech. Roundtable, 1991—; vis. scholar, advisor Health and Welfare Unit, Inst. for Econ. Affairs, London; vis. scholar Green Coll. Oxford (Eng.) U., 1994—; chmn. Nat. Fund for Med. Edn., 1994—; dir. English Speaking Union, Indpls.; gov. Soc. Indiana Pioneers; lectr. in field. Contbr. articles to profl. jours. Pres. Eli Lilly and Co. Found., 1976—88; pres., chmn. bd. Indpls. Health Inst., 1988—91; trustee Kenyon Coll., Gambier, Ohio, Ind. Hist. Soc.; pres. bd. trustees Boston Biomed. Rsch. Inst.; chmn. Nat. Fund for Med. Edn., 1996—; bd. dirs. Carnegie Coun. on Ethics and Internat. Affairs, 1985—92; accredited nongovtl. observer rep. to UN Goodwill Found. Ind. Inc., 1987—95; bd. dirs. Sta. WFYI Pub. TV, Indpls., 1983—91, Indpls. Mus. Art, Am. Symphony Orch. League, 1987—92, Nat. Health Coun., 1984—91, Pub. Affairs Coun., Washington, Nat. Fund for Med. Edn.; bd. advisors Christian Theol. Sem., N.C. Schl Arts, Bishops Sch., LaJolla, Calif.; chmn. bd. dirs. Ind. Repertory Theatre, 1979—85; vice chmn., exec. com., bd. dirs. Indpls. Symphony Orch. and Ind. State Symphony Soc., 1977—91; chmn. task force on fine arts Commn. for Future of Butler U.; chmn. exec. com. Pan Am. Econ. Leadership Conf. 10th Pan Am. Games, Indpls.; mem. Chgo. Coun. on Fgn. Rels.; bd. govs. Soc. Ind. Pioneers; trustee Boston Biomed. Rsch. Inst., 1991—. Fellow: The Hudson Inst. (sr. adj. Indpls.); mem.: Inst. Medicine NAS, Ind. Soc. Pioneers (bd. govs.), NAM (vice-chmn. health policy com. 1987—91, bd. dirs.), Literary Club Indpls., Reform Club London, Traders Point Hunt Club, N.Y. Yacht Club, Edgartown Golf Club, Chappaquiddick Beach Club, Crooked Stick Golf Club, Lambs Club, Contemporary Club, Woodstock Club, Yacht Club, Edgartown Yacht Club, Naples (Fla.), Met. Club (Washington). Office: Butler U Coll Bus Adminstrn 4600 Sunset Ave Indianapolis IN 46208-3487 Fax: 317-940-9455.

DAVIS, EDMOND RAY, lawyer; b. Glendale, Calif., Sept. 4, 1928; s. Archie Allen and Eve Mae (Hoover) D.; m. Ruby Evelyn Davis, Oct. 17, 1954; children: Phillip A., Sandra A. Ed., Pepperdine Coll.; JD, U. Calif., San Francisco, 1952. Bar: Calif. 1952, U.S. Dist. Ct. (cen. dist.) Calif. 1952. Assoc. Bailie, Turner & Sprague, 1955-60; trust counsel Security Pacific Nat. Bank, 1960-67; ptnr. Overton, Lyman & Prince, L.A., 1967-87, Brobeck, Phleger & Harrison, L.A., 1987-99, Davis & Whalen, Pasadena, Calif., 1999—. Chmn. legal adv. com. San Marino Unified Sch. Dist., 1981—; mem. legal com. Music Ctr. Found., Performing Arts Council, Los Angeles County, 1980—; trustee WM Group of Funds. Chmn., pub. adminstr. Pub. Guardian Adv. Commns., Los County Bd. Suprs., 1974-76; bd. dirs. Braille Inst. Am., Inc., 1974—, Children's Bur. So. Calif., Children's Bur. Found., WM Group of Funds, Mut. Funds; pres. Calif. Jaycees, 1962. With U.S. Army, 1952-54. Recipient Alumni award Pepperdine Coll., 1962. Fellow Am. Coll. Trust and Estate Counsel (chmn. Calif. chpt. 1981-86); mem. Internat. Acad. Estate and Trust Law (academician), State Bar of Calif. (chmn. estate planning, trust and probate law sect. 1977-78), L.A. County Bar Assn. (exec. com., probate and trust law sect. 1986-89, Arthur K. Marshall award Probate and Trust Law sect. 1991), Order of Coif, Calif. Club, Chancery Club. Office: Davis & Whalen LLP 553 S Marengo Ave Pasadena CA 91101-3114 E-mail: edavis@daviswhalen.com.

DAVIS, EDWARD BERTRAND, retired federal judge, lawyer; b. W. Palm Beach, Fla., Feb. 10, 1933; s. Edward Bertrand and Mattie Mae (Walker) D.; m. Patricia Lee Klein, Apr. 5, 1958; children: Diana Lee Davis, Traci Russell, Edward Bertrand, III. JD, U. Fla., 1960; LLM in Taxation, N.Y. U., 1961. Bar: Fla. 1960. Pvt. practice, Miami, 1961-79; counsel High, Stack, Lazenby & Bender, 1978-79; U.S. dist. judge So. Dist. Fla., 1979-2000; assoc. Ackerman Senterfitt, 2000; chair state wide litig. practice. Served with AUS, 1953-55. Mem. Fla. Bar Assn., Dade County Bar Assn. Office: Akerman Senterfitt Suntrust Internat Ctr One SE 3d Ave 28th Fl Miami FL 33131 Fax: 305-374-5095. E-mail: edavis@akerman.com.

DAVIS, E(DWARD) MARCUS, lawyer; b. Atlanta, Nov. 24, 1951; s. Edward Martin and Marcine (McConnell) D.; m. Sue Fouquet; children: Edward Clark, Hannah Morgan. AB in Econs., Duke U., 1973; JD, U. Ga., 1976. Bar: U.S. Supreme Ct. 1981. Ptnr. Davis, Zipperman, Kirschenbaum & Lotito, Atlanta, 1983—. Contbr. articles to profl. jours. Mem. ABA, ATLA, Ga. Trial Lawyers Assn., Ga. Criminal Def. Lawyers Assn., Nat. Bd. Trial Advocacy (cert.), Am. Bd. Profl. Liability Attys. (cert.), Lawyers Club of Atlanta. Presbyterian. Avocations: boating, painting, horses. Office: Davis Zipperman Kirschenbaum & Lotito 918 Ponce De Leon Ave NE Atlanta GA 30306-4212 E-mail: marc@dzkl.com.

DAVIS, EDWARD WILSON, business administration educator; b. Thomaston, Ga., Aug. 4, 1935; s. James Royland, Jr. and Hazel (Bass) D.; m. Patricia Gail Forrest, Oct. 20, 1962; children: Matthew Wilson, Edward Royland. BS in Mech. Engring, Ga. Inst. Tech., 1957, MS in Indsl. Engring, 1959; postgrad., Swiss Fed. Inst. Tech., 1957-58; MPhil, Yale U., 1967, PhD, 1968. Project leader Ops. Research, Inc., Washington, 1960-64; asst. prof. Harvard Bus. Sch., Cambridge, Mass., 1968-73; vis. asso. prof. Sloan Sch. Mgmt., M.I.T., Cambridge, 1973-74; assoc. prof., then prof. U. N.C., Chapel Hill, 1974-78; prof. Grad. Sch. Bus. Adminstrn., U. Va., Charlottesville, 1978—, Oliver Wight prof. bus. adminstrn., 1984—, Isidore Horween rsch. prof., 1991-96. Cons. various pvt. and public cos., U.S. and Europe. Author: Case Studies in Material Requirements Planning, 1978; co-author: Project Management with PERT & CPM, 3d edit., 1983; editor: Project Management, 1974, 2d edit., 1982. Council mem. Pilgrim Congregation Ch., 1972-74; cub scout and boy scout leader Occoneechee council Boy Scouts Am., 1974-77. IBM faculty fellow in internat. bus., 1976 Mem. Am. Mgmt. Assn., Inst. Mgmt. Scis., Am. Inst. Indsl. Engrs., Project Mgmt. Inst., Am. Inst. Decision Scis., Am. Prodn. and Inventory Control Soc. (dir. Ednl. and Research Found., presdl. award 1974, 89), U. Va. Raven Soc., Westminister Canterbury of the Blue Ridge (bd. dirs. 2000—). Presbyterian. Office: PO Box 6550 Charlottesville VA 22906-6550 E-mail: ewd@virginia.edu.

DAVIS, EGBERT LAWRENCE, III, lawyer; b. Winston-Salem, NC, Dec. 30, 1937; s. Egbert Lawrence Jr. and Eleanor (Layfield) D.; m. Alexandra Holderness, Aug. 25, 1962; children: Alexandra Davis Hipps, Egbert L. IV, Lucinda Davis, Pamela Davis. AB, Princeton U., 1960; LLB, Duke U., 1963; MBA, George Washington U., 1966. Bar: N.C. 1963. Assoc. Womble, Carlyle, Sandridge & Rice, Winston-Salem, N.C., 1965-70, ptnr., 1970-82, Raleigh, N.C., 1982-97, of counsel, 1997—. Sec. Wachovia Realty Investments, Winston-Salem, 1969—82. Mem. editl. bd. Duke U. Law Jour., 1963. Chmn. N.W. Environ. Preservation Com., Inc., Winston-Salem, 1980; chmn. bd. trustees N.C. Bapt. Hosp., Winston-Salem, 1981—82; chmn. N.C. Family Bus. Forum, 1993—94; co-chmn. Raleigh Wake Leadership Found., 2002—; mem. state coun. N.C. Prison Fellowship, 1994—97; exec. com. NC Found. for Econ. Edn., 1996—, Ea. Ctr. for Regional Devel., 1996—97; bd. dirs. N.C. chpt. Coastal Conservation Assn., 1997—; rep. N.C. Ho. of Reps., Raleigh, 1970—74; senator N.C. Senate, Raleigh, 1974—78; bd. dirs. Ctr. for Citizenship, Enterprise and Govt., 2003—. Named Citizen of Yr. Winston-Salem Mayor's Com. on Employment of the Handicapped, 1971, Young Man. of Yr. Winston-Salem Jaycees, 1972; recipient Freedom Guard award N.C. Jaycees, 1973, U.S. Jaycees, 1973. Mem. N.C. Bar Assn. (bd. govs. 1979-82), Raleigh Rotary Club (pres. 1986-87). Presbyterian. Avocations: reading, writing, tennis, biking, fishing. Office: Womble Carlyle Sandridge PO Box 831 Raleigh NC 27602-0831

DAVIS, ELBA LUCILA, veterans affairs nurse; b. San Juan, P.R., Feb. 25, 1945; d. Eladio Millan and Fidencia Walker; m. Joseph Edward Davis; children: Pauly Lucille, Joelyne Lucille. BS Mgmt., Columbian Union Coll., 1995; Cosmetology degree, Hollywood Acad., College Park, Md., 1988; Principles of Real Estates degree, Prince Georges C.C., Largo, Md., 2001. RN P.R., 1971. Student aide Columbus Hosp., N.Y.C., 1963—64; med. asst. Dr. Durruthy's Office, Bronx, NY, 1964; officinist P.R. Lottery, Rio Piedras, 1965—67; nurse Saint Martin's Hosp., Rio Piedras, PR, 1971, Carolina (P.R.) Mcpl. Hosp., 1971—76, Walter Reed Army Med. Ctr., Silver Spring, Md., 1976—80; cosmetologist Hair Cuttery, Wheaton, Md., 1993—93; nurse VA Med. Ctr., Washington, 1980—. Unit preceptor VA Med. Ctr., Washington, 1985—, chairperson edn. IV Team, 2001—, rep. safety com., 1995—96, rep. product com., 1995—96, rep. standard of care com., 1992—94, rep. quality assurance com., 1981—83, rep. scheduling com. IV Team, 2001—. Actor: (video prodn.) Annual Infection Control Review Video, 1997, (Video) VA Med. Ctr. BCMA Sys./Japanese Prodn., 2001; (films) The Replacements, 1999. Active Wild Life Defendant, Washington, 2001; RN Anthrax Hotline Channel 9 News on Anthrax, Washington, 2001. Mem.: Fed. Women's Program, Washington DC Nurses Assn. Mem. Seventh Day Adventist. Avocations: reading, bicycling, exercise, crafts, singing.

DAVIS, ELENA DENISE, accountant; b. Rome, NY, June 24, 1953; d. Robert Frederick and Arlene Ruth (Fravor) Vrooman; m. Joseph E. Davis, Dec. 24, 1975 (div. Nov. 1988); children: JoAnna Lynn, Robert George, Crystal Leigh. AS, Jefferson C.C., Watertown, N.Y., 1975; BSBA, BS in Acctg., Orlando Coll.,

1995; MBA in Acctg., Fla. Met. U., 2001. Staff acct., asst. mgr. Vrooman's Tire & Rd. Svc. Inc., Adams, N.Y., 1975-89; claim assoc. Hartford Ins., Maitland, Fla., 1989-97; acct. Raybob Plumbing Co. Inc., Orlando, 1997-98, Ctrl. Sweeping Svc., Inc., Winter Garden, Fla., 1998-99; staff acct., office mgr. Engelmeier Roofing & Sheet Metal Co., Inc., Lockhart, Fla., 1999—; acct. Oil Fla. Active Boy Scouts Am., Girl Scouts Am., PTA; Sunday sch. tchr. Methodist Ch., 1984-89. Home: PO Box 721 Ocoee FL 34761-0721

DAVIS, ELLA DELORES, special education educator, elementary school educator; b. Quitman, La., July 19, 1957; d. Gencie Lee and Bessie (J.) D. BA, La. Tech. U., 1979; MS, Grambling State U., 1989. Tchr. lang. arts, social studies and leisure time activities Jackson Parish Sch. Bd., Jonesboro, La., 1982—. Mem. Spl. Edn. Coun. Jonesboro, 1991-93. Author: The Power of Jesus--An Enlightening Story of Incidences That Happened in My Life and How Jesus Interceded, 1989, Behavior Booklet, 1992, A Complete Guide to Setting Up a Special Education Program, 1992, Special Education Lesson Plan Booklet, 1992, My Math Fact Booklet, 1992, My Word Booklet, 1993, Pictorial of Life Photo Album Inserts to Girls and Boys, 2000, Be A Success, 2001; inventor health and beauty aid products, variety other products. Mem. exec. bd. NAACP, Jonesboro, 1992—; mem. 5th Dist. Black Caucus, Monroe, La., 1990—, Jonesboro Beautification Bd., 1993—. Mem. La. Assn. Educators. Democrat. Baptist. Avocations: volleyball, basketball, cooking, travel, reading. Home: 271 Sugar Creek Rd Quitman LA 71268-1313

DAVIS, ERIC KEITH, professional baseball player; b. L.A., May 29, 1962; m. Erica D. Davis. Baseball player Cin. Reds, 1980—91, L.A. Dodgers, 1991—93, Detroit Tigers, 1993—94, Cin. Reds, 1996, Balt. Orioles, 1997—98, St Louis Cardinals, 1998—2001, San Francisco Giants, 2001—02. Named Comeback Player of Yr., Nat. League, 1996; named to All-Star Team, 1987, 1989, Silver Slugger Team, 1987, 1989, Nat. League All-Star Team, Sporting News, 1987, 1989; recipient Gold Glove award, Nat. League, 1987—89. Achievements include playing in World Series, 1990.

DAVIS, ERIC LYLE, political scientist, educator, college administrator; b. Boston, Aug. 12, 1952; s. Samuel Joseph and Esther Pearl (Litman) D.; m. Kathleen Louise Jesseman, June 29, 1985. BA, Brown U., 1973; MA, Stanford U., 1975, PhD, 1978. Asst. prof. Middlebury (Vt.) Coll., 1980-84, assoc. prof., 1984-89, prof., 1989—, dean acad. programs, 1991-93, dean acad. planning, 1993-95, v.p. info. tech., 1995-97, sec., 1997—. Mem. Phi Beta Kappa. Office: Middlebury Coll Old Chapel Middlebury VT 05753 E-mail: ericd@middlebury.edu.

DAVIS, ERROLL BROWN, JR., utility executive; b. Pitts., Aug. 5, 1944; s. Erroll Brown and Eleanor Margaret (Boykin) D.; m. Elaine E. Casey, July 13, 1968; children: Christopher, Whitney Diploma in elec. engring., Carnegie-Mellon U., 1965; MBA in Fin., U. Chgo., 1967. Corp. fin. staff Ford Motor Co., Detroit, 1969-73, Xerox Corp., Rochester, N.Y., 1973-78; v.p. fin. Wis. Power and Light Co., Madison, 1978-82, v.p. fin and pub. affairs, 1982-84, exec. v.p., 1984-87, pres., 1987, pres., CEO, 1988-98; pres. WPH Holdings, 1990—98; pres., CEO Alliant Energy, Madison, 1998—, chmn., 2000—. Bd. dirs. BP plc, PPG Industries; mem. adv. bd. Fed. Res. Bank of Chgo. Active Selective Svc. Bd., Madison, 1982-2001; mem. bd. regents U. Wis., 1987-94; bd. dirs. United Way Dane County, 1984-89, chmn. bd. dirs., 1987; life trustee Carnegie Mellon U., chmn. bd. trustees, 2000—; bd. dirs. Competitive Wis., 1989—, Ednl. Comm. Bd., 1992-94; chmn. Start Smart of Dane County. Mem. Am. Soc. Corp. Execs., Wis. Mfg. and Commerce (bd. dirs. 1986—, chmn. 1994-95), Am. Gas Assn. (bd. dirs. 1990-95), Electric Power Rsch. Inst. (bd. dirs. 1990—), Assn. Edison Illuminating Cos. (bd. dirs. 1993—), Edison Electric Inst. (bd. dirs. 1995—, chmn. 2002-03, DOE electricity adv. bd.). Avocations: golf, biking. Office: Alliant Energy 4902 N Biltmore Ln Madison WI 53718

DAVIS, EVAN ANDERSON, lawyer; b. N.Y.C., Jan. 18, 1944; s. Richard T. and Charlotte (Upham) D.; m. Mary Carroll Rothwell; children: Sara Mei-Ping, Charlotte Zhong Xue. BA, Harvard U., 1966; JD, Columbia U., 1969. Bar: N.Y. 1970, U.S. Dist. Ct. (so. dist.) N.Y. 1973, U.S. Ct. Appeals (2d cir.) 1973, U.S. Dist. Ct. (ea. dist.) N.Y., 1978, U.S. Supreme Ct. 1979. Law clk. to judge U.S. Ct. Appeals (D.C. cir.), 1969-70; law clk. to Justice Potter Stewart U.S. Supreme Ct., 1970-71; gen. counsel N.Y.C. Budget Bur., 1971-72; chief consumer protection div. N.Y.C. Law Dept., 1972-74; task force leader, impeachment inquiry staff U.S. Ho. of Reps., 1974; assoc. Cleary, Gottlieb, Steen & Hamilton, N.Y.C., 1975-78, ptnr., 1979-85, 91—; counsel to gov. of N.Y., 1985-90. Vice chmn., bd. dirs. Fund for N.Y.C., 1982-85; trustee Columbia U., 1993—, mem. exec. com., 1994—, chair bd. Fin. com., 1999—, vice chair bd., 2001—. Editor-in-chief Columbia Law Rev., 1968-69. Treas. Sch. for Field Studies, 1991-95; dir. Franklin and Eleanor Roosevelt Inst., 1993—; mem. exec. com., 1994-2002; dir. Mus. of Hudson Highlands, 1991—, Storm King Sch., 1991-98; bd. visitors Helen Hayes Hosp., 1992-98, mem. coun. fgn. rels.; co-chairperson N.Y. Fair Elections Project, 1998—. Recipient Hopkins medal St. David's Soc., N.Y., 1988, Bruckner medal Fed. Bar Coun., 1990, Aquarium Environ. award Wildlife Conservation Soc., 1995, Milton Gould award for outstanding advocacy Office Appellate Defender, 1998, award Brennan Ctr., 1999, Law and Soc. award N.Y. Lawyers for the Pub. Interest, 2000, 1844 award New York Correctional Assn, 2001. Mem. ABA (ho. of dels. 1983-85, 91-93, 2000-02, chmn. spl. com. youth edn. for citizenship 1986-88, chmn. standing com. pub. edn.), Assn. Bar City N.Y. (chmn. exec. com. 1982-83, v.p. 1983-84, pres. 2000-02), Legal Aid Soc. (v.p. 1983-85, 97-2000, exec. com. 1992-2000), Am. Law Inst., Coun. of Fgn. Rels., N.Y. State Bar Assn. (com. on stds. of atty. conduct 1992—, commn. on middle income access to legal svc. 1995—). Home: 15 E 9th St New York NY 10128 Office: Cleary Gottlieb & Hamilton 1 Liberty Plz New York NY 10006-1470

DAVIS, EVELYN Y. editor, writer, publisher, investor; b. Aug. 16; d. Herman H. and Marian (Witteboom) DeJong; m. William Henry Davis, 1957 (div. 1958); m. Marvin Knudsen, 1969 (div. 1970); m. Walter O. Froh Jr., 1991 (div. 1994). Student, Western Md. Coll., George Washington U., N.Y. Inst. Fin. Editor, pub., Highlights and Lowlights, 1964— . Pres. Evelyn Y. Davis Found., 1989—; mem. adv. bd. George Washington U. Med. Ctr.; hon. bd. govs. Art Inst. of Chgo. Fellow JFK Ctr. for Performing Arts. Mem.: Smithsonian Benefactors Cir., Andrew Carnegie Soc. (life), George Washington U. Club (life), Capitol Hill Club (life). Home: Watergate East 2510 Virginia Ave NW Washington DC 20037-1904 Office: Highlights and Lowlights Watergate Office Bldg 2600 Virginia Ave NW Ste 215 Washington DC 20037-1905 *To me power is greater than love, and I did not get where I am by standing in line, nor by being shy.*

DAVIS, FERD LEARY, JR., law educator, lawyer, consultant; b. Zebulon, N.C., Dec. 4, 1941; s. Ferd L. and Selma Ann (Harris) D.; m. Joy Baker Davis, Jan. 25, 1963; children: Ferd Leary III, James Benjamin, Elizabeth Joy. BA, Wake Forest U., 1964, JD, 1967; LLM, Columbia U., 1984. Bar: N.C. 1967. Editor Zebulon (N.C.) Record, 1958; tchr. Davidson County Schs., Wallburg, N.C., 1966; ptnr. Davis & Davis and related law firms, Zebulon and Raleigh, N.C., 1967-76; asst. pros. Wake County Dist. Ct., Raleigh, 1968-69; town atty. Town of Zebulon, 1969-76; founding dean Campbell U. Sch. Law, Buies Creek, N.C., 1975-86, prof. law, 1975—. Dir. Inst. to Study Practice of Law and Socioecon. Devel., 1985—; chmn. The Davis Cons. Group, Inc., Buies Creek, 1987—; pres. LAWLEAD/NIELLP, 1998—; cons. U. Charleston, W.Va., 1979; vis. scholar Ctr. for Creative Leadership, 1993. Assoc. editor Wake Forest U. Law Rev. Trustee Wake County Pub. Librs., 1971-75, Olivia Raney Trust, 1969-71; mem. N.C. State Dem. Exec. Com., 1970-72, N.C. Gen. Statutes Commn., 1977-79, Commn. on the Future of N.C., 1980-83; dir., Howard Meml. Christian Edn. Fund, Raleigh Bus. and Tech. Ctr., NC BarCares. 1st Lt. USAR, 1959-66. Babcock scholar Wake Forest U., 1963-67; Dayton Hudson fellow Columbia U., 1982-83. Fellow Coll. Law Practice Mgmt.; mem. ABA, N.C. Bar Assn., N.C. State Bar, Rotary, Phi Delta Phi, Delta Theta Phi, Omicron Delta Kappa. Democrat. Office: LAWLEAD/NIELLP PO Box 4280 Buies Creek NC 27506-4280

DAVIS, F(RANCIS) KEITH, civil engineer; b. Bloomington, Wis., Oct. 23, 1928; s. Martin Morris and Anna (Weber) D.; m. Roberta Dean Anderson, May 25, 1957; 1 child, Mark Francis. BSCE, S.D. State U., 1950. Registered profl. engr., Mo., Ind., Nebr., Mich., Colo., Ariz., Oreg. With firm Howard, Needles, Tammen & Bergendoff, Kansas City, Mo., 1950—, asst. chief structural designer, 1960-65, project mgr., sect. chief, 1965-76, dep. chief structural engr., 1976-79, chief engr., 1979—. Mem. bd. advisers N.W. Kans. Area Vocat. Tech. Sch., 1977-80, chmn., 1979-80. With U.S. Army, 1951-53. Fellow ASCE; mem. NSPE, Mo. Soc. Profl. Engrs., Am. Ry. Engring. Assn. (tech. com. 1981—), Homestead Country Club. Home: 5024 Howe Dr Shawnee Mission KS 66205-1465 Office: PO Box 419299 1201 Walnut St Kansas City MO 64106-2117 E-mail: kdavis@hntb.com.

DAVIS, FRANCIS RAYMOND, priest; b. Washington, Feb. 10, 1920; s. Frank Raymond and Ruth Madeline (Donovan) D.; B.A., St. Bernard's Sem., Rochester, N.Y., 1941; M.L.S., Cath. U. Am., 1953. Ordained priest Roman Cath. Ch., 1945; asst. pastor St. Ambrose Ch., Rochester, 1945-50; prof. lit. St. Bernard's Sem., 1950-51, librarian, 1950-69, prof. speech., 1958-67; pastor Our Lady Lourdes Ch., Elmira, N.Y., 1969-78; pastor St. Mary's Ch., Dansville, N.Y., 1978-80, St. Patrick's Ch., Corning, N.Y., 1980-90. Mem. Chemung county gen. edn. bd. Diocese of Rochester, 1971-78; mem. exec. com. Chemung County (N.Y.) Council Aging, 1972-76; mem. adv. com. Chemung County Office for Aging, 1973-78; mem. exec. com. Ecumenical Preaching Mission, 1977-78; bd. dirs. All Saints' Acad., Corning, 1986-90, founder. Fellow Internat. Biog. Assn.; mem. ALA, Cath. Library Assn. (officer sem. sect. 1958-61), Ch. and Synagogue Library Assn. (nominating com. 1979), Elmira Vicinity Ministerial Assn. (officer 1972-73). Author articles and book revs. Address: 155 State St Corning NY 14830-2534

DAVIS, FRANK DANIEL, retired journalist; b. Brookville, Pa., Dec. 30, 1925; s. Frank and Essie (Martz) D.; m. Beverley Anne Smith, Feb. 25, 1950; children: Blake M., Mark J., Sally A., Lynn E., Timothy T., Wendy B., Quentin M. BA in Journalism, Pa. State U., 1947; MA in Journalism, Northwestern U., 1948. Dir. publicity and info. Pa. Human Rels. Commn., Harrisburg, 1957-86; reporter The Tribune-Democrat, Johnstown, Pa., 1948-57; ret. Pres. Friendship Force Grtr. Harrisburg, 1995. Named to Pa. Voter Hall of Fame, Commonwealth Pa. Dept. State, 1998. Mem. NAACP (pres. Johnstown chpt. 1956, sec. Grtr. Harrisburg chpt. 1993-94), Soc. Profl. Journalists (membership chmn. Ctrl. Pa chpt. 1975-80). Avocations: slide photography, gardening, travel. Home: 200 Gettysburg Pike Mechanicsburg PA 17055-8016

DAVIS, FRANK TRADEWELL, JR., lawyer; b. Atlanta, Feb. 2, 1936; s. Frank T. and Sue (Burnett) D.; m. Winifred Storey, June 23, 1961; children: Frank, Frederick, Gordon. AB, Princeton U., 1960; JD, George Washington U., 1963; LLM, Harvard U., 1964. Bar: Ga. 1963, D.C. 1966, U.S. Ct. Appeals (5th cir.) 1963, U.S. Ct. Appeals (11th cir.) 1982, U.S. Supreme Ct. 1968. Assoc. Hansell, Post Brandon & Dorsey, Atlanta, 1964-67; ptnr. Hansell & Post, Atlanta, 1968-77, 79-86, Long, Aldridge & Norman, Atlanta, 1986—. Ptnr., gen. counsel Pres.'s Reorgn. Project Office of Pres., 1977-79; vis. instr. U. Ga. Law Sch., 1964-66, Ga. State U. Law Sch., 1988-90; vis. prof. Emory U. Law Sch., 1992—. Author: Business Acquisitions, 1977, (2d edit.), 1982; contbr. articles to legal jours. Bd. dirs. Nat. Inst. Justice, 1980—81, Westminster Schs., 1969—, chmn. bd. dirs., 1984—89; bd. dirs.. Va. Sem., 1980—94, exec. com., 1985—89; mem. Atlanta Charter Commn.; chmn. Atlanta Crime Commn., 1977; mem. bd. councilors Carter Presdl. Ctr., 1988—; chmn. Rotary Ednl. Found. Atlanta; commr. Atlanta Regional Commn., 1999—; sr. warden All Saints' Episcopal Ch., 1982, 2002, vestry, 2000—. Lt. USN, 1960—62. Fellow Am. Bar Found.; mem. Am. Law Inst., Atlanta C. of C. (bd. dirs. 1975-77), Piedmont Driving Club (Atlanta), Capital City Club (Atlanta), Cedar Creek Racquet Club (Cashiers, N.C.), The Army and Navy Club (Washington), Rotary (pres. Atlanta chpt. 1990-91, bd. dirs., sec. 1988-89, chmn. bd., 1991-92, chmn. Ednl. Found. 1997—). Home: 2500 Peachtree Rd Atlanta GA 30305-5609 Office: 303 Peachtree St NE Ste 5300 Atlanta GA 30308-3264 E-mail: ftdjr@earthlink.net.

DAVIS, FRANK WAYNE, lawyer; b. Ada, Okla., Aug. 24, 1936; s. Roscoe Gladstone and Neva Dell (Peck) D.; m. Kay Diane Higginbotham, Aug. 12, 1961; children: David, Paul. Student, U. Ill., Urbana, 1956-57; BA, East Cen. U., 1958; LLB, U. Okla., Norman, 1959. Bar: Okla. 1959, U.S. Dist. Ct. (we. dist.) Okla. 1965, U.S. Ct. Appeals (10th crct.) 1976. Acting postmaster U.S. Postal Service, Ada, 1959-61; assoc. Denny W. Falkenburg, Medford, Okla., 1961; atty. Logan County, Guthrie, Okla., 1961-65; sole practice Guthrie, 1965—83, 1988—; ptnr. Davis and Hudson, Guthrie, 1985-88. Mcpl. judge City of Guthrie, 1974-78; rep. State of Okla., Oklahoma City, 1978—; vice chmn. judiciary com. Okla. Ho. of Reps., 1981-82, 89, 91—; minority fl. leader, 1982-86, asst. minority fl. leader, 1986-90. Del. gen. conf. United Meth. Ch., Portland, Oreg., 1976; del. Rep. Nat. Convs., 1984, 96, alt. del., 2000; scoutmaster Boy Scout Troop # 850, Guthrie, 1961-2000; chmn. Logan County Reps., Guthrie, 1964-69. Recipient Silver Beaver award Boy Scouts Am., 1978. Mem. Okla. Bar Assn., Logan County Bar Assn. (pres. 1972-73), Gideons. Lodges: Lions, Masons. Methodist. Avocations: fishing, stamp collecting, farming, oil and gas production. Office: 115 N Division St Guthrie OK 73044-3240 also: 509 State Capitol Bldg Oklahoma City OK 73105 Home: 17300 Valley Crst Edmond OK 73003-6770

DAVIS, FRED, journalist, educator; b. Columbia, S.C., Feb. 14, 1947; s. Nathaniel Lewis Sr. and Arneatha Pearl (Robinson) D.; m. Joan Sineta Walker, Jan. 14, 1967; children: Alex LaMar, Kevin Alexander. BS in English Edn., N.C. A&T State U., 1969. City/coun. reporter WFMY-TV/CBS, Greensboro, N.C., 1969-70; govtl. reporter WJRT-TV/ABC, 1970-74, dir. documentaries and pub. affairs, 1974-75; anchor-reporter WMAL-TV (WJLA-TV/ABC), Washington, 1975; various positions in field to reporter, news editor WRC-TV/NBC News, Washington, 1975; gen. assignment, news program svc. reporter KNBC-TV/NBC News, Burbank, Calif., 1976; writer/reporter KHJ-TV/Ind., Hollywood, Calif., 1976-78; anchor/editor WIS-TV/NBC, Columbia, S.C., 1978-80; asst. news dir., sr. producer WJXT-TV/CBS, Jacksonville, Fla., 1980-81; staff writer Jacksonville Jour./Fla. Pub. Co., 1981; news dir. ABC Direction Radio Network/ABC News, N.Y.C., 1981-88; weekly commentator CBS-owned radio stas., 1992; self-syndicated columnist S.C. newspapers, 1992—; Disting. prof. mass media mgmt. Wash. State U., Pullman, 1995-97; columnist The Seattle Times, The Spokesman-Rev., 1996—98. Adj. prof. Edward R. Murrow Sch. of Comm., Wash. State U., Pullman, 1997—2000; cons./host Sta. KWSU-TV (PBS), 1997—; owner media svcs./broadcast news consultancy, 1989—; vis. lectr. Benedict Coll., Columbia, 1979—80, Columbia, 1990, Coll. Journalism U. S.C., 1987, Coll. Journalism & Mass Comm., U. Nebr., Lincoln, 1997—99; mem. Journalism and Mass Comm. del. to China, Citizens Ambassador Program, 1996, Journalism and Mass Comm. del. to Italy, Switzerland, Austria, Citizens Ambassador Program, 1997, Journalism and Mass Comm. del. to S. Africa, Citizens Ambassador Program, 1999; expert media witness Libel Def. Resource Ctr., San Diego, 1997; del. People to People Internat., Russia, 1998, Finland, 98; cons., host KWSU-TV, KUON-TV, 1997; cons., writer The Gallup Org., Lincoln, Nebr., 1999—; del. News World conf., Barcelona, 1999; lectr. Coll. Journalism & Mass. Comm., U. Nebr., Lincoln, 1997—99, U. Nebr., Lincoln, 1999—; adj. instr. Coll. Journalism & Comm., 2001. Contbr. articles; provider (news commentaries) CBS-owned radio stas., N.Y., L.A., Chgo., Phila., San Francisco, Detroit, Mpls., columnist (newspaper) The Seattle Times, 1996—97, The Royal Gazette, Bermuda, 1996—97, The Spokesman-Rev., 1996—97, prodr./cons. (global bus. report) Bermuda Broadcasting Co., 2000—01, writer (jour.) Jacksonville Bus. Jour., 2001, prodr./moderator ("Socratic" Roundtables TV series) WJCT-TV (PBS), Jacksonville, Fla., 2001. Bd. visitors, N.C. A&T State U., Greensboro, 1988—; del. Russia and Finland People to People Internat., 1998. Recipient award, Leadership Flint (Mich.), 1973, Internat. Radio Festival of N.Y., 1983—88, Ohio State award, ABC Radio, 1986, award, Nat. Press Club, 1984, 1985, Comm. Excellence to Black Audiences award of distinction, ABC Dir./Radio Network, 1987, b'nai b'rith Edward R. Murrow Brotherhood award, 1986, Disting. Alumni award, Nat. Assn. for Equal Opportunity in Higher Edn., 1988, Disting. Acheivement award, Mass Media Mngmt. Studies, Coll. Liberal Arts, Wash. State U., 1996. Mem.: U.S. Tennis Assn. (USTA), Broadcast Edn. Assn., Assn. for Edn. in Journalism and Mass Comm., S.C. Press Assn., Nat. Assn. Black Journalists, Acad. TV Arts and Scis., Am. Fedn. TV and Radio Artists, Radio-TV News Dirs. Assn., Internat. Platform Assn., PGA Ptnrs., Broadcast Edn. Assn., Assn. for Edn. in Journalism and Mass Comm., Nat. Geog. Soc., Soc. Profl. Journalists, Nat. Assn. Black Journalists, Acad. TV Arts and Scis., Am. Fedn. TV and Radio Artists, Radio-TV News Dirs. Assn., Internat. Platform Assn., PGA Ptnrs. (charter mem., charter), U.S. Tennis Assn., U.S. Golf Assn., The Folio Soc., Planetary Soc., Nat. Geog. Soc., The Folio Soc., S.C. Press Assn., U.S. Golf Assn., Planetary Soc., Alpha Phi Alpha, Alpha Phi Alpha. Baptist. Avocations: gourmet cooking, racquetball, golf, tennis, barbecue judging. Office: Davis Media Svcs & Syndication LLC/ U Fla Coll Journalism & Comm PO Box 56741 Jacksonville FL 32241-6741 E-mail: fdav444@prodigy.net., dms444@mediaone.net.

DAVIS, FREDERICK ATHIE, management executive; b. Detroit, Apr. 9, 1938; s. Leonard Athie Davis and Edna Irene Smith Smalley; m. Patricia Ann O'Keefe, Oct. 12, 1957; children: Laurel A. Smith, Lynnette A., Harner, Leah A. Davis-Bellucci, Lucynda A. Thrushman. Student, St. Clair Community Coll., 1973, U.S. Power Squadron, 1974-75, U.S.C.G. Auxiliary, 1981-85. Lic. internat. radio operator; lic. capt. USCG Master; comml. towing endorsement. Owner, operator Lake Appliance Sales and Svc., Belleville, Mich., 1959-62; svc. technician RCA Svc. Co., Ferndale, Mich., 1962-66; owner, operator Home Appliance Svc. Co., Port Austin, Mich., 1966-83; police officer Village Port Austin, 1968-78; owner, operator TMS Mfrs. Rep., Mich., 1985-88; sales rep., test boat operator Henry H. Smith and Co., various locations, Mich. and Fla., 1985-88; pres. Thumb Marine Inc., Charter and Salvage, Port Austin, 1970—; owner, capt. Miss Port Austin Perch Charter Boat, Port Austin, 1983—; owner, operator Assistance Towing Svc., 1991—; marine cons. Club Marine Boat/U.S. (Lloyds of London), Fla., 1989—. State Mich. instr. Boating and Snowmobile H.S., 1972-78; instr. U.S. Power Squadron, Bad Axe, 1975-80, USCG Aux. B S & S Classes, Port Austin, 1981-85, flotilla 15-09 Comdr., 1981-83, div. 15 vice capt., 1985. Boating safety columnist Fla. Keys Angler, Mich. Out-of-Doors, Huron Daily Tribune, Woods N Water News, Bay City Times; freelance writer Powerboat, Sea Mag., Boating, Heartland Boating, Boating World, Trailer Boats, Lakeland Boating, BoatMotor Dealer, Marina Dockage, Go Boating, Mid Am. Boating, Gt. Lakes Angler. Mem. Port Austin Village Coun., 1975-77; vol. fireman Village of Port Austin, 1970-96, ambulance attendant, 1970-75; mem. ad hoc com., bd. dirs. Thumb Area Gt. Lakes State Bottomland Preserve Huron County, 1984-88. Recipient Life Saving awards Port Austin Village Coun., Huron County Sheriff's Dept., Pub. Svc. commendation USCG, 1991. Mem.: Mich. Charterboat Assn., Nat. Charterboat Assn., Thumb Area Charter Capts. Assn., Boating Writers Internat., Port Austin C. of C. (v.p. 1972, 1983—84, pres. 1991), Port Austin Boat Club. Avocations: boat restoration, lake and ocean cruising, pleasure boating, ocean fishing, shrimping. Home and Office: Thumb Marine Inc PO Box 340 Port Austin MI 48467 also: PO Box 1866 Key Largo FL 33037-1866 E-mail: padavis@avci.net.

DAVIS, FREDERICK BENJAMIN, retired law educator; b. Bklyn., Aug. 21, 1926; s. Clifford Howard and Anne Frances (Forbes) D.; m. Mary Ellen Saecker, Apr. 21, 1956; children: Judith, Robert, James, Mary. AB, Yale U., 1948; JD, Cornell U., 1953; LLM with honors, Victoria U. of Wellington, New Zealand, 1955. Bar: N.Y. 1953, Mo. 1970, Ohio 1981. Assoc. Engel Judge & Miller, N.Y.C., 1953-54; instr. U. Pa. Law Sch., 1955-56; asst. prof. NYU, 1956-57, U. S.D., 1957-60, assoc. prof., 1960-62, Emory U., 1962-63, prof., 1963-66, U. Mo.-Columbia, 1966-70, Edward W. Hinton prof. law, 1970-81, Edward W. Hinton prof. emeritus, 1981—; dean, prof. law U. Dayton Sch. Law, 1981-86; dean, prof. Memphis State U., 1987-92, prof., 1992-98, prof., dean emeritus, 1998—. Cons. adminstrv. procedure Mo. Senate, 1974-77; vis. prof. Wake Forest U. Sch. Law, 1980, 86-87, U. Wis., 1960, George Washington U., 1965, Tulane U., 1966, U. Mo.-Kansas City, 1973, U. Ky., 1977. Contbr. numerous articles, comments, revs., notes to profl. jours. Served with USNR, 1944-46. Mem. ABA (coun. sect. adminstrv. law 1969-75), Am. Law Inst., Rotary Club (Memphis Ctrl. chpt.), Summit Club. Republican. Episcopalian. E-mail: freddyandmary@aol.com.

DAVIS, FREDERICK CHARLES, county official; b. Cedar Rapids, Iowa, Nov. 26, 1934; s. Charles Clinton Davis and Marietta Leone Ross-Davis; m. Geraldine Marie Nix-Davis, July 31, 1959; children: Gloria, Vicki, Katherine, Marlene. BBA, Nat. U., 1983. Test technician Audio Devices, Santa Ana, Calif., 1957-59; calibration technician IRC, Manhattan Beach, Calif., 1959-61; semiconductor test technician Std. Semiconductors, Santa Ana, 1961-62; metrology lab. technician, lead Northrop Corp., Anaheim, Calif., 1962-70; asst. mgr. Trader Joe's Markets, Fullerton, Calif., 1970-75; Major subcontract adminstr. Northrop Corp., Hawthorne, Calif., 1975-91; county supr. Butte County, Oroville, Calif., 1997—. Citizens adv. com. Butte County Assn. Govt., Oroville, 1993-94, Butte County for Budget Solutions, Chico, Calif., 1994-96; chmn. Magalia (Calif.) Ridge Mcpl. Adv. Coun., 1992-93, chair Butte County Bd. Supr., 1997-98, vice-chmn., 1999; founder, pres. Butte Libr. Found. With USAF, 1953-57. Mem. Nat. Assn. Counties, Calif. State Assn. Counties (bd. dirs.). Republican. Avocations: cruises, photography, golf. Office: Butte County 25 County Center Dr Oroville CA 95965-3316 Fax: 530-872-6339. E-mail: fredngeri@aol.com.

DAVIS, GARRY (S. GARETH DAVIS), b. Bar Harbor, Maine, July 27, 1921; s. Meyer and Hilda (Emery) D.; m. Audrey Peters, April 10, 1950 (div.); 1 child, Kristina Star; m. Esther Peter, June 4, 1962 (div.); children: Troy Alaric, Athena Veronica, Kim Gregory. Student, Carnegie Inst. Tech., Pitts., 1940-41; D Geo-dialectics/World Law, East-West U. of Brahma Vidya, Fernhill, India, 1987. Actor, N.Y.C., 1940-52; founder, pres. Internat. Registry World Citizens, Paris, 1949; founder, world coord. World Govt. of World Citizens, Ellsworth, Maine, 1953; founder, pres. World Svc. Authority, Washington, 1954, cons., 1975—; pub. World Citizen News, —. Danny Kaye's understudy: Let's Face It, 1941; 2d comedy lead: Three to Make Ready, 1946; actor: Bless You All, 1951, Stalag 17, 1953, B'way, Road and London Co. 2d comedy lead; summer stock: Deertrees Theatre, Harrison, Maine, Bucks County Playhouse, Bucks County, Pa., Uncle Willie (with Menascha Skulnik, Road), 1956, 1776, Dinner Theatre, Burnbrae, Md., My Fair Lady, Cmty. Theatre, Ellsworth, Maine, Col. Pickering; founder, dir. World Govt. Inst., 1998; founder, pub. World Govt. House, 2001; wing comdr. World Govt. Air Force. Author: The World is My Country, 1960, World Government, Ready or Not!, 1985, Passport to Freedom, 1992, Dear World, 2000, World Citizen in the Holy Land, 1997. Candidate for mayor, Washington, 1986; candidate for U.S. president, 1988; founder World Citizen Found., 1996; coord. World Syntegrity Project, 1993. 1st. lt. U.S. Air Corps, 1941-46, B-17 bomber pilot. Fellow Fortean Soc.; mem. Navion Soc., Aircraft Owners & Pilots Assn. Avocations: tennis, skiing, videotaping, computer networking, flying. Home: 6 Ledoux Ter South Burlington VT 05403-6442 Office: World Svc Authority 1012 14th St NW Washington DC 20005-3406 Fax: (802) 862-3744. E-mail: world/law@globalnetisp.net.

DAVIS, GENE, public relations professional, state legislator; b. Salt Lake City, July 2, 1945; s. John Albert and Glenna Rachel (Cameron) D.; m. Penny Lou Hansen, Mar. 9, 1971; children: James, Pamela. Cert. electronic engring., Radio Operational Engring., Burbank, Calif., 1963; LLB, LaSalle Ext. U., Chgo., 1974. Announcer KNAK Radio, Salt Lake City, 1965-75; prodn. continuity dir. KALL Radio AM/FM, Salt Lake City, 1976-86; owner G. Davis Advt., Pub. Rels., Salt Lake City, 1986-91; pub. rels. prof. Valley Mental Health, Salt Lake City, 1990—; mem. Utah Senate, Dist. 3, Salt Lake City, 1998—. Treas. Comm. Fed. Credit Union, Salt Lake City, 1981-86. Vice chair East County Recreation Bd., Salt Lake City, 1991—2000; rep. Utah State House of Reps., Salt Lake City, 1986—98; mem. Utah State Senate, Salt Lake City, 1998—, mem. bus., labor & human svcs. com., exec. appropriations com., coun. of state govt.- health capacity task force. Mem. Sugar House Rotary Club, Sugar House Cmty. Coun. (chmn. 1984-85). Democrat. Mem. Lds Ch. Avocations: golf, gardening, politics. Home: 865 Parkway Ave Salt Lake City UT 84106-1704 Office: Valley Mental Health 5965 S 900 E Salt Lake City UT 84121-1794 E-mail: gened@vmh.com.

DAVIS, GENE, retired civil engineer; b. Lower Peach Tree, Ala., Apr. 21, 1935; s. Edgar Thomas and Una (Smith) D.; m. Betty Marie Davidson; children: Jean Marie Davis, Jenifer Davis Cerny, Joanna Davis Palladino, James Andrew Davis. BSCE, U. Ala., 1958; MS in Mgmt., Naval Postgrad. Sch., 1969; cert., Armed Forces Staff Coll., 1974. Commd. ensign USN, 1958, advanced through grades to Capt., 1980; resident engr. Navy Project Office, Cape Canaveral, Fla., 1960-63, Dir. of Constrn. in South East Asia, Bangkok, Thailand, 1963-65; program mgr. Pacific divsn., Naval Civil Engring., Honolulu, 1965-68; exec. officer Naval Constrn. Bat. 121, Gulfport, Miss., 1968-70; dir. constrn. planning Hdqrs., Naval Civil Engring., Washington, 1974-76; comdg. officer Naval Constrn. Bat. 133, Gulfport, 1976-78; chief of staff Naval Constrn. Regiment, Port Hueneme, Calif., 1978-81; comdr. officer Pub. Works Ctr., Great Lake, Ill., 1981-83; vice comdr. Pacific divsn., 1983-86; dir. constrn. Diego Garcia, 1986-87; retired USN, 1987; sr. group engr. Martin Marietta, Orlando, 1987-92; ops. mgr. Brown & Root Inc., Houston, 1992-2001; civil engr. cons., 1997-98;

v.p. RSI, Inc., 1997-98; ret., 2001. Author: Analysis of the Imperial Iranian Navy Construction Program, 1974. Mem. ASCE, Soc. Am. Mil. Engrs. (pres. Diego Garcia post 1992), USN Inst. Republican. Roman Catholic. Home: PO Box 535 Thomasville AL 36784-0535 E-mail: GeneDavis65@usnx.com.

DAVIS, GENE H. music educator; b. Jennings, La., Jan. 9, 1939; s. Alvin and Hazel Davis; m. Bettye Davis; children: Harrel, Shana, Derrion. BS in Music, Grambling Coll., 1963; MusM, Northwestern State U., Natchitoches, La., 1973. Music choir dir. Vernon HS, Leesville, La., 1963—69, Leesville HS, 1969—70; music dir. choir and band Hornbeck (La.) HS, 1970—84, Vernon Mid. Sch., Leesville, 1984—. Mem. libr. bd. Vernon Parish, 1996—; founder Vernon Parish Cmty. Choir, Leesville, music dir., 1970—. Recipient commendation, La. State Rep. John R. Smith, 1999, Gene Davis Day, Leesville, La., 1999. Mem.: La. Music Educators Assn., Am. Choir Dirs. Assn., Music Educators Nat. Conf. Home: 130 Carver Dr Leesville LA 71446 Office: Leesville Leader Leesville LA 71446

DAVIS, GEORGE CULLOM, historian; b. Aurora, Ill., May 2, 1935; s. George Cullom and Mary Elizabeth (Scripps) D.; m. Marilyn Louise Whittaker, June 22, 1957 (div. Mar. 1974); children: Catherine, Lesa, Charles; m. Ann Elizabeth Chapman, May 27, 1976. AB, Princeton U., 1957; MA, U. Ill., Urbana, 1961, PhD, 1968; Dr of History (hon.), Lincoln Coll., 1999; Diploma of Honor, Lincoln Meml. U., 1995; DHL (hon.), Knox Coll., 2000. Instr. Punahou Sch., Honolulu, 1957-59, U. Ill., Urbana, 1962-64; asst. prof. Ind. U., Bloomington, 1964-70, assoc. dean, 1967-70; assoc. prof. Sangamon State U., Springfield, Ill., 1970-74, prof., 1974-95; prof. emeritus, 1995—; prof. history U. Ill.-Springfield, 1974—; dir., sr. editor Lincoln Legal Papers Documentary Edit., 1988—. Bd. dirs. Bank One, Springfield; cons. John Nuveen & Co., Chgo., 1989—, Meml. Med. Ctr., Springfield, 1991—. Author: History With a Tape Recorder: An Oral History Handbook, 1972, 4th edit., 1985; co-author: Oral History: From Tape to Tape, 1977, Bench and Bar on the Illinoir Frontier, 1979, The Prairie Bondman, 1996, Memorial Days, 1997; editor: Bicentennial Studies in Sangamon History, 1973-78; co-editor: The Public and the Private Lincoln: Contemporary Perspectives, 1979, Abraham Lincoln Association Papers, 1981-86, The Law Practice of Abraham Lincoln: Complete Documentary Edit. (DVD-ROM), 2000; contbr. numerous articles to profl. jours.; editl. advisor Scholar Book Revs. on CD-ROM, 1991-93. Del. Dem. Nat. Conv., 1972; pres. Springfield Pub. Schs. Found., 1987-88. Recipient Pelzer award Orgn. Am. Historians, 1962, award of Merit Ill. State Hist. Soc., 1975, Writer of Yr. award Friends of Lincoln Libr., 1989; Fulbright Rsch. scholar, 1987-88; fellow Newberry Libr., 1977, NEH/Woodrow Wilson Found. Inst., 1980, NEH Summer Inst. on Pub. History, 1984, Studs Terkel award Ill. Humanities Coun., 2002; grantee Ill. Bicentennial Commn., 1974-75, Ill. State Libr., 1975, 79-81, Ill. Legis. Coun., 1979-87, Ill. Humanities Coun., 1980-82, NEH, 1990-92, 94—, Nat. Hist. Publs. and Records Commn., 1990—, Ill. Bar Found., 1990-91, Ency. Brit., 1991, Shelby C. Davis Found., 1991—, William Nelson Cromwell Found., 1992—. Mem. Manuscript Soc., Assn. for Documentary Editing (chmn. constitution com. 1990-94, pres. 1997-98), Ill. Coalition of Libr. Advocates (bd. dirs. 1982-84), Ill. Humanities Coun. (bd. dirs. 1983-89, vice chair 1985-87, chair 1987-89), Ill. State Hist. Soc. (v.p. 1974-75, 82-83, bd. dirs. 1979-82, exec. com. 1979-82, adv. bd. 1994—), Sangamon County Hist. Soc. (bd. dirs. 1971-74, 79-82, v.p. 1981-82, 90-91, pres. 1991-92), Orgn. Am. Historians (treas. 1984-93), Oral History Assn. (nominating com. 1978-79, 85-87, colloquium program com. 1978, chmn. nat. workshop 1979, nat. coun. 1980-85, v.p. 1982-83, pres. 1983-84), Abraham Lincoln Assn. (bd. dirs. 1977—, chmn. publs. com. 1981-87, v.p. 1984-86, pres. 1995-96). Democrat. Home: 2624 E Lake Shore Dr Springfield IL 62707-5533 Office: Lincoln Legal Papers Old State Capitol Springfield IL 62701

DAVIS, GEORGE DONALD, executive land use policy consultant; b. Oneida, N.Y., Nov. 19, 1942; s. Pearl Floyd and Kathrine Virginia (Connolly) D.; m. Anita Face Riner, June 26, 1976; children: Maria Lisa, Brett Hollis, Sarah Bessie, Lara Emily; stepchildren: Andrea G. Riner, Joel S. Riner. BS in Forestry, SUNY, 1964; postgrad., Cornell U., 1971. Forester, pub. land adminstr. U.S. Forest Svc. Dept. Agr., Colo., 1964-68; ecologist Gov. N.Y. State Temp. Study Commn. on Future of Adirondacks, 1969-71; pvt. land use and natural resources cons. Ithaca, N.Y., 1971; dir. planning Adirondack Park Agy., Ray Brook, N.Y., 1971-76; exec. dir. Wilderness Soc., Washington, 1976-77; spl. asst. U.S. Forest Svc., Washington, 1977-79; dep. forest supr. Idaho Panhandle Nat. Forests, Coeur d'Alene, 1979-82; land use, natural resource cons. Wadhams, N.Y., 1982-94; program dir. Adirondack Coun., 1983-88; exec. dir. Adirondack Land Trust, 1984-88; prin. Davis Assocs., 1988—. Pres. Ecol. Sustainable Devel., Inc., 1994—97; coord. Global Assocs. in Sustainable Devel., 1997—2002; project dir. Land Use Policy and Allocation Program for Lake Baikal Watershed in Russia, 1991—93, Lake Hovsgol/Selenge River Wateshed in Mongolia, 1992—94, Ussuri River Watershed in Russian Far East and China, 1993—97, Altai Retai Rep., Russia, 1994—97; exec. dir. Gov. Commn. on Adirondacks in the 21st Century, 1989—90; mem. environ. task force Rockefeller Bros. Fund; mem. Hudson Basin project task force Rockefeller Found. Co-author: The Unfinished Agenda, 1977, Developing a Land Conservation Strategy, 1987; author: Ecosystem Representative as a Criterion for World Wilderness Designation, 1987, 2020 Vision: Fulfilling the Promise of the Adirondack Park, 1988, Completing the Adirondack Wilderness System, 1990, The Lake Baikal Region in the Twenty-First Century: A Model of Sustainable Development or Continued Degradation?, 1993, A Comprehensive National Program of Sustainable Land Use Policies for the Lake Hovsgol-Selenge River Watershed, 1994, A Sustainable Land Use and Allocation Program for the Ussuri/Wusuli River Watershed and Adjacent Territories, 1996; contbr. to profl. publs. Active Gov. N.Y. State Forest Industry Task Force, 1987-89, N.Y.-New Eng. Gov. Task Force on No. Forest Lands, 1988-90. MacArthur fellow, 1989—. Roman Catholic. Home and Office: 2482 N 32d St Springfield OR 97477-7900 E-mail: davisassoc1@aol.com. *The basic goal of my life has been to promote land and natural resource stewardship, through direct action and example, to help insure that our planet's resources are more equitably distributed among members of the present generation and are sufficient for future generations.*

DAVIS, GEORGE EDWARD, industrial designer; b. Hugo, Okla., July 3, 1928; s. Silas William and Florence Elva (White) D.; m. Betty Sue Walker, July 21, 1951; children: Susan Elizabeth, Laura Ellen. Student, U. Tex., 1946-49; BA, Art Ctr. Coll. Design, L.A., 1956. Registered interior designer, Tex. Staff designer Friedrich Refrigeration Co., San Antonio, 1957; design dir. comml. divsn. Woodarts Co., Houston, 1958-59; staff designer Brede, Inc., Houston, 1960-61; designer, co-founder Concept Planners and Designers, Houston, 1962-64; mgr. archtl. dept. Lockheed-Calif. Co., NASA Manned Spacecraft Ctr., Clear Lake, Tex., 1965-66; staff designer office products divsn. Litton Industries, Austin and San Antonio, 1967-68; staff designer Clegg Design Group, San Antonio, 1969-76; ind. design cons. San Antonio, 1977—. Interior designer for USAA, San Antonio, 1991-2001; dir. Systemics, Inc., San Antonio, Christian Bookmark, Inc., San Antonio, 1972-88. Trustee, San Antonio Christian Sch., 1973-82, chmn. bd., 1979-80; bd. elders Christ Presbyn. Ch., San Antonio, 1982-85; mem. Zoning Commn., City of Castle Hills, 1983-93, mem. City Coun., 1993-94, mem. Archtl. Rev. Com., 1995-2001. Served with USAF, 1950-54. Decorated DFC, Air medal with 3 oak leaf clusters. Mem. AIA (profl. affiliate), Tex. Soc. Architects (profl. affiliate, award of merit 1968). Home: 205 Wisteria Dr Castle Hills TX 78213-2109 Office: PO Box 13385 San Antonio TX 78213-0385

DAVIS, GEORGE KELSO, nutrition biochemist, educator; b. Pitts., July 2, 1910; s. Ross Irwin and Jennie (Kelso) D.; m. Ruthanna Wood, Jan. 25, 1936; children— Dorothy Jeanne (Mrs. Arthur C. Aikin, Jr.), Mary Ellen (Mrs. W. Edgar Benedict), Ruthanna Marie (Mrs. Donald W. Davidson), Virginia Kay (Mrs. John M. Fedison), Robert Wyatt, George William. BS, Pa. State U., 1932; PhD, Cornell U., 1937. Research asst. Cornell U., 1932-37; research asst. prof. chemistry Mich. State U., 1937-42; prof. nutrition, animal nutritionist U. Fla., Gainesville, 1942-79, prof. emeritus, 1979—, dir. nuclear scis., 1960-65, dir. biol. scis., 1965-70, dir. research, 1970-75; prof. human nutrition U. Hawaii, 1985. Mem. Fla. Nuclear Commn.; chmn. Internat. Biol. Program Sect. Use and Mgmt. Biol. Resources, U. Fla. Council Oak Ridge Asso. Univs.; cons. minister agr., Costa Rica, univs. Costa Rica, Buenos Aires, San Marco, Peru, U. Agraria, Peru, Sao Paulo, Brazil, FAO, Dept. Agr., OEA-INTA, Argentina, Dept. Health, Edn. and Welfare, Nutrition Found., Fla. Dept. Agr.; mem. food and nutrition bd., com. animal nutrition, internat. biol. program com. Nat. Acad. Sci.-NRC, also chmn. bd. agr. and renewable resources, 1980-82; dir. human nutrition research grants program U.S. Dept. Agr., 1977-79; rev. bds. NSF, Nat. Acad. Scis., NIH; U. Fla. Faculty lectr., 1960; hon. prof. U. Chile, 1961— ; Wellcome vis. prof. U. Ill., 1978; pres. Nat. Nutritional Consortium, 1977-78 Editor: (with A.E. Harper) Nutrition in Health and Disease and International Development. Mem. editorial bd. Jour. Animal Sci.; contbr. articles to profl. jours., chpts. books. Recipient Faculty award Fla. Blue Key, 1958, Disting. Faculty award U. Fla., 1960, Scientist of Yr. award Mus. Sci. and Industry Fla, 1981, Disting. Alumnus award Pa. State U., 1982, Disting. Achievement award U. Fla., 1996, George F. Hixson award 1997. Fellow Am. Inst. Nutrition (chmn. com. nutrition and trace elements 1961-64, nat. exec. com. jour. 1961, Borden award 1964, C.A. Elvehjem award 1985, mem. council 1971-74, pres. 1975-76, chmn. fellows com. 1984-92); mem. NAS, AAAS, Am. Inst. Biol. Scis. (chmn. S.E. regional coun. biol. satellite programs 1965-72), Am. Chem. Soc. (sec.-treas. Fla. 1955, chmn. 1958, Fla. award 1956, Kenneth A. Spencer award 1980, chmn. Frasch awards com. 1980-91), Am. Soc. Animal Sci. (nat. v.p. 1961-62, sec. So. sect. 1960-61), Am. Soc. Biol. Chemists, Soc. Exptl. Biology and Medicine, Am. Dairy Assn., Am. Nuclear Soc., Soc. for Environ. Geochemistry and Health (pres. 1976-77), Fedn. Am. Socs. Exptl. Biology (chmn. pub. affairs com. 1975-77), Internat. Union Nutrition Scis. (chmn. U.S. nat. com., pres. XII Internat. Nutrition Congress), Sao Paulo Vet. Soc. (hon.), Peruvian Vet. Assn. (hon.), Kiwanis, Sigma Xi (pres. Fla. 1956-57), Alpha Zeta, Phi Lambda Upsilon, Gamma Sigma Delta, Phi Eta Sigma, Phi Sigma, Gamma Sigma Epsilon, Phi Kappa Phi, Blue Key. Home: 2903 SW 2nd Ct Gainesville FL 32601-9057 E-mail: davis.gk@worldnet.att.net.

DAVIS, GEORGE LINN, banker; b. Des Moines, July 9, 1934; s. James Cox and Elizabeth (Linn) D.; m. Anne Roberts, May 1955 (div. Jan. 1967); children: James, Elliott, George Linn; m. Mary Elizabeth Graham, Apr. 27, 1968; children: Stephen, Thomas. BA, Yale U., 1956; MBA, Harvard U., 1958. Sr. v.p. Citibank NA, N.Y.C., 1958-81; exec. v.p. First Chgo. Corp., Chgo., 1981-87; Citicorp/Citibank group exec. N.Am. Fin. Group, N.Y.C., 1987-90; chmn. Scarborough Ptnrs., Inc., N.Y.C., 1990—; pres., CEO, bd. dirs. 1st Am. Bankshares Inc., Washington, 1990-91. Bd. dirs. Sealy Inc.; CEO Banco de Venezuela Internat., Syscon Inc.; chmn. Emex, Inc. Trustee Central Park Conservancy; chmn. Nat. Stroke Assn. Mem. Robert Morris Assocs., Assn. Equipment Lessors (bd. dirs. 1974-76), Chgo. Club, Glenview Club, Sleepy Hollow Country Club, Univ. Club. Republican. Office: Scarborough Partners Inc 450 Park Ave Fl 6 New York NY 10022-2605 E-mail: GD@JFLPartners.com.

DAVIS, GLENN CRAIG, psychiatrist; b. Columbia, Mo., Apr. 26, 1946; s. Morris S. and Dorothy (Hall) Davis; children: Jason Michael, Galen Brent. BA, Reed Coll., 1968; MD, Duke U., 1972. Diplomate Am. Bd. Psychiatry and Neurology. Intern, then resident Duke U. Med. Ctr., Durham, N.C., 1972-75; clin. assoc. NIMH, Bethesda, Md., 1975-77, chief of drug abuse unit, biological psychiatry br., 1977-79; assoc. prof. U. Tenn. Ctr. Health Scis., Memphis, 1979-81; assoc. prof. then prof. Sch. of Medicine Case Western Reserve U., Cleve., 1981-87; dir. psychiat. rsch. to chief of staff Cleve. VA Med. Ctr., 1981-87; chair psychiatry Henry Ford Med. Ctr., Detroit, 1987-92; v.p. behavioral svcs. Henry Ford Health System, Detroit, 1991-94, v.p. acad. affairs, 1992—2001, chief med. officer suburban regions, 1996-98, assoc. dean Case Western Reserve U., 1993—2001; prof. psychiatry Case Western Reserve U., Cleve., 1994—2001; pres. Am. Bd. Psychiatry & Neurology, Deerfield, IL; dean coll. of human medicine Mich. State U., East Lansing, Mich., 2001—. Clin. prof. U. Mich. Sch. Medicine, Ann Arbor, 1988—2001. Author numerous scientific rsch. papers and book chpts.; contbr. articles to profl. jours. Lt. comdr. USPHS U.S. Army, 1975—79. Fellow Am. Psychiat. Assn., Am. Psychopathological Assn.; mem. AAAS, AMA, Biol. Psychiatry, Am. Bd. Psychiatry and Neurology (dir. 1996—, pres. 2000), Am. Bd. Med. Specialties, Sigma Xi, Alpha Omega Alpha. Office: Mich State U A-110 East Fee Hall East Lansing MI 48824 E-mail: gdavis@msu.edu.

DAVIS, GORDON RICHARD FUERST, retired biologist, translator; b. Prince Albert, Sask., Can., Apr. 5, 1925; s. Louis James Davis and Nora Sylvia Fuerst; m. Marie Bérengère Pauline Bérubé, May 25, 1949 (sep. 2003); children: Joseph Richard Kevin (dec.), Elyse Bruce, Marie Raymonde Joceline, Marie-Thérèse Danielle. B.Sc. in Zoology with honors, McGill U., 1948, M.Sc., 1949, PhD, 1952. Agrl. scientist biol. control unit Can. Dept. Agr., Que., 1948-52, research officer research br., 1952-65, research scientist research br., 1965-85; translator Co-Operators Fin. Svcs. Ltd., Regina, Sask., Can., 1987-90; pres., mng. dir. Triple-D Translation Svcs., Regina, Sask., 1990-95. Mem. Div. III sci. curriculum com. Sask. Dept. Edn., 1974-80 Contbr. articles to profl. jours. Bd. trustees Saskatoon Catholic Bd. Edn., 1974-77; mem. Sask German Council, Inc., rep to Concordia German Language Sch., 1986-87, v.p., 1986-87. Served with Royal Can. Navy Vol. Res., 1944-45. Carpenter Teaching fellow, 1950-51 Mem. Nutrition Soc. Can. (sec. 1973-77, v.p. 1979-80, pres. 1980-81), Can. Fedn. Biol. Socs. (dir. 1973-77, 80-81, hon. sec.-treas. 1980-84), Sask. Geneal. Soc., Regina Geneal. Soc., Can.'s Nat. History Soc., Prince Albert Hist. Soc., Alzheimer Soc. Saskatchewan. Roman Catholic. Home: 2345 Broad St Apt 507 Regina SK Canada S4P 1Z1 E-mail: r.davis@accesscomm.ca. *A knowledge of as many areas of learning as possible and a general understanding of related and unrelated fields helps to push back the limitations of our horizons; a dedication to one goal at a time; a desire to improve the environment for the general good and acknowledgement by future inquirers of the value of the contributions that one has made: all provide their own opportunities in a hostile world.*

DAVIS, GRAY (JOSEPH GRAHAM DAVIS), former governor; b. N.Y.C., Dec. 26, 1942; m. Sharon Ryer, Feb. 20, 1983. BA cum laude, Stanford U., 1964; JD, Columbia U., 1967. Chief of staff to Gov. Jerry Brown State of Calif., Sacramento, 1975—81, mem. Calif. State Assembly, 1983—87, state contr., 1986-94, lt. gov., 1995-99, gov., 1999-2003. Chmn. Housing and Community Devel. Com., Calif. Coun. on Criminal Justice, Franchise Tax Bd., State Lands Commn.; mem. Bd. Equalization, State Tchrs. Retirement System, Pub. Employees Retirement System, Nat. Coun. Institutional Investors; U. Calif. Regent, Calif. State U. trustee; mem. intergovtl. policy adv. com. on trade Office of U.S. Trade Rep. Founder Calif. Found. for the Protection of Children. Democrat.*

DAVIS, GREGORY THOMAS, marine surveyor; b. Evergreen Park, Ill., Jan. 19, 1952; s. Bernard Thomas and Helen Therese (Keehan) D.; m. Christine Ellen Luka, Aug. 25, 1975; children: Brian Thomas, Bonnie Jean. BA, Coll. of Santa Fe, 1973. Cert. marine surveyor, fire and explosion investigator, bd. cert. forensic examiner. Adjuster Gen. Adjustment Bur., Chgo., 1973-74; marine surveyor Graham Miller Ltd., London, 1974-76; marine surveyor, pres. Davis and Co. Ltd., Lisle, Ill., 1977—. Guest lect. Tec Core, Wheeling, Ill., 1990—; mem. ad hoc com. on marine fuel U.L. Marine, Northbrook, Ill., 1986—; mem. Am. Bd. Forensic Examiners. Contbr. articles to profl. jours. Parents adv. bd. U. San Diego, 2000-2001. Mem. Nat. Assn. Marine Surveyors (chmn. ins. com. 1982-95, chair yachts and small crafts tech. com. 2000—), Am. Boat and Yacht Coun. (bd. dirs. 1999—), Nat. Fire Protection Assn. (permanent mem. 303 com. 1997—), Am. Soc. for Non-destructive Testing, Nat. Assn. Fire Investigators, Internat. Assn. Arson Investigators, Internat. Assn. Marine Investigators, Soc. of Naval Architects and Marine Engrs. (mem. 0-45 panel 1997—), Nat. Marine Mfrs. Assn. (mem. boating industry risk mgmt. com., edn. com.). Avocations: computer, boats, fishing, golf. Office: Davis and Co Ltd 1989 University Ln Ste I Lisle IL 60532-4132 E-mail: gdavis@daviscoltd.com.

DAVIS, GWENDOLYN LOUISE, air force officer, English educator; b. Toledo, Dec. 8, 1951; d. Robert Louis and Marietta Beatrice (Sautter) Davis; m. Barry Dennis Fayne, Jan. 6, 1979 (div. Feb. 2001); children: Ashleigh Elizabeth, Zachary Alexandur-John. BFA, So. Meth. U., 1972; MEd, U. North Tex., 1978; MA, U. Denver, 1987. Cert. tchr., Tex., Ala.; cert. secondary tchg. Am. Montessori Soc. Substitute tchr., Toledo and Dallas, 1972-73; film dir. Channel 39 Christian Broadcasting Network, Dallas, 1973-75; engr., air operator Channel 40 Trinity Broadcasting Network, Tustin, Calif., 1978; commd. 2d lt. USAF, 1978, advanced through grades to maj., 1989, ret., 1995; mgr. western area Hdqrs. USAFR Officers Tng. Corp., Norton AFB, Calif., 1979-81; chief tng. systems support Hdqrs. Air Force Manpower Pers. Pentagon, Washington, 1981-84; pers. policies officer J1, Orgn. of Joint Chiefs of Staff Pentagon, Washington, 1984-85; asst. prof. English, dir. forensics USAF Acad., Colorado Springs, Colo., 1987-92; adj. faculty mem. dept. English Auburn U., Montgomery, Ala., 1994-95; adj. faculty mem. dept. arts and scis. Troy State U., Montgomery, 1994-96; dir. Bullock County HS Learning Ctr., Union Springs, Ala., 1995-96; tech. and acad. tchr. Ctr. for Advanced Tech. Booker T. Washington Magnet H.S., Montgomery, 1996; tchr. speech and English Mountain Brook H.S., Birmingham, Ala., 1997-98; tchr. humanities Joseph Bruno Montessori Acad., Birmingham, 1998-2000; upperschool director Sacred Heart Church Sch., 2000-2001, ednl. cons., 2001—02; founder, dir. Shiloh Village Montessori H.S., 2002—. Assoc. editor Airpower Jour., Maxwell AFB, Ala., 1992-94, mil. doctrine analyst, 1994-95; chmn. mil. affairs Jr. Officer's Coun., Norton AFB, 1981; invited spkr. in field; chmn. program devel. com. for nat. orgn. Cross Exam. Debate Assn., 1990-91. Contbr. articles to profl. jours. Teacher, mem. choir, soloist various chs., 1973; chair publicity com. Birthright, Inc., Woodbridge, Va., 1983. Named Command Jr. Officer of Yr., Hdqrs. USAFR Officers Tng. Corps, 1979. Mem. Nat. Parliamentary Debate Assn. (co-founder, editor Parliamentary Debate jour. 1992-95), Am. Montessori Soc., Phi Upsilon Omicron. Avocations: reading, antiques, sight-seeing, family. Home: 4978 Overton Rd Birmingham AL 35210 E-mail: gwendavis1@aol.com.

DAVIS, H. ALAN, retired airline captain, consultant; b. Knoxville, Tenn., Apr. 24, 1932; s. Fred Edwin Davis and Rose Lee (Perrin) Davis Williams; m. Betty Jean Carter, June 11, 1951; children: Cynthia Lynn Davis Roper, Linda Susan Davis Williamson, Scott Alan. BS, Jackson Coll., Honolulu, 1965; disting. grad., Indsl. Coll. of Armed Forces, 1970; M of Arts in Teaching, Rollins Coll., 1972; EdD, Nova U., 1980. Cert. FAA in airline transport. Commd. 1st sgt. USAF, 1951, advanced through grades to maj., 1972; dir. ops., chief pilot Sky Safari Air Travel Club, Orlando, Fla., 1972-73; co. check airman, capt. Rich Internat. Airways, Miami, Fla., 1979-85; dept. chmn., tchr. Maynard Evans High Sch., Orlando, 1973-85; co. check airman, line capt. Trans Air Link Corp., Miami, 1985-92; with ops. dept. Walt Disney World, Orlando, Fla., 1992-94; chief pilot Hemisphere Internat. Airlines, Miami, 1994-96; ret., 1996; entertainment ops. staff Walt Disney World, 1996—. Air Santo Domingo line capt. APA Internat., 1992-93. Recipient Nat. Achievement award, Am. Soc. Aerospace Edn., 1980. Mem.: DAV (life), VFW (life), Retired Officers Assn., Aircraft Owners and Pilots Assn., Quiet Birdmen, Masons, Shriners. Republican. Avocations: golfing, hunting, fishing. Home: 8208 Banyan Blvd Orlando FL 32819-4145

DAVIS, HARLEY CLEO, retired career officer; b. Van Buren, Ark., May 7, 1941; s. Aleta (Johnson) D.; m. Patricia Ann White, Mar. 9, 1985. BS, Ark. Tech. U., 1963; MA, Ea. Ky. U., 1972; exec. devel. program, U. N.H., 1987. Commd. 2d lt. U.S. Army, 1963, advanced through grades to maj. gen., 1993; platoon leader 1st Bn., 50th inf., 2d Armored Div., 1963; various assignments, 1963-80; comdr. 3d Bn., 5th Spl. Forces Group, Ft. Bragg, N.C., 1980-82; chief leadership br. Hdqrs. Dept. of the Army, Washington, 1982-84; chief of staff JFK Spl. Warfare Ctr. and Sch., Ft. Bragg, 1985-86; comdr. 5th Spl. Forces Group, Ft. Campbell, Ky., 1987-89; asst. comdt. JFK Spl. Warfare Ctr. and Sch., Ft. Bragg, 1989-91; dep. commdg. gen. U.S. Army Sp. Ops. Command, Ft. Bragg, 1991-92; comdg. gen. U.S. Army Spl. Forces Command (Airborne), Ft. Bragg, 1992-95; dep. commdg. gen. Fifth U.S. Army (west), Ft. Lewis, Wash., 1995-97. Decorated DSM with oak leaf cluster, Legion of Merit, Soldier's Medal, Bronze Star with two oak leaf clusters, Air medal with with oak leaf cluster. Office: 1001 Connecticut Ave NW Ste 1035 Washington DC 20036

DAVIS, HARRY REX, political science educator; b. Ozona, Tex., Nov. 9, 1921; s. Rex Otis and Mima (Gowin) D.; m. Ruth Elizabeth Greenlee, Sept. 6, 1947; children: Peter Gowin, Scott Andrew, Martha Greenlee. BA summa cum laude, Tex. Christian U., 1942; AM, U. Chgo., 1949, PhD, 1951; postdoctorate, Union Theol. Sem., 1952-53. Teaching fellow Tex. Christian U., 1945-46; mem. faculty dept. govt. Beloit (Wis.) Coll., 1948-90, assoc. prof., 1956-59, prof., 1959-90, chmn. dept., 1959-84, prof. emeritus, 1990—. Cons. ch. and soc. dept. World Council Chs., 1969. Author: (with others) Small City Government, 1962, Colleges and Commitments, 1971; Editor: (with others) Reinhold Niebuhr on Politics, 1960. Active Beloit City Coun., 1959-60, Beloit Bd. Ethics, 1975-81, Wis. Gov.'s Coun. on Jud. Selection, 1983-86, Beloit Bd. Health, 1996-2002, chmn., 1996-98; chmn. Beloit Dem. Com., 1956, 61-63; local mgr. campaigns congl. candidates. With USAAF, 1942-45. Ford faculty fellow, 1952-53; Social Sci. Research Council grantee; Rockefeller Found. grantee. Mem. Midwest Polit. Sci. Assn. (sec.-treas. 1959-65, mem. exec. coun. 1966-68), Am. Polit. Sci. Assn. (chmn. Burdette award com. 1979), Am. Soc. Polit. and Legal Philosophy, Soc. Christian Ethics. Democrat. Presbyterian (elder, coun. on ch. and society 1965-72, Gen. Assembly commr. 1991). Office: Beloit Coll Dept Government Beloit WI 53511 Home: 2423 Stonehedge Ln Beloit WI 53511-6727

DAVIS, HEATHER LYNNE, communications officer; b. Wilmington, Del., Aug. 29, 1967; d. Gary Wendel and Suzanne Delores Davis; m. José Felix Padua, Dec. 19, 1957. BA in english, Hollins U., 1989; MA in creative writing, Syracuse U., 1992. Devel. officer Internat. Rsch. & Exchanges Bd., Wash., 1993—96, editor, 1996—98; dir. found. rels. Nat. Women's Law Ctr., Wash., 1998—2000; comm. Manoff Group, Inc., Wash., 2000—. Tchg. asst. Syracuse U., 1989—91; adj. instr. Montgomery Coll., Rockville, Md., 1995—96. Bd. mem. Friends of the Torpedo Factory Art Ctr., Alexandria, Va., 2002—; tutor Wright to Read Program, Alexandria, 2001—; sponsor Women for Women Internat., Wash., 1998—. Mem.: Global health Coun. Avocations: writing, travel, web site devel..

DAVIS, HELEN GORDON, former state senator; b. N.Y.C., 1926; m. Gene Davis; children: Stephanie, Karen, Gordon. BA, Bklyn. Coll.; postgrad., U. South Fla., 1967-70. Tchr. High Sch. Commerce, N.Y.C., Hillsborough High Sch., Tampa, Fla.; grad. asst. U. South Fla., 1968; mem. Fla. Ho. of Reps. (1st woman to be elected in 1974 from Hills Co., 1st woman to chair the legis. delegation), 1974-88; state senator, 1988-92; mem. Fla. Supreme Ct. Commn. on Gender Bias in the Cts., 1988-90, Fla. Supreme Ct. Commn. on Mediation and ArbitratioN, 1987—. Chmn. senate appropriations subcom. human svcs., mem. rules com., internat. trade and econ. devel. com., health and rehab. svcs. com. Jud. chmn. Local Govt. Study Commn. Hillsborough County (Fla.), 1964; mem. Tampa Commn. on Juvenile Delinquency, 1966-69, Mayor's Citizens Adv. Com., 1966-69, Quality Edn. Commn., 1966-68, Gov.'s Citizen Com. for Ct. Reform, 1972, Hillsborough County Planning commn., 1973-74; mem. Gov.'s Commn. on Jud. Reform, 1976; mem. employment com. Commn. Cmty. Rels., 1966-69; by-laws chmn. Arts Coun. Tampa, 1971-74; 1st v.p. Tampa Symphony Guild, 1974; bd. dirs. U. South Fla. Found., 1968-74, Stop Rape, 1973-74; founder Ctr. for Women, Tampa, 1978; past pres. PTA; active adv. commn. Nat. Child Care Action Campaign, Nat. Ctr. for Crime and Delinquency; chair Hillsborough Dem. Exec. Com., also pres. Recipient U. South Fla. Young Democrats Humanitarian award, 1974, Diana award NOW, 1975, Woman of Achievement in Arts award Tampa, 1975, Tampa Human Rels. award, 1976, Hannah G. Solomon Citizen of Yr., 1980, St. Petersburg Times/Fla. Civil Liberties award, 1980, Friend of Edn. award, 1981, Fla. Alliance for Responsible Parenting award, 1981, Humanitarian award Judeo-Christian Clinic, 1984, Fla. Network of Runaway Youth award, 1985, Ctr. for Women Leader-advocate Friend award, 1985, Nat. Assn. Juvenile Ct. Judges Appreciation award, 1987, AAUW Leadership award, 1987, Hillsborough County Halfway House appreciation award, 1988, Martin Luther King award City of Tampa, 1988, Nat. Fedn. Dem. appreciation, 1989, Dept. Legal Affairs appreciation, 1990, Superwoman award Mus. Sci. and Industry, 1990, Nat. Childcare Merit award Nat. Assn. Sch. Psychologists, 1992, Am. Judicature award Am. Judicature Assn., 1993, Woman of Courage award City of Tampa, 2000; named Fla. Motion Picture and TV Outstanding Legislator, 1990; named to Fla. Women's Hall of Fame, 1999. Mem. LWV (pres. Hillsborough County 1966-69, lobbyist, Fla. adminstrn. of justice chmn. 1969-74), Am. Arbitration Assn., Hills County Expy. Authority, Fla. Supreme Ct. Commn. Arbitration. Democrat. Home: 45 Adalia Ave Tampa FL 33606-3301 Fax: 813-253-0393. E-mail: hegordav@aol.com.

DAVIS, HENRY ARNOLD, automotive company executive; b. Memphis, Mar. 3, 1964; s. James Arthur and Eddie Lee Davis; m. Tanya K. Davis; children: Tamala R., Jeffrey T., Jorel T., Tatiana J., Tiffany J. BSEE, Yale U., 1986; MBA, Stanford U., 1992. Ops. analyst Allied Signal Aerospace, Torrance, Calif., 1992-93, sr. ops. analyst, 1993; engagement mgr. Allied Signal, Inc., Morristown, N.J., 1994; mgr. new bus. devel. Allied Signal Comml. Avionics sys., Olathe, Kans., 1995, distbn. mgr., 1995-96; dir. procurement Rockwell Automotive, Troy, Mich., 1996-97; plant mgr. Meritor Automotive, Canal Fulton, Ohio, 1997-99; v.p. Materials Aultman Health Found., Canton, Ohio,

1999-2000; ops. mgr. Fed. Mogul Corp., Sumter, SC, 2000—03; divsn. ops. mgr. Eaton Corp., Marshall, Mich., 2003—. Vol. coach East Palo Alto Mid. Sch., Palo Alto, Calif., 1992; mem. alumni schs. com. Yale U.; mem. Stanford GSB Alumni; bd. dirs. Boy Scouts Am.; bd. trustees Detroit C. of C. Mem.: Nat. Black MBA Assn., Sumter C. of C. Indsl. Assn. Avocations: golf, tennis, skiing, reading, chess. Home: 8148 Waterwood Dr Kalamazoo MI 49048 Office: Eaton Corp 1101 W Hanover St Marshall MI 49068 E-mail: henryadavis@eaton.com.

DAVIS, HENRY BARNARD, JR., lawyer; b. East Grand Rapids, Mich., June 3, 1923; s. Henry Barnard and Ethel Margaret (Turnbull) D.; m. Margaret Lees Wilson, Aug. 27, 1946; children: Caroline Dellenbusch, Laura Davis, George B. BA, Yale U., 1945; JD, U. Mich., 1950; LLD, Olivet Coll., 1983. Bar: Mich. 1951, U.S. Dist. Ct. (we. dist.) Mich. 1956, U.S. Ct. Appeals (6th cir.) 1971, U.S. Supreme Ct. 1978. Assoc. Allaben, Wiarda, Hayes & Hewitt, 1951-52; ptnr. Hayes, Davis & Dellenbusch PLC, Grand Rapids, Mich., 1952—2002, Davis & Davis Law Office PLC, Grand Rapids, 2002—. Mem. Kent County Bd. Commrs., 1968-72; mem. Cmty. Mental Health Bd., 1970-94, past chmn.; trustee, sec. bd. Olivet Coll., 1965-91, trustee emeritus, 1991—; bd. dirs. Jr. Achievement Grand Rapids, 1960-65; chair Grand Rapids Historic Preservation Com., 1977-79; trustee East Congregational Ch., 1979-81. Served with USAAF, 1943-46, Philippines. Mem. ABA, Mich. Bar Assn., Grand Rapids Round Table (pres. 1969), Masons. Republican. Home: 30 Mayfair Dr NE Grand Rapids MI 49503-3831 Office: 535 Fountain St NE Grand Rapids MI 49503-3421 E-mail: hbdavis@mac.com.

DAVIS, HENRY JEFFERSON, JR., former naval officer; b. Quincy, Fla., May 6, 1929; s. Henry and Sara Jewell (Davis) D.; m. Ernestine Hunt Tully, June 8, 1955; children: Frances Cornelia Davis Wallington, Jessica Leigh Davis Coughlin, H.J. Davis V, George Walton Davis II. Student, U. Fla., 1947-48; BS, Fla. State U., 1952; postgrad., U.S. Naval Acad., 1949-51; MS, U.S. Naval Postgrad. Sch., 1962. Commd. ensign U.S. Navy, 1952, advanced through grades to rear adm., 1977; comdg. officer Naval Security Group Activity, Winter Harbor, Maine, 1968-70; asst. chief of staff to comdr. in chief U.S. Pacific Fleet, dir. Naval Security Group Pacific, 1973-76; chief Nat. Security Agy., Pacific, cryptologic adv. to comdr. in chief Pacific, 1976-77; asst. dir. plans and resources Nat. Security Agy., 1977-79, dep. dir. ops., 1979-82, ret., 1982. Mgmt. cons. State of Fla. Info. Resource Commn., 1984-92. Mem. Gadsden County (Fla.) Sch. Bd., 1984—94, chmn., 1988—91, 1993—94; mem. Quincy-Gadsden Airport Authority, 1994—2001; trustee The Bapt. Coll. of Fla., 1994—2001; bd. dirs. Fla. Sch. Bd. Assn., 1990—92, Gadsden Arts Inc., 1996—2002. Decorated Def. Superior Service medal, Bronze star, Def. Meritorious Service medal, others. Baptist.

DAVIS, HERBERT OWEN, lawyer; b. Washington, June 11, 1935; s. Owen Stier and Claudie Lea (Pointer) D.; children: Herbert O. Jr., Ann P., Paul B. BA, U. N.C., 1957; JD, Duke U., 1960. Bar: N.C. 1960, U.S. Dist. Ct. (mid. dist.) N.C. 1960. Assoc. Smith Moore Smith Schell & Hunter, Greensboro, NC, 1960—66, ptnr., 1966—86, Smith Helms Mulliss & Moore, Greensboro, 1986—2002, Smith Moore LLP, Greensboro, 2002—. Editor in chief Duke Law Jour., 1959—60. Mem. ABA, N.C. Bar Assn., Greensboro Country Club, Greensboro City Club (bd. dirs.), The Carolina Club, Phi Beta Kappa. Home: 2303 Danbury Rd Greensboro NC 27408-5123 Office: Smith Moore LLP 300 N Greene St Ste 1400 Greensboro NC 27401-2171 E-mail: bert.davis@smithmoorelaw.com.

DAVIS, HIRAM JOE, public school administrator; b. Spartanburg, S.C., Feb. 13, 1930; s. Flake Revere and Dolorus Jane (Haigler) D.; m. Anna Jane Ripley, Mar. 16, 1951; children: Alan Joe, Kendal Jay. AB, Asbury Coll., 1951; MEd, Kent State U., 1957. Cert. supt., prin., supervisor, tchr. Elem. sch. tchr., Antrim, Ohio, 1951-52; tchr. Auburn Elem. Sch., Chagrin Falls, Ohio, 1952-57; prin. Kenston Elem. Schs., Chagrin Falls, Ohio, 1957-62; prin., dir. of 16 schs. Firestone Rubber Plantation, Harbel, Liberia, West Africa, 1962-64; asst. high sch. prin. Orange Schs., Pepper Pike, Ohio, 1964-66, prin. Brady Mid. Sch., 1966-84; interim prin. Kenston Schs., Chagrin Falls, Ohio, 1984-98. Past bd. mem. Am. Inst. Fgn. Study, Greenwich, Conn., 1968-84, prin. summer sch. groups to Europe, 1968-82; attendee White House Conf. on Edn.; owner JD Mailboxes. Chmn. trustees Garfield Meml. United Meth. Ch., Pepper Pike, mem. p.p.r. com., mission com.; vol. traveling libr. for Geauga County Pub. Libr. to Amish schs.; scoutmaster troop 1 Liberian Boy Scouts and Boy Scouts Am., Harbel, Liberia, 1962-64; summer session missionary svc. Liberia, 1985, Kenya, 1987; founder Chagrin Valley Jr. Athletic Conf. Mid. Schs. Recipient Dedicated Svc. award Chagrin Valley Jr. Athletic Conf., Garfield Meml. award for dedicated svc. in all areas of churchmanship, Harry Denman Evangelism award for lay leader United Meth. Ch. Conf., Cmty. Svc. award Fedn. Orange Cmties. Mem. NEA (life dept. Nat. Elem. Sch. Prin.), Kiwanis (George F. Hixson award 1964; pres. Lander Cir. 1969-70). Avocation: raising registered belgians.

DAVIS, HOWARD JEFFREY, lawyer; b. Phila., Oct. 2, 1955; s. Herbert U. and Elma G. Davis; m. Barbara Salter, Aug. 10, 1980; children: Sara, Amanda, Eliza. BA, Princeton U., 1977; JD, U. Chgo., 1980. Assoc. Schnader, Harrison, Segal & Lewis, Phila., 1980-83, Kleinbard, Bell & Brecker, Phila., 1984-85, ptnr., 1986-98, mng. ptnr., 1999—. Guest lectr. Pa. Bar Ins., Phila., 1994—; bd. dirs. Robert Filter Group, GDG Internat., Inc., JJB Group. Trustee Fed. Jewish Agys., Phila., 1993—, mem. exec. com., 1996—, mem. com. seventy; bd. dirs. Phila. Geriatric Ctr., 1996—, Com. of Seventy, 2003—. Recipient Young Leadership award, Fedn. Jewish Agys., 1992. Mem.: ABA (corp. sect.), Phila. Bar Assn., Pa. Bar Assn. Avocations: golf, tennis, reading. Home: 440 W Chestnut Hill Ave Philadelphia PA 19118-3712 Office: Kleinbard Bell & Brecker 1900 Market St Ste 700 Philadelphia PA 19103-3573 Business E-Mail: hdavis@kleinbard.com.

DAVIS, HOWARD TED, engineering educator; b. Hendersonville, N.C., Aug. 2, 1937; s. William Howard and Gladys Isabel (Rhodes) D.; m. Eugenia Asimakopoulos, Sept. 15, 1960 (dec. July 1996); children: William Howard II, Maria Katherine; m. Catherine Asimakopoulos, Mar. 9, 2000. BS in Chemistry, Furman U., 1959; PhD in Chem. Physics, U. Chgo., 1962. Postdoctoral fellow Free U. of Brussels, 1962-63; asst. prof. U. Minn., Mpls., 1963-66, assoc. prof., 1966-69, prof., 1969-80, prof., head chem. engring. and materials sci., 1980-95, dean Inst. Tech., 1995—, Regent's prof., 1997—. Editor: Springs of Creativity, 1981; author: Statistical Mechanics of Phases, Interfaces and Thin Films, 1995, (with K. Thomson) Linear Algebra and Linear Operators in Engineering, 2000; contbr. over 500 articles to sci. and engring. jours. Fellow Sloan Found., 1967-69, Guggenheim Found., 1969-70. Mem. AAAS, AIChE (Walker award for excellence in pubs. 1990), NAE, Am. Chem. Soc., Soc. Petroleum Engrs., Minn. Fedn. Engring. Socs. (Disting. Engr. 1998). Democrat. Methodist. Avocations: tennis, golf, reading, movies. Home: 1822 Mount Curve Ave Minneapolis MN 55403-1018 Office: U Minn 421 Washington Ave SE Minneapolis MN 55455-0373 E-mail: davis@itdean.umn.edu.

DAVIS, H(UMPHREY) DENNY, publisher; b. Fayette, Mo., May 8, 1927; s. Lionel Winchester and Sarah Elizabeth (Denny) D.; m. Barbara Ellen Hartsgrove, June 6, 1954; 1 child, Thomas Shackelford. Student, Central Meth. Coll., Fayette, 1944-45, 46-47; BJ, U. Mo., 1949. Reporter, wire editor S.E. Missourian, Cape Girardeau, 1949-54; corr. UPI, Oklahoma City, Tulsa, Denver, 1954-55, exec. Albuquerque, 1955-56, bur. mgr. Lima, Peru, 1955-58, mgr. for Brazil Rio de Janeiro, 1958-68; mgr. no. div. Latin Am. Mexico City, 1968-75; regional exec. Charlotte, N.C., 1975-78; founder, owner pub. Wood Creek Corp., Fayette, 1978—; editor Fayette Advertiser and Democrat-Leader, Fayette, 1984—2001. Author profl. manual; contbr. articles to mags. and newspapers. Chmn. Fayette Planning and Zoning Commn., 1980-87; chmn. Howard County Rep. Cen. Com., Fayette, 1982-98; pres. Franklin or Bust, Inc., Fayette, 1988-2000; mem. Santa Fe Trail Nat. Hist. Trail Nat. Adv. Coun., 1991-97. With USN, 1945-46, 50-51. Mem. NRA, Santa Fe Trail Assn., Fayette Area Heritage Assn. (v.p. 1989-91), Am. Legion. Republican. Episcopalian. Avocation: local history. Home: 400 N Church St Fayette MO 65248-1125 Office: Wood Creek Corp PO Box 132 Fayette MO 65248-0132 E-mail: hddavis@mcmsys.com.

DAVIS, IAN, management consulting firm executive; B in Politics, Philosophy and Econs., Oxford (Eng.) U. With Bowater (paper mfg. firm), McKinsey & Co., London, 1979—, head, London office, mng. dir., 2003—. Office: McKinsey & Co No 1 Jermyn St London SW1Y 4UH England also: McKinsey & Co 55 E 52d St 21st fl New York NY 10022

DAVIS, IRVIN, advertising, public relations, broadcast executive; b. St. Louis, Dec. 18, 1926; s. Julius and Anna (Rosen) D.; m. Adrienne Bronstein, Apr. 25, 1968; 1 child, Jennifer Alison. BSBA, Washington U., 1950; postgrad., St. Louis U., 1952; D Humanities (hon.), Nat. Coll., 1981. Pres. Clayton-Davis & Assoc., Inc., St. Louis, 1953—, Admiral Broadcasting Corp., St. Louis, 1983—. C.p., bd. dirs. Nat. Acad. TV Arts and Scis., 1982—; bd. dirs. Truman Bank; pres. Galtex Broadcasting; pres. Celebrities Prodns. Author: (books) Room for Three, Comprehensive Tng. in Advt. and Pub. Relations; producer (film) Family Album, 1974, Use It in Good Health, Charlie, 1975. Pres. Child Assistance Program, 1986—92; v.p. Boys and Girls Town Mo., St. James, 1976—99, Make Today Count, 1985—86; bd. dirs. Jackie Joyner Kersee Found., 1997—2001, Crusade Against Crime, St. Louis, 1984—; v.p. St. Louis Artists Guild, 2002—. Sgt. USAF, 1945—47, PTO. Recipient Freedom Found. award, 1975, Internat. Film and TV Festival award, 1973-75, Internat. Broadcasting award Hollywood Advt. Club, 1965, 77, 82, 83, Cinegolden Eagle award Coun. on Internat. Non-Theatrical Events, 1975, Nat. Emmy award, 1991. Mem.: Am. Fedn. TV and Radio Arts, Am. Med. Writers Assn., Pub. Rels. Soc. Am. (accredited), St. Louis Club, Press Club, Advt. Club. Office: Clayton-Davis & Assoc Inc 7777 Bonhomme Ave Ste 900 Saint Louis MO 63105-3697

DAVIS, J. MAC, lawyer, state judge; b. Washington, Apr. 5, 1952; s. Glenn Robert and Kathryn Janet (McFarlane) D.; m. Kristi Schuepp, June 5, 1976; children: Glenn Walter, Carl William, Ann Elizabeth. BA with honors, U. Wis., 1973; JD cum laude, U. Mich., 1976. Bar: Wis. 1976. Ptnr. Love, Brown, Love, Phillips & Davis Law Firm, Waukesha, Wis., 1976-82, Phillips & Davis Law Firm, Waukesha, 1982-90; mem. Wis. Senate, Madison, 1983-90; cir. ct. judge Waukesha, Wis., 1990—. Faculty Nat. Jud. Coll., Reno, 1994—95, Wis. Jud. Coll., Wis., 1990—; parliamentarian, mem. legis. com. Wis. Jud. Conf. Mem. Nat. Conf. Commrs. on Uniform State Laws, 1983—90; chmn. Waukesha County Sheriff's Grievance Com., 1979—90; active Mental Health Assn. Waukesha County, 1976—, past pres.; pres. Glenn Davis Charitable Found., Waukesha, 1978—; bd. dirs. United Way in Waukesha County, 1993—96; vol. judge Wis. Jud. Coll.; mem. exec. com. Waukesha County Rep. Com., 1976—90. Recipient George Washington award Freedom's Found. at Valley Forge, 1970. Mem.: Wis. Vol. Trial Judges Assn. (vice chair 2001—), Waukesha County Bar Assn. (bd. dirs. 2001—), Wis. Bar Assn. Office: Waukesha County Courthouse 515 W Moreland Blvd Waukesha WI 53188-2428

DAVIS, JACK WAYNE, JR., publishing executive; b. Toledo, Ohio, May 21, 1947; s. Jack Wayne and Virginia (Moore) D.; m. Amélie Claiborne Matthews, June 24, 1977; 1 child, Claiborne Levering. Grad., Harvard Coll., 1969. Mng. editor Figaro, New Orleans, 1972-73; reporter, columnist, asst. city editor, city editor Item, New Orleans, 1973-80; metro editor The Times - Picayune, New Orleans, 1980-83; assoc. metro editor, night metro editor, metro editor The Chgo. Tribune, 1983-87; editor, v.p. Daily Press, Newport News, Va., 1987-94, pres., pub., CEO, 1994-98; pres. Tribune Interactive Inc., 1998—99, pub.,v.p. planning, 1999—2000; pres., pub. CEO The Hartford Courant, Hartford, Conn., 2000—. Frank Knox fellow U. Rajasthan, India, 1971, Profl. Journalism fellow Stanford U., 1977-78. Mem. Wadsworth Atheneum Mus. of Art (bd. dirs.), Metro Hartford Regional Econ. Alliance, The Antiquarian and Landmarks Soc., The Pirate's Alley Faulkner Soc., Hartford Courant Found., Hartford's Camp Courant. Avocations: sculling, reading. Office: Hartford Courant 285 Broad Street Hartford CT 06115-2510

DAVIS, JAMES ALLAN, gerontologist, educator; b. Portland, Oreg., May 20, 1953; s. Alfred Jack and Anne (Dickson) D.; m. Lois Carol Lindsay, Dec. 17, 1978; children: Sarah Elizabeth, Matthew Simon. BS, U. Oreg., 1975, MS, 1976, EdD, 1980. State mental health gerontologist Oreg. Mental Health Div., Salem, 1978-80; project dir. Oreg. Long Term Care Tng. Project, Salem, 1979-80; tng. specialist Nat. Assn. Area Agys. on Aging., Washington, 1981; asst. dir. for internships and vol. svc. exptl. learning programs U. Md., 1981-86, mem. rsch. and instructional faculty, 1982-86; com. adminstr. Oreg. State Human Resources Com., Salem, 1987; exec. dir., legis. dir. Oreg. State Coun. Sr. Citizens, Salem, 1987—2002; program coord. for sr. mental health care Oreg. Sr. and Disabled Svc. Div., Salem, 1989—2001; pres. James A. Davis and Assocs. Inc., Portland, 1991—; state project dir. Oreg. Assn. RSVPs, 1995—. Vis. asst. prof. Ctr. for Gerontology, U. Oreg., 1990-92; co-chair Audio-Visual Program, Internat. Congress Gerontology, 1985; nat. gerontology acad. adv. panel, Nat. Hosp. Satellite Network, 1983-85; presenter nat. confs. on aging, health care, exptl. edn., age stereotyping; lobbyist United Srs. Oreg., Oreg. State Coun. Sr. Citizens, Oreg. State Denturist Assn., Oreg. State Pharmacist Assn., Oreg. Soc. Physician Assts., Oreg. Legal Techs. Assn., Oreg. Dental Lab. Assn., Wash. Denturist Assn., Nat. Denturist Assn.; adj. asst. prof. Urban Studies Inst. on Aging, Portland State U., 2003—. Co-author: TV's Image of the Elderly, 1985; contbg. editor Retirement Life News, 1988-92; sr. issues editor Sr. News, 1989-96; contbr. articles to profl. jours.; producer, host approximately 400 TV and radio programs. Founding pres. Oreg. Alliance for Progressive Policy, 1988-89; co-chair mental health com., vice chair legis. com., Gov.'s Commn. on Sr. Svcs., 1988-89; exec. coun., media chair Human Svcs. Coalition Oreg., 1988-89; bd. dirs. Oreg. Health Action Campaign, 1988-92; 2d v.p., bd. dirs. Oreg. State Coun. for Sr. Citizens, 1977-80, 90-92, Oreg. Medicaid Com., 1996—; co-chair Oreg. Medicare/Medicaid Coalition, 1995—, Oreg. Long Term Care Campaign, 1996-98; mem. Gov's. Task Force for Volunteerism, State of Md., 1983-84, State Legis. Income Tax Task Force, 1990; vice chair Oreg. State Bd. Denture Technology, 1991-96; mem. com. for assessment on needs for volunteerism, Gov.'s Vol. Coun., State of Md., 1984-86; project dir. Oreg. Assn. Ret. and Sr. Vol. Programs, 1995—; mem. exec. bd. dirs. Oreg. Advocacy Coalition of Srs. and People with Disabilities, 1997—; chmn., bd. dirs. Oreg. Campaign for Patient Rights, 1997—. Recipient Disting. Svc. award City of Salem, 1980, Spl. Human Rights award, 1981, Svc. award U. Md., 1984, Hometown U.S.A. award Community Cable TV Producers, 1988, Disting. Svc. award Oreg. State Coun. Sr. Citizens, 1991. Mem.: Oreg. State Coun. of Sr. Citizens (Disting. Svc. of Sr. award 2000), Alzheimers Assn. of Oreg. (Pub. Policy award 2000), Nat. Denturist Assn. (exec. dir. 1982—89), Gerontol. Soc. Am. (mental health task force 1982—84, co-chmn. 1983—84), Nat. Assn. State Mental Health Dir. (nat. exec. com. 1978—80, vice chmn. 1979—80, spl. cons.81 1981—82, mem. aging div., co-chmn. nat. program com. 1984—87, nat. media chair 1985—92), Nat. Gray Panthers (nat. exec. com. 1984—87, nat. bd. dirs. 1984—92, program co-chmn. nat. biennial conv. 1986, nat. health task force 1981—, co-chmn. 1983—84, chmn. mental health subcom. 1981—86, editor Health Watch 1982—84, state program developer Oreg. chpt. 1979—80, 1989, lobbyist 1987—, gov.'s patient protection work group 2000—01). Democrat. Office: James A Davis and Assocs Inc 1020 SW Taylor St Ste 610 Portland OR 97205-2506 E-mail: davisjasr@aol.com.

DAVIS, JAMES FRANCIS, lawyer; b. Chester, Pa., Mar. 14, 1947; s. Paul Lamoyne and Kathryn Cora (Stump) D.; m. Patricia Ann Hewson, Aug. 7, 1971; children— Michael Brandon, Victoria Ashley. B.A., Columbia Coll., 1969; J.D., Villanova U., 1972. Bar: Del. 1973, Pa. 1973, U.S. Dist. Ct. Del. 1973, U.S. Ct. Appeals (3d cir.) 1983. Jud. law clk. Superior Ct. New Castle County, Wilmington, Del., 1972-73; assoc. Biondi & Babiarz, Wilmington, 1973-79, Morris, Nichols, Arsht & Tunnell, Wilmington, 1979-83; counsel, Hercules, Inc., Wilmington, 1983—99, chief counsel Aqualon Divsn., 1999—. Mem. Del. Bar Assn. (sec. comml. law sect. 1983-84). Republican. Roman Catholic. Home: 138 Marcella Rd Wilmington DE 19803-3451 Office: Hercules Inc Hercules Plz Wilmington DE 19894-0001

DAVIS, JAMES HENRY, retired psychology educator; b. Effingham, Ill., Aug. 6, 1932; s. Kenneth E. and Forest (Naylor) D.; m. Elisabeth Bachman, June 27, 1954; children— Stephen J., Kristin E., Leah E. BS, U. Ill., 1954; MA, Mich. State U., 1958, PhD, 1961. Asst. instr. psychology Mich. State U., East Lansing, 1959-60; instr. psychology Miami U., Oxford, Ohio, 1960-61, asst. prof. psychology, 1961-65, assoc. prof. psychology, 1965-66; vis. assoc. prof. psychology Yale U., New Haven, 1966-67, U. Ill., Champaign, 1967-68, assoc. prof., 1968-70, prof. psychology, 1970-97, prof. emeritus psychology, 1997. Fellow Ctr. for Advanced Study in Behavioral Scis., 1987-88. Author: Group Performance, 1969; editor: (with W. Brandstatter and H.C. Schuler) Dynamics of Group Decisions, 1978, (with W. Brandstatter and G. Stocker-Kreichgauer) Group Decision Making, 1982, (with G.M. Stephenson) Progress in Applied Social Psychology, Vol. I, 1981, Vol. II, 1984, (with Erich Witte) Understanding Group Behavior, Vol. 1 and Vol. 2, 1996; contbr. articles to profl. jours. Served with U.S. Army, 1954-56 Fellow AAAS, Am. Psychol. Soc.; mem. Psychonomic Soc., Midwestern Psychol. Assn., Soc. Exptl. Social Psychologists, Soc. for Judgment and Decision Making, Soc. Math. Psychology, Sigma Xi Home: 10 Lake Park Rd Champaign IL 61822-7101 E-mail: jdavis@s.psych.uiuc.edu.

DAVIS, JAMES HORNOR, III, lawyer; b. Clarksburg, W.Va., Oct. 9, 1928; s. James Hornor II and Martha (Maxwell) D.; m. Ouida Caldwell, July 1, 1950; children— James Hornor IV, Lewis Caldwell. AB, Princeton U., 1950; LL.B., U. Va., 1953. Bar: W.Va. 1953. Ptnr. firm Preston & Davis, Charleston, 1953-65, Spilman, Thomas, Battle & Klostermeyer, Charleston, 1965-86; of counsel Campbell, Woods, Bagley, Emerson McNeer & Herndon, Charleston, 1987—. Mem. W.Va. Ho. of Dels., 1961-62, W.Va. Senate, 1963-66; pres. Dingess-Rum Properties, Inc. Hon. trustee Ea. Mineral Law Found. Served with USAF, 1953-55. Fellow ABA (life); mem. Am. Law Inst. (life), Am. Judicature Soc. (dir. 1978-81), W.Va. Jud. Coun. (chmn. 1973-81), W.Va. Bar Assn. (pres. 1985-86), Kanawha County Bar Assn., Nat. Coun. Coal Lessors (chmn. 1980—), W.Va. Mfrs. Assn. (chmn. 1973-75, hon. dir.) Democrat. Episcopalian. Office: Campbell Woods Bagley et al PO Box 2393 Charleston WV 25328-2393

DAVIS, JAMES LEE, lawyer; b. High Point, N.C., May 2, 1940; AB with high honors, Guilford Coll., 1968; JD with honors, U. N.C., 1971. Bar: N.C. 1971. With Ward and Smith P.A., New Bern, N.C. Charles A. Dana scholar. Mem. N.C. State Bar, N.C. Bar Assn. (chmn. real property sect. coun. 1981-82), Craven County Bar Assn. (pres. 1978-79), Order of Coif. Office: Ward and Smith PA PO Box 867 1001 College Ct New Bern NC 28562-4972 E-mail: jld@wardandsmith.com.

DAVIS, JAMES MCCOY, retired real estate executive; b. Columbus, Ohio, Oct. 19, 1914; s. James McCoy and Laura Victoria (Smith) D.; m. Phyllis Ruth Rowe, Jan. 24, 1948; children: Perine Davis Ceperley, Linda Davis Bryson, Carol, Paul, Jamie Davis Micalizzi. BBA, Ohio State U., 1937; postgrad., Union Theol. Sem., N.Y.C., 1937-39; BD, Oberlin Grad. Sch. Theol., 1942; MA, Columbia U., 1947, EdD, 1952; MDiv (hon.), Vanderbilt U., 1973. Minister First Congl. Ch., Ravenna, Ohio, 1939-42; field exec. Congl. Christian Com. War Victims and Services, N.Y.C., 1942-43; counselor for internat. services U. Wash., Seattle, 1948-54; dir., assoc. prof. U. Mich., Ann Arbor, 1954-64; v.p. Inst. Internat. Edn., N.Y.C., 1964-67; provost U.S. Internat. U., San Diego, 1967-70; pres. Northwestern Mich. Coll., Traverse City, 1970-73; realtor James M. Davis, San Diego, 1974-77; pres. James M. Davis Inc. & Assocs., San Diego, 1977—. Contbr. articles to profl. jours. Pres. World Affairs Coun., San Diego, 1981-83; chmn. bd. Consumer Credit Counselors, San Diego, 1988-89; mem. San Diego County Grand Jury, 1990-91; v.p. Baja Presbyn. Missions, 1994-2000. Capt. U.S. Army, 1943-46. Decorated Bronze Star with oak leaf cluster. Mem. Nat. Assn. Fgn. Student Affairs: Assn. Internat. Educators (life, pres. 1959-60), Calif. Assn. Realtors (bd. dirs. 1978-79, 88), San Diego Assn. Realtors (com. chmn. 1978-79, 88), Soc. Mayflower Descs., Rotary. Republican. Presbyterian. Avocations: community service, travel. Home: 4906 Pacifica Dr San Diego CA 92109-2311

DAVIS, JAMES NORMAN, neurologist, neurobiology researcher; b. Dallas, Oct. 24, 1939; s. Moses and Ruth (Grossman) D.; m. Frances Isabel Cantor, May 1, 1965; children— Amanda, Adam, Joanna. BA, Cornell U., 1961, MD, 1965. Diplomate Am. Bd. Neurology and Psychiatry. Intern Bellevue Hosp., N.Y.C., 1965-66; rsch. assoc. Lab. Chem. Pharmacology Nat. Heart Inst.-NIH, Bethesda, Md, 1966-68; resident Duke U., 1968-69, asst. prof., 1972-77, assoc. prof. medicine and pharmacology, 1977-80, prof. medicine, 1980-92, prof. pharmacology, 1987-92, prof. neurobiology, 1989-92; prof., chmn. dept. neurology SUNY, Stony Brook, 1992—; resident in neurology Cornell U.-N.Y. Hosp., 1969-72, North Shore Hosp., 1971; instr. neurology Cornell U., 1969-71; Fulbright fellow U. Goteborg, Sweden, 1972. Contbr. articles to profl. jours. Served with USPHS, 1966-68 Mem. Am. Neurol. Assn., Soc. Neurosci., Am. Soc. Pharmacology and Exptl. Therapeutics, Am. Acad. Neurology, N.C. Soc. Neurosci. (pres. local chpt. 1981-82). Democrat. Jewish. Home: 45 Southgate Rd Setauket NY 11733-1540 Office: SUNY Neurology Dept Hsc T12 020 Stony Brook NY 11794-0001

DAVIS, JAMES O(THELLO), physiology educator; b. Tahlequah, Okla., July 12, 1916; s. Zemry and Villa (Hunter) D.; m. Florrilla Louise Sides, Dec. 27, 1941; children: Janet Ruth, James Lawrence. MA in Zoology, U. Mo., 1939, PhD, 1942, BS in Medicine, 1943; MD, Washington U., 1945. Intern Barnes Hosp., St. Louis, 1945-46; investigator Lab. Kidney and Electrolyte Metabolism, Nat. Heart Inst., Bethesda, Md., 1949-57, chief sect. on exptl. cardiovascular disease, 1957-66; asso. prof. physiology Temple U. Sch. Medicine, Phila., 1955-56; vis. asso. prof. physiology Johns Hopkins Sch. Medicine, 1961-64; vis. prof. physiology U. Va. Sch. Medicine, 1964; prof., chmn. dept. physiology U. Mo. Sch. Medicine, Columbia, 1966-82, prof. emeritus, 1982—. Mem. editorial bd. Am. Jour. Physiology, 1961-63, 66-69, Endocrinology, 1962-65, Circulation Research, 1962-66, 71-76, 78-81, Hypertension, 1979-80. Served with AUS, 1943-45; Served with USPHS, 1946-66. Recipient AMA Golden Apple award for teaching U. Mo., 1968, Sigma Xi Rsch. award U. Mo., 1971, Modern Medicine Disting. Achievement award, 1973, Alumni gold medal U. Mo., 1973, Volhard award, 1974, CIBA award for hypertension rsch., 1975, Carl J. Wiggers award, 1976, citation of merit U. Mo. Sch. Medicine, 1981, Disting. Alumnus award Coll. Arts & Scis. U. Mo., 1993; James O. Davis Disting. Professorship in Cardiovascular Rsch. established in his honor, U. Mo. Sch. Medicine, 1987; James O. Davis Disting. Lectureship in Cardiovascular Sci. established in his honor, U. Mo. Sch. Medicine, 1995; named Hon. Sesquicentennial Prof. U. Mo., 1989. Mem. Am. Heart Assn. (mem. med. adv. council, vice chmn. council for high blood pressure research 1970-72, chmn. council 1972-74), Am. Physiology Soc. (council 1974-78, steering com. circulation group 1978-81, pres. circulation sect. 1981), Endocrine Soc., Soc. Exptl. Biology and Medicine, Nat. Inst. Health Extramural Program, Assn. Physiology Dept. Chairmen (council 1971-74), Inter-Am. Soc. Hypertension (council 1978-80), Internat. Soc. Hypertension (pres. 1980-82), Nat. Acad. Scis., Sigma Xi, Alpha Omega Alpha. Home: 612 Maplewood Dr Columbia MO 65203-1764

DAVIS, JAMES ROBERT, cartoonist; b. Marion, Ind., July 28, 1945; s. James William and Anna Catherine (Carter) D.; m. Jill Carol Davis; 1 son, James Alexander. BS, Ball State U., Muncie, Ind., 1967. Artist, Groves & Assocs., advt., Muncie, 1968-69; asst. to cartoonist: Tumbleweeds comic strip, 1969-78; cartoonist: Garfield comic strip, 1978— ; TV script Here Comes Garfield, 1982, Garfield on the Town, 1983 (Emmy award 1984), Garfield in the Rough, 1984 (Emmy award 1985), Garfield's Halloween Adventure, 1985 (Emmy award 1986), Garfield in Paradise, 1986, Garfield Goes Hollywood, 1987, The Garfield Christmas Special, 1987; author: Garfield at Large, 1980, Garfield Gains Weight, 1981, Garfield Bigger Than Life, 1981, Garfield Weighs In, 1982, Garfield Takes the Cake, 1982, Garfield Treasury, 1982, Here Comes Garfield, 1982, Garfield Sits Around the House, 1983, Garfield Second Treasury, 1983, Garfield Eats His Heart Out, 1983, Garfield Tips the Scale, 1984, Garfield Loses his Feet, 1984, Garfield: His Nine Lives, 1984, Garfield Makes It Big, 1985, Garfield Rolls On, 1985, Third Garfield Treasury, 1985, Garfield Out to Lunch, 1986, The Unabridged, Uncensored, Unbelieveable Garfield Book, 1986, Garfield Food for Thought, 1987, The 4th Garfield Treasury, 1987, The Garfield Cat Naming Book, 1988, Garfield Chews the Fat, 1989, The 5th Garfield Treasury, 1989, Happy Birthday, Garfield, 1989, Garfield, Tiens Bon La Rampe, 1989, Garfield's Longest Catnap, 1989, Garfield The Big Star, 1989, Garfield in the Park, 1989, Garfield and the Tiger, 1989, Mini-Mysteries featuring Garfield, 1990, Garfield: The Me Book: A Guide to Superiority, How to Get It, Use It, and Keep It, 1990, Garfield's Judgement Day, 1990, Garfield's Feline Fantasies, 1990, Garfield Stories, 1990, Garfield on the Farm, 1990, Garfield Hangs Out, 1990, Garfield Goes to Waist, 1990, The Sixth Garfield Trasury, 1991, Garfield: The Truth About Cats, 1991, Garfield: Seasons Greetings, 1991, Garfield Thanksgiving Special, 1991, Garfield Takes Up Space, 1991, Garfield Says a Mouthful, 1991, Garfield Gets a Life, 1991, Garfield's Ghost Stories, 1992, Garfield Vacation Greetings, 1992, Garfield Learns About Thoughtfulness: Don't Be Late!, 1992, Garfield Learns About Planning: Surprize Party, 1992, Garfield Learns About Money: Money Madness!, 1992, Garfield Learns About

Fire Safety: Where's the Fire?, 1992, Garfield Learns About Cooking: Any Cat Can Cook, 1992, Garfield Learns about Conservation: Endangered Odie?, 1992, Garfield Keeps His Chin Up, 1992, Garfield By the Pound, 1992, Garfield Birthday Greetings, 1992, The Seventh Garfield Treasury, 1993, Garfield's Big Fat Hairy Joke Book, 1993, Garfield Takes His Licks, 1993, Garfield Hits the Big Time: His 25th Book, 1993, Garfield's Tales of Mystery, 1994, Garfield's Night Before Christmas, 1994, Garfield's Insults, 1994, Garfield's Haunted House: And Other Spooky Tales, 1994, Garfield's Furry Tales, 1994, Garfield's Big Fat Scary Joke Book, 1994, Garfield's Big Fat Holiday Joke Book, 1994, Garfield Insults, Put-Downs, 1994, Garfield Fat Cat, 1994, Garfield Discovers America, 1994, Garfield's Son of Big, Fat Hairy Jokes, 1994, Big Hairy Garfield, 1994, Garfield, The Easter Bunny?, 1995, Garfield's Stupid Cupid: And Other Silly Stories, 1995, Garfield Fat Cat 3 Pack, 1995, Garfield Dishes It Out, 1995, Mr. Potato Head, 2001. Mktg. Hall of Fame award Am. Mktg. Assn., 1982; recipient Disting. Alumnus award Am. Assn. State Colls. Univs. Mem. Nat. Cartoonists Soc. (Best Humor Strip of 1981, 86, Segar award 1985, Cartoonist of Yr. 1990), Newspaper Comics Council. Protestant. Republican. Office: Universal Press Syndicate 4520 Main St Ste 700 Kansas City MO 64111-7701

DAVIS, JAMES THOMAS, lawyer; b. Uniontown, Pa., Oct. 17, 1951; s. Norman J. and Thelma (Solomon) D.; m. Martha Russin, Sept. 4, 1976; children: Cara Catherine, Jeremy James, Adina Ann, Jacob Jamail, Kalie Marie. BA, California (Pa.) State Coll., 1973; JD, Duquesne U., 1976. Bar: Pa. 1976, U.S. Dist. Ct. (we. dist.) Pa. 1976, U.S. Supreme Ct. 1984; cert. criminal and civil trial advocate Nat. Bd. Trial Advocacy. Asst. dist. atty. Fayette County, Pa., 1977-83; ptnr. firm Davis & Davis, Uniontown, 1976— Adj. faculty California (Pa.) U. Mem. ATLA, Pa. Trial Lawyers Assn. Democrat. Eastern Orthodox. Office: Davis & Davis PO Box 1163 Uniontown PA 15401-1163 E-mail: jdavis@davisanddavislaw.com.

DAVIS, JAMES WESLEY, university program administrator, artist, writer, composer; b. L.A., Oct. 9, 1940; s. Charles Wesley and Hazel Virginia (Porter) D.; m. Linnea Sharsmith, Mar. 31, 1962 (div. 1978); children: Marc Jerome, Timothy Andrew; m. Ellen Alva Hales, Oct. 6, 1990. BA in Edn., Calif. Coll. Arts & Crafts, Oakland, 1964; BFA, Calif. Coll. Arts & Crafts, 1965; MFA, U. Colo., 1967, MA, 1970. Lectr. art dept. U. Ark., Fayetteville, 1967-96; prof. art dept. Western Ill. U., Macomb, 1969-81; instr. art dept. U. Colo., Denver, 1981; dir. performance art prodns. Denver, 1981-83; head art dept. East Tex. State U., Commerce, 1983-88; chair art dept. Ind. State U., Terre Haute, 1988-89; dir. inter-arts ctr. San Francisco State U., 1989—2002, prof. art dept., 2002—. Bd. dirs. Paul Dresher Ensemble, San Francisco, 1994—. Exhibited in over 100 mus. exhbns. worldwide, 1984—; represented in permanent collections over 20 museums; contbr. to profl. jours.; composer over 50 musical works; performer in field. Recipient purchase awards 8 museums worldwide, 1970—, award Swarovski Internat., Belgium, 1968, award Phelan Commn., Oakland, 1975. Office: San Francisco State U Art Dept 1600 Holloway Ave San Francisco CA 94132-1722

DAVIS, JANET MARIE GORDEN, secondary education educator; b. Springfield, Mo., Jan. 6, 1938; d. Ura Arlond and Evelyn Ruby (Nickols) Gorden; m. Benjamin George Davis, June 21, 1980; children: Leslie Anne, John Nathan. BS, S.W. Mo. U., 1960, MA, 1969; PhD, U. Md., 1992. Tchr. Springfield Schs., 1960-64; instr. USAFE-U. Md., Germany, 1965-67, S.W. Mo. U., Springfield, 1969-70; tchr., dept. chair Baltimore County, 1977—. Cons. in internat. edn. World Relief Corp., Wheaton, Ill., 1984; asst. prof. Balt. Internat. Coll., 1993-95. Author: For the Love of Literature: A Survey of Fiction, 1989, For the Love of Literature: Reading and Writing Nonfiction, 1989. Fulbright fellow, Eng., 1980-81. Mem. Dickens Fellowship, Fulbright Assn., Phi Kappa Phi. Baptist. Avocations: piano, animal rights, victorian poetry, hymnology. Home: 6580 Madrigal Ter Columbia MD 21045-4628

DAVIS, JAY M. wholesale distribution executive; With Nat. Distbg. Co., Atlanta, 1970—, pres., COO, 1991—97, pres., CEO, 1997—2003, chmn., CEO, 2003—. Office: Nat Distbg Co Inc 1 National Dr SW Atlanta GA 30336*

DAVIS, JEAN LERCHE, writer; d. Delbert Lerche and Doris Koch Lerche Dietrich. AA, Southeastern Iowa C.C., Burlington, Iowa, 1971; BA, Western Ill. U., 1973. Freelance writer, Atlanta, 1996—99; med. writer WebMD, Atlanta, 1999—, WebMD Med. News Svc. Author: (brochure) Rollins Pavillion brochure, Emory Hospital (Target award for Excellence, 1997). Vol. Hands-On Atlanta, Atlanta, 1999—2002. Mem.: Atlanta Press Club, Am. Med. Writers Assn. (writer, editor 1996—97, chpt. program chmn. 1998—99, chpt. pres. 1999—2000). Avocations: tennis, travel. Office: WebMD 1175 Peachtree St NE Atlanta GA 30361 E-mail: jdavis3@webmd.net.

DAVIS, JEAN REYNOLDS, music educator, author, poet, composer; b. Cumberland, Md., Nov. 1, 1927; d. Foster Ray and Wilhelmina Barrick Reynolds; m. Warren Hirst Davis, Jr., Dec. 9, 1949 (div. Mar. 1975); children: Mark Reynolds, Stephen Scott. MusB magna cum laude, U. Pa., 1949. Pvt. tchr. piano, theory, composition, counterpoint, Phila., 1942—. Editl. cons. in piano tchg. materials Music Pubs. Holding Corp., N.Y.C., 1959-65; tchr. music appreciation Trenton (N.J.) State Prison, 1974; piano instr. Haverford (Pa.) Friends' Sch.; contest adjudicator tchr. orgns., Phila. Author: A Hat on the Hall Table, 1967, To God with Love, 1968, Parish Picnic, 1970, poetry; composer: 2 operas, 2 symphonies, ballet for young people, numerous piano, vocal and orchestral works. Recipient Thornton Oakley medal for distinctive achievement in creative arts, Benjamin Franklin medal for Outstanding Svc., award of merit U. Pa. Cultural Olympics. Mem. Am. Coll. Musicians, Music Tchrs. Nat. Assn., Am. Soc. Composers, Authors and Pubs., Nat. Guild Piano Tchrs., Phila. Music Tchrs. Assn. Episcopalian. Avocations: cooking, drama, public speaking, social commentary. Home: 901 Montgomery Ave Apt 104 Bryn Mawr PA 19010-2854

DAVIS, JEREMY MATTHEW, chemist; b. Bakersfield, Calif., Aug. 5, 1953; s. Joseph Hyman and Mary (Pavetto) D.; m. Bernadette Sobkiewicz, Aug. 28, 1976 (div.); children: Andrew Jeremy, Christopher Peter. BS in Biol. Scis., U. Calif., Irvine, 1974; M in Pub. Adminstrn., Calif. State U., Long Beach, 1983. Chemist I, II, Orange County Water Dist., Fountain Valley, Calif., 1977—84, supervising chemist, 1984—. Papers in field; TV appearance contestant on Jeopardy, 2001. Lay eucharistic minister St. Margaret of Scotland Episcopal Ch., San Juan Capistrano, Calif., St. John the Divine Episcopal Ch., Costa Mesa, Calif. Named Lab. Person of Yr., Calif. Water Environment Assn., Santa Ana River Basin, 1984. Mem. MENSA, Toastmasters Internat. (pres. Watermeisters club 1996, 99, gov. founder's dist. area C-5, 1999-2001, gov. divsn. C 2001-2002). Office: Orange County Water Dist PO Box 8300 Fountain Valley CA 92728-8300 E-mail: jdavis@ocwd.com., jermedavis@hotmail.com.

DAVIS, JERRY RAY, retired railroad company executive; b. Sylvan Grove, Kans., June 30, 1938; s. Ralph Jacob and Clara Willamine (Jennsen) D.; m. Patricia L. Stauffer, Sept. 12, 1958; children: Richard, Roger, Anthony, Randall. MS in Mgmt., MIT, 1976. Telegrapher Union Pacific R.R., Salina, Kans., 1957-59, telegrapher, dispatcher Kans., Colo., 1959-65; asst. supt. safety and courtesy Union Pacific R.R., Kansas City, 1968, trainmaster Utah div. Salt Lake City, 1969-71, trainmaster Idaho div. Idaho Falls, 1971-73, asst. to gen. supt. transp. Omaha, 1973, asst. supt. Oreg. div. Portland, 1973-74, supt. Utah div. Salt Lake City, 1974-75, asst. gen. supt. transp. Omaha, 1976-78, gen. supt. eastern dist., 1978, asst. v.p. ops., 1979-81, v.p. ops., 1981-86, exec. v.p. ops., 1986-89; pres. CSX Rail Transport, Jacksonville, Fla., 1989-91, exec. v.p. ops., 1991-92, exec. v.p. ops., COO, 1992—. Mem. adv. coun. USO; active Luth. Social Svcs. Mem. Am. Assn. R.R. Supts., Ry. Fuel and Oper. Officers Assn., First Coast Mfrs. Assn., Nat. Freight Transp. Assn., TPC, River Club, San Jose Country Club. Republican. Lutheran. Home: 2131 E Alameda Ave Denver CO 80209-2710

DAVIS, JESSICA G. clinical geneticist, pediatrician; b. Bklyn., Apr. 3, 1934; d. Nathan S. and Sylvia (Teplitz) Grosof; m. Andrew R. Davis, June 17, 1956; children: Jennifer Davis Hall, David. BA, Wellesley Coll., 1955; MD, Columbia U., 1959. Diplomate Am. Bd. Med. Genetics. Intern pediatrics St. Luke's Hosp.-Columbia U.; fellow Albert Einstein Coll. Medicine Yeshiva U., N.Y.C., 1961-68, instr. Albert Einstein Coll. Medicine, 1962, asst. prof. Albert Einstein Coll. Medicine, 1968-74; assoc. prof. clin. pediatric Coll. Medicine Cornell U., N.Y.C., 1974—. Cons. March of Dimes, N.Y.C., 1974—, Hastings Inst., Garrison, N.Y., 1979—; mem. sickle cell adv. com. NIH. Contbr. articles to profl. jours. Recipient numerous grants. Fellow: Am. Coll. Med. Genetics (founding fellow, CME officer); mem.: N.Y. Acad. Medicine, Coun. Regional Genetics Network (pres. 1991—94), Am. Soc. Human Genetics. Office: Weill Med Coll Cornell U Presbyn Hosp 525 E 68th St Rm HT150 New York NY 10021-4870 E-mail: jgdavis@mail.med.cornell.edu.

DAVIS, JIM, congressman, lawyer; b. Oct. 11, 1957; m. Peggy Bessent; children: Peter, William. BA, Washington and Lee U., 1979; JD, U. Fla., 1982. Pvt. practice law, Tampa, Fla., 1982-88; ptnr. Bush, Ross, Gardner, Warren and Rudy, Tampa, Fla., 1988; mem. Fla. Ho. of Reps., 1988-97, majority leader; mem. U.S. Congress from 11th Fla. dist., 1997—; mem. budget com., house adminstrn. com., internat. rels. com.; mem. Ho. Energy and Commerce Com., 2003—; co-chair New Dem. Coalition. Democrat. Office: 409 Cannon Ho Office Bldg Washington DC 20515-0001*

DAVIS, JIMMY FRANK, assistant attorney general; b. Lubbock, Tex., June 14, 1945; s. Jack and Fern Lisemby D.; m. Joyce Zelma Hart, Nov. 6, 1976; children: Jayme Leigh, Julee Ellen. BS in Edn., Tex. Tech. U., 1968; JD, U. Tex., 1972. Bar: Tex. 1972, U.S. Supreme Ct. 1975, U.S. Dist. (no dist.) Tex. 1976, U.S. Ct. Appeals (5th cir.) 1976, U.S. Ct. Appeals (11cir.) 1981. Asst. criminal dist. atty. Lubbock County, 1973—77, adminstrv. asst., 1976-77; county and dist. atty. Castro County, Tex., 1977-92; asst. atty. gen. State of Tex., 1993—; mem. forms com. Atty. Gen. Office, 1999—2001. Mem. State Bar of Tex. (com. admissions dist. 16 1974-78, dist. 13 1983-92, govt. lawyers sect., coun. mem. 1991-92), Tex. Dist. and County Attys. Assn., Lubbock County Jr. Bar Assn. (pres. 1977), Tex. Tech. Ex Students Assn. (dist. rep. 1981-84, bd. dirs. 1985-90), Coll. of State Bar of Tex. (continuing legal edn. 1984-93), Kiwanis of Lubbock (pres. 1977), Kiwanis of Dimmitt (pres. 1981), Delta Theta Phi. Office: PO Box 2747 916 Main St Suite 900 Lubbock TX 79408

DAVIS, JO, naturopath, hypnotherapist; b. Pecos, Tex., Jan. 6, 1937; d. Johnnie Rex and Laura (Swann) D.; children: Cassandra Ann, Charles Rex. AA in Nursing, N.Mex. State U., 1992; BSc in Nutrition, Clayton Coll. Naturahealth, 1995, MSc in Nutrition, 1996; DD, Am. Inst. Theology, 1996; PhD in Nutrition, Clayton Coll. Naturahealth, 1997; PhD in Hypnotherapy, Am. Pacific U. Diplomate Am. Psychotherapy Assn.; cert. hypnotherapist; RN, Kans., Mo., Tex., N. Mex. Asst. coord. Carlsbad Hospice, Inc., N. Mex., 1992-98; prin., owner Natural Health Training and Resource Ctr., Carlsbad, N. Mex., 1994-98; dir. New Directions, Inc., Oak Grove, Mo., 1999—. Cons. Westbrooke Chiropractic, Lee's Summit, Mo., 1999—, Chiropractic Physicians, Independence, Mo., 1999—; instr. Continuing Edn. RNs, Tex.; cert. trainer Neuro-Linguistic Programming, Inst. for Time Line Therapy Tng. Contbr. articles to newspapers; newsletter editor, 1994-96. Mem. Internat. Good Neighbor Coun., Mex., U.S.A., 1994-96; pres. Wildlife Rescue, Inc., Carlsbad, 1992-96; ordained minister Reverend Universal Life Ch. Named N. Mex. Woman of Yr. State of N. Mex., 1992. Mem. Internat. Guild Hypnotists, Am. Assn. Univ. Women, Am. Bd. Hypnotherapy, Am. Holistic Health Assn., Nat. Audobon Soc., The Nature Conservancy, Order of Eastern Star. Avocations: raising horses, shaman studies, native am. culture. Home and Office: 8311 S Hillside School Rd Oak Grove MO 64075-8245 E-mail: dr.davis@micro.com.

DAVIS, JO, nurse, aromatherapist, writer, professional speaker, small business owner; b. St. Louis, Feb. 9, 1947; d. Jesse Marshall Davis and JoAnn (Charlsie Mae) (Skaggs) McCants; children: Jo Alice Gallagher, Andrew W. Lingle, Jr., James M. Lingle, Daniel V. Lingle, Elizabeth K. Nash. *Fourth-great grandfather, John Rankin Davis, born in Maryland, migrated to Virginia. In 1811 relocated to Missouri, married Sarah Jane Pearsall of Tennessee. Three Davis generations farmed near Lakewood, Missouri, on Davis Crossing road, named for the family. Father, Jesse Marshall Davis, invented the magnet on the can opener in the 1940's, during employment at Swing-A-Way Mfg. Co. Mother, Jo Ann (Skaggs-McCants) Davis, born in Steele, MO, was a writer. She relocated to St. Louis after graduation; worked at Firmin Desloge Hospital, (St. Louis University Hospital), as a nurse. Maternal grandparents, Mae Henderson Skaggs and John J. Skaggs, were from Tennessee.* AS in Sci. and Liberal Arts, Forest Park Coll., 1976—82; studied, State Fair Coll., 1980—81, U. Mo., Columbia, 1981, Kirkwood Coll., 1993; grad., Pacific Inst. Aromatherapy, 2000. Lic. practical nurse, Mo.; internat. cert. aromatherapist Calif., Mo., Ill., 2000. Nurse, Mo., 1982—; columnist Driving Force Mag./Pollard Pub., Ala., 1996—2001; nurse/aromatherapist Madison Med. Ctr., Fredericktown, Mo., 2000—; creator, tchr. safe driving U.S. Dept. Transp., U.S. Dept. Commerce, Bur. Census, Mo.; pvt. duty nurse Am. Nursing Resources, St. Louis; interior designer Transart Corp., Inc., St. Louis; owner, operator pest control co. Exterm Pest Control, St. Louis; over-the-road truck driver CRST, Cedar Rapids, Iowa, 1993—97, Henderson Trucking, Salem, Ill., Celadon Trucking, Indpls., USX-press, Chattanooga; census taker U.S. Dept. Commerce, Bur. Census; aromatherapeutic cons. Mo., 2000—. Aromatherapeutic cons., Mo., 2000—; internat. profl. speaker (motivational, writing, single parenting, repercussions of domestic abuse). Author: (poetry collection) Wings, 1998, Motivational Seven Steps to Assuming Responsibility, 1999; author: (as J. Marshall Davis) The Write to Kill, 1999; author: Tribal Dancer (Hon. Mention); editor: The Scene Newspaper; author: (booklet abused women victims of domestic violence) used in shelters and support groups, singer (actress) stage. Leader Girl Scouts Am., Overland, Mo., 1972—73, Boy Scouts Am., Sedalia, Mo., 1981—82. Named Most Valued Leader, Boy Scouts Am., Sedalia, 1982; recipient Presenter's award for serving as a role model, 18th Nat. Women's Tng. Program, New Horizons, St. Louis, 1985, Safety Essay Grand award, T.T.C., Inc., Salem, Ill., 1994, Pres. award for literary excellence, Iliad Press, 1997, 1st, 2nd, 3d Pl. writing contest, State Fair Coll., Cert. of Achievement, Profl. Speaking Tng. program, Wis., 1999. Mem.: Toastmasters, Soc. Children's Book Writers and Illustrators, Truck Writers Nat. Assn., Internat. Women's Writers Guild, Nat. Writers Union, Mo. Women of Today, Mo. Nurse's Assn., Nat. Geog. Soc., Phi Theta Kappa (Xi Epsilon). Methodist. Achievements include research in a natural cure for HIV as well as studying effects of essential oils on illness and the human body. Avocations: horseback riding, ice skating, free hand climbing, photography, violin. Home: Rt 1 Box 171A Arcadia MO 63621

DAVIS, JO ANN S. congresswoman; b. Rowan County, N.C., June 29, 1950; m. Charles E. Davis II; children: Charlie, Chris. Attended, Hamtpon Roads Business Coll. Mem. Va. State Legis., 1998-2001, mem. gen. laws com., mem. health welfare & insts., mem. sci. & tech. com., mem. claims com, mem. Chesapeake and its tributaries com.; mem. U.S. Congress from 1st Va. dist., 2001—; mem. armed svcs. com., govt. reform com., internat. rels. com. Republican. Mem. Assembly Of God Ch. Office: 1123 Longworth Ho Office Bldg Washington DC 20515-4601*

DAVIS, JOAN, English language educator; b. N.Y.C., June 7, 1948; d. John Patrick and Marian McInerney; m. William George Davis, July 24, 1971. BA, Coll. St. Rose, 1970; M, Binghamton U., 1976. English tchr. Owego Free Acad., NY, 1970—, chair English dept., 1991—99, English lang. arts coord. grades 6-12, 1999—2002; adj. instr. English Syracuse Univ., 1987—. Chair curriculum com. Mid. States Assn. Evaluation Vis. Team, 1993. Mem. Tioga County (N.Y.) Planning Bd., 1982-88. Mem. N.Y. State English Coun. (Tchr. Excellence award 1991, regional co-dir. 1997-2002), Nat. Coun. Tchrs. English, Delta Kappa Gamma Soc. Internat. Avocations: reading, gardening, skiing. Office: Owego Free Acad 1 Sheldon Guile Blvd Owego NY 13827-1095 E-mail: jdavis@oagw.stier.org.

DAVIS, JOEL, publisher; b. Chgo., Apr. 5, 1934; s. Bernard George and Sylvia (Friedman) D.; m. Carol Sue Barnett, Aug. 3, 1958; children: Charles Michael, Andrew Barnett, Jonathan William. BA, Brown U., 1957; student, Columbia U., summer 1953. With Davis Publs., Inc., N.Y.C., 1957-92, exec. v.p., 1959-68, pres., 1969-92, Sylvia Porter's Personal Fin. Mag. Co., 1982-89, Woodworker, Inc., Westport, Conn., 1993-95; ptnr. Davis/Herschbein & Assocs., L.L.C., Westport, 1996—; pres. Archtl. Designs, Inc., Westport, 1996—. Bd. dirs. Mut. N.Y., Money Series Fund Inc. Nat. chmn. univ. fund Brown U., 1965—68; bd. dirs. Brit. Am. Ednl. Found., 1977—80; mem. exec. com. gen. devel. coun. Brown U., 1962—77, Young Pres. Orgn., 1971—83; vice chmn. Brown Devel. Coun., 1968—69; regional dir. Assoc. Alumni Brown U., 1965—67, trustee, mem. corp., 1968—73; mem adv. and exec. com. Brown U., 1971—73, chmn. budget and fin. com., 1971—73, chmn. nat. alumni schs. program, 1982—85; trustee Westport Pub. Libr., 1992—2001; pres. Westport Libr. Adv. Coun., 2001—03; trustee Brookfield Craft Ctr., 1992—94; pres. Westport Pub. Libr., 1997—99. Mem. Am. Arbitration Assn. (mem. nat. panel), Mag. Pubs. Am. (bd. dirs. 1969-94, sec. 1979-81, vice chmn. mktg. com. 1969-73, mem. exec. com. 1971-88, mem. fin. com. 1974-88, chmn. membership com. 1975-91), Brown Club (mem. N.Y.C. bd. govs. 1963-69), Weston Field Club. Home: 15 Crooked Mile Rd Westport CT 06880-1124 Office: Archtl Designs Inc 274 Riverside Ave Westport CT 06880-4808 E-mail: prez@architecturaldesigns.com

DAVIS, JOHN ADAMS, JR., electrical engineer, roboticist, corporate research executive; b. Winston-Salem, N.C., May 26, 1944; s. John Adams and Jean Elizabeth (Bowles) D.; m. Sharon Kay Hammons, Dec. 19, 1965; 1 child, Heather Noelle. BSEE with honors, N.C. State U., 1971; MS in Engring., Fla. Tech. U., 1976; MBA, Loyola Coll., Balt., 1980. Design engr. Martin Marietta Corp., Orlando, Fla., 1971-76, sr. program mgr. Glen Burnie, Md., 1988-89; sr. engr., project mgr. Gould, Inc., Glen Burnie, Md., 1976-79, program mgr., 1984-88; mgr. data systems Bendix Corp., Columbia, Md., 1979-81; corp. ops. mgr. Vector Automation, Inc., Balt., 1981-82; dir., div. mgr. Ill. Inst. Tech. Rsch. Inst., Chgo., 1982-83; gen. mgr. Marine Systems div., dir. corp. bus. area Eastport Internat., Inc., Upper Marlboro, Md., 1989-93; pres. JADE Rsch. Corp., Severna Park, Md., 1993—. Pres., cons. Bustech Co., Severna Park, 1982-84; gen. mgr. Small Bus. Innovative Resource Ctr., 1987—; leading expert on U.S. Govt.'s Small Bus. Innovative Rsch. Program; speaker profl. confs. Contbr. articles to profl. jours. Bd. dirs. Cape Arthur Community Improvement Assn., Severna Park, 1981-82, 89-90; mem. Md. Gov.'s Com. to Elect Sch. Bd., 1982. Sgt. USAF, 1965-68, Vietnam. Recipient USAF Commendation medal. Mem. AIAA, IEEE (bd. dirs. 1978-79), Am. Def. Preparedness Assn., Assn. U.S. Army, Assn. Proposal Mgmt. Profls., Hazardous Materials Controls Rsch. Inst., Am. Nuclear Soc., Marine Tech. Soc. (remotely operated vehicle com.), Assn. Unmanned Vehicle Systems (bd. trustees 1993-96, Mem. of Yr. 1991, tech. co-chmn. nat. conf. and exhbn. 1991, 92, 93, v.p. Capitol chpt.), Tau Beta Pi, Eta Kappa Nu. Republican. Presbyterian. Avocations: snow and water skiing, boating, swimming, ch. choir, chess. Office: JADE Rsch Corp 5 Linda Ln Severna Park MD 21146-3234

DAVIS, JOHN CHARLES, lawyer; b. Kansas City, Mo., Mar. 4, 1943; s. Ralph B. Jr. and Helen M. (Schneider) D.; m. C. Jane Reusser, June 18, 1966; children: Tracy A., Matthew S. BA, U. Kans., 1965; JD, U. Mich., 1968. Bar: Mo. 1968, Kans. 1983. Ptnr. Stinson, Mag & Fizzell, P.C., Kansas City, 1968—. Chmn. Fed. Estate Tax Symposium, 1986-87. Chmn. Bacchus Found., Kansas City, 1974; bd. dirs. Crittenten, Kansas City, 1988-94, vice chmn., 1990-92; trustee Schutte Found., Kansas City, 1986—, UMKC, 1989—, treas., 1994-96, counsel, 1996—; trustee Village Presbyn. Ch. Found., chmn., 1991-93; elder Village Presbyn. Ch., 1994-97; bd. dirs. Gamma O Edn. Found., 1991—, Heart of Am. Counsel, Boy Scouts Am., 1995—, exec. com., 1996—; dir. John Cty. C.C. Found., 2000—. Fellow Am. Coll. Trust and Estate Counsel (by-laws com. 1987-96, chmn. 1996-99, 2002-, program com. 1993-96); mem. ABA, Mo. Bar Assn., Kans. Bar Assn., Estate Planning Soc. Kansas City (pres. 1990-91), Nelson-Atkins Mus. Soc. Fellows, Kansas City Club (v.p. 1989-90), Indian Hills Country Club (Mission Hills, Kans.), Rotary, Gamma Omicron (pres., bd. dirs. 1979-85). Presbyterian. Avocations: squash, Hopi art, marklin trains, travel, photography. Home: 6421 High Dr Shawnee Mission KS 66208-1935 Office: Stinson Morrison Hecker LLP Ste 2600 1201 Walnut St Kansas City MO 64106

DAVIS, JOHN EDWARD, music educator, musician; b. Omaha, Nebr., July 7, 1954; s. William Edward and Dorothy Ann Davis; m. Susan Lynn Aronovici, June 10, 1990; children: Evan William, Andrew Russell. MusB magna cum laude, San Francisco State U., 1990, MusM, 1991; D in Musical Arts, U. Ariz., 1997. Saxophonist San Francisco Saxophone Quartet, 1980—87, Nuc. Whales Saxophone Orch., Santa Cruz, Calif., 1987—91; grad. tchg. asst. San Francisco State U., 1990—91, U. Ariz., Tucson, 1991—94, grad. rsch. asst., 1994—95; asst. prof. of music Berry Coll., Mt. Berry, Ga., 1995—2001, assoc. prof. music, 2001—; flutist Rome (Ga.) Symphony Orch., 1995—. Arranger (musical arrangement) Brandenburg Concerto No. 3: For Flute Choir. J. S. Bach, 1998, String Quartet No. 4, K. 157: For Saxophone Quartet. W. A. Mozart, 1999, Three Madrigals: For Flute Quartet or Flute Choir Orlando di Lasso, 1999, Concerto Grosso, Op. 3, No. 8: For Flute Choir. Antonio Vivaldi, 1999, Quartet in C Minor, Op. 18, No. 4: For Saxophone Quartet L. van Beethoven, 1999, Quartet, No. 58, Op. 54, No. 2: For Saxophone Quartet Franz Josef Haydn, 1999, Divertimento, K. 138: For Flute Choir W. A. Mozart, 1999, Lady Radnor's Suite: For Flute Choir. C. Hubert H. Parry, 1999, Sheep May Safely Graze: For Saxophone Sextet, 2000, Intermezzo, Op. 118, No. 2: For Flute Choir Johannes Brahms, 2000, Souvenir de Porto Rico: For Flute Choir. Louis Moreau Gottschalk, 2000, Gloria, from Missa Tu Es Petrus: For Flute Choir. Palestrina, 2000, Trio in G Major, Op. 53, No. 1: For Flute Trio, 2000, Concerto Grosso, Op. 6, No. 3: For Flute Choir. G. F. Handel, 2000, What Wondrous Love: For Flute Choir, 2001, Finale, from Serenade, Op. 22: For Flute Choir Antonin Dvorak, 2001, Allegro, from Sinfonia Concertante: For Flute Choir. J. C. Bach, 2001, Tarentelle Styrienne: For Flute Choir, 2002, I Need Thee Every Hour. Robert Lowry, 2002; arranger: musical arrangement Enigma Variations: For Flute Choir, Edward Elgar, 2003; saxophonist (recording) Thar They Blow. Nuclear Whales Saxophone Orchestra. Whaleco Music, Whalin'. Nuclear Whales Saxophone Orchestra, Bach/Mozart. The San Francisco Saxophone Quartet, The San Francisco Saxophone Quartet; contbr. articles to profl. jours. Recipient ASCAP Std. award, ASCAP, 1999, 2000, 2001, 2002, 2003; Conducting Fellow, Conductors Inst. SC., 1998. Mem.: ASCAP, Music Educators Nat. Conf., Nat. Flute Assn., Nat. Assn. Coll. Wind and Percussion Instrs., Coll. Music Soc., Pi Kappa Lambda, Phi Mu Alpha. Presbyterian. Avocations: photography, aviation, bicycling, tennis. Office: Berry College 11 Berry College Mount Berry GA 30149 Home: 121 E Clinton Dr Rome GA 30165 Home Fax: 706-238-7847; Office Fax: 706-238-7847. E-mail: jdavis@berry.edu.

DAVIS, JOHN EUGENE, restaurant executive, beverage company executive, disc jockey; b. Buffalo, Aug. 27, 1948; s. Stanley and Dorothy (Svennson) D.; m. Carolyn Elizabeth Cummings, June 14, 1969; children: John, Jady. AA, Niagara County C.C., 1968; BA, Oneonta State U., 1970; MS, Russell Sage Coll., 1974. Tchr. Schenectady (N.Y.) City Sch. Dist., 1970-92; pres. PJ's Bar-B-Q, Inc., Saratoga Springs, N.Y., 1986—, Sarasoda, Inc., Saratoga Springs, 1998—. Active Rep. Chairman's Club, Saratoga Springs. Mem. Nat. Restaurant Assn., N.Y. State United Tchrs., Schenectady Fedn. Tchrs., Greater Saratoga C. of C., United Restaurant Hotel Tavern Assn. of N.Y. State, Nat. Rifle Assn., N.Y. State Restaurant Assn., Lions (Lion of the Yr. 1984-85). Methodist. Avocations: physical fitness, boating, fishing, football. Home: 1 Kaydeross Ave Saratoga Springs NY 12866-8736 Office: PJ's Bar-B-Q Inc RR 9 Saratoga Springs NY 12866-9809 E-mail: pjsbbq@aol.com, sarasodas@aol.com.

DAVIS, JOHN F., III, travel company executive; married; 3 children. BSBA, Tex. Christian U., Ft. Worth. Pres. Mid-South Drilling Co.; co-founder 800-FLOWERS; founder ATC Comm.; launched TravelWeb.com, 1994; pres., CEO Dallas-based Pegasus Solutions, Inc. Bd. dirs. Dallas Visitors, Convs. Bur., TRX, Inc. Campaign dir., treas. re-election campaign Senator John G. Tower, 1978. Named one of People of Yr., Travel Agt. Mag., 1991, one of bus. travel industry's 25 Most Influential Execs., 1994, 95, 97, 98, 99, Agt. of Change, Computerworld, 1995, one of 25 Most Influential People in Meetings Industry, Meeting News, 1997, Person of Yr. in Interactive Travel, Interactive Travel Report, 1998; named to 1999 list of top 75 execs. in the hotel industry Lodging mag., Travel Industry Hall of Fame, Bus. Travel News, 1999. Office: care Pegasus Sys Inc 3811 Turtle Creek Blvd Ste 100 Dallas TX 75219-4461

DAVIS, JOHN HERSCHEL, surgeon, educator, retired; b. Coraopolis, Pa., May 11, 1924; s. John Herschel and Fern (Pew) D.; m. Peggy Lou Seyler, Sept. 7, 1946; children: Karen LaRue, Wendy Sue, Halle Rive. Student, Allegheny Coll., 1942-43; MD, Western Res. U., 1948. Diplomate: Am. Bd. Surgery. Intern Univ. Hosps., Cleve., 1948-49, resident, 1955-56; asst. prof. surgery Western Res. U., Cleve., 1956-59, assoc. prof. surgery, 1959-64, prof., 1964-69; dir. surgery Cleve. Met. Hosp., 1966-69; prof. dept. surgery U. Vt., Burlington, 1969—; prof. emeritus retired, 1999. Dir. Am. Bd. Surgery, Phila., Am. Bd. Emergency Medicine, East Lansing, Mich., Am. Trauma Soc., Chgo., 1978— ; chmn. surgery sect. NIH, Washington, 1982— Editor: Current Concepts of Surgery, 1965, Jour. of Trauma, 1974, Clinical Surgery, 1987, Essentials of Clinical Surgery, 1991; Am. editor: Brit. Jour. Injury; editorial bd.: Medfact; corr. editor: Journal de Traumatologie, Jour. Injury. Mem. Bar. Rev. Com. Vt. Supreme Ct., 1982. Served to capt. U.S. Army, 1950-53. Recipient William

Peck Rsch. award Western Res. U., 1961; recipient Surgeon of Year award Nat. Safety Coun., N.Y.C., 1979 Fellow ACS (Scudder Oration award 1979, Disting. Svc. award 1991); mem. AAAS, Am. Assn. for History of Medicine, Am. Surg. Assn., Am. Assn. Surgery Trauma, Am. Burn Assn., Am. Fedn. Clin. Rsch., Am. Heart Assn., Am. Trauma Soc., Central Soc. Clin. Rsch., Central Surg. Soc., Chittenden County Med. Soc., Collegium Internationale Chirurgiae Digestivae, Digestive Disease Found., Eastern Surg. Soc., Halsted Soc., Internat. Soc. for Burn Injuries, Italian Surg. Rsch. Soc., Nat. Rsch. Coun. of Nat. Acad. Scis., New Eng. Soc. for Vascular Surgery, New Eng. Surg. Soc. (Nathan Smith award 1997), N.Y. Acad. Scis., Soc. Internationale de Chirurgie, Soc. Exptl. Biology and Medicine, Soc. Med. Cons. to Armed Forces, Soc. Surgery Alimentary Tract, Soc. Surg. Chairmen, Soc. for Vascular Surgery, Surg. Biology Club II, Vt. State Med. Soc. (Disting. Svc. award 1990), Allen O. Whipple Med. Soc., Sigma Xi, Alpha Omega Alpha Clubs: Ethan Allen (Burlington). Republican. Home: 21 Ridgewood Dr Burlington VT 05401-2625

DAVIS, JOHN JAMES, religion educator; b. Phila., Oct. 13, 1936; s. John James and Cathryn Ann (Nichols) D.; m. Carolyn Ann. BA, Trinity Coll., Dunedin, Fla., 1959, DD (hon.), 1968; MDiv, Grace Coll. & Grace Theol. Sem., Winona Lake, Ind., 1962, ThM, 1964, ThD, 1967. Instr. Grace Coll. & Grace Theol. Sem., 1963-65, prof. of Old Testament, 1965—, exec. v.p., 1976-82, pres., 1986-93; exec. dean Near East Sch. Archaeology, Jerusalem, 1970-71. Area supr. Tekoa Archeol. Expdn., Jordan, 1968, 70, Raddana Expdn., Jordan, 1974, Heshbon Expdn., Jordan, 1976, Abila Archeol. Expdn., Jordan, 1982, 84, Khirbet el-Maqatir Expdn., Israel, 2000. Author: Paradise to Prison, 1975 (Book of Yr.), The Perfect Shepherd, 1979 (Book of Yr.), 16 other books. Chmn., bd. dirs. Kosciusko Comty. Hosp., 1994-2000. Recipient Gold award United Way, 1980, Conservation award Barbee Property Owners Assn., 1983; named Outdoor Writer of Yr., Ind. Dept. Natural Resources, 1986, to the Koscivsko County Rep. Hall of Fame, 1992. Mem. Am. Schs. of Oriental Research, Near East Archeol. Soc., Outdoor Writers Assn., Hoosier Outdoor Writers Assn. (pres. 1984-86). Avocations: fishing, hunting, photography. Home: PO Box 557 Winona Lake IN 46590-0557 Office: Grace Theol Sem 200 Seminary Dr Winona Lake IN 46590-1224

DAVIS, JOHN MACDOUGALL, lawyer; b. Seattle, Feb. 20, 1914; s. David Lyle and Georgina (MacDougall) D.; m. Ruth Anne van Arsdale, July 1, 1939; children: Jean, John, Bruce, Ann, Margaret, Elizabeth. BA, U. Wash., 1936, LLB, JD, 1940. Bar: Wash. 1940. Assoc. Poe, Falknor, Emory & Howe, Seattle, 1940-45; pvt. practice Seattle, 1945-46; ptnr. Davis & Riese, Seattle, 1946-48, Emory, Howe, Davis & Riese, Seattle, 1948-50, Howe, Davis & Riese, Seattle, 1951-53, Howe, Davis, Riese & Aiken, Seattle, 1953-58, Howe, Davis, Riese & Jones, Seattle, 1958-68, Davis, Wright, Todd, Riese & Jones, Seattle, 1969-85; of counsel Davis, Wright & Jones, Seattle, 1985-89, Davis Wright Tremaine, Seattle, 1990—. Lectr. U. Wash. Law Sch., 1947-52. Bd. dirs. Virginia Mason Hosp., Seattle, 1952-79, pres., 1970-72; bd. dirs. Pacific Sci. Ctr., 1971-90, dir. emeritus, 1991—, past pres., past chmn.; trustee Whitman Coll., 1971-86, chmn., 1983-86; bd. dirs. Blue Cross Wash. and Alaska, 1982-89, Diabetic Trust Fund, 1954—, Wash. Student Loan Guaranty Assn., 1978-83; mem. adv. bd. Chief Seattle council Boy Scouts Am.; mem. Mercer Island Sch. Bd., 1956-66. Served with USNG, 1931-34. Recipient Disting. Eagle Scout award, 1982 Mem. ABA, Wash. State Bar Assn. (merit award 1965), Seattle-King County Bar Assn. (pres. 1960-61), Order of Coif, Rainier Club (Seattle), The Mountaineers Club, Phi Delta Phi, Alpha Delta Phi. Clubs: Rainier (Seattle). Presbyterian. Avocation: mountain climbing. Home: 9104 Fortuna Dr #3305 Mercer Island WA 98040-3166 Office: Davis Wright Tremaine 2600 Century Sq 1501 4th Ave Ste 2600 Seattle WA 98101-1688

DAVIS, JOHN ROWLAND, university administrator; b. Mpls., Dec. 19, 1927; s. Roland Owen and Dorothy (Norman) D.; m. Lois Marie Falk, Sept. 4, 1947; children— Joel C., Jacque L., Michele M., Robin E. BS, U. Minn., 1949, MS, 1951; postgrad., Purdue U., 1955-57; PhD, Mich. State U., 1959. Hydraulic engr. U.S. Geol. Survey, Lincoln, Nebr., 1950-51; instr. Mich. State U., 1951-55; asst. prof. Purdue U., 1955-57; lectr. U. Calif., Davis, 1957-62; hydraulic engr. Stanford Rsch. Inst., South Pasadena, Calif., 1962-64; prof. U. Nebr., Lincoln, 1964-65, dean coll. engring. and architecture, 1965-71, faculty rep. intercollegiate athletics; prof., head dept. agrl. engring. Oreg. State U., Corvallis, 1971-75, instl. athletic rep., 1972-87, dir. Agrl. Expt. Sta., assoc. dean Sch. Agr., 1975-85, dir. spl. programs Office of Academic Affairs, assoc. dir. athletics, 1987-89, prof. emeritus, assoc. dir. athletics, 1989—. Governing bd. Water Resources Research Inst., 1975-85; dir. Western Rural Devel. Center, 1975-85, Agrl. Research Found., Jackman Inst.; cons. Stanford Research Inst., Dept. Agr., Consortium for Internat. Devel.; dir. Engrs. Council Profl. Devel., 1966-72; pres. Pacific-10 Conf., 1978-79. Contbr. articles to profl. jours. Mem. budget commn. City of Corvallis, 2003—. With USNR, 1945-46. Fellow Am. Soc. Agrl. Engrs. (dir. 1971-73, Agrl. Engr. Yr. award Pacific N.W. region 1974), NCAA (v.p. 1979-83, sec.-treas. 1983-85, pres. 1985-87), Heartland Humane Soc. (pres. bd. dirs. 2002). Home: 2940 NW Aspen St Corvallis OR 97330-3307 Office: Oreg State U Gill Coliseum Corvallis OR 97331 E-mail: john.r.davis@att.net.

DAVIS, JOHN WARREN, real estate broker; b. York, Pa., Feb. 14, 1946; s. Frank Asbury Jr. and Lillian Margaret (Billings) D. BA in Polit. Sci., Drake U., 1968; AA in Real Estate, San Diego City Coll., 1976; MS in Acquisition and Contract Mgmt., West Coast U., 1987; postgrad., Walden U., 1992—. Real estate sales staff, 1972-79; clk. GS 3 Naval Ocean Sys. Ctr., 1979-80; contract intern, contract adminstr. Office of Naval Rsch., 1980-84; contract specialist, warranted ordering officer Gen. Svc. 1102-11 Naval Weapons Sta., 1984-86; contract specialist Gen Svc. 1102-12 Navy Space Sys. Activity, 1986-88; procurement analyst Gen Svc. 102-12 COMNAVAIRPAC, 1988-98; def. contract mgr. Def. Contract Mgmt. Command, 1998—; sr. v.p. Azan Corp. Group, San Diego. Del. San Diego State U. to the Nat. Acad. Conf. for Contract Mgmt. Educators, 1991, 92, 93; profl. cons. Computer Applications, Inc., 1992; mem. tech. program com., chairperson for electronic data interchange Soc. of Logistics Engrs., 1995; mem. Golden Hill planning com. City of San Diego; adj. instr. San Diego State U., chmn. curriculum rev. com. for acquisitiion. Author, Paperless Contracting, The EDI Revolution, 1995, contbr. articles to profl. publs. With U.S. Army, Vietnam, 1968-72. Fellow Nat. Contract Mgmt. Assn. (cert. profl. contract mgr.); mem. ABA (mem. sub-com. pub. law sector, sub-com. on intellectual property), SAR (nat., Calif. and San Diego chpts.), Am. Arbitration Assn. (nat. panel mem.), Soc. Govt. Meeting Planners (v.p. San Diego chpt.), Soc. Logistics Engrs., San Diego Athletic Club, San Diego Writers and Editors Guild, Author's Guild (past pres.); rsch. bd. adv. Am. Bio. Inst. Episcopalian. Avocations: swimming, traveling. Home: PO Box 620657 San Diego CA 92162-0657 Office: Azan Corp Group 900 F St San Diego CA 92101

DAVIS, JOHN WILLIAM, government science and engineering executive; BSME, U. Tex., 1957; MSME, So. Meth. U., 1962; PhD in Aerospace Engring., Okla. State U., 1972. Aerodynamics design engr., sr. and lead wind tunnel engr. Chance Vought Corp., Grand Prairie, Tex., 1957-61; chief gas dynamics sect. Marshall Space Flight Ctr. NASA, Huntsville, Ala., 1961-75, exptl. investigations br. chief Ames Rsch. Ctr., 1975-80; dir. Propulsion Wind Tunnel Facility Calspan Corp./Arnold Engring. Devel. Ctr. Ops., Arnold AFB, Tenn., 1980-87, v.p., gen. mgr., 1987-1994; vice pres., gen. mgr. Micro Craft Tech./Arnold Engring. Devel. Ctr.Ops., Arnold AFB, Tenn., 1994, chief engr. micro crafttech., 1994-95, AEDC chief scientist, 1995—. Exec. dir. U. Tenn./Calspan Ctr. Aerospace Rsch.; bd. dirs. U. Tenn./Calspan Ctr. Space Transp. and Applied Rsch. Contbr. 38 articles to profl. jours. Bd. dirs. Tenn. Valley Aerospace Region, Hands-On Sci. Ctr., trustee, chmn. fin. com. Recipient Ground Testing award Am. Inst. of Aeronautics and Astronautics, 1994 Fellow AIAA (Ground Testing award 1994, mem. ground testing and simulation tech. com., mem. honors and awards subcom., 1992, liaison officer to thermophysics tech. com.), Arnold Engring. Devel. Ctr., Internat. Test and Evaluation Assn., Air Force Assn., Nat. Mgmt. Assn., Supersonic Tunnel Assn. (past pres., sec., mem.-at-large, exec. bd. dirs.). Office: Arnold Engring Devel Ctr-CN 1099 Avenue C Ste 106 Arnold AFB TN 37389-9010

DAVIS, JON L. logistics consultant; b. Louisiana, Mo., Mar. 1, 1934; s. Lloyd Israel Davis and Mary Isabelle (Cory) Stone; m. Rita Marie Pitts, July 21, 1957; children: Michael Louis, Catherine Faith, Laurie Marie. BSBA magna cum laude, U. Albuquerque, 1977. Cert. profl. logistician. Enlisted USAF, 1956, advanced through grades to col., 1979, ret., 1985; col., dep. comdr. maintenance 479th Tactical Tng. Wing, Holloman AFB, N.Mex., 1979-81, 67 Tactical Reconaissance Wing, Bergstrom AFB, Tex., 1981-83; col., dir. logistics USAF Operational Test & Evaluation Ctr., Kirtland AFB, N.Mex., 1983-85; asst. v.p. Los Alamos Tech. Assocs., Albuquerque, 1985-2000; logistics cons. Albuquerque, 2000—. Author Air Force manuals. Mem. Austin-Bergstrom Community Coun., Austin, Tex., 1981-83, Alamogordo (N.Mex.) Mil. Adv. Com., 1980-81. Decorated Legion of Merit, D.F.C., 12 Air medals. Mem. Intl. Soc. of Logistics (sr. mem., chpt. chmn. 1991), Internat. Test & Evaluation Assn., USAF Logistics Officers Assn., Air Force Assn. (life mem.), Red River Valley Assn. Republican. Home and Office: 9706 Camino Del Sol NE Albuquerque NM 87111-1510 E-mail: jdavis502@comcast.net.

DAVIS, JONNI K. secondary school educator, writer; b. Crane, Tex., May 22, 1956; d. Norman E. and Emily Bradford; m. George Jefferson Davis; 1 child, Patrick. BA, Baylor U., 1978. Cert. tchr.secondary edn.-English/History. Tchr. English and drama Teague (Tex.) H.S., 1979—81; tchr. English James Martin H.S., Arlington, Tex., 1985—87; tchr. Brit. lit./English and leadership Arlington H.S., 1987—. Co-facilitator, site-based decision making com. Arlington H.S., 1994—97, varsity cheerleader sponsor, 1994—95, dir. sr. class variety show, 1994—, student leadership advisor, 1999—, class of 2005 lead sponsor, 2001—. Author: ParenTime Educational Video Series, Harris Hospital-Methodist, 1983; dir.: (educational videos) ParenTime I, 1983, ParenTime II - Feeding Your Baby, 1983 (Bronze Quill award for excellence in comm. IABC Ft. Worth, 1983). Mem.: Okla. Writers' Fedn., Inc. (contest category chair 2001), United Educators' Assn., Baylor Alumni Assn. (life). Methodist. Avocation: writing.

DAVIS, JOSEPH LLOYD, educational administrator, consultant; b. Crawfordsville, Iowa, May 4, 1927; s. Whitfield and Jane (Lloyd) D.; m. Margaret Florence Cooper, Dec. 28, 1949; children: Stephen Joseph, Thomas Whitfield, Jane Ellen. BSc, Ohio State U., 1949, MA, 1955, PhD, 1967. Reporter Ohio State Jour., 1943-49, 52-53; tchr. Morey Jr. H.S., Denver, 1949-52, Central H.S., Columbus, Ohio, 1953-54; asst. dir. adminstrv. rsch. Columbus Public Schs., 1954-56, dir. publs. and public info., 1956-60, exec. asst. to supt., 1960-64, asst. supt. spl. svcs., 1964-77, supt. of schs., 1977-82; exec. dir. Ohio Coun. Vocat. Edn., 1985-96. Past pres. Columbus Rotary; adj. prof. Ohio State U., 1983—; founder, dir. emeritus Ohio State U. Nat. Acad. for Supt.; cons. and author in field. Mem., bd. trustees Interprofl. Commn. Ohio, 1999—, Kids Voting/Ctrl. Ohio Region, 1999—; mem., past pres. Friends Bd. WOSU AM, FM and TV, Ohio State U., Columbus, 1986—98, 2000—. With USN, 1945—46, with USN, 1950—51. Recipient award for civic leadership Columbus Area C. of C., 1980, Liberty Bell award Columbus Bar Assn., 1980; named to Pub. Schs. Hall of Fame, Columbus, Ohio, 1993. Mem. Am. Assn. Sch. Adminstrs. (disting. svc. award 1989). Nat. Sch. Pub. Rels. Assn. (pres.'s award 1980), Assn. for Career and Tech. Edn., Ohio Assn. for Career and Tech. Edn., Buckeye Assn. Sch. Adminstrs., Nat. Soc. Study Edn., Horace Mann League, Ohio State U. Alumni Assn. (leadership consortium 2003—), Rotary (Rotarian of Yr. award 1994), Torch Club Columbus, Phi Delta Kappa, Epsilon Pi Tau (laureate 1994, Disting. Svc. award 2000), Kappa Delta Pi, Omicron Tau Theta. Presbyterian. E-mail: jdavis59@columbus.rr.com.

DAVIS, JOSHUA MALCOLM, lawyer, educator; b. Worcester, Mass., May 11, 1965; s. William Merritt and Jessica Ann (Hoffmann) Davis; m. Susan Marysol Flink, Aug. 11, 1991; children: Emerson Jacob, Malcolm Christopher. BA, Swarthmore Coll., 1987; JD, U. Chgo., 1991. Bar: Mass. 1992; U.S. Ct. Appeals (10th cir.), 1992; U.S. Dist. Ct. (Mass.), 1993; U.S. Ct Appeals (1st cir.), 1993; U.S. Supreme Ct., 1995; U.S. Ct. Appeals (2d cir.), 1997. English tchr. St. Paul's Sch., Concord, NH, 1987—88; law clerk Hon. Stephanie K. Seymour U.S. Ct. Appeals (10th cir.), Tulsa, 1991—92; assoc. Hill & Barlow, Boston, 1992—99, mem., 1999—2002, chair employment practice group, 2000—02; dir. Goulston & Storrs, Boston, 2002—. Tchg. asst. torts Harvard Law Sch., Cambridge, Mass., 1997, part-time lectr. law, Northeastern U. Sch. Law, 1998—. Mem. ABA, Mass. Bar Assn., Boston Bar Assn., Am. Employment Law Coun., Order of Coif. Democrat. Avocations: golf, reading. Office: Goulston & Storrs 400 Atlantic Ave Boston MA 02110-2607 E-mail: jdavis@goulstonstorrs.com.

DAVIS, JOY LEE, English language educator; b. N.Y.C., Apr. 3, 1931; d. William Henry and Genevieve (Rhein) Belknap; m. Peter John King, Aug. 26, 1955 (div. Feb. 1985); children: William Belknap King, Russell Stuart King; m. John Bradford Davis, Jr., July 5, 1986. AB, Wellesley Coll., 1952, AM, 1953; PhD, Rutgers U., 1968; postgrad., Oxford (Eng.) U., 1978. Tchr. English Dana Hall Sch. for Girls, Wellesley, Mass., 1953-54; instr. English U. Mo., Columbia, 1954-55, Boston U., 1955-56; tchr. English Brookline (Mass.) High Sch., Spartanburg (S.C.) High Sch., 1956-60; prof. English Ohio Wesleyan U., Delaware, 1966-71, Hamline U., St. Paul, 1972-74, U. Minn., Mpls., 1974-77, Coll. St. Thomas, St. Paul, 1977-88; lectr., dir. Joy Davis Seminars, St. Paul, 1988—. Author: Everything But: An Education Memoir, 1999, The Hero in Literature: Prometheus to Prufrock, 2003; pub. poetry in New World Writing and Crisp Pine Anthology; lit. criticism in Midwest Quar., 1993, Jour. Grad. Liberal Studies, 1996. Wellesley Coll. scholar, 1952. Mem. AAUW (bd. dirs., v.p. ways & means, 2003—, Svc. awrd St. Paul br. 1983), Midwest MLA, Mpls. Inst. Fine Arts, Minn. Club (bd. dirs. 1982-88), New Century Club (bd. dirs., spl. subjects chmn.) Schubert Club (bd. dirs., chmn. mus. com.), Wellesley Coll. Club (regional campaign com.), Delta Kappa Gamma. Republican. Presbyterian. Avocations: reading, travel, creative cuisine. Home and Office: 4312 Pond View Dr Saint Paul MN 55110-4155

DAVIS, JUDY, actress; b. Perth, Australia, Apr. 23, 1955; m. Colin Friels, 1984; children: Jack, Charlotte. Student, Nat. Inst. Dramatic Art, Sydney, Australia. Appearances include: (film) High Rolling, 1976, My Brilliant Career, 1979 (Best Actress Sammy award Australian Film and TV Awards 1979, Best Actress award Brit. Acad. Film and TV Arts 1981, Best Newcomer Brit. Acad. Film and TV Arts 1981), Hoodwink, 1981 (Best Supporting Actress Sammy award Australian Film and TV Awards 1981), Winter of Our Dreams, 1981 (Best Actress Sammy award Australia Film and TV Awards 1981), Heatwave, 1982, The Final Option, 1983, A Passage to India, 1984 (Acad. award nominee for best actress 1984), Kangaroo, 1986, High Tide, 1987, Georgia, 1988, Alice, 1990, Impromptu, 1991, Barton Fink, 1991, Naked Lunch, 1991 (Best Supporting Actress award N.Y. Critics Cir. 1991), Where Angels Fear to Tread, 1991, Husbands and Wives, 1992 (Acad. award nominee for best supporting actress 1992), The Ref, 1994, The New Age, 1994, Children of the Revolution, 1996, Absolute Power, 1996, Blood and Wine, 1996, Deconstructing Harry, 1996, Celebrity, 1997, The Echo of Thunder, 1998, Gaudi Afternoon, 2000, The Man Who Sued God, 2001; (TV movies) A Woman Called Golda, 1982 (Emmy award nominee 1982), The Merry Wives of Windsor, 1982, Rocket to the Moon, 1986, One Against the Wind, 1991, Serving in Silence: The Margarethe Cammermeyer Story, 1995 (Emmy award), Swimming Upstream, 2001;(telemovie) Coast to Coast, 2002; (TV miniseries) Water Under the Bridge, 1982; (stage) Lulu (Frank Wedekind), Piaf (Pam Gem), Insignificance (Terry Johnson), 1982, Echo of Thunder (Emmy nomination), 1997, (TV prodn.) Dash & Lily, 1997 (Emmy nomination), A Cooler Climate, 1998, Me and My Shadows, 2000 (Golden Globe award, Am. Screen Actors award, Golden Satellite award, Broadcast Critics Choice award, Am. Film Inst. award, Emmy award). Office: care Shanahan Mgmt PO Box1509 Darlinghurst NSW 1300 Australia

DAVIS, JULIA MCBROOM, college dean, speech pathology and audiology educator; b. Alexandria, La., Sept. 29, 1930; d. Guy Clarence and Addie (McElroy) McBroom; m. Cecil Ponder Davis, Aug. 25, 1951 (div. 1981); children: Mark Holden, Paul Houston, Anne Hamilton; m. David G. Reynolds, Aug. 26, 1987. BA, Northwestern State U., Natchitoches, La., 1951; MS, U. So. Miss., 1965, PhD, 1966. Asst. prof. U. So. Miss., Hattiesburg, 1966-69, assoc., 1969-71; assoc. prof. Southwestern State U., Hammond, 1971; faculty U. Iowa, Iowa City, 1971-87, prof., chmn. dept. speech pathology and audiology, 1980-85, assoc. dean Coll. Liberal Arts, 1985-87, dir. Speech and Hearing Ctr., 1979-80; dean Coll. Social and Behavioral Scis. U. South Fla., Tampa, 1987-90, assoc. provost, 1990-91; dean Coll. Liberal Arts, U. Minn., Mpls., 1991-96, prof., 1991-97. Author (with Edward J. Hardick) : Rehabilitative Audiology for Children and Adults, 1981; editor: Our Forgotten Children, 3d edit., 2001; assoc. editor: Jour. Speech Hearing Research, 1975—77, Jour. Speech Hearing Disorders, 1982—83. Pres., bd. of trustees Minn. Foun. for Better Hearing & Speech; bd. trustees Mpls. Found., Ballet Arts of Minn., Johnson County Crisis Ctr., Am. Speech-Lang.-Hearing Assn. Found.; bd. dirs. Crisis Intervention Ctr. Fellow Am. Speech-Lang.-Hearing Assn. (cert. in clin. competence in audiology, chmn. program com. 1980-81, found. trustee 2001-), Iowa Speech and Hearing Assn. (v.p.-liaison 1972-73, honors 1985); mem. Acad. Rehabilitative Audiology (pres. 1979-80), Iowa Conf. for Hearing Impaired (pres. 1975-76), Sigma Xi. Democrat. Methodist. Home: 55 Rita Lyn Ct Iowa City IA 52245-3504

DAVIS, JULIAN MASON, JR., lawyer; b. Birmingham, Ala., July 30, 1935; s. Julian Mason Sr. and Madeline (Harris) D.; m. June Carolyn Fox, Aug. 11, 1957; children: Karen Madeline, Julian Mason III. BA, Talladega (Ala.) Coll., 1956; JD, SUNY, Buffalo, 1959. Bar: Ala. 1960, U.S. Dist. Ct. (no. dist.) Ala. 1961, U.S. Ct. Appeals (5th crct.) 1961, U.S. Tax Ct. 1979, U.S. Ct. Appeals (11th crct.) 1981, U.S. Dist. Ct. (mid. dist.) Ala. 1989, U.S. Supreme Ct. 1993. With Sirote & Permutt P.C., Birmingham. Bd. dirs. Protective Indsl. Ins. Co., Birmingham, chmn. bd., 1988—; bd. dirs. Energen Corp., Birmingham. Mem. ABA, Nat. Bar Assn., Ala. Bar Assn. (bar commr. 1987-96), Birmingham Bar Assn. (sec., treas. 1978-79, pres. 1984-85). Democrat. Avocations: golf, reading. Office: Sirote & Permutt PC 2311 Highland Ave S Birmingham AL 35205-2972 E-mail: mdavis@sirote.com.

DAVIS, KAREN, fund executive; b. Blackwell, Okla., Nov. 14, 1942; d. Walter Dwight and Thelma Louise (Kohler) Padgett; 1 child, Kelly Denise Collins. BA, Rice U., 1965, PhD, 1969. Asst. prof. econs. Rice U., 1969-70; econ. policy fellow Social Security Adminstrn. Brookings Instn., Washington, 1970-71, rsch. assoc., 1971-74, sr. fellow, 1974-77; dep. asst. sec. for planning and evaluation, health HEW, Washington, 1977-80; adminstr. health resources adminstrn. USPHS, Washington, 1980-81; prof. Johns Hopkins U., Balt., 1981-92; chmn., 1983-92; exec. v.p. Commonwealth Fund, N.Y.C., 1992-94, pres., 1995—. Mem. Physican Payment Rev. Commn., 1986-94; dir. Commonwealth Fund Commn. on Elderly People Living Alone, 1985-91; vis. lectr. Harvard U., 1974-75; mem. nat. adv. com. Agy. for Health Care Rsch. and Quality, 1999—. Author: National Health Insurance: Benefits, Costs and Consequences, 1975, Health and the War on Poverty, 1978, Medicare Policy: New Directions for Health and Long-Term Care, 1986, Health Care Cost Containment, 1990. Mem. Inst. Medicine, Phi Beta Kappa. Democrat. Methodist. Home: 200 E 62 St New York NY 10021 Office: The Commonwealth Fund The Harkness House 1 E 75th St New York NY 10021-2692 E-mail: kd@cmwf.org.

DAVIS, KAREN SUE, hospital nursing supervisor; b. Owensboro, Ky., June 5, 1950; d. Robert J. and Mona F. (Urlaub) D. Diploma, Deaconess Sch. Nursing, 1971. RN, Ky.; cert. in pediatric nursing; cert. PALS. Charge nurse pediatrics Daviess County Hosp., 1971-89; clin. supr. pediatrics 11-7 shift Owensboro Mercy Health Sys. Parish Campus, 1989—. Republican. Lutheran. Avocations: needlework, reading, traveling, cooking, decorating. Home: 686 N Fairview Ct Rockport IN 47635

DAVIS, KATHERINE HELENE, vocalist, educator; b. Chgo., Feb. 25, 1953; d. Ethel Campbell and Wesley Davis; m. Caleb Dube; 5 children. Singer, vocalist various locations, Chgo., 1982—. Actor Kuumba Theater, Chgo., 1982—88. Singer: These Men Look Good to Me, Excuse Me, 1984. Grantee Neighborhood Arts Program grant, Dept. of Cultural Affairs, City of Chgo., 2000—01. Mem.: Assn. Profl. Orch. Leaders. Avocation: travel. Home: 1609 W Estes #3W Chicago IL 60626 Home Fax: 773-761-6356. Personal E-mail: Matessoul@aol.com.

DAVIS, KATHRYN WASSERMAN, foundation executive, writer, lecturer; b. Phila., Feb. 25, 1907; d. Joseph and Edith (Stix) Wasserman; m. Shelby Cullom Davis, Jan. 4, 1932; children: Shelby M. Cullom, Diana Davis Spencer, Priscella Alden (dec.). BA, Wellesley Coll., 1928; MA, Columbia U., 1931; D of Polit. Sci., U. Geneva, 1934; law degree (hon.), Columbia U., 1997. Researcher Coun. on Fgn. Rels., N.Y.C., 1934-36, State of Pa., Phila., 1936-37; writer and lectr. on fgn. affairs N.Y., 1937—; ptnr. Shelby Cullom Davis & Co., N.Y.C., 1985—; pres. The Shelby Cullom Davis Found., N.Y.C., 1985—. Lectr. on fgn. affairs. Author: Soviets at Geneva, 1934. Trustee Wellesley Coll., 1983— ; v.p. Women's Nat. Rep. Club, 1976—, chmn. internat. affairs com.; bd. govs. Harvard U., mem. vis. com. Russian studies, 1986—; past pres. LWV. Recipient life achievement award Women's Nat. Rep. Club, 1990, gold medal for disting. svc. to humanity Nat. Inst. Social Scis., 1990, Claire Booth Luce medal Heritage Found., 1991, Plymouth Com. award Mayflower Soc., 1992, Life Accomplishment award Internat. House, 1995. Mem. Cosmopolitan Club (N.Y.C., com. fgn. visitors), Sleepy Hollow Club (Scarborough N.Y.), N.Y. Harbor Club, Seal Harbor Club (Maine), Jupiter Island Club (Hobe Sound, Fla.), The Everglades Club, Inc (Palm Beach, Fla.), Knickerbocker Club, Univ. Club. Avocations: skiing, tennis, swimming, travel. Home: PO Box 689 Hobe Sound FL 33475-0689 Office: Shelby Cullom Davis & Co LP 609 5th Ave New York NY 10017-1021

DAVIS, KEIGH LEIGH, aerospace engineer; b. Mitchell, S.D., Oct. 6, 1954; d. Clarence Ralph and Katherine Lee Schilling; m. Glenn Nickerson Davis, Nov. 24, 1992; 1 child, Tasha Clare Marie. BS in Aerospace Engring. & Mechanics, U. Minn., 1976; MS in Aerospace Engring., U. Dayton, 1983. Stability and control project engr. Flight Stability and Control Br., USAF, Wright Patterson AFB, Ohio, 1976-85, E-3/Joint Stars Program Office, Wright Patterson AFB, 1985-86; lead stability, control & flying qualities project engr. Advanced Tactical Fighter Program, Wright Patterson AFB, 1986-88, Advanced Tactical Fighter Sys. Program Office, Wright Patterson AFB, 1988-90; stability and control project engr. Joint Tactical Autonomous Weapon Sys. Program Office, Wright Patterson AFB, 1990-91; lead br. engr. Flight Stability and Control Br., Wright Patterson AFB, 1991-94; stability and control tech. specialist Flight Mechanics Br., Wright Patterson AFB, 1993—. Chmn. MIL-STD-1797 pilot-in-the-loop oscillation update team ASC/ENFT, Wright Patterson AFB, 1992-95, responsible engr. for flying qualities of piloted aircraft mil. std., 1992—, mil. handbook, 1997—; co-chmn. USAF flying qualities devel. process team, 1995—. Mem. AIAA (sr.), Nat. Mgmt. Assn., Soc. Women Engrs. (life), Order of Ea. Star (pres.).

DAVIS, KEITH EUGENE, psychologist, educator, consultant; b. Clifton, N.C., May 15, 1936; s. Ted Eugene and Mary Flossie (Rol) D.; m. Dorothy Ann Reeves, Feb. 23, 1968; 1 child, Kristin Lee; children from previous marriage: Rachel, Rebecca, Jessica. BA, Duke U., 1958, PhD, 1963. Instr. psychology Princeton U., 1961-62; asst. prof. U. Colo., Boulder, 1962-67, assoc. prof., 1967-70; prof., chmn. dept. psychology Livington Coll., Rutgers U., New Brunswick, N.J., 1970-73; prof. U.S.C., Columbia, 1973—; adj. prof. health adminstrn., health promotion/edn. U. S.C., Columbia, 1991—, univ. provost, 1974-78; chair dept. psychology U.S.C., Columbia, 1994-96; founder The Paradigm Group, mgmt. cons. mem. population study sect. Nat. Inst. Child Health and Human Devel., 1973-76; mem. mental health rsch. edn. rev. com. NIMH, 1979—, chmn., 1980-83; mem. NSF social psychology grant rev. panel, 2002-; chmn. State Plan Adv. Com., S.C. State Dept. Mental Health, 1976-78; pres. past participants Greater Columbia Forum, 1975-76. Author: Advances in Experimental Social Psychology, 1963; author, editor: Advanced in Descriptive Psychology, 1981; editor: The Social Construction of the Person, 1985; co-editor: Stalking: Perspectives on Victims and Perpetrators, 2001; contbr. to Theoretical Perspectives on Personal Relationships, 1993; assoc. editor: Personal Relationships, 1993-97; exec. editor Jour. Social Psychology; contbr. some 100 articles to profl. jours. Bd. dirs. Columbia Area Mental Health Ctr., 1976-82, chmn. bd. dirs., 1981. Woodrow Wilson fellow, 1958-59, So. Fellowships Fund fellow, 1958-61. Fellow APA, Am. Psychol. Soc.; mem. Am. Sociol. Assn., Internat. Assn. Relationships Rsch. (program chair 1992), Mind Assn., Nat. Coun. Family Rels., Soc. Descriptive Psychology (1st pres. 1979-81), Phi Beta Kappa, Omicron Delta Kappa. Home: 1808 Catawba St Columbia SC 29205-3010 Office: U SC Dept Psychology Columbia SC 29208-0001

DAVIS, KENNETH WAYNE, English language educator, business communication consultant; b. Chariton, Iowa, June 22, 1945; s. Wayne Pitman and Jeanne Frances (West) Davis; m. Bette Hargrove, Nov. 28, 1970; children: Cassandra Alice, Evan Thomas. BA, Drake U., 1967; MA, Columbia U., 1968; PhD, U. Mich., 1975. From asst. prof. English to assoc. prof. U. Ky., Lexington, 1975-88; assoc. prof. to prof. Ind. U.-Purdue U., Indpls., 1988—, dept. chair, 1998-2001; edn. dir. Am. Cabaret Theatre, 2001—. Bus. cons., Lexington, 1977-88; pres. Komei, Inc., 1994—. Author: Better Business Writing, 1983, (with others) Business Communication for the Information Age, 1988, Rehearsing the Audience, 1988, (with others) Writing: Process, Product, and Power,

1993; prodr.: 2001: Lessons in Leadership videoconf., 1991; numerous other books and articles. Bd. dir. Shepherd's House, Inc., Lexington, 1986-88, Waycross Camp and Conf. Ctr., 1995-2000, World Trade Club Ind., 1998-2001. Sgt. US Army, 1968-71. Woodrow Wilson fellow, 1967; recipient Faculty Service award Nat. Univ. Continuing Edn. Assn., 1987. Mem.: ASTD, Assn. Profl. Comm. Cons. (bd. dirs. 2003—), Assn. Bus. Comm. (bd. dirs. 2003—), Toastmasters Internat., Hon. ORder Ky. Col. Episcopalian. Avocations: theater, travel. Office: Ind U-Purdue U Dept English 425 University Blvd Indianapolis IN 46202-5148

DAVIS, KENNETH LEON, psychiatrist, pharmacologist, medical educator; b. N.Y.C., Sept. 10, 1947; married, 1972; 2 children. BA, Yale U., 1969; MD, Mt. Sinai Med. Sch., 1973. Diplomate Am. Bd. Psychiatry and Neurology. Intern Stanford U., 1973-74, resident, 1973-76, life sci. rsch. assoc., 1975-76; rsch. assoc. Stanford Psych. Clin., 1974-79; asst. dir. Stanford Psych. Clin. Rsch. Ctr., VA Med. Ctr., 1975-79; clin. psychiat. cons. Santa Clara Valley Med. Ctr., 1976-79; chief dept. psychiat. VA Med. Ctr., 1979-87; assoc. prof. psychiatry and pharmacology Mt. Sinai Sch. Medicine, 1979-84; dir. schizophrenia biol. rsch. ctr., 1981-91; prof. Mt. Sinai Sch. Medicine, 1984—, chair dept. psychiatry, 1987—, Esther and Joseph Klingenstein prof., 1994—. Editor Alzheimer's Disease and Associated Disorders, Biol. Psychiatry, Clin. Neuropharmacology, Harvard Review of Psychiatry, Internat. Jour. Geriatric Psychiatry, Internat. Jour. Geriatric Psychopharmacology, Jour. Geriatric Psychiatry & Neurology, Jour. Psychiatric Rsch., Jour. Am. Geriatrics Soc., Schizophrenia Rsch., Neuropsychopharmacology, Jour. Exptl. Cognitive and Behavioral Neurosci., Molecular Psychiatry, Sociedade de Psiquiatria Do Rio Grande Do Sul; author, co-author over 500 sci. articles. Recipient A. E. Bennett Clin. Sci. Rsch. award, 1977, Saul Horowitz Jr. Meml. award, 1977-78, Solomon Silver award, 1981, Joel Elkes Internat. award ACNP, 1986, Daniel H. Efron Excellence in Rsch. award, 1990, Rita Hayworth award Alzheimer's Assn., 1991, Lifetime Sci. award Inst. Advanced Sci. in Immunology and Aging, 1992. Mem. NAS, Am. Coll. Neuropsychopharmacology, Am. Psychiat. Assn. (APA/KEMPF award 1999), Soc. Biol. Psychiatry (Gold medal award 1999, APA awd. Rsch. in Psychiatry, 2001), Inst. of Medicine of NAS. Achievements include research in the biological basis of senile dementia of the Alzheimers' type, and schizophrenia. Office: Mount Sinai School of Medicine Dept Psychiatry 1 Gustave L Levy Pl New York NY 10029-6500 E-mail: kenneth.davis@mssm.edu.

DAVIS, KIMBERLY BROOKE, art gallery director; b. L.A., 1953; BFA, Pratt Inst., N.Y.C., 1975; postgrad., Hunter Coll., N.Y.C. Dir. Bernard Jacobson, L.A., 1979-84, N.Y.C., 1983, L.A. Louver, Venice, Calif., 1985—. Office: L A Louver 45 N Venice Blvd Venice CA 90291-4127 E-mail: kimberly@lalouver.com.

DAVIS, KIRK STUART, lawyer; b. Olean, N.Y., Dec. 30, 1957; s. Robert DeWitt and Joan Gracie Davis; m. Aileen Stewart, Dec. 24, 1982. BS, Stetson U., 1979, JD, 1982. Bar: Fla. 1983, U.S. Dist. Ct. (mid. dist.) Fla. 1983. Lawyer Greene, Mann, Rowe, St. Petersburg, Fla., 1983-84, Greene & Mastry, P.A., St. Petersburg, 1984-91, Elias & Davis, P.A., Clearwater, Fla., 1991-94, Annis, Mitchell, Tampa, Fla., 1995-97, Akerman Senterfitt, Tampa, 1997—. Mem. Fla. Bar Assn. (chair health law sect. 1992-93, chair health law cert. com. 1998-99). Avocation: golf. Office: Akerman Senterfitt 100 S Ashley Dr Ste 1500 Tampa FL 33602-5314

DAVIS, LANCE ALAN, research and development executive, metallurgical engineer; b. Ridley Park, Pa., Nov. 19, 1939; s. Earl W. and Ruth Naomi (Lentz) D.; m. Susan Ruth Kroesser, July 28, 1962; children: Susan, Virginia, Lance Jr. BS in Metall. Engring., Lafayette Coll., 1961; M in Engring., Yale U., 1963, PhD, 1966. Applied scientist research staff Yale U., New Haven, Conn., 1966-68; staff physicist Allied Chem. Corp., Morristown, N.J., 1968-74, mgr. strength physics, 1974-78, mgr. Metglas Devel. sect., 1978-80; dir. materials lab. Allied Corp., Morristown, 1980-84; v.p. R&D, Allied-Signal, Inc., Morristown, 1984-94; dir. Office of Tech. Transition Dept. Defense, 1994-99; exec. dir. NAE, Washington, 1999—. Contbr. numerous articles to profl. jours., chpts. to books; co-inventor 6 patents. Mem. AIME, NAE, Am. Soc. for Metals, Am. Phys. Soc., Materials Research Soc., Sigma Xi, Phi Beta Kappa, Tau Beta Pi. Home: 4006 Ellicott St Alexandria VA 22304-1012 Office: Nat Acad Engring 2101 Constitution Ave NW Washington DC 20418-0007 E-mail: ldavis@nae.edu.

DAVIS, LANCE BARROW, lawyer, municipal judge; b. St. Joseph, Mo., May 3, 1954; s. William True, Jr. and Virginia (Motter) D.; divorced; 1 child, William Truett. Diploma, Cornell U., 1976; JD, Calif. Western U., San Diego, 1979. Bar: Mo. 1987, D.C. 1984, U.S. Supreme Ct. 1998. Staff mem. Sen. Thomas F. Eagleton, Washington, 1972, Ho. Judiciary Com./Impeachment Inquiry Staff, Washington, 1974, Sen. Stuart Symington, Washington, 1976; law clk. to presiding justice James H. Meredith U.S. Dist. Ct., St. Louis, 1979-80; ptnr. Bartlett Joint Ventures I & II, Wichita, Kans., 1980-85; assoc. Lamb & Ochs, Washington, 1986-87; asst. prosecuting atty. Buchanan County, St. Joseph, 1987-89; ptnr. Wilcox, Houts & Davis, St. Joseph, 1989-94; pvt. practice law, 1994—; mcpl. judge 5th Jud. Dist., Easton, Mo., 1990—; city atty. Amazonia. Pres. Main St., St. Joseph, Inc., 1990-93, Buchanan County Dem. Club, 1988—; fin. coun. Mo. State Dem. Party, 1985; counsel Fed. Emergency Mgmt. Agy., Nat. Def. Exec. Res., Washington, 1989—. Recipient Progress award St. Joseph Devel. Corp., 1991. Mem. ABA, Mo. Bar Assn., D.C. Bar Assn., Masons. Episcopalian. Avocations: percussion, hist. preservation. Office: 510 N 4th St Saint Joseph MO 64501-1740

DAVIS, LANCE EDWIN, economics educator; b. Seattle, Nov. 3, 1928; s. Maurice L. and Marjorie Dee (Seibert) D.; m. Susan Elizabeth Gray, Dec. 2, 1977; 1 child, Maili. BA, U. Wash., Seattle, 1950; PhD (Ford Found. dissertation fellow summer 1956), Johns Hopkins U., 1956. Teaching asst. U. Wash., 1950-51, 52-53; teaching asst., then instr. Johns Hopkins U., 1953-55; from instr. to prof. econs. Purdue U., 1955-62; mem. faculty Calif. Inst. Tech., Pasadena, prof. econs., 1968—, Mary Stillman Harkness prof., 1980—; rsch. assoc. Nat. Bur. Econ. Rsch., 1979—. Author: The Growth of Industrial Enterprise, 1964; co-author: The Savings Bank of Baltimore, 1956, American Economic History: The Development of a National Economy, 2d rev. edit, 1968, Institutional Change and American Economic Growth, 1971, Mammon and the Pursuit of Empire: The Political Economy of British Imperialism, 1860-1912, 1987, Internat. Capital Markets and Economic Growth 1820-1914, 1994, In Pursuit of Leviathan: Technology, Institutions, Productivity and Profits in American Whaling, 1816-1906, 1997, Evolving Financial Markets and Foreign Capital Flows: Britain, the Americas, and Australia, 1870-1914, 1999; co-editor: American Economic Growth: An Economist's History of the United States, 1971; mem. bd. editors Jour. Econ. History, 1965-73, Explorations in Economic History, 1984-88, THESIS, Theory, and History of Econ. and Social Instns. and Structures, with Soviet and Western Scholars, 1991—. With USNR, 1945-48, 51-52. Recipient Arthur Cole prize Econ. History Assn., 1966, Alice Hanson Jones prize, 1998, Sanwa Monograph prize Ctr. for Japan-U.S. Bus. and Econ. Studies, 1995, Libr. Co. Phila. program in early Am. economy and society prize, 2000; Ford Found. Faculty fellow, 1959-60; Guggenheim fellow, 1964-65; fellow Ctr. for Advanced Study in Behavioral Scis., 1985-86. Fellow Am. Acad. Arts and Scis.; mem. Coun. 1 Rsch. Econ. History (chmn. 1973-74, 75-76), Econ. History Assn. (pres. 1978-79, trustee 1980-82, Alice Hanson Jones prize 1998), Anglo-Am. Hist. Assn. (gov. 1978-80), Econs. Inst. (policy and adv. bd. 1984-87), Cliometric Soc. (trustee 1993-97). Home: 1746 Grevelia St South Pasadena CA 91030-2753 Office: Calif Inst Tech Humanities And Social Scis Dv Pasadena CA 91125-0001 E-mail: led@hss.caltech.edu.

DAVIS, LARRY MICHAEL, air force officer, healthcare manager, consultant; b. Lodi, Ark., Mar. 30, 1947; s. Harmon Odell and Jeanice (White) D.; m. Linda Ruth Blanchard, Mar. 22, 1969; children: Elizabeth Blanchard, Brooke Alison. BS, U. Ark., 1969; MA, Pepperdine U., 1978; postgrad., USAF Air U., 1975, 83-84. Commd. 2nd lt. USAF, 1969, advanced through grades to col., 1985; navigator, instr. navigator 596th Bombardment Squadron; radar navigator 62d Bombardment Squadron, 1971-75; instr. navigator, asst. curriculum mgr. 450th Flying Tng. Squadron, Mather AFB, Calif., 1975-76; asst. navigator sect. chief Standardization and Evaluation divsn. 323rd Flying Tng. Wing, Mather AFB, Calif., 1976-78; air ops. staff officer Tng. Analysis div. HQ Air Tng. Command, Randolph AFB, Tex., 1978-79; chief navigation tng. HQ Air Tng. Command, Randolph AFB, Tex., 1979-81; air ops. officer 99th Strategic Reconnaissance Squadron Beale AFB, Calif., 1982-83; wing chief of inspection 9th Strategic Reconnaissance Wing, 1983-84; reconnaissance ops. staff officer, reconnaissance emergency war order plans officer, chief reconnaissance plans divsn. HQ Strategic Air Command, Offutt AFB, Nebr., 1984-87; comdr. 3550th USAF Recruiting Squadron, Indpls., 1987-89; comdr. 3555th USAF Recruiting Squadron Milw., 1988; dep. comdr. 3501st USAF Recruiting Group, Hanscom AFB, Mass., 1989-91; health-care cons., customer svc. mgr. Electronic Data Systems, Indpls., 1991-96; mgr. provider rels. Unisys Corp., Frankfort, Ky., 1996-97, mgr. client svcs. Tallahassee, 1997; mgr. network devel. and provider rels. Healthplan Southeast, Tallahassee, 1997-99; program adminstr. Medicaid program devel. Agy. for Health Care Adminstrn. State of Fla., Tallahassee, 1999-2000; dir. vet. svcs. Leon. Co., Tallahassee, 2003—. Decorated D.F.C., Air medal with three oak leaf clusters. Mem. Mil. Officers Assn., Air Force Assn., Rotary (mem. health sharing com. 1989-90), Blue Key, Alpha Zeta, Alpha Gamma Rho. Baptist. Avocations: golf, tennis. Home: 2844 Whittington Dr Tallahassee FL 32309-8214 E-mail: lldavis01@earthlink.net.

DAVIS, LAURA ANN, executive coach, trainer, facilitator; b. Wilmington, Del., Dec. 30, 1959; d. James W. and Jean E. (Sachtjen) D. BA in Sociology of Health Care with high honors, U. Del., 1981; MBA in Mktg., Emory U., 1985. Credit-collection analyst Chase Manhattan Bank, Wilmington, 1982-84; retail store supr. Exxon Co., Dallas, 1985-86, project dir. new product devel., 1986—; Equifax Inc., Atlanta, 1986-91, dir. industry mktg., 1991-92; mktg./tng. mgr. United Parcel Svc., 1992-94; sr. cons., exec. coach Pantelis Inc., Decatur, 1997—; pres. Laura A. Davis & Assocs., Inc., 1997—; exec. coach, leadership devel. cons. Adj. prof. Mercer Univ., 1988—; participant numerous seminars and profl. tng. courses in field. Contbg. author: A Guide to Getting It: Self-Esteem. Recipient MBA Merit scholarship, Emory U., 1983-85, Sociology Award for Excellence, Alpha Kappa Delta, 1981. Mem. ASTD, Ga. Speakers' Assn., World Future Soc., Sierra Club, Orgn. Change Alliance, Internat. Coaching Fedn. Avocations: hiking, acting, reading, public speaking, skiing. Home and Office: 2270 Sanford Rd Decatur GA 30033-5525 E-mail: coachlad@bellsouth.net.

DAVIS, LAURA ARLENE, retired foundation administrator; b. Battle Creek, Mich., Apr. 14, 1935; d. Paul Bennett and Daisy E. (Coston) Borgard; m. John R. Davis, Aug. 7, 1955; children: Scott Judson, Cynthia Ann Davis Welker. BS, Ctrl. Mich. U., 1986. Sec. Mich. Loan Co., Battle Creek, 1952-56; legal sec. Ryan, Sullivan & Hamilton, Battle Creek, 1957-64; exec. sec. W.K. Kellogg Found., Battle Creek, 1965-76, adminstrn./program asst., 1976, fellowship dir., 1977, asst. v.p. adminstrn., asst. corp. sec., 1978-84, v.p. corp. affairs, corp. sec., 1984-95, spl. asst. to pres., CEO, 1996-97. Cons. Mich. State U., 1998—. Pres. bd. dirs. Charitable Union, Battle Creek, 1983-85; mem. allocations panel United Way of Battle Creek, 1983, v.p. cmty. rels., 1990-91, 1st v.p., 1994, pres. of bd., 1995-97; bd. dirs. Battle Creek Gas Co., 1988—, Riding for the Handicapped Cheff Ctr., 1991-96, sec., 1992; trustee Binder Park Zoo; mem. adv. coun. Argubright Bus. Coll., 1989-90; mem. Visionquest 5000, 1989; mem. selection com. Cmty. Leadership Acad.; bd. dirs. Coun. Mich. Founds., 1994-97; mem. membership com. Recipient Athena award C. of C., Cmty. Svc. award J.C. Penney. Mem. Adminstrv. Mgmt. Soc. (pres. chpt. 1982-83), Am. Mgmt. Assn., Nat. Touring Network (bd. mem. 1997-99, sec. 1998-99), Battle Creek C. of C. Home: 101 Brighton Park Battle Creek MI 49015-9615

DAVIS, LAWRENCE EDWARD, church official; b. Louisville, Aug. 14, 1939; s. George Edward and Isabel (Gerow) D.; m. Joan Cynthia Rhodes, June 20, 1959 (dec. Mar. 1984); children: Terri L., Todd E., Cynthia Davis Kennedy, Wendy J.; m. Barbara Irene Oldford, Mar., 1985. BS, Nyack Coll., 1961; MDiv, New Brunswick Theol. Sem., 1968; DDiv (hon.), King Coll., 1991. Pastor Christian Missionary Alliance, Detroit; exec. pastor World Presbyn., Livonia, Mich., 1974-82; stated clk. Evang. Presbyn. Ch., Livonia, 1981—. Adj. prof. Reformed Theol. Sem., Jackson, Miss., 1988—. Mem. Nat. Assn. Evangelicals (bd. adminstrn. 1983—). Presbyterian. Home: 38646 Silken Glen Dr Northville MI 48167-8960 Office: Ward Presbyn Ch 4000 Sixth Mile Rd Northville MI 48167

DAVIS, LAWRENCE JAMES, editor, writer; b. Seattle, July 2, 1940; s. Maurice Nelson and Eula Jane (Randall) D.; m. Barbara Frances Ball, Sept. 23, 1962 (div. Apr. 1994); children: Jeremy, Gabriel, Barbara, Tina. BA summa cum laude, Stanford U., 1962. Rschr. CBS, N.Y.C., 1963; writing fellow Stanford (Calif.) U., 1963-64; mgr. Sterling Wine & Liquor, Bklyn., 1966-68; program dir. U. Rochester, N.Y., 1972-90; contbg. editor Harper's Mag., N.Y.C., 1981—. Contbg. editor Book World, N.Y.C., 1972-73. Author: Whence All But He Had Fled, 1968, Cowboys Don't Cry, 1969, A Meaningful Life, 1971, Walking Small, 1973. Recipient Gerald Loeb award Loeb Found., 1983, Champion Tuck award Dartmouth U., 1984, Nat. Mag. award Assn. Am. Mag. Pubs., 1991, William Allen White award U. Kans., 1995. Mem. Century Assn. Democrat. Episcopalian. Avocations: cooking, travel, architecture, gardening. Home and Office: 138A Dean St Brooklyn NY 11217

DAVIS, LAWRENCE WILLIAM, radiation oncologist; b. N. Braddock, Pa., Sept. 5, 1935; s. William Paul Davis and Julia Helen Zukas; children: James G., Karen E. BS, Juniata Coll., Huntington, Pa., 1957; MA, U. Pa., 1969; MBA, Temple U., 1984; MD, Georgetown U., 1961. Diploamte Am. Bd. Radiology (trustee 1981-95, asst. exec. dir. radiation oncology 1994—); lic. physician Pa., Md., N.Y., Ga. Asst. instr. radiology U. Pa., Phila., 1962-66, instr. radiology, 1966, 68-69, asst. prof. radiology, 1969-72, assoc. prof. radiology, 1972-75; prof. radiation therapy Thomas Jefferson Sch. Medicine, 1975-84; prof. and chmn. radiation oncology Albert Einstein Coll. Medicine, Bronx, 1984-91, Emory U., Atlanta, 1991—. Cons. Armed Forces Radiobiology Rsch. Inst., Bethesda, 1968-70; exec. com. of med. staff Montefiore Med. Ctr., 1984-87, 1990-91, div. coun., 1988-89; prof. svc. com. Phila. div. Am. Cancer Soc., 1970-75. Contbr. numerous articles to profl. jours.; assoc. editor Internat. Jour. Radiation Oncology, 1986—; editorial bd. Neuro Oncology, 1989-99, assoc. editor, 1991—; editorial bd Am. Jour. Clin. Oncology, 1991—. Capt. USAF, 1966-68. Fellow Am. Cancer Soc., Phila., 1963-64, NIH, 1964-66, Am. Cancer Soc. traineeship, 1968-71 Fellow Am. Coll. Radiology; mem. AMA, AAAS, Am. Assn. Cancer Rsch., Am. Coll. Radiology (commn. on radiation oncology 1981-90, bd. chancellors 1993-99), Am. Soc. Therapeutic Radiology and Oncology (chmn. bd. 1988-89, pres. 1987-88), Am. Coll. Hosp. Adminstrs., Am. Mgmt. Assn., Am. Radium Soc. (pres. 1992-93), Am. Soc. Clin. Oncology, Med. Assn. Atlanta, N.Y. Acad. Scis., Ga. State Med. Soc., Ga. State Radiol. Soc., Radiation Rsch. Soc., Radiol. Soc. N.Am., Alpha Omega Alpha. Office: Emory Clinic 1365 Clifton Rd NE Atlanta GA 30322-1013 E-mail: davis@radonc.emory.org.

DAVIS, LEON, oil company executive; b. Arkansas City, Kans., Nov. 15, 1918; s. Miriam Kahan; m. Elene Meyer Davis, July 19, 1952; children: Lynn, Lance, Ross, Evan. BA, U. Okla., 1940. Co-owner Davis Bros., Tulsa and Houston, 1945—. Chmn. bd. Alliance S.B.I.Co. Co., Tulsa. Chmn. Okla. Civil Rights Commn., 1966; co-founder, chmn. Interferon Found., Houston, 1979-90; pres. Urban League, Tulsa, 1964; bd. dirs. M.D. Anderson Hosp. Col. USAAF, 1940-48. Mem. Kiwanis (pres. 1965.). Avocation: tennis. Home: 502 Thamer Ln Houston TX 77024-6920 Office: Davis Bros 1221 Mckinney St Ste 3100 Houston TX 77010-2009 E-mail: leondavis@davisbros.com.

DAVIS, LEONARD, violist; b. Willimantic, Conn., May 19, 1919; s. Maurice and Clara (Klemer) D.; m. Frieda Reisberg, Dec. 7, 1946. D, Juilliard Grad. Sch., 1941. With NBC Symphony Orch. under Toscanini, 1946—50; violist, prin. violist N.Y. Philharm. Orch., N.Y.C., 1949-91; mem. faculty Manhattan Sch. Music, N.Y.C., 1985—; editor Internat. Music Co.; prin. violist, rec. orchs., 1950—. Concert artist in U.S., Europe, and the Orient; tchr., clinician, master classes various conservatories worldwide, 1970—; recs. include complete J.S. Bach solo Suites for Viola. Contbr. articles to profl. jours. Juilliard Grad. Sch. fellow, 1937-41. Mem. Am. Viola Soc., Am. String Tchr. Assn. Jewish. Avocations: poetry writing, painting, chamber music. Home: 165 West End Ave Apt 21P/R New York NY 10023

DAVIS, LEONARD, physiatrist; b. N.Y.C., Oct. 28, 1936; s. Alex and Mollie Davis; m. Enid Glantz, July 6, 1963; children: Kimberly, Glenn. BS cum laude, Bklyn. Coll., 1958; MD, SUNY, Bklyn., 1962. Diplomate Am. Bd. Phys. Medicine and Rehab. Intern Long Island Coll. Hosp., 1962-63; resident NYU Rusk Inst., 1965-68; attending physiatrist Beth Israel Med. Ctr., N.Y.C., 1968—, dir. rehab., 1983-89; assoc. prof. rehab. Mt. Sinai Sch. Medicine, to 1993, Albert Einstein Coll. Medicine, 1994—, chief phys. medicine and rehab. Contbr. articles to profl. jours. Chmn. bd. Internat. Nursery Sch., Queens, N.Y. Capt. USAF, 1963-65. Mem. N.Y. Soc. Phys. Medicine and Rehab. (pres. 1981-82), N.Y. Acad. Medicine (chmn. exec. com. sect. phys. medicine and rehab. 1983-84), Am. Acad. Phys. Medicine and Rehab., Assn. Acad. Physiatrists, Am. Acad. Electrodiagnostic Medicine. Avocations: hiking, revolutionary war history, photography, history of world war i. Office: Beth Israel Med Ctr 1st Ave and 16th St New York NY 10003

DAVIS, LEWIS, architectural firm executive; Adv. to the pres. on design and planning Univ. of Pa., Pa., 1970—80; founder Davis Brody Bond, LLP, 1952—. Vis. critic Harvard, Princeton, Mass. Inst. of Tech., Mass., Univ. of Pa., Pa., RI Sch. of Design, RI, Univ. of Ill., Ill.; Davenport prof. of Arch. Yale Univ. Design, Waterside and Riverbend housing complexes, New York City, US Pavilion in the 1970 World's Fair, Osaka, Japan. Recipient AIA Arch. Firm Award, Louis Sullivan Award for Arch., Nat. Inst. of Arts and Letters' Arnold W. Brunner Award, 3 consecutive nat. awards, Am. Inst. of Arch. Mem.: Cooper Union Sch. of Arch. (faculty mem. for 25 yr.), Bd. of Overseers, Univ. of Pa. Sch. of Design and Planning. He participated in the planning and design of facilities for major corp. such as ARCO, Corning Glass Works, Philip Morris, IBM, AT&T, and Hallmark; hosp. such as New York's Mem. Sloan-Kettering Cancer Center and Mt. Sinai; and Univ. such as Cornell, Cornell Coll. of Vet. Med., Princeton, Brown, Columbia and Harvard Med. Sch. The firm's scope of work has also included the restoration of the Bronx Zoo, and the NY Pub. Libr. Office: Davis Brody Bond LLP 315 Hudson St 9th Fl New York NY 10013*

DAVIS, LEWIS U., JR., lawyer; b. Pitts., Mar. 25, 1950; s. Lewis Uber and Myrtle Elizabeth (Otte) D.; children: Shannon Lynn, Christin Lynn; m. Laraine Frazzini, May 22, 1993; 1 child, Laura Fitzgerald. BS in Engring. summa cum laude, Lehigh U., 1972; JD summa cum laude, Cornell U., 1975. Bar: Pa. 1975, U.S. Dist Ct. (we. dist.) Pa. 1975, U.S. Ct. Appeals (3d cir.) 1978. Assoc. Buchanan Ingersoll, Pitts., 1975-82, ptnr., shareholder, 1982—, v.p. tech., chief technology officer, 1994—. Contbr. articles to profl. jours. Mem. ABA, Am. Bankruptcy Inst., Pa. Bar Assn. Avocations: computers, tennis, golf. Office: Buchanan Ingersoll One Oxford Centre 301 Grant St Fl 20 Pittsburgh PA 15219-1410

DAVIS, LINCOLN, congressman; b. Sept. 13, 1943; m. Lynda Compton; three children. BS in Agronomy, Tenn. Tech. U. Mem. Tenn. Ho. of Reps. 92nd-93rd Gen. Assemblies, 1980—84, Tenn. Senate 100th Gen. Assembly, 1996—2002, Dem. majority whip, vice-chmn. transp. com., mem. senate environment, conservation, tourism coms., 1996-98, Tenn. Senate 101st Gen. Assembly, 1998—2002; mem. U.S. Ho. of Reps. from 4th Tenn. dist., 2003—. Mayor, Town of Byrdstown, 1978-82; former mem. Upper Cumberland Devel. Dist., Upper Cumberland Human Resource Agy., LBJ&C Devel. Corp. Mem. Tenn. Jaycees (past state pres.). Office: 504 Cannon HOB Washington DC 20515-4204 E-mail: sen.lincoln.davis@legislature.state.tn.us.*

DAVIS, LINWOOD LAYFIELD, lawyer; b. Winston Salem, NC, Jan. 24, 1940; s. Egbert Lawrence Jr. and Eleanor (Layfield) D.; m. Martha Hannah Hatch, June 23, 1963; children: Hannah Anne, Jane Elizabeth, Linwood Jr., Susannah. AB cum laude, Princeton U., 1962; JD, Duke U., 1967. Bar: N.C. 1967, N.C. Supreme Ct., 1967, U.S. Tax Ct., 1973, U.S. Dist Ct. (mid. dist.) N.C., 1975, U.S. Ct. Appeals (4th cir.) N.C., 1975, U.S. Claims Ct., 1980. Assoc. Womble Carlyle Sandridge & Rice PLLC, Winston-Salem, N.C., 1967-74, mem., 1974—. Revenue laws study com. N.C. Legis. Rsch. Commn., 1979-81. Active Leadership Winston-Salem, 1990; vice-chmn. campaign United Way Forsyth County, 1976, campaign chmn., 1977, bd. dirs., 1976-78; chmn. new dimensions campaign Arts Coun., Inc., 1979-80, bd. trustees, 1979-84; bd. dirs. Forsyth Health Planning Coun., 1970-76, chmn., 1973-75, Amos Cottage, 1969-78, pres., 1971-73; bd. dirs. Children's Ctr. Physically Handicapped, 1967-78, v.p., 1969-71; bd. dirs. Crisis Control Ministry, Inc., 1975-78, N.C. Outward Bound Sch., 1982-88, N.C. Citizens for Bus. and Industry, 1987-94, 96—; deacon First Bapt. Ch., 1973—, mem. children's ctr. com., 1973, long range planning com., 1973-74, mem. stewardship chmn., 1976, bd. trustees, 1980 82, 86-88, chmn., 1981-82, mem. charter and bylaw com., 1990—; adv. com. Reynolds Health Ctr., 1975-78; bd. trustees N.C. Bapt. Hosp., 1985-88, 91-94, 96-99, 2001—, bldg. com., investment com., exec. com., chmn. trustees, 1999; trustee N.C. Bapt. Hosp. Sch. Pastoral Care Found., Inc., 1978-82; bd. dirs. Med. Ctr. Wake Forest Univ. Baptist, 1990-93, 96-99, vice-chmn., 1992, chmn., 1993, 97; trustee N.C. Sch. Arts, 1977-85; adv. coun. Wake Forest U. Planned Giving, 1988-90, chmn., 1988-89; chmn. capital campaign for new bldg. N.C. Bapt. Found., 1988-89; nat. chmn. Duke U. Law Sch. Ann. Fund, 1991-92; bd. vis. Wake Forest U. Divinity Sch., 1997—. 1st lt. USAR, 1962-64. Recipient Disting. Svc. award Winston-Salem Jaycees, 1973, Forsyth Duke U. Alumni Assn., 1984. Fellow Am. Coll. Trust and Estate Coun.; mem. ABA (bus. law sect., sect. taxation, com. exempt orgns., real property, probate and trust law sect.), N.C. State Bar Assn., Forsyth County Bar Assn. (pres. 1997-98), Winston-Salem Rotary Club, Greater Winston-Salem C. of C. (bd. dirs. 1983-87), Princeton U. Alumni Assn. Winston-Salem (pres., past chmn. local ann. giving and schs. com., class of 62 agt. 1992-97, exec. com. alumni coun. 1993-95, alumni assn.). Office: Womble Carlyle Sandridge & Rice PLLC One W Fourth St Winston Salem NC 27101

DAVIS, LISA CORINNE, artist; b. Balt., Jan. 22, 1958; d. Robert Clarke and Elaine C. (Carsley) D.; m. Colin Murray Cathcart, Oct. 25, 1986; children: G. Davis Cathcart, Corinne Davis Cathcart. BFA, Pratt Inst., 1980; MFA, CUNY, 1983. Asst. prof. School of Art, Yale U., New Haven, 1997—. One-man shows include June Kelly Gallery, N.Y.C., Print Club, Phila., 1993, 2d St. Gallery, Charlottesville, Va., 1994, Mcpl. Gallery, Atlanta, 1994, Halsey Gallery, Charleston, S.C., 1994, Dell Pryor Galleries, Detroit, 1994, Project Room Bronx Coun. on the Arts, N.Y., 1996; group shows include Inroads Gallery, N.Y.C., 1984, U.S. Capitol Bldg., Washington, 1986, The Schenectady Mus., N.Y., 1986, Ridge St. Gallery, N.Y.C., 1987, 88, Christie's, N.Y.C., 1989, 90, Artist's Space, N.Y.C., 1990, 91, Okeanos Gallery, Berkeley, Calif., 1992, Pyramid Atlantic Workshop, Washington, 1992, Print Club, Phila., 1992, Granary Books, N.Y.C., 1993, Kenkeleba Gallery, N.Y.C., 1993, Orgn. Ind. Artists, N.Y.C., 1993, Art in General, N.Y.C., 1993, 94, The Bronx Mus. Arts, 1993, 96, Butters Gallery, Portland, Oreg., 1993, Barrett House Galleries, Poughkeepsie, N.Y., 1994, Gallery Annext, N.Y.C., 1994, City Without Walls, Newark, 1994, Papermill, N.Y.C., 1995, Ctr. Contemporary Art, Newark, 1996. Regional fellow Mid-Atlantic Arts Found., 1992, fellow NEA, 1995-96, artists' fellow N.Y. Found. for Arts, 1997, 2000. Studio: 323 West 39th St New York NY 10018

DAVIS, LOIS ANN, computer specialist, educator; b. Thermopolis, Wyo., Nov. 29, 1945; d. Hester Oliver and Ruth Louise (Baker) Davis; m. Harold W. Wright, Dec. 22, 1969 (div. 1988); children: Geraldine Ann, Harold W. III. BS in Bus. Edn. cum laude, U. Wyo., 1968, MS in Bus. Edn., 1988. Cert. office automation profl., Wyo. Instr. Lander (Wyo.) Valley High Sch., 1968-70, Cath. Sch., Chandler, Ariz., 1970-71; part-time instr. Casper (Wyo.) Coll., 1981-83, instr. bus. div., 1983-94, network support specialist, acad. computing, 1994-95, acting dir. acad. computing, 1995-96, dir. acad. computing, 1996—. Textbook reviewer Prentice-Hall, Englewood, N.J., 1989-91; co-dir. Casper Regional Tech. Ctr., 1999-2000; mem. computer sys. adv. bd. Casper Coll., 1995-2002; chair Casper Coll. Adminstrv. Alliance, 1996-97. Author: Electronic Communications, 2d edit., 1996. Bd. dirs. Murie Audubon Choir Nat. Audubon, 1995—97. Mem. Office Systems Rsch. Assn. (conf. co-chair 1999), Wyo. Bus. Edn. Assn. (sr. rep. 1991-92), Beta Gamma Sigma (life), Phi Kappa Phi (life). Avocations: cross-country skiing, hiking, gardening, reading. Home: 1514 Jim Bridger Ave Casper WY 82604-3186 Office: Casper Coll Academic Computing 125 College Dr Casper WY 82601-4612

DAVIS, LORRAINE JENSEN, writer, editor; b. Omaha, Apr. 2, 1924; d. Theron R. and L. Mildred (Henkel) Jensen; m. Richard Morris Davis, Apr. 4, 1959 (dec.); 1 child, Laura Jensen. BA, U. Denver, 1946. Copywriter Glamour mag., N.Y.C., 1946-54, prodn. editor, 1954-61, Vogue Children mag., N.Y.C., 1963-66. Writer, assoc. features editor, Vogue mag., N.Y.C., 1966-77; mng. editor, writer women's news column, 1977-88; editorial dir. Condé Nast Books, 1988-91; editor: Vogue Living and Food Guide, 1975; editorial cons.: Vogue Beauty and Health Guide, 1979-82; editor: Cooking with Colette (by Colette Rossant), 1975, Fairchild Dictionary of Fashion (by Charlotte Calasibetta),

1975, English translation Paul Bocuse's French Cooking, 1977. Recipient Disting. Citizen award Alpha Gamma Delta, 1981 Mem. NOW, Phi Beta Kappa. Democrat. Episcopalian. Home: 200 Leeder Hill Dr Apt 538 Hamden CT 06517-2729

DAVIS, LOURIE IRENE BELL, computer education and information systems specialist; b. Las Vegas, N.Mex., Apr. 8, 1930; d. Currie Oscar and Minnie I. (Rodgers) Bell; m. Robert Eugene Davis, Aug. 21, 1950; children: Judith Anne, Robert Patrick, (adopted) Jaime Alleyn, (adopted) Flint Christopher. BS, West Tex. U., 1959; student, Ea. N.Mex. U., 1947-49, U. Tulsa, 1980-81. Cert. elem. tchr., 4th grade, music grades 3-12, Canute, OK, 1947-1951; cert. elem. tchr. grades 5&6, LA and SS, Amarillo, Tex., 1959-65; cert. elem. tchr. 6th grade, LA & SS, Tulda, OK, 1966-68. Tchr. lang. arts, social studies, music grades 4-6, Tex., 1959—65; programmer/analyst Blue Cross/Blue Shield Okla., Tulsa, 1972-75, Nat. Bank Tulsa, 1968—71; mgr. sys. Blue Cross/Blue Shield Okla., Tulsa, 1977-81, dir. info. sys., 1981-82, mgr. project control, 1983, mgr. info. ctr., 1984-85, mgr. profl. cons. and tng., 1985-87; faculty devel. coord. CAID Okla. State U., Okmulgee, 1987-90; dir. Region 8 Intertel, Inc., Tulsa, 1987—91, adminstrv. officer, 1991-95, pres., CEO, 1995-2000, treas., CFO, 2001—. Sys. curriculum coord., computer sci. instr. Tulsa Jr. Coll., 1975-76, mem. computer sci. adv. bd., 1976-83, adj. instr., 1977-83, 93-94; computer bus. and edn. cons. Davis Cons., 1991-2002; mem. steering com. US Senate bus. adv. bd., 1981-88; ind. cons., Tulsa, 1987; lectr. computer assisted instr. Success League of Innovation Conf., St. Louis, 1989, Music Users Group Conf., U. Tenn., Chattanooga, 1989, Pres.'s Day Des Moines Area C.C., 1990. Mem. budget panel United Way Tulsa, 1981-87, Allocations Exec. Com. Appreciation award, 1987; mem. US Rep. Presdl. Task Force, 1982-93, Rep. Nat. com., 1983-91; mem. Holy Family Sch. Bd., 1991-95, nominating com. chair, 1993, sec., 1993-95. Recipient Internat. Merit award Assn. Sys. Mgmt., 1980, 84; winner League of Innovation for C.C.S. Competition, IBM, 1989. Mem.: NEA, AAUW, NAFE, Okla. Edn. Assn., Tulsa Classroom Tchrs. Assn., Higher Edn. Acad. Coun. of Okla., Tulsa Area Sys. Edn. Assn. (recorder 1980—81), Intertel (nat. acceptance com. chair 1978, dir. region VIII 1987—91, membership officer 1991—95, pub. Integra, Jour. of Intertel 1992—2002, chmn. bd. 1995, 2000, treas. 2001— lifetime mem. and appreciation award 1997), Habitat for Humanity, Arbor Day Found., Sierra Club, Mensa, Alpha Chi. Republican. Mem. Unity Ch. of Christianity. Home and Office: Davis Cons 2403 W Oklahoma St Tulsa OK 74127-3027 E-mail: LourieD@aol.com.

DAVIS, LOYD EVAN, defense industry marketing professional; b. Newark, Ohio, Apr. 10, 1939; s. Paul Edwin and Eleanor Amanda (Loyd) D.; m. Delores Madeline Wells, Nov. 10, 1959 (div. 1975); children: Mark Evan, Geoffrey Scott; m. Judith Ann Lambert, Sept. 15, 1977; 1 child, James Richard. BS in Elec. Engring., Okla. State U., 1963, MS in Elec. Engring., 1968. Commd. 2d lt. USAF, 1964, advanced through grades to maj., 1974; served in various locations, then ret. U.S. Air Force, 1979; mem. sr. profl. staff Dynatrend, Inc., Arlington, Va., 1979-82; mktg. mgr. govt. systems sector Harris Corp., Alexandria, Va., 1982-87; mktg. mgr. E-Systems Melpar Div., Falls Church, Va., 1987-90; mem. sr. profl. staff Adroit Systems, Inc., Alexandria, Va., 1990-95; bus. devel. cons. L3 Comms Corp., Salt Lake City, 1996—. Mem.: Armed Forces Comm. Electronics Assn., Air Force Assn., Nat. Def. Indsl. Assn., Assn. U.S. Army, Mt. Vernon Amateur Radio Club (pres. 1987—88), Davis County Amateur Radio Club (v.p. 1997), Woodbridge Wireless Club (pres. 1972—73, 1988—89), Masons (sec. 2003—, worshipful master 2002). Republican. Methodist. Avocation: ham radio. Home: 1476 Madera Hills Dr Bountiful UT 84010-1523 Office: L3 Comms Corp Comm Systems West 640 North 2200 West Salt Lake City UT 84116-2925 E-mail: loyd.e.davis@l-3com.com.

DAVIS, LUTHER, writer, producer; b. N.Y.C., Aug. 29, 1921; s. Charles Thomas and Henriette (Roesler) D.; m. Dorothy deMilhau, Nov. 3, 1943 (div. 1961); children: Noelle, Laura Duval. BA, Yale U., 1938. Author: (play) Kiss Them for Me, 1945, (libretto with Charles Lederer) Kismet (Tony award 1953); prodr. Timbuktu, 1978 (Tony nomination 1979), (libretto) Grand Hotel, 1989 (Tony nomination 1990), 15 solo screenplays including The Hucksters, 1946, A Lion Is in the Street, 1950, Across 110th Street, 1972; author, prodr. Lady in a Cage, 1964; numerous TV series, pilots and episodes. Served to maj. USAAF, 1942-45, CBI, ETO. Recipient Tony award, 1953. Mem. Dramatists Guild Am., Writers Guild Am.-West, League Am. Theaters and Prodrs., Acad. Motion Picture Arts and Scis., PEN.

DAVIS, LYNN ETHERIDGE, political scientist, educator; b. Miami, Fla., Sept. 6, 1943; d. Earl DeWitt and Louise (Featherston) Etheridge. BA, Duke U., 1965; MA, Columbia U., 1967, PhD, 1971; DHL (hon.), Va. Theol. Sem., 2000. Lectr. Miles Coll., Birmingham, Ala., 1966-67; asst. prof. polit. sci. Barnard Coll., Columbia U., N.Y.C., 1970-74; rsch. assoc. Internat. Inst. for Strategic Studies, London, 1973; program analysis staff Nat. Security Council, 1974; asst. prof., lectr. dept. polit. sci. Columbia U., 1974-76; prof., staff mem. Senate Select Com. on Intelligence, 1975-76; dep. asst. sec. of def. for policy plans and nat. security affairs Office of the Under Sec. for Policy, Dept. Def., Washington, 1977-79, asst. dep. under sec. for policy planning, 1979-81; rsch. Internat. Inst. Strategic Studies, London, 1981-82; prof. national security affairs National War Coll., Washington, 1982-85; dir. studies Internat. Inst. Strategic Studies, London, 1985-87; hon. sr. rsch. fellow, dept. war studies Kings Coll., London, 1988-90; rsch. fellow John Hopkins Fgn. Policy Inst, Paul H. Nitze Sch. Advanced Internat. Studies, 1988-91; v.p. army rsch. divsn., dir. Arroyo Ctr. RAND, Santa Monica, Calif, 1991-93, sr. fellow Washington, 1997—2001, sr. polit. scientist, 2001—; under sec. for arms control and internat. security affairs Dept. State, Washington, 1993-97. Author: The Cold War Begins, Soviet American Conflict Over Eastern Europe, 1974. Woodrow Wilson fellow, 1965-66, 69-70, 81-82; Columbia U. fellow, 1965-66, 68-69; recipient David D. Lloyd prize Harry S. Truman Library, 1976 Mem. Coun. on Fgn. Rels., Phi Beta Kappa. Home: 827 S Lee St Alexandria VA 22314-4333 Office: RAND 1200 S Hayes St Arlington VA 22202-5050 E-mail: Lynn_Davis@rand.org.

DAVIS, LYNN HARRY, secondary education educator; b. Jamestown, N.Y., Mar. 6, 1949; s. Harry Lynn and Marjorie Ellen (Greenwood) D.; m. Patricia Ann Carapella; 1 child, Matthew Michael. BS, SUNY, Fredonia, 1971. Cert. tchr., N.Y. Sci. tchr. West Genesee Sch. Dist., Camillus, N.Y., 1972—, adult edn. computer tchr., 1985-91, sci. curriculum coord., 1988—; tech. support specialist Teaching Ctr. Syracuse U., 1991—98; adult edn. computer tchr. Syracuse U. Teaching Ctr., 1984—86. Chmn. Sci. Bldg., West Genessee Sch. Dist., 1983-88, coord. sci. curriculum, 1988—. Contbr. numerous articles to profl. jours. Strategic planning com. mem. West Genesee Cen. Schs.; fundraiser United Way, Syracuse, 1978-81, YMCA, Syracuse, 1981; mem. Friends of Zoo, 1987-98. Mem. ASCD, N.Y. State United Tchrs. (del. 1980-85, 97-2000), Am. Fed. of Tchrs., Nat. Sci. Tchrs. Assn., West Genesee Tchrs. Assn. (v.p. for negotiations 1979-85, sec. 1986—, newsletter editor 1986—, webmaster 1997— (numerous awards)). Avocations: golf, photography, computers. Home: 14 Blackwood Dr Liverpool NY 13090-3764 Office: West Genesee Cen Sch Dist Ike Dixon Rd Camillus NY 13031-9619 Personal E-mail: davis@twcny.rr.com.

DAVIS, MAGGIE (MARIE HILL), writer; b. Norfolk, Va. d. George Blair and Dorothy Austin (Mason) Hill; children: Stuart, Richard, David, Cambren. Advt. copywriter Young and Rubicam, N.Y.C.; asst. in rsch. to chmn. dept. psychology Yale U., New Haven. Instr. creative writing courses Yale U.; guest writer/artist Internat. Cultural Ctr., Hammamet, Tunisia. Author: The Far Side of Home, 1992, Daggers of Gold, 1993, Moonlight and Mistletoe, 1993, The Amethyst Crown, 1994, Blood Red Roses, 1991 (named Best Medieval Novel by Romantic Times mag.), A Christmas Romance, 1991 (dramatized as CBS Sunday Night Movie 1994), Eagles, 1980, The Sheik, 1977, Rommel's Gold, 1971, Enraptured, 1999, Masquerade, 1999, Strangers in the Night, 2000, Out of the Blue, 2002, Stage Door Canteen, 2003; feature writer Atlanta Jour. Constn.; contbr. articles and short stories to Ga. Rev., Cosmopolitan, Ladies Home Jour., Good Housekeeping, Holiday, Venture mags. Named Ga. Author of Yr., 1963; recipient Silver Pen award Affaire de Coeur Mag., 1987, Lifetime Achievement award Romantic Times Mag., 1987. Mem. Medieval Acad. Am., Authors Guild, Romance Writers of Am., Pub. Rels. Soc. Am., Acad. Am. Poets, Women's Polit. Caucus, Caledonian Club. Democrat. Mem. Soc. Of Friends. Avocations: hiking, swimming. E-mail: madav1@aol.com.

DAVIS, MAGGIE L. elementary teacher; b. Bastrop, La., July 13, 1939; m. Killion C. Davis II, May 1, 1961. BA, U. Calif, 1982, postgrad.; PhD, Grambling State U., 1961. Cert. elem. tchr. Tchr. Berkeley (Calif.) Unified Sch. Dist., 1987—. Head supr. Willie Youth Field O.E.S., 1983—. Mem. Alpha Kappa Alpha (sec. 1959), NCNW. Lodges: Pride Alameda, O.E.S. (worth matron 1983—), Queen Sheba L.K.T. (fin. sec. 1982—), Queen Adah Grand Chpt. (grand recorder 1984—, fin. sec. 1983—). Democrat. Baptist. Avocations: sewing, reading, solving puzzles, swimming, tennis. Office: 1501 Harmon St Berkeley CA 94703-2619

DAVIS, MAMIE (DENISE DAVIS), writer; b. Florence, SC, July 28, 1943; divorced; 1 child, Jacqueline Barksdale. Cert. IBM data entry, N.Y.C., 1981. From clk grade 2 to prin. admin. assoc. NYC Civil Svc., 1962—86; freelance writer, composer N.Y.C. and, SC, 1986—. Tchg. coord., cons. NYC-DSS/HRA, 1980—86; stock actor Pilgrim Dramatic Playhouse. Author: Agency Procedures: Lust and Corruption, 2002, (novel and screenplay) Jessie's Folly, 2000, (plays) So Many Drops of Rain (showcased at NATAS), over 30 short stories; actor: numerous feature films, (Off-Broadway plays) Medea, Damn That Miss Anne, The Nurse, Civil Rights Worker. Mem.: ASCAP. Avocations: fashion design, dressmaking, book cover design.

DAVIS, MARC I. journalist, writer; b. Chgo., Nov. 12, 1934; s. Sol and Rose (Schwartz) Davis; children: Kevin, Laura. Student, U. Ill., 1952—53, Roosevelt U., 1953—54, NYU, 1957—58. Copy clerk Chgo. Tribune, 1952—55; feature editor Fort Bliss (Tex.) News, El Paso, 1955—57; assoc. editor World News Map of Week, Chgo., 1958; gen. assignment reporter El Paso Herald-Post, Tex., 1959—60; editor Physician's Mgmt., Chgo., 1960—63; owner, operator, entrepreneur Adv.-Pub. Rels. Consultancy, Chgo., El Paso, 1963—80; tchr. art Suburban Fine Arts Ctr., Highland Park, Ill., 1970—75; copy supr. Bradford Exch., Chgo., 1980—93. Contbr. writer Chgo. Tribune, Chgo. Sun-Times, Ency. Britannica, Ad Week, Crain's Chgo. Bus.; author: (novels) Spector, 1970, Dirty Money, 1992; author: (contbr.) books, articles, nat. pubs., Harvard Med. Sch. web site; reporter City News Bur., Chgo., El Paso Herald Post. With U.S. Army, 1955—57, Fort Buss, Tex. Nominee Shamus award, Pvt. Eyewriters Am. Independent. Avocation: painting.

DAVIS, MARGARET BRYAN, paleoecology researcher, educator; b. Boston, Oct. 23, 1931; AB, Radcliffe Coll., 1953; PhD in Biology, Harvard U., 1957; DSc (hon.), U. Minn., 2002. NSF fellow dept. biology Harvard U., Cambridge, Mass., 1957-58; dept. geosci. Calif. Inst. Tech., Pasadena, 1959-60; rsch. fellow dept. zoology Yale U., New Haven, 1960-61, prof. biology, 1973-76; rsch. asoc. dept. botany U. Mich., Ann Arbor, 1961-64, assoc. rsch. biologist Gt. Lakes Rsch. divsn., 1964-70, rsch. biologist, assoc. prof. dept. zoology, 1966-70, rsch. biologist, prof. zoology, 1970-73; head dept. ecology and behavioral biology U. Minn., Mpls., 1976-81, prof. dept. ecology, evolution and behavior, 1976-82, Regents prof. ecology, 1983—2000. Vis. prof. Quaternary Rsch. Ctr., U. Wash., 1973; vis. investigator environ. studies program U. Calif., Santa Barbara, 1981-82; adv. panel ecology NSF, 1976-79; sci. adv. com. biology, behavior and social scis., 1989-91; adv. panel geol. record of global change, NRC, 1991-92, planetary biology com., 1981-82, global change com; 1987-90, mem. screening com. in plant scis., internat. exch. of persons com., 1972-75, sci. and tech. edn. com., 1984-86, vis. rsch. scientist scholarly exch. com. NAS/NRC, People's Republic China, mem. grand challenges in environ. sci. com., 1999-2000; U.S. nat. com. internat. Union Quaternary Rsch., 1966-74; bd. trustees Inst. for Ecosys. Studies, 2000—. Mem. editl. bd. Quaternary Rsch., 1969-82, Trends in Ecology and Evolution, 1986-92, Ecosystems, 2000—. Recipient Sci. Achievement award Sci. Mus. Minn., 1988, alumnae Recognition award Radcliffe Coll., 1988, Nevada medal, 1993, Merit award Bot. Soc. Am., 1998, award for Contbn. Grad. Edn., U. Minn., 1999. Fellow: AAAS, Geol. Soc. Am., Am. Acad Arts and Scis.; mem.: NAS, Am. Quaternary Assn. (councillor 1969—70, 1972—76, pres. 1978—80, Dist. Career award 2001), Brit. Ecol. Soc. (hon.), Am. Soc. Naturalists (hon.), Ecol. Soc. Am. (pres. 1987—88, Eminent Ecologist award 1993), Nature Conservancy (bd. dirs. Minn. chpt. 1979—85), Internat. Assn. Gt. Lakes Rsch. (bd. dirs. 1970—73), Sigma Xi, Phi Beta Kappa. Office: U Minn Dept Ecology Evolution & Behavior 100 Ecology Bldg 1987 Upper Buford Cir Saint Paul MN 55108-1051

DAVIS, MARGARET THACKER, retired critical care, medical and surgical nurse; b. Greensboro, N.C., June 7, 1925; d. Tiller Foltz and Lucy Wright (Spencer) Thacker; m. Joe Southard Davis, Feb. 4, 1961; 1 child, Dana Lee. Diploma in nursing, Baylor U., Dallas, 1947; student, Ea. N.Mex. U., Roswell, 1978. RN, N.Mex., Tex., Fla. Office nurse Drs. Britt & Cafaro, St. Augustine, Fla., 1947-50, Dr. Robert J. Rowe, Dallas, 1950-61, Dr. F.A. English, Roswell, 1964-74; charge nurse post anesthesia care unit Ea. N.Mex. Med. Ctr., Roswell, 1990-91, ret., 1991. Named Employee of Month, Ea. N.Mex. Med. Ctr., 1985. Mem. ANA, Am. Soc. Post Anesthesia Nurses (charter), Post Anesthesia Nurses Assn. N.Mex. (bd. dirs. 1980-86, sec. 1986-87, legis. com. 1989-90), N.Mex. Nurses Assn. (dist. 5 sec. 1983-85, 91-93, pres. 1986-88, bd. dirs. 1988-90, 92-94, 96-98, membership chmn. 1988-90, chmn. nominating com. 1990, Nurse of Yr. award 1989, search for excellence award 1990, dist. 5 honored nurse 1995), Baylor U. Sch. Nursing Alumni Assn. E-mail: maggied53@aol.com.

DAVIS, MARGUERITE HERR, judge; b. Washington, Nov. 12, 1947; d. Norman Phillip and Margaretha Joanna Herr; m. James Riley Davis, June 20, 1970; children: Amy Marguerite, Christine Riley. AA with honors, St. Petersburg J. Coll., Clearwater, Fla., 1966; BA with honors, U. of South Fla., 1968; JD with honors, Fla. State U., 1971. Bar: Fla. 1971, U.S. Dist. Ct. (no. dist.) Fla. 1971, U.S. Dist. Ct. (mid. dist.) Md. 1985, U.S. Ct. Appeals (11th cir.) 1985, U.S. Supreme Ct. 1986. Atty. workers compensation div. U.S. Dept. Labor, Tallahassee, 1971; sr. legal aide Fla. Supreme Ct., Tallahassee, 1971-85, exec. asst. to Hon. Chief Justice Alderman, 1982-84; ptnr. Swann & Haddock, Tallahassee, 1985-87, Katz, Kutter, Haigler, Alderman, Davis & Marks, Tallahassee, 1987-93; judge Dist. Ct. of Appeal (1st dist.) Fla., Tallahassee, 1993—. Mem. editl. bd. Trial Advocate Quar., 1991-93; contbr. chpts. to books. Mem. ABA, Fla. Bar Assn. (Tallahassee chpt., appellate ct. rules com. 1995—, appellate ct. rules com. chair, 1995-97, grievance com., disciplinary rev. com., chmn. supreme ct. local rules adv. com., jud. cir. grievance com., rules of jud. adminstrn. 1995-99, chair 1997-98, chair jud. evaluation com. 1999-2000, chair 2001-03, exec. coun. appellate advocacy sect.), Fla. State Fed. Jud. Coun. (exec. dir. 1985—), Tallahassee Women Lawyers, Fla. Def. Lawyers Assn. (amicus curiae com.), Fla. Supreme Ct. Hist. Soc., Am. Arbitration Assn. (ad hoc com. stds. for appellate practice cert.), Altrusa Club of Tallahassee (treas. 1971-76), Fla. State U. Alumni Assn. (bd. dirs. 1975-76), Jud. Mgmt. Coun. (appellate ct. workload and jurisdiction com. 1996—, chair appellate rules liaison com., appellate practice and advocacy sect. 1996-98), Univ. So. Fla. (bd. dirs. Alumni Assn. 1999), Phi Theta Kappa. Methodist. Avocations: quilting, sewing, knitting, running, reading.

DAVIS, MARK HEZEKIAH, JR., electrical engineer; b. Knoxville, Tenn., Oct. 5, 1948; s. Mark Hezekiah and Grace Carson (Owens) D.; m. Susan Nakamura, July 14, 1977; children: Michell Grace, Kelli Michelle, John Micheal. BSEE, U. Tenn., 1972, MS, 1973. Devel. engr. Westinghouse Electric Corp. - U.S. ACE, Pitts. and Oakridge, 1969-76; sr. rsch. engr. N.L. Petroleum Svc., Houston, 1977-79; mgr. rsch. and devel. Advanced Ocean Systems divsn. Hydril Corp., Houston, 1980-81; engring. mgr. Schlumberger Corp., Sugarland, Tex., 1981-82; dir. electronics devel. Tech. for Energy Corp., Knoxville, 1982-84; mgr. digital signal processing N.E.C. Electronics, Mountain View, Calif., 1984-88; dir. comm. Executon Info. Systems, Stamford, Conn., 1988-93; dir., v.p. engring. C.S.I. Telecom, Palm Springs, Calif., 1993—. Pres. N.W. Houston United Civic Assn., 1980-82. Robert Miller scholar, 1971; U. Tenn. Nat. Alumni scholar, 1972; U.S. AEC grantee, 1973. Mem. IEEE (sr.), Am. Soc. Engring. Edn., Optical Soc. Am., Electro-Chem. Soc., Marine Tech. Soc., Soc. Photo-Optical Instrumentation Engrs. Achievements include: current work in fiber optic sensors and comm. systems and high temperature electronics in geosci.; subspecialties: ocean engineering; fiber optics. Home: 15422 Winding Moss Dr Houston TX 77068-3813 Office: CSI Telecom 4505 California Ave Ste 206 Long Beach CA 90807 E-mail: heze@aol.com.

DAVIS, MARK LOFLAND, II, retired educator, farmer, photographer, financial consultant; b. East Orange, N.J., July 30, 1928; s. Frank Wilson and Anna Josephine (Titus) D.; m. Marjorie Ann Pittinger Cron, Dec. 19, 1954. BS, Lehigh U., 1954; M in Forestry, Duke U., 1960; postgrad., U. Del., 1966-74, Del. State U., 1987-90. Cert. tchr., Del. Fire dist. forester Bur. of Land Mgmt., Palmer, Alaska, 1960-64, rehab. forester Canon City, Colo., 1964-66; tchr. Milford (Del.) Sch. Dist., 1966-73; asst. prin. Sussex Vo-Tech. Ctr., Georgetown, Del., 1973-86, youth advisor, 1986-90; account exec. Dean Witter Reynolds, Dover, Del., 1990-95; CEO Images Captured by Davis, Inc., Del. Cons. forester Davis Enterprises, Milford, Del., 1968-90; owner, operator Davis Dexter Farms, Ellendale, Del., 1966—; dealer AI Root Co., Medina, Ohio, Milford, Del., 1969-90. Coord., designer Cmty. Park Assn., Palmer, 1962-64; chairperson Forestry and Agr. 1st State RC&D Coun., Dover, 1986-86, 86-90, chairperson, mem. coun., 1990—; vol. Alumni Admissions Outreach Lehigh U., 1994—. With U.S. Army, 1948-51. S. Hallett DuPont fellow U. Del., 1967; recipient Voice of Democracy award VFW, 1988-89, 89-90. Mem. Irish Soc. Del., Sussex Vo-Tech. Retirees, Am. Dexter Cattle Assn. (hon. life, pres. 1974-78, editor newsletter 1974-78), Am. Vocat. Assn. (life), Vocat. Indsl. Club Am. (hon. life), Am. Mustang and Burro Assn. (state coord. greater Delmarva chpt. 1996—, nat. dir.), Profl. Photographers of Am., Profl. Photographers of Del. (parlimentarian), Diamond Disciples, Inc. Avocations: farming, foreign travel, photography, camping. Office: Images Captured by Davis Inc 18655 Piper Ln Ellendale DE 19941-9710 Fax: (302) 422-5370. E-mail: MarkLDavis@prodigy.net.

DAVIS, MARK MURRAY, lawyer; b. East Grand Rapids, Mich., Nov. 13, 1963; s. Thomas Bruce and Susan (Murray) D. BS, Mich. State U., 1986; JD, Marquette U., 1989; M in Environ. Law, Vt. Law Sch., South Royalton, 1990. Bar: Wis. 1989, Mich., U.S. Dist. Ct. (we. dist.) Mich. 1990, U.S. Ct. Appeals (11th cir.) 2000. Atty. Vt. Office atty. Gen., Montpelier, 1989-90; asst. regional counsel Hazardous Waste br. U.S. EPA, Atlanta, 1990-92, CERCLA br. U.S. EPA, Atlanta, 1992-95; ptnr. Varnum, Riddering, Schmidt & Howlett,LLP, Grand Rapids, Mich., 1995—. Mem. East Grand Rapids Planning Commn., 1997—; bd. dirs. Western Mich. Environ. Action Coun., 1997—, Alternatives in Motion. Mem. ABA (sec. natural resources, energy and environ. law), Wis. Bar Assn., Mich. Bar Assn., Grand Rapids Bar Assn. Office: Varnum Riddering et al Bridgewater Pl PO Box 352 Grand Rapids MI 49501-0352 E-mail: mmdavis@varnumlaw.com.

DAVIS, MARTHA ALGENITA SCOTT, lawyer; b. Houston, Oct. 1, 1950; d. C.B. Scott and Althea (Lewis) Scott Renfro; m. John Whittaker Davis, III, Aug. 21, 1976 (dec. Oct. 1997); children: Marthea, John IV. BBA, Howard U., 1971, JD, 1974. Bar: Tex. 1974, U.S. Dist. Ct. (so. dist.) Tex. 1975, U.S. Ct. Appeals (5th cir.) 1976, U.S. Supreme Ct. 1980. Tax atty. Shell Oil Co., Houston, 1974-79; counsel Port of Houston Authority, 1979-89; sr. v.p., cmty. affairs officer JP Morgan Chase & Co., 1989—; ptnr. Burney, Edwards, Hall, Hartsfield & Scott, Houston, 1975-78; bd. dirs. Unity Nat. Bank. Bd. dirs. Houston Citizens Chamber, 1980-90, Neighborhood Ednl. Ctr., Houston, 1983-87, Peoples' Workshop to Performing Arts; coord. Operation Big Vote, Washington, 1984-85; mem. planning commn. City of Houston, 1987-91; founding chair Houston Downtown Mgmt. Corp., 1991-92; pres. Greater Houston Women's Found., 1996-98; chair Third Ward Redevel. Coun., 1998. Recipient Achievement award Greek Coun., Houston, 1973; Houston's Most Influential Black Women award Black Experience Mag., Five Young Outstanding Houstonians award Houston Jr. C. of C., 1989; named one of Houston Ten Women of Distinction, Chrones and Colitis Found. and The Houston Press, 1993, one of Women on the Move, Houston Post, 1994. Mem. Nat. Bar Assn. (pres. 1990-91, sec. 1983-88, chmn. voter edn./registration com. 1985-86, Pres. award 1993, 94), Black Women Lawyers Assn. (vice chair 1983-84, Profl. Achievement award 1984), Houston Lawyers Assn. (bd. dirs. 1977-78, 85-89, pres. 1988-89), The Links (nat. and western parliamentarian 1994, Houston parliamentarian). Baptist. Office: JP Morgan Chase & Co 14 CBBE-93 PO Box 2558 Houston TX 77252-2558

DAVIS, MARTIN CLAY, lawyer, professor; b. Tulsa, Okla., Dec. 12, 1947; s. James William and Vera Ruby (Hatcher) D.; m. Rebecca Jo Strong, Aug. 22, 1970; children: Christopher James, Jennifer Alice. BA, U. Ark., 1970; JD, Vanderbilt U., 1973. Bar: Tex. 1973, U.S. Tax Ct. 1985, cert. specialist estate planning, probate law State Bar Tex. Assoc. atty. Gary, Thomasson, Hall & Marks, Corpus Christi, Tex., 1973-77, partner, 1977-94, Davis, Hutchinson & Wilkerson, LLP, Corpus Christi, Tex., 1994—. Adj. prof. Corpus Christi (Tex.) State U., 1980-83, 87, Tex. A&M U.-C.C., 1993; bd. dirs. Corpus Christi Estate Planning Coun. (pres. 1985-86); pres. Am. Assn. Individual Investors, Corpus Christi subchpt., 1995-96; lectr. various profl. assns. Assoc. Editor: Vanderbilt Law Rev., 1972-73. Pres. Family Counseling Svc., Corpus Christi, 1984; trustee, chmn. United Meth. Ch., 1998; bd. dirs. South Tex. Cmty. Fund. Recipient Leadership award, Corpus Christi C. of C., 1980. Fellow, Tex. Bar Found., Am. Coll. Trust & Estate Counsel; mem. ABA (subcom. chmn. taxation sect., 1975-80), State Bar Tex. (estate planning and probate law adv. commn., taxation sect.; planning com. advanced estate planning and probate course, 1982, 85, 91, planning com. wills and probate inst. 1985, 87, 88, com. to revise the Tex. Trust Act), Order of the Coif. Avocations: tennis, basketball, teaching. Office: Davis Hutchinson & Wilkerson LLP Frost Bank Plz Ste 1270 Corpus Christi TX 78470

DAVIS, MARVIN ARNOLD, manufacturing company executive; b. St. Louis, Nov. 16, 1937; s. Sam and Pauline (Neuman) D.; m. Trudy Brenda Rein, Aug. 11, 1968; children: Julie, Jeffrey. BS in Chem. Engring., Washington U., St. Louis, 1959; MBA in Fin.and Mktg., Washington U., 1966. Lead engr. Standard Oil Calif., San Francisco, 1962-64; product mgr. Shell Chem. Co., N.Y.C., 1966-69; group controller Pfizer, Inc., N.Y.C., 1969-75; exec. v.p. Good Hope Industries, New Orleans, 1975-77; pres., chief exec. officer Reed Industries, Inc., Stone Mountain, Ga., 1978-79; pres. Sentrex Ltd., Atlanta, 1977-82; v.p. Sentry Ins., 1982-84; chmn., CEO Petrowax PA Inc., 1991-93, Datamax Corp., 1996—; cons., pres. Grisanti Galef Goldress, 1984-97, mng. ptnr., 2001—. Chmn., CEO Petrowax PA, Inc., 1992-94, Signal Apparel Corp., 1993-94; chmn. Folger Adams Corp., Simplicity Pattern Co., Pandick Press; instr. Farleigh Dickinson U., 1968-71; lectr. Washington U., 1966, 77; cons. in field; bd. dirs. Wherehouse Enterntainment Corp., Fairlanes Bowling Corp., Cellu-land Corp., Northwest Pipe and Casing Co., Z Axis Corp., Crown Crafts Corp., Turn Around Mgmt. Assn., Cherokee Corp.; pres. AMA Fund, Inc. Author: The Profit Prescription, 1985, Turnaround, 1987, The Turnaround Formula, 2002. Served to lt. USNR, 1959-62. Recipient scholarship Washington U., 1959, fellow, 1968. Mem. DeKalb C. of C., Citrus Club, Beta Gamma Sigma, Alpha Chi Sigma. Jewish. Office: Grisanti Galef and Goldress 333 Sandy Springs Cir #106 Orlando FL 32808-1089

DAVIS, MARY ANN, graphic artist; b. Indianapolis, Oct. 7, 1954; d. Lloyd Farnsworth Neely and Laverne Frances Tragesser; m. Charles Anthony Davis, Oct. 17, 1976. BFA, Ind. U., 1976. Creative design specialist Meridian Ins., Indianapolis, 1983—91; pres. Davis Graphic Design, Indianapolis, 1991—. Exhibitions include Nashville Path (Gov.'s award, 2002). Mem.: Ind. Plein Air Painters (bd. dirs. 2001—03), Herron Alumni Assn. (pres. 2000—02). Office: Davis Graphic Design 5335 N Tacoma Suite 8 Indianapolis IN 46220 Home Fax: 317-254-1293; Office Fax: 317-254-1293. Personal E-mail: dgd@indy.net. E-mail: dgd@indy.net.

DAVIS, MARY BRONAUGH, music educator; b. Kansas City, Kans, June 28, 1937; d. John Esme and Martha Lucinda (Wilson) Bronaugh; m. William D. Davis, Jr., Jan. 1, 1983. AB, William Jewell Coll., Liberty, Mo., 1959; MA, Conservatory Music, U. Mo., Kansas City, 1974. Cert. tchr. piano. Piano tchr. Leshosky Music Store, Gladstone, Mo., 1959-61; organist Pres. Hotel, Kansas City, 1965-67; piano tchr. Maple Woods C.C., Kansas City, 1972-81; ind. piano/organ tchr. Gladstone, Mo., 1962—; min. music, organist Barry Christian Ch., Kansas City, 1960—. Mem. Music Tchrs. Nat. Assn. (bd. dels. 1995-96), Am. Guild Organists (youth chair Greater Kansas City chpt. 2003—, Mo. Fedn. Music Clubs (handbell chair 1999-2003, Ch. Musician of Yr. 1998, 99), Mo. Music Tchrs. Assn. (pres. 1995-96), Kansas City Music Tchrs. Assn. (pres. 1988-90), Federated Music Tchrs. Greater Kansas City (pres. 1969-70, 84-85). Home: 1400 NE 76th Ter Kansas City MO 64118-1907

DAVIS, MARY BYRD, conservationist, researcher; b. Cardiff, Wales; came to U.S., 1947; d. John Dymond and Joanna Inger (Falconer) Byrd; m. Robert Minard Davis; children: Carol, John. BA, Agnes Scott Coll., 1958; MA, U. Wis., 1968, PhD, 1972; MLS, Simmons Coll., 1974. Acquisitions libr. No. Mich. U., Marquette, 1974-75; asst. libr. Georgetown (Ky.) Coll., 1975-78; libr. U. Ky., Lexington, 1978-83; freelance writer and editor Georgetown, 1983-90, 93—; staff writer, office mgr. Earth First Jour., Canton, N.Y., 1990; co-founder

and pub. Wild Earth, Canton, N.Y., 1991-92, assoc. editor Richmond, Vt., 1993—; dir. Yggdrasil Inst., Georgetown, Ky., 1994—. Author: The Military Civilian Nuclear Link, 1988, Guide de L'Industrie Nucleaire Francaise, 1988, The Green Guide to France, 1990, Going Off the Beaten Path: An Untraditional Travel Guide to the U.S., 1991, Old Growth in the East: A Survey, 1993, La France nucléaire: matières et sites, 1997, 2002, The U.S. Enrichment Establishment 1999, 1999; co-author: Les Déchets nucléaires militaires Français, 1994; editor: Eastern Old-Growth Forests: Prospects for Rediscovery and Recovery, 1996, Eastern Old-Growth Notes, 1997-2000. Bd. dirs. Centre de Documentation et de Recherche sur la Paix et les Conflits, Lyon, France, 1989—, Wildlands Ctr. for Preventing Roads, Missoula, Mont., 1996-99. Mem. Nat. Writers Union, Sierra Club (editor energy report 1986-87, exec. com. Cumberland chpt. 1982-84), Phi Beta Kappa. E-mail: mdavis@old-growth.org.

DAVIS, MARY ELIZABETH, speech pathologist, educator, counselor; b. Larned, Kans., July 1, 1930; d. LeRoy D. and Katheryn (Herndon) Harris; m. W.G. Davis, Apr. 3, 1969; children: Pamela Koch, Michelle Dalton; 1 stepchild, Wendy Garton. BA, Calif. State U., Fresno, 1959, MA, 1982. Cert. resource specialist, speech pathologist tchr., deaf tchr., counselor, Calif. Dir. recreation and occupl. therapy Wyo. State Hosp., Evanston, 1956-58; tchr. Fresno Unified Sch. Dist., 1960-80, Barton County C.C., Great Bend, Kans., 1990-98. Bd. dirs. Larned Historical Soc., Santa Fe Trail Ctr., Larned, Kans., 2001—. Mem. Am. Counseling Assn., Nat. Bd. Cert. Counselors. Home: 534 W 4th St Larned KS 67550-3410

DAVIS, MARY GEORGIA, music educator; b. Indpls., May 18, 1942; d. Richard P. and Mary L. (Brokaw) D.; 1 child, Melissa Anne. MusB, U. Colo., 1964; MusM, U. N.Mex., 1968; D of Musical Arts, U. Colo., 1972. Dir. music 1st Congrl. Ch., Albuquerque, 1964-68, Boulder, Colo., 1968-73; dir. music arts Littleton (Colo.) United Meth. Ch., 1973-77; dir. arts 1st Plymouth Congrl. Ch., Engelwood, Colo., 1977—; tchr. music pvt. practice, 1964—; owner Music Design, Highlands Ranch, Colo., 1990—. Composer Columbine, 1973, Vocabulary for Peace, 1984, Words of a Believer, 1982, Who Got Called? 1999; arranger Custom Midi Tracks, 1990—, Brass and Organ Arrangements. Mem. Music Tchrs. Am. Choral Dirs. Assn., Nat. Assn., Colo. Music Tchrs. Assn., Choristers Guild. Mem. United Ch. Christ. Avocations: camping, skiing, fishing, travel, 4x4. Home: 1395 Northridge Rd Highlands Ranch CO 80126-2515 Office: 1st Plymouth Congrl Ch 3501 S Colorado Blvd Englewood CO 80110-4211

DAVIS, MARY HELEN, psychiatrist, psychoanalyst, educator; b. Kingsville, Tex., Dec. 2, 1949; d. Garnett Stant and Emogene (Campbell) D. BA, U. Tex., 1970; MD, U. Tex., Galveston, 1975; grad. in adult and child psychoanalysis, Inst. for Psychoanalysis, Chgo., 1982-92. Cert. Nat. Bd. Med. Examiners, Am. Bd. Psychiatry and Neurology, Child and Adolescent Psychiatry. Intern, then resident in psychiatry SUNY, Buffalo, 1975-78; fellow in child psychiatry U. Cin., 1978-80; asst. prof. Med. Coll. Wis., Milw., 1980-89, clin. assoc. prof., 1989-93; med. dir. adolescent treatment unit Milw. Psychiat. Hosp., 1981-86, Schroeder Child Ctr., 1986-89; pvt. practice, 1989-93; med. dir. Devereux-Victoria (Tex.) Psych. Residential Treatment Ctr., 1993-94; pvt. practice Lancaster, Pa., 1995—. Cons. Milw. Mental Health Cons., 1980-93, Children's Svc. Soc., Milw., 1982-93, Cath. charities, Harrisburg, Pa., 1996—, Sch. Dist. Lancaster, 1998—. Bd. dirs. Next Generation Theatre, Milw., 1988-90, Next Act Theatre, Milw., 1990-92, Lancaster Guidance Ctr., 2002--. Mem. Am. Psychiat. Assn., Am. Soc. Adolescent Psychiatry, Am. Med. Women's Assn., Assn. for Child Psychoanalysis, Am. Psychoanalytic Assn. Baptist. Avocations: science fiction, music, computers, crochet.

DAVIS, MARY W. ALLEN, medical secretary; b. Athens County, Ohio; d. William Henry Sr. and Emma Cornelia (Stovall) Allen; m. O. William Davis, Jan. 21, 1946 (dec. Sept. 1979); children: William Thomas Davis, Barbara Ellen Davis Whitaker. BS in Commerce, Ohio U., 1944. Cert. med. asst. Head war bond divsn. payroll dept. Tenn. Eastman Co., Oak Ridge, Tenn., 1944-46; med. sec., office mgr. Office Dr. William H. Allen, Jr., Nelsonville and Athens, Ohio, 1956-96. Co-compiler, author: Nelsonville in Pictures, 1988 (C. of C. Person of Yr. 1989); compiler, officer: Automobile Tour of Historic Nelsonville, 1994; co-compiler: 15 vols. Athens Messenger newspaper obituaries Athens County, Ohio starting from 1900 newspapers. Ann. reunion chmn. Athens (Ohio) High Sch., 1990—. Named All Ea. Tenn. Women's Basketball team selection, 1945; named to Honorable Order of Ky. Colonels, 2001; recipient citizenship award, VFW, 1989, Cert. of Appreciation, Athens County Genealogy Soc., 1999. Mem.: Nelsonville C. of C. (pres. 1980—82), Stovall Family Assn. (pres. 1988—2002, pres. emeritus 2002—), 17th Century Colonial Dames, United Daus. of the Confederacy, Ohio Fedn. Women's Clubs (jr. dir. 1956—58, treas. 1966—74, 2d v.p. 1974—76, 1st v.p. 1976—78, pres. 1978—80, co-chmn. circulation dept. Quar. Mag. 1984—2000, chmn. trustees Annette Phelps Lincoln Scholarship 1993—, chmn. circulation dept. Quar. Mag. 2000—), Gen. Fedn. Women's Clubs (com. mem. 1980—, chmn.), Rotary (pres. 1993—94, 1997—98, 2001—02, 2002—03, Paul Harris fellow 1997). Avocations: volunteering for community service, genealogy, collecting historical pictures and articles, scrapbooking. Home: 15979 State Route 691 Nelsonville OH 45764-9432 E-mail: mwadavis@frognet.net.

DAVIS, MICHAEL, medical educator; b. Bronxville, N.Y., Nov. 14, 1942; s. Pearce and Lucia D.; children: Nathaniel, Alexander. BA, Northwestern U., 1965; PhD, Yale U., 1969. Rsch. assoc. Yale U. Sch. Medicine, New Haven, 1969-70, asst. prof., 1970-75, assoc. prof., 1975-84, prof., 1984-98, 1998—; Robert W. Woodruff prof. psychiatry Emory U. Sch. Medicine, Atlanta, 1998—. Contbr. more than 200 articles to profl. jours.;, author 65 book chpts. USPHS Rsch. Scientist award NIMH, 1975-79, 80-85, 85-90, 90-95, 95-99; Sterling fellow Yale U., 1969. Fellow Am. Psychol. Assn., Am. Psychol. Soc., Am. Coll. Neuropsychopharmacology, AAAS; mem. Soc. for Neurosci., Soc. for Psychophysiology, Phi Beta Kappa. Office: Emory U Sch Medicine Dept Psychiatry 1639 Pierce Dr Rm 4311 Atlanta GA 30322-0001 E-mail: mdavis4@emory.edu.

DAVIS, MICHAEL CHASE, retired aerospace industry executive, retired military officer; b. Fullerton, Calif., Oct. 12, 1931; s. Arthur Elling Davis and Mary Stafford (O'Brien) Greene; m. Jacqueline L. Watkins, Dec. 6, 1976; children from previous marriage: Michael Chase Jr., Mark Stafford. BS, U.S. Naval Acad., 1953; SM, ScD, MIT, 1961. Commd. ensign USN, 1953, advanced through grades to capt., 1971; design supt. Mare Island Naval Shipyard, Calif., 1966-68; sys. analyst Office Asst. Sec. Def., Washington, 1968-70; ship design dir. Trident Submarine and Aegis Warships, Naval Sea Sys. Command, Arlington, Va., 1970-75; comdg. officer David Taylor Naval Ship Rsch. and Devel. Ctr., Bethesda, Md., 1975-77; ret., 1977; program mgr. Sci. Applications, Inc., Arlington, 1977-79; program mgr., dir. Sea Shadow Stealth Ship and other marine programs, Lockheed Martin Missiles and Space Co., Sunnyvale, Calif., 1979-96; pub. Ovarian Cancer Internet Website, 1996-99. Decorated Legion of Merit, 1977; recipient DAR award for seamanship, 1953, D.W. Taylor award for sci. achievement, 1963, award for sci. achievement Bur. Ships, 1963, Joint Svc. commendation Sec. Def., 1970. Mem.: IEEE, US Naval Inst. Republican. Address: HC2 Box 2441 Tecumseh MO 65760 E-mail: anchor@townsqr.com.

DAVIS, MICHAEL J. judge; b. 1947; BA, Macalester Coll., 1969; JD, U. Minn., 1972; LLD (hon.), Macalester Coll., 2001. Law clk. Legal Rights Ctr., 1971-73; with Office Gen. Counsel Dept. Health, Edn. and Welfare, Social Security Adminstrn., Balt., 1973; criminal def. atty. Neighborhood Justice Ctr., 1974, Legal Rights Ctr., 1975—78; pub. defender Hennepin County, 1978-83; judge Hennepin County Mcpl. Ct., 1983-84, Hennepin County Dist. Ct. (4th jud. dist.), 1984-94; atty., commr. Mpls. Civil Rights Commn., 1977-82; judge U.S. Dist. Ct. Minn., St. Paul, 1994—. Constnl. law instr. Antioch Mpls. C.C., 1974; criminal def. trial practice instr. Nat. Lawyer's Guild, 1977; trial practice instr. William Mitchell Coll. Law, 1977-81, Bemidji Trial Advocacy Course, 1992, 93; adj. prof. U. Minn. Law Sch., 1982—, Hubert H. Humphrey Sch. Pub. Affairs, 1990; instr. Minn. Inst. Legal Edn., Civil Trial Practice Inst., 1991-92; lectr. FBI Acad., 1991, 92. Mem. Minn. Superior Ct. Racial Bias Task Force, 1990—93, U.S. Dist. Ct.; chmn. Pretrial Release & Bail Evaluation Com., 1997—. Recipient Outstanding Alumni award Macalester Coll., 1989, Good Neighbor award WCCO Radio, 1989, Disting Svc. award William Mitchell Coll. of Law, 2000. Mem. ABA, Nat. Bar Assn., Minn. Minority Lawyers Assn., Am. Inns. of Ct., Fed. Bar Assn., Fed. Judges Assn., Hennepin County Bar Assn., Minn. State Bar Assn., Minn. Lawyers Internat. Human Rights Com. (past mem. bd. dirs.), Internat. Acad. Trial Judges, Nat. Assn. for Pub. Interest Law (bd. dirs.), 8th Cir. Jury Instruction Com., U.S. Assn. Constitutional Law. Office: US Dist Ct Minn 300 S 4th St Ste 14E Minneapolis MN 55415-2251 E-mail: mjdavis@mnd.uscourts.gov.

DAVIS, MICHAEL RICO, county official; b. Charlotte, N.C. s. Lawrence Kenneth and Myrtle Elizabeth (Antrum) D. BA, U. N.C., 1979; MPA, Calif. State U., 1994, MA, 1996. Intern, adminstrv. asst. to majorit floor leader Calif. Assembly, L.A., 1980-81, field rep. assemblywoman Maxine Waters, 1983-86, adminstrv. asst., 1986-89; adminstrv. asst., dist. dir Congresswoman Maxine Waters, L.A., 1990-92; sr. counselor Optimist Homes & Ranch, Inc., L.A., 1981-83; sr. dep. 2nd dist. to Yvonne Burke L.A. County Bd. Suprs., L.A., 1993—. Author: Minorities in Business, 1997. Spl. asst. Jesse Jackson for President, L.A., 1984; dir. GOTV Tom Bradley for Mayor, L.A., 1989; del. Dem. Nat. Convention, N.Y., 1992, 2000, regional dir. Bill Clinton for President, L.A., 1991-92; bd. dirs. Tng. Rsch./Head Start, L.A., 1984—; mem. black adv. com. L.A. Police Commn., 1984-87; mem. presdl. selection com. Charles Drew Med. U., L.A., 1997; mem. nat. steering com. Al Gore for Pres. of U.S., 1999—. Named to Outstanding Young Men of Am., 1981, 96, Young Leader, Am. Swiss Found., 1998. Mem. Am. Soc. Pub. Adminstrn. mem. nat. coun. 2002—, v.p. L.A. Met. chpt. 2000-02), So. Calif. Mediation Assn., Kappa Alpha Psi (historian 1977-78, Outstanding Achievement 1978, regional dir. 1978-79, Man of Yr. 1979, chmn. social action 1997, bd. dirs. we. province 1982-84, contbr. to jour.), Phi Alpha Delta. Democrat. Home: PO Box 19672 Los Angeles CA 90019-0672 Office: LA County Bd Suprs 500 W Temple St Los Angeles CA 90012-2713

DAVIS, MICHAEL STEVEN, lawyer; b. Brookline, Mass., Aug. 1, 1947; s. Ralph and Beatrice (Levy) D.; m. Madelyn O. Davis, Aug. 16, 1970; children: Gregory, Adam, Bethany. AB, U. Rochester, 1969; JD cum laude, Boston U., 1972. Bar: N.Y. 1973, U.S. Dist. Ct. (so. and ea. dists.) N.Y. 1974, U.S. Ct. Appeals (2d cir.) 1974, U.S. Supreme Ct. 1979, U.S. Ct. Claims, 1980. Assoc. Chadbourne & Parke, N.Y.C., 1972-82; sr. counsel corp. litigation Am. Internat. Group, N.Y.C., 1982-88; ptnr. Zalkin, Rodin & Goodman, LLP, N.Y.C., 1988-99, Zeichner, Ellman & Krause, LLP, N.Y.C., 1999—. Asst. adj. prof. C.W. Post Ctr., L.I. U., Glen Cove, N.Y., 1975-79. Editor Boston U. Law Rev., 1970-72. Mem. Citizens Ctr. for Children of NY, Inc., 1978—87; trustee The Harvey Sch., Katona, NY, 1994—97; pres. Pelham (NY) Jewish Ctr., 1986—88; v.p. Sinai Free Synagogue, 2003—. Mem. ABA, Assn. Bar City of N.Y., Am. Arbitration Assn., ARIAS, Huguenot Bridge Club. Democrat. Office: Zeichner Ellman & Krause LLP 575 Lexington Ave New York NY 10022-6102 E-mail: mdavis@zeklaw.com.

DAVIS, MICHELE, federal agency administrator; b. Louisville, Ky. BS in Fgn. Svc., Georgetown U., Washington, 1988; M in Econs., Am. U. Economist Citizens for Sound Economy; economist minority leader staff Joint Econ. Com. Washington; chief spokesperson majority leader's office; advisor house Rep. leadership; comms. dir. house majority leader Dick Armey, 1997—2001; asst. sec. pub. affairs U.S. Dept. Treasury, Washington, 2001—. Republican. Office: US Dept Treasury Pub Affairs 1500 Pennsylvania AveNW Washington DC 20220

DAVIS, MONIQUE D. (DEON DAVIS), state legislator; b. Chgo., Aug. 19, 1936; d. James and Constance (Dutton) McKay; divorced; children: Robert Jr., Monique C. Conway. BS in Edn., Chgo. State U., 1967, MS in Guidance and Counseling, 1976. Tchr. Chgo. Bd. Edn., 1967-86, coordinator, 1986—; mem. Ill. Ho. of Reps. from 27th dist., 1987—, vice chmn. elem. and secondary edn. com. Mem. legis. com. Chgo. Area Alliance Black Sch. Edn., 1982-84, Independent Voters of Ill.-Independent Precinct Orgns., Chgo., 1982-83; coordinator 21st ward, Citizens for Mayor Washington, 1985, 87. Recipient GRIT award Roseland Womens Orgn., 1987; named a Tchr. Who Makes a Difference PTA, 1978, 85, 2002 March Monique Davis Named best Legislature of the year by Chicago Area Proseet Mem. Chgo. Area Tchrs. Alliance (chmn.), Christian Bd. Edn. (bd. dirs. 1978-82), Phi Delta Kappa. Mem. United Ch. of Christ. Office: Ill Ho of Reps 2040-j Stratton Bldg Springfield IL 62706-0001*

DAVIS, MORRIS SCHUYLER, astronomer; b. Bklyn., Dec. 14, 1919; s. Nathan Samuel and Helen (Gross) D.; m. Dorothy Irene Hall, May 26, 1945; children: Glenn Craig, Elizabeth Davis Nyblade, Cynthia Louise Davis, Deborah Susan Davis, Katherine Davis Stalberg, Martha Davis Werlen. BA, Bklyn. Coll., 1946; MA, U. Mo., 1947; PhD, Yale U., 1950. Dir. Computer Ctr., Yale U., New Haven, 1956-66, also research assoc. astronomy; pres. dir. Triangle Univs. Computation Ctr., Research Triangle Park, N.C., 1966-70; Morehead prof. astronomy U. N.C., Chapel Hill, 1970-85, Morehead prof. astronomy emeritus, 1985—. Fellow AAAS; mem. Univ. Research Assn. (trustee 1977-83, exec. editor Celestial Mechanics 1985-89), Am. Astronom. Soc., Internat. Astron. Union. Unitarian Universalist. Home: 404 N Estes Dr Chapel Hill NC 27514-7629 Office: U NC CB#3255 Dept Physics and Astronomy Phillips Hall 039A Chapel Hill NC 27599-0001 E-mail: morrisdavis@mindspring.com.

DAVIS, MULLER, lawyer; b. Chgo., Apr. 23, 1935; s. Benjamin B. and Janice (Muller) D.; m. Jane Lynn Strauss, Dec. 28, 1963 (div. July 1998); children: Melissa Davis Muller, Muller Jr., Joseph Jeffrey; m. Lynn Straus, Jan. 23, 1999. Grad. with honors, Phillips Exeter (N.H.) Acad., 1953; BA magna cum laude, Yale U., 1957; JD, Harvard U., 1960. Bar: Ill. 1960, U.S. Dist. Ct. (no. dist.) Ill. 1961. Practice law, Chgo., 1960—; assoc. Jenner & Block, 1960-67; ptnr. Davis, Friedman, Zavett, Kane, MacRae, Marcus & Rubens, 1967—. Lectr. continuing legal edn., matrimonial law and litigation; legal adviser Michael Reese Med. Rsch. Inst. Coun., 1967-82; co-chair com. to study and recommend a comprehensive rules design for the domestic rels. divsn. Circuit Ct. of Cook County, Ill., 2003—. Author: (with Sherman C. Feinstein) The Parental Couple in a Successful Divorce, 1984; Illinois Practice of Family Law, 1995, (with Jody Meyer Yazici), 5th edit., 2003; contbg. author Marriage, Health and the Professions, 2002; mem. editl. bd. Equitable Distbn. Jour., 1984—; contbr. articles to law jour. Bd. dirs. Infant Welfare Soc., 1975-96, hon. bd. dirs., 1996—, pres., 1978-82; co-chmn. gen. gifts 40th and 45th reunions Phillips Exeter Acad., chair class capital giving, 1994-98, 50th reunion gift com. Yale Class Coun. 2002—. Capt. U.S. Army, Ill. N.G., 1960-67. Fellow Am. Acad. Matrimonial Lawyers (bd. mgr. Ill. chpt. 1996-99), Am. Bar Found.; mem. ABA, FBA, Ill. Bar Assn., Chgo. Bar Assn. (matrimonial com. 1968-83, sec. civil practice com. 1979-80, vice chmn. 1980-81, chmn. 1981-82), Am. Soc. Writers on Legal Subjects, Chgo. Estate Planning Coun., Legal Aid Soc. (vice chmn. matrimonial bar 1991-95, (vice chmn. 1995-97, chmn. 1997-99, co-chair Com. to Study and recommend a comprehensive Rules Design for the Domestic Rels. Div., Circuit Ct. of Cook County, Ill., 2003-), Lawyers Club Chgo., Tavern Club, Lake Shore Country Club, Chgo. Club. Republican. Jewish. Home: 161 E Chicago Ave Apt 34 E Chicago IL 60611-2601 Office: Davis Friedman Zavett Kane MacRae Marcus & Rubens 140 S Dearborn St Ste 1600 Chicago IL 60603-5288 E-mail: mdavis@davisfriedman.com.

DAVIS, NATHAN CHILTON, federal agency administrator; b. St. Albans, N.Y., May 2, 1954; s. Nathan Chilton Davis and Ferne Irene Snyder; m. Deborah Laurie Nygaard, Apr. 15, 1973; children: Nathan Chilton III and Richard Randall (twins), Jaime Rae, Evan Michael. AS, U. Calif., San Diego, 1979; BS, Kensington U., 1994; grad., USDA Grad. Sch., 2000. Cert. emergency paramedic, arson investigator, auditor. Fire chief, paramedic Salton City Svcs., Salton Sea, Calif., 1975-78; emergency paramedic City of San Bernardino/Riverside, Calif., 1978-79; detention officer U.S. Immigration, El Centro, Calif., 1981-83, physician asst., 1983-85, tng. administrator Laguna Niguel, Calif., 1985-87, dep. asst. regional commr., 1987-88, officer in charge El Centro, 1988-95, asst. chief enforcement officer Washington, 1995—. Instr. Fed. Law Enforcement Tng. Ctr., U.S. Dept. Justice, 1985; course developer U.S. Immigration Svc., 1986; arson investigator Riverside (Calif.) County FireDept., 1975; pres. Fed. Exec. Bd., 1991-95; chair Career Opportunity Program Adv. Coun., 1993. Author: Executive Protection, 1984, revised, 1994, Detention Operations, 1985, Corporate Violence, 1993, Leader's Guide to Office Management, 1994; numerous tng. programs. Capt. U.S. Army, 1980-88. Recipient Life Saving medal Salton Cmty. Svcs., 1980, Army Commendation award Dept. Def., 1987, Performance award, 1994 (v.p. Al Gore), commendation, 1995; nominated Innovation in Am. Govt. award JFK Sch. of Bus., Harvard U., 1994, Ins. Commrs. award for excellence, 1994. Mem. Am. Correctional Assn. (gold), Am. Assn. Correctional Psychology. Avocations: flying, writing, travel, scuba diving, teaching. Home: 9594 Basilwood Dr Manassas VA 20110-7926 Office: US Immigration 425 I St NW Washington DC 20536-0001

DAVIS, NATHAN JOSEPH, academic administrator, music educator; b. Davis, Calif. s. Martin David and Virginia Whiteford Davis; m. Elise Margrethe Midelfort, July 14, 1979; children: Peter, Emma. BA, NYU, New York, NY, 1981—85; MA, Montclair State U., Montclair, NJ, 1978—79; Ph. D, NYU, New York, NY, 1980—85. Provost Tri-College U., Fargo, ND, 2000—; music educator Minn. State U., Moorhead, Minn., 1990—.

DAVIS, NATHANIEL, humanities educator; b. Boston, Apr. 12, 1925; s. Harvey Nathaniel and Alice Marion (Rohde) D.; m. Elizabeth Kirkbride Creese, Nov. 24, 1956; children: Margaret Morton Davis Mainardi, Helen Miller Davis Presley, James Creese, Thomas Rohde. Grad., Phillips Exeter Acad., 1942; AB, Brown U., 1944, LLD, 1970; MA, Fletcher Sch. Law and Diplomacy, 1947, PhD, 1960; postgrad. Russian lang. and area, Columbia, Cornell U., Middlebury Coll., 1953-54, U. Central de Venezuela, 1961-62, Norwich U., 1989. Asst. history Tufts Coll., 1947; joined U.S. Fgn. Service, 1947; 3d sec. Prague, Czechoslovakia, 1947-49; vice consul Florence, Italy, 1949-52; 2d sec. Rome, 1952-53, Moscow, USSR, 1954-56; Soviet desk officer State Dept., 1956-60; 1st sec. Caracas, Venezuela, 1960-62; acting Peace Corps dir., Chile, 1962; spl. asst. to dir. Peace Corps, 1962-63, dept. assoc. dir., 1963-65; U.S. minister to Bulgaria, 1965-66; sr. staff Nat. Security Coun. (White House), 1966-68; U.S. amb. Guatemala, 1968-71, Chile, 1971-73; dir. gen. Fgn. Service, 1973-75, asst. sec. of state for African affairs, 1975; U.S. amb. Switzerland, 1975-77; State Dept advisor and Chester Nimitz prof. Naval War Coll., 1977-83, lectr., 1991—; Alexander and Adelaide Hixon prof. humanities Harvey Mudd Coll., Claremont, Calif., 1983—2002, faculty exec. com., 1986-89, acting dean of faculty, 1990, emeritus prof., 2002—. Lectr. in field. Author: The Last Two Years of Salvador Allende, 1985, Equality and Equal Security in Soviet Foreign Policy, 1986, A Long Walk to Church: A Contemporary History of Russian Orthodoxy, 1995, 2d edit., 2003. Mem. ctrl. com. Calif. Dem. Party, 1987—90, 1991—, mem. exec. bd., 1993—, mem. bus. and profl. caucus, 1992; mem. L.A. County Dem. Ctrl. Com., 1988—90, 1992—, regional vice chmn., 1994—96; del. Dem. Nat. Conv., 1988, 1992, 1996, 2000; del. So. Calif. conf. United Ch. of Christ, 1986—87. Lt. (j.g.) USNR, 1944—46. Recipient Cinco Aguilas Blancas Alpinism award, Venezuelan Andean Club, 1962, Disting. pub. Svc. award, USN, 1983, Elvira Roberti award for outstanding leadership, Los Angeles County Dem. Com., 1995, spl. merit award (as author), So. Calif. Motion Picture Coun., 1998, Prism award for nat., state, county and local svcs., Jerry Voorhis Claremont Dem. Club, 1999; Fulbright scholar, Moscow, 1996—97. Mem.: AAUP (pres. Claremont Coll. chpt. 1992—96, 1998), Am. Acad. Diplomacy, Coun. on Fgn. Rels., Am. Fgn. Svc. Assn. (bd. dirs., vice chmn. 1964), Cosmos Club, Phi Beta Kappa. Home: 1783 Longwood Ave Claremont CA 91711-3129 Office: Harvey Mudd Coll 301 E 12th St Claremont CA 91711-5901

DAVIS, NICHOLAS HOMANS CLARK, finance company executive; b. N.Y.C., Dec. 1, 1938; s. Feltz Cleveland and Loraine Vanderpool (Homans) D.; children from previous marriage: Loraine, Helen, Alexandra, Eleanor; m. Brenda Jean Molen, Dec. 18, 1982; children: Nicholas, Elizabeth. BA in Geology with honors, Princeton U., 1961; MBA in Fin., Stanford U., 1963. Chartered fin. analyst. Research analyst Fahnestock & Co., N.Y.C., 1963-67; mgr. research Andresen & Co., N.Y.C., 1967-71; dir. research Boettcher & Co., Denver, 1971-75; v.p. corp. fin. White Weld & Co., Denver, 1975-78; v.p. asset mgmt. Paine Webber Co., Denver, 1978-92; pres. Mont. Investment Advisors, Inc., Bozeman, 1991—. Trustee, investment officer Thenen Found., Montclair, N.J., 1966—. Dir. chair of comp com. Appleton Papers, Inc. Mem. Riverside Country Club, Rotary. Avocations: skiing, flyfishing, deepwater voyaging, writing, backpacking. Home: 85 Limestone Meadows Ln Bozeman MT 59715 Office: Mont Investment Advisors Inc 104 E Main St # 416 PO Box 7090 Bozeman MT 59771-7090 E-mail: mintnd@aol.com.

DAVIS, NORMAN M. poet, writer; b. Phila., Oct. 13, 1936; s. Milton B. and Esther P. Davis; m. Linda Crane, July 24, 1990. BA in English, Am. U., 1958. Reporter UPI, Washington, 1966—67; editor Bur. Nat. Affairs, Inc., Washington, 1967—71; freelance writer, editor Washington, 1971—82, Chgo., 1991—96; clk. office inspector gen. U.S. Dept. HUD, Chgo., 1982—91; admin. asst., office mgr. United Blood Svcs., Chgo., 1996—98; gen. mgr., editor, writer Linda Crane Prodn., Blue Island, Ill., 1994—2001, Caribou, Maine, 2001—. Author: The Complete Book of U.S. Coin Collecting, 1971, 2d edit., 1976, Amusing, Holmes!, 1992, numerous poems; contbr. articles to profl. jours. With USN, 1958—62. Mem.: Maine Writers & Publ. Alliance. Democrat. Unitarian Universalist. Office: NMD Products 168 Grimes Mill rd Caribou ME 04736

DAVIS, OLLIE WATTS, musician, educator; b. Oak Hill, W.Va, Dec. 20, 1957; s. Matthew Julius Payne and Ramona Sereta Ross; m. Harold Dwayne Davis, Aug. 2, 1980; children: Kirstie Elisabeth, Jonathan Dwayne, Ashley Michelle, Charity Christian. BS, W.Va. Inst. Tech., 1979; MusM, U. Ill., 1982, D in Musical Arts, 1988; MA, W.Va U., 1987. Music tchr. Kanawha County Sch., Charleston, W.Va., 1979—80; lectr. Ill. State U., Normal, Ill., 1985—86; asst. prof. U. Ill., Urbana, 1988—94, assoc. prof., 1995—. Author: (novels) Talks My Mother Never Had With Me, Volume I & II, 1999—2002. Mem.: Nat. Arts and Letters Soc., Sigma Alpha Iota. Avocations: reading, interior decorating. Office: U Ill 2136 Music Bldg 1114 W Nevada Urbana IL 61801

DAVIS, OTTO ANDERSON, economics educator; b. Florence, S.C., Apr. 4, 1934; s. Otto and Pauline (Anderson) D.; m. Carolyn Quinn, Dec. 26, 1962; children— Craig, Wendy, Ross. AB, Wofford Coll., 1956; MA, U. Va., 1957, PhD, 1960. Asst. prof. econs. Grad Sch. Indsl. Adminstrn., Carnegie-Mellon U., Pitts., 1960-65; assoc. prof. Grad Sch. Indsl. Adminstrn. Carnegie-Mellon U., 1965-67, prof., 1967-68, prof. polit. economy Sch. Urban and Public Affairs, 1968-81, W.W. Cooper univ. prof. econs. and pub. policy, 1981—, assoc. dean, 1968-75, dean, 1975-81; rsch. dir. Pa. Tax Commn., 1979-82. Bd. visitors Air U., Maxwell AFB, 1980-83. Contbr. book revs. and articles to profl. jours. Fellow Econometric Soc.; mem. Public Choice Soc. (pres. 1970-72), Assn. Public Policy Analysis and Mgmt. (policy council, pres. 1982-83), Am. Econ. Assn., Am. Polit. Sci. Assn., Am. Soc. Public Adminstrn. Office: Carnegie-Mellon U Dept Social Decision Scis Porter Hall # 223F Pittsburgh PA 15213-3890 E-mail: od0a@andrew.cmu.edu.

DAVIS, OWEN KIDDER, physician, reproductive endocrinologist; b. N.Y.C., Aug. 16, 1956; s. Stephen Edward and Joyce Baldwin (Kidder) D.; m. Marianne Alida Gawain, Nov. 19, 1983; children: Zoe Catherine, Alida Ashby. BA, Swarthmore Coll., 1978; MD, Bowman Gray Sch. Medicine, 1982. Diplomate Am. Bd. Ob-gyn., Am. Bd. Reproductive Endocrinology. Intern, resident N.Y. Hosp., Cornell Med. Ctr.; fellow Brigham and Women's Hosp., Boston; instr. Harvard U., Boston, 1986-88; assoc. prof. Cornell U. Med. Coll., N.Y.C., 1988—; assoc. ob-gyn. Brigham & Women's Hosp., Boston, 1986-88; assoc. attending ob-gyn. N.Y. Hosp., 1988—. Acting chief gynecology Cornell Med. Ctr., assoc. dir. In Vitro Fertilization. Contbr. articles to profl. jours. Bd. dirs., med. dir. Am. Infertility Assn.; chair instl. rev. bd. N.Y. Presbyn. Hosp.; chief of gynecology Cornell Med. Ctr. John Lockwood Meml. fellow Swarthmore Coll., 1978. Fellow: N.Y. Acad. Medicine (sec. sect. ob-gyn. 1991—92), Am. Coll. Ob-Gyn.; mem.: AMA, Soc. for Reproductive Endocrinologists, Soc. Assisted Reproductive Tech. (pres.-elect, exec. com., past chair practice com.), Am. Soc. for Reproductive Medicine (legis. monitor, practice com., govt. rels. com. 1987—), Alpha Omega Alpha. Avocations: music, travel, tennis. Office: Cornell U Med Coll 525 E 68th St New York NY 10021-4872 Home: 165 E 72d St Apt 16A New York NY 10021

DAVIS, PAMELA BOWES, pediatric pulmonologist; b. Jamaica, N.Y., July 20, 1949; d. Elmer George and Florence (Welsch) Bowes; m. Glenn C. Davis, June 28, 1970 (div. Mar. 1987); children: Jason, Galen. AB, Smith Coll., 1968; PhD, Duke U., 1973, MD, 1974. Internal medicine intern Duke Hosp., 1973-74, resident in internal medicine, 1974-75; sr. investigator NIAMD/NIH, Bethesda, Md., 1977-79; asst. prof. U. Tenn. Coll. Medicine, Memphis, 1979-81, Case Western Res. U. Sch. Medicine, Cleve., 1981-85, assoc. prof., 1985-89, prof., 1989—, Arline H. and Curtis F. Garvin Rsch. prof., 2002—, chief pediatric pulmonary divsn., 1985—, vice chmn. rsch. dept., 1994-96. Pres. Am. Fedn. for Clin. Rsch., Thorofare, NJ, 1989—90; trustee Rsch. Am, Arlington, Va.,

1989—90; mem. adv. coun. Nat. Inst. Diabetes, Digestive and Kidney Diseases, 1992—96; mem. bd. sci. counselors NHLBI, 2001—. Contbr. articles to profl. jours. Chmn., med. adv. coun. Cystic Fibrosis Found., Bethesda, 1988-90. Named to, Clevel. Med. Hall of Fame, 2001; recipient Samuel Rosenthal award in acad. pediat., 1996, Maurice Saltzman award, Mt. Sinai Health Care Found., 1998, Smith Coll. medal, 2001, Rainmaker of Yr., Edn. Rsch. Northeast Ohio Live Mag., 2002. Fellow ACP; mem. Am. Pediatric Soc., Am. Acad. Pediatrics, Am. Physiol. Soc., Am. Thoracic Soc., Am. Soc. Gene Therapy, Biophys. Soc., Soc. for Pediatric Rsch., Phi Beta Kappa, Sigma Xi, Alpha Omega Alpha. Office: Rainbow Babies/Child Hosp 2101 Adelbert Rd Cleveland OH 44106-2624 E-mail: pbd@po.cwru.edu.

DAVIS, PAMELA MARIE, administrative analyst; b. New Orleans, Jan. 22, 1961; d. David James Davis Sr. and Anita Hurst Davis. B in Pub. Adminstrn., Loyola U., 1983. Adminstrv. analyst divsn. housing and neighborhood devel. City of New Orleans, 1988—2002, prin. analyst divsn. housing and neighborhood devel., 2003—; civil svc. trainer Civil Svc. Dept., New Orleans, 1991—. Mem. City Civil Svc. Commn., New Orleans, 1999—. Contbr. (employee newsletters) The Link/Our Beat, 1999—. Lector St. Peter Claver Ch., New Orleans, 1971—, lector tng. coord., 1991—, chairperson worship commn., 1988—92; assoc. mem., pres. St. Vincent de Paul Conf., New Orleans, 1994—99; del. Nat. Black Cath. Congress, 1992; mem. parish coun. St. Peter Claver Ch., New Orleans, 1985—97; bd. dirs. Outstanding Young Ams., 1996—98. Named one of Outstanding Young Women of Am., 1983, 1988; recipient Order of St. Louis medallion, Archdiocese of New Orleans, 1988, Hibernia Merit award, Bur. Govtl. Rsch., 1997. Mem.: Legion of Mary (assoc.). Democrat. Roman Catholic. Avocations: reading, playing table tennis, traveling. Office: Divsn Housing and Neighborhood Devel 1340 Poydras St 10th Fl New Orleans LA 70112

DAVIS, PATRICIA M. educator; b. Lloydminster, Alberta, Can., Nov. 16, 1932; d. George E. and Edith May (Kent) McKerihan; m. Harold M. Davis, Dec. 17, 1958 (dec. Dec. 24, 1971); children: Harold Neal, Rosemary Anne. BA, Dallas Bapt. Coll., 1981; MA, U. Tex., Austin, 1988, PhD, 1994. From grass roots worker to materials cons., tchr. trainer Summer Inst. Linguistics/Min. Edn., Peruvian Amazon region, 1963-84; literacy trainer Summer Inst. Linguistics, England, 1970, 88, U. Oreg. 1985-88; internat. literacy educator and edn. cons. Summer Inst. Linguistics, Dallas, 1995—. Literacy trainer, Ethiopia, 1992, Kenya, 1994, 97, U. ND, 1995, 98-99, Singapore, 1995, Asia, 1997, Peru, 1997-98, 2000, The Philippines, 1999, Dallas, 2000, East Africa, 2001, 2002, Panama, 2003. Author: Cognition and Learning, 1991, La enseñanza del castellano como segunda lengua entre los grupos etnolingüísticos de la Amazonia, 1997, Los machiguengas aprenden a leer, 2002; co-author: Bilingual Education: An Experience in Peruvian Amazonia, Spanish edit., 1979, English edit., 1981. Mem. Internat. Reading Assn., Comparative and Internat. Edn. Soc., Alpha Chi, Kappa Delta Pi, Phi Kappa Phi. Avocations: sewing, entertaining, reading anthropology. Office: SIL Internat 7500 W Camp Wisdom Rd Dallas TX 75236-5639

DAVIS, PAUL B. mechanical engineer, civil engineer, retired; b. N.Y.C., Jan. 20, 1909; s. Samuel and Esther (Schwartz) D.; m. Sally Vogel (dec.), Nov. 24, 1932; children: Gerald Joseph, Audrey Thea Coll; m. Beatrice Fibus, Aug. 17, 1999. Student, Poly. U. N.Y., 1928. Engring. draftsman Mcpl. Pub. Works, N.Y.C., 1929-41; asst. engr. Bd. Water Supply, N.Y.C., 1941-42; sr. designer to asst. supt. design hydro/nuc/fossil fuel electric generating stas. Ebasco Svcs., Inc., N.Y.C., 1942—66; mgr. Spanish projects Ebasco Overseas Corp., Madrid, 1966-72; project engring. mgr. Burns & Roe, Hempstead, N.Y., 1973-76; ednl. coord. Argonne Nat. Lab., Argonne, Ill., 1977. Dir. Poinciana Condominium Assn., Lake Worth, Fla., 1979-86. Mem. NSPE (life), N.Y. State Soc. Profl. Engrs., Nat. Wildlife Fedn., The Nature Conservancy, Sierra Club, Zionist Orgn. Am., World Jewish Congress, B'nai B'rith. Avocations: spanish culture, oil painting, bridge, swimming. Home: 3520 Whitehall Dr Apt 303 West Palm Beach FL 33401-1072

DAVIS, PAUL JOSEPH, endocrinologist; b. Chgo., Oct. 28, 1937; s. Paul Albert and Maxine Lydia (Mason) D.; m. Faith Ainsworth Baker, Dec. 8, 1962; children: Matthew, John, Sarah. BA magna cum laude, Westminster Coll., 1959; MD cum laude, Harvard U., 1963. Intern Bronx Municipal Hosp. Center, 1963-64, resident in medicine, 1964-67; clin. assoc. NIH, Bethesda, Md., 1967-69, sr. staff assoc., 1969-70; head endocrinology div. Balt. City Hosps., 1970-75; prof. medicine, head endocrinology div. SUNY, Buffalo Med. Sch., 1975-90, also vice chmn. dept. medicine; prof., chmn. dept. medicine Albany Med. Coll., Albany Med. Ctr., N.Y., 1990-99, sr. assoc. dean for clin. rsch., 1998—; chief med. svc. VA Med. Ctr., Buffalo, 1980-90; dir. Clin. Rsch. Inst. of Wadsworth Ctr. N.Y. State Dept. Health and Albany Med. Coll., 2000—. Mem. merit rev. bd. endocrinology VA; bd. dirs. Am. Bd. Internal Medicine; dir. Ordway Rsch. Inst., Albany, N.Y., 1999—. Trustee Westminster Coll., Fulton, Mo., 2000—. Fellow ACP (gov. Upstate N.Y. region), Gerontol. Soc.; mem. Am. Fedn. Med. Rsch., Am. Soc. Biochemistry and Molecular Biology, Am. Thyroid Assn. (bd. dirs., pres. 1997-98), Endocrine Soc., Bd. Sci. Counselors, Nat. Inst. Aging. Achievements include research and publs. on mechanisms of action of thyroid hormone, effects of aging on endocrine function. Home: 35 Old South Rd West Sand Lake NY 12196-2104 Office: Clin Rsch Inst Mailcode 54 47 New Scotland Ave Albany NY 12208-3412 E-mail: pjdavis@albany.net.

DAVIS, PAUL ROBERT, investment manager, portfolio manager; b. Lynn, Mass., Mar. 17, 1964; s. Harold S. and Diane Aida Davis; m. Liane D'Alessandro, Oct. 12, 1991. AB, Dartmouth Coll., 1986; MBA, Harvard U., 1991. Assoc. cons. Monitor Co., Cambridge, Mass., 1985-86, cons., 1986-88, project mgr., 1988-89; v.p., prin. Yeager Wood & Marshall, N.Y.C., 1990-96, CFO, 1991-94; mng. dir. Hagler, Mastrovita & Hewitt, Boston, 1996-98; mng. dir., chief investment officer pvt. client group David L. Babson & Co., Cambridge, 1998—. Mem. Harvard Club N.Y., Assn. Investment Mgmt. and Rsch. (CFA, Chartered Investment Counselor), Dartmouth Alumni Assn. (leadership agt. 1988—), Boston Econ. Club. Avocation: offshore ocean yacht racing. Office: David L Babson & Co One Memorial Dr Cambridge MA 02142

DAVIS, PETER FRANK, filmmaker, author; b. Santa Monica, Calif., Jan. 2, 1937; s. Frank and Tess (Slesinger) D.; m. Johanna Mankiewicz, Sept. 13, 1959 (dec. July 1974); children— Timothy, Nicholas; m. Karen Zehring, June 10, 1979 (div. Dec., 1995); children: Jesse, Antonia; m. Alicia Anstead, July 4, 2003; stepchild: Kristen Anstead. AB magna cum laude, Harvard U., 1957. Editorial asst. N.Y. Times, N.Y.C., 1958-59; writer, interviewer Sextant Film Prodns., N.Y.C., 1961-64; writer, assoc. producer NBC News, N.Y.C., 1964; writer, producer CBS News, N.Y.C., 1965-72; freelance filmmaker N.Y.C., 1972-82; freelance writer, 1976—. Vis. lectr. various univs., 1974-75. Documentary cons. Pumping Iron, 1978, Gilda Live, 1980; writer, prodr.: (TV documentaries) The Heritage of Slavery, 1968, The Battle of East St. Louis, 1969, The Selling of the Pentagon, 1971 (Emmy award 1971, Peabody award 1971, Writers Guild Am. award 1971, George Polk award 1971); prodr. The Best Hotel on Skid Row, 1990; writer Age 7 in America, 1991; prodr., writer JACK, 1993; assoc. prodr., writer (documentary) Hunger in America, 1968 (Writers Guild Am. award 1968); dir., prodr.: (films) Hearts and Minds, 1974 (Oscar award 1975), Middletown, 1982; co-writer (TV film) Haywire, 1980; contbg. editor Esquire Mag., 1985-92; author: Hometown, 1982, Where is Nicaragua?, 1987, If You Came This Way, 1995; also articles in The Nation, Esquire, New York Woman, TV Guide, New York Times mag. Served with AUS, 1959-60. Recipient Saturday Rev. award, 1970, 71, Peace and Friendship among Nations medal, 2003; Poynter fellow Yale U., 1971, assoc. fellow, 1972—. Mem. Writers Guild Am., Authors Guild Am. Democrat. Home and Office: PO Box 357 Castine ME 04421-0357

DAVIS, PHILIP J. mathematician; b. Lawrence, Mass., Jan. 2, 1923; s. Frank and Annie (Shrager) D.; m. Hadassah Finkelstein, Jan. 2, 1944; children: Abigail, Frank, Ernest, Joseph. BS, Harvard U., 1943, PhD, 1950; PhD honoris causa, Roskilde U., Denmark, 1997. Chief numerical analysis sect. Nat. Bur. Standards, Washington, 1958-63; prof. applied math. Brown U., Providence, 1963-92; prof. emeritus, 1993—. Author: Lore of Large Numbers, 1961, Interpolation and Approximation, 1963, Numerical Integration, 1967, 3.1416 and All That, 1969, The Schwarz Function, 1974, Circulant Matrices, 1979, The Mathematical Experience, 1981 (Am. Book award 1983), The Thread, 1981, Descartes' Dream, 1986, No Way, 1987, Thomas Gray, Philosopher Cat, 1988, The Spiral of Theodorus, 1993, Thomas Gray in Copenhagen, 1995, Mathematical Encounters of the Second Kind, 1996, The Education of a Mathematician, 2000. Recipient Math. award Washington Acad. Scis., 1960, Chauvenet prize Math. Assn. Am., 1963, Lester R. Ford award, 1983, George Polya award, 1987, Math. Comm. award, 1997. Mem. Math. Assn. Am., Am. Math. Soc. Home: 175 Freeman Pkwy Providence RI 02906-4620 Office: Brown Univ Applied Math Dept Providence RI 02912-0001 E-mail: philip_davis@brown.edu.

DAVIS, RACHEL LEE MOSTERT, advertising executive; b. Arkadelphia, Ark., Sept. 8, 1952; d. James Lawrence and Dorothy Marie (Diamond) Mostert; m. Richard Lawrence Davis, Nov. 17, 1979 (div. 1997). BS in Advt., U. Tex., 1975. Account exec. DBG&H Unltd., Inc., Dallas, 1975—76, sr. account exec., 1976—78, v.p., 1979—80; co-owner Oldfield Davis, Inc., Dallas, 1980—90, prin., 1990—. Bd. dirs. Sales and Mktg. Coun., Dallas, 1978—80, Hist. Lakewood Found., 1990—91, Old City Park, 1994—96. Mem. The Phorum Presbyn. Hosp. of Dallas, 1991—, exec. com., 1994—96, chmn., 1999—2000; mem. Pres.'s leadership coun. Tex. Health Resources, 2000—; project chmn. Jr. League Dallas, 1987—88, 1993—94, chmn. edn. com., 1990—91, bd. dirs., 1990—93, 1994—96, chmn. pub. rels. com., 1991—92, adminstrv. v.p., exec. com., 1992—93, chmn. nominating com., 1995—96, chmn. membership com., 1994—95; mem. adv. coun. Hist. Preservation League, 1994—95; bd. dirs. Dallas Summer Musicals Guild, 2000—; graphics chmn. Swiss Ave. Hist. Dist. Assn., Dallas, 1986—89, 1992. Recipient 1st Family Pl. Partners Card Champion award, 1999. Mem.: Dallas Advt. League, Greater Dallas C. of C. (com. for disting. women leaders lecture series 1991—92), Dallas Press Club (bd. dirs. 1996—98, chmn. Gridiron Gala 1996, 1997), Kappa Kappa Gamma. Presbyterian. Office: Oldfield Davis Inc 2910 N Hall St Dallas TX 75204

DAVIS, RANDY LEE, soil scientist; b. L.A., Nov. 23, 1950; s. Willie Vernon and Joyce Christine (Manes) D. AA, Yuba Community Coll., 1972; BS in Soils and Plant Nutrition, U. Calif., Berkeley, 1976. Vol. soil scientist U.S. Peace Corps, Maseru, Lesotho, 1976-79; soil scientist Hiawatha Nat. Forest, Sault Saint Marie, Mich., 1979-86; project soil scientist Bridger-Teton Nat. Forest, Jackson, Wyo., 1986-91, forest soil scientist, 1991-97, soil and water program leader, 1997-2001; nat. soils program leader USDA Forest Svc., Washington, 2001—. Detailed soil scientist Boise (Idaho) Nat. Forest, 1989, 92, Mendocino (Calif.) Nat. Forest, 1996, San Bernardino (Calif.) Nat. Forest, 1999; detail assignment Nat. Burned Area Emergency Rehab. program leader Washington, 2000, 2002-03; acting nat. program leader Wetland and Riparian Program, USDA Forest Svc., 2002—. Editor Soil Classifiers newsletter; contbr. articles to profl. jours. Pres. Sault Community Theater, Sault Saint Marie, 1984-86. Mem. Am. Chem. Soc., Soil Sci. Soc. Am., Soil and Water Conservation Soc. (bd. dirs. 1991-92, chpt. pres. 1993-97), Am. Water Resources Assn., Internat. Soc. Soil Sci., Soc. for Range Mgmt. Methodist. Home: 208 12th SE Washington DC 20003 Office: USDA Forest Svc 1400 Independence, SW Washington DC 20250-1103 Personal E-mail: randyd83001@yahoo.com. Business E-Mail: rdavis03@fs.fed.us.

DAVIS, RAYMOND, JR., physical chemistry researcher; b. Washington, Oct. 14, 1914; s. Raymond D. and Ida Rogers (Younger) D.; m. Anna Marsh Torrey, Dec. 4, 1948; children: Andrew Morgan, Martha Safford Davis Kumler, Nancy Elizabeth Davis Klemm, Roger Warren, Alan Paul. BS, U. Md., 1937, MS, 1939; PhD, Yale U., 1942; DSc, U. Pa., 1990, Laurentian U., 1997, U. Chgo., 2000. Chemist Dow Chem. Co., Midland, Mich., 1937-38, Monsanto Chem. Co., Dayton, Ohio, 1946-48; sr. chemist Brookhaven Nat. Lab., Upton, N.Y., 1948-84; rsch. prof. dept. physics and astronomy U. Pa., Phila., 1984—. Contbr. articles to profl. jours. Served with USAAF, 1942-46. Recipient Boris Prejel prize N.Y. Acad. Scis., 1955, award for nuc. applications in chemistry Am. Chem. Soc., 1979, Pontecorvo prize Inst. for Nuclear Rsch., Russia, 2000, Wolf prize for physics Israel, 2000, Nat. Medal of Sci., 2001, Nobel prize for physics, 2002, Benjamin Franklin medal for physics, 2003. Mem. AAAS, NAS (Comstock prize 1978), Am. Phys. Soc. (Tom W. Bonner prize 1988, W.K.H. Panofsky prize 1992), Am. Geophys. Union, Am. Astron. Soc. (Beatrice M. Tinsley prize 1994, George Ellery Hale prize 1996). Office: U PA Dept Physics and Astronomy Philadelphia PA 19104

DAVIS, REX DARWIN, business consultant; b. Skiatook, Okla., June 11, 1924; s. Ivan Francis and Ruth Mae (Nabors) D.; m. Amelia Roberts Fry, Apr. 14, 1979; children by previous marriage: Deborah Ruth, Kathleen Marie. LLB, U. Okla., 1949; postgrad., Princeton U., 1966. Exec. asst. to asst. regional commr. Bur. Alcohol Tobacco and Firearms, Cin., 1962-66, asst. regional commr., 1966-70, dir. Washington, 1970-78; pres. Nat. Assn. Beverage Importers, Inc., Washington, 1978-85, Delta Cons., Inc., Washington, 1985-95; pres., chief exec. officer New Europe Wines, Inc., 1991-95. Exec. dir. Pres.'s Forum of Beverage Alcohol Industry, 1990-2001; chmn. Lic. Beverage Info. Coun., Washington, 1981-85, Internat. Fedn. Wine & Spirits, Paris, 1982-85. Author: Federal Searches and Seizures, 1964 Vice chmn. Sky Ranch Found., Washington, 1983-85; pres. Treas. Hist. Assn., 1978-79. 1st lt. USAAF, 1943-45. Decorated Purple Heart, Air medal; recipient Chevalier de Merite Agricole French Gov., 1983, award for exceptional svc. Dept. Treasury, 1978, Meritorious Svc. award 1977, Lifetime Achievement award Bur. Alcohol, Tobacco, Firearms, 2001; named Fed. Employee of Yr. Cin. chpt. Fed. Bus. Assn., 1965; Meritorious award William A. Jump Found., 1959. Mem. Am. Soc. Assn. Execs., Okla. Bar Assn., Pi Kappa Alpha, Internat. Club, Princeton Club. Avocations: golf, tennis, snorkeling, stamp collecting. Home and Office: Delta Cons Inc 311 10th St SE Washington DC 20003-2130

DAVIS, REX LLOYD, insurance company executive; b. Des Moines, Dec. 29, 1929; s. Leon Mack and Mercedes Johanna (Lamar) D.; m. Sally JoAnne Richard, Apr. 14, 1952; children: Kristine Lynn, Craig Thomas, JD, Drake U., 1952. Bar: Iowa, U.S. Dist. Ct. Iowa, U.S. Supreme Ct.; C.P.C.U. C.L.U. With Employers Mut. Casualty Co., Des Moines, 1954-66, regional v.p. Phila., 1966-72; exec. v.p. Ranger Ins. Co., Houston, 1972-75, pres., 1975-84; pres., chief operating officer Ranger Ins. Mgrs., Ranger Internat. Ins. Ltd., Ranger County Mut.; atty.-in-fact Ranger Lloyds, Houston, 1975-84; pres., chief operating officer Rex L. Davis & Assocs., Inc., 1984—; chmn. United Republic Reins. Co., 1986-92, also bd. dirs. Mem., Houston Bar Assn., Soc. CPCUs, Soc. CLUs, Lakeside Country Club (Houston), Petroleum Club (Houston), Delta Theta Phi. Office: Rex L Davis & Assocs 2450 Fondren Rd Ste 102 Houston TX 77063-2320

DAVIS, RICHARD BRADLEY, internal medicine, pathology educator, physician; b. Iowa City, Iowa, Nov. 6, 1926; s. Bradley Nelson and Gladys Mae (Fairbanks) D.; m. Jean Nixeen Anderson, June 22, 1957; children— Janet, Stephen, Catharine. BS, Yale U., 1949; MD, State U. Iowa, 1953; PhD, U. Minn., 1964. Intern Mary Fletcher Hosp., Burlington, Vt., 1953-54, resident, 1954-56; instr. U. Minn., Mpls., 1959-64, asst. prof. medicine, 1964-69; vis. investigator Sir William Dunn Sch. Pathology, Oxford, Eng., 1964-65, MRC Blood Coagulation Research Unit, Churchill Hosp., Oxford, 1965; asso. prof. medicine U. Nebr., Omaha, 1969-73, prof. medicine, 1973-94, acting dir. div. hematology, 1974-76, prof. pathology, 1976-94, dir. hematology div., 1976-79, emeritus prof. internal medicine, 1994—. Contbr. articles to sci. publs. Served with U.S. Army, 1945-46. Borden Undergrad. Med. Research grantee, 1953; USPHS career devel. awardee, 1961-69 Fellow A.C.P., Central Soc. Clin. Research, Am. Fedn. Clin. Research, Am. Soc. Exptl. Pathology, N.Y. Acad. Scis., Am. Assn. History of Medicine Soc. Exptl. Biology and Medicine, Am. Soc. Hematology, Royal Micros. Soc., Internat. Soc. Haemostasis and Thrombosis, Omaha Mid-West Clin. Soc., Sigma Xi, Alpha Omega Alpha, Phi Beta Pi, Theta Kappa Psi. Home: 103 Woodhall Spa Williamsburg VA 23188-9138 E-mail: rbd@visi.net.

DAVIS, RICHARD CALHOUN, dentist; b. Manhattan, Kans., Jan. 4, 1945; s. William Calhoun and Alison Rae (Wyland) D.; Danna Ruth Ritchel, June 13, 1968; 1 child, Darin Calhoun. Student, Ariz. State U., 1963-65, BA, 1978, U. Ariz., 1966; DDS, U. of Pacific, 1981. Retail dept. head Walgreens, Tucson, 1965-66, mgmt. trainee Tucson, San Antonio, 1967-70, asst. store mgr. Baton Rouge, 1970-72; field rep. Am. Cancer Soc., Phoenix, 1972-74; dept. head Lucky Stores, Inc., Tempe, Ariz., 1976-78; practice dentistry specializing in gen. dentistry Tucson, 1981—. Bd. dirs. Home Again, Inc. Chmn. bd. Capilla Del Sol Christian Ch., Tucson, 1984. Fellow Internat. Congress Oral Implantologists, Am. Coll. Oral Implantology, Am. Soc. Osseointegration; mem. ADA, Acad. Gen. Dentists, Am. Straight Wire Orthodontic Assn., Am. Assn. Functional Orthodontics, Sleep Disorders Dental Soc., So. Ariz. Bus. Assn. (treas. 1998), N.W. Dental Study Club, Tucson Advanced Cosmetic Study Club, Optimists (past pres. N.W. club, preceptorship in dental implantology), Elks. Republican. Mem. Christian Ch. (Disciples Of Christ). Avocations: golf, skiing, watersports, fishing, camping. Office: 2777 N Campbell Ave Tucson AZ 85719-3101

DAVIS, RICHARD CARLTON, rehabilitation services administrator; b. Salem, Mass., June 10, 1948; s. William Montgomery and Ruth Wiley (Durkee) D.; m. Patricia Lynn Paquette, Apr. 6, 1974; children: Susannah, Amanda, Adam. BA, Concord Coll., 1969; postgrad., U. Iowa. Orientation tchr. Iowa Dept. for the Blind, Des Moines, 1971-73, rehab. tchr., 1973-77, rehab. counselor, 1977-80, sr. svc. specialist, 1980-86; so. area supr. N.Mex. Commn. for the Blind, Alamogordo, 1987-91, orientation ctr. adminstr., 1987-92; asst. commr. State Svcs. for the Blind, Minn. Dept. of Econ. Security, St. Paul, 1992-2000; cons. on blindness and rehab. Circle Pines, Minn., 2000—; asst. dir. BLIND, Inc., Mpls., 2000—. Cons. Nebr. Svcs. for the Visually Impaired, Lincoln, 1980, Am. Printing House for the Blind, Louisville, 1992. Coord./vol. field svc. rep. Job Opportunities for the Blind, Balt., 1979-86; chair, vice chair Mayor's com. for the Handicapped, Alamogordo, 1990-92; bd. dirs. White Sands Press Club (treas., 1998-1990), Alamogordo, 1988-92. Recipient Silver award United Way, 1991, over 100% Goal award, 1990, Founders award N.Mex. Commn. for the Blind, 1992, Wayne E. Bonnell award Nat. Fedn. of the Blind, 1982, Gov.'s commendations, 1998, 2000, Cert. of Appreciation, Red Lake Nation's divsn. Rehab. Svcs. Mem. Nat. Coun. of State Agencies for the Blind (bd. dirs. 1994-98, treas. 1999-2000), Coun. of State Adminstrs. of Vocat. Rehab., Nat. Fedn. of the Blind (Des Moines Chpt. award 1983), Alamogordo Rotary Club. Avocations: camping, canoeing, snowshoeing, woodworking. Home: 136 Canterbury Rd Circle Pines MN 55014-1777

DAVIS, RICHARD E. lawyer; b. Canton, Ohio, Mar. 14, 1950; m. Nan A Sponseller. BA, Coll.of Wooster, Ohio, 1972; MA, U. So. Calif., L.A., 1973; JD, U. So. Calif., 1976. Bar: Ohio 1976, Fla. 1998, cert.: Nat. Acad. Elder Law Attys. (elder law atty.) 2001. Ptnr. Day, Ketterer, Raley, Wright, Ltd., Canton, Ohio, 1982—97; dir. Krugliak, Wilkins, Griffiths & Dougherty Co., LPA, Canton, 1998—. Mem. editl. bd. advisors Probate Law Jour. of Ohio, Cleve., 2000—; nat. bd. advisors Wealth Transfer Planning, N.Y.C., 1998—. Chmn. adminstrv. bd. Faith United Meth. Ch., North Canton, 1991—92; v.p. endowment Canton Symphony Orch., 1999—2001, trustee The Wilderness Ctr., Wilmot, 1997—2001, Pathway Caring for Children, Canton, 1993—99, Student Loan Found., North Canton, 1984—97, YMCA of Ctrl. Stark County, Canton, 1999—2001, Downtown Canton Assn., Canton, 1984—88; adult leader Boy Scouts of Am., North Canton, 1982—2000. Fellow: Am. Coll. of Trust & Estate Counsel; mem.: ABA (member of various committees 1976—2001), Land Trust Alliance, Stark County Bar Assn. (various committees 1976—2001), Ohio State Bar Assn. (bd. govs. 1998—), The Fla. Bar, Nat. Acad. f Elder Law Attys., Akron-Canton Estate Planning Forum, Rotary (pres. 1990—91). Office: Krugliak, Wilkins, Griffiths & Dougherty 4775 Munson NW Canton OH 44718 Office Fax: 330-497-4020. Business E-Mail: redavis@actec.org.

DAVIS, RICHARD EARL, lawyer; b. Jackson, Mich., Aug. 13, 1951; s. Richard Allen and Velva Elizabeth (England) D.; m. Paula Hurst, Dec. 9, 1972; children: Richard Seth, Tessa Rebecca. BA, U. So. Fla., 1973, MA, 1975; JD cum laude, Stetson U., 1977. Bar: Fla. 1978, U.S. Ct. Appeals (11th cir.), U.S. Dist. Ct. (mid. dist.) Fla.; bd. cert. city, county and local govt. law Fla. Bar; cert. circuit civil mediator. Asst. county atty. Hillsborough County, Fla., 1978-85; assoc. Holland & Knight, Tampa, Fla., 1985-88, ptnr., 1988-96, Richard E. Davis, P.A., Tampa, Fla., 1997—. Adj. prof. St. Leo U.; lectr. in field. Mem. ABA, Hillsborough County Bar Assn., Fla. Bar Assn., Stetson Lawyers Assn., Tampa Downtown Partnership, Phi Kappa Phi, Phi Sigma Alpha. Office: 220 E Madison St Ste 512 Tampa FL 33602-4826 E-mail: tpaland@earthlink.net.

DAVIS, RICHARD EDMUND, facial plastic surgeon; b. Washington, Apr. 7, 1958; BS, U. Ga., 1981, MS, 1983; MD, Med. Coll. Ga., 1987. Diplomate Am. Bd. Otolaryngology, Am. Bd. Facial Plastic and Reconstructive Surgery. Intern U. N.C., Chapel Hill, 1987-88, resident in otolaryngology, 1988-92; fellow, instr. Oreg. Health Sci. U., Portland, 1992-93; asst. prof. facial plastic and reconstructive surgery U. Miami (Fla.) Sch. Medicine, 1993-99, assoc. prof. facial plastic and reconstructive surgery, 1999—. Mem. staff VA Med. Ctr., Portland, Oreg., 1992-93, Jackson Meml. Hosp., Miami, 1993—, VA Med. Ctr., Miami, 1993—. Mem. AMA, Am. Acad. Otolaryngology Head and Neck Surgery, Am. Acad. Facial Plastic and Reconstructive Surgery (Sir Harold Gilies award 1993), Fla. Soc. Facial Plastic and Reconstructive Surgery. Office: U Miami Hosp and Clinic 1475 NW 12th Ave Ste 4027 Miami FL 33136-1002

DAVIS, RICHARD ERNEST, engineer; b. San Francisco, Nov. 20, 1936; 1 child, Richard Jr.; m. Sharon L. Buss, Aug. 26, 1961; children: Dawn, Michelle. BS in Engring., Calif. State Poly. U., San Luis Obispo, 1967. Facilities engr., energy conservation engr. Naval Weapons Ctr., China Lake, Calif., 1967-77; solar program coordinator U.S. Dept. Energy, Oakland, Calif., 1977-78; program mgr. Solar Energy Research Inst., Golden, Colo., 1978-80; engring. specialist Holmes & Narver, Mercury, Nev., 1980-90; engring. specialist nuclear waste Nev./Yucca Mountain Project Raytheon Svcs., Mercury, 1990-93; constrn. engr. mgr. Fluor Daniel, Inc., 1993-96; city constrn. mgr. Fluor Daniel Telecom, 1996-97, constrn. mgr., project engr. prison constrn., 1997-99; owner Amargosa Cons., 1999—. Contbr. articles to profl. jours. Served with USAF, 1954-62. Avocations: hiking, camping. Home and Office: 3968 Egar Rd Golden Valley AZ 86413

DAVIS, RICHARD FRANCIS, city government official; b. Providence, Aug. 18, 1936; s. Walter Francis and Mary Elizabeth (Gearin) D.; m. Virginia Catherine Oates, Aug. 27, 1960; children: Walter Douglas, John Richard, Theresa Catherine. BS, U. Ark., Little Rock, 1964; student city and regional planning, MIT, summer, 1964; postgrad., Carnegie Mellon U., 1973. Planner Met. Area Planning Commn., Little Rock, 1964-66; mem. Met. Planning Commn. Kansas City, Mo., 1966-67, dir. econs., 1967-69, dir. ops., 1969-71; exec. dir. Mid-Am. Regional Council, Kansas City, 1972-77; gen. mgr. Kansas City Area Transp. Authority, 1977-2000; instr. city planning U. Mo., Kansas City, 1973-74; Planning commr. City of Gladstone, Mo., 1967-69, 81-90, city councilman, 1969-71, mayor, 1971-72, chmn. park bd., 1972-76, mem. bd. zoning adjustment, 1993—; bus. devel. Olsson Assocs., 2002—. Mem. Gladstone Econ. Betterment Coun., 2003—; mem. Clay County (Mo.) Indsl. Devel. Commn., 1972-77, Coun. on Edn., Kansas City, 1974-82, treas., chmn. interdist. rels. com.; bd. dirs. Mo. Pub. Transit Assn., 1979-2000, pres., 1987-89, 1999-2000; bd. dirs. Kans. Pub. Transit Assn., 1979-2000; trustee Black Econ. Union, 1984-88; bd. dirs., treas. Heart of Am. United Way Vol. Ctr., 1985-87. Mem. coun. advisers, Major League Baseball Players Trust for Children, 2000—; v.p. Brooktree Homeowners Assn., 1979-80; mem. Total Transp. adv. com., MidAmerica Regional Coun., 1977-2000, chmn. transit adv. com., 1997-2000; mem. Northland Regional C. of C., 2000-. Served with USAF, 1955-59. Recipient Transp. Svc. award Kansas City chpt. Conf. of Minority Transit Officials, 1987. Mem. Am. Soc. Pub. Adminstrn. (pres. Kansas City chpt. 1980, Pub. Adminstr. of Yr. award 1973, L.P. Cookingham award 1991), Am. Planning Assn., Am. Pub. Transit Assn. (bd. dirs. 1980-93, 94—, mem. govtl. affairs and legis. steering com., v.p. mgmt. and fin. com. 1984-86, v.p. govt. affairs com. 1991-93, Outstanding Pub. Transp. Mgr. award 2000), Kansas City Royal Lancers (bd. dirs. 2001—, v.p. 2001-02, pres. 2002-03). Home: 3612 NE Brooktree Cir Kansas City MO 64119-2229

DAVIS, RICHARD FRANK, former state legislator, research scientist; b. Ann Arbor, Mich., Sept. 9, 1945; s. Paul E. and Irmagene (Blair) D.; m. Constance Ann Meeker, 1966; children: Robert, Joanna, Stephen. BS, Case Inst. Tech., 1967; postgrad., U. Wis., 1967-69; PhD, Yale U., 1972. Rsch. assoc. EI DuPont, Wilmington, Del., 1972-2000; sr. rsch. assoc., 2000—; rschr. agr. products dept. DuPont, 1972—; mem. Dist. 26 Del. State Ho. of Reps., 1983-98, chmn. corrections com., 1984-92, mem. pub. safety com., 1984-92, mem. judiciary com., 1984-92, mem. appropriations com., 1984-92, chmn. appropriations com., 1993-98, co-chmn. joint fin. com., 1993-98. Former chmn. bd. CONTACT, Wilmington; pres. Mariners Watch Maintenance Corp., 2002—. Mem. Nat. Conf. of State Legislatures, 1982-98, chmn. Fiscal, oversight, and intergovtl. affairs com., 1997-98; chmn. bd. dirs. Mark Inc. Ministries, 1997—; bd. dirs. Del. Coalition for Literacy, 1999—, chmn., 2001—; bd. dirs. Del. Mentor Program, 1999—, v.p. bd., 2002-03; bd. dirs. Civic League New Castle County,

1999—, v.p., 2002—; treas. Bear Glasgow Civic Coun., 2002-2003. Post-doctoral fellow Ohio State U., 1972. Mem. Am. Chem. Soc., Am. Legis. Exch. Coun. (Outstanding State Legislator, 1984-98), Nat. Right to Life. Address: 200 Stewards Ct Bear DE 19701-2296

DAVIS, RICHARD HUNT, JR., historian; b. Highland Park, Mich., Sept. 30, 1939; s. Richard Hunt and Helen Grace Davis; m. Jeanne Elizabeth Gruber, May 28, 1939; children: Richard Francis, Jonathan Edward. BA, Grinnell Coll., 1961; MA, U. Wis., 1965, PhD, 1969. Prof. history, now prof. emeritus U. Fla., Gainesville, 1967—, dir. Ctr. for African Studies, 1979—88, dir. internat. studies and programs, 1993—94. Author: Encyclopedia of African History and Culture, Volumes 4&5, (monograph) Bantu Edn. and the Edn. of Africans in South Africa, 1972; editor: Mandela, Tambo, and the African Nat. Congress, 1991, Apartheid Unravels, 1991. Sec. U. Pk. Neighborhood Assn., Gainesville, 2001—03; troop leader Boy Scouts Am., Gainesville, 1978—88; com. mem. So. Africa Fulbright Rev. Com., Coun. for Internat. Exch. of Scholars, Washington, 2001—03. Sr. Fulbright scholar, Coun. for Internat. Exch. Scholars, 1999, Woodrow Wilson fellow, Woodrow Wilson Found., 1961—62, NDEA Title VI Fgn. Lang. fellow, U.S. Dept. Edn., 1964—66, Younger Humanist fellow, Nat. Endowment for the Humanities, 1973—74. Mem.: United Faculty Fla. (treas., v.p. 1972—78), African Studies Assn. (editor African Studies Rev. 1980—88), Am. Hist. Assn. Presbyterian. Avocations: travel, reading, politics, family. Home: 1812 NW 6th Ave Gainesville FL 32603 Office: Univ Florida History Dept PO Box 117320 Gainesville FL 32611-7320

DAVIS, RICHARD JOEL, lawyer, former government official; b. N.Y.C., Mar. 27, 1946; s. Herbert H. and Sylvia (Ginesin) D.; m. Nancy R. Davis. BA, U. Rochester, 1966; JD, Columbia U., 1969. Bar: N.Y. 1970. Law clk. to Judge Jack B. Weinstein, U.S. Dist. Ct. for Eastern Dist. N.Y., 1969-70; asst. U.S. atty. So. Dist. N.Y., 1970-73; task force leader Watergate Spl. Prosecution Force, Washington, 1973-75; assoc. Weil, Gotshal and Manges, N.Y.C., 1976-77, partner, 1981—; asst. sec. of the treasury for enforcement and ops. Dept. Treasury, Washington, 1977-81; instr. in trial advocacy Harvard U.; instr. Nat. Inst. Trial Advocacy. Co-author: American Hostages in Iran, 1988. Mem. Task Force on Ops. of Phila. Police Force, 1986, Task Force on Use and Security of Central Park, 1989; mem. Mayor's Commn. on Police Corruption, 1995—, chmn. 1996—; chmn. Randall's Island Sports Found. Mem. ABA, Legal Aid Soc. N.Y.C. (v.p. 1987-91, bd. dirs. 1987-92), Citizens Union (bd. dirs. 1991-97, vice chmn. 1993-97), Boys Harbor (bd. dirs. 1993—, co-chmn. lawyers com. on violence 1994-98, bd. dirs. parks coun. 1994—). Office: Weil Gotshal & Manges 767 5th Ave New York NY 10153-0119

DAVIS, RICHARD MALONE, economics educator; b. Hamilton, N.Y., June 2, 1918; s. Malone Crowell and Grace Edith (McQuade) D. AB, Colgate U., 1939; MA, Cornell U., 1941, PhD, 1949. From instr. to assoc. prof. econs. Lehigh U., Bethlehem, Pa., 1941-54; assoc. prof. econs. U. Oreg., Eugene, 1954-62, prof., 1962-83, prof. emeritus, 1983—. Contbr. articles to profl. jours. Served with U.S. Army, 1942-45, CBI. Mem. Phi Beta Kappa. Republican. Home: 1040 Ferry St Apt 503 Eugene OR 97401-3332 Office: Univ Oreg Dept Econs Eugene OR 97403

DAVIS, RICHARD OLIVER, obstetrician-gynecologist, educator; b. Athens, Ga., 1947; MD, Med. Coll. Ga., 1973. Diplomate Am. Bd. Ob-gyn., Am. Bd. Maternal and Fetal Medicine. Intern U. Ala. Hosp., Birmingham, 1973-74, resident ob-gyn., 1974-77, fellow fetal and maternal medicine, 1979-81; prof. ob-gyn. U. Ala., Birmingham, 1982—; attending physician in ob-gyn. U. Ala. Hosp., Birmingham, 1977—, divsn. dir. maternal-fetal medicine, 1997-2000. Fellow ACOG; mem. AMA. Office: U Ala Hosp Dept Ob-Gyn OHB 451 619 19th St S Birmingham AL 35249-7333 E-mail: richardd@uab.edu.

DAVIS, RICHARD OWEN, lawyer; b. Tucson, June 26, 1949; s. Charles Owen and Elaine Germaine (Neller) D.; m. Wendy Ellen Hottel, Sept. 5, 1981; children: Kelly, Richard. BS, Purdue U., 1971; JD, Fordham U., 1975; LLM in Taxation, Georgetown U., 1992. Bar: N.J. 1975, D.C. 1978. Legal editor Prentice-Hall, Inc., Englewood Cliffs, N.J., 1975-76; supervisory sr. tax specialist Peat Marwick, Roanoke, Va., 1982-83; asst. br. chief IRS, Washington, 1976-82, 84-92; assoc. prof. Susquehanna U., Selinsgrove, Pa., 1993—. Home: 108 Deerfield Ct Selinsgrove PA 17870-8617 Office: Susquehanna Univ Selinsgrove PA 17870 E-mail: rdavis@susqu.edu.

DAVIS, RICHARD RALPH, lawyer; b. Houston, July 28, 1936; s. William Ralph and Virginia (Allison) D.; m. Christina R. Zelkoff, June 1, 1974; 1 child, Virginia Lee Allison. BA, Yale U., 1962, LLB, 1965; MBA, Columbia U., 1965. Bar: N.Y. 1966. Law clk. FAA, Washington, 1964; assoc. Chadbourne & Parke, N.Y.C., 1965-73, ptnr., 1974-83; sr. v.p., gen. counsel Inspiration Resources Corp., N.Y.C., 1983-91; sr. v.p., sec., gen. counsel Bessemer Securities Corp./Bessemer Trust Co., NA, N.Y.C., 1991—. With U.S. Army, 1956-59. Mem. ABA. Home: 1185 Park Ave Apt 6-g New York NY 10128-1309 E-mail: davis@bessemer.com.

DAVIS, RICHARD WATERS, lawyer; b. Rocky Mount, Va., July 9, 1931; s. Beverly Andrew and Julia (Waters) D.; m. Mary Alice Woods; children: Debra, Julie, Richard Jr., Bob, Bev. B, Hampden-Sydney Coll., 1951; LLB, U. Richmond, 1959. Bar: Va. 1959. Pvt. practice, Radford, Va., 1959—. Dist. judge City of Radford, 1962-80; mem. Pub. Defenders Commn. Va., 1993—, chmn. 2002-; mem. Va. State Bar Coun., 1989-95; assoc. prof. bus. law Radford U.; lectr. Va. Trial Lawyers Assn. Fellow Am. Coll. Trial Lawyers, Am. Bar Found., Va. Law Found. (fellows coun. 1992-98); mem. ABA. Va. Bar Assn. Home: 101 5th St Radford VA 24141 Office: PO Box 3448 Radford VA 24143-3448

DAVIS, ROBERT J. internet company executive; BSc summa cum laude, Northeastern U.; MBA with high distinction, Babson Coll.; D in Comml. Sci. (hon.), Bentley Coll., 1999. From mem. staff to pres., CEO Lycos, Waltham, Mass., 1995—. Bd. dirs. Boston Coll. H.S., The Greater Boston C. of C., Mass. Interactive Media Coun., The Man. com. Office: Lycos 400-2 Totten Pond Rd Waltham MA 02451-2000

DAVIS, ROBERT BARRY, technician, religious studies educator; b. Greenville, S.C., June 30, 1953; s. Robert Berry and Alda Lowe (Wilson) D.; m. Terry Denise Merritt Hippensteel (div.); children: David Barry, Terry Lee; m. Barbara Anne Scott (div.); m. Tracey Lynn Simpson, Apr. 18, 1999. B in Biblical Studies, Logos Christian Coll., Jacksonville, Fla., 1996; master's in Theological Studies, Logos Christian Coll., 2001, postgrad., 2002—. Technician Delta Mills, Piedmont, S.C., 1979-89, 94-95, 1999, Fabri-Kal, Greenville, 1989-93; asst. tchr. Child Devel. Ctr. New Life Christian Fellowship, Greenville, 1996-98; acad. dean, instr. Logos Bible Coll., 1996-98; technician Hitachi U.S., Greenville, S.C., 1999—. Minister Ind. Ministry, 1978—; radio minister, Simpsonville, S.C., 1997. Author: Hebraic Perspectives of the Gospel, 1995, Little Nut to a Tree of Life, 1997, Feasts of the Lord, 1998, God's Purposes for the Feasts, 2000, Deeper Look at the Feasts, 2000, Jewish/Christian Differences, 2000, Intimacy In The Song of Songs, 2000, Christianity Daughter of Judaism, 2001, Jesus At Twelve, 2002. Republican. Avocations: hiking, camping. Home and Office: 200 Sleepy Hollow Rd Piedmont SC 29673-7614 E-mail: barrydavis@mindspring.com.

DAVIS, ROBERT EDWARD, retired communication educator; b. Wichita, Kans., Apr. 2, 1931; s. Edward Lorenzo and Dorrinda Belle (Packer) D.; m. Jacqueline Peggy Baas, Aug. 22, 1955 (div. 1979); children: Robert J., Sarah J., James E.; m. Martha Toni Merrill, Jan. 8, 1983. BA, U. No. Iowa, 1953; MA, U. Iowa, 1956, PhD, 1965. Instr. Grundy Ctr. (Iowa) High Sch., 1953-54; asst. to dir. radio and TV U. No. Iowa, Cedar Falls, 1954-58; lectr., instr. dept. speech and theatre Hunter Coll., N.Y.C., 1961-63, 65-66; asst. prof. dept. speech U. Mich., Ann Arbor, 1966-69; from assoc. prof. to prof. and chmn. dept. cinema and photography So. Ill. U., Carbondale, 1969-74; prof. and chmn. Dept. Radio-TV-Film, U. Tex., Austin, 1974-87, John T. Jones Jr. Centennial prof. in communication, 1987-89, now emeritus, 1989—. Mem. Pacific Grove Planning Commn., 1999—. Author: Response to Innovation, 1976; co-producer, dir. (film) Maple Sugar Farmer, 1973 (7 nat. and internat. awards); writer, performer, dir., producer over 1000 edn1. radio and tv programs; contbr. articles to profl. jours. Mem. Pacific Grove City Coun., 1990-98; mayor pro-tem Pacific Grove, 1994-98; bd. dirs. Heritage Soc. Pacific Grove, 2001—. Republican. Methodist. Avocations: travel, photography. Home: 1212 Del Monte Blvd Pacific Grove CA 93950-2029 E-mail: rtdavis@aol.com.

DAVIS, ROBERT EDWARD, state supreme court justice; b. Topeka, Aug. 28, 1939; s. Thomas Homer and Emma Claire (Hund) D.; m. Jana Jones; children: Edward, Rachel, Patrick, Carolyn, Brian. BA in Polit. Sci., Creighton U., 1961; JD, Georgetown U., 1964. Bar: Kans. 1964, U.S. Dist. Ct. Kans. 1964, U.S. Tax Ct. 1974, U.S. Ct. Mil. Appeals 1965, U.S. Ct. Mil. Review, 1970, U.S. Ct. Appeals (10th cir.) 1974, U.S. Supreme Ct. 1982. Pvt. practice, Leavenworth, Kans., 1967-84; magistrate judge Leavenworth County, 1969-76, county atty., 1980-84, judge dist. ct., 1984-86; judge Kans. Ct. Appeals Jud. Br. Govt., Topeka, 1986-93; justice Kans. Supreme Ct., Topeka, 1993—. Lectr. U. Kans. Law Sch., Lawrence, 1986-95. Capt. JAGC, U.S. Army, 1964-67, Korea. Mem. Am. Judges Assn., Kans. Bar Assn., Leavenworth County Bar Assn. (pres. 1977), Judge Hugh Means Am. Inn of Ct. Charter Orgn. Lawrence. Roman Catholic. Office: 301 W 10th Ave Topeka KS 66612

DAVIS, ROBERT G. insurance executive; degree, MBA, U. Tex. Acct. exec. E.F. Hutton & Co., L.A.; chmn., CEO MBank, Brownville, Tex., MCorp (acquired by Banc One), San Antonio, 1985-89; chief credit officer Bank One Tex.; pres., CEO Bank One Columbus, 1991-95, Banc One Credit Corp., 1995-96; chmn., pres., CEO USAA, San Antonio, 1996—. Office: USAA 9800 Fredericksburg RD San Antonio TX 78288

DAVIS, ROBERT GLENN, research scientist; b. Pitts., May 16, 1951; s. Glenn Ruthven and Roberta (McClurg) D. BS in Chemistry, Pa. State U., 1973; PhD in Organic Chemistry, Purdue U., 1979. Postdoctoral assoc. U. Vt., Burlington, 1979-81; asst. prof. chemistry Temple U., Phila., 1981-84; editor, indexer Inst. Sci. Info., Phila., 1984-85; sr. rsch. scientist Uniroyal Chem. Co., Inc., Middlebury, Conn., 1985—. Active The Nature Conservancy, Middletown. John and Elizabeth Holmes Teas scholar Pa. State U., University Park, 1973. Mem. AAAS, Am. Assn. Pharm. Scientists, Am. Chem. Soc. (chmn. New Haven sec. 1990-91), Phi Lambda Upsilon, Phi Kappa Phi, Nat. Honor Soc., Sigma Xi. Achievements include 9 patents; discovery of herbicide Pantera. Home: 151 Andrew Ave Apt 49 Naugatuck CT 06770-4327

DAVIS, ROBERT LARRY, lawyer; b. Lubbock, Tex., June 6, 1942; s. R. H. and Bernice (Pray) D.; m. Peggy Saunders, Jan. 23, 1965; children: Lee Michael, Melissa Lynn. BA, Rice U., 1964; LLB (with honors), U. Tex., 1967. Bar: Tex. 1967, U.S. Dist. Ct. (We. dist.) Tex. 1969, U.S. Dist. Ct. (So. dist.) Tex. 1989. Assoc. Royston Rayzor & Cook, Houston, 1967-68; from assoc. to ptnr. Brown McCarroll, Austin, Tex., 1968—. Bus. sect. coord., mem. mgmt. com.; parliamentarian, mem. exec. com. Downtown Revitalization Task Force, Austin, 1978-80. Mem., past pres. Boys Club of Austin and Travis County, 1981—; trustee Eanes Ind. Sch. Dist., Austin, 1986-93, pres., 1990-93. Mem.: Assn. Atty. Mediators (pres. Ctrl. Tex. chpt. 1995). Methodist. Avocations: sports, music, reading. Home: 3607-3 Pinnacle Rd Austin TX 78746 Office: Brown McCarroll 1400 One Congress Plz III Congress Austin TX 78701 E-mail: rdavis@mailbmc.com.

DAVIS, ROBERT LAWRENCE, lawyer; b. Cin., Apr. 5, 1928; s. Bryan and Henrietta Elizabeth (Weber) D.; m. Mary Lee Schulte, June 14, 1952; children: Gregory, Randy, Jenny, Bradley. BA, U. Cin., 1952; JD with honors, Salmon P. Chase Coll. Law, 1958. Bar: Ohio 1958, U.S. Supreme Ct. 1966. Assoc. Trabert & Gay, Cin., 1958-62; ptnr. Trabert, Gay & Davis, Cin., 1962-68, Gay, Davis & Kelly, Cin., 1969-71; pvt. practice Cin., 1972—. Lectr. Mt. St. Joseph Coll. 1972-82; arbitrator Am. Arbitration Assn.; assoc. adj. prof. Salmon P. Chase Coll. Sch. Law, 1969-80; lectr. Good Samaritan Hosp. Sch. Nursing, 1960-71. Pres. bd. trustees Cmty. Ltd. Care Dialysis Ctr., 1978-86; mem. Hamilton County Ohio Hosp. Commn., 1986, Kidney Found. Greater Cin., 1989, 92. Served to capt. U.S. Army, 1946-48, 52-53. Decorated Bronze Star medal, Army Commendation medal. Fellow Am. Coll. Trial Lawyers (state chmn. 1994-95); mem. Ohio Bar Assn., Cin. Bar Assn. (John P. Kiely Professionalism award 2002), Am. Bd. Trial Advs. (adv., pres. Cin. chpt. 1996), Lawyers Club (pres. 1962-63), Order of Curia, KC, Phi Delta Theta, Phi Alpha Delta, Sigma Sigma, Omicron Delta Kappa. Home: 9969 Voyager Way Cincinnati OH 45252-1962 Office: 3600 Carew Tower Cincinnati OH 45202 E-mail: rdavis@choice.net.

DAVIS, ROBERT LEACH, retired government official, consultant; b. Torrington, Conn., July 20, 1924; s. Clarence Adelbert and Ruth Mabel (Leach) D.; m. Lorraine Lillian Szabla, Sept. 16, 1950; children: Russell, Cynthia, Vicki, Scott, Gregg. BA in Psychology, U. Mich., 1949. Claims examiner Social Security Adminstrn., Chgo., 1950-52; investigator and personnel specialist U.S. CSC, Chgo., 1952-67; personnel dir. U.S. Post Office Region, Chgo., 1967-71; div. chief, asst. bur. dir. U.S. CSC, Washington, 1971-78; dep. asst. sec. for adminstrn. and mgmt. Dept. Labor, Washington, 1978-82. Served with AUS, 1943-46. Decorated Purple Heart. Democrat. Unitarian-Universalist. Home: 3420 Cordley Lake Rd Pinckney MI 48169 E-mail: rdavis3330@aol.com.

DAVIS, ROBERT NORMAN, hospital administrator; b. July 30, 1938; s. Norman DuBois and Geraldine Elizabeth (Sliker) D.; m. Elizabeth Ann Paine, June 15, 1985; children: Keith Robert, Kathryn Beth, Karl Thomas. BSCE, Pa. State U., 1960; MS in Mgmt., Rensselaer Poly. Inst., 1970. Dir. plant ops. Am. Hosp. Assn., Chgo., 1964-68; dir. mgmt. engring. Hosp. Assn. of N.Y., Albany, 1968-72; assoc. exec. dir. United Hosp., Portchester, N.Y., 1973-75; regional mgr. Arthur Young & Co., N.Y.C., 1975, Medicus Sys. Corp., Nashville, 1976-79; assoc. adminstr. Vanderbilt U. Hosp., Nashville, 1979-81; adminstr. Meml. divsn. Charleston (W.Va.) Area Med. Ctr., 1981-83; prin. Ernst & Young Health Care, 1996-2001; pres. Resource Devel. Assocs., Hendersonville, Tenn., 2001—. Contbr. articles to profl. jours. Bd. dirs., treas. Mid. Tenn. Youth Soccer Inc., 1979-82. With M.S.C., USAF, 1960-63. Fellow Am. Coll. Healthcare Execs., Hosp. Info. Mgmt. Sys. Soc. (dir. 1972-75, hon. fellow 1985). Baptist. Home: 116 Hidden Pt Hendersonville TN 37075-5541 E-mail: bobdavis777@aol.com

DAVIS, ROBERT PAUL, physician, educator; b. Malden, Mass., July 3, 1926; s. Samuel and Sarah (Lemberg) D.; m. Ruby Black, Sept. 5, 1953; children—Edward L., John R., Elizabeth A. AB cum laude, Harvard U., 1947, MD magna cum laude, 1951, A.M., 1955; A.M. (ad eundem), Brown U., 1967. Diplomate: Am. Bd. Internal Medicine, subsplty. bd. nephrology. Intern Peter Bent Brigham Hosp., Boston, 1951-52, asst. medicine, 1952-55, sr. asst. resident physician, 1955-56, chief resident physician, 1956-57; jr. fellow Soc. of Fellows Harvard, 1952-55; asst. medicine Harvard Med. Sch., 1956-57; asst. prof. medicine U. N.C., 1957-59, Albert Einstein Coll. Medicine, 1959-66, assoc. prof., 1967; career scientist Health Research Council, N.Y.C., 1962-67; asst. vis. physician Bronx Mcpl. Hosp. Center, 1959-65, assoc. vis. physician, 1966-67; physician in chief Miriam Hosp., Providence, 1967-71, dir. renal and metabolic diseases, 1974-79; prof. med. sci. Brown U., 1967-84, prof. emeritus, 1984—, chmn. sect. in medicine div. biol. and med. scis., 1971-74. Vis. scientist Ins. Biol. Chemistry of U. Copenhagen, 1965-66; past mem. corp. Butler Hosp., Jewish Family and Children's Service; mem. sci. adv. council N.E. Regional Kidney Program; vice chmn. R.I. Advisory Commn. Med. Care and Edn. Found.; chmn. med. adv. bd. R.I. Kidney Found.; past bd. dirs. Associated Alumni Brown U.; mem. med. adv. bd. New Eng. sect. Am. Liver Found., 1986-90; trustee New Eng. Organ Bank, Boston, 1969—, treas., 1970— ; pres. End-Stage Renal Disease Coordinating Coun. Network 28, New Eng., 1978-79 Assoc. editor: R.I. Med. Jour, 1971-80; contbr. articles to profl. jours. Served as ensign USNR, 1944-46; as lt. (j.g.) M.C. 1951. Traveling fellow Commonwealth Fund, 1965-66; Willard O. Thompson Meml. traveling scholar A.C.P., 1965 Fellow AAAS, ACP; mem. Am. Fedn. Clin. Research, Am. Soc. Transplantation (com. on infrathoracic organs 2003—), Harvey Soc., Biophys. Soc., N.Y. Acad. Medicine, Am. Heart Assn., N.Y. Acad. Sci., Am. Soc. Cell Biology, Soc. Gen. Physiologists, Am. Physiol. Soc., Am. Soc. Artificial Internal Organs, Internat. Soc. Nephrology, Clin. Diabetes Assn. R.I. (pres. 1970-71), Providence, R.I. med. socs., Am. Soc. Nephrology, Am. Soc. Pediatric Nephrology, Soc. for Health and Human Values, Am. Philos. Assn., Phi Beta Kappa, Sigma Xi. Home: 75 Prospect St Providence RI 02906-1330 Office: Brown U Ste 400B 245 Waterman St Providence RI 02906-5215

DAVIS, ROBIN JEAN, state supreme court justice; b. Boone County, W.Va., Apr. 6, 1956; m. Scott Segal; 1 child, Oliver. BS, W.Va. Wesleyan Coll., 1978; MA in Indsl. Rels., JD, W.Va. U., 1982. With Segal & Davis L.C., 1982-96; justice W.Va. Supreme Ct. of Appeals, 1996—, chief justice, 1998—2002. Mem. W.Va. U. Law Inst., W.Va. Bd. of Law Examiners, 1991—. Contbr. articles to W.Va. Law Rev. Mem. ABA, Assn. of Trial Lawyers of Am., Kanawha County Bar Assn., Am. Acad. Matrimonial Lawyers. Office: Supreme Ct of Appeals Bldg 1 Rm E 301 State Capitol Charleston WV 25305*

DAVIS, ROGER EDWIN, lawyer, retired discount chain executive; b. Lakewood, Ohio, Dec. 29, 1928; s. Russell G. and Irma (Aboline) D.; m. Eva Grace Keeler, July 25, 1953 (div. Feb. 1980); children: Susan Lee, Lisa Ann, Steven Russell; m. Yvonne L. Berich, June 1, 1980. AB, Harvard U., 1950; LL.B., U. Mich., 1953. Bar: Mich. 1953. Pvt. practice, Detroit, 1955-60; assoc. Langs, Molyneaux & Armstrong, 1955-60; counsel Avis Enterprises, 1961-62; with legal dept. S.S. Kresge Co. (now Kmart Corp.), 1963-70, v.p., gen. counsel, sec., 1970-85, sr. v.p., gen. counsel, sec., 1985-91, ret., 1991. Served with AUS, 1953-55. Mem. State Bar Mich., Fla. Bar, Pine Lake Country Club (pres. 1991), Bonita Bay Club. E-mail: rogeredavis@worldnet.att.net.

DAVIS, ROGER LEWIS, lawyer; b. New Orleans, Jan. 27, 1946; s. Leon and Anada A. Davis; m. Annette Vucinich; 1 child, Alexandra. BA, Tulane U., 1967; MA, UCLA, 1969; PhD, UCLA, 1971; JD, Harvard U., 1974. Bar: Calif. 1974. Assoc. Orrick, Herrington & Sutcliffe, L.L.P., San Francisco, 1974-79, ptnr., 1980—, chmn. pub. fin. dept., 1981—. Mem. mcpl. fiscal adv. com. Mayor of San Francisco; tech. adv. com. Calif. Debt & Investment Adv. Commn. Fellow: Am. Coll. Bond Counsel (bd. dirs.); mem.: ABA (tax sect., mem. com. tax exempt financing), Calif. Pub. Securities Assn. (bd. dirs. 1998—, infrastructure subcom. of state strategic com. on terrorism), Nat. Assn. Bond Lawyers (mem. com. profl. responsibility and securities law and disclosure). Office: Orrick Herrington & Sutcliffe LLP 400 Sansome St San Francisco CA 94111-3143 E-mail: rogerdavis@orrick.com.

DAVIS, RON LEE, clergyman, author; b. Carroll, Iowa, Oct. 17, 1947; s. David Clarence and Elizabeth Regina (Thompson) D.; m. Shirley Louise O'Connor, Aug. 31, 1973; children: Rachael LeeAnn, Nathan Paul. BA cum laude, Tarkio (Mo.) Coll., 1969; MDiv cum laude, Dubuque (Iowa) Theol. Sem., 1971; DDiv, Bethel Theol. Sem., St. Paul, 1977. Ordained to ministry Presbyn. Ch., 1971. Chaplain Minn. Vikings, Mpls., 1975-80; assoc. pastor Hope Presbyn. Ch., Mpls., 1971-80; sr. pastor First Presbyn. Ch., Fresno, Calif., 1981-86, Community Presbyn. Ch., Danville, Calif., 1986-91; tchr. Bible Oakland (Calif.) A's, 1990-91; writer, 1983—. Invited speaker at gen. sessions and confs. and on TV. Author: Gold in the Making, 1983, A Forgiving God in an Unforgiving World, 1984, Healing Life's Hurts, 1986, A Time for Compassion, 1986, Courage to Begin Again, 1988, Mistreated, 1989, Becoming a Whole Person in a Broken World, 1990, Mentoring, 1990. Mem. pres.'s adv. coun. Fellowship of Christian Athletes; bd. dirs. Youth for Christ, cen. Calif., 1982-85, Fresno Pacific Coll., 1983-84. Recipient award for outstanding leadership State Bar; named to Outstanding Young Men of Am. Avocation: running. Home: 562 Via Appia Walnut Creek CA 94598-2225 Office: Calif Home Loans 1850 San Miguel Dr # 100 Walnut Creek CA 94596

DAVIS, RONALD P. secondary school administrator; b. McKees Rocks, Pa., Dec. 15, 1970; s. Paul H. and Loretta M. (Crenshaw) Davis. BS in Edn., Slippery Rock U., 1992, MA in Student Personnel, 1994; EdD, Nova Southeastern U., 1999. Head camp counselor Boys and Girls Club, Pitts., 1989-93; resident advisor dept. residence edn. Slippery Rock (Pa.) U., 1991-94, grad. asst. Office Student Life, 1993-94; tchr. Stranahan H.S., Ft. Lauderdale, Fla., 1994-99, athletic dir., 1995-99; pres. Visions in Edn., Plantation, Fla., 1995-99; vice prin. Gateway Regional H.S., Woodbury Heights, N.J., 1999-2001, prin., 2001—, Palmyra (N.J.) Adult H.S., 2000-01. Speaker in field. Contbr. articles to profl. jours. Mem. Masons. Democrat. Lutheran. Avocations: baseball, football, animals, dancing, travel. Home: 26 Charles III Dr Glassboro NJ 08028-2836

DAVIS, ROSWITA BEATE, architectural engineer; b. Ranzau, Germany, Sept. 27, 1945; came to U.S., 1966; d. Heinz Otto and Erika (Waht) Neander; 1 child, Erika Neander. Archtl. Draftsperson, Trade and Tech. Coll., Unna, Whestphalen, 1963. Lic. engr., Germany. Chmn. bd. Interior Design Assoc., 1978-81; sr. facilities engr. Ford Aerospace and Comm. Corp., 1981-85. Author: (poetry) Assorted Lives, 1996; (poetry anthologies) Seasons to Come, 1995 (award 1995), Beyond the Stars, 1996 (award 1996), A Tapestry of Thoughts (award 1996), Best Poems of 1996 (award 1996); (novel) Stones That Lie, 1996. Named one of Famous Poets of 20th Cent., Famous Poet Soc. Avocations: reading, writing, dining out, real estate investing and managing. Office: 8992 E Calle Diego Tucson AZ 85710-7324

DAVIS, ROY KIM, otolaryngologist, health facility administrator; b. Logan, Utah, Jan. 20, 1947; m. JoNell Davis; children: Kimberly, Roy Neal, Tamralyn, Cynthia Joy, Mindy Anne, Ricks Eric. BS magna cum laude, Utah State U., 1972; MD, U. Utah, 1975. Diplomate Am. Bd. Otolaryngolgoy. Resident in prespecialty surgery Madigan Army Med. Ctr., 1975-76, resident in otolaryngology, 1976-79; fellow Boston U., Boston, 1979-80; instr. surgery Uniformed Svc. U. Health Sci., Bethesda, Md., 1980-81, asst. prof. surgery, 1981-83; asst. chief otolaryngology svc. Walter Reed Army Med. Ctr., 1980-83; from asst prof. to assoc. prof. U. UT, Salt Lake City, 1983-85; chief otolaryngology head and neck surgery S.L. VA Med. Ctr., Salt Lake City, 1986-93, 99—; dir. John A. Dixon Laser Inst. U. UT, Utah, 1993-98. Adj. prof. comm. disorders U. Utah, 1993—, prof. surgery, 1993; course instr. Am. Acad. Otolaryngology; scientific dir. Rocky Mountain Cancer Data System, 1985-96; mem. head and neck com. SW Oncology Group, 1985—; vis. prof. Madigan Army Medical Ctr., 1980, Brooke Army Medical Ctr., 1981, Tripler Army Medical Ctr., 1982, U. N.C., 1986, U. Tex., 1988, Szent-Gyorgyi Albert Univ., Szeged, Hungary, 1989, First Pavlov Medical Inst., Leningrad, USSR, 1990, Univ. Keil, Germany, 1990, Georg-August U., Gottingen, Germany, 1990, 96, Wilhelm-Pieck Univ. Rostock, Germany, 1990, U. Indonesia, Jakarta, 1995, Bowman-Gray Med. Sch.-Wake Forest U., 1996; Univ. of Iowa, 1997, Cairo Un., 2001-2002; guest examiner Am. Bd. Otolaryngology, 1994-95, 99. Co-author numerous books and book chpts.; contbr. articles to profl. jours. Mem. Jon A. Huntsman Cancer Inst. Fellow Am. Acad. Otolaryngology, Am. Laryngological Assn., Am. Soc. Laser Medicine and Surgery, Am. Coll. Surgeons, Am. Soc. Head and Neck Surgery; Soc. Univ. Otolaryngolgoists, Utah Soc. Otolaryngology, Am. Laryngo., Rhinol. & Otol. Soc., Sec. of Am. Bronchoesophagol. Assoc., Soc. Univ. Otolaryngologists, Alpha Epsilon Delta, Am. Laryngo. Assn. Office: Otolaryngology Head & Neck Surgery 3c134A U Utah Hlth Scis Ctr Salt Lake City UT 84132-0001 E-mail: r.kim.davis@hsc.utah.edu.

DAVIS, ROY WALTON, JR., lawyer; b. Marion, N.C., Jan. 15, 1930; s. Roy Walton and Mildred Gertrude (Wilson) D.; m. Madeline Burch Combs, Sept. 10, 1955; children: R. Walton III, Madeline Trent, Rebekah Wilson, Sally Fielding. BS, Davidson Coll., 1952; JD with honors, U. N.C., 1955. Bar: N.C. 1955, U.S. Dist. Ct. (we. dist.) N.C. 1960, U.S. Ct. Appeals (4th cir.) 1963. Ptnr. Davis & Davis, Marion, 1959-60; from assoc. to ptnr. and pres. Van Winkle, Buck, Wall, Starnes & Davis, Asheville, N.C., 1960—. Lectr. in field. Contbr. articles to profl. publs. Chancellor Episc. Diocese of Western N.C., 1980—. With U.S. Army, 1956-59. Fellow: Internat. Soc. Barristers, Am. Coll. Trial Lawyers (state chair 1994—96), Am. Bar Found.; mem.: ABA (Ho. of Dels. 1989—92, ins. practice and litig. sects.), N.C. Assn. Def. Attys., N.C. State Bar (pres. 1985—86, trustee IOLTA 1987—93, bd. law examiners 2002—), N.C. Bar Assn. (chmn. young lawyers divsn. 1965—66, chair adminstrn. of justice task force 1999—2002, Gen. Practice Hall of Fame), Order of the Coif. Democrat. Home: 359 Country Club Rd Asheville NC 28804-2639 Office: Van Winkle Buck Wall Starnes & Davis 11 N Market St Ste 300 Asheville NC 28801-2932

DAVIS, RUSSELL C. career officer; Student pilot tng., Graham Air Base, Fla., Vance AFB, Okla., 1958-60; BA in Gen. Edn., U. Nebr., Omaha, 1963; JD, Drake U., 1969; student, Air Command and Staff Coll., 1973, Indsl. Coll. Armed Forces, 1979, Harvard U., 1989. Commd. 2d lt. USAF, 1960, advanced through grades to lt. gen., 1998; strategic bombardment pilot 4347th Combat Crew Tng. Wing, McConnell AFB, Kans., 1960; various pilot assignments USAF, 1960-68; flight comdr. 124th Tactical Fighter Squadron Iowa Air NG, Des Moines, 1968-70; air ops. officer 132d Tactical Fighter Group Iowa Air NG, Des

Moines, 1970-77, officer in charge Command Post, 132d Tactical Fighter Wing, 1977-78; dep. comdr. ops. Hdqs. Iowa Air NG, Des Moines, 1978-79; dep. chief manpower and personnel Air NG Support Ctr., Andrews AFB, Md., 1979-80; exec. to chief NG bur., Pentagon, Washington, 1980-82, vice chief, 1995-98, chief Arlington, Va., 1998—; wing comdr. 113th Tactical Fighter Wing D.C. Air NG, Andrews AFB, 1982-90; Air NG asst. to comdr. Tactical Air Command, Langley AFB, 1990-91; comdg. gen. D.C. NG, Washington, 1991-95. Former mem. bd. trustees Drake U. Decorated D.S.M., Legion of Merit with oak leaf cluster, Small Arms Expert Marksmanship Ribbon. Recipient Roy Wilkins Achievement award NAACP, 1984, Air Force Assn. Svc. award Air Force Assn. Hdqs., 1985; scholar Tuskegee U., 1956-58; Ira Eaker fellow Tony Anthony chpt. Air Force Assn., 1988. Office: NGB/CV 1411 Jefferson Davis Hwy Arlington VA 22202-3231

DAVIS, RUSSELL HADEN, consultant; b. Washington, Nov. 26, 1940; s. Walter Haden Davis and Virginia (Russell) Edge; m. Iva Lee Crocker, 1964; children: Brandon Denise, Haden Arnold. BA, U. Va., 1962; MDiv, Union Theol. Sem., N.Y.C., 1965; ThM, So. Bapt. Theol. Sem., Louisville, 1966; STM, Union Theol. Sem., N.Y.C., 1978, PhD, 1986. Ordained to ministry So. Bapt. Ch., 1961, endorsed to chaplaincy Alliance of Baptists in the USA, 2000. Clin. chaplain Ky. State Reformatory, LaGrange, 1966-71, Ctrl. State Hosp., Milledgeville, Ga., 1971-77; assoc. minister The Riverside Ch., N.Y.C., 1977-86; asst. prof. psychiatry and religion Union Theol. Sem., N.Y.C., 1986-91; mem. faculty Blanton-Peale Grad. Inst. Pastoral Psychotherapy, N.Y.C., 1989-91; dir. Psy-Law, N.Y.C., 1989-91; asst. prof. U. Va., 1994, assoc. prof., 1994-95; pvt. practice pastoral psychotherapy, 1974-98; exec. dir. Assn. for Clin. Pastoral Edn., Inc., Decatur, Ga., 1995-98; pres. Legacy Group Internat., 1998—; founder sch. clin. pastoral edn. Sentara Norfolk (Va.) Gen. Hosp., 2001—. Author: Freud's Concept of Passivity, 1993; also articles. Founder Sch. of Clin. Pastoral Edn., Sentara Hosps., Norfolk, Va., 2001; bd. dirs. Tidewater Pastoral Counseling Svcs., Norfolk, Va., 2001—, Inst. for Relationship Therapy, NY, 1981—88, Counseling Ctr., Riverside Ch., NY, 1978—82. Named Ky. Col., State of Ky., 1970; fellow Union Theol. Sem., 1979-81, rsch. grantee, 1987-90; fellow Oaklawn Found., 1980. Mem.: Assn. of Profl. Chaplains (bd. cert. chaplain 1974—99), Assn. Clin. Pastoral Edn. (cert. supr.). Office: Sch Clin Pastoral Edn Sentara Norfolk Gen Hosp 600 Gresham Dr Norfolk VA 23507 E-mail: legacy@5pillars.com

DAVIS, RUTH A. federal agency administrator; b. Phoenix, May 28, 1943; BA, Spelman Coll., 1966; MSW, U. Calif., Berkeley, 1968. Consular officer, Kinshasa, Zaire, 1969-71, Nairobi, Kenya, 1971-73, Tokyo, 1973-76, Naples, Italy, 1976-80; spl. asst. internat. affairs Mayor of Washington, 1980-82; sr. watch officer ops. ctr. Dept. State, 1982-84, chief tng. and liaison, bur. pers., 1984-86; consul gen. Barcelona, 1987-91; amb. to Benin, 1992-96; prin. dept. asst. Sec. State. for Consular Affairs U.S. Dept State, Washington, 1995-97, dir. nat. fgn. affairs tng. ctr., 1997—2001; dir. gen. of foreign serv. U.S. Dept. State, Washington, 2001—. Mem. sr. seminar Fgn. Svc. Inst., 1992. Office: US Dept State Bureau of Human Resources 2201 C St NW Washington DC 20520 Office Fax: 202-647-5080.

DAVIS, RUTH CAROL, pharmacy educator; b. Wilkes-Barre, Pa., Oct. 27, 1943; d. Morris David Davis and Helen Jane Gillis. BS, Phila. Coll. Pharmacy and Sci., 1967; PharmD, Ohio State U., 1970; AA in Elec. Engring., ITT Tech. Inst., 1999. Cert. pharmacist, Pa., Md. Mgr. pharmacist Fairview Pharmacy, Etters, Pa.; mgr., pharmacist Neighborcare Pharmacy, Balt.; dir. ambulatory svcs. Rombro Health Svcs., Balt.; tchr., pharmacist Boothwyn Pharmacy, Phila.; pharm. cons. Nat. Rx Svcs. of Pa.; Eagle Managed Care, 1996; pharmacist Pharmastat Inc., 1996—; pharmacy supr. Johns Hopkins Hospice Pharmacy, 2000—; asst. prof. pharmacy Anne Arundel C.C., 2001—. Adj. prof. Essex C.C., 1999, Balt. City C.C., 2000. Republican. Baptist. Avocations: music, reading. Home and Office: 75 Lion Dr Hanover PA 17331-3849

DAVIS, RUTH MARGARET (MRS. BENJAMIN FRANKLIN LOHR), technology management executive; b. Sharpsville, Pa., Oct. 19, 1928; d. W. George and Mary Anna (Ackermann) D.; m. Benjamin F. Lohr, Apr. 29, 1961. BA, Am. U., 1950; MA, U. Md., 1952, PhD, 1955, CMU, 1978, U. Md., 2000. Statistician FAO, UN, Washington, 1946-49; mathematician Nat. Bur. Standards, 1950-51; head ops. rsch. div. David Taylor Model Basin, 1955-61; staff asst. Office Dir. Def. Rsch. and Engring. Dept. Def., 1961-67; asso. dir. rsch. and devel. Nat. Libr. Medicine, 1967-68; dir. Lister Hill Nat. Center for Biomed. Communications, 1968-70; dir. Inst. for Computer Scis. and Tech. Nat. Bur. Standards, 1970-77; dep. undersec. def. for rsch. and engring., 1977-79; asst. sec. resource applications U.S. Dept. Energy, 1979-81; chmn., pres., CEO Pymatuning Group Inc. FMR, 1981-2000. Chmn. Aerospace Corp., 1994—2001; lectr. U. Md., 1955—57, Am. U., 1957—58; vis. prof. computer sci. U. Pa., 1969—72; adj. prof. U. Pitts.; mem. Md. Gov.'s Sci. Adv. Coun., 1971—77; chmn. nat. adv. coun. Elec. Power Rsch. Inst., 1975—76. Contbr. articles to profl. jours. Recipient Rockefeller Tech. Mgmt. award, 1973, Fed. Woman of the Yr. award, 1973, Systems Profl. of Yr. award, 1979, Disting. Svc. medal, U.S. Dept. Def., 1979, U.S. Dept. Energy, 1981, Gold medal, 1981, Ada A. Lovelace award, 1984, Disting. Alumnus award, U. Md., 1993; inducted into Computer News Hall of Fame, 1988. Fellow AIAA, Soc. for Info. Display; mem. AAAS, Am. Math. Soc., Math. Assn. Am., Nat. Acad. Engring. (counselor), Nat. Acad. Pub. Adminstrn., Nat. Acad. Arts and Scis., Washington Philos. Soc., Sigma Pi Sigma, Tau Beta Pi. Office: Pymatuning Group Inc 1500 N Beauregard St Ste 101 Alexandria VA 22311-1878 E-mail: rmdavis5@aol.com. *The rapid rate of change in our lives due principally to technology and changing personal values makes adaptability and flexibility key ingredients to success. The one essential invariant of success is integrity, accompanied by compassion.*

DAVIS, RUTH MARIE, writer, retired other: health services; d. Avalon Hines and Henry Allen Sisler, Ralph Tucker (Stepfather); m. Daniel Newton Davis, Jr., Sept. 2000; m. Michael Fox, Sr. (div. 1986); children: Michael Fredric Fox II, Stephanie Marie Fox. Veteran's Rep. Accredidation Calif. Dept. of Veteran's Affairs Nat. Svc. Office, 1994, Veterans Services Rep. Accrediation The Am. Legion, 1994, Completion of Advanced Pay Grade Program USNR, 1993. Veteran's services rep. Yuba-Sutter County Veteran's Services Office, Marysville, Calif., 1979—2000. Bd. of directors Yuba County Employee's Assn., Local Number 1, Yuba City, 1991—92, All Valley Veteran's, Marysville, 1998—2000, Yuba-Sutter Counties Veteran's Meml. Com., Marysville, 1998—2001. Author: (novels) The Reclamation Project, (poem) Family Ties, (short stories) Protecting Your Karma, (poem) A Pl. They Call Vietnam, Mother's Arms, Brother's For All Eternity. With USNR, 1992—96. Recipient Recognition of Disting. Meritorious Svc., VFW, 1999, Cert. of Appreciation, Yuba-Sutter Veteran's Meml. Com., 2000. Mem.: NRA, Soc. for Creative Anachronism. Republican. Mem. Christian Ch. Avocations: creative writing, scuba diving, medieval recreation, garment design. Personal E-mail: rthegreat@yahoo.com.

DAVIS, SAMUEL, hospital administrator, educator, consultant; b. N.Y.C., Sept. 30, 1931; s. Morris and Ethel (Levowitz) D.; m. Ellen Darce Kalker, June 16, 1957; children: Joseph Evan, Thomas Adam, Jonathan Edward, Jessica Ann. BA, CCNY, 1952; MS, Columbia U., 1957. Acct. Roosevelt Hosp., N.Y.C., 1954-55; relief adminstr. Meml. Center Cancer and Allied Diseases, N.Y.C., 1955-56; adminstrv. resident, then adminstrv. asst. to dir. and dir. ambulatory care services Roosevelt Hosp., 1956-59; mem. adminstrv. staff Hillside Hosp., Glen Oaks, N.Y.C., 1959-72, exec. v.p., 1970-72; exec. cons. L.I. Jewish-Hillside Med. Center, New Hyde Park, N.Y., 1972; exec. pres. Mt. Sinai Hosp., Mpls., 1972-75, dir. N.Y.C., 1975-81, pres., 1981-85; sr. v.p. Mt. Sinai Med. Center, N.Y.C., 1975-77, exec. v.p., 1978-84; pres. EcuMed, N.Y.C., 1984-85; prin. Sam Davis & Assocs., Rye, N.Y., 1986—; sr. dir. Delta Cons. Group, N.Y.C., 1990-98; assoc. prof. adminstrv. medicine Mt. Sinai Med. Sch., 1975-79, acting chmn., 1977-79, Edmond A. Guggenheim prof. health care mgmt., chmn. health care mgmt., 1979-84, disting. service prof. health care mgmt., 1984—; adj. prof. health care adminstrn. Baruch Coll., CUNY, 1978-87; prof. mgmt., clin. prof. Sch. Pub. Health Columbia U., 1988—; cons. health care strategy and orgnl. change, 1976—; pres. Sam Davis & Assoc., 1999—. Dir. health care research, The Ctr. for Mgmt., CUNY; vice chmn. bd. dirs. Hennepin County (Minn.) Health Coalition, 1973-75; mem. health adv. com. Minn. Met. Health Bd., 1974-75; mem. Hennepin County Health and Social Services Adv. Bd., 1974-75. Author: Decision Analysis in Hospital Administration, 1974; contbr. articles to profl. jours. Trustee Mpls. Fedn. Jewish Service, 1973-75; chmn. health and welfare div. N.Y.C. Fedn. Jewish Philanthropies, 1975-76; trustee, mem. exec. com. Montefiore Med. Ctr., Bronx, N.Y., 1985—. Served with AUS, 1952-54. Recipient Humanitarian award NCCJ, 1984; fellow social studies and humanities CCNY, 1952; WHO fellow, 1970; sr. fellow Wharton Sch. U. Pa., 1986—. Fellow Am. Coll. Hosp. Adminstrs., Am. Pub. Health Assn.; mem. Am. Assn. Hosp. Planning, Am., Am. Acad. Dramatic Arts (bd. dirs., exec. com.), N.Y. State hosp. assns., Am. Mgmt. Assn., Herman Biggs Soc. Office: Sam Davis & Assocs 74 Greenhaven Rd Rye NY 10580-2210 E-mail: sd.a@att.net.

DAVIS, SARA LEA, pharmacist; b. Knoxville, Tenn., Aug. 1, 1951; d. Horace William and Margaret Jewel (Hill) D. BS in Liberal Arts, U. Tenn., 1973; BS in Pharmacy, U. Tenn., Memphis, 1976, PharmD, 1977. Asst. mgr. Pharmaco Nuclear, Inc., Chgo., 1977-79; nuclear pharmacist Kansas City, Mo., 1979, Bapt. Meml. Hosp., Memphis, 1979-83; asst. mgr. Syncor, Inc., Washington, 1983-84; staff pharmacist Rite Aid Corp., Knoxville, 1984—2002, pharmacist-in-charge, 1987—. Rep. 3d High Country Nuclear Medicine Conf., Vail, Colo., 1983; mem. adv. bd. V.I.P. Home Nursing & Rehab., Knoxville, 1985-86. Active Leconte Exec. Women's Coun. Mem. Am. Pharm. Assn., Acad. Pharm. Sci. (sect. nuclear pharmacy), Soc. Nuclear Medicine, Memphis Bus. and Profl. Women's Assn. (bd. dirs. 1982-83), Club Leconte, U. Tenn. Century Club, Mortar Bd., Phi Beta Kappa, Phi Kappa Phi, Rho Chi, Alpha Lambda Delta. Baptist. Office: Rite Aid Pharmacy 508 E Tri County Blvd Oliver Springs TN 37840-2018

DAVIS, SARAH IRWIN, retired English language educator; b. Louisburg, N.C., Nov. 17, 1923; d. M. Stuart and May Amanda (Holmes) D.; m. Charles B. Goodrich, Nov. 18, 1949 (div. 1953). AB, U. N.C., 1944, AM, 1945; PhD, NYU, 1953. Teaching asst. English dept. NYU, 1948-51; tchr. English Elizabeth Irwin High Sch., N.Y.C., 1951-53; editor coll. texts Henry Holt, N.Y.C., 1953-55; editor coll. texts, enclopedias McGraw-Hill, N.Y.C., Rome, 1953-60; asst. prof. English Louisburg (N.C.) Coll., 1960-63, Randolph-Macon Woman's Coll., Lynchburg, Va., 1963-70, assoc. prof. English, 1970-75, chairperson Am. studies, 1971-87, prof. English and Am. studies, 1975-87, ret., 1987. Contbr. articles to profl. jours. Mem. MLA, Am. Studies Assn., N.C.-Va. Coll. English Assn. (various coms.), Franklin County Hist. Soc. (pres. 1989-94). Address: Carol Woods 139 750 Weaver Dairy Rd Chapel Hill NC 27514

DAVIS, SARAH JANE, health care professional; b. Cheyenne, Wyo., Feb. 8, 1949; d. Frederick Eugene and Bernice (Deaver) Fowler; m. David Allen Davis, Dec. 21, 1968 (div. 1973); 1 child, Jacoby. BS in Healthcare, 2003. Key punch operator San Antonio Coll., 1967-70; with personnel dept. Bapt. Meml. Hosp., San Antonio, 1970-71; key punch operator Frost Bank, San Antonio, 1971-72; mgr. Stop and Go, Inc., San Antonio, 1971-72; asst. dir. facilities mgmt. S.W. Tex. Meth. Hosp., San Antonio, 1973—; med. ctr.ops. mgr. Meth. Hosp., San Antonio, Cmty. Hosp. & Meth. Womens & Childrens Hosp., San Antonio. Mem. Nat. Fire Protection Assn. Avocations: needle work, reading, psychology. Office: SW Tex Meth Hosp 7700 Floyd Curl Dr San Antonio TX 78229-3979

DAVIS, SCOTT JONATHAN, lawyer; b. Chgo., Jan. 8, 1952; s. Oscar and Doris (Koller) D.; m. Anne Megan, Jan. 4, 1981; children: William, James, Peter. BA, Yale U., 1972; JD, Harvard U., 1976. Bar: Ill. 1976, U.S. Dist. Ct. (no. dist.) Ill. 1976, U.S. Ct. Appeals (7th cir.) 1977, U.S. Ct. Appeals (8th cir.) 1986. Law clk. to judge U.S. Ct. Appeals (7th cir.), Chgo., 1976—77; assoc. Mayer, Brown, Rowe & Maw, Chgo., 1977—82, ptnr., 1983—. Bd. editors: Harvard Law Rev., 1974—76; contbr. articles to profl. jours. V.p. Chgo. Police Bd. Home: 838 W Belden Ave Chicago IL 60614-3236 Office: Mayer Brown Rowe & Maw 190 S La Salle St Ste 3100 Chicago IL 60603-3441

DAVIS, SCOTT MICHAEL, director, music educator; b. Pitts., Apr. 22, 1976; s. James Earl Collins, Jr. and Lynda Sue Quickel. BS in Music Edn., Pa. State U., 1999. Cert. instr. 1 in music edn. Pa. Substitute music tchr. Punxsutawney (Pa.) Area Schs., 1999—2000; band dir. Leisure City K-8 Ctr., Homestead, Fla., 2000—. Mem.: Pa. Music Educators Assn., Fla. Bandmasters Assn., Fla. Music Edn. Assn., Music Educators Nat. Conf., United Tchrs. Dade (bldg. steward 2001—02). Democrat. Avocations: tennis, travel, music. Home: 8600 SW 212th St #105 Miami FL 33189 Office: Leisure City K-8 Ctr 14950 SW 288th St Homestead FL 33033 Office Fax: 305-247-5179. Personal E-mail: scottdavis_76@hotmail.com. E-mail: smdavis100@yahoo.com.

DAVIS, SHARON EILEEN, congressional staff member; b. Washington, Feb. 21, 1951; d. Carl Clell and Bernadette M. (Leach) D.; m. Albert C. Eisenberg, Jan. 10, 1976; children: Matthew, Alex. BA in Sociology, Hollins Coll., 1973; MPA, George Mason U., 1993. Legis. clk. Com. on Interstate and Fgn. Commerce U.S. Ho. of Reps., Washington, 1975-80, chief clk., adminstrv. asst. Com. on Energy and Commerce, 1981-94, chief minority clk. Com. on Energy and Commerce, 1995—; campaign mgr. Va. Ho. of Dels. mem. Karen Darner, 1990. Bd. visitors George Mason U., Fairfax, Va., 1993-97, alumnae rep., 1996-97, past chair com. EEO/affirmative action, 1995-96; bd. dirs., chmn. Arlington (Va.) Infant and Child Edn. Ctr., 1983-90; bd. dirs. Wakefield H.S. Found., Arlington, 1990—; chair Arlington County Dem. Com., 1981-85; pres. Va. Young Dems., 1977-78; mem. Arlington Partnership for Children, Youth and Families, 1999—; candidate Arlington County Sch. Bd., 1999—; mem. Arlington Pub. Schs. Adv. Coun. on Instrn., 2000—, chair, 2003—; bd. dirs. YMCA, Arlington, 2002, Cmty. Residences, Inc., 2001-. Named Outstanding Young Dem. of Va., Va. Young Dems., 1976-77; Dominion Va. Power fellow Orensen Inst. for Polit. Leadership, U. Va.. Home: 817 N Irving St Arlington VA 22201-2007 E-mail: sharon.davis@mail.house.gov.

DAVIS, SHARON GAIL, nursing assistant; b. Pana, Ill., Sept. 4, 1952; d. Richard Paul Stewardson and Edith Lucille (Beckett) Read; m. Joe Phillips, Sept. 13, 1993 (dec. Feb. 20, 1998); m. Samuel Lee Davis, Mar. 6, 1999; children: Nathan Johnson, Annette Johnson, Kenneth Kimmel, Elizabeth Bennett, George. Cert. nursing asst., Ill. Coll., 1998. Cert. nursing asst. Sullivan (Ill.) Nursing Home, 1991—92, 1998—99, Ill. Masonic Home, Sullivan, 1992—93, Heartland Christian Village, Neoga, Ill., 1999—. Mem.: Lit. Soc. Poets (life awards 1993—98). Avocations: horseback riding, writing, playing piano. Home: 759 Elm St Neoga IL 62447

DAVIS, SHELBY MOORE CULLOM, investment executive, consultant; b. Phila., Mar. 20, 1937; s. Shelby Cullom and Kathryn (Wasserman) D.; m. Wendy Ann Adams, June 20, 1959 (div. 1975); children: Andrew, Christopher, Victoria; m. Gale Abbie Lansing, Apr. 17, 1976; children: Lansing, Alida, Edith. AB with honors, Princeton U., 1958. V.p. in charge equity rsch. Bank of N.Y., N.Y.C., 1958-66; founding ptnr. Davis, Palmer & Biggs, N.Y.C., 1966-78; sr. v.p. Fiduciary Trust Co., N.Y.C., 1978-83, cons., 1983-98; pres. various mut. funds Davis Selected Advisers, Santa Fe, 1983-98, also dir. all mut. funds, 1969-78, 83-98. Contbr. articles to Fin. Analysts Jour. Bd. dirs., trustee Beekman Downtown Hosp., N.Y.C., early 1960s; bd. dirs. Am. Cancer Soc., N.Y.C., early 1970s; trustee United World Coll., 1988—, Teton Sci. Sch., 2001—; mem. adv. bd. Coll. of the Atlantic, 1999—. Mem. N.Y. Soc. Security Analysts (bd. dirs. 1965), Univ. Club, River Club (N.Y.C.), Harbor Club (Seal Harbor, Maine), Tuxedo Club (Tuxedo Park, N.Y.), Jupiter Island Club, Jackson Hole Golf and Tennis Club. Republican. Avocations: skiing, hiking, travel, swimming, tennis. Home: PMB 25185 PO Box 20000 Jackson WY 83001-7000 Office: Davis Advisors PO Box 1688 Santa Fe NM 87504-1688 E-mail: shelby@dsaco.com.

DAVIS, SHELTON HAROLD, sociologist, educator; b. Pitts., Aug. 13, 1942; s. Robert Davis and Fannie Secher; m. Mary Clare Gubbins, July 20, 1979; children: Rebecca Anne, Peter Daniel. Student, London Sch. Econs., 1963—64; BA, Antioch Coll., 1965; PhD, Harvard U., 1970. Lectr. social anthropology Harvard U., Camrbdige, Mass., 1971—73; founder, dir. Indigena, Inc., Berkeley, Calif., 1973—75, Anthropology Resource Ctr., Boston, 1975—84; sr. sociologist The World Bank, Washington, 1987—92, prin. sociologist social policy and resettlement divsn., environment dept., 1993—98, sector manager-L.Am. and Caribbean region, social devel. unit, 1998—. Bd. dirs. Plumsock Fund, South Woodstock, Vt.; adj. asst. prof. anthropology MIT, Cambridge, 1976—79, Boston U., 1979—82; adj. prof. L.Am. studies program, Edmund A. Walsh sch. of fgn. svc. Georgetown U., Washington, 1992—; vis. lectr. social anthropology Fed. U. Rio de Janeiro, 1969—70. Author: Victims of the Miracle: Development and the Indians of Brazil, Land Rights and Indigenous Peoples: The Role of the OAS Inter-American Commission on Human Rights, La Tierra de Nuestros Antepasados: Estudio de la Herencia y la Tenencia de la Tierra en el Altiplano de Guatemala; editor: Antropologia do Direito:Estudo Comparativo de Categorias de Divida e Contrato, (albums) Social Exclusion and Poverty Reduction in Latin America and the Caribbean Region; contbr. articles to profl. joursl and monographs. Fellow, NIMH, US Pub. Health Svc., 1965—69; grantee, Am. Coun. Learned Socs. and Social Sci. Rsch. Coun., 1981, J. Roderick MacArthur Found., 1984—86, World Bank Rsch. Com., 1996—98, World Bank Learning and Leadership Ctr., 1996; scholar, OAS Inter-Am. Commn. Human Rights, 1984—86. Jewish. Avocations: walking, hiking, travel, visiting art museums, listening to jazz and latin music. Home: 608 Highland Ave Falls Church VA 22046 Office: The World Bank 1818 H St NW Washington DC 20433 Office Fax: 202-676-9373. Personal E-mail: sdavis2@worldbank.org. E-mail: sdavis2@worldbank.org.

DAVIS, SHIRLEY HARRIET, social worker, editor; b. Brookline, Mass., June 27, 1922; d. Jacob and Matilda (Goldberg) Freedman; m. Edward H. Davis, Nov. 11, 1943; children: Anita Maureen Davis Winn, Lawrence Paul. AB, Calvin Coolidge Coll., 1944; postgrad., Simmons Sch. of Social Work, 1944-45. Social worker Travelers Aid of N.Y., N.Y.C., 1944-48; dir. Community Svc. Workshop of Woodmere (N.Y.) Acad., 1966-70; v.p. for program and membership West End Aux. Peninsula Hosp. Ctr., Edgemere, N.Y., 1973-80; dir. Family Practice Playroom Coll. Medicine, Downstate Med. Ctr., Bklyn., 1977-83; officer mgr. Edward H. Davis, M.D., Loxahatchee, Fla., 1983-93; dir. publicity and pub. rels. Fla. Atlantic Region of Hadassah, 1994—. Publ. com. Am. Jewish Congress Genetics of Breast Conf., 1997; publ. chair Walk for Better Health Fla. Atlantic Region Hadassah, 1998—, ann. spring conf. Fla Atlantic Region of Hadassah, 1995—. Editor: Hadassah of Wellington Fla., 1990-93. V.p. membership Hadassah of Wellington, 1992-94, bulletin bus. mgr.; dir. publicity and pub. rels., bd. dirs. Fla. Atlantic Region of Hadassah, 1994—; chair Fla. Atlantic Region of Hadassah Women's Health Symposium, 1996, 97, 98, 99, 2000, publicity chair Check It Out Breast Cancer Awareness Program, 1999—; chair Women's Health Symposium, 2000. Wellington chpt. honoree Fla. Atlantic Region of Hadassah ann. Woman of Valor awards, 1996, honoree Fla. Atlantic Region of Hadassah 13th Ann. Spring Conf. for Excellence in Publicity and Pub. Rels., 1998; recipient Nat. Hadassah Love of a Lifetime award, 1996, Nat. Hadassah Best Health Symposium Nation First Pl. award for Woman's Health Symposium, 1998. Republican. Jewish. Avocation: amateur radio. Home: 10601 Firewood Ct West Palm Beach FL 33414-8522 E-mail: hadpublict@aol.com.

DAVIS, SID, journalist; b. Youngstown, Ohio, Nov. 13, 1927; s. Morris and Hilda (Friedman) D.; m. Barbara J. Flint, July 21, 1960; children: Lawrence Jay, Morse Robert. BS, Ohio U., 1952. News reporter Sta. WJEH, Gallipolis, Ohio, 1950-51; news dir. Sta. WKBN, Youngstown, 1952-59; White House corr. Westinghouse Broadcasting Co., Washington, 1959-68, chief Washington news bur., 1968-77; dir. news NBC News, Washington, 1977-79, bur. chief, 1979-80, v.p. and bur. chief, 1980-82, sr. Washington corr., 1982-87; dir. office programs Voice Am., 1987-94; Direct News and other worldwide programming for VOA's English and 45 othe langs. Guest scholar Brookings Instn., Washington, 1994-96; lectr., writer on media and presidency, 1996-97; mem. nat. adv. bd. Close-up Found.; writer, lectr. on media and the presidency and TV's impact on pub. policy, 1997—. Producer: eyewitness account Kennedy assassination Dialogue on Dallas, 1963; dir. coverage all maj. news stories in U.S., presdl. trips abroad. Served with USN, 1946-48. Recipient L.J. Horton award Ohio Univ., 1996; named Sigma Delta Chi Outstanding Journalism Grad. Ohio U., 1952 Mem. White House Corrs. Assn., Radio and TV News Dirs. Assn., Nat. Press Club, Cosmos Club, Fed. City Club, Sigma Delta Chi, Omicron Delta Kappa, Tau Kappa Alpha. Achievements include covering Khrushchev's tour U.S., 1959, U.S. space launchings, 1960-63, Kennedy tours abroad as pres., Johnson's travels as pres., Ford trips to China, USSR, Asia, and Europe; one of three reporters aboard Air Force One to witness swearing in of Pres. Johnson in Dallas, polit. reporting and analysis of major nominating convs., campaigns and elections beginning in 1960, including extensive travel with all Presdl. candidates, directing news coverage for VOA of Gulf War crisis, 1991-92.

DAVIS, SIDNEY L. journalist; b. Boston, Aug. 6, 1935; s. Philip Davis and Bessie Schiller; m. Marlene C. (Levy), Dec. 23, 1958; children: Lynne Weinstein, Susan Costa. AA, Boston U., 1956, BS, 1958. Writer Larkin Publs., Boston, 1958-70, editor, 1970-82, publisher, 1983-91, group publisher, 1991—. Spkr. various confs. and orgns. Bd. visitors Berklee Coll. Music, Boston, 1995—. Recipient Hon. Lifetime Dir. award, Am. Music Conf., 2002. Mem. Masons, B'nai Brith, Sigma Delta Chi, Kappa Tau Alpha. Home: 14 Imrie St Randolph MA 02368-1522 Office: Larkin Publs 50 Brook Rd Needham MA 02494-2929

DAVIS, STANFORD MELVIN, engineering executive, internet consultant; b. Camden, N.J., June 12, 1941; s. Winford and Rose Marie (Rich) D.; m. Pamela Davis, Nov. 25, 1967 (div. 1980); children: Peter, Shawna; m. Laura A. Rudolph, Feb. 21, 1987. AB, BSEE, Rutgers U., 1964; postgrad., UCLA, 1967; MBA, U. Portland, 1974. Elec. engr. RCA, Van Nuys, Calif., 1966-68; project engr. Tek, Wilsonville, Oreg., 1968-79; S/W mgr. Tektronix, Wilsonville, 1979-81, mgr. mktg., 1981-83; founder, v.p. engring. Concept Technologies, Portland, 1983-86; mgr. engring. program INTEL, Hillsboro, Oreg., 1986-87, product line mgr., 1987-88; engring. mgr. Graphic Printing div. Textronix, Wilsonville, Oreg., 1989-95; pres. Straight-on Industries, Beaverton, Oreg., 1995-98; tech. cons. Pres. Internet Profls. Northwest; v.p. sales, mktg. PDX Web; sr. mgr. Storepartners.com; bus. devel. mgr. Netropole Inc.; spkr. on E-commerce, Your Business on the Web, 1999-2000, internet mktg. PSU Macromedia Daze, 2000; spkr. in field. Patentee in field. Served to capt. U.S. Army, 1964-66. Recipient Outstanding Product award Datapro, Delran, N.J., 1985. Mem. Internet Profls. N.W., Software Assn. Oreg., Portland City Club (Pres.'s award 1996). Avocations: skiing, gardening, camping, tennis, fishing. Home and Office: PO Box 1488 Beaverton OR 97075-1488 E-mail: stand@straight-on.com., stan@netropole.com.

DAVIS, STANLEY NELSON, hydrologist, educator; b. Rio de Janeiro, Aug. 6, 1924; s. Nelson Caryl and Mary Faye (Caulkins) D.; m. Barbara Jean Wickham, Apr. 14, 1949 (div.); children: Gerald Nelson, Ruth Ann, Darlene Grace, Randall Wayne, Betty Jean, Nancy Faye.; m. Augusta G. Felty, Feb. 12, 1982; children— Tara Devi, Locana Kamala BS in Geology, U. Nev., 1949; MS, U. Kans., 1951; PhD, Yale, 1955. Geologist U.S. Bur. Reclamation, 1949, Mo. Geol. Survey, 1952, 53, 55; instr. U. Rochester, 1953-54; mem. faculty Stanford, 1954-67, prof. geology, 1965-67, U. Mo., 1967-73, chmn. dept., 1969-72; asso. dean Coll. Arts and Scis., 1972-73; prof. geology Ind. U., Bloomington, 1973-75; prof. hydrology U. Ariz., Tucson, 1975—, head dept. hydrology and water resources, 1975-79. Vis. prof. U. Chile, Santiago, 1960-61; tchr. Bowling Green U., summer 1963, Princeton, summer 1965, U. Hawaii, fall 1966; instr. U. Oriente in Venezuela, summer 1967-68, 72; lectr. Am. Geol. Inst.; mem. East Greenland Expdn., Arctic Inst. N. Am., summer 1959; cons. to govt. and industry, 1955— Author: Hidrogeología, 1961, (with R.M. DeWiest) Hydrogeology, 1966, (with P. Reitan and R. Pestrong) Geology, Our Physical Environment, 1976, (with D.J. Campbell, H.W. Bentley, T.J. Flynn) Ground Water Tracers, 1984; also articles. Served with AUS, 1943-46, PTO. Fellow AAAS, Geol. Soc. Am. (O.E. Meinzer award 1989), Am. Geophys. Union; mem. Assn. Ground Water Scientists and Engrs., Soc. Econ. Paleontologists and Mineralogists, Sigma Xi. Home: 6540 W Box Canyon Dr Tucson AZ 85745-9681 Office: U Ariz Dept Hydrology & Water Resou Tucson AZ 85721-0001 E-mail: sndavis@u.arizona.edu.

DAVIS, STEPHEN, football player; b. Mar. 1, 1974; m. Virginia Davis; children: Dentia, Sherrell, Stephen Davis Jr. Degree in vocat. edn., Auburn. Profl. football player Washington Redskins, 1996—. Office: 21300 Redskins Park Dr Ashburn VA 20147

DAVIS, STEPHEN DRAKE, lawyer; b. Andrews, Tex., Jan. 17, 1957; s. J. Frank and Patricia Ann (Harrison) D.; m. Susan Diane Schindler; children: Matthew W., Kelly A., Ross H. BSChE, La. State U., 1979; JD, U. Tex., 1981. Bar: Tex. 1982. Assoc. Vinson & Elkins L.L.P., Houston, 1982-89, ptnr., 1990—, adminstrv. head Singapore office Singapore, 1995-2001, Asia-Pacific liaison, 2002—, energy practice exec. com., 2002—. Chmn. Students Awareness Com., Houston, 1988-89; mem. Offshore Lawyers Liaison Com., Singapore, 1996-2000. Author reviews, spkr. confs. Instr. Coll. Rep. Nat. Com.,

1977-79, mem. 1977-78; state chmn. La. Coll. Reps., 1977-78; participant coalition for the preservation of Hilshire Village, 1989; dir. Passages, Inc., Houston, 1992-94. Scholar Soc. Petroleum Engrs., 1975-76, La. State U. top 100 scholar, 1975-78, Nat. Merit scholar, 1975-79; named Houston Young Lawyer's Assn. outstanding com. leader, 1987, Asia Leading Lawyer, 1996-2003, 20 Best Energy and Natural Resources Lawyers in World, 2000, 25 Best Project Fin. Lawyers in World, 2002. Mem. ABA, Tex. Bar Assn., Inter-Pacific Bar Assn. Office: Ste 2300 1001 Fannin Houston TX 77002 E-mail: sdavis@velaw.com.

DAVIS, STEPHEN EDWARD FOLWELL, banker; b. Auckland, N.Z., July 12, 1964; s. George Folwell and Elizabeth Ann (Strother) D. BA, Harvard Coll., 1987. Rsch. intern The Brookings Instn., Washington, 1984; sales intern Lotus Devel. Corp., Cambridge, Mass., 1986-87; fin. analyst Salomon Bros. Inc., N.Y.C., 1987-89; interest rate swap trader Kidder Peabody & Co., N.Y.C., 1989-90; derivatives trader Deutsche Bank AG, N.Y.C., 1990-95; proprietary trader Dai-Ichi Kangyo Bank, Ltd., 1995-96; head derivatives trading Hypo Bank AG, N.Y.C., 1996-97; pres. Nuuanu Real Estate Investors, Honolulu, 1997—. Researcher book: The Ultimate Insiders, 1989. Homesteading coord., dir. Crimson Impact Inc., N.Y.C., 1991-95; treas. The Quadrille Soc., N.Y.C., 1991—; vol. Habitat for Humanity, 2002. JFK Sch. Govt. grantee, 1984; Lindsay Exeter Meml. scholar, 1983. Mem. Fgn. Policy Assn., Harvard Club of N.Y. Avocations: foreign policy, golf, running. Address: 1330 Ala Moana Blvd # 2407 Honolulu HI 96814-4231 E-mail: sdavis@post.harvard.edu.

DAVIS, STEPHEN HOWARD, applied mathematics educator; b. N.Y.C., Sept. 7, 1939; s. Harry Carl and Eva Leah (Axelrod) D.; m. Suellen Lewis, Jan. 15, 1966. BEE, Rensselaer Poly. Inst., 1960, MS in Math, 1962, PhD in Math., 1964; BSc honoris causa, U. Western Ont., 2001. Research mathematician Rand Corp., Santa Monica, Calif., 1964-66; lectr. in math. Imperial Coll., London U., 1966-68; asst. prof. mechanics and materials sci. Johns Hopkins U., 1968-70, assoc. prof., 1970-75, prof., 1975-78; prof. engring. sci. and applied math. Northwestern U., 1979—, Walter P. Murphy prof., 1987—, McCormick Sch. prof., 2000—. Dir. Ctr. for Multiphase Fluid Flow and Transport, 1986-88; cons. in field; vis. prof. math. Monash U., Australia, 1973; vis. prof. chem. engring. U. Ariz., 1977; vis. prof. aerospace and mech. engring., 1981; vis. scientist Institut für Aerodynamik-ETH, Zurich, Switzerland, 1971; vis. scientist Dept. Math. Ecole Polytechnique Federale, Lausanne, Switzerland, 1984, 85, vis. prof. 1987, 88, 91; mem. U.S. Nat. Com. for Theoretical and Applied Mechanics, 1978-87. Asst. editor Jour. Fluid Mechanics, 1969-75, assoc. editor, 1975-89, editor-in-chief, 2000—; contbr. articles to profl. jours. Recipient Alexander von Humboldt award, 1994, Fluid Dynamics prize Am. Phys. Soc., 1994, G.I. Taylor medal Soc. for Engring. Sci., 2001. Fellow Am. Phys. Soc. (chmn. divsn. fluid dynamics 1978-79, 87-88, councillor divsn. fluid dynamics 1980-82); mem. NAE, Am. Acad. Arts and Scis., Soc. Indsl. and Applied Math. (coun. 1983-87), Sigma Xi, Pi Mu Epsilon. Home: 1199 Edgewood Rd Lake Forest IL 60045-1308 Office: Northwestern U McCormick Sch Engring/Applied Scis Sheridan Rd Evanston IL 60208-0001

DAVIS, STERLING EVAN, television executive; b. Mpls., Feb. 10, 1941; s. Lyman Eugene and Ruby Elizabeth (Larson) D.; m. Bonnie S. Taylor, Jan. 15, 1977; children: Evan, Emily, Robin. BA, Taylor U., 1963; postgrad., U. So. Calif., L.A., 1968-70. Chief engr. Metrotape, Hollywood, Calif., 1974-78; v.p. ops. The Vidtronics Co., Hollywood, 1978; chief engr. Telemation Prodns., Seattle, 1978-82; dir. ops. Sta. KTVU, Inc., Oakland, Calif., 1982-98; v.p. engring. Cox Broadcasting, Atlanta, 1998—. Bd. dirs. Easter Seals Soc. Lt. USN, 1963-67, Vietnam. Mem. IEEE, Soc. Motion Picture & TV Engrs., Audio Engring. Soc., Soc. Broadcast Engrs. Office: Cox Broadcasting PO Box 105357 Atlanta GA 30348-5357 E-mail: sterling.davis@cox.com.

DAVIS, STEVE, state legislator; b. Sept. 22, 1949; m. Carol Keck; children: Shane, Shelly. Student, Lewis and Clark C.C., So. Ill. U. Hwy. commr. Wood River Twp., Ill., 1981-94; former mem., treas. Madison County Dem. Cen. Com.; Ill. state rep. Dist. 111, 1995—. Mem. Aging, Appropriations-Edn., Environ. and Energy and Transp. Coms., 1995—, Ill. Ho. of Reps.; draftsman R. W. Booker and Assocs., 1970; sr. civil engr. Sterling Engring. Co., 1970-73, Volz Engring. and Survey, 1973-75, PHO Inc., 1975-78; operator Amoco Oil Co., 1978-80; pres. Steve Davis and Assocs., 1980-82. Bd. dirs. Family Svc. and Vis. Nurse Assn. Mem. Moose, Am. Legion (post 214), Ill. Legis. Sportsmans Caucus. Office: 2 Terminal Dr Ste 18B East Alton IL 62024-2289*

DAVIS, STEVEN M. architectural firm executive; With Davis Brody Bond, 1982, ptnr., 1988 . Vis. critic Harvard U., U. of Pa., Parsons Sch. of Design, CUNY. Office: Davis Brody Bond LLP 315 Hudson St 9th Fl New York NY 10013 Fax: 212-633-4762.*

DAVIS, STEVEN MICHAEL, air force officer, test pilot; b. Everett, Wash., Nov. 6, 1961; s. Raymond A. and Leila E. Davis; m. Margaret Louise Cleaver, Sept. 2, 1992. BS in Physics, USAF Acad., 1984; MS in Aerospace Engring., U. So. Calif., 1991, MS in Systems Mgmt., 1996. Commd. 2nd lt. USAF, 1984, advanced through grades to lt. col., 2000; KC-10A aircraft comdr. 6th Air Refueling Squadron, March AFB, Calif., 1990-91, KC-10A instr. pilot, 1991; wing tactics officer 22d Air Refueling Wing, March AFB, Calif., 1991-92; student test pilot USAF Test Pilot Sch., Edwards AFB, Calif., 1992-93; chief test pilot 418th Flight Test Squadron, Edwards AFB, Calif., 1993-95; ops. officer Detachment 1, 46th Ops. Group, Hurlburt Field, Fla., 1995-98; chief test pilot Air Mobility Warfare Ctr., Ft. Dix, NJ, 1998—2001; program mgr. Airborne Laser Sys. Program Office, Kirkland AFB, N.Mex., 2001—. Dir. BBD Liquidation Corp., Redlands, Calif., 1994-99. Sec. Inland Empire Space Group, Riverside, Calif., 1991-93. Decorated Air medal, 1991, Lt. Gen. Bobby Bond Memorial Aviator Awd., 1997, NDIA Air Force Tester of the Year, 1997, Meritorious Svc. Medal, 1998, AMC Test Dir. of Yr., 1999. Mem. AIAA, Soc. Exptl. Test Pilots, Nat. Space Soc. Avocations: rebuilding automobiles, remodeling houses, hockey, scuba diving, bicycling.

DAVIS, SUE ELLEN H. elementary and secondary music educator; b. Girard, Ohio, May 26, 1952; d. Edgar J. and Jane A. (O'Brien) Harris; 1 child, Heidi Elizabeth. BM, Youngstown (Ohio) State U., 1975, MS in Edn./Sch. Counseling, 1985. Cert. counselor, music tchr. K-12, sch. counselor. Tchr. vocal music, kindergarten-12th grade Girard City Schs. Grant coord. Tng. Ohio Parents for Success, Girard City Schs. Active in ch. and community orgns.; co-founder Cmty. Band, 2002. Mem. NEA, Ohio Edn. Assn., Girard Edn. Assn., Nat. Assn. Tchrs. Singing (high sch. div. competition judge), Music Educators Nat. Conf., ASCD, Ohio Sch. Counselor Assn., Ohio Career Devel. Assn., Ohio Assn. Counseling and Devel., Eastern Ohio Counselor's Assn., Ohio Assn. Counselor Educators and Suprs., Ohio Coll. Pers. Assn., Ohio Mental Health Counselors Assn., Ohio Assn. for Specialists in Group Work, Phi Delta Kappa, Delta Kappa Gamma, Sigma Alpha Iota.

DAVIS, SUSAN A. congresswoman; b. Cambridge, Mass., Apr. 13, 1944; m. Steve, 1970; children: Jeffrey, Benjamin. Degree in Sociology, U. Calif., Berkeley; MA in Social Work, U. N.C. Social worker; exec. dir. Aaron Price Fellowship Program, 1990-93; served Calif. State Assembly, 1994-2000; congresswoman Calif. 53rd Dist., 2000—; mem. Ho. Com. on Veteran Affairs. Mem. Congressional com. House Armed Svcs., Edn. and Workforce; chaired Women's Caucus for Senate and Assembly, Consumer Protection, Govt. Efficiency, Econ. Devel. com.; created and co-chaired Select com. on Adolescence. Mem. San Diego City Sch. Bd., 1983-1992, pres. and v.p.; pres. League of Women Voters San Diego., Democrat. Office: 1224 Longworth House Office bldg Washington DC 20515*

DAVIS, SUZY, information center owner; b. Duncan, Okla., July 19, 1936; d. Elmer Arvin and Reba Dorril (Johnson) Gilstrap; m. Francis Jerome Dillard, Jan. 22, 1955 (div. May 1975); children: Jeri S., Lawrance A., Joe P., Marie E.; m. William Thomas Davis, Dec. 20, 1984 (dec.). Grad. high sch., Newman, Calif., 1954. Guest lectr. Calif. State U., Long Beach, 1986, 89, model Riverside, 1988-90, San Bernardino, 1988—, Cmty. Coll., San Bernardino, 1988—, Robert E. Wood Watercolor Workshop, Palm Springs, Calif., 1990, U. Nev., Las Vegas, 1993-95, Cheyenne C.C., North Las Vegas, 1993-95, Las Vegas Art Mus. Studio, 1994-95; owner, operator Nudist Info. Ctr., North Las Vegas, Nev., 1984-92; prodn. coord. Heritage Video, Las Vegas, 1992; bd. dirs. Beachfront USA, Moreno Valley. Bd. dirs. Callen-Davis Meml. Fund, Moreno Valley, Calif., 1988—, Western Sunbathing Assn., Studio City, Calif., 1989-92; active adopt-a-hwy. Western Sunbathing Assn., Victorville, Calif., 1990-92, Earth Week (city clean-up), Daggett, 1990. Named as part of Family of Yr., Western Sunbathing Assn., 1986, for Membership Increase by Percentage, Am. Sunbathing Assn., 1986, Woman of the Yr., Am. Sunbathing Assn., 1992; recipient Glen Eden award Am. Sunbathing Assn., 1986. Mem. Am. Assn. Nude Recreation (life), Western Sunbathing Assn. (life). Avocations: dancing, reading, coin collecting, stamp collecting.

DAVIS, TAMMIE LYNETTE, assistant principal; b. Kingsport, Tenn., Jan. 17, 1961; d. James T. and Gertrude (Bridges) D. BS in Music Edn., Tenn. Technol. U., 1983; MEd in Ednl. Leadership, East Tenn. State U., 1992. Cert. tchr., Tenn. Chorus and orchestra director John Sevier Mid. Sch., Kingsport, 1983—2001; asst. prin. Jefferson Elem. Sch., Kingsport, 2001—. Chmn. dept. fine arts John Sevier Mid. Sch., 1987, 91-93, 98-2000, chmn. adv. bd., 1991-93; participant Music Educators Nat. Conf., 1981—, Tenn. Arts Acad., 1993. Violist Kingsport Symphony Orch., 1979-89, 92-94, bd. dirs., 1987-89; violist Johnson City Symphony Orch., 1995—; mem. (hammered dulcimer folk group) Wire Kwire, Kingsport, 1986—. Designated Career Ladder Tchr. III, State of Tenn., 1992; named one of Outstanding Music Educators, Gov.'s Sch. for Arts, Tenn., 1990. Mem. NEA, ASCD, Tenn. Edn. Assn., Am. String Tchrs. Assn., Kingsport Edn. Assn. (treas. 1992-94, pres.-elect 1994-95, pres. 1995-96), Nat. Assn. for Preservation and Perpetuation of Storytelling, Tenn. Assn. for Preservation and Perpetuation of Storytelling, Bays Mountain Dulcimer Soc. (pres. 1988-90). Avocations: collecting figurines, reading, writing, performing folk music, flea marketing. Home: 2021 Pendragon Rd Kingsport TN 37660-3432 Office: Jefferson Elem Sch 2216 Westmoreland Kingsport TN 37660

DAVIS, TERESANN WELLER, social worker; b. Sharon, Pa., Mar. 9, 1946; d. Frank and Teresa (Phelan) Weller; m. Ronald E. Davis, Nov. 24, 1972 (div. 1979); 1 child, Jeanne Marie Reighard. BA, Youngstown State U., 1969; MSSA, Case Western Res. U., 1978. Lic. ind. social worker, profl. clin. counselor, Ohio. Therapist Child and Adult Mental Health Ctr., 1969-72; social worker, supr. adult svcs. Valley Counseling, Warren, Ohio, 1973—. Bd. dirs. Someplace Safe, Warren, Rape Crisis Team, Warren; mem. adv. bd. Warren Health Dept.; mem. Child Abuse and Neglect Team, Warren; mem. Pleasant Valley Ecumenical Ch. Mem. NASW. Avocations: reading, youth baseball.

DAVIS, TERRELL, former professional football player; b. San Diego, Oct. 28, 1972; Student, Long Beach State U., U. Ga. Running back Denver Broncos, 1995—2002; player AFC Championship Game, 1997, Super Bowl, 1997, Pro Bowl, 1996, 1997. Named Sporting News NFL-Pro Team Running Back, 1996, 1997. Office: Denver Broncos 13655 Broncos Pkwy Englewood CO 80112-4150

DAVIS, TERRI JUDITH, television producer, writer; b. Pitts., Feb. 9, 1961; d. Louis Jr. and Shirley Merle (Riley) D. Student, Columbia Coll., Chgo., 1979-80, UCLA, 1980-83, Fashion Inst. Tech., N.Y.C., 1983. Assoc. prodr. John & Leeza, 1993, exec. prodr. Manu Dibango and Hugh Masakela Live, 1994, In Their Eyes, 1996; prodr.: Marilu, 1995, The RuPaul Show, 1995, Loveline, 1996, Interior Motives, 1997—2000 (Emmy nomination for Best Show, 1997), The Christopher Lowell Show (Emmy nomination for Best Show, 1999); show prodr., field dir. : Area Style Network; prodr.: Design on a Dime HGTV; writer Season to Taste, 1995. Pres. so. Calif. chpt. St. Jude Children's Rsch. Hosp., 1995-96. Mem. AFTRA, Emmy, NAFE. Democrat. Avocations: fundraising, fashion design, fiction. Office: Jude Entertainment Ste 306 401 S Cochran Ave Los Angeles CA 90036-3351

DAVIS, TERRY HUNTER, JR., lawyer; b. Charlottesville, Va., Mar. 19, 1931; s. Terry Hunter and Mattie May (Parsons) D.;m. Mary Jane Irwin, Sept. 3, 1960; 1 child, Terry Hunter III. BA, Va. Mil. Inst., 1953; LLB, U. Va., 1958. Bar: Va. 1958, N.Y. 1959. Assoc. Thacher, Proffitt, Prizer, N.Y.C., 1958-60; law clk. Chief U.S. Dist. Judge, Norfolk, Va., 1960-61; assoc., ptnr. Taylor, Gustin, Harris, Norfolk, 1961-88; ptnr. Harris, Fears, Davis, Lynch & McDaniel, Norfolk, 1988—. Contbg. author Virginia Lawyer's Basic Practice Handbook, 1964. Chmn. Norfolk Electral Bd., 1971-72. 1st lt. U.S. Army, 1953-55. Mem. ABA, Va. Bar Assn., Va. State Bar (com. mem. 1972-73), Norfolk/Portsmouth Bar (com. chmn. 1962-63), SAR (treas. 1962-64), Kiwanis. Republican. Episcopalian. Avocations: jogging, tennis. Home: 7451 N Shore Rd Norfolk VA 23505-1770 Office: Harris Fears Davis Lynch & McDaniel PO Box 12756 Norfolk VA 23541-0756 E-mail: tdavis@aol.com.

DAVIS, THERESA MARY, education educator, artist; b. Alliance, Ohio, Feb. 26, 1954; d. Robert Roland and Josephine Cecalia (Marhefky) Montgomery; m. Jan Gibbson Davis, Oct. 25, 1996; m. Fredrick Alan Young, July 31, 1971 (dec. July 7, 1978); children: Dustin Alan, Jeremy Matthew. BA Hist. and Religion, Mt. Union Coll., Alliance, Ohio, 1995; MA Hist., Univ. Akron, Akron, Ohio, 2000. Mgr. Pets & More, Sault St. Marie, Mich., 1971—72; new bus. mgr. First Nat. Bank of Alliance, Alliance, Ohio, 1974—78; owner, trainer Down to Earth Quarter Horses, Alliance, Ohio, 1979—90; tchg. asst. Univ. Akron, Akron, Ohio, 1996—98; educator Stark County Sch., Stark County, Ohio, 1998—2000; tchg. asst. Univ. Akron, Akron, Ohio, 2000—. Contbr. articles to profl jour. Recipient Rob and Viola Dunn Bible award, Mt. Union Coll., Ohio, 1993, Grand Ol' Army Rep. award, 1994; scholar Martin Scholarship, Univ. Akron, 1996—2002. Mem.: Orgn. Am. Historians, Phi Chi (Delta Chi Chptr.) (sec. 1996—98, 2000—). Democrat. Avocation: art. Home: 9737 McCallum Ave Alliance OH 44601 Office: Univ Akron Arts and Sci Bldg Akron OH

DAVIS, THOMAS HILL, JR., lawyer; b. Raleigh, NC, June 11, 1951; s. Thomas Hill and Margie Wayne (Perry) D.; m. Julia Dee Wilson, May 31, 1980; children: Thomas Hill III, Alexander Erwin, Julia Hadley, Hunter McDowell. BA, N.C. State U., 1973; JD, Wake Forest U., 1976. Bar: N.C. 1976, U.S. Dist. Ct. (ea. and middle dist.) N.C. 1976, U.S. Ct. Appeals (11th cir.) 1982, U.S. Ct. Appeals (4th cir.) 1986, U.S. Supreme Ct. 1979. Reporter Winston-Salem (N.C.) Jour., 1974-76; asst. atty. N.C. Dept. Justice, Raleigh, 1976-88; gen. ptnr. Poyner & Spruill, Raleigh, 1988—. Arbitrator Am. Arbitration Assn., 1990—; lectr. Campbell U. Sch. Law, Buies Creek, N.C., 1992. Supplement editor: Construction Litigation, 1992; contbg. author: Public & Private Contracting in North Carolina, 1985, North Carolina Adminstrative Law, 1996; contbr. articles to profl. jours. Active NC R.R. Legis. Study Commn., Raleigh, 1985—87; pres. Badger-Iredell Found.; bd. dirs. Juvenile Diabetes Rsch. Found. Capt. N.C. State Def. Militia, 1993—. Mem. N.C. Bar Assn. (Appreciation award 1989), Wake County Bar Assn. (VLP award 1995), North Hills Club, Lions. Democrat. Presbyterian. Avocations: fly fishing, wing shooting, photography, tennis. Home: 608 Blenheim Pl Raleigh NC 27612-4943 Office: Poyner & Spruill 3600 Glenwood Ave Raleigh NC 27612-4945 E-mail: thdavis@poynerspruill.com.

DAVIS, THOMAS M., III, congressman; b. Minot, N.D., Jan. 5, 1949; m. Peggy Davis; 3 children. BA in Polit. Sci., Amherst Coll., 1971; JD, U. Va., 1975. Page U.S. Senate, 1964-67; pvt. practice, 1975-79; v.p., gen. counsel Advanced Techs., 1979-90; mem. Mason Dist., 1979-91; mem. then chmn. Fairfax County Bd. Suprs., 1980—94; gen. counsel PRC, Inc., 1990-94; mem. U.S. Congress from 11th Va. dist., 1995—; mem. energy and commerce com., govt. reform com.; chmn. Nat. Rep. Congress. Com., govt. reform subcom., 2001—. Served in Va. Nat. Guard, Army Nat. Guard, U.S. Army. With U.S. Army, with USAR, with Va. Nat. Guard. Mem.: Baileys Crossroads Rotary Club (charter mem., past pres.). Republican. Office: US House Reps 2348 Rayburn Ho Office Bldg Washington DC 20515-4611*

DAVIS, THOMAS PAUL, music educator, choral director; b. Wellsboro, Pa., Aug. 2, 1953; s. Waldo Ray and Jane Kathryn (Foley) D. B of Music Edn., Nyack Coll., 1976; postgrad. studies, Pa. State U., 1976. Band dir. Juniata Valley H.S., Alexandria, Pa., 1976-79; choral dir. Westmont-Hilltop H.S., Johnstown, Pa., 1979-81, Titusville (Fla.) H.S., 1981—. So. divsn. chmn. for male choirs Am. Choral Dirs. Assn., 1991-97; cast choir dir. Walt Disney World Co., 1988-93. Music dir. St. Luke's Prebyn. Ch. Titusville, 1983-87, Merritt Island (Fla.) Presbyn. Ch., 1991—. Mem. Fla. Music Educators Assn. (mentor program 2001), Fla. Vocal Assn. (bd. mem. 1986-89, 99—, superior Choral Ratings 1984-85, 87-2002), Nat. Choral Dirs. Assn. (divsn. chmn. 1991-97), Music Educators Nat. Conf., Phi Delta Kappa. Democrat. Avocation: travel. Office: Titusville HS 150 Terrier Trl Titusville FL 32780 E-mail: davist2@brevard.k12.fl.us.

DAVIS, THOMAS PINKNEY, secondary school educator; b. Seminole, Okla., Oct. 10, 1956; s. George Pinkney and Flora Elizabeth (Bollinger) D.; m. Leslie Anne Workman, Jan. 26, 1990; children: Brianna Elizabeth, Mary Katherine, James Pinkney, Robert McKenzie, Victoria Anne; stepchildren: Christopher Lee, Jennifer Dawn, Matthew Joseph, Daniel Jacob, Joshua Issiac Beene. BS with Honors, BA with Honors, East Cen. U., Ada, Okla., 1979. Dir. math. lab. East Cen. U., 1991-92; tchr., chair math. dept. Roosevelt (Okla.) High Sch., 1992-93; tchr. math., chair math. dept. Keota (Okla.) High Sch., 1993-2000; tchr., chair math. dept. Spade (Tex.) Ind. Sch. Dist., 2000—. Book reviewer Jour. Assn. of Lunar and Planetary Observers/The Strolling Astronomer; adj. instr. Connors State Coll., 1998-99; rsch. assoc. Fermi Nat. Accelerator Lab., 1999. Reviewer Sci. Books and Films, 1986—. Fellow Brit. Interplanetary.Soc., Soc. Antiquaries of Scotland; mem. AIAA, Am. Astronautical Soc., Assn. Lunar and Planetary Observers, Nat. Coun. Tchrs. Math., Okla. Coun. Tchrs. Math., Okla. Acad. Sci., Alpha Chi, Pi Gamma Mu. Republican. Episcopalian. Home: Glazner House PO Box 10 Spade TX 79369-0010 Office: Spade Ind Sch Dist PO Box 69 Spade TX 79369-0069 E-mail: tp_davis@yahoo.com.

DAVIS, THOMAS W. investment bank executive; b. Doylestown, Pa., Oct. 23, 1953; s. Clarence J. and Phyllis D; m. Linda J., Aug. 2, 1975; children: Christin, Whitney, Kaitlyn. BA, Johns Hopkins U., 1975; MBA, U. Chicago, 1977. Sr. v.p. Merrill Lynch & Co., N.Y.C., 1993-95, sr. v.p. head investment banking, 1995-97, exec. v.p./pres. corp. and institutional clients, 1997—2001, chmn., 2001—. Adv. coun. U. Chgo. Grad. Sch. Bus., 1999—. Bd. dirs. Choral Soc. Westchester, Scarsdale, N.Y., 1996—. Recipient award for Academic Excellence, U. Chgo., 1977. Mem. Phi Beta Kappa. Avocations: coaching, golf, reading. Office: Merrill Lynch & Co 250 Vesey St New York NY 10080-0002

DAVIS, THOMAS WILLIAM, computer company executive; b. Belvidere, Ill., Mar. 14, 1946; s. Thomas William and Charlotte Ann (Schildgen) D.; m. Lyndel Etta Schuettpelz, Apr. 3, 1971; 1 child, Bryan William. BSEE, Milw. Sch. Engring., 1968; MSEE, U. Wis., Milw., 1971. Registered profl. engr., Wis. From asst. prof. to assoc. prof. elec. engring. Milw. Sch. Engring., 1971-75, head computer engring. tech., 1975-77, prof. 1976-94, chmn. dept. elec. engring., 1977-84, dean rsch., 1981-84, dean acads. and rsch., 1984-87, v.p. academics, dean faculty, 1987-89, sr. v.p. 1989-94; exec. v.p. Super Steel Products Corp., Milw., 1994-96, sr. v.p., 1996-98; pres. Milw. Rehab. Ctr., 1997—; pres. Prophet Tech. LLC, 1998—; lectr. U. Wis., Milw., 1973-76. Author: Problems in Measurements, 1968, (textbooks) Computer Aided Analysis, 1973, Introduction to Interactive Programs, 1978, Experimentation with Microprocessor Applications, 1981; patentee in field. Warning and comms. officer Ozaukee County Emergency Govt., Wis., 1981-82; sgt. reserves Grafton Police Dept., Wis., 1976-2001; corp. mem. svcs. Curative Rehab. Ctr, Gov.'s Quality Improvement Task Force, Gov.'s Sci. and Tech. Coun.; bd. dirs. Jagemann Stamping, Amalga Composites Co, Curative Care Network Svcs., Inc.; past pres. Milw. Coun. Engring. and Sci. Socs., MSOE Alumni Assn., Inc. Mem. IEEE (sr., student activity dir. 1972-73), Engrs. and Scis. Milw. (past pres.), Robotics Internat., Soc. Mfg. Engrs. (sr.), Milw. Sch. Engring. Alumni Assn. (achievement award 1968, 25th ann. Outstanding Alumnus award 1993, pres. 1997-98), UWM Alumni Assn. (outstanding alumnus award 1995), Wis. Soc. Profl. Engrs. (past pres. Milw. chpt.), Phi Kappa Phi, Tau Alpha Pi, Eta Kappa Nu. Avocation: flying, amateur radio. Home: 5590 Gray Log Ct Grafton WI 53024-9622 Office: Prophet Technologies 1550 N Prospect Ave Milwaukee WI 53202-6501 Business E-Mail: tom@prophettechnologies.com.

DAVIS, TOM IVEY, II, management executive; b. New Bern, N.C., Feb. 14, 1946; s. Tom Ivey and Carrie Best (Tyson) D.; m. Linda Ann Sawyer, Mar. 9, 1968; children: Tom Ivey III, Matthew Curtis. BS, BA, East Carolina U., 1976. CPA, N.C. Bus. mgr. Davis Oil Co., New Bern, 1973-76; acct. to supr. sr. acct. Peat Marwick Mitchell & Co, CPA, Raleigh, N.C., 1976-80; chief fin. officer HCM, Inc., Va. Beach, Va., 1980-82, ATC Petroleum, Inc., Wilmington, N.C., 1982-83; v.p. fin., chief fin. officer Brian Ctr. Mgmt. Corp., Hickory, N.C., 1983-84, exec. v.p., chief oper. officer, 1984-95; pres. T.J. Ivey & Co., Hickory, 1996-97; sr. v.p. bus. devel. Svc. Master Diversified Health Svc., 1998, sr. v.p., CFO, 1998-99, exec. v.p., COO, 1999-2000; pres., CEO Forest Hill Investors, LLC, 2000—. Bd. dirs. BB&T, Hickory Bd. dirs. Luth. Nursing Homes, Inc., 1995—, Catawba Valley chpt. ARC, 1994 97; mem. bd. visitors Lenoir-Rhyne Coll., 1995-2001. With USNR, 1973-94. Mem. AICPA, N.C. Assn. CPAs, Tenn. Assn. of CPAs, Catawaba County C. of C. (small bus. adv. coun. 1989). Republican. Lutheran. Avocations: reading, off-road driving, camping. Office: 6799 Great Oaks Rd Ste 250 Germantown TN 38138 E-mail: tdavis2@ltcmgt.com.

DAVIS, TROY ARNOL, reflexologist, hypnotherapist; b. Quitman, Tex., Apr. 5, 1921; Student, Am. Inst. Reflexology, Am. Inst. Med. Hypnoanalysts. Cert. reflexologist; cert. hypnotherapist. Practice reflexology and hypnotherapy, Karnes City, Tex. Contbr. articles to profl. pubs.; songwriter "A Country Stayin' Free," 2002, poet. Served with USN, WWII. Recipient Presdl. medal of merit, Presdl. Task Force. Mem. Internat. Soc. Poets. Home: PO Box 295 Karnes City TX 78118-0295

DAVIS, VERA, elementary school educator; b. Cornish, N.H., Sept. 16, 1940; d. Francis Edward and Alice Cone (Parkhurst) Williams; m. John T. Davis, July 3, 1968; 1 child, William Guy. BS, Castleton (Vt.) State Coll., 1962; M in Reading, Coll. St. Joseph, Rutland, Vt., 1992. Cert. tchr. Tchr. 2d grade Town of Cavendish, Proctorsville, Vt., Title I tchr., 1996—. Mem. NEA, Vt. Edn. Assn. Home: 66 Main St Ludlow VT 05149-1113

DAVIS, VICTOR ALLEN, JR., executive magistrate; b. Kans City, Mo, July 23, 1946; s. Victor Allen and Polly Jean (Porterfield) Davis; m. Joycelyn Ann Davis, Aug. 9, 1969; children: Melissa Ann, Aimee Leigh. BA cum laude, Kans. State U., Mo., 1968; JD, Kans. State U., 1971. Bar: Kans./ US Dist. Ct. Kans. 1971. Assoc. Weary, Davis, Henry, Struebing & Troup, Junction City, Kans., 1971—73, ptnr., 1973; officer, dir. Junction City Abstract & Title Co.; magistrate US Dist. Ct. Kans., 1973. Contbr. articles. Recipient Nat. Civilian Leader of Yr. Award, Armed Svc. Dept., YMCA/USA. Mem.: Kans. Law Rev.Bd. (tech. editor 1970—71), US Magistrates Coun. (Junction City, C of C bd. of dir. 1985—), Geary County Bar Assn., Kans. Bar Assn., ABA, Leadership Kans., various ch. bd. commn., George Smith Libr. (chmn. bd. trustees), United Way Junction City (bd. dir. 1979, 1985), Armed Svc. YMCA (chmn. bd. 1979—81), Junction City Jaycees (pres. 1978), Lions. Republican. Meth. Office: 819 N Washington St Junction City KS 66441-2446

DAVIS, VIRGINIA, trade show producer; b. Waycross, Ga., Nov. 14, 1933; d. Arthur Lewis and Mina (Hyers) Davis; m. Edward Anthony Carfano, July 3, 1954 (div. June 1976). Adminstrv. asst. Mills Music Ltd., N.Y.C., 1960-67; v.p. Edward Carr Prodns., Ltd., N.Y.C., 1990-96; owner Virginia Davis Trade Shows, Convs., Meetings, N.Y.C. and Phoenix, 1973—; asst. at trade shows and press confs. William Campeau Pub. Rels., 1983—. Democrat. Avocations: reading, dancing, yoga, animals. Home: 5301 W Camelback Rd Sun City AZ 85351

DAVIS, W. HOWARD, retired oral and maxillofacial surgeon; b. L.A., Sept. 21, 1926; s. T. Howard Davis; m. E. Jane Davis, Dec. 11, 1945; children: David, Christopher. DDS, U. So. Calif., L.A., 1948. Cert. Am. Bd. Oral and Maxillofacial Surgery. Resident oral surgery U. So. Calif.-L.A. County Med. Hosp., 1948-50; assoc. oral surgeon Dr. A.O. Hubbell, Long Beach, Calif., 1950-54, Dr. Harlan Apfel, San Pedro, 1956-57; pvt. practice oral surgeon Bellflower, Calif., 1957—. Co-editor: Reconstructive Preprosthetic Oral and Maxillofacial Surgery, 1986, 2nd edit., 1995; contbr. chpts. to books and articles to profl. jours. Lt. USN, 1954—56. Fellow Am. Assn. Oral Maxillofacial Surgeons (various coms. 1954—); mem. ADA, Calif. Dental Soc., Harbor Dental Soc., Rotary Club (pres.). Avocation: golf. Office: 14343 Bellflower Blvd Bellflower CA 90706-3135

DAVIS, W. JEREMY, dean, law educator, lawyer; b. Pitts., Apr. 13, 1942; s. Winthrop Neuffer and Eleanor (Power) D.; m. Jacqueline Dvoracek, June 11, 1966; children: Jeremy Michael, Sarah Elizabeth. BSBA, U. Denver, 1964, JD, 1970; LLM, Yale U., 1980. Bar: Colo. 1970, N.D. 1973. Pvt. practice law, Denver, 1970-71; asst. prof. U. N.D., Grand Forks, 1971-74, assoc. prof., 1975-82, dean, prof. law, 1983—2002, gen. counsel, 1993-2000, dir. legal affairs, 2000—02; dean, Sutin prof. law Appalachian Sch. of Law, 2003—. With

U.S. Army, 1965-68. Fellow Bush Found., 1979-80. Mem. State Bar Assn. N.D. (bd. govs. 1982-2002), N.D. Trial Lawyers Assn. (bd. govs. 1986-2002). Home: PO Box 1008 Grundy VA 24614 Office: Rt 83 Slate Creek Rd PO Box 2825 Grundy VA 24614 E-mail: wjd@asl.edu.

DAVIS, WANDA ROSE, lawyer; b. Lampasas, Tex., Oct. 4, 1937; d. Ellis DeWitt and Julia Doris (Rose) Cockrell; m. Richard Andrew Fulcher, May 9, 1959 (div. 1969); 1 child, Greg Ellis; m. Edwin Leon Davis, Jan. 14, 1973 (div. 1985). BBA, U. Tex., 1959, JD, 1971. Bar: Tex. 1971, Colo. 1981, U.S. Dist. Ct. (no. dist.) Tex. 1972, U.S. Dist. Ct. Colo. 1981, U.S. Ct. Appeals (10th cir. 1981), U.S. Supreme Ct. 1976. Atty. Atlantic Richfield Co., Dallas, 1971; assoc. firm Crocker & Murphy, Dallas, 1971-72; prin. Wanda Davis, Atty. at Law, Dallas, 1972-73; ptnr. firm Davis & Davis Inc., Dallas, 1973-75; atty. adviser HUD, Dallas, 1974-75, Air Force Acctg. and Fin. Ctr., Danver, 1976-92; co-chmn. regional Profl. Devel. Inst. Am. Soc. Mil. Comptrollers, Colorado Springs, Colo., 1982; chmn. Lowry AFB Noontime Edn. Program, Exercise Program, Denver, 1977-83; mem. speakers bur. Colo. Women's Bar, 1995—, Lowry AFB, 1981-83. Mem. fed. ct. liaison com. U.S. Dist. Ct. Colo., 1983; mem. Leaders of the Fed. Bar Assn. People to People Del. to China, USSR and Finland, 1986. Contbr. numerous articles to profl. jours. Bd. dirs. Pres.'s Coun. Met. Denver, 1981-83; mem. Lowry AFB Alcohol Abuse Exec. Com., 1981-84. Recipient Spl. Achievement award USAF, 1978; Upward Mobility award Fed. Profl. and Adminstrv. Women Denver, 1979, Internat. Humanitarian award CARE, 1994. Mem. Fed. Bar Assn. (pres. Colo. 1982-83, mem. nat. coun. 1984—, Earl W. Kintner Disting. Svc. award 1983, 1st v.p. 10th cir. 1986-97, Internat. Hummanitarian award CARE, 1994), Zach Found. for Burned Children (award 1995), Colo. Trial Lawyers Assn., Bus. and Profl. Women's Club (dist. IV East dir. 1983-84, Colo. pres. 1988-89), Am. Soc. Mil. Comptrollers (pres. 1984-85), Denver south Met. Bus. and Profl. Women's Club (pres. 1982-83), Denver Silver Spruce Am. Bus. Women's Assn. (pres. 1981-82; Woman of Yr. award 1982), Colo. Jud. Inst., Colo. Concerned Lawyers, Profl. Mgrs. Assn., Fed. Women's Program (v.p. Denver 1980), Colo. Woman News Community adv. bd. 1988—), Dallas Bar Assn., Tex. Bar Assn., Denver Bar Assn., Altrusa, Zonta, Denver Nancy Langhorn Federally Employed Women (pres. 1979-80). Christian.

DAVIS, WAYNE ALTON, computer science educator; b. Ft. Macleod, Alta., Can., Nov. 16, 1931; s. Frederick and Anna Mary (Barr) D.; m. Audrey M. Zorolow, July 17, 1959 (div. 1989); children: Fredrick M., Peter W., Timothy M.; m. Patricia Ruth Syme, Mar. 24, 1990. BSE, George Washington U., 1960; MSc, U. Ottawa, 1963, PhD, 1967. Sci. officer Def. Resch. Bd., Ottawa, Ont., 1960-68; research scientist Dept. Comms., Ottawa, 1968-69; vis. scientist NRC, Ottawa, 1975-76; assoc. prof. U. Alta., Edmonton, 1969-77, prof. computing sci., 1977-91, prof. emeritus, 1991—, acting chmn. computing sci., 1982-83; acting dir. Alta. Centre for Machine Intelligence and Robotics, 1988-89. Lectr. U. Ottawa, 1965-69; sessional lectr. Carleton U., 1967; cons. Editor: The Barrs of Ardenville, 1978; editor Procs. Graphics Interface, 1994, 95, 96, 97, 98. Grantee NRC, 1970-78; rsch. grantee Natural Scis. and Engring. Rsch. Coun., 1978-92; strategic grantee Natural Scis. and Engring. Rsch. Coun., 1981-83; grantee Def. Rsch. Bd., 1974-76; hon. prof. Harbin Shipbldg. Engring. Inst., China, 1985. Mem. Can. Info. Processing Soc. (pres. 1978-79), Can. Human Computer Comms. Soc. (pres. 1981-96), Can. Soc. Computational Study of Intelligence (treas. 1976-86), Faculty Club. Anglican. Home: Box 817 605-21st St Fort Macleod AB Canada T0L 0Z0 Office: U Alta Dept Computing Sci Edmonton AB Canada T6G 2E8 E-mail: davis@cs.ualberta.ca.

DAVIS, WENDELL, JR., lawyer; b. N.Y.C., June 22, 1933; m. Penelope Case, May 17, 1969; children: Jennifer C., Virginia W. Hartung, Peter T. AB cum laude, Harvard U., 1954, LL.B. cum laude, 1961. Bar: Conn. 1961, N.Y. 1963, U.S. Dist. Ct. (so. and ea. dist.) N.Y. 1964, U.S. Dist. Ct. Conn. 1966, U.S. Ct. Appeals (2d cir.) 1966, U.S Ct. Appeals (5th cir.) 1972, U.S. Supreme Ct. 1973. Law sec. to Justice Charles D. Breitel, N.Y.C., 1964-65; ptnr. Scheuermann & Davis and predecessor firms, N.Y.C., 1975-78, 92-00, Emmet, Marvin & Martin, N.Y.C., 1978-91. Pres. Carnegie Hill-90th St. Inc., 1977-80 Bd. dirs. United Way Larchmont, 1984-91. Lt. USNR, 1957. Mem. Am. Law Inst., Assn. Bar City N.Y., Harvard Club, Univ. Club Larchmont (gov. 1991-94, pres. 1993-94). Home: 28 Huguenot Dr Larchmont NY 10538-1935

DAVIS, WESLEY D. psychologist, educator; b. Shreveport, La., May 13, 1934; s. Homer E. and Fannie G. Davis; m. Lora C. Davis, June 10, 1963 (div. Nov. 10, 1970); children: Evon Michelle, Elizabeth Ann. BA, Hardin-Simmons U., Abilene, Texas, 1956; MA, Baylor U., Waco, Texas, 1957; postgrad., U. Colo., 1958—62; PhD, Fla. State U., Tallahassee, 1985. Cert. tchr. Fla. Asst. prof. psychology Hendrix Coll., Conway, Ark., 1957—59; staff psychologist Colo. State Hosp., 1962—63; staff pschologist Leon County Mental Health Ctr., Tallahassee, 1963—70, Atlantic Mental Health Ctr., Virginia Beach, 1970—75; dir., evaluation services Escambia County Pub. Schools, Pensacola, Fla., 1975—. Adj. prof. ednl. leadership U. West Fla., Pensacola, 1990—93; adj. prof. pschology Troy State U., Pensacola, Fla., 1993—98; psychol. evaluations Divsn. Vocat. Rehab., Tallahassee, also Virginia Beach, Va., 1963—75. Contbr. editls. and articles to various jours. Recipient Pres.'s award, Fla. Ednl. Rsch. Coun., 1999, An Apple from the Tchr. award, Escambia Edn. Assn., 2002. Mem.: Fla. Assn. Test Adminstrs. (bd. dirs. 1992—95), Fla. Ednl. Rsch. Coun. (pres. 1999—2000), Fla. Ednl. Rsch. Assn., Phi Kappa Phi. Democrat-Npl. Southern Baptist. Achievements include research citations in The American Psychologist. Office: Escambia County Public Schools 30 E Texar Drive Pensacola FL 32503-2902 Office Fax: 850-429-2963. E-mail: wdavis@escambia.k12.fl.us.

DAVIS, WILLIAM E. utility executive; With Niagara Mohawk Holdings, Inc., CEO, chmn. bd. dirs., 1993—2002; chmn. bd. dirs. Nat. Grid USA, 2002—. Office: 300 Erie Blvd W Syracuse NY 13202-4250

DAVIS, WILLIAM EUGENE, judge; b. Winfield, Ala., Aug. 18, 1936; s. A. L. and Addie Lee (Lenahan) Davis; m. Celia Chalaron, Oct. 3, 1963. JD, Tulane U., 1960. Bar: La. 1960. Assoc. Phelps Dunbar Marks Claverie & Sims, New Orleans, 1960—64; ptnr. Caffery Duhe & Davis, New Iberia, La., 1964—76; judge U.S. Dist. Ct., Lafayette, La., 1976—83, U.S. Ct. Appeals (5th Cir.), Lafayette, 1983—. Mem.: ABA, Maritime Assn. U.S., La. Bar Assn. Republican. Office: US Ct Appeals 800 Lafayette St Ste 5100 Lafayette LA 70501-6883

DAVIS, WILLIAM GRENVILLE, lawyer, former Canadian government official; b. Brampton, Ont., Can., July 30, 1929; s. Albert Grenville and Vera M. (Hewetson) D.; m. Helen MacPhee, 1953 (dec. 1962); children— Neil, Nancy, Catherine, Ian; m. Kathleen Mackay, 1963; 1 dau., Meg. BA, U. Toronto, 1951; grad., Osgoode Hall Law Sch., 1954; LLD (hon.), Waterloo Luth. U., 1963, Western Ont. U., 1965, U. Toronto, 1967, McMaster U., 1968, Queen's U., 1968, Windsor U., 1969; DU (hon.), Ottawa U., 1980; LHD (hon.), Yeshiva U., N.Y., Nat. U. of Ireland, U. Tel Aviv. Bar: Ont. 1955. Ptnr. Davis, Webb and Hollinrake, Brampton, 1955-59; mem. Provincial Parliament Ont. from Peel Riding, 1959, 63, Peel North Riding, 1967, 71, Brampton Riding, 1975; 2d vice-chmn. Hydro-Electric Power Commn. of Ont., 1961-62; minister of edn. Province of Ont., 1962-71, also minister of univ. affairs, 1964-71, premier, 1971-85; apptd. spl. envoy on acid rain by prime minister of Can., 1985-86; of counsel Torys LLP, Toronto, 1986—. Apptd. mem. Privy Coun. Queen Elizabeth II, 1982—; vice chmn. internat. adv. coun. Power Corp. Can.; bd. dirs. 1st Am. Title Ins. Co., NIKE Can. Ltd., Magellan Aerospace Corp., St. Lawrence Cement, 1st Am. Title Co., BPO Properties Ltd., Home Capital Group Inc., Magna Entertainment Corp. Author: Education in Ontario, 1965, Building an Educated Society, 1816-1966, 1966, other publs. Leader Progressive Conservative Party, 1975-81. Recipient Order of Ont. award; named Companion, Order of Can. Mem. Can. Bar Assn., Ont. Bar Assn., Albany Club, Kiwanis, Masons. Mem. United Ch. Office: Torys The Maritime Life Tower Toronto ON Canada M5K 1N2

DAVIS, WILLIAM HOWARD, lawyer; b. Monmouth, Ill., May 24, 1951; s. Orville Francis and Alice Gertrude (Hennenfent) D.; m. Susan Claire Parris, April 11, 1981; children: Benjamin Patrick, Jackson Mitchell, Claire Marie. BA with honors, U. South Fla., 1974; JD with high honors, Fla. State U., 1977. Bar: Fla. 1977, U.S. Dist. Ct. (no. dist.) Fla. 1977, U.S. Dist. Ct. (mid. dist.) Fla. 1986, U.S. Ct. Appeals (11th cir.) 1986, U.S. Supreme Ct. 1993. Assoc. Thompson, Wadsworth, Messer & Rhodes, Tallahassee, 1977-80; ptnr. Wadsworth & Davis, P.A., Tallahassee, 1980—2002; of counsel Messer, Caparello and Self, PA, Tallahassee, 2003—. Instr. legal writing Fla. State U., 1976-77; mem. Fla. Supreme Ct. Commn. on Professionalism, 2002—. Editor notes and comments Fla. State U. Law Rev., 1976-77. Bd. dirs. Legal Aid Found., Inc., 1980-81, Fla. Legal Svcs., Inc., 1988-96, pres., 1993; pres. student govt., chmn., state coun. student body pres. State U. Sys. Fla., 1973-74. Mem. Acad. Fla. Trial Lawyers, Nat. Assn. Criminal Def. Lawyers, Fla. Bar (2d cir. judge nominations commn. 1986-90, chmn. 2d cir. jud. grievance com. 1988-90), Fla. Bar Found. (bd. dirs. 1993-94, 97—, sec.-treas. 2002—, chmn. legal assistance to poor grant com. 1993—, exec. com. 2000—), Tallahassee Bar Assn. (bd. dirs. 1982-88, pres. 1986-87), Fla. Assn. Criminal Def. Lawyers (coalition juvenile justice), Am. Inns of Ct. (master of bench emeritus, exec. com. Tallahassee 1994-96), Coalition for Juvenile Justice, Cath. Charities (bd. dirs. Tallahassee region 1995-2002, pres. 1999-2001), Gulf Winds Track Club, Capital Tiger Bay Club, Omicron Delta Kappa, Phi Sigma Alpha. Home: 914 Mimosa Dr Tallahassee FL 32312-3012 Office: Messer Caparello & Self PA 215 S Monroe St Ste 701 Tallahassee FL 32301 Office Fax: 850-222-0720.

DAVIS, WILLIAM L. publishing company executive; BA in Polit. Sci., Princeton U., 1965. With Sears, Roebuck and Co.; pres. Appleton Electric; group v.p. Emerson, 1983—85, pres. skills divsn., 1985—88, exec. v.p., 1988—93, sr. exec. v.p., 1993—95, head process control group, 1995, CEO, chmn., 1997—. Office: RR Donnelley & Sons Co 77 W Wacker Dr Fl 19 Chicago IL 60601-1604

DAVIS, WILLIAM TERRY, software engineer, technology manager; b. Canonsburg, Pa., Apr. 28, 1954; s. William Glen and Dorothy Jane (Bright) D. BS, California (Pa.) State Coll., 1976; postgrad., Pa. State U., 1976; MS, U. Pitts., 1979. Teaching asst. Pa. State U., State College, 1976, U. Pitts., 1977-79; sr. engr. Union Switch & Signal R & D, Pitts., 1978-85; product devel. specialist Dun & Bradstreet, Dunsgate, N.Y.C., 1986-91; mgr. software dept. Casco, Signal Ltd., Shanghai, 1991-92; tech. officer Chem. Bank, Banklink, N.Y.C., 1993-94; product devel. specialist Dun & Bradstreet, N.Y.C., 1986-91, sr. application developer, 1994-97, mgr. voice/fax/email delivery sys., 1997—2002. Discussion panel mem. Transpac Symposium, Balt., 1984; spkr. Assn. Am. Railroads, Toronto, Ont., 1983, and Boston, 1984, Internat. Rail Congress, Brussels, 1985. Contbr. articles to profl. jours. Avocations: bicycling, skiing, playing piano, keeping a journal. Home: 450 Clinton St Apt 3B Brooklyn NY 11231-3413

DAVIS, WILLIAM WALTER, recruiter, trainer; b. Pewee Valley, Ky., Jan. 5, 1946; s. B.E. Garvey and Clara Virginia (Gordon) D. BA, U. Louisville, 1967. Vol. cmty. devel. U.S. Peace Corps, Colombia, 1967-69; coord. Man. region Can. Univ. Svcs. Overseas, Winnipeg, 1978-79, nat. bd. dirs., 1979; devel. educator Sask. Cross-Cultural Centre, Inc., Saskatoon, Can., 1979-88; coord. tng. and tech. assistance So. Empowerment Project, Inc., Maryville, Tenn., 1988—. Mem. Can. Union Pub. Employees, Winnipeg, 1976-78, local 3012, Sask., 1984-85, pres. dist. coun., 1986-87; founding mem. Nat. Organizers Alliance, Washington, 1992. Mem. editl. com. NOA's Ark, 1994-97; columnist Appalachian Reader, 1998-2002; contbr. articles to profl. jours. Named Ky. Col., 1967; Windcall resident Common Counsel Found., 1998. Avocations: genealogy, gardening. Home: 1525 Barbra Estates Dr Seymour TN 37865-3637 Office: So Empowerment Project Inc 343 Ellis Ave Maryville TN 37804-5824 E-mail: walterdavis@chartertn.net., souempow@bellsouth.net.

DAVIS, YVONNE D. county official; b. Orange, N.J., Sept. 21, 1947; d. William J. and Alice-Ruth Patterson; m. Royce Davis; children: Shannon K., Sarah K. BA in Spanish, Montclair State Coll., Upper Montclair, N.J., 1975; cert. pub. mgmt., Kean Coll., Union, N.J., 1982; cert. equal employment, Rutgers U., 1984. Bilingual family svc. worker dept. citizen svcs. Essex County Divsn. Welfare, Newark, 1971-78, family svc. supr., 1978-81, adminstrv. analyst, 1981-83, prin. personnel technician, 1983-86, pers. mgr., supr. prin. pers. technician, 1984—, adminstrv. dep. dir. welfare, 1992-93, dir. dept., 1994-95, pers. mgr., 1995-99, chief pers. and labor rels., 1999, dep. dir. welfare, 2000—. Mem. exec. bd. Essex County Minority Employees Assn., Newark, 1984-85; mem. employment coun. Tng., Inc., Newark; mem. Essex County Adv. Bd. on Status of Women; mem. Coordinating Coun. for Social Svcs., Essex County, N.J.; mem. Essex County Ins. Commn.; mem. Essex County Juvenile Justice Detention Ctr. Policy Reform Task Force, 1997—; active Epilepsy Found. Am., Trenton; vol. Isaiah Ho. Homeless Shelter, 2000. Recipient Excellence in Personnel Mgmt. award Essex County Minority Employees Assn., 1986, Excellence in Spanish award Nat. Assn. Tchrs. Spanish, 1964, 65, Excellence in French award Nat. Assn. Tchrs. French, 1965, Recognition award United Way, 1984-2000; cert. of appreciation U.S. Dept. Treas., 1984, tng. cert. N.J. Div. Civil Rights, 1988. Mem. NAFE, NAACP, Am. Mgmt. Assn., Am. Assn. Affirmative Action, Nat. Assn. Pub. Sector Equal Opportunity Officers, Nat. Assn. Negro Bus. and Profl. Women Inc., Mcpl. Career Women Newark Inc. Democrat. Baptist. Avocations: photography, theater workshop. Office: Essex County Dept Citizen Svcs Divsn Welfare Admin Offices 18 Rector St 9th Fl Newark NJ 07102-4512

DAVIS-GOFF, ANNABEL, writer; b. Ireland, Feb. 19, 1942; came to U.S., 1971; d. Sir Ernest Davis-Goff and Cynthia O'Connor; children: Max, Jenny. Author: (family memoir) Walled Gardens, 1989, (novel) The Dower House, 1997; editor: (anthology) The Literary Companion to Gambling, 1996; author: (novel) This Cold Country, 2002.

DAVIS-IMHOF, NANCY LOUISE, retired elementary school educator; b. Stamford, Conn., Feb. 17, 1940; d. Ernest A. and Margaret (Carlson) Davis; m. William A. Imhof, Nov. 17, 1962 (div. Dec. 1989); children: Samuel, Jacqueline, Susan. BA, Barnard Coll., 1962; MEd, George Mason U., 1975. Cert. tchr., Va. Tchr. Arlington (Va.) Pub. Schs., 1975-2001. Freelance photographer. Mem. family life edn. com., Arlington Pub. Schs., 1990-91; mem. ad hoc com. on future of T.J. Community Ctr., 1991; mem. Commn. on Aging, Arlington County, 2002; mem. vestry St. Georges Episcopal Ch., Arlington, 1987-90; charter bd. mem. Arlington Learning Retirement Inst., 2002. Arlington Sch. System grantee, 1988-89, 99-2000, 00-01. Mem. NEA, Va. Edn. Assn., Arlington Edn. Assn. (sch. rep. 1989, 90). Democrat. Avocation: triathlons. Home: 894 N Ohio St Arlington VA 22205-1530

DAVIS-JEROME, EILEEN GEORGE, principal; b. N.Y.C., Nov. 10, 1946; d. Rennie and Flora May (Compton) George; m. Bruce Davis, Aug. 8, 1970 (div. 1978); m. Frantz Jerome, Sept. 7, 1982; 1 child, Thais Davis. BFA, Pratt Inst., 1968; MA, CUNY, 1971, PD, 1990; EdD, Nova Southeastern U., 1998. Lic. ednl. adminstr., prin., instrn. specialist, N.Y. Tchr. fine arts Herbert Lehman High Sch., Bronx, N.Y., 1971-75; tchr. English/fine arts Jr. High Sch. 131, Bronx, 1975-76; tchr. English Jr. High Sch. 22, Bronx, 1976-79; tchr. fine arts Andrew Jackson High Sch., Cambria Heights, N.Y., 1979-83, coord. art dept., 1986-92; admissions counselor Fashion Inst. Tech., SUNY, N.Y.C., 1983-85; coord. Queensborough Coll. Project Prize, Bayside, N.Y., 1991-92; project dir. Andrew Jackson Magnet High Sch., Cambria Heights, N.Y., 1993—, project dir. Humanities and the Arts, 1994—; ednl. adminstr. Queens High Sch. Office, N.Y.C. Pub. High Schs., Corona, N.Y., 1993-94; prin. Humanities and the Arts Magnet H.S., Cambria Heights, NY, 1994—. Coord. internat. studies Friends of Jackson High Sch., Cambria Heights, 1986-93, equal opportunity coord., 1989-92; exam asst. N.Y. C. Bd. Edn., Bd. Examiners, Bklyn., 1983-87; curriculum/career cons. Fashion Inst., SUNY, Detroit, Washington, Phila., 1983-86. Curriculum writer N.Y. State Project to Implement Career Edn., 1975, N.Y. State Futuring, 1984; proposal writer Magnet Sch. Funding, 1993; author: Resource Book, 1989. Mem., speaker Cambria Heights Civic Assn., 1983; mem. N.Y. Urban League, N.Y.C.; vol. Mayor's Vol. Action/Alpha Sr. Cr., Cambria Heights, 1984; vol. Black Spectrum Theatre Co., 1983-86; mem. coord. coun. h.s. divsn. N.Y.C. Bd. Edn., 1997—; v.p. for edn. Madam C.J. Walker Found., 2001—. Named Educator of Yr., NAACP/ACT-SO, N.Y.C., 1992; recipient Recognition award, Black Spectrum Theatre Co., 1983, Speakers award, N.Y.C. Bd. Edn. Open Doors, 1983—84, Black Exec. Exch. Program Nat. Urban League, N.Y.C., 1984, Developer Grant award, Impact II Grant, N.Y.C., 1989, Laurelton Club Prol. award, 1996, Disting. Educator award, L.I. br. Nat. Assn. Univ. Women, 2001, Life Membership award, NAACP, N.Y.C., 2001, Excellence in Edn. award, Omega Psi Phi, 2002. Mem. ASCD, N.Y. State Art Tchrs. Assn., N.Y.C. Art Tchrs. Assn. (v.p., sec. 1983-85, cert. 1983-86), Cultural Heritage Alliance (assoc., Recognition award 1986), Greater Queens Chpt. The Links, Inc., Delta Sigma Theta (chair arts and letters 1991-97, Golden Life award 1991), Phi Delta Kappa (Disting. Cert. 1994). Democrat. Episcopalian. Avocations: painting, travel, dance, writing, theater. Office: Magnet HS Humanities and the Arts 20701 116th Ave Jamaica NY 11411-1038

DAVIS-KALUGIN, DORINNE SUE, audiologist; b. East Orange, N.J., Mar. 29, 1949; d. William Henry and Evelyn Doris (Thorp) Taylor; children: Larissa Louise, Peter Alexander; m. Eric S. Kalugin. BA, Montclair State Coll., 1971, MA, 1973. Cert. tchr. of hearing impaired, speech correctionist, tchr. speech and drama, supr. nursery sch. endorsement, N.J. Ednl. audiologist Kinnelon (N.J.) Bd. Edn., 1972-94, kindergarten tchr., 1994-97; ednl. audiologist Inst. for Career Advancement, Inc., 1980-82, Dover Gen. Hosp., 1984-86; pres. Hear You Are, Inc., 1987-98, Davis Ctr. Hearing Speech and Learning, Inc., Budd Lake, NJ, 1998—2002; with Davis Ctrs., Inc., 2002—. Adj. prof. Kean Coll., Union, NJ, 1993—95. Mem. NEA, Internat. Orgn. Educators Hearing Impaired, Am. Speech and Hearing Assn. (cert. clin. competence in audiology), Am. Acad. Audiology, N.J. Speech and Hearing Assn., N.J. Edn. Assn., Ednl. Audiology Assn. (past pres.). Methodist. Home: 51 King Rd Landing NJ 07850-1308 Office: Davis Ctrs Inc 98 Rt 46W Budd Lake NJ 07828

DAVISON, AUDREY M. lawyer, consultant; b. Flasher, N.D., Dec. 30, 1919; d. Frank and Laura Wyman Colegrove; m. John Roats, June 5, 1938 (div. June 1949); 1 child, Gary Charles Roats; m. Kenneth Bradley Davison (dec.); 1 child, Nelson Bradley. BA in Music, U. Wash., 1950; MA, Stanford U., 1963; JD, San Francisco Law Sch., 1992. Rsch. assoc. Vets. Hosp. and Stanford U., Palo Alto, Calif., 1965—67; sr. clin. lab. scientist Cmty. Hosp. of Los Gatos/Saratoga, Calif., 1973—85, San Jose Med. Group, 1986—94; cons. in environ. law Seattle, 1994—. Rsch. scientist VA, Palo Alto, 1967—73; instr. DeAnza C.C., Cupertino, Calif., 1974—79. Organizer citizen participation for preservation of foothills, Santa Clara County, Calif., 1970—75. Mem.: Assn. Women in Sci. (bd. dirs. Seattle chpt. 1997—99, co-chair outreach com.), Toastmasters Internat. (Dist. 2 officer 1997—, Area 3 Gov. 1997—, com. chair Success/Leadership Program 1998—99, Outstanding Mem. cert. and pin 1998). Achievements include development of 2.5% agarose column separation of anti-hemophilic globulin separation from frozen human plasma. Home: 320 Valley St #5 Seattle WA 98109

DAVISON, CALVIN, retired lawyer; b. Norwood, Ohio, Jan. 9, 1932; s. Emberson and Hazel Hildreth (Jenz) D.; m. Carole Ann Sawyer, Apr. 3, 1971; 1 child, Douglas Sawyer. AB cum laude, Miami U., Oxford, Ohio, 1953; JD cum laude, Harvard U., 1959. Bar: D.C. 1959, U.S. Dist. Ct. D.C. 1959, U.S. Ct. Appeals (D.C. cir.) 1959, U.S. Ct. Appeals (6th cir.) 1973, U.S. Ct. Appeals (2d cir.) 1979, U.S. Ct. Appeals (4th cir.) 1991, U.S. Supreme Ct. 1964. Assoc. Pogue & Neal, Washington, 1959-65, ptnr., 1965-67, Jones, Day, Reavis & Pogue, Washington, 1967-79, Crowell & Moring, Washington, 1979-97. Contbr. articles to profl. jours. Lt. j.g. USN, 1953-56 Mem. ABA, D.C. Bar Assn., Univ. Club. Avocations: swimming, tennis. Home: 4950 Quebec St NW Washington DC 20016-3231

DAVISON, DANIEL P. retired banking executive; b. N.Y.C., Jan. 30, 1925; s. F. Trubee and Dorothy (Peabody) D.; m. Catherine Cheremeteff, June 27, 1953; children: Daniel P. Jr., George P., Henry P. BA, Yale U., 1949; JD, Harvard U., 1952. Assoc. White & Case, N.Y.C., 1952-55; exec. v.p. Morgan Bank, N.Y.C., 1955-79; chmn., CEO U.S. Trust, N.Y.C., 1979-90; chmn. Christie's, N.Y.C., 1990-94, Burlington No. Sante Fe R.R., Fort Worth, 1996-97. Treas. Florence Gould Found., N.Y.C., 1983—. Recipient Legion of Honor, France. Mem. Piping Rock Yacht Club, Seawanhaka Yacht Club, N.Y. Yacht Club. Republican. Episcopalian. Avocations: sailing, fishing, hunting. Home: 90 Peacock Ln Locust Valley NY 11560-1019 Office: c/o US Trust 114 W 47th St New York NY 10036-1510

DAVISON, EDWARD JOSEPH, electrical engineering educator; b. Toronto, Ont., Can., Sept. 12, 1938; s. Maurice and Agnes (Quinlan) D. Assoc., Royal Conservatory of Music, Toronto, 1957; BA, U. Toronto, 1960, MA, 1961; PhD, Cambridge U., 1964, Sc.D., 1977. Asst. prof. dept. elec. engring. U. Toronto, 1964-66, assoc. prof., 1968-74, prof. dept. elec. engring. and computers, 1974-2000, Univ. prof., 2001—. Asst. prof. dept. elec. engring. and computer scis. U. Calif., Berkeley, 1966-67; dir. Elec. Engring. Consociates Ltd., Toronto, 1977—; elected Hon. prof. of Beijing Inst. of Aeronautics and Astronautics, 1986; pres. Elec. Engring. Consociates, Ltd., Toronto, 1997-99. Assoc. editor: Jour. Automatica, 1974-87, Jour. Large Scale Systems: Theory and Applications, 1979-90, Jour. Optimal Control and Methods, 1983— ; cons. editor IEEE Transactions on Automatic Control, 1985. Contbr. numerous articles infield to profl. jours. Athlone fellow, 1961-63; E.W.R. Steacie Meml. fellow, 1974-77; Killam Rsch. fellow, 1979-80, 81-83; named to U. Toronto Engring. Alumni Hall of Distinction, 2003; recipient Killam Engring. prize Can. Coun., 2003. Fellow Royal Soc. Can., IEEE (v.p. Control Systems Soc. 1979-80, mem. adminstrv. com. 1977-83, dir. Soc. mag. 1980-82, assoc. editor jour. Trans. on Automatic Control 1974-76, editl. adv. bd. IEEE Procs. 1980-81, Centennial medal 1984, elected disting. mem. 1984); mem. IEEE Control Systems Soc. (pres.-elect 1982-83, pres. 1983-84, Hendrik W. Bode Lectr. prize 1997), Profl. Engrs. Ont. (cons. engr. 1979—), Internat. Fedn. Automatic Control (vice chmn. theory com. 1978-87, chmn. 87-90, Quazza medal 1993, vice chmn. tech. bd. 1990-93, coun. mem. 1990-96, vice chmn. IFAC policy com. 1996-99, IFAC adminstrv. and fin. com. 1999—, IFAC Outstanding Mem. Svc. award 1996), Russian Acad. Nonlinear Scis. Office: U Toronto Dept Elec Engring-Computers Toronto ON Canada M5S 1A4 E-mail: ted@control.utoronto.ca.

DAVISON, ELIZABETH JANE LINTON, education educator; b. Las Cruces, N.Mex., Mar. 9, 1931; d. Melvy Edgar Linton and Clara Virginia Hale; m. Curwood Lyman Davison, Jan. 29, 1954; 1 child, Lawrence. BS, N.Mex. State U., 1957; postgrad., U. N.Mex.; Grad., Norris Sch. Real Estate, Albuquerque, 1984. Cert. tchr., N.Mex., Oreg.; cert. real estate agt., N.Mex., appraiser. Sec., treas. C.L. Davison, Md., Pa., 1975-88, 1975-88; ind. real estate contractor Century 21, Las Cruces, 1984-85; ret. Albuquerque Pub. Schs., 1957-60, 64-68; pres. Sun Dial Enterprises, 1984-95; tchr. Beaverton Pub. Schs., 1960-64. Mem. NEA, Legis. Coun., N.Mex. Albuquerque Classroom Tchrs. Inter-City Coun. (v.p.), AAUW, Phi Delta Kappa (Svc. key). Home: 3013 Cumberland Dr San Angelo TX 76904-6108

DAVISON, HELEN IRENE, secondary education educator, counselor; b. Oskaloosa, Iowa, Dec. 19, 1926; d. Grover C. and Beulah (Williams) Hawk; m. Walter Francis Davison, June 20, 1953 (div.); 1 child, Linda Ellen. BS in Zoology, Iowa State U., 1948; MS in Biol. Sci., U. Chgo., 1951; MA in Ednl. Psychology and Counseling, Calif. State U., Northridge, 1985. Med. rsch. technician U. Chgo. Med. Sch., 1951-53; tchr. sci. Lane High Sch., Charlottesville, Va., 1953-55; med. rsch. asst. U. Va. Med. Sch., Charlottesville, 1955-56, U. Mich., Ann Arbor, 1956-60; tchr. sci. Monroe High Sch., North Hills, Calif., 1966-98, chmn. sci. dept., 1990-91, sch. site coun., 1993-94, ret., 1998. Rsch. technician Los Alamos Sci. Labs., summer 1954; part-time counselor psychotherapy Forte Found., Encino, Calif., 1987-92, Tarzana, Calif., 1993-2000, Northridge, Calif., 2000—. V.p. San Fernando Valley chpt. Am. Field Svc., 1980-81; vol. counselor Planned Parenthood Am., L.A., 1982-88. NSF fellow, 1985-86. Mem. Calif. Tchrs. Assn., Calif. Assn. Marriage and Family Therapists, Iowa Acad. Sci. (assoc.), AAUW. Avocations: traveling, history, cooking.

DAVISON, IRWIN STUART, lawyer; b. Hazelton, Pa., Feb. 17, 1942; s. Julius S. and Gertrude (Kempner) D.; m. Ilene F. Hershinson, Nov. 24, 1966; children— Jill, Joshua. B.A., Lafayette Coll., 1963; J.D., Bklyn. Law Sch., 1966. Bar: N.Y. 1967, U.S. Dist. Ct. (so. and ea. dist.) N.Y. 1969, U.S. Supreme Ct. 1971. Dir. criminal justice projects Addition Services Agy., N.Y.C., 1975, asst. commr., 1975-76, gen. counsel, 1976-77; counsel Office of Substance Abuse Services, City of N.Y., 1977-78; dep. gen. counsel Dept. Health, city of N.Y., 1978-80, gen. counsel, 1980— . Chmn. Zoning Bd. Appeals, Mt. Vernon, 1982— . Mem. N.Y. County Lawyers Bar Assn. Home: 92 Frederick Pl Mount Vernon NY 10552-2331

DAVISON, KENNETH EDWIN, American studies educator, genealogist; b. East Cleveland, Ohio, May 4, 1924; s. Gordon Edwin and Mildred K. (Smith) D.; m. Virginia Nell Rentz, June 14, 1959; children: Robert Edwin, Richard Allen. AB, Heidelberg Coll., 1946; AM, Western Res. U., 1951, PhD, 1953. Asst. prof. history, polit. sci. Heidelberg Coll., Tiffin, Ohio, 1952-56, assoc.

prof. polit. sci., 1956-59, prof., 1959-64, prof. history, dir. gen. edn. program, 1964-67, prof., chmn. Am. studies dept., 1967-83, prof., chmn. history and Am. studies dept., 1983-89, emeritus prof. history and Am. studies, 1989—. Vis. prof. Am. studies Bowling Green State U., 1972-75, 89, 93; cons. Tiffin Hist. Trust, 1976-89, trustee 2000—; pub. hist. and cons. in field. Author: Cleveland and the Civil War, 1962, The Presidency of Rutherford B. Hayes, 1972, The American Presidency: A Guide to Bibliographical Sources, 1983, (with others) Ohio's Heritage, 1984, rev. edit., 1989, 92, 95; editor: (with others) Ohio History Resource Guide, 1991; guest editor: Ohio History, 1968; editor Hayes Hist. Jour., 1976-82; book rev. editor Presdl. Studies Quar., 1978-86, book rev. counselor, 1986-88; contbg. author Collier's Ency., 1964, 68, Am. Educator's Ency., 1965; contbr. articles to profl. jours. Chmn. Heidelberg Cmty. Lecture and Concert Series, 1956—63, Ohio com. for pub. programs in humanities, 1973—80, exec. com., 1973—80; chmn. Tiffin-Seneca Bicentennial Commn., 1974—77, 1987—89; bd. dirs. Seneca County Mus., 1976—90, Seneca County Mus. Found., 1990—98, Heritage Village Bd., 1992—93; mem. lay bd. Mercy Hosp., 1983—86; trustee Ohio Preservation Alliance, 1992—96, Heritage Ohio/Downtown Ohio, Inc., 2003—; historian Roadtrek Internat., 1996—98, 2002—; presdl. adv. com. Ohio Bicentennial, 1999—; elder Presbyn. ch., 1991—93, 2003—. Recipient Ohioana Libr. Book award, 1973; grantee, Am. Philos. Soc., 1963—64, NEH summer seminar, 1978, 1981, 1987, Can. Embassy Faculty Enrichment, 1979—81, Gerald R. Ford Found., 1983, Ohio Humanities Coun., 2002, 2003. Mem. Orgn. Am. Historians, Ohio-Ind. Am. Studies Assn. (pres. 1965, 66), Am. Assn. State and Local History (cert. of commendation 1993), So. Hist. Assn., Ohio Acad. History (editor newsletter 1971-74, pres. 1986-87, Disting. Svc. award 1989), Am. Studies Assn. (nat. exec. coun. 1968-78, nat. treas. 1973-78), Ohio Hist. Soc. (rsch. adviser 1968-75, bd. trustees ex officio 1986-87), Ctr. for Study of Presidency (bd. editors 1974-98), Presidency Rsch. Group, Nat. Geneal. Soc., Palatines to Am., Ohio Geneal. Soc. (trustee-at-large 2000-01), Seneca County Geneal. Soc. (FGS del.), Ohio Assn. Hist. Socs. and Mus. (trustee at-large 1986-92, exec. com. 1991-92), Tiffin Hist. Trust (Preservation award 1998), Pi Kappa Delta, Phi Alpha Theta. Home: 125 Hampden Park Tiffin OH 44883-3344

DAVISON, PETER HUBERT, editor, poet; b. N.Y.C., June 27, 1928; s. Edward and Natalie (Weiner) D.; m. Jane Auchincloss Truslow, Mar. 7, 1959 (dec. July 1981); children: Edward Angus, Lesley Truslow; m. Joan Edelman Goody, Aug. 11, 1984. AB magna cum laude, Harvard U., 1949; Fulbright scholar, St. John's Coll., Cambridge (Eng.) U., 1949-50. Page U.S. Senate, 1944; asst. editor Harcourt, Brace & Co., 1950-51, 53-55; asst. to dir. Harvard U. Press, 1955-56; assoc. editor Atlantic Monthly Press, 1956-59, exec. editor, 1959-64, dir., 1964-79, sr. editor, 1979-85; poetry editor Atlantic Monthly, 1972—; editor Peter Davison Books Houghton Mifflin Co., Boston, 1985-98, poetry editor, 1985-98. Mem. adv. bd. Nat. Transl. Ctr., 1965-68; policy panelist in lit. Nat. Endowment for Arts, 1980-83; Phi Beta Kappa Vis. Scholar, 1989-90. Author: (poems) The Breaking of the Day, 1964, The City and the Island, 1966, Pretending to Be Asleep, 1970, Dark Houses, 1971, Walking the Boundaries, 1974, A Voice in the Mountain, 1977, Barn Fever and Other Poems, 1981, Praying Wrong: New and Selected Poems, 1957-1984, 1984, The Great Ledge, 1989, The Poems of Peter Davison 1957-1995, 1995, Breathing Room, 2000 (prose) One of the Dangerous Trades: Essays on the Work and Workings of Poetry, 1991; autobiography Half Remembered, 1973, rev. edit., 1991, The Fading Smile, Poets in Boston From Robert Frost to Robert Lowell to Sylvia Plath, 1955-60, 1994; editor: Hello, Darkness: The Collected Poems of L.E. Sissman, 1978, The World of Farley Mowat, 1980; contbr. poems, articles to numerous mags., anthologies. Trustee Fountain Valley Sch., 1967-75; mem. corp. Yaddo, 1978— . Served with AUS, 1951-53. Winner competition Yale Series Younger Poets, 1963; recipient Poetry award Nat. Inst. Arts and Letters, 1972, James Michener award Acad. Am. Poets, 1981, New Eng. Book award for Lit. Excellence New Eng. Booksellers Assn., 1995, Mass. Book award, 2001. Fellow Am. Acad. Arts and Sci.; mem. Phi Beta Kappa. Clubs: Examiner, St Botolph (Boston); Harvard (N.Y.C.). Office: The Atlantic Monthly 77 N Washington St Ste 500 Boston MA 02114-1916

DAVISON, RICHARD, physician, educator; b. Buenos Aires, Nov. 7, 1937; came to U.S., 1966; s. Charles Edward and Matilde (Muller) D.; m. Lisette Glusberg, July 1, 1965; 1 child, Sebastian. MD, U. Buenos Aires, 1963. Diplomate Am. Bd. Internal Medicine, Am. Bd. Cardiovascular Diseases, Am. Bd. Critical Care Medicine. Intern Inst. Med. Rsch., Buenos Aires, 1964; resident Passavant Meml. Hosp., Chgo., 1966-68, chief resident, 1968-69; cardiology fellowship VA Hosp., Chgo., 1969-71; asst. prof. Northwestern U. Sch. Medicine, Chgo., 1973-81, assoc. prof., 1981—, chief sect. critical care medicine, 1982—, chief sect. cardiology, 1988-92; dir. med. intensive care area Northwestern Meml. Hosp., Chgo., 1973—2003. Contbr. articles to profl. jours. Recipient Thrombolysis in Myocardial Infarction award NIH. Fellow Am. Coll. Cardiology, Am. Coll. Physicians, Council of Clin. Cardiology (Am. Heart. Assn.), Soc. Critical Care Medicine; mem. Am. Heart Assn., Alpha Omega Alpha. Office: Northwestern Meml Hosp Divsn Critical Care 201 E Huron St Galter 10-240 Chicago IL 60611-2908

DAVISSON, MELVIN THOMAS, consulting engineer; b. Dec. 23, 1931; s. David Earl and Leona Caroline (Haas) Davisson; m. Marlene Elaine Krumeich, May 14, 1955; children: James Preston, Diana Marie, Teresa Lynn, Kathleen Elaine. BCE, U. Akron, 1954; MS, U. Ill., 1955, PhD, 1960. Registered profl. engr., Ohio, Ill., structural engr., Ill. Structural engr. Clark, Dietz Assn., Urbana, Ill., 1955—56; rsch. asst., instr. U. Ill., Urbana, 1956—59, asst. prof., 1960—63, assoc. prof., 1963—71, prof. civil engring., 1971—81; cons. engr. M.T. Davisson, Cons. Engring., Champaign, Ill., 1958—. Chmn. to various tech. coms. Contbr. articles to profl. jours. Recipient Alfred A. Raymond award, Raymond INternat. Bilders, 1958. Mem.: NSPE, ASTM, ASCE (Collingwood prize 1964), Deep Found. Inst. (Disting. Svc. award 1990), Internat. Soc. Soil Mechanics and Found. Engring., Am. Ry. Engring. Assn., Am. Concrete Inst., Sigma Xi. Home and Office: 15 Lake Park Rd Champaign IL 61822-7132

DAVIS-SUTTON, ROSILAND, secondary school educator; d. Wilbur James Davis and Brenda Louise Griffin-Davis; 1 child, Victoria Brianna Sutton. BA in Psychology, U North Tex., 1995; MA with honors in Human Resources Devel., Webster U, 2001. Sales assoc. Advanced Telemarketing, Irving, Tex., 1995—96, Mobile Comm., Dallas, 1996—98; sales Dillards, Irving, Tex., 1998—99; asst. training HR Coord. Citizens Comm., Dallas, 1999; site rep. Webster U, Columbia, SC, 1999—2002; instr. aide Pleasant Grove High Sch., Texarkana, Tex., 2003—. Counselor Mayar's Summer Youth Employment, Dallas, 1998. Mem.: Soc. Human Resources Mgmt., Optimist Club, Jack & Jill Club, Phi Delta Kappa, Alpha Kappa Alpha (Hospitality and Edn. Comm.). Home: PO Box 6892 Texarkana TX 75505

DAVIT, FRANK TORINO, accountant; b. Rockford, Ill., June 20, 1961; s. Torino and Ernestina Davit. BS in Accountancy, No. Ill. U., 1983. CPA. Managerial acct. Ingersoll Engrs., Inc., Rockford, 1984-88, ptnr.-in-charge acct. and fin. svcs., 1988-92, CFO, 1992—2001, Implementation Svcs. LLC, 2002—. Mem.: Inst. Mgmt. Accts. (Rockford chpt.). Avocations: golf, collecting sports memorabilia. Home: 6594 Rolling Hedge Ln Rockford IL 61108-5625 Office: Bourton Group and Implementation Svcs 11350 N Meridian Indianapolis IN 46032-2913

DAVY, MICHAEL FRANCIS, civil engineer, consultant; b. Springfield, Mo., Mar. 24, 1946; s. Philip Sheridan and Caecilia Magdelen (Thiemann) D.; m. Joyce Kay Young, Aug. 17, 1968; children: Mark Sheridan, Katherine Ann, Jennifer Mary. BS, U. Wis., 1969. Diplomate Am. Acad. Environ. Engrs. Project engr. Davy Engring. Co., La Crosse, Wis., 1969-74, v.p., 1975-88; mgr. Davy Labs., La Crosse, 1975—; pres. Davy Engring. Co., La Crosse, 1989—. Dir. St. Francis Med. Ctr., 1993-95, Wis. Mfrs. and Commerce, 1995-98, Wells Fargo Bank-LaCrosse, 1998—. Mem. Gov.'s Clean Water Task Force, 1988-89; bd. dirs. Gateway Area coun. Boy Scouts Am., La Crosse, 1973—, pres. exec. bd., 1989—91; bd. dirs. La Crosse Family YMCA, 2000—. Disting. Eagle Scout, 1988, Silver Beaver Gateway Area Coun., 1987. Mem. NSPE (nat. bd. dirs. 1987-93), ASCE (Young Engr. Yr. 1980), Wis. Soc. Profl. Engrs. (Engr. Yr. 1987,pres. 1984-85, sec. 1980-82, Young Engr. Yr. 1976), Wis. Assn. Consulting Engrs. (bd. dirs. 1987-90), Profl. Engrs. in Pvt. Practice (vice chmn. 1981-83, Merit award 1990), LaCrosse Country Club (dir. 1993-99, pres. 1997-99). Roman Catholic. Avocations: swimming, boating. Home: 615 23rd St N La Crosse WI 54601-3853 Office: Davy Engring Co 115 6th St S La Crosse WI 54601-4153

DAVY, WILLIAM ALLEN, account executive; b. Montpelier, Vt., July 23, 1955; s. William Allen and Lorraine Mae (Pariezo) D.; m. Katherine Gourdine-Davy, Jan 14. 1999; children: Jordan Katherine, Jaden Gourdine. BBA, Lynn U., Boca Raton, 1978. Technician V.R. Dental Studio, Falls Church, Va., 1983-87; acct. rep. AT&T, Reston, Va., 1987-88, sys. cons. Vienna, Va., 1988-91, design specialist Oakton, Va., 1991-96; sr. design specialist Lucent Tech., Reston, Va., 1996-97, sr. tech. rep., 1997-2000; sr. acct. exec. Expanets, Reston, Va., 2000—01. Pres. Jordan Pub., Reston. Va., 1999—. Author: Let Justice Be Done, 1999. Recipient Grand Slam award, AT&T, 1990. Mem. Soc. Profl. Journalists, Nat. Writers Union. Office: # 369 11654 Plaza America Dr Reston VA 20190 E-mail: w.davy@att.net.

DAW, HAROLD JOHN, lawyer, director; b. N.Y.C., July 6, 1926; s. Joseph and Dorothy (Dannenberg) D.; m. Meryl Kann, Sept. 25, 1960. AB, Union Coll., 1950; LL.B., Columbia U., 1954. Bar: N.Y. 1955. Assoc. Shearman & Sterling, N.Y.C., 1954-62, ptnr., 1962-89. Served with USN, 1944-46, ETO. Mem. ABA, N.Y. State Bar Assn., Bar Assn. City N.Y., Phi Beta Kappa Clubs: University. Home: 15 Buena Vista Dr Westport CT 06880-6602

DAWDY, W. DAVID, pediatrician; b. Highland, Ill., Aug. 9, 1940; s. William Dressor and Florine (Kersey) D.; m. Janice Finke; children: Michael, Cathleen. BA in chemistry, Greenville (Ill.) Coll., 1962; MD, U. Ill., Chgo., 1966. Diplomate Am. Bd. Pediatrics. Resident in pediatrics Columbus (Ohio) Children's Hosp., 1969-71; Pvt. practice Westerville, Ohio, 1972—; rotating intern Wayne County HOsp., Eloise, Mich., 1996-97. Cons. Access Health, Broomfield, Colo., 1993—, Physician Continuing Med. Edn., 1990—. Capt. U.S. Army, 1967-69. Mem. Ohio State Med. Assn. (edn. chmn. 1997—), Children's Practicing Pediatricians (pres. 1999, chmn. bd. 2000). Free Methodist. Avocations: tennis, bicycle touring. Office: Associated Pediatrics Inc 801 Eastwind Dr Westerville OH 43081-3303

DAWE, JAMES ROBERT, lawyer; b. Bristol, Conn., Aug. 12, 1945; s. John Grosvenor and Madeline Rose Dawe; m. Mary Gardner, July 5, 1970; children: Emily, Jeremy, Sarah. BA, Lehigh U., 1967; M City Planning, San Diego State U., 1974; JD, U. San Diego, 1976. Bar: Calif. 1976, U.S. Dist. Ct. (so. dist.) Calif. 1976. Atty. Seltzer Caplan McMahon Vitek, San Diego, 1976—. Chair Urban Librs. Coun., Evanston, Ill., 1993-94, San Diego Pub. Libr. Commn., 1986-94; past chair Libr. Calif. Bd., Sacramento, Downtown San Diego Partnership, San Diego City Mgr. Ballot Com.; chair San Diego Pub. Libr. Found.; vice chair, steering com. Downtown San Diego Ctr. City Cmty. Plan Update. Mem. ABA (real property sect.), Urban Land Inst., Calif. Bldg. Industry Assn. (legal action com.). Office: Seltzer Caplan McMahon Vitek 750 B St Ste 2100 San Diego CA 92101-8177

DAWES, ALAN S. automotive company executive; B in Applied Math., Harvard U., 1977, MBA, 1981. Asst. treas. Chase Manhattan Bank, 1977-80; fin. analyst GM, N.Y.C., 1981-83, mgr. overseas borrowings, 1984, dir. overseas fin. analysis, 1985, dir. financing, investments and fin. planning, 1986, gen. dir. Treasurer's Office, 1987, asst. treas., 1988-91, asst. comptr. Detroit, 1991; fin. dir. Automotive Components Group, 1992; GM v.p., gen. mgr. Delphi Chassis Systems (formerly Delco Chassis Systems); CFO Delphi Chassis Systems, 1998; CFO, exec. v.p. Delphi Automotive Systems Corp., Troy, Mich., 1998—. Named Fin. Exec. of Yr. Automotive News Industry All Stars, 1999. Mem. Harvard Bus. Club. Office: Delphi Automotive Systems Corp 5725 Delphi Dr Troy MI 48098-2815

DAWES, DOMINIQUE, Olympic athlete; b. Silver Spring, Md., Nov. 20, 1976; BS, U. Md., 1999. Mem. U.S. Olympic Team, Barcelona, 1992, Atlanta, 1996. Named U.S.A. Gymnastics Athlete of Yr., 1993, Sportsperson of Yr., USA Gymnastics, 1994, 3d pl. team, Olympic Games, Barcelona, Spain, 1992, 2d pl. all around and floor exercise, 1st in vault and balance beam, 3d uneven bars, Coca Cola Nat. Championships, Salt Lake City, 1993, 2d in uneven bars and balance beam, World Gymnastics Championships, Birmingham, Eng., 1993, 1st pl. in all around, vault, balanve beam and floor exercise, McDonald's Am. Cup, Orlando, Fla., 1994, 1st pl. in all around, vault, uneven bars, balance beam and floor exercise, Cola Cola Nat. Championships, Nashville, 1994, 1st pl. in all around, NationsBank World Team Trials, Richmond, Va., 1994, 2d pl. team, World Championships, Dortmund, Germany, 1994, 1st pl. in uneven bars and floor exercise, 3d pl. in balance beam, Coca Cola Nat. Championships, New Orleans, 1995; recipient Arch McDonald award, Touchdown Club Washington, 1995, McDonald's Balancing It All award, 1995, Harry P. Iba Citizen Athlete award, 1995, Gold medal Team Competition, Olympic Games, Atlanta, 1996. Avocations: reading, dancing, acting. Office: care USA Gymnastics Pan Am Plz 201 S Capitol Ave Ste 300 Indianapolis IN 46225-1058

DAWES, ROBERT LEO, mathematician, consultant; b. Big Spring, Tex., Mar. 5, 1945; s. William Robert and Josephine Melloo (Duflot) D.; m. Rosemary Mae Nelson, Oct. 10, 1970; children: Sara Michelle, Karen Melissa. BS in Math., Tex. Tech U., 1966, MS in Math., 1968; PhD in Math., U. Tex., 1977. Mem. tech. staff Tex. Instruments, Inc., Dallas, 1975-81; sr. specialist E-Systems, Inc., Garland, Tex., 1981-85; pres. Martingale Rsch. Corp., Allen, Tex., 1985-94, QED Corp., Bedford, Tex., 1995—; asst. prof. math. Hampton (Va.) U., 2002—. Founder, chair Metroplex Inst. Neural Dynamics, Dallas, 1986-90. Mem. city coun. City of Parker (Tex.), 1987-99. Lt. USNR, 1968-71. Mem. IEEE (sr., chmn. Dallas chpt., Acoustics, Speech and Signal Processing Soc. 1988), Internat. Neural Network (chair math. and theory spl. interest group 1990-92). Avocation: quantum mechanics. Home: 521 River Gate Rd Chesapeake VA 23322

DAWES, ROBYN MASON, psychology educator; b. Pitts., July 23, 1936; s. Norman H. and Zita (Hill) D.; children by previous marriage: Jennifer, Molly. BA in Philosophy, Harvard U., 1958; MA in Clin. Psychology, U. Mich., 1960, PhD in Math. Psychology, 1963; PhD (hon.), U. Goteborg, Sweden, 1999. Rschr. Ann Arbor (Mich.) VA Hosp., 1962-67; lectr. U. Mich., Ann Arbor, 1963-66, asst. prof., 1966-67; assoc. prof. psychology U. Oreg., Eugene, 1967-71, prof., 1971-85, co-head dept. psychology, 1972-73, acting head, 1979-80, head, 1981-85; prof. psychology Carnegie Mellon U., 1985—, head dept. social and decision scis., 1985-90, 95-96, univ. prof., 1992—, Charles J. Queenan Jr. univ. prof., 1997—. Rsch. scientist Oreg. Rsch. Inst., Eugene, 1967-76, v.p., 1973-74; NATO lectr., The Hague, The Netherlands, 1968; vis. prof. U. Calif., Santa Barbara, 1975-75; cons. numerous insts. and orgns.; Olof Palme vis. prof. U. Stockholm and U. Goteborg, 1999. Author: Fundamentals of Attitude Measurement, 1972, Rational Choice in an Uncertain World, 1988 (William James book award div. gen. psychology Am. Psychol. Assn.), House of Cards: Psychology and Psychotherapy Built on Myth, 1994, paperback edit., 1996, Irrationality in Everyday Life, How Pseudo-Scientists, Lunatics and the Rest of Us Systematically Fail to Think Rationally, 2001, paperback edit., 2003; co-author: (with C.H. Coombs and A. Tversky) Mathematical Psychology: An Elementary Introduction, 1970, (with R. Hastie) Rational Choice in an Uncertain World, (2d edition), 2001; contbr. articles to profl. jours; mem. editl. bds., cons numerous profl. jours. and publs. Rackham Summer fellow, 1961, James McKean Cattell Sabbatical fellow, 1978-79; del. NAS, USA-USSR Acad. Scis. Seminar Decision Making, Moscow-Tblisi, USSR, 1979; fellow Ctr. Advanced Study in Behavioral Scis., 1980-81, Ctr. for Rationality and Interactive Decision Making The Hebrew U. of Jerusalem, 1994. Fellow AAAS, Am. Acad. Arts and Scis., Am. Psychol. Soc., Am. Assn. Applied and Preventive Psychology (exec. bd. 1991—); mem. Oreg. Psychol. Assn. (pres. 1984-85), Am. Statis. Assn., Pub. Choice Soc., Psychometric Soc., West Coast Small Group Rsch. Soc. (pres. 1977-78), Judgement and Decision Making Rsch. Soc. (chmn. exec. bd. 1988, exec. bd. 1994-95), Soc. Advancement of Socio-Econs. (exec. bd. 1991-98—), Sigma Xi, Phi Kappa Phi (sr.). Office: Carnegie Mellon U Dept Social & Decision Scis Pittsburgh PA 15213 *It took a while to understand the wisdom of Herodotus to "take good counsel with (ourselves); for even if the event turns out contrary to one's hopes, still one's decision was right"--always drawing support from the knowledge that the future is uncertain.*

DAWICKI, DOLORETTA DIANE, analytical chemist, research biochemist, educator; b. Fall River, Mass., Sept. 13, 1956; d. Walter and Stella Ann (Olszewski) D. BS, S.E. Mass. U., 1978; PhD, Brown U., 1986. Rsch. assoc. Meml. Hosp. R.I., Pawtucket, 1986-92; asst. prof. Brown U., Providence, 1986-96; rsch. assoc. VA Med. Ctr., Providence, 1992-96; quality control tech. svcs. prin. scientist Genzyme Corp., Framingham, Mass., 1996—. Contbr. articles to profl. jours. Mem. AAAS, Am. Soc. for Biochemistry and Molecular Biology, Parenteral Drug Assn. Achievements include research on in vivo antiplatelet mechanism of action of the clinical agent dipyridamole, endothelial cell injury, effects of nucleotides on leukocyte-endothelial cell interaction, assay development, optimization, and validation to monitor drug identity, safety, and efficacy; product testing and quality control release of commercial therapeutic finished drug products. Home: 3 Odyssey Ln Franklin MA 02038-2460 Office: Genzyme Corp PO Box 9322 Framingham MA 01701-9322 E-mail: dale.dawicki@genzyme.com.

DAWKINS, JIMMIE ANGELA, art educator; b. Ft. Oglethorpe, Ga., Sept. 24, 1942; d. James Harold and Neva Valeria (Dauley) Dawkins; m. Melville Madden Drake, Feb. 14, 1964 (div. Feb. 1967); 1 child, John Michael. BA Visual, Auburn U., Ala., 1964; MFA, Pratt Inst., Bklyn., 1970. Graphic designer Obata Studio, Tokyo, 1965-67; studio asst. Richard Rogers Inc., NYC, 1970-71; tchg. asst. Art Students League, NYC, 1972-73; instr. U. Ala., Huntsville, 1974-75, adj., 1975—; assoc. prof. art Ala. A&M U., Normal, 1975—. One-woman shows Artist's Workshop and Gallery, Huntsville, 1976, Meridian (Miss.) Mus. Art, 1977, Ala. A&M U., 1977, 79, 86, 94, Stillman Coll., Tuscaloosa, Ala., 1978, Athens Coll., 1979, U. North Ala., 1982, U. Ala., Huntsville, 1986, The Gallery at Nativity, 1989, 92, also others; 3-person show Huntsville Hilton, 1994; exhibited in numerous group shows, including Ala. A&M U., 1976-80, 82, 85, 86, 87, 89, 95, 96, 2003, Anniston (Ala.); Mus. Natural History, 1983, Jacksonville (Ala.) State U., 1984, Auburn (Ala.) U., 1985, U. North Ala., 1986, U. Ala., Birmingham, 1986, U. Ala., Huntsville, 1989, North Ala. Coll., 1989, Huntsville Art League, 1994, Connie Ulrich's Gallery, 1994, Huntsville Mus. Art, 1995, Holland Smith Gallery, 1996; represented in permanent collections Pratt Inst., Bklyn., Huntsville Mus. Art, also numerous pvt. collections; pub.: Drawing from the Center: The Art of Representing Life, 2000. Named to Outstanding Young Women of Am., 1978; John Carroll Meml. scholar Art Students League, 1967; Grad Art Fellowship Fund award Pratt Inst., 1970; NEH fellow, 1977, Fulbright-Hays fellow, 1981, 93. Episcopalian. Avocations: early music, performing on recorders, harpsichord and viola da gamba. Office: Alabama A&M Univ Dept Art Normal AL 35762 E-mail: jdawkins@aamu.edu.

DAWN, CLARENCE ERNEST, history educator; b. Chattanooga, Dec. 6, 1918; s. Fred Hartman and Hettie Lou (Gibson) D.; m. Pansie Mozelle Dooley, July 8, 1944; children: Julia Anne, Carolyn Louise. BA, U. Chattanooga, 1941; MA, Princeton U., 1947, PhD, 1948. Instr. history U. Ill., Urbana, 1949-52, asst. prof., 1952-55, assoc. prof., 1955-60, prof., 1960—, prof. emeritus, 1989—, dir. U. Ill. Tehran Rsch. Unit, Iran, 1972-74. Fellow Inst. Advanced Studies, Hebrew U., Jerusalem, 1981-82 Author: From Ottomanism to Arabism, 1973; contbr. articles to profl. jours. Served with AUS, 1942-46, with U.S. Army, 1951-52. Social Sci. Rsch. Coun. World Area fellow, 1948-49; fellow joint com. on Near and Mid. East Social Sci. Rsch. Coun. and Am. Coun. Learned Socs., 1966-67; Fulbright-Hays fellow, 1966-67. Mem. Mid. East Studies Assn., Mid. East Inst. Home: 1628 72d Ave SE Mercer Island WA 98040

DAWN, JESSE ANSON, writer, composer; b. Abington, Pa., May 17, 1944; s. William Craige Wolfersberger and Jesse Eibren; children: Jesse, Leonino. Student, Phila. Coll. of Arts. Author, columnist Positive Prodns., 1975—; song-writer World Changing Books and Records, Hawaii, 1991—. Author: Never Old, 1993, The Rejuvenator's Bible, 1999. Organizer numerous music cmty. events, 1993—. With U.S. Army, 1965—67, Vietnam. Recipient award for content, Nat. Assn. Ind. Pubs., 1994. E-mail: youthdawn@cs.com.

DAWODU, SEGUN TOYIN, sports medicine physician, physiatrist; b. Ilorin, Nigeria, Oct. 13, 1960; arrived in U.S., 1995; s. Michael O. Dawodu and Sarat Dawodu-Bamidele; m. Egbe Monisola Osifo; 1 child, Zainab; m. Florence O. Aigbogun, Oct. 2, 1992 (div. June 23, 1996); children: Osamudiamen, Sarat. MD, U. Ibadan, Nigeria, 1984. Diplomate Am. Bd. Phys. Medicine And Rehab., Am. Bd. Electrodiagnostic Medicine, Royal Coll. Surgeons of Edinburgh, Faculty of Med. Informatics, Am. Bd. Ind. Med. Examiners, cert. Fedn. State Med. Bds.; Ednl. Commn. for Fgn. Med. Grads. Resident physician orthop. surgery and trauma Royal Coll. Surgeons, London, 1992—96; resident physician phys. medicine and rehab. Albany (N.Y.) Med. Ctr., 1996—2000; clin. instr., attending physician traumatic brain injury and stroke rehab. Mt Sinai Med. Ctr., N.Y.C., 2000—01; med. dir., sole proprietor Pmrehab Pain and Sports Medicine Assocs., Herndon, Va., 2001—. Module tutor, med. informatics Royal Coll. Surgeons Edinburgh, Scotland, 2002—; mem. instn. ethics com. Albany Med. Ctr., 1997, mem. internal rev. com. for urology dept., 99, chief resident dept. phys. medicine and rehab., 1999—2000. Contbr. articles to profl. jours. Asst. sec. Assn. Resident Doctors, U. Benin Tchg. Hosp., Benin-City, Nigeria, 1984—85; pub. rels. officer Nigerian Med. Students Assn., Lagos, 1981—82; Nigerian rep. Internat. Fedn. Med. Students' Assns. Confs., Austria, 1981—83. Named Outstanding Pub. Rels. Officer, Nigerian Med. Students Assn., 1982; scholar Nat. Physical Medicine and Rehab. scholar, Rhone-Poulenc Rhone Pharms., 1999. Fellow: Am. Acad. Electrodiagnostic Medicine, Am. Acad. Phys. Medicine and Rehab.; mem.: AMA, Internat. Spinal Injection Soc., Fairfax County Med. Soc., Internat. Soc. Phys. Medicine and Rehab., Am. Med. Informatics Assn., Rosicrucian Order (Amorc), Am. Mensa. Office: Pmrehab Pain & Sports Medicine Associate 3048 Mitchellville Rd Bowie MD 20716 Office Fax: 301-218-5016. Personal E-mail: segun@dawodu.com. Business E-Mail: drdawodu@pmrehab.com.

DAWOOD, MOHAMED YUSOFF, obstetrician, gynecologist; b. Singapore, Sept. 13, 1943; came to U.S., 1974; s. Sheikh and Fatimah (Hussein) D.; m. Firyal Sultana Khan, July 14, 1978; children: Fatimah Sultana, Fauzia Sultana, Firdaus Sultana, Hassan Yusoff. MB, ChB, U. Sheffield, Yorkshire, Eng., 1968, MD, 1974; M of Medicine with gold medal, U. Singapore, 1972. Diplomate Am. Bd. Obstetrics and Gynecology, Am. Bd. Reproductive Endocrinology. Lectr. U. Singapore, 1973—74; first asst. in ob-gyn. U. Melbourne, 1974; from instr. to assoc. prof. ob-gyn. Cornell U. Med. Coll., N.Y.C., 1974—79; prof. ob-gyn. U. Ill., Chgo., 1979—90; Berel Held prof. ob-gyn. and reproductive scis. U. Tex. Med. Sch., Houston, 1990—2001; prof., chmn. dept. ob-gyn. Morehouse Sch. Medicine, Atlanta, 2001—. Study sect. mem. NIH Child and Human Devel., 2000—; cons.; editl. cons., reviewer in field. Author: Green's Gynecology, 1990, Dysmenorrhea, 1981, Premenstrual Syndrome and Dysmenorrhea, 1985, Oxytocin, vol. 2, 1984, Prostaglandin Inhibition in Obstetrics and Gynecology, 1983; mem. editl. bd. Fertility and Sterility, 2000—, Current Obstetrics and Gynecology, 1988-2000; contbr. articles to profl. jours. Recipient Gold medal Jaycee Jr. C. of C. Singapore, 1973. Fellow ACS, ACOG, Internat. Coll. Surgeons, Am. Gynecol. & Obstet. Soc., Royal Coll. Ob-Gyn. (Edgar Gentilli prize 1974, Gold medal 1973); mem. Endocrine Soc. Achievements include research in steroid endocrinology and chemotherapy of trophablastic diseases, prostaglandins in the causation of menstrual cramps and relief by blocking prostaglandins; role of oxytocin in human parturition, bone-depleting effect of GnRH agonists during treatment of endometriosis; presence of neurohypophyseal peptides in primate and human ovaries; regulation of primate corpus luteum. Office: Morehouse Sch Medicine Dept Ob-gyn 720 Westview Dr SW Atlanta GA 30310 E-mail: mdawood@msm.edu.

DAWSON, ADAM, private investigator; b. N.Y.C., May 4, 1950; s. Martin and Renee D.; m. Constance Jo Stewart, Oct. 21, 1950. BA, Syracuse Univ., N.Y., 1972. Lic. private investigator, Calif. Press sec. U.S. Congressman M. Blouin, Washington, 1977-78; reporter Evening News, Annapolis, Md., 1978-79, Daily News, L.A., 1979-84; L.A. bureau chief Orange County Register, Santa Ana, Calif., 1984-88; city editor Journal Tribune, Biddeford, Maine, 1988-89; owner Dawson Ryan Assocs., L.A., 1989—. Sr. instr. UCLA Extension, L.A., 1981-91. Mem. sports advisory coun. City Santa Monica, Calif., 1996—. Named Best Investigative Reporting Valley Press Club, L.A., 1982, named Best Investigative Series Orange County Press Club, 1986. Office: Dawson Ryan Assocs 12021 Wilshire Blvd # 846 Los Angeles CA 90025-1206

DAWSON, CINDY MARIE, lawyer; b. Oklahoma City, May 3, 1960; d. Alva Glenn and Ethel Estelle Horner; m. Ronnie L. Dawson, July 14, 1977; children: Kristina Lee Ann, Kathryn DeeAnn, Shaunna Renee. AA, Rose State Coll., Midwest City, Okla., 1993; BBA, U. Ctrl. Okla., 1994, postgrad., 1997—; JD, Oklahoma City U., 1997. Bar: Okla. 1997. Leasing agt. Brentwood Apts., Shawnee, Okla., 1988; bus. advisor Triple H Constrn., Eufaula, Okla., 1989-96; pvt. practice atty. Edmond, Okla., 1997-2000; asst. dist. atty. Shawnee, Okla., 2000—01; pvt. practice atty. Eufaula, 2001—. Mem.: ATLA, Legal Aid Western

Okla., Okla. Criminal Def. Lawyers Assn., Okla. Trial Lawyers Assn., Okla. Bar Assn., Eufaula Alumni Assn., Phi Delta Phi. Avocations: reading, cooking, sports, travel. Office: 112 Selmon Rd Eufaula OK 74432 E-mail: dawsonpc@hotmail.com.

DAWSON, DENNIS RAY, lawyer, manufacturing company executive; b. Alma, Mich., June 19, 1948; s. Maurice L. and Virginia (Baker) D.; m. Marilynn S. Gordon, Nov. 26, 1971; children: Emily Lynn, Brett Thomas. AA, Gulf Coast Coll., 1968; AB, Duke U., 1970; JD, Wayne State U., 1973. Bar: Mich. 1973, U.S. Dist. Ct. (ea. dist.) Mich. 1973, U.S. Dist. Ct. (we. dist.) Mich. 1975. Assoc. Watson, Wunsch & Keidan, Detroit, 1973-75; mem. Coupe, Ophoff & Dawson, Holland, Mich., 1975-77; staff atty. Amway Corp., Ada, Mich., 1977-79; corp. counsel Meijer, Inc., Grand Rapids, Mich., 1979-82; sec., corp. counsel Tecumseh Products Co., 1982-92; corp. counsel, asst. sec. Holnam Inc., Dundee, Mich., 1992-93; v.p., gen. counsel, sec. Denso Internat. Am. Inc., Southfield, Mich., 1993-2000, sr. v.p., gen. counsel, sec., 2000—. Exec. com. Bank of Lenawee, Adrian, Mich., 1984-93, also bd. dirs.; adj. prof. Aquinas Coll., Grand Rapids, 1978-82; govt. regulation and litigation com. Outdoor Power Equipment Inst. Inc., Washington, 1982-92. Trustee Herrick Meml. Hosp., 1988-91, Tecumseh Civic Auditorium, 1986-89; mem. adv. coun. Montessori Children's House and Acad., Adrian, 1987-93. Mem. ABA, Mich. State Bar Assn., Am. Soc. Corp. Secs., Am. Corp. Counsel Assn., Mich. Mfrs. Assn. (lawyers com. 1987-92), Lenawee C. of C. (bd. dirs. 1988-92). Office: Denso Internat America Inc PO Box 5133 24777 Denso Dr Southfield MI 48034-5244

DAWSON, DIXIE TUTTLE, mathematics consultant; b. Breckenridge, Mo., Dec. 23, 1946; d. William Dale and Doris Tuttle; m. James Edwin Dawson, Apr. 15, 1973; children: Cherie, Devin. BS in Math., Sci., N.W. Mo. State U., 1968; postgrad., UCLA, 1971-74; MEd, Pepperdine U., 1979. Tchr. math. Richmond (Mo.) High Sch., 1968-70, Long Beach (Calif.) Jr. High Sch., 1970-80; math. cons. Long Beach, 1980—. Part-time prof. edn. Calif. State U., Dominguez Hills, Long Beach, 1997—; speaker CMC Math. Conf., 1980-89. Mem. Nat. Coun. Tchrs Math. (Calif. math. coun. so. sect.), Computer Users in Edn. Office: Long Beach Unified Sch Dist 1515 Hughes Way Long Beach CA 90810-1839 E-mail: ddawson@lbusd.k12.ca.us.

DAWSON, DONALD ANDREW, mathematics educator, researcher; b. Montreal, Que., Can., June 4, 1937; s. William Norman Cecil and Frances Malcolm (Andrew) D.; m. Elizabeth Jean Hilton, May 9, 1964; children: Michael, Suzanne. BSc, McGill U., Montreal, 1958, MSc, 1959; PhD, MIT, 1963. Sr. engr. Raytheon Corp., Bedford, Mass., 1962—63; assoc. prof. McGill U., 1963—70; prof. Carleton U., Ottawa, Canada, 1970—99; dir. The Fields Inst. for Rsch. in Math. Scis., Toronto, Canada, 1996—2000; prof. emeritus Carleton U., 1999—. Assoc. editor: Electronic Jour. of Probability, 1998; contbr. articles to profl. jours. Fellow Inst. Math Stats. (assoc. editor Annals of Probability jour. 1987-90), Internat. Stats. Inst., Royal Soc. Can.; mem. Can. Math. Soc. (co-editor in chief jour. 1988-93), Can. Statis. Soc., Am. Math. Soc., Bernoulli Soc. (adv. bd. stochastic processes application 1982—, pres. 2003–). Avocations: cross-country skiing, walking, music appreciation. Office: Sch Math and Statis Carleton U Ottawa ON Canada K1S 5B6 E-mail: ddawson@math.carleton.ca.

DAWSON, EARL BLISS, obstetrics and gynecology educator; b. Perry, Fla., Feb. 1, 1930; s. Bliss and Linnie (Calliham) D.; m. Winnie Ruth Isbell, Apr. 10, 1951; children: Barbara Gail, Patricia Ann, Robert Earl, Diana Lynn. BA, U. Kans., 1955; postgrad., Bowman Gray Sch. Medicine, 1957-59; MA, U. Mo., 1960; PhD, Tex. A&M U., 1964. Rsch. instr. dept. ob-gyn. U. Tex. Med. Br., Galveston, 1963-65, rsch. asst. prof., 1965-68, rsch. assoc. prof., 1968-89, assoc. prof., 1989—. Cons. Interdeptl. Com. on Nutrition for Nat. Def., 1965-68, Nat. Nutrition Survey, 1968-69. Author: Effect of Water Borne Nitrites on the Environment of Man; contbr. numerous articles to profl. jours., chpts. to books. Scoutmaster Boy Scouts Am., 1969—. With USNR, 1947-52. Nutrition rsch. fellow, 1960-61; scholar NSF, 1961-62; rsch. fellow NIH, 1962-63. Mem. Am. Inst. Nutrition, Am. Soc. Clin. Nutrition, Am. Coll. Nutrition, Am. Fertility Soc., Soc. Exptl. Biology and Medicine, Soc. Environ. Geochemistry and Health, Tex. Acad. Scis., N.Y. Acad. Scis., Mic-O-Say Club (Kansas City, Mo.), Sigma Xi, Phi Rho Sigma. Baptist. Achievements include research on prenatal nutrition, male fertility, epidemiology of lithium in Texas, biochemical changes associated with pre-menstrual syndrome. Home: Apt 8 3431 S Peach Hollow Cir $D Pearland TX 77584-8006 Office: U Tex Med Br Dept Ob-Gyn Galveston TX 77550

DAWSON, EDWARD JOSEPH, merger and acquisition executive; b. Rochester, Pa., Apr. 1, 1944; s. Ralph Edward and Evelyn May (Riggle) D.; m. Lynda Sue Weir, 1975; 5 children. BS in Indsl. Mgmt., Carnegie Mellon U., 1966; MBA in Fin., U. Chgo., 1968. Lic. security broker/dealer, real estate broker. Computer systems analyst, corp. fin. analyst Tex. Instruments Corp., Dallas, 1968-70, product planning mgr. digital systems divsn., 1970-72, mgr. comml. equipment bus. objective, 1972-74, mgr. mktg. electronic watch divsn., 1975-76, mgr. mktg. home video systems, 1976-77; sr. v.p. ops. and mktg. Capital Alliance Corp., Dallas, 1977-80, exec. v.p. merger ops., 1980-81, chmn. bd., CEO, pres., 1981—. Sec. M&A Internat., 1988, v.p., 89, 96, pres., 90, 97; mem. faculty Bus. Leadership Ctr. So. Meth. U., 1999—; mem. entrepreneurship adv. coun. Carnegie Mellon U., 1998—. Author: 4 books. Pres. Marina del Rey Homeowners Assn., 1982-84. Mem. Omicron Delta Kappa, Beta Theta Pi. Mem. Ch. of Christ. Home: 818 Stratford Dr Southlake TX 76092-7109 Office: Capital Alliance Corp 2777 N Stemmons Fwy Ste 1220 Dallas TX 75207-2293 E-mail: ed.dawson@cadallas.com.

DAWSON, ELIZABETH ANN, marketing professional; b. Kansas City, Mo., May 30, 1967; d. Jerry Lee and Emily Ann Dawson. BSBA, Washington U., Kansas City, Mo., 1989; MBA, Rockhurst U., 1994. Mktg. rsch. assoc. Quality Controlled Svcs., Kansas City, Mo., 1989—90; mktg. rsch. dir. KC Pub., Kansas City, Mo., 1990—95; sr. cons. Sunflower Group, Overland Park, Kans., 1995—98; mktg. dir. Healthy Kansas City, 1998—2002, Ozanam Home for Boys, Kansas City, 2002—. Sec. bd. dirs. Health Resource Ptnrs., Kansas City, 2000—; bd. dirs. Hage Endowment, 2d Presbyn. Ch., Kansas City, Mo., 1999—. Mem.: Cmty. Assn. Nonprofit Bus. Execs., Nonprofit Comms. Network (bd. dirs., program v.p. 2002—), Am. Mktg. Assn. Presbyterian. Avocations: home restoration, needlecrafts, travel, reading. Office: Healthy Kansas City Ozanam 8150 Wornall Rd Kansas City MO 64114 Office Fax: 816-508-3535. E-mail: bd3573@cornerstonesofcare.org.

DAWSON, GAIL ALESIA, management educator; b. Phila., Pa., Oct. 8, 1964; d. Thomas Isiah and Juna Bernice Dawson; m. Rick Cooper, Aug. 9, 1997. BSBA, Fla. A&M U., 1986; MBA, Drexel U., 1992—92; PhD in Bus. Adminstrn., U. of South Fla., 2001. Prodn. supr. in tng. GM Flint Assembly, Mich., 1986—87; scheduling coord. GM Ft. Wayne Assembly, Ind., 1987—89, GM Tarrytown Assembly, 1989—90; mgmt. cons. Price Waterhouse, Washington, 1992—95; asst. prof. mgmt. U. of Tenn., Chattanooga, 2000—. Bd. dirs. Girls Inc., Chattanooga, 2003; coun. mem. Women's Coun. on Diversity, Chattanooga, 2001—03. Mem.: Soc. for Advancement of Mgmt., Soc. for Human Resource Mgmt., So. Mgmt. Assn., Acad. of Mgmt., Nat. Black MBA Assn. (life), Beta Gamma Sigma. Office: U Tenn 615 Mc Callie Ave Chattanooga TN 37403 Home Fax: 423-425-4158; Office Fax: 423-425-4158. Personal E-mail: gail-dawson@utc.edu. E-mail: gail-dawson@utc.edu.

DAWSON, HARRY (TERRY) SAMUEL, JR., policy analyst/advisor, consultant; b. Washington, Nov. 14, 1946; s. Harry Samuel and Gladys Penny (Eavey) Dawson; m. Barbara Ann Bogle, Sept. 1, 1969; children: Brett Allan, Sean Eric. BS Aero Engring., Univ. Md., Coll. Pk., Md., 1969; MS Engring. Adminstrn., The George Washington Univ., Washington, 1972; DEng, Univ. Md., Coll. Pk., Md., 1978. Sr. engr., project mgr. System Planning Corp., Arlington, Va., 1974—80, The Analytic Sci. Corp., Arlington, Va., 1980—83; sr. staff, engring. advisor Space Com., US House of Rep., Washington, 1983—95; dir., strategic assessment Rockwell Space Divsn., Downey, Calif., 1995—96, dir. vision and change, 1996—97; chief-of-staff, chief strategist $5 billion Boeing prop. team Boeing, Houston, 1997—98, dir. space shuttle safety and quality, 1998—. A space policy advisor Bill Clinton-Presdl. Campaign, Washington, 1992; founder, dir., treas. NSC Scientific and Ednl. Found., Washington, 1979—; founder, dir. Nat. Space Soc., Washington, 1974—90. Recipient 20 plus sci. fair awards, NASA/Air Force/Army/Navy, Md, 1960—64, Young Engr. Prize, Washington Soc. of Engr., 1969. Mem.: AIAA (policy adivosr bd. 1981—82), Nat. Space Soc. (life), Nat. Space Club (pres. 1976—77). Ch. Of Christ. Achievements include authored a major defense assessment for Carter and Reagan White House; significant Space Policy leadership roles, 1983-95; played major leadership in Challenger accident investigation by Congress, 1993-94; lead unprecedented effort to establish unified Space launch policies in 6 House/Senate Com. 1998—; established Space Shuttle safety and quality office in Boeing (builder of Orbiter fleet). Avocations: travel, movies, do-it-yourself projects. Home: 4615 Jade Green Ct Houston TX 77059

DAWSON, HORACE GREELEY, JR., former diplomat, government official; b. Augusta, Ga., Jan. 30, 1926; s. Horace Greeley Dawson; m. Lula M. Cole, Aug. 30, 1953; children: Horace Greeley III, Horace Gregory. AB, Lincoln (Pa.) Coll., 1949, LLD (hon.), 1990; AM, Columbia U., 1950; PhD, Iowa State U., 1960. Instr. English So. U., Baton Rouge, 1950-53; assoc. prof., dir. pub. rels. N.C. Cen. U., Durham, 1953-62; joined U.S. Fgn. Svc., 1962; svc. in Uganda, Nigeria; mem. sr. seminar in fgn. policy Fgn. Svc. Inst., 1970-71; amb. to Botswana, 1979-83; dep. examiner Dept. State, U.S. Fgn. Svc., 1982-84; dir. equal opportunity and civil rights USIA, 1985-89; program dir. Sch. Comm. Howard U., Washington, 1989-90, dir. Patricia Roberts Harris program in pub. affairs, 1990-94, asst. to pres. for pub. affairs and comms., 1994-95, dir. Ralph J. Bunche Internat. Affairs Ctr., 1996—. Vis. prof. U. Lagos, Nigeria, 1966-67, U. Md., 1971-79; bd. dirs. Ctr. for the Pub. Policy and Diplomacy Lincoln U. Author: Handbook for High School Newspaper Advisors, 1961, The Relationship Between Business and Government in Japan, 1980; contbr. chpt. to: Exporting America, Essays on American Studies Abroad; contbr. articles to profl. publs.; co-editor: New Dimensions in Higher Education, 1961; mng. editor Coll. Lang. Assn. Jour., 1957-60. Chmn. pro tem, sr. bd. stewards Met. AME Ch., 1988-98. With AUS, 1944-46. Mem. NAACP, Am. Fgn. Svc. Assn., Coun. Fgn. Rels., Fgn. Student Svc. Coun. (bd. dirs.), World Affairs Coun. (bd. dirs.), Assn. Black Am. Ambs. (former pres., chmn.), Alpha Phi Alpha World Policy Coun. Office: Bunche Internat Affairs Ctr Howard U 2218 6th St NW Washington DC 20059-0001

DAWSON, HOWARD ATHALONE, JR., federal judge; b. Okolona, Ark., Oct. 23, 1922; m. Marianne Atherholt, Feb. 2, 1946; children: Amy, Suzanne. BS in Commerce, U. N.C., 1946; JD, George Washington U., 1949. Bar: D.C. 1949, Ga. 1958. Pvt. practice, Washington, 1949-50; atty. civil div. Office Chief Counsel, IRS, 1950-53, asst. regional counsel Atlanta region, 1953-56, regional counsel, 1957, asst. chief counsel adminstrn., 1958-62; judge U.S. Tax Ct., Washington, 1962—, chief judge, 1973-77, 83-85, sr. judge, 1985—; prof. law, dir. grad. tax program U. Balt. Sch. Law, 1986-89. David Brennan Disting. prof. law U. Akron Sch. Law, spring 1986; Disting. adj. prof. law U. San Diego Sch. Law, spring 1991. Served with AUS, 1943-45, ETO; capt. Res. Mem. ABA, D.C. Bar Assn., Fed. Bar Assn., Chi Psi, Delta Theta Phi. Office: US Tax Court 400 2nd St NW Washington DC 20217-0002

DAWSON, JAMES CLIFFORD, environmental science educator, geologist; b. Toronto, Ont., Can., Apr. 19, 1941; arrived in US, 1961; s. Clifford and Winifred Mary (Tadman) D.; m. Caroline Weiss, June 12, 1971. AA, Mt. San Antonio Coll., 1963; BA, UCLA, 1965, MS, 1967; PhD, U. Wis., 1970. Asst. prof. geology SUNY, Plattsburgh, 1970-74, assoc. prof., 1974-80, prof. environ sci., 1980-91, univ. disting. svc. prof., 1991—. Pres. Nat. Assn. State Bds. Edn., 1998. Chmn. Adirondack Land Trust, Inc., Elizabethtown, N.Y., 1984-89; bd. dirs. Adirondack Coun., Elizabethtown, 1982-2000; pres. Assn. for Protection of Adirondack, Schenectady, N.Y., 1982-83; mem. exec. coun. Lake Champlain Com., Inc., Burlington, Vt., 1976-98, bd. regents N.Y. State, 1993—. Mem.: AAAS, Am. Assn. Petroleum Geologists, Am. Geophys. Union, Geol. Soc. Am., Sigma Xi. Home: 2 Birchwood Dr Peru NY 12972-2600 E-mail: james.dawson@plattsburgh.edu.

DAWSON, JAMES RICHARD, fire and safety engineer; b. Fond du Lac, Wis., July 1, 1936; s. Cecil V. and Helen (Greider) D.; m. Martha Bromley, June 10, 1959; children: Heather Joy Dawson Cudworth, Jamie Dawson Strebing. Cert. safety profl., master fire fighter. With Mut. Fire Inspection Bur. New Eng., Salem, Mass., 1959-61, Home Ins. Co., Milw., 1961-65; safety dir. Amron Corp. divsn. Gulf and Western Co., Waukesha, Wis., 1965-69; fire and safety engr. Ind. U., Bloomington, 1969-2000, ret., 2000. CEO, trustee Bloomington Twp., 1979-98. Mem. Am. Soc. Safety Engrs., Fedn. of Fire Chaplains, Ind. Vol. Fireman's Assn., Fraternal Order Police. Republican. Methodist. E-mail: jrdawson@indiana.edu.

DAWSON, JOHN FREDERICK, retired architect; b. Stambaugh, Mich., Sept. 4, 1930; s. Frederick John and Myrtle (Olson) D.; m. Ruth Jennette Opland, May 8, 1954; children: Craig Frederick, Cindy Paulette. BArch, U. Mich., 1953. Registered arch., Mich., Md., D.C. Instr. U. Mich., 1956-60, asst. prof. architecture, 1960-63; dir. govtl. affairs AIA, Washington, 1963-65; v.p. Louis C. Kingscott & Assos. Inc., Washington and Kalamazoo, 1965-70; pres. Development Services, Inc., Kalamazoo, 1970-72; exec. v.p. Spanpark Corp., Kalamazoo, 1972-75; mgmt. cons. to architects, 1975-76; dir. adminstrn. Bus. and Instl. Furniture Mfrs. Assn., 1976-77; owner Solar Unltd., 1977-82; pres. Solar Solutions, Inc., 1980-84; v.p. tech. svcs. Maxam Tech., Inc., 1984-87; sr. architect David Volkert & Assoc., 1988-89; v.p. adminstrn. Edmunds & Hyde, Inc., 1989; architect/preservation officer facilities mgmt. divsn., dir. Exec. Office of the Pres., Washington, 1990-95; hist. pres. cons. Turner Constrn. Co., 1997-98; hist. architecture cons. Ft. Bliss, Tex., 1999—. Preservation inspection cons. Turner Constrn. Co., 1997-98; vice chmn. Kalamazoo Energy Policy Adv. Com., 1980-82 Pres. Whitley Park Condo. Assn., 1997-98, bd. dirs., 1997-99. With AUS, 1953-55. Home: HCI Box 265 Eagle Harbor MI 49950 E-mail: jfd97481@aol.com.

DAWSON, JOHN JOSEPH, lawyer; b. Binghamton, N.Y., Mar. 9, 1947; s. Joseph John and Cecilia (O'Neill) D. BA, Siena Coll., 1968; JD, U. Notre Dame, 1971. Bar: Ariz. 1971, Nev. 1991, Calif. 1993, D.C. 1994, N.Y. 1996. Nat. practice group chair, bankruptcy and creditors rights practice group Quarles & Brady Streich Lang LLP, Phoenix. Reporter local rules ct. U.S. Bankruptcy Ct. for Dist. Ariz.; atty. rep. U.S. Ct. Appeals (9th cir.), 1992-95 Co-author: Advanced Chapter 11 Bankruptcy, 1991. Fellow Ariz. Bar Found.; mem. State Bar Ariz. (chmn. bankruptcy sect. 1976-77, 80-81), Am. Bankruptcy Inst., Comml. Law League Am. Republican. Roman Catholic. Avocations: sports, reading, movies, travel, writing. Office: Quarles & Brady Streich Lang LLP Renaissance One Two North Central Ave Phoenix AZ 85004-2391 E-mail: jdawson@quarles.com.

DAWSON, KAREN OLTMANNS, nursing educator; b. El Centro, Calif., Mar. 14, 1947; d. Victor Roy and Lois Louise Oltmanns; m. Arthur B. Dawson, Sept. 13, 1970; children: David, Jonathan, Stephen, Matthew, Anna-Lisa. BSN, UCLA, 1969; postgrad., U. Calif., Irvine, 1980; MA, U. Colo., Denver, 1992. Cert. instr. nursing Calif., Colo., pub. health nurse, early childhood spl. edn. instr. Staff nurse, maternal-child Swedish Med. Ctr., Englewood, Colo., 1986-92, parent educator, 1983—; nurse, spl. edn. tchr. Cherry Creek Acad., 1995-97—; adminstr. early intervention ctr. for children with spl. needs, 1997-98; dir., v.p. A. Dawson Tutoring, Inc., 1998—; dir. Children's World ARAMARK Ednl. Svcs. Clin. instr. Aurora Pub. Schs. Vocat. Ctr., C.C. of Denver, Arapahoe C.C., Littleton, Colo.; spl. edn. tchr. Hope Ctr., Denver, 1992-93. Spl. edn. tchr. United Cerebral Palsy Assn., Denver, 1993-95. Mem. Neonatal ICU Connections Task Force, Swedish Med. Ctr. Colo. Consortium for Preterm Infant Devel.

DAWSON, KATON, political organization administrator; b. Columbia, S.C., 1956; married; 2 children. Businessperson auto parts firm; chmn. S.C. Rep. Party, 2002—. Office: SC Rep Party 1508 Lady St Columbia SC 29201

DAWSON, LESLIE NARYNE, quality assurance professional; d. Naryne Fowler; children: Donald Bernard Lignore, Jr., Donna Leslie Callaghan, Robert Anthony Lignore, Brian William. B of Journalism, Pub. Rels., U. Ctrl. Fla., 1998. Office mgr. Farber & Halligan, P.C., Media, Pa., 1976—80; computer operator Wing Pubs., Folsom, 1986—88; dept. adminstrv. asst. Martin Marietta Elec. Systems, Orlando, Fla., 1988—90; quality assurance engring. adminstr. Siemens Westinghouse Power Corp., 1990—. Cons. Jr. Achievement, Orlando, 1999—2002; coord. Orlando UCF Shakespeare Guild, Orlando, 1999—2002; mem. Friends of Winter Pk. Meml. Hosp., Winter Park, 2001—02; participant Ctrl. Fla. Helpline, 1999—2000; coord. Shepherd's Hope, 1999—2001; singer Voices of Valencia, 2000—02. Mem.: Phi Theta Kappa (assoc.).

DAWSON, LEWIS EDWARD, minister, retired military officer; b. Louisville, Oct. 26, 1933; s. Lewis Harper and Zelma Ruth (Hocutt) D.; m. Margaret Ellen Poor, July 29, 1956; children: Edward Rhodes, David Harper, Deborah Louise, Virginia Ruth. BA, Baylor U., 1954; MDiv, So. Bapt. Sem., 1960; postgrad., Presbyn. Sch. Christian Edn., 1977—. Ordained to ministry So. Bapt. Conv., 1960. Pastor Finecastle (Va.) Bapt. Ch. and Zion Hill Bapt. Ch., 1960-63, First So. Bapt. Ch., Great Falls, Mont., 1963-67; commd. capt. USAF, 1967, advanced through grades to col., 1983; chaplain McCoy AFB, 1967-69, PhuCat AB, Vietnam, 1969—70, Sheppard AFB, 1971-73, RAF, Chicksands, Eng., 1973-76, Keesler AFB, 1977-79; sr. chaplain Ankara (Turkey) Air Sta., 1979-81; mem. USAF Chaplain Res. Bd. Maxwell AFB, 1981-84; sr. chaplain Wright-Patterson AFB, 1984-87, Elmendorf AFB, Alaska, 1987-89, ret., 1989; assoc. dir. mil. chaplaincy Home Mission Bd., Atlanta, 1989-93; assoc. to dir. chaplaincy divsn. Home Mission Bd., So. Bapt. Conv., Alpharetta, Ga., 1994-97; pastoral ministries assoc. First Bapt. Ch., Jonesboro, 1997-99; ret., 1999. Clk. Triangle Bapt. Assn., 1965-66; chmn. Mont. Indian mission com. Mont. So. Bapt. Fellowship, 1965-66, treas., 1965-66. Mem. exec. coun. Save the Children Fund, Shefford, Eng., 1973-76. Decorated Bronze Star, Meritorious Svc. medal with 4 oak leaf cluster, Legion of Merit, Air Force Commendation medal. Home: 1926 Coventry Way Jonesboro GA 30236-2688 E-mail: LDawson797@aol.com. *When the weapons of war are exploding all around you as well as when you are secure at home with family, God is with you. God is in the logistics business, supplying all that people need as we make ourselves available to God.*

DAWSON, MARY E. b. Halifax, N.S., Can., June 23, 1942; d. Thomas Paul and Florence Margaret (Thurston) McMillan; m. Peter Dawson, Aug. 30, 1969; children: David, Emily. BA in Philosophy with honors, McGill U., 1963, BCL, 1966; DESD, U. Ottawa, 1968; LLB, Dalhousie U., 1970. Tax rschr. Revenue Can., Ottawa, 1967-68, legal counsel, 1968-69; tchg. fellow Dalhousie U., 1969-70; legis. drafter Dept. of Justice, Ottawa, 1970-79, assoc. chief legis. counsel, 1980-86, asst. dep. minister pub. law, 1986-88, assoc. dep. minister, 1988—. Mem. adv. bd. Ctr. Rsch. and Edn. Women and Work, Sch. Bus., Carleton U. Recipient Lynn William Jacobs Q.C. award, 1965, 1978; scholar, McGill U., 1960. Mem.: Ont. Bar, Que. Bar, N.S. Bar, Internat. Bar Assn. (chmn. govt. law com. 1998—2002, mem. coun. 2002—). Avocations: nordic skiing, swimming, theater, reading. Home: 97 Reid Ave Ottawa ON Canada K1H 1T1 Office: Dept Justice Rm EMB-4175 Ottawa ON Canada K1A 0H8 E-mail: mary.dawson@justice.gc.ca.

DAWSON, MARY RUTH, curator, educator; b. Highland Park, Mich., Feb. 27, 1931; d. John Elson and Olga Josephine (Down) D. BS, Mich. State Coll., 1952; postgrad., U. Edinburgh, 1952-53; PhD, U. Kans., 1957. Instr. zoology Smith Coll., 1958-61; asst. program dir. NSF, Washington, 1961-62; mem. staff Carnegie Mus., Pitts., 1962—, curator, 1971—, chmn. earth sci. div., 1973-97, acting dir., 1982-83, curator emeritus, 2003. Adj. prof. earth scis. U. Pitts., 1971—. Recipient Arnold Guyot award Nat. Geog. Soc., 1981, Woman in Sci. award Chatham Coll., 1983; named Disting. Dau. Pa., 1987; Dr. Hum, Chatham Coll., 1999, Fulbright scholar, 1952-53; fellow AAUW, 1958-59; research grantee NSF, 1961-62, 65—; recipient Romer-Simpson Medal Soc. Vertebrate Palentology. Fellow Geol. Soc. Am., Arctic Inst. N.Am.; mem. Soc. Vertebrate Paleontology (hon.; v.p. 1972-73, pres. 1973-74), Paleontol. Soc., Paläontologische Gesellschaft, Bernese Mountain Dog Club Am., Am. Soc. Mammalogists, Phi Beta Kappa. Achievements include research and publication on Tertiary Lagomorpha, 1957—, early Tertiary Holarctic rodents, 1960—, Arctic paleontology, 1975—. Office: Carnegie Mus 4400 Forbes Ave Pittsburgh PA 15213-4080

DAWSON, MIMI WEYFORTH, public policy consultant; b. St. Louis, Aug. 31, 1944; d. Francis Griffin and Jeanne (Gething) Weyforth; m. Rhett Brewer Dawson, Jan. 15, 1976; 2 children: Elizabeth Stuart, Andrew Brewer. AB, Washington U., St. Louis, 1966. Press sec., legis. asst. to Rep. James Symington, Mo. Dist., 1973; pres. sec., chief staff Sen. Bob Packwood, Oreg., 1973-81; commr. FCC, Washington, 1981-87; dep. Sec. U.S. Dept. of Transportation, Washington, 1987-89; sr pub. policy cons. Wiley, Rein and Fielding LLP, Washington, 1989—. Apptd. U.S. Holocaust Meml. Coun., 1992-98; adj. fellow Ctr. for Strategic and Internat. Studies. Mem. Atlantic Coun. U.S. (bd. dirs. 1995—). Republican. Roman Catholic. Office: Wiley Rein and Fielding LLP 1776 K St NW Washington DC 20006-2304 E-mail: mdawson@wrf.com.

DAWSON, NORMA ANN, lawyer; b. Detroit, Sept. 11, 1950; d. Emmett Chamberlain and B. Louise Dawson. BA, Pa. State U., 1971; JD, U. Mich., 1974. Bar: Calif. 1979, U.S. Dist. Ct. (cen. dist.) Calif. 1979, U.S. Ct. Appeals (9th cir.), 1979, U.S. Supreme Ct. 1984, U.S. Dist. Ct. (so. dist.) Calif. 1991, U.S. Dist. Ct. (ea. and no. dists.) Calif. 1993. Compliance atty. Penncorp Fin., Inc., Santa Monica, Calif., 1980-87; assoc. Mathon & Rosensweig, Beverly Hills, Calif., 1987-89, Stone & Hiles, Beverly Hills, 1989-94; pvt. practice L.A., 1994—. Judge pro tem L.A. Cts., 1989—. Editor: Making A Difference: Stories By and About Lawyers Who Have, 1999. Bd. dirs. Open Fist Theatre Co., Hollywood, Calif., 1991-94. Mem. Calif. State Bar (probation monitor 1984-96), Los Angeles County Bar Assn., Beverly Hills Bar Assn. (mandatory fee arbitrator 1984—), Women Lawyers Assn. L.A. Office: 2286 E Carson St PMB 310 Long Beach CA 90807-3044

DAWSON, PATRICIA LUCILLE, surgeon; b. Kingston, Jamaica, W.I., Sept. 30, 1949; came to U.S. 1950. d. Percival Gordon and Edna Claire (Overton) D.; children: Alexandria Zoe, Wesley Gordon. BA in Sociology, Allegheny Coll., 1971; MD, N.J. Med. Sch., Newark, 1977; MA in Human and Orgn. Devel., The Fielding Inst., 1996, PhD in Human and Orgnl. Sys., 1998. Membership dir. N.J. ACLU, Newark, 1972; resident in surgery U. Medicine and Dentistry N.J. N.J. Med Sch., 1977-79; Virginia Mason Med. Ctr., Seattle, 1979-82; pvt. practice specializing in surgery Arlington, Wash., 1982-83; dir. med. staff diversity Group Health Coop., Seattle, 1993-98, staff surgeon, 1983-98; pvt. practice Seattle, 1998—. Author: Forged by the Knife—The Experience of Surgical Residency from the Perspective of a Woman of Color. Fellow ACS, Seattle Surg. Soc.; mem. Physicians for Social Responsibility, Assn. Women Surgeons, Wash. Black Profls. in Health Care, NOW. Avocations: fiction, walking, cooking. Office: Providence Comp Breast Ctr Jefferson Twr 1600 E Jefferson St Ste 300 Seattle WA 98122-5645

DAWSON, PAULA DAYL, oncological nurse; b. Mount Airy, N.C., Apr. 30, 1956; d. Walter Samuel Dawson and Sybil Ann (Adkins) Anderson. AAS in Nursing, Surry C.C., Dobson, N.C., 1992. RN, N.C. Instr. Miller-Motte Bus. Coll., Winston-Salem, N.C., 1992-93; hematology-oncology staff nurse Wake Forest U. Bapt. Med. Ctr. Comprehensive Cancer Ctr., Winston Salem, N.C., 1992-98, asst. clin. nurse mgr., 1998—. Mem. Shared Governance Steering Com., Wake Forest U. Bapt. Med. Ctr., Winston-Salem, 1996-97. Vol. instr. first aid, safety and disaster svcs., Surry Count chpt ARC, Mt. Airy, N.C., 1992—, bd. mem., co-chair disaster svcs., 1997-98; basic cardiac life support instr. Am. Heart Assn., Winston-Salem, 1994—. Mem. Oncology Nursing Soc. (cert. oncol. nurse), Piedmont Triad Oncology Nursing Soc., Nat. League of Nursing, N.C. Nurses Assn. Democrat. Avocations: flower gardening, reading, photography, walking, needlework. Office: Wake Forest U Bapt Med Ctr Medical Center Blvd Winston Salem NC 27157 E-mail: ddawson@tcia.net.

DAWSON, PETER HENRY, telecommunications components executive; b. Derby, Eng., May 28, 1937; arrived in Can., 1961; s. Leslie Thomas and Beatrice Mary (Shaw) D.; m. Marilyn Ann McLellan, Aug. 24, 1963; children: Jennifer, Kathryn. BSc, U. London, 1958, PhD, 1961. Postdoctoral fellow Nat. Rsch. Coun., Ottawa, Canada, 1961—63; rsch. scientist GE Co., Schenectady, NY, 1963-69; rsch. prof. Laval U., Que., Can., 1969-74; rsch. officer Nat. Rsch. Coun., Ottawa, 1974-86, lab. dir., 1986-90, dir.-gen., 1990—98, mgr. semiconductor based R&D, 1990-98; pres. Iridian Spectral Techs., Ottawa, 1998—2001, chmn., 2002—. Bd. dirs. Ionalytics Inc. Editor, author: Quadrupole Mass Spectrometry and Its Applications, 1974; contbr. over 100 articles to profl. jours.; patentee in field. Avocations: photography, crafts. Office: Iridian Spectral Techs 1500 Montreal Rd Ottawa ON Canada K1A OR6 E-mail: p-m.dawson@sympatico.ca.

DAWSON, PETER JOHN, pathologist, educator; b. Feb. 17, 1928; came to U.S., 1960; s. Sydney and Bertha (Richards) D.; m. Nancy Sexton Taylor, Apr. 10, 1953 (div. 1969); m. Elizabeth Ann Coombs, Mar. 1, 1982. BA, Cambridge U., 1949, MA, 1953, MB, BCh, 1952, MD, 1960. Diplomate Am. Bd. Pathology. Intern Royal Berkshire Hosp., Reading, Eng., 1952-53, Victoria Hosp. for Children, London, 1953; resident St. George's Hosp., London, 1953-54, Royal Postgrad. Med. Sch., 1954—55, 1959; vis. asst. prof. U. Calif., San Francisco, 1960-62; lectr. U. Newcastle, Eng., 1962-64; assoc. prof. U. Oreg., Portland, 1964-67, prof. pathology, 1967-76; prof. pathology, dir. lab. surg. pathology U. Chgo., 1977-89; prof. pathology and lab. medicine U. South Fla., Tampa, 1989-99; chief pathology and lab. svcs. James Haley VA Hosp., Tampa, 1994-99; prof. emeritus U. South Fla., Tampa, 1999—. Contbr. articles to profl. jours. Fellow Royal Coll. Pathologists; mem. Chgo. Pathology Soc. (v.p. 1984-86, pres. 1986-88), Internat. Acad. Pathology, Am. Assn. Cancer Rsch., Am. Assn. Pathologists. Episcopalian. Avocation: sailing. E-mail: agildaws@aol.com.

DAWSON, PHILIP, history educator; b. Ann Arbor, Mich., Nov. 28, 1928; s. John Philip and Emma Van Nostrand (McDonald) D.; m. Ellen Greene, Feb. 6, 1954 (div. Oct. 1980); children: John, Elizabeth; m. Evelyn Raskin, Jan. 23, 1981 (dec. Sept. 1995); m. Kathryn Callaghan, Jan. 18, 1997. BA, U. Mich., 1950, MA, 1951; PhD, Harvard U., 1961. Reporter The Washington Post, 1953-55; tchg. fellow in history Harvard U., Cambridge, Mass., 1957-59, 60-61, instr. history, 1961-64; asst. prof. history Stanford (Calif.) U., 1964-70, assoc. prof. history, 1970-73; prof. history Bklyn. Coll. CUNY, 1973-98. Author: Provincial Magistrates and Revolutionary Politics in France, 1789-1795, 1972; co-editor: The French Revolution and the Meaning of Citizenship, 1993; contbr. articles to profl. jours. Fellow NEH, 1987-88. Mem. Soc. des Etudes Robespierristes, Soc. de l'Histoire de Paris et de l'Ile-de-France, Soc. for French Hist. Studies. Home and Office: 56 7th Ave New York NY 10011-6672 E-mail: phdawson@nyc.rr.com.

DAWSON, ROBERT EDWARD, SR., ophthalmologist; b. Rocky Mount, N.C., Feb. 23, 1918; s. William and Daisy (Wright) D.; m. Julia Belle Davis, Mar. 10, 1950; children: Dianne Elizabeth, Janice Elaine, Robert Edward, Melanie Lorraine. BS, Clark Coll., 1939; MD, Meharry Med. Coll., 1943. Diplomate Am. Bd. Ophthalmology (examiner 1979-82). Intern Homer G. Phillips Hosp., St. Louis, 1943-44, resident, 1944-46; preceptor Duke Hosp., Durham, N.C., 1946-50, hosp. instr., 1947-61, clin. instr. ophthalmology, 1968-70; pvt. practice Durham, 1946-55, 57-88; mem. attending staff ophthalmology Lincoln Hosp., Durham, 1946-55; cons. ophthalmology N.C. Cen. U. Health Svc., Durham, 1950-64; chief ophthalmology and otolaryngology Lincoln Hosp., Durham, 1959-76; mem. attending staff ophthalmology Watts Hosp., Durham, 1966-76; mem. attending staff ophthalmology, v.p. med. staff Durham County Gen. Hosp., 1976-88; med. dir. Lincoln Hosp., Durham, 1968-70; lectr. ophthalmology Lincoln Hosp. Sch. Nursing, Durham, 1948-56; clin. assoc. Duke U., Durham, 1969-75; clin. asst. prof. ophthalmology Duke U. Eye Ctr., Durham, 1975-87, scholar in residence, 1991—, cons. in ophthalmology, 1987-89. Instr. ophthalmology Duke Hosp., 1948-67; chair dept. opthalmology 3310th Hosp., Scott AFB, Belleville, Ill., 1956-57; mem. N.C. Adv. Com. on Med. Assistance, 1972-85; mem. adv. bd. N.C. State Commn. for Blind, 1965-75; mem. Gov.'s Adv. Com. Med. Assistance; regional surg. dir. Eye Bank Assn. Am., Inc., 1968-79. Mem. Durham Coun. Human Rels., 1967-69; mem. Pres. Com. on Employment of Handicapped, 1971-79; bd. dirs. Durham County Tb Assn., 1950-54, Better Health Found., 1960-66, Durham Community House, 1966-68, Lincoln Community Health Ctr., Am. Cancer Soc., Durham United Fund, Durham County Mental Health Ctr., 1976-79, Found. for Better Health of Durham County Gen. Hosp., 1975-79; bd. dirs., v.p. Nat. Soc. Prevention of Blindness; trustee Durham Acad., 1969-72, Durham County Gen. Hosp.; life trustee Meharry Med. Coll.; trustee emeritus N.C. Cen. U., Mut. Savs. & Loan; mem. bd. mgmt. Meharry Med. Coll. Alumni Assn.; bd. assocs. Greensboro Coll., N.C.; co-founder, chmn. bd. dirs. Lincoln Pvt. Diagnostic Clinic; bd. visitors Clark Coll., Atlanta. Served as maj., M.C., USAF, 1955-57. Recipient Disting. Svc. award Clark Coll., 1984, Nat. Assn. Equal Opportunity in Higher Edn., 1985, Physician of Yr. award Old North State Med. Soc., 1981, Meritorious Svc. Highest award, 1991, Durham N.C. City of Medicine highest award for cmty. svc., City of Medicine Cmty. Svc. award, Durham, NC, 2002, Trailblazer in Ophthalmology award Nat. Med. Assn., 2001. Fellow ACS, Acad. Ophthalmology; mem. AMA, Nat. Soc. to Prevent Blindness (v.p.), Am. Assn. Ophthalmology, Soc. Eye Surgeons, Nat. Med. Assn. (trustee 1971-80, pres. 1979-80, Disting. Service award 1983), Pan Am. Med. Assn. (diplomate), Old North State Med. Soc. (pres. 1966-67), Durham Acad. Medicine (pres. 1967-68), NAACP (life), Durham Bus. and Profl. Chain, C. of C., Meharry Nat. Alumni Assn. (past pres.), Alpha Omega Alpha, Alpha Phi Alpha (past pres.), Sigma Pi Phi (pres.), Chi Delta Mu (pres.). Democrat. Mem. A.M.E. Ch. (stewards bd. 1968—). Mason (33d degree, Shriner). Club: Toastmasters (pres. 1969-70). Home: 817 Lawson St Durham NC 27701-4534 Office: 817 E Lawson St Durham NC 27701-4534

DAWSON, ROY EDWARD, academic advisor; b. Denver, Aug. 6, 1946; s. Walter Raymond and Bernice Sarah (McGregor) D.; m. Norma Jean Roach, June 4, 1968 (div. Apr. 1987); children: Jeffery Lee, David Allen; m. Kathleen Lameiro, Sept. 4, 1993. AS, C.C. of Denver, Lakewood, 1975; BA, U. Colo., 1977, MA, 1991; PhD, U. Colo., Denver, 2002. Staff engr. Midwest Rsch. Inst., Golden, Colo., 1982-87; biology instr. U. Colo., Boulder, 1991-93, Denver, 1993-99, acad. advisor Boulder, 1999—. Contbr. articles to profl. jours. Vol. City and County of Boulder, 1979-86; mem. Lamm-Wirth Rocky Flats Comm., Denver, 1980-87, chmn., 1986-87. With USN, 1964-68, Vietnam. Recipient William H. Burt award U. Colo. Mus., Boulder, 1991; decorated Nat. Def. Svc. medal, Vietnam Svc. medal with two bronze stars, Rep. of Vietnam Campaign medal. Avocations: hiking, cross country skiing, sea kayaking. Office: Univ Colo Acad Advising Ctr Woodbury Arts & Scis 290 UCB Boulder CO 80309-0290

DAWSON, STEPHEN EVERETTE, lawyer; b. Detroit, May 14, 1946; s. Everette Ivan and Irene (Dresser) D.; m. Consiglia J. Bellisario, Sept. 20, 1974; children: Stephen Everette Jr., Gina C., Joseph J. BA, Mich. State U., 1968; MA, U. Mich., 1969, JD, 1972. Bar: Mich. 1972, U.S. Dist. Ct. (ea. dist.) Mich. 1972, U.S. Supreme Ct. 1978, U.S. Ct. Appeals (6th cir.) 1980. Assoc. Dickinson, Wright, Moon, Van Dusen & Freeman, Detroit, 1972-79; ptnr. Dickinson, Wright, PLLC, Bloomfield Hills, Mich., 1979—. Adj. prof. law U. Detroit, 1986-88. Mem. ABA, Am. Coll. Real Estate Lawyers, Mich. State Bar Assn. (mem. coun. real property law sect. 1986-93, chair 1992-93, land title stds. com. 1999—), Mich. State Bar Found., Phi Beta Kappa. Republican. Avocations: jogging, reading. Office: Dickinson Wright PLLC 38525 Woodward Ave Ste 2000 Bloomfield Hills MI 48304-5092 E-mail: sdawson@dickinsonwright.com.

DAWSON, STUART OWEN, landscape architect, urban designer; b. Urbana, Ill., Apr. 27, 1935; s. Alva Owen and Mildred (Kemp) Dawson; m. Virginia Wilson (div. July 1968); children: Julie Dawson Orsatti, Emilie Dawson Carter, Mark Owen; m. Ellen Washington, Oct. 24, 1970. BFA in Landscape Architecture, U. Ill., 1957; MFA in Landscape Architecture, Harvard U., 1958. Registered landscape architect 30 states. Draftsman U. Ill., Urbana, 1955-56; draftsman, designer Sasaki, Walker, Assocs., Watertown, Mass., 1957-58, assoc., 1959-62; prin. Sasaki, Dawson, DeMay and Assocs., Watertown, 1962-70; v.p., prin. Sasaki & Assocs., Watertown, 1970—. Advisor The Waterfront Ctr., Washington; adv. bd. Riley Inst., Charleston, SC; resident Am. Acad. Rome, 1976; instr. Harvard Grad. Sch. Design, 1990—93, U. Ill., Urbana, 1997. Prin. works include Deere and Co. Corp. Hdqs., Moline, Ill., TRW Corp. Hdqs., Lindhurst, Ohio, McDonalds Corp. Hdqs., Oak Brook, Ill., Brown Forman Corp. Hdqs., Louisville, Downtown and Waterfront, Newburyport, Mass., Arts Dist., Dallas, Betty Marcus Park, Rice U., Houston, Tex. Med. Ctr., Enid Haupt Garden, The Smithsonian Inst., The Kennedy Ctr., Washington, Fountain Plaza, Buffalo, Boston Waterfront Pk. and Long Wharf, Christian Sci. Ctr., Boston, Charleston Waterfront Pk., Charleston, S.C., Maritime Ctr., Detroit River Waterfront Park, Boulder Mall, Boulder, Colo., Frito-Lay Corp. Hdqs., Plano, Tex., Capitol City Landing and Riverfront, Indpls., Scioto Riverfront and COSI, Columbus, Ohio, Fed. Campus, Oklahoma City, Doosan Meml. Park, Seoul, Korea, Cin. Waterfront Park. Mem. corp. Hurricane Island Outward Bound Sch., Rockland, Maine; founding commr. Boston Landmarks; juror Salem Witch Trial Tercentenary Meml. Competition. 1st lt. U.S. Army, 1958—60. Fellow: Am. Soc. Landscape Architects (design awards jury 1985, chmn. 1986—, juror coun. of fellows 1989—91, Gold medal 1999); mem.: Reading Rm. York Harbor, Maine, Harvard Faculty Club, York Golf and Tennis Club. Avocations: sailing, drawing, dog sledding, fly fishing, skiing, golf. Home: Big Pine Island PO Box 1113 York Harbor ME 03911-1113 Office: Sasaki Assocs Inc 64 Pleasant St Watertown MA 02472-2316

DAWSON, SUZANNE STOCKUS, lawyer; b. Chgo., Dec. 29, 1941; d. John Charles and Josephine (Zolpe) Stockus; m. Daniel P. Dawson Sr., Sept. 1, 1962; children: Daniel P. Jr., John Charles, Michael Sean. BA, Marquette U., 1963; JD cum laude, Loyola U., Chgo., 1965. Bar: Ill. 1965, U.S. dist. Ct. (no. dist.) Ill. 1965. Assoc. Kirkland & Ellis, Chgo., 1965-71, ptnr., 1971-82, Arnstein & Lehr, Chgo., 1982-89, Foley & Lardner, Chgo., 1989-94; spl. counsel publicly held corps. Glenview, Ill., 1995-97; corp. counsel Baxter Healthcare Corp., Deerfield, Ill., 1997-98, sr. counsel, 1998—. Mem. various coms. United Way Chgo.; corp. adv. bd. Sec. State of Ill., 1973; past mem. bd. advisors Loyola of Chgo. Law Sch.; trustee Lawrence Hall Youth Svcs., Chgo., 1983-98, pres., 1991-93, chair 1993-96; mem. adv. bd. Cath. Charities Chgo., 1985—, chair north suburban regional adv. bd., 2002—; mem. exec. com., bd. governance Notre Dame High Sch., Niles, Ill., 1990-97. Recipient Founder's Day award Loyola U., 1980, St. Thomas More award Loyola of Chgo. Law Sch., 1983. Mem. ABA, Am. Arbitration Assn. (appointed mem. nat. panel of comml. arbitrators 1996—), Ill. Bar Assn. Roman Catholic. Avocations: piano, choir singing, gardening, skiing, gourmet cooking. Home: 2113 Valley Lo Ln Glenview IL 60025-1724 Office: Baxter Healthcare Corp One Baxter Pkwy Deerfield IL 60015-4633 E-mail: suzanne_dawson@baxter.com.

DAWSON, TED MURRAY, neurologist, educator; b. Idaho Falls, Idaho, Apr. 19, 1959; s. Oliver Murray and Goldy Dawson; m. Valina Lynn Dawson, June 14, 1986. BS, Mont. State U., 1981; MD, PhD, U. Utah, 1986. Diplomate Am. Bd. Med. Examiners, Am. Bd. Psychiatry and Neurology. Intern in medicine U. Utah Affiliated Hosps., Salt Lake City, 1986-87; resident in neurology Hosp. of U. Pa., Phila., 1987-90; tchg. and rsch. asst. dept. pharmacology U. Utah, Salt Lake City, 1984-86; asst. instr. dept. neurology U. Pa., Phila., 1989, instr., 1989-90; postdoctoral fellow, sr. clin. fellow dept. neurosci. Johns Hopkins U., Balt., 1990-92, instr. dept. neurosci. and neurology, 1992-93, asst. prof. dept. neurology and neurosci., 1993-96, assoc. prof., 1996—2000, prof. neurology, neurosci., cellular and molecular medicine, 2000—; co-dir. Parkinson's Disease Ctr., 1996—2002; dir. Parkinson's Disease and Movement Disorder Ctr., 2002—. Dir. Morris K. Udall Parkinson's Disease Rsch. Ctr. Excellence, 1998—; co-dir. neuroregenerational repair program Inst. for Cell Engring. Contbr. articles to profl. jours. Mem. AMA, AAAS, Am. Acad. Neurology, Am. Fedn. Clin. Rsch., Soc. Neurosci., Molecular Medicine Soc., Am. Neurol. Assn. Office: Johns Hopkins U Carnegie 214 600 N Wolfe St Baltimore MD 21287-0005

DAWSON, VIRGINIA SUE, retired newspaper editor; b. Concordia, Kans., June 6, 1940; d. John Edward and Wilma Aileen (Thompson) Morgan; m. Neil S. Dawson, Nov. 28, 1964; children: Shelley Diane Dawson Sedwick, Lori Ann Dawson Hughes, Christy Lynn. BS in Home Econs. and Journalism, Kans. State U., 1962. Asst. publs. editor Ohio State U. Coop. Extension Svc., Columbus, 1962-64; home editor Ohio Farmer mag., Columbus, 1964-78; food editor Columbus Dispatch, 1978—2000, ret. Recipient Commn. award Ohio Poultry Assn., 1980. Mem. Assn. Food Journalists. Avocations: biking, running, reading, cooking.

DAWSON, WILLIAM RYAN, zoology educator; b. Los Angeles, Aug. 24, 1927; s. William Eldon and Mary (Ryan) D.; m. Virginia Louise Berwick, Sept. 9, 1950; children: Deborah, Denise, William. Student, Stanford, 1945-46; BA, UCLA, 1949, MA, 1950, PhD, 1953; DSc, U. Western Australia, 1971. Faculty zoology U. Mich., Ann Arbor, 1953-94, prof., 1962-94, D.E.S. Brown prof. biol. scis., 1981-94, chmn. div. biol. scis., 1974-82, dir. Mus. Zoology, 1982-93, D.E.S. Brown prof. emeritus, 1994—. Lectr. Summer Inst. Desert Biology, Ariz. State U., 1960-71, Maytag prof., 1982; rschr. Australian-Am. Edn. Found., U. Western Australia, 1969-70; Carpenter lectr. San Diego State U., 1996; mem. Speakers Bur., Am. Inst. Biol. Sci., 1960-62; mem. adv. panel NSF environ. biology program, 1967-69; mem. adv. com. for rsch. NSF, 1973-77; adv. panel NSF regulatory biology program, 1979-82; mem. R/V Alpha Helix New Guinea Expdn., 1969; chief scientist R/V Dolphin Gulf of Calif. Expdn., 1976; mem. R/V Alpha Helix Galapagos Expdn., 1978. Editorial bd.: Condor, 1960-63, Auk, 1964-68, Ecology, 1968-70, Ann. Rev. Physiology, 1973-79, Physiol. Zoology, 1976-86; co-editor: Springer-Verlag Zoophysiology and Ecology series, 1968-72; assoc. editor: Biology of the Reptilia, 1972, Birds of N.Am., 1997—. Served with USNR, 1945-46. USPHS Postdoctoral Research fellow, 1953; Guggenheim fellow, 1962-63; Recipient Russell award U. Mich., 1959, Distinguished Faculty Achievement award, 1976; Wheeler Lectr. U. N.D., 1986. Fellow AAAS (council del. 1984-86), Am. Ornithol. Union (Brewster medal 1979); mem. Soc. Integrative Comparative Biology (pres. 1985), Am. Physiol. Soc., Ecol. Soc. Am., Cooper Ornithol. Soc. (hon., Painton award 1963, Miller Rsch. award 1996), Phi Beta Kappa, Sigma Xi, Kappa Sigma. Home: 1376 Bird Rd Ann Arbor MI 48103-2351 E-mail: wrdawson@umich.edu.

DAY, ADRIENNE CAROL, artist, art educator; b. Jackson, Miss., Dec. 13, 1955; d. Robert Maxwell and Phyllis Mary (Roberts) D. BFA, U. Okla., 1986; MFA, Ariz. State U., 1990. Adj. instr. Mesa (Ariz.) C.C., 1990; artist-in-residence Arts Coun. Okla., Okla. City, 1991—; vis. lectr. dept. art U. Ctrl. Okla., Edmond, 1993-98; adj. prof. art Okla. City U., 1996—; adj. asst. prof. U. Okla. Coll. Liberal Studies, Norman, 1997—2001; art specialist Western Village Acad., Oklahoma City, 2001—. Coord., organizer Suite Okla. exchange portfolio, 1997. One-woman shows include Ariz. State U., Tempe, 1990, Individual Artists of Okla. exhbn., Okla. City, 1993, ARC Gallery, Chgo., 1995, Leslie Powell Gallery, Lawton, Okla., 1996, U. Southeastern Okla., Durant, 1998; exhibited in group shows at Ariz. State U., Tempe, 1989 (purchase award), Guadalupe Cultural Arts, Ctr., San Antonio, 1989 (cash award), Greenville (N.C.) Mus. Art, 1989, Ind. U., 1989, Shemer Art Ctr. and Mus., Phoenix, 1990, Kirkpatric Ctr. Gallery, Okla. City, 1991, Okla. City Art Mus., 1992, Fla. State U. Mus., Tallahassee, 1993, Corcoran Sch. Art, Washington, 1994-97, U. Ctrl. Okla. Faculty Exhibit, Edmond, 1994-97, Austin Peay U., Clarksville, Tenn., 1994, I.A.O/M.A.R.S. Exchange Exhibit, Phoenix, 1995, Alexander Hogue Gallery, U. Tulsa, Okla., 1997, Truman State U., 1998, Columbia (Mo.) Coll., 1998, Morgan Gallery, Kansas City, 2000, Wichita, Kans., 2001; represented in permanent collections Haarmann and Reimer Corp., Germany, Corcoran Mus., Washington, U. Ctrl. Okla., Fred Jones Mus., Carol Reese Mus., East Tenn. State, U. Tenn., Knoxville, Miss. State U., U. Texas, Tyler, Fellers & Co., Okla. City, U. Fla., Gainsville, Bradley U., Peoria, Ariz. State U., Ohio U., Athens, Brigham Young U., U. Utah, U. Alberta. Recipient Letzeiser Gold medal U. Okla. Sch. Art, Norman, 1987, Abraham and Bessie Lehrer Meml. award Ariz. State U., 1989, faculty purchase award Presdl. Ptrns. U. Ctrl. Olka., Edmond, 1995; first alt. Fourth Annual Nathan Cummings Travel fellow Ariz. State U., 1989; Artist Project grantee Ariz. Commn. on the Arts, 1991, Sudden Opportunity grantee Okla. Visual Arts Coalition, Okla. City, 1992. Democrat. Home and Office: PO Box 6354 Norman OK 73070-6354

DAY, ANGELA RIDDLE, occupational health nurse, educator; b. Greenville, SC, Oct. 23, 1963; d. Earl C. and Sandra Riddle; m. Herbert Day, May 26, 1984; 2 children. BSN, Clemson U., 1985. RN, SC; cert. occupational health nurse specialist; cert. occup. hearing conservationist, pulmonary function tech., CPR, first aid instr. Staff nurse St. Francis Hosp., Greenville, 1985-86; dir. occup. health nursing, ednl. coord. North Hills Med. Ctr., Greenville, 1986-94; occupational health nrse BMW Mfg. Corp., Greer, SC, 1994-96; cons. in field, 1996—; cons. Safety Components Fabric Tech., Inc., Greenville, 2002—. Mem. Am. Assn. Occupational Health Nurses, SC State Assn. Occup. Health Nurses (com. chmn.). E-mail: akrday215@msn.com.

DAY, ANN ELIZABETH, artist, educator; b. Valetta, Malta, June 1, 1927; came to U.S., 1940; d. John Dwight and Joyce Elizabeth (Marett) Harvey; m. George Frederick Day, Oct. 23, 1948 (div. Oct. 1979); children: Georgianna Day Ludcke, John F., David S.; m. Donald Monturean Mintz, Dec. 30, 1980. BA, Mt. Holyoke Coll., 1948. Asst. to dir. advanced studies Nat. Ctr. Atmospheric Rsch., Boulder, Colo., 1962-67; edn. dir. Waterloo (Iowa) Recreation and Arts Ctr., 1967-76; curator edn. svcs. Utah Mus. Fine Arts, Salt Lake City, 1976-80; lectr. art history YMHA of N.J., Wayne, 1982—, RSVP, Paramus, N.J., 1994—, Art History Tours of France, Tour de France, Ltd., 1994—, Classic Residence, Teaneck, N.J., 1995—, Belleville (N.J.) Libr., 1995—, Montclair (N.J.) Adult Sch., 2001—, Teaneck (N.J.) Sr. Ctr., 2003—; freelance artist Ringwood, N.J., 1982—; represented by Nathans Gallery, West Paterson, NJ. Vice chair, panelist Fed. State Ptnrship., NEA, Washington, 1972-77; mem. exec. com. Nat. Assn. Community Arts Agys., Washington, 1975-77. Author of poems; represented in permanent collections Utah Mus. of Fine Arts, also U.S. and abroad. Recipient Silver medal Utah Watercolor Soc., Salt Lake City, 1976, Lake Mohawk Club award Sussex County Art Assn., Sparta, N.J., 1992, 93, Best in Show award Sussex County Art Assn., 1997, Artists Mag. award (NWS juried exhibition), 1996. Mem. Nat. Watercolor Soc., N.J. Watercolor Soc. (Heimrod award for NJWSC exhibit 1991), Phi Beta Kappa. Democrat. Avocations: walking, swimming, collecting tribal art. Home and Office: 117 Cedar Rd Ringwood NJ 07456-1800

DAY, ANNE WHITE, retired nurse; b. Cin., July 9, 1926; d. Pinkney McGill and Anna Pearl (Glendenning) White; m. Raymond Eric Parker, Mar. 6, 1948 (div. 1969); children: Douglas McGill, Stephanie Morse. Diploma, Christ Hosp. Sch. Nursing, Cin., 1947. RN, Ohio; cert. chem. dependency nurse Consol. Assn. Nurses in Substance Abuse. Staff nurse to asst. head nurse Holmes divsn. U. Cin., 1948-84; nursing supr. Villa Hope Extended Care Facility, Cin., 1970-72; staff nurse Hillenbrand Nursing Home, Cin., 1980-82, Emerson A. North Hosp., Cin., 1982-94. Vol. Group Against Smoke Pollution, Cin., 1989—; donor Zoo, Cin., 1989—, Voters for Choice, Ohio, 1989—, Ams. for Non-Smokers Rights, Calif., 1989—, Action on Smoking or Health, 1989—, Stop Teenage Addiction to Tobacco. Mem. DAR (life). Episcopalian. Avocations: swimming, reading, knitting, crocheting, pattern dancing.

DAY, ANTHONY, book critic, journalist; b. Miami, Fla., May 12, 1933; s. Price and Alice (Alexander) D.; m. Lynn Ward, June 25, 1960; children— John, Julia (dec.). AB cum laude, Harvard U., 1955, postgrad. (Nieman fellow), 1966-67; L.H.D. (hon.), Pepperdine U., 1974. Reporter Phila. Bull., 1957-60, 1960-69, chief Washington bur., 1969; chief editorial writer L.A. Times, 1969-71, editor editorial pages, 1971-89, sr. corr., 1989-95; contbg. writer L.A. Times Book Review, 1995—. Mem. Signet Soc. Harvard, Asia Soc., Santa Fe Coun. Internat. Rels.

DAY, BURNIS C. artist, educator; b. Hepzibah, W.Va. s. Jeff Monroe and Willie Etta (Porter) D. Student, Art and Design Coll., Detroit, 1964—66, Famous Artists Sch., Westport, Conn., 1965—67; AAS, Oakland C.C., Farmington Hills, Mich., 1969. Keyliner and photostat operator Freuhauf Corp., Detroit, 1970-71; art dir. Urban Screen Process, Detroit, 1971-73; instr. art Pittman's Galleries, Inc., Detroit, 1973-74; art assoc. Cal Summers' House of Art, Detroit, 1971-77; with 21st Century Video, Detroit; free-lance advt. and painting, Detroit, 1977—. Instr. art Wayne County C.C., 1985—98, St. Scholastica Summer Day Camp, Detroit, 1995—98; juror Mich. State Fair, Detroit, 1992, Arts for Parks, Jackson Hole, Wyo., 1994; field videographer Inst. for Survey Rsch., Temple U., Phila., 1992—93; instr. painting on TV satellite UAW-Chrysler Nat. Tng. Ctr., Detroit, 1995—99; panelist Mich. Arts and Humanities Touring Dir., 2000—03. One-man shows include Pittman Galleries, Detroit, 1981, exhibited in group shows at The Gallery Tanner, L.A., 1984, The Laramie Art Guild, Wyo., 1979, The N.Mex. Art League, 1979, Nat. Theatre, Lagos, Nigeria, 1977, Represented in permanent collections Detroit Inst. Arts, City of N.Y., U. Utah Mus. Fine Arts, Mus. No. Ariz., Mus. Art, Ponce, P.R., Las Vegas Art Mus., Kauai Regional Libr., Lihue, Hawaii, Former Pres. Bill Clinton's Pvt. Collection from the White House, Washington County Mus. Fine Arts Md., U. Mont. Mus. Fine Arts, N.Mex. Highlands U., Ft. Smith (Ark.) Art Ctr., Fisk U. Art Galleries, Tenn., Hofstra U. Mus., N.Y., Mus. City N.Y., Oprah Winfrey's pvt. collection, Chgo., Mus. of Art and Archaeology, Univ. Mo.-Columbia, Univ. S.D. Art Galleries, Charles B. Goddard Ctr. for the Visual and Performing Arts, Ardmore, Okla.; author: Burnis Calvin Day's Neogeometric Paintings (His Travels, Insight on Art and Artists), 2003. Vol. svc. camera operator pub. access program Comcast Cable TV, 1988. Recipient various awards for art, including 1st place award for mural People's Art and Detroit Recreation Dept., 1976, 2d place, 1977, cert. of recognition U.S. Zone Com., Lagos, Nigeria, 1977. Achievements include since the late 1990's I have est. a neogeometric sch. of art internat. Avocations: nature, outdoors, Go. Office: PO Box 0255 Detroit MI 48231 0255 Personal E-mail: burnisday@yahoo.com.

DAY, DAVID OWEN, lawyer; b. Long Beach, Calif., Apr. 3, 1958; s. Robert Owen and Linda Sue (Weaver) D.; m. Vicki Temple Butler, Sept. 24, 1980; children: Candi, Chad, Charles, Chase, Catelyn. BA magna cum laude, E. Tenn. State U., 1980; JD with high honors, U. Tenn., 1984. Bar: Tenn. 1984, U.S. Dist. Ct. (mid. dist.) Tenn. 1984, U.S. Ct. Appeals (6th cir.) 1990, U.S. Supreme Ct. 1990; cert. civil trial specialist, Nat. Bd. Trial Advocacy and Tenn. Commn. on Continuing Legal Edn. and Specialization. Assoc. Law Office of Donald G. Dickerson, Cookeville, Tenn., 1984-87; ptnr. Dickerson and Day Attys. at Law, Cookeville, 1987-90; pvt. practice Cookeville, Tenn., 1990—. Lectr. Bank Adminstrv. Inst., 1990, Tenn. Bankers Assn., 1993, Tenn. Consol. Ret. Sys., 1996, Am. Inst. Banking, 1996. Asst. editor Tennessee Law Review, 1982-83. Frederick T. Bonham scholar U. Tenn., 1981, Harold C. Warner scholar U. Tenn., 1982, Carl W. Miller scholar U. Tenn., 1983. Mem. ABA, ATLA, Tenn. Trial Lawyers Assn., Putnam County Bar Assn., Tenn. Bar Assn., Phi Kappa Phi, Alpha Lambda Delta. Ch. of Jesus Christ of Latter-day Saints. Avocations: song writing, singing, playing basketball, pub. speaking, traveling. Home: PO Box 704 Cookeville TN 38503-0704 Office: 19 S Jefferson Ave Cookeville TN 38501-5911

DAY, DAVID VAUGHAN, psychology educator; b. Albany, Feb. 20, 1956; s. Donald Joseph and Evelyn Kay Day; children: Meghan children: Emerson. BA, Baldwin-Wallace Coll., 1983; MA, PhD, U. Akron, 1988. Asst. prof. psychology La. State U., Baton Rouge, 1988—91, Pa. State U., University Park, 1991—96, assoc. prof. psychology, 1996—2001, prof. psychology, 2002—. Adj. rsch. scientist Ctr. for Creative Leadership, Greensboro, 1998—2002; pres., bd. dirs. Collegian, Inc., State College, 1992—2000. Contbr. Grantee, W.K. Kellogg Found., 1998—2003. Fellow: APA, Soc. for Indsl. and Orgnl. Psychology; mem.: Soc. for Orgnl. Behavior, So. Mgmt. Assn., Acad. Mgmt. Home: 2548 Sleepy Hollow Dr State College PA 16803 Office: Pa State U 126 Bruce V Moore Bldg State College PA 16802 Office Fax: 814-863-7002. Personal E-mail: dvd111@juno.com. Business E-Mail: dvd1@psu.edu.

DAY, DONALD SHELDON, lawyer; b. Boston, Nov. 3, 1924; s. Israel and Frances (Goldberg) D.; m. Edythe Greenberg, July 8, 1945; children— Clifford L., Richard J., Halee Beth. BA, Bates Coll., 1946; LLB, Cornell U., 1948. Bar: N.Y. 1948. Past chmn. bd. Saperston and Day P.C., Buffalo, 1979-96; pres. World Union for Progressive Judaism, 1988-95. Bd. dirs. various corps. Gen. chmn. United Jewish Fund Campaign, Buffalo, 1971-73, 75; past co-chmn. Western N.Y. chpt. NCCJ; past pres. United Jewish Fedn. Buffalo; past chmn. bd. Childrens Hosp. Buffalo, Union Am. Hebrew Congregations; trustee Forest Lawn Cemetery and Crematory, Hebrew-Union Coll. With AUS, 1942-45. Mem. Am., N.Y. State, Erie County bar assns., Order of Coif, Phi Kappa Phi. Jewish (past pres. temple). Office: Hiscock & Barclay 3 Fountain Plz Buffalo NY 14203-1486

DAY, EDWARD FRANCIS, JR., lawyer; b. Portland, Maine, Nov. 4, 1946; s. Edward Francis and Anne (Rague) D.; m. Claire Ann Nicholson, June 27, 1970; children: Kelley Ann, John Edward. BA, St. Anselm Coll., 1968; JD cum laude, U. Maine, 1973; LLM in Taxation, NYU, 1976. Bar: N.J. 1973, U.S. Dist. Ct. N.J. 1973, U.S. Tax Ct. 1974, N.Y. 1981. Assoc. Hannoch, Weisman, Stern & Besser, Newark, 1973-74, Carpenter, Bennett & Morrissey, Newark, 1974-78, ptnr., 1979-93, sr. ptnr., 1994-98, of counsel, 1999—. Instr. employee benefits and comml. law The Am. Coll., Valley Forge, Pa., 1981-82; exec. v.p., gen. counsel Main Steel Polishing Co., Inc., Tinton Falls, N.J., 1999—. Editor Maine Law Rev., 1972-73. Mem., vice-chmn. Allenhurst (N.J) Bd. Adjustment, 1983-85; mem., vice-chmn. Allenhurst Planning Bd., 1985-87; mem. Nat. Ski Patrol, Denver, 1985—; scoutmaster Monmouth coun. Boy Scouts Am., Ocean Twp., 1987-90; mem. 10th Mountain Divsn. Assn., Aspen, Colo., 1996—, Appalachian Mt. Club, Boston, 2003—. Served in U.S. Army, 1968-70. Named One of Outstanding Young Men of Am., 1979; Ford Found. scholar, 1966-68. Mem.: ABA, Appalachian Mountain Club (Boston), Estate Planning Coun. No. N.J., Essex County Bar Assn., N.J. Bar Assn., Forsgate Country Club (Jamesburg, N.J.), Jersey Coast Club of Red Bank (v.p. 1976—77), Deal (N.J.) Golf and Country Club (bd. dirs. 1985—92, sec. 1991—92), Am. Legion. Roman

Catholic. Avocations: golf, skiing, piano. Home: 225 Spier Ave Allenhurst NJ 07711-1120 Office: Carpenter Bennett & Morrissey 3 Gateway Ctr Newark NJ 07102-4079 also: Main Steel Polishing Company Inc 2 Hance Ave Eatontown NJ 07724-2726

DAY, EMERSON, physician; b. Hanover, N.H., May 2, 1913; s. Edmund Ezra and Emily Sophia (Emerson) D.; m. Ruth Fairfield, Aug. 7, 1937 (dec. Oct. 1994); children: Edmund Perry, Robert Fairfield, Nancy, Bonnie, Sheryl; m. Germaine Scherman, Sept. 24, 1999. BA, Dartmouth Coll., 1934; MD, Harvard U., 1938. Intern Presbyn. Hosp., N.Y.C., 1938- 40; fellow in cardiology Johns Hopkins U., 1940-42; asst. resident medicine N.Y. Hosp., 1942; med. dir. internat. divsn. Trans World Airline, N.Y.C., 1945-47; asst. prof. preventive medicine and pub. health Cornell U. Med. Coll., 1947-50, assoc. prof. clin. preventive medicine and pub. health, 1950-54, prof. preventive medicine Sloan Kettering divsn., 1954-64; chmn. dept. preventive medicine Meml. Hosp., N.Y.C., 1954-63; dir. Strang Cancer Prevention Clinic, 1950-63; mem., chief divsn. preventive medicine Sloan-Kettering Inst., N.Y.C., 1954-64; cons. in geriatrics Cold Spring Inst., Cold Spring-on-Hudson, N.Y., 1952-57; dir. N.Y.C. Dept. Health Cancer Detection Center, 1947-50, Strang Clinic/Meml. Sloan Kettering Cancer Ctr., 1950-63, PMI-Strang Clinic, 1963-69; pres. Preventive Medicine Inst., Strang Cancer Prevention Ctr., 1969—; hon. pres., mem. bd. trustees Preventive Medicine Inst., 1969—; v.p., med. dir. Medequip Corp., 1969-76, sr. med. cons., 1976-82; med. v.p. Health Mgmt. Internat., Inc., 1982-84; med. dir. Physicians for Med. Cost Containment, Inc., 1984-94; prof. medicine Northwestern U. Med. Sch., 1976-81, prof. emeritus, 1981—; assoc. dir. Northwestern U. Cancer Center, 1976-81; med. dir. Portes Cancer Prevention Center, 1978-79; attending physician Northwestern Meml. Hosp., 1976-81, vis. physician, 1981-99. Lectr. Cook County Grad. Sch. Med., 1977-90; mem. Northwestern U. Med. Assocs., 1980-81; med. dir., chmn. dept. internal medicine Chgo. Splty. Hosp. and Med. Center, 1981-84; hon. staff physician Evanston, Glenbrook hosps., 1976-99; attending physician, mem. med. bd. James Ewing Hosp., Meml. Hosp., N.Y.C., 1950-64; founder, sr. mem. PMX Med. Group, N.Y.C., 1956— 70; adj. prof. biology N.Y. U., 1965-70; mem. cancer detection com. Internat. Union Against Cancer, 1954-70; pres. N.Y.C. div. Am. Cancer Soc., 1963-64; med. cons. Medidata Health Services, Inc., 1986-90. Contbr. numerous articles to profl. jours. Dir. Am. Found. for Children and Youth. Served as flight surgeon ATC USAAF, 1942-45. Recipient Bronze medal Am. Cancer Soc., 1956, professorship in early detection Ill. divsn., 1976-79, Lifetime Achievement award Strang Cancer Prevention Ctr., 2003. Fellow ACP, N.Y. Acad. Medicine, N.Y. Acad. Scis. (pres. 1965), APHA, Am. Occupl. Med. Assn., Am. Geriatrics Soc., Internat. Acad. Cytology (hon.); mem. AMA, Am. Soc. Cytopathology (founder, pres. 1958, hon., Papanicolaou award 1978), Am. Soc. Preventive Oncology, Internat. Health Evaluation Assn., Soc. for Advanced Med. Sys. (founding dir. 1969-81), Am. Assn. Med. Sys. and Informatics (founding dir. 1981-84), Harvey Soc., Chgo. Clin. Ethics Program (charter), Century Assn. (N.Y.C.), Ill. Med. Soc., Chgo. Med. Soc., Med. Cons. Svcs. Assn., Dartmouth Club of N.Y.C. (award 1955), Phi Beta Kappa, Alpha Omega Alpha, Zeta Psi. Home and Office: 19 Pinewood Vlg West Lebanon NH 03784-3122 E-mail: Gerry.day@mailstation.com.

DAY, GREGORY LYNN, music educator; b. Galesburg, Ill., Oct. 18, 1955; s. Harold Edwin and Norma Ferne Day; m. Margaret Marie Dusa, May 19, 1990; 1 child, Ann Marie. MusB Edn., Augustana Coll., 1977; MusM Edn., No. Ill. U., 1979. Cert. tchr. Ill. Music educator/choral dir. Sterling (Ill.) Sch. Dist., 1977—79, Geneseo (Ill.) Sch. Dist., 1979—82, AlWood Sch. Dist., Woodhull, Ill., 1982—84, Flossmoor (Ill.) Sch. Dist., 1984—. Composer 34 original choral pieces. Choir dir. St. Jude Cath. Ch., New Lenox, Ill., 1996. Mem.: NEA, Music Educators Nat. Conf., Flossmoor Edn. Assn., Ill. Edn. Assn., Am. Choral Dirs. Assn., Ill. Music Educators Assn. Roman Catholic. Avocations: astronomy/cosmology, home electronics. Home: 1849 Harvard Ln New Lenox IL 60451 Office: Parker Jr HS 2810 School St Flossmoor IL 60422

DAY, GREGORY THOMAS, lawyer; b. L.A., Apr. 17, 1964; s. Arthur John and Margaret Genevieve Day. BA in History, Humboldt State U., 1986; JD, U. Oreg., 1995. Bar: Oreg. 1995. Atty. Hydes & Day, Canyon City, Oreg., 1995-98, Davis, Adams & Day, Grants Pass, Oreg., 1998—. With U.S. Army, 1987-92, Oreg. Army N.G., 1992—. Mem. Am. Legion, Elks, Delta Sigma Phi. Republican. Office: Davis Adams & Day 600 NW 5th St Grants Pass OR 97526-2024 E-mail: gregoryd@roguefirm.com.

DAY, HOWARD WILMAN, geology educator; b. Burlington, Vt., Nov. 17, 1942; s. Wilman Forrest and Virginia Louise (Morton) D.; children: Kristina, Sarah, Susan; m. Judy Lynn Blevins. AB, Dartmouth Coll., 1964; MS, Brown U., 1968, PhD, 1971. From asst. prof. to assoc. prof. geology U. Okla., Norman, 1970-76; from asst. prof. to prof. geology U. Calif., Davis, 1976—, chmn. dept., 1990-96. Co-editor Jour. Metamorphic Geology, 1985-92; contbr. articles to profl. jours. Fulbright fellow, Norway, 1964, Alexander von Humboldt fellow, Fed. Republic Germany, 1977. Fellow Geol. Soc. Am., Mineral Soc. Am.; mem. Am. Geophys. Union. Office: U Calif Dept Geology Davis CA 95616 E-mail: hwday@ucdavis.edu.

DAY, JAMES, television executive; b. Alameda, Calif., Dec. 22, 1918; s. James Magee and June (Reeve) D.; m. Beverley Anne Hare, Apr. 12, 1943; children: Meredith Johnson, Douglas Craig, Alan Kent, James Ross. BA, U. Calif., Berkeley, 1941; postgrad., Stanford U., 1951; LHD (hon.), Newark State Coll., Newark, N.J., 1972. Dir. pub. svc. NBC, San Francisco, 1946-49; radio specialist Civil Info. & Edn. Sect./Supreme Commdr. Allies/Pacific, Tokyo, 1949-51; dep. dir. Radio Free Asia, San Francisco, 1951-53; pres., gen. mgr. KQED (TV-FM), San Francisco, 1953-69; pres. Nat. Ednl. TV, N.Y.C., 1969-71, WNET-TV, N.Y.C., 1971-73; prof. radio, TV Bklyn. Coll., CUNY, N.Y.C., 1976-89, prof. emeritus, 1989—; pres. Publivision, Inc., N.Y.C., 1973—. Pres. Timely Prodns. for TV, N.Y.C., 1989—; founding dir. Children's TV Workshop, Pub. Broadcasting Svc., Internat. Pub. TV Screening Conf., Comm. Improvement, Inc. Author: The Vanishing Vision: The Inside Story of Public Television, 1995, interviewer: (TV) Kaleidoscope, 1954-69, Day at Night, 1973-74, Conversations with Eric Hoffer, 1967, Conversations with Arnold Toynbee, 1968. Capt. U.S. Army, 1941-46. Recipient Robert C. Kirkwood award, San Francisco Found., 1966, Golden Plate award, Am. Acad. Achievement, Dallas, 1968, 50th Anniversary Dirs. award, Ohio State U., Columbus, 1986; resident scholar Rockefeller Study Ctr., Bellagio, Italy, 1978. Mem. Internat. Inst. Comm., Soc. Profl. Journalists. Avocations: photography, swimming. Home: 115 E 86th St New York NY 10028-1057 Office: Publivision Inc One Lincoln Pla New York NY 10023 E-mail: jdayny@aol.com.

DAY, JAMES MACDONALD, lawyer, educator; b. Stamford, Conn., June 19, 1930; s. James and Catherine MacDonald (Clark) Day; m. Carolyn Payne, Sept. 6, 1955; children: Catherine Ouida, James M. BA magna cum laude, Piedmont Coll., 1956; LLB, Am. U., Washington, 1959. Bar: D.C. 1960, Am. Samoa 1971. Dir. office of hearings and appeals Dept. Interior, Washington, 1970—73, chmn. oil import appeals bd., 1973, adminstr. mining enforcement and safety adminstrn., 1974—76; ptnr. Cotten, Dat & Doyle, Washington, 1976—. Adj. prof. oil and gas law Am. U., 1984—. With U.S. Army, 1950—52. Recipient Outstanding Svc. award, Dept. Interior, 1973. Mem.: ABA, Rocky Mountain Mineral Law Inst., Bar Assn. Am. Samoa. Republican. Presbyn. Office: 1899 L St NW Suite 1200 Washington DC 20036

DAY, JAMES MCADAM, JR., lawyer; b. Detroit, Aug. 18, 1948; s. James McAdam and Mary Elizabeth (McGibbon) D.; m. Sally Marie Sterud; children: Cara McAdam, Brenna Marie, Michael James. AB, UCLA, 1970; JD magna cum laude, U. Pacific, 1973. Bar: Calif. 1973, U.S. Dist. Ct. (no. dist.) Calif. 1973, U.S. Ct. Appeals (9th cir.) 1975. Assoc. Downey, Brand, Seymour & Rohwer, Sacramento, 1973-78, ptnr., 1978—, chmn. natural resources dept., 1985—90; mng. ptnr. Downey, Brand, Seymour & Rohmer, Sacramento, 1990—94, chmn. nat. resources dept., 2002—, mng. ptnr., 1997—2001. Contbr. articles to profl. jours. Pres., bd. dirs. Sacramento Soc. for Prevention of Cruelty to Animals, 1976-79, Children's Home Soc. of Calif., Sacramento, 1979-85; bd. dirs. Sta. KXPR/KXJZ, Inc. Pub. Radio, Sacramento, 1984-94, chmn., 1990-93; bd. dirs. Calif. State Libr. Found., 1995-2000, chmn., 1995-2000. Mem. ABA (natural resources sect. 1998), Calif. Bar Assn. (exec. com. 1985-89, chmn. real property law sect. 1988), Rocky Mountain Mineral Law Found., Sacramento Petroleum Assn., Calif. Mining Assn., U. Pacific McGeorge Law Sch. Alumni Assn. (bd. dirs. 1980-83). Avocations: yacht racing and cruising, fishing. Office: Downey Brand Seymour & Rohwer 555 Capitol Mall Fl 10 Sacramento CA 95814-4504

DAY, JAMES SANDERS, history educator; b. Chitose AFB, Japan, Oct. 23, 1956; s. Herschel Harold and Edith Louise (Sanders) D.; m. Patricia René Davis, May 3, 1981; children: Abigail René, Mary Afton. BS in Engring., U.S. Mil. Acad., 1979; MA in History, U. Ga., 1989; diploma, U.S. Army Command Coll., 1993; PhD in History, Auburn U., 2002. Commd. 2d lt. U.S. Army, 1979, advanced through grades to maj.; asst. prof. history U.S. Mil. Acad., West Point, N.Y., 1989-92; ret. U.S. Army, 1995; instr. history Marion (Ala.) Mil. Inst., 1995-96, Judson Coll., Marion, 1996-99, U. Montevallo, 1997—, Auburn U., Montgomery, 1999-2000. Contbr. articles to profl. jours. Recipient Nat. Collegiate Edn. award, 1996. Mem. Am. Hist. Assn., Orgn. Am. Historians, So. Hist. Assn., Soc. for Historians Tech., Assn. Ala. Historians, Phi Kappa Phi, Phi Alpha Theta. Baptist. Avocations: running, handball, stock investments, tole painting, woodworking. E-mail: dayjs@montevallo.edu.

DAY, JOHN ANTHONY, JR., pulmonologist; b. Washington, Sept. 7, 1949; s. John Anthony and Marcia (O'Brien) Day; m. Jane Marie Doyle, July 9, 1983; children: Margaret Eugenie, Nicholas Paul, Helen Elizabeth. AB, Harvard Coll., 1973; MD, Cornell U., 1981. Diplomate Am. Bd. Critical Care Medicine, Am. Bd. Internal Medicine. Intern, resident in internal medicine Vanderbilt U. Hosp., Nashville, 1981-84; instr. medicine Brown U., Providence, 1984-85, fellow in pulmonary medicine, 1985-87; attending physician Carney Hosp., Boston, 1987-93; asst. prof. medicine U. Mass. Med. Sch., Worcester, 1993—. Attending physician St. Vincent Hosp., Worcester, 1993—, Day Kimball Hosp., Putnam, Conn. Fellow: Am. Coll. Chest Physicians; mem.: Am. Thoracic Soc. Home: 44 Spring St Shrewsbury MA 01545-2357 Office: 346 Pomfret St Putnam CT 06260

DAY, JOHN ARTHUR, lawyer; b. Madison, Wis., Sept. 21, 1956; s. John Donald and Elinor Roletta (Heath) D. BS, U. Wis., Platteville, 1978; JD, U. N.C., 1981. Bar: Tenn. 1981, U.S. Dist. Ct. (mid. dist.) Tenn. 1981, U.S. Ct. Appeals (6th cir.) 1982, civil cert. Nat. Bd. Trial Advocacy 1991. Assoc. Dault Cummings Conners & Berry, Nashville, 1981-86, ptnr., 1987-92; shareholder Branham & Day, P.C., 1993—. Mem. Civil Justice Reform Act adv. group U.S. Dist. Ct. (mid. dist.) Tenn., 1991-95; mem. Tenn. Supreme Ct. Commn. on Continuing Legal Edn. and Specialization, 2001—. Co-author: Tennessee Law of Comparative Fault, 1997, 2d edit., 2002; founder, editor Tenn. Tort Law Letter, 1995—; contbr. articles to profl. jours. Com. mem. Cohn Roundtable, Nashville, 1988; assoc. Harry Phillips Inn of Ct., 1990-92, Tenn. John Marshall Inn of Ct., 1999—. Fellow Am. Coll. Trial Lawyers; mem. Tenn. Trial Lawyers Assn. (bd. govs. 1984-85, treas. 1985-89, v.p. 1989-93, pres. 1993-94, chair legal edn. com. 1985-86, chair legis. com. 1987-90, CLE com. 1984-97, pub. rels. com. 1986-88, long range planning com. 1991-93), Assn. Trial Lawyers Am. (Tenn. pub. rels. rep. 1986-87, people's law sch. com. co-chair 1986-88, pub. rels. com. 1986-91, chair 1988-89, edn. com. 1987-88, pub. affairs com. 1987-89, publs. com. 1990-93, vice chmn. 1991-93, co-chair 1992-93, key person com. 1987-89, nursing home litigation group 1985-89, chmn. 1987-89, mem. exec. com. 1994-95, chair pres.'s coun. 1994-95), Nashville Bar Assn. (bd. dirs. 1998-2000, circuit and chancery ct. com. chair 1989, fee disputes com. 1984-85, 87, vice chmn. 1988, chmn. 1989), Lawyers Involved for Tenn. (trustee 1988—), Tenn. Bar Assn. (mem. litigation sect. coun. 1989-90), Nat. Bd. Trial Advocacy (bd. dirs. 1998—, stds. com. 1998—, v.p. 2001-02, pres.-elect 2002-03), Tenn. Justice Ctr. (bd. dirs. 1999—). Democrat. Home: 608 Good Springs Rd Brentwood TN 37027-5173 Office: Branham & Day PC PO Box 40592 Nashville TN 37204

DAY, JOHN DENTON, retired company executive, cattle and horse rancher, breeder, trainer, wrangler, actor, educator; b. Salt Lake City, Jan. 20, 1942; s. George W. and Grace (Denton) Jenkins; m. Susan Hansen, June 20, 1971; children: Tammy Denton Wadsworth, Jeanett B. Barber. Student, U. Utah, 1964-65; BA in Econs. and Bus. Adminstrn. with high honors, Westminster Coll., 1971. Riding instr., wrangler Uinta wilderness area U-Ranch, Neola, Utah, 1955-58; wrangler, riding instr. YMCA Camp Rodger, Kamas, Utah, 1957; stock handler, driver, ruffstock rider Earl Hutchinson Rodeo Contractor, Idaho, 1959; with Mil. Data Cons., Inc., L.A., 1961-62, Carlseon Credit Corp., Salt Lake City, 1962-65; sales mgr. sporting goods Western Enterprises, Salt Lake City, 1965-69; founder Rockin d Ranch, Millcreek, Utah, 1969; ski instr. Brighton (Utah) Ski Sch., 1969-71; Western rep. PBR Co., Cleve., 1969-71; owner, founder, pres. John D. Day, mfrs. reps., 1972—; dist. sales rep. Crown Zellerbach Corp., Seattle and L.A., 1971-73; dist. sales mgr. Surfonics Engrs., Inc., Woods Cross, Utah, 1976-78, Garland Co., Cleve., 1978-81; pres., founder Dapco paper, chem., instl. food and janitorial supplies, Salt Lake City, 1973-79; rancher Heber, Utah, 1976-90, horse tng. facility, horsemanship sch. and ranch, Temecula, Calif., 1984-90, St. George, Utah, 1989-99; pres., founder John D Day Greeting Cards and Art Works, 1990—; horse training Horsemanship Sch., Quarter Horse Breeding Facility, Yerington, Nev., 1999—. Sec. bd. Acquadyne, 1974, 75. Actor, dir., prodr. (movies) The Big Sky, 1952, Rebel Without a Cause, 1955, Devils Brigade, 1967, Coyote Summer, 1995, (videos) Someday Soon, 1993, A Tour of Snows Canyon, 1993, All For the Love of Horse, 1982-83, Stallion Management, 1985, others; tv spls. and commls., Chev., Palmer, The Osmonds, others; contbr. articles to jours., including Western Artist. Group chmn. Tele-Dex fund raising project Westminster Coll.; founder, supr. vol. group Day's Rangers, 1990-99; vol. Dixie Nat. Forest, 1989-94, USDA Forest Svc.; 1st U.S. wilderness ranger USDA, US Forest Svc., Dixie Nat. Forest, Pine Valley Ranger Dist., Pine Valley Mountain Wilderness, So. Utah, 1994-99; vol. State of Nev. Ft. Churchill State Hist. Pk. & Pony Express Tr., 1999-. With AUS, 1963-64. Recipient grand nat. award Internat. Custom Car Show, San Diego, 1962, Award of Excellence Winternationals Nat. Hot Rod Assn., 1962-63, Key to City, Louisville, 1964, Champion Bareback Riding award, 1957, Vol. award USDA Forest Svc., 1991, 92, 93, nominated U.S. Vol. award, Safety award Dixie Nat. Forest, P.V.R.D., 1992-99; recipient Outstanding Performance award USDA, 1995, 98, Cert. Appreciation, 1997, DNF Outstanding Svc. award, 1997, Pine Valley Mountain Wilderness award, Nev. State Parks, Cert. of Appreciation Vol. Svc., 2000-2002, Fort Churchill State Historic Park, 2000-2002; Dally team roping heading and heeling champion, 1982. Mem. Internat. Show Car Assn. (co-chmn. 1978-79), Am. Quarter Horse Assn. (life, Horseback Riding Program 5000 Hour award 2002), Profl. Horseman Assn. (high point reining champion 1981, awarded Nat. Reining Horse Assn. Bronze, qualified for world championship, Dodge, Toyota Fall Futurite Circuit Champion Working Cowhorse 1994-95, World Championship Show qualifier and participant Oklahoma City Sr. Cutting 1994), Intermountain Quarter Horse Assn. (sr. reining champion 1981, champion AMAT reining 1979-81), Utah Quarter Horse Assn. (state champion AMAT reining 1979, 80, AMAT barrel racing 1980, working cowhorse champion 1982, trained working cowhorse and rider champion 1992, 98, trained amateur reining horse and rider champion 1996, open cutting res. champion 1993-95, 97, open cutting champion 1994, Menlove Dodge Toyota Fall Futurity circuit champion working cowhorse, 1994-95, open working cowhorse champion & broadmare halter champion 1995, Rose cir. working cowhorse champion 1995, 98, Rose Cir. Open working cowhorse champion, showed cir. champion Brodmare at Halter Rose cir. open cutting champion 1996, 97, bd. dirs. 1992-94, trained amateur barrel racing and amateur pole bending horse and rider 1998, State Reserve Champion amateur cutting horse and rider), Profl. Cowhorseman's Assn., Nat. Cutting Horse Assn. (affiliate), Profl. Cowhorseman's Assn. (world champion team roping, heeling 1986, 88, high point rider 1985, world champion stock horse rider 1985-86, 88, world champion working cowhorse 1985, PCA finals open cutting champion, 1985-88, PCA finals 1500 novice champion 1987, PCA finals all-around champion 1985-88, inducted into Hall of Fame 1988, first on record registered Tex. longhorn cutting contest, open champion, PCA founder, editor newsletter 1985-89, pres. 1984-88), World Rodeo Assn. Profls. (v.p. Western territory 1989-98, judge nat. high sch. rodeo, cutting horse and rodeo queen contest, 1990—, hon. life v.p. Western Terr. U.S. 1998—), Future Farmers Am. (horse judge 2003—), Nevada Quarter House Assn. (mem. com., Am. Quarter House Assn., Ride 2000, "Let Freedom Ride", Fall Circuit 2000 Open Cutting Champion), Nev. Quarter Horse Assn. (Summer Circuit Champion), 2002.

DAY, JOHN SIDNEY, management sciences educator; b. Newton, Mass., Oct. 13, 1917; s. Franklin Everett and Marion (Guild) D.; m. Barbara Jane Felch, Nov. 20, 1940; children: John Sidney, Stephen L. Student, Tufts U., 1935-37, Oxford Sch. Bus. Adminstrn., 1939; MBA with distinction, Harvard U., 1950, D.C.S., 1956; D. in Mgmt. (hon.), Purdue U., 1993. Asst. to pres. C. Carlson Co., Boston, 1939-40, 45-46; instr. Oxford Sch. Bus. Adminstrn., Cambridge, Mass., 1946-48; rsch. asst. Harvard Grad. Sch. Bus. Adminstrn., Cambridge, Mass., 1950-51, rsch. assoc., 1951-53, asst. prof., 1953-56; assoc. prof. Purdue U., Lafayette, Ind., 1956-59, prof. indsl. mgmt., 1959-83, dean Krannert Grad. Sch. Mgmt., 1969-78, v.p. for devel., 1978-83, Krannert prof. mgmt., 1983-86, v.p. emeritus, 1986—. Author: (with L. Bollinger) Management of New Enterprises, 1952, Subcontracting Policy in the Airframe Industry, 1956, (with P. Donham) New Enterprise and Small Business Management, 1960. Bd. dirs. Purdue Rsch. Found., 1980-83; mem. Tippecanoe County (Ind.) chpt. ARC, 1968-74, chmn., 1974; treas. Tippecanoe County Easter Seal Soc., 1972-78; mem. West Lafayette Econ. Devel. Commn., chmn., 1975-83; mem. nat. adv. coun. Boy Scouts Am., 1976-78; trustee Joint Coun. on Econ. Edn., 1976-78; pres. Oak Point Cmty. Assn., Inc., 1980-86; bd. dirs. Home Hosp., 1972-78, pres., 1977; bd. dirs. Am. Assemblies Collegiate Schs. Bus., 1974-78, pres., 1977-78. Served to col. USMCR. Decorated Bronze Star (2); Baker scholar; Ford Found. fellow, 1959-60; named Hon. Sec. of State Ind.; receipent Sagamore of the Wabash. Mem. 1st Marine Divsn. Assn., Masons, Rotary. Home and Office: 25 River Mead Rd Peterborough NH 03458 E-mail: josidday@rivermead.org.

DAY, JULIAN C. retail executive; BA, MA, Oxford U.; MBA, London Bus. Sch. Sr. engagement mgr. McKinsey & Co., 1980-85; v.p., European devel. mgr. Chase Manhattan Bank, 1985-87; exec. mgmt. cons. Kohlberg, Kravis, and Roberts, 1987-93; exec. v.p., CFO Safeway, Inc., 1993-98, Sears, Roebuck and Co., Hoffman Estate, Ill., 1999—2002; pres, COO Kmart Corp., 2002—03, pres, CEO, 2003—. Office: Kmart Corp 3100 W Big Beaver Rd Troy MI 48084*

DAY, KATHLEEN PATRICIA, financial planner; b. West Palm Beach, Fla., Nov. 16, 1947; d. John I. and Lorraine A. (Risavy) Simmons; m. Bryan Patrick Day, Sept. 20, 1969; children: Kevin Kristopher, Amy Teresa. BS in Med. Tech., U. Fla., 1969; MBA, Fla. Internat. U., 1980. Cert. Fin. Planner; Chartered Fin. Analyst. Credit analyst corp. lending Southeast Bank NA, Miami, Fla., 1981-83; fin. cons. in pvt. practice Miami, 1983-87; pres. Integrated Asset Mgmt. Inc., Miami, 1987-88, Enrichment Group Kathleen Day and Assoc., Inc., 1989—, 2001—. Mem. CFP Nat. Bd. Practice Stds., 2000-01; pres. The Enrichment Group, Inc., 2001—; mem. Capstone Group, LLC, 2001—. Bd. dirs. Delphi Found., Miami, 1985-88. Mem. Fin. Planning Assn., Assn. Investment Mgmt. and Rsch., Capstone Group. Avocations: sailing, snow skiing. Office: The Enrichment Group 7355 SW 87th Ave Ste 300 Miami FL 33173-3565 E-mail: kathleen@theenrichmentgroup.com.

DAY, KEVIN THOMAS, banker, community services director; b. London, Aug. 24, 1937; came to U.S., 1957; s. William Stanley and Mary Ann (Hook) D.; m. Mary Violet Scheuber, Aug., 1960. BA, Brisbane Tech. Coll., Queensland, Australia, 1957. Pres. Americana Investments, San Francisco, 1960-63; stockbroker Sutro and Co., San Francisco, 1963-66; regional v.p. Am. Express Investment Co., San Francisco, 1966-70; dir. mktg. ITT Fin. Svcs., N.Y.C., 1970-78; pres. Exec. Assocs., Reno, Nev., 1978-83, First Interstate Bank Found., Reno, 1983-1991; exec. dir. Cath. Community Svcs., Reno, 1991—. Chmn. Nev. Fgn. Trade Zone, Reno, 1986-91, Desert Rsch. Inst., Reno. Pres. Econ. Devel. Authority, Reno, 1985, Nev. Mus. Art, 1989-91; mem. exec. com. Western Indsl. Nev., Reno, 1985-90; commr. Nev. Commn. on Econ. Devel., Carson City, 1987-90. Named Man of Yr., Reno mag., 1988, Torch of Liberty award, 1989; named to Nev. Order of Silver Spur, 1990. Republican. Roman Catholic. Avocations: adventure travel, wilderness camping, art collecting. Home: 4835 Pinesprings Dr Reno NV 89509-6504 Office: Cath Community Svcs 500 E 4th St Reno NV 89512-3316

DAY, L. B. management consultant; b. Walla Walla, Wash., Sept. 16, 1944; s. Frank Edmond and Geraldine Eloise (Binning) D. BS, Portland State Coll., 1966; MBA, George Washington U., 1971. Design mktg. cons. Leadership Resources Inc., Washington, 1970-71; faculty mem. USDA Grad. Sch. of Spl. Programs, Washington, 1971-74; dir. Office of Employee Devel. Oreg. Dept. Transp., Salem, 1972-75; prin. Day-Henry Assoc. Inc., Portland, Oreg., 1975-78, Day-Floren Assocs. Inc., Portland, Oreg., 1978-95, LB Day & Co., Portland, Oreg., 1996—. Cons. Allergan, Applied Materials, AMD, Intel Corp., Fujitsu, Radisys, VLSI Tech., Inc., Pharmacia & Upjohn, RadiSys, Triquint, Sumco USA, others; adj. prof. Willamette U. Grad. Sch. Adminstrn., Salem, Oreg. Grad. Inst.; bd. dirs. Microchip Tech., Inc.; mem. adv. bd. Sch. Mgmt. Willamette U., 2001. Author: The Supervisory Training Program, Performance Management, Team-Oriented Management, 1989, Leading Change, 1999, Leading Teams, Building Great Companies; contbr. articles to profl. jours. With U.S. Army, 1967-70. Scottish Rite fellow George Washington U., 1970. Avocations: marathon runner, horseback riding, civil war. Office: L B Day & Co Inc 806 SW Broadway Fl 11 Portland OR 97205-3333 E-mail: lb@lbday.com.

DAY, LEE MONROE, agriculture economics educator; b. Thayer, Iowa, Feb. 25, 1923; s. Samuel Gordon and Helen Swindler D.; m. Joan Meredith Day, Sept. 8, 1948; children: Michael Gordon, Meredith Lee Garrison. BS, Iowa State U., 1947, MS, 1948; PhD, U. Minn., 1953. Asst. prof. U. Wis., Madison, Wis., 1950-55; agrl. economist U.S. Dept. Agrl., St. Paul, 1955-61, agrl. economist Office of the Sec. Washington, 1961-67; prof. agrl. econ. Pa. State U., State coll., Univ. Pk., Pa., 1967-74; head dept. agrl. econ. and rural Sociology Pa. State U., Univ. Pk., Pa., 1969-74; dir. N.E. Regional Ctr. for Rural Devel., Ithaca, NY, 1975-85; prof. emeritus Cornell U., Ithaca, 1988—. Mem., chmn. planning commn. Village of Lansing, Ithaca, NY, 1985-88; v.p., pres., bd. dirs. North Myrtle Beach Citizens Assn., 1990-98; bd. dirs. Horry County Solid Waste Authority, Conway, SC, 1995-98, Dem. committeeman, Ferguson Township, Pa. Mem. Am. Agrl. Econs. Assn., NE Agrl. Econs. Coun. (life, disting. mem.), Iowa State Alumni Assn., Am. Legion, Farmhouse Fraternity. Democrat. Avocations: traveling, golfing, bridge. Home: 3301-944 Shellers Bend State College PA 16801 E-mail: ldays@adelphia.net.

DAY, LINCOLN HUBERT, demographer, educator; b. Ames, Iowa, Jan. 7, 1928; s. John Armstrong and Vera Hills Day; m. Alice Taylor, Nov. 26, 1952; children: Thomas Hills, Caroline Day Santesteban. BA, Yale U., 1949; MA, Columbia U., 1951, PhD, 1957. Instr., asst. prof. sociology Mt. Holyoke Coll., South Hadley, Mass., 1955—58; asst. prof. sociology Princeton (NJ) U., 1958—59; rsch. assoc. Bur. Applied Social Rsch. Columbia U., N.Y.C., 1958—62; vis. fellow in demography Australian Nat. U., Canberra, 1962—64, sr. fellow in demography, 1973—94; rsch. assoc. Sch. Pub. Health Harvard U., Boston, 1964—65; assoc. prof. pub. health and sociology Yale U., New Haven, 1965—70; chief demographic and social stats. br. UN, N.Y.C., 1970—73; Hofstee fellow Netherlands Interdisciplinary Demographic Inst., Den Haag, 1994. Co-author (with Alice Taylor Day): Too Many Americans, 1964; co-author: (with A.J. Jaffe) Disabled Workers in the Labor Market, 1964; author: Analysing Population Trends, 1983, The Future of Low-Birthrate Populations, 1992; co-editor (with D.T. Rowland): How Many More Australians?, 1988; co-editor: (with Ma Xia) Migration and Urbanization in China, 1994; contbr. numerous articles to profl. jours. Bd. dirs. Ctr. for Arms Control and Non-Proliferation, Washington. Cpl. U.S. Army, 1953—55. Fellow, Fulbright Found., 1968; scholar-in-residence, Bellagio (Italy) Study and Conf. Ctr., 1990. Mem.: Am. Sociol. Assn., Sustainable Population Australia, Nature and Soc. Forum, European Assn. for Population Studies, Internat. Union for Sci. Study of Population, Population Assn. Am., Amnesty Internat., Coun. for a Livable World, ACLU, Cosmos Club. Democrat. Avocations: travel, politics. Home: 2124 Newport Pl NW Washington DC 20037-3001

DAY, LUCILLE LANG, museum administrator, educator, writer; b. Oakland, Calif., Dec. 5, 1947; d. Richard Allen and Evelyn Marietta (Hazard) Lang; m. Frank Lawrence Day, Nov. 6, 1965 (div. 1970); 1 child, Liana Sherrine; m. Theodore Herman Fleischman, June 23, 1974 (div. 1985); 1 child, Tamarind Channah Fleischman; m. Richard Michael Levine, Aug. 25, 2002. AB, U. Calif., Berkeley, 1971, MA, 1973, PhD, 1979; MA, San Francisco State U., 1999. Tchg. asst. U. Calif., Berkeley, 1971-72, 75-76, rsch. asst., 1975, 77-78; tchr. sci. Magic Mountain Sch., Berkeley, 1977; specialist math. and sci. Novato (Calif.) Unified Sch. Dist., 1979-81; instr. sci. Project Bridge Laney Coll.,

Oakland, 1984-86; sci. writer and mgr. precoll. edn. programs Lawrence Berkeley Nat. Lab., 1986-90, life scis. staff coord., 1990-92, mgr. Hall of Health, Children's Hosp. and Rsch. Ctr. at Oakland, 1992—. Lectr. St. Mary's Coll. Calif., Moraga, 1997—2000. Author: numerous poems, articles and book reviews; author: (with Joan Skolnick and Carol Langbort) How to Encourage Girls in Math and Science: Strategies for Parents and Educators, 1982; author: (poetry) Self-Portrait with Hand Microscope, 1982, Fire in the Garden, 1997, Wild One, 2000, Lucille Lang Day, Greatest Hits, 1975-2000, 2001, Infinities, 2002. Recipient Joseph Henry Jackson award in lit., San Francisco Found., 1982; Grad. fellow, NSF, 1972—75. Mem.: Soc. Pub. Health Edn. (No. Calif. chpt.), Math./Sci. Network, Nat. Assn. Sci. Writers, No. Calif. Sci. Writers Assn., Phi Beta Kappa, Iota Sigma Pi. Home: 1057 Walker Ave Oakland CA 94610-1511 Office: Hall of Health 2230 Shattuck Ave Berkeley CA 94704-1416 E-mail: lucyday@hallofhealth.org., lucyday@earthlink.net.

DAY, M. JOANNA, accountant, foundation administrator; b. Cleve., Sept. 8, 1936; d. Joseph C. and Margaret (Peters) T.; m. Milton Clifford (div.); 1 child, Gregory Alan ; m. Allan W. Day, Nov. 4, 1960; 1 child, Lisa Adrienne. BS in Acctg., Garfield Sr. Coll., 1979. CPA. Contr. Micromenex, Willoughby, Ohio, 1976-80, LCNE, Perry, Ohio, 1980-83, Mid-Con Corp., Indpls., 1983-86, Capital Industries, Indpls., 1986-92; sr. dir. fin. Indpls. Pub. Transp., 1992-94, sr. dir. acctg., 1994-97; fiscal dir. United Way, Indpls., 1997—. Home: 10705 Birch Tree Cir Indianapolis IN 46236-8195

DAY, MARGARET ANN, research librarian, information specialist; b. Butler, Pa., Nov. 15, 1941; d. Edwin James and Helen Louella (Christy) Longwell; m. Donald Emery Day, Dec. 15, 1961; children: Catherine Anne (dec.), Donna Lau, Donald Edwin. BS in Edn. magna cum laude, Clarion U. Pa., 1972, MS in LS, 1986. Cert. tchr., profl. libr., Pa.; lic. real estate salesperson, Pa. Substitute tchr. Karns City (Pa.) Area Schs., 1976, 79-85; grad. asst. Clarion U. Pa., 1985-86; libr., info. specialist Interactive Media Corp., Butler, Pa., 1987—94. Real estate sales assoc. Ed Shields, Realtor, Butler, 1994. Pres. Bruin (Pa.) Borough Coun., 1984. DAR, Breth and Wahr scholar, 1959. Mem. Beta Phi Mu. Avocations: reading, gardening, sewing, cooking and nutrition, continuing education. Home: PO Box 85 Bruin PA 16022-0085 Office: Interactive Media Corp 292 Three Degree Rd Butler PA 16002-3860

DAY, MARY, artistic director, ballet company executive; b. Wash. Trained by Lisa Gardinier; ArtsD (hon.), Shenandoah Conservatory; DHL (hon.), Mount Vernon Coll. Co-founder Washington Sch. of Ballet, 1944—; founder Washington Ballet, 1976—. Named Washingtonian of Yr., Washingtonian mag.; recipient Mayor's award, Woman of Achievement award, WETA TV, Met. Dance award, Founders award, Cultural Alliance, Excellence in Teaching Chautauqua Dance award, sr. Svcs. Disting. award IONA. Office: Washington Ballet 3515 Wisconsin Ave NW Washington DC 20016-3085

DAY, MARY ANN, medical/surgical nurse; b. Covington, Tenn., Apr. 9, 1944; m. George Day, Jan. 17, 1980; children: Maurice, Michele, Shawn, Corey. AAS, Joliet (Ill.) Jr. Coll., 1989; BSN, Lewis U., 1995; student, U. St. Francis, 1998—. RN, Ill.; cert. emergency nurse pediat. course. Staff nurse Michael Reese Hosp., Chgo., 1989-91, MacNeal Hosp., Berwyn, Ill., 1991-99, Westlake Hosp., Melrose Park, Ill., 1999—; adj. faculty/LPN program Triton Coll., River Grove, Ill., 1996—, instr. RN continuing edn. course, 1998—; asst. patient care mgr. St. Joseph Hosp., Joliet, Ill., 1999—; IV therapist Ctrl. Dupage Hosp., Winfield, Ill., 1999—; nursing supr. St. Anthony's Hosp., Chgo., 2001—. Mem. diversity task force com., Westlake Hosp., 1999; instr. in nursing assistance Waubonsee Coll., 2002. Nominee Black Profl. Female scholarship, Minority Student of Yr., 1989. Avocations: classical music, classical pianist. Home: 6 Puffin Cir Bolingbrook IL 60440-1236 Office: IL E-mail: mhoneyday@aol.com.

DAY, MARY JANE THOMAS, cartographer; b. Connors, New Brunswick, Can., Oct. 12, 1927; d. Angus and Delina (Michaud) Thomas; m. Howard M. Day, July 1, 1949 (dec. April 27, 2003); children: Laurie Anne Day Greene, Angus Howard. BS in Geography, U. Md., 1974, BS in Bus. & Mgmt., 1977. Meteorol. aide Hangar 8 Eastern Airlines, N.Y.C., 1946-47, U.S. Weather Bur., Washington, 1948-50; cartographic aide U.S. Navy Hydrographic Office, Suitland, Md., 1950-57, cartographer, 1957-62, U.S. Navy Oceanographic Office, Suitland, 1962-72, Def. Mapping Agy., Suitland/Brookmont, 1972-93; ret., 1994. Cartographer USNS Harkness, 1978, Indonesian Naval Personnel, Jakarta, Indonesia, 1981-82. Compiled, wrote and published; The Descendants of John Thomas of Connors, N.B., 1988; author numerous poems. Mem. Andrews Officers Club (Md.). Avocations: travel, genealogy, foreign languages. Home: 3532 28th Pky Temple Hills MD 20748-2922

DAY, MARY LOUISE, volunteer; b. LaGrange, Ill., May 22, 1917; d. Kenneth Farwell Burgess and Louise Frances Todd; m. J. Edward Day, July 2, 1941; children: Geraldine Day Zurn, Mary Louise Day Himmelfarb, James E. Jr. (dec.). AB, Vassar Coll., 1939. Bd. dirs. YWCA, Washington, 1962-80, chmn. internat. fair, 1966, 82; active YWCA World Svc. Coun.; mem. adv. bd. The Hospitality Info. Svc., Washington, 1964—, chmn., 1969-71; chmn. women's bd. Am. Heart Assn., Washington, 1981-83; mem. Smithsonian Women's Com., Washington, 1982—. Democrat. Home: 5804 Brookside Dr Bethesda MD 20815-6667

DAY, MELVIN SHERMAN, information and telecommunications company executive; b. Lewiston, Maine, Jan. 22, 1923; s. Israel and Frances (Goldberg) D.; m. Louisa Walker; children: Cynthia Day Solganick, Wendy Day Young, Robert Marshall. BS, Bates Coll., 1943; postgrad., U. Tenn., 1953-54. Chemist Metal Hydrides Inc., Beverly, Mass., 1943-44, Tenn. Eastman Corp., Oak Ridge, 1944-46; sci. analyst AEC, Oak Ridge, 1946-48, asst. chief tech. info. svc. extension, 1950-56, chief, 1956-58, dir. tech. info. div. Washington, 1958-60; dep. dir. Tech. Info. and Ednl. Programs Office, NASA, Washington, 1960-61, dir. Sci. and Tech. Info. div., 1961-67, dep. asst. adminstr. tech. utilization, 1967-70; head Office Sci. Info. NSF, Washington, 1970-72; dep. dir. Nat. Libr. Medicine, HEW, Bethesda, Md., 1972-78; dir. Nat. Tech. Info. Svc. Dept. Commerce, 1978-82; v.p. Info. Tech. Group, 1982-84, Rsch. Publs., 1984-86; sr. v.p. Herner & Co., 1986-88; pres. M. Day Cons. Internat., Inc., Arlington, 1988—; exec. v.p. BIIS Corp., Herndon, 1991-94, GlobeNet Holding Corp., 1994-97. Cons. IAEA, 1960; adviser OECD, 1970, 75; U.S. mem. OECD info. policy group; U.S. mem. NATO Tech. Info. Panel, 1960-70, 79-82, chmn., 1970; chmn. com. on sci. and tech. info. Fed. Coun., 1970-72, chmn. com. on intergovtl. sci. rels., 1969-70, chmn. sci. info. exch. adv. bd., 1963-69, mem. chem. abstracts adv. bd., 1964-68; mem. Fed. Libr. Com., 1968-78, chmn. exec. bd., 1973-75; trustee Found. Ctr. 1972-78, trustee emeritus, 1991—; U.S. mem. adv. com. on librs., documentation and archives UNESCO; pres. abstracting bd. Internat. Coun. Sci. Unions, 1977-83; bd. dirs. Internat. Coun. for Sci. and Tech. Info., 1983—, Inst. for Internat. Info. Programs, 1985-88; trustee Engring. Info., Inc., 1981-84, bd. dirs., 1993-98; del. numerous panels; cons., adviser and lectr. in field; mem. adv. com. HHS Health Svcs. Rsch. Dissemination and User Liaison, 1990-92, also mem. dissemination com. Mem. editorial bd. Health Comm. and Informatics, 1977-80, Infomediary, 1990-93, Yearbook of the Database Info. Industry, 1990-91, Bull. of Am. Soc. Info. Sci., 1977-80 Bd. visitors U. Pitts. Grad. Sch. Info. Sci., 1977-83. With U.S. Army, 1944-46. Recipient Exceptional Svc. medal NASA, 1971, Superior Svc. award USPHS, 1976. Fellow AAAS, Nat. Fedn. Abstracting and Info. Svcs. (hon. fellow); mem. Am. Soc. Info. Sci. (chmn. internat. rels. com. 1972-75, pres. 1975-76, coun. 1975-77, editorial bd. bull.), Am. Chem. Soc., Spl. Libr. Assn., Am. Soc. Cybernetics (bd. dirs. 1975-79), Venezuelan Acad. Scis. (hon. corr.), Internat. Coun. Sci. and Tech. Info. (hon., disting. svc. award 1997), Cosmos Club. Home: 4309 Chesapeake St NW Washington DC 20016-4509 E-mail: melday1269@aol.com.

DAY, MICHAEL GORDON, information technology executive, educator; b. Madison, Wis., July 30, 1951; s. Lee Monroe and Joan (Meredith) D.; m. Donna Kay Corl, May 26, 1979 (div. Apr. 1986); children: Thomas Lee, Anne Elizabeth; m. Carol Ann Stefanko, Apr. 12, 1997. BA, Pa. State U., 1973; JD, George Washington U., 1976. Bar: Pa. 1976. Assoc. Alan Ellis, Esq., State College, Pa., 1976-77; pvt. practice State College, Pa., 1977-85; with Profl. Planning Cons., State College, Pa., 1985-86, Century Fin. Svcs., State College, Pa., 1986-96; solutions expert Netscape, 1996-99; dir. Info. Tech. Inst./Shepherd Coll., Shepherdstown, W.Va., 1999—. Instr. bus. law Pa. State U., University Park, 1978-79, instr. continuing legal edn., 2002; counsel Boccardo Law Firm, San Jose, Calif., 1983, Rees Law Firm, Washington, 1983; sr. v.p. Century Mortage Corp., 1991-96. Chmn. Com. to Elect Mel Hodes Senator, Pa., 1982, Dem. Com., State College, 1982-84; active Exec. Com. Centre County, 1982-84, United Pennsylvanians, 1982-83; gen. counsel CLEAN, 1982-85; v.p. Mt. Nittany Conservancy, 2000-02; candidate for Pa. Ho. Reps., 1980; candidate for dist. justice 49th Dist. Pa., 1977. Mem. Lions Paw Alumni Assn. (pres. 1999-2001), Parmi Nous, Omicron Delta Kappa, Delta Sigma Rho. United Ch. Of Christ. Office: 400 W Stephen St Martinsburg WV 25401 E-mail: michael@michaelday.org.

DAY, PETER RODNEY, geneticist, educator; b. Chingford, Essex, Eng., Dec. 27, 1928; came to U.S., 1963; m. Lois Elizabeth Rhodes, May 26, 1951; children: Susan Catherine, Rupert Peter, William Rodney. BS in Botany, Birkbeck Coll., Eng., 1950; PhD, U. London, 1954. Sr. scientific officer John Innes Inst., Hertford, Eng., 1957-63; assoc. prof. Ohio State U., Columbus, 1963-64; chief, genetics dept. Conn. Agrl. Expt. Sta., New Haven, 1964-79; dir. Plant Breeding Inst., Cambridge, Eng., 1979-87; prof. genetics, dir. Rutgers U., New Brunswick, NJ, 1987—2002, prof. emeritus, 2002—. Sec. Internat. Genetics Fedn., 1984-93; trustee Internat. Ctr. for Maize and Wheat Improvement, Mexico City, 1986-92; chmn. Mng. Global Genetic Resources Bd. on Agrl., NAS, Washington, 1986-93. Author: Genetics of Host-Parasite Interaction, 1974; co-author: (with J.R.S. Fincham) Fungal Genetics, 1963, (with H.H. Prell) Plant-Fungal Pathogen Interaction, 2001. Commonwealth Fund fellow U. Wis., 1954-56; Guggenheim Meml. fellow U. Queensland, 1972. Home: 394 Franklin Rd New Brunswick NJ 08902 E-mail: day@aesop.rutgers.edu.

DAY, RICHARD ALLEN, chemistry educator; b. Kellogg, Iowa, Apr. 4, 1931; s. Clarence Hodson and Della (Mendenhall) Day; m. Lyn Tibbits, Aug. 19, 1956; children: Eric, Sylvia. Student, William Penn Coll., 1949-50; BS, Iowa State U., 1953; Phd, MIT, 1958. Rsch. assoc. MIT, Cambridge, 1957-59; asst. prof. chemistry U. Cin., 1959-63, assoc. prof. chemistry, 1963-68, prof. chemistry, 1968—, prof. biol. chemistry Coll. of Medicine, 1972—. Faculty rep. to U. Cin. Bd. Trustees, 1990-93; exec. com. Ohio Valley Chromatography Symposium; bd. dirs. DataChem, Inc., Indpls., BioCin Inc., Cin. Patentee in field. Recipient numerous grants. Fellow AAAS; mem. Am. Chem. Soc. (chmn. Cin. sect. 1982-83), Am. Soc. Mass Spectrometry, Am. Soc. Microbiology, Am. Soc. Biochem. & Molecular Biology, Protein Soc. E-mail: richard.day@uc.edu.

DAY, RICHARD EARL, lawyer, educator; b. St. Joseph, Mo., Nov. 2, 1929; s. William E. and Geneva C. (Miller) D.; m. Melissa W. Blair, Feb. 2, 1951; children: William E., Thomas E. BS, U. Pa., 1951; JD with distinction, U. Mich., 1957. Bar: Ill. 1957, D.C. 1959, S.C. 1980. Assoc. Kirkland & Ellis, Chgo., 1957-58, Howrey Simon Baker & Murchison, Washington, 1958-61; asst. prof. law U. N.C., Chapel Hill, 1961-64; assoc. prof. Ohio State U., Columbus, 1964-66, prof., 1966-75, U. S.C., Columbia, 1975-76, 80-86, dean, 1977-80, John William Thurmond chair disting. prof. law, 1986-99, disting. prof. law emeritus, 1999—. Cons. U.S. Office Edn., 1964-66; course dir. Ohio Legal Ctr. Inst. Columbus, 1970-75; vis. prof. law U. Southampton (Eng.), fall 1988. Author: The Intensified Course in Antitrust Law, 1972, rev. edit., 1974; book rev. editor Antitrust Bull., 1968-71, adv. bd., 1971—; adv. bd. Antitrust and Trade Regulation Report, 1973-76, Jour. Reprints for Antitrust Law and Econs., 1974—. Ohio commr. Nat. Conf. on Uniform State Laws, 1967-75, S.C. commr., 1977-80; mem. Ohio Gov.'s Adv. Coun. Internat. Trade, 1972-74, S.C. Jud. Coun., 1977-80; chmn. S.C. Appellate Def. Coun., 1977-80, S.C. Com. Intellectual Property and Unfair Trade Practices Law, 1981-87. Lt. USNR, 1952-55. Named John William Thurmond Disting. Prof. Law. Mem. ABA, S.C. Bar Assn. (bd. govs. 1977-80), Am. Law Inst. Methodist. Home: 204 Saint James St Columbia SC 29205-3074 Office: U SC Law Ctr Main And Green Sts Columbia SC 29208-0001

DAY, RICHARD PUTNAM, marketing, strategic planning and employee benefits consultant, arbitrator; b. Hartford, Conn., Feb. 13, 1930; s. Godfrey Malbone and Sheila (Wilson) D.; m. Patricia Ann Brady, Jan. 26, 1957; children: Richard Jr., Stephen, Thomas, Gregory, Katharine, Martha, Ward, Emily. Student, The Choate Sch., 1948; AB, Middlebury Coll., 1952. With group field sales Conn. Gen. Life Ins. Co., Hartford, Detroit, Toledo, Phoenix, 1952-61; dir. sales group Bankers Life Nebr. (name changed to Ameritas Life Ins. Corp.), Lincoln, 1961-73, v.p. group, 1973-87, exec. v.p. group, 1987-91, exec. v.p. bus. devel., 1991-93; prin. R.P. Day Consulting, Paradise Valley, Ariz., 1993—. Dir. Nat. Health Care Svcs., Jacksonville, Fla., 1988-95. Trustee, pres. bd. Madonna Profl. Care Ctr., Lincoln, 1970-80, trustee Lincoln Gen. Hosp., 1980. Lt. USN, 1952-56. Mem. VFW, Internat. Soc. Cert. Employee Benefit Specialists (bd. dirs. pres. governing coun., chmn. bd. 1986), Am. Soc. CLUs, Internat. Found. Employee Benefit Plans, Profl. Ins. Mass-Mktg. Assn., Mass-Mktg. Ins. Inst., Nat. Assn. Dental Plans, Am. Legion, Retired Officers Assn., Country Club of Lincoln, Scottsdale Country Club, Blue Key Honor Soc., Phi Kappa Tau. Republican. Episcopalian. Avocation: golf. Home: 6530 N 61st St Paradise Valley AZ 85253 E-mail: daypvaz@aol.com.

DAY, ROBERT ANDROUS, English language educator, former library director, editor, publisher; b. Belvidere, Ill., Jan. 18, 1924; s. Floyd Androus and Mabel May (Dorn) D.; m. Betty Lucy Johnson, Aug. 27, 1949; children—Nancy, Barton, Robin BA, U. Ill., 1949; MS, Columbia U., 1951. Librarian, Sci. and Tech. div. Newark Pub. Library, 1951-53; librarian, editor Inst. Microbiology Rutgers U., 1953-60, dir. Coll. of South Jersey Library, 1960-61; mng. editor Am. Soc. Microbiology, Washington, 1961-80; dir. ISI Press, Phila., 1980-86; v.p. Inst. for Sci. Info., Phila., 1984-86; prof. English, U. Del., Newark, 1986-2000, prof. emeritus, 2000—. Tchr. sci. writing; pub. cons. NSF, NIH, others Author: How to Write and Publish a Scientific Paper, 1979, 5th edit., 1998, Scientific English: A Guide for Scientists and Other Professionals, 1992, 2d edit., 1995. With USAAF, 1943-46. Mem. AAAS, Coun. Science Editors (chmn. 1977-78), Soc. Scholarly Pub. (pres. 1982-84), Am. Med. Writers Assn., Soc. Tech. Comm., European Assn. Sci. Editors, Assn. Tchrs. Tech. Writing. Home: 77 Ritter Ln Newark DE 19711-5174 E-mail: bday@udel.edu.

DAY, ROBERT DWAIN, JR., foundation executive, lawyer; b. Stockton, Calif., Dec. 14, 1950; s. Robert Dwain and June Rita Day; m. Carol Robin Tyler; children: Leslie Carroll, Ryan Tyler. BS, Va. Tech., 1974; JD, U. S.C., 1977. Bar: S.C. 1977, D.C. 1978. Forester USDA Forest Svc., Washington and Columbia, S.C., 1973-77; dir. resource policy Soc. Am. Foresters, Bethesda, Md., 1977-81; resident fellow Resources for the Future, Washington, 1981-82; exec. dir. Renewable Natural Resources Found., Bethesda, 1982—; corp. sec. RNRF Title Holding Corp., 1997—. Cons. Office of Tech. Assessment U.S. Congress, Washington, 1981-82; mem. nat. task force Soc. Am. Foresters, Bethesda, 1982-83; advisor The Conservation Found., Washington, 1978-79; mem. adv. coun. Coll. Natural Resources, Utah State U., 1992-96, Va. Tech., 1999—; mem. nat. awards coun. for environ. sustainability Renew Am. Inc., 1997-98; del. Afghanistan-Am. Summit on Recovery and Reconstruction, Washington, 2002. Author policy analysis column Jour. of Forestry, 1977-81; editor: Renewable Resources Jour., 1982—. Appt. by county exec. to 9/11 Econ. Impact Panel Montgomery County, 2001. Mem. AAAS, D.C. Bar Assn., Soc. Am. Foresters, Soil and Water Conservation Soc., Environ. Law Inst., Coun. Engring. and Sci. Soc. Execs., Montgomery County Soc. for Assns. (exec. com. 1992-94, 98—, vice chmn. 1999-2000, chmn. 2000). Home: 2191 Canterbury Way Potomac MD 20854-6105 Office: Renewable Natural Resources 5430 Grosvenor Ln Ste 220 Bethesda MD 20814-2193

DAY, ROBERT MICHAEL, oil company executive; b. Winnfield, La., Jan. 28, 1950; s. Robert Neal and Virginia Ruth (Franklin) D.; m. Noelie Barron, Dec. 20, 1975; children: Robert Michael Jr., Brionne. BS, La. State U., 1976; MBA, U. Houston-Clear Lake, 1989. Roustabout, floorman Global Marine Drilling Co., Houston, 1976-77; sales engr. NL Baroid Petroleum Svcs., Houston, 1977-78; drilling technician East Tex. div. Exxon Co., USA, Houston, 1978-79, sr. drilling technician Southeastern div. New Orleans, 1979-81, drilling supt., 1981-84, drilling supt. hdqrs. Houston, 1984-89, drilling supt. Offshore div. New Orleans, 1989-91; ops. supr. hdqrs. drilling Exxon Co., Internat., Houston, 1991-99; sr. ops. supr. Exxon Mobil Devel. Co. Drilling, Houston, 2000—. Contbr. articles to profl. jours. Ruling elder Clear Lake Presbyn. Ch., Houston, 1987-88. With U.S. Army, 1969-73. Mem.: Soc. Petroleum Engrs., Soc. of 1st Inf. Divsn., Masons. Republican. Home: 20730 Chappell Knoll Dr Cypress TX 77433-5510

DAY, ROBERT WILLIAM, geotechnical engineer; b. Frankfurt, Germany, Nov. 3, 1955; s. Norman Charles and Jean Joann (Kole) D.; m. Deborah Ann Cozort, Feb. 20, 1982; 1 child. B of Civil Engring., Villanova U., 1976, M of Civil Engring., 1978; M of Civil Engring, Engr.'s degree, MIT, 1981. Registered profl. engr. Airz., Calif., Nev. Civil engr. Shell Oil Co., 1978; teaching, rsch. asst. MIT, 1978-81; staff engr. San Diego Soils Engring., 1981-82; chief geotech. engr. Am. Geotech., 1984—. Fm ASCE, Am. Soc. Testing & Materials. Office: Am Geotech 5764 Pacific Center Blvd San Diego CA 92121-4207

DAY, ROBERT WINSOR, preventive medicine physician, researcher; b. Framingham, Mass., Oct. 22, 1930; s. Raymond Albert and Mildred (Doty) Day; m. Jane Alice Boynton, Sept. 6, 1957 (div. Sept. 1977); m. Cynthia Taylor, Dec. 16, 1977; children: Christopher, Nathalia, Natalia, Julia. Student, Harvard U., 1949-51; MD, U. Chgo., 1956; MPH, U. Calif., Berkeley, 1958, PhD, 1962. With USPHS, 1956-57; resident U. Calif., Berkeley, 1958-60; research specialist Calif. Dept. Mental Hygiene, 1960-64; asst. prof. Sch. Pub. Health and Sch. Medicine UCLA, 1962-64; dep. dir. Calif. Dept. Pub. Health, Berkeley, 1965-67; prof., chmn. dept. health services Sch. Pub. Health and Community Medicine, U. Wash., Seattle, 1968-72, dean, 1972-82, prof., 1982—; pres., dir. Fred Hutchinson Cancer Rsch. Ctr., Seattle, 1981-97, pres., dir. emeritus, 1997—, mem. pub. health scis., 1997—. Mem. Nat. Cancer Adv. Bd., 1992—98, Nat. Cancer Policy Bd., 1996—2000; chief med. officer Epigenomics, Inc.; sci. dir. Internat. Consortium Rsch. Health Effects Radiation; cons. in field. Fellow: APHA, AAAS, Am. Coll. Preventive Medicine; mem.: Am. Assn. Cancer Insts. (bd. dirs. 1983—87, v.p. 1984—85, pres., chmn. bd. dirs.), Assn. Schs. Pub. Health (pres. 1981—82), Am. Assn. Cancer Rsch., Am. Soc. Preventive Oncology, Am. Soc. Clin. Oncology. Office: 1872 E Hamlin St Seattle WA 98112 E-mail: dlcllc@attbi.com.

DAY, ROLAND BERNARD, retired chief justice state supreme court; b. Oshkosh, Wis., June 11, 1919; s. Peter Oliver and Joanna King (Wescott) D.; m. Mary Jane Purcell, Dec. 18, 1948; 1 dau., Sarah Jane. BA, U. Wis., 1942, JD, 1947. Bar: Wis. 1947. Trainee Office Wis. Atty. Gen., 1947; assoc. mem. firm Maloney & Wheeler, Madison, Wis., 1947-49; 1st asst. dist. atty. Dane County, Wis., 1949-52; partner firm Day, Goodman, Madison, 1953-57; firm Wheeler, Van Sickle, Day & Anderson, Madison, 1959-74; legal counsel mem. staff Sen. William Proxmire, Washington, 1957-58; justice Wis. Supreme Ct., Madison, 1974-95, chief justice, 1995-96. Mem. Madison Housing Authority, 1960-64, chmn., 1961-63; regent U. Wis. System, 1972-74 Served with AUS, 1943-46. Mem. ABA, State Bar Wis., Am. Trial Lawyers Assn., Ygdrasil Lit. Soc. (pres. 1968), Madison Torske Klubben, Masons (33rd degree). Mem. United Ch. of Christ. Clubs: Madison, Madison Lit.

DAY, RONALD RICHARD, retired financial executive; b. York, Pa., Nov. 14, 1934; s. Russell Aldinger and Rosa Ellenora (Reever) D.; m. Patricia Glee Duncan, Nov. 24, 1956. BS in Econs., Lebanon Valley Coll., Annville, Pa., 1956; postgrad., U.S. Army Fin. Sch., Indpls., 1957, Lehigh U., 1961. Mgr. cost control and sys. Mack Trucks, Inc., Allentown, Pa., 1963-67; mgr. cost acctg. Am. Chain divsn. Acco Babcock Co., York, 1967-70, divsn. contr., 1970-82, v.p. fin. and acctg. Chain and Forged Products Group, 1982-89; pres., sr. v.p., contr., chief fin. officer AAA So. Pa., 1990—; ret., 2001. Committeeman York County Rep. Party, 1972-74; bus. chmn. York County chpt. Am. Heart Assn., 1987-89. Served to 1st lt. U.S. Army, 1957-59. Mem. York Area C. of C., Internat. Platform Assn., Lafayette Club, Outdoor Country Club, Masons, Shriners, Order of DeMolay (mem. adv. bd. 1975-89), Rotary (sec. West York club 1988-92, pres. 1993-94). Lutheran. Avocations: golf, hunting, fishing, boating, travel. Home: 2430 Ramblewood Rd York PA 17404-3941

DAY, RONALD ELWIN, consulting executive; b. Randolph, Vt., Dec. 15, 1933; s. John Ellis and Esther Murle (Tabor) D.; m. Elizabeth Jean McKeage, June 26, 1955; children: Gary Alan, Kathi Ellen, Judy Anne, Jeffrey Evan. AA, Pasadena City Coll., 1958, student, 1958-59; BA, U. Calif., Santa Barbara, 1961; MBA, UCLA, 1962. Internal auditor North Am. Aviation, Downey, Calif., 1962—64; sys. and procedures mgr. Proto Tool Co., L.A., 1964—65; computer programmer First Nat. Bank, Boston, 1966—67, project mgr., 1967—73, sys. analyst, 1974—77, sys. planning com. chmn., trust divsn., 1977—89, trust info. mgmt. sys. adminstr., 1977—89; pres. Edge Sys. Projects, Inc., North Reading, Mass., 1990—2002. With USAF, 1952-56. Mem. Soc. Advancement of Mgmt., U.S. Ski Assn., Nat. Geog. Soc., Boston Computer Soc., Assn. Sys. Mgmt., Alpha Gamma Sigma. Republican. Home and Office: 2 Bigham Rd North Reading MA 01864-2904

DAY, RUSSELL CLOVER, state agency administrator; b. Concord, N.H., June 29, 1943; s. Alan C. and Lois M. (Huntington) D.; m. Carol Ann Tasker, July 9, 1965; children: Jennifer Marie, Jeffrey Russell. BA, New England Coll., 1965; postgrad., Fairfield U., 1965, U. N.H., 1965-67; M in Human Svcs. Adminstrn., Antioch U., Keene, N.H., 1978. Examiner State of N.H. Soc. Security Disability Determination Svc., Concord, 1969-73, supr., 1973-81, dep. dir., 1981-85, adminstr., 1985—. Trustee New England Coll., 1987-89; mem. supervisory com. N.H. Fed. Credit Union, chairperson, 1995-97, bd. dirs., 1997—. Recipient Vol. Achievement award N.H. Credit Union League, Edward Filene award, Social Security Commrs. Citation, 2000, Assoc. Commrs. Citation, 2000, Excellence in Govt. award Greater Boston Fed. Exec. Bd., 2002. Mem. Nat. Coun. Disability Determination Dirs. (exec. com. 1991-94), Masons, Lions Club (pres. 1983-84, chmn. region I, dist. 44-N 1995-96, Melvin Jones fellow 2000), New Eng. Coll. Alumni Assn. (chmn. 1987-89). Republican. Congregationalist. Avocations: fishing, boating, stamp collecting, photography. Home: 73 Wallace Rd Goffstown NH 03045 Office: Social Security Disability Determination Svc PO Box 452 Concord NH 03302-0452 E-mail: rcday2@aol.com.

DAY, SANDY J. painter, writer; b. Clinton, Ind., Nov. 12, 1938; Student, Mpls. Sch. Art. City mural, The Watcher, 1998. Mem. Mayor's Culture Commn., Anderson, Ind., 1996—. Recipient Purchase award, Minnetrista Cultural Ctr., 1998. Mem.: Watercolor Soc. Ind. (signature award 1998), Hoosier Salon (featured artist 2002), Ind. Artists Club. Home: 3461 E 250 N Anderson IN 46012-9433

DAY, STACEY BISWAS, physician, educator; b. London, Dec. 31, 1927; came to U.S. 1955, naturalized 1977. s. Satis B. and Emma L. (Camp) D.; m. Ivana Podvalova, Oct. 18, 1973; 2 children. MD, Royal Coll. Surgeons, Dublin, Ireland, 1955; PhD, McGill U., 1964; DSc, Cin. U., 1971. Intern King's County Hosp., SUNY Downstate Ctr., 1955-56; resident fellow in surgery U. Minn. Hosp., 1956-60; hon. registrar St. George's Hosp., London, Eng., 1960-61; lectr. exptl. surgery McGill U., Montreal, Que., Can., 1964; asst. prof. exptl. surgery U. Cin. Med. Sch., 1968-70; assoc. dir. basic med. rsch. Shriner's Burn Inst., Cin., 1969-71; from asst. to assoc. prof. pathology, head Bell Mus. Pathobiology U. Minn., Mpls., 1970-74; dir. biomed. comm. and med. edn. Sloan-Kettering Inst., N.Y.C., 1974-80; mem. Sloan-Kettering Inst. for Cancer Rsch., 1974-80; mem. adminstrv. coun., field coordinator, 1974-75; prof. biology Sloan Kettering divsn. Grad. Sch. Med. Sci. Cornell U., 1974-80; clin. prof. medicine divsn. behavioral medicine N.Y. Med. Coll., 1980-92; prof. biopsychosocial medicine, chmn. dept. community health U. Calabar (Nigeria) Sch. Medicine, 1982-85; prof. internat. health, dir. Internat. Ctr. for Health Scis. Meharry Med. Coll., Nashville, 1985-89, dir. WHO Collaborating Ctr. ICHS, 1987-89; founding dir. WHO Collaborating Ctr., Nashville, 1987-89, emeritus dir., 1989; adj. prof. family and cmty. medicine U. Ariz. Coll. Med. Scis., Tucson, 1985-89; univ. prof. internat. health U. Calabar, Nigeria, 1989—; permanent vis. prof. med. edn. Oita Med. Univ., Japan, 1992-99. Arris and Gale lectr. Royal Coll. Surgeons, England, 1972; vis. lectr., Ireland, 72; vis. prof. U. Bologna, 1977, Kyushu, Japan, 90, U. Mauritius, 1991, Bratislava U., 1991, U. Tokyo, Japan, 1992—93, U. Nagasaki, Japan, 1992—93, Beijing, 1993; vis. prof. health comm. U. Santiago, Chile, 1979—80, Colombo, Sri Lanka, 1996; vis. prof. Oncologic Rsch. Inst., Tallinn, Estonia, 1976, All India Insts. Health, 1976, U. Maidugari, 1982, Veclore U., India, 1996, De Quito, Ecuador, 1996; vis. acad. Oxford (Eng.) U., 1993—95; moderator med. cartography and computer health Harvard U., 1978, Acad. Scis., Czech Republic, 1987, Australia, 88; Fulbright prof. Charles U., Czech Republic, 1989; prof. (hon.) Coll. Health Scis. U. San Francisco de Quito (Ecuador), 1996; cons. Pam Am. Health Assn., 1974—90, U.S.-USSR Agreement for Health Cooperation, 1976, WHO Collaborating Ctr. Meharry Med. Coll., Nashville, 1985, NAFEO/USAID, 1986—89; mem. expert com. for health, manpower devel.

WHO, 1986—90, cons. divsn. strengthening health care resources, 1987—90, UN-FSSTD, 1987, AID/Joint Memorandum of Understanding W. Africa, Kenya, 1987—89, South Africa, 1987—89, Sudan, 1985—89; cons. to dean med. coll. faculty med. and health scis. ABHA, Asir, Saudi Arabia, 1981; cons. to dir. High Tatras symposia Post Grad. Med. Inst., Bratislava, 1990—; cons. to rector U. Autónoma Agraria Antonio Narro, Saltillo, Mexico, 1987—89; pres., chmn. Pub. Cultural and Ednl. Prodns., Montreal, Canada, 1966—85; bd. dirs., v.p. Am. Sci. Activities Mario Negri Found., 1975—80; bd. dirs. Internat. Health, African Health Consultancy Svc., Nigeria, Ekologia & Zivot, Slovakia; founding chmn. (hon.), bd. dirs. Lambo Found. U.S.; v.p., trustee Cancer Relief Found., Calabar; pres., exec. dir. Internat. Found. Biosocial Devel. and Human Health, 1978—86, chmn., 1986—; mem. Medzinárodny Poradny Vybor Nadácie Ekológia Zivot, Slovakia, 1995—; cons. Inst. Health, Lyfford Cay, Bahamas, 1981, Govt. Cross River State, Nigeria, Itreto State and H.H. Obong of Calabar, Nat. Bd. Advisors, Am. Biog. Inst., 1982—; cons. cmty. health and health comms. Navaho Nation, Sage Meml. Hosp., Ganado, Ariz., 1984; founder, cons. Primary Self-Health Clinics, Oban, Ikot Oku Okono and Ikot Imo, Nigeria, 1982—84; cons. High Tatras Internat. Health Symposia, Slovakia, 1990—; apptd. ab. Gov. State of Tenn., 1986—; adj. clin. prof. medicine N.Y. Med. Coll.; prof. (hon.) Colegio Ciencias Salud U. San Francisco, Quito, 1965—; vis. prof. U. San Francisco, 1996. Author: (verse) Collected Lines, 1966, (plays) By the Waters of Babylon, 1966, (verse) American Lines, 1967, (plays) The Music Box, 1967, Three Folk Songs Set to Music, 1967, Poems and Etudes, 1968, (novels) Rosalita, 1968, The Idle Thoughts of a Surgical Fellow, 1968, Edward Stevens-Gastric Physiologist, Physician and American Statesman, 1969, Letters to Ivana from Calabar, 2001, (novella) Bellechasse, 1970, A Leaf of the Chaatim, 1970, Ten Poems and a Letter from America for Mr. Sinha, 1971, Curling's Ulcer: An Experiment of Nature, 1972, Tuluak and Amaulik: Dialogues on Death and Mourning with the Inuit Eskimo of Point Barrow and Wainwright, Alaska, 1974, East of the Navel and Afterbirth: Reflections from Rapa Nui, 1976, Health Communications, 1979, The Biopsychosocial Imperative, 1981, What Is Survival: The Physician's Way and the Biologos, 1981, Developing Health in the West African Bush, 1995; author: (in Czech) Moudrost Samuraju, 1998; author: Selected Poems and Embers of a Medical Life, 1999, In the Shadow of the Bush - Letters from Calabar, 1999-2000, 2000, Vitaesophia of Integral Humanism, 2001, The Klacelka in a Slavic Woodland, 2003; editor: Death and Attitudes Toward Death, 1972, Membranes, Viruses and Immune Mechanisms in Experimental and Clinical Disease, 1972, Ethics in Medicine in a Changing Society, 1973, Communication of Scientific Information, 1975, Trauma: Clinical and Biological Aspects, 1975, Molecular Pathology, 1975; editor: (with Robert A. Good) (series) Comprehensive Immunology, 9 vols., 1976—80; editor: Cancer Invasion and Metastasis-Biologic Mechanisms and Therapy, 1977, Some Systems of Biological Communication, 1977, Image of Science and Society, 1977, What Is A Scientist?, 1978, Sloan Kettering Inst. Cancer Series, 1974—80; editor: (with K. Inokouchi) Selections from the Chronicle of the Hagakure as Wisdom Literature: The Way of The Samurai of Saga Domain, 1993; editor-in-chief, mem. editl. bd. Health Communications and Informatics, 1974—80, editor in chief The American Biomedical Network: Health Care System in America Present and Past, 1978, A Companion to the Life Sciences, Vol. 1, 1979, A Companion to the Life Sciences, Vol. 2, Integrated Medicine, 1980, A Companion to the Life Sciences, Vol. 3, Life Stress, 1981, Advance to Biopsychosocial Health, 1984, editor in chief, mem. editorial bd. Health Communications and Biopsychosocial Health; editor (with others): Cancer, Stress and Death, 1979, 2nd edit., 1986; editor: Computers for Medical Office and Patient Management, 1981, Readings in Oncology, 1980, Biopsychosocial Health, 1981, Primary Health Care Guidelines: A Training Manual for Community Health, 2nd edit., 1986; editor: (with T.A. Lambo) Contemporary Issues in International Health, 1989; sr. editor, with Salat and others Health and Quality of Life in Changing Europe in the Year 2000, 1992, sr. editor, with H. Koga Hagakure-Spirit of Bushido, 1993, sr. editor, with K. Inokuchi Selections from the Chronicles of the Hagakure as Wisdom Literature: The Way of the Samurai of Saga Domain, 1993, sr. editor, with Salát Health Management, Organization, and Planning in Changing Eastern Europe, 1993, sr. editor, with M. Kobayashi and K. Inokuchi, in Japanese The Medical Student and the Mission of Medicine in the Twenty First Century, 1995, sr. editor The Wisdom of Hagakure, 1996, Developing Health in the West African Bush, 2 parts, 1995, Letters of Owen Wagensteen to a Surgical Fellow: with a memoir, 1996, Man and Mu: The Cradle of Becoming and Unbecoming, 1997, Czech Caesura: Golden Prague and the Black Years (Notes from Diaries 1970-1990), 1998, Moudrost Samuraju Trigon (in Czech), 1998, Poems and Embers of a Medical Life, 1998, The Surgical Treatment of Ischaemic Heart Disease with An Account of the Coronary and Intercoronary Circulation in Man and Animals, 1999, Introduction-Comprehensive Medicine (Oriental-Occidental Overview), 2000, Letters to Ivana from Calabar, 2001, Purkynje Address and Other Health Care Lectures Czechoslovakia 1989-1999, 2002, Pliskova's Butterflies-When God Says Enough, 2003, mem. editl. bd. Annual Reviews on Stress, Jour. Stress, cons. editl. bd. Comprehensive Medicine (Japan), Wilhelm Von Humboldt Über Die Unter Dem Namen Bhagavad Gita with commentary, 2001, Purkyne Address and Other Healthcare Lectures, 1989-1999; co-editor: various publs.; contbr. articles; prodr.: TV and health edn. programs, 1982—85, (TV film) Onchocerciasis - River Blindness in Africa, 1988. Served with Brit. Army, 1946-49. Recipient Moynihan medal Assn. Surgeons Gt. Britain and Ireland, 1960, Reuben Harvey triennial prize Royal Coll. Physicians, Ireland, 1957, Arris and Gale award Royal Coll. Surgeons, Eng., 1972, disting. scholar award Internat. Communication Assn., 1980, Sama Found. medal, 1982, disting. citation Hagakure Soc., 1992, Nat. Svc. medal Royal Brit. Legion, 1993; named to Hon. Order Ky. Cols., 1968; named Chieftan Ntufam Ajan of Oban Ejagham People, Cross River State, Nigeria, 1983; hon. prof. Del Colegio De Ciencas De La Salud De La Universidad San Francisco De Quito, 1996; recipient Chieftan Obong Nsong Idem Ibibio Nigeria, 1983, Mgbe (Ekpe) honor Nigeria, commendation WHO address Fed. Govt. Nigeria, Calabar, 1983, Leadership in Internat. Med. Health citation Pres. U.S., 1987, WHO medal, 1987, Agromedicine citation Commr. of Agr., State of Tenn., 1987, Assembly citation State of N.Y., 1987, Citation Congl. Record., 1987; Maestro Honorifo, U. Autonoma Agraria, Coahuila, Mex., 1987; presented Key to the City of Nashville, 1987; recipient Vice-Chancellor's Citation and Presentation for Primary Health Care Teaching in Nigeria, U. Calabar, 1988; Pamétni medal Postgrad. Med. Coll., Prague, 1991, Gold medal U. of Bratislava, 1991, Disting. Citation Hagakure Rsch. Soc., Japan, 1992, Nat. Svc. medal Royal Brit. Legion, 1993, Citation Commendation from Pres. Kyoto Prefectural U. Medicine, Japan, 1993, Citation Commendation on Contbn. to Med. Edn. from Pres. Oita Med. U., Japan, 1997; addresses presented by people of Ikot Imo, Nsit Anyang, Oban, 1982-84, Commendation from King of Calabar, 1984; Ciba fellow Can., 1965; Stacey Day Ward named in his honor by Fed. Min. and Gov. of Cross River State, Calabar Med. Ctr., Nigeria, 1986; charter mem. U.S. Normandy Com., 1988; 1st fgn. hon. mem. Hagakure Res. Soc. (Samurai), Kyushu, Japan, 1991. Fellow: African Acad. Med. Scis. (founder), African Acad. Sci., World Acad. Arts and Scis., Japanese Found. for Biopsychosocial Health (internat. hon. fellow and most disting. mem.), Zool. Soc. London Royal Micros. Soc., Royal Soc. Health; mem.: APHA, AMA, AAS, Adelaide Hosp. Soc. (Ireland), Soc. Med. Geographers USSR, Am. Rural Health Assn. (v.p. internat. sci. affairs, bd. dirs.), Am. Anthrop. Assn., Am. Inst. Stress (bd. dirs.), Am. Assn. History Medicine, N.Y. Acad. Scis., Can. Authors Assn., Internat. Burn Assn., Am. Burn Assn. Home: 6 Lomond Ave Chestnut Ridge NY 10977 E-mail: biosocmed@aol.com. *I have tried to assimilate all that is good in many cultures and to bring about a synthesis of these expressions in my own life and writings. It is as if I must find a third eye that can see what is best in all men, to integrate them newly into a changing world, and to be as much a releasing force as to be an absorbing force. This direction, I believe, commits one to an unceasing philosophy to unlearn and to relearn.*

DAY, STOCKWELL BURT, government official; b. Barrie, Ont., Can., Aug. 16, 1950; s. Stockwell and Gwendolyn (Gilbert) D.; m. Valorie Martin Day, Oct. 2, 1971; children: Logan, Luke, Ben. Auctioneer, Alta., Can., 1972-74; dir. Teen Challenge Outreach Ministries, Edmonton, Alta., 1974-75; contractor Comml. Interiors, Alta., 1976-78; sch. adminstr./asst. pastor Bentley (Alta) Christian Centre, 1978-85; mem. Legis. Assembly Alta. Legis., Edmonton, 1986—, govt. caucus whip, 1989-92, govt. house leader, 1994-97, min. of labor, 1992-96, min. of family and social svcs., 1996-97, provincial treas., acting premier, 1997-2000; leader The Can. Alliance, Calgary, 2000—01, sr. critic fgn. affairs, 2002—. Chmn. Alta. Tourism Edn. Coun., Edmonton, 1987-89, Premier's Coun. on Family, Edmonton, 1990-92. Mem. Red Deer Rotary, Red Deer Legion (assoc.). Avocations: tennis, roller blading, backpacking, reading. Office: Ofcl Opposition 491 W Block Ho of Commons Ottawa ON Canada K1A 0A6

DAYA, JACKIE, publishing company executive; Sr. v.p., CFO Cahners Pub. Co., Newton, Mass., 1999; exec. v.p. Robert Barghaus, 1999—2000; sr. v.p., fin. adminstrn. Hasbro Interactive, 2000—. Office: Hasbro Interactive 50 Dunham Rd Beverly MA 01915-1894

DAYA MATA, SRI (FAYE WRIGHT), clergywoman; b. Salt Lake City, Jan. 31, 1914; d. Clarence Aaron and Rachel (Terry) Wright. Grad. high sch., 1931. Ordained to ministry Self-Realization Fellowship, 1935. Min. Self-Realization Fellowship, L.A., 1935—, bd. dirs., 1941—, sec., 1944-45, treas., 1945-71, lectr., 1952—; pres. brs. U.S., Can., Mex., S.Am., Europe, Africa, Asia, Australia and New Zealand Self-Realization Fellowship/Yogoda Satsanga Soc. of India, 1955—. Gemeinschaft der Selbst-Verwirklichung, 1974—, Self Realization Inst. of Va., Inc., 1981—. Author: (books) Only Love, 1976, Finding the Joy Within You, 1990, Enter The Quiet Heart, 1998; (videocassettes) Security in a World of Change, 1989, Him I Shall Follow, 1997, Living in the Love of God, 2002; contbr. articles to mags. Pres. Yogoda Satsanga Homeopathic Mahavidyalaya, Yogoda Satsanga Mahavidyalaya, Yogoda Satsanga Vidyalaya, Yogoda Satsanga Kanya Vidyalaya, Yogoda Satsanga Sangeet Kala Bharati, Yogoda Satsanga Shilpa Kala Bharati, Yogoda Satsanga Balkrishnalaya, Yogoda Satsanga Sevashram Hosp., Worldwide Prayer Circle, others. Home and Office: Self-Realization Fellowship 3880 San Rafael Ave Los Angeles CA 90065-3298

DAYE, CHARLES EDWARD, law educator; b. Durham, N.C., May 14, 1944; s. Eccleasiastes and Addie Lula (Roberts) D.; m. Norma Lowery, Dec. 19, 1976; stepchildren: Clarence L. Hill, III, Tammy H. Roundtree. Student, N.C. Central U., 1966; JD, Columbia U., 1969. Bar: N.Y. 1970, D.C. 1971, N.C. 1975, U.S. Supreme Ct. 1979. Assoc. Dewey, Ballantine, Bushby, Palmer & Wood, N.Y.C., 1969; law clk. U.S. Ct. Appeals (6th cir.), 1969-70; assoc. Covington & Burling, Washington, 1970-72; prof. law Sch. Law U. N.C., Chapel Hill, 1972-81, 85—, Henry Brandis prof. law, 1991—. Dean, prof. law Sch. Law, N.C. Central U., Durham, 1981-85; cons. N.C. Dept. Adminstrn., 1975; mem. Triangle Housing Devel. Corp., 1973—, chmn. 1977-93; chair N.C. Poverty Project, 1990—, pres. Law Sch. Admission Coun., 1990-93. Author: (with Mandelker et al) Housing and Community Development, 1981, 2d edit., 1989, 3rd edit., 1999, (with Morris) N.C. Law of Torts, 2d edit., 1999; contbr. articles to profl. jours. Mem. ABA (mem. commn. on minorities in the profn. 1990-95), N.C. Assn. Black Lawyers (Lawyer of Yr. 1980, pres. 1976-78, exec. sec. 1979-99), N.C. Bar Assn. Democrat. Baptist. Home: 3400 Cambridge Rd Durham NC 27707-4508 Office: Univ NC Law Sch Chapel Hill NC 27599-0001 E-mail: cdaye@email.unc.edu.

DAYES, LLOYD ALBERT, neurosurgeon, minister; b. Kingston, West Indies, Feb. 15, 1929; arrived in U.S., 1953; s. Samuel George Dayes and Legonia Edith Nicholson; m. Thelma Yvonne Goldsmith, 1957; children: Darlene, Albert, Michelle. Ministerial program, West Indies Coll.; BA, Pacific Union Coll., Napa, Calif., 1955; MD, Loma Linda Univ. Sch. of Medicine, L.A., 1959; postgraduate edn., Mt. Sinai Med. Ctr., N.Y., 1985, Oxford Univ., Oxford, Eng., 1993. Lic. Med. Coun. of Can., 1960, cert. Am. Bd. of Neurol. Surgery, 1967. Resident Montreal Neurol. Inst. McGill U., 1960—65, demonstrator in neuropathology, 1962; instr. in neurosurgery Loma Linda Univ., Loma Linda, Calif., 1965—66, asst. prof. neurosurgery, 1966—78, assoc. prof. neurosurgery, 1978—88, prof. of neurosurgery, 1988; attending neurosurgeon Loma Linda Univ. Med. Ctr., Loma Linda, Calif., 1965—, Riverside Gen. Hosp., Riverside, Calif., 1965—, Loma Linda Cmty. Hosp., Loma Linda, Calif., 1978—. Acting chmn. divsn. of neurosurgery Loma Lina Univ. Med. Ctr., Loma Linda, Calif., 1989—89. Contbr. scientific papers to over 27 conf., articles to profl. jour. Ethics com. Loma Linda Univ., 1988—90; welcome com. CNS, 1978; admission com. Loma Linda Univ., 1986—92, cirriculm com., 1975—78, utilization review com., 1988—90; coord.-med. student neurogurgical rotation and electives Loma Linda Univ. Sch. of Medicine, 1995—99. Recipient Univ. Alumnus of the Yr. award, Loma Linda Univ., 2001; Jesse Noyes Found. Fellowship, N.Y., 1955—59. Fellow: The Royal So. of Medicine, Am. Acad. of Neurol. and Orthopedic Surgeons, Am. Coll. of Surgeons, Am. Coll. of Nagiology, Internat. Coll. of Angiology, Internat. Coll. of Surgeons; mem.: Am. Soc. of Forensic Medicine (neurosurgery divsn.), N. Am. Skull Base Soc., The Joint Sec. on Neurtrauma and Critical Care, Am. Soc. of Law and Medicine, Calif. Neurol. Soc., N.Y. Acad. of Sci., Am. Assn. Tissue Banks, AAAS, Am. Chem. Soc., Am. Coll. of Legal Medicine, Congress of Neurol. Surgeons, Canadian Neurol. Soc., L.A. Soc. of Neurology and Psychiarty, Calif. Med. Assn., Pan Am. Med. Assn., San Berardino County Med. Soc., Sigma XI, Alpha Omega Alpha Honor Med. Soc. Achievements include research in magnesuim and its influence on Cerebal Vasospasm; elec. events triggering Cardiac Arrhythmia; Catecholamines and the Cerebrogenci-Cardiac interrelationships; pituitary-Thyroid Dysfunction with Cardiac interface; A search for the killer - Gliob;astoma Multiforme. Avocations: gardening, rosarian. Office: Ch Ogrn 11234 Anderson Loma Linda CA 92354

DAYMON, JOY JONES, school psychology specialist; b. Prescott, Ark. d. Coy A. and Alma E. (Honea) Jones; m. Jack C. Daymon, May 3, 1947; children: Jim, Michael, David, Deborah. BA, Long Beach State Coll.; MS in Ednl. Psychology, U. So. Calif., 1974; student, UCLA. Cert. elem. tchr., sch. psychologist specialist, Ark.; lic. profl. counselor, Ark. Tchr. Redondo Beach (Calif.) Sch. Dist.; ednl. examiner El Dorado (Ark.) Schs. Adj. instr. So. Ark. U., Magnolia; presenter workshop on assessment of severe and multi-handicapped various state and nat. convs. Author: Rabbit Pancakes, 1995, Princess Diana the Lamb to the Slaughter, 2002. Mem. NASP (state del., 1984-86), APA, Ark. Psychol. Assn. (treas. 1978-80), Ark. Sch. Psychologists Assn. (state del.), Ark. Counseling Assn., Nat. Bd. Cert. Counselors, Ark. Assessment in Counseling (pres., 1980-81), Delta Kappa Gamma (pres. 1986-87), Phi Delta Kappa. Home: 2202 N Wyatt Dr El Dorado AR 71730-9262 Office: 108 Randolph El Dorado AR 71730

DAYNARD, RICHARD ALAN, law educator; b. NYC, July 19, 1943; s. David M. and Sarah (Weidenbaum) D.; m. Carol S. Iskols, Aug. 9, 1975; children: David J., Gabriela C. BA, Columbia U., 1964, MA in Sociology, 1970; JD, Harvard U., 1967; PhD in Urban Studies and Planning, MIT, 1980. Bar: N.Y. 1967, U.S. Ct. Appeals (6th cir.) 1986, U.S. Supreme Ct. 1986, U.S. Ct. Appeals (11th cir.) 1987, U.S. Ct. Appeals (5th cir.) 1996. Law clk. 2d cir. U.S. Ct. Appeals, N.Y.C., 1967-68; tchg. fellow Columbia U., N.Y.C., 1968-69; asst. prof. law Northeastern U., Boston, 1969-71, assoc. prof. law, 1971-73, prof. law, 1973—. Lectr. Tufts Med. Sch., Boston, 1975—89; dir. law and obesity project Pub. Health Advocacy Inst., 2002—; lectr. and cons. in field. Editor-in-chief Tobacco Products Litigation Reporter, 1985—; assoc. editor: Tobacco Control: An Internat. Jour., 1998—; contbr. articles to profl. jours. Chmn. Tobacco Products Liability Project, Boston, 1984—; pres. Group Against Smoking Pollution of Mass., Boston, 1983—, Clean Indoor Air Ednl. Found., Boston, 1983-92, Tobacco Control Resource Ctr., Inc., Boston, 1993—; pres. Stop Teenage Addiction to Tobacco, 1996-98; chair lay adv. bd. Flight Attendants Med. Rsch. Inst., 2003—. Mem. ABA, Am. Pub. Health Assn., Law and Soc. Assn., Phi Beta Kappa. Home: 90 Commonwealth Ave Boston MA 02116-3040 Office: Northeastern U Sch Law 400 Huntington Ave Boston MA 02115-5005 E-mail: r.daynard@neu.edu.

DAYS, DREW S., III, lawyer, law educator; b. 1941; m. Ann Ramsay Langdon, 1966; children: Alison, Elizabeth. Degree in Eng. Lit. with honors, Hamilton Coll., 1963; LLB, Yale U., 1966. Bar: Ill. 1966, N.Y. 1970. Assoc. Cotton, Watt, Jones & King, Chgo., 1966-67; vol. Peace Corps., Honduras, 1967-69; assoc. counsel NAACP Legal Def. Fund, N.Y.C., 1969-73, 75-77; assoc. prof. Temple U., 1973-75; asst. atty. gen. Dept. of Justice, Washington, 1977—80; assoc. prof. Yale U., New Haven, 1981-86, prof., 1986-93, Alfred M. Rankin chair Law Sch., 1991; solicitor gen. Dept. Justice, Washington, 1993-96; of counsel Morrison & Foerster LLP, 1997—. Dir. Schell Ctr. for Internat. Human Rights Yale U. Law Sch., 1988-93. Bd. dirs. John D. and Catherine T. MacArthur Found., Petra Found., Hamilton Coll. Mem. Am. Law Inst., Am. Bar Found., Am. Acad. Arts and Scis., Am. Acad. Appellate Lawyers, Coun. on Fgn. Rels., Inter-Am. Dialogue. Office: Yale Law Sch PO Box 208215 New Haven CT 06520-8215 E-mail: drew.days@yale.edu.

DAY-SALVATORE, DEBRA LYNN, medical geneticist; b. Hoboken, N.J., Oct. 23, 1953; m. Francis P. Salvatore, Sr., Dec. 24, 1988. BA in Biology, Harvard U., 1975; MS in Pharmacology, NYU, 1979, PhD in Pharmacology, 1982; MD, Case Western Res. U., 1986. Diplomate Am. Bd. Med. Genetics, Am. Bd. Pediats. Grad. fellow dept. pharmacology NYU Med. Ctr., 1978-79; sr. rsch. asst. dept. medicine Case Western Res. U., Cleve., 1979-82, rsch. assoc. dept. molecular biology and microbiology, 1982-84; pediatric and adolescent medicine resident Cleve. Clinic Found., 1986-89; med. genetics fellow Robert Wood Johnson Med. Sch., New Brunswick, N.J., 1990-91, asst. prof. pediatrics, 1990—, coord. perinatal genetics dept. ob-gyn., 1991-92, dir. divsn. reproductive and perinatal genetics dept. ob-gyn., 1992—, asst. prof. ob-gyn. and reproductive scis. and pediatrics, 1992—, acting chief divsn. clin. genetics, dept. ob-gyn. and reproductive scis., 1993—; physician Robert Wood Johnson Univ. Hosp., New Brunswick, 1990—, St. Peter's Med. Ctr., 1992—, chief divsn. clin. genetics, 1996—. Mem. genetic adv. bd. N.J. State Dept. Health's Parental and Child Adv. Com.; mem. med. adv. bd. Cryo-Cell Internat. Genetics editor Jour. of Perinatology, 1993—; contbr. articles, abstracts to profl. jours. Cons. N.J. Interagency Adoption Coun. Mem. AAAS, AMA, Am. Acad. Pediatrics (mem. N.J. chpt.), Am. Soc. Cell Biology, Am. Soc. Human Genetics, Human Genetics Assn. N.J. (mem. legis. com.), N.Y. Acad. Sci. Office: Saint Peter's Univ Hosp 254 Easton Ave # 4410 New Brunswick NJ 08901-1766

DAYSON, DIANE HARRIS, superintendent, park ranger; b. N.Y.C., Feb. 14, 1953; d. Robert Gene and Dessie Lee (Osborne) Harris; m. Kevin Maurice Dayson, Sept. 15, 1978; children: Dayna Renee, Kyle Ryan. BA in Early Secondary Edn. and Am. History, SUNY, Cortland, 1975; MS, NYU, 2000; Sr. Exec. Svc. grad., U.S. Dept. Interior, 2000. With Nat. Pk. Svc. U.S. Dept. Interior, 1975—, law enforcement ranger, 1977-79, concessions specialist, 1979-81, site mgr. Nat. Pk. Svc., 1984-87, supt. Nat. Pk. Svc. Oyster Bay, N.Y., 1987-90, Morristown, N.J., 1990-93, Hyde Park, N.Y., 1993-95; supt. Statue of Liberty Ellis Island, N.Y.C., 1996—. Adj. prof. NYU Wagner Sch. of Pub. Adminstrn.; ambassador to Amsterdam, 1998; ambassador on geneology to Paris, France, 2000, Bremehaven, Germany, 2000, San Marino, Italy, 1997. Active United Way, Dutchess County; exch. steward, Manchester, Eng., 1994; bd. dirs. Christian Ministry in Nat. Parks, 1997—. Mem. NAFE, Oyster Bay C. of C. Republican. Roman Catholic. Avocations: travel, knitting, reading. Office: Statue of Liberty Ellis Island Liberty Is New York NY 10004-1467

DAYTON, CHARLES KELLY, lawyer; b. Belvidere, Ill, May 16, 1939; s. Charles F. and Marie Dayton; children: Michael, James. BA, Dartmouth Coll., 1961; JD, U. Mich., 1964. Bar: Minn. 1964, Wis. 1988. Ptnr. Gray Plant Mooty & Bennet, Mpls., 1964-71; legal dir. Minn. Pub. Interest Rsch. Group, Mpls., 1971-72; founding ptnr. Pepin Dayton Herman & Graham, Mpls., 1973-88; ptnr. Leonard, St. & Deinard, Mpls., 1988—2002; dir. Graywolf Press, Minn. Adj. prof. U. Minn. Law Sch., Mpls., 1983-84. Dir. Environ. Law and Policy Ctr., Chgo., 1996—; bd. dir. Elmer L. and Eleanor Andersen Found., St. Paul, 1997, Nat. Coun. on Sci. and the Environ., Washington, 1992—; Minn. Ctr. for environ. Advocacy; pathways; Mn. League of Cons. Voters. Named Environmentalist of Decade, Northstar chpt. Sierra Club, 1982, Pro Bono Vol. award Minn. Ctr. for Environ. Advocacy, Disting. Svc. award Minn. Justice Found., 1997. Mem. Hennepin County Bar Assn. (chair environ. law com. 1994-99). Avocations: sailing, cross country skiing, canoeing. Office: Minn Ctr for Environ Advocacy 29 E Exchange St Paul MN 55101 Home: 2235 Scudder St Saint Paul MN 55108-1919

DAYTON, DEANE KRAYBILL, translation company executive; b. Marion, Ind., May 24, 1949; s. Wilber Thomas and Donna Irene (Fisher) D.; m. Carol Mae Noggle, June 2, 1969; 1 child, Christopher Thomas. BA in Chemistry Edn., Ind. Wesleyan U., 1970; MS in Teaching, Randolph-Macon U., 1974; MS in Instrnl. Tech., PhD in Instrnl. Tech.,, 1976. Sci. tchr., chair sci. dept. Jessamine County Jr. High Sch., Nicholasville, Ky., 1970-73; asst. prof. instructional tech. sch. edn. U. Va., Charlottesville, 1976-77; grad. asst., teaching asst. Ind. U., Bloomington, 1973-76, asst. prof. instrnl. tech. Sch. Edn., 1977-83, dir. prodn. svcs. audio-visual ctr., 1979-83; dir. media div. CDC, Atlanta, 1981; v.p. cons. svcs. Ednl. Techs., Inc., Charlotte, N.C., 1983-85; exec. mgr. documentation and lang. transl. Intergraph Corp., Huntsville, Ala., 1985-98; v.p. worldwide ops. Berlitz GlobalNET, Princeton, NJ, 1998—2002; sr. v.p. interpretations Bowne Global Solutions, Washington, 2002—. Cons. trainer George Meany Ctr. Labor Studies, Silver Spring, 1978-82; cons., developer Discover Pl., Charlotte, 1984-86; tng. developer First Union Bank, Charlotte, 1982-85, United Carolina Bank, Monroe, N.C., 1984; cons. Anacomp, Sarasota, Fla., 1982-84. Co-author: Planning and Producing Instructional Media, 1985; producer (film) Computer Graphics for Communication, 1982; contbr. articles to profl. jours. Chairperson exhibits com. North Ala. Sci. Ctr., Inc., Huntsville, 1990-92. Recipient Young Scholar award AV Comm. Rev./Ednl. Resources Info. Ctr., 1977. Mem. ASTD, Nat. Soc. for Performance and Instrn., Soc. for Tech. Comm., Assn. for Ednl. Comm. and Tech. (pres. media design and prodn. divsn. 1982, James W. Brown award 1986). Avocation: developing computerized science museum exhibits. Home: 188 Carter Rd Princeton NJ 08540-2103 Office: Bowne Global Solutions 1730 Rhode Island Ave NW Washington DC 20036 E-mail: deane.dayton@bowneglobal.com., dkdayton@attglobal.net.

DAYTON, JEAN, elementary school principal; b. Belleville, Ill., Jan. 6, 1957; d. Charles John and Marjorie Jane Hempen Mueth; m. Michael Louis Dayton, Oct. 26, 1996. BS in Spl. Edn. & Elem. Edn., So. Ill. U., 1980, MS in Spl. Edn., 1993; PhD in Edn., St. Louis U., 1998. Tchr. spl. edn. Cmty. Consol. Sch. Dist. 110, Fairview Heights, Ill., 1980-92, behavior devel. coord., 1992-93; spl. edn. advisor So. Ill. U., Edwardsville, 1993-98; supr. spl. edn. program Cmty. Unit Sch. Dist. #10, Collinsville, Ill., 1998-2000; prin. Caseyville (Ill.) Elem. Sch., 2000—. Leader Tchr. Support Team, St. Clair County, Ill., 1989-91; mem. Transition Planning Com., St. Clair County, 1992-93. Tchr. in space applicant NASA, Cape Canaveral, Fla., 1985. Mem. Coun. Exceptional Children. Office: Caseyville Elem Sch 433 S 2d St Caseyville IL 62232

DAYTON, KATHLEEN G. clinical research coordinator; b. San Bernardino, Calif., June 22, 1963; d. Ronald Jack and Carol Bernice (Walton) Kelly; m. Darren R. Dayton, Jan. 4, 1999; children: Amanda May, Andrea René. Diploma, United Health Careers, San Bernardino, Calif., 1984. Hemodialysis nurse San Bernardino Valley Dialysis, San Bernardino, 1984-94; staff nurse Blood Bank San Bernardino/Riverside Counties, San Bernardino, 1994-96; rsch. nurse Ariz. Rsch. and Edn., Phoenix, 1996—2003; hospice case mgr. RTA Hospice, Phoenix. Mem. ACRP, Am. Nephrology Nurses Assn., Nat. Kidney Found. E-mail: research@uswest.net.

DAYTON, MARK, senator; b. Mpls., Jan. 26, 1947; 2 children: Eric, Andrew. Grad. cum laude, Yale U., 1969. Tchr. gen. sci. N.Y.C. Pub. Sch., 1969-71; counselor, adminstr. Social Svc. agency, Boston, 1972-76; legis. asst. to Minn. Senator Walter Mondale; staff mem. for Govr. Rudy Perpich, Minn., 1977; commr. econ. devel. State of Minn., 1978, commr. energy and econ. devel., 1983, state auditor, 1990, U.S. senator, 2001—. Mem. Senator Paul Wellstone's re-election campaign, 1995-96; agr., armed svcs., rules, gov. affairs com., state of Minn. Democrat. Office: SR-346 Russell Senate Office bldg Washington DC 20510*

DAYTON, NICK A. pharmaceutical executive; b. San Antonio, Tex., Dec. 25, 1956; s. Lewis A. and Mildred A. Dayton; m. Marcia L. Cunningham, Oct. 5, 1991; children: Alexandra, Isabelle. BA, St. Edward's U., Austin, Tex., 1978; MA in Orgnl. Mgmt., U. Phoenix, 1995; D of Bus. Adminstrn., U. Sarasota, 1999. Cert. grad. cert. in competitive intelligence. Mfg. mgr. Abbott Labs., Austin, 1982—89, plant QA mgr. - HPD Mountain View, Calif., 1989—93, site quality assurance mgr. - ADD Santa Clara, Calif., 1993—96, dir. quality assurance - HPD Abbott Park, Ill., 1996—2001, dir. corp. quality assurance, 2001—. Profl. advisor for grad. students DePaul U., Chgo., 1996—2002; mem. editl. rev. bd. Jour. cGXP Compliance, Royal Palm Beach, 1997—2002; tech. adv. bd. Mantra Software Corp., Westborough, 1998—2002; cert. trainer - situational leadership Ken Blanchard Assocs., Chgo., 1996—2002. Contbr. articles to profl. jours. Mem.: AAUP, Assn. for Advancement of Med. Instrumentation (com. on infusion pumps 1999—2002), Regulatory Affairs Profls. Soc., Soc. Competitive Intelligence Profls., Parenteral Drug Assn. (v.p. Midwest chpt. 1999—2001, mem. core team electronic records, electronic signatures working group 1999—2002), Am. Soc. Quality. Roman Catholic. Avocations: research, travel, training, teaching, consulting. Home: 1180 Harlan

Ct Lake Forest IL 60045 Office: Abbott Labs 100 Abbott Park Rd North Chicago IL 60064-6088 Home Fax: 847-735-0117; Office Fax: 847-938-4422. Personal E-mail: nickdayton@msn.com. Business E-Mail: nick.dayton@abbott.com.

DAZE, ERIC, professional hockey player; b. Montreal, Can., July 2, 1975; Selected 4th found NHL entry draft Chgo. Blackhawks, 1993; left wing Beauport QMJ Hockey League, 1992-95; right wing Chgo. Blackhawks, 1995—. Named to QMJ Hockey League All-Star first team, 1993-94, 94-95. Recipient Can. Hockey League Most Sportsmanlike Player of Yr. award, 1994-95, Frank J. Selke Trophy, 1994-95; named Sporting News Rookie of Yr., 1996. Office: c/o Chicago Blackhawks 1901 W Madison St Chicago IL 60612-2459

DCAMP, CHARLES BARTON, educator, musician; b. Feb. 16, 1932; s. Glenn Franklin and Nina Clarice (Larson) Dc.; m. Ruth Joyce MacDonald, June 27, 1953; children: James Charles, Douglas Kevin, David Michael, Richard Manley, Paul Frederick, Jon Barton; 15 grandchildren. BS, U. Ill., 1956, MS, 1957; PhD, U. Iowa, 1980. Tchr. Watervliet (Mich.) Pub. Sch., 1958-61; tchr. music United Twp. H.S., East Moline, Ill., 1961-63; band dir. Pleasant Valley (Iowa) Schs., 1963-74; prof. music St. Ambrose U., Davenport, Iowa, 1974-97; prof. emeritus, 1997—; dir. bands, chmn. divsn. fine arts, chmn. dept. music St. Ambrose U., Davenport, Iowa. Guest dir., adjudicator festivals, music contests, Iowa, Ill., Minn.; prodr. Quad-City Music Guild, 1973-77, music dir., 1967—; chmn. Iowa All-State Band, 1971-74; instr. woodwinds Bemidji State U. Band Camp, 1967-92. Editor: Iowa Music Educator mag., 1978-80; pub. arrangements for concert band; contbr. articles to profl. jours. Mem. Riverdale Vol. Fire Co., 1966-75, pres., 1971-73; founder, 1st condr. Quad-City Wind Ensemble, 1987—; choirmaster Bettendorf Presbyn. Ch. Choir, 1982-94. With AUS, 1952-55. Recipient Karl King Disting. Svc. award Iowa Bandmasters, 1987, Disting. Svc. to Music Edn. award Iowa Music Educators Assn., 1995; named to Quad City Music Guild Hall of Fame, 1997. Mem. Iowa Bandmasters Assn. (past pres., Karl King Disting. Svc. award 1987), Coll. Band Dirs. Nat. Assn., Music Educators Nat. Conf., Iowa Music Educators (pres., past pres., Disting. Svc. award 1995), Am. Fedn. Musicians, Am. Philatelic Soc., Nat. Band Assn. (Iowa state chmn.), Quad City Stamp Club (editor newsletter 1993-98), Masons (sec. Brubaker Lodge 2000—, Grand Musician Grand Lodge Iowa 2000-01), Hi-12 (Davenport chpt., sec. 1999—), Shriners (Kaaba shrine), Davenport York Rite, Scottish Rite, Phi Mu Alpha Sinfonia, Phi Delta Kappa, Tau Kappa Epsilon. Republican. Methodist. Home: 803 W Rusholme St Davenport IA 52804-1927 Office: Saint Ambrose U Music Dept Davenport IA 52803

DE, DEVASMITA, research aquarist; b. Calcutta, India, Nov. 6, 1966; d. Kamal Chandra and Sheila D.; m. Arijit Das, June 2, 1990. BS, U. Calcutta, 1990; MS in Human Ecology, Vrije U., Brussels, 1994. Aquarist J.G. Shedd Aquarium, Chgo., 2000—; lead rsch. aquarist project seahorse McGill U., Montreal, Can., 2001—. Recipient Internat. Cert. Human Ecology, 1994. Mem. AAAS. Avocations: astronomy, reading, cookery, swimming, classical music. Office: JG Shedd Aquarium 1200 S Lake Shore Dr Chicago IL 60605

DE ABREU, SUE, elementary educator; b. Honolulu, Dec. 29, 1947; d. Lawrence and Mary (Jones-Howard) de Abreu-Morris; 1 child, Steven. AA, Gulf Coast Coll., Panama, 1967; BA, Fla. State U., 1971; BS, Harvard U., 1968; MS, Ga. So. Coll., 1984; MA, U. West Fla., 1985. Cert. art edn. tchr. K-12th, elem. tchr., sci. specialist 5th-6th grades, Fla. Reading specialist Craig Elem. Sch., Vail, Colo., 1980; tchr. sci. 7th-8th grade Ludowic County Schs., Jesup, Ga., 1981-84; tchr. sci. 5th-6th grade Gulf County Pub. Schs., Port St. Joe, Fla., 1985-98. State judge Fla. State Sci. and Engring. U. Fla, instr.; spl. news cons. Time Mag., 2001. Inventor Learning Through Creative Designs series, 2000. Chmn. Gulf County-N.W. Fla. chpt. Nat. Dem. Senatorial Com., 2001; pres. DeAbreu Plantation Nurseries; landscape designer, pres. Abreu Landscaping Design Svcs. Recipient Outstanding Fla. Artist award, Fedn. Fla. Women's Clubs Am., 2000-01. Mem. NEA, ASCD, Nat. Art Edn. Assn., Nat. Middle Sch. Assn., Nat. Wildlife Fedn. (Gulf County dir.), Wewahitchka Fedn. Women's Club (v.p. 1994-96).

DEACHMAN, ROSS VARICK, lawyer; b. Plymouth, N.H., Mar. 13, 1942; s. W. John Deachman and H. Annie Griffin; m. Nancy L. Stone, Aug. 30, 1964; children: Amy E., William John IV. BA, U. N.H., 1964; JD, Boston U., 1967. Assoc. Burns, Bryant, Hinchey & Nadeau, Dover, N.H., 1967-70; ptnr. Murphy and Deachman, Plymouth, 1971-74; owner Deachman Law Office, Plymouth, 1974-89; ptnr. Deachman & Cowie, P.A., Plymouth, 1989—. Dir., sec. N.H. Bar Assn., 1975-80; pres. Grafton County Bar Assn., 1980. Author: Bi-Centennial of the Grafton County Bar Association, 1993; editor: 25th Reunion Class of 1964, 1989. Moderator Town of Holderness, N.H., 1988—; sch. bd. mem. Pemi-Baker Co-op Sch. Dist., Plymouth, 1989—. Office: Deachman & Cowie PA PO Box 96 66 Main St Plymouth NH 03264-1451

DEACON, DAVID EMMERSON, business executive; b. Toronto, Ont., Can., July 22, 1949; s. Donald Mac Kay and Florence (Campbell) D.; m. Kathryn Robinson (divorced); m. Mary Cecilia Eberle, July 23, 1982 (divorced). Student, Brock U., St. Catherines, Ont., 1968-70, Casa Sch. Fine Arts, Paris, 1970-71. Chmn. election orgn. Liberal Party Ont., Toronto, 1973-75; chmn., editor polit. alerts F.H. Deacon, Hodgson Inc., Toronto, 1975-79, v.p. retail sales, 1979-84; gen. mgr. Porsche div. VW Can., Toronto, 1984-87; pres. Deacon Day Advt., Toronto, 1988-94; chmn. Lowe SMS, Toronto, 1994-96; mng. dir., COO, CFO Padulo Integrated, Toronto, 1996-2000; ptnr. Investment Profile, Inc., Toronto, 2000—; pres. Azure Dynamics Corp., 2001—. Illustrator: (poetry) Sun Street, 1970; records include Over the Line, 1994, The Iron Clock, 1996, Stranger in the Morning, 1999; narrator Discovery Channel prodn. Frontiers of Construction, 2001, 02, 03. Chmn. campaign tng. Fed. Liberty Party, 1977-79; pres. Ont. Liberal Party, 1983-85; chmn. Ont. campaign John Turner Leadership, 1984. Winner Can. Endurance Racing championship Can. Automobile Sport Club, 1980. Mem. Toronto Club. Avocations: skiing, tennis, windsurfing, sailing. E-mail: ddeacon@azuredynamics.com.

DEACON, JOHN C. lawyer; b. Newport, Ark., Sept. 26, 1920; BA, U. Ark., 1941, JD, 1948. Bar: Ark. 1948. Ptnr. Barrett & Deacon, Jonesboro, Ark. Commr. from Ark. to Nat. Conf. Commrs. on Uniform State Laws, 1966—, chmn. exec. com., 1977-79, pres. 1979-81. Recipient Ark. Outstanding Lawyer-Citizen award, 1973. Fellow Am. Coll. Trial Lawyers, Internat. Acad. Trial Lawyers (bd. dirs. 1978-84), Southwestern Legal Found. (trustee 1975-95, chmn. Research Fellows 1983-85); mem. Craighead County Bar Assn. (pres. 1968-69), N.E. Ark. Bar Assn. (pres. 1966-68), Ark. Bar Assn. (pres. 1970-71), ABA (chmn. sect. bar activities 1967-68, Ark. del. 1967-79, bd. govs. 1980-83, 92-93, chair sr. lawyers divsn. 1994-95), Am. Counsel Assn. (pres. 1974-75), Am. Bar Found. (pres. 1994-96), Internat. Assn. Def. Counsel, Nat. Assn. R.R. Trial Lawyers, Delta Theta Phi. Office: PO Box 1700 Jonesboro AR 72403-1700 also: Barrett & Deacon PA Union Planters Bank Building 300 S Church St Jonesboro AR 72401-2911 E-mail: jdeacon@barrettdeacon.com.

DEACON, SHARON RAE, clinical psychologist; b. Whittier, Calif., Dec. 23, 1942; d. Ray O. and Frieda (Tierney) Kathol; children: John, Brian, Greg, Sylinda. BA, U. So. Calif., 1964, PhD, 1969. Lic. clin. psychologist. Pvt. practice, Glendale, Calif., 1968—; behavioral scientist L.A. County Dept. Mental Health, 1969—; dir. S.R. Deacon & M.M. Parent Psychol. Inst. Learning, 1994—. Author: (films) Dance Therapy, 1971, Emotional Development, 1978, (comic book) Yogi Bear on Earthquakes, 1984, (with others) Discipline With Love, 1977; contbr. articles to profl. jours. Active ARC, L.A., 1973— (Spotlight award 1985). NIMH grantee, 1965-68; rsch. grantee U. So. Calif., 1968. Mem. APA, Calif. Psychol. Assn., L.A. County Psychol. Assn., Nat. Register, Glendale Area Mental Health Profl. Assn. (pres.). Avocations: family outings, fishing, swimming. E-mail: raedeacon@aol.com.

DEACY, THOMAS EDWARD, JR., lawyer; b. Kansas City, Mo., Oct. 14, 1918; s. Thomas Edward and Grace (Scales) D.; m. Jean Freeman, July 10, 1943 (div. 1988); children: Bennette Kay Deacy Kramer, Carolyn G., Margaret Deacy Vickrey, Thomas, Ann Deacy Krause; m. Jean Holmes McDonald, 1988. JD, U. Mo., 1940; MBA, U. Chgo., 1949. Bar: Mo. 1940, Ill. 1946. Practice law, Kansas City, 1940-42; ptnr. Taylor, Miller, Busch & Magner, Chgo., 1946-55, Deacy & Deacy, Kansas City, 1955—. Lectr. Northwestern U., 1949-55, U. Chgo., 1950-55; dir., mem. exec. com. St. L.-S.F. Ry., 1962-80; dir. Burlington No. Inc., 1980-86; mem. U.S. team Anglo-Am. Legal Exchange, 1973, 77. Mem. Juv. Protective Assn. Chgo., 1947-55, pres., bd. dirs., 1950-53; mem. exec. bd. Chgo. coun. Boy Scouts Am., 1952-55; pres. Kansas City Philharmonic Orch., 1961-63, chmn. bd. trustees, 1963-65; trustee Sunset Hill Sch., 1963-73; trustee, mem. exec. com. u. Kansas City, 1963—; trustee Mo. Law Sch. Found., pres., 1973-77, Kans. chpt. The Nature Conservancy, 1994-99. Capt. AUS, 1942-45. Fellow Am. Coll. Trial Lawyers (regent 1968—, treas. 1973-74, pres. 1975-76), Am. Bar Found; mem. Am. Law Inst., Jud. Conf. U.S. (implementation com. on admission of attys. to fed. practice 1979-86), ABA (commn. standards jud. adminstrn. 1972-74, standing com. fed. judiciary 1974-80), Ill. Bar Assn., Chgo. Bar Assn., Mo. Bar, Kansas City Bar Assn., Lawyers Assn. Kansas City, Chgo. Club, La Jolla (Calif.) Country Club, La Jolla Beach and Tennis Club, Kansas City Club, Kansas City Country Club, River Club, Q.E.B.H. Sr. Hon. Soc. of Mo. Univ., Beta Gamma Sigma, Sigma Chi. Home: 2724 Verona Cir Shawnee Mission KS 66208-1265 Office: 920 Main St Ste 1900 Kansas City MO 64105-2010 E-mail: ted@deacylaw.com.

DE AGOSTINO, SERGIO, engineering educator; b. Rome, Jan. 17, 1961; arrived in U.S., 1990; s. Elio and Delia De Agostino. Degree, U. Rome, 1987, PhD, 1992; Masters, Brandeis U., 1994. Rsch. assoc. U. Rome, 1994—2000; asst. prof. Armstrong Atlantic State U., Savannah, Ga., 2000—. Mem.: AAUP, IEEE, Assn. Computing Machinery. Avocations: music, guitar, movies, theater. Home: 12300 Apache Ave Savannah GA 31419 Office: Armstrong Atlantic State U 11935 Abercorn St Savannah GA 31415 Office Fax: 912-921-2083. Business E-Mail: agos@armstrong.edu.

DEAK, CHARLES KAROL, chemist; b. Budapest, Hungary, Sept. 26, 1928; came to U.S., 1955, naturalized, 1961; s. Karoly and Ida (Benes) D.; m. Jenny Bocinski, Apr. 9, 1958; children: James, Christine. BS, Eotvos Coll., Budapest, 1948; student, Sorbonne, Paris, 1949; postgrad., Wayne State U., 1957-61. Cert. prof. chemist; bd. cert. forensic examiner. With Frankel Co., Inc., Detroit, 1957-73, quality control mgr., 1968-71, mgr. tech. svcs., 1971-73; pres. Analytical Assocs., Inc., Detroit, 1973-92, C.K. Deak Tech. Svcs., Inc., Warren, Mich., 1992—. Patentee in chem. firefighting agts. and dense metal separation. Fellow ASTM, Am. Inst. Chemists; mem. Am. Chem. Soc., Am. Soc. Metals, Assn. Analytical Chemists, Photog. Soc. Am., Internat. Brotherhood Magicians. Roman Catholic. Home: 29844 Wagner Dr Warren MI 48093-8635 E-mail: ckdeak@aol.com.

DEAK, ISTVAN, historian, educator; b. Szekesfehervar, Hungary, May 11, 1926; came to U.S., 1956, naturalized, 1962; s. Istvan and Anna (Timar) D.; m. Gloria Gilda Alfano, July 4, 1959; 1 dau., Eva., U. Budapest, 1945-48; student, Sorbonne, 1950-51, U. Md., Munich, W. Ger., 1953-55; MA, Columbia U., 1958, PhD, 1964. Journalist, librarian and bookseller, Budapest, Paris and Munich, 1945-56; instr. history Smith Coll., 1962-63; mem. faculty Columbia U., 1963—, prof. history, 1973-93, Seth Low prof. History, 1993-97, emeritus prof., 1997—. Mem. Inst. Advanced Study, Princeton, N.J., fall 1981; pres. Conf. on Slavic and East European History, 1985. Author: Weimar Germany's Left-Wing Intellectuals: A Political History of the Weltbühne and Its Circle, 1968, The Lawful Revolution: Louis Kossuth and the Hungarians, 1848-1849, 1979, Hungarian edit., 1983, 2d edit., 1994, German edit., 1989, Beyond Nationalism: A Social and Political History of the Habsburg Officer Corps, 1848-1918, 1990, German edit., 1991, 2d edit., 1995, Hungarian edit., 1993, Italian edit., 1994, Essays on Hitler's Europe, 2001, Hungarian edit., 2003; co-editor: Eastern Europe in the 1970's, 1972, Everyman in Europe: Essays in Social History, 2 vols., 2d edit., 1981, 3d edit., 1989, The Politics of Retribution in Europe: World War II and its Aftermath, 2000. Recipient Lionel Trilling Book award Columbia U., 1979 George Washington award Hungarian-Am. Assn., 1999; German Acad. exch. fellow, 1960-61; Guggenheim fellow, 1970-71; Fulbright-Hays travel fellow, 1973, 84-85; fellow Woodrow Wilson Ctr. for Scholars, Washington, 1985 Mem. Hungarian Acad. Scis., Am. Hist. Assn., Am. Assn. Advancement Slavic Studies (Wayne S. Vuchinich Book prize). Home: 410 Riverside Dr New York NY 10025-7974 Office: Columbia U 1209 B Internat Affairs Bldg New York NY 10027

DEAKIN, JAMES, writer, former newspaperman; b. St. Louis, Dec. 3, 1929; s. Rogers and Dorothy (Jeffrey) D.; m. Doris Marie Kanter, Apr. 14, 1956; 1 son, David Andrew. AB, Washington U., St. Louis, 1951. Mem. staff St. Louis Post-Dispatch, 1951-81, Washington corr., 1953-80, White House corr., 1955-80; adj. assoc. prof. journalism George Washington U., 1981-87. Fellow Woodrow Wilson Internat. Ctr. for Scholars, 1980-81 Author: The Lobbyists, 1966, Lyndon Johnson's Credibility Gap, 1968, Straight Stuff, 1984, A Grave for Bobby, 1990; co-author: Smiling Through the Apocalypse, 1971, The Presidency and The Press, 1976, The American Presidency, Principles and Problems, vol. II, 1983, The White House Press on the Presidency, 1983; contbr. numerous articles to mags. Recipient Disting. Alumnus citation Washington U., 1973, Merriman Smith award for White House reporting, 1977; Markle Found. grantee, 1981 Mem. White House Corrs. Assn. (pres. 1974-75) Home and Office: 4 Burr Ave Barrington RI 02806-4205

DEAKTOR, DARRYL BARNETT, lawyer; b. Pitts., Feb. 2, 1942; s. Harry and Edith (Barnett) D.; children: Rachael Alexandra, Hallie Sarah. BA, Brandeis U., 1963; LLB, U. Pa., 1966; MBA, Columbia U., 1968. Bar: Pa. 1966, Fla. 1980, N.Y. 1980. Assoc. firm Goodis, Greenfield & Mann, Phila., 1968-70, ptnr., 1971; gen. counsel Life of Pa. Fin. Corp., Phila., 1972; asst. prof. U. Fla. Coll. Law, Gainesville, 1972-74, assoc. prof., 1974-80; with Mershon, Sawyer, Johnston, Dunwody & Cole, Miami, Fla., 1980-81, ptnr., 1981-84, Walker Ellis Gragg & Deaktor, Miami, 1984-86, White & Case LLP, Miami, 1987-95, White & Case LLC, Johannesburg, 1995-2000, Palo Alto, Calif., 2000—01, ret. ptnr., 2002—. Mem. Dist. III (Fla.) Human Rights Advocacy Com. for Mentally Retarded Citizens, 1974-78, chmn., 1978-80; mem. adv. bd. Childbirth Edn. Assn. Alachua County, Fla., 1974-80; mem. resource devel. bd. Mailman Ctr. for Child Devel., 1981-88. Mem. Fla. Bar. Mailing: 5216 Sunshine Canyon Dr Boulder CO 80302-8753

DEAKYNE, WILLIAM JOHN, library director, musician; b. Harrisburg, Pa., June 25, 1936; s. William John and Hazel (Brown) D. MusB, U. Hartford, 1961; MLS, Villanova U., 1962; Diploma in French, Berlitz Sch., Phila., Stamford, Conn., 1967, 69. Cert. libr., N.J., Mass., N.Y., Wash. Dir. Meuser Meml. Libr., Easton, Pa., 1962-64; dir. Coyle Free Libr., Chambersburg, Pa., 1964-65, Free Libr. Springfield Twp., Phila., 1965-68, Darien (Conn.) Libr., 1968-78, East Lyme (Conn.) Libr., 1979—. Founding mem. Libraries-on-Line, Inc., 1983. Organist, pianist (composed Jeu de Clochette, 1964); contbr. articles to profl. jours. V.p. East Lyme C. of C., Niantic, Conn., 1985; founding mem. Librs. on Line, 1983; mem. Am. Cathedral of the Holy Trinity, Paris, 1998—; charter mem. Founders Planned Giving Soc., U. Hartford, 1996—. Mem. ALA (del. to Internat. Fedn. Libr. Assn. meetings Chgo., Copenhagen 1969), Les Amis de Vielles Maisons. Democrat. Avocation: promoting English pipe organs in the U.S., restoration of pipe organs in France. Home: Westchester Dr East Lyme CT 06333 Office: East Lyme Pub Libr 39 Society Rd Niantic CT 06357-1100

DEAL, CHARLES RAYMOND, anesthesiologist; b. St. Petersburg, Fla., Jan. 30, 1932; s. Louis Calvin and Katherine Estes (Benton) D.; m. Rose Maxine Michalove, Dec. 29, 1960; children: Charles Raymond Jr., James Michael. BS in Pharmacy, U. Fla., 1953; MD, U. Miami (Fla.), 1969. Diplomate Am. Bd. Anesthesiology. Intern Jackson Meml. Hosp., Miami, 1969-70, resident in Anesthesiology, 1970-72; pvt. practice Tallahassee, Fla., 1972—. Fellow Am. Coll. Anesthesiologists; mem. Am. Soc. Anesthesiologists, Captial Med. Soc., Fla. Med. Soc., Fla. Soc. Anesthesiologists. Office: 2173 Centerville Pl Tallahassee FL 32308-4356

DEAL, ERNEST LINWOOD, JR., banker; b. Florence, Ala., Jan. 5, 1929; s. Ernest Linwood and Nell W. (Willingham) D.; m. Mary Cooper, Dec. 27, 1952; children: Theresa Lynn, Sarah Street, Matthew Cooper, Jennifer Willingham. Student, Florence State Coll., 1947-49; BS, U. Ala., 1952; postgrad., Southwestern Grad. Sch. Banking, So. Meth. U., 1961. V.p. Tex. Commerce Bank, Houston, 1956-65; sr. v.p. Capital Nat. Bank, Houston, 1965-71; pres., CEO Fannin Bank, Houston, 1971-82, chmn., CEO, 1982; chmn., chief exec. officer InterFirst Bank, Houston, 1983, First City Nat. Bank (name changed to First City Tex.), Houston, 1984-88; sr. chmn. First City Tex., Dallas, 1988-91, chmn. bd. dirs., pres., CEO Austin, 1991-92; chmn. adv. bd. Frost Nat. Bank-Austin, 1993—. Bd. dirs. Houston Trust Co. Bd. visitors M.D. Anderson Hosp., Houston, 1971—; bd. dirs. Phi Gamma Delta Ednl. Found., 1996—; past chmn. Houston Pks. Bd., Houston Aviation Com.; chmn. local organizing com. U.S. Olympic Festival, 1986; Tex. state chmn. U.S. Olympic Com., 1989-93, S.W. regional chmn., 1993—, nat. fin. com.; past chmn. bd. trustees, life trustee Kinkaid Sch.; trustee Southwestern Grad. Sch. Banking. Lt. USNR, 1952-55. Mem. U. Ala. Alumni Assn., Houston C. of C. (bd. dirs., exec. com.), Am. Bankers Assn. (governing coun., state v.p., govt. rels. coun. 1977-82, v.p. 1978-79), Tex. Bankers Assn. (bd. dirs.), Assn. Res. City Bankers (chmn. golf com.), Houston Country Club, Preston Trail Golf Club (Dallas), Austin Country Club, Phi Gamma Delta (bd. trustees 1990-96), Delta Sigma Pi, Omicron Delta Kappa, Phi Kappa Delta (bd. trustees 1996—). Republican. Presbyterian. Office: Frost Nat Bank-Austin PO Box 1727 816 Congress Ave Austin TX 78701-2442

DEAL, GORDON RICHARD, music educator, musician, real estate agent; b. Chgo., ., Nov. 17, 1959; s. Gordon R. Deal, Sr. and Edna J. Deal; m. Deborah A. Pisha, Apr. 10, 1964; 1 child, Carolyn G. MusB, Am. Conservatory Music, Chgo., 1981; MusM, Sherwood Conservatory Music, Chgo., 1985. Studio piano tchr. D & G Music Co., Joliet, Ill., 1976—, concert pianist, 1985—; adj. piano faculty Moody Bible Inst., Chgo., 1999—. Mgr. Majestic Pets, Inc., Evergreen Park, Ill., 1975—94; min. music Oak Lawn (Ill.) Alliance Ch., Oak Lawn, Ill., 1981—85; real estate salesperson Coldwell Banker Honig-Bell, Joliet, Ill., 2001—. Musician: (musical arrangements) Majestic Piano Praise. Recipient Gt. SW Piano Masters Competition, Moraine Valley C.C., 1985. Mem.: Music Tchrs. Nat. Assn., Ill. State Music Tchrs. Assn., Joliet Music Tchrs. Assn. (sec. 1999—2001). R-Consevative. Avocations: photography, hiking, golf. Personal E-mail: richard@richarddeal.com.

DEAL, JOSEPH MAURICE, academic administrator, art educator, photographer; b. Topeka, Aug. 12, 1947; s. Percy Harold and Laura Jean (Close) D.; m. Christine Adkin Bertelson, Aug. 8, 1981 (div. 1987); 1 child, Meredith Ivy; m. Betsy Sara Ruppa, July 20, 1991. BFA, Kansas City Art Inst., 1970; MA, U. N.Mex., 1975; MFA, U. N. Mex., 1978. Dir. exhbns. Internat. Mus. Photography at George Eastman House, Rochester, N.Y., 1975-76; prof. art U. Calif., Riverside, 1976-89, assoc. dean, 1986-89; dean Sch. Art Washington U., St. Louis, 1989-99; provost R.I. Sch. Design, Providence, 1999—. Mem. overview panel visual arts program Nat. Endowment for Arts, Washington, 1990-93, panel chair, 1992-93. Subject of book: Joe Deal: Southern California Photographs 1976-86, 1992, Between Nature and Culture, Photographs of the Getty Center by Joe Deal, 1999. Fellow Nat. Endowment for the Arts, 1977, 80, John Simon Guggenheim Found., 1983. Mem. Coll. Art Assn. (sec. bd. dirs. 1997—). Office: Rhode Island School Design 2 College St Providence RI 02903-2717 E-mail: jdeal@risd.edu.

DEAL, KEVIN PAUL, furniture designer; b. Chg., Oct. 3, 1956; s. Paul Sydney Deal and Bernice Lorraine Chowning-Deal; m. Nancy Kaye Ream, Oct. 1, 1988 (div. Jan. 1993); 1 child, Veronica Victoria. AS in fire sci., Crafton Hills Coll., 1997, AS in emergency med. svc., 1998. Owner Wood Dr., San Diego, 1984—90; owner, furniture repair Wood Magic, Riverside, 1990—2003; firefighter, EMT Riverside County Fire Dept., Calif., 1994—99; owner Deal Aviation, Riverside, 2002—03. Scholarship chmn. San Diego Fine Woodworkers, 1987—90. Designer (aviation design) SPAD 13 Drawings, 2002; author: (paper) UR, Home of the Ziggurat, 1997. Mem.: Smithsonian Inst., Nat. Geographic Soc., Exptl. Aircraft Assn., Archeol. Inst. of Am., Valley Coll. Fencing Club, Alpha Gamma Sigma (life). Roman Catholic. Achievements include invention of mini sander, 2002. Avocations: archaeology, history, archery, sailing, swordsmith. Office: Kevin Deal P O Box 701 Riverside CA 92502

DEAL, NATHAN J. congressman, lawyer; b. Millen, Ga., Aug. 25, 1942; m. Sandra Dunagan; children: Jason, Mary Emily, Carrie, Katie. BA, Mercer U., 1964, JD, 1966. Atty., 1968—; asst. dist. atty. N.E. cir. Hall County, Ga., 1970-71, judge, juvenile court, 1971-72; mem. Ga. State Senate, 1981—93, pres. pro tempore, 1991—93; mem. U.S. Congress from 10th Ga. Dist., 1993—. Mem. com. on commerce, subcoms. on energy and power, telecomm. and fin., commerce, trade and hazardous materials. Capt. JAGC, U.S. Army, 1966-68. Republican. Office: US Ho Reps 2437 Rayburn Hob Washington DC 20515-1009*

DEAL, TIMOTHY, association executive, former diplomat; b. St. Louis, Sept. 17, 1940; s. Edward F. and Loretta (Fuemuller) D.; m. Jill Brady, Sept. 5, 1964; children; Christopher, Bart. BA, U. Calif., Berkeley, 1962; postgrad., San Francisco State Coll., 1964-65, Am. U., 1972-73. With Am. Embassy, Tegucigalpa, Honduras, 1966-68, Warsaw, Poland, 1969-72, econ. counselor London, 1981-85; various fgn. svcs. assignments Dept. State, Washington, 1972-76; sr. staff mem. NSC, The White House, Washington, 1976-81; dep. U.S. rep. to U.S. Mission to OECD, Paris, 1985-88; dir. office Ea. European/Yugoslav affairs Dept. State, 1988-89; spl. asst. to pres. for nat. security affairs NSC, The White House, 1989-92; minister, dept. chief of mission Am. Embassy, London, 1992-96; ret., 1996; sr. v.p. U.S. Coun. for Internat. Bus., Washington, 1996—. Bd. dirs. Banner Life Ins. Co., William Penn Life Ins. Co., Legal and Gen. Am. Capt. U.S. Army, 1963-65. Avocations: theater, cinema, sports. Home: 5721 Macarthur Blvd NW Washington DC 20016-5304 Office: 1030 15th St NW Ste 800 Washington DC 20005-2633

DEAL, WILLIAM BROWN, physician, educator, author, medical school dean; b. Durham, N.C., Oct. 4, 1936; s. Harold Albert and Louise (Brown) D.; m. April Autrey, May 2, 1998; children: Kimberly Deal Wolpert, Kathleen Louise. AA, Mars Hill Coll., 1956; AB, U. N.C., 1958, MD, 1963. Intern in medicine U. Fla. Hosp., Gainesville, 1963-64, asst. resident, 1966-68, fellow in infectious diseases Gainsville, 1968—69, chief resident, instr. dept. medicine Gainesville, 1969-70; asst. prof. dept. medicine U. Fla., 1970-73, assoc. dean Coll. of Medicine, 1973-77, assoc. prof. dept. cmty. health and family medicine, 1973-75, assoc. prof. dept. medicine, 1973-75, prof., 1975-88, acting dean Coll. of Medicine, 1977-78, dean Coll. of Medicine, v.p. clin. affairs, 1978-88, clin. prof. medicine, 1988—; assoc. dean, prof. medicine U. Ala. Sch. of Medicine, 1991-96, sr. assoc. dean, prof. medicine, 1996-97, dean, 1997—; interim CEO UAB Health Sys., 1998-99; v.p. medicine U. Ala., Birmingham, 2000—. Pres. Maine Med. Ctr. Found., Portland, Maine, 1988—90; asst. to sr. v.p. AMA, 1980; lectr. Northwestern U., 1980; vis. clin. tutor City Hosp. U. Edinburgh, Scotland, 1967; bd. dirs. U. Ala. Health Sys., UAB Health Svcs. Found., Callahan Eye Found. Hosp., UAB Med. West, Children's-Women's Health Sys. Contbr. articles to numerous profl. jours. Fellow: ACP, Royal Soc. Medicine; mem.: AMA (chmn. governing coun. sect. on med. schs. 1986—87, liaison com. on med. edn. 1982—87, exec. com. AAMC 1986—88), Nat. Com. Fgn. Med. Edn./Accreditation, Med. Assn. of the State of Ala., Jefferson County Med. Soc., Nat. Rural Health Assn., Ala. Rural Health Assn., Zool. Soc. of Ala., Noble Order of the Flea, Alpha Omega Alpha (bd. dirs. 1986—95, pres. 1993—95), Beta Theta Pi, Phi Chi. Office: Sch of Med FOT 1203, UAB Birmingham AL 35294-0001

DEAL, WILLIAM THOMAS, school psychologist; b. Dec. 18, 1949; s. Richard Lee and Rheta Lucille (Gerber) D.; m. Paula Nespeca, AUg. 5, 1972. BS, Bowling Green State U., 1972; MA, John Carroll U., 1977; postgrad., Kent State U., 1979—. Sci. tchr. Westlake Schs., 1972-76; intern sch. psychologist Garfield Heights Schs., 1976-77; sch. psychologist, 1977—; pvt. practice psychology, 1982-84. Alternate mem. adv. council Cuyahoga COunty Spl. Edn. Svc. Ctr., 1977—. Recipient Cert. of Recognition, Garfield Heights Bd. Edn., 1980; Outstanding Achievement award Cleve. Assn. for Children with Learning Disabilities, Inc., 1980; named Psychologist of Yr., Cleveland Sch., 1990. Mem. Nat. Assn. Sch. Psychologists, United Teaching Profession, Ohio Sch. Psychology Assn., Cleve. Assn. Sch. Psychologists, Phi Delta Kappa. Republican. Methodist. Home: 5290 Kings Hwy Cleveland OH 44126-3059 Office: 4900 Turney Rd Cleveland OH 44125-2501

DE ALESSI, ROSS ALAN, lighting designer; b. San Francisco, Apr. 16, 1955; s. August Eugene De Alessi and Angela Maria (Caredio) Leonard; m. Susan Tracey Stearns, Aug. 11, 1990; 1 child, Chase Arthur. BFA, Stephens Coll., 1978. In-house lighting designer GUMP'S, San Francisco, 1981-84; prin. Ross De Alessi & Assoc., San Francisco, 1984-87, Luminae Lighting Design, San Francisco, 1987-93; prin., co-founder Ross De Alessi Lighting Design, Seattle, 1993—. Works include GUMP'S Christmas Windows, San Francisco (award of Distinction Gen. Electric, 1986, Spl. Citation 1989, Edwin F. Guth award Illuminating Engring. Soc. 1989, 90), TAB Products Showroom, L.A. (award of

Distinction Gen. Electric 1987), St. Augustine's Ch., Pleasanton, Calif. (Sect. award Illuminating Engring. Soc. 1988), L.A. Quinta (Calif.) Resort Plz. Fountains (award of Excellence Gen. Electric 1988, Paul Waterbury award Illuminating Engring. Soc. 1989), McKesson Bldg. Lobby, San Francisco (award of excellence Gen. Electric 1988, Edwin F. Guth award Illuminating Engring. Soc. 1989), Brown & Bain, Phoenix (Merit award Gen. Electric 1989), Saxe Gallery, San Francisco (Edwin F. Guth award Illuminating Engring. Soc. 1989), Plz. Pk., San Jose, Calif. (Paul Waterbury Spl. Citation Illuminating Engring. Soc. 1990), The Palace Fine Arts, San Francisco (Edison Award Gen. Electric 1990, Paul Waterbury award Illuminating Engring. Soc. 1991, award of Excellence Internat. Assn. Lighting Designers 1991), Le Touessrok, Island of Mauritius (Merit award Gen. Electric 1993, Sect. Award Illuminating Engring. Soc. 1994, Paul Waterbury award 1994), St. Patrick's Sem., Menlo Park, Calif. (Edison award Gen. Electric 1993, Edwin F. Guth award Illuminating Engring. Soc. 1994, Citation Internat. Assn. Lighting Designers 1994), Palace of the Lost City, Republic of Boputhatswana (Award of Merit Gen. Electric 1992, Paul Waterbury award Internat. Assn. Lighting Designers 1993), Wells Fargo Bank-Flagship Bank, San Francisco (award of excellence Gen. Electric 1992, Merit award Illuminating Engring. Soc. 1993, citation Internat. Assn. Lighting Designers 1993), Santa Barbara County Courthouse, Santa Barbara (Paul Waterbury award Illuminating Engring. Soc. 1995, award of excellence Internat. Assn. Lighting Designers 1995), City of Bridges, Cleve. (Edison award 1995, Paul Waterbry award Illuminating Engring. Soc. 1997), MGM Grand Gateway of Entertainment, Las Vegas (award of excellence Gen. Elec. 1998, Edwin F. Guth award Illuminating Engring. Soc. 1999, Merit award Internat. Assn. Lighting Designers 1999), Helsinki Master Plan-Esplanade (Edison award 1999, Award of Distinction, Illuminating Engring. Soc. 2000, Merit award Internat. Assn. Lighting Designers), Space Needle (award of excellence Gen. Electric 2000, Illuminating Engring. Soc. 2001, Merit award Internat. Assn. Lighting Designers 2001), Forth Bridge (award of excellence Internat. Assn. Lighting Designers 2002), Montecasino (Merit award Gen. Electric 2001, Sect. award Internat. Assn. Design awards 2002). Mem. Internat. Assn. Lighting Designers (lighting cert.), Nat. Coun. on the Certification Lighting Profls., Illuminating Engring. Soc., Washington Athletic Club. Avocations: scuba diving, traveling. Office: Ross De Alessi Lighting Design 2815 2nd Ave Ste 280 Seattle WA 98121-3217

DEALEY, LYNN TOWNSEND, artist; b. Smithfield, NC, July 16, 1954; d. John Sims and Rebecca Barnes Townsend; m. Russell Edward Dealey, May 4, 1985. BS in Health Edn. cum laude, U. NC, Greensboro, 1976; AS in Advt. Design, Art Inst. Ft. Lauderdale, 1977. Mem. adv. bd. Artreach, Dallas, 1991—92; spkr. in field. Illustrator: A Coon Creek Chronicle, 1992; mural, tiger exhibit Dallas Zoo, 1998. Recipient various awards, recognition for charity work, United Way, U. Tex., Austin, others, 1997—. Mem.: Dallas Country Club, Dallas Social Dir. Avocations: science, biology, cartooning, travel, cooking. Office: PO Box 191406 Dallas TX 75219

DEALY, JOHN MICHAEL, chemical engineer, educator; b. Waterloo, Iowa, Mar. 23, 1937; s. Milton David and Ruth Marion (Dorton) D.; m. Jacqueline Dery, Aug. 22, 1964; 1 child, Pamela. BS, U. Kans., 1958; MS, U. Mich., 1959, PhD, 1963; postdoctoral fellow, 1964. Asst. prof. chem. engring. McGill U., Montreal, Que., Can., 1964-67, assoc. prof., 1967-72, prof., 1972—, chmn. dept., 1993-94; dean engring., 1994-99. Cons. indsl. rheology and polymer processing Author: 4 books on melt rheology and plastics processing; contbr. articles. Fellow: Can. Acad. Engring., Royal Soc. Can., Soc. Plastics Engrs.; mem.: Soc. Rheology (pres. 1987—89), Sigma Xi, Theta Tau, Tau Beta Pi. Home: 315 Roslyn Ave Montreal QC Canada H3Z 2L7 Office: McGill U Chem Engring Dept 3610 University St Montreal QC Canada H3A 2B2 E-mail: john.dealy@mcgill.ca.

DEAMER, MICHAEL LYNN, mayor, lawyer, accountant; b. Aurora, Ill., Apr. 8, 1946; s. Jack C. and Jean A. (Purdie) Deamer; m. Evelyn M. Warren, Sept. 12, 1969; children: Michelle, Tracy, Debbie, Robin, Michael. BA in Acctg., U. Utah, 1970, JD, 1973. CPA Utah; bar: Utah 1973, U.S. Ct. Appeals (9th and 10th cirs.), U.S. Tax Ct. 1973, U.S. Supreme Ct. 1976. Asst. atty. gen. State of Utah, Salt Lake City, 1974-76, chief dep. atty. gen., 1976-80; ptnr. Randle Deamer & Lee PC, Salt Lake City, 1980—2002; mayor of Centerville, Utah, 2002—. Adj. prof. mgmt. and bus. law U. Utah, 1983—86. Recipient Silver Beaver award, Boy Scouts Am., 1996. Mem.: Kiwanis (pres. 1995—96, Hixson award). Republican. Office: Randle Deamer & Lee PC 139 E South Temple Ste 330 Salt Lake City UT 84111-1169 E-mail: ulaw@xmission.com.

DE AMORIM, VALDIVIA VÂNIA SIQUEIRA, translator; b. Recife, Brazil, June 17, 1944; d. Francisco Targino and Angelica (Lucas) De Siqueira; m. Jimmie Willis Beauchamp (div. 1970); 1 child, Angélica R. Beauchamp-Ringeisen; m. João Mendonca de Amorim Filho, 2002. BS in Journalism, CEUB, 1978; MA in Portuguese and Spanish Lit., NYU, 1992. Registered profl. journalist. Social comm. sec. Office of Brazilian Presidency, Brasilia, Brazil, 1984-90; Portuguese translator Family Court, N.Y.C., 1993; translator, broker asst. Josephthal Lion & Ross, N.Y.C., 1995, U.S. Securities and Futures, N.Y.C., 1996—99; in flight translator, internat. flight attendent Am. Airlines. Reporter, corr. Revista Aerea, N.Y.C., 1984—; founder, tchr. Lang. Sch. Multi Lingua, Brazil; tchr. Portuguese and Spanish, Sigma Delta Pi, Purdue U., Ind., 1982-84, NYU, 1990-92. Author: Stigma, Saga for a New World, 1000-2003, 2003. Founder literary hour NYU; liberal artist Lafayette Art Mus., 1982-84. Mem. NYU Alumni, C. of C. of the Rockways (exec. dir. 1998). Presbyterian. Avocations: oil painting, piano, horseback riding, boating/fishing.

DEAN, BARTHOLOMEW CRISPIN, anthropology educator; b. London, Dec. 18, 1963; s. Warwick Randal Dean, Stella Keeper Dean; m. Michelle Ann Elizabeth McKinley; children: Maxwell Eric Amauta, Isadora Ursula, Gideon Jack Malachi. PhD, Harvard University, Cambridge MA, 1987—95; M.Phil, Oxford University, Oxford, UK, 1985—87; BA, Washington University, St. Louis, MO, 1982—85. Instr. dept. anthropology Harvard U., Cambridge, Mass., 1994—95; asst. prof. dept. anthropology U. Kans., Lawrence, 1995—2002; co-founder, dir. rsch. Amazonian People''s Resources Initiative (APRI), 1995—2002; coord., foundingf mem. grad. program Amazon studies U. Nacional Mayor San Marcos, Lima, Peru, 1999—2000. Asst. curator U. Kans, Mus. Anthropology, Lawrence, 1995—2002; rev. editor Cultural Survival Quarterly: World Report on the Rights of Indigenous Peoples & Ethnic Minorities, Cambridge, 1995—2002; mem. editl. bd. Amazonía Peruana (Centro Amazónico de Antropología y Aplicacíon Práctica), Lima, 2000—03. Editor: At the Risk of Being Heard: Identity, Indigenous Rights & Postcolonial States., 2003; co-editor: Handbook of Latin American Studies, 1999—2002. Fellow, Royal Anthropological Inst. Gt. Brit. & Ireland, 1998—99, Coldsmiths Coll., U. London. Fellow: Royal Anthropological Institute of Great Britain and Ireland; mem.: American Association of University Professors, Council for Museum Anthropology, Latin American Studies Association, American Ethnological Society, American Anthropological Association. Avocation: travel, book collecting, meditation. Office: University of Kansas Department of Anthropology, 622 Fraser Lawrence KS 66045 Office Fax: 785-864-5224. Business E-Mail: bdean@ukans.edu.

DEAN, BEALE, lawyer; b. Ft. Worth, Feb. 26, 1922; s. Ben J. and Helen (Beale) D.; m. Margaret Ann Webster, Sept. 3, 1948; children: Webster Beale, Giselle Liseanne. BA, U. Tex., Austin, 1943, LLB, 1947. Bar: Tex. 1946, U.S. Dist. Ct. (no., so, we. and ea. dists.), U.S. Cir. Ct. (5th and 11th cirs.) 1952, U.S. Supreme Ct. 1954. Asst. dist. atty., Dallas, 1947-48; assoc. Martin, Moore & Brewster, Ft. Worth, 1948-50; mem. Martin, Moore, Brewster & Dean, 1950-51, Pannell, Dean, Pannell & Kerry (and predecessor firms), 1951-65; ptnr. Brown, Herman, Scott, Young & Dean, Ft. Worth, 1965-71, Brown, Herman, Scott, Dean & Miles, Ft. Worth, 1971-98, Brown, Herman, Dean, Wiseman, Liser & Hart, LLP, Ft. Worth, 1998—2003, sr. counsel, 2003—. Spl. asst. Atty. Gen. Tex., 1959-61. Regent Nat. Coll. Dist. Attys., 1985—. With AUS, 1942-45, ETO. Mem. ABA, Bar Assn. Fifth Fed. Cir., Ft. Worth-Tarrant County Bar Assn. (past pres. 1971-72, Blackstone award 1991), Am. Coll. Trial Lawyers, State Bar Tex. (dir. 1973-75), Am. Bar Found., Tex. Bar Found. (charter mem.), Ft. Worth Boat Club, Ridglea Country Club, Ft. Worth Club. Presbyterian. Office: 200 Ft Worth Club Bldg Fort Worth TX 76102-4905

DEAN, BURTON VICTOR, management educator; b. June 3, 1924; BS, Northwestern U., 1947; MS, Columbia U., 1948; PhD, U. Ill., 1952. Mathematician U.S. Dept. Def., Washington, 1952-55; rsch. mathematician Ops. Rsch., Inc., Silver Spring, Md., 1955-57; prof. ops. rsch. Case Western Res. U., Cleve., 1957-85, chmn. dept., 1965-76, 79-85; prof., chmn. dept. orgn. and mgmt. San Jose (Calif.) State U., 1985—2001, dir. entrepreneurial forum, 1987; dir. Silicon Valley Ctr. for Entrepreneurship, 2002—. Program dir. Vis. Scholars in Orgn. and Mgmt., San Jose State U., 1986-87, Vis. Scholars in Mfg. Mgmt., 1988-89, Total Quality Mgmt. Cert. Program, 1992-98; dir. Entrepreneurial Forum, Sept., 1987, expts. in mfg. Calif. Conf. Tech. Grant, 1989-92, Total Quality Mgmt. Implementation Inst., 1993; rsch. assoc., chair and vice-chair rsch. assocs. policy oversight com. Internat. Inst. Surface Transp. Policy Studies, 1993—, co-dir. Colloquium on Planning for Surface Transportation and Land Use, 1995; dir. Mgmt. Tng. Program Project Divsn. Worker's Compensation Calif. Dept. Indsl. Rels., 1995-96, Tech. Comml. Assistance Project Calif. State U. Inst., 1996; assoc. Inst. Pub. Adminstrn., N.Y.C. and Washington, 1972-79; ops. rsch. assoc. Booz, Allen and Hamilton, Cleve., 1972-79; chmn. adv. bd. Sourcenet Corp., 1986-87; vis. prof. Stanford U., 1985, Israel Inst. Tech., 1962-63, U. Louvain, Belgium, Tel Aviv U., Ben-Gurion U., Israel, 1978; sci. adv. bd. Advanced Bio-Systems, Inc., 1984-85, Applied Imaging Corp., 1987-89, Telecom Inc., 1987-90; vis. scholar U. Calif., Berkeley Haas Sch. Bus., 1993, Stanford U. Sch. Engring., 1993; bd. dirs. Environ. Bus. Cluster; cons. in field; adv. com. No. Calif. Mfg. Extension Ctr., 1994-2001; Workforce Silicon Valley Collaborative Coun., 2000, Santa Clara Valley Mfg. Group, 1995-96; mem. Integrated Water Resources Plan Stakeholder Process Santa Clara Water Dist., 1996-2000; dir. Incubator Without Walls, San Jose State U. Cmty. Outreach Partnership Ctr., 1997-2001; co-gen. chair INFORMS, 2002. Author: Applications of Operations Research in Research and Development, 1963, 2d. edit., 1978, Mathematics of Modern Management, 3d. edit., 1967, Instructor's Manual, 1966, (with others) Industrial Inventory Control, 1972, (with Joel Goldhar) Management of Research and Innovation, 1981, Project Management: Methods and Studies, 1985, (with John Cassidy) Strategic Management: Methods and Studies, 1990, 2d edit., 1991, Japanese edit., 1992; editor Jour. of Bus. Venturing, 1985-93, Jour. of Engring. and Tech. Mgmt., 1989-2001, Prodn. and Ops. Jour., 1990-2000, Studies in Mgmt. Sci. and Systems, 1974—, (books) Textbooks in Operations Research, 1980-84, Studies in Operations Research, 1970-73; assoc. editor Ops. Rsch. Letters, 1981-84, Jour. Ops. Rsch. Soc. India, 1968-74; dept. editor IEEE Trans. on Engring. Mgmt. Dept. Quality, Tech. and Innovation, 1985-98(mgmt. 1999-2002); contbr. articles to profl. jours., chpts. to books. Recipient Centennial scholar medal Case Inst. of Tech., 1981, Outstanding Faculty Rsch. award Coll. of Bus., San Jose State U., 1994. Fellow AAAS (v.p., chmn. indsl. sci. and tech. sect. 1971, 76, chair nominations com. 1997-98); mem. IEEE (vice chmn. seminars 1986-88, founder Cleve. chpt. 1984, editorial bd. 1968-2002, Centennial medal 1984), Am. Prodn. and Inventory Control Soc. (Santa Clara acad. laison 1986-89), Am. Math. Soc., Inst. Mgmt. Scis. (editor Mgmt. Sci. jour. 1970-86, assoc. editor 1990-98, coun. mem. 1973-85, roundtable laiason panel 1983-84), Ops. Rsch. Soc. Am., Inst. Mgmt. Sci., Coll. of Innovation Mgmt. and Entrepreneurship (founder, chmn. 1987-89, coun. 1989-92), Am. Soc. Quality Control (Santa Clara Valley chpt., bd. dirs. 1992-94), Acad. Mgmt., Calif. U. Prodn. and Ops. Mgmt. Soc. (co-founder 1988, v.p./pres.-elect 1991-92, pres. 1992-93, bd. dirs. 1993-96), Calif. Coun. Quality (founder 1991-92), Prodn. and Ops. Mgmt. Soc., Sigma Xi, Beta Gamma Sigma, Omega Rho (founder 1977, hon. ops. rsch., historian 1978-82, exec. com. 1977-82, 84-86, v.p. 1978-80, pres. 1980-82, v.p. mtgs. 1996-97). Office: San Jose State U Bus Coll Dept Orgn & Mgmt San Jose CA 95192-0070 Home: 520 Lowell Ave Palo Alto CA 94301-3815

DEAN, CAROLE LEE, film company executive; b. Dallas, Mar. 23, 1939; d. Roy Webster and Dorothy Lee Dean; children: Richard Dean, Carole Joyce. Student, UCLA. Pres. Studio Film and Tape, L.A., 1969-2000, N.Y.C., 1970-2000, Chgo., 1994=2000, From the Heart Prodn., L.A., 1992—. Prodr., host Health Styles, 1994-97; author: Heal Thyself, 1999, Art of Funding Your Film, 2003. Mem. Nat. Arts Club. Republican. Avocations: skiing, equestrian. E-mail: caroleedean@worldnet.att.net.

DEAN, CHRYSTELL FETTY, women's health nurse, educator; b. Roswell, N.Mex., Jan. 17, 1956; d. Harold Russell and Wanda Jewell (Goldsmith) Fetty; m. Doyle W. Dean (dec. Oct. 1998); children: Merette Whitney, Rigele Wesley. AAS, Rose State Coll., 1979; BSN, U. Cen. Okla., 1981. Cert. breast feeding educator Okla. State Dept. of Health; cert. pediat. advanced life support. Staff nurse labor and delivery Okla. Meml. Hosp., Oklahoma City, 1981-84, Norman (Okla.) Regional Hosp., 1983-87, Hillcrest Health Ctr. (name now St. Michael Hosp.), Oklahoma City, 1987—2002; clin. instr. obstetrics ADN program and med.-surg. nursing Oklahoma City C.C., 1992—2002, nurse practitioner, lab cons.; faculty DeMarge Sch. Practical Nursing. Item writer, exam. devel. Nat. Cert. Corp. for Obstet., Gynecol. and Neonatal Nursing Spltys., Chgo., 1992—; panel mem. for item rev. Nat. Coun. Licensure Exam., 1994; presenter in field; author, presenter test item constrn. and evaluation faculty Oklahoma City C.C.; prof. nursing Rose State Coll., Midwest City, Okla., 2002—. Mem. Okla. Inst. for Child Adv., Oklahoma City, 1989—. Mem. Assn. Women's Health, Obstetrics and Neonatal Nurses (cert.), Nat. Cert. Corp. (cert. in-patient obstetrics). Avocation: travel. Home: 2408 SW 111th St Oklahoma City OK 73170-3246 E-mail: cdean@rose.edu.

DEAN, DAVID ALLEN, lawyer; b. Chattanooga, Tenn., Jan. 14, 1948; s. William Berry and Elizabeth (Connor) D.; 1 child, Hillary Diane. BBA, So. Meth. U., 1969; JD, U. Tex.-Austin, 1973. Bar: Tex. 1973. Asst. dir. Tex. Office Comprehensive Health Planning, Austin, 1973; adminstrv. asst. Gov. Tex., Austin, 1974; legal counsel Gov. Briscoe, State of Tex., Austin, 1975-78, to Gov. Clements, 1979-81; sec. state State of Tex., Austin, 1981-83; ptnr. Winstead, McGuire, Sechrest & Minick, Dallas, (now Winstead, Sechrest & Minick) 1983-93, chmn. pub. law sect., PAC com., bus. devel. com., also bd. dirs., 1994—; shareholder David A. Dean & Assocs., P.C., Dallas, 1994—; pres. Transp. Strategies, Inc., Dallas; pres., CEO Dean Internat., Inc., Dallas, 1994—, Innovative Transp. Strategies, Dallas, 1994—; lectr. in field. Editor: Texas Campaign and Financial Disclosure Manual, 1984; Election Study of Fifty States, 1982. Author: Gubernatorial Parole Policies, 1980. Contbr. articles to Tex. Bus. and Comml. Quar., 1981-83, Dallas Bus. and Profl. Rev. Exec. dir. Gov.'s Criminal Justice Div., Austin, 1980-81, Crime Stoppers Adv. Council, 1979-81; chmn. State Fed. Voter Fraud Task Force, 1982; chmn. Gov.'s Task Force on Health and Human Services, 1975-79, Nat. Gov.'s Health Consortium, 1977-78; trustee Dean Learning Ctr., Dallas, 1970—, mem. exec. com., chmn. nominating com., 1970—; bd. dirs. Girlstown U.S.A., 1973-85, Greater Dallas Crime Commn., 1983—, chmn., 1985-88, former mem. exec. com., past chmn. legis. com.; mem. Interstate Oil Compact Commn., Austin, 1979-83, State Bd. Canvassers, Austin, 1981-83; mem. spl. interim com. Criminal Justice System Tex., Austin, 1981; co-chmn., mem., chmn. subcom. pub. disclosure, polit. funds, and lobby regulations Pub. Servant Stds. Conduct Adv. Com., Austin, 1981-83; v.p., mem. Dallas Challenge Task Force, bd. dirs., 1983-88, mem. exec. com., 1983-88; mem. long-range planning com. St. Mark's Sch. Tex., Dallas, 1983-84; mem. exec. com. bd. dirs., chair pub. policy Nat. Crime Prevention Coun., Washington, 1984—; co-chmn., chmn. legis. com., mem. exec. com. Mayor's Criminal Justice Task Force, City of Dallas, 1985-88; mem. Greater Dallas Ahead, Inc., 1985-86, U.S Marshall Selection Com., 1986-87; mem. exec. com. Tex. Criminal Justice Task Force, Austin, 1986-90, vice-chmn., chmn. legis. com., 1986-90; mem. Citizen's Adv. Com. Long-Range Water Supply Study, City of Dallas, 1988-90; mem. Task Force Pub. Utility Regulation, State of Tex., Austin, 1989-90; mem. adv. bd. Dallas United, 1990-92; commr. Pres.'s Commn. Model State Drug Laws, Washington, 1992-93; co-chair Dallas host com. N.Am. Free Trade Agreement Negotiations, 1992; subcom. chmn. fin. com. Ursuline Acad. Dallas, 1992—, mem. bd. of dad's club, 1992—; co-chmn. Dallas Meml. Ctr. Holocaust Studies, Dallas, 1993; mem. mktg. com. Dallas/Ft. Worth Internat. Airport, 1994—; trustee Meth. Med. Ctr., Dallas, 1992, mem. quality rev. com., 1992, mem. long range planning com., 1992; bd. dirs. Swiss Ave. Ctr. Pastoral Care and Family Counseling, Dallas, 1983-88, Cotton Bowl Coun., Dallas, 1984-89, Tex. Bus. Hall of Fame, Dallas, 1988-90, Dallas Summer Musicals, 1992, Nat. Alliance Model State Drug Laws, 1993, mem. exec. com., 1993; sec. bd. dirs. St. Paul Hosp. Found., Dallas, 1985-88. Served with Tex. Air N.G., 1975. Recipient Spl. Recognition award Dallas City Coun., Mayor of Dallas, 1992. Mem. Am. Prosecutors Rsch. Inst., Tex. Bar Assn. (mem., chmn. spl. com. study Tex. election laws 1982-83), ABA, Dallas Bar Assn., Ctrl. Dallas Assn. (mem. exec. com. bd. dirs., mem. govtl. and legal affairs com.), Ducks Unltd., Am. Quarter Horse Assn., Greater Dallas C. of C. (chmn. N.Am. Free Trade Agreement initiatives, former chmn. pub. affairs divsn., past chmn. state govtl. affairs com., former bd. dirs., past mem. exec. com.), U. Tex. Ex-Students Assn. (life), Sigma Alpha Epsilon. Methodist. Clubs: Idlewild, Terpsichorean, Rainbo lake, Tower, Salesmanship Club (Dallas). Office: David A Dean & Assocs PC 8080 Park Ln Ste 600 Dallas TX 75231-5911

DEAN, DENNIS RICHARD, language educator; b. Belvidere, Ill., May 29, 1938; s. Edwin Wendell and Ruth Alden Dean; m. Susan Thach, June 15, 1968 (div. June 1985). AB in English, Stanford U., 1960, AM in English, 1962; PhD in English, U. Wis., 1968. Prof. English and humanities U. Wis. Parkside, Kenosha, 1967-92; vis. rsch. prof. Istanbul (Turkey) Tech. U., 1993-94; ind. scholar, 1995—. Sr. Fulbright lectr. Chonnam Nat. U., Kwangju, Korea, 1977. Author: James Hutton and the History of Geology, 1992, Gideon Algernon Mantell: A Bibliography with Essays, 1998, Gideon Mantell and the Discovery of Dinosaurs, 1999 (transl. into Japanese 2000); contbr. articles to profl. jours. With U.S. Army, 1962-64. Recipient History of Geology award, Geol. Soc. Am., 2002. Fellow Geol. Soc. London, Edinburgh Geol. Soc.; mem. History of Sci. Soc., Brit. Soc. History of Sci., Hist. of Earth Scis. Soc. (counsellor 1999-2000). Avocations: reading, collecting, travel. Home: 834 Washington St Evanston IL 60202

DEAN, DORSEY EDWARD, retired engineer; b. Akron, Ohio, Apr. 14, 1927; s. Clark Bolin and Cohen Lulu (Talbott) D.; m. Marian Louise Johns, Dec. 20, 1947; children: Linda Suzanne, Richard Thomas, Sheri Lynn, James Edward. BS with distinction, U. Akron, 1949. Registered profl. engr., Calif. Statis. quality control mgr. N.Am. tire plants Firestone Tire and Rubber Co., Akron, 1949-58; sr. quality/reliability engr. Canaveral ops. Martin Co., Cape Canaveral, Fla., 1958-60; rsch. mathematician RCA Internat. Missile Test Project, Patrick AFB, Fla., 1960-70; sr. quality engr., quality supr. Gen. Dynamics Space Sys. Divsn., Cape Canaveral, 1971-89; ret. Chmn. quality control and mgmt. adv. com. Brevard C.C., Cocoa, Fla., 1969-77; advisor Space Congress, Cocoa Beach, Fla., 1985-97. Author: (booklet) Firestone Quality, 1956. Pres. Convair Mgmt. Assn., Cape Canaveral, 1978; v.p. Merritt Towers Condo. Assn., Merritt Island, Fla., 1997—. With USN, 1945-46. Recipient Engr. of Yr. award Fla. Engring. Soc., 2000. Fellow Am. Soc. Quality (cert. quality engr., cert. reliability engr., nat. bd. dirs. 1967-71, regional exec. dir. 1968-71, chmn. Cape Canaveral sect. 1977-78), Canaveral Coun. Tech. Socs. (chmn. 1984, 96, Engr. of Yr. 2000). Republican. Presbyterian. Achievements include development of statistical quality control and reliability engineering techniques in the tire, space, photographic, electronic and computer industries. Home: 300 S Sykes Creek Pkwy # 806 Merritt Island FL 32952-3324 E-mail: dorseydean@juno.com.

DEAN, DOUG, state representative; Mem. Colo. Gen. Assembly, speaker of the house, 2000—. Office: 200 E Colfax Rm 246 Denver CO 80203 E-mail: dougdean1@aol.com.

DEAN, EDWIN BECTON, entrepreneur; b. Danville, Va., Feb. 7, 1940; s. Edwin Becton and Lois (Campbell) D.; m. Deirdre Anne Jacovides, Aug. 16, 1964; children: Jennifer E., Kristin R., Brian N. BS in Physics, Va. Poly. Inst. and State U., 1963, MS in Math., 1965; postgrad., George Washington U., 1974-77; cert. profl. study engring. mgmt., Old Dominion U., 1998. Technician, assoc. engr. Johns Hopkins U. Applied Physics Lab., Laurel, Md., 1959-64; physicist, mathematician, electronic engr., and ops. rsch. analyst Naval Surface Warfare Ctr., Silver Spring, Md., 1964-79; owner, mgr. Gen. Bus. Svcs. and Beta Systems, Virginia Beach, Va., 1979-84, Virginia Beach Communique Inc., Virginia Beach, Va., 1980-81; registered rep. First Investors Corp., Arlington, Va., 1971-85; dir. Tips Club of Virginia Beach, Inc., 1980-82; computer specialist Naval Supply Systems Command, Norfolk, Va., 1982-83; head cost estimating office NASA Langley Rsch. Ctr., Hampton, Va., 1983-90, tech. resource mgr. Space Exploration Initiative Office, 1990-94, sr. rsch. engr. multidisciplinary optimization br., 1994-98; owner The DFV Group, Virginia Beach, Va., 1996-98; pres. The DFV Group, Inc., Virginia Beach, 1999—2002. Presenter in field. Contbr. articles to profl. jours. NASA fellow, 1963-65. Mem. IEEE, Assn. for Computing Machinery, Internat. Soc. Parametric Analysts (past chmn. bd. dirs.), Am. Soc. for Quality Control, Am. Assn. Cost Engrs., Internat. Neural Network Soc., Am. Math. Soc., QFD Inst., Sigma Pi Sigma, Pi Mu Epsilon, Phi Kappa Phi. E-mail: tradermax@att.net.

DEAN, EDWIN ROBINSON, economist, educator, consultant; b. South Bend, Ind., July 25, 1933; s. William Stover and Eleanor (Hatcher) D.; m. Emily Rebecca Finlay, Feb. 2, 1963; children: Gabrielle N., Natalie R. BA in Philosophy magna cum laude, Yale U., 1955; postgrad., Gokhale Inst. Politics-Econs., Poona, India, 1955-56; PhD in Econs., Columbia U., 1963. Instr., then asst. prof. econs. Columbia U., N.Y.C., 1960-68; assoc. prof. Queens Coll., CUNY, 1968-72; program dir. Am. Friends Svc. Com., N.Y.C., 1970-73; supervisory equal opportunity specialist in econs. U.S. Commn. on Civil Rights, 1973-80; sr. assoc. Nat. Inst. Edn., Washington, 1980-83, acting asst. dir., 1983; supervisory economist Bur. Labor Stats., Washington, 1983-85, chief div. productivity rsch., 1985-89, assoc. commr. Office Productivity and Tech., 1989-99, ret., 1999; adj. prof. econs. George Wash. U., Washington, 2000—. Cons. to World Bank, 2001-03; mem. exec. com. Conf. Rsch. Income and Wealth, 1994-2000; chair working party industry stats. OECD, 1998-2000. Author: The Supply Responses of African Farmers: Theory and Measurement in Malawi, 1966, Plan Implementation in Nigeria, 1962-66, 1972; contbg. author: The Challenge Ahead: Equal Opportunity in Referral Unions, 1976, Non-referral Unions and Equal Employment Opportunity, 1982; editor: The Controversy over the Quantity Theory of Money, 1965, Education and Economic Productivity, 1984; contbr. articles to profl. jours. Recipient Julius Shiskin award, Nat. Assn. Bus. Econs., 2000; fellow Howland travel fellow, Yale U., 1955, Seager fellow in econs., 1956, 1957, William Bayard Cutting travel fellow, Columbia U., 1958, NSF, 1961—62; grantee rsch., Columbia U. Coun. for Rsch. in Social Scis., 1964, Rockefeller Found., Ibadan, Nigeria, U.S., 1965—67; scholar, Yale U., 1951—55. Mem.: Am. Econ. Assn. Unitarian Universalist.

DEAN, GARY NEAL, artist, architect; b. Alexandria, Va., Sept. 19, 1953; s. Louie Franklin Dean. BS in Architecture, U. Ill., 1977. Registered architect, Calif., Tex., Ill., N.Y., Fla., Vt., N.C., Wis., Iowa, Ark, Ga., Md.; cert. Nat. Coun. Archtl. Registration Bds.; registered interior designer, Ill., Tex. Designer, draftsman SRGF, Inc. Architects, Springfield, Ill., 1977-79; project mgr. Sarti-Huff Archtl. Group, Inc., Springfield, 1979-82; architect Henningson, Durham & Richardson, Inc., Dallas, 1982-84; prodn. mgr. Bogard, Guthrie & Ptnrs., Inc., Dallas, 1984-85; mgr., project architect Archtl. Designers, Inc., Dallas, 1985-87; pvt. practice architecture Dallas, 1987—; prin. Kaiser Gochnauer Ltd., 1987—; v.p., ptnr. Designhaus, Inc., 1989-94; project dir. Hard Rock Cafe Internat., Inc., Orlando, Fla., 1994—; pvt. practice Orlando, 1995—; prin. Gary N. Dean, Arch. V.p., ptnr. Designhaus, Inc., 1989-94; project dir. Hard Rock Cafe Internat., Inc., Orlando, Fla., 1994-95; project mgr. Sverdrup Facilities, Inc., 1997-2002. Prin. works include State of Ill. Capitol, LaCima Club, Las Colinas, Tex., Hackberry Creek Country Club, Las Colinas, Renaissance Club, Phoenix, Creve Coeur Club, Peoria, Ill., Millennium, Hard Rock Cafe Retail Store, N.Y.C., Hard Rock Cafe, Singapore, Atlanta, Miami, Fla., Madrid, Nashville, San Antonio, N.Y.C., Copenhagen, Myrtle Beach, S.C., Taipei, China, Seoul, Korea, Walt Disney World Epcot Millennium World Communities Pavilion & Events Facility, MGM Icon Hat & Hand, MGM One Man's Dream. Home: 4232 Winderlakes Dr Orlando FL 32835

DEAN, GEOFFREY, book publisher; b. Newcastle-upon-Tyne, Eng., Sept. 18, 1940; s. Thomas Craig and Mildred Catherine (Hoggard) D.; m. Philma Marina Patterson, Aug. 10, 1963; children: Andrea Samantha, Christopher Michael. BA, U. Toronto, 1961. With McGraw-Hill Co. Can. Ltd., 1961-66, coll. editor, 1962-66; sales mgr. Methuen Publs., Toronto, 1966-70; v.p. mktg. Van Nostrand Reinhold Ltd., Toronto, 1970-76; pres., dir. John Wiley & Sons. Can. Ltd., Toronto, 1976-86; cons. Geoffrey Dean Enterprises, 1986—; pres. Tech. Instrnl. Products Inc., 1987-88, Scriptographic Communications Ltd., Toronto, 1989-91. Dir. Youth Employment Svc., Toronto, 1995-2000; mem. adv. bd. on sci. pub. Nat. Rsch. Coun. Can., 1982-84; chmn. Book and Periodical Coun., 1988-89; mem. project assessment com. Book Pub. Industry Devel. Program, Govt. Can., 1987-91; internat. cons. Dept. of Edn., Rep. of Philippines, 1996-97. Bd. dirs. Can. Diabetes Assn., 1987-89. Mem. Can. Book Pubs. Coun. (pres. 1983), Ont. Bus. Edn. Assn. (hon. pres. 1982-84), Rotary. Home and Office: 801-75 Wynford Heights Cr Toronto ON Canada M3C 3H9

DEAN, GEORGE ALDEN, advertising executive; b. Chgo., June 2, 1929; s. George Abiathar and Velma Clio (Shields) D.; children: George Alden, Diane Flach; m. Jane Kentnor Pratt, Apr. 12, 1975. BA, Princeton U., 1952; MBA, Harvard U., 1956. With DFS, Dorland Worldwide Inc., N.Y.C., 1956—, mgmt. supr., 1970—, exec. v.p., 1968-88. Co-chair Women's Campaign Sch., Yale U. Sch. Law. Bd. dirs. United Home Care, Women's Campaign Fund, 1993—, Shubert Theatre, Conn. Coalition Against Gun Violence, UNIFEM Conn., 2000--; fin. chmn. Mauwehu coun. Boy Scouts Am., 1968-73; bd. visitors Babcock Sch. Wake Forest U.; founder 50/50 by 2000; trustee YWCA, Bridgeport. Decorated Bronze Star. Episcopalian. Home: Southport, Conn. Died Jan. 10, 2003.

DEAN, H. CLARK, retired civil engineer, professional genealogist; b. Evanston, Ill., Jan. 22, 1931; s. Herbert Franklin and E(lla) Frances (Clark) D.; m. Mary Margaret McHugh, Aug. 20, 1960; children: Merrick Stephen McHugh, Nancy Lauck Dean Cacioppo. BSCE, Swarthmore Coll., 1953; MBA, U. Chgo., 1964. Registered profl. engr., Pa.; registered structural engr., Ill.; cert. genealogist Bd. for Cert. Genealogists. Engr. Pratt & Whitney, East Hartford, Conn., 1954; jr. engr. Modjeski & Masters, Harrisburg, Pa., 1954, engr., 1956-61, Harza Engring. Co., Chgo., 1961-67, asst. to v.p., 1967-72, asst. project mgr., 1972-74, project mgr., 1974-76, asst. dept. head, 1976-80, dept. head, 1980-97; ret., 1997. Contbr. articles to geneal. publs., including Am. Genealogist., Nat. Geneal. Soc. Quar., New Eng. Hist. and Geneal. Register, N.Y. Geneal. and Biog. Record. With C.E., U.S. Army, 1955-56. Mem. ASCE (life), New Eng. Hist. and Geneal. Soc., Nat. Geneal. Soc., Soc. Mayflower Descs. in Ill. (treas. 1967-70, bd. assts., 1990-98, gov. 1998-2001), Order Founders and Patriots Am., Ill. Soc. War of 1812, Assn. Profl. Genealogists, North Suburban Geneal. Soc. (pres. 1976), Sheridan Shore Yacht Club (Wilmette, Ill.). Avocation: sailing. Home: 422 Kelling Ln Glencoe IL 60022-1113

DEAN, HOWARD, former governor; b. N.Y.C., Nov. 17, 1948; s. Howard Brush and Andrea (Maitland) D.; m. Judith Steinberg; children: Anne, Paul. BA, Yale U., 1971; MD, Albert Einstein Coll. Medicine, 1978. Intern, then resident in internal medicine Med. Ctr. Hosp. Vt., 1978-82; practice medicine specializing in internal medicine Shelburne, Vt.; mem., house edn. com., mcpl. corps. and elections com., rules com. Vt. House of Reps., Montpelier, 1983-86, asst. minority leader, 1985-86; lt. gov. State of Vt., Montpelier, 1986-91, gov., 1991—2003. Asst. clin. prof. medicine U. Vt. Coll. Medicine. Bd. dirs. Vt. Developmental Capabilities Council, U. Vt. Council, Vt. Adv. Commn. Intergovtl. Affairs, Vt. State Bd. Nat. Forests; founder Vt. Youth Conservation Corps; sponsor Long Trail Preservation Fund. Democrat. Home: 325 S Cove Rd Burlington VT 05401-5447 Office: PO Box 1228 Burlington VT 05402*

DEAN, HOWARD M., JR., food company executive; b. 1937; married. BBA, So. Meth. U., 1960; MBA, Northwestern U., 1961. With Dean Foods Co., Inc., Franklin Park, Ill., 1955—, internal auditor, 1965—68, asst. to v.p. fin., 1968—70, pres., 1970—89, CEO, 1987—, chmn., 1989—. Served to lt. (j.g.) USN, 1962—65. Office: Dean Foods Co 3600 River Rd Franklin Park IL 60131-2185

DEAN, JACK, protective services official; b. Denton, Tex., June 16, 1937; AA, Tyler (Tex.) Jr. Coll.; ed. hwy. patrol program, Tex. Dept. Pub. Safety, 1960. With Tex. Hwy Patrol, Pecos, Tex., 1961-64, Tyler, Tex., 1964-70, Tex. Rangers, McAllen, 1970-74, sgt. Waco, 1974-78, capt. San Antonio, 1978-93; U.S. marshal U.S. Cts., Western dist. Tex., 5th cir., San Antonio, 1994—. Mem. Tex. Ranger Found., Tex. Sheriffs Assn., Masons. Office: Office of US Marshal John H Woods US Courthouse 655 E Durango Blvd San Antonio TX 78206-1100

DEAN, JACK PEARCE, retired insurance company executive; b. Shreveport, La., Aug. 26, 1931; s. James Albert and Nina (Smith) D.; m. Elizabeth Anne Tillman, June 5, 1952; children— Linda Susan Dean Ratchford, Cynthia Anne Dean Thomas, James David BS in Bus. Adminstrn., Acctg., La. Tech. U., Ruston, 1951. C.P.A. Audit supr. Peat, Marwick, Mitchell & Co., C.P.A.s, New Orleans and Jackson, Miss., 1958-63; treas. Lamar Life Ins. Co., Jackson, 1963-64, v.p., treas., 1964-68, sr. v.p., treas., 1968-73, pres., 1973-89, also dir.; v.p. Lamar Life Corp., 1972-73, pres., 1973-83, chmn. bd. dirs., 1983-88. Dir. Am. Coun. of Life Ins., Washington, 1978-81, chmn. Life Ins. Polit. Action Com., 1981-84; pres. Jackson C. of C. 1986, bd. dirs. 1974-76, 1981-87; bd. dirs. Health Ins. Assn. Am. 1985-88; chmn. Miss. Life & Health Ins. Guaranty Assn., 1985-88. Pres. United Way of Capital Area, Jackson, 1975, v.p., 1974, campaign chmn., 1973; pres. Goodwill Industries of Miss., Jackson, 1972. Named Outstanding Alumnus of Yr., Coll. of Adminstrn. and Bus., La. Tech. U., 1974; recipient Service to Humanity award Miss. Coll., 1978, Vol. Activist award D.H. Holmes/Germaine Monteil, 1987. Mem. AICPA, Soc. La. CPA, Rotary Lodge Jackson. Baptist. Avocations: genealogy, personal computer, swing era recorded music collection. Home: 110 Country Club Dr Madison MS 39110-8809 E-mail: JackPDean@aol.com.

DEAN, JAMES BENWELL, lawyer; b. Dodge City, Kans., May 23, 1941; s. James Harvey and Bess (Benwell) D.; m. Sharon Ann Carver, Sept. 1, 1962 (div. 1991); m. Patricia A. Bostick, Aug. 23, 1993 (div. 1999); children: Cynthia G. Dean Vosburgh, James M.; m. Gail M. Cohen, Sept. 21, 2002. Student, Southwestern Coll., 1959-60, U. Colo., 1961; BA, Kans. State U., 1962; JD, Harvard U., 1965. Bar: Colo. 1965, U.S. Dist. Ct. Colo. 1965, U.S. Tax Ct. 1966, Nebr. 1971, U.S. Ct. Appeals (10th cir.) 1971. From assoc. to ptnr. Tweedy & Mosley, Denver, 1965-71, Kutak Rock Cohen Campbell Garfinkle & Woodward, Omaha, 1971-73; ptnr. Mosley, Wells & Dean, Denver, 1973-77, Kutak Rock & Huie, Denver, 1977-81, James B. Dean, P.C., Denver, 1981-91, Dean, McClure, Eggleston & Husney, Denver, 1991-95, James B. Dean, PC, Denver, 1995-2000, Dean & Stern, LLC, Denver, 2001—; spl. asst. atty. gen. State of Colo., Denver, 1989—. Lectr. U. Ark. Law Sch., Fayetteville, 1982-86, C.C. Aurora, Colo., 1996-97. Co-editor Agricultural Law Jour., 1979-84; contbr. articles to profl. jours. Recipient Erwyn E. Witte Colo. Cooperator award, Colo. Coop. Coun., 1996. Mem.: Am. Agrl. Law Assn. (pres.-elect 1985—86, pres. 1986—87, bd. dirs. 1981—83, strategic planning com. 2000—01, Disting. Svc. award 1989), Denver Bar Assn., Colo. Bar Assn. (sec. agrl. law sect. 1991—94, bd. dirs. 1989—2001), Nebr. Bar Assn., ABA (advisor bd. forum com. on rural lawyers and agrl. bus. 1983—89). Republican. Avocations: photography, woodworking, hiking, piano. Office: 4155 E Jewell Ave Ste 703 Denver CO 80222-4511 E-mail: jim@deanandstern.com.

DEAN, JAMES WENDELL, military officer, nurse; b. Hamtramck, Mich., Apr. 29, 1948; s. Albert Jack and Kathleen Elizabeth (Freeman) D.; m. Iris Viola Rankine, Sept. 10, 1971; children: James W. Jr., Christopher N., Veronica V. AS in nursing, Wayne County Community Coll., Detroit, 1975; BSN, B in Natural Sci., Madonna Coll., Livonia, Mich., 1980; MBA, U. Devonshire. RN, Pulmonary Function tech., audiometric tech.; cert. occupational health nurse specialist. Charge nurse Lakeside Gen. Hosp., Detroit, 1975-76, Detroit Gen. Hosp., 1976-77; nursing instr. Automated Acad., Detroit, 1976-77; occupl. health nurse GM-Cadillac Motor Co., Detroit, 1977-83, Walt Disney World, Orlando, 1983-84; supr. occupl. health nurse Dept. of Def., USN, Orlando, 1984-87; occupl. health nurse/infection control & immunotherapy nurse VA, Orlando, 1987—. Crime watch patrolman Buena Ventura Lakes Crimewatch, Kissimmee, Fla., 1986. Lt. col. USAFR. Recipient sustained superior performance award Dept. Def., Orlando, 1985, 86, presdl. unit citation USAF, Wurtsmith AFB, Mich., 1968. Mem. ANA, Assn. Profls. Infection Control, Fla. Nurses Assn., Nurses Orgn. Va. (chpt. rep. 1988—), Cen. Fla. Occupational Health Nurses Assn. (v.p. 1985-86), Res. Officers Assn., AMVETS Post #30, Am. Legion, VFW. Democrat. Baptist. Avocations: bicycling, shuffleboard, horseshoes. Home: 612 Redwood Ct Kissimmee FL 34743-9028

DEAN, JEAN BEVERLY, artist; b. South Paris, Maine, Aug. 23, 1928; d. Henry Dyer and Doris Filena (Judd) Small; m. Samuel Lester Dean. AS, Becker Coll., Worcester, Mass., 1948; AA, Edison Coll., Ft. Myers, Fla., 1980. Artist, Ft. Myers, 1963—. (one-woman shows) Edison C.C. Gallery, Ft. Myers, Joan Ling Gallery, Gainesville, Fla., Berry Coll., Mt. Berry Ga., Gallery 10, Asheville, N.C., Sanibel Gallery, Fla., 1993, Barrier Island Group for the Arts, Sanibel, 1994, 1996, Sanibel Gallery, 1995, Gallery Mido, Belleview Mido Resort, Belleair, Fla., 1996, No. Trust Bank, Ft. Myers, 1996, Lee County Alliance of the Arts, 1996, Art League of Manatee County, Fla., 1996, Naples Libr., 1997, Sy Zy Gy Gallery, Ft. Myers, 1998, 2000, Barnes and Noble, 2000, Captiva Civic Assn., Fla., 2000, So. Co. Ctr. for the Arts, Ft. Myers, Fla., 2000, Viva Gallery, Captiva, Fla., 2000, Broadway Palm Dinner Theatre, Ft. Myers, Fla., 2001, Art House, 2002, Tower Gallery, Sanibel, Fla., 2002, exhibited (group shows) S.E. Painting and Sculpture Exhbn., Jacksonville, Fla., Southeastern Ctr. for Contemporary Art, Ybor City, S.W. Fla. Internat. Airport, 1991, 1995, Ctr. Art Show, St. Petersburg, Fla., 1991, Ridge Juried Art Show, Winter Haven, Fla., 1992, Artists Group, Sarasota, 1992, Women's Caucus for Art, 1993, Polk Mus., Lakeland, Fla., 1993, Daytona Mus., Fla., 1994, Women's Caucus Art Nat. Show, San Antonio, 1995, Capitol Gallery, Tallahassee, 1995, Women's Caucus Art State Show, Sarasota, 1995, Women's Caucus for Art, Miami, 1996, 1998, Fla. Artist Group, Winter Haven, 1996, Jacksonville Art Mus., 1998, Edison Coll., Ft. Myers, 1999, Fla. So. Coll., Lakeland, 1999, Art Ctr., St. Petersburg, Fla., 1999, Viva Gallery, Captiva, Fla., 2000, Charlotte County Nat., Fla., 2000, Nat. Exhibit, Winter Haven, Fla., 2000, The Capitol, Tallahassee, Fla., 2001, Venice Art Ctr., 2001, Captiva Art Ctr., 2001; Exhibited in group shows at Charlotte County National, Fla., 2002, Alliance of the Arts, Ft. Myers, Fla., 2002—03, Barrier Island Group for the Arts, Sanibel, Fla., 2002, Gallery on Broadway, Ft. Myers, Fla., 2002, Represented in permanent collections Am. Embassy, exhibited in group shows at Florida Gulf Coast U., Ft. Myers, 2003, Represented in permanent collections Madrid, Edison Coll., Ft. Myers, Fla., First Fed. Savs. and Loan, Ft. Myers, Naples, Fla., NCNB Bank, Tampa, Health Park, Ft. Myers, Clara Barton House, Washington, Hirshhorn Collection, one-woman shows include Albert Judd Gallery, Southington, Conn., 2002, Crossed Palms Gallery, Boreelia, Fla., 2002, exhibited in group shows at Bonita Arts Ctr, Bonita Springs, Fla., 2003. Active Lee County Alliance for Arts, 1994-2003; chair invitational com. Barrier Island Group for Arts, Sanibel, 1994-99; founder Open Doors Lee County Alliance of the Arts, Fla., 1990—. Recipient more than 100 awards. Mem. Nat. Mus. Women in the Arts (charter mem.), Fla. Artists Group. Democrat. Unitarian Universalist. Home: 17643 Captiva Island Ln Fort Myers FL 33908-6115

DEAN, JOHN F. retired school system administrator; b. Bridgeport, Conn., Nov. 15, 1926; s. James Henry and Mary McKay Dean; m. Katherine Nisbet, Aug. 28, 1949; children: Karol M. Hicks, Brian R. BS in Edn., U. So. Calif., 1950; MA, Calif. State U., 1955; EdD, U. So. Calif., 1966. Tchr. Newport Beach (Calif.) Sch. Dist., 1950-56, elem. sch. prin., 1956-61, dir. curriculum, 1961-69; dean Orange Coast C.C., Costa Mesa, Calif., 1969-70; prof. edn. Whittier (Calif.) Coll., 1970-91; supt. of schs. Orange County Dept. Edn., Costa Mesa, 1991-2001, emeritus, 2001—. Author: Teaching in America, 1978. Bd. dirs. Hoag Meml. Hosp., Newport Beach, Calif., 1972—2003. With USN, 1944—46. Republican. Presbyterian. Avocation: professional writing. Home: 1136 Highland Dr Newport Beach CA 92660-5618

DEAN, JOHN GUNTHER, diplomat; b. Germany, Feb. 24, 1926; came to U.S., 1939, naturalized, 1944; s. Joseph and Lucy (Askenaczy) D.; m. Martine Duphenieux, Dec. 26, 1952; children: Catherine Dean Curtis, Paul, Joseph. BS magna cum laude, Harvard U., 1947, MA, 1950; Doctorate, U. Paris, 1949. With ECA, Am. embassy, Paris, 1950-51, Am. embassy, Brussels, 1951-53, asst. econ. commr. Saigon, 1953-56; polit. officer Am. Embassy, Laos, 1956—58; consul Am. consulate, Togo, 1959-60; chargé d'affaires Am. Embassy, Mali, 1960-61; with Dept. State, Washington, 1961-65; polit. officer Am. Embassy, Paris, 1965—69; regional dir. CORDS in Central Vietnam, 1970-72; dep. chief mission Am. Embassy, Laos, 1972—74, amb. to Cambodia, 1974—75, Denmark, 1975—78, Lebanon, 1978—81, Thailand, 1981—85, India, 1985—88. Adv. U.S. delegation to UN, 1963; now mem. adv. bds. several nat. and internat. cos. and instns. Served to 2d lt. AUS, 1944-46. Fellow Center for Internat. Affairs Harvard, 1969-70 Mem.: Harvard (N.Y.C.); Kenwood Golf and Country (Washington). Office: 29 Blvd Jules Sandeau 75116 Paris France Home: Chalet Crettaz BP 1318 1936 Verbier Valais Switzerland E-mail: johnmartinedean@aol.com.

DEAN, JOHN RANDALL, financial consultant, general building contractor; b. Detroit, Mar. 9, 1932; s. William Harry and Ada Elizabeth Dean; m. Shirley Grace Dean, Dec. 24, 1956 (div. July 1972); children: Leslie Kim, Randall Kent. BSEE, Lawrence Inst. Tech., 1953; postgrad., UCLA. Mgr. ground support divsn. Airesearch Mfg. Co., L.A., 1953-60; mgr. command[ ]and power dept. Lockheed Missile & Space Divsn., Van Nuys, Calif., 1960-63; gen. mgr. Signet Sci. Co., Burbank, Calif., 1963-67; v.p. United Capital Planners, Beverly Hills, Calif., 1967-70; regional mtkg. mgr. Weston Hydraulics, Panarama City, Calif., 1970-97; fin. cons., pres., bd. dirs. Nat. Mktg. & Fin., Inc., South Lake Tahoe, Calif., 1993—. Real estate salesman Unique Realty Assn., Woodland Hills, Calif., 1970-72; fin. planner Unimet Fin. Svcs., L.A., 1972-75; owner, pres., bd. dirs. Sierra Note, Inc., 1994—, Sierra Sunset Mktg., Inc., 1994—, High Sierra Mktg., Inc., 1994—. Sierra Constrn. Svcs., Inc., 1994—. Named Top Ins. Salesman for 1970, Hartford Life & Accident Co. Avocations: remodeling, woodworking, hiking, cross-country skiing. Office: Nat Mktg & Fin Inc PO Box 9580 South Lake Tahoe CA 96158-2580

DEAN, K. MATTHEW, elementary school educator; b. Evansville, Ind., Oct. 13, 1952; s. Robert Sheridan and Mae Blanche (Carlisle) D. BS, U. So. Ind., 1974; MS, Ind. U., 1980. Tchr. elem. sch. Bend Gate Sch., Henderson, Ky., 1974-2001. Treas. Tri-State Amateur Radio Soc., Evansville, 1992-95, Friends of Angel Mounds, Evansville, Ind., 1996-98. Fellow Delta Arts Acad.; mem. Ky. Edn. Assn., Kappa Delta Pi. Avocations: amateur radio, woodcarving, photography, history, travel. Home: 1540 S Boeke Rd Evansville IN 47714 E-mail: absolam1@juno.com.

DEAN, LEANN FAYE LINDQUIST, librarian; b. Benson, Minn., Oct. 25, 1948; d. Lawrence Axel and Leonora Olivia (Nybakke) Lindquist; m. James Allen Dean, Aug. 20, 1971 (div. 1996); children: Sonja Leonore, Trevor Lawrence. BA, Concordia Coll., Moorhead, Minn., 1969; MA in Libr. Sci., U. Minn., 1976; MA in Polit. Sci., U. S.D., 1991. Libr. Litchfield (Minn.) Jr. High Sch., 1969-76; asst. dir. Buckham Meml. Libr., Faribault, Minn., 1976-83; libr. Black Hills State Coll., Spearfish, S.D., 1983-85; libr. Sch. Bus. U. S.D., Box Elder, 1985-87; dir. learning svcs. Nat. Coll., Rapid City, S.D., 1987-91; head of public svcs. Briggs Library, U. Minn., Morris, 1991—. Ch. libr. Litchfield Zion Luth. Ch., Our Saviors Ch., Faribault, Our Saviors Ch., Spearfish, South Canyon Luth. Ch., Rapid City. Democrat. Lutheran. Home: 7 S Court St Morris MN 56267-1613

DEAN, LESLIE ALAN (CAP DEAN), economist, consultant; b. Indpls., June 18, 1940; s. Henry Lloyd and Margaret Ann (Pfafman) Dean; m. Jeanne Louise Lambert, Apr. 14, 1962; children: David Richard, Laura Elizabeth. BA, U. Ill., 1963, MA, 1966; postgrad., U. Pitts., 1968-69. Internat. loan analyst Bank Calif., San Francisco, 1970; joined Fgn. Svc., 1970; devel. officer U.S. AID, Washington, 1970, 77-79, Vientiane, Laos, 1971-75, Kathmandu, Nepal, 1975-77, Islamabad, Pakistan, 1979-83, Dar Es Salaam, Tanzania, 1983-85, asst. mission dir. Lusaka, Zambia, 1985-87, mission dir. sr. fgn. svc., 1988-90, office dir. Washington, 1990-92, mission dir. Pretoria, South Africa, 1992-96, dep. asst. adminstr. Africa Bur. Washington, 1996-98; dir. integrated devel. programs sub-Saharan Africa Internat. Found. Edn. & Self Help, Phoenix, 1999—2003, dir. ops., 2003—. Elder, chair mission com. Pinnacle Presbyn. Ch., 2002—. Capt. USAF, 1964—68. Mem.: Phi Eta Sigma. Avocations: swimming, reading, travel. Office: IFESH 5040 E Shea Blvd Ste 260 Scottsdale AZ 85254-4687 E-mail: capdean@ifesh.org.

DEAN, MICHAEL J. lobbyist, consultant; b. Detroit, Oct. 2, 1947; s. Ray Donald and Joanne Rae (Roth) Dean. PhD, George Washington U., 2002. Lobbyist Machinist Union, Washington; polit. cons. The Dean Group, Cape Coral, Fla. Dir. Cape Coral Dems., Fla.; CEO Dean & Volkers Comm., Cape Coral, Fla. Mem.: CCDC (exec. dir. 2002—). Home: CollBSE 23rd Fl Melbourne FL 32940

DEAN, MICHAEL M. lawyer; b. Phila., Jan. 7, 1933; BA, Antioch Coll., 1954; JD cum laude, U. Pa., 1957. Bar: Pa. 1957. Fulbright fellow U. London, 1962-63; ptnr. Wolf, Block, Schorr & Solis-Cohen, Phila., 1966-2000, of counsel, 2000—. Dir. Univ. City. Sci. Ctr., Phila., 1993—, chmn., 2000—02. Bd. dirs. emeritus Ctrl. Phila. Devel. Corp., 1996—, pres., 1987—90, chmn., 1990—95; counsel, bd. dirs., exec. com., chmn. endowment trust Diagnostic and Rehab. Ctr., Phila., 1980—; exec. com., bd. dirs., sec. Ctr. City Dist., 1990, solicitor, 1991—. E-mail: mdean@wolf.block.com.

DEAN, ODELL JOSEPH, JR., urologist, educator; b. Nashville, Mar. 9, 1958; s. Odell Joseph and Barbara Jean (Crowther) D. BS, Howard U., 1979; MD, La. State U., New Orleans, 1983. Diplomate Am. Bd. Urology. Resident in surgery and urology Howard U. Hosp., Washington, 1984-86; resident in urology Tulane U. Med. Ctr., New Orleans, 1986-89, fellow in renal transplantation, 1989-91; asst. prof. surgery and urology U. Mo., Columbia, 1991-93; asst. prof. urology Tulane U., 1993-95; attending urologist Columbia Healthcare Sys., Tex., 1996—. Cons. Ellis Fischel Cancer Ctr., Columbia, 1991-93, Tulane Cancer Ctr., 1993-95; med. edn. adv. com. Tulane Med. Sch., 1994-95; residency program dir. Tulane dept. urology, 1994-95; assoc. rsch. fellow NIH, Bethesda, 1979-80; mem. prostate cancer adv. com. Tex. Dept. Health, 1996—. Contbr. articles to profl. jours. Advisor Neighborhood Youth Corps, New Orleans, 1980-91; sr. cons. Total Cmty. Action, New Orleans, 1993-95; pres. Am. Cancer Soc., Angelina County, Tex., 1998—. Grantee Atrium Med., 1989, Medtronic, 1989, Searle Pharms., Chgo., 1992, Pfizer Pharms., 1994. Fellow ACS; mem. Am. Urological Assn., Soc. Univ. Urologists, S.W. Oncology Group, Angelina County Med. Soc., Assn. Acad. Minority Physicians. Roman Catholic. Avocations: computer scis., tennis. Office: Ste 104 302 Medical Park Dr Lufkin TX 75904 E-mail: ojdean@cox-internet.com.

DEAN, PAUL JOHN, magazine editor; b. Pitts., May 11, 1941; s. John Aloysius and Perle Elizabeth (Thompson) D.; m. Jo-ann Tillman, Aug. 19, 1972 (div. Mar. 1981); children: Jennifer Ann, Michael Paul. Student engring., Pa. State U., 1959-60. Gen. mgr. Civic Ctr. Honda Co., Pitts., 1965-68, Washington-Pitts. Cycle Co., Canonsburg, Pa., 1968-70; nat. svc. mgr. Yankee Motor Co., Schenectady, 1970-73. Competition congressman Am. Motorcyclist Assn., 1971, 72, trustee, sec. bd., 1988-91, chmn., 1991-97; bd. dirs. AMA ProRacing, 1997—; adv. bd., guest speaker L.A. Trade Tech. Coll., 1974-90; trustee Am. Motorcyclist Heritage Found., 1990-91. Engring. editor Cycle Guide mag., Compton, Calif., 1973-74, editor-in-chief, 1974-80, editorial dir., 1980-84; editor-in-chief Cycle World mag., Newport Beach, Calif., 1984-88, editorial dir. Cycle and Cycle World mags., 1988-92; v.p., editorial dir. Cycle World Mag. Group, 1992—; author manuals. Served with AUS, 1964-65. Named to, Nat. Motorcycle Mus. and Hall of Fame, 2002. Home: 5915 Arabella St Lakewood CA 90713-1203 Office: Hachette Filipacchi Media US 1499 Monrovia Ave Newport Beach CA 92663-2752 E-mail: CW1Dean@aol.com.

DEAN, RICHARD ANTHONY, mechanical engineer, engineering executive; b. Bklyn., Dec. 22, 1935; s. Anthony David and Anne Mylod Dean; m. Sheila Elizabeth Grady, Oct. 5, 1957; children: Carolyn Anne, Julie Marie, Richard Drews. BSME, Ga. Inst. Tech., 1957, MSME, U. Pitts., 1963, PhDME, 1970. Registered profl. engr., Calif. From jr. engr. to mgr. thermal and hydraulic engring. Westinghouse Nuclear Energy Sys., 1959-70; v.p., tech. dir. water reactor fuels General Atomics, San Diego, 1970-74, v.p. uranium and light water reactor fuel, 1974-80, sr. v.p., 1980-92; pres. Leading Edge Engring., San Diego, 1993—; pres., CEO Cutting Edge Products, Inc., San Diego, 1997—. Cons. U.S. Congress Office Tech. Assessment. 1st lt. U.S. Army, 1957-59. Mem. AAAS, ASME (former chmn. nuclear fuels tech. com.), Am. Nuclear Soc. (gen. chmn. annual meeting 1993), Global Found. (bd. advisors), Internat. Thermonuclear Experimental Reactor (adv. bd.). Achievements include the develpoment of commercial nuclear power stations; advanced the understanding of boiling heat transfer phenomena; invention of advanced nuclear fuel assembly. Home: 6699 Via Estrada La Jolla CA 92037-6432 Office: Leading Edge Engring # 313 13240 Evening Creek Dr San Diego CA 92128 E-mail: leeinc@cts.com.

DEAN, RICHARD HENRY, surgeon, educator; b. Radford, Va., June 16, 1942; s. Howard Lee and Minnie Yates (Crowder) D.; children: Richard Lancaster, Harrison Blaylock, Howard Lee Alexander, Williams Cabler. BA, Va. Mil. Inst., 1964; MD, Med. Coll. Va., 1968. Diplomate Am. Bd. Surgery (bd. dirs. 1993—), Am. Bd. Gen. Vascular Surgery, Am. Bd. Plastic Surgery. Surg. intern Vanderbilt U. Hosp., 1968-69, surg. asst. resident, 1969-73, chief. surg. resident, 1973-74, asst. prof. surgery sch. medicine, 1975-77, assoc. prof. surgery, 1977-81, prof. surgery, 1981-86, head divsn. vascular surgery sch. medicine, 1978-86; vascular rsch. fellow, instr. surgery Northwestern U. Hosp, 1974-75; Richard T. Meyers prof. and chmn. surgery Bowman Gray Sch. Medicine Wake Forest U., Winston-Salem, NC, 1987-89, dir. divsn. surg. scis., chmn. dept. gen. surgery Bowman Gray Sch. Medicine, 1989-97, sr. v.p. health affairs, 1997—2001; dir. Wake Forest U. Baptist Med. Ctr., 1997—; pres. Wake Forest U. Health Scis., 2001—. Vis. prof. U. Vienna, Austria, 1980, U. NSW, Sydney, Australia, 1982, U. Queensland, Brisbane, Australia, 1984, U. Rochester (N.Y.) Med. Ctr., 1986, 2nd Internat. Symposium on Ischemia, Madrid, 1986, U. Health Scis., Bethesda, Md., 1987, East Carolina U., Greenville, N.C., 1987, Ga. Bapt. Med. Ctr., Atlanta, 1988, Roanoke (Va.) Meml. Hosp., 1988, Ea. Va. Med. Sch., Norfolk, 1988 (two lectures), Mayo Clinic, Rochester, Minn., 1989, Med. Coll. Va., Richmond, 1990, W.Va. U. Health Sci. Ctr., Charleston, 1990, Va. Vascular Soc., Hot Spring, 1990, First All-Union Congress Cardiovascular Surgery, Moscow, 1990, Carolinas Heart Inst., Charlotte, 1991, U. Miami Sch. Medicine, 1991, Allegheny Gen. Hosp., Pitts., 1992, Northwestern U. Med. Sch., Chgo., 1992, U. Minn., Mpls., 1992, Nat. Naval Med. Ctr., Bethesda, 1992, Emory U. Sch. Medicine/Emory Hosp., Atlanta, 1992, Internat. Symposium Hosp. Universitario, Madrid, 1993, Ruprect-Karls-Universitat Heidelberg, Germany, 1993, La. State U. Med. Ctr., Shreveport, 1993, U. N.C., Chapel Hill, 1993, U. Man., Winnipeg, Can., 1993, U. Cin. Med. Ctr., 1993; Paul Dudley White vis. prof. U. Sao Paulo and Campinas, Brazil, 1982; Deryl Hart lectr. Duke U. Med. Sch., 1991; mem. Coun. on Cardio-Thoracic and Vascular Surgery, 1990-91; dir. Am. Bd. Plastic Surgery, 1995—; guest lectr. in field. Editor: (with J.A. O'Neill Jr.) Vascular Disorders of Childhood, 1983, (with W.P. Ritchie and G. Strele Sr.) General Surgery, 1994, (with J.S.T. Jao and D.C. Brewster) Current Diagnosis and Treatment in Vascular Surgery, 1995; mem. editl. bd. Jour. Vascular Surgery, Annals of Vascular Surgery; contbr. numerous chpts. to books and articles to sci. and profl. jours. Recipient Superior Performance award, 1997. Fellow: ACS (N.C. chpt., cardiovascular com. 1987), Am. Heart Assn. (stroke coun., coun. high blood pressure rsch.); mem.: AMA, Nat. Libr. Medicine (bd. regents 2001—), H. William Scott, Jr. Soc. (sec. 1982—87, pres. 1988—89), S.E. Surg. Congress, So. Surg. Assn. (v.p. 1997—98), So. Med. Assn., Forsyth-Stokes-Davie County Med. Assn., So. Assn. Vascular Surgery (program com. 1982—85, exec. coun. 1985—88, pres.-elect 1988—89, pres. 1990—91), Va. Surg. Assn. (hon.), So. Calif. Vascular Surgery Soc. (hon.), Assn. Acad. Surgery (exec. coun. 1978—80, nominating com. 1980), Soc. Vascular Surgery (publs. com. 1992—, recorder), Soc. Univ. Surgeons, Internat. Soc. Surgery, Internat. Soc. Cardiovascular Surgery (vis. prof. First Sci. Congress 1992), Am. Surg. Assn. (adv. membership com. 1991—), Am. Bd. Surgery (cons. com. on vascular surgery 1986—92, dir. 1993—). Home: 268 S Pine Valley Rd Winston Salem NC 27104 Office: Wake Forest U Sch Medicine Medical Center Blvd Winston Salem NC 27157-0001

DEAN, ROBERT BRUCE, architect; b. Brockton, Mass., Jan. 15, 1949; s. Robert George and Marjorie Gertrude (O'Donnell) D.; m. Mary Hood Hoskinson, June 18, 1977; children: Robert Maxwell, Anne, Claire. BA, U. Pa., 1971; MArch, Columbia U., 1976. Registered architect, N.Y., Conn. Staff architect Skidmore, Owings & Merrill, Architects, N.Y.C., 1976-77; job capt. Stephen Jacobs & Assn., N.Y.C., 1977-78; staff architect Johnson-Burgee Architects, N.Y.C., 1978-79; pvt. practice architecture N.Y.C. and Syracuse, 1979-85; project architect Robert A.M. Stern Architects, N.Y.C., 1985-86; pres. Dean Design, Inc., New Canaan, Conn., 1986—. Adj. assoc. prof. Columbia U., N.Y.C., 1978-83; asst. prof. Syracuse U., 1980-84. Contbr. articles to profl. jours. Bd. dirs. Redding Hist. Soc.; mem. Planning Commn. Town of Redding, Dem. Town com. Grantee Syracuse U. 1982, grantee Nat. Endowment Arts, 1983-84; William Kinne Fellow, 1976. Mem. AIA, Conn. Soc. Architects. Democrat. Congregationalist. Avocation: american cultural and commercial history. Office: Dean Design Inc 111 Cherry St New Canaan CT 06840-5530 E-mail: rdean@deandesign.net.

DEAN, ROBERT FRANKLIN, insurance company executive; b. Houston, Nov. 1, 1942; s. Claude Nathan and Nellie Gladis (Davis) D.; m. Kathy Copeland, Aug. 16, 1963 (div. Jan. 1970); 1 child, Robert Franklin Jr.; m. Betsy Ellen Kniehl, Sept. 20, 1975 (dec. Jan. 1994); children: James, Kyle, Courtney Elizabeth; m. Charlene Harmon Sailors, Feb. 25, 1995 (div. Dec. 1999). BBA in Bus. Mgmt., U. Houston, 1968. Cert. safety profl. Safety engr. Gulf Ins. Group, Houston, 1968-69, Indsl. Indemnity Ins., Houston, 1969-75; loss control mgr. Crum & Forester Ins. Group, Houston, 1975-78; sr. mktg. cons. Aetna Ins.

Co., Houston, 1978-80; v.p. mktg. div. Stanley Ins., Houston, 1980-81; pres., chief exec. officer Dean & Draper Ins. Agy. Inc., Houston, 1981—. Head football coach Alief Youth Assn., Houston, 1975-81; mem. steering com. Rep. Party, Houston, 1988; bd. trustees Harris County Impact Political Action Com., 1991-96. Recipient Cert. of Appreciation, Spring Br. Sch. Dist., 1985, Outstanding Svc. award Tex. Automotive Assn., 1985; named Agt. of the Yr., Travelers Ins. Co., 1999. Mem. Am. Soc. Safety Engrs. (cert. com. on edn. Houston chpt. 1975-76), Houston Gemini Automation Group (bd. dirs. Houston chpt. 1989-90, pres. 1990-92), Ind. Ins. Agts. of Am. (bd. dirs. Houston chpt. 1991-96), Houston Assn. of Ins. Agts. (legis. com. 1993-94, mem. recreation com., charitable events bd. liaison, bd. dirs. charitable found.), Gemini User of Am. Republican. Episcopalian. Avocations: golf, health, motorcycling, choir, swimming. Office: Dean & Draper Ins Agy 3131 W Alabama 4th Fl Houston TX 77098 E-mail: bdean@deandraper.com.

DEAN, ROBERT STUART, lawyer; b. N.Y.C., Mar. 22, 1952; s. Leo J. and Sonia (Margolin) D.; m. Lynn W.L. Fahey, July 31, 1983; children: Alexander, Benjamin. BA, Northwestern U., 1973; diploma in advanced internat. studies, Johns Hopkins U., Bologna, Italy, 1974; JD, NYU, 1977. Bar: N.Y. 1978, U.S. Dist. Ct. (ea. and so. dists.) N.Y. 1979, U.S. Ct. Appeals (2d cir.) 1979, U.S. Supreme Ct. 1986. Assoc. appellate counsel Criminal Appeals Bur., Legal Aid Soc., N.Y.C., 1977-79, sr. supervising atty., 1979-97; atty.-in-charge Ctr. for Appellate Litigation, N.Y.C., 1997—. Adj. asst. prof. law NYU Sch. Law, N.Y.C., 1995—97; adj. prof. law Bklyn. Law Sch., N.Y.C., 1998—2003. Co-author: New York Pretrial Criminal Procedure, 1996. Mem. New York County Lawyers Assn., Assn. Bar City N.Y. Office: Ctr for Appellate Litigation 74 Trinity Pl New York NY 10006-2003

DEAN, RONALD GLENN, lawyer; b. Milw., Feb. 18, 1944; children: Elizabeth Lucile, Joshua Henry. BA, Antioch Coll., 1967; JD, U. Wis., 1970. Bar: Wis. 1970, Calif. 1971. Assoc. Mink & Neiman, L.A., 1971; ptnr. Margolis, McTernan, Scope & Sacks, L.A., 1974-77; pvt. practice Pacific Palisades, 1977—. Mem. judge pro-tem program L.A. County Bar, 1978-91; judge pro tem Beverly Hills Mcpl. Ct., 1980-90; arbitrator L.A. Superior Ct., 1980—, L.A. County Fee Dispute Panel, 1979-86, 94—, Santa Monica Mcpl. Ct., 1980-2001; referee for disciplinary matters State Bar Ct., 1980-88, supervising referee, 1984-88, rev. dept. 1988-90, judge pro tem 1990 94. Bd. dirs. Pacific Palisades Residents Assn., 1983-2001, pres., 1985-88; counsel to Pacific Palisades Cmty. Coun., 1983-92, 2000—, C. of C. rep. to Cmty. Coun., 1995-2000; mem. Councilman's Citizen Adv. Com. to Develop Pacific Palisades Civic League, 1987-89; exec. bd. pacific Palisades Dem. Club, 1990-2003, pres., 1991, 96; mem. Palisades P.R.I.D.E., 1996—, pres., 1997-98, bd. dirs. Fellow Coll. Labor and Employment Lawyers, Am. Coll. Employee Benefit Counsel (charter, bd. dirs. 2000—); mem. Am. Arbitration Assn. (panel 1974-95), ABA (co-chmn. employee benefits com., labor sect., bd. sr. editors Employee Benefits Law 1995-98, plaintiff co-chair, nat. insts. subcom.), BNA Pension and Benefits Reporter (adv. bd. 1995—, co-chair sr. editors book Employee Benefits Law), Wis. Bar Assn., Calif. State Bar (chmn. pension and trust benefits com. of labor sect. 1984), L.A. County Bar Assn., Antioch Alumni Assn. (dir. 1982-88), Pacific Palisades (Calif.) C. of C. (bd. dirs. 1995-2000). Office: 15135 W Sunset Blvd Ste 280 Pacific Palisades CA 90272-3735 E-mail: rdean@74erisa.com.

DEAN, THOMAS EUGENE, music educator, consultant; b. Washington, Nov. 8, 1959; s. Joseph Rober Dean and Joanne Mary Bielefeld, Camille Dean (Stepmother) and Gilbert E. Bielefeld(Stepfather); m. Trisha Ann Ferko, Nov. 5, 1983; children: Heather Marie, Holly Nicole. BS in Music Edn., West Chester (Pa.) U., 1982, MusM in Music Edn., 1993. Cert. tchr. Del., 2002. Music educator The Eisenhower Sch., Levittown, Pa., 1982—83, Twin Spring Farm Day Sch., Ambler, Pa., 1983—84, Dover (Del.) HS, 1984—. Mem. leadership team for vpac commn. Dept. of Edn., Dover, Del., performance indicator com. mem. Choral dir. Parkersford Bapt. Ch., Pa., 1983—84; choir dir. Wyoming (Del.) United Meth. Ch., 1984—85. Recipient Director's award for Notable Contbn., Fiesta-val Invitational Music Festivals, 1992, 1993, 1996. Mem.: Kent County Music Educators Assn. (assoc.; treas. 1990—94), Music Educators Nat. Conf. (assoc.), Del. Music Educators Assn. (assoc.; editor 1995—2002, chorus chmn. 1988—90, choir chmn. 2000—02, web master 1995—2002), Pi Kappa Lambda. Republican. Roman Catholic. Home: 3 Stewart Court Dover DE 19904 Office: Dover High School 1 Pat Lynn Drive Dover DE 19904 Office Fax: 302-672-1565. Personal E-mail: tdean@capital.k12.de.us. E-mail: tdean@capital.k12.de.us.

DEAN, WILLIAM EVANS, aerospace industry executive; b. Greenville, Miss., July 6, 1930; s. George Thomas Dean and Martha Myrtle (Evans) Carlton; m. Dorothy Sue Hamilton, Oct. 14, 1953; children: Janet Lea, Jody Anne, Justin H. B in Aero. Engring., Ga. Inst. Tech., 1952; MBA, Pepperdine U., 1970; grad., USAF Air Command and Staff Coll., 1970. FAA cert. airplane and instrument flight instr. Commd. officer USAF, 1952, advanced through grades to maj., 1962; divsn. mgr., dir. Rockwell Internat. Corp., L.A., 1962-67, v.p., divsn. gen. mgr., 1967-80; exec. v.p. Acurex Corp., Mountain View, Calif., 1981-82, pres., COO, 1982-83, pres., CEO, 1983-90, vice chmn., 1990-91; assoc. dir. Ames Rsch. Ctr. NASA, Moffett Field, Calif., 1991-93, dep. ctr. dir., 1994-97; v.p., dir. Univs. Space Rsch. Assn., Columbia, Md., 1997—2002; founder, mng. dir. The Dean Group, LLC, Santa Ana, Calif., 2002—. Lectr. Calif. State U., Chico, 1988, Santa Clara U., 1993-98. Contbr. articles on gen. mgmt. and aero. engring. to profl. jours. Bd. dirs. NCCJ, San Jose, Calif., 1984-97, co-chmn., 1988-91; bd. dirs. Santa Clara County Mfg. Group, San Jose, 1984-91, vice-chmn., 1988-91; bd. dirs. Saddleback Community Coll., Mission Viejo, Calif., 1976-77, United Fund, Orange County, Calif., 1971; United Way, Santa Clara County, San Jose, 1985-91; vice-chmn., bd. advisors Leavey Sch. Bus., Santa Clara U., 1987-97, vice chmn., 1989-91; tech. com. Orange County Bus. Coun., 1998-2000. Decorated Air Force Commendation medal with oak leaf cluster; recipient Spl. Svc. award United Way, 1986, NASA Astronaut Personal Achievement award, 1972, 84, Outstanding Contbn. to Manned Exploration of the Moon award, 1972, Medal for Outstanding Leadership, 1995, Group Achievement awards, 1995, Disting. Svc. medal, 1997; Silver Knight of Mgmt. award Nat. Mgmt. Assn., 1978, Commendation Cert. Calif. State Assembly, 1986, Pres.' award Santa Clara U., 1993; named Disting. Alumnus award Woodward Acad., 1999, Ga. Inst. Tech., 1995; inducted to Engring. Hall of Fame, Ga. Inst. Tech., 1997. Fellow AIAA (bd. dirs. 1979-86, 91-95, Space Shuttle award 1984), Internat. Acad. Astronautics (Paris), Am. Astron. Soc., Nat. Space Soc.; mem. Am. Electronics Assn. (edn. found. 1982-88), Aircraft Owners and Pilots Assn., Air Force Assn., Armed Forces Comm. and Electronics Assn. Republican. Baptist. Office: The Dean Group 13422 Laurinda Way Santa Ana CA 92705-1926 E-mail: wdean1@comcast.net.

DEANE, DEBBE, psychologist, journalist, editor, consultant; b. Coatesville, Pa., July 30, 1950; d. George Edward and Dorothea Alice (Martin) Mays; widowed; children: Theo, Vonisha, Lorise, Voniece. AA in Psychology, Mesa Coll., 1989; BA Psychology, San Diego State U., 1993; MA in Psychology, Nat. U., 1995; postgrad., U.S. Internat. U., 1995—. Announcer Sta. KBPI, Denver, 1969-70, Sta. WKXI, Jackson, Miss., 1970-72; news anchor Sta. WNGE-TV, Nashville, 1973-76; news dir. Sta. KLDR, Denver, 1976-78; host, reporter Sta. KMGH-TV, Denver, 1978-81; news anchor, editor Sta. KHOW, Denver, 1978-79; news & pub. affairs dir. Sta. KLZ, Denver, 1979-80, Sta. KCBQ, San Diego, 1980-82; news anchor Sta. KOGO, San Diego, 1983-84; news anchor, reporter Sta. KCST-TV, San Diego, 1984-87; dir. comm. Omni Corp., San Diego, 1987—; news anchor Sta. KFI, L.A., 1990-91; sr. psychiat. therapist Behavioral Health Group, San Diego, 1993—. Media liaison United Negro Coll. Fund, San Diego, 1990-92; dir. comm. United Chs. of Christ, San Diego, 1989-92; cons. San Diego Assn. Black Journalists, 1985-92, San Diego Coalition Black Journalists, 1985-92; cons. in field. Campaign fin. analyst San Diego County Registrar of Voters, San Diego, 1990; cons. San Diego County Office Disaster Preparedness, 1990-91, Nu Way Youth Ctr. & Neighborhood House, Inc., San Diego, 1991-92; counselor Project STARRT, San Diego, 1991-92; cons. United Way Home Start, Inc. Family Self-Sufficiency Program, 1996—; cons. and program coord. San Diego Healthy Start, Inc., 1997—, Samuel L. Gompers Secondary Inst. Math., Sci. & computer Tech., 1997—. Recipient San Diego Black Achievement award Urban League, 1989, Best News Show & Spot News award San Diego Press Club, 1985, Golden Mike award So. Calif. Broadcast Assn., L.A., 1986; named one of Top 25 Businesswomen Essence Mag., 1978, Outstanding Humanitarian Worldvision, 1993, Outstanding Humanities Alumna Mesa Coll., 1993, Woman of the Year. Mem. AFTRA, APA, Am. Psychol. Assn., Am. Women in Radio & TV, Women in Comm., Black Students Sci. Orgn. (sec. 1989-91), Africana Psychol. Soc. (media coord. 1990-92), Psi Chi. Democrat. Achievements: first African-Am. in U.S. lic. to teach radio & TV broadcast prodn. Home: 3545 Valley Rd No 1 Bonita CA 91902-4164 E-mail: debbedeane@worldnet.att.net.

DEANE, ELAINE, lawyer; b. Washington, Sept. 10, 1958; d. William Francis Goode and Elizabeth Anne (Downes) Deane. AB, U. Calif., Berkeley, 1980; JD, U. San Francisco, 1986. Bar: Calif. 1986. Assoc. Parkinson, Wolf, Lazar & Leo, L.A., 1985-89, Peltit & Martin, San Francisco, 1989-91, Frandzel & Share, San Francisco, Calif., 1992-93, Arter & Haddon, San Francisco, 1994—. Mem. Calif. Bar Assn., L.A. County Bar Assn., Century City Bar Assn., Beverly Hills Bar Assn., San Francisco Bar Assn., Lawyers' Com. for Urban Affairs, Sierra Club, Amnesty Internat., Wilderness Soc., Greenpeace. Avocations: ballet, theatre, environment. Office: Arter & Haddon 2 Embarcadero Ctr Lbby 4 San Francisco CA 94111-3822

DEANE, JAMES GARNER, magazine editor, conservationist; b. Hartford, Conn., Apr. 5, 1923; s. Julian Lowrie and Miriam (Grover) D. BA, Swarthmore Coll., 1943. Mem. editorial staff Washington Star, 1944-60, edn. editor, 1952-57, classical recs. critic, 1952-60; ind. researcher, vol. in conservation activity, 1961-68; assoc. editor Nat. Parks Mag., 1968-69, editor, 1969; asst. editor The Living Wilderness, Washington, 1969-71, exec. editor, 1971-75, editor, 1975-81; editor Defenders mag., Washington, 1981-2001, editor emeritus, 2001; v.p. Defenders of Wildlife, Washington, 1997-2001. Washington corr. Mus. Courier, 1945-55; contbg. editor High Fidelity mag., 1953-55; mem. com. transp. environ. rev. process Transp. Research Bd. NRC, 1974-77; Am. co-chmn. Can. U.S. Environ. Coun., 1975-81. Bd. dirs. Arctic Internat. Wildlife Range Soc., 1979—; trustee Com. of 100 on Federal City, 1967-90, 1st vice chmn., 1967-69; chmn. Potomac Valley Conservation and Recreation Council, 1967. Served with AUS, 1946-47. Recipient award Edn. Writers Assn., 1956, Public Service award Washington Newspaper Guild, 1956, Charles Carroll Glover award Nat. Park Service, 1967 Home: 111 Audubon Rd Leeds MA 01053 Address: PO Box 104 Leeds MA 01053 E-mail: jdeane@the-spa.com. *Protection of as many as possible of the remaining wild places and, with them, of the marvelous diversity of living species on our crowding planet is one of the imperatives of our time. This need can be met only by developing worldwide understanding of its crucial importance. That is the challenging task of the nature-conservation movement. I find it exhilarating to be making some contribution, however modest, to the accomplishment of that task through the techniques of journalism.*

DEANE, KAREN PEKLO, retail executive; b. Rocky Mount, NC, June 1, 1961; d. Joseph William and Marilyn Janelda (Murdoch) P. BS in Mktg., U. West Fla., 1987. Dept. mgr. trainee Gayfers, Pensacola, Fla., 1984-88, asst. sr. buyer Mobile, Ala., 1988-89, dept. mgr. and buyer Ridgeland, Miss., 1989-92; dept. mgr. Marshall Fields, Schaumburg, Ill., 1992-95; dep. mgr. Sears, Pensacola, Fla., 1995-98, mdse. analyst Hoffman Estates, Ill., 1998-2000, dist. mktg. mgr. NYC, 2000—03, 2002—. Sears Store Gen. Mgr., 2003-present, Mem. Jr. League of NYC, Pensacola Ski Club. Republican. Roman Catholic. Avocations: golf, tennis, skiing. Home: 121 Margie Dr, Apt 204 Warner Robins GA 31093 Office: Sears 2930 Watson Blvd Centerville GA 31028 E-mail: ksp12345@aol.com.

DEANE, LELAND MARC, plastic surgeon; b. N.Y.C., June 18, 1952; s. Maurice Allen and Barbara Elaine (Ushkow) D.; m. Danielle Anne Sheft, Nov. 21, 1993; 1 child, Ashby Bennett, Galen Ames. BS, Union Coll., 1974; MD, SUNY, Bklyn., 1978. Diplomate Am. Bd. Surgery, Am. Bd. Plastic Surgery. Intern, then resident in surgery New Eng. Med. Ctr., 1978-83; resident in plastic surgery Ea. Va. Grad. Sch. Medicine, 1983-85; fellow in hand surgery Jefferson Med. Coll., 1986; pvt. practice L.I. Plastic Surg. Group P.C., Garden City, N.Y., 1986—. Mem. surg. rev. com. Winthrop U. Hosp., Mineola, N.Y., 1986—, mem. resident edn. com., 1992—; instr. surgery Cornell Med. Coll., 1989—. Contbr. articles to profl. jours. Advisor Mothers of Super Twins, L.I., 1995—. Grantee So. Med. Assn., 1984. Fellow ACS, Am. Acad. Pediat.; mem. Am. Soc. Plastic and Reconstructive Surgeons, Northea. Soc. Plastic Surgeons, N.Y. Regional Soc. Plastic and Reconstructive Surgery, Seawanhaka Corinthian Yacht Club, N.Y. Yacht Club. Office: LI Plastic Surg Group PC 999 Franklin Ave Garden City NY 11530-2913

DEANE, LEON, retired company executive; b. Balt., Sept. 27, 1915; s. Joseph and Ida (Ellison) D.; m. Laura Wolk, Oct. 30, 1952; children: Stephen Ellison, Ida Susan. Grad. H.S., Balt. Musician USN Band and Orch., Washington, 1935-37, Balt. (Md.) Symphony Orch., 1938-39; mgr. Calvert Credit Corp., Washington, 1940-47; prin. govt. contract negotiator Gallant Engring. Co., Washington, 1948-49; pres. Fidelity Sound Co., Washington, 1950-85. Seaman 1st class USN, 1935-37. Democrat. Avocations: music, boating, sports. Home: 6912 Granby St Bethesda MD 20817-6038

DEANE, RICHARD HUNTER, JR., lawyer, former federal judge; b. Oct. 18, 1952; BA, U. Ga., 1974, JD, 1977; LLM, U. Mich., 1979. Bar: Ga. 1977. Asst. U.S. atty. No. Dist. Ga., 1980-88; chief gen. crimes sect. U.S. Attys. Office, 1988-91, chief criminal divsn., 1991-94; magistrate judge U.S. Dist. Ct. (no. dist.) Ga., Atlanta, 1994-98; U.S. atty. No. Dist. Ga., Atlanta, 1998—2002; with Jones Day, Atlanta, 2002—. Office: Jones Day 303 Peachtree St Ste 3500 Atlanta GA 30308

DEANGELIS, CATHERINE D. pediatrics educator; b. Scranton, Pa., Jan. 2, 1940; m. James C. Harris. BA, Wilkes Coll., 1965; MD, U. Pitts., 1969; MPH, Harvard U., 1973. Diplomate Nat. Bd. Med. Examiners, Am. Bd. Pediat.; RN Pa., N.Y. Intern in pediat. Children' Hosp., Pitts., 1969—70; resident in pediat. Johns Hopkins Hosp., Balt., 1970—72, teaching fellow pediat. dept. internat. health Sch. Pub. Health, 1972; pe liatrician Roxbury Comprehensive Health Clinic, Boston, 1972—73; asst. prof. pediat. Coll. Physicians and Surgeons, asst. prof. health svc. adminstrn. Sch. Pub. Health Columbia U., 1973—75; mem. staff divsn. pediatric ambulatory care, dir. med. edn. Child Care Project Columbia Presbyn. Med. Ctr., 1973—75; asst. prof. pediat. Sch. Medicine U. Wis., 1975—77, assoc. prof. pediat. Sch. Medicine, 1977—78; dir. ambulatory pediatric svcs. U. Wis. Hosps., 1975—78; assoc. prof. pediat. Johns Hopkins Sch. Medicine, 1978—85; dir. pediatric primary care and adolescent medicine Johns Hopkins Hosp., 1978—84, co-dir. adolescent pregnancy program, 1979—82; with dept. health svcs. adminstrn. and dept. internat. health Johns Hopkins Sch. Hygiene and Pub. Health, 1980—90; dir. residency tng. dept. pediat. Johns Hopkins Hosp., 1983—90, dir. divsn. gen. pediat. and adolescent medicine, 1984—90; deputy chmn. dept. pediat. Johns Hopkins Sch. Medicine, 1983—90, prof. pediat., 1986—, assoc. dean acad. affairs, 1990—93, sr. assoc. dean acad. affairs and faculty, 1993—94, vice dean acad. affairs and faculty, 1994—99; editor Jour. AMA, 2000—. Mem. Gov.'s Task Force to Evaluate Health Care in Wis. State Prisons, 1975—78; chmn. ambulatory care com. U. Wis. Hosp., 1976—78; mem. med. sch. admissions com. U. Wis. Sch. Medicine, 1976—78, chmn., 1977—78; mem. exec. coun. dept. pediat. and Children's Ctr. Johns Hopkins U. Sch. Medicine, 1982—90, chmn. fin. com. dept. pediat., 1984—85, chmn. assoc. prof.'s promotion com., 1985—88, chmn. com. developing Women's Health Ctr. at Johns Hopkins Med. Instns., 1993—; mem. Md. Gov.'s Task Force on Women's Health, 1993—, chair, 1994—; mem. search com. U. Wis., 1976, Johns Hopkins Sch. Medicine, 1984, 88, 92, 93; mem. nat. rev. com. for accreditation of nurse practitioners Am. Nurses' Assn., 1975—79, co-chmn., 1977; mem. peer rev. com. nurse practitioner programs divsn. nursing Health Resources Agy., Dept. HEW, 1979—81. Author: Basic Pediatrics for the Primary Care, 1984; editor: An Introduction to Clinical Research, 1990; editor: (with others) Principles and Practice of Pediatrics, 1990, 1994; assoc. editor Pediatric Annals, 1990—, editor Archives of Pediatrics and Adolescent Medicine, 1993—. Cons. Robert Wood Johnson Found., 1973—; mem. adv. group on improving outcomes for children Pew Charitable Trusts, 1991—92; mem. adv. panel medicine Pew Health Profn.'s Commn.; mem. nat. adv. com. Robert Wood Johnson Clin. Scholars Program, 1992—; mem. steering com. Rural Health Planning, Wis. Recipient George Armstrong award, Ambulatory Pediatric Assn., scholarship, Acad. Adminstrn. and Health Policy, Assn. Health Ctrs., 1993; fellow NIH, 1973. Fellow: APHA, Am. Acad. Pediat. (govt. affairs com. 1984—88, chpt. III youth com. N.Y. chpt. 1974—75, chmn. adolescent com. Md. chpt. 1981—84); mem.: Soc. Adolescent Medicine, Am. Bd. Pediat. (examiner 1986—, long-range planning com. 1990—91, chmn. long-range planning com. 1992—, bd. dirs. 1990—, fin. com. 1991—, sec., treas. 1993—95, chair-elect 1995—96, chair 1996, search com. 1990), Am. Pediatric Soc. (sec., treas. 1989—), Alpha Omega Alpha. Address: JAMA 515 N State St Chicago IL 60610-4325 Office: Johns Hopkins Sch Medicine 720 Rutland Ave Ste 106 Baltimore MD 21205-2109

DE ANGELIS, JUDY, anchorwoman; b. Passaic, N.J., Oct. 1, 1949; d. Fredrick and Patricia (Zollo) De An.; m. Barry Sheffield, Aug. 28, 1977; children: Alexader, Katelin, Corrine. Student, Hart Sch. Music, Hartford, Conn., 1968-69; BA in Speech and Drama, U Hartford, 1971; MA in Edn., Montclair State U., 1973. Lic. 3d class operator FCC. Anchor Sta. WALK-AM-FM, Patchogue, N.Y., 1978-79, Sta. WGBB-FM, Freeport, N.Y., 1979-80, Sta. WKJY-FM, Hempstead, N.Y., 1980, Sta. WHLI, Hempstead, 1980, Sta. WCBS-FM, N.Y.C., 1980-81; reporter, anchor Sta. WNBC, N.Y.C., 1981-88; morning anchor Sta. WINS, N.Y.C., 1988—; co-owner Sheffield Studios, Mahwah, N.J. Freelance anchor The Source, 1982-88; freelance anchor NBC Radio Network, 1982-888, host talk-net, 1989-90; news anchor HBO Entertainment, 1988; indsl. voice-over Odyssey Prodns., N.Y.C., 1981-88; comml. voice-over DWJ, Ridgewood, N.J., 1994—, Gourvitz Comm., N.Y.C., 1995—; cons. Media Placement Svcs., Glen Rock, N.J., 1994—. Author: (documentary) Child Abuse: The Darker Side of Growing Up, 1982 (Olive awrd N.Y.C. Coun. of Chs., 1983; appeared on Broadway in Rockabye Hamlet, 1976. Lectr. on broadcasting all ednl. levels, 1985—; dir. religious edn. Christ Episcopal Ch., Ridgewood, 1995—; troop leader Girl Scouts U.S.A., 1994—. Recipient award for pub. svc. N.Y. Deadline Club,, 1982, spl. citation Office N.Y.C. Comptr., 1983; name Best Radio Newscaster, N.Y. AIR, 2000, 01. Mem. AFTRA, Actors Equity, Ramapo-Bergen Animal Refuge. Democrat. Avocations: carpentry, swmming, gardening, crossword puzzles, sailing. Office: 1010 WINS Radio 888 7th Ave New York NY 10106-0001

DEANGELIS, MICHELE F. school system administrator; b. Boston; d. Carmine and Maria C. Parziale; m. Arthur DeAngelis, Feb. 27, 1971 (dec. Sept. 1987). BS in Edn., U. Mass., Boston, 1960; MEd, Boston U., 1964; cert. advanced grad. study edn. adminstrn., Northeastern U., 1976, EdD in Ednl. Adminstrn., 1986; cert. nat. supt.'s acad., George Washington U., Am. Assn. Sch. Adminstrs., 1992; postgrad., Harvard U., 1993—. Cert. supt. schs., asst. supt. schs., adminstr. spl. edn., reading supr. and specialist, prin. Classroom tchr. Somerville (Mass.) Pub. Schs., 1960-64; reading specialist Dept. Def. Schs., Germany, 1964-67; reading supr. Prince George's County Schs., Bowie, Md., 1967-69; sch. adminstr. cen. office Tewksbury (Mass.) Pub. Schs., 1969—; owner, operator Candelabra Restaurant, Malden, Mass., 1970-72; chief exec. officer Mish Art Diamond Tool Co., Inc., Woburn, Mass., Paterson, N.J., 1973-84; cons. Ednl. Enhancement Assn., Inc., Woburn, 1986—. Adv. bd. mem. Merrimack Edn. Collaborative, Chelmsford, Mass., 1979—, Camp Paul for Handicapped Children, Chelmsford, 1988-90, Harvard U. Prins. Ctr., Cambridge, Mass., 1991—; mem. Mass. Bar Assn. Juvenile Justice Conf. Task Force, 1991—, Blue Ribbon Sch. Task Force, 1991—, high sch. accreditation team New Eng. Assn. Schs. and Colls., 1991, 93, 97; bd. dirs. Juvenile Justice Task Force, Greater Lowell Area, Mass., 1990—; steering com. mem. Merrimack Valley Coalition for Children, Lawrence, Mass., 1990—; ctrl. office rep. Harvard U. Prins. Ctr., 1991-93, adv. counil; mem. Harvard Supts. Round Table, 1999—. Cand. Sch. Com., Somerville, 1969; mem. Ward 2 Civic Assn., Somerville, 1969-80; campaign worker Reelect Mary Tomeo Campaign, Somerville, 1971-75, Elect George Spartichino Campaign, Cambridge, 1990; fnds Sturbridge Village, 1987—; mem. community svc. com. Mass. Bar Assn., 1992—. Recipient commendation Mass. State Dept. Edn., 1985, cert. Appreciation Lowell Task Force Recognition Support Attendant Day Care Program, 1990, cert. Appreciation Mass. Commr. Office Children., letter Appreciation Mass. Bar Assn., 1991, cert. Appreciation, Tewksbury Pub. Schs., 1991, 92, 93. Mem. ASCD, Internat. Reading Assn., Coun. Exceptional Children, N.E. Coalition of Ednl. Leaders, Mass. Adminstrs. for Spl. Edn., Am. Assn. Sch. Adminstrs., Hamilton Reservoir Assn, Kappa Delta Pi, Pi Lambda Theta. Avocations: pianist, drama prodn., travel. Home: 255 Lexington St Woburn MA 01801-5925 Office: Tewksbury Pub Schs 139 Pleasant St Tewksbury MA 01876-2789 Fax: 978-640-7878. E-mail: mdeagelis@tewksbury.mec.edu.

DE ANGELIS, ROSEMARY ELEANOR, actress; b. Bklyn., Apr. 26, 1933; d. Francis and Antoinette (Donofrio) De A.; m. Kenneth Richard Bridges, Sept. 12, 1965 (div. 1983); 1 child, Laurel Ann. BA, Empire State Coll., 1998. Appeared in plays Spinning the Butter, Over The River and Through the Woods, Queen and the Rebels, High Time, Six Characters in Search of an Author, Mrs. Klein (Barrymore award 1993), The Paradise Kid, In the Summer House, The Transfiguration of Benno Blimpie (Drama Desk award-Best Actress), N.Y. Sharespeare Fest. (with Joseph Papp dir.), numerous others; appeared in movies Frequency, Hit and Runway, Two Family House, The Wanderers, Enormous Changes at the Last Minute, Nothing Lasts Forever, Out of Darkness, Household Saints, Mamma Mia, Angie, Two Bits, The Juror; appeared in TV shows 100 Centre St., Guiding Light, As The World Turns, Monkey, Monkey, The Death of Ivan Ilyich, P.B.S. Theatre in Am., Baker's Dozen, The Equalizer, Law and Order; co-writer (screenplay) Burning Intentions, 1992-99; director: Shadow Boxers, 1998; author: The Nightingales; author numerous poems. Recipient residency award, Edna St. Vincent Millay writer's colony. Mem. AFTRA, SAG, Actors Equity Assn. Avocations: painting, photography.

DE ANTONI, EDWARD PAUL, lab administrator; b. San Francisco, Mar. 7, 1941; s. Attilio Mario and Zita Elizabeth (Lolich) DeA.; m. Karen Dolores Thode, Jan. 22, 1966; children: Marc Edward, Christopher Earl. AB, U. San Francisco, 1962; PhD, Cornell U., 1971. Vol. Peace Corps, Turkey, 1964-66; sr. analyst Planning Bur. State of S.D., Pierre, 1973-76; dir. health planning Dept. Health, 1976-81; asst. dir. Assoc. Sch. Bds. S.D., 1981-84; dir. cancer control program Colo. Dept. Health, 1986-90; rsch. dir. Cancer Ctr., Porter Meml. Hosp., Denver, 1991-92; chair genitourinary cancer control Southwest Oncology Group, 1991-97; rsch. dir. Prostate Cancer Edn. Coun., 1991-97; asst. prof. urology Health Sci. Ctr., U. Colo., Denver, 1992-99, sr. instr., 2000—, sr. instr pathology/urology, 2001—. Woodrow Wilson fellow, 1962-63; ESEA fellow, 1966-69 E-mail: ed.deantoni@uchsc.edu. *The life of the mind, inspired by a classic liberal education and by a faith in truth, has been a major force in my life. I realize, however, that such learning enriches most when it is embedded in a life of practical affairs, when it enlivens my relationships with others, and when it is used to seek a good beyond myself.*

DEAN-ZUBRITSKY, CYNTHIA MARIAN, psychologist, researcher; b. Urbana, Ill., Oct. 27, 1950; d. William Bonaparte and Lois (Doran) Dean; m. John Jay Zubritsky, Sept. 15, 1979; 1 child, Grant Doran. BA, Ind. U., 1972; M in Psychology, Pa. State U., 1978; PhD, Temple U., 1989. Counselor New Castle (Pa.) Youth Devel. Ctr., 1972-76; dir. Ill. Family Edn. Ctr., Danville, 1976-77; researcher Pa. State U., University Park, 1977-78, 89—; film cons. Ill. Devel. Disabilities Council, Springfield, 1978; psychologist Atkins House, York, Pa., 1978-82; quality assurance specialist Pa. Office Mental Retardation, Harrisburg, 1982-84; dir. tng. and staff devel. Pa. Office Mental Health, Harrisburg, 1984-89; pvt. practice psychology Harrisburg, 1989—. Bd. dirs. children and youth svcs. Vermilion County Mental Health Program, Danville, 1975-77; psychologist Loysville (Pa.) Youth Devel. Ctr., 1981-82; tchr. Danville Community Coll., 1975; cons. U. Ill., Urbana, 1976, Danville Sch. System, 1975-76; asst. prof. dept. psychiatry U. Pa., 1989—; rsch. alliance for mentally ill Pa., 1989-92. Vol. ARC, 1967-87, YWCA, 1970-89; mem. Pa. Task Force on Mental Health: Women, Harrisburg, 1986-87. Fed. rsch. grantee NIMH, CSAD, AOA; Human Resource Devel. grantee NIMH, 1985-88, Office of Substance Abuse Prevention grantee, 1992-97, Pew Charitable Trust grantee, 1997—, SAMHSA grantee, 1997—. Mem. Internat. Psychogeriatric Assn., Nat. Assn. State Mental Health Program Dirs., Gerontol. Soc. Am., Am. Soc. Aging, Am. Horticulture Soc., Phi Delta Kappa, Phi Mu. Republican. Presbyterian. Avocations: horticulture, interior design. Office: U Pa Dept Psychiatry Philadelphia PA 19104

DEAR, JOHN, priest; b. Elizabeth City, N.C., Aug. 13, 1959; s. David and Margaret D.. BA in History, Duke U., 1981; MDiv, Grad. Theol. Union, Berkeley, Calif., 1992; M in Theology, Grad. Theol. U., Berkeley, Calif., 1993. Ordained priest Roman Cath. Ch., 1993. Asst. pastor St. Aloysius' Ch., Washington, 1993—94; exec. dir. Sacred Heart Ctr., Richmond, Va., 1995—96; prof. Fordham U., Bronx, NY, 1997; exec. dir. Fellowship of Reconciliation, Nyack, NY, 1998—2001. Chaplain Red Cross, N.Y.C., 2001; activist for non-violence. Author: Oscar Romero and the Nonviolent Struggle for Justice,

Our God is Nonviolent: Witnesses in the Struggle for Peace and Justice, The Sacrament of Civil Disobedience, Seeds of Nonviolence, The Sound of Listening, Disarming the Heart: Toward a Vow of Nonviolence, The God of Peace: Toward a Theology of Nonviolence, Peace Behind Bars: A Journal from Jail, Jesus the Rebel, Living Peace, Mary of Nazareth, Prophet of Peace; editor: The Vision of Peace: Faith and Hope in Northern Ireland: The Writings of Nobel Laureate Mairead Maguire, The Road to Peace: Writings on Peace and Justice by Henri Nouwen, And the Risen Bread: The Selected Poems of Daniel Berrigan, 1957-1997, Mohandas Gandhi: Selected Writings, Apostle of Peace: Essays on honor of Daniel Berrigan. Home: Box 516 Springer NM 87747

DEAR, PETER ROBERT, historian, educator; b. Portsmouth, Hampshire, United Kingdom, Mar. 3, 1958; s. John Leslie and Marjorie Rhoda (Halsted) Dear; m. Pauline Carpenter Dear, Feb. 17, 1958. PhD, Princeton U., 1984. Temp. lectr. Imperial Coll., London, 1984—85; rsch. fellow Gonville & Caius Coll., Cambridge, England, 1985—86. Prof. history Cornell U., Ithaca, NY, 1986—. Author: (academic book) Mersenne and the Learning of the Schools; editor: The Lit. Structure of Sci. Argument; author: Discipline and Experience (Ludwik Fleck Prize, 1998); editor: The Scientific Enterprise in Early Modern Europe; author: Revolutionizing the Sciences (Watson Davis Prize, 2002). Recipient Ludwik Fleck Prize (best book), Soc. for Social Studies of Sci., 1998, Davis Prize (best book for gen. audience), History of Sci. Soc., 2002; fellow Guggenheim Fellowship, John Simon Guggenheim Meml. Found., 2000. Mem.: Brit. Soc. for the History of Sci., Soc. for Social Studies of Sci., History of Sci. Soc. Office: Cornell Univ Dept History McGraw Hall Ithaca NY 14853

DEAR, RONALD BRUCE, social work educator; b. Phila., Sept. 23, 1933; s. John David and Margaret (McDade) D.; 1 child, Bruce. BA, Bucknell U., 1955; honors cert., U. Aberdeen, Scotland, 1955; MSW, U. Pitts., 1957; PhD in Social Work, Columbia U., 1972. Cert. social worker, N.Y., Wash. Chief social worker Mental Hygiene Cons. Svc., Aberdeen Proving Ground, Md., 1958-60; chief Neuropsychiat. Clinic, 7th Inf. Divsn., Korea, 1960-61; residence dir. Horizon House, Inc., Phila., 1961-64; prof. U. Wash., Seattle, 1970—. Vis. prof. U. Bergen, Norway, 1984, U. Trondheim, Norway, 1996; faculty lobbyist U. Wash., 1983-85, 88-91, faculty pres., 1993-95; master tchr. Coun. on Social Work Edn., 1991, 93, 94, 97; mem. adv. bd. Internat. Population and Family Assocs. Author: Social Welfare Policy: Trends and Issues, 6th edit., 2001; editor: Poverty in Perspective, 1973; mem. editl. bd. Columns, 2001—, The Social Policy Jour., 2002—; mem. editl. adv. com. Columns, 2001—; contbr. articles to profl. jours. and encys. Apptd. by gov. to income assistance adv. com., 1987-93, to adv. com. for Dept. S ocial and Health Svcs., 1980-83, Human Svcs. Policy Ctr., 1996—, adv. com. Wash. State Econ. Svcs., 1996—; mem nat. adv. bd. Influencing State Policy, 1997—; appeared in centennial program of Columbia U. Sch. of Social Work, 1998. 1st lt. U.S. Army, 1957-61. Mem. NASW (Social Worker of Yr. Wash. chpt. 1981, mem. staff legis. N.Y.C. chpt. 1968-69), Acad. Cert. Social Workers, Coun. on Social Work Edn. Avocations: travel in over 45 countries, photography, hiking. Home: 7328 16th Ave NE Seattle WA 98115-5737 Office: U Wash Sch Social Work 4101 15th Ave NE Seattle WA 98105-6250

DEARBORN, MAUREEN MARKT, speech and language clinician; b. Brockton, Mass., Jan. 19, 1948; d. Francis Joseph and Marjorie Agnes (White) M.; m. James Clement Bovin, Nov. 6, 1970 (div. June 1973); m. David C. Dearborn, Jan. 14, 1989. BA in Speech Pathology and Audiology, U. Mass., 1970; MA in Ednl. Psychology, Am. Internat. Coll., Springfield, Mass. Speech and lang. clinician Holyoke (Mass.) Pub. Schs., 1970—. Chmn. Holyoke Cancer Crusade, 1985; voter registration chmn. Holyoke Dem. Com., 1987; chmn. deaconesses 2d Congl. Ch. Holyoke. Mem.: DAR (historian Eunice Day 1984—), Mass. Tchrs. Assn., Mass. Speech, Hearing and Lang. Assn., Am. Speech, Hearing and Lang. Assn. (continuing edn. adv. bd. 1988—91, congl. action contact 1988—90), Holyoke Tchrs. Assn., Hampden County Tchrs. Assn. (pres. 1981, 1987, sec. 1982, v.p. 1984—86, treas. 1988—), Dorchester Hist. Soc., Wrenthan Hist. Soc., Assn. for Gravestone Studies, Friends of the Libr. Coun. (treas. 1992—2000), Mass. Geneal. Soc., New Eng. Hist. and Geneal. Soc. Avocations: bicycling, antiques, genealogy, aerobics. Home: 257 W Franklin St Holyoke MA 01040-2210 Office: Holyoke Pub Schs 57 Suffolk St Holyoke MA 01040-5015

DEARDEN, ROBERT JAMES, pharmacist; b. Phila., Sept. 25, 1932; s. Raymond Francis and Genevieve (Hendershot) D.; m. Marie Elizabeth Harrell, Aug. 21, 1954; children: Cherylanne, James, Jeanette, Denise. BS in Pharmacy, Temple U., 1955. Registered community pharmacist, Fla., N.J., Pa. Pharmacist, mgr. Merck Sharp and Dohme, Phila., 1955-57, Roman Pharmacy, Phila., 1957-63; pharmacist Phila. Polio Immunization Drive, 1963; pharmacist, pres. Barclay Pharm. Surg. Corp., Cherry Hill, N.J., 1964-83; pharmacist, mgr. Eckerd Drug Corp., Clearwater, Fla., 1983-95; with Cardinal Health Network, 1995—. Preceptor Fla. State Bd. Intern Program, Sarasota, 1986-95. V.p., treas. Wedgewood Lakes Condo. Assn. Mem. Am. Pharm. Assn., Fla. Pharm. Assn., Nat. Audubon Soc., Kappa Psi. Republican. Roman Catholic. Avocations: attending major league baseball spring training, travel, swimming, bicycling. Home: 5202 Wedgewood Ln Sarasota FL 34235-7020

DEARDOFF, R. BRUCE, automotive executive; b. Apr. 2, 1948; BS, Fordham U, N.Y.C. CEO Island Lincoln-Mercury Group, 1985—. Office: Island Lincoln-Mercury 1850 E Merritt Island Cswy Merritt Island FL 32952-2665*

DEARING, REINHARD JOSEF, city official; b. Bamberg, Fed. Republic of Germany, May 1, 1947; m. Michele Jack, Feb. 14, 1967 (div. Oct. 1980); 1 child, Lauren; m. Patricia Lee Pollack, Jan. 2, 1982; 1 child, Bradford. AA, La. State U., Baton Rouge, 1968, BA, 1975, MA, 1977, postgrad., 1979; PhD, Northwestern U., 2003. CPM, Tulane U., 1989. Adminstrv. officer La. Nat. Bank, Baton Rouge, 1972-75; teaching asst. La. State U., 1975-79; adj. asst. prof. U. So. Miss., Natchez, 1977-79; chief of staff, chief adminstrv. officer City of Slidell, La., 1979—. Cons. La. Mcpl. Assn., Baton Rouge, 1985-87. Author: The Waffen-SS: A Representative Study, 1977, General James Dearing and the Cause of the Confederacy, 2001, SS General Karl Wolff and his Italian Odyssey, 2003; contbr. articles to profl. jours. Mem. Gov.'s Mcpl. Policy Task Force, PJPHS sch. bd. Officer U.S. Army, 1968-72. Decorated Silver Star, col. La. State Guard; named Hon. State Senator, La. Mem. La. Mcpl. Assn., Nat. League Cities, St. Tammany Mcpl. Assn., Am. Pub. Works Assn., La. State Alumni Assn. (dir. 1985-87), Assn. U.S. Army, Am. Legion, Internat. City Mgrs. Assn., Mil. Order of the Stars and Bars, Sons of Confederate Vets., Lions. Republican. Avocations: historic research, Civil War reenacting, fencing, racquetball, jogging. Office: City of Slidell PO Box 828 Slidell LA 70459-0828 E-mail: RDearing@cityofslidell.org.

DEARINGER, DAVID B. art historian, curator; b. Versailles, Ky., May 22, 1950; s. John Arthur Dearinger and Anna Louise Lane. BA, U. Ky., 1972; MA in Am. Studies, CUNY, 1983, MPhil in Art History, 1986, PhD in Art History, 1993. Flight svc. mgr., flight attendant Trans World Airlines, 1973-88; rsch. asst. Nat. Acad. Design, N.Y.C., 1985-88, asst. curator, 1988-89, assoc. curator, 1993-96, acting dir., 1996-97, chief curator, 1996—; adj. lectr. dept. art history Hunter Coll., N.Y.C., 1988, Queens Coll., Flushing, N.Y., 1988-89; archives technician Archives of Am. Art Smithsonian Instn., N.Y.C., 1989-93; instr. Fashion Inst. Tech. SUNY, 1989-91, adj. asst. prof., 1991—; adj. lectr. art dept. Bklyn. Coll., 1990-91, Adelphi U., Garden City, N.Y., 1991; lectr. Am. arts course Sotheby's Ednl. Studies, N.Y.C., 1991-92. Author: Rave Reviews: American Art and its Critics, 1826-1925, 2000; co-author: (with William H. Gerdts) Masterworks of American Impressionism from the Pfeil Collection, 1992, Faces of Justice: The Portraits of John Marshall, 2001; contbg. author: May Family Collection of American Paintings, 1988, An American Collection, 1989, Prix de Home, 1991, The Internat. Atlas of Western Art History, 1994, Nature Observed, Nature Interpreted Nineteenth-Century Am. Landscape Drawings and Watercolors from the Nat. Acad. of Design and the Cooper-Hewitt Mus. Nat. Design Mus., 1995, Permanent Collection Catalogue Addison Gallery Am. Art, Phillips Acad., Andover, Mass., 1996, 150 Yrs. of Phila. Still-Life Painting, 1997, All Things Bright and Beautiful: California Impressionist Paintings, 1998, Selections from the Permanent Collecton of Am. Art, New Britain (Conn.) Mus. Am. Art, 1998, Am. Nt. Biography, 1998, Ency. New Eng. Culture, 1999; contbr. articles to profl. jours. Grantee Luce Found., 2000, Lucelia Found., 2000; dissertation fellow Luce Found., 1989-90, 90-91. Democrat. Avocations: genealogy, body building. Office: Nat Acad Design 1083 Fifth Ave New York NY 10128

DE ARMAS, FREDERICK ALFRED, foreign language educator; b. Havana, Cuba, Feb. 9, 1945; came to U.S., 1959, naturalized, 1968; s. Alfredo and Ana Maria (Galdos) De A. BA magna cum laude, Stetson U., DeLand, Fla., 1965; PhD (Carnegie fellow 1965-68), U. N.C., 1968. Mem. faculty La. State U., Baton Rouge, 1968-88, prof. Spanish, 1978-88, acting chmn. dept., 1979-80, dir. grad. studies, 1980-85; prof. Spanish and comparative lit. Pa. State U., 1988-91, Disting. prof. Spanish and comparative lit., 1991-98, Edwin Erle Sparks prof. Spanish and Comparative Lit., 1998-2000, fellow Inst. for Arts and Humanities, 1989-2000; prof. Spanish U. Chgo., 2000-01, Andrew W. Mellon prof. of humanities, 2001—. Vis. assoc. prof. U. Mo., Columbia, summer 1977, vis. prof., fall 1986; vis. prof. Duke U., spring 1994. Author: The Four Interpolated Stories in the Roman Comique, 1971, Paul Scarron, 1972, The Invisible Mistress, 1976, The Return of Astraea, 1986, The Prince in the Tower, 1993, Heavenly Bodies, 1996, A Star-Crossed Golden Age, 1998, Cervantes, Raphael and the Classics, 1998, also articles; editor: Pa. State U. Studies in Romance Literatures, 1991-2001; co-editor: European Literary Careers, 2002; mem. editorial adv. bd. Bull. Comediantes, 1981—, Hispanófila, 1981-88, 2001—, PMLA, 1985-89, Hispania, 1993-95, Jour. Interdisciplinary Lit. Studies, 1993—, S. Atlantic Rev., 2003—; assoc. editor South Central Rev., 1987-89, Comparative Literature Studies, 1989-2001. NEH grantee, summer 1979; NEH fellow, 1985, 95, summer inst., 1989, dir. summer inst., 1994, dir. summer seminar, 2003. Mem. MLA, Comparative Lit. Assn., Renaissance Soc. Am., Am. Assn. Tchrs. Spanish and Portuguese, Assn. Internat. Hispanistas, Hispanic Soc. Am. (corr.), Cervantes Soc. Am. (v.p. 2003—). Office: U Chgo Dept Romance Lang 1050 E 59th St Chicago IL 60637 E-mail: fdearmas@uchicago.edu.

DEASON, HEROLD MCCLURE, lawyer; b. Alton, Ill., July 24, 1942; s. Ernest Wilburn and Mildred Mary (McClure) D.; m. Wilma Lee Kaemmerle, June 18, 1966; children: Sean, Ian, Whitney. BA, Albion Coll., 1964; JD, Northwestern U., 1967. Bar: Mich. 1968. Assoc. Bodman, Longley & Dahling, LLP, Detroit, 1967-74, ptnr., 1975—. City atty. Grosse Pointe Pk., Mich., 1978—. Vice chmn. Detroit, Windsor Freedom Festival, 1978-92; bd. dirs. Spirit of Detroit Assn., 1980—. Recipient Spirit of Detroit award, Detroit City Coun., 1986. Mem. ABA, Mich. Assn. Mcpl. Attys. (pres. 1995-97), Detroit Bar Assn., Can.-U.S. Bus. Assn. (v.p. 1997—), Grosse Pointe Yacht Club (commodore 1992-93), Detroit Racquet Club, Windsor Club, Clinton River Boat Club. Home: 1044 Kensington Ave Grosse Pointe Park MI 48230-1437 Office: Bodman Longley & Dahling 100 Renaissance Ctr 34th Fl Detroit MI 48243-1001 E-mail: hdeason@bodmanlongley.com.

DEASY, CORNELIUS MICHAEL, architect; b. Mineral Wells, Tex., July 19, 1918; s. Cornelius and Monetta (Palmo) D.; m. Lucille Laney, Sept. 14, 1941; children— Diana, Carol, Ann. B. Arch., U. So. Calif., 1941. Practice architecture, Los Angeles, 1946-76, partner, Robert D. Bolling, 1960-76; Prin. works include prin. offices student union, Calif. State U., Los Angeles.; Author: Design for Human Affairs, 1974, Designing Places for People, 1985. Vice pres. Los Angeles Beautiful; dir. Regional Plan Assn. Commr., Los Angeles Bd. Zoning Appeals, 1973— . Recipient numerous design awards, Nat. Endowment Arts award, 1983. Fellow AIA (past pres., dir. So. Calif. chpt., chmn. com. research) Home and Office: Davenport Creek Farm 4979 Davenport Creek Rd San Luis Obispo CA 93401-8109

DEASY, WILLIAM JOHN, construction, marine dredging, engineering and mining company executive; b. N.Y.C., June 22, 1937; s. Jeremiah and Margaret (Quinn) D.; m. Carol Ellyn Lemons, Feb. 1, 1963; children: Cameron, Kimberly. BS in Civil Engring, Cooper Union, 1958; LLB, U. Wash., 1963. With Morrison Knudsen Corp.- Boise, Idaho, 1964-88, v.p. N.W. region, 1972-75, v.p. mining, 1975-78, group v.p. mining, 1978-83, exec. v.p. mining, shipbuilding and mfg., 1983-84, pres., chief operating officer, 1984-85, pres., chief exec. officer, bd. dirs., 1985-88; vice chair, pres., CEO, bd. dirs. T.L. James & Co., New Orleans, 1991-99; chmn. bd. T.L. James & Co., 1999—. Mem. adv. bd. Sundt Cos., Inc.; chmn. endowment com., trustee Loyola U., New Orleans. Mem. La. Com. of 100. Mem. Moles. Home: 2427 Camp St Apt C New Orleans LA 70130-5645 Office: T L James & Co Inc PO Box 20115 New Orleans LA 70141-0115 E-mail: wjdeasy@bellsouth.net.

DEATER-DECKARD, KIRBY, psychology educator, researcher; b. Peoria, Ill., Apr. 2, 1967; s. Loren and Mary Jane Deckard; m. Keirsten Deater-Deckard, Aug. 31, 1990; 1 child, Anna. BA, Pa. State U., 1988; MA, PhD, U. of Va., 1994. Post-doctoral fellow Vanderbilt U., Nashville, 1994—95; rsch. scientist Social, Genetic and Devel. Psychiatry Rsch. Ctr., Inst. of Psychiatry, London, 1995—98; assoc. prof. Dept. of Psychology, U. of Oreg., 1998—. Contbr. articles to profl. jours. Elder of session Wetsminster Presbyn. Ch., Eugene, Oreg., 2001—. Rsch. grant, NSF, 1999—2002, Joseph Rowntree Found., 1998—2000, Rsch. Grant, Nat. Inst. of Child Health and Human Devel., 2002—, Pre-doctoral Tng. Grant fellowship, NIMH, 1991—93. Mem.: Am. Psychol. Soc., Soc. for Rsch. in Child Devel., Phi Beta Kappa.

DEATHERAGE, EDWARD L. psychologist; b. LA, Jan. 20, 1941; s. William A. Deatherage and Fannie M. Wallace-Deatherage; children: Amy L. Treece, Eric A. Treece. BA, Loma Linda U., Calif., 1971; MA in Psychology, Pepperdine U., 1974; PhD in Psychology, U.S. Internat. U., San Diego, 1977. Diplomate and Fellow Am. Bd. of Med. Hypnotherapists, 1987, Am. Bd. of Med. Psychotherapists and Diagnosticians, 1988. Clin. dir. Beverly Enterprises, San Bernardino, Calif., 1975—77; clin. resident psychology Wright Patterson AFB Med. Ctr., 1977—78; staff psychologist Fairchild AFB Med. Ctr., Wash., 1978—81; clinic dir., psychologist Psychol. Svcs., Spokane, Wash., 1981—91; clinic dir. North Idaho Counseling Svc., Ctr. for Awareness, Post Falls, Idaho, 1993—. Mem. Spokane County Cmty. Services Adv. Bd., Wash., 1981—85. Capt. USAF, 1977—81. Mem.: Am. Coun. of Hypnotist Examiners, Am. Psychol. Soc., APA. Independent. Office: Ctr for Awareness 601 E Seltice Way Ste 209 Post Falls ID 83854 Office Fax: 208-773-6739.

DEATHERAGE, WILLIAM VERNON, lawyer; b. Drumright, Okla., Apr. 17, 1927; s. William Johnson and Pearl Mae (Watson) D.; m. Priscilla Ann Campbell, Sept. 16, 1932; children: Thomas William, Andrea Susan. BS, U. Oreg., 1952, LLB with honors, 1954. Bar: Oreg. 1954, U.S. Dist. Ct. Oreg. 1956. Ptnr. Frohnmayer, Deatherage, Pratt, Jamieson & Clarke & Moore, Medford, Oreg., 1954—. Bd. dirs. Oreg. Law Inst., U. Oreg. Found. With USN, 1945-48. Mem. Am. Coll. Trial Lawyers, Internat. Acad. Trial Lawyers, Delta Theta Phi, Rogue Valley Country Club (pres. 1988), Rogue River Valley Univ. Club. Democrat. Episcopalian. Address: 2592 E Barnett Rd Medford OR 97504-8345 E-mail: fdfirm@fdfirm.com.

DEATON, BEVERLY JEAN, nursing administrator, educator; b. Plainview, Ill., Oct. 15, 1942; d. Charles Byron Kirby and Wilma Irene Crocket Kirby Novy; m. John H. Deaton, May 18, 1963; children: Mary Kathryn Deaton Lovejoy, Amy Christine Deaton Williams. Diploma, St John's Hosp. Sch. Nursing, Springfield, Ill., 1963; BSN, So. Ill. U., Edwardsville, 1986, MSN, 1994. RN Ill., cert. inpatient obstet. nursing, ACLS instr. Maternity staff nurse St. Francis Hosp., Litchfield, Ill., 1971-76, maternity supr., 1976-81, dir. maternity, 1981—2001, dir. quality svcs., risk mgmt., 2001—; legal nurse cons., 2000—. Childbirth educator, 1975—2001; presenter at cmty. and profl. orgn. confs.; fetal monitor instr.-trainer Assn. Women's Health, Obstetric and Neonatal Nurses, 1991—. Named Nurse of Yr., March of Dimes, Chgo., 1994, March of Dimes Springfield, Ill. Region, 2002. Mem.: AWHONN (vice chair Ill. sect. 1995—96, dist. VI 1997, nat. bd. dirs. 1999—), Sigma Theta Tau. Christian. Avocations: travel, photography. Home: PO Box 374 Litchfield IL 62056-0374 Office: St Francis Hosp PO Box 1215 Litchfield IL 62056-0999

DEATON, CHARLES MILTON, lawyer; b. Hattiesburg, Miss., Jan. 19, 1931; s. Ivanes Dean Deaton and Martha Sarah Elizabeth Fortenberry; m. Mary Dent Dickerson, Aug. 15, 1951; children: Diane Rossi, Dara Rogers, Charles M., Jr. BA, Millsaps Coll., 1949-51, 55-56; JD, U. Miss., 1959. Legis. asst. U.S. Ho. of Reps., Washington, 1957; assoc. Brewer, Deaton & Bowman, Greenwood, Miss., 1958—; mem. Miss. Ho. of Reps., Jackson, 1960-80, appropriations chmn., 1976-80; city atty. City of Greenwood, Miss., 1970-84; adminstrv. asst. to Govs. Wm. Winter, B. Allain State of Miss., Jackson, 1980-88; bd. dirs. Bank of Commerce, Greenwood. Recipient Miss Conservationist of Yr. award The Nature Conservancy, Jackson, 1991, Nat. Oak Leaf award, Arlington, Va., 1992, Sports Hall of Fame award Millsaps Coll., Jackson, Alumnus of Yr. award, 1995, others. Mem. ABA, The Nature Conservancy, Miss. Wildlife Heritage Commn., others. Avocations: cooking, hunting, fishing, conservation, gardening. Office: Brewer Deaton & Bowman PO Drawer B Greenwood MS 38935

DEATON, FAE ADAMS, clinical social worker, counselor; b. Phila., Feb. 19, 1932; d. Charles Sizemore and Dorothea Lucia (Adams) Deaton; children: Dorothea Fae Stein Krause Scott, Caroline Louise Stein Collins, Erich Charles Stein. MusB, Salem Coll., 1953; postgrad., Oxford U., Eng., 1961—63, U. Alaska, 1968—69, Wright State U., 1971—73; MS in Edn., Old Dominion U., 1975; MSW, Norfolk State U., 1980; postgrad., Santa Clara U., 1980, Elizabeth City State U., 2000—. Diplomate Am. Bd. Social Workers, Am. Bd. Clin. Social Workers; lic. clin. social worker, Va., N.C.; lic. profl. counselor, Va.; lic., cert. Del Giacco art therapist. Tchr. music, Mifflin, Ohio, 1953—54; h.s. supr. USN Dependents Sch., Argentia, Canada, 1956—57; tchr. USAF Dependents Sch., Croughton, England, 1960—63, Upper Heyford, England, 1963—64; mag. editor Scott AFB, Ill., 1966—67; mem. staff Hist. and Fine Arts Mus., Anchorage, 1968—70; publicity chmn., mem. publicity staff Alaska Council on Arts, 1969—70; counselor Youth Svcs. Bur., Dayton, Ohio, 1973; engring. rsch. aide Wright Patterson AFB Biophysics Lab., Dayton, 1973; writer Dayton Daily News, 1973; field rsch. aide Am. Inst. Rsch., Palo Alto, Calif., 1974—75; counselor, patient advocate Norfolk (Va.) Free Clinic, 1975—76; adminstrv. asst. econs. dept. Old Dominion U., Norfolk, 1975—76; tchr., counselor Blessed Sacrament Sch., Norfolk, 1976—77; mem. mental health team, young adolescent unit, milieu therapist Portsmouth (Va.) Psychiat. Ctr., 1977—79, mem. children's unit, 1979—80; child, adult, family and marital therapist sexual trauma treatment Ctr. Psychiatrists/Portsmouth Psychiat. Ctr., 1980—82; mem. psychology faculty Tidewater C.C., Virginia Beach, Va., 1987—88; therapist, social worker children's svcs. sexual trauma treatment unit Cmty. Mental Health Ctr. and Psychiat. Inst. Dept. Psychiatry, Eastern Va. Med. Sch., Norfolk, 1983—88; dir., psychotherapist Hampton Roads Psychotherapy Assocs. and Childhood Trauma Treatment Ctr., Norfolk, 1988—95; mem. lt. gov.'s taskforce on sexual victimization prevention Va., 1992—95; lead clin. social worker Edenton unit Albemarle Mental Health Ctr., 1995—99; ind. clin. social worker, pvt. practice Elizabeth City, NC, 1999—; mem. Edenton DSS Cmty. Resource Coms., 1999—2001. Cons. Families United, Norfolk, Va., 2001—02; lectr. Elizabeth City State U., 2003—; intern Mus. of Albemarle, 2003; adj. faculty social works dept. Elizabeth City State U., 2003—. Contbr. papers and lectures various confs. and tng. programs in U.S., 1967—. Mem. Tidewater Profl. Assn. on Child Abuse, 1978—82, pres., 1981—82; mem. Tidewater Rape Info. Svcs., Norfolk, 1978—88; adminstr./author, bd. dirs. Sexual Abuse Helpline of Tidewater, 1979—95; mem. VBDSS Sexual Abuse Treatment Team, 1979—82; mem. adhoc com. Nat. Coalition on Sexual Abuse, 1980—81; pres. Tidewater Alliance on Sexual Abuse, 1984—87; mem. admissions/release bd. Norfolk Lakehouse Girls Detention Home, 1978—79; program chmn. Conf. Internat. Yr. of the Child, Norfolk, 1979; mem. Middle Atlantic Coalition on Sexual Victimization of Children, 1980—83, sec., 1981—82; mem. Virginia Beach Dept. Social Services Multi Discipline Team, 1983—86, Norfolk Com. for Prevention of Child Abuse, 1983—95; chmn. task force spl. children Children's Art Center, Norfolk, 1979—81; co-chmn. Gov.'s Child Abuse sub-com.; chmn. Families United Va., Inc., 1980—95; sponsor/coord. Virginia Beach chpt. Parents United, chmn. quality assurance com., regional chairperson mid.-Atlantic chpts., 1987—92; chmn. 20th Anniversary, Norfolk, 1991; historian Alaska Artists Guild, 1969—70; mem. Elmendorf AFB Sch. Bd., 1967—68; state dir. parents United Inc., Va., 1979—92, Famlies United, Tidewater, 1992—95; mem. Messiah concert Evelyn Johnson Cmty. Singers, 2000—; vol. Hampton Rds. Naval Mus., 2001—, USS Wis., 2001—; clarinetist Pensacola H.S. Marching Band, 1946—47, Newport Symphony Orch., 1948—49; mem. choir Mount Lebanon AME Zion Ch.; mem. campus and worship commn. Christ Episcopal Ch., 2003—; Sunday Sch. pianist Warrenton Presbyn. Ch., 1946—47; mem. Salem Coll. Chorus, 1949—53, Salem Chapel Quartet, 1952—53, Base Chapel Choir, RAF, Croughton, 1961—64, jr. choir dir., 1962—64; mem. Trinity Luth. Ch. Choir, Norfolk, 1970; bd. dirs. Tidewater Alliance on Sexual Abuse, 1981—88, Tidewater Assembly on Family Life, 1981—82, Va. chpt. Nat. Com. on Prevention of Child Abuse, 1981—82, Parents Anonymous of Va., 1984—86, Norfolk Little Theater, 1977—78; bd. mem. Parents United Internat., San Jose, Calif., 1987—92. Recipient Spl. recognition award Peninsular Task Force on Sexual Abuse Child Abuse for work contbr. to the wellbeing of children and family, Gov.'s award for work in child/sexual abuse, Norfolk, Va. Mem. NASW, Am. Profl. Soc. on Abuse of Children (life), Calif. Profl. Soc. on Abuse of Children (life), Nat. League Am. Pen Women, Elizabeth City Hist. Neighborhood Assn., So. Christian Leadership Conf., Children's Home Soc. N.C. (support group sec.). Office: 205 E Fearing St Elizabeth City NC 27909-4815 E-mail: faedeaton@hotmail.com.

DEATS, SUZANNE, writer, editor, artist; b. Abilene, Tex., Nov. 14, 1937; d. Otto and Susan Reynolds Deats; m. Benny J. Bedford, Aug. 27, 1960 (dec. Jan. 19, 1978); children: Aaron Bedford, John Bedford. BA in Fine Arts, U. N.Mex., 1981. Juror Santa Fe Art Festival, Main St. Show, Ft. Worth, Cowley Coll., Kans. Contbr. articles to periodicals; author, editor: Voices in New Mexico Art, 1996; author: (book) Earl Bliss, 1999, Evelyne Boren: Joie de Vivre, 1998, The Life and Art of William Vincent, 1997; co-author: Interior Furnishings Southwest, 1992; prodn. editor: book The New Mexico Millennium Collection, 2000, 2001, Kent Ullberg: Monuments to Nature, 1998, novel Shannon, 1998, book Artist en Route, 1997; one-woman shows include Hill's Gallery, Santa Fe, Ten Craftsmen, Albuquerque, Odessa Coll., Tex., Sombraje, Santa Fe, exhibited in group shows at Happy World Enterprises, Japan; prodn. editor: Voices in New Mexico Art, 1996. Mem.: Mensa. Avocations: fiction, design, cooking, travel.

DEAVENPORT, EARNEST W., JR., chemical executive; b. Macon, Miss. BS chem. engring., Mississippi State U.; MA in Mgmt., MIT. Chem. engr. Eastman Chem. Co., 1960, pres. Carolina divsn., 1982; asst. gen. mgr. Eastman Chem. Divsn., 1985; v.p. Kodak, 1985, pres. and group v.p., 1989; chmn., CEO Eastman Chem., Kingsport, Tenn., 1994—. Chmn. Am. Plastics Coun.; bd. dir. First Am. Corp. Alfred P. Sloan fellow MIT; recipient Exec. Excellence award Chem. Mgmt. and Resources Assn., 1995. Mem. Chem. Mfg. Assn. (bd. dir. 1994—), Soc. Chem. Industry (exec. com. Am. section), NAE. Office: Eastman Chem Co PO Box 511 Kingsport TN 37662-5000

DEAVER, PHILLIP LESTER, lawyer; b. Long Beach, Calif., July 21, 1952; s. Albert Lester and Eva Lucille (Welton) D. Student, USCG Acad., 1970-72; BA, UCLA, 1974; JD, U. So. Calif., 1977. Bar: Hawaii 1977, U.S. Dist. Ct. Hawaii 1977, U.S. Ct. Appeals (9th cir.) 1978, U.S. Supreme Ct. 1981. Assoc. Carlsmith, Wichman, Case, Mukai & Ichiki, Honolulu, 1977-83, ptnr., 1983-86, Bays, Deaver, Lung, Rose & Baba, Honolulu, 1986, mng. ptnr., 1986-95. Contbr. articles to profl. jours. Bd. dirs. Parents and Children Together, 1993—2003, v.p. 2000-2002, chmn. bd., 2003-. Mem. ABA (forum com. on the Constrn. Industry), AIA (affiliate Hawaii chpt.), Am. Arbitration Assn. (arbitrator). Home: 2471 Pacific Heights Rd Honolulu HI 96813-1029 Office: Bays Deaver Lung Rose and Baba PO Box 1760 Honolulu HI 96806-1760 E-mail: pdeaver@legalhawaii.com.

DEBAETS, TIMOTHY JOSEPH, lawyer, legal educator; b. South Bend, Ind., Aug. 16, 1949; s. Joseph H. and Dorothy (Marshall) DeB. BA, Columbia U., 1971; JD, Duke U., 1975. Bar: N.Y. 1976, U.S. Dist. Ct. (so. and ea. dists.) N.Y. 1976. Assoc. Simpson Thacher & Bartlett, N.Y.C., 1975-79, Pavia & Harcourt, N.Y.C., 1979-83, Stults & Marshall, N.Y.C., 1983-90, Cowan, DeBaets, Abrahams & Sheppard, N.Y.C., 1990-91, ptnr., 1991—. Asst. adj. prof. NYU Sch. of Arts, N.Y.C., 1984, Sch. of Continuing Film, Video & Edn. dept. of film and video and broadcasting, 1991. Mem. editl. bd. Duke Law Jour., 1974-75; contbr. articles to jours., lectr., panelist in field. Bd. dirs. Dance Theatre Workshop, N.Y.C., 1981-91, Vol. Lawyers for the Arts. Served with USAR, 1971-77. Mem. ABA (forum com. on entertainment and sports industry 1980—), N.Y. State Bar Assn. (mem. spl. com. on copyright laaw 1981—, chmn. 1984-87, exec. com. sect. on entertainment and sports law 1988—, treas. 1994—, vice chmn. 1996—), Assn. Bar City N.Y. (mem. spl. com. on entertainment and sports law 1980-84, art law com. 1986-89, sports law 1993-95, entertainment law 1997-99), Copyright Soc. U.S. Office: Cowan DeBaets Abrahams & Sheppard 40 W 57th St New York NY 10019-4001

DEBAKEY, ERNEST GEORGE, physician, surgeon; b. Lake Charles, La., Feb. 17, 1912; s. Shaker and Raheega DeB.; m. Marsha Lauder, Apr. 8, 1999; 1 child, Elizabeth. BS Pharmacy, Tulane U., 1931, MD, 1939. Diplomate Am.

Coll. Surgeons. Intern Charity Hosp., New Orleans, 1939-40, resident, 1941-42, 45-48; resident thoracic surgery Washington U., St. Louis, 1940-41; pvt. practice Mobile, Ala., 1948-93. Prof. emeritus surgery Tulane U., 1949—, U. South Ala., Mobile, 1973—; staff dept. surgery Mobile Infirmary Med. Ctr., Providence Hosp., Springhill Meml. Hosp., USA-Doctors. Chmn. DeBakey Fund Drug Edn. Program, Mobile, 1992—, DeBakey Fund Perioperative Nursing Continuing edn., 1989-93, DeBakey awards excellence perioperative nursing. Major USAF, 1942-45, CBI. Recipient award excellence Mobile Infirmary Med. Ctr., 1993; named Physician of Yr. Mobile County Med. Auxiliary, 1993; dept. surgery Mobile Infirmary Med. Ctr. named DeBakey Surg. Ste. in his honor, 1988, Ernest G. DeBakey Charitable Found., 1997; inducted Ala. Healthcare Hall of Fame, 2001. Fellow Am. Coll. Surgeons; mem. Ala. Thoracic Soc. Republican. Episcopalian. Office: 1729 Springhill Ave Mobile AL 36604-1411

DEBAKEY, LOIS, science communications educator, writer, editor; b. Lake Charles, La. d. S. M. and Raheeja (Zorba) DeBakey. BA in Math., Tulane U., MA in Lit. and Linguistics, 1959, PhD in Lit. and Linguistics, 1963. Asst. prof. English Tulane U., 1963—64; asst. prof. sci. communication Tulane U. Med. Sch., 1963-65, assoc. prof. sci. communication, 1965-67, prof. sci. comm., 1967-68, lectr., 1968-80, adj. prof., 1981-92; prof. sci. comm. Baylor Coll. Medicine, Houston, 1968—. Mem. biomed. libr. rev. com. Nat. Libr. Medicine, Bethesda, Md., 1973-77, bd. regents, 1981-86, cons., 1986—, co-chmn. permanent paper task force, 1987—, lit. selection tech. rev. com., 1988-93, chmn., 1992-93, outreach planning panel, 1988-89; dir. courses in med. comm. ACS and other orgns.; trustee DeBakey Med. Found., 1995--; exec. coun. Commn. on Colls. So. Assn. Colls. and Schs., 1975-80; mem. nat. adv. coun. U. So. Calif. Ctr. Continuing Med. Edn., 1981, steering com. Plain English Forum, 1984, founding bd. dirs. Friends Nat. Libr. Medicine, 1985—, chmn. med. media award of excellence com. FNLM, 1992—, adv. com. Soc. for Preservation English Lang. Lit., 1986, Nat. Adv. Bd. John Muir Med. Film Festival, 1990-92, The Internat. Health and Med. Film Festival, Acad. of Judges, 1992-93; mem. adv. coun. U. Tex. at Austin Sch. Nursing Found., 1993—; cons. legal writing com. ABA, 1983—, Ency. Brit. Biomed. and Health Database, 1999--; former cons. Nat. Assn. Std. Med. Vocabulary; pioneered instruction in sci. comm. in med. sch. Sr. author: The Scientific Journal: Editorial Policies and Practices, 1976; co-author: Medicine: Preserving the Passion, 1987; Medicine: Preserving the Passion in the 21st Century, 2003; mem editl. bd.: Tulane Studies in English, 1966-68, Cardiovascular Research Center Bull., 1971-83, Health Communications and Informatics, 1975-80, Forum on Medicine, 1977-80, Grants Mag, 1978-81, Internat. Jour. Cardiology, 1981-86, Excerpta Medica's Core Jours. in Cardiology, 1981—, Health Comm. and Biopsychosocial Health, 1981-82, Internat. Angiology, 1985—, Jour. AMA, 1988-2002; mem. usage panel Am. Heritage Dictionary, 1980—; cons. Webster's Med. Desk Dictionary, 1986; editl. advisor Ency. Brit.; contbr. articles on biomed. comm. and sci. writing, literacy, also other subjects to profl. jours., books, encys., and pub. press. Active Found. for Advanced Edn. in Sci., 1977—. Recipient Disting. Svc. award, Am. Med. Writers Assn., 1970, Bausch & Lomb Sci. award, 1st John P. McGovern award, Med. Libr. Assn., 1983, Outstanding Alumna award, Newcomb Coll., 1994. Fellow Am. Coll. Med. Informatics, Royal Soc. for Encouragement of Arts, Mfrs., and Commerce; mem. Internat. Soc. Gen. Semantics, Med. Libr. Assn. (hon.), Coun. Biology Editors (dir. 1973-77, chmn. com. on editl. policy 1971-75), Coun. Basic Edn. (spl. com. writing 1977-79), Assn. Tchrs. Tech. Writing, Dictionary Soc. N.Am., Nat. Assn. Sci. Writers, Soc. for Health and Human Values, Com. of Thousand for Better Health Regulations, Golden Key, Phi Beta Kappa. Office: Baylor Coll Medicine 1 Baylor Plz Houston TX 77030-3411

DEBAKEY, MICHAEL ELLIS, cardiovascular surgeon, educator, scientist; b. Lake Charles, La., Sept. 7, 1908; s. Shaker Morris and Raheeja (Zorba) DeBakey; m. Diana Cooper, Oct. 15, 1936; children: Michael Maurice, Ernest Ochsner, Barry Edward, Denis Alton; m. Katrin Fehlhaber, July 1975; 1 child, Olga Katarina. BS, Tulane U., 1930, MD, 1932, MS, 1935; more than 50 hon. degrees from prestigious univ. throughout the world. Diplomate Nat. Bd. Med. Examiners, Am. Bd. Surgery, Am. Bd. Thoracic Surgery. Intern Charity Hosp., New Orleans, 1932—33, asst. surgery, 1933—35, U. Strasbourg, France, 1935—36, U. Heidelberg, Germany, 1936; instr. surgery Tulane U., New Orleans, 1937—40, asst. prof., 1940—46, assoc. prof., 1946—48; prof., chmn. dept. surgery Baylor Coll. Medicine, 1948—93, Disting. svc. prof., 1968—, v.p. med. affairs, 1968—69, CEO, 1968—69, pres., 1969—79, Olga Keith Wiess prof. of surgery, 1981—, chancellor, 1978—96, chancellor emeritus, 1996—; pres. The DeBakey Med. Found., 1961—; dir. Nat. Heart Blood Vessel Rsch. Demonstration Ctr., Baylor Coll. Medicine, 1974—84; dir. DeBakey Heart Ctr., Baylor Coll. Medicine, 1985—. Surgeon-in-chief Ben Taub Gen. Hosp., 1963—93; sr. attending surgeon Meth. Hosp.; clin. prof. surgery U. Tex. Dental Br.; cons. surgery VA Hosp., U. Tex. M.D. Anderson Cancer Ctr., St. Luke's Hosp., Tex. Children's Hosp., Tex. Inst. Rehab. and Rsch., Houston, Brooke Gen. Hosp., Brooke Army Med. Ctr., Ft. Sam Houston, Tex., Walter Reed Army Hosp., Washington, D.C.; mem. med. adv. com. Office Sec. Def., 1948—50; mem. task force med. svcs. Hoover Commn., 1949; founding bd. dirs. Friends of Nat. Libr. of Medicine, 1985—; mem. bd. regents Nat. Libr. of Medicine, 1956—60, 1994—98, chmn., 1959, 98; past mem. nat. adv. heart coun. NIH; mem. Nat. Adv. Health Coun., 1961—65, Nat. Adv. Coun. Regional Med. Programs, 1965—, Nat. Adv. Gen. Med. Scis. Coun., 1965, Program Planning Com., Com. Tng., Nat. Heart Inst., 1961—; mem. civilian health and med. adv. coun. Office Asst. Sec. Def.; chmn. Pres.'s Commn. Heart Disease, Cancer and Stroke, 1964; mem. adv. coun. Nat. Heart Lung and Blood Inst., 1982—87; chmn. Found. Biomedical Rsch., 1988; trustee, v.p. Baylor Med. Found.; adv. Dag Hammarskjöld Med. Sci. Prize Com.; trustee Baylor Coll. Medicine, 1996; fgn. adj. prof. Karolinska Inst., 1997. Author (with Robert A. Kilduffe): Blood Transfusion, 1942; author: (with Gilbert W. Beebe) Battle Casualties, 1952; author: (with Alton Ochsner) Textbook of Minor Surgery, 1955; author: (with T. Whayne) Cold Injury, Ground Type, 1958; author: A Surgeon's Visit to China, 1974, The Living Heart, 1977, The Living Heart Diet, 1985, The Living Heart Brand Name Shopper's Guide, 1992, The Living Heart Guide to Eating Out, 1993, The New Living Heart Diet, 1996, The New Living Heart, 1997; editor: Yearbook of surgery, 1958—70; chmn. adv. editl. bd.: Medical History of World War II, founding editor: Jour. Vascular Surgery, 1984—88; contbr. over 1600 articles to med. jours. Disting. mem. U.S. Army Med. Dept. Rgt., 1989; cons. to Surgeon Gen., 1946—. Col. Office Surgeon Gen. U.S. Army, 1942—46, now Col. Res. U.S. Army. Decorated Legion of Merit, 1945; named in his honor Michael E. DeBakey Dept. Surgery, Baylor Coll. Medicine, 1999, in his honor Michael E. Debakey Heart Inst. Kan., Hays Med. Ctr., 1999, in his honor Michael E. DeBakey Internat. Surgery Chair, Uniformed Svc. Univ. Health Sci., 2000, in his honor Michael E. DeBakey Inst. Comparative Cardiovascular Sci. and Biomedical Devices, Tex. A&M Univ., 2000, innumerable honors and awards including Leader in Medicine, AMA, 1997, charter mem., Tex. Sci. Hall Fame, 2001; named an inductee Space Tech. Hall Fame, 1999; named one of 200 Most Influential People in Telemedicine, Ctr. Pub. Svc. Comm., 1996, Top Ten Heroes, Millenium Soc., 1996; named to Health Care Hall of Fame, Modern Healthcare, 1996, Houston Hall Fame, 1999, Sci. in Tex. Hall Fame, 2000; recipient Rudolph Matas award, 1954, Disting. Svc. award, Internat. Soc. Surgery, 1958, Modern Medicine award, 1957, Leriche award, Internat. Soc. Surgery, 1959, Great medallion, U. Ghent, 1961, Grand Cross, Order Leopold, Belgium, 1962, Albert Lasker award for clin. rsch., 1963, Order of Merit Chile, 1964, St. Vincent prize med. scis., U. Turin, 1965, Centennial medal, Albert Einstein Med. Ctr., 1966, Gold Scalpel award, Internat. Cardiology Found., 1966, Eleanor Roosevelt Humanities award, 1969, Meritorious Civilian Svc. medal, Office Sec. Def., 1970, Medal of Freedom with Distinction Presdl. award, 1969, Inst. Med. Nat. Acad. Sci., 1981, Theodore E. Cummings award, 1987, Nat. Med. of Sci. award, 1987, First Issue Michael DeBakey medal, ASME, 1989, Inaugural award, Scripps Clinic and Rsch. Found., 1989, DeBakey-Bard Chair in Surgery, Baylor Coll. of Medicine, 1990, Disting. Svc. award, Am. Legion, 1990, Lifetime Achievement award, Found. for Biomed. Rsch., 1991, Maxwell Finland award, Nat. Found. for Infectious Diseases, 1992, Acad. of Athens award, 1992, Pres. Disting. Svc. award, Baylor Coll. Medicine, 1992, Gibbon award, Am. Soc. Extracorporeal Tech., 1993, named in his honor Michael E. DeBakey Libr. Svc. Outreach award, Friends of the Nat. Libr. Medicine, 1993, Alton Ochsner award relating smoking to health, 1993, Thomas Jefferson award, AIA, 1993, Lifetime Achievement award, Am. Heart Assn., 1994, prize for basic biomed. rsch., Giovanni Lorenzini Med. Fedn., 1994, Disting. Svc. award, Tex. Soc. Biomed. Rsch., 1994, Heart Saver award, Save A Heart Found., Cedars-Sinai Med. Ctr., 1994, Honor award, United Meth. Assn. Health & Welfare Ministries, 1995, Michael E. DeBakey chair in Pharm., Baylor Coll. Medicine, 1995, Nat. Order of Medicine Vasco Nunez de Balboa, Panama, 1995, Pub. Svc. award, AIAA, 1997, Boris Petrovsky Internat. Surgeons award, 1997, Premio Giuseppe Corradi award, Bevagna, Italy, 1997, Rotary Nat. award, 1997, Sesquicentennial medal, Tulane Coll., 1997, Fire of Genius award, So. Utah U., 1997, Commonwealth Trust award for invention and sci., 1997, Michael E. DeBakey Heart Inst. Wis. named in his honor, Kenosha Hosp. and Med. Ctr., 1992, Michael E. DeBakey, M.D. award for Excellence in Visual Edn. named in his honor, 1993, DeBakey Scholar in Cardiovasc. Scis. MD-PhD Program named in his honor, Baylor Coll. Medicine, 1994, Michael E. DeBakey, MD Excellence in Rsch. award named in his honor, 1994, dedication of Northwestern U. Med. Sch. book, 1995, Michael E. DeBakey H.S. Health Professions named in his honor, 1996, Med. Ctr. of LA Found. Inaugural Spirit of Charity award, 1998, Leader in Medicine honor, AMA, 1997, John P. McGovern Lecture award, Cosmos Club Found., 1998, Lifetime Achivement award, Rsch. Am., 1998, Michael E. DeBakey Presdl. Excellence award named in his honor, 1998, Mus. Health and Med. Sci. Lifetime Membership award, 1999, Disting. Svc. award, Soc. Vascular Surgery, 1999, Sci. Achievement award, Am. Assn. Thoracic Surgery, 1999, inaugural Michael E. DeBakey award contbns. to Am.'s Health, AIA, 1999, Bicentennial Living Legends award, Libr. Congress, 2000, Lifetime Achievement Outstanding Alumnus award, Tulane Med. Alumni Assn., 2000, Tall Texan award, Muscular Dystrophy Assn., 2001, Invention Yr., DeBakey Ventricular Assist Device, NASA, 2001, Mendal Medal award, Villanova U., Pa., 2001, Living Legend award, World Artificial-Organ, Immunology, Transplant Soc., Ottawa, Can., 2001, Inspired Leadership award, Am. Bible Soc., 2001, Wall of Honor tribute for lifetime contributions, 2002, Lifetime Achievement award, Internat. Health and Med. Film Festival, 2002, Golden Hippocrates Internat. Prize for Excellence in Medicine, Horev Med. Ctr., Haifa, Israel and Iraeli Minister Health, 2003, Ben Taub Humanitarian award, Harris County Hosp. District Found., 2003. Fellow: Internat. Acad. Cardiovascular Scis. (hon.), Am. Coll. Cardiology (hon.), Royal Coll. Physicians and Surgeons of U.S. (hon. disting. fellow 1992), Inst. of Medicine Chgo. (hon.); mem.: AMA (Hektoen Gold medal 1954, Disting. Svc. award 1959, Hektoen Gold medal 1970), AAAS, Uniformed Svc. Alumni Assn. (life hon.), Internat. Soc. Surgery, Soc. Univ. Surgeons, Assn. Internat. Vascular Surgeons (pres. 1983), Internat. Cardiovascular Soc. (pres. 1958, pres. N.Am. chpt. 1964), Am. Assn. Thoracic Surgery (pres. 1959), So. Surg. Assn. (pres. 1989-90, chmn. coun. 1995—), Am. Surg. Assn. (pres. 1989, Disting. Svc. award 1981), Soc. Vascular Surgery Lifeline Found. (pres. 1989), Soc. Vascular Surgery (pres. 1954), Am. Heart Assn., Royal Soc. Medicine, Assn. Française de Chirurgie (hon.), Med. Libr. Assn. (hon.), Hellenic Surg. Soc. (hon.), Mex. Acad. Surgery (hon.), Telemedicine 200 Ctr. for Pub. Svcs., Acad. of Athens, University Club (Washington), Houston Club (hon.), Alpha Omega Alpha, Sigma Xi (William Procter prize for sci. achievement 1995). Episcopalian. Achievements include development of roller pump universally used in heart-lung machine; Dacron artificial arteries and Dacron-velour arteries as surgical replacement of diseased arteries; first successful patch-graft angioplasty; fundamental concept of therapy in arterial disease; left ventricular bypass pump for cardiac assistance and first successful clinical application; first successful resection and graft replacement of fusiform aneurysm; establishment of Meth. DeBakey Heart Ctr., Meth. Hosp., Houston, 2001; establishment of DeBakey USU Brigade, 2001; establishment of Michael E. DeBakey award for Long-life Well-lived in Svc. to Mankind, Huffington Ctr. on Aging, 2001; establishment of Michael E. DeBakey Scholarship in Grad. Sch. Biomedical Sci., Baylor Coll. Medicine, 2001; establishment of Michael E. DeBakey Journalism award, Found. Biomedical Rsch., 2002. Office: Baylor Coll Medicine 1 Baylor Plz Houston TX 77030-3411

DEBAKEY, SELMA, science communications educator, writer, editor, lecturer; b. Lake Charles, La. BA, postgrad., Newcomb Coll., Tulane U., New Orleans. Dir. dept. med. communication Ochsner Clinic and Alton Ochsner Med. Found., New Orleans, 1942-68; prof. sci. communication Baylor Coll. Medicine, Houston, 1968—; editor Cardiovascular Research Ctr. Bull., 1970-84. Mem. panel judges Internat. Health and Med. Film Festival, 1992. Author: (with A. Segaloff and K. Meyer) Current Concepts in Breast Cancer, 1967; past editor Ochsner Clinic Reports, Selected Writings from the Ochsner Clinic; contbr. numerous articles to sci. jours., chpts. to books. Named to Tex. Hall of Fame. Mem. AAAS, Soc. Tech. Communication, Assn. Tchrs. Tech. Writing, Am. Med. Writers Assn. (past bd. dirs.; publ., nominating, fellowship, constn., bylaws, awards, and edn. coms.), Council Biol. Editors (past mem. trn. in sci. writing com.), Soc. Health and Human Values, Modern Med. Monograph Awards Com., Nat. Assn. Standard Med. Vocabulary (former cons.). Office: Baylor Coll Medicine 1 Baylor Plz Houston TX 77030-3411

DEBARBADILLO, JOHN JOSEPH, metallurgist, management executive, metal products executive; b. York, Pa., Jan. 27, 1942; s. John Joseph and Esta Dorothy (Knaub) deB.; m. Marianne Kathryn Kissane, Aug. 28, 1965; children: Christine, Elena. BS in Metallurgy, Lehigh U., 1963, MS in Metallurgy, 1965, PhD in Metallurgy and Materials Scis., 1967. Rsch. metallurgist Paul D. Merica rsch. lab. Inco Ltd., Suffern, N.Y., 1967-70, sect. mgr., 1970-82, dept. mgr., 1982-84; asst. to v.p. tech. Inco Alloys Internat., Huntington, W.V., 1984, mgr. R & D, 1984-88, dir. R&D planning, 1989-93; mgr. process improvement, 1993-96; mgr. aerospace materials and process devel. Inco Alloys Internat., Huntington, W.Va., 1996—. Mem. tech. rev. bd. Generic Rsch. Ctr., U.S. Bur. Mines, Washington, 1985—93; mem. materials engring. tech. adv. com. W.Va. U., Morgantown, 1989—; chmn. W.Va. adv. bd. exptl. program to stimulate competitive rsch., 1994—98; mem. W.Va. Sci. and Tech. Adv. Coun., 1996—; v.p., bd. dirs. Specialty Metal Processing Consortium, 1998—. Editor: Sulfide Inclusions in Steel, 1974, Solid State Powder Processing, 1990, Structural Applications of Mechanical Alloying, 1990, 2d edit., 1993; contbr. articles to profl. jours.; patentee in field. V.p. Jaycees, Warwick, N.Y., 1972-78. Fellow Am. Soc. for Metals; mem. AIME (Hunt award 1977), Sigma Xi. Democrat. Roman Catholic. Avocations: competitive swimming, gardening. Office: Spl Metals Corp PO Box 1958 Huntington WV 25720-1958 Fax: 304-526-5973. E-mail: jdebarba@smcwv.com.

DE BARBIERI, MARY ANN, nonprofit management consultant; b. Winston-Salem, N.C., May 1, 1945; d. Robert Carroll and Annie Louise (Neal) Hutcherson; m. Alfredo Emanuelle De B.; children: Maria Luisa, Riccardo Roberto. BA in Theatre Arts, Mary Washington Coll., 1967; student, Herbert Berghof Studio, 1967-69. With J. Walter Thompson, N.Y.C., 1967-68; asst. to producer Norman Twain Prodns., N.Y.C., 1968-69, Contemporary Theatre Co., N.Y.C., 1971-74; co. mgr. Folger Theatre Group, Washington, 1974-77, bus. mgr., 1977-80; mng. dir. Shakespeare Theatre at the Folger, Washington, 1980-90; performing arts cons. Alexandria, Va., 1990-92; dir. The Found. Ctr., Washington, 1992-94; pres. De Barbieri and Assocs., 1994—. Adj. prof. arts mgmt. grad. program Am. U., 1994—; treas. League of Washington Theatres, 1983-86; chair selection com. The Washington Post/Washington Coun. Agys. Award for Excellence in Nonprofit Mgmt., 1997, 98, 99, mem. selection com. 1996-99, The Washington Post Grants in the Arts, 1997—; curriculum design cons. Choral Mgmt. Inst. of Chorus Am., 2002-03; presenter in field. Bd. dirs. Washington Area Lawyers for Arts, 1984-94; bd. dirs. Cultural Alliance Greater Washington, 1986-96, v.p., 1990-96; bd. dirs. Nat. Soc. Fundraising Execs., 1993-96, v.p. edn., 1995, treas., 1996; bd. dirs. Washington Coun. Agys., 2000—; chair Performing Arts Coun., Alexandria, Va., 1981-84; founder, first chair Alexandria Commn. for Arts, 1984-88, theatre commr., 1984-94; contbr. to study of downtown stages for new theatre in Washington, 1985; v.p., bd. dirs. Cultural Alliance Greater Washington, 1990-96; mem. panel Va. Commn. for the Arts, 1990-96. Recipient Outstanding Svc. to Theatre Community award League of Washington Theatres, 1990. Office: 3812 Fort Worth Ave Alexandria VA 22304-1709 E-mail: debarasso@aol.com.

DEBARDELEBEN, JOHN THOMAS, JR., retired insurance company executive; b. Ft. Benning, Ga., Aug. 28, 1926; s. John Thomas and Erin Gautier (Howard) DeB.; m. Martha Evelyn Graves, Sept. 24, 1946 (div. Mar. 1989); children: John T. III, Charles G., Eve Lamar; m. Florence Barbara Kaiser, Oct. 7, 1989. BA, Vanderbilt U., 1947. C.L.U., Am. Coll., 1963. Agt., asst. mgr. N.Y. Life Ins. Co., Nashville and Chattanooga, 1951-56, gen. mgr. Knoxville, Tenn., Savannah, Ga. and Montgomery, Ala., 1957-70, regional v.p. Chgo., 1971-76, v.p. N.Y.C., 1976-78, sr. v.p., 1978-82, exec. v.p., 1982-89. Mem. Rep. County Com., Montgomery, Ala., 1963-64; active Crusade of Mercy, Chgo., 1972-75, United Way of Tri-State, N.Y.C., 1979-81. Recipient First Founder's award Health Ins. Assn. Am., 1988. Mem. Nat. Assn. Life Underwriters, Am. Soc. C.L.U.s, Gen. Agts. and Mgts. Conf., Health Ins. Assn. Am. (mem. fed. programs com. 1985-89, chmn. 1987-88, Founder's award 1988), Rotary Club, Montgomery, Chgo. C. of C. Home: 1628 Balihai Ct Gulf Breeze FL 32563-2787

DEBARLING, ANA MARIA, language educator; b. Del Rio, Tex., Apr. 30, 1938; d. Octauiano and Guadalupe Dominguez; m. Peter Wesley Barling, June 4, 1968 (div. Oct. 1988); children: Laura Blanche, Wesley Peter. BA, San Jose State U., 1968, M in Hispanic Lit., 1970; DEd, U. Pacific, 2001. Cert. sch. administrn. Calif. Secondary tchr. Fremount Union H.S. Dist., Sunnyvale, Calif., 1968—94, dir. gifted edn., 1980—83; lang. prof. West Valley Coll., Saratoga, Calif., 1994—. Cons. Edn. Testing Svcs., San Antonio, 1992—; bilingual proficiency testing City of Morgan Hill and Campbell, Calif., 1995—. Editor: (booklet) Gifted & Talented Education, 1991. Mem. Latina Leadership, San Jose, 1988—, Immigration Edn. Task Force, Santa Clara, Calif., 1999—. Mem.: Am. Tchrs. Fgn. Lang., Faculty Assn. C.C. Democrat. Roman Catholic. Home: 373 Redwood Ave Santa Clara CA 95051 Office: West Valley Coll 14000 Fruitvale Ave Saratoga CA 95070 E-mail: and_maria_de_baring@wuv.edu.

DEBARTOLO, EDWARD JOHN, JR., professional football team owner, real estate developer; b. Youngstown, Ohio, Nov. 6, 1946; s. Edward J. and Marie Patricia DeBartolo; m. Cynthia Ruth Papalia, Sept. 27, 1968; children: Lisa Marie, Tiffanye Lynne, Nicole Anne. Student, U. Notre Dame, 1964—68. With Edward J. DeBartolo Corp., Youngstown, Ohio, 1960—, v.p., 1972—76, exec. v.p., 1976—79, chief adminstrv. officer, 1979—94; pres., CEO, 1995—; owner San Francisco 49ers, 1977—97; chmn. bd. DeBartolo Realty Corp., 1994—; chmn., CEO DeBartolo Entertainment, Inc. Mem. Nat. Cambodia Crisis Com., 1980—; adv. coun. Nat. Assn. People with AIDS, 1992; trustee Youngstown State U., 1974—77; nat. adv. coun. St. Jude Children's Rsch. Hosp., 1978—, local chmn., 1979—80; chmn. local fund drive Am. Cancer Soc., 1975—; chmn. 19th Ann. Victor Warner award, 1985, City of Hope's Spirit of Life Banquet, 1986; apptd. adv. coun. Coll. Bus. Adminstrn. U. Notre Dame, 1988; bd. dirs. Cleve. Clinic Found., 1991; lifetime mem. Italian Scholarship League. With U.S. Army, 1969. Recipient Man of Yr. award, St. Jude Children's Hosp., 1979, Boy's Town of Italy in San Francisco, 1985, Sportsman of Yr. award, Nat. Italian Am. Sports Hall of Fame, 1991, Cert. of Merit, Salvation Army, 1982, Warner award, 1986, Silver Cable Car award, San Francisco Conv. and Visitors Bur., 1988, NFL Man of Yr. award, Football News, 1989, Svc. to Youth award, Cath. Youth Orgn., 1990, Hall of Fame award, Cardinal Mooney High Sch., 1993. Mem.: Internat. Coun. Shopping Ctrs., Dapper Dan Club (bd. dirs. 1980—), Fonderlac Country Club, Tippecanoe Country Club. Office: Edward J DeBartolo Corp PO Box 9128 Youngstown OH 44513-0128 *Personal philosophy: Success in business and sporting competition relies on the same basic ingredients--hire the best qualified people and then provide them with the leadership and best resources to accomplish the task.*

DEBARTOLO, HANSEL MARION, JR., otorhinolaryngology surgeon; b. Aurora, Ill., May 13, 1947; s. Hansel Marion and Rosemary (Boetto) D.; m.Susan Elizabeth Debartolo, June 26, 1977; children: Doré, Hansel III, Merrit, Janae, Raquel. BA cum laude, U. Minn., 1969; MD, Loyola U., Chgo., 1972; JD, William Howard Taft U. Diplomate Am. Bd. Otolaryngology, Nat. Bd. Med. Examiners, Am. Acad. Anti-Aging. Fellow in surgery Mayo Clinic., Rochester, Minn.; fellow in otorhinolaryngology Geisinger Clinic, Danville, Pa.; former chief of staff AmSurg, Joliet, Ill. Ptnr. Chgo. White Sox, H.M.D., Racing Stables, Chgo. Metro TV, Sportsvision, CETUS Internat., Granada Cosmisky Parks Assocs., Hard Master Recording; CEO H.M.D. Devel.; attending surgeon dept. surgery Delnor Cmty. Hosp., Geneva; former chmn.; attending surgeon Mendota (Ill.) Hosp.; bd. examiner Am. Acad. Anti-Aign. Contbr. articles to profl. jours. Dir. Debartolo Rsch. Found. Fellow Deafness Research Assn. (life.), Am. Acad. Otorhinolaryngology (legis. key physician Ill., mem. bd. govs.), Chgo. Larynigol. and Otological Soc., Am. Rhinologic Soc., Am. Acad. Anti-Aging Medicine, Priestly Surgical Soc., Drs. Mayo Soc. Life; mem. AAAS, Am. Acad. Advancement Medicine, Ill. Soc. Opthalmology and Otolaryngology (exec. council, sec.-treas., chief editor proceedings), Pa. Acad. Ophthalmology and Otolaryngology. Clubs: Aurora Country. Roman Catholic. Avocations: tennis, skiing, golf, cycling, amateur radio station operator. Home: 20 Dorchester Ct Aurora IL 60506-9139 Office: Debartolo Clinic 11 Debartolo Dr Sugar Grove IL 60554-9584 Fax: (630) 859-1830. E-mail: dr@debartoloclinic.com.

DEBARTOLO-YORK, DENISE, sports team executive; m. John C. York II; 4 children. Grad., Notre Dame U. Team pres. Pitts. Penguins; exec. v.p. personnel and corp. mktg./comm. The Edward J. Bartolo Corp., vice chmn., 1994; chmn. The Edward J. DeBartolo Corp. Supporter DeBartolo Family Found. Mem. fin. adv. bd. Ursuline Sisters; mem. MADD; recognized for contbn. to St. Charles Elem. Sch., Boardman, Ohio. Office: care San Francisco 49ers 4949 Centennial Blvd Santa Clara CA 95054-1229

DEBBINK, THOMAS MASON, management educator; b. Bay City, Mich., June 12, 1957; s. John Dirk Debbink, Jean Debbink; m. Jonnie Mack Myers, Dec. 19, 1999; m. Katrina Witt, Aug. 19, 1978 (div. Nov. 1994); children: John, Erik. BA cum laude, Albion Coll., 1980; MS in Mfg. Mgmt., Kettering U., 1990; PhD of Bus. Adminstrn., U. Cin., 2001. Cert. cert. quality engr., Am. Soc. Quality Control, 1991. Mgr. GM, 1980—92; actor Toledo Repertoire Theatre, 1999—2000; asst. prof. mgmt. Tiffin (Ohio) U. Bd. dirs. Toledo Sch. for Arts. Mem.: Acad. Mgmt., Rotary Internat. Avocation: sailing. Home: 234 S Monroe St Tiffin OH 44883

DEBEAR, RICHARD STEPHEN, library planning consultant; b. N.Y.C., Jan. 18, 1933; s. Arthur A. and Sarah (Morrison) deB.; m. Estelle Carmel Grandon, Apr. 27, 1951; children: Richard, Jr., Diana deBear Fortson, Patricia deBear Talkington, Robert, Christopher, Nancy deBear Naski. BS, Queens Coll., CUNY, 1953. Sales rep. Sperry Rand Corp., Blue Bell, Pa., 1954-76; pres. Libr. Design Assocs., Plymouth, Mich., 1976-97, Am. Libr. Ctr., Plymouth, 1981—. Bldg. cons. to numerous librs., 1965—; mem. interior design program profl. adv. com. Wayne State U. Mem. ALA, Mich. Libr. Assn. (oversight com. Leadership Acad. 1990—). Office: Am Libr Ctr Inc 1149 S Main St Plymouth MI 48170-2213 E-mail: ddebear@americanlibrary.com.

DE BEARN, GASTON, XIV, pharmaceutical company executive, consultant; b. Paris, June 2, 1939; s. Gaston XIII de Bearn and Frances Georgette Moss; m. Anne Hoagland, Dec. 19, 1964 (div. Oct. 1979); children: Celine, Gaston XV, Marc, Marie-Rose, Rene; m. Ann McCormick, May 28, 1982; children: Justin, Colleen. Student, Georgetown U., 1957-59; BSS in Govt., Fairfield U., 1961; JD, LLD, Am. U., 1964. Prof. staff, mem. U.S. Senate Senate Govt. Ops. Com., Washington, 1957-61; trust officer U.S. Trust Co., N.Y.C., 1965-69; asst. dir. fed. affairs Hoffmann-La Roche, Inc., Washington, 1970-96; pres. Washington Liaison Group LLC, Vienna, Va., 1997—. Chmn. Evergreen Farm Arch. Control Com., Haymarket, Va., 1989—. Mem. SAR (Empire State chpt.), Capital Soc., Capitol Hill Club. Avocations: history, genealogy, political science, golf. Home: 3819 Delashmitt Dr Haymarket VA 20169-1819 Office: Washington Liaison Group LLC Ste 1350 8000 Towers Crescent Dr Vienna VA 22182-2700

DEBEAUBIEN, HUGO H. lawyer; b. Detroit, Sept. 20, 1948; s. Phillip Frances and June (Hesse) deB.; m. Mary Lazenby, Apr. 30, 1977; 1 child, Hugo Samuel. BS in Bus., Fla. State U., 1970; JD, Stetson U., 1973. Bar: Fla. 1973, U.S. Dist. Ct. (mid. dist.) Fla. 1974, U.S. Supreme Ct. 1978, U.S. Ct. Appeals (11th cir.) 1981. Asst. state atty. Fla. 9th Jud. Cir. Ct., Orlando, 1973-76; ptnr. Drage, deBeaubien, Orlando, 1976-79; ptnr., pres. Drage, deBeaubien, Knight & Simmons, Orlando, 1980-87, Drage, deBeaubien, Knight, Simmons, Romano and Neal, Orlando, 1987-98; ptnr. Drage, deBeaubien, Knight, Simmons, Mantzaris and Neal, Orlando, 1999—; pres. deBeaubien, Knight, Simmons, Mantzaris and Neal LLP, 2002—. Lectr. Fla. Bar Assn., 1981-83; bd. dir. Fla. Citrus Sports Assn., 1996—; dir. Princeton Charter Sch., 2000-03. Mem. ATLA, Nat. Assn. Criminal Def. Lawyers, Fla. State U. Alumni Assn. (bd. dirs. 1986-93, sec. 1993-94, treas. 1995-96, v.p. 1996-97, chmn.-elect 1997-98, chmn. 1998-99), Univ. Center Club Tallahassee, Country Club Orlando. Republican. Methodist. Avocations: golf, tennis. Home: 1125 Belleaire Cir Orlando FL 32804-6703 Office: deBeaubien Knight Simmons Mantzaris & Neal LLP 322 N Magnolia Ave Orlando FL 32801-1609 E-mail: hdeBeaubien@dbksmn.com.

DE BELLIS, ROBERT HENRY, physician, medical educator; b. N.Y.C., Aug. 8, 1930; s. Vincent and Filomena (De Giorgio) De B. BS, Queens Coll., 1951; MD, Columbia U., 1958. Intern medicine Jacoby Hosp., 1958-59, resident medicine, 1959-61; from assoc. to assoc. prof. Coll. Physicians and Surgeons, Columbia U., N.Y.C., 1964—. Mem. adv. bd. N.Y. State Soc. Hematology and Oncology. Mem. Am. Soc. Clin. Oncology, Am. Soc. Hematology. Office: Coll Physicians & Surgeons 161 Fort Washington Ave New York NY 10032 3713

DEBELLO, MARGUERITE CATHERINE, oncological nurse; b. Detroit, Nov. 25, 1964; d. Frank J. Jr. and Gail C. (Hahn) Fisher; m. David DeBello, Aug. 10, 1985; children: Anthony, Daniel, Matthew, Christian, Nicholas. Diploma, Hurley Med. Ctr. Sch. Nursing, Flint, Mich., 1985; BSN, U. Mich., Flint, 1990; MSN, Oakland U., 1997. Cert. oncology nursing. Clin. nurse Harper Hosp., Detroit, 1985-92, case mgr. extender, 1992-98; adj. nursing faculty Oakland C.C., Rochester, Mich., 1998—. Mem. Oncology Nursing Soc., Sigma Theta Tau (Theta Psi chpt.). E-mail: MDeBelloRN@aol.com.

DEBENEDETTI, CARLO, entrepreneur; b. Turin, Italy, Nov. 14, 1934; Student, Polytech. U., Turin, Italy; PhD (hon.), Wesleyan U., 1986. Chmn., CEO Gilardini, Turin, Italy, 1972-76; CEO Fiat, Turin, 1976; vice-chmn., CEO Ing. C. Olivetti and Co., Ivrea, Italy, 1978-83, chmn., CEO, 1983-96. Bd. dirs., vice-chmn., CEO Compagnie Industriale Riunite; founder Euromobiliare; chmn., CEO Cofide; chmn. Sogefi; dir. Ctr. Strategic Internat. Studies, Washington; mem. European Adv. Com., N.Y. Stock Exchange; bd. dirs. Valeo, Pirelli, Fd. L'Espresso Named Cavaliere del Lavoro Republic of Italy, 1983, Officier, Légion d'Honneur Republic of France, 1987. Mem. Royal Swedish Acad. Engrng. Scis., Confindustria (v.p. 1983). Office: CIR SpA Via Ciovassino 1 20121 Milan Italy E-mail: cdebenedetti@cirgroup.it.

DEBENEDETTI, PABLO GASTON, chemical engineering educator; b. Buenos Aires, Mar. 30, 1953; came to the U.S., 1980; U.S. citizen; s. Sergio Isaias and Francine Fanny (Lehmann) D.; m. Silvia Irene Strauss, July 11, 1987; children: Gabriel Alejandro, Dina Sonia. BS in Chem. Engrng., Buenos Aires U., 1978; MS, MIT, 1981, PhD, 1985. Rsch. engr. O de Nora Impianti Elettrochimici, Milan, Italy, 1978-80; asst. prof. dept. chem. engrng. Princeton (N.J.) U., 1985-90, assoc. prof., 1990-94, prof. chem. engrng., 1994—, dept. chair, 1996—, class of 1950 prof., 1998—. Vaughan lectr. Calif. Inst. Tech., 1992; Katz meml. lectr. City Coll. CUNY, 1997; Wohl meml. lectr. U. Del., 1997; Cary lectr. Ga. Inst. Tech., 1998; Berkeley lectr. in chem. engrng. U. Calif., Berkeley, 2003. Author: Metastable Liquids Concepts and Principles, 1996; mem. editl. bd.: Jour. Supercritical Fluids, 1988—, supercritical Fluid Sci. and Tech., 1995—, Jour. Chem. Engrng. Data, 1996—, Revs. in Chem. Engrng., 1999—, Chem. Engrng. Edn., 2000—, Indsl. and Engrng. Chem. Rsch., 2001—, Physica A, 2001—; contbr. articles to profl. jours. including Journ. Chem. Physics, Jour. Phys. Chemistry, Nature, Phys. Rev. Letters, Molecular Physics, Am. Inst. Chem. Engr. Jour., others. Named NSF Presdl. Young Investigator, 1987; European Econ. Cmty. fellow, 1978, Camille and Henry Dreyfus Tchr. scholar, 1989, Guggenheim fellow, 1991, Nat. Acad. Engrng., 2000, Prausnitz award 2001. Mem.: AAAS, NAE, Am. Phys. Soc., Am. Chem. Soc., Am. Inst. Chem. Engrs. (Profl. Progress award 1997), Sigma Xi. Achievements include rsch. in protein processing and separations with supercritical fluids; thermodynamics of supercritical fluids and mixtures; thermodynamics of supercooled and glassy water; thermodynamics and statistical mechanics of metastable systems; thermodynamics of polyamorphic phase transitions; structure, dynamics, and thermodynamics of glasses. Office: Princeton U Dept Chem Engrng Princeton NJ 08544-0001

DE BENEDICTIS, DARIO, lawyer, arbitrator, mediator; b. Providence, Aug. 22, 1918; s. Anthony and Efra (Bassani) DeB.; m. Leanna May Carlson, July 22, 1950; Marc, Don, Gail. AB, U. Calif., Berkeley, 1946; JD, Harvard U., 1949. Bar: Calif., 1949, U.S. Supreme Ct., 1962. Draftsman, title examiner Calif. Pacific Title Co., Redwood City, 1936-38, 39-46; law sec. to Judge Clifton Mathews U.S. Circuit Ct., San Francisco, 1949-50; ptnr. Thelen, Marrin, Johnson and Bridges, San Francisco, 1950-88, of counsel, 1989-93. Instr. San Francisco Law Sch., 1949-53, lectr. U. Calif. Bus. Sch. Extension, 1965-72, Golden Gate U., San Francisco, 1973-75; lectr., author Fed. Publs., Washington, 1978-89; judge pro tem Mcpl. Ct., San Francisco, 1980-97; chmn. 27 dispute review bds. Caltrans, 1996—; mem. Dispute Resolution Bd. Found. Contbg. author to handbooks on constrn. practices. Bd. dirs. Legal Aid Soc., San Francisco, 1952-88, Camron-Stanford House Preservation Assn., 1992-94; mem. Calif. Pub. Works Contract Arbitration Com., panel of arbitrators. Capt. U.S. Army, 1942-46, PTO, lt. col. USAR, 1946-62; ret. Mem. ABA, FBA, Calif. Bar Assn., San Francisco Bar Assn., Coutra Costa County Bar Assn., Am. Arbitration Assn. (nat. panel arbitrators, nat. panel mediators, panel Large Complex Case Program-Constrn., Disting. Svc. award for outstanding contbn. in area of comml. disputes 1990), Soc. Profls. in Dispute Resolution, Calif. Dispute Resolution Coun., Assoc. Gen. Contractors Calif. (Assocs. Achievement award 1992, legal adv. com. lifetime achievement award 1999). Home and Office: 1200 Rockledge Ln Apt 3 Walnut Creek CA 94595-2877 Fax: 925-280-0601.

DE BERARDINIS, CHARLES ANTHONY JOSEPH, physician; b. Passaic, N.J., July 1, 1961; children: Matthew, Sarah, Hannah. BA in Biology, Ithaca Coll., 1983; DO, U. Medicine and Dentistry NJ, 1989. Diplomate Nat. Bd. Osteo. Med. Examiners. Resident in internal medicine Kennedy Meml. Hosp., Stratford, NJ, 1990—92; fellow in cardiology Deborah Heart & Lung Ctr., Browns Mills, NJ, 1992—96; attending cardiologist, asst. dir. cardiac catheterization lab. Deborah Heart and Lung Ctr., Brownsmills, NJ, 1996; dir. Cardiac Catheterization Lab. So. Ocean County Hosp., 2003—. Fellow Am. Coll. Cardiology; mem. Am. Osteo. Assn., Am. Coll. Osteo. Internists (diplomate, bd. cert. internal medicine, cardiology and interventional cardiology). Office: Deborah Heart & Lung Ctr Trenton Rd Browns Mills NJ 08015

DEBERRY, FISHER, college football coach; b. Cheraw, S.C., June 9, 1938; m. LuAnn DeBerry; children: Joe, Michelle BA, Wofford Coll., 1960. Coach, tchr. high schs., S.C., 6 yrs.; asst. football coach Wofford Coll., Spartanburg, S.C., 2 yrs., Appalachian State Coll., Boone, N.C., 9 yrs.; quarterbacks coach Air Force Acad., USAF Acad., Colo., 1980-81, offensive coord., 1981-83, head football coach, 1984—. Led teams in Ind. Bowl, 1984, Blue Bonnet Bowl, 1985, Freedom Bowl, 1987, Liberty Bowl, 1989-92, Copper Bowl, 1995, Las Vegas Bowl, 1997. Motivational spkr. to religious and corp. groups; fund raiser Easter Seals, March of Dimes, Salvation Army; chmn. Am. Heart Assn. Named Western Athletic Conf. Coach of Yr., 1985, 95, Nat. Coach of Yr., 1985. Mem. Fellowship Christian Athletes. Office: Hdqs USAF Acad 2304 Cadet Dr Ste 200 U S A F Academy CO 80840-5099

DEBEVOISE, A. CLAY, artist; b. Morristown, N.J., May 4, 1954; s. Thomas M. and Ann (Taylor) D.; m. Linda J. Derick, Oct. 13, 1979 (div. Jan. 1987); children: Nell M. Derick-Debevoise, Marie Calin. BA, Trinity Coll., Hartford, Conn., 1975; MFA, Sch. Visual Arts, N.Y.C., 1993. Adj. faculty Sch. Visual Arts, N.Y.C., 1994-96, Internat. Ctr. Photography, N.Y.C., 1996, San Francisco Art Inst., 1999; founder ArtHop.com, 2002. Exhibited in solo shows at Trinity Coll., Artworks Gallery, Pulse Art, N.Y.C., Brecht Forum, N.Y.C., others; exhibited in group shows at Cooper Union, N.Y.C., Ctrl. Arts Collective, Tucson, Bannister Gallery/R.I. Coll., Providence, Wadsworth Atheneum, Hartford, Real Art Ways, Hartford, Austin State U., Nacogdoches, Tex., So. Exposure, San Francisco, Neuberger Mus., Purchase, N.Y., Fuller Mus., Brockton, Mass., 1999, ISEA, Paris, 2000, Siggraph 2001, L.A.; represented in collections N.Y. Bklyn Mus. Art, Columbus (Ohio) Mus. Art., Fogg Art Mus., Harvard U. Art Mus., Cambridge, Mass., N.Y. Pub. Libr., Cin. Art Mus., Wadsworth Atheneum, Hartford, Conn., others; contbr. articles to profl. jours. Mem. Am. Assn. Museums, YLEM. E-mail: Clay@ClayDebevoise.com.

DEBEVOISE, DICKINSON RICHARDS, federal judge; b. Orange, N.J., Apr. 23, 1924; s. Elliott and Josephine (Richards) D.; m. Katrina Stephenson Leeb, Feb. 24, 1951; children: Kate, Josephine Debevoise Davies, Mary Debevoise Rennie, Abigail D. Byrne. BA, Williams Coll., 1948; LLB, Columbia U., 1951. Bar: N.J. 1953, U.S. Supreme Ct. 1956. Law clk. to Hon. Phillip Forman, chief judge U.S. Dist. Ct. for Dist. N.J., 1952-53; assoc. firm Riker, Emery & Danzig, Newark, 1953-56; partner firm Riker, Danzig, Scherer, Debevoise & Hyland, Newark, 1957-79; judge U.S. Dist. Ct. for N.J., 1979—; adj. prof. constitutional law Seton Hall U., 1992-94. Pres. Newark Legal Services Project, 1965-70; chmn. N.J. Gov.'s Workmen's Compensation Study Commn., 1972-73; mem. N.J. Supreme Ct. Adv. Com. on Jud. Conduct, 1974-78; chmn. N.J. Disciplinary Rev. Bd., 1978-79; mem. Lawyers Adv. Com. for 3d Circuit, 1975-79, chmn., 1979; chmn. N.J. Legal Services Adv. Council, 1976-78 Asso. editor: N.J. Law Jour, 1959-79. Trustee Ramapo Coll., N.J., 1969-73, chmn. bd., 1971-73; trustee Williams Coll., 1969-74, Fund for N.J., 1985—; trustee Hosp. Ctr. at Orange, N.J., v.p., 1975-79; pres. Democrats for Good Govt., 1956-60, active various presdl., senatorial, gubernatorial campaigns; active St. Stephens Episcopal Ch. Sgt. U.S. Army, WWII, 1st lt. Korean War. Decorated Bronze Star. Fellow Am. Bar Found.; mem. ABA, N.J. Bar Assn., Fed. Bar Assn. (v.p. 1976), Assn. Fed. Bar State N.J. (v.p. 1977-79), Essex County Bar Assn. (treas. 1960-64, trustee 1968-71), Am. Law Inst., Judicature Soc., Columbia Law Sch. Assn. (bd. dirs., pres. 1992-94). Office: US Dist Ct PO Box 999 Newark NJ 07101-0999

DEBEVOISE, FRANCINE (FRANKE DEBEVOISE), artist; b. Northport, NY, Mar. 27, 1929; d. Harold Johnson Pidgeon and Alice Conklin Miles; m. Kenneth Hall DeBevoise, July 4, 1952; children: Mark Alan, Jill. BS, Hartwick Coll., 1951; student, Art Students League, N.Y.C., 1969-71. One-woman shows include Johnson & Johnson Corp. Hdqtrs., 1986, Lenoir Rhyne Coll., Hickory, N.C., 1996, Georgian Ct. Coll., Lakewood, N.J., 2000, others; exhibited in group shows at Catharine Lorillard Wolfe Art Club, 1973-2003, Bergen County Artists Guild, Paramus, N.J., 1977, Allied Artists of Am., N.Y.C., 1977, others; commd. oil portraits, 1979—. Mem.: N.J. Am. Artists Profl. League (John Grabach award 2002), Am. Artists Profl. League, Catharine Lorillard Wolfe Art Club (hon.; bd.dirs. 1981—89, bd. dirs. 1992—2003, historian 1994—2003, Anna Hyatt Huntington Bronze medal 1975, Anna Hyatt Huntington Horse's Head trophy 1983, Margaret Dole Portrait award 1993). Home: 9 Haytown Rd Lebanon NJ 08833

DE BEVOISE, LEE RAYMOND, editor, writer; b. Paterson, N.J., Aug. 24, 1948; m. Sharon De Bevoise; children: Suzanne, Richard (dec.). Student, Glassboro State Coll., 1968; ASN, Cumberland C.C., Vineland, N.J., 1974; student, Stockton State Coll., 1981; MS in Comm. summa cum laude, La Salle U., 1996. RN, N.J. Editor The Artery Millville (N.J.) Hosp., 1970-73; staff instr. ARC, Phila., 1981—; v.p. De Bevoise & Assocs., Friend, Nebr., 1993—. Adj. prof. La Salle U., 1996—; editor, webmaster www.fishdreams.com, 1997—; clin. info. sys. liaison Bryan Home Health Care Svc., Lincoln, 1998—. Columnist The Daily Jour., Millville, N.J., 1990-97; field editor Disabled Outdoors mag., Grand Marais, Minn., 1994-97; editor The South Jersey Angler Mag., Vineland, N.J., 1996-97; editor www.ci.friend.ne.us, 2000. Asst. advisor Med. Explorer Post, Millville, 1971-72; trustee Millville Day Care Ctr., 1974-77; co-chmn. adv. com. State Assemblyman Salmon, Millville, 1986-89; trustee, deacon, treas. Open Bible Bapt. Ch., Millville, 1986-95; choir dir., elder Friend Berean Ch., Friend, Nebr., 2000—; dir. pub. rels., Meadowwood Environ. Sanctuary, Millville, 1990-97, S.J. Sportsmen's Jamboree, Maurice River Twp., N.J., 1990-96; chmn., emcee Friend Talent Show, 1999—. With USN, 1969-70. Recipient 1st place award Bi-centennial Photography, 1976. Mem. Boat Writers Internat., Boating Writers Internat., Kodak Profl. Network, Internat. Freelance Photographers Orgn., Internat. Webmasters Assn., Mason-Dixon Outdoor Writers Assn. (Gatco Best Mag. column award, Pete Greer Meml. award 1st runner up for best black and white photography), HTML Writers Guild, Internat. Webmasters Assn. Avocations: personal computers, fishing, shooting sports, environmental concerns, boating. Home: 607 S Pine St Friend NE 68359-1534 Office: De Bevoise & Assocs 607 S Pine St Friend NE 68359-1534 E-mail: lee@fishdreams.com.

DEBIAGI, ANNA LILLIAN, retired educator; b. N.Y.C., July 21, 1930; d. Giovanni-Battista and Michelina (Caramanna) Pollara; m. Giovanni DeBiagi, Nov. 19, 1955; children: Gianni Deo, Maria-Michelina Cologera. BA, CUNY, 1952; MA, Columbia U., 1957; postgrad., L.I. U., 1977. Tchr. Massapequa (N.Y.) Pub. Schs., 1953-87. Exhibited in Massapequa Pub. Libr.; group shows in Huntington, Babylon. Tchr. Ch. St. John the Bapt., Bronx, 1952-54, supt. 1954-56; instr. CPR, Am. Heart Assn., 1976-78; tchr. rep. PTA; arts & culture bd. City of Pembroke Pines, Fla., 1999-2001; active Friends Libr., 1999—; artist sel. panel Southwest Libr. Acad. Village, Pembroke Pines, 1999; co-founder Culture Vultures, 2001—. Mem. AAUW (chmn. 1964-65, pres. 1977-79, chmn. 1981-96, Commendation award 1982, Eleanor Roosevelt Found. name grant 1990; v.p. membership 1998-2000), Am. Italian Hist. Soc., Hist. Soc. Massapequas, Massapequa Fedn. Ret. Tchrs., Art League of L.I., Pequa Art Assn., Wantagh Arts Coun. Avocations: writing poetry, painting, music, needlework. Home: 662 SW 159th Dr Pembroke Pines FL 33027-1145 E-mail: adebiagi@bellsouth.net.

DE BIAS, DENNIS ANTHONY, physician; b. Meadowbrook, Pa., Aug. 7, 1960; BS in Biology, St. Joseph's U., 1982; MD, Jefferson Med. Coll., 1986. Diplomate Am. Bd. Family Practice. Physician West Norriton (Pa.) Family Practice, 1989-94; physician, med. dir. Matthew Brooke Family Practice, Birdsboro, 1994-96; physician Phoenixville (Pa.) Family Medicine, 1996—2003. Physician Delphi Family Health Ctr., 2003—. Fellow Am. Acad. Family Practice; mem. AMA, Pa. Med. Soc., Montgomery County Med. Soc., Alpha Omega Alpha, Alpha Sigma Nu. Office: Delphi Family Health Ctr Ste 400 1000 Gravel Pike Schwenksville PA 19473-4499

DEBIASI, ROBERTA LYNN, physician, medical educator; b. Falls Church, Va. BA summa cum laude with distinction in Psychology, Boston U., 1988; MD, U. Va., 1992. Lic. infectious diseases subspecialty Am. Bd. of Pediats., cert. Am. Bd. Pediats., lic. physician Nat. Bd. Med. Examiners, 1993, med. lic. Colo. State, 1999, Colo. State, 1996. Intern in pediat., 1992—93; fellow pediat. infectious diseases U. Colo. Health Scis. Ctr., Children's Hosp., Denver, 1996—99, asst. prof. divsn. pediat. infectious diseases, dept. neurology, 1999—; physician, assoc. investigator Vets. Adminstrn. Hosp., Denver, 1999—; resident in pediat., supr. PICU, NICU, Ward U. Calif. at Davis Med. Ctr., Sacramento. Contbr. articles to profl. jours., chpts. to books. Recipient NIH Physician-Scientist award, NIH, 2002—07, Rsch. Enrichment Award Program fellowship, VA, 1999—2001, Trustee scholarship, Boston U., 1988; fellow Rsch. Enrichment award, VA, 1999—2001; grantee Rsch. Career Devel. award, 2002. Mem.: Am. Acad. of Pediat., Infectious Diseases Soc. of Am. (Young Investigator award 2000—02), Pediatric Infectious Diseases Soc., Am. Soc. for Microbiology, Am. Soc. for Virology, Raven Soc., Phi Beta Kappa, Alpha Phi. Office: U Colo Health Scis Ctr Dept Pediats and Neurology Divsn Infecti 4200 E 9th Ave Denver CO 80262 Office Fax: 303-393-5271. E-mail: roberta.debiasi@uchsc.edu.

DEBICKI, ANDREW PETER, foreign language educator; b. Warsaw, June 28, 1934; came to U.S., 1948, naturalized, 1955; s. Roman and Jadwiga (Dunin) D.; m. Mary Jo Tidmarsh, Dec. 29, 1959 (dec. 1975); children: Mary Beth, Margaret; m. Mary Elizabeth Gwin, May 16, 1987. BA, Yale U., 1955, PhD, 1960. Instr. Trinity Coll., Hartford, Conn., 1957—60; asst. prof. Grinnell Coll., Iowa, 1960—62, assoc. prof., 1962—66, prof., 1966—68; prof. Spanish U. Kans., Lawrence, 1968—76, Univ. Disting. prof., 1976—. Dir. Hall Ctr., 1989-93; dean Grad. Sch. and Internat. Programs, 1993-2000; dir. NEH summer seminars 1976, 78, 89, 2003. Author: La poesia de Jose Gorostiza, 1962, Estudios sobre poesia espanola contemporanea, 1968, 81, Damaso Alonso, 1970, 74, La poesia de Jorge Guillen, 1973, Poetas hispanoamericanos contemporaneos: Punto de vista, perspectiva, experiencia, 1976, Poetry of Discovery, 1982, 87, Angel Gonzalez, 1989, Spanish Poetry of the Twentieth Century, 1994, 97; contbr. articles to various publs. Guggenheim fellow, 1970-71, 80, Nat. Humanities Ctr. fellow, 1980, 92-93, Am. Coun. Learned Socs. fellow, 1966-67, NEH sr. rsch. fellow, 1992-93; ADFL Career award 1999. Mem. MLA (exec. coun. 1989-93), Am. Assn. Tchrs. Spanish and Portuguese. Home: 1445 Applegate Ct Lawrence KS 66049-2937 Office: U Kans Dept of Spanish/Portuguese Lawrence KS 66045-0001 E-mail: adebicki@ukans.edu.

DE BLASI, CAMILLE E. advocate, counselor; b. Paterson, NJ, July 3, 1968; d. Joachim Thomas and Lucille Alicia De Blasi. BA, U. N.Mex, Albuquerque, NM, 1990; MA, Wash. State U., Pullman, WA, 1992. Dir. Ctr. Life Principles, Redmond, Wash., 1993—; dir. edn. Human Life Wash., Redmond, Wash., 1993—; adj. prof. speech communication NW Coll., Kirkland, Wash., 2001—. Hosp. counselor Group Health Hosp., Redmond, Wash., 2001—. Co-author (book) Healing the Culture. Lobbyist Human Life Wash., Olympia, Wash., 1993—2001. Master: Being With (dir. 2001—); mem.: Modestly Yours (founder, dir. 2002—). Roman Catholic. Office: Center forLife Principles 2601 151 Place NE Redmond WA 98052

DE BLASI, TONY (ANTHONY ARMANDO DE BLASI), artist; b. Alcamo, Italy, Jan. 1, 1933; came to U.S., 1938, naturalized, 1959; s. Frank and Josephine (Frisella) De B.; m. Eva Machauf; children from previous marriage: Keith, Eric. Student, Art Students League, N.Y.C., 1957-59; BA, U. R.I., 1961; MFA, Ind. U., 1963; student of William Leete, Kingston, R.I., 1959-61; student of James McGarrell, Bloomington, Ind., 1961-63; student William Bailey and Dr. Albert Elsen, student of Rudy Pozzatti,, Bloomington, 1961-63; also others. Chmn., instr. dept. art Washington and Jefferson Coll., Washington, Pa., 1963-66; prof. painting and drawing Mich. State U., East Lansing, 1966-86; instr. Sch. Visual Arts, N.Y.C., 1988-90. One-man shows of paintings 1963—, including Kresge Art Mus., Mich. State U., East Lansing, 1969, 72, 76, Spectrum Gallery, N.Y.C., 1968, 69, 71, 73, Detroit Art Inst., 1972, Razor Gallery, N.Y.C., 1975, 77, Western Mich. U., Kalamazoo, 1979, Wake Forest U., Winston-Salem, N.C., 1980, Urban Inst. Contemporary Art, Grand Rapids, Mich., 1981, Andrews U., Berrien Springs, Mich., 1983, Louis K. Meisel Gallery, N.Y.C., 1985, 87, 88, 89, 91, 93, 95, Hokin Kaufman Gallery, Chgo., 1988, Hokin Gallery, Bay Harbor Island, Fla., 1990, 92, SUNY Fine Arts Gallery, Oneonta, N.Y., 1998; numerous group shows 1963— including Mus. of Modern Art, Penthouse Gallery, N.Y.C., 1968, Henri Gallery, Washington, 1968, 70, Riverside Mus., N.Y.C., 1970, Spectrum Gallery, 1970, 71, Eastern Mich. U., Ypsilanti, 1972, Corcoran Gallery, Washington, 1973, Razor Gallery, N.Y.C., 1975, 77, 78, 79, Grand Rapids Art Mus., 1980, Neill Gallery, N.Y.C., 1980, Detroit Inst. Arts, 1969, 70, 82, Ball State U. Gallery, Muncie, Ind., 1983, Louis K. Meisel Gallery, N.Y.C., ann. 1984-90, N.J. Ctr. Visual Arts, Summit, 1985, 69th Regement Armory, N.Y.C., 1988, Islip Art Mus., N.Y., 1993, Jaffe Baker Blau Gallery, Boca Raton, Fla., 1995, Dorothy Blau Gallery, Bay Harbor Island, Fla., 1997, Heuser Art Ctr. Gallery, Bradley U., Peoria, Ill., 2001; represented in permanent collections Detroit Art Inst., Ind. U. Mus. Fine Arts, Bloomington, Ulrich Mus. Art, Wichita, Kans., Rose Art Mus., Brandeis U., Waltham, Mass., City Nat. Bank, Detroit, Greenfield Energy Corp., L.A., Best Products Co. Inc., Richmond, Kresge Art Mus., East Lansing, Mich., also numerous pvt. collections; represented by Louis K. Meisel Gallery, N.Y.C., 1984-96, Dorothy Blau Gallery, Bay Harbor Island, Fla., 1997—. Served with USN, 1951-55. Recipient Albert Kahn Assoc. Archs. and Engrs. prize, 1969, Founders Purchase prize (1st prize), Detroit Art Inst., 1970, Mich. Fine Arts Competition award of excellence, Birmingham-Bloomfield Art Ctr., 1982; grantee, Tiffany Found., 1966, Individual Artist grantee, Mich. Coun. for Arts, 1983. E-mail: tonydeblasi@hotmail.com.

DE BLASIO, MARIA P. physician; b. Naples, Italy, May 4, 1940; came to U.S., 1967; d. Agnello and Sophia (Recchia) de B. BA, St. Jeanne D'Arc Coll., Naples, 1958; MD, U. Naples, 1966; M in Piano and Composition, San Pietro A Maiella, Conservatory of Music, 1963. Resident Mt. Vernon (N.Y.) Hosp., 1967-72, Union Hosp., Bronx, N.Y., 1972, Misericordia Hosp., Bronx, 1968; fellow U. Pa., Phila., 1972; attending physician Our Lady of Mercy, Bronx, N.Y., 1982—, St. Barnabas Hosp., Bronx, N.Y., 1981—. Med. dir. Jean Jugan Residence, Bronx. Named Best Physician of Yr., New Yorker mag., 1996, N.Y. mag., 2002. Mem. AMA, Bronx County Med. Soc., N.Y. State Med. Soc. Avocations: concerts, opera, reading. Home: 2226 Valentine Ave Bronx NY 10457-1106 Office: 3065 Grand Concourse Bronx NY 10468

DE BLASIS, JAMES MICHAEL, artistic director, producer, stage director; b. N.Y.C., Apr. 12, 1931; s. James and Sarah (de Felice) de B.; m. Ruth Hofreuter, Aug. 25, 1957; 1 child, Blythe. BFA, Carnegie Mellon U., 1959, MFA, 1960. Mem. drama faculty Carnegie Mellon U., 1960-62; head drama dept. Onondaga C.C., Syracuse, N.Y., 1963-72; head Opera Workshop, Syracuse, 1969-70; adv. of opera Corbett Found., Cin., 1971-76; gen. dir. Cin. Opera Assn., 1973-87, artistic dir., 1988-96. Internat. ind. stage dir. of opera, 1962—; pvt. coach, Dramatic Interpretation of Operatic Roles, 1995—. Artistic advisor, Pitts. Opera, Inc., 1979-83. With U.S. Army, 1951-53. Recipient award Omicron Delta Kappa, 1959, Alumni award Bellaire High Sch., 1974, award in arts adminstrn. Gov. Ohio, 1989, Post/Corbett award for performing artist Corbett Found./Cin. Post, 1989. Mem. Actors Equity, Am. Guild Mus. Artists, Drama Alumni Carnegie Mellon U., Beta Theta Pi, Omicron Delta Kappa. Republican. Episcopalian.

DEBNEY, GEORGE C. mathematical physicist; b. Beaumont, Tex., Feb. 19, 1939; BA, Rice U., 1961; PhD, U. Tex., 1967. Analyst TRW, Houston, 1966-68, prof. math. Va. Tech., Blacksburg, 1968-85; sr. mathematician ANSER, Arlington, Va., 1985-87; sr. scientist Schafer Corp., Arlington, Va., 1987-89, SAIC, Arlington, Va., 1989—. Contbr. more than 25 articles on relativity and gravitation to profl. jours. Rsch. fellow Soc. for Engrng. Edn., 1975, 76. Mem. AIAA, Am. Phys. Soc., Math. Assn. Am. Achievements include research in defense techniques, performance, architecture, technology, and systems engineering. Office: SAIC/CSF 1755 Jeff Davis Hwy Ste 809 Arlington VA 22202 E-mail: debneyg@saic.com.

DEBO, VINCENT JOSEPH, lawyer, manufacturing company executive; b. Bklyn., Feb. 14, 1940; s. George and Letitia (Ruggiero) D.; m. Linda Mellucci, June 25, 1966; 1 child, Jennifer Lynn. BS, Fordham U., 1961, JD, 1964. Bar: N.Y. 1965, U.S. Dist. Ct. (so. and ea. dists.) N.Y. 1967, U.S. Tax Ct. 1969, U.S. Ct. Appeals (2d cir.) 1967, U.S. Supreme Ct. 1969. Assoc. various law firms, N.Y.C., 1964-70; corp. counsel Bangor Punta Corp., Greenwich, Conn., 1970-73; from asst. gen. counsel, asst. sec. to v.p., gen. counsel Internat. Rheem Mfg. Co., N.Y.C., 1973—. Dir., officer various corp. subs. and joint ventures. Mem. ABA (subcoms.). Home: 4 Greenlea Ct Westport CT 06883-3016 Office: Rheem Mfg Co 405 Lexington Ave Fl 22D New York NY 10174-0307 Business E-Mail: vdebo@rheemny.com.

DEBOCK, RONALD GENE, real estate company executive; b. Buckley, Wash., Sept. 12, 1928; m. Donna J. DeBock, Sept. 24, 1949; children: Beverly J. DeBock Satter, Gary, Janice. BA, N.W. Coll., Kirkland, Wash., 1953; MDiv., Western Evangelical Sem., Portland, Oreg., 1960; AA, Tacoma (Wash.) C.C., 1979; PhD, Calif. Grad. Sch. Theology, Glendale, 1979. Ordained minister Assemblies of God Ch., 1953-96. Commd. ensign USNR, 1957, advanced through grades to lt. comdr., 1971, chaplain, 1958-71; founder, owner Rainier Rentals (now Ranier Rentals & Sa;es), Puyallup, Wash., 1975—, Fireball Publs., Puyallup, 1993—. Instr. Am. sign lang. Cmty. Ednl. Opportunity, Orting, Wash., 1995-96. Author: Practice What You Preached, 1993. Active Aloha Hotel Chapels Ministry, Honolulu, 1988-96; bd. dirs. Romanian Renewal Internat., 1993-96, v.p., 1995-96; del. Pierce County Rep. Conv.; charter mem. Rep. Presdl. Task Force. Decorated Vietnam Cross of Gallantry with palm; recipient Delta Epsilon Chi award, 1975, Paul Harris award Rotary, 1992. Mem. Wash. Assn Realtors, Inc., Puyallup C. of C., Mil. Chaplains Assn. USA, VFW, DAV. Avocations: deep sea fishing, oriental languages.

DEBOER, BERNICE MARY, nurse; b. Chicago Heights, Ill., Mar. 25, 1939; d. Domenic C. and Bernice J. (Bodkins) Gestout; m. David John DeBoer, Oct. 26, 1963; children: Christine B., David D. Diploma in nursing, St. Agnes Sch. Nursing, Fond du Lac, Wis., 1960; BSN, Alverno Coll., 1989. RN, Wis.; cert. parish nurse Marquette U. RN VA, Wood, Wis., 1960-61; clin. nurse IV St. Joseph's Hosp., Milw., 1961-97; parish nurse Elmbrook Meml. Hosp., Brookfield, Wis., 1994—2001; ret., 2001. Assessor of students Alverno Coll., Milw., 1989—; mem. parish nurse adv. bd. Covenant Healthcare, Milw.; spkr. in field. Contbr. and editor: A Manual of Laboratory and Diagnostic Tests, 4th edit., 1992, 5th edit., 1996, 6th edit., 2000, Common Laboratory and Diagnostic Tests, 1st edit., 1995, 2d edit., 1999, Documenting Care, Communication, The Nursing Process and Documentation Standards, 1991. Advisor to Archdiocese of Milw., Parish Health Ministries; mem. adv. bd. Archdiocese of Milw. Office for Women, spiritual mentor. Roman Catholic. Avocations: reading, retreat work, hiking, camping, writing, travel. Home: N77W15955 Hunters Ridge Cir Menomonee Falls WI 53051-7436

DE BOER, PIETER CORNELIS TOBIAS, mechanical and aerospace engineering educator; b. Leiden, Netherlands, May 21, 1930; s. Pieter and Willemina (Zuydam) deB.; m. Joan Lieshout, June 7, 1956; children: Maarten P., Claire E., Yvette E. MechE degree, Delft U. Tech., 1955; PhD in Physics, U. Md., 1962. Rsch. asst., assoc. Tech. U. Delft, 1954-55; rsch. assoc. U. Md.,

1957-62, rsch. asst. prof., 1962-64; asst. prof. Cornell U., 1964-68, assoc. prof., 1968-74; prof. Sibley Sch. Mech. and Aerospace Engring., Cornell U., 1974—2000, assoc. dir., 1982-91; prof. Sibley Sch. Mech. and Aerospace Engring., Cornell U. Grad. Sch., Ithaca, NY, 2000—. Tech. staff Aerospace Corp., 1963, 65, 67, 95, 97, 99, Ford Motor Co., 1971-73, gas turbine div. GE Co., 1978-78, Commissariat Atomic Energy, Grenoble, France, 2000-01; vis. prof. von Karman Inst. for Fluid Dynamics, Belgium, 1968, Cornell Aero. Lab., Buffalo, 1969, Tech. U. Delft, 1985-86; tech. staff ; cons. Conelec, Elmira, N.Y., Allied Chem., Inc., Mt. Clemens, Mich., Inst. for Def. Analyses, Arlington, Va., others. Mem. Am. editor Applied Sci. Rsch., 1987-98; contbr. articles to profl. jours. With Dutch Army, 1955-57. NATO fellow, 1968. Fellow AIAA (assoc.); mem. ASME, AAUP, Am. Phys. Soc., Am. Soc. Engring. Edn., Royal Inst. Engrs. (The Netherlands), Royal Netherlands Acad. Scis. (corr.), Golden Key, Finger Lakes Cycling Club, Finger Lakes Runners Club, Cayuga Nordic Ski Club (pres.), Sigma Xi, Pi Tau Sigma, Sigma Pi Sigma. Office: Cornell U Sibley Sch Mech Aerospace Upson Hall Ithaca NY 14853

DEBOIS, JAMES ADOLPHUS, lawyer; b. Oklahoma City, Dec. 23, 1929; s. James D. and Catherine (Bobo) DeB.; m. Mary Catherine Watkins, Aug. 4, 1951; children: James Adolphus Jr., Catherine Cecile, Annette Marie. B.A. in Liberal Arts, Okla. State U., 1951; LL.B., Okla., U., 1955. Bar: Okla. 1954, U.S. Dist. Ct. (ea. dist.) Okla. 1955, U.S. Dist. Ct. (we. dist.) Okla. 1959, Mo. 1963, N.Y. 1965, U.S. Ct. Appeals (8th cir.) 1969, Calif. 1971, U.S. Ct. Appeals (9th cir.) 1971, U.S. Ct. Appeals (D.C. cir.) 1975, U.S. Supreme Ct. 1976. Atty. Southwestern Bell Telephone Co., Oklahoma City, 1959-63, St. Louis, 1963-64, gen. atty., Oklahoma City, 1965-67, gen. solicitor, St. Louis, 1967-70; atty. AT&T, N.Y.C., 1964-65, gen. atty., 1976, gen. atty., Basking Ridge, N.J., 1976-78, assoc. gen. counsel, 1978-83, v.p. law, 1985-93; v.p. legal dept. Pacific Tel. and Tel. Co., San Francisco, 1970-71, v.p., gen. counsel, 1971-76; v.p., gen. counsel, sec. AT&T Info. Systems Inc. (formerly Am. Bell Inc.), Morristown, N.J., 1983-85. Retired April, 1993. Lt. USAF, 1951-53, Korea. Mem. ABA (chmn. pub. utility law sect. 1985-86), Calif. Bar Assn., San Francisco Bar Assn. (sect. chmn. corp. law dept. 1975). Episcopalian. Club: Baltusrol (bd. govs. Springfield, N.J. 1982—). Office: AT&T 131 Morristown Rd Rm 2014A Basking Ridge NJ 07920-1655

DE BOLD, ADOLFO J., pathology and physiology educator, research scientist; b. Paraná, Argentina, Feb. 14, 1942; arrived in Can., 1968; s. Adolfo E.G. and Ana (Patriarca) deB.; m. Mercedes L. Kuroski; children: Adolfo A., Alejandro J., Cecilia I., Gustavo A., Pablo G. B.Sc. (hon.), Faculty Chem. Sci., Cordoba, Argentina, 1968; M.Sc. in Pathology, Queen's U., Kingston, Ont., 1971, PhD in Pathology, 1973. Cert. clin. chemist. Demonstrator in physics Nat. U. Cordoba, 1961-62, demonstrator normal and path. histology, 1964-67; resident, chief resident Nat. Hosp., Clinicas, Cordoba, 1966-68; asst. prof., lab. scientist Queen's U. and Hotel-Dieu Hosp., Kingston, 1974-82, assoc. prof., 1982-85, prof., 1985-86; prof. pathology and physiology U. Ottawa, Ont., Can., 1986—. Bd. dirs. research U. Ottawa Heart Inst. at Ottawa Civic Hosp., 1986—. Discovered Atrial Natriuretic Hormone, 1981, patented, 1986; contbr. over 100 sci. articles and chpts. to books in field. Bd. dirs. Heart Inst., Ottawa, 1986-93. Decorated officer Order of Can.; recipient Queen Elizabeth II Golden Jubilee medal, Gairdner Internat. award Gairdner Found., Toronto, 1986, Manning Prin. award Manning Found., Alta., Can., 1986, Sci. Achievement award Am. Soc. Hypertension, 1986, rsch. achievement award Can. Cardiovasc. Soc., 1986, CIBA award Am. Heart Assn., 1994; Disting. Rsch. Prof. award Ont. Heart and Stroke Found. Fellow Royal Soc. Can.(McLaughin medal of excellence in rsch. 1988), Royal Coll. Physicians and Surgeons (Can.), AAAS; mem. Can. Hypertension Soc., Am. Soc. for Hypertension, Internat. Soc. Hypertension (Rsch. Achievement award), Internat. Soc. Heart Rsch., Am. Sect. Can. Fedn. Biol. Socs., Histochem. Soc., U.S. Acad. Pathology, Can. Acad. Pathology, Am. Soc. Cell Biology, Can. Soc. Cell Biology, Internat. Acad. Pathology, Am. Assn. Pathology, Fedn. Am. Soc. Exptl. Biology, Microscopial Soc. Can., Soc. Exptl. Biology and Medicine, Can. Soc. Anatomy, N.Y. Acad. Sci. Roman Catholic. Avocation: classical guitar. Office: U Ottawa Heart Inst 40 Ruskin St Ottawa ON Canada K1Y 4W7 E-mail: adebold@ottawaheart.ca.

DEBOLD, JOSEPH FRANCIS, psychology educator; b. Boston, Nov. 3, 1947; s. Joseph Francis and Patricia (Miltimore) DeB.; m. Carol Lynn Hook, Dec. 20, 1969. AB, UCLA, 1969; PhD, U. Calif., Irvine, 1976. Trainee U. Calif. NICHD Devel. & Reproductive Biology, Irvine, 1971-75; instr., rsch. assoc. Mich. State U., East Lansing, 1975-77; asst. prof. Carnegie-Mellon U., Pitts., 1977-79, Tufts U., Medford, Mass., 1979-83, assoc. prof., 1983-91, chmn. dept. psychology, 1990-93, prof., 1991—, chmn. dept. psychology, 2002—; vis. rsch. assoc. Children's Hosp. Med. Ctr., Boston, 1981-85. Advisor NSF, Washington, 1989-92. Mem. editorial bd. Hormones and Behavior, 1987-92; contbr. articles to profl. jours., chpts. to books. Grantee NSF, 1986-99, Nat. Inst. Alcoholism and Alcohol Abuse, 1980-2002, Biomed Rsch. Support Program, 1990-91. Mem. AAAS, Soc. for Neurosci., Nat. Assn. Advisors for Health Professions, N.Y. Acad. Scis., Rsch. Soc. on Alcholism, Sigma Xi, Psi Chi. Avocations: motorcycling, tennis, volleyball. Office: Tufts U Dept Psychology 490 Boston Ave Medford MA 02155

DE BONO, LUELLA ELIZABETH, music educator; b. Argyle, Iowa, May 15, 1920; d. Albert Fred and Bessie Mae (Langwith) Haffner; m. Charles De Bono, July 26, 1947; 1 child, Douglas. MMus, Sherwood Conservatory Music, Chgo., 1945; M in Counseling and Guidance, U. St. Thomas, St. Paul, 1966; postgrad., U. Minn. Lic. music instr. of keyboard, voice and instrumental. Dir. music Am. Girl's Coll., Assiut, Egypt, 1945-48; music tchr. Argyle Pub. Sch., 1949-54; instr. music MacPhail Coll. Music, Mpls., 1956-66; counselor various pub. schs., Minn., 1966-82; pvt. music instr. Eden Prairie, Minn., 1982—. Profl. accompanist and pianist; adjudicator state music contests, Mpls., 1958—. Nat. honor soc. advisor St. Paul Pk. H.S., 1966-68; Am. field svc. adviser St. Paul Pk. H.S.; counselor Am. Youth Hostel Camp, Europe, 1946. Presbyterian. Avocations: animals, showing horses, volunteering. Home: 17325 Pioneer Trail Eden Prairie MN 55347-3403

DEBONT, JAN, cinematographer, director; b. Eindhoven, Noord-Brabant, Netherlands, Nov. 22, 1943; Cinematographer: (films) White Slave, 1969, Drop-out, 1969, The Baby in the Tree, 1969, Diary of a Hooker, 1971 Joao, 1972, Turkish Delight, 1973, Keetje Tippel, 1975, Max Havelaar, 1976, Private Lessons, 1981, Roar, 1981, I'm Dancing as Fast as I Can, 1982, Cujo, 1983, All the Right Moves, 1983, Bad Manners, 1984, The Fourth Man, 1984, The Jewel of the Nile, 1985, (with Donald E. Thorin) Mischief, 1985, Flesh and Blood, 1985, Ruthless People, 1986, The Clan of the Cave Bear, 1986, Jumpin' Jack Flash, 1986, Who's That Girl?, 1987, Leonard, Part 6, 1987, Die Hard, 1988, Bert Rigby, You're a Fool, 1989, Black Rain, 1989, The Hunt for Red October, 1990, Flatliners, 1990, Lethal Weapon 3, 1992, Shining Through, 1992, Basic Instinct, 1992, (TV movies) Sadat, 1983, The Ray Mancini Story, 1985, Parker Kane, 1990; (TV series) Tales from the Crypt ("Split Personality"), 1992 (CableACE award nomination best direction of photography 1992); dir.: (films) Speed, 1994, Twister, 1996, Speed 2: Cruise Control (also prodr.), 1997, The Haunting (also exec. prodr.), 1999, Lara Croft Tomb Raider: The Cradle of Life, 2003; prodr. only: SLC Punk!, 1999, Minority Report, 2002, Equilibrium, 2002, Thought Crimes, 2003. Office: The Gersh Agency 232 N Canon Dr Beverly Hills CA 90210-5302

DE BOOR, CARL, mathematician; b. Stolp, Germany, Dec. 3, 1937; m. Matilda C. Friedrich, Feb. 6, 1960 (div. Sept. 12, 1984); children: C. Thomas, Elisabeth, Peter, Adam; m. Helen L. Bee, Jan. 2, 1991. Student, Universitaet Hamburg, 1956-59, Harvard U., 1959-60; PhD, U. Mich., 1966. Rsch. mathematician Gen. Motors Research Labs., 1960-64; asst. prof. math., computer sci. Purdue U., 1966-68, assoc. prof., 1968-72; prof. math., computer sci. U. Wis.-Madison, 1972—2003. Vis. staff mem. Los Alamos Sci. Labs., 1970-95. Author: (with S. Conte) Elementary Numerical Analysis, 1972, 1980, A Practical Guide to Splines, 1978, 2001, (with J.B. Rosser) Pocket Calculator Supplement for Calculus, 1979, (with K. Höllig and S. Riemenschneider) Box Splines, 1993. Named John Von Neumann lectr. Soc. Indsl. and Applied Math., 1996. Fellow Am. Acad. Arts and Scis.; mem. Nat. Acad. Engring., NAS, Soc. Indsl. and Applied Math., Polish Acad. Sci., Leopoldina, Phi Beta Kappa. Office: PO Box 1076 East Sound WA 98245 E-mail: carl@deBoor.de.

DE BORCHGRAVE, ARNAUD, editor, writer, lecturer; b. Brussels, Oct. 26, 1926; s. Count Baudouin and Audrey (Townshend) de B.; m. Dorothy Solon, Apr. 1950; 1 child, Arnaud; m. Eileen Ritschel, Mar. 31, 1959; 1 child, Trisha; m. Alexandra D. Villard, May 10, 1969. Student, Maredsous, Belgium, 1936-39, King's Sch., Canterbury, Eng., 1940-42. Free-lance writer, Eastern Europe, 1946-47; staff United Press, Western Europe, 1947-51; mgr. Benelux Countries, 1949-51; European Corr. Newsweek, Paris, North Africa, Middle East, Indo-China, 1951-54, fgn. editor, sr. editor, 1955-59, chief fgn. corr., 1959-62, mng. editor internat. edits., 1962-63, chief Newsweek Corr., 1964-80; columnist, TV host; sr. assoc. Ctr. for Strategic and Internat. Studies, 1981-85; editor in chief The Washington Times and Insight Mag., 1985-91; dir. Transnat. Threats Initiative, sr. advisor Ctr. for Strategic and Internat. Studies, Washington, 1991—; pres., CEO, UPI, Washington, 1999-2001. Editor-at-large, Washington Times and UPI, 2001—. Served with Brit. Royal Navy, 1942-46. Decorated commandeur de l'Ordre de Leopold II, Medaille Maritime Belge; recipient Medal of Honor Def. Council, 1980, Medal of Honor World Bus. Council, 1981, Washington Dateline award Soc. Profl. Journalists, also numerous awards for fgn. reporting. Mem. Am. Soc. Newspaper Editors, Internat. Press Inst., Inter-Am. Press Assn., Coun. on Fgn. Rels., Racquet and Tennis Club, Met. Club, Econ. Club of Washington, Nat. Press Club. Home: 2801 New Mexico Ave NW Washington DC 20007-3921 Office: Ctr for Strategic and Internat Studies 1800 K St NW Washington DC 20006-2202

DEBOW, JAY HOWARD CAMDEN, public relations executive; b. Flushing, N.Y., Sept. 21, 1932; s. Thomas Howard and Dorothea (Camden) DeB.; m. Audrey Ellison, May 4, 1957 (div. 1985); children: Stacy, Carolyn, Jennifer, Hollis; m. Suzanne Hayat, Nov. 12, 1986. AB, U. Ga., 1955. Reporter Athens (Ga.) Banner Herald, 1954; news writer UPI, N.Y.C., 1955; v.p. pub. rels. Merrill Anderson Co., N.Y.C., 1956—60; founder, pres. Jay DeBow & Ptnrs., Inc., N.Y.C., 1960—89; pres. Jay DeBow & Ptnrs. Omnicom Pub. Rels. Network, N.Y.C., 1990—92; founder, mng. prin. The Energy Team, 1993—; mng. ptnr. DeBow Mellow Palmer Group, LLC. Chair Jay DeBow & Ptnrs., Inc., 1992—; chmn. bd. advisors Salvation Army Manhattan. Recipient Ad Week Nat. Mktg. Program award, 1990, Cipra award Inside PR Mag., 1991. Mem. Nat. Investor Rels. Inst. (former chmn. govt. affairs com., ethics com., mem. steering com., sr. Investor Rels. Roundtable), Pub. Rels. Soc. Am. (Silver Anvil award 1991), Internat. Inst. Comms., Counselors Acad., Internat. Pub. Rels. Assn., N.Y. Soc. Security Analysts, Assn. Investment Mgrs., Soc. Profl. Journalists, Nat. Press Club (Washington), Met. Club (N.Y.C.; bd. govs., chmn., mem. com.). Home: 530 Park Ave Apt 6J New York NY 10021-8015 E-mail: jaydebow@aol.com.

DEBOW, THOMAS JOSEPH, JR., advertising executive; b. N.Y.C., May 18, 1936; s. Thomas Joseph DeBow and Evelyn Francis (Brooks) Menck; m. Rosalinda Angelini, Sept. 9, 1961; children: Yvette, Thomas J III, Walter Brooks. V.p. McCann Ericson, N.Y.C., 1965—69; dir. Young and Rubicam, N.Y.C., 1969—71; pres. Curry DeBow, N.Y.C., 1971—74; v.p. BBDO, N.Y.C., 1974—76; pres. DeBow Comm. Ltd., N.Y.C., 1976—95, chmn., 1995—; mng. ptnr. Global Card Mktg., LLC, 2001—. Mem. Cystic Fibrosis Found., dir., 1988—; vice chmn. Len Cariou Entreprolebrity Golf Tournament, 1990; vice chmn. children's legacy com. Franciscan Sisters of the Poor Found., 1996—. Mem.: Progresive Era Assn., Friar's Sunshine Com. (chmn. 1987—, Friar of Yr. 1990), N.Y. Athletic Club, Knollwood Country Club. Home: 55 E 86th St New York NY 10028-1059 Office: DeBow Comm Ltd 850 7th Ave Ste 605 New York NY 10019-5230 E-mail: Tom@DeBow.com.

DE BRANGES DE BOURCIA, LOUIS, mathematics educator; b. Paris, Aug. 21, 1932; s. Louis and Diane (McDonald) deB.; m. Tatiana Jakimow, Dec. 17, 1980; 1 child, Konstantin. BS, MIT, 1953; PhD, Cornell U., 1957. Prof. Purdue U., Lafayette, Ind., 1962-88, disting. prof. of math., 1989—. Fellow Sloan Found., 1963-66, Guggenheim Found., 1967-68; recipient Humboldt prize Alexander Humboldt Found., 1986-88, Ostrowski prize Alexander Ostrowski Found., 1989. Home: Hameau de l'Yvette Batiment D Chemin des Graviers F-91190 Gif Sur Yvette France Office: Purdue U Dept Math Lafayette IN 47907-2067 E-mail: branges@math.purdue.edu.

DEBRECZENY, PAUL, Slavic language educator, writer; b. Budapest, Hungary, Feb. 16, 1932; came to U.S., 1960; s. Zsigmond and Margit Ibolya (Csanady) D.; m. Gillian Marjorie Butterworth, Oct. 30, 1959; children: Louise, Martin. BA in Russian Studies, Eotvos U., Budapest, 1953, BA in Hungarian Studies, 1955; PhD in Russian Lit., U. London, 1960. Research assoc. Inst. Lit. Studies, Hungarian Acad. Scis., Budapest, 1955-56; trans. editor Pergamon Press, Oxford, Eng., 1959-60; from asst. to assoc. prof., dept. chmn. Tulane U., New Orleans, 1960-67; assoc. prof. U. N.C., Chapel Hill, 1967-74, prof., chmn., 1974-79, prof. Slavic langs., 1979-83, Alumni disting. prof. Russian and comparative lit., 1983-99, prof. emeritus, 1999—, chmn. humanities divsn., 1984-86; dir. Ctr. for Slavic, Eurasian and East European Studies U. N.C.-Duke U., Chapel Hill, 1991-94. Author: Nickolay Gogol and His Contemporary Critics, 1966, Temptations of the Past, 1982, The Other Pushkin, 1983, 2d rev. edit. in Russian, 1996, Social Functions of Literature: Alexander Pushkin and Russian Culture, 1997; translator: The Captain's Daughter and Other Stories by Alexander Pushkin, 1992; translator, editor: Literature and National Identity, 1970, Alexander Pushkin's Complete Prose Fiction, 1983; editor: Chekhov's Art of Writing: A Collection of Critical Essays, 1977, American Contributions to the Ninth International Congress of Slavists, Vol. 2: Literature, 1983; editor: Russian Visual and Narrative Art: Varieties of Seeing, 1994; mng. editor: The Pushkin Journal, 1993-96, the Pushkin rev., 1997-98. Awarded Golden Key City of New Orleans, 1967. Mem. AAUP, MLA, Am. Assn. Tchrs. Slavic and East European Langs. (v.p. 1978-79), Am. Assn. for Advancement of Slavic Studies, So. Conf. on Slavic Studies (v.p. 1979, pres. 1980, Sr. Scholar award 1987), N.Am. Pushkin Soc. (pres. 1993). Democrat. Home: 304 Hoot Owl Ln Chapel Hill NC 27514-2743 Office: U NC Dept Slavic Langs Chapel Hill NC 27599-3165 E-mail: pdebrecz@email.unc.edu.

DEBREU, GERARD, economics and mathematics educator; b. Calais, France, July 4, 1921; arrived in U.S., 1950, naturalized, 1975; s. Camille and Fernande Decharne Debreu; m. Françoise Bled, June 14, 1945; children: Chantal, Florence. Student, Ecole Normale Supérieure, Paris, 1941—44, Agrégé de l'Université, France, 1946; DSc, U. Paris, 1956; Dr. Rerum Politicarum honoris causa, U. Bonn, 1977; D. Scis. Economiques (hon.), U. Lausanne, 1980; DSc (hon.), Northwestern U., 1981; Dr. honoris causa (hon.), U. des Scis. Sociales de Toulouse, 1983, Yale U., 1987, U. Bordeaux I, 1988. Rsch. assoc. Centre Nat. De La Recherche Sci., Paris, 1946—48; Rockefeller fellow, 1948—50, 1948—50, 1948—50; rsch. assoc. Cowles Commn., U. Chgo., 1950—55; assoc. prof. econs. Cowles Found., Yale, 1955—61; fellow Ctr. Advanced Study Behavioral Scis., Stanford U., 1960—61; vis. prof. econs. Yale U., 1961; prof. U. Calif., Berkeley, 1962—, prof. Miller Inst. Basic Rsch. in Sci., 1973—74, prof. math., 1975—84, prof. emeritus, 1985—. Guggenheim fellow, vis. prof. Ctr. Ops. Rsch. and Econometrics, U. Louvain, 1968—69, vis. prof., 1971, 72, 88; Erskine fellow U. Canterbury, Christchurch, New Zealand, 1969, Christchurch, 87, vis. prof., 73; Overseas fellow Churchill Coll., Cambridge, England, 1972; Plenary address Internat. Congress Mathematicians, Vancouver, 1974; vis. prof. Cowles Found. for Rsch. in Econs., Yale U., 1976, U. Bonn, 1977; rsch. assoc. Cepremap, Paris, 1980; faculty rsch. lectr. U. Calif., Berkeley, 1984—85, Class of 1958 chair, 1986—; vis. prof. U. Sydney, Australia, 1987; lectr. in field. Author: Theory of Value, 1959, Mathematical Economics: Twenty Papers of Gerard Debreu, 1983; assoc. editor: Internat. Econ. Rev., 1959—69, mem. editl. bd.: Jours. Econ. Theory, 1972—, SIAM Jours. on Applied Math., 1976—79, Jours. of Complexity, 1985—, Games and Econ. Behavior, 1989—, Econ. Theory, 1991, mem. adv. bd.: Jours. Math. Econs., 1974—, corr.: Math. Intelligencer, 1983—84. With French Army, 1944—45. Decorated Chevalier de la Légion d'Honneur, Commandeur de l'Ordre Nat. du Mérite, Officier Le Légion d'Honneur; named sr. U.S. Sci. awardee, Alexander von Humboldt Found., 1977; recipient Nobel Prize in Econ. Scis., 1983, Berkeley Citation, 1991. Fellow: AAAS, Am. Econ. Assn. (disting. fellow 1982, pres.-elect 1989, pres. 1990), Econometric Soc. (mem. coun. 1964—72, Fisher-Schultz lectr. 1969, exec. com. 1969—72, pres. 1971, mem. coun. 1978—85, exec. com. 1980—82); mem.: NAS (chmn. sect. econ. scis. 1982—85, com. human rights 1984—90, chair class V behavioral and social scis. 1989—92, mem. Coun. of NAS of USA 1993—), Berkeley Fellows, French Acad. Scis. (fgn. assoc.), Am. Philos. Soc.

DE BRIER, DONALD PAUL, lawyer; b. Atlantic City, Mar. 20, 1940; s. Daniel and Ethel de B.; m. Nancy Lee McElroy, Aug. 1, 1964; children: Lesley Anne, Rachel Wynne, Danielle Verne. BA in History, Princeton U., 1962; LL.B. with honors, U. Pa., 1967. Bar: N.Y. 1967, Tex. 1977, Utah 1983, Ohio 1987. Assoc. firm Sullivan & Cromwell, N.Y.C., 1967-70, Patterson, Belknap, Webb & Tyler, N.Y.C., 1970-76; v.p., gen. counsel, dir. Gulf Resources & Chem. Corp., Houston, 1976-82; v.p. law Kennecott Corp. (former subs. BP America Inc.), Salt Lake City, 1983-89; assoc. gen. counsel BP America Inc., Cleve., 1987-89; gen. counsel BP Exploration Co. Ltd., London, 1989-93; exec. v.p., gen. counsel Occidental Petroleum Corp., L.A., 1993—. Bd. dirs. L.A. Philham., L.A., 1995—; mem. adv. bd. govs. Riviera Country Club, 2002—. Lt. USNR, 1962—64. Mem. Calif. Club, Adv. Bd. Gov., Riviera Tennis Club. Home: 699 Amalfi Dr Pacific Palisades CA 90272-4507 Office: Occidental Petroleum Corp 10889 Wilshire Blvd Los Angeles CA 90024-4201

DE BRIGARD, EMILIE, anthropologist, consultant; b. N.Y.C., Dec. 11, 1943; d. A. Lincoln and Ruth Emilie (Jaeger) Rahman; m. Raul de Brigard, June 11, 1966; 1 child, George. BA, Harvard Coll., 1963; MA, U. Calif., 1972. Guest curator dept. of film Mus. of Modern Art, N.Y.C., 1972-73; asst. to dir. human studies film archives Smithsonian Instn., Washington, 1975-77; prin. programmer Margaret Mead Film Festival Am. Mus. Natural History, N.Y.C., 1977-78; faculty Harvard Summer Sch., Cambridge, Mass., 1980-86; pres. Internat. Film Seminars, Inc., N.Y.C., 1981-83; vis. lectr. dept. anthropology Yale U., New Haven, Conn., 1989-91; pres. Soc. for Visual Anthropology, Washington, 1995-97, FilmResearch, Higganum, Conn., 1970—. Cons. Choreometrics Project, N.Y.C., 1970-73; mem. Comité Internat. des Films de l'Homme, Paris, 1977—. Author: (books) The History of Ethnographic Film, 1971, Anthropological Cinema, 1973, Cine Antropológico, 1978; producer (film) Margaret Mead: A Portrait by a Friend, 1978. Trustee Wadsworth Atheneum, Hartford, Conn., 2000—; corporator Conn. Inst. for the Blind-Oak Hill, Hartford, Conn., 1996—; bd. dir. Friends of the Ixchel Mus., Guatemala, 2003—. Recipient scholarship Harvard U., Cambridge, Mass., 1963-64, fellowship, Yale U., New Haven, Conn., 1987-88; grantee: Wenner-Gren Found., N.Y.C., 1970-72, Tinker Found., N.Y.C., 1976. Fellow Am. Anthrop. Assn., Royal Anthrop. Inst.; mem. Soc. Woman Geographers, Harvard Alumni Assn. (dir. 2002-2005, Hiram S. Hunn award 2002), Town and County Club, Harvard Club of So. Conn. (v.p. 1995—), Saturday Morning Club. Avocation: costume and textiles. Home: 285 Riverside Dr Apt 7E New York NY 10025-5227 Office: FilmResearch 8 Christian Hill Rd Higganum CT 06441-4030 E-mail: debrigard@att.net.

DEBRINCAT, SUSAN JEANNE, nutritionist; b. Detroit, Oct. 7, 1943; d. Lloyd Brode and Florence Claire (Majewski) Greenleaf; m. Raymond Frank DeBrincat, June 19, 1965; children: David Lloyd, Mark Joseph. BS magna cum laude, Mich. State U., 1965. Cert. med. technologist, Am. Soc. Clin. Pathologists. Med. technologist Harper Hosp., Detroit, 1965-66, South Macomb Hosp., Warren, Mich., 1966; art teacher YWCA, Berkley, Mich., 1969-80; master coord. Shaklee Corp., West Bloomfield, Mich., 1977—, lifetime master, 1990—, sr. master coord., fascilitator for pacific inst., 1997—. Nutritional counselor, fashion, color, image, makeup counselor, mgmt. and leadership trainer, motivational spkr. for Shaklee Corp.; interior designer. Painter oil, acrylic, watercolors. Mem. Rep. Nat. Com. Pres.'s Club, Found. Club, Phi Kappa Phi, Delta Zeta. Roman Catholic. Avocations: painting, art and antiques, reading, travel.

DEBRUCE, PAUL, agricultural food products company executive; Founder DeBruce Grain Inc., Kansas City, Mo., 1978, CEO, 1978—; also DeBruce Grain de Mex., Queretaro.*

DE BRUHL, A. MARSHALL, writer, editor, publishing consultant; b. Woodfin, N.C., Nov. 3, 1935; s. Arthur Marvin and Janie Myra (Wright) De B. AB, Duke U., 1958. Editor U. Pa. Press, 1963-64; editl. staff Crowell-Collier Macmillan, 1964-67; with Charles Scribner's Sons, N.Y.C., 1967-85, mng. editor Dictionary Sci. Biography, Dictionary of Middle Ages, v.p., dir. Reference Book divsn.; then sr. v.p. Scribner Book Cos., Inc.; with Doubleday Pub. Co., N.Y.C., 1986-88; exec. editor Anchor Press; cons. editor HarperCollins, 1988-91, Henry Holt, 1992-94. Author: Sword of San Jacinto: A Life of Sam Houston, 1993; co-editor: International Thesaurus of Quotations, 1996. Lt. (j.g.) USNR, 1959-62. Mem. PEN, Authors Guild, Century Assn. Clubs: Century Assn. Address: 148 Elk Mountain Rd Asheville NC 28804 E-mail: dres1945@aol.com.

DEBS, BARBARA KNOWLES, former college president, consultant; b. Eastham, Mass., Dec. 24, 1931; d. Stanley F. and Arline (Eugley) Knowles; m. Richard A. Debs, July 19, 1958; children: Elizabeth, Nicholas. BA, Vassar Coll., 1953; PhD, Harvard U., 1967; LLD, N.Y. Law Sch., 1979; LHD, Manhattanville Coll., 1985. Freelance translator editor Ency. of World Art divsn. McGraw-Hill Pub., N.Y.C., 1959-62; from asst. prof. to prof. Manhattanville Coll., Purchase, N.Y., 1968-86, pres., 1975-85; trustee, chmn. collections com. N.Y. Hist. Soc., 1985-87, pres., CEO, 1988-92; cons. non-profit orgns. pvt. practice, 1992—. Contbr. articles on Renaissance and contemporary art to profl. publs. Mem. N.Y. Coun. Humanities, 1978-85; mem. Westchester County Bd. Ethics, 1979-84; trustee N.Y. Law Sch., 1979-89; trustee Geraldine R. Dodge Found., 1985—; bd. dirs. Internat. Found. for Art Rsch., 1985-92; trustee Com. Econ. Devel., 1985-94, Bklyn. Mus. Art, 1996—; mem. Coun. Fgn. Rels., 1983—; mem. exec. bd. Bard Ctr. for Decorative Arts, 1995—; bd. govs. Fgn. Policy Assn., 1996-2002; hon. trustee Manhattanville Coll., 1996—, Midori Found., 1998—. AAUW Nat. fellow and Ann Radcliffe fellow, 1958-59; Am. Council Learned Socs. grantee, 1973; Fulbright fellow, Pisa, Italy, 1953, U. Rome, 1954. Mem. Am. Coun. on Edn. (chmn. commn. acad. affairs 1977-79), Young Audiences (nat. dir. 1977-80), Renaissance Soc. Am., Coll. Art Assn., Phi Beta Kappa. Clubs: Cosmpolitan, Century Assn.

DEBS, RICHARD A. investment banker; b. Providence, Oct. 7, 1930; s. Abraham George and Madge (Fatool) D.; m. Barbara Knowles, July 19, 1958; children: Elizabeth Anderson, Nicholas. BA summa cum laude, Colgate U., 1952; postgrad. (Fulbright scholar), Cairo U., 1952-53; MA, Princeton U., 1956, PhD, 1963; LLB, Harvard U., 1958, grad. Advanced Mgmt. Program, 1973. Bar: N.Y. 1960. Researcher joint project Harvard-Princeton, 1958-59; with Fed. Res. Bank of N.Y., N.Y.C., 1960-76, legal dept., 1960-64, asst. counsel, 1964-69, sec. of bank, 1965-69, v.p. govt. bonds and securities, 1969-72, v.p. loans and credits, 1969-72, v.p. open market ops., 1972, sr. v.p., 1973, 1st v.p., chief adminstrv. officer, 1973-76; alt. mem. Fed. Open Market Com., 1973-76; mng. dir. Morgan Stanley & Co., Inc., 1976-87; pres. Morgan Stanley Internat. Inc., 1976-87; chmn. R.A. Debs & Co., 1987—; adv. dir. Morgan Stanley, 1987—; chmn. The Malaysia Fund Inc., 1987—. Bd. dirs. Gulf Internat. Bank, London, Mizuho Corp. Bank, Mizuho Securities Co.; advisor Bank Julius Baer, 1987—, United Gulf Group (Kuwait), 1987—, Dai-Ichi Mut. Life, Tokyo, 1988—, Nissho Iwai Corp., Tokyo, 1990—; chmn. com. fiscal agy. ops. Fed. Res. System, 1969-76; mem. Fed. Res. Steering Com. on Payments Mechanism, 1973-76, Fed. Res. Steering Com. on Internat. Banking, 1973-76; allied mem. N.Y. Stock Exchange, also chmn. adv. com. internat. capital markets; mem. com. multinat. enterprises U.S. coun. Internat. Bus.; mem. internat. capital markets adv. com. Fed. Res. Bank of N.Y.; mem. Nat. Commn. on Pub. Svc. (The Volcker Commn.); mem. Overseas Devel. Coun.; mem. U.S. Office Pers. Mgmt. Task Force on Pay Reform; mem. World Bank Adv. Group on Pvt. Sector Devel.; mem. bus. adv. coun. European Bank for Reconstrn. and Devel., Russian-Am. Banking Forum; mem. Carnegie Commn.; mem. Take Stock in Am. Com., 1973-76; mem. Egypt-U.S. Bus. Coun.; mem. adv. coun. Near Eastern program Princeton U.; mem. N.Y. State Savs. Bond Com., 1973-76; adv. coun. Am. Inst. Banking, 1973-76. Contbr. articles on internat. banking to profl. publs. Chmn. emeritus, trustee Carnegie Hall; bd. dirs. Fedn. Protestant Welfare Agys., Inst. Internat. Edn.; trustee Carnegie Endowment for Internat. Peace, Am. Univs. Field Staff; trustee Am. U., Beirut, vice chmn., 1981-94, chmn., 1994—; bd. dirs. Am. Council on Germany; mem. vis. com. Middle East Center Harvard U., 1976-82, mem. vis. com. Ctr. for Internat. Affairs; mem. Group of 30, Reuters Carnegie Global Pub. Policy Group, 1999—; also mem. exec. com. Bretton Woods Com.; U.S. chmn. U.S.-Saudi Arabia Bus. Coun. Mem. ABA (com. Middle Eastern law), Assn. Bar City N.Y., Coun. Fgn. Rels., C. of C. U.S. (internat. policy com., chmn. subcom. on internat. econ. devel. 1979-87), Egyptian Am. C. of C. (chmn.), N.Y. C. of C. and Industry, Japan Soc., Asia Soc., Fgn. Policy Assn. (bd. govs.), Econs. Club, Century Assn. (N.Y.C.), Larchmont Yacht (N.Y.), River Club, Phi Beta Kappa Assocs. Office: Morgan Stanley & Co 1221 Ave of Americas New York NY 10020-1001

DEBUNDA, SALVATORE MICHAEL, lawyer; b. Phila., June 17, 1943; s. Salvatore and Marie Ann (Carilli) DeB.; children: Lauren, David. BS in Econs., U. Pa., 1965, JD, 1968. Bar: Pa. 1968, U.S. Supreme Ct. 1977. Law clk. to justice Phila. Ct. of Common Pleas, 1968-69; asst. gen. counsel ARA Services, Inc., Phila., 1969-74; sr. assoc. Cohen, Verlin, Sherzer & Porter, Phila., 1974-75; v.p., sec., gen. counsel AEL Industries, Inc., Montgomeryville, Pa., 1975-80; v.p., gen. counsel Cooper Assocs., Inc., Marlton, N.J., 1980-81; v.p. cable TV devel. Greater Media, Inc., East Brunswick, N.J., 1981-85; ptnr., chmn. media/entertainment law group Fox, Rothschild, O'Brien & Frankel, Phila., 1985-91; shareholder, dir. Pelino & Lentz, PC, Phila., 1991—. Mem. ABA, Pa. Bar Assn., Phila. Bar Assn., Fed. Comm. Bar Assn. Avocations: sports, owning thoroughbred horses. Office: Pelino & Lentz PC 1650 Market St One Liberty Pl 32d Fl Philadelphia PA 19103-7393

DE BURLO, COMEGYS RUSSELL, JR., investment advisor, educator; b. Phila. s. Comegys Russell and Margaret (Whitehurst) de B.; m. Edith Power Thatcher; children: Jane Thatcher, Charles Russell, John Todd. BS, Swarthmore Coll.; MBA, U. Pa.; DBA, Harvard U. Past CFO Tufts U., v.p., prof., treas., hon. treas. V.p. Ednl. Testing Svc., Princeton, N.J.; dir. UST Corp., NIH, Nat. Cancer Inst., Cancer Program Adv. Com., Cancer Rsch. Ctrs. Rev. Com., Am. Coun. on Edn., Com. on Taxation; pres., prin. The de Burlo Group Inc., 1987—. Past adv. com. No. Calif. Cancer Program; past mem. sci. adv. com. U. N.Mex. Cancer Treatment Ctr., Ohio State U. Comprehensive Cancer Ctr., 1983-97; pres. Mass. Assn. Schs. and Colls.; trustee Cambridge Friends Sch., Belmont Hill Sch., Moses Brown Sch., Lincoln Sch., BB&N Sch.; bd. mgrs. New Eng. Yearly Meeting; trustee Obadiah Brown/Sarah Swift Fund; commr. pub. trust funds. With USNR. Fellow Royal Hort. Soc.; mem. Assn. for Investment, Mgmt. and Rsch., Boston Security Analysts Soc., Internat. Assn. for Comparative Rsch. on Leukemia and Related Diseases (treas.), Am. Rhododendron Soc. (asst. treas. Mass. chpt.), Harvard Club, Green Mountain Club, Appalachian Mountain Club, Tau Beta Pi. Office: 50 Federal St Boston MA 02110-2500 E-mail: edith@bloomberg.net.

DEBUS, ALLEN GEORGE, history educator; b. Chgo., Ill., Aug. 16, 1926; s. George Walter William and Edna Pauline (Schwenneke) D.; m. Brunilda Lopez-Rodriguez, Aug. 25, 1951; children: Allen Anthony George, Richard William, Karl Edward. BS, Northwestern U., 1947; A.M., Ind. U., 1949; PhD, Harvard U., 1961; postgrad., U. Coll. London, 1959-60; D.Sc. h.c., Cath. U. Louvain, 1985. Research chemist Abbott Labs., North Chicago, Ill., 1951-56; asst. prof. U. Chgo., 1961-65, assoc. prof. history, 1965-68, prof., 1968-78, Morris Fishbein prof. history sci. and medicine, 1978-96, Morris Fishbein prof. emeritus, 1996—; dir. Morris Fishbein Ctr. for Study History Sci. and Medicine, 1971-77. Disting. vis. prof. Ariz. ctr. for medieval and renaissance studies Ariz. State U., 1984; vis. prof. Inst. Chemistry, U. São Paulo, Brazil, 1990; mem. internat. adv. com. Tel-Aviv U. The Cohn Inst. History and Philosophy of Sci. and Ideas, Ctr. for History and Philosophy of Sci. of Hebrew U. of Jerusalem; mem. internat. adv. bd. Annali dell'Istituto e Museo di Storia della Scienza di Firenze; cons. lit. and sci. curriculum Ga. Inst. Tech. Author: The English Paracelsians, 1965, 66, (with Robert P. Multhauf) Alchemy and Chemistry in the 17th Century, 1966, The Chemical Dream of the Renaissance, 1968, 2d edit., 1972, Science and Education in the 17th Century, 1970, (with Brian Rust) The Complete Entertainment Discography, 1973, 2d rev. edit., 1989, The Chemical Philosophy, 2 vols., 1977, 2d edit., 2002, Japanese transl., 1999, Man and Nature in the Renaissance, 1978, 15th rev. edit., 1995, Italian transl., 1982, Spanish transl., 1985, 86, 2d edit., 1995, Japanese transl., 1986, Chinese transl., 1988, 2000, Greek transl., 1997, Robert Fludd and His Philosophical Key, 1979; Science and History: A Chemist's Appraisal, 1984, Chinese tranl., 1999, Chemistry, Alchemy and the New Philosophy, 1550-1700, 1987, The French Paracelsians: The Chemical Challenge to Medical and Scientific Tradition in Early Modern France, 1991, 2002, Paracelso e la Tradizione Paracelsiana, 1996, Chemistry and Medical Debate: Van Helmont to Boerhaave, 2001; editor: World Who's Who in Science from Antiquity to the Present, 1968, Science, Medicine and Society in the Renaissance, 2 vols, 1972, Medicine in Seventeenth-Century England, 1974; editor reprint: Theatrum Chemicum Britannicum (1652), 1967, John Dee's Mathematicall Praeface (1570), 1975; editor: (with Ingrid Merkel) Hermeticism and the Renaissance: Intellectual History and the Occult in Early Modern Europe, 1988, (with Michael T. Walton) Reading the Book of Nature: The Other Side of the Scientific Revolution, 1998; essayist: Festschrift: Experiencing Nature: Essays for Allen G. Debus (edited by Paul Theerman and Karen Parshall, 1997); mem. bd. adv. editors Physis Rivista internazionale de storia della scienza, Nuncius, The 16th Century Jour.; adv. editor: History of Science; hon. bd. editors Incognita; programmed 3 records released by Smithsonian Instn. Music of Victor Herbert, 1979; contbr. articles to profl. jours.; patentee in field. Social Sci. Rsch. Coun. fellow, 1959-60; Fulbright fellow, 1959-60; Fels Found. fellow, 1960-61; Guggenheim fellow, 1966-67; overseas fellow Churchill Coll. Cambridge (Eng.) U., 1966-67, 69; mem. Inst. Advanced Study Princeton, N.J., 1972-73; NEH fellow Newberry Libr., Chgo., 1975-76; fellow Inst. for Rsch. in Humanities U. Wis., Madison, 1981-82, NEH, 1987, Folger Shakespeare Libr., Washington; rsch. grantee Am. Philos. Soc., 1961-62, Wellcome Trust, 1962, NIH, 1962-70, 74-75, 77-78, 92-97, NSF, 1961-63, 71-74, 80-83, Am. Coun. Learned Socs., 1966, 70, 71. Fellow AAAS (mem. electorate nominating com., sect. L 1974-77, chmn. com. 1974); mem. History of Sci. Soc. (council 1962-65, 87-90, program chmn. 1972, Pfizer award 1978, Sarton medal 1994, Disting. lectr. 1996), Soc. Study Alchemy and Early Chemistry (mem. council 1967—), Am. Assn. for History Medicine (program com. 1975), Brit. Soc. for History Sci., Internationale Paracelsus Gesellschaft, Am. Chem. Soc. (asso. mem. history of chemistry div., exec. com. 1969-72, Dexter award 1987), Soc. Med. History of Chgo. (sec.-treas. 1971-72, v.p. 1972-74, pres. 1974-76, mem. council), Académie Internat. d'Histoire de la Medecine, Société Internationale d'Histoire de la Medecine, Academie Internat. d'Histoire des Scis. (corr. 1971, membre effectif 1991), Am. Inst. History of Pharmacy (Edward Kremers award 1978, adv. panel hist. activity 1979-81, awards com. 1981—), Am. Soc. Reformation Research, Assn. Recorded Sound Collections., Midwest Junto for History of Sci. (pres. 1983-84), Academia das Ciencias de Lisboa. Office: U Chgo Dept History Chicago IL 60637 E-mail: adebus@midway.uchicago.edu.

DEBUS, ELEANOR VIOLA, retired business management company executive; b. Buffalo, May 19, 1920; d. Arthur Adam and Viola Charlotte (Pohl) D. Student, Chown Bus. Sch., 1939. Sec. Buffalo Wire Works, 1939-45; home talent prodr. Empire Producing Co., Kansas City, Mo.; sec. Owens Corning Fiberglass Buffalo; pub. rels. and publicity Niagara Falls Theatre, Ont., Can.; pub. rels. dir. Woman's Internat. Bowling Congress, Columbus, Ohio, 1957-59; publicist, sec. Ice Capades, Hollywood, Calif., 1961-63; sec. to contr. Rexall Drug Co., L.A., 1963-67; bus. mgmt. acct. Samuel Berke & Co., Beverly Hills, Calif., 1967-75, Gadbois Mgmt. Co., Beverly Hills, 1975-76; sec., treas. Sasha Corp., L.A., 1976-92; former bus. mgr. Dean Martin, Eleanor Powell, Debbie Reynolds, Shirley MacLaine. Contbr. articles to various mags. Mem.: Am. Film Inst. Republican.

DEBUSK, MANUEL CONRAD, lawyer, business executive; b. Grosvenor, Tex., June 13, 1914; s. Elias C. and Ollie (Lewis) DeB. BA, Tex. Technol. Coll., 1933; LL.B., So. Meth. U., 1941. Bar: Tex. 1942. Adminstrv. asst. FHA, Washington, Dallas, 1934 41; spl. agt. FBI, 1941-46; partner DeBusk & DeBusk, Dallas, 1946—. Mem., chmn. coordinating bd. Tex. Colls. and Univs., 1969-70; Chmn. Dallas County Dem. Party, 1967-71; bd. dirs., chmn. bd. regents Tex. Technol. Coll., 1959-65; pres. DeBusk Found., Assn. Small Founds.; mem. Coun. on Founds. Mem. Tex. Bar Assn., Tex., Nat. mortgage bankers assns., Nat. Lefthanded Golf Assn. (past pres.), Cosmopolitan Internat. (past internat. pres.) Home: 7365 Elmridge Dr Dallas TX 75240-3623 Office: 2089 N Collins Blvd Richardson TX 75080-2664 *One's yardstick, whether business or avocation, must be to leave the world a better place that it was before you touched it.*

DE BUSTROS, ANDRÉE CHINIARA, physician; b. Damascus, Syria, Feb. 13, 1955; d. Jean and Noha (Dib) Chiniara; m. Serge Nicolas De Bustros, June 21, 1981; children: Paul, Christina. BS in Biology and Chemistry, Am. U. Beirut, 1976, MD, 1980; MPH, U. Ill., Chgo., 1992. Diplomate in internal medicine, endocrinology and metabolism Am. Bd. Internal Medicine. Asst. prof. oncology and medicine Johns Hopkins U., Balt., 1986-91; sect. head, endocrinology Christ Hosp., Oak Lawn, Ill., 1992—; clin. assoc. prof. medicine U. Ill., Chgo., 1994—. Contbr. chpts. to books, articles to profl. jours. Dalland fellow Am. Philos. Soc., 1983-85; Clin. Scientist awardee Johns Hopkins U., 1986-88. Mem. Am. Diabetes Assn., The Endocrine Soc., Alpha Omega Alpha, Delta Omega. Avocations: reading, music, bicycling, travel. Office: Christ Hosp 4440 W 95th St Oak Lawn IL 60453-2699 E-mail: andree.debustros@advocatehealth.com.

DECAMINADA, JOSEPH PIO, retired insurance company executive; b. Gebo, Wyo., Oct. 17, 1935; s. Pio and Ida (Franch) D.; m. Genevieve Caputo, Aug. 30, 1958; 1 child, Joseph BA magna cum laude, St. Francis Coll., 1956; JD, St. John's U., 1959; postgrad., Harvard U., 1978-79. CPCU, CLU; chartered fin. cons. From corp. sec. to sr. v.p., sec. Atlantic Mut. Ins. Co., Centennial Ins. Co., N.Y.C., 1971-86, exec. v.p., sec., 1986-96. Past chmn. bd. dirs. CPCU-Harry J. Loman Found., Motor Vehicle Accident Indemnification Corp., N.Y. Property Ins. Underwriting Assn., Ind. Fedn. N.Y. Contbr. articles to profl. jours. Bd. dirs. Coll. Mt. St. Vincent, Riverdale, NY. Decorated Knight of Malta; recipient Brotherhood award NCCJ, 1991; named Ins. Man of Yr. Recovery Forum, 1978; Anglo-Am. fellow B.D. Cooke & Ptnrs., Ltd., London, 1966. Mem. Soc. CPCU (nat. pres. 1984-85, Disting. Svc. award 1989, Eugene A. Toale Meml. award N.Y. chpt. 1974), Soc. CLU. Home: 3 Ridgecrest N Scarsdale NY 10583-2013

DECAMPS, CHARLES MICHAEL, lawyer; b. Arlington, Va., Oct. 14, 1950; s. Charles Modeste and Loraine (Seward) DeC.; children: Sarah Hopkins, Christopher Duff, William Michael. BA with honors, U. Va., 1972, JD, 1975. Bar: Va. 1975, U.S. Dist. Ct. (ea. dist.) Va. 1975, U.S. Dist. Ct. (we. dist.) Va. 1975, U.S. Ct. Appeals (4th cir.) 1975. Law clk. U.S. Dist. Ct. (we. dist.) Va., 1975; assoc. Cabell, Paris, Lowenstein & Bareford, Richmond, Va., 1976-86; ptnr., dir. Sands, Anderson, Marks & Miller, Richmond, 1986—. Chmn. regional com. Young Lawyers Conf., Va. State Bar, 1978-84. Active Am. Cancer Soc., Richmond, 1978-81, United Givers Fund, Richmond, 1981-83; com. mem. St. James Ch., Richmond, 1980-82, vestryman, 1989-92, chmn. mission and outreach com., 1990, sr. warden, 1991; mem. Leadership Metro Richmond, 1991; bd. dirs. Richmond Ambulance Authority, Inc,. 1990—; bd. dirs. Historic Monument Ave. and Fan Dist. Found., Inc., Richmond, 1983-93; bd. dirs. Fan Dist. Assn., 1984-87; pres. West Richmond Little League, 1993-94. Mem. ABA, Richmond Bar Assn., Va. Bar Assn., Westwood Club (Richmond), Phi Beta Kappa, Omicron Delta Kappa. Episcopalian. Avocations: sports, running, tennis. Home: 8963 Wishart Rd Richmond VA 23229-7158 Office: Sands Anderson Marks & Miller PO Box 1998 Richmond VA 23218-1998

DE CANI, JOHN STAPLEY, statistician, educator; b. Canton, Ohio, May 8, 1924; s. John Mustin and Ada Louise (Stapley) deC.; m. Jessie Montrose Farr, Dec. 17, 1955 (dec. Sept. 1969). BS, U. Wis., 1948; MBA, U. Pa., 1951, PhD, 1958. Mem. faculty U. Pa., Phila., 1948—, assoc. prof. stats., 1963-72, prof., 1972-95; prof. emeritus, 1995—; chmn. dept. stats. U. Pa., 1972-78. Cons. USN, 1957—, NAACP., 1967—, EEOC, 1976— Author: (with R. C. Clelland) Basic Statistics, 1973; contbr. articles to profl. jours. Served with USAAF, 1943-45. Recipient Distinguished Teaching award Lindbach Found., 1964; recipient Wharton disting. teaching award, 1978, 95, 97; Fulbright grantee Norway, 1959-60 Fellow: Royal Stats. Soc., Am. Statis. Assn.; mem.: Biometric Soc., Inst. Math. Statistics. Home: 226 W Rittenhouse Sq Apt 1715 Philadelphia PA 19103

DE CARO, BARBARA ANN MARY, health and physical education educator; b. Rockaway, N.Y., Mar. 15, 1948; d. Irwin Hess and Anna Marie (Kiely) Stilwell; m. Laurence T. De Caro, July 28, 1973; children: Laurence T. Jr., Scott A. BA, Montclair (N.J.) State Coll., 1970, MA, 1978. Cert. health and phys. edn. tchr., N.J., adapted phys. edn., drivers edn., family life edn., adminstrn. and supervision. Tchr. Pascack Hills High Sch., Montvale, NJ, 1970—, softball coach, 1971-76, basketball coach, 1971-78, adolescent intervention counselor, 1985-86, advisor student govt., 1990-99, class advisor, 1988, 1994, 2001. Advisor NCCJ, Princeton, N.J., 1983-98; mem. Hillsdale Bd. of Health, 1990-, v.p., 1991, pres., 1996-; chairperson Hillsdale Sch. and Community Task Force, 1986-92; European group leader EF Ednl. Tours, 1999—. Co-author: Family Life Education Curriculum, 1982—. Mem. Bergen County Task Force on Crimes Against Children, Montvale, 1982-84; coord. Pascack Valley Regional High Sch. Phys. Edn. Articulation, Montvale, 1983-84, Jump Rope for Heart, Am. Heart Assn., Montvale, 1986-, Adolescent Suicide Awareness, Montvale, 1985-86; sec. Pascack Valley Am. Heart Assn., 1987-88. Recipient Vol. of Yr. award Hillside Bd. Health, 1998. Mem. N.J. Edn. Assn., ASCD, Nat. Coun. on Family Rels., AAHPERD, N.J. Assn. for Health, Phys. Edn., Recreation and Dance (v.p.-elect 2000-2001, v.p. 2001, peer coord. 1996—, peer mediation trainer 1994—, instr. crisis prevention inst. 1997—, internal coord. mid. states evaluation com. 1998-2003, mem. diversity coun. 2000-02, character edn. coord. 2002--). Avocations: tennis, crafts. Office: Pascack Hill High Sch Grand Ave Montvale NJ 07645

DE CAROLIS, PHILIP JOSEPH, space designer, educator; b. N.Y.C., Oct. 17, 1934; s. Ercole and Angelina Valentina De Carolis; m. Ruth Mary Hart, Jan. 30, 1954; children: Donna Marie, Philip Eric, Christopher Hart. Student, Acad. Aeronautics, Elmhurst, N.Y., 1953—55; BPS, SUNY, Saratoga Springs, 1992, MA, 1997; PhD in Edn., U. San Jose, Costa Rica, 1999. Human factors designer Avionics Rsch. Corp., Hempstead, NY, 1955—57, AMF Engring. Lab., Greenwich, Conn., 1957—60; indsl. designer AMF Corp. Hdqs., N.Y.C., 1960—62; design dir. SDI Corp., Long Island City, NY, 1962—72; prin. De Carolis Designs Ltd., N.Y.C. and Northport, NY, 1972—. Mem. adv. bd. Am. Bd. Diplomates in Pharmacy, N.Y.C., 1971—73. Contbr. articles to profl. jours. Pres. Northport Hills Civic Assn., 1971. Named to Alumni Honor Roll, SUNY, 2001; recipient Design and Engring. Innovation award, Internat. CES, Las Vegas, 2001, 2003. Master: F&AM; mem.: Am. Soc. Furniture Designers (bd. dirs. 2002—), Indsl. Designers Soc. Am. Achievements include creation of children's promenades for N.Y. Philharmonic Young People's Concerts; numerous design patents for collection of A/V furniture. Avocations: sculpting, painting, teaching. Office: De Carolis Designs Ltd 154 Waterside Rd Northport NY 11768 Fax: 631-261-0939. E-mail: philip.decarolis@esc.edu.

DÉCARY, ROBERT, judge; b. Montreal, Que., Can., May 26, 1944; s. Jacques M. Décary. BA, Coll. Brebeut, Montreal, 1963; LLL, U. Montreal, 1966; LLM, U. London, 1968. Bar: Quebec 1967. Polit. asst. Sec. State External Affairs, Ottawa, Ont., Can., 1970-73; lawyer Deschênes, de Grandpré, Montreal, 1973-80, Noël, Décary & Assocs., Hull, Que., 1980-90; judge Fed. Ct. Appeal, Ottawa, Ont., Can., 1990—. Contbr. essays to publs. Mem. Can. Bar Assn. (coun.). Office: Fed Ct Appeal Supreme Ct Bldg Ottawa ON Canada K1A 0H9

DE CASTRO, BRENDA J. artist, webmaster; b. Fullerton, Calif., Dec. 27, 1961; d. Joe Claire and Shirley Ann Thompson; m. Luis de Castro; children: Ana Christina, Luis Fransisco;children from previous marriage: Shalina Marie Hamlet, Bryce Edwin Vitus, Nicholas Alan Vitus. Artist B.J. de Castro Art Studio, Simi Valley, Calif., 1976—, webmaster, 1997—2003, owner, artist, 2001—. Publication, Thinking, one-man exhibition, Art Expo L.A. Recipient Fine Arts - Realism Award, Ln. County, Oreg., 1997, Artist of the Month, Mosiacs Art Gallery, 1999, Award, Art Space 2000, 2001. Mem.: Artists Exch., Nat. Assn. Fine Artists. Office: BJ de Castro Art Studio 625 Eisenhower Way Simi Valley CA 93065 E-mail: bj@bjdecastro.com.

DE CASTRO, HUGO DANIEL, lawyer; b. Panama City, Panama, Sept. 12, 1935; came to U.S., 1947; s. Mauricio Fidanque and Armida Rebecca (Salas) de C.; m. Isabel Shapiro, July 25, 1958; children: Susan M., Teresa A., Andrea L., Michele L. BSBA in Econs. cum laude, UCLA, 1957, JD summa cum laude, 1960. CPA Calif.; bar: Calif. 61. Prin. de Castro, West, Chodorow, Glickfeld & Nass Inc., L.A., 1961—. Lectr. UCLA, 1962-67, 68, counsel to dean Law Sch., 1963—; commr. tax adv. com. State Bar Calif. Editor UCLA Law Rev., 1959-60, Taxation for Lawyers, 1971-88; contbr. articles to profl. jours. Trustee Stephen S. Wise Temple, Jewish Fedn. Cmty. Found.; trustee, bd. dirs., chmn. fin. com. UCLA Found.; bd. dirs. Western L.A. Found.; bd. dirs. Hebrew Union Coll.; bd. govs. Trustee Endowment Trusts. Mem. ABA chmn. taxation subcom.), ACLU, L.A. County Bar Assn., Beverly Hills Bar Assn. (bd. dirs. Law Found.), L.A. C. of C. (former chmn., dir.), L.A. World Affairs coun., Am. Jewish Com., Del Rey Yacht Club (Calif., former dir., officer), Founders of Music Ctr., Las Hadas Country Club (Mex.), Pi Lambda Phi. Office: de Castro West Chodorow et al 10960 Wilshire Blvd Ste 1400 Los Angeles CA 90024-3702

DECATUR, RAYLENE, museum director; Pres., CEO Denver Mus. of Nature & Sci. (formerly Denver Mus. of Natural History), 1995—. Office: Denver Mus of Nature & Sci 2001 Colorado Blvd Denver CO 80205-5732

DECELL, HAL C. federal agency administrator; m. Jane DeCell; children: Caroline, Clayton, Charles. BA, Tulane U., 1971; JD, George Mason U., 1981. Bar. D.C. 1981. Past legis. dir., Washington; past press sec.; past spl. projects dir.; past chief staff, adminstrv. asst. to congressman Jamie L. Whitten, chmn. house appropriations com. Ho. of Rep.; asst. sec. congl. and intergovtl. rels. Dept. HUD, Washington, 1995-2000. Office: Farm Credit Adminstrn 1501 Farm Credit Dr Mc Lean VA 22102-5090 E-mail: decellh@fca.gov.

DE CELLES, CHARLES EDOUARD, theologian, educator; b. Holyoke, Mass., May 17, 1942; s. Fernand Pierre and Stella Marie (Shooner) De C. *Professor DeCelles currently has three sons in college. Christopher, 23, graduated Summa Cum Lade from St. Joseph's University, Philadelphia, where he was a Board of Trustees' Scholar (full tuition) and earned the Bachelor of Science degree in physics. He is presently pursuing a master's degree in software engineering at the University of Scranton. Mark, 20, a Shahan Scholar at the Catholic University of America, is a junior pursuing a bachelor's degree with majors in mathematics and religion. Salvador, 19, is a freshman at the University of Scranton and holds a Dean's Scholarship. He is working toward a bachelor's degree in computer engineering.* BA, U. Windsor, Ont., Can., 1964; MA in Theology, Marquette U., Milw., 1966; PhD, Fordham U., 1970; MA in Religion, Temple U., Phila., 1979. m. Mildred Manzano Valdez, July 17, 1978; children: Christopher Emanuel, Mark Joshua, Salvador Isaiah. Mem. faculty Dunbarton Coll. of Holy Cross, Washington, 1969-70, Marywood Coll. (became Marywood U., 1997), Scranton, Pa., 1970—, prof. religious studies, 1980—. Mem. bd. examiners U. Calicut, Kerala, India, 1985—86; subject specialist Accrediting Commn. of Distance Edn. and Tng. Coun., 1995; moderator Students Organized to Uphold Life, Marywood Coll., 1982—; co-chmn. Task Force Social Justice and Environment, 1992—93, corrector off-campus degree program, 1977—, dept. scribe, 1995—. Author: Paths of Belief, Vol. 2, 1977, prin. co-author rev. edit., 1987; The Unbound Spirit: God's Universal Sanctifying Work, 1985, Jesus: The Eternally Begotten of the Father as Human Being, 1993; editor Biographical Directory Cath. Acad. Scis. in U.S.A., 1994, Science and Religion in Dialogue, 1999; also pamphlets, articles, book revs., guest editorials, columns, letters, occasional columnist Nat. Cath. Register, 1983-87, The Dunmorean, 1996-97; regular columnist The Catholic Observer, 1996—; contbr. articles to profl. jours., mags. and newspapers. Mem. Ecumenism and Inter-faith Commn., Diocese of Scranton, 1992—, Ecumenical Leadership Com., 1999—; bd. dirs. Scranton UN Assn., 1974-75, chmn. UN Day, 1974; mem. ProLife prep. Commn. Scranton Diocesan Synod, 1984-85; mem. Filipino-Am. Assn. N.E. Pa., 1984-91, pub. rels. officer, 1985-91, editor newsletter, 1988-91; bd. dirs. Scranton chpt. Pennsylvanians for Human Life, 1983—, v.p., 1994—; leader Cath. Charismatic Prayer Group, Scranton, 1970-76; pack com. mem. Boy Scouts, Scranton, 1990-95, Cath. religious emblems counselor, 1993-96; chmn. prolife com. Immaculate Conception parish, 1994—. Recipient cert. of appreciation, U.S. Cath. Conf., 1976, Disting. Svc. award, UN Assn. U.S., 1974, Svc. award, Filipino-Am. Assn. N.E. Pa., 1990, cert. appreciation, Boy Scouts Am., 1991, 1992, 1993, 1994, 1995, Defender of Life cert. of appreciation, Susan B. Anthony List, 2003, several athletic awards for rd. running yearly, 1987—96, multiple awards for speed walking, 1990—96, 2000—02, admitted to the Order Cor Mariae, Marywood Coll., 1990, invested knight, Equestrian Order of the Holy Sepulchre of Jerusalem, 1994; Fordham U. Presdl. scholar, 1966—68. Mem. Cath. Acad. Sci. U.S.A. (pub. com. 1991—, chmn. program com. 1993-96, chmn. pub. com. 1997-2001, v.p. 1997—), Coll. Theology Soc. Am., Men of the Sacred Heart (Scranton chpt.), Scranton Organized Area Runners, Wyoming Valley Striders, Theta Alpha Kappa (chpt. moderator 1982—). Roman Catholic. Home: 923 E Drinker St Dunmore PA 18512-2644 Office: Marywood U Dept Religious Studies Scranton PA 18509-1598 E-mail: decelles@es.marywood.edu. *What the world needs is compassion. It needs me to climb out of the confines of my own little ego and embrace humankind: humanity created not in my image but God's - including the senile man, the habitual alcoholic, the AIDS victim, the starving Somalian, the abused woman, the child in the womb.*

DECESARE, DONALD E. broadcasting executive; b. Jersey City, Mar. 6, 1947; s. Emilio D. and Anita T. DeCesare; m. Catherine M. Fahey, June 20, 1970; 1 child, Elizabeth Ann. BA, U. Pitts., 1967; MA, U. Conn., 1969. News dir. Sta. WGCH-AM, Greenwich, Conn., 1972—74; reporter Westinghouse Broadcasting Corp., N.Y.C., 1974—76; writer CBS News divsn. CBS Inc., N.Y.C., 1976—78, news editor, 1978—80, fgn. prodr., 1980—83, sr. fgn. prodr., 1983—85, mgr. N.Y./New England bur., 1985—87, fgn. editor, 1987—89, v.p. news coverage, 1989—90, v.p. ops., 1990—96; v.p. CBS News, 1990—96; pres. Crossroads Comm. of Old SaybrookLLC, Norwalk, Conn., 1996—, Crossroads Comm. / Enterprises; owner/operator WMRD-AM, Middletown, Conn., 1996—, WLIS-AM, Old Saybrook, Conn., 1996—. Bd. dirs. Middlesex County United Way, Norwalk Symphony Soc. Recipient Columbia DuPont award Columbia U., 1989; Overseas Press Club award, 1990. Mem.: Conn. Pub. Access Network (bd. dirs.), Conn. Broadcasters Assn. (bd. dirs.), Old Saybrook C. of C. (bd. dirs., pres. 2002—). Avocations: latin american art, furniture making, computers. Office: Crossroads Comm LLC 157 N Seir Hill Rd Norwalk CT 06850-1333 also: PO Box 1150 777 River Rd Middletown CT 06457-3922 also: PO Box 1420 77 Springbrook Rd Old Saybrook CT 06475-1225 E-mail: don@wliswmrd.net.

DECHAINE, DEAN DENNIS, lawyer; b. Lake Oswego, Oreg., Dec. 12, 1936; s. Bennet Dennis and Hazel Pearl (Vose) DeC.; m. Joan Carolyn Mann, Sept. 29, 1963; children: Michael, Beth, Eve. BS, Portland State U., 1959; LLB, U. Va., 1964. Bar: Va. 1964, Oreg. 1964, Wash. 1986, U.S. Dist. Ct. Oreg. 1964, U.S. Dist. Ct. (we. dist.) Wash. 1986, U.S. Ct. Appeals (9th cir.) 1966, U.S. Ct. Internat. Trade 1996. Rsch. asst. to U.S. senator from Oreg. Richard L. Neuberger, Washington, 1959-60; legis. asst. to U.S. senator from Oreg. Hall S. Lusk, Washington, 1960; ptnr. Miller Nash LLP, Portland, 1964—. Sec., legal counsel World Forestry Ctr., Portland, 1965—. Contbr. article to profl. jour. Chair Portland State U. Alumni Assn., 1967-68, Portland State U. Alumni Bd., 1986-89; scoutmaster Boy Scouts Am., Lake Oswego, 1983 86; program chair continuing legal edn. Oreg. State Bar, 1971; chair aviation sect. 1989-90, chair admiralty sect., 1983-84, 1997-99. With U.S. Army, 1960-61. Mem.: Maritime Law Assn. U.S. (proctor). Home: 443 Country Club Rd Lake Oswego OR 97034-2107 Office: Miller Nash LLP 111 SW 5th Ave Ste 3400 Portland OR 97204-3655 Fax: 503-224-0155. E-mail: dean.dechaine@millernash.com.

DE CHAMPEAUX DE LABOULAYE, DENNIS, computer scientist; BS in Math., U. Amsterdam, The Netherlands; PhD in Math., U. Leiden, The Netherlands. Rschr. U. Amsterdam, 1970-82; assoc. prof. Tulane U., New Orleans, 1982-84; staff engr. ADAC Labs., San Jose, Calif., 1984-86; engr., scientist Hewlett-Packard, Palo Alto, Calif., 1986-93; sr. SW cons. Rational, Santa Clara, Calif., 1993-94; cons. Scopus, Emeryville, 1994, Libr. U. Calif., Berkeley, 1994, NET, Redwood City, Calif., 1994, McKesson, San Francisco, 1995, Nat. Semiconductor, Santa Clara, 1995-96, KLA, San Jose, 1996, AllTell, San Jose, 1996, Kaiser Permanente, Oakland, Calif., 1996, KLA, San Jose, 1997, Sabre Decision Systems, Ft. Worth, 1997—98, Fireman's Fund, Novato, Calif., 1998, Sprint, Dallas, 1999, Blue Cross and Blue Shield, Jacksonville, 1999; pres. New Channel, Redwood City, Calif., 2000, Onto00 Inc., 2001—. Mem. AAAI, Assn. Computing Machinery, Sigart.

DE CHAMPLAIN, VERA CHOPAK, artist, painter; b. Kulmbach, Germany, Jan. 26, 1928; d. Nathaniel and Selma (Stiefel) Florsheim; m. Albert Chopak de Champlain, 1948. Student, Art Students League, N.Y.C., 1950-60; spl. studies with Edwin Dickinson, 1962-64. Art. dir., tchr. Emanuel Ctr., N.Y.C., 1967—. One person shows Consulate Fed. Rep. Germany, N.Y.C., 1986, Fusco Gallery, N.Y.C., 1982, B. Altman Gallery, N.Y.C., 1982; group shows include Munich, Germany, 1966, Rudolph Gallery, Woodstock, N.Y., 1967, Artists Equity Gallery, N.Y.C., 1970-77, Lever House, N.Y.C., 1974, 80, 85, 88, Avery Fisher Hall-Cork Gallery, N.Y.C., 1970, 82, 83, 84, 87, 89, 94, 99, Fountainbleau Gallery, N.Y.C., 1972, 73, 74, NYU, 1978, Met. Mus., 1979, Muriel Karasik Gallery, Westhampton Beach, N.Y., 1980, Lever House, N.Y.C., 1990, Broome St. Gallery, N.Y.C., 1991, 92, 93, 94, 95, Cornell U. Med. Libr., 1995, 96; represented in permanent collections Butler Inst. Am. Art, Youngstown, Ohio, Ga. Mus. Art, Athens, Slater Mus., Norwich, Conn., Webster Coll., St. Louis, Evansville Mus. Arts & Sci., Ind., Smithsonian Instn., Archives Am. Art,

Washington, Jacob Javits Fed. Bldg., N.Y., Permanent Mission of the Netherlands to UN, NYU-Grey Art Gallery, NYU, 1996. Recipient award in portrait painting, Hainesfalls, N.Y., 1965, First Prize-World award, Acad. Italia, Parma, 1985, 87; subject of TV interview, 1984; presented to Queen Elizabeth of England, 1991. Fellow Royal Soc. Arts (London); mem. Artists Equity Assn. N.Y., Arts Students League (life), Nat. Soc. Arts and Letters (art chmn. 1969—), Woman Pays Club, Liederkranz City Club N.Y. (trustee 1979—), Kappa Pi (life). Home: 230 Riverside Dr New York NY 10025-6105 Office: 230 Riverside Dr New York NY 10025-6105

DECHANO, LISA M, geographer, educator; d. David F. and Cynthia C. DeChano. BS, Juniata Coll., 1993; MS, U. ND, 1994; MA, Ohio U., 1997; PhD, SW Tex. State U., 2000. Asst. prof. Calif. State Poly. U., Pomona, 2000—01, Western Mich. U., Kalamazoo, 2001—. Assoc. editor (jour.) Rsch. in Geog. Edn.; contbr. articles to profl. jours. Grantee, Tchg. and Learning with Tech., Western Mich. U., 2002—. Mem.: Assn. of Am. Geographers (mem. publications com. 2001—, vice chmn. Environ. Perception and Behavioral Geography Splty. group 2003), Gamma Theta Upsilon, Omega Omega. Office: Western Mich U Dept Geography 3521 Wood Hall Kalamazoo MI 49008 Office Fax: 269-387-3442. E-mail: ldechano@wmich.edu.

DECHANT, VIRGIL C. retired fraternal organization administrator; b. Antonino, Kans., Sept. 24, 1930; s. Cornel J. and Ursula (Legleiter) D.; m. Ann Schafer, Aug. 20, 1951; children: Thomas, Daniel, Karen, Robert. Hon. degree, Pontifical Coll. Josephinum, Columbus, Ohio, St. Anselm's Coll., Manchester, N.H., St. Leo's Coll., Fla., Mt. St. Mary's Coll., Emmitsburg, Md., St. John's U., S.I., N.Y., Providence Coll., Sacred Heart U., Bridgeport, Conn., Pontifical U. Santo Tomas, Manila, Assumption Coll., Worcester, Mass., Albertus Magnus Coll., New Haven; hon. degree, St. Thomas U., St. Paul, Kans. Newman Coll., Wichita, Franciscan U., Steubenville, Ohio, Benedictine Coll., Atchison, Kans., St. Thomas U., Fredericton, N.B., Can., Dallas U. With KC, 1948—63, dir., asst. supreme sec., supreme master 4th degree, 1963, supreme sec., 1967-77, supreme knight, CEO, 1977—2000. Appointee Pontifical Coun. for the Family, 1982—; consultor, Pontifical Coun. for Social Comm., 1990—; hon. councilor of state, Vatican City State, 2001; mem. Coun. of Superindency, Inst. for Works of Religion (Vatican Bank), 1990—. Bd. dirs. Nat. Shrine Immaculate Conception, Washington; past bd. dirs. Pontifical Coll. Josephinum, Columbus; trustee Cath. U. Am.; commr. Christopher Columbus Quincentenary Commn. for founding of Ams., 1992; apptd. auditor Snyod Am., 1997. Decorated Knight St. Gregory the Great promoted to comdr. with Star elevated to Knight Grand Cross, Knight Grand Cross Equestrian Order Holy Sepulchre, Holy Land Pilgrim Shell, Knight Grand Cross Order Pius IX, Knight Sovereign Mil. Order of Malta; named one of Gentleman of His Holiness, Pope John Paul II, 1987; appointed to Extraordinary Synod of Bishops in Vatican, 1985, Synod of Bishops on Laity, 1987, Synod of Bishops for Am., 1997; recipient Cross of Merit with Golden Star of Holy Sepulchre of Jerusalem, 1990.

DECHAR, PETER HENRY, artist; b. N.Y.C., Apr. 19, 1942; s. Edouard and Diane D.; m. Natasha Gratcheva, Apr. 23, 1999; 1 child, Antonina. Prin. Peter Dechar Inc. Archtl. Furniture. Exhibited one-man shows, Cordier & Ekstrom Gallery, N.Y.C., 1967, 69, 75, Twentieth Century Art from the Rockefeller Collection, N.Y.C., 1969, Mus. Modern Art, N.Y.C., 1969, group shows, Larry Aldrich Mus., Ridgefield, Conn., 1967, Krannert Art Mus., 1967, Whitney Mus. Art, N.Y.C., 1967, 69; represented in permanent collections, Mus. Modern Art, N.Y.C., Whitney Mus. Art, N.Y.C., Larry Aldrich Mus., Ridgefield, Conn., Walker Art Ctr., Fiberglass Tower Art Collection, Julien Levy Collection, Chase Manhatten Collection, Rockefeller Collection.

DE CHASTELAIN, A(LFRED) JOHN G(ARDYNE) D(RUMMOND), Canadian army officer, diplomat; b. Bucharest, Rumania, July 30, 1937; emigrated to Can., 1955, naturalized, 1962; s. Alfred George G. and Marion Elizabeth (Walsh) de C.; m. MaryAnn Laverty, Sept. 9, 1961; children: Duncan John, Amanda Jane. Student, Fettes Coll., Edinburgh, Scotland, 1950-55, Mt. Royal Coll. Calgary, Can., 1956; BA with honors in History, Royal Mil. Coll., Can., 1960; grad., Brit. Army Staff Coll., 1966; D in Mil. Sci. (hon.), Royal Mil. Coll. Can., 1996; LLD in Conflict Resolution (hon.), Royal Rds. U., 2001. Commd. 2d lt. Can. Army, 1960, advanced through grades to gen., 1989; comdg. officer 2d Bn. Princess Patricia's Can. Light Inf., 1970-72; comdr. Can. Forces Base, Montreal, Que., 1974-76; comdr. Can. Contingent UN Force in Cyprus, 1976-77; comdt. Royal Mil. Coll. Can., Kingston, Ont., 1977-80; comdr. 4th Can. Mechanized Brigade Group, Lahr, Fed. Republic Germany, 1980-82; dir. Gen. Land Doctrine Nat. Def. Hdqrs., Ottawa, 1982-83; dep. comdr. Mobile Command, St. Hubert, Que., 1983-86; asst. dep. min. pers. Nat. Def. Hdqrs., Ottawa, Ont., Can., 1986-88, vice chief of Def. Staff, 1988-89, chief of Def. Staff, 1989-93; Can. amb. to U.S. Washington, 1993. Past v.p. Scouts Can.; chief Defence Staff, 1994-95; mem. internat. Body on Decommissioning of Arms in No. Ireland, 1995-96; mem. ind. chmn. No. Ireland Peace Talks, 1996-98; chmn. Ind. Internat. Commn. on Decommissioning of Arms in No. Ireland, 1997—. Decorated comdr. Order Mil. Merit (Can.), officer Order of Can., comdr. Order St. John of Jerusalem, comdr. Legion of Merit (U.S.), Companion of Honour (U.K.); recipient Hellenic Commendation medal of Merit and Honor (Greece), Vimy award, Conf. Def. Assocs. Mem. Dominion of Can. Rifle Assn. (past pres.), Royal Scottish Country Dance Soc., St. Andrew's Soc., Royal Mil. Coll. Club, Royal Can. Legion, Royal Can. Mil. Inst, Col. of the Regiment, PPCLI, 2000-2003 Home: 170 Acacia Ave Ottawa ON Canada K1M 0R3 E-mail: ajgd.dec@sympatico.ca.

DECHER, RUDOLF, physicist, researcher; b. Wuerzburg, Ger., Aug. 22, 1927; came to U.S., 1960, naturalized, 1967; s. Hermann Alexander and Karola (Krenig) D.; m. Christa Anna Hort, Jan. 7, 1956 (dec. July 1999); children: Peter H., Marianne C. M in Physics, U. Wuerzburg, W. Ger., 1950, PhD in Physics, 1954. Research scientist Dynamit AG, Troisdorf, W. Ger., 1955-60; with NASA Marshall Space Flight Ctr., Huntsville, Ala., 1960-94; retired NASA, 1994; chief astrophysics div., space sci. lab. NASA Marshall Space Flight Ctr., 1970-86, asst. dir. space sci. lab., 1986-89, chief astrophysics div., space sci. lab., 1989-93, asst. dir. space sci. lab., 1993-94; prin. rsch. scientist Ctr. for Space Plasma & Aeronomic Rsch Inst. for Space Physics, Astrophysics & Edn., U. Ala., Huntsville, 1995—. Recipient Exceptional Service medal NASA, 1977 Mem. Am. Phys. Soc., AIAA. Roman Catholic. Home: 718 Owens Dr SE Huntsville AL 35801-2034

DECHERD, ROBERT WILLIAM, newspaper and broadcasting executive; b. Dallas, Apr. 9, 1951; s. Henry Benjamin Jr. and Isabelle Lee (Thomason) D.; m. Maureen Healy, Jan. 25, 1975; children: William Benjamin, Audrey Maureen. AB cum laude, Harvard U., 1973. Exec. v.p. Dallas Morning News, 1980-83, A.H. Belo Corp., Dallas, 1981-84, pres., chief operating officer, 1985-86, chmn., chief exec. officer, 1987-94, chmn., pres. and CEO, 1994—, also bd. dirs. Dir. Kimberly-Clark Corp., 1996—. Pres. Dallas Symphony Assn., 1979-80, Dallas Symphony Found., 1984-86, St. Mark's Sch., Tex., 1988-91; chmn. Dallas Parks Found., 1985-87, Dallas Soc. Profl. Journalists, 1978; trustee Tomas Rivera Policy Inst., 1992—; incorporator, pres. Freedom. of Info. Found. Tex., 1978. Recipient Disting. Svc. award Dallas Jaycees, 1985, Am. Newspaper Exec. of Yr. award Adweek mag., 1985, citation of honor AIA, 1988, Seymour Preston award Nat. Assn. Ind. Schs. Coun. Advancement and Support Edn., 1989, James Madison award Freedom of Info. Found. Tex., 1989, Henry Cohn Humanitarian award Anti-Defamation League, 1992, Freedom of Speech award The Media Inst., 1998; named to the Tex. Bus. Hall of Fame, 1995; recipient St. Mark's Disting. Alumnus award, 1998. Mem. Tex. Soc. Architects (hon.), Newspaper Assn. Am. (mem. exec. bd. 1992-96). Office: A H Belo Corp PO Box 655237 Dallas TX 75265-5237

DE CHERNEY, ALAN HERSH, obstetrics and gynecology educator; b. Phila., Feb. 13, 1942; s. William Aaron and Ruth (Hersh) DeC.; m. Deanna Faith Saver, June 26, 1966; children: Peter, Alexander. BS in Natural Scis., Muhlenberg Coll., 1963; MD, Temple U., 1967; MA (hon.), Yale U., 1985. Diplomate Am. Bd. Ob.-Gyn. (examiner 1984—, bd. dirs. 1995—), Am.Bd. Reproductive Endocrinology (bd. dirs. 1988-94), Nat. Bd. Med. Examiners (examiner 1987-90). Intern in gen. medicine U. Pitts., 1967-68; resident in ob-gyn. U. Pa., Phila., 1968-72, instr. dept. ob-gyn, 1970-72; asst. prof. ob-gyn. Yale U. Sch. Medicine, New Haven, 1974-78, assoc. prof., 1979-84, prof., 1984-91, John Slade Ely prof. ob-gyn, 1987-92, dir. div. reproductive endocrinology, dept. ob-gyn, 1982-92, lectr. dept. biology, 1985-92; Louis E. Phaneuf prof., chmn. dept. ob-gyn. Tufts U. Sch. Medicine, 1992-96; prof. dept. ob-gyn. UCLA, 1996—. Editor (in chief): Fertility and Sterility, 1996—. Maj. U.S. Army, 1972—74. Recipient Disting. Alumni award Temple U., 1989, 2002, Muhlenberg Coll., 1994. Fellow ACOG, Am. Fertility Soc. (pres. 1994-95), Am. Assn. History of Medicine, Soc. for Assisted Reproductive Tech. (pres. 1987-88), Soc. Reproductive Endocrinologists (pres. 1988), Soc. Reproductive Surgeons (charter, pres. 1991), Endocrine Soc., European Soc. Human Reproductions and Embryology, Soc. Gynecologic Surgeons, Soc. for Study of Reproduction, Soc. Gynecologic Investigation (pres. 1994-95). Office: UCLA Sch Medicine Dept Ob/Gyn 27-177 CHS Mail Code 174017 10833 Le Conte Ave Los Angeles CA 90095-3075

DECHERNEY, DEANNA SAVER, interior designer; b. Phila., Mar. 5, 1943; d. Martin and Bessie (Pitkoff) Saver; m. Alan Hersh DeCherney, June 26, 1965; children: Peter, Alexander, Nicholas. BFA, Univ. of the Arts, 1966. Designer Paul Planert Design Assocs., Pitts., 1967-68; assoc. designer Temple U., 1969-72; dir. interiors P.A.E., Tokyo, 1972-74; pres. The Nat. Design Service, Woodbridge, Conn., 1981-91, Weston, Mass., 1991-96. Instr. Paier Coll. Art, 1975-91, chmn. interior design dept., 1989-91; instr. Post Coll., 1987-89; mem. adv. bd. New Eng. Sch. Art & Design, Boston, 1993-94, trusteee, 1995—; mem. devel. bd. Boston Archtl. Ctr., 1993. Editl. dir. Design Times Mag., 1998-03, dir. at large, 1984-2003. Chmn. Vassar Coll. Parents and Friends Devel. Com., 1992; bd. dirs. Chamber Orch. of New Eng., 1975-88, The Neighborhood Music Sch., 1979-85; bd. dirs. Fider Visitors, 1991-98; trustee Univ. of the Arts, 1999—; pres. Friends of the Fulfillment Fund, 2000-02. Mem. Am. Soc. Interior Designers (pres. Conn. chpt. 1983-84, 87-88, v.p. N.E. region 1989-91), Interior Design Edn. Coun., Conn. Acad. Arts and Scis., Internat. Interior Deesign Assn. (v.p. residential design 1995-98, internat. v.p. residential design 1991, 92, 96, 97, 98), Friends of The Fulfillment Fund. (pres. 1999-2000). Address: 10720 Chalon Rd Los Angeles CA 90077-3315 E-mail: decherney@aol.com.

DECHERNEY, GEORGE STEPHEN, research scientist, research facility administrator, pharmaceutical executive; b. Wilmington, Del., June 16, 1952; s. Herman George and Grace Antoinette (Lewis) DeC.; m. Cleonice Anne DiSabatino, June 9, 1992; children: Elizabeth, Constance, Sarah, Elliot. BA, Columbia U., 1974; MD, Temple U., 1978; MPH, Columbia U., 1998. Instr. Vanderbilt U., Nashville, 1983-84; asst. prof. Uniformed Svcs. U., Bethesda, Md., 1985-89; dir. Diabetes and Metabolic Ctr., Wilmington, 1989-99; clin. assoc. prof. Thomas Jefferson Univ., Phila., 1989—, chief clin. pharmacology, endocrinology Christiana Care Health Sys., Newark, 1990-2000, dir., 1990-2000; assoc. prof. biology U. Del., 1991—; exec. v.p. clin. ops. PRA Internat., McLean, Va., 2000—. Invited internat. speaker 50th anniversary Greenslopes Hosp., Brisbane, Australia; bd. dirs. Wilmington Charter Sch. Math. and Sci., 1996—. Editor-in-chief Del. Med. Jour., 1998-2000; editor Good Clin. Practice Jour., 2000—. Trustee Christiana Care HealthSystem, 1998—. Maj. USAF, 1986-89. Mem. AMA, Am. Diabetes Assn. (pres. Del. affiliate 1990-95), N.Y. Acad. Scis., Endocrine Soc., Am. Soc. Quality (regional councilor 1998-2000). Achievements include research in endocrinology, in diabetes mellitus, in aerospace medicine. Office: PRA Internat 824 Market St Ste 809 Wilmington DE 19801

DE CHIARO, JOHN PAUL, music educator; b. Bronx, N.Y., Jan. 19, 1953; s. Arnold and Lucille De Chiaro. BS Music Edn, Kean U., 1975; MA, NYU, 1981. Music tchr. Edgewater (N.J.) Pub. Schs., 1975—76; guitar instr. Delbarton Sch., Morristown, NJ, 1976—81; prof. guitar Coll. St. Elizabeth, Convent Station, NJ, 1976—81, U. So. Miss., Hattiesburg, 1981—. Dir. Hattiesburg Youth Orch., 1981—87, Pine Belt Guitar Symposium, Hattiesburg, 1985—; founder Elmo & Mary Glenn Harrison Guitar Scholarship, U. So. Miss., 1986. Performer: (4 CD set) The Complete Works of Scott Joplin on Guitar, 1999; performer: (CDs) Christmas on Guitar, 1987, Sounds of Christmas on Guitar, 1985, The Guitar on Broadway, 1992, Soundscapes - The Mississippi Guitar Quartet, 2003, The Wedding Album, 2001; author: The Complete Works of Scott Joplin, 2001; performer: for Pope John Paul II, 6 solo recitals, Carnegie Hall, 2 solo recitals, White House; musician: (solo recitals) Carnegie Hall. Recipient Young Artist of Yr. award, Musical Am. Mag., 1982. Mem.: Music Tchrs. Nat. Assn., Lions. Roman Catholic. Avocations: running, model railroad, model airplanes. Home: 44 Chadlee Rd Hattiesburg MS 39401 Office: U So Miss Box 5081 Hattiesburg MS 39406

DECI, EDWARD LEWIS, psychologist, educator; b. Clifton Springs, N.Y., Oct. 14, 1942; s. Charles Henry and Janice Margaret (Upchurch) Deci. AB, Hamilton Coll., 1964; postgrad., London Sch. Econs., 1965; MBA, U. Pa., 1967; PhD, Carnegie-Mellon U., 1970. Postdoctoral fellow Stanford U., 1973-74; mem. faculty U. Rochester, NY, 1970—, chair dept. psychology, 1993-94, prof. psychology, 1978—; pvt. practice psychotherapy, 1975—; pres. Inst. for Rsch. and Reform in Edn., 1995-97, chmn., 1997—. Orgnl. cons., 1970—; lectr., cons., Bulgaria, Canada, Germany, Israel, Japan, Norway, Italy, Poland, Sweden, England, Jordan, Thailand, Australia, Finland, Spain. Author: (book) Intrinsic Motovation, 1975, The Psychology of Self-Determination, 1980; co-author: Industrial and Organizational Psychology, 1977, Intrinsic Motivation and Self-Determination in Human Behavior, 1985, Why We Do What We Do, 1995. Pres. Monhegan Mus. Assn., 1984—; trustee Monhegan (Maine) Conservation Assocs., 1982—89, 1992—95. Grantee NIMH, 1977—78, 1989—94, NSF, 1981—83, Nat. Inst. Child Health and Human Devel., 1986—89, 1990—96. Fellow: APA, Am. Psychol. Soc. Office: U Rochester Psychology Dept Rochester NY 14627 E-mail: deci@psych.rochester.edu.

DECIL, STELLA WALTERS (DEL DECIL), artist; b. Indpls., Apr. 26, 1921; d. William Calvin and Hazel Jean (Konkle) Smith; m. John W. Walters, June 19, 1940 (div. Sept. 1945); m. Casimir R. Decil, Feb. 6, 1965. Grad., Indpls. Acad. Comml. Art, 1939, John Heron Art Inst., Indpls., 1941. Staff artist William H. Block Co., Indpls., 1945-50, art dir., 1952-62, Frank R. Jelleff Co., Washington, 1950-51, Diamonds Dept. Stores, Phoenix, 1962-67; freelance artist, 1967-70. Painting instr. various art groups in Ariz.-N.Mex, 1970—, Phoenix Art Mus., 1975—77; mem. visual arts bd. Prescott Fine Arts Assn., 1990—2000; curator Mature Eye Bi-Ann. Prescott (Ariz.) Fine Arts Assn., 1996—2000; instr. Mountain Artists Guild, Prescott, 1995—97. One-woman shows include Cave Creek, Carefree, Scottsdale, Ariz., N.Mex., exhibited in group shows, Phoenix, Scottsdale, Las Cruces, N.Mex, Hoosier Salon, Folger Gallery, Indpls., Mammen II Gallery, Scottsdale, Thompson Gallery, Garelick Gallery, in pvt. collections, Represented in permanent collections Continental Bank, Humana Hosp., Pueblo Grande Mus., VA Med. Ctr., Prescott, Mayo Ctr. Women's Health, Scottsdale, Proctor Bank Vt., Bank Rio Grande, Las Cruces. Past pres. Scottsdale Art League, 1973. Named Ad Woman of Yr., Indpls. Ad Club, 1958; recipient Maxine Cherrington Meml. award, Hoosier Salon, 1973. Mem.: No. Ariz. Watercolor Assn., Ariz. Artists Guild, Ariz. Watercolor Soc. (Royal Scorpion Status, past pres.). Home: 9460 E Towago Dr Prescott Valley AZ 86314-7140

DECIUTIIS, ALFRED CHARLES MARIA, oncologist, television producer; b. N.Y.C., Oct. 16, 1945; s. Alfred Ralph and Theresa Elizabeth (Manko) deCiutiis; m. Catherine L. Gohn. *Family originated in Aquila. Key dates in family history include: 893, first ranked among the nobles of Italy; In 1140, at the assizes of Ariano, merged by Roger II with the Campaneschi; 1527, merger of Italian and Spanish branches; 1629, created "Princes of the Holy Roman Empire"; 1711, ancestor Giovanni Nocerino, discovered remains of Herculaneum; 1860, numbered among Garibaldi's 1000; 1901, Count Salvatore de Ciutiis, translated work leading to Concordate of 1929; 1920s, Count Vincenzo de Ciutiis appointed ambassador to Spain by Italy; Count Vincente de Ciutiis, Count of Madrid, assassinated in Spanish Civil War. The family has both Italian and Spanish branches. Paternal grandfather awarded the order of the Holy Spirit and buried in a church in Naples dedicated to the nobles of Spain. He was also responsible for the renovation of the Church of Santa Chiara in Naples, which was nearly destroyed in World War II. Around the turn if the century, the Marquesa of Salerno was also a Ciutus. A paternal cousin, Msgr. Vincenzo de Ciutus, would regularly preside at the famous festival of San Gennero in Naples.* BS summa cum laude, Fordham U., 1967; MD, Columbia U., 1971. Diplomate Am. Bd. Internal Medicine, Am. Bd. Med. Oncology. Intern N.Y. Hosp.-Cornell Med. Ctr., N.Y.C., 1971-72, resident, 1972-74; fellow in clin. immunology Meml. Hosp.-Sloan Kettering Cancer Ctr., N.Y.C., 1974-75, fellow in clin. oncology, 1975-76, spl. fellow in immunology, 1974-76; guest investigator, asst. physician exptl. hematology Rockefeller U., N.Y.C., 1975-76; pvt. practice specializing in med. oncology L.A., 1977—. Mem. med. adv. com. Olympics, 1984; co-founder Medtrina Med. Ctr., Torrance, Calif., physician asst. supr., 1984; mem. fgn. policy leadership project Ctr. Internat. Affairs, Harvard, Ill. *On a professional level Dr de Ciutiis was privileged to participate in the care of numerous celebrities. These included such luminaries as Dr. Ralph Bunche, Nobel Laureate and former ambassador of the U.S. to the U.N.; Madam Chiang Kai-Shek; Lady Bailey of Leeds Castle in Kent; Mrs. Payson, the former owner of the N.Y. Mets; Aristotle and Hercules Onassis; Christine Nicharos (Ford); actor and Academy Award winner, Melvyn Douglas; choreographer Bob Fosse; former Arkansas governor Winthrop Rockefeller; Zero Mostell, Norton Simon; Roy Rogers, Mr. Fredrick Wacker and Martha Mitchell, among many other notables. His close friends include, the late Pulitzer Prize winner and actor Jason Miller and the late Lasker award winner Dr. Robert A. Good.* Host cable TV shows, 1981—, med. editor Cable Health Network, 1983—, Lifetime Network, 1984—; syndicated columnist: Coast Media News, 1980; prodr.: numerous med. TV shows; contbr. articles to profl. jours. Mem. gov. bd. med. coun. Italian-Am. Found.; mem. Italian-Am. Civic Com., L.A., 1983, Cath. League Civil and Rel. Liberty, World Affairs Coun., L.A., Boston Mus. Fine Arts, Met. Mus.; founder Italian-Am. Med. Assn., 1982; co-founder Italian-Am. Legal Alliance, L.A., 1982—; mem. UCLA Chancellor's Assocs. Served to capt. M.C. U.S. Army, 1972—74. Leukemia Soc. Am. fellow, 1974—76. Fellow: ACP, Internat. Coll. Physicians and Surgeons; mem.: AAAS, AMA (Physician's Recognition award 1978—80, 1982—85, 1986—89, 1989—91, 1991—94, 1994—96, 1996—), Am. Soc. Hematology (emeritus), Internat. Platform Assn., Drug Info. Assn., Chinese Med. Assn., Am. Geriat. Soc., Am. Pub. Health Assn., N.Y. Acad. Sci. (life), Internat. Health Soc., Am. Union Physicians and Dentists, Los Angeles County Med. Assn., Calif. Med. Assn., Am. Soc. Clin. Oncology, Mensa, Smithsonian Instn., Nat. Geog. Soc. (life), Fondazione Giovanni Agnelli, Nature Conservancy, Nat. Wildlife Fedn., Sigma Xi, Alpha Omega Alpha, Phi Beta Kappa. Achievements include first to 1st comprehensive clinical description of chronic fatigue syndrome as a neuro-immunologic acquired disorder. Office: PO Box 384 Agoura Hills CA 91376-0384

DECK, DARRELL (CHESTER DECK), minister, historian; b. Ogden, Ind., Feb. 6, 1933; s. George Chester and Hildreth Geneve (McIntyre) Deck; m. Betty June Marsh, Aug. 22, 1954; children: David Marshall, Deborah June, Darlene Michelle. AB, Johnson Bible Coll., 1955; student, Christian Theol. Sem.; certificate, Inst. Pastoral Care, 1962. Ordained minister Ind., 1952. Minister Fountaintown Christian Ch., Fountaintown, Ind., 1952—54, Guyton Christian Ch., Guyton, Ga., 1954—63, Rocky Ford Christian Ch., Rocky Ford, Ga., 1954—71, Tusculum Christian Ch., Tusculum, Ga., 1954—63, First Christian Ch., Sylvania, Ga., 1963—71, Rogersville, Tenn., 1971—73, Raleigh Christian Ch., Rushville, Ind., 1973—76, Countryside Christian, Shirley, Ind., 1996—. Revivalist, 1952—; lectr. in field; trustee Mahoning Valley Christian Svc. Camp; mem. coun. of seventy Johnson Bible Coll.; mem. Nat. Trust Historic Preservation. Contbr. articles to profl. jours., columns in newspapers. Organizer Malcom Grass Meml. Park, Shirley, Ind., 1987, Jane Ross Reeves Octagon House Found., 1987—; dir. Centennial, Shirley, Ind., 1990; restoration coord. Kof P Bldg., Greenfield, Ind., 2000, Jane Ross Reeves Octagon House, Shirley, Ind., 2002—; tour dir. Town of Shirley; bd. mem. Bd. Zoning Appeals, Hancock, Ga., 1985—2001; bd. dir. Hancock County Parks Bd. Recipient Spark Plug award, U.S. Jaycees, 1968, David L. Estell Civic award, 1999, Preservation award, Greenfield Historic Landmarks, 2001. Mem.: Shirley Ministerial Assn., Nat. Trust Historic Preservation, Ind. Archivists Soc., Hancock County Hist. Soc. Avocations: farming, developing, refinishing, restoration, antiques. Home: 105 Main St PO Box 69 Shirley IN 47384

DECK, JUDITH Z. adult nurse practitioner; b. Washington, Dec. 22, 1941; Student, Yale U., 1968-69; BS, SUNY, Buffalo, 1965, MS, 1990. Staff nurse Alaska Psychiat. Inst., Anchorage, 1966; nurse in burn unit Emergency Hosp., Buffalo, 1969-70; nurse Gateway, Williamsville, N.Y., 1971, 82-88; nurse practitioner Buffalo VA Med. Ctr., 1990-91, Millard Fillmore Hosp., Buffalo, 1992-97, Ob/Gyn. Assocs. of Western N.Y., 1993, Buffalo Gen. Hosp., 1993-95, Bros. of Mercy Nursing and Rehab. Ctr., Clarence, N.Y., 1996-2000; staff nurse Night Call, PC, Amherst, NY, 2000—; nurse practitioner U. Buffalo Rsch. Found., 2001—. Recipient S. Mouchly Small award, 1965, Silver Key, SUNY Buffalo, 1962, Panhellenic award, 1959. Mem. N.Y. State Coalition Nurse Practitioners, Am. Acad. Nurse Practitioners, Sigma Theta Tau. Office: WHI SUNY at Buffalo 65 Farber Hall Buffalo NY 14214 E-mail: judithzdeck@aol.com.

DECK, RICHARD ALLEN, political scientist, consultant, writer, human rights activist; b. Concord, N.H., May 6, 1953; s. Herbert Heller Jr. and Eleanor DuVall (Deyo) D.; m. Jo Ann Marie Passariello, Nov. 15, 1986. Student, Ripon Coll., 1972-73, Waseda U., Japan, 1974-75; BA in Polit. Sci. and East Asian Studies summa cum laude with honors, Macalester Coll., 1977; cert. Urban and Regional Planning and Design, Harvard U., 1978; Grad. Cert. in Brit. Fgn. Policy, Oxford (Eng.) U., 1980; MA in Econs. in Pub. Policy & Adminstrn., U. Manchester (Eng.), 1982; M in City Planning, U. Calif., Berkeley, 1982; AM in Polit. Sci., Stanford U., 1985; MALS, Dartmouth Coll., 1994; PhD in Polit. Sci., Stanford U., 1997. Internat./intercultural rels. seminar leader Assn. of Current English Keio U., Japan, 1975; mag writer and interviewer The English Jour., Japan, 1975; rschr. writer Dem. Farmer Labor Party, Minneapolis, 1976; survey rchr. and analyst Project on Volunteerism Adelphi U., L.I., 1978; legis. analyst rschr. Assembly Edn. Com. New York St. Assembly, Albany, 1979; co-chair external affairs Grad. Assembly U. Calif., Berkeley, 1981-82; fellow internat. peace and security studies Social Sci. Rsch. Coun. and John D. and Catherine T. MacArthur Found., Southeast Asia, 1986-88; vis. joint fellow nat. and internat. security U. So. Calif. and UCLA, 1989; rsch. fellow and project coord. Asian Regionalization Asia/Pacific Rsch. Ctr., Stanford U. and The Asia Found. San Francisco, Calif., 1991-92; v.p. Catalyst Concepts, Berkeley, 1992-2000, pres., 2001—; founding dir. Asia/Pacific Reg. Policy Rsch. Inst., Berkeley and Emeryville, 1998—; prodr., dir. Asian Democracy and Human Rights Webcasting Sta. Alliance for Reform and Democracy in Asia, Berkeley and Emeryville, Calif., 2001—. Social sys. dir. and bd. dir. U. Calif. Space Working Group, U. Calif., Berkeley, 1979-80, 81-82; grad. rep. from Berkeley campus for the student body pres. coun. U. Calif. (systemwide), 1981-82; tchg. asst. Stanford (Calif.) U., 1983, 86, mem. grad. studies com., 1983-84, head tchg. asst., 1984, observer Project Peace and Coop. Asia-Pacific Region, 1984, mem. internat. rels. sr. faculty search com., 1985-86, co-instr., 1991; seminar group discussion leader, M.A.L.S. Colloquium on Ctrl. Amer., Darmouth Coll., 1984; lectr. and participant World Affairs Coun. No. Calif., study group on the Assn. of So. East Asian Nat., San Francisco, 1985; participant Project Soviet Internat. Behavior, U. Calif., Berkeley and Stanford U., 1985-86; lectr. Inst. S.E. Asian Studies, 1988, Nat. U. Singapore, 1988, Asean Insts. Conf. on U.S.-Asean Relations, Singapore, 1988; conf. participant and delegate 40th Anniv. Commemoration of the Signing of the United Nat. Charter in San Francisco, 1985; ofcl. observer U.S. del. Pacific Econ. Cooperation Coun., PECC Gen. Meeting/Conf., San Francisco, 1992; global media dir. U.S.-S.E. Asian Alliance for a Dem. Asia, Cambridge, Mass., 1998-2000; cons. Def. & Diplomacy, The Newshour with Jim Lehrer, PBS-TV, Washington and Arlington, Va., 2000; panelist and spkr. Good Governance and Dem. Reform in Asia-Ideals in Action, Press Conf. and Staff Briefing, Congl. Human Rights Caucus, Washington, 2001; mem. Nat. Bus. Adv. Coun., Washington, 2002—; cons. Lawyer's Com. on Human Rights, N.Y.C., 2003, Nat. Dem. Inst. Internat. Affairs, Washington, 2003, Sweden-Singapore Initiative for Democracy, Olaf Palme Inst., Swedish Internat. Liberal Ctr., Jarl Hjalmarsson Found., Stockholm, Singapore Dem. Party, 2003—; spkr., lectr. in field. Author: U.S. official delegation "Dialogue Partners" session, First ASEAN Economic Congress, ASEAN Chambers of Commerce and Industry, and the Institute of Strategic and International Studies, 1987, Fourth ASEAN Institutes Conference on the Association of Southeast Asian Nations and the United States, 1988; (with others) Peace, Conflict, and Strategic Cultures in the Asia-Pacific Region, 1999 (nominee Kiriyama Pacific Rim book prize), (with others) The Singapore Puzzle, 1999 (nominee Kiriyama Pacific Rim book prize), Strategic Cultures in the Asia-Pacific Region, 1999 (paper edit., nominee Kiriyama Pacific Rim book prize); contbr. to profl. articles; mem. edtl. bd., edtl. writer, polit. corr., and polit. feature writer The Stanford Daily, 1982-83; rschr. and writing cons. The Concept of Relationship in International Politics, 1989-90; contbr. papers to various organizations; interview subject (TV) Friday Background, Current Affairs Unit, Singapore Broadcasting Corp., 1987, Berita (Evening news), RTM (Malaysian govt. network), 1987, Official Questionner of Malaysian Prime Minister Mahathir bin Mohamad, Iseas Singapore Lecture, Inst. of Southeast Asian Studies, 1988; (film) co-narrator and co-interviewer The Pennsylvania Underground: The Sanctuary Movement and Illegal Ctrl. Am.

Refugees in Philadelphia, 1986; (newspaper) Internat. Herald Tribune, Republic of Singapore, 1987, (radio) The Michael Fay Caning Affair, The World Tonight with Phil Till Show, Radio Can., Vancouver, 1994; spl. contbr. Asiaweek newsmag., Hong Kong, 1998. Del. candidate N.H. Pres. Preferences Primary, Dem. Nat. Conv., Keene, 1972, Calif. Pres. Primary, Stanford, 1984, Berkeley, 1992; candidate N.H. Constl. Conv., Keene, 1974; city and campus chairperson Calif. Dem. Pres. Primary Campaign, Stanford U. and Palo Alto, Calif., 1984, 92; chmn. N.H. Govs.' Youth Hwy. Safety Adv. Com., 1972; staff intern Minn. Dem. Farmer Labor Party Hdqs., 1976; bd. dirs. U. of Manchester Postgrad. Soc. (UK), 1980-81; conf. participant and del. 40th Anniversary Commemoration of the Signing of the UN Charter in San Francisco: Conf. Assessing the UN After 40 Years, UN Assn. San Francisco and World Affairs Coun. No. Calif., 1985; spl. fellowship coord. Open Soc. Inst., N.Y.C., 1997-98, 2000; interim chairperson panel of experts and resource persons on Asian democratization Alliance for Reform and Democracy in Asia, Washington, 2000-2001; co-chair Assn. Scholars and Rschrs. for Asian Dem. Studies, Alliance for Reform and Democracy in Asia, Bangkok and Washington, 2001—; co-dir. Asia Democracy Index Project, Alliance for Reform and Democracy in Asia, Osaka, Japan, Melbourne, Australia, Berkeley/Emeryville, Calif., 2001—. Recipient World Affairs Coun. Staff award, 1985, Nat. Small-Bus. Legis. Leadership Achievement award Bus. Adv. Coun., Washington, 2002; Nat. Forensics League scholar Ripon Coll., 1972-73; Harry Sherman scholar Macalester Coll., 1976-77; John W. Searle Meml. scholar Macalester Coll., 1976-77, Outstanding Sr. award, Minnesota Jaycees, College Court of Honor, 1977; N.Y. State Assembly Grad. Scholar fellow, 1979; Roothbert Fund fellow U. Calif., Berkeley, 1979-80, 81-82; Inst. Internat. Edn. scholar Oxford U., 1980; Rotary Internat. Grad. fellow U. Manchester, 1980-81; Lasker scholar U. Calif., Berkeley, 1981-82; Newhouse fellow U. Calif., Berkeley, 1981-82; Eisenhower Meml. Grad. scholar Stanford U., 1982-83; AMVETS scholar Stanford U., 1982-86; Stanford U. Grad. fellow 1982-86; MALS Grad. fellow Dartmouth Coll., 1984, 86; UN Assn. and World Affairs Coun. scholar, 1985; Fgn. Lang. and Area Studies grantee U.S. Dept. Edn., 1985; SSRC/MacArthur found. fellow in Internat. Peace and Security, N.Y.C., N.Y., and Chicago, 1986-88; USC-UCLA Vis. Joint fellowship in Nat. and Internat. Security, L.A., 1989; rsch. fellow Asia/Pacific Rsch. Ctr. Stanford U. and the Asia Found., San Francisco, 1991-92; co-nominee (with Dr. Chee Soon Juan, Singapore) Nobel Peace Prize, 1999-2003. Mem. Internat. Studies Assn. (presenter 1998), Assn. Asian Studies, Acad. Polit. Sci., Am. Polit. Sci. Assn., Pi Kappa Delta, Phi Alpha Theta, Pi Sigma Alpha, Phi Beta Kappa. United Ch. of Christ. Avocations: reading novels and screenplays, viewing films. Office: Catalyst Concepts PO Box 8393 Berkeley CA 94707-8393

DECKEL, A. WALLACE, psychiatry educator; b. Boston, Apr. 21, 1952; s. Albert Wallace and Doris E. Deckel; m. Martha P. Deckel, Sept. 8, 1990; children: Matthew, Alan, Raymond. BS, Boston Coll., 1974; MS, Boston U., 1977; PhD, Uniform Svc. U. Health Scis., 1985. Bd. cert. neuropsychologist Am. Bd. Profl. Neuropsychology. Clin. neuropsychologist Kessler Inst. for Rehab., East Orange, N.J., 1985-86; instr. Johns Hopkins U. Sch. Medicine, Balt., 1983-85; assoc. prof. psychiatry N.J. Med. Sch., U. Medicine and Dentistry N.J., Newark, 1986-91; assoc. prof. psychiatry and neurosci. U. Conn. Med. Sch., Farmington, 1992—. Cons. Danbury Ch. of Christ, other religious orgns. Contbr. sci. articles to profl. jours. Bd. dirs. Conn. Huntington's Disease Assn., 1997-98. Grantee State of Conn., 1997—, Hartford Found. for Giving, 1998, Hartford Hosp., 1998—, Patterson Trust Fund, 2001—. Mem. Am. Coll. Profl. Neuropsychology, Conn. Neuropsychol. Soc., Soc. for Neurosci. Avocations: exercise, cetacean research.

DECKELBAUM, NELSON, lawyer; b. Washington, Apr. 1, 1928; s. Fred and Rose (Egber) D.; m. Louann Jacobs, Oct. 19, 1952; children: David Alan, Todd Stuart. BS, Georgetown U., 1950, JD, 1952. Bar: D.C. 1952, Md. 1957, U.S. Supreme Ct. 1966. Practice law, Washington, 1952—; sr. ptnr. Deckelbaum Ogens & Raftery, Chartered, 1974—. Staff mem. Commn. on Govt. Security, 1956; dir. Independence Savs. Bank. Chmn. Democratic precinct, Montgomery County, Md., 1958. Served with USAF, 1952-54. Named in Best Lawyers in Am. Fellow Am. Coll. of Bankruptcy; mem. Am., Md., D.C. bar assns., Am. Judicature Soc., Georgetown Univ. Alumni Assn., Woodmont Country Club, Univ. Club (pres. 1994-95), D.C. Real Estate Commn. Home: 4200 Massachusetts Ave NW Apt 115 Washington DC 20016 Office: Deckelbaum Ogens & Raftery 3 Bethesda Metro Ctr Bethesda MD 20814-5330 E-mail: ndeckelbaum@deckelbaum.com.

DECKER, CHARLES RICHARD, investment executive; b. Murphysboro, Ill., Mar. 13, 1937; s. Ernest George and Joyce Ellen (Gibson) D.; m. Jeanine Ann Cowell, June 6, 1959; children: Ann Marie Britt, Lynn Rochelle Lake, Charles Ernest BBA, U. Miss., 1959; MBA, Ind. U., 1962, EdD, 1968; cert., Harvard U., 1981. Cert. fin. planner, 1990. Asst. prof. Ill. State U., Normal, 1968-70, chmn. dept. bus. adminstrn., 1970-74; dean sch. bus. Millikin U., Decatur, Ill., 1974-80, provost, v.p., 1980-86, Grover M. Hermann prof. bus. policy, 1986-98; ptnr. Black Watch Investment Mgmt., 2002—. Investment mgr., bd. dirs. John Warner Fin. Svcs. Inc., 1996-2002. Contbr. articles to profl. jours. Bd. dirs. Decatur Civic Ctr., 1984-92, vice chmn., 1986-87, chmn., 1987-92; bd. dirs. United Way of Decatur and Macon County, 1984-87, Boys Club, Decatur, 1980-82; mem. exec. bd. Lincoln Trails Coun. Boy Scouts Am., 1988-93, SME chair, 1989-91, v.p., 1990-93. Mem. North Cent. Assn. Acad. Deans (pres. 1984-85), C. of C. (bd. dirs. 1976-79, v.p. 1979), Alpha Lambda Delta, Phi Delta Kappa, Phi Kappa Phi, Omicron Delta Kappa, Sigma Chi. Avocations: photography, tennis, biking, golf. Home: 1740 Illini Dr Decatur IL 62521-9169

DECKER, CRAIG J. German educator, translator, researcher; b. Newark, July 26, 1956; s. Russell W. and Clara A. Decker; m. Susanne Adams Fetherolf; children: Andrew R. Decker-Fetherolf, Grace D. Decker-Fetherolf. BA, Bates Coll., 1974—78; MA, U. Calif., Irvine, 1980, PhD, 1986. Tchg. asst. and assoc. U. Calif., Irvine, 1978—83; instr. German Oreg. State U., Corvallis, 1983—84, Bates Coll., Lewiston, Maine, 1984—86, asst. prof. German, 1986—92, assoc. prof. German, 1992—99, prof. German, 1999—. Editl. bd. Modern Austrian Lit., 2000—; del. assembly mem. (regional rep. New Eng. and Ea. Can.) MLA, New York, 2003—. Editor: (literary anthology) Austrian Identities: Portraits in Twentieth-Century Prose; translator: (novels) Stone's Paranoia (by Peter Henisch); editor: (ency.) Encyclopedia of Modern Drama, author numerous scholarly articles. Recipient Article Prize, German Academic Exch. Svc./German Studies Assn., 1991; fellow Summer Seminar Fellowship, Nat. Endowment Humanities, 1985; grantee, German Academic Exch. Svc., 1979. Faculty Rsch. Grants, Bates Coll., 1990, 1993, 1997, 1999, Faculty Travel Grant, 2002. Mem.: MLA, Modern Austrian Lit. and Culture Assn., German Studies Assn., Am. Assn. Tchrs. of German, Phi Beta Kappa. Office: Bates Coll 3 Andrews Rd Lewiston ME 04240 Office Fax: 207-786-8331. E-mail: cdecker@bates.edu.

DECKER, CYNTHIA J. SCHAFER, community and occupational health nurse; b. Easton, N.Y., July 4, 1950; d. Frederick Phillip III and Mary Louise (Whelden) Schafer; m. Charles Robert Decker, Jr., Feb. 23, 1974. Diploma, Samaritan Hosp. Sch. Nursing, Troy, N.Y., 1972; BS in Health Care Mgmt., Empire State Coll., 1995. RN, N.Y.; cert. QMRP. Head nurse, medication nurse Samaritan Hosp., 1972-73; nurse operating and recovery rooms, med.-surg. floor Community Hosp. Schoharie County, Cobleskill, N.Y., 1973-78; coord., field nurse Upjohn HealthCare Svcs., Albany, N.Y., 1978-84; program nurse sheltered workshop Schoharie County Assn. Retarded Children, Schoharie, N.Y., 1984-93, health svcs. adminstr., 1993-99; nurse, gen. practice physician's office, Central Bridge, N.Y., 1999—. Article 81 ct. evaluator, 1995. Sec. Schoharie County Sheriff's Tactical Search and Rescue Force, 1995. Mem. N.Y. State Mental Retardation-Devel. Disabled Nurses Assn. (rec. sec. 1987-88, 90-92, seminar com., past mem. newsletter com.), Samaritan Hosp. Sch. Nursing Alumni Assn.

DECKER, GILBERT FELTON, consultant; b. Marietta, Ga., June 23, 1937; s. Felton Ambrose and Mary Irene (Pettyjohn) D.; children: Carlyle F., Donna L., Michael T. BSEE, Johns Hopkins U., 1958; MS, Stanford U., 1966. Systems engr. Sylvania Electronics Products, Mountain View, Calif., 1964-66; program mgr. ESL, Inc., Sunnyvale, Calif., 1966-69, v.p. engring., 1969-75, v.p. ops., 1975-77, pres., 1978-82; v.p. new ventures TRW Inc., 1982-85; pres. Penn Central Fed. Systems Co., 1985-90; pres., chief exec. officer Acurex Corp., Mountain View, Calif., 1990-93; asst. sec. rsch. devel. and acquisition Dept. Army, Washington, 1994-97; exec. v.p. Walt Disney Imagineering, Glendale, Calif., 1998—2001; pvt. cons., 2002—. Chmn. fund-raising com. Jobs for Progress, Inc., fund-raising div. United Way, Army Sci. Bd., 1987-89; mem. engring. adv. bd. Johns Hopkins U. Served with U.S. Army, 1958-64. Mem. Am. Electronics Assn. (mem. exec. com.), Santa Clara County Mfrs. Group (dir.), Res. Officers Assn., Assn. U.S. Army, Air Force Assn., Assn. Old Crows, Army Sci. Bd. (chmn.), Am. Def. Preparedness Assn., Tau Beta Pi, Eta Kappa Nu, Pi Tau Sigma.

DECKER, JAMES LUDLOW, management consultant; b. Batavia, N.Y., Nov. 5, 1923; s. James Ludlow and Ruth Adeline (Peard) D.; m. Bette Wilson Botzler, Jan. 31, 1997. B of Aero. Engring., Rensselaer Poly. Inst., 1944; postgrad. Textron Advanced Mgmt. Program, Harvard U., 1974. Registered profl. engr., Md. With The Martin Co., Balt., 1944-67; dep. mgr. Lunar Module, Apollo Office, NASA, Houston, 1963; program mgr. surface effect ship program U.S. Navy, Washington, 1967-72; v.p., gen. mgr. Bell Aerospace Can., Grand Bend, Ont., 1972-74; prin. J.L. Decker, Baldwin, Md., 1974—. Guest lectr. AIAA, 1972-79, Can. Aeros. and Space Inst., 1973-79, George Washington U., 1974, Royal Aero. Soc., 1972, Aero. Engring. Rensselaer Poly. Inst., 1990—; cons. USN, Maritime Adminstrn., USCG, NRC Can., Can. Coast Guard, various corps., 1972—. Contbr. articles to profl. jours.; patentee in field. Pres., Greenbrier Cmty. Assn., 1956-57; regional chmn. Rensselaer Fund, 1982; mem. Congl. Subcom. to Rev. NASA Adv. Com. Utilization, 1987; mem. pres.'s adv. coun. Meredith Coll., 1999. Buffalo Alumni scholar, 1941-44, N.Y. State Regents scholar, 1941-44, Rensselaer Alumni fellow, 1991. Fellow AIAA (assoc.), mem. Soc. Naval Archs. and Marine Engrs., Am. Soc. Naval Engrs., Rensselaer Soc. Engrs., N.Y. Acad. Sci., Patroons of Rensselaer, Cosmos Club (Washington), Towson Golf and Country Club, Sigma Xi, Tau Beta Pi. Republican. Baptist. Address: 1 Shawnery Ct Baldwin MD 21013-9657

DECKER, JOHN FRANCIS, lawyer, educator; b. Sherrill, Iowa, May 15, 1944; s. Lawrence and Loretta (Hefel) D. BA, U. Iowa, 1967; JD, Creighton U., 1970; LLM, NYU, 1971, JSD, 1979. Bar: Calif. 1973, U.S. Dist. Ct. (no. dist.) Calif. 1973, Ill. 1978, U.S. Dist. Ct. (no. dist.) Ill. 1980, U.S. Ct. Appeals (7th cir.) 1981. Asst. prof. law DePaul U. Coll. Law, Chgo., 1971-73, assoc. prof., 1974-79, prof. law, 1979—, coord. extern program, 1978—. Counsel R.E. Robbins Law Firm, Stockton, Ill., 1978-79; vis. prof. U. San Francisco Sch. Law, 1980; reporter Ill. Jud. Conf., Chgo., 1981—. Author: Prostitution: Regulation and Control, 1979, Revolution to the Right, 1982, The Investigation and Prosecution of Arson, 1999, Illinois Criminal Law: A Survey of Crimes and Defenses, 3d edit., 2000; contbr. articles to profl. jours.; staff editor Creighton Law Rev., 1969-70. Recipient award of Distinction, DePaul Law Rev., 1978, Excellence in Teaching, DePaul U., 1999. Mem. ABA, Assn. Trial Lawyers Am. Democrat. Roman Catholic. Home: 306 Maple Ave Elmhurst IL 60126-2333 Office: DePaul Univ Coll of Law 25 E Jackson Blvd Chicago IL 60604-2289 E-mail: jdecker1@depaul.edu.

DECKER, JOHN WILLIAM, steel company executive; b. Cleve., July 15, 1948; s. James William and Betty Erdmann (Smith) D.; m. Elaine Marie Metz, Aug. 30, 1971; children: Amanda Elaine, Gregory John. BS, Lincoln Meml. U., 1966-70; MEd, Kent (Ohio) State U., 1970-72. Cert. tchr., adminstr., Ohio. Elem. tchr. Parma (Ohio) City Schs., 1970-78; corp. sec., treas. Decker Steel & Supply, Inc. (formerly Decker Reichert Steel & Supply, Inc.), Cleve., 1978-83, v.p., 1983-85, pres., chmn., chief exec. officer, 1985—. Mem. Am. Theater Orgn. Soc.; Playhouse Square Vol. Group; co-chmn. cmty. fin. com. Parma City Schs., 1994—97; apptd. Parma Bd. Edn., 1997, elected, 1998—2001, v.p., 1999—, pres., 2000—01; ruling elder Parma South Presbyn. Ch., Parma Heights, Ohio, 1979—81, 1983—92, 1996—, clk. of session, 1983—94, chmn. fin. com., 1995—96, chmn. properties coun., 1997—2000, adminstrv. coun. chairperson, 2001. Mem. Greater Cleve. Growth Assn. Lodges: Masons. Republican. Avocations: choral group singing, pipe organ playing, repair and building, collecting antique telephones, collecting victorian lighting. Home: 9634 Greenbriar Dr Cleveland OH 44130-4756 Office: 4500 Train Ave Cleveland OH 44102-4515

DECKER, JOSEPHINE I. health clinic official; b. Barling, Ark., May 24, 1933; d. Ralph and Ada A. (Claborn) Snider; m. William Arlen Decker, Feb. 4, 1952; 1 child, Peter A. BS in Health Mgmt., Kennedy Western U., 1986, MS in Bus. Adminstrn., 1987. With Southwestern Bell Tel. Co., Ft. Smith, Ark., 1951-52, Sparks Med. Found. (formerly Holt Krock Clinic), Ft. Smith, 1952—, bus. adminstr., 1970—; reg. dir. Sparks Med. Found., Ft. Smith, 1999—. Bd. dirs. Sparks Credit Union, Bost Found., Crisis Ctr. for Women, Sparks Women's Ctr., Leadership Ft. Smith; mem. adv. coun. Northside H.S., Southside H.S., Ft. Smith, Ft. Smith Girls Shelter, Ft. Smith Credit Bur. Mem. Credit Women Internat., Soc. Cert. Consumer Credit Execs. Office: Sparks Med Plaza 1500 Dodson Ave Fort Smith AR 72901-5128 E-mail: jdecker@sparks.org., decker02@quixnet.net.

DECKER, KATE DELANO-CONDAX See DELANO-CONDAX, KATE

DECKER, LARRY E, education educator; b. Cottage Grove, Oreg., Dec. 13, 1940; s. Edward LeRoy and Lila I. (Strong) D.; m. Virginia Ann Pyle, June 1, 1962; children: Weston E., Wendy A. BS, U. of Oregon, 1965, MS, 1967; PhD, Mich. State U., 1971. Cmty. outreach Lane County Youth Project, Eugene, Oreg., 1964—65; instr. U. of Oreg., Eugene, Oreg., 1967—70; mott intern Nat. Ctr. for Cmty. Edn., Flint, Mich., 1970—71; dir. cmty. edn. St. Louis Pk. Pub. Sch., St. Louis Pk., Minn., 1971—73; prof., assoc. dean U. of Va., Charlottesville, 1993—95; eminent scholar chair Fla. Atlanta U., 1995—. Cons., com. mem. Charles S. Mott Found., Flint, Mich. Author: Community, Education and Social Impact Perspective, 1983, Home-School-Community, 1988, Building Learning Communities, 1990, Community Education Across America, 1990, Educational Restructuring and the Community Education Process, 1992, Grantseeking: How to Find a Funder and Write a Winning Proposal, 1993. Bd. dirs. Nat. Cmty. Edn. Assn., Fairfax, Va., 1966—, Internat. Cmty. Edn. Assn., Fairfax, Va., 1974—; cons. US Dept. of Edn., Washington DC, 1977—. Charles S. Mott Found. grantee, 1993; recipient Nat. Contbr. award Nat. Community Edn., Washington, 1986. Mem. Nat. Community Edn. Assn. (bd. dirs., chair). Avocations: travel, fishing, bird watching. Office: Coll of Edn, Fla Atlantic University 777 Glades Rd Boca Raton FL 33431 Office Fax: 561-297-3618. E-mail: ldecker@fau.edu.

DECKER, MALCOLM DOYLE, insurance agent; b. Springfield, Mo., Sept. 10, 1946; s. Doyle Vancle and M. Evelyn (Barton) D.; m. Janis Kay Mount, June 1, 1968; children: Matthew William, Carrie Elizabeth. BS in Edn., S.W. Mo. State U., 1969. CLU, ChFC. Tchr., coach Camdenton (Mo.) Sch. Sys., 1971-75; agt. State Farm Ins. Cos., Lebanon, Mo., 1975-78, 99—, agy. mgr., 1978-95, agy. field cons., 1995-98, agy. adminstrv. asst. Columbia, Mo., 1999—, agt. Camdenton, Mo., 1999—. Pres. Laclede County Sheltered Workshop, Lebanon, 1978-81; mem. Lebanon Park Bd., 1982-83, pres., 1983; mem. Lebanon R-3 Sch. Bd., 1983-89; mem. Lebanon Babe Ruth Baseball World Series, 1985-95, exec. dir., 1991-94. 1st lt. U.S. Army, 1969-71, Vietnam. Mem. South West Mo. State Univ. Alumni (alumni bd., pres. 1996), Optimist Club (pres. 1975, 2002), Masons (honor master 1983), Scottish Rite, Shriners. Southern Baptist. Avocations: flying, golf. Office: PO Box 650 Camdenton MO 65020-0650

DECKER, MARY DURYEA, retired educator, community volunteer; b. Portland, Oreg., Mar. 17, 1928; d. Oliver Martin Nisbet, MD and Lois Marguerite (Mangus) Nisbet; m. Richard Adrian Duryea, Aug. 23, 1950 (dec. Apr.1958); 1 child, Maria Duryea; m. Edward Albert Decker, Jan. 28, 1967. BS in Speech and Sociology, Northwestern U., 1950; MA in Speech and Edn., Stanford U., 1961. Cert. adminstr., counselor, instr., Calif. cmty. colls. Social worker, supr. City of Austin, Tex., 1950-54; med. social worker Monterey (Calif.) County Hosp., 1955-57; instr. speech, counseling San Jose (Calif.) City Coll., 1961-62; residence hall dir. Stanford (Calif.) U., 1962-65; dean students Scripps Coll., Claremont, Calif., 1965-69; asst. vice chancellor U. Calif., San Diego, 1969-75; chief student svcs. officer 3 campuses San Diego C.C. Dist., 1976-88; project mgr. Combined Case Mgmt., Lincoln County, Oreg., 1991-93. Mem., chair chief student svc. offices Region X, Calif. C.C. Chancellor's Office, 1976-88; mem. Gov.'s Coun. on Nutrition and Volunteerism, 1978-80. Mem., pres. Vol. Bur. San Diego, 1970-72; mem., v.p. United Way, San Diego, 1971-78; bd. dir., v.p. Girl Scouts San Diego, 1976-88; trustee North Lincoln Health Dist., Lincoln City, Oreg., 1990—, chair bd., 1995-97; vice chair Gov.'s Coun. Alcohol and Drug Programs, Salem, Oreg., 1994-99; bd. dir. Oreg. Pacific Area Health Ed. Ctr., Newport, 1992-99; mem. statewide adv. com. Area Health Edn. Ctr. Program, 1999—; apptd. by gov. to bd. trustees Oreg. Health and Sci. U., 2001—. Recipient grant Ford Found., 1985-88. Mem. Univ. Club Portland. Republican. Presbyterian. Home: PO Box 721 Lincoln City OR 97367-0721

DECKER, MICHAEL H. government agency administrator; BBA in Bus. Adminstrn., U. Notre Dame; MA in Govt./Nat. Security Studies, Georgetown U.; MS in Strategic Intelligence, Def. Intelligence Coll. Commd. 2d lt. USMC, advanced through grades, NBC def. officer, asst. BLT ops. officer, commanding officer Co. G BLT 2/6, security force/marine security guard officer Security br., asst. ops. officer/liaison officer 26th Marine amphibious unit, asst. intelligence officer 13th Marine Expeditionary Unit, sr. intelligence analyst 7th MEB and I MEF, asst. dir. intelligence; sr. systems engr. Delfin Systems; dep. program mgr. for long-range info. networked comm. svcs. Sci. Applications Internat. Corp. Decorated Bronze Star medal, Navy Commendation medal, Marine Corp Commendation medal. Office: CMC (PAC) HQ USMC Pentagon Rm 5E 671 2 Navy Annex Washington DC 20380-1775

DECKER, MICHAEL LYNN, lawyer, judge; b. Oklahoma City, May 5, 1953; s. Leroy Melvin and Yvonne (Baird) D. BA, Oklahoma City U., 1975, JD, 1978; grad., Nat. Jud. Coll., U. Nev., Reno, 1990. Bar: Okla. 1978, U.S. Ct. Appeals (10th cir.) 1979, U.S. Dist. Ct. (we. dist.) Okla. 1985, U.S. Supreme Ct. 1994. Assoc. Bay, Hamilton, Lees, Spears, and Verity, Oklahoma City, 1978-80; assoc. dir. devel. Oklahoma City U., 1980-81, asst. dean, Sch. of Law, 1981-82; sr. oil and gas adminstrv. law judge Okla. Corp. Commn., Oklahoma City, 1982-92, sr. asst. gen. counsel oil and gas conservation, 1992-95, deputy gen. counsel oil and gas conservation, 1995—. Campaign staff intern U.S. Senator Henry Bellmon's Re-election Campaign, 1974; mem. Civil Arbitration Panel, U.S. Dist. Ct. (we. dist.) Okla., 1985—; seminar spkr. Am. Inst. Profl. Geologists (Okla. sect.), 1985, Conf. on Consumer Fin. Law, Oil and Gas Law Inst., 1999-2001; mem. dean's adv. com. Oklahoma City U. Law Sch., 1986; mem. sys. rev. bd. Okla. Corp. Commn., 1990-93, mem. process mgmt. rev. team, 1995-96; lectr. adminstrv. law Vanderbilt U. Sch. Law, 1993, lectr. oil and gas regulatory practice Okla. U Coll. Law, 2003; mem. legal and regulatory affairs com. Interstate Oil and Gas Compact Commn., 2000—, mem. coun. state oil and gas attys., 2001-, chair, 2003, mem. revision subcom. Model Oil and Gas Conservation Act, Interstate Oil and Gas Compact Commn., 2003. Trustee Oklahoma City U., 1989—91, mem. alumni bd. dirs., 1986—2000; mem. com. of twenty Oklahoma City Art Mus., 1987—95, co-chair omelette party, 1990; vol. Contact Teleminister, Oklahoma City, 1986—91; Okla. Corp. Commn., 1990; mem. Class XI Leadership Oklahoma City, 1993; area rep. Okla. Mozart Festival, Bartlesville, 1988—; pres. alumni assn. Oklahoma City U., 1988—92; mem. adminstrv. bd. St. Luke's United Meth. Ch., 1988—92, chair missions com., 1993—94; mem. nat. alumni bd. dirs. Oklahoma City U., 2000—, also mem. devel. com., long range planning com., adminstrv. liaison com., and student rels. com.; bd. dirs. Eldercare Access Ctr., Inc., 2001—03, Contact Teleminister, Oklahoma City, 1987—90, March of Dimes Western Okla., 1990—93. Mem.: Oklahoma City Mineral Lawyers Soc., Okla. County Bar Assn. (exec. com. young lawyers sect. 1978—82, mem. law day com. 1979—88, chmn. law day luncheon spkr. com. 1979—88), Okla. Bar Assn. (mineral law sect., environ. law sect.), Raymer Soc. for the Arts (bd. dirs., Lindsborg, Kans. 1999—, sec. 2002—), Lions, Lambda Chi Alpha (Outstanding Alumnus award 1983, treas. bldg. corp. 1984—89, pres. 1989—91), Phi Alpha Delta. Republican. Home: 2008 NW 44th St Oklahoma City OK 73118-1902 Office: Okla Corp Commn State Capitol Complex Jim Thorpe Bldg PO Box 52000 Oklahoma City OK 73152-2000 E-mail: bloomin2@cox.net.

DECKER, PETER RANDOLPH, rancher, former state official; b. N.Y.C., Oct. 1, 1934; s. Frank Randolph and Marjorie (Marony) D.; m. Dorothy Morss, Sept. 24, 1972; children: Karen, Christopher, Hilary. BA, Middlebury Coll., Vt., 1957; MA, Syracuse U., 1961; PhD, Columbia U., 1974. Tchr. Cate Sch., Carpinteria, Calif., 1961-63; sr. writer Congl. Quar., Washington, 1963-64; asst. to pres. Middlebury (Vt.) Coll., 1964-67; staff asst. Sen. Robert Kennedy, Washington, 1967-68; corr. AP, Laos, Vietnam, 1970; instr./lectr. Columbia U., N.Y.C., 1972-74; asst. prof. Duke U., Durham, N.C., 1974-80; owner, operator Double D Ranches, Ridgway, Colo., 1980—; commr. agr. State of Colo., Denver, 1987-89; pres. Decker & Assocs., Denver, Colo., 1989—. Dir. Nat. Western Stock Show, Denver, 1990—; bd. dirs. Fed. Res. Bd. Kansas City, Denver, 1992-98; bd. dirs. Western Colo. Bank, Montrose; pres. Telluride Bancorp, Inc., 1990-97; mem. adv. bd. Crow Canyon Archeol. Ctr., Fulcrum Press. Author: Fortunes and Failures, 1978, Old Fences, New Neighbors, 1998; contbr. articles to profl. jours. and mags. Trustee Middlebury Coll., 1988-96, Colo. Commn. on Higher Edn., 1985-93; chmn. Ouray County Dem. Party, 1982-85; chmn. Ouray County Planning Commn., 1981-85; chmn. Colo. Endowment Humanities, 1982-85; chmn., bd. trustees Ft. Lewis Coll., 2002—. Lt. U.S. Army, 1957-60, capt. Res., 1960-67. English Speaking Union scholar, 1952-53; Nat. Endowment for Humanities fellow Yale U., 1977-78, Rockefeller Found. fellow, 1979-80. Mem. Nat. Cattlemen's Assn., Colo. Livestock Assn., Denver Athletic Club, Elks, Colo. Author's League, Angler's Club (Key Largo, Fla.), Columbia U. Club (N.Y.C.). Democrat. Home: 395 Race St Denver CO 80206-4118

DECKER, PETER WILLIAM, academic administrator; b. Grand Rapids, Mich., Mar. 20, 1919; s. Charles B. and Ruth E. (Thorndill) D.; m. Margaret I. Stainthorpe, June 10, 1944; children: Peter, Marilyn, Christine, Charles. BS, Wheaton Coll., 1941; postgrad., Northwestern U., 1942-43, U. Mich., 1958-60; DSc, London Inst. Applied Rsch., 1973; LLD, 1975; DSTh, Midwestern Baptist Bible Sem., 1995. Withadvtg. dept. Hotels Windermere, Chgo., 1942; with Princess Pat Cosmetics, Chgo., 1943; market rsch. investigator A.C. Nielson Co., Chgo., 1944-48; pres. Peter Decker Constrn. Co., Detroit, 1948-60; sales mgr. Century Chem. Products Co., Detroit, 1961-62, vice pres., 1962-63, pres., 1963-75; sr. ptnr. G & D Advtg. Assocs., 1967-78; vice pres., treas., exec. dir. Christian Edn. Advancement, Inc., 1975-95; registrar, instr. N.T. Greek Missions and Theology Birmingham Bible Inst., MI, 1973-86; prof. Midwestern Baptist Coll., 1984—, dir. student fin. aid, 1984—. Trustee Midwestern Baptist Coll., 1985—, mem. exec. com., 1984—, asst. to pres. 1985-90, treas. 1991-95; bd. dirs., prof., trusteeMidwestern Bapt. Bible Sem., 1995—, vice pres. Midewestern Bapt. Bible Seminary Grad. Sch., 1998—. Author: Gettin to Know New Testament Greek, Christology, The Pauline Epistles. Scoutmaster, Boy Scouts of Am., 1956-61, neighborhood commr., 1961-66, merit badge counselor, emeritus, 1979—; mem. Bd. Rev. Beverly Hills, Mich., 1957-63; chmn. Bd. Rev. Southfield Twp., Mich., 1964-67; past pres., Beverly Hills Civic Assn., 1956, bd. dirs., 1953-57, pres., 1958-59; trustee, deacon, Birmingham Mich. Bible Inst., instr. Bible Inst.; bd. dirs. Mich. Epilepsy Ctr. and Assn., 1957-71, exec. com., 1962-67. Recipient Arrowhead Honor awd. Boy Scouts Am., 1965. Mem. AAAS, ASTM, Mich. Edn. Assocs., Inc (exec. com. 1994—, treas. 1994-95), Detroit Soc. Model Engrs. (pres. 1958, 62, bd. dirs. 1955-71), Chem. Splty. Mfg. Assn., Nat. Geog. Soc., Internat. Platform Assn., The Heritage Found., Smithsonian Instn. Assocs., Archaeol. Inst. Am., Bibl. Archaeol. Soc., Bible-Sci. Assn., Creation Rsch. Soc., Mich. Student Fin. Aid Assn., Midwest Assn. Student Fin. Aid Adminstrs. Republican. Avocations: biographies, writings of great christians. Home: 32210 Rosevear St Beverly Hills MI 48025-3921 Office: Midwestern Baptist Coll 825 Golf Dr Pontiac MI 48341-2379

DECKER, RAYMOND FRANK, technology transfer executive, metal products executive, scientist; b. Afton, N.Y., July 20, 1930; s. Bernett Hurd and Mildred (Bisbee) Decker; life ptnr. Mary Birdsall, Dec. 27, 1951; children: Susan, Elizabeth, Catherine, Laura. BS, U. Mich., 1952, MS, 1955, PhD, 1958. With Inco Ltd., 1958-82, v.p. corp. tech. and diversification ventures, 1978-82; v.p. rsch. and corp. rels. Mich. Technol. U., Houghton, 1982-86; pres., CEO Univ. Sci. Ptnrs., Inc., 1986-98; pres. ASM Internat., 1986-87; founding chmn. Thixomat, Inc., 1988—, also bd. dirs.; founding chmn. Wavemat, Inc., 1987-88. Bd. dirs. Spl. Metals Corp.; adj. prof. Poly. Inst. Bklyn., 1962—66, NYU, 1968, U. Mich., 1997—; cons. KMS Fusion, Inc., Howmet turbine Components, Alcoa, GE, GM, 1985—; Van Horn Disting. lectr. Case-Western Res. U., 1975; mem. materials adv. bd. NASA, 1969, Nat. Bur. Stds., 1973, NSF, 1985—86; mem. Nat. Materials Adv. Bd., 1982—88; mem. exec. com. Strategic Hwy. Rsch. Program, 1986—93; long-range planning com. Metall. Soc., 1985—87, State Rsch. Fund Panel Mich., 1983—86; chmn. rsch. & tech. coordinating com. Fed. Hwy. Adminstrn., 1995—98; trustee Foundry Ednl. Found., 1975—77, Welding Rsch. Coun., 1975—80; chmn. bd. trustees Mich. Energy

and Resource Rsch. Assn., 1985—86; keynote spkr. on superalloys Seven Springs Conf., 1980, NAE, 1980—. Author: (book) Strengthening Mechanisms in Nickel-Base Superalloys; editor: Maraging Steels. Chmn. alumni com. dept. material sci. and engrng. U. Mich., Ann Arbor, chmn. class of 1952 reunion; chmn. Ch. Coun., 2001—. Recipient IR-100 award, 1964, Sesquicentennial award, U. Mich., 1967, Disting. Grad. award, 1994, Innovation award, Mobile Computing, 1999, Inc 500 award, 1999. Fellow: Am. Soc. Metals Internat. (chmn. materials sys. and design divsn. 1971—73, trustee 1976—79, chmn. organizing com. World Materials Congress 1988, Campbell Meml. lectr. 1985, chmn. diamond decade com. 1980—81, hon. mem. 1991, Alpha Simga Mu lectr. 2001, Gold medal 1981); mem.: NAE, AAAS, AIME (lectr. Inst. Metals divsn. 1973, R. F. Mehl medal 1973). Congregationalist. Achievements include co-inventing maraging steels, Thixomolding machine. Home: 3065 Provincial Dr Ann Arbor MI 48104-4117 E-mail: rdecker@thixomat.com.

DECKER, RICHARD KNORE, lawyer; b. Lincoln, Nebr., Sept. 15, 1913; s. Fred William and Georgia (Kilmer) D.; m. Fern Iona Steinbaugh, June 12, 1938. AB, U. Nebr., 1935, JD, 1938. Bar: Nebr. 1938, U.S. Supreme Ct. 1941, D.C. 1948, Ill. 1952. Trial atty. antitrust div. Dept. Justice, 1938-52; ptnr. Lord, Bissell & Brook, Chgo., 1953-84, of counsel, 1984—. Trustee Village of Clarendon Hills (Ill.), 1960-64; chmn. bd. elders Community Presbyn. Ch., Clarendon Hills, 1963-66; mem. Union Ch. of Hinsdale; chmn. bd. Community House, Hinsdale, Ill., 1976, Robert Crown Ctr. for Health Edn., Hinsdale, Ill., 1981-83, also bd. dirs, 1976—. With USNR, 1942-45, lt. comdr. ret. Mem. ABA (chmn. antitrust sect. 1971-72), Ill. Bar Assn. (gov. 1969-73, chmn. antitrust sect. 1964-66), Chgo. Bar Assn. (chmn. antitrust law com. 1956-59), The Lawyers Club Chgo., Hinsdale Golf Club (pres. 1968). Republican. Home: 196 Pheasant Hollow Dr Burr Ridge IL 60527 Office: 115 S La Salle St Ste 2900 Chicago IL 60603-3801

DECKER, ROBERT OWEN, history educator, clergyman; b. Lafayette, Ind., Nov. 6, 1927; s. Samuel Owen and Helen Dale (Noble) D.; m. Margaret Ann Harris, May 30, 1948; 1 child, Terry Lynn Decker DeIulis. AB, Butler U., 1953; AM, Ind. U., 1958; PhD, U. Conn., 1970. Ordained to ministry Congregational Ch., 1990. Instr. City of LaPorte (Ind.) Schs., 1956—59, Ctrl. Conn. State U., New Britain, 1959-63, asst. prof., 1963-73, assoc. prof., 1973-77, prof. history, 1977-89, prof. emeritus, 1989—. Editor manuscripts Wesleyan U. Press, 1977-89; advisor NEH, 1977-89, Connecticut River Found. Author: Whaling Industry of New London, 1973, The Whaling City: A History of New London, 1976, A Student Guidebook to American History, 1983, Hartford Immigrants, 1987, The New London Merchants, 1986, Cromwell, Connecticut 1650-1990: The History of A River Port Town, 1991; contbr. articles and book revs. to profl. jours. Mem. Christian Activities Coun., Hartford, 1965—, pres., 1972-74, 76-78, historian, 1983—, life mem., 1996—; bd. dirs. Hartford Inner City Exch., 1971-81, chmn. bd., 1977-80; chmn. state legis. adv. com. Conn. Devel. Disabilities Coun., 1973-75; evaluator programs Conn. Humanities Coun.; historian Rocky Hill (Conn.) Congl. Ch., 1985-89, Conn. 350th Com., 1985-89; justice of peace, Rocky Hill, 1985-89, 2000—, constable, 1986-89, 2002—, apptd. town historian, 1988—; mem. Assn. Conn. Mcpl. Historians, 1988—, membership sec., 1994—, pres., 1996-97; pastor Eagle Rock Congl. Ch., 1989-93, Bozrah Centre Congl. Ch., 1994-95, supply pastor, 1995-2001; mem. exec. bd. Conn. Congl. Christian Chs., 1995-2001; pastor Barkhamstead Ctr. Congl. Ch., 2001—; mem. UCC Hist. Com., 1989-92, Rep. Town Comm., Rocky Hill, 2000—; dir. Old Towne Tourism Dist. Conn., 1989-90; justice of peace, 1998—. Served with U.S. Army, 1946-52. Asian Studies grantee, 1959; Am. Studies grantee, 1959; Danforth grantee, 1962; Munson Maritime grantee, 1961; Smithsonian Inst. grantee, 1963; recipient Pierport Edwards award, 2003. Mem. Orgn. Am. Historians, Am. Hist. Assn., New Eng. Hist. Assn., Conn. Hist. Assn., Assn. for Study of Conn. History, AAUP, New London County Hist. Soc., Am. Waldensian Aid Soc. (pres. Hartford chpt. 1986-89), Masons (Master Stepney Lodge 1990, 92, Master's award 1992, Arthur E. Warner award 1996, Master Silas Deans Lodge 2001—02, Grand Chaplain 1997-2003, High Priest Delta chpt. 1998-99, Knight Mason 1998—, master Philosophic Lodge Rsch., worshipful master 2000-01, Master's award 2001, 2002, eminent comdr. 2001—02, thrice illustrious master Walcott Coun. I 2000-01, high priest 2001—02, assoc. grand prelate, 2002-), Royal Arch Masons. Republican. Congregationalist (life deacon). Home: 2623 Main St Rocky Hill CT 06067-2507 Office: Fellowship Conn Congl Chs 277 Main St Hartford CT 06106-1818 E-mail: robertowendecker@world.net.att.net.

DECKER, SUSAN, Internet company executive; BS, Tufts U.; MBA, Harvard U. Cert. Charterd Fin. Analyst. With Donaldson, Lufking & Jenrette (DLJ), 1986—2000, publ. and advtsg. rsch. anlayst, global head rsch.; CFO, sr. v.p. fin. and adminstrn. Yahoo!, Sunnyvale, Calif., 2000—. Apptd. to acctg. stds. adv. coun. Fin. Acctg. Fedn. Office: Yahoo! 701 1st Av Sunnyvale CA 04089*

DECKER, WALTER JOHNS, toxicologist; b. Tannersville, N.Y., June 13, 1933; s. H. Russell and Leola May (Coons) D.; m. Barbara Allen Hart, Aug. 19, 1961; children: Karl Hart, Reid Johns, Sam Travis. BA, SUNY, Albany, 1954, MA, 1955; PhD, George Washington U., 1966. Commd. 2d lt. U.S. Army, 1955, advanced through grades to lt. col., 1970, ret., 1975; assoc. prof. U. Tex. Med. Br., Galveston, 1976-83; pres. Toxicology Cons. Svcs., El Paso, Tex., 1984-97. Adj. clin. prof. Tex. Tech. U., El Paso, 1991—. Contbr. articles to jours. Clin. Toxicology, Vet. and Human Toxicology, Toxicology and Applied Pharmacology, others. Mem. sci. rev. panel Nat. Libr. Medicine's Hazardous Substance Data Bank, Bethesda, Md., 1985-2000; chair steering com. West Tex. Poison Ctr., El Paso, 1994-96. Recipient Aesculapius award, Tex. Med. Assn., 1977, Career Achievement award, Am. Acad. Clin. Toxicology, 2001. Fellow: Am. Acad. Clin. Toxicology (Career Achievement award 2001); mem.: Soc. Toxicology. Episcopalian. Achievements include research in toxicology. E-mail: bdecker273@earthlink.net.

DECKER, WAYNE LEROY, meteorologist, educator; b. Patterson, Iowa, Jan. 24, 1922; s. Albert Henry and Effie (Holmes) D.; m. Martha Jane Livingston, Dec. 29, 1943; 1 dau., Susan Jane. BS, Central Coll., Pella, Iowa, 1943; postgrad., UCLA, 1943-44; MS, Iowa State U., 1947, PhD, 1955. Meteorologist U.S. Weather Bur., Washington and Des Moines, 1947-49; mem. faculty U. Mo. at Columbia, 1949—, prof. atmospheric sci., 1958-67, prof., chmn. dept. atmospheric sci., 1967-91; prof. emeritus U. Mo., Columbia, 1992—; dir. coop. inst. applied meteorology U. Mo. at Columbia, 1985-92; cons. climatologist, 1992—. Chmn. com. climatic fluctuations and agrl. prodn. NRC, 1975-76; bd. dirs. Council for Agrl. Sci. and Tech., 1978-85, mem. exec. com., 1981-85; chair organizing com. 16th Internat. Congress Biometeorology. Fellow Am. Meteorol. Soc.; mem. Internat. Soc. Biometeorology (treas. 1990-99), Am. Geophys. Union, Am. Agronomy Soc., Sigma Xi, Gamma Sigma Delta. Home: 1007 Hulen Dr Columbia MO 65203-1414 Office: U Mo 116 Gentry Hall Columbia MO 65211-7040

DECKER, WILLIAM ALEXANDER, editor; b. Williamsport, Pa., Feb. 20, 1952; s. John Christian and Elizabeth (Talley) Decker; m. Cynthia Morris, Aug. 8, 1981; children: Kurtis William, Laura Elizabeth. BA, Bucknell U., 1974; MA, Wheaton Grad. Sch., 1979, Luth. Northwestern Theol. Sem., 1987. News reporter Grit Newspaper, Williamsport, Pa., summers 1970-73; mgr., editor publicity dept. Wycliffe Bible Translators and Summer Inst. of Linguistics, Republic of Philippines, 1974-76, 1983-85; editor Town and Country Newspaper, Seneca, Ill., 1979-82; asst. editor Am. Luth. Ch., Mpls., 1986-87; asst. to editor Luth. Partners Evang. Luth. Ch. in Am., Chgo., 1988-94; mng. editor Luth. Partners Evangelical Luth. Ch. in Am., Chgo., 1994—. Mem. Associated Ch. Press, Washington, 1988—; assoc. in ministry Evang. Luth. Ch. in Am., Chgo., 1988—. Organizer, fundraiser, walker CROP (hunger) Walk, Des Plaines, 1990—; mem. Arthritis Found., Chgo., 1992—; adult religious edn. tchr. Luth. Congregations, 1979—; H.S. youth leader N.W. Cmty. Youth Min., 2000—, bd. dirs., 2002—. Mem. Bread for the World, Concord Coalition, Common Cause. Avocations: piano, bicycling, singing, swimming. Home: 619 Yale Ct Des Plaines IL 60016-2332 E-mail: wdecker@elca.org.

DECKERS, PETER JOHN, dean; b. Boston, Feb. 13, 1941; married, 1964; 7 children. BA cum laude, Coll. of the Holy Cross, 1962; MD cum laude, Boston U., 1966. Diplomate Nat. Bd. Med. Examiners, Am. Bd. Surgery. Med. intern Boston City Hosp., 1966—67; jr. asst. resident gen. surgery Boston U. Med. Ctr., Univ. Hosp., 1967—68; clin. assoc. surgery br. Nat. Cancer Inst., NIH, Bethesda, 1968—70; resident gen. surgery Boston U. Med. Ctr., U. Hosp., 1971, UPSHS trainee in acad. surgyer, 1971—72, resident in gen. surgery, 1972—73, chief resident in gen. surgery, 1973—74; staff surgeon Boston City Hosp., 1974—84; asst. to assoc. prof. surgery Boston U. Sch. Medicine, 1974—78; dean U. Conn. Sch. of Medicine, 1995—2000, dean sch. of medicine and exec. v.p. health affairs, 2000—. Attending staff gen. surgery John Dempsey Hosp./U. Conn. Health Ctr., 1984—, VA Med. Ctr., 1984-89; sr. staff dept. surgery Hartford Hosp., 1984—; program dir. Hartford Hosp.-U. Conn. Integrated Surg. Residency Program, 1984-94; dir. divsn. of gen. surgery Hartford Hosp., 1984-87; sr. staff dept. surgery New Britain Gen. Hosp., 1989—, Dept. Surgery, Mt. Sinai Hosp., 1989—, St. Francis Hosp. and Med. Ctr., 1988—; chmn. dept. surgery Hartford Hosp., 1987-94, Murray-Heilig prof., chmn. dept. surgery U. Conn. Sch. of Medicine, 1987-95; surgeon-in-chief John Dempsey Hosp., 1990-94; program dir. U. of Conn. Integrated Gen. Surg. Residency Tng. Program, 1990-94; interim dean, 1992-94; exec. v.p. for clin. affairs U. Conn. Health System, 1994-95; exec. v.p. for physician practice orgn. U. Conn. Health System, 1995—. Editl. bd. Breast Surgery: Index and Reviews, 1993, Surg. Oncology, 1991; contbr. numerous articles to profl. jours. Recipient First Prize James Ewing Resident Rsch. award, 1971; recipient numerous grants. Mem. Transplantation Soc., Am. Assn. for Cancer Rsch., Eastern Coop. Oncology Group, Assn. for Acad. Surgery, Am. Assn. for Cancer Edn., Am. Fedn. for Clin. Rsch., Mass. Med. Soc., Am. Radium Soc. (exec. com. 1989-91), Am. Soc. of Clin. Oncology, Soc. of Surg. Oncology (mem. coms.), Soc. of Univ. Surgeons, New England Cancer Soc. (pres. 1993, pres.-elect, 1992, exec. coun. 1991-94), Boston Surg. Soc., Societe Internationale de Chirurgie, Bay State Health Care, Soc. for the Surgery of the Alimentary Tract, New England Surg. Soc. (treas. 1996-98, pres. 1999), Assn. of Program Dirs. in Surgeons (pres.-elect 1990-91, pres. 1991-92), Conn. State Med. Soc. (mem. cancer coordinating com. 1990-91), Am. Cancer Soc. (Hartford chpt.), Connecticare, Hartford County Med. Assn., Soc. of Surg. Chmn. Home: 44 Heritage Dr Avon CT 06001 Office: Univ of Conn Health Ctr 263 Farmington Ave Farmington CT 06030-3800 E-mail: deckers@nso.uchc.edu.

DECKERT, MYRNA JEAN, small business owner, consultant; b. McPherson, Kans., Nov. 4, 1936; d. Francis J. and Grace (Killion) George; m. Ray A. Deckert, Sept. 29, 1957; children: Rachelle, Kimberly, Charles, Michael. AA, Coll. of Sequoias, 1956; BBA, U. Beverly Hills, 1983, MBA, 1984. Youth dir. Asbury Meth. Ch., El Paso, Tex., 1960-63; teen program dir. YWCA, El Paso, 1963-69, assoc. exec. dir., 1969-70, CEO, 1970—2002; chair strategic planning com. Tex. Dept. Pub. and Regulatory Svcs., 1994-97; owner, prin. MJD and Assocs., 2002—. Cons. to nonprofits. Pres. Exec. Forum, 1991—92; commr. Housing Authority City of El Paso, 1989—92; former chair bd. trustees Columbia Med. Ctr. East, 1992—97; deans adv. com. Tex. Tech. Med. Ctr.; past trustee Dues/High Tower Found.; chair Leadership EP, 1994—95; past mem. Tex. Challenge Adv. Com., 1998; chair Change Initiative Com., 1998—2000; adv. dir. M.D. Anderson Hosp., Houston; co-chair El Paso Ind. Sch. Dist. Bd. Com., 2000; mem. City of El Paso Bond Com., 1999—2000; mem. nat. coordinating bd. YWCA of the USA, 2002—, chair global campaign; bd. dirs. Chase Bank of Tex., El Paso, Blue Cross/Blue Shield Tex., 1999—. Recipient Hannah Soloman Cmty. Svc. award Nat. Coun. Jewish Women, Sertoma Club award Svc. to Mankind, 1974, Cmty. Svc. award League United L.Am. Citizens, 1980, Humanitarian award, 1994, Vol. Svc. award Vol. Bur., 1984, Merit award Adalante Mujer, 1986, Social Svc. award KVIA/Sunturians, 1986, Excellence award Nat. Assn. YWCA Execs., 1990, Racial Justice award YWCA of the U.S.A., 1991, Disting. Svc. award Rotary of El Paso, 1997, Citizen of Yr. award Greater El Paso Assn. Realtors, 1998; named Woman of Yr., AAUW, 1975, Dir. of Yr., United Way El Paso County, 1985, First Lady of El Paso, Beta Sigma Phi, 1991, One of 10 Most Influential Women, El Paso Times, 1995, Citizen of Yr., Mil. Order of World Wars, 1996; inducted into El Paso Women's Hall of Fame, 1990, El Paso Hist. Soc. Hall of Honor, 1995, Hall of Fame/Coll. of Sequoias, 1995, Hall of Honor, 1996, Jr. Achievement Bus. Hall of Honor, 1998, Bravo award LWV, 1999; named Citizen of Yr., El Paso Bd. Realtors, 1999; Conquistador award, City of El Paso, 2002; named El Pasoan of Yr., 2003. Mem.: Rotary (v.p. El Paso club 1990—93). Methodist. Home: 4276 Canterbury Dr El Paso TX 79902-1352 E-mail: mjdeckert@aol.com., mdeckert@ywcaelpaso.org.

DECKO, KENNETH OWEN, trade association administrator; b. New Haven, Aug. 7, 1944; s. Charles C. and Frances D.; m. Marilyn Seaver, Oct. 21, 1972; children: Kurt, Amy. Student, Duke U.; JD, U. Conn., 1969. With Conn. Bus. and Industry Assn., Hartford, 1970—, pres., 1981—. Served with USAR, 1969-70. Office: 350 Church St Hartford CT 06103-1106

DECKROSH, HAZEN DOUGLAS, retired state agency educator and administrator; b. Defiance, Ohio, Apr. 13, 1936; s. Lawrence L. and Martha L. Deckrosh; m. Carol Ann Everett, Nov. 25, 1970; children: Stephanie, Todd, Douglas, Nadia Nicole. BS, Ohio No. U., 1959; MEd, U. Toledo, 1980. Cert. tchr., Ohio. Phys. edn. and history tchr., coach Waynesfield (Ohio)-Goshen Jr. High Sch., 1959-61; coach, history, phys. edn. tchr. Coshocton (Ohio) Sacred Heart High Sch., 1961-63; health-phys. edn. tchr., coach West Holmes Jr. High Sch., Millersburg, Ohio, 1965-70; tchr. history and govt., coach Elida High Sch., 1970-73; occupational work experience tchr.-coord., coach Spencerville (Ohio) High Sch., 1973-77; occupational work edn. tchr., coord. Four County Vocat. Sch., Archbold, Ohio, 1977-82, 99—; vocat. supr. Jefferson County Vocat. Sch., Steubenville, Ohio, 1986-87; occupational work experience tchr., coord. Ohio Dept. of Youth Svcs., Columbus, 1987-94; ret., 1994. Pres. DYS Coordinators, Columbus, 1990-94; ski instr. Swiss Valley, Mich., 1995—; GED instr. Correction Ctr. Northwest Ohio. Editor: Threaded Fasteners, 1987; contbr. articles to profl. publs. Mem. Am. Youth Hostels, Lima, 1972—. Mem. NEA, Ohio Edn. Assn., Am. Vocat. Assn., Ohio Vocat. Assn., Occupl. Work Experience Coords. Assn. (state adv. coun., Lima rep. 1977-80, Columbus rep. 1991-94), Full Gospel Bus. Men's Fellowship Internat., Gideons Internat. (treas., then sec.), 5th Dist. Ofcls. Assn. (v.p., rules interpreter), Capitol West Umpires Assn. (rules interpreter 1991-93), Lima Umpires Assn. (sec.-treas. 1973-77), Ret. Tchrs. Assn. (pres.), Alpha Sigma Phi. Republican. Avocations: sports officiating, high school and college sports, teaching skiing. Home: 12265 County Road 150 Montpelier OH 43543-9613

DECONDO, ANTHONY PAUL, SR., elementary school educator; b. Paterson, N.J., Sept. 4, 1940; s. Luigi DeCondo and Anna Catherine DiGrazia; m. Camille Catherine DeRosa, Aug. 25, 1962; children: Anthony, Michael, Louis. BS in Edn., Seton Hall U., 1962; MA in Adminstrn. and Supervision, William Paterson U., 1985. Tchr. Five/Six Sch., Hackensack, NJ, N.K. Parker Sch., Hackensack, NJ, Maple Hill Sch., Hackensack, NJ; guidance counselor Broadway Sch., Hackensack, NJ, tchr., Midland Sch., Rochelle Park, NJ. Dir. summer arts program Hackensack Bd. Edn., 1993—2001. Author: (textbook) New Jersey Adventure, 2000. Mem.: NEA, Archaeol. Soc. N.J., Bergen County Edn. Assn., N.J. Edn. Assn. Avocations: archaeology, writing, photography. Home: 33 Kipp Ave Elmwood Park NJ 07407

DE CORDOVA, HECTOR ARMANDO, artist, consultant, art educator; b. N.Y., N.Y., May 13, 1931; s. Armando Luis de Cordova and Margarita Umpierre; 1 child, Daniel de Cordova. Degree in interior arch., Parson Sch. Design, 1958. Self employed, NY, 1958—, 1958—, 1958—. Pres., v.p. Artists Alliance East Hampton, NY, 1991—99; bd. dirs. OLA, South Fork, L.I., N.Y., 2003—, East End Arts Coun., L.I., N.Y., 2003—. With USN, 1951—55, Korea. Mem.: Artists Alliance East Hampton (pres. 1995—99), Salmagundi Club, Nat. Arts Club. Avocations: kayaking, travel. Home: South Dr Sag Harbor NY 11963 Fax: 631-725-9326. E-mail: joyhect@aol.com.

DECOSTA, BENJAMIN, airport executive; BA in Physics, Queens Col.; JD, NY Law Sch., 1975. With Port Authority NY, 1972—78; chief of staff, personnel and labor relations City of NY, 1978—83; gen. mgr. Newark Int. Airport, NJ, 1994—98; gen. mgr. aviation Hatsfield Int. Airport, Atlanta, 1998—. Office: Dept Aviation Hatsfield Internat Airport 6000 N Terminal Pkwy, PO Box 20509 Atlanta GA 30320*

DECOSTA, PETER F. chemical engineer; b. New Bedford, Mass. s. Anthony and Deolinda (DeSouza) DeC. BS with distinction, U. Mass., 1962; MA, U. Conn., 1966; cert., U. R.I., 1968; MS, MIT, 1970; cert., Boston U., 1979, Northeastern U., 1980; profl. engrng. degree, U. Wis., 1981. Chemist Portsmouth Naval Shipyard, N.H., 1962-64; chemistry, physics, math. tchr. Apponequet H.S., Lakeville, Mass., 1964-66; quality assurance engr. U.S. FDA, Boston, 1966-71, systems analyst Washington, 1970-71, U.S. EPA, Washington, 1971-75; ops. rsch. analyst U.S. Army Natick (Mass.) Rsch., Devel. and Engrng. Ctr., 1976-83, phys. scientist, 1983-86, gen. engr., 1986-2000; ind. cons. engr., 2000—. Part-time instr. Northeastern U., Boston, 1987—, Worcester (Mass.) Poly. Inst., 1984-90, Mass. Bay Community Coll., Wellesley, 1983-2000. Contbr. articles to profl. jours. Planner, Planning Bd. City of New Bedford, Mass., 1975; mem. ch. activities, charities; mem. Leadership Cir. WGBH-TV (PBS), Boston, 1992, WBUR-AM/FM (NPR), Boston, 1997; charter mem. U.S.S. Constn. Mus., 1992; mem. John F. Kennedy Presdl. Libr. Found., Nat. Trust for Hist. Preservation. Commonwealth scholar U. Mass., 1958-62, City of New Bedford scholar, 1958-62, Allied Chem. Co. scholar, 1960-62; U. Conn. teaching fellow, 1964-65, NSF fellow Boston Coll., 1965, Advanced Engrng. fellow MIT, 1969-70, NSF/AAAS fellow MIT, 1984; recipient Natick Comdr.'s award U.S Army Natick Rsch., Devel. and Engrng. Ctr., 1981, 86, Cold War Recognition cert. U.S. Dept. Def., 2000, Gulf War Desert Storm Recognition cert. U.S. Amry, 1991. Fellow Am. Inst. Chemists; mem. AIChE (cert.), AAUP, AAAS, Future Techs. Inst., Am. Chem. Soc., Geol. Soc. Am., Planetary Soc., Mus. Sci., John F. Kennedy Presdl. Libr. Found., Libr. of Congress Assocs. (charter mem.), Smithsonian Nat. Assocs., Old Dartmouth Hist. Soc. (New Bedford Whaling Mus.), Children's Mus., MIT Faculty Club, MIT Club Southeastern Mass., Nature Conservancy, Sigma Xi, Alpha Chi Sigma, Phi Lambda Upsilon. Avocations: gemology, coin and stamp collecting.

DECOTIS, RUTH JANICE, career planning administrator, educator; b. Lebanon, N.H., July 3, 1949; d. David Gilman Fowler and Olive Leonie Greenwood; m. Terry L. DeCotis, Sept. 2, 1967; children: Gregory, Curtis, Erin. AS magna cum laude in Sec. Sci., Plymouth State Coll., 1989, BS magna cum laude in Adminstrn. Mgmt. & Comm., 1995, MEd magna cum laude in Counselor Edn. & Human Rels., 1998. Sec. Equity Pub., Orford, NH, 1969—79; sec. social sci. dept. Plymouth State Coll., Plymouth, NH, 1980—86, from program asst. to academic & career adv. ctr., 1986—. Travel agt. Plymouth Travel, Plymouth, 1991—. Co-author: Great Jobs for Math Majors, 1998. Mem.: Assn. for Psychol. Type, Nat. Academic Adv. Assn., Nat. Soc. Experiential Edn., Am. Counseling Assn. Avocations: travel, antiques, restoration of old homes. Office: Plymouth State Coll Academic & Career Adv Ctr 17 High St MSC 44 Plymouth NH 03264 Fax: 603-535-2528. E-mail: rdecotis@mail.plymouth.edu.

DECOURCEY, CATHERINE MAUREEN, special education educator; d. Anne G and Richard J DeCourcey. BA, Grinnell Coll., 1978—82; MEd, U. of Tex., 1996—98; PhD, U. of Tex. at Austin, 1998—2003. Texas Teacher Certificate Tex. Bd. of Edn., 1992, Teaching Certificate Iowa, 1982, Illiinois, 1983. Spl. edn. tchr. Ridgeway Acad., 1983—84; tchr. Maywood Pub. Schools, Maywood, Ill., 1984—86; writing asst. Nat. Coll. of Edn., 1986—87; spl. edn. tchr. Chgo. Pub. Schools, 1988—92, Austin Ind. Sch. Dist., Austin, Tex., 1992—99; tchg. asst. U. of Tex., 1999—2003, field experience facilitator, 2000—; intern St. Edward's U., Austin, Tex., 2003. Cooperating tchr. Chgo. Pub. Schools, Chgo., 1988—92; mentor tchr. Austin Ind. Sch. Dist., Austin, Tex., 1996—99; guest lectr. U. of Tex., 1997—2000; chairperson, campus adv. coun. Austin Ind. Sch. Dist., 1996—97. Recipient Tex. Excellence Tchg. award, The Ex Students' Assn. and the Cabinet of Coll. Councils of the U. of Tex. at Austin, 2001; Annie Webb Blanton scholarship, Alpha State of Delta Kappa Gamma Internat., 2000—01. Mem.: Coun. for Exceptional Children, Am. Ednl. Rsch. Assn., Pi Lambda Theta, Kappa Delta Pi, Delta Kappa Gamma.

DECOURSEY, THOMAS ERIC, physiologist, educator; b. Ames, Iowa, July 16, 1951; s. Wesley F. and Verda I. (Grove) DeC.; m. Carolyn Garver; children: Audrey G., Jillian Z. BA summa cum laude, McPherson Coll., 1974; PhD, U. Cin., 1979. Asst. prof. physiology Rush Presbyn. St. Luke's Med. Ctr., Chgo., 1985-90, assoc. prof., 1990-98, prof., 1998—. Co-dir. Pulmonary Patch Clamp Ctr., 1985—. Mem. editl. bd. Am. Jour. Physiology, 1990—, Jour. Gen. Physiology, 1994-97; contbr. articles to profl. jours. Albert J. Ryan Found. fellow, Cin., 1976-79; hon. rsch. fellow U. Glasgow, 1980-81. Mem. Biophys. Soc., Am. Physiol. Soc., Soc. Gen. Physiologists. Democrat. Achievements include research on ion channels in non-excitable cells. Office: Rush Med Ctr Dept Molecular Biophysics and Physiology 1750 W Harrison St Chicago IL 60612-3824

DE COURTEN-MYERS, GABRIELLE MARGUERITE, neuropathologist; b. Fribourg, Switzerland, Aug. 8, 1947; came to U.S., 1979; d. Maurice Edmond and Margrit (Wettstein) De Courten; m. Ronald Elwood Myers, Apr. 18, 1981; 1 child, Maximilian. BSBA, Akademikergemeinschaft, Zurich, Switzerland, 1967; MD, U. Zurich, 1974. Resident in psychiatry Hopital Psycho-Geriatrique, Gimel, Switzerland, 1974-75; resident in pediatrics U. Hosp. Zurich, 1977; resident in neuropathology U. Hosp. of Lausanne, Switzerland, 1976-78; rsch. assoc. NIH, Bethesda, Md., 1979-80; fellow in neuropathology Coll. of Medicine U. Cin., 1980-83, asst. prof. neuropathology Coll. of Medicine, 1983-88, assoc. prof. neuropathology Coll. of Medicine, 1988-89, tenured assoc. prof. Coll. of Medicine, 1989—. Cons. Vets. Affairs Med. Ctr., Cin., 1983—, Children's Hosp. Med. Ctr., Cin., 1984—, Good Samaritan Hosp., Cin., 1990—. Grantee VA, 1985—, NIH, 1986-90, 93—, Am. Heart Assn., 1991-94, Am. Diabetes Assn., 1995. Mem. AAAS, Am. Assn. Neuropathologists, Am. Acad. Neurology, AAUP, Soc. Acad. Emergency Medicine, Soc. Exptl. Neuropathology. Office: U Cin Coll of Medicine Dept Pathology PO Box 670529 231 Bethesda Ave Cincinnati OH 45267-0529 E-mail: gabrielle.decourten@uc.edu.

DECRANE, ALFRED CHARLES, JR., petroleum company executive; b. Cleve., June 11, 1931; s. Alfred Charles and Verona (Marquard) DeCrane; m. Joan Elizabeth Hoffman, July 3, 1954; children: David, Lisa, Stacie, Stephanie, Sarah, Jennifer. BA, U. Notre Dame, 1953; JD, Georgetown U., 1959; LHD (hon.), Manhattanville Coll., 1990; DJD (hon.), U. Notre Dame, 2002. Cert. Va. Bar, 1959, D.C. Bar, 1959, Tex. Bar, 1961, N.Y. Bar, 1966. Legal dept. Texaco, Inc., Houston, 1959—65, N.Y.C., 1964—66, asst. to vice chmn. bd., 1965—67, asst. to chmn. bd., 1967—68, gen. mgr. producing dept. Eastern hemisphere, 1968—70, v.p., 1970—76, sr. v.p., gen. counsel, 1976—77, sr. v.p., dir., 1977—78, exec. v.p., 1978—83, pres., 1983—86, chmn. bd. dirs., 1987—96, chmn., chief exec. officer, 1993—96. Bd. dirs. Harris Corp., Corn Products Internat., U.S. Global Leaders Growth Fund, Ltd. Life trustee U. Notre Dame. 1st lt. USMC, 1954—55. Mem.: ABA (sect. sec. 1964—67). Achievements include co-founder Natural Resources Law Jour. mineral law sect. Office: PO Box 1247 Greenwich CT 06836-1247

DECREASE, WILLIAM MAURICE, total quality management consultant; b. Shenandoah, Pa., Sept. 25, 1928; s. Nicholas and Estelle (Cusatis) DeC.; m. Alberta A. Bindi, Aug. 3, 1952; children: Dean W., Drew D., Lynn M. BS in Chemistry, Pa. State U., 1951; postgrad. in Biochemistry, U. Chgo., 1954; postgrad. in Mgmt., Case Western Res. U., 1970. Rsch. chemist Continental Can Co., Chgo., 1954-58; asst. mgr. R&D Lord Corp., Erie, Pa., 1958-70, mgr. mktg., 1970-80, divsn. mgr., 1980-85, mgr. corp. quality, 1985-88; pres. William DeCrease & Assocs., Erie, Pa., 1988—. Chief cons. Total Quality Mgmt. Inst., Erie, 1992-95; cmty. quality cons. World Wide Communities, U.S., Europe, Can., Mex., 1990-95; pres. Adhesive and Sealant Coun., Washington, 1980-81. Contbr. articles to profl. jours.; 17 patents in field. Pres., founder Erie Excellence Coun.; bd. dirs. World Ctr. for Cmty. Excellence, Erie; chmn. Erie Area C. of C., 1991-92. Cpl. U.S. Army, 1952-54. Recipient Highest Achievement award Erie Excellence Coun., 1991, Chamber award Erie Area C. of C., 1994. Mem. Am. Soc. for Quality Control. Republican. Avocations: golf, gardening. Home and Office: William DeCrease and Assocs 205 W 42nd St Erie PA 16508-3030

DECROCE, ALEX, state legislator; b. Morristown, N.J., June 10, 1936; m. Betty Lou Bisson, 1994; 3 children. Student, Seton Hall U. Chmn. Morris County (N.J.) Rep. Com., 1971-72, freeholder, 1984-89, dir., 1986—; mem. Morris County Bd. Elections, 1973-82, chmn., 1977-81; assemblyman N.J. State Assembly, 1989—, dep. spkr., 1994—; chmn. transp., labor N.J. RR & Transp. Mus. Commn., 1994—; prin. Gallo-DeCroce, Inc., Parsippany-Troy Hills; pres. Gal-Lex & Tedesco. Recipient Legislator of Yr. award Transp. Am. Legis. Exch. Coun., 1992, Appreciation award Coun. Spl. Transp., 1993, Legis. award Utility-Transp. Contractors, 1993. Mem. Morris, West Essex and Parsippany C. of C., Rotary (Outstanding Citizen of Parsippany 1991). Address: 101 Gibraltar Dr Ste 2-d Morris Plains NJ 07950-1287*

DECROSTA, SUSAN ELYSE, graphic designer; b. Cambridge, Mass., Aug. 28, 1956; d. Joseph Mario and Gertrude Ermelinda (Galligani) DeC. BFA, Mass. Coll. Art, 1980. certified art tchr., supr. Graphic artist Nixdorf Computer

Corp., Burlington, Mass., 1981-86; lead artist, illustrator Raytheon Co., Andover, Mass., 1986-94; graphic designer Raytheon Svc. Co., Burlington, Mass., 1994—; artist, illustrator Rivers, Trainor, Doyle, Providence, 1987. Freelance graphic artist, 1980—; guest speaker to design and illustration students Northeastern U., 1992. Publ. (graphic design U.S.A. mag.), 2000 (Am. Graphic Design award, 2003). Vol. AIDS Action Com., Boston; bd. dirs. Jeannette Neill Dance Scholarship Program, Boston, 1999—. Recipient Excellence award Soc. Tech. Communications & Art Direction, 1986, Am. Graphic Design award Graphic Design USA, 2000. Mem.: Women's Initiative Network, Art Alumni Assn. Avocations: dancing, painting. Office: Raytheon Svc Co 2 Wayside Rd Burlington MA 01803-4607 E-mail: susan_e_decrosta@raytheon.com., susandecrosta@rcn.com.

DECROW, KAREN, lawyer, author, lecturer; b. Chgo., Dec. 18, 1937; d. Samuel Meyer and Juliette (Abt) Lipschultz; m. Alexander Allen Kolben, 1960 (div. 1965); m. Roger DeCrow, 1965 (div. 1972, dec. 1989). BS, Northwestern U., 1959; JD, Syracuse U., 1972; DHL (hon.), SUNY, Oswego, 1994. Bar: N.Y., U.S. Dist. Ct. (no. dist.) N.Y. Resorts editor Golf Digest mag., Evanston, Ill., 1959-60; editor Am. Soc. Planning Ofcls., Chgo., 1960-61; writer Ctr. for Study Liberal Edn. for Adults., Chgo., 1961-64; editor Holt, Rinehart, Winston, Inc., N.Y.C., 1965; textbook editor L.W. Singer, Syracuse, N.Y., 1965-66; writer En. Regional Inst. for Edn., Syracuse, 1967-69, Pub. Broadcasting System, 1977; tchr. women and law, 1972-74; nat. bd. mem. NOW, 1968-77, nat. pres., 1974-77, also nat. politics task force chair; cons. affirmative action; pvt. practice, 1974—. Lectr. topics including law, gender, internat. feminism to corps., polit. groups, colls. and univs., U.S., Can., Mex., Finland, China, Greece, former USSR; nat. coord. Women's Strike for Equality, 1970; moot ct. judge, 1974–; N.Y. State del. Internat. Women's Yr., 1977; originator Schs. for Candidates; participant DeCrow-Schlafly ERA Debates, from 1975; founder (with Robert Seidenberg, MD) World Woman Watch, 1988; gender issues advisor Nat. Congress for Men; mem. Task Force on Gender Bias. Author: (with Roger DeCrow) University Adult Education: A Selected Bibliography, 1967, American Council on Education, 1967, The Young Woman's Guide to Liberation, 1971, Sexist Justice, 1974, First Women's State of the Union Message, 1977, (with Robert Seidenberg) Women Who Marry Houses: Panic and Protest in Agoraphobia, 1983, Turkish edit., 1988, 2d Turkish edit., 1989, United States of America vs. Sex: How the Meese Commission Lied About Pornography, 1988, (with Jack Kammer) Good Will Toward Men: Women Talk Candidly About the Balance of Power Between the Sexes, 1994; editor: The Pregnant Teenager (Howard Osofsky), 1968, Corporate Wives, Corporate Casualties (Robert Seidenberg, MD), 1973; contbr. articles to USA Today, N.Y. Times, L.A. Times, Chgo. Tribune, Nat. Law Jour., Women Boston Globe, Vogue, Mademoiselle, Ingenue, Newsday, Chgo. Sun Times, Penthouse, Washington Post, L.A. Times Mag., Policy Review, Miami Herald, Internat. Herald Tribune, Social Problems, Houston Chronicle, Pitts. Press, Nat. NOW Times, Syracuse U. Mag., San Francisco Chronicle, Civil Rights Quar., Women Lawyers Jour., other newspapers, mags.; regular columnist: Syracuse New Times; columnist N.Y. Times Spl. Features; recording: Opening Up Marriage, 1980. Hon. trustee Elizabeth Cady Stanton Found.; active Hon. Com. to Save Alice Paul's Birthplace; Liberal party candidate for Mayor of Syracuse, 1969. Recipient Profl. Recognition award for best newspaper column Syracuse Press Club, 1990, 94, 95, 96, 2000, Best Column award, 1994-95, 99, 2001, 02, Best Column award N.Y. Press Assn., 1991-92, 95, award Barnard Coll., Vet. Feminists of Am. and the Barnard Ctr. for Rsch. on Women, Woman of Achievement/Distinction award Gov. George E. Pataki, 1998; Svc. to Soc. award Northwestern U. Alumni Assn., 2002, Achievement award The Post-Standard, Syracuse, 2003. Mem. NOW (pres.), Onondaga County Bar Assn. (profl. ethics com.), N.Y. Women's Bar Assn. (ctrl. N.Y. chpt. pres. 1989-90, jud. screening com., Joan L. Ellenbogen Founder's award 2003), N.Y. Bar Assn., ACLU (Ralph E. Kharas Disting. Svc. in Civil Liberties award 1985), Elizabeth Cady Stanton Found. (trustee), Working Women's Inst. (bd. advisors), Syracuse Friends Chamber Music, Atlantic States Legal Found., Yale Polit. Union (hon. life), Nat. Congress Men (gender issues advisor), Mariposa Edn. and Rsch. Found., Nat. Coun. Children's Rights (adv. panel), Wilderness Soc., Northwestern U. Alumni Assn., Women's Inst. Freedom Press, Art Inst. Chgo., Nat. Women's Polit. Caucus, Theta Sigma Phi. Address: 7599 Brown Gulf Rd Jamesville NY 13078-9636 *I feel especially lucky to be able to participate, as Holmes said, in the passion of our times. The movement to create equality between women and men is the most interesting and exciting during this period in history. My goal is a world where the gender of a baby will have little or no relevance to future pursuits or pleasures - personal, political, economic, social, or professional. It is exhilarating to watch society change in that direction.*

DECUIR, WINSTON G., SR., lawyer; b. Baton Rouge, Aug. 17, 1948; s. Maurice and Loffie Decuir; m. Barbara Conant, June 17, 1970; children: Winston Jr., Jason, Brandon. BS, Xavier U., New Orleans, 1970; JD, La. State U., 1975. Bar: La. Asst. atty. gen. La. Dept. Justice, Baton Rouge, 1975—89; ptnr. Decuir & Clark, Baton Rouge, 1989—. Judge ad hoc Baton Rouge City Ct., 1995. Named Practitioner of the Yr., Louis Martenet Soc., 1995; recipient Award of Merit, NAACP-La., 1999. Democrat. Roman Catholic. Home: 961 Castle Kirk Baton Rouge LA 70808 Office: Decuir & Clark 1961 Government St Baton Rouge LA 70806

DEDE, BONNIE AILEEN, librarian, educator; b. Racine, Wis., Mar. 21, 1942; d. Edward Charles and Gracebelle Roeber; children: Suzan A., Ercan M. BA, U. Mich., 1963, MA, 1966, AM in LS, 1968; cert., U. Ill., 1970. Various positions U. Mich. Libr., Ann Arbor, 1967—88, head spl. formats cataloging, 1988—99, adj. lectr. sch. info., 1989—, head monograph cataloging prodn., 1999—. Mem. part-time faculty libr. and info. sci. program Wayne State U., Detroit, 1993—; vis. lectr. Grad. Sch. Libr. and Info. Sci. U. Ill., Urbana-Champaign, 2003—; cons. Gale Rsch., Detroit, 1993; reviewer Am. Reference Books Ann., 1992—; cons. grant projects OCLC, 1991—92, 1994—96. Mem. editl. bd. MC, Jour. Acad. Media Librarianship, 1992-2002. Grantee Title II-B, U.S. Office Edn., 1970, faculty-libr. coop. rsch. grantee Coun. on Libr. Resources, 1986-88, access grantee NEH, 1990-93. Mem. ALA, Alpha Lambda Delta, Beta Phi Mu (pres. Mu chpt. 1991-96). Office: U Mich 100 Hatcher Libr North Ann Arbor MI 48109-1205

DEDEAUX, PAUL J. orthodontist; b. Pass Christian, Miss., Feb. 22, 1937; s. Mack and Harriet D.; m. Janet Louise Harter, June 29, 1971; children: Michele, Kristen, Kelly. BA, Dillard U., 1959; DDS, Howard U., 1963; MS, Fairleigh Dickinson U., 1975. Pvt. practice, Washington, 1976-93, Santa Ana, Calif., 1976-93; instr. Howard U., Washington, 1967-69; dental dir. Dr. Martin Luther King Health Ctr., Bronx, N.Y., 1969-70, dentist, 1970-76; chief dentist Calipatria State Prison, Calif., 1993-96, Calif. Med. Facility, Vacaville, 1996—. Instr. Howard U., Washington, 1967-69; cons. Hostos C.C., Bronx, 1971-76; mem. adv. panel Dental Econs. mag., 1976; adj. assoc. prof. Columbia U., N.Y.C., 1970-72. Contbr. articles to profl. jours. Capt. U.S. Army, 1963-67, USAR, 1975—, col., 1985—, comdr., 1994-97, ret. 1997. Mem. Am. Assn. Orthodontists, Pacific Coast Soc. Orthodontists, ADA, Calif. Dental Assn., Assn. Mil. Surgeons of U.S. Democrat. Methodist. Avocations: photography, fishing. Home: 940 Celestine Cir Vacaville CA 95687-7853 Office: Calif Med Facility PO Box 2000 1600 California Dr Vacaville CA 95687

DEDERICK, ROBERT GOGAN, economist; b. Keene, NH, Nov. 18, 1929; s. Frederic Van Dyck and Margaret (Gogan) D.; m. Margarida N. Magalhaes, Aug. 24, 1957; children: Frederic, Laura, Peter. AB, Harvard U., 1951, AM, 1953, PhD, 1958; postgrad., Cornell U., 1953-54. Econ. research mgr. New Eng. Mut. Life Ins. Co., Boston, 1957-64; assoc. economist No. Trust Co., Chgo., 1964, v.p., assoc. economist, 1965-69, v.p., economist, 1969-70, sr. v.p., chief economist, 1970-81, exec. v.p., chief economist, 1983-94, econ. cons., 1994—; mem. panel of econ. advisers Congl. Budget Office; mem. econ. adv. bd. U.S. Commerce Dept., 1968-70, 75-76, 83-85, asst. sec. commerce for econ. affairs, 1981-82, under sec. commerce for econ. affairs, 1982-83; prin. RGD Econs., Hinsdale, 1994—. Fellow: Nat. Assn. Bus. Economists (pres. 1973—74, governing coun. 1969—75); mem.: Internat. Conf. Comml. Bank Economists, Am. Bankers Assn. (alumni coun.), Harvard Discussion Group Indsl. Economists, Conf. Bus. Economists (chmn. 1984—85), Capital Hill Club (Washington), Hinsdale Golf Club, Harvard Club (Chgo., Boston, Cape Cod), Econ. Club (Chgo.). Home: 113 S County Line Rd Hinsdale IL 60521-4722 Office: RGD Economics 113 S County Line Rd Hinsdale IL 60521-4722 also: Northern Trust Company 50 S Lasalle St Chicago IL 60675-0001 E-mail: dederick_robert@ntrs.com.

DEDERICK, RONALD OSBURN, lawyer; b. Chgo., Aug. 26, 1935; s. Clint Goddard and Isabel Lucille (Osburn) D.; m. Dorothy Hope Spence; children: Cynthia Rae Dederick Stroili, Kenneth Scott. BA, U. Va., 1957, JD, 1962. Bar: N.Y. 1962, U.S. Dist. Ct. (so. dist.) N.Y. 1964, Conn. 1969, U.S. Dist. Conn. 1970, U.S. Supreme Ct. 1990. Assoc. Sullivan & Cromwell, N.Y.C., 1962—69; ptnr. Durey & Pierson, Stamford, Conn., 1969—79, Day, Berry & Howard, Stamford and Greenwich, 1979—. Bd. dirs. Vol. Action Coun., Stamford, 1972-79, Guardianship Advocacy Resource Program, Inc., Stamford, 1984-2000; trustee, sec. West Conn. Multiple Sclerosis Soc., 1985-99; chair Greenwich (Conn.) Arts Coun., 1990-94. Capt. USNR, ret. Fellow Am. Bar Found.; mem. ABA (chair multistate com. 1984-87), Conn. Bar Assn. (chair probate sect. 1988-90), Conn. Bar Found. (James W. Cooper fellow), Stamford Regional Bar Assn. (bd. dirs. 1982-88), Internat. Bar Assn., Internat. Acad. Estate and Trust Law, Rotary (pres. Stamford 1980-81, Paul Harris fellow 1984), Milbrook Club (pres. 1980-81). Republican. Presbyterian. Avocations: golf, fishing. Office: Day Berry & Howard LLP One E Putnam Ave Greenwich CT 06830 Home: 1440 Laurel View Dr Virginia Beach VA 23451 E-mail: rdederick@dbh.com.

DEDMAN, BERTRAM COTTINGHAM, retired insurance company executive; b. Columbia, Tenn., Dec. 24, 1914; s. Bertram Cottingham and Mary Ella (Fariss) D.; m. Rainsford Bayard MacDowell, June 16, 1938; children: Rainsford Dedman Olson, Ella. AB, U. of South, Sewanee, Tenn., 1937; JD, George Washington U., 1941. Bar: Tenn. 1941, D.C. 1977. Trial atty. Antitrust Div., Dept. Justice, Washington, 1941-54, Texaco, Inc., Los Angeles, 1954-57; asst. counsel, asso. gen. counsel, gen. counsel Ins. Co. of N.Am., Phila., 1957-70; v.p., gen. counsel INA Corp. (now CIGNA Corp.), Phila., 1968-77; v.p., sec. INA Corp., 1975-79. Editor, contbr.: Merger of Insurance Companies, 1966. Served with USNR, 1944-47. Mem. Am., Fed., Tenn., Phila. bar assns., Am. Judicature Soc., Internat. Assn. Ins. Law (past pres. U.S. chpt.) Home: 500 Elmington Ave Nashville TN 37205-2513

DEDMAN, BILL, journalist; b. Chattanooga, Oct. 14, 1960; s. Harold C. and Bobbye (Griswold) Dedman; m. Pamela J. Belluck, Sept. 5, 1993; 1 child, Justin. Student, Wash. U., St. Louis, 1978—81. Reporter Warrensburg (Mo.) Star-Jour., 1981, Blue Springs (Mo.) Examiner, 1981—82, Chattanooga Free Press, 1983, Chattanooga Times, 1984—86, Knoxville News-Sentinel, 1986—87, Atlanta Journal-Constitution, 1987—89, Washington Post, 1989—91; fellow Freedom Forum Media Studies Ctr. Columbia U., N.Y.C., 1992—93; contbg. writer Mother Jones Mag., 1993—94; dir. computer-assisted reporting AP, 1994—97; writer N.Y. Times, 1997—. Hearst vis. fellow U. Md. Coll. Journalism, 1993—94; lectr. Northwestern U. Author: (book) The Color of Money: Home Mortgage Lending Practices Discriminate Against Blacks, 1988; contbr. Recipient Pulitzer Prize for investigative reporting, 1989, Robert F. Kennedy Journalism award grand prize, 1989, Worth Bingham prize, 1989, numerous others. Mem.: Investigative Reporters and Editors (bd. dirs. 1990—96, award 1989).

DEDMAN, ROBERT HENRY, sales executive; b. Rison, Ark., Feb. 15, 1926; s. Robert Henry and Cornelia D.; m. Nancy McMillan, Dec. 6, 1952; children: Robert H. Jr., Patricia Dedman Dietz. BA, U. Tex., 1946, BS, LLB, U. Tex., 1948; LLM, So. Meth. U., 1953. Foun., chmn. ClubCorp Inc., Dallas, 1957—; mem. State Hwy. Commn., Austin, Tex., 1981-85, 87-91. Adv. dir. Stewart Info. Svcs., 1989—. Chmn. bd. trustees, So. Meth. U., Dallas, 1993-96, active, 1976—. Named to Tex. Bus. Hall of Fame, 1987, Entrepreneur of Yr., Dallas, 1980, Marketer of Yr., Dallas, 1986; recipient Horatio Alger award, Washington, 1989. Republican. Methodist. Avocations: tennis, golf. Office: ClubCorp Inc Ste 700 3030 Lyndon B Johnson Fwy Dallas TX 75234-7763

DEDO, DOUGLAS DONALD, physician; s. Homer H. and Dorothy (Gregg) D.; m. Kathy Crawford Dedo; children: Susan, Cynthia, Rebecca, Andrew. BA, U. Kans., 1965; MD, Northwestern U., 1969. Diplomate Am. Bd. Otolaryngology, Am. Bd. Cosmetic Surgery, Am. Bd. Facial Plastic Surgery; lic. physician, Fla. Intern Univ. Hosp., Jackson, Miss., 1969-70; resident in gen. surgery St. Luke's Hosp., St. Louis, 1970-71; resident in otolaryngology Washington U. Sch. Medicine, St. Louis, 1971-75, instr. otolaryngology, head and neck surgery, 1975-79; clin. asst prof. otolaryngology, head and neck surgery U. Miami Sch. Medicine, 1978—; pvt. practice, 1977-97; with Harbour ENT Assocs., 1997—. Staff Good Samaritan Hosp., West Palm Beach, Fla., St. Mary's Hosp., Jackson Meml. Hosp., Miami, Wellington Regional Med. Ctr., West Palm Beach. Contbr. articles to profl. jours. Mem.: AMA, Am. Assn. Cosmetic Surgery, Palm Beach County Med. Soc. (pres. 1996—97), Fla. Med. Assn., Fla. Soc. Otolaryngology, Am. Acad. Cosmetic Surgery (pres. 1999—2000), Am. Acad. Facial Plastic and Reconstructive Surgery, Am. Acad. Otolaryngology. Presbyterian. Office: Palm Beach Inst Cosmetic Surgery & Longevity Ste C303 11211 Prosperity Farms Rd Palm Beach Gardens FL 33410-3401 E-mail: dedo_md@prodigy.net.

DEDONATO, DONALD MICHAEL, obstetrician, gynecologist; b. Bridgeport, Conn., Apr. 25, 1952; s. Michael Anthony and Mary Jane (Zawacki) DeDonato; m. Susan Mary Naulty, June 15, 1974; children: Mark Dominic, David Nicholas. BA in Chemistry cum laude, Coll. Holy Cross, 1974; MD, Loyola U., Maywood, Ill., 1977. Intern Loyola Foster McGaw Hosp., Maywood, Ill., 1977-78; resident Ohio State U. Hosp., Columbus, Ohio, 1978-81; ob-gyn. Ob-Gyn. Assocs., Arlington Heights, Ill., 1981-87, DeDonato, Goodnough and Geittmann, Ob-Gyn., Arlington Heights, 1987-92; pres., CEO N.W. Women's Cons., Arlington Heights, 1993—. Clin. instr. Northwestern U. Med. Ctr., Chgo., 1981—; chmn. dept. ob-gyn. N.W. Cmty. Healthcare, 1998—2000. Mem. alumni bd. Loyola Stritch Sch. of Medicine, Maywood, Ill. Recipient CIBA award. Mem. AMA, Am. Assn. Med. Colls. (Loyola rep.), Chgo. Med. Soc., Ill. State Med. Soc., Am. Bd. Ob-Gyn., Am. Assn. Gyn. Laparoscopists, Garden Camera (pres. 1985-86, 92-93), Phi Beta Kappa, Alpha Sigma Nu. Avocation: photography. Office: NW Womens Cons 1630 W Central Rd Arlington Heights IL 60005-2407

DEDRICK, KENT GENTRY, retired physicist, researcher; b. Watsonville, Calif., Aug. 9, 1923; s. Frederick David and Matilda (Redman) D.; 1 child, Susan Marie. BS in Chemistry and Physics, San Jose (Calif.) State U., 1946; MS in Phys. Scis., Stanford U., 1949, PhD in Theoretical Physics, 1955. Rsch. assoc. U. Mich., Ann Arbor, 1954-55, Stanford U., 1955-62; math. physicist Stanford Rsch. Inst., Menlo Park, Calif., 1962-75; cons. scientist Atty. Gen.'s Office State of Calif., Sacramento, 1976-80; with marine tech. safety dept. State Lands Commn., Sacramento, 1980-81, rsch. specialist, 1981-92; cons. scientist phys. and environ. scis., 1992—. Contbr. articles to profl. jours.; composer instrumental and vocal works, 1978—. Pres. Com. for Green Foothills, Palo Alto, Calif., 1972-74; founding co-chmn. So. Crossing Action Team, San Francisco Bay area, 1970-72, chmn. Bayfront com. Sierra Club, Palo Alto, 1967-72. Mem. Am. Phys. Soc., Am. Geophys. Union, Soc. Wetland Scientists, Sigma Xi. Achievements include co-discovery of mathematical theorem on Lagrange and Taylor series. Home: 1360 Vallejo Way Sacramento CA 95818-3450 E-mail: Kgdedrick@earthlink.net.

DE DUVE, CHRISTIAN RENÉ, chemist, educator; b. Thames-Ditton, Eng., Oct. 2, 1917; s. Alphonse and Madeleine (Pungs) de Duve; m. Janine Herman, Sept. 30, 1943; children: Thierry, Anne, Françoise, Alain. MD, U. Louvain, Belgium, 1941, PhD, 1945, MSc, 1946; PhD (hon.), U. Turin, 1969, U. Leiden, 1970, U. Sherbrooke, 1970, U. Lille, 1973, Cath. U. Santiago, Chile, 1974, U. René Descartes, Paris, 1974, State U. Liege, 1975, State U. Ghent, 1975, Gustavus Adolphus Coll., St. Peter, Minn., 1975, U. Rosario, Argentina, 1975, U. Aix-Marseille II, 1979, U. Keele, 1982, Katholieke U. Leuven, 1984, Karolinska Inst., Stockholm, 1986, U. Montreal, 1992, Rockefeller U., 1997. Lectr. physiol. chemistry faculty medicine Cath. U. Louvain, 1947—51, prof., head dept. physiol. chemistry, 1951—85, emeritus prof., 1985—. Prof. biochem. cytology Rockefeller U., N.Y.C., 1962—74, Andrew W. Mellon prof., 1974—88, prof. emeritus, 1988—; vis. prof. Albert Einstein Coll. Medicine, Bronx, NY, 1961—62, Chaire Francqui State U. Ghent, 1962—63, Free U., Brussels, 1963—64, State U., Liège, 1972—73, Facultés U. Notre-Dame de la Paix, Namur, 1990—91; Mayne guest prof. U. Queensland, Brisbane, Australia, 1972; pres. Internat. Inst. Cellular and Molecular Pathology, Brussels, 1974—91. Mem. editl. bd.: Subcellular Biochemistry, 1971—87, Preparative Biochemistry, 1971—80, Molecular and Cellular Biochemistry, 1973—80. Conseil d'adminstrn. Fonds Nat. de la Rsch. Sci., 1958—61; conseil de gestion Fonds de la Rsch. Sci. Médicale, 1959—61, commn. sci., 1958—61; com. experts Conseil Nat. de la Politique Sci., 1958—61; adv. bd. Ciba Found., 1960—85; adult devel. and aging rsch. and tng. rev. com. Nat. Inst. Child Health and Devel., NIH, 1970—73; adv. com. for med. rsch. WHO, 1974—79; sci. adv. com. Max Planck-Inst. for Immunbiology, 1975—78, Ludwig Inst. Cancer Rsch., 1985—91, Mary Imogene Bassett Rsch. Inst., 1986—90, Clin. Rsch. Inst. Montreal, 1986—; biology adv. com. N.Y. Hall of Sci., 1986—; adv. sci. com. Basel Inst. for Immunology, 1989—93. Recipient Prix des Alumni, 1949, Prix Pfizer, 1957, Prix Francqui, 1960, Prix Quinquennal Belge des Scis. Médicales, Belgium, 1967, Merit award, Gairdner Found. Internat., Can., 1967, Dr. H.P. Heineken prize, The Netherlands, 1973, Nobel prize for physiology or medicine, 1974, Theobald Smith award, Albany Med. Coll., 1981, Jimenez Diaz award, 1985. Fellow: AAAS; mem.: NAS, Soc. Belge Physiology, N.Y. Acad. Scis., Internat. Soc. Cell Biology, European Cell Biology Orgn., European Molecular Biology Orgn., European Assn. Study Diabetes, Koninklyke Acad. voor Geneeskunde, German Acad. der Naturforscher Leopoldina, Soc. Belge Biochim. (pres. 1962—64), Soc. Chimie Biologique, Am. Soc. Cell Biology (coun. mem. 1966—69, E.B. Wilson award 1989), Pontifical Acad. Sci., Am. Soc. Biol. Chemists, Am. Philos. Soc., Biochem. Soc. (Harden award 1978), Am. Chem. Soc., Royal Acad. Belgium, Royal Acad. Medicine, German Assn. for Cell Biology (assoc.), Acad. Europaea (assoc.), Acad. Scis. d'Athénes (assoc.), Acad. Scis. Paris (assoc.), Royal Soc. Can. (assoc.), Royal Soc. London (assoc.), Am. Acad. Arts and Scis. (assoc.), Sigma Xi. Office: Rockefeller U 1230 York Ave New York NY 10021-6399 also: ICP 75 Ave Hippocrate B-1200 Brussels Belgium

DEE, FRANCIS X. lawyer; b. N.Y.C., July 13, 1944; BA, Manhattan Coll., 1966; JD, Cath. U. Am., 1969; LLM in Labor Law, NYU, 1975. Bar: N.Y. 1970, N.J. 1972, U.S. Supreme Ct. 1981. Atty. NLRB, 1969-72; labor counsel Litton Industries, 1972-76; sr. ptnr. Carpenter, Bennett & Morrissey, Newark, 1976—. Fellow Am. Coll. Trial Lawyers (N.J. state chmn. 1999-01), Internat. Acad. Trial Lawyers, Coll. Labor and Employment Lawyers, Am Bar Found.; mem. ABA (litigation sect., com. on devel. law under nat. labor rels. act labor and employment law sect. 1975—), N.Y. State Bar Assn. (litig., labor and employment law sects.), N.J. State Bar Assn. (litig. sect., del. to gen. coun. 1985-92, exec. bd. 1983-92, mgmt. co-chair com. on practice and procedure under nat. labor rels. act 1980-83, sec. labor employment law sect. 1987-89, vice chmn. 1989-91, chmn. 1991-92), Essex County Bar Assn., Trial Attys. of N.J., Fed. Bar Assn. Office: Carpenter Bennett & Morrissey Three Gateway Ctr 100 Mulberry St Fl 17 Newark NJ 07102-4004

DEE, IVAN RICHARD, book publisher; b. Chgo., Mar. 11, 1935; s. Jack Arthur and Jeanette Rose (Melcher) D.; m. Sandra Cohen, June 21, 1959 (div. 1973); m. Phyllis Kirz, Aug. 3, 1977 (div. 1981); m. Barbara Burgess, Apr. 15, 1989; children: Alexander, Sara, Jacob, Gabriel. BJ, U. Mo., 1956, MA, 1957. Pres. Ardivan Press, Macon, Ga., 1960-61; v.p., editor-in-chief Quadrangle Books, Chgo., 1961-72; assoc. editor Chgo. Tribune Book World, Chgo., 1972-73; exec. editor Pubs.-Hall Syndicate, Chgo., 1973-74; editor-in-chief Chicagoan Mag., Chgo., 1974-75; dir. pub. affairs Michael Reese Hosp. and Med. Ctr., Chgo., 1975-89; pres. Ivan R. Dee, Inc., Chgo., 1989—. V.p. South Side Planning Bd., Chgo., 1975-89; commr. Chgo. Baseball League, 1978-00. Lt. (j.g.) USN, 1957-60. Office: Ivan R Dee Inc 1332 N Halsted St Chicago IL 60622-2624

DEE, JAMES PHILLIP, human resources consultant; b. Phila., Nov. 16, 1927; s. Nicholas M. and Lillian (Townsend) D'Addarie; m. Anneliese Zintel, June 30, 1958; 1 child, James P. Jr. AB, U. Fla., 1948; MA, U. Mo., 1950; PhD, Ohio State U., 1957. Asst. prof. Syracuse (N.Y.) U., 1959-63; assoc. prof. Pa. State U., 1963-67; prof. Bowling Green State U., 1967-69; dir. mgmt. devel. Ingersoll-Rand Co., 1969-72; project mgr. Internat. Labor Orgn., Nigeria, 1972-74; chief field ops. tng. br. UN Indstl. Devel. Orgn., Vienna, Austria, 1974-87; mng. dir. Human Resources Devel. Internat., Vienna, 1987—. Contbr. articles to profl. jours. Home and Office: Linke Wienzeile 158/33 A-1060 Vienna Austria

DEE, RONDA, poet, photographer; b. Bronx, NY, May 6, 1943; d. Maurice Dee and Rachel Hoffer. AA, Manhattan CC, NYC, 1974; BS, NYU, 1976. Sec. Book of Knowledge, NYC, 1962—78; private tutor, head start tchr. City Coll., 1962—72; tchr. k-3 N.W. Harlee Elem. Sch., Dallas, 1977; sec. City of Dallas, 1977, 1982; adminstr. sec. Contact Dallas, 1980—82; journalist Brookhaven Sch. News, Dallas, 1987, Richland Chronicle, Dallas, 2003—. Actress Piquaresque Players, Dallas, 1977; founder Day Award for Scholastic Achievement, 1976; artist Ward Nasse Gallery, NYC, 1995; featured reader Barnes & Noble Booksellers, 2000—02. Exhibitions include Brookhaven Coll., Dallas, 1988; photographer (book) Photograph: Walls of New York City, Internat. Lib. of Congress, 2002; author-photographer: Parallex, 2002—03; contbr. poem, to literary jours.; photographer (photography show) 9/11 Meml. Photography Show From The Heart of New York: Wells Fargo Bldg. Plano, Tex., Richland Coll., 2002—03. Mem. Concerned Citizens Pesticide Control, Dallas, 2003—. Recipient Juried Art Contest winner for Party Animal, Brookhaven Coll., 1986. Mem.: Poetry Soc. Am., Sierra Club, Phi Theta Kappa. Avocations: camping, theater, films, exercise. Home: PO Box 823478 Dallas TX 75382-3478

DEE, SCOTT ALLEN, veterinarian, researcher; b. Rochester, Minn., Sept. 27, 1958; s. Richard Walter and Pauline Kay (Anderson) D.; m. Lisa Ann Bell, Oct. 9, 1993; children: Nicholas, Ellen. BA in Biology, Gustavus Adolphus Coll., 1981; MS in Veterinary Microbiology, U. Minn., 1985, DVM, 1987, PhD in Vet. Medicine, 1996. Diplomate Am. Coll. Vet. Microbiologists. Vet., ptnr. Swine Health Ctr., Morris, Minn., 1987-99; assoc. prof. in swine medicine U. Minn. Coll. of Vet. Medicine, 1999—. Mem. adv. bd. Swine Health and Prodn., St. Paul, 1991—, Boehringer-Ingelheim Vetmedica, St. Joseph, Mo., 1992—, Pfizer Animal Health, Lee Summit, Mo., 1994—; spkr. Internat. Porcine Reproductive and Respiratory System Conf., Ploufragan, 1999, Copenhagen, 1995, St. Paul, 1992, Rome, 2003, World Vet Congress, Lyon, 1999; internat. syposium on swine disease eradication del. Conf. Rsch. Workers, St. Paul, 1995-2000, invited spkr., 2001-02; assoc. tenure prof. dept. clin. and population scis. Coll. Vet. Medicine, U. Minn., mem., chair com. on admissions and scholastic standing, 2000—. Author: Veterinary Clinics of North America: Swine Reproduction, 1992, Current Veterinary Therapy III, 1993, Diseases of Swine, 9th edit., 2003, Merck Veterinary Manual, 8th edit., 1997, Current Veterinary Therapy IV, 1998, Diseases of Swine, 1999; splty. editor Compendium Continuing Edn., 1995, Herd Health, 2001; contbr. more than 75 articles to profl. jours. Recipient First Decade award Gustavus Adolphus Coll., 1991, Allen D. Leman Sci. in Practice award, 1996, Disting. Alumni Cert., U. Minn. Coll. Vet. Medicine, 1996, Dist. Alumni Lect., U. Minn. CVM, 1997. Mem. AVMA (Practitioner Rsch. award 1998), Am. Assn. Swine Practitioners (Swine Practitioner of Yr. 1996). Office: U Minn Coll Vet Medicine 385 Animal Sci/Vet Medicine Bldg 1988 Fitch Ave Saint Paul MN 55108-6009

DEEB, LARRY CHARLES, pediatric endocrinologist, epidemiologist; b. Tallahassee, Fla., July 2, 1947; s. Charles Hobeica and Carol Anna (Goll) D.; m. Josephine Marie Sutter, Oct. 7, 1978; children: Michael Larry, Laura Elizabeth. BA, Emory U., 1969, MD, 1973. Diplomate Am. Bd. Pediatrics. Pediatric resident U. Minn., Mpls., 1973-75, endocrine fellow, 1975-77, epidemiologist Ctrs. for Disease Control, Atlanta, 1977-80; pediatric endocrinology Childrens Clinic, Tallahassee, Fla., 1980—. Epidemiologist cons. State of Fla., Tallahassee, 1980—; clin. prof. U. Fla., Gainesville, 1980—; med. dir. Diabetes Ctr. at Tallahassee; epidemiologist NIH, Bethesda, Md., 1988-93; bd. dirs. Fla. Camp for Children and Youth with Diabetes. Mem. editl. bd. practical Diabetes, 1987—, Clin. Diabetes, 1988-92, 96—, Meml. Rey Med. Ctr., 1992—, Diabetes Spectra, 1992; contbr. articles to profl. jours. Lt. comdr. USPHS, 1965-77. Fellow Am. Acad. Pediatrics, Lawson Wilkins Pediatric Endocrinology Soc., Internat. Soc. Pediatric and Adolescent Diabetes, Am. Assn. Clin. Endocrinologists; mem. Am. Diabetes Assn. (Fla. chpt. bd. dirs. 1981—), Internat. Diabetes Fedn. (life), Rotary. Episcopalian. Home: 2307 Trescott Dr Tallahassee FL 32308-0929 Office: Children's Clinic 2416 E Plaza Dr Tallahassee FL 32308-5384 E-mail: lcdeeb@attglobal.net.

DEEB, MARY-JANE, editor, educator; b. Alexandria, Egypt, Aug. 27, 1946; came to U.S., 1973; d. Alix and Stephanie (Klanscek) Anhoury; m. Marius K. Deeb, Sept. 27, 1969; 1 child, Hadi K. BA in Sociology, Am. U., Cairo, 1967, MA in Sociology, 1972; PhD in Internat. Rels., Johns Hopkins U., 1987. Rsch. assoc. Ford Found., Beirut, 1972-73; cons. UN Econ. Commn. for Western Asia, Beirut, 1980, UNICEF, Beirut, 1980-81; project dir. U.S. AID, Beirut, 1982-83;

asst. professorial lectr. George Washington U., Washington, 1988-89, 93, 97, Georgetown U., Washington, 1991, 94; asst. prof. Am. U., Washington, 1989-94, adj. assoc. prof., 1994—; editor Mid. East Jour., Washington, 1995-98; Arab world area specialist Libr. of Congress, Washington, 1998—. External reviewer for grant proposals U.S. Inst. Peace, Washington, 1991, 92, 97; testified on subcom. on Africa fgn. rels. com. U.S. Ho. of Reps., 1991, 92, 98; testified before the select com. on intelligence, U.S. Senate, 1996; testified on fgn. rels. com. U.S. Senate, 1997, UN Monitor of Algerian legislative elections, 1997; dir. Algeria program Corp. Coun. on Africa. Author: Libya Since the Revolution, 1982, Libya's Foreign Policy, 1991; co-editor: Hasib Sabbagh from Palestinian Refugee to Citizen of the World, 1996, Cocktails and Murder on the Potomac, 2001; novel rev. editor Internat. Jour. Mid.-East Studies, 1989-94; contbr. articles, revs. to profl. jours. and encys., and chpts. to books; interviewed on numerous TV programs, including CBS Evening News, ABC News, NBC Nightly News, CNN Headline News, Fox Morning News, PBS, and in news publs., including N.Y. Times, Washington Post, Time mag., L.A. Times, The Christian Sci. Monitor, U.S.A. Today, Boston Globe, Tokyo Shimbum, Yomouri, others. Mem. UN Assn., Am. Polit. Sci. Assn., Internat. Studies Assn., Mid. East Studies Assn. N.Am., Women's Caucus for Polit. Sci., Am.-Tunisian Assn. (exec. bd. 1989—), Hannibal Club (founding mem. 1999), World Affairs Coun., Women in Fgn. Policy. Roman Catholic. Office: Libr Congress African and Middle Ea Divsn Jefferson Bldg 101 Independence Ave SE Washington DC 20540-0002 E-mail: mdee@loc.gov.

DEEB, RULA ANSELMO, environmental engineer; d. Anselmo Deeb and Sana Sadaka; m. Marwan Nader, Aug. 16, 1997. BS, Warren Wilson Coll., Asheville, N.C., 1991; MS, U. Calif., Berkeley, 1994, PhD, 1999. Instr., extension program U. Calif., Berkeley, Calif., 1999—; lectr. Stanford U., Menlo Park, Calif., 1999—2000; postdoctoral rschr. U. Calif., Berkeley, Calif., 1999—2000; sr. project engr. Malcolm Pirnie, Inc., Emeryville, Calif., 2000—. Mem.: Am. Geophys. Union, Assn. Environ. Engring. and Sci. Profs., Nat. Ground Water Assn., Water Environment Fedn., Groundwater Resources Assn. Calif. Home: 512 Matisse Ct Walnut Creek CA 94597 Office: Malcolm Pirnie Inc 2000 Powell St Suite 1180 Emeryville CA 94608 Office Fax: 510-596-8855. Personal E-mail: ruladeeb@hotmail.com. E-mail: rdeeb@pirnie.com.

DEEDS, ROBERT CREIGH, lawyer, state legislator; b. Richmond, Va., Jan. 4, 1958; s. Robert Livingston Deeds Jr. and Emma Lewis (Tyree) Hicklin; m. Pamela Kay Miller, Feb. 10, 1981; children: Amanda Jane, Rebecca Lewis, Austin Creigh, Susannah Kemper. BA, Concord Coll., Athens, W.Va., 1980; JD, Wake Forest U., 1984. Bar: Va. 1984, U.S. Dist. Ct. (we. dist.) Va. 1988. Assoc. Carter, Craig & Bass, P.C., Danville, Va., 1984-85, John C. Singleton, Warm Springs, Va., 1985-87; ptnr. Singleton & Deeds, Warm Springs, Va., 1988-99; mem. Va. Ho. of Dels., 1992—2001, Va. Senate, 2001—; sole practice R. Creigh Deeds, P.C., Hot Springs, Va., 2000—. Commonwealth atty. Bath County, Va., 1988-92; chmn. Dem. Caucus, Va. Ho. Dels., 2000-01. Bd. dirs. Va. Mus. Frontier Culture. Mem. Va. State Bar, Allegheny-Bath Bar Assn., Va. Trial Lawyers Assn., Va. Assn. Commonwealth's Attys. (bd. dirs. 1989-91). Democrat. Presbyterian. Avocation: fishing. Office: R Creigh Deeds PC Drawer D Hot Springs VA 24445 E-mail: rcdeeds@tds.net.

DEEDS, WILLIAM CHARLES, university dean, executive; b. Gt. Bend, Kans., Jan. 4, 1951; s. Charles Bruce and Gertrude Belle Deeds; m. Pamla Kay Hoadley, May 27, 1978; children: Charles Hoadley, MacKenzie Walter. BA, Wichita State U., 1974; MS, Kans. State U., 1977, PhD, 1979. Rsch. psychologist U.S. Army Rsch. Inst., Alexandria, Va., 1979-81; dir. Human Resources Certificate program Moravian Coll., Bethlehem, Pa., 1981-83, prof. psychology, 1981-2000, chmn. dept. psychology, 1989-90, assoc. dean acad. affairs, 1990-98, dean acad. affairs, 1998-2000; v.p. acad. affairs, dean of coll. Morningside Coll., Sioux City, Iowa, 2000—. Contbr. articles to profl. jours. Recipient Lindback award Lindback Found., 1988; grantee NIMH, 1974-78. Mem. Am. Psychol. Soc., Midwestern Psychol. Assn., Soc. Indsl. and Orgnl. Psychology, Am. Conf. Acad. Deans, Lions, Psi Chi. Home: 4705 Old Lakeport Rd Sioux City IA 51106 Office: Morningside Coll 1501 Morningside Ave Sioux City IA 51106 E-mail: deeds@morningside.edu.

DEEG, EMIL WOLFGANG, manufacturing company executive, physicist; b. Selb, Germany, Sept. 20, 1926; came to U.S., 1967, naturalized, 1975; s. Fritz and Trina (Poehlmann) D.; m. Hedwig M.S. Kempf, Aug. 25, 1953; children: Wolfgang, Martin, Bernhard, Renate. Dipl. Physiker, U. Wuerzburg, 1954, Dr. rer. nat., 1956. Rsch. asst. Max Planck Inst., Wuerzburg, 1954-59; mem. tech. staff Bell Telephone Labs., Allentown, Pa., 1959-60; rsch. assoc. Jenaer Glaswerk Schott U. Gen., Mainz, Germany, 1960, dir. rsch., 1960-65; assoc. prof. physics and solid state sci. Am. U., Cairo, 1965-67; mgr. ceramic rsch. Am. Optical Corp., Southbridge, Mass., 1967-71, mgr. materials rsch., 1971-73, dir. process and materials rsch., 1973-75, dir. inorganic materials R&D, 1975-77, tech. adviser, 1977-78; sr. scientist Anchor Hocking Corp., Lancaster, Ohio, 1978-79, mgr. materials R&D, 1979-80; mgr. glass tech. Bausch & Lomb, Rochester, N.Y., 1980-82; mgr. glass and fiber devel. Mead Office Sys., Richardson, Tex., 1982-84; project mgr. AMP, Inc., Harrisburg, Pa., 1984-92. Cons., Lemoyne, Pa., 1992-2002; mem. Internat. Commn. on Glass, 1963-81, Internat. Commn. for Optics, 1964-66; cons. NASA Spacelab Program, 1971-78; expert witness on glass product patent litigation German Patent Office, 1978-81. Author: (with H. Richter) Glas im Laboratorium, 1966; editor AMP Jour. Tech., 1993-98; patentee in field; contbr. chpts. to books, articles to profl. jours. Pres. PTA, Woodstock, Conn., 1970-71; committeeman Mohegan coun. Boy Scouts Am., 1967-73; trustee Woodstock Acad., 1971-78; overseer Old Sturbridge Village, Inc., 1972-81; chmn. Optical Info. Ctr., Southbridge, 1976-77. With German Army, 1944-45. Fellow Am. Ceramic Soc. (emeritus); mem. Optical Soc. Am. (emeritus), Nat. Inst. Ceramic Engrs., Internat. Tech. Inst. (inductee Hall of Fame for Engring., Sci. and Tech. 1988), Engrs. Soc. Pa. (dir. 1996-98), Lions (pres. Woodstock chpt. 1975, zone chmn. dist. 23 C, Lions Internat. 1976-78). Home and Office: 501 Ohio Ave Lemoyne PA 17043-1525 E-mail: ewdeeg@att.net.

DEEGAN, JOHN, JR., academic administrator, researcher; b. Elizabeth, N.J., Nov. 18, 1944; s. John and Margaret (Pignataro) D.; m. Anita Hope Rochelle, Dec. 19, 1964; children: Michael J., Matthew B. Student, Monmouth Coll., West Long Branch, N.J., 1962-64; BS, Evangel Coll., Springfield, Mo., 1967; MA, U. Mich., 1969, PhD, 1972. Asst. prof. Rice U., Houston, 1972-75, U. Rochester, N.Y., 1975-80, assoc. prof., 1980; spl. asst. to dep. adminstr. EPA, Washington, 1980; dir. Love Canal Project, 1980-82; assoc. dean Sch. Pub. Health U. Ill., Chgo., 1982-86, acting dean, 1983-85; prof. U. No. Iowa, Cedar Falls, 1986-89, dean Coll. Social and Behavioral Scis., 1986-89; provost, v.p. acad. affairs, prof. U. So. Maine, Portland, 1989-94; dean coll., v.p. acad. affairs, prof. Westminster Coll., New Wilmington, Pa., 1994—2002; pres., prof. St. Andrews Presbyn. Coll., Laurinburg, NC, 2002—. Cons. EPA, 1983-86; trustee Ill. Cancer Coun., 1983-86; bd. dirs. Leopold Ctr. for Sustainable Agr. State of Iowa, 1987-89. Contbr. articles to sci. jours. Recipient EPA Bronze medal award, 1982; U. Rochester fellow in preventive medicine, 1979, Acad. Adminstrn. fellow Am. Coun. on Edn., 1986-87. Mem. AAAS, APHA, Am. Chem. Soc., Sigma Xi, Delta Omega. Democrat. Presbyterian. Avocations: fishing, golfing. Office: Office of the President St Andrews Presbyn Coll Laurinburg NC 28352

DEEGAN, MARY JO, sociology educator; b. Chgo., Nov. 27, 1946; d. William James and Ida May (Scott) Deegan; life ptnr. Michael Ray Hill. AS, Lake Mich. Coll., 1966; BS, Western Mich. U., 1969, MA, 1973; PhD, U. Chgo., 1975. Asst. prof. U. Nebr., Lincoln, 1975-80, assoc. prof., 1980-89, prof., 1989—. Med. trainee U. Chgo. Ctr. for Health Adminstrn., 1972-75; grad. asst. Western Mich. U., 1969-71; del. Conf. on Directions in Health Econs., New Orleans, 1972. Author: Jane Addams and Men of the Chicago School, 1892-1918, 1988 (Choice award, 1989), American Ritual Dramas, 1989, Race, Hull House, and the University of Chicago, 2002; editor: Women in Sociology, 1991, American Ritual Tapestry, 1998, Play, School and Society, 1999, Essays on Social Psychology, 2001, The New Woman of Color, 2002, Women at the Hague, 2003; co-editor: Women and Disability, 1985, Women and Symbolic Interaction, 1987, Feminist Ethics in Social Research, 1989, With Her in Ourland, 1997; co-editor: (with C.P. Gilman) The Dress of Women, 2002; co-editor: On Art, Labor, and Religion, 2003; series editor Women & Sociological Theory, 2001; contbr. articles to profl. jours. Mem.: Harriet Martineau Sociol. Soc., Internat. Sociol. Assn., Am. Sociol. Assn. (Disting. Scholarly Career award in history of sociology 2002). Office: Dept Sociology 711 Oldfather Hall U Nebraska Lincoln NE 68588-0324

DEEKLE, PETER VAN, library director; b. N.Y.C., May 30, 1946; s. William Cleveland and Marian Elizabeth (Maynard) D.; m. Barbara Eugenia Maier, Aug. 8, 1970; children: Lee Christina, Glenna. BA in English, U. Pa., 1968; MS in Libr. and Info. Sci., Drexel U., 1973; DEd, Temple U., 1987. Asst. extension svcs. libr. Montgomery County/Norristown (Pa.) Pub. Libr., 1971-73; assoc. dir. libr. Allegany Community Coll., Cumberland, Md., 1973-77; head nonprint media svcs. U. Md. Librs., College Park, 1977-81; asst. dean acad. affairs, chmn. instrl. resources div. Harrisburg Area Community Coll., 1981-88; libr., dir. honors program Susquehanna U., Selinsgrove, Pa., 1988-93; dir. Madeleine Clark Wallace Libr., Wheaton Coll., Norton, Mass., 1993-2000; dean libr. svcs., dir. honors program Roger Williams U., Bristol, R.I., 2000—. Chair com. interlibr. cooperation-comprehensive planning coun. State Libr. Pa., 1982-83; chair Consortium R.I. Acad. Rsch. Libr., 2003—. Vol., English tchr. Peace Corps, Iran, 1968-70; mem. preservation adv. com. Mass. Bd. Libr. Commn., 1999-2000; mem. tchg. and learning task force Mid. States Assn. Colls. and Schs., 1998-99. Mem. ALA, Assn. Coll. and Rsch. Librs., Mid. State Assn. Colls. and Schs. (cons. commn. higher edn. accreditation team visits), New Eng. Assn. Schs. and Colls. (cons. accreditation team visits), Pa. Libr. Assn. (pres. 1990-91), Md. Assn. Cmty. and Jr. Colls. (chair learning resources divsn. 1977, mem. Mass. master plan for libraries 1993-95, chair Southeast Mass. coop. libraries 1995-97, co-chair LAMA fund raising/fund fare exch. com. 1997-99). Office: Roger Williams U One Old Ferry Rd Bristol RI 02809

DEEL, FRANCES QUINN, retired librarian; b. Pottsville, Pa., Mar. 9, 1939; d. Charles Joseph and Carrie Miriam (Ketner) Q.; m. Ronald Eugene Deel, Feb. 5, 1983. BS, Millersville State Coll., 1960; M.L.S., Rutgers U., 1964; M.P.A., U. West Fla., 1981. Post librarian U.S. Army Armor (Desert Tng. Ctr.), Ft. Irwin, Calif., 1964-66; staff librarian Mil. Dist. of Washington, 1966-67; supervisory librarian 1st Logistical Command, APO San Francisco, 1967-68; tech. process specialist Naval Edn. and Tng. Supervisory Command, Washington, 1968-77, Pensacola, Fla., 1968-77; chief tech. library USAF Armament Lab., Eglin AFB, Fla., 1977-81; dir. command libraries Air Force Systems Command (Andrews AFB), Washington, 1981-92; mem. exec. adv. council Fed. Library and Info. Network, Washington, 1985-86, libr. Air Force Dist. of Washington (Bolling AFB), Washington, 1992-94; dir. Navy Dept. Libr., Washington, 1994; ret., 1994. Mem. ALA (dir.-at-large armed forces libraries sect. Chgo. 1983-86), Spl. Libraries Assn., D.C. Library Assn. Roman Catholic. Home: 99 Country Club Dr W Destin FL 32541-4433

DEELY, MAUREEN CECELIA, community health nurse; b. Washington, Feb. 8, 1960; d. Thomas Michael and Felice R. (Alvarez) Deely. AA, Montgomery Coll., 1984. Staff RN Phi Szabo PG Count/Detention Ctr., Upper Marlboro, Md., 1984-85, Sands Nursing Svcs. Inc., Silver Spring, Md., 1985-86, Windsor HomeCare Inc./Alliance Against AIDS, Washington, 1988-89; community health nurse Montgomery County Health Dept., Silver Spring, 1989—. Mem. adv. com. cmty. programs clin. rsch. Washington Regional AIDS Program, 1990—; chmn. adv. bd. Women's Interagency HIC Study Nat. Cmty., 1997—2000; mem. AIDS adv. com. Montgomery Hospice Soc., 1993; panelist, field reviewer develop treatment improvement protocol Ctr. Substance Abuse Treatment, 1993; mem. cmty. adv. bd. Nat. Women's Interagency HIV Study, 1993; alt. rep. adv. bd. Washington Area Consortium. Nat. WIHS, 1994, nat. rep.; rep., cmty. adv. bd. Nat. Cmty. Adv. Bd. Nat. WIHS; spkr. Bur. NAPWA-Nat. Assn. People with AIDS. Mem. nat. adv. bd. rev. and synthesis HIV/AIDS related consumer/client level evaluations Health Resources Svcs. Adminstrn.; recuperative care coord. homeless, 1998; co-chair Suburban Md. HIV Care Consortium, 1998; mem. health care and corrections task force and panel Met. Washington Coun. Govts.; mem. Healthcare for Homeless Montgomery County, Md., 1999; v.p., sec. Suburban Md. HIV/AIDS Alliance, 1996, pres., 1997—98; mem. Cmty. Adv. Bd. Food and Friends, 1997, Suburban Md. HIV Prevention Regional Work Group, 1997; bd. dirs. PWA coms. Md., Inc., 1997—98. Recipient Cheryl D. Friedman award, Montgomery County HHS, 1995, Outstanding Svc. award, Montgomery County Dept. Correction and Rehab., 1996, Carol Johnson Meml. Cmty. Svc. award, 2001. Mem.: Am. Pain Soc.

DEEM, GEORGE, artist; b. Vincennes, Ind., Aug. 18, 1932; s. George C. and Laura (Bobe) D. Student, Vincennes U., 1951-52; BFA, Sch. Art Inst. Chgo., 1958. Instr. painting Sch. Visual Arts, N.Y.C., 1965-66, Leicester (Eng.) Coll. Art and Design, 1966-67, U. Pa., 1968; artist in residence Evansville (Ind.) Mus. Arts and Scis., 1979; vis. artist Ill. State U., Normal, 1982, Branson Sch., Ross, Calif., 1995. Sec. exec. com. MacDowell Colony Fellows, 1982-87. One man shows Allan Stone Gallery, N.Y.C., 1963, 64, 65, 66, 68, 69, 75, 77, Sneed Gallery, Rockford, Ill., 1968, 69, 72, 76, 80, Merida Gallery, Louisville, 1966, 68, 69, 78, 83, Indpls. Mus. Art, 1974, Witte Meml. Mus., San Antonio, 1975, Evansville (Ind.) Mus. Arts and Sci., 1979, Greenberg Gallery, St. Louis, 1979, On View Downtown Gallery, Indpls., 1986, Evansville (Ind.) Mus. Arts and Sci., 1993, Harn Mus. Art, U. Fla., Gainesville, 1993, Mitchell Mus. Art, Mt. Vernon, Ill., 1993, Polk Mus. Art, Lakeland, Fla., 1994, Ind. State Mus., Indpls., 1994, Eckert Fine Art Gallery, Indpls., 1994, Capricorn Gallery, Bethesda, Md., 1994, Wichita (Kans.) Ctr. for Arts, 1994, Nancy Hoffman Gallery, N.Y.C., 2000, Mus. Arts and Sci., Evansville, Ind., 2001, Pavel Zoubok Gallery, N.Y.C., 2002; group shows include Whitney Mus. Am. Art, N.Y.C., 1978, Pa. Acad. Fine Arts, 1981, Allentown (Pa.) Art Mus., 1983, Ft. Wayne (Ind.) Mus. Art, 1984, Nancy Hoffman Gallery, N.Y.C., 1985, 86, 87, 88, 89, 90, 91, 94, 98, Flint (Mich.) Inst. Arts, 1993, Nassau County Mus. of Art, Roslyn Harbor, N.Y., 1994; Museum of Art, U. of Oregon, Eugene, 1996, Pavel Zoubok/Mary Delahoyd Gallery, N.Y.C., 1998, Nassau County Mus. of Art, Roslyn Harbor, N.Y., 2000, Allan Stone Gallery, N.Y.C., 2000, Miami U. Art Mus., Oxford, Ohio, 2002, Herbert F. Johnson Mus. Art, Ithaca, N.Y., 2002; represented in permanent collections Indpls. Mus. Art, Evansville Mus. Arts and Sci., Stiftung Ludwig, Aachen, Germany, Vassar Coll. Art Gallery, Mus. Fine Arts, Houston, Miami U. Art Mus., Oxford, Ohio, Weatherspoon Art Gallery U. N.C., Greensboro, Chase Manhattan Bank, N.Y.C., Cleary Gottlieb Steen & Hamilton, N.Y.C., 1st Nat. Bank Boston, Ariz. State U. Art Mus., Tempe, Hallmark Cards, Inc., Kansas City, Mo., State Russian Mus., St. Petersburg, Mus. of Modern Art, San Francisco, Am. Gen. Fin., Inc., Evansville, Ind., Wellington Mgmt. Co., Boston; commns. Nutter, McLennen & Fish, Boston, 1988, Paul, Weiss, Rifkind, N.Y., 1989, Mirage Resorts, 1998; subject of video profile, 1993 ; Art School: An Homage To The Masters, paintings by George Deem, introduction by Irene McManus, Thames and Hudson, LTD., London, 1993, Chronicle Books, San Francisco, 1993; contbr. articles to profl. jours. Served with U.S. Army, 1953-55. Home and Office: 10 W 18th St New York NY 10011-4606

DEEMER, ALBERT EARL, social worker, director; b. USSR, Nov. 10, 1912; came to U.S., 1921; s. Barney and Rose Deemer; m. Estelle Soffen, June 28, 1940; 1 child, Lee Bruce. AB, U. Pitts., 1934, MSW, 1937. Caseworker Juvenile Ct., Pitts., 1936-38; caseworker, supr., asst. dir. Jewish Children's Bur., Chgo., 1938-48; regional dir. Joint Distbn. Com. Midwest, N.Y.C., 1948-50; case cons. Jewish Family Svc., Kansas City, Mo., 1950-53; exec. dir. Jewish Family Svc. Assn., Buffalo, 1953-87, exec. dir. emeritus, 1987-90, ret., 1990. Cons. Erie County Dept. Mental Health, Buffalo, 1962-64; peer reviewer Coun. Accreditation, Family & Children's Assn., N.Y.C., 1983-86. Mem. Mayor's Com. Alcoholism, Buffalo, 1965; arbitrator Dispute Settlement Ctr. Better Bus. Bur., Buffalo, 1987—; bd. dirs. Rsch. and Planning Coun., 1972—80, Family SVc. N.Am.; pres. Meals on Wheels Buffalo and Erie Counties, 1979—81, bd. dirs., 1979-86; bd. dirs., pres. Found. for Crisis Svc., 1988; treas. Crisis Svcs., Buffalo, 1986—88, bd. dirs., 1988; vol. Sr. Ctr. Town of Tonawanda, Buffalo, 2001—. 2d lt. U.S. Army, 1943—45. Recipient Outstanding Vol. Svc. award Meals on Wheels Buffalo, 1981, statuette Found. for Crisis SVcs., 1988. Mem. NASW (cert., editor newsletter N.Y. chpt., western div. 1991—, chair N.Y. State chpt. western div., western N.Y. div. Lifetime Achievement award 1993, N.Y. state chpt., 1993), Nat. Assn. Vocat. Svcs. (bd. dirs. 1970-80), Jewish War Veterans U.S.A. Avocations: golfing, bridge, securities studies.

DEEN, HUGH GORDON, physician, neurological surgeon; b. Columbus, Ga., Dec. 10, 1953; s. Hugh Gordon, Sr. Deen and Martha (Holliday) Ecker; m. Ruth Elaine Boyd, Aug. 20, 1977; children: Joseph, Ruth. SB in Chemistry, MIT, 1974; MD, U. South Ala., Mobile, 1978. Diplomate Am. Bd. Neurol. Surgery. Intern U.S. Naval Hosp., Portsmouth, Va., 1978—79, attending neurosurgeon San Diego, 1984—88; resident Mayo Clinic, 1979—84, cons., chair dept. neurol. surgery, 1988—. Assoc. prof. Mayo Med. Sch., Rochester, Minn., 1996—. Mem. editl. bd. Mayo Clinic Procs., 1996-, Practical Revs. in Neurosurgery; contbr. numerous articles to profl. jours. Regional chair MIT ednl. coun. MIT, 1996—, alumni rep., 1991—. Capt. U.S. Navy, 1974—. Fellow ACS; mem. Am. Assn. Neurol. Surgeons, Congress Neurol. Surgeons, N.Am. Spine Soc., Soc. Neurochirurgie de Langue Francaise, Alpha Omega Alpha, Neurosurgical Soc. Am. Episcopalian. Office: Mayo Clinic Jacksonville 4500 San Pablo Rd Jacksonville FL 32224

DEEN, JAMES ROBERT, nuclear engineer; b. Dallas, Mar. 1, 1944; s. James Young and Dorothy Faye Deen; m. Katy James Pavlidou, Aug. 14, 1971; children: Dorothy, Christina, David, Joshua, Priscilla, Joy. B in Engring. Sci., U. Tex., 1966, BSME, 1970, PhD, 1973. Registered profl. engr., Calif. Sr. engr. Gen. Electric, San Jose, Calif., 1972-76; asst. nuclear engr. Argonne (Ill.) Nat. Lab, 1976-81, nuclear engr., 1981—. Mem. Am. Nuclear Soc. Republican. Mem. Evang. Free Ch. Avocation: classical music instrn. Home: 593 Cambridge Way Bolingbrook IL 60440-1047 Office: Argonne Nat Lab 9700 Cass Ave Lemont IL 60439-4803

DEERFIELD, DAVID WILEY, II, chemist; b. Topeka, Kans., Sept. 1, 1955; BS in Chemistry, U. Kans., 1977; PhD of Chemistry, U. Minn., 1984. Postdoctoral rsch. assoc. U. N.C., Chapel Hill, 1984-88; sci. specialist Pitts. Supercomputing Ctr., 1988—, coord. biomed. application group, 1988—, mgr., 1988—, dir. biomedical initiative, 1988—. Mem. AAAS, Am. Chem. Soc., Assn. Computing Machinery, N.Y. Acad. Scis. Avocation: photography. Office: Pittsburgh Supercomputing 4400 5th Ave Pittsburgh PA 15213-2617

DEERING, ALLAN BROOKS, retired soft drink company executive; b. Chappaqua, N.Y., Apr. 1, 1934; s. Clarence and Muriel (Lee) D.; m. Carol Ann Werle, Apr. 14, 1957; children: Peter Brooks, Andrew Werle. BA, Columbia U., 1956. Systems analyst IBM Corp., White Plains, N.Y., 1956-58; EDP mgr. R.H. Donnelly Corp., N.Y.C., 1958-68; dir. systems and data processing W.R. Grace & Co., N.Y.C., 1968-76, asst. v.p., 1975; dir. info. systems SCM Corp., N.Y.C., 1976-81; dir. mgmt. info. svcs. Pepsi Co., N.Y.C., 1981-86, v.p. mgmt. info. svcs., 1986—2000. Mem. Mayor's Industry Adv. Bd. for Data Processing, N.Y.C., 1978, adv. bd. Pace U. Sch. Computer Sci., Omicron. Mem. Data Processing Mgmt. Assn., Soc. Mgmt. Info. Systems (bd. dirs.), N.Y. Computer Execs. Roundtable, Grocery Mfrs. Am. (chmn. systems com.), Rocky Point Club, Old Greenwich Yacht Club, Milbrook Club. Home: 3 Perkley Ln Riverside CT 06878-2309 E-mail: abdeering@snet.net.

DEERING, ANNE-LISE, artist, retired real estate salesperson; b. Oslo, June 20, 1935; d. Reidar Ingolf Dahlsrud and Dagny Elfrida (Grönneberg) Nilsen; m. Reginald Atwell Deering, Oct. 20, 1956 (div. July 1992); children: Eric, Mark, Linda. Norman. BA in Art, Pa. State U., 1977, postgrad., 1990—91. Rsch. asst. Yale U., New Haven, 1955-57; ceramic artist/potter State College, Pa., 1977-98. Real estate agt. Coldwell Banker Univ. Realty, State College, 1992-93, Century 21 Corman Assocs., State College, 1993-99; artist mem. Art Alliance Ctrl. Pa., 1977-2000. Editor Ctrl. Pa. Guild of Craftsmen newsletter, 1994; exhibited in group shows at Newark Mus., 1990, Montain Top Gallery, Cresson, Pa., 1998, Pen and Brush Gallery, N.Y.C., 1998, 99, 2000, 01, Queensborough C.C., 2000, FIDEM, Weimar, Germany, 2000, FIDEM, Paris, 2002, ANA, Colorado Springs, 2001, Penn State U., 2002, Wroclav, Poland, 2002, AMSA mems. exhibit, Nat. Ornamental Metal Mus., Memphis, 2003. Mem. visual arts adv. com. Ctrl. Pa. Festival of Arts, 1989-93, co-chair, 1991-93, jury and rules co-chmn. for sidewalk sales com., 1993-97. Mem.: Internat. Fedn. Medal Art, Wash. Potters Assn. (bd. dirs. 2000—), Art Alliance Ctrl. Pa. (chair mems. juried exhibit 1978, bd. dirs. 1978—79, participant Gallery Shop 1989—99, steering com. 1994—97), Am. Medallic Sculpture Assn. (newsletter editor 2000—03, co-chmn. Hands Across the Sea Am./Polish Medals Exhibit 2001—02, sec. 2001—), Am. Mus. Women in Arts (charter), Ctrl. Pa. Guild Craftsmen (pres. 1986—87, 1993—94), Pa. Guild Craftsmen (bd. dirs. 1980—83, v.p. 1985, bd. dirs. 1985—98, v.p. 1991, 1992, coord., chair ann. Christmas sale). Avocations: photography, music, sailing, gardening, wine making. Home: 24229 92nd Ave W Edmonds WA 98020-6503 E-mail: superpotr@aol.com.

DEERING, FRED ARTHUR, retired insurance company executive; b. Winfield, Kans., Jan. 12, 1928; s. Frederick A. and Lucile (Phillips) D.; m. Isabell Staufenberg, June 14, 1949; m. Elizabeth Kimball MacMillan, Apr. 12, 1979; children: Anne Deering Buchanan, Kate. BS, LLD, U. Colo., 1951; LHD (hon.), Loretto Heights Coll., 1984. Bar: Colo. 1951. Assoc. firm Gorsuch, Kirgis, Campbell, Walker & Grover, Denver, Denver, 1951-54; ptnr. Gorsuch, Kirgis, Campbell, Walker & Grover, Denver, 1954-62; v.p., gen. counsel Security Life of Denver, 1962-66, pres., CEO, 1966-82, chmn., CEO, 1982-91, chmn., 1991-93; chmn. exec. com., 1994-95; bd. dirs. ING Am. Ins. Holdings, Inc., 1991—2000; chmn., CEO, dir. Midwestern United Life Ins. Co., 1983-89, Halifax Life Ins. Co., Toronto, 1985-88; vice-chmn. bd. Invesco Funds Group, 1990—2003, chmn., 1968-90. Instr. Am. Inst. Banking, 1953-57; guest lectr. Colo. Sch. Law, 1958-59. Editor-in-chief Rocky Mountain Law Rev. Trustee Loretto Heights Coll., 1968-88, chmn. bd. dirs., 1968-84, chmn. emeritus, 1984-88; bd. dirs. Wallace Village for Children, 1968-78, Met. United Fund, 1969-71, Porter Hosp., 1970-79, U. Colo. Found., 1972-75; mem. adv. com. Met. Assn. for Retarded Children, Denver, 1970-71, Denver Rsch. Inst., 1972-76; trustee Huebner Found., 1980-85, St. Mary's Acad., Denver, 1989-95, 97—; bd. dirs. Inst. Internat. Edn., Denver, 1986-92, Nat. Western Stock Show, 1990-96, Invesco, Global Health Scis. Fund, Ptnrs. for Health, Fin. Designs Ltd. With U.S. Army, 1946-47. Named Colo. Businessman of Yr. Alpha Kappa Psi, 1977, Disting. Law Alumnus, U. Colo., 1982. Mem. ABA, Colo. Bar Assn., Denver Bar Assn., Am. Judicature Soc., Colo. Life Conf., Life Office Mgmt. Assn. (bd. dirs. 1977-81, 82-85, chmn. 1983-84), Denver C. of C., Met. Denver Execs. Club (pres. 1970-71), Cherry Hills Country Club (bd. dirs. 1973-76, pres. 1975-76), Wigwam Club, Bang-a-Way Club, The Oaks Country Club, Univ. Club. Order of Coif, Sigma Alpha Epsilon. *My life has been influenced more by a handful of people than by events or any other factors. Therefore, I am inclined to think that the lives of others may be more important than anything else in shaping our own careers and destinies.*

DEERING, RONALD FRANKLIN, librarian, minister; b. Paxton, Ill., Oct. 6, 1929; s. Minor Franklin and Grace Gilmour (Perkins) D.; m. Geraldine Gibbons, June 27, 1953 (dec. Jan. 1965); m. Edith Ann Proctor, June 12, 1966; children: Mark David, Daniel Timothy. BA summa cum laude, Georgetown (Ky.) Coll., 1951; MDiv, So. Bapt. Theol. Sem., 1955, PhD, 1962; MLS, Columbia U., 1967. Ordained to ministry So. Bapt. Conv., 1950. Pastor 1st Hilltop Bapt. Ch., North College Hill, Ohio, 1949-50; instr. in Bible Georgeton (Ky.) Coll., 1950-51; pastor Blue River Bapt. Ch., Salem, Ind., 1954-59; instr. Greek, N.T. So. Bapt. Theol. Sem., Louisville, 1958-61, theol. libr., 1962-95, assoc. v.p. for acad. resources, 1995—. Chmn. So. Bapt. Hist. Commn., Nashville, 1987-90; interim pastor 31 chs. in Ind., Ky., 1961-90; del. Bapt. World Alliance, Miami, Fla., Toronto, Ont., Can., L.A., 1965, 80, 85. Contbr. articles to profl. jours. Eli Lilly Theol. Librarianship grantee, 1967. Mem. AAUP, ALA, Southeastern Libr. Assn., Am. Theol. Libr. Assn. (nat. pres. 1984-85), Ky. Libr. Assn., Phi Alpha Theta, Beta Phi Mu, Sigma Tau Delta. Democrat. Home: 3111 Dunlieth Ct Louisville KY 40241-2937 E-mail: rondeering@bellsouth.net.

DEERING, THOMAS PHILLIPS, retired lawyer; b. Winfield, Kans., Feb. 15, 1929; s. Frederick Arthur and Lucile (Phillips) D.; m. Marilyn Marie Anderson, Sept. 6, 1952; children: Thomas P. Jr., Robert E., Paul A. BS, U. Colo., 1951, LLB, 1956. Bar: Oreg. 1956, Colo. 1956, U.S. Dist. Ct. Oreg. 1956. Assoc. Hart Spencer McCulloch Rockwood & Davies (now Stoel Rives), Portland, Oreg., 1956-62; ptnr. Stoel Rives LLP, Portland, 1962—99; ret., 1999. Mem. Western Pension and Benefits Conf., 1989—; mem. faculty Am. Law Inst.-ABA, 1985-96. Co-author: Tax Reform Act of 1986, 1987. Bd. dirs. Girl Scouts Columbia River Coun., Portland, 1961-70; trustee, moderator First Unitarian Ch., Portland, 1967-70; trustee, pres. Catlin Gabel Sch., Portland, 1970-76; bd. dirs., v.p. ACLU, Portland, 1966-71, 73-80; chmn. Multnomah County Task Force on Edgefield Manor, Portland, 1972-75; bd. dirs., treas. Portland Art Mus., Contemporary Arts Coun., 1986-88; mem. City County Task Fore on Svc. Evaluation, Portland, 1982-85, Citizen's Adv. Com. West Side Corridor Project, Portland, 1988-93; bd. govs. Pacific N.W. Coll. Art, 1991-2000, 2002-, chair,

1996-2000, chair presdl. search com. 2002-2003; mem. collections com. Portland Art Mus., 1992-96; trustee Oreg. Coll. Art and Craft Endowment, Portland, 1991-97. With U.S. Army, 1952-54. Recipient Disting. Mem. award Western Pension and Benefits Conf., 1999. Fellow Am. Coll. Tax Coun., Am Coll. Benefits Counsel (emeritus); mem. ABA (tax sect., EB com. 1989-2000), City Club of Portland (bd. govs. 1968-70, 2000—). Democrat. Avocations: hiking, skiing, sailing, reading. Home: 5235 SW Burton Dr Portland OR 97221-2517 Office: Stoel Rives LLP 900 SW 5th Ave Ste 2600 Portland OR 97204-1268 E-mail: tpdeering@stoel.com., tomdeering@attbi.com.

DEERMAN, RUTH GILLETT, sales professional, flying instructor; b. El Paso, Tex., June 17, 1915; d. Otis Theodore and Katie Yvette (Textor) Gillett; m. Charlie Luther Deerman, Nov. 25, 1933 (dec. June 1992). Student, U. Tex., El Paso, 1966. Flight instr. Border Aviation, El Paso, 1944; flight and ground instr. S.W. Air Rangers, El Paso, 1968; beauty cons. Mary Kay Cosmetics, El Paso, 1969-70, ind. sales dir., 1970-75, ind. sr. sales dir., 1975—. Tchr. flying and ground sch., 1945—; accident prevention councilor FAA, 1972-80. Bd. dirs. Am. Cancer Soc., 1957-67; pres. Providence Meml. Hosp. Aux., 1960-61; past treas. Womans Club El Paso; past bd. dirs. YWCA, El Paso; past pres. Women's Missionary Union, 1st Bapt. Ch. Named Tex. Flying Farmers State Queen, 1955; winner All Woman Transcontinental Air Race, 1954; inducted into El Paso Aviation Hall of Fame, 1983; honored with granite plaque Internat. Forest of Friendship, 1977; recipient Jimmie Kolp award for contbg. to aviation and 99s, 1975. Mem. NAFE, Nat. Assn. Flight Instr., 99s (lic. women pilots, past internat. pres.), Whirly Girls (Whirly Girl # 78), Silver Wings, El Paso Aviation Assn. (v.p. 1947), 66s (founder), Clowns of Am. Internat., El Paso C. of C. (coms. woman's dept.), PEO, Ladies Oriental Shrine Am. (FAA accident prevention councilor 1972-80), Daus. of Nile (queen 1951-52), Order Ea. Star (worthy matron 1945). Republican. Avocations: bowling, golf. Home and Office: 405 Camino Real Ave El Paso TX 79922-2003

DEERSON, ADELE SHAPIRO, lawyer, educator; b. N.Y.C., July 14, 1924; d. Samuel and Marion (Pestreich) Shapiro; m. Nathan Deerson, Sept. 8, 1946 (dec. 1992); children: Bruce Alan, Jayne Ellen; m. Paul Berg, Oct. 23, 1999. BA, Hunter Coll., 1944; JD magna cum laude, Bklyn. Law Sch., 1946, JSD magna cum laude, 1949. Bar: N.Y. 1946. Atty. Henry H. Salzberg, N.Y.C., 1946-49; trial counsel Cosmopolitan Mut., N.Y.C., 1959-78; sole practice Nassau County, N.Y., 1949—; asst. prof. N.Y. Inst. Tech., 1968, assoc. prof., 1969-78, prof. law, 1978—. Profl. no-fault arbitrator, N.Y., 1988—; arbitrator Am. Arbitration Assn., Small Claims Ct., Civil Ct., Dist. Ct. Nassau, N.Y. Author: Learning Manual Business Law, 1978; staff editor Jour. Legal Svcs. Edn. Recipient Cert. of Appreciation Judges Civil Ct., Queens, 1977, N.Y.C. Family Ct. 1977. Mem. Queens County Bar Assn., Nassau County Bar Assn., Nat. Bus. Law Tchrs., Am. Arbitration Assn., Nassau-Suffolk Women's Bar Assn., B'nai B'rith (v.p. 1956-58), Philonomic, Delta Mu Delta. Home: 7612 176th St Flushing NY 11366-1514 E-mail: asdeerson@yahoo.com.

DEERY, HUGH GUNNER, II, physician; b. Indpls., July 20, 1949; s. Hugh Gunner and Josephine Mabel (Hirsbrunner) D.; m. JoAnne Kathryn Didier, Nov. 28, 1970; children: Hugh Gunner III, Ryan Patrick, Christopher Didier, Kathryn Ann. BS, U. Ill., 1971; MS, No. Ill. U., 1973; MD, Rush Med. Coll., Chgo., 1977. Diplomate in internal medicine and infectious diseases Am. Bd. Internal Medicine. Postgrad. tng. in internal medicine Los Angeles County/U. So. Calif. Med. Ctr., L.A., 1977-79; postgrad. in internal medicine U. Mich., Ann Arbor, 1979-80, fellow in infectious diseases, 1980-82; practice in infectious diseases Burns Clinic, Petoskey, Mich., 1982-99, No. Mich. Infectious Diseases, Petoskey, 1999—. Contbr. articles to profl. jours. John G. Searle fellow, 1980. Fellow ACP, Infectious Diseases Soc. Am. (Clinician's award 2002); mem. AMA, Mich. State Med. Soc., No. MIch. Med. Soc., Am. Soc. for Microbiology, Soc. Healthcare Epidemiology Am., Mich. Infectious Diseases Soc., Internat. Soc. for Travel Medicine, Beta Beta Beta. Home: 7889 Indian Garden Rd Petoskey MI 49770-8709 Office: No Mich Infectious Diseases 560 W Mitchell St Ste 350 Petoskey MI 49770-2277

DEES, BOWEN CAUSEY, institute executive, retired; b. Batesville, Miss., July 20, 1917; s. John Simeon and Ida Lea (Causey) D.; m. Sarah Edna Sanders, Aug. 25, 1937 (dec. 1999); 1 child, Sarah Edna; m. Dorothea Regina Simoneau, Sept. 24, 2001. AB, Miss. Coll., 1937, DSc (hon.), 1963; PhD, NYU, 1942; LLD, Lehigh U., 1976, Phila. Coll. Textiles and Sci., 1979; DSc (hon.), Temple U., 1981. Prof. physics Miss. Coll., 1943-44; instr. elec comms. Radar Sch., MIT, 1944-45; asst. prof. physics Rensselaer Poly. Inst., 1945-47; physicist, then div. chief sci. and tech. div., gen. hdqrs. SCAP, Tokyo, 1947-51; program dir. fellowships NSF, 1951-56, dep. asst. dir. sci. personnel and edn., 1956-59, asst. dir., 1959-63, assoc. dir. for edn., 1963-66, assoc. dir. planning, 1963-66; v.p. U. Ariz., 1966-68, provost acad. affairs, 1968-70; pres. Franklin Inst., Phila., 1970-82, pres. emeritus, 1982—. Adv. com. U.S. Army Command and Gen. Staff Coll., 1967-69; sci. info. coun. NSF, 1970-74; mem. Sci. Manpower Commn., Washington, 1976-79; U.S. co-chmn. U.S.-Japan Com. on Sci. Cooperation, 1981-87. Author: Fundamentals of Physics, 1945, The Allied Occupation and Japan's Economic Miracle, 1997; contbr. articles to profl. jours. Mem. Cosmos (Washington). E-mail: bcdees2@aol.com.

DEES, C. STANLEY, lawyer; b. Tulsa, June 24, 1938; AB, Princeton U., 1960; LLB, U. Va., 1963. Bar: Va. 1963, D.C. 1964. Ptnr. McKenna, Long & Aldridge LLP, Washington. Lectr. U. Va. Law Sch. Contbr. articles to profl. jours. Trustee Legal Aid Soc. D.C., 1970-83, pres., 1978-80; mem. Va. Dem. Ctrl. Com., 1971-74. Fellow Am. Bar Found.; mem. ABA (chmn. fed. cts. com. 1977-78, jud. remedies com. 1978-80, program com. 1980-81, coun. mem. 1981-84, sec. 1984-85, vice-chmn. pub. contract law sect. 1985-86, chmn. pub. contract law sect. 1987-88), U.S. Ct. Fed. Claims Bar, D.C. Bar (vice-chmn. 1974-75, chmn. 1975-77, steering com., govt. contracts and litigation divsn.), Va. State Bar, Coun. Def. and Space Indsl. Assns. (chmn. 1991-93), Nat. Security Indsl. Assn. (v.p. 1983-90, trustee 1990-96), D.C. Bar Found. (adv. com.), Order of Coif.

DEES, JULIAN WORTH, retired academic/research administrator; b. Henderson, N.C., Feb. 20, 1933; s. Charles Andrew and Gertrude Elizabeth (Lancaster) D.; m. Bernita June Funk, Aug. 29, 1954; children: Sandra Eileen Dees Anthony, Mark Alan, Gregory Linn. BS in Radio Engring., Tri-State U., Angola, Ind., 1953, BS in Adminstrv. Engring., 1954; MSEE, U. Cin., 1955. Registered profl. engr., Ga. Microwave engr. IT&T Labs., Ft. Wayne, Ind., 1955-60; project mgr., sr. engr. Martin Marietta Corp., Orlando, Fla., 1960-71; dir. electromagnetic lab. Ga. Inst. Tech., Atlanta, 1971-80, assoc. v.p. rsch., dir. office contract adminstrn., prin. rsch. engr., 1980-98. Asst. sec., asst. treas Ga. Tech. Rsch. Corp., Atlanta, 1980-98; bd. dir. Coun. on Rsch. & Tech., Washington. Contbr. articles to jours. in field; patentee in field. Named Author of Yr., Martin Marietta Corp., 1965. Fellow IEEE (Engr. of Yr. Orlando chpt. 1968); mem. Soc. Rsch. Adminstrs. (sr.), Coun. on Govtl. Rels., Nat. Coun. Univ. Rsch. Adminstrs. Avocations: woodworking, judging barbeque cook-offs. Home: 2128 Rosser Pl Stone Mountain GA 30087-1517

DEES, LAFON CARABO, brokerage house executive; b. Bennettsville, S.C., Aug. 13, 1937; s. Willie Ray and Allie Lee Dees; m. Winston Clark, June 15, 1963; 1 child, Kimberly Dees Earle. BBA, Wofford Coll., 1959. Factory rep. Armstrong World Ind., 1962-69, gen. sales mgr. Stewart Co., Dallas, 1969-72; factory rep. Lane Co., Atlanta, 1982; sr. v.p. investments Robinson Humphrey/Salomon Smith Barney, Atlanta, 1983—. Trustee Charitable Trust. 1st lt. U.S. Army, 1959-62. Mem. Buckhead Club. Republican. Methodist. Avocations: sports, reading, music, travel. Home: 5465 New Wellington Close NW Atlanta GA 30327

DEES, MORRIS SELIGMAN, JR., lawyer; b. Shorter, Ala., Dec. 16, 1936; s. Morris Seligman and Annie Ruth (Frazer) D.; m. Elizabeth Breen; children: Morris Seligman III, John Fuller, Ellie. BS, U. Ala., 1958, LLB, 1960. Bar: Ala. 1960. Chmn. bd. Fuller and Dees Pub., Inc. (merged with Times Mirror), 1960-69; ptnr. Levin and Dees, 1969-71; chief trial counsel So. Poverty Law Ctr., Montgomery, Ala., 1971—. Pres. Funding Group, 1983—; instr. criminal law Jones Law Sch., 1960-62; vis. fellow John F. Kennedy Sch. Govt., Harvard U.; elected fellow U. Pa. Law Sch., 1988. Author: (with Steve Fiffer) A Season for Justice, 1991, also made-for-TV movie, NBC, 1991. Dir. nat. fund raising McGovern for Pres., 1972; nat. fin. chmn. Carter for Pres., 1976; nat. fin. dir. Kennedy for Pres., 1980; trustee Miles Coll. Named One of 10 Outstanding Young Men Am. U.S. Jaycees, 1967; recipient Outstanding Svc. for Human Rights award Tuskegee Inst., 1976, Trial Lawyer of Yr. award Trial Lawyers for Pub. Justice, 1987, Pub. Svc. Achievement award Common Cause, 1988, Justice award So. Christian Leadership Conf., 1989. Mem. ABA (Young Lawyers Disting. Svc. award 1987), Ala. Bar Assn., Direct Mail Mktg. Assn. (bd. dirs., Showmanship award 1968), Beta Gamma Sigma. Unitarian (pres. ch. 1968). Home: Rolling Hills Rnch Mathews AL 36052 Office: So Poverty Law Ctr 400 Washington St Montgomery AL 36104-4344*

DEES, SANDRA KAY MARTIN, psychologist, research scientist; b. Omaha, Apr. 18, 1944; d. Leslie B. and Ruth Lillian (May) Martin; m. Doyce B. Dees. BA magna cum laude, Tex. Christian U., 1965, MA, 1972, PhD, 1989. Cert. Montessori Soc., 1977. Adminstrv. asst., rsch. coord. Hosp. Improvement Project, Wichita Falls (Tex.) State Hosp., 1968-69; caseworker adoptions Edna Gladney Home, Ft. Worth, 1970-71; psychologist Mexia (Tex.) State Sch., 1971-72; sch. psychologist Ft. Worth Ind. Sch. Dist., 1971-78, program evaluator, 1978-86; pvt. counselor, 1986-88; rsch. scientist Tex. Christian U., Ft. Worth, 1989—, mem. adj. faculty, 1991-92, mem. grad. faculty, 1994—. Bd. dirs Because We Care, Ft. Worth, 1988-97, Hill Sch., 1994—. Contbr. articles to profl. jours. Dallas TCU Women's Club creative writing scholar, 1962-64, Virginia Alpha scholar, 1963; NASA rsch. asst., 1965-67; USPHS trainee, 1967-68. Mem. APA, Am. Ednl. Rsch. Assn., Mental Health Assn., Mortar Board, Mensa, Sigma Xi, Alpha Chi, Phi Alpha Theta, Psi Chi, Phi Delta Kappa. Home: 29 Bounty Rd W Fort Worth TX 76132-1003 Office: Tex Christian U Dept Psychology Fort Worth TX 76129-0001 E-mail: s.dees@tcu.edu.

DEES, TOM MOORE, II, internist; b. Dallas, Mar. 4, 1931; s. Tom Hawkins and Maida Elizabeth (Board) D.; m. Suzanne Settle, Feb. 20, 1971; children: Tom Moore III, David Walsh. BA, Johns Hopkins U., 1952; MD, Southwestern Med. Sch., 1956. Intern Bellevue Hosp., N.Y.C., 1957, resident, 1958-59; rsch. fellow in cardiology Southwestern Med. Sch., Dallas, 1961; internist, ptnr. pvt. practice medicine MedProvider, Dallas, 1962—. Dir. and mng. ptnr. Swiss Ave. Med. Bldg., Dallas, 1984—; clin. asst. prof. medicine Southwestern Med. Sch., Dallas, 1962—; assoc. attending physician Baylor Med. Ctr., Dallas, 1962—. Mem. dist. commn. Boy Scouts Am., Dallas, 1963-72; mem. ofcl. bd. Highland Park Meth. Ch., Dallas, 1963-72. Capt. USAF, 1959-61. Mem. ACP (life), AMA, Am. Soc. Internal Medicine, Johns Hopkins U. Alumni Assn. (pres. North Tex. chpt 1964-68), Tex. Club of Internists (pres. 1992-93). Republican. Avocations: hunting, fishing, gardening. Home: 3649 Stratford Ave Dallas TX 75205-2810 Office: 3434 Swiss Ave Ste 420 Dallas TX 75204-6292

DEES, WILLIAM LESLIE, veterinary medicine educator; b. Dallas, July 14, 1949; s. W. Daulby and Corinne E. Dees; m. Rose M. Dees, Mar. 24, 1973; children: Leslie C., William B. BS in Animal Sci., Tex. A&M U., 1971, MS in Animal Sci., 1979, PhD in Anatomy, 1982. Postdoctoral fellow U. Tex. Southwestern Med. Ctr., Dallas, 1982-86; prof. Coll. of Vet. Medicine, Tex. A&M U., College Station, 1986—. Neuroendocrinology adv. panel NSF, Washington, 1995-98; cons., grant rev. panels NIH, Washington, 1993—; rschr. Tex. A&M U., 1986—. Contbr. articles to profl. jours. Rsch. grants NIH, 1983—; recipient Award for Rsch. Excellence Pfizer, Inc., 1996, Rsch. award Carrington Labs., 1989, Rsch. Scientist Devel. award NIH, 1987-97. Mem. Endocrine Soc., Soc. for Neurosci., Internat. Soc. of Neuroendocrinology. Office: Tex A&M U Dept Vet Anatomy University Dr College Station TX 77843-0001

DEESE, E(THEL) HELEN, English educator; b. San Diego, Sept. 15, 1925; d. Clyde Thomas and Ethel (Findlay) Smith; m. Rupert Julian Deese, Mar. 4, 1951; children: Rupert Thomas, Mary Ann, Franklin William, Richard Samuel. BA, U. Calif., Riverside, 1968, MA, 1970, PhD, 1977. Lectr. U. Calif., Riverside, 1977-79, 81-83, Calif. State Poly. U., Pomona, 1979-81; assoc. prof. English Mt. St. Mary's Coll., Los Angeles, 1983-89; Fulbright lectr. Hungary, 1989-90, 1990-91. Critic So. Calif. drama, Shakespeare Bull., N.Y.C., 1985—; author: Robert Lowell: A Reference Guide, 1982; editor: Robert Lowell: New Essays on the Poetry, 1986, Critical Essays on Wallace Stevens, 1988, William Carlos Williams, 1989; contbr. articles to profl. jours. Mem. MLA, Internat. Fedn. for Theatre Rsch., Assn. of Lit. Scholars and Critics, Shakespeare Assn. Democrat. Unitarian Universalist. Home: 601 E Baseline Rd Claremont CA 91711-2237 Office: Univ of Calif Dept English 906 University Ave Riverside CA 92521-0323

DEETS, DWAIN AARON, retired aerospace technology executive; b. Bell, Calif., Apr. 16, 1939; s. Kenneth Robert and Mildred Evelyn (Bergman) D.; m. Catherine Elizabeth Meister, June 18, 1961; children: Dennis Allen, Danelle Alaine. AB, Occidental Coll., 1961; MS in Physics, San Diego State U., 1964; ME, UCLA, 1978. Rsch. engr. Dryden Flight Rsch. Ctr. NASA, Edwards, Calif., 62-78, 79-85, hdqrs. liaison engr. Washington, 1978-79, mgr. Edwards, 1979-85; dir. rsch. engring. Dryden Flight Rsch. Ctr., Edwards, 1990-96, dir. aerospace projects, 1996-97, dir. flight rsch. R&T, 1997-99; hdqrs. mgr. flight rsch. NASA, Washington, 1988-89; ret., 1999. Chmn. Reusable Launch Vehicles Non-Advocate Rev., 1995-96. Contbr. articles to profl. jours. Recipient Exceptional Svc. medal NASA, 1988, Pres. Rank award SES, 1998, Founders award Atheists United, 2002 Fellow AIAA (assoc., Wright Bros. lectr. aeros. 1987); mem. Soc. Automotive Engrs. (chmn. aerospace control and guidance systems com. 1988-90), Toastmasters, Antelope Valley Symphony Orch. and Master Chorale (bd. dirs.). Democrat. E-mail: dad2wrk@antelecom.net.

DEETS, RICHARD M. secondary school educator, consultant; s. Richard M. Deets, Sr. and Mary E. Deets; m. Susan W. Wise; 1 child, Michelle R. Choate. BA, Calif. State U., L.A., 1975; MA, Calif. State U., Northridge, 2000. Cert. resource specialist Calif., 1998, edn. adminstrn. Calif., 2000. Coord. coop. edn. L.A. Unified Sch. Dist., 1982—85, tchr., 1986—96, dean, 1996—2000, title I coord., 2000—01, resource specialist, 2001—. Author: (poetry) Poetic Divesities. Ednl. programs chair Sierra Madre (Calif.) Search and Rescue Team, 1989—2003; pres. Employment and Tng. Assn. Calif., L.A., 1983—84. Named Coord. of the Yr., Vocat. Industry Clubs Am., 1982. Mem.: EDUCARE (assoc.), Phi Delta Kappa (assoc. 20 Yr. Svc. 2003). Republican. Episcopalian. Achievements include first to On-site study of Soviet Union Space Program. Avocations: mountain climbing, writing poetry, reading, mentor for high school students. Office: Los Angeles Unified School District 9229 Haskell Ave North Hills CA 91343

DEFATO, JOAN, librarian; b. Bklyn., Apr. 23, 1935; d. John Matthew and Frances Cecelia (Irwin) DeFato. AB in Botany, Barnard Coll., 1956; MS in Libr. Svc., Columbia U., 1957. Asst. med. librarian Equitable Life Assurance Soc., N.Y.C., 1957—59; librarian Boyce Thompson Inst. Plant Rsch., Yonkers, NY, 1959—73; plant sci. librarian Los Angeles County Arboretum and Botanic Garden, Arcadia, Calif., 1973—. Bd. dirs., rec. sec. Pacific Hort. Found., 1987—. Recipient Billie Connor award, Spl. Librs. Assn., So. Calif. chpt., 1995. Mem.: So. Calif. Hort. Soc. (membership sec., bd. dirs. 1986—), Coun. on Bot. and Hort. Librs. (pres. 1983—84, Charles Robert Long award of merit 2002). Office: Los Angeles County Arboretum & Botanic Garden 301 N Baldwin Ave Arcadia CA 91007-2697 E-mail: joan.defato@arboretum.org.

DEFAZIO, LYNETTE STEVENS, dancer, choreographer, educator, chiropractor, author, actress, musician; b. Berkeley, Calif., Sept. 29, 1930; d. Honore and Mabel J. (Estavan) Stevens; children: J.H. Panganiban, Joanna Pang. Student, U. Calif., Berkeley, 1950-55, San Francisco State Coll., 1950-51; studied classical dance teaching techniques and vocabulary with Gisella Caccialanza and Harold and Lew Christensen, San Francisco Ballet, 1952-56; D in Chiropractic, Life-West Chiropractic Coll., San Lorenzo, Calif., 1983; cert. techniques of tchg., U. Calif., 1985; BA in Humanities, New Coll. Calif., 1986. Lic. chiropracter, Mich.; diplomate Nat. sci. Bd.; eminence in dance edn., Calif. C.C. dance specialist, std. svcs., childrens ctrs. credentials Calif. Dept. Edn., 1986. Contract child dancer Monogram Movie Studio, Hollywood, Calif., 1938-40; dance instr. San Francisco Ballet, 1953-65; performer San Francisco Opera Ring, 1960-67; performer, choreographer Oakland (Calif.) Civic Light Opera, 1963-70; dir. Ballet Arts Studio, Oakland, 1960; tchg. specialist Oakland Unified Sch. Dist., 1965-80; fgn. exch. dance dir. Academie de Danses-Salle Pleyel, Paris, 1966; instr. Peralta C.C. Dist., Oakland, 1971—, chmn. dance dept., 1985—. Cons., instr. ext. courses UCLA, Dirs. and Suprs. Assn., Pitts. Unified Sch. Dist., 1971-73, Tulare (Calif.) Sch. Dist., 1971-73; rschr. Ednl. Testing Svcs., HEW, Berkeley, 1974; resident choreographer San Francisco Childrens Opera, 1970—, Oakland Civic Theater; ballet mistress Dimensions Dance Theater, Oakland, 1977-80; cons. Gianchetta Sch. Dance, San Francisco, Robicheau Boston Ballet, TV series Patchwork Family, CBS, N.Y.C.; choreographer Ravel's Valses Nobles et Sentimentales, 1976. Author: Basic Music Outlines for Dance Classes, 1960, Basic Music Outlines for Dance Classes, rev., 1968, Teaching Techniques and Choreography for Advanced Dancers, 1965, Basic Music Outlines for Dance Classes, 1965, Goals and Objectives in Improving Physical Capabilities, 1970, A Teacher's Guide for Ballet Techniques, 1970, Principle Procedures in Basic Curriculum, 1974, Objectives and Standards of Performance for Physical Development, 1975, Techniques of the Ballet School, 1970, Techniques of the Ballet School, rev., 1974, The Opera Ballets: A Choreographic Manual Vols. I-V, 1986; assoc. music arranger: Le Ballet du Cirque, 1964, assoc. composer, lyricist: The Ballet of Mother Goose, 1968; choreographer Valses Nobles Et Sentimentales (Ravel), Transitions (Kashevaroff), 1991, The New Wizard of Oz, 1991, San Francisco Children's Opera (Gingold), Canon in D for Strings and Continuo (Pachelbel), 1979, Oakland Cmty. Orch. excerpts from Swan Lake, Faust, Sleeping Beauty, 1998, Rodeo, Alameda Coll. Cultural Affairs Program, 2000, dancer solo dancer Three Stravinsky Etudes, Alameda Coll. Cultural Affairs Program, 1999, appeared in Flower Drum Song, 1993, Gigi, 1994, Fiddler on the Roof, 1996, The Music Man, 1996, Sayonara, 1997, Bye Bye Birdie, 2000, Barnum, the Circus Musical, 2001; musician (violinist): Oakland Cmty. Concert Orch., 1995—; condr. Gil Gleason:. Bd. dirs. Prodrs. Assocs., Inc., Oakland, 1999—. Recipient Foremost Women of 20th Century, 1985, Merit award San Francisco Children's Opera, 1985, 90. Mem. Calif. State Tchrs. Assn., Bay Area Chiropractic Rsch. Soc., Profl. Dance Tchrs. Assn. Home and Office: 4923 Harbord Dr Oakland CA 94618-2506 E-mail: balletarts@bigplanet.com.

DEFAZIO, PETER A. congressman; b. Needham, Mass., May 27, 1947; m. Myrnie Daut. BA in Econs. and Polit. Sci., Tufts U., 1969; postgrad., U. Oreg., 1969-71, MS in Pub. Adminstrn./Gerontology, 1977. Aide to U.S. Rep. Jim Weaver, 1977-82; sr. issues specialist, caseworker, dist. field office U.S. rep. Jim Weaver, 1977-78, legis. asst. Washington office, 1978-80, dir. constituent services, 1980-82; mem. commn. representing Springfield Lane County (Oreg.) Commn., 1982-86; mem. U.S. Congress from 4th Oreg. dist., Washington, 1987—; mem. resources com., water and power subcom.; mem. transp. and infrastructure com., ranking mem. water resources and environ. subcom. Mem. Lane County Econ. Devel. com., Intergovtl. Relations com.; bd. dirs. Eugene-Springfield Met. Partnership; Lane County Dem. precinct person, 1982—. Served with USAFR. Mem. Assn. of Oreg. Counties (legis. com.), Nat. Assn. of Counties (tax and fin. com.). Democrat. Office: US Ho of Reps 2134 Rayburn Ho Office Bldg Washington DC 20515-0001*

DE FEE, NICOLE RENEÉ, education educator; d. William Arthur and Karen Horton Defee. BA, North Ga. Coll. and State U., 1998; MA, Austin Peay State U., Tenn., 2000; PhD, U. of Nebr., 2000—. Doctoral student, tchg. asst. U. of Nebr., Lincoln, 2000—. Mem.: Soc. of Early Americanists, Modern Langs. Assn. Avocations: running, travel. E-mail: nrd@unlserve.unl.edu.

DEFEIS, ELIZABETH FRANCES, law educator, lawyer; b. N.Y.C. d. Francis Paul and Lena (Amendola) D. BA, St. John's U., 1956, JD, 1958, JSD (hon.), 1984; LLM, NYU, 1971; postgrad., U. Milan, Italy, 1963-64, Inst. Internat. Human Rights, 1991. Bar: N.Y. 1959, U.S. Dist. Ct. (fed. dist.) 1960, U.S. Dist. Ct. (so. dist.) N.Y. 1961, U.S. Supreme Ct. 1965, U.S. Dist. Ct. (ea. dist.) N.Y. 1978, N.J. 1983. Asst. U. S. atty. So. Dist. N.Y., Dept. Justice, 1961-62; atty. RCA Corp., 1962-63; assoc. Carter, Ledyard & Milburn, N.Y.C., 1963-69; atty. Bedford Stuyvesant Legal Svcs. Corp., 1969-70; prof. law Seton Hall U., Newark, 1971—, dean Sch. Law, 1983-88. Vis. prof. St. Louis U. Sch. Law, 1988, St. John's U. Sch. Law, 1990, 2001, U. Milan, Italy, 1996; Fulbright-Hays lectr., Iran, India, 1977-79; lectr. Orgn. Security and Cooperation in Europe, Russia, Turkmenistan, Tajikistan, Azerbaijan; vis. scholar Ctr. Study of Human Rights, Columbia U., 1989; project dir. TV series Women and Law, 1974-80; narrator TV series Alternatives to Violence, 1981; mem. com. women and cts. N.J. Supreme Ct., 1982-95; trustee Legal Svcs. N.J., 1983-88; mem. 3rd Cir. Task Force on Equality in the Cts., 1995-98; tech. cons. on Constitution of Armenia, 1992-95; project dir. T.V. series Pub. Internat. Law.; legal expert Armenia election OSCE, 1998. Chair Albert Einstein Inst., Boston, 1995—2001. Fulbright-Hays scholar Milan, Italy, 1963-64, Fulbright-Hays, Orgn. for Security and Cooperation in Europe scholar, Armenia, Russia, Italy, 1996; Ford Found. fellow, 1970-71. Mem. ABA, Nat. Italian Am. Bar Assn., Columbian Lawyers Assn., Assn. of Bar of City of N.Y. (internat. law com., coun. internat. affairs), N.J. Bar Assn., Nat. Italian Am. Found. Office: Seton Hall U Law Sch One Newark Ctr Newark NJ 07102 E-mail: defeisel@shu.edu.

DEFELICE, EUGENE ANTHONY, physician, medical educator, author, consultant, magician; b. Beacon, N.Y., Dec. 24, 1927; s. Domenick and Louise (Grippo) DeF. BS, Columbia U., 1951; MD, Boston U., 1956. Ciba fellow, lectr. pharmacology Boston U. Sch. Medicine, 1954-57; intern Newton (Mass.) Wellesley Hosp., 1957; practice medicine specializing in internal medicine North Miami, Fla., 1958-61; asst. dir. clin. rsch. Warner Lambert Rsch. Inst., Morris Plains, N.J., 1961-64; dir. clin. rsch. Bristol Labs. (now Bristol Meyers Squibb), Syracuse, N.Y., 1965-66, Sandoz Inc. (now Novartis Inc.), East Hanover, N.J., 1967-68, exec. dir. clin. research, 1969-70, dir. sci. affairs and comml. devel., 1970-74, dir. corp. sci. devel., 1974, v.p. corp. sci. devel., 1974-77, v.p. internat. med. rsch., med. advisor, 1977-83. Prof. biochemistry, microbiology and pub. health, dir. rsch. New Eng. Coll. Pharmacy, 1956-58; practice in medicine, cons. in medicine and med. rsch., Morristown, N.J., 1961-87, East Schodack and Albany, N.Y., 1988—; clin. assoc. prof. medicine Coll. Medicine and Dentistry N.J.-Rutgers Med. Sch., 1977-84; clin. prof. medicine UMD-Robert Wood Johnson Med. Sch., 1985—; clin. prof. anesthesiology UCLA, 1978-83. Co-author: Angiotensin Converting Enzyme Inhibitors, 1987, Prostaglandins, Platelets, Lipids: New Developemnts in Atherosclerosis, 1981, Health and Obesity, 1983, Beta Blockers in the Treatment of Cardiovascular Diseases, 1984, The Pharmacological Treatment of Cardiovascular Diseases, 1986; author: Web Health Info. Resource Guide, 2001, Breast Cancer, 2002, Overweight, Obesity and Health, 2002, Nutrition and Health, 2003; mem. internat. editl. com. Triangle, Sandorama, 1977—81; contbr. numerous articles to profl. jours.; cons. to editor. Served with U.S. Army, World War II. Named hon. citizen of Italy; named to Notable Italian-Am. Hall of Fame. Fellow Am. Geriat. Soc., Acad. Psychosomatic Medicine; mem. Soc. Am. Magicians, Internat. Brotherhood Magicians; emeritus mem. numerous profl. socs. Home and Office: PO Box 9160 Albany NY 12209-0160 *Success in life comes from constancy of purpose, diligent work, living according to sound moral and religious principles, and having faith and hope in the future. Helping to make the world a better place to live in, autographing one's work in excellence, and doing good by others are the rewards which bring happiness.*

DEFELICE, JAMES L. writer; b. N.Y.C., Aug. 23, 1956; s. Louis and Eileen DeFelice; m. Debra Scacciaferro, Sept. 10, 1984; 1 child, Robert J. BA, Marist, 1977; MA, SUNY, 1981. Author: Coyote Bird, 1992, War Breaker, 1993, The Silver Bullet, 1995, The Iron Chain, 1995, The Golden Flask, 1996, Havana Strike, 1997, Brother's Keeper, 2000, Cyclops One, 2003; author: (with Dale Brown) Dreamland, 2001, Nerve Center, 2002, Razor's Edge, 2003, Piranha, 2003; author: (with Stephen Coonts) Deep Black, 2003; author: (short fiction in anthologies) The Man Who Got Khrushchev-First to Fight, 1999, In the Hunter's Shadow-First to Fight, 1999, Come to Earth-First to Fight II, 2001, Refugees-First to Fight II, 2001, Cain-A Date That Will Live in Infamy, 2001, Lazarus-Alternate Gettysburgs, 2002, Wolf Flight-Victory, 2003. Personal E-mail: jdchester@aol.com.

DE FELITTA, FRANK PAUL, producer, writer, director; b. N.Y.C. s. Pat and Genevieve (Sibilio) De F.; m. Dorothy Gilbert; children: Eileen Raymond. Student, U. N.C., New Sch. Social Research, 1948. Dir.-writer, CBS, 1950-57, dir. programming, Nat. Telefilms Assos., 1959-61, producer, writer, dir., NBC, from 1962, producer, dir., writer, Universal Studios, 1968-69; film documentaries include Music of the South, 1955; sci. series Conquest, 1957; natural sci. series Adventure, 1953-55; hist. series Odyssey, 1958, The Chosen Child, 1962 (Writers Guild award), Emergency Ward, 1962 (Emmy award), Experiment in Excellence, 1963 (Sch. Bell award), Battle of the Bulge, 1964, The Stately Ghosts of England, 1964, The World of the Teenager, 1966 (Robert J. Flaherty award), Pearl Harbor, 1966 Golden Eagle award; dir., author: films Trapped, 1973, The Two Worlds of Jennie Logan, 1979 (Silver Halo award), Killer in the Mirror, 1986, Scissors, 1990; dir.: film Dark Night of the Scarecrow, 1981; (Brotherhood award of Nat. Conf. Christians and Jews for film Mississippi- A Self Portrait, George Washington Honor medal of Freedoms Found. for film The American Image.); Author: films The First of January, 1970, The Savage Is

Loose, 1971, Audrey Rose, 1977, The Entity, 1981; novels Oktoberfest, 1972, Audrey Rose, 1975, The Entity, 1978, Sea Trial, 1980, For Love of Audrey Rose, 1982, Golgotha Falls, 1984, Funeral March of the Marionettes, 1990, A Swift Death to Critics, 2000. Recipient Peabody award, 1954, 63, Thomas Alva Edison award, 1958, 2 Gold Eagle awards Coun. on Internat. Non-Theatrical Events. Mem. Writers Guild Am., Dirs. Guild Am.

DEFENDI, VITTORIO, medical research administrator, pathologist; b. Treviglio, Italy, Nov. 16, 1928; married, 1955; 3 children. MD, U. Pavia, 1951. Instr. pathology dept. U. Pavia, 1951-52; pathologist virus sect. Lederle Labs., N.Y.C., 1956-58; assoc. pathologist Med. Sch., U. Pa., 1958-64, assoc. prof., 1964-68, Wistar prof., 1968-74; prof. pathology, chmn. dept. pathology Sch. NYU Sch. Medicine, N.Y.C., 1974—. Brit. Coun. scholar Postgrad. Med. Sch., U. London, 1952-53; Fulbright fellow Med. Sch., U. Vt., 1953-54; rsch. fellow Detroit Inst. Cancer Rsch., 1954-56; assoc. mem. Wistar Inst., 1958-64, mem. staff, 1964-74; rsch. prof. Am. Cancer soc., 1973—. Leukemia Soc. scholar, 1962-66. Mem. Am. Soc. Cell Biology, Am. Soc. Exptl. Pathology, Histochem. Soc., Am. Assn. Immunology, Am. Assn. Cancer Rsch. Achievements include research in viral oncology; tumor biology; mechanism of immunological defense. Office: NYU Sch Medicine Dept Pathology 550 1st Ave New York NY 10016-6402 E-mail: vittorio.defendi@med.nyu.edu.

DEFEO, PHILLIP D. brokerage house executive; BA in econ. and internat. fin., Iona Coll. Opers. mgr. Procter and Gamble; sr. v.p. internat. securities divsn. Bankers Trust Co., London; mng. dir. worldwide equities opers. Lehman Bros.; sr. v.p. and mem. oper. com. FMR Corp.; exec. v.p. & dir. mktg. and customer svc. Cedel Internat.; pres. and CEO Van Eck Assocs. Corp.; chmn. and CEO Pacific Exch., San Francisco, 1999—. Bd. dirs. Computershare Ltd., 2000—. Office: Pacific Exch 115 Sansome St San Francisco CA 94104*

DE FERRARI, GABRIELLA, curator, writer; b. Tacna, Peru, June 3, 1941; came to U.S., 1959, naturalized, 1964; d. Armando and Delia De Ferrari; children: Nathaniel, Gabriella, Jeppson. BA, St. Louis U., 1962; MS, Tufts U., 1965; MA, Harvard U., 1981. Dir. Inst. Contemporary Art, Boston, 1975-77; acting curator Busch Reisinger Mus., Harvard U., Cambridge, Mass., 1978-79; asst. dir. for curatorial affairs and program Fogg Art Mus., 1979-82. Cons. editor Travel and Leisure; mem. bd. visitors Harvard U. Art Museums, Cambridge, Mass.; trustee New Sch. U., N.Y.C., Wadsworth Atheneum, Hartford, Conn. Author: A Cloud on Sand, 1990, Gringa Latina A Woman of Two Worlds, 1995. Office: 10 Jay St New York NY 10013-2861

DEFEVER, SUSANNA ETHEL, English language educator; b. Manistee, Mich., May 11, 1934; d. Arthur Theodore and Florence Marie Christine (Larson) Mason; m. Charles J. Defever, Aug. 1, 1959; children: Keith S., Kristin E. AB, Cen. Mich. U., 1956; MA, Wayne State U., 1963; postgrad., Mich. State U., 1957, 58. Cert. secondary education tchr. 1959. Tchr. English, journalism, drama Lakeview High Sch., St. Clair Shores, Mich., 1956-65; tchr. English, composition St. Clair County C.C., Port Huron, 1965-70, part time tchr., 1971-77, prof. English, composition, 1977-95. Conf. planning Liberal Arts Network Devel. (LAND) for Consortium of Mich. Cmty. Coll., 1990—93, v.p., conf. chmn., 1994—95, pres., 1995—96, chair LAND millennium award for innovative team tchg., 1999—; dir. writing workshops for K-12 tchrs. Sanilac County Intermediate Sch. dist., 1987, 88, writing workshops for K-12 tchrs. Sanilac County Intermediate Sch. Dist., 1992, Cheboygan Otsego Presque Isle Intermediate Sch. Dist., 1989, 90, Port Huron Area Schs., 1991; mem. adv. com. Mich. Proficiency Exam, 1992—96; exec. com. Mich. Writing Projects, 1987—93; reviewer English Edn., 1993—2001. Editor: The Heritage of Ira, 1990, An Enduring Heritage, 1992; scholar, lectr. Let's Talk About It series, Mich. Libr. Assn., 1987-93, NEH/Modern Poetry series, St. Clair County Libr., 1994, spkr. Whitehills Book Club, East Lansing, 1987—; contbr. articles to profl. jours.; presenter workshops; pub. poet. Founding mem. Marge Boal Drama Festival; newsletter editor, SC4 Retirees 2000-, pres. 2003—; bd. dirs. SC4 Friends of the Arts, Marine City Concert Series, St. Clair County Cmty. Mental Health Authority, 2000—, Devel. Disabled Adv. Coun., 2002—; Anderson music com. St. Clair Cmty. Found., 2001—. Recipient Disting. Faculty award, 1983, Disting. faculty award, 1989, Nat. Inst. Staff Orgn. Devel. Excellence Award for Tchg., U. Austin, 1992, LAND Leadership award, 2000, Beacon grant, 1991—92, Sperry grant, 1994. Mem.: NEA, Cmty. Coll. Humanities Assn., Mich. Coun. Tchrs. English (regional coord. 1979—85, v.p. 1986—87), Mich. Coll. English Assn. (newsletter chmn., editor 1989—91, v.p. 1992), Nat. Coun. Tchrs. English (judge 1983—2002, assoc. chmn. local conv. arrangements 1984, local arrangements com. 1997), SC4 Retirees (pres. 2003—), Delta Kappa Gamma (sec. 1992—94, scholarship chair 2000—02), Phi Theta Kappa (hon.).

DEFFAA, CHIP, jazz critic; b. New Rochelle, N.Y., May 18, 1951; s. Louis Philip and Alberta (Saby) D. AB, Princeton U., 1973. Jazz critic N.Y. Post, N.Y.C., 1986—. Author: Swing Legacy, 1989, Voices of the Jazz Age, 1990, In the Mainstream, 1992, Traditionalists and Revivalists in Jazz, 1993, (with David Cassidy) C'mon Get Happy, 1994, Jazz Veterans, 1995, Blue Rhythms, 1996; editor F. Scott Fitzgerald: The Princeton Years, 1997. Trustee Princeton Tiger Mag., 1983—. Finalist for Excellence in Recorded Sound Rsch. award Assn. for Recorded Sound Collections, 1991; recipient Deems Taylor award ASCAP, 1993. Mem. Nat. Acad. Recording Arts & Scis., Am. Theatre Critics Assn., The Drama Desk. Avocations: music, theater, hiking, reading. Home: 50 Quartz Ln Paterson NJ 07501-3345 E-mail: watergap18@aol.com.

DEFFENBAUGH, RALSTON H., JR., immigration agency executive, lawyer; b. Oakland, Calif., Apr. 12, 1952; s. Ralston H. and Marion F. (Funda) D.; m. Miriam Ruth Boraas, Oct. 24, 1976; children: Natalie, Carl. BA, U. Colo., 1973; JD, Harvard U., 1977. Bar: Colo. 1977. Atty. Ireland, Stapleton & Pryor, Denver, 1977-80; asst. to gen. sec. Lutheran World Fedn., Geneva, 1981-85; dir. Luth. Office for World Community, N.Y.C., 1985-90; pres. Luth. Immigration & Refugee Svc., N.Y.C., 1991—. Legal advisor Luth. Bishops and Coun. of Chs., Namibia, 1989-90. Recipient Arnold E. Carlson award Gustavus Adolphus Coll., St. Peter, Minn., 1991, Graven award Wartburg Coll., 1994, Sylvester Michelfelder award Trinity Luth. Sem., 1995. Office: Luth Immigration & Refugee Svc 700 Light St Baltimore MD 21230-3850

DEFFINA, THOMAS VICTOR, lawyer, consultant; b. N.Y.C., Mar. 14, 1942; s. Philip Anthony and Antoinette (Napoli) D. BA, St. John's U., Jamaica, N.Y., 1964, JD, 1967. Bar: N.Y. 1967, U.S. Dist. Ct. (so. and ea. dists.) N.Y. 1968, U.S. Ct. Customs and Patent Appeals 1968. Assoc. Manton, Giaimo, P.C., N.Y.C., 1968-74; Anthony L. Schiavetti Law Practice, N.Y.C., 1974-77; ptnr. Deffina & Blau, P.C., N.Y.C., 1977-86, Deffina, Rosner & Nocera, N.Y.C., 1986—; trial cons. Employers Ins. Wausau, N.Y.C., 1977—, Aetna Casualty and Surety, N.Y.C., 1986; group coun. Mut. Ins. Co., N.Y.C.; talk show panelist Readers Digest Lifeline, Nat. Pub. Svc. TV, 1982. Mem. ABA, N.Y. State Bar Assn., N.Y. State Trial Lawyers Assn. Republican. Roman Catholic. Club: Downtown Athletic. Home: 8 Mountain Run Boonton NJ 07005-8709 Office: Deffina & Blau 377 Broadway New York NY 10013-3907

DEFFNER, NORMAN FRED, dermatologist; b. Kansas City, Mo., June 5, 1936; s. Oscar August and Elsie Adele (Liebers) D.; m. Janet Sue Swaim, Aug. 24, 1963; children: Patricia, Brian, Mark. BS, U. Wis., River Falls, 1958; MS, U. Wis., Madison, 1964, MD, 1968; MS, U. Minn., 1972. Intern Gunderson Clinic, La Crosse, Wis., 1968-69; resident in dermatology Mayo Clinic, Rochester, Minn., 1969-72; dermatologist, Cutis, S.C., Wausau, Wis., 1972-77; chief of staff Wausau Hosp., 1976-77; pvt. practice, Wausau, 1977—. Physicians adv. com. North Ctrl. Health Protection Plan, Wausau, 1986-92. With N.G., 1955—63. Fellow Am. Acad. Dermatology; mem. AMA, Wis. Dermatol. Soc. (sec.-treas. 1983-84, pres. 1984-85), Marathon County Med. Soc. (pres. 1986-88), Wausau C. of C. Avocations: gardening, fishing, hunting.

DEFFRY, FRANK M. retired marriage and family therapist; b. Chgo., July 4, 1938; s. Harry and Mary Josephine Deffry. BS, U. San Francisco, 1985; M in Family Therapy, Calif. Family Study Ctr., 1987; PhD in Psychology, Calif. Grad. Inst., 1995. Dir. drug recovery program Pathway Recovery House, San Jose, Calif., 1971—73; counselor VA Hosp., L.A., 1973—77; pvt. practice group therapist Westwood, Calif., 1977—85; interventionist Employee Assistance Program McDonald Douglas/Vista Treatment Ctr., Calif., 1985—95; clin. supr. St. Joseph's Hosp., Burbank, Calif., 1985—90; pvt. practice addiction specialist Santa Monica, Calif., 1985—2000; ret. Expert in addictions. Author three novels and several books of poetry. With USMC, 1956—58. Mem.: Alcoholics Anonymous (sec., treas.). Avocations: jazz, reading, films, travel, motorcycling. Home: Apt 6 829 Ocean Park Blvd Santa Monica CA 90405

DEFIELD, CHARLEEN K. accountant; b. Oakland, Calif., Nov. 5, 1950; d. Donald Norbert and Carleen Charlotte (Sappenfield) D. BS, Calif. State U., Hayward, 1974, MBA, 1979. CPA, Calif. 1987, Mont. 1992; cert. tchr., Calif., 1979. Acct. King White and Danielson CPAs, San Leandro, Calif., 1974-76, City of Oakland Park and Recreation, Oakland, Calif., 1977-78; asst. prof. Calif. State U. Sonoma, Rohnert Park, 1979-84; dir. Inst. for Sml. Bus. Devel., Rohnert Park, 1980-82; owner, coach Golden Visions Coaching, Castro Valley, Calif., 1995-98; instr. Holy Names Coll., Oakland, 1991—2001; owner CPA firm Castro Valley, Calif., 1978—2001. Author: (newsletters) Quarterly Tax News, 1977-99. Regent Piedmont chpt. DAR, 1991—93, chaplain, 1997—99; bd. dirs. DCPC Found., 2002—03. Mem.: Golden Gate Enrolled Agts. (bd. dirs. 1987—93, pres. 1991—92), Nat. Soc. Enrolled Agts., Calif. Soc. CPAs. Republican. Presbyterian. Avocations: history, genealogy, ballroom dancing, historic costuming, travel. Office: PO Box 1746 Brentwood CA 94513

DEFILIPPI, GEORGE, retired air force officer; b. Mobile, Ala., Sept. 6, 1947; s. George and Margaret Josephine (Lazzari) DeF.; m. Patricia Naismith McAdam, July 21, 1969; children: Jocelyn, Gwendolyn, Geoffrey, James. BS, USAF Acad., Colorado Springs, 1969; MS, Air Force Inst. Technology, Dayton, Ohio, 1977. Enlisted USAF, 1969, advanced through ranks to col., exec. sec., program mgr. Scientific Adv. Bd., 1984-86, chief tng. divsn. 602d Tactical Air Control Wing Davis Mountain AFB, Ariz., 1986-88, cmdr. 22d Tactical Air Support Tng. Squadron, 1988-89, cmdr. 23d Tactical Air Support Squadron, 1989-90, cmdr. Air Liaison Office XVIII Airborne Corps Ft. Bragg, N.C., 1991-93, cmdr. Air Liaison Office to 3d Rep. Korea Army Uijongbu, Korea, 1992-93, mil. staff specialist Undersec. Def. Acquisition & Tech. Washington, 1993-96, mil. asst. to dir. strategic tactical systems, 1996-99; ret., 1999; field dir. mil. requirements Northrop Grumman Life Support, Arlington, Va., 1999—. Vol. Arlington Emergency Winter Shelter, 1993-99, v.p., 1993-2000; mem. Arlington Com. of 100, 1994—; vestryman St. George's Episcopal Ch., 1996-99, Stephen min., leader, 1999—. Mem. Assn. Unmanned Vehicle Sys. (bd. dirs. Capitol chpt. 1993-97), Air Force Assn. (Steele chpt. sec. VPOPO(operations) and newsletter editor 1999—). Episcopal. Avocations: jogging, swimming. Office: Northrop Grumman Life Support 1000 Wilson Blvd Ste 2300 Arlington VA 22209 E-mail: defilippi@northropgrumman.com.

DEFINO, JOSEPH FRANCIS, lawyer; b. Newark, Feb. 18, 1952; s. Frank and Marie D. AB, Bucknell U., 1974; JD, Tulane U., 1977. Bar: N.J. 1977, Fla. 1979, D.C. 1980. Jud. clk. Hon. Thomas F. Shebell, Jr., JSC, Monmouth County, N.J., 1977-78; atty. Morgan & Falvo, West Long Branch, N.J., 1978-81, Anschelewitz, Barr, Ansell & Bonello, Oakhurst, N.J., 1981-84, Falvo, Bonello, Moriarty & Steiger, Oakhurst, N.J., 1984-86, Jacobowitz, Grabelle, Defino & Latimer, Oakhurst, 1986—. Chmn. early settlement panel Monmouth Vicinage Superior Ct. N.J.; prosecutor Wall Twp., 1997-2003. Mem. ABA, ATLA, N.J. Bar Assn., Monmouth Bar Assn. (chmn. family law com. 1997-99, trustee 2001—). Republican. Avocation: fishing. Office: Jacobowitz Grabelle Defino Latimer & Fradkin PO Box 609 Oakhurst NJ 07755-0609

DEFIORE, PERRY DENNIS, academic administrator, business owner; b. Allentown, Pa., Dec. 22, 1947; s. Nicholas Samuel and Beatrice Marie (McClellan) D.; m. Leslie Irene Tucker (div. Aug. 1978); children: Perry Jr., Sheryl; m. Blanca Lilia Treviño, Mar. 30, 1980; children: Andrew, Michael, Monica, Franklin. Student, Federated Tax Schs., LaSalle U., Ins. Adjusters Sch., Miami, Fla., Cleve. Inst., Newspaper Inst., Foley-Belsaw Inst., U. Regiomontana, Monterrey, Mex., Stratford Inst., Harcourt Inst. Dept. mgr. C&S Bank, Albany, Ga., 1969-70; supr. Brown Group, various locations, 1970-74, U.S. Shoe, various locations, 1974-85; mgr. Whiddon's, Dallas, 1985-90; jr. high sch. prin. Instituto Columbia S.C., Monterey, 1990—; founder, CEO Soc. Internat. de Cientificos Juveniles. Pres. Math & Sci., Monterrey, 1992—95; mem. Proyecto Jason, Monterrey, 1996—; developer ednl. programs in field. Author textbooks for bilingual schs.; developer ednl. programs in field; author: Escape From Progress, 1986. Staff sgt. USMC, 1965-68. Mem.: Jason Acad. (internat. facilitator), N.Y. Acad. Scis., Soc. Internacional Cientificos Juveniles (founder). Lutheran. Avocations: golf, fishing, astrophysics. Home: Colonia Loma Larga Loma Florida #100 Monterrey Nuevo Leon Mexico Office: Inst Columbia SC Enrique Herrera # 2305 San Pedro Garza García Garza Mexico E-mail: perryblanca@yahoo.com.

DEFLEUR, LOIS B. university president, sociology educator; b. Aurora, Ill., June 25, 1936; d. Ralph Edward and Isabel Anna (Cornils) Begitske; m. Melvin L. DeFleur (div.) AB, Blackburn Coll., 1958; MA, Ind. U., 1961; PhD in Sociology, U. Ill., 1965; HHD (hon.), U. Alaska, 1999. Asst. prof. sociology Transylvania Coll., Lexington, Ky., 1963-67; assoc. prof. Wash. State U., Pullman, 1967-74, prof., 1975-86, dean Coll. Liberal Arts, 1981-86; provost U. Mo., Columbia, 1986-90; pres. Binghamton U., SUNY, 1990—. Disting. vis. prof. USAF Acad., 1976-77; vis. prof. U. Chgo., 1980-81; bd. dirs. Energy East Corp., HealthNow, N.Y. Author: Delinquency in Argentina, 1965; (with others) Sociology: Human Society, 3d edit. 1981, 4th edit., 1984, The Integration of Women into All Male Air Force Units, 1982, The Edward R. Murrow Heritage: A Challenge for the Future, 1986; contbr. articles to profl. jours. Mem. Wash. State Bd. on Correctional Svcs. and Edn., 1974-77, State of N.Y. Edn. Dept. Curriculum and Assessment Coun., 1991-94, Trilateral Task for N.Am. Ednl. Collaboration, USIA, 1993-95. Recipient Disting. Alumni award Blackburn Coll., 1991, Chief Exec. Leadership awrd Coun. for Advancement and Support of Edn., 1999, Civic Leadership award Greater Binghamton C. of C., 2003, Woman of Distinction award Girl Scout Coun., 2002; grantee NIMH, 1969-79, NSF, 1972-75, Air Force Office, 1978-81. Mem. NCAA (pres. commn. 1996, exec. com. 1997-98), Am. Sociol. Assn. (publs. com. 1979-82, nominations com. 1984-86, coun. mem. 1987-90), Pacific Sociol. Assn. (pres. 1980-82), Coun. Colls. of Arts and Scis. (bd. dirs. 1982-84, pres. 1985-87), Aircraft Owners and Pilots Assn., Internat. Comanche Soc., Nat. Assn. State U. and Land-grant Colls. (exec. com. 1990-93, chair coun. of pres. 1994-95, chmn. bd. dirs. 1996-97), Am. Coun. Edn. (bd. dirs. 1994-2000, v.p. chair-elect 1997-98, chair bd. dirs. 1998-99), Consortium Social Sci. Assns. (bd. dirs. 1993-96). Office: Binghamton U Office of Pres PO Box 6000 Binghamton NY 13902-6000

DEFLEUR, MARGARET H. communications educator; b. Toledo, Nov. 29, 1949; d. Bart Anthony and Elizabeth Paula (Poch) Hanus; m. Melvin Lawrence DeFleur, Dec. 29, 1978. BA, U. Miami, Coral Gables, Fla., 1984, MBA, 1987; PhD, Syracuse U., 1994. Adj. prof. Syracuse U., 1992; asst. prof. Boston U., 1994-2000, assoc. prof., 2000—; vis. scholar Harvard U., 1996-98. Dir. Health Comm. Program, Boston U., 1997—. Author: Computer-Assisted Investigative Reporting: Development and Methodology, 1997; contbr. articles to profl. jours. Mem. Assn. for Edn. in Mass Comm. and Journalism, Nat. Comm. Assn. Home: 20 Burnett Rd Southborough MA 01772-1467 Office: Boston U Coll Comm 640 Commonwealth Ave Boston MA 02215-2422

DE FOLIART, GENE RAY, retired entomologist, researcher, educator; b. Stillwater, Okla., June 24, 1925; s. Jess Henry and Ruby Marie De Foliart; m. Florence Louise Ball, Jan. 29, 1950 (dec. Feb. 4, 1998); children: David William, Sharon Kay, Linda Suzanne. BS, Okla. State U., 1942—48; PhD, Cornell U., 1948—51. Asst. prof. U. of Wyo., 1951—56, assoc. prof., 1956—59, U. of Wis., 1959—66, prof., 1966—91, prof. emeritus, 1991—. Cons. Ctr. for Disease Control, Atlanta, 1969—69; chair, dept. of entomology U. of Wis., 1968—76; study sect., tropical medicine and parasitology NIH, 1975—79; grant cons. Can. Dept. of Health and Nat. Welfare, Ottawa, 1977—89; chair, dept. of entomology U. of Wis., 1982—83. Contbr. Ensign U.S Naval Aviation, 1943—45, Various Locations. Recipient Hoogstraal Medal for outstanding achievement in med. entomology, Am. Soc. of Tropical Medicine and Hygiene, 1998; Rsch. grants on Mosquitoes/Arboviruses, NIH, 1966—90. Mem.: Entomol. Soc. of Am. (chair, sect. of med. entomology 1971—72). Achievements include helping to pioneer western world interest in insects as a global food resource; contributed to discoveries relative to transovarial transmission of arboviruses by mosquitoes. Avocations: reading, travel. Home: 6 South Kenosha Drive Madison WI 53705 Office: U of Wis 1630 Linden Drive Madison WI 53706

DE FONVILLE, PAUL BLISS, monument and library administrator; b. Oakland, Calif., Mar. 3, 1923; s. Marion Yancey and Charlotte (Bliss) de F.; m. Virginia Harpell, June 17, 1967. Student, Calif. Poly. U., 1942-44, Michael Chekhov Group, 1947-52. Founder, pres. Cowboy Meml. and Libr., Caliente, Calif., 1969—; tchr. outdoor edn. Calif. State U., Bakersfield, 1980. Life mem. Presdl. Task Force, Washington, 1984—, Rep. Senatorial inner circle, Washington, 1989—, Nat. Rep. Congl. Com., Washington, 1990—, Rep. Nat. Com., 1987—, U.S. Senatorial Club, 1988—, Rep. Senatorial Commn., 1991, Presdl. Election Registry, 1992; del. Presdl. Trust, 1992; mem. Presdl. Commn. Am. Agenda; affiliate Lake Isabella Bd. Realtors, 1993; hon. marshall Lake Isabella, Kern County Christmas Parade, 1993. Recipient Slim Pickens award Calif. State Horsemen, 1980, Marshall-Working Western award Rose Parade, Pasadena, 1980, recognition Kern County, 1984, proclamations Mayor of Bakersfield, 1984, 85, Govt. of Calif., 1984, resolution Calif. Senate, 1988, Calif. Assembly, 1990, Presdl. Order of Merit, 1991, Congl. Cert. of Merit, 1992, Rep. Presdl. Legion of Merit award, 1992, Rep. Presdl. Legion of Merit award, 1992, document Gov. of Calif., 1993, Rep. Nat. Com. Cert. Recognition, 1992, Rep. Presdl. adv. Commn. Cert. award, 1993, Congl. Cert. Appreciation, 1993, Cert. Commendation Washington Legal Found., 1993, Rep. Presdl. award, 1994, Rep. Congl. Order of Liberty, 1993, Internat. Order of Merit medal, 1993, 20th Century award for achievement, 1993, Rep. Senatorial Medal of Freedom, 1994, Ronald Reagan Eternal Flame of Freedom medal and cert., 1995, Cmty. Svc. and Profl. Achievement medal, 1995, World Lifetime achievement award ABI-USA, 1996, Millennium medal of Freedom, 1999. Mem. SAG, NRA, Calif. State Horsemen (life), Equestrian Trails (life), Forty Niners (life), Calif. Rep. Assembly, Heritage Found., Cowboy Turtles Assn. (life), Rodeo Cowboys Assn. (life), Pro Rodeo Cowboys Assn. (life), Internat. Platform Assn., Lake Isabella C. of C., Kern County C. of C. Baptist. Avocations: heritage, horses, cowboys, mountain men, indians. Home: 40371 Cowboy Ln Caliente CA 93518-1405

DEFOOR, J. ALLISON, II, lawyer; b. Coral Gables, Fla., Dec. 6, 1953; s. James Allison Sr. and Marjorie (Keen) DeF.; m. Terry Ann White, June 24, 1977; children: Melissa Anne, Mary Katherine, James Allison III. BA, U. So. Fla., 1976; JD, Stetson U., 1979; MA, U. So. Fla., 1979; postgrad., Harvard U., 1989; STD, So. Fla. Ctr. Theol. Studies, 1999, MDiv, 2001, postgrad., 2002—. Bar: Fla. 1979, U.S. Dist. Ct. (so. dist.) Fla. 1980, U.S. Ct. Appeals (5th cir.) 1981, U.S. Ct. Appeals (11th cir.) 1982. Asst. pub. defender, 1979—80; asst. state's atty. 16th Cir., Key West, Fla., 1980—83, dir. narcotics task force, 1981—83; judge Monroe County, Plantation Key, Fla., 1983—87; assoc. Cunningham, Albritton, Lenzi, Warner, Bragg & Miller, Plantation Key, 1987—89; sheriff Monroe County, Fla., 1989—90; sr. v.p. CEO Wackenut Monitoring Systems Inc., Coral Gables, Fla., 1991—92; gen. counsel, sec. HEM Pharm. Corp., Phila. and Key Largo, 1992—93; ptnr. Hershoff, Lupino DeFoor & Gregg, Tavernier, Fla., 1993—99; Everglades policy coord. State of Fla., Office of Gov., Tallahassee, 1999—2000; gen. counsel Tidewater Cons, Inc., Tallahassee, 2000—02; state coord. EarthBalance, Inc., Tallahassee and North Port, 2002—; of counsel Hershoff, Lupino & Mulick, Tavernier, Fla., 2000—. Adj. faculty St. Leo Coll., Key West, 1980-81, U. So. Fla., Ft. Myers, 1981-82, Fla. Internat. U., Miami, 1985, U. Miami Law Sch., 1985-99, Fla. A&M U., 1999-2001; faculty Nat. Jud. Coll., Reno, Nev., 1985-86; lectr. Yale U., 2000, U. Pa. Law Sch., 2000. Editor U. Miami Law Rev., 1985; author: DeFoor & Schultz, Fla. Civil Procedure Forms with Practice Commentary, 1989, Odet Philippe, Peninsular Pioneer, 1997 (Safety Harbor Mus., Fla.). Trustee Coun. for Sustainable Fla., Fla. Dispute Resolution Consortium, Kairos Horizon, Collins Ctr. for Pub. Policy, Fla. C. of C.; pres. Mus. of Fla. History Found., 2000—01, Coun. for Sustainable Fla., 2001—03; chmn. Monroe County Rep. Exec. Com., 1987—88, 1994, state committeeman, 1994—99; mem. Fla. Rep. Exec. Com., 1995—99; del. Rep. Nat. Conv., 1992; Rep. nominee Lt. Gov. of Fla., 1990; chmn. Wakulla County Rep. Exec. Com., 2001—; vice chmn. Rep. Party of Fla., 2003—. Named one of Five Outstanding Young Men in Fla., Jaycees, 1984, Ten Outstanding Young Men in Am., Jaycees, 1985; recipient Merit award Fla. Crime Prevention Commn., 1982, Leadership Fla. Class V, Chmn.'s award Fla. Audubon, 1997. Mem. ABA, Fla. Bar (bd. govs. 1995-97), Mensa, Ocean Reef Club (Key Largo, Fla.), Islamorada Fishing Club, Key West Yacht Club, Explorer's Club (New York), Gov.'s Club. Republican. Episcopalian. Avocations: scuba diving, sailing, golf. Home: 359 River Plantation Rd Crawfordville FL 32327-1517 Office: Earth Balance 200 W College Ave Ste 311-D Tallahassee FL 32301

DEFORCE, DIETER LUCIËN DANIËL, research scientist, educator; b. Menen, Belgium, July 7, 1971; s. Arnaut Deforce and Yvette Delbecque; m. Ann Katrien Paula Vercruysse, Apr. 3, 1999. PharmD, U. Gent, Gent, Belgium, 1994, PhD in Pharm. Scis., 1999. Postdoctoral fellow Belgian Am. Ednl Found. U. Calif., San Diego, 1999-2000; sci. rschr. postdoctoral fellow U. Gent, 2000—01, prof., 2001—. Author: Advances in Chromatography, 2000; contbr. articles to profl. jours., chpts. to books; inventor in field. Recipient Belgian Am. Ednl. Found. and D. Collen fellow Belgian Am. Ednl. Found., 1999. Mem. Am. Assn. Pharm. Scientists. Home: Kortrijksestraat 3 Kuurne 8520 Belgium Office: U Gent Harelbekestraat 72 Ghent 9000 Belgium Fax: 32 9 220 6688. E-mail: dieter.deforce@ugent.be.

DEFORD, FRANK, sportswriter, television and radio commentator, author; b. Balt., Dec. 16, 1938; s. Benjamin F. Deford Jr. and Louise (McAdams) Deford; m. Carol Penner, Aug. 28, 1965; children: Christian McAdams, Scarlet Faith. BA, Princeton U., 1962. Writer Sports Illustrated mag., N.Y.C., 1964-89, 98—; editor, pub. The Nat. Sports Daily, N.Y.C., 1989-91; contbg. editor Newsweek, 1991-93, 96-98, Vanity Fair, 1993-96. Commentator Nat. Pub. Radio, Washington, 1980—, Cable News Network, N.Y.C., 1980—86, NBC Sports, N.Y.C., 1986—89, ESPN Radio, N.Y.C., 1991—98, HBO, N.Y.C., 1994—. Author: Five Strides on the Banked Track, 1971, There She Is, 1971, Cut 'n' Run, 1972, The Owner, 1976, Big Bill Tilden: The Triumphs and the Tragedy, 1976, Everybody's All-American, 1982, Alex: The Life of a Child, 1983, The Spy in the Deuce Court, 1986, The World's Tallest Midget, 1987, Casey on the Loose, 1989, Love and Infamy, 1993, The Best of Frank Deford, 2000, The Other Adonis, 2001, An American Summer, 2002; author: (screenplay) Trading Hearts, 1988. Trustee Cystic Fibrosis Found., Washington, 1973—, chmn., 1984—99, chmn. emeritus, 1999—. Named Sportswriter of Yr., Nat. Assn. Sportswriters and Sportscasters, 1982, 1984, Sportswriter Hall of Fame, 1998, Nat. Mag. Writer of Yr., Wash. Journalism Rev., 1987, 1988, Best U.S. Sportswriter, Am. Journalism Rev., 1992; recipient 1st Winner award for Excellence in Sport Journalism Ctr. for Study of Sport in Soc., Northeastern U., 1985, Disting. Svc. to Journalism award, U. Mo., 1987, Emmy award for TV Writing and Commentary, 1988, George Foster Peabody award for Documentary Writing, 1999, Sportswriter of Yr., Nat. Assn. Sportswriters and Sportscasters, 1985, 1986, 1987, 1988, Nat. Mag. Award for Profiles, 1999. Democrat. Episcopalian. Home and Office: PO Box 1109 Greens Farms CT 06838-1109 E-mail: frank6de@aol.com.

DEFORD, RUTH I. music educator; b. Lawrence, Kans., Dec. 8, 1946; d. Donald D. DeFord and Leora M. Adams DeFord; m. Mahesh K. Kotecha, Aug. 20, 1977; children: Vicram Cyrus, Vijay Roy. MusB, BA, Oberlin (Ohio) Coll. Conservatory Music, 1968; PhD, Harvard U., 1975. Asst. prof. SUNY, Geneseo, NY, 1975—77; prof. Hunter Coll. and Grad. Ctr. CUNY, N.Y.C., 1977—. Contbr. chapters to books, articles to profl. jours. Office: Music Dept Hunter Coll 695 Park Ave New York NY 10706

DEFOREST, ADAMADIA, pediatric virologist; b. Harrisburg, Pa., July 16, 1933; d. Theodore David and Laura Arabelle (Davis) D. BA, Hood Coll., 1955; MS, Wash. State U., 1957; PhD, Temple U., 1968. Diplomate Am. Bd. Med. Microbiology. Instr. dept. pediatrics Temple U. Sch. Medicine-St. Christopher's Hosp. for Children, Phila., 1967-70, asst. prof., 1970-78, assoc. prof., 1978-97; assoc. prof. dept. pathology and lab. medicine MCP-Hahnemann Sch. Medicine, 1999—. Cons. N.Am. Biols., Inc., Miami, Fla., 1993-95; mem. adv. panel FDA, Washington, 1985—. Author: Chemical Sterilization, 1973, Infection Control, 1990, Pulmonary Disease in Children, 1994. Treas. Cheltenham Camera Club, 1999—. Fellow Am. Acad. Microbiology: mem. APHA (governing coun. 1990-96, Difco award 1989); mem. Am. Soc. Microbiology, Pan Am. Soc. for Clin. Virology (governing coun. 1992-96). Lutheran. Avocation: photography. Office: St Christopher's Hosp for Children Erie Ave at Front St Philadelphia PA 19134 E-mail: ada@navpoint.com.

DE FOREST, SHERWOOD SEARLE, agricultural engineer, agribusiness services executive; b. Ames, Iowa, Sept. 20, 1921; s. Frank Ray and Clara Maud (Searle) De F.; m. Virginia Mary Flynn, June 20, 1947; children: David, Debra, Denise, Kimberly. Student, U. Cin., 1939-40; BS, Iowa State U., 1943, MS, 1947. Instr. agrl. engring. Iowa State U., 1946-47, extension agrl. engr., 1947-52; engring. editor Successful Farming mag., Des Moines, 1952-59; with USX, Pitts., 1959-77, mgr. agrl. equipment mktg., 1964-70, indsl. rep., 1970-77; v.p., assoc. The Montgomery Group, Inc., Tallahassee, Fla., 1977-96; pollution prevention engr. Fla. Dept. Environ. Protection, Tallahassee, 1996-99; owner De Forest Agri-Serivces, Tallahassee, Fla., 1977-99. Pres. Ginande Corp., 1986-91; tech. transfer project leader No. Agrl. Energy Center, Sci. and Edn. Adminstrn., U.S. Dept. Agr., Peoria, Ill., 1980-81; cons. Pakistan, 1984, Portugal, 1985, 86; mem. indsl. and profl. adv. com. Coll. Engring. Pa. State U., 1966-71; mem. NE Regional Agrl. Research Planning Com., 1970-72; mem. Fla. Gov.'s Continuing Care Adv. Coun., 1996-2000. Contbg. author: Power to Produce, U.S. Dept. Agr. Yearbook, 1969, Steel in Agriculture, 1966; Pub. TravelHost of Pitts. mag., 1982-83; tech. editor Soc. Automotive Engrs. Internat., 1987-89; numerous articles to Successful Farming Mag. Served to 1st lt. USAAF, 1942-46. Recipient Am. Soc. Agrl. Engrs.-Metal Bldg. Mfrs. Assn. award for disting. work in advancing knowledge and sci. of farm bldgs., 1964 Fellow: Am. Soc. Agrl. Engrs. (pres. 1975—76); mem.: Fla. Life Care Residents Assn., Inc. (chpt. pres. 1999—2002, state bd. dirs. 2001—, state treas. 2003—). Presbyterian (ruling elder). Achievements include patents in field. Home and Office: 4173 Covenant Ln Tallahassee FL 32308-5766 E-mail: sdeforesthsd@earthlink.net.

DEFOREST, WALTER PATTISON, III, lawyer; b. Ft. Sill, Okla., Dec. 4, 1944; s. Walter P. Jr. and Mary E. (Miller) DeF.; m. Anna Thun. BA, U. Pitts., 1966; JD, Harvard U., 1969. Bar: Pa. 1970, U.S. Ct. Appeals (2d and 3d cirs.) 1973, U.S. Ct. Appeals (4th, 5th and D.C. cirs.) 1978, U.S. Ct. Appeals (10th cir.) 1981, U.S. Ct. Appeals (11th cir.), U.S. Ct. Appeals (7th cir.) 1986, U.S. Ct. Appeals (fed. cir.) 1995, U.S. Supreme Ct. 1974, W.Va. 1997, Ohio 2001. Assoc. Reed, Smith, Shaw & McClay, Pitts., 1969—77, ptnr., 1978—93, DeForest Koscelnik Yokitis & Kaplan, Pitts., 1994—2003, 2003—. Instr. Grad. Sch. Indsl. Adminstrn. Carnegie Mellon U., Pitts., 1974-75. Mem. adv. com. Big Bros. and Big Sisters Western Pa., Pitts., 1984—; bd. dirs. Pa. Small Bus. Advocacy Coun., Harrisburg, 1984-89, 92. Mem. ABA (litigation, labor sects.), Pa. Bar Assn. (litigation, labor sects.), Allegheny County Bar Assn. (litigation sect., fed. ct. sect.). Office: DeForest Koscelnik Yokitis & Kaplan 3000 Koppers Bldg 436 7th Ave Pittsburgh PA 15219-1826

DEFOTIS, GARY CONSTANTINE, chemical physicist, educator; b. Chgo., June 30, 1947; s. Nicholas Constantine and Leona Irene (Szymanowski) DeF. BSc in Chemistry, U. Ill., 1968; PhD in Phys. Chemistry, U. Chgo., 1977. Postdoctoral rsch. assoc. U. Ill., Chgo., 1977-78; asst. prof. Mich. State U., East Lansing, 1978-80, Coll. William and Mary, Williamsburg, Va., 1980-84, assoc. prof., 1984-89, prof. chemistry, 1989-92, Garrett-Robb-Guy prof. chemistry, 1992—97, 2002—. Reviewer various jours., funding agys. Contbr. articles to sci. jours. Grantee NSF, others; recipient Outstanding Faculty award, Commonwealth of Va., 1998. Mem. Am. Phys. Soc., Am. Chem. Soc. (Rsch. in Undergrad. Instn. award 1997), Coun. on Undergrad. Rsch., Phi Beta Kappa. Achievements include discovery of the 3D-XY-ferromagnet in an insulating system; development of systems exhibiting unique magnetic phase diagrams. Office: Coll William and Mary Dept Chemistry PO Box 8795 Williamsburg VA 23187-8795

DE FRANCESCO, JOHN BLAZE, JR., public relations consultant, artist, writer; b. Stamford, Conn., May 22, 1936; s. John Blaze and Mae (Matyscyk) DeF.; m. Louise C. Terlizzo, Nov. 1, 1958 (div. 1983); children: Daryl, Jay, Dana, Dorian; m. Diana Picchietti, Oct. 20, 1990. BS, U. Conn., 1958. Sr. v.p. Daniel J. Edelman, Inc., Chgo., 1967-77; exec. v.p. Ruder Finn & Rotman, Inc., Chgo., 1977-85; prin., CEO DeFrancesco/Goodfriend Pub. Relations, 1985-2001; exec. v.p. L.C. Williams & Assoc., Chgo., 2001—03; prin. DeFrancesco Artist and Writer, 2003—. Bd. dirs. Ill. Divsn. Vocat. Rehab., 1976-78; mem. pub. rels. adv. bd. Gov.'s State U., 1994-98. Comdr. USN, 1958-67; comdr. USNR; ret. 1979. Recipient 3 Silver Anvil awards Pub. Rels. Soc. Am., 6 Golden Trumpet awards Publicity Club, Chgo. Mem. Pub. Rels. Soc. Am., Navy League U.S., Mil. Officer Assn. Am. Roman Catholic. Home and Office: 18785 Saint Andrews Dr Monument CO 80132-8824

DE FRANCESCO, JOHN KENNETH, foreign language educator; b. Phila., July 26, 1932; s. John and Anna (Giove) de F. BA, LaSalle Coll., 1955; AM, Middlebury Coll., 1956; postgrad., U. Wis., 1957-58, U. Rome, 1961, U. Florence, Italy, 1962; ABD, Rutgers U., 1963; postgrad., U. Rome, 1964, U. Perugia, Italy, 1990. Tchr. Phila. Pub. Sch., 1955-56; grad. asst. U. Wis., Madison, 1957-58; dir. lang. lab LaSalle U., Phila., 1958-60, asst. prof., 1959-67; assoc. prof. Camden County Coll., Phila., 1967-69, prof., 1969—2001, chmn. Fgn. Lang., 1968—2001, prof. emeritus, 2002; lectr. Cabrini Coll., Radnor, Pa., 1965-68. Lectr. Rutgers U., New Brunswick, NJ, 1962-63; prof. Emeritus, 2001. Recipient award for tchg. excellence Camden County Coll., 1980, U. Tex., Austin, 1989; scholar Middlebury Coll., 1952, 53, 55, 56, U. Wis., 1957-58, Rutgers U., 1962-63; Fulbright grantee, Rome and Florence, 1961-62; Fulbright-Hays grantee U. Rome, 1964; Govt. of Italy study grantee U. Perugia, 1990; spl. award 1983), Am Assn. Tchr. Italian (pres. Del. Valley chpt. 1990-94, 96-2000, spl. award 1994, 99, award of excellence 2000). Mem. MLA (bd. dir. Phila. sect. 1979-83, 90-94, 1996-2000), Am. Commn. Tchr. Fgn. Langs., Am. Assn. Tchr. Spanish and Portuguese (pres. Phila. and Vicinity chpt. 1979-83, spl. award 1983), Am Assn. Tchr. Italian (pres. Del. Valley chpt. 1990-94, 96-2000, spl. award 1994, 99, award of excellence 2000), Camden Co. Coll. Faculty Assn. (pres. 1969-71, Spl. award 1971, commencement spkr. 1991, Pres. medal 2000), Fulbright Alumni Assn. (bd. dir. Phila. area 1998—), Sons of Italy (trustee Benvenuto lodge 1995-2002, hist. 1998-2000, state del. 1997-01, v.p. 2001—, trustee dist. 5 1999-2001), Commn. Italians in Fgn. Countries (bd. counselors 1998—), Overbrook Farms Club, Overbrook Italian-Am. Club, Phila. Area Spanish Educators (charter), Nat. Italian Am. Found., Unione Regionale Abruzzese (bd. dir.), Smithsonian Assn., Pi Delta Phi. Roman Catholic. Avocations: travel, classical music, dancing. Home: 6491 Sherwood Rd Philadelphia PA 19151-2416

DEFRANCESCO, MARK STEPHEN, physician; b. New Haven, Conn., Dec. 16, 1949; s. James Joseph and Josephine Elizabeth DeF.; m. Helen Mary Ouellette, May 4, 1984; children: Christopher, Erin, Bethany, Kaitlin. BA, Yale U., 1971; MD, U. Conn., 1980; MBA, U. New Haven, 1997. Diplomate Am. Bd. Ob. Gyn. Pvt. practice physician Ctr. for Women's Health, Waterbury, Conn., 1984—, pres., 1997—; co-med. dir. Women's Health Conn., Inc., Avon, Conn., 1997—, chief med. officer, 1999—. Dir. Women's Health Conn., Avon, Conn., 1997—; lectr. in field. State rep. Conn. State Legislature, Hartford, 1973. Recipient Disting. Grad. award Nat. Cath. Edn. Assn., 1996, knight of honor Notre Dame H.S., West Haven, Conn., 1998; grantee Eli Lilly & Co., 1999. Fellow ACOG (officer, vice chair Conn. sect. 1997-99, chair 2000—), Am. Coll. Surgeons; mem. New England Ob-gyn. Soc. (coun. mem.), Conn. State Med. Soc. (mem. maternal morbidity and mortality com.). Avocations: golf, computers, reading. Office: Ctr for Women's Health 60 Westwood Ave Waterbury CT 06708-2460 Fax: 203-578-3824. E-mail: markdefran@aol.com., mark.defrancesco@womenshealthusa.com.

DEFRANCIS, SUELLEN MARIA, interior architect; b. Bklyn., Sept. 21, 1946; d. Joseph Agustino and Mary DeF.; m. James D. Block, Apr. 23, 1965 (div. 1983); children: Melissa, Louis, Maximillian. BS, CCNY, 1982; BArch, CUNY, 1982, MS in Urban Design, 1983. Designer John Burgee Architects, N.Y.C., 1985-86; prin., owner Suellen DeFrancis Archtl. Interiors, Scarsdale, 1986—. Real estate investment advisor; lectr. Iona Coll., New Rochelle, N.Y., in field of architecture. Major projects include N.Y. Yacht Club, N.Y.C., Nippon Steel, N.Y.C., Mitsubishi Estate Housing, Ashiya, Japan, Asahi Breweries, Kobe, Japan, Sakikawa residences, Tokyo, Atlanta, and N.Y.C., Okada residences, Iwaki, Japan, N.Y.C., Met. Tower, N.Y.C., Genex Hdqs., N.Y.C., Hilcrest by Hilton, Tarrytown, N.Y., The Castle Restaurant and Inn, Tarrytown, Berkshire Place Hotel, N.Y., IBM Milford (Conn.) Campus, archtl. restoration 1923 Young Apts. Bldg., Scarsdale, N.Y.; works pub. in (book) 100 Designers' Favorite Rooms, 1993, 1st and 3d edits., (mag.) Kukan, Japan, N.Y. Times, Wall St. Jour. Trustee St. Christopher's-Jennie Clarkson Childcare Svcs., Inc. Recipient del Gaudio award N.Y. Soc. Architects, 1982; AIA scholar, 1982. Mem. AIA (assoc., N.Y.C. AIA interiors com.), Internat. Interior Design Assn., Internat. House of Japan, Far East Soc. Architects and Engrs., Nippon Club, Cosmopolitan Club (N.Y.C.). Avocations: travel, tennis. Office: PO Box 247 Scarsdale NY 10583-0247

DEFRANCO, BONIFACE FERDINAND LEONARD (BUDDY DEFRANCO), clarinetist, bandleader; b. Camden, N.J., Feb. 17, 1923; m. Joyce O. Yount; 1 child, Charles Lee. Student, Mastbaum Music Sch., Phila. Alto saxophonist, solo clarinetist Johnny Scat Davis Band, on tour, 1939, Gene Krupa Orch., on tour, 1941-42, Charlie Barnett Orch., on tour, 1943; solo clarinet Tommy Dorsey Orch., on tour, 1944-48, Count Basie Septet, on tour, 1950; bandleader Buddy DeFranco Orch., 1951; featured clarinetist Jazz at the Philharm. All Star Tours, worldwide, 1952-54; condr. Glenn Miller Orch., 1966-74; leader, guest artist The Buddy DeFranco Group, Panama City, Fla., 1974—. Performer, clinician Yamaha Music Corp., Grand Rapids, Mich., 1973—; clinician, judge various univs., 1950—. Author: Buddy DeFranco Hand in Hand with Hanon, 1996, Buddy DeFranco on Jazz Improvisation, 1973, Mel Bay Presents Modern Jazz Compositions and Studies for the Clarinet, 1983; rec. artist numerous albums including Hark: Buddy DeFranco Meets the Oscar Peterson Quartet, 1994, Chip Off the Old Bop, 1994, You Must Believe in Swing, & Nobody Else But Me, with Metropole Orch., 1997, Flying Fingers of Art Tatum and Buddy DeFranco, Cross Country Suite with Nelson Riddle (Grammy award 1956), Mr. Lucky, Mood Indigo, Chicago Fire with Buddy DeFranco and Terry Gibbs, George Gershwin Songbook with Oscar Peterson, Buddy DeFranco/Dave McKenna. Do Nothing 'Till You Hear From Us, 1999. Named #1 Jazz Clarinetist over 45 times Downbeat mag., Metronome mag., Playboy Mag. All Stars-All Stars, Ency. Jazz Musicians poll. Fellow Nat. Assn. Jazz Educators; mem. ClariNetowrk (bd. dirs. 1980—), ASCAP. Home (Summer): 978A Colorado Ave Whitefish MT 59937-3413 Address: 22525 Coral Ave Panama City FL 32413-3047 E-mail: harkii@hotmail.com.

DE FREITAS, GABRIEL FERNANDES, surgical oncologist; b. New Bedford, Mass., Oct. 7, 1934; s. John and Mary (Costa) de F.; m. Sylvia Eileen Anderson, June 24, 1961; children: Laurie, Elisabeth, Geoffrey. AB, Brown U., 1956; MD, Boston U., 1960. Resident in gen. surgery and otolaryngology Boston U. Med. Ctr., 1961-67; fellow oncology Meml. Sloan Kettering Cancer Ctr., N.Y.C., 1967-69; pvt. practice surg. oncology Phoenix, 1969-89; staff surgeon gen. surgery VA Med. Ctr., Alexandria, La., 1989-90, chief of surgery Hot Springs, S.D., 1990-91; gen. surgeon Riverwood Clinic, Wisconsin Rapids, 1991-93; surg. oncologist Lorain (Ohio) Cmty., St. Joseph Regional Health Ctr., 1993-96, Knoxville (Tenn.) Breast Ctr., 1996-98; pvt. practice Phoenix, 1998-2000; ret., 2000. Capt. U.S. Army, 1962-63. Fellow ACS; mem. Soc. Surg. Oncology, Soc. Head and Neck Surgeons, Am. Radium Soc., Am. Soc. Clin. Oncology, Am. Soc. Breast Disease, Am. Soc. Breast Surgeons. Avocations: music, art, gardening, egyptology.

DE FRIES, JOHN CLARENCE, behavioral genetics educator, researcher; b. Delrey, Ill., Nov. 26, 1934; s. Walter C. and Irene Mary (Lyon) De F.; m. Marjorie Jacobs, Aug. 18, 1956; children: Craig Brian, Catherine Ann. BS, U. Ill., 1956, MS, 1958, PhD, 1961. Asst. prof. U. Ill., Urbana, 1961-66, assoc. prof., 1966-67; rsch. fellow U. Calif., Berkeley, 1963-64; assoc. prof. behavioral genetics and psychology U. Colo., Boulder, 1967-70, prof., 1970—, dir. Inst. for Behavioral Genetics, 1981-2001. Author: (with G.E. McClearn) Introduction to Behavioral Genetics, 1973, (with Plomin and McClearn) Behavioral Genetics: A Primer, 1980, 4th edit., 2001, (with R. Plomin) Origins of Individual Differences in Infancy, 1985; (with R. Plomin and D.W. Fulker) Nature and Nurture During Infancy and Early Childhood, 1988, Nature and Nurture During Middle Childhood, 1994, (with R. Plomin, I.W. Craig and P. McGuffin) Behavioral Genetics in the Postgenomic Era, 2003, (with S.A. Petrill, R. Plomin and J.K. Hewitt) Nature, Nurture and the Transition to Early Adolescence, 2003; co-founder Behavior Genetics jour., 1970, mem. editl. adv. bd. 1st lt. U.S. Army, 1957-65. Grantee in field. Fellow AAAS (sect. J), Internat. Acad. for Rsch. in Learning Disabilities; mem. Am. Psychol. Soc., Am. Soc. Human Genetics, Behavior Genetics Assn. (sec. 1974-77, pres. 1982-83, Th. Dobzhansky award for outstanding rsch. in field 1992), Internat. Dyslexia Assn., Rodin Remediation Acad. and Found. Office: U Colo Inst Behavioral Genetics 447 UCB Boulder CO 80309-0447

DEFRIES, RUTH S. earth system scientist, researcher; b. Washington, Oct. 20, 1956; d. Myron G. DeFries and Tamar D. Lieberman; m. Jitendra N. Bajpai, Nov. 23, 1980; children: Triveni, Avinash Bajpai. BA summa cum laude, Washington U., St. Louis, 1976; PhD, Johns Hopkins U., 1980. Rschr. India Inst. Tech., Bombay, 1980—83; sr. project officer Nat. Rsch. Coun., Washington, 1983—91; assoc. rsch. scientist U. Md., College Park, 1991—99, assoc. prof., 1999—. Mem.: Ecol. Soc. Am. (Aldo Leopold Leadership fellow 2001), Am. Geophys. Union. Office: U Md Geography Dept College Park MD 20742 Office Fax: 301-314-9299. Business E-Mail: rd63@umail.umd.edu.

DE FRIESE, GORDON H. health services researcher; b. Trion, Ga., Apr. 25, 1942; BS, Middle Tenn. State U., 1963; MA, U. Ky., 1966, PhD, 1967. Instr. dept. behavioral sci. U. Ky. Med. Ctr., Lexington, 1966—67; asst. prof. sociology and social psychology Cornell U., Ithaca, NY, 1969—71; rsch. assoc. Cecil G. Sheps Ctr. for Health Svcs. Rsch. U. N.C., Chapel Hill, 1971—, asst. prof. sociology, 1971—77, asst. prof. family medicine Sch. Medicine, 1973—75, clin. assoc. prof. dept. epidemiology Sch. Pub. Health, 1978—82, assoc. prof. Sch. Medicine, 1976—82, prof. Sch. Medicine, 1982—, prof. Sch. Pub. Health, 1982—, prof. dept. dental ecology Sch. Dentistry, 1986—, co-dir. Robert Wood Johnson Found. Clin. Scholars Program, 1986—2000. Adj. asst. prof. Sloan Inst. Hosp. Adminstrn.; dir. U.S. Army Armor Sch. Electives Divsn., Fort Knox, Ky., 1967—69; co-dir. Comprehensive Health Planning Tng. Program of the Dept. of Sociology and City and Regional Planning and the Sloan Inst. Hosp. Adminstrn. Cornell U., Ithaca, NY, 1969—71; co-dir. grad. program in med. sociology Dept. Sociology U. N.C., Chapel Hill, 1971—76, dir. Cecil G. Sheps Ctr. for Health Svcs. Rsch., 1973—2000; pres., CEO N.C. Inst. Medicine; cons. and presenter in field; numerous other career related activities. Author (with B.D. Barker): Assessing Dental Manpower Requirements: Alternative Approaches for State and Local Planning, 1982; editor (with J.W. Bawden): Planning for Dental Care on a Statewide Basis: The North Carolina Dental Manpower Project, 1981; editor: (with T.C. Ricketts, J.S. Stein) Methodological Advances in Health Services Research, 1989; editor: Health Svcs. Rsch., 1983—96; co-editor (spl. issue): Jour. Family and Cmty. Health, 1982; assoc. editor: Social Forces, 1971—76, Drugs in Health Care, 1974—76, Jour. Health and Social Behavior, 1985—87, Am. Jour. Health Promotion, 1986—92, mem. editl. bd.: Health Care Mgmt. Rev., 1977—93, Med. Care, 1980—83, Internat. Jour. Health Scis., 1980—, Jour. Gerontology: Med. Scis., 1989—91, Comparative Health Policy: Nations, States, Cmtys., 1993—, book rev. editor: Health Svcs. Rsch., 1979—84; contbr. chapters to books, articles to profl. jours. Fellow: N.Y. Acad. Medicine; mem.: APHA (med. care sect.), Soc. for Gen. Internal Medicine, Found. for Health Svcs. Rsch. (bd. dirs. 1982—94, pres. 1986—87), Assn. for Health Svcs. Rsch. (bd. dirs. 1982—90, pres.-elect 1983—85, pres. 1985—86), Inst. Medicine, Sigma Xi. Office: Dept Social Medicine Med Sch Wing D U NC Campus Box 7240 Chapel Hill NC 27599-7240

DEFUSCO OCHAL, MARY THERESA, lawyer; b. Conshohocken, Pa., USA, Nov. 8, 1957; d. Domenico and Antonetta DeFusco; m. Leon Joseph Ochal, Dec. 26, 1981; children: Amanda Ochal, Leon Joseph III Ochal, Elizabeth Ochal, Domenic Ochal. JD, Temple U. Sch. of Law, 1982; BA, U. of Penn., 1979. Staff atty. Defender Assoc. of Phila., 1982—87; dep. chief Mcpl. Ct. Unit Defender Assoc. of Phila., 1987—95; dir. of training and recruitment Unit Defender Assoc. of Phila., 1995—; asst. in law Temple U. Sch. of Law, Philadelphia, Pa., 1992—; asst. faculty team leader Nat. Inst. for Trial Advocacy, 1992—96. Coun. bd. The Birth Ctr., Bryn Mawr, Pa., 1996—, pres. bd., 1992—96, bd. mem., 1989—92. Author: (article in manual) Criminal Law Practice & Procedure in Phila., 1989. Recipient St. Thomas More Award, St. Thomas More Soc. of Phila., 2000, Cesare Beccaria award, Crimnial Justice Section of Phila. Bar & Justinian. Soc., 1997, The Polsky Cup, Polsky Moot Ct. Judges, 1981, The Maria Rosa award, Am. Inst. for Italian Culture, 1979. Office: Defender Association of Philadelphia 1441 Sansom St Philadelphia PA 19102 E-mail: mdefusco@philadefender.org.

DEGENHARDT, ROBERT ALLAN, architectural firm executive, engineering executive; b. Kearney, Nebr., May 29, 1943; s. Robert Franklin and Florence Elizabeth (Spohnheimer) D.; m. Elizabeth Scholl; children: Barry, Christopher, Kathleen. BSME, U. Nebr., 1965, MSME, 1968. Registered profl. engr., D.C. and all states except Alaska and Hawaii. Project engr. Davis & Wilson Architects and Engrs., Lincoln, Nebr., 1964-68, White Sands (N.Mex.) Missile Range, 1968-70, Sundstrand Aviation, Rockford, Ill., 1970-74; dir. engring. Davis, Fenton, Stange, Darling, Architects and Engrs., Lincoln, 1974-77; v.p. mech. engring. Durrant Engrs. Inc., Madison, Wis., 1977-1980; dir. mech. engring . Ellerbe Assocs. Inc., Mpls., 1980-82, dir. archtl./engring. svcs., 1982-83, v.p., dir. ops., 1983-85; sr. v.p., dir. Ellerbe Becket Inc., Washington, 1985-89; exec. v.p., COO Ellerbe Becket Co., Mpls., 1989-93, pres., COO, 1993-94, pres., CEO, 1994-98, CEO, 1998-2001, pres., 2001—; sr. v.p. 3D Internat., Houston. Mem. Ctr. for Ethical Bus. Cultures, 1993—. 1st lt. U.S. Army, 1968-70. 1st lt. U.S. Army, 1968—70. Mem. Constrn. Industry Roundtable, U.S. C. of C. (internat. polic com.), Sigma Xi, Pi Tau Sigma. Republican. Lutheran. Avocations: fly fishing, backpacking, fly-fishing.

DEGENHART, ANNE ELIZABETH, music educator; b. Peoria, Ill., Aug. 1, 1976; d. Lillard Bates and Susan Kay Twitty; m. Shawn Thomas Degenhart, Dec. 22, 2001; 1 child, Aidan Rahe Metz. MusB in Vocal Performance, Bradley U., 1998; M in Music Edn., Ill. State U., Normal, 2001. Cert. instr. Kindermusik Internat., 2003. Pvt. vocal instr., Metamora, Ill., 1998—; gen. music instr., choral dir. St. Mark's Cath. Grade Sch., Peoria, 1998; cantor St. Mark's Cath. Ch., Peoria, 1998—2001, children's choir dir., 1998—2001; grad. asst. Ill. State U., Normal, 1999—2001; gen. music instr., choral dir. Elmwood (Ill.) Cmty. Schs., 2002—02; music tchr. St. Philomena Cath. Grade Sch., Peoria, 2003—. Dir., instr. Summer Music Camp, Peoria, 2000—01. Actor: cmty. theatre. Clemenceau Music scholar, Bradley U., Dr. Richard P. Wolf Meml. scholar, arts scholar, Cornstock Cmty. Theatre. Mem.: Peoria Area Music Tchrs. Assn., Music Tchrs. Nat. Assn. Republican. Roman Catholic. Avocations: travel, home remodeling, reading, hiking. Home: 322 N Lafayette Metamora IL 61548 Personal E-mail: degen22@mtco.com.

DE GENNARO, RICHARD, retired library director, library advisor; b. New Haven, Mar. 2, 1926; s. Ralph and Acquilina (Pedicini) De G.; m. Birgit M. Erikson, June 12, 1953; children: Ralph, George, Christina. BA, Wesleyan U., 1951, MA, 1960; MS in LS, Columbia U., 1956; postgrad., Univs. Paris, Madrid and Perugia, 1951-55; grad. Advanced Mgmt. Program, Harvard U., 1971; DHL (hon.), Wabash Coll., 1991. Jr. acct. Atlas Constructors, Morocco, 1952-53; reference librarian N.Y. Pub. Libr., 1956-58, dir., 1987-90, successively reference librarian, asst. dir., assoc. univ. librarian systems devel., sr. assoc. univ. librarian Harvard U. Libr., 1958-70; dir. librs. U. Pa., 1970-86, adj. prof. English, 1979-86; libr. Harvard Coll., 1990-96. Vis. prof. Grad. Libr. Sch., U. So. Calif., 1968-69; cons. libr. bldgs., tech. and mgmt.; mem. overseers com. to visit libr., Harvard U.; cons. MIT, Johns Hopkins U.; mem. adv. bd. Chem. Abstracts Svc., 1967-70; mem. Palinet bd. Union Libr. Catalogue, 1970—; mem. com. internat. sci. and tech. info. programs NAS-NRC, 1977-79; mem. Mellon Found. JSTOR Bd., 1995—; sr. libr. advisor JSTOR; mem. governing bd. Rsch. Librs. Group, 1979-89, sr. vis. fellow, 1980-81, chmn., 1984-95; Bowker lectr., 1979; Lazerow lectr., 1984. Author: Shifting Gears, Information Technology and the Academic Library, 1984, Libraries, Technology, and the Information Marketplace, Selected Papers, 1987; contbr. articles to profl. jours. Bd. dirs. Ctr. for Rsch. Librs., 1977-81; trustee U. Pa. Press, 1978-82. With USN, 1942-46. Recipient Disting. Alumnus award Wesleyan U., 1991; Hugh Atkinson award, 1993; named Acad. Rsch. Libr. of Yr., 1991; Coun. Libr. Resources fellow, 1971; Rockefeller Found. Ctr. fellow, Bellagio, Italy, 1981; info. tech. fellow U. Edinburgh, 1984. Mem. Assn. Rsch. Librs. (pres. 1975, dir. 1973-76), ALA (pres, info. sci. and automation div. 1975), Am. Soc. Info. Soc. (Melvil Dewey medal 1986), Century Assn. Club, Grolier Club, Harvard Club. Home: Unit 1414 988 Blvd Of The Arts Apt 1414 Sarasota FL 34236-4838

DE GENNES, PIERRE-GILLES, physicist, educator; b. Paris, Oct. 24, 1932; Ed, PhD, Ecole Normale Superieure. Rsch. scientist Centre d'Etudes Nucleaires de Saclay, 1955-59; prof. solid state physics U. Paris, Orsay, 1961-71; prof. Coll. de France, Paris, 1971—; dir. Ecole de Physique et Chimie, Paris, 1976—2002; sci. adv. for chem. physics Rhodia, France, 1999—. Author: (book) Superconductivity of Metals and Alloys, 1965, The Physics of Liquid Crystals, 1973, Scaling Concepts in Polymer Physics, 1979, Simple Views on Condensed Matter, 1992—2003, Les Objets Fragiles, 1994, Gouttes, Bulles Perles et Ondes, 2002, Petit Point, 2002. Ensign French Navy, 1959—61. Recipient Nobel prize in physics, 1991. Mem.: AAAS, Russian Acad. Sci., Nat. Acad. Scis., Brazilian Acad. Scis., Ukranian Acad. Scis., Royal Soc., Dutch Acad. Scis., Académie des Sciences. Avocations: drawing, hiking. Office: Institut Curie Sect Biophysique 11 Rue P Curie 75005 Paris France E-mail: pgg@curie.fr.

DEGENSHEIN, JAN, architect, planner; b. Bklyn., Sept. 15, 1946; s. Harry and Beverly (Oppenheimer) D.; m. Lynne Sheren, Sept. 1, 1968 (div. Mar. 1978); 1 child, Britta; m. Nadja Hoyer-Booth, June 1, 1980 (sep. Sep. 2002); children: Oleg, Anya. BS Archtl. Scis., Washington U., 1967; BArch, MS in Planning, Pratt Inst., 1970; postgrad., CUNY, 1979-84. Registered architect, N.Y., N.J., Conn., Pa., Vt.; cert. NCARB. Assoc. architect R.C. Weinberg & Assocs., N.Y.C., 1968-70, Seiler Nakrosis Kerner, Liberty, N.Y., 1970-72; v.p. Degan Enterprises Inc., New City, N.Y., 1973-78; pres., prin. Jan Degenshein Architect-Planner, New City, 1975-83; pres. Degenshein Denker Assocs. P.C., Nyack, N.Y., 1983-88, Degenshein Denker Bodnar P.C., Nyack, 1988-91; prin., pres. Jan Degenshein Architects-Planners, Nyack, N.Y., 1991—. Guest critic Pratt Inst. Sch. Architecture, 1982, CCNY Sch. Architecture, 1990. Author: Atlantic-Schermehorn Corridor, 1970. Chmn., com. mem. Rockland County (N.Y.) Art in Pub. Places, 1987-1998; v.p., trustee Blue Rock Sch., West Nyack, 1989-95; mem. bd. advisors Martin Luther King Multi-Purpose Ctr., Spring Valley, N.Y., 1991—; vol., mem. bd. advisors, bd. dirs. Vol. Counseling Svcs., New City, 1994-2002; mem. environ. adv. coun. U.S. Rep. Benjamin Gilman, 1993-96; mem. campaign cabinet Arts Fund for Rockland, Rockland County, 1990-92; mem. N.Y. State Bldg Ofcls. Conf., 1994—, Interfaith Forum on Religious Art and Architecture, 1983—, Arts Coun. of Rockland, 1986—; nominating com. Rockland County coun. Girl Scouts U.S., 1991-94; coord. Leadership Rockland Econ. Devel. Day, 1995-2000, bd. dirs., 1995-2002, sec., 1999-2002, mem. selections com., fin. com.; mem. Rockland Mcpl. Planning Fedn., 1990—, assoc. dir., 1997—; bd. dirs.Housing Action Coun., 1998-2001, exec. bd., 1999-2001; mem. retention and expansion com.Rockland Econ. Devel. Corp., 1996—, cert. recognition, 1999. Recipient archtl. excellence award Orange County Bd. Realtors, 1988, 89, Rockland County Execs. Arts award, 1995; winner Arts Coun. of Rockland poetry competition, 2002; named Bus. Man of Yr., Nat. Rep. Congl. Com., 2002, Bus. Leader of Yr., Rockland Jour. News, 2003. Mem. AIA (honor award for archtl. excellence Westchester/Mid-Hudson 1987, 88, 92, 94, 96, 2000; cmty.design awards; Rockland County Beautification award. 1992, 94 Rockland County Legislature Cert. of Recognition, 1999, Am. Inst. Cert. Planners, Am. Planning Assn., Rockland County Builders Assn. (Assoc. of Yr. 1978, Builder of Yr. 1980), Leadership Rockland (dir. 1994—, pres. alumni assn. 1994-96, sec. 1999—),Rockland Bus. Exchange (v.p., pres. membership com. 1993-97), Rockland Coalition for Democracy and Freedom (dir. 1995), Am. Forum for Global Edn. (advisor 1995-97) Hist. Soc. Rockland, Computer and Telecom. Initiative Rockland (chairperson nominating com. 1996, bd. dirs. 1997-2001), Rockland Bus. Assn. (mem. svcs. com. 1996, chair amb.'s com. 1996-98, comms. and advocacy com. 1997—, bd. dirs. 1997-2001, chmn. affordable housing com. 2001—), Nyacks C. of C. (v.p. 1988-89), Rotary Internat. Avocations: graphic arts, cooking, golf, writing. Office: 205 S Broadway Nyack NY 10960-4425 E-mail: Jan@Degenshein.com.

DE GEORGE, LAWRENCE JOSEPH, diversified company executive; b. N.Y.C., May 6, 1916; s. Frank Phillip and Frances (Cavallo) DeG.; m. Florence A. Efel, Dec. 18, 1943; children: Lawrence F., Peter R. BSEE, Princeton U., 1936; MS, MIT, 1938; PhD in Advanced Math., Columbia U., 1939. Assoc. prof. elec. engring. Columbia U., 1938-39; field engr. Radio Engring. Lab., N.Y.C., 1939-41; pres. Times Wire and Cable Co., Inc., div. Internat. Silver Co., Wallingford, Conn., 1946; also v.p., dir. Times Wire and Cable div., 1958-64, pres., 1964-68; v.p., dir. Insilco Corp., Meriden, Conn., 1968-72, exec. v.p., 1972-77, vice chmn., 1976-77; chmn., pres. Times Fiber Communications, Inc., Meriden, 1977-84, chmn., chief exec. officer, 1985-92, LPL Techs. Inc., Wallingford, Conn., 1985-97, Amphenol Corp., Wallingford, Conn., 1987-97;

chmn., CEO DeG Capital Ptnrs. Ltd., Wallingford. Dir. Travelers Equities Fund, Inc., Hartford, Conn. Lt. comdr. USNR, 1941-46. Mem.: Club Collette, Admirals Cove Yacht Club, City Club, Palm Beach Yacht Club. Republican. Home: 176 Spyglass Ln Jupiter FL 33477-4037 Office: DeG Capital Ptnrs Ltd Ste 410 140 Intracoastal Pointe Dr Jupiter FL 33477-5094

DEGERSTROM, JAMES MARVIN, retired engineering executive; b. Owosso, Mich., Aug. 9, 1933; s. John Marcellus and Emma Judith (Folkadahl) Degerstrom; m. Ann Blandford, July 3, 1964. BSME, Mich. State U., 1955; MBA, DePaul U., 1966. Cert. plant engr. Adminstrv. asst. Sunbeam Corp., Chgo., 1955-61; mfg. supt. Internat. Register Co., Inc., Chgo., 1961-65; sr. engr. Kitchens of Sara Lee, Inc., Deerfield, Ill., 1965-71; pres. Edmanson Bock Caterers, Chgo., 1972; mgr. bldg. ops. Jewel Cos., Inc., Barrington, Ill., 1972-81; dir. plant ops. Copley Meml. Hosp., Aurora, Ill., 1981-86, Little Co. Mary Hosp., Evergreen Park, Ill., 1986-88; dir. facilities Oak Park Hosp., 1988-89; mgr. plant engring. Honeywell, Inc., Joliet, Ill., 1989-90; dir. facilities mgmt. S. Suburban Hosp. of Adv. Health Care Sys., Hazel Crest, Ill., 1990-98, Oak Brook, Ill., 1990—98; ret., 1998. Bd. dirs., treas. Credit Union Kitchens of Sara Lee, 1966—70. With USAF, 1957—65. Mem.: Am. Inst. Plant Engrs. (sec. 1977—79, pres. chpt. 5 1991), Am. Inst. Indsl. Engrs., Toastmasters (pres. 1981, dist. officer 1982, area gov. 1982, lt. gov. 1983—84, dist. gov. 1984—85). Home: 102 Knollwood Ct Oak Brook IL 60523-1518 E-mail: jaandegerstrom@aol.com.

DE GETTE, DIANA LOUISE, congresswoman, lawyer; b. Tachikawa, Japan, July 29, 1957; came to U.S., 1957; d. Richard Louis and Patricia Anne (Rose) De G.; m. Lino Sigismondo Lipinsky de Orlov, Sept. 15, 1984; children: Raphaela Anne, Francesca Louise. BA magna cum laude, The Colo. Coll., 1979; JD, NYU, 1982. Bar: Colo. 1982, U.S. Dist. Ct. Colo. 1982, U.S. Ct. Appeals (10th cir.) 1984, U.S. Supreme Ct. 1989. Dep. state pub. defender Colo. State Pub. Defender, Denver, 1982-84; assoc. Coghill & Goodspeed, P.C., Denver, 1984-86; sole practice Denver, 1986-93; of counsel McDermott & Hansen, Denver, 1993-96; mem. Colo. Ho. of Reps., 1992-96, asst. minority leader, 1995-96; mem. U.S. Congress from 1st Colo. dist., 1997—; mem. commerce com. Editor: (mag.) Trial Talk, 1989-92. Mem. Mayor's Mgmt. Rev. Com., Denver, 1983-84; resolutions chair Denver Dem. Party, 1986; bd. dirs. Root-Tilden Program, NYU Sch. Law, N.Y.C., 1986-92; bd. trustees, alumni trustee Colo. Coll., Colorado Springs, 1988-94. Recipient Root-Tilden scholar NYU Sch. Law, N.Y.C., 1979, Vanderbilt medal, 1982. Mem. Colo. Bar Assn. (bd. govs. 1989-91), Colo. Trial Lawyers Assn. (bd. dirs., exec. com. 1986-92), Colo. Women's Bar Assn., Denver Bar Assn., Phi Beta Kappa, Pi Gamma Mu. Democrat. Avocations: reading, backpacking, gardening.*

DE GEUS, AART J. computer software company executive; MSEE, Swiss Fedn. Polytech Inst.; PhD Electrical Engring., So. Meth. U. Chmn., CEO Synopsys, Mountain View, Calif. Vice chmn., edn. supporter Silicon Valley Mfrs. Group; vice chmn. Electronic Design Automation Consortium. Fellow: IEEE (Indsl. Pioneer award). Office: Synopsys 700 E Middlefield Rd Mountain View CA 94043-4033

DEGEUS, WENDELL RAY, photographer; b. Des Moines, Feb. 1, 1948; s. Raymond G. and Thelma Z. (Hollingsworth) DeG. A. in Photography, Hawkeye Inst. Tech., 1973. Cert. EMT, basic trauma life support., PHTLS. Lab mgr., head tech. Midwest Photo Svc., Galesburg, Ill., 1975-80; sr. prodn. specialist TGS Tech. Inc./EROS Data Ctr., Sioux Falls, S.D., 1980-92, Hughes STX Corp/EROS Data Ctr., Sioux Falls, S.D., 1992-98; with Raytheon Corp./Eros Data Ctr., 1998—. Basic life support/CPR instr. Am. Heart Assn. Vol. Hot Line 58, Crisis Intervention, Galesburg, 1977-78; mem. Minnehaha County Rescue Squad, Sioux Falls, 1988—. Mem. Nat. Assn. Emergency Med. Technicians, S.D. EMT Assn. (state tng. officer dist. 2 1993-99). Democrat. Mem. Wesleyan Ch. Avocations: nature photography, bicycling, music, ham radio operation. Home: 819 N Walts Ave Sioux Falls SD 57104-2238 E-mail: wdegeus_1@lycos.com.

DEGHETT, STEPHANIE COYNE, writer, educator; b. Saranac Lake, N.Y., Aug. 31, 1951; d. Ward Robert and Alice Mae (Marshall) C.; m. Victor John DeGhett, Aug. 2, 1980; 1 child, Torie Rose. BA magna cum laude, SUNY, Potsdam, 1976; MA, U. Vt., 1981. Asst. coord. Sch.-within-a-Sch. Potsdam Coll., 1977; manuscript reviewer ABT Assocs., Cambridge, Mass., 1978; cons. Grad. Studies Office/SUNY, Potsdam, 1978; ednl. coord. CETA Title VI Projects, Potsdam, 1978; grad. tchg. fellow U. Vt., Burlington, 1979-81; prof., writing program SUNY, Potsdam, 1981—. Poetry editor: Blueline mag., 1987—; contbr. short story, poetry, ; showed photographs Del Bello Gallery, Toronto, 1991. Reading vol. Lawrence Ave. Elem. Sch., Potsdam, 1995—; bd. dirs. Environ. Mgmt. Coun., Canton, N.Y., 1984-86. Mem. Nat. Coun. Tchrs. English, Assn. Tchrs. Advanced Composition, SUNY Writers Coun. Democrat. Episcopalian. Avocations: skiing, gardening, photography, birding. Home: 25 Wheeler Rd Potsdam NY 13676-3404 Office: SUNY at Potsdam Pierrepont Ave Potsdam NY 13676

DEGHETTO, KENNETH ANSELM, engineering executive, construction executive; b. Clifton, N.J., Apr. 1, 1924; s. Anselm and Linda (Zanetti) DeG.; m. Helen Zschack, Nov. 5, 1944; children: Donna, Glenn. BS, U.S. Mcht. Marine Acad., 1943; B.Mech. Engring., Rensselaer Poly. Inst., 1950. Registered profl. engr., N.Y., N.J., Wash., Fla., Alaska. With Foster Wheeler Corp., Livingston, N.J., 1951-96, dir., 1972-96, v.p., 1973-76, exec. v.p., 1976-84, chmn. bd., 1983-87, Foster Wheeler Internat. Corp., Livingston, N.J., 1975-85, also bd. dirs. Bd. dirs. adv. brd., Mack-Cali Realty Corp.; chmn. KDG Internat. Cons. Mem. Rensselaer Sch. of Engring. adv bd., nat. chmn. U.S. Mcht. Marine Acad. Kings Point Challenge; chmn. Am. Found. for U. of the W.I.; vice-chmn. Bus. Coun. for Internat. Understanding. Lt. USNR, 1943-46. Fellow ASME, Brit. Inst. Mech. Engrs.; mem. Nat. Assn. Corrosion Engrs., Sigma Xi, Tau Beta Pi, Tau Pi Sigma. Clubs: Royal and Ancient Golf (St. Andrews, Scotland); Montclair (N.J.) Country, Brit. Engring. Golfing Soc. (capt. 1990). Lutheran. Home: 42 Cornell Dr Livingston NJ 07039-5518 Office: KDG Internat Cons 139 E McClellen Ave Livingston NJ 07039

DEGIGLIO, MICHAEL A. food products executive; Pres. Agro Dynamics subs. EcoScience Corp., East Brunswick, N.J., pres., CEO, 1995—, Village Farms LP, Eatontown, NJ, 1990—. Office: EcoScience Corp 7 Christopher Way Eatontown NJ 07724-3325 also: Village Farms LP 7 Christopher Way Eatontown NJ 07724 Fax: 732-676-3031.

DEGIOIA, JOHN J. university president; b. Orange, Conn. m. Theresa Miller DeGioia; 1 child, John Thomas. BA in English, Georgetown U., 1979, PhD in Philosophy, 1995. Asst. to the pres. Georgetown U., Washington, 1982—85, dean of student affairs, 1985—92, assoc. v.p., chief adminstrv. officer, 1992—95, v.p., 1995—98, lectr., mem. faculty, 1995—, sr. v.p., 1998—2001, pres., 2001—. Mem. adv. group COFHE Quality Mgmt.; mem. com. for presdl. responsibilities in student life Assn. Cath. Colls. and Univs.; participant Forum for Higher Edn.; bd. dirs. Fund for Edn. in South Africa, Washington Found. for Psychiatry. Named one of Young Leaders of the Acad., Change mag., 1998; recipient Chmn.'s award, Georgetown Alumni Admissions Program, 1997. Office: Georgetown U Office of the Pres 204 Healy Hall Box 571789, 37th and O Streets, NW Washington DC 20057

DEGIOVANNI-DONNELLY, ROSALIE FRANCES, biology researcher, educator; b. Bklyn., Nov. 22, 1926; d. Frank and Rose (Quartuccio) DeGiovanni; m. Edward Francis Donnelly, Sept. 23, 1961; children: Edward F. Jr., Francis M. BA, Bklyn. Coll., 1947, MA, 1953; PhD, Columbia U., 1961. Adj. prof. microbiology and genetics George Washington U., Washington, 1968—; rsch. biologist FDA, Washington, 1968-88. Contbr. articles to profl. jours. Recipient Merit award FDA, 1970. Mem. AAAS, AAUW, Italian Cultural Soc., Environ. Mutagen Soc., N.Y. Acad. Scis., Am. Soc. Microbiology, McLean Indoor Club, Sigma Xi, Sigma Delta Epsilon. Democrat. Roman Catholic. Avocations: theater, swimming, tennis, travel, photography. Home: 1712 Strine Dr Mc Lean VA 22101-4744 Office: George Washington U Microbiology Dept Washington DC 20052-0001 E-mail: edndol@earthlink.net.

DEGIUSTI, DOMINIC LAWRENCE, medical science educator, academic administrator; b. Treviso, Italy, Mar. 30, 1911; came to U.S., 1916, naturalized, 1925; s. Angelo L. and Angela (DeNegri) DeG.; m. Dianna Dobrzechowski, June 28, 1974; children— Lenore (Mrs. Antoine Noujaim), Angelo, Peter. BS, Coll. of St. Thomas, St. Paul, 1936; MS, U. Mich., 1938; PhD (DuPont fellow), U. Wis., 1943. Instr. Coll. of St. Thomas, 1936-38, asst. prof., 1942-43, 46-47; asst. in helminthology U. Mich. Biol. Sta., 1939-41, 46-51; instr., asst. prof. NYU Coll. Medicine, N.Y.C., 1943-46; research assoc. U. Minn. Coll. Medicine, 1946-47; asst. prof. Catholic U. Am., Washington, 1947-49; assoc. prof. dept. biology Wayne State U., Detroit, 1949-57, prof. dept. biology and Sch. Medicine dept. comparative medicine, 1957-81, prof. emeritus, 1981—, chmn. dept. biology, 1967-72, chmn. dept. comparative medicine, 1978-79. Mem. staff dept. pathology Detroit Gen. Hosp. Hutzel Hosp. Markle Found. fellow to Central Am., 1945; Fulbright Research fellow to Naples, Italy Zool. Sta., 1952; La. State U. fellow to Caribbean, 1957 Fellow N.Y. Acad. Scis., AAAS, Am. Inst. Fishery Research Biologists; mem. Am. Soc. Parasitologist (mem. council 1964-67), Am. Soc. Tropical Medicine and Hygiene, Am. Soc. Zoology, Am. Soc. Protozoology, Am. Micros. Soc. (mem. council 1963-69, v.p. 1965, pres. 1966), Helminthology Soc. Washington, Mich. Acad. Sci., Arts and Letters, Mich. Entomol. Soc. (pres. 1954), Sigma Xi. Home: 50295 Brockton Ct Macomb MI 48044-6108

DEGNAN, JAMES HENRY, physicist; b. Norristown, Pa., July 18, 1947; s. James Henry and Madeleine Mary (Bennis) D.; m. Elizabeth Teresa Castillo, Aug. 8, 1970 (div. May 21, 1984); children: James Henry, Michelle Teresa; m. Rikki Layne Quintana, May 15, 1988; 1 child, Siobhan Kathleen. BS in Physics, St. Joseph's U., Phila., 1969; MS in Physics, U. Pitts., 1972, PhD in Physics, 1973. Physicist GS-13 Air Force Weapons Lab., Kirtland AFB, N.Mex., 1978-85; physicist GS-14 Phillips Lab. (formerly Air Force Weapons Lab.), Kirtland AFB, 1985-94, physicist GS-15, 1994—. Adj. prof. U. N.Mex., Albuquerque, 1980-83; tech. adv. group Def. Nuclear Agy., Washington, 1992-95; presenter in field. Contbr. over 42 articles to profl. jours. Capt. USAF, 1973-78, Lt. Col. USAFR, 1978—. Mem. IEEE (sr. mem., session chmn. 1991, 93, 95), Am. Phys. Soc. Republican. Roman Catholic. Achievements include rsch. in feasibility of electromagnetic implosion of spherical metal shells, advances in compact torus, plasma flow switch, plasma gun, Z-pinch, and plasma compression technology. Office: Air Force Rsc Lab AFRL/DEHP 3550 Aberdeen Ave SE Kirtland Afb NM 87117-5776 E-mail: james.degnan@kirtland.af.mil.

DEGNAN, JOHN JAMES, III, physicist; b. Phila., Dec. 10, 1945, s. John James Jr. and Ruth Dolores (Vece); m. Adele Susan Henry, June 27, 1969; children: Adam John, Andrew Paul. BS in Physics, Drexel U., 1968; MS in Physics, U. Md., 1970, PhD in Physics, 1979. Student trainee NASA Goddard Space Flight Ctr., Greenbelt, Md., 1964-67, physicist, 1968-72, sr. physicist, 1972-79, sect. head, 1979-89, dep. mgr. crustal dynamics project, 1989-93, head space geodesy and altimetry projects office, 1993-96, head geosci. tech. office, 1996—2003; chief scientist Sigma Space Corp., Lanham, Md., 2003—. Instr. Drexel U., Phila., 1967-68; assoc. mem. Adv. Group on Electron Devices, 1980-85, dep. mem. 1985-89; adj. prof. physics Am. U., Washington, 1988-93; chmn. CSTG SLR/LLR Subcommn., 1992-98, chmn. Internat. Laser Ranging Svc. Governing Bd., 1998-2002; tech. bd. Wegener, 1992—2000, chmn., 2000—; mem. Am. Geophys. Union Steering Com. for Geodesy, 1998—, CSTG Exec. Bd. Contbr. articles to profl. jours. Mem. Common Cause, Annapolis, Md., 1970—; v.p., treas. Pasadena Theatre Co., Md., 1982-84. Drexel Bd. Trustees scholar, 1963; recipient Marple-Newtown Sch. Dist. Hall of Fame award, Disting. Alumnus, 1989, Moe I. Schneebaum Meml. award for engring. NASA/GSFC, 1987, Tsiolkovsky medal, 2002. Fellow Internat. Assn. Geodesy; mem. IEEE (sr.), Optical Soc. Am., Am. Phys. Soc., Am. Geophys. Union (steering com. geodesy 1998—), Planetary Soc., Internat. Laser Comm. Soc. (charter), Nat. Space Club, Sierra Club, Sigma Pi Sigma, Sigma Pi. Roman Catholic. Home: 928 Barracuda Cove Ct Annapolis MD 21401-4719 Office: Sigma Space Corp 9801 Greenbelt Rd Ste 103 Lanham MD 20706 E-mail: John.Degnan@sigmaspace.com.

DEGNAN, JOHN MICHAEL, lawyer; b. Mpls., Apr. 2, 1948; s. John F. and Lorraine A. Degnan; m. Barbara B. Degnan; children: Michael Gene Carland, John Patrick, Amy Marie, David Charles. BA, U. Minn., 1970; JD, William Mitchell Coll. Law, 1976. Bar: Minn. 1976, U.S. Dist. Ct. Minn. 1976, U.S. Ct. Appeals (8th cir.) Minn. 1976, U.S. Supreme Ct. 1976. Ins. underwriter Marsh & McLennan, Mpls., 1973-76; lawyer Bassford, Lockhart, Truesdell & Briggs, P.A., Mpls., 1976—2003, Murnane, Conlin, White & Brandt, St. Paul, 2003—. Lectr. in field. Bd. dirs. Hennepin County Pub. Libraries, 1980-84, Storefront Youth Action, 1981-83, Mediation Ctr., 1991—. 1st lt. U.S. Army, 1971-72, Vietnam. Fellow: Am. Bd. Trial Advocates, Am. Coll. Trial Lawyers; mem.: ABA, Am. Soc. Law and Medicine, Def. Rsch. Inst., Minn. Def. Lawyers Assn. (bd. dirs. 1986—, pres. 1990—91), Am. Bd. Trial Advocates, Nat. Bd. Trial Advocacy (cert. civil trial specialist), Hennepin County Bar Assn. (professionalism com.), Minn. State Bar Assn. (ins. com., lectr. convs. 1984—85, civil trial cert. governing coun., cert. trial specialist), Richfield Jaycees (past pres.). Avocations: running, tennis, golf, boating, sports. Office: Murnane Conlin White & Brandt 1800 US Bank Corp Piper Jaffray Tower 444 Cedar St Saint Paul MN 55101

DEGNITZ, DOROTHY ELSIE, retired nurse; b. Wis., Aug. 13, 1936; d. Fredrick William and Elsie Emily (Lawrenz) D. BSN, Northwestern U., 1959; cert., Frontier Sch. Nursing, 1968; diploma in nursing edn., Armidale (Australia) Coll., 1981; MA in Social Sci., Azusa (Calif.) Pacific U., 1986. RN, Wis. Instr. psychiat. nursing Sch. Nursing, Evanston (Ill.) Hosp., 1960-66; missionary nurse tchr. Bd. for Mission Svcs., St. Louis, 1966-67, 68-70, 1971-87; nursing supr. infirmary and nights Bethesda Luth. Home and Svcs., Watertown, Wis., 1987-94, part-time staff nurse, 1994-2001; part-time parish nurse Good Shepherd Luth. Ch., Watertown, 1999—; ret., 2001—. Mem. Nat. League for Nursing, Wis. Nurses Assn. Home: 1202 S 9th St Watertown WI 53094-6604

DE GOGORZA, PATRICIA, sculptor, educator; b. Detroit, Mar. 17, 1936; d. Maitland and Julia Harlow (Brodt) de G.; m. Dadi Wirz, Aug. 7, 1958 (div. Dec. 1962); 1 child, Paulo; m. James Edward Gahagan, Apr. 18, 1963 (dec. July 1999); 1 child, Sharon. BA, Smith Coll., 1958; MA, Goddard Coll., 1975. Cert. justice of the peace Vt., 2002. Asst. prof. art Bard Coll., Annandale, N.Y., 1966-69; drawing instr. U. Vt., Burlington, 1980-81; instr. Vt. Studio Ctr., Johnson, 1984—; sculpture instr. The Carving Studio, West Rutland, Vt., 1987—. Johnson State Coll., 1996, Arts Workshop, Akaroa, New Zealand, 1999—. Chair sculpture dept. Goddard Coll., Plainfield, Vt., 1973-74, 78-79; faculty MFA program Vt. Coll., Montpelier, 1992-93; instr. Vt. Clay Studio, Montpelier, 1994-97, Arts Workshop, Alkaroa, New Zealand, 1999—, Sculpture Workshop, Alcaroa, 200—, Clay Figure Study Workshop, Barre, Vt., 2002-03. One-woman shows include Sculpin Gallery, Martha's Vineyard, 1973, Bundy Mus., Waitsfield, Vt., 1982, Dibden Gallery, Johnson (Vt.) State Coll., 1984, Moonbrook Gallery, Rutland, Vt., 1984, A.V.A. Gallery, Hanover, N.H., 1985, Wood Art Gallery, Montpelier, 1988, Hillyer Gallery, Smith Coll., Northampton, Mass., 1989, Brown Libr., Craftsbury, Vt., 1999, exhibited in group shows at Carving Studio Sculptors in Vt., 1988—97, Helen Day Art Ctr., Stowe, Vt., 1986—98, So. Vt. Art Ctr., Manchester, 1993—97, West Branch Sculpture Gardens, Stowe, 1994—98, Akaroa Mus., New Zealand, 1999, Wood Art Gallery, Montpelier, 2000—03, Studio Place Arts, Barre, Vt., 2001—. Represented in permanent collections Sun/Moon Cycle granite sculpture Johnson State Coll., Riverbirds marble sculpture Marble St. Sculpture Pk., West Rutland, Pegasus marble sculpture Burlington City Bike Path, Mermaid, Merman and Dolphin 2 marble sculptures, Tree of Life, State of Vt. Pavilion Bldg., Montpelier, numerous pvt. collections and pvt. sculpture commns. Bd. dirs., pres. Art Resource Assn., Montpelier, 1976-84; chair Dem. Party, Woodbury, Vt., 1982—; art organizer, tchr. Rural Sch. Devel. Program, Woodbury, 1972-74; violinist I Vt. Philharm. Orch., 1979—, Montpelier Chamber Orch., 1997—, Contra Dance Band, 1998—. Mem. Internat. Sculpture Ctr., Art Resource Assn., Carving Studio. Democrat. Avocations: violin, gardening. Home and Office: 1580 Dog Pond Rd East Calais VT 05650-8134

DEGRAFF, HELEN MARIE, artist; b. Oran, Iowa, Feb. 27, 1928; d. LeRoy and Ethel May (Ramsey) Cosselman; m. Joseph Richard Palmer, June 9, 1952 (div. May 1973); children: William Joseph, Carole Lynn; m. Victor M. DeGraff, June 29, 1976. Grad. h.s., Oran, 1945. Portrait artist pvt. art studio, Elmhurst, Ill., 1960-74; art show dir. West Suburban Alliance, Wheaton, Ill., 1970-75; asst. promotional dir. Yorktown Shopping Ctr., Villa Park, Ill., 1971-73; office mgr., art editor V.I.P. Internat. Ednl. Films, Oak Brook, Ill., 1973-74; co-owner, artist Sands of Time Studio, Cobden, Ill., 1980—. Juror, art show judge, Chgo., 1965-75; art instr. pvt. studio, Elmhurst, Ill., 1975-80. Group exhbns. in watercolor and pastel in numerous locations, 1966—; contbr. poetry Best New American Poets, 1984, American Poetry Anthologies, 1985, 86, The Hand of Destiny, 1998 (Editor's Choice award Outstanding Achievement in Poetry 1998); represented in permanent collection St. Luke's Med. Ctr. Avocations: reading, music.

DEGRANDIS, RONALD WAYNE, music educator; b. Drexel Hill, Pa., Feb. 6, 1951; m. Janet K. Hardy, July 25, 1998; children: Sarah J. Hardy, Rebekah L. Hardy. MusB in Edn., Temple U., 1973; MusM in Edn., West Chester (Pa.) U., 1978. Cert. tchr. PA, 1973. Band, orch., jazz band dir. Shawnee Mid. Sch., Easton, Pa., 1979—; instrumental music tchr., coord. Tower Hill Sch., Wilmington, Del., 1974—79; instrumental music tchr. Gt. Valley Sr. HS, Malvern, Pa., 1973—74. Prin. viola Allentown (Pa.) Symphony Orch., 1979—; solo violist Assumption B.V.M. Ch. Contemporary Ensemble, Bethlehem, Pa. Composer: (songs) Northampton County 250th Anniversary March, Tracy Sch. Trilogy in 3 movements. Mem.: NEA, Pa. Music Educators Assn., Music Educators Nat. Conf., AFM Local 45. Home: 1915 Dartford Road Bethlehem PA 18015 Office: Shawnee Middle School 1010 Echo Trail Easton PA 18040 Personal E-mail: rongovla@fast.net.

DEGRANDPRE, CHARLES ALLYSON, lawyer; b. Manchester, N.H., July 7, 1936; s. Arthur Vital and Andrea Amanda (L'Etoile) DeG. AB, Clark U., 1958; JD, U. Mich., 1961. Bar: N.H. 1961, U.S. Dist. Ct. N.H. 1964, U.S. Supreme Ct. 1969. Dir. McLane, Graf, Raulerson & Middleton, P.A., Portsmouth, N.H., 1968—. Trustee, chair Smith Found., Manchester, 1986—; bd. dirs. Greater Piscataqua Cmty. Found., 1990-97. Author: Probate Law and Procedure, 1990, 2d edit., 1996, Wills, Trusts and Gifts, 1992, 3d edit., 1997. Chmn. bd. trustees Canterbury Shaker Village, 1992—97; bd. trustees Strawbery Banke Mus., 1997—2003; trustee, chair Smith Found., Manchester, NH, 1986—99; bd. dirs. N.H. Bar Found., 1997—; bd. dirs.. Greater Piscataqua Cmty. Found., 1990—97, Seacoast Land Trust, 1997—2002. Recipient N.H. Vol. of Yr. award Office of Gov., Concord, N.H., 1982. Fellow: Am. Coll. Trust and Estate Coun; mem.: N.H. Bar Assn. (Pres.'s award 1983, 2001). Avocations: hiking, reading, wine. Home: 60 Pleasant Point Dr Portsmouth NH 03801-5265 Office: McLane Graf Raulerson & Middleton 10 Pleasant St PO Box 459 Portsmouth NH 03802-0459 E-mail: cdegrandpre@mclane.com.

DE GRASSI, LEONARD, art historian, educator; b. East Orange, N.J., Mar. 2, 1928; s. Romulus-William and Anna Sophia (Sannicolo) DeG.; m. Dolores Marie Welgoss, June 24, 1961; children: Maria Christina, Paul. BA, U. So. Calif., 1950, BFA, 1951, MA, 1956; postgrad., Harvard U., 1953, Istituto Centrale del Restauro di Roma, 1959-60, U. Rome, 1959-60, UCLA, 1970-73. Tchr. art Redlands (Calif.) Jr. High Sch., 1951-53, Toll Jr. High Sch., Glendale, Calif., 1953-61, Wilson Jr. High Sch., Glendale, 1961; mem. faculty Glendale Coll., 1962—, prof. art history, 1974-92, chmn. dept., 1972, 89, prof. emeritus, 1992—. Tchr. Cite U., Paris, 1992, Istituto /Schuola Leonardo da Vinci, Florence, Italy, 1992. Prin. works include: (paintings) high altar at Ch. St. Mary, Cook, Minn., altar screen at Ch. St. Andrew, El Segundo, Calif., 1965-71, 14 Stas. of the Cross Ch. St. Mary, Cook, Minn., altar screen at Ch. of the Descent of the Holy Spirit, Glendale, 14 Stas. of the Cross at Ch. of St. Benedict, Duluth, Minn; also research, artwork and dramatic work for Spaceship Earth exhbn. at Disney World, Orlando, Fla., 1980. Decorated Knight Grand Cross Holy Sepluchre, 1974, knight St. John of Jerusalem, 1976, knight Order of Merit of Republic of Italy, 1973 Cross of Merit, 1984, 89; recipient J. Walter Smith Svc. award, 2001, numerous commendations; named First Disting. Faculty, 1987, Outstanding Educator of Am., 1971. Mem. Art Educators Assn., Am. Rsch. Ct. Egypt, Tau Kappa Alpha, Kappa Pi, Delta Sigma Rho. Office: 1500 N Verdugo Rd Glendale CA 91208-2809

DEGRAW, JOSEPH IRVING, JR., chemist, consultant; b. Washington, D.C., May 26, 1933; s. Joseph Irving and Gladys Margarite DeGraw; m. Ruth Jean Klees, May 4, 1957; children: Ronald Wayne, Sharon Rae. BS in Chemistry, U. Calif., Berkeley, 1956; PhD in Organic Chemistry, Stanford U., 1961. Rsch. organic chemist Merck & Co., Rahway, NJ, 1956—57, Stanford Rsch. Inst., Menlo Park, Calif., 1957—63, sr. organic chemist, 1963—74, program mgr. med. chemistry, 1974—80, dir. medicinal chemistry, 1980—90, assoc. dir. bioorganic chemistry, 1990—94; faculty assoc. U. Mont., Missoula, 1996—. Biomed. cons. Stanford Rsch. Inst., Menlo Park, Calif., 1983—95; mem. grant rev. filariasis WHO, Geneva, 1978; mem. grant rev. study sect. NIH, Washington, 1980—88. Contbr. articles to profl. jours.; mem. editl. bd.: Current Medicinal Chemistry, 1996—. Mem.: Am. Chem. Soc. (medicinal chemistry). Achievements include patents for new drugs; new drug inhibitors of folate biosynthesis; 5 clinically active anticancer, new analgesic, nonaddictive analog of morphine in preclinical development. Avocations: skiing, bowling, golf, hiking, woodworking. Home: 1255 Snowbowl Rd Missoula MT 59808 Office: U Mont Chem/Pharm Missoula MT 59807

DEGREGORI, THOMAS ROGER, economics educator, consultant; b. Cleve., May 5, 1935; s. James Victor and Mary Ann (Tambascio) DeG.; m. Gayle Sutherland, Oct. 22, 1960; children: Alice Eve, James Veblen, Roger Sutherland. BA in Philosophy and Govt., U. N.Mex., Albuquerque, 1959, MA in Econs., 1960; PhD in Econs., U. Tex., 1965. Vis. lectr. in econs. U. Khartoum, Sudan, 1962-63; from instr. to asst. prof. Case Inst. of Tech., Cleve., 1963-67; from asst. prof. to prof. U. Houston, 1967—. Mem. devel. studies program U.S. AID, Washington, 1978, mem. rsch. adv. com., 1987—; vis. lectr. Dhaka (Bangladesh) U., 1988; cons. and lectr. in field. Author: Technology and Economic Development in Africa, 1969, A Theory of Technology, 1985, (with others) Economic Development: The Cultural Context, 1969, Agriculture and Modern Technology, 2001, The Environment, Our Natural Resources and Modern Technology, 2002, Bountiful Harvest, 2002, others; contbr. numerous articles to profl. jours. Mem. Am. Coun. on Sci. and Health (bd. dirs.). Home: 2327 Goldsmith St Houston TX 77030-1129 Office: U Houston Dept Econs 4800 Calhoun Rd Houston TX 77204-5019

DEGROAT, DIANE, illustrator, author children's books; b. Newton, NJ, May 24, 1947; BFA, Pratt Inst., Bklyn., 1969. Designer, art dir. Holt, Rineholt, Winston, N.Y.C., 1969-72; freelance author, illustrator, 1972—. Author, illustrator: Roses Are Pink, Your Feet Really Stink, 1996, Trick or Treat, Smell My Feet, 1998, Happy Birthday to You, You Belong in a Zoo, 1999, Jingle Bells, Homework Smells, 2000, Annie Pitts, Burger Kid, 2000, We Gather Together -- Now Please Get Lost!, 2001, Good Night, Sleep Tight, Don't Let the Bedbugs Bite, 2002, Liar, Liar, Pants on Fire, 2003; illustrator: Little Rabbit's Loose Tooth, 1975, A Turkey for Thanksgiving, 1991, Dr. Ruth Talks to Kids, 1993; exhbns. include Am. Inst. Graphic Arts, Art Dirs. Club, Soc. Illustrators. Mem. Soc. Children's Book Writers & Illustrators, Authors Guild. Office: Harper Collins Children's Books 1350 Ave of the Americas New York NY 10019-4703 E-mail: dianedegroat@comcast.com.

DEGROAT, WILLIAM CHESNEY, pharmacology educator; b. Trenton, N.J., May 18, 1938; s. William Chesney and Margaret (Welch) deG.; m. Dorothy Marion Albertson, June 13, 1959; children: Allyson L., Cynthia L., Jennifer L. BSc, Phila. Coll. Pharmacy and Sci., 1960, MSc, 1962; PhD, U. Pa., 1965, postgrad., 1965-66, Australian Nat. U., Canberra, 1966-67. Vis. research fellow John Curtin Sch. Med. Research, Canberra, 1967-68; asst. prof. U. Pitts. Med. Sch., 1968-72, assoc. prof., 1972-77, prof. pharmacology, 1977—, acting chmn. dept. pharmacology, 1978-80, adj. prof. pharmacy, 1978-88, prof. psychology, 1982-86, mem. ctr. of neurosci., 1984—, prof. dept. behavioral neurosci., 1986-94, prof. dept. neurosci., 1995-96. Vis. prof. U. Coll., London, 1998; mem. neurobiology study sect. NIH, 1983-88; vis. scientist NIAAA-NIH, 1989-90. Mem. editl. bd. Jour. Pharmacology and Exptl. Therapeutics, 1975—, Jour. Autonomic Nervous Sys., 1979—, assoc. editor, 1985-94, Neurourology and Urodynamics, 1982—, Am. Jour. Physiology, 1983-94, Life Scis., 1993—, Urology, 1996-98, Current Opinion in Central and Peripheral Nervous System Investigational Drugs, 1999—; editl. cons. profl. jours.; contbr. articles to profl. jours., chpts. in books. NSF fellow, 1962-63; pharmacology fellow Riker Pharm. Co., 1966-67; NSF fellow, 1966-67; recipient research Career Devel. award NIH, 1972-77, NIH Merit award, 2000. Fellow: AAAS; mem.: Internat. Soc. for Autonomic Neurosci. (exec. v.p.), Am. Autonomic Soc., Am. Motility Soc., Soc. for Basic Urologic Rsch., Internat. Med. Soc. of Paraplegia, Urodynamics Soc. (Lifetime Achievement award 1995), Am. Gastroent. Assn., Internat. Brain Rsch. Orgn., Soc. for Neurosci. (treas. 1994—95), Am. Soc. Pharmacology and Exptl. Therapeutics (award for exptl. therapeutics 2003),

N.Y. Acad. Scis., Rho Chi, Sigma Xi. Republican. Methodist. Home: 6357 Burchfield Ave Pittsburgh PA 15217-2732 Office: U Pitts Med Sch W-1352 Biomed Sci Tower Terrace St Pittsburgh PA 15213 E-mail: degroat@server.pharm.pitt.edu.

DEGROFF, RALPH LYNN, JR., investment banker; b. Balt., Oct. 23, 1936; s. Ralph Lynn and Marion (Day) D.; m. Marion Parsons Sinwell, Feb. 4, 1989. AB, Princeton U., 1958; MBA, U. Va., 1960. With Dillon, Read & Co. Inc., N.Y.C., 1961-81, v.p., 1970-74, sr. v.p., 1974-81; mng. dir. Donaldson, Lufkin & Jenrette, 1981-94. Past bd. dirs. Interstate Gen. Corp., The Ryland Group, Regency Corp.; bd. dirs. Wagner Bros. Containers Inc., The Winthrop Trust Co.; trustee Holland Soc. N.Y. With U.S. Army, 1960-61. Mem. Soc. of the Cin., Soc. Colonial Wars, Md. Club, Elkridge Club, Hillsboro Club. Presbyterian. Address: 7 Gracie Sq New York NY 10028-8001 Home: 2002 Ridgecrest Ct Baltimore MD 21204

DEGROOT, LESLIE JACOB, medical educator; b. Ft. Edward, N.Y., Sept. 20, 1928; BS, Union Coll., 1948; MD, Columbia U., 1952. Intern, asst. resident in medicine Presbyn. Hosp., N.Y.C., 1952-54; health physician Nat. Cancer Inst., 1954-55; physician U.S. Mission, Afghanistan, 1955-56; clin. and research fellow medicine Mass. Gen. Hosp., Boston, 1956, 58-60, resident, 1957-58, asst., 1960-64, asst. physician, 1964-66; assoc. prof. exptl. medicine MIT, 1966-68, assoc. dir. dept. nutrition and food sci. Clin. Research Ctr., 1966-68; prof. endocrinology Pritzker Sch. Medicine, U. Chgo., 1968—, chief thyroid study unit, 1968—, chief endocrinology sect., 1980-87. Mem. Cancer Inst. clin. fellow, 1954-55 Mem. Assn. Am. Physicians, Am. Thyroid Assn., Endocrine Soc., Am. Soc. Clin. Investigation, Am. Fedn. Clin. Research Office: Univ Chgo Med Ctr MC3090 5841 S Maryland Ave Chicago IL 60637-1463 E-mail: ldegroot@medicine.bsd.uchicago.edu.

DEGROOT, MARY A. social welfare administrator; BA, Met. State Coll., 1981; BS, S.D. State U., Brookings, 1974; postgrad., Harvard U., 1992. Fin. analyst AT&T, Mountain Bell, Denver, 1981—87; pres. Cmty. Health Charities Colo., Denver, 1997—. Bd. dirs. Young American's Bank, Denver. City councilwoman City and County of Denver; pres. Colo. Women's Health Care Coalition, Denver; treas. Colo. Consumer Health Initiative, Denver, 2000—03; mem. pub. policy com. Alzheimer's Assn., Denver, 1998—2003. Office: Cmty Health Charities Colo Ste 341 1777 S Bellaire Denver CO 80222

DEGROOT, TIMOTHY, finance educator; b. Windsor, Ontario, Canada, Feb. 14, 1960; s. Bert and Beatrice DeGroot; m. Bonnie Brown, Aug. 28, 1982; children: Alison, Joyce, Mackenzie, Kellen, Cassidy. MBA, Fla. State U., 1993; PhD, U. Fla., 1997. Prof. Okla. State U., Stillwater. Contbr. articles to profl. jours. Mem.: Soc. for Indsl. and Orgnl. Psychology (assoc.), Acad. Mgmt. (assoc.). Office: Okla State Univ College of Business Stillwater OK 74078-4011 E-mail: drivingthenet@yahoo.com.

DE GROOTE, ROBERT DAVID, general and vascular surgeon; b. Hackensack, N.J., Aug. 30, 1951; s. Emiel and Filomena Lillian (Candio) De G. BS in Biology, Fordham U., 1973; MD, Autonomous U. Guadalajara, Jalisco, Mex., 1978. Diplomate Am. Bd. of Surgery. Resident gen. surgery U. Medicine and Dentistry N.J. Med. Sch., Newark, 1979-84, fellow critical care medicine, 1981-82, fellow vascular surgery, 1984-86; fifth pathway St. Joseph's Hosp., Paterson, N.J., 1978-79; attending surgeon Hackensack (N.J.) Med. Ctr., 1986—. Contbr. articles to Surgery, Stroke, Archives of Surgery, Annals of Vascular Surgery. Named Man of Yr., Lyndhurst, N.J. chpt. Italian-Am. Nat. Svc. Orgn., 1993, Top Doctor in New York, New York Mag., Top Doctor in N.J., N.J. Monthly. Fellow ACS; mem. AMA, Internat. Soc. for Cardiovascular Surgery, Soc. for Critical Care Medicine, Ea. Vascular Soc. Roman Catholic. Office: 83 Summit Ave Hackensack NJ 07601-1262 E-mail: rdegroote@aol.com.

DEGRYSE, BERNARD, cell biologist; s. Claude Degryse and Pierrette Taddei; m. Maddalena de Virgilio, Apr. 23, 2001. PhD in Cell Biology and Microbiology, U. Aix-Marseille II, France, 1993. Head chem. lab. Caleb Brett Co., Port de Bouc, France, 1990—91; postdoctoral fellow Labs. de Biochimie Médicale and U38 INSERM, Marseille, France, 1993—94, Molecular Genetics, Dept. of Cell Biology and Functional Genetics, DIBIT, U. Vita-Salute San Raffaele, Milan, 1996—99; rsch. assoc. Dept. of Genetics and Micro-organism Biology, U. of Milan, 1999—2000, Divsn. of Vascular Biology, Dept. of Cell Biology, The Scripps Rsch. Inst., La Jolla, Calif., 2000—. Mem. internat. reviews panel Med. Sci. Monitor Jour., 2002—. Achievements include patents for Inhibitor or antagonist of HMG1 protein used for the cure of vascular disorders; patents pending in field of agonist and antagonistic peptides of the urokinase receptor (UPAR): stimulators and inhibitors of cell migration. Office: The Scripps Rsch Inst 10550 N Torrey Pines Rd La Jolla CA 92037 Office Fax: 858-784-7353. E-mail: degryse@scripps.edu.

DEGUIRE, MARK ROBERT, materials scientist, educator; b. Chgo., Apr. 4, 1958; s. Robert LeRoy and Eleanor Marie (Perrella) DeG.; m. Eileen Ann Joyce, May 23, 1981; children: Audrey, Jeannette, Adam, Ruth. BS, U. Ill., 1980, MS, 1982; PhD, MIT, 1987. Teaching asst. U. Ill., Urbana-Champaign, 1980-82; rsch. asst. MIT, Cambridge, 1982-87; affiliated faculty mem. Yeager Ctr. Electrochem. Scis., Cleve., 1987—; Nord asst. prof. Case Western Res. U., Cleve., 1987-90, asst. prof. dept. materials sci. and engring., 1990-93, assoc. prof., 1993—. Session chmn. ann. meetings Am. Ceramic Soc., 1989, 91, 93, 94, 98, 2000, 03, program co-chair, 2001-02; symposium co-organizer Am. Ceramic Soc., 2002, 2003, Material Rsch. Soc., 1999; guest scientist Max Planck Institut Metallforschung, Stuttgart, Germany, 1996-97; invited mem. peer rev. panels NSF, NASA, Dept. Energy; cons. Erico Products, Lubrizol Corp., others; reviewer Jour. Am. Ceramic Soc., Phys. Rev., Jour. Applied Physics, other profl. jours. Contbr. articles to refereed jours.; co-editor conf. proc. vols. Organic-Inorganic Hybrid Materials, Nanostructured Materials and Nanotechnology. Mem. Am. Ceramic Soc., Materials Rsch. Soc., Keramos, Am. Soc. Metals Internat. Roman Catholic. Achievements include patents (co-author) for solution synthesis of ceramics, thin film deposition process for ceramics; co-discovery of phenomenon of normal-state magnetic alignability of oxide superconducting particles. Office: Case Western Res Univ Dept Materials Sci/Engring 10900 Euclid Ave Dept Cleveland OH 44106-7204

DEGUTIS, DOROTHEA LYNN, psychiatrist; BS in Edn., Northwestern U., Evanston, Ill., 1975; MD, U. Ill., Chgo., 1984. Resident Michael Reese Hosp., Chgo., 1984-87, Children's Meml. Hosp., Chgo., 1987-89; pvt. practice, 1989—; med. dir. Thresholds, Northfield, Ill., 1990-98; dir. child psychiatry Old Orchard Hosp., Skokie, Ill., 1991-93; psychiatrist Advocate Health Sys., Chgo., 1993—. Adv. bd. CHGIR Willpower Thresholds, 1999—. Recipient Achievement award APA Psychiatric Svc., Thresholds, Ill. Fellow Am. Acad. Child and Adolescent Psychiatry. Office: 5225 Old Orchard Rd Ste 45 Skokie IL 60077-1027

DEHAAN, JOHN DAVID, forensic specialist; BS, U. Ill., Chgo., 1969; PhD, Strathclyde U., Glasgow, Scotland, 1995. Criminalist Alameda County Sheriff, Pleasanton, Calif., 1970—74, Calif. Dept. Justice, Sacramento, 1974—83, criminalist supr., 1987—98; phys. scientist U.S. Treasury Dept., San Francisco, 1983—87; forensic scientist Fire-Ex Forensics, Vallejo, Calif., 1998—. Author: Kirk's Fire Investigation, 2002; co-author: Forensic Fire Reconstruction, 2003. Recipient P.W. Allen award, Forensic Sci. Soc. U.K., 2000. Fellow: Am. Acad. Forensic Sci. (Paul Kirk award 2003), Am. Bd. Criminalists; mem.: Internat. Assn. Arson Investigators, Calif. Assn. Criminalists (pres. 1983—84), Forensic Sci. Soc. (dipl. fire investigation 1993). Avocations: vintage sports cars, toy trains. Office: Fire-Ex Forensics Inc 3505 Sonoma Blvd #20-314 Vallejo CA 94590

DE HAAN, KAREN L. lawyer, accountant; b. Long Beach, Calif., Mar. 24, 1968; d. John Maurice De Haan and Linda Louise Hanna. BS, N.E. Mo. State U., 1990; acctg. cert., Northwestern U., 1994; JD, U. Louisville, 1998. Bar: Ky. 1998, 2001. CPA, Ill. Sec. Lazar & Karasick, MD, Evanston, Ill., 1991-95; assoc. Goldberg & Simpson, Louisville, 1998—2000, Sommer and Barnard, 2001—. Acct. Chilton & Medley, Louisville, part-time 1999. Mem. devel. bd. Actor's Theater, Louisville, 1998-2000. Mem. ABA, AICPA, Ky. Bar Assn., Ill. CPA Soc., Louisville Bar Assn., Women Lawyers Assn., Ind. Bar Assn., Brandeis Soc., Phi Beta Phi. Office: Sommer and Barnard Monument Cir 4000 Indianapolis IN 46240 Home: Apt 231 8619 Lake Clearwater Ln Indianapolis IN 46240-7725

DE HAAN-PULS, JOYCE ELAINE, sales account representative, educator; b. Grand Rapids, Mich., Dec. 22, 1941; d. Harry Herman and Dorothy Elaine (Kikstra) De Haan; children: Bruce Todd, Daniel Lane, Christy-Anne Sara Elizabeth Puls. Student, Calvin Coll., 1960-61; BS with honors, Grand Valley State U., Yugoslavia, 1978; M in Instnl. Tech., Wayne State U., Siedman Grad. Coll., 1986; M in Comms., Wayne State U., 1986. Owner, operator Joyce Elaine's Beauty Parlor, Grandville, Mich., 1960-64; asst. assessor City of Hudsonville, Mich., 1978; dir. displaced homemaker program Women's Resource Ctr., Grand Rapids, 1979-81; visual products rep. 3M Corp., Grand Rapids, 1982-85, sr. account rep. Detroit, 1985-89, regional sales mgr. S.E. Mich., 1989-93; v.p. mktg. TransContinental Traders, Ltd., Detroit, 1993—. Adj. prof. Baker Bus. Coll., Muskegon, Mich., 1999—, Davenport U., Grand Rapids, 2000—; mem. Ottawa County (Mich.) CETA Adv. Bd.; bd. dirs. Downtown Day Care Ctr., Grand Rapids, 1972. Mem. Preservation Wayne, Detroit Internat. Vis. Coun. Recipient Cert. of Appreciation Bishop of Saigon, Vietnam, 1969; Top Sales rep. 3M/US, 1983, VIP, 1983, 84, 85, 86, 87, 88, 89; Phillip Morris scholar, 1975. Mem.: NAFE, Rental Property Owners Assn., Am. Soc. Pub. Adminstrn., Grand Rapids Coun. on World Affairs, Nat. Assn. Fgn. Students, Wayne State U. Alumni Assn. (mem. steering com. 2001—), Hist. Indian Village Assn. Republican. Home: PO Box 567 White Cloud MI 49349-0567 E-mail: JEPuls@aol.com.

DE HAAS, DAVID DANA, emergency physician; b. Hollywood, Calif., May 31, 1956; S. Martin and Norma (Deutsch) De H.; m. Mary Danuta Przybylowski, June 27, 1982; children: Lindsay Alexandra, Heather Brittany, Lance Austin. BS in Biochemistry, UCLA, Westwood, Calif., 1979; MD, Chgo. Med. Sch., 1983. Diplomate Am. Bd. Internal Medicine, Am. Bd. Emergency Medicine, Nat. Bd. Med. Examiners; cert. provider advanced trauma life support, ACLS, Pediatric Advanced Life Support, BCLS, Med. Disaster Response, instr. ACLS, Pediatric Advanced Life Support, Med. Disaster Response. Resident emergency medicine/internal medicine Kern Med. Ctr., Bakersfield, Calif., 1983-87; assoc. med. dir. Family Care Med. Assocs., Huntington Beach, Calif., 1987—; emergency physician Anaheim (Calif.) Meml. Hosp., 1988—; asst. clin. prof. medicine dept. internal medicine U. Calif.-Irvine Med. Ctr., Orange, 1989—; emergency physician St. Bernardine Med. Ctr., San Bernardino, Calif., 1991—; ptnr. Calif. Emergency Physicians Med. Group, San Bernardino, 1991—. Expert reviewer Med. Bd. Calif.; affiliate faculty ACLS, Pediatric Advanced Life Support, Am. Heart Assn.; vice chmn. dept. emergency medicine St. Bernardine Med. Ctr., ACLS dir., dir. quality assurance/continuous quality improvement dept. emergency medicine; mem. edn. com. Med. Disaster Response; ptnr.Calif. Emergency Physician Med. Group. Fellow ACP, Am. Coll. Emergency Physicians; mem. AMA, Calif. Med. Assn., Orange County Med. Soc., Soc. Orange County Emergency Physicians (bd. dirs.), Assn. Clin. Faculty U. Calif., Irvine Coll. Medicine. Avocations: pin collecting, gardening, reading, 1st edit. book collecting, western Americana. Home: 26882 Via La Mirada San Juan Capistrano CA 92675-4935 Office: St Bernardine Med Ctr 2101 N Waterman Ave San Bernardino CA 92404-4836

DEHAAS, JOHN NEFF, JR., retired architecture educator; b. Phila., July 4, 1926; s. John Neff and Sadie Lavinia (Hagel) DeH.; m. C. Bernice Wallace, Dec. 27, 1950; children: Kenneth Eric, Jocelyn Hilda. BArch, Tex. A&M U., 1948, MEd, 1950. Registered architect, Mont. Instr. Tex. A&M U., College Station, 1948-50, U. Tex., Austin, 1950-51; successively instr. to prof. Mont. State U., Bozeman, 1951-80. Supervisory architect Historic Am. Bldgs. Survey, summers San Francisco, 1962, Bozeman, 1963, 65, Milw., 1969; cons. Mont. Historic Preservation Office, Helena, 1977-78, mem. rev. bd., 1968-79. Author: Montana's Historic Structures, Vol. 1, 1864, Vol. 2, 1969, Historic Uptown Butte, 1977; editor quar. newsletter Mont. Ghost Town Preservation Soc., 1972— Bd. dirs. Mont. Assn. for Blind, Butte, 1984-95. Recipient Centennial Preservation award Mont. Historic Preservation Office, 1989, Dorothy Bridgman award for Outstanding Svc. to the Blind Montana Assn. for the Blind, 1990. Fellow AIA (com. on historic resources 1974—); mem. Mont. Hist. Soc. (trustee's award 1989). Republican. Methodist. Home: 1021 S Tracy Ave Bozeman MT 59715-5329

DEHART, ROY LYNCH, physician, educator; b. Grayson, Ky., Jan. 18, 1936; s. Sanford Bomar and Gladys Lillian (Lynch) D.; m. Ella Julia Goodlett, Aug. 8, 1957; children: Evelyn Judith, John Sanford. BS, U. Tenn., Knoxville, 1957; D in Medicine, U. Tenn., Memphis, 1960; MPH, Johns Hopkins U., 1965; MS, George Washington U., 1974. Cert. aerospace medicine, occpl. medicine Am. Bd. of Preventive Medicine, Am. Bd. of Family Practice. Comdr. Armstrong Aerospace Med. Rsch. Lab., Wright-Patterson AFB, Ohio, 1976-80, USAF Sch. of Aerospace Medicine, Brooks AFB, Texas, 1980-83; pres. Indsl. Medicine Employers Svc., Inc., Tulsa, Okla., 1983-85; dir. divsn. occpl. and environ. medicine U. Okla. Health Sci. Ctr., 1985-94, chmn. dept. of family and preventive medicine, 1993-98; dir. Ctr. for Occupl. and Environ. Medicine Vanderbilt U., 1999—. Bd. dirs., past pres. Am. Coll. Occupational and Environ. Medicine; med. dir. OHA Inc., 2002—; mem. Presdl. Adv. Bd. on Health of Nuclear Workers, 2001—; mem. com. on long duration space flight Nat. Acad. Medicine, 2002—. Author: Fundamentals of Aerospace Medicine, 1986, 3d. edit., 2002; contbr. chpts. to books. Moderator of the bd. Christian Ch., Edmond, Okla., 1997; Col. USAF, 1959-83. Decorated Bronze Star USAF, Air Medal, Legion of Merit with two Oak Leaf Clusters; recipient George E. Schafer award, 2002. Fellow Am. Coll. Preventive Medicine (pres. 1993-95, Disting. Svc. award 1998), Am. Coll. Occpl. Environ. Medicine (pres. 1992-93, Robert A. Kehos award of merit 1995, William S. Knudson award 1998), Aerospace Med. Assn. (Eric Liljencrantz award 2002, American Acad. Family Practice, Internat. Acad. Aviation and Space Medicine; mem. Soc. Tchrs. Family Medicine. Avocations: recreational travel, theatre, religious activities, reading, management information systems. Home: 12 Thorndale Ct Nashville TN 37215-6146 E-mail: rdehart118@aol.com.

DEHAYES, DANIEL WESLEY, management executive, educator; b. Columbus, Ohio, Sept. 23, 1941; s. Daniel Wesley and June Rosiland (Page) DeH.; married Lisa A. Gregoline; children: Sarah Baxter, Benjamin Wesley. BA in Math. and Computer Sci., Ohio State U., 1963, MBA, 1964, PhD in Bus. Adminstrn., 1968. Asst. prof. systems analysis Naval Postgrad. Sch., Monterey, Calif., 1967-69; asst. prof. sch. bus. Ind. U., Bloomington, Ind., 1969-72, assoc. prof.sch. bus., 1972-79, prof. sch. bus., 1979—, dean of acad. computing, 1981-86, asst. v.p. info. tech., 1987-88; dir. Ctr. For Entrepreneurship and Innovation, Ind. U., Bloomington, 1989-98. Exec. dir. Inst. Rsch. on the MIS, 1989-92, chmn. exec. edn., 1992-93; cons. in field. Textbook author; contbr. articles to profl. jours. Served to capt. U.S. Army, 1967-69 Recipient fellowships and grants Mem. Decision Scis. Inst., Acad. Mgmt. Republican. Methodist. Office: Indiana University Kelley School of Business Bloomington IN 47405

DEHMELT, HANS GEORG, physicist, educator; b. Germany, Sept. 9, 1922; arrived in U.S., 1952, naturalized, 1962; s. Georg Karl and Asta Ella (Klemmt) Dehmelt; m. Diana Elaine Dundore, Nov. 18, 1989; 1 child from previous marriage, Gerd. Grad., Graues Kloster, Berlin, Abitur, 1940; D Rerum Naturalium, U. Goettingen, 1950; D Rerum Naturalium (hon.), Ruprecht Karl-Universitat, Heidelberg, 1986; DSc (hon.), U. Chgo., 1987. Postdoctoral fellow U. Goettingen, Germany, 1950—52, Duke U., Durham, NC, 1952—55; vis. asst. prof. U. Wash., Seattle, 1955, asst. prof. physics, 1956, assoc. prof., 1957—61, prof., rsch. physicist, 1961—. Cons. Varian Assocs., Palo Alto, Calif., 1956—76. Contbr. articles to profl. jours. Recipient Humboldt prize, 1974, award in Basic Rsch., Internat. Soc. Magnetic Resonance, 1980, Rumford prize, Am. Acad. Arts and Scis., 1985, Nobel prize in Physics, 1989, Nat. medal of Sci., 1995; grantee NSF, 1958—. Fellow: Am. Phys. Soc. (Davisson-Germer prize 1970); mem.: NAS, Am. Optical Soc., Am. Acad. Arts and Scis., Sigma Xi. Home: 1600 43rd Ave E Seattle WA 98112-3205 Office: U Wash PO Box 35-1560 Seattle WA 98195-1560

DEHMLOW, ECKEHARD VOLKER, education educator, educator; b. Berlin, May 25, 1933; s. Friedrich and Melitta (Goede) D.; m. Sigrid Moehl, May 23, 1958; children: Henrietta, Marvin, Carola. Student, Earlham Coll., Richmond, Ind.; Dipl-Chem, Free U. Berlin, 1959; DrRerNat, Tech. U. Berlin, 1961. Postdoctoral asst. Yale U., New Haven, 1961-62; sci. asst. Tech. U. Berlin, 1963-68, prof., 1969-79; full prof. U. Bielefeld, 1979-98, prof. emeritus, 1998—. Guest prof. MIT, Cambridge, 1971, U. East Anglia, Norwich, Eng., 1975, U. Okla., Norman, 1978, U. Kyoto, Japan, 1986, Leningrad State U., USSR, 1989, South Africa, 1992. Author: (with wife) Phase Transfer Catalysis, 3d edit., 1993; contbr. numerous articles to profl. jours. Mem. Gesellschaft Deutscher Chemiker, Royal Soc. Chemistry, Am. Chem. Soc. Home: Rahnsdorfer Weg 2 D-33619 Bielefeld Germany Office: Fakultaet Fuer Chemie Universitaet Bielefeld D-33615 Bielefeld Germany E-mail: dehmlow@post.uni-bielefeld.de.

DEHN, FRANCIS XAVIER, lawyer, journalist; b. Bronx, N.Y., Aug. 12, 1957; s. Francis X. and Irene (Canning) D. BSFS in Internat. Politics, Georgetown U., 1979; JD, Harvard U., 1983; MS in Journalism, Columbia U., 1991. Bar: N.Y. 1985. Atty. Webster & Sheffield, N.Y.C., 1985-90; reporter Sta. WPDE-TV, Florence/Myrtle Beach, S.C., 1991-93; atty. Gersten, Savage, Kaplowitz & Curtin, 1993-95; reporter Court TV, 1995-97; ptnr. Jacobs, deBrauwere & Dehn LLP, 1998—2001; mem. Smith Dornan & Shea, PC, N.Y.C., 2002—. Vis. asst. prof. Newhouse Sch. Pub. Comm. Syracuse U., 2002—; adj. prof. law Pace U., White Plains, NY, 2003—. Orgn. dir. O'Rourke for Gov. campaign, 1986. Mem. Phi Beta Kappa. Roman Catholic. Office: Smith Dornan & Shea PC 355 Lexington Ave New York NY 10017 E-mail: fdehn@sds-law.com.

DEHN, JAMES KEITH, financial advisor; b. Buffalo, Jan. 29, 1957; s. Earl Sylvester and Kathryn Agnes (Pericak) D.; m. Cathleen Patterson, June 27, 1981. BA, Walsh U., 1979; MBA, SUNY, Buffalo, 1981; postgrad., NYU, 1996. Sales rep. Indsl. Metals, Inc., North Canton, Ohio, 1980-97; fin. advisor Prudential Securities, N.Y.C., 1997-2000; fin. advisor pvt. client group UBS PaineWebber, N.Y.C., 2000—. Exec. prodr. (video) Getting to Know the Unique Behavioral Capabilities of the Newborn, 1987. Co-founder Friends of Footpath Footpath Dance Co., Cleve., 1988-90, bd. trustees, 1990-91. Recipient Heritage Home Renovation award Cleve. Heights Cmty. Congress, 1990. Mem. Alumni Assn. SUNY Buffalo, Nat. Trust Historic Preservation. Avocations: tennis, sailing, culinary arts, historical preservation. Office: UBS PaineWebber 140 Broadway 24th Fl New York NY 10005

DEHNER, JOSEPH JULNES, lawyer; b. Cin., Nov. 28, 1948; s. Walter Joseph and Bess (Humphries) D.; m. Noel Julnes, Nov. 19, 1983; children: Holly Julnes, Sara Julnes. AB, Princeton U., 1970; JD, Harvard Law Sch., Cambridge, Mass., 1973. Bar: Ohio 1973, U.S. Dist. Ct. (no. and so. dists.) Ohio 1975, Fla. 1986, U.S. Dist. Ct. (ca. dist.) Ky. 1988, U.S. Ct. Internat. Trade 1992. Law clk. to judge U.S. Court Appeals, Cleve., 1973-75; assoc. Kyte, Conlan, Wulsin & Vogeler, Cin., 1975-78, Frost Brown Todd LLC, Cin., 1978—; chmn. Universal Transactions Inc., 1991-95. Co-mgr. Ukraine Investments Ltd., 1995-99. Author: Structured Settlements and Periodic Payment Judgments, 1986, A Guide to Soviet Businesspeople on American Business Law, 1991, Doing Business in Russia, 1992, Dispute Resolution and China, 1994, A Foreign Investors Guide to Ukraine, 1995; contbr. articles to profl. publs. Sec., v.p. Cin. Preservation Assn., 1978-86; mem. Cin. Planning Commn., 1984-85; pres. Charter Com. Greater Cin., 1982-86; chmn. Cin.-Kharkiv Sister City Project, 1988-91; trustee Princeton U., 1970-74, Ohio Hist. Soc., 1974-78; chancellor Episcopal Diocese of So. Ohio, 1997—. Mem. ABA (vice chair internat. litigation com.), Pub. Investors Arbitration Bar Assn., Ohio State Bar Assn. (chmn. internat. law com. 1989-91), Cin. Bar Assn., Sixth Cir. Jud. Conf. Episcopal. Avocations: tennis, family, reading. Home: 822 Yale Ave Terrace Park OH 45174-1258 Office: Frost Brown Todd LLC 2200 PNC Ctr 201 E 5th St Ste 2200 Cincinnati OH 45202-4182

DEHORATIUS, RAPHAEL JOSEPH, rheumatologist; b. Phila., Sept. 16, 1942; s. Pasquale P. and Edith R. DeH.; children: Nicole, Danielle. BS, St. Joseph's U., Phila., 1964; MD, Jefferson Med. Coll., 1968. Med. intern Jefferson Med. Coll., Phila., 1968-69, asst. prof. medicine, 1976-78, assoc. prof. medicine, 1978-82; med. resident U. N.Mex., Albuquerque, 1969-70, rheumatology fellow, 1972-74, asst. prof. medicine, 1974-76; prof. medicine Hahnemann U., Phila., 1982-92, Jefferson Med. Coll./Thomas Jefferson U., Phila., 1992—. Contbr. articles to profl. jours./publs. Maj. USAF, 1970-72. Recipient Lupus Rsch. grant Commonwealth of Pa., Arthritis Rsch. grant. Fellow: ACP, Am. Coll. Rheumatology (chmn. profl. meetings 1988—91, edn. coun. 1988—91, v.p. 2000—01, pres.-elect 2001—02, pres. 2002—); mem.: Am. Fedn. Clin. Rsch., Assn. Am. Immunologists. Home: 210 W Crystal Lake Ave Apt 160B Haddonfield NJ 08033-3157 Office: Thomas Jefferson Univ 613 Curtis Bldg 1015 Walnut St Philadelphia PA 19107-5005

DEHORITY, MIRIAM A. (MIRIAM NEWMAN), artist; b. Hampton, Ga., Jan. 6, 1928; d. David Johnson and Ethel (Sloan) Arnold; m. William Truslow Newman, Feb. 12, 1954 (dec.); children: David Arnold Newman, William Truslow III Newman; m. Edward Havens DeHority, Jr., Jan. 1, 1984. BA, Agnes Scott Coll., 1949; student, Atlanta Sch. Art, 1953-55, Ga. State U., 1959-60, Chatov Studios, 1961-63. One-woman shows include Water Color Soc. Ala., Mont., 1963 (1st award), Am. Water Color Soc.-Nat. Acad. Galleries, NYC, 1966, Patricia Cloutier Gallery, 2000, 2002, 2 person show, Heath Gallery, Atlanta, 1968, Soc. Fine Arts, Palm Beach, Fla., 1999, Soc. of 4 Arts, Palm Beach., 1999, Patricia Cloutier Gallery, 2002, William Truslow Newman III, exhibited in group shows at Atlanta Art Assocs., 1958—62, High Mus. Art, Atlanta, 1965, 1971, Soc. Contemporary Art, Mobile, Ala., 1969, Mus. Arts and Sci., Macon, Ga., 1972, Heath Gallery, 1972, Swan Coach House Gallery, Atlanta, 1983, 1988, Patricia Cloutier Gallery, Jupiter, Fla., 1992, 1999—2000, Lighthouse Gallery, Jupiter, 1997, represented in permanent collections. Founding pres. Members Guild High Mus., Atlanta, 1966; bd. dirs. High mus. Art, Atlanta, 1966-67, Atlanta Arts Alliance, 1966-67, Jr. League of Atlanta, 1958-68. Recipient First award Ala. Water Color Soc., 1963. Avocations: gardening, cooking, design, tennis, golf.

DEHOVITZ, JACK ALAN, physician, educator, health facility administrator; b. Oceanside, Calif., Aug. 12, 1952; s. Bernard and Ruth (Senturia) DeH. BS, U. Calif., Davis, 1974; MPH, U. Tex., Houston, 1975; MD, U. Tex., Galveston, 1980. Diplomate Am. Bd. Internal Medicine, Am. Bd. Preventive Medicine, Am. Bd. Infectious Disease. Intern medicine St. Vincent's Hosp. and Med. Ctr., N.Y.C., 1980-81; asst. resident medicine N.Y. Hosp.-Cornell Med. Ctr., N.Y.C., 1981-82; Strang fellow in pub. health Cornell U. Med. Coll., N.Y.C., 1983-85; fellow in internat. medicine, infectious diseases N.Y. Hosp., N.Y.C., 1983-85; asst. med. dir. Spellman Ctr. of HIV Disease, N.Y.C., 1985-88; asst. prof. Cornell U. Med. Coll., N.Y.C., 1985—2000, SUNY, Bklyn., 1985-91, assoc. prof., 1991—2000, dir. AIDS Prevention Ctr., 1988-93, dir. HIV Ctr., 1993—, prof., 2000—. Cons. infectious diseases N.Y. State Dept. Health, Albany, 1989-91; cons. Czech Min. Health, Prague, 1990-92. Editor AIDS Manual, 1988, HIV Infection in Women, 1995; contbr. articles to profl. jours. Mem. organizing com. Czech-Am. Med. Com., Prague, 1990. Fellow ACP, N.Y. Acad. Medicine, Infectious Diseases Soc. Am.; mem. APHA, N.Y. Soc. Tropical Medicine, Internat. AIDS Soc. Jewish. Office: SUNY Health Sci Ctr Bklyn 450 Clarkson Ave Box 1240 Brooklyn NY 11203-2056

DEICKEN, RAYMOND FRIEDRICH, neuropsychiatrist, clinical neuroscientist; b. Honolulu, June 28, 1957; s. Raymond T. and Miriam (Ogata) D. AB, MS, Stanford U., 1980; MD, U. Calif., San Francisco, 1984. Diplomate Nat. Bd. Med. Examiners, Am. Bd. Psychiatry and Neurology. Resident physician U. Calif., San Francisco, 1984-88, rsch. fellow, 1988-91, asst. prof. psychiatry, 1991-97, assoc. prof., 1997—; staff physician VA Med. Ctr., San Francisco, 1991—. Lectr. in field. Reviewer manuscripts Biol. Psychiatry, 1987—, Psychiatry Rsch., 1992—; contbr. articles to profl. jours. Alumni mentor Stanford U. Student Alumni Mentor Program, 1993—. Recipient Young Investigator award Nat. Alliance for Rsch. on Schizophrenia and Depression, 1992, 94, Ind. Investigator award, 2000, Stanley Found. rsch. award Nat. Alliance for Mentally Ill, 1997, 98, VA Physician Rsch. Assoc. Career Devel. award, 1991-95; Dista fellow Soc. Biol. Psychiatry, 1991. Mem. AMA, Soc. for Neuroscience, Soc. Biol. Psychiatry, Internat. Soc. Magnetic Resonance in Medicine, Am. Psychiat. Assn., Internat. Soc. Neuroimaging in Psychiatry, Collegium Internat. Neuro-psychopharmacologicum, Internat. Soc. for Affective Disorders, N.Y. Acad. Scis. Episcopalian. Home: 197 Carnelian Way San Francisco CA 94131-1780 Office: Dept Veterans Affairs Med Ctr 4150 Clement St San Francisco CA 94121-1545 E-mail: deicken@itsa.ucsf.edu.

DEIDESHEIMER, ANNAMARIA, English educator; d. Harold Jacob and Mary Ann Deidesheimer. BA, Immaculata Coll., 1986; MA, Villanova U, 1994; student, 2003—. Cert. tchg. Fla., Pa., N.Y. English tchr. Pine Crest Prep. Sch., Ft. Lauderdale, Fla., 1990—2000; adj. English instr. Jefferson Cmty. Coll., Watertown, NY, 2000—, SUNY, Potsdam, 2001—. Chairperson Broward Debate Assn., Ft. Lauderdale, 1993—95. V.p. cmty. Affairs Broward Young Democrats, Fla., 1997—98; editor Donkey Tales Newsletter Broward County Young Democrats, Fla., 1997—98; precinct leader com. mem. Broward Democratic Exec. Cmty., Fla., 1995—99. Mem.: Onondaga County Bar Assn., Nat. Counil of English Tchr., Modern Language Assn. (assoc.). Democrat. Cath. Avocations: gardening, writing, photography. Home: 238 Flower Ave West Watertown NY 13601

DEIGHTON, LEN, author; b. London, Feb. 18, 1929; Author: The Ipcress File, 1962 (motion picture U.S., 1963), Horse Under Water, 1963, U.S. edit. 1968, Funeral in Berlin, 1964 (motion picture U.S., 1965), Ou Est le Garlic/Basic French Cooking, 1965, 2d edit., 1979, U.S. edit., 1977, Action Cook Book, 1965, Cookstrip Cook Book, 1966, Billion Dollar Brain, 1966 (motion picture U.S., 1966), An Expensive Place to Die, 1967, Len Deighton's Dossier, 1967, Only When I Larf, 1968 (motion picture U.S., 1968), Bomber, 1970 (radio drama U.S., 1970), U.S. Edit. of Declarations of War, 1971, Close-Up, 1972, Spy Story, 1974 (motion picture U.S., 1974), Eleven Declarations of War, 1975, Yesterday's Spy, 1975, Twinkle, Twinkle, Little Spy, 1976, Catch a Falling Spy, 1976, Fighter, 1977, U.S. edit., 1978, SS-GB, 1978, U.S. edit., 1979, Blitzkrieg, 1979, U.S. edit., 1980, XPD, 1981, Goodbye Mickey Mouse, 1982, Berlin Game, 1983, Mexico Set, 1984, London Match, 1985, Winter: A Berlin Family 1899-1945, 1987, U.S. edit., 1988, Spy Hook, 1988, Spy Line, 1989, Spy Sinker, 1990, Basic French Cookery Course, 1990, ABC of French Food, 1989, U.S. edit., 1990, MAMista, 1991, City of Gold, 1992, Violent Ward, 1993, Blood, Tears & Folly, 1993, Faith, 1994, U.S. edit., 1995, Hope, 1995, U.S. edit., 1996, Charity, 1996; co-author: The Assassination of President Kennedy, 1967, Airshipwreck, 1978, U.S. edit., 1979, Battle of Britain, 1980, 2d edit., 1990, U.S. edit., 1980; (13-part TV series) Game, Set & Match, 1985. Office: care Jonathan Clowes Ltd 10 Iron Bridge House London NW1 8BD England E-mail: jonathanclowes@aol.com.

DEIHL, MICHAEL ALLEN, federal agency administrator; b. Bluffton, Ind., Apr. 22, 1952; s. Robert W. and Betty J. (Miller) D.; m. Deborah Ann Crabb, June 16, 1973; 1 child, Samantha Lynn. BSEE, Colo. State U., 1974. East slope area mgr. ECPO Bur. Reclamation, Loveland, Colo., 1981-85, chief com. and control divsn., ECPO, 1985-87; chief maintenance divsn. Hoover Dam Bur. Reclamation, Boulder City, Nev., 1987-90; project mgr. Alaska Power Adminstrn., Dept. Energy, Juneau, 1990-92, dir. power divsn., 1992, adminstr., 1992-95; adminstr. Dept. Energy Southwestern Power Adminstrn., Tulsa, 1995—. Office: Southwestern Power Admin 1 W 3rd St Tulsa OK 74103-3502

DEIHL, SUSAN GALYEN, historic preservationist; b. Columbus, Miss., May 22, 1973; d. James Bruce Galyen, Jr. and Janice Greear Galyen; m. Joshua John Joseph Deihl; children: Cole children: Grayson. BA, U. Va., 1995; M Hist. Preservation, U. Ga., 1998. Intern Hist. Preservation Soc. Durham, 1997; nat. register asst. Paul Hardin Kapp, AIA, Galax, Va., 1997; preservation planner/grants coord. Mass. Hist. Commn., Boston, 1999—2000; asst. to revolving fund dir. Preservation NC, Raleigh, NC, 2000—01. Mem., vol. Preservation N.C., 2001—02; mem. Capital Area Preservation, Raleigh, NC, 2001—02, Va. Hist. Soc., Richmond, Va., 1995—2002, Colonial Williamsburg Found., Williamsburg, Va., 1993—2002, Nat. Trust for Hist. Preservation, Washington, 1990—2002. Mem.: Student Hist. Preservation Soc. (v.p. 1997—98), Nat. Honor Soc. Hist. Preservation. Home: 1211 Mordecai Drive Raleigh NC 27604

DEIKMAN, EUGENE LAWRENCE, lawyer; b. Denver, Nov. 27, 1927; s. Herman and Eva (Lader) D.; m. Dolores Korosec, 1952 (div. 1964); children: Diana Wong, Jill, Alan; m. Doris A. Walker, Sept. 2, 1967 (div. May 1984); 1 child, Jane; m. Roberta Brozovich, May 21, 1998. LLB, U. Colo., 1951. Bar: Colo. 1953, U.S. Dist. Ct. Colo, 1955, U.S. Ct. Appeals (10th cir.) 1956. Ptnr. Menin & Deikman, Denver, 1954-59, Montfort, Wilson & Deikman, Denver, 1959-62; pvt. practice Denver, 1962-79; pres. Eugene Deikman, P.C., Denver, 1979—. Cons. Crusade for Justice, Denver, 1972-79. Mem., co-founder Mus. Contemporary Art/Denver, 1996--. Mem. Colo. Bar Assn., Nat. Lawyers Guild (founder Denver chpt., Founder cert. 1987). Democrat. Avocations: painting, art collecting, photography, skiing. Office: 1700 Broadway Ste 1200 Denver CO 80290-1201 Fax: 303-861-4310. E-mail: gdeikman@aol.com.

DEILY, LINNET FRAZIER, federal agency administrator; b. Dallas, June 20, 1945; d. William Harold and Ruth (White) Frazier; m. Myron Bonham Deily, Apr. 18, 1981. BA, U. Tex. Austin, 1967; MA, U. Tex. Dallas, 1976. Banking officer, asst. v.p., v.p. Republic Bank, Dallas, 1975—80, sr. v.p., 1980—81; v.p. First Interstate Bancorp, L.A.., 1981—83; sr. v.p., divsn. mgr. First Interstate Bank, L.A.., 1983—84; past sr. v.p., CFO, pres. First Interstate Bank Ltd. Vice chmn., pres. Charles Schwab Corp., San Francisco; bd. dirs. First Interstate Inst., L.A. Mem.: Univ. Club L.A. (fin. com.). Office: Exec Off of the Pres US Trade Repr 600 17th St NW Washington DC 20508-4801

DEININGER, DAVID GEORGE, judge; b. Monroe, Wis., July 9, 1947; s. Wilbur Emerson and Anna Emilie (Karlen) D.; m. Mary Carol Nussbaum, June 4, 1969; children: Jonathan David, Christopher Jacob, Emilie Joanne. BS, U.S. Naval Acad., 1969; JD, U. Wis., 1978. Bar: Wis. 1978, Ill. 1978, U.S. Dist. Ct. (we. dist.) Wis. 1978. Ptnr. Benkert, Spielman, Asmus & Deininger, Monroe, 1978-87; legislator Wis. State Assembly, Madison, 1987-94; of counsel Brennan, Steil, Basting & MacDougall, S.C., Monroe, 1988-94; cir. ct. judge Green County, 1994-96. Active Monroe Sch. Bd., 1986-89, Monroe Theatre Guild, 1980—; chmn. Green County Rep. Cen. Com., Monroe, 1982-84. Lt. USN, 1969-75. Mem. Green County Bar Assn. (pres. 1982-83), Wis. State Bar Assn., Am. Legion, VFW, Optimists (pres. Monroe chpt. 1984-85). Avocations: bridge, cross country skiing, boating. Home: 2615 Golf View Court Monroe WI 53566-3646 Office: Ct Appeals Dist IV Madison WI 53703-3330

DE IORIO, LUCILLE THERESA, social worker; b. Utica, N.Y., Mar. 7, 1926; d. Patsy and Elizabeth (Graziano) De I. BA, Syracuse U., 1949, MSW, 1969. Cert. social worker, N.Y. Caseworker Oneida County Dept. Social Svcs., Utica, 1952—65, case supr., 1965-90, tng. supr., 1969-70, dir. staff devel., 1970—. Mem. NASW, Acad. Cert. Social Workers, N.Y. State Assn. for Human Svcs., Staff Devel. Assn. N.Y. State. Republican. Roman Catholic. Avocations: writing, collection character dolls. Home: 1306 Sherman Dr Utica NY 13501-5313 Office: 800 Park Ave Utica NY 13501-2939

DEIOTTE, MARGARET WILLIAMS TUKEY, nonprofit consultant, grants writer; b. Lafayette, Ind., Mar. 6, 1952; d. Ronald B. and Elizabeth A. (Williams) Tukey; m. Charles E. Deiotte, Sept. 11, 1971 (dec.); children: Raymond, Karl, Ronald. Student, U. Wash., 1969-72, 77-79. V.p., treas. Logical Systems, Inc., Colorado Springs, 1982-86; v.p. CEDSYS, Inc., Colorado Springs, 1987-92; pres. Penrose Enrichment Program Found., Colorado Springs, Colo., 1988-89; free lance tech. and grant proposal writer, 1990—; dir. Rexall Showcase Internat., Boca Raton, Fla., 1994—. Conf. coord. Colo. Assn. Ptnrs. in Edn., 1994; editor Am. Boarding Kennels Assn., 1995-98; owner Outside The Box, 1996—, presenter seminar Pikes Peace Pace Conf., 1991, 92; presenter 20th annual nat. conf. Am. Boarding Kennels Assn. Mem. adv. bd. gifted and talented Sch. Dist. 11, 1989—, mem. dist. II found. bd., 1997—, OS/CR adv. coun. dist. II, 1999—2001; pres. Penrose Elem. PTA, 1989—91; 1st v.p. El Paso Coun. PTA, 1990—91, treas., 1991—92; mem. grants commn. Colo. State PTA, 1990—91; coach Odyssey of the Mind, 1990, 1991—92, 1995—96; mem. dist. accountability com. Sch. Dist. 38, 1993—94; accountability chmn. Lewis-Palmer Mid. Sch.; mem. gifted and talented com. Sch. Dist. # 38; mem. parent bd., internat. baccalaureate Palmer High Sch., Colorado Springs, Colo., 1994—97, treas., 1995—96, pres., 1996—97; bd. dirs. YMCA Youth Leadership Inst., 1990—92, 1992—93. Mem.: Assn. Fundraising Profls., Assn. Fundraising Profls. Home and Office: 1221 Mount View Ln Colorado Springs CO 80907-4722

DEISENHOFER, JOHANN, biochemistry educator, researcher; b. Zusamaltheim, Bavaria, Germany, Sept. 30, 1943; arrived in U.S., 1988, naturalized, 2001; s. Johann and Thekla (Magg) D.; m. Kirsten Fischer-Lindahl, June 19, 1989. Diploma in Physics, Technische U., Munich, 1971, PhD, 1974, Doctor habilis, 1987. Postdoctoral fellow Max-Planck Inst. Biochemie, Martinsried, Fed. Republic of Germany, 1974-76, staff scientist, 1976-88; investigator Howard Hughes Med. Inst., Dallas, 1988—; prof. biochemistry U. Tex., Dallas, 1988—. Contbr. over 75 sci. papers to profl. publs. Recipient Nobel prize for chemistry, 1988; co-recipient Biol. Physics prize Am. Phys. Soc., 1986, Otto Bayer prize, 1988; decorated The Knight Commander's Cross (Badge and Star) Of the Order of Merit of Germany, 1990, Bavarian Order of Merit, 1992. Mem. AAAS, NAS, Am. Crystallographic Assn., German Biophys. Soc., Protein Soc., Biophys. Soc., Academia Europaea, German Acad. Natural Scientists Leopoldina. E-mail: Johann.Deisenhofer@UTSouthwestern.edu.

DEISLER, PAUL FREDERICK, JR., retired oil company executive; b. El Paso, Tex., Jan. 20, 1926; s. Paul Frederick and Jeanie Donnelly (Monroe) D.; m. Ellen Louise Bardwell, June 15, 1950; children: Jane Ellen, Paul Conrad, Julia Monroe. BS in Chem. Engring, Tex. A&M U., 1948; MS, Princeton U., 1949, PhD, 1952. With Shell Oil Co., 1952—69, v.p. transp. and supplies, 1969-71; dir. supply and refining Compañía Shell de Venezuela, 1971-73; v.p. Chem. Co., Houston, 1973-74; v.p. research and engring. products Shell Oil Co., Houston, 1974-76, v.p. health, safety and environment, 1976-86; dir. Chem. Industry Inst. Toxicology, 1975-86; ret., 2003. Chmn. adv. coun. dept. chem. engring. Princeton U., 1978-81; vis. exec. prof. Sch. Bus., U. Houston, 1986-90, mem. curriculum adv. bd. Inst. Corp. Environ. Mgmt., 1992-93; exec. com. sci. adv. bd. EPA, 1986-94, cons., 1994-2000; environ. adv. coun. Rohm and Haas Co., 1989-93; adj. prof. environ. risk assessment U. Tex. Sch. Pub. Health, 1990-94; policy com. Ctr. for Global Studies, Houston Advanced Rsch. Ctr., The Woodlands, Tex., 1992-98; chair policy com. Houston Advanced Rsch. Ctr., The Woodlands, 1995-96. Editor: Reducing the Carcinogenic Risk in Industry, 1984; area editor for health and environ. risk analysis Risk Analysis: An Internat. Jour., 1997, 98; author articles on environ. health risk assessment and mgmt. Bd. dirs. ARC, Houston, 1975-80; chmn. fin. com. Houston Sci. Fair, 1974-76; alumni councilor, trustee Tex. A&M Research Found., 1977-99, trustee; bd. dirs. Tex. Inst. for Advancement of Chem. Tech., 1988-2000; mem. governing coun. Inst. for Bus., Ethics and Pub. Issues, U. Houston, 1987-90. Served with USN, 1944-46, PTO. Fellow Soc. Risk Analysis (pres. 1986-87); mem. AAAS, AIChE, N.Y. Acad. Scis., U.S. Naval Inst., Assn. Princeton Grad. Alumni (bd. dirs. 1976-79), Am. Petroleum Inst. (chmn. health, environ. and safety gen. com. 1983-84), Am. Chem. Soc., Soc. for Regulatory Toxicology and Pharmacology, Sigma Xi, Tau Beta Pi, Phi Kappa Phi. Address: PO Box 5819 Austin TX 78763-5819 E-mail: sinprisa@earthlink.net.

DEISSLER, ROBERT GEORGE, fluid dynamicist, researcher; b. Greenville, Pa., Aug. 1, 1921; s. Victor Girard and Helen Stella (Fisher) D.; m. June Marie Gallagher, Oct. 7, 1950; children— Robert Joseph, Mary Beth, Ellen Ann, Anne Marie BS, Carnegie Inst. Tech., 1943; MS, Case Inst. Tech., 1948; PHD, Case Western Res. U., 1989. Researcher Goodyear Aircraft Corp., Akron, OH, 1943-44; aero. rsch. scientist NASA Lewis Rsch. Ctr., Cleve., 1947-52, chief fundamental heat transfer br., 1952-70, staff scientist, sci. cons. fluid physics, 1970-94, disting. rsch. assoc., 1994—. Fellow Lewis Rsch. Acad., 1983—; staff scientist sr. level emeritus, 1994. Author: Turbulent Fluid Motion, Taylor and Francis, 1998; contbr. articles to profl. jours.; areas of rsch. fluid turbulence, turbulent heat transfer, turbulent solutions of equations of fluid motion, nonlinear dynamics and chaos, meteorol. and astrophysical flows, radiative heat transfer in gases, heat transfer in powders. Served as lt. (j.g.) USNR, 1944-46 Recipient NACA/NASA Exceptional Svc. award, 1957, Outstanding Publ. award, 1978, Wisdom Soc. award of honor, 2000; Lewis Rsch. Acad. fellow, 1983—. Fellow AIAA (Best Paper award 1975, Tech. Achievement award 1981), ASME (Heat Transfer Meml. award 1964, Max Jacob Meml. award 1975, Wisdom Hall of Fame 2000); mem. Am. Phys. Soc., Sigma Xi. Roman Catholic. Avocations: violin, reading, walking, natural theology. Home: 4540 W 213th St Fairview Park OH 44126-2106 Office: NASA Glenn Rsch Ctr 21000 Brookpark Rd Cleveland OH 44135-3191 *It is desirable that research be fundamentally based, even when it is undertaken with a view toward an application. Then the research will likely be worthwhile, regardless of whether or not the application materializes.*

DEITCH, D. GREGORY, meteorologist; b. Gettysburg, Pa., Aug. 22, 1953; s. Druid Cassatt and Betty Jane (Ridinger) D.; m. Judith Arline Brown, Sept. 1, 1990; 1 stepchild, Kevin Miller. BS in Astronomy, Villanova U., 1975; BS in Meteorology, U. Utah, 1978, MS in Meteorology, 1981. Meteorologist intern Nat. Earth Satellite Svc., Anchorage, 1979, Honolulu, 1980; meteorologist at Amundsen-Scott South Pole Sta. ITT Antarctic Svcs., 1981-82; operational and ballistics meteorologist U.S. Army Atmospheric Scis. Lab., White Sands Missile Range, N.Mex., 1982-90; meteorologist in climatology Air Force Combat Climatology Ctr., Asheville, NC, 1990-98; meteorologist Air Force Tech. Application Ctr., Patrick AFB, Fla., 1998—. Team chief Ft. Huachuca (Ariz.) Meteorol. Team, 1985. Mem. Am. Meteorol. Soc. Republican. Avocations: physical fitness, photography, numismatics, travel. Home: 1197 Walnut Grove Way Rockledge FL 32955-4696

DEITERS, SISTER JOAN ADELE, psychoanalyst, nun, chemistry educator; b. Cincinnati, Apr. 28, 1934; d. Alfred Harry and Rose Catherine (Rusche) D. BA, Coll. Mt. St. Joseph, Cin., 1963; PhD, U. Cin., 1967; M in Christian spirituality, Creighton U., Omaha, 1985. Joined Sisters of Charity, Roman Cath. Ch., 1952; cert. psychoanalyst, Westchester Inst. for Tchg. in Psychoanalysis and Psychotherapy, 2000. Prof. chemistry Coll. Mt. St. Joseph, Cin., 1969-78; Matthew Vassar Jr. chair Vassar Coll., Poughkeepsie, NY, 1978-96. Contbg. articles to profl. jour. Mem. Am. Chem. Soc., Sisters of Charity, Sigma Xi; Nat. Assn. for Advancement of Psychoanalysis. Home: 73A Raymond Ave Poughkeepsie NY 12603-3117 Office: 39 Collegeview Ave Poughkeepsie NY 12603-2415

DEITRICH, RICHARD ADAM, pharmacology educator; b. Monte Vista, Colo., Apr. 22, 1931; s. Robert Adam and Freda Leona (Scott) D.; m. Mary Margaret Burkholder, Jan. 29, 1954; children: Vivian Gay, Leslie Lynn, Lori Christine. BS, U. Colo., 1953, MS, 1954, PhD, 1959. Postdoctoral fellow, then instr. Johns Hopkins U., Balt., 1959-63; asst. prof., then assoc. prof. U. Colo., Denver, 1963-76, prof. pharmacology, 1976—, sci. dir. Alcohol Rsch. Ctr., 1977—. Vis. prof. U. Berne, Switzerland, 1973-74. Editor: Development of Animal Models, 1981, Initial Sensitivity to Alcohol, 1990; contbr. over 100 articles to sci. publs. Pres. Mile High Coun. on Alcoholism, Denver, 1972-73; moderator 1st Universalist Ch., Denver, 1979. With U.S. Army, 1954-56. Grantee Nat. Inst. Alcoholism, 1977—, Nat. Inst. Communicative Disease and Stroke, 1963, numerous others. Mem. Rsch. Soc. on Alcoholism (pres. 1981-83), Internat. Soc. Biomed. Rsch. on Alcoholism (treas. 1986-94), Am. Soc. Pharmacology, Am. Soc. Biol. Chemistry. Avocations: photography, fishing, camping. Office: Univ Colo 4200 E 9th Ave Denver CO 80220-3700

DEITRICK, WILLIAM EDGAR, lawyer; b. N.Y.C., July 30, 1944; s. John English and Dorothy Alice (Geib) D.; m. Emily Jane Posey, June 22, 1968; children: William Jr., Elizabeth, Peter. BA, Johns Hopkins U., 1967; JD, Cornell U., 1971. Bar: Ill. 1972, U.S. Dist. Ct. (no. dist.) Ill. 1972, U.S. Ct. Appeals (7th cir.) 1976, D.C. 1981. Ptnr. Gardner, Carton and Douglas, Chgo., 1972—85; sr. v.p., dep. gen. counsel, mgr. litigation divsn. Continental Bank N.A., 1985—91; ptnr. Mayer, Brown, Rowe & Maw, Chgo., 1991—. Contbr. articles to profl. jours. Trustee North Shore Country Day Sch., 1992-97; gov. mem. Shedd Aquarium; With U.S. Army, 1968-70. Mem. ABA, Ill. Bar Assn., Chgo. Bar Assn., Johns Hopkins U. Alumni Assn. (class agt. 1967-95), Cornell Law Sch. Chgo. Alumni Assn. (chmn. 1985-87), Legal Club, Univ. Club Chgo. (bd. dirs.), Indian Hill Club (Winnetka, Ill.). Home: 365 Greenwood Ave Glencoe IL 60022-2045 Office: Mayer Brown Rowe & Maw 190 S La Salle St Ste 3100 Chicago IL 60603-3441

DEITZ, SUSAN ROSE, columnist; b. Far Rockaway, N.Y., Mar. 21, 1934; d. Emanuel and Florence Jean (Goodstein) Davis; m. Morris J. Mandelker, Nov. 29, 1975; 1 child, Scott Richard; m. Richard Alan Deitz, Dec. 22, 1958 (dec. 1967). Student, Smith Coll., Barnard Coll., N.Y.C., Art Students League, Stella Adler Theater Studio. Advice columnist L.A. Times Syndicate, 1975-2000; syndicated columnist Creators Syndicate, 2000—. Faculty New Sch., N.Y.C., 1977-79; radio personality, 1979; columnist Prodigy Svcs., White Plains, N.Y., 1987-93; spkr. satellite conf. NAFE, 1990; lectr. L.A. Times Syndicate Spkrs. Bur.; guest expert iVillage.com. Author: Valency Girl, 1976, Single File, 1989, paperback edit., 1990. Honored Single Parent Resource Ctr., N.Y.C., 2001. Mem. Women in Comm. (Outstanding Member award 1984), Authors Guild, Newspaper Features Assn., Overseas Press Club (elect.), Smith Coll. Club. Achievements include being resident expert fidget.com., southJersey.com, Lipetnights.com, divorceinteractive.com, ivillage.com.

DEJACK, JACQUELINE ELVADEANA, artist, educator; b. St. Louis, Oct. 9, 1938; d. John Allen and Margie Louise (Cooksey) Williams; m. James Patrick DeJack (dec. June 1994); children: Jennifer Lynn, John Patrick. Student, St. Louis U, 1966-67, Webster Coll., 1978-79; AA, East Ctrl. U., 1979; student, U. Mo., 1998. Lic. real estate agt., Mich.; cert. broker sales and tchr. broker, Mo. Sales staff Hudsons Dept. Store, Detroit, 1957; with First Fed. Savs., Detroit, 1961-62; cons. to libr. dir. St. Louis U., 1965-66; bank cons., ins. mgr. Willston (Mo.) State Bank, 1967-68; co-founder, broker, cons. Tri County Real Estate, Pacific, Mo., 1971-89; pvt. practice artist and writer Jacqueline's Affordable Graphics, Pacific, Mo., 1993-2001; broker, sales Hickenbotham Real Estate, 2000-2001. Fine art tchr., cons. Six Flags Over Mid-Am., Eureka, Mo., summer 1982. Supr. youth corp. St. Louis U., 1964; bd. mem. U. Mo., St. Louis, 1980; mem. Sears (Mich.) Writer's Guild, 1987. Mem. Cadillac Artis Guild, Phi Theta Kappa. Avocations: writing, art, histary research, music, swimming.

DEJAMMET, ALAIN, diplomat; Perm. rep. of France to UN, N.Y.C., 1995—, pres. Security Coun., 1999—. Office: Perm Mission of France to UN 1 Dag Hammarskjöld Plz 245 E 47th St Fl 44 New York NY 10017-2201

DE JANOSI, PETER ENGEL, research manager; b. Pecs, Hungary, June 26, 1928; came to U.S., 1947; s. Paul E. and Kitty de Janosi; m. Monica Reis, Nov. 30, 1963; children: Paul, Nicholas, Alexander. BA, Conn. Wesleyan U., 1950; MA, U. Mich., 1951, PhD, 1956; PhD (hon.), Budapest U. Econs., 1997. Economist Standard Oil Co. of N.J., N.Y.C., 1956-62; program officer in charge Ford Found., N.Y.C., 1962-80; v.p. Russell Sage Found., N.Y.C., 1980-90; dir. Internat. Inst. Applied Systems Analysis, Laxenburg, Austria, 1990-96; sr. advisor Lead Internat., N.Y.C., 1998—. Mem. adv. coun. Cornell U. Coll. of Human Ecology, Ithaca, N.Y., 1985-90; mem. goven. coun. Internat. Inst. for Applied Systems Analysis, Laxenburg, Austria, 1987-90; mem. exec. com. The Internat. Fedn. of Insts. of Advanced Studies, 1993-96; governing bd. Inst. Internatl. Global Environ. Strategies, Japan, 1997—, Grad. Faculty New Sch. U. Recipient Cross of Honor first class Republic of Austria, golden decoration Province and City of Vienna. Mem. Coun. on Fgn. Rels., Century Assn. Home: 5 Leroy Pl Chappaqua NY 10514-3207 E-mail: dejanosi@aol.com.

DE JARNETTE, JAMES E. psychoanalyst; b. Atlanta, Mar. 22, 1948; s. Charles Nathan and Sarah (Phillips) de J. BA, Shorter Coll., 1970; MA, West Ga. U., 1971; PhD, Sussex (Eng.) Coll., 1973; PhD in Psychoanalysis, Shefferton U., England, 2002; PhD in Psychology (hon.), Cosmopolitan U. and Rsch. Inst., 2002. Diplomate Am. Coll. Forensic Examiners, Am. Coll. Forensic Medicine, Am. Bd. Med. Psychotherapists, Am. Acad. Experts in Traumatic Stress, Am. Bd. Profl. Disability Cons., Am. Bd. Psychol. Specialties, Am. Psychotherapy Assn. Pvt. practice, Beverly Hills, Calif., 1973—; pres. S.W. Counseling Svc., Inc., 2001—. Fellow: Am. Grief Assn., Am. Orthopsychiat. Assn. (life); mem.: APA, So. Calif. Biofeedback Soc. (bd. dirs.), Am. Soc. Clin. and Exptl. Hypnosis, Calif. Assn. Marriage and Family Therapists, Am. Psychotherapy Assn. (bd. dirs.), Alpha Pi Omega, Pi Gamma Nu. Avocations: writing, reading. Office: 8306 Wilshire Blvd Ste 2662 Beverly Hills CA 90211 E-mail: mindspa@pacbell.net.

DEJESUS, ONOFRE T, chemist; s. Artemio U and Lucia Tolentino DeJesus; m. Peggy A. Harless, Jan. 1, 1981; children: Melanie J, Melissa M. PhD, Va. Tech, 1980. Rsch. assoc. U. of Chgo., Chicago, Ill., 1981—83; rsch. asst. prof. U. Of Chgo., Chicago, Ill., 1983—87; asst. prof. U. of Wis. Med. Sch., Madison, Wis., 1987—93, assoc. prof., 1993—2002, prof., 2002—; asst. chemist Argonne Nat. Lab., Argonne, Ill., 1986—87. Rsch. asst. Philippine Atomic Rsch. Ctr., Quezon City, Philippines, 1971—75; vis. chemist Brookhaven Nat. Lab., Upton, Long Island, NY, 1975—76. Achievements include development of PET imaging agents for dopamine system.

DEJEWSKI, DEBORAH ELIZABETH, pharmacist; b. Phila., Mar. 15, 1972; d. Salvatore P. and Carol A. Dejewski. BS in Sci., Phila. Coll. Pharmacy and Sci., 1995. Lic. pharmacist, Pa. Pharmacist Consumer Value Stores, Phila., 1995, Drug Emporium, Phila., 1995-98, Acme Markets, Inc., Downingtown, Pa., 1998-2000; with Yo! Sci., Norristown, 2000, Sci. Staffing, King of Prussia, Pa., 2000—01, Centocor, Wayne, Pa., 2001—. Vol. St. Vincent's Orphanage, Phila., 1997. Mem.: Drug Info. Assn., Am. Pharm. Assn.

DE JONG, CONSTANCE A. artist; b. San Diego, Dec. 21, 1950; d. Rolland and Rita De Jong. BS in Edn., Bowling Green State U., 1972; MA, U. N.Mex., 1975, MFA, 1981. Asst. prof. art U. N.Mex., Albuquerque, 1989-95, assoc. prof., 1995—. Lectr. Bezalel Acad. Art, Jerusalem, Israel, 1994, jak art 2001, Jakarta, Indonesia, Albuquerque Mus., N.Mex., 2003—. One woman show at Albuquerque Mus., 2003; exhibited in shows at Mus. of Fine Arts, Mus. of N.Mex., 2001-02, Univ. Art Mus., U. N.Mex., 1999, Cedar Rapids Mus. of Art, Iowa, 1998, Sheldon Meml. Art Gallery, U. Nebr., 1997, SITE, Santa Fe, 1996, Linda Durham Gallery, Santa Fe, 1995, Albuquerque Mus., 1995, Mulvane Art Mus., Topeka, 1991, 93, John Davis Gallery, N.Y.C., 1989, Mus. Fine Arts, Santa Fe, 1987, Roswell Mus., 1984, Salina (Kans.) Art Ctr., 1983, Tyler (Tex.) Art Mus., 1982, others; sculptures in collections at Albuquerque Fine Arts Mus., Mulvane Art Mus., Kans., Mus. N.Mex., Fisher-Landau Ctr., N.Y.C., Mus. N.Mex. Vol. Animal Humane Soc., Albuquerque, 1998. Named Outstanding Tchr. of Yr., U. N.Mex., 1994; Nat. Endowment for Arts fellow, 1982, U. N.Mex. rsch. grantee, 1980, 97, N.Mex. Arts Commn. grantee, 1979. Mem. Albuquerque Zen Ctr. Avocation: scuba diving. Office: U NMex Dept Art And Art Hist Albuquerque NM 87131-0001

DE JONG, DAVID SAMUEL, lawyer, educator; b. Washington, Jan. 8, 1951; s. Samuel and Dorothy (Thomas) De J.; m. Tracy Ann Barger, Sept. 23, 1995; children: Jacob Samuel, Franklin Joseph. BA, U. Md., 1972; JD, Washington and Lee U., 1975; LLM in Taxation, Georgetown U., 1979. Bar: Md. 1975, U.S. Dist. Ct. Md. 1977, U.S. Tax Ct. 1977, U.S. Ct. Appeals (4th cir.) 1978, U.S. Supreme Ct. 1979, D.C. 1980, U.S. Dist. Ct. D.C. 1983, U.S. Ct. Claims, U.S. Ct. Appeals (fed. cir.) 1983; CPA, Md.; cert. valuation analyst. Atty. Gen. Bus. Svcs., Inc., Rockville, Md., 1975-80; ptnr. Stein Sperling Bennett De Jong Driscoll & Greenfeig, PC, Rockville, 1980—. Adj. prof. Southea. U., Washington, 1979-85, Am. U., Washington, 1983-2002; instr. U. Md., College Park, 1986-87, Montgomery Coll., Rockville, 1983; mem. character com. 7th Appeals Cir. Md. Ct. of Appeals. Co-author: (ann. book) J.K. Lasser's Year-Round Tax Strategies, 1989—; editor Notes and Comments, Washington and Lee U. Law Rev., 1974-75. V.p. Seneca Whetstone Homeowners Assn., Gaithersburg, Md., 1981-82, pres. 1982-83. Mem. ABA, AICPA, Am. Assn. Atty.-CPAs (bd. dirs. 1997—, sec. 1998-99, treas. 1999-2000, v.p. 2000-02, pres. elect 2002-2003, pres. 2003—), Md. Bar Assn., Montgomery County Bar Assn. (chmn. tax sect. 1991-92, treas. 1996-97), D.C. Bar Assn., Md. Assn. CPAs, D.C. Inst. CPAs, Nat. Assn. Cert. Valuation Analysts, Inst. Bus. Appraisers, Md. Soc. Accts., Phi Alpha Delta. Office: 25 W Middle Ln Rockville MD 20850-2214

DE JONG, GORDON FREDERICK, education educator, consultant; b. Berea, Ky., Aug. 6, 1935; s. Frederick Henry and Elizabeth (Devries) De Jong; m. Caroline Jane Miller, July 1, 1961; children: Judith Kristen, Gregory Gordon, Graham Austin. BA, Ctrl. Coll., Pella, Iowa, 1957; MA, Univ. Ky., Lexington, Ky., 1960, PhD, 1963. Instr. Univ. Ky., Lexington, Ky., 1961—63; asst. prof., full prof. Pa. State Univ., Univ. Pk., Pa., 1963—91; sr. fellow East-West Ctr., Honolulu, 1978—79; vis. faculty Netherlands Grad. Sch. in Demography, 1994; disting. prof, dir., grad. program in demography Pa. State Univ., Pa., 1992—. Dir. Population Rsch. Inst., Pa. State Univ., Pa., 1974—76, Pa., 1982—88; rsch. cons. Govt. Thailand, Philippines, South Africa, 1983—; editor, demography Population Assn. of Am., Washington, 1987—90. Editor: (acadmic book) Migration Decision Making, 1981, Social Demography, 1972; contbr. articles to profl. jour. Demographic advisor Exec. officers and Legislators Commonwealth of Pa., 1980—; Task Force on Aging, mem. Atty. Gen. Pa., 1993—2000. Mem.: Faculty Senate, Pa. State Univ., Popluation Assn. of Am. (chair), Am. Sociol. Assn. (chair). Achievements include research in 25 competitively awarded rsch. grants in demography issues internat; expert

scholar on immigration and internat. migration; Founder and dir. of grad. program in demography, Pa. State Univ. Avocations: music, sports. Office: Population Rsch Inst 506 Oswald Tower University Park PA 16802

DEJONG, H. WILLIAM, health educator; b. Flagstaff, Ariz., Dec. 19, 1950; s. Henry William and Dorothy Rose (Cooney) DeJ.; m. Maureen Ann Kelley, June 18, 1988; children: Christene A., Margaret M., H. William. AB summa cum laude, Dartmouth Coll., 1973; MA, Stanford U., 1975, PhD, 1977. Dir. evaluation Ctr. for Health Comm., Boston, 1987-90; ind. cons. Wayland, Mass., 1990—; lectr. health comm. Harvard Sch. Pub. Health, Boston, 1995-2001; dir. Higher Edn. Ctr. for Alcohol and Other Drug Prevention, Newton, Mass., 1995—; prof. Boston U. Sch. Pub. Health, 2001—. Author: Preventing Interpersonal Violence Among Youth, 1994, Setting and Improving Policies for Reducing Alcohol and Other Drug Problems on Campus, 1996, The Media and the Message: Lessons Learned from Past Public Service Campaigns, 1998. Bd. dirs. Mothers Against Drunk Driving, Irving, Tex., 1993-96; mem. bd. visitors Rockefeller Ctr., Dartmouth Coll., Hanover, N.H., 1991-95, 96-99; governing mem. Mass. Tobacco Control Oversight Coun., Boston, 1994-98. Recipient Bronze Apple award Nat. Ednl. Media Network, 1997. Mem. APHA, Phi Beta Kappa. Home: 29 Rice Spring Ln Wayland MA 01778-3515 Office: Boston U Sch Pub Health 715 Albany St Boston MA 02118 E-mail: wdejong@bu.edu

DE JONGHE, LUTGARD C. educator; m. Lynn S. Sargent; children: Erika S., Jessica S. BS in Chem. Engring., HTI, Antwerp, Belgium, 1961; MS in Metallurgy, U. Del., 1968; PhD, U. Calif., Berkeley, 1970. Tech. staff Nuc. Rsch. Inst., Mol, Belgium, 1963—65; rsch. fellow Harvard U., Cambridge, Mass., 1970—73; asst. and assoc. prof. Cornell U., Ithaca, NY, 1973—78; sr. scientist Lawrence Berkeley Nat. Lab., Berkeley, Calif., 1978—; prof. materials sci. and engring. U. Calif., Berkeley, 1978—. Chmn. PolyPlus Battery Co., Berkeley, 1991—. Mil. svc., 1961—63. Named Sr. U.S. Scientist, A.v. Humboldt Found., 1990. Fellow: Am. Ceramic Soc. (R.M. Fulrath award 1985). Office: Univ Calif Berkeley 324 Hearst Mining Bldg MSE Berkeley CA 94720 Office Fax: 510-486-4881. E-mail: dejonghe@lbl.gov.

DE JONG-POMBO, TERESA MARIA, concert pianist, educator; b. Seattle, June 1, 1961; d. Pieter Nicolaas and Maria Josefa de Jong; m. Diego Pombo, July 8, 1989; children: Stefania Camila Pombo, Natalia Maria Pombo, Matthew Paul Pombo. MusB in Piano Performance summa cum laude, U. of So. Calif., L.A., 1983, MusM in Piano Performance, 1988; Konzertfach Diplom, Hochschule fuer Musik und darstellende Kunst, Vienna, 1988. Lic. cmty. coll. tchr. Calif., 1989. Pvt. piano instr., Fountain Valley, Calif., 1976—; asst. lectr. keyboard dept. U. of So. Calif., L.A., 1983—85; lectr. piano dept. The Colburn Sch. of Performing Arts, L.A., 1989—; lectr. keyboard dept. Orange Coast Coll., Costa Mesa, Calif., 1999—. Guest lectr. presenting a seminar on piano pedagogy Universidad Javeriana (U. Javeriana), Bogota, Colombia, 1989; guest artist, presenting performances and master classes Pa. Acad. of Music, Lancaster, 1998; panelist at conv. Music Teachers Nat. Assn., L.A., 1999; adjudicator various music competitions, 1990—; recitalist Fulbright Commn., Boesendorfer Hall, Wiener Neudorf, Leon de Greiff Auditorium, Seal Beach Chamber Music Series, Christ Ch. by the Sea, Huntington Beach Arts Associates and many others, Various Cities, Calif., 1974—; piano soloist in concerto appearances Orange Coast Coll. Symphony Orch., Costa Mesa, Calif., 1989—. Contbr. Grantee Fulbright grantee, Fulbright Commn., 1985—86; scholar Carnation scholar, U. of So. Calif., 1979—83. Mem.: Calif. Assn. of Profl. Music Tchrs., Music Tchrs. Assn. of Calif. (br. vice-president 1993—94), Music Tchrs. Nat. Assn., Pi Kappa Lambda (life), Phi Kappa Phi (life). Roman Catholic. Avocations: skiing, travel. Home: 9177 Nadine River Cir Fountain Valley CA 92708 Personal E-mail: tdejongpombo@socal.rr.com.

DE KANTER, ELLEN ANN, English and foreign language educator; b. Spokane, Wash., Mar. 10, 1926; d. George L. and Alison P. (Christy) Tharp; m. Scipio de Kanter, Feb. 2, 1949 (dec.); children: Scipio, Georgette, Robert, Adriana. BA, Mexico City Coll.-U. of Ams., 1947; MEd, U. Houston, 1972, MA in Spanish, 1974, EdD, 1979. Dir. bilingual edn., prof. U. St. Thomas, Houston, dir. bilingual edn., 1979—. Contbr. articles to profl. jours. Grantee 11 Tchr. Tng. Grants, U. of St. Thomas, 1986—. Mem. Nat. Assn. Bilingual Edn. (chmn. 1989 conf., program chair 1993 conf.), Houston Area Assn. Bilingual Edn. (pres. 1987-88), Inst. Hispanic Culture (bd. dirs. 1989-90). Home: 3015 Meadowview Dr Missouri City TX 77459-3308 Office: U St Thomas 3800 Montrose Blvd Houston TX 77006-4626 E-mail: dekanter@stthom.edu.

DEKARSKE, STEVEN RONALD, purchasing agent; b. Sheboygan, Wis., Aug. 20, 1955; s. Ronald H. and Marilyn J. DeKarske; m. Caron H. Rigotti, May 29, 1976; children: Melissa, Craig. BA, Lakeland Coll., 1998. Purchasing mgr. Kenro Inc., Fredonia, Wis., 1992-99, Lakeshore Tech. Coll., Cleveland, Wis., 1999—. Chmn. purchasing officers com. Wis. Tech. Coll., 1999—; chmn. Wis. Indianhead, Lakeshore, and Midstate Tech. Colls. Consortium Desktop and Sys. Procurement Team, Cleveland, 1999-2000; participating mem. WILM Consortium Fin. Peoplesoft Implementation Team, Cleveland, 1999—. Past treas. St. Paul Luth. Ch., Sheboyan, Immanuel Luth. Ch., Sheboyanl; past coach Sheboygan Luth. H.S. Debate Team, Sheboygan North H.S. Debate Team; past asst. coach Sheboygan North H.S. Forenics Team. Mem. Nat. Inst. Govtl. Purchasing, Nat. Assn. Purchasing Mgmt., Wis. Assn. Pub. Purchasers. Lutheran. Avocations: swimming, traveling, tutoring, cooking. Home: PO Box 516 Sheboygan WI 53082 Office: Lakeshore Tech Coll 1290 North Ave Cleveland WI 53015 Office Fax: 920-693-3635. E-mail: peanutt99@msn.com., Steven.DeKarske@gotolte.edu.

DEKAY, MICHAEL L. decision science educator; b. Starkville, Miss., Mar. 29, 1963; s. H. T. and Martha E. DeKay; m. Judith A. Hartman, July 20, 1997; children: McKenzie, Addison. BS, Calif. Inst. Tech., 1985; MS, Cornell U., 1987; MA, PhD, U. Colo., 1994. Rsch. and tchg. asst. dept. chemistry Cornell U., Ithaca, NY, 1985—86; rsch. asst. dept. psychology U. Oreg., Eugene, 1987—89; rsch. and tchg. asst. dept. psychology U. Colo., Boulder, 1989—94; health svcs. rsch. specialist, postdoctoral fellow VA Med. Ctr. and Dept. Ops. and Info. Mgmt., U. Pa., Phila., 1994—96; assoc. prof. engring. and pub. policy and decision sci. Carnegie Mellon U., Pitts., 1996—. Author: (book chpt.) Improving Regulation: Cases in Environment, Health, and Safety, 2001. Grantee, NSF, 2001—, NSF and EPA, 1999—. Mem.: APA, Soc. for Risk Analysis, Soc. for Med. Decision Making (Lee Lusted prize 1995), Soc. for Judgment and Decision Making, Brunswik Soc. (New Investigator award 1993), Am. Psychol. Soc. Office: Carnegie Mellon U HJ Heinz Sch Pub Policy Pittsburgh PA 15213-3890

DEKEN, JEAN MARIE, librarian, archivist; b. St. Louis, Apr. 5, 1953; d. Cornelius John and Loretta Frances (McGuire) D.; m. James Roger Reed, Jan. 2, 1981. BA in English summa cum laude, Washington U., 1974, MA in English, 1976; M in Libr. Info. Sys., San Jose State U., 2002. Cert. archivist Acad. Cert. Archivists. Archivist Mo. Botanical Garden, St. Louis, 1975-78; mgmt. analyst Nat. Archives and Records Svc., St. Louis, 1978-81, supervisory archives specialist, 1981-82; instr. of English St. Louis Community Coll., St. Louis, 1982-83; curator John W. Barriger III collections St. Louis Merc. Libr., 1983-85; libr. Ralston Purina, St. Louis, 1985-86; mgr. libr. svcs. Maritz, Inc., St. Louis, 1986-87; supervisory archivist Nat. Archives and Records Adminstrn., St. Louis, 1987-96; archivist Stanford U. Stanford Linear Accelerator Ctr., 1996—. Author: Henry Shaw: His Life and Legacy, 1977, Stanford Linear Accelerator Center, Celebrating 40 Years: A Photo Hitory, 2002; contbr. articles to profl. jours. Mem. Spl. Librs. Assn., Midwest Archives Conf., Soc. Am. Archivists, Soc. Calif. Archivists (bd. mem.), Western Archives Inst. Avocation: swimming. Office: Stanford U Stanford Linear Accelerator Ctr 2575 Sand Hill Rd MS82 Menlo Park CA 94025

DE KENESSEY, STEFANIA MARIA, composer; b. Budapest, Hungary, Oct. 6, 1956; came to U.S., 1967; d. Zoltan Elek and Stefania Ivanova Kenessey; m. Andrew Henry Chapman, June 20, 1976; children: Dora Rosalia, Jordan Spencer. BA, Yale U., 1976; MFA, Princeton U., 1978, PhD, 1984. Prof. music New Sch. U., N.Y.C., 1980—2000, artist-in-residence, 2001—. Founder, artistic dir. The Derriere Guard, N.Y.C., 1997—. Composer: (Operas) The Monter Bed, The Other Wise Man, (orchestra) Cutting Loose, Manned Flight, Wintersong, Summer Nights, (chamber) Shades of Darkness, Beating Down, Magic Forest Dances, Sunburst, (songs) High Summer, In Memoriam, Autumn Elegy, The Muse Is Not Amused, The Daughters of Odessa, Girl in the Mirror, Jumping Jacks, Mothers and Daughters, Elizabethan Lyrics, (films) Art Under the Radar, The Last Angry Man, The Passing, (albums) Shades of Dark, Shades of Light, Two By three, Sunbursts, Sing for the Cure, An American Sampler, The Orchestra According to the Seven. Meet the Composer grantee, 1990—. Mem. ASCAP (Std. Music award 1990—), Nat. Assn. Composers (sec. East Coast chpt. 1985-92), Internat. Alliance for Women in Music (founding pres. 1993-94), Am. Women Composers (pres. 1990-93). Avocations: novels, poetry, theater, visual and fine arts. Home: 171 W 71st St Apt 2A New York NY 10023 Office: 27 West 67th St Studio 1FW New York NY 10023 E-mail: dekeness@att.net.

DEKIEFFER, DONALD EULETTE, lawyer; b. Newport, R.I., Nov. 8, 1945; s. Robert and Melissa (Hibberd) deKieffer; m. Nancy Kishida, June 27, 1970; 1 child, Nathan Hiroyuki. BA, U. Colo., 1968; JD, Georgetown U., 1971. Bar: U.S. Supreme Ct. 1982, U.S. Ct. Appeals (D.C. cir.) 1971, U.S. Dist. Ct. D.C. 1971, U.S. Ct. Claims 1971, U.S. Ct. Internat. Trade 1971. Mem. profl. staff Senate Rep. Policy Com., Washington, 1969—71; assoc. Collier, Shannon, Rill & Edwards, 1971—74; ptnr. Collier, Shannon, Rill, Edwards & Scott, 1974—80, deKieffer, Berg & Creskoff, 1980; gen. counsel U.S. Trade Rep., 1981—83; ptnr. Plaia, Schaumburg & deKieffer, 1983—84, Pillsbury, Madison & Sutro, 1984—92, deKieffer, Dibble & Horgan, 1992—. Mem. Presdl. Transition Team, 1980—81. Author: How to Lobby Congress, 1981, Doing Bus. with the USA, 1984, Doing Bus. with Romania, 1985, Doing Bus. in the U..S., 1985, Doing Bus. with the New Romania, 1991, Internat. Bus. Traveler's Companion, 1992, How Lawyers Screw Their Clients, 1996, The Citizen's Guide to Lobbying Congress, 1997. Mem.: ABA, Fed. Bar Assn., D.C. Bar Assn., Internat. Antitrust Soc., Am. Soc. Internat. Law. Office: deKieffer & Horgan 729 15th St NW Ste 800 Washington DC 20005-2105 E-mail: ddekieffer@dhlaw.com.

DEKKER, EUGENE EARL, biochemistry educator; b. Highland, Ind., July 23, 1927; s. Peter and Anne (Hendrikse) D.; m. Harriet Ella Holwerda, July 5, 1958; children: Gwen E., Paul D., Tom R. AB, Calvin Coll., 1949; MS, U. Ill., 1951, PhD, 1954. Instr. U. Louisville Med. Sch., 1954-56; instr. biol. chemistry U. Mich. Med. Sch., Ann Arbor, 1956-58, asst. prof., 1958-65, assoc. prof., 1965-70, prof., 1970-94, assoc. chmn. dept., 1975-88, emeritus prof., 1994—. Served with USN, 1945-46 Mem. AAAS, Am. Chem. Soc., Am. Soc. Biol. Chemists, Am. Soc. Plant Physiologists, Oxygen Soc., Protein Soc., Sigma Xi, Phi Lambda Upsilon. Mem. Christian Reformed Ch. Home: 4001 Glacier Hills Dr Apt 126 Ann Arbor MI 48105-3655 Office: U Mich Med Sch Dept Biol Chemistry Ann Arbor MI 48109-0606

DEKKER, GEORGE GILBERT, literature educator, literary scholar, writer; b. Long Beach, Calif., Sept. 8, 1934; s. Gilbert J. and Laura (Barnes) D.; m. Linda Jo Bartholomew, Aug. 31, 1973; children by previous marriage: Anna Allegra, Clara Joy, Ruth Siobhan, Laura Daye. BA in English, U. Calif.-Santa Barbara, 1955; MA in English, 1958; M.Litt., Cambridge U. (Eng.), 1961; PhD in English, U. Essex (Eng.), 1967. Lectr. U. Wales, Swansea, 1962-64; lectr. in lit. U. Essex, 1964-69, reader in lit., 1969-72, dean Sch. Comparative Studies, 1969-71; assoc. prof. English Stanford (Calif.) U., 1972-74, prof., 1974—, chmn. dept., 1978-81, 84-85, Joseph S. Atha prof. humanities, 1988—, dir. program in Am. Studies, 1988-91, assoc. dean grad. policy, 1993-96. Author: Sailing After Knowledge, 1963, James Fenimore Cooper the Novelist, 1967; Coleridge and the Literature of Sensibility, 1978, The American Historical Romance, 1987; editor: Donald Davie: The Responsibilities of Literature, 1983. Nat. Endowment Humanities fellow, 1977; Inst. Advanced Studies in Humanities fellow U. Edinburgh (Scotland), 1982; hon. fellow, Clare Hall Cambridge, 1997, Stanford Humanities Ctr., 1997. Mem. Am. Lit. Assn. Democrat. Office: Stanford U Dept English Stanford CA 94305 *Over the past forty years I have divided my personal and professional life between the U.S. and Britain— not England alone, but Ireland, Scotland and Wales, too. This experience has given the distinctive stamp to my work as a teacher and writer, making me as much at home with Scott as with Hawthorne, with a British as well as an American university. I am currently completing a book-length study of relationships between British tourism and the Romantic novel, 1760-1830.*

DEKKERS, MARIJN, electronics executive; b. The Netherlands; PhD in Chem. Engring., U. Eindhoven, The Netherlands. Rsch. scientist R&D Ctr. GE, Schenectady, NY, various operating positions, 1985—95; joined AlliedSignal, 1995; pres. electronics materials divsn. Honeywell Internat. (formerly Allied-Signal), Sunnyvale, Calif.; COO Thermo Electron Corp., Waltham, Mass., 2000—. Contbr. articles to profl. jours. Achievements include patents in field. Office: Thermo Electron Corp PO Box 9046 81 Wyman St Waltham MA 02454-9046

DEKMEJIAN, RICHARD HRAIR, political science educator; b. Aleppo, Syria, Aug. 3, 1933; came to U.S., 1950, naturalized, 1955; s. Hrant H. and Vahede V. (Matossian) D.; m. Anoush Hagopian, Sept. 19, 1954; children: Gregory, Armen, Haig. BA, U. Conn., 1959; MA, Boston U., 1960; Middle East Inst. cert., Columbia U., 1964, PhD, 1966. Mem. faculty SUNY, Binghamton, 1964-86; prof., chmn. dept. polit. sci. U. So. Calif., Los Angeles, 1986-90, prof. internat. bus. Marshall Sch. Bus.; also master Hinman Coll., 1971-72. Lectr. Fgn. Svc. Inst., Dept. Def., Dep. State, 1976-87; vis. prof. Columbia U., U. Pa., 1977-78; cons. Dept. State, AID, USIA, UN, Dept. Def. Author: Egypt Under Nasir, 1971, Patterns of Political Leadership, 1975; Islam in Revolution, 1985, 2nd edit., 1995, Ethnic Lobbies in U.S. Foreign Policy, 1997, Troubled Waters: The Geopolitics of the Caspian Region, 2001, The Just Prince: A Manual of Leadership, 2003; contbr. articles to profl. jours. Pres. So. Tier Civic Ballet Co., 1973-76. Served with AUS, 1955-57. Mem. Am. Polit. Sci. Assn., Middle East Inst., Middle East Studies Assn., Internat. Inst. Strategic Studies, Skull and Dagger, Pi Sigma Alpha, Phi Alpha Theta. Office: U So Calif Dept Polit Sci Los Angeles CA 90089-0044 E-mail: dekmejia@usc.edu.

DE KOK, DANIEL JOHN, music educator; b. Holland, Mich., Feb. 13, 1960; s. Paul Wesley and Olga Katherine De Kok; m. Nancy Ann Brooks, Sept. 9, 1963; children: Daniel John, Sarah Margaret, Natalie Rose. MusB, U. of Mich., 1978—82; MusM, Western Mich. U., 1985—87. Asst. band dir. Edinburg Jr. H.S., Tex., 1982—83; sr. choir dir. Prince of Peace Luth. Ch., Grand Rapids, 1987—88; dir. of music All Saints Regional Sch., Phillipsburg, NJ, 1990—92; tchr. of music Plainfield Bd. of Edn., NJ, 2000—03; dir. Performing Arts Acad. Kensington H.S., Phila., 2003—. Actor: (production) The Music Man; musical director (production) The Merry Widow, Brigadoon, Jesus Christ Superstar, Carnival; singer: (concerts) Bach Choir of Bethlehem PA; musical director (production) The Merry Widow. Mem. Northampton County Rep. Com., Easton, 2000—02. Scholar Tchg. Guitar Workshop, Music Educators Nat. Conf./GAMA/NAMM, 2002. Mem.: Phi Mu Alpha Sinfonia, Nat. Scrabble Assn. (winner, Detroit Tournament 1982), Acacia Frat. Republican. Roman Catholic. Avocations: guitar, Scrabble, gourmet cooking. Home: 1807 Lehigh St Easton PA 18042 Office: Kensington HS 2051 E Cumberland St Philadelphia PA 19125 Personal E-mail: djdekok@yahoo.com.

DEKOK, DAVID, writer, reporter; b. Holland, Mich., July 17, 1953; s. Paul W. and Olga (Kilian) DeK.; m. Lisa W. Brittingham, Oct. 1, 1988; children: Elizabeth B., Lydia B. BA, Hope Coll., Holland, 1975. Reporter The News-Item, Shamokin, Pa., 1975-87, The Patriot-News, Harrisburg, Pa., 1987—. Cons. PBS documentary Centralia Fire, 1982-83; guest lectr. Bucknell U., Lewisburg, Pa., 1988-97. Author: Unseen Danger: A Tragedy of People, Government and Centralia Mine Fire, 1986, republished, 2000. Del. Mich. Dem. Conv., 1972; mem. St. Stephen's Episcopal Sch. Bd., 1999—, chmn. tech. com. Recipient Keystone Press award Pa. Newspaper Pubs. Assn., 1979, 86, 87, 90, 99, Pub. Svc. award AP Mng. Editors of Pa., 1981, Janus award Mortgage Bankers Am., 1992. Mem. Investigative Reporters and Editors, Nat. Press Club (Freedom of the Press award 1995), Soc. Profl. Journalists (pres. ctrl. Pa. chpt. 1989-91, Spotlight award 1995), Newspaper Guild, Nat. Writers Union. Episcopalian. Home: 113 Conoy St Harrisburg PA 17104-1608 E-mail: ddekok@comcast.net.

DEKOK, ROGER GREGORY, career officer; b. Kenosha, Wis., Jan. 10, 1947; s. Roger Gerritt Dekok and Hazel Deloris (Wilkinson) Busche; m. Carolyn Susan Flinkow, June 15, 1968; children: Kristen Laura, Ryan Matthew. BA in Math., U. Wis., 1968; MS in Sys. Mgmt., Air Force Inst. Tech., 1979, postgrad., 1978-79; attended, Air War Coll., 1983-84. Commd. 2d lt. USAF, 1968, advanced through grades to lt. gen., 1995, space sys. staff officer HQ, 1979-83, dir. space plans HQ Air Force Space Command Maxwell AFB, Ala., 1983-84, dir. space programs Nat. Security Coun., White House Washington, 1987-88, spl. asst. to Pres., Nat. Security Coun., White House, 1988, comdr. 1st Space Wing Peterson AFB, 1989-90, comdr. 50th Space Wing Falcon AFB, Colo., 1990-93; dir. plans HQ Air Force Space Command USAF, Peterson AFB, 1993-95; dir. ops. U.S. Space Command, Peterson AFB, 1995-96; comdr. Space and Missle Systems Ctr., L.A., 1996-98; dep. chief of staff for plans and programs USAF-Pentagon, Washington, 98—; vice comdr. U.S. Space Commd, Peterson AFB, 2000—. Recipient Nat. Space Achievement award Nat. Rotary Club, 1987, James V. Hartinger award for career space achievement NSIA, 1995. Mem. Air Force Assn., Nat. Space Club (bd. govs. 1988-89, 96—). Lutheran. Avocations: golf, skiing, tennis, personal computing. Office: USAF/VC 150 Vandenberg St Ste 1104 Peterson AFB CO 80914-4020

DEKOSKY, STEVEN TRENT, neurologist; b. Camden, N.J., Mar. 23, 1947; s. Aaron and Evelyn (Gorlen) DeK.; m. Beverly Nelson; children: Allison. Lauren. AB in Psychology, Bucknell U., 1968; MD, U. Fla., 1974. Diplomate in neurology Am. Bd. Psychiatry and Neurology. Post-doctoral fellow, instr. neurology U. Va. Sch. Medicine, Charlottesville, 1978-79; asst. prof. neurology, anatomy U. Ky. Coll. Medicine, Lexington, 1979-85; grad. faculty U. Ky. Grad. Sch., Lexington, 1981-90; assoc. prof. anatomy and neurology U. Ky. Coll. Medicine, Lexington, 1985-90, interim chmn. dept. neurology, 1985-87; prof. psychiatry U. Pitts. Sch. Medicine, 1990—, prof. neurology, neurobiology, 1990—, grad. faculty, 1991—, interim chair dept. neurology, 2000—01, chair dept. neurology, 2002—. Vis. prof. psychology U. Calif., Irvine, 1983; co-dir. Alzheimer's disease rsch. ctr. U. Pitts. Med. Ctr., 1990-94, dir., 1994—, U. Ky. Med. Ctr., 1985-90; task force on Alzheimer's disease State of Ohio, Columbus, 1986-92; med. sci. adv. bd. Alzheimer's Assn., 1992—; dir. behavioral neurology of aging tng. program U. Pitts., 1990—. Mem. Am. Neurol. Assn. (Presd. award 1988), Am. Acad. Neurology, Am. Soc. Neurochemistry, Am. Heart Assn. (stroke coun.), N.Y. Acad. Scis., Soc. Neurosci., Soc. Exptl. Neuropathology (councillor 1990-92), Behavioral Neurology Soc., Am. Bd. of Psychiatry and Neurology. Office: U Pitts 3471 5th Ave Ste 811 Pittsburgh PA 15213-2593 E-mail: dekoskyst@upmc.edu.

DEKOSTER, HEINZ ADOLPH, retired technology consultant; b. Heidelberg, Germany, Apr. 11, 1919; came to U.S., 1959; s. Godfried and Maria Elisabeth de Koster; m. Martha M. Hoerdt, July 27, 1942; children: Alexander P., Beatrix E. MSEE, Acad. Tech. Scis. and Arts, Rotterdam, The Netherlands, 1939; PhD in Applied Physics, U. Heidelberg, 1945. Head indsl. controls Hasler A.G., Switzerland, 1952-59; indsl. controls specialist Allen Bradley Inc., Milw., 1959-61; staff scientist ITT-Kellogg, Palo Alto, Calif., 1961-63; head applied physics dept. Gen. Time Corp., Stamford, Conn., 1963-68; v.p. engring., dir. Seggos Industries/Kenilworth R&D Corp., Stamford, 1968-75; technology cons., 1975-90; ret., 1990. Contbr. numerous articles to profl. jours.; patentee in field. Mem. IEEE (sr.), Am. Phys. Soc., N.Y. Acad. Scis. Home: 19 Woodway Rd Unit # 5 Stamford CT 06907-1459

DE KOSTER, JOHN G. lawyer; b. Berea, Ohio, May 23, 1950; s. Lucas J. and Dorothea L. De Koster; m. Glenda F. Alons, Aug. 19, 1972; children: Lucas, Philip. BS in Polit. Sci., Iowa State U., 1972; JD, U. Colo., 1975. Bar: Iowa 1975, U.S. Supreme Ct. 1978. Atty., advisor U.S. Dept. of Interior, Washington, 1975-79; ptnr. De Koster & De Koster, Hull, Iowa, 1979—. Bd. dirs. Iowa State Bank, Hull, Mut. Fire and Auto Ins. Co., Cedar Rapids. Pres. Hull Cmty. Found., 1999—. Named Citizen of Yr. Hull Bus. and Profl. Club, 1997, Employer of Yr., 2002; recipient Cmty. Svc. award Modern Woodmen, Hull, 1987. Fellow Iowa State Bar Found.; mem. Iowa State Bar Assn. (bd. govs. 1994-99), Sioux County Bar Assn. (pres. 1996-98), Kiwanis. Office: De Koster & De Koster 1102 Main St PO Box 801 Hull IA 51239-0801

DEKREY, RAMONA, medical/surgical nurse, educator; b. Tappen, N.D., Nov. 15, 1929; d. Floyd and Rose (Colsrud) Billington; m. Arthur DeKrey, July 23, 1950 (dec. Dec. 17, 1997); children: Lee, Nan, Eve. AD, RN, Dickinson (N.D.) U., 1976; BSN, Mary U., Bismarck, N.D., 1982. RN cert. tchr., N.D., cert. med./surgical nurse, geriatrics nurse, psychiatric nurse. Charge nurse, med./surg., ICU Hettinger (N.D.) Hosp., 1976—82; chair person, tchr. LPN Nursing Program Ft. Berthold Jr. Coll., Newtown, ND, 1982—85; adj. tchr. Otero Jr. Coll., La Junta, Colo., 1985—90; head nurse, supr. VA Hosp., Ft. Lyon, Colo., 1985—97. Columnist Tips and Time Savers, LPN Bimonthly mag., 1985—2001, RN Mag., Bent County Dem. newspaper. Mem. Red Cross local Coord. Disaster Team; mem. interdenominational missionary health care team Karen Hill Tribes, Thailand; legis. mem. Area Agy. on Aging; sec. Las Animas City Tree Bd.; vol. health educator Sr. Opportunity Ctr., '; vol. hospice nurse, 1985—2002; deaconness Presbyn. Ch. Mem.: AARP (vice chairperson), Nat. Assn. Ret. Federal Employees (sec.), Sisterhood Prominent Ext. Order, Nat. Nurses Honor Soc. Avocations: hiking, poetry, travel. Home: PO Box 572 Las Animas CO 81054-0572

DEKU, AFRIKADZATA, international, French, English and Afrikan-centric Continental Afrikan scholar, researcher, author, publisher, educator; b. Kadjebi, Ghana, Dec. 13, 1949; m. Yayra Deku; children: Mawunyo, Aku Sika, Mawulolo, Afrikamawuse, Afrikamawuedem, Afrikaworlanyo. BA with honors, U. Cape Coast, Ghana, 1977; MSc, U. Ife, Nigeria, 1981; diploma, Inst. Internat. D'Adminstrn. Pub., Paris, 1983; MPhil, U. Paris XI, Sorbonne, 1983, PhD, 1985. Lic. mediator, arbitrator, negotiator. Ind. post-doctoral rsch. scholar U. Denver, 1986-87; founder, chief exec., prof. pan-Afrikan studies Afrikan Culture Inst., 1987—; vis. assoc. prof. Afrikan history Clark Atlanta U., 1990-91; vis. assoc. prof. Africana studies Morris Brown Coll., Atlanta, 1990; vis. assoc. prof. Afrikan culture, continuing edn. dept. Ga. State U., 1990; pub. The Afrikan Truth, 1994—, Continental Afrikan Pubs., 1990—. Vis. prof. French and Afrikan lit. Wofford Coll., Spartanburg, S.C., 1988-89, Converse Coll., Spartanburg, 1989; trainer, guest speaker Clemson U. 4-H Operation Pride, 1994—; ACT ESL placement test fairness reviewer and cons., 2000; participant ACT ESL Teleconf., 2000; resident guest artist Kennedy Middle Sch., Aiken, S.C., 1997, Jackson (S.C.) Mid. Sch., 1998, S.C. Writers Ann. Workshop Conf. Faculty, Manuscript Evaluator; poetry judge Pan-Afrikan Poetry Recitals, Myrtle Beach, 1998; founder, bd. chmn. Afrikamawu Miracle Mission made up of: Continental Afrikan Devel. Authority, KADA, Continental Afrikan Govt. Implementation Authority, KAGO, and Continental Afrikan Culture Promotions Authority, KAFO; guest artist Spartanburg Internat. Festival, 1999, Ea. Lit. Fellowship, Clinton, S.C., 1999, Greenville (S.C.) Internat. Festival Cultural Awareness summer jubilee, 2001, Greenville Summer Jubilee Festival for the Arts, 2001; guest author Lee County Young Authors Ann. Conf., Bishopville, S.C., 1999; lectr., spkr. and cons. in field. Author: (poetry) We Are All Continental Afrikans, 1991, Sacred Verses For My Afrikan Queens, 1992, Sacred Afrikan Spiritual Power From Within, 1993, Agbenoxevie Menye, Ablodesafui, Agbedefu (Ewe poetry), Courage, Mere Afrique, Cris de Tonnerre, Coups de Marteau, A Toi le Paradis de Ma Langue (Afrikan Poetry in French); (plays) No Where is Heaven, Breaking the Bloody Sword of Apartheid, (rsch. books) L'Union Continentale Africaine, vols. 1-3, 1986, Continental Afrikan Power Now, 1987, The Afrikan-Centric Perspective of the Afrikan World Crisis, 1988, Continental Afrikan Manifesto, 1999, Continental Afrikan Power in Figures, 1989, The Afrikan Gospel of Total Happiness Now and Always, 1991, The Power of Afrikan-Centricity, 1992, AFRIKAMAWUNYA or the Holy Afrikan Bible, 1997, Continental Afrika: From Two Hundred Million Seasons to the Present, 1994, The Power and Benefits of Continental Afrikan Culture, 1994, How to Be a Continental Afrikan Again, 1994, Positive Self-Knowledge Technology, 1994, Positive Goal Achievement Technology, 1994, Positive Problem-Solving Technology, 1996, Positive Decision-Making Technology, 1999, I Want To Tell You Why, 1995, From Eagle to Chicken and Back, 1995, Continental Afrikan Constitution of the Continental Afrikan Republic, 1998—; Why the World Bank /IMF/UN etc. Are a Curse Rather Than a Blessing to Afrika, 2001, The Afrikan Origin of Humanity, 2001, Behold Your Continental Afrikan Savior Afrikadela Is Born, 2001, Still Slaves in the "Land of the Free," 2001, Passing Our ABC Test of our Afrikan-Centricity, 2001, The Dates Western Powers do not want us to Know About, 2001, Authentic Continental Afrikan Name Book, 2001; spkr. in field. Founder Afrikan-Centricity Movement, Continental Afrikan Govt. Orgn., Continental Afrikan Found., Continental Afrikan Devel. Authority. Grantee S.C. Arts Commn., 1990-91; scholar Ghana Govt., 1970-72, 73-77, Commonwealth, 1975, 77, 78, French Govt., 1982-85; recipient OYO State Bursary award, 1980-81, Spartanburg, S.C. Arts Coun. award, 1989-90, S.C. Arts Commn. grant, 1990-91. Mem. ABA, Am. Arbitration Assn., S.C. Coun. for Mediation and Alternative Dispute Resolution, Internat. Biog. Assn., Internat. Platform Assn., French PhD Holders Assn.,

African Studies Assn., African Heritage Studies Assn., Am. Polit. Sci. Assn. Home: 182 Stribling Cir Spartanburg SC 29301-1651 also: Box 209 Dansoman Accra Ghana E-mail: afrikalion@aol.com.

DEKUYPER, MARY HUNDLEY, non-profit consultant; b. Syracuse, N.Y., Feb. 23, 1939; d. Edwin Graves and Edna Thompson (Smith) Hundley; m. Frederick Timothy DeKuyper, June 17, 1961; children: Gordon, Sarah. AB, Wellesley Coll., 1960. Adminstr. Calvert Sch., Balt., 1960-65; cons., 1981—. Cons. Assn. Governing Bds., Washington, 1992—, BoardSource, Washington, 1992—; nat. chair vols. ARC, 2000—. Author: Trustee Handbook, 1998, 2003. Pres. Bryn Mawr Sch. Bd., 1984—88; mem. exec. com. Planned Parenthood Md., 1989—98, chair nominating com., 1989—90, chair devel. com., 1990—92, chair strategic planning com., 1992—94, vice chair bd., 1990—96, chair com. bd. devel., 1994—96, vice chair, 1997—98; chair bd. dirs. ARC Greater Chesapeake and Potomac Blood Region, 1992—94, chair bd. devel. com., 1994—96, ex-officio, 1997—99, bd. dirs., 1999—2000; exec. com. ARC Ctrl. Md. chpt., 1989—92, chair blood svcs. com., 1988—92, vice chair bd., 1990—92, chair transition com., 1991, vice chair bd., 1996, chair bd., 1996—98, hon. bd. dirs., 1999—; pub. support com. ARC Nat. Bd. Govs., 1993—99, ex-officio, 2000—, vice chair biomed. svcs. bd., 1994—96, vice chair audit com., 1996—99, history and edn. ctr. adv. bd., 1996—, exec. com., 1996—99, ex-officio, 2000—; pres. nat. bd. Girls, Inc., 1986—90, chair nat. adv. com. trustee edn. project, 1992—95, trustee educator, 1995—; bd. dirs. United Way of Ctrl. Md., 1996—, mem. exec. com.; bd. dirs. Union Meml. Hosp. Found., 1999—2001, Planned Parenthood Md. Found., 1997—2000; vol. Ctrl., 2000, Far Hills Country Day Sch., 2000—, Clara Barton Fed. Credit Union, 2001—; Trustee Enoch Pratt Free Libr., Balt., 2002—; mem. fin. commn. Episcopal Diocese Md., 1993—97, chair program and budget com., 1995—98. Named to, Md.'s Top 100 Women, 1996, 2002; recipient William J. Casey award, 1989, Mary H. DeKuyper Trustee Svc. award, Bryn Mawr Sch., 1989, Exemplary Cmty. Svc. award, Health and Welfare Coun., 1990, Mary H. DeKuyper award, ARC Greater Chesapeake and Potomac Blood Region, 1994, Clementine Peterson award, United Way Ctrl. Md., ARC Nat. Harriman award, 2000. Mem. Jr. League Balt. (pres. 1975-77, Sustainer award 1988), Hamilton St. Club (treas. 1991-95), Wellesley Coll. Club. Democrat. Episcopalian. Home: 4422 Underwood Rd Baltimore MD 21218-1150 Office: ARC 2025 E St NW Washington DC 20006 E-mail: dekuyperm@usa.redcross.org deluyper@ix.netcom.com.

DE LA BANDERA, ELNA MARIE, interpreter, translator; b. Rahway, N.J., Apr. 30, 1936; d. Laertes Gardner and Clara (Hansen) Fortenbaugh; m. Jorge Luis de la Bandera, Dec. 13, 1963; children: Jorge Luis Jr., Cristina Renee. BA in Spanish with honors, Colby Coll., 1958; MA in Spanish translation, Rutgers U., 1991. Cert. Spanish interpreter U.S. Cts., 1987; accredited translator Am. Translators Assn. Spanish-English, 1987, English-Spanish, 1988. Sec., translator U.S. Fgn. Svc., Argentina, Uruguay, 1959-63; translator Inter-Am. Coun. Commerce and Prodn., Montevideo, Uruguay, 1966-67; freelance interpreter, translator U.S. and Peru, 1968-86; sr. editor Princeton (N.J.) Internat. Translations, 1980-83; sec. Wysoker, Glassner & Weingartner, New Brunswick, N.J., 1984-86; translator, interpreter, test adminstr. N.J. Judiciary, Trenton, 1986-96, cons., 1997-98, part-time employee, 1998—. Mem. temp. faculty Rutgers U., New Brunswick, 1986, 91; cons., coord. interpreting svcs. State of Mass., 1988; cons. on ct. interpreter cert. State of Wash., 1990; oral examiner Fed. Ct. Interpreter Cert. Project, 1989, 93, 2002, 03; cons. Nat. Ctr. for State Cts., 1994-95, 98—. Mem. Nat. Assn. Judiciary Interpreters and Translators, Am. Translators Assn., Phi Sigma Iota, Alpha Delta Pi. Republican. Presbyterian. Avocations: golf, boating, writing, travel. Home: 103 Fairway Blvd Monroe Township NJ 08831-2716 Home (Winter): 3706 SE 18th Pl Cape Coral FL 33904-5094 E-mail: elliedelaB@msn.com.

DELABRE, KEVIN MICHAEL, religious organization executive; b. Kankakee, Ill., May 25, 1952; s. Richard Victor Sr. and Theresa Ann (Marlaire) D.; children: Heather, Aaron. AA, Kankakee C.C., 1972; BA, Govs. State U., 1974, M in Pub. Service, 1980. With Kankakee Fed. Savs. and Loan Assn., 1973-96, mgr. investment svcs., 1983-96, ins. risk mgr., 1985-87, security officer, 1989-96; dir. devel. Cath. Diocese Joliet, Ill., 1996—, risk mgr., 1999—, cemeteries dir., 2000—01, mem. retirement bd., 1998—. V.p. bd. dirs. Green Garden Mut. Ins. Co., investment com. chmn., 1999—. Chmn. sustaining membership program Kankakee Trials Dist. Boy Scouts Am., 1981-83, dist. chmn., 1984-85, exec. mem. Rainbow Coun., 1984-86; chmn. fin. com. St. George's Ch., 1985-88, choir dir., 1985-99; mem. Dist. 258 Sch. Bd., 1985-97, Bishop McNamara H.S. Bd., 1997-2000; past bd. v.p. Kankakee Area spl. Edn. Coop., 1995-97, mem., 1993-96; vol., Rialto Theatre, Joliet, Ill., 2003—. Mem. Nat. Cath. Stewarship Coun. Roman Catholic. Avocations: golf, guitar, wood working. Home: 2038 Manico Ct Unit 301 Crest Hill IL 60435- Office: Diocese Joliet St Charles Pastoral Ctr 402 S Independence Blvd Romeoville IL 60446-2264

DELACAMPAGNE, CHRISTIAN H. humanities educator; b. Dakar, Senegal, Dec. 23, 1949; arrived in U.S., 1998; s. Jacques Delacampagne and Anne-Marie Sarrazin; m. Emilia Crespo, Mar. 31, 1975 (div. 1986); 1 child, Manuel Delacampagne Crespo; m. Ariane Ateshian, May 28, 1999. Agrégé de philosophie, Ecole Normale Supérieure, Paris, 1972; Docteur D'Etat ès Lettres et Scis. Humaines (hon.), U. Paris I, 1982. Prof., France, 1974—80; cultural attaché French Embassies, various locations, 1981—97; prof. Conn. Coll., New London, 1998—2000, Tufts U., Medford, Mass., 2000—02, Johns Hopkins U., Balt., 2002—. Author: A History of 20th Century Philosophy, 1999. Recipient Ordre des Arts et Lettres, French Govt., 1992, Ordre Nat. du Mérite, 1995. E-mail: cdelacampagne@aol.com.

DE LA CANCELA, VICTOR, psychologist; b. Bronx, N.Y., Dec. 18, 1952; s. Luis Fernandez and Guillermina (Ortiz) De La C. BA cum laude, CCNY, 1974, MPhil, 1979, MPH, 1995, PhD, 1981. Diplomate in clin. psychology Am. Bd. Profl. Psychology; Lic. marriage, family and child counselor, Calif.; lic. psychologist, Calif., Mass., N.Y.; cert. health svcs. provider, Mass.; cert. HIV counselor, N.Y. Intern, clin. fellow Med. Sch. Harvard U., 1977-79; supervising psychologist Boston City Hosp., 1979-81; dir. outpatient svcs. San Fernando Valley Cmty. Mental Health Ctr., Van Nuys, Calif., 1982-83; dir. Latino mental health Cambridge (Mass.) Hosp., 1983-85; dir. family svcs. Brookside Cmty. Health Ctr., Boston, 1985-88; dir. cmty. programs Dr. S.C. Fuller Cmty. Mental Health, Boston, 1988-89; sr. v.p. N.Y.C. Health and Hosps. Corp., 1990-95; asst. clin. prof. Coll. Physicians and Surgeons Columbia U., N.Y.C., 1990-2000, assoc. clin. prof., 2000—. Asst. in psychology Beth Israel Hosp., Boston, 1979—81; network supr. Boston City Hosp., 1983—89; assoc. psychologist Brigham and Women's Hosp., Boston, 1985—88; asst. prof., psychologist Columbia-Presbyn. Med. Ctr., N.Y.C., 1990—96; instr. Harvard Med. Sch., Boston, 1979—81, lectr., 1983—88, U. Mass., Boston, 1985—89; cons. Puerto Rican Youth Devel. Leadership, Boston, 1983—86, Concilio Hispano Cambridge, Inc., 1988—90, Martha Eliot Health Ctr., Boston, 1989—90, Boriken Health Ctr., NY, 1995, Bronx Ctr. Cmty Svcs., 1995, Ctr. for Substance Abuse Prevention, SAMHSA, 1995—, Ctr. for Substance Abuse Treatment, 1996, Tremont-Crotona Family Day Care Ctrs., 1998—99; pres., CEO Salud Mgmt. Assocs., Riverdale, NY, 1995—; psychologist Comprehensive Habilitation Svcs., NY, 1995—99; clin. adminstr. Gateway Counseling Ctr., Bronx, NY, 1996—99; dir. behavioral health svcs. Correctional Health Svcs. N.Y.C. Health and Hosps. Corp., 1999; dir. orgnl. devel. Tremont-Crotona Child Devel. Ctr., 1999—2001, dep. exec. dir., 2001—; faculty Beth Israel Med. Ctr. Residency in Urban Family Practice, 2000—01; res. in family practice Wyckoff Med. Ctr., 2002—; officer in charge Behavior Health Svcs, Mills Troop Med. Clin., Fort Dix, NJ, 2003—; faculty clin. psychopharmacology program Mass Sch. of Profl. Psychology, 2003—. Contbr. numerous articles to profl. jours. Capt. Med. Svcs. Corps, USAR. Recipient Pres. Svc. award, N.Y. Assn. Black Psychologists, 1990, Outstanding Contbn. award, 1991, U.S. Surgeon Gen.'s cert. of appreciation, 1993, Alumni Svc. award, CCNY, 2001. Fellow: APA (commr. 1994—96, pres. clin. psychology of ethnic minorities sect. 1999, bd. govs. 2000—02, Coll. Profl. Psychology cert. oversight com. 2002—, cert. HIV-AIDS trainer, com. on profl. practices and stds., 5th ann. achievement award), Soc. Clin. Psychology, Soc. Psychol. Study of Social Issues, Network for Multicultural Tng. in Psychology, Acad. Clin. Psychology, Soc. Pub. Health Edn., Prescribing Psychologists Register (diplomate, regional dir., outstanding PIONEER leadership award), Am. Orthopsychiat. Assn.; mem.: Latino Behavioral Health Network, Assn. Hispanic Mental Health Profls., Nat. Puerto Rican Policy Network, Nat. Hispanic Psychol. Assn. (pres. 1986—90, Outstanding Contbn. award 1989, Exemplary Leadership and Svc. 1990), Am. Soc. Advancement of Pharmacotherapy (chair ethnopharmaco-therapy com. 2000—, bd. dirs. 2001—). Home: 6 Diane Ct Cortlandt Manor NY 10567 Office: Salud Management Assocs Highpoint-on-the-Hudson Bronx NY 10463-1020

DELACATO, JANICE ELAINE, learning consultant, educator; b. Bklyn., June 6, 1926; d. Frode Siegfried and Vilma (Rils) Fernstrom; m. Carl Henry Delacato, June 20, 1951; children: Elizabeth Delacato Putnam, Carl Henry, David Fernstrom. AB, Bryn Mawr Coll., 1948. Tchr. Rydal Hall, Ogontz Sch., Pa., 1948-49, The Spence Sch., N.Y.C., 1949-50, Chestnut Hill Acad., Phila., 1950-52; co-dir. The Chestnut Hill Reading Clinic, Phila., 1951-65, Delacato & Delacato Cons. in Learning, Phila., 1972-88; mgr. Morton (Pa.) Book Store, 1972-88; co-dir. The Delacato & Delacato Conf. Autism & Learning Disabilities, 1979-82. Editor newsletter Temple U. Med. Ctr. Women's Aux., Phila., 1953-65; class editor Bryn Mawr Coll. Alumnae Bull., 1966-79. Chmn. fund-raising com. Springside Sch., 1969-71; treas. Main St. Fair Antiques Booth, Chestnut Hill Hosp., 1965-77. Recipient Main St. Fair award Chestnut Hill Hosp., 1972. Mem. AAUW, Phila. Cricket Club. Republican. Unitarian Universalist. Home: Apt 1014 Lincoln Woods 9801 Germantown Pike Lafayette Hill PA 19444

DE LA CRUZ, CAROLINA, pharmacist; b. Havana, Cuba, Dec. 22, 1962; d. Harold and Yolanda (Morlote) De La C. BS, Rutgers U., Newark, N.J., 1984, Arnold & Marie Schwartz Coll. Pharmacy, Bklyn., 1987. Pharmacist Midtown Drugs, Kearny, N.J., 1987-89, ShopRite Pharmacy, Hasbrouck Heights, N.J., 1989—; fin. rep. Primerica Fin. Svcs., Paramus, NJ, 1999—. Avocations: hiking and the outdoors, travel, reading, skiing, natural medicine. Office: Primerica Fin Svcs 15 Essex Rd 5th Fl Paramus NJ 07652

DELA CRUZ, JOSE SANTOS, retired state supreme court justice; b. Saipan, Commonwealth No. Mariana Islands, July 18, 1948; s. Thomas Castro and Remedio Sablan (Santos) Dela C.; m. Rita Tenorio Sablan, Nov. 12, 1977; children: Roxanne, Renee, Rica Ann. BA, U. Guam, 1971; JD, U. Calif., Berkeley, 1974; cert., Nat. Jud. Coll., Reno, 1985. Bar: No. Mariana Islands, 1974, U.S. Dist. Ct. No. Mariana Islands 1978. Staff atty. Micro. Legal Svcs. Corp., Saipan, 1974-79; gen. counsel Marianas Pub. Land Corp., Saipan, 1979-81; liaison atty. CNMI Fed. Laws Commn., Saipan, 1981-83; ptnr. Borja & Dela Cruz, Saipan, 1983-85; assoc. judge Commonwealth Trial Ct., Saipan, 1985-89; state supreme ct. chief justice Supreme Ct. No. Mariana Islands, 1989-95; retired, 1995. Mem. Conf. of Chief Justices, 1989-95, Adv. Commn. on Judiciary, Saipan, 1980-82; chmn. Criminal Justice Planning Agy., Saipan, 1985-95. Mem. Coun. for Arts, Saipan, 1982-83; chmn. Bd. of Elections, Saipan, 1977-82; pres. Cath. Social Svcs., Saipan, 1982-85. Mem. No. Marianas Bar Assn. (pres. 1984-85). Roman Catholic. Avocations: golf, reading, walking. *There is an inherent goodness in every person, no matter how bad that person may appear. Recognizing that goodness in each gives us hope that the future of mankind will not be destructive.*

DELAFUENTE, CHARLES, lawyer, educator, journalist; b. N.Y.C., Oct. 6, 1945; s. Maurice and Rose (Schulder) De La F.; m. Jill Rosenfeld, Apr. 8, 1979; children: Marc, Carla. Student, Queens Coll., Flushing, N.Y., 1962-66; BA, SUNY, Albany, 1979; JD cum laude, Yeshiva U., N.Y.C., 1981. Bar: N.Y. 1982, D.C. 1985. Night city editor N.Y. Post, N.Y.C., 1969-78; assoc. Herzfeld & Rubin, N.Y.C., 1981-83; atty. Fed. Jud. Ctr., Washington, 1984-85; fgn. desk editor UPI, Washington, 1985-87; asst. city editor Daily News, N.Y.C., 1987-90; asst. mng. editor Times Union, Albany, N.Y., 1990-94; dep. met. editor Daily News, N.Y.C., 1949-95; editor Record, Troy, N.Y., 1995-96; ptnr. Forman & De La Fuente, Latham, N.Y., 1997-98; staff editor N.Y. Times, 1998—. Del. N.Y. State Fair Trial/Free Press Com., Albany, 1994-96; adj. prof. George Washington Coll. Law, Washington, 1985-87, Cardozo Law Sch. Yeshiva U., 1989-90. Mem. Order of Barristers.

DE LA FUENTE RAMIREZ, JUAN RAMON, Mexican government official, academic administrator; b. Mexico City, Sept. 5, 1951; married; 3 children. MSc, U. Minn.; postgrad. psychiatry, Mayo Clinic. Prof. Nat. Nutrition Inst.; rschr. Mex. Inst. Psychiatry; dir. health rsch. program U.N.A.M., mem., 1980, dir. med. faculty, 1991—94, health sec., 1994; sec. health Govt. of Mex., Washington, 1995—99; served in Cabinet as rector U.N.A.M., 1999; rector Nat. Autonomous U. Mex., 2002—; chief resident U. Minn. Vis. prof. several fgn. univs. Author books on health rsch. Vol. internat. health orgns.; investigator Nat. Inst. Nutrition, Mex. Inst. Psychiatry, Mexico City. Recipient Eduardo Liceaga prize, Nat. Acad. Medicine. Mem.: Internat. Assn. Univ. Office: U Nat Autonoma Mex DGSCA Circuito Exterior Ciudad U Delegacion Coyoacan Distrito Federal CP 04510 Mexico

DE LA GARZA, LUIS ADOLFO, lawyer; b. Mission, Tex., Nov. 22, 1943; s. Adolfo and Carmen (Barrera) de la G.; m. Sherry Lynn Hatcher, Apr. 12, 1974; children: Miguel, Gabriel, Lucas. BBA, U. Tex., 1966; MBA, U. Hawaii, 1972; JD, U. Tex., 1975. Bar: Tex. 1975. Counsel El Paso Natural Gas Co., Tex., 1975-78; sr. counsel El Paso Co., Houston, 1978-81; sr. atty., asst. sec. Valero Energy Corp., San Antonio, 1981-87, v.p. corp. rels., 1987-97, PG&E Gas Transmission-Tex. Corp., San Antonio, 1997-2000; ptnr. Holland & Knight, LLP, San Antonio, 2001—03. Co-founder, pres., CEO Texen Power Co., 2000. Chmn. March of Dimes San Antonio Walk Am., 1996, 97; bd. dirs., chmn. Latino leadership for the libr. campaign San Antonio Pub. Libr. Found.; bd. dirs. Tex. Equal Access to Justice Found., comms. com., 1994-2003; bd. dirs. Valero Polit. Action Com., San Antonio, 1984-97, chmn., 1987-97; bd. dirs. Valero Fed. Credit Union, 1987-88; bd. dirs. World Affairs Coun., San Antonio, 1987, exec. com., 1988-90; scout leader Boy Scouts Am., San Antonio, 1984-2003; mem. Witte Coun., Witte Com., San Antonio Mus. Assn., 1985-90; bd. dirs., chmn. United Way Tex., mem. pub. policy com., 2000-03; bd. dirs. Tex. Civil Justice League; mem. bus. adv. coun. U. Tex., San Antonio; commr. Tex. Equal Acces Justice Commn., 2001-2003. Capt. USMC, 1966-72, Vietnam. Decorated Air medal with 15 oak leaf clusters; named One of the Hundred Most Influential Hispanics in Am. Hispanic Bus. Mag., 1990, One of the Corp. Elite in Am. Hispanic Mag., 1990-2000; recipient Breaking Barriers award Nat. Hispanic Employees Assn., 1993, Vol. of Yr. March of Dimes 1998. Fellow Tex. Bar Found.; mem. Tex. Bar Assn., San Antonio Bar Assn. (chmn. corp. counsel sect. 1986-88), Greater San Antonio C. of C. (govtl. affairs, edn. coun. steering com., bd. dirs. 1987-90), Southside C. of C. (bd. dirs. 1989-90), San Antonio Hispanic C. of C. (bd. dirs. 1989-91). Methodist. Office: Tex Power Co LLC 8940 Wurzbach Rd San Antonio TX 78240 Fax: 210-615-1340. E-mail: ldelagarza@texaspower.com.

DE LA GUARDIA, MARIO FRANCISCO, electrical engineer; b. Havana, Cuba, Dec. 4, 1936; came to U.S., 1979; s. Mario D. and Catalina (Basconcillos) de la G.; m. Nery Esther Agudo, Aug. 23, 1970; 1 child, Mario Felix. BS in Elec. Engring., U. Havana, 1963; M of Applied Sci., U. Waterloo, Ont., Can., 1976. Registered profl. engr., Fla. Assoc. prof. U. Havana, 1964-67; researcher Acad. Scis. Cuba, Havana, 1967-71; design engr. Braun S.A., Madrid, 1971-73, Nat. Cash Register Can. Ltd., Waterloo, 1976-79; sr. engr. Coulter Electronics, Inc., Hialeah, Fla., 1979-80; programmer project systems Burroughs Corp., Coral Springs, Fla., 1980-81; prin. engr. Racal Milgo, Inc., Sunrise, Fla., 1981-90; sr. software engr. Beckman Coulter, Inc., Miami, Fla., 1991-99; software cons. Next Generation Sys. Corp., Miami, 2000—. Patentee in field. Active Childreach, 1976—. Mem. IEEE. Republican. Roman Catholic. Avocations: personal computers, swimming. Home: 13211 SW 39th Ter Miami FL 33175-3235 Office: Next Generation Sys Corp 13211 SW 39th Ter Miami FL 33175-3235 E-mail: nxgsystems@bellsouth.net.

DE LAGUNA, FREDERICA, anthropology educator emeritus, writer, publisher; b. Ann Arbor, Mich., Oct. 3, 1906; d. Theodore and Grace Mead (Andrus) de L. AB, Bryn Mawr Coll., 1927; PhD, Columbia U., 1933; LHD (hon.), U. Alaska, 1982. Asst., field dir. U. Pa. Mus., Phila., 1931-35; assoc. soil conservationist U.S. Soil Conservation Svc., 1936; lectr. anthropology Bryn Mawr (Pa.) Coll., 1938-41, asst. prof., 1941-42, 46-49, assoc. prof., 1949-55, prof. anthropology, 1955-75, William R. Kenan, Jr. prof. emeritus, 1975—. Pub., Frederica de Laguna Northern Books Pub.; vis. lectr., vis. prof. U. Pa., U. Calif., Berkeley, Bryn Mawr Coll.; hon. curator Am. sect. U. Pa. Mus., 1983—. Author: The Thousand March: Adventures of an American Boy with Garibaldi, 1930, The Archaeology of Cook Inlet, Alaska, 1934, 1975, The Arrow Points to Murder, 1937, 1999, Fog on the Mountain, 1938, Frederica de Laguna, 1995; co-author (with Kaj Birket-Smith): The Eyak Indians of the Copper River Delta, Alaska, 1938, Prehistory of North America as Seen From the Yukon, 1947, Chugach Prehistory: The Archaeology of Prince William Sound, 1956, 1967, The Story of a Tlingit Community, 1960; co-author: (with others) The Archaeology of the Yakutat Bay Area, Alaska, 1964, Under Mount Saint Elias: The History and Culture of the Yakutat Tlingit, 1972, Voyage to Greenland: A Personal Initiation Into Anthropology, 1977, 1995, Tales from the Dena, 1995, Travels Among the Dena: Exploring Alaska's Yukon Valley, 2000; editor: Selected Papers from the American Anthropologist 1888-1920, 1960, 1976, The Tlingit Indians (George Thornton Emmons), 1991, reprint, 2002; advisor, participant documentary film More Than Words, 1994, subject of documentary film Reunion Under Mt. St. Elias, 1996, subject spl. exhibit Pratt Mus., Homer, Alaska, 2000. Lt. comdr. USNR, 1942-45. Recipient Lindback award for disting. tchg., Bryn Mawr Coll., 1975, Rochester Mus. award and fellow, 1941, Inaugural award Contbn. to Alaska History award, Alaska Hist. Soc., 2001, Lucy Wharton Drexel medal for archaeology, U. Pa. Mus., 1999; fellow, Columbia U., 1930—31, NRC, 1936—37, Rockefeller Found., 1945—46, Wenner-Gren Found., 1949—50, Social Sci. Rsch. Coun., 1962—63; grantee, Am. Philos. ., Arctic Inst. of N.Am., 1973, Bryn Mawr Coll., NEH, NSF, U. Pa. Mus., Wenner-Gren Found. for Anthrop. Rsch. Fellow AAAS; mem. Am. Anthrop. Assn. (pres. 1966-67, Disting. Svc. award 1986), Arctic Inst. N.Am. (hon. life), NAS, Soc. for Am. Archaeology (1st v.p. 1949-50, 50th Ann. award 1986), No. Studies Assn. (internat. secretariat, hon. pres. 1991—), Phila. Anthropology Soc. (pres. 1939-40), Alaska Anthrop. Assn. (hon. life, award for lifetime contbn. to Alaskan anthropology 1993), Homer (Alaska) Natural History Soc. (hon. life, Silver Trowel award), Before Columbus Found. (Am. Lifetime Book award 1995). Democrat. Home and Office: 3300 Darby Rd # 1310 Haverford PA 19041-1067

DELAHANTY, CARLOS ANTHONY, industrial engineer; b. Scottsdale, Ariz., May 3, 1965; s. Carlos Victor and Mary Martha (Santa Marina) D. BS in Indsl. Engring., Ariz. State U., 1991. Indsl. engr. Intel Corp., Chandler, Ariz., 1993, Gaylord Container Corp., Glendale, Ariz., 1994; project scheduling engr., planning cons. Lockwood Greene Engrs., Phoenix, 1994-95; project scheduling engr. Honeywell Air Transp. Sys., Phoenix, 1996; indsl. engring. cons. Knight Architects Engrs. Planners, Inc., Phoenix, 1997; project and cost control engr. Honeywell Indsl. Automation and Control, Phoenix and Houston, 1997-99; project controls engring. dept. mgr. Gcss Graphic Sys., Westmont, Ill., 1999-2000; indsl. engr., master scheduler Intel Corp., Albuquerque, 2000—. Mem. Inst. Indsl. Engrs., Project Mgmt. Inst., Alpha Pi Mu. Roman Catholic. Avocation: amateur bowling. Home: 201 Country Club Dr SE Apt 1713 Rio Rancho NM 87124-0419 Office: Intel Corp 4100 Sara Rd Rio Rancho NM 87124 E-mail: Anthony.Delahanty@Intel.com., anthonydelahanty@aol.com.

DELAHANTY, LINDA MICHELE, dietitian; b. Boston, Feb. 8, 1957; d. John Joseph and Helen Mary (Salami) D.; m. Paul Joseph Gorski, June 14, 1987. BS summa cum laude, U. Mass., 1978; MS summa cum laude, Boston U., 1980. Adminstrv. dietitian Joslin Diabetic Camp, Charlton, Mass., 1978; nutritional research asst. Lemuel Shattuck Hosp., Jamaica Plain, Mass., 1979; nutrition educator Home Med. Service-Univ. Hosps., Boston, 1980, Boston City Hosp., 1980-81; clin. dietitian Mass. Gen. Hosp., Boston, 1981-88, researcher Diabetes Ctr., 1983—, nutrition counselor, 1988—. Nutrition coord. Diabetes Control and Complications Trial, NIH, 1987—93, co-investigator Diabetes Prevention Program, 1996—2002; co-investigator LOOK AHEAD (Action for Health in Diabetes), 1999—; cons. New Eng. Diabetes and Endocrinology Ctr., Brookline, Mass., 1985—86; panelist NIH Consensuc Devel. Conf., Bethesda, Md., 1986, Am. Diabetes Assn. Consensus Statement on Self Monitoring of Blood Glucose, 1993; expert panelist TV series Doctors on Call, 1997; assoc. lectr. Harvard U. Geriatric Edn. Ctr., 1984—89; instr. Med. Sch. Harvard U., Cambridge, 2002—. Mem. editl. bd. Diabetes Spectrum, 1994-96, Diabetes Forecast, 2001—, Jour. Am. Dietetic Assn., 2002--; contbr. articles to profl. jours. Recipient Charles H. Best medal for Disting. Svc., Am. Diabetes Assn., 1994, Rschrs. award Am. Dietetic Assn., 1998, Mary P. Huddleston award, 2002; named Young Dietitian of Yr. Am. Dietetic Assn., 1984. Mem. Mass. Area Rehab. Dietitians (co-chair 1983-84), Diabetes Care and Edn. Practice Group (sec. 1985-87), Mass. Gerontol. Nutrition Practice Group (chair 1984-85), Mass. Dietetic Assn. (chair community dietetics div. 1983-84, coun. on practices), Am. Dietetic Assn. (area coord. gerontol. nutrition and dietetic practice group 1988-90). Roman Catholic. Avocations: skiing, photography, travel. Home: 18 Saybrook Rd Framingham MA 01701-7835 Office: Mass Gen Hosp Diabetes Ctr 50 Staniford St Ste 340 Boston MA 02114-2620 E-mail: ldelahanty@partners.org.

DELAHANTY, REBECCA ANN, school system administrator; b. South Bend, Ind., Oct. 18, 1941; d. Raymond F. and Ann Marie (Batsleer) Paczesny; m. Edward Delahanty, June 22, 1963; children: David, Debbie. BA, Coll. of St. Catherine, Minn., 1977; MA, Coll. St. Thomas, Minn., 1983; PhD, Ga. State U., 1994. Cert. in adminstrn. and supervision Ga. Initiator, tchr. gifted kindergarten Dist. 284 Sch., Wayzata, Minn., 1977-83; gifted kindergarten coord. St. Barts Sch., Wayzata, 1983-85; prin. Dabbs Loomis Sch., Dunwoody, Ga., 1987-91; asst. to supt. Buford (Ga.) City Schs., 1993-98, supt., 1998-99; prof. Ga. State U., 1999-2000; ednl. cons.,, 2000—; adv. bd. U. Saint Thomas, Coll. Edu., 2001—. Staff devel. adv. coun. Ga. Contbr. Mem. adv. bd. Coll. Edn. U. St. Thomas, 2001—. Mem.: ASCD, Minn. Coun. Gifted and Talented, Minn. Assn. Gifted Children, Nat. Assn. Gifted Children, Am. Ednl. Rsch. Assn., Omicron Gamma, Phi Delta Kappa.

DELAHAYE, ALFRED NEWTON, retired journalism educator; b. West Baton Rouge Parish, La., June 4, 1929; s. Alfred and Lillian (Hebert) D. BA in Journalism, La. State U., 1949, MA in Journalism, 1951; PhD in Journalism, U. Mo., 1970. Mng. editor Houma (La.) Courier, Terrebonne Press, 1953-57; dir. pub. info. Nicholls State U., Thibodaux, La., 1957-67, 83-90, disting. prof. journalism, 1984-90, prof. emeritus journalism, 1990—; instr. journalism U. Mo., Columbia, 1967-69. Contbr. news stories, editls. to profl. publs. Mem. Soc. Profl. Journalists, Assn. for Edn. in Journalism and Mass Comm., La. State U. Journalism Alumni Assn. (founding pres. 1954), Phi Kappa Phi (founding pres. Nicholls chpt. 1974). Democrat. Roman Catholic. Avocations: reading, travel. Home: 610 Fairway Dr Thibodaux LA 70301-3726 Office: Nicholls State U Dept Mass Cmn Thibodaux LA 70310-0001 E-mail: maco-ad@Nicholls.edu.

DE LA HOUSSAYE, BRETTE ANGELO-PEPE, electronics engineer, researcher; b. L.A., Aug. 20, 1960; s. Wilbert Joseph de la Houssaye and Paula Marie (Jones) Colby. BSEET, Devry Inst. Tech., 1989. Pvt. practice, Calif., 1990—. Mem. IEEE, Am. Phys. Soc., Nat. Trust Historic Preservation, Am. Mus. Natural History. Achievements include discoveries of an alternate method for calculating work, using Newton's second Law of Motion and work energy theorem. Home: 7719 Goodland Ave North Hollywood CA 91605-2041

DELAHUNT, BRETT, pathologist; b. Wellington, New Zealand, Feb. 20, 1950; s. John Joseph Delahunt; m. Susan Anne Kirk. BSc with honors, Victoria U., 1972; B of Med. Sci., U. Otago, New Zealand, 1976, MB ChB, 1978, MD, 1995. Resident med. officer Wellington Hosp., 1979-80; lectr. in pathology U. Otago, 1980-86, sr. lectr. in pathology, 1986-94, assoc. prof., 1994-96, prof., 1996—, chmn. dept. pathology Wellington Sch. Medicine, 1995—; dep. dean Wellington Sch. Medicine, 1998—. Prin. med. advisor St. John Ambulance, New Zealand, 1993-97; bd. mgmt. Wellington Free Ambulance Svc., 1986-96; mem. nat. civil def. health planning com. Ministry of Civil Def., 1992—; mem. cancer reporting adv. group Ministry of Health, New Zealand; cons. pathologist New Zealand Cancer Registry Ministry of Health, 1997—; chair scientific adv. com. Wellington Med. Rsch. Found., 1997—, Ministry of Fgn. Affairs, NZ Com. for Dissemination of Humanitarian Law, 1998—; govt. appointee Med. Lab. Technologists Registration bd., 2000-. Editor: New Zealand Aid Manual, 1994, 2d edit., 1995, Manual of Use and Interpretation of Pathology Tests; contbr. over 150 articles to profl. jours. Recipient Svc. medal New Zealand Ambulance, 1991; created Knight Order of St. John, 1995, Knight of the Order St. Lazarus, New Zealand, 1999. Fellow Royal Coll. of Pathologists of Australia (editor); mem. New Zealand Soc. of Pathologists (v.p. 1991-93, pres. 1996—), Internat. Soc. of Urol. Pathology (v.p. Australasia 1995-98, sec. 1998—), Cancer Soc. New Zealand (chair nat. scientific adv. com.). Office: Wellington Sch Medicine Sch Medicine PO Box 7343 Wellington South New Zealand Business E-Mail: bd@wnmeds.ac.nz.

DELAHUNT, WILLIAM D. congressman; b. Quincy, Mass., July 18, 1941; s. Bill Sr. and Ruth Delahunt; children: Kirstin, Kara. BA, Middlebury Coll., 1963; JD, Boston Coll., 1967. Asst. clk. Norfolk Superior Ct., 1968—70; legal counsel Quincy Police Dept., 1970; pvt. practice law, 1971-75; dist. atty. State of Mass., 1975—96; mem. 105-108th Congresses from 10th Mass. dist., 1997—; mem. judiciary resources com. 105th Congress from 10th Mass. dist. Mem. Quincy City Coun., 1971; mem. Mass. Ho. of Reps., 1973-75, asst majority leader. With USCGR, 1963-71. Democrat. Office: 1317 Longworth House Washington DC 20515-2110*

DELAHUNTY, JOSEPH LAWRENCE, state senator, business investor; b. Portland, Maine, June 5, 1935; s. Joseph Edward and Jane (Faulkner) D.; m. Gail Ruth Ruppert, Sept. 2, 1961; children: Deborah Baker, Joseph Jr., Devin, Brian, William. Student, Bryant Coll., 1955-57. Store mgr. W.T. Grant Co., Wethersfield, Conn., 1957-75, dist. mgr., regional mgr.; owner, pres. Windham Nurseries & Florist Inc., 1975-83; pres. Car-Del Property Mgmt. Co., 1983—; owner, pres. Fireside Inn motel, Salem, N.H., 1985-87, Delahuntys Auto-Wash, Salem, 1988—; mem. N.H. State Senate, Concord, 1986-98, pres., 1995-98; owner Delahunty's Nursery, Wyndham, N.H. Senate majority leader N.H. State Senate. Mem. Salem Bd. Selectmen. Served with U.S. Army, 1958-60. Republican. Roman Catholic. Home: 14 Old Farm Rd Salem NH 03079-1278 Office: Delahuntys Nursery 41 Range Rd Windham NH 03087-2003

DE LA IGLESIA, FELIX ALBERTO, pathologist, toxicologist; b. Cordoba, Argentina, Nov. 27, 1939; s. Andres Avelino and Rosalia (Figueroa) De La Iglesia; m. Graciela Moreno, May 19, 1964; children: Felix Andres, Jose Vicente, Alberto Victor, Michele, Stephanie. MD, U. Cordoba, 1964. Dir. Warner-Lambert Rsch. Inst., Toronto, Ont., 1972-79; dir. toxicology Warner-Lambert/Parke-Davis, Ann Arbor, Mich., 1979-83; v.p. pathology and exptl. toxicology Parke-Davis Pharm. Rsch., Ann Arbor, Mich., 1983-2000; v.p. preclin. worldwide safety Parke-Davis R&D, 1983—2000; prof. pathology U. Toronto Sch. Medicine, 1981—. Adj. prof. toxicology, prof. pathology U. Mich. Med. Sch. Pub. Health, 1982—; cons. pharm. rsch. and devel., 2000—; founder, prin. FIP-Consulting, Mich., 2001—; founder, sr. cons. Cambridge Biotech. Ltd., 2001—; mem. sci. adv. bd. Cellomics, Pitts., Waratah Pharma, Boston; founder, chief sci. officer QRxPharma Pty Ltd., Sydney, Australia, 2002. Author: Molecular Biochemistry of Human Disease, 1985, Drug Toxicokinetics, 1993, Drug-Induced Hepatotoxicity, 1996. Served to 1st lt. Argentine Army Inf., 1954-56. Fellow Acad. Toxicological Scis. Avocations: collecting antique microscopes, vintage sports cars, commercial real estate development. Home and Office: 2307 Hill St Ann Arbor MI 48104-2651

DE LA MAZA, LUIS M. pathology educator; b. Ribadesella, Asturias, Spain, Aug. 12, 1943; came to U.S., 1968; s. Tomas A. and Maria de los Angeles (Fernandez) de la M.; m. Maria M. de la Maza; children: Michael, Helen. MD, Faculty of Medicine, Madrid, 1966; PhD, U. Minn., 1974. Prof. pathology U. Calif., Irvine, 1979—. Author: Color Atlas Microbiology, 1997, (jour.) Infection and Immunity, 1983—. Mem. AAAS, Am. Soc. Microbiology. Office: U Calif Dept Pathology Med Sci I Rm D440 Irvine CA 92697-4800

DE LA MORANDIERE, BRICE, finance executive; b. Paris, Mar. 15, 1965; m. Valerie, Oct. 15, 1988; children: Achille, Aziyade, Zelie. Diplome, D'Etudes Approfondies U. Paris, 1989, L'Institut d'Etudes Politiques de Paris, 1988. Fin. analyst Carnaud, Paris, 1988-89; fin., mgr. CMB Packaging, Oxford, England, 1989-92; fin. dir. Carnaudmetalbox, Istanbul, Turkey, 1992-96; group controller Carnaudmetalbox Splty. Cans, Paris, 1996-97; CFO Christian Dallaz, Paris, Phila., 1997—2001, Bacou-Dalloz, 2001—. Recipient Alexander E. Loeb award, 2000. Home: 412 Righters Mill Rd Penn Valley PA 19072 Office: Bacou-Dalloz 1150 First Ave Ste 400 King Of Prussia PA 19406 Fax: 610-728-1960. E-mail: bdelamorandiere@bacou-dalloz.com.

DELAND, MICHAEL REEVES, energy executive; b. Boston, Dec. 13, 1941; s. Frank Stanton and Susan Robertson (Reeves) D.; m. Jane Slocum, Aug. 18, 1973; children: Stanton, Melissa, Holly. AB, Harvard U., 1963; JD, Boston Coll., Newton, Mass., 1969; PhD (hon.), Taegu (South Korea) U., 1998. Bar: Mass. 1970, U.S. Supreme Ct. 2000. Mgr. U.S. Congl. campaign, Concord, Mass., 1970; staff asst. to pres. U. Mass., Boston, 1971; chief enforcement br. EPA, Boston, 1971-76, regional adminstr., 1983 89; environ. counsel Environ. Rsch. Tech., Concord, 1976-83; chmn. Pres. Coun. on Environ. Quality, Washington, 1989-93; vice chmn. Am. Flywheel Systems Inc., Washington, 1993-2000. Bd. adv. HYDRO Que., 1993-96. Chmn. bd. Nat. Orgn. on Disability, 1990—; vice-chmn. World Com. on Disability, 1996—; bd. dirs. Assoc. Harvard Alumni, 1977-79, Mgmt. Inst. Environ and Bus., 1990-96, World Resources Inst., 1997—, Boston Globe Newspaper Co., 1998-2003; mem. corp. Woods Hole Oceanographic Instn., 1993-2002; trustee Noble and Greenough Sch., Dedham, Mass., 1976-82; vestryman Trinity Episcopal Ch., Boston, 1976-78, St. John's Ch. Lafayette Sq., Washington, 1998-2002. Lt. (j.g.) USN, 1963-65. Recipient award Mass. Audubon Soc., 1986, Spl. Achievement award Nat. Wildlife Fedn., 1989. Mem. The Country Club (Brookline, Mass.), Beverly Yacht Club, Met. Club, Chevy Chase Club, Phi Beta Kappa (hon.). Republican. Avocation: sailing. Home: 4901 Loughboro Rd NW Washington DC 20016-3456 Office: 910 16th St NW Ste 500 Washington DC 20006-2903 Fax: 202-833-4174.

DELANEY, ATIMA CHUMPA, pediatrician; Cert. Am. Bd. of Pediat. Attending physician Children's Hosp., Boston, 1996—. Fellow: Am. Acad. of Pediat.

DELANEY, HERBERT WADE, JR., lawyer; b. Leadville, Colo., Mar. 30, 1925; s. Herbert Wade and Marie Ann (Garbarino) DeL.; m. Ramona Rae Ortiz, Aug. 6, 1953; children: Herbert Wade III, Paula Rae, Bonnie Marie. BSBA, U. Denver, 1949, LLB, 1951. Bar: Colo. 1951, U.S. Supreme Ct. 1959. Pvt. practice, Denver, 1953-64, 1965-91, 94—; mem. firm DeLaney and Sandven, P.C., 1992-94; faculty U. Denver, Colo., 1960-61, 89; ptnr. DeLaney & West, Denver, 1964-65. Capt. JAG's Dept., USAF, 1951-53. Mem. Colo. Bar Assn., Denver Bar Assn., Am. Legion, Masons, Elks, Phi Alpha Delta. Office: 2609 S Quebec Unit 12 Denver CO 80231

DELANEY, JOHN ADRIAN, mayor; b. Lansing, Mich., June 29, 1956; s. James Edward and Mary Ann (Langius) D.; m. Gena Barrett, Sept. 6, 1980; children: William Langius, Adrian Anne, Marye Margaret, James Barrett. BA in History, U. Fla., 1977, JD, 1981. Bar: Fla. 1981. With State Atty.'s Office, Jacksonville, Fla., 1981-91; chief asst. state atty. Jacksonville, Fla., 1986-91; gen. counsel City of Jacksonville, 1991-92, 94-95, chief of staff, mayor, 1992-94, mayor, 1995—. Mem. Leadership Jacksonville, 1986, Leadership Fla.-13; chmn. St. Paul's Episcopal Sch. Bd. Mem. Inns of Ct., Fla. Blue Key (pres. 1980), Rotary, Delta Upsilon. Roman Catholic. Avocation: camping. Home: 110 Bowles St Jacksonville FL 32266-4917 Office: Office of the Mayor 117 W Duval St, St James Bldg, City Hall Jacksonville FL 32202-3429

DELANEY, JOHN CHARLES, pharmaceutical company executive; b. Englewood, N.J., Dec. 3, 1953; s. James Martin and Jean Gloria D.; m. Anne Mirabito, June 8, 1980 (wid. Mar. 1990); children: Kevin, Megan; m. Kari J. Gavic, Apr. 20, 1993; children: Kiandra, Walker, Ayden. BA in Social Sci., Dominican Coll., Blauvelt, N.Y., 1978; MBA in Fin., U. New Haven, 1983. Fiduciary acct. Mfrs. Hanover Trust Co., N.Y.C., 1978-81; fin. analyst Burroughs, Danbury, Conn., 1981-83, Mobil Oil Co., Stratford, Conn., 1983-85; cost acct. Boehringer Ingelheim Pharms., Ridgefield, Conn., 1985—, mgr. budgets, sales and mktg., 1985—, mgr. specialty markets, 1985—, area mgr., managed care Stillwater, Minn., 1985—, area dir., managed care, 1985—. Sgt. U.S. Army, 1972-75. Decorated Army Commendation medal U.S. Army. Mem. Acad. Managed Care Pharmacy. Avocations: sports, music. Home and Office: 2425 Overlook Ct N Stillwater MN 55082-1565 E-mail: jdelaney@rdg.boehringer-ingelheim.com.

DELANEY, JOHN MARTIN, JR., lawyer; b. Alton, Ill., Aug. 14, 1956; s. John Martin and Joan Margaret (Galloway) D.; m. Julia Ann Spurgeon, Nov. 23, 1984; children: Margaret Louise, Victoria Jane, John M. III. BA, St. Louis U., 1978, JD, 1981. Bar: Ill. 1981, U.S. Dist. Ct. (so. dist.) Ill. 1985, Mo. 1990, U.S. Dist. Ct. (ea. dist.) Mo. 1990. Law clk. Madison County Cts., Edwardsville, Ill., 1978-79, Dunham Boman & Leskera, East St. Louis, Ill., 1980-81; asst. states atty. Madison County States Atty.'s Office, Edwardsville, 1981-84; assoc. Allen, Mendenhall & Assocs., Alton, Ill., 1985-89, Allen, Meyer, Mendenhall, Hackett & Delaney, 1989-90, Allen, Mendenhall, Delaney & Assocs., 1990-92, Smith, Allen, Mendenhall, Delaney & Assocs., 1992-96, Law Office of John Delaney, 1996—. Instr. criminal law and procedure Lewis and Clark C.C., Godfrey, Ill., 1986—. Bd. dirs. Cen. Bapt. Bd., Collinsville, Ill., 1982-83, Blue Knights Law Enforcement, Edwardsville, 1983-85; trustee Godfrey Village & Township, 1993-99. Named to Outstanding Young Men Am. U.S. Jaycees, 1983. Mem. Ill. State Bar Assn., Madison County Bar Assn., Alton-Wood River Bar Assn. Roman Catholic. Office: Law Office of John Delaney 346 W Saint Louis Ave East Alton IL 62024-1148 E-mail: reywal@yahoo.com.

DELANEY, JOHN WHITE, lawyer; b. Springfield, Mass., Feb. 28, 1943; s. Frank T. and Emily (White) D.; m. Betsey Secor; children: Erin, Elizabeth. AB, Harvard U., 1964, JD, 1967. Bar: Mass. 1967, U.S. Dist. Ct. Mass. 1968. Staff asst. to U.S. senator Leverett Saltonstall, Washington, 1966; law clk. Mass. Superior Ct., Boston, 1967-68; asst. atty. gen. State of Mass., Boston, 1968-69; legis. asst. Gov. Commonwealth of Mass., Boston, 1969-73; asst. sec. consumer affairs and bus. regulation Commonwealth of Mass., 1973-76; exec. dir. Boston Mcpl. Rsch. Bur., 1976-80; dir. govt. and community affairs Bank of Boston, 1980-89; sr. ptnr. Hale and Dorr, Boston, 1989—. Dir. New England Legal Found., Boston, 1986—. Dir. Robert F. Kennedy Action Corps, Boston, 1973-92; sec. Coordinating Com., Boston, 1984-87; trustee, mem. exec. com. Mass. Taxpayers Found., Boston, 1986—; trustee Boston Mcpl. Rsch. Bur., 1991—; mem. adv. coun. The Trustees of Reservations, 1993-99, 2000—; dir. Greater Boston C. of C., 1992—; pres. Friends of RFK Children's Action Corps, Inc., 1996—; dist. rep. Dedham (Mass.) Town Meeting, 1986—. Fellow Mass. Hist. Soc. Office: Hale and Dorr LLP 60 State St Boston MA 02109-1800

DELANEY, KEVIN FRANCIS, retired naval officer, consulting firm executive; b. Wolcott, Conn., Sept. 23, 1946; s. John Delaney; m. Patricia Delaney, June 8, 1968; children: Kelly, Diana, Seana. BS in Engring., U.S. Naval Acad., Annapolis, Md., 1968; M in Bus., George Washington U., 1977; postgrad., MIT, 1984, Harvard U., 1993. Commd. USN, 1968, advanced through grades to rear admiral, 1991, ret., 1998; commdg. officer Heli Anti-Sub Squadron 32, Norfolk, Va., 1980-82, 82-84; air ops. officer USS Guadal Canal, 1984-86; commdg. officer HSL-31, wing comdr. Helo Sea Control Wing 3, Mayport, 1987; commdg. officer Naval Air Sta., Jacksonville, Fla., 1989-91; comdr. shore activities U.S. Atlantic Fleet, Norfolk, Va., 1993-94; dir. shore installation mgmt. Chief Naval Ops., Washington, 1994-95; comdr. Navy Region S.E. Jacksonville, 1995-98; exec. v.p. Coggin Automotive Group, Jacksonville, Fla., 1998-2000; exec. v.p., COO HealthScreen Am., Jacksonville, Fla., 2000—02; pres., CEO Delaney & Assocs. Consulting, Mil. Reunions Inc.; pres. Futura Sales Inc. Bd. mem. 12 Who Care Selection Com., Jacksonville, 1995--, Vol. Jax, Inc., Jacksonville, 1995-98, Childrens' Haven, Orange Park, Fla., 1995-98; chmn. Navy/Marine Corp. Relief Soc., Jacksonville, 1995-98; bd. dirs. Salvation Army, United Way, USO, YMCA, Jr. Achievement, N.E. Fla. Safety Coun., World Affairs Coun., Freedoms Found.; vice chmn. Toyota Gator Bowl; chair United Way N.E. Fla.; pres. Ronald McDonald House; bd. govs., pres. Fla. C.C. Jacksonville Found. Mem. Fla. C. of C. (exec. com.), Rotary (pres. 2000), N.E. Fla. Safety Coun. (exec. treas.). Home: 4551 Swilcan Bridge Ln N Jacksonville FL 32224-5618 Office: Delaney and Assocs 9428 Baymeadows Rd Ste 580 Jacksonville FL 32256 E-mail: kdelaney@military-reunions.com.

DELANEY, MARION PATRICIA, retail executive; b. Hartford, Conn., May 20, 1952; d. William Pride Delaney Jr. and Marian Patricia (Utley) Murphy. BA, Union Coll., Schenectady, N.Y., 1973. Adminstrv. asst. N.Y. State Assembly, Albany, 1973-74; account exec. Foote, Cone & Belding, N.Y.C., 1974-78; sr. account exec. Dailey & Assocs., L.A., 1978-81; pub. rels. cons. NOW, Washington, 1981-83; account supr. BBDO/West, L.A., 1983-85; v.p. Grey Advt., L.A., 1985-87, San Francisco, 1987-89; sr. v.p. McCann-Erickson, San Francisco, 1989-95; sr. v.p., dir. advt./mktg. comms. Bank of Am., San Francisco, 1995-99; mng. dir. doodlebug LLC, San Anselmo, Calif., 2001—; cons. Brand Strategy, 1999—2000. Del. Dem. Nat. Conv., San Francisco, 1984; bd. dirs. JED Found., Hartford, Conn., 1989—, Easter Seals Soc., Bay Area, 1995-97. Mem. NOW (v.p. L.A. chpt. 1980-83, pres. 1984, advisor 1985-87), Marin Assn. Female Execs., Contemporary Ceramics Studio Assn., Am. Splty. Toy Retailers Assn., Hobby Industries Assn., Toy Industry Assn., San Anselmo C. of C. Congregationalist. Home: 11 Gary Way Fairfax CA 94930-1002

DELANEY, MARY ANNE, retired theology studies educator; b. Waltham, Mass., Feb. 15, 1926; d. Thomas Joseph and Mary Teresa (Berry) D. BA, Regis Coll., 1953; MEd, U. Mass., Boston, 1973; MDiv, Andover Newton Theol. Sch., Newton Ctr., Mass., 1978. Tchr. various schs., Mass., 1953-73; pastoral counselor Boston City Hosp., 1974-76; dir. pastoral care Cape Breton Hosp., Sydney River, Canada, 1978-81, Nova Scotia Hosp., Dartmouth, 1981-86, Misericordia Hosp., Edmonton, Canada, 1986-91; pastoral counselor Assn. Pastoral Edn., Waltham, Mass., 1992-96, Emmanuel Coll., Boston, 1996—2001; supr. pastoral edn. Leland Retirement Home, Waltham, 1992—2001; ret., 2001. Vice chair bioethics consultative svc. Misericordia Hosp., Edmonton, 1987-91; vis. scholar Andover Newton Theol. Sch., 1991-92. Trustee Pastoral Inst., Halifax, N.S., Can., 1981-86; mem. commn. on ecumenism Archdiocese of Halifax, 1982-86; mem. of the Congregation of Sisters of St. Joseph, Boston, 1945—. Mem. Can. Assn. Pastoral Edn. (cert. com. 1987-91), Assn. for Clin. Pastoral Edn. (cert. supr., accreditation com. 1993-98, cert. com. 1998-2001). Roman Catholic. Avocations: international travel, classical music, international travel, classical music, art, reading. Home and Office: 16 Cutter St Waltham MA 02453-5911 E-mail: sr.marydelaney@mediaone.net.

DELANEY, MATTHEW SYLVESTER, mathematics educator, academic administrator; b. Ireland, Nov. 26, 1927; s. Joseph C. and Elizabeth M. (Bergin) D.; came to U.S., 1947, naturalized, 1952; student St. John's Coll., 1947-51; BA, Immaculate Heart Coll., L.A., 1958; MS, Notre Dame U., 1960; PhD, Ohio State U., 1971. Ordained priest Roman Cath. Ch., 1951; assoc. pastor L.A. Cath. Diocese, 1951-55; instr. math., physics Pius X High Sch., Downey, Calif., 1955-58, vice prin., 1960-62; instr. math. Immaculate Heart Coll., L.A., 1962-65, asst. prof., 1965-72, assoc. prof., 1972-76, prof., 1976— ; asst. acad. dean, 1973-78; dean acad. devel. Mt. St. Mary's Coll., L.A., 1978-82, acad. dean, 1978-91; prof. math., 1991—, prof. emeritus, 1996—. NSF grantee, 1959-60, 61. Achievements include: Formal recognition of the eponyms, "Delaney Sets" and "The Delaney Symbol" in the disciplines of discrete geometry and math. crystallography, 1985. Mem. Internat. Union Crystallography, Am. Math. Soc., Math. Assn. Am., N.Y. Acad. Scis.. Democrat. Contbr. articles to math. publs., profl. jours. Home: Apt 32C 13700 El Dorado Dr Seal Beach CA 90740-3843 Office: Mount Saint Mary's Coll 12001 Chalon Rd Los Angeles CA 90049-1526

DELANEY, MICHAEL FRANCIS, lawyer; b. Washington, Jan. 22, 1948; s. Donald J. and Evelyn A. (Edwards) D.; m. Sally E. Jenkins, July 30, 1977 (div. Nov. 1984); 1 child, Patrick Neal; m. Kathleen Lynette Gibbons, Feb. 22, 1986; children: Rebecca Marie, Laura Margaret. BA, U. Kans., 1969, JD, 1976. Bar: Mo. 1976, U.S. Dist. Ct. (we. dist.) Mo. 1976, U.S. Ct. Appeals (8th cir.) 1978, U.S. Ct. Appeals (10th cir.) 1979. Assoc. Spencer, Fane, Britt & Browne, Kansas City, Mo., 1976-81, ptnr., 1982—, mng. ptnr., 1992—93, exec. com., 2000—. Lectr. law U. Kans., Lawrence, 1977-78, 92-93. Articles editor U. Kans. Law Rev., 1975. Active Kansas City Tomorrow, 1982; mem. steering com. Kansas City Vets. Meml. Fund, 1984-88; vol. citizen rev. agy. rels. com. United Way, Kansas City, 1984—; co-chmn. Heartland Labor and Employment Conf., 1988—; bd. mem. Harwycke Homes Assn. Capt. U.S. Army, 1969-73, Vietnam. Mem. ABA, Mo. Bar Assn., Kans. City Met. Bar Assn., Lawyers Assn. Kansas City, Edn. Law Assn., Nat. Sch. Bds. Assn., Mo. Coun. Sch. Attys., U. Kans. Law Soc. (bd. govs. 1988-92), Kansas City Tomorrow Alumni Assn. (bd. dirs. 1990-94). Democrat. Roman Catholic. Home: 5710 W 130th St Overland Park KS 66209-3645 Office: Spencer Fane Britt & Browne 1000 Walnut St Ste 1400 Kansas City MO 64106-2140 Business E-Mail: mdelaney@spencerfane.com.

DELANEY, MORGAN D. physician, educator; b. Alexandria, Va., July 16, 1946; s. Martin Donohue Delaney and Maude Shackleford Owens-Delaney. BA in German, U. Va., 1967, MD, 1971. Diplomate Am. Bd. Internal Medicine, Am. Bd. Pulmonary Disease. Resident in internal medicine Emory U., Atlanta, 1971-72, George Washington U. Med. Ctr., Washington, 1972-74, chief resident in internal medicine, 1974-75, fellow in pulmonary diseases, 1975-77, asst. prof. medicine, 1978-85; asst. prof. medicine U. Miami, Fla., 1977-78; dir., intro. to clin. medicine Dade-Monroe Lung Assn., 1982—; assoc. prof. medicine George Washington U. Med. Ctr., Washington, 1985—, dir. practice of medicine course, 1992—, dir., divsn. Pulmonary Diseases, 1997—2002. Dir. Dade-Monroe Lung Assn., Miami, 1977-78, D.C. Lung Assn., 1979-81; adv. bd. Mus. Early So. Decorative Arts, 2000-. Pres. Hist. Alexandria (Va.) Found., 1983—; mem. Bd. Archtl. Rev., Alexandria, 1980-83, Hist. Alexandria Resources Com., 1988-94, Mayor's Task Force on Design Rev. Guidelines, Alexandria, 1991-93; mem. Mayor's Task Force on Historic Easements; mem. Mayor;s Task Force on the Alexandria Acad.; mem. exec. com. Historic Alexandria Antiques Show, 1999--. Recipient Disting. Tchr.'s award, George Washington U., 1995. Mem. Am. Thoracic Soc., Am. Coll. Chest Physicians, D.C. Thoracic Soc. (exec. com. 1985-89), Med. Soc. D.C., AOA Med. Honor Soc., Phi Beta Kappa. Avocations: historic preservation, architectural history, american decorative arts, american domestic history, gardening. Home: 202 King St Alexandria VA 22314-3210 Office: George Washington U 5-405 2150 Pennsylvania Ave NW Washington DC 20037-3201 E-mail: mdelaney@mfa.gwu.edu.

DELANEY, PAMELA DELEO, foundation administrator; b. Providence, May 14, 1947; d. Raymond S. and Anna A. Santulli DeLeo; m. Carroll J. Delaney Jr., Sept. 12, 1970; 1 child, Carroll J. III. BA, Newton (Mass.) Coll., 1969; MA, Rutgers U., 1970; M in Philosophy, Columbia U., 1978. Dept. sec., asst. to police commr. N.Y.C. Police Dept., 1971 80, dir. civilian programs, 1980-83; pres. N.Y.C. Police Found., 1983—. Chmn. N.Y.C. Civilian Complaint Review Bd, 1974-83; mem. N.Y.C. cmty. Bd., 1998-02. Office: NYC Police Found 345 Park Ave New York NY 10154-0004 E-mail: pdelaney@nycpolicefoundationl.org.

DELANEY, ROBERT FINLEY, columnist, political sociologist, lecturer; b. Fall River, Mass., Aug. 2, 1925; s. Joseph Patrick and Mary Gertrude (Finigen) D.; m. Mary Elizabeth Flynn, Jan. 21, 1950; children: Mary Ellen, Flynn, Nancy, Carrie, Deirdhre, Sarah; m. Patricia Ann Riley, Jan. 21, 1984. Student, Dartmouth Coll., 1943; B.N.S., Holy Cross Coll., 1946; postgrad., Harvard U., 1946, U. Vienna, 1956; MA, Boston U., 1948; BSL.S., Cath. U. Am., 1955; D.H.L. (hon.), U. Mass., 1981. Fgn. service info. officer Dept. of State, 1950—69; asst. dir. USIA, Washington, 1968-69; dir. Edward R. Murrow Center Public Diplomacy Fletcher Sch., Tufts U., Boston, 1969-70; pres. Thunderbird Grad. Sch. Internat. Mgmt., Phoenix, 1970-71; Milton Miles prof. internat. relations U.S. Naval War Coll., Newport, RI, 1971—81; pres. Michael W. Moynihan Public Affairs, Washington and N.Y., 1981—83; chmn. RFD, Inc., Newport, 1983-91; sr. policy advisor U.S. Space Sta., NASA, 1994-97; adj. prof. internat. mgmt. Salve Regina U., Newport, 1972-78; pres. Global Scis., Ltd., 1985-89; pub. affairs cons. Esso S.A. Author: Your Career in Foreign Service, 1957, Literature of Communism in America, 1958, The Psychology of Terror, 1980, Terror as a Tactic, 1988; editor: This is Communist Hungary, 1959, First Fifty Years of American Public Diplomacy, 1969, International Communications and the New Diplomacy, 1970, The Fourth Estate: The Impact of the Media on National Security Decision-Making, 2002. Incorporator Newport Hosp., 1979-82; mem. Rochambeau Bicentennial Commn., 1979-80; bd. advisors Salve Regina Coll., 1973-77; naval aide to Gov. of R.I., 1976-81; R.I. press sec. Edward Kennedy primary campaign, 1980. Served to capt. USNR, 1943-81, PTO, Vietnam. Decorated Air medal (U.S.), Medal of Merit (Vietnam); Knight (Chev.) of St. Lazarus (KSL), Mil. and Hospitaller Order of Jerusalem; recipient citation for Inter-am. Cooperation Orgn. Am. States, 1965, Volker Found. award, 1954-55, Superior Service award Dept. State, 1962, Disting. Service award, 1965. Mem. Pub. Rels. Soc. Am., Am. Fgn. Service Assn., Pres.' Assn., Am. Mgmt. Assn., Navy League, Naval War Coll. Found., Inter Univ. Seminar on Armed Forces, Delta Phi Epsilon, Alpha Sigma Nu. Clubs: N.Y. Yacht (N.Y.C.), Reading Room (Newport), Dacor House, Met., Nat. Press (Washington). Roman Catholic. Home: 28 Elm St Newport RI 02840-2405

DELANEY, ROBERT PATRICK, librarian, writer; b. Miles City, Mont., Mar. 16, 1961; s. Alfred John and Ann Lois (D'Ambrosia) D. AAS in Broadcast Comm., Suffolk County C.C., 1982; BA in English magna cum laude, Dowling Coll., 1985; MSLS, L.I. U., 1987. Grad. asst. Southampton (N.Y.) Campus Libr., L.I. U., 1986-87, libr., 1987—, Babylon (N.Y.) Pub. Libr., 1987-88; librarian Farmingdale (N.Y.) Campus Libr., Poly. U., 1988, C.W. Post Campus Libr., L.I. U., Brookville, N.Y., 1989—. Author: Dreamfinder, 1986, Nightfawn and the Gleam, 1989, Brightblossom and the Gleam, 1990, The Sinking Star, 1990, Sex and the Single Elf, 1993, The Quiet and Fertile Plain, 1995, There Goes the Neighborhood, 1997, Back to Camelot, 2001. Mem. Suffolk County Libr. Assn., Film Music Soc., Internat. Arthurian Soc. Avocations: Shakespeare, poetry, filmscores, Arthurian legends, mythology. E-mail: www.geocities.com/Broadway/1906. Home: 34 University Dr Lake Ronkonkoma NY 11779-1905

DELANEY, ROBERT VERNON, logistics and transportation executive; b. Passaic, N.J., Mar. 16, 1936; s. Edward Aloysius and Helen Margaret (Gauthier) D.; m. Elissa Ornato, June 15, 1963; children: Edward, James. BBA, NYU, 1963, MBA, 1966; postgrad., St. Louis U., 1967-69, Am. U., 1971-72. Registered practitioner Surface Transp. Bd. formerly ICC. Transp. mgr. Nabisco, N.Y.C., 1958-62; distbn. mgr. Monsanto Co., St. Louis, 1963-70; dir. phys. distbn. Md. Cup Corp., Owings Mills, 1970-74; mgr. internal cons. Pet Inc., St. Louis, 1974-78; mgr. distbn. planning Internat. Paper Co., N.Y.C., 1978-83; sr. v.p. Leaseway Transp. Co., Cleve., 1983-87; practice leader for transp. Arthur D. Little, Inc., Cambridge, Mass., 1988-89; exec. v.p. Cass Info. Sys., St. Louis, 1990—. Founder Warehousing Edn. and Rsch. Coun., Oak Brook, Ill., 1977; bd. dirs. Pvt. Carrier Conf., Inc.; faculty Acad. Advanced Traffic, 1966; guest lectr., frequent spkr. edn1. and profl. orgns. Co-author Transportation Strategies for the Eighties, 1982, The Distribution Handbook, 1984; mem. editl. rev. bd. Transportation Quar., Internat. Jour. Phys. Distbn. and Materials Mgmt.; contbr. articles to newpapers and bus. pubs. Mem. transp. com. The New England Coun., Boston, 1978-82. St. Louis Regional Commerce & Growth Assn., 1975-78; bus. advisor Norman Thomas H.S., N.Y.C., 1979-82. Staff sgt. U.S. Army, 1953-56. Recipient Salzberg Medallion award for transp., Syracuse U., 1988. Mem. Am. Soc. Transp. and Logistics (cert., Joseph Scheleen award for excellence 1992), Coun. Logistics Mgmt. (exec. com. 1976-84, sec. 1983-84, Disting. Svc. award 1981), Nat. Coun. Phys. Distbn. Mgmt. (John Drury Sheahan Disting. Svc. award 1981), Nat. Press Club (Washington, author ann. State of Logistics report). Republican. Avocation: education. Office: Cass Info Systems 13001 Hollenberg Dr Bridgeton MO 63044-2410 Business E-Mail: bdelaney@cassinfo.com.

DELANEY, ROBERT VINCENT, former gas company executive, economic development consultant; b. N.Y.C., Oct. 1, 1934; s. Charles Peter and Alice Mary (O'Rorke) D.; m. Marie Josephine Monaco, Oct. 13, 1956; children: Robert Vincent, Richard Clement, Charles John, Christopher Raymond, Elizabeth Marie. BS in Acctg., Fordham U., 1956; grad. advanced mgmt. program, Harvard U., 1979. Tax mgr. Bklyn. Union Gas Co., 1965-66, personnel mgr., 1966-71, asst. v.p. human resources, 1971-75, v.p. engring., 1975-81, sr. v.p. customer ops., 1981-88, group sr. v.p., chief adminstrv. officer, 1988-90; prin. CPS Cons., N.Y.C., 1990—. Chmn. bd. Greater Jamaica Devel. Corp., N.Y.C.; bd. dirs. Queens Overall Econ. Devel. Corp., N.Y.C., Comprehensive Devel., Inc.; faculty advisor N.Y.C. Tech. Coll., 1968-92. Bd. dirs. Jr. Achievement N.Y., 1972-78, Coop. Edn. Commn. N.Y.C., 1977-82, N.Y. Hall Sci., N.Y.C., 1983-92, Queens Symphony Orch., 1981-91; pres. Harvard AMP Class of 1979, Cambridge; pub. mem. Bd. Cert. for Profl. Engrs. and Land Surveyors State of N.Y., Albany, 1977-87. Capt. arty., U.S. Army, 1957. Recipient Outstanding Svc. award Jr. Achievement, 1980, Disting. Citizen award Queens Symphony Orch., 1980, Bus. Friends of Arts award Borough of Queens, 1984, merit award Am. Legion, 1985, leadership award Greater Jamaica Devel. Corp., 1997, Disting. Svc. award Manhattan Comprehensive Night and Day H.S., 2001. Mem. Am. Gas Assn. (taxation com. 1962-64, customer acctg. com. 1965-67, chmn. pers. com. 1970-73, chmn. fin. and adminstrv. sect. 1982-83, award of merit 1979), Harvard Bus. Sch. Club of N.Y. (bd. dirs.), Harvard U. Club, Bklyn. Club, Beta Gamma Sigma. Republican. Roman Catholic. Avocations: tennis, stickball (three sewer hitter). Home and Office: 1025 Fifth Ave New York NY 10028-0134

DELANEY, TIM, sociologist, educator; s. Thomas James and Mary Elizabeth (Ryan) Delaney. AAS, Cayuga CC, Auburn, NY, 1977; BS, SUNY, Brockport, 1979; MA, Calif. State U.-Dominguez Hills, Carson, CA, 1990; PhD, U. Nev., Las Vegas, 1994. Asst. prof. Canisius Coll., Buffalo, 1998—. Editl. adv. bd. Collegiate Press, San Diego, 2001. Author: (book) Community, Sport and Leisure, 2001, Classical Social Theory: Investigation and Application, 2003; editor: Values, Society & Evolution, 2002. Elected polit. ofcl. Dem. Party, Erie County, NY, 2000; voter registration vol. All polit. parties, Buffalo & Los Angeles, 1988; media expert Pub. Rels., Canisius Coll., Buffalo, 1988. Recipient Cert. of Appreciation, Russian Acad. of Scis., 1999, Moscow State U., 2001. Mem.: North Am. Soc. for Sociology of Sport, Pacific Sociol. Assn., Phi Kappa Phi, Alpha Kappa Delta. Avocations: running, weightlifting, writing, travel, improving social awareness. Home: 265B Evans St Apt #2 Buffalo NY 14221 Office: Canisius Coll 2001 Main St Buffalo NY 14201 E-mail: delaneyt@canisius.edu.

DELANO, LESTER ALMY, JR., b. New Bedford, Mass., Nov. 28, 1928; s. Lester A. and Beatrice (Thomas) D.; m. Margaret Dent (div.); 1 child, Leslie Ann; m. Helaine Shipper; children: Oliver Evan, Peter Franklin. Student, Amherst Coll., Brown U.; MA, U. Chgo. Mktg. cons., Chgo., 1950-54; v.p. North Advt., Inc., Chgo., 1955-60; pres. Dodge & Delano, Inc., N.Y.C., 1961-71, Tinker, Dodge & Delano, Inc., 1971-76; chmn., chief exec. officer Tinker, Campbell-Ewald Inc., N.Y.C., 1976-77; pres. Campbell-Ewald Internat., London, Eng., 1977-80, Marschalk Campbell-Ewald Worldwide, N.Y.C., 1980-85; chmn. exec. com. Lowe Marschalk Worldwide, 1986-87; exec. dir. The Lowe Group PLC, N.Y.C., 1987—2002; CEO Octagon Worldwide, 2001—02. Author: Creative Advertising Planning. Served with USN, 1945-48. Home: 115 Central Park W New York NY 10023-4153 E-mail: delano@speakeasy.net.

DELANO, VICTOR, retired naval officer; b. Washington, Dec. 20, 1919; s. Harvey and Marcia (Murdock) D.; m. Jacqueline Stinson (dec. 1990); children: Katherine Delano Jahnig, Harvey II. BSEE with distinction, U.S. Naval Acad., 1941; MS in Physics, MIT, 1949; postgrad., Indsl. Coll. Armed Forces, 1961-62. Ensign USN, 1941, advanced through grades to capt., 1959; staff comdr. 2d Fleet, 1956-58, Atlantic Fleet, 1963-65; chief of staff Atlantic Amphibious Force, 1966-67; with Office Chief of Naval Ops., 1967-69; ret., 1969; pres. Wichita Eagle-Beacon Pub., 1970-71. V.p., treas. Naval Hist. Found., Washington, 1980-99; trustee Naval Acad. Found.; trustee, bd. dirs. Avon (Conn.) Old Farms Sch., 1980-92, 95—; bd. dirs. Friends Nat. Zoo, Washington, 1971-80, Episc. Ctr. for Children, Washington, 1975-84, 88-94, Kingsbury Ctr., Washington, 1986-95. Decorated Legion of Merit (2), Bronze Star, Purple Heart. Mem. Naval Inst., Naval Acad. Alumni Assn., Mil. Order Carabao, Pearl Harbor Survivors Assn., Chevalier du Tastevin, Chevy Chase Club, Metropolitan Club (Washington), Army-Navy Club, Las Campanas Club (Santa Fe), Eagle Creek Golf and Country Club (Naples, Fla.), Burning Tree Club. Avocation: golf. Home: 760 Waterford Dr Apt 201 Naples FL 34113-8013 also: 5610 Wisconsin Ave Apt 1409 Chevy Chase MD 20815-4439

DELANO-CONDAX, KATE (KATE DELANO-CONDAX DECKER), marketing and public relations executive; b. Phila., Mar. 23, 1945; d. John and Laura Foster (Delano) C. Student, Sweet Briar Coll., 1964—66, U. St. Andrews, Scotland, 1966-67. Legis. aide to Sen. Samuel J. Ervin, Jr. Subcom. Separation of Powers, Com. on Judiciary U.S. Senate, Washington, 1970-73; ptnr. U.S. Trade Trip to People's Republic China, 1973; assoc. producer, asst. dir. KYW-TV, Phila., 1973-74; account exec. Aitkin, Kynett Pub. Rels., Phila., 1975-77, ICPR Pub. Rels., N.Y.C., 1977-79; dir. pub. rels. Am. Heritage Pub. Co., Inc., N.Y.C., 1979-81; account exec. Howard J. Rubenstein Pub. Rels., Inc., N.Y.C., 1981-82; rsch. assoc. Nordeman Grimm Exec. Search Firm, N.Y.C., 1982-84; pres. Kate Delano Condax & Assocs. Mktg., N.Y.C., 1984-89; nat. dir. mktg. and pub. rels. Allmilmo Corp., Fairfield, N.J., 1989-92. Mktg. and media cons.; exec. dir. Philadelphia 100; pres. Pet Bulls, Inc., bd. dirs. The Eldercare Project, 1998—. Author: Horse Sense: Cause and Correction of Problems, 1979, 2d edit. rev., 1990, Riding: A Guide for New Riders, 1995, 120th edit., 2003, 101 Training Tips for Your Dog, 1994, 13th edit., 2002. Probono housing counselor to elderly, N.Y.C., 1980—; bd. dirs. ex officio, mktg. dir. Interfaith Caregivers; dir. pub. affairs Recording for the Blind & Dyslexic, Princeton, N.J., 1995-97; exec. dir. Elder Project: Creating a Living Environment for the Elderly, 1997—. Mem. Brit. Horse Soc. (instr.), Am. Horse Shows Assn. (judge ex-officio), Soc. Mayflower Descs., Nat. Soc. Colonial Dames Am., Coffee House Club N.Y. Office: 314 E Central Ave Moorestown NJ 08057-3637

DELAP, BILL JAY, engineer, consultant; b. Paola, Kans., Nov. 3, 1931; s. Wilbur Jay and Wilma Pauline (Carpenter) D.; m. Angela Ellen Irwin, Feb. 21, 1957; children: Deven Kelly, Dawn Denise. BS in Petroleum Engring., Kans. U., 1954; LLB, LaSalle Extension U., 1966. Registered profl. engr. Engr. Panhandle Eastern Corp., Kansas City, Mo., 1954-56, product engr. Liberal, Kans., 1956-57, div. engr. Springfield, Ill., 1957-69, reg. engr. Liberal, 1969-71, area supt., 1971-73, region mgr. Brighton, Colo., 1973-86; prin. engr. 4-D Triangle Co., Hudson, Colo., 1986—. Bd. mem. Cottonwood Svcs. Corp., Denver, 1989—. Co-author: Natural Gas Storage Fields, 1964. Mem. Greater Brighton Area COFC, 1978. Mem. Nat. Soc. Profl. Engrs. (pres. northern chpt. 1976), Soc. Petroleum Engrs., Grand Lodge AF&AM. Republican. Baptist.

DELAP, J. Q., JR., gas company executive; b. Liberal, Kans., May 29, 1948; s. J.Q. and Estella Fern (Cook) D.; m. Ellen Rubin, Oct. 22, 1983; children: J.Q. (Jake), Tiffani Jaye. BSME, Rose-Hulman Inst., 1970; MBA, Pepperdine U., 1978. Engr. Panhandle Eastern Pipeline Co., Kansas City, Mo., 1970-74; mgr. hydrocarbon sales Anadarko Prodn. Co., Houston, 1974-76; mgr. gas liquids acquisition No. Gas Products Co., Houston, 1976-77; mgr. gas supply Gulf Coast region Farmland Industries, Inc.; crude oil rep. Gulf Coast region CRA, Inc., Houston, 1977-79; pres. La. Energy and Devel. Corp., New Orleans, 1979-92, Loutex Energy Inc., 1980-92, Delta Gas Inc., 1980-92, La. State Gas Corp., 1981-92, Gas Systems Network, Inc., 1981-92, NorthCan Energy, Inc., 1981-92; founder, owner ENERGY Internat. Corp., 1992—. Bd. advisors Rose-Hulman Inst., 1980. Mem. ASME, Am. Gas Assn., La. Gas Assn. (bd. dirs.), Natural Gas Men of Houston, Am. Petroleum Inst., Ind. Prodrs. Assn. Am., Tex. Ind. Prodrs. and Royalty Owners, Pipeliners Assn. of Houston, Houston Energy Fin. Group, Houston Prodrs. Forum, Natural Gas Men of New Orleans, Petroleum Club (Houston). Presbyterian. Home: 2115 Forest Falls Dr Kingwood TX 77345-1778 Office: PO Box 6690 Kingwood TX 77325-6690 E-mail: jqdelap@flash.net.

DELAP, TONY, artist; b. Oakland, Calif., Nov. 4, 1927; s. Truman Henry and Catherine (Yontz) D.; m. Kathleen Rose Campbell, Dec. 27, 1964; children—Kelly Rose, Jack Henry. AA, Menlo Jr. Coll., 1947; student, Claremont Grad. Sch., 1947-49. Prof. U. Calif. at Irvine, 1965-91. Exhibited group shows, San Francisco Mus., Oakland Mus., Whitney Mus., U. Ill., Mus. Modern Art N.Y., L.A. County Mus., Pasadena Mus., one man shows, Dilexi Gallery, San Francisco, 1963, 67, Robert Elkon Gallery, N.Y.C., Felix Landau Gallery, L.A., 1966, 68, U. Calif. at Irvine, Nicholas Wilder Gallery, L.A., 1972, 74, 76, Calif. Inst. Tech., 1974, Calif. State U., Long Beach, 1974, John Berggruen Gallery, San Francisco, 1972, 76, Jan Turner Gallery, L.A., 1987, 89, 91, Modernism Gallery, San Francisco, 1986, 89, 92, 96, Klein Gallery, Chgo., 1985, Beatrix Wilhelm Gallery, Stuttgart, Germany, 1992, Gudrun Spielvogel Gallery, Munich, 1993, Works Gallery, Santa Ana, Calif., 1992, Allene Lapides Gallery, Santa Fe, N.Mex., 1992, Mark Moore Gallery, Santa Monica, Calif., 1994-95, 98, Calif. State U., Fullerton, 1994, Peter Blake Gallery, Laguna Beach, 2000, 2002, ony DeLap Retrospective Ex. at OCMA, Newport Beach, 2000, San Jose Mus. of Art, 2001; represented in permanent collections: Whitney Mus., Mus. Modern Art N.Y.C., Walker Art Inst., Tate Gallery, London, Long Beach Mus. Art, Los Angeles County Mus. Art, Santa Barbara (Calif.) Mus. Art, Newport Harbor Art Mus., Newport Beach, Calif., Guggenheim Mus., N.Y.C. Address: 225 Jasmine St Corona Del Mar CA 92625-3035

DELAPA, JUDITH ANNE, business owner; b. Bad Axe, Mich., Feb. 1, 1938; d. John Vincent and Ellen Agatha (Peters) McCormick; m. James Patrick DeLapa, Jan. 10, 1959; children: Joseph Anthony, James P. II, John M., Gina M. BS, Mich. State U., 1959, MA, 1985. Tchr. various schs., Mich., 1959-64; co-founder Saluto Foods Corp., Benton Harbor, Mich., 1963-76; founder Earthtone Interiors, St. Joseph, Mich., 1977-82, High Impact Mktg. Svcs., Grand Rapids, Mich., 1987—2002. Mktg. rsch. and mgt. cons., writer various clients, nationwide. Author: High-Impact Business Strategies, 1993, The McCormick-DeLapa Family Cookbook, 1997, A Place Called Ireland, 2000, Was That Really Us God?, 2001. Past vice chair exec. bd. Grand Rapids Symphony Orch.; bd. dirs., pres. The Samaritan Found.; bd. dirs. Grand Rapids Art Mus. Judith A. DeLapa Perennial Garden named in her honor Mich. State U. Avocations: reading, travel, theater. Office: High Impact Mktg Svcs 2505 E Paris Ave SE Grand Rapids MI 49546-6100

DE LA PAZ, LUCIA, social worker, consultant; b. N.Y.C., Dec. 27, 1960; d. William and Leocadia De La Paz. BS in Edn., SUNY, Old Westbury, 1982; MSW, Fordham U., 1988. Cert. in theory and practice of psychotherapy; lic. social worker Bd. Edn., N.Y.C. Caseworker, supr. Adminstrn. for Children's Svcs., Jamaica, N.Y., 1985-90, tng. devel. specialist, 1990-95, child welfare specialist supr., 1995-96; med. social worker Med. Assistance Program, N.Y.C., 1995-97, Montefiore Home Health Agy., Bronx, N.Y., 1995-99; cons. Local 371 Union, N.Y.C. Mem. NASW, Coalition of Labor Union Women, Labor Coun. for Latin Am. Advancement, Old Westbury Alumni Assn. Avocations: travel, swimming, reading. Office: NYC Adminstrn for Children's Svcs 92-31 Union Hall St Jamaica NY 11433

DE LA PEDRAJA, RENÉ ANDRÉS, history educator; b. Havana, Cuba, Nov. 26, 1951; came to U.S., 1960; s. Rafael Angel and Ludmila Emma (Toman) De La P.; m. Beatriz Reyes, June 14, 1975; 1 child, Jaroslav Andrés. BA, U. Houston, 1973; MA, U. Chgo., 1974, PhD, 1977. Rsch. prof. Sch. Econs. U. de los Andes, Bogotá, Colombia, 1976-85; asst. prof. history Kans. State U., Manhattan, 1986-89, Canisius Coll., Buffalo, 1989-92, assoc. prof. history, 1992-97, prof., 1997—. Author: Historia de la Energía en Colombia 1537-1930, 1985, Fedemetal y la Industrialización de Colombia, 1986, Energy Politics in Colombia, 1989, The Rise and Decline of U.S. Merchant Shipping in the Twentieth Century, 1992 (CHOICE Outstanding Acad. Book award ALA 1994), Historical Dictionary of the U.S. Merchant Marine and Shipping, 1994, Oil and Coffee, 1998, Latin America Merchant Shipping in the Age of Global Competition, 1999. Mem. Am. Hist. Assn. (life), L.Am. Studies Assn., Conf. on Latin Am. Hist. (life). Democrat. Roman Catholic. Avocations: movies, architectural homes, travel. Home: 47 Argyle Park Buffalo NY 14222-1205 Office: Canisius Coll Dept History 2001 Main St Buffalo NY 14208-1035 E-mail: delapedr@canisius.edu.

DE LA PENA, CORDELL AMADO, pathologist; b. Honolulu, Apr. 30, 1934; s. Eusebio de Guzman Awanan and Virginia Uyeno de Costa; m. Linda Laron Lapuz, Apr. 1, 1957; children: Leslie, Nina, Cordell Amado. MD, U. Santo Tomas, Manila, 1958. Diplomate Am. Bd. Anatomy and Clin. Pathology (subcert. in hematology); cert. Am. Bd. Infection Control. Intern St. John's Hosp., Lowell, Mass., 1960-61; resident New Britain (Conn.) Gen. Hosp., 1963-67; pathologist St. Mary's Hosp., Clarksburg, W.Va., 1967, Union Protestant Hosp., Clarksburg, 1967, United Hosp. Inc., Clarksburg, 1967-78, pres. med. staff, 1974—, bd. dirs., chief pathologist, dir. lab. and blood bank, 1978—; dir. lab. SWJMH and Webster Spring Meml. Hosp., 1998—. Cons. VA, St. Joseph's Stonewall Jackson Meml. hosps.; asst. prof. pathology W. Va. Sch. Medicine, 1980-81, dir. 1997—, clin. prof. pathology Sch. Medicine and Osteo. Sch. Medicine; clin. prof. med. tech. Fairmont State Coll.; pres. Harrison County Cancer Soc., 1974-76; bd. dirs. W.Va. United Health Sys., 1997--. Fellow Coll. Am. Pathologists (ho. of dels. 1982-86. 88--), Am. Soc. Clin. Pathologists, Am. Soc. Hematology; mem. Internat. Acad. Pathology, Am., W.Va. (state councillor 1981-85, pres. 1987-88), med. assns., W.Va. Pathol. Soc. (treas. 1975-77, pres.-elect 1977-80, pres. 1980-81), Harrison County Med. Soc. (treas. 1977-78, pres. 1980-81), W.Va. State Soc. Hematology (pres. 1980-81), W.Va. Assn. Blood Banks (pres. 1982—), Assn. Philippine-Am. Pathologists (pres. 1981-83), Nat. Skeet Shooting Assn., W.Va. Bird Dog Club (pres. 1972), W.Va. Assn. Blood Banks (pres. 1982-83), Orgn. State Med. Assns., Orgn. State Med. Assn., Masons (pres.). Home: 209 Candlelight Dr Clarksburg WV 26301-9725 Office: United Hosp Clarksburg WV 26301

DE LA PIEDRA, JORGE, orthopedic surgeon; b. Peru, Feb. 11, 1923; came to U.S., 1960, naturalized, 1963; s. Luis G. and Rosa M. (Quinones) de la P.; m. June M. Daugherty, May 1, 1955; children: Ana Maria, Jorge Antonio, James Michael. Grad., U. de San Marcos, Lima, Peru, 1942, MD, 1960. Diplomate Am. Bd. Orthopedic Surgery, Am. Bd. Profl. Disability Cons. Intern Army Hosp., Lima, 1951-52; rotating intern Augustana Hosp., Chgo., 1952-53; resident in orthopedic surgery St. Francis Hosp., Peoria, Ill., 1953-54, Charlotte (N.C.) Meml. Hosp., 1954-57; fellow in orthop. divsn. Duke U. Hosp., 1956-57; acting chief orthopedic dept. Social Security Adminstrn. Hosp. 1, Lima, 1958-59; orthopedic surgen Mullens (W.Va.) Hosp., 1960-66; practice medicine specializing in orthopedic surgery, Princeton, W.Va., 1966—; mem. staff Princeton Cmty. Hosp., 1966—. Served with Peruvian Army, 1951-52. Recipient award Disting. Physicians of Am. Fellow Internat. Coll. Surgeons, Am. Acad. Disability Evaluating Physicians; mem. AMA (Physician's award 1969, 72-74, 77, 80, 84), W.Va. State Med. Assn., Mercer County Med. Soc., Am. Fracture Assn., So. Med. Soc., Latin Am. Soc. Orthopedic Surgeons, Orthopedic Rsch. and Edn. Found. (life), Peruvian Acad. Surgery, So. Orthopedic Soc., W.Va. Orthopedic Soc., Peruvian Am. Med. Soc., Nat. Assn. Disability Evaluating Physicians (charter), K.C. Roman Catholic.

DELAPLAINE, GEORGE BIRELY, JR., newspaper editor, cable television executive; b. Frederick, Md., Dec. 9, 1926; s. George B. and Ruth (Carty) D.; m. Elizabeth Barker, Aug. 12, 1955; children: George III, James, Edward, John. BBA, Johns Hopkins U., 1948. From reporter to publisher Frederick News-Post, 1949—; v.p. Frederick Brick Works, Inc., 1989—. Chmn. bd. GSComms.; bd. dirs. DeCorp Ams., Inc. Named Honorary Am. Farmer, Nat. Future Farmers Am., 1987; recipient Disting. Eagle Scout award, 1997, Md. Entrepreneur of the Yr. award, Ernst & Young, 1999, Silver Beaver Scout award, 2002. Mem. Kiwanis, Eagles, Jaycees, Masons. Republican. Episcopalian. Office: Great Southern Enterprises PO Box 3829 Frederick MD 21705-3829

DELAPLANE, SISTER MARJORIE MARIE, music educator; b. Chgo., June 28, 1923; d. Harry Leslie and Margaret Elizabeth (Kleinert) D. MusB, Siena Heights Coll., 1949; MusM, U. Mich., 1954. Tchr. St. Mary Elem. Sch., Kingman, Ariz., 1944-51; prin. St. Joseph Sch., Bronxville, N.Y., 1951-53; tchr. music Mt. St. Mary Acad., St. Charles, Ill., 1953-54, Dominican High Sch., Detroit, 1954-57, Hoban High Sch., Cleve., 1957-58; dir. music Regina High Sch., Wilmette, Ill., 1958-62, Aquinas High Sch., Chgo., 1962-65, Mildoon High Sch., Rockford, Ill., 1965-69; tchr. music Our Lady Knock, Calumet City, Ill., 1969-70; assoc. instr. Ind. U., Bloomington, 1970-72; instr. piano Am. Conservatory Music, Chgo., 1972-81, South Suburban Coll., South Holland, Ill., 1981—2002, Sherwood Cons. Music, Chgo., 1982—. Lectr., recitals at local colls. Mem. Soc. Am. Musicians, Ill. State Music Tchrs. Assn., Chgo. Area Music Tchrs. Assn. (pres. 1988-90). Home: 701 Locust Rd 1E Wilmette IL 60091-2217 Office: Regina Dominican Piano Studio 701 Locust Rd Fine Arts Bldg Wilmette IL 60091

DE LA RENTA, OSCAR, fashion designer; b. Santo Domingo, Dominican Republic, July 22, 1936; s. Oscar and Maria Antonia (deFiallo) de LaR.; m. Francoise de Langlade, Oct. 31, 1967 (dec. 1983); 1 adopted child, Moises; m. Anne E. de la Renta, Dec. 26, 1989. Student, Santo Domingo U., Academia de San Fernando, Madrid. Mem. staff Balenciaga's AISA, Madrid; asst. to Antonio Castillo at Lanvin, Paris, 1961-63; chief designer Elizabeth Arden, N.Y.C., 1963-65; chief designer, chmn. bd. dirs. Oscar de la Renta, Ltd., N.Y.C., 1965—; designer Pierre Balmain, Paris, 1993—. Bd. dirs. La Casa del Nino Orphanage and Sch., Santo Domingo, Met. Opera, Carnegie Hall, Thirteen/WNET, Hispanic Designers, Spanish Inst. Decorated Order Juan Pablo Duarte, Order Cristobal Colon (Dominican Republic); recipient Coty awards, 1967, 68, Golden Tiberius award, 1968, Lifetime of Achievement award The Coun. of Fashion Designers of Am., 1990, Neiman-Marcus award, 1968, Fragrance Found. award 1991, Living Legend award Am. Soc. Perfumers, 1995, Lifetime Achievement award Hispanic Heritage Soc., 1996; named to Coty Hall of Fame, 1973. Mem. Coun. Fashion Designers Am. (bd. dirs.). Office: Oscar de la Renta Ltd 550 7th Ave Fl 8 New York NY 10018-3207

DELARGE, MARIE P. director; b. Lafayette, La., June 21, 1951; d. Oran and Edolia Prejean; m. Wayne M. DeLarge, Feb. 10, 1973; children: Angelle, Ashley, Wayne II, Marcus. BA, Dillard U., 1969; EdM, U. New Orleans, 1976, PhD, 2003. Reading lab asst. Dillard U., New Orleans, 1974—77; instr. Xavier U., New Orleans, 1978—88, dir. reading lab, 1988—92, dir. Aetna Project, 1992—94, dir. Upward Bound, 1994—. Active All Congregations Together, New Orleans, 1990—95. Avocations: cooking, reading. Office: Xavier Univ Dir Upward Bound 7325 Palmetto Box 41B New Orleans LA 70125-1009

DE LARIOS, DORA, artist; b. L.A., Oct. 13, 1933; d. Elpidio and Concha (Martinez) De L.; 1 child, Sabrina. BFA, U. So. Calif., 1957. Tchr. ceramics UCLA, 1979, U. So. Calif., L.A., 1959; curator 1st internat. ceramic exhbn., L.A., 1988. Ceramic artist, commd. work for site specific areas, including Montage Resort and Spa, Laguna Beach, Calif., 2003; over 40 major works located in Tahiti, Hawaii, Japan, N.J., Fla., pvt. resdl. projects. Democrat. Avocations: reading, collecting cook books, cooking, drawing edwin the rabbit. Studio: 8560 Venice Blvd Los Angeles CA 90034-2549

DE LA RIVA, MYRIAM ANN, artist; b. Mexico City, Mex., Oct. 8, 1940; arrived in U.S., 1989; d. Adolfo De La Riva and Marianne Kayser; m. Conrado Gallegos, Feb. 26, 1961; children: Conrado Bernardo, Aileen, Eugenio Eduardo. Grad. in Fine Arts, IberoAm. U. V.p. World Coun. Visual Artists, Mexico City, 1994—96; bd. dirs. Latin Am. Art Mus. One-woman shows include, 1988—2002, exhibited in group shows, 1988—2002, prin. works include mural Today XXist Century. Vol. Tamayo Comtemporary Art Mus., Mexico City, 2000—03, Munal Mus., San Carlos, 2000—02; mem. Miami Art Mus., 1991—98, Nat. Mus. Women in Arts, 1991—98, Global Culture Ctr., 1991—98. Recipient 1st prize, Sor Juana Found. Mex.-Lebanon Inst. Cultural, 1998, 3d prize, Francisco Goitia prize, 1994, Francisco Goitia prize, Ateneo del Anahuac, 1991, 1992. Mem.: Assn. Artac Aiap-Unesco, Soc. Mex. de Artistas Plasticos. Home: 10150 SW 139 Ct Miami FL 33186 Office: Delariva Bosque de Guayacanes #57 11700 Mexico City Mexico E-mail: delarivamyriam@hotmail.com

DE LA ROCHA, CARLOS A. retired physician; b. Santo Domingo, Dominican Republican, Aug. 12, 1934; s. Carlos A. and Germania (Contin) de la R.; m. Penelope Lynn Lansing, May 20, 1961; children: C. Andrew, Maria L., Michael J., David L., Alicia M., Juan A. MD, Univ. de Santo Domingo, 1958. Diplomate Am. Bd. Surgery. Rotating intern City Hosp. at Elmhurst, Queens, N.Y., 1958-59; asst. resident surgery Albert Einstein Med. Ctr., Phila., 1959-60, Ellis Hosp., Schenectady, N.Y., 1960-62, chief resident surgery, 1962-63; tchg. fellow surgery St. Clares Hosp., Schenectady, 1963-65; asst. attending surgeon St. Clares and Ellis Hosps., 1965-69, attending surgeon, 1969-98; ret., 1998. Chmn. tissue unit Ellis Hosp., 1985-90; mem. Ellis Hosp. Found. Bd., 1988-94. Fellow Am. Coll. Surgeons; mem. Am. Soc. Gen. Surgeons, N.Y. State Soc. Surgeons, N.Y. State and County Med. Soc. Republican. Roman Catholic. Avocations: travel, classical music. Home: 44 Van Voast Ln Scotia NY 12302-9621 also: PO Box 1397 Schenectady NY 12301-1397 E-mail: delarochac@hotmail.com.

DE LA ROCHA, RAQUELLE, lawyer, educator; b. L.A., Mar. 11, 1958; m. Daniel J. Bussel; children: Sarah, Hannah, Eli Javier. BA in Philosophy cum laude, UCLA, 1983, JD, 1987. Bar: Calif. 1987, U.S. Dist. Ct. (ctrl., no. and so. dists.) Calif., 1987, Ct. of Appeals (9th cir.) 1987. Legal clk. to Hon. Elwood Lui Calif. Ct. Appeal; atty. O'Melveny & Myers, L.A., 1987-89; supervising atty. Saperstein & Seligman, L.A., 1989; trial counsel State Bar Calif., L.A., 1990, sr. litigator, 1991; lectr. Sch. Law, UCLA, 1991-96; of counsel Ballard, Rosenberg & Golper, Universal City, Calif., 1996-2001; ptnr. Lamb & Baute, L.A., 2001—03; adj. prof. Pepperdine Sch. of Pub. Policy, Malibu, Calif., 2003—. Mem. L.A. Police Commn., 1999-2001, v.p., 2000-01, pres., 2001; commr. Calif. Parks Commn., 2001—, vice chair, 2003—; vis. asst. prof. UCLA, 1996-2002. Mem. L.A. City Commn. Status Women, 1990-91; trustee L.A. chpt. Leukemia Soc. Am., 1990-91; judge pro tem E. L.A. Mcpl. Ct., 1990-94; mem. program adv. com. UNICEF, 1991; commr. L.A. Bd. Civil Svc. Commrs., 1991-93, v.p., 1992-93; commr. Calif. Fair Polit. Practices Commn., 1993-95; bd. dirs. Treepeople, 1993-94; pres. L.A. City Ethics Commn., 1995-97, v.p., 1998-99; mem. governing bd. Encino/Tarzana Regional Med. Ctr., 1997-2001; mem. Calif. Adv. Commn. on Domestic Violence, 2001 Named Woman of the Future Comision Feminil L.A., 1995, Woman of the Yr. Mex. Am. Opportunity Found., 1996; recipient Lintz award San Fernando Valley Bar Assn., 2000. Mem. ABA (mem. standing com. election law 1998-2001), Mex. Am. Bar Assn. L.A. (bd. dirs. 1992), UCLA Law Alumni Assn. (bd. dirs. 1993-97). Office: Pepperdine Sch Pub Policy 24255 Pacific Coast Hwy Malibu CA 90263 E-mail: raquelle.delarocha@pepperdine.edu.

DE LARROCHA, ALICIA, concert pianist; b. Barcelona, May 23, 1923; d. Eduardo and Teresa (De La Calle) de L.; m. Juan Torra, June 21, 1950; children: Juan, Alicia. Grad. (prize extraordinary, Gold medal), Acad. Marshall, Barcelona; MusD (hon.), U. Ann Arbor, 1979, Middlebury Coll., 1981, Carnegie-Mellon, 1985. Debut, Barcelona, 1929, solo recitalist, concert pianist maj. orchs. in, Europe, U.S., Can., Cen. and S.Am., South Africa, New Zealand, Australia, Japan; dir. Acad. Marshall, 1959—; rec. artist: Hispavox, CBS, Decca, London; records; (Grammy awards 1974, 75, 88, 91, nominations 1967, 75, 77, 82, 84, 90, 91, 92, 93, 1st Gold medal Merito a la Vocacion 1973), Spanish Encores, Spanish Fireworks, Spanish Music (I-IV). Recipient Harriet Cohen Internat. Music award, 1956, Franz Liszt award, 1989, Principe de Asturias award 1994, UNESCO award 1995; Paderewski Meml. medal, 1961; Grand prix du Disque Acad. Charles Cros, 1960, 74; Edison award, 1968, 78, 89, Ondas award, Spain, 1992, 2000; decorated Civil Merit Order, 1962, Isabel la Catolica, Spain, 1972; hon. academician Bayerische Akademie der Schönen Künste, Munich; Real Academia Bellas Artes San Fernando, Madrid, Real Academia de Bellas Artes, Granada, R.A.BB.AA Sant Jordi, Barcelona; comdr. dans l'Ordre des Arts et des lettres, Paris, Fundación Guerrero Spanish Music award, 1999, Spanish Arts Tchr. nat. award, 2000. Mem. Musica en Compostela (dir.), Hispanic Soc. Am. (corr.), Internat. Piano Archives (hon. pres.) Office: Farmaceutic Carbonell 46-48 Atic Barcelona 08034 Spain also: Columbia Artists Mgmt Inc care Wilford Div 165 W 57th St New York NY 10019-2201

DE LASA, JOSÉ M. lawyer; b. Havana, Cuba, Nov. 28, 1941; came to U.S., 1961; s. Miguel and Conchita de Lasa; m. Maria Teresa Figueroa, Nov. 23, 1963; children: Maria Teresa, José, Andrés, Carlos. BA, Yale U., 1968, JD, 1971. Bar: N.Y. 1973. Assoc. Cleary, Gottlieb, Steen & Hamilton, N.Y.C., 1971-76; legal dept. Bristol-Myers Squibb Co., N.Y.C., 1976-94; sr. v.p., sec. and gen. counsel Abbott Labs., 1994—. Lectr. internat. law, various locations. Bd. dirs. Am. Arbitration Assn., The Resource Found., Chgo. Coun. Fgn. Rels., The Stovir Found. Mem. ABA, Assn. of Bar of City of N.Y., Assn. Gen. Counsel, North Shore Gen. Counsel Assn., Ill. State Bar Assn. Roman Catholic. Office: Abbott Laboratories D-364 AP6D-2 100 Abbott Park Rd North Chicago IL 60064-3500

DELATEUR, BARBARA JANE, medical educator; b. Hoquiam, Wash., Nov. 17, 1936; Student, Marylhurst (Oreg.) Coll., 1954-56; BS in Philosophy, St. Louis U., 1959; MD, U. Wash., 1963, MSc, 1968. Cert. Am. Bd. Phys. Medicine and Rehab.; lic. physiatrist, Wash., Md. Rotating intern U. Hosp., U. Wash., 1963-64; resident dept. phys. medicine and rehab. U. Hosp., 1964-67; instr. dept. phys. medicine and rehab. U. Wash. Sch. Medicine, 1967-68, asst. prof., 1968-71, assoc. prof., 1971-76, prof. dept. rehab. medicine, 1976-93; prof., dir. dept. phys. medicine and rehab. Johns Hopkins U. Sch. Medicine, Balt., 1993—, Lawrence Cardinal Shehan chair phys. medicine and rehab., 1993—, joint prof. health policy & mgmt. Sch. Hygiene & Pub. Health, 1994—; acting physiatrist-in-chief Rehab. Medicine Svc. Harborview Med. Ctr., Seattle, 1970-72, physiatrist-in-chief, 1972-93; dir. Muscular Dystrophy Clinic Meml. Hosp., Yakima, Wash., 1979-88; dir. dept. phys. medicine and rehab. Johns Hopkins Hosp., Balt., 1993—; med. dir. dept. rehab. medicine Good Samaritan Hosp., Balt., 1993—. Vis. prof. dept. rehab. medicine and dept. internal medicine SUNY, Syracuse, 1988; cons. physiatrist Johns Hopkins Geriatrics Ctr., Johns Hopkins Bayview Med. Ctr., Balt., 1994—; vis. lectr. dept. phys. medicine Coll. Medicine, Ohio State U., 1985; Arthur Grant lectr. U. Tex., San Antonio, 1992; Marquette lectr. Jefferson Med. Coll., Phila., 1993; spkr. various univs. and orgns.; pres. Phys.Medicine and Rehab./Edn. and Rsch. Found., 1990-94; mem. governing coun. sect. rehab. hosps. and programs Am. Hosp. Assn., 1993—; mem. adv. bd. Wash. State Divsn. Vocat. Rehab., 1979-84. Contbr. articles to profl. jours.; mem. editl. bd. Archives Phys. Medicine and Rehab., 1978-84, Health After 50, Johns Hopkins Hosp., 1994—; reviewer Jour. Am. Geriatrics Soc., 1994—. Recipient Elizabeth and Sidney Licht award for sci. writing, 1990, Excellence in Tchg. award N.J. Med. Sch., 1992, Excellence in Rsch. Writing award Assn. Acad. Physiatrists and Am. Jour. Phys. Medicine and Rehab., 1992, Golden Goniometer award Phys. Medicine and Rehab.

Residents, 1995, Labe Scheinberg award, Meeting of Consortium of MS Ctrs., Portland, Oreg., 1995. Fellow Am. Acad. Phys. Medicine; mem. AMA, Am. Acad. Phys. Medicine and Rehab. (bd. govs. 1983-90, v.p. 1986-887, pres-elect 1987-88, pres. 1988-89, past-pres. 1989-90, Disting. Clinician award 1998), NAS, Am. Burn Assn., Am. Congress Rehab. Medicine, Assn. Acad. Physiatrists (Disting. Academician award 1998), Internt. Assn. for Study of Pain, King County Med. Assn., Northwest Assn. Phys. Medicine and Rehab. (pres. 1974-76), Gerontol. Soc. Am. (clin. medicine sect.), Wash. State Med. Assn. Office: JHPM & R Good Samaritan Profl Bldg 5601 Loch Raven Blvd Ste 406 Baltimore MD 21239-2905

DE LA TORRE, JORGE IGNACIO, plastic surgeon, educator; b. Kansas City, Mo., Dec. 14, 1963; s. Jorge German and Julia (McDermott) de la Torre; m. Carol Beauchamp, June 22, 1996; children: Mary Margaret, Anna Cristina, Jorge Augustin. BA, U. Tex., Austin, 1986; MD, U. Tex., Houston, 1991. Resident St. Joseph Hosp., Houston, 1991-96, Nassau County Med. Ctr., East Meadow, N.Y., 1996-98; fellow U. Ala., Birmingham, 1998-99, asst. prof. plastic surgery, 1999—2003, assoc. prof. plastic surgery, 2003—; dir. Ctr. Advanced Surg. Aesthetics, sect. chief Birmingham VA Med. Ctr. Contbr. articles to profl. jours. Mem. media host com. Econ. Summit Indsl. Nations, Houston, 1990; mem. vol. com. Rep. Nat. Conv., Houston, 1992. Fellow: ACS; mem.: AMA, Am. Soc. Reconstructive Microsurgeons, Am. Soc. Plastic Surgeons, Am. Soc. Laser Medicine and Surgery, Am. Cleft Palate Assn., Am. Burn Assn. Avocations: skiing, music, biking. Home: 204 Main St Mountain Brook AL 35213-2506 Office: U Ala Birmingham 510 20th St South FOT 1164 Birmingham AL 35294-3411

DE LA TORRE, ROGER ANIBAL, surgeon; b. Cuba, Dec. 26, 1957; s. Rogelio A. and Amalia de la Torre. BA cum laude, Notre Dame (Ind.) U., 1979; MD, Ind. U., Indpls., 1986. Diplomate Am. Bd. Surgery. Resident gen. surgery Mt. Sinai Med. Ctr., 1986-91; gen. ptnr. de la Torre/Scott, Wentzville, Mo., 1991—; chief of surgery Doctors Hosp., Wentzville, 1991—2002, pres. med. staff, 1996; clin. asst. prof. surgery U. Mo.-Columbia Sch. Medicine, 1996—; mem. staff Advanced Laparoscopic Tng. Ctr., Atlanta, 1994—, Mo. Laser Inst., St. Louis, 1993—. Mem. med. adv. bd. C.R. Bard, Inc., Billerica, Mass., 1994—, Gen. Surg. Innovations, Palo Alto, Calif., 1994—; clin. adv. bd. MicroSurge, Inc., Needham, Mass., 1995—; hernia adv. bd. U.S. Surg. Corp., Norwalk, Conn., 1993—; presenter in field various orgns. Contbr. articles to profl. jours. Fellow ACS, Internat. Coll. Surgeons; mem. AAAS, Am. soc. Bariatric Surgery, Am. Soc. Gen. Surgeons, N.Y. Acad. Scis. Achievements include patents on surgical mesh with semi-rigid border, surgical instruments for tying a knot in a length of suture at a remote location, magazine for loading needle onto stitching instrument and for loading suture onto a suture dispensing instrument, Laparoscopic Access Port for surgical instrument or the hand. Office: Gen Laproscopic & Vascular Surgery Vascular Surgery 600 Medical Dr Ste 202 Wentzville MO 63385-3426

DE LATTRE, CANDACE LORRAINE, singer, voice teacher; b. Flint, Mich., Jan. 3, 1950; d. Eugene Charles and Lorraine (Kithcart) DeL. MusB in Vocal Pedagogy, Mich. State U., 1973, MusM in Voice, 1975; Specialist in Music, U. Mich., 1989; postgrad., Am. Inst. Musical Studies, Graz, Austria, 1979. Cert. in voice tech. McClosky Inst. Voice Therapy, 1997. Voice instr. Flint Sch. Performing Arts, 1976-96; asst. prof. voice and musicology Oreg. State U., Corvallis, Oreg., 1982-83; dir. Opera Workshop, vocal instr. Marygrove Coll., 1999—2002; vocal technician McClosky Inst. of Voice, 1997—, sec., 1999—; voice instr. Oakland U., 2001—, Cranbrook Sch., 2001—. Dir. opera workshop Flint Inst. Music, 1977—81, U. Mich., Ann Arbor, 1978—80, dramatic coach, vocal therapist, 1987—89, Flint Sch. Performing Arts, 1987—96, dir. advanced curriculum program, 1991—96; master class presenter Glassboro (NJ) U., 1981, Iowa State U., Ames, 1986, Ames, 89, Flint Pub. Schs., 1988; 1st Am. examiner in voice Royal Conservatory of Music, Toronto, 1994—; mem. edn. and outreach com., bd. dirs. Mich. Opera Theatre, 1994—; founder De Lattre Inst. Vocal Arts (DIVA!) and OperaDIVA!, 1997—2001; dir., planner Opera Camp, Mich. Opera Theatre, 2000—. Appeared in numerous operas and concerts in Austria, 1979, Mich. Opera Theatre, 1981, 89, 99, 2000, Kalamazoo Opera, 1984, Pacific N.W. Wagner Festival, 1985, Chamber Opera Chgo., 1985, Hill Auditorium, Ann Arbor, 1989, Flint Symphony, Rochester Symphony, Japan Symphony, Warren Symphony, 1981—, others. Asst. chmn. William C. Byrd Young Artist Competition, Flint, 1980-86, chmn., 1986-89; mem. cdn. adv. com. bd. dirs. Mich. Opera Theatre, Detroit, 1994—. Recipient 1st Place award Met. Opera awards, Cleve., 1979, Portland, 1982, Internat. Opera Competition, 1985, Bronze medallion, chant opera Concours Internat. d'Execution Musical, 1979, Benneche award for Wagnerian Singing, Liederkranz Found., 1981. Mem.: Opera Am., Am. Guild Mus. Artists, Nat. Assn. Tchrs. Singing, Mensa, St. Cecilia Soc. (v.p. 1978—80, grantee 1979). Mem. Baha'i Faith. Avocations: computers, visual arts, designing jewelry.

DELATY, SIMONE, retired language educator; b. Valenciennes, France, Jan. 17, 1939; came to U.S., 1963; d. Georges and Hélène (Lagarde) D.; m. Joseph Szertics, Dec. 8, 1962 (div. 1978); 1 child, Claire Szertics. Lic. ès-Lettres, U. Grenoble, France, 1962; D in Comparative Lit., U. Bordeaux, 1970. Instr. French Bowling Green U., Bowling Green, Ohio, 1964-67, U. Iowa, Iowa City, 1968-69, asst. prof. French, 1969-76, assoc. prof. French, 1976-86, prof. French, 1986—96; ret., 1996; owner, operator of Simone's Plain and Simple-Artisan Bread and Farm Fresh Products, Wellman, Iowa, 1996—. Author: L'héritage espagnol de José-Maria de Heredia, 1975, Oeuvres poétiques complètes de J.M. de Heredia, 1984. Grantee Am. Philos. Soc., 1976, Am. Coun. Learned Socs., 1976. Mem.: MLA.

DELAUDER, WILLIAM B. academic administrator; Dean arts and scis. N.C. Agrl. and Tech. State U., Greensboro, until 1987; pres. Del. State U., Dover, 1987—. Office: Del State U Office of Pres 1200 N Dupont Hwy Dover DE 19901-2202

DELAUGHTER, THOMAS GLENN, finance educator, consultant, academic administrator; b. New Orleans, La., Apr. 3, 1948; s. Thomas Jefferson and Lurlean Waldrup DeLaughter; m. Grace Noel Tatum, June 20, 1998; 1 child, Madeline Elizabeth Costa. PhD in Bus. Adminstrn., Fla. State U., 1995; MBA, Miss. Coll., 1989, BA, 1971. Vis. asst. prof. U. Fla., Gainesville, 1996—; asst. prof. bus. adminstrn. Flagler Coll., St. Augustine, Fla., 1998—. Author: (book) Gator Marketing, management.org. Elder Presbyn. Ch., Hernando, Miss., 1979—81. Recipient Tchr. of Yr., BACC U. Fla., 1997. Mem.: Acad. Mgmt. Episcopalian. Avocation: golf. Office: Flagler Coll 74 King St Saint Augustine FL 32084 E-mail: doc@flagler.edu.

DELAURA, DAVID JOSEPH, English language educator; b. Worcester, Mass., Nov. 19, 1930; s. Louis and Helen Adeline (Austin) DeL.; m. Ann Beloate, Aug. 19, 1961; children: Michael Louis, Catherine, William Beloate. AB, Boston Coll., 1955, A.M., 1958; PhD, U. Wis., 1960. Mem. faculty U. Tex. at Austin, 1960-74, prof. English, 1968-74; Avalon Found. prof. humanities, prof. English U. Pa., Phila., 1974-99, chmn. dept., 1985-90, univ. ombudsman, 1993-97. Author: Hebrew and Hellene in Victorian England: Newman, Arnold, and Pater, 1969; editor: Victorian Prose: A Guide to Research, 1973; contbr. chpts. to books, articles and revs. to profl. publs. Mem. MLA Assn. (ann. award for outstanding article 1964). Home: 31 Orchard Ln Villanova PA 19085-1133 E-mail: ddelaura@sprynet.com.

DELAURO, ROSA L. congresswoman; b. New Haven, Conn., Mar. 2, 1943; m. Stanley Greenberg. Student, London Sch. Econs. & Polit. Sci., 1962-63; BA in History and Polit Sci. cum laude, Marymount Coll., 1964; MA in Internat. Politics, Columbia U., 1966. Tng. assoc. Community Progress Inc., New Haven, Conn., 1967-69; instr. in internat. rels. Albertus Magnus Coll., 1967-68; adminstrv. asst. Nat. Urban Fellows, 1969-72, asst. dir., dir., 1972-75; city coord. Carter-Mondale Presdl. Campaign, New Haven, 1976; exec. asst. Mayor Frank Logue, New Haven, 1976-77, campaign mgr., 1977; exec. asst., devel. adminstr. City of New Haven, 1977-79; campaign mgr. Chris Dodd for U.S. Senate, 1979-80, 86; adminstrv. asst. U.S. Senator Christopher J. Dodd, Washington, 1981-87; state dir. Mondale-Ferraro Presdl. Campaign, N.J., 1986; ptnr. DeLauro-Geller, 1987-88; regional dir. Dukakis for Pres. Campaign, N.Y., N.J., Con., 1988; exec. dir. EMILY's List, 1989; mem. U.S. Congress 3rd Conn. dist., 1991—; mem. house appropriations com.; chief dep. minority whip. Del. to Dem. Nat. Conv., 1984; bd. dirs. Pax Ams. Past pres. New Haven Arts Coun. Assoc. fellow Timothy Dwight Coll., Yale U.; recipient Leadership award Am. Com. on Italian Migration. Mem. Nat. Italian-Am. Found., Dem. Women for Progress. Democrat. Office: US House of Reps 2262 Rayburn Ho Office Bldg Washington DC 20515-0703 also: District Office 59 Elm Street New Haven CT 06510*

DELAWIE, HOMER TORRENCE, retired architect; b. Santa Barbara, Calif., Sept. 24, 1927; s. Fred Ely and Gertrude (Torrence) D.; m. Billie Carol Sparlin (div. 1969); m. Ethel Ann Mallinger, Sept. 3, 1973; children: Gregory, Claire, Shandell, Tracy, Stephanie, Scott. BS in Archtl. Engring., Calif. Poly. State U., San Luis Obispo, 1951. Registered architect, Calif. Pvt. practice architecture, San Diego, 1958-61; founder, CEO Delawie Wilkes Rodrigues Barker & Bretton Assocs., San Diego, 1961—98, ret., 1998, ptnr. emeritus, 1998—. Mem. Planning Commn., City of San Diego, 1969-82; adv. bd. KPBS Pub. TV. Recipient Award of Merit Calif. chpt. Am. Inst. Planners, Lay Citizens award Phi Delta Kappa, 1975, award Calif chpt. Am. Planning Assn., 1982; named Disting. Alumnus, Calif. Poly. State U., 1972. Fellow AIA (over 60 design awards 1973—, Architects Svc. award Calif. coun. 1973, spl. award San Diego chpt. 1978, Pub. Svc. award Calif. coun. 1981, Outstanding Firm award San Diego chpt. 1986, Calif. Coun. Lifetime Achievement award 1998). Democrat. Home: 2749 Azalea Dr San Diego CA 92106-1132 Office: Delawie Wilkes Rodrigues Barker & Bretton Assocs 2265 India St San Diego CA 92101-1725

DELAY, THOMAS D. (TOM DELAY), congressman; b. Laredo, Tex., Apr. 8, 1947; s. Charles Ray and Maxine (Wimbish) DeL.; m. Christine Furrh, Aug. 26, 1967; 1 child, Danielle BS, U. Houston, 1970. Gen mgr. Redwood Chem., Houston, 1970-73; owner, operator Albo Pest Control, Stafford, Tex., 1973-84, pres., 1984—; mem., appropriations com. vice chmn. adminstrn. com., chmn. budget and oversight of transp. com. Tex. Ho. of Reps., Austin, 1979-84; mem. 99th-108th Congresses from 22d Tex. dist., 1985—; mem. HUD com. 99th-106th Congresses from 22d Tex. dist., mem. appropriations com., majority whip; house majority leader 108th Congress. Mem. appropriations and pub. health coms. Tex. Ho. of Reps.; mem. Grace Caucus, Washington, 1985— ; mem. U.S.-Mexico Interparliamentary Del., Washington, 1985-86; mem. Republican study com. Sci. and Tech. Task Force, 1985-86; mem. Rep. research com. Regulatory Reform Caucus, 1985-86. Bd. dirs. Youth Opportunities Unltd., Houston; precinct chmn. Republican Party, Simonton, Tex., 1974-78; Gala chmn. Ft. Bend County "War on Drugs" Coalition, 1987; adv. bd. CloseUp Found.; active drug abuse and rehab. ctr. Odyssey House, Tex; adv. bd. Joint Ctr. for Urban Mobility Research, Houston; mem. Ft. Bend Arts Adv. Council. Recipient Legislator of Yr. award Tex. Assn. to Improve Distbn., 1983; ABC's Outstanding Legislator for the 67th Session Leadership award Young Conservatives of Tex., 1984; Nat. Security Leadership award Coalition Peace Through Strength, Washington, 1985-90; Freshman Class Rep., U.S. House GOP Com. on Coms., Washington, 1985-86; Golden Bulldog award Watchdog of the Treasury, 1985-90. Mem. Congl. Leaders for a Balanced Budget, Greater Houston Pest Control Assn. (former pres.), Tex. Pest Control Assn. (bd. dirs.), Southwest Energy Council, Am. Legis. Exchange Council, Nat. Conf. State Legislators, Fort Bend County Fair Assn. (life) Clubs: Sweetwater Country (Sugar Land, Tex.); Fort Bend 100. Lodges: Rotary. Republican. Baptist. Avocations: hunting; skiing; golf. Office: US Ho of Reps 242 Cannon House Office Bldg Washington DC 20515-4322*

DELBANCO, NICHOLAS FRANKLIN, English educator, writer; b. London, Aug. 27, 1942; came to U.S., 1948; s. Kurt and Barbara Gabriele Delbanco; m. Elena Greenhouse, Sept. 12, 1970; children: Francesca Barbara, Andrea Katherine. AB, Harvard U., 1963; MA, Columbia U., 1966. Mem. faculty Bennington (Vt.) Coll., 1966-85; prof. English Williams Coll., Williamstown, Mass., 1983, Skidmore Coll., Saratoga Springs, N.Y., 1984; Robert Frost Collegiate prof. English U. Mich., Ann Arbor, 1985—. Dir. MFA in writing program U. Mich., 1985—; vis. prof. Iowa U. Writer's Workshop, Iowa City, 1980; vis. adj. prof. Columbia U., N.Y.C., 1981, 96-98; founding dir. Bennington Writing Workshops, 1978-85; chair fiction panel Nat. Book Awards, N.Y.C., 1997; vis. fellow Woodrow Wilson Nat. Found., Princeton, N.J., 1981—. Author: Group Portrait: Conrad, Crane, Ford, James & Wells, 1983, The Writer's Trade, 1990, Running in Place: Scenes from the South of France, 1991, In the Name of Mercy, 1995, Old Scores, 1997, What Remains, 2000, others; editor: Stillness and Shadows, 1985, Speaking of Writing, 1990, Bernard Malamud on Life and Art, 1996, others. Mem. ant. adv. bd. Share Our Strength, Writers Harvest, Washington, 1994—; mem. governing bd. Mich. Journalism Fellows Program, 1990—; mem. Arts Am. U.S. Info. Agy., Washington, 1992. Fellow Nat. Endowment for Arts, 1973, 82, J.S. Guggenheim Meml. Found., 1980; nominee Mich. Author of the Yr., Mich. Assn. Librs., 2002. Fellow Internat. Am. Studies and Lang. Faculty Salzburg; mem. Authors Guild, Authors League, PEN, Century Assn., Signet Soc., Phi Beta Kappa. Home: 428 Concord Rd Ann Arbor MI 48104-1706 Office: U Mich Hopwood Rm Angell Hall Ann Arbor MI 48109 E-mail: delbanco@umich.edu.

DELBANCO, THOMAS LEWIS, medical educator, researcher; b. London, Dec. 7, 1939; came to U.S., 1948; s. Kurt and Barbara Gabriele (Bernstein) D.; m. Jill Martin Behrens, Dec. 13, 1964; children: Steven, Suzanne, Jennifer. BA, Harvard U., 1961; MD, Columbia U., 1965. Diplomate Am. Bd. Internal Medicine. Intern in medicine Bellevue Hosp., N.Y.C., 1965-66, resident, 1967-68, Presbyn. Hosp., N.Y.C., 1966-67; chief resident Harlem Hosp. Ctr., N.Y.C., 1968-69; mem. staff, dir. div. gen. medicine and primary care Beth Israel Hosp., Boston, 1971—2002; Richard and Florence Koplow - James Tullis prof. gen. medicine and primary care Harvard Med. Sch., 2000—. Dir. Picker/Commonwealth Program Patient-Centered Care, 1987-94; chmn. Picker Inst., 1994-2000; mem. coun. APHA, 1983-85; mem. program com. Inst. Medicine, NAS, 1991-94. Editor: 4 books; contbr. numerous articles to profl. jours. Vice chmn. United Way Mass. Bay, Boston, 1987-91; co-dir. Learning Through Drama Program, Lexington, Mass., 1982-90; bd. dirs. Health Commons Inst., 1994-2001. Maj. U.S. Army, 1969-71. Robert Wood Johnson Health Policy fellow Inst. Medicine, 1977-78. Master ACP; mem. Am. Fedn. Clin. Rsch., Soc. Gen. Internal Medicine (pres. 1986-87, councillor), Nat. Pub. Health and Hosps. Inst. (bd. dirs.). Jewish. Avocation: violin. Office: Beth Israel Deaconess Med Ctr 330 Brookline Ave Boston MA 02215-5400 E-mail: tdelbanc@bidmc.harvard.edu.

DELBENE, KURT, information technology executive; B in Indsl. Engring., U. Ariz.; MA, Stanford U.; MBA, U. Chgo. Software devel. AT&T Bell Lab.; mgmt. cons. McKinsey & Co.; from mgr. to v.p. authoring & collaboration svc. group Microsoft, Redmond, Wash., 1992, v.p. authoring & collaboration svc. group. Office: One Microsoft Way Redmond WA 98052-6399

DEL BONO, IRENE LILLIAN (IRENE STONE GUILD DEL BONO), lawyer; b. Milford, Mass., May 27, 1949; d. Roy Prescott and Sara Lucretia (Snyer) Stone; children: Gregory Howe Jr., Daniel David. BS in Criminal Justice, Westfield State Coll., 1989; JD, Boston U., 1991, MA in Hist. Preservation, 1992. Bar: Mass. 1991, U.S. Supreme Ct. 1996, U.S. Dist. Ct. Mass. 2000. Asst. atty. gen. Office Atty. Gen., Boston, 1992-2001; dir. land acquisition and protection State Mass. Dept. Environ. Mgmt., 2001—. Active Framingham Hist. Soc. Mem. Mass. Bar Assn. (property law sect.), Mass. Conveyancer's Assn., Nat. Trust Hist. Preservation, N.E. Legal Preservation Network, U.S. Supreme Ct. Hist. Soc., Danvers Alarm List Co. Avocations: writing, bicycling, hiking, internet. Home: 24 Nern St Natick MA 01760-3527 Office: State Mass Dept Environ Mgmt Land Acquisition/Protection 251 Causeway St Boston MA 02114 E-mail: delbonoandlaw@hotmail.com.

DELBOURGO, JOËLLE LILY, publishing executive; b. Alexandria, Egypt, Sept. 10, 1953; came to U.S., 1960; d. Edward Daniel and J. Andrée (Domergue) D.; m. Lewis Foster Patton, May 16, 1976 (div. May 1996); children: Caroline Emily, Andrew David. Student, Vassar Coll., 1970-72; BA, Williams Coll., 1974; MA, Columbia U., 1975. Editorial asst. Bantam Books, N.Y.C., 1975-76, asst. editor, 1976-78, assoc. editor, 1978-80; sr. editor Ballantine Del Rey Fawcett Ivy Books div. Random House Inc., N.Y.C., 1980-81, exec. editor, 1981-83, editor-in-chief, 1983-86, v.p., editor-in-chief trade books, 1986-89, editor-in-chief hard cover books and trade paperback, 1990-95; v.p., editl. dir. HarperCollins, N.Y.C., 1996, sr. v.p., assoc. publ., editor-in-chief, 1997-99; CEO, pres. Joëlle Delbourgo Assocs. Inc. Lit. Mgmt., Pub. Cons., 1999—. Columbia faculty fellowship, 1974-75. Mem. Women's Media Group, Phi Beta Kappa. Office: 450 7th Ave Ste 3004 New York NY 10123-3004 E-mail: joelle@delbourgo.com.

DEL CALVO, ALBERTO C. educational association administrator, lawyer; b. Havana, Cuba, Feb. 11, 1923; arrived in U.S., 1960; s. Francisco del Calvo and Emilia (Martinez) del calvo; m. Mirza G. del Calvo, May 14, 1952; children: Alberto Hector, Jorge Alberto. PhD in Law, Havana U., Cuba, 1946; MA in Spanish, Mt. St. Mary's Coll., L.A., 1969. Pres., scholarship coord. Cuban Am. Tchrs. Assn., Downey, Calif., 2000—. Office: Cuban American Tchrs Assn 9727 Garnish Dr Downey CA 90240-3002

DEL CERRO, GERARDO, sociologist, researcher; b. Burgos, Spain, Feb. 22, 1966; s. Gerardo del Cerro-Rueda and Herminia Santamaria. BA, Logic and Philosophy of Sci., U. Autonoma, Madrid, 1989; MA, Sociology, New School for Social Research, New York City, 1992—94; MA, Music Theory and Piano Performance, Real Conservatory of Music, Madrid, 1996; PhD, Urban Planning, New School for Social Research, New York, 1992—97. Assoc. rschr. Spanish Ministry of Edn., Madrid, 1990—92; project area leader National Sci. Found. Gateway Program, N.Y.C., 1997—2002; dir. assessment and innovation The Cooper Union for Advancement of Sci. and Art, N.Y.C., 1999—. Prof. of Sociology U. Madrid, 1995—96; social sci. analyst PREMDAM, Madrid, Spain, 1994—96; rsch. cons. Burgos City Hall, Burgos, Spain, 2001—02. Contbr. articles to profl. jours. Pres. Music Soc. Coll. Mayor Ximenez de Cisneros, Madrid, 1986—89. Recipient Alumni Assn. award, Coll. Mayor Ximenez de Cisneros, 1991, Vis. Scholarship, Skidmore Coll., 1989-90; fellow, New Sch. for Social Rsch., 1993, Univ. Autonoma de Madrid, 1984 through 1989. Mem.: New York Acad. of Scis., Soc. for Social Implications of Tech., Am. Soc.of Engring. Edn., World Future Soc. Avocation: languages. Office: The Cooper Union 51 Astor Place New York NY 10003 Business E-Mail: cerro@cooper.edu.

DEL CHIARO, MARIO ALDO, art historian, archeologist, etruscologist, educator; b. San Francisco, Apr. 22, 1925; s. Casimiro and Elisa (Bianchi) A.; m. Christina Falkman, Sept. 13, 1958; children: Kari Louise, Marco Claudio, Paola Christina. AB, U. Calif.-Berkeley, 1950, MA, 1951, PhD, 1956. Teaching asst. art history U. Calif. at Berkeley, 1950-51, 55, Univ. fellow in art, 1951-52; John Wesley Britton traveling fellow in classics, 1952-53; Met. Mus. Art fellow, 1953-54; grantee Am. Numismatic Soc. Seminar, 1954; faculty U. Calif., Santa Barbara, 1956—, prof. art history, 1966-94, prof. emeritus, 1994; chmn. dept. U. Calif.-Santa Barbara, 1969-72; Mem. archeol. staff for excavations in Turkey, Yugoslavia, Egypt, Sicily and Italy; dir. U. Calif.-Santa Barbara archeol. expdns. to, Tuscany, Italy. Author: The Genucilia Group: A Class of Etruscan Red-Figured Plates, 1957, Etruscan Red-Figured Vase-Painting at Caere, 1974, The Etruscan Funnel Group: A Tarquinian Red-Figured Fabric, 1974; exhbn. catalogues Greek Art in Private Collections of Southern California, 1963, Etruscan Art from West Coast Collections, 1967, Roman Art in West Collections, 1973, Etruscan Ghiaccio Forte, 1976, Re-exhumed Etruscan Bronzes, 1981; Classical Art, Sculpture in the Santa Barbara Mus. Art, 1984; editor: Corinthiaca, Studies in Honor of Darrell A. Amyx, 1986; contbr. book revs. and articles to profl. jours. Decorated Cavaliere Ufficiale Order of Merit (Italy); recipient Internat. award in archaeology, Tutto Maremma, Italy, 1990; grantee, Am. Philos. Soc., 1957, 1975, NEH, 1977; Prix de Rome fellow, Am. Acad. in Rome, 1958—60, Sr. Faculty fellow, Humanities Inst. U. Calif. at Berkeley, 1967—68. Mem. Archeol. Inst. Am., Explorers Club, Istituto Studi Etruschi ed Italici, Florence, Deutsches Archäologisches Inst., Istituto Archeologico Rome, European Acad. Scis. and Art, Salzburg, Phi Beta Kappa. Home: Hope Ranch 1376 Estrella Dr Santa Barbara CA 93110-2418

DELCO, EXALTON A., JR., retired biology educator; b. Houston, Sept. 4, 1929; BA, Fisk U., 1949; MS, U. Mich., 1950; PhD, U. Tex., 1962; LLD (hon.), Huston-Tillotson Coll., 1986. Assoc. to prof. biology Huston-Tillotson Coll., Austin, Tex., 1963—68, v.p. acad. affairs, 1967—85, Austin C.C., 1985—93; spl. asst. to pres. U. Tex., Austin, 1995—96, adj. prof., 2001—. Contbr. chapters to books. Bd. dirs. Travis County MHMR Ctr., Austin, 1992—, Salvation Army, Austin, 1989—, Austin Symphony Soc., 1990—. Fellow: Tex. Acad. Sci., AAAS; mem.: Kiwanis (pres. 1984—86). Achievements include discovery of vocalization in a species of fish and a new species of freshwater fish parasite. Avocation: woodworking, reading, travel. Home: 1805 Astor Place Austin TX 78721

DEL COLLE, PAUL LAWRENCE, communications administrator, educator; b. Lynn, Mass., Dec. 16, 1950; s. Alfiero Luigi and Doris Claire (Rich) D.; m. Ellen Mary Ambrose, May 26, 1979 (div. 2001). BA, Holy Cross Coll., 1972; MS, Boston U., 1975; PhD, NYU, 1990. News dir. Sta. WGNG, Providence, 1972-73; writer, assoc. prodr. Boston U. Prodns., 1974-76; instr. comms. Iona Coll., New Rochelle, N.Y., 1976-80; asst. prof. comms. William Paterson Coll., Wayne, N.J., 1980-83, Marist Coll., Poughkeepsie, N.Y., 1983-90; pres., owner D.C. Media Cons., 1981-93; asst. prof. comms. Coll. of Mt. St. Vincent, Riverdale, N.Y., 1991-95; journalism lectr. NYU, 1995; sr. media analyst Forbes for Pres., Inc., 1995-96; media analyst John McLaughlin and Assocs., 1996-97; pres. sec. Yonkers (N.Y.) Pub. Schs., 1997-98; comm. project mgr. Integrated Supply Chain, IBM, Somers, N.Y., 1998-99; assoc., media rels exec. fin. rels. bd. BSMG Worldwide, 1999—. Judge news/documentary divsn. Emmy awards NATAS, 1988—; sr. media split. Bliss Gouverneur & Assocs., N.Y.C.; cons. in field. Writer TV show The Pennant Chase, 1988; writer, announcer (radio spots) Thanks to You, 1986, (video news releases) Positalker/Grand Union, 1982; writer (book review) Review of Broadcasting: An Introduction, 1981, Review of Writing News for Broadcast, 1981, (mag. article) Bicentennial Burger Boutique, 1975; contbg. book reviewer Bookscapes, 1994-96. Cons. United Way of Dutchess County, Poughkeepsie, 1984-92; vol. Mental Health Assn., 1983-97, Am. Heart Assn., Poughkeepsie, 1989—, Am. Diabetes Assn., 1998—. Recipient Scholarship Internat. Radio/TV Found., 1988, 90, 94, Grad. Assistantship Boston U., 1973-74; named Outstanding Young Men in Am., 1981; tchg. fellow Poynter Inst. for Media Studies, St. Petersburg, Fla., 1993. Roman Catholic. Avocations: gardening, baseball memorabilia. Home: 13 Oxford Rd # 1 Hastings On Hudson NY 10706 E-mail: paul@blisspr.com.

DE LEEUW, FRANK, economist; b. Amsterdam, The Netherlands, Sept. 18, 1930; arrived in US, 1935; s. Henry and Rachel (Souhami) de L.; m. Louise Wilbur Mason, 1952; children: David, Peter, Nicholas, Benjamin. BA, Harvard U., 1951, MPA, 1953, PhD, 1965. Asst. economist Fed. Res. Bank, San Francisco, 1953-56; economist, sect. chief Fed. Res. Bd., Washington, 1956-69; vis. prof. SUNY, Buffalo, 1968-68; sr. staff mem. Urban Inst., Washington, 1969-75; asst. dir. Congl. Budget Office, Washington, 1975-77; chief statistician Bur. Econ. Analysis U.S. Dept. Commerce, Washington, 1978-91; cons. IMF, 1991—2000. Lectr. Howard U., Washington, 1969-71; prof. Kiev (Ukraine)-Mohyla U., 1997. Author: Operating Costs in Public Housing, 1971, (with others) The Web of Urban Housing, 1975; contbr. articles to profl. jours. Mem. Am. Econ. Assn., Soc. Govt. Economists, Conf. on Rsch. in Income and Wealth (chmn. 1972-74). Home: 97 College Ave Poughkeepsie NY 12603

DELEHANT, RAYMOND LEONARD, botanist, educator; b. New Haven, June 30, 1937; s. John Patrick and Dorothy Barbara (Luft) D. BS, So. Conn. State U., 1959, MS, 1964; postgrad., U. Colo., 1965, U. Calif., Berkeley, 1966, U. Vt., 1967. Permanent cert. tchr., Conn. Instr. botany So. Conn. State U., New Haven, part-time 1964-71; sci. tchr. jr. high sch. Bd. Edn., North Haven, Conn., 1959-95, emeritus, 1995—. Cons. textbook program Rand McNally Co., 1974; sci. fameworks curriculum com. Conn. State Dept. Edn., 1995—; fellow Conn. Acad. Math., Sci. and Tech., 1996; project com. cons. Conn. Acad. Math., Sci. and Tech., Conn. Sci. Assessment Project, project mgr. Camp dir. nature sect. Boy Scouts Am., summers 1953, 57, 64, merit badge counselor Quinnipiac coun. New Haven, 1964-70; asst. ranger West Rock Nature Ctr., New Haven, 1956, 58; rep. Citizens Pk. Coun., New Haven, 1974-75; chmn. bd. trustees Park Oaks Sr. Comm. Assn., New Haven, 1964—; trustee St. John the Bapt. Parish, 2002--. NSF fellow 1966, 67; recipient Eagle Scout award, Boy Scouts Am., 1955. Mem. Nat. Sci. Tchrs. Assn. (mem. program com. 1999 conv.), Conn. Sci. Tchrs. Assn. (life; bd. dirs. 1964-67, treas. 1967-75, v.p. 1975-80, pres. 1980-84, 95-97, Conn. Sci. Educator Fellow award 2000, editor newsletter 1999—). Roman Catholic. Avocations: photography, hiking, camping, wood carving, home repairs. Home: 122 Dorrance St Hamden CT 06518-3342

DELENER, NEJDET, college dean, marketing and international business educator; b. Bursa, Turkey, Oct. 29, 1952; came to U.S., 1976; s. Mehmet and Fatma Delener; m. Nese Delener, July 21, 1978; children: Berent, Berker. Postgrad. diploma, Oxford (Eng.) Poly. Inst., 1976; MBA, NYU, 1978, advanced profl. cert., 1981; PhD, CUNY, 1987. Adj. lectr. Baruch Coll., CUNY,

N.Y.C., 1981-83; asst. prof. Hofstra U., Hempstead, N.Y., 1983-89; assoc. prof. St. John's U., Jamaica, N.Y., 1989-99, prof. mktg. and internat. bus., 1999—, assoc. dean acad. affairs, 1997—. Vis. lectr. Erasmus U., Rotterdam, The Netherlands, 1988; internat. mktg. cons. Ellington Duval Inc., N.Y.C., 1992—; strategy cons. Marriott Corp., N.Y.C., 1986-87. Author: Strategic Planning and Multinational Trading Blocs, 1999; editor: Ethics in International Marketing, 1995; contbr. articles to profl. jours. Excellence in Tchg. scholar, 1997; rsch. prof. Nat. Advt. Found., 1996; U.S. Dept. Edn. grantee, 1996-98. Fellow Beta Gamma Sigma; mem. Global Bus. and Tech. Assn. (founder, exec. pres. 1998—), Acad. Bus. Adminstrn. (v.p. 1992-96, Leadership award 1994), Am. Mktg. Assn., Acad. Mktg. Sci. (Rsch. award 1991), N.E. Bus. and Econs. Assn. (v.p. 1998—, Rsch. award 1994). Avocations: travel, theater, soccer, swimming. Office: St John's U Coll Bus Peter J Tobin Coll of Bus 8000 Utopia Pkwy Jamaica NY 11439-0001

DELEO, JAMES A. state legislator; b. Chgo., Aug. 10, 1951; m. Ann Filishio, 1991. Ed., Loop Jr. Coll., DePaul U. Real estate salesman; mem. from 16th dist. Ill. Ho. of Reps., 1985-92; mem. Ill. State Senate, 1993—. Mem. Joint Civic Com. Italian-Ams. Office: 6839 W Belmont Ave Chicago IL 60634-4646 also: Senator 10th Dist 323 Capitol Bldg Springfield IL 62706*

DE LEON, ANTONIO CARMELO, JR., internist, cardiologist; b. Manila, July 16, 1933; came to U.S., 1957; MD, U. Philippines, Manila, 1956. Diplomate Am. Bd. Internal Medicine, Am. Bd. Cardiovascular Diseases. Intern Philippines Gen. Hosp., Manila, 1955-56, resident in internal medicine, 1956-57; resident in cardiology Phila. Gen. Hosp., 1957-59; resident in medicine Georgetown Hosp., Washington, D.C., 1959-60, fellow in medicine, 1962-63; instr. in medicine Georgetown U., Washington, 1963-66, asst. prof. in medicine, 1966-72, assoc. prof. in medicine, 1972-77, prof. in medicine, 1977-82; clin. prof. medicine, chief cardiologist Coll. Medicine-Tulsa U. Okla., 1983—. Med. dir. Cardiovasc. Inst.; dir. continuing med. edn. St. John Med. Ctr., Tulsa. Fellow ACP, Am. Coll. Cardiologists, Am. Coll. Chest Physicians, Am. Heart Assn.; mem. Am. Coll. Physician Execs. Office: 1923 S Utica Ave Tulsa OK 74104-6520

DE LEON, LIDIA MARIA, magazine editor; b. Havana, Cuba, Sept. 10, 1937; d. Leon J. and Lydia (Diaz Cruz) de L. BA in Communications cum laude, U. Miami, Coral Gables, Fla., 1979. Staff writer Miami Herald, Fla., 1978-79; editorial asst. Halsey Pub. Co., Miami, 1980-81, assoc. editor, 1981, editor, 1981—, editor Delta Sky mag., 1983-95. Mem. Am. Soc. Mag. Editors, Am. Assn. Travel Editors, Golden Key, Sigma Delta Chi. Roman Catholic. Avocation: tennis. Office: 12550 Biscayne Blvd # 212 Miami FL 33181

DELEON, PATRICK HENRY, lawyer; b. Waterbury, Conn., Jan. 6, 1943; s. Patrick and Catherine (Dzubay) D.; m. Jean Louise Murphy; children: Patrick Daniel Nainoa, Katherine Malia Malie. BA, Amherst Coll., 1964; MS, Purdue U., 1966, PhD in Clin. Psychology, 1969; MPH, U. Hawaii, 1973; JD, Catholic U., 1980. Bar: Hawaii 1981, U.S. Dist. Ct. Hawaii 1983, U.S. Ct. Appeals (9th cir.) 1983; diplomate Am. Bd. Profl. Psychology, Am. Bd. Forensic Psychology. Tng. psychologist Peace Corps Tng. Ctr., Hilo, Hawaii, 1969-70; staff psychologist Diamond Head Mental Health Ctr., Hawaii State Hosp., Honolulu and Kaneohe, Hawaii, 1970-73; adminstrv. asst. U.S. Senator Daniel K. Inouye, Washington, 1973—. Fellow APA (pres. 2000, assoc. editor Am. Psychologist Jour. 1981—, editor Profl. Psychology Rsch. and Practice 1995-2000), Hawaii Psychol. Assn. (Disting. Svc. award 1981), Hawaii Bar Assn. Democrat. Home: 5701 Wilson Ln Bethesda MD 20817 Office: care Senator D K Inouye Us Senate Washington DC 20510-0001

DE LEON, SERGIO LEON, protective services official; b. Ft. Worth, Sept. 10, 1971; s. Sergio and Susana De Leon; m. Frances Granados, Apr. 27, 2002; 1 child, Alena Susana. Degree in Polit. Sci., Tex. Wesleyan U., 1998. Constable precinct 5 Tarrant County, Ft. Worth, 2001—. Cons. in field, Fort Worth, Tex., 1992—2000. Pres. Alamo Heights Neighborhood Assn., Ft. Worth, 1999; mem. Dem. Leadership Coun., Washington, 2002. Grantee, North Ctrl. Tex. Coun. Govts., 2003. Mem.: Lambda Kappa Kappa (life; v.p. 1997—98). Roman Catholic. Avocations: jogging, hunting, fishing, reading, weightlifting. Home: 4413 Geddes Ave Fort Worth TX 76107 Office: Precinct Five Constable's Office 300 W Belknap Fort Worth TX 76196 Home Fax: 817-884-3292; Office Fax: 817-884-3292. Personal E-mail: deleon1@hotmail.com. E-mail: sdeleon@tarrantcounty.com.

DE LEON, SYLVIA A. lawyer; b. Corpus Christi, Tex., Mar. 2, 1950; BA, Briarcliff Coll., 1972; JD, U. Tex., 1976. Bar: Tex. 1976, D.C. 1977. Ptnr. Akin, Gump, Strauss, Hauer & Feld LLP, Washington. Adj. prof. law Georgetown U. law ctr., 1988-90; bd. dirs. (pres. apptd. senate confirmed) Amtrak, Nat. Railroad Passenger Corp., 1994—, vice chmn. 2003-, chair corp. strategy com. Bd. trustees U. Tex. Law Sch. Found. 2002-, U. Tex. Law Assn., 1985-89, 92-96, 2000-03, U. Tex. Devel. Bd., 1996—, bd. dirs. Washington Ballet, 2001-; coord. issues transp. Clinton-Gore Presdl. Transition Team, 1992; presdl. appointee Nat. Commn. Ensure Strong Competitive Airline Industry, 1993, White House Conf. on Travel and Tourism. Mem. Bar Assn. D.C., State Bar Tex. (chmn. fed. law and regulations com. 1984-87), Nat. Civil Aviation Rev. Commn. Office: Akin Gump Strauss Hauer & Feld Ste 400 1333 New Hampshire Ave NW Washington DC 20036-1564

DE LEONARDIS, NICHOLAS JOHN, bank executive, financial lecturer, educator; b. Chgo., Nov. 13, 1929; s. John and Marie (Janik) De L.; m. Mary Ellen Kloss, Aug. 17, 1957; children: Deborah Marie, Valerie Ann, Nicolette Mary, Regina Ellen, John Paul. BS, De Paul U., 1951, MA, 1968. Salesman Asher J. Goldfine & Co., Chgo., 1953-55; mem. trust dept. staff First Nat. Bank, Chgo., 1955-63, with mcpl. sales dept., 1963-78, v.p. Money Market Ctr., 1978-80, v.p., chmn. money market com., 1980-85; sr. v.p., treas. La Salle Nat. Bank, subs. Algemene Bank Nederland, N.V., 1985-90; sr. v.p., chmn. asset and liability com. La Salle Nat. Corp.; exec. in residence dept. fin. De Paul U., Chgo., 1990—, lectr., 1968-78, dir. DePaul-People's Republic of China Project, 1990-95. Lectr. MBA program De Paul, Hong Kong, 1997—2000; guest lectr. bankers' seminars, 1992—99; grad. sch. banking U. Wis., Madison, 1980—87; mem. Gov.'s task force on Future of Mental Health in Ill., 1986—87; cons. to Polish bankers, Warsaw, 1993—99; mem. com. specialist assignment and evaluation Chgo. Stock Exch., 1993—2003; commn. rev. state's mental health code, 1988; adv. com. devel. disabilities Ill. Dept. Mental Health and Devel. Disabilities, 1993—2000. Contbr. articles to profl. publs. Trustee, past chmn. Found. Hearing and Speech Rehab., Chgo., 1968-92; pres. Dixon (Ill.) Assn. Retarded Citizens, 1984-2003. With USMC, 1952—53, Korean War. Mem. Union League Chgo., Heidelberg Club Internat., Delta Mu Delta, Beta Gamma Sigma.

DELERAY, ARTHUR LOYD, chemist, educator; b. Sonora, Calif., June 27, 1936; s. Dudley Early and Alta Loyd Deleray; children: Mark Arthur, Michael Howard. BSChemE, U. Calif., Berkeley, 1959; MA, MS in Engring., Princeton U., 1962, PhD in Chem. Engring., 1966. Sr. staff scientist MB Assocs., San Ramon, Calif., 1964—70; prof. Chabot Coll., Hayward, Calif., 1970—76, Livermore, Calif., 1976—88, Las Positas Coll., Livermore, Calif., 1988—. Cons. solar energy, Livermore, 1978—; pres. acad. senate Chabot Coll., Livermore, 1987—89, Las Positas Coll., Livermore, 1991—92. Mem.: Sigma Xi. Achievements include patents in field. Avocations: skiing, tennis, hiking, reading. Home: 274 Sierra Dr Walnut Creek CA 94596-4850 Office: Las Positas Coll 3033 Collier Canyon Rd Livermore CA 94551 Business E-Mail: adeleray@clpccd.cc.ca.us.

DE LERNO, MANUEL JOSEPH, electrical engineer; b. Jan. 8, 1922; s. Joseph Salvador and Elizabeth Mabry (Jordan) De L.; m. Margery Ellen Eaton, Nov. 30, 1946 (div. Oct. 1978); children: Diane, Douglas. BEE, Tulane U., 1941; MEE, Rensselaer Poly. Inst., 1943. Registered profl. engr., Ill., Mass. Devel. engr. indsl. control dept. Gen. Electric Co., Schenectady, N.Y., 1941-44; design engr. Lexington Electric Products Co., Newark, N.J., 1946-47; asst. prof. elec. engring. Newark Coll. Engring., 1948-49; test engr. Maschinenfabrik Oerlikon, Zurich, Switzerland, 1947-48; application engr. Henry J. Kaufman Co., Chgo., 1949-55; pres. Del Equipment Co., Chgo., 1955-60; v.p. Del-Ray Co., Chgo., 1960-67; pres. S-P-D Svcs. Inc., Forest Park, Ill., 1967-81, S-P-D Industries, Inc., Berwyn, Ill., 1981—2001, S-P-D Inc., Schaumburg, Ill., 2001—. Mem. standards making coms. Nat. Fire Protection Assn. Internat. Lt. (j.g.) USNR, 1944-45. Fellow Soc. Fire Protection Engrs.; mem. IEEE (sr. life), Ill. Soc. Profl. Engrs., Am. Water Works Assn. Home: 36w760 Stonebridge Ln Saint Charles IL 60175-4931 Office: 1161 Tower Rd Schaumburg IL 60173 E-mail: manny@spdinc.com.

DELERY, FERDINAND JOSEPH, III, aerospace transportation executive; b. New Orleans, Dec. 27, 1949; s. Ferdinand Joseph Delery, Jr. and Marie Cates Delery; m. Aida Valeria Alexander, July 21, 1978 (div. Nov. 17, 1983); children: Kiana Marie, Dominique Inez, Tiopol O'Neillia. BA in Polit. Sci., Journalism, U. New Orleans, 1971. Reporter New Orleans States-Item, 1969—71; city hall reporter Daily Record Newspaper, New Orleans, 1971—73; reporter WWL-TV, New Orleans, 1973—74; soc. editor La. Weekly Newspaper, New Orleans, 1974—75; media dir. Orleans Parish Prison, New Orleans, 1975—79; thermal protection sys. Lockheed Martin Aerospace, New Orleans, 1980—, safety coord., 1980—. Author: I Have A Dream, How To Drive 'Em Crazy; editor (pub.): (newsletter) Delery Gazette, 1986—. Team leader Rep. Nat. Com., New Orleans, 1997—2003. Scholar Herbert Lehman Fund scholar, La. State U., 1971. Mem.: Writers Club Press. Roman Catholic. Home: 2655 Lavender St New Orleans LA 70122 Office: Delery Gazette PO Box 26862 New Orleans LA 70186-6862 Personal E-mail: fdelery@bellsouth.net. E-mail: fdelery@bellsouth.net.

DELEUZE, MARGARITA, artist; b. Caracas, Miranda, Venezuela, May 11, 1943; arrived in US, 1982, naturalized, 1992; d. Ivor Hauck and Margarita Schnell; m. Felipe Silén, July 3, 1964 (div. Nov. 1982); children: Anabella, Margarita; m. Eric Charles Deleuze, Nov. 12, 1988. AAS, Bennett Coll., 1962. Recipient Arts awards Venezuelan VAAUW, Caracas, 1971, 72, San Francisco Mus. Contemporary Hispanic Art award, 1998, Premio Nosotros award, ALAS, Miami, 2000, Artistic Achievement award Five Part Nat. Juried Competition, Artscape Naples, Fla.; named Dressage Nat. Champion, Venezuelan Riding Fedn., Caracas, 1972, 73, 74, 75. Mem. World Wildlife Fund, Nat. Audubon Soc., Humane Soc. Broward County, Defenders Wildlife, Cousteau Soc., Nat. Mus. Women in Arts. Avocations: photography, gardening, traveling, music, gourmet cooking. Home: 2698 Cypress Ln Weston FL 33332-3423 Studio: MD Fine Arts Studio 2698 Cypress Ln Weston FL 33332-3423 E-mail: margarita@deleuze.com.

DELFINO, JOSEPH JOHN, environmental engineering sciences educator; b. Port Chester, N.Y., 1941; s. John J. and Frances C. Delfino; m. Dorothy Delfino; children: Janelle, Justin. BS in Chemistry, Holy Cross Coll., 1963; MS in Chemistry, U. Idaho, 1965; PhD in Civil and Environ. Engring. & Water Chemistry, U. Wis., 1968. From instr. to assoc. prof. chemistry USAF Acad., Colorado Springs, Colo., 1968-72; sect. head, tech. mgr. IBT & Nalco Environ. Sci., Northbrook, Ill., 1972-74; sect. head environ. scis. Wis. State Lab. Hygiene, Madison, 1974-82; from asst. prof. to assoc. prof. U. Wis., Madison, 1974-80, assoc. dir. water resources ctr., 1977-78, prof. civil and environ. engring., 1980-82; prof. environ. engring. sci. U. Fla., Gainesville, 1982—, affiliate prof. chemistry, 1990—, chmn. dept. environ. engring. sci., 1990—99, interim chmn., 2002—03, affiliate prof. natural resources and environment, 1994—, interim dir. Ctr. for Wetlands and Water Resources, 1995. Adv. bd. Fla. State U. Sys. Ctr. for Solid and Hazardous Waste Mgmt., 1996-99, 2002—, Ctr. Environ. Studies, 1996-99; bd. dirs. Univ. Athletic Assn., Inc.; adj. faculty U. Colo., Colorado Springs, 1969-71, Ill. Inst. Tech., Chgo., 1973; com. on tech. World Fedn. Engring. Orgns., v.p. N.Am. 1999-2002. Writer, co-originator, chief tech. advisor documentary Fla. Water Story, Sta. WEDU-TV, Tampa, Fla.; contbr. articles on water chemistry, environ. scis. and engring. to profl. publs. Mem. Citizens Environ. Quality Coun., Northbrook, Ill., 1972-74; mem. Mercury Tech. Adv. Com., State of Fla., 1991-93; mem. Alachua County Air Quality Commn., Fla., 1999; mem. T.M.D.L. tech. adv. com. Fla. Dept. Environ. Protection, 1999-2000. Capt. USAF, 1968-72. Recipient Pub. Svc. award Univs. Coun. on Water Resources, 1990. Fellow AAAS; mem. Am. Chem. Soc. (exec. com. environ. chem. divsn. 1973-76, editor Envirofacs environ. chem. divsn. 1973-76, student awards com. environ. chem. divsn. 1995-97, com. on environ. improvement 1998-2001, Cert. of Merit environ. chem. divsn. 1991), Am. Soc. Civil Engring., Nat. Assn. State U. and Land Grant Colls. (ecology sect., exec. com. 1998-2001), Assn. Environ. Engrs. and Sci. Profs. Office: U Fla Dept Environ Engring Scis PO Box 116450 310 Black Hall Gainesville FL 32611-6450

DEL FOSSE, CLAUDE MARIE, aerospace software executive; b. Paris, June 27, 1940; came to the U.S., 1963; s. Guy and Gabrielle (Bouyges) D.F.; m. Genevieve Juliette Des Devises, Dec. 23, 1971; children: Laurent Fabrice, Olivier Andre, Oriane Gabrielle. Diploma in Engring. Ecole Nat. Supérieure, d'Arts et Métiers, Paris, 1963; MS, Calif. Inst. Tech., 1964; MBA, U. Paris, 1966. Software engr. Soc. d'Info. Appliquée, Paris, 1964-67, Control Data Corp., L.A., 1968-69; sr. tech. staff CACI, Inc., L.A., Washington, 1969-78, v.p., div. mgr. Washington, 1979-84; cons., chief scientist Bite, Inc., Washington, 1984-86; mgr. program devel. Software Productivity Consortium, Reston, Va., 1986-89, v.p. tech. transfer Herndon, Va., 1989-95, v.p. mem. programs, 1995—. Bd. dirs. Winter Simulation Conf., 1979-82, gen. chmn., 1981. Bd. dirs. Lincolnia Park Recreational Club, Alexandria, Va., 1981, 82, 88; bd. dirs. Shenandoah Ridge Owners Assn., Wintergreen, Va., 1996-98, 99-2001, pres., 1998-2001. NATO fellow, 1964, Fulbright fellow, 1964. Mem. AFCEA, AIAA, Tech. Transfer Soc. Avocations: tennis, skiing. Home: 5229 Chippewa Pl Alexandria VA 22312-2023 E-mail: claude@delfosse.com.

DELFS, ANDREAS, conductor, musical director; b. Flensburg, Germany; Grad., Hamburg Conservatory, 1981; MA, Juilliard Sch., 1984. Staff conductor Lüneburg Stadttheater; music dir. Hamburg U. Orch.; musical asst. Hamburg State Opera; guest conductor Bremen State Theater, 1981; dir. Pitts. Youth Symphony; resident conductor Pitts. Symphony, 1986-90; music dir. Orch. Suisse Jeunes, 1984-95, Bern Opera, 1991-94; conductor N.Y. City Opera, 1995-96; music dir. Milw. Symphony Orch., 1997—; gen. music dir. Hannover State Opera and Orch. Guest condr. Phila. Orch. at Carnegie Hall, 1998, London Philharm., 1997, Dallas Symphony Orch., 1997, Houston Symphony, 1996—98, Junge Deutsche Philharmonic, Germany, 1995—98, Bern Symphony Orch., Minn. Orch., Detroit Symphony, Rochester Philharm. Bruno Walter scholar, Juilliard Sch., Steinburg fellow, Pitts. Symphony. Office: Milw Symph Orch 330 E Kilbourn Ave Ste 900 Milwaukee WI 53202-3141*

DELGADO, CLARA S. English language education specialist; b. Dayton, Ohio, Sept. 26, 1952; d. Paul and Jo Ellen (Wilson) Liesenhoff; m. Raúl Escalón, Sept. 18, 1977 (div. Sept. 1988); 1 child, Tania; m. Máximo Delgado, Feb. 23, 1990; stepchildren: Max Brian, Bridget Patricia. Degree in Spanish lit., U. Valencia, Spain, 1972-74; BA, Murray State U., 1974; MA, Wright State U., 1984. Instr. Global Sch. of Idioms, Valencia, 1972-74; instr., interim dir. ESL program Miami U., Greenville, Ohio, 1974-77; instr. English Inst., Reynosa, Mexico, 1978; outreach worker La Raza Unida, Dayton, 1979; instr., acting dir. The English Lang. and Multicultural Inst., Dayton, 1982-86, dir., 1986—. Cons. to member schs. Southwestern Ohio Coun. Higher Edn., Dayton, 1985—; cons., presenter Ohio Pub. Sch. Systems, 1985—; cons. Dayton ESL Providers, 1985—; presenter numerous cross-cultural, communication and management workshops and seminars, 1984—. Author: (book and cassette program) Speaking American English, 1985 (Program of Yr. award 1986), Hispanics in the U.S.A., 1991, (CD-ROM) Speak Fluent American English, 2000, (test and classroom materials) Ohio Language Assessment for Non-Native Speakers, 2002. Founder, vol. instr. Spanish/English GED (Gen. Edn. Devel.) Program, Dayton, 1979-84; founding mem., vol. Project READ (Reading Edn. for Adults in Dayton), 1988—; founding dir. La Casa del Pueblo, Dayton, 1975-78; vol. emergency translator Vol. Bank/Dayton Cts., 1982—. Named one of Top 10 Women in Greater Dayton Area, Dayton Daily News, 1992. Mem. NAFE, Nat. Assn. Fgn. Student Affairs, Bus. and Profl. Women, Tchrs. of English to Speakers of Other Langs., Assn. Ind. Colls. and Schs. (cons./evaluator 1989—), Dayton Coun. World Affairs, Nat. Image. Avocations: aerobics, creative writing, reading. Office: English Lang and Multi- Cultural Inst 300 College Park Ave Rm 117 Dayton OH 45469-0001

DELGADO, DWIGHD D(UBIED), company executive; b. Mayaguez, P.R., June 5, 1950; s. Ramon T. Delgado-Murphy and Rosalina (Ortiz) Delgado; m. Laurel Lee Waters, Feb. 1986; stepchildren: Jennifer Leigh, Sarah Noel. B in Inds. and Sys. Engring., Ga. Inst. Tech., 1977; M in Engring. Mgmt., George Washington U., 1997. Specialist in materials and prodn. control Lighting Bus. Group, Gen. Electric Co., Cleve., 1977-81, prodn. engr. incandescent lamps, 1979-81, mgr. shop ops. Halogen unit, 1981-83, mgr. shop ops. splty. unit, 1983-84; mgr. spl. projects GE Ceramics, Gen. Electric Co., Pepper Pike, Ohio, 1984; ops. mgr. ECOM de Mex., SA de CV (Gen. Electric Tech. Svcs. Co.), Ciudad Juarez, Chihuahua, Mex., 1984-86; mgr. new processes and equipment programs prodn. divsn. GE Lighting, Gen. Electric Co., 1987, sr. project mgr. tech. divsn., 1987-88, resident engring. mgr., 1989-91, tech. leader, 1990-91; dir. fabrication Fusion Sys. Corp., Rockville, Md., 1991-94, dir. mfg., 1994-96, Fusion UV Sys., Spectris, plc, Gaithersburg, Md., 1996-99, v.p. mfg., 2001—03, v.p. ops., 2003—. Founder, sole mem. Strategic Ops. Solutions, LLC, 2000—; pres., bd. dirs. Strategic Path and Engring., Inc., 2001—. Mem. U.S. Chess Fedn. Mem. Am. Inst. Indsl. Engrs. (sr.; bd. dirs. 1980-83, v.p. student and external affairs 1983-84, pres.-elect 1984-85, Chpt. Devel. Excellence award 1980), Am. Soc. for Quality Control (sr.; cert. quality engr. 1986), Aircraft Owners and Pilots Assn. (pvt. pilot lic. 1998), AirLifeLine, Sports Car Club Am. (autocross, pit crew), U.S. Sailing Club (basic keelboat cert., basic cruising cert., bareboat cruising cert.). Roman Catholic. Avocations: flying, sailing, auto racing, chess. Home: 9443 Hickory View Pl Gaithersburg MD 20886-1409 E-mail: dwighd@aol.com., ddelgado@fusionuv.com.

DELGADO, JANE, health executive, writer; b. Havana, Cuba, June 17, 1953; d. Juan Lorenzo Delgado Borges and Lucila Aurora Navarro Delgado; m. Mark A. Steo, May 15, 1999; 1 child, Elizabeth A. Steo. BA, SUNY, New Paltz, 1973; MA, NYU, 1975; MS, W. Averell Harrimann Sch., 1981; PhD in Clin. Psychology, SUNY, Stony Brook, 1981. Children's talent coord. Children's TV Workshop, 1973-75; rsch. asst. SUNY, Stony Brook, 1975-79; social sci. analyst U.S. Dept. Health and Human Svcs., 1979-83, health policy advisor, 1983-85; pres., CEO Nat. Alliance for Hispanic Health, 1985—; pvt. practice in psychology, 1979—. Bd. dirs. Nat. Health Coun., 1986—97, Carter Ctr. Mental Health Taskforce, 1991—2000, Patient Safety Inst., 2001—; trustee The Kresge Found, 1997—, Found. Child Devel., 1989—97. Author: Salud! A Latina's Guide to Total Health, 1997, 2d edit., 2002. W.K. Kellogg Found. Nat. fellow, 1988, NIMH fellow, 1975-79; recipient Surgeon Gen.'s award, 1992; recipient Health & Sci. Latina Excellence award, 1995; named SUNY Alumna of Yr., 1993 Mem. Hispanics in Philanthropy (bd. dirs. 1997-2000). Office: Nat Alliance for Hispanic Health 1501 16th St NW Washington DC 20036-1401

DELGADO, JORGE A. soil scientist; b. Bayamon, P.R.; s. Juan Delgado and Luz Delia Colon; m. Ida M. De Leon, Dec. 28, 1983; children: Jorge A. Jr., Ana Maria, Maria Alejandra, Maria Del Pilar. BS, U. P.R., Mayaguez, 1982; MS, La. State U., 1984, PhD, 1987. Cert. profl. soil scientist Am. Soc. Agronomy /Soil Sci. Soc. Am., 2000, profl. agronomist Am. Soc. Agronomy/Soil Sci. Soc. Am., 2000, profl. crop scientist Am. Soc. Agronomy/Soil Sci. Soc. Am., 2000. Scientist Ctr. for Energy and Environ. Rsch., U. P.R., Rio Piedras, 1987—89; natural sci. prof. Interamerican U., Bayamon, 1988—91; advisor Dept. Agr. P.R., San Juan, 1989—92; soil scientist USDA-Agrl. Rsch. Svc., Ft. Collins, Colo., 1992—. Faculty affiliate soil and crop scis. Colo. State U., Ft. Collins, 1996—. Editor: (spl. issue) Nutrient Mgmtm. in the USA: Jour. Soil Water Conservation, Jour. Comms. Soil Sci. Plant Analysis; contbr. articles to profl. jours. Mem.: Soil Sci. Soc. Am., Am. Soc. Agronomy, Soil and Water Conservation Soc. (pres. publ. bd. Jour. Soil Water Conservation 2001—, chair elect divsn. S-06, rsch. editor Jour. Soil Water Conservation 2001—03, Cert. of appreciation for outstanding svc. to the publ. bd. 2002, chpt. commendation 2002, Presdl. citation 2000, 2002), Sigma Xi, Gamma Sigma Delta. Office: USDA-Agrl Rsch Svc Fed Bldg PO Box E 301 S Howes Fort Collins CO 80522 Office Fax: 970-490-8213. E-mail: jdelgado@lamar.colostate.edu.

DELGADO, ORLANDO, import company executive; b. Miami, Fla., May 12, 1968; s. Enrique Antonio and Maria Luisa D.; m. Lourdes Maria Buigas, May 6, 1995; children: Orlando Delgado Jr., Alexis Michele. AA, Miami Dade Cmty. Coll., Miami, 1988; BS, Barry Univ., 1990. Sr. acct. coord. South Fla. Export, Miami, 1987-91; sr. acct. mgr. Tire Kingdom, Coral Springs, Fla., 1991-92; transport dir. Sugarman Assocs., Miami, 1992-93; supr. export ops. & logistics Coulter Corp., Miami, 1993-96; dir. regional export & logistics Honeywell Inc. Latin Am. Divsn., Sunrise, Fla., 1996—. Mem. S. Fla. Roundtable Coun. of Logistics Mgmt. Republican. Roman Catholic. Avocations: golf, fishing, parenting. Office: Honeywell Inc Latin Am Divsn Ste 420 480 Sawgrass Corporate Pkwy # 200 Sunrise FL 33325-6235

DELGADO, RAMON LOUIS, educator, author, director, playwright, lyricist; b. Dec. 16, 1937; s. Eloy Vincent and Hildegard (Chapman) D. BA, Stetson U., 1959; MA, Baylor U., 1960; MFA, YAle U., 1967; PhD, So. Ill. U., 1976. Tchr. Lyman H.S., Longwood, Fla., 1960-62; mem. faculty Chipola Jr. Coll., Marianna, Fla., 1962-64, Ky. Wesleyan Coll., 1967-72, Hardin-Simmons U., 1972-74, So. Ill. U., 1974-76, St. Cloud (Minn.) State U., 1976-78; prof. speech and theater Montclair State U., Upper Montclair, NJ, 1978—2003. Evaluator N.J. Teen Arts Festival, 1980, 81; judge Am. Theatre Assn. Coll. Theater Festival, 1980, 82, 83, 84, 85, N.J. Teen Galaxy Competition, 1984. Playwright: Waiting for the Bus, 1968, Once Below a Lighthouse, 1972, The Jerusalem Thorn, 1979, A Little Holy Water, 1983, Stones, 1983, The Flight of the Dodo, 1990, Remembering Booth, 1997, The Iron Corset, 1999, Consider the Phoenix, 2000; editor: The Best Short Plays, 1981-89; author: Acting with Both Sides of Your Brain, 1986; contbr. articles to profl. jours. Sec. Forest St. Manor Condo Assn., 1997-99; bd. dirs. 12 Miles West Theatre, 2000-2002. Recipient Samuel French Play award, 1966, U. Mo. Play award, 1971, 75, playwriting awards Am. Coll. Theatre Festival, 1976, 77, 78, Grand prize Music City Song Festival contest, 1988, 7 hon. mentions, 1989; Midwest Profl. Playwrights fellow, 1978; Ford Found. grantee, 1961; playwright-in-residence INTAR, 1980 Mem. Dramatists Guild, Assn. for Theatre in Higher Edn., Nat. Theatre Conf., Theta Alpha Phi, Phi Kappa Phi. Democrat. Home: 16 Forest St Apt 107 Montclair NJ 07042-3519

DELGADO BARRIO, FRANCISCO JAVIER, president supreme court of Spain; Pres. Tribunal Supremeo, Madrid, 1996—. Office: Tribunal Supremo Plaza de la Villa de Paris 28004 Madrid Spain Fax: 341-319-4767.

DEL GIUDICE, LEON LOUIS, auctioneer; b. Rome, Sept. 24, 1917; s. Cassiodoro and Francesca (Giovannucci) Del G.; m. Frankye L. Van Swearingen, Oct. 3, 1948. BS, BA, Trinity Coll., Hartford, Conn., 1938. Chemist, metallurgist Union Drawn Steel Corp., Hartford - East Hartford, Conn., 1938-43; owner Chop House Restaurant, Hartford, 1943-45; chief metallurgist Republic Steel Corp., East Hartford, 1945-46; owner, appraiser, auctioneer Plus Del's Studios, Wethersfield, Conn., 1948—. With U.S. Army, 1946-48. Mem. Masons (master, 32 deg.). Methodist. Avocations: art, lecturing, teaching, restoring. Home and Office: 144 Avery Hts Hartford CT 06106-4264

DEL GIUDICE, LUISA, folklorist, ethnologist, historical institution administrator, educator; b. Terracina, Latina, Italy, July 30, 1956; d. Alberto Del Giudice and Liliana Caracuzzo; m. Edward Fowler Tuttle; children: Elena Tuttle, Giulia Tuttle. PhD, UCLA, 1987. Dir. Italian Oral History Inst., L.A., 1994—2002. Vis. prof. UCLA, 1995—2001. Editor: (book) Studies in Italian American Folklore, 1993 (Fulbright fellow, 1992), Imagined States: National Identity, Utopia and Longing in Oral Cultures, 2001; author: Cecilia: Testi e contesti di un canto narrativo tradizionale, 1995; editor: (anthology) Italian Traditional Song, 1989, (book) Western Gerusalem: University of California Studies on Tasso, 1984. Fellow: Ctr. for Medieval & Renaissance Studies, UCLA (assoc.); mem.: Am. Folklore Soc., Folklore Studies Assn. Can., Slow Food Internat., Société Internationale d'Ethnologie et Folklore (exec. 2001—05), Kommission für Volksdichtung (pres. 2000—05). Episcopalian. Office: Italian Oral History Inst PO 241553 Los Angeles CA 90024-1553 Business E-Mail: luisadg@humnet.ucla.edu.

DEL GIZZO, SUZANNE, language educator; b. Summit, NJ, June 14, 1971; d. Giovanni del Gizzo and Robin Hall; m. Timothy W. McGraw, Dec. 12, 2000. BA, NYU, 1993; MA, U. Chgo., 1994; PhD, Tulane U., 2003. Lectr. Tulane U., New Orleans, 1997—2000, U. Md., College Park, 2000—, Georgetown U., Washington, 2002—. Author: Going Home: Hemingway, Primitivism and Identity, 2003; contbr. articles to profl. jours. Recipient Hemingway grant, JFK Libr., Boston, 1999; grantee, Tulane U., 1999. Mem.: MLA, Hemingway Soc. (Smith-Reynolds Founders fellow 2002), Modernist Studies Assn.

DEL GRECO, ALBERT LOUIS, JR., former football player; b. Providence, Mar. 2, 1962; m. Lisa, June 14, 1986; children: Erica, Trey, Derrick. BS in Bus. Transp., Auburn. Football player Greenbay Packers, 1984—87, Phoenix Cardinals, 1988—90, Houston Oilers, 1991—96; kicker Tennessee Titans, Nashville, 1997—2000; assist. coach Birmingham Steeldogs, 2002—. Participant recording NFL Anthem song for charity We're All in This Together, 1998. Active Make-A-Wish Found., Multiple Sclerosis Found. Named best golfer among athletes in other profl. sports Golf Mag., winner five NFL Cadillac Classics, 1993-96, 99; leads NFL in field goal percentage, 1995—. Office: Birmingham Jefferson Convention Complex 2100 Richard Arrington Jr Blvd N Birmingham AL 35203*

DEL GUERCIO, LOUIS RICHARD MAURICE, surgeon, educator, company executive; b. N.Y.C., Jan. 15, 1929; s. Louis and Hortense (Ardengo) Del G.; m. Paula Marie Helene de Vautibault, May 18, 1957; children: Louis, Francsca, Paul, Catherine, Maria, Michelle, Christopher, Anthony. BS, Fordham U., 1949; MD, Yale U., 1953. Diplomate: Am. Bd. Surgery, Am. Bd. Thoracic Surgery. Intern Columbia-Presbyn. Med. Center, N.Y.C., 1953-54; resident St Vincent's Hosp., N.Y.C., 1954-58, Cleve. City Hosp., 1958-60; practice medicine specializing in thoracic surgery, 1960—; mem. faculty Albert Einstein Coll. Medicine, N.Y.C., 1960-71, assoc. prof., 1966-70, prof. surgery, 1970-71, dir. Clin. Research Center-Acute, 1967-71; dir.; clin. prof. surgery N.J. Coll. Medicine, Newark, 1971-76; prof. surgery N.Y. Med. Coll., N.Y.C., 1976—, chmn. dept., 1976—2001, emeritus prof. surgery, 2001—; chief surgery Westchester County Med. Center, 1976—. Cons. surgeon other hosps.; mem. surg. study sect. NIH, 1970-74; mem. com. on shock NRC-Nat. Acad. Scis., 1969-71; mem. merit rev. bd. VA, 1971-74; mem. health care tech. study sect. Dept. HHS, 1980-84; cons. Nat. Ctr. Health Services Research, 1980-84; chmn. bd. dirs. Daltex Med. Scis., Inc. Author: (with B.G. Clarke) Urology, 1956, The Multilingual Manual for Medical History Taking, 1972, (with S.G. Hershey, R. McConn) Septic Shock in Man, 1971; editor-in-chief Critical Care Monitor, 1980-85, Complications in Surgery, 1990—; contbr. articles to med. jours.; patentee in field. With Mcht. Marine, 1946-47; with AUS, 1949-51; col. med. dept. USAR, 1990—. Recipient award in medicine Fordham U. Alumni Assn., 1974, Gold award Am. Acad. Pediats., 1973, Humanitarian award Boys' Towns of Italy, 1994; Am. Thoracic Soc. fellow, 1959-60; grantee Health Rsch. Coun. N.Y., 1965-71, NIH, 1962-71. Fellow ACS, Coll. of Critical Care Medicine; mem. Am. Trauma Soc. (founding mem.), Soc. Critical Care Medicine (founding mem., pres. 1976), Am. Surg. Assn., Am. Physiol. Soc., Soc. Univ. Surgeons, French Nat. Acad. of Surgery, Equestrian Order of Holy Sepulchre of Jerusalem. Home: 14 Pryer Ln Larchmont NY 10538-4021 Office: NY Med Coll Dept Surgery Valhalla NY 10595 *Adaptability and the determination of what is possible are the keys to personal success and contentment.*

DELHOMME, BEVERLY ANN, lawyer; b. New Orleans, Sept. 24, 1954; s. August Nevle and Shelby (Bourgeois) DelH.; m. Bertis Little. Cert. in radiologic tech., Charity Hosp. Sch., New Orleans, 1972-74; BS magna cum laude in Biology, William Carey Coll., 1980; JD, U. Houston, 1984. Bar: Tex. 1984, La. 1985, U.S. Dist. Ct. (no. dist.) Tex. 1985. X ray technician VA Hosp., New Orleans, 1974-79; assoc. Richard Martin PC, Dallas, La., 1985, Paul A. Lockman PC, Dallas, 1986-88; ptnr. DelHomme & Skrepnek (name now DelHomme & Assocs.), Dallas, 1986—, 1986—. Editor Houston Jour. Internat. Law, 1983-84. Vol. ARC, 1970-81. Prudential Life Ins. Health Law scholar U. Houston Law Ctr., 1983; recipient 10 Yrs. Svc. award ARC, Chalmette, La., 1980. Mem. ABA, Am. Trial Lawyers Assn., Tex. Trial Lawyers Assn., La. Bar Assn., Dallas Bar Assn., Dallas Trial Lawyers Assn. Episcopalian. Avocation: water skiing. Office: DelHomme & Assocs 415 Oakwood Tower 3626 N Hall St Dallas TX 75219-5107 E-mail: tjtnsly@aol.com.

DELI, ANNE TYNION, marketing executive; b. Milw., Apr. 18, 1956; m. Steven F. Deli; 2 children. BA in History and French, Georgetown U., 1978. Acct. exec. Dancer Fitzgerald Sample, N.Y.C., 1978-80; acct. supr. Grey Advt., N.Y.C., 1980-82; v.p. Wells Rich Greene, N.Y.C., 1982-84; sr. v.p. Lawrence Charles Free, N.Y.C., 1984-86; prin. Anspach Grossman Portugal, N.Y.C., 1986-88; sr. v.p. Siegel & Gale, N.Y.C., 1988-93; v.p., global mktg. Harley-Davidson, Inc., Milw., 1993-95; pres., founder North River Strategies, Milw./Chgo., 1995—2000; owner Orlando Harley-Davidson, 2000—. Dir. Milw. Zool. Soc.; bd. dirs. Chgo. Shakespeare Theatre, 2001—02, Orlando Mus. Art, 2002—. Republican. Avocations: world travel, decorative arts, golf. Office: 30 S Wacker Dr Ste 2318 Chicago IL 60606-7405

DELI, STEVEN FRANK, business investment and development executive; married; 1 child. BA in Econs., Northwestern U., 1973; MBA, Harvard U., 1977. Staff mem. comml. and real estate banking dept. Continental Ill. Nat. Bank, Chgo., 1973-75; investment banker Warburg Paribas Becker Inc., Chgo., 1977-84; mng. dir., head corp. fin. Dean Witter Reynolds, Inc., Chgo., 1984-92; founder, chmn., CEO Harley-Davidson Fin. Svcs., Inc., 1992-99; founder, chmn. Unicorn Fin. Svcs., Inc., 1997-2000; CEO H-D Am. Rd. LLC, Orlando, Fla., 2000—. Mem. fin. com. and gov. mem. Chgo. Symphony Orch.; mem. Chgo. Com. of the Chgo. Coun. on Fgn. Rels. and Mid-Am. Com.; past sr. warden, vestryman Christ Ch., Winnetka, Ill. Mem. Chgo. Club (past bd. dirs.), Econ. Club Chgo., Indian Hill Club, Commonwealth Club, Eldorado Country Club, Country Club of Orlando. also: 3770 37th St Orlando FL 32805 E-mail: stevendeli@aol.com.

D'ELIA, CHRISTOPHER FRANCIS, marine biologist, educator; b. Bridgeport, Conn., Aug. 7, 1946; s. Francis G. and Marian Frances (Wakeman) D'Elia; m. Jennifer Anne Hunnicutt, June 10, 1973; 1 child, Tallmadge Wakeman. AB, Middlebury Coll., 1968; PhD, U. Ga., 1974. Postdoctoral scholar UCLA, 1974; vis. asst. prof. U. So. Calif., L.A., 1975; Noyes postdoctoral fellow Woods Hole (Mass.) Oceanog. Inst., 1975-77; from asst. prof. to assoc. prof. Chesapeake Biol. Lab. U. Md., Solomons, 1977—88, prof., 1988-99, SUNY, Albany, 1999—, v.p. rsch., 1999—2002, prof. biology and pub. adminstrn. and policy, 2002—. Dir. biol. oceanography program NSF, Washington, 1987—89, mem. adv. panel ocean scis. divsn., 1982—84; dir. Md. Sea Grant Coll., 1989—98; mem. rsch. planning adv. group, priorities workgroup Chesapeake Bay Program, 1989—91, mem. sci. and tech. adv. com., 1993—98; cons. to govt. and industry, 1976—; regional rep. Coastal Resources Adv. Com. Md., 1982—83; mem. adv. com. Md. Sea Grant program, 1980—86; chmn. Mid-Atlantic Regional Marine Rsch. Bd., 1991—96; mem. sci. adv. bd. ecol. processes and effects com., marine monitoring com. EPA, 1991; mem. Leadership Md., 1997. Mem. editl. bd. Limnology and Oceanography, 1983—86; contbr. articles to profl. jours. Bd. dirs. Hudson River Found., 1998—; acad. adv. com. Indsl. Rsch. Inst., 2001—; bd. dirs. Great Lakes Consortium, 2000—. Grantee, ERDA, 1976, EPA, 1978—82, Dept. Energy, 1979, NOAA, 1989—98, NSF, 1979—; Disting. Patrick scholar, Acad. Natural Scis., 1982—83. Fellow: AAAS; mem.: Great Lakes Rsch. Consortium (bd. gov. 1999—), Indsl. Rsch. Inst. (mem. acad. advancment com. 2001—), Coun. Soc. Pres. (sec. 1993—96, treas. 1997, chmn.-elect 1998, chmn. 1999, past chmn. 2000), Coun. Sea Grant Dirs. (chmn.-elect, chmn. budget com. 1994), Sea Grant Assn. (pres. 1991—92, chmn. fed. rels. com. 1992—93, pres. 1999), N.Y. Acad. Sci., Nat. Assn. State Univs. and Land Grant Colls. (co-chmn. bd. dirs. 1994—95, coun. grad. rsch. and grad. edn. exec. com. 2000—01, bd. oceans and atmosphere, mem. exec. com., chmn. edn. com., chmn. spl. task force reorganization), Nat. Assn. Environ. Profs. (bd. dirs. Md. 1985—86), Internat. Soc. Reef Studies, Estuarine Rsch. Fedn. (v.p. 1989—91, pres. 1991—93, past pres. 1993—95), Ecol. Soc. Am. (chmn. pub. affairs com. 1989—91, vice chmn. 1991—92), Am. Soc. Limnology and Oceanography, Am. Chem. Soc., Cosmos Club, Sigma Xi. Avocations: sailing, skiing, private pilot. Office: SUNY Dept Biol Scis 1400 Washington Ave Albany NY 12222-0100 E-mail: cdelia@albany.edu.

DELIA, CLAUDE WILLIAM, retired physician, pathologist; b. Medford, Mass., July 24, 1924; s. T. P. and Rose (Daiute) D.; m. Jeanne Wetmore, Aug. 2, 1949 (dec. Sept. 2002); children: Nancy Ann Delia Minter, Deborah Delia Webster, Pamela Egan, Patricia J. Campbell. Student, Harvard U., 1946; MD, Yale U., 1950. Diplomate Am. Bd. Pathology. Dir. lab. Conway Hosp., S.C., 1960-97; ret., 1997. Mem. adv. bd. First Citizens Bank, Conway. Served U.S. Army, 1943—46, WWII, maj. U.S. Army, 1950—60, Korean Conflict. Fellow Coll. Am. Pathologists, Am. Soc. Clin. Pathologists; mem. AMA, Japanese-Am. Soc. Pathologists, S.C. Med. Assn., N.Y. Acad. Scis., Conway Hosp. Found. (mem. ethics com. 2001—). Republican. Avocations: reading, writing. Home: River Bend 407 Sasser Ln Conway SC 29527-7659

D'ELIA, NICHOLAS, secondary school educator; b. N.Y., Sept. 22, 1959; s. Mario John and Angela Rose (Puma) D'Elia; m. Carolyne Gilroy, Aug. 24, 1984; children: Nicole, Michael, Philip. *Father Mario D'Elia has been a pioneer in the field of dental prosthetics since 1953. Conducting his work at Memorial Sloan Kettering Hospital in New York City he has contributed to the recovery of countless cancer patients. Parents Mario and Angela D'Elia have celebrated 49 years of marriage. Wife Carolyne has continued her endeavors in finance and insurance.* BA, CUNY, 1981. V.p. prodn. Flying Tiger Comm., N.Y.C., 1981-84; prodr., dir. Merrill Lynch Video Network, N.Y.C., 1985-89; freelance dir. N.Y.C., 1980-90; prodr., dir. Rainbow TV Prodns., Inc., N.Y.C., 1990—94; tchr. Holy Name Sch., Bklyn., 1995—2001, New Utrecht HS, Bklyn., 2001—. Freelance dir. TV Generation, 1982 (U.S.A. Cable Video of the Week, 1983); freelance video engr. ABC Sports, 1981-85, ABC DayTime, N.Y.C. and remote locations, 1983-85, MacNeil-Lehrer News Hour, N.Y.C., 1983-85, CBS News, N.Y.C. and remote locations, 1983-84. *Production Assisting on motion pictures such as MY OLD MAN, 1979 (TV); SPLASH, 1983; WITHOUT A TRACE, 1983; CONCRETE BEAT, 1983 preceded a period of technical work in TV and video. Currently a Social Studies teacher, past TV experience is brought into the classroom, This includes coverage of the 1984 Reagan reelection campaign; the Stock Market Crash of 1987; the development and direction of three live weekly financial TV news shows for Merrill Lynch. Previously published in Video Magazine and most recently Cable in the Classroom Magazine (April 2001), authored article on the integration of TV and the Internet in the classroom.* Writer, producer (corp. mktg. tape) You Must Remember This..., 1989 (AVCA Bronze award, 1989). Mem. NATAS, Internat. TV Assn. Roman Catholic. Avocations: performing and fine arts, scuba diving, auto racing. Office: New Utrecht HS 1601 80th St Brooklyn NY 11214

DELIFORD, MYLAH EAGAN, mathematics educator; b. Chgo., Nov. 7, 1948; d. Charles L.G. Eagan and Shirley R. (Bennett) Lewis; m. Albert Deliford Jr., Nov. 27, 1971 (div. Dec. 1984). BS in Edn., Chgo. State U., 1969; MA in Math., Northea. U., 1977. Tchr. Chgo. Bd. Edn., 1969—. Mem. Math. Assn. Am., Nat. Coun. Tchrs. Math., Nat. Alliance Black Sch. Educators, Chgo. Elem. Tchrs. Math. Club, Met. Math. Club Chgo., Ill. Coun. Tchrs. Math., Benjamin Banneker Assn. Democrat. Roman Catholic. Home: 7467 N Ridge Blvd Chicago IL 60645-1902 Office: Dunbar Vocat Career Acad 3000 S King Dr Chicago IL 60616-3452 E-mail: mdeliford@enc.K12.il.us.

DELIGNE, PIERRE RENÉ, mathematician; b. Brussels, Oct. 3, 1944; s. Albert and Renée (Bodart) D.; m. Elena Vladimirovna Alexeeva, Sept. 9, 1980; children: Natalia, Alexis. Licence en mathématiques, ULB (Université Libre de Bruxelles), Brussel, 1966, PhD in Mathematics, 1968. Jr. scientist Fond National de la Recherche Scientifique Belgium, Brussel, 1967-68; vis. mem. Institut des Hautes Etudes Scientifiques, Bures sur Yvette, France, 1968-70; permanent mem. Inst. des Hautes Etudes Scientifiques, Bures sur Yvette, France, 1970-84; prof. Inst. for Advanced Study, Princeton, N.J., 1984. Editor Pub. Math. Institut des Hautes Etudes Scientifiques, 1970; contbr. articles to profl. jours. Recipient Fields medal Internat. Math. Union, 1978; Crafoord prize, 1988. Mem. Associé Etranger Academie des Sciences, AAAS (fgn. hon.), Royal Belgian Acad. Office: Inst for Advanced Study Sch Mathematics Einstein Dr Princeton NJ 08540 E-mail: deligne@math.ias.edu.

DELIMAN, ROBERT MICHAEL, surgeon; b. Braddock, Pa., Mar. 11, 1928; m. Renate Marie; children: Belle, Darwin, Michael. MD, George Washington U., 1953. Diplomate Am. Bd. Surgery. Intern Highland (Calif.) Alameda County Hosp., 1953-54; resident Kaiser Found. Hosp., Oakland, Calif., 1954-55, City Hope Med. Ctr., Duarte, Calif., 1958-59, Long Beach (Calif.) VA Hosp., 1959-62; surgeon So. Calif. Surg. Med. Group Inc., Arcadia, 1962-98. Surgeon Meth. Hosp., Arcadia, 1962-98, City Hope Med. Ctr., Duarte, Santa Teresita Hosp.(v.p. med. affairs, bd. dirs. 1995-99); pres. So. Calif. Physicians Coun.; former bd. dirs. L.A. County Found. Medical Care; former med. dir. Mid Valley Physicians, Greater Pacific HMO. Recipient commendation for exemplary record of civic leadership, Calif. Senate, 2001. Fellow ACS, Am. Coll. Physician Execs., Am. Coll. Angiology; mem. Soc. Clin. Vascular Surgery, L.A. Surg. Soc. Office: 324 W Walnut Ave Monrovia CA 91016-3346

DE LIO, ANTHONY PETER, lawyer; b. Bklyn., 1928; s. David V. and Margaret M. De L.; m. Marie DiTrani, 1952; children: Anthony P., Donna Marie Maistros, Lois Anne Cromwell. BS in Physics, Poly Inst. Bklyn., 1953; JD with honors, George Washington U., 1957. Bar: D.C. 1957, Conn. 1958, U.S. Dist. Ct. Conn. 1958. With patent dept. Bendix Corp., Washington, 1954-56; patent advisor U.S. Navy Dept., Washington, 1957; assoc. Blair & Spencer, Stamford, Conn., 1957-60; ptnr. Spencer, Rockwell & Bartholow, Stamford, 1960-62, Rockwell & De Lio, New Haven, 1962-64, De Lio & Montgomery, New Haven, 1964-81, De Lio and Libert, New Haven, 1981-84, De Lio & Assocs., New Haven, 1984-91, De Lio & Peterson, New Haven, 1991—. Lectr. in field. Contbr. articles to legal jours. Chmn. Hamden Planning and Zoning Commn., 1969-81; alt. commr. Hamden Zoning Bd. Appeals, 1981-85. Served with USMC, 1946-48. Mem. ABA, Am. Intellectual Property Law Assn., Conn. Intellectual Property Law Assn., Internat. Intellectual Property Law Assn., New Haven Country Club, Amity Club (New Haven), Alpha Phi Delta. Democrat. Roman Catholic. Office: 121 Whitney Ave New Haven CT 06510-1242 E-mail: delpet@delpet.com.

DE LISA, JOEL ALAN, rehabilitation physician, rehabilitation research executive; b. Seattle, Mar. 18, 1942; s. Joseph Phillip and Alice Georgia (Jensen) DeL.; m. Janet Hopper, July 25, 1971. BS in Zoology, Wash. State U., 1964; MD, U. Wash., 1968, MS, 1976. Diplomate Am. Bd. Phys. Medicine and Rehab. (chmn. 1993-98); diplomate spinal cord injury medicine. Intern St. Josephs Hosp., Phoenix, 1968-69; resident in phys. medicine and rehab. U. Wash., Seattle, 1972-75; med. dir., chief med. officer Kessler Inst. Rehab., West Orange, N.J., 1987-93; sr. v.p., chief med. officer Kessler Rehab. Corp., West Orange, 1994-2000; pres., CEO Kessler Med. Rehab. Rsch. and Edn. Corp., West Orange, 1998—. Prof., chmn. dept. phys. medicine and rehab. Univ. Medicine and Dentistry N.J., Newark, 1987—, interim dean, 2000; chmn. dept. phys. medicine and rehab. St. Barnabas Med. Ctr., Livingston, N.J., 1990-98; spkr. Taiwan Nat. U. Hosp., 1995, 23d ann. meeting Korea Acad. Rehab. Medicine, 1995. Author: Manual of Nerve Conduction Velocity and Clinical Neurophysiology, 1998, Principles and Practice of Rehabilitation Medicine, 1998; editor: Jour. Spinal Cord Medicine, 1999—. Mem. AMA, Assn. Acad. Physiatrists, Am. Acad. Phys. Medicine and Rehab., Am. Congress Rehab. Medicine, Am. Paraplegic Soc. (hon., pres. Jackson Heights chpt. 1989-91, Excellence award 1995). Office: Kessler Med Rehab Rsch and Edn Corp 1199 Pleasant Valley Way West Orange NJ 07052-1424

DE LISI, JOANNE, media consultant, educator; b. Bklyn. d. Louis Anthony and Maria Anna De Lisi. BA, Hunter Coll., 1972, MA, 1977; postgrad., NYU. Cert. tchr. N.Y. Asst. instr. Hunter Coll., N.Y.C., 1974-75; instr. NYU, N.Y.C., 1974-78; cons. communication N.Y.C., 1976—; instr. Bklyn. Coll., 1978-82, dir. forensics, 1981-82, asst. dir. acad. prep. program, 1980-82; adj. lectr. City U. Sys., N.Y.C., 1983-91. Profl. entertainer, 1953—75; faculty advisor Alpha Tau Omega, Bklyn. Coll., 1980—82. Contbr. articles to profl. jours., poems to anthologies, radio programs, newspapers. Mem. adv. bd. N.Y. State Senator Serphin Maltese. Recipient Nat. award of excellence, POW/MIA, Am. Legion Aux., 1995, Nat. award, USO and Savs. Bonds Jr. Activities Am. Legion Aux., 1996—98, Vets. Affairs, 1998—2000. Mem.: Metro N.Y. Database Internet Users Group, Fencers Am., Hunter Alumni Orgn., Am. Legion (pub. rels. officer Queens County 1991—93, treas. 1991—2001, v.p., girls state chmn. 1993—94, pub. rels. officer, newsletter editor, sec. Leonard unit 1993—94, pres. 1994—95, judge Forensics Tournament 1995—2003, del. N.Y. state Dept. Conv. 1995, nat. security chmn., jr. activity chmn., pub. rels. dir. 1996—98, pres. unit 104 1996, 10th dit. sgt-at-arms, sec., v.p. 2001—03), Kappa Delta Pi. Roman Catholic. Avocations: antique collector, travel, jewelry making, fencing dir. Office: Wyckoff Heights Sta PO Box 370029 Brooklyn NY 11237-0029

DE LISIO, STEPHEN SCOTT, lawyer, director, pastor; b. San Diego, Dec. 30, 1937; s. Anthony J. and Emma Irving (Cheney) DeL.; m. Margaret Irene Winter, June 26, 1964; children: Anthony W., Stephen Scott, Heather E. Student, Am. U., 1958-59; BA, Emory U., 1959; LLB, Albany Law Sch., 1962; LLM, Georgetown U., 1963. Bar: N.Y. 1963, D.C. 1963, Alaska 1964. Practice law, Fairbanks, Alaska, 1963-71, Anchorage, 1972-96; asst. dist. atty. Fairbanks, 1963-65; assoc. McNealy & Merdes, 1965-66; lectr. U. Alaska, 1965-67; ptnr. Staley, DeLisio & Cook, 1966-93, DeLisio, Moran, Geraghty & Zobel, Inc., 1994—2003. Bd. dirs. Woodstock Property Co., Inc., Pasit Inc., Challenger Films Inc.; vice chmn. Crosstown CBMC, 1986—87, chmn., 1987—88, 1990—91, area coord., 1987—92; city atty., Fairbanks, 1967—70, Barrow, 1969—72, Ft. Yukon and North Pole, 1970—72; past sec. U. Alaska Heating Corp., Inc.; past sec.-treas. Trans-Alaska Electronics, Inc., Baker Aviation, Inc.; former arbitrator, mem. Alaska regional coun. Am. Arbitration Assn. Author: (with others) Law and Tactics in Federal Criminal Cases, 1964. Past pres. Tanana Valley State Fair Assn.; past v.p. Fairbanks Mental Health Assn., Fairbanks United Good Neighbors Fund; bd. dirs. Anchorage Cmty. Chorus, 1975—77, Common Sense for Alaska, 1987—94, Alaska chpt. Lupus Found., 1989—96; chmn. bd. Alaska Voluntary Health Assn., 1993—96; former bd. dirs. Greater Fairbanks Cmty. Hosp. Found.; met. dir. Christian Businessmen's Outreach, 1993—94, bd. dirs. Anchorage, 1985—92; met. dir. Alaska Christian Businessmen's Com. U.S.A., 1994—2000; rep. precinct committeeman, 1970—76; chmn. Alaska Rep. Rules Com. Anchorage Rep. Com, 1973; v.p. We the People, 1977—79; vice chmn. Alaska Libertarian Party, 1983—84; mem. nat. com. Libertarian Party, 1982—85; deacon Anchorage Bible Fellowship, 1986—90, elder, pastor, 1990—; Alaska coord. Crown Ministries, 1991—93. Recipient Jaycee Disting. Service award, 1968 Mem. Am. Trial Lawyers Assn., Am. Judicature Soc., Alaska Bar Assn., D.C. Bar Assn., Anchorage Bar Assn., Spenard Bar Assn. (pres. 1975-77), U.S. Jaycees (past dir.), Alaska Jaycees (past pres.), Fairbanks Jaycees (past pres.), Chi Phi, Pi Sigma Phi, Woodstock Golf Inc. Club (pres. 1984—). Home: 5102 Shorecrest Dr Anchorage AK 99502-1329 Office: Anchorage Bible Fellowship 7348 Abbott Loop Rd Anchorage AK 99507 Office Fax: 907-522-9079. E-mail: cbmcak@alaska.net. *A well-defined sense of values and the courage and determination to adhere to it is as essential to a life of purpose and fulfillment, as the rising of the sun is to life on this planet. The challenge is to develop values that are as relevant to the changes of tomorrow as to the reality of the now and the past. The "situation ethics" approach is as disastrous as a smashed rudder on a storm tossed vessel. The Way, the Truth and the Life is found only in Christ Jesus.*

DELL, CHRISTOPHER WILLIAM, ambassador; b. June 1956; BA, Columbia Univ., 1978; MS, Oxford U., 1980. Various positions with U.S. Fgn. Svc.; dep. dir. Office of Regional Polit. Affairs, Bur. of European and Can. Affairs, 1994—96; dep. chief of mission U.S. Embassy, Sofia, Bulgaria, 1997—2000; chief of mission U.S. Office, Pristina, Kosovo, 2000—01; U.S. amb. to Angola, 2001—. Author: (novels) The Fork in the Road, 2001. Recipient Order of the Madara Horseman, First Degree, Rep. of Bulgaria, 2000, Kellett fellowship, Columbia U., 1978. Office: DOS Amb 2550 Luanda Pl Washington DC 20521*

DELL, MICHAEL JOHN, lawyer; b. N.Y.C., Aug. 18, 1954; Sidney Samuel and Ethel Rachel (Tannenholtz) D.; m. Lisa Ellen Rothschild, Aug. 24, 1980; children: Benjamin Reuben, Joshua Matthew, Rebecca Talia. BA, Oxford U., 1975; JD magna cum laude, Harvard U., 1978. Bar: N.Y. 1979, U.S. Dist. Ct. (no. so., ea., and we. dists.) N.Y., U.S. Ct. Appeals (2d, 3d, 7th, and 8th cirs.), U.S. Supreme Ct. Law clk. to judge Stanley A. Weigel U.S. Dist. Ct. Calif., San Francisco, 1978-79; assoc. Kramer, Levin, Nessen, Kamin & Frankel, N.Y.C., 1979-85, ptnr., 1986—. Editor and assoc. editorial dir. Harvard Law Rev., 1976-78. Mem. ABA, Bar Assn. of City of N.Y. Avocations: family, travel, swimming, writing. Office: Kramer Levin Naftalis & Frankel LLP 919 3rd Ave Rm 3803 New York NY 10022-3902 E-mail: mdell@kramerlevin.com.

DELL, MICHAEL S. computer company executive; b. Houston, Feb. 1965; s. Alexander and Lorraine D.; m. Susan Lieberman, Oct. 23, 1989. Student, U. Tex., 1983-84. Founder Dell Computer Corp. (formerly PC's Ltd.), Austin, 1984—, now chmn., CEO. Author: Direct From Dell: Strategies that Revolutionized an Industry, 1999. Recipient Entrepreneur of Yr. award Inc. Mag., 1990, Customer Satisfaction award JD Power, 1991, 93; named CEO of Yr. Fin. World Mag., 1993, Chief Exec. of Yr. Chief Exec. Mag., 2001, One of Top-Ten Most Powerful People in Bus. Forture Mag., 2003. Office: Dell Computer Corp 1 Dell Way Round Rock TX 78682-0001*

DELL, RALPH BISHOP, pediatrician, researcher; b. Mt. Village, Alaska, July 31, 1935; s. Elwin B. and Elizabeth B. (Bishop) D.; m. Kathryn M. Bownass, June 17, 1957 (div. Dec. 1982); children: Laura, Kenneth; m. Karen K. Hein, Aug. 28, 1983; stepchildren: Ethan Hein, Molly Hein. BA, Pomona Coll., 1957; MD, U. Pa., 1961. Diplomate Am. Bd. Pediatrics. Intern and resident Children's Hosp. Med. Ctr., Boston, 1961-63; NIH postdoctoral fellow Coll. Physicians and Surgeons, Columbia U., N.Y.C., 1963-66, assoc., 1966-67, asst. prof. pediatrics, 1967-72, assoc. prof., 1972-78, prof., 1978-97; Dir. Inst. for Lab. Animal Rsch., NRC, Washington, 1997-2000, ret., 2000. Author 3 books, 100 research papers; co-inventor amino acid solution. Recipient Research Career Devel award NIH, 1966-71, Career Scientist award Health Research Council N.Y., 1972-75; Fogarty Sr. Internat. fellow NIH, 1975-76. Mem. Am. Pediat. Soc., Am. Physiologic Soc., Am. Soc. Clin. Investigation, Soc. for Pediat. Rsch., Assn. for Computing Machinery, Am. Assn. Accreditation Lab. Animal Care (coun. on accreditation). Democrat. Home: PO Box 607 Jacksonville VT 05342 E-mail: rbdelle@direcwag.com.

DELL, ROBERT CHRISTOPHER, geothermal sculptor, scenic artist; b. Nyack, N.Y., Feb. 22, 1950; s. Edward John and Laurel Jean (McGrath) D.; children: Robert Carroll, Malcolm Vincent, Terrence Edwardl; m. Siena Gillan Porta, May 30, 1986. BS in Edn., SUNY, Oneonta, 1972; MFA in Sculpture, SUNY, New Paltz, 1975. Mem. arch. and cmty. appearance bd. rev. Orangetown, N.Y., 1979-2001, vice-chmn., 1987—, mem. planning bd., 2001—; dir. visual arts Vriesland W. Hudson Art Ctr., Pearl River, N.Y., 1978-80, artist-in-residence, 1980; guest spkr. Cooper Union, N.Y.C., 1994, MIT, 1994, 97, Harvard U., 1995, Nassau C. C., 1999, Akureyri Art Mus., 1999, Ireland Art Acad., 2001; rsch. fellow Ctr. Advanced Visual Studies MIT, 1993-95, rsch. affil., 1995-97; vis. artist Akureyri Sch. Visual Art, 1999. Solo shows include Vorpal Gallery, Chgo., 1978, N.Y.C., 1981, 88, San Francisco, 1985, New Acquisitions Gallery, Syracuse, 1983, Blue Hill Cultural Ctr., Pearl River, N.Y., 1987, 98-99, Am. Cultural Ctr., Reykjavik, Iceland, 1988, geothermal sculpture installation, Krisuvik, Iceland, 1988, Mid-Hudson Arts and Sci. Ctr., Poughkeepsie, N.Y., 1992, Castle and Old Faithful, Grotto Geyser Groups Yellowstone Nat. Park, Wyo., 1996, Reykjavik Art Mus. Harbour House, 2001, Akureyri Art Mus., Iceland, 1999, Geysir, Haukadal, Iceland, 1999, Kresge Oval MIT, 1997 group shows include Meyeroff Gallery, Md. Inst. Art, Balt., 1980, Thronja Gallery, Springfield, Mass., 1984-93, 14 Sculptors Gallery, N.Y.C., 1985, 94, New Acquisitions Gallery, 1982-87, SUNY, New Paltz, 1987, MIT Mus., Cambridge, Mass., 1990-91, Siegel Gallery, Lehigh U., Bethlehem, Pa., 1991-92, Barbara Gibson Gallery, Nyack, N.Y., 1992, Perlan, Reykjavik, (permanent geothermal sculpture installation), 1991—, Galleri Ofeigur, Reykjavik, 1993-94, MIT Mus./Ctr. Advanced Visual Studies MIT, 1994, Tisch Gallery Tufts U., Mass., 1995, Carpenter Ctr. Visual Arts Harvard U., Cambridge, Mass., 1995, ArtSpace Gallery, New Jersey City (N.J.) U., 1998-99, Firehouse Art Gallery Nassau C. C., Garden City, N.Y., 1999, Galleri Fold, Reykjavik, 1998-99; permanent collections include Fulbright Commn., Reykjavik, Syracuse U., Mus. Fine Art, Springfield, Mass., MacDowell Colony, Peterborough, N.H., SUNY, Town of Orangetown (N.Y.); subject of video Hitavaetur MIT, Circumstantial Prodns., 1991, News Story, Frettir, geothermal sculpture State TV Iceland, 1993-96; scenic artist motion pictures, TV shows; master scenic artist One Life to Live ABC, 1988-99 (Daytime Emmy award 1995); author: Hitavaettur and The Implications of Geothermal Sculpture, 2000. Fellow MacDowell Colony, 1980, Am. Scandinavian Found., 1999-00; Collaboration Art, Sci. and Tech. grantee Syracuse U., 1978, NYSCA grantee, 1986, Fulbright sr. rsch. fellow, 1988, Ptnrs. of Ams. grantee, 1993, grantee Robert E. Brennan Found., 1993, Waterloo Found. Arts, 1994, Coun. Arts at MIT, 1997, N.Y. Found. for the Arts grantee, 2001. Home: 421 Washington St Tappan NY 10983-2703

DELL, ROBERT MICHAEL, lawyer; b. Chgo., Oct. 4, 1952; s. Michael A. and Bertha Dell; m. Ruth Celia Schiffman, May 29, 1976; children: David, Michael, Jessica. BGS, U. Mich., 1974; JD, U. Ill., 1977. Bar: U.S. Dist. Ct. (no. dist.) Ill. 1977, U.S. Ct. Appeals (7th cir.) 1977, U.S. Dist. Ct. (no. dist.) Calif. 1990. Law clk. to justice U.S. Ct. Appeals (7th cir.), Chgo., 1977—79; assoc. Latham & Watkins, Chgo., 1982—85, ptnr., 1985—, mng. ptnr. San Francisco office, 1990—94, firm chmn. and mng. ptnr., 1995—. Home: 19 Tamal Vista Ln Kentfield CA 94904-1005 Office: Latham & Watkins 505 Montgomery St Ste 1900 San Francisco CA 94111-2552

DELL, STEPHEN OWEN, neurosurgeon; b. N.Y.C., June 13, 1944; s. Joseph Bernard and Laura Rachel (Lubowitz) D.; m. Julia Anne Walsh, Jan. 17, 1972; children: Elizabeth, Emily, Rebecca, Joseph. AB, Harvard U., 1964; postgrad., Oxford (Eng.) U., 1965-66; MA, Princeton U., 1967; MD, NYU, 1972. Intern, resident U. Calif., San Francisco, 1972-74; chief Friends' Hosp., Kaimosi, Kenya, 1974-75; resident N.Y. Neurol. Inst., N.Y.C., 1975-79; instr. Tufts U., Boston, 1979-82; neurosurgeon Spine Clinic New Eng., Epsom, N.H., 1992—, Brookdale Hosp., Bklyn., 1990-91; founder Med. Diagnostics, Burlington, Mass., 1984-95; dir. Lifesource, Hooksett, N.H., 1992—; founder Neuromuscular Cons., Epsom, N.H., 1992—, Oakland, Calif., 1995—. Vis. sr. lectr. U. Zimbabwe, 1992, U. Ghana, 1994, U. Cayetano Heredia, Lima, Peru, 1996. Contbr. articles to sci. jours. Fellow Rockefeller Found., 1982. Mem. FIENS, Am. Assn. Neurol. Surgeons, Congress Neurol. Surgeons, Soc. Pediatric Neurosurgery. Unitarian Universalist. Avocations: skiing, mountaineering, reading, family, sports. Home: 125 Woodland Way Piedmont CA 94611-3839 Office: Neuromuscular Cons 411 30th St Ste 508 Oakland CA 94609-3303

DELL, THOMAS CHARLES, nurse anesthetist; b. Port Huron, Mich., May 28, 1959; s. John W. and Lois M. (Bell) D.; children: Adam, Aubree, Andrea. AS, St. Clair County Community Coll., Port Huron, Mich., 1979; BSN, No. Mich. U., 1981; BS, Mercy Coll. Detroit, 1985; MS, Gooding Inst. Nurse Anethesia, Panama City, Fla., 1998. RN, Mich.; cert. nurse anesthetist. Nurse Marquette (Mich.) Gen., 1981-83, Mercy Hosp., Port Huron, 1983-85, nurse anesthetist, insvc. coord., 1985-88; nurse anesthetist Saber Salisbury and Assoc., Southfield, Mich., 1988—; chief nurse anesthetist McKenzie Meml. Hosp., Sandusky, Mich., 1989-98; clin. and didactic instr. U. Mich./Hurley Med. Ctr. Sch. Nurse Anesthesia, Flint, 1998—2001; staff nurse anesthetist Marlette (Mich.) Cmty. Hosp., 2001—. Mem. Am. Assn. Nurse Anesthetists, Mich. Assn. Nurse Anesthetists. Avocations: table tennis, bicycling, trumpet playing.

DELL, WARREN FRANK, II, management consultant; b. Louisville, Aug. 8, 1945; s. George Justus and Opal Lee (Roberts) D.; m. Theresa LoParco, July 11, 1970; child, Stacy Lee. BS, Northeastern U., 1968; MBA, Iona Coll., 1973. Cert. mgmt. cons. Systems analyst Am. Can Co., Greenwich, Conn., 1968-69; cons. Info. Techniques, Inc., Norwalk, Conn., 1969-70; systems analyst Colgate Palmolive, N.Y.C., 1970-72, supr. mktg. stats., 1972-73, mgr. forecast and adminstrn., 1973-77; cons. Case and Co., Stamford, Conn., 1977-80, prin., 1980-83, sr. ptnr., dir., 1983-85; prin. Cresap, a Towers Perrin Co., N.Y.C., 1985-86, v.p., 1986-90; pres. Dellmart & Co., Stamford, Conn., 1989—. Contbr. articles to profl. jours. Bd. dirs. JSL Perekrivstok, Stamford (Conn.) Golf Authority, Stamford (Conn.) Hist. Soc. Mem. Coun. Logistics Mgmt., Warehouse Edn. Rsch. Coun., Food Distbn. Rsch. Soc., Am. Philatelic Soc., Inst. Mgmt. Cons., Comite Internat. Des Entreprises A Succursates. Republican. Avocations: stamp collecting, golf, travel. Office: Dellmart & Co 125 Hardesty Rd Stamford CT 06903-4327 E-mail: wfdell2@msn.com.

DELLACORTE, CHRISTOPHER, engineer, tribologist; b. Port Jefferson, N.Y., Dec. 10, 1963; s. Franklin Alfred and Suzanne DellaCorte; m. Patricia DellaCorte. BS, Case Western Res. U., 1986, MS, PhD, Case Western Res. U., 1987. Rsch. engr. Case Western Res. U., Cleve., 1986-87, NASA, Cleve., 1987—. Contbr. over 50 articles to profl. jours. Bd. dirs. Medina (Ohio) County Bd. Mental Retardation and Devel. Disabilities, 1992-96. Mem. ASME (Burt L. Newkirk award 1996, conf. planning com. 1995—), Soc. Tribologists and Lubrication (assoc. editor, solid lubricants com. chair 1989-92). Avocations: mechanical devices, technical history, natural history. Office: NASA Glenn Rsch Ctr MS 23-2 21000 Brookpark Rd Cleveland OH 44135-3191*

DELLA-GIUSTINA, JO-ANN SUBOTIN, lawyer; b. Springfield, Mass., Sept. 6, 1951; d. Joseph Augustus and Jennie Delores (Subotin) Della-G. BA, Clark U., 1972; MA, Columbia Coll., Chgo., 1983; JD, Chgo.-Kent Coll. Law, 1987; ABD in Criminal Justice, CUNY, 2002. Bar: Ill. 1987, Mass. 1996, N.Y. 1998, U.S. Dist. Ct. (no. dist.) Ill. 1987, N.Y. 1998. Tchr. S.W. Ind. Sch. Dist., San Antonio, 1976-78, Malcolm X Coll., Chgo., 1978-80; dir. pub. rels. H&R Block, Chgo., 1983-85; asst. corp. counsel City of Chgo., 1987-89; sr. atty. Office of Cook County Pub. Defender, Chgo., 1989-90; judicial law clk. to Justice David Cerda Ill. Appellate Ct., Chgo., 1990-98. Cons. Am. Planning Assn., Chgo., 1990—98; bd. dir. loan repayment and assistance program ITT Chgo., 1995—97, mem. exec. com. criminal justice PhD program, 2001—02; mem. curriculum com. criminal justice PhD program CUNY, 1999—2001, graduate tchg. fellow, 2001—, mem. exec. com. PhD program, 2001—02; adj. asst. prof. John Jay Coll., 2001—; presenter in field. Author: Blossom of the Flower, 1990; author (legal jour.) Land Use Law and Zoning Digest, 1990-98; contbr. articles to profl. jours. Pres. Greenwood Ct. Condominium Assn., Chgo., 1989-98. Mem. Justinian Soc. Lawyers, Nat. Assn. Women Lawyers (named Outstanding Law Grad. 1987), Women in Film (programs com. 1992-94), Acad. Criminal Justice, Acad. Criminal Justice Scis., Nat. Women's Studies Assn., Am. Soc. Criminology, Nat. Italian-Am. Bar Assn., Order of Coif. Avocations: travel, reading. Home and Office: 41-41 41st St 5E Long Island City NY 11104 E-mail: jdella@earthlink.net.

DELLAGLORIA, JOHN CASTLE, city attorney, educator; b. NYC, June 29, 1952; s. Arthur A. and Marianne Dellagloria; divorced; 1 child, Rebecca; m. Marilyn Castle Dellagloria, Sept. 25, 1988; 1 child, Caitlin. BA in English Lit., SUNY, Binghamton, 1976; JD, U. Miami, 1979. Bar: Fla. 1979, N.Y. 1986, U.S. Ct. Appeals (11th cir.) 1981, U.S. Dist. Ct. (so. dist.) Fla. 1980, U.S. Supreme Ct. Rsch. asst. 3rd Dist. Ct. Appeal, Miami, Fla., 1980-81; assoc. Cassel & Cassel PA, Miami, 1981-82; dep. city atty. City of North Miami Beach, Fla., 1983-86; city atty. City of South Miami, Fla., 1986-90; chief dep. city atty. City of Miami Beach, Fla., 1990-96; city atty. City of North Miami, Fla., 1995—; gen. counsel Miami Beach Housing Authority, 1997-2000, South Miami Cmty. Redevel. Agy., 1998—2002. Lectr. Sch. Profl. Devel., U. Miami, 1982-88, dir. paralegal program, 1984-86, lectr. Sch. Bus., 1989—, lectr. real property program; lectr. govt. law sect. Fla. Bar; moderator Rachlin, Cohen & Holtz, Ann. Govt. Law Symposium, 1996—. Com. person Parrot Jungle Com., Pinecrest, Fla., 1998. Mem. Eugene P. Spellman Am. Inn of Ct. (alumnus). Democrat. Jewish. Avocation: long distance running. Office: City of North Miami 776 NE 125th St North Miami FL 33161-5654 E-mail: catdel@hotmail.com.

DELLAGNENA, GAIL LYNN, computer programmer analyst, consultant; b. Akron, Ohio, Oct. 19, 1956; d. George McInnes Massie and Iva Gena Ridgeway. BA in Polit. Sci., Kent State U., 1977. Programmer PACCAR, Seattle, 1990, Boeing, Seattle, 1991-92; cons. Computer People, Portland, 1992-94; programmer Fred Meyer, Portland, Oreg., 1994-98, Oreg. Dental Svcs. Health Plan, Portland, 1998-99; cons. E-Core Tech., Portland, 2000, ADECCO, Portland, 2000—. Democrat. Presbyterian. Avocations: biking, aerobics, hiking, reading. E-mail: g.dellagnena@worldnet.att.net.

DELLAPA, GARY J. aviation consultant; Budget dir., Miami Dade Co. Miami Internat. Airport, 1980—85, asst. co. mgr., 1985—93, aviation dir., 1993—2001; assoc. 9 Left Aviation Mgt. Assocs. Inc., Miami, 2001—. Office: 9 Left Aviation Assocs Red Bird Ctr, # 219 5783 SW 40th St Miami FL 33155-5301

DELLARIPA, CHRISTINE M. nursing care administrator; b. Hartford, Conn., 1948; d. Louis M. and Mary G. (Aszklar) D. Diploma, Middlesex Meml. Hosp., Middletown, Conn., 1970. RN, Conn. Staff-charge nurse Mt. Sinai Hosp., Hartford, Conn., 1970-76; staff/charge nurse John Dempsey Hosp. of U. Conn. Health Ctr., Farmington, 1976-80, asst. nurse mgr. ICU, 1980-89, interim nurse mgr. ICU, 1983-84, 87-88; home health nurse Kimberly Quality Care, Farmington, 1990-91; nursing care coord. U. Conn. Health Ctr., Farmington, 1991—. Recipient Alumnae Assn. award Middlesex Meml. Hosp., 1970, Middlesex Meml. Hosp. Sci. award, 1968. Mem. AACN, Am. Assn. Office Nurses, Nat. League for Nursing. Office: U Conn Health Ctr Univ Med Group 263 Farmington Ave Farmington CT 06030-0002

DELLA ROCCA, GREGORY JOHN, orthopaedic surgeon; b. Albany, NY, Sept. 8, 1969; s. John Stephen and Marcia Rose Della Rocca. BS, Cornell U., 1992; PhD, Duke U., 1998, MD, 1999. Instr. Princeton Rev., Chapel Hill, N.C., 1995-98; orthopaedic resident Barnes-Jewish Hosp., St. Louis, 1999—. Mem. med. policy action com., com. on minority affairs, med. adv. com. Duke U. Med. Ctr., Durham, 1995-96, instnl. rev. bd., 1994-95. Recipient Sulzer award, Orthop. Rsch. and Edn. Found., 2002, Resident Leadership Forum award, Am. Orthop. Assn., 2003. Mem. Pi Kappa Phi (vice archon 1991). Avocations: soccer, downhill skiing. E-mail: dellaroccag@msnotes.wustl.edu.

DELLA ROCCO, KENNETH ANTHONY, lawyer; b. Bridgeport, Conn., Sept. 5, 1952; BA, Sacred Heart U., Fairfield, Conn., 1974; JD, U. Bridgeport, 1982. Bar: Conn. 1983, U.S. Dist. Ct. Conn. 1985, N.Y. 1988, U.S. Supreme Ct. 1991. Assoc. Cummings & Lockwood, Stamford, Conn., 1982-88; from asst. gen. counsel to v.p. Melville Corp., Rye, NY, 1988—93, v.p. legal affairs, gen. counsel, 1993—95; counsel Cacace, Tusch & Santagata, Stamford, 1996—2002; ptnr. Martin, Lucas & Chioffi LLP, Stamford, 2003—. Mem. Conn. Bar Assn., Regional Bar Assn. Office: Martin Lucas and Chioffi LLP 1177 Summer St Stamford CT 06905

DELLAS, MARIE C. retired psychology educator and consultant; b. Buffalo; d. Theodore Andrew and Katherine (Callos) D. BS cum laude, State U. Coll., Buffalo, 1945; MEd, U. Buffalo, 1967; PhD, SUNY, Buffalo, 1970. Asst. editor Urban Edn. Jour., Buffalo, 1966-67; rsch. asst. SUNY, Buffalo, 1967-69; asst. prof. psychology Ea. Mich. U., Ypsilanti, 1969-73, assoc. prof., 1973-79, prof., 1979-93. Mem. adv. bd. Inst. Study Children and Families, 1983-93. Author: Dellas Identity Status Inventory, 1979, 81, Creative Thinking Applied to Problem Solving Manual, 1993; contbr. articles to profl. jours.; mem. bd. editors Midwestern Ednl. Researcher, 1980-87, Urban Edn. Jour., 1977-94. Recipient Josephine N. Keal award Women's Commn., 1980, 85, 86; Grad. Rsch. grantee Ea. Mich. U., 1980-84. Mem. APA, Am. Ednl. Rsch. Assn., Nat. Assn. Gifted Children, Midwestern Ednl. Rsch. Assn., Midwestern Psychol. Assn., Mich. Acad. Gifted, Am. Assn. Univ. Women, Women's Coun. Cleveland Mus. of Art, Pi Lambda Theta. Home and Office: 2201 Acacia Park Dr Apt 312 Lyndhurst OH 44124-3840

DELLAS, ROBERT DENNIS, investment banker; b. Detroit, July 4, 1944; s. Eugene D. and Maxine (Rudell) D.; m. Shila L. Clement, Mar. 27, 1976; children: Emily Allison, Lindsay Michelle BA in Econs., U. Mich., Ann Arbor, 1966; MBA, Harvard U., Cambridge, 1970. Analyst Burroughs Corp., Detroit, 1966-67, Pasadena, Calif., 1967-68; mgr. U.S. Leasing, San Francisco, 1970-76; pres., dir. Energetics Mktg. & Mgmt. Assn., San Francisco, 1978-80; sr. v.p. E.F. Hutton & Co., San Francisco, 1981-85; prin. founder Capital Exchange Internat., San Francisco, 1976—. Gen. ptnr. Kanland Assocs., Tex., 1982, Claremont Assocs., Calif., 1983, Lakeland Assocs., Ga., 1983, Americal Assocs., Calif., 1983, Chatsworth Assocs., Calif., 1983, Walnut Grove Assocs., Calif., 1983, Somerset Assocs., N.J., 1983, One San Diego Assocs., Calif., 1984, Big Top Prodns., L.P., Calif., 1994. Bd. dirs., treas. Found. San Francisco's Archtl. Heritage. Mem. U.S. Trotting Assn., Calif. Harness Horse Breeders Assn. (Breeders award for Filly of Yr. 1986, Aged Pacing Mare, 1987, 88, Colt of Yr. 1990), Calif. Golf Club San Francisco. Office: Capital Exch Internat 1911 Sacramento St San Francisco CA 94109-3419

DELLERE, DIANA MARIE, school psychologist; b. Colby, Kans., Apr. 2, 1968; d. Alvin Dale and Lois Marie (Towns) D. AA, Colby (Kans.) C.C., 1988; BS, Ft. Hays State U., 1990, MS, 1992; EdS, 1994. Cert. sch. psychologist, Kans. Sch. psychologist Wichita (Kans.) Pub. Schs., 1993—. Big sister Big bros./Big Sisters, Wichita, 1997—. Mem. Nat. Assn. Sch. Psychologists, Kans. Assn. Sch. Psychologists (editor 1995-97, 99-2000, assoc. editor 1998-99), Wichita Sch. Psychology Assn. (sec., pres. 1999-2000). Republican. Roman Catholic. Avocations: reading, crafts, quilting, sewing, children. E-mail: dmdpsych@msn.com.

DELLEUR, JACQUES WILLIAM, civil engineering educator; b. Paris, Dec. 30, 1924; came to U.S., 1952, naturalized, 1957; s. Georges Leon and Simone (Rossum) D.; m. DeLores Ann Horne, June 18, 1957; children: James Robert, Ann Marie. Civil and Mining Engr., Nat. U. Colombia, 1949; MS in Civil Engring., Rensselaer Poly. Inst., 1950; D.Engring. Sci., Columbia U., 1955. Civil engr. R.J. Tipton and Assocs., 1950-52; from research asst. to instr. civil engring. and engring. mechanics Columbia U., 1952-55; mem. faculty Purdue U., 1955-95, prof. hydraulic engring. and hydrology, 1963-95, prof. emeritus hydraulic engring., 1995—, head hydromechanics and water resources area, 1965-76, head hydraulic and systems engring. area, 1981-90, 91-92; assoc. dir. Purdue U. Water Resources Rsch. Ctr., 1971-89, acting dir., 1983. Rschr. fluid mechanics U. Grenoble, Fance, 1961-62, hydrology and environ. fluid mechanics French Nat. Hydraulics Lab., Chatou, France, 1968-69, 76-77, statis. hydrology U. Brussels, Belgium, 1991; NSF sr. exch. scientist U. Grenoble, France, 1983-84; vis. prof. U. Quebec, Canada, 1996—, Vrije U., Brussels, 1991—; mem. sci. coun. Revue des Sciences de L'eau/Water Scis. Sci. Interest Group/Nat. Inst. Sci. Rsch., Quebec, 1988—; vis. lectr. Ecole Polytechnique Federale de Lausanne, Switzerland, 1991, 93, 95, 97; coord. Consortium of U.S. and European Cmty. Univs. for Scholar and Multimedia Exchs. in Environ. and Water Resources Engring. and Scis., 1998-2003. Author and co-author 2 books on statis. hydrology; co-author book on urban hydorlogy; editor: Handbook of Groundwater Engineering, 1999; assoc. editor: Handbook of Civil Engineering, 1995, 2d edit., 2002; assoc. editor Jour. Hydraulic Engring., 2003--, also articles, reports in field. Recipient Type 2 award, Environ. and Water Resources Inst., 2003. Fellow Ind. Acad. Sci.; mem. ASCE (Freeman fellow 1961-62, chmn. fluid dynamics com. 1964-66, task com. mechanics of turbulence 1964-69, task com. hydraulics of bridges 1963-68, task com. on rehab. urban drainage infrastructure 1988-90, co-chmn. task com. on urban drainage rehab. & techniques 1990-94, chmn. com. urban water resources 1994-95, chmn. com. sediment movement in urban drainage sys. 1998-2003, internat. bd. advisors Jour. Hydrologic Engring. 1996—, Svc. to the Profession award 2000, Ven Te Chow Hydrology award 2002), Am. Geophys. Union (chmn. urban hydrology com. 1978-83), Am. Water Resources Assn., Am. Soc. Engring. Edn., Internat. Assn. Hydraulic Rsch. (U.S. del. joint com. on urban storm drainage with Internat. Assn. Water Quality 1987-93), Internat. Assn. Sci. Hydrology, Ind. Water Resources Assn. (Charles Harold Bechert award 1992). Home: 124 Mohican Pl West Lafayette IN 47906-2159 Office: Purdue U Sch Civil Engring 550 Stadium Mall Dr West Lafayette IN 47907-2051

DELLIBOVI, ALFRED A. bank executive; b. Queens, N.Y., Feb. 1, 1946; m. Elizabeth Power; children: Robert, Christine. BA, Fordham Coll., 1967; MPA, Baruch Coll., 1973. High sch. tchr.; mem. N.Y. State Assembly, Albany; adminstr. N.Y. region Urban Mass Transp. Adminstrn., U.S. Dept. Transp., N.Y.C., 1981-84, dep. adminstr. Washington, 1984-87, adminstr., 1987-89; deputy sec. HUD, Washington, 1989-92. Roman Catholic.

DELLI COLLI, HUMBERT THOMAS, chemist, product development specialist; b. Utica, N.Y., July 8, 1944; s. Cyril Thomas and Carol Dolores (Fragola) D.; m. Judith Eleanor Maloney, June 24, 1967; 1 child, Kristin Anne. BS in Chemistry, Clarkson Coll., 1966, PhD, 1971. Phys. chemist Edgewood Arsenal, Md., 1971-73; rsch. scientist Westvaco Corp., Charleston, S.C., 1973-75, devel. mgr. agrichems. and polychems. dept., 1975-84, devel. mgr. new tech., polychems. dept., 1984-91; mgr. agrl. chem. devel. Westvaco Polychems., Charleston, SC, 1991-2000; bus. mgr. agrl. chems and mineral techs.., polychems. dept. Mead Westvaco Corp., Charleston, SC, 2001—02; bus. mgr. agrl. chems. and mineral tech. Polychems. dept. Weadwestvaco, 2002—. Cons. U.S. Army Chem. Systems Lab., Aberdeen, Md., 1971—. Contbr. articles to profl. jours.; patentee in field. Pres. Mcpl. Bd. Health, Goose Creek, S.C., 1974-75; mem. Berkeley County (S.C.) Water and Sewer Authority, 1978-79; mem. vestry bd. St. Thomas Ch., North Charleston, S.C., 1986—. With U.S. Army, 1970-73; capt. USAR, 19773-92, Operation Desert Storm, 1991. Grantee NDEA, 1966, Clarkson Coll., 1962, 66; Uniroyal Undergrad. scholar, 1962, N.Y. State Regents scholar, 1962. Mem. AAAS, N.Y. Acad. Sci., Am. Chem. Soc., So. Weed Sci. Soc., N. Cen. Weed Control Conf., S.C. Sci. Council (adv. bd. mem.), Weed Sci. Soc. Am. Lodges: KC, Ducks Unltd. Republican. Roman Catholic. Avocations: black powder firearms, hunting, fishing, woodworking, wine collecting. Home: 7 Campanella Ct Charleston SC 29406-8606 Office: Westvaco Polychems PO Box 118005 Charleston SC 29423-8005 Fax: 843-746-8165. E-mail: htdelli@westvaco.com.

DELLIFIELD, DENNIS L. conductor; b. Oberlin, Ohio, Oct. 13, 1948; s. Maynard L. and Wilma E. Dellifield; m. Marilee Hefner, May 8, 1971; children: David, Jonathan. BA, Bluffton Coll., Bluffton, OH, 1968—71; MS, U. of Dayton, Dayton, OH, 1971—75. Asst. marching band dir. Bluffton H.S., Bluffton, Ohio, 1967—68, Elida H.S., Elida, Ohio, 1968—71; condr. of bands Allen East H.S., Lafayette, Ohio, 1971—. Secondary consulting com. mem. Bluffton Coll., Bluffton, Ohio, 1980—89; dir. Lafayette cmty. chorus, Lafayette, Ohio, 1978—; educator English Luth. Ch., Bluffdon, Ohio, 1975—. Author: (book) Band Ten Hut!. Bd. mem., bd. of pub. affairs Lafayette village coun., Lafayette, Ohio. Recipient Outstanding Alumni, Bluffton Coll., 1991, Tchr. Of The Yr., Sam's Club of Am., 1998, Who's Who Ammo Tchr., Nominating Com., 7 times. Mem.: Nat. Band Assn., Ohio Music Educators Assn., Music Educators Nat. Conf. Independent. Lutheran. Avocations: research, research, research, collecting first additions. Office: Allen East High School 105 North Washington Street Lafayette OH 45854 Office Fax: 419-649-8900.

DELLINGER, ANNE MAXWELL, law educator; b. Omaha July 19, 1940; d. William Hampton and Margaret Mary (Jackson) Maxwell; m. Walter Estes Dellinger, June 12, 1965; children— Hampton Yeats, Andrew King. Student Randolph Macon Woman's Coll., 1958-60; B.A., U. N.C., 1962; M.A., Tulane U., 1964; J.D., Duke U., 1974. Bar: N.C. 1974, U.S. Supreme Ct. 1991. Tech. writer, editor Equitable Life Assurance Soc., N.Y.C., 1964-65; instr. English U. Miss., Oxford, 1966-68; assoc., asst. prof. pub. law and govt. U. N.C., Chapel Hill, Prof., 1974—; spl. asst. to dir. FBI, Washington, 1980-81; cons. health coms. N.C. Gen. Assembly, 1983. Author: North Carolina School Law: The Principal's Role, 1980; A Legal Guide for North Carolina School Board Members, 1978; editor Health Law Bull., Inst. Govt., 1982—; gen. editor. author chpt. Healthcare Facilities Law, 1991; counsel Hogan & Hartson, Washington, D.C., 1993-95; contbr. articles to profl. jours. Mem. Order Coif, Assn. Women Faculty U. N.C. (pres. 1984-85), N.C. Soc. Health Care Attys. (pres. 1984-85), Phi Beta Kappa. Democrat. Home: 604 E Franklin St Chapel Hill NC 27514-3822 Office: Inst Govt Univ NC Cb # 3330 Chapel Hill NC 27599-0001

DELLINGER, CHARLES WADE, minister; b. Lincolnton, N.C., Feb. 25, 1949; s. Coy Hillard Dellinger and Lorene (Russ) Harbinson; m. Sarah Lynn Baxter, July 20, 1969; children: Sarah Beth, Charles Matthew. AA, Gardner-Webb Coll., 1969, BA cum laude, 1971; MDiv, S.E. Bapt. Sem., 1975, D of Ministry, 1983. Ordained to ministry Bapt. Ch., 1969. Pastor Roseland Bapt. Ch., Lincolnton, N.C., 1969-71; assoc. pastor, pastor Temple Bapt. Ch., Gastoma, N.C., 1971-74; pastor Mulls Meml. Bapt. Ch., Shelby, N.C., 1975-87; sr. pastor Old Town Bapt. Ch., Winston-Salem, N.C., 1987-98, First Bapt. Ch., Hudson, N.C., 1998—. Bd. dirs. Gardner-Webb Coll., Bolling Springs, N.C., 1980-84, 86-90; assoc. chaplain Cleveland Meml. Hosp., Shelby, 1985-87. Author: Personal Mementos, 1990, A Study in Theodily: A Preventive Tool in Grief Ministry. Bd. dirs. Boy Scouts Am., Winston-Salem, 1989—, dist. advancement chmn., 1990—; moderator Kings Mountain Bapt. Assn., Shelby, 1985-87; chmn. ministry coun., Bapt. State Conv., Raleigh, 1987-88. Recipient Disting. Citizen award State of N.C., 1973. Mem. Am. Family Counselors, Am. Assn. Christian Counselors (charter). Democrat. Baptist. Avocations: golf, fishing, hunting, reading. Home: 109 Optimist Ave Hudson NC 28638-2124 *A precious gift called "life" has been given to us. How we use that gift will bring blessing or curse. The length of life matters little. The honor to the giver comes if the gift is used for blessing.*

DELLOFF, STEFAN T. lawyer; b. N.Y.C., Apr. 15, 1942; AB, Rutgers U., 1963; JD, NYU, 1972. Bar: N.J. 1972. Revenue officer IRS, N.Y.C., 1966-72; exec. asst. Motivation and Tng. Programs, Fair Lawn, N.J., 1972—; pvt. practice, Fair Lawn, 1972—. Office: 518 Essex Pl Fair Lawn NJ 07410-1012

DELLO JOIO, NORMAN, composer; b. N.Y.C., Jan. 24, 1913; s. Casimir and Antoinette (Garramone) Dello J.; m. Barbara Bolton, 1974; children: Victoria, Justin, Norman. Student, All Hallows Inst., 1926-30, Coll. City N.Y., 1932-34, Inst. Mus. Art, 1936, Juilliard Grad. Sch., 1939-41, Yale Sch. Music, 1941; Mus.D. (hon.), Colby Coll., Lawrence Coll., U. Cin., 1967, St. Mary's Coll., 1969, Susquehanna U., 1980. Tchr. composition Sarah Lawrence Coll., 1945-50, Mannes Coll. Music, 1952—; commentator Met. Opera broadcasts; dean Sch. for the Arts, Boston U., 1972-78. Mem. rsch. adv. coun. U.S. Office Edn.; adv. coun. State U. N.Y., Potsdam; chmn. policy com. contemporary music Ford Found. Composer: Ballet On Stage, 1944; piano and chorus Jubilant Song, 1945, Piano Sketchers, 2000, A Dream, 2000, Ricercari; for piano and orch., 1946, Variations- Chaccone-Finale, 1947, Diversion of Angels; dance, 1948, Concertante for Clarinet and Orch, 1949, New York Profiles; for orch., 1949, The Triumph of St. Joan; opera, 1950, Psalm of David; chorus and strings and brass orch., 1950, Song of Affirmation; soprano, chorus strings and brass, narrator, orch., 1950, Somebody's Coming; chorus and piano, The Tall Kentuckian; score for musical play, 1952, Song of the Open Road; chorus, 1952, (opera) The Ruby, 1953, The Lamentation of Saul, Baritone solo orch., 1954, The Trial at Rouen, 1955, Mediations on Ecclesiastes, 1956 (Pulitzer prize 1958), Air Power, symphonic suite, 1956, Ballad of the 7 Lively Arts, 1957, To St. Cecilia mixed chorus and brass, 1958, (opera) Blood Moon; also: Variations and Fantasy for Piano and Orchestra, 1961; (love songs) There is a Lady Sweet and Kind, Why So Wan, Pale Lover, Let Me Count the Ways, Meeting at Night; score Songs of Adieu, The Orch. Louvre, NBC TV, 1965 (Emmy award), Beyond Every Horizon; for Symphonic band Antiphonal Fantasy; organ, brass, strings, 1965, Songs of Walt Whitman for Orch. and Chorus, 1966, Capriccio; for piano, 1968, Fantasies on Theme of Haydn (orchestra), 1968, Time of Snow; ballet, 1968, Proud Music of the Storm; chorus, brass, organ, 1967, Days of the Modern; chorus, brass, percussion, 1968, Evocations; Variants on Medieval Tunel Band, 1965, chorus, orch., 1970, Psalm of Peace; chorus, organ, french horn, trumpet, 1971, Mass; chorus, organ, brass Concertante for Wind Instruments, 1972, Of Crows and Clusters; chorus and piano, 1972, Suite for Flute and Piano, 1973, Suite for Clarinet and Piano, 1973, Suite for Organ, 1973, Folio for Piano, 1973, Lyric Fantasies for Viola and Strings, 1973, The Poet's Song, 1973, Leisure, 1973, Songs of Abelard (band and voice) Mass to the Blessed Virgin; organ and chorus, 1974, Satiric Dances; band, 1974, Stage Parodies; piano 4 hands, 1974, Mass of the Eucharist in honour of Pope John XXIII; organ, brass, strings and chorus, 1975, Notes from Tom Paine; chorus and piano, 1975, Colonial Variants; orch., 1976, Southern Echoes, 1976, Colonial Ballads; band, 1977, As of a Dream; orch., soloists, chorus, narrator and dancers, 1978, Sonata for Trumpet and Piano, 1978, Songs of Remembrance; voice solo and orch., 1978, Salute to Scarlatti; piano, 1978, The Psalmist's Meditation; chorus and piano, 1978, Variations; piano, 1980, Hymns Without Words; chorus and piano, 1979, Ballabili; dances for orch., 1981; chorus and piano Love Songs at Parting, 1982; string orch. East Hampton Sketches, 1983; piano and 4 hands Song at Springtide, 1984; concert band Aria and Roulade, 1983; chorus and concert band Let Us Sing a New Song, 1984, concert band Metaphrase, 1985, orch. Variants on a Bach Chorale, 1985, piano Introduction and Fantasies, 1985, Short Intervallic Etudes for Piano, 1986, Sing a Song Universal for chorus and piano, 1987, Nativity for chorus, soloists and orch., 1987, The Quest, 1990, mixed chorus and piano, A Memory: Men's Chorus and Piano, 1991, Songs of Memory, 1991, Variants on a Medieval Tune, 1993, Reflections on an Ancient Hymn for chamber orch., 1996, Salute to the Orch. Chamber Orch. Player, 1997, chamber orchestra Divertimento, 1997, Reflections on an Ancient Tune, 1997, piano 2 Songs Without Words, 1997, String Quartet, "Lyrical Interludes," 1998, concert band Fantasies, The Vigil for Mixed Chorus and Brass Instruments, band arrangement Jubilant Song, (music for TV series) Air Power, Directimento for Chamber Orch., 1997, mixed chorus and piano Passing Strangers, 2002; Lyrical Movement for string orch., 1995; Lyrical Interludes-string quartet Simple Sketches for piano, 2000, chorus and piano Dreamers, 2000, chorus and piano Passing Strangers, 2002, concert band City Scenes, 2003. Chmn. planning com. Ford Found.; Bd. dirs. Am. Music Center. Recipient Elizabeth Sprague Coolidge award, 1937; recipient Town Hall Composition award, 1941, N.Y. Music Critics Circle award, 1949, 58, Pulitzer prize for music, 1957, Emmy award for TV Score, Lifes Achievement award, Nat. Band Dirs. Assn., 2003; Grants and Scholarships in name of Norman Dello Joio awarded to Choral Soc. East Hampton students, 2003; Guggenheim fellow, 1943-44; Am. Acad. Arts and Letters grantee, 1945. Mem. Nat. Acad. Arts and Letters (coun.), Broadcast Music, Devon Yacht Club. Home: PO Box 154 East Hampton NY 11937-0154 *Whatever recognition I have received for my creative work, I owe for the most part, to an understanding mother and disciplinarian father. In this, my 70th year, I give thanks for a loving wife, a composer son whose music I feel will be an extension of myself into the future, and a son who is an Olympic equestrian of whom I am proud.*

DELLON, A. LEE, plastic surgeon; b. Bronx, N.Y., Apr. 18, 1944; s. Alfred and Irene (Samuels) D.; divorced; children: Evan, Glenn, Brian. BA, Johns Hopkins U., 1966, MD, 1970. Prof. plastic surgery and neurosurgery Johns Hopkins U. Sch. Medicine, Balt.; prof. plastic surgery U. Ariz.; prof. of plastic surgery Univ. of Maryland. Author 3 books in field; contbr. over 325 articles to profl. publs. Home: 102 Cotswold Rd Baltimore MD 21210 Office: 3333 N Calvert St Ste 370 Baltimore MD 21218-2864

DELL'OSSO, LOUIS FRANK, neuroscience educator; b. Bklyn., Mar. 16, 1941; s. Frank and Rose (Perrone) Dell'O.; m. Aquilina Marie Ferlo, May 22, 1965 (div. 1976); single ptnr. Charlene Hale Morse, Sept. 30, 1977. BEE, Bklyn. Poly. Inst., 1961, postgrad., 1961-63; PhD, U. Wyo., 1968. Co-dir. Ocular Motor Neurophysiology Lab. VA. Med. Ctr., Miami, Fla., 1972-80; asst. prof. biomed. engring. and surgery U. Miami, 1970-72, asst. prof. neurology, 1972-75, assoc. prof. neurology, 1975-79, prof. neurology, 1979-80; dir. Ocular Motor Neurophysiology Lab. VA Med. Ctr., Cleve., 1980—; prof. neurology and biomed. engring. Case Western Res. U., Cleve., 1980—. Cons. Westinghouse Research Lab, Pitts, 1966-67, 70-71, Mt. Sinai Hosp., Miami, Fla., 1972-75. Bd. dirs. Vineland Galloway Civic Assn., Miami, 1973-76. Grantee NIH, 1971-77, VA Med. Ctr., 1972—, NSF, 1970. Fellow N.Am. NeuroOphthalmology Soc.; mem. IEEE, Engring. in Medicine and Biology Soc. (sr., chpt. chmn. 1977-78), Assn. Rsch. in Vision and Ophthalmology, Soc. Neurosci., NY Acad. Scis., Train Collectors Assn., CCCC Rod & Gun Club. Democrat. Home: 2356 Tudor Dr Cleveland OH 44106-3212 E-mail: lfd@cwru.edu.

DELLUMS, RONALD V. former congressman, health facility administrator; b. Oakland, Calif., Nov. 24, 1935; m. Cynthia Lewis; 4 children. AA, Oakland City Coll., 1958; BA, San Francisco State Coll., 1960; MSW., U. Calif., 1962. Psychiat. social worker Calif. Dept. Mental Hygiene, 1962-64; program dir. Bayview Community Ctr., San Francisco, 1964-65; from assoc. dir. to dir. Hunters Point Youth Opportunity Ctr., 1965-66; planning cons. Bay Area Social Planning Coun., 1966-67; dir. concentrated employment program San Francisco Econ. Opportunity Coun., 1967-68; sr. cons. Social Dynamics, Inc., 1968-70; mem. 92nd-104th Congresses from 9th Calif. Dist., 1971-98; former chmn. house com. on D.C.; former mem. permanent select com. on intelligence; chmn. house armed svcs. com., 1993; pres. Healthcare Internat. Mgmt., Washington, 1998—2001; sr. ptnr. Dellums, Brauer, Halterman & Assocs., Washington, 2001—. Lectr. San Francisco State Coll., U. Calif., Berkeley; mem. U.S. del. North Atlantic Assembly, ranking minority mem. Nat. Security Com.; former chmn. Congl. Black Caucus, Calif. Dem. Congl. Del. Author: Defense Sense: The Search For a Rational Military Policy, 1983, Lying Down with the Lions, 2000. Mem. Berkeley City Coun., 1967-71. With USMCR, 1954-56. Democrat. Office: Dellums Brauer Halterman & Assocs 1201 Pennsylvania Ave NW Ste 300 Washington DC 20004-2436

DELMAIN, FRED, industrial psychologist; b. San Francisco, Jan. 18, 1924; s. F. Del Mugnaio and Lillia Belluomini; m. Jeanne Ball. PhD, U. Chgo. Psychologist, Oakland, Calif. Inventor of brain probe; originator indsl. bus. psychology for execs., psychokinesis expander. Author 3 books on bridge, Hand Pattern System, Valuation Analysis, Bridge Theory; contbr. poetry to various publs. Lt. (j.g.) USN, 1943—46. Named to, Bridge Hall of Fame. Avocation: bridge (grandmaster). Home: 185 Alta Rd Oakland CA 94618 E-mail: delmain.com@juno.com.

DELMAR, EUGENE ANTHONY, architect; b. Gallitzin, Pa., June 8, 1928; s. Frank and Viola (Bocci) DiMaria; m. Bettie Hardin, Apr. 7, 1951; children: Diana, Daniel, David. B.Arch., Columbia U., 1954; M.Arch. in Urban Design, Catholic U. Am., 1971. Architect Ronald S. Senseman, FAIA, Washington, 1954-59; pres. Eugene A. Delmar, Silver Spring, Md., 1959-93, Delmar Architects, P.A., Olney, Md., 1993—. Mem. vis. com. Sch. Architecture U. Md., 1975. Important works include Electrophysics Lab., Columbia, Md., Montgomery County Jud. Ctr., Natatorium, Washington, Charlotte Hall Vets. Retirement Home, Denton Courthouse/Multi-Svc. Ctr., Brooke Grove Elem. Sch., F. Douglass H.S., Springbrook H.S., Rocky Hill Mid. Sch., Blake H.S., Francis Scott Key Elem. Sch., Rockville Nursing Home, Treatment and Learning Ctr., G. James Gholson Midl Sch., Cora L. Rice Elem. Sch. Ednl. Complex, Huntingtown H.S. Mem. code enforcement bd. Dept. Econ. and Community Devel. Md., 1973-76; mem. Montgomery County Beautification Com., 1965, Montgomery County Sign Rev. Bd., 1968-71; bd. dirs. Rockville Nursing Home. Served to 2d lt. C.E., U.S. Army, 1946-48. Recipient Disting. Service award U.S. Jaycees, 1964, E.B. Morris Disting. Service award, 1976 Fellow AIA (First award design 1966, award of merit for design Potomac Valley chpt. 1966, bd. dirs. Potomac Valley chpt. 1992-97); mem. Md. Soc. Architects (pres. 1972-73), Sigma Chi. Clubs: Silver Spring Lions (pres. 1978-79), Columbia University. Office: Delmar Architects PA 3411 Olandwood Ct Ste 205 Olney MD 20832-1488

DELMAR, EVELYN EMAN See **EMAN DELMAR, EVELYN**

DELMARRE, DAVID, formulation scientist; b. Valence, France (incl. Monaco), July 4, 1969; s. Nicole Clerembault and Bernard Dion(Stepfather). PhD, ENS Cachan, 1998. Post doc UBC, Vancouver, Canada, 1998—2001; sr. formulation scientist BioDelivery Sciences Internat., Newark, 2001—. Achievements include research in drug delivery. Personal E-mail: david.delmarre@verizon.net.

DELMORO, RONALD ANTHONY, elementary school principal; b. N.Y.C., June 14, 1948; s. Alfred and Ann Delmoro; m. Denna Loeb Delmoro, Dec. 27, 1987; children: Nicole, Ronald, Daniel, Stephen. BA in History, Iona Coll., 1970; MS in Edn., New Paltz State U., 1972; prof. diploma, Fordham U., 1975. Elem. sch. tchr. Yorktown Sch., Yorktown Heights, N.Y., 1970-75, 76-80, secondary sch. tchr., 1975-76, pub. sch. adminstr., 1980—. Adj. prof. Mercy Coll., Dobbs Ferry, N.Y., 1997—. Author: Handbook for Site Based Decision Making in Elementary Schools, 1990. Religion instr. St. Patrick's Ch., Yorktown, 1970-80; dir. teen ctr. Parks and Recreation, Yorktown, 1972-80, dir. men's football, 1982—. Mem. ASCD, Yorktown Adminstrs. and Supervisors (pres. 1989—), Nat. Assn. of Elem. and Secondary Sch. Prins. Roman Catholic. Avocations: research, sports, photography. Home: 2377 Rela Ln Yorktown Heights NY 10598-3844 Office: Brookside Sch 2285 Broad St Yorktown Heights NY 10598-3814

DEL NEGRO, JOHN THOMAS, lawyer; b. Springfield, Mass., Oct. 2, 1948; s. Angelo Antonio and Marguerite (Garofalo) Del N.; m. Linda Anne Mayberry, July 6, 1973. BA, George Washington U., 1970; JD, Cornell U., 1975. Bar: Conn. 1975, U.S. Dist. Ct. Conn. 1978, U.S. Tax Ct. 1981. Assoc. Murtha, Cullina, Richter & Pinney, Hartford, Conn., 1975-81, ptnr., 1982-95, Del Negro & Feldman, LLC, Hartford, 1995—. Author: (with Levenson) Depreciation and Investment Tax Credits, 1983. Bd. dirs. Conn. Opera Assn., 1990-2003, Watkinson Sch., 1992-2000. Mem. ABA, Conn. Bar Assn. (tax exec. com. 1992-2002). Office: Del Negro & Feldman LLC Goodwin Sq 225 Asylum St Hartford CT 06103-1524 E-mail: jdelnegro@dfctlaw.com.

DELNICK, MARTHA JOYCE, retired elementary education educator; b. Muncie, Ind., July 17, 1939; d. Doyt Randall and Susan (Straley) Whiteman; m. Jerry Spencer, July 6, 1962 (div. 1967); children: Jay Dee, Todd Alan. BA, Ball State U., 1970, MA, 1975; postgrad., Mich. State U., U. Mich. Cert. tchr., Mich. Tchr. Bennett Elem. Sch., Marion, Ind., 1965-67; tchr. elem. sch. Grand Rapids (Mich.) Pub. Schs., 1970-77, reading cons., 1977-87, tchr. compensatory edn., 1987-96, itinerant tchr. Title I, 1996-2001. Tchr. Acad. Summer Success Acad., 1991-95; presenter Compensatory Edn. Parent Orgn., Grand Rapids, 1980-89, Jefferson Sch. Family Math. program, Grand Rapids, 1992; mem. Mich. Math. Insvc. Project K-2, 1991-92, 3-6, 1992-93, math. svc. trainer Compensatory Edn. Tchrs. and Paraprofls., 1991-93; in-svc. MEAP trainer Grand Rapids Pub. Sch. Tchrs., 1995-2001—. Author curriculum materials. Mem. NEA (life), Mich. Edn. Assn. (life), Grand Rapids Edn. Assn. (rep. 1985-90, sch. bd. contact 1986-88), Mich. Reading Assn., Mich. Coun. Tchrs. Math. Mem. United Ch. of Christ. Avocations: sewing, crafts, cooking. Home: 6211 Woodwater Ave NE Belmont MI 49306-9255

DELNIK, ALEXANDER, business development executive, consultant; b. Zhitomir, Ukraine, Nov. 10, 1961; came to U.S., 1991; s. Yefim and Bera (Nevelskaya) D. MS, Civil Engring. Inst., Kiev, Ukraine, 1983, PhD, 1987; MBA, UCLA, 1997. Registered profl. engr., Calif. Engr. Civil Engring. Inst., Kiev, 1987-88, sr. rschr./lectr., 1988-91; engr./lab. supr. Soil Tech, Inc., Temecula, Calif., 1991-93; project mgr. Dames & Moore, Inc., L.A., 1993-98; mgr. strategic planning and new bus. devel. Edison Internat., Rosemead, Calif., 1998—. Editor: English-Russian-Ukrainian Geotechnical Dictionary, 1992; contbr. articles to profl. jours.; editl. bd. Ukrainian Jour. of Found. Engring., 1990-92. Recipient Diploma of Sr. Rschr., Coun. Ministers of USSR, 1990; Ministry of Higher Edn. Lenin's scholar, 1982-83, grantee, 1989-91. Achievements include research and development of numerical techniques to simulate soil-structure interaction; major design and construction projects worldwide; risk management, strategic planning and development of major business opportunities for a leading energy company. Home: 12745 Sarah St Studio City CA 91604 E-mail: alex.delnik@usa.net.

DELO, ELLEN SANDERSON, lawyer; b. Nassawadox, Va., Nov. 29, 1944; d. Robert G. and Daisy B. (Hitchens) Sanderson; m. Arthur C. Delo Jr., Mar. 20, 1971; 1 child, Marjorie Cotton Delo. BA, U. Richmond, 1966; JD, Rutgers U., 1977; LLM, NYU, 1985. Bar: N.J., 1977, U.S. Dist. Ct. N.J., 1977, U.S. Tax Ct., 1987, U.S. Ct. Appeals (2nd cir.) 1997, D.C. 1999, N.Y. 1999. Law clk. to Hon. John J. Geronimo N.J. Superior Ct., 1977-78; assoc. Lamb Hutchinson Chappell Ryan & Hartung, Jersey City, 1978-80, Chasan Leyner Holland & Tarrant, Jersey City, 1980-84, Stryker Tams & Dill, Newark, 1985-92, ptnr., 1993-98; exec. compensation assoc. Bachelder Law Offices, N.Y.C., 1998—2002, of counsel, 2002—. Lectr. on tax issues. Contbr. articles to profl. jours. Lay reader Ch. St. Andrew and Holy Communion, South Orange, N.J. Democrat. Episcopalian. Avocation: animal welfare organizations and activities. Home and Office: 340 Montrose Ave South Orange NJ 07079-2439 E-mail: esdelo1@aol.com.

DE LOACH, BERNARD COLLINS, JR., retired physicist; b. Birmingham, Ala., Feb. 19, 1930; s. Bernard Collins and Ada Blanche (Moore) De L.; m. Annie Ruth Wilson, Aug. 24, 1951; children: Linda Louise, Bernard Collins III. BS in Physics, Auburn U., 1951, MS in Physics, 1952; PhD in Physics, Ohio State U., 1956. Mem. tech. staff AT&T Bell Labs., Holmdel, N.J., 1956-63, supr. Murray Hill, N.J., 1963-66, dept. head, 1966-89, ret., 1989. Courtesy prof. engring. sci. U. Ctrl. Fla., Orlando, 1993—. Author tech. papers and lectures; patentee in field. Recipient Stuart Ballantine medal Franklin Soc., 1975, Vladimir Karapetoff award Eta Kappa Nu, 2003. Fellow IEEE (David Sarnoff medal 1975, co-recipient Engring. Excellence medal, 1993). Avocations: gardening, jogging, fishing.

DELOACH, ROBERT EDGAR, corporate executive; b. Daytona Beach, Fla., Jan. 6, 1939; s. Ollie Newman and Sally Gertrude (Schrowder) DeL. Student, U. Alaska-Anchorage, 1967-69, Alaska Meth. U., 1970, Pacific Luth. U., 1972. Lic. elec. engr. and adminstrs., Alaska, 1979; lic. pvt. pilot, real estate broker, ins. agt. Former chmn. bd. Alaska Stagecraft, Inc., Anchorage; pres. BG Systems Co., BG Tax & Acctg., Inc., The Electric Doctor, Inc., Apollo Travel, Inc.; former pres. Coastal Electronics, Inc.; former owner-mgr. Bargain Towne, Anchorage. Active Anchorage Cmty. Theatre, Anchorage Theater Guild. Mem. Assn. Ind. Accts., Internat. Assn. Theatrical Stage Employees and Moving Picture Machine Operators U.S. (past pres. local 770), Ind. Elec. Contractors Assn., Internat. Assn. Elec. Insps. Home: PO Box 520569 Big Lake AK 54481-8469

DELOACHE, WILLIAM REDDING, pediatrician; b. Camden, S.C., Mar. 27, 1920; s. William Redding and Louise Blakeney (Zemp) DeL.; m. Bond Davis, Sept. 7, 1943; children: Frances D., William Redding Jr. Student, Furman U., Greenville, S.C., 1937-38; BA, Vanderbilt U., 1941, MD, 1943. Diplomate Am. Bd. Pediatrics; lic. Tenn. Healing Arts.; cert. med. examiner, S.C. Intern pediatrics Vanderbilt Hosp., Nashville, 1944, resident pediatrics, 1947-48, N.C. Bapt. Hosp., Bowman Gray, Winston-Salem, 1948-49; pvt. practice Greenville, S.C., 1949-53; ptnr. Christie Pediatric Group, Greenville, 1953-72; dir. nurseries Greenville Hosp. Sys., 1972-77, dir. med. edn., 1977-82; assoc. exec. dir. Am. Bd. Pediatrics, Chapel Hill, N.C., 1982-87, ofcl. examiner, 1976-90. Assoc.,sr. assoc. Greenville Meml. Hosp., Greenville Hosp. Sys., 1994-92; mem. pediatric staff St. Francis Hosp., Greenville, 1949-92; assoc. prof. pediatrics Med. U. S.C., 1973-87; mem. bd. Vanderbilt U. Med. Ctr., Nashville, 1985-91, mem. adv. bd., 1991—. Contbr. articles to profl. jours. Elder Fourth Presbyn. Ch., Greenville. Capt. U.S. Army, 1944-46. Mem. AMA, Am. Acad. Pediatrics (career achievement award S.C. chpt. 1987), Greenville County Med. Soc. (pres. 1971), S.C. Med. Assn., So. Soc. Pediatric Rsch., So. Perinatal Assn., Greenville C. of C. (bd. mem.), Rotary Club (mem. bd. 1976—), Greenville Country Club, Poinsett Club. Avocations: woodworking, gardening, travel, tennis. Home: 72 Round Pond Rd Greenville SC 29607-3717 E-mail: billdel@charter.net.

DELOATCH, CHERYL LEE, communications company executive; b. Murfreesboro, N.C., Dec. 30, 1963; d. Gilbert Lee and Susie Monger Deloatch. BA, U. N.C., 1988, MEd, 1993. Instr. Roanoke-Chowan C.C., Ahoskie, N.C., 1988-90; tchr. N.C. Pub. Schs., 1990-97; radio broadcaster Mortenson Broadcasting, Raleigh, 1998; tech. svc. specialist MCI World Comm., Cary, NC, 1998—2002. TV news asst. Sta. WRAL-TV 5, Raleigh, 1997-98; radio broadcaster Hertford Broadcasting, Ahoskie, N.C., 1988; writer, editor various cos., 1987—. Sec. Sunday sch. Mt. Sinai Bapt. Ch., Como, N.C., 1990-96; active Adopt-A-Student Program Weldon Elem. Sch., 1991-92; media vol. Spl. Olympics World Summer Games, 1999. Mem. Internat. Assn. of Bus. Communicators, N.C. Writers Network, Journalism Alumni and Friends Assn., Gen. Alumni Assn., N.C. Assn. of Govt. Info. Officers, N.C. Assn. of Educators. Avocations: reading, writing, music, movies and restaurants, theatre.

DE LOERA, DAVID F. religious studies educator; b. Hammond, Ind., June 26, 1940; s. Francisco Velasco and Dorthy Akin De Loera; m. Shirley Juanita Cook, Oct. 26, 1968. BDiv, St. Bonaventure, Lake Forest, Ill., 1963; M, U. Metaphysics, L.A., 1985; PhD, U. Metaphysics, 1990. Ordained Nat. Metaphysics Inst., 1983. Rancher, Augs, N.Mex., 1967—68, 1979—; retailer, 1979; founder, pres. Asclepiads AHOA, Calumet City, Ill., 1984—. Therapist Asclepiads AHOA, Hammond, 1983—; lectr. AHOA, Milw., 1984; book reviewer Llewellyn, St. Paul, 1990—. Author: Asclepiad Corp., 1985. Unitarian. Avocation: biblical and religious comparative research. Office: Asclepiads AHOA PO Box 95 Calumet City IL 60409 E-mail: doctorasclepius@juno.com.

DEL OLMO, FRANK, newspaper editor; b. L.A., May 18, 1948; s. Francisco and Margaret Rosalie (Mosqueda) D.; m. Karen Margaret King, Feb. 6, 1970 (div. Sept. 1982); 1 child, Valentina Marisol; m. Magdalena Beltran-Hernandez, Nov. 10, 1991; 1 child, Francisco Manuel. Student, UCLA, 1966-68; BS magna cum laude in Journalism, Calif. State U., Northridge, 1970. Reporter-intern L.A. Times, 1970-71, gen. assignment reporter, 1971-80, columnist, editorial bd., 1980-90, deputy editor, 1990-98, assoc. editor, 1998—. Instr. Chicano Studies, Calif. State U., 1970-71; contbg. editor Race Relations Reporter, Nashville, 1973-75; on-air host, writer "Ahora" Sta. KCET-TV, L.A., 1974; chief writer, rschr. KNBC, 1975; bd. contbrs., freelance reporter Nuestro Mag., 1976-81; program co dir. Summer Program Minority Journalists, 1990, faculty mem. 1979, vis. faculty mem. 1978, 80-83, 85, 89; vis. prof. Dow-Jones Newspaper Fund U. So. Calif. Sch. Journalism, 1975, bd. dirs. Numerous lectrs., presentations at colls., univs. Named Senior Faculty of Summer Program Minority Journalists Inst. Journalism Edn.; recipient Emmy award, 1976, Sigma Delta Chi Achievement award, 1982, Profl. Achievement award UCLA Alumni, 1990, Pulitzer Prize, 1984; Nieman fellowship Harvard U., 1987-88. Office: Los Angeles Times 202 W 1st St Los Angeles CA 90012-4105

DELONG, DAVID G. architect, urban planner, educator; Bachelors, U. Kans.; M in Architecture, U. Pa., 1963; PhD in Arch. History, Columbia U., 1976. With Conklin & Rossant, N.Y.C.; restoration arch. Harvard-Cornell Archeol. Expn., Sardis, Turkey, 1967—68; sr. designer, then assoc. John Carl Warnecke & Assocs., N.Y.C., 1969—74; prof., chair grad. program hist. preservation Columbia U., N.Y.C., U. Pa., Phila., 1984—96. Bd. dirs. Frank Lloyd Wright Bldg. Conservancy, Phila. Hist. Preservation Corp., Nat. Coun. Preservation Edn.; dir. Preservation Alliance Greater Phila.; J.M. Fitch resident in hist. preservation Am. Acad., Rome, 1997; cons. in field. Author: Bruce Goff: Toward Absolute Architecture, Historic American Buildings: Texas, 2 vols., Calif., 4 vils., New York, 8 vols., The Architecture of Bruce Goff: Buildings and Projects, 1916-74; co-author: Frank Lloyd Wright: Designs for an American Landscape, Louis I. Kahn: In the Realm of Architecture (AIA Internat. Frank Lloyd Wright and the Living City Book award); editor: Working with Mr. Wright: What It Was Like, Wright in Hollywood: Visions of a New Architecture; co-editor: American Architecture: Innovation and Tradition; co-author: Out of the Ordinary: Robert Venturi, Denise Scott Brown and Associates. Fellow Fulbright, 1967—68, Chettle Vis., U. Sydney, 1992, Guggenheim, 1997—98; scholar vis., Getty Ctr. History Art and Humanities, 1989. Mem.: Soc. Arch. Historians (dir.). Office: U Pa Grad Program Hist Pres 115 Meyerson Hall Philadelphia PA 19104-6311

DELONG, DEBORAH, lawyer; b. Louisville, Sept. 5, 1950; d. Henry F. and Lois Jean (Stepp) D.; children: Amelie DeLong, Samuel Prentice. BA, Vanderbilt U., 1972; JD, U. Cin., 1975. Bar: Ohio 1975, Ky. 1999, U.S. Dist. Ct. (so. dist.) Ohio 1975, U.S. Ct. Appeals (Fed. cir.) 1990, (11th cir.), 1995, U.S. Ct. Appeals (6th cir.) 1991, U.S. Supreme Ct. 1982. Assoc. Paxton & Seasongood, Cin., 1975-82, ptnr., 1982-88, Thompson, Hine & Flory, 1989—2001. Contbr. articles to profl. jours. Bd. dirs. Cin. Opera, Cin. Shakespeare Festival, Clovernook Ctr. for the Blind. Mem. ABA, Ohio State Bar Assn., Cin. Bar Assn., Arbitration Tribunal U.S. Dist. Ct., Ohio, 1984. Republican. Episcopalian. Office: Dinsmore & Shohl LLP 1900 Chemed Ctr 255 E Fifth St Cincinnati OH 45202-4089

DELONG, DONALD R. accountant; b. Muskegon, Mich., Sept. 3, 1946; m. Susan K. Jourden; children: Kristy, Andrew. BS in Acctg., Ferris State U., Big Rapids, Mich., 1968. CPA, Mich. Staff acct. Alexander Grant & Co., Muskegon, 1970—75; co-founder Brickley DeLong, P.C., Muskegon, 1975—, mng. ptnr., pres., 1985—. Pres. Shoreline Land Co.; ptnr. KIMA Properties, Bluffton Bay Estates; mem. acctg. com. Mich. Dept. Edn., 1986-98; mem. adv. com. various cos. Co-author: State of Michigan School Accounting Manual, 1989. Officer Bluffton Bay Estates Condo Assn., 1999—; trustee McGraft Ch., Muskegon, 1995—99, treas., 1995—; bd. dirs., pres. YMCA, Muskegon, 1991. Acting sgt. U.S. Army, 1968—70. Mem. Mich. Assn. CPAs (state acctg. com. 1982-94). Office: Brickley DeLong PC PO Box 999 500 Terrace Plz Muskegon MI 49443

DE LONG, JACOB EDWARD, real estate broker; b. Syracuse, N.Y., Oct. 5, 1939; s. Jacob Edward (dec.) and Eva Ann (Sposato) D. (dec.); children: Edward Andrew, Michael Anthony, Sean Michael (dec.). Grad. high sch., Fayetteville, N.Y. Sales rep. Ill. Shade Div., Slick Airways, Chgo., 1963-67; dir. mktg. Bean Bros. Inc., Walton, N.Y., 1967-71; real estate sales Longley Jones Assoc., Syracuse, 1971-73, Radclif Real Estate, Syracuse, 1973-76; comml. real estate J. Edward De Long Real Estate, Syracuse, 1976 80, Eagan Real Estate Inc., Syracuse, 1980—. Pres. bd. dir. The Andrew Nelson Self Help Ctr., Syracuse. Fund raiser, Friends of the Burnet Park Z00, Syracuse, 1986. Sgt. USAF, 1957-62. Mem. N.Y. State Bd. Realtors, Onandaga Bd. Realtors, Onondaga Ski Club, Syracuse Ski Hawks, Am. Legion, Rotary. Republican. Roman Catholic. Office: Eagan Real Estate Inc 1208 James St Syracuse NY 13203-1324 also: Eagan Real Estate Inc 1 Telergy Pkwy East Syracuse NY 13057 E-mail: edelong2002@aol.com.

DELONG, JAMES CLIFFORD, air transportation executive; b. N.Y.C., Jan. 29, 1940; s. Mary (Oles) DeL.; m. Nancy L. Hill; children: Andrew Hill, Theodore James. BS, Colgate U.; MA, U. Calif. Asst. mgr. Wichita Midcontinent Airport, 1970, airport mgr., 1971-74; asst. mgr. Houston InterContinent Airport, 1975-77, airport mgr., 1980-85, Houston Hobby Airport, 1978-79; dep. dir. dept. aviation Houston Dept. Aviation, 1986-87; dir. aviation Phila. Divsn. Aviation, 1987-93, Denver Divsn. Aviation, 1993-98; gen. mgr. Reg. Airport Authority of Louisville and Jefferson County, Ky., 1998—. Bd. dirs. Phila. Conv. and Vis. Bur., 1992-93. Pilot, USAF, 1963-70. Mem. Am. Assn. Airport Execs. (bd. dirs. 1989), Internat. Civil Aviation Orgn. (helicopters panel 1985—), Airport Operators Internat. (bd. dirs. 1990, info. sys. com. 1988, chmn. tech. com. 1979), Airport Coun. Internat. (bd. dirs., chmn. 1996), Nat. Transp. Rsch. Bd. (exec. bd. dirs. 1992-95), Variety Club Internat. (bd. dirs. 1992-93). Avocations: classical guitar, restoration antique autos, motorcycling. Office: Louisville Intl Airport Regional Airport Authority PO Box 9129 Louisville KY 40209-0129

DELONG, JANICE AYERS, education educator; b. Bedford, Va., May 8, 1943; d. Lloyd Edward and Minnie Hilda (Updike) Ayers; m. Elmer Mason Nance, Aug. 22, 1964 (dec. May 16, 1968); m. Robert Edward DeLong, Dec. 3, 1970; children: Michael Anthony, Tonya Lynne, Kara Susanne; 1 stepchild, Kimberly Beth. BA, Lynchburg Coll., 1965, MEd, 1970, MEd, 1987; postgrad., Shenandoah U., 1994. Tchr. Bedford (Va.) County Sch. System, 1965-68; social worker Dept. Social Svcs., Bedford, 1969-70; tchr. Longwood Ave. Christian Sch., Bedford, 1976-80, Timberlake Christian Sch., Lynchburg, Va., 1980-85; instr. Liberty U., Lynchburg, Va., 1985—. Presentor at numerous reading and children's lit. workshops. Co-author: Core Collection for Small Libraries, 1997, Contemporary Christian Authors, 2000, Young Adult Poetry: A Survey and Theme Guide, Redwall: A Study Guide, 2003. Mem. choir Flat Creek Bapt. Ch., Lynchburg, 2000—. Mem. Internat. Reading Assn., Nat. Coun. Tchrs. English, Appalachain Tchrs. Network, Tchrs. and Writers Collaborative, Kappa Delta Pi (Golden Apple award 1990). Republican. Baptist.

DELONG, LANCE ERIC, physics educator, researcher; b. Denver, Nov. 12, 1946; s. Robert Earl and Svea Virginia (Selander) DeL.; m. Michele Denise Arranaga, Dec. 30, 1977 (div. Mar. 1983); m. Mary Jane Gorham, Sept. 1983; children: Kristin Ann, Rebecca Jane, Eric Zachary, Tyler Gorham BA, U. Colo., 1968; MS, U. Calif., San Diego, 1969, PhD, 1977. Asst. prof. physics U. Va., Charlottesville, 1977—79; asst. prof. U. Ky., Lexington, 1979—83, assoc. prof., 1983—2001, prof., 2001—. Scientist-in-residence materials sci. and tech. divsn. Argonne (Ill.) Nat. Lab., 1985—86, faculty rsch. participant, 1986—89; mem. user group high-flux isotope reactor Oak Ridge (Tenn.) Nat. Lab., 1983—; rsch. assoc. Ames (Iowa) Lab., 1984—; expert divsn. materials rsch. NSF, Washington, 1988, program dir. low temp. physics, 89; vis. scholar U. Calif., San Diego, 2002; co-founder, bd. dirs. Lev Tech Inc., 2001—. Co-editor procs. of Rare Earth Rsch. Confs., 1986, 88, 93, 96; contbr. over 95 articles to profl. jours. Recipient rsch. opportunity award Rsch. Corp., 1988; Cottrell rsch. grantee, 1983, rsch. grantee U.S. Dept. Energy, 1981-84, 88-89, 96—, NSF, 1991—. Mem. Am. Phys. Soc., Am. Assn. Physics Tchrs. Avocations: physical conditioning, soccer, rugby. Office: U Ky Physics and Astronomy Lexington KY 40506-0001

DELONG, LAWRENCE ALBERT, former legislative official; b. Cooperstown, N.Y., Nov. 18, 1941; s. Albert Stanford and Dorothy Shires (Smith) DeL.; 1 child, Carl Albert (dec.). BA, Hamilton Coll., 1963. Staff assoc. for health and social svcs. N.Y. State Assembly, Albany, 1970-76, dep. dir. program and com. staff, 1976-89, coord. recruitment and tng., 1989-96; rsch. dir. N.Y. Joint Legis. Com. on Pub. Health, Albany, 1969-70; intern, rsch. assoc. N.Y. Office of Legis. Rsch., Albany, 1963-64, 68-69. Editor: Officers of the Town of Worcester, 1964, A Bicentennial History of the Town of Worcester, 1997, The DeLongs of Worcester, New York and Associated Families, 2000, Conversations, 2001, Historian, Town of Worcester, 1961-1964, 2000. Commr., pres. Ea. N.Y. Connie Mack Baseball League, Latham, N.Y., 1972—; co-founder Worcester Hist. Soc., Inc., 1970; trustee Maple Grove Cemetery Assn., 1999-2003; chmn. Town of Worcester Planning Bd., 2001-2003. Lt. USN, 1964-68, Vietnam. Recipient Peter A. Keyrouze award Ea. N.Y. Connie Mack Baseball League. Mem.: Upper N.Y. State Amateur Baseball Assn. (sec. 1996—2003). Democrat. Methodist. Avocations: stamp, coin and license plate collecting, hiking, amateur baseball, family history. Home: 238 Grooms Rd Clifton Park NY 12065-6213 E-mail: ldelong@nycap.rr.com.

DELONG, RONALD, artist, educator; b. Bethlehem, Pa., Nov. 18, 1949; s. Kermit and Mary Jane Delong. BS in Art Edn., Kutztown U., 1972, MEd in Art Edn., 1988. Tchr. Northwestern Lehigh S. Dist., New Trifoll, Pa., 1972-95, Palisades Sch. Dist., Kintnersville, Pa., 1979-83; mgr. art edn. Binney & Smith, Inc., Easton, Pa., 1995—; prof. Moravian Coll., Bethlehem, Pa., 1996—. Author, editor: Teacher Resource Guide, 1985-97, Crayola Dream Makers, 1995-00. Pres. Lehigh Art Alliance, 1976-79; bd. dirs. Allentown (Pa.) Art Mus., 1997-00, Mayfair Art Festival, Allentown, 1997-00. Mem. Pa. Art Edn. Assn. (pub. chair 1985-97, pres.-elect 1998-00). Home: 2908 Rockdale Rd Slatington PA 18080-4013 Office: Binney and Smith Inc 1100 Church Ln Easton PA 18040-6638

DE LORCA, LUIS E. public school administrator, educator, speaker; b. L.A., Oct. 18, 1959; children: Nicholus A. and Angelus M. (twins). AA, Rio Hondo Jr. Coll., Whittier, Calif., 1983; BA, Calif. State Poly. U., 1989; MA in Humanities, Calif. State U., Dominguez Hills, 1997; tchg. credential, Nat. U., 1997; adminstrv. credential, U. So. Calif., 1998, D. Football coach various high schs., So. Calif., 1980; pub. rels. dir. Calif. Poly Pomona Music Dept., 1987-89; pres. Exclusive Concepts, L.A., 1987-89; lifeguard L.A. City Recreation Dept., 1980-87; tchr. English Cathedral H.S., L.A., 1989-90; tchr., rsch. specialist Whittier (Calif.) Union H.S., 1990; founder, dir. The Learning Advantage Ctr., Whittier, 1991—; elem. tchr. St. Paul of the Cross Sch., La Mirada, Calif., 1993-95; CEO New Ednl. Wave Inc., Whittier, 1994—; tchr. L.A. County Office Edn., 1995-98; asst. prin. Bassett Unified Sch. Dist., 1998-2000; prin. Franklin Mid. Sch., Long Beach (Calif.) Unified Sch. Dist., 2000—. Active Big Bros. of Am., Sierra Club Mem. Assn. Calif. Sch. Adminstrs., Whittier C. of C., Cousteau Soc., Phi Delta Kappa (exec. bd. dirs., v.p. projects). Democrat. Avocations: scuba, martial arts, swimming, handball, skiing. Home: 11323 Gradwell St Lakewood CA 90715 E-mail: LDelorca@lbusd.k-12.ca.

DELORENZO, DAVID JOSEPH, retired public relations executive; b. Auburn, N.Y., Nov. 25, 1932; s. Joseph Robert and Marie (Hahn) DeL.; m. Margaret Mae Pinckney, July 21, 1956; children: David William, Mary Beth DeLorenzo Waldo. Student public schs., Auburn. With lab. Gen. Electric Co., Auburn, 1951, 54-57; asst. bur. chief Elmira Star Gazette, 1957-58; bur. chief Syracuse (N.Y.) Post Standard, 1958-66; polit. writer, city hall reporter Auburn Citizen-Advertiser, 1966-71, asst. sports editor, 1971-77; editor Bowling mag. Am. Bowling Congress, Greendale, Wis., 1977-81, asst. mgr. pub. relations dept., 1981-82, mgr. pub. relations dept., 1982-96; ret. Sports chmn. Cayuga County (N.Y.) March of Dimes, 1965-77. Served with USCG, 1951-54. Recipient writing awards including 5 1st place awards Cayuga County Fire-Police Assn., 1960-65; Journalism award Auburn Police Benevolent Assn., 1974; First place writing award Profl. Bowlers Assn., 1982; Bowling Mag. writing awards. Mem. Bowling Writers Assn. Am. (pres. 1974-75, meritorious service award 1976, exec. dir. 1997-98), Mid-Am. Bowling Writers (pres. 1986-88). Democrat. Roman Catholic. Home: # 1101 4900 Brittany Dr S Apt 1101 Saint Petersburg FL 33715-1644 E-mail: pegdadelo@aol.com. *Fortunate most aptly describes my life. With little background, I first was accepted as a newspaperman which led to being editor of a national publication and eventually to my former position of public relations manager of the world's largest sports membership organization. I sincerely appreciate the confidence so many others had in me through the years.*

DELORENZO, DAVID W. J. human resources consultant; b. Auburn, N.Y., Jan. 15, 1957; s. David J. and Margaret M. (Pinckney) DeL.; m. Jacquelyn DeLorenzo, Sept. 16, 2000; 1 child, David C. AAS, Cayuga County C.C., Auburn, 1978; BS n Bus., SUNY, 2003; diploma in environ. health/battlefield, flight nurse, Brooks AFB Sch. Aerospace Med., San Antonio. Cert. occupl. hearing conservationist, EMT-D, ACLS, BLS and first aid instr.; cert. hazardous material tech., spirometry NIOSH; bd. cert. occupl. health nurse specialist Am. Bd. Occupl. Health Nurses; FAA lic. pvt. pilot. RN, trauma ICU S.U.H. Upstate Med. Ctr., Syracuse, N.Y.; RN ICU Niagara Falls (N.Y.) Meml. Med. Ctr.; RN, surgical ICU VA Med. Ctr., Buffalo, N.Y.; mgr. human resources, Worldwide Midrange Engrg. health cons. Cummins Engring. Co., Inc., Columbus, Ind.; v.p., COO, Western Niagara Physician, P.C., Western N.Y. Occupl. Medicine, P.C. Active Jamestown Area Safety Coun., Chautauqua County Health Coalition. Lt. col. USAFR. Decorated Meritorious Svc. medal with one oak leaf cluster, Air Force Commendation medal; recipient USAF Suggestion award, Armed Forces Volunteerism medal; Andrew Murphy Meml. scholar, Flight Nurse Honor Grad. scholar. Mem. Soc. Human Resource Mgmt., Am. Occupl. Health Nurses, N.Y. State Assn. Occupl. Health Nurses, Northeastern Assn. Occupl. Health Nurses, Res. Officers Assn. (life mem.). Home: 3517 Palmer Rd Ransomville NY 14131-9689

DE LORENZO, ROBERT ALLAN, emergency physician; b. N.Y.C., Sept. 15, 1963; MD, Albany (N.Y.) Med. Coll., 1990. Diplomate Am. Bd. Emergency Medicine. Commd. 2d. lt. U.S. Army, 1985, advanced through grades to lt. col, 1996; intern Wright State U., Dayton, Ohio, 1990-91, resident Emergency Medicine, 1990-93, fellow Emergency Medicine, 1993-94; staff Dept. Emergency Medicine Darnall Army Comty. Hosp., Ft. Hood, Tex., 1994-97; assoc. residency dir. Brooke Army Med. Ctr., Ft. Sam Houston, Tex., 2000—01. Asst. prof. Tex. A&M U., 1994-97; assoc. clin. prof. Uniformed Svcs. U., Bethesda, Md.; instr. Acad. Health Scis., Ft. Sam Houston, Tex., 1997-2000; dir. San Antonio Uniformed Svcs. Health Edn. Consortium Residency in Emergency Medicine, 2001—. Author: Tactical Emergency Care, 1999, Weapons of Mass Destruction: Emergency Care, 2000. Mem. Am. Coll. Emergency Physicians, Assn. Mil. Surgeons of the U.S., Nat. Assn. Emergency Med. Svc. Physicians, Soc. Acad. Emergency Medicine, Sigma Xi. E-mail: Robert.DeLorenzo@amedd.army.mil.

DELORENZO, ROBERT JOHN, neurologist, molecular neuroscientist; b. Clifton, N.J., June 26, 1947; s. Sylvio A. and Johanna DeL.; m. Lorisa Mernette DeLorenzo, June 16, 1973; children: Brock, Grant, Shanelle. PhD in Neuropharmacology, Yale U., 1973, MD, MPH, Yale U., 1974. Diplomate Am. Bd. Psychiatry and Neurology. Asst. prof. neurology Yale Med. Sch., New Haven, 1977-80, assoc. prof. neurology, 1980-85; prof., chmn. neurology Va. Commonwealth U., Richmond, 1985-2000; George Bliley prof. neurology U. Med. Coll. Va., Richmond, 1988—, prof. molecular biophysics and biochemistry, 1985—, prof. pharmacology and toxicology, 1985—, dir. neurosci. rsch. facility, 1985—2000, Directorship STAR Scientific, Chester, Va., 1998—, chmn. bd., 1998-2000, CEO, 1999-2000. Author: Total Child Care, 1982; contbr. articles to profl. jours. Bd. trustees The Found. for Excellence and Ethics and Medicine, N.Y.C., 1999—, The Grass Found., Boston, 1993-97; profl. adv. bd. Epilpsy Found. of Am., Landover, Md., 1990-95. Recipient Jacob Javits award NIH, 1986, Dixon Woodbury Rsch. award U. Utah, 1994, Disting. Neuroscientist award La. State U., 1993. Fellow Am. Acad. Neurology, Am. Neurol. Assn.; mem. Am. Epilepsy Soc. (Milken award 1998), Soc. of Neurosci., Epilepsy Found. Am. (pres. profl. adv. bd. 1993-95, Jodi Folch Pi award 1984), Am. Soc. Neurochemistry. Avocations: running, antiques and rare books, culinary activities. Office: Med Coll of VA PO Box 980599 Richmond VA 23298 E-mail: rdeloren@hsc.vcu.edu.

DE LORENZO, WILLIAM E. foreign language educator; BA in Spanish and Speech, Montclair State Coll., 1959, MA in Speech and Drama, 1964; PhD in Fgn. Lang. Edn. and Tchr. Edn., Ohio State U., 1971. Tchr. Spanish various locations, N.J.; asst. prof. Spanish, Montclair State Coll.; assoc. prof. emeritus, coord. fgn. lang. edn./2d lang. edn. U. Md., College Park. Organizer, co-dir. symposium for fgn. lang. tchr. candidates. Recipient Florence Steiner award, 1992. Mem. Am. Coun. on Tchg. Fgn. Langs. (charter). Office: U Md Dept Curriculum-Instrn Harold Benjamin Bldg Rm 2311 College Park MD 20742-0001

DELOREY, JOHN ALFRED, printing company executive; b. Malden, Mass., July 13, 1924; s. John Alfred and Alice Gertrude (Collins) D.; m. Ann M. Abbott, Dec. 27, 1952; children— Debra Ann, Michael John, David Abbott BS in Econs., Boston Coll., 1950; MBA, Harvard U., 1953. Plant mgr. Container Corp. Am., Renton, Wash., 1965-69, mgf. mgr. Carol Stream, Ill., 1969-73, gen. mgr. St. Louis, 1973-77, Carol Stream, 1977-81, v.p., divsn. gen. mgr. St. Louis, 1981-82; exec. v.p. W.F. Hall Printing Co., Chgo., 1982-87; v.p. Container Corp. Am., 1987-93; pres. DeLorey & Assocs., Oak Brook, Ill., 1993—. Dir. Container Corp. Am. Polit. Action Com., Chgo., 1981-86. Author: (with others) Consumer Packaging, 1953 Served to maj. USAF, 1942-53, ETO. Decorated DFC, Air medal with 3 oak leaf clusters, European Theater medal with 3 battle stars. Mem.: Paperboard Packaging Assn. (dir. midwest region 1977—81), Boston Coll. Club (Naples, Fla.), Kensington Country Club, Harvard Bus. Club, Butterfield Country Club. Avocations: golf, swimming, skiing, bridge, reading. Home and Office: DeLorey & Assocs 194 Briarwood Loop Oak Brook IL 60523-8714

DELORME, MICHAEL, toxicologist, researcher; b. Detroit, Mich., Dec. 18, 1966; s. Lawrence and Carolyn DeLorme; m. Holly Hodgins, June 18, 1994; 1 child, Evan. BS, Wayne State U., 1985—89, MS, 1991—94, PhD, 1994—99. Registered Medical Technologist Am. Soc. for Clin. Pathology, Ill., 1989. Med. technologist Damon Clin. Laboratories at the Detroit Med. Ctr., 1989—90, Cottage Hosp., Grosse Point Farms, Mich., 1990—94; grad. rsch. asst. II Wayne State U., Detroit, 1994—99; postdoctoral fellow CIIT Centers for Health Rsch., Rsch. Triangle Pk., NC, 1999—2002; rsch. toxicologist - inhalation group DuPont Haskell Lab., Newark, Del., 2002—. Contbr. articles to profl. jours. AIHA Found. scholarship, Am. Indsl. Hygiene Assn., 1996. Mem.: Soc. of Toxicology, Am. Indsl. Hygiene Assn. Office: DuPont Haskell Lab PO Box 50 Newark DE 19714 Office Fax: 302-366-6420. E-mail: michael.p.delorme@usa.dupont.com.

DELOYHT-ARENDT, MARY ISOBEL, artist; b. Independence, Mo., Mar. 10, 1927; d. Frank Howard and Edith Isobel Strickland; m. William Joseph Arendt; children: Tracey McKee, Tammy Strnatka. AA, Columbia Coll., 1946; BA in Fine Arts, U. Mo., 1949. Group exhibits include Brea Art Ctr., Conejo Valley Mus., San Bernardino County Mus., West Bend Gallery, Western Colo. Ctr., Grady Gammage Auditorium, Ariz. State U., Tex. U., San Antonio, Goddard Art Ctr., Ardmore, Okla., Waldorf Astoria, N.Y.C., Utah State U., Gonzaga U., Ad Gallery, Spokane, The Casino, Avalon, Calif.; represented in pvt. collections Am. Embassy, Geneva, Valley Nat. Bank, Empire Machinery, Giant Industries, First Interstate Bank, Thunderbird Bank, Ariz. Biltmore, Marriott Camelback Inn; represented by S.R. Brennen, Scottsdale, Ariz., Courtyard Gallery, New Buffalo, Mich., Gold Nugget Gallery, Wickenburg, Ariz, Timmons Courtyard Gallery, Rancho Sante Fe, Calif.; included in books: Spash Three, 1994, Painting with the White of Your Paper, 1994, Make Your Watercolors Look Professional, 1997, The Best of Flower Painting, 1997, Splash 5, 1998, Keys to Painting Fruit and Flowers, 2000, Splash 7, 2001, The Language of Landscape, 2002, also numerous mags. Mem. Nat. Watercolor Soc. (signature), Ariz. Watercolor Soc. (Royal mem.), Ariz. Artists Guild (past pres., life mem.), Plein Air Painters Am. (signature), 22x30 Profl. Critique Group, Tucson Plein Air Painters (hon.). E-mail: mdawatercolor@juno.com.

DELP, WILBUR CHARLES, JR., lawyer; b. Cedar Rapids, Iowa, Oct. 26, 1934; s. Wilbur Charles and Irene Frances (Flynn) D.; m. Patricia Lynn Vesely, June 22, 1963; children: Marci Lynn, Melissa Kathryn, Derek Charles. BA, Coe Coll., 1956; LL.B., NYU, 1959. Bar: Ill. 1960, U.S. Supreme Ct. 1962. Assoc. Sidley Austin Brown & Wood, Chgo., 1959—68, ptnr., 1968—. Lectr. securities law seminars With USAF, 1959-65. Mem. ABA (securities com.), Chgo. Bar Assn., Lawyers Club (Chgo.), Mid-Day Club (Chgo.), Phi Beta Kappa, Phi Kappa Phi. Home: PO Box 97 Wayne IL 60184-0097 Office: Sidley Austin Brown & Wood Bank One Plz Chicago IL 60603-0001 E-mail: wdelp@sidley.com.

DEL PAPA, FRANKIE SUE, former state attorney general; b. 1949; BA, U. Nev.; JD, George Washington U., 1974. Bar: Nev. 1974. Staff asst. U.S. Senator Alan Bible, Washington, 1971—74; assoc. Law Office of Leslie B. Grey, Reno, 1975—78; legis. asst. to U.S. Senator Howard Cannon, Washington, 1978—79; ptnr. Thornton & Del Papa, 1979—84; pvt. practice Reno, 1984—87; sec. of state State of Nev., Carson City, 1987—91, atty. gen., 1991—2002. Active Nev. Women's Fund; bd. dirs. Sierra Arts Found.; adv. com. Trust for Pub. Land. Democrat.*

DELPAR, HELEN, historian; b. N.Y.C., May 10, 1936; d. Nicholas Delpar and Dolores Ricaurte. BA, Douglass Coll., New Brunswick, N.J., 1957; MA, NYU, 1961; PhD, Columbia U., N.Y.C., 1967. Asst. prof. history Ind. State U., Terre Haute, Ind., 1967—69, Fla. State U., Panama Canal Zone, 1969—73; prof. history U. Ala., Tuscaloosa, 1974—. Author: (book) Red Against Blue, 1981, The Enormous Vogue of Things Mexican, 1992; co-author: Reference Guide to Latin American History, 2000. Office: Univ of Alabama Dept History Box 870212 Tuscaloosa AL 35487

DELPARIGI, ANGELO, research scientist; b. Matera, Italy, Nov. 7, 1961; arrived in U.S., 1999; s. Mario and Antonietta DelParigi. Degree in medicine and surgery, U. of Bari, Italy, 1993; degree in nutrition, U. of Bari, 1996. Resident U. of Bari, Med. Sch., Italy, 1996—99; rsch. fellow NIH, Phoenix, 1999—. Sci. rsch. NIH, Phoenix, 1999—. Contbr. articles to profl. jours. Vol. various causes and orgns. Recipient award, Am. Coll. of Nutrition, 2000. Mem.: Endocrine Soc. (assoc.), Am. Soc. Nutritional Scis. (assoc.). Achievements include research in Brain activity in humans in hunger, taste, and satiation; Gene expression in human brain of obese and lean donors. Office: NIH Rm 5-41A 4212 N 16 St Phoenix AZ 85016 Office Fax: 602-200-5335. E-mail: adelpari@mail.nih.gov.

DELPESCO THORNTON, NANCY ROSE, artist, educator; b. Bklyn., May 2, 1939; d. Alphonse Joseph and Margery Dora (Thompson) Bolduc; m. Andrew Del Pesco, Aug. 8, 1959 (div. July 1966); children: Belinda, Robin, Todd (dec.), Nancy, James; m. Stephen Wayne Thornton, Mar. 16, 1990. Owner, operator Lindenmuth Gallery, Rockport, 1973-76, DelPesco Needlepoint Design, Rockport, Mass., 1975-76, Workingman's Gallery, Santa Barbara, Calif., 1977-79, retail lingerie store and women's home party bus., Santa Barbara, 1980-83, Women's Painting Co., Santa Barbara, 1983-89, DelPesco Fine Arts, Santa Barbara, Calif., and Wash., 1989-97, Fernandina Beach, Fla., 1997—. Demonstrating artist Ritz Carlton Hotel, Amelia Island, Fla., 1998-2000, Del Pesco Fine Art Gallery, Fernandina Beach, Fla., 2000—; owner AdLib Greetings/art cards storefront, Fernandina Beach, 1997—. Author: (children's books) Over the Garden Wall, 1997, It's OK to be Different, 1997, Best Buddies, 1998; contbr. art to Best of Acrylics by the Rockport Publishers, 1996. Tchr. art mental hosp., Essex, Mass., 1974-75, city jail, Essex, 1974-75; counselor Battered Women's Ctr., Santa Barbara, 1979-80. Mem. Valley Artists Guild (treas. 1994-95, pres. 1995-96, Gold medal 1994, Best of Show 1995), Valley Watercolor Soc. (exhibit chmn. 1995-96, sec. 1996-97, Best of Show 1996), Amelia Island Art Assn. Avocations: dancing, walking, reading, helping others. Home: 2328 Sadler Rd # 2B Fernandina Beach FL 32034-3047 Studio: DelPesco Fine Arts 13 N 4th St Fernandina Beach FL 32034-4123 E-mail: nancy@artbydelpesco.com.

DELPH, DONNA JEAN (DONNA MAROC), education educator, consultant, university administrator; b. Hammond, Ind., Mar. 7, 1931; d. Edward Joseph and Beatrice Catherine (Ethier) Maroc; m. Billy Keith Delph, May 30, 1953 (div. 1967); 1 child, James Eric. BS, Ball State U., 1953, MA, 1963, EdD, 1970. Cert. in ednl. adminstrn./supervision, reading specialist, Ind.; cert. elem. sch. tchr., Ind., Calif. Elem. tchr. Long Beach (Calif.) Community Schs., 1953-54; elem. tchr., reading specialist, asst. dir. elem. edn. Hammond Pub. Schs., 1954-70; prof. edn. Purdue U. Calumet, Hammond, 1970-84, 88-90, prof. emeritus, 1990—, head dept. edn., dir. tchr. edn., 1984-88. Cons. pub. schs., Highland, Ind., 1970-88, Gary, Ind., 1983-88, East Chicago, Ind., 1987-88, Hammond, 1970-88; speaker/workshop presenter numerous profl. orgns., Hammond, 1964—; mem. exec. coun. Nat. Coun. Accreditation Tchr. Edn., 1991-97. Author: (with others) Individualized Reading, 1967; contbr. articles, monographs to profl. jours. Bd. dirs. Bethany Child Care and Devel. Ctr., Hammond, 1972-77. Recipient Outstanding Teaching award Purdue U. Calumet, 1981. Mem. Assn. Tchr. Educators, Assn. for Supervision and Curriculum Devel. (rev. coun. 1987-91, bd. dirs. 1974-85), Internat. Reading Assn., Ind. Reading Profs. (pres. 1985-86), Pi Lambda Theta. Office: Purdue Univ Calumet Dept Education Hammond IN 46323 E-mail: delnjohn@otherside.com.

DELPH, KATHLEEN ANNE, foundation administrator, development director; b. L.A., May 30, 1956; d. Joseph Michael and Edna Mae (Salem) Nassany; m. Stephen Alan Delph, Aug. 29, 1981; children: Brittany, Taylor. BA, U. Calif., Irvine, 1980. Dir. found. and corp. devel. Intefnat. Bible Soc., Colorado Springs, Colo., 1995-98, Compassion Internat., Colorado Springs, 1998-99, devel. dir., 1999—2001, donor rels. dir., 2001—. Cons. in field. Participant Nat. Prayer Breakfast, Washington, 2000, 2001; presenter, participant The Leadership Luncheon, Colorado Springs, 2000, The Grant Seekers Foru, Colorado Springs, 1996-99; adv. com. Colorado Springs Pregnancy Ctr., 2001; mem., presenter Evang. Devel. Ministries, 1998-99. Mem. Christian Stewardship Assn., Nat. Assn. Fundraising Execs., Christian Mgmt. Assn. Avocations: skiing, reading, cooking. Office: Compassion Internat 12290 Voyager Pkwy Colorado Springs CO 80921

DEL PRADO, SERGIO, professional soccer team executive; b. Havana, Cuba; arrived in U.S., 1962; m. Leslie Del Prado; children: Monica, Eric. BS in Bus. Adminstrn., Calif. State U., Long Beach. Formerly with L.A. Kings/Nat. Hockey League, dir. mktg., corp. acct. mgr., 1997-92, Hispanic broadcast mgr., 1992-94, corp. account mgr., dir. mktg.; gen. mgr. L.A. Galaxy, 1999—. Office: care LA Galaxy 1010 Rose Bowl Dr Pasadena CA 91103-2864

DELPRETE, PIERO GIUSEPPE, botanist, curator, educator; b. Villanova Monferrato, Italy, Feb. 19, 1958; s. Francesco Delprete and Antonietta Beccaria. BS, U. Calif., Davis, 1990; PhD, U. Tex., Austin, 1996. Herbarium asst. curator U. Calif., Davis, 1987-90, U. Tex., Austin, 1990-96, N.Y. Bot. Garden, Bronx, 1996—. Adj. prof. botany, CUNY, N.Y.C., 1996—; assoc. editor (scientific jour.) Brittonia, N.Y.C., 1996—. Mem. Bot. Soc. L.Am., Bot. Soc. Brazil, Internat. Assn. Plant Taxonomy. Avocations: writing biographies and historical explorations, music. Office: NY Botanical Garden 200th St & Southern Blvd Bronx NY 10458-5126 Fax: 718-817-8648. E-mail: pdelprete@nybg.org.

DEL RASO, JOSEPH VINCENT, lawyer; b. Phila., Dec. 21, 1952; s. Vincent and Dolores Ann (D'Adamo) Del R.; m. Anne Marie McGloin, Apr. 17, 1982; children: Joseph Vincent Jr., Katherine Anne, Marianna. BS in Acctg., Villanova U., 1974, JD, 1983. Bar: Pa., 1983, Fla. 1988. Exec. v.p. Belgrade Constrn., Inc., Wayne, Pa., 1974-80; atty. SEC, Washington, 1983-85; assoc. Dechert, Price & Rhoads, Washington, 1986-88; ptnr. Holland & Knight, Ft. Lauderdale, Fla., 1988-92, Stradley, Ronon, Stevens & Young, Phila., 1992-98, Pepper Hamilton LLP, Phila., 1998—. Gen. counsel, bd. dirs. Nat. Italian-Am. Found.; chair bd. trustees Am. Univ., Rome. Co-editor-in-chief Villanova Jour. Law and Investment Mgmt. Sec. of bd. consultors Villanova U. Sch. Law; bd. dirs. Justinian Found.; mem. Columbus Citizens Found., N.Y. Mem. ABA, Aronimink Golf Club. Republican. Roman Catholic. Office: Pepper Hamilton LLP 18th & Arch Sts 3000 Two Logan Sq Philadelphia PA 19103

DEL RIO, JACK, professional football coach, former professional football player; b. Castro Valley, Calif., Apr. 4, 1963; m. Linda Del Rio; children: Lauren, Hope, Aubrey, Luke. Student, U. So. Calif., 1985. Linebacker New Orleans Saints, 1985—86, Kansas City Chiefs, 1987—88, Dallas Cowboys, 1989—91, Minn. Vikings, Eden Prairie, 1992-95; asst. strength coach New Orleans Saints, 1997, linebackers coach, 1998, Balt. Ravens, 1999—2001; def. coord. Carolina Panthers, 2002; head coach Jacksonville Jaguars, 2003—. Selected to Pro Bowl, 1994. Office: 1 ALLTEL Stadium Pl Jacksonville FL 32202*

DEL ROSARIO, ANNA ANTONIO, director; EdM, Teachers Coll., Columbia U., 1999. Admissions officer UCLA, Los Angeles, Calif., 1994—97; asst. dir. student affairs The Juilliard Sch., New York, NY, 1999—2000; undergrad. student affairs officer UC Berkeley, 2001—.

DEL ROSARIO, MARIANO BORAS, JR., artist; b. Naga, The Philippines, Nov. 20, 1955; came to US, 1981; s. Mariano Platon Sr. and Rosita (Boras) Del R. BFA, U. The Philippines, 1978; MFA, Md. Inst. Coll. of Art, 1983. Instr. Art Students League of NY One-person shows include The Cultural Ctr. of Philippines, 1981, Soho Ctr. Visua Artists, NYC, 1988, OK Harris Gallery, NYC, 1988, 91, 93, 96, 98, West Galle ry, Metro-Manila, The Philippines, 1996; exhibited in mus. shows at Mus. Philippine Art, Manila, 1980, Balt. Mus. Art, 1983, Queens Mus. Art, NY, 1987, 89, Bronx Mus. Arts, NY, 1989, Butler Inst. Am. Art, Youngstown, Ohio, 1995, Cultural Ctr. Philippines, Manila, 1997; exhibited in group shows at Asian Pacific Am. Studies Inst. Gallery, NYU, 1999, Rotunda Gallery, Bklyn., 1999. Recipient Thirteen Artists award, Cultural Ctr. The Phillippines, 1978, Bklyn. Cmty. Access TV/Rotunda Gallery Artist Residency, Bklyn., 1999; fellow, Glassell Sch. Art, 1983—84, Asian Cultural Coun., 1996—97; grantee, Pollock-Krasner Meml. Found., 1989—90, Emerge 2000, ALJIRA/ A ctr. for contemporary art,/ Newark, NJ, 2001, Pollock-Krasner Meml. Found., 2000. Home: 175 Willoughby St Apt 12L Brooklyn NY 11201-5410

DEL ROSARIO, RUBEN, mechanical engineer, researcher; b. Ponce, P.R., Aug. 3, 1967; s. Ruben Del Rosario Ramos and Elba Torres; m. Diana Del Rosario, June 24, 1990; 1 child, Natalia Cristina. BSME, U. of P.R., Mayaguez, 1990; MS in Indsl. Engring., Cleve. State U., 1993. Registered profl. engr., Ohio. Rsch. engr. Ohio Aerospace Inst., Brookpark, Ohio, 1990; rsch. test engr. NASA John H. Glenn Rsch. Ctr., Cleve., 1990—96, asst. project mgr. for emmisions reduction, 1996—98, mgr. of aeropropulsion components rsch. facilities, 2002—03, interagy. coord. mgr. for aeronautics, 2003—. Commr. City of Berea Planning Commn., Ohio, 1995—2001; mem. City of Berea Charter Rev. Commn., 1994—95; chair NASA Glenn Hispanic Adv. Coun., 1997—2000. Recipient NASA Equal Opportunity medal, 2001. Mem.: AIAA (exec. sec. of turbine engine testing working group 2000—02), Soc. of Hispanic Profl. Engrs. (v.p. ne ohio chpt. 1992—95). Office: NASA John H Glenn Research Center 21000 Brookpark Rd MS 6-8 Cleveland OH 44135 E-mail: ruben.delrosario@grc.nasa.gov.

DEL RUSSO, ALESSANDRA LUINI, retired law educator; b. Milan, Jan. 2, 1916; d. Avvocato Umberto and Candita (Recio) Luini; m. Carl R. del Russo, Apr. 12, 1947; children: Carl Luini, Alexander David. PhD in History with honors, Royal U., Milan, 1939; SJD summa cum laude, Royal U., Pavia, Italy, 1943; LLM in Comparative Law, George Washington U., Washington, 1949. Bar: Md. 1956, Md. Ct. Appeals, Ct. of Appeals (Milano) 1947, U.S. Ct. Appeals (D.C. cir.) 1950, U.S. Supreme Ct. 1955. Legal adviser Allied Mil. Govt. and Ct., Milan, 1945-46, U.S. Consulate Gen., Milan, 1946-47; pvt. practice Washington, Bethesda, Md., 1950-58; atty. adviser Legis. Ref. Libr. of Congress, Washington, 1958-59; atty. U.S. Commn. on Civil Rights, Washington, 1959-61; prof. Howard U. Sch. Law, Washington, 1961-81, dir. grad. program, 1972-74, prof. emerita, 1981—; adj. prof. Stetson U. Coll. Law, St. Petersburg, Fla., 1980-95, adj. prof. emerita, 1995—. Professorial lectr. George Washington U. Law Ctr., 1970-80; mem. legal cons. com. U.S. Commn. on Status of P.R., Washington, 1965-66; lectr. in field. Author: International Protection of Human Rights, 1971; editor and chmn. of symposium on International Law of Human Rights, Howard U. Sch. of Law, Washington, 1965; contbr. numerous articles to internat. and Am. profl. jours. Rsch. grant Howard U., 1963. Mem. ABA, Brit. Inst. Internat. and Comparative Law, Am. Soc. Internat. Law. Republican. Roman Catholic. Achievements include 1st woman to receive LLM in Comparative Law from George Washington U. Home: 400 Ocean Trail Way Apt 908 Jupiter FL 33477-5527

DEL SESTO, JANICE MANCINI, opera company executive; Gen. dir. Boston Lyric Opera Co., Boston, Mass. Office: Boston Lyric Opera Co 45 Franklin St Boston MA 02110-1301

DELSON, ELIZABETH, artist; b. N.Y.C., Aug. 15, 1932; d. Julius and Emmy (Haas) Pfannmuller; m. Sidney L. Delson, Sept. 10, 1955; children— Karen Lee, Sara Jeanne, Matthew Robert. BA, Smith Coll., 1954; MA, Hunter Coll., 1972. Instr. graphic arts Pratt Inst., 1962-66 Shows include USIA Traveling Exhibit, 1962-64, Bklyn. Mus. Nat. Print Exhbn., 1966, others; one-woman shows Hicks Street Gallery, 1964, L.I. U., 1969, 74, Paerdegat Libr., 1971, 74, Park Gallery, 1973, Brownstone Gallery, 1974, 84, Clayton & Liberatore, 2002; group shows include Hudson Guild, 1982, 83, 88, 90, 92, 98, 2000, Cork Gallery, 1987, 88, 89, 91, 92, 94, 98, 2003, Broome Street Gallery, 1992, 95, 96, 2000, 01, 02, Lever Ho., 1985, 91, 98, Millenium Gallery, 2000, others; represented in permanent collections N.Y. Pub. Libr., L.I. U., So. Ill. U., Columbia U., Boston Pub. Libr., Bklyn. Mus. Mem. Soc. Am. Graphic Artists, Contemporary Artists Guild (treas. 1980—), Audubon Artists (Medal of Honor for graphics 1961, Gold Medal of Honor 1996, Pen and Brush 1st prize for graphics 2001), Artists Alliance East Hampton (co-treas. 2001—). Address: 29 Orkney Rd East Hampton NY 11937-1313

DELSON, SIDNEY LEON, architect; b. Chgo., Apr. 10, 1932; s. Robert and Evelyn (Fistel) D.; m. Elizabeth Pfannmuller, Sept. 10, 1955; children: Karen Lee, Sara Jeanne, Matthew Robert. BArch, Pratt Inst., 1959. Registered architect, N.Y. Archtl. draftsman Irving G. Kay, N.Y.C., 1957-59; project architect William B. Tabler Assocs., N.Y.C., 1959-62; architect-designer Union Carbide Corp., Tarrytown, N.Y., 1962-64; archtl. dept. head Metcalf and Eddy Engrs., N.Y.C., 1965-66; devel. adminstr. N.Y. State Facilities Devel. Corp., N.Y.C., 1966-80, dir. design, 1980-91; pvt. practice architecture Bklyn., 1991-99, East Hampton, N.Y., 1999—. Editor: Design Procedure Manual, 1986, 2d edit., 1988, 3d edit., 1991. Mem. Community Planning Bd. Bklyn., 1968-71, vice chmn., 1971; chmn. adv. com. Bklyn. Mus. Community Gallery, 1970-73.

Served as sgt. U.S. Army, 1951-53. Fellow AIA; mem. N.Y. State Assn. Architects (bd. dirs. 1982-85, 89, sec.-treas. 1988, Matthew W. DelGaudio award 1992), Am. Cons. Engrs. Coun. (peer rev. 1987—), Am. Arbitration Assn. (panelist 1971—). Home and Office: 29 Orkney Rd East Hampton NY 11937-1313

DEL TIEMPO, SANDRA KAY, sales executive; b. Willoughby, Ohio, Nov. 21, 1962; d. Charles Soloman and Lacey Marie (Webb) Eggers; m. Robert Joseph Craig, June 28, 1986 (div. Jan. 1993); 1 child, Misty Marie Mangus; m. Robert David Del Tiempo, Feb. 14, 1995; stepchildren: Jaime Brandon, Joseph David Del Tiempo. AAB cum laude, Shawnee State U., 1985; BBA summa cum laude, Ohio U., 1987; postgrad., Pepperdine U., 1998-2000. From ter. mgr. to sales mgr. ARA Cory, San Diego, 1988-90; sales rep. Rsch. Inst. Am., Riverside, Calif., 1990-92, 96-00, regional sales mgr. So. Calif., L.A., 1992-95, leader's coun. Culver City, 1996-2000, pres. bd. dirs., 1996-97, asst. mgr., 1997, 1999-2000, corp. acct. mgr., 1997-2000; mem. sales adv. bd. RIA/CLR Group (formerly Rsch. Inst. Am.), Culver City, 1998-2000; sr. v.p. Media Strategy Lawnmower Media, Culver City, 2000; sr. account exec. SAP Am., Irvine, Calif., 2000—. Cons. Video Ave., Paradise Pizza, Chillicothe, Ohio, 1987-88; sales rep. to corp. acct. mgr. Rsch. Inst. Am. Orange County, L.A., 1990-2000. Active Girl Scouts U.S., Menifee, 1988 92, Jr. All Am. Football. Mem. NAFE, NOW, Phi Kappa Phi, Phi Theta Kappa, Delta Mu Delta. Democrat. Avocations: travel, reading, jazz. Home: 6732 E Ashler Hills Cave Creek AZ 85331-3130 Office: CCH Inc 2700 Lake Cook Rd Riverwoods IL 60015 E-mail: sdeltiempo@yahoo.com.

DEL TORO SOTO, JAIME, psychiatrist; b. Guanica, P.R., Feb. 9, 1947; s. Jaime Del Toro Rodríguez and Adoración Soto Arroyo; m. Adalina Feliciano Santiago, Aug. 8, 1970; children: Adaime, Jaime Javier, Jorge Javier. BS, U. P.R., 1969; MD, Zaragoza U., Spain, 1976. Diplomate Am. Bd. Forensic Medicine. Intern in gen. medicine Bayamon Regional Hosp., PR, 1977—78; resident in psychiatry P.R. Inst. Psychiatry, San Juan, 1979—82, clin. instr., 1982—90, co-dir. Outpatient Clin., 1985—86, asst. clin. prof., 1990—. Acting med. adminstr. Psychiat. Ctr. P.R., San Juan, 1982—92; co-dir., clin. officer Inst. Psychaitry and Human Behavior, San Juan City Hosp., 1987—90; cons. and lectr. in field, 1992—; pvt. practice, 1992—. Mem.: Am. Psychiat. Assn., Am. Bd. Disability Analysts, Am. Coll. Forensic Examiners, Colegio Med. Cirujanos P.R., P.R. Psychiat. Soc. Avocations: saltwater sportfishing, anthropology. Office: Psychiat Ctr PR 652 Ave M Rivera Ste 3195 San Juan PR 00918-4261

DEL TUFO, ROBERT J. lawyer, former US attorney, former state attorney general; b. Newark, Nov. 18, 1933; s. Raymond and Mary (Pellecchia) Del T.; m. Katherine Nouri Hughes; children: Barbara, Ann, Robert, David. BA cum laude in English, Princeton U., 1955; JD, Yale U., 1958. Bar: N.J. 1959. Law sec. to chief justice N.J. Supreme Ct., 1958-60; assoc. firm Dillon, Bitar & Luther, Morristown, N.J., 1960-62, ptnr., 1962-74; asst. prosecutor Morris County, N.J., 1963-65; 1st asst. prosecutor, 1965-67; 1st asst. atty. gen., 1974-77; dir. criminal justice, 1976-77; U.S. atty. Dist. of N.J., Newark, 1977-80; prof. Rutgers U. Sch. Criminal Justice, 1979-81; ptnr. firm Stryker, Tams & Dill, 1980-86, Hannoch Weisman, 1986-90; atty. gen. State of N.J., 1990-93; ptnr. Skadden, Arps, Slate, Meagher & Flom, N.Y.C. and Newark, 1993—; commr. N.J. State Commn. of Investigation, 1981-84. Instr. bus. law Fairleigh-Dickinson U., 1964; mem. N.J. State Bd. Bar Examiners, 1967-74; mem. criminal law drafting com. Nat. Conf. Bar Examiners, 1972-2002; bd. dirs. Nat. Ctr. for Victims of Crime, 1995-2003; Nat. Italian Am. Found., 1995-2003, Integrity Inc., 1995—, John Cabot U. in Rome, 1997—, Legal Svcs. N.J., 2000—. IOLTA, 1994-99, N.J. Pub. Interest Law Ctr., 1996-99, Daytop Village Found., 1998—, Planned Parenthood, 1998-99; mem. com. on character N.J. Supreme Ct., 1982-84; spl. master, fed. jail onvercrowding litigation, Essex County, 1989-90; trustee Boys and Girls Clubs of Am., 2000—. Bd. editors Yale U Law Jour; contbr. articles to profl. jours. Mem. law enforcement adv. com. County Coll. of Morris, 1970-85; mem. Morris County Ethics Com., 1968-71, Morris County Jud. Selection Com., 1970-72, Essex County Jud. Selection Com., 1982-84; v.p., mem. exec. com. United Fund of Morris County, 1966-70; chmn. Morris Twp. Juvenile Conf. Com., 1963-74; bd. dirs. Nat. Found. March of Dimes, 1966-68, Vis. Nurse Assn. Morris County, 1963-70, Morristown YMCA, 1970-74; trustee Boys & Girls Club Am., 1999—, Atty.'s Fund for Client Protection, 1999—; trustee Newark Acad., 1976-95, 97—2002, pres. bd. dirs. 1983-87; bd. regents St. Peter's Coll., 1979-85. Fellow Am. Bar Found.; mem. Am., N.J., Morris County bar assns., Nat. Dist. Attys. Assn., Yale Law Sch. Assn. (exec. com. 1978-84), Order of Coif. Home: 13 Ober Rd Princeton NJ 08540-4917 Office: Skadden Arts Slate Meagher & Flom One Newark Ctr Newark NJ 07102 also: 4 Times Sq New York NY 10036-6522 E-mail: rdeltufo@skadden.com.

DELTUVIA, JOHN JOSEPH, JR., systems and procedural analyst; b. New Brunswick, N.J., Dec. 9, 1962; s. John Joseph and Margaret Helen Deltuvia. AA in Humanities, Ocean County Coll., Toms River, N.J., 1982; BA in Polit. Sci., Livingston Coll., 1985; AAS in Computer Sci., Ocean County Coll., Toms River, N.J., 1987; BA in Computer Sci., Thomas Edison State Coll., Trenton, N.J., 1991. Cert. Reiki practitioner. MIS technician N.J. Divsn. Pub. Welfare, Trenton, 1986-88; sys. mgr. Monmouth County Probation Dept., Freehold, N.J., 1988-97; programmer Dezine Healthcare Solutions, East Brunswick, N.J., 1997-99; sys. and procedures analyst Adminstrv. Office N.J. Cts., Trenton, 1999—. Mem. Assoc. Bodywork and Massage Profls. Avocations: reading, web design. Fax: 609-984-3630 and 978-389-6136. Home: 1300 Violet Ln Jackson NJ 08527 Office: Adminstrv Office NJ Cts PO Box 976 Trenton NJ 08625 E-mail: john.deltuvia@judiciary.state.nj.us., jjd@sillious.net.

DELUCA, ANTHONY J. civilian military employee; b. N.Y.C., Apr. 29, 1946; s. Joseph Anthony and Jean (Trentalange) DeL.; m. Mary Alaimo, June 18, 1967; children: Renee, Joseph, Regina. B in Econs., Fordham U., 1967; M in Pub. Adminstrn., Troy State U., 1976. Cert. Acquisition Profl. Level III. USAF procurement officer Eglin AFB, Fla., 1967-72, civil svc. various positions with the deputy for procurement and mfg., 1972-78; procurement analyst USAF mem. Fed. Acquistion Regulation Project Office, 1978-79; supervisory procurement analyst Hdqs. Air Force Syss. Command, Andrews AFB, Md., 1979-82, advanced from first command competition advocate to deputy Air Force competition advocate gen., 1984-87; first civilian competition advocate gen. Office of the Asst. Sec. of the Air Force (Acquistion), Washington, 1987; dir. Air Force Office Small and Disadvantaged Bus. Utilization, Washington, 1990-2001; pres. INTECS Internat., Alexandria, Va., 2001—. Ira Eaker fellow Air Force Assn.; recipient Meritorious Civilian Svc. award, Exceptional Civilian Svc. award, Presdl. Disting. Rank award, Presdl. Meritorious Rank award, Minority Participation Program award Latin Am. Mgmt. Assn., Fed. Advocate award SBA, Frances Perkins award, Applause award; named Advocate of Yr., Small Disadvantaged Bus. Mem. Sr. Exec. Assn., Air Force Assn. Roman Catholic. Avocations: biking, music. Office: INTECS International Inc 5500 Cherokee Ave Ste 410 Alexandria VA 22312-2321

DE LUCA, ANTHONY JAMES, psychoanalyst, theologian; b. N.Y.C. s. James Carl and Antoinette (Scarano) DeL. BA, St. John's U., 1957; STB, Cath. U. Am., 1961; BS, Queens Coll., 1963; MA, Fordham U., 1965, PhD, 1971; MA, St. John's U., 1973; cert. psychoanalysis/psychotherapy, Postgrad. Ctr. Mental Health, 1975; postdoctoral studies, Georgetown U., 1997-98, Princeton U., 1999—. lic. clin. psychologist, Pa.; marriage counselor, N.J.; sch. psychologist, N.Y., N.J. Asst. prof. philosophy and psychology Notre Dame Coll., N.Y.C., 1967-71, Fordham U., N.Y.C., 1972-73; exec. dir. Am. Inst. for Creative Living, Inc. Bklyn., S.I., N.Y., Morrisville, Pa., East Brunswick, N.J., 1972—. Assoc. pastor Bklyn Diocese, Roman Catholic Ch., 1961-67, cons. Marriage Tribunal, 1967—; UN rep. for Ch.; spl. UN advisor to Kyrgyzstan at UN and Washington Embassy; dean Internat. Sch. for Mental Health Practitioners, S.I. and Pa.; cons. N.Y.C. Police Dept., 1980—; dir., producer S.I. Cmty. TV; standing conf. for Oriental Orthodox Ch., Oriental Orthodox Roman Catholic Cons., Joint Eastern/Oriental Orthodox Commn., U.S.A., 1999—. Author: Freud and Future Religious Experience, 1976. Vicar gen. Sts. Peter & Ignatius mission Malankara Syrian Orthodox Ch., 1998; mediator Civil Ct. City of N.Y., 1998; rector Ignatius U., Indpls. Fellow Am. Orthopsychiat. Assn.; mem. APA, Am. Philos. Assn., Am. Sociol. Assn., Am. Group Psychotherapy Assn., Am. Assn. Marriage and Family Therapists (supr.), Am. Found. Religion and Psychiatry, Alzheimer's Assn. (bd. dirs.), Coun. Register Health Providers in Psychology. Home: 2295 Victory Blvd Staten Island NY 10314-6625 E-mail: ignatiusu@aol.com.

DE LUCA, CARLO JOHN, biomedical engineer, educator; b. Bagnoli del Trigno, Italy, Oct. 12, 1943; came to the U.S., 1973; s. John and Josephine (De Blasio) DeL.; m. Christine M. Rafferty. B in Applied Sci., U. B.C., Can., 1966; MS, U. N.B., Can., 1968; PhD, Queen's U., 1972. Lectr. U. N.B. Computing Ctr., Fredericton, 1968; lectr. biomed. engring. unit Queen's U., Kingston, Ont., Can., 1969-70, lab. instr. dept. anatomy, 1970-71, lectr. dept. anatomy, 1971-72, asst. prof. dept. anatomy, 1972-73; lectr. MIT, Cambridge, Mass., 1973—. Rsch. assoc. in orthopaedic surgery Children's Hosp. Med. Ctr., Harvard U. Med. Sch., Boston, 1973-79, prin. rsch. assoc. in orthopaedic surgery, 1979-84, dir. Neuromusclar Rsch. Lab., 1980-84; adj. assoc. prof. biomed. engring. Boston U., 1977-84, prof. biomed. engring., 1984—, rsch. prof. neurology, 1985—, dir. NeuroMuscular Rsch. Ctr., 1984—, chmn. dept. biomed. engring., 1986; dean Coll. Engring., Boston U., 1986-89; founder, pres. DelSys, Inc., 1993—; cons. Liberty Mut. Rsch. Ctr., Hopkinton, Mass., 1973-94; rsch. mem. Harvard-MIT divsn. health sci. and tech., 1978-84; affiliated scientist New Eng. Regional Primate Ctr., 1977-87; mem. nat. and internat. coms.; apptd. dir. Inst. for Disability Prevention and Wellness, U. Medicine and Dentistry of N.J., 1999; mem. Nat. Adv. Coun. for Biomed. Imaging and Engring., 2002—. Founding editor-in-chief Jour. Electromyography and Kinesiology, 1990; mem. editl. bds. sci. jours.; co-author: Muscles Alive; contbr. articles on biomed. engring. and neurophysiology to sci. publs. Founder, pres. Neuromuscular Rsch. Found., 1985—. Recipient Volvo award Internat. Soc. for Study of Lumbar Spine, 1989, Wartenweiler Lecture award Internat. Soc. Biomechanics, 1993, Stuart Reiner Meml. Lectr. award Am. Assn. Electrodiagnostic Medicine, 1994, United Cerebral Palsy Found. Tech. award, 1999; named to Italian Cultural Ctr. Hall of Fame, Vancouver, Can., 1991; Ont. Govt. fellow, 1969-70; grantee RSA, VA, NIH, NASA, U.S. Army, USAF. Fellow IEEE, Am. Inst. Med. and Biol. Engring. (founding fellow 1993, Basmajian Lectr. award 1998); mem. AAAS, Biomed. Engring. Soc., Internat. Soc. Electrophysiol. Kinesiology (sec. gen. 1976-80, sec. 1980-84, v.p. 1985-88, pres. 1988-92), Can. Med. and Biol. Engring. Soc., Soc. Neuro-Sci., Orthopaedics Rsch. Soc., Dante Alighieri Soc. (bd. govs. 1986-88), Mass. Tech. Park Corp. (bd. govs. 1987-90), Harvard Club Boston, Sigma Xi. Home: 107 Livingston Rd Wellesley MA 02482-7308 Office: Boston U NeuroMuscular Rsch Ctr 19 Deerfield St Boston MA 02215-1904 E-mail: cjd@bu.edu.

DELUCA, DOMINICK, medical educator, researcher; BA in Bacteriology, UCLA, 1969, PhD in Microbiology, 1974. Predoctoral fellow NIH dept. bacteriology UCLA, 1970—74, rsch. asst. dept. bacteriology, 1974; postdoctoral fellow Leukemia Soc. Am., Walter and Eliza Hall Inst., Parkville, Australia, 1974—77; scientist cancer biology program Frederick (Md.) Cancer Rsch. Ctr., 1977—80; asst. prof. biochemistry Med. U. SC, Charleston, 1980—85, assoc. prof. biochemistry, 1985—90; assoc. prof. microbiology and immunology U. Ariz., Ariz., 1990—. Mem. pub. policy com. Ariz. Diabetes Control Coun., 1997—2001, chmn., 1999—2001; mem. AIDS rsch. program basic scis. rev. panel U. Calif., 1996—99; mem. brain disorders and clin. neuroscis. study sect. NIH, 1999—. Mem. editl. adv. bd.: Devel. and Comparative Immunology, 1995—2002; contbr. articles to profl. jours., chpts. to books. Recipient Developing Scholar award, Health Scis. Found. Med. U. S.C., 1987, Rsch. award, NIH, 1983, 1986, 1989, 2002, NASA, 1999, Juvenile Diabetes Rsch. Found., 1988, 1998, 2001, 2003, Ariz. Disease Control Rsch. Commn., 1992, 1996, 1998, 2000, 2003, Am. Diabetes Assn., 1995, 2002. Mem.: Ariz. Cancer Ctr., Southeastern Immunology Conf. (pres.-elect 1982—83, pres. 1983—84, bd. dirs. 1985). Office: U Ariz Dept Micro Immuno PO Box 245049 Tucson AZ 85724-5049

DE LUCA, EVA, vocalist, writer, composer, entrepreneur, designer, inventor; d. John Adolph De Luca and Rosa Maria Litrenta; m. Alfred A. Sirna, May 11, 1975 (dec. Dec. 1984); m. Russell Frederick Du Laux, Dec. 24, 1985. Student, Peabody Inst., 1936-37, Juilliard Sch., 1943-44, Marymount Coll., 1985; Doctorate (hon.), Dewey Internat. Consortium, 1999. Pres. Eva De Luca Co., N.Y.C., 1950, Greeting Scrolls, Ltd., N.Y.C., 1960; cons. Creative Consultations, N.Y.C., 1994; mem. adv. bd. Humanity Against Hatred, N.Y.C., 1992-96; CEO/creative dir. Ideas Unlimited U.S.A., 2001. Profl. operatic debut Phila. La Scala Opera Co.; European opera debut La Boheme and Madama Butterfly; starred in 1st rec. of La Rondine (Puccini) for Columbia Records, 1955; author poetry. Com. mem. Women's Nat. Rep. Club, N.Y.C., 1978-85; active Italian Welfare League, N.Y.C., 1978, Met. Opera Guild, N.Y.C., 1979. Recipient Editor's Choice award for outstanding achievement in poetry Nat. Libr. Poetry, 1997, awarded 2 design patents Mirror-View Measuring Stick, 1972. Mem. The Famous Poets Soc., The Russian Nobility Assn. in Am., Inc. (benefit com. mem.), Sovereign Order of Orthodox Knights Hospitaller of St. John of Jerusalem (dame comdr.). Roman Catholic. Achievements include patents for mirror-view measuring stick, personal dental aid; inventor in field; patents for personal dental aid. Avocations: reading, political campaign activity, theater, opera. Home: FDR Sta Box 477 New York NY 10150-0477

DELUCA, JAMES PATRICK, graphic arts and advertising educator, consultant; b. N.Y.C., Aug. 21, 1933; s. Ignazio and Filomena (Romano) D.; m. Teresa Maria Iraggi, Oct. 1, 1960; 1 child, Teresa Maria. AAS, N.Y.C. Community Coll., 1960; BS, NYU, 1963, MA, 1964; EdD, Nova U., 1976. Mem. faculty dept. graphic arts and advt. tech. Ctr. for Advt. Printing & Pub. N.Y.C. Tech. Coll., 1960—; chair dept. N.Y.C. Tech. Coll., 1970-84, prof., chair dept. graphic arts, 1970—; pvt. practice mgmt. cons. to edn. and bus. N.Y. Nat. lectr. on Norman Rockwell, illustrator; asst. examiner N.Y.C. Bd. Edn., 1969, advisor, 1969; ednl. and tech. advisor Graphic Arts, Inc., Pitts., 1967—; co-chair print evaluation sect. Tech. Assn. Pulp and Paper Industry, 1969; mem. ednl. com. The Graphic Arts Tech. Found., 1970—; advisor various pubs. Contbr. articles to profl. jours.; developer grants, 1970—; presenter numerous confs., programs. Trustee Goudy Soc., Am. Printing History Assn.; past pres. Club Printing House Craftsmen. Recipient Gamma Gold Key award GET, 1972, Elmer G. Voigt award Graphic Arts Tech. Found., 1977, Navigators Graphic Arts award Navigators Graphic Arts Assn. N.Y., 1978, James H. Branhey award Printing Mgrs. Assn. Am., 1978, Horace Hart award Graphic Arts Tech. Found., 1982, Soderstrom Soc. Award, 1983, James J. Rudisill award Edn. Council on Graphic Arts, 1978, Van Hanswyk Jasser award Craftsmen, 1978, Man of Year award Lithographic Industries Met. N.Y., 1980, others; named Man of Yr. Printing Tchrs. Guild, 1987. Mem. NEA, Am. Assn. Higher Edn., Am. Assn. Community and Jr. Colls., Am. Tech. Assn., Internat. Graphic Arts Edn. Assn., Printing Industries Am., Nat. Assn. Printers Lithographers (Nat. Key Employee award 1982), Assn. Graphic Arts Assn. N.Y., Am. Vocat. Assn., Am. Mus. Natural History, Smithsonian Hist. Soc., Navigators Graphic Arts Assn. (pres.). Home: 621 8th Ave New Hyde Park NY 11040-5405 Office: CUNY NY Tech Coll 621 8th Ave New Hyde Park NY 11040-5405

DELUCA, MICHAEL, film company executive; Pres. prodn. and devel. New Line Cinema, L.A., now pres., COO of prodn. Office: New Line Cinema 116 N Robertson Blvd Fl 2D Los Angeles CA 90048-3103 also: 888 7th Ave Fl 20 New York NY 10106-0001

DELUCA, PATRICK PHILLIP, pharmaceutical scientist, educator, administrator; b. Scranton, Pa., Sept. 7, 1935; m. Judy Beitzel, June 16, 1956; children: Paul, Thomas, Patrick, Donald, Michelle, Michael. BS in Pharmacy, Temple U., 1957, MS in Pharmacy, 1960, PhD in Pharmacy (SKF W.G. Karr fellow), 1963. Analytical chemist SKF Co., 1957-59; instr., rsch. assoc. Temple U., 1959-62; sr. rsch. pharmacist CIBA Co., Summit, N.J., 1963-66, plant mgr., 1966-69, dir., 1969-70, Cormedics Corp., Somerville, N.J.; faculty U. Ky., 1970—; prof., assoc. dean U. Ky. Coll. Pharmacy, 1972-87, dir. ctr. for pharmaceutical sci. and tech., 1987-88, chmn. faculty pharm. scis., 1998-2000. Pharm. sci. adv. com. FDA; cons. to pharm. industry and FDA. Editor-in-chief: Jour. Pharm. Devel. and Tech., 1995—99; contbr. more than 190 articles to sci. and profl. jours. Mem., pres. parish pastoral coun. Christ the King Cathedral, 1996—99. Recipient Leo G. Penn award Temple U., 1957, Lunsford-Richardson Pharmacy Rsch. award Richardson Merrell Co., 1960, 62, Best Paper Toward Advancement Indsl. Pharmacy award N.J. Pharmacy Discussion Group, 1965, Disting. Alumni award Temple U., 1989, Outstanding Educator award in U.S., 1974, Sturgill Rsch. award U. Ky., 1995; also numerous grants. Fellow: Am. Assn. Indian Pharm. Scientists, Acad. Pharm. Sci. (pres. 1979—80), Am. Assn. Pharm. Scientists (editor-in-chief PharmSciTech electronic jour. 1999—, bd. dirs. 1986—88, Rsch. Achievement award 1988, Outstanding Manuscript award in pharm. devel. and technology 1998, Outstanding Educator award 2000, Sullivan medallist at UK 2001, Ky Pharmacist of Yr. 2002, Outstanding Manuscript award in pharm. tech. 2002, Swintosky Disting. lectr. 2003), Inst. for Advanced Biotech. (sr.); mem.: Am. Soc. Enteral and Parental Nutrition, N.Y. Acad. Sci., Am. Soc. Hosp. Pharmacists (Rsch. award 1975), Parenteral Drug Assn. (Rsch. Achievement award 1975), Am. Pharm. Assn., Rho Chi, Sigma Chi. Achievements include research in pharmaceutical technology and novel drug delivery. Home: 3292 Nantucket Dr Lexington KY 40502-3269 Office: U Ky Coll Pharmacy Rose St Lexington KY 40536-0001

DELUCA, PAUL MICHAEL, retired physician, surgeon; b. Troy, N.Y., Jan. 19, 1917; s. Michael Ercole and Helen (Fitzpatrick) DeL.; m. Dorothy G. Gardner, Feb. 18, 1943 (dec. May 1990); children: Paul Michael, Lynda, Albert, John, Susan, Lisa, Joanne. BS in Biology, Holy Cross Coll., 1939; MD, Albany Med. Coll., 1943. Practiced medicine specializing in neurosurgery; ret. Capt. USAF, 1952-54. Mem. Elks, Am. Legion. Roman Catholic. Avocations: hunting, fishing, gardening. Home: 508 N Oak Ave Endicott NY 13760-4149

DELUCA, RONALD, former advertising agency executive, consultant; b. Reading, Pa., Oct. 28, 1924; s. Nicola and Grace (Carabello) DeL.; m. Lois Ann Hall, Nov. 27, 1952; children: Christine, Diane, Patricia, Maria, Lisa, Nicholas. Certificate comml. art, Pratt Inst., 1949; B.F.A., Syracuse U., 1951; BA, New Sch. Social Research, 1966. Artist J.C. Penney, N.Y.C., 1951-52; designer Remington Rand, N.Y.C., 1952-53; art dir. Roy S. Durstine (advt.), N.Y.C., 1954-56, Kenyon & Eckhardt (advt.), N.Y.C., 1956-66; head creative group Grey Advt., N.Y.C., 1966-67; with Kenyon & Eckhardt Advt., N.Y.C., 1967-85, exec. v.p., vice chmn., 1976-85; pres. Bozell Jacobs, Kenyon & Eckhardt, N.Y.C., 1986-89, vice chmn., 1989-91; cons., 1991—. Founder, v.p. Hancock Cmty. Edn. Found., 1998—. Home and Office: PO Box 551 Hancock NY 13783-0551

DE LUCA, THOMAS GEORGE, lawyer; b. Jersey City, Dec. 28, 1950; s. Michael Anthony and Estelle Theresa (Wickiewicz) De L.; m. Annette Catherine Pandolfo, Aug. 16, 1975; children: Michele, Thomas, Rachel. BS in Econs., St. Peters Coll., Jersey City, 1972; JD, Seton Hall U., 1978. Bar: N.J. 1978, U.S. Dist. Ct. 1978, N.Y. 1981, U.S. Dist. Ct. (so. and ea. dists.) N.Y. 1981, U.S. Ct. Appeals (2d cir.) 1986, U.S. Ct. Appeals (3d cir.) 1987, U.S. Claims Ct. 1989, U.S. Dist. Ct. (we. dist.) N.Y. 1990, U.S. Dist. Ct. (no. dist.) N.Y. 1991, U.S. Supreme Ct. 1987. Supervising underwriter Fireman's Fund Ins. Cos., Newark, 1972-77; assoc. Sellar, Richardson & Stuart, Newark, 1978-80, Postner & Rubin, N.Y.C., 1980-84, ptnr., 1985-93, De Luca & Forster, Cranford, N.J., 1994—. Mem. ABA, N.J. Bar Assn., N.Y. County Lawyers Assn. Roman Catholic. Home: 14 Kilmer Dr Colonia NJ 07067-1213 Office: De Luca and Forster 11 Commerce Dr Cranford NJ 07016-3501 E-mail: delucafor@aol.com.

DELUCCA, LEOPOLDO ELOY, otolaryngologist, head and neck surgeon; b. Santurce, P.R., Nov. 1, 1952; s. Leopoldo Claudio and Laura Iris (Juncos) Delucca; m. Judith Lynn McClellan, June 11, 1977; children: Lauren Denise, Gina Fay. Pre-med. degree, U. P.R., 1973; MD, Jefferson Med. Coll., Phila., 1977. Diplomate Am. Bd. Otolaryngology. Otolaryngologist Ft. Dodge (Iowa) Med. Ctr., 1981-86; practice medicine specializing in otolaryngology Ft. Dodge, 1986—. Active med. staff Trinity Regional Hosp., Ft. Dodge, 1981—, chief of surgery, 1985—, pres. med. staff, 1991—; vol. faculty Coll. Osteo. Medicine and Surgery, Des Moines, 1981-82. Bd. dirs. Trinity Regional Hosp., 1993-99; Comedia Musica Players guitarist First Covenant Ch. Praise Band; guitarist and tenor Sonshine Singers. Fellow ACS, Am. Acad. Otolaryngology-Head and Neck Surgery, Am. Acad. Facial Plastic and Reconstructive Surgery. Republican. Roman Catholic. Avocations: guitar, singing, crosswords. Home: 2626 Woodland Dr Fort Dodge IA 50501-7130 Office: Physicians Office Bldg 200 Kenyon Rd Ste 200 Fort Dodge IA 50501-5762 E-mail: iaoto@dodgenet.com.

DELUCE, RICHARD DAVID, lawyer; b. Nanaimo, B.C., Can., Oct. 3, 1928; came to U.S., 1929; s. Robert and Myrtle (Hickey) DeL.; m. Joanne Strang, Sept. 10, 1955; children: David S., Amy Jane Eigner, Daniel R. AB, UCLA, 1950; JD, Stanford U., Palo Alto, Calif., 1955. Bar: Calif., 1955, U.S. Dist. Ct. (no. dist.) Calif. 1955, U.S. Ct. Appeals (9th cir.) 1955, U.S. Dist. Ct. (cen. dist.) Calif. 1956, U.S. Supreme Ct. 1963, U.S. Dist. Ct. (so. dist.) Calif. 1972. Rsch. atty. Calif. Supreme Ct., San Francisco, 1955-56; assoc. Lawler, Felix & Hall, L.A., 1956-62, ptnr., 1962-90, Arter, Hadden, Lawler, Felix & Hall, L.A., 1990—2003. Co-author: California Civil Writ Practice, 2d edit., 1987. Capt. U.S. Army, 1951-53, Korea. Fellow Am. Coll. Trial Lawyers, Am. Bar Found.; mem. Calif. Club. Home: 3617 Paseo Del Campo Palos Verdes Estates CA 90274-1161

DE LUCIA, FRANK CHARLES, physicist, educator; b. St. Paul, June 21, 1943; s. Frank Charles and Muriel Ruth (Rinehart) D.; m. Shirley Ann Wood, June 25, 1966; children: Frank Charles, Elizabeth Ann. BS, Iowa Wesleyan Coll., 1964; PhD, Duke U., 1969. Instr., research assoc. Duke U., Durham, N.C., asst. prof., assoc. prof.; program mgr. Army Research Office, Research Triangle Park, N.C.; prof. Duke U., Durham, chmn. physics dept.; prof., chmn. dept. physics Ohio State U., Columbus, 1990-98, prof., 1998—. Recipient Max Planck Rsch. prize, 1992, William F. Meggers award, 2001; named Disting. rsch. scholar, 1999, Disting. Univ. prof., 2000. Mem. Am. Phys. Soc., IEEE, Optical Soc. Am., Phi Beta Kappa. Office: Ohio State U Dept Of Physics Columbus OH 43210

DELUCIA, GENE ANTHONY, government administrator, computer company executive; b. Methuen, Mass., Feb. 20, 1952; s. Antonio Gitano and Carmen Theresa (Carpenito) DeL. BS, Boston Coll., 1973; MBA, Northeastern U., 1980. Project mgr. Delphi div. Arthur D. Little Inc., Lowell, Mass., 1975-78, gen. mgr. eastern region, 1978-80; systems devel. mgr. Wang Labs. Inc., Lowell, 1980-83; pres., CEO Computer Innovations Inc., Lowell, 1983-86; pres. Corp. Investment Bus. Brokers, North Andover, Mass., 1986-88; v.p. Maximus Inc., Falls Church, Va., 1988-90, div. pres., 1990-96; pres. Strategic Visions Inc., Indian Rocks Beach, Fla., 1996—. Mem. AOPA. Avocations: skiing, racquetball, electronics, flying, golf. Home and Office: 518 Harbor Dr N Indian Rocks Beach FL 33785-3117

DELUE, STEVEN MULLER, political scientist, educator; b. Chgo., Mar. 6, 1945; s. William DeLue and Dorothy Pokedoff; m. Karen Doering, Aug. 3, 1968; children: Erik Nathaniel, Dana Daniel, Anna Renee. BA, U. Ill., 1967; MA, U. Wash., 1969, PhD, 1971. Instr. polit. sci. U. Wash., Seattle, 1971—72; asst. prof. U. North Fla., Jacksonville, 1972—77, assoc. prof., 1977—83, prof., 1983—, chair polit. sci., 1977—83; prof., chair dept. polit. sci. Miami U., Oxford, Ohio, 1983—94, assoc. dean Coll. Arts and Sci., 1994—2003, sr. assoc. dean, 2003—. Author: Political Obligation in a Liberal State, 1989, Political Thinking, Political Theory and Civil Society, 1997, Polit. Thinking, Polit. Theory and Civil Soc., 2002; contbr. articles to numerous profl. jours.; author: transl. into Arabic, 2003. Campaign worker Dem. candidates. Recipient NEH award, 1976, 79, 81, 82, 87. Mem. Am. Polit. Sci. Assn., Assn. Am. Colls. and Univs. (campus rep.), Phi Kappa Phi. Jewish. Avocations: running, reading, travel. Home: 714 Melissa Dr Oxford OH 45056 Office: Miami U 143 Upham Hall Oxford OH 45056 E-mail: deluesm@muohio.edu.

DELUGACH, ALBERT LAWRENCE, journalist; b. Memphis, Oct. 27, 1925; s. Gilbert and Edna (Short) D.; m. Bernice Goldstein, June 11, 1950; children: Joy, David, Daniel, Sharon. B.J., U. Mo., 1951. Reporter Kansas City (Mo.) Star, 1951-60, St. Louis Globe Democrat, 1960-69, St. Louis Post Dispatch, 1969-70; investigative reporter Los Angeles Times, 1970-89. Served with USNR, 1943-46. Recipient Pulitzer prize for spl. local reporting, 1969, Gerald Loeb award for disting. bus. and fin. journalism, 1984 Home: 4313 Price St Los Angeles CA 90027-2815

DELUGO, ERNEST MARIO, JR., electrical engineer; b. N.Y.C., Sept. 25, 1950; s. Ernest M. and Irma (Maisonett) DeL.; m. Yolanda Garcia, Oct. 17, 1991; children: Jessica, Lisa, David. BSEE, Polytech. U. N.Y., 1971; MBA in Fin., U. Conn., 1995; postgrad. tech. and product strategy, MIT/Sloan, 1999; MSc in Info. Sys. Engring., Poly. U., 2002. Cert. cogeneration engr., project

mgr. Field engr. General Elec. Co., N.Y.C., 1971-75, elec. engr. Schenectady, N.Y., 1975-81; constrn. engr. Burns & Roe, Oradell, N.J., 1977; sr. control sys. engr. Bechtel Power, Ann Arbor, Mich., 1981-84; sr. elec. engr. General Elec. Co., Schenectady, 1984-86, prin. engr., 1986-88, v.p. Stamford, Conn., 1988-92; sr. v.p., dir. projects and bus. devel. Ridgewood (N.J.) Power Corp., 1992-94; pres., mng. dir., project mgr. DeLugo Tech. LLC, Bethel, Conn., 1994—. Author: Project Management: Managing the Investors' Perspective, 1995; contbr. articles to profl. jours. Recipient Project Mgmt. award, Gov. of South Korea, 1979. Mem.: IEEE, Assn. Energy Engrs., Am. Mgmt. Assn., Project Mgmt. Inst., Computer Soc., Assn. of Computing Machinery. Avocation: model railroading. Home: 18 Payne Rd Bethel CT 06801-1239 Office: Delugo Techs LLC 18 Payne Rd Bethel CT 06801-1239 Fax: 203-792-5496. E-mail: erniedelu1@aol.com.

DELUHERY, PATRICK JOHN, state legislator; b. Birmingham, Ala., Jan. 31, 1942; s. Frank B. and Lucille (Donovan) D.; m. Margaret Morris, 1973; children: Allison, Norah, Rose. BA with honors, U. Notre Dame, 1964; BSc in Econs. with honors, London Sch. Econs., 1967. Legis. asst. U.S. Senator Harold Hughes, Washington, 1969-74, U.S. Senator John Culver, Washington, 1975; asst. prof. econs. and bus. adminstrn. St. Ambrose U., Davenport, Iowa, 1975—. Mem. Iowa State Senate, 1979—; ins. agt., 1989—. Democrat. Roman Catholic. Home: 11839 100th Ave Davenport IA 52804-9110 Office: Iowa Senate Statehouse Des Moines IA 50319-0001 E-mail: pdeluhery@saunix.sau.edu., patrick_deluhery@legis.state.ia.us.

DELUISE, VINCENT PAUL, ophthalmologist; b. N.Y.C., Jan. 11, 1952; BS in Bioengineering, Princeton U., 1973; MD, Cornell U., 1977. Diplomate Am. Bd. Ophthalmology. Intern H.C. Moffitt Hosp. U. Calif., San Francisco, 1977-78; resident Bascom Palmer Eye Inst., U. Miami Sch. Medicine, 1978-81; fellow Proctor Found. in Ophthalmology, U. Calif., San Francisco, 1981-82; corneal fellow Ophthalmic Cons. N.W., Seattle, 1982; asst. attending opthalmologist New York Hosp., N.Y.C., 1982—; attending ophthalmologist West Haven (Conn.) VA Hosp., 1982—; clin. instr. dept. ophthalmology Yale U. Sch. Medicine, New Haven, 1982—; clin. asst. prof. ophthalmology U. Conn. Health Sci. Ctr., Farmington, 1982—; attending opthalmologist, chmn. dept. ophthalmology St. Mary's Hosp., Waterbury (Conn.) Hosp., 1982—; ptnr., dir. cornea unit OptiCare Eye Health Ctr., Waterbury, Conn., 1982—. Adj. asst. prof. dept. ophthalmology Cornell U. Med. Coll., N.Y.C., cornea moderator New England Ophthal. Soc., 1991. Editorial bd. Ocular Therapy; contbr. articles to profl. jours. Med. adv. bd. Sjogren's Syndrome Found. Fellow ACS, Am. Acad. Ophthalmology (Honor award 1989, Sr. Honor award 2001); mem. Castroviejo Soc., Contact Lens Assn. Ophthalmologists, Ocular Microbiology and Immunology Group, Rsch. to Prevent Blindness, Phi Beta Kappa. Office: 87 Grandview Ave Waterbury CT 06708-2514

DELUKE, DEAN M. oral surgeon; b. Schenectady, N.Y., Jan. 16, 1952; s. Dominick J. and Virginia D. (Anderson) DeLuke; m. Theresa S. Slowey, Oct. 6, 1984; 1 child, Deanna Marie. BA, St. Michaels Coll., Burlington, Vt., 1974; DDS, Columbia U., 1978. Diplomate Am. Bd. Oral and Maxillofacial Surgery. Pvt. practice oral and maxillofacial surgery, Schenectady, 1982—; chief dept. dentistry St. Clare's Hosp., 1989—93. Cons. Sunnyview Hosp., Schenectady, 1982—2000, VA Med. Ctr., Albany, NY, 1988—2001; pres. N.Y. State Soc. Oral and Maxillofacial Surgeons, 1994; mem. nat. adv. bd. OMS Nat. Ins. Co., 1994—. Contbr. articles to profl. jours. Trustee Albany (N.Y.) Acad. for Girls, 1996—; bd. dirs. St. Clares Hosp. Found., Schenectady, NY, 1987—93, Oral and Maxillofacial Surgery Polit. Action Com., 1996—98. Fellow: Internat. Assn. Oral and Maxillofacial Surgeons, Am. Assn. Oral and Maxillofacial Surgeons (del. 1992—96), Am. Coll. Dentists; mem.: Am. Assn. Dental Cons., Am. Med. Writers Assn., Am. Cleft Palate-Craniofacial Assn. Avocations: skiing, boating. Home: 25 Robinwood Dr Clifton Park NY 12065 Office: 1070 Nott St Schenectady NY 12308

DELUNA, D.N. literary educator; b. L.A., Dec. 16, 1959; Student, Santa Monica Coll., 1978; BA summa cum laude, U. So. Calif., 1980, MA in English, 1984; PhD in English, Johns Hopkins U., 1993. Tchg. asst. U. So. Calif., 1981, writing tutor, 1983; tchg. asst. in contemporary Am. Letters Johns Hopkins U., Balt., 1992, lectr. in New Asian Am. and Latino writing, 1993, lectr. in intro. to fiction and poetry writing, 1993—, lectr. in contemporary Asian Am. fiction, 1994—. Part-time instr. bilingual Spanish-English elem. sch., 1978. Author revs., articles, conf. papers. Mem. MLA, Am. Soc. for Eighteenth-Century Studies, Milton Soc. Am., Am. Journalism Historians Assn., Bibliographical Soc. Am. Home: Colonnade Condos 3801 Canterbury Rd Baltimore MD 21218-2370 Office: Johns Hopkins U Writing Seminars Baltimore MD 21218

DE LUNG, JANE SOLBERGER, independent sector executive; b. Anniston, Ala., July 9, 1944; d. Samuel and Margaret Polk (Oldham) S.; m. Harry Leonard De Lung, Apr. 23, 1965 (div. 1972); m. Charles F. Westoff, May 2, 1997. BA in History, Emory U., 1966; MA in Urban Planning, Roosevelt U., Chgo., 1972. Exec. asst. Cook County Legal Assistance, Chgo., 1967-69; asst. dir. family planning Am. Coll. Ob-Gyn, Chgo., 1969-71; v.p. Ill. Family Planning Coun., Chgo., 1971-80; asst. commr. Chgo. Dept. Pub. Health, 1981-82; pres. Pub. Solutions, Princeton, N.J., 1982-88, Population Resource Ctr., N.Y.C., 1988—. Bd. dirs. Planned Parenthood Mercer County, Trenton, N.J., 1986-96, Population Resource Ctr., 1989—, Trenton Head Start, 1993—; mem. adv. bd. dept. sociology Princeton U., 1991—; mem. Nat. Adv. Com. UN Assn. of USA, 1998—. Mem. APHA, AAUW, LWV, Internat. Union Scientific Study of Population, Population Assn. Am., UN Assn. of U.S.A. Democrat. Episcopalian. Office: Population Resource Ctr 15 Roszel Rd Princeton NJ 08540-6248 E-mail: jdelung@prcnj.org.

DE LURGIO, STEPHEN ANTHONY, management educator; b. St. Louis, June 27, 1945; s. Louis J. and Amelia Barbara (Machler) De L.; m. Ina C. Kimmel, Nov. 10, 1969; children: Stephen A. II, Patrick M. BSME, U. Mo., 1967; MBA, St. Louis U., 1971, PhD, 1976. Design engr. Emerson Electric, St. Louis, 1967-70; project engr. Coinco Inc., St. Louis, 1970-74; asst. prof. mgmt. U. Ill., Springfield, 1974-76; prof. mgmt. U. Mo., Kansas City, 1976—. Co-author: (books) Quantitative Models for Business Decisions, 1980, Forecasting Systems for Operations Management, 1991, Forecasting Theory, 1998; contbr. articles to profl. jours. Bd. dirs. Animal Health Inst., St. Louis, 1985—. U. Kansas City Faculty fellow U. Kansas City Trustees, 1986. Fellow Am. Prodn. and Inventory Control Soc. (chmn. 1984-89, mem. Cert. Com. 1984-89); mem. The Inst. of Man Sci., Inst. of Indsl. Engrs., Internat. Inst. of Forecasters, Decision Scis. Inst. Avocation: trout/fly fishing. Office: U Mo Bloch Sch Bus Kansas City MO 64110 E-mail: sad@forecast.umkc.edu.

DE LUTIS, DONALD CONSE, investment adviser, consultant; b. Rome, N.Y., Apr. 25, 1934; s. Conse R. and Mary D.; m. Ruth L.; 1 child, Dante. BS in Econs., Niagara U., 1956; MBA, Boston Coll., 1962. V.p. John Nuveen & Co., Inc., San Francisco, 1968-74; acct. exec. Dean Witter & Co., London, 1975-77; sr. investment officer Buffalo Savs. Bank, N.Y., 1978-80; exec. v.p. Robert Brown & Co., Inc., San Francisco, 1980-89, Capitol Corp. Asset mgmt., 1989-91; exec. v.p., dir. Pacific Securities, Inc., San Francisco, 1980-91; mng. dir. Coast Ptnrs. Securities, Inc., 1998-99; chmn. Orrell Capital Mgmt., Inc., 1991-98, 2000—. Commr. San Francisco Bay Conservation and Devel. Commn., 1983-93, State of Calif. Commn. Housing and Community Devel., 1974-77. Served with USAF, 1957-58. Mem. Nat. Assn. Bus. Economists, San Francisco Bond Club. Republican. Roman Catholic.

DEL VALLE, CEZAR JOSE, artist, writer, theatre historian; b. Washington, Apr. 14, 1945; s. Cezar and Ida Marie (MacIntosh) Del V.; m. Irene Dorthea DuVal, Sept. 1963 (div. Aug. 1968); m. Darleen Jeanette Travers, Sept. 21, 1968 (div. June 2001); 1 child, Corinne. Grad. high sch., Suitland, Md., 1963. Co-owner Talking of Michaelangelo Gallery, Washington, 1973; former historian The Broadway Theatre Inst.; cons. film dept Mus. Modern Art, NYC, 2002—. Concert promoter MacIntosh Prodns., Alexandria, Va., 1976-78; performers agt., Alexandria and N.Y.C., 1976-82; lectr. Smithsonian Instn., Washington, 1973, North Va. Community Coll., 1973, N.Y. Coun. for Humanities, 2000; curator 11th Ann. Invitational Art Show, Annapolis, Md., 1973; lectr. Mus. of Holography, N.Y.C., 1988-91; bd. dirs. Nebreuko Theatre Co., 1984; artist-in-residence Pawtucket, R.I., 1994; lectr., walking tours for librs. and hist. socs.; cons. in theatre history. Exhibited in over 17 solo exhbns., 115 group shows, including L.I. U., Bklyn., 1974, 89, Cameravision, L.A., 1981, Wolfe St. Gallery, Alexandria, Va., 1973-75, Belanthi Gallery, Bklyn., 1982; group shows include Cleve. Photographic Workshop, 1981, 89, Mus. of Hudson Highlands, Cornwall-on-Hudson, N.Y., 1983, Transamerica's Celebrate the Athlete, L.A., 1984, Photospiva '91, Joplin, Mo., 1991, OIA Artists Salon, N.Y.C., 1991, Newark Mus., 1992, Monmouth Mus., Lincroft, N.J., 1993, Barron Arts Ctr., Woodbridge, N.J., 1993, William's Art Ctr., Rutherford, N.J., 1993, Gallery 450, N.Y.C., 1993, Printmaking Coun. N.J., Somerville, 1994, Galleri 8, Portland, Oreg., 1994, Rotunda Gallery, NYC, 1998, Salon Exhbn., NYC, 1998, Gallery 128, NYC, 1999, Sperone Westwater Gallery, NYC, 2002, Rotunda Gallery, Bklyn., 2002, AIR Gallery Group Ex, NYC, 2003; represented in permanent collections Kinsey Inst., Ind. U., Word Craft, Redwood City, Calif., Tampa (Fla.) Mus. of Art, numerous pvt. collections; work pub. in photographic annual; contbr.: Brooklyn Film, 2002; contbr. articles to profl. jours. Columnist Alexandria Port Packet, 1976; bd. dirs. Tuesday Evening Hour, 1996—; chmn. bd. Tuesday Evening Hour. Mem. Bklyn. Hist. Soc., Theatre Hist. Soc. Am., Bklyn. Coord. Coun. for Preservatio of Neighborhood History, Cinema Theatre Assn. Great Britain, Art Deco Soc. N.Y. Avocations: cooking, travel, theatre. Home: 433 16th St 1R Brooklyn NY 11215-5820

DEL VALLE, MIGUEL, state legislator; b. P.R., July 24, 1951; m. Lupe; 4 children. BA, MA, Northeastern Ill. U. Mem. dist. 2 Ill. State Senate, 1987—; chmn. consumer affairs, vice chmn. com. and econ. devel., mem. appropriations II, higher edn., revenue and elections and reapportionment coms. also: Ill State Senate Capitol Bldg Springfield IL 62706-0001*

DELWICHE, WILLIAM ARTHUR, economist, researcher; b. La Planta, Md., Aug. 24, 1976; s. Raymond Arthur and Margaret Anne (Thiebaud) Delwiche; m. Andrea Rose Guryel, May 30, 1999. BA in Econs., U. Md., 1999. Asst. economist Robert W. Baird and Co., Milw., 1999—. Mem. bd. edn. St. Lucas Elem. Sch., Milw., 2001. Republican. Lutheran. Avocations: reading non-fiction, gardening. Home: 1302 N 58th St Milwaukee WI 53208 Office: Robert W Baird and Co Fl 24 777 E Wisconsin Ave Milwaukee WI 53202 E-mail: wdelwiche@rwbaird.com.

DELY, STEVEN, aerospace company executive; b. N.Y.C., July 16, 1943; m. Kristine Jon Kolbe, June 7, 1975; 1 child, Jonathan Laurence. BBA, CCNY, 1966; JD, Bklyn. Law Sch., 1968; postgrad. program mgmt. devel., Harvard U., 1970. Bar: N.Y. 1972, U.S. Supreme Ct. 1983. Corp. counsel, dir. personnel services Grumman Allied Industries Inc., Garden City, N.Y., 1971-75, gen. counsel, sec., 1976-78; v.p. human resources Melville, N.Y., 1979-82; dir. human resources Grumman Corp., Bethpage, N.Y., 1982-85; v.p. resources and adminstrn. Grumman Electronics Systems div., Bethpage, 1985-86; v.p., asst. to chmn. bd. Grumman Corp., Bethpage, 1986-91, v.p. exec. staff, 1991-92, sr. v.p. exec. staff, corp. sec., 1993-94; co-founder Dispute Resolutions Inc., Huntington, N.Y., 1998—. Capt. U.S. Army, 1969-71.

DEMAIN, ARNOLD LESTER, microbiologist, educator; b. N.Y.C., Apr. 26, 1927; s. Henry and Gussie (Katz) D.; m. Joanna Kaye, Aug. 2, 1952; children: Pamela Robin Demain McCloskey, Jeffrey Brian. BS, Mich. State U., 1949, MS, 1950; PhD, U. Calif., Berkeley, 1954; Doctorate (hon.), U. Leon, Spain, 1997, Ghent (Belgium) U., 1999, Technion-Israeli Inst. Tech., 2000, Mich. State U., Muenster, Germany, 2000, Muenster (Germany) u., 2003. Rsch. asst. U. Calif., Davis, 1952-54; rsch. microbiologist Merck & Co., Inc., Danville, Pa., 1954-56, Rahway, N.J., 1956-65, founder, head of dept. ferm. microbiology, 1965-69; prof. of ind. microbiology MIT, Cambridge, 1969—2001; fellow Charles A. Dana Rsch. Inst., Drew U., Madison, NJ, 2001—. Author or editor 10 books; contbr. 477 articles to profl. jours. With USN, 1945—47. Recipient Hotpack award Can. Soc. Microbiology, 1978, Rubro award Australian Soc. Microbiology, 1978, Indsl. Microbiology award Italian Pharm. Assn., 1989, Hans Knoll meml. award, Germany, 1990, G. Mendel award Czech Acad. Sci., 1998, Andrew Jackson Moyer award USDA, 1998. Mem.: NAS, Am. Chem. Soc. (Marvin Johnson biotech. award), Am. Soc. Microbiology (Waksman award N.J. br. 1975, Biotech. award 1990, Disting. Svc. award 1994, Alice C. Evans award 1998, hon. mem. N.E. br. 1999), Soc. Indsl. Microbiology (pres. 1990, Charles Thom award 1978, Waksman Tchg. award 1995), Hungarian Acad. Sci., Mex. Acad. Sci., Croatian Soc. Biotech. (hon.), Czech Soc. Microbiology (hon.), Soc. Actinomycetes Japan (hon.), French Soc. Microbiology (hon.). Achievements include 21 patents; elucidation of biosynthetic pathway to penicillins and cephalosporins; recognition of phenomenon of biochemical regulation of secondary metabolism; discovery of role of lysine and amino adipic acid in penicillin biosynthesis. Office: Drew Univ RISE HS-330 Madison NJ 07940

DE MAIN, JOHN, orchestra musical director; b. Youngstown, Ohio, Jan. 11, 1944; BMus, Juilliard Sch. Music, 1966, MusM, 1968; studies in conducting with, Leonard Bernstein, Peter Adler. Assoc. condr. St. Paul Chamber Orch., 1972-74; music dir. Tex. Opera Theater, 1974-76; former music dir. Houston Grand Opera, Opera Omaha; artistic dir. Madison Symphony Orch. & Opera, Wis., 1993—. Prin. guest condr. Chautauqua Opera Inst., 1985. Rec. performances: Piano Concerto (Frances Thorne), 1975, Porgy and Bess, 1976, Nocturnes (Miriam Gideon), 1978. Finalist Grand Prix, 1977; recipient Julius Rudel award, 1971, Grammy award, 1977; Juilliard Sch. Music scholar, 1964—68. Office: Madison Symphony Orch 6314 Odana Rd Madison WI 53719 Home: 52 White Oaks Ln Madison WI 53711-6216*

DEMAIO, BARBARA PATRICIA, social worker; b. Bronx, N.Y., Oct. 29, 1940; d. Alphonse Joseph and Elizabeth Elsie (Vogel) DeM.; children: Antonio Joseph, Damon Luis. AAS in Human Svcs., Rockland C.C., 1971; BSW summa cum laude, Fairleigh Dickinson U., 1973; MSW, Yeshiva U., 1975, postgrad., 1981. Cert. social worker; qualified clin. social worker; diplomate. Counselor developmentally disabled ARC, Pomona, 1971-73; counselor foster care Abbott House, Tarrytown, N.Y., 1973-74; psychiat. social worker Mental Health Outpatient Clinic, Pomona, 1974-75; dir. med. social work Dept. Hosps. Robert Yeager Health Ctr., Pomona, N.Y., 1975—. Instr. Yeshiva U. Gerontol. Inst., 1981; cons. Skilled Nursing Facility, 1980; rape crisis counselor, 1983; adj. prof. Albany State U.; field instr. Fordham U., Dominican Coll., St. Thomas Aquinas Coll., Fairleigh Dickinson U., Rockland C.C., 1975—. Mem. NASW, Acad. Cert. Social Workers, Westchester-Rockland Health Care Social Work Assn., Phi Sigma Omicron, Phi Omega Epsilon. Avocations: reading, art, music, home design. Office: Dr Robt L Yeager Health Ctr Dept Hosps Bldg A Pomona NY 10970

DE MALLET BURGESS, THOMAS, opera director, music educator; b. Barnstaple, N. Devon, Eng., June 15, 1964; arrived in U.S., 2000; s. Brian Leslie Burgess and Dawn de Mallet Morgan; m. Fiona Mary McAndrew, Aug. 17, 1996; 1 child, Iseult Sophie de Mallet Burgess. BA in Philosophy and Modern Langs. with honors, postgrad., Oxford (Eng.) U., 1987—. Freelance opera dir. Royal Opera House, London, Guildhall Sch. Music and Drama, London, English Touring Opera, London, Royal Acad. Music, London, Wexford Festival Opera, Ireland, Mälmo (Sweden) Opera and Music Theatre, 1987—, others; prof. opera U. Cin. Conservatory of Music, 2000—. Artistic dir. Opera Shop, London, 1988—91; mng. dir. Blood and Honey Prodns., London, 1989—93; cons. dept. edn. English Touring Opera, London, 1994—98. Author: The Singing and Acting Handbook, 2000. Recipient 1st Pl. award, Nat. Opera Assn., 2001, 2002. Mem.: Dirs. Guild Gt. Britain. Avocation: gardening. Office: U Cin Conservatory Music PO Box 210003 Cincinnati OH 45221 Business E-Mail: demallth@uc.edu.

DEMANN, MICHAEL MARCUS, psychologist; b. Mpls., June 1, 1932; s. George S. and Mary Hazel (Short) DeM; m. Carol. L. Knutson, Feb. 10, 1961; children: James G., Susan M., John P. BA, U. Minn., 1955, MA, 1958, PhD, 1960. Staff mem. VA Hosp., Mpls., 1960-61; cons. psychologist Rohrer, Hibler and Replogle, Mpls., 1961-65; pvt. practice cons. psychologist, Mpls., 1965—. Bd. dirs. Internat. Graphics Corp., Mpls.; cons. Social Security Adminstrn, Mpls., 1966-67. Bd. dirs. Opportunity Workshop, Mpls., 1962-69; bd. govs. St. Mary's Jr. Coll., Mpls., 1973. With M.S., U.S. Army, 1950-52. Mem. APA, Minn. Psychol. Assn. (exec. coun. 1971-73), Am. Legion. Home: 10437 W Riverview Dr Eden Prairie MN 55347-4920

DE MAR, LEODA MILLER, designer; b. N.Y.C., May 26, 1929; d. Benjamin and Malvina (Altman) Miller; m. Robert Mathis de Mar, Dec. 30, 1955 (div. Jan. 1985); children: Victoria, Miller Mathis, Charles David. Diploma, Parson's Sch. of Design, N.Y.C., 1946-49; postgrad., Parson's Sch. of Design, Eng., France, Italy, 1949, NYU, 1950-53. Designer Joseph B. Platt, Indsl. Design, N.Y.C., 1950-53; instr. textiles Parson's Sch. Design, N.Y.C., 1953-55; freelance designer various companies, N.Y.C., 1956-62; designer Leoda de Mar, Inc., N.Y.C., 1962-74; designer, advt. cons. Woodson Wallpapers, N.Y.C., 1975-85; fabric and wallcovering designer, advt. cons. Richard E. Thibaut, Inc., Irvington, N.J., 1985—. Designer 1st wallpaper collection Pippin Papers, N.Y.C., 1954, 1st wallpaper collection Woodson Wallpapers, 1955, own collections Richard E. Thibaut, Inc., 1985—, fabric and wallcovering designs featured in various popular mags.; contbr. articles to mags. Recipient Creativity award Art Direction mag., 1981. Avocations: pets, gardening, cooking. Home and Office: 350 Riversville Rd Greenwich CT 06831-3255

DEMAR, LEON KENNETH, dermatologist; b. Phila., Aug. 18, 1945; s. Leon and Sarah Kessler (Dein) Glassman; m. Christina Margaret Hift, Oct. 30, 1989; children: Jonathan, Alexander. BA, Haverford Coll., 1967; MD, NYU, 1973. Diplomate Am. Bd. Dermatology. Intern medicine Manhattan VA Hosp., N.Y.C., 1973-74; resident dermatology Stanford (Calif.) U. Med. Ctr., 1974-75; resident, chief resident dermatology Columbia-Presbyn. Med. Ctr., N.Y.C., 1975-77; pvt. practice N.Y.C., 1977—; asst. clin. prof. dermatology Columbia U., N.Y.C., 1977—. Mem. attending staff Lenox Hill Hosp., Columbia Presbyn. Med. Ctr., St. Lukes-Roosevelt Hosp., Beth Israel Hosp., N.Y.C. Fellow Am. Acad. Dermatology; mem. Am. Soc. Dermatol. Surgery, Am. Soc. Pediat. Dermatology, Am. Soc. Laser Surgery, Internat. Soc. Dermatol. Surgery, N.Y. County Med. Soc. Office: 985 5th Ave New York NY 10021-0142

DEMARCHI, ERNEST NICHOLAS, retired aerospace executive; b. Lafferty, Ohio, May 31, 1939; s. Ernest Constante and Lena Marie (Cireddu) D.; m. Carolyn Marie Tracz, 1960; children: Daniel Ernest, John David, Deborah Marie; m. Sharon Titherley, 1996. BME, Ohio State U., 1962; MS in Engring., UCLA, 1969. Registered profl. engr., Ohio; registered profl. cert. mgr. Exec. N.Am. Aviation/Rockwell/Boeing, 1962—2002; ret., 2002. Mem. Apollo, Skylab and Apollo-Soyuz missions design team in electronic and elec. systems, mem. mission support team for all Apollo and Skylab manned missions, 1962-74, mem. Space Shuttle design team charge elec. systems equipment, 1974-77, in charge Orbiter Data Processing System, 1977-81, in charge Orbiter Ku Band Communication and Radar System, 1981-85, in charge orbitor elec. power distbr., displays, controls, data processing, 1984-87, in charge space based interceptor flt. exper., 1987-88, kinetic energy systems, 1988-90, ground based interceptor program, 1990-97, dep. program mgr. Nat. Missile Def. Program, 1997-2000, assoc. dep. program mgr. Space Shuttle Program, 2000-02. Recipient Apollo Achievement award NASA, 1969, Apollo 13 Sustained Excellent Achievement Snoopy award, 1971, Exceptional Svc. award Rockwell Internat., 1972, Outstanding Contbn. award, 1976, NASA ALT award, 1979, Shuttle Astronaut Snoopy award, 1982, Pub. Svc. Group Achievement award NASA, 1982, Rockwell Pres.'s award, 1983, 87. Mem. AIAA, ASME, Nat. Mgmt. Assn., Assn. U.S. Army, Varsity O Alumni Assn. Home: 8227 E Hillsdale Dr Orange CA 92869-2440

DEMARCO, RALPH JOHN, real estate developer; b. N.Y.C., Mar. 22, 1924; s. Frank and Mary (Castriota) DeM.; m. Arlene Gilbert, July 1, 1945; children: Sheryl DeMarco Grahn (dec.), Stephen, Laura DeMarco Wilson. BA, Claremont Men's Coll., 1956. Assoc. John B. Kilroy Co., Riverside, Calif., 1960-64, also mgr. ops. Riverside and San Bernardino counties, 1960-64; v.p. Marcus W. Meairs Co., 1964-67; pres. Diversified Properties, Inc., Riverside, 1967-72; v.p. Downey (Calif.) Savs. and Loan Assn., 1972-75; exec. v.p. DSL Svc. Co., 1972-75; pres. Interstate Shopping Ctrs., Inc., Santa Ana, Calif., 1975-87; exec. dir. comml. devel. Lewis Homes Mgmt. Corp., Upland, Calif., 1987-89; pvt. practice San Diego, 1989—. Mem. City of Riverside Planning Commn., 1955-59; mem. Airport Commn., 1960-70; mem. Urban Land Inst. 1st lt. USAF, 1942-45. Mem. Internat. Coun. Shopping Ctrs. Home: 44-489 Town Center Way # D 273 Palm Desert CA 92260-2723 Office: 1125 Linda Vista Dr Ste 107 San Marcos CA 92069-3819

DE MARCO, THOMAS JOSEPH, periodontist, educator; b. Farmingdale, N.Y., Feb. 12, 1942; s. Joseph Louis and Mildred Nora (Cifarelli) De M.; children: Todd Gordon, Kristin Alice, Lisa Anne. BS, U. Pitts., 1962; D.D.S., 1965; PhD, certificate in Periodontology, Boston U., 1968; cert. in fin. planning, Coll. Fin. Planning, Denver, 1976. Certificate in clin. hypnosis. Practice dentistry specializing in periodontics and implants, Cleve., 1968—; mem. staff Met. Gen. Hosp., Cleve., Univ. Hosp., Cleve., VA Hosp., Cleve.; asst. prof. periodontics and pharmacology Case-Western Res. U., 1968-70, assoc. prof., 1970-73, prof., 1973-84; asso. dean Case-Western Res. U. (Sch. Dentistry), 1972-76, dean, 1976-84; pvt. practice periodontia, 1984—. Author review books in dentistry, book on fin. planning, also articles on periodontology, pharmacology, fin. planning. Grantee Air Force Office Sci. Research, 1969; grantee Upjohn Co., 1970; grantee Columbus Dental Mfg. Co., 1971. Mem. Am. Acad. Periodontology, Internat. Assn. Dental Research, Am. Soc. for Preventive Dentistry (past pres. Ohio chpt.) Home: 12370 Rockhaven Rd Chesterland OH 44026-2744 Office: 29001 Cedar Rd Cleveland OH 44124

DE MARE, GEORGE, author; b. Denver, Nov. 11, 1912; s. J.S. and Marie de Mare; m. Mercedes Moore; children: Gregory, Malcolm, Gilbert, Adrienne. BA, Yale U., 1936. Dir. comms. and publs. Price Waterhouse, 1956-70. Com. on social and econ. improvement White House, 1965. Author: The Empire, 1956, Ruling Passion, 1957, Sybille, 1988, Corporate Lives, 1976 (main selection Fortune Book club), Communicating at the Top, 1986, 101 Ways to Protect Your Job, 1988. Fellow Internat. Assn. of Bus. Communicators (former pres.), N.Y. Assn. of Bus. Editors (former pres.), Indsl. Comms. Coun. (former dir.). Home: 75 Main St Saugerties NY 12477-1125

DE MARGITAY, GEDEON, acquisitions and management consultant; b. Budapest, Hungary, Mar. 6, 1924; came to U.S., 1953, naturalized, 1958; s. Joseph and Anne (de Bessenyei) de M.; m. Virginia Varet Martin, Dec. 30, 1963. Student, U. Budapest Grad. Sch. Econs., 1941-44, Ecole des Scis. Politiques, Paris, 1946-48. With N.Y. Times, 1947-50, 54-61; with European info. divsn. Mut. Security Agy., 1950-53; chief exec. Magnum Photos, Inc., N.Y.C., 1961-63; with Time Inc., 1964-75, dir. mktg. svcs. Time/Life TV, 1975; dir. broadcast and corp. planning NBC, 1975-78; acquistions and mgmt. cons. N.Y.C., 1978—. Co-author: Broadcasting: The Next Ten Years, 1977. Mem. Assn. for Sys. Mgmt., Internat. Radio-TV Soc., World Future Soc., Am. Acad. Polit. and Social Sci. Republican. Presbyterian. Address: 65 E 96th St New York NY 10128-0730

DE MARIA, ALFRED ANTHONY, neurologist; b. Sewickley, Pa., Mar. 27, 1952; s. Alfred Anthony and Helen Josephine (Goray) De M.; m. Katherine Grace Bridge, June 25, 1977; children: Genevieve Camille, Gabrielle Christine. BA, Johns Hopkins U., 1973; MD, Ohio State U., 1976. Diplomate Am. Bd. Psychiatry and Neurology. Intern N.C. Baptist Hosp., Winston-Salem, 1976-77; resident in neurology N.C. Meml. Hosp., Chapel Hill, 1977-80; fellow in EEG Mayo Clinic, Rochester, Minn., 1980-81; attending physician Neurol. Assocs., Columbus, Ohio, 1981-92, Wilmington (N.C.) Health Assocs., 1993—. Med. dir. EEG lab. Riverside Meth. Hosp., Columbus, Ohio, 1981-92; med. dir. sleep lab. Cape Fear Meml. Hosp., Wilmington, 1993—. Host (TV show) Second Opinion, 1996—. Mem. Am. Acad. Neurology, Am. Sleep Disorders Assn., Am. EEG Soc., Am. Epilepsy Soc., Nat. Stroke Assn., Nat. Headache Found., Nat. Assn. Physician Broadcasters. Avocations: music, skiing. Office: Wilmington Health Assocs 1202 Medical Center Dr Wilmington NC 28401-7307

DE MARIA, ANTHONY JOHN, electrical engineer; b. Santa Croce, Italy, Oct. 30, 1931; came to U.S., 1935; s. Joseph and Nicolina (Daddona) De M.; m. Katherine M. Waybright, Aug. 29, 1953; 1 dau., Karla Kay. BS in Elec. Engring., U. Conn., 1956, PhD in Elec. Engring., 1965; MS, Rensselaer Poly. Inst., 1960. Acoustic research engr. Andersen Lab., West Hartford, Conn., 1956-57; magnetic research engr. Hamilton Standard Div. United Techs. Corp., Windsor Locks, Conn., 1957-58; asst. dir. rsch. electronics and photonics United Techs. Rsch. Ctr., East Hartford, Conn., 1958-94; founder, chmn., CEO DeMaria ElectroOptics Sys., Inc., Bloomfield, Conn., 1994-2001, chief scientist Coherent Laser divsn., 2001—; rsch. prof. Photonics Rsch. Ctr. U. Conn., Storrs, 1994-98; pres. TeraBit Commns., LLC, 2001—. Instr. electronics U. Hartford, 1957-60; adj. prof. physics Rensselaer Poly. Inst. Grad. Ctr., Hartford, 1970-77; lectr. in lasers UCLA, 1974-82; mem. adv. group on electronic devices Dept. Def., 1977-86, chmn., 1980-85; mem. evaluation com. on electromagnetic tech. Nat. Bur. Standards, 1977-79; mem. Ctr. Elec. and Electronic Engring.,

1979-83; mem. LANL Adv. Com. for Chemistry and Laser Sci., 1985-92. Author: Lasers, Vol. III, 1972, Vol. IV, 1976; Contbr. articles to profl. jours. Mem. Air Force Sci. Adv. Bd., 1981-86. Recipient Disting. Alumnus award U. Conn., 1978, Disting. Engring. award, U. Conn., 1983, Davies medal and award Rensselaer Poly. Inst., 1980, Air Force Meritorious medal for civilian svc., 1986. Fellow IEEE (editor Jour. Quantum Electronics, Morris N. Liebman meml. award 1980), SPIE (bd. dirs. 1995—, v.p. 2002, pres. 2003), Optical Soc. Am. (v.p. 1979, pres. 1981, chmn. bd. editors 1986-89, Frederic Ives medal 1988), Am. Phys. Soc.; mem. NAE (Farichild Disting. scholar 1982-83, Calif. Inst. Tech.), NAS, Conn. Acad. Scis. and Engring. (pres. 1994-99). Address: Coherent DEOS 1280 Blue Hills Ave Bloomfield CT 06002-5304

DEMARIA, ANTHONY NICHOLAS, cardiologist, educator; b. Elizabeth, N.J., Jan. 12, 1943; s. Anthony and Charlotte DeMaria; m. Delores Horn; children: Christine, Anthony, Jonathon. BA, Coll. Holy Cross, 1964; MD, N.J. Coll. Medicine, 1968; hon. degree, Kagawa Med. U., Japan, U. Bordeaux, France. Diplomate Am. Bd. Internal Medicine, Am. Bd. Cardiovascular Disease, Am. Bd. Cardiovascular Medicine. Intern St. Vincent Hosp., Worcester, Mass., 1968-69; resident USPHS Hosp., Staten Island, N.Y., 1969-71; fellow cardiology U. Calif., Davis, 1969-73, asst. prof. medicine, 1972-77, assoc. prof. medicine, 1977-81, prof. medicine, 1977-81; prof. medicine, chief cardiology div. U. Ky., Lexington, 1981-92; dir. Ky. Heart Inst., Lexington, 1989—; prof. medicine, chief cardiology U. Calif. Sch. Medicine, San Diego, 1992—, vice chmn. internal medicine, 1998—2001, med. dir. cardiovascular ctr., Judith and Jack White chair cardiovascular medicine. Mem. rev. bds. Vets. Adminstrn. Med. Research Merit in Cardiovascular Studies, Nat. Inst. Health, NSF, NIH, NHLBI, U. Calif., U.S. FDA; chmn. Diagnostic Radiology Study Sect. NIH; vice-chmn. dept. medicine U. Calif., San Diego, 1998—. Mem. editl. bd. Am. Heart Jour., Am. Jour. Cardiac Imaging, Circulation, Am. Jour. Cardiology, Jour. Am. Coll. Cardiology, Health News from New Eng. Jour. Medicine; editor-in-chief Jour. Am. Coll. Cardiology, 2001—; assoc. editor Jour. Club, Cardiology, Jour. Am. Coll. Cardiology; editl. cons. Am. Jour. Physiology, Annals Internal Medicine, Archives Phys. Medicine and Rehab., Catheterization and Cardiovascular Diagnosis, Jour. Clin. Investigation, New Eng. Jour. Medicine; contbr. numerous articles to profl. jours. ; host Cardiology Update, Lifetime Med. TV. Recipient Humanitarian award Theodore and Susan Cummings, 1978, Disting. Alumnus award Coll. Medicine and Dentistry of N.J., 1988, Echocardiography award Tufts U., 1988, award of excellence Am. Acad. Med. Adminstrs., 1994, William Harvey award Am. Med. Writers Assn., 1996; named one of Best Doctors in Am., Best Heart Specialist in U.S. Good Housekeeping mag., 1996; Golden Empire Heart Assn. grantee, Am. Heart Assn grantee, Ky. Heart Assn. grantee, Vet. Adminstrn. grantee, Nat. Heart, Lung and Blood Inst. grantee; teaching scholar Am. Heart Assn. Fellow ACP, Am. Coll. Cardiology (chmn. 27th ann. scientific session 1978, cardiovascular procedures com., govt. rels. com., v.p. elect 1986, pres. elect 1987-88, pres. 1988—, active various coms., Young Investigator award 1976), Am. Coll. Chest Physicians; mem. Am. Heart Assn. (bd. dirs. work evaluation unit Yolo Sierra chpt., Ky. chapter, active various coms., Teaching scholar 1979-82), Am. Fedn. Clin. Rsch., Yolo County Med. Socs., Am. Inst. Ultrasound in Medicine (bd. dirs.), Am. Soc. Echocardiography (bd. dirs. 1975-87, v.p. 1983-85, pres. 1985-87, assoc. editor), N.Am. Soc. for Cardiac Radiology, Assn. U. Cardiologists. Roman Catholic. Office: U Calif Med Ctr 225 Dickinson St Ste 360 San Diego CA 92103-1910

DEMARIA, JOSEPH CARMINUS, lawyer; b. Phila., June 21, 1947; s. Joseph and Mary A. DeMaria. AB in Politics, St. Joseph's Coll., Phila., 1969; JD, Villanova U., 1972. Bar: Pa. 1972, U.S. Dist. Ct. (ea. dist.) Pa. 1972, U.S. Ct. Appeals (3rd cir.) 1982, U.S. Supreme Ct. 1982, Conn. 1988. Staff atty. Southeastern Pa. Transportation Authority, Phila., 1972-78; mng. atty. Aetna Life and Casualty, Phila., 1978-87, asst. v.p., staff counsel ops. Hartford, Conn., 1987-91; claim counsel Aetna Life & Casualty, Phila., 1991-96; pvt. practice Phila., 1972—. Mem. Montgomery Bar Assn., Pa. Bar Assn., John Peter Zenger Law Soc., German Am. Police Assn., German Soc. Pa., Am.-Italian Soc. Phila., Justinian Soc., FOP. Republican. Roman Catholic. Avocations: tennis, music, science fiction, classical automobile collecting. Home and Office: 237 Weadley Rd King Of Prussia PA 19406-3746 Fax: 610-337-7807.

DEMARIA, MICHAEL BRANT, psychologist; b. Norwalk, Conn., Apr. 23, 1962; s. Francesco and Jacqueline (Campbell) DeM.; m. Kathleen Jean Kies, July 4, 1992; 1 child, Danielle. BA in Psychology magna cum laude, BA in Philosophy magna cum laude, U. West Fla., 1982; MA in Psychology, Duquesne U., Pitts., 1983, PhD in Clin. Psychology, 1987. Lic. clin. psychologist, Fla.; registered play therapist; diplomate in expressive therapy. Doctoral intern Bapt. Hosp. and Lakeview Ctr., Pensacola, Fla., 1985-86; resident Clin. Psychology Assn., Pensacola, 1986-88, clin. psychologist, 1988-89; founder, clin. psychologist, pres., clin. dir. DeMaria and Assoc., Pensacola, 1989—. Founder, dir. Ontos: A Center for Being; therapist Counseling Ctr. Point Park Coll., Pitts., 1983-84, Ctr. Tng. and Rsch. in Psychology Duquesne U., 1983-86, instr. Psychology Dept., 1983-85, rsch. asst., 1983-85; faculty assoc. U. West Fla., 1985—; cons. Adolescent Stress Ctr. Bapt. Hosp., Pensacola, 1985-89, IMPACT Program, 1986-88, Child Protection Team, 1986-89; cons./expert witness State Atty. Office, Pensacola, Renascence Recovery Ctr., Anchorage Counseling Svcs., Community Drug & Alcohol Commn., Rivendale Hosp.; speaker in field Author: Horns and Halos: Towards the Blessing of Darkness, 1992, Ever Flowing on: On Being and Becoming Oneself, 2001; contbr. articles to The Humanistic Psychologist, Internat. Jour. of Play Therapy, Art and Psychotherapy: An International Jour. Mem. Fla. Legis. Task Force on Child Abuse and Neglect Reports, 1988-90. Recipient Merit scholarship Dept. Psychology, Dept. Philosophy U. West Fla., Alumni Found. scholarship, Disting. Alumni award, 1992. Mem. APA, Soc. for Personality Assessment, Assn. for Play Therapy, Southeastern Psychol. Assn., Fla. Psychol. Assn. (treas. 1989—), Psi Chi, Phi Kappa Phi. Avocations: music, writing, poetry, drumming, native american flute. Office: 512 E Zaragoza St Pensacola FL 32501-6155 E-mail: efo@ontos.org.

DE MARIE, ANTHONY JOSEPH, lawyer; b. Buffalo, May 10, 1928; s. Joseph and Josephine (Radice) DeM.; m. Rose Galluzzo, July 23, 1955; children— Michael, Janice, Gregory, Lynda. J.D., U. Buffalo, 1955. Bar: N.Y. 1956, U.S. Dist. Ct. (we. dist.) N.Y. 1960, U.S. Ct. Appeals (2d cir.) 1982. Ptnr., Dixon & De Marie, Buffalo, 1956— . Dir., Neighborhood Legal Services of Erie County, Buffalo, 1971-74. Served with AUS, 1946-48, 50-51. Mem. Erie County Bar Assn. (past bd. dirs.), Trial Lawyers Assn. Erie County (past pres., gov.) N.Y. State Bar Assn., Fla. Bar Assn., N.Y. State Trial Lawyers Assn., Assn. Trial Lawyers Am., Western N.Y. Trial Lawyers Assn. Republican. Roman Catholic. Club: Transit Valley Country. Office: De Marie & Schoenborn PC 800 Convention Tower Buffalo NY 14202-3174

DE MARINO, DONALD NICHOLSON, international business executive, former federal agency administrator; b. Greensburg, Pa., Sept. 28, 1945; s. Thomas C. and Sue Eleanor (Nicholson) De M.; m. Caroline Mack, Dec. 27, 1967 (div. 1981); children: Christopher Tyson, Benjamin Nicholson; m. Betsy Reiver, July 18, 1981; children: Alexander Reiver, William McCurdy. BA, U. Pa., 1967. Dir. Mack & Nicholson, West Chester, Pa., 1972-76; bus. cons. The Nicholson Group, Inc., N.Y.C., 1976-81; sr. project officer U.S.-Saudi Arabian Joint Commn. on Econ. Cooperation, Riyadh, Saudi Arabia, 1981-84, dir., 1985-87; mgr. Litton Industries Offset Investment Programs, Riyadh, 1984-85; sr. project adviser The Arab Investment Co., Riyadh, 1985; internat. bus. cons., prin. De Marino Assocs., Coatesville, Pa., 1987-88; dep. asst. sec. Africa, Near East and South Asia U.S. Dept. Commerce, Washington, 1989-90; U.S. advisor Tata Group of India, 1991—; chmn. Nat. U.S.-Arab C. of C., 1991—; pres. De Marino Assocs., Inc., 1992—. Lectr. Wharton Sch. Advanced Mgmt. Program, 1994-96; nat. adv. com. Mid. East Policy Coun.; chmn. Arab-Fgn. C. of C., 1999-2000; bd. dir. Merchant Bridge & Co., Ltd.; founding dir. US-Iraq Bus. Coun. Mem. nat. adv. bd. Mid. East Policy Coun. Decorated Chevalier, Sovereign Mil. Order of Temple of Jerusalem; recipient Disting. Svc. award Govt. of Saudi Arabia, 1987. Mem. Sovereign Mil. Order Temple Jerusalem (chevalier templars), Arab-Fgn. C. of C. (chmn. 1999-2000), Racquet Club, Mask and Wig Club. Republican. Presbyterian. Home: 43 Longview Rd Coatesville PA 19320-4311 Office: PO Box 791 Unionville PA 19375-0791

DEMARK, ROBIN KAY, librarian; b. Elmira, N.Y., Oct. 5, 1961; d. John Jr. and Betty E. (Makowiec) DeM. BA in Psychology, East Carolina U., 1984, MLS in Libr. and Info. Sci., 1993. Cert. libr., N.C. Tchr. asst. East Carolina U., Greenville, N.C., 1991-93, reference asst. Joyner Libr., 1992-93; bus./reference libr. Wayne County Pub. Libr., Goldsboro, N.C., 1993-95; reference libr. Pope Air Force Base Libr., 1995—2001, Seymour Johnson AFB, NC, 2001—. Cons., tutor, instr., computer rschr., Goldsboro, 1993—. Author: (manual) An Introduction to Computerized Resources and Database Searching in an Academic Library, 1993. Recipient Festival Event and Mgmt. cert. Strom Thurmond Inst., 1994. Mem. Goldsboro C. of C. (rep. for bus. dept. Wayne County Pub. Libr. 1994—). Democrat. Roman Catholic. Avocation: entertaining. Home: PO Box 592 Goldsboro NC 27533-0592 Office: Seymour Johnson AFB 4 Fighter Wing Pub Affairs Seymour Johnson AFB NC 27531 E-mail: robin.demark@seymourjohnson.af.mil.

DEMARK-WAHNEFRIED, WENDY, nutritionist, researcher; b. Detroit, Jan. 31, 1956; d. Rudolph and Helen Demark; m. Gene Arthur Wahnefried, Feb. 16, 1980; children: Nicholas Jay, Petra Justine. BS, U. Mich., 1978; MS, Tex. Women's U., 1980; PhD, Syracuse U., 1988. Reg. dietitian; lic. dietitian/nutritionist. Assoc.cancer control rsch. Duke U. Med. Ctr., Durham, NC, 1991—92; asst. prof. medicine, asst. dir. Stedman Ctr. Nutritional Studies, 1993-97, assoc. prof. surgery, 1997—. Contbr. articles to profl. jours. Preventive Oncology Acad. Award Grantee Nat. Cancer Inst., 1993—; recipient investigator award Cancer Rsch. Found. Am., 1993, instnl. award Am. Cancer Soc., 1993. Mem.: Am. Dietetic Assn. (Young Dietitian Yr. award 1983, Susan G. Komen Prof. of Survivorship 2002—). Avocations: cross-country skiing, ice skating, gardening, ballroom dancing, hiking. Home: 105 Birkhaven Dr Cary NC 27511-8942 Office: Duke U Med Ctr PO Box 3707 Durham NC 27710-0001

DE MARNEFFE, BARBARA ROWE, historic preservationist; b. Boston, June 2, 1929; d. H S Payson and Florence Van Arnhem (Cassard) Rowe; m. James Hopkins, Oct. 9, 1954 (div. 1969); m. Francis de Marneffe, 1969; stepchildren: Peter, Daphne, Colette. BA, Vassar Coll., 1952. Tchr. Chapin Sch., N.Y.C., 1952-54; adminstrv. asst. to dean Sch. of Indsl. Mgmt. MIT, Cambridge, Mass., 1959-60; asst. pub. rels. dir. Peter Bent Brigham Hosp., Boston, 1960-61, pub. rels. dir., 1961-63; pub. rels. cons. Diabetes Found. and Joslin Clinic, Boston, 1963-64; pub. rels. dir. McLean Hosp., Belmont, Mass., 1964-68; mgr. pub. affairs Cambridge (Mass.) C. of C., 1975-78; pres. de Marneffe Selections, Cambridge, 1978-90. Trustee Edith Wharton Restoration, Inc, 1999; chair Edith Wharton Restoration, Inc., 2002—; corporator Brookline Savings Bank, Mass., 1995—. Contbr. articles to profl jours. Trustee Archives Am Art Smithsonian Inst, Washington, 1983—99, trustee coun, 1999—2000; officer, bd dirs Family Counseling Serv Cambridge, 1969—78; trustee Peterborough Players, NH, 1983—89, docent NC Mus Art, Raleigh, 1992—93; chair Friends of Pain Ctr Mass Gen Hosp, Boston, 1995—99; mem adv coun Farnsworth Art Mus, Rockland, Maine, 1995—98; state comitteewoman Mass Rep, 1977—80; exec secy Cambridge Rep City Comt, 1956—57; pub relations dir Peabody for Congress Campaign, Newton, Mass., 1968; vestry Emmanuel Episcopal Ch, Dublin, NH, 1995—; comt mem Ellis Mem Settlement House Antiques Show, 1968—89; bd dirs Friends McLean Hosp, Belmont, Mass., 1967—89, Friends Frances Lehman Loeb Art Ctr, Vassar Col, 2001—, Nat Comt Treatment Intractable Pain, Washington, 1980—90. Mem.: Jewelers Am Inc, Vassar Club (pres Boston chpt 1989). Avocations: medicine, business, politics, historic preservation, decorative arts. Home: 126 Coolidge Hl Cambridge MA 02138-5522

DE MARNEFFE, FRANCIS, psychiatrist, hospital administrator; b. Brussels, May 7, 1924; arrived in England, 1940; came to U.S., 1950; s. Armand Gustave and Esther Magdalen (Loveday) de M.; m. Nancy Marie Edmonds, Aug. 5, 1955 (div. Sept. 1967); children: Peter Loveday, Daphne Elizabeth, Colette; m. Barbara Rowe Hopkins, Dec. 5, 1969. MB, BS, U. London, 1950. Diplomate Am. Bd. Psychiatry and Neurology. Intern Muhlenberg Hosp., Plainfield, N.J., 1950-51; asst. resident in psychiatry Mass. Gen. Hosp., Boston, 1952; teaching fellow in psychiatry Med. Sch. Harvard U., Boston, 1955-56, rsch. fellow, 1955-56; resident in psychiatry McLean Hosp., Belmont, Mass., 1953-54, staff psychiatrist, 1955-90, cons. psychiatrist, 1990—, gen. dir., 1962-87, gen. dir. emeritus, 1987—, pres., CEO McLean Health Svcs., Inc., 1986-89; med. dir. Holly Hill Mental Health Svcs., Raleigh, N.C., 1990-93. Instr. psychiatry Med. Sch. Harvard U., 1961-66, lectr. 1966—; mem. accreditation coun. psychiat. faciltities Joint Commn. on Accreditation of Hosps., Chgo, 1979-84, mem. tech. adv. com., 1979-84, chmn. accreditation, 1970-72, mem. coun., 1970-79; adminstr. McLean divsn. Hall-Mercer Hosp., Phila., 1969-87; v.p. Hall-Mercer Hosp., 1980-87; exec. v.p. Belmont programs Mass. Gen. Hosp., Boston, 1986-87; clin. prof. psychiatry U. N.C., Chapel Hill, 1991-93; assoc. cons. prof. psychiatry Duke U. Med. Sch., 1991-93, v.p. Wake County Mental Health Assn., 1992-93, med. staff Rex Hosp., Raleigh, N.C., 1993; mem. Corp. Ptnrs. Health Care Inc., Boston, 1994—; trustee working group McLean Hosp., 1996, co chair on com. on expanding svcs. and revs.; cons. Exec. Svcs. Corps., Boston, 1996—. Author: (non-fiction) Introduction to Adolescent Patients in Transition, 1974; author: (contbg.) The Changing Mental Health Scene, 1976; author: Last Boat From Bordeaux, 2001; mem. editl. bd. (jour.) McLean (Hosp.) Jour., 1976—90. Trustee Guidance Camps, Inc., Boston, 1968-90, Preschool, Inc., Cambridge, Mass., 1961-62, Concord Acad. Mass., 1975-78, Nat. Assn. Pvt. Psychiat. Hosps., Washington, 1982-85, 93-94, McLean Hosp. Corp., Belmont, 1985-87; mem. Corp. of Family Svc. Assn. Greater Boston, 1978-81; hon. trustee Concord Acad., 1978—; bd. dirs. Mass. chpt. Nat. Com. for Prevention of Child Abuse, Boston, 1979-81, Health Planning Coun. Greater Boston, 1972-76; chmn. med. divsn. United Way, 1986; mem. Mass. Gen. Hosp. Corp., 1988-94, coll. Des Conseillers of French Libr. & Cultural Ctr., Boston, 1995-99; bd. dirs. Friends of McLean, 1995—, 1st v.p., 1997-99, pres., 1999—; chmn. Boston chpt. French Heritage Soc. (formerly Friends of Vieilles Maisons Françaises), 2000—. Served as flying officer RAF, 1943-46. Recipient Presdl. award Nat. Assn. Pvt. Psychiat. Hosps., 1991. Fellow: Am. Coll. Mental Health Adminstrn., Mass. Med. Soc., Royal Coll. Psychiatrists, Am. Coll. Psychiatrists, Am. Psychiat. Assn. (life), Royal Coll. Physicians (licentiate); mem.: Eng. Ctrl. Neuropsychiat. Hosp. Assn. (pres. 1986—87), Royal Coll. Surgeons, The Royal Air Force Club (London), Lake (Dublin, N.H.) Club, Thames Rowing Club (London), Cambridge Boat Club, Leander (Henley-on-Thames, Eng.) Club, Harvard of Boston, Somerset (Boston) Club, The Country Club (Brookline). Home: 126 Coolidge Hl Cambridge MA 02138-5522 Office: McLean Hosp 115 Mill St Belmont MA 02478-1048

DE MARR, MARY JEAN, English language educator; b. Champaign, Ill., Sept. 20, 1932; d. William Fleming and Laura Alice (Shauman) Bailey. BA, Lawrence Coll., 1954; MA, U. Ill., 1957, PhD, 1963; postgrad., U. Tuebingen, 1954-55, Moscow State U., 1961-62. Asst. prof. English Willamette U., 1964-65; asst. prof. English Ind. State U., 1965-70, assoc. prof., 1970-75, prof., 1975-95, prof. emerita English and women's studies, 1996—. Author: Colleen McCullough: A Critical Companion, 1996, Barbara Kingsolver: A Critical Companion, 1999, Kaye Gibbons: A Critical Companion, 2003; co-author: Adolescent Female Portraits in the American Novel, 1961-81: An Annotated Bibliography, 1983, The Adolescent in The American Novel Since 1960, 1986; Am. editor: Annual Bibliography of English Language and Literature, 1979-90; editor, contbr. In the Beginning: First Novels in Mystery Series, 1995. Recipient Fulbright assistantship, 1954—55, Dove award, Popular Culture Assn., 1996, Midam. award, Soc. for the Study of Midwestern Lit., 2000. Mem.: ACLU, AAUP, MLA, Modern Humanities Rsch. Assn., Phi Kappa Phi, Phi Beta Kappa. Home: 594 Woodbine Terre Haute IN 47803-1760 E-mail: mjd594@msn.com.

DEMARS, JUDITH M. elementary educator; b. Cleve., Mar. 17, 1947, d. Edward C. and Ann J. (Sedivy) Nau; m. Gordon DeMars, Mar. 10, 1973; 1 child, Darren Jay. BS in Edn., Cleve. State U., 1969; MA in Edn., Baldwin Wallace Coll., Berea, Ohio, 1984; PhD, U. Akron, 1990. Cert. tchr. Nat. Bd. Edn., early childhood generalist Nat. Bd. Edn. Tchr. Garfield Heights City Sch., Ohio; tchr. 2d and 3d grades Warrensville Heights City Sch., Ohio; tutor developmental reading, 6th-8th grades Medina, Ohio; tutor Chpt. I reading, 1st and 2d grade, multiage tchr. Highland Local Schs., Medina. Ohio Reads coord. Sharon Elem.; presenter in field. Rsch. on beginning reading methods. Mem. adv. com. Medina County Tchrs. Acad. Martha Holden Jennings grantee. Mem. Internat. Reading Assn. (Ohio coun.), Assn. for Supervision and Curriculum Devel., Assn. for Childhood Edn. Internat. Home: 6704 Kennard Rd Medina OH 44256-8559

DE MARTIN, COLLEEN DIANNE, college official, interior designer, consultant; b. Detroit, Mar. 18, 1950; d. F. Robert and Jeanne Claire Maxwell; m. Gerald John De Martin (div. 1984); children: Jessica Marie, Timothy Robert. BS in Interior Design and Home Econs., Ea. Mich. U., 1972; MA in Housing and Interior Design, Wayne State U., 1975; postgrad., Liberty U., 1991-97. Cert. Mich. Hypnosis Assn. Program coord. interior design U. Minn. Tech. Coll., Crookston, 1977-84; instr. interior design Calif. Poly. State U., San Luis Obispo, 1984-89, Wayne State U., Detroit, 1990-93; counselor, student advisor Ross Tech. Inst., Ann Arbor and Taylor, Mich., 1993-96; program dir. interior design, student advisor Baker Coll., Auburn Hills, Mich., 1994—. V.p., historian Ctrl. Coast Interior Designers, 1983-85; CAD coord., kitchen designer Grahl's Kitchen & Bath, Woodhaven, Mich., 1990-91; hist. cons. Avila Lighthouse Restoration/Harbor Commn., Avila Beach, Calif., 1987-88, Hart House Restoration, Santa Maria, Calif., 1988-89; com. me., organizer State Conf. East Faces West, San Luiis Obispo, 1986; asst. counselor Job Tng. Placement Assn., Southgate, Mich., 1995; owner Maxwell Design Cons., Grosse Ile, Mich., 1996—; spkr. Stroheim & Rohamm, Troy, Mich., 1998. Editor slide/tape series The French Monarchy: The Study of French Furnishings, 1981. Handbell player El Morro Nazarene Ch., Los Osos, Calif., 1987-89, dir. children;s handbell, 1988; panel participant on teenage drugs Grosse Ile TV, 1996; tour hostess Garden Club, Grosse Ile, 1998; instr., advisor Habitat for Humanity, Auburn Hills, 1999. Recipient outstanding svc. award Distributive Edn. Clubs Am., 1981, Interior Design Club, U. Minn., 1984, Am. Soc. Interior Designers, 1985; scholar Presbyn. Ch. U.S.A., 1968-69. Mem. Interior Design Soc. (profl. mem., edn. rep. 1975—). Mem. Nazarene Ch. Avocations: basket weaving, paper making, sewing, piano. Home: 28731 Elbamar Dr Grosse Ile MI 48138-2070 Office: Baker Coll 1500 University Dr Auburn Hills MI 48326-2642

DEMARTINI, FRANK THOMAS, film company executive, lawyer; b. Oyster Bay, N.Y., Feb. 23, 1962; s. Frank Anthony and Grace Marie (Lombardi) DeM. AB, Syracuse U., 1983; JD cum laude, Touro Coll., Huntington, N.Y., 1986. Bar: Calif. 1986. Atty. Edwin J. Richards & Assocs., Santa Anna, Calif., 1986-88; prin. v.p. Pentalpha Film Group, Hollywood, Calif., 1987-89; atty. Lewis & Co., Santa Monica, Calif., 1988; owner Martin and DeMartini Law Firm, L.A., 1988-92; ptnr. Anderson & DeMartini, 1992-98; owner Palladin Film Group, 1994-98; ptnr. Barab, Anderson, Barton, DeMartini, Kline and Coate LLP, Beverly Hills, 1996-97; owner, CEO Frank DeMartini Prodns. (was DeMartini/Anderson Prodns., now Swingin' Prodns., LLC), L.A., 1998—; prodn. exec. NuImage, Inc., 1999—. Cons. Dianne Bridget Beatty, L.A., 1987-89, Ashton Nolley, 1987-90, Dy Sharr Music Pub., 1988-92, Beholder Film corp., 1989-92, ALB Prodns., Inc., 1989—. Prodr.: Motel Blue, 1997, The Replacement, 1999, aka The Alternate, Crocodile, 2000, Spiders, 2000, Crocodile 2 aka Death Roll, 2000, Quicksand, 2001, In the Shadow of the Cobra, 2001; assoc. prodr. Crystal Lake, 1990, Loving Deadly, 1994, asst. prodr. (tv show) The Laughter Co., 1986, Peroxide Passion, 2001; co-exec. prodr. : Viad, 2003. Asst. committeeman Nassau County Rep. Com., Salisbury, N.Y., 1985-86. Mem. ABA (tax entertainment com.), Producer's Guild of Am. Roman Catholic. Avocations: music, theater. Office: Swingin' Prodns LLC 3765 Motor Ave # 710 Los Angeles CA 90034-6403 E-mail: frankyd@hollwood.org.

DEMARTINI, ROBERT JOHN, business executive, entrepreneur; b. N.Y.C., Apr. 4, 1919; s. Andrew John and Regina Louise (Bosetti) D.; m. Carol Elaine Bauer, Feb. 5, 1945; children: Nancy Demartini Warner, David, Regina Demartini Carter. BS, MIT, 1941. Registered profl. engr., Mass. Textile engr. Russell Mfg. Co., Middletown, Conn., 1941-43; textile application engr. Gen. Electric Co., Schenectady, 1943-51; with Huyck Corp., 1951-79, exec. v.p. internat. ops., 1973-79; dir. King Fifth Wheel Corp., 1977-82; pres. Demartini Devel. Industries, 1979—; gen. ptnr. REICO Ltd., 1980-86. Adj. prof. N.C. State U., 1980-87. Contbr. articles to profl. jours.; patentee in field. Exec. advisor U. N.C. Sch. Bus. Adminstrn., 1985—87; chmn. Flat Rock CCRC Project, 1993—95; bd. dirs. N.C. World Trade Coun., 1976—79, Ctr. for New Bus. Devel., 1979—82. Mem. Kenmure Golf Club, Seabrook Island Club. Office: 215 Pineholt Ln Flat Rock NC 28731-9767

DEMARTINO, ANTHONY GABRIEL, cardiologist, internist; b. Bronx, N.Y., Oct. 7, 1931; s. Agostino and Vincenzina (Clarizia) DeM.; m. Marlene Mignone, Aug. 8, 1964; children: Anthony Augustin, Laura Jean. BS cum laude, Iona Coll., 1953; MD, SUNY, 1957. Diplomate Nat. Bd. Med. Examiners, Am. Bd. Internal Medicine (cardiovascular disease). Intern U. divsn. Kings County Med. Ctr., Bklyn., 1957-58, med. resident, 1960-62; fellow cardiopulmonary Cornell U., N.Y. Hosp., 1962-64; acting chief medicine Fordham divsn. Misericordia Fordham Affiliation, Bronx, 1964-65; physician in charge cardiac lab. Misericordia-Fordham Affiliation, 1965-69; attending physician dept. medicine and cardiology Our Lady of Mercy Med. Ctr., Bronx, 1967-95, sr. physician, 1995—, mem. med. bd., 1985-93; asst. attending The Presbyn. Hosp., N.Y.C., 1998—. Attending physician dept. medicine and cardiology Lawrence Hosp., Bronxville, N.Y., 1977-97, sr. attending physician, 1997—, mem. med. bd., 1989-94, sec., treas. med. bd., 1996-97, assoc. dir. dept. medicine, 1993-97; practice medicine, specializing in cardiology and internal medicine, Bronx and Bronxville, 1964—; v.p. med. bd. Misericordia Hosp. Med. Ctr., Bronx, 1973-75, pres., 1975-77; clin. asst. prof. medicine N.Y. Med. Coll., 1971—; hon. police surgeon N.Y.C.; asst. attending physician presbyn. Hosp., N.Y., 1996—; asst. in medicine Columbia U., N.Y.C., 1996—. Mem. editl. bd. N.Y. Med. Quar., 1980-84; contbr. articles to profl. jours. Trustee Misericordia Hosp., 1977-83; sec., treas. med. bd. Lawrence Hosp., 1996-97. Served to capt., M.C., U.S. Army, 1958-60. Nat. Heart Inst. fellow, 1962-64. Fellow ACP/Am. Soc. Internal Medicine, Am. Coll. Cardiology, Coun. Clin. Cardiology of Am. Heart Assn., Am. Coll. Chest Physicians, N.Y. Cardiol. Assn.; mem. AMA, Westchester County, N.Y. County Med. Soc., Am. Coll. of Med. Roman Catholic. Office: 77 Pondfield Rd Bronxville NY 10708-3809

DE MASSA, JESSIE G. media specialist; BJ, Temple U.; MLS, San Jose State U., 1967; postgrad., U. Okla., U. So. Calif. Tchr. Palo Alto (Calif.) Unified Sch. Dist., 1966; librarian Antelope Valley Joint Union High Sch. Dist., Lancaster, Calif., 1966-68, ABC Unified Sch. Dist., Artesia, Calif., 1968-72; dist. librarian Tehachapi (Calif.) Unified Sch. Dist., 1972-81; media specialist, free lance writer, 1981—; assoc. Chris DeMassa & Assocs., 1988—. Author: (novel) The Haunting and Murder in Aruba, 2002; contbr. articles to profl. jours. Mem. Statue of Liberty Ellis Island Found., Inc.; charter supporter U.S. Holocaust Meml. Mus., Washington; supporting mem. U.S. Holocaust Meml. Coun., Washington; mem. Nat. Trust for Hist. Preservation. Named to Nat. Women's Hall of Fame, 1995. Fellow Internat. Biog. Assn.; mem. Calif. Media and Libr. Educators Assn., Calif. Assn. Sch. Librs. (exec. coun.), AAUW (bull. editor chpt., assoc. editor state bull., chmn. publicity, 1955-68), Nat. Mus. Women in Arts (charter), Hon Fellows John F. Kennedy Libr. (founding mem.), Women's Roundtable of Orange County, Nat. Writer's Assn. (so. Calif. chpt.), Calif. Retired Tchrs. Assn. (Harbor Beach divsn. 77), The Heritage Found., Claremont Inst., Nat. Women's History Mus. (charter mem.), Libr. of Congress (nat. charter mem.). Home: 9951 Garrett Cir Huntington Beach CA 92646-3604 E-mail: jdwriter10@aol.com.

DE MASTRY, JOHN A. engineer; b. Columbus, Ohio, Nov. 12, 1930; s. Anthony John and Helen Luticia (Harrison) De M.; m. Alice Joan Ptacek, Sept. 4, 1954; children: Michael, Mary, Jean, Joseph, Patricia. BSc, Ohio State U., 1953. Project engr. Battelle Meml. Inst., Columbus, Ohio, 1956-62; project leader Battelle Mml. Inst., 1962-63, assoc. div. chief, 1963-68, tech. rep., 1968-70; sr. engr. Westinghouse Electric Corp., Pitts., 1970-74; asst. mgr. Fla. Power & Light Co., Miami, 1974-80, mgr., 1980-88, staff engr., 1988-93; retired; cons. in nuclear fuel cycles, 1993—. Contbr. articles to profl. jours. Fellow Am. Nuclear Soc.; mem. ASME. Republican. Roman Catholic. Avocations: photography, sports. Home and Office: 9036 Gardens Glen Cir West Palm Beach FL 33418-4535

DEMATTEO, GLORIA JEAN, financial counselor; b. Perth Amboy, N.J., May 23, 1943; d. John J. and Helena (Elias) Kancz; m. Ronald D. DeMatteo, Feb. 20, 1965 (div. Nov. 1987); children: Douglas J., Keith G. Student, Berkeley Sch., 1961. CLU. Exec. sec. Rhodia Inc., New Brunswick, N.J., 1961-65; real estate saleswomen Mid-Jersey Realty, East Brunswick, N.J., 1974-79; pntr. Realty World Garden of Homes, East Brunswick, 1979-81; spl. agt. Prudential Ins. Co. Am., Iselin, N.J., 1981-2000; agt. Rahway (N.J.) Savs. and Ins. Agy., Inc., 2000—01; account exec. retirement svcs. divsn. Citistreet Travelers Educators Retirement, Woodbridge, NJ, 2002—. V.p. Belcourt Condo Assn.,

North Brunswick, N.J., 1987-88. Mem. Nat. Assn. Life Underwriters (nat. sales achievement award, nat. quality award), Soc. Fin. Svc. Profls., Prudential Leaders Club. Avocations: bridge, hiking, dancing, theater. Home: 463 Andover Pl East Brunswick NJ 08816-5121 Office: 581 Main St Woodbridge NJ 07095 E-mail: gdematteo@citistreetonline.com.

DEMATTEO, RONALD PAUL, surgeon; b. Pitts., Jan. 7, 1965; s. Ronald C. and Donna A. DeM.; m. Allyson F., Sept. 9, 1995; 1 child, Siena. BA, Johns Hopkins U., 1986; MD, Cornell U., 1990. Diplomate Am. Bd. Surgery. Resident in gen. surgery Hosp. U. Pa., Phila., 1990-97; fellow in surg. oncology Meml. Sloan-Kettering Cancer Ctr., N.Y.C., 1997-99, asst. attending surgeon, 1999—. Contbr. rsch. articles to med. jours. Recipient Nat. Rsch. Svc. award NIH, 1994-96. Fellow ACS (assoc., study chair oncology group 1999—); mem. Am. Assn. Cancer Rsch., Soc. Surgery Alimentary Tract, Cum Laude Hon. Soc., Alpha Omega Alpha, Phi Beta Kappa. Office: Meml Sloan-Kettering Cancer Ctr 1275 York Ave New York NY 10021-6094 E-mail: dematter@mskcc.org.

DEMATTIES, NICHOLAS FRANK, artist, art educator; b. Honolulu, Oct. 19, 1939; s. Ernest and Florence Adele (Sutherl) deM.; children by previous marriages— Seth, Nicholas II. BA, Calif. State U., Long Beach, 1964; MS, Ill. Inst. Tech., 1967. Instr. San Diego State Coll., 1967-69; asst. prof. Mt. St. Marys Coll., Los Angeles, 1969-70; guest lectr. U. Oreg., 1972; vis. asst. prof. Albion (Mich.) Coll., 1973-74; asst. prof. art Ariz. State U., Tempe, 1974-77, assoc. prof., 1977—. Founder, dir. Pacific N.W. Graphics Workshop, Cheshire, Oreg., 1970-75. One-person shows Suzanne Brown Gallery, Scottsdale, 1981, No. Ariz. U. Flagstaff, 1983, Collier Gallery, Scottsdale, 1986, 88, The Studio, 1991, 92, 94, Bentley Gallery, Scottsdale, Ariz., 1994, Wenniger Gallery, Rockport, Mass., 1994; exhibited in group shows Portland (Oreg.) Art Mus., 1985, Tucson Mus. Art, 1984, 91, 93, Missoula (Mont.) Mus. Art, 1985, Plains (Minn.) Art Mus., 1985, Phoenix Art Mus., 1983, Laguna Gloria Art Mus., Austin, Tex., 1984, LaGrange Nat. XVI, Ga., 1991 Jurors award), Washington and Jefferson Nat. Painting Show, Pa., 1991, Smith Mus., Springfield, Mass., 1991, Mitchell Gallery, Md., 1991, No. Ariz. U. Art Mus., Flagstaff, 1991, Biennial, Fuller Art Ctr., N.M., 1991 (cash award, best of show, purchase award Contemporary Arts Ctr., New Orleans 1992), McNeese Nat., Lake Charles, La., 1992 (purchase award), San Bernardino (Calif.) County Mus., 1993, N.Mex. Art Langue, Albuquerque, 1994 (hon. mention), Olin Fine Arts Ctr., Washington, Pa., 1994, Lafayette (La.) Art Gallery, 1994, Montreal (Que., Can.) Internat. Exhbn., 1994 (spl. mention 1994), W. & J. Nat. Painting Show, Washington, Pa. (cash award); represented in permanent collections, Los Angeles County Mus. Art, Bklyn., Mus. Art, Phoenix Art Mus., Bibliotheque Nat. de Paris, Libr. Served with USAF, 1956-60. Oreg. Arts Commn. fellow, 1972, Western States Arts Found. fellow, 1979; recipient cash award Tex. Fine Art Assn., 1984, Bennial award Tucson Mus. Art, 1984, 88. Studio: 8131 N 18th St Phoenix AZ 85020-3938

DEMAUSE, LLOYD, psychohistorian; b. Detroit, Sept. 19, 1931; s. Leon and Martha (Koren) DeM.; m. Susan Hein; children: Neil, Jennifer, Jonathan. Student, GM Inst., 1948-52; AB, Columbia U., 1957, postgrad., 1957-61, Nat. Psychol. Assn. for Psychoanalysis, 1959-60. Founder Atcom Inc. (pub.), 1959; chmn. bd., dir. Inst. for Psychohistory; pub. Psychohistory Press; mem. faculty N.Y. Center for Psychoanalytic Tng. Editor, author: Jimmy Carter and American Fantasy, The History of Childhood, The New Psychohistory, A Bibliography of Psychohistory, Foundations of Psychohistory, Reagan's America: The Emotional Life of Nations; editor: Jour. Psychohistory. With AUS, 1952-54. Mem. Internat. Psychohist. Assn. (pres.). Home and Office: Inst for Psychohistory 140 Riverside Dr New York NY 10024-2605 E-mail: psychhst@tiac.net.

DEMBER, WILLIAM NORTON, retired psychologist, educator; b. Waterbury, Conn., Aug. 8, 1928; s. David and Henrietta Dember; m. Cynthia Fox, Dec. 21, 1958; children: Joanna, Laura, Gregory. AB, Yale U., 1950; MA, U. Mich., 1951, PhD, 1955. Instr. dept. psychology U. Mich., 1954-56; asst. prof. Yale U., 1956-59; faculty U. Cin., 1959-98, prof. psychology, 1965-98, asst. dean, grad. sch., 1965-67, head dept. psychology, 1968-76, 79-81, dean Coll. Arts and Scis., 1981-86, disting. rsch. prof., 1989, prof., dean emeritus, 1998; ret. Author: Psychology of Perception, 1960, 2d edit., 1979, Visual Perception, 1964, General Psychology, 1970, 2d edit., 1984, Exploring Behavior and Experience, 1971, Spontaneous Alternation Behavior, 1989; contbr. articles to profl. jours. Fellow APA, Am. Psychol. Soc.; mem. Midwest Psychol. Assn. (pres. 1976). Achievements include developing and testing theory of motivation applying to behavior of human beings and animals; rsch. in visual metacontrast, optimism/pessimism, and sustained attention. Home: 920 Oregon Trl Cincinnati OH 45215-2536 E-mail: Drsdember@aol.com.

DEMBICER, EDWIN HERBERT, retired lawyer; b. June 12, 1928; s. Sam and Rose (Weinstein) Dembicer; m. Phyllis Rita Meyerowitz, Oct. 19, 1952; children: Leslye R. Geller, Tracy S. LLB, N.Y. Law Sch., 1950. Bar: N.Y. 1950. Assoc. Louis L. Berko, N.Y.C., NY, 1950—51, Martin M. Kolbrener, N.Y.C., 1953—55; sole practice N.Y.C., 1955—57; ptnr. Dembicer & Lederer, Bklyn., 1957—92, ret., 1992. Assembly dist. leader Dem. Party, Hewlett, NY, 1965. With U.S. Army, 1951—53. Mem.: N.Y. State Trial Lawyers Assn., Am. Judges Assn., Am. Arbitration Assn. (arbitrator 1973—92), Masons (master 1966). Home: 11186 Green Lakes Dr Boynton Beach FL 33437-1470 E-mail: dembicee@bellsouth.net.

DEMBLING, PAUL GERALD, lawyer, former government official; b. Rahway, N.J., Jan. 11, 1920; s. Simon and Fannie (Ellenbogen) D.; m. Florence Brotman, Nov. 22, 1947; children: Ross Wayne, Douglas Evan, Donna Stacy. BA, Rutgers U., 1940, MA, 1942; JD, George Washington U., 1951. Bar: D.C. 1952. Grad. asst., teaching fellow Rutgers U., 1940-42; economist Office Chief Transp., Dept. Army, 1942-45; since practiced in Washington; indsl. relations NACA, 1945-51, spl. counsel, legal adviser, gen. counsel, 1951-58; asst. gen. counsel NASA, 1958-61, dir. legis. affairs, 1961-63, dep. gen. counsel, 1963-67, gen. counsel, 1967-69, chmn. bd. contract appeals, 1958-61, vice chmn. inventions and contbns. bd., 1959-67; mem. and alt. rep. U.S. del. UN Legal Subcom. Com. on Outer Space, 1964-69; gen. counsel GAO, 1969-78; partner Schnader, Harrison, Segal & Lewis, Washington, 1978-93, sr. counsel, 1994—2002. Prin. author NASA Act, 1958; professorial lectr. George Washington U. Law Sch., 1965-86; lectr. Am. Grad. U., 1978-2000. Co-author: Federal Contract Management, 1988, Essentials of Grant Law Practice, 1991; editor in chief Fed. Bar Jour., 1962-69; contbr. articles to profl. jours. Recipient Meritorious Civilian Service award War Dept., 1945; Disting. Service medal NASA, 1968; Nat. Civil Service League award, 1973 Fellow: AIAA (chmn. com. law and sociology 1969—71), Nat. Acad. Pub. Adminstrn., Nat. Contract Mgmt. Assn. (bd. advisers 1973—98), Fed. Bar Found. (life); mem.: FBA (nat. coun. 1963—, pres. Capitol Hill chpt. 1977—78, nat. sec. 1978—79, pres.-elect 1981—82, nat. pres. 1983—84, bd. dirs. bldg. corp. 1989—, fellow (life)), ABA (coun., pub. contract law sec. 1983—84, vice chmn. 1984—85, chmn. elect 1985—86, chmn. 1986—87), Internat. Inst. Space Law (pres. Am. assn. 1970—72, Internat. Astronaut. Fedn. award 1992), Procurement Roundtable (bd. dirs. 1984—, vice chmn. 1988—), D.C. Bar (mem. steering com. govt. contracts and litigation sect. 1989—95), Nat. Lawyers Club, Cosmos Club, Phi Delta Phi. Home: 11625 Pamplona Blvd Boynton Beach FL 33437-4077 Office: Schnader Harrison Segal & Lewis 1300 I St NW Washington DC 20005-3314 E-mail: pfdemb@webtv.net.

DEMBO, DONALD HOWARD, cardiologist, medical administrator, educator; b. Balt., Jan. 27, 1931; s. Sydney Harry and Yetta (Bank) D.; m. Leatrice Cohen, Aug. 10, 1952; children: Steven Jay, Michael Brian Dembo, Susan Ann Weinstein. BA, Johns Hopkins U., 1951; MD, U. Md., 1955. Diplomate Am. Bd. Internal Medicine, Am. Bd. Cardiovascular Disease. Internship Sinai Hosp., Balt., 1955-56; residency in medicine Univ. Hosp., Balt., 1956-58; asst. cardiologist in chief U.S. Army Hosp., Frankfurt, Germany, 1958-60; fellow in cardiology Univ. Hosp., 1960-61; chief of cardiology Md. Gen. Hosp., Balt., 1961-91, Good Samaritan Hosp., Balt., 1975-95; assoc. physician in chief, vice chair of medicine Sinai Hosp., 1995-99; asst. prof. medicine Univ. Md., 1970-91, Johns Hopkins Univ., 1991—; pres. Cen. Md. Cardiology, Balt., 1976-95; med. dir. Johns Hopkins Cardiology, Timonium, Md., 1999—. Contbr. articles to profl. jours. Trustee Cardiopulmonary Resuscitation, Inc., 1975-77; chmn. adv. bd. Easton Waterfowl Festival, Easton, Md., 1990-93. Capt. U.S. Army, 1958-60. Recipient Bronze, Silver & Gold award Am. Heart Assn. (Md. affiliate), Svc. award Md. Gen. Hosp., Svc. award Good Samaritan Hosp., Disting. Physician award Sinai Hosp., AMA Hero in Medicine award, 2001; Cardiology tchg. scholar Hopkins/Sinai Internal Med. Program. Fellow: ACP, Am. Heart Assn. (Md. affiliate pres. 1971—72), Am. Coll. Chest Physicians, Am. Coll. Cardiology (trustee 1990—97, sec./treas. 1997—99, gov. elect Md. chpt. 1999—2000, gov. Md. chpt. 2000—03); mem.: Med. Chi, Md. State Med. Assn. (pres. 1994—95), Balt. City Med. Soc. (pres. 1996—97), Md. Soc. Cardiology (pres. 1976—78). Democrat. Jewish. Avocations: fishing, boating, swimming, tennis, fly fishing, photography. Home: 9430 Bantry Road Easton MD 21601 Office: 110 W Timonium Rd Ste 2C Lutherville Timonium MD 21093-7303 E-mail: ddembo@jhmi.edu., dhdembo@aol.com.

DEMBOWSKI, FREDERICK LESTER, educational administrator, educator, consultant; b. Syracuse, N.Y., July 17, 1948; s. Frederick L. and Jean Marie (Oswald) D.; m. Rhona Dembowski; children: Kirsten, Erika. BS, SUNY, Oswego, 1970, MS, 1972; EdD, U. Rochester, 1978. Asst. prof. SUNY, Albany, 1979-84, assoc. prof. ednl. adminstrn., 1984—, dir. Ednl. Mgmt. Inst., 1985—; prof., coord. PhD program Lynn U., Fla., 2000—02, chmn. dept. ednl. adminstrn., 1995—2000, assoc. dean, 2002—. Cons. AID, Washington, 1984—; dep. chief party Somtad Project, Usaid/Somalia, Africa, 1988-90. Author: School/Effective Sch. Dist. Mgmt., 1999, School Finance Management, 1983, Effective School District Management, 1999; editor: Administrative Uses of Microcomputers, 3 vols., 1984; contbr. articles to profl. jours., chpts. to books. Mem. Am. Sch. Bus. Ofcls. (chmn. mgmt. com. 1982—, outstanding rschr. award 1985), Am. Edn. Fin. Assn., Am. Ednl. Rsch. Assn., Am. Assn. Sch. Adminstrs., Phi Delta Kappa. Roman Catholic. Avocations: travel, fishing, diving. Office: Lynn U Coll Edn Boca Raton FL 33431 E-mail: fdembowski@lynn.edu.

DEMBOWSKI, PETER FLORIAN, foreign language educator; b. Warsaw, Dec. 23, 1925; arrived in U.S., 1966, naturalized, 1974; s. Wlodzimierz and Henryka (Sokolowski) D.; m. Yolande Jessop, June 29, 1954; children: Anne, Eve, Paul. BA with honors, U. B.C., 1952; Doctorat d'Universite, U. Paris, France, 1954; PhD, U. Calif. at Berkeley, 1960. Instr. French U. B.C., 1954-56; asst. prof. French U. Toronto, 1960-63, assoc. prof., 1963-66; mem. faculty U. Chgo., 1966-95, prof. French, 1970-95, Disting. Svc. prof., 1989-95, prof. emeritus, 1995—, dean students div. humanities, 1968-70, chmn. dept. Romance langs. and lits., 1976-83, resident master Snell-Hitchcock halls, 1973-79; vis. mem. Sch. Hist. Studies Inst. Advanced Study Princeton, N.J., 1979-80. Author: La Chronique de Robert de Clari, 1963, Jourdain de Blaye, 1969, Ami et Amile, 1969, La Vie de sainte Marie l'Egyptienne, 1977, Jean Froissart and his Meliador, 1983, Jean Froissart, Le Paradis d'Amour et l'Orloge Amoureus, 1986, Erec et Enide, 1994, L'Estrif de Fortune et Vertu, 1999. Served with Polish Army, 1944-46. Decorated Cross of Valor, Cross of Service with swords (Poland), Chevalier des Palmes Academiques (France); Guggenheim fellow, 1970-71; Danforth Found. assoc., 1976-84 Fellow Am. Acad. Arts and Scis.; mem. Société de Linguistique Romane (councillor 1995-99), Medieval Acad. Am. (councillor 1980-82). Office: U Chgo Dept Romance Langs and Lit 1050 E 59th St Rm 205B Chicago IL 60637-1559

DEMBROW, DANA LEE, lawyer; b. Washington, Sept. 29, 1953; parents: Daniel William and Catherine Louise (Carder) D. BA, Duke U., 1975; JD, George Washington U., 1980. Bar: D.C., Md., W.Va. Law clk. D.C. Superior Ct., Washington, 1979-80; assoc. Smink & Scheuermann, Washington, 1980-81, Reback & Parsons, Washington, 1981-82, Howard M. Rensin, Hyattsville, Md., 1984-86; mem. com. on constitutional and adminstrv. law Md. Ho. of Dels., 1986-92; mem. jud. com. Md. State Legis., 1993—. Chair county affairs com., Montgomery Del., 1994—; can. for congress, Md.'s 4th Congl. Dist., 1992; chair subcom. on civil law and procedure House Judiciary Com., 1994—, chair Intergovernmental Affairs Com., Southern Legis. Conference, 1999-2000. Chair Colesville Strawberry Festival, 1998, 99. Office: 220A Lowe House Office Bldg Annapolis MD 21401 E-mail: dana_dembrow@house.state.md.us., del.dem.@erols.com.

DEMENCHONOK, EDWARD VASILEVICH, philosopher, linguist, researcher, educator; b. Vitebsk, Belarus, Jan. 1, 1942; came to U.S., 1992; s. Vasiliy Ivanovich Demenchonok and Olga Stanislavovna Plovinskaya; m. Sondra Marisa Franceil, July 1, 1993; children: Anna, Leonid. BA in Music, Mus. Coll., Minsk, Belarus, 1961; MA in Russian and Spanish, Moscow State U. Lomonosov, 1969; PhD, Russian Acad. Scis., Moscow, 1977. Rschr., then sr. rschr. Inst. Philosophy Russian Acad. Scis., 1970-95; assoc. prof. Moscow State U. Lomonosov, 1982-84; prof. Moscow State Pedagogic U., 1991-92; prof. Spanish Am. dept. Acad. Slavic Culture, Moscow, 1991-92; assoc. prof. Spanish Brewton-Parker Coll., Mt. Vernon, Ga., 1994-95; assoc. prof. fgn. langs. Ft. Valley (Ga.) State U., 1995—. Vis. rschr. Acad. Scis. Cuba, 1978, 79, 83; vis. prof. U. INCCA Colombia, Bogota, 1988-90, Spanish U. Ga., Athens, 1992-93; lectr. in field. Author: Contemporary Technocratic Thought in the U.S.A., 1984; (in Spanish) América Latina en la Época de la Revolución Científico-Téchnica, 1990, Filosofía en el Mundo Contemporaneo, 1990, Filosofía Latinoamericana: Problemas y Tendencias, 1990; editor: Problems of Philosophy and Culture in Latin America, 1983, Contemporary Catholic Philosophy, 1985, New Tendencies in Western Social Philosophy, 1988; contbr. articles to profl. jours., chpts. to books. Mem. MLA (participant convs. 1992, 93, 99), L.Am. Studies Assn. (participant XVIII congress 1994), Am. Philos. Assn., Internat. Soc. Universal Dialogue, Russian Philosophical Soc., Assn. Cultural Rschrs. Russia, Assn. for Philosophy and Liberation, Southeastern Coun. Latin Am. Studies, Soc. for Iberian and L.Am. Thought. Russian Orthodox. Avocation: music. E-mail: demenche@usa.net.

DE MENIL, LOIS PATTISON, historian, philanthropist; b. NYC, May 15, 1938; d. Charles Krone and Julia Anne (Hasson) Pattison; m. Georges Francois Conrad de Menil, Aug. 3, 1968; children: John-Charles, Joy-Alexandra, Benjamin, Victoria. AB, Wellesley Coll., 1960; diploma, Inst. d'Etudes Politiques, Paris, 1962; Lic. in Law, U. Paris, 1962; PhD, Harvard U., 1972. Pres. D. M. Found., N.Y.C., 1986—. Bd. dirs. AXA Nordstern Art Ins. Corp.; counsellor to Ministry of Culture, Romania, 1997—2001; mem. Coun. Fgn. Rels., 1976—, Inst. for Strategic Studies, London, 1978—, French Inst. Internat. Rels., Paris, 1980—, U.S. Coun. on Germany, N.Y.C., 1978—, Festival d'Automne, Paris, 1997—. Author: Who Speaks for Europe?, 1978; editor, translator: The African Unity Movement, 1965, French Foreign Policy under De Gaulle, 1967. Internat. coun. Mus. Modern Art, NYC, 1975—; vis. com. to art mus. Harvard U., Cambridge, Mass., 1977—; vice-chair bd. dirs. Dia Ctr. for Arts, N.Y.C., 1985—96; vice-chair trustees coun. Nat. Gallery Art, Washington, 1988—97; bd. dirs. World Monuments Fund, N.Y.C., 1990—, Groton Sch., 1991—, NASDAQ Found., 2000—; co-chair Ctr. for Khmer Studies, 1998—2002, pres., chair, 2003—; bd. dirs., pres., chair Coun. Am. Overseas Rsch. Ctrs., 2003—. Fulbright scholar, France, 1960-62; Ford Found. fellow, 1966-68. Mem. Century Assn., Univ. Club, River Club, Harvard Club, Fishers Island Country Club, Phi Beta Kappa. Episcopalian. Avocations: art, skiing, tennis, adventure travel. Home: 120 E 70th St New York NY 10021-5007 Office: D M Found 149 E 63rd St New York NY 10021-7405

DE MENT, IRA, judge; b. Birmingham, Ala., Dec. 21, 1931; s. Ira J. and Helen (Sparks) De M.; m. Ruth Lester Posey; 1 child, Charles Posey. AS, Marion Mil. Inst., 1951; AB, U. Ala., 1953, LLB, 1958, JD, 1969. Bar: Ala. 1958, U.S. Dist. Ct. (mid. dist.) Ala. 1958, U.S. Ct. Appeals (5th cir.) 1958, U.S. Supreme Ct. 1966, U.S. Dist. Ct. (so. dist.) Ala. 1967, U.S. Dist. Ct. D.C. 1972, U.S. Ct. Appeals (D.C.) 1972, U.S. Tax Ct. 1972, U.S. Customs and Patents Appeals 1976, U.S. Dist. Ct. (no. dist.) Ala. 1977, U.S. Ct. Appeals (11th cir.) 1981, U.S. Ct. Mil. Appeals 1972. Law clk. Sup. Ct. Ala., 1958-59; asst. atty. gen. State of Ala., 1959, spl. assty. atty. gen., 1966-69, 81-92; asst. U.S. atty. Montgomery, Ala., 1959-61; pvt. practice, 1961-69, 77-92; U.S. dist. judge (mid. dist.) Ala., 1992—. Acting U.S. atty. Mid. Dist. Ala. 1969, U.S. atty., 1969-77; asst. atty., legal advisor to police and fire depts. City of Montgomery, 1965-69; inst. Jones Law Sch., 1962-64; instr. Montgomery Police Acad., 1964-77; lect. constl. Ala. Police Acad., 1971-75; instr. law enforcement U. Ala., 1967, mem. adj. faculty New Coll., 1974-75, adj. prof. psychology, 1975-92; spl. counsel to Gov. State Ala., 1980-88, gen. counsel Commn. on Aging, 1980-82. Lt. col. USAR, 1953-74; maj. gen. USAFR ret. Decorated Legion of Merit, DSM, others; recipient Disting. Svc. award Internat. Assn. Firefighters, 1975, Rockefeller Pub. Svc. award Woodrow Wilson Sch. Pub. and Internat. Affairs Princeton U., 1976; named Alumnus of Yr. Marion Mil. Inst., 1988, Significant Sig award Sigma Chi Fraternity, 1998, Judicial Award of Merit Ala. State Bar, 1998, Marion Mil. Inst. Disting. Alumnus award, 2003. Mem. ABA, Fed. Bar Assn., D.C. Bar Assn., Ala. Bar Assn. (mem. editl. adv. bd. The Alabama Lawyer 1966-72), Am. Judicature Soc., Nat. Assn. Former U.S. Attys., Phi Alpha Delta. Republican. United Methodist. Clubs: Masons, Shriners. Address: PO Box 2149 Montgomery AL 36102-2149 also: 1 Church St Montgomery AL 36104 Fax: 334-954-3681. E-mail: Ira_DeMent@almd.uscourts.gov.

DEMENT, JAMES ALDERSON, JR., lawyer; b. Clinton, Okla., Sept. 11, 1947; s. James Alderson and Ruby (Weaver) DeM.; m. Sally Anne Wylder, June 6, 1970; children: Stephen, Suzanne, Jonathan. BA summa cum laude, Tex. Christian U., 1969; JD in Internat. Affairs, Cornell U., 1972. Bar: N.Y. 1973, Tex. 1974. Assoc. Alexander & Green, N.Y.C., 1972-73, Baker Botts, LLP, Houston, 1977-85, ptnr., 1998—; ptnr., chmn. corp. tax and internat. sect. Butler & Binion, LLP, Houston, 1985-97. Adj. prof. U. Houston, 1987-88; dir. Houston World Affairs Coun. 2002—. Mem. edtl. rev. bd. The Internat. Lawyer, 1987-94. Trustee Houston Ballet Found., 1989-96, Brazos Presbyn. Homes, Inc., 1990-96. Capt. USAF, 1973-77. Fellow Tex. Bar Found.; mem. State Bar Tex. (internat. law sect., chmn. 1989-90), Internat. and Comparative Law Ctr. Southwestern Legal Found. (adv. coun. 1986—), Houston Bar Assn. (internat. law sect., pres. 1989-90). Presbyterian. Office: Baker Botts LLP 910 Louisiana St Houston TX 77002-4995 E-mail: james.dement@bakerbotts.com.

DEMENT, WILLIAM CHARLES, medical researcher, medical educator; b. Wenatchee, Wash., July 29, 1928; s. Charles Frederick and Kathryn (Severyns) Dement; m. Eleanor Weber, Mar. 23, 1956; children: Catherine Lynn, Elizabeth Anne, John Nicholas. BS, U. Wash., 1951; MD, U. Chgo., 1955, PhD, 1957. Bd. cert. in clin. polysomography. Intern Mt. Sinai Hosp., N.Y.C., 1957—58, rsch. fellow dept. psychiatry, 1958—63; assoc. prof. dept. psychiatry and behavioral scis. Stanford U., 1963—67, prof., 1967—; dir. Stanford Sleep Disorders Clinic and Lab., 1970—, Sleep Rsch. Lab., Stanford, Calif., 1963—. Chmn. U.S. Surgeon Gen.'s Joint Coord. Coun., Project Sleep, 1979—, Nat. Commn. on Sleep Disorders Rsch., 1990—92. Author: Some Must Watch While Some Must Sleep, 1972, The Sleep Watchers, 1992; editor-in-chief: Sleep, 1977—, mem. editl. bd.: Neurobiology of Aging, 1982—. Recipient medal, Intra-Sci. Rsch. Found., 1981, Disting. Svc. award, U. Chgo. Med. Alumni Assn., 1978. Mem.: Am. Physiol. Soc., Am. EEG Soc., Western EEG Soc., Soc. Neuroscience, Psychiat. Rsch. Found., Inst. Medicine of NAS, Assn. Sleep Disorders Ctrs. (pres. 1982, Nathaniel Kleitman prize), Sleep Rsch. Soc. (founder). Office: Stanford Sleep Disorders Ctr 701 Welch Rd Ste 2226 Palo Alto CA 94304-1711

DEMENTIS, KATHARINE HOPKINS, retired interior designer; b. Indpls., Dec. 20, 1922; d. Stephen Francis and Margaret Bell (Yeager) Hopkins; m. Gilbert X. Dementis, Feb. 1, 1953; children: Mary Margaret Dementis O'Dwyer, Stephen Ezra Hall. Student, John Herron Art Sch., 1941-44; BS, U. Wis., 1971. Interior designer L.S. Ayres and Co., Indpls., 1945-51; pres. Ariz. Questers, Phila., 1991-93; ret., 1993. Mem.: DAR, Union Hills Country Club. Republican. Presbyterian. Avocations: artist, decorator, antique collecting. Home: 12830 Castlebar Dr Sun City West AZ 85375-3270

DEMENY, PAUL GEORGE, demographer, researcher; b. Nyiregyháza, Hungary, Dec. 24, 1932; s. József Demény and Margit Iványi; m. Lynn Hall, Sept. 7, 1962; children: Lylla Carter, John. BA, U. of Budapest, Hungary, 1955; PhD, Princeton U., N.J., 1961. Asst. prof., economics and rsch. assoc. Princeton U., NJ, 1961—66; assoc. to full prof. econs. U. of Mich., Ann Arbor, 1966—69; prof. econs. U. of Hawaii, Honolulu, 1969—73; dir. east-west population inst. East-West Ctr., Honolulu, 1969—73; v.p. The Population Coun., N.Y.C., 1973—88, disting. scholar New York, 1989—. Founding editor Population and Devel. Rev., N.Y.C., 1975—. Co-author: (book) Regional Model Life Tables and Stable Populations; co-editor: Population and Development, Encyclopedia of Population. Pres. Population Assn. of Am., Washington, 1986. Recipient External Mem., Hungarian Acad. of Scis., 2001, Laureate, Internat. Union for the Sci. Study of Population, Paris, 2003. Mem.: Princeton Club of N.Y. (assoc.). Home: 4 Alden Rd Greenwich CT 06831 Office: The Population Coun One Dag Hammarskjold Pl New York NY 10017 Office Fax: 212-755-6052. Personal E-mail: pauldemeny@hotmail.com. E-mail: pdemeny@popcouncil.org.

DEMER, MARGARET ELIZABETH, lawyer; b. Cleve. BS in Edn., Kent State U., 1941; LLB, JD, Ind. U., 1958. Bar: Ind. 1958, Ohio 1959. Pvt. practice law, Cleve., 1958—. Pers. specialist U.S. Govt., Washington, 1979-82. Sgt. Women's Army Corps, 1942—46. Mem. Garfield Heights Womens Club. Republican. Mem. United Ch. of Christ. Mem. United Ch. Of Christ. Home and Office: 11429 Bradwell Rd Garfield Heights OH 44125-3505

DEMERATH, JULIE ELLEN, music educator; b. Neenah, Wis., Mar. 14, 1955; d. Donald W. and Helen Marie Demerath; m. Dennis Carl Brei, Jan. 11, 1976 (div. Nov. 9, 1994); children: Lucie Elizabeth Brei, Nikkolaus Richard Brei, Kateri Barbara Brei, Delora Helene Brei, Geoffrey Carl Brei, Josef Xavier Brei. EdM Instrumental, U. of Wis., 1973—77; MA in Sacred Music and Liturgy emphasis in Conducting, St. Joseph Coll., Rensselaer, Ind., 1998—2001. Lic. tchr. instrumental music edn. State of Wis. Dept. of Pub. Instrn., 1995. Pvt. music studio tchr. self-employed, Cornell, Menasha, Eau Claire, and Boyd, Wis., 1978—; music dir. St. Olaf Parish, Eau Claire, 1995—2001; dir. of liturgy Congregation of the Sisters of St. Agnes, Fond du Lac, Wis., 2003—. Composer: (liturgical for choir, assembly and piano) Eucharist Without Walls, (hymn) The Cross, (mass for cantor, assembly & piano) Mass in Honor of Blessed Kateri; dir.: (service recital) An Evening Svc. of Epiphany; researcher: diocesan report Native Am. Liturgical Music, research paper The life of William Byrd and Thorough Analysis of Surge Illuminare, The life of Antonio Vivaldi and thorough Analysis of the Beatus Vir movement of his Psalm 112 - RV598; author: (jour. article) Singing Liturgy, Singing Justice, Shaping Ch.; composer: (voice and piano) Psalm 8; arranger (choral) Veni; translator (arranger): (choral) Stunned to Silence. Pres. PTA, Cornell, 1988—92; music dir. St. Olaf Parish, Eau Claire, 1995—2001; religious edn. tchr. Holy Cross parish and St. Olaf parish, Cornell and Eau Claire, 1984—2001; world youth day adult leader Diocese of LaCrosse, Cornell, 1993—93, music dir. Eau Claire, 1997—97, Chippewa Valley Chpt. of the Am. Guild of Organists, Eau Claire, 2001—01; pres. and commn. chair Coun. of Cath. Women, Cornell, Chippewa and La Crosse, 1988—93; adjudicator Wis. Sch. Music Assn., Madison, 1978—2003. Recipient Degree of Distinction, Nat. Forensic League, 1973; grantee Edn. Grant, Chippewa Valley Chpt. of the Philanthropic Edn. Orgn., 2001; scholar La Crosse Diocesan Lay Formation, Diocese of La Crosse, 1999, 2000, 2001. Mem.: Music Teacher's Nat. Assn. (assoc.), Am. Choral Directors Assn. (assoc.), Nat. Assn. of Pastoral Musicians (assoc.). Roman Catholic. Avocations: travel, fine dining. Office: Congregation of the Sisters of St Agnes 320 County Road K Fond du Lac WI 54935 Personal E-mail: juliedem@msn.com.

DEMERATH, NICHOLAS JAY, III, sociology educator; b. Boston, Nov. 10, 1936; s. Nicholas J. and Helen Louise (Titus) D.; m. Judith Wood Richie, June 25, 1960; children: Loren Roberts, Peter Wells, Benjamin Burroughs. AB magna cum laude, Harvard U., 1958; MA, U. Calif., Berkeley, 1962, PhD, 1964. Instr. to prof. sociology U. Wis., 1962-72; exec. officer Am. Sociol. Assn., Washington, 1970-72; prof., chmn. sociology U. Mass., Amherst, 1972—. Vis. prof. Yale U., 1992, Harvard U., 1993. Author: Social Class in American Protestantism, 1965 (with R.A. Peterson) System, Change and Conflict, 1967, (with P.E. Hammond) Religion in Social Context, 1968, (with M.T. Aiken and G. Marwell) Dynamics of Idealism, 1971, A Tottering Transcendence, 1974, (with K.F. Schuessler and O.N. Larsen) Social Policy and Sociology, 1974, (with G. Marwell) Sociology: Perspectives and Applications, 1976, (with Rhys H. Williams) A Bridging of Faiths, 1992, (with P.D. Hall, T. Schmitt, R.H. Williams) Sacred Companies. 1997, Crossing the Gods, 2000; book rev. editor: Am. Sociol. Rev., 1965-68. Rsch. fellow, grantee Danforth Found., 1965, NIMH, 1960-62, New World Found., 1966; Lilly Endowment grantee for church-state rsch., 1983—; Fulbright Indo-Am. fellowship to India, 1993. Mem. Am. Sociol. Assn. (chmn. publs. com. 1975-77, chmn. endowment com. Am. Sociol Found. 1984-88), Eastern Sociol. Soc. (v.p. 1975, pres. 2000-01), Soc. for Sci. Study Religion (pres. 1997-99), Assn. for the Soc. of Religion (pres. 2003—), Amherst Nickwits (fixtures sec.). Democrat. Home: 30 Harris Mountain Rd Amherst MA 01002-3521 E-mail: demerath@soc.umass.edu.

DEMERDASH, NABEEL ALY OMAR, electrical engineer; b. Cairo, Apr. 26, 1943; came to U.S., 1966; s. Aly Omar and Aziza D.; m. Esther Adel Feher, Feb. 22, 1969; children: Yvonne, Omar, Nancy. BScEE with 1st class honors, Cairo U., 1964; MSEE, U. Pitts., 1967, PhD, 1971. Tchg. asst. in elec. engring. Cairo

U., 1964-66, U. Pitts., 1966-68; engr. Westinghouse Electric Corp., Pitts., 1968-72; asst. prof. elec. engring. Va. Poly. Tech. Inst. and State U., Blacksburg, 1972-77, assoc. prof. elec. engring., 1977-81, prof., 1981-83; prof. dept. elec. and computer engring. Clarkson U., Potsdam, N.Y., 1983-94; prof., chmn. dept. elec. and computer engring. Marquette U., Milw., 1994-97, prof. dept. elec. and computer engring., 1994—. Cons. Sundstrand Corp., Rockford, Ill., 1985-98. Contbr. articles to profl. jours. Recipient Cert. of Recognition, NASA, 1979, Cert. of Tchg. Excellence, Va. Poly. Inst. and State U., 1980, Tchr. of Yr. award, Beta Omicron chpt. Eta Kappa Nu, Marquette Univ., 2003. Fellow IEEE (subcom. chmn. 1988-92, 94-97, Nikola Tesla award 1999); mem. IEEE Power Engring. Soc. (disting. lectr. 1987—, Elec. Machinery Com. prize paper award 1993, working group award 1994, PES prize paper award 1993, working group award 1994), Indsl. Electronics Soc. (Disting. Spkr. program 1990—), Electromagnetics Acad. Achievements include development of three dimensional finite element vector potential and coupled 3D vector potential-scalar potential methods of solution of electromagnetic fields in electric devices; time-stepping coupled finite element-state space computer simulation models and design of electronically operated/controlled AC and DC motor drives. Office: Marquette Univ Elec Computer Engring Dept PO Box 1881 Milwaukee WI 53201-1881 E-mail: nabeel.demerdash@marquette.edu.

DE MERE-DWYER, LEONA, medical illustrator; b. Memphis, May 1, 1928; d. Clifton and Leona (McCarthy) De M.; m. John Thomas Dwyer, May 10, 1952; children: John, DeMere, Patrice, Brian, Anne-Clifton DeMere Dwyer, McCarthy-DeMere Dwyer. BA, Rhodes Coll., Memphis, 1949; MSc, U. Memphis, 1984; PhD, Kennedy-Western U., 1990. Lic. embalmer, funderal dir. Med. artist McCarthy DeMere, Memphjis, 1950-80; pres. Aesthetic Med. & Forensic Art, 1984—; speech therapist Memphis, 1950-82. Lectr. on med. art univs., confs., assns.; cons. in prostheses Vocat. Rehab. Svcs., in plastic surgery, 2001; elected expert witness in funeralization Nat. Forensic Ctr. Author: AIDS; Care of Health Care Workers in the Workplace; contbr. articles to profl. jours. Bereavement counselor, organizer Ladies of St. Jude, Memphis, 1960; active Brooks Art Gallery League of Memphis; emm. God's Unfinished Bus. com. Temple Israel; vice dir. Tellico Hist. Found., 1980; mem. exec. bd. Chickasaw coun. Boy Scouts Am.; active Rep. campaign coms. Recipient Disting. Svc. award Gupton-Jones Coll. Mortuary Sci., 1981, Silver medal Sons of the Am. Revolution medal, 1985, Martha Washington medal. Mem. Nat. Forensic Ctr. (expert witness funeralization 1991—), Fedn. Internat. d'Automobile (internat. car racing 1972, lic.), Assn. Med. Illustrators, Am. Assn. Med. Assts., Emergency Dept. Nurses Assn., Am. Physicians Nurses Assn., Am. Soc. Plastic and Reconstructive Surgeons Found. (guest mem. cons.), Women in Law (chmn. assocs.), Exec. Women Am., Brandeis U. Women, DAR (1st v.p. regent 1980), UDC (pres. Nathan Bedford Forrest chpt.), Cotton Carnival Assn. (chairperson children's sect. 1968-70), Tenn. Club, Royal Matron Amaranth (Faith Ct.), Sertoma (1st female mem. Memphis, elected pres. 1989-90), Pi Sigma Eta, Kappa Delta (adv.), Kappa Delta Pi. Home: 1000 Murray Hill Ln Apt 304 Memphis TN 38120-2668

DEMERITT, KELLY ANNE, accountant; b. Atchison, Kans., Oct. 13, 1971; d. James Edward and Raynette Louise U.; m. Glenn Keith DeMeritt, July 3, 1999; 1 child, Mason. BS in Acctg. and Bus., Baker U., 1993; MBA, Benedictine Coll., 1999. Sr. acct. Berberich Trahan & Co., P.A., Topeka, Kans., 1993-95; dir. fin. City of Atchison, 1995—. Adj. prof. Benedictine Coll., Atchison, 1998-99. Recipient Winning with Teamwork Atchison Area C. of C., 1999. Mem. Kiwanis Club of Atchison (pres. 1999-2001), Govt. Fin. Officers Assn. (Disting. Budget Presentation award, Cert. of Achievement for Excellence in Fin. Reporting), Assn. of Govt. Accts. Office: City of Atchison 515 Kansas Ave Atchison KS 66002 Fax: 913-367-3654. E-mail: kellyd@cityofatchison.com.

DEMERS, ELIZABETH ANNE, education educator; b. Windsor, Ontario, Canada, July 13; d. Roland Joseph and Annie Hamilton (Drummond) Demers. BA in Acctg., U. of Waterloo, 1989; M in Acctg., U. Waterloo, 1990; PhD Bus. Admin., Stanford U., 2000, M.S. Stats., 1997. Asst. mgr. fin. adv. Price Waterhouse, Toronto, Canada, 1992—93; rsch. asst. grad. sch. of bus. Stanford U., 1994—99; asst. prof. Simon Sch. of Bus. U. of Rochester, 1999—. Author: (research article) Jour. of Fin. Econ., 2002, Review of Acctg. studies, 2000, Jour. of Acctg. Rsch., 2001. Grantee Rsch. Grant, CIMA, 2001, Fellowship, Soc. of Mgmt. Acctg. of Can., 1994—98. Mem.: Am. Fin. Assn., Am. Academic Acctg. Assoc. Office: Simon Sch Bus U Rochester Rochester NY 14627 E-mail: lizdemers@simon.rochester.edu.

DEMERS, JUDY LEE, former state legislator, university dean; b. Grand Forks, North Dakota, June 27, 1944; d. Robert L. and V. Margaret (Harming) Prosser; m. Donald E. DeMers, Oct. 3, 1964; div. Oct. 1971; 1 child, Robert M.; m. Joseph M. Murphy, Mar. 5, 1977; div. Oct. 1983. BS in nursing, U. N.D., 1966; M in Edn., U. Wash., 1973, post grad., 1973-76. Pub. health nurse Govt., Wash., DC, 1966-68; Combined Nursing Svc., Mpls., 1968-69; instr. pub. health nursing U. N.D., Grand Forks, ND, 1969-71; assoc. dir. Medex program, 1970-72; rsch. assoc. U. Wash., Seattle, 1973-76; dir. family nurse practitioner program, 1977-82; dir. under grad. med. edn., 1982-83; assoc. dir. rural health, 1982-85; mem. N.D. Ho. of Reps., 1982-92; assoc. dean, 1983—; mem. N.D. Senate, 1992-2000. Cons. health manpower devel. staff, Honolulu, 1975-81, Assn. Physician asst. programs, Washington, 1979-82; site visitor cons., AMA Com. Allied Health Edn. Accreditation, Chgo.,1979-81. Author: Educating New Health Practitioners, 1976; mem. editl. bd.: P.A. Jour., 1976-78; contbr. articles to profl. jours. Sec., bd. dirs. Valley Health, Grand Forks, N.D., 1982—; mem. exec. com., bd. dirs. Agassiz Health Systems Agy., Grand Forks, 1982-86; mem. N.D. State Daycare Adv. Com., 1983-93, Mayor's Adv. com. on Police Policy, Grand Forks, 1983-85, N.D. State Foster Care Adv. Com., 1985-87, N.D. State Hypertension Adv. Com., 1983-85, Gov.'s Com. on DUI and Traffic Safety, 1985-91, State wide Adv. Com. on AIDS, 1985-90; bd. dirs. Casey Found., Families First Initiative, 1988-97, Comprehensive Health Assn. N.D., 1993-95, United Health Found., 1990-97, Northern Valley Mental Health Assn., 1994-00, bd. dir., Grand Forks Girl's and Women's Hockey Assn., 1999-2002; bd. dirs., sec.-treas., exec. com., program com., fundraising com., sec.-treas. Devel. Homes, 1999—; adv. bd. Mountainbrooke (formerly Friendship Place), 1992-96; adv. com. Ruth Meiers Adolescent Ctr., Grand Forks, 1988-2002, Altru Health Sys. Corp. Bd., 1997—; mem. Commn. on Future Structure of VA Health Care, 1990-91; bd. dirs. Red River Valley Cmty. action Program, 1991—; mem. Resource and Referral Bd. Dirs., 1990—; caring coun. N.D. Blue Cross and Blue Shield Caring Program for Children, 1995-99; coun. mem. N.D. Health Task Force, 1992-94; healthcare subcom. Northern Gt. Plains Econ. Devel. Commn., 1995-96; adv. com. on telecomms. and healthcare FCC, 1996; mem., chmn. Grand Forks City and County Bd. Health, 2000—. Recipient: Pub. Citizen of Yr. Award, N.D. chpt., Nat. Assn. Social Workers, 1986, Golden Grain Award, N.D. Dietetic Assn., 1988, Person of Yr. Award, U. N.D., Law Women Caucus, 1990, Legislator of Yr. award North Valley Labor Coun., 1990, N.D., Martin Luther King Jr. Award, 1990, Legislator of Yr. Award, Mental Health Assn., N.D., 1993, N.D. Libr. Assn. Legislator of Yr., 1999, Friend of Medicine Award N.D. Med. Assn., 1999, Legislator of Year Award, N.D. Pub. Employees Assn., 1999, Friend of Counseling Award, N.D. State Counseling Assn., 2000, Legislative Svc. Award, ARC of N.D., Friend of Higher Edn. Award, AAUP, 1995. Mem. N.D. Nurses Assn., Alpha Lambda Delta, Sigma Theta Tau, Pi Lampda Theta. Home: Unit 92 N 2200 S 29th St Apt 92N Grand Forks ND 58201-5869 Office: UND Sch Medicine PO Box 9037 501 N Columbia Rd Grand Forks ND 58202-9037 E-mail: jdemers@medicine.nodak.edu.

DEMERS, NANCY KAE, nursing educator; b. Manchester, NH, Oct. 18, 1938; d. Paul E. and Nellie (Matijas) Watts; m. Raymond Joseph Demers, Feb. 13, 1960; children: Paula, John, Diane. RN, Elliot Hosp. Sch. Nursing, Manchester, N.H., 1959; BSN, St. Anselm Coll., 1969; MSN, Boston U., 1978; postgrad., Nova U., 1994—. Social and health educator NH Youth Devel. Ctr., Manchester, 1969—74; dir. nursing svcs. Hanover Hill Nursing Home, Manchester, 1974—75; asst. prof. St. Anselm Coll., Manchester, 1974-82; maternal and child health coord. Concord (N.H.) Hosp., 1982-83; assoc. prof. NH Tech. Coll., Manchester, 1983—88; prof. nursing NH Cmty. Tech. Coll., Manchester, 1988—2000; adminstr. Regency Nursing Care, LLC, Bedford, NH, 2000—. Panel item writer Nat. Coun. Licensure Exam, 1993; developer evaluation component for an ongoing AIDS edn./prevention program for youths between the ages of 14 and 19, Claremont Coll. and Fed. U. Ceara, Brazil. Recipient Ptnrs. of the Ams. award W.K. Kellogg Found., 1996. Mem. N.H. Am. Diabetes Assn. (bd. mem. 1988-93, Disting. Svc. award 1993), N.H. Nurse Educators, N.H. Ptnrs. of Americas (corr. sec. 1992—, travel awards 1991, 93, 95, Internat. award 1996), Transcultural Nursing, Sigma Theta Tau. Home and Office: 501 Route 101 Bedford NH 03110-4710

DEMERTZOGLOU, PINDARO EPAMINONDA, systems administrator, education educator; s. Epaminoudas Pindaros and Gesthimani Prodromos Demertzoglou; m. Sofia Anestis Theodoridou, Aug. 4, 2002. BS, Am. Coll. of Thessaloniki, Greece, 1995; MBA, Rensselaer Poly. Inst., N.Y., 1998, MS, 2001; postgrad., SUNY. Network database adminstr. Am. Coll. of Thessaloniki, Greece, 1995—96; database developer Aristotelian U., Thessaloniki, Greece, 1996; bus. mgr. The Design Works, Troy, NY, 1997; database developer Rensselaer Poly. Inst., Troy, NY, 1997—98, database specialist, 1999—2001, sr. sys. adminstr., 2001—. Adj. mis faculty Rensselaer Poly. Inst., Troy, NY, 2000—, Union Coll., Schenectady, NY, 2003—. Scholar Tuition Scholarship, Am. Coll. of Thessaloniki, 1994—95, Rensselar Poly. Inst., 1997—98. Mem.: Am. Mgmt. Assn., AAUP, N.Y. State Sheriffs' Assn. Inst., Inc. (hon.). Home: 100 McChesney Ave B-12 Troy NY 12180 Office: Rensselaer Polytechnic Inst 110 8th St Pitts 2224 Troy NY 12180 Personal E-mail: demerp@hotmail.com. E-mail: demerp@rpi.edu.

DEMERY, DOROTHY JEAN, secondary school educator; b. Houston, Sept. 5, 1941; d. Floyd Hicks and Irene Elaine Burns Clay; m. Leroy W. Demery, Jan. 16, 1979; children: Steven Bradley, Rodney Bradley, Craig Bradley, Kimberly Bradley. AA, West L.A. Coll., Culver City, Calif., 1976; AS, Harbor Coll., Wilmington, Calif., 1983; BS in Pub. Adminstrn., Calif. State U., Carson, 1985; MS in Instructional Leadership, Nat. U., San Diego, 1991. Cert. real estate broker, tchr. math. and bus. edn., bilingual tchr., crosscultural lang. and acad. devel.; lang. devel. specialist. Eligibility social worker Dept. Pub. Social Svcs., L.A., 1967-74; real estate broker Dee Bradley & Assocs., Riverside, Calif., 1976—; tchr. math L.A. Unified Sch. Dist., 1985-91; math/computer sci. tchr. Pomona (Calif.) Unified Sch. Dist., 1991—. Adj. lectr. Riverside C.C., 1992—93; mem. Dist. Curriculum Coun./Report Card Task Force, Pomona, 1994—; del. rep. assembly NEA, 1991—2003. Chairperson Human Rights Com., Pomona, 1992—, sec. steering com., 1993—, adv. bd., 1993—; mem. polit. action com. Assoc. Pomona Tchrs., 1993-94. Recipient Outstanding Svc. award Baldwin Hills Little League Assn., L.A., 1972. Mem.: Calif. Tchrs. Assn. (state coun. 2000, chair site base, chair dept. math.), Associated Pomona Tchrs. (site base chairperson, math. chairperson 1994—, nominee to Nat. Coun. Tchrs. of Math. 2001, bd. dirs. 1998—), Aux. Nat. Med. Assn., Nat. Coun. Tchrs. Math., Nat. Bus. Assn. Avocations: hiking, tennis, walking. Office: Simons Middle School 900 E Franklin Ave Pomona CA 91766-5362

DEMETER, STEVEN, neurologist, medical publishing company executive; b. Budapest, Hungary, Jan. 12, 1947; came to U.S., 1957; s. Arpad and Ilona (Wiesner) D.; m. Diane Simkin, Jan. 8, 1984; children: Sara, Nikki. BS, CUNY, 1969; MD, N.Y. Med. Coll., 1973. Diplomate Am. Bd. Psychiatry and Neurology. Intern Beth Israel Med. Ctr., N.Y.C., 1973-74; neurology resident Albert Einstein Coll. Medicine, Bronx, N.Y., 1974-77; inst. neurology N.Y. Med. Coll., N.Y.C., 1977-79; fellow in behavioral neurology U. Iowa Coll. Medicine, Iowa City, 1979-81; fellow Ctr. for Brain Rsch., U. Rochester (N.Y.) Sch. Medicine, 1981-84, instr. neurology, 1982-84, asst. prof. Ctr. for Brain Rsch., 1984-87, asst. prof. neurology, 1987-89, clin. asst. prof., 1989-91, clin. assoc. prof., 1991-93; pres. MedLink Corp., San Diego, 1990—; assoc. clin. prof. neurosci. U. Calif., San Diego, 1995—. Neurology cons. Rochester Psychiat. Ctr., 1985-91 Contbr. numerous articles to med. jours. Grantee Scottish Rite Schizophrenia Rsch. Found., 1987-90, Whitehall Found., 1990-93, NIH, 1991-94. Fellow Am. Acad. Neurology, Royal Soc. Medicine (London); mem. AAAS, Soc. for Neurosci., Tourette Syndrome Assn. (med. adv. bd. 1985-93, bd. dirs. 1987-93). Office: MedLink Ste 120 10393 San Diego Mission Rd San Diego CA 92108-2134

DEMETREON, DAIBOUNE ELAYNE, minister; b. Brunswick, Maine, Aug. 5, 1945; d. James Demetreon and Grace Lewis; m. James Allison Devine, Mar. 3, 1986; children from previous marriage: William Anthony Decker, James Steven Decker; 6 grandchildren. Degree, Unity Sch. Practical Christianity & Ordination, 1975; postgrad., Rio Salado Coll., 1992; BA in Psychology, Ottawa U., 1994, MA in Profl. Counseling, 1999. Ordained min. Unity Ch., 1975; cert. practitioner Neuro-Linguistic Program. Sr. min. Unity of Ann Arbor, Mich., 1975-77, Unity of Boulder, Colo., 1977-78, Unity of Colorado Springs, 1980-86, Unity of Scottsdale, Ariz., 1989-95. Chmn. World of One Fellowship, Colorado Springs, 1986—, pastoral counselor, Scottsdale, 1989—; adv. bd. dirs. Boulder (Colo.) Psychiat. Inst., 1977-78; campus min. U. Mich., Ypsilanti, 1975-77; conductor workshops chaplains program U.S. Army, Ft. Carson; vol. Am. Fgn. Svcs., 1996—. Author, narrator audio tape Transformations, 1985; host talk show God and You, 1983; contbr. articles to profl. publs. Chem. dependency counselor St. Luke's Hosp., 1993-96; Am. Fgn. Svc. vol., 1996—; counselor/advocate for children at risk, Scottsdale, Ariz., 1999—. Avocations: gardening, sewing, hiking, camping, sculpture. Office: World of One Fellowship 269 SW Winterpark Cir Lees Summit MO 64081-4010

DEMETRESCU, MIHAI CONSTANTIN, research scientist, educator, computer company executive; b. Bucharest, Romania, May 23, 1929; came to U.S., 1966; s. Dan and Alina (Dragosescu) D.; m. Agnes Halas, May 25, 1969; 1 child, Stefan. M.E.E., Poly. Inst. of U. Bucharest, 1954; PhD, Romanian Acad. Sci., 1957. Prin. investigator Rsch. Inst. Endocrinology Romanian Acad. Sci., Bucharest, 1958-66; rsch. fellow dept. anatomy UCLA, 1966-67; faculty U. Calif.-Irvine, 1967-83, asst. prof. dept. physiology, 1971-78, assoc. rschr., 1978-79, assoc. clin. prof., 1979-83; v.p. Resonance Motors, Inc., Monrovia, Calif., 1972-85; pres. Neurometrics, Inc., Irvine, 1978-82, Lasergraphics Inc., Irvine, 1982-84, chmn., CEO, 1984—. Mem. com. on honor degrees U. Calif.-Irvine, 1970-72. Contbr. articles to profl. jours.; patentee in field. Postdoctoral fellow UCLA, 1966. Mem. IEEE (sr.), Am. Physiol. Soc. Republican. Home: 8 Sunset Hbr Newport Coast CA 92657-1706 Office: 20 Ada Irvine CA 92618-2303 E-mail: Dr.D@lasergraphics.com.

DEMETRION, JAMES THOMAS, art museum director; b. Middletown, Ohio, July 10, 1930; s. Tom and Susie (Tsifiklis) D.; m. Barbara Parrish, 1954; 1 child, Elaine. BS in Edn., Miami U., 1952; hon. doctorate, Simpson Coll., 1984. Curator Pasadena Art Mus., Calif., 1964-66, dir., 1966-69, Des Moines Art Ctr., 1969-84, Hirshhorn Mus. & Sculpture Garden, Washington, 1984—2001. Cons. bd. trustees Noguchi Found., 2002—; mem. Mus. adv. panel Nat. Endowment for Arts, 1973-76, co-chmn., 1974-76; mem. IRS Art Adv. Panel, 1983-86. Mem. Assn. Art Mus. Dirs. (treas. 1976-77, pres. 1979-80). Office: Hirshhorn Mus-Sculpture Garden Independence Ave At 7th St SW Washington DC 20560-0001

DEMETRIOS, archbishop; b. Thessaloniki, Greece, 1928; Degree with honors, U. Athens, 1950, ThD in Theology, 1977; PhD in Philosophy with distinction, Harvard U., 1972. Ordained priest Greek Orthodox Ch., 1964. Elected titular bishop, aux. bishop to Archbishop of Athens, Vresthena, Greece, 1967; disting. prof. Biblical studies and Christian origins Holy Cross Greek Orthodox Sch. of Theology, Brookline, Mass., 1983-93; elected Archbishop of Am. Greek Orthodox Ch. in Am., 1999—. Vis. prof. New Testament Harvard Divinity Sch. Author: Authority and Passion, 1987, The Transcendent God of Eugonostos, 1991, Christ, the Pre-Existing God, 1992. Office: Greek Orthodox Archdiocese of Am 8-10 E 79th St New York NY 10021

DEMHARTER, CHERYL ANN MARIE, foreign language educator, former administrator; b. New Orleans, May 20, 1955; d. Anton Irwin and Liliane Irene (Auger) D.; m. Ashraf F. Fouad, May 26, 1990; children: Anthony, Edward. BA magna cum laude, U. New Orleans, 1975; MA, Tulane U., 1978, PhD, 1981. Grad. tchg. asst. Tulane U., New Orleans, 1977-80, vis. instr. French, 1980-81; asst. prof. French U. Tex., Austin, 1981-86; dir. fgn. lang. programs MLA, Assn. Depts. Fgn. Langs., N.Y.C., 1986-88; vis. asst. prof. French U. Iowa, Iowa City, 1989-90; owner FrenchSounds, LLC, Farmington, Conn., 1997—. Adj. lectr. French U. Hartford, West Hartford, 1999—2002. Recipient summer stipends U. Tex. Rsch. Inst., 1982, 85, NEH, 1982; faculty enrichment grantee Can. Govt., 1984, faculty rsch. grantee, 1985. Mem. Am. Assn. Tchrs. French, Internat. Soc. Phonetic Scis., Am. Coun. Tchrs. Fgn. Langs., Rocky Mountain MLA, N.E. MLA, Assn. Can. Studies in the U.S., N.E. Coun. Que. Studies, So. Coun. Francophone Studies (2d v.p. 1985-86), Alliance française de Hartford, Phi Kappa Phi. E-mail: FrenchSounds@comcast.net.

DEMICHAEL, MARK JOSEPH, physical education educator, baseball coach; b. Barberton, Ohio, Apr. 13, 1966; s. Joseph L. and Gladys Esther DeMichael; m. Kimberly Cubie, July 29, 1989; children: Ashley Lynette, Kasey Rene. MEd, Azusa Pacific U., 1993. Cert. tchr. Mass. Prof. phys. edn. Ind. Wesleyan U., Marion, 1996—, head baseball coach, 1996—. Dir. baseball camp Ind. Wesleyan U., Marion, 1996—; chair regional baseball NAIA, Olathe, Kans., 2002—. Vol. Salvation Army, Marion, Ind., 1999—2003. Recipient Baseball Coach of the Yr., Commonwealth Coast Conf., 1996, 1997. Mem.: Ind. Assn. Health Phys. Edn. Recreation Dance (assoc.; state sport com. 2002—03, dir. higher edn. 2000—03), Am. Assn. Health Phys. Edn. Recreation Dance (assoc.). Republican. Avocations: travel, movies. Office: Indiana Wesleyan University 4201 S Washington St Marion IN 46953 Office Fax: 765-677-2328. E-mail: mark.demichael@indwes.edu.

DE MICHELE, O. MARK, utility company executive; b. Syracuse, N.Y., Mar. 23, 1934; s. Aldo and Dora (Carno) De M.; m. Faye Ann Venturin, Nov. 8, 1957; children: Mark A., Christopher C., Michele M., Julianne; m. Barbara Joan Stanley, May 22, 1982; 1 child, Angela Marie. BS, Syracuse U., 1955; hon. doctorate, No. Ariz. U., 1997. Mgr. Seal Right Co., Inc., Fulton, N.Y., 1955-58; v.p., gen. mgr. L.M. Harvey Co. Inc., Syracuse, 1958-62; v.p. Niagara Mohawk Power, Syracuse, 1962-78, Ariz. Pub. Svc., Phoenix, 1978-81, exec. v.p., 1981-82, pres., CEO, 1982-97, also bd. dirs.; pres., CEO Greater Phoenix Econ. Coun., 1997-98; chmn., CEO Urban Realty Ptnrs. LLC, 1998—. Bd. dirs. Ont. Power Generation. Pres. Jr. Achievement, Syracuse, 1974-75, Phoenix, 1982-83, United Way Ctrl. N.Y., Syracuse, 1978, Ariz. Opera Co., Phoenix, 1981-83, Phoenix Symphony, 1984-86, United Way Phoenix, 1985-86, Ariz. Mus. Sci. and Tech., 1988-90; pres. Childrens Action Alliance, 1989-92; chmn. Valley Sun United Way, 1984-86, Phoenix Econ. Coun., 1991-94; chmn. Morrison Inst. Pub. Policy at Ariz. State U.; chmn. Ariz. Cities in Schs., 1994-97, Nat. Environ. Edn. Found., 1997—; pres. Episcopal Cmty. Svc. Found. Named Outstanding Young Man of Yr., Syracuse Jaycees, 1968, Phoenix Man of Yr., Phoenix Ad Club, 1992; recipient Humanitarian award Nat. Conf., 1995. Mem. Phoenix C. of C. (chmn. bd. 1986-87). Clubs: Phoenix Country, Ariz. (Phoenix). Republican. Home: 1536 Glorietta Blvd Coronado CA 92118-2306 Office: Urban Realty Ptnrs LLC 2415 E Camelback Rd Ste 700 Phoenix AZ 85016-4245 E-mail: mdemichele@aol.com.

DEMIDOV, VADIM V. biotechnologist, writer; b. Novosibirsk, Russia, July 10, 1954; arrived in U.S., 1994; s. Valery S. Demidov and Klaudya I. Babkina; m. Lyudmila G. Romaschenko, Nov. 18, 1985 (div.); 1 child, Julia; m. Inna Verba, Mar. 21, 1987. MS in Phys.-Chem. Engring., Moscow Phys-Tech. Inst., 1977; PhD in Biophysics, Inst. Molecular Genetics, Moscow, 1980. Jr. rschr. Rsch. Inst. for Biol. Testing of Chem. Compounds, Moscow, 1980—85; rschr. Moscow Inst. Biotech., 1985—87; sr. rschr. Inst. Mineralogy, Geochemistry and Crystallochemistry of Rare Elements, 1987—90, Inst. Molecular Genetics, Moscow, 1990—93; vis. asst. rsch. prof. dept. biology George Mason U., Fairfax, Va., 1993; vis. rsch. prof. Panum Inst. Copenhagen U., 1993—94; sr. rsch. assoc., group leader Ctr. for Advanced Biotech., dept. biomed. engring. Boston U., 1994—; mem. editl. bd. Trends Biotech., 2003. Participant 3 sci. ecol. expeditions on peninsulas Kamchatka and Taimyr and Russian Far East, 1990—92; mem. internat. working group experts on planetary protection, 1991—92; mem. sci. bd. on problem of gene targeted drugs Russian Acad. Sci., 1992—93. Contbr. articles to profl. jours., chapters to books; reviewer: jours. in field. Recipient Silver medal, All-Union Nat. Exhbn. Econ. Achievements, Moscow, 1988; grantee, Russian State Com. Natural Resources and Environment, 1991—93. Mem.: N.Y. Acad. Sci. Avocations: travel, art collecting. Office: Ctr Advanced Biotech Boston U 36 Cummington St 2d Fl Boston MA 02215

DEMIERI, JOSEPH L. retired bank executive; b. N.Y.C., Aug. 31, 1940; s. Leo A. and Frances (Garone) DeM.; m. Anne Patricia McCue, May 15, 1965. BBA, Tex. A&M U., 1962. C.P.A., N.Y. With Peat, Marwick, Mitchell & Co., N.Y.C., 1962-68; v.p., controller City Investing Co., N.Y.C. and Beverly Hills, Calif., 1968-82; exec. v.p. Motown Industries, Los Angeles, 1982-84; chmn., CEO Calif. Millworks Corp., Valencia, 1985-95; sr. v.p., CFO Western Security Bank, Burbank, Calif., 1995—2002. Home: 6259 Ebbtide Way Malibu CA 90265-3608

DEMILES, EDWARD, agent; b. Indpls., Sept. 22, 1962; s. Lee Henry and Gearldine (Woolridge) DeM. BA in Bus., U.S. Army Sch. Adminstrn., 1982. Lic. agt. Am. Fedn. Musicians. V.p. Festival City Prodns., Indpls., 1978-81; founder, chief exec. officer Sahara Records & Filmworks Co., Chgo., 1981—, The Edward DeMiles Co., Chgo., Dallas, Indpls., 1984—, pub. rels/promotions dir. Dallas, 1984—, entertainment agt., 1987—. Tv producer Black Knight Prodns., Indpls., 1980-81; prodn. coord. USO Presents Suzanne Somers Show, Karlsrule, West Germany, 1982; concert promoter In Clubhouse Promotions, Oklahoma City, 1984-85. Mem. Am. Fedn. Musicians. Office: The Edward DeMiles Co 10th Fl S627 28 E Jackson Bldg Chicago IL 60604

DE MILLE, BARBARA MUNN, writer, former English literature educator; b. Buffalo, Feb. 24, 1932; d. Carl Alfred Munn and Helen Shelden Stout; m. William De Mille, Sept. 11, 1952. BA magna cum laude, SUNY, Buffalo, 1970, MA, 1975, PhD, 1978. Adj. prof. SUNY, Albany, 1978-80; prof. Jinan U., Guangzhou, China, 1980-81; asst. prof. Coll. William and Mary, Williamsburg, Va., 1981-85; weekly commentator N.E. Pub. Radio, Albany, 1993-95. Contbr. articles to jours. and mags. NEH fellow Cornell U., 1986; grantee Vogelstein Found., 1987. Mem. Phi Beta Kappa.

DEMILLE, DALE ESTHER, medical/surgical nurse, educator; b. New Britain, Conn., Nov. 3, 1953; d. Jared Armand Tofani and Esther Constance Tofano; m. Richard Kenneth DeMille, July 24, 1993 (div.); m. Robert John Zdankiewicz, June 8, 1974 (div.); children: Kristen Leigh Zdankiewicz Martin, Eric Robert Zdankiewicz. Assocs. degree, Greater Hartford C.C., 1990; BS in Nursing, Cen. Conn. State U., 1993; MS in Nursing, U. of Hartford, 2001. RN Conn., cert. CCRN, AACN. Nurse critical care New Britain Gen. Hosp., 1990—2000, cardiovasc. angiographic radiology nurse, 1999—, nurse med. telemetry, 2002—. Std. setting Exelsior Coll., Albany, NY, 2002—, exam item writer, 2002—; manuscript reviewer Prentice-Hall, Pearson Edn., Livonia, Mich., 2002—; adj. faculty U. Conn., Storrs, 2001—02, Quinnipiac U., Hamden, Conn., 2001—02. Topical spkr. New Britain Gen. Hosp.'s Instl. Ethics Com.'s Pub. Ethics Com. Meeting, New Britain, 2001. Scholar, Greater Hartford Region Soroptimist Internat., 1989, Arthur C. Banks, Jr. Found., 1990, AAUW, 1990. Mem.: AACN, Am. Nurses' Assn., Sigma Theta Tau. Conservative. Avocations: antiques and collectibles, singing, furniture restoration, hot-air ballooning. Personal E-mail: ddemille53@yahoo.com.

DEMILLE, DIANNE LYNNE, mathematics educator, administrator; b. Dundas, Ontario, Can., Mar. 21, 1948; d. Leslie Benjamin and Helen Isobel (Don) DeMille; m. Tate Stanley Casey, June 16, 1971 (div. June, 1975); 1 child, Marie Anne; m. Thomas John Camacho, Aug. 30, 1980 (div. June, 1999); children: Patricia Suzanne, Tara Lynne. BA in Math., Whittier Coll., 1970, secondary tchg. credential, 1972; PhD, Walden U., 2000. Math. tchr. Mater Dei H.S., Santa Ana, Calif., 1972-79, Santa Ana (Calif.) H.S., 1979; instr. math. Coast C.C., Costa Mesa, Calif., 1979-81; math. tchr., mentor tchr. Downey (Calif.) Unified, 1979-93; specialist Orange County Dept. Edn., Costa Mesa, 1993—2002, coord. math. and assessment NSF CO-PI project, 2002—. Coord. assessment/Golden State exams, devel. algebra/Geometry/h.s. math., 1983—; cons., presenter confs., Orange County Dept. Edn., Costa Mesa, 1986—, Calif. State Dept. of Edn., Sacramento, 1989—; chief math devel. team Calif. Learning Assessment Sys.; chief reader, table reader Golden State Math. Exam.; mem. devel. team, chief reader Calif. State Regional Lead Assessment, coord. devel. team, 1996—; reviewer Am. Coll. Testing. Author: Batch Basic, 1973; author and project specialist (series of books and workshops) So. Calif. Regional Algebra Project Focus on Algebra, Focus on Geometry, 1989—, (units in book) Math A, Investigating Mathematics, 1989. Recipient Wright Bros. Innovative Tchrs. award, Rockwell Co., L.A., 1991; grantee Rockwell Co., 1992. Mem. ASCD, Am. Sch. Counselors Assn., Nat. Coun. Tchrs. Math., Nat. Coun. Suprs. Math., Calif. Math. Coun., Assn. Calif. Sch. Adminstrs., Phi Delta Kappa. Home: #101 1700 W Cerritos Ave Anaheim CA 92804 Office: Orange County Dept Edn 200 Kalmus Dr Costa Mesa CA 92626-5922 E-mail: d.demille@verizon.net.

DEMILLE, NELSON RICHARD, writer; b. N.Y.C., Aug. 23, 1943; s. Huron and Antonia (Panzera) DeM.; children: Lauren, Alex. BA in Polit. Sci. and History, Hofstra U., 1970, LHD (hon.), 1989; DLitt (hon.), L.I. U., 1993; LDH (hon.), Dowling Coll., 1997. Freelance writer, 1973—. Judge Book-of-the-Month Club. Author more than 12 novels, including By the Rivers of Babylon, 1978, Cathedral, 1981, The Talbot Odyssey, 1984, Word of Honor, 1985, The Charm School, 1988, The Gold Coast, 1990, The General's Daughter, 1992, Spencerville, 1994, Plum Island, 1997, The Lion's Game, 2000, Up Country, 2002; co-author: Mayday, 1998; contbr. short stories to mags. 1st lt. U.S. Army, 1966-69. Decorated Air medal, Bronze Star, Vietnamese Cross of Gallantry; recipient Estabrook award Hofstra U. Mem. Mystery Writers Am., Author's Guild, Mensa. Roman Catholic.

DEMING, CLAIBORNE P. oil industry executive; Positions in law, prodn., exploration, mktg., land depts. Murphy Oil, El Dorado, Ark., 1979; v.p., 1988; v.p. petroleum ops., 1988; exec. v.p., COO, 1992; mem. exec. com.; also bd. dirs.; mgr. land and contracts Murphy Oil USA Inc., 1988-92; pres., 1992-93. On assignment Ocean Drilling and Exploration Co. (ODECO, now Murphy Exploration & Production Co.), New Orleans. Office: Murphy Oil 200 Peach St El Dorado AR 71730

DEMING, DAVID, geologist, educator; b. Terre Haute, Ind., Mar. 18, 1954; s. Leo Reese and Adela Deming; m. Jerry Adams Deming, Sept. 11, 1982; children: John, Joseph. BA, Purdue U., 1976; BS, Ind. U., Indpls., 1983; PhD, U. Utah, 1988. Postdoctoral rsch. assoc. La. State U., Baton Rouge, 1989—90; NRC postdoctoral fellow U.S. Geol. Survey, Menlo Park, Calif., 1990—91; prof. geology and geophysics U. Okla., Norman, 1992—. Adj. scholar Okla. Coun. of Pub. Affairs, Oklahoma City, 1999—, Nat. Ctr. Policy Analysis, Dallas. Author: (book) Introduction to Hydrogeology, 2001; editor (history editor): (jour.) Ground Water, 2002—; mem. editl. bd.: Petroleum Geosci., Geothermics. Coun. mem. Soc. Sci. Exploration. Mem.: Am. Assn. Petroleum Geologists, Am. Geophys. Union. Office: Dept Geology U Okla 100 E Boyd St Rm 810 Norman OK 73019 Office Fax: 405-325-3140. Business E-Mail: ddeming@ou.edu.

DEMING, RUST M. ambassador; b. Oct. 1941; m. Kristen Deming; 3 children. Diploma, Rollins Coll., 1964; Postgrad. Diploma, Stanford U., 1981. Former polit. officer U.S. Embassy, Tunisia, 1966; dir. Office of Japanese Affairs, Washington, 1991—93; dep. chief of mission Japan, 1993—96; Charge d'Affaires, ad interim, 1996—97; prin. dep. asst. sec. for East Asian and Pacific Affairs U.S. Embassy, Tunisia, 1998—2000; U.S. amb. to Rep. of Tunisia, 2001—. Recipient Civilian Meritorious awards, U.S. Def. Dept., 1995—97. Office: DOS Amb 6360 Tunis Pl Washington DC 20521

DEMING, THOMAS EDWARD, publishing company executive; b. Chgo., May 5, 1954; s. Anthony A. and Josephine (Andracki) Dziurdzik; m. Mary Ann Jadowic, May 15, 1976; children: Mark Thomas, Emily Marie, William Joseph. BS in Acctg., De Paul U., 1976, MBA, 1986. CPA, Ill. Acct. Arthur Andersen & Co., Chgo., 1975-81; asst. contr. Scott, Foresman & Co., Glenview, Ill., 1981-83, v.p., contr., 1983-88, v.p. fin., 1988-89, v.p. fin. and adminstrn., 1990; treas. Macmillan/McGraw-Hill Sch. Pub. Co., Lake Forest, Ill., 1990-91, v.p., treas., 1991-92, Harper Collins Pubs., N.Y.C., 1992-95; v.p. fin. Harper Collins Pubs., Inc., N.Y.C., 1995-96; v.p. fin. planning & ops. McDougal Littell Pub., Inc., Evanston, Ill., 1996—; corp. v.p. McDougal Littell parent co. Houghton Mifflin, 1996—. Mem. Fin. Execs. Inst., Am. Inst. CPA's, Ill. Soc. CPA's, DePaul U.'s Ledger & Quill, Beta Alpha Psi, Delta Mu Delta, Beta Gamma Sigma. Avocations: golf, skiing. Office: McDougal Littell Inc 909 Davis St Evanston IL 60201

DEMING, WILLIS RILEY, lawyer; b. Ada, Ohio, Nov. 28, 1914; s. Cliffe and Okla (Riley) D.; m. Dorothy Arline Hill, 1950 (div. 1971); children: Susan Elizabeth, Deborah Anne Gunst, David Riley; m. Constance S. Mori, 1971 (div. 1986); m. Olive Plunkett Rose, 1994 (dec. 1999). BA, Ohio State U., 1935, JD, 1938. Bar: Ohio 1938, Calif. 1947, D.C. 1957. Pvt. practice, Columbus, Ohio, 1938-39; casualty claim examiner Am. Surety Co., N.Y.C., 1939-41; chief bds. and claims rev. br. San Francisco Port of Embarkation, 1946-47; atty. Treadwell and Laughlin, San Francisco, 1947-54, Brobeck, Phleger & Harrison, San Francisco, 1954-56, Washington, 1956-60; pvt. practice Washington, 1961-62; atty. Matson Nav. Co., San Francisco, 1962—71, gen. counsel, 1967-71, 74-92; v.p., sec., gen. counsel Alexander & Baldwin, Inc., Honolulu, 1968-74; sr. v.p., gen. counsel Matson Nav. Co., San Francisco, 1974—92. Served to lt. col. AUS, 1941-46; col. U.S. Army, ret. Mem. ABA, State Bar Calif., Soc. for Asian Art (pres. 1995-97), Claremont Country Club (Oakland). Home: 5649 Country Club Dr Oakland CA 94618-1715 E-mail: wrdeming@hotmail.com.

DEMING, WILLOUGHBY HOWARD, education educator; b. Washington, Apr. 5, 1956; s. Andrew S and Maidee Coffman Deming; m. Lauren Wellford; children: David Wellford, Jonathan Walker. BA, Coll. of William and Mary, 1974—78; MA, U. of Chgo., 1978—79, PhD, 1979—91. Assoc. prof. U. of Portland, Oreg., 1998—. Office: U of Portland 5000 N Willamette Blvd Portland OR 97203 Office Fax: 503-943-7803. E-mail: deming@up.edu.

DEMINT, JAMES WARREN, congressman, marketing professional; b. Greenville, S.C., Sept. 2, 1951; s. Thomas Eugene and Betty (Rawlings) Batson; m. Deborah Henderson, Nov. 6, 1951; children: Jake, Ginger, Timothy, Donna. BS in Comm., U. Tenn., 1973; MBA, Clemson (S.C.) U., 1979. Sr. sales rep. Scott Paper Co., Greensboro, N.C., 1973-75; writer Henderson Advt., Greenville, 1975-81; v.p. Leslie Advt., Greenville, 1981-83; CEO, pres. The Demint Mktg. Group, Greenville, 1983—; mem. U.S. Congress from 4th S.C. dist., 1999—; mem. edn. and workforce com., small bus. com., transp. and infrastructure com. Speaker, workshop leader, Success 88 Small Bus. Admin. and So. Bell 1988. Chmn. bd. Greensville Vocat. Rehab. Ctr. 1986, Christian Bus. Men's Com., 1983, Mitchel Rd. Christian Acad., 1988, 1st v.p. Speech, Hear and Learning Ctr., 1986. Mem. Greenville C. of C., S.C. C. of C., Rotary. Republican. Presbyterian. Avocations: sailing, running, biking, tennis, music.*

DE MIRANDA, FABRIZIO, b. Naples, Italy, Oct. 30, 1926; s. Domenico and Vera (Padula) De M.; m. Maria Chiara Piciocchi, Feb. 18, 1952. D of Civil Engring., U. Naples, 1950. Chief engr. Finsider SpA, Milan, 1957-67; mem. Studio de Miranda Assocs., Milan, 1968—. Assoc. prof. Politecnico U., Milan, 1965-96; chmn. Coll. Tecnici Dell'Acciaio, Milan, 1970-73. Contbr. articles to profl. jours. Home: via Settembrini 3 20124 Milan Italy Office: Studio De Miranda Assocs via Settembrini 2 20124 Milan Italy Fax: +39 02 29 41 52 10. E-mail: stdma@tin.it.

DEMIRCI, ALI, microbiological and food engineer; b. Aug. 3, 1964; PhD, Iowa State U., 1992. Rsch. assoc. Iowa State U., Ames, 1994—99; asst. prof. Pa. State U., University Park, Iowa, 1999—2002. Achievements include patents in field. Office: Pa State U 231 Agricultural Engineering Bldg University Park PA 16802 Office Fax: 814-863-1031. Business E-Mail: demirci@psu.edu.

DEMISSIE, YEMANE I. filmmaker; Student, UCLA. Dir. acquisitions Prodr. Svcs. Group, Inc., L.A. and London, 1987—92. Filmmaker : (exhibitions include) Mannheim-Heidelberg Film Festival, 1997; Internat. Festival Visual Arts, 1997; Vues d'Afrique, 1997; Seattle Internat. Film Festival, 1997; Fribourg Film Festival, 1997; Internat. Film Festival Rotterdam, 1997; Hamptons Internat. Film Festival, 1997; M-NET All Africa Film Awards, 1997 (Paulin Vieyra Merit award for outstanding work in cinema); Pitts. Film Festival, 1998; Third Internat. Film Festival, 1998; Midnight Sun Film Festival, 1998; Urban World Film Festival, 1998; L.A. Pan African Film Festival, 1999; Mus. Fine Arts, 1999; CineVegas Internat. Film Festival, 1999; Cascade Festival of African Films, 2000; Inst. Contemporary Art, 2000; Axed at the Rectory, 1986; History of the Cave, Part I, 1986; Uncle Vanya, 1986; Kentu, 1987; Three Kinds of Light, 1987; Testify!, 1988; Bicycle Encounter, 1988; African Artists Series, 1993. Recipient Federico DeLaurentis award, L.A., Cert. of award for outstanding achievement in African film, U. Calif. San Diego, Hon. Mention, Urban World Film Festival, Nantes Mayor's award, Nantes Festival des 3 Continents, European Union Spl. Mention, Pan African Film and TV Festival, Burkina Faso, Spl. Jury prize and COE prize, So. African Film Festival, Zimbabwe, First Pl. award, Nat. Black Programming Consortium; fellow John Simon Guggenheim Meml. Found. fellow, 1999, Nat. Resources fellow, Calif. Arts Coun. Artists fellow; grantee Nat. Black Programming Consortium Prodn., ind. film and videomaker grantee, Am. Film Inst.

DEMITA, GERALDINE, librarian; b. N.Y.C., July 30; d. Michael DeMita and Philomina Pastore. BA, Nazareth Coll., 1973; MLS, Pratt Inst., 1975. Cert. libr., N.Y. Librarian Franklin Nat. Bank, N.Y.C., 1974, Seagrams & Co., N.Y.C., 1975-77, GM, N.Y.C., 1978-80, Queens Borough Pub. Libr., N.Y.C., 1982—. Tutor Children's Devel. Fund, N.Y.C., 1990-91. Rsch. book: Swelling Tide, 1998. Mem. Meadows Spa, North Shore Tennis and Racquet Club, Wildwood Pool and Tennis Club. Roman Catholic. Avocations: tennis, reading, music, jogging, gardening.

DEMITCHELL, TERRI ANN, law educator; b. San Diego, Apr. 10, 1953; d. William Edward and Rose Annette (Carreras) Wheeler; m. Todd Allan DeMitchell, Aug. 14, 1982. AB in English with honors, San Diego State U., 1975; JD, U. San Diego, 1984; MA in Edn., U. Calif., Davis, 1990; EdM, Harvard U., 1997. Bar: Calif. 1985, U.S. Dist. Ct. (so. dist.) Calif. 1985; cert. elem. tchr., Calif. Tchr. Fallbrook (Calif.) Union Elem. Sch. Dist., 1976-86; adminstrv. asst. gen. counsel San Diego Unified Sch. Dist., 1984; assoc. Biddle and Hamilton, Sacramento, 1986-88; instr. U. N.H., 1990-93. Teaching asst. U. Calif., Davis, 1987. Author: The California Teacher and the Law, 1985, The Law in Relation to Teacher, Out of School Behavior, 1990, Censorship and the Public School Library: A Bicoastal View, 1991; contbr. chpt. to book. Mem. Calif. Bar Assn., Am. Bar Assn. Office: Apt 2207 10 Chestnut St Exeter NH 03833-1878

DEMITCHELL, TODD ALLAN, education educator, educator; b. Portsmouth, Va., Aug. 9, 1947; s. Wilfred E. and Mary Anna (Hughes) DeM.; m. Terri A. Wheeler, Aug. 14, 1982. BA, U. La Verne, 1969, MA, 1973; EdD, U. So. Calif., 1979; MA, U. Calif., Davis, 1990. Tchr. Pomona (Calif.) Unified Sch. Dist., 1969-71, South Bay Union Elem. Sch. Dist., Imperial Beach, Calif., 1974-75, lead tchr., 1975-78; asst. prin. Fallbrook (Calif.) Union Elem. Sch. Dist., 1978-80, prin., 1980-83; supt., prin. Pauma (Calif.) Sch. Dist., 1983-86; dir. pers. and labor rels. Travis (Calif.) Unified Sch. Dist., 1986-89; postdoctoral vis. scholar, rsch. asst. Nat. Ctr. Ednl. Leadership Harvard U., Cambridge, Mass., 1989-90; asst. prof. U. N.H., Durham, 1990-96, coord. grad. studies, 1993-95, assoc. chair dept. edn., 1995-96; assoc. prof., 1996—00; prof., chair dept. edn., 2001—; assoc. prof., chair dept. ednl. leadership/spl. edn. Sonoma State U. Design team Sch. Leaders Acad., N.H., 1991-93. Co-author: Teacher Unions and TQE: Building Quality Labor Relations, 1994, The Limits of Law-Based School Reform: Vain Hopes and False Promises, 1997; mem. authors com. Education Law Reporter; contbr. more than 90 articles to profl. jours., chpts. to books. Recipient Jim Rubovitz award, New Eng. Ednl. Rsch. Orgn., 2003. Mem. ASCD, Am. Ednl. Rsch. Assn., Edn. Law Assn. Office: U NH Morrill Hall Durham NH 03824

DEMITRA, PAVOL, hockey player; b. Dubnica, Slovakia, Nov. 29, 1974; Drafted left wing/ctr., 1993—96; traded left wing/ctr. St. Louis Blues, 1996—. Mem. Slovia Hockey Team Winter Olympics, Nagano, Japan, 1998. Office: c/o St Louis Blues 1401 Clark Ave Saint Louis MO 63103-2700

DEMKO, CATHY, artist, art educator; b. Chgo., July 8, 1944; d. Jean S. Badiaco; m. E. Ramon Nelson; 1 child, Patricia Ann Jedike. Student, Art Inst., Chgo., Cape Cod Sch. of Art, Scottsdale Artist Sch., Design Masters of Calif.; BBA, Tempe Bus. Coll., 1983. Artist Marion Helpers, Stockbridge, Mass., 1992—, USCG, Washington. Tchr. Mesa (Ariz.) Parks and Recreation, 1983—85, Collier County Recreational Bd., Naples, Fla., 1985—92, Snowflake Gallery, Wilmington, Vt., 1992—96, Collier County Pub. Schools, Naples, 1996—98, Marco Island Art League, Marco Island, Fla., 1997—. Exhibitions include Studio Art Gallery, Marco Island, Fla., 1986—2001, Nat. Wildlife Gallery Am., Carmel, Calif., 1986—90, Panache Art Gallery, 1990—92, Mendocino Gallery in Calif., 1990—92, Galerie Internat., Marco Island & Naples, Fla., 1991—2002, Mangrove Art Gallery, Marco Island, Fla., 1993—98, Lucky's Wave (So. Waters award, 2000), scratch board, Preening Egret, 1999 (Audubon award, 2001), exhibitions include Orange Blossom Express, 2000 (R.R. Excellency award, 2000), one-woman shows include Golden Gecko Art Gallery, Sedona, Ariz., 2003, Rookery Bay Field Guide, 1998. Tchr. Sr. Citizens Recreational Activities, Naples, 1982—2002; artist Christian Womens Assn., Marco Island, 1982—2002. Mem.: Am. Soc. Marine Artists (assoc.), Plein Air Painters (assoc.), Art League of Marco Island (assoc.), Am. Women Artists (assoc.). Avocations: travel, writing, nature. Home: 1225 Skyline Dr Naples FL 34114-8290 Office: Snowflake Gallery 1225 Skyline Dr Naples FL 34114

DEMKO, GEORGE JOSEPH, geographer; b. Catasauqua, Pa., Apr. 10, 1933; s. George and Anna (Scarba) D.; m. Jeanette Edwina Small, Aug. 29, 1959; children: Megan, Kerstin. BS, West Chester U., 1958; MS, So. Ill. U., 1959; PhD, Pa. State U., 1964; postgrad., Moscow State U., USSR; DSc (hon.), Shawnee State U. of Ohio, 1995. Instr. Pa. State U, State College, 1963-64; asst. prof. Ind. U., Bloomington, 1964-65; prof. Ohio State U., Columbus, 1965-83; program dir. Geography and Regional Sci., NSF, Washington, 1983-84; The Geographer, dir. Office of The Geographer, State Dept., Washington, 1984-89; dir. Rockefeller Ctr. for Social Scis., Dartmouth Coll., Hanover, N.H., 1989-95, prof. geography, 1989—. Cons. Internat. Research and Exchanges Bd., Princeton, N.J., 1970-95, NASA, 1979-80, Microsoft Corp., 1992—; head subcomm. on geography, US/USSR, Princeton, 1980-91; adj. prof. Charles U., Prague, Czech Republic. Author: The Russian Colonization of Kazakhstan, 1966, Kazakh transl., 1998, Discovery in Geography, 1980, Regional Development in East and West Europe, 1986, Perspectives on Soviet Geography, 1980, Geography in the USSR and U.S.: A Spectrum of Views, 1992, Why In The World: Adventures in Geography, 1993, Populations at Risk in America, 1995, Reordering the World: Geopolitical Perspectives on the 21st Century, 1995; contbr. numerous articles to profl. jours. Sgt. USMC, 1951-54, Korea. Named Outstanding Alumnus, W. Chester (Pa.) U., 1980, University Fellow, Pa. State U., State College, 1986; recipient numerous grants and awards for research and teaching from the Nat. Sci. Found., Rockefeller Found., Gold Medal award for scholarly contbns. Charles U., Prague, Czech Republic, 1998, others. Mem. Assn. Am. Geographers (pres. 1986-88), Am. Assn. for Advancement of Slavic Studies (exec. dir. 1969-74), Kennan Inst. for Advanced Russian Studies (acad. advisor 1982-86), Russian Geog. Soc. (hon.). Avocations: sailing, squash, piano. Office: Dartmouth Coll Dept Geography Hanover NH 03755 E-mail: george.demko@dartmouth.edu.

DEMLER, FREDERICK RUSSEL, minerals economist, commodities broker; b. Lebanon, Pa., Apr. 6, 1953; s. Lewis Frederick and Arline (Hertzog) D.; m. Linda Kass, Aug. 26, 1976; children: Todd, Scott. BS in Mineral Econs., Pa. State U., 1976, PhD in Mineral Econs., 1980. Researcher Resources for the Future U.S. Bur. of Mines, 1976-78, NSF, 1978-80; instr. mineral econs. Pa. State U., University Park, 1979-80; sr. planning analyst, corp. planning Exxon Minerals Co., N.Y.C., 1980-83; 1st v.p., commodities, minerals economist Drexel Burnham Lambert, N.Y.C., 1983-90; 1st v.p., mineral economist Paine Webber, Inc., N.Y.C., 1990-93; global mgr. metals, mineral economist Man Financial, N.Y.C., 1993—. Media spokesperson; mem. strategic mgmt. bd., bd. dirs. Am. Copper Coun. Contbr. numerous articles to trade and profl. publs. V.p., coach Travel Soccer, Upper Mketide Twp. Mem. AIME, The Futures Industry Assn., Pa. State U. Alumni Assn., Pa. State Football Lettermen's Club, Chi Phi. Home: 18 Timber Knolls Dr Washington Crossing PA 18977-1000 Office: Man Financial 717 Fifth Ave 9th Fl New York NY 10022 E-mail: fred@manfinancial.com.

DEMME, JONATHAN, actor, director, producer, writer; b. Rockville Centre, N.Y., Feb. 22, 1944; m. Joanne Howard; children: Raymona, Brooklyn; m. Evelyn Purcell (div.). Ed., U. Fla. With Avco Embassy Films, 1966, Pathe Films, 1966-67; with publicity dept. United Artists, 1968-69; writer Film Daily, 1966-68. Co-screenwriter, dir. (film) Caged Heat, 1974, Crazy Mama, 1975, Fighting Mad, 1976; story developer: Black Mama White Mama, 1975; dir.: Citizen's Band, 1977, Last Embrace, 1979, Melvin and Howard, 1980 (Best Dir. award), Swing Shift, 1983, Stop Making Sense, 1984, Swimming to Cambodia, 1987, Married to the Mob, 1988, The Silence of the Lambs, 1991 (Best Dir. Acad. award 1991), Cousin Bobby, 1992, Philadelphia, 1993, Mandela, 1996, Beloved, 1998, Storefront Hitchcock, 1998, The Truth About Charlie, 2002; dir., co-prodr. Something Wild, 1986, prodr. Miami Blues, 1990, exec. prodr. Devil in a Blue Dress, 1995; dir., actor : That Thing You Do!, 1996; dir., prodr. The Agronomist, 2003; dir.(TV movie): Who Am I This Time?, 1982, (documentary film) Accumulation with Talking Plus Water Motor; (music videos) UB40, Chrissie Hynde, Sun City Video of Artists United Against Apartheid, Suzanne Vegad, A Family Tree; prodr.: Haiti: Dreams of Democracy, Women & Men 2 (A Domestic Dilemma)., (music video) Murder, Inc. (Bruce Springsteen), 1995. Mem.: Dirs. Guild Am. also: Clinica Estetico 127 W 24th St Fl 7 New York NY 10011-1914 Office: c/o Robert Newman Internat Creative Management 8942 Wilshire Blvd Beverly Hills CA 90211*

DEMMITT, JOYCE MILLER, management consultant; b. Pitts., Dec. 13, 1946; d. Kenneth William and Virginia (Booker) Miller; m. Paul Joseph Demmitt, Oct. 22, 1983; children: Louisa Dorothy, Daniel Kenneth. BA, Gettysburg Coll., 1968; MLS, U. Md., 1975. Reference libr. Howard County Libr., Columbia, Md., 1970-75, br. mgr., 1975-78, reader's adv. coord., 1978-81, head adult svcs., 1981-86, head info. svcs., 1986-96, assoc. dir. pub. svc., 1996—2001. Mem. exec. bd. libr. assoc. tng. program Cooperating Librs. of Ctrl. Md., 1997—; spkr. in field. Contbr. chpts. to books. Pres. alumni chpt. U. Md. Coll. Libr. and Info. Sci., 1985-86; chair bd. dirs. Careerscope, Howard County, 1985-87; exec. bd. Assn. Cmty. Svcs., Howard County, Md., 1994-97; stakeholder Howard County United Vision, 1999; bd. dirs. Health Improvement Leadership Team, Howard County, 1996-99; chair Howard County Childcare Task Force, 1987; bd. dirs. Howard County Commn. on Aging, 2002—. Grantee Md. Divsn. Libr. Devel. and Svcs., 1981—. Mem. ALA, Md. Libr. Assn. (pres. 1995-96), bd. mem. Howard County Comm. on Aging, 2002—. Democrat. Avocations: training, public speaking, child advocacy, piano. E-mail: joycedem@aol.com.

DEMMLER, ALBERT WILLIAM, JR., retired editor, metallurgical engineer; b. Pitts., Feb. 21, 1929; s. Albert William and Hester Louisa (Dye) Demmler; m. Donna Lou Frederick, Feb. 16, 1957 (dec. Nov. 2001); children: Richard Frederick, Keith Alan(dec.), Diane Leslie, Debra Lynn. PhB in Liberal Arts, U. Chgo., 1948; BSMetE, U. Mich., 1951, MSMetE, 1952, PhD, 1955. Rsch. engr. Alcoa Rsch. Labs., New Kensington, Pa., 1955-68; registered rep. Butcher & Singer, Pitts., 1968-74; exec. searcher Reese Assoc., Pitts., 1974-76; assoc. editor Soc. Automotive Engrs. Inc. Mags., Warrendale, Pa., 1976-90, sr. editor, 1990-99, ret., 1999. Patentee in field. Mem. NRA, Soc. Automotive Engrs., Am. Soc. Metals Internat., Hypnotism Soc. Pa., Tarentum Dist. Sportsmens Club, Pa. Rifle and Pistol Assn., Pa. Gun Collectors Assn., Crowfoot Rod & Gun Club, Mensa, Tau Beta Pi, Phi Lambda Upsilon, Sigma Xi. Democrat. Presbyterian. Avocations: competitive rifle, pistol, hypnosis. Home: 132 Glenview Dr New Kensington PA 15068-4900

DEMMLER, JOHN HENRY, retired lawyer; b. Pitts., June 20, 1932; s. Ralph Henry and Catherine (Hollinger) D.; m. Janet Rice, July 20, 1957; children: Richard H., Ralph W., Carol L. BA, Princeton U., 1954; LLB cum laude, Harvard U., 1959. Bar: Pa. 1960, U.S. Dist. Ct. (we. dist.) Pa. 1960. Assoc. Reed Smith Shaw & McClay, Pitts., 1959-65, ptnr., 1966-93, of counsel, 1994—. Dir. Duquesne Light Co., Pitts., 1977-90. Trustee Shady Side Acad., Pitts., 1969-75, 77—, vice chmn., 1980-84, chmn., 1984-87; chmn. Fox Chapel Borough Zoning Hearing Bd., 1993—. Mem. Pa. Bar Assn. (pub. utility law sect. 1976—), Fox Chapel Golf Club, HYP-Pittsburgh Club. Republican. Episcopalian. Home: 102 Foxtop Dr Pittsburgh PA 15238-2202 Office: Reed Smith LLP 435 6th Ave Pittsburgh PA 15219-1886

DEMMON, TERRI LYNN, educational consultant, educator; d. Max A. and Doris J. Wallace; m. Douglas Dean Demmon, Jr., Sept. 7, 1990; children: Derek E., Amir M Rahemi-Demmon. EdD, Ind. U., Bloomington, IN, 1996—2001. Higher Education Distance Educator Ind. Unviersity, 1997; Teaching License Ind. State Bd. of Higher Edn., 1986. Instrnl. strategies cons. Ind. U. South Bend, South Bend, Ind., 1999—; instr. IVY Tech State Coll., South Bend, Ind., 1988—97. V.p. of ednl. programs Parents Without Partners, South Bend, Ind., 1985—89; v.p. Ind. State Teacher's Assn. - Student Educators, Indianapolis, Ind., 1985—86. Recipient Who's Who Among America's Teachers, Who's Who, 1994, 1996, 1998; grantee Assessment Grant, Ind. U., 2003. Home: 53240 Glenwood Rd Dowagiac MI 49047-9497 Office: Ind U So Bend 1700 Mishawaka Ave Northside 242 South Bend MI 46554 Office Fax: 574-239-5003. Personal E-mail: tdemmon@locallink.net. E-mail: tdemmon@iusb.edu.

DEMMY, TODD LYLE, surgeon; b. Phila., May 29, 1960; s. Merlyn Ray and Claire Mildred D.; m. Maryellen Boyle, Oct. 19, 1985; children: Tara, Michael. BS, Pa. State U., 1981; MD, Jefferson Med. Coll., 1983. Diplomate Am. Bd. Thoracic Surgery, Am. Bd. Surgery. Assoc. prof. of surgery U. Mo., Columbia, 1991—2002; chief thoracic oncology Ellis Fischel Cancer Ctr., Columbia, Mo., 1994—2002; chair thoracic surgery Roswell Park Cancer Inst., Buffalo, 2002—. Co-dir. cardiac transplant program U. Mo., Columbia, 1991-2002. Recipient Thoracic Surgery Dirs. Assn. award Soc. Thoracic Surgeons, 1983. Mem. ACS (sec. Mo. chpt. 1989-99, v.p. 1999-2000, pres. 2000-01). Republican. Roman Catholic. Avocations: piano, computer programming, tennis, swimming. Office: Elm and Carlton St Buffalo NY 14263 E-mail: todd.demmy@roswellpark.org.

DEMOFF, MARVIN ALAN, lawyer; b. L.A., Oct. 28, 1942; s. Max and Mildred (Tweer) D.; m. Patricia Caryn Abelov, June 16, 1968; children: Allison Leigh, Kevin Andrew. BA, UCLA, 1964; JD, Loyola U., L.A., 1967. Bar: Calif. 1969. Asst. pub. defender Los Angeles County, 1968-72; ptnr. Steinberg & Demoff, L.A., 1973-83, Craighill, Fentress & Demoff, L.A. and Washington, 1983-86; of counsel Mitchell, Silberberg & Knupp, L.A., 1987—2002; mng. dir. Neuberger Berman LLC, L.A., 2002—. Mem. citizens adv. bd. Olympic Organizing Com., L.A., 1982-84; bd. trustees Curtis Sch., L.A., 1985-94, chmn. bd. trustees, 1988-93; sports adv. bd. Constitution Rights Found., L.A., 1986—. Mem. ABA (mem. forum com. on entertainment and sports), Calif. Bar Assn., UCLA Alumni Assn., Phi Delta Phi. Avocations: sports, music, art. Office: Neuberger Berman LLC 1999 Ave of the Stars Los Angeles CA 90067

DEMOLEN, RICHARD LEE, historian; b. Hartford, Wis., Aug. 19, 1938; s. Raymond A. and Helen A. (Desimowich) D. AB in History, U. Mich., 1962, MA, 1963, PhD, 1970. Asst. prof. history Drury Coll., Mo., 1966-67, Ithaca (N.Y.) Coll., 1967-70; rschr., writer, editor Folger Shakespeare Libr., Washington, 1970-93. Author: The Spirituality of Erasmus of Rotterdam, 1987, Richard Mulcaster and Educational Reform in the Renaissance, 1991; editor: Richard Mulcaster's Positions, 1971, Erasmus of Rotterdam: A Quincentennial Symposium, 1971, Erasmus, 1973, The Meaning of the Renaissance and Reformation, 1974, One Thousand Years: Western Europe in the Middle Ages, 1974, Essays on the Works or Erasmsus, 1978, Leaders of the Reformation, 1984, Religious Orders of the Catholic Reformation, 1994. Sr. Fulbright scholar U. London, 1974-75; Younger Humanist fellow NEH, 1971-72, fellow Folger Shakespeare Libr., Newberry Libr., Huntington Libr.; rsch. grantee Am. Philos. Soc., NEH. Mem. Renaissance Soc. Am., Erasmus of Rotterdam Soc. (founder), Am. Cath. Hist. Assn., Friends of St. Thomas More. Roman Catholic. Home: 330 River Front Dr Reno NV 89523

DEMOND, JEFFREY STUART, cable television and telecommunications executive; b. Morristown, N.J., June 27, 1955; s. Marvin Harry DeMond and Lois Ann (Worrell) Kramer; m. Helene Regina Sullivan, Dec. 24, 1987; children: Brendan, Christopher. BS, U. Ala., 1978. CPA, N.Y. Sr. mgr. Peat, Marwick, Mitchell & Co., N.Y.C., 1978-85; exec. v.p., CFO Bresnan Comm. Inc., White Plains, N.Y., 1985—. Lectr., adj. prof. Hunter Coll., N.Y., 1984-85. Composer various popular music, 1974—; performer Sailcat record album Cathouse, 1976. Named an Outstanding Musician, Nat. Assn. Jazz Educators, 1978, Outstanding Jazz Soloist, Stan Kenton Coll. All-Star Orch., 1978. Mem. AICPA, Nat. Cable and Telecomm. Assn. (fin. com.), N.Y. State Soc. CPA, Beta Gamma Sigma. Avocations: guitar, performing, composing music. Office: Bresnan Comm Inc 777 Westchester Ave White Plains NY 10604-3103 E-mail: jdemond@bresnan.com., jdemond@optonline.net.

DEMONSABERT, WINSTON RUSSEL, chemist, consultant; b. New Orleans, June 12, 1915; s. Joseph Francis and Davida Elizabeth (Gullett) deM.; m. Eleanor Ray Ranson, Aug. 8, 1955; 1 child, Winston Russel. BS in Chemistry, Loyola U., New Orleans, 1937; MA in Edn., Tulane U., 1945, PhD in Chemistry, 1952. Asst. prof. Loyola U., New Orleans, 1948-49, assoc. prof., 1949-55, prof., 1955-66; chief chemist Nat. Ctr. for Disease Control, Dept.

Health and Human Svcs., Atlanta, 1966-69; chief contract liason br. Nat. Ctr. for Health Svcs. Rsch., 1969-73; chief extramural programs Bur. Drugs FDA, Rockville, Md., 1973-79; scientist adminstr. office of interagy. sci. coordination Office of Commr., FDA, after 1979; now cons., govt. liaison environ. chemistry and toxicology. Assoc. prof. Tulane U., 1957-58; research chemist Am. Cyanamid Co., 1957-58; vice-chmn. Interagy. Testing Com., 1982. Contbr. to Ency. Americana, Ency. Chemistry, also profl. jours. Committeeman Boys Scouts Am., New Orleans and Atlanta; mem. curriculum coms. New Orleans Pub. Sch. Bd., 1965. Fellow AAAS, Am. Inst. Chemists (chmn. La. chpt. 1958-60, chmn. Ga. chpt. 1968-69, pres. D.C. chpt. 1982-83); mem. Am. Chem. Soc. (past chmn. La. sect.). Roman Catholic. Achievements include research in environmental effects (detection, prevention and treatment) of toxic wastes, pesticides and air pollution, and zirconium chemistry. Home and Office: 4317 Lake Trail Dr Kenner LA 70065-1541

DEMONTE, CLAUDIA ANN, artist, educator; b. Astoria, N.Y., Aug. 25, 1947; d. Joseph James and Ammeda Ellen (Heiss) DeM.; m. William Edward McGowin, May 28, 1977. BA, Coll. Notre Dame, 1969; MFA, Cath. U., 1971. Instr. Bowie State Coll., Md., 1971-72, Prince Georges C.C., Largo, Md., 1972; prof. dept. art U. Md., College Park, 1972—. Dir. Art Workshops, New Sch. Social Rsch., N.Y.C., 1980-94; USIA artist in residene (Sofia) Bulgaria, 1982; mem. art bd. Queens Coll., N.Y. Selected exhbns.: Corcoran Gallery of Art, 1976, Contemporary Arts Center, New Orleans, Cranbrook Acad., 1978, Marianne-Deson Gallery, 1979, Miss. Mus., Fort Worth Mus., Washington Project for the Arts, 1980, Marion Locks Gallery, Miami Dade Gallery, Xochipilli, 1981, 86, 95, New Sch. Social Research, 1982, Queens Mus., N.Y., Stamford Mus., Conn., Gallery 121, Antwerp, Belgium, 1985, Gracie Mansion Gallery, N.Y., 1987, Brentwood Art Gallery, St. Louis, 1987, Nina Freunenheim Gallery, Buffalo, N.Y., 1987, Internat. Rev. of the Arts Arsenal, Amalfi, Italy, 1987, Esbo Mus., Helsinki, Finland, 1988, Evanston (Ill.) Art Ctr., 1989, Gracie Mansion Gallery, N.Y., Barbara Gillman Gallery, Miami, 1991, 92, 94, Gallery 86, Lodz, Poland, Slow Art, Painting in N.Y. Now, P.S. 1 Mus., N.Y., 1991, Haggerty Mus., Wis., 1993, Nina Freudenheim Gallery, Buffalo, 1994, Leedy Voulkos Gallery, Kansas City, Mo., 1996, Panaroma Gallery, Barcelona, Spain, Silpakorn U., Bangkok, 1997, Retrospective, Choklalfabuken, Malmo, Sweden, 1998, Liesbeth Lip Gallery, Rotterdam, The Netherlands, 1999, Retrospective Rosemont Coll., Pa., 2000, U. New Eng. Tucson Mus., Ariz., 2001, Mus. of S.W., Midland, Tex., 2002, Internat. Mus. of Women, San Francisco, 2003; pub. collections include Indpls. Mus., Stamford Mus., Miss. Mus., Prudential Life Ins., Hyatt-Regency, Chem. Bank, Best Products, U. Md., Mus. Modern Art, New Orleans Mus., Minn. Mus., Grand Rapids Mus., Mich., UCLA, Corcoran Gallery of Art, Bklyn. Mus., Indpls. Mus., Bass Mus., Tucson Mus., Boca Raton Mus.; author: (with Judy Bachrach) The Height Report, 1983, (pomegranate) Women of the World: A Global Collection of Art, 2000; commissioned works include: U. No.Iowa, 2003. Mem. art bd. Queens (N.Y.) Coll. Recipient award Am.-Italian Assn., 1971, Head Balt. Bus., 1972, Creative award Me., 1974, 77, 83, 87; N.Y. Found. for the Arts fellow, 1989—, N.Y.C. Dept. Cultural Affairs Art in Pub. Places Sculpture Commn., 1991, N.Y.C. Dept. Cultural Affairs Mural Commn. fellow 1993, sculpture commn. N.Y.C. Dept. Cultural Affairs, 1997, N.Mex. State Art Commn., Sculpture Commn., Socorro, 1998, U. No. Iowa Commn., 2003, Gund Found. grant, 1998, Ancohrage Found. of Tex. grant, 1999. Democrat. Home: 96 Grand St New York NY 10013-2633 E-mail: mcmonte2@aol.com., demonte@umd.edu.

DE MONTEBELLO, PHILIPPE LANNES, museum administrator; b. Paris, May 16, 1936; came to U.S., 1951, naturalized, 1955; s. Roger L. and Germaine (de Croisset) de M.; m. Edith Bradford Myles, June 24, 1961; children: Marc, Laure, Charles. BA magna cum laude, Harvard U., 1961; MA, NYU Inst. Fine Arts, 1963; LL.D. (hon.), Lafayette Coll., 1979; D.H.L. (hon.), Bard Coll., 1981; D.F.A. (hon.), Iona Coll., 1982. Assoc. curator European paintings Met. Mus. Art, N.Y.C., 1963-69; dir. Mus. Fine Arts, Houston, 1974-77; vice dir. for curatorial and ednl. affairs Met. Mus. Art, 1974-77, acting dir., 1977-78, dir., 1978-99, dir., CEO, 1999—. Mem. adv. coun. depts. art and archaeology Columbia U.; mem. Fogg, Fellow, Fogg Mus., Harvard U. Author: Peter Paul Rubens, 1969; mem. editorial bd. Internat. Jour. of Mus. Mgmt. and Curatorship. Trustee, NYU Inst. Fine Arts. Served to 2d lt. AUS, 1956-58. Decorated chevalier Legion d'Honneur (France), Encomienda de Numero de la Orden Isabel la Catholica (Spain), officier Ordre de Leopold (Belgium), Knight Commdr. Pontifical Order of St. Gregory the Great, Comdr. Order of Arts and Letters, 2001; recipient NYU Grad. Sch. Alumni Achievement award, 1978, gold medal Nat. Inst. Soc. Sci., 1989, The Spanish Inst., 1992, Rebekah Kohut award Nat. Coun. Jewish Women, 1993, NYU Alumni Assn. Disting. Alumni award, 1998, Living Landmark award NY Landmarks Conservancy, 2001, Mayoral Proclamation, 2002, Nat. Endowment for the Arts, Nat. Medal of Arts, 2003; Woodrow Wilson fellow, 1961-62; Gallatin fellow, 1981. Mem. Assn. Art Mus. Dirs. (works of art com.), Mus. Coun. N.Y.C., Am. Fedn. of the Arts (trustee, exec. com.), Am. Assn. Mus. Avocations: collecting old master drawings, chess, tennis. Home: 1150 5th Ave New York NY 10128-0724 Office: The Met Mus of Art 1000 5th Ave New York NY 10028-0113

DEMONTIGNEY, JAMES MORGAN, health services administrator; b. Wilkes-Barre, Pa., Aug. 2, 1947; s. James DeMontigney and Elizabeth Morgan-DeMontigney; m. Sharon Ann Frake-DeMontigney, Dec. 11, 1971; children: Rachelle Ann, Marc James. BA in Polit. Sci., U. Tenn., 1969, MSW, 1975. Caseworker Burlington County Welfare, Mt. Holly, N.J., 1969-71; parole officer N.J. Bur. Parole, Trenton, 1971; social worker N.J. Divsn. Pub. Welfare, Hamilton Township, 1971-73, N.J. Divsn. Youth and Family Svcs., Trenton, 1973, 75-78, casework supr. Camden, 1981-83, rsch. assoc. Bur. Rsch. Trenton, 1983-85, stds. and procedures technician, 1986-87; social worker N.J. Divsn. Med. Assistance and Health Svcs., Trenton, 1978-79, social work supr., 1979-81, field svc. supr. Woodbury, 1987, program devel. specialist Bur. Home and Cmty. Svcs. Trenton, 1987—2002; care mgmt. coord. Sr. Care Mgmt. Inc., Pennington, NJ, 2002—. Cons. Emmanuel Cancer Found., Scotch Plains, NJ, 2002—. Advisor Strength to Love, Inc., Mt. Holly, 1992—97; mem. Citizens Concerned for Mt. Holly, 1998—2000; case work cons. Emmanuel Cancer Found., Scotch Plains, NJ; mem. Mt. Holly (N.J.) Twp. Rep. Com., 1983—, chmn., 1985—; mcpl. coord. Reagan for Pres. Campaign, Mt. Holly, 1984, Bush for Pres. Campaign, Mt. Holly, 1988, 1992, Saxton for Congress Campaign, Mt. Holly, 1988, 1990, 1992, 1994, 1996, 1998, 2000; phonebank coord. Kean for Gov. Campaign, Burlington County, NJ, 1985; mcpl. coord. Saxton for Congress Campaign, Mt. Holly, 2002, Allen, Faulkner, Williams Campaign, Mt. Holly, 1997, Daniels, Ruuolo Campaign, 1999, Franks for Senate Campaign, 2000, Franks for Gov. Campaign, 2001, Whitman for Gov. Campaign, 1993, 1997, Schundler for Gov. Campaign, 2001, Allen for Senate Campaign, 2002; mem. Mt. Holly Twpl. Planning Bd., 1986—93; chmn. Mt. Holly Twp. Planning Bd., 1990—96; mem. Mt. Holly Bd. Ethics, 1986—92; mem. adv. com. Burlington County Cmty. Devel. Block Grant, 1998—99, 1999—2000, 2001—02, 2002—03. Mem. Cmty. Workers Am., Mt. Holly Twp. Rep. Club (charter mem. 1983—, pres. 1984, 89, 90, 91), Comm. Workers Am. Avocations: antiques, collectables, coins, stamps, sports. Home: 305 Ridgway St Mount Holly NJ 08060-1443 Office: Sr Care Mgmt Inc Road 23 Rte 31N Ste A 30 Pennington NJ 08534 E-mail: demontig4@directv.internet.com.

DEMOPULOS, HAROLD WILLIAM, lawyer; b. Providence, RI, Jan. 14, 1924; s. George K. and Grace (Loures) D.; m. Frances Scorzoni, June 10, 1967; children— Amelia Hannah, Abigail Mary. BA, Brown U., 1948; JD, U. Miami, 1952. Bar: Fla. 1952, RI 1953, US Dist. Ct. (so. dist.) Fla. 1952, US Dist. Ct. RI 1953. Sole practice, Providence and Bristol, RI, 1953—; Patentee in field. Clk. RI State Senate Jud. Com., 1953-54; atty. labor rels. bd. RI Dept. Labor, 1968-70; mem. dist. adv. coun. SBA, 1970-78, mem. adv. bd. State of RI Briston County Cable Area; probate judge Town of Bristol (RI), 1973-74; bd. dir. Bristol Land Trust Corp. Pres., Bristol C. of C., 1970s; mem. corp. Roger Williams Univ., Bristol; v.p. Bristol Art Mus., 1970s; treas., bd. dir. Coggeshall Farm Mus. Inc.; incorporator, bd. dir. Prepaid Legal Service Corp. RI With US Army, 1942-46. Mem. RI Bar Assn. (pres. 1984—), ABA, Fla. Bar Assn., R.I. Law Inst. (bd. dir.), RI Law Found., Order of Ahepa (pres. Sophocles chpt. 1958, dist. gov. 1966-67). Rotary, Brown Club (pres. RI 1975). Republican. Greek Orthodox. Office: Westminster Square Bldg 10 Dorrance St Ste 634 Providence RI 02903-2018

DEMOREST, ALLAN FREDERICK, retired psychologist; b. Omaha, Dec. 20, 1931; s. Byron Peter and Minerva Gladys (Heine) D.; 1 child, Steven M. BA, U. Omaha, 1957; MA, U. Mich., 1959, postgrad., 1960. Lic. psychologist, Iowa, Nat. Register Health Svc. Providers. Counselor Mayor's Com. on Skid Row Problems, Detroit, 1959-61; psychologist Macomb County Schs., Mt. Clemens, Mich., 1961-64; chief psychologist Jasper County Mental Health Ctr., Newton, Iowa, 1964-68; exec. dir. North Cen. Iowa Mental Health Ctr., Ft. Dodge, 1968-75; pvt. practice Ft. Dodge, 1968-85; psychologist Iowa Luth. Hosp., Des Moines, 1985-87; clin. dir. United Behavioral Systems, Des Moines, 1987-94, sr. psychologist, 1994-96; cons. pvt. practice, Des Moines, 1996 . Adj. prof. psychology Buena Vista U., Ft. Dodge, 1974—. Contbr. articles on rational therapy to profl. jours. Founding bd. dirs. Rape and Sexual Assault Victim Program, Ft. Dodge, 1976-85, Family Violence Ctr., Ft. Dodge, 1976-85, Youth Shelter Svcs., Ft. Dodge, 1979. With U.S. Army, 1952-54, Korea. Recipient appreciation award Community Mental Health Ctrs. Assn., 1968, community svc. award Iowa Dept. Human Svcs., 1985. Fellow Albert Ellis Inst.; mem. APA., Iowa Psychol. Assn., Adminstrv. Mgmt. Soc. (pres. Ft. Dodge 1979-80, 84-85), Iowa Assn. for Advancement Psychology (pres. 1984, appreciation award 1988), Elks (exalted ruler 1979, trustee 2002). Home and Office: 4225 Hickman Rd Des Moines IA 50310-3334 E-mail: ademorest@aol.com. *Honesty and integrity are the greatest personal assets of a human being.*

DEMOREST, MARK STUART, lawyer; b. Chambley, France, Mar. 14, 1957; came to U.S., 1960; s. Raymond Phillip and Maud Jane D.; m. Patricia Louise Button, July 28, 1979; children: Melissa, Matthew, Kristin, Kevin, Ryan. AB magna cum laude, Harvard U., 1979; JD magna cum laude, U. Mich., 1983. Bar: Mich. 1983, U.S. Dist. Ct. (ea. dist.) Mich. 1983, U.S. Ct. Appeals (6th cir.) 1984, U.S. Ct. Appeals (7th cir.) 1986, U.S. Supreme Ct. 1993, U.S. Dist. Ct. (cen. dist.) Ill. 1995, U.S. Ct. Appeals (4th cir.) 1995, U.S. Dist. Ct. (we. dist.) Mich. 1996, U.S. Dist. Ct. (ea. dist.) Wis. 2003. Assoc. Dykema Gossett, Detroit, 1983-85, Simpson & Moran, Birmingham, Mich., 1985-87; ptnr. The Robert P. Ufer Partnership, Bloomfield Hills, Mich., 1987-92, Hainer, Demorest & Berman, P.C., Troy, Mich., 1993-98; pvt. practice, 1998—. Mem. ABA, State Bar Mich., Harvard Club Ea. Mich. (schs. com.), Order of Coif. Methodist. Avocations: lacrosse, other sports. Office: Ste 100 19853 W Outer Dr Dearborn MI 48124-2066 E-mail: mdemorest@rileyhurley.com.

DEMOREST, STEVEN MCGREGOR, music educator; b. Detroit, Aug. 24, 1959; s. Allan Frederick and Laurel Perkins Demorest; m. Karen Leslie Tollenaar, July 12, 1996; children: Jessica Marie Tollenaar-Olive, Claire McGregor. BA in Music (cum laude), Luther Coll., Decorah, IA, 1981; MusM. in Choral Conducting, Westminster Choir Coll., 1983; PhD in Curriculum and Instrn., U. Wisconsin, 1989. Asst. prof. music edn. U. North Tex., Denton, Tex., 1989—93; assoc. prof. music edn. U. Wash., Seattle, 1993—; condr. NW Chamber Chorus, Seattle, 1997—. Author: Building Choral Excellence; CD, Wassail!, Coronation Anthems; contbr. articles to profl. jours. Mem.: Euro. Soc. Cognitive Sci. of Music (consulting editor 2001—02), Perception & Cognition Spl. Rsch. Interest Group (chair 1992—96), Music Educators Nat. Conf., Am. Choral Dirs. Assn. Achievements include research in psychology of music; sight-singing pedagogy; neuromusical rsch. Avocations: golf, travel. Office: University of Washington School of Music Box 353450 Seattle WA 98195-3450 Personal E-mail: demorest@u.washington.edu. E-mail: demorest@u.washington.edu.

DE MORI, RENATO, computer science educator, researcher; b. Milan, Aug. 5, 1941; PhD, Poly. U., Turin, Italy, 1967. Prof., chmn. U. Turin, 1977-79, prof., 1979-84; prof., chmn. Concordia U., Montreal, Que., Can., 1984-85; dir. Sch. Computer Sci. McGill U., Montreal, Que., Can., 1986-95, prof., 1995-96; v.p. rsch. Centre Recherche Informatique Montreal, 1987-94; prof. U. Avignon, France, 1997—. Mem. Nat. Scis. and Engring. Council Can., 1983-89; assoc. Can. Inst. Advanced Rsch. Author: Computer Models of Speech, 1983; editor: Computer Perceptions, 1982, Spoken Dialogs with Computers, 1998; contbr. over 100 articles to profl. jours. Fellow IEEE Computing Soc.; mem. Assn. Computing Machinery (chief editor speech communication). Office: U d'Avignon Lab Info BP1228 339 Chemin Menajeries 84911 Avignon CEDEX 9 France E-mail: renato.demori@lia.univ-avignon.fr.

DEMOS, VASILIKIE POLYTIMY, sociology educator; b. Charleston, S.C., Feb. 20, 1947; d. James John and Catherine James Demos; m. Frederick William Peterson, June 18, 1983; stepchildren: Kristin, Karl, Caleb. BA, Towson State Coll., 1969; MA, U. Toledo, 1971; PhD, U. Notre Dame, 1978. Asst. prof. sociology U. Minn., Morris, 1977-87, assoc. prof. sociology, 1987-97, prof. sociology, 1997—2003, prof. emeritus, 2003—. Bd. mem. Immigration History Rsch. Ctr., U. Minn., Mpls., 1989—; hon. vis. prof. U. NSW, Australia, 1990-91. Editor: (book series) Advances in Gender Research, 1994—. Bd. mem. Morris Pub. Libr. Bd., 1996-99. Recipient NEH Summer Seminar awards, Raleigh, N.C., 1978, Stanford, Calif., 1984, Bush Sabbatical Program award Bush Found., U. Minn., Mpls., 1992. Mem. Am. Sociol. Assn., Sociologists for Women in Soc. (pres. 1993-94), North Ctrl. Sociol. Assn. (pres. 1995-96, Aida Tomeh Disting. Svc. award 2001). Greek Orthodox. Avocations: sewing, cooking. Office: Univ Minn Morris MN 56267

DEMOSS, HAROLD RAYMOND, JR., federal judge; b. Houston, Tex., Dec. 30, 1930; s. Harold R. and Jessy May (Cox) DeMoss; m. Judith Phelps; children: Harold R. III, Louise Holland. BA, Rice U., 1952; LLB, U. Tex., 1955. Bar: Tex. Assoc. Bracewell & Patterson, Houston, 1957—61, ptnr., 1961—91; judge U.S. Ct. of Appeals (5th cir.), Houston, 1991—. Chmn. bd. Tex. Bill of Rights Found., Houston, 1969—70; pres. Tanglewood Homeowners Assn., 1987; area chmn. Bush Congl. Campaign, 1968; mem. platform group Bush for Pres., Washington, 1988; rsch. analyst Bush/Quayle campaign, 1988; dist. del.-at-large Rep. Nat. Conv., Houston, 1980, alt. del.-at-large, 1984, 1988; Harris County vice chmn. Tower Senate campaign, Houston, 1972, Ford/Dale campaign, 1976; Harris County chmn. Loeffler for Gov. Primary, 1986; Harris County co-chair Regan/Bush campaign, 1980, 1984; Tex. state chmn. Bush for Pres. Primary, 1979—80, Tex. vice chmn., 1988; del. Rep. State Conv., Houston, 1968; vestryman St. Martin's Episcopal Ch., Houston, 1968—72; mem. exec. bd. Episcopal Diocese Tex., 1983—86, chmn. planning com., 1985—88, del. Diocesan Conv., 1976—88; bd. dirs. Amigos de las Americas, 1974—76. Sgt. U.S. Army, 1955—57. Fellow: Tex. Bar Assn. (life); mem.: ABA, Tex. Assn. Def. Counsel (bd. dirs. 1972—74), Houston Bar Assn. (bd. dirs. 1969—71, 1st v.p. 1972—73), Maritime Law Assn. U.S., Am. Judicature Soc., Internat. Bar Assn., The Houston Club. Avocations: fishing, waterskiing. Office: Bob Casey US Courthouse 515 Rusk St Ste 12015 Houston TX 77002-2605

DEMOSS, JON W. insurance company executive, lawyer; b. Kewanee, Ill., Aug. 9, 1947; s. Wendell and Virginia Beth DeMoss; m. Eleanor T. Thornley, Aug. 9, 1969; 1 child, Marc Alain. BS, U. Ill., 1969, JD, 1972. Bar: Ill. 1972, U.S. Dist. Ct. (cen. dist.) Ill. 1977, U.S. Supreme Ct. 1978, U.S. dist. Ct. (no. dist., trial bar) Ill. 1983. In house counsel Assn. Ill. Electric Coop., Springfield, 1972-74; registered lobbyist Ill. Gen. Assembly, Springfield, 1972-74; asst. dir. Ill. Inst. for CLE, Springfield, 1974-85; exec. dir. Ill. State Bar Assn., 1986-94; pres., CEO ISBA Mut. Ins. Co., Chgo., 1994—. Bd. dirs. Bar Plan Surety & Fidelity Co., St. Louis, 1999-. Bd. dirs. Springfield Symphony Orch., 1982-87, Ill. Inst. for CLE, 1986-89, Nat. Assn. of Bar Related Ins. Cos., 1989, pres., elect., 1998-99, pres. 1999-2000; bd. dirs. Lawyers Reins. Co., 1997—; bd. visitors John Marshall Law Sch., 1990—. Capt. U.S. Army, 1972. Fellow Am. Bar Found. (life, co-chmn. projects to prepare Appellate Handbook 1978, 90), Ill. Bar Found. (life, bd. dirs. 1983-85); mem. ABA (ho. of dels. 1979-85, 89, 91, 93-94), Nat. Conf. Bar Pres., Am. Judicature Soc. (bd. dirs. Ill. state chpt., treas. 2002-), Ill. State Bar Assn. (pres. 1984-85, bd. govs. 1975-85, chmn. com. on scope and correlation of work 1982-83, chmn. budget com. 1983-85, chmn. legis. com. 1983-84, 85, chmn. com. on merit selection of judges 1977, del. long-range planning conf. 1977, 78, liaison to numerous coms. and sects.), Chgo. Bar Assn., Lake County Bar Assn., U. Ill. Coll. Dean's Club, La Chaine des Rotisseurs (Chgo.), Ordre Mondial des Gourmet Degustateurs (Chgo.), Les Gourmets (Chgo.). Home: 180 Norwich Ct Lake Bluff IL 60044-1914 Office: ISBA Mutual Ins Co 223 W Ohio St Chicago IL 60610-4101 Business E-Mail: jon.demoss@isbamic.com.

DE MOTT, BENJAMIN HAILE, educator, author; b. Rockville Centre, N.Y., June 2, 1924; s. D. Gerard and Janet (Sanders) DeM.; m. Margaret Jane Craig, June 22, 1946; children— Joel, Thomas, Benjamin, Megan. BA, George Washington U., 1949; PhD, Harvard, 1953; MA, Amherst Coll., 1960; D.Litt., Franklin and Marshall Coll., 1970; LLB, Union Coll., 1975. Teaching fellow Harvard, 1950; from instr. to Mellon prof. humanities Amherst (Mass.) Coll., 1951—; columnist Harper's, 1962-64, 81—, Am. Scholar, 1962-64, Atlantic Monthly, 1973-80. Prof. Mass. Inst. Tech., 1962; Fulbright prof. Birmingham (Eng.) U., 1965; vis. prof. Utah U., 1966, Yale, 1968-70; writer Nat. Ednl. TV, 1964; also cons.; mem. Columbia Seminar Am. Civilization; cons. Office Edn., Carnegie Commn. on Future Pub. Broadcasting; cons. Soc. Mag. Writers, Nat. Inst. Edn., N.Y. State Arts Council, Nat. Endowment for Arts, Am. Council Learned Socs., Council Grad. Schs., Danforth, Rockefeller founds; Aspen Inst. Edn. dept. Amalgamated Clothing Workers Union, AFL-CIO; exec. com. Tchrs. and Writers Collaborative, N.Y.C.; seminar dir. Nat. Endowment for Humanities, 1973-74, 76-77, 78-79 Author: novels The Body's Cage, 1959, A Married Man, 1968; essays Hells & Benefits, 1962, You Don't Say, 1966, Supergrow, 1969, Surviving the Seventies, 1971, Scholarship for Society, 1974, America in Literature, 1977, Close Imagining, 1982, The Imperial Middle, 1990, The Trouble with Friendship, 1996, Killer Woman Blues, 2000; Bd. editors: essays College English, 1964-70; contbg. editor: essays Sat. Review, 1972-73, Atlantic Monthly, 1977—; Contbr. articles to profl. jours. Bd. acad. advisers Marlboro Coll., 1963-65; mem. Presdl. Adv. Council Women's Ednl. Programs, 1975-76, Gov.'s Council Arts and Humanities, 1974-77; bd. dirs. Mass. Found. Humanities in Pub. Affairs, 1974— ; mem. exec. bd. Fedn. Humanities Programs, 1979— ; trustee Nat. Humanities Faculty; mem. selection com. Guggenheim Found., 1975— . Recipient Harbison award for distinguished teaching Danforth Found., 1969; Guggenheim fellow, 1964, 69 Mem. PEN, Nat. Book Critics Circle, Modern Lang. Assn., Phi Beta Kappa. Clubs: Century. Home: PO Box 356 Worthington MA 01098-0356

DE MOTT, MARIANNE, educator, artist, craftsperson, space designer; b. New Rochelle, NY, June 5, 1932; d. Monroe Van Wart and Mathilde Ann De Mott. Student, Coll. New Rochelle, 1950-53; student Sch. Modern Dance, Henry St. Playhouse, N.Y.C., 1958-61; BA, Hunter Coll./CUNY, 1969, postgrad., 1969-71. Cert. tchr., N.Y. Westchester county dir. girls and women's activities Cath. Youth Orgn., Yonkers, NY, 1953-54; tchr. phys. edn. and English, Sacred Heart of Mary Acad./Mother Butler Meml. H.S., Bronx, N.Y., 1954-65; tchr. art Harrison (N.Y.) Jr. Sr. H.S., 1970-71; art tchr., designer, craftsperson Studio of Art, Deming, N.Mex., 1973—. Lectr. on art history, gems and minerals; theater set designer. Designer jewelry with macrame and beads, gems and minerals; painter, creator wood sculptures; finder, exhibitor gems and minerals; lapidarist; photographer. Founder, rschr. Apache Hts. Homeowners Assn., Deming, 1979—88; asst. sec. Cooke's Peak Vol. Fire Dept., Deming, 1993—97; co-founder, life mem. Deming Arts Coun., bd. dirs., 1989—, exhbn. com., 1994—99; chmn. Arts in the Park, 1992—94; chmn. performance com., county-wide youth art show, 1989—; chmn. Arts in the Park, 2003. Named Coach of Yr., Cath. Youth Orgn., 1962, Cert. of Appreciation for Promoting Cmty. Arts and Cultural Activities, Gov. of N.Mex., 1976, Cert. of Appreciation, Deming Arts Coun., 1994, 2000. Mem.: Am. Fedn. Gem and Mineral Socs. (Bull. Editors Hall of Fame 2000—), Deming Gem and Mineral Soc. (sec. 1974—79, bd. dirs. 1985—89, bull. editor 1991—98, libr. 1999—), Kingdom of the Sun Art Assn., Rocky Mountain Fedn. Gem and Mineral Socs. Republican. Roman Catholic. Avocations: visual and performing arts and cultural events, rockhounding, gardening, swimming. Home and Office: 4320 Cherokee Trl NW Deming NM 88030-8307

DEMOULAS, TELEMACHUS A. retail grocery company executive; b. 1923; married. With DeMoulas Supermarkets, Inc., Tewksbury, Mass., 1954—, now pres., treas., CEO. Office: DeMoulas Supermarkets Inc 875 East St Tewksbury MA 01876-1495

DE MOURA CASTRO, LUIZ C. musician, educator; b. Rio deJaneiro, Mar. 16, 1941; arrived in U.S., 1969; s. Luis G. De Moura Castro and Maria Passos; m. Bridget M. Unna, Apr. 1, 1967; children: Marilia, Beatriz, Iracema, Helena. Grad. summa cum laude, Escola Nacional de Musica, Rio de Janeiro, 1965, Conservatory Brasiliera de Rio de Janeiro, 1965; grad. cert., Liszt Acad. Music, Budapest, 1967. Prof. piano Pro Arte Seminarios de Musica, Rio de Janeiro, 1967—; assoc. prof. piano Tex. Christian U., Ft. Worth, 1969—79; prof. piano, the Harrt Sch. U. Hartford, Conn., 1979—; prof. piano Conservatory of Girona, Catalonia, 1980—88, Conservatory of Barcelona, Spain, 1987—93. Vis. prof. piano Cath. U. Am., Washington, 1994—; chair piano dept. JP Carrero Music Sch., Barcelona, 1990—; vis. prof. piano Pro Arte Seminarios de Musica, Rio de Janeiro, 1990—; bd. dirs. World Piano Pedagogy Conf., Am. Liszt Soc.; adjudicator Fulbright Scholarships, N.Y.C., 1998—, Van Cliburn Internat. Piano Competition, Ft. Worth, Md. Internat. Piano Competition, Can. Nat. Piano Competition; co-founder summer music courses, Girona and Vilaller, Spain. Musician: (CDs) Schenker Fantasie Op. 2, 1986, Villa-Lobos Musica para Piano, 1987, Flor Amorasa Songs and Dances of Brazil, 1989, Milonga del Angel, 1990, Cuba Piano, 1991, Liszt Funerailles, Consolations, 1992, Marlos Nobre, 1993, Liszt Two Piano Music, Vol. 1, 1994, Liszt Two Piano Music, Vol. 2, 1994, Transfigurations Liszt: religious music, 1994, A la recherche du temps Romantics, 1994, Bachianas Bach/Franck/Villa-Lobos, 1995, Dolly French 4 hand music, 1995, O brilho e a sombra Chopin, 1995, Villa-Lobos, 1996, Amor Cigano Brahms 4 hand music, 1996, Grazioso Brahms Clarinet Sonatas, 1996, Ginastera, Vol. 1 Complete works, 1998, Ginastera, Vol. 2 Complete works, 1998, Chopin Nocturnes, Vol. 1, 1998, Brasil 500 Oswald Piano Quintet, 1999, Rachmaninov Concerto # 3 Variations, 1999, Songs and Dances of Brazil, 1999, Rachmaninov Ste. Op. 11, 1999, Rachmaninov Concerto #2, 1999, Chopin Nocturnes Vol. 2, 1999, Serie Musica Brasiliera Vol. 2, 2000, Modinha, 2001, Schubert 4 Hand Music, 2003. Recipient Citation, South Windsor, State of Conn., 2001, nominated for Latin Grammy for Brazilian CD Modinha, 2002. Mem.: Brazilian Liszt Soc. (co-founder), Hartford Piano Soc. (co-founder), Music Tchrs. Nat. Assn., Pi Kappa Lambda. Roman Catholic. Home: 38 E Woodhaven Dr Avon CT 06001

DEMPSEY, ANDREW FRANCIS, JR., lawyer; b. Newark, Jan. 18, 1941; s. Andrew Francis and Veronica (White) D.; m. Mary Teresa McTague, Aug. 1, 1964; children— : Moira, Sheila, Andrew, Peter. B.A., St. Bonaventure U., 1962; J.D., Cath. U. Am., 1968. Bar: D.C. 1968, Md. 1974, U.S. Dist. Ct. Md. 1976, U.S. Ct. Claims, 1970, U.S. Ct. Appeals (4th cir.) 1976, U.S. Ct. Appeals (D.C. cir.) 1968, U.S. Supreme Ct. Ptnr. Hudson & Creyke, Washington, 1969-74; v.p., gen. counsel Intercounty Constrn., Balt. and Ft. Lauderdale, Fla., 1974-77; ptnr. Sullivan & Beauregard, Washington, 1977-82; chief exec. officer, mng. ptnr. Dempsey, Bastianelli, Brown and Touhey, Chartered, Washington, 1982—91; of counsel Seyfarth, Shaw, Fairweather & Geraldson, Washington, 1994-97; pres., CEO, Beacon Hill Devel. LC, Def. Resources Internat. LLC; dir. Constructibility Cons., Washington; mem. NRC, Nat. Acad. Sci., U.S. Nat. Com on Tunneling Tech. Editor Cath. U. Law Rev., 1967-68. Served to capt. USMCR, 1962-72. Mem. ABA, D.C. Bar Assn., Md. State Bar Assn., Am. Arbitration Assn. (nat. panel arbitrators), Catholic U. Law Sch. Alumni Soc. (pres. 1982-85), Sea Pines Country Club (Hilton Head Island, S.C.). Home: 13304 Beall Creek Ct Potomac MD 20854-1117 Office: Dempsey Deliberto 555 Fairmount Ave Baltimore MD 21286 E-mail: drewdempsey@att.net.

DEMPSEY, B. artist; b. Ada, Okla., Nov. 24, 1926; d. John Benjamin Foster and Alma Lula Hubbard; m. Loyd Dempsey, Apr. 21, 1949; children: Ronny DeWayne, Johnny DeWight, Loyd Raymond, Novelia Dianne, Kevin Wendell. Diploma, Byng H.S., Ada, 1945. Sec. First Nat. Bank, Ada, 1945, Ada Welfare Dept., 1946; sorter/packer Hazel-Atlas Glass Co., Ada, 1946-48; tailor, seamstress S & Q Clothiers, Ada, 1971-86. Exhibited in group shows at Okla. State Capitol, 1981-93, Festival of Lights, Oklahoma City, 1983-86, Folklife Festival Art Show, Oklahoma City, 1983-86, Oklahoma City Meml. Bldg.; exhibits in 12 area shows annually. Mem. Ada Artists Assn. (publicity chair), Magic Brush Art Guild (publicity chair), Holdenville Soc. Painters. Democrat. Baptist. Avocations: church choir, sewing and painting crafts, creative doll making. Home: 921 Williams St Ada OK 74820-1822

DEMPSEY, BERNARD HAYDEN, JR., lawyer; b. Evanston, Ill., Mar. 29, 1942; s. Bernard H. and Margaret C. (Gallagher) D.; m. Cynthia T. Dempsey; children: Bernard H. III, Matthew B., Kathleen N., Rose Maureen G., Alexandra C., Anastasia M. BS, Coll. Holy Cross, 1964; JD, Georgetown U., 1967. Bar: Fla. 1968, D.C. 1979. Law clk. to chief judge U.S. Dist. Ct. (mid. dist.) Fla., 1967-69; asst. U.S. Atty. Mid. Dist. Fla., 1969-73; pvt. practice Orlando, Fla., 1973—; spl. asst. to U.S. Atty. Mid. Dist. Fla., 1974. Lectr. in field. Contbr. articles to profl. jours. Recipient John Marshall award U.S. Dept. Justice, 1972, U.S. Atty's Outstanding Performance award 1970-73. Mem.: ATLA, ABA, Orange County Bar Assn., Am. Arbitration Assn., Fed. Bar Assn., Fla. Bar Found., Am. Judicature Soc., Fla. Bar Assn., Nat. Employment Lawyers Assn.,

U.S. Attys. Assn. for Mid. Dist. Fla., Fla. Assn. Criminal Def. Lawyers, Nat. Assn. Criminal Def. Lawyers, Winter Park (Fla.) Racquet Club, Univ. Club (Orlando), Delta Theta Phi. Republican. Roman Catholic. Office: Dempsey & Sasso Bank of America Ctr 390 N Orange Ave 27th Fl Orlando FL 32801-1643 E-mail: bhd@dempseyandsasso.com.

DEMPSEY, CECELIA See BYRNE-DEMPSEY, CECELIA

DEMPSEY, CEDRIC W. former sports association administrator; b. Apr. 14, 1932; m. June Dempsey, Aug. 22, 1953; children: Linda, David, Marcia. BA in Phys. Edn. and History, MA in Edn., Albion Coll.; PhD in Phys. Edn., U. Ill.; LLD (hon.), Albion Coll. Grad. asst., asst. football and basketball coach, head tennis coach Albion (Mich.) Coll., 1954-56, head basketball & cross country coach, phys. edn. instr., 1959-62, dean of men, 1962-63; grad. asst., counselor profl. students, dir. placement svc. U. Ill., Urbana, 1956-59; asst. basketball coach, supr. undergrad. health, phys. edn. & recreation, asst. prof. U. Ariz., Tucson, 1963-65, asst. dir. health, phys. edn., recreation & athletics, assoc. prof., 1965-67, dir. athletics, 1982-93; dir. athletics, chair phys. edn. & recreation U. of the Pacific, Stockton, Calif., 1967-79; dir. athletics San Diego State U., 1979, U. Houston, 1979-82; pres. NCAA, Overland Park, Kans., 1993—2002. Sec.- treas. exec. com. NCAA, adminstrn. com., coun. and joint policy bd., chair budget subcom., mem. numerous other coms. Recipient Kathy Miller Courage award Phoenix Press Box Assn., 1988, Disting. Alumni award Albion Coll., 1993; named to Albion Coll. Inaugural Hall of Fame, 1989, U. Pacific Sports Hall of Fame, 1991.

DEMPSEY, DAVID ALLAN, company official; b. Eglin AFB, Fla., Sept. 5, 1957; s. David Leroy and Marguerite (Thomas) D.; m. Debra Kay Gross, Jan. 22, 1982; children: Nakia, Elisabeth, David. AS in Restaurant Mgmt., C.C. of Air Force, Maxwell AFB, Ala., 1987, AS in Contracts Mgmt., 1989; BS in Logistics Sys. Mgmt., Colo. Tech. U., 1995. Cert. lay spkr. United Meth. Ch. Postal asst. U.S. Postal Svc., Wilmington, Del., 1974-75; enlisted man USAF, 1975, advanced through grades to master sgt., 1991; ret., 1995; sr. subcontract adminstr. TRW, Inc., Colorado Springs, Colo., 1995-98; contract mgr. Harris Tech. Svcs. Corp., Colorado Springs, Colo., 1998-2000; sr. contract adminstr. Lockheed Martin Info. Tech., Colorado Springs, 2000—. V.p. TRW Colorado Springs Employee Assn., 1998. Pres. bldg. accountability com. Evans Elem. Sch., Colorado Springs, 1993—; vol. dist. 49 sch.-bus. alliance Jr. Achievement, 1999—, 1st vice chair, 2001; apptd. Colo. Minority Bus. Coun. by Gov. Owens, 2001; mem. Colorado Springs Leadership Inst., 2001; treas. Cropwalk for Hunger Colorado Springs, 2001; sec. El Paso County Dem. Com., 1999—; publicity chair El Paso County Dem. Club, 2001—; bd. dirs. No. Chs. Care, 2001—02; coord. D-Day, Share Colo. Ctrl. United Meth. Ch., Colorado Springs, 1993—, treas. missions/outreach com., 1999—, co-coord. interfaith hospitality network, 1999, coord. interfaith hospitality network, 2000—; Sunday sch. tchr., cert. lay spkr. Rocky Mountain Conf., 1994—; chmn. bd. dirs. No. Chs. Care, 2001; bd. dirs. Food for Thought, 1999—, v.p., 2000—; sec., bd. dirs. African-Am. Youth Leadership Conf.; bd. dirs. Homeward Pikes Peak, 2003—, Tobacco Edn. and Prevention Partnership, 2002—03; mem. Mt. Olive Coll. Alumni Assn., Mt. Olive, NC, Pikes Peak Urban League, Colorado Springs. Mem.: NAACP (1st v.p. Colorado Springs br. 2003—), ACLU, Hispanic C. of C. (bd. dirs. 2000—), Ret. Enlisted Assn., Noncommd. Officers Assn. (chmn. 1995), Nat. Contract Mgmt. Assn. (publicity chmn. 1996—98, employment chmn. 1996—98, chpt. pres. 1998—99, nat. dir. 1999—2001), Black Leadership Forum, So. Colo. Bus. Links (co-chair 2000—01), Toastmasters (v.p. 1994—95, pres. 1995). Avocations: reading, watching movies, volunteering. E-mail: tripled@pcisys.net.

DEMPSEY, EDWARD JOSEPH, lawyer; b. Lynn, Mass., Mar. 13, 1943; s. Timothy Finbar and Christine Margaret (Callahan) D.; m. Eileen Margaret McManus, Apr. 15, 1967; children: Kristen A. Stolfi, Katherine B. Aydin, Shelagh E., James P. AB, Boston Coll., 1964; JD, Cath. U. Am., 1970. Bar: D.C. 1970, Conn. 1982. Assoc. Arent, Fox, Kintner, Plotkin & Kahn, Washington, 1970-72, Akin, Gump, Strauss, Hauer & Feld, Washington, 1972-75; supervisory trial atty. EEOC, Washington, 1975-79; assoc. Whitman & Ransom, Washington, 1979-81, Farmer, Wells, McGuinn & Sibal, Washington, 1981-82; ptnr. Farmer, Wells, Sibal & Dempsey, Washington, Hartford, Conn., 1983-84; dir. indsl. rels. and labor counsel United Technologies Corp., Hartford, 1985—. Capt. USNR (ret.). Fellow Coll. Labor and Employment Lawyers; mem. ABA. Office: United Techs Bldg Hartford CT 06101

DEMPSEY, JACQUELINE LEE, special education director; b. Pitts., Jan. 4, 1951; d. Alexander and Catherine (Rankin) D. BS, Edinboro (Pa.) State Coll., 1972, MEd, 1974; PhD, U. Pitts., 1983. Tchr. Allegheny Intermediate Unit, Pitts., 1975-77, master tchr., 1977-78, instructional advisor, 1978-81, project dir., 1981-86, program adminstr., 1985-86; exec. dir. The Early Learning Inst., Pitts., 1986-95; pres. Early Childhood Internat., Pitts., 1995—. Guest field reviewer Exceptional Children, 1989-95. Chair Pa. Early Intervention Interagy. Coord. Coun., 1992-93; mem. Gov.'s Commn. on Children and Families, 1992-93. Mem. Coun. for Exceptional Children, Early Intervention Providers Assn. Pa. (vice chair 1986-88), Pitts. Area Coun. Adminstrv. Women in Edn. (pres. 1985-86), Phi Delta Kappa. Office: Early Childhood Internat 46 Walnut St Pittsburgh PA 15205-3117

DEMPSEY, JAMES RAYMON, industrial executive; b. Red Bay, Ala., Oct. 4, 1921; s. Newman W. and Maude (Berry) D.; m. Dolores Barnes, Jan. 19, 1943 (dec. Sept. 1997); children: Susan, David Barnes, Anne. Student, U. Ala., 1937-39; BS, U.S. Mil. Acad., 1943; MS, U. Mich., 1947, D of Engring. (hon.), 1964. Commd. 2d lt. U.S. Army, 1943; advanced through grades to lt. col. USAF, 1951; with photo reconnaissance squadron Eng., France, World War II; squadron comdr., 1945; guided missiles project officer, then chief guided missile projects (Research and Devel. Directorate, Air Force Hdqrs.), 1948- 49; exec. officer to (Dep. Chief Staff for Devel.), 1950-51; chief project sect. (Air Force Missile Test Center), Patrick AFB, Fla., then operations officer missile test range, 1951-53, resigned, 1953; asst. to v.p. planning Convair div. Gen. Dynamics Corp., 1953-54; dir. Gen. Dynamics Corp. (Atlas program), 1954-57; mgr. Gen. Dynamics Corp. (Convair-Astronautics div.), 1957-58; v.p. Gen. Dynamics Corp. (Convair div.), 1958-61; sr. v.p. Gen. Dynamics Corp.; pres. Gen. Dynamics Astronautics, 1961-65, Gen. Dynamics Convair, 1965-66; v.p. missiles, space and electronics group Avco Corp., 1966-68, v.p., group exec. govt. products group, 1968-75; pres. Digital Broadcasting Corp., 1978-79; mng. partner J.J. Finnigan Industries, Duluth, Ga., 1978-85; pres. Southeastern Rail Car Co., 1986-89; pvt. investor, 1990—. Trustee Phoenix Series Fund, 1968-91, Big Edge Series Fund, 1985-91, Phoenix Multi-Portfolio Fund, 1989-91, Precious Metal Holdings, 1980-93, Keystone Internat., 1987-93; chmn. bd. Transatlantic Capital Corp., Transatlantic Investment Corp., 1984-86; mem. spl. com. on space tech. NASA. Decorated Air Medal with clusters, D.F.C. U.S.; Croix de Guerre France); Dist. Graduate Award, US Military Acad., 2002. Fellow AIAA, Am. Astronaut. Soc.; mem. Air Force Assn. (bd. dirs. 1958-59, Dist. Grad. award 2002), Burning Tree Club, Congl. Country Club. Home and Office: 4081 Ridgeview Cir Mc Lean VA 22101-5809

DEMPSEY, JERRY EDWARD, retired service company executive; b. Landrum, S.C., Oct. 1, 1932; s. Adolphus Gerald and Willie Ceyattie (Lee) D.; m. Harriet Coan Calvert; children: Jerrie E., Harriet R., Margaret. BS, Clemson U., 1954, LLD (hon.), 2001; MBA, Ga. State Coll., 1968. With Borg-Warner Corp., Chgo., 1956-84, gen. mgr. York divsn., 1972-77, exec. v.p., 1977-79, pres., COO, 1979-84; sr. v.p. Waste Mgmt. Inc., Oak Brook, Ill., 1984-93; chmn., CEO PPG Industries, Inc., Pitts., 1993-97, chmn., 1997. Bd. dirs. Navistar, Eastman Chem. Co. Dean's adv. coun. Sch. Engring. Clemson U., chmn. pres.'s adv. coun.; bd. dirs. Pitts. Theol. Sem., Greenville Symphony, Greater Greenville Forum. Named Bus. Leader of Yr., Oak Brook (Ill.) Jaycees, 1989; recipient Bronze award Fin. World, 1989, 90, Pres.'s award Clemson U., 1990, Disting. Svc. award, 1992, Horatio Alger award, 1995, Am. Heritage award Anti-Defamation League, 1995, Disting. Alumni award Ga. State U., 1999. Mem. ASHRAE, Melrose Club, Duquesne Club (dir.), Thornblade Country Club, Greenville Country Club, Fox Chapel Golf Club. Office: PPG Industries Inc 1 Ppg Pl Pittsburgh PA 15272-0001

DEMPSEY, JOAN, federal agency administrator; BA Polit. Sci., So. Ark. U.; MA Pub. Adminstrn., U. Ark. Deputy dir. Gen. Defense Intelligence Program Staff; dir. Mil. Intelligence Staff, Nat. Mil. Intelligence Prodn. Ctr.; acting asst. sec. defense Command, Control, Comm. and Intelligence; deputy asst. sec. Defense for Intelligence and Security; deputy dir. cmty. mgmt. CIA, Washington, 1997—. With USN. Office: DDCI/CM Intelligence Cmty Washington DC 20505

DEMPSEY, MARY A. library commissioner, lawyer; m. Philip Corboy, Sept. 4, 1992. BA(hon.), St. Mary's Coll., Winona, Minn., 1975; MLS, U. Ill., 1976; JD, De Paul U., 1982. Ill. Bar, 1982. Libr. Hillside Pub. Libr., Ill., 1976-78; assoc. Reuben and Proctor, Chgo., 1982-85; assoc. gen. counsel Michael Reese Hosp. and Med. Ctr., Chgo., 1985-86; pvt. practice Chgo., 1987-89; counsel Sidley and Austin, Chgo., 1990-93; commr. Chgo. Pub. Libr., 1994—. Adj. prof. law DePaul U. Coll. Law and Health Inst., Chgo., 1986-90; spl. counsel Chgo. Bd. Edn., 1987-89; mem. adv. bd. Dominican U. Grad. Sch. Libr. and Info. Sci., River Forest, Ill. Mem. State Street Commn., Chgo.; bd. dir. Big Shoulders Fund (for inner city Cath. sch.), Urban Libr. Coun.; trustee DePaul U., Chgo.; mem. Ill. State Libr. Adv. Coun. State libr. scholar in Ill. Mem. Chgo. Bar Assn., Chgo. Network. Office: Chgo Pub Libr 400 S State St Chicago IL 60605-1203

DEMPSEY, RAYMOND LEO, JR., radio and television producer, moderator, writer; b. Providence, June 18, 1949; s. Raymond Leo Sr. and Louise Veronica (Gambuto) D.; m. Patricia Batchelder (div. 1984); children: Joab, Jahdeam, Deezsha, Nathaniel, Talitha. BA in Liberal Arts, R.I. Coll., 1973; cert., Blake Computer Programming Inst., 1977; cert. in Bus., U. R.I., 1979; cert., Billy Graham Sch. Evangelism, Ashville, N.C., 1989; postgrad., Harvard U., Roger Williams U., Bryant Coll., Bristol C.C., C.C. R.I., Providence Coll. Lic. real estate agt., R.I.; lic. radio sta. operator FCC; cert. secondary tchr., videographer, contractor, R.I. Writer local and nat. publs., 1980—88; producer, moderator Chapter & Verse TV, Sta. RICA-TV, Providence, 1983—; tchr. R.I. Pub. High Schs., Providence and Cranston, 1988; producer, moderator radio programs Ch. Focus and People, Sta. WRIB, East Providence, 1989—. Bd. dirs. Blessing, Inc., Providence; spl. corr. Songtime U.S.A. Radio Network, 1988—, spl. reporter, spl. contbr., 1991; host Straight Talk, Sta. WKRI, 1989, dir. World Exch., 1991-93; co-host The Bible Answer Program, Sta. WARV, 1986; judge The Ace Awards, 1992, Cable Ace Awards, 1992; interviewer Gallup Poll, 1987; trainee N.E. Law Enforcement Officers Assn., 1991; elector Radio Hall of Fame, 1993, Stellar Awards, 1993; nursing asst. nursing homes, R.I., 1979; pvt. nurse's asst. R.I. Hosp., 1979; patient attendant R.I. Mental Hosp.; papers placed in permanent reference res. Brit. Libr., London, N.Y.C. Pub. Libr., Libr. Congress, Washington; donated reference libr. U. Steubenville, Ohio, 1995; preliminary judge Audio Pub. Assn. awards, 1996—. Dancer R.I. Coll. Dance Co., 1969; actor: The Wig and Mask Society of La Salle Acad., 1965. Bd. dirs. R.I. Right to Life, Cranston, 1973—; witness R.I. Gen. Assembly, 1973—, R.I. Bd. Health, 1973—; vol. ARC, R.I. Hosp.; registrar voters State of R.I., 1980, 91, 92; del. Rep. Nat. Conv. 1980; sponsor World Vision, Pasadena, Calif., 1981—, Compassion Internat., Colo. Springs, Colo., 1989—; chief boys instr. karate Mattson Acad., Providence, 1968-71; mem. Providence Sci. Outreach of Brown U.; del. Gov.'s Conf. on Libr. and Info. Svcs., 1991; elector White House Conf. on Libr. and Info. Svcs.; Justice of Peace, 1991; regional rep. Students Against Vietnam War, 1971, Taxpayers Action Network, 1991; ptnr. Food for the Hungry, 1984—; del. Ellen McCormack for Pres., 1976; vol. U.S. Fish and Wildlife Svc., R.I. Hosp., Providence, 1975, Providence Amb. Clinic, 1975; elected Rep. City Com. and Rep. State Ctrl. Com.; chmn. Issues and Rsch. Com. Rep. party Providence; numerous collection donations to libraries and Archdiocese of N.Y., 1975—; ret. dir. Ground Zero, Citizens Against Govt. Waste; donator Vt. Hist. Soc., Brattleboro, 1975, Dominican Phillips Meml. Libr., Providence Coll., 1975, reference libr. Brown U., 2001, Cranston (RI) Pub. Libr., 2001, The Master's Sem., Calif., 2001, Joseph Stanton Meml. Libr., NYC, 2001. Named One of Top 4 Local Cable TV Prodrs. in Nation, Nat. Assn. Local Cable Programming, 1987, ofcl. Jerusalem Pilgrim, State of Israel, 1990, Ptnr. in Philanthropy, 1995; recipient 2 Internat. Angel awards for excellence in Cable TV presentations, 1991, cert. U.S. SBA, 1990, Diamond award, 1992, 1st prize for excellence in pub. affairs in R.I. and Mass., 1992, Achievement award Dale Carnegie Orgn., 1992, 1st pl. award Mastermedia: The Spotlight award, 1993; nominated for J.C. Penney Golden Rule award. Mem. AAAS, ASCD, NRA, Am. Math. Soc., Coll. Sci. Tchrs., Sons Union Vets., Nat. Assn. H.S. Tchrs. English, Evangel. Theol. Soc., Soc. for Coll. Tchrs., Nat. Assn. Edn. of Young Children, Nat. Assn. Tchg. Sci., Modern Poetry Assn., Am. Soc. Oriental Rsch., Archaeol. Inst. Am., R.I. Assn. for Edn. Young Children, R.I. Assn. for Supervision and Curriculum Devel., Mental Health Assn. R.I., N.Y. Acad. Scis., Internat. Press Assn. (founding mem.), Nat. Geog. Soc., Nat. Assn. Broadcasters, Modern Poetry Assn., Nat. Assn. Radio Talk Show Hosts, Nat. Acad. Cable Programming, Near East Archaeol. Soc., Internat. Platform Assn., Nat. Assn. Tchrs. Sci., Jewish TV Inst. (charter), Smithsonian Air and Space Mus., Smithsonian Instn. (assoc.), Royal Inst. Pub. Health and Hygiene London (affiliate), Bread for the World, Evangs. for Social Action, Mus. Heritage Soc., Interscholastic Inst., Libr. Co. Phila., John Russell Bartlett Soc. (Brown U.), Intertel, Mensa, USCG Aux., Golden Key, Abraham Lincoln Soc., Internet Soc., Rel. Heritage Am., Providence Athenaeum, Toastmasters Internat., R.I. Pilots Assn., Phi Theta Kappa. Avocations: scuba diving, marksmanship, archaeology. Home and Office: PO Box 41000 Providence RI 02940-1000 *Orthodoxy presumes orthopraxy, and correct knowledge must precede correct action; yet anything minus love equals zero.*

DEMPSEY, THOMAS JOSEPH, retired postmaster; b. Centralia, Pa., Mar. 16, 1945; s. William Anthony and Helen Agnes (Dewey) D.; m. Grace Mary Sewa, Nov. 24, 1973; children: Brian, Thomas Joseph Jr., Kevin. Grad., Postal Svc. Acad., Potomac, Md., 1984. Cert. postmaster trainer U.S. Postal Svc. Clk. U.S. Postal Svc., Centralia, 1968-77, mail carrier Girardville, Pa., 1977-79, postmaster Locustdale, Pa., 1979-81, Centralia, 1981-84, Girardville, 1984-2000, officer-in-charge selection bd. Lancaster, Pa., 1992-99, mem. postmaster selection bd. and customer svc. bd., 1994-99; ret., 2000. Author: History of Centralia, 1992. Sec. Centralia Ambulance Svc., 1970-73. Mem. Nat. Assn. Postmasters U.S., Nat. League Postmasters, Hist. Soc. Schuylkill County, KC. Democrat. Roman Catholic. Avocations: genealogy, history, fishing. Home: 204 W Main St Girardville PA 17935-1706 E-mail: tdemps@ptd.net.

DEMPSTER, BARRY (EDWARD), writer, poet; b. Toronto, Ont., Can., Jan. 17, 1952; s. Albert Edward and Helen Florence (Robinette) D.; m. Karen Ruttan, Sept. 26, 1981. Student, Centennial Coll., 1972-75. Lectr. poetry workshops League Can. Poets and Writers Union Coun. Author: Fables for Isolated Men, 1982, Globe Doubis, 1983, Real Places and Imaginary Men, 1984, David and the Daydreams, 1985, Writing Home, 1989, Positions To Pray In, 1989, The Unavoidable Man, 1990, Letters From a Long Illness With the World, The D.H. Lawrence Poems, 1993, The Ascension of Jesse Rapture, 1993, Fire and Brimstone, 1997, The Salavation of Desire, 2000; co-author: Best Canadian Stories, 1980, Third Impressions, 1982; editor: Tributaries, An Anthology: Writer to Writer, 1978; contbr. to anthologies; book rev. and poetry editor. Recipient Confedn. Poets prize, 1995, Scarborough Bicentennial award of merit, 1996, Petra Kerney Poetry prize, 2002. Mem. League Can. Poets, Writers' Union Can. Avocations: writing film criticism, travel, music, gardening, bicycling. Address: 45 French Cres Holland Landing ON Canada L9N 1J8 E-mail: dempster@passport.ca.

DEMPSTER, MURRAY WAYNE, academic administrator, religion educator, minister; b. Melville, Sask., Can., June 27, 1942; came to U.S., 1965; s. Raymond Daniel Rudolph and June (Bellamy) Rynbend; m. Coralie Faith Erickson, Sept. 26, 1964; 1 child, Marlon Murray. Ministerial diploma, N.W. Bible Coll., Can., 1963; BA in Bibl. Studies summa cum laude, So. Calif. Coll., 1968; MA in Social Ethics, U. So. Calif., 1969, PhD in Social Ethics, 1980. Ordained to ministry Assemblies of God, 1965. Asst. min. Cen. Pentecostal Ch., Edmonton, Alta., Can., 1963-65; assoc. min. 1st Assembly of God, Long Beach, Calif., 1965-68; dean of men So. Calif. Coll., Costa Mesa, 1969-70, campus pastor, 1970-71, asst. prof. religion, 1971-78, assoc. prof., 1980-87, prof. social ethics, 1987—99; provost Vanguard U. (formerly So. Calif. Coll.), 1999—2000; pres. Vanguard U., 2000—. Vis. prof. Fuller Theol. Sem., Pasadena, Calif., 1980—; Pentecostal lectr. Regent Coll., Vancouver, B.C., Can., 1988; Staley lectr. Southeastern Coll., Lakeland, Fla., 1991. Co-author: Salt and Light: Evangelical Political Thought in Modern America, 1989; author: (with others) Pastoral Problems in the Pentecostal-Charismatic Movement, 1983; co-editor: Called and Empowered: Global Mission in Pentecostal Perspective, 1991, Agora mag., 1977-81; mem. editorial adv. bd.: The Study of Philosophy, 3d edit., contbr. articles to religious jours. Mem. instl. rev. team Calif. State Dept. Edn., 1984, 86. Recipient Outstanding Faculty award Associated Student Body, So. Calif. Coll., 1981-82; scholar So. Calif. Coll., 1967-68, U. So. Calif., 1968-69; Layne Found. fellow U. So. Calif., 1971-74. Mem. Soc. for Pentecostal Studies (2d v.p. 1989, 1st v.p., program chair ann. meeting 1990, pres. 1990-91), Am. Acad. Religion, Soc. for Sci. Study of Religion, Soc. Christian Ethics, Soc. Christian Philosophers. Democrat. Home: 2 Toulon Laguna Beach CA 92677-5429 Office: Vanguard U Pres Office 55 Fair Dr Costa Mesa CA 92626-6520

DEMSETZ, HAROLD, economist, educator; b. Chgo., 1930; BA, U. Ill., 1953; MBA, Northwestern U., 1954, PhD in Econs., 1959. Prof. econs. U. Chgo., 1963-71; sr. rsch. fellow Hoover Instn., Stanford, Calif., 1971-77; prof. econs. UCLA, 1971—, Arthur Anderson Alumni prof. bus. econs, 1988-95, emeritus, 1995—. Author: Economic, Legal, and Political Dimensions of Competition, 1982, The Organization of Economic Activity, Vol. I, 1988, Vol. II, 1989, The Economics of the Firm, 1995; contbr. numerous articles, book chpts. Fellow AAAS; mem. Mont Pelerin Soc., Am. Econs. Assn., WEA Internat. (pres. 1996). Office: UCLA Dept Econs 405 Hilgard Ave Los Angeles CA 90095-9000 E-mail: hdemsetz@ucla.edu.

DEMUNBRUN-HARMON, DONNE O'DONNELL, retired family physician; b. St. Paul, Aug. 26, 1926; d. Francis Joseph and Julia (Hoffmann) O'Donnell; m. Truman Weldon DeMunbrun, Mar. 17, 1948 (dec. Aug. 1996); children: Michael J., Steven M., Julie F., Suzanne B.; m. Donald Laurance Harmon, Aug. 26, 1997. BS, U. Ky., 1948, MS, 1949; MD, U. Louisville, 1954. Diplomate Am. Bd. Family Practice. Rotating intern St. Anthony Hosp., Louisville, 1955—56; pvt. practice Louisville, 1956—85; med. dir. St. Mary and Elizabeth Hosp., Louisville, 1971—76, Parkway Med. Ctr., Louisville, 1976—99, Family Health Ctrs., Louisville, 1985—90; ret., 1999. Case reviewer Health Care Rev., Louisville, 1995-96; criteria writer Nat. Health Svc., Louisville, 1995-96; asst. clin. prof. family practice, U. Louisville Med. Sch., 1987-90. Pres. Jacques Timothe Boucher Sieur de Montburn Heritage Soc., Nashville, 1996-97. Recipient mayor's citation Cify of Louisville, 1990, proclamation of tribute Jefferson County, Ky., 1990. Mem.: Jefferson County Med. Soc. (life; v.p. 1976—77), Ky. Acad. Family Practice (life), Ky. Med. Assn. (life; del.), Am. Acad. Family Practice (life), Filson Club, Execs. Club, Univ. Club, Sigma Pi Sigma, Pi Mu Epsilon, Alpha Lambda Delta. Avocations: gardening, reading, travel, family, dogs. Home: 2001 Deals Branch Dr Louisville KY 40206-2902 E-mail: d2d.harmon@att.net.

DE MUNIZ, PAUL J. state supreme court justice; Judge Oreg. Ct. Appeals, 1990—2001; justice Oreg. Supreme Ct., 2001—. Author (with others): Immigrants in Courts, 1999. Office: Supreme Ct 1163 State St Salem OR 97301*

DEMURO, PAUL ROBERT, lawyer; b. Aberdeen, Md., Mar. 21, 1954; s. Paul Robert and Amelia C. DeMuro; m. Susan Taylor, May 26, 1990; children: Melissa Taylor, Natalie Lauren, Alanna Leigh. BA summa cum laude, U. Md., 1976; JD, Washington U., 1979; MBA, U. Calif., Berkeley, 1986. CPA Md.; bar: Md. 1979, U.S. Dist. Ct. Md. 1979, DC 1980, U.S. Dist. Ct. DC 1980, U.S. Tax Ct. 1981, U.S. Ct. Appeals (4th cir.) 1981, Calif. 1982, U.S. Dist. Ct. (no. dist.) Calif. 1982, U.S. Dist. Ct. (ea. dist.) Calif. 1986; cert. healthcare compliance. Assoc. Ober, Grimes & Shriver, Balt., 1979-82; ptnr. Carpenter et al, San Francisco, 1982-89, McCutchen, Doyle, Brown & Enerson, San Francisco, 1989-93, Latham & Watkins, San Francisco, 1993—. Author: The Financial Managers Guide to Managed Care and Integrated Delivery Systems, 1995, The Fundamentals of Managed Care and Network Development, 1999; co-author: Health Care Mergers and Acquisitions: The Transactional Perspective, 1996, Health Care Executives' Guide to Fraud and Abuse, 1998; editor, contbg. author: Integrated Delivery Systems, 1994, article and rev. editor: Washington U. Law Quar., 1975—76. Mem. San Francisco Mus. Art, 1985—. Fellow: Healthcare Fin. Mgmt. Assn. (bd. dirs. No. Calif. chpt. 1990—93, nat. principles and practices bd. 1992—95, vice chair 1993—95, nat. bd. dirs. 1995—97, mem. exec. com. 1996—97, chair compliance officers forum adv. coun. 1998—2000, sec. 1999—2001, bd. dirs. No. Calif. chpt. 1999—, mem. nominating com. 2001—02, pres.-elect 2001—02, mem. governance com. 2002—03, pres. 2002—03); mem.: AICPA, ABA (chair transactional and bus. health care interest group 1998—2000, chair programs com. 2000—02, governing coun. 2000—, chmn. mem. and mktg. com. 2002—, vice chair coord. com. diversity 2002—, budget officer 2003—, fin. officer 2003—, health law sect.), Healthcare Compliance Assn. (cert. in health care compliance), Am. Coll. Healthcare Execs., Med. Group Mgmt. Assn. (cert. med. practice exec.), Am. Health Lawyers Assn. (task force best practices in advising clients 1998—99, fraud and abuse and self-referral substantive law com. 1998—, task force on ENRON 2002), Calif. Bar Assn., L.A. County Bar Assn. (health law sect.). Republican. Office: Latham & Watkins 505 Montgomery St Ste 1900 San Francisco CA 94111-2552 E-mail: paul.demuro@lw.com.

DEMUTH, ALAN CORNELIUS, lawyer; b. Boulder, Colo., Apr. 29, 1935; s. Laurence Wheeler and Eugenia Augusta (Roach) DeM.; m. Susan McDermott; children: Scott Lewis, Evan Dale, Joel Millard. BA magna cum laude in Econs., U. Colo., 1958, LLB cum laude in Gen. Studies, 1961. Bar: Colo. 1961, U.S. Dist. Ct. Colo. 1961, U.S. Ct. Appeals (10th cir.) 1962. Assoc. Akolt, Turnquist, Shepherd & Dick, Denver, 1961-68; ptnr. DeMuth & DeMuth, Denver, 1968—. Conf. atty. Rocky Mountain Conf. United Ch. of Christ, 1970-95; bd. dirs. Friends of U. Colo. Libr., 1978-86; bd. dirs., sponsor Denver Boys Inc., 1987-93, sec., 1988-89, v.p., 1989-90, pres., 1992-93; bd. dirs. Denver Kids, Inc., 1993—, Children's Ctr. for Arts and Learning, 1995—; mem. bd. advisors Lambuth Family Ctr. of Salvation Army, 1994—, chmn., 1994—; bd. advisors Metro Denver Salvation Army, 1988—, vice chmn. 1994-96. Mem. ABA, Colo. Bar Assn., Denver Bar Assn., Denver Rotary (bd. dirs. 1996-98), Phi Beta Kappa, Sigma Alpha Epsilon, Phi Delta Phi. Republican. Mem. United Ch. of Christ. Office: DeMuth & DeMuth 990 S High St Denver CO 80209-4551

DEMUTH, NINA LEWIS, engineering company executive; b. Benton, Ill., July 14, 1921; d. William Henry and Agnes Clara (Landreth) Lewis; m. Herbert Willard Demuth, Feb. 16, 1947; 1 child, Nina Dale (dec.). Student, Nassau Coll., 1976—. With Barbour Co., Inc., St. Louis, 1939-47; pres. Demuth Co., Garden City, N.Y., 1948—, Demuth Service Corp., Garden City, 1955—, Demuth Devel. Corp., Garden City, 1958. Contbr. Mem. adv. com. on nutrition N.Y. Hosp., Cornell Med. Coll., 1986—2002, Meml. Sloan-Kettering Cancer Ctr., Rockefeller U. Named to WLIW-21 Gala 2002 Celebrating Women Who Make a Difference; recipient Women Who Make a Difference honor, WLIW-21, 2002. Mem.: Found. for Pharm. Scis. (incorporator 1979, pres. 1979—83, 2000—, bd. dirs., treas. 1984—), Parenteral Drug Assn. (bd. dirs. 1977—79), Huguenot Soc. Methodist. Office: 6 Sunset Ln Garden City NY 11530-4310 E-mail: hndemuth@aol.com.

DEMUTH, VIVIENNE BLAKE MCCANDLESS, artist, illustrator; b. Nutley, N.J., Mar. 8, 1916; d. George Wilbur and Hazel Metcalfe Blake; m. Henry DeMuth, July 3, 1935 (div. Sept. 1957); children: Simon (dec.), Vivienne, Shelley, David; m. George Warren McCandless, May 12, 1984 (dec. May 1995). Diploma, Am. Sch. Design, 1932, 33. Designer, artist Norcross Pub. Co., N.Y.C. and West Chester, Pa., 1936-40, 50-75; designer, illustrator Fisher Price Toys, East Aurora, N.Y., 1957-80; freelance book illustrator many pub. cos., 1992-94. Mem. newspaper panel cmty. newspapers Cape Cod, Mass.; artist, crafts tchr. presch. Cape Cod Mus. Natural History, Brewster, Mass., 1994—. Illustrator: Little Golden Book A to Z, 1945, Pre-School Science, 1996, many others. Mem. Nature Conservancy, Mass. Audubon Soc., Cape Cod Mus. Natural History (artist environ. posters). Avocations: early childhood education, grandchildren, cooking, travel, reading. Home: 2300 Herringbrook Rd PO Box 983 North Eastham MA 02651-0983 E-mail: vivienne@c4.net.

DEMUZIO, VINCE THOMAS, state legislator; b. Gillespie, Ill., May 7, 1941; s. Vince and Catherine McKnight (Murphy) D.; m. Deanna Joan Clemonds, June 23, 1962; children: Bradley, Stephanie. BA, Sangamon State U.; MA, U. Ill., Springfield, 1996; JD (hon.), Lewis and Clark C.C. Investigator Office of Sec. of State, Springfield, Ill.; exec. dir. Ill. Valley Econ. Devel. Corp., Carlinville; mem. Ill. State Senate, Springfield, 1974—, asst. majority leader, 1983-92, asst. minority leader, 1992—2003, majority leader, 2003—. State ctrl. committeeman 20th Congl. Dist., Springfield, 1982-2002; state chmn. Ill. Dem. Ctrl. Com., 1986-90; precinct committeeman Macoupin County Dem. Ctrl. Com., Carlinville, 1992—, chmn., 1992—. Named Friend of Agriculture Ill. Extension Adviser's Assn., 1993, Legislator of Yr. Ill. Edn. Assn., 1976;

recipient Ill. Agriculture award Ill. Assn. Vocat. Agriculture Tchrs., 1993. Mem. K. of C., Elks. Roman Catholic. Avocations: historical, biographical and political reading. Office: 323 Capitol Bldg Springfield IL 62706-0001*

DEMY, TIMOTHY JAMES, military chaplain; b. Brownsville, Tex., Dec. 6, 1954; s. Millard Nile and Pauline Juanita (Owen) D.; m. Lyn Elizabeth Evans, Aug. 26, 1978. BA, Tex. Christian U., 1977; ThM, Dallas Theol. Sem., 1981, ThD, 1990; MA, U. Tex. at Arlington, 1994, Salve Regina U., 1990, Naval War Coll., 1999. Commd. lt. jr. grade USN, 1981, advanced through grades to cmdr., 1993. Adj. instr. Naval War Coll., Newport, R.I., 1996—; co-dir. Ctr. for the Am. Family, Springfield, Va., 1995—. Co-author: When the Trumpet Sounds, 1995, The Coming Cashless Soc., 1996, Suicide: A Christian Response, 1998, Winning the Marriage Marathon, 1999, Genetic Engineering: A Christian Response, 1999, The Return, 1999, Politics and Public Policy: A Christian Response, 2000, In the Name of God, 2002; contbr. articles to profl. jours. Mem. Nat. Assn. Evangelicals, Evangelical Theol. Soc., Soc. Biblical Lit., Ctr. for Bioethics and Human Dignity, Orgn. Am. Historians, Naval Order U.S. Avocations: reading, cartography, animals. Office: 7 Ellen Rd Middletown RI 02842-5504 E-mail: lynd1@mindspring.com.

DENABURG, CHARLES L(EON), lawyer; b. Birmingham, Ala., June 5, 1934; s. Joe and Ethel (Levy) D.; m. Jan Barber, July, 1983; children: Lorraine, Edmond, David Todd. BS, U. Ala., 1954 JD, 1956. Bar: Ala. 1956. Sr. ptnr. Najjar Denaburg, P.C. and predessor firms, Birmingham, 1960—; panelist various seminars continuing legal edn. U. Ala., Tuscaloosa, 1965—. Capt. USAF, 1956-59. Fellow Am. Coll. of Bankruptcy (cert. creditors rights specialist); mem. ABA, Ala. State Bar Assn., Birmingham Bar Assn., Comml. Law League Am. Home: 3537 Mill Run Rd Birmingham AL 35223-1427 Office: Najjar Denaburg 2125 Morris Ave Birmingham AL 35203-4274

DENACO, PARKER ALDEN, state official, lawyer, arbitrator; b. Bangor, Maine, Apr. 19, 1943; s. Alden F. and Pauline N. Denaco; m. Gayle Gernert Denaco, May 23, 1989. BA in History and Govt., U. Maine, 1965, MBA, 1975; JD, Washington and Lee Univ., 1968; postgrad., Air Command and Staff Coll., 1981. Bar: Maine 1968, U.S. Dist. Ct. Maine 1968, U.S. Ct. Mil. Appeals. Assoc. atty. Eaton & Peabody, Bangor, Maine, 1968—69; exec. officer and adj. 100 MP Bn, Ft. Bragg, NC, 1969—70; provost marshal US Army, Inchon, Republic of Korea, 1970—71; exec. dir. Maine Labor Rels. Bd., Augusta, 1972—88; adj. grad. instr. Thomas Coll., Waterville, Maine, 1977—80; state staff judge advocate Maine Air N.G., Augusta, ME, 1973-86; vis. prof. in constl. law U. Maine, 1990—91; hon. fac. mem. USAF Judge Advocate Gen. Sch., Maxwell AFB, Ala.; exec. dir. N.H. Pub. Employee Labor Rels. Bd., 1991—2003. Contbr. articles to profl. jours. Bd. dirs. Acad. Collective Bargaining Info. Svc., 1979-82; bd. dirs., founding mem. and dir. Pub. Employment Rels. Svcs., 1978-81; bd. dirs. New Eng. Consortium of State Labor Rels. Agys., 1978-2003; neutral pub. mem. Com. on Pub. Sector Bargaining, ABA, 1974—; neutral chair, 1987-01, mem. Alternate Dispute Resolution Section, ABA, 1998—; mem. Boston Adv. Coun., Am. Arbitration Assn., 1978—; elected Nat. Acad. Arbitrators, 1987; Judicial Divsn., ABA, 1998—, Nat. Conf. of Admin. Law Judges; corporator Maine Savs. Bank, 1982-84; law coun. Washington and Lee Univ., 1988-92. Served to capt. U.S. Army, 1969-73, to col. Air NG and USAFR, 1973-95. Recipient Harmon award. USAF, 1986, Legion of Merit, 1990, Disting. Svc. award ABA, 2001. Fellow Coll. Labor and Employment Lawyers (chmn. First Circuit Com., 2003); mem. ABA (Disting. Svc. award 2001), Assn. Labor Rels. Agys. (pres. 1978-79), Maine Bar Assn. (labor sect. co-chmn. 1980-85), N.H. Bar Assn. (chmn. labor and employment law sect. 2002-03) Soc. Profls. in Dispute Resolution (charter), Indsl. Rels. Rsch. Assn., Nat. Acad. Arbitrators, Res. Ofcrs. Assn. (life), N.G. Assn. of U.S. (life), Phi Delta Phi, Beta Gamma Sigma. Address: 1465 Hooksett Rd Unit 11 Hooksett NH 03106-1861 also: PO Box 227 Lincolnville ME 04849-0227 Fax: 603-268-0914. E-mail: denaco4adr@yahoo.com.

DEN ADEL, RAYMOND LEE, classics educator; b. Pella, Iowa, Apr. 23, 1932; s. John J. and Nellie (DeGeus) D. BA, Ctrl. Coll., 1954; MA, U. Iowa, 1959; PhD, U. Ill., 1971. Latin tchr. Pella H.S., 1954-55; grad. student Am. Acad., Rome, 1960, Vergilian Sch., Cumae, Italy, 1960, 73; fellow U. Iowa, Iowa City, 1957-58, tchg. asst., 1962-63; Latin and English tchr. Proviso West H.S., Hillside, Ill., 1958-62; v.p. Proviso Ednl. Assn., 1960-61; grad. student Am. Sch. Classical Studies, Athens, 1961, site participant, 1989-90; fellow, asst. and instr. in classics U. Ill., Urbana, 1963-67; dir. Ill. H.S. Latin Conf., 1967; faculty, chair classics dept. Rockford (Ill.) Coll., 1967—97, chair div. lang. and lit., 1971—74, prof., 1975—97, 1997—. Lectr. Ctr. for Learning in Retirement Rock Valley Coll., 2001—03. Bd. dirs. Rockford Cmty. Concert Assn., 1979-85; mem. Burpee Museum of Natural Hist. (life) mem. exec. com. Archaeol. Inst. Am., (life), governing bd., 1990-96, trustee, 1990-94, v.p., 1994-96, Disting. Svc. award, 1997. With CIC, U.S. Army, 1955-57. Fulbright grant, Italy, 1960; named Vol. of Yr., Source Program, Rockford, 1983, Outstanding Coll. Latin Tchr. in Ill., 1987, Outstanding Fgn. Lang. Tchr. in Ill., 1989. Mem.: AAUP (pres. Rockford chpt. 1974—76, Ill. coun. 1977—80, sec. 1984—86, v.p. 1988—89), AIA (Ctrl. Ill. Soc. sec.-treas. 1966—67, coun. 1966—98, Rockford Soc. pres. 1968—70, 1972—74, 1991—93, sec. 1993—94, v.p. 1998—99), Classical Soc. Am. Acad. Rome (sec. 1990—93), Ill. Coun. Tchg. Fgn. Langs., Fulbright Alumni Assn., Biblical Archaeol. Soc., Ill. Classical Conf. (v.p. 1968—69, pres. 1969—70), Am. Assn. Dutch-Am. Studies, Vergilian Soc. Am. (life; sec. 1978—80), Classical Assn. Mid. West and South (life; 1st v.p. 1980—81), Am. Philol. Assn. (life Field Scholarship award 1961), Am. Classical League (life; nat. coun. 1969—82, Scholarship award 1960), Chgo. Classical Club (pres. 1977—79), Rotary (bd. dirs. Rockford chpt. 1987—89, dist. gov. rep. 1989—91, bd. dirs. Rockford chpt. 1991—95, v.p. 1992—93, pres. 1993—94, dist. gov. rep. 1994—97, gov. dist. 6420 1997—98, chair past dist. gov. coun. 1998, Paul Harris 711 Club, bd. dirs. 2002—, Svc. Above Self award Rockford Club and Dist. 6420 1989, Paul Harris fellow, benefactor 1982), Chi Gamma Iota, Phi Sigma Iota, Phi Beta Kappa (v.p. 1988—89, triennial coun. 1988—, pres. Eta Ill. chpt. 1989—92), Eta Sigma Phi (nat. exec. sec. 1974—78), Sigma Tau Delta. Presbyterian. Avocations: photography, travel, reading, philately, music. Home: 701 Broadway St Pella IA 50219

DENAPOLI, PAUL FREDERICK, investment manager; b. Newton, Mass., Feb. 1, 1952; s. Paul A. and Katherine (Kvale) deN. BS, U. N.H., 1981. CFP; registered investment advisor, registered securities prin. Founder AVS Prodns., Salem, Mass.; regional sales mgr. Structures Unltd., Manchester, N.H.; planner Cornerstone Fin., Waltham, Mass.; investment mgr. Liberty Securities, Boston; sr. partner Atlantic Advisor Grp., Peabody, Mass.; br. mgr. New Eng. Adv. Group, Peabody, Mass. No. Colo. campaign mgr. McGovern for Pres., Ft. Collins, 1972; judge Carrol Ctr. for the Blind, Boston, 1995; fundraiser various Dem. campaigns; active Foster Parents Plan & Christian Children's Fund. Mem. Inst. CFPs, Corinthian Yacht Club (Marblehead). Avocations: skiing, mountain biking, sports car racing, sailboat racing. Home: 83 School St Groveland MA 01834

DENARDIS, LAWRENCE J. academic administrator; Pres. U. New Haven, West Haven, Conn., 1991—. Office: U New Haven Office of President 300 Orange Ave West Haven CT 06516-1916

DENARO, ANTHONY THOMAS, psychiatrist; b. N.Y.C., Aug. 9, 1929; s. Joseph and Maria (DeGennaro) Denaro; m. Mitsuru Suzuki, Nov. 23, 1963. BS, CCNY, 1960; MD, U. Okla., 1969; MPA, U. Hartford, 1981. Diplomate Nat. Bd. Med. Examiners, Am. Bd. Psychiatry, Am. Bd. Gen. Psychiatry and Child Psychiatry, Adminstrv. Psychiatry. Intern Nassau County Med. Ctr., East Meadow, N.Y., 1969-70; resident in child psychiatry U. Pa., Phila., 1970-72, resident in gen. psychiatry, 1972-74; dir. child psychiatry U. Conn. Health Ctr., Farmington, 1974-78; dir. adolescent unit Natchaug Psychiat. Hosp., Willamantic, Conn., 1978-80; assoc. dir. child and adolescent service Mt. Sinai Hosp., Hartford, Conn., 1980-82; assoc. dir. child and adolescent psychiatry Elmcrest Psychiat. Inst., Portland, Conn., 1982-84; dir. outpatient psychiatry Woodhull Med. and Mental Health Ctr., N.Y.C., 1984-85; dir. child and adolescent psychiatry First Hosp. Wyoming Valley, Kingston, Pa., 1985-98; med. dir. child and adolescent behavioral health svcs. Ea. Conn. Health Network, Inc., 1998—; med. dir. Child Devel. Clinic, Scranton, Pa., 1999-2001; dir. child and adolescent svcs. First Hosp. Wyoming Valley, Kingston, 2001—. Asst. prof. dept. psychiatry U. Conn. Sch. Medicine, Farmington, 1974-83. With U.S. Army, 1947-49. Fellow Am. Acad. Child and Adolescent Psychiatry; mem. AMA, Am. Psychiat. Assn., Am. Assn. Psychiat. Adminstrs., Northeastern Pa. Psychiat. Soc. (pres. 1990-91), Phi Beta Kappa. Republican. Office: First Hosp Wyoming Valley 562 Wyoming Ave Kingston PA 18704

DENARO, CHARLES THOMAS, lawyer; b. Phila., Aug. 16, 1953; s. Anthony Carmen and Alfia Dorothy (Nucifora) D.; m. Carol Anne Lewis, Apr. 24, 1983; children: Kristin Anne, Samantha, Kandace. BA, Villanova U., 1975, JD, 1978. Bar: Pa. 1978. Gen. counsel Pilgrim Life Ins. Co., Folcroft, Pa., 1979-87; exec. v.p. Pilgrim Ins. Group, Folcroft, 1987-93; corp. counsel Corp. Life Ins. Co., West Chester, Pa., 1993-94; sec., assoc. gen. counsel Reliance Standard Life Ins. Co., Phila., 1995—, asst. v.p., sec., dep. gen. counsel, 1999—. Bd. dirs. Pilgrim Life Ins. Co., Folcroft, Delphi Project Found. Mem. ABA, Pa. Bar Assn., Assn. Trial Lawyers Am. Republican. Roman Catholic.

DENARO, GREGORY, lawyer; b. Rochester, N.Y., Dec. 10, 1954; m. Nancy Cardiff; children: Adrienne, Gregory, Madeline. BA, U. Rochester, 1976; JD, U. Miami, 1979. Bar: Fla. 1979, U.S. Dist. Ct. (so. dist.) Fla. 1979, U.S. Ct. Appeals (5th and 11th cirs.) 1981, U.S. Supreme Ct. 1984, N.Y. 1985, U.S. Dist. Ct. (mid. dist.) Fla. 1986, U.S. Ct. Appeals (D.C. cir.) 1989, U.S. Dist. Ct. (we. dist.) Tex. 1990, U.S. Ct. Appeals (4th cir.) 1992. Pub. defender Dade County, Miami, Fla., 1979 82; sr. ptnr. Gregory C. Denaro P.A., Miami, 1982—. Advisor nat. mock trial U. Miami Law Sch., 1984—. Mem. ABA (criminal law sect.), Dade County Bar Assn., Assn. Trial Attys., Nat. Assn. Criminal Def. Lawyers, Fla. Assn. Criminal Def. Lawyers (bd. dirs.). Office: Coconut Grove Bank Bldg 2701 S Bayshore Dr Ste 605 Coconut Grove FL 33133-5360 E-mail: gdenaro@bellsouth.net.

DE NATALE, ANDREW PETER, lawyer; b. Bklyn., July 7, 1950; s. Peter E. and Mary (Tamberino) DeN.; m. Lynn Susan Kennedy, July 28, 1973; children: Andrew, Christopher. BS in Econs., U. Pa., 1972; JD, Fordham U., 1975. Bar: N.Y. 1976, U.S. Dist. Ct. (so. dist.) N.Y. 1976, U.S. Dist. Ct. (ea. dist.) N.Y. 1977, U.S. Ct. Appeals (2d cir.) 1978, U.S. Supreme Ct. 1979, U.S. Dist. Ct. (no. dist.) N.Y. 1982. Assoc. Krause, Hirsch & Gross, N.Y.C., 1975-79, Stroock & Stroock & Lavan, N.Y.C., 1980-83, ptnr., 1984-91, White & Case, N.Y.C., 1991—. Contbr. numerous articles to newspapers and profl. jours. Mem. ABA, N.Y. Yacht Club, Seawanhaka Corinthian Yacht Club. Office: White & Case LLP 1155 Avenue Of The Americas New York NY 10036-2787

DENAVIT, JACQUES, retired physicist; b. Paris, Oct. 1, 1930; came to U.S., 1952; s. Georges and Marie (Arnould) D.; m. Catherine Dahlinger, Aug. 6, 1954; children: George, Paul, Mary. Degree in Gen. Math./Physics, U. Paris, 1952; MSEE, Northwestern U., 1953, PhD in Mech. Engring., 1956. Asst. prof. Northwestern U., Evanston, Ill., 1958-61, assoc. prof., 1961-66, prof. mech. and nuclear engring., 1966-82; rsch. physicist plasma physics divsn. Naval Rsch. Lab., Washington, 1969-71; rsch. physicist Lawrence Livermore Nat. Lab., Livermore, Calif., 1982-93. Author: (with R.S. Hartenberg) Kinematic Synthesis of Linkages, 1964; contbr. numerous articles on plasma physics and computer simulation to profl. jours. Fellow Am. Phys. Soc. Home: 3536 Gresham Ct Pleasanton CA 94588-3431 E-mail: jacdenavit@aol.com.

DENBO, ALEXANDER, retired bank executive; JD-LLB, Dickinson Sch. Law, 1932. Bar: N.J., 1934, U.S. Supreme Ct., 1952. Judge Mcpl. Ct., Burlington City, N.J., 1943-52, Burlington County Dist. Ct., 1952-55; exec. v.p. Mechanics Nat. Bank, 1954-55; pres. First Nat. State Bank West Jersey (formerly Mechanics Nat. Bank), 1955-77. Cons. trust dept. Fidelity Bank & Trust Co. N.J.; commr. Supreme Ct., 1938; former solicitor Willingboro Twp., Florence Twp., Pemberton Twp., Bordentown Twp., Edgewater Park Twp., Beverly Housing Authority, Burlington Twp., Fieldsboro Borough; bd. dirs. Beverly Bldg. Loan Assn., MacAndrews & Forbes Co. Treas. County of Burlington, N.J., 1944-52; solicitor bd. edn. Twp. Pemberton Edgewater Park Sewerage Authority; v.p. N.J. Divsn. Am. Cancer Soc., 1945; pres. Burlington County Cancer Soc., 1945; past chmn. bond drives ARC, United Jewish Appeal; past trustee Rancocas Valley Hosp., Zurbrugg Hosp. N.J., Dickinson Sch. Law, Carlisle, Pa.; mem. citizens adv. com. City of Burlington, 1967; dir. Burlington County Coll. Found.; pres. Temple B'Nai Israel, Burlington, 1967; mem. Burlington City Indsl. Com.; chmn. Am. Jewish Com., Burlington County; bd. govs. Greater Trenton Symphony Assn.; Burlington County cmty. coun. McGuire Air Force Base; past mem. Com. Labor Mgmt. Rels., Burlington City; past mem. adv. com. N.J. League Municipalities; past mem. Legis. Com. Revision Election Laws, 1944; past mem. law enforcement com. Gov.'s Fire Safety Conf., 1948; treas. bldg. fund. com. St. Mary's Hall Doane Acad. Recipient Citizenship award Jewish War Vets. U.S., 1953, Citation, Borough of Fieldsboro, 1960, Mayor and Coun. Burlington Twp., 1973, Borough Fieldsboro, Edgewater Park Twp., Bd. Edn. Borough Fieldsboro. Mem. ABA, Burlington County Bar Assn. (pres. 1956), N.J. State Bar Assn., Am. Judicature Soc., Am. Arbitration Assn. (nat. panel), Burlington Trade Assn. (sec. 1937), Assn. U.S. Army (pres. Fort Dix chpt. 1976), Burlington County Hist. Soc., Jr. Order Mechanics, B'nai B'rith, Kiwanis (pres. 1945), Burlington Lodge, Moose, Tall Cedars Lebanon, Elks. Achievements include naming of sch. the Alexander Denbo Sch. Home: Burlington, NJ. Died Oct. 12, 2001.

D'ENCARNACAO-BRADLEY, AJA A. supervisor; b. Riverside, Calif., May 4, 1972; d. Frederico and Dorothy Mae d'Encarnacao; m. Dwayne M. Bradley, Mar. 9, 2002; children: Christian, Sky. AA in Humanities, Riverside Cmty. Coll., 1994; BA in Social Sci., Calif. State U, San Bernadino, 1998; AS in Early Childhood Studies, Riverside Cmty. Coll., 2001. Internship San Bernardino (Calif.) Superior Ct., 1997; social svc. coord. NAACP, Riverside, Calif., 1999, site supr., 1999, Riverside (Calif.) County Office of Edn., 1999—; internship - Summer R.C.C. Early Childhood, 1999. Program dir. cert., 2001; reg. Profl. Growth Adv. County Comm. on Tchg. Credentialing, Calif. Chairperson Students For Peace & Social Justices Riverside Cmty. Coll., 1991. Mem.: Blue Print for Vol. Diversity. Christian. Avocations: serving the Lord, writing, civil rights, law. Home: 24109 Fir Ave 92553 Office: 3939 13th St Riverside CA 92502

DENCE, EDWARD WILLIAM, JR., lawyer, banker; b. Newport, R.I., Feb. 25, 1938; s. Edward William and Dorothea Margaret (Conway) D.; m. Claire A. Guertin, Nov. 14, 1970; children: Suzanne Lynn, Christine Anne. AB summa cum laude, Providence Coll., 1959; LL.B., Harvard U., 1963. Bar: Mass. 1963, R.I. 1965. Atty. New Eng. Electric System, 1963-68; sec., gen. counsel Fleet Boston Fin. Corp., Providence, 1968-85, v.p., mem. mgmt. com., 1980-85, Ropes & Gray, Providence, 1985-92, Edwards & Angell, Providence, 1992—. Mem. stockholders' adv. com. Fed. Res. Bank, Boston, 1976-77 Mem. R.I. Commn. Inter-Govtl. Rels., 1970-71; chmn. Sargent Rehab. Ctr., 1991-92; bd. dirs. R.I. Pub. Expenditure Coun., 1969-85, R.I. Bar Found.; mem. Providence Roman Cath. Diocesan Bd. Edn., 1970-73; trustee, chmn. audit com., chmn. compensation com. St. Joseph Hosp.; trustee So. New Eng. Rehab. Ctr. Named One of Outstanding Young Men in Am., 1972 Mem. R.I. Bar Assn., Boston Bar Assn. (program chmn. banking com.). Home: 1485 High Hawk Rd East Greenwich RI 02818-1364 E-mail: edence@ealaw.com.

DENCH, JUDITH OLIVIA, actress; b. York, Eng., Dec. 9, 1934; d. Reginald Arthur and Eleanora Olave (Jones) D.; m. Michael Williams, Feb. 5, 1971; 1 child, Tara Cressida Frances. Student, Ctrl. Sch. Speech Tng.; LittD (hon.), Warwick U., 1978, York U., 1983. Theatrical appearances include: (Old Vic) Hamlet, Midsummer Night's Dream, Twelfth Night, 1957-58, The Importance of Being Earnest, As You Like It, Romeo and Juliet, 1959-61; (Venice Festival) Romeo and Juliet (Paladino d'Argentino), 1961; (Royal Shakespeare Co., Stratford) The Cherry Orchard, Measure for Measure, Midsummer Night's Dream, A Penny for a Song, 1961-62; (Oxford Playhouse) The Alchemist, The Three Sisters, Romeo and Jeanette, 1964; (Oxford and London) The Promise, 1966-67; (London) Sally Bowles in Cabaret, 1968; (Royal Shakespeare Co., London) Twelfth Night, A Winter's Tale, London Assurance, 1970; (Royal Shakespeare Co., Stratford) The Merchant of Venice, The Duchess of Malfi, 1971; tour of Japan with Twelfth Night, 1972; (London) London Assurance, 1973; (Oxford and London) The Wolf, 1974; (London) The Good Companions, 1974-75, The Gay Lord Quex, 1975; (Royal Shakespeare Co., Stratford) Much Ado About Nothing, The Comedy of Errors, Macbeth (SWET Best Actress award for Lady Macbeth), King Lear, 1976-77; Cymbeline, 1979; (Royal Shakespeare Co., London) Pillars of the Community, The Way of the World, 1977-78, (Aldwych) Juno and the Paycock (SWET Best Actress award, Evening Std. Drama award for best actress, Plays and Players award for Best Actress, Variety Club award Actress of Yr.), 1981, A Kind of Alaska, The Importance of Being Earnest (Std. Best Actress award, Plays and Players award for best actress), Pack of Lies (Plays and Players award, SWET Best Actress award), Mr. and Mrs. Nobody, 1988, Antony and Cleopatra (Olivier award, Evening Std. Drama award, Drama mag. award), Gertrude in Hamlet, The Cherry Orchard, 1989, 90, The Blough and the Stars, The Sea, Coriolanus, 1992, The Gift of the Gorgon, 1992-93, The Seagull, 1994, Filumena in London, 1998, Amy's View in New York, 1999, The Royal Family, 2001, The Breath of Life, 2002; dir. plays Much Ado About Nothing, Look Back in Anger, The Boys from Syracuse, Romeo and Juliet; TV appearances include: Major Barbara, Talking to a Stranger (Best TV Actress of Yr. award 1967), Jackanory, Luther, Nieghbours, Marching Song, Days to Come, The Comedy of Errors, Macbeth, Village Wooing, Love in a Cold Climate, A Fine Romance, The Cherry Orchard, Going Gently, Saigon, Mr. and Mrs. Edgehill, 1988 (ACE award), Ghosts, Make and Break, Behaving Badly, Can You Hear Me Thinking, Torch, Absolute Hell (Oliver award Best Actress 1996), As Time Goes By: films: He Who Rides a Tiger, A Study in Terror, Four in the Morning (Brit. Film Acad. Most Promising Newcomer award 1965), A Midsummer Night's Dream, The Third Secret, Dead Cert, Wetherby, 1985, A Room with a View, 84 Charing Cross Road, A Handful of Dust (Brit. Acad. Film and TV Arts award 1989), Henry V, 1989, Jack & Sarah, 1994, Golden Eye, 1995, A Little Night Music, 1995 (Oliver award Best Actress in a Musical 1996), Mrs. Brown (Brit. Acad. Film and TV Arts Sctoland award 1997, Critics Circle Film award 1997, Golden Globe award for best actress 1997, Acad. award nomination 1997), Amy's View, 1997 (Critics Circle Drama award 1997), Tomorrow Never Dies, 1997, Shakespeare in Love, 1998 (Acad. award Best Supporting Actress 1998), Tea With Mussolini, 1999, The World is Not Enough, 1999, The Last of the Blond Bombshells, 2000, Chocolat, 2000, Iris, 2002 (BAFTA award best actress), The Shipping News, 2002, The Importance of Being Ernest, 2002, Die Another Day, 2002. Recipient Rothermore award for lifetime achievement, 1997, Critics Circle award for outstanding svc. to the arts, Acad. Award for Best Supporting Actress for Shakespeare in Love, 1999, Tony Award for Best Actress in Amy's View; decorated Order Brit. Empire; Dame Comdr. Brit. Empire; named UK Entertainment Personality of Yr. Variety, 1999, Walpole medal, N.Y., 2000, Benjamin Franklin medal, Royal Soc. Arts, London, 2000, Golden Globe award for best supporting actress in Chocolat, 2000; BAFTA fellow, 2001. Mem. Religious Soc. Friends.

DENCKER, LESTER J. lawyer; b. Milw., Apr. 27, 1914; s. Charles W. and Barbara M. (Haubert) D.; m. Cecilia F. Wellington, June 17, 1944. PhB, Marquette U., 1938, JD, 1940. Bar: Wis. 1940, U.S. Dist. Ct. (ea. and we. dists.) Wis. 1940, U.S. Supreme Ct. 1954, U.S. Ct. Appeals (7th cir.) 1973. Pvt. practice, Milw. Treas. Milw. Bar Found. Mem. Wis. regional bd. Nat. Conf. for Cmty. Justice, from 1999; Pres. adv. coun. to mayor City of Milw., 1954, sec. mcpl. mass transp. com., 1954—55, mem. July 4 com., 1957—62; chmn. bd. trustees Milwaukee County War Meml. Corp., 1989; pres. Upper Fond du Lac Capitol Drive Advancement Assn., 1958—60. Recipient Disting. Pub. Svc. award Milwaukee County Bd. Suprs., 1994, Standing Ovation award Greater Milw. Conv. and Visitors Bur., 1997; knight comdr. Equestrian Order of Holy Sepulchre of Jerusalem, 1985. Mem. ABA, Am. Judicature Soc., State Bar Assn. Wis. (emeritus), Milw. Bar Assn. (chmn. spkrs. bur. 1957-59, memls. com. 1964-94, Spl. Svc. award 1998), St. Thomas More Lawyers Soc. (pres. 1974), CBI Vets. Assn. (co-founder, 1st nat. comdr. 1948-49), Marquette U. Law Alumni Assn. (pres. 1953-54), VFW (life), Elks. (exalted ruler Milw. 1965), Lions (pres. Milw. 1954), Am. Legion (commdr. 1999-2000). Home: Milwaukee, Wis. Died Oct. 7, 2002; Milw..

DENDAHL, JOHN, political organization administrator; Chmn. Rep. Party N.Mex., Albuquerque, 1994—. Office: Rep Party NMex 2901 Juan Tabo Blvd NE Ste 116 Albuquerque NM 87112-1885 Fax: 505-292-0755.

DENDINGER, WILLIAM J. career officer, chaplain; BA in Philosophy and English, Immaculate Conception Sem., 1961; MA in Theology, Aquinas Inst., 1964; MS in Counseling, Creighton U., 1969; student, Squadron Officer Sch., 1973; postgrad., Sch. Applied Theology, 1978; student, Air War Coll., 1987. Commd. capt. USAF, 1970, advanced through grades to maj. gen., 1997; base chaplain Maxwell AFB, Ala., 1970-72, Yokota Air Base, Japan, 1972-74; cadet wing chaplain USAF Acad., Colorado Springs, Colo., 1974-78; base chaplain Osan Air Base, S. Korea, 1979-80, Mather AFB, Calif., 1980-82; mem. chaplain resource bd. USAF Chaplain Svc. Inst., Maxwell AFB, 1982-85; base chaplain Hahn Air Base, W. Germany, 1985-88; plans and programs officer then chief plans/programs div. Office Air Force Chief Chaplains, Bolling AFB, D.C., 1988-93; command chaplain Hdqs. Air Combat Command, Langley AFB, Va., 1993-95; dep. chief Air Force Chaplain Svc. Hdqs. USAF, Washington, 1995-97, chief Air Force Chaplain Svc., 1997—. Decorated Legion of Merit with oak leaf cluster. Named Prelate of Honor with title of Rev. Monsignor, His Holiness Pope John Paul II, 1994. Office: HQ USAF/HC 112 Luke Ave SW Ste 316 Bolling AFB DC 20332-5113

DENDLER, ROYCE, painter, sculptor, writer; b. Berwick, Pa., Jan. 14, 1941; s. Ralph and Fay Dendler; m. Sue Deming (div. June 1969); m. Olga Dendler; 1 child, C. BA, Gettysburg Coll., 1962; BFA, MFA, Yale U.; PhD, NYU, 1969. Home and Studio: 5012 Mount Rd Bristol VT 05443

DENDY, MARK, choreographer; BFA, N.C. Sch. Arts, 1983. Past young artist scholar Am. Dance Festival; founder Mark Dendy, Dance and Theatre, N.Y.C., 1983—. Performer: (plays) In Between; choreographer (films) Franchesca Page, 1997, theatre Ballet I, 1990, Symmetries, 1994, Les Biches, 1997, Roman (1) Dream Analysis, Afternoon and the Faunes, 1998. Recipient Sustained Achievement in Arts award, Nat. Soc. Arts and Letters; NEA choreographer fellow. Office: 279 E Houston St Apt 2B New York NY 10002-1033

DENEEN, PATRICK JOHN, political scientist, educator; b. Hartford, Conn., July 21, 1964; s. Richard P. and Irene M. (Dionne) Deneen; m. Inge M. Herre, Aug. 7, 1993; children: Francis Carey, Adrian John, Alexandra Marie. BA in English, Rutgers U., 1986, PhD in Polit. Sci., 1995. Spl. adv. to dir. U.S. Info. Agy., Washington, 1995-97. Educator Princeton (N.J.) U., 1997—. Author: The Odyssey of Political Theory, 2000. Recipient Leo Strauss award Am. Polit. Sci. Assn., 1995, fellow Earhart Found., 1999, 2001-02, scholar Pew Evangelical, 1999-2000. Office: Dept Politics Princeton U Princeton NJ 08544-0001 E-mail: pdeneen@princeton.edu.

DENEGALL, JOHN PALMER, JR., construction executive; b. Tarrytown, N.Y., Mar. 21, 1959; s. John P. Sr. and Edna D. (Kirkaldy) Denegall; m. Johnnie Lou Jarrett, Feb. 27, 1982 (div.); children: John P. III, Revisa Taylor. Student, Westchester C.C., Vahalla, N.Y., 1977-80. Notary Pub.: N.Y. 2001. Mgr. Elmsford (N.Y.) Raceway Inc., 1976-80, Radio Shack, Yorktown Heights, NY, 1980—81; ins. claims adjuster Liberty Mut. Ins. Co., N.Y.C., 1981-85; sr. ins. claims rep. Crum & Forster Comml. Ins., N.Y.C., 1985-96; v.p., risk mgr. City Wide Asphalt Paving Co. Inc., Bklyn., 1996-99; v.p. Nico Asphalt Paving Inc., Bklyn., 1999—. Arbitrator Ins. Arbitration Forum, N.Y.C., 1986; pres. Denegall Properties, Inc., Jamaica, NY, 1986—89, Eva's Laundry Inc., Bronx, NY, 1989—94. Republican. Presbyterian. Avocations: bicycling, auto racing, basketball. E-mail: nicoasphaltjohn@aol.com.

DENEGRE, GEORGE, lawyer; b. New Orleans, Oct. 10, 1923; s. Thomas Bayne and Alma (Baldwin) D.; m. Gayle Stocker, Oct. 4, 1950; children: Stanhope Bayne-Jones, Gayle Stocker Felchlin, George, John Gayle. BA, Yale U., 1943; LLB, Tulane U., 1948. Bar: La. 1948. With firm Chaffe, McCall, Toler & Philips, 1948-49; assoc. Jones, Walker Waechter, Poitevent, Carrère & Denègre, New Orleans, 1949-52; ptnr. Jones, Walker, Waechter, Poitevent, Carrère & Denègre, 1951—2002. Sec., dir. Canal Barge Co., Inc., 1951-2002; sec., dir. Cen. Gulf Lines, Inc., 1958-99; sec. Internat. Shipholding Corp., 1978-99; dir. G.H. Tichenor Antiseptic Co., 1966-2002. Bd. dirs. Met. Crime Commn., 1966-02, Eugenie and Joseph Jones Family Found., 1963-93, Bus. Task Force for Edn., New Orleans Neighborhood Devel. Found., 1989-90, New Orleans Regional Med. Ctr., La. Assn. Mental Health, 1953-77, pres., 1960-61; bd. dirs., sec., exec. com., pres. World Trade Ctr.; bd. govs. Tulane Med. Ctr., 1969-83, vice-chmn., 1977-82, chmn., 1983; vice-chmn., bd. adminstrs. Tulane U., 1980-93; bd. dirs. Chamber New Orleans and River Region, chmn., 1991; vice-chmn. bd. dirs. Met. Arts Fund, 1989-90, New Orleans Coun.-Navy League U.S.; bd. dirs., sec. Bus. Coun., 1986-2001; mem. bd., exec. com. Pub. Affairs Rsch. Coun.; sec. La. Coun. for Fiscal Reform, 1987-96; bd. commrs. Downtown Devel. Dist., 1989-95, chmn., 1992; co-chmn. Mayor's Found. for Edn., 1987-91; chmn. Mayor's Com. for Charity Hosp.; founding mem. La.

Partnership for Innovation and Tech. Metrovision Partnership; sec. bd. dirs. Orleans Intercmty. Coun.; vice-dean Consular Corps, 1988-91; Com. 100, 1993-95, Select Com. on Revenues and Expenditures in La. Future (SECURE), 1993-95; adv. bd. Coll. Bus. Adminstrn., U. New Orleans, 1994-96; mem. Com. for Better New Orleans. Lt. USNR, 1943-46. Hon. Consul of India, 1977-2002; Rex, King of Carnival, 1986. Mem. La. Bar Assn., New Orleans Bar Assn., Maritime Bar Assn., Boston Club of New Orleans, Pickwick Club, La. Club, New Orleans Country Club, Stratford Club. Home: 1525 Webster St New Orleans LA 70118-6134 Office: Jones Walker Waechter Poitevent Carrere Denegre 201 Saint Charles Ave New Orleans LA 70170-5100 E-mail: gdenegre@joneswalker.com.

DENENBERG, HERBERT SIDNEY, journalist, lawyer, former state official; b. Omaha, Nov. 20, 1929; s. David Aaron and Fannie (Rothenberg) Denenberg; m. Naomi N. Glushakow, June 22, 1958. BS, Johns Hopkins U., 1958; JD, Creighton U., 1954; LLM, Harvard U., 1959; PhD, U. Pa., 1962; LLD, Allentown Coll. St. Francis de Sales, 1989; LHD, Spring Garden Coll., 1992. CLU, CPCU. Mem. firm Denenberg & Denenberg, Omaha, 1954—55; asst. prof. ins. U. Iowa, Iowa City, 1962, Wharton Sch. Fin. and Commerce, U. Pa., 1962—65, assoc. prof., 1965—68, Harry J. Loman prof. ins., 1968—73; commr. ins. State of Pa., 1971—74; commr. Pa. Pub. Utility Commn., 1975; columnist Phila. Bull., 1975—79; consumer columnist Phila. Daily News, 1979—81, Phila. Jour., 1981—82, Del. County Daily and Sunday Times, 1987—90, Bucks County Courier Times, 1987—90, Pottstown Mercury, 1988—94, Burlington County Daily Times, 1987—90, Reading Eagle, 1989—, Doylestown Patriot, 1991—, Citizen's Choice of Wilkes-Barre, Pa., 1992—, Mainliner, 1992—94, Auto Insider, 1992—93, Collector's Guide, 1992—93, New Chester Jour., 1992—94, Del. County Bus. Monthly, 1993—96, Hellenic News, 1993—, 1994, Phoenixville, Phoenix, 1994—96, Eastern Poconos Cmty. News, 1999—; editor The Denenberg Report Orgn., 1999—; consumer and investigative reporter Adelphia Cable Update Cable Sys., 1999—2000, Sta. WCAU-TV (NBC), Phila., 1975—98; talk show host Sta. WCAU-AM CBS, Phila., 1976—80; consumer reporter WLVT-TV (PBS), 2001—. Columnist Sales and Mktg. Mag., 1976—80, Ins. Monitor, Hyderalnd, India; regular on Real People NBC-TV, 1979—80; consumer reporter Nat. Pub. Radio, 1979; spl. counsel, rsch. dir. Pres.'s Nat. Adv. Panel on Ins. in Riot-Affected Areas., 1967—68; spl. adviser to Gov. Pa. on consumer affairs, 1974—75; assoc. dir. Wis. Ins. Laws Rev. Project, 1966—71; cons. Dept. Labor, 1965—68, Coop. Devel. Adminstrn., PR, 1967—68, John F. Kennedy Ctr., Washington, 1966—71, Small Bus. Adminstrn., 1968—71, Dept. Justice, 1969, FTC, 1968, Dept. Transp., 1969—70, State of Nev., 1969—71, Alaska Legislature, 1976, U.S. Commn. Civil Rights, 1977—78, Concerned Physicians for Patient Care; spl. cons. to Mayor Washington, 1968—69; mem. Bd. of Health Promotion and Disease Prevention of Inst. Medicine NAS, 1973—74, mem., 1973—; vis. prof. law Temple U.; adj. prof. ins., info. sci. and tech. Cabrini Coll., 1999—; rsch. fellow Sapio Inst. Interactive Learning, 1999—. Author (with others): (book) Risk and Insurance, 2d edit., 1973; author: (with Spencer L. Kimball) Insurance Government and Social Policy, 1969; author: (with J.R. Ferrari) Life Insurance and/or Mutual Funds, 1967; author: (with S.L. Kimball) Mass Marketing of Property and Liability Insurance, 1970; author: The Insurance Trap, 1972, Shopper's guide to Surgery, 1972, Shopper's Guide to Dentistry, 1973, Shopper's Guide to Insurance on Mobile Homes, 1973, A Citizens Bill of Hospital Rights, 1973, Shopper's guide to Bankruptcy, 1974, Shopper's guide Book, 1974, Herb Denenberg's Smart Shopper's Guide, 1980, Shopper's guide to Medical Equipment, 1990, A Consumer's Guide to Herbal Medicines, 1999, Guide to Selecting a Pharmacist, 1999; columnist, mem. editl. bd. Caveat Emptor, 1971—79, mem. adv. bd. medicine and health newsletter The Dr.'s People, 1989—93. Mem. adminstrv. bd. S.S. Huebner Found., 1968—71; pres. Am. Risk and Ins. Assn., 1969—70; Dem. candidate U.S. Senate, 1974; bd. dirs. Consumers Union, 1973—76; bd. trustees Ctr. for Proper Medication Use, 1994—. 1st lt. JAGC U.S. Army, 1955—58. Named to Phila. Press Club Hall of Fame, 1995; recipient awards for articles, Jour. Risk and Ins., Lambert award, 1972, Nat. Press Club award, 1976, 1977, 1980, 1984, 1988, Journalism award, Am. Osteo. Assn., 1976, Am. Chiropractors Assn., 1977—80, 1988, citation, Columbia U., Media award, ATLA, 1986, Enterprise Reporting award, Phila. Press Club, 1986, 1987, 1999, Pub. Svc. award, 1987, 1989, 1996, 1997, 1999, Best Feature award, 1995, 1996, 1997, Spot News award, 1999, award for lifetime achievement, 1998, Gov.'s Hwy. Safety award, State of Pa., 1997, Enterprise Reporting award, Pa. AP, 1988, Nat. Headliner award, 1987—88, 1990, 1992, 40 Emmy awards, Best TV Pub. Svc. award, Soc. Profl. Journalists, 1987, 1988, 1990, 1992, 1993, 1994, 1998, 1999, TV Feature award, 1989, 1994, 1995, 1996, 1997, 1998, TV Mag. Feature award, 1989, 1992, Best Media Criticism, 1990, 1993, Best Investigation, 1990, 1992, 1993, 1994, 1995, 1996, 1997, 1998, 1999, Best Health and Sci. Report, 1995—99, Breaking News award, 1998, Outstanding Media Consumer Svc. award, Consumer Fedn. Am., 1990, Sam Beber Disting. AZA Alumnus award, B'nai B'rith, 1990, Outstanding Citizen award, Firemen's Assn. Pa., 1991, Consumer of Yr. award, Pa. Assn. Weights and Measures, 1991, Phila. award integrity in journalism, 1988, Award of Excellence in legal reporting and analysis, Am. Bd. Trial Advocates, 1996, Award of Lifetime Achievement, Phila. Press Club, 1998, Award for Excellence in Legal Reporting and Analysis, Am. Bd. Trial Advocates, 1996, Phila. Press Club award for lifetime achievement, 1998, others, Am. Bd. Trial Advocates award, 1996. Mem.: ABA (life), Internat. Assn. Ins. Law (v.p. sci. sect. Am. chpt. 1967—71), Med. Soc. Access to Physicians (blue ribbon panel Phila. County 1998—), Am. Risk and Ins. Assn. (2nd v.p. 1967—68, bd. dirs. 1967—71, pres. 1969—70), Montgomery County Bar Assn., Pa. Bar Assn., Old Clunker Club (founder, pres. 1982—). Home: PO Box 7301 Saint Davids PA 19087-7301 E-mail: hdenenberg@aol.com. *Our governmental system is designed to make politicians fat and special interests groups rich. Government has become our number "one" consumer fraud. As a government official, educator, and author I have attempted to make government work for people instead of for special interests and politicians only. I have been willing to make waves and rock boats. I have tried to show that government can help people.*

DENERY, DALLAS G. aeronautical engineer, researcher; b. Detroit, May 10, 1939; s. Herman and W. L. (Dallas) Denery; m. Sharon K. Keegan, July 13, 1963; children: Dallas G. II, Celia A., John P. BS in Engring., U. Mich., 1962; MS in Engring., U. Washington, 1965; PhD, Stanford U., 1971. Aerospace engr. Boeing Co., Seattle, 1962—66, NASA Ames Rsch. Ctr., Moffett Field, Calif., 1966—81, chief guidance and naval br., 1981—95, dep. chief aviation sys. divsn., 1995—. Dr. Hugh L. Dryden Meml. fellow, Nat. Space Club, 1979. Fellow: AIAA; mem.: Sigma Xi. Achievements include development of avionics for two-segment noise abatement approaches, method for extracting parameter estimates from dynamic sys. that is insensitive to initial parameter estimates and air traffic control automation. Home: 12611 Larchmont Ave Saratoga CA 95070 Office: NASA Ames Rsch Ctr MS 210-4 Moffett Field CA 94035 Fax: 650-604-0752. Personal E-mail: denery@msn.com.

DENES, AGNES C. environmental artist; b. Budapest, Hungary, 1931; Student, CCNY, New Sch. Social Research, Columbia U., 1964-66; DFA, Ripon Coll., 1994. Lectr. NYU, 1971, CUNY, 1972, 76Oberlin (Ohio) Coll., 1973, N.Y. Inst. Tech., N.Y.C., 1973, Corcoran Sch. Art, Washington, 1973, 74, U. Mass. Amherst, 1974, Ohio Wesleyan U., Delaware, 1974, Pratt Inst., N.Y.C., 1974, 76, 81, Ohio State U., Columbus, 1974, Moore Coll. Art, Phila., 1974, San Francisco Art Inst., 1975, 76, Kensington Arts Assn., Toronto, 1975, U. Calif., Berkeley, 1976, 90, U. Akron, Ohio, 1976, San Jose (Calif.) State U., 1976, Pratt Inst., N.Y.C., 1976, Newport Harbor Art Mus., Newport Bch., Calif., 1976, 81, Rutgers U., New Brunswick, N.J., 1976, Temple U., Phila., 1977, Art Gallery, Toronto, 1977, UCLA, 1978, Birmingham Poly. Inst., Eng., 1978, Rochester (N.Y.) Inst. Tech., 1979, St. Laurence U., Canton, N.Y., 1980, 82, Hunter Coll., N.Y.C., 1980, 81, MIT, Cambridge, Mass., 1980, Skidmore Coll., Saratoga Springs, N.Y., 1980, Wabash Coll., Crawfordsville, Ind., 1983, Miami (Fla.)-Dade C.C., 1984, Harvard U., Cambridge, Mass., 1984, Cooper Union Advancement Sci. and Art, N.Y.C., 1985, U. Hawaii, Honolulu, 1985, 1993, U. Genoa, Italy, 1986, Nat. Inst. Fine Arts, Guadalajara, Mex., 1986, U.N.D., Grand Forks, 1989, Architects House, Moscow, 1990, Fla. State U., Tallahassee, 1991, Royal Acad., Stockholm, 1992, Fine Arts Acad., Helsinki, Finland, 1992, Cornell U., Ithaca, N.Y., 1993, SUNY Albany, 1993, Great Hall, Cooper Union, 1993, 99, 2000, Boston U., 1994, Tufts U, Medford, Mass., 1995, Kansas City Art Inst. Mo., 1995, SUNY Potsdam, N.Y., 1996, U. Sao Paulo, Brazil (Visual Arts Congress), 1996, San Franciso Art Inst., 1997, N. Tex. U., Denton, 1997, Modern Art Mus., Ft. Worth, Tex., 1997, Centro Studi Americani, Rome, Italy, 1998, Pusan Met. Mus., Korea, 1998, Chinese Cultural Ctr., N.Y., 1999, Fort Asperen Found., Holland, 2000, Bayly Art Mus., U. Va., Charlottesville, 1999, Carnegie Mellon U., Pittsburgh, 1999, Russian State U. Humanities, Moscow, 2001, Modern Art Mus., Ft. Worth, Tex., 2002, Herron Sch. Art, U. Ind., Indianapolis, 2003, CAA Coll. Art Assn.Conf., N.Y., 2003, Haggerty Mus. Art, Marquette U., Milwaukee, 2003, Naples Mus. Art, Fla., 2004; vis. critic sch. archtecture U. Pa., 1991; tchr. art Sch. Visual Arts, N.Y.C., 1974-79, San Francisco Art Inst., 1976, Skowhegan (Maine) Sch. Painting and Sculpture, 1979, Universita degli Studi di Genoa, Italy, 1986, Hartford (Conn.) Art Sch., 1988; speaker at numerous global confs. One-person shows include Columbia U., N.Y.C., 1965, Ruth White Gallery, N.Y.C., 1968, A.I.R. Gallery, N.Y.C., 1972, Ohio State U., Columbus, 1974, Corcoran Gallery Art, Washington, 1974, Stefanotty Gallery, N.Y.C., 1975, U. Akron, Ohio, 1976, Newport Harbor Art Mus., Newport Beach, Calif., 1976, Rutgers U., 1976, 112 Green St. Gallery, N.Y.C., 1977, Temple U., 1977, Centre Culturel Americain, Paris, 1978, Franklin Furnace, N.Y.C., 1978, Ikon Gallery, Birmingham, Eng., 1978, Amerika Haus, Berlin, 1978, Studio d'Arte Cannaviello, Milan, 1979, Inst. Contemporary Art, London, 1979, Gallerie Aronowitsch, Stockholm, 1980, Galleriet, Lund, Sweden, 1980, Elise Meyer Gallery, N.Y.C., 1980, 81, MIT, 1980, Kunsthalle, Nurnberg, Germany, 1982, No. Ill. U. Art Gallery, Chgo., 1985, U. Hawaii Art Gallery, 1985, Ricardo Barreto Arte Contemporaneo, Guadalajara, Mex., 1986, Arts Club Chgo., 1990, Anselmo Alvarez Galeria de Arte, Madrid, Spain, 1990, Cornell U., Ithaca, N.Y., 1992, Wynn Kramarsky, N.Y.C., 1994, Joyce Goldstein Gallery, N.Y., 1995 & 1997, Gibson Gallery, SUNY Potsdam, N.Y., 1996, View Gallery, N.Y., 1997, Gallerie Il Bulino, Rome, 1998, Samek Gallery, Bucknell U., Lewisburg, Pa., 2003, Herron Sch. Art, Indiana U., 2003, Haggerty Mus. Art, Marquette U., Milwaukee, 2003, Naples Art Mus., Fla., 2004; group exhbns. include Hundred Acres Gallery, N.Y.C., 1970, Nat. Acad. Galleries, N.Y.C., 1970, 80, Dwan Gallery, N.Y.C., 1970, Jewish Mus., N.Y.C., 1970, Finch Coll. (N.Y.) Mus., 1971, Whitney Mus. Art, N.Y.C., 1971, 73, 76, Mus. Modern Art, Buenos Aires, 1971, Mus. Fine Arts, Santiago, Chile, 1971, Inst. Contemporary Art, Lima, Peru, 1971, NYU, 1972, Albion Coll., Mich., 1972, N.Y. Cultural Ctr., N.Y.C., 1972, 73, Kent State U., 1972, Oberlin Coll., 1972, N.Y. Inst. Tech., N.Y.C., 1972, Bklyn. Mus., 1972, 76, 80, Kunsthaus, Hamburg, Germany, 1972, Pace Coll., 1973, 78, Mus. Modern Art, 1973, 77, Kunstverein, Berlin, 1973, Calif. Inst. Arts, Valencia, Calif., 1973, Wadsworth Atheneum, Hartford, Conn., 1973, Kunsthalle, Cologne, 1974, Indpls. Mus., Ofart, Ind., 1974, San Francisco Mus. Art, 1974, Stadtisches Mus., Leverkusen, Germany, 1975, Grey Art Gallery N.Y.U., 1975, Inst. Contemporary Art, U. Pa., Phila., 1975, Michael C. Rockefeller Arts Ctr., Fredonia, N.Y., 1976, Arts Gallery, New South Wales, Sydney, Australia, 1976, Mus. Natural Hist., N.Y.C., 1977, Documenta VI, Kassel, Germany, 1977, Cleve. State U., 1977, Venice Biennale, Italy, 1978, 80, Yale U. Art Gallery, New Haven, 1978, Leo Castelli Gallery, N.Y.C., 1978, Rose Esman Gallery, N.Y.C., 1978, 79, Nat. Gallery, Wellington, Australia, 1978, Mus. Contemporary Arts, Brisbane, Australia, 1978, Seibu Art Mus., Tokyo, 1979, Gallerie AIX, Stockholm, 1979, Ackland Art Mus., Chapel Hill, N.C., 1979, Kunstmuseum, Berne, Switzerland, 1979, Mus. Ludwig, Cologne, 1979, Gulbenkiam Found., Lisbon, Portugal, 1979, Museo Espanol de Arte Contemporaneo, Madrid, 1979, Tel Aviv Mus., 1979, Vienna Mus. des 20 Jahrhunderts, Austria, 1979, New Mus., N.Y.C., 1980, Albright Coll., Reading, Pa., 1980, 81, Wright State U., Dayton, Ohio, 1980, U. Pa., 1980, Kunstforeninger Mus., Copenhagen, 1980, Biblioteca Nacional, Madrid, 1980, Musee Nat. d'art Moderne, Paris, 1980, Museo de Arte Contemporanea, Brazil, 1980, Rutgers U., 1981, 86, Hofstra U., N.Y.C., 1981, 92, Aldrich Mus. Contemporary Art, Ridgefield, Conn., 1981, Palais des Beaux Arts, Brussels, 1981, U. Colo. Art Galleries, Boulder, 1981, Toledo (Ohio) Mus. Art, 1981, Galerie Nacional de Arte Moderna, Lisbon, 1981, New Gallery Contemporary Art, Cleve., 1981, Galleriet, Lund, Sweden, 1982, Nat. Acad. Design, N.Y.C., 1982, Va. Commonwealth U., Richmond, 1982, John Michael Kohler Art Ctr., Sheboygan, Wis., 1982, San Francisco Mus. Modern Art, 1983, Osaka U. Arts, Japan, 1983, Tacoma (Wash.) Art Mus., 1983, Nat. Mus. Art, Smithsonian Inst., Washington, 1984, 85, San Antonio Mus. Assn., 1984, Dayton (Ohio) Art Inst., 1984, Rhona Hoffman Gallery, Chgo., 1984, Germans van Eck Gallery, N.Y.C., 1984, Bard Coll., N.Y., 1984, 90, Ronald Feldman Fine Arts, N.Y.C., 1984, Am. Inst. Arts & Letters, 1985, 86, Moderna Museet, Stockholm, 1985, Rosemont (Pa.) Coll., 1985, Bass Mus. Art, Miami Bch., Fla., 1985, Winnipeg (Can.) Art Gallery, 1985, Anchorage (Alaska) Hist. & Fine Arts Mus., 1985, U. Minn., Duluth, 1985, Stamford (Conn.) Mus., 1985, Nurnburg, Kunsthalle, Germany, 1986, Print Club, Phila., 1986, Museo de Artes Moderno La Tertulia, Cali, Colombia, 1986, Santa Maria di Castello, Genoa, Italy, 1986, Ethnographic Mus., Belgrade, Yugoslavia, 1986, Nat. Acad. Design, N.Y.C., 1987, Circulo de Bellas Artes, Madrid, 1987, Kolnischer Kunstverein, Cologne, 1987, Goteborgs Kontsmuseum, Sweden, 1987, Sonya Henie-Neils Onstad Found., Hovikodden, Norway, 1987, Minn. Mus. Art, St. Paul, 1987, Kjarvalsstadir, Reykjavik, Iceland, 1987, Circulo de Bellas Artes, Madrid, 1987, Museu de Arte, Sao Paulo, Brazil, 1987, Cin. Art Mus., 1989, Denver Art Mus., 1989, 91, Pa. Acad. Fine Arts, Phila., 1989, L.I. U., Brookville, N.Y., 1989, Brandeis U., Waltham, Mass., 1991, Mus. Contemporary Art, Helsinki, Finland, 1992, The Mus. Tampere, Finland, 1992, Art Gallery, Hamilton, Can., 1992, Expo '92, Moguer, Spain, 1992, Laumeier Sculpture Park & Gallery, St. Louis, 1993, Dallas Mus. Nat. Hist., 1993, Epad, La Defénse, Paris, 1993, Tufts U., Medford, Mass., 1995, Rutgers U., 1996, Staatsgalerie, Stuttgart, Germany, 1997, Am. Acad., Rome, Biennale dei Parchi, Palazzo delle Esposizione, Rome, Wexner Ctr. for Arts, Ohio State U., Pusan Met. Arts Mus., Korea, 1998, Mus. Contemporary Art, L.A., 1999, Simmons Visual Art Ctr., Grenau U., Gainesville, Ga., 1998, Nat. Mus. Women in Arts, Washington D.C., 1999, Mus. Contemporary Art (MOLA), Los Angeles, 1999, Contemporary Art Mus., Houston, 2000, Huntington Gallery, Mass.Coll. Art, Boston, 2000, Boulder Mus. Contemporary Art, Colo., 2000, Mus. Modern Art, N.Y.C., 2000 & 2001, Museo D'Art Contemporani (MACBA), Barcelona, 2000, Hayward Gallery, London, 2000, Achim Möller Gallery, N.Y., 2000, Denver Art Mus., Colo., 2000, Cooper Union Sch. Engring., N.Y., 2000, Ft. Asperen Found., The Netherlands, 2000, Venice Biennale, Italy, 2001, Herter Callery, U. Mass., Amherst, 2001, Göteborgs Internationalle Konstbiennal, Sweden, 2001, Gallery L, Moscow, 2001, Internat. Art Biennal, Buenos Aires Museo Nacional de Bellas Artes, Argentina, 2002, Ringling Sch. Art & Design, Sarasota, Fla., 2002, Contemporary Art Ctr., Cincinnati, Ohio, 2002, House of Docs Gallery, Sundance Film Festival, Utah, 2002; commns. and installations include Artpark, Lewiston, N.Y., 1977, 79, Container Corp. Am., Chgo., 1979, Manhattan Pub. Art Fund, N.Y.C., 1982, Dept. Cultural Affairs, Genoa, Italy, 1986, First Nat. Bank Chgo, N.Y.C., 1986-87, Am.- Scandinavian Found, Sweden, 1988-89, NSW Masterplan City of Berkeley, Calif., 1988-91, City of Chgo. Pub. Art Program, 1990-91, Internat. Ctr. Preservation Wild Animals, Columbus, Ohio, 1990-93, Ministry Environment & United Nations, Tree Mountain, Pinsiö gravel pit, Ylöjarvi, Finland, 1992-96, Mahtesh Ramon Crater, Israel, 1995, Mus. Contempory Art, Helsinki, Finland, 1992, Sheep, Am. Acad. Rome, Italy, 1998, A Forest for Australia, Melbourne, 1998, Poetry Walk, U. Va. Art Mus., Charlottesville, 2000, Nieuwe Hollandse Waterline, Ft. Asperen Found., Holland, 2000, Göteborgs Internat. Konstbiennal, Sweden, 2001, Venice Biennale, Italy, 2001; author: Paradox and Essence, 1976, Sculptures of the Mind, 1976, Isometric Systems in Isotropic Space: Map Projections, 1979, Book of Dust -- The Beginning and the End of Time and Thereafter, 1989, Notes on a Visual Philosophy in Symmetry-Unifying Human Understanding, 1986. Creative Artists Pub. Svc. grantee N.Y. State Coun. Arts, 1972, 74, 80, Visual Arts Program grantee, N.Y. State Coun. Arts, 1979, 84, The Thord-Gray Meml. Fund, Rsch. and Devel. grantee Am.-Scandinavian Found., 1987, Herbert F. Johnson Mus. Art Purchase prize Richard A. Florscheim Art Fund, 1992; Individual Artists fellow NEA, 1974, 75, 81, 89, Collaboration in Art, Sci. and Tech. fellow Syracuse U., 1977, Deutscher Akademischer Austausdienst fellow Berlin, 1978, Rsch. fellow Ctr. Advanced Visual Studies, MIT, 1980, Studio for Creative Inquiry, Carnegie-Mellon U., 1993—, fellow Carnegie Mellon U., 1993, Courant Inst., 1996, Am. Acad., Rome, Prize Fellow, 1998, 4 fellowships Nat. Endowment; recipient Nat. Drawing Competition Purchase prize Rutgers U., 1974, Internat. Women's Yr. award Internat. Women's Art Festival, 1975-76, Berthe Von Moschzisker prize Print Club, 1980, The Ann and Donald McPhail award Print Club, 1982, Hassam and Speicher Fund Purchase award Am. Acad. Arts & Letters, 1985, The Eugene McDermott Achievement award MIT Coun. for Arts, 1990, Young Lawyers Pub. Art award Chgo. Bar Assn., 1992, Watson award, 1999. Address: 595 Broadway New York NY 10012-3222

DENES, MICHEL JANET, physical therapist, rehabilitation consultant; b. Detroit, Apr. 29, 1950; d. Seymore Bernard and Clarine (Stierer) Swartz; m. George Denes, Jan. 22, 1984; 1 child, Zachary Todd. BS in Phys. Therapy, U. Mich., 1972. Cert. phys. therapy, neuro-devel. treatment in adult hemiplegia. Staff phys. therapist Sinai Hosp. of Detroit, 1972-77, supr., phys. therapist, 1977-78, chief phys. therapy supr., 1979-88; phys. therapist Rehab. Physicians, P.C., Birmingham, Mich., 1989; phys. therapy cons. closed head injury program Spl. Tree Rehab. Sys., Birmingham, 1989-98; program devel. coord. Great Lakes Rehab. Hosp., Southfield, Mich., 1998—. Adj. instr. Coll. Allied Health Professions Wayne State U., Detroit, 1982—90; lectr. in field. Mem.: Am. Acad. Oral Medicine, Neurodevel. Treatment Assn. Avocations: tennis, travel, gardening, art, interior decorating. Office: Great Lakes Rehab Hosp 22401 Foster Winter Dr Southfield MI 48075-3724

DENES, RONNI CAROL, academic administrator; d. Herbert Spencer and Sylva S. (Srybnik) Shernoff; m. Steven George Denes, June 6, 1974; 1 child, Jesse Steven. BA, Am. U., 1968; MA, Columbia U., 1974. Tchr., curriculum developer N.Y.C. Bd. Edn., Bronx, 1968-80, policy analyst, writer, cons. N.Y.C., 1981-85; advt./pub. relations copywriter, cons. N.Y.C., 1981-84; dir. comm. Nat. Action Coun. for Minorities in Engring., Inc., N.Y.C., 1985-88, v.p. comm. and pub. relations, 1989-90, v.p. comm. and pub. affairs, 1991-93, v.p. rsch., policy and pub. affairs, 1994-96, sr. v.p. rsch. and ops. and asst. corp. sec., 1997-2000; v.p. external affairs The Cooper Union for Advancement of Sci. and Art, N.Y.C., 2000—. Dir. Oak Ridge (Tenn.) Assoc. Univs., 1999—, Jr. Engring. and Tech. Soc., 1985-96; commr. Engring. Workforce Commn., Washington, 1994-2000; com. on diversity engring. workforce Nat. Acad. Engring., Washington, 2000—. Editor: (with G. Campbell Jr. and C. Morrison) Access Denied: Race, Ethnicity and the Scientific Enterprise, 2000; editor-in-chief NACME Rsch. Letter, 1994-2000; contbr. articles to profl. jours.; exec. prodr. A New Institutional Vision, Nat. Tech. U., 1993, The Challenge: A Kid's Introduction to Engineering, NACME, 1993, America 2000: Education for a Competitive Workforce, PBS, La., 1992. Adv. bd. Houston Alliance for Minority Participation, 1999-2000; mem. study panel for sci. and engring. data 2000 NSF, Washington, 1999—; dir. East Harlem Coll. and Career Counseling Program, N.Y.C., 1986-88. Recipient Creativity '86 award Art Direction Mag., 1986, Apex award for pub. excellence Comm. Concepts, 1987; NSF grantee, 1994, 99. Mem. Am. Assn. Engring. Socs. (bd. govs., del. to engrs. pub. policy coun. 1994-2000), Commn. on Profls. in Sci. and Tech. (commr. 1996-2000). Avocations: skiing, travel, film, novels. Office: The Cooper Union for Advancement Sci/Art External Affairs 30 Cooper Sq New York NY 10003

DE NESNERA, ALEXANDER PETER, psychiatrist; b. Montclair, N.J., Feb. 9, 1957; s. Peter and Olia (Donn) de N.; m. Susan Carter Jarvis, May 30, 1987; 1 child, Christopher Lewis. Student, Johns Hopkins U., 1974-75; BA in Biology, NYU, 1978; diploma med. scis., St. George's U., Grenada, 1983; MD, Dartmouth Coll., 1986; cert. in med. mgmt., Carnegie-Mellon U., 2001. Diplomate Nat. Bd. Med. Examiners; diplomate Am. Bd. of Psychiatry and Neurology; cert. geriat. Psychiatry, Am. Bd. Addiction Psychiatry; cert. forensic psychiatry. Escort interpreter U.S. Dept. State, Washington, 1978-86; research asst. Rockefeller U., N.Y.C., 1980-81; resident in psychiatry Dartmouth Hitchcock Med. Ctr., Hanover, N.H., 1986-90; asst. med. dir. Weekend Intoxicated Driver Intervention Program, Hanover, 1987-88, med. dir., 1988-89; cons. psychiatrist Hanover Terrace Nursing Home, 1988-89; cons. psychiatrist Alzheimer's disease clinic Mary Hitchcock Meml. Hosp., Hanover, 1988-89; staff psychiatrist Nashua (N.H.) Brookside Hosp., 1988-90; asst. prof. psychiatry Dartmouth Coll., 1990—; staff psychiatrist New Hampshire Hosp., 1990—, pres. med. orgn., 2000—; dir. forensic psychiatry fellowship N.H. Hosp., 2001—. Asst. clerkship dir., med. student tchg. Dartmouth Med. Sch., 1990—; cons. psychiatrist secure psychiat. unit Dept. Corrections, N.H. State Prison, 1997—; bd. examiner Am. Bd. Psychiatry and Neurology, 1998; forensic psychiatry fellowship dir. N.H. Hosp., 2001—; bd. dirs. N.H. br. Nat. Alliance for the Mentally Ill. Mem.: Nat. Alliance for the Mentally Ill (bd. dirs. N.H. br. 2002—), N.H. Psychiat. Soc. (treas. 1997—, pres. 2000—02), Am. Coll. Physician Execs., Am. Psychiat. Assn., Beta Lambda Sigma. Avocations: reading non-fiction history books, softball, hockey. Office: New Hampshire Hosp 36 Clinton St Concord NH 03301-2359 E-mail: adenesne@dhhs.state.nh.us.

DE NEUFVILLE, PIERRE, retired brokerage house executive; b. Paris, Sept. 15, 1924; came to U.S., 1974; s. Andre and Jacqueline (de Villeneuve) de N.; 1 child, Oliver. BA, Sorbonne U., 1946. Asst. v.p. LaCruz, Linares, Spain, 1947-50; USAF liaison Coca-Cola Internat., Paris, 1950-54; mgr. sales promotion France-Presse, Paris, 1954-56; mgr. Hayden Stone, Paris, 1956-64; resident ptnr. Bache and Co., Paris, 1964-73; internat. v.p. Lehman Bros., N.Y.C., 1973-87; mgr. internat. dept. Balis, Zorn, Gerard Inc., N.Y.C., 1987-89; ret., 1989; writer. Author: The Half Wit, 1987, The Red Star, 1987. Counsel to co-chmn. U.S. Senate/Congress Peace Through Strength, Washington, 1987—. Served to brig. gen. Free French Army. Decorated Medaille Militaire, 3 Croix de Guerres France; recipient U.S. Presdl. Order of Merit. Sufi. Club: Yacht Club de France. Avocations: philosophy, writing, sailing.

DE NEUFVILLE, RICHARD LAWRENCE, engineering educator; b. N.Y.C., May 6, 1939; s. Lawrence Eustace and Adeline de N.; m. Virginia Lyons; children: Robert, Julie. SB, SM, MIT, 1961, PhD, 1965; Dr. h.c (hon.), Tech U., Delft, 2002. Asst. prof. to assoc. prof. dept. civil engring. MIT, Cambridge, Mass., 1965-75, prof., chmn. Tech. and Policy Program, 1975-2000, prof. engring sys., 2000—. Vis. prof. U. Calif., Berkeley, 1974—76, London Grad. Sch. Bus., 1973, Ecole Centrale de Paris, 1981—82; mem. vis. com. U. Va., Charlottesville, 1987; adj. prof. Ecole Nationale des Ponts et Chausees of Paris, 1988—, U. Bristol, England, 1992—99; vis. prof. Australian Bur. Transport and Comml. Econs., 1995; mem. vis. com. Tech. U., Delft, Eindhoven and Utrecht, The Netherlands, 1996—97; vis. prof. Harvard U., 2000—; advisor Alta. Heritage Fund for Sci. and Engring. Rsch., 2000—, B.C. Leading Edge Found., 2003; adj. prof. Ecole Hassania des Travaux Publics of Casablanca, 2000—01, MBA des Ponts, 2000—; vis. prof. Balliol Coll., Oxford U., 2001; sr. rsch. assoc., life mem. Clare Hall Coll., Cambridge U., 2002—; mem. Netherlands Rev. on Engring. Sys., 2002—; sr. rsch. assoc. Judge Inst. Author: Airport Systems Planning, Design and Management, 2003, Applied Systems Analysis, 1990, Airport Systems Planning, 1976, Systems Planning and Design, 1979, Systems Analysis for Engineers and Managers, 1971; editor Jour. Transp. Rsch., 1975-86, Jour. Air Transport Mgmt., 1993—, Intnerat. Jour. Tech. Policy and Mgmt., 1999—. Bd. dirs. Geographic Data Tech., 1982-90, Urban Data Processing, 1970-80, Ecole Bilingue, French-Am. Internat. Sch. of Boston, 1992-97; trustee Kennedy Meml. Trust (U.K.), 1993-98; Consejo del Rector, Universidad Anahuac del Sur, Mexico, 1999. 1st lt. C.E., U.S. Army, 1961-62. White House fellow, 1964-65, Guggenheim fellow, 1973, U.S.-Japan Leadership fellow, 1990, Class of 1960 fellow, 2000; recipient Sys. Sci. prize NATO, 1974, Risk and Ins. prize Risk and Ins. Soc., 1976, Alpha Kappa Psi award, 1985, Engring. Excellence award Australia Instn. Engrs., 1986, Irwin Sizer award, 1988, FAA prize for tchg. excellence, 1990, Chevalier de l'Ordre des Palmes Academiques, 1999. Mem. ASCE, AAAS, Ops. Rsch. Soc. Am., Brit.-N.Am. Com., Am. Alpine Club, Cambridge Boat Club, Cambridge Skating Club, Cambridge Tennis Club, Internat. House of Japan. Office: MIT Rm E40-245 Cambridge MA 02139 E-mail: ardent@mit.edu.

DENEVAN, WILLIAM MAXFIELD, geographer, prehistorian, ecologist; b. San Diego, Oct. 16, 1931; s. Lester W. and Wilda M. D.; m. Patricia Sue French, June 21, 1958; children: Curtis, Victoria. PhD, U. Calif., Berkeley, 1963. Faculty dept. geography U. Wis., Madison, 1963-94, prof., 1972-94, chmn. dept., 1980-83, dir. L.Am. Ctr., 1975-77, prof. emeritus, 1994—. Author/co-author: The Upland Pine Forests of Nicaragua, 1961, The Aboriginal Cultural Geography of the Llanos de Mojos of Bolivia, 1966, The Biogeography of a Savanna Landscape, 1970, Adaptive Strategies in Karinya Subsistance, Venezuelan Llanos, 1978, Campos Elevados en los Llanos Occidentales de Venezuela, 1979, Cultivated Landscapes of Native Amazonia and the Andes, 2001; editor/co-editor: The Native Population of the Americas in 1492, 1976, Pre-Hispanic Agricultural Fields in the Andean Region, 1987, Swidden-Fallow Agroforestry in the Peruvian Amazon, 1988, Hispanic Lands and Peoples, 1989, Las Chacras de Coporaque, 1994; contbr. articles to profl. jours. With USN, 1953-55. Grantee Fulbright, 1957, NRC, 1961-62, Ford Found., 1965-66, NSF, 1972-73, 84-86, Nat. Geog. Soc., 1985-86, NEH, 1989-90; Guggenheim fellow, 1977-78. Mem. Assn. Am. Geographers (Honors award 1987), Am. Geog. Soc., Am. Anthrop. Assn., Soc. for Am. Archaeology, Am. Acad. Arts and Scis. E-mail: sbden@saber.net.

DENG, DONNA Y. urologist, surgeon; BA, U. Calif., Berkeley, 1993; MD, U. Calif., Davis, 1998. Lic. Calif., 2000. Resident U. Calif., San Francisco, 1998—. Contbr. articles to profl. jours. Mem.: Am. Urol. Assn. Office: UCSF Dept Urology 400 Parnassus Ave A633 San Francisco CA 94143

DENG, FAN, research scientist; b. Putian, Fujian, China, Dec. 11, 1964; m. Li Sun, Jan. 2, 1992; 1 child, Yu. BS, Fujian Agr. U., China, 1984; MS, Anhui Agr. U., 1991; PhD, U. Tsukuba, Japan, 1996. Postdoctoral rsch. assoc. Internat. Rsch. Ctr. for Agr. Scis., Ministry of Agr., Tsukuba, Japan, 1996; domestic rsch. fellow Sci. and Tech. Agy., Tsukuba, 1996—99; postdoctoral rsch. scientist Mich. Tech. U., Houghton, 1999; rsch. scientist Va. Poly. Inst. and State U., Blacksburg, 1999—2002; rsch. fellow Donald Danforth Plant Sci. Ctr., St. Louis, 2002—. Contbr. Recipient Outstanding Rsch. award, Weed Sci. Soc. of Japan, 1999; Japan Ministry of Edn. scholar, 1992—96. Mem.: AAAS, Chinese Assn. for Sci. and Tech. (Va. chpt. pres. 2001—02, Agr. Soc. pres. 2002), Internat. Tea Sci. and Culture Soc. (standing bd. mem. 1999—2002), Asian-Pacific Weed Sci. Soc. Achievements include patents for technology of natural tea soft drink processing; 4-counerate CoA ligase is the active site of plant growth regulators. Home: 974 N Warson Rd R2023 Saint Louis MO 63132-2918

DENGER, MICHAEL LOUIS, lawyer; b. Davenport, Iowa, Sept. 8, 1945; s. Ralph Henry and Bernice Marie (Cederberg) D.; m. Mary Elizabeth Colbert, Aug. 30, 1969; children: Lorna Marie, Mary Catherine, Rachel Anne. BS with highest distinction, Northwestern U., 1967; JD cum laude, Harvard U., 1970. Bar: D.C. 1970, U.S. Ct. Appeals (D.C. cir.) 1971, U.S. Supreme Ct. 1978. Assoc. atty. Sutherland, Asbill & Brennan, Washington, 1970-76, ptnr., 1976-92, Gibson, Dunn & Crutcher LLP, Washington, 1992—. Adj. prof. law Washington and Lee U., 2000—; speaker on antitrust, trade regulation numerous groups. Bd. editors Antitrust Report, 1992—; contbr. articles to profl. jours. Mem. nat. adv. coun. Northwestern U. Sch. Comm., Evanston, Ill., 1990—. 2nd lt. USAR, 1970. Mem. ABA (vice chair antitrust law sect. 1985-86, sec. antitrust law sect. 1988-91, chair-elect antitrust law sect. 1991-92, chair antitrust law sect. 1992-93, chair edit. bd. antitrust sect. Federal and State Price Discrimination Law 1991, co-editor in chief antitrust sect. State Antitrust Practice and Statutes 3 vols. 1990, vice chair edit. bd. antitrust sect. Antitrust Law Devels. 2d edit. 1984), Columbia Country Club (Chevy Chase, Md.). Republican. Roman Catholic. Avocations: tennis, collecting military miniatures, military history, bridge. Home: 5802 Kirkside Dr Chevy Chase MD 20815-7118 Office: Gibson Dunn & Crutcher LLP 1050 Connecticut Ave NW Ste 900 Washington DC 20036-5306

DENGLER, ROBERT ANTHONY, professional association executive, educator; b. Upper Darby, Pa., Aug. 23, 1947; s. Anthony William and Harriet Josephine (Schneider) D.; m. Renee Faith Aird, Oct. 26, 1985. BS, Drexel U., 1970, MBA, 1972; MS in MIS, Benedictine U., 2000, postgrad., 2000—. Cert. assn. exec., mtg. profl. Cons. orgn devel. Abinton Hosp., Abington, 1970—73; dir. tng. & edn. Parkview Meml. Hosp., Ft. Wayne, Ind., 1973-76; dir. human resource mgmt. Americana Healthcare Corp., Chgo., 1976-82; corp. mgr. Human Resource Tng. and Devel. Means Svc. Inc., Chgo., 1982-83; dir. physician services West Suburban Hosp. Med. Ctr., Oak Park, Ill., 1983-85; assoc. dir. Assoc. Equipment Distributors, Oak Brook, Ill., 1985-88; exec. v.p. Internat. Reprographic Assn., Oak Brook, 1988-92; exec. dir. Data Processing Mgmt. Assn., Park Ridge, Ill., 1993-94; pres. R.A. Dengler & Assocs., 1994—; exec. dir. Nat. Assn. Med. Staff Svcs., Lombard, Ill., 1996-98; engring. leadership devel. adminstr. Commonwealth Edison/Exelon Corp., 2001—03. Adj. instr. orgn. behavior Aurora (Ill.) U.; adj. instr. mgmt. info. sys. Hawaii Pacific U., Honolulu. Capt. USAR, 1972-80. Mem. Inst. Mgmt. Cons., Project Mgmt. Inst., Am. Soc. Assn. Execs., Acad. of Mgmt., Midwest Acad. Mgmt., Orgn. Devel. Network, Orgn. Devel. Inst., Mensa. Home and Office: 294 Lionel Rd Riverside IL 60546-2204

DENHAM, BRYAN ERROL, communications educator; b. Belleville, Ill., Feb. 8, 1967; s. Charles William Denham Jr. and Deanna Mary Gregory. BA, Ind. U., 1989; MA, Calif. State U., Fullerton, 1993; PhD, U. Tenn., 1996. Asst. prof. S.W. Mo. State U., Springfield, 1997-99; Charles Campbell assoc. prof. sports comm. Clemson (S.C.) U., 1999—. Co-author: Introduction to Journalism, 2001; contbr. articles to profl. jours. Mem. Assn. for Edn. in Journalism and Mass Comm., Am. Polit. Sci. Assn., Am. Assn. for Pub. Opinion Rsch., Nat. Comm. Assn., N.Am. Soc. for the Sociology of Sport, Midwest Assn. for Pub. Opinion Rsch. Avocations: Americana, films. Home: 854 Issaqueena Trail #1007 Central SC 29630 Office: Clemson Univ 412 Strode Tower Clemson SC 29634 E-mail: bdenham@clemson.edu.

DENHAM, CAROLYN HUNTER, academic administrator, statistics educator; b. Abilene, Tex., Sept. 21, 1945; d. J. C. and Mary (Balch) Hunter; m. Robert Edwin Denham, June 3, 1966; children: Jeffrey, Laura. BA, U. Tex., 1966; MEd, Boston Coll., 1967, PhD, 1971. Prof. ednl. rsch. Calif. State U., Long Beach, 1971-88, assoc. dean grad. studies and rsch., 1983-88; prof. ednl. rsch. Calif. State Poly. U., Pomona, 1988-92, assoc. v.p. for acad. programs, 1988-92; dir. Nat. Ctr. Social Work and Edn. Collaboration Fordham U., N.Y.C., 1992—. Appointed mem. Calif. Commn. on Tchr. Credentialing, 1976-80; statis. cons. sch. fin. case, 1973-74. Co-editor: Time to Learn, 1980 (Best in Eric award 1980); editor The Generator, 1978—; cons. editor Jour. Pers. in Edn., 1986—; mem. rsch. adv. coun. Handbook on Tchr. Edn.; contbr. articles to profl. jours. Trustee Westridge Sch., Pasadena, Calif., 1985-89, Cushing Acad., Claremont Grad. Sch.; bd. dirs. Lincoln Found. and Inst., Cambridge, Mass., Access Devel. Corp., The Constn. Works, Children's Aid Soc., Inst. Internat. Edn.; advisor ednl. policy for gubernatorial campaigns. Am. Coun. on Edn. fellow, 1988. Mem. Am. Edn. Rsch. Assn. (sec. Div. G 1982-84), Nat. Coun. on Measurement on Edn., L.A. Women's Found. (charter founder). Democrat. Espicopalian. Avocations: reading, cooking, hiking, aerobic dancing.

DENHAM, EARL LAMAR, lawyer; b. Biloxi, Miss., July 1, 1947; s. Earl Lamar and Ruby (Young) D.; children: Katherine Elizabeth, Rachel Ann, Israel Anderson, Nathan Levi, Earl Lamar III; m. N.A. Hema Malini; children: Judith Jaya, Sachika Braka, Arya Tova. BS, U. Miss., 1969, JD, 1972. Bar: Miss. 1972, U.S. Dist. Ct. (no. and so. dists.) Miss. 1972, U.S. Ct. Appeals (5th cir.) 1978, U.S. Supreme Ct. 1978. Assoc. Hurlbert & O'Barr, Biloxi, 1972-73; ptnr. Levi & Denham, Ltd., Ocean Springs, Miss., 1973—99. Capt. USAR, 1970-78. Mem. ABA, ATLA (sustaining), Nat. Assn. Criminal Def. Lawyers, Miss. Trial Lawyers Assn., Miss. Bar Assn., Ocean Springs Yacht Club (bd. govs. 1988), Southern Trial Lawyers Assn. Democrat. Jewish. Avocations: sailing, hunting. Office: Denham Backstrom & Assoc Ltd 424 Washington Ave PO Box 596 Ocean Springs MS 39566-0596

DENHAM, FREDERICK RONALD, management consultant; b. Middlebrough, Eng., Oct. 21, 1929; s. Frederick and Gladys (Tattersall) D.; m. Lynn Hughes, Sept. 19, 1953; children— John, Gillian, Michael. B.Sc., U. Durham, Eng., 1950, PhD, 1953; MBA, U. Buffalo, 1960. Registered profl. engr., Ont. cert. mgmt. cons. Sci. officer Def. Research Bd., Ottawa, Ont., Can., 1953-54; indsl. engr. Ford Motor Co. of Can., Ltd., Windsor, Ont., 1954-56; asst. supt. Union Carbide Can., Welland, Ont., 1956-61; cons. Thorne, Stevenson & Kellogg, Toronto, Ont., 1961-67; v.p. Stevenson, Kellogg, Ernst & Whinney, 1967-89; vice chmn. Peat, Marwick, Stevenson & Kellogg, Toronto, 1989-94; pres. Ron Denham & Assocs., Inc., 1994—; dir. Proctor & Redfern, Ltd., 1994—, A.T. Kearney, Toronto, 1994—. Prof. Faculty Adminstrv. Studies York U., 1967-71 Trustee North York Bd. Edn., 1974-78. Fellow Engring. Inst. Can., Inst. Cert. Mgmt. Cons. Ont. (pres. 1982-83), Masons, Rotary (dist. gov. 1993-94). Anglican. Home and Office: 15 Danville Dr North York ON Canada M2P 1H7 E-mail: ron.denham@atkearney.com.

DENHAM, JEFFREY, state senator; b. Nov. 05; BS, Calif. Poly. State U., San Luis Obispo. Agrl. businessman; cand. dist. 28 Calif. Ho. of Reps, 2000; mem. dist. 12 Calif. State Senate, 2002—. Mem. Agriculture and Water Resources Com., Banking, Commerce and Internat. Trade, Edn. Com.; vice chair Environ. Quality Com.; mem. Natural Resources and Wildlife Com., Vets. Affairs Com. Served with USAF. Republican. Mailing: State Capitol Rm 4090 Sacramento CA 95814 Office: 2824 Park Ave Merced CA 95340*

DENHAM, PAUL, technology sales and marketing executive; b. Oklahoma City, Okla., Jan. 19, 1960; BS in Elec./Sys. Engring., U.S. Naval Acad., 1982. Mktg. rep. IBM Sales and Distbn., Charleston, S.C., 1987-89, client mgr., 1989-93; personal software mktg. team leader IBM Personal Software Products Divsn., Charleston, 1993-95; competitive software strategy IBM Software Group, Somers, N.Y., 1995-96; mktg. programs exec. IBM Internet Divsn., Tarrytown, N.Y., 1996-97; nat. sales mgr. IBM Advanced Tech. Migrations, IBM, White Plains, N.Y., 1997-99; WW channels mgr. IBM Global E-commerce Solutions, IBM Global Industries, White Plains, 1999-2000; worldwide e-commerce mgr. IBM.COM, White Plains, 2000-2001, mgr. world wide merchandising, 2001—02, mgr. tech. strategy, 2002—. Mem. adv. bd. Carolina Film Alliance, Charleston, 1998—; dir. strategic ops. Naval Res. Unit Comdr. Submarine Force, Atlantic Fleet, Norfolk, Va., 1998—2001; dir. manpower Naval Res. Unit Comdr., 2001—02; OIC Navy personnel comd. pers. 9 comp 106. Spl. guest TV show Computer Chronicles, 1995; TV co-host Inside Tech., 1994-95; radio host regular weekly program Inside Tech., 1994-95. Lt. USN, 1982—87, dir. strategic ops., unit comdr. submarine force Atlantic fleet USNR, 1998—2001, Norfolk, Va., dir. manpower, unit comdr. USNR, 2001—, OIC Navy personnel command pers 9 comp 106 USNR, 2002—. Mem. AFTRA, U.S. Naval Acad. Alumni Assn. Avocations: screenwriting, photography, painting, running, cycling, weight training. Office: IBM COM 1133 Westchester Ave White Plains NY 10604-3599

DENHAM, PAUL RAYMOND, construction executive; b. Camden, N.J., June 13, 1962; s. Francis Kennedy and Margeret Mary Denham; m. Mary Byrd Glass; children: Paul Tucker, Thomas Christian, Leighton Byrd, Lapsley Glass. BSME, U. Va., 1984; M in Engring. Adminstrn., George Washington U., 1987. Lic. profl. engr., Va.; lic. master HVAC. Project engr. Babcock & Wilcox, Lynchburg, Va., 1984-89; v.p. So. Air, Inc., Lynchburg, 1989-99. Bd. dirs. Met. Lynchburg Red Cross; pres. Paul Munro PTA, Lynchburg, 1999. Mem. ASHRAE. Episcopalian. Avocations: woodworking, golf, watersports. Office: So Air Inc 2655 Lakeside Dr Lynchburg VA 24501-6944 Fax: 804-385-9081.

DENHAM, ROBERT EDWIN, lawyer, investment company executive; b. Dallas, Aug. 27, 1945; s. Wilburn H. and Anna Maria (Hughes) Denham; m. Carolyn Hunter, June 3, 1966; children: Jeffrey Hunter, Laura Maria. BA, U. Tex., 1966; MA, Harvard U., 1968, JD, 1971. Bar: Calif. 1972. Assoc. Munger Tolles and Olson, L.A., 1971—73; ptnr. Munger Tolles Olson, L.A., 1973—85, 1992—93; mng. ptnr. Munger Tolles and Olson, L.A., 1985—91; chmn., chief exec. officer Salomon Inc, N.Y.C., 1992—97; ptnr. Munger Tolles and Olson, L.A., 1998—. Pres. Pasadena (Calif.) Ednl. Found., 1977—79; trustee Poly. Sch. Pasadena, 1989—93, v.p. bd. trustees, 1991—93; trustee New Sch. Social Rsch., 1995—, Natural Resources Def. Coun., 1992—; adv. bd. of the pres. Calif. State U., Sonoma, 1993—; trustee The Conf. Bd., 1994—, Russell Sage Found., 1997—; pub. mem. Ind. Stds. Bd., 1997—; former co-chmn. Subcoun. on Capital Allocation of the Competitiveness Policy Coun.; former mem. Bipartisan Commn. on Entitlement and Tax Reform; former U.S. rep. to the Asia Pacific Econ. Coun. Bus. Adv. Coun.; mem. bus. sector adv. group on corp. governance OECD; trustee Cathedral Corp. Diocese of L.A., 1986—92; bd. dirs. Pub. Counsel, L.A., 1981—84, United Way, N.Y.C., 1994—97, U.S. Trust Co., AMKOR Tech., Inc. Mem.: ABA, L.A. County Bar (bus. and corps. exec. com. 1985—), State Bar Calif. Democrat. Episcopalian. Avocations: soccer, cooking. Office: Munger Tolles and Olson 355 S Grand Ave # 3500 Los Angeles CA 90071-1560

DENHARDT, DAVID TILTON, molecular and cell biology educator; b. Sacramento, Feb. 25, 1939; s. David Burton and Edith (Tilton) D.; m. Georgetta Louise Harrar, July 1, 1961; children: Laura Jean, Kristin Ann, David Harrar. BA in Chemistry with high honors, Swarthmore Coll., 1960; PhD in Biophysics, Calif. Inst. Tech., 1965. Instr. biol. labs Harvard U., 1964-66, asst. prof., 1966-70; assoc. prof. biochemistry McGill U., Montreal, Que., Can., 1970-77, prof., 1977-80; prof. biochemistry, microbiology and immunology, dir. Cancer Research Lab., U. Western Ont., London, 1980-88; prof. biol. scis. Rutgers U., New Brunswick, N.J., 1988—, chmn., 1988-95, dir. Bur. Biol. Rsch., 1988-95, dir. cell devel. biology grad. program, 1991-94. Mem. sci. adv. bd. Ctr. for Advanced Biotech. and Medicine, Piscataway, N.J., 1988-91, 1988-91. Editor: Jour. Virology, 1977-87, Gene, 1985-93, Exptl. Cell Rsch., 1994—; assoc. editor: Jour. Cellular Biochemistry, 1994—; mem. editorial bd. Jour. Cancer Rsch. Methods and Clin. Oncology, In Vivo Internat. Jour. Fellow AAAS, Am. Acad. Microbiology, Royal Soc. Can.; mem. Am. Cancer Soc., Am. Soc. Biol. Chemists, Am. Microbiol. Soc., N.Y. Acad. Scis., Am. Soc. Cell Biology, Phi Beta Kappa. Office: Rutgers U Nelson Biol Labs 604 Allison Rd Piscataway NJ 08854-8000 E-mail: denhardt@biology.rutgers.edu.

DENHOLTZ, ELAINE GRUDIN, literature educator, writer; b. NJ; d. Maurice and Lillian (Sachs) Grudin; m. Melvin Denholtz; children: Jeffrey, Steven, Lisa. BA, Bucknell U.; MA, Seton Hall U. Adj. prof. English Fairleigh Dickinson U., Madison, NJ, 1966—. Author: (plays) The Highchairs, 1977, (book) How to Save Your Teeth & Money, 1977, The Dental Facelift, 1981, Having It Both Ways, 1981, Playing for High Stakes, 1986, Balancing Work & Love, 2000, The Zaddik, 2001; contbr. articles to profl. publs. Named to, N.J. Lit. Hall of Fame; recipient numerous lit. and dramatic awards, grants. Mem.: Phi Beta Kappa. Avocation: swimming. Office: Fairleigh Dickinson U Madison Ave MDBO-01 Madison NJ 07940

DE NICOLA, PETER FRANCIS, photographic distributor; b. N.Y.C., Oct. 28, 1954; s. Louis Joseph and Nancy Eleanor (Maddi) DeN.; m. Charlotte Rebecca White, Sept. 2, 1998. BS, NYU, 1976, MBA, 1978. Pres., founder P.F. DeNicola, Inc., Stamford, Conn., 1976-84; acct. Main Hurdman, N.Y.C., Conn., 1978-81; tax mgr. Gen. Signal Corp., Stamford, Conn., 1981-83, Emery Air Freight Corp., Wilton, Conn., 1983-85; dir. taxes A.I. Internat. Corp., N.Y.C., Conn., 1985-88; tax mgr. Siemens Corp., N.Y.C., 1989-91; sr. tax analyst Fuji Photo Film U.S.A., Inc., Elmsford, N.Y., 1991-93, assoc. tax mgr., 1994-98, tax mgr., 1999—. Author: Legal Liability of Tax Return Preparers, 1978; contbr. articles to tax and investment periodicals. Recipient Ferdinand W. Lafrentz acctg. award, 1977 CPA, Conn., N.Y. Mem. Tax Soc. NYU, Assn. MBA Exec., Am. Mgmt. Assn., Stamford Tax Assn. (sec.-treas. 1988-89, v.p. 1989-90, treas. 1999—), Nat. Assn. Acct., NYU Commerce Alumni Assn. (dir. 1978-96, corr. sec. 1978-79, rec. sec. 1979-81, chmn. budget com. 1987-88, chmn. Annual Bus. Conf. 1988-89, chmn. alumni admissions coun. 1989-96), AICPA (fed. tax and tax acctg. com. 1984—), NY Soc. CPA (fed. and state tax com. 1983-85, depreciation and investment tax credit com. 1986-87), Conn. Soc. CPA, Tax Exec. Inst. (bd. dir.), Round Table Assn. of US (co-founder 1986, nat. treas. 1987-88, 90-92, nat. pres. 1988-89, del. to internat. convention, 1987, 88), Estate Planning Coun. Westchester County, Round Table 3 of Greenwich (Conn.) (dir. 1984-90, 1985-86, pres. 1986-88), Internat. Platform Assn., Princeton Club, Rockefeller Ctr. Club (NYC), Soundview Club, Long Ridge Club (Stamford), Saw Mill River Racquet Club (Mt. Kisco, NY), St. James's Club (Antigua), Capitol Hill Club (Washington), NY Athletic Club, Pelham (NY) Country Club. Republican. Roman Catholic. Home: PO Box 4637 Stamford CT 06907-0637 Office: Fuji Photo Film USA Inc 200 Summit Lake Dr Valhalla NY 10595 E-mail: peterd7510@aol.com., peter_denicola@fujifilm.com.

DENIGRIS, CAROLE DELL CATO, artist; b. N.Y.C., May 26, 1936; d. Frederick and Elsie Helen (Dell) Cato; m. Daniel Anthony DeNigris, June 30, 1957; children: Daniel Cary, Carole Lynn. Student, Hunter Coll., 1954-57; studied with Richard Lippold, William Baziotes,, 1954-57, studied Oriental art with Diana Kan, 1969-75; grad., Silva Mind Control. Buyer, salesperson Ethel Allan, Stamford, Conn., 1976-79; asst. mgr., buyer Jean Hutchinson, Greenwich, Conn., 1977-85; dir. Decker Studio and Art Gallery Ltd., Glenville, Conn., 1985-88; mgr. Odetta-Women's Fine Apparel, Greenwich, 1988-90; freelance fragrance model Guerlain of Paris, Stamford, 1990—. One-woman shows include Greenwich Hosp., 1995, Greenwich (Conn.) Beauty Salon and Spa, 2003, 2 person show, Town and Country Club, Hartford, Conn., 2001, exhibited in group shows at Hammond Mus., North Salem, N.Y., Ferguson Libr., Stamford, Hurlbert Gallery, Greenwich, Wilton (Conn.) Libr., Greenwich Art Soc., Conn. Cmty. Bank, Greenwich, Old Bergen Art Guild, 1977—78, Hobe Sound (Fla.) Art Gallery, Pen and Brush Club, N.Y.C., Port Chester (N.Y.) Libr., Greenwich YWCA. Pres. Newcomers of Port Chester, 1969-70. Mem. Oriental Brush Artists Guild (v.p. 1995-96, pres. 1996-98, publicity chairperson, advisor to pres., asst. treas. art exhibit com., asst. hostess art exhibit com.). Republican. Avocations: mycology, methaphysics. Home: 12 Nutmeg Dr Greenwich CT 06831-3211

DENIOUS, JON PARKS, retired publishing executive; b. Buffalo, Apr. 5, 1939; s. Wilbur Franklin Jr. and Nancy (Parks) D.; m. Sharon Marie Fee, June 17, 1963; children: Timothy, Elizabeth. Owner Durango (Colo.) Printing and Graphics, 1985-90; publ. Silverton Standard and The Miner, Colo., 1990-99; ret., 1999. Mem. Nat. Newspaper Assn., Colo. Press Assn. Avocations: walking, reading. E-mail: denious@frontier.net.

DENIOUS, SHARON MARIE, retired publisher; b. Rulo, Nebr., Jan. 27, 1941; d. Thomas Wayne and Alma (Murphy) Fee; m. Jon Parks Denious, June 17, 1963; children: Timothy Scot, Elizabeth Denious Cessna. Grad. high sch. Operator N.W. Pipeline co., Ignacio, Colo., 1975-90; pub. The Silverton Standard & The Miner, Colo., 1990-99. Avocations: reading, hiking. E-mail: denious@frontier.net.

DENIRO, MARY LYN S. lawyer; b. Salt Lake City, Feb. 15, 1959; d. Ted Gordon and Marilyn Valoe (Butcher) Symes; m. Dan DeNiro. BS magna cum laude, U. Utah, 1980; JD magna cum laude, Fordham U., 1992. Bar: N.Y. 1993. Exec. asst. to chmn. ASARCO Inc., NYC, 1983-91, legal asst., 1991-92; jud. clk. US Dist. Ct. (ea. dist.), Bklyn., 1992-93; assoc. Davis Polk & Wardwell, NYC, 1993-99; v.p., legal counsel Zurich Centre Group, NYC, 1999—2003; v.p. Counsel Ace Capital Re Inc., 2003. Mem. Order of Coif, Phi Kappa Phi, Phi Eta Sigma. Office: Ace Fin Svc 1325 Ave of the Americas New York NY 10019

DE NIRO, ROBERT, actor; b. N.Y.C., Aug. 17, 1943; s. Robert and Virginia DeNiro; m. Diahnne Abbott; children: Raphael Eugene, Drina. Studied acting with, Stella Adler, Lee Strasberg. Motion pictures appearances include The Wedding Party, 1969, Hi, Mom!, 1970, Jennifer On My Mind, 1971, Bloody Mama, Born to Win, 1971, The Gang That Couldn't Shoot Straight, 1971, Bang the Drum Slowly, 1973, Mean Streets, 1973, The Godfather, Part II, 1974 (Acad. award best supporting actor), The Last Tycoon, Taxi Driver, 1976, New York, New York, 1900, 1977, The Deer Hunter, 1978, Raging Bull, 1980 (Acad. award best actor), True Confessions, 1981, The King of Comedy, 1982, Once Upon a Time in America, 1984, Falling in Love, 1984, Brazil, 1984, The Mission, 1985, Angel Heart, 1987, The Untouchables, 1987, Dear America: Letters Home From Vietnam, 1987 (documentary), Midnight Run, 1988, (also exec. prodr.) We're No Angels, 1989, Jacknife, 1989, Stanley & Iris, 1990, Goodfellas, 1990, Awakenings, 1991 (Acad. award nomination), Backdraft, 1991, Cape Fear, 1991, Guilty By Suspicion, 1991, Mistress, 1992, Night and the City, 1992, Mad Dog and Glory, 1993, This Boys Life, 1993, (also dir.) A Bronx Tale, 1993, Mary Shelley's Frankenstein, 1994, Casino, 1995, Heat, 1995, The Fan, 1996, Marvin's Room, 1996, Sleepers, 1996, (also prodr.) Wag the Dog, 1997, Copland, 1997, Great Expectations, 1998, 15 Minutes, 1999, Analyze This, 1999, Flawless, 1999 (also prodr.), The Adventures of Rocky and Bullwinkle, 1999 (also prodr.), Lenny Bruce: Swear to Tell the Truth, 1998 (TV, voice), 15 Minutes, 2001, The Score, 2001 (also dir.), City by the Sea, 2002, Analyze That, 2002; prodr.: Entropy, 1999, About a Boy, 2002; co-prodr. Thunderheart, 1992; theater roles include Strange Show, 1982; exec. prodr.: (TV) Tribeca, 1993, (film) Faithful, 1996, Nasty Driver, 2000, Meet the Parents, 2000, Conjugating Niki, 2000. Recipient Hasty Pudding award Harvard U. 1979, D.W. Griffith award for best actor, 1990. Office: Creative Artists Agy 9830 Wilshire Blvd Beverly Hills CA 90212-1825*

DENISE, THEODORE CULLOM, philosophy educator; b. Whitewater, Wis., Mar. 9, 1919; s. Malcolm F. and Margaret E. (Lawrence) D.; m. Kathleen W. Cowles, Oct. 4, 1942; children: Patricia Denise White, Theodore Cullom (dec.). BA, U. Mich., 1942, MA, 1947, PhD, 1955. Teaching fellow U. Mich., 1946-48; mem. faculty Syracuse U., 1948—, assoc. prof. philosophy, 1959-64, prof. philosophy, 1964-89, prof. emeritus philosophy, 1989—, chmn. dept., 1959-72, chmn. humanities depts., 1973-76; dir. liberal studies Inst. Univ. Adminstrs., 1961-63; dir. of semester in Italy, 1967-68, 76-77; dir. grad. studies in philosophy, 1976-84; mem. editl. com. Univ. Press, 1972-78. Author/editor: (with others) Great Traditions in Ethics, 1953, The Social Writings of Bertrand Russell, 1955, Contemporary Philosophy and Its Origins, 1967, Retrospect and Prospect, 1956; contbr. articles to philos. jours. Served with AUS, 1942-46. Mem. Assn. Symbolic Logic, Am. Philos. Assn., Alpha Kappa Lambda. Home: 8 Cranberry Ln Easthampton MA 01027 Office: Syracuse U Dept Philosophy Syracuse NY 13244-0001 Personal E-mail: teddenise@juno.com.

DENISH, DIANE D. lieutenant governor; d. Libby Donley and Jack Daniels; m. Herb Denish; 3 children. Assoc. pub., bus. devel. and advt. sales Starlight Pub. Ltd., Albuquerque Living and NMex. Monthly, Albuquerque; state chmn. N.Mex Dem. Party, 1999—2001; former owner Target Group; lt. gov. State of Nev., 2003—. Address: 1301 San Pedro Albuquerque NM 87110 Office: State Capitol, Ste 417 Santa Fe NM 87501

DENISON, BARRY REED, human rights association executive; b. Ft. Sumner, N.Mex., June 1, 1957; s. Shell Davenport and Melva Ogden Denison; m. Deborah DeYoung DeYoung, Apr. 13, 1959; children: Bethany Paige, Kelly Nicole, David Reed. BA, Oral Roberts U., 1980, MBA, 1983. Dir. student outreach Oral Roberts U., Tulsa, Okla., 1979—83; exec. dir. Trinity Outreach Internat., Tulsa, 1982—2002; fin. mgr. Bridges for Peace, Jerusalem, 1995—2002, nat. dir., COO, 1996—2000, dir. for internat. devel., 2000—02; exec. dir. Internat. Third World Leaders Assn., Nassau, 2002—. Cons. Reed & Assocs. Ltd., Nassau, 1996—2001; rep. to UN ECOSOC WOLMI, Kingston, Jamaica, 1997—2003; dir. Americas Internat. Banking Corp, Nassau, 1998—2001. Rep. UN ECOSOC ITWLA & WOLMI, Geneva, 1996—2002; internat. spokesperson Bridges for Peace, Jerusalem, 1996—2002. Protestant Evangelical Charismatic. Office: International Third World Leaders Assoc Diplomat Center - Carmichael Highway Nassau Jamaica Office Fax: 1-242-361-2260. E-mail: itwla@bfmmm.com.

DENISON, CYNTHIA LEE, accountant, tax specialist; b. Hyannis, Mass., Feb. 1, 1956; d. Gordon Avery Denison, Elizabeth Theresa Bourque-Denison; children: Randall Wayne Brown, Shaun Avery Brown, Kelly Joseph Brown. BS in Bus. Adminstrn., Hawaii Pacific U., 1990. Office mgr., tax preparer H&R Block, Fayetteville, NC, 1979—83; asst. acct., acctg. supr. Dept. of Def. Acctg. and Fin., Germany, 1984—86; revenue agt. IRS, Bailey's Crossroads, Va., 1990—91, taxpayer rep., 1991—97, lead tax specialist, 1997—2000, sr. tax specialist, taxpayer rep., 2000—. Electronic filing No. Va. coord. IRS, Bailey's Crossroads, 1998—. Unoffical scoutmaster and cubmaster, den mother, com. mem., counselor Boy Scouts Am., Honolulu, 1986—90; football, baseball, soccer coach Moral, Recreation & Welfare, Honolulu, 1986—90; baseball coach Youth Sports, Spring Lake, NC, 1981—83. Mem.: AAUW, Statue of Liberty/Ellis Island Soc., Smithsonian Instn., Nat. Preservation Soc., Nat. Geog. Soc., Denison Soc., Nat. Geneal. Soc., New Eng. Hist. and Geneal. Soc. Avocations: genealogy, historic preservation, animal preservation, reading, crafts. Home: 2909 Marsala Ct Woodbridge VA 22192 Personal E-mail: cyndidenison1@msn.com.

DENISON, JAMES DICKEY, broadcasting executive; b. Clarendon, Tex., July 1, 1926; s. Dallas D. and Gladys (Condron) D.; m. Jo Beth Huser, June 27, 1965; children: Jack D., P. Dianne, Robert Ladd, Kathryn Anne Denison (Kit). Student, McMurry Coll., 1943, 46, U. Tex., 1947-49; BArch, U. Houston, 1952. Contracting engr. Am. Bridge div. U.S. Steel, Houston, 1952-60; co-owner, v.p. Globe Equipment Rental, Houston, 1961-67; owner, operator B & B Steel, Hobbs, N.Mex., 1967-73; co-owner, chief exec. officer VLA Fabrication div. Structures, Inc., Hobbs, 1973-79; owner, operator Denison's Photography, Kingwood, Tex., 1979-82, Sta. KKTC-FM, Brownfield, Tex., 1985-96. Chmn. N.Mex. State Highway Commn., 1974-79; congl. aide U.S. Congressman Harold Runnels, N.Mex., 1971-72. Served with USN, 1944-46, PTO. Mem. Brownfield C. of C. Lodges: Rotary (v.p. Hobbs club 1971-72). Democrat. Methodist. Avocations: photography, fishing. Home: 1002 E Cardwell Brownfield TX 79316-4608

DENISON, MARY BONEY, lawyer; b. Wilmington, N.C., June 8, 1956; d. Leslie Norwood Jr. and Lillian (Bellamy) Boney; children: Mary Catesby Bellamy, James Wholley IV. AB, Duke U., 1978; JD, U. N.C., 1981. Bar: N.Y.

1982, U.S. Dist. Ct. (so. and ea. dists.) N.Y. 1983, U.S. Ct. Appeals (2d cir.) 1984, DC 1988, U.S. Dist. Ct. DC 1988, U.S. Ct. Appeals (DC cir.) 1988. Assoc. Law Office William G. Kaelin, N.Y.C., 1981-82, Smith, Steibel, Alexander & Saskor, N.Y.C., 1982-86, Graham & James, Washington, 1986-91, ptnr., 1992-96, Farkas & Manelli PLLC, Washington, 1996-2000, Manelli, Denison & Selter, PLLC, Washington, 2001—. Vol. Legal Aid Soc., N.Y.C., 1983—86. Mem.: ABA, Internat. Trademark Assn. (vice chair treaty analysis com. 2000—01, chair treaty analysis com. 2001—, bd. dirs. 2003—), French Am. C. of C. Washington (treas. 1991—97). Democrat. Episcopalian. Office: Manelli Denison & Selter 2000 M St NW Ste 700 Washington DC 20036-3364 E-mail: mdenison@mdslaw.com.

DENISON, RICHARD EUGENE, retired agricultural services company executive; b. Harrisburg, Pa., Aug. 24, 1932; s. Benjamin C. and Viola M. (Cramer) D.; m. Peggy A. Koskinas, Apr. 19, 1958; children: Richard E. Jr., Carol Denison Brame. BS, Pa. State U., 1954. Cert. agrl. cons. Asst. store mgr. Grange League Fedn., Youngsville, Pa., 1957-59; grain buyer Quaker Oats, Shiremanstown, Pa., 1959-62; assoc. editor, advt. salesman Pa. Farmer, Harrisburg, 1962-68, mgr., 1968-70, Pa. Farm Bur. Farm Mgmt. Svcs., Camp Hill, Pa., 1970-86; gen. mgr. Pa. Farm Bur. Mems. Svcs. Corp., Camp Hill, Pa., 1986-92; assoc. adminstr. Pa. Farm Bur., Camp Hill, 1992-94. Pres. Pa. State Agrl. Adv. Coun., University Park, Pa., 1988-90, mem. 1984-94; mem. Pa. Adv. Coun. on Vocat. Edn., Harrisburg, 1982-85, Pa. Farm Show Com., Harrisburg, 1970-82. Com. mem. Keystone area coun. Boy Scouts Am., Mechanicsburg, Pa., 1945—, v.p., 1995-98; trustee Shiremanstown United Meth. Ch., 1977-87, adminstrv. bd. dirs., 1960-87; chmn. adv. bd. Mechanicsburg Rainbow Assn., 1975-80; scouting coord. Ctrl. Pa. Conf. United Meth. Ch., 1998-99, fin. and adminstrn. com.. With USAF, 1955-57. Recipient Silver Beaver award Boy Scouts Am., 1977, award of merit, 1982, God and Svc. Recognition award, 1986, Disting. Commr. award, 1990, James E. West Fellowship award, 1994, Grand Cross of Color award Internat. Order of Rainbow for Girls, 1979, Dairy and Animal Sci. Disting. Animal Sci. Alumnus award Pa. State U., 1998. Mem.: Am. Soc. Agrl. Cons., Coll. Agr. Alumni Soc. (bd. dirs. 1997—2000), Zembo Shrine, Masons (Daniel Carter Beard Masonic Scouter award 2003), Harrisburg Consistory, Henry P. Armsby Honor Soc. Republican. Avocations: golf, scouting, hiking, gardening. Home: 1783 Springwillow Dr Mechanicsburg PA 17055

DENISTON-TROCHTA, GRACE MARIE, educator, artist; d. Leopold and Amalie (Hotarek) Henzl; m. James Trochta; children: Paul Michael and Maria Suzanne Deniston. BA in Elem. Edn., U. Mich., 1962; MA in Art Edn., U. Iowa, 1984; PhD in Curriculum and Instrn & Art Edn., U. Wis., 1995. Cert. tchr art edn., elem. edn., Wis. 6th grade tchr. Colegio Franklin Roosevelt, Peru, 1963-64; art tchr., dept. chair St. Katharine /St. Mark's Sch., Bettendorf, Iowa, 1975-82; art tchr. U. Chgo. Lab. Sch., The Dewey Sch., 1984-87, Graland Country Day Sch., Denver, 1987-88, Sewickley Acad., Pa., 1988-89, Greenfield Pub. Sch. Dist., Wis., 1990-91; adminstr. People's Rep. China vis. scholar exchange program U. Wis., Madison, 1982-84, career counselor, placement cons., tchg. asst., lectr. dept. art, 1989-96; asst. prof. art U. No. Iowa, Cedar Falls, 1996-98, U. Wis., Oshkosh, 1998—2001; editl. cons. Visual Arts Rsch., 2000—. Co-advisor Student Art Educator's Assn., 1996-98. Exhibited in group shows at U. Chgo. Lab. Sch., 1986, Women's Caucus for Art, Meml. Union, U. Wis., Madison, 1992, Milw. War Meml., 1992, Milw. Inst. Art and Design, 1993, Electronic Gallery, Chgo., 1993; contbg. author: Real-World Readings in Art Ed., 2000; contbr. articles. Mem.: Women's Caucus for Art, U.S. Soc. for Edn. Through Art, Seminar for Rsch. Art Edn., Caucus on Social Theory and Art Edn. (comms. coord., exec. bd. 1998—2000), Nat. Art Edn. Assn., Am. Edn. Rsch. Assn. Home: 5912 Running Deer Trl Mc Farland WI 53558-9053

DENKE, CONRAD WILLIAM, motion picture producer; b. Cottonwood, Ariz., July 23, 1947; s. Lee Ernest and Barbara Ann (Russell) D.; m. Laura Lee Nielson; children: Alexander, Elisabeth. BA in Radio-TV Communications and Psychology, U. Wash., 1969. Dir. Sta. KCTS-TV, Seattle, 1967-69; dir. producer Cinema Assocs., Seattle, 1973-78; pres. Am. Motion Pictures, Seattle, 1978—2002; CEO Victory Studios, Seattle, 2002—. Bd. dirs. Am. Cinema Found., Whidbey Island Films; ptnr. Post Solutions, 2003—; publ., founder Highdef Mag., 2002—. Dir., producer: (indsl. documentary) Tunnels Under Chicago, 1981 (Chris award 1981, Gold award, Silver award, Cine Golden Eagle award, 1981); dir. (ednl. documentary) More Than Bows and Arrows, 1978 (Best Western Documentary 1978); producer: (TV series) Adventures on Sinclair Island, 1986, (talk show series) Teens Talk, (PBS documentary) Educations Wars, 1996, National Desk, 1997, 99. Mormon bishop, stake presidency. With USAF, 1969-73. Recipient Cine Golden Eagle award Council on Internat. Nontheatrical Events, 1977, 79, 89, 95, Silver Cindy award Info. Film Producers Am., 1977, 98, Gold Camera award U.S. Indsl. Film Festival, 1978, Telly award, 1989, 95, 97, 2 Telly's, 1998, 3 Gold awards Emerald City awards, 1997, 2000, World medal N.Y. Film Festival, 1998, 2 Aegis awards, 1998, 2 Aurora awards, 1998, Nat. ITVA award, 2000, Silver Screen award 2000. Mem. Internat. TV Assn. (dir. Seattle chpt. 1980-90, chpt. pres. 1983-84, chmn. HD Consortium for Nat. Assn. TV Program Execs., Silver Reel, 1986, Gold Reel 1997), Wash. Motion Picture Coun. (pres. 1992-96), Assn. Ind. Comml. Prodrs. (v.p. N.W. chpt. 1985-87, pres. 1987-90), Am. Cinema Found. in L.A. (bd. dirs., v.p. 1994—), Prodrs. Guild Am. Republican. Formed E Pluribus Unum Films in 2000. Office: Victory Studios 2247 15th Ave W Seattle WA 98119-2417 E-mail: conrad@victorystudios.com.

DENKE, PAUL HERMAN, retired aircraft engineer; b. San Francisco, Feb. 7, 1916; s. Edmund Herman and Ella Hermine (Riehl) D.; m. Beryl Ann Lincoln, Feb. 10, 1940; children: Karen Denke Mottaz, Claudia Denke Tesche, Marilyn Denke Oliver. BCE, U. Calif.-Berkeley, 1937, MCE, 1939. Registered profl. engr., Calif. Stress engr. Douglas Aircraft Co., Santa Monica, Calif., 1940-62, mgr. structural mechanics Long Beach, Calif., 1962-65, chief sci. computing, 1965-71, chief structures engr. methods and devel., 1972-78, chief scientist structural mechanics, 1979-84, staff mgr. Boeing fellow, 1985-2000; ret. Mem. faculty dept. engring. UCLA, 1941-50. Author numerous tech. papers. Assoc. fellow AIAA; mem. Soc. Automotive Engrs. (Arch T. Colwell merit award 1966, IAE Outstanding Engr. merit award 1985), Sigma Xi, Chi Epsilon, Tau Beta Pi. Democrat. Achievements include pioneering and developing finite element method of structural analysis. Home: 1800 Via Estudillo Palos Verdes Peninsula CA 90274-1908 E-mail: pauldenke@earthlink.net.

DENKER, HENRY, playwright, author, director; b. N.Y.C., Nov. 25, 1912; s. Max and Jennie (Geller) D.; m. Edith Rose Heckman, Dec. 5, 1942. LL.B., N.Y. Law Sch., 1934. Bar: N.Y. 1935. Practiced law, N.Y.C., 1935-38; exec. Research Inst. Am., N.Y.C., 1936-37; tax cons. Standard Stats. subs. Standard and Poor, N.Y.C., 1937-39. Lectr. dramatic writing Am. Theatre Wing, 1961-63, Coll. of the Desert. Writer, dir., prodr.: (radio series) The Greatest Story Ever Told, N.Y.C., 1947-57; author: (Broadway plays) Time Limit, 1956, A Far Country, 1961, Venus at Large, 1962, A Case of Libel, 1964, What Did We Do Wrong, 1968, Something Old, Something New, 1976, Horowitz and Mrs. Washington, 1979; (off-Broadway) The Name of the Game, 1967, A Sound of Distant Thunder, 1969, The Headhunters, 1974, CurtainCall, 1999; (screenplays) The Heartfarm, 1970, The Hook, Twilight of Honor, Time Limit, A Time for Miracles, 1980, Outrage, 1984; writer, dir., prodr. numerous TV dramas, 1950-66; TV spls. include Give Us Barrabas, 1964, Neither Are We Enemies, 1971, The Choice, The Court Martial of Lietenant Calley, Mother Seton, 1980, Love Leads the Way, 1985, Outrage, 1986, Case of Libel, 1986; author: I'll be Right Home Ma, 1949, My Son, The Lawyer, 1950, Salome, Princess of Galilee, 1954, That First Easter, 1956, The Director, 1970, The Kingmaker, 1972, A Place for the Mighty, 1973, The Physicians, 1975, The Experiment, 1976, The Starmaker, 1977, The Scofield Diagnosis, 1977, The Actress, 1978, The Error Judgement, 1979, Horowitz and Mrs. Washington, 1979, The Warfield Syndrome, 1981, Outrage!, 1982, The Healers, 1983, Kincaid, 1984, Love Leads the Way, 1985, A Case of Libel, 1985, Robert, My Son, 1985, Judge Spencer Dissents, 1986, The Choice, 1987, The Retreat, 1988, A Gift of Life, 1989, Payment in Full, 1990, Doctor on Trial, 1991, Labyrinth, 1994, This Child is Mine, 1995, To Marcy, With Love, 1996, A Place for Kathy, 1997, The Third Day, 1999, Benjie, 1999, Class Action, 2000, Clarence, 2002. Recipient Peabody award, 1949; Christopher award, 1953; Emmy award, 1948 Mem. Acad. TV Arts and Scis. (coun.), Authors League (coun.), Dramatists Guild (coun. 1967-69), Authors Guild, Writers' Guild. Jewish. Address: 241 Central Park W New York NY 10024-4530 E-mail: hwdenker@aol.com.

DENKEWALTER, KIM RICHARD, lawyer; b. Chgo., May 7, 1948; s. Walter and Doris A. (Gast) D. BA, Loyola U., Chgo., 1971; JD, U. Ill., Chgo., 1974. Bar: Ill. 1974, U.S. Dist. Ct. (no. dist.) Ill. 1974, U.S. Ct. Appeals (7th cir.) 1977, U.S. Supreme Ct. 1979. Ptnr. Abramovic, Denkewalter & Ryan, Chgo., 1974-79; pres. Denkewalter & Assocs., 1979-85, Denkewalter, Angelo & Minkow, 1986-97, Paramount Developers, Inc., 1997-98; real estate broker Chgo., 1978—. Mem. Hoopis Fin. Group, Northfield, Ill.; guest lectr. Am. Coll. Emergency Physicians, Rosemont, Ill., 1979-84. Served with USAR, 1970-76. Named hon. EMT-A, Ill. Dept. Pub. Health, 1983. Mem. ATLA, ABA, Ill. State Bar Assn., Chgo. Bar Assn., Ill. Real Estate Lawyers Assn., Mission Hills Country Club, The Men's Golf Assn. (bd. dirs., v.p. 1997-98, 2002—). Home: 1762 Sienna Ct Wheeling IL 60090-6747 Office: Denkewalter & Angelo 5215 Old Orchard Ste 1010 Skokie IL 60077 Office Fax: 847-583-2255. E-mail: krdlaw@aol.com.

DENKO, JOANNE D. psychiatrist, writer; b. Kalamazoo, Mich., Mar. 29, 1927; d. John S. and Marian Mildred (Boers) Decker; m. Charles Wasil Denko, June 17, 1950; children: Christopher Charles, Nicholas Charles, Timothey Charles. BA summa cum laude, Hope Coll., 1947; MD, Johns Hopkins U., 1951; MS in Psychiatry, U. Mich., 1963. Lic. psychiatrist Md., Ill, Mich., Ohio. Pvt. practice, Columbus, Ohio, 1961-68; staff psychiatrist Fairview Hosp., Cleve., 1968-97, Cleve. Clinic Health Systems, 1997—2003, Luth. Hosp., Cleve., 1998—2002; pvt. practice Rocky River, Ohio, 1968—2003. Cons. Juvenile Diagnostic Ctr., Columbus, 1967—68, VA Hosp., Cleve., 1968—72, Cmty. Mental Health Ctrs., Greater Cleve., 1974—80; clin. instr. Case Western Res. U., Cleve., 1981—83; adj. prof. Geneva Coll., Beaver Falls, Pa., 2001—. Author: Through the Keyhole at Gifted Men and Women, 1977; author: (pen name Victoria C.G. Greenleaf) A Handful of Ashes: One Mother's Tragedy, 2001, Fighting the Good Fight: One Family's Struggle against Adolescent Alcoholism, 2002, Into a Mirror and Through a Lens: Forty Poems on the Mother/Child Relationship from Conception to Marriage, 2003; author: (monograph) The Psychiatric Aspects of Hypoparathyroidism, 1962; contbr. articles to profl. jours.; author: poetry, 1960—. Mem. AAAS (reviewer children's books), Cleve. Astron. Soc. (bd. dirs. 1984-86, 96-98), Mensa (Cleve. area br. pres. 1986-87), Great Books Discussion Group (Rocky River, chmn. 1985-92, 94—), Kiwanis Internat. Russian Orthodox. Achievements include naming sexual deviance klismaphilia; research in special problems of adults of high intelligence, educating gifted girls, teenage alcoholism, mental illness in pre-literate peoples, psychiatric aspects of lupus, antisocial personality disorder, adolescent alcoholism. Home and Office: 21160 Avalon Dr Cleveland OH 44116-1120 E-mail: joannedenko@hotmail.com.

DENLINGER, EDGAR JACOB, electronics engineering research executive; b. Lancaster, Pa., June 17, 1939; s. Victor Jacob and Marian Alice (Shoemaker) D.; m. Cynthia Della Wilson, June 24, 1967; children— Crystal Shereen, Craig Wesley BS in Engring. Sci., Pa. State U., 1961; MSE.E., U. Pa., 1964, PhD in E.E., 1969. Research engr. Applied Research RCA, Camden, N.J., 1961-65; research assoc. Moore Sch. U. Pa., Phila., 1965-67; mem. tech. staff MIT Lincoln Lab., Lexington, Mass., 1967-73, RCA Labs, Princeton, N.J., 1973-83, group head signal conversion systems research, 1983-87; group head microwave systems rsch. David Sarnoff Research Ctr., Princeton, N.J., 1987-92, sr. mem. tech. staff, 1992—. Adj. prof. dept. elec. engring. Drexel U., Phila., 1982-88. Contbr. articles to profl. jours. Patentee microwave devices and circuits Mem. Hickory Acres Civic Assn., East Windsor, N.J., 1973-81 Recipient Achievement award David Sarnoff Rsch. Ctr., Princeton, 1979, 94. Fellow IEEE (treas. sect. 1980-83, vice chmn. 1984, chmn. 1985) Lodges: Mason, Tall Cedars, Shriners. Republican. Presbyterian. Avocations: music, swimming. Home: 7 Wheatston Ct Princeton Junction NJ 08550-1936

DENLINGER, JOHN KENNETH, journalist; b. Lancaster, Pa., Mar. 25, 1942; s. John Emory and Elizabeth (Smith) D.; m. Nancy Dodson, July 29, 1995; children: Lauri, Scott. BS in Econs, Pa. State U., 1964. Mem. staff Pitts. Press, 1964-66; mem. staff Washington Post, 1966—; sports columnist, 1975-90. Author: For the Glory, 1994; co-author: Athletes for Sale, 1975, Redskin Country: From Baugh to the Super Bowl, 1983, Golf: The Mind Game, 1990, Tennis: The Mind Game, 1991, Skiing: The Mind Game, 1993. Named to U.S. Basketball Writers Assn. Hall of Fame, 2001. Office: The Washington Post 1150 15th St NW Washington DC 20071-0002

DENLINGER, VICKI LEE, secondary school physical education educator; b. Dayton, Ohio, June 13, 1961; d. David Lee and Barbara Ann (Zimmerman) D.; 1 child, David Micheal. Student, Ohio State U., 1979-82; BS in Edn., Wright State U., 1982-85; postgrad. studies, Miami U., Oxford, Ohio, 1986-87, U.S. Sports Acad., Daphne, Ala., 1996-97, U. Dayton, 2001—. Cert. phys. edn. and health tchr., Ohio; lic. athletic trainer, Ohio. Student athletic trainer Wright State U., Dayton, Ohio, 1983-85; asst. athletic trainer Oakwood (Ohio) City Sch., 1984-86; grad. asst. athletic trainer Miami U., Oxford, Ohio, 1986-87; subst. tchr. Oakwood City Sch., Kettering Moraine City Schs., Ohio, 1987-89; athletic trainer Kettering Moraine City Schs., Kettering, Ohio, 1987-96, tchr., 1989—; owner InnerPrize, Kettering, 1996—. Pub. spkr. Greater Dayton Athletic Trainers, 1987—, InnerPrize, 1996—; advisor Kettering Fairmont Student Athletic Trainers Assn., Kettering Moraine City Schs., 1989—96; facilitator Student Assistance Support Group, Kettering-Moraine City Schs., 1994—2000; instr. Kettering Awareness Tobacco Edn. Program, 1997—2001; advisor Students Against Destructive Decisions, 1997—. Mem. PTA Assns. of various Kettering-Moraine Pub. Schs., 1989-00; co-dir. Kettering 24-Hour Relay Challenge, 1999. Named Jaycee of the Month Region E, 1996, Ohio Jaycees, Most Outstanding Write-Up of the First Quarter, 1996, Ohio Jaycees. Mem. NEA, ASCD, Nat. Athletic Trainer's Assn. (cert. athletic trainer), Ohio Athletic Trainers Assn., Greater Dayton Athletic Trainers Assn., Nat. Strength and Conditioning Assn., Internat. Weight Lifting Assn. (cert. weight trainer), Ohio Edn. Assn., Kettering Edn. Assn., Ohio Assn. for Health, Phys. Edn., Recreation and Dance, Am. Coll. Sports Medicine, Nat. Fedn. Interscholastic Coaches Edn. Program/Am. Coaching Effectiveness Program, Sports First Aid Instr. Avocations: Christian studies, fitness, personal devel. and sports, athletics. Home: 3489 Valleywood Dr Kettering OH 45429-4234 Office: Kettering Fairmont HS 3301 Shroyer Rd Kettering OH 45429-2635 E-mail: denlingerv@aol.com.

DENLOW, MORTON, federal magistrate judge; b. 1947; BA, Washington U., 1969; JD, Northwestern U., 1972. Pvt. practice, Chgo., 1972-96; sr. lectr. Loyola U. Sch. Law, 1983-95; adj. prof. trial advocacy Northwestern U. Sch. Law, 1990-91; magistrate judge U.S. Dist. Ct. (no. dist.) Ill., 1996—. With USAR, 1970-76. Office: US Dist Ct 219 S Dearborn St Ste 1356 Chicago IL 60604-1802 Fax: 312-554-8547.

DENMAN, JAMES BURTON, lawyer; b. Brownwood, Tex., Nov. 15, 1947; s. James Burton and Margaret Gwendolyn D.; m. Donna Van Tuyle, Feb. 18, 1978; children— Tuyle, Lindsay. A.A., Porterville Jr. Coll., 1968; B.S., Calif. State U.-Fresno, 1970; J.D., Samford U., 1973. Bar: Fla. 1974. Ptnr., assoc. Dolan, Denman & Gramling, P.A., Fort Lauderdale, 1975-78; prin. James B. Denman & Assocs., P.A., Fort Lauderdale, 1978-80; ptnr. Bunnell, Denman & Woulfe, P.A., Fort Lauderdale, 1980— . Bd. dirs. Bethany Christian Sch., Fort Lauderdale, 1984. Mem. Assn. Trial Lawyers Am., Acad. Fla. Trial Lawyers. Democrat. Lutheran. Clubs: Lauderdale Yacht, Tower. Home: 1940 NE 59th St Fort Lauderdale FL 33308-2446 Office: Bunnell Denman & Woulfe PA 888 E Las Olas Blvd Fl 4 Fort Lauderdale FL 33301-2272

DENMAN, NICHOLAS WERNER, insurance executive; b. Rottenberg, Germany, Jan. 27, 1946; came to U.S., 1953; s. Charles Newton and Hilda D.; m. Barbara Jean Schlitz, Oct. 12, 1968; children: Stephen, Lara, Shawn, Nicole. BA, Kent (Ohio) State U., 1974; Assoc. Degree in Claims, Risk Mgmt., Loss Control Mgmt. CPCU, CFP, cert. fund specialist. Supr. Sugardale Meats, Canton, Ohio, 1968-69; patrolman Canton Police Dept., 1969-73; security officer Kent State U., North Canton, 1970-74; claims adjuster Nationwide Ins., Canton, 1974-80, mgr. claims, 1980-83, ins. rep. Shreve, Ohio, 1983—. Dir. Shreve Bus. Assn., 1986—, pres., 1998-2002. With U.S. Army, 1964-67. Decorated Silver Star, Bronze Star medals. Mem. Soc. CPCU's, Internat. Assn. Fin. Planners, Am. Legion, Vietnam Vets. Am., Masons, KC. Republican. Roman Catholic. Avocation: photography. Home: 2539 Timothy Pl Wooster OH 44691-9185 Office: PO Box 507 Shreve OH 44676-0507 E-mail: denmann@nationwide.com.

DENMARK, BERNHARDT, manufacturing executive; b. Bklyn., June 6, 1917; s. William M. and Kate (Lazarus) D.; m. Muriel Schechter, Sept. 22, 1943; children: Richard J., Karen. AB, NYU, 1941; postgrad., Am. U., 1941-42, Nat. Inst. Pub. Affairs, 1941-42. Vice pres. sales Telecoin Corp., N.Y.C., 1946-49; v.p. sales Internat. Latex Corp., N.Y.C., 1949-55; mgr. mktg. Playtex Co., N.Y.C., 1955-59, v.p., gen. mgr. family products div., 1959-63, v.p. mktg., 1963-65; pres. Playtex Co. Playtex div., 1965-67, Internat. Playtex Corp., N.Y.C., 1968-69, chmn. bd., 1969; exec. v.p., dir., mem. exec. com. Glen Alden Corp., N.Y.C., 1969-72; pres. Bevis Industries, Inc., White Plains, N.Y., 1972-76, Bus. Mktg. Corp. for N.Y.C., 1977-78; chmn. Denmark, Donovan & Oppel Inc., N.Y.C., 1978-85; chmn. bd. dirs. Advanced Photonix, Inc., Camarillo, Calif., 1992—, Xsirius, Inc., Camarillo, 1992—. Bd. dirs. Stanley Warner Corp., Schenley Industries, BVD Corp., Kleinerts Inc., Advanced Photonics Inc. Served to capt. AUS, 1942-46. Mem.: Fairview Country (Greenwich, Conn.); City Athletic (N.Y.C.). Home: 870 United Nations Plz Apt 34B New York NY 10017-1820

DENMARK, DARRON B. compliance specialist; b. Hollywood, Fla., May 7, 1968; s. Ellen D and Henry R Taylor(Stepfather). BA in Pub. Adminstrn., Fla. Meml. Coll., Miami, 1999; MA in Orgnl. Mgmt., U. of Phoenix, Ft. Lauderdale, Fla., 2001; MPA in Pub. Adminstrn. (Pub. Policy), Clark Atlanta U., Atlanta, 2003. Appeals analyst United Healthcare of Ga., Atlanta, 1997—2001; complaince specialist Emory U., Atlanta, 2001—. With USAR, 1987—95. Mem.: Nat. Forum for Black Pub. Adminstrs. (assoc.). Democrat. Home: 305 Avery Glen Decatur GA 30030 Office: Emory University 1256 Briarcliff Rd 4th Flr Atlanta GA 30306 Personal E-mail: dbdenm@aol.com.

DENN, CYRIL JOSEPH, financial advisor; b. Mankato, Minn., Jan. 23, 1948; s. Bertram Henry and Hildegard M. (Drummer) D.; m. Sandra Lee Jones, Oct. 22, 1966 (div. 1970); m. Darlene Kay Wittrock, Apr. 19, 1974; children: Darcy Ann, Amanda Kay, Cassandra Jo. BS, Mankato State U., 1977, 5-yr. cert., 1982; ChFC, Am. Coll., 1985. CLU, 1982. Factory laborer Kato Engring. Co., Mankato, 1971—74; sales rep. Met. Life, Mankato, 1974—76, sales mgr., 1976—79, sales rep., 1979—82, mktg. specialist Aurora, Ill.; 1982—83, br. mgr. Sioux Falls, SD, 1983—84, sales rep., 1984—86; regional mgr. Cath. Aid Assn., St. Paul, 1986—89; mgr. Prudential Ins. Co., Sioux Falls, 1989—91, Aberdeen, SD, 1992—94; asst. mgr. Farm Bur. Fin. Svcs., Aberdeen, 1995—96; fin. advisor Bus., Estate, Retirement & Ins. Planning, Mankato, 1996—2000; fin. svcs. exec., fin. planner MetLife Fin. Svcs., Mankato, 1997—2000; fin. svcs. rep. Denn Ins. & Fin. Svcs., 2000—. Mem. St. Clair (Minn.) Pub. Sch. Bd., 1981-83. With U.S. Army, 1968-71. Fellow: Life Underwriters Tng. Coun.; mem.: Farmamerica (devel. com., mktg. com., programs com., amb. program 2003—), Ea. S.D. Soc. Fin. Svc. Profls. (pres. 1992—93, video teleconf. coord. 1992—96), Mankato Area Chamber and Conv. Bur. (bus. devel. com. 1996—2001, bus. devel. chair 2000—01), Am. Legion, Leave-A-Legacy Mankato Area (chmn. mem. com. 2000—), S.D. Planned Giving Coun. (steering com. 1994—95, chair 1995—2001, v.p. programs), Soc. Fin. Svc. Profls. (profl. achievement in cont. edn. com. 1991—94, midwest liaison team 1992—2000, mem. devel. com. 1994—97), S.D. Assn.-NAIFA (chmn. life underwriters tng. coun. 1993—96), Aberdeen Assn.-NAIFA (bd. dirs. 1992—96, sec.-treas. 1994—95, pres. elect 1995—96), Gen. Agy. Mgrs. Assn. (career devel. award 1994), Sioux Falls Assn.- NAIFA (bd. dirs. 1991—92, edn. chmn., co-chmn. life underwriting tng. coun.), Midwest Pony of Americas Club (pres. 1988—91, horse show chmn. 1989), S.D. Ponies of Americas Club (bd. dirs. 1986—97, pres. 1987—89). Republican. Roman Catholic. Avocations: horses, reading.

DENN, MORTON MACE, chemical engineering educator; b. Passaic, N.J., July 7, 1939; s. Herbert Paul and Esther (Taub) D; m. Vivienne Roumani; children: Matthew Philip, Susannah Rachel, Rebekah Leah. BS in Engring., Princeton U., 1961; PhD, U. Minn., 1964, DSc (hon.), 2001. Postdoctoral fellow U. Del., Newark, 1964-65, from asst. prof. to prof. Chem. Engring., 1965-77, Allan P. Colburn prof., 1977-81; prof. U. Calif., Berkeley, 1981-99, chmn. dept. chem. engring., 1991-94. Harry Pierce prof. chem. engring. Technion, Israel Inst. Tech., Haifa, 1979-80; Chevron Energy prof. chem. engring. Calif. Inst. Tech., 1980; vis. prof. chem. engring. U. Melbourne, Australia, 1985; program leader for polymers Ctr. for Advanced Materials Lawrence Berkeley Nat. Labs., 1983-99; vis. Forchheimer prof. Hebrew U., Israel, 1998-99; disting. prof. chem. engring. City Coll. CUNY, 1999—, prof. physics, 2001—, Albert Einstein prof. sci. and engring., 2001—, dir. Benjamin Levich Inst. for Physico-Chem. Hydrodynamics, 2000—. Author: Optimization by Variational Methods, 1969, (co-author) Introduction to Chemical Engineering Analysis, 1972, Stability of Reaction and Transport Processes, 1975, Process Fluid Mechanics, 1980, Process Modeling, 1986; co-editor Chemical Process Control, 1976; contbr. numerous articles to profl. jours., author book chpts. Guggenheim fellow, 1971-72; William M. Lacey lectr. Calif. Inst. Tech., 1979, Fulbright lectr., 1979-80; Peter C. Reilly lectr. Notre Dame U., 1980; Bicentennial Commemoration lectr. La. State U., 1984; Arthur Kelly lectr. Purdue U., 1987; Stanley Katz lectr. CCNY, 1990, other lectureships. Fellow AAAS, AIChE (editor jour. 1985-91, Profl. Progress award 1977, William H. Walker award 1984, Warren K. Lewis award 1998, Inst. lectr. 1999); mem. NAE, Am. Soc. Engring. Edn. (chem. engring. divsn. lectureship award 1993), Soc. Rheology (editor jour. 1995—, Bingham medal 1986), Brit. Soc. Rheology, Polymer Processing Soc., Am. Phys. Soc., Sigma Xi. Office: Levich Inst City Coll CUNY 1M Steinman Hall New York NY 10031 E-mail: denn@ccny.cuny.edu.

DENNANY, KELLY, mechanical engineer, test engineer; b. Kalamazoo, Sept. 26, 1972; d. Robert Dale Jr. and Debra Lee Dennany. BS in Mech. Engring., GMI Engring. and Mgmt. Inst., Flint, MIch., 1995. ABS lab. sr. test engr. Continental Teves, Auburn Hills, Mich., 1995—. Mem. Soc. Automotive Engrs. Republican. Baptist. Avocations: rubber stamping, cooking, crafts.

DENNARD, ROBERT HEATH, engineering executive, scientist; b. Terrell, Tex., Sept. 5, 1932; s. Buford Leon and Loma (Heath) Dennard; m. Jane Bridges; children: Robert(dec.), Amy, Holly. BSEE, So. Methodist U., 1954, MSEE, 1956; PhD, Carnegie Inst. Tech., 1958. Staff engr. IBM, Yorktown Heights, NY, 1958—63; rsch. staff mem. IBM Rsch. Ctr., Yorktown Heights, NY, 1963—71, group mgr., 1971—79, fellow, 1979—. Contbr. articles; patentee (scientific works) in field, including basic dynamic RAM memory cell. Named Inventor of Yr., N.Y. Intellectual Property Law Assn., 1995; named to Nat. Inventors Hall of Fame, 1997; recipient Nat. medal of Tech., Pres. U.S., 1988, Harvey prize, Technion-Israel Inst. Tech., 1990, Aachener and Munchener prize for tech. and applied sci., 2001. Fellow: IEEE (Edison medal 2001); mem.: Am. Philos. Soc., NAE. Avocation: Scottish country dancing.. Office: IBM Rsch Ctr PO Box 218 Yorktown Heights NY 10598-0218

DENNEEN, JOHN PAUL, lawyer; b. N.Y.C., Aug. 18, 1940; s. John Thomas Denneen and Pauline Jane Ludlow; m. Mary Veronica Murphy, July 3, 1965 (dec. Dec. 2000); children: John Edward, Thomas Michael, James Patrick, Robert Andrew, Daniel Joseph, Mary Elizabeth. BS, Fordham U., 1963; JD, Columbia U., 1966. Bar: N.Y. 1966, U.S. Ct. Appeals (2d cir.) 1974, U.S. Dist. Ct. (so. and ea. dists.) N.Y. 1975, Mo. 1987. Assoc. Seward & Kissel, N.Y.C., 1966-75; sr. v.p., gen counsel, sec. GK Techs., Inc., Greenwich, Conn., 1975-83; exec. v.p., gen. counsel, sec. Chromalloy Am. Corp., St. Louis, 1983-87; ptnr. Bryan Cave LLP, St. Louis, 1987-99; exec. v.p. corp. devel. and legal affairs, sec. NuVox, Inc., St. Louis, 1999—. Mem. ABA, Internat. Bar Assn., N.Y. State Bar Assn., N.Y.C. Bar Assn., Bar Assn. Met. St. Louis. Office: NuVox Inc Ste 500 16090 Swingley Ridge Rd Chesterfield MO 63017-6029

DENNEHY, BRIAN, actor; b. Bridgeport, Conn., July 9, 1939; m. Jennifer Dennehy; 3 children from previous marriage. Grad., Columbia U.; postgrad., Yale U. Appeared in motion pictures Semi-Tough, 1977, F.I.S.T., 1978, Foul Play, 1978, Butch and Sundance: The Early Days, 1979, 10, 1979, Little Miss Marker, 1980, Split Image, 1982, First Blood, 1982, Never Cry Wolf, 1983, Gorky Park, 1983, Twice in a Lifetime, 1985, Silverado, 1985, Cocoon, 1985, F/X, 1986, Legal Eagles, 1986, Best Seller, 1987, The Belly of an Architect, 1987, Return to Snowy River, 1988, Miles from Home, 1988, Cocoon: The Return, 1988, The Last of the Finest, Seven Minutes, Presumed Innocent, 1990, F/X 2, 1991, Gladiators, 1991, Midnight Movie, 1993, Gilligan's Island: The Movie, 1997, Tommy Boy, 1995, The Stars Fell on Henrietta, 1995, Romeo and Juliet, 1996, Dish Dogs, 1998, Out of the Cold, 1999, Deep River, Finders, Keepers, Looking for Mr. Goodbar, Summer Catch, 2001, Stolen Summer, 2002; theatre appearances include Streamers, off-Broadway, 1976, The Rat in

the Skull, Wisdom Bridge Theatre, Chgo., 1985, The Cherry Orchard, Bklyn. Acad. Music, 1988, The Iceman Cometh, Goodman Theatre, Chgo., 1990, Says I, Says He, Sea Plays, Bus Stop, Julius Caesar, Ivanov, The Front Page, Translations, Galileo, A Touch of the Poet, Goodman Theatre, Chgo., MacBeth, Romeo & Juliet, 1996, Long Days Journey into Night (Tony award winner for best actor), 2003; appeared in TV series Big Shamus, Little Shamus, 1979, Star of the Family, 1982-83, Birdland, 1993-94, (BBC series) Nostromo, 1995, A Season in Purgatory, 1996, Undue Influence, 1996, Larry McMurty's Dean Man Walk, 1996; numerous movies for TV including Annie Oakley, Showtime Cable TV Tall Tales and Legends series, 1985, Acceptable Risk, 1986, HBO prodn. The Lion of Africa, 1987, Perfect Witness, 1989 (Cable Ace nominee), The Last of the Finest, 1990, Shattered Vows, 1993, Murder in the Heartland, 1993 (Emmy nomination, Supporting Actor - Miniseries or Special, 1993), Prophet of Evil, 1993, Foreign Affair, 1993 (CableAce award, Best Actor in a movie or miniseries), Rising Son, Bloodfeud, Evergreen, Acceptable Risks, The Terrorist, A Rumor of War, In Broad Daylight, The Last Place on Earth, Teamster Boss: The Jackie Presser Story, Birdland, Leave of Absence, Jack Reed: An Honest Cop, Final Appeal, Pride and Extreme Prejudice, (miniseries) A Killing in a Small Town, 1990 (Emmy nominee for Outstanding Supporting Actor), To Catch a Killer, 1991 (Emmy nominee, Am TV awards nominee), The Burden of Proof, 1992 (Emmy nominee for Outstanding Supporting Actor), A Season in Purgatory, 1996, Nostromo, 1996, Dead Man's Walk, 1996, Day One, Undue Influence, 1996, Jack Reed: Death and Vengeance, 1996, ; dir., co-writer, actor, co-exec. prodr.: (TV movies) Jack Reed: Champion of the Cheap Homicide, Jack Reed: A Killer Amoungst Us, Jack Reed: One of Our Own, Shadow of A Doubt, Jack Reed: A Search for Justice, Jack Reed: Death and Vengeance, 1996, Netforce, 1999, Too Rich: The Secret Life of Doris Duke, Fail Safe, 2000, A Season on the Brink, 2002, Death of a Salesman (also prodr.), 2000 Served with USMC, Vietnam Won 1999 Tony Award, Best Actor, Drama, Death of a Salesman. Office: care Susan Smith & Assocs 121 N San Vicente Blvd Beverly Hills CA 90211-2303

DENNEHY, RAYMOND LEO, philosopher, educator; b. San Francisco, Aug. 31, 1934; s. Joseph Patrick and Mary Agnes Dennehy; m. Maryann Dennehy, Aug. 4, 1990; children: Mark, Bridget, Andrea, Rosalind. BA, in Philosophy, U. San Francisco, 1962; postgrad., U. Calif., Berkeley, 1962—64; PhD in Philosophy, U. Toronto, 1973. Asst. prof. philosophy U. Santa Clara, Calif., 1966—72; instr. philosophy West Valley C.C., Saratoga, Calif., 1972—74; asst. dean, lectr. philosophy U. San Francisco, 1974—79, assoc. prof. philosophy, 1979—85, prof. philosophy, 1985—. Founding mem., tchr. St. Ignatius Inst., U. San Francisco, 1976—2001, Campion Coll., San Francisco, 2002—. Author: Reason & Dignity, 1981, Anti-Abortionist at Large, 2002; editor: Christian Married Love, 1981. With USN, 1954—58, PTO. Recipient Human Life award, San Francisco United for Life, 1999. Mem.: Nat. Assn. Scholars, Am. Soc. for Bioethics and Humanities, Fellowship of Cath. Scholars (bd. dirs. 1984—87), Am. Cath. Philos. Assn. (exec. com. 1983—86), Am. Maritain Assn. (pres. 1986—94). Republican. Roman Catholic. Office: Univ San Francisco Philosophy Dept 2130 Fulton St San Francisco CA 94117

DENNER, MELVIN WALTER, retired life sciences educator; b. North Washington, Iowa, Aug. 27, 1933; s. Norbert William and Petronella Nettie (Eischeid) D.; m. N. Anne Greer, June 19, 1965; children: Mark Andrew, Michael Alan (twins). BS, Upper Iowa U., 1961; MS (NSF fellow), U. Ky., 1963; PhD, Iowa State U., 1968. Asst. prof. life scis. U. So. Ind., Evansville, 1968-71, assoc. prof., 1971-76, prof., 1976-95, Disting. prof., 1989-90, premed. advisor, chmn. dept., 1969-95, assoc. chmn. div. scis. and math., 1975-77, acting chmn. div. scis. and math., 1976-77, chmn., 1979-87; dean Sch. of Sci. and Engring. Tech., 1994; coord. univ. self-study U. So. Ind., Evansville, 1976, 86, 96; ret., 1996. Eucharistic minister Corpus Christi Ch., 1981—; panelist Ind. Com. Higher Edn., 1993. Contbr. articles to profl. jours.; editor USI Ret newsletter. Vice chmn. Iowa Young Dems., 1958-60; bd. dirs. Deaconess Hosp. Allied Health Programs, chmn. radiation tech. adv. com., 1987-95; bd. dirs. Evansville Mus. Arts and Scis.; mem. alumni adv. bd. U. So. Ind., 1982—; spl. minister Corpus Christi Ch., 1981—; mem. facilcom. Ludington (Mich.) H.S., 2000—. With USN, 1953-57. Named Ind. Prof. of Yr., 1989, Sagamore of the Wabash, 1989; NSF fellow 1962, 64, NIH fellow, 1966-67, Alumni Achievement fellow, 1967-68. Fellow AAAS (film critic); mem. Internat. Soc. Invertebrate Pathology (founding), Am. Soc. Parasitologists, Am. Micros. Soc. (nat. treas.), North Ctrl. Assn. Colls. and Secondary Schs. (visitation team 1976-94), Am. Inst. Biol. Scis., Sigma Xi (pres. So. Ind. chpt.), Sigma Zeta. Home: 215 S Lakeshore Dr Apt 20 Ludington MI 49431-2076 *The greatest gift we can have on earth is knowledge, for in knowledge we have truth.*

DENNERY, LINDA, newspaper publishing executive; b. Phila., July 7, 1947; V.p., gen. mgr. Times-Picayune, New Orleans, 1987—97, pres., mem. of advisory bd., 1997—99; pub. Star-Ledger, Newark, 1999—. Bd. dirs. Kingsley House, Touro Infirmary, Bur. Govtl. Rsch., So. Newspaper Pub. Assn., Internat. Women's Forum. Mem.: bd. of dir. of Kingsley House, Touro Infirmary, Bureau of Governmental Research, Southern Newspaper Pub. Assoc., International Women's Forum. Office: Star Ledger 1 Star Ledger Plz Newark NJ 07102-1200*

DENNETT, LISSY, sculptor; b. Vienna, May 3, 1926; came to U.S., 1939; d. Joseph and Margaret (Friedlander) Weiss; m. Leonard Dennett, Dec. 21, 1947; children: Steven E., Ronald B., Richard A. BA in Art/design, Bklyn. Coll., 1948; postgrad., Queens Coll., 1952-53, Hunter Coll., 1954. Tchr. K-6, art specialist N.Y.C. Bd. Edn., 1952-72; sculptor Great Neck (N.Y.) adult program, 1988—. Sculpture shown in many exhbns. including Nassau County Mus. Fine Arts, Roslyn, N.Y., Grace Bldg., N.Y.C., Designer Showcase, Sands Point, N.Y., Westchester C.C. Gallery, Valhalla, N.Y., Unitarian Ch., White Plains, N.Y. Pres. Kensington Civic Org., Great Neck, 1980-88; bd. dirs. North Shore Cmty. Arts Coun., 1980—; mem. art adv. com. Great Neck Ctr. for Visual and Performing Arts, 1993—. Recipient Salmagundi award, N.Y.C., 1980, 82; Stanley Altman Stone award, Cera-Cast Art Foundry award, Mamaroneck Artists Guild, Port Washington Art Adv. Coun. award for Sculpture, Alexander Rappaport Meml. award for Sculpture. Mem. Artists Network of Great Neck (pres. 1989-95, 99-2001), Nat. Assn. Women Artists (jury 1988-90, 95-97), Contemporary Sculptors Guild (exhbn. chair 1983-85), Visual Arts Alliance of L.I. (rec. sec. 1990-96), Sculptors Inc. (pres. 1985-89). Home: 10 Canterbury Rd Apt 1C Great Neck NY 11021-2611 E-mail: lissywd@aol.com.

DENNEY, DWIGHT LEE, engineer; b. Arvin, Calif., Aug. 17, 1954; s. Daryle R. and Roberta L. (McElroy) D.; m. Diana L. Harris, June 15, 1974; children: Daniel L., Deborah L. BA in Physics and Math., Point Loma Nazarene Coll., 1976; PhD in Physics, Iowa State U., 1982. Postdoctoral fellow Ames Lab./Iowa State U., 1982-83; sr. prin. sys. engr. Raytheon Missle Sys., Tucson, 1983—; pvt. part-time cons. DLD, 1991—. Bd. dirs. Ninth St. Christian Sch., Upland, Calif., 1990-94. Mem. Am. Phys. Soc., Soc. Photo-Optical Instrumentation Engrs. Achievements include copyright on infrared target and background simulation; patent on realtime infrared image generation and realtime seeker simulation. Home: 3629 W Sunbright Dr Tucson AZ 85742-1137 Office: Raytheon Missile Systems PO Box 11337 Tucson AZ 85734-1337

DENNEY, LAURA FALIN, insurance company executive; b. Knoxville, Tenn., Sept. 23, 1948; d. Jack Gordon and Marilyn Frances (Ramsey) Falin; m. Richard Earl Buchanan, Feb. 14, 1970 (dec. Oct. 1972); m. Peter Michael Denney, Sept. 6, 1978. BS, East Tenn. State U., 1970. From underwriting asst. to regional territory mgr. Safeco Ins. Co., Atlanta, 1971—2000, personal bus. mgr., 2000—01, mgr. personal lines underwriting, 2001—. Counselor St. Patrick's Episc. Ch., Dunwoody, Ga., 1983-86. Republican. Mem. Ch. Of God. Avocations: golfing, reading, decorating. Office: Safeco Ins Co 2055 Sugarloaf Cir Duluth GA 30097-4932

DENNICK, LORI ANN (LORANDEN), artist, model, actress; b. Cannonsburg, Pa., Feb. 8, 1962; d. Albert William and Mary Alice (Baldwin) D. AS, Pa. Comml. Bus. Coll., Washington, 1987; BA, U. Md., 1992; MFA, Hunter Coll., N.Y.C., 1999. Freelance artist, Pitts., 1992—; editor, art dir. Common Ground, Pitts., 1995-96; talent developer Main Line Models, McKeesport, Pa., 1999-2000; plus size model Main Line Inc., McKeesport, 1999-2000; model Dreams and Desires, 2003—, All Star Mgmt., 2003. Art exhibitor St. Art, Pitts., 1993—; model Shaun Internat. of Ill., Elegant Extras; model for catalogs; extra The Mothman Prophecies, 2001, The Clearing, 2003. Artist Free to Do Anything, 1999, Flying Goddess, 1999, Heart Attack, 1999 (Best of Show 1999), Content Goddess, 1999; role of Beverly in Sorrow is My Sister, 2003. Mem. daffodil days com. Am. Cancer Soc., Pitts., 1999. Named Miss 16 Plus-Model of Yr., Miami, Fla., 1995, Ms. Plus Internet World, 2002, Ms. Elegant Pa., 2002, Ms. Plus Pa., 2002, Miss Pa. Galaxy, 2002, Miss Pa Galaxy, 2003, Miss Am. Rose McKeesport City Queen, 2003, Ms. Picture Perfect Pa., 2003; recipient Ms. McKeesport Am. States, 2003. Mem.: AFTRA, Models United (dir. plus size models divsn.), Internat. High IQ Soc. Democrat. Presbyterian. Avocations: theater arts, travel, painting, jewelry design. E-mail: loranden1@gopittsburgh.com.

DENNIES, SANDRA LEE, city official; b. Buffalo, Dec. 26, 1951; d. Norman John and Shirley Edith (Dils) D.; m. Robert Francis Gilbane, Sept. 21, 1974 (div. Apr. 1987); children: Brandon Michael, Gianpatrick. AS in Dental Hygiene, U. Bridgeport, Conn., 1972, BS in Dental Hygiene Edn., 1973; MS in Health Scis., So. Conn. State U., 1979. Dental hygienist various orgns., New Haven, 1972-73, Leonard B. Zaslow, DDS, Westport, Conn., 1973-81; lectr. U. Bridgeport, 1973-76; planner City of Bridgeport, 1977-79, planning asst., 1979-81; grants dir. City of Stamford, Conn., 1981—. Sec. Com. on Emergency Med. Disaster Planning, Bridgeport, 1978-79; dir., dep. dir. Stamford Coliseum Authority, 1982-91; dep. dir. Stamford Film Commn., 1986-88. Editor, chief Hy-Light Jour., 1973-76. Mem. Stamford Youth Planning and Adv. Bd., 1981-91, Stamford Youth Svc. Bur., 1991-95, United Way Corp., Stamford, 1986-93; pres., sec. Alcohol and Drug Abuse Coun., 1987-92; mem. bd. Christian Outreach North Stamford Congl. Ch., 1988-92, 95-2000, mem. pastoral rels. com., 1995—; mem. Coun. Chs. and Synagogues Assembly, Stamford, 1989; pres. Stamford Mcpl. Supervisory Employees Union, 1991-99, mem. 1981—; v.p., sec. Stamford Sch. Readiness Found., 1998—. Democrat. Avocations: piano, clarinet, guitar, skiing. Home: 171 Shadow Ridge Rd Stamford CT 06905-1813 Office: City of Stamford 888 Washington Blvd PO Box 10152 Stamford CT 06904-2152 E-mail: sandra171@aol.com.

DENNIN, JOSEPH FRANCIS, lawyer, former government official; b. N.Y.C., June 9, 1943; s. William Wilfred and Kathryn L (Sever) D.; m. Sandra Earl Peek, Dec. 28, 1968; children: Theresa Michel, Allison Kathleen, James Joseph. BA with great distinction, Stanford U., 1965, JD, 1968; postgrad., U. Helsinki, Finland, 1968-69. Bar: Calif. 1969, N.Y. 1970, D.C. 1986, U.S. Supreme Ct. 1985, U.S. Ct. Appeals (fed. cir.) 1987, Ct. Internat. Trade 1987. Assoc. Simpson, Thacher & Bartlett, N.Y.C., 1969-75; counsel U.S. Senate Intelligence Com., Washington, 1975-76; staff asst. to Pres. White House, Washington, 1976-78; dir. ops. U.S. Internat. Trade Commn., Washington, 1978-79; dep. assoc. atty. gen. Dept. Justice, Washington, 1979-81; dep. asst. sec. for fin., investment and svcs. Dept. Commerce, Washington, 1981-82, dep. asst. sec. for Africa, the Near East and South Asia, 1982-84, asst. sec. for internat. econ. policy, 1984-86; ptnr. internat. dept. McKenna & Cuneo, L.L.P., Washington, 1986—. Bd. dirs. U.S.-Taiwan Bus. Coun.; mem. bd. advisors N.Am. Free Trade and Investment Report; mem. N.Am. Free Trade Agreement Article 19 Panel. Gen. editor Law and Practice of the World Trade Orgn. Fulbright grantee Inst. Internat. Edn., 1968 Mem. ABA. Home: 5108 Nahant St Bethesda MD 20816 2336

DENNIN, ROBERT ALOYSIUS, JR., pharmaceutical research scientist; b. Newark, Mar. 5, 1951; s. Robert Aloysius Sr. and Elizabeth Jane (Cooney) D. B in Biology, Montclair State Univ., 1975, M in Biology, 1976. From asst. scientist II to sr. clin. rsch. coord. Hoffmann La Roche, Inc., Nutley, N.J., 1977-96, mgr. clin. ops. drug supply, 1996—. Rschr. in AIDS and cancer. Contbr. chpt. in book and articles to profl. jours. Vol. Nat. Guard Militia Mus., NJ. Mem. AAAS, Am. Soc. for Microbiology, N.Y. Acad. Scis. Avocation: guitar. Office: Hoffmann-LaRoche Inc 340 Kingsland St Nutley NJ 07110-1199 E-mail: robert_a.dennin_jr@roche.com.

DENNING, EILEEN BONAR, management consultant; b. Chester, Pa., June 24, 1944; d. Michael Bonar and Lucille J. Denbroeder. Postgrad., Greenwich U. Pres. Denning and Co., Castro Valley, Calif., 1975—. Mem. adv. bd. Diablo Valley Coll. bus. div.; faculty adv. bd. Am. Inst. Banking. Designed and developed mgmt. tng. programs for various banks in California. Coord. Castro Valley Earthquake Preparedness, 1980—; fundraiser Castro Valley Schs., 1976—. Mem. Nat. Women's Polit. Caucus. Avocation: raising and training great pyrenees and german shepherd dogs. Home and Office: Apt 42 3419 Washington St Lemon Grove CA 91945-2571 E-mail: eileendenning2@cox.net.

DENNING, KAREN CRAFT, finance educator; b. Pitts., Mar. 23, 1952; d. Edward Harvey and Esther Naomi Craft; m. John Thomas Denning; children: Naomi Liza, Chloe, Lacey. AB, Cornell U., 1974; PhD, U. Pitts., 1986. Lectr., asst. prof. Case Western Res. U., Cleve., 1985—88; prof. W.Va. U., Morgantown, 1988—2003, Fairleigh Dickinson U., 2003—. Editor: e-Jour. Social Studies, 2002—; contbr. articles to profl. jours. Bd. dirs. Katz Grad. Sch. Bus. Ph.D. Alumni Bd., Pitts. Grantee Internat. Programs Instrnl. Tech. grantee, W.Va. U., 1998—99. Mem.: Am. Fin. Assn., So. Fin. Assn., Midwestern Fin. Assn., Ea. Fin. Assn., Fin. Mgmt. Assn., 20th Century Club, Beta Gamma Sigma (pres. 1998). Presbyterian. Avocations: travel, piano, reading, skiing.

DENNING, MICHAEL MARION, marketing professional, educator; b. Durant, Okla., Dec. 22, 1943; s. Samuel M. and Lula Mae (Waitman) D.; m. Suzette Karin Wallance, Aug. 10, 1968 (div. 1979); children: Lila Monique, Tanya Kerstin, Charlton Derek; m. Donna Jean Hamel, Sept. 28, 1985; children: Caitlin Shannon, Meghan O'Donnell. Student, USAF Acad., 1963; BS, U. Tex., 1966, Fairleigh Dickinson U., 1971; MS, Columbia U., 1973; PhD, Kingsfield U., 1998. Mgr. systems IBM, White Plains, N.Y., 1978-79, mgr. svc. and mktg. San Jose, Calif., 1979-81; nat. market support mgr. Memorex Corp., Santa Clara, Calif., 1979-81, v.p. mktg., 1981-82; v.p. mktg. and sales Icot Corp., Mountain View, Calif., 1982-83; exec. v.p. Phase Info. Machines Corp., Scottsdale, Ariz., 1983-84, Tricom Automotive Dealer Systems Inc., Hayward, Calif., 1985-87; pres. ADS Computer Svcs., Inc., Toronto, Ont., Can., 1985-87, Denning Investments, Inc., Palo Alto, Calif., 1987, Pers. Solutions Group, Inc., Menlo Park, Calif., 1990-96, Crystal Rsch. Corp., Scottsdale, Ariz., 1997-98; pres., CEO, Landtech Environmental Inc., Scottsdale, Ariz., 1998-99; pres. Impulse Response Group, Inc., Phoenix, 2002—. Adj. prof. Arizona State U. Coll. Bus., Tempe, 1997—; chmn. Exec. Com. Emerging Entrepreneurs, Scottsdale, Az., 1998—. With USAF, 1962-66; Vietnam. Mem. Rotary, Phi Beta Kappa, Lambda Chi Alpha (pres. 1965-66). Republican. Methodist. Office: Impulse Response Group Inc 501 N 44th St Phoenix AZ 85008 E-mail: michael.denning@asu.edu.

DENNING, PETER JAMES, computer scientist, engineer; b. N.Y.C., Jan. 6, 1942; s. James Edwin and Catherine M. (Manton) D.; m. Dorothy Elizabeth Robling, Jan. 24, 1974; children— Anne, Diana. BEE, Manhattan Coll., 1964, ScD (hon.), 1985; MS in Elec. Engring., MIT, 1965, PhD, 1968; LLD (hon.), Concordia U., 1984; PhD (hon.), Pace U., 2002. Asst. prof. elec. engring. Princeton U., 1968-72; assoc. prof. computer scis. Purdue U., 1972-75, prof., 1975-84, head dept., 1979-83; dir. Rsch. Inst. Advanced Computer Sci. NASA Ames Rsch. Ctr., Mountain View, Calif., 1983-90, rsch. fellow, 1990-91; assoc. dean, chair of computer sci. dept. George Mason U., 1991-97, dir. Ctr. for New Engr., 1993-98, vice provost for continuing profl. edn., 1997-98, univ. coord. for process reengring., 1998-2000, spl. asst. to v.p. for info. tech., 2000—02, chair of technology coun., 2001—02; prof., chmn. computer sci. dept. Naval Postgrad. Sch., 2002—, dir. Cebrowsku Inst. Info. Suoeriority and Innovation, 2003—. Co-founder CSNET, 1981; bd. dirs. Charles Babbage Inst., 2000—, Ctr. for Nat. Software Studies, 1996—; mem. tech. adv. bd. Sequent Computer Corp., 1985-91, Hewlett-Packard Labs., 1989-93. Author: Professional Development Seminars, 1968—, also textbooks and numerous rsch. papers; columnist Am. Scientist mag., 1985-93. Recipient Outstanding Faculty award Princeton U. Engring. Assn., 1971, Best Paper award Am. Fedn. Info. Processing Socs., 1972, Disting. Svc. to Computing Rsch. award Computing Rsch. Assn., 1989, Centennial Engring. award Manhattan Coll., 1992, Commonwealth Va. Outstanding Educator award, 2003; NSF fellow, 1964-67. Fellow IEEE, AAAS, Assn. for Computing Machinery (pres. 1980-82, Karl Karlstrom Outstanding Educator award 1996, Outstanding Contbn. award 1998, Outstanding Computer Sci. Educator award 1999), Am. Soc. for Engring. Edn., Assn. for Computing Machinery (chmn. publs. bd. 1992-98, chmn. edn. bd. 1998—, dir. info. tech. profession initiative 1999-2001, editor-in-chief Computing Surveys 1977-79, Comm. ACM 1983-92, Best Paper award 1968, Recognition of Svc. award 1974, Disting. Svc. award 1989), N.Y. Acad. Scis.; mem. Sigma Xi, Eta Kappa Nu, Tau Beta Pi. Office: Naval Postgrad Sch Code CS Monterey CA 93943 E-mail: pjd@nps.navy.mil.

DENNIS, ANTHONY JAMES, lawyer; b. Manchester, Conn., Feb. 11, 1963; BA cum laude, Tufts U., 1985; JD, Northwestern U., Chgo., 1988. Bar: Conn. 1988, DC 1989, US Dist. Ct. Conn. 1988. Assoc. Robinson & Cole, Hartford, Conn., 1988-89; atty. Aetna, Inc., Hartford, 1989-92, counsel, 1992—. TV and radio talk show guest. Author: The Rise of the Islamic Empire and the Threat to the West, 1996, Letters to Khatami: A Reply to the Iranian President's Call for a Dialogue Among Civilizations, 2001, Osama Bin Laden: A Psychological and Political Portrait, 2002; co-author: Healthcare Antitrust: Strategies for Changing Provider Organizations, 1994; contbr. articles to profl. jours. Mem. Conn. Bar Assn. (subcom. chmn. 1990-93, exec. com. 1990—, com. chmn. 1990—, treas. 1993-94, vice-chmn. 1994-95, chmn. 1995-99), D.C. Bar Assn., Am. Health Lawyers Assn., KC (past grand knight). Office: Aetna Inc 151 Farmington Ave Hartford CT 06156-3124 E-mail: dennisaj@aetna.com.

DENNIS, CARL, poet; Artist in residence SUNY Buffalo. Instr. creative writing Warren Wilson Coll. Author: Practical Gods, Ranking the Wishes. Recipient Ruth Lilly prize, Poetry Mag. and Modern Poetry Assn., 2000, Pulitzer prize, 2002; fellow, Guggenheim Found., Nat. Endowment for Arts. Office: SUNY Buffalo 306 Clemens Hall N Campus Buffalo NY 14260

DENNIS, DIANE JOY MILAM, retired architect; b. Jacksonville, Fla., Oct. 8, 1925; d. Robert Richerson Milam, Meriel Lapham Wilson; m. Thomas Gordon Dennis, Nov. 9, 1974 (dec. Apr. 1999). Grad., Bennington Coll., 1943—47; MArch, Columbia U., 1949—55; studied landscape arch., Harvard U., 1978. With several archtl. firms, N.Y.C.; with Edward Ruekel Stone on Kennedy Ctr. bldg. Mem.: AIA. Home: 47 E 64th St Apt 10A New York NY 10021

DENNIS, DONNA FRANCES, sculptor, art educator; b. Springfield, Ohio, Oct. 16, 1942; d. Donald Phillips and Helen Frances (Hogue) D. BA in Art, Carleton Coll., 1964; student, Coll. Art Studies Abroad, Paris, 1964-65, Art Students League, N.Y.C., 1965-66. Instr. Skowhegan Sch. Painting and Sculpture, Maine, 1982, Sch. Visual Arts, N.Y.C., 1983-90, SUNY, Purchase, 1984-85, 87, Princeton U., N.J., 1984; assoc. prof. SUNY Purchase Coll., 1990-96; prof. SUNY, 1996—, Doris and Karl Kempner disting. prof., 2001—03. One-woman shows include Holly Solomon Gallery, N.Y.C., 1976, 80, 83, 98, Contemporary Arts Ctr., Cin., 1979, Neuberger Mus. of SUNY-Purchase, 1985, Univ. Gallery, U. Mass., Amherst, 1985, Bklyn. Mus., 1987, Del. Art Mus., Wilmington, 1988, Indpls. Mus. Art, 1991-98, Sculpture Ctr., N.Y.C., 1993, Dayton Art Inst., 2003; exhibited in group shows Venice Biennale, Italy, 1982, 84, Whitney Mus., N.Y.C., 1979, 81, Tate Gallery, London, 1983, Hirshhorn Mus., Washington, 1979, 84, Biennial of Pub. Art, Neuberger Mus., 1997, Asheville (N.C.) Mus. Art, 1998, experiencenter, Dayton Art Inst., Dayton, Ohio; permanent commissions include decorative fence P.S. 234, N.Y.C., I.S. 5, Queens, N.Y., Wonderland Sta., MBTA, Boston, North Plaza, Klapper Hall, Queens Coll., Queens, N.Y., Am. Airlines Terminal, Terminal One, Kennedy Airport, N.Y.C. Recipient Art award for excellence in design N.Y.C. Art Commn., 1987, Art award Am. Acad. and Inst. of Arts and Letters, 1984, Bessie Set Design award, 1992; grantee N.Y. State Creative Artists, 1975, 81, N.Y. Found. for Arts, 1985, 92; fiscal sponsorship, N.Y. Found. for Arts, 2002-; fellow Guggenheim Found., 1979, NEA, 1977, 80, 86, 94, Pollock-Krasner award, 2001. Democrat. Home: 131 Duane St New York NY 10013-3850

DENNIS, ELIZABETH P. social worker, therapist, consultant; b. Spokane, Wash., Aug. 31, 1949; d. Joe E. and Carol Virginia (Glen) H.; m. David R. Dennis (div. Sept. 1981); children: Natasha, Michael. BA in Psychology, U. Tex., 1972, MSSW, 1987. Lic. master social worker, advanced clin. practitioner; lic. marriage and family therapist. Rehab. tchr. Criss Cole Rehab. Ctr., Austin, Tex., 1978-85; social worker Austin Community Nursery Sch., Austin, Tex., 1987-88, Charter Lane Hosp., Austin, Tex., 1988-89; contract therapist Austin Child Guidance Ctr., Austin, Tex., 1987-89, therapist/grant coord., 1989—2000, intake and program dir., 2000—02; blind children's cons. Tex. Commn. for the Blind, Austin, 2002—. Vol. Polit. Action Orgns., Austin, Tex. Grantee: Kappa Gamma Rehab., 1986, Delta Sigma Theta, Bernice Milburn Moore, U. Tex., 1986, Bus. and Profl. Women, Washington, 1986, Victor and Myra Ravel, U. Tex., 1987; named Austin Social Worker of Yr., 2002. Mem. NASW, Nat. Assn. Marriage and Family Therapists, Phi Kappa Phi. Democrat. Avocations: gardening, reading, traveling. Office: Tex Commn for the Blind 4800 N Lamar Blvd Austin TX 78756

DENNIS, EVERETTE EUGENE, JR., foundation executive, educator, writer; b. Seattle, Aug. 15, 1942; s. Everette Eugene and Kathryn Marie (Platt) D.; m. Emily Thompson Smith, 1987. BS, U. Oreg., 1964; MA, Syracuse U., 1966; PhD, U. Minn., 1974; postdoc., Harvard U., 1978-79. Info. officer dept. mental health State of Ill., Chgo., 1966-68; asst. prof. Kans. State U., Manhattan, 1968-72; asst. prof., assoc. prof. then prof. U. Minn., Mpls., 1972-81, dir. grad. program. Sch. Journalism and Mass Communication, 1978-81; prof., dean Sch. Journalism U. Oreg., Eugene, 1981-84; founding exec. dir. Freedom Forum Media Studies Ctr. Columbia U., N.Y.C., 1984-96; also v.p., 1989-94; sr. v.p., 1994-97; exec. dir. Internat. Consortiums Univs., 1996-97; founding pres. Am. Acad. in Berlin, 1996-2000; Felix E. Larkin disting. prof. Grad. Sch. of Bus., Fordham U., 1997—; COO Internat. Longevity Ctr., 1999—. Head Project on Future of Journalism and Mass Communication Edn.; trustee Internat. Mus. Photography at Eastman House, Rochester, N.Y., Internat. Inst. Communications, London, Ctr. Internat. Journalists. Reston, Va.; councillor Am. Antiquarian Soc., Worcester, Mass. Author, editor 42 books including: The Magic Writing Machine, 1971, Other Voices: The New Journalism in America, 1973, Justice Hugh Black and the First Amendment, 1978, Enduring Issues in Mass Communication, 1978, The Media Society, 1978, Reporting Processes and Practices, 1981, New Strategies for Public Affairs Reporting, 1983, Basic Issues in Mass Communication, 1984, Reshaping the Media, 1989, Media Freedom and Accountability, 1989, The Cost of Libel, 1989, Media Debates, 1991, 4th edit., 2002, Understanding Mass Communication, 7th edit. 2002, Media and the Environment, 1991, Beyond the Cold War, 1991, Of Media and People, 1992, Demystifying Media Technology, 1993, Higher Education in the Information Age, 1993, America's Schools and the Mass Media, 1993, Radio-The Forgotten Medium, 1995, The Culture of Crime, 1995, American Communication Research, 1996, Publishing Books, 1997, Media and Public Life, 1997, Media and Children, 1996, Media-Black and White, 1996, Media and Congress, 1997, Media and Democracy, 1998; editor-in-chief Media Studies Jour. 1987-96; contbr. articles to profl. jours. Summer fellow Stanford U., 1969, East-West Communication Inst., Hawaii, 1976; liberal arts fellow in law, Harvard U., 1978-79, vis. Nieman fellow, 1980, John F. Kennedy Sch. Govt. rsch. fellow, 1981, John Henry Newman fellow Fordham U., 2002-03 recipient H. Kreighbaum Under 40 award for nation's outstanding journalism educator, 1982, U. Oreg. Webfoot award, 1985, Disting. Svc. award U. Oreg., 2002, Global Media Rsch. award Ctr. for Global Media, 2002; inducted to Oreg. Journalism Hall of Fame, 2001. Fellow Am. Orthopsychiat. Assn.; mem. Assn. Edn. in Journalism & Mass. Comms. (pres. 1983-84), Am. Polit. Sci. Assn., Internat. Comm. Assn., Soc. Profl. Journalis ts, Internat. Mass Comm. Rsch. Soc., Internat. Inst. Comm., Coun. Fgn. Rels.; Clubs: Century Assn. (N.Y.), Harvard Club (N.Y.). Office: ILC-USA 60 E 86th St New York NY 10028-1009 also: Fordham U 113 W 60th St New York NY 10023-7404

DENNIS, FRANK GEORGE, JR., retired horticulture educator; b. Lyons, N.Y., Apr. 12, 1932; s. Frank George and Corinne Isabel (Smith) D.; m. Katharine Ann Merrell, June 5, 1954. BS in Agriculture, Cornell U., 1955, PhD in Pomology, 1961. Postdoctoral fellow NSF, Gif-sur-Yvette, France, 1961-62; asst. prof. Cornell U., Geneva, N.Y., 1962-68, assoc. prof., 1968—, Mich. State U., East Lansing, 1968-72, prof., 1972-96; ret., 1996. Contbr. articles to profl. jours. Fulbright fellow, Morocco, 1990. Fellow Am. Soc. for Hort. Sci. (v.p. 1985-86, Gourley award 1985, sci. editor HortScience 1997-2000); mem. Internat. Soc. Hort. Sci. (chmn. working group 1984-90), Sigma Xi. Office: Mich State U Dept Horticulture East Lansing MI 48824-1325 E-mail: fgdennis@msu.edu.

DENNIS, GARY C. neurosurgeon, educator; b. Washington, Dec. 27, 1950; s. Creed and Yvonne (Bush) C.; children: Gary Jr., Gina, Gregory. BA, Boston U.; MD, Howard U. Intern Johns Hopkins Hosp., Balt., 1976-77; residency Baylor Coll. of Medicine Affiliated Hosp., Houston, 1977-81; chief of neurosurgery Kern Med. Ctr., Bakersfield, Calif., 1981-83; clin. assoc. prof. U. Calif., San Diego, 1981-85; chief of neurosurgery Howard U., Washington, 1984—, asst. prof surgery, 1984-90, assoc. prof., 1990—; attending physician DC Gen. Hosp., Washington, 1990—. Vis. lectr. neurosurgery Johns Hopkins Sch. Med., 1980-98; surg. cons. D.C. Gen . Hosp., 1986-89; mem. Mayors Commn. to oversee Med. Examiners Office, Washington, 1990, Mayors Transition Team for Health, Washington, 1990; mem. D.C. Commn. on Jud. Disabilities and Tenure, 2000—; mem. Sec.'s Adv. Com. on Regulatory Reform, 2001-02; chmn. bd. Delmarva Found. D.C.; mem. Bd. Med. Edn. for South African Blacks, 2002—. Mem. Practicing Physicians Adv. Coun., Health Care Fin. Agy., Washington, 1991-99, Com. on Health Care Reform, Cong. Black Caucus, Washington, 1994—; bd. dirs. Am. Liver Found., 1999-2002; mem. D.C. Health Care Reform Commn. Named One of Top Drs. S.E. Area, Washingtonian Mag., 1995. Fellow ACS; mem. Med. Soc. D.C. (pres. 1996-98, chmn. bd. dirs. 1998-99, alt. del. to AMA 2001), Nat. Med. Assn. (pres.-elect 1997—, pres. 1998-99), Am. Assn. Neurol. Surgeons (mem. chair 1994-95), Nat. Med. Assn. (trustee 1992-97, 98—, pres. 1998), Howard U. Med. Alumni Assn. (pres. 2002--). Avocations: music, outdoor cooking, fishing. Office: Howard U Hosp 2041 Georgia Ave NW Washington DC 20060-0001 E-mail: gcdennis@pol.net.

DENNIS, GREGORY JAMES, music educator, secondary school educator; b. 1947; s. William James and Anita Esther D.; m. Diane Rae Lien, 1969; children: Daniel Charles, Joel Andrew. BS in Choral Music Edn., U. Wis., Platteville, 1969; MM in Choral Music Edn., U. Mich., 1998. Cert. tchr. Mich., Wis. Tchr. choral, instrumental and gen. music Lowell Jr. HS Flint (Mich.) Pub. Schs., 1969—74, Flint Ctrl. HS, 1974—76, Flint Ctrl. HS and Flint Fine Arts HS, 1976—77, Mt. Horeb (Wis.) HS, 1977—2000; choral dir. Edgewood Coll., Madison, spring 1997. Sr. lectr. U. Wis., Platteville, 2000—; chair, coord., sect. leader Wis. Honors Project/Wis. Sch. Music Assn., Madison, 1987-99; dir. Mt. Horeb Chorale, 1986—, Masterworks Chorale and Orch., 1996-2001; dir. Madison Boy Choir, 1991-93, Iowa County Scenic Sounds Male Chorus, 1988-2000, Platteville Chorale, 2001—. Bd. dirs. Song of Norway, Ltd., Mount Horeb, 1989-92. Falhauber scholar U. Wis.-Platteville, 1967. Mem. Am. Choral Dirs. Assn., Internat. Thespian Soc., Mich. Sch. Vocal Assn. (bd. dirs. 1975-77), Wis. Music Educators Assn. (bd. dirs. 1982-84), Wis. Choral Dirs. Assn. (bd. dirs. 1994-96, actor, dir., choreographer), Lions. Roman Catholic. Avocations: model railroading, flower gardening, house plants, music, travel. Office: Univ Wis 1 University Plz Platteville WI 53818 E-mail: dennisg@uwplatt.edu.

DENNIS, HELEN MARION, gerontologist, educator; b. Lansdale, Pa, Aug. 27, 1940; d. Eric and Hedy (Gruenberg) Gutman; m. Lloyd B. Dennis, Dec. 1, 1963; children: Lauren, Susan. BA, Pa. State U., 1962; MA, Calif. State U., Long Beach, 1976. Asst. coordinator data analysis George Washington U., Washington, 1965-69; project dir., lectr. Andrus Gerontology Ctr. U. So. Calif., Los Angeles, 1976—; dir. Andrus Inst., Andrus Gerontology Ctr. U. So. Calif., 1995-98; project dir. The Conf. Bd., NYC, 1988-90; weekly columnist Copley Paper--Daily Breeze, 2001—. Bd. dir. Temple Menorah, Redondo Beach, Calif., 1981-92, pres. 1992-95; mem. LA Coun. Careers Older Am., 1985-90; mem. adv. bd. Project Reinvest, Coro Found., LA, 1985; pres. Career Encores, 1991-93; bd. dir. Ctr. Health Care Rights, Excellence in Tchg. Award, 1998 USC Andrus Assoc., Univ. of So. Calif. Recipient Francis Townsend award, Calif. State U., 1999, Disting. Tchr. award, Assn. of Gerontology in Higher Edn., 2003. Mem. Internat. Soc. Pre-Retirement Planners (nat. pres. 1986-87, pres. So. Calif. chpt. 1983-85, editl. bd.), Am. Soc. Aging, Gerontol. Soc. Am., Nat. Coun. on Aging, RSVP (v.p. 1997-2000). Home and Office: 347 Via El Chico Redondo Beach CA 90277-6757

DENNIS, JACK BONNELL, computer scientist, educator; b. Elizabeth, N.J., Oct. 13, 1931; SB, SM, MIT, 1954, ScD in Elec. Engring., 1958. Asst. prof. elec. engring. MIT, Cambridge, 1959-65, assoc. prof., 1965-69, prof. computer sci. and engring., 1969-87; prof. computer sci. and engring. emeritus, 1987—; pres. Dataflow Computer Corp., 1987-2000. Chief scientist Acorn Networks, 1996-2001. Recipient Eckert-Mauchly award IEEE Assn. for Computing Machinery, 1984 Fellow IEEE, Assn. for Computing Machinery. Office: MIT Lab for Computer Sci 200 Technology Sq Cambridge MA 02139-3539

DENNIS, JAMES LEON, judge; b. Monroe, La., Jan. 9, 1936; s. Jenner Leon and Hope (Taylo) Dennis; children: Stephen James, Gregory Leon, Mark Taylo, John Timothy. BS in Bus. Adminstrn, La. Tech. U., Ruston, 1959; JD, La. State U., 1962; LLM, U. Va., 1984. Bar: La. 1962. Assoc. firm Hudson, Potts & Bernstein, Monroe, 1962—65, ptnr., 1965—72; judge 4th Dist. Ct. La. for Morehouse and Ouachita Parishes, 1972—74, La. 2d Circuit Ct. Appeals, 1974—75; assoc. justice La. Supreme Ct., 1975—95; coord. La. Constnl. Revision Commn., 1970—72; del., chmn. judiciary com. La. Constnl. Conv., 1973; judge U.S. Ct. Appeals Fifth Cir., New Orleans, 1995—. Chmn. La. Commn. on Bicentennial U.S. Constn.; mem. La. Ho. of Reps., 1968—72. With U.S. Army, 1955—57. Mem.: ABA (com. on appellate practice), 4th Jud. Bar Assn., La. Bar Assn., Rotary. Methodist. Office: US Courthouse 600 Camp StRm 219 New Orleans LA 70130-3425

DENNIS, JOHN DAVISON, minister; b. Pitts., Sept. 18, 1937; s. John Wellington and Helen Isabella (Davison) D.; m. Nancy Schumacher, Jan. 7, 1967; children: Michael, Andrew. AB, Wesleyan U., 1959; BD, Princeton Theol. Sem., 1962, ThM, 1965. Ordained to ministry United Presbyn. Ch. (USA), 1962. Asst. pastor First Presbyn. Ch., Germantown, Pa., 1962-69, sr. pastor Corvallis, Oreg., 1969—. Exch. min. St. Columba's Presbyn. Ch., Johannesburg, Republic of South Africa, 1978. Chaplain Germantown Hosp., 1965-69; west coast dean Presbyn. Young Pastors Seminars, 1983-85; pres. Madison Ave. Task Force, 1975-77, pres. Corvallis Community Improvement, Inc., pres. USSR Sister City Assn., 1989-90; founder Corvallis Fish Emergency Aid Svc., 1969-76; trustee Ecumenical Ministries of Oreg., 1989-98, chmn. bd. dirs. 1996-98; bd. dirs. United Way of Benton County, 1986-90; candidate U.S. Congress from Oreg. 5th dist., 1988; asst. squash coach Princeton Univ., 1959-62. Recipient Spl. Achievment award City of Corvallis, 2002; fellow Aspen Inst., 1987; Pacific coast doubles squash champion, 1972-73. Mem. Rotary (charter mem., dir. local club, Rotarian of Yr. 1998). Home: 2760 NW Skyline Dr Corvallis OR 97330-6518 Office: 114 SW 8th St Corvallis OR 97333-4546 E-mail: church@1stpres.org.

DENNIS, KIMBERLY OHNEMUS, philanthropy consultant; b. Waltham, Mass., Aug. 3, 1957; d. Clifford Andrews and Jeanne (Kelley) Ohnemus; m. William Cullen Dennis, Aug. 20, 1991; children: D. William, Jesse Kelley. BA in Sociology, Bowdoin Coll., 1979. Child protective caseworker Maine Dept. Human Svcs., Caribou, Maine, 1979-80; adminstrv. asst. John M. Olin Found., N.Y.C., 1980-81, program officer, 1984-88; dir. of program devel. Pacific Rsch. Inst., San Francisco, 1988-89; dir. of public affairs Inst. for Humane Studies, Fairfax, Va., 1989-91; exec. dir. Philanthropy Roundtable, Indpls., 1991-96; philanthropy cons. Indpls., 1996—; exec. dir. D&D Found., Indpls., 1998—; dir. Nat. Rsch. Initiative, Am. Enterprise Inst., 2002—. Commn. mem. Nat. Commn. on Philanthropy and Civic Renewal, Washington, 1996-97; bd. dir. W.H. Brady Found., 1997-2003, Maggie Valley, NC, Ind. Women's Forum, 1999-2003. Mem. Polit. Economy Rsch. Ctr., Bozeman, Mont., 1991-2000, chmn. bd., 1996-2000; adv. bd. Donner Found. New Leadership Fellows Program, N.Y.C., 1995-97; judge Acton Inst. Samaritan Awards, Grand Rapids, 1994-97; pres. bd. dirs. Donors Trust, 1999—; trustee Earhart Found., 2002--; bd. dirs. The Philanthropy Roundtable, 2002--. Mem. The Phila. Soc. Republican. Office: D&D Found 1150 17th St NW Washington DC 20036- E-mail: dennisko@aol.com.

DENNIS, PATRICIA LYON, adult education educator; b. Rockford, Tenn., June 13, 1933; d. Howard Stanton and Dora Hester (Maynard) Lyon; m. Norman Bryan Dennis Jr., Jan. 12, 1957 (dec. Jan. 1985); children: Sarah Dennis Banks, Rebecca Dennis Hampton. BS, George Peabody Coll., 1955; MA, U. Mo., 1977; postgrad., Auburn U., 1972-73, U. Kans., 1982-92, U. Mo., Kansas City, 1994, 96. Cert. tchr.; cert. libr. media specialist, Kan; elem. classroom tchr., N.C., Mich., Mo., Ala. 3d grade tchr. Ray Street Elem. Sch., High Point, N.C., 1955-56; kindergarten and 3d grade tchr. Wurtsmith Dependent Sch., Clark AFB, Philippines, 1957-59; spl. reading tchr., 1st grade tchr. McDonald Elem. Sch., K.I. Sawyer AFB, Mich., 1961-63; kindergarten tchr. Gladden Elem. Sch., Richards-Gebaur AFB, Mo., 1964-65; 2d grade tchr., libr. Goose AFB Dependent Sch., Labrador, 1965-67; 2d grade tchr. Edgewood Acad., Wetumpka, Ala., 1969-70; 1st and 4th grade tchr. Trinity Christian Day Sch., Montgomery, Ala., 1970-72; 2d and 3d grade tchr. Fairview Elem. Sch., Olathe, Kans., 1974-77; libr. media specialist Wash. Elem. Sch., Olathe, Kans., 1977-99; instr. continuing edn. Johnson County C. C., Overland Pk., Kans., 1999—. Pres. Pre-Sch. Bd., Gunter AFB, 1968-69; children's choir dir. Leawood (Kans.) Bapt. Ch., 1979-84, Sunday sch. dept. dir., 1987-88, ch. libr., 1990-93; bd. dirs. Scholarship Pageant, Kansas City, 1988-96; chaperone, traveling companion Miss Am.-Kans. Scholarship Pageant, Pratt, Kans., 1989-98; commr., book rev. com. Kans. State Reading Cir. Commn., Topeka, 1985-91, 94-96, 97-99; primary subcom. chairperson Kans. State Reading Circle, 1998-99. Mem.: MLA, NEA, Kans. Reading Assn., Kans. Assn. Sch. Librs. (presenter 1990—97), Olathe Culture Group (v.p. 2002—), Sigma Alpha Iota (treas. 1954), Alpha Delta Kappa (sec. 1999—2002, pres. 2002—, mem. cmty. scholarship bd. 2002—03). Republican. Baptist. Avocations: harp, piano, voice, dance, physical fitness. Home and Office: 10525 Chesney Ln Olathe KS 66061-2775

DENNIS, PETER RAY, environmental corporate executive; b. Milw., Nov. 21, 1938; s. Raymond Wilbur and Elizabeth Susan (Oliver) D.; m. Mary Joan Dennis, July 22, 1977; children: Matthew Lee, Rebecca Ann. BS, U. Wis., 1962, LLB, 1964. Bar: Wis. 1964, U.S. Dist. Ct. (we. dist.) Wis. 1964. Pres. Peter R. Dennis & Assocs., Madison, Wis., 1961-66, Neoflex Rubber, Co., Madison, Wis., 1966-68; Poly-R Corp., 1966-68; cons. Chas. R. Feldstein Co., Chgo., 1968-73; exec. v.p. Idrex, Inc., Chgo., 1973-86; pres. Hazardnet, Inc., Chgo., 1986-95, Geomar, Inc., 1994-96; treas., exec. v.p., sec. Opti-Med., Ltd., 1996—. Dir. Frankfort (Ill.) Devel. Corp., 1988-91, St. Peters United Ch. of Christ, Frankfort, 1989-92. Mem. ABA (corp. sec. 1964—), Wis. Bar Assn., Air Waste Mgmt. Assn. (Lake Mich. sec. 1990-94), Ill. Mfrs. Assn. (environ. com. 1973-85), Masons, Shriners. Avocations: hunting, fishing, wood carving. Office: Opti-Med Inc 212 W Sycamore St Sycamore IL 60178 Home: 212 W Sycamore St Sycamore IL 60178

DENNIS, RALPH EMERSON, JR., lawyer; b. Marion, Ind., Dec. 19, 1925; s. Ralph Emerson Sr. and Martha Elnora (Bahr) D.; m. Virginia Lea Harter, June 19, 1949 (dec. Oct. 1981); children: Nancy J. Barefoot, Kathleen Ann Tolk, Amel Joseph, Mary Elizabeth Saler, Ralph E. III; m. Barbara Grose, May 31, 1985. BS, Dartmouth Coll., 1946; JD, Ind. U., 1950. Bar: Ind. 1950, U.S. Supreme Ct. 1971. Sr. ptnr. Dennis, Cross, Raisor, Jordan & Marshall, P.C., Muncie, Ind., 1956-80, Dennis, Raisor, Wenger & Haynes, P.C., Muncie, 1980-85, Dennis & Wenger, P.C., Muncie, 1985-86, Dennis, Wenger & Abrell, P.C., Muncie, 1986—. Chmn. bd. dirs. Lift-A-Loft Corp., Muncie. City judge, Muncie, 1951-59, city atty., 1964-67; trustee Muncie Community Schs., 1960-63. With USN, 1944-46. Recipient Disting. Service award, Muncie Jaycees, 1959, Good Govt. award, Muncie Jaycees, 1959. Mem. ABA, Ind. Bar Assn. Clubs: Del. Country (Muncie). Lodges: Elks, Masons. Republican. Lutheran. Home: 411 N Greenbriar Rd Muncie IN 47304-3117 Office: Dennis Wenger & Abrell PC 324 W Jackson St Muncie IN 47305-1625

DENNIS, RUTLEDGE M. sociology educator, researcher; b. Charleston, SC, Aug. 16, 1939; s. David and Ora Jane (Porcher) D.; children: Shay Tchaka, Imaro Marlin Aki, Kimya Nuru, Zuri Sanyika. BS, S.C. State U., 1966; MA, Wash. State U., 1969, PhD, 1975. Dir. Black studies program Va. Commonwealth U., Richmond, 1971-78, assoc. prof. dept. sociology, 1978-89; Commonwealth prof. dept. sociology George Mason U., Fairfax, Va., 1989—, prof. dept. sociology, 1992—. Co-dir. sociology grad. program George Mason U.; coord. Southeastern Regional African Seminar, Richmond-Charlottesville, 1973-76; del. Ea. Va. Internat. Consortium, 1972-77; pres. Assn. Black Sociologists, 1981-83; founder Rutledge Dennis Found. for Human Devel., Ctr. for African Am. Culture and Leadership; co-founder African-Am. Acad. Co-author: The Politics of Annexation, 1982; editor: JAI Press Series in Race and Ethnic Relations, 1990—, Racial and Ethnic Politics, 1994, The Black Middle Class, 1995, W.E.B. Du Bois: The Scholar as Activist, 1996, Black Intellectuals, 1997, Oliver C. Cox, 2000, Marginality and Society: Issues in Class, Race, and Gender, 2003; co-editor: The Afro-Americans, 1976, Race and Ethnicity in Research Methods, 1993, Race and Ethnicity: Comparative and Theoretical Approaches, 2003. Housing commr. Richmond Redevel. and Housing Authority, 1977-80; bd. dirs. Housing Opportunities Made Equal, Richmond, 1976-80. With U.S. Army, 1960-63. Fellow Fgn. Affairs scholar, 1965; recipient Cmty. Svc. award Boys Clubs Am., 1976; named Outstanding Educator of Am., 1975; recipient Reise-Melton Cultural award, 1980, Disting. Leadership award Afro-Am. Studies Program, 1991, Nat. Black Monitor Family and Cmty. award 1985, Va. Commonwealth U., 1991, Pres.'s award S.C. State U., 1966, Jewish Educators award, 1998, Joseph Himes award for Disting. Scholarship, 2001, Ba'Alay Keriyah Soc., 2003, others; grantee Ford Found., 1970, NEH, 1978, NIMH, 1980-81; 25th Ann. lectr. African-Am. studies program Va. Commonwealth U., 1996, others. Mem. Am. Sociol. Assn., Soc. Study Social Problems, So. Sociol. Soc., Ea. Sociol. Soc. (chmn. minorities com. 1992-96), Assn. Black Sociologists (pres. 1981-82, 82-83, chmn. hist. and archives com., 2002-, Leadership award 1995), African Heritage Soc., Sigma Xi, Omicron Delta Kappa, Alpha Phi Alpha (Acad. Excellence award 1985), Alpha Kappa Mu, Alpha Kappa Delta. Office: George Mason U Dept Sociology Anthrop Fairfax VA 22030

DENNIS, SHAY, social worker; b. Pullman, Wash., Dec. 10, 1970; s. Rutledge Melvin and Sarah Helen Dennis; m. Wendy Krystal Evans, Sept. 18, 1999; children: Shay, Justin, Desireé, Shaphan, Cierra. BS in Psychology, Hampton U., 1992. Sex abuse counselor Genesis, Richmond, Va., 1997—2000; rehab. counselor Dept. Juvenile Justice, Richmond, 2001—02; social worker Dept. Mental Health, Richmond, 2002—. Dir., owner Youth Advocacy Svcs., Richmond, 2001—. Democrat. Avocations: working with juveniles and dysfunctional households, family, church activities, basketball. Office: Youth Advocacy Svcs 1213 Greystone Ave Richmond VA 23224 E-mail: shaydenn@qwickconnet.net.

DENNISON, DONALD LEE, lawyer; b. Dec. 5, 1932; s. Robert Irving and Hannah W. Dennison; m. Tina L. Dennison, Feb. 12, 1955; children: Scott A., Carol R., David R. BSME, Carnegie Inst. Tech., Pitts., 1955; JD, George Washington U., 1961. Bar: Va. 1969, U.S. Supreme Ct. 1965, U.S. Ct. Appeals (fed. cir.) 1969, Md. 1968, D.C. 1962, U.S. Ct. Appeals (4th cir.) 1970. Examiner U.S. Patent Office, Washington, 1957-60; ptnr. Dennison & Dennison, Washington, 1960-66, Dennison, Meserole, Pollack & Scheiner, Arlington, Va., 1966-98, Dennison, Meserole, Scheiner & Schultz, 1999-2000, Dennison, Scheiner, Schultz and Wakeman, 2000—01, Dennison, Schultz and Dougherty, 2002—. Pres. Met. Washington Soccer Referees Assn., 1980-83; v.p. Mid-Atlantic D.O.G.S., Inc. Search and Rescue Unit. 1st lt. U.S. Army, 1954-57. Mem. Internat. Trademark Assn., European Cmty. Trademark Assn. Republican. Home: 11209 Farmland Dr North Bethesda MD 20852-4521 Office: Dennison Schultz & Doughterty 1745 Jefferson Davis Hwy Arlington VA 22202-3402 E-mail: ddennison@dennisonlaw.com.

DENNISON, GEORGE MARSHEL, academic administrator; b. Buffalo, Ill., Aug. 11, 1935; s. Earl Fredrick and Irene Gladys (McWhorter) D.; m. Jane Irene Schroeder, Dec. 26, 1954; children: Robert Gene, Rick Steven. AA, Custer County (Mont.) Jr. Coll., 1960; BA, U. Mont., 1962, MA, 1963; PhD, U. Wash., 1967. Asst. prof. U. Ark., Fayetteville, 1967-68; vis. asst. prof. U. Wash., Seattle, 1968-69; asst. prof. Colo. State U., Fort Collins, 1969-73, assoc. prof., 1973-77, assoc. dean Coll. Arts, Humanities and Social Sci., 1976-80, prof., 1977-87, acting acad. v.p., 1980-82, acting assoc. acad. v.p., 1982-86, assoc. acad. v.p., 1987; provost, v.p. acad. affairs Western Mich. U., Kalamazoo, 1987-90; pres. U. Mont., Missoula, 1990—. Cons. U.S. Dept. Justice, 1976-84; bd. dirs. Inst. Medicine and Humanities, Missoula, Internat. Heart Inst. Mont., Missoula. Author: The Dorr War, 1976; contbr. articles to jours. in field. Bd. dirs. Kalamazoo Ctr. for Med. Studies, 1989-90; bd. dirs. Missoula Rocky Mountain Coll., Billings, Mont. Campus Compact. With USN, 1953-57. ABA grantee, 1969-70; Colo. State U. grantee, 1970-75, Nat. Trust for Hist. Preservation grantee, 1976-78; U.S. Agy. for Internat. Devel. grantee, 1979—; Colo. Commn. on Higher Edn. devel. grantee, 1985. Mem. Am. Hist. Assn., Orgn. Am. Historians, Am. Assn. Higher Edn., Am. Soc. for Legal History. Avocations: handball, cross-country skiing. Office: U Montana Office of The Pres Univ UH 109 Missoula MT 59812-0001

DENNISON, GERARD FRANCIS, economic analyst; b. Lewiston, Maine, Aug. 3, 1948; s. Alfred Alexandre Jr. and Regina Violet (Routhier) D.; m. Patricia Elaine Potter, June 24, 1989; stepchildren: Rochelle Elizabeth Riordan, Melanie Lois Wentworth. BS BA, Thomas Coll., 1970, MBA, 1986. Lic. stockbroker, Maine. Sr. econ. analyst Maine Dept. Labor, Lewiston, 1971—. Mem. confs. in field. City councilor City of Auburn, Maine, 1994—2000; corporator, bd. dirs., mem. various coms. Auburn-Lewiston Boys/Girls Club; corporator Auburn Pub. Libr; mem. cmty. bldg. com. United Way; mem. mem. Kittyhawk Indsl. Park Com.; chair Enhanced Cmty. Policing Com.; mem. adv. coun., planning com. Lewiston-Auburn Coll.; chair Auburn Indsl. Park Site Selection Com.; mayor's rep. Auburn Sch. Com., Lewiston Auburn Edn. Coalition; dir. Auburn Exch. Club; dir. exec. com. Androscoggin Valley Coun. of Govts.; coord. Androscoggin County campaign for Gov. Angus S. King Jr., 1998; mentor Togolese Refugee Family Resettlement Program; mem. long range planning task force Auburn Pub. Libr.; mem. Androscoggin County Budget Rev. Com.; bd. dirs. Franco-Am. Heritage Ctr.; mem. John Baldacci Gubernatorial Campaign, 2001—02; bd. dirs. Lewiston-Auburn Econ. Growth Coun., Lewiston-Auburn R.R. Mem. USA Forum Francophone des Affaires, Auburn Exch. Club, Auburn Bus. Devl. Corp., Am. Legion, Poland Spring Country Club. Democrat. Roman Catholic. Avocations: golf, reading. Home: 28 7th St Auburn ME 04210-5633 Office: Maine Dept Labor 5 Mollison Way Lewiston ME 04240-5805 E-mail: gerard.dennison@maine.gov., gerry.dennison@verizon.net.

DENNISON, RAMONA POLLAN, special education educator; b. Floydada, Tex., Jan. 19, 1938; d. William C. and Anne M. (Tivis) Pollan; m. Bob Dennison, Oct. 12, 1956; 1 child, Tajquah. BS, MEd, E. Cen. U., 1972, cert. in psychometry, 1974, lic. in profl. counseling, 1975. Lic. psychometrist, profl. counselor. Tchr. Konawa (Okla.) Pub. Sch., 1972—. Mem. NEA, DAR, PEO, Okla. Edn. Assn., Okla. Assn. Children of Learning Disabilities, Konana Edn. Assn., Lic. Profl. Counselor Assn., Nat. Assn. Children Learning Disabilities, E. Cen. Alumni Assn., Tanti Study Club, Oak Hills Country Club, Delta Kappa Gamma, Phi Delta Kappa. Democrat. Baptist. Avocations: tennis, bridge, walking, cooking, gardening. Home: 18326 County Rd 1542 Ada OK 74820-3072

DENNISON, ROBERT ABEL, III, civil engineer; b. Herkimer, N.Y., Sept. 2, 1951; s. Robert A. and Ruth (Friesen) D.; m. Marilyn Smith, June 21, 1981; children: Andrew, Christopher. AAS, Westchester Community Coll., 1974; BCE, Manhattan Coll., 1978. Registered profl. engr., N.Y., N.H. Dep. commr. Putnam County Dept. Hwy., Carmel, NY, 1983-85; bridge mgmt. engr. region 8 N.Y. State Dept. Transp., Poughkeepsie, 1985-92, bur. dir. Albany, 1992—98, regional dir., 1998—. Town engr. Town of Kent, N.Y., 1983-90; mem. AASHTO subcom. on design, 1993-98. Contbr. articles to Pub. Works Mag. Arbitrator Am. Arbitration Assn., White Plains, N.Y., 1986—. Home: 122 Wilson Ave Kingston NY 12401-2030

DENNISON, RONALD WALTON, engineer; b. San Francisco, Oct. 23, 1944; s. S. Mason and Elizabeth Louise (Hatcher) D.; m. Deborah Ann Rutter, Aug. 10, 1991; children: Ronald, Frederick. BS in Physics and Math., San Jose State U., 1970, MS in Physics, 1972. Physicist, Memorex, Santa Clara, Calif., 1970-71; sr. engr. AVCO, San Jose, Calif., 1972-73; advanced devel. engr. Perkin Elmer, Palo Alto, Calif., 1973-75; staff engr. Hewlett-Packard, Santa Rosa, Calif., 1975-79; program gen. mgr. Burroughs, Westlake Village, Calif., 1979-82; dir. engring., founder EIKON, Simi Valley, Calif., 1982-85; sr. staff technologist Maxtor Corp., San Jose, 1987-90; dir. engring. Toshiba Am. Info. Systems, 1990-93, cons. engr., 1994—; materials. Author tech. publs. Served to sgt. USAF, 1963-67. Mem. IEEE, Am. Vacuum Soc., Internat. Soc. Hybrid Microelectronics, Internat. Disk Drive Equipment and Materials Assn. Republican. Methodist. Mem. Aircraft Owners and Pilots Assn., Internat. Comanche Soc. Home: 4050 Soelro Ct San Jose CA 95127-2711 E-mail: ron@rondennison.com.

DENNISON, STANLEY SCOTT, retired forest products company executive, consultant; b. Mitchelville, Md., Sept. 1, 1920; s. Ralph Stanford and Cora Adeline (Scott) D.; m. Sharon Lee Johnson, June 1, 1983; 1 stepchild, Whitney C. Maddox; children by previous marriage: Judith Dennison Tucci (dec.), Joan Dennison Daffron, Joyce Dennison Bischoff. Ed., Columbia Union Coll., 1938; BS, MBA, Calif. Western U., 1979, PhD, 1982. Operative builder Dennison Co., 1939-43; traffic rep. U.P. R.R., 1943-49; v.p. Arlington Millwork, Va., 1949-52, Internat. Filling Machine Co., Petersburg, Va., 1952-57, Atlanta Oak Flooring Co., 1957-62; regional mgr. Ga.-Pacific Corp., Portland, Oreg., 1962-70, v.p., 1970-78, sr. v.p., 1978-82, exec. v.p., 1982-85; exec. mgmt. cons., 1985—. Past trustee Stonehill Coll., U. Portland, Calif. Western U.; bd. dirs. Aquinas Ctr. Theology at Emory U., Atlanta. Mem. Capital City Club (Atlanta), Commerce Club (Atlanta), Alpha Kappa Psi. Democrat. Roman Catholic. Home: 5255 Glenridge Dr NE Atlanta GA 30342-1353 E-mail: drssd@atl.mediaone.net.

DENNISON, TERRY ALAN, investment consultant; b. Milw., Jan. 8, 1947; s. Willard Lawrence and Delphia Marie (Willis) D.; m. Lynn Celeste Kovacic, Mar. 30, 1974. BA, U. Wis., 1969, MBA, 1972. CPA, Ill. V.p. sys. devel. Ins. Computing Corp., Madison, Wis., 1971-72; v.p., mgr. investment tech./investment analytical svcs. div. Continental Ill. Nat. Bank & Trust Co., Chgo., 1972-84; v.p., mgr. date processing divsn. Wilshire Assocs., Santa Monica, Calif., 1984-87; prin. Mercer Investment Cons., Inc., L.A., 1988—. Mem. AICPA, Ill. Soc. CPAs. Office: Mercer Investment Cons Inc 777 S Figueroa St Los Angeles CA 90017-5800

DENNISON-LEONARD, SARAH, lawyer; b. Seattle, Oct. 6, 1962; d. David Christian III and Mary Louise (Dunker) Henny; m. Charles Edward Leonard, Oct. 22, 1988; children: Carlie, Gaela. BA, Smith Coll., 1986; JD, Stanford U., 1994. Bar: Oreg. 1994. Crew coach U. Mass., Amherst, 1987-88; dir. health svcs. Hampshire County chpt. ARC, Northampton, Mass., 1989-90; assoc. Stoel Rives LLP, Portland, Oreg., 1994-98; ptnr. Krogh & Leonard, Portland, 1998—. Spkr. in field. ECAC scholar-athlete, 1986. Mem. ABA, Oreg. State Bar Assn., Phi Beta Kappa. Avocations: parenting, sports, hiking. Office: Krogh & Leonard 506 SW 6th Ave Ste 750 Portland OR 97204-1555

DENNISTON, BRACKETT BADGER, III, lawyer; b. Oak Park, Ill., July 23, 1947; s. Brackett Badger Jr. and Frances Ann (Jones) D.; m. Kathleen Foley, Aug. 2, 1975; children: Alexandra, Brackett Badger IV, Elizabeth. AB, Kenyon Coll., 1969; JD, Harvard U., 1973. Bar: Mass. 1974, U.S. Dist. Ct. Mass. 1975, U.S. Dist. Ct. (we. dist.) Tex. 1987, U.S. Ct. Appeals (1st cir.) 1975, U.S. Ct. Appeals (D.C. cir.) 1976, U.S. Ct. Appeals (7th cir.) 1978, U.S. Ct. Appeals (10th cir.) 1981, U.S. Supreme Ct. 1981. Law clk. to judge U.S. Ct. Appeals for 9th Cir., Honolulu, 1973-74; assoc. Goodwin, Procter & Hoar, Boston, 1974-81, ptnr., 1981-82, 86-93, mem. exec. com., 1990-93; chief major frauds unit U.S. Atty.'s Office, Boston, 1982-86; chief legal counsel Gov. of Mass., Boston, 1993-96; v.p., sr. counsel litigation GE, Fairfield, Conn., 1996—, also chmn. policy compliance rev. bd. Class chmn. Kenyon Coll., Gambier, Ohio, 1979-90, trustee, 2000—; mem. Duxbury (Mass.) Zoning Bd. Appeals, 1980-92, chmn., 1984-90, dir. New England Legal Found., 1998- (vice chair 2003-). Recipient Dir.'s award for superior achievement U.S. Dept. Justice, 1986, alumni award Kenyon Coll., 1991-96. Mem. Mass. Bar Assn. (chmn. coun. jud. adminstrn. sect. 1989-90, jud. adminstrv. coun. 1987-90, 95-96, criminal justice sect. 1986—, litig. sect. 1988—), trustee, Boston Bar Found., 2002-. Office: GE Co 3137 Easton Tpke Fairfield CT 06432-1008 E-mail: brackett.denniston@corporate.ge.com.

DENNISTON, JEANNIE L. lawyer; b. Jackson, Miss., May 3, 1951; d. Verne Leroy Culbertson and Mabel Jean Bunge; m. Michael Edward Denniston, (div. Aug. 1999); 1 child, Sara Elizabeth. BS, U. Ozarks, 1973; JD, U. Ark., Little Rock, 1994. Office mgr. McGuire-Smith, Little Rock, 1976-79; mortgage banker Worthen Bank & Trust, Little Rock, 1979-84; constrn. loan officer City Nat. Bank, Ft. Smith, Ark., 1984; adminstrv. asst. ERC properties, Ft. Smith, 1984-91; pvt. practice law Morrilton, Ark., 1994-98; dep. prosecuting atty. Conway County, Morrilton, 1997-98; assoc. Gordon, Caruth & Virden, Morrilton, 1998—. Instr. 100 Proof Inc., Morrilton, 1997-2000. Mem. Morrilton Planning and Zoning Commn., 1996-99; bd. dirs. Safe Place Inc., Morrilton, 1995-96, Main St. Morrilton Inc., 1996-97. Mem. ABA, Ark. Bar Assn., Ark. Trial Lawyers Assn., Ark. Assn. Women Lawyers, Conway County Bar Assn.,

Morrilton Area C. of C. (treas. 1999, 2d v.p. 2000, 1st v.p. 2001, bd. dir. 1997-98), Kiwanis Baha'i. Baha'I. Avocations: scuba diving, needlework. Office: Gordon Caruth & Virden PLC PO Box 558 105 S Moose St Morrilton AR 72110-3425

DENNISTON, MARJORIE MCGEORGE, retired elementary school educator; b. Coraopolis, Pa., Mar. 21, 1913; d. Chauncey Kirk and Elsie (George) McGeorge; m. Delbert Dicks Denniston, Dec. 25, 1942 (dec. 1973); 1 child, Robert Bruce. Student, Ohio U., 1931-33; BA, Westminster Coll., 1936; postgrad., U. Kans., 1959, Western Ill. U., 1962, 64. Elem. tchr. county schs., West Pittsburg, Pa., 1936-42, New Castle Sch. System, Pa., 1942, 51-78. Pres. Newcastle NEA, 1965-67; vol. aid Pa. Assn. Retarded Children, Jameson Hosp., Law County Home, 1984-96; trustee, elder Presbyn. Ch., New Castle, 1986-92, v.p. Ch. Women United, 1990-94. Named First Lady of New Castle, 1989, Outstanding Woman of Yr. for Community Svc. Jr. Woman's Club, 1990, Disting. Alumni Achievement Cmty. Svc. award Westminster Coll., 1990. Mem. AAUW, LWV (sec. New Castle chpt. 1986—), Coll. Club (parliamentarian), Woman's Club (parliamentarian Lawrence County fedn. 1984—, sec. 1986-88), Woman's Club of New Castle (parliamentarian 1990-99), Fedn. Jrs. (v.p. 1994-96), Pa. Assn. State Retirees (v.p. local chpt. 1994—), Cmty. Ch. Women Lawrence County (parliamentarian 1995—), Delta Kappa Gamma. Republican. Avocations: photography, coin and rock collecting, volunteering, book reviewing, travel. Home: 331 Laurel Blvd New Castle PA 16101-2523

DENNISTON, MARTHA KENT, business owner, author; b. Phila., Feb. 8, 1920; d. Samuel Leonard and Elizabeth (Cryer) Kent; m. Edward Shippen Willing, May 14, 1942 (div. 1972); children: Peter, Matthew, Thomas, Stephen; m. George C. Denniston, July 5, 1974. BA, Bryn Mawr (Pa.) Coll., 1941; MA, U. Wash., Seattle, 1965. Clinic dir. Population Dynamics, Seattle, 1973-84; pvt. practice investor, 1950—; resort owner Ecologic Pl., Port Townsend, Wash., 1972—. Sec. bd. dirs. Ctr. for Population Communications, N.Y.C., 1983-86. Author: Beyond Conception, Our Children's Children, 1971, (poems) The Bladed Quiet, 1994. Bd. dirs. Population Action Coun., Washington, 1977-80. Mem. Nat. Soc. Colonial Dames Am. Avocations: genealogy, environmental concerns. Home: 45 Robbins Rd Nordland WA 98358-9607

DENNY, BREWSTER CASTBERG, retired university dean; b. Seattle, Sept. 5, 1924; s. Merle Wilson and Margaraith (Castberg) D.; m. Patricia Virginia Sollitt, June 14, 1950; 1 child, Maria Janet. AB, U. Wash., 1945; MA in Law and Diplomacy, Tufts U., 1948, PhD, 1959. Instr. Mass. Inst. Tech., 1948-52; with Office of Sec. of Def., 1952-60; profl. staff mem. Sub-Com. on Nat. Policy Machinery, US Senate, 1960-61; asso. prof. pub. affairs U. Wash., 1961-64, prof. pub. affairs, 1964—, 1st dir. Grad. Sch. Pub. Affairs, 1962-68, 1st dean, 1968-80, dean emeritus, 1980—, chmn. marine affairs bd., 1972-79, prof. Am. diplomatic history, 1991—. US rep. to 23d Gen. Assembly UN, 1968; cons. RAND Corp., 1961-68; mem. vis. com. dept. govt. Harvard U., 1967-72; mem. Presdl. Adv. Coun. on Intergovtl. Pers. Policy, 1971-74; chmn. Gov. Task Force on Exec. Orgn., 1968-72; presdl. mem. US-PR Commn. on Status of PR, 1964-66; mem. bd. sci. and tech. in devel. NAS, 1976-81, co-chmn. Korean com. on sci. and tech., 1977-82; mem. Rsch. and Edn. Adv. Panel to Compt. Gen. US, 1979-2000. Author: Seeing American Policy Whole, 1985; contbr. to Am. Polit. Sci. Rev., Sci., Pub. Adminstrn. Rev.; author, co-author, editor articles, books, chpt., and reports. Trustee 20th Century Fund, 1975—, vice chmn., 1982-86, chmn., 1986-94; co-chair Children's Budget Coalition, 1991—. Mem. AAAS (com. on new directions 1975-78, charter mem. com. on sci. and pub. policy 1968-72, com. on arms control 1980-88), ASPA, UN Assn. USA (nat. policy panel on UN capabilities in the 1970s 1970-71), Nat. Acad. Pub. Adminstrn., Am. Hist. Assn., Coun. Fgn. rels., Nat. Assn. Sch. Pub. Affairs and Adminstrn. (pres. 1968-69). Home: 2021 1st Ave Apt F12 Seattle WA 98121-3113

DENNY, COLLINS, III, lawyer; b. Richmond, Va., Dec. 5, 1933; s. Collins Jr. and Rebecca (Miller) Denny; m. Anne Carples, June 28, 1957; children: Collins IV, William R., Katharine D. Joyce. AB, Princeton U., 1956; LLB, U. Va., 1961. Bar: Va. 1961, U.S. Dist. Ct. (ea. dist.) Va. 1962, U.S. Ct. Appeals (4th cir.) 1962, U.S. Tax Ct. 1971, U.S. Ct. Claims 1976. Assoc. Denny, Valentine & Davenport, Richmond, 1961-67; ptnr. Mays & Valentine LLP, Richmond, 1967-2000, mng. ptnr., 1992-93; gen. counsel, corp. sec. Coastal Lumber Co., Weldon, NC, 1980—2003; ptnr. Troutman, Sanders, Mays & Valentine LLP, Richmond, 2001. Gen. counsel Bear Island Timberlands Co., LLC, Ashland, Va., 1985—99, Bear Island Paper Co., LLC, 1989—2000. Contbr. chapters to books, articles to profl. jours. Lt. USNR, 1956—66. Mem.: ABA (chmn. exempt orgns. subcom., tax. sect. 1971—86), Richmond Feeder Cattle Assn. (pres. 1972—77), Va. Forestry Assn., Va. Tax Rev. (adv. bd. 1978—2002), Va. State Bar (com. chmn. 1981—83), Va. Bar Assn. (chmn. jr. bar 1965—66), Princeton Alumni Assn. Va. (pres. 1974—78), Va. Country Club, Deep Run Hunt Club (pres. 1987—88), Richmond-First Club (pres. 1969—70). Episcoplian. Avocations: horse sports, tree farming, agriculture. Office: TroutmanSanders 1111 E Main St PO Box 1122 Richmond VA 23218-1122

DENNY, DALLAS, psychological examiner; b. Asheville, N.C., Aug. 18, 1949; d. Richard and Ruby Lee Denny; m. Lynneda Roberts Dec. 24, 1971 (div. 1977). BS in Psychology, Sociology, Mid. Tenn. State U., 1974; MA in Psychology, U. Tenn., 1979; postgrad., Vanderbilt U., 1984-86, Ga. State U., 1993—94. Lic. psychol. examiner Tenn., 1980. Ho. mgr. Home 2, Inc., Nashville, 1977-80; protective svcs. field worker Tenn. Dept. Human Svcs., Nashville, 1979-80; relief ho. mgr. Com-Care, Inc., Greeneville, Tenn., 1981-82; computer programmer Vanderbilt U., Nashville, 1983, Duplex Software, Franklin, Tenn., 1984; psychol. examiner Greene Valley Devel. Ctr., Greenville, 1986-90; behavior specialist DeKalb Cmty. Svc. Bd., Stone Mountain, Ga., 1990—. Founder, exec. dir. Am. Ednl. Gender Info. Svcs., Decatur, Ga., 1990-98. Author: Gender Dysphoria: A Guide to Research, 1994, Current Concepts in Transgender Identity, 1998; acquisitions editor Empathy Mag., 1993-94; editor-in-chief Chrysalis Mag., 1990-98; editor Transgender Tapestry Jour., 1999—; contbr. articles to profl. jours. Sec. Atlanta Pride, 1994—95; sr. advisor to Atlanta Mayor Bill Campbell on gay, lesbian, bisexual and transgender issues, 1996—98; dir. Fantasia Fair, 2001—; founder Real Life Experience, Inc. Mem. Gender Edn. and Advocacy (bd. dirs. 1999—), Outreach Inst. Gender Studies (bd. dirs. 2000—). Office: Gender Edn and Advocacy PO Box 33724 Decatur GA 30033-0724 E-mail: aegis@gender.org.

DENNY, JAMES M. health care services company executive; Chmn. Pearle Heath Svcs. Inc., Dallas. Address: Pearl Health Svcs Inc 2534 Royal Ln Dallas TX 75229-3417 Office: Gilead Sciences Inc 333 Lakeside Dr Foster City CA 94404

DENNY, JERA CECILIA JANE ELIZABETH, musician, graphics designer; d. Stewart Duane Sayre and Dorothy Jane Campbell; m. Struan Alexander Oglanby, May 29, 1986 (div. Apr. 1997). Cert. in audio arts and scis., Ctr. for Media Arts, 1986. Mgr. Evergreen Rec., N.Y.C., 1987—89, Shakedown Sound, N.Y.C., 1989; owner, art dir. The Mad Hand Arts, Graphics and Design, N.Y.C., 1991—; owner, prodr., sound engr. 2 Frank Studios, Forest Hills, NY, 1995—; mgr. Bass Hit/M.A.W. Studios, N.Y.C., 1997—98. Owner, pub. Howard Beale Music, N.Y.C., 2002—. Writer, performer, prodr.: record album/CD Sister Atom Cloud, 1996, Dog Days, 1998, Circus Physics, 2002. Mem.: ASCAP.

DENNY, JOHN BERNARD, biochemist, educator; b. San Antonio, Mar. 15, 1953; s. Charles Harvey and Dorothy Luke D.; m. Callise Ollom, Oct. 5, 1996; children: Bryan Thomas Denny, Kathleen Denny, William Reese, Gene Reese. BS, U. Tex., 1975; MA in Pharmacology, U. Tex., Dallas, 1977; PhD in Biochemistry, U. Fla., 1982. NIH postdoctoral fellow Rockefeller U., N.Y.C., 1982-85; asst. prof. U. Tex., San Antonio, 1989-96, rschr. Health Sci. Ctr., 1996—. Author: Cancer Cell Organelles, 1981, Membrane Receptors, 1984; contbr. articles to profl. jours. Recipient Tom Slick award in biochemistry and molecular biology Tom Slick Found., 1991. Mem. Rho Chi. Office: U Tex Health Sci Ctr Dept Ophthalmology 7703 Floyd Curl Dr San Antonio TX 78284-6200 E-mail: DENNY@UTHSCSA.edu.

DENNY, JUDITH ANN, retired lawyer; b. Lamar, Mo., Sept. 18, 1946; d. Lee Livingston and Genevieve Adelpha (Falke) D.; m. Thomas M. Lenard, May 29, 1976; children: Julia Lee, Michael William. BA, La. Tech. U., 1968; JD, George Washington U., 1972. Bar: D.C. 1973. Asst. spl. prosecutor Watergate Spl. Prosecution Force, Washington, 1973-75; pros. atty. U.S. Dept. Justice, Washington, 1975-78; dir. div. compliance U.S. Office Edn. HEW, Washington, 1978-80; acting asst. insp. gen. for investigations U.S. Dept. Edn., Washington, 1980; dep. dir. policy and compliance, office of revenue sharing U.S. Dept. Treasury, Washington, 1980-83, counselor to gen. counsel, 1983-89; insp. gen. ACTION, Washington, 1989-94; cons. Fed. Quality Inst., 1994-95. Mem. D.C. Bar Assn. Home: 2816 Arizona Ter NW Washington DC 20016-2642

DENNY, MARY CRAVER, state legislator, rancher; b. Houston, July 9, 1948; d. Kenneth and Lois (Skiles) Craver; m. Henry William Denny, Jan. 26, 1969 (div. Aug. 1990); 1 child, Bryan William. Student, U. Tex., 1966—70; BS in Elem. Edn. magna cum laude, U. North Tex., 1973. Cert. tchr. Tex. Owner, mgr. Craver Ranch, Aubrey, Tex., 1973—; mem. Tex. Ho. of Reps., Austin, 1993—. Mem. numerous other civic orgns.; del. state and nat. Rep. convs., 1972—; chmn. Denton (Tex.) County Rep. Com., 1983—91; bd. dirs. Tex. Fedn. Rep. Women, 1988—92, 1994—96, Tex. Com. Humanities, 1990, YMCA, Denton, 1985—; life mem. pres.'s coun. U. N. Tex., Denton, 1974—, chmn., 1983; mem. Denton Benefit League, 1976—, Denton Arts Coun., 1986—. Named Outstanding Rep. Vol., Denton County Rep. Com., 1985, Outstanding Alumna in Edn., U. N. Tex. Coll. Edn., 1993; named one of 10 Outstanding Rep. Women, Tex. Fedn. Rep. Women, 1991. Mem.: Nat. Conf. State Legislature, Am. Legis. Exch. Coun., Ariel Club, Delta Zeta. Episcopalian. Avocations: swimming, bridge. Address: 8684 FM 2153 Aubrey TX 76227-3029 Office: PO Box 2910 Austin TX 78768-2910 also: 1001 Cross Timbers Rd Flower Mound TX 75028 E-mail: mary.denny@house.state.tx.us.

DENNY, RICHARD ALDEN, JR., retired lawyer; b. Atlanta, Oct. 13, 1931; s. Richard Alden and Maybeth Sullivan (Graham) D.; m. Margaret Hunt, Aug. 1954; children: Margaret Denny Dozier, Richard Alden III, Dallas Hunt, Lee Denny Griffith. BA, Washington and Lee U., 1952; LLB, Emory U., 1954. Bar: Ga. 1954. Assoc. King & Spalding, Atlanta, 1954-60, ptnr., 1960-92. Chmn. bd. Met. Atlanta Crime Commn., 1972-73; bd. dirs. Woodruff Arts Ctr., 1991-97, life trustee, 1997—; bd. dirs. High Mus. of Art, Atlanta, 1971—, chmn., 1991-94; bd. dirs. Lovett Sch., Atlanta, 1969—, chmn., 1980-83, emeritus trustee, 1999—. Mem. Lawyers Club Atlanta (pres. 1972-73), Atlanta Lawyers Found. (chmn. 1976-77), Washington and Lee Alumni Assn. (pres. 1980-81), Piedmont Driving Club (pres. 1982-84), Peachtree Golf Club, Omicron Delta Kappa. Episcopalian. Office: King & Spalding Ste 4900 191 Peachtree St NE Atlanta GA 30303-1740

DENNY, WILLIAM MURDOCH, JR., investment management executive; b. Schenectady, N.Y., June 10, 1934; s. William Murdock and Ione Elizabeth (Lundy) D.; m. Delores Gay Shillady, June 11, 1966; children: Ellen Gay, Nancy Beth, Linda Ann. ScB in Chemistry, Brown U., 1958; MBA in Fin., Drexel U., 1974. Mem. mgmt. staff chem. spltys. divsn. Pennwalt Corp., Phila., 1961-73; pres. Denny Fin. Enterprises, Paoli, Pa., 1974—. Chmn. mgmt. com. Houston-Leon County Coal Co. Interests, Crockett, Tex., 1987-2002; winegrower Clover Mill Farm Vineyards, LLC, Chester Springs, Pa., 1998—. Bd. dirs. United Way of North Central Chester County, 1980-83. Lt. comdr. USN, 1959-61. Mem. Fin. Analysts Fedn., Fin. Analysts Phila., Navy League U.S., Corinthians Assn. (Phila. fleet capt. 1996-97, sec. 2002-03), Phi Kappa Psi, Brown U. Club (pres. 1979-81, Phila.), Aronimink Golf Club (Newtown Square, Pa.), Yacht Club of Hilton Head Island (S.C.), Sea Pines Club. Home: Clover Mill Farm Chester Springs PA 19425 Office: PO Box 458 Paoli PA 19301-0458

DENOMMÉ, ROBERT THOMAS, foreign language educator; b. Fitchburg, Mass., May 17, 1930; s. George Edward and Sara (Richards) D. BA, Assumption Coll., Worcester, Mass., 1952; MA, Boston U., 1953; Grad. Diploma, Sorbonne, U. Paris, 1959; PhD, Columbia U., 1962; LHD, Assumption Coll., 2001. Instr. in French St. Joseph's Coll., Phila., 1956-60; asst. prof. French U. Va., Charlottesville, 1962-64, U. Chgo., 1964-66; assoc. prof. French U. Va., Charlottesville, 1966-70, prof. French, 1970—, Douglas Huntly Gordon prof. French lit., 1991—, prof. and chmn. French dept., 1977-89. Vis. prof. French U., Orléans, France, 1978. Author: The Naturalism of G. Geffroy, 1963, Nineteenth Century French Romantic Poets, 1969, French Parnassian Poets, 1972, Le Conte de Lisle, 1973, Alfred de Vigny, 1985. Decorated officier Order de Palmes Académiques (France); recipient All-Univ. Tchg. award U. Va. Bd. Visitors, 1994, Fulbright scholar, France, 1959. Mem. MLA (sec., chmn. 1971-72), Am. Assn. Tchrs. French, South Atlantic MLA (pres., past pres.), Assn. Internationale Études Françaises (Paris), Société des Amis d'Alfred de Vigny (Paris), Colonnade Club (Charlottesville), Phi Beta Kappa (hon., Beta Va. chpt.). Roman Catholic. Avocations: reading, classical music. Home: 119 Cameron Ln Charlottesville VA 22903-1707 Office: Univ Va Dept French 302 Cabell Hall Charlottesville VA 22903-3196

DENOON, DAVID BAUGH HOLDEN, economist, educator, consultant; b. Toledo, Apr. 12, 1945; s. Clarence E. and Eleanor (Kratz) D. BA, Harvard U., 1966; M.P.A., Princeton U., 1968; PhD, MIT, 1975. Asst. to chmn. Pa. State Bd. Edn., 1968; program economist U.S. AID, Dept. of State, Jakarta, Indonesia, 1969-71; asst. to pres. Nat. Bur. Econ. Research, N.Y.C., 1971-72; from asst. prof. to prof. politics and econs. NYU, 1975—; v.p. U.S. Export-Import Bank, Washington, 1978-79; dep. asst. sec. U.S. Dept. Def., Washington, 1981-82, cons., 1982-91, U.S. Dept. State, Washington, 1992-93. Bd. dirs. NCast Corp., Sunnyvale, Calif. Author: Devaluation Under Pressure: India, Indonesia, and Ghana, 1986, Real Reciprocity-Balancing U.S. Economic and Security Policies in the Pacific Basin, 1993, Ballistic Missile Defense in the Post-Cold War Era, 1995; editor, contbr.: The New International Economic Order: A U.S. Response, 1979, Constraints on Strategy: The Economics of Western Security, 1986, Changing Capital Markets and the Global Economy, 1988. Mem. Bucks County Land Use Task Force, 1975—78; active Bucks Rep. Party, 1976—; trustee Goucher Coll., Balt. Mem.: Fgn. Policy Assn. (bd. dirs.), Internat. Inst. for Strategic Studies, Internat. Studies Assn., Coun. Fgn. Rels., Am. Polit. Sci. Assn., Am. Econ. Assn., Asia Soc., Cosmos Club (Washington), Harvard Club (N.Y.C.). Home: 3609 Creamery Rd Wycombe PA 18980 Office: NYU 269 Mercer St New York NY 10003 E-mail: david.denoon@nyu.edu.

DE NOTO, THOMAS J. chemical engineer; b. Rochester, N.Y., Apr. 2, 1943; s. Felice and Sarah De Noto; m. Donna De Noto. BSChemE, U. Rochester, 1964, MSChemE, 1967, PhDChemE, 1972. Vis. scholar U. Calif., Berkeley, 1967—70; from engr. to sr. prin. engr. Polaroid, Cambridge, Mass., 1971—98. Pres. bd. dirs. Sandia Consortium, Ala., 1997—2000; pres., chmn. bd. dirs. rsch. group Leadership for Mfg. MIT, Cambridge, 1996—99. V.p. S. Lexington (Mass.) Civic Assn., 1996—98, pres., 1998—. Scholar, NATO, Eng., 1976, NATO, Turkey, 1978. Achievements include patent for method of rendering photographs writeable. Avocations: skiing, hiking. Home: 288 Concord Ave Lexington MA 02421-8105 Office: Polaroid Corp 1 Upland Dr Norwood MA 02062

DENSEN, PAUL MAXIMILLIAN, former health administrator, educator; b. N.Y.C., Aug. 1, 1913; s. Charles Edwin and Carrie (Weinberg) Densen; m. Elizabeth A. Reed, Dec. 19, 1939; children: Rebecca E., Peter. AB, Bklyn.Coll., 1934; D.Sc., Johns Hopkins U., 1939; MA (hon.), Harvard U., 1968. From instr. to assoc. prof. preventive medicine Vanderbilt U. Med. Sch., 1939—46; chief div. med. research statistics VA, Washington, 1946—49; assoc. prof., then prof. biometry Grad. Sch. Pub. Health, U. Pitts., 1949—54; dir. div. research and statistics Health Ins. Plan Greater N.Y., 1954—59; dept. commr. N.Y.C. Dept. Health, 1959—66; dept. adminstr. N.Y.C. Health Services Adminstrn., 1966—69; dir. Harvard Center Community Health and Med. Care, 1968—85; prof. community health Harvard Sch. Pub. Health, 1968—85, prof. emeritus, 1985—. Fellow: AAAS, APHA, Am. Statis. Assn.; mem.: Inst. Medicine of NAS, Am. Epidemiol. Soc. Home: PO Box 405 165 Fremont Rd Sandown NH 03873-2204

DENSLEY, COLLEEN T. principal; b. Provo, Utah, Apr. 12, 1950; d. Floyd and Mary Lou (Dixon) Taylor; m. Steven T. Densley, July 23, 1968; children: Steven, Tiffany, Landon, Marianne, Wendy, Logan. BS in Elem. Edn., Brigham Young U., 1986, MEd in Tchg. and Learning, 1998. Cert. in elem. edn., K-12 adminstrn. Utah. Substitute tchr. Provo Sch. Dist., 1972-85, curriculum specialist, 1999-2001; tchr. 6th grade, mainstreaming program Canyon Crest Elem. Sch., Provo, 1985—94; instructional facilitator Campus Crest Elem., 1994—99; prin. Wasatch Elem. Sch., Provo, 2001—. Tchr. asst., math. tutor Brigham Young U., 1968—69; attendee World Gifted and Talented Conf., Salt Lake City, 1987, Tchr. Expectations and Student Achievement, 1988—89, Space Acad. for Educators, Huntsville, Ala., 1992; supr. coop. tchr. for practicum tchrs., 1987—90; co-chmn. accelerated learning and devel. com.; trainee working with handicapped students in mainstream classroom, 1989; mem. elem. sch. lang. arts curriculum devel. com., 90; mem. task force Thinking Strategies Curriculum, 1990—91; extensions specialist gifted and talented, 1990—91; math, 1991—; master tchr. Nat. Tchr. Tng. Inst., 1993. Co-author: (curricula) Provo Sch. Dist.'s Microorganism Sci. Kit, 1988, Arthropod Sci. Kit, 1988, Tchg. for Thinking, 1990—, PAWS Presents the Internet and the World Wide Web, 1997. Named Utah State Tchr. of the Yr., 1992; recipient Honor Young Mother of Yr. award, State of Utah, 1981. Mem.: NEA, Provo Edn. Assn. (Tchr. of the Yr. 1991—92), Internat. Space Edn. Initiative (adv. bd.), Utah Coun. Tchrs. Math., Utah Edn. Assn., Nat. Coun. Tchrs. Math. Republican. Mem. Lds Ch. Office: Wasatch Elem Sch 1080 N 900 E Provo UT 84604 E-mail: colleend@provo.EDU.

DENSLOW, DEBORAH PIERSON, primary education educator; b. Phila., May 2, 1947; d. Merrill Tracy Jr. and Margaret (Aiman) D.; m. James Tracy Grey III, Nov. 24, 1972 (div. Dec. 1980); 1 child, Sarah Elizabeth. BS, Gwynedd Mercy Coll., 1971; MA, Marygrove Coll., Detroit, 2000. Tchr. Willingboro (N.J.) Bd. Edn., 1971—. Union rep. Burlington County Edn. Assn., Willingboro, 1981-82, ednl. adv. Nat. Constitution Ctr., Phila., 2002-.; mem. task force for reoganization Morrisville Sch. Dist., 1991-92. Mem. Borough Coun., Morrisville, 1988—94, pres., 1992—94, rep. candidate, 1986; borough chmn. Am. Cancer Soc., 1986—87; sec. bd. dirs. Morrisville Free Libr., 1988—90, bd. dirs., 1988—2001; mem. Morrisville Mcpl. Authority, chmn., 1994—95, 1996—2000, asst. sec., treas., 1995—96, 2001; judge City Gardens Contest The Pa. Horticultural Soc., Phila., 2002; committeewoman 1st ward Morrisville (Pa.) Rep. Com., 1986—98. Mem. NEA, N.J. Edn. Assn., Willingboro Edn. Assn. (union rep. 1981-82, alt. union rep. 1988-89), Parents without Ptnrs. (bd. dirs. Mercer County chpt. 1981-82, sec. 1982-84), Bucks County Boroughs Assn. (bd. dirs. 1989—, v.p. 1990-92, pres. 1992-93), Pa. Mcpl. Authorities Assn. (profl. devel. com. 2000-2001). Presbyterian. Avocations: swimming, sailing. Home: 1 Garrett Lne Willingboro NJ 08046

DENSMORE, ANN, speech pathology/audiology services professional, audiologist, writer; b. L.A., Nov. 24, 1941; d. Ray B. and Margaret M. (Walsh) D.; children: Kristin Ann, Jennifer Ann. BS cum laude, UCLA, 1963; MA in Communicative Disorders, Calif. State U., 1975; student, Cape Cod Conservatory Arts, 1977-79; EdM in Human Devel. and Psychology, Harvard U., 1991; EdD, Clark U., 1997. Cert. in speech-lang. pathology and audiology, in clin. competence. Cons., owner Child Talk. AAUW fellow Harvard U., 1990-91, Clark U., 1992-94. Clark U. fellow, 1992-94. Office: 4 Militia Dr Ste 15 Lexington MA 02420 E-mail: ann_densmore@post.harvard.edu.

DENSMORE, DOUGLAS WARREN, lawyer; b. Jan. 30, 1948; s. Warren Orson and Lois Martha (Ery) D.; m. Janet Roberta Broadley, Oct. 26, 1973; children: Bradley Wythe, Andrew Fitz Douglas. AB, Coll. of William and Mary, Williamsburg, Va., 1970; JD cum laude, U. Toledo, 1975. Bar: Ohio 1976, US Dist. Ct. (no. and so. dist.) Ohio, Va. 1980, US Dist. Ct. (ea. and we. dist.) Va. 1980, US Ct. Appeals (4th cir.) 1980, US Supreme Ct., 1997, US Bankruptcy Ct. (we. dist.) Va., 2002. Assoc. Gertner, Barkan & Robon, Toledo, 1975-77, Shumaker, Loop & Kendrick, Toledo, 1977-79; corp. counsel Dominion Bankshares Corp., Roanoke, Va., 1979-80; assoc. Woods, Rogers, Muse, Walker & Thornton, Roanoke, Va., 1980-84; ptnr. Woods, Rogers & Hazlegrove, Roanoke, Va., 1984-96, Flippin, Densmore, Morse and Jessee, Roanoke, Va., 1996—. Co-author: Examining the Increase in Federal Regulatory Requirements and Penalties: Is Banking Facing Another Troubled Decade?, 1995; contbr. articles to profl. jour. Decorated Venerable Order St. John (Eng.), Companion of the O'Conor Don (Ireland), knight grand cross Royal Order of Don Carlos I (Portugal), knight grand cross Order of St. Catherine, knight comdr. of justice Order of St. Lazarus, first class Order of Polonia Restituta (Poland), knight grand cross Order St. Stanislas (Poland), knight grand cross Order of the Temple, knight comdr. Order of Crown of Thorns, knight grand cross Order of St. Michael and St. George, knight grand cross Orthodox Order St. John, knight Order of St. John, Knights of Malta, knight grand cross Order of Holy Cross of Jerusalem, knight grand cross with collar Order of St. Gregory, knight grand cross Order of St. Stephen, Royal Ukranian Order of St. Vladimir the Great, knight grand cross Greek Order of St. Denis of Zante, Order of the White Eagle. Master: Masons (jr. deacon 1992, 32 degree); fellow: Baskerville Soc. (U.K.); mem.: ABA (banking law com. 1988—, Uniform Comml. Code com. 1988—), The Business Leadership Fund (bd. of dir. 2003), Roanoke Bar Assn. Found. (pres. 2002—03), Bar Assn. City of Roanoke (bd. dirs. 1998—, pres. 2001—02), Va. Bar Assn. (Corp. Code com. 1984—), New Century Venture Ctr. (bd. dirs. 2003—), Scottish Soc. Va. Highlands (bd. dir. 1992—2000), Roanoke Regional C. of C., New Century Tech. Coun. (bd. dir. 1997—), Vet. Corps Art NY, English Speaking Union, Augustan Soc., Army-Navy Union, Brit. Manorial Soc. (Lord of Stratford St. Andrew), Soc. of St. George, Royal Overseas Club (London), Farmington Country Club (Charlottesville, Va.), Roanoke Country Club, Shenandoah Club (Roanoke), Rotary, Royal Order of Scotland, Shriners, Kiwanis Internat. Episcopalian. Avocations: golf, gardening, reading. Office: Flippin Densmore Morse & Jessee Ste 1800 First Union Tower Roanoke VA 24011-3315 E-mail: densmore@flippindensmore.com.

DENSON, G. ROGER, critic, writer, scriptwriter; b. Buffalo, Feb. 2, 1956; s. Hinton B. and Laraine J. (Schultz) D. BA in Arts and Humanities, SUNY, Buffalo, 1978. Curator dance, performance art, video and film Hallwalls Ctr. Art, Buffalo, 1978-80, dir. exhbns., drawings, paintings and sculpture, 1980-82; curatorial dir. Jayne H. Baum Gallery, N.Y.C., 1986-88; freelance critic and writer on art and culture, 1989—. Freelance curator, The New Mus., N.Y.C., 1981, The Alternative Mus., N.Y.C., 1987. Author: Capacity: History, The World and The Self, with Essays by Thomas McEvilley; contbr. articles to profl. jours. Bd. dirs. Alternative Mus., 1986-92, Gallery Assn. N.Y., 1981-87. Recipient Emerging Artist award NEA, 1982-83, Zoetrope award: Top Twelve Screenwriters in Am., 2001, Miramax Pictures Project Greenlight. Top 250 Screenwriters in the U.S., Chesterfield Writers' Film Project (Paramount Pictures). Mem.: Internat. Assn. Art Critics. Home: 131 W 15th St Apt 23 New York NY 10011-6757

DENSON, WILLIAM FRANK, III, lawyer; b. Birmingham, Ala., Aug. 1, 1943; s. William Frank Jr. and Martha Jane (Wilson) D.; m. Deborah Lynn Davis, July 6, 1974; 1 child, Patricia Lynn Pyle. BA, U. Montevallo, 1965; JD, Emory U., 1968. Bar: Ala. 1968. Atty. Spain, Gillon, Riley, Tate & Ansley, Birmingham, 1969-73; atty., asst. sec., sec. Vulcan Materials Co., Birmingham, 1973-88, sec., asst. gen. counsel, 1988-92, v.p., sec., asst. gen. counsel, 1992-94, v.p. law, sec., 1994-98, sr. v.p. law, sec., 1998-99, sr. v.p., gen. counsel, sec., 1999—. Trustee U. Montevallo, 1987-99; bd. dirs. Glenwood Mental Health Svcs., 1990-96. Mem. ABA, Ala. State Bar, Country Club of Birmingham, Willow Point Country Club (Alexander City, Ala.), Kiwanis Club Birmingham. Republican. Episcopalian. Avocations: golf, reading, travel. Home: 3215 E Briarcliff Rd Birmingham AL 35223-1304 Office: Vulcan Materials Co 1200 Urban Center Dr Birmingham AL 35242-2545

DENT, CEDRIC CARL, musician, educator; b. Detroit, Sept. 24, 1962; s. Edward Samuel and Barbara Eloise Dent; m. Beverly Dawn Hayes, Dec. 6, 1987; 1 child, Cedric Carl. MusB in Choral Music Edn., U. Mich., 1985; MusM in Music Theory and Arranging, U. Ala., 1987; PhD in Music Theory, U. Md., 1997. Co-prodr., co-arranger, performer Take 6 vocal ensemble, Nashville, 1985—. Songwriter, pub. Broadcast Music Inc., 1988—; Roy Acuff chair of excellence in the creative arts Austin Peay State U., Clarksville, Tenn., 1999; host Music to my Ears Nat. Pub. TV WDCN, Nashville, 2000; mem. chancellor's disting. fellows series U. Calif., Irvine, 2001. Composer: (songs) Soon One Morn, 2002; prodr.(songwriter): (recorded performance) The Dream, 1999. Nominee Grammy Award for best instrumental arrangement accompanying a vocal, Nat. Acad. Recording Arts and Scis., 1990, Dove award for urban recorded song of the yr., Gospel Music Assn., 1999, Grammy award for best jazz vocal performance, Nat. Acad. Recording Arts and Scis., 2000. Mem.: AFTRA, Phi Kappa Phi. Avocations: reading, church music, jogging. Home: 1810 Ashmore Ct Mount Juliet TN 37122

DENT, EDWARD DWAIN, lawyer; b. Ft. Worth, Dec. 23, 1950; BA, Tex. Christian U., 1973; JD, St. Mary's U., Tex., 1976. Bar: Tex., U.S. Dist. Ct. (no. and so. dists.) Tex., U.S. Supreme Ct. Atty., ptnr. Kugle, Stewart, Dent, Frederick, Ft. Worth, 1979-89; founder Dent Law Firm, Ft. Worth, Dallas, 1990—. Bd. dirs. West Side Little League. Recipient Hist. Preservation Award, Tarrant County Hist. Soc., 1992. Mem. ATLA, Pres.'s Club (life), U.S. Supreme Ct. Hist. Soc., Tex. Trial Lawyers (bd. dirs. 1989-2002, Tarrant County Trial Lawyers (bd. dirs. 1988-89, officer 1989), Trial Lawyers for Pub. Justice, Ft. Worth Club, Colonial Country Club, Million Dollar Advocacy Soc. (life). Democrat. Office: Dent Law Firm 1120 Penn St Fort Worth TX 76102-3417

DENT, EDWARD EUGENE, manufacturing company specialist; b. Charleston, W.Va., Oct. 14, 1948; s. Eugene Franklin and Delcie Marie (Harper) D.; m. Karen Sue Smith, Nov. 21, 1968; children: Jason Edward, Joseph Andrew. BA, W.Va. Inst. Tech., 1973; MA, Va. State U., 1988; cert. in labor, Ind. U., 2001. Cert. tchr., W.Va., Va. Fin. mgr. Ray Broyhill Ford, Hopewell, Va., 1973-75; bus. mgr. sales Strosnider Chevrolet, Inc., Hopewell, 1975-78; adminstr. crafts Brown & Root Constrn./Engrs., Richmond, Va., 1978-80; process spinning operator Kevlar spinning ops. E.I. duPont de Nemours & Co., Richmond, 1981—2001, process operator Kevlar, 2001—. Chem. process operator Tyvek Union rep.; union pres. ARWI-DuPont. Author: Race Relations in Hopewell, Va. 1635-1932, 1988, Betrayal: Employee Relations at DuPont, 1981-1994, 1995. Active Va. Hist. Soc. Sgt. U.S. Army, 1967-69, Vietnam. Sgt. U.S. Army, 1967—69, Vietnam. Decorated Combat Inf. badge, Army Commendation medal with oak leaf cluster. Mem. Soc. First Inf. Divsn. (Big Red One), Am. Legion, Va. state U. Alumni (pub. rels. officer Chesterfield chpt. 1989-91), Phi Alpha Theta (alumni, treas. W.Va. Inst. Tech. chpt. 1972-73), Alpha Chi. Baptist. Avocations: reading, travel, teaching, fishing, writing. Home: 4487 Cypress Creek Dr Prince George VA 23875

DENT, FREDERICK BAILY, former mill executive, former ambassador, former secretary of commerce; b. Cape May, N.J., Aug. 17, 1922; s. Magruder and Edith (Baily) D.; m. Mildred C. Harrison, Mar. 11, 1944 (dec.); children: Frederick Baily, Mildred Hutcheson, Pauline Harrison, Diana Gwynn, Magruder Harrison. BA, Yale U., 1944. With Joshua L. Baily & Co., Inc., N.Y.C., 1946-47; with Mayfair Mills, Arcadia, SC, 1947—, 2003, pres., 1958-88, treas., 1977—2001, chmn., 1998—2001, also bd. dirs. Sec. Dept. Commerce, Washington, 1973-75, amb., spl. rep. for trade negotiations, 1975-77; bd. dirs. Joshua L. Baily & Co. Chmn. Spartanburg County Planning and Devel. Commn., 1960-72; trustee Spartanburg Day Sch., Brevard Music Ctr.; past mem. corp. Yale U. Lt. USNR, 1943-46, PTO. Named Laureate, S.C.; named to S.C. Hall of Fame, Laureate, S.C., S.C. Bus. Hall of Fame, Textile Hall of Fame. Mem. Spartanburg Area C. of C. (chmn. 1991). Episcopalian. Home: 221 Montgomery Dr Spartanburg SC 29302-3443

DENT, JEFFREY, music educator; b. Berwick, Pa., Apr. 17, 1959; s. Jay P. and Theresa M. Dent; m. Jane A. Strunk, July 17, 1982; children: Thomas R., Susan J. B Music Edn., Mansfield U., Pa., 1981. Music educator Jersey Shore Middle Sch., Jersey Shore, Pa., 1990—, Hanover Area Schs., Wilkes Barre, Pa., 1984—90, East Lycoming Schs., Hughesville, Pa., 1981—84. Leader Boy Scouts of Am., Lock Haven, Pa., 1991—96; mem. bd. Millbrook Playhouse, Mill Hall, Pa., 1995—; mem. Knights of Columbus, Lock Haven, Pa., 1995—. Mem.: Pa. Music Educators, Nat. Judges Assn. Office: Jersey Shore Middle Sch 601 Thompson St Jersey Shore PA 17740

DENT, THOMAS AUGUSTINE, lawyer, educator; b. N.Y.C., Aug. 28, 1920; s. Darby Thomas and Mary Margaret (Goggins) D.; m. Virginia Michels, Apr. 21, 1951; children— Francis W. Koupash, Marie Dent Scofield, Marc Thomas. BA, Queens Coll., 1942; JD, Bklyn. Law Sch., 1948, LLM, 1957. Bar: N.Y. 1949, U.S. Dist. Ct. (so. dist.) N.Y. 1949, U.S. Dist. Ct. (ea. dist.) N.Y. 1980, U.S. Ct. Appeals (2d cir.) 1980. Assoc. Dayton & D'Amato, Bayside, N.Y., 1950-54; sole practice, Flushing, N.Y., 1954-55; ptnr. Dent & Witschieben and predecessor Dent, Goldblum & Witschieben, Flushing, 1955-78, Garden City, N.Y., 1978— ; adj. assoc. prof. bus. law Queens Coll., Flushing, 1962-88; asst. dist. atty. Queens County, Kew Gardens, 1964-66; arbitrator Civil Ct. City N.Y., Kew Gardens, 1981-91. Pres. Child Guidance Ctr. No. Queens, Flushing, 1959-62; counsel Udalls Cove Preservation Com., Inc., Douglaston, N.Y., 1979— . Lt. USN, 1943-46; PTO. Mem. Bar Assn. Nassau County, Queens County Bar Assn., Queens Coll. Alumni Assn. (pres. 1951-53, trustee 1974—). Democrat. Roman Catholic. Clubs: North Hills Country (Manhasset, N.Y.). Rotary (pres. local club 1955-56, dist. gov. 1976-77). Home: 25025 41st Rd Flushing NY 11363-1712 Office: Dent & Witschieben 821 Franklin Ave Garden City NY 11530-4519

DENTEN, CHRISTOPHER PETER, lawyer; b. Oakland, Calif., Apr. 23, 1964; s. Richard and Waltraud Denten; m. Mary McLaughlin, May 18, 1996; 1 child, Aiden. BA, U. Calif., Berkeley, 1986; JD, U. San Francisco, 1990; LLM in Tax, Golden Gate U., 2003. Bar: Calif. 1991, U.S. Dist. Ct. (no. dist.) Calif. 1991, U.S. Ct. Appeals (9th cir.) 1991; CPA, Colo.; notary public. Tax profl. KPMG Peat Marwick, Oakland, 1988-92; sr. tax analyst Cisco Sys., Inc., San Jose, Calif., 1992-97; assoc. gen. counsel, dir. legal affairs and taxation Network Assocs., Inc. (formerly McAfee, Inc.), Santa Clara, Calif., 1997—2002; gen. counsel iManage, Inc., Foster City, Calif., 2003—. Bd. dirs. Network Assocs. fgn. subs., 2000-02; gen. counsel iManage, Inc., Foster City, Calif., 2003—. Named to Outstanding Young Men of Am., 1982; Brother Gary Stone Meml. scholar, 1982. Mem. AICPA, Santa Clara Bar Assn., San Mateo County Bar Assn., Nat. Notary Assn., U. Calif. Berkeley Alumni Assn., U. San Francisco Law Sch. Alumni Assn., Network Assocs. Pres. Club. Republican. Roman Catholic. Avocations: marathons, golf, art, travel. Home and Office: PO Box 117932 Burlingame CA 94011-7932

DENTI, JOSEPH RAYMOND, music educator, director; b. Erie, Pa., May 1, 1976; s. Joseph Patrick and Sandra Machusko Denti. BS in Music Edn., Duquesne U., 1998, MusM in Music Edn., 2002; student in Edn., George Mason U., 2003—. Cert. tchr. Commonwealth of Pa., 1998. Dir. of instrumental studies Charleroi (Pa.) Area Sch. Dist., 1998—2000, Carlynton Sch. Dist., Carnegie, Pa., 2000—02, Hopewell Sch. Dist., Aliquippa, Pa., 2002—03. Tchr. Duquesne U., Pitts., 1998—2003, cons., 2000—02. Contbr. articles to profl. jours. Recipient Am. Legion award, St. Louise de Marillac, 1990. Mem.: Pa. Fedn. of Contest Judges, Am. Orff Soc. Assn., Dalcroze Soc. of Am. Three Rivers Chpt., Tubists Universal Brotherhood Assn., Pa. Music Educators Assn., Music Educators Nat. Conf., Mu Phi Epsilon, Pi Kappa Lambda, Omicron Delta Kappa. Republican. Roman Catholic. Avocations: golf, reading, travel, basketball, baseball. Home: 1265 Tidewood Drive Bethel Park PA 15102 Personal E-mail: aven493@yahoo.com.

DENTINGER, RONALD LEE, comedian, speaker, freelance writer; b. Milw., Feb. 14, 1941; s. William Cassel and Kathryn Faye (Ritzman) D.; m. Kaylee Ann Kasten, Aug. 28, 1965; children: Ronald Lee Jr., Joann Jean. Officer Milw. Police Dept., 1962-67; dist. mgr. Am. Automobile Assn., Madison, Wis., 1967-71; gen. mgr. Don Q Inn, Dodgeville, Wis., 1971-85; comedian, spkr. Dodgeville, 1976—. Humorist quoted in comedy mags., books; jokes sold to Rodney Dangerfield Joan Rivers, The Tonight Show, Saturday Night Live, 20/20 Show, Time Mag.; author: (with others) The Art of Communication, The Great Communicators II, (joke books) Down Time, How to Argue with Your Spouse. Pres. Hidden Valley Tourism Region, Wis., 1984. Named Funniest Person in Wis., Showtime-TV Network, 1985. Mem. Nat. Spkrs. Assn., Wis. Profl. Spkrs. Assn., Wis. Soc. Assn. Execs., Dodgeville C. of C. (pres. 1984). Home and Office: PO Box 151 Dodgeville WI 53533-0151

DENTLER, ANNE LILLIAN, artist; b. Pitts., Oct. 13, 1937; d. Bailey Kent and Anna Wilhelmina Schaefer; m. Gary Morgan, July 13, 1957 (div. Mar. 1975); children: Gary, Sherree, Mitch; m. David Daniel Dentler, Aug. 14, 1976; stepchildren: David, Jr., Joseph Charles. Degree in journalism, Pa. State U., 1974; postgrad., McNeese U., 1984, 85, 86, postgrad., 1998-2000; degree in art, Pa. State U., 2002. Clk.- typist Westinghouse Electric, Beaver, Pa., 1956, 57, 58; clk. (part time) J.C. Penney, Baden, Pa., 1974-76; rschr. survey analysis Penn State U., University Park, Pa., 1973-74; dep. prothonotary Beaver County Govt., 1974—78; dep. magistrate Pa. State Govt., Baden, 1976-80. Profl. artist, workshop instr., Pa., La.; with arts immersion program Calcasieu Arts & Humanities, Lake Charles, La., 1989; illustrator, conceptual artist Vol. Ctr. Southwest La., 1989-95; artist in residence Calcasieu Parish Schs., Lake Charles, 1990; assoc. mem. Women in the Arts, Washington, 1995; instr. continuing edn. portraiture McNeese U., Lake Charles, 1998—. Illustrator: Jean Lafitte, Louisiana Buccaneer, 1990—, Rhythmic Alphabet; author: Portraiture...in Plain Language, 1993, First Step Arithmetic, 1994, My Sister, My Friend, 1994, Birds Gotta Fly, 1995, Many Hats, Many Faces, 1996. Bd. dirs. Associated La. Artists, 1984—, Gateway Found., Lake Charles, 1988, Martin Luther King Coalition, Lake Charles, 1993. Recipient Best of Show award Arts and Humanities Coun., Southwest La., 1986; named Artist of Yr., Gateway Found., 1988. Mem. Assoc. La. Artists (founder 1984, pres. 1984, 85, 86, sec. 1990, workshop instr. 1986-99, 2000—), Beaumont Art League, New Orleans Art Assn., New Brighton Art Assn. Democrat. Baptist. Avocation: traveling. Studio: Annie's Artworks 2223 W Sale Rd Lake Charles LA 70605-7946

DENTLER, ROBERT ARNOLD, sociologist, educator; b. Chgo., Nov. 26, 1928; s. Arnold E. and Jennie (Munsen) D.; m. Helen Hosmer, Sept. 7, 1950; children: Deborah, Eric, Robin. BS, Northwestern U., 1949, MA, 1950, Am. U., 1954; PhD, U. Chgo., 1960. Reporter Chgo. City News Bur., 1949; tchr. Pomfret Sch., 1950-52; intelligence officer U.S. Govt., 1952-54; instr. Dickinson Coll., 1954-57; fellow U. Chgo., 1957-59; rschr. U. Kans., 1959-61; asst. prof. Dartmouth Coll., 1961-62; mem. faculty Tchrs. Coll., Columbia U., N.Y.C., 1962-72, prof. sociology, dep. dir. to dir. Ctr. for Urban Edn., 1966-72; dean Sch. Edn., Boston U., 1972-79; sr. sociologist Abt Assocs., Cambridge, Mass., 1979-83; prof. sociology U. Mass., Boston, 1983-92; sr. fellow McCormack Inst. Pub. Affairs, 1993-94; faculty assoc. Trotter Inst., 1994—2001; dir. Inst. for Learning and Teaching U. Mass., Boston, 1987, acting dean Coll. Edn., 1988. Author: (with Peter Rossi) The Politics of Urban Renewal, 1961, (with Nelson W. Polsby and Paul A. Smith) Politics and Social Life, 1963, (with Phillips Cutright) Hostage America, 1963, (with B. Mackler and M.E. Warshauer) The Urban R's: Race Relations as the Problem in Urban Education, 1967, Major American Social Problems, 1967, (with M.E. Warshauer) Big City Dropouts and Illiterates, 1967, American Community Problems, 1967, Major Social Problems, 1973, Urban Problems, 1977, (with M.B. Scott) Schools on Trial: An Inside Account of the Boston School Desegregation Case, 1981, (with D.C. Baltzell and D.J. Sullivan) University on Trial, 1983, (with A.L. Hafner) Hosting Newcomers, 1997, Practicing Sociology, 2001, The Looking-Glass Self: A Memoir, 2002; editor Sociol. Practice Rev., 1989-92. Home: 11 Childs Rd Lexington MA 02421-4517 Office: U Mass Dept Sociology Boston MA 02125-3393

DENTON, CAROL FORSBERG, retired training systems designer; b. Boston, Mar. 5, 1937; d. Algot Oscar and Isabelle Marie (Flynn) Forsberg; m. Earle Lewis Denton; children: Susan E., Kathleen E. Denton Pierson. BS in Geology, U. Okla., 1959; MAT in Counseling, Rollins Coll., Winter Park, Fla., 1970, postgrad., 1971. Cert. sci. tchr., counselor, Fla. Counselor U. Okla., Norman, 1958-59; sci. tchr. Lee County Bd. Pub. Instruction, Ft. Myers, Fla., 1960-61; counselor U. Fla., Gainsville, 1961-62; tchr. Seminole County bd. Instruction, Sanford, Fla., 1965-69; pers. mgmt. specialist Naval Tng. Device Ctr., Orlando, Fla., 1969-73, ednl. specialist, 1973-93; head advanced instrnl. systems br. Naval Air Warfare Ctr. Tng. Sys. Divsn., Orlando, Fla., 1993-99, Dept. of Navy Aquisition Profl. Cmty., 1995-2000. Mission pilot, observer, tchr. Civil Air Patrol, Orlando, 1965-75; mem. Joint Svc. Action Group ICW, Pentagon, Washington, 1986—; steering com. Intersvc./Industry Tng. Sys. and Edn. Conf., Orlando, 1991-94, chair, 1994, patrol officer, 2000—; mem. Navy Adv. Group, Interactive Courseware, Washington, 1986-99. Contbr. articles to profl. jours. Human rels. commn. City of Orlando, 1972-75; bd. dirs. Fairwinds Fed. Credit Union, Orlando, 1987—, chmn. bd. dris., 1999—; apptd. Army Arlington Ladies personal rep. for Army Chief of Staff, Washington, 1984-86. Recipient Civilian Exemplary Svc. award, 1995, Dept. of Navy Civilian Meritorious Svc. award, 1999, Paul Harris award Rotary Internat., 2003. Mem. Ctrl. Fla. Human Factors Soc. (pres., bd. dirs. 1978-80), Altrusa Internat. (pres. Orlando chpt. 1978-82), Sigma Xi, Kappa Delta Pi. Republican. Presbyterian. Achievements include research in interactive courseware and distance learning training capabilities. Home: 1017 Gran Paseo Dr Orlando FL 32825-8330

DENTON, D. KEITH, management educator; b. Paducah, Ky., June 28, 1948; s. Derward and Bonnie Denton; children: Shane, Taylor. BS, Murray State U., 1971; M in Pub. Adminstrn., Memphis State U., 1974; PhD, So. Ill. U., 1981. Supr. Shelby Pre-Casting, Memphis, 1971-72; safety engr. Md. Casualty Corp., Memphis, 1972-76; instr. Draughn's Bus. Coll., Paducah, 1977; safety trainer Union Carbide Corp., Paducah, 1977-78; prof. So. Ill. U., Carbondale, 1978-83, S.W. Mo. State U., Springfield, 1983—. Cons. Small Bus. Research Ctr., Springfield, 1985—, Springfield Remfg. Corp., 1986. Author: Safety Management, 1982; (with others) Safety Performance, 1985, Quality Service in America, 1989, The Production Game, 1990, Handling Employee Complaints, 1990, Horizontal Management, 1991, The Service Trainer, 1992, Recruitment Retention and Employee Relations, 1992, Did You Know?, Fascinating Facts and Fallacies, 1994, Enviro-Management: How Companies Turn Pollution Cost into Profits, 1994, The Toolbox for the Mind, 1999, Empowering Intranets, 2002; contbr. over 150 articles to profl. jours. Mem. Acad. Mgmt., Nat. Assn. Purchasing, Am. Soc. Prodn. and Inventory Control, Inst. Indsl. Engrs. Office: SW Mo State U 901 S National Ave Springfield MO 65804-0088

DENTON, DEREK ASHWORTH, medical researcher, medical scientist; b. Launceston, Tasmania, Australia, May 27, 1924; s. Arthur A. and Catherine (Edwards) D.; m. Margaret Catherine Dame Scott, Mar. 13, 1953; children: Matthew, Angus. MBBS, Melbourne U., 1947. Haley Rsch. Fellow Walter and Eliza Hall Inst., Melbourne, 1948; med. rsch. fellow, sr. med. rsch. fellow Nat. Health and Med. Rsch. Coun., Melbourne, 1948—, prin. med. rsch. fellow, 1970; founding dir. Howard Florey Inst. Exptl. Physiology and Medicine, Melbourne, 1971-89, emeritus dir., 1990—; pres. Howard Florey Biomed. Found., Melbourne, 1997—. Bd. dirs. David Syme Ltd. Pubs. "The Age", 1984-93; 1st v.p. Internat. Union of Physiol. Scis., 1983-89 (chmn. nominating com. and com. on commns. 1986-93), mem. jury Albert and Mary Lasker Found. awards in med. sci., 1979-90; fgn. assoc. NAS of U.S., 1995; adj. scientist Southwest Found. Biomed. Rsch., San Antonio, 1994—; foreign assoc. Inst. de France Acad. des Scis., 2000. Author: The Hunger for Salt, 1982, The Pinnacle of Life: Consciousness in Animals and Humans; editor: Olfaction and Taste, 1985. Fellow Royal Soc. (London), Royal Coll. Physicians (hon., London and Australia), Am. Physiol. Soc. (hon.), AAAS (hon., fgn.); mem. Royal Swedish Acad. Scis. (fgn. med. mem.). Avocations: wine, tennis, fly fishing. Home: 816 Orrong Rd Toorak 3142 Melbourne Australia Office: U Melbourne Howard Florey Inst Exptl Physiology Medi Parkville 3052 Australia E-mail: dad@hfi.unimelb.edu.au.

DENTON, FRANK M. newspaper editor; b. Tulsa, Mar. 30, 1945; s. Frank McCray and Eydith (Langley) D.; m. April Murphy, June 18, 1983 (div. 2000); children: Langley Sara, Allegra Murphy. BA, U. Tex., 1968; MS, Columbia U., 1970; MBA, U. Wis., 1994, PhD, 1996. Sportswriter Austin Am. Statesman, 1964-66; reporter Stuart Long News Svc., Austin, Tex., 1966-69, Anniston (Ala.) Star, 1970-72, Cin. Enquirer, 1972-75; asst. lifestyle editor Detroit Free Press, 1976-78, lifestyle editor, 1978-81, asst. mng. editor, 1981-86; editor Wis. State Journal, Madison, 1986—. Bd. dirs. Mid-Am. Press Inst. Mem. Am. Soc. Newspaper Editors (bd. dirs.), Phi Kappa Phi. Home: 3046 Irvington Way Madison WI 53713-3414 Office: Wis State Journal 1901 Fish Hatchery Rd Madison WI 53713-1297 E-mail: fdenton@madison.com.

DENTON, JOAN CAMERON, reading consultant, former educator; b. Chgo. d. Wallace William and Ruth Elizabeth (Nothof) Cameron; m. Robert Eastman Denton, Aug. 16, 1958; children: Marianne, Lynn, Robert. BS in Edn., Northwestern U., Evanston, Ill., 1954; MS in Spl. Edn. and Reading, U. Nebr., Omaha, 1982. Tchr. English and social studies Berwyn (Ill.) Pub. Schs.; tchr. devel. and advanced secondary reading Omaha Pub. Schs., reading diagnostician; lead tchr. Reading Svcs.; reading cons. Scholastic, Inc. Former mem. external visitation team/reading Boys Town Schs., Omaha Pub. Schs.; supr. summer literacy ctr., instr. U. Nebr., Omaha; mem. instrl. dist. coms.; former mem. rev. bd. Reading Tchr.; co-chair Metro Reading Coun. Lit. Project Listening Libr.; mem. reading leadership team, cons. gifted reading study Omaha Pub. Schs.; coord. OPS/AT&T Reading Pioneers Assisting Literacy in Schs. Program, mem. cons. team. Co-author computer-based reading comprehension course for Ind. Study H.S., U. Nebr. Coll. Continuing Edn. Chmn. Operation Sch. Bell, Assistance League Omaha; bd. dirs. Munro-Meyer Women's Guild, Sacred Hearth Sch. Guild. Recipient Disting. Alumni award U. Nebr. Coll. Edn., Omaha, 1998. Mem. AAUW, NEA, Nebr. Edn. Assn., Omaha Edn. Assn., Internat. Reading Assn., Nebr. Reading Assn., Met. Reading Coun., Phi Delta Kappa, Alpha Xi Delta. E-mail: denton@tconl.com.

DENTON, KATHRYN M. merchant banker, writer; b. Elyria, Ohio, Apr. 7, 1959; d. Alfred Glenn and Esther M. (Paul) Cummings; children: Samuel T Denton IV, Benjamin J., Brenda Anne, Lori Christine Miller. BS, Wash.U., St. Louis, 1988. Mgr. (developers and dbas) Fed. Res. Bank, St. Louis, 1993—96, tech. relationship mgr., 1997—2002, dist. tech. coord., 2002—; writer www-.gantthead.com, 2001—. Tech. writer www.ganttnead.com, 2001—. Author: (book) The Search of a Lifetime, Corporate Russian Roulette. Nat. coord. Adoption Registration Coalition, 1996—2003; lead St. Louis Area Adoption and Reunion Survivors, 2001—03; advisor St. Louis City Schools Work Study Program, 2002—03. Mem.: Fed. Res. Bank Toastmasters Club (pres. 2003, named Advanced Toastmaster 2002). Avocations: photography, French horn, guitar, trumpet, bicycling. Personal E-mail: kdentonH@ix.netcom.com.

DENTON, MEDONA BONNER, research chemistry educator; b. Beaumont, Tex., June 15, 1944; s. Harold and Julia (Bonner) D. BS in Chemistry, BA in Psychology, Lamar State Coll. Tech., 1967; PhD in Chemistry, U. Ill., 1972. Asst. prof. chemistry U. Ariz., Tucson, 1971-76, assoc. prof., 1976-80, prof., 1980—. Cons. Lawrence Livermore (Calif.) Lab., Baird Corp., Bedford, Mass., DOW Chem. Corp., Midland, Mich.; bd. dirs. Root Corp., Houston, Denco Research, Tucson. Editor: Jour. Automatic Chemistry, Chemometrics and Intelligent Lab. Systems, 1986; contbr. articles to profl. jours.; inventor in field. Alfred P. Sloan Research fellow, 1976-80. Mem. Am. Chem. Soc., Soc. Applied Spectroscopy (chmn. Ariz. chpt. 1977-78, nat. program com. 1978-79, Lester W. Strock award 1991), Instrument Soc. Am., Sigma Xi, Phi Lambda Upsilon, Alpha Chi Sigma. Avocations: scuba diving, skiing, spleunking, racing autos.

DENTON, MICHAEL JOHN, research economist, energy risk expert, financial engineer, finance company executive; b. Kokomo, Ind., July 31, 1955; s. John Louis and Marguerite (Layden) D. BSE in Interdisciplinary Engring., Purdue U., 1977; MBA in Fin. and Internat. Bus., U. Chgo., 1981; MA in Econs., U. Ariz., 1994, PhD, 1997. Registered profl. engr., Ind. Mech. engr. Sargent & Lundy, Engr., Chgo., 1977-80; field project engr. Amoco Oil Co., Chgo., 1980-83; sr. assoc. Theodore Barry & Assoc., L.A., 1983-85; mng. assoc. Metzler & Assoc., Deerfield, Ill., 1986-92, tech., electric markets rsch. Econ. Sci. Lab. U. Ariz., Tucson, 1992-95; prin. Utilities Internat., Inc., Chgo., 1994-96; v.p. ION Cons., Chgo., 1997-2000; v.p. N.Am. strategic consulting Caminus Corp., NYC, 2000—01; sr. v.p. Energy Anal., NYC, 2002—. Bd. advisors Internat. Found. for Rsch. in Exptl. Econ. Mem.: Profl. Risk Mgrs. Internat. Assn., Econ. Sci. Assn., Am. Econ. Assn. Avocations: scuba, running, Go, enology. Home: 2216 E 5th St Tucson AZ 85719-5207 Office: 825 3rd Ave New York NY 10022 E-mail: michael.denton_81@gsbalum.uchicago.edu.

DENTON, RAY DOUGLAS, insurance company executive; b. Lake City, Ark., May 16, 1937; s. Ray Dudney and Edna Lorraine (Roe) D.; m. Cheryl Emma Borchardt, Mar. 9, 1964; children: Ray D., Derek St. Clair, Carter Lee (dec.). BA, U. Mich., 1964, postgrad., 1969—70, Wayne State U., 1964—65, JD, 1969. Claims rep. Hartford Ins. Co., Crum & Forster, Detroit, Am. Claims, Chgo., 1962-73; ptnr. Chgo. Metro Claims, Oak Park, Ill., 1974-75; founder, pres. Ray D. Denton & Assocs., Inc., Hinsdale, Ill., 1975—. Insurance company executive; b. Lake City, Ark., May 16, 1937; s. Ray Dudney and Edna Lorraine (Roe) D.; BA, U. Mich., 1964, postgrad., 1969-70; JD, Wayne State U., 1969, postgrad., 1964-65. m. Cheryl Emma Borchardt, Mar. 9, 1964; children: Ray D., Derek St. Clair, Carter Lee (dec.). Claims rep. Hartford Ins. Co., Crum & Forster, Detroit, and Am. Claims, Chgo., 1962-73; partner Chgo. Metro Claims, Oak Park, Ill., 1974-75; founder, pres. Ray D. Denton & Assocs., Inc., Hinsdale, Ill., 1975—. Mem. Pi Kappa Alpha, Phi Alpha Delta. Office: 930 N York Rd Ste 14 Hinsdale IL 60521-2993 E-mail: cherayden@msn.com.

D'ENTREMONT, EDWARD JOSEPH, infosystems engineer, educator; b. Lynn, Mass., June 25, 1954; s. Joseph Albenie and Gertrude Grace (Flattery) D'E. BA in Math., Salem State Coll., 1976; MS in Applied Math., Northeastern U., 1982. Floor supr. Jordan Marsh co., Peabody, Mass., 1972-76; sci. programmer Electronics Corp. Am., Cambridge, Mass., 1977, Sulivan and Cogliano, Waltham, Mass., 1977; software engr. Raytheon Svc. Co., Burlington, Mass., 1977-86, Baytheon Missile Sys. divsn., Bedford, Mass., 1986-96, Desktop Data Inc., Burlington, Mass., 1995-98; prin. software engr. Newsedge Corp., Burlington, 1998—2002, Dialog Corp., Burlington, 2002—. Instr. Fitchburg State Raytheon Inst., Tewksbury, Mass, 1986-96, U. Lowell, Mass., 1991-2001; sr. software engr. Raytheon Co.; instr. continuing edn. Salem State Coll., 1993-95. Campaign worker presdl. campaigns, 1968-72, city coun., state rep., Lynn, 1976, Dukakis for Gov., Lynn, 1982; vol. tech. com. Aborn Elem. Sch. Mem. IEEE, Am. Math. Soc., Math. Assn. Am., Soc. for Indsl. and Applied Math., IEEE Computer Soc., N.Y. Acad. Scis., Assn. Computing Machinery, St. Mary's H.S. Alumni Assn., Salem State Coll. Alumni Assn., Northeastern U. Alumni Assn., Lexington Racquet and Swim Club. Democrat. Roman Catholic. Home: 50 York Rd Lynn MA 01904-1130

DENUNZIO, RALPH DWIGHT, investment banker; b. White Plains, N.Y., Nov. 17, 1931; s. Frank and M. Winifred (Sandbach) DeN.; m. Jean A. Ames, Sept. 25, 1954; children: David Ames, Peter Dwight, Thomas Richard. AB, Princeton U., 1953. With Kidder, Peabody & Co., Inc., N.Y.C., 1953-87, exec. v.p., 1968-77, pres., 1977, chief exec. officer, 1980-87, chmn., chief exec. officer, 1986-1987, also dir. Bd. dirs. Fed. Express Corp., Memphis, Harris Corp., Melbourne, Fla., Nike, Inc., Beaverton, Oreg.; bd. govs. N.Y. Stock Exch., 1968, vice chmn. bd., 1969-71, chmn. bd., 1971-72. Past pres. bd. trustees Deerfield (Mass.) Acad.; past pres. bd. trustees Greenwich (Conn.) Country Day Sch.; past trustee Princeton U. Mem. Securities Industry Assn. (past chmn. 1980-81), Bond Club (N.Y.C.) (past pres., gov.), Links Club (N.Y.C.), Princeton Club (N.Y.C.), N.Y. Yacht Club, Stanwich Club (Greenwich), Riverside Yacht Club (Conn.), John's Island Club (Vero Beach, Fla.). Republican. Roman Catholic. Home: Bridle Path Ln Riverside CT 06878 Office: Harbor Point Assocs Inc 375 Park Ave Ste 2602 New York NY 10152-2699

DENUZZO, RINALDO VINCENT, pharmacy educator; b. Cleve., Oct. 21, 1922; s. Luigi and Domenica Mary (Razzano) DiNuzzo; m. Lucy Bernadine Sneed, June 29, 1946; 1 child, Lisa Ann. BS, Albany Coll. Pharmacy, 1952; MS in Edn., SUNY-Albany, 1956; LHD, Union U., 2003. Registered pharmacist, N.Y., Fla., Vt. Prof. pharmacy N.Y. Coll. Pharmacy, Albany, 1952—, adminstrv. asst., 1963-80. Pharmacist N.Y., Fla., Vt., 1968-95; sr. pharmacist inspector N.Y. State Dept. Health, 1966-95; field dir. Market Measures, Inc.; chmn. tech. pharmacy adv. com., 1977-95; lectr. drug product substitution and generic drugs; notary public. Author: Ann. Albany Coll. Pharmacy Prescription Survey, 1956—84, Substitution, The New York State Experience, 1980, RX Services, XIII Winter Olympic Games, 1980, Ann. DeNuzzo Prescription Survey, 1985—96, Imapct of One-Line Prescription Form on Generic Drug Use, 1987, Cipro, Vasotec, Volatren Post Biggest Gains, 1987, Using the Right Tools to Achieve Personal Success, 1990, Personal Selling, 1991, Annual Survey Tracks Drug Prescribing Trends, 1990, Consumer Prescription Prices Increase, 1991, Changes in Dental Prescribing, 1991, How to Reduce Prescription Medical Costs, 1992, Are Dental Prescriptions a Viable Target for RPhs?, 1992, Financial Success: A Challenge for the Future, 1996, A National Drug Expert Is Needed, 1999, Down Memory Lane, 1999, 2002, What Graduates Need to Know: A Prescription for the Future Financial Success: ACP's Reflection of Progress 1881-2001; A Brief Written and Pictorial History, 2001; editor: Albany Coll. Pharmacy Alumni News, 1961—81; mem. editl. bd. MMM, 1977—80. Instr. first aid, responding to emergencies CPR ARC; mem. East Greenbush Ctrl. Sch. Dist. Bd. Edn., 1974—92, v.p., 1975—76, pres., 1976—78, 1991—92, East Greenbush Edn. Found.; chmn. Albany Coll. Pharmacy Faculty, 1987—89, com. on coms., 1984—87, promotions com., 1989—92, exec. com., grievance com., chair strategic planning steering com., 1995—96; faculty affairs chmn. and rev. Albany Coll. Pharmacy, 1990—94; sr. student status com., faculty ombudsman Albany Coll. Pharmacy Faculty, 1991—2002, mission statement com., 1995; mem. adv. bd. Merrell-Dow Hosp., 1987; sec.-treas. Union U. Pharmacy Coll. Coun., 1970—80; com. on coms. Albany Coll. Pharmacy Faculty, 1996—97; mem. profl. adv. com. Albany Vis. Nurses Assn.; mem. rev. panel on prescription payment rev. commn. Office Tech. Assessment U. S. Congress, 1988; mem. ethics panel Siena Coll., 1992; mem., dir. Rensselaer County Taxpayers Assn.; cons. pharmacist, coord. pharm. svcs. XIII

Olympic Winter Games, Lake Placid, NY, 1980; liaison Health Sys. Mgmt. degree Joint MS with Union Coll. With U.S. Army, 1941—46, with USAF, 1946—47, capt. M.C., pharm. officer USAFR, 1948—63, ret. USAFR, 1982. Named Francis J. O'Brien Pharmacy Man of Yr., 1979, 2002; recipient 25 Yr. Svc. citation, ARC, 30 Yr. Svc. citation, Svc. plaque, East Greenbush Ctrl. Sch. Dist., 25 Yr. Svc. award, N.Y. State Dept. Health, Disting. Svc. citation, Rensselaer County Taxpayers Assn., established L. Sneed DeNuzzo Sch., Concord Coll., W.V. Mem.: AAUP (pres. 1978—), AARP, Albany Coll. Pharmacy Alumni Assn. (exec. dir. 1965—86, disting. svc. medal 1975), N.Y. State Pub. Employees Fedn., N.Y. Sch. Bd. Assn., N.Y. State Pharm. Soc., Am. Pharm. Assn., Am. Assn. Colls. Pharmacy (sec.-treas., coun. faculties 1979—80, chmn. elect 1982—83, chmn. 1984—87, dir. 1984—89, roundtable presentation ann. meeting 1996, del. ann. meeting 1997), USA Air Muse, 46th and 72nd Recon. Assn., Nat. Italian-Am. Found. (coun.), Officers Club (West Point, N.Y.), Albany Coll. Pharmacy Pres.'s Club (chmn. bd. 1962—87), Kappa Psi (dep. grand coun. Beta Delta chpt., sec.-treas., Albany grad.), Army Five Star, Beta Delta (ann. Rinaldo V. DeNuzzo lucnheon 1988—). Republican. Roman Catholic. Home: 19 Alva St East Greenbush NY 12061-2027 Office: 106 New Scotland Ave Albany NY 12208-3425 E-mail: reutterd@acp.com.

DENVER, EILEEN ANN, magazine editor; b. N.Y.C., Nov. 16, 1942; d. Daniel Joseph and Katherine Agnes (Boland) D.; m. Duncan C. Stephens, July 2, 1988. BA, Coll. New Rochelle, 1964; certificate, Radcliffe Sch. Pub., 1964; MA, Ind. U., 1967. Editorial asst. Mass. Inst. Tech. Tech. Review, Boston, 1965-66; instr. English St. Peter's Coll., Jersey City, 1967-70; assoc. editor, writer Am. Home mag., N.Y.C., 1971-75; asst. editor Consumer Reports, Mt. Vernon, N.Y., 1975-77, asst. mng. editor, 1977-79, mng. editor, 1979-91, exec. editor, 1991-96, dir. editl. ops., 1997-2000, assoc. editl. dir./exec. editor, 2000—. Office: Consumer Reports 101 Truman Ave Yonkers NY 10703-1044

DENYES, JAMES RICHARD, industrial engineer; b. Detroit, Oct. 9, 1948; s. Heyward Thornton and Rosalie (Blair) D.; m. Pamela Brothers, Jan. 1, 1994; children: Amy Cheryne, Laura Michelle. BS in Indsl. Engring. and Ops. Rsch., Va. Tech. U., 1970. Indsl. engr., prodn. control engr., distbn. foreman Allied Chem. Corp., Moncure, N.C., 1970-72; quality control engr. Duke Constrn. Co., Norfolk, Va., 1972-75; command indsl. engr., staff indsl. engr. Navy Manpower and Material Analysis Ctr., Atlantic, Norfolk, 1975-84; head mgmt. engring. dept., Navy Manpower Analysis Ctr., Norfolk, 1981-84; dir. Navy Sch. Work Study, Navy Manpower Engring. Ctr., Norfolk, 1984-88; mgr. indsl. engring. Navy Manpower Analysis Ctr., Chesapeake, Va., 1988-89; dir. Navy Sch. Manpower Mgmt., 1989-94; head dept. tng. Navy Occupational Safety, Health and Environ. Tng. Ctr., 1994—. Co-founder Idea Assocs., 1983-94. Author: Work Smarter Not Harder--Methods Improvement Workbook, 1991; leadership staff Work Simplification Confs., 1992. Treas. Va. Orgn. to Keep Abortion Legal, 1977-79, bd. dirs., 1979-81; fin. adv. NOW, 1975-76; pres. B.M. Williams Elem. Sch. PTA, 1982-83, 1st v.p., 1983-84, 1st v.p., pres., 1984-85; mem. stds. of quality planning coun. Chesapeake Pub. Schs., 1982-83; pres. Crestwood Elem. Sch. PTA, 1986-87; founder, head steering com. couples group Unity Renaissance Ch., 1998, bd. dirs., 1998-2002, sec. 1998-99, v.p., 2000, 2003, pres., 2001, trustee, 2003—; bd. dirs. Hampton Roads Quality Mgmt. Coun., 1989-91. Mem. ASTD (bd. dirs. 1992-97, exec. v.p. 1993-94, pres. 1995), Am. Inst. Indsl. Engrs. (sr.; bd. dirs. 1977-91, prs. chpt. 1980-81, 88-89), Improvement Inst. (trustee 1982-85, 86-88, pres. 1989-92, Pres.'s Cup 1985), Creative Problem Solving Inst. (leadership staff 1985—, Leadership Svc. and Commitment award 1999), Va. Congress Parents and Tchrs. (hon. life)., Pi Delta Epsilon. Home: 1187 Lawson Cove Cir Virginia Beach VA 23455-6807

DENYS, ERIC HELI, neurologist; b. Brugge, Belgium, Apr. 19, 1940; m. Sonja S. Declercq. BS, U. Leuven, 1962, BA in Philosophy, 1965, MD, 1966, MS in Sports Medicine, 1969. Diplomate Am. Acad. Neurology. Intern U. Paris and Marburg A/D Lahn, 1965-66; resident in neurology U. Leuven, Belgium, 1966-69, Stanford (Calif.) U. and Mayo Clinic, 1969-71; Muscular Dystrophy Assn. fellow Inst. Med. Scis. Pacific Med. Ctr., San Francisco, 1974-76; assoc. dir. ALS and Neuromuscular Rsch. Ctr. Pacific Med. Ctr., San Francisco, 1980-89, dir. electromyography lab. dept. neurology, 1980-93. Assoc. clin. prof. neurology U. Calif., San Francisco, 1994—, pres. assn. clin. faculty, 2000; cons. San Francisco Free Clinic, 1994—; dir. inst. neurol. scis. Med. Rsch. Inst. San Francisco Pacific Presbyn. Med. Ctr., 1986-89, co-dir., 1984-86, trustee med. rsch. inst., 1984-89, dir. edn. and trng., 1979-80. Contbr. articles to profl. jours. Fellow Am. Bd. Electrodiagnostic Medicine, Am. Acad. Neurology; mem. Am. Assn. Electrodiagnostic Medicine, San Francisco Neurol. Soc. (pres. 2001-2002), San Francisco Med. Soc., Calif. Med. Assn., Assn. Calif. Neurologists. Office: Calif Pacific Med Ctr Dept Neurology 2100 Webster St Ste 110 San Francisco CA 94115-2374

DENYSYK, BOHDAN, international consultant; b. Kornberg, Germany, Feb. 13, 1947; came to U.S., 1949; s. John and Maria (Zelenewich) D.; m. Halina Bubela, June 28, 1969; children: Maria H., Danya L., Adrienne Y., Alexis M. BS, Manhattan Coll., 1968; MS, Cath. U. Am., 1971; PhD, Union Inst. (formerly Union for Experimenting Colls. and Univs.), Cin., 1981. Project mgr. Naval Weapons Lab., Dahlgren, Va., 1968-72; scientist Naval Med. Research Inst., Bethesda, Md., 1972-75; program mgr. Naval Surface Weapons Ctr., Dahlgren, 1975-78; dept. head E.G. & G. Inc., Rockville, Md., 1978-81; dep. asst. sec. U.S. Dept. Commerce, Washington, 1981-83; dir. civil programs IBM Corp., 1983-86; pres. DLR Assocs., Arlington, Va., 1972-80, 83—, Global U.S.A., 1986—, also owner, bd. dirs. Mem. Congl. Adv. Panel on China, 1985—; bd. dirs. Mazak Corp.; mem. Def. Sci. Bd., 1990—. Contbr. articles to profl. jours. Mem. Presdl. Transition Team, Washington, 1991; regional dir. Rep. Nat. Com., 1980; dir. pub. rels. Ukrainian Nat. Info. Svc., 1976-80; mem. Pres.'s Export Coun., 1981—, Presdl. Awards Commn., 1986-87; exec. dir. Md. Reagan-Bush Campaign, 1984, Bush-Quayle Campaign, 1992; mem. nat. policy forum Fgn. Affairs Coun., 1995—; pres. Phi Mu Alpha Sinfonia, 1967-68; nat. dir. for coalitions Dole for U.S. Pres. Campaign, 1987-88; dep. polit. dir. Dole for Pres., 1995-96; regional polit. dir. Gov. Bush for Pres. 2000, 1999—; mem. Bush-Cheney Transition Team, 2001; mem. sr. commn. on nat. security CSIS, 2000-2001; mem. Marsland State Info. Tech. Bd., 2003—. Navy fellow, 1969-72; Regents scholar, 1964-68 Fellow N.Y. Acad. Sci.; mem. AIAA, AAAS, Am. Def. Preparedness Assn., Am. Phys. Soc. Republican. Roman Catholic. Avocations: scuba, skiing, running. Office: Global USA Inc 2121 K St NW Ste 650 Washington DC 20037-1825

DENZLER, JAMES WYATT, pharmacist; b. Marion, Va., Jan. 30, 1958; s. Roger Vincent Denzler and Helen Margaret Lambert Williams. BS in Biology, East Tenn. U., 1981, U. Minn., 1988. Registered pharmacist, Va., Calif., N.Y. Pharmacist Longs Drugs, Santa Barbara, Calif., 1988-90, Thrifty Drugs, Santa Barbara, 1990-91, Eckerd/Revco, Virginia Beach, Va., 1991-2000, Norfolk (Va.) Gen. Hosp., 1998—; pharmacist mgr. Rite Aid, Virginia Beach, Va., 2000—. Pres., owner Denzler Corp., Norfolk, 1996—; diabetes educator, mem. AADE, 2000—; adj. faculty Hampton U., 2001. Mem. Am. Pharm. Assn., Aubudon Soc., U.S. Table Tennis Assn., Pi Kappa Alpha (chpt. pres.), Phi Delta Chi (chpt. pres.). Avocations: birding, table tennis, weightlifting, photography. Office: Rite Aid 5795 Princess Anne Rd Virginia Beach VA 23462 E-mail: jamz9260@aol.com.

DEO, NARSINGH, computer scientist, educator; b. Raniganj, Bihar, India, Jan. 2, 1936; s. Bihari Lal and Durga (Modi) Jee; m. Karen Ruth Baier, June 29, 1968. BS, Patna U., India, 1956; Dip. I.I.Sc., Indian Inst. Sci., 1959; MS, Calif. Inst. Tech., 1960; PhD, Northwestern U., 1965. Assoc. electronic engr. Burroughs Electro Data divsn., 1960-62; sr. engr. Jet Propulsion Lab., Pasadena, 1966-69, mem. tech. staff, 1969-71; v.p. Britt Electronics Corp., Santa Monica, Calif., 1968-69; asst. prof. elec. engring. Calif. State Coll., 1971; assoc. prof. elec. engring. Indian Inst. Tech., Kanpur, 1971-74, prof., head computer ctr., 1975-77; prof. Wash. State U., Pullman, 1977-87, chmn. dept. computer sci., 1980-84; Millican chair prof. U. Ctrl. Fla., Orlando, 1986—; dir. Ctr. Parallel Computation, 1989—. Electronics design cons. Ctr. Behavior Therapy, Beverly Hills, Calif., 1967—71; mem. faculty engring. ext. UCLA, 1965—68; vis. assoc. prof. U. Ill., Urbana; vis. prof. Wash. State U., Pullman, 1974—75, ETH, Zurich, Switzerland, 1993, Australian Nat. U., Canberra, 1996, Chuo U., Tokyo, 2002; vis. faculty IBM Thomas J. Watson Rsch., Yorktown Heights, NY, 1984, Oak Ridge Nat. Lab., 1994. Author: 4 textbooks; contbr. scientific papers to profl. jours. Recipient Fla. Gov.'s award, 1989; grantee, NSF, U.S. Dept. Transp., Army Rsch. Office, U.S. Army's PM-TRADE, Fla. High Tech. and Industry Coun. Fellow: IEEE, Assn. Computing Machinery. Achievements include patents in field. Home: 3901 Orange Lake Dr Orlando FL 32817-1637 E-mail: deo@cs.ucf.edu.

DEONES, JACK E. corporate executive; b. Mankato, Minn., Sept. 21, 1931; s. Nicholas H. and Beatrice R. (Viste) D.; m. Cleo Pat Peters, May 29, 1955; children— Gregg N., Alexa M. BSS, St. Mary's Coll., 1953; JD, Yale U., 1956. Bar: Minn. 1956, N.J. 1974. Spl. agt. FBI, 1960-62; atty. Pfizer, Inc., 1962-65; div. counsel Honeywell, Inc., 1965-69; asst. gen. counsel Foster Wheeler Corp., Livingston, N.J., 1969-77, corp. sec., 1977-96, v.p., 1984-96; chmn., pres. Castlerock Assocs., Parsippany, N.J., 1996—. Dir. York Internat. Corp., Briarcliff Assocs., Inc. Served with USN, 1956-60. Mem. ABA, N.J. Bar Assn., Minn. Bar Assn. Home: 59 Briarcliff Rd Mountain Lakes NJ 07046-1304 Office: Castlerock Assocs PO Box 6133 Parsippany NJ 07054-7133

DEORCHIS, FRANKIE JUANITA, forester, writer; b. Hawkins, Tex., Dec. 10, 1920; d. E. Whitney and Bura Moseley Moore; m. M. E. DeOrchis, June 27, 1948; children: Vincent Moore, Diane Frances Vogth-Eriksen, Douglas F. BS, Columbia U., 1948. Bookkeeper Civil Svc., Washington, 1942—44; law office mgr. DeOrchis & Ptnrs., N.Y.C., 1982—84; forest mgr., 1980—. Republican. Avocations: travel, reading, cooking, entertaining, charity work. Home: 50 Shore Rd Old Greenwich CT 06870

DEORCHIS, VINCENT MOORE, lawyer; b. NYC, Aug. 25, 1949; s. Mario E. and Frankie (Moore) DeO.; children: Vincent Scott, Dana Lauren. BA, Fordham Coll., 1971, JD, 1974. Bar: N.Y. 1975, U.S. Dist. Ct. (so. and ea. dists.) N.Y. 1975, U.S. Ct. Appeals (2d cir.) 1975, U.S. Supreme Ct. 1985, U.S. Ct. Appeals (3d cir.) 1989, U.S. Dist. Ct. (so. dist.) Tex. 1992, U.S. Ct. Appeals (4th cir.) 1996. Assoc. Haight, Gardner, Poor & Havens, N.Y.C., 1974-84; ptnr. DeOrchis, Walker & Corsa, LLP, N.Y.C., 1997—2002, DeOrchis & Ptnrs. LLP, NYC, 1984—. Co-author: Attorney's Practice Guide to Negotiations, 1985. Pres. North Stratmore Civic Assn., Manhasset, N.Y., 1978-82. Mem. ATLA, ABA (com. on maritime litig.), Inter-Pacific Bar Assn., Maritime Law Assn. (former bd. dirs., rep. to Comite Maritime Internat.), Assn. Transp. Practitioners, N.Y. County Lawyers Assn. (com. on maritime and admiralty law), Propeller Club U.S. Avocation: sailing. Office: DeOrchis and Ptnrs LLP 61 Broadway Fl 26 New York NY 10006-2802

DEORIO, ANTHONY JOSEPH, surgeon; b. Chgo., June 27, 1945; s. Joseph John and Catherine Marie Deorio; m. Janet Ann Balskus, Jan. 10, 1970; children: Joseph, Catherine. BS, Loyola U., Chgo., 1967; MD, Loyola U., Maywood, Ill., 1971. Diplomate Am. Bd. Surgery. Intern St. Joseph Hosp., Chgo., 1971-72; resident in surgery Loyola Med. Ctr., Maywood, 1972-76, clin. instr. surgery, 1976-77, asst. prof. surgery, 1977—; pvt. practice Resurrection Hosp., Chgo., 1977—, dir. surg. edn., 1977—, chmn. dept. surgery, 1984-88, sec. med. staff, 1986-88. Assoc. examiner Am. Bd. Surgery, 1993, 96. Contbr. articles to profl. jours. Fellow ACS (com. on applicants 1990—); mem. AMA, Ill. Med. Soc., Chgo. Med. Soc., Chgo. Surg. Soc., Ill. Surg. Soc., Alumni Assn. Stritch Sch. Medicine (bd. govs.), Columbian Club, KC, Blue Key, Alpha Omega Alpha. Roman Catholic. Avocations: model railroads, sports, fishing. Office: 7447 W Talcott Ave Chicago IL 60631-3745

DEORIO, JAMES KEITH, orthopedic surgeon; b. Dearborn, Mich., June 25, 1948; s. Milo L. and Gertrude A. DeOrio; m. Rita M. Genaw, Feb. 13, 1971; children: Matthew, Mark, Maric. MD, George Washington U., 1977. Diplomate Am. Bd. Orthopedic Surgery. Commd. USAF, 1970, advanced through ranks to col., ret., 1986; assoc. prof. Uniformed Svc. U. of the Health Sciences, Bethesda, Md., 1984—; chair, dept. of orthopedics Mayo Clinic, Jacksonville, Fla., 1986—2001; asst. prof. of orthopedics Mayo Med. Sch., Jacksonville, Fla., 1990—; med. dir., outpatient surgery ctr. Mayo Clinic, Jacksonville, Fla., 1995—2001, dir., foot and ankle fellowship program, 1999—2003. Cons. to surgeon gen. USAF, 1994; asst. editor Foot and Ankle Internat. Fellow: Am. Acad. of Orthop. Surgeons; mem.: Soc. of Air Force Clin. Surgeons, Duval County Med. Soc., Fla. Orthopaedic Soc., Am. Orthop. Foot & Ankle Soc. Home: 7865 James Island Trail Jacksonville FL 32256 Office: Mayo Clinic 4500 San Pablo Rd Jacksonville FL 32224 Office Fax: 904-953-2005.

DEOUL, KATHLEEN BOARDSEN, publishing executive; b. New London, Conn., May 5, 1944; d. Harry Kostrope Boardsen and Elizabeth (Conti) Dunham; m. Neal Deoul, June 20, 1982; 1 child, Shannon Rae. Grad. high sch., New London. Br. mgr. Qwip Sys. divsn. Exxon, Balt.; br. ops. mgr. Exxon Office Sys., Pitts., 1977-82, owner, pres. Bus. Quars., Crystal City, Va., 1983-95, Wellness Alternatives, Balt., 1993—, Cassandra Books, LLC, 2001. Author: (book) Cancer Cover-up, 2001. Mem. adv. bd. Network Mktg. Lifestyles Mag.; mem. Team Diamond; co-chair Found. Alternative Cancer Treatments. Mem.: Pres.'s Club Nikken, Inc. (Distbr. of Yr. 1999—2000), Pres.'s Club Exxon. Avocations: venture capitalist, travel, writing, interior decorating, public speaking. E-mail: kathleendeoul@comcast.net.

DEOUL, NEAL, electronics company executive; b. N.Y.C., Feb. 27, 1931; s. George and Pearl (Hirschfeld) D.; m. Bernice Kradel, Dec. 25, 1955 (div.); children; Cara Jan, Stefani Neva, Evan Craig; m. Kathleen B. Davis, June 20, 1982; 1 child, Shannon Rae. BS in Physics, CCNY, 1952; JD, Bklyn. Law Sch., 1959. Bar: N.Y. 1960. Engr. Signal Corps., U.S. Army, Evans Signal Lab., Belmar, N.J., 1952-55, Airborne Instruments Lab., Deer Park, N.Y., 1955-56; sales mgr. FXR, Inc., Woodside, L.I., 1956-60; pres. Microwave Dynamics Corp., Plainview, L.I., 1960-61, Paradynamics, Inc., Huntington Station, N.Y., 1961-64; mgr. Servo Corp. Am., Hicksville, N.Y., 1964-66; v.p. Trio Labs., Inc., Plainview, 1966-69; exec. v.p. Microlab/FXR, Livingston, N.J., 1969-74; pres. Neal Deoul Assocs., Balt., 1974—. Chmn. Found. for Alternative Cancer Treatments, Balt., 2000—. Mem. IEEE (sr.), N.Y. State Bar Assn., Md. Bar Assn., Young Pres.'s Orgn., Profl. Group Engring. Mgmt., Am. Arbitration Assn. Home and Office: 2 Bellchase Ct Baltimore MD 21208-1300

DEPACE, NICHOLAS LOUIS, physician; b. Nutley, N.J., Oct. 18, 1953; s. Nicholas Frank and Rose (Piro) DeP.; m. Marilyn Tomaro, Jan. 17, 1981. BS, Seton Hall U.; MD, N.J. Sch. Medicine, Mt. Sinai, N.Y.C.; internal medicine cardiology, Hahnemann U., Phila. Diplomate Am. Bd. Internal Medicine and Cardiology. Intern in internal medicine Overlook Hosp., Summit, N.J., Columbia U., N.Y.C., 1978-79; resident internal medicine, fellow in cardiology Hahnemann Med. Coll. and Hosp., Phila., 1979—83; practice medicine specializing in internal and cardiology medicine Phila., 1982—; with radio Sta. WPEN, Phila., 1990—2001; clin. prof. medicine Thomas Jefferson U. Hosp., 1997—; chief divsn. preventive cardiology Grad. Hosp., 1996-97; dir. heart repair program Phila. Heart Inst., Presbyn. Med. Ctr., Phila., 1993-95; dir. Jefferson Heart Ctr. South, 1997—. Co-author: The Heart Repair Manual; mem. editl. bd. Am. Jour. Cardiology. Fellow Am. Coll. Cardiology, Am. Coll. Chest Physicians; mem. Phila. Coll. Physicians. Republican. Roman Catholic. Avocations: reading, writing, travel, sports. Office: 188 Fries Mill Rd Ste N2 Turnersville NJ 08012-2055 also: 2422 24 S Broad St Philadelphia PA 19145

DE PALMA, BRIAN RUSSELL, film director, writer; b. Newark, Sept. 11, 1940; s. Anthony Fredrick and Vivenne (Muti) DeP.; m. Gale Anne Hurd, July 21, 1991; daughter, Lolita. BA, Columbia Coll., 1962; MA, Sarah Lawrence Coll., 1964. Dir. and writer: short film Woton's Wake, 1963 (Rosenthal Found. award 1963); documentary films Dionysus in '69, 1970, The Responsive Eye, 1966; feature films include Murder a la Mod, 1968, Greetings, 1968 (Silver Bear Berlin Film Festival award 1969), The Wedding Party, 1969, Hi Mom, 1970, Get to Know Your Rabbit, 1972, Sisters, 1973, Phantom of the Paradise, 1974 (Grand prize 1975), Obsession, 1976, Carrie, 1976 (Avoriaz prize 1977), The Fury, 1978, Home Movies, 1979, Dressed to Kill, 1980, Blow Out, 1981, Scarface, 1983, Body Double, 1984, Wise Guys, 1986, The Untouchables, 1987, Casualties of War, 1989, Bonfire of the Vanities, 1990, Raising Cain, 1992, Carlito's Way, 1993, Mission Impossible, 1996, Snake Eyes, 1998, Mission to Mars, 2000, Femme Fatale, 2002 Office: Paramount Pictures Lubitsch Annex # 119 5555 Melrose Ave # 119 West Hollywood CA 90038-3197*

DEPALMA, RALPH GEORGE, surgeon, educator; b. N.Y.C., Oct. 29, 1931; s. Frank and Maria (Sibilio) deP.; m. Maleva Tankard, Sept. 17, 1955; children: Ralph L., Edward F., Maleva B., Malinda G. AB, Columbia U, 1953; MD, NYU, 1956. Diplomate Am. Bd. Surgery, Am. Bd. Vascular Surgery. Resident in surgery Univ. Hosps., Cleve., 1962-64; from instr. to prof. surgery Case Western Res. U., Cleve., 1964-80; prof., chmn. surgery U. Nev., Reno, 1980-82, George Washington U. Sch. Medicine, Washington, 1982-92; Lewis B. Saltz prof. of surgery George Washington U. Med. Ctr., Washington, 1992-94; prof. surgery, vice-chmn. dept. surgery, assoc. dean U. Nev., Reno, 1994-2000; nat. dir. surgery Dept. Vets. Affairs, Washington, 2000—; prof. surgery Uniformed Svsc. U. Health Scis., Bethesda, Md., 2000—. Editor: (with J.M. Giordano) Reoperative Vascular Surgery, 1987, Basic Science of Vascular Surgery, 1988; assoc. editor: Haimovici Vascular Surgery: Principles and Techniques, 1989; co-editor: Basic Science in Vascular Disease, 1997; assoc. editor Internat. Vascular Surgery, Internat. Jour. Impotence Rsch.; contbr. articles to profl. jours. Stroke liaison nat. chpt. Am. Heart Assn., 1992-94; bd. dirs. Reno Chamber Orch., 1999-2000. Capt. USAF, 1958-61. Grantee USPHS, 1974-82. Fellow ACS; mem. Cleve. Vascular Soc. (pres. 1977-78), Rocky Mt. Vascular Soc. (pres. 1981-82), Am. Surg. Assn., Soc. Vascular Surgery, Washington Acad. Surgery (sec. 1991-92, v.p. 1992-93, pres. 1993-94), Am. Venous Forum (sec. 1991-94, bd. dirs. found. 1992-95), Am. Coll. Healthcare Execs. (assoc.), 1996, Cosmos Club (admissions com. 1992-94, awards com. 2001, chair 2003—), Western Vascular Soc., Prospectors Club Reno. E-mail: rgdepalma@mall.va.gov.

DEPALO, WILLIAM ANTHONY, JR., Latin American studies educator; b. N.Y.C., July 17, 1941; s. William Anthony and Elsie Elizabeth (Reighton) DeP.; m. Deborah Jean Borgmann, Dec. 30, 1983; children: Lee Kevin, Christopher Patrick, Brian William, Katherine Elizabeth. BS in Microbiology, N.Mex. State U., 1963; MA in History, U. Okla., 1971; student, Interam. Def. Coll., Ft. McNair, Washington, 1985-86; PhD in Latin Am. Studies, U. N.Mex., 1994. Commd. 2d lt. U.S. Army, 1963, advanced through grades to col., 1985; comdr. 1st Bn., 10th Infantry, Ft. Carson, Colo., 1983-85, 4th Psychol. Ops. Group, Ft. Bragg, N.C., 1986-89, U.S. Army Sch. of the Ams., Ft. Benning, Ga., 1989-91; adj. prof. U. N.Mex., Albuquerque, 1995—. Author: The Mexican National Army, 1997; contbr. The United States and Mexico at War, 1998. Decorated Silver Star, Bronze Star for Valor, Purple Heart (2), Legion of Merit (3). Mem. Albuquerque Coun. Fgn. Rels. Republican. Roman Catholic. Avocations: triathlons, running, cycling. Home: 4009 Shenandoah Pl NE Albuquerque NM 87111-4157 Office: U NMex Latin Am-Iberian Inst Albuquerque NM 87131-0001 E-mail: wdepalo@aol.com.

DE PAN, HARRY MCCARTHY, retired surgeon; b. Glens Falls, N.Y., July 13, 1923; MD, Cornell U., 1947. Cert. surgeon, 1955. Intern Hartford Hosp., 1947-48, resident surgeon, 1948-49, 52-54, Hosp. Spl. Surgeons, N.Y.C., 1949-50; resident thoracic surgeon Cedarcrest Hosp., Newington, Conn., 1958-59; sr. attending surgeon Glens Falls N.Y. Hosp. Mem. AMA, ACS, DAGS. Home: 10 Pershing Rd Queensbury NY 12804-2537

DEPAOLA, DOMINICK PHILIP, academic administrator; b. Bklyn., Dec. 29, 1942; s. Dominick and Marie (DeStefano) DeP.; m. Rosemary Elizabeth Femiano, Aug. 2, 1969; 1 child, Alexis Junc. BS, St. Francis Coll., 1964; DDS, NYU, 1969; PhD, MIT, 1974; ScD (hon.), Baylor U., 1995; PharmD (hon.), Mass. Coll. Pharmacy and Health Scis., 2002. Assoc. prof. Va. Commonwealth U., Med. Coll. Va., Richmond, 1974-78; dean Dental Sch. U. Tex. Health Sci. Ctr., San Antonio, 1983-87, interim dean Grad. Sch. Biomed. Scis., 1986-87; dean Dental Sch. U. Medicine and Dentistry N.J., Newark, 1988-90; pres., dean Baylor Coll. Dentistry, Dallas, 1990-96; pres. Tex. A&M Univ. Sys.-Baylor Coll. Dentistry, Dallas, 1996-97; pres., CEO Forsyth Inst., Boston, 1998—; prof. Harvard U. Sch. Dental Medicine, Boston, 1999—. Mem. Nat. Adv. Dental Rsch. Coun. for Nat. Inst. Dental Rsch., 1996-2000; mem. dental adv. com. Pew Commn. for Health Professions, 1991; chair, bd. dirs. Oral Health Am., 1999-2000; bd. dirs. Block Drug Co.; mem. Commn. on Dental Accreditation, 1992-97. Recipient Presdl. award San Antonio Dist. Dental Soc., 1987, Alumni Achievement award NYU Coll. Dentistry, 1993. Fellow Am. Acad. Oral Medicine (hon.); mem. ADA, Am. Inst. Nutrition, Am. Assn. Dental Schs. (past pres. 1989-91), Am. Soc. for Clin. Nutrition (chair pub. info. com. 1995—), Am. Soc. Nutritional Scis. (chair pub. info. com. 1995—), Am. Assn. Dental Rsch. (v.p. 2002), Internat. Assn. Dental Rsch., Hispanic Dental Assn. (hon.), Am. Dietetic Assn. (hon.), Rsch.!Am (bd. dirs.). Avocations: skiing, racquetball, tennis, golf, reading. Office: Forsyth Inst 140 Fenway Boston MA 02115-3799 E-mail: ddepaola@forsyth.org.

DEPAOLI, GERI M. (JOAN DEPAOLI), artist, art historian; b. June 8, 1941; m. Alexander DePaoli, July 4, 1961; children: Alexander Mark, Michael Alexander. BA, U. Md., 1974, MA, 1978; student, U. Calif., Davis, 1965-68. Art history educator, artist, curator slides and photos Nat. Mus., Bangkok, Thailand, 1968-71; art prof. Montgomery Coll., Rockville, Md., 1978-82; cons. oriental slide and photo collection Princeton U., 1983-84; lectr. Princeton Sch. Visual Arts, 1986-90; curator The Mus. Art, Ft. Lauderdale, Fla., 1986; dir. Coun. for Creative Projects, N.Y.C., 1989-91; faculty artworks Princeton Sch. Visual Arts, 1984-91; exec. dir. EducArt Projects Inc., Davis, Calif., 1991—. Cons. in field. Author: Emmy Lou Packard: A Woman and a Century, 1998, Barbara Spring, Populations from the Collective Unconscious, 1998, Donna Billick: Making Art out of Stone, 1999, Clayton Bailey: Happenings in the Circus of Life, 2000; editor (exhbn. catalog): Elvis & Marilyn: 2 X Immortal, Rizzoli, 1994; author (ednl. resource guide) Elvis & Marilyn: 2 X Immortal, 1994, (ednl. program) Images of Power, 1994, video prodr. Images of Power: Balinese Paintings made for Gregory Bateson and Margaret Mead, 1994, editor/co-curator (exhbn. catalog) Transcending Abstraction, 1986, reviewer ArtMatters Newspaper, Phila., 1987—90, author-curator The Trans Parent Thread: Asian Philosophy in Recent Am. Art, 1990, contbg. author Art of Calif. Mag.; one-woman shows include E.W. Gallery, Bethesda, Md., 1978, Upstairs Gallery, Kingston, N.J., 1982, Gallery at the Purple Barge, N.Y.C., 1984, The Art Gallery, Kingston, 1985, Back Door Gallery, Princeton, 1986, Campion Gallery of Art, 1987, AT&T Corp. Gallery, Princeton, 1989, Rider Coll. Gallery, Lawrenceville, N.J., 1990; also numerous group shows. Councilor Nat. Abortion Rights Action League, 1989—. Recipient award for excellence in pub., Office of Pres. of U.S., 1969. Fellow Soc. for Arts Religion and Contemporary Culture; mem. Assn. Ind. Historians of Art (v.p. 1988—), Coll. Art Assn., Princeton Rsch. Forum, Nat. Coalition of Ind. Scholars, Sierra Club, Greenpeace. Buddhist. Avocations: skiing, philosophy discussion groups, intellectual history. Office: EducArt Projects Inc PO Box 267 Davis CA 95617-0267

DEPAOLIS, POTITO UMBERTO, food company executive; b. Mignano, Italy, Aug. 28, 1925; arrived in U.S., 1966, naturalized, 1970; s. Giuseppe A. and Filomena (Macchiaverna) DePaolis; m. Marie A. Caronna, Apr. 10, 1965. Vet Dr, U. Naples, 1948; Libera Docenza, Ministero Pub. Istruzione, Rome, 1955. Prof. food svc. Vet. Sch., U. Naples, Italy, 1948—66; asst. prof. A Titre Benevole Ecole Veterinaire Alfort, Paris, 1956; vet. inspector U.S. Dept. Agr., Omaha, 1966—67; sr. rsch. chemist Grain Processing Corp., Muscatine, Iowa, 1967—68; v.p., dir. prod. devel. Reddi Wip, Inc., L.A., 1968—72; with Kubro Foods, L.A., 1972—73, Shade Foods, Inc., 1975—; pres. Vegetable Protein Co., Riverside, Calif., 1973—, Tima Brand Food Co., 1975—, Dr. Tima Natural Foods, 1977—. Contbr. articles in field to profl. jours. Fulbright scholar, Cornell U., Ithaca, N.Y., 1954, British Coun. scholar, U. Reading, Eng., 1959—60, postdoctoral rsch. fellow, NIH, Cornell U., 1963—64. Mem.: AAAS, Greater L.A. Press Club, Italian Press Assn., Biol. Sci. Assn. Italy, Vet. Med. Assn., Italian Assn. Advancement Sci., Inst. Food Technologists ("Seminatore D'oro" as best soccer referee for all Italy). Achievements include patents in field. Home: Bel Air 131 Groverton Pl Los Angeles CA 90077-3732 Office: 236 Lasky Dr Beverly Hills CA 90112 also: 6878 Beck Ave North Hollywood CA 91605-6205 E-mail: drtima@aol.com.

DEPAOLO, RONALD FRANCIS, editor, writer; b. Jamaica, N.Y., July 12, 1938; s. Francis Edward and Evelyn Helen (Turck) deP.; m. Meredith Nell Mass, Aug. 12, 1967; children— Britton, Damon, Baird. BA cum laude, Moravian Coll., Bethlehem, Pa., 1964; MS, Northwestern U., 1965. Reporter, corr., writer Life mag., 1965-70; news editor, corr. Business Week mag., 1970-72; freelance writer and editor, 1972-76; editor-in-chief, asst. pub. I-AM mag., N.Y.C., 1976-78; sr. editor Boardroom Reports, N.Y.C., 1978-80; editor-in-chief M.D. Mag., N.Y.C., 1980-84; editor, pub. Kirkus Revs., N.Y.C., 1984-87. Pres. Rock Lodge Devel. Corp., 1987—; adj. prof. communications Ramapo Coll., Mahwah, N.J., 1974-75 Author: Russia and the Independent States, 1992, The Presidency from A to Z, 1998, Elections from A to Z, 1998,

Guide to Congress, 1999; contbr.: Encyclopedia of American Political History, 2001. Served with AUS, 1957-59, 60-61. Home: Hawks' Dance Farm 175 Rock Lodge Rd Stockholm NJ 07460 E-mail: oakine@nji.com.

DEPAOLO, ROSEMARY, dean, academic administrator; b. Bklyn., July 17, 1947; d. Nunzio and Edith (Spano) DeP.; m. Dennis B. Smith, 1977 (div. 1983); m. T. Frederick Wharton, 1984. BA, CUNY, Flushing, 1970; MA, Rutgers U., 1974, PhD, 1979. Asst. prof. to prof., dir. Ctr. for Humanities Augusta (Ga.) Coll., 1975-90; asst. dean Coll. Arts and Sci. Ga. So. U., Statesboro, 1990-93; dean Coll. Arts and Scis. Western Carolina U., Cullowhee, N.C., 1993-97; pres. Ga. Coll. and State U., Milledgeville, 1997—2003; chancellor U. North Carolina, Wilington, NC, 2003—. Office: 601 S College Rd Wilmington NC 28403-3297*

DE PAPP, ZSOLT GEORGE, endocrinologist; b. Windsor, Ont., Canada, Oct. 27, 1933; arrived in U.S., 1938; s. John L. E. and Emmy (Birgling) de Papp; children from previous marriage: Anne, John, Erika. AB, Dartmouth Coll., 1955; MD, U. Rochester, 1959. Diplomate in internal medicine, geriatrics, endocrinology and metabolism Am. Bd. Internal Medicine. Intern Strong Meml. Hosp., Rochester, NY, 1959-60, asst. resident in medicine, 1960-61, fellow in endocrinology, 1964-65; assoc. resident in medicine Yale New Haven Hosp., 1963-64, attending physician, 1978-79; head primary care ctr. St. Raphael's Hosp., New Haven, 1976-78; chief assoc. medicine U. Rochester Sch. Medicine, 1980; head endocrine unit Highland Hosp., Rochester, 1980—. Capt. U.S. Army, 1961—63. Lutheran. Office: Highland Hosp 1000 South Ave Rochester NY 14620-2782 E-mail: zdePmd@frontiernet.net.

DEPARLE, NANCY-ANN MIN, former federal agency administrator, lawyer; b. Rockwood, Tenn., Dec. 17, 1956; m. Jason DeParle. BA, U. Tenn., 1978; JD, Harvard U., 1983; BA, MA, Balliol Coll., Oxford U., Eng., 1981. Past pvt. practice in law; commr. human svcs. Gov. Ned McWherter State of Tenn., 1987-89; past assoc. dir. health and pers. White House OMB, Washington; administr. Health Care Financing Adminstrn. HHS, Washington, 1997—2000; mem. board of dir. Cerner Corp., Kansas City, Mo., 2001—. Rhodes scholar, 1979-81. Office: Cerner Corp 2800 Rockcreek Pkwy Kansas City MO 64117

DEPAUL, ANTHONY KENNETH, lawyer; b. Chester, Pa., Feb. 9, 1938; s. Samuel DePaul and Lucille DiNicola; m. Joanne J. Machristie, June 30, 1984. BA, Widener U., 1959; JD, Georgetown U., 1962. Bar: Pa., U.S. Dist. Ct. D.C. 1964, U.S. Ct. Mil. Appeals 1968, U.S. Supreme Ct. 1975. Pub. defender, Media, Pa., 1970-75; pro bono def. counsel for indigent accused Phila., 1970—90. Instr. U.S. Mil. Acad., West Point, N.Y., 1965-70; prof. law Widener U., Chester, Pa., 1970-90, St. Joseph's U., Phila., 1972-92; solicitor mcpl. fire cos., 1970-90. With JAGC U.S. Army, 1966—70. Recipient Alumni Achievement award, Widener U. Mem.: Pa. Trial Lawyers Assn., Pa. Bar Assn., Phila. Bar Assn. Home: Gen Delivery Honey Brook PA 19344

DE PAUW, GOMMAR ALBERT, priest, educator; b. Stekene, Belgium, Oct. 11, 1918; came to U.S., 1949, naturalized, 1955; s. Desiré and Anna (Van Overloop) De P. Diplomate Classical Humanities, Coll. St. Nicholas, Belgium, 1936; JCB, U. Louvain, 1943, JCL, 1945; Juris Canonici Dr., Catholic U. Am., 1953. Ordained priest Roman Cath. Ch., 1942. Parish priest, chaplain Cath. Social Action, Ghent, Belgium, 1945-49, N.Y.C., 1949-52; successively prof. moral and fundamental dogmatic theology and canon law sem. div., assoc. prof. philosophy coll. div. Mt. St. Mary's Coll., Emmitsburg, Md., 1952-65, dean studies maj. sem. div., 1954-64, mem. council adminstrn., 1957-65. Theol. adviser II Vatican Ecumenical Council, 1962-65; founder-pres. Cath. Traditionalist Movement, Inc., 1964—. Author: The Educational Rights of the Church, 1953, The Rebel Priest, 1965, The Traditional Roman Catholic Mass, 1977, Bishops on War and Peace, 1983, The Traditional Requiem Mass, 1989, The Challenge of Peace Through Strength, 1989, Keep The Faith-Reagan Dicta, 2000; co-author: New Catholic Ency.; Dictionary of the Bible, Ephemerides Theologicae Lovanienses; editor: Sounds of Truth and Tradition, Quote... Unquote; producer Latin weekly radio mass, daily internet mass, various religious phonograph records, audio and video cassettes. With Belgian Army inf. M.C., 1939-45, World War II Resistance and Free Polish Forces. Decorated Honor Cross (Free Polish Forces); recipient Achievement Citation, U.S. Army. Mem. AAUP, Internat. Platform Assn., Cath. Theol. Soc., Am. Canon Law Soc. Am., Am. Security Coun., Am. Cath. Philos. Assn., Nat. Cath. Ednl. Assn., Univ. Prof. for Acad. Order. Home and Office: Cath Traditionalist Movement 210 Maple Ave Westbury NY 11590-3117 Fax: 516-333-7535. *Especially since my founding of the Catholic Traditionalist Movement in 1964 has made me somewhat "controversial," I draw great inspiration from two sayings adorning the walls of my office. One, attributed to Davy Crockett: "Be sure you're right. Then go ahead!" The other, quoting Saint Athanasius: "If the whole world goes against the truth, then Athanasius must go against the whole world!" And when living by those axioms becomes heavy at times, I just brace myself and coin another one of my own: "It's better to be right alone, than to be wrong with a thousand others!"*

DEPERSIO, RICHARD JOHN, otolaryngologist, plastic surgeon; b. Oak Ridge, Tenn., July 10, 1949; s. John Dominick DePersio and Genevieve (Kellerman) Weinberg; m. Melissa Eddlemon, Nov. 23, 1994; children: Lauren Elizabeth, Katherine Genevieve, Gerard Edward, Richard John, Robert James. BS with honors, U. Tenn., Knoxville, 1971; MD, U. Tenn., Memphis, 1974. Diplomate Am. Bd. Facial, Plastic and Reconstructive Surgery, Am. Bd. Otolaryngology. Intern City of Memphis Hosps., 1975; surgery resident Meth. Hosp., Memphis, 1976-77; otolaryngology resident U. Tenn., Memphis, 1977-80; pvt. practice Knoxville Otolaryngology Facial Surgery Clinic, 1980—, Ear, Nose and Throat, Greater Knoxville. Clin. assoc. prof., U. Tenn. Dept. Surgery, Knoxville, 1980—; chmn. surgery, St. Mary's Med. Ctr., 2003—. Pres. Knoxville Acad. Medicine Found., 2002—. Fellow: ACS, Am. Head and Neck Soc., Am. Soc. Laser Medicine and Surgery, Am. Acad. Aesthetic and Restorative Surgery, Am. Rhinologic Soc., Am. Soc. TMJ Surgeons, Am. Acad. Otolaryngology-Head and Neck Surgery, Am. Acad. Cosmetic Surgery, Am. Acad. Facial, Plastic and Reconstructive Surgery; mem.: AMA, Trustee Tennesee Med. Assoc. (assoc. 2002—05), Knoxville Acad. Medicine Found., Knoxville Acad. Medicine (pres.-elect 1998, pres. 1999, 2002), Tenn. Med. Assn. (v.p. 2000, bd. trustees 2002—). Roman Catholic. Avocations: tennis, golf, basketball. Home: 6805 Shadow Ridge Dr Knoxville TN 37918-9530 Office: Greater Knoxville ENT Assocs Ste 200 1515 St Mary's St Knoxville TN 37917-4540

DE PETRO, THOMAS GERARD, librarian, educator; b. Omaha, Oct. 16, 1954; s. Alfred Salvatore and LaVaughn (Jewell) D.P. BA, U. Colo., 1978; MLS, U. Tex., 1985. Libr. I Jefferson County Pub. Libr., Lakewood, Colo., 1979-84; teaching asst. U. Tex., Austin, 1985; libr. II Houston Pub. Libr., 1985-88; libr. NASA Johnson Space Ctr., Houston, 1988-89; engring. libr. Wichita State U., 1990-98, Tex. A&M, 1999—2003; rep. STN Internat., Karlsruhe, Germany, 2003—. Mem. Am. Soc. for Engring. Edn., ALA, Spl. Librs. Assn. Avocations: swimming, running, short-wave radio, foreign languages. Office: Tex A&m U College Station TX 77843-0001

DE PEW, DAVID PHILIP, advertising executive, consultant, lecturer; b. St. Louis, June 18, 1930; s. Ralph and Roberta Dorthea (Scattergood) De P.; m. Joyce Ann Moran, Aug. 15, 1952; 1 child, David John. BJ in Advt., U. Mo., Columbia, 1956; postgrad., Roosevelt U., Chgo., 1968. Cert. bus. communicator. News writer Caterpillar Tractor Co., Peoria, Ill., 1956-58; account exec. Thomson Advt., Peoria, 1959-61; v.p., client svcs. mgr. Marsteller, Inc., Chgo., 1961-69; v.p., account group supr. Bozell & Jacobs, Inc., Chgo., 1970-78; v.p., Ptnr. Winfield Advt. Agy., St. Louis, 1977-88; v.p., account mgr. Adamson Advt. Agy., St. Louis, 1988-93; cons., lectr. Advance Mktg. Group, Washington, Mo., 1993—. Author mag. column Case Histories in Mktg., 1985-86; creator/copywriter various advt. campaigns. Advt. program mgr. Peoria Pub. Schs., 1960; precinct capt. Republican Party, Matteson, Ill., 1968. Mem. SAR, St. Louis Bus. Mktg. Assn. (pres. 1984), Nat. Korean War Vets. Assn. (pub. info. officer 1994-96, bd. dirs.), Korean War Vets. Assn. St. Louis (bd. dirs. 1992-2002), Elks Club, Pi Kappa Alpha, Alpha Delta Sigma. Republican. Methodist. Avocations: skeet/trap shooting, golf, antique clock restoration, flying. Home: 4 Jason Ridge Dr Washington MO 63090-4142 Office: Advance Mktg Group 4 Jason Ridge Dr Washington MO 63090-4142 E-mail: dpdepew@fidnet.com.

DEPEW, SPENCER LONG, lawyer; b. Wichita, Kans., June 6, 1933; s. Claude I. and Frances Ann (Bell) D.; m. Donna Wolever, Dec. 28, 1957; children: Clifford S., Sally F. AB, U. Wichita, 1955; LLB, U. Mich., 1960. Bar: Kans.; U.S. Dist. Ct. Kans.; U.S. Supreme Ct. Mem. Depew and Gillen, LLC, Wichita. Mem. Interstate Oil and Gas Compact Commn., Oklahoma City. With U.S. Army, 1955-57, Germany. Mem. IPAA, Kans. Ind. Oil and Gas Assn. Home: 6322 E English St Wichita KS 67218-1802 Office: Depew and Gillen LLC 151 N Main St Ste 800 Wichita KS 67202-1409

DEPINO, CHRIS ANTHONEY, state legislator; b. New Haven, July 10, 1952; s. Salvatore and Angela (Salemme) DeP.; m. Arlene Marie Porto, May 19, 1978; children: Angela, Joanna. AS in Edn., South Ctrl. C.C., New Haven, 1983. Condr. Metro-North Commuter R.R., N.Y.C., 1972-80. 83—, train master, 1980-83; mem. Conn. Ho. of Reps., Hartford, 1992—2000; chmn. Conn. Rep. Com., 1996—2003. Commr. Water Pollution Control Authority, New Haven, 1989-93; mem. New Haven Bd. Aldermen, 1990-93; chair., Conn. Republican Party. Fed. Transp. Adminstrn. urban mass transp. planning fellow, 1982. Mem. Annex Young Men's Assn., St. Andrew Apostle Soc., UTU, Metro-North Commutr R.R. President's Club. Republican. Roman Catholic. Avocations: playing jazz harmonica, bicycling, swimming, music instructingg. Home: 1354 Dean St New Haven CT 06512-4000*

DEPKEN, CRAIG A., II, economics educator; b. Tenn., Aug. 22, 1969; s. Craig A. and Geraldine R. Depken; m. Linda M. D'Hoore, 1996. AB in Econs., U. Ga., 1991, PhD in Econs., 1996. Assoc. prof. econs. U. Tex., Arlington, 1996—. Contbr. articles to profl. jours. Mem. Am. Econ. Assn., So. Econ. Assn., Western Econ. Assn., Blue Key Nat. Honor Soc. Avocation: golf. Office: U Tex Arlington Dept Econs PO Box 19479 Arlington TX 76019-0001 E-mail: depken@uta.edu.

DE POL, JOHN, artist; b. N.Y.C., Sept. 16, 1913; s. Joseph Zangrando and Theresa (Mariani) DeP.; m. Thelma June Roth, May 31, 1946; 1 dau., Patricia Gail. Student, Art Students League N.Y., Sch. Tech., Belfast, No. Ireland. Free lance wood engraver, printmaker, illustrator prints represented permanent collections, Cin. Mus., Library of Congress, N.Y. Pub. Library, Met. Mus. Art, Syracuse U. Library, others.; creator of, Woodcut Soc., presentation print, 1952, Miniature Print Soc., 1952, Albany Print Club, 1958, 59; [illegible], N.Y. Printers Wall of Fame, 1980. With USAAF, 1943-45. Recipient Richard Comyn Eames Mus. purchase prize, 1952, Kate W. Arms Meml. prize, 1955, 56, Albany Print Club Purchase prize, 1968, John Taylor Arms Meml. prize NAD, 1968, Ralph Fabri prize NAD, 1999, others; named Academician Nat. Acad. Design Fellow Cleve. Med. Libr. Assn. (hon.); mem. Art Students League (life), Soc. Am. Graphic Artists, Albany Print Club, Rowfant Club Cleve. (hon.), The Typophiles (hon.). Address: 770 Anderson Ave Apt 18K Cliffside Park NJ 07010

DE POUZILHAC, ALAIN DUPLESSIS, advertising executive; b. Sete, Herault, France, June 11, 1945; s. Pierre and Jeanine (Caffarel) de P.; m. Carole de Pouzilhac, Sept. 6, 1969; children: Edouard, Cedric, Philippine. Asst. advt. mgr. Publicis, Paris, 1968; advt mgr. DDB, Paris, 1968-75; exec. v.p. Havas Conseil, Neuilly, France, 1976-82, chmn., CEO, 1982-87, HDM, Neuilly and Puteaux, France, 1987-89, Eurocom, Neuilly, 1989—, EURO RSCGWW, Neuilly, France, 1991, Havas Advt., 1996—, Havas, 2002. Avocations: soccer, rugby. Home: 21 rue de Miromesnil 75008 Paris France Office: Havas 2 Allee De Longchamp 92150 Suresnes France E-mail: alain.de-pouzilhac@havas.com.

DEPP, JOHNNY, actor; b. Owensboro, Ky., June 9, 1963; s. John and Betty Sue D.; m. Lori Anne Allison (div.). Guitarist; ex-member bands the Flame, the Kids, Rock City Angels, 1985; actor TV series 21 Jump Street, 1987-90; actor films Nightmare on Elm Street, 1984, Private Resort, 1985, Platoon, 1986, Cry-Baby, 1990, Edward Scissorhands, 1990, Freddy's Dead: The Final Nightmare, 1991, American Dreamers, 1992, Benny & Joon, 1993, What's Eating Gilbert Grape, 1993, Ed Wood, 1994, Arizona Dreamer, Don Juan DeMarco, 1995, Dead Man, 1995, Nick of Time, 1996, Donnie Brasco, 1997, The Astronaut's Wife, 1998, L.A. Without a Map, 1998, Fear and Loathing in Las Vegas, 1998, The Source, 1999, The Ninth Gate, 1999, The Libertine, 1999, Just to Be Together, 1999, The Astronaut's Wife, 1999, Sleepy Hollow, 1999, The Source, 1999, The Man Who Cried, 2000, Chocolat, 2000, Blow, 2001, From Hell, 2001, Pirates of the Caribbean: The Curse of the Black Pearl, 2003, Once Upon A Time in Mexico, 2003; writer, dir., actor: The Brave, 1997; TV movies include Slow Burn, 1986; TV guest appearance The Vicar of Dibley, 1994. Office: 9100 Wilshire Blvd Ste 725E Beverly Hills CA 90212-3441*

DEPPA, TIMOTHY WAYNE, electrical engineer; b. Seattle, Dec. 21, 1955; s. Duane Arthur and Velma Marie (Houchin) D.; m. Sarah Elizabeth McNaughton, July 21, 1984; children: Brian, Jeffrey, Lisa. BSEE, Columbia U., 1980; MSEE, U. Calif., 1981. Mem. tech. staff AT&T Bell Labs., 1980-90; mgr. data comms. Okidata, 1990-96, sr. mgr., systems engr., 1996—, dir. systems engring., 2000—. Mem. IEEE, N.Y. Acad. Scis., Multi-Function Products Assn. (bd. dirs. 1997—, pres. 1999—), Internat. Color Consortium, Tau Beta Pi, Eta Kappa Nu. Achievements include patents for network printer quick configuration, host-based printing system, network printer discovery and aging, object oriented design for network printing. Home: 18 Buxton Rd Cherry Hill NJ 08003-2104 E-mail: tdeppa@okidata.com.

DEPPE, HENRY A. insurance company executive; b. S.I., N.Y., July 1, 1920; s. Herman and Marie Deppe; m. Florence Chieffo, Aug. 8, 1943; children: Katherine, Marlaina, Lynda. Student, Cornell Sch. Hotel Adminstrn., 1943. CLU. Agt. Travelers Life Ins. Co., White Plains, N.Y., 1946-49; dist. mgr. Mass. Life Ins. Co., White Plains, 1949-57; gen. agt. Guardian Life Ins. Co., White Plains, 1956-87; pres. Nat. Pension Svc., Inc., White Plains, 1957-85, chmn. bd., CEO, 1985-87, chmn. bd., pres., CEO Boca Raton, Fla., 1985—. Bd. dirs. YOREC Corp.; mem. faculty CLU Inst., 1985—; guest lectr. N.Y. State Trial Lawyers Assn., Fairleigh Dickinson Pension Inst., IRS, C.W. Post Tax Inst., various other profl. assns. and ednl. instns. Pres. Young Republicans Club of Westchester County (N.Y.), 1954-55, Ossining (N.Y.) PTA, 1963-64, Multiple Sclerosis Soc. Westchester, 1964, 65; pres. Estate Planning Coun. of Westchester; founder Tax Inst., Iona Coll., co-chmn. inst., 1976-78; bd. dirs. ARC, Westchester County, N.Y., 1984-88, Boy Scouts Am., Westchester County, 1988—; pres., bd. dirs. N.Y. Fertility Rsch. Found., 1985-89; active. Boca Raton Mus. of Art, 1990, bd. dir., v.p., 1991-93, pres. 1993-95, chmn. capital campaign, chmn. endowment com. Recipient Nat. Sales Achievement award, 1966; Fred E. Hamilton award, 1975; David Ben Gurion Friendship award, 1975; Guest of Honor award United Jewish Appeal Fedn., 1978; Leadership award State of Israel, 1979; Disting. Citizen award, Westchester-Putnam Coun. Boy Scouts Am., 1986; Palm Beach County's Leading Men award Cystic Fibrosis Found., 2002; The Henry A. Deppe Chair for pension studies in his honor The Am. Coll. of Chartered Life Underwriters. Assn. Advanced Life Underwriters, Am. Pension Conf., Am. Soc. Pension Actuaries, Am. Soc. C.L.U.s, Life Underwriters Assn. Westchester (pres. 1949-50), Nat. Assn. Pension Cons. and Adminstrs. (treas.), Fertility Rsch. Assn. (pres. bd. dirs. 1982-83), Nat. Assn. Health and Welfare Plans, Million Dollar Round Table (life mem.), Golden Key Soc. (founder), Top of Table, Ten Million Dollar Forum, Rsch. Agys. Group, Boca Raton Hotel and Country Club, Boca Golf and Tennis Club, Westchester Country Club, Royal Palm Yacht and Country Club (rear commodore). Home and Office: Nat Pension Svc 1629 Royal Palm Way Boca Raton FL 33432-7439

DEPPE, PAUL RICHARD, electrical engineer, engineering test pilot; b. Indpls., June 28, 1954; s. Roger George Deppe and Beatrice Anna Altendorfer; m. Martha Grace Moritz, Mar. 12, 1983 (div. 1996); children: Richard, Carolyn; m. Yvonne Jeanette Cabrera, Aug. 9, 1998; 1 child, Colette. BSEE with honors, U.S. Naval Acad., 1976. Commd. ensign USN, 1976, advanced through grades to lt. comdr., 1984; transferred to USNR, 1988, hon. discharge, 2001; engring. test pilot Veridian Engring., Buffalo, 1988—. Mem. Sigma Xi. Office: Veridian Engring 150 N Airport Dr Buffalo NY 14225

DEPPERSCHMIDT, THOMAS ORLANDO, economist, consultant; b. St. Louis, Dec. 3, 1935; s. Robert O. and Marcella C. (Meier) D.; m. Bertha Marie Waldman, Nov. 28, 1957; children: M. Susan, Mark, Joel, Andrew, Amy, Joan. AB, Ft. Hays (Kans.) State U., 1958; PhD, U. Tex., 1965. Asst. prof., then asso. prof. W. Tex. State U., Canyon, 1961-66; prof. econs. Memphis State U., 1966—2001, prof. emeritus, 2001—, chmn. dept., 1977-83. Research assoc. study N.Y.C. elevator industry, 1996. Co-author: Encyclopedia of Economics, 1974, Assessing Family Loss in Wrongful Death Litigation, 1999; editor: Financial Policies in Transition, 1968; author over 40 tech. treatises. With AUS, 1954-56. Mem.: Soc. Litigation Economists, Am. Acad. Econ. and Fin. Experts (bd. dirs.), Nat. Assn. Forensic Economists, Am. Econ. Assn. Home and Office: 1957 Mt Repose Germantown TN 38139-3443 E-mail: tdpprsch@memphis.edu.

DEPPISCH, PAUL VINCENT, data communications executive; b. Madison, Wis., Dec. 15, 1950; s. Vincent Francis and Evelyn Catherine (Eichmeier) D. Cable splicing foreman GTE Calif., Santa Monica, 1968-73; gen. foreman DataCom Inc., Santa Monica, 1973-78; sr. project mgr. A.I.D.C.O., North Hollywood, Calif., 1978-84; cons. Systex Group Ltd., Phoenix, 1984-90; pres. Ambient Data Tech. Inc., Upland, Calif., 1990-2001. Founder, dir. Boogere Prodns. Internat., Santa Monica, 1973—; bd. dirs. Systex Group Ltd. Min. Universal Life Ch., Modesto, Calif. Mem. Bldg. Industry Cons. Svc., Inc., C. of C., L.A. World Affairs Coun. Avocations: hunting, fishing, community service. Home: PO Box 1712 Santa Monica CA 90406-1712 Office: PO Box 564 Rancho Cucamonga CA 91729-0564 E-mail: paul.deppisch@verizon.net.

DEPRA, ALAN JAY, mechanical engineer; b. Johnstown, Pa., Dec. 30, 1959; s. Alfred Dominic and Janet Lou Depra. BSME, U. Pitts., 1981, MS in Mfg. Engring., 1998, MS in Indsl. Engring., 2001; MBA, St. Francis U., 2003. Registered profl. engr., DC, Ga., Md., N.J., N.Y., N.C., Ohio, Pa., Va., W.Va., Del. Mech. cons. H. F. Lenz Cons. Engrs., Johnstown, 1981—84; sr. engr. Gen. Pub. Utilities, Inc., Johnstown, 1994—2000, Reliant Energy Inc., Johnstown, 2000—03, Johnstown Engring. Assocs. Inc., 2003—. Mem.: ASME, Assn. Facilities Engring. (cert. plant engr.), Am. Soc. Metals, Soc. Mfg. Engrs. (cert. mfg. engr., cert. enterprise integrator, cert. engring. mgr.). Achievements include development of computer assisted furthest neighbor, nearest neighbor clustering heuristic for optimization of classical vehicle routing problems; computer simulations to optimize classical uncapacitated facility location problems; computer simulations to optimize equipment placement and relocation during heat exchanger tube welding and rolling processes; an advanced product design process model that effectively combines the use of quality function deployments with design for manufacturing and design for assembly techniques. Avocation: motorcycle touring. Home: 131 Breck Ln Johnstown PA 15901-2010 Office: Johnstown Engring Assocs Inc 310 Belmont St Ste 2 Johnstown PA 15904

DEPREIST, JAMES ANDERSON, conductor; b. Phila., Nov. 21, 1936; s. James Henry and Ethel (Anderson) DePriest; m. Betty Louise Childress, Aug. 10, 1963; children: Tracy Elisabeth DePriest, Jennifer Anne DePriest; m. Ginette Grenier, July 19, 1980. BS, U. Pa., 1958, MA, 1961, LHD (hon.), 1976; student, Phila. Conservatory Music, 1959—61; LHD (hon.), Reed Coll., 1990, Portland State U., 1993; MusD (hon.), Laval U., Quebec City, Can., 1980, Linfield Coll., 1986, Juilliard, 1993; DFA (hon.), U. Portland, 1983, Pacific U., 1985, Willamette U., 1987, Drexel U., 1989, Oreg. State U., 1990; D of Arts and Letters (hon.), St. Mary's Coll., Moraga, Calif., 1985; HHD (hon.), Lewis and Clark U., 1986. Am. specialist music for State Dept., 1962—63; condr.-in-residence Bangkok, 1963—64; condr. various symphonies and orchs., 1964—; condr., music dir. Oreg. Symphony, Portland, 1980—. Prin. artistic adv. Phoenix Symphony; permanent cond. designate Tokyo Met. Symphony Orch. Condr.: Am. debut with N.Y. Philharm., 1964, asst. condr. to Leonard Bernstein N.Y. Philharm. Orch., 1965—66, prin. guest condr. Symphony of New World, 1968—70, European debut with Rotterdam Philharm., 1969, Helsinki Philharm., 1993, assoc. condr. Nat. Symphony Orch., Washington, 1971—75, prin. guest condr., 1975—76, music dir. L'Orch. Symphonique de Que., 1976—83, Oreg. Symphony, 1980—, prin. guest condr. Helsinki Philharm., 1993, music dir. Monte Carlo Philharm., 1994, appeared with Phila. Orch., 1972, 1976, 1984—85, 1987, 1990, 1992—94, Chgo. Symphony, 1973, 1990, 1992, 1994, Boston Symphony, 1973, 1997—99, Cleve. Orch., 1974, condr.: Am. premiere of Dvorak's First Symphony, N.Y. Philharm., 1972, chief condr. Malmö Symphony, 1991—94; author: (poems) This Precipice Garden, 1987, The Distant Siren, 1989. Trustee Lewis and Clark Coll., 1983—. Decorated Insignia of Comdr. of Order of Lion of Finland; recipient 1st prize gold medal, Dimitri Mitropoulos Internat. Music Competition for Condrs., 1964, Merit citation, City of Phila., 1969, medal, City of Que., 1983; grantee, Martha Baird Rockefeller Fund for Music, 1969. Fellow: Am. Acad. Arts and Scis.; mem.: Royal Swedish Acad. Music. Office: Oreg Symphony 921 SW Washington St Ste 200 Portland OR 97205-2800*

DEPRIEST, C(HARLES) DAVID, engineering executive, retired military officer; b. Mount Pleasant, Pa., Oct. 18, 1938; s. Charles Leonard and Elizabeth Carolyn (Hoover) DeP.; m. Blanca Reinoso Rivas, July 1, 1960 (div.); children: Lisa Lynn Nees, Diane Cokerdem DePriest, David Eric; m. Marlena J. Brechtel, Aug. 1, 2001 (dec.). BSEE with distinction, Air Force Inst. Tech., 1974, MS in Electro-Optics, 1975. Cert. profl. logistician Soc. Logistics Engrs. Enlisted USAF, 1959, advanced through grades to col., 1984, squadron navigator, 1964-68, squadron radar navigator, wing flight examiner Wright-Patterson AFB, Ohio, 1968-72; chief missile guidance br. USAF armament lab., Eglin AFB, Fla., 1975-79; program element monitor, dep. chief, avionics & armament divsn. air staff HQ USAF, Washington, 1979-83; chief engring. divsn. material mgmt. directorate Warner-Robins ALC, Ga., 1984-86; dir. intercommand electronic warfare aero. systems divsn. Wright-Patterson AFB, 1986-88; dir. plans and ops. AF electronic combat office USAF, Wright-Patterson AFB, 1988-91; ret., 1991; mgr. Warner Robins applications dept. The Analytic Scis. Corp., Inc., Warner Robins, Ga., 1992-97; pres. DePriest Assocs., Inc., Warner Robins, 1997—. Decorated DFC, Legion of Merit, Air medal with silver oak leaf cluster, Meritorious Svc. medal with two bronze oak leaf clusters. Mem.: IEEE (sr.), Soc. Logistics Engrs., Air Force Assn., Mensa, Rotary, Assn. Old Crows, Tau Beta Pi. Office: DePriest Assocs Inc 110 Park Dr Warner Robins GA 31088-5167 E-mail: cddeprie@ix.netcom.com.

DEPRIMO, GAETANO MANFRED, b. Weiden, Germany, July 19, 1948; s. Joseph Gaetano and Erna DeP. AB in Math., U. Calif., Berkeley, 1969; MA in Math., U. Calif., 1971. Instr. in math. Medgar Evers Coll./CUNY, Bklyn., 1971-76; lectr. in math. Montgomery Coll., Rockville, Md., 1976-78; instr. in math. Kankakee (Ill.) C.C., 1978-81, City Coll. of San Francisco, 1982-89, dept. chair, math., 1989-92, instr. in math., 1992—. Apptd. mem. Calif. Math. Project, 1987-93, elected to Calif. Math. Project exec. com., 1989-93; cons. Southwestern Coll. Maths. Acad., Chula Vista, Calif., 1989-93, NSF funded San Francisco Unified Sch. Dist. Urban Systemic Program, 2000-02. Chair steering com. Alliance for C.C. Ednl. Leadership, San Francisco, 1988; co-dir. math. achievement through systemic support grant program funded by Calif. Postsecondary Edn. Com., Dwight D. Eisenhower Profl. Devel. Program, San Francisco, 1995-99. Mem.: Faculty Assn. Calif. C.C.s, Math. Assn. Am., Nat. Coun. Tchrs. of Math., Calif. Math. Coun. C.C. (treas. 1987—90, Disting. Svc. award, Tchg. Excellence award 2002), Calif. Math. Coun., Am. Fedn. Tchrs., Am. Math. Soc., Am. Math. Assn. of Two-Yr. Colls. Roman Catholic. Avocations: reading, music. Office: City Coll of San Francisco 50 Phelan Ave San Francisco CA 94112-1821 E-mail: gdeprimo@ccsf.edu.

DE QUEIROZ, MARCIO S. engineering educator; b. Rio de Janeiro, July 12, 1966; BSEE, Fed. U. of Rio de Janeiro, 1990; MS in Mech. Engring., Pontifical Cath. U. of Rio de Janeiro, 1993; PhD in Elec. Engring., Clemson U., 1997. Rsch. assoc. U. of Va., Charlottesville, 1997—98; vis. asst. prof. Poly. U., Bklyn., 1998—2000; asst. prof. La. State U., Baton Rouge, 2000—. Author book in field; contbr. articles, book chpts., papers to profl. publs. and confs. Mem.: ASME (assoc.), IEEE (assoc.; assoc. editor Transactions on Sys., Man, and Cybernetics 2001—). Office: La State U Dept Mech Engring Baton Rouge LA 70803-6413 E-mail: dequeiroz@me.lsu.edu.

DERBES, ALBERT JOSEPH, III, lawyer, accountant; b. New Orleans, Mar. 18, 1940; s. Albert Joseph Jr. and Marcelle (Jourdan) D.; m. Shirley Brown, June 8, 1963; children: Albert Joseph IV, Eric Joseph. BBA, Tulane U., 1963, JD, 1966. Bar: La., Tex., U.S. Tax Ct., U.S. Supreme Ct., U.S. Ct. Appeals (5th cir.), U.S. Dist. Ct. (ea., mid. and we. dists.) La., U.S. Dist. Ct. (ea. dist.) Tex.; CPA, La., Miss., Ga., Fla. Ptnr. Derbes & Derbes, CPAs, New Orleans, 1964-69, Trahan, Kernion, & Derbes, CPAs, New Orleans, 1970-78, Hurdman & Cranston, CPAs, New Orleans, 1978-79, Main, Hurdman, CPAs, New Orleans, 1979-82, Windhorst, Pastorek & Gaundry, Attys. at Law, Harvey, La., 1982-88, Derbes & Co., CPAs, Metairie, La., 1982—2003; pvt. practice, 1988-95; with

The Derbes Law Firm, LLC, Metairie, 1995—. Capt. USAF, 1966-69. Mem. ABA, AICPAs, La. State Bar Assn., La. Soc. CPAs, Miss. Soc. CPAs, Nat. Assn. State Bds. of Accountancy (bd. dirs. 1983-84, v.p. 1984-85, pres. 1986-87). Republican. Roman Catholic. Avocations: fishing, reading. Office: 3027 Ridgelake Dr PO Box 8176 Metairie LA 70011-8176 E-mail: ajderbesiii@derbeslaw.com.

DERBES, DANIEL WILLIAM, manufacturing executive; b. Cin., Mar. 30, 1930; s. Earl Milton and Ruth Irene (Grauten) D.; m. Patricia Maloney, June 4, 1952; children: Donna Ann, Nancy Lynn (dec.), Stephen Paul. BS, U.S. Mil. Acad., 1952; MBA, Xavier U., Cin., 1963. Devel. engr. AiResearch Mfg. Co., Phoenix, 1956-58; with Garrett Corp., L.A., 1958-80, v.p., gen. mgr., then exec. v.p., 1975-80, dir., 1976-87; pres. Signal Cos., Inc., La Jolla, Calif., 1980—82, Signal Advanced Tech Group, 1982—83, Allied-Signal Internat. Inc., 1985-88; exec. v.p. Allied-Signal, Inc., Morristown, N.J., 1985-88; pres. Signal Ventures, Solana Beach, Calif., 1990—. Chmn. bd. dirs. WD-40 Co.; bd. dirs. Sempra Energy. Exec. bd. nat. coun. Boy Scouts Am., 1981-95; trustee U. San Diego, 1981—, vice-chmn., bd. trustees, 1990-93, chmn., 1993-96. With AUS, 1952-56. Republican. Roman Catholic. Office: Signal Ventures 777 S Pacific Coast Hwy Ste 107 Solana Beach CA 92075-2623

DERBEZ BAUTISTA, LUIS ERNESTO, secretary of foreign affairs of Mexico; b. Mexico City, June 14, 1949; Degree in econs., San Luis Potosí Autonomous U., Mex.; M in Econs., U. Oreg.; PhD in Econs., Iowa State U. With World Bank, dir., supr., multilateral econ. assistance, strucural adjustment programs, ind. cons., 1997—2000, Inter-Am. Devel. Bank, Washington, 1997—2000; prof. Grad. Sch. Bus. Mgmt. ITESM, Monterrey, Mexico, dir. econometric studies unit and econs. dept.; various acad. positions including acad. vice rector U. Ams., Cholula, Mexico; sec. economy Govt. of Mex., 2000—03, sec. foreign affairs, 2003—. Office: Ministry of Fgn Affs Ricardo Flores Magnon 2 CP 06954 Mexico City Mexico*

DERBY, ERNEST STEPHEN, federal judge; b. Boston, July 10, 1938; s. Elmer Goodrich and Lucy (Davis) D.; m. Gretel Hanauer, June 10, 1961 (dec. Oct. 2000); children: Anne Gray, Michael Stephen; m. Carolyn Schwenk, May 11, 2002. AB with distinction, Wesleyan U., 1960; LLB cum laude, Harvard U., 1965. Bar: Md. Ct. Appeals 1965, U.S. Dist. Ct. Md. 1966, U.S. Ct. Appeals (4th cir.) 1968, U.S. Supreme Ct. 1973. Law clk. to presiding justice U.S. Dist. Ct. Md. and U.S. Ct. of Appeals 4th cir., 1965-66; assoc. Piper & Marbury, Balt., 1966-71, ptnr., 1973-87; asst. atty. gen. Atty. Gen. Md., 1971-73; judge U.S. Bankruptcy Ct., Balt., 1987—. Adj. faculty U. Md. Sch. Law, 1987, 90-99. Pres. Dismas Ho., Balt. Inc., 1969—; trustee Enoch Pratt Free Libr., Balt., 1977-93. Fellow Am. Coll. Bankruptcy, Md. Bar Found.; mem. Md. State Bar Assn., Anne Arundel County Bar Assn., Paca/Brent Am. Inn of Ct. (pres. 1993-94). Office: US District Court US Courthouse 101 W Lombard St Ste 9442 Baltimore MD 21201-2906

DERBY, STEVEN LEO, lawyer; b. Lackawanna, N.Y., May 4, 1964; s. Leo Edward and Bernadette Muriel D.; m. Debbie Anuskiewicz, Oct. 17, 1992; children: Kevin Robert, Alison Bernadette, Nicholas Leo. BA in French and Govt., St. Lawrence U., Canton, N.Y., 1986; JD, Golden Gate U., 1990. Bar: Calif. 1990, U.S. Dist. Ct. (no. dist.) Calif. 1990. Law clk. Evans, Farber & Cipinko, San Francisco, 1988-90, 1990-92; assoc. Law Offices of Paul B. Engler, Walnut Creek, Calif., 1992—2002, The Derby Law Firm P.C., 2002—. Mock trial judge Golden Gate U., San Francisco, 1990—. Contbr. articles to profl. jours. Vol. Vol. Legal Svcs., San Francisco, 1992—, AIDS Action Legal Program, San Francisco, 1999, Atty.'s Reference Panel, Concord, 1992—; panel mem. KRON Action Com., Daly City, Concord, Calif., 1998-99. Mem. ATLA, Consumers Attys. Calif., Contra Costa City Bar Assn. (judge pro temp 1998, mediator 1998). Democrat. Roman Catholic. Avocations: baseball, carpentry, bowling, tennis. Home: 2460 Overlook Dr Walnut Creek CA 94596-3009 Office: Derby Law Firm PC Ste 350 200 Pringle Ave Walnut Creek CA 94596 Office Fax: 925-937-4273.

DERBY, STEVEN R. foundation administrator; b. Abington, Pa., Jan. 10, 1948; s. Robert E. and Betty Jane D.; m. Marilyn Lane Derby, Dec. 20, 1969; children: Michael R., Peter J. BS in Econs., U. Pa., Phila., 1969, MBA, 1973; Cert., Def. Lang. Inst., West Coast, Monterey, Pa., 1971. Asst. v.p. U. Pa., 1973—88; v.p. Temple U., Phila., 1988—94; sr. cons. Schultz & Williams, Inc., Phila., 1994—97; v.p. The Riddle HealthCare Found., Media, Pa., 1997—. Chair, bd. devel. com. Rocky Run YMCA, Media, Pa., 1997—2003. Specialist 6 U.S. Army, 1969—75, Pedricktown, NJ. Mem.: Soc. Performing Arts (chair dvel. com. 2002—03), Nat. Soc. Fund Raising Execs. (chmn.), Assn. Fund Raising Profls. Office: The Riddle HealthCare Found 1068 W Baltimore Pike Media PA 19063 Office Fax: 610-891-3421. E-mail: sderby@riddlehospital.org.

DERBYSHIRE, WILLIAM WADLEIGH, language educator, translator; b. Phila., Dec. 30, 1936; s. Roger S. and Arline (Wadleigh) Derbyshire; m. Kathleen Derbyshire (div. 1981); children: Ann, Wesley, Lee. BA, U. Pa., 1958, MA, 1959, PhD, 1964. Cert. Russian-English translator. Instr. U. Pa., Phila., 1959-61; asst. prof. Lycoming Coll., Williamsport, Pa., 1961-63, SUNY-Binghamton, Vestal, NY, 1964-69; assoc. prof. Rutgers U., New Brunswick, NJ, 1969-76, prof., 1976-94; freelance translator, 1994—. Cons. Thomas Edison Coll., Trenton, NJ, 1981—94. Author: (book) Reference Grammar of Slovene, 1993, A Learner's Dictionary of Slovene, 2002; contbr. articles to profl. jours. Active Gov.'s Coun. Ethnic Affairs, NJ, 1992—94. Fulbright fellow, 1972—73, N.J. Dept. Higher Edn. fellow, 1984—85, Rsch. grantee, Dept. Edn., Washington, 1989—90, 1995—96. Mem.: Am. Translators Assn., Soc. Slovene Studies (treas. 1982—86, sec. 2002—), Am. Assn. Tchrs. Slavic and Eastern European Langs. (pres. 1985—86), Am. Assn. Advancement Slavic Studies (bd. dirs. 1986—89). Avocation: opera. E-mail: wwdslovene@aol.com.

DERCHIN, MICHAEL WAYNE, portfolio manager and financial analyst; b. N.Y.C., Aug. 17, 1942; s. James and Rose (Minenberg) D.; m. Dary Bret Ingham, Dec. 29, 1970; children: Taylor-Leigh, Danielle-Ashlin Lacey. BA, Bklyn. Coll., 1964; MBA, CCNY, 1966; postgrad., Syracuse U., 1966-69. Sr. analyst Am. Airlines, N.Y.C., 1969-70; dir. mktg. Pan Am. World Airways, N.Y.C., 1970-74, Am. Airlines, N.Y.C., 1974-79; v.p. Oppenheimer & Co., Inc., N.Y.C., 1979-82, First Boston Corp., N.Y.C., 1982-88; mng. dir. Drexel Burnham Lambert, N.Y.C., 1988-90; sr. v.p., dir. rsch., chmn. stock selection com. Nat. West Securities, N.Y.C., 1990-95; mng. dir. Tiger Mgmt., 1995-2000; founder, pres. JetCap, Fair Haven, N.J., 2000—, Derchin Mgmt., N.Y.C., 2002—. Columnist Travel Weekly, N.Y.C., 1984-90; spl. guest Wall St. Week, Owings Mills, Md., 1982-90, guest MacNeil Lehrer Newshour, N.Y., 1985; expert witness U.S. Senate Aviation subcom., 1984; lectr. Travel Research Assn., N.Y.C., 1981-84. Named to first team All Am. Analysts Instnl. Investor mag., 1983, 90, stock picker, 1995. Mem. N.Y. Soc. Security Analysts, N.Y. Airline Analysts Soc. (chmn. mem. com. 1985, pres. 1986-87), Wings Club, Travel Tourism Rsch. Assn., Nat. Arts U. Club (N.Y.C.), Union League Club (N.Y.C.), Navesink Country Club (Rumson, N.J.). E-mail: michael@derchin.com.

DERDERIAN, HOVNAN, church official; b. Beirut, Dec. 1, 1957; Student, Sem. of Catholicossate Cilicia, Antelias, Lebanon, 1983, Sem. Holy See of Etchmiadzin, Armenia; B of Theology, U. Oxford, Eng., 1983, M of Theology, 1987. Ordained celibate priest, 1980; ordained bishop, 1990, ordained archbishop, 1993. Pastor Holy Trinity Armenian ch., Toronto, Ont., Can., 1984-90; primate of diocese, bishop Armenian Ch. of Can., 1990-93, archbishop, 1993-94; v.p. Can. Coun. Chs., 1994—; primate Armenian Ch. Can. Mem. Armenian Ch. Office: Diocese Armenian Ch Can 615 Stuart Outremont QC Canada H2V 3H2 Fax: 514-276-9960. E-mail: adiocese@aol.com.

DERE, WILLARD HONGLEN, internist, educator; b. Sacramento, Jan. 8, 1954; s. William Janson and Bessie Lon (Joe) D.; m. Julia Mei Lum, June 18, 1978; children: Melissa Ellen, Kathryn Elizabeth. AB, U. Calif., Davis, 1975, MD, 1980. Intern Health Sci. Ctr., U. Utah, Salt Lake City, 1980-81, resident, 1981-83; instr. internal medicine, geriatrics U. Utah, Salt Lake City, 1985-87, asst. prof., 1987-89; rsch. fellow U. Calif., San Francisco, 1983-85; asst. prof. Ind. U. Sch Medicine, Indpls., 1989-98; clin. assoc. prof. Ind. U. Sch. Medicine, Indpls., 1998—; clin. rsch. physician Lilly Rsch. Labs., Indpls., 1989-91, dir. European regulatory affairs, 1991-94, dir. endocrine rsch., 1994-98, exec. dir. global clin. rsch., 1998-2001, v.p. gen. medicine, 2002—. Dir. emergency rm. VA Med. Ctr., Salt Lake City, 1985-86; cons. U. Utah Student Health Svc., Salt Lake City, 1985-89, acting dir., 1987-88. Editor: Practical Care of the Ambulatory Patient, 1989; Contbr. articles to profl. jour. Hon. assoc. investigator VA, San Francisco, 1984. Mem. ACP, AAAS, Am. Soc. Bone and Mineral Rsch., Assn. Osteobiology. Presbyterian. Achievements include rsch. in adrenocortical function in AIDS, oncogene regulation in thyroid cells, multi-center antibiotic trials, drug safety, health economics, selective estrogen receptor modulators, osteoporosis. Office: Lilly Corp Ctr Lilly Rsch Labs Ctr Indianapolis IN 46285-0001 E-mail: wdere@lilly.com.

DEREBERY, MARY JENNIFER, otolaryngologist; m. Gregory Edward Spahr; children: Alexandra J. Spahr, Madison C. Spahr. MD, U. Tex., Galveston, 1979. Diplomate Am. Bd. Otolargyngology. Otologist Ho. Ear Clinic, L.A., 1986—. Med. adv. bd. Sertoma Internat., Kansas City, Mo., 1998—2002. Grantee, NIH. Fellow: ACS, Triologic Assn., Am. Acad. Otolaryngic Allergy (Golden Apple 2000, Pres.'s award 2001), Am. Neurotologic Soc., Am. Acad. Otolaryngology Head and Neck Surgery (pres.-elect 2002—), Am. Otologic Soc. Office: Ho Ear Clinic 2100 W 3rd St Los Angeles CA 90057 Office Fax: 213-484-5900.

DEREGIBUS, WILLIAM, artist; b. Mount Kisco, N.Y., May 21, 1954; s. Cleo and Diana (Douglass) DeR.; m. Surin Rungpanich, Oct. 30, 1986. BFA, Cornell U., Ithaca, N.Y., 1978. Artist, illustrator, N.Y., Bangkok, 1978-86, 88—; gen. mgr. Vegas Hotel, Hua Hin, 1986-88. Illustrator: (books) Franklin and Sterling Hill Mines, N.J.-the World's Most Magnificent Mineral Deposits, 1995, The Silver Surf, 1995; painter, artist: (oil portrait) Mr. & Mrs. Edmund C. Lynch III, 1986, Aspen East: Home of D.H. Koch, Southampton, N.Y., 1993; curator Nassau County Ctr. for Cultural Devel., Muttontown, N.Y., 1996; mineral art included in the Steidle Mineral Art Collection/Pa. State U.; mural Village Club, Sands Point, N.Y. Recipient Peacock Showcase award Visual Arts Alliance of Long Island, 1991. Episcopalian. Avocations: chess, martial arts, skiing, mineralogy, asian studies. Home: Piping Rock Rd Locust Valley NY 11560

DEREGNIER, RAYE-ANN ODEGAARD, physician, researcher; b. Waukesha, Wis., Aug. 2, 1958; d. Clarke and Rita Odegaard; m. Matthew James deRegnier. BA, Northwestern U., Ill., 1980; MD, Med. Coll. of Wis., 1984. Pediatric resident Children's Med. Ctr., Dallas, 1984—87; pediatric hospitalist Baylor Med. Ctr., Dallas, 1987—88; neonatal fellow U. of Minn., Mpls., 1988—91; asst. prof. of pediat. Bowman Gray Sch. of Medicine, Winston-Salem, NC, 1991—93; asst. prof. Children's Hosp. St. Paul, Univ of MN, Mpls. St. Paul, 1993—2001; assoc. prof. of pediat. Northwestern U., Chgo., 2001—. Med. dir. Devel. Clin., Prentice Women's Hosp., Chgo., 2001—. Contbr. several pediat. jours. Mem.: Soc. for Infant Studies, Soc. for Rsch. in Child Devel., Am. Acad. of Pediat., Soc. for Pediatric Rsch. Office: Neonatology Rm 404B PWH 333 E Superior St Chicago IL 60305 Office Fax: 312-926-7014.

DE REINECK, MARIE, interior designer; b. Ellington, Mo. d. Thomas Otto and Lessie (Deen) Buford; m. Baron Radu de Reineck, Mar. 30, 1933; 1 child, Claire; m. Radu Romanesco, Dec. 8, 1970. BS, Fordham U., 1941; grad., N.Y. Sch. Interior Design. Freelance interior designer, 1941—. Tchr. interior design Finch Coll., N.Y.C., 1946-61, NYU, N.Y.C., 1949-54; founder Claymar Sch. Design, 1948-55. Author: How to Decorate Your Home, 1954. Mem. Am. Inst. Decorators, AIA/Am. Archtl. Found. (allied mem.). Republican. Roman Catholic.

DEREMEE, RICHARD ARTHUR, physician, educator, researcher; b. Red Wing, Minn., July 4, 1933; s. Arthur Eugene and Anna Helen (Vinquist) DeR.; m. E. Lucille Fogelstrom, Mar. 17, 1956; children— Lisa C., Brita L., Bo A. BA, Gustavus Adolphus Coll., 1955; BS, MD, U. Minn., 1959. Diplomate Am. Bd. Internal Medicine. Intern William Beaumont Gen. Hosp., El Paso, 1959-60; resident Mayo Clinic, Rochester, Minn., 1962-66, fellow in internal medicine and pulmonary disease, 1962-66, cons. in internal medicine and pulmonary disease, 1966—; assoc. prof. medicine Mayo Med. Sch., Rochester, 1977-83, prof. medicine, 1983-96; ret., 1996. Friedrich Wegener Meml. lectr. Lübeck, Germany, 1992. Contbr. numerous articles to profl. jours. Served as capt. M.C., U.S. Army, 1959-62 Recipient cert. of achievement U.S. Army, 1962; Judson Daland travel award Mayo Found., 1966; Alumni citation Gustavus Adolphus Coll., 1982; named to Red Wing H.S. Wall of Honor, 2000. Fellow ACP, Am. Coll. Chest Physicians; mem. Am. Thoracic Soc. Republican. Lutheran. Home: 2209 5th Ave NE Rochester MN 55906-4017 E-mail: radrst@aol.com.

DEREMER, SUSAN RENÉ, artist; b. Atlanta, June 29, 1959; d. Lewis Emmett Rhoden and Beth Lee (Perkins) Keener; m. Randall Eugene Deremer, Apr. 7, 1990. Student, Inst. Fine Arts, Rio de Janeiro, 1977-78; BFA, U. Ga., 1982; postgrad., Atlanta Law Sch., 1987-88. Art dir. Exec. Printing, Inc., Marietta, Ga., 1988-90; graphic artist IBM, Atlanta, 1992-93; pres. Deremer Studio, Inc., Atlanta, 1993—; instr. painting Douglasville Sch. Art. Illustrator/author: (book): Atlanta, An Historical Sketchbook, 1998; author: (newsletter) Folio, 1997-99; one-woman shows include South Cobb Arts Alliance, Inc., Mableton, Ga., 1992, Smyrna (Ga.) Libr., 1996, The Art Place-Mt. View, Marietta, Ga., 1999; exhibited in group shows 21st Ann. Atlanta Artists Club Mems. Traveling Show, 1993, 22d Ann., 1994, Atlanta Artist Club Show, 1994, Fine Arts Soc. of Kennesaw, Ga., 1995, Portrait Soc. of Atlanta, 1994-99; represented in permanent collections Zoo Atlanta, Bapt. Student Ctr., U. Ga., Athens, Robert L. Osborne H.S., Marietta, Glitsch Process Sys., Roswell, Ga.; featured in Pastel Artist Internat. mag., 2002. Mem. student adv. bd. High Mus. of Art, Atlanta, 1976-77, Ga. Gov.'s honors program Ga. State Bd. Edn., Macon, 1976. Recipient 1st pl. award Ga. Scholastic Press Assn., 1977, 2d pl. award Semana de Arte, 1977, Award of Excellence, Printing Industry Assn. of Ga., 1989. Mem. Am. Artists Profl. League Inc. (69th Grand Nat. Exhibition 1997, 70th Grand Nat. Exhibition 1998), Portrait Soc. Atlanta, Inc. (pres. 1997-99), Am. Soc. Portrait Artists, Am. Soc. Classical Realism, Portrait Inst. N.Y. (charter). Presbyterian. Office: The Portrait Group PO Box 8067 Reston VA 20195-1967 E-mail: redsrd@peoplepc.com.

DERENSIS, PAUL, lawyer; b. Boston, July 3, 1944; s. Pardo and Tatiana (Dramorska) D.; m. Sheila B., Aug. 25, 1968 (div. 1983); children: Allyson, Jennifer, Heather, Karen, Will; m. Linda A. Fraze, Oct. 6, 1990; children: Parker L., Lindsey A. BA, Harvard U., 1966, JD, 1969. Bar: N.Y. 1970, Mass. 1975, U.S. Supreme Ct. 1982, U.S. Ct. Appeals (2nd cir.) 1975, U.S. Ct. Appeals (1st cir.) 1976), U.S. Dist. Ct. (so. and ea. dists.) N.Y. 1971, U.S. Dist. Ct. Mass. 1975. Assoc. Poletti Freidin Prashker Feldman & Gartner, N.Y.C., 1969-75; dir./shareholder Powers & Hall Profl. Corp., Boston, 1975-84; dir., shareholder Deutsch Williams Brooks DeRensis & Holland, P.C., Boston, 1984—. Essex County atty., Mass., 1987-92; town counsel Town of Nantucket, 1986—, Town of Randolph, 1990—, Town of Cohasset, 1996—, Town of Carlisle, 1999—, Town of Canton, 2003—, town of Wilmington, 2003—. Contbr. articles to profl. jours. Mem. Planning Bd. Town of Sherborn (Mass.), 1990-93, mem. bd. of selectmen, 1996—, chmn., 1997-2002; mem. Sherborn Housing Partnership, Woodhaven Study Com., 1989-96; chmn. Sherborn Groundwater Protection Com., 1992-96, mem. adv. com., 1994-95,chmn s.w. water area protection adv. com., 1995-98. Mem. ABA, Assn. Bar City N.Y., Mass. Bar Assn., Boston Bar Assn., Mass. Assn. City Solicitors and Town Counsel. Office: Deutsch Williams Brooks DeRensis & Holland 99 Summer St Fl 13 Boston MA 02110-1235

DERESIEWICZ, HERBERT, mechanical engineering educator; b. Brno, Czechoslovakia, Nov. 5, 1925; s. William and Lotte (Rappaport) D.; m. Evelyn Altman, Mar. 12, 1955; children: Ellen, Robert, William. BME, CCNY, 1946; MS, Columbia U., 1948, PhD, 1952. Sr. staff engr. Applied Physics Lab., Johns Hopkins U., 1950-51; mem. faculty Columbia U., N.Y.C., 1951—, prof. mech. engring., 1962-94, chmn. dept. mech. engring., 1981-87, 90-93, emeritus, 1994—. Cons. stress analysis, vibrations, elastic contact, wave propagation, mechanics of granular and porous media. Fulbright sr. research scholar, Italy, 1960-61, Fulbright lectr., Israel, 1966-67; vis. prof., Israel, 1973-74. Editor Columbia Engring. Rsch., 1975-92; contbr. articles to profl. jours. Served with AUS, 1946-47. Univ. fellow Columbia U., 1949-50. Home: 336 Broad Ave Englewood NJ 07631-4304

DE REVERE, DAVID WILSEN, retired professional society administrator; b. Englewood, N.J., Nov. 13, 1937; s. Wilbur L. and Ethel M. (Gilchrist) De R.; m. Ellen B. Tompkins, June 7, 1958; children: Mark S., Roger T. BA, Colgate U., 1959; MDiv, Yale U., 1963. Cert. master chaplain Internat. Conf. Police Chaplains. Sr. pastor 1st Ch. of Christ in Saybrook, Old Saybrook, Conn., 1963-85; exec. dir. Internat. Conf. Police Chaplains, Destin, Fla., 1985—2003. Author, editor: Chaplaincy in Law Enforcement, 1989. Chaplain Old Saybrook (Conn.) Dept. Police Svcs., 1964-85, FBI, 1991—. Home: 408 Spanish Moss Tr Destin FL 32541

DERFLER, EUGENE L. real estate agent, former state legislator; b. Portland, Oreg., May 24, 1924; s. Leo and Jessie E. (Tatom) D.; m. Thelma M. Brekke, Aug. 14, 1944; children: Judith Lynne, Dennis Gene, Richard Henry. Grad., Pensacola Naval Aviator Sch.; student, W. Wash. Coll. Mgr. Firestone Tire & Rubber Co., Tillamook, Oreg., 1946-52; owner Nico Furniture & Appliance Co., Salem, Oreg., 1952-81; broker Coldwell Banker, Salem, 1982—; mem. Oreg. Ho. of Reps., Salem, 1989-94, Oreg. Senate, Salem, 1995—2002, Northwest Power and Conservation Council, Oreg., 2003—. Pres. Transit System fpr Salem, 1981-84; chmn. Marion County Juvenile Service Commn., Salem, 1983-87; bd. dirs. YMCA, Salem, 1984-85. Lt. USN, 1943-46. Republican. Avocations: photography, jogging, hiking. Office: Coldwell Banker Mountain West 1011 Commercial St NE Salem OR 97301-1049 also: NW Power & Conserv Council 851 SW 6 Ave Ste 1100 Portland OR 97204*

DERGALIS, GEORGE, artist, educator; b. Athens, Greece, Aug. 31, 1928; s. Demetrios and Zina Dergalis; m. Margaret Murphey; 1 child by previous marriage, Alexis. MFA, Acad. Belle Arti, Rome, 1951; diploma, Boston Museum Sch., 1956-59. Instr. Boston Mus. Sch., 1961-69, De Cordova Mus., Lincoln, Mass., 1961-94; pvt. instrn. Wayland, Mass., 1969—; chmn., curator Festival Bostonians for Art and Humanity, 1976; chmn. curator prisom art Inst. Contemporary Art Boston, 1975-76; artist-in-residence Ptnrs. of Ams., Colombia, 1979; lectr. Helicon, Harvard U., 1981; juror Once is Not Enough, Cambridge Art Assn., 1994. One-man shows include Woodstock Gallery, London, 1974, Cámera de Comercio de Medellin, Columbia, 1980, Galesburg (Ill) Civic Art Ctr., 1985, Hotel Meridien, Boston, 1987, Wayland Art/Space, 1994; exhibited in group shows Danforth Mus., Framingham, Mass., 1988-90, Mus. Fine Arts, Boston, 1989 (Merit award), Boston Pub. Libr., 1994-95, South Shore Art Ctr., 1994, Boston Corp. Art, 1995—, Indpls. Art Ctr., 2000-01, Mass. State House and Commonwealth Mus., Boston, 2000, Springfield Art Mus., 2002, Foothills Art Ctr., 2003others; represented in permanent collections at Loomis and Sayles, Boston, Scudder, Stevens and Clark, Boston, Novartis, Hale & Dorr, Boston, Decordova Mus. Lincoln, Mass., Alliance Capital Mgmt., N.Y., Museo de Zea, Colombia, U.S. Army Ctr. Mil. History, Washington, also pvt. collections; book It's All in Your Head, 1991, Rocky Mountain NH Watermedia Exhbn., Foothills Art Ctr., Golden Co., 2003, Author, Art of War, 2002. Trustee, Graham Jr. Coll., 1971; hon. dir. Boston Ballet, 1971. With USAF, 1951-54. William Paige scholar, 1959; recipient Prix de Rome, 1951, Civilian merit award U.S. Army Hist. Soc., 1969, Gold medal Accademia Italia delle Arte, 1980, Merit award Mus. of Fine Arts, 1989, Best of Show award Commonwealth of Mass., 2000, Juror's award Watercolor USA, 2002. Mem. Internat. Sculpture Assn., Internat. Sculpture Ctr., Alumni Assn. Boston Mus. Sch. (pres., 1966-67), Copley Soc. Boston (v.p., art chmn. 1978, Excellence in Technique award 1978), DeCordova Mus. Corp. Pigm. Home: 72 Oxbow Rd Wayland MA 01778-1009

DERGARABEDIAN, PAUL, energy and environmental company executive; b. Racine, Wis., Jan. 19, 1922; s. John and Mary (Hirmizian) D.; m. Mary A. Jansouzian, Dec. 27, 1947; children— Celeste, Claudia, Clarice, Paul. BS, U. Wis., 1948, MS, 1949; PhD (Shell Oil fellow), Caltech, 1952. Br. head U.S. Naval Weapons Center, Pasadena, Calif., 1952-55; lab. dir. TRW Systems, Redondo Beach, Calif., 1955-72; staff dir. TRW Systems (Energy Systems group), 1974-80; dir. The Aerospace Corp., El Segundo, Calif., 1972-74, 80-89, tech. cons., 1989—. Vis. prof. aeros. Caltech, 1971-72; founder, dir. Frontier Savs. & Loan; cons. in field. Served with USAAF, 1943-46. Fellow Inst. Advancement of Engring., Am. Astron. Soc. (dir. 1971—, nat. pres. 1969-71); mem. Phi Beta Kappa, Sigma Xi. Democrat. Armenian Apostolic. Club: Stereophonic of So. Calif. (pres. 1967-69). Home: 22401 Canyon Crest Dr Mission Viejo CA 92692-4548 E-mail: sysanalcon@compuserve.com. *As a scientist I have been moderately successful - and lucky - in doing what people in my field would consider creative work. The greatest contribution to this success, I feel, has been methodology which was gleaned from certain teachers and associates. If I have done the same for someone else, that would be the greater success.*

DE RHAM, CASIMIR, JR., lawyer; b. N.Y.C., Sept. 5, 1924; s. Casimir and Lucy Lathrop (Patterson) de Rham; m. Elizabeth Moran Evarts, June 9, 1945; children: Elizabeth Morgan, Henry Casimir, Rufus Patterson, Jeremiah Evarts. Student, Yale U., 1943-44; AB, Harvard U., 1946, JD, 1949. Bar: Mass. 1949, U.S. Dist. Ct. Mass. 1949. Assoc. Palmer & Dodge, Boston, 1949-51, 52-55, ptnr., 1956-94, of counsel, 1994—. Dir. Cambridge Trust Co., Cambridge Bancorp, 1967-99, hon. dir., 1999-2002. Trustee Mount Auburn Hosp., Cambridge, Mass., 1962-93, pres., 1966-77, chmn. bd. dirs., 1977-80, treas., 1993—, The Mount Auburn Found., Inc., 1985-91, 93-96, Commonwealth Sch., Boston, 1958-2002, chmn. bd. dirs., 1966-87, sr. adv. com., 2002—, St. Mark's Sch., Southborough, Mass., 1962-74, Cambridge Cmty. Found., 1985—; overseer, dir. Boys and Girls Clubs of Boston Inc., 1956-93, sec., 1973-93, sr. adv. bd., 1993—; dir. Ctr. for Blood Rsch. Inc., Boston, 1964-90, clk., 1964-84, hon. trustee, 1990—; trustee, sec. Sterling and Francine Clark Art Inst., Williamstown, Mass., 1973-95, hon. trustee, 1995—; dir. Women's Ednl. and Indsl. Union, Boston, 1975-98; dir., treas. Florence Evans Bushee Found., Boston, 1982-94; trustee Campbell & Hall Charity Fund, Boston, 1981—; dir. Olivetti Found. Inc., Boston, 1960—, treas., 1983-94, clk., 1960-94; trustee Little Harbor Chapel, Portsmouth, N.H., 1959—; fin. adv. com. Cambridge Hist. Soc., 1980-91, chmn., 1988-90; chmn. Cambridge Rep. City Com., 1954-58; mem. Mass. Rep. State Com., 1960-69; alt. del. Rep. Nat. Conv., 1964, 68; mem. exec. com. Permanent Fund Soc., The Boston Found., 1993-94. Capt. USMCR, 1943-46, 51-52. Mem. ABA, Mass. Bar Assn., Boston Bar Assn., Cambridge-Arlington-Belmont Bar Assn. (pres. 1982-83), Am. Bar Found., St. Botolph Club (Boston), The Country Club (Brookline, Mass.), Masons (Harvard Lodge), Am. Legion. Episcopalian. Avocations: reading, tennis, politics. Home: 47 Lakeview Ave Cambridge MA 02138 3255 Office: Palmer & Dodge Prudential Ctr 111 Huntington Ave Boston MA 02199-7613 E-mail: cderham@palmerdodge.com.

DER-HOUSSIKIAN, HAIG, linguistics educator; b. Cairo, Aug. 16, 1938; s. Vagharsh and Adrine (Karalian) Der-H.; m. Gaylynne Hall, Aug. 27, 1961. Student, Am. U., Cairo, 1957-59; BA, Am. U., Beirut, 1961, MA, 1962; PhD, U. Tex., 1969. Research assoc. U. Dar-es-Salaam, Tanzania, 1966-67; asst. prof. linguistics U. Fla., Gainesville, 1967-72; dir. linguistics, 1971-72, 84-85; assoc. prof. U. Fla., Gainesville, 1972-77, dir. Ctr. for African Studies, 1973-79, prof., 1977—2003, chmn. dept. African and Asian langs. and lits., 1982-91, prof. emeritus, 2003—. Mem. grad. council U. Fla., 1988-91; sr. Fulbright lectr. Universidade de Luanda, Angola, 1972-73, Universite du Benin, Lome, Togo, 1979-81; vis. prof. African linguistics U. Zimbabwe, Harare, 1989; panelist, grant proposal reviewer U.S. Dept. Edn., Washington, 1976—; USIA Acad. Specialist Grant cons. to U. De Ouagadougou, Burkina Faso, 1981; USIA Acad. Specialist Grant lectr. U. Marien Ngouabi, Brazzaville, Congo, May-Aug. 1988; occasional grant proposal evaluator Social Sci. and Humanities Coun. Can. Author: TEM, Grammar Handbook, 1980, TEM, Communication and Culture, 1980, TEM, Special Skills, 1980; contbr. chapters to books; co-editor: Language and Linguistics Problems in Africa, 1977; compiler: A Bibliography of African Linguistics, 1972, reviewer: African Book Publ. Rev., 1996—. ACTION grantee, 1980-81. Mem. MLA (African Linguistics bibliographer 1967-74), Linguistics Soc. Am., African Studies Assn., Southeastern Conf. on Linguistics, Phi Kappa Phi. Armenian Apostolic. Avocations: reading, hiking, traveling. Office: U Fla Dept African Asian Langs and Lit 470 Grinter Hall Gainesville FL 32611-2037 Mailing: Univ Station PO Box 14105 Gainesville FL 32604-2105

DERICCO, LAWRENCE ALBERT, college president emeritus; b. Stockton, Calif., Jan. 28, 1923; s. Giulio and Agnes (Giovacchini) DeR.; m. Alma Mezzetta, June 19, 1949; 1 child, Lawrence Paul. BA, U. Pacific, 1949, MA, 1971, LLD (hon.), 1987. Bank clk. Bank of Am., Stockton, 1942-43; prin. Castle Sch. Dist., San Joaquin County, Calif., 1950-53; dist. supt., prin. Waverly Sch. Dist., Stockton, 1953-63; bus. mgr. San Joaquin Delta Jr. Coll. Dist., Stockton, 1963-65, asst. supt., bus. mgr., 1965-77, v.p. mgmt. services,

1977-81; pres., supt. San Joaquin Delta Coll., 1981-87, pres. emeritus, 1988—. Mem. Workforce Investment Bd. With AUS, 1943-46, PTO. Mem. NEA, Calif. Tchrs. Assn., Native Sons of Golden West (past pres.), Phi Delta Kappa Office: 6847 N Pershing Ave Stockton CA 95207-2524 E-mail: ldericco@softcom.net.

DERICKSON, STANLEY LEWIS, minister, writer; b. Lexington, Nebr., Feb. 19, 1940; s. George Henry and Mary LeOra Derickson; m. Faith Louann Diefenbach, Feb. 28, 1964; children: Stanley L. II, Laurie Lynn, Timothy James. BA, Denver Bapt. Bible Coll., 1973; ThB, Western Bapt. Bible Coll., Salem, Oreg., 1978; ThM, Trinity Theol. Sem., Newburgh, Ind., 1980; PhD, Trinity Theol. Sem., 1981. Ordained to ministry Berean Ch., 1976. Missionary WEF Ministries, 1982-87; tchr. Frontier Sch. of Bible, LaGrange, Wyo., 1987-91; interim pastor Immanuel Bapt. Ch., Salem, Oreg., 1996-97; pastor Roberts Cmty. Ch., 1999-2000; pastor-at-large, 2000—. Author: Mr. D.'s Notes on Theology, 1993, Mr. D.'s Notes on Missions, 1998, Mr. D.'s Notes on Regeneration, 1998, Mr. D.'s Notes on Lots or Other Things, 1999, Mr. D.'s Notes on I Timothy, 2000, Mr. D's Notes on Zeal, 2002, Dr. D's Notes on Colossians, 2003; contbr. articles to Bapt. Bulletin, Voice mag. With USN, 1958-62. E-mail: mrd@thedericksons.com.

DE RIOS, MARIA ESTELA, engineering company executive; d. Julio Lopez Jr. and Guillermina Lopez Esquer; m. Miguel Riós, Sept. 2, 1967; children: Miguel III, Benjamin Tomás, Eva Angelica, Magdalena Anastasia. BA in Math. and Chemistry, U. N.Mex., 1980. Student asst. U. Md., College Park, 1968—71; contracts specialist Pub. Svc. Co. N.Mex., Albuquerque, 1980—86; cons. U. N.Mex., Albuquerque, 1988; owner, acting dir. pers., sec. bd. dirs. Orion Internat. Techs., Albuquerque, 1986—. Mem. nat. adv. bd. Mfg. Extension Partnership, NIST, 1997—. Chmn. N.Mex. Mfg. Extension Partnership, 2000—; bd. dirs. Hispanic Culture Found., 1999—; mem. Gov.'s Bus. Adv. Coun. State of N.Mex., 1996—2001; mem. Econ. Forum, 1995—; bd. dirs. found. Robert O. Anderson Grad. Sch. Mgmt., U. N.Mex., 1996—98; mem. cmty. adv. coun. Coll. Engring. U. N.Mex., 1995—96. Mem.: Nat. Contract Mgmt. Assn. (program chmn. 1990—91, pres.-elect 1991—92, pres. 1992—93, nat. bd. dirs. 1992—94), U.S.-Mex. C. of C. (dir. N.Mex. office, v.p. Rocky Mountain chpt, bd. dirs. 1996—), Hispano C. of C., N.Mex. Women's Forum (v.p. 2002). Democrat. Roman Catholic. Home: 10067 Los Cansados NW Albuquerque NM 87114

DE RIOS, MARLENE DOBKIN, medical anthropologist, educator; b. N.Y.C., Apr. 12, 1939; d. Bernard and Anne Dobkin; m. Yando Rios, Nov. 7, 1969; 1 child, Gabriela. BA in Psychology, Queens Coll., 1959; MA in Anthropology, NYU, 1962; PhD, U. Calif., Riverside, 1972. Lic. marriage and family therapist, 1986. Prof. anthropology Calif. State U., Fullerton, 1969-2000, prof. emeritus, 2000—; assoc. clin. prof. dept. psychiatry U. Calif., Irvine, 1989—; health sci. adminstr. NIMH, Rockville, Md., 1980-81. Author: Hallucinogens-Cross Cult Perspective, 1984, Visionary Vine, 1984, Amazon Healer, 1992, LSD, Spirituality and the Creative Process, 2003; contbr. over 200 sci. articles to profl. jours. Mem.: APA. Office: 2555 E Chapman Ave Ste 407 Fullerton CA 92831

DERIVAN, MARY COLLINS, nursing consultant, oncological nurse; b. NYC, Apr. 2, 1939; d. John Francis and Anne Frances (Connaire) Collins; m. Albert T. Derivan, July 4, 1961; children: Janice, Nancy, Linda, Donna. BSN, Hunter/Bellevue, 1960; MSN, Villanova U., 1987. Advanced cert. RN, MSN, AOCN. Staff nurse Vis. Nurse Svc. N.Y., N.Y.C., 1960-61, Vis. Nurse Assn. Plainfield, N.J., 1961-62; head nurse St. Francis Hosp., Jersey City, N.J., 1962-63; instr. St. Francis Hosp. Sch. Nursing, Jersey City, N.J., 1963-64; dir. insvc. edn. Yonkers (N.Y.) Gen. Hosp., 1964-65; staff nurse Naval Med. Ctr., New London, Conn., 1968, Stella Maris Hospice, Towson, Md., 1979-80; asst. dir. nursing Wayne (Pa.) Nursing Ctr., 1981-82; staff nurse Fitzgerald Mercy Hosp., Darby, Pa., 1982-83, nurse mgr., 1983-90, nurse educator, 1990-99; ret., 1999; nursing cons., 1999—; parish nurse coord. Ch. of St. Andrew, Newtown, Pa., 2000—; staff oncology nurse St. Mary Med. Ctr., Langhorne, Pa., 2001—02. Bd. dirs. Delaware County unit Am. Cancer Soc., 1988—2000. Presenter in field. Vol. Am. Home Missions Owingsville Ky., 1991. Recipient Quality of Life for Rehabilitation award Del. County Unit, 1997, Nightingale award of Pa., Chairperson of Yr. Lower Bucks County ARC, 2002. Mem. Oncology Nursing Soc. (founding mem., co-chair program com., chair nominating com. Penns Wood chpt.). Roman Catholic. Avocations: reading, traveling, writing. Home: 779 Linton Hill Rd Newtown PA 18940-1207

DE RIVAS, CARMELA FODERARO, psychiatrist, hospital administrator; b. Cortale, Italy, Nov. 25, 1920; came to U.S., 1935, naturalized, 1942; d. Salvatore and Mary (Vaiti) Foderaro; m. Aureliano Rivas, Oct. 30, 1948; children: Carmen, Norma, Sandra, David. Student, U. Pa., 1940-42; MD, Women's Med. Coll. Pa., 1946. Diplomate: Am. Bd. Psychiatry and Neurology. Intern women's Med. Coll. Pa. Hosp., 1946-47; gen. med. resident Chestnut Hill Hosp., Phila., 1947-48; gen. practice Tex., 1948-49; mem. staff Norristown (Pa.) State Hosp., 1949-63, supt., 1963-70, dir. family planning, 1979-87, clin. dir. spl. assignments, 1979-82; assoc. psychiatry U. Pa., 1963-75. Psychiatrist Penn Found. Mental Health, Sellersville, Pa., 1970—72; dir. intake coping svcs. Ctrl. Montgomery Mental Health/ Mental Retardation Ctr., Norristown, Pa., 1972—77, med. dir., 1977—82, psychiatrist, 1980—82; cons. surveyor Health Care Fin. Adminstrn., 1987—2001; dir. program evaluation Norristown State Hosp., 1979—82, med. dir., 1982—87. Named to Hall of Fame S. Phila. H.S., 1968; recipient citation Women's Med. Coll. Pa., 1968, Amita achievement award, 1976, achievement award Grad. Club Phila., 1976; named Woman of Yr. Pa. Fedn. Bus. and Profl. Women, 1979. Disting. life fellow Am. Psychiat. Assn., Pa. Psychiat. Soc. (rep. assembly of dist. brs. 1979-88); mem. AMA, Phila. Psychiat. Soc. (councilor), Montgomery County Med. Soc. (bd. dir., past pres.), Pa. Med. Soc. (chmn. adv. com. to aux. 1981-88, mem. ho. of dels., mem. commn. on med. edn. 1991-94, mem. com. on continuing med. edn. 1994-98). Home: Dunwoody Village-CH 112 3500 W Chester Pike Newtown Square PA 19073-4101

DERKSEN, CHARLOTTE RUTH MEYNINK, librarian; b. Newberg, Oreg., Mar. 15, 1944; BS in Geology, Wheaton (Ill.) Coll., 1966; MA in Geology, U. Oreg., 1968, MLS, 1973. Faculty and libr. Moeding Coll., Ootse, Botswana, 1968-70, head history dept., 1970-71; tchr. Jackson (Minn.) Pub. High Sch., 1975-77; sci. libr. U. Wis., Oshkosh, 1977-80; libr. and bibliographer Stanford (Calif.) U., 1980—. Acting chief scis., 1985-86, head Sci. and Engring. Librs., 1992-97. Contbg. author: Union List of Geologic Field Trip Guidebooks of North America; contbr. articles to profl. jours. Mem. ALA, Western Assn. Map Librs., Geosci. Info. Soc. (v.p. 1997-98, pres. 1998-99), Am. Geol. Inst. (soc. coun. 2000-02), Geol. Soc. Am. (publ. com. 2002—), Cartographic Users Adv. Coun. (chair 1988-90), GeoRef Adv. Bd. (chair 1998—). Republican. Lutheran. Home: 128 Mission Dr East Palo Alto CA 94303-2753 Office: Stanford U Branner Earth Scis Library Stanford CA 94305 E-mail: cderksen@stanford.edu.

DERLACKI, EUGENE L(UBIN), otolaryngologist, physician; b. Chgo., Mar. 16, 1913; s. Walter and Jadwiga (Pamulowna) D. BS, Northwestern U., 1936, MD, 1939; postgrad. otolaryngology, Rush Med. Coll., 1940, U. Ill., 1941-42. Diplomate: Am. Bd. Otolaryngology. Intern Cook County Hosp., Chgo., 1939-40, jr. resident, 1941, sr. resident, 1942-43; sr. attending staff Northwestern Meml. Hosp., 1946—2002; prof. otolaryngology Northwestern U. Med. Sch., 1957—2002, now prof. emeritus, 2002—. Contbr. articles to profl. jours. Past pres. Am. Hearing Research Found. Served with M.C. AUS, 1943-46. Mem. AMA, Am. Acad. Otolaryngology (past pres.), Coll. Allergists, Am. Otol. Soc. (past pres.), Am. Laryngol., Rhinol. and Otol. Soc. Home: 700 W Fabyan Pkwy Apt 22A Batavia IL 60510-1479 Office: Northwestern Med Faculty Found 675 N Saint Clair St Chicago IL 60611-5975

DERMAN, CYRUS, mathematical statistician; b. Phila., July 16, 1925; s. Samuel and Bessie (Segal) D.; Martha Winn, Feb. 24, 1961; children: Adam Jason Winn (dec.), Hester Beth Rebecca. AB, U. Penn., 1948, A.M., 1949; PhD, Columbia U., NYC., 1954. Instr. Syracuse U., Syracuse, NY, 1954-55; faculty Columbia U., NYC, 1955—, prof. ops. rsch. NYC., 1965-94; prof. emeritus, 1994. Vis. prof. Israel Inst. Tech., Haifa, 1961-62, Stanford, 1965-66; vis. prof. U. Calf., Davis, 1975-76, U. Calif., Berkeley, 1979 Author: (with Morton Klein) Probability and Statistical Inference for Engineers, 1959, Finite State Markovian Decision Processes, 1970, (with Leon Gleser and Ingram Olkin) A Guide to Probability Theory and Application, 1973, Probability Models and Applications, 1980, 2d edit., 1994, (with Sheldon Ross) Statistical Aspects of Quality Control, 1996. With U.S. Navy, 1943-46. Recipient John von Neumann Theory prize, INFORMS, 2002. Fellow Inst. Math. Statistics, Am. Statis. Assn. Achievements include research and publs. on theory of Markov chains, Brownian motion, statis. inference, mgmt. sci. and ops. research. Home: 15 Pond Hill Rd Chappaqua, NY 10514-2531 Office: Columbia U Mudd Bldg New York NY 10027

DERMANIS, PAUL RAYMOND, architect; b. Jelgava, Latvia, Aug. 2, 1932; came to U.S., 1949; s. Pauls and Milda (Argals) D. BArch, U. Wash., 1955; MArch, MIT, 1959. Registered architect, Wash. Architect John Morse & Assocs., Seattle, 1961-62; assoc. Fred Bassetti & Co., Seattle, 1963-70; arch. Ibsen Nelsen & Assocs., Seattle, 1970-71; ptnr. Streeter/Dermanis & Assocs., Seattle, 1973-97; owner Paul Dermanis Archs., 1997—. Designs include Sunset house (citation 1984), treatment plant, 1992. Mem. Phinney Ridge Neighborhood Assn., Seattle, 1985—. With USN, 1955-57. Mem. AIA, Apt. Assn. Seattle and King County, U. Wash. Alumni Assn., MIT Club of Puget Sound, Phi Beta Kappa, Tau Sigma Delta. Democrat. Lutheran. Avocations: skiing, painting, photography. E-mail: pdermanis@aol.com.

DERMARDEROSIAN, DIRAN ROBERT, rug cleaning company executive; b. Boston, Oct. 29, 1940; s. Kevork George and Vartouhi (Belekian) DerM. BS, Curry Coll., Milton, Mass., 1964; MS, Emerson Coll., Boston, 1969. Vice prin. Billerica (Mass.) Sr. High Sch., 1975-86; pres. Brookline Rug Cleaning Co., Inc., Needham Heights, Mass., 1987—. Mem. Curry Coll. Alumni Assn., Emerson Coll. Alumni Assn., Billerica Elks. Avocations: boating, gardening. Home: 325 Hunnewell St Needham MA 02494-1340 E-mail: poreeg@aol.com.

DERMKSIAN, GEORGE, cardiologist; b. NYC, Nov. 10, 1927; s. Yervant Edward and Mariam Dermksian; m. Tamara Manookian Dermksian, June 13, 1954; children: Gregory Edward, Jeffrey Vahe. AB, Columbia Coll., N.Y.C., 1948; MA, Columbia U., 1950; MD, Cornell U., 1954. Diplomate Nat. Bd. Med. Examiners, Am. Bd. Internal Medicine. Intern St. Lukes Hosp. Ctr., NYC, 1954—56, resident in internal medicine, 1958—60; pvt. practice, 1960—2000; sr. attending physician and cardiologist emeritus St. Luke's/Roosevelt Hosp. Ctr., NYC, 2000—; clin. prof. medicine Coll. Physicians and Surgeons, Columbia U., NYC, 1994—. Cons. flight surgeon, lectr. USAF Sch. Aviation Medicine, Randolph AFB, Tex., 1956—58; physician Union Theol. Sem., N.Y.C., 1960—70, Collegiate Sch., N.Y.C., 1962—92; med. staff St. Luke's/Roosevelt Hosp. Ctr., NYC, 1960—; faculty Columbia U. Coll. Physicians & Surgeons, NYC, 1960—. Contbr. Mem. N.Y. State Senate Adv. Com. on Legis. Issues, 1985; vol. physician Airlift Project (Armenian Earthquake), 1988; bd. dirs. Am. Assn. to Aid Armenian Nat. Sanatarium in Lebanon, 1986—90, Armenian Am. Med. Philanthropic Fund, 1990—. Capt. USAF, 1956—58. Recipient Mosby Scholarship Book award for scholastic excellence, Cornell U. Med. Coll., 1954, Cert. of Merit for outstanding clin. and rsch. contbns., USAF Sch. Aviation Medicine; scholar Alumni scholar, Boston U. Med. Sch., 1951—52. Fellow: ACP, Am. Heart Assn., N.Y. Acad. Medicine; mem.: Begg Honor Soc. (hon.), Alpha Omega Alpha. Armenian Apostolic. Avocations: collecting books with illustrated prints 1930-1950, collecting American stamps and coins, American Indian sculptures, fishing, exercise. Home and Office: 1115 5th Ave New York NY 10128-0100

DERMODY, WILLIAM CHRISTIAN, biomedical consultant; b. Lompoc, Calif., Sept. 22, 1941; s. William Frederick and Ann Drusilla Dermody; m. Lynne Heringer, Sept. 19, 1964; 1 child, Christina. BS, Calif. State Polytechnic U., 1964; MS, Utah State U., 1968, PhD, 1970. Postdoctoral fellow Cornell U., Ithaca, N.Y., 1969-70; sr. rsch. physiologist Parke-Davis & Co., Ann Arbor, Mich., 1970-76; sect. head cancer markers Frederick (Md.) Cancer Rsch. Ctr., 1976-81; dir. biotech. Am. Dade, Miami, Fla., 1981-84; mktg. mgr. ICN Biomed./Miles Sci., Lyle, Ill., 1984-86; mgr. tech. resources Difco Labs., Ann Arbor, 1986-88; assoc. dir. sci. Am. Type Culture Collection, Rockville, Md., 1988-90; pres. Bio World Assoc., Gaithersburg, Md., 1990—. Adj. prof. U.Miami Cancer Ctr., 1982-84, Fla. Internat. U., Miami, 1982-84; proposal reviewer Advanced Tech. Program, NIST, Gaithersburg, 1995—; mem. steering com. Molecular Biology Ctr., Wayne State U., Detroit, 1987-88; pub. spokesperson to civic and sci. orgns. Pres. Homeowners Assn., North Potomac, Md., 1990-92. Grantee NSF, 1967-70. Mem. Alpha Zeta. Avocation: antiques. Home and Office: 405 Christopher Ave Apt 34 Gaithersburg MD 20879-3539 E-mail: cldermody@aol.com.

DERN, JOHN ANDREW, language educator; b. Southampton, Pa., May 19, 1965; s. Charles Henry and Germaine Elizabeth Dern; m. Patricia Ann Yerkes, Oct. 10, 1992; 1 child, John Robert. BA, Temple U., 1988, M in Liberal Arts, 1992; PhD, Lehigh U., 1998; cert. completion, U. London, 1992. Bus. writer Bucks County Courier Times, Levittown, Pa., 1989—90; instr. English Temple U., Phila., 1991—99; lectr. English Gwynedd-Mercy Coll., Gwynedd Valley, Pa., 1999—. Lectr. English Pa. State U., Abington, 1997—98. Author: Martians, Monsters and Madonna: Fiction and Form in the World of Martin Amis, 2000; author: (essay) The Edgar Allan Poe Rev., 2001, Pennsylvania English, 2002. Vol. Graeme Park Pa. Historic Site, Horsham, 2001—. Mem.: Pa. Coll. English Assn., Nat. Coun. Tchrs. English, Coll. English Assn., Poe Studies Assn., Modern Lang. Assn. Avocations: writing, play Highland bagpipes, movies, old time radio shows. Office: Gwynedd-Mercy College Gwynedd Valley PA 19437

DERNER, CAROL A. retired librarian; b. Evansville, Ind., May 12, 1934; d. Jacob Christopher and Catherine Loretta (Grant) Niedhammer; m. George Bendix Derner, May 4, 1957. BA in Am. Lit., Ind. U., 1956, MA in Libr. Sci., 1958. Children's libr. Monroe County Pub. Libr., Bloomington, Ind., 1958-59, Pub. Librs. of Lake County, Merrillville, Ind., 1959-60; sch. libr. Valparaiso (Ind.) Cmty. Schs., 1960-63; head popular libr. Gary (Ind.) Pub. Libr., 1963-64, head extension dept., 1964-67; head libr. Elmwood Park (Ill.) Pub. Libr., 1968-76; asst. dir. Lake County Pub. Libr., Merrillville, 1976-85, dir., 1985-99. Adj. faculty Ind. U. Sch. Libr. and Info. Sci., Bloomington, 1982-94. Contbr. articles to profl. jours. Mem. edn. com. N.W. Ind. Forum, Portage, 1992-99; mem., sec. Ednl. Referral Ctr., Highland, Ind., 1996-99. Named Woman of Yr., Merrillville Bus. and Profl. women, 1990. Mem. ALA (coun. 1983-87), Ind. Libr. Fedn. (Libr. of Yr. 1997), Exec. Coun., Altrusa Club of Ind. Dunes (pres. 1998-99). Avocations: reading, travel, antiques. Home: 2558 Shellsburg Ave Henderson NV 89052-6442 E-mail: caderner@aol.com.

DE ROCCO, ANDREW GABRIEL, physicist, educator; b. Westerly, R.I., July 31, 1929; s. Joachim and Ida Lovat De R.; 1 son, J. Lovat. BS (Merit scholar), Purdue U., 1951; MS, U. Mich., 1953, PhD (Du Pont fellow), 1956; postdoctoral fellow, NRC, 1956-57. Mem. faculty U. Mich., Ann Arbor, 1957-62; vis. prof. U. Colo., Boulder, 1962-63; prof. molecular physics U. Md., College Park, 1963-79; First Disting. vis. prof. USAF Acad., 1975-76; vis. prof. Tufts U., 1968, 69; dean of faculty and Coll. prof. natural scis. Trinity Coll., Hartford, Conn., 1979-84; pres. Denison U., Granville, Ohio, 1984-89; dir. ind. coll. challenge program Ohio Bd. Regents, Columbus, 1988-89; cons. Ohio Found. Ind. Colls., 1989-91; commr. higher edn. State of Conn., Hartford, 1991-99; sr. fellow New England Bd. of Higher Edn., 1999—, sr. moderator ednl. leadership program. Mem. staff phys. scis. lab., div. computer research and tech. NIH, 1969-79; cons. Bendix Corp., Office of Sec. Def., Inst. for Def. Analysis, IBM, Dana Found., NIH, C.A. Johnson Found., Alfred E. Sloan Found., Am. Coun. on Edn., Assn. Am. Colls., Nat. Sci. Found., North Cent. Assn. Colls. and Secondary Schs.; pres. Nat. Collegiate Honors Coun., 1977-78. Contbr. numerous articles to profl. jours., chpts. to books; editorial cons., Acad. Press, Cambridge Univ. Press, Harper & Row, Holt, Rinehart & Winston, others. Bd. dirs. Greater Washington Coun. for Clean Air, 1967-71; mem. village coun. Friendship Heights, Chevy Chase, Md., 1974-76; bd. dirs. World Affairs Ctr., Conn., Innovations, Inc., CHESLA, Conn. Student Loan Found., Edn. Commn. of the States, Ednl. Leadership Program; chmn. bd. New Eng. Bd. Higher Edn., Shaliko Theatre Co., N.Y.C.; bd. dirs. MetaArts, Sci. Ctr. Conn.; pres. North Coast Athletic Conf., 1986-88; bd govs. Rackham Sch. Grad. Studies, U. Mich.; mem. dean's adv. coun. Sch. Sci., Purdue U.; pres. bd. dirs. Chamber Music Plus, 2001-03; chmn. bd. Conn. Acad. for Edn. in Sci., Math., Tech., 2002--; bd. incorporators Hartford Sch. Art, 2003—; trustee Barbieri Endowment Italian Studies. Recipient William Raney Harper medal, 1988, Disting. Alumnus award Purdue U., 1999, Disting. Svc. award Conn. Innovations, 1999; NRC fellow, 1956-57; Am. Cancer Soc. fellow, 1956-57; NATO sr. fellow, 1964. Fellow: AAAS, Random Soc.; mem.: Conn. Acad. Sci. and Engring., State Higher Edn. Exec. Officers (exec. com.), Engring. Acad. So. New Eng. (bd. govs.), Md. Acad. Scis. (sci. coun. 1970—79), Am. Assn. Physics Tchrs. (com. internat. edn.), Biophys. Soc., Am. Phys. Soc., Am. Chem. Soc., Ohio Found. Ind. Colls. (exec. com.), The Compact for Faculty Diversity (nat. adv. com.), Omicron Delta Kappa, Sigma Pi Sigma, Delta Rho Kappa, Phi Lambda Upsilon, Sigma Xi. Office: New England Bd of Higher Edn 45 Temple Pl Boston MA 02111-1305 Fax: (617) 338-1577. E-mail: agdr731@aol.com.

DEROCCO, EMILY STOVER, federal agency administrator; BA Journalism, Pa. State U.; JD, Georgetown U., 1982. Bar: D.C. 1983. Exec. dir. Nat. Assn. State Workforce Agys.; asst. sec. employment and tng. adminstrn. U.S. Dept. Labor, Washington, 2001—. Office: US Dept Labor 200 Constitution Ave NW Washington DC 20210

DEROCHE, KATHLEEN SAMROW, elementary educator, mathematics consultant; b. De Ridder, La., Sept. 29, 1952; d. Joseph Earl and Thekla Agnes (Meyer) Samrow; m. Nolan Joseph Deroche Jr., Aug. 7, 1971; children: Christopher, Juanita, Matthew, Sarah. BS in Elem. Edn., Nicholls State U., 1978, MEd, 1996. Cert. elem. edn. La., spl. edn. La., supr. La. Elem. sch. tchr. St. James Pub. Schs., Lutcher, La., 1977—, asst. principal, 2002—. Coord. St. James River Camp, 2002—; tutor, Gramercy, La., 1973—75, Gramercy, 2000—01; curriculum writer Nicholls State U. Region 3, Thibodaux, La., 1996—98; Fulbright Meml. tchr., Japan, 1998. Contbr. articles to profl. jours. Lectr. family life com. mem. St. Joseph Ch., Paulina, La., 1996-97; mem. quilt com., maypole coord. Centennial Com., Gramercy, Lutcher, 1993, 95; team leader La. Alliance Sch. Reform. Phys. edn. grantee STAR Enterprises, Convent, La., 1992, math. edn. grantee, 1993, sci. edn. grantee, 1994; recipient Presdl. Excellence award sci. & math. NSF, 1994, Making the Grade Tchr. award Freeport/McMoran & WVUE-TV, New Orleans, 1995, Excellence in Math Tchg. award La. Assn. Tchrs. Math., Baton Rouge, La., 1993, Greater New Orleans Math. Tchrs., 1993. Mem. Nat. Coun. Tchrs. Math. (cons. 1992—), La. Assn. Educators, St. James hist. Soc. (Hist. award 1994, ednl. chairperson 1985—), Phi Delta Kappa, Delta Kappa Gamma (v.p., pres. 1990-94), Phi Kappa Phi. Roman Catholic. Avocations: sewing, craftmaking, reading, quilting. Home: 2861 Admirals Landing St Paulina LA 70763-2504 Office: Gramercy Elem Sch PO Box 1518 Gramercy LA 70052-1518

DE ROCHE, LINDA LEE, English language educator; b. South Bend, Ind., Mar. 31, 1952; d. William Joseph and Lois May (Wilburn) Claycomb; m. John David Pelzer, Mar. 16, 1974 (dec. Apr. 1997), m. Stéphane De Roche, July 5, 2001. BA, Ball State U., 1974; MA, U. Notre Dame, 1976, PhD, 1984. Asst. prof. English Ball State U., Muncie, 1980-82, 83-88; prof. English Wesley Coll., Dover, Del., 1988—. Author: Mary Higgins Clark, 1995, Erich Segal, 1997, Student Companion to F. Scott Fitzgerald, 2000, Revisiting Mary Higgins Clark, 2003. Mem. Del. Humanities Coun., Wilmington, 1990-95. Collaborative Rsch. grantee Fulbright Commn., Eng., 1986. Mem. MLA, N.E. MLA. Avocations: travel, herb gardening, needlework. Office: Wesley Coll 120 N State St Dover DE 19901-3835 E-mail: derochli@wesley.edu.

DE ROCHER, DENISE D. social sciences educator; b. Spokane, Wash., Mar. 3, 1961; d. Robert Earl Oehlschlaeger and Gay Marie DeRusha; 1 child, Danelle Marie Black. BA in English Lit., Lewis Clark State Coll., 1989; MA in Polit. Sci., Wash. State U., 1992. Cert. tchr. Mont., Idaho. H.S. tchr. White Pine Sch. Dist., Deary, Idaho, 1992—94, Belt Sch. Dist., Mont., 1996—97; bookkeeper Sleeping Lady Retreat, Leavenworth, Wash., 1999—2000; H.S. tchr. White Pine Sch. Dist., Deary, Idaho, 2000—01. Mem.: Acad. Polit. Sci., Nat. Dem. Party, Art Mus. Women, Holocaust Meml. Mus. Democrat. Judaism. Avocation: international issues: politics, economics, social issues. Home: 635 SE Side St Pullman WA 99163 Office: White Pine Sch Dist 371 S Main St Troy ID 83871

DE ROE DEVON, The Marchioness See GERRINGER, ELIZABETH

DE ROEST, JAN MARIE, mental health counselor; b. Seattle, Wash., Oct. 9, 1965; d. Stanley Robert and Glenna Muriel (Bennett) Hagedorn; m. Gary Eugene De Roest, Apr. 26, 1987. BS in Microbiology, Oreg. State U., 1987; MA in Counseling Psychology, Lewis and Clark Coll., 1996; postgrad., Pacific U., 2001—. Med. asst. Met. Clinic, Portland, Oreg., 1987-89; rsch. asst. Oreg. Health Sci. U., Portland, 1989-90; med. asst. Portland Clinic, 1991-92; rsch. asst. VA Med. Ctr., Portland, 1992-93; med. asst. Neighborhood Health Clinic, Portland, 1995-96, master's intern, 1995-96, Delaunay Family of Svcs., Portland, 1995-96; geriatric mental health specialist Unity, Inc., Portland, 1997-2001. Mem.: APA, Oreg. Gerontol. Assn., Oreg. Psychol. Assn., Am. Soc. Aging, Am. Mental Health Counseling Assn., Am. Aging and Devel. Assn., Am. Counseling Assn., Lewis and Clark Alumni Assn. Democrat. Roman Catholic. E-mail: jderoest@attbi.com.

DERON, EDWARD MICHAEL, lawyer; b. Detroit, Dec. 18, 1945; m. Jana Lene Berlenbach, Aug. 12, 1977. BS, Wayne State U., 1968, JD cum laude, 1972; LLM in Taxation, NYU, 1973. Bar: Mich. 1972, U.S. Ct. Appeals (6th cir.) 1973, U.S. Tax Ct. 1974. Assoc. Evans & Luptak, Detroit, 1973-79, ptnr., 1980—. Contbr. chpt. to book. With U.S. Army, 1969-71, ETO, Germany. Mem.: ABA, Nat. Com. on Planned Giving, Fin. and Estate Planning Coun. Met. Detroit, Detroit Met. Bar Assn. (co-chmn. taxation com. 1984—86), Mich. Bar Assn. (taxation sect., chmn. estates and trusts com. 1994—96, taxation sect. coun. 1996—99, editor Mich. Tax Lawyer 1998—99, sec. 1999—2000, treas. 2000—01, vice-chmn. 2001—02, chmn. 2002—03), KC, Rotary, Detroit Athletic Club. Office: Evans & Luptak 7457 Franklin Rd Ste 250 Bloomfield Hills MI 48301 also: 18720 Mack Ave Ste 220 Grosse Pointe Farms MI 48236 E-mail: ederon@evansluptak.com.

DEROSA, DAVID FRANCIS, finance educator, trading company executive; b. Glen Ridge, NJ, July 20, 1950; s. Frank J. and Michelle A. DeRosa; m. Sibylle Schubach, May 23, 1986; children: Julia, Francesca. AB in Econs., U. Chgo., 1972, PhD in Fin. and Econs., 1978. Dir. fgn. exch. Swiss Bank Corp., N.Y.C., 1993-96; lectr. in fin. U. Chgo. Grad. Sch. Bus., 1995-96; mng. ptnr. Quadrangle Investments, Greenwich, Conn., 1996-97; pres. DeRosa Rsch. and Trading, New Canaan, Conn., 1997—; dir. MidWest ISO, 1998—. Adj. prof. fin. Yale U. Sch. Mgmt., New Haven, 1996—; fellow Yale Ctr. for Internat. Fin.; pres., owner Commodity Trading Advisor, 1997—; bd. dirs. Rubicon Fund Mgmt., BlueCrest Capital Internat.; rschr., cons., spkr. in field. Author: Options on Foreign Exchange, 1992, 2nd edit., 1999, Managing Foreign Exchange Risk, 1996, Currency Directives, 1998, In Defense of Free Capital Markets-The Case Against a New International Financial Architecture, 2001; contbr. articles to profl. jours. Avocation: financial columnist. E-mail: derosa@derosa-research.com.

DE ROSA, EOLO, otolaryngologist; b. Balt., 1923; s. Ulysses and Maryann (Grieco) De R.; m. Loraine Holt, June 4, 1961 (wid. Aug. 1983); m. Joyce Johnson, May 18, 1986. BS, Harvard U., 1945; MD, U. Montreal, 1951. Diplomate Am. Bd. Otolaryngology. Intern U. Montreal, 1950-51; resident in internal medicine Beverly Hosp., 1951-52; resident in surgery Luth. Med. Ctr., N.Y.C., 1967-68; resident in otolaryngology St. Luke's Hosp., N.Y.C., 1968-71; clin. asst. prof. otolaryngology Brown U., Providence, 1990; chief ENT dept. VA Med. Ctr., Providence, 1990—. Med. examiner Social Security Adminstrn. Fellow Am. Bd. Otolaryngology, Am. Coll. Plastic and Facial Surgery, Am. Coll. Surgeons, Mass. Med. Soc.; mem. New Eng. Otolaryngol. Soc. Mem. Soc. Of Friends. Office: 22 Paton Rd Shrewsbury MA 01545-5623

DEROSA, FRANCIS DOMINIC, chemical company executive; b. Seneca Falls, N.Y., Feb. 26, 1936; s. Frank and Frances (Bruno) DeR.; m. Vivian DeRosa, Oct. 24, 1959; children: Kevin, Marc, Terri. Student, Rochester Inst. Tech., 1959-61; BS, MBA, Chadwick U.; PhD, City U. L.A. Cert. med. photographer. CEO Advance Paper & Equipment Supply Inc., Mesa, Ariz., 1974—, Pottery Plus Ltd., Mesa, 1984—, Advance Tool Supply Inc., Mesa, 1989-94. Vice chmn. bd. adjustments City of Mesa, 1983-89, bd. dirs. dept. parks and recreation, 1983-86; pres. Christ the King Mens Club, 1983-84; bd. dirs. Mesa C. of C., 1983-88. Mem. Ariz. Sanitary Supply Assn. (pres. 1983-84), Internat. Sanitary Supply Assn. (coord. Ariz. chpt. 1994-96, sec. bd. 1994-96), Gilbert, Ariz. C. of C. (bd. dirs., v.p. 1992-96, pres. 1996-97, sec. internat. bd. 1994-96), Gilbert Heights Owners Assn. (pres. 1992-93), Mesa Country Club, Calif. Yacht Club, Santa Monica (Calif.) Yacht Club, Rotary (pres. Mesa Sunrise chpt. 1987-88, Paul Harris fellow 1988), Masons (32 degree, pres. 1973), Sons of Italy (pres. 1983-84), Shriners. Avocations: music,

physical fitness, sailing, golf. Home: 513 E Horseshoe Ave Gilbert AZ 85296-1705 Office: Advance Paper & Maintenance Supply Inc 33 W Broadway Mesa AZ 85210-1505 E-mail: frank26phd@aol.com.

DE ROSA, GUY PAUL, orthopedic surgery educator; b. Napoleon, Ohio, Oct. 25, 1939; married. BS, Notre Dame U., 1961; MD, Ind. U., 1965. Diplomate Am. Bd. Orthopedic Surgery. Resident in gen. surgery Sch. Medicine, Ind. U., Indpls., 1965—66, resident in orthopedic surgery, 1966—70; fellow in pediat. orthopedics Hosp. for Sick Children, London, 1969—70; asst. prof. orthopedic surgery Sch. Medicine, Ind. U., Indpls., 1970—76, assoc. prof., 1976—82, dir. undergrad. edn. dept. orthopedic surgery, 1972—, chief neuromuscular disease, 1972—, coord. Garceau-Wayu Lectureships dept. orthopedic surgery, 1975—, dir. Cerebral Palsy Clinic, 1978—88, orthopedic cons. Hemophilia Clinic, 1978—91, prof. orthopedic surgery, 1981—, orthopedic cons. Rheumato-Orthopedic Clinic, 1984—, chmn. dept. orthopedic surgery, 1986—95; exec. dir. Am. Bd. Orthopaedic Surgery, Chapel Hill. Attending physician Wishard Meml. Hosp., Indpls., 1970—95, Ind. U. Med. Ctr., Indpls., 1970—95, James Whitcomb Riley Hosp. for Children, Indpls., 1970—95; coord. Ctrl. Ind. and So. Ind. State Bd. Health Programs, Scoliosis and Sch. Screening, 1977; mem. orthop. surgery steering com. Children's Cancer Study Group, 1990; mem. residency rev. com. for orthop. surgery Accreditation Coun. for Grad. Med. Edn., 1990—; vis. prof. Children's Hosp., Columbus, Ohio, 1977, St. Joseph Hosp., Ft. Wayne, Ind., 1977, Miami Valley Hosp., Dayton, Ohio, 1978, Dayton, 82, Dayton, 85, Dayton, 86, Deaconess Hosp., Evansville, Ind., 1980, Bloomington (Ind.) Hosp., 1982, U. Tex., Galveston, 1982, U. Mo. Med. Ctr., Columbia, 1983, Southwestern Mich. Area Health Edn. Ctr., Kalamazoo, 1985, Newington (Conn.) Children's Hosp., 1988, Children's Hosp. Med. Ctr., Akron, Ohio, 1992; and numerous others; active Hemophilia Med. Adv. Coun., 1978—; presenter in field. Contbr. articles. Bd. dirs. United Cerebral Palsy, 1973—85, Hemophilia Found., 1978—, New Hope of Ind., 1984—86, mem. long range planning com., 1984—85, mem. task force on serving brain injured, 1988; bd. dirs. Ind. Found. Hand Surg. Rsch. and Edn., 1989—95; mem. adv. bd. Head Injury Found., 1995, Children's Limb Found., 1992—; mem. pub. rels. and promotion com. Ind. Gov.'s Coun. on Phys. Fitness and Sports Medicine, 1986—92, mem. promotion com., 1988—92; dir. State of Ind. Orthop. Rsch. and Edn. Found., 1993, bd. trustees, 1994. Maj. USAF, 1970—72. Recipient Ensminger award for rsch. in trauma, 1967, Willis Gatch award, 1968; grantee grantee in field. Mem.: 20th Century Orthop. Assn., Internat. Soc. Orthop. Surgery and Traumatology, Scoliosis Rsch. Soc. (mem. edn. com. 1985—), Russell Hibbs Soc., Pediat. Orthop. Soc. N.Am. (mem. com. on fellowships 1986—92, bd. dirs. 1990—92, 2d v.p. 1994, 1st v.p. 1995, pres. 1996), Mid-Am. Orthop. Assn. (chmn. program com. 1986—87, bd. dirs. 1986—, sec. 1990—93, 2d v.p. 1993—94, 1st v.p. 1994—), Marion County Med. Soc., Acad. Orthop. Soc. (mem. undergrad. edn. com. 1983—87), Clin. Orthop. Soc., Assn. Orthop. Chmn., Ind. State Med. Soc., Ind. Orthop. Soc. (mem. exec. com. 1986—95), Am. Orthop. Foot and Ankle Soc. (mem. com. biomechanics 1982—84, mem. program com. 1985—), Am. Acad. Cerebral Palsy and Devel. Medicine, Am. Acad. Orthop. Surgeons (mem. com. undergrad. edn. 1976—83, chmn. 1979—83, mem. com. pediat. orthopedics 1988—94, mem. subcom. on spine 1990, mem. subcom. on pediats. program com. 1992, mem. coun. clin. resources 1993—94), Am. Acad. Pediats., Am. Fracture Assn. (Wellmerling award 1982), Am. Orthop. Assn. (mem. nominating com. 1988—89, del.-at-large exec. com. 1988—89, mem. com. on N.Am. traveling fellowship 1989—93, mem. com. planning and devel. 1991—, 2d pres.-elect 1994—), AMA, Am. Bd. Orthopedic Surgery (oral examiner 1983—, site investigator residency rev. com. 1983—, mem. credentials com. 1990—93, bd. dirs. 1990—, mem. oral examinations com. 1990—, mem. grad. edn. com. 1990—, mem. oral recert. examination com. 1992—93, mem. practice audit com. 1992—93, rep. alt. 1992—93, ACS adv. coun. 1992—94, sec. 1993—94, mem. cert. renewal com. 1993—94, mem. fin. com. 1993—94, mem. exec. com. 1993—94, vice chmn. residency rev. com. 1994—, chmn. 1995—97), Spectators Orthop. Letters Club, Little Orthop. Club, Orthop. Letters Club, Alpha Epsilon Delta, Alpha Omega Alpha. Office: Am Bd Orthopedic Surgery 400 Silver Cedar Ct Chapel Hill NC 27514-1585

DE ROSA, WILLIAM THOMAS, internist, hematologist, oncologist; b. Newark, Nov. 1, 1953; DO, Kirksville Coll. Osteo., 1980. Diplomate Am. Bd. Internal Medicine, Am. Bd. Hematology, Am. Bd. Oncology. Intern USPHS Hosp., Staten Island, N.Y., 1980-81; resident in internal medicine Morristown (N.J.) Meml. Hosp., 1983-85; fellow in hematol. oncology Yale U. Sch. Medicine, New Haven, 1985-88; pvt. practice Morristown. Mem. staff Morristown Meml. Hosp. Fellow Am. Coll. Physicians; mem. Am. Soc. Hematology, Am. Soc. Clin. Oncology. Office: Carol G Simon Cancer Ctr PO Box 1089 100 Madison Ave Morristown NJ 07960-6136 E-mail: william.derosa@ahsys.org.

DE ROSE, SANDRA MICHELE, psychotherapist, educator, supervisor, administrator; b. Beacon, N.Y. d. Michael Joseph Borrell and Mabel Adelaide Edic Sloane; m. James Joseph De Rose, June 28, 1964 (div. 1977); children: Stacey Marie, Harrison Marquisa. Diploma in nursing, St. Luke's Hosp., 1964; BA in Child and Community Psychology, Albertus Magnus Coll., 1983; MS in Counseling Psychology with honors, Century U., 1986, PhD in Counseling Psychology with honors, 1987. Gen. duty float nurse St. Luke's Hosp., Newburgh, N.Y., 1964-65; pvt. practice New Haven, 1975—; supr. nurses Craig House Hosp., Beacon, N.Y., 1986-94; dir. staff devel., team dir. divsn. outpatient treatment svc. Conn. Mental Health Ctr., New Haven, 1986-94; dir. edn., 1994-95; clin. instr. Sch. Nursing Yale U., New Haven, 1979-84, clin. instr. dept. psychiatry, 1989-96; dir. edn. outpatient divsn. Conn. Mental Health Ctr., New Haven, 1994-95. Clin. dir. Comprehensive Psychiat. Care, Norwich, Colchester and Willimantic, Conn., 1994-96; group practice Comprehensive Psychiat. Care, Norwich, Conn., 1995-2003, Alternative Paths, Yalesville, Conn., 1995-97. Mem. AAUW, ANA (cert.), Conn. Nurses Assn., Conn. Soc. Nurse Psychotherapists, Assn. for Advancement Philosophy and Psychiatry, New Haven C. of C., Sigma Theta Tau, Delta Mu, Alpha Sigma Lambda. Avocations: music, theater, antiques, interior design/architecture, traveling. Office: 5210 Prospect St New Haven CT 06511-2186 also: 200 W Town St Norwich CT 06360-2112

DEROSIER, ARTHUR HENRY, JR., historian; b. Norwich, Conn., Feb. 18, 1931; s. Arthur Henry and Rose (Raymond) DeR.; m. Linda Preston Scott, Dec. 26, 1979; children: Deborah Ann, Marsha Carol, Brett Preston Scott, Melissa Estelle. BS, U. So. Miss., 1953; MA, U. S.C., 1955, PhD, 1959. Asst. prof. history The Citadel, 1956—57, Converse Coll., Spartanburg, SC, 1957—59; asst. prof. U. So. Miss., 1959-60, assoc. prof., 1960-64, prof., 1964-65; assoc. prof. history U. Okla., 1965-67, asst. dean, Grad. Coll., 1966-67; dean Grad. Sch., prof. history East Tenn. State U., Johnson City, 1967-72, v.p. for adminstrn., 1972-74; vice chancellor for acad. affairs, prof. history U. Miss., 1974-76, vice chancellor, 1976-77; pres. East Tenn. State U., 1977-80, Coll. of Idaho, Caldwell, 1980-87, Rocky Mountain Coll., Billings, Mont., 1987—2002; historian We. Heritage Ctr., Billings, 2002—, CEO and sr. fellow, 2002—. Pres. Ind. Colls. of Mont., 1992-2002; vis. prof. history U. Mass., summer 1964; ednl. TV series on Am. history, 1966-72; bd. dirs. Rocky Mountain Bank. Author: Through the South with a Union Soldier, 1969, The Removal of the Choctaw Indians, 1970, (with others) Four Centuries of Southern Indians, 1975, Forked Tongues and Broken Treaties, 1975, Appalachia: Family Traditions in Transition, 1975, Pioneer Trails West, 1985, Institutional Revival: Case Histories, 1986; contbr. articles to hist. jours. Active numerous Indian philanthropies; commr. U.S. Senate Commn. Oneline Chile Protection, 1999—2001; mem. Idaho Commn. on Pardons and Parole, 1985—87; mem. adv. com. on apprenticeship U.S. Dept. of Labor, 2003—; bd. dirs. Deaconess Med. Ctr., 1988—92. With1952 USAF, 1948. So. fellow, 1958; Am. Philos. Soc. grantee, 1964 Mem. Am. Hist. Assn., Orgn. Am. Historians, So. Hist. Assn., Western Hist. Assn., Nat. Assn. Ind. Colls. and Univs. (fin. com. higher edn. 1990-97), Coun. Ind. Colls., Western Ind. Colls. Fund, Nat. Assn. Sch. and Coll. of United Meth. Ch. (chmn. com. on internat. edn. 1993-96, bd. dirs. 1994-97), Phi Beta Kappa. Home: 1809 Mulberry Dr Billings MT 59102-0601 Office: Western Heritage Ctr 2822 Montana Ave Billings MT 59101 E-mail: derosier@rocky.edu. *I continue to believe in higher education and note again that a college is a place where educational opportunities are available for all who treasure learning. The testing, challenging, and expanding of the mind is our primary responsibility, and we should be graded on how successfully we complete that task. A college is also an integral part of society. It helps us develop and clarify ideals and goals; it challenges us to develop a civilized set of principles; and it affords us an opportunity to test those principles and goals in the greater society. And it must teach us to approach life with a sense of humor. We are human: we are capable of significant achievements and bumbling failures. An educated person learns to live with both, allowing success and failure to meet each other with good grace and a smile.*

DE ROSIER, DAVID JOHN, biophysicist, educator; b. Milw., Feb. 22, 1939; s. Herman Francis and Adell Marie De Rosier; children: Elizabeth Anne, Charles David. BS, U. Chgo., 1961, PhD, 1965. Postdoctoral fellow Lab. Molecular Biology, Cambridge, England, 1965-69; asst. prof. chemistry U. Tex., Austin, 1968-72, assoc. prof., 1972-73; assoc. prof. physics Brandeis U., Waltham, Mass., 1973-78, prof., 1978-79, prof. biology, 1979—, chmn. grad. program biophysics, 1978-79, 80-83, chmn. dept. biology, 1984-87, Abraham S. and Gertrude Burg prof. life scis., 1993—. Mem. study sci. NIH, 1983-86; chmn. Gordon Rsch. Conf., 1989; Bacaner rsch. lectr. U. Minn., 1990, Tom Garrar lectr., 1993; Blakeslee lectr. Smith Coll., 1996; Schmidt lectr. Weizmann Inst., 1998; dir. W.M. Keck Inst. for Cellular Visualization; Miller vis. prof. U. Calif., Berkeley. Assoc. editor Jour. Molecular Biology, 1988-93; mem. editl. bd. Jour. Cell Biology, 1988-91, 96-99, Current Opinion in Structural Biology, 1991—, Biophys. Jour., 1999-2002. Coordinator Mason-Rice Community Sch., Newton, Mass., 1975-77. Recipient Merit award, NIH, 1991, Alexander Hollaender award, Nat. Acad. Scis., 2001; fellow, Air Force Office Sci. Rsch., 1965, Am. Cancer Soc., 1966, NSF, 1967, Guggenheim Found., 1987; grantee, NIH, 1970—. Fellow: AAAS, Biophys. Soc. (coun., exec. bd., Elizabeth Robert Cole award 1993), Am. Soc. Microbiology (divsn. J lectr. 2000); mem.: Nat. Acad. Scis., Am. Acad. Arts and Scis., Am. Soc. Cell Biologists, Microscopic Soc. Am. Home: 27 Chesterfield Rd Waltham MA 02454-2343 Office: Brandeis U MS029 Rosenstiel Ctr Waltham MA 02465 E-mail: derosier@brandeis.edu.

DE ROSSET, WILLIAM S. physicist; b. Chgo., Apr. 1, 1942; s. Armand John and Ruth (Bailey) de Rosset; m. Marian Marian Rose Kerr, June 26, 1971; children: William K., Lauren E., Armand J. BA in Physics, Johns Hopkins U., 1964; MS in Physics, U. Ill., 1966, PhD in Physics, 1970. Chief lethal mechanisms br. Army Rsch. Lab., Aberdeen Proving Ground, Md., 1985—99, phys. scientist, 1999—. Home: 214 Hemlock Ln Aberdeen MD 21001-2405

DE ROSSI, JULIE ANNE, music promoter, entrepreneur, freelance editor, retail consultant; b. Houston, Jan. 4, 1960; d. Robert B. and Dorothy Gean (Weempe) Hyde; 1 child: Aaron James Hehr. Student, U. St. Thomas, Houston, 1977, Portland C.C., The Dalles, Oreg., 1984-85; AA, North Seattle C.C., 1987. Cert. window fashions profl. assoc., specialist, master Window Fashions Cert. Program. Prin., CEO Interiors by JAG, Houston, 1990—; owner Motherland Entertainment Group, www.motherland.cc, 2001—. Mem. design coun. Mus. Fine Arts, Houston; mem. Friends of AFRO POP, North Am. World Music Coalition, kaft.org. Bus. ptnr. Hough Elem. Found. and Sch.; patron Pilchuck Glass Sch. Mem. NAFE, Window Fashions Edn. and Design Resource Network, Greater Vancouver C. of C. (liaison bus. and edn. partnership 1992—, amb. 1993-95), Inst. Managerial and Profl. Women. Avocations: furniture and landscape design, jewelry design, art collecting, travel, music. E-mail: survivorgal@hotmail.com.

DEROUCHEY, BEVERLY JEAN, investment company executive; b. Kenosha, Wis., Sept. 3, 1958; d. Dean Rodney and Doris May (Rasch) DeR. BS in Bus. Mgmt., U. Wis., 1982; MBA in Fin., Cornell U., 1984. Chartered fin. analyst, 1993; lic. NASD-series 2-7-63-65. Acctg. asst. Kenosha (Wis.)-News Pub. Corp., 1979-81; polit. intern Office of Congressman Les Aspin, Racine, Wis., 1982; teaching asst. Cornell U., Ithaca, N.Y., 1983; audit intern Coopers and Lybrand, Syracuse, N.Y., 1983; staff cons. Peterson & Co., N.Y.C., 1984-86; assoc. Salomon Bros., N.Y.C., 1986-90, v.p., 1991; assoc. investment officer Dartmouth Coll., Hanover, N.H., 1992-94; v.p., dir. asset allocation CTC Consulting, Portland, Oreg., 1995; investment mgr. Constellation Investments, Inc., Balt., 1996-97; dir. rsch. Paradigm Cons. Svcs. LLC, Quechee VT. and Clifton NJ., 1998-2000; founder, mng. dir. Long Trail Capital LLC, Quechee, Vt., 2000—. Alumni phonathons Cornell U., Ithaca, N.Y. and N.Y.C., 1982-87, co-chair new donor com., 1985-87; active Rep. Senatorial Inner Circle. Cornell U. scholar, 1982-84, BPW scholar, 1977, 82-83, AAUW scholar, 1981. Mem. Am. Film Inst., N.Y. Soc. of Security Analysts, Assn. for Investment Mgmt. and Rsch., Bus. and Profl. Women (bd. dirs. 1991-92), Film Soc. Lincoln Ctr., Quechee (Vt.)-Lakes Landowners' Assn. Republican. Lutheran. Avocations: tennis, golf, travel, writing. Home: PO Box 1309 Quechee VT 05059-1309 E-mail: bderouchey@hotmail.com.

DEROUIN, JAMES GILBERT, lawyer; b. Eau Claire, Wis., July 11, 1944; BA cum laude, U. Wis., 1967, JD, 1968. Bar: Wis. 1968, Ariz. 1986. Ptnr. Steptoe & Johnson LLC, Phoenix, Ariz.; atty. Meyer, Hendricks, Victor, Osbonn & Maledon, Phoenix, Ariz.; ptnr. Dewitt, Ross & Stevens, Madison, Wis. Polychlorinatedbyphenol chair Wis. Dept. Natural Resources, 1976-78; mem. spl. com. on solid waste mgmt. Wis. Legis. Coun., 1976-79, ad hoc com. on hazardous waste mgmt., 1980-82, spl. com. on groundwater mgmt.; mem. Wis. Dept. Nat. Resources Metallic Mining Coun., 1978-85; chair Phoenix Environ. Quality Commn., 1986, Phoenix Environ. Quality Com., 1989-92; mem. Ariz. Govs. Regulatory Review Coun. 1986—; co-chair Ariz. Dept. Environ. Quality/Ariz. Dept. Water Resources Groundwater Task Force, 1996-97; mem. nat. adv. coun. superfun subcom. EPA. Chair. State Bar Ariz. (environ. and nat. resources law sect. 1989-90). Office: 201 E Washington St # 1600 Phoenix AZ 85004-2382

DEROUSIE, CHARLES STUART, lawyer; b. Adrian, Mich., May 24, 1947; s. Stuart J. and Helia I. (Juntunen) DeR.; m. Patricia Jean Fetzer, May 31, 1969; children: Jennifer, Jason. BA magna cum laude, Oakland U., 1969; JD magna cum laude, U. Mich., 1973. Bar: Ohio, 1973, U.S. Dist. Ct. (so. dist.) Ohio 1974. Ptnr. Vorys, Sater, Seymour and Pease, LLP, Columbus, Ohio, 1973—. Trustee Ballet Met., Inc., Columbus, 1978-90, pres., 1986-88; trustee Gladden Community House, Columbus, 1975-81, pres., 1979-81; mem. Children's Hosp. Devel. Bd., Columbus, 1987—, pres. 1995-96; trustee Elder Choices of Ctrl. Ohio, Columbus, 1989-95, Heritage Day Health Ctrs., Columbus, 1992-98. Fellow Columbus Bar Found.; mem. ABA, Am. Health Lawyers Assn., Columbus Bar Assn., Ohio Bar Assn., Order of Coif. Office: Vorys Sater Seymour and Pease LLP PO Box 1008 52 E Gay St Columbus OH 43215-3161

DEROUX, DANIEL GRADY, artist; b. Juneau, Alaska, Oct. 25, 1951; s. Harold Edward DeRoux and Mary Elizabeth (Rice) Quist; m. JoAnn Marie Grady, Aug. 16, 1992; children: Eric, Katie. Curator of exhibits Alaska State Mus., Juneau, 1978-79; set designer Perseverance Theatre, Douglas, Alaska, 1988-91; owner Gallery Still Russian and Alaskan Contemporary Art, Juneau, 1991-92. Artist, 1971—. Solo exhbns. include Natsoulas/Novelozo Gallery, Davis, Calif., 1989, Czar's Summer Palace, St. Petersberg, Russia, 1992, Somar Gallery, San Francisco, 1992, Mercer-Hood Gallery, Seattle, 1994, Ft. Mason Ctr., San Francisco, 1995; exhibited in group shows at Fourth Florence Biennale Exhibit of Contemporary Art, Florence, Italy, 2003, 1st Western States Arts Found. Nat., 1979. Recipient Gold medal for most accomplished artist, Bronze medal in Mixed Media, L.A. Internat. Art Competition, 1984, Third Place award N.Y. Internat. Art Competition, 1988; named Best of Show, Calgene West Coast Art Competition, Calif., 1988. Home: 19191 Randall Rd Juneau AK 99801-8209

DEROW, PETER ALFRED, publishing company executive; b. Boston, Apr. 18, 1940; s. Harry A. and Ruth D. (Dimond) Derow; m. Ruth C. Joffe, June 13, 1965; children: Jonathan, Polly, James. BA cum laude, Harvard U., 1963, MBA, 1965. Pres. Newsweek, Inc., N.Y.C., 1976-77; sr. v.p., dir. CBS, Inc., N.Y.C., 1977-78; v.p., dir. The Washington Post, 1978-81; chmn. Newsweek, Inc., N.Y.C., 1978-81; pres. CBS Pub. Group, N.Y.C., 1981-86; v.p. CBS, Inc., N.Y.C., 1981-86; pres. Goldmark Industries, N.Y.C., 1987-88; sr. v.p. Reed Pub. USA, Stamford, Conn. and Newton, Mass., 1988; pres. Instl. Investor, Inc., N.Y.C., 1988-97; dir. 101 Comm., LLC, Chatsworth, Calif., 1999—; CACI, Inc., Arlington, Va., 2000—. Dir. GlobalSpec, Troy, NY, 1999—, Mediamap, Inc., Watertown, Mass., 2000—, Netscan, Inc., Falls Church, Va., 2000—, Moore Med., Inc., New Britain, Conn., 2001—. Author: Successful Publishing on Campus, 1966; mem. editorial bd. Harvard Bus. Rev., 1981-95. Avocations: tennis, sculling, reading, bicycling. Home: PO Box 534 Bedford NY 10506-0534 Office: 19th Fl 6 E 43rd St New York NY 10017 Fax: (212) 286-8046. E-mail: derow@mindspring.com.

DERR, ALLEN R. lawyer; b. Sandpoint, Idaho, Apr. 5, 1928; BA in Journalism, U. Idaho, 1951, JD, 1959; student, U. Ill., 1955-56. Bar: Idaho 1959, U.S. Dist. Ct. Idaho 1959, U.S. Cir. Ct. (9th cir.) 1964, U.S. Supreme Ct. 1971. Asst. atty. gen. State of Idaho, 1959-60; pvt. practice Boise, 1960—. Spkr., lectr., master ceremonies, radio and TV panelist; chair info. com. Idaho State Bar, 1992—, founder Citizen's Law Acad. Editor and asst. exec. dir. Tau Kappa Epsilon Nat. Mag.; contbr. articles to profl. jours. Adv. bd. U. Idaho Law Sch.; past state pres. Young Dem. Club for Idaho. Recipient Disting. Svc. award, Tau Kappa Epsilon, 1955; named Alumnus of Yr. T.K.E., 1999, Idaho Freedom award ACLU, 2002, Professionalism award Idaho State Bar, 2002. Mem.: Idaho Citizen's Law Acad., Am. Legion (past comdr.), Idaho State Bar Assn. (Professionalism award 2002), Idaho Trial Lawyers Assn. (founder), Idaho Press Club (bd. dirs.). Achievements include won historic Supreme Court decision in Reed v. Reed recognizing discrimination against women for the first time; featured in book Days of Destiny by James McPherson. Home: Penthouse 1005 199 N Capitol Blvd Boise ID 83702-5982 Office: PO Box 1006 Boise ID 83701-1006

DERR, BRUCE WOODS, information technology executive; b. Williamsport, Pa., Dec. 12, 1948; s. Harold Schmucker Jr. and Shirley Anne DeHaas; m. Susan S. Wadley, Dec. 28, 1971 (div. Mar. 1989); children: Shona Snow, Laura Woods; m. Catherine Scott-Derr, Aug. 3, 1991. BA, Syracuse (N.Y.) U., 1970, MA, 1973, PhD, 1979. Anthropology prof. Eisenhower Coll., Seneca Falls, 1978-82, Syracuse (N.Y.) U., 1976-88, info. studies prof., 1985-94, sr. programmer, analyst, 1987-89, info. ctr. mgr., 1989-93, lead UNIX cons., 1993-95; systems engring. mgr. Applied Theory Comms., Syracuse, 1995-98; sr. tech. project mgr. Emory U., Atlanta, 1998—2001; assoc. dir. info. tech. AtheroGenics, Inc., Atlanta, 2001—. Cons. Support Technologies, Inc., Atlanta, 1998. Author: The Growing Abundance of Food and Poverty in a North Indian Village, 1979. Bd. dirs. Open Hand Theatre, Syracuse, 1994—96, Glens at Powers Ferry Homeowners Assn., 2002—. Mem. IEEE, Nat. Coun. of Univ. Rsch. Adminstrs. (ERA V program com. 1999, region III ERA com. 1999, pres.'s coun. tech. 2000), Fed. Demonstration Partnership, Inst. Validation Studies, Drug Info. Assn. Episcopalian. Avocations: reading, body building, driving, music, movies. Office: AtheroGenics Inc 8995 Westside Pkwy Alpharetta GA 30004 E-mail: bderr@atherogenics.com.

DERR, THOMAS SIEGER, religion educator; b. Boston, June 18, 1931; s. Thomas Sieger and Mary Ferguson (Sebring) D.; children: Peter Bulkeley, Laura Seely, Mary Williams, Erin Vincent, Philip Henry; m. Linda Vincent, Feb. 14, 1986. AB, Harvard U., 1953; MDiv, Union Theol. Sem., 1956; PhD, Columbia U., 1972. Ordained to ministry, United Ch. of Christ, 1956. Researcher World Council Chs., 1961-62; asst. chaplain Stanford U., Calif., 1956-59, Smith Coll., Northampton, Mass., 1963-65, asst. prof. religion, 1965-71, assoc. prof., 1972-77, prof., 1977—. Cons. World Coun. Chs., 1965—; dir. Inst. on Religion in Pub. Life, N.Y.C.; mem. complemental faculty Rush Med. Coll., Chgo., 1979-84. Author: The Political Thought of the Ecumenical Movement, 1972, Ecology and Human Need, 1975, Church, State and Politics, 1981, Barriers to Ecumenism: The Holy See and the World Council of Churches on Social Questions, 1983, Believable Futures of American Protestantism, 1988, Creation at Risk? Religion, Science, and Environmentalism, 1995, Environmental Ethics and Christian Humanism, 1996; contbr. articles to profl. jours. Danforth Found. grantee, 1959-60, 65-66; Inst. for Advanced Study of Religion U. Chgo. fellow, 1981. Soc. for Christian Ethics. Home: 60 Harrison Ave Northampton MA 01060-2911 Office: Smith Coll Dept Religion Northampton MA 01063-0001 E-mail: tderr@smith.edu.

DERR, WILLIAM JAMES, retired non-commissioned officer; b. Catawissa, Pa., Oct. 24, 1934; s. Cyrus Sylvester and Dorothy Mae Derr; m. Marie Louise Parise, Oct. 27, 1956; children: Tina Marie, Theresa Ann. Grad. with GED, 1957. Enlisted U.S. Army, 1951, advanced through grades to SFC E-7, 1967, ret., 1972; warehouse supt. Pa. Liquor Control Bd., Harrisburg, Pa., 1972—94, ret., 1994; with U.S. Army, Republic of Korea, 1951—54, 1958—61, 1963—64, 1968—71, 1971—72. Author: Righteousness or Iniquity, 2001. Mem. retiree coun. U.S. Army, Carlisle Barracks, Pa., 1984—; vol. ombudsman Dept. of Aging, Carlisle, Pa., 1999—2000. SFC E-7 USAR, 1951—67. Decorated Army meritorious Unit Commendation, Vietnam Gallantry Cross with bronze palm., Vietnam Civil Action medal with Silver Star, Army Commendation Medal with Oak Leaf Cluster, Nat. Defense Svc. Medal with Bronze Star, Korean Svc. Medal, Vietnam Service Medal with Silver Star, UN Svc. Medal (Korea), Republic of Vietnam Campaign Medal. Mem.: VFW (life), Disabled Am. Vet. (life), Nat. Assn. for Uniformed Svc. (life), Mechanicsburg Lions Club (pres. 2000—01, Lion of Yr. 2001—02), Am. Legion (life). Avocations: world travel, hunting, fishing, reading, gardening. Home: 8 Cumberland Dr Mechanicsburg PA 17050

DERRICK, JOHN MARTIN, JR., electric company executive; b. Washington, Mar. 14, 1940; s. John M. and Audrey (Robey) D.; m. Linda Denhofer, Oct. 14, 1961; 1 child, Mark Frederick. BSEE, Duke U., 1961; postgrad., George Washington U., 1969. Registered profl. engr., D.C., Md. Various engring. positions Potomac Electric Power Corp., Washington, 1965-70, then mgr. various depts., then exec. v.p. and chief oper. officer, chmn., CEO, 1998—. Pres. Duke Club Washington, 1974-75, Bethesda (Md.) Lions Club, 1978-79; trustee Md. Nature Conservancy; gov. Wesley Theol. Sem; chmn. YMCA, 1995-96, Jr. Achievement, 1994-95. Lt. (j.g.) USN, 1962-65. Mem. IEEE, NSPE, Washington Bldg. Congress (pres. 1985-86), Edison Electric Inst., U.S. Energy Assn. (chmn.). Republican. Methodist. Avocations: boating, tennis, golf. Office: Potomac Electric Power Co 1900 Pennsylvania Ave NW Washington DC 20068-0002

DERRICK, MALCOLM, physicist; b. Hull, Eng., Feb. 15, 1933; came to U.S., 1963, naturalized, 1976; s. Arthur Henry and Gladys (Hopkinson) D.; m. Kathleen Allen, 1957; 1 child, Matthew; m. Christa Zars Baumgardner; 1966; m. Eva Krebbers, 1995. B.Sc. with 1st class honours, U. Birmingham, 1954, PhD, 1959; MA, Oxford U., 1961. Instr. Carnegie Inst. Tech., 1957-60; asst. prof. Oxford U., 1960-63; asst. physicist Argonne (Ill.) Nat. Lab., 1963-67, sr. physicist, 1967—, dir. high energy physics div., 1974-81. Vis. prof. U. Minn., 1969-70, Univ. Coll., London, 1972-73; adv. com. Stanford U. Accelerator Center, Fermi Nat. Accelerator Lab.; mem. high energy physics adv. panel Dept. Energy. Author numerous research papers on high energy physics. Fellow Am. Phys. Soc. Home: 20 Equestrian Way Lemont IL 60439-9785 Office: Argonne Nat Lab Bldg 362 Argonne IL 60439 E-mail: mxd@hep.anl.gov. *The opportunity to spend a lifetime's career investigating the Fundamental physical basis of matter is one that has been given to relatively few people. Such research requires large and expensive accelerators and particle detectors and so can only be funded by government agencies. It is to the credit of the United States that such support has been generously given, and the resulting revolution in our understanding of nature is the outstanding intellectual achievement of our times.*

DERRICK, WILLIAM DENNIS, retired physical plant administrator, consultant; b. San Diego, Feb. 7, 1946; s. Charles Woodrow and Catherine Elizabeth (McCormick) D.; m. Lynda Ray Adams, June 15, 1964 (div. 1971); children: Tod Sean, Shannon Kay, Nicole Dione, Johnathon Robert; m. Frances C. Bouck, Nov. 19, 1979; children: Kaila June Warner, Bryan Charles. Student, U. Nebr., 1971-72, 73-74, U. Mont., 1974-77, 98-99, Internat. Corr., 1966-67, 81, Battelle Meml. Inst., 1985, Project Mgmt. Inst., 1986-95, 98—. Elec. draftsman City of Lincoln (Nebr.) Light Dept., 1964-65; asst. engr. to adjutant gen. Nebr. N.G. State of Nebr., Lincoln, 1965-66; owner, mgr., archtl. draftsman Lumberman's Plan Svc., Inc., Lincoln, 1966-70; owner, mgr. Lenny's Lounge, Missoula, Mont., 1978-80; engring. technician, constrn. insp., adminstr. USDA/Helena (Mont.) Nat. Forest, 1980-83; facilities project mgr. pub. office bldgs. div. City and County of Denver, 1984-86; supt. bldgs. and grounds Denver Pub. Libr., 1986-91; dir. phys. plant Red Rocks C.C., Lakewood, Colo., 1991-94; CEO Derrick, Inc., Stevensville, Mont. Mem. Local Govt. Study Commn., Stevensville, Mont., 1974; bd. dirs. Lewis and Clark County Fair Bd., Helena, Mont., 1979-83; candidate U.S. Ho. of Reps., 1999—. Mem. Project Mgmt. Inst. (cert. project mgr. prof. #619, v.p. programs Denver chpt. 1986-89, pres. 1990-91, v.p. pub. rels. 1992-93, bd. dirs., ex-officio). Avocations: computer technology, videography, photo journalism, ind. entrepenuerism, golf. Home: PO Box 401 Stevensville MT 59870-0401 E-mail: wder789456@msn.com.

DERRICKSON, DENISE ANN, secondary school educator, educator; b. Seaford, Del., Sept. 20, 1956; d. William Hudson and Patricia Ann (Adkins) D. BS, James Madison U., 1978; MEd in Counseling and Human Devel., George Mason U., 1990, MEd in Curriculum & Instrn., 1994. Social studies instr. Brentsville Dist. High Sch., Nokesville, Va., 1978-91, Woodbridge (Va.) Sr. High Sch., 1991-99. Faculty liaison Parent-Tchr. Action Coun., 1990-91; prin.'s adv. coun., 1994-96. Vol. Childrens Hosp., Washington, 1983-86, Action in the Community through Svc., Inc.-Helpline, Manassas, Va., 1988-92. Recipient Cert. Appreciation Prince William County Sch. Bd., 1989, Outstanding Educator award Va. Govs. Sch., 1990, ACTS-Helpline Outstanding Vol. Svc. award, 1990; presented with U.S. Flag Armed Svcs. Hall of Honor at the dedication of the U.S. Women's Meml., 1998. Mem. NEA, AAUW, ASCD, VFW, Am. Assn. Curriculum Devel., Nat. Soc. for Study of Edn., Va. Edn. Assn., Va. Assn. Supervision and Curriculum Devel., Prince William Edn. Assn., Internat. Platform Assn., Kappa Delta Phi, Phi Delta Kappa. Avocations: sewing, crafts, travel.

DERRICKSON, SHIRLEY JEAN BALDWIN, elementary school educator; b. Balt., Aug. 7, 1943; d. James Francis and Dorothy Elizabeth (Jubb) Baldwin; m. Ernest Hughes Derrickson, Aug. 19, 1978. BA, Knox Coll., 1965; MEd, Goucher Coll., 1969; postgrad., Towson State U., 1970-77. Cert. profl. status elem. tchr., Del. Tchr. Howard Park Elem. Sch., Balt., 1969-70, Lida Lee Tall Learning Resource Ctr., Towson (Md.) State U., 1970-83, Selbyville (Del.) Mid. Sch., 1983-84, East Millsboro (Del.) Elem. Sch., 1984—, lead tchr. in sci., 1995—. Fgn. affairs chmn. Dagsboro (Del.) Century Club, 1990-96, sec., 1986-88; sec. Dagsboro Rep. Club, 1986-88; active Friends of Prince George's Chapel, 1994—, Del. Sr. Olympics, 1998-2002, Nat. Sr. Olympics, 1999. Recipient Washington Regional scholarship, 1961-64. Mem. NEA, Del. State Edn. Assn., Indian River Edn. Assn., PTO, Grace United Meth. Ch. Republican. Methodist. Avocations: canoeing, sailing, golf, tennis, volleyball. Office: East Millsboro Elem Sch 500 E State St Millsboro DE 19966-1199

DERRICKSON, WILLIAM BORDEN, manufacturing executive; b. Milford, Del., May 30, 1940; m. Patricia Jean Hayes, Feb. 1, 1964; children: Stephen Russel, Michael Scot BSEE, U. Del., 1964; diploma, Harvard Bus. Sch., 1979. Registered profl. engr. Supr. elec. maintenance Delmarva Power, Salisbury, Md., 1964-68; instrumentation engr. Hercules, Inc., Wilmington, Del., 1968-69, Sun Shipbldg., Chester, Pa., 1969-70; dir. project Fla. Power & Light Co., Juno Beach, Fla., 1970-84; sr. v.p. Pub. Svc. Co. N.H., Manchester, 1984-85; pres. New Hampshire Yankee Electric Co., Seabrook, 1985-87; pres., COO WPD Assocs., Inc., 1986-88, Quadrex Corp., Campbell, Calif., 1988-89, chmn. bd., CEO, 1989-93; also chmn. bd. dirs.; chmn. bd., CEO QES Inc., Palm City, Fla., 1994—, IBEX Engring. Svcs., Palm City, 1995—2002. Nuclear advisor Tenn. Valley Authority Bd. Dirs., 1987. Contbr. articles to profl. publs. Named Constrn. Man of Yr. ENR/McGraw-Hill Publs., 1984 Mem. NSPE, Am. Nuclear Soc., Project Mgmt. Inst., N.H. Soc. Profl. Engrs., Internat. Platform Assn., Rep. Senatorial Inner Circle. Republican. Avocations: golf, travel, numismatics, piano. Home: 1864 SW Saint Andrews Dr Palm City FL 34990-2208 Office: IBEX Engring Svcs PO Box 2078 Palm City FL 34991-7078

DERSH, RHODA E. management consultant, business executive; b. Phila., Sept. 10, 1934; civ; d. Maurice S. and Kay (Wiener) Eisman; m. Jerome Dersh, Dec. 23, 1956; children: Debra Lori, Jeffrey Jonathan. BA, U. Pa., 1955; MA, Tufts U., 1956; MBA, Manhattan Coll., 1980. Interpreter Consul of Chile, 1954-57; various teaching and staff positions Albright Coll., Mt. Holyoke Coll., Amherst Coll., Marple Newtown Sch., 1957-58; pres., chief exec. officer Profl. Practice Mgmt. Assocs., Reading, 1976—, Pace Inst., Reading, 1981—, Pace Mgmt., Inc., 1983—;, 1984-90. Mem. regional adv. bd. First Union Bank, 1998—. Author: The School Budget is Your Business, 1976, Business Management for Professional Offices, 1977, The School Budget: It's Your Money, It's Your Business, 1979, Improving Public School Management Practices, 1979, Part-Time Professional and Managerial Personnel: The Employers View, 1979; contbr. articles to profl. jours. Bd. dirs. Pa. State Bd. Pvt. Lic. Schs., 1987-93; cons. dir. pub. sch. budget study project City of Reading, 1967-78, chmn. comprehensive community plan task force, 1973-75; chmn. pub. svc. cons. project 1980-90; panel chmn. budget allocations United Way, 1974-76; del. White House Conf. on Children Youth, 1970; co-founder World Affairs Coun., Reading and Berks County, 1963-65; chmn. Berks County Com. for Children Youth, 1968-72; commr. Trial Ct. Nominating Commn. of Berks County (Pa.), 1982-84; bd. dirs. United Way of Berks County, 1984-89; chmn. programs Leadership Berks, 1986-87; bd. dirs. Reading Ctr. City Devel. Corp., Berks Bus.-Edn. Coalition Corp., 1991—; mem. Greater Berks Devel. Bd., 1998—. Recipient Trendsetter award YWCA, 1985. Mem. AAUW (ednl. found. grant.), LWV, Pa. Assn. Pvt. Sch. Bus. Adminstrs. (bd. dirs. 1985-89), Berks County C. of C. (bd. dirs. 1983-86, chmn. edn. com. 1983-85), Am. Acad. Ind. Cons. (pres. 1978-80), Reading and Berks C. of C (Entrepreneur of Yr. 1985), Rotary (bd. dirs. Reading, Pa., chpt. 1989-90). Office: 606 Court St Reading PA 19601-3542

DERSHAW, D. DAVID, radiologist; b. Phila., Dec. 10, 1948; s. Samuel and Lucille D. BA, Trinity Coll., 1970; MD, Jefferson Med. Coll., 1974. Diplomate Am. Bd. Radiology, Am. Bd. Diagnostic Radiology. Intern Beth Israel Hosp., N.Y.C., 1974-75; resident in diagnostic radiology N.Y. Hosp.-Cornell Med. Ctr., N.Y.C., 1975-78; fellow Jefferson Hosp., Phila., 1978-79; radiologist Meml. Sloan-Kettering, N.Y.C., 1981—, dir. breast imaging, 1991—; assoc. prof. radiology Cornell U. Med. Coll., N.Y.C., 1989-96, prof., 1996—. Chmn. N.Y. Breast Cancer Adv. Coun., 1991-2000; dir. Am. Coll. Radiology-Armed Forces Inst. Pathology Mammography Program, Reston, Va., 1993-94, 97—. Contbr. articles to profl. jours. Fellow Am. Coll. Radiology (breast task force 1993-94, 96—, chair com. on stereotaxic accreditation 1995-2002), Soc. Breast Imaging (exec. bd. 1997—, pres. 2003—); mem. Radiol. Soc. N.Am., N.Y. Roentgen Soc. (exec. bd. 2000-02), Am. Roentgen Ray Soc., N.Y. Met. Breast Group. Office: Meml Sloan-Kettering Ctr 1275 York Ave New York NY 10021-6094

DERSHEM, LARRY DOUGLAS, lawyer, author; b. Dayton, Ohio, May 11, 1948; s. William Aaron and Helen Marie (Ullery) D.; m. Hoa Thuy Le, July 5, 1980; children: Michelle Le, Kristin Lynn. AB, UCLA, 1973; MLS, U. Calif., Berkeley, 1974; JD, U. San Diego, 1978. Bar: Calif. 1979, U.S. Dist. Ct. (so. dist.) Calif. 1979. Catalog libr. U. San Diego Sch. Law, 1974-77; assoc. law libr. San Diego County Law Libr., 1977-87; dir. law libr. Nat. Univ. Sch. Law, San Diego, 1987-93; br. svcs. libr. Los Angeles County Law Libr., L.A., 1993-94; reference libr., computer rsch. specialist U. San Diego Sch. Law, 1994-97; dir. classificaton standards Lexis Nexis, Miamisburg, Ohio, 1997—2000; pvt. practice San Diego, 1979-97, 2001—. Author: California Legal Research Handbook, 1995; compiler loose-leaf books Libr. of Congress. With USNR, 1968-69. Mem. Am. Assn. Law Librs., San Diego County Bar Assn., So. Calif. Assn. Law Librs. Republican. Avocations: computer programming, piano, drums. Office: Dershem & Assocs 12707 High Bluff Dr 2d Fl San Diego CA 92130 E-mail: larry.dershem@timesaver.net.

DERSHOWITZ, ALAN MORTON, lawyer, educator; b. Bklyn., Sept. 1, 1938; s. Harry Dershowitz and Claire Dershowotz; m. Carolyn Cohen; children: Elon Marc, Jamin Seth, Ella Kaille Cohen Dershowitz. BA magna cum laude, Bklyn. Coll., 1959, LLD, 2001; LLB magna cum laude, Yale U., 1962; MA (hon.), Harvard Coll., 1967; LLD (hon.), Yeshiva U., 1989; PhD (hon.), Haifa U., 1993; LLD (hon.), Syracuse U., 1997, Hebrew Union Coll., Monmouth Coll., Bklyn. Coll., 2001. Bar: D.C. 1963, Mass. 1968, U.S. Supreme Ct. 1968. Law clk. to chief judge David L. Bazelon, U.S. Ct. Appeals, 1962—63; to justice Arthur J. Goldberg, U.S. Supreme Ct., 1963—64; mem. faculty Harvard Law Sch., 1964—, prof. law, 1967—, Felix Frankfurter Prof. of Law, 1993—; fellow Ctr. for Advanced Study of Behavioral Scis., 1971—72. Cons. to dir. NIMH, 1967—69, Pres.'s Commn. Civil Disorders, 1967, Pres.'s Com. Causes Violence, 1968, NAACP Legal Def. Fund, 1967—68, NIMH's Pres.'s Commn. Marijuana and Drug Abuse, 1972—73, Coun. on Drug Abuse, 1972—, Ford Found. Study on Law and Justice, 1973—76; rapporteur Twentieth Century Fund Study on Sentencing, 1975—76. Author (with others): Psychoanalysis, Psychiatry and the Law, 1967, Criminal Law: Theory and Process, 1974, The Best Defense, 1982, Reversal of Fortune: Inside the von Bulow Case, 1986, Taking Liberties: a Decade of Hard Cases, Bad Laws and Bum Raps, 1988, Chutzpah, 1991, Contrary to Popular Opinion, 1992, The Abuse Excuse, 1994, The Advocate's Devil, 1994, Reasonable Doubts, The Vanishing American Jew, 1997, Sexual McCarthyism: Clinton, Starr and the Emerging Constitutional Crisis, 1998, Just Revenge, 1999, The Genesis of Justice, 2000, Supreme Injustice, 2001, Letters to a Young Lawyer, 2001, Shouting Fire, 2002; contbr. articles to profl. jours., with others: America Declares Independence, 2003, with others: America Declares Independence, 2003; editor-in-chief: Yale Law Jour., 1961—62. Chmn. civil rights com. New England region Anti-Defamation League, B'nai B'rith, 1980—85; bd. dirs. ACLU, 1968—71, 1972—75, Assembly Behavioral and Social Scis. at NAS, 1973—76. Fellow Guggenheim, 1978—79. Mem.: Order of Coif, Phi Beta Kappa. Jewish. Office: Harvard Law Sch 1575 Massachusetts Ave Cambridge MA 02138-2801

DERSHOWITZ, NATHAN ZEV, lawyer; b. Bklyn., May 5, 1942; s. Harry and Claire (Ringel) D.; m. Marilyn Barlach, Dec. 29, 1963; children— Adam, Rana. Grad. Bklyn. Coll., 1963; J.D., NYU, 1966. Bar: N.Y. 1966, U.S. Ct. Appeals (1st, 2d, 3d, 5th, 6th, 7th, 8th, 11th, D.C. and fed. cirs.), U.S. Supreme Ct. Atty., Legal Aid Soc., N.Y.C., 1966-69; assoc. Stroock & Stroock & Lavan, N.Y.C., 1969-73, Greenbaum, Wolff & Ernst, N.Y.C., 1974-77; bd. dirs. Commn. Law and Social Action, Am. Jewish Congress, N.Y.C., 1977-83; sr. ptnr. Dershowitz & Eiger, N.Y.C., 1983-86; gen. counsel Pearl, N.Y.C. and Washington, 1981— ; spl. prof. Hofstra U. Law Sch., Hempstead, N.Y., 1979. Contbr. articles to profl. jours. Mem. ch. state com. ACLU, N.Y., 1980-84. Home: 2 Tudor City Pl New York NY 10017-6800 Office: Dershowitz & Eiger 225 Broadway New York NY 10007-3001

DERSHWITZ, MARK, anesthesiologist, researcher; b. Dearborn, Mich., Jan. 27, 1955; s. Arthur and Tillye (Segel) D.; m. Renée Margot Goetzler, Sept. 13, 1986. BA in Chemistry, Oakland U., 1974; PhD, Northwestern U., 1982, MD, 1983. Diplomate Am. Bd. Anesthesiology. Intern Carney Hosp., Boston, 1983; resident Mass. Gen. Hosp., Boston, 1984-86, rsch. fellow, 1986-88, staff anesthesiologist, 1988—2000; instr. Harvard U., Cambridge, Mass., 1987-90, asst. prof., 1990-97, assoc. prof., 1997—2000; prof., vice chair anesthesiology, prof. biochemistry and molecular pharmacology U. Mass., Worcester, Mass., 2000—; staff anesthesiologist U. Mass. Meml. Health Care, 2000—. Author: The MGH Board Review of Anesthesiology, 1998; contbr. articles to profl. jours. NIH rsch. grantee, 1986-88. Mem. Am. Soc. Anesthesiologists, Internat. Anesthesia Rsch. Soc., Am. Soc. Pharmacology and Exptl. Therapeutics, Am. Soc. for Clin. Pharmacology and Therapeutics, Assn. Univ. Anesthesiologists. Jewish. Achievements include research on the clinical pharmacology of intravenous anesthetics, sedatives, and antiemetics. Home: 33 Wildwood Dr Sherborn MA 01770 1102 Office: Dept Anesthesiology U Mass 55 Lake Ave N Worcester MA 01655

DERSTADT, RONALD THEODORE, health care administrator; b. Detroit, June 9, 1950; s. Theodore Edward and Dorothy J. (Semko) D.; m. J. Gail Adamson, June 9, 1990. BA, U. Detroit, 1971; M of Hosp. Healthcare Adminstn., Xavier U., 1975. Mgr. shared svcs. Bethesda Hosp. North, Cin., 1975-76; asst. adminstr. McCullough-Hyde Meml. Hosp., Oxford, Ohio, 1977-79; pres. Hospice of Cin., Inc., 1979-82; dir. strategic planning St. Francis-St. George Hosp., Cin., 1982-84; v.p. Mgmt. Dynamics, Inc., Cin., 1984-85; sr. v.p. St. Francis-St. George Mgmt. Co., Cin., 1986-88; v.p. Franciscan Health System of Cin., 1988-91; dir. hosp. affairs ChoiceCare, Cin., 1991-95; CEO Medquest, Owensboro, Ky., 1995-98; COO Ctr. for Chem. Addictions Treatment, Cin., 1998—. Vice-chmn., bd. dirs. Franciscan Health Network, Cin., Franciscan Health Ventures, Cin. Treas., bd. dirs. Ohio Easter Seals Soc., Columbus, 1987-93; bd. dirs. S.W. Ohio Easter Seal Soc., Cin., 1986-92; adv. bd. Dater Jr. H.S., Cin., 1984-88. Fellow Am. Coll. Healthcare Execs.; mem. Healthcare Fin. Mgmt. Assn., Am. Hosp. Assn., Ohio Hosp. Assn. Avocations: boating, golf, radio control model building. Home: 7363 Dogtrot Rd Cincinnati OH 45248 Office: 830 Ezzard Charles Dr Cincinnati OH 45214-2525

DERTHICK, ALAN WENDELL, architect, architectural firm executive; b. Johnson City, Tenn., July 6, 1931; s. Lawrence Gridley and Helda Lee (Hannah) Derthick; m. Jane Bailey, Dec. 22, 1958; children: Mark Alan, Steven John. BArch, Auburn U., 1954. Registered arch., Tenn., Ga., Ala. Ptnr. Derthick, Henley & Wilkerson Archs., Chattanooga, 1960—. Prin. works include Miller Pl., 1989 (Honor award), Hunter Mus. Art, 1977 (Honor awards), 1994, Chattanooga Pub. Libr., 1977 (Honor award), 1992, Hamilton County Cts. Bldg., 1992, Alexian Village, 1993, 2003, Covenant Transport Nat. Hdqrs., 1997, 2000, Chattanoooga Conv. Ctr., 2003, EPB Garage, 2003, TVPPA, 2002, Hardy Sch., 2001. Chmn. Chattanooga Codes Rev. Bd., 1975—95, Mayor's Better Schs. Task Force, Chattanooga, 1984—85, Hamilton County Codes Appeals Bd., 1999—2003; pres. 1st Christian Ch., 1978, 1984, 1998, 1999, 2000. With USAF, 1954—56. Recipient Honor award, Nat. Concrete Reinforcing Steel Inst., 1977. Mem.: AIA (pres. Chattanooga chpt. 1966, 1972, Honor award 1989, Gulf States Regional Nat. Honor award 1961, 1977, 1978), Tenn. Soc. Archs. (pres. 1991), Mountain City Club. Home: 602 Marr Dr Signal Mountain TN 37377-2228 Office: Derthick Henley Wilkerson 1001 Carter St Chattanooga TN 37402-5014

DERTIEN, JAMES LEROY, librarian; b. Kearney, Nebr., Dec. 14, 1942; s. John Ludwig and Muriel May (Cooley) D.; m. Elaine Paulette Mohror, Dec. 26, 1966; children— David Dalton, Channing Lee AB, U. S.D., 1965; MLS, U. Pitts., 1966; MPA, U. S.D., 1995. Head librarian Mitchell Pub. Library, S.D., 1966-67; head librarian Sioux Falls Coll., S.D., 1967-69; acting dir. libraries U. S.D., Vermillion, 1969-70; head librarian Vets. Meml. Pub. Library, Bismarck, N.D., 1970-75, Bellevue Pub. Library, Nebr., 1975-81; libr. dir. Siouxland Librs., S.D., 1981—. Pres., bd. dirs. Vol. and Info. Ctr., Sioux Falls, 1991-93. Mem. ALA, Mountain Plains Library Assn. (pres. 1978-79, editor newsletter 1982—), S.D. Library Assn. (pres. 1986-87). Lodges: Rotary. Unitarian Universalist. Avocations: backpacking, reading, fishing. Home: 2501 S Kiwanis Ave Apt 303 Sioux Falls SD 57105-0161 Office: Siouxland Librs 201 N Main Ave Sioux Falls SD 57104-6002 E-mail: jimd@siouxland.lib.sd.us.

DERUYTER, MARILYN, real estate broker; b. Canandaigua, N.Y., May 8, 1942; d. Ernest Robert and Alice Zereda Mason Prober; m. Paul C. DeRuyter, Dec. 29, 1961 (div. July 1990); children: Kristin M. Walters, Paul R. Grad., high sch., Shortsville, N.Y., 1960, Real Estate Inst., 1982. Cert. residential specialist; grad. Real Estate Inst. Exec. sec. Red Jacket Tel., Shortsville, 1966-72; paralegal David G. Retchless Esq., Clifton Springs, N.Y., 1972-80; real estate broker M. DeRuyter Real Estate, Shortsville, 1978—. Recipient Sales Master Gold and Zenith awards for Sales Excellence. Mem.: Clifton Springs Rotary, Lions. Avocations: reading, shopping, family. Home: 74 E Main St Clifton Springs NY 14432 E-mail: mderuyte@rochester.rr.com.

DERVAN, JOHN PATRICK, cardiologist; b. Boston, Aug. 3, 1950; s. Peter Brendan and Ellen (Comer) D. BS, Boston Coll., 1972; MD, St. Louis U., 1976. Diplomate Am. Bd. Internal Medicine, also Sub-bds. Cardiovascular Disease, Critical Care Medicine, Interventional Cardiology. Intern Faulkner Hosp., Boston, 1976-77, jr. and sr. resident, 1977-79, chief resident in internal medicine, 1979-80; fellow cardiology Beth Israel Hosp., Boston, 1980-83; instr. medicine Harvard Med. Sch., Boston, 1982-83; clin. asst. prof. medicine Jefferson Med. Coll., Phila., 1983-85, asst. prof. medicine, 1985-86, SUNY, Stony Brook, 1986-93, assoc. prof. medicine, 1993-98, clin. assoc. prof. medicine, 1998—. Dir. cardiac catheterization lab. Univ. Hosp., SUNY, Stony Brook, 1986-98, dir. interventional cardiology, 1986-98. Fellow Am. Coll. Cardiology, Soc. Cardiac Angiography and Intervention; mem. ACP, Soc. Critical Care Medicine, Am. Heart Assn. Office: North Suffolk Cardiology Assocs Ste #1 2500 Nesconset Hwy Stony Brook NY 11790-2561

DERVAN, PETER BRENDAN, chemistry educator; b. Boston, July 28, 1945; s. Peter Brendan and Ellen (Comer) D.; m. Jackqueline K. Barton; children: Andrew, Elizabeth. BS, Boston Coll., 1967; PhD, Yale U., 1972. Asst. prof. Calif. Inst. Tech., Pasadena, 1973-79, assoc. prof., 1979-82, prof. chemistry, 1982-88, Bren prof. chemistry, 1988—; chmn. div. chemistry & chem. engring., 1994—. Adv. bd. ACS Monographs, Washington, 1979-81 Mem. adv. bd. Jour. Organic Chemistry, Washington, 1981—; mem. editorial bd. Bioorganic Chemistry, 1983—, Chem. Rev. Jour., 1984—, Nucleic Acids Res., 1986—, Jour. Am. Chem. Soc., 1986—, Acct. Chem. Res., 1988—, Bioorganic Chem. Rev., 1988—, Bioconjugate Chemistry, 1989—, Jour. Med. Chemistry, 1991—, Tetrahedron, 1992—, Bioorganic and Med. Chemistry, 1993—, Chemical and Engineering News, 1992—; contbr. articles to profl. jours. A.P. Sloan Rsch. fellow, 1977; Camille and Henry Dreyfus scholar, 1978; Guggenheim fellow, 1983; recipient Arthur C. Cope Scholar award 1986, Maison de la Chimie Found. prize, 1996. Fellow Am. Acad. Scis.; mem. NAS, Am. Chem. Soc. (Nobel Laureate Signature award 1985, Harrison Howe award 1988, Arthur C. Cope award, 1993, Willard Gibbs medal, 1993, Rolf Sammet prize, 1993, William H. Nichols medal 1994, Kirkwood medal 1998, Alfred Bader award 1999), Inst. Medicine (Remsen award 1998, Linus Pauling medal 1999, Richard Tolman medal 1999), French Acad. Scis. (fgn., Tetrahedron prize 2000); mem. Am. Philos. Soc. (Harvey prize 2002). Office: Calif Inst Tech 1201 E California Blvd Pasadena CA 91125-0001

DERVIN, BRENDA LOUISE, communications educator; b. Beverly, Mass., Nov. 20, 1938; d. Ermina Diluiso; adopted d. John Jordan and Marjorie (Sullivan) D. BS, Cornell U., 1960; MA, Mich. State U., 1968, PhD, 1972; PhD (hon.), U. Helsinki, 2000. Pub. info. asst. Am. Home Econ. Assn., Washington, 1960-62; pub. info. specialist Ctr. Consumer Affairs, U. Wis., Milw., 1962-65; instr., rsch. and teaching asst. dept. communications Mich. State U., E. Lansing, 1965-70; asst. prof., Sch. Info. Transfer Syracuse (N.Y.) U., 1970-72; asst. to assoc. prof. U. Wash., Seattle, 1972-85; prof. comm. Ohio State U., Columbus, 1985—. Co-author: The Mass Media Behavior of the Urban Poor, 1980; editor: Rethinking Communication, 1989, Communication A Different Kind of Horserace, 2003, Sense-making Methodology Reader, 2003; editor Progress in Communication Sci., 1981-92; contbr. articles to profl. jours. Grantee U.S. Office Edn., 1974-76, Calif. State Libr., 1974-84, Nat. Cancer Inst., 1984, Ameritech, 1992. Fellow Internat. Communication Assn. (pres. 1986-87); mem. Internat. Assn. Mass Communications Rsch. (governing coun. 1988-97). Home: 4269 Kenridge Dr Columbus OH 43220-4157 Office: Ohio State U 3016 Derby 154 N Oval Mall Columbus OH 43210-1330 E-mail: dervin.1@osu.edu.

DERYUGA, VYACHESLAV O. nuclear physicist, computer scientist, consultant; b. Krasny Liman, Ukraine, Mar. 9, 1955; s. Okeksiy D. and Polina P. Deryuga; m. Larisa P. Kolomiets, July 28, 1978 (div. Nov. 1984); 1 child, Anna Dotsenko; m. Vera B. Smirnova, Apr. 18, 1986; 1 child, Polina. BSc, Kharkov (Ukraine) State U., 1978; MSc, Kharkov State U., 1978; PhD, Kharkov (Ukraine) State U., 1982. Vis. rschr. Joint Inst. for Nucler Rsch., Dubna, Russia, 1978-81; sr. rsch. scis. Kharkov State U., 1981-86, assoc. prof., sr. rsch. scientist, 1992—97; assoc. prof., head dept. Kharkov Inst. Zootechniques and Vet. Medicine, 1986-92; cons. Computer Tech., Inc., NYC, 1997—2002; project leader Morgan Stanley, NYC, 2002—. Mem. coun. Soc. for Sci. Edn. Knowledge, Kharkov, 1986-91; docent USSR Bd. Edn., 1991; fellow James Beard Found. Author: Physics, 1993; contbr. articles to sci. jours., including Instruments and Exptl. Techniques, Nuclear Physics, Jour. Physics, Hyperfine Interactions. Mem. IEEE (sr.), IEEE Computer Soc. (sr.), Ukrainian Phys. Soc. Inventor of electro-hydraulic desintegrator of microorganisms; research on acoustic effects of high-current electron beams; pioneering work in design of computer programs for automated spectra processing; design and implementation of automated customer account transfer service. E-mail: deryuga@computer.org.

DERZAW, RICHARD LAWRENCE, lawyer; b. N.Y.C., Mar. 6, 1954; s. Ronald Murray and Diana (Diamond) D.; m. Susan Katz, 1993. BA magna cum laude, Fairleigh Dickinson U., 1976; JD, Ohio No. U., 1979. Bar: Fla. 1979, U.S. Dist. Ct. (so. dist.) Fla. 1981, U.S. Ct. Appeals (5th cir.) 1981, U.S. Ct. Appeals (11th cir.) 1981, U.S. Ct. Appeals (2d cir.), 1988, N.Y. 1982, N.C. 1995, U.S. Dist. Ct. (so. dist.) N.Y. 1985, U.S. Dist. Ct. (ea. dist.) N.Y., 1986, U.S. Tax Ct. 1986, U.S. Supreme Ct., 1988. Sole practice, Boca Raton, Fla., 1979-82, N.Y.C., 1982—. Mem. ABA, N.Y. State Bar Assn., N.C. Bar Assn., Fla. Bar Assn., Am. Arbitration Assn., Assn. of Bar of City of N.Y., Fed. Bar Coun., Lions of Boca Raton (treas. 1981-82), Phi Alpha Delta, Phi Zeta Kappa, Phi Omega Epsilon. Office: 477 Madison Ave New York NY 10022 E-mail: derzlaw@aol.com.

DERZON, GORDON M. hospital administrator; b. Milw., Dec. 28, 1934; married. BA, Dartmouth Coll., 1957; MHA, U. Mich., 1961. Adminstrv. resident Bklyn. Hosp., 1960-61, adminstrv. asst., 1961-63, asst. exec. dir., 1963-65, exec. dir., 1966-67, State U. Hosp., Bklyn., 1967-68, Kings County Hosp. Center, Bklyn., 1968-74; CEO U. Wis. Hosps. and Clinics, Madison, 1974-2000; assoc. prof. SUNY, 1967-74; clin. prof. U. Wis., now emeritus prof. Bd. dirs. Ind. Living, MATC Found., Madison Cmty. Health Ctr. Hospice, Combat Blindness Found., Ctr. Health Emotions. Contbr. articles to profl. jours. Mem. Am. Hosp. Assn. (past chmn. pub. gen. hosp. sect.). Home: 3440 Topping Rd Madison WI 53705-1439 Office: U Wis Hosp & Clinics 600 Highland Ave Madison WI 53792-0001 E-mail: gm.derzon@hosp.wisc.edu.

DE SA E SILVA, ELIZABETH ANNE, secondary school educator; b. Edmonds, Wash., Mar. 17, 1931; d. Sven Yngve and Anna Laura Elizabeth (Dahlin) Erlandson; m. Claudio de Sá e Silva, Sept. 12, 1955 (div. July 1977); children: Lydia, Marco, Nelson. BA, U. Oreg., 1953; postgrad., Columbia U., 1954-56, Calif. State U., Fresno, 1990, U. No. Iowa, 1993; MEd, Mont. State U., 1978. Cert. tchr. Oreg., Mont. Med. sec., 1947-49; sec. Merced (Calif.) Sch. Dist., 1950-51; sec., asst. Simon and Schuster, Inc., N.Y.C., 1954-56; tchr. Casa Roosevelt-União Cultural, São Paulo, Brazil, 1957-59, Coquille (Oreg.) Sch. Dist., 1978-96; music tchr. Cartwheels Presch., North Bend, Oreg., 1997—99, 2001. Tchr. piano, 1967—78; instr. Spanish Southwestern Oreg. C.C., Coos Bay, 1991—94; pianist/organist Faith Luth. Ch., North Bend, Oreg., 1995—2002, New Life Luth. Ch., Florence, Oreg., 2002—; vocal soloist, 1996—; voice tchr., 1997—99. Chmn. publicity Music in Our Schs. Month, Oreg. Dist. VII, 1980-85; sec. Newcomer's Club, Bozeman, Mont., 1971. Quincentennial fellow U. Minn. and Found. José Ortega y Gasset, Madrid, 1991. Mem. AAUW (sec., scholarship chmn., co-pres., pres., treas., editor newsletter), Nat. Trust Hist. Preservation, Am. Coun. on Tchg. Fgn. Langs., Am. Assn. Tchrs. Spanish and Portuguese, Nat. Coun. Tchrs. English, Music Educators Nat. Conf., Oreg. Music Educators Assn., Oreg. Coun. Tchrs. English, Confedn. Oreg. Fgn. Lang. Tchrs., VoiceCare Network. Democrat. Avocations: swimming, walking, travel, drama. Home: PO Box 1807 Florence OR 97439

DESAI, ANITA, writer; b. Mussoorie, India, June 24, 1937; came to U.S., 1987; d. D.N. and Toni (Nime) Mazumdar; m. Ashvin Desai, Dec. 13, 1958; children: Rahul, Tani, Arjun, Kiran. BA, Delhi U., 1957. Tchr. Smith Coll., Mount Holyoke Coll.; prof. of writing MIT, Cambridge, 1993—2002. Author: Cry, the Peacock, 1963, Voices in the City, 1965, Bye-Bye Blackbird, 1968, The Peacock Garden, 1974, Where Shall We Go This Summer?, 1975, Cat on a Houseboat, 1976, Fire on the Mountain, 1977, Games at Twilight and Other Stories, 1978, Clear Light of Day, 1980, The Village by the Sea, 1982, In Custody, 1985, Baumgartner's Bombay, 1989, Journey to Ithaca, 1995, Fasting, Feasting, 1999, Diamond Dust and Other Stories, 2000. Recipient Winifred Holtby prize Royal Soc. Lit., 1978, Sahitya Acad. award, 1979, Guardian award for children's book, 1982, Lit. Lion award N.Y. Pub. Libr., 1993, Neil Gunn fellowship Scottish Arts Coun., 1994, Moravia prize, Italy, 1999; Girton Coll. and Clare Hall fellow Cambridge U., Eng. Fellow Am. Acad. Arts and Letters (hon.), Royal Soc. Lit. Eng. Home: Rogers Coleridge and White Ltd 20 Powis Mews London W11 1JN England

DESAI, CAWAS JAL, business executive; b. Bombay, 1938; came to U.S. 1968; s. Jal Tehmurasp and Dina Jal Desai; m. Kamal Aspy Cavina, 1963; children: Darius, Adil. B in Commerce and Econs., U. Bombay, 1959, LLB, 1962. Chartered acct., India. Ptnr. Dalal, Desai & Kumana, Bombay, 1963-68; sr. acct. Arthur Young & Co., N.Y.C., 1968-69, acting mgr., 1970-71; with Pechiney Group, 1971-92; contr. Guggenheim Corp., Jersey City, 1971-73; mgr. acctg. and audit Pechiney World Trade (USA), Inc., N.Y.C., 1973-74, dir. acctg., 1974-75, contr., 1976-81; controller Pechiney Trading Internat., 1981-84; v.p. control Pechiney World Trade (U.S.A.), Inc., N.Y.C., 1985-87; exec. v.p. Guggenheim Corp., North Bergen, N.J., 1987-92, COO, 1991-92; exec. v.p. Accumed, Inc., 1993-97; sr. dir. acctg. and ops. Novasoft Info. Tech. Corp., Lawrenceville, N.J., 1998-2000; v.p. fin. Savant Consulting Group, Edison, NJ, 2000—. Pres. Zoroastrian Assn. Pa. and N.J., 1979-81. Fellow Inst. Chartered Accts. Republican. Avocations: reading, numismatics. Home: 661 Nancy Rd Yardley PA 19067-1975 E-mail: cdesai@savantinc.com.

DESAI, GAUTAM T. physician; b. Bulawayo, Zimbabwe, Jan. 7, 1946; s. Thakorbhai and Manjula Desai, m. Maya Desai, June 28, 1970; children: Nirav, Seema. MB BS, Baroda Medical Coll., Baroda, Gujrat, India, 1970. Diplomate Am. Bd. Internal Medicine and Pulmonary Diseases. Intern Queens (N.Y.) Hosp. Ctr., 1972-73, med. resident in internal medicine, 1973-75; fellow in pulmonary medicine Queens Hosp. Ctr., 1975-77; attending physician Lincoln

Hosp., Bronx, N.Y., 1977-78; pvt. practice, Randolph, N.J., 1978—. Fellow Am. Coll. Chest Physicians; mem. N.J. Med. Soc., Morris County Med. Soc., N.J. Sleep Soc. Avocations: tennis, travelling, bridge, ballroom dancing. Office: 447 Rt 10 Ste 2 Randolph NJ 07869 also: 653 Willow Grove St # 2700 Hackettstown NJ 07840 Fax: (908) 852-7404. E-mail: gdesai@juno.com.

DESAI, HIREN D. software engineer; b. Amravati, India, Oct. 24, 1959; came to U.S., 1982; s. Deovrat R. and Nilly D. Desai; m. Ketki H. Desai, Dec. 9, 1990; children: Rahul, Meera, Priya. BTech in Electronics Engring., Varanasi (India) Inst. Tech., 1982; MS in Computer Sci., U. Ctrl. Fla., 1985; MBA, Emory U., 1995. Systems mgr. Ultra Pink, N.Y.C., 1985-86; systems cons. Granada Systems Design, N.Y.C., 1987-90; sr. software engr. Estek Products-Kodak, Charlotte, N.C., 1990-92; project mgr., sr. mem. tech. staff Bellsouth Telecom., Atlanta, 1992-98; mng. prin. cons. Oracle Cons. Svcs., Atlanta, 1998—. Recipient Mktg. Faculty Honor award and Decision & Info. Analysis award Emory U., Atlanta, 1996. Mem. IEEE, IEEE Computer Soc., Telephone Pioneers Am., Beta Gamma Sigma. Avocation: chess. Home and Office: 11650 Dunhill Place Dr Alpharetta GA 30005-6716 E-mail: hkdesai@worldnet.att.net.

DESAI, KIRTIDA D. medical educator; b. Jan. 3, 1969; MB BS, Govt. Med. Coll., Surat, Gujarat, India, 1992. Intern U. Miss. Med. Ctr., Jackson, 1993-94, resident in psychiatry, 1994-97, clin. asst. prof., 1997—; staff psychiatrist Miss. State Hosp., Whitfield, 1999—. Address: 628 Sherringham Ct Ridgeland MS 39157-4194 Office: Mississippi State Hosp Whitfield MS 39193

DESAI, MAULIK BHARAT, emergency physician; b. Ahmedabad, Gujarat, India, Jan. 3, 1964; s. Bharat Chiman and Sudha Bharat Desai; 1 child, Tanya Maulik. B Medicine and Surgery, NHL Mcpl. Med. Sch., Ahmedabad, 1981—86; MD, KM Sch. P.G. Medicine, Ahmedabad, 1990, Cornell U., 1997. Diplomate Am. Bd. Internal Medicine. Resident in internal medicine, 1995—97; cons. physician, internist Physicians Affiliated Care, Owensburo (Ky.) Mercy Health Sys., 1997—98, St. Mary's at Warrick, Booneville, Ind., 1997—98; cons. emergency physician Trigg Comb Hosp., Cadiz, Ky., 1999—, Muhlenberg Cmty. Hosp., Greenville, Ky., 1999—, Med. Ctr., Scottsville, Ky., 1999—; dir. emergency/ambulatory care Minor Emergency Ctr., Owensboro, 1999—; dir. emergency medicine Logan Meml. Hosp., Russellville, Ky., 2000—. Chief cons. physician Mehta Hosp. and ICU, Ahmedabad, 1991—95; chief cons. physician, advisor Sanand (India) Civil Hosp., 1991—95; chief investigative physician Gujarat Med. Coun., 1989—91; investigative physician Invest, U. South Fla., Tampa, 1998—2000. Vol. physician Ahmedabad, Sanand med. camps, 1990—95, Lions, Rotary and Round Table orgns., Owensboro Free Med. Clinic, 1997—99. Fellow: Am. Soc. Internal Medicine; mem.: ACP, AMA, Gujarat Med. Coun. (life), Indian Med. Coun. (life), Am. Assn. Physicians from India (life). Hindu. Avocations: reading, music, travel, sports. Office: Logan Meml Hosp 1625 S Nashville Rd Russellville KY 42276

DESAI, NIRANJAN A. chemical engineer; b. Pune, Maharashtra, India, Feb. 20, 1978; s. Anil M. and Snehal A. Desai. B of Engring., U. Pune (India), 1999; MS, Pa. State U., University Park, 2001; postgrad., Carnegie Mellon U., Pitts., 2003—. Engr. Carrier Corp., United Technologies Corp., Syracuse, NY, 2001; advanced engr. Siemens Westinghouse Power Corp., Pitts., 2002—. Grad. rsch. asst. Pa. State U., University Park, 2000—01, grad. tchg. asst., 2000. Nat. Talent Search scholar, Nat. Coun. of Ednl. Rsch. and Tng., 1993. Mem.: SAE Internat., Mensa, Tau Beta Pi. Office: Siemens Westinghouse Power Corp 1310 Beulah Road Pittsburgh PA 15235 E-mail: niranjan.desai@siemens.com.

DESAI, NITIN DAYALJI, international organization official; b. Bombay, July 5, 1941; s. Dayalji M. and Shantaben Desai; m. Aditi Gupta, Apr. 28, 1979; children: Kartikeya, Nandan. BA with honors, U. Bombay, 1962; MSc in Econs., London Sch. Econs., 1965. Econs. lectr. Liverpool (Eng.) U., 1965-67, Southampton (Eng.) U., 1967-70; cons. Tata (India) Econ. Consultancy Svcs., 1970-73; cons., adviser Planning Commn. Govt. of India, 1973-85, sr. adviser Brundtland Commn., 1985-87, spl. sec. Planning Commn., 1987-88, sec., chief econs. adviser Min. of Fin., 1988-90; dep. sec. gen. UNCED UN, Geneva, 1990-92, undersec. gen. for Pehuj coordination and sustainable devel. N.Y.C., 1993-97, undersec. gen. for econ. and social affairs, 1997—. Office: UN DC2-2320 New York NY 10017

DESAI, SIMA S. internist; d. Suresh K. and Lata S. Desai. BS in Biology, BA in Chemistry, U. N.Mex., 1990, MD, 1994. Intern Oreg. Health and Sci. U., Portland, 1994—95, resident internal medicine, 1995—97, chief resident internal medicine, 1997—98, asst. prof. medicine, 1998—, adj. prof. Sch. Dentistry, 2001—. Mem.: ACP (chair assocs. coun. 2000—03), Soc. Hosp. Medicine, Soc. Gen. Medicine.

DESAI, VEENA BALVANTRAI, obstetrician and gynecologist, educator; b. Karvan, Gujarat, India, Oct. 5, 1931; came to U.S., 1973; d. Balvantrai P. and Maniben (Vashi) Desai; m. Vinay D. Gandevia, Sept. 19, 1964. MBBS, Seth G.S. Med. Coll., Bombay, 1957, MD, 1961. Jr. resident Bombay U., 1957-59; house officer gyn. Chalmer's Hosp., Edinburgh, Scotland, 1962-63; registrar ob-gyn. Neath (U.K.) Gen. Hosp., 1963-64, Scunthorpe (U.K.) Gen. Hosp., 1964-66; chief resident ob-gyn. St. John (Can.) Gen. Hosp., 1973-74; attending ob-gyn. Portsmouth (N.H.) Hosp., 1975-84; assoc. prof. Boston U., 1985-86; sr. staff ob-gyn. Santa Clara (Calif.) Valley Med. Ctr., 1986-87; mem. sr. staff ob-gyn. West Anaheim (Calif.) Med. Ctr., 1988-98, chief dept. ob-gyn., 1992-93, vice chief of gen. med. staff, 1994—95; ob/gyn Bay State Med. Ctr., Springfield, Mass., 1998—; chief ob-gyn. Mercy Med. Ctr., Springfield, 2002—. Assoc. clin. prof. ob-gyn. U. Calif., Irvine, 1990-98; pres. Desai Med. Corp., Anaheim, 1989—. Chmn.'s advisor Nat. Security Coun.; charter mem. Presdl. Task Force; mem. Rep. Party Inner Cir., 1984-2001. Recipient Presdl. Medal of Merit, 1982, award Spl. Congl. Adv. Bd., 1984, Order of Liberty, U.S. Congress, 1995, Medal of Freedom, U.S. Senate, 1994, medal Ronald Wilson Reagan Eternal Flame of Freedom, 1996, Millennium Medal of Freedom, Rep. Senate, 1999. Fellow ACS, Internat. Coll. Surgeons, Am. Coll. Ob-Gyn., Western Mass. Ob-Gyn. Soc. (pres. 2002—), Royal Coll. Ob-Gyn. (chmn. Am. rep. com. 1997-2002), mem. Buena Park Rotary (pres. 1994, chair internat. svc. 1992-93), Rep. Inner Cir. Avocations: latchhook work, internat. politics, traveling. Home: 35 Sean Louis Cir West Springfield MA 01089-4547

DE SAINT PHALLE, PIERRE CLAUDE, lawyer; b. N.Y.C., July 21, 1948; s. Thibaut and Rosamonde (Frame) de Saint P. BA, Trinity Coll, 1970; JD, Columbia U., 1973. Bar: N.Y. 1974, U.S. Ct. Appeals (2d cir.) 1975, U.S. Dist. Ct. (so. and ea. dist.) N.Y. 1975, D.C. 1982. Assoc. Davis Polk & Wardwell, N.Y.C., 1973-82; European Office, 1976-77; ptnr. N.Y.C., 1983—. Asst. gen. counsel U.S. Synthetic Fuels Corp., Washington, 1980-81. Mem. ABA, N.Y.C. Bar Assn., Internat. Bar Assn. River Club, Quoque Field Club, Quoque Beach Club, Nat. Golf Links of Am. Roman Catholic. Office: Davis Polk & Wardwell 450 Lexington Ave Fl 31 New York NY 10017-3982

DE SAINT PHALLE, THIBAUT, investment banker, educator, lawyer, financial consultant; b. Tuxedo Park, N.Y., July 23, 1918; s. Fal and Marie (Duryee) de Saint P.; m. Rosamond Frame, Jan. 12, 1946 (dec. 1960); children: Fal, Pierre, Thérèse; m. Elene Canrobert Isles, June 21, 1965 (div. 1983); children: Marc, Diane; m. Mariana M. Smith, April 24, 1983. Student, Harvard U., 1935-37; AB, Columbia U., 1939, JD, 1941. Bar: N.Y. 1942, D.C. 1984, U.S. Supreme Ct. 1945. Assoc. Chadbourne, Wallace, Parke & Whiteside, N.Y.C., 1941-50; ptnr., head corp. law dept. Lewis & McDonald, N.Y.C., 1950-58; v.p., treas. Becton, Dickinson and Co., Rutherford, N.J., 1958-62, dir., 1958-67; sr. ptnr. Coudert Bros., N.Y.C., 1962-66, of counsel, 1966-77, Vorys, Sater, Seymour & Pease, Washington, 1983-86. Ltd. ptnr. Dean Witter & Co., pres. Dean Witter Overseas Fin. Corp., N.Y.C., 1967-68; investment banker Stralem, Saint Phalle & Co., Inc., N.Y.C., 1968-70, vice chmn. bd. dirs., 1968-70; mem. faculty, prof. internat. fin. and law Centre d'Etudes Industrielles, Geneva, 1971-76; dir. Export-Import Bank U.S., Washington, 1977-81; Scholl chair internat. bus. Georgetown U. Center Strategic and Internat. Studies, 1981-83; chmn. Saint Phalle Internat. Group, 1985—. Author: The Dollar Crisis, 1963, Multinational Corporations, 1976, U.S. Productivity and Competitiveness in International Trade, 1980, Trade Inflation and the Dollar, 1981, rev. edit., 1984, The Federal Reserve, an Intentional Mystery, 1985; contbr. numerous articles on internat. fin. and trade to profl. jours. Lt. comdr. USNR, 1942—46. Decorated Navy Commendation medal, Bronze Star, Legion d'Honneur (France). Mem.: ABA, Jockey Club, Met. Club. Roman Catholic. Home and Office: Saint Phalle Internat Group PO Box 2038 Boca Grande FL 33921 Fax: 941-964-4436.

DE SALME, JOHN W. retired music educator, music association administrator; b. Corpus Christi, Tex., May 12, 1935; s. Orrin Richard and Martha Frances de Salme; m. Margaret Clare Brown, Nov. 27, 1983; children: John W., Robert E., Suzanne E. de Salme-Kaiser. MusB, U. Iowa, 1957, MA, 1960, MFA, 1967. Iowa permanent profl. cert. Dir. of bands Orange Grove (Tex.) H.S., 1957—59, Iowa Valley Cmty. Schs., Marengo, 1960—62; music dept. chair, dir. of bands West H.S., Iowa City, 1968—93; music dir., prin. condr. Ea. Iowa Brass Band, Mt. Vernon, 1992—2001; v.p., contest contr. N.Am. Brass Band Assn., 2000—. Music adjudicator Iowa H.S. Music Assn., Boone, 1960—; trombonist Corpus Christi Symphony Orch., 1955—59; guest condr. Iowa City Cmty. Band, 1966—76. Mem.: NEA, Iowa Bandmasters Assn., Music Educators Nat. Conf., N.Am. Brass Band Assn., Am. Sch. Band Dirs. Assn. Avocations: bicycling, outdoor sports, archery, philately, photography. Home: 3718 Cottage Res Rd NE Solon IA 52333 Office: NAm Brass Band Assn 3718 Cottage Res Rd NE Solon IA 52333 E-mail: jwdesalme@aol.com.

DE SALVA, CHRISTOPHER JOSEPH, lawyer, consultant; b. Milw., June 16, 1950; s. Salvatore Joseph and Elaine Mae De S.; m. Erika Marie De Salva, May 24, 1975; 1 child, Jessica Anne. BA in Polit. Sci., St. Vincent Coll., 1972; JD summa cum laude, Am. Coll. Law, 1987; MBA, Calif. Coast U., 1993, postgrad., 1994. Bar: Calif. 1994, U.S. Dist. Ct. (ctrl. dist., so. dist.) Calif. 1995, U.S. Ct. Fed. Claims 1995, U.S. Tax Ct. 1995, U.S. Supreme Ct. 2000. Founder, owner C.J. De Salva & Assocs. Investment and Mktg. Svcs. of La Quinta (now C.J. De Salva & Assocs., La Quinta, 1979—; pvt. practice La Quinta, Calif., 1994-98, Indio, Calif., 1994—, San Diego, 1996-98. Ceo, pres. The Kings Vault Gallery, Inc., 1985; adj. faculty property law Am. Coll. Law, Brea, Calif., 1989-90, 92-95; life and disability ins. agent C.J. De Salva Ins. Agency 1978—; real estate broker De Salva Realty Calif., 1980—, realtor, 1985-94; tax cons., preparer Christopher De Salva Tax Cons.; cons. Christopher De Salva Bus. and Mgmt. Cons.; lectr. property law. Am. Coll. Law. Author: NAFTA, The Hidden Agenda, 1995. 1st lt. USMC, 1974-77. Recipient Am. Jurisprudence scholarship award Am. Coll. Law. Mem. ABA, Assn. Trial Lawyers, Vietnam Era Vet., Vet. of Latin Am., Nat. Soc. Pub. Accts (cert. 1984), Calif. Bar Assn. Avocations: music, sports, writing songs, flying. Office: 45-902 Oasis St Ste D Indio CA 92201

DE SALVA, SALVATORE JOSEPH, retired pharmacologist, toxicologist; b. N.Y.C., Jan. 14, 1924; s. Nicola Carlo and Frances Agnes (Caldarella) De S.; m. Elaine Mae Radloff, June 14, 1948; children: Salaine Claire De Salva Bonanne, Christopher Joseph, Stephanie De Salva Farrelly, Steven William, Gregory Vincent, Peter Nicholas, Philip Anthony, Deidre De Salva Berry. BS, Marquette U., 1947, MS, 1949; postgrad., U. Ill., Chgo., 1951-53; PhD, Stritch Sch. Medicine, Loyola U., Chgo., 1958. Research and teaching asst. Marquette U., Milw., 1947-49; research biochemist Milw. County Gen. Hosp., 1954; instr. U. Ill., Chgo., 1951-52; asst. prof. Chgo. Coll. Optometry, 1951-53; pharmacologist Armour Pharm. Lab., Chgo, 1953-59; sect. head Colgate Palmolive Co., Piscataway, N.J., 1959-66, sr. research assoc., 1966-72, mgr., 1972-76, assoc. dir. research for pharmacology and toxicology, 1976-83, dir. research pharmacology and toxicology, 1983-88, worldwide ops. dir., 1988-90, corp. dir. human and environ. safety worldwide, 1990-92; pres. Salva Cons. Svcs., Somerset, N.J., 1992-99; ret. 1999. Lectr. Loyola U., 1957-59; mem. technician tng. N.J. Council for Research and Devel., Rutgers U., 1969-72. Editor: Symposium for Biomedical Electronic Instrumentation, 1965; contbr. articles to profl. jours.; patentee in field; current work in pharmaco-toxicology of flourides, sequestering agts. and surfactants, nitrosamine risk assessment, alternative safety testing method devel., safety of triclosan and use in dental therapeutic products. Mem. Park Forest (Ill.) Mosquito Abatement Program, 1952-55, Franklin Twp. (N.J.) Sch. Bd., 1969-70, Somerset (N.J.) Bd. Health, 1965-67, Cath. Youth Orgn., Somerset; v.p. Cedar Hill Swim Club, Somerset; active Boy Scouts Am., Somerset, 1965-67; trustee Franklin Twp. Day Care Ctr., 1969. Served with USN, 1942-46. Mem. AAAS, Soc. Exptl. Biology and Medicine, Am. Soc. Pharmacology and Exptl. Therapeutics, Soc. Toxicology, Internat. Union Pharmacology (toxicology sect.), N.Y. Acad. Scis., Internat. Soc. Regulatory Pharmacology and Toxicology, Internat. Soc. Study of Xenobiotics, Sigma Xi. Roman Catholic. Home: 83 Demott Ln Somerset NJ 08873-1604

DESALVO, JOSEPH SALVATORE, economics educator, researcher; b. Jacksonville, Fla., Aug. 6, 1938; s. John S. and Mary (Costas) DeS.; m. Sandra Ann Birdseye, June 8, 1960; children: Debra Ellen, John Marion. BA in Econs., U. Fla., 1960, MA in Econs., 1961; PhD in Econs., Northwestern U., 1968. Rsch. economist The Rand Corp., Santa Monica, Calif., 1967-71; assoc. prof. U. Wis., Milw., 1971-75, dept. chmn., 1972-74; vis. rsch. prof. Cath. U. Mons, Belgium, 1974-75; prof. U. Wis., Milw., 1975-83; dir. Ctr. for Econ. & Mgmt. Rsch., U. South Fla., Tampa, 1984-89, prof., 1983—, dept. chmn. 1998-03; Author-editor: Perspectives on Regional Transportation Planning, 1975; contbr. articles to profl. jours., chpts to books. Econs.-in-Action fellow Case Inst. Tech., 1962; Univ. fellow Northwestern U., 1963-64. Mem. Am. Econ. Assn., So. Econs. Assn., Reg. Sci. Assn., Am. Real Estate & Urban Econs. Assn., So. Regional Sci. Assn. Home: 4850 Osprey Dr S Apt 201 Saint Petersburg FL 33711-4696 Office: U South Fla Dept Econs Tampa FL 33620

DESANCTIS, ROMAN WILLIAM, cardiologist, educator; b. Cambridge Springs, Pa., Oct. 30, 1930; s. Vincent and Margherita (Marini) DeSanctis; m. Ruth Ann Foley, May 7, 1955; children: Ellen Ruth, Lydia Marie, Andrea Jean, Marcia Louise. BS summa cum laude, U. Ariz., 1951, DSc (hon.), 1999; MD magna cum laude, Harvard U., 1955; DSc (hon.), Wilkes Coll., 1984, U. Ariz., 1998. Diplomate Am. Bd. Internal Medicine, Sub Bd. Cardiovasc. Diseases. Successively intern, asst. resident, sr. resident in medicine Mass. Gen. Hosp., Boston, 1955—56, successively intern, asst. resident, sr. resident in medicine, 1958—60, fellow in cardiology, 1960—62; dir. CCU, 1967—80, dir. clin. cardiology, 1980—98, emeritus, 1998—, physician, 1970—. Mem. faculty Harvard U. Med. Sch., 1964—, Evelyn and James Jenks and Paul Dudley White prof. medicine, 1998—. Co-author: Cardiac Clinico-Pathological Conferences of the Mass. Gen. Hosp., 1972, The Practice of Cardiology, 1989; contbr. articles to med. jours. Officer M.C. USNR, 1956—58. Decorated Order of Dynasty of Alouite Morocco; recipient Excellence in Clin. Tchg. award, Harvard U. Med. Sch., 1990, Centennial Achievement award, U. Ariz., 1989, Alumni Achievement award, U.S. Army, 2001. Fellow: ACP (master of the coll. 1994), Am. Coll. Cardiology (Gifted Tchr. award 1991, Disting. Fellow award 1999); mem.: Am. Clin. and Climatol. Soc., New Eng. Cardiovasc. Soc. (pres. 1979—80), Assn. Univ. Cardiologists, Inst. Medicine, Assn. Am. Physicians, Am. Heart Assn. (David Littmann award 1996, Paul Dudley White award 1999), Knights of Malta, Aesculapian Club, Winchester Country Club. Roman Catholic. Home: 5 Thoreau Cir Winchester MA 01890-3340 Office: Mass Gen Hosp 15 Parkman St # 467 Boston MA 02114-3117

DE SANCTIS, VINCENT, college president; b. Paterson, N.J., July 13, 1941; s. Vincent and Helen (Ruocco) De S.; m. Francine Barone, Aug. 19, 1967; children: Gregory, Stephanie. BA in Social Studies, William Paterson Coll., 1963; MA in Social Studies, Montclair State U., 1966; EdD in Adminstrn. and Supervision, Rutgers U., 1970. Tchr., dept. chmn. Passaic County Tech. and Vocat. High Sch., Wayne, N.J., 1963-68; rsch. asst. Grad. Sch. Edn. Rutgers U., New Brunswick, N.J., 1968-69; asst. dir. Adult Edn. Resource Ctr. Montclair State Coll., Upper Montclair, N.J., 1969-70, dir. Adult Edn. Resource Ctr., 1970-72, dir. HEW region II adult continuing edn. staff devel. project, 1972-75; dean community edn. Pa. Coll. Tech., 1975-78; asst. prof. Sch. Edn. So. Ill. U., Edwardsville, 1978-82; campus exec. officer Pa. State U.-Shenango Valley, Sharon, 1982-87; pres. Warren County Community Coll., Washington, N.J., 1988—. Title III reader U.S. Dept. Edn. Mem. editorial bd. Adult Literacy and Basic Edn., 1977-82, Pitman Learning Series CBTE, 1978-79, Setting the Pace, 1980-82; editorial cons. Career Edn. quarterly, 1979-80; contbr. articles to profl. jours. Chmn. Commn. Adult Basic Edn., 1974; evaluator 70 001, Inc., 1979; mem. Warren County Human Rels. Commn. Mem. Am. Assn. C.C.s, Country C.C. Pres.'s Assn. N.J., Coun. County Colls. N.J. (chair fin. com. 1988-96), Adult Edn. Assn. (cert. leadership), Rotary (chair youth exch. program Belvidere chpt.). Avocations: running, birding, reading. Home: 830 Lopatcong St Belvidere NJ 07823-2012 Office: Warren County Community Coll 475 State Route 57 W Washington NJ 07882-4343

DESANDO, JOHN ANTHONY, retired humanities educator; b. Rochester, N.Y., Sept. 23, 1940; s. Carl James and Marie Louise (Notebaert) DeSando; children: Erik, Courtney, Rachel, Jessica, Thea, Gabrielle. BA, Georgetown U., 1962; MA, PhD, U. Ariz., 1972. Asst. prof. English Norwich U., Northfield, Vt., 1967-74; dir. student activities U. Mass., Boston, 1975-77; dean of students U. Maine, Fort Kent, 1978-79; v.p. acad. affairs Franklin U., Columbus, Ohio, 1980—2002, prof. humanities, ret., 2002. Critic TV program World Film Classics TV series, Columbus, 1990—2003; vice chmn. Film Coun. Greater Columbus, 2000—02; bd. dirs. Spillman Co.; co-host It's Movie Time, WCBE-FM, 2001—. Assoc. editor: Movies on Media Handbook, 1994—; cinema series host Columbus Mus. Art; prodr.: (TV series) World Film Classics, 1998; co-host It's Movie Time, 2001—. Chair humanities divsn. Columbus Internat. Film Festival, 1994—2001; tech. advisor Ohio Humanities Coun., 1995—2001. Recipient Communicator award of Excellence, 2002, Silver Microphone award, 2003. Mem.: MLA, Nat. Coun. Tchrs. English, Nat. Euchre Players Assn. (bd. dirs. 1982—, bd. dirs. literacy coun. 1997—99), Ohio State U. Photography and Cinema Alumni Soc. (bd. dirs. 1997—), Kiwanis (pres. 1994—95). E-mail: desandoj@franklin.edu.

DE SANTIS, CHRISTOPHER CHARLES, education educator, writer; b. Longmont, Colo., 1966; BA, Lewis and Clark Coll., 1987—89; MA in African-Am. studies, U. of Wis.-Madison, 1989—90; PhD in english, U. of Kans., 1992—97. Asst. prof. of am. and african-american lit. Westfield State Coll., Mass., 1997—99; asst. prof. of african-am. and am. lit. Ill. State U., 1999—2002, assoc. prof. of african-am. and am. lit., 2002—. Office: Illinois State University Campus Box 4240 Normal IL 61790 E-mail: ccdesan@ilstu.edu.

DE SANTIS, MARK, osteopathic physician; b. Amityville, N.Y., Jan. 2, 1954; s. Vera De S.; m. Elizabeth Anne King, July 15, 1989; children: Mark Anthony, Matthew Robert. AS in Phys. Sci., Nassau C.C., 1975; BS in Nuclear Medicine, C.W. Post Coll., 1982; MS in Med. Biology, L.I. U., 1991; DO, Kirksville Coll. Osteo. Med., 1993. Registered nuclear medicine technologistl cert. diagnostic radiology resident, Harlam Hosp., N.Y.C., 2002. Asst. Brookhaven Nat. Lab., Upton, N.Y., 1978-87; staff nuclear medicine technologist Sloan-Kettering Meml. Med. Ctr., N.Y.C., 1977-78; asst. radiophysicist, nuc. cardiology tech. L.I. Jewish Med. Ctr., New Hyde Park, N.Y., 1978-88; med. intern Massapequa Gen. Hosp., Seaford, N.Y., 1993-94; osteopathic radiology resident St. Barnabas Hosp., Bronx, N.Y., 1994-95; nuclear medicine resident VA Med. Ctr., Northport, N.Y., 1995-97; forensic radiology cons. Suffolk County Med. Examiners, 2000—. Clin. instr. Sch. Allied Health Profls., Stony Brook U. Health Sci. Ctr., SUNY, 1986-87; medicine clerkship aerospace flight surgeon tng. course NASA, 1993. Contbr. articles to profl. publs. Founder Oil 4 Kids Project. With USN, 1982. Recipient Still Kickin' Editor award KCOM. Mem. Am. Osteo. Assn., Soc. Nuclear Medicine, Am. Roentgen Ray Soc., Am. Osteo. Coll. Radiology. Avocations: computer programming, flying, restoring antique autos, piano. Home: 55 Lincoln Blvd Bethpage NY 11714-5517

DE SANTIS, SYLVIA, library director; b. Palmer, Mass., Mar. 27, 1920; d. Ezio DeS. and Josephine Alonzo. BA in Chemistry, Mt. Holyoke Coll., 1942. Chem. rsch. libr. Jackson Lab., E.I. DuPont, Wilmington, Del., 1942-43, Naugatuck (Conn.) Chem., 1944-45, libr. dir., 1944—49, Monson (Mass.) Free Libr. & Reading Room Assoc., 1949-97; retired, 1997. Cons. in field. Mem. Monson Arts Coun.; Trustees of Reservations Mass. Mem.: Nat. Audubon Soc., Monson Hist. Soc., Western Mass. Libr. Club. Avocations: collecting art, books, photography, gardening. Home: PO Box 358 Monson MA 01057-0358

DE SANTIS, VINCENT PAUL, historian, educator; b. Birdsboro, Pa., Dec. 25, 1916; s. Antonio and Martha Mae (Templin) DeS.; m. Helene O'Brien, June 24, 1946; children— Vincent, Edmund, Philip, John; m. Margaret Lois Lambert, May 13, 1978. BS, West Chester U., Pa., 1941; PhD, Johns Hopkins, 1952. Mem. faculty U. Notre Dame, 1949—, prof. history, 1962—, chmn. dept., 1963-71. Vis. prof. Johns Hopkins, 1954, Bklyn. Coll., 1961, Georgetown U., 1962, U. Genoa, 1967-68, U. Queensland, Australia, 1976, 79, 88, U. Victoria, Can., 1986, 88-90. Author: Republicans Face the Southern Question, 1959, The Shaping of Modern America, 1877-1916, 1973, 2d edit., 1977, Gilded Age Presidents, 1979, President Carter and Human Rights, 1982, The Shaping of Modern America, 1877-1920, 1989, 3rd edit., 2000; co-author: Our Country, 1960, Roman Catholicism and the American Way of Life, 1960, America's Ten Greatest Presidents, 1961, The Democratic Experience, 1963, 68, 73, 76, 81, The Gilded Age, 1968, America Past and Present, 1968, American Foreign Policy in Europe, 1969, America's Eleven Greatest Presidents, 1971, Six Presidents from the Empire State, 1974, The Heritage of 1776, 1976, The Impact of the Cold War, Reconsiderations, 1977, A History of United States Foreign Policy, 4th edit, 1980, Region, Race and Reconstruction, 1982, Popular Images of American Presidents, 1988, The American Presidents, 2000; compiler The Gilded Age, 1973; editor Forum Press Series in American History. Mem. Cath. Commn. on Intellectual and Cultural Affairs. Served to capt. AUS, 1941-45. Recipient R.D.W. Connor award N.C. Lit. and Hist. Assn., 1959, award Am. Philos. Soc., 1955, 62, 63, Disting. Alumni award West Chester State Coll., 1970; Guggenheim fellow, 1960-61; Fulbright lectr., 1967-68, 79, 91-92; Henry E. Huntington grantee, 1973; Radcliffe Coll. grantee, 1982 Mem. Orgn. Am. Historians, Nat. Geog. Soc., Soc. Am. Historians, Am. Cath. Hist. Assn. (pres. 1963-64), Am. Hist. Assn., Soc. for History Edn., Soc. for Historians of Am. Fgn. Rels., So. Hist. Assn., Am. Studies Assn., AAUP, Nat. Audubon Soc., Edward Frederick Sorin Soc., No. Ind. Hist. Soc., Phi Alpha Theta. Home: PO Box 562 Notre Dame IN 46556-0562

DE SANTO, DONALD JAMES, psychologist, educational administrator; b. Bklyn., July 5, 1942; s. Vincent James and Rose Ann (Dowd) DeS.; m. Loretta DePippo, Aug. 25, 1962; children: Dolores, Jennifer, Marisa. BA cum laude, St. Francis Coll., N.Y., 1964; MA in Clin./Child Psychology, St. John's U., 1966; profl. diploma, 1976; hon. degree, Oglala Lakota Coll., 1999. Asst. law libr. rsch. asst. Dewey, Ballantine, Bushby, Palmer & Wood, N.Y.C., 1960-64; rsch. asst. St. John's U., N.Y.C., 1964-65, tchg. fellow, 1965-66; project dir. 2 federally funded grants, 1975-76; dir. The Rugby Sch., Freehold, N.J., 1977—. People to People amb. to Cuba, 2001. Contbg. editor Channels jour. spl. educators, 1986-90, 96—. Mem. Nat. Trust Historic Preservation; mem. Youth Guidance; mem. Youth Guidance Com., Freehold, 1983—, chmn. econ. devel. com., 1984-86; mem. Econ. Devel. Com., Freehold, 1983-87; mem. Zoning Bd Adjustment, Freehold, 1985-86; commr. Lake Topanemus Commn., 1990-94; Rep. campaign chmn., Freehold, 1990, 91; bd. dirs. Monmouth County Transp. Assn., 1990, 91-92; mem. U.S. Selective Svc. Bd., 1991—; apptd. Selective Svc. Commn., 1992; v.p. Freehold Rep. Club, 1991-92; mem. adv. bd. Congl. Awards Com., 1994-98; mcpl. chmn. Freehold Borough Rep. Party, 1995; appt. Rep. Nat. Com., 1995; participant, amb. People to People, Beijing, 1995, Cuba, 2000; mem. exec. bd. Monmouth County Mental Health Assn. Recipient Fire Prevention medal, N.Y.C., 1954, citation for outstanding contbn. to arts in edn. N.J. Commr. Edn., 1981, Pres. award Assn. Schs. and Agys. for the Handicapped, 1995-96, N.J. Very Spl. Arts award, 1996, N.J. Gov's. Arts in Edn. award, 1996; Title VIb Fed. grantee, 1972-78. Mem. NRA (life), APA (pub. rels. com. div. 16), Nat. Assn. Pvt. Schs. Exceptional Children, Coun. Exceptional Children, N.J. Assn. Schs. and Agys. for Handicapped (sec., conf. chmn. 1983-84, pub. rels. chmn. 1984-86, Pres. award 1995-96, Legacy of Caring award 2002), Nat. Soc. Psychologists in Mgmt., Assn. for Help Retarded Children, Monmouth County Hist. Assn., N.J. Assn. Children With Learning Disabilities, Nat. Assn. Pvt. Schs. Exceptional Children, Optimists, Monmouth County Mental Health Assn. (bd. dirs.), Elks, Nat. Assn. Sch. Psychologists, Psi Chi, Phi Delta Kappa. Roman Catholic. Home: 222 Park Ave Freehold NJ 07728-2006 Office: care Rugby Sch at Woodfield PO Box 1403 Belmar NJ 07719-1403 E-mail: Poppled@aol.com.

DESANTO, JAMES JOHN, lawyer; b. Chgo., Oct. 12, 1943; s. John Joseph and Erminia Asunda (Cassano) DeS.; m. Denise Clare Caneva, Feb. 3, 1968; children: Carrie Ann, James Thomas, John Joseph. BA, U. Ill., 1965; JD, DePaul U., 1969. Bar: Ill. 1969, U.S. Dist. Ct. (no. dist.) Ill. 1969, U.S. Ct. Appeals (7th cir.) 1972, U.S. Supreme Ct. 1974; cert. mediator 19th Jud. Circuit, Ill., 1996. Asst. state's atty., Waukegan, Ill., 1969-72; assoc. Finn, Geiger & Rafferty, Waukegan, 1972-74; ptnr. Rawles, Katz & DeSanto, Waukegan, 1975-80; pvt. practice, Waukegan, 1980-88; sr. ptnr. DeSanto & Bonamarte, Waukegan, 1988-91; pvt. practice, Libertyville, Ill., 1991—, James J. DeSanto and Assocs., 1992-99; ptnr. DeSanto, Morgan & Mittelman, Libertyville, 1999—. Lectr. in trial technique and practice Ill. Inst. for CLE and

Ill. Bar Assn.; lectr. in bus. law Coll. of Lake County, 1974-84; bd. dirs. Ill. State Bar Assn. Mut. Ins. Co., 1989—, chair com. on fin. and investment 1995-97, 2000-01, sec./treas., 1999—, 2d v.p., 2001-02, 1st v.p., 2002—, chmn. bd. dirs., 2003—. Co-editor Tort Trends newsletter, 1988-91. Trustee Village of Libertyville, 1991-93; chairperson parish pastoral coun. St. Joseph's Ch., Libertyville, 2000-02. Fellow Ill. Bar Inst.; mem. ATLA, State Bar Assn. (mem. ad hoc com. profl. quality in practice of law, 1995—, ins. law sect. coun., 2001—), Ill. State Bar Assn., Lake County Bar Assn. (sec. 1979-80, 2d v.p. 1991-92, pres. 1993-94), Lake County Trial Lawyers Assn. (sec. 1985—), Jefferson Inns of Ct., Libertyville Rotary (pres. 1990-91). Avocations: golf, fishing. Home: 1209 St William Dr Libertyville IL 60048-1275 Office: 712 Florsheim Dr Libertyville IL 60048-5270 E-mail: desanto@iconnect.net.

DESAULNIERS, RENE GERARD LESIEUR, retired optometrist; b. Danielson, Conn., Oct. 21, 1922; s. Egide A. and Rose (Regis) D.; children: Suzanne Rose Bauzys, Maureen Frances Russe, Michelle Elizabeth Van Haagen, Thomas Benedict, John Christopher. Grad., U.S. Army Mil. Intel. Sch.; student, Georgetown U., 1943, Boston U., 1944; OD, Pa. Coll. Optometry, 1948; grad., Joe Brinkman Profl. Umpire Sch., Fla. Lic. optometrist Conn., Fla., R.I. Individual practice optometry, Putnam, Conn., 1948-98; ret., 1998. Externship Gessel Inst. Child Devel. Yale U., 1964-92; past pres. Conn. Bd. Examiners in Optometry, 1957-91; past pres. Internat. Assn. Bd. Examiners in Optometry; past pres. Nat. Bd. Examiners in Optometry, 1975-85. Life mem., former nat. dir. Am. Optometric Found.; past pres. Putnam Little League; 2d pres. Quinnebaug Valley Assn. for Retarded, 1963; past mem. Putnam Sch. Bd.; chmn. DK Hosp. Devel. Fund, 1984—85. Lt. U.S. Army, 1943—46, maj. inf. USAR, 1946—63. Recipient Sam Levitt Meml. award, 1948; named Conn. Optometrist of Yr., 1989. Fellow: Nat. Acad. Practices (Disting. Practitioner), Am. Acad. Optometry; mem.: Nat. League Umpires Baseball, Conn. Assn. Optometrists, Am. Optometric Assn., New Eng. Coun. Optometrists (chmn. 42nd Congress), Conn. Approved Baseball Umpires (ea. bd. past pres. 1981—82), Am. League Umpires Baseball (vision cons.), Am. Legion (baseball com., VFW commn.), Elk, KC (4th degree), Omega Delta. Home: 41 Grove St Putnam CT 06260-2107

DE SAUSSURE, RICHARD LAURENS, JR., retired neurosurgery educator; b. Dec. 29, 1917; s. Richard Laurens and Margaret Hamilton De Saussure; m. Phyllis H. Falk; children: Alexis Laurens, Richard Laurens III, Denise Anita. AB, U. Va., 1939, MD, 1942. Diplomate Am. Bd. Neurol. Surgery (sec. 1970-73). Dean U. Tenn., Memphis, 1980-88; intern U. Va. Hosp., 1942-43, resident neurosurgery, 1946-47, 48-49; resident Cin. Gen. Hosp., Memphis, 1947-48; chief neurol. surgery VA Hosp., Memphis, 1949-50; mem. Semmes Murphy Clinic, 1951-82; instr. to prof. neurol. surgery U. Tenn., Memphis, 1950-88, dean, 1980-88, prof. emeritus, 1988—. Contbr. articles to med. jours. Maj. M.C., U.S. Army, 1943-46. Named Disting. Neurosurgeon, South Neurol. Surgery Soc., 1990; recipient Harvey Cushing medal Am. Assn. Neurol. Surgery, 1995. Republican. Episcopalian. Avocations: photography, golf, chess. Home: 4290 Heatherwood Ln Memphis TN 38117-2302 E-mail: DeSRichard@aol.com.

DE SAVORGNANI, ADRIANE ALDRICH, health care administrator, nurse; b. Boston, Dec. 17, 1940; d. Merritt James Aldrich and Edith Carolyn (Borrebach); m. Luciano de Savorgnani, Aug. 1, 1979 (dec. Aug. 2002); children: Andrew, Alexia, Miranda. AB, Radcliffe Coll., 1962; diploma in nursing coord. program, Radcliffe Coll./Mass. Gen Hosp, 1965; MPH, U. Hawaii, 1974; DBA, Nova U., 1992. RN, Hawaii; cert. nursing adminstrn. advanced. Clin. nurse Dept. Public Health, Washington, 1966-67; staff nurse pediat., obstetrics, nursery, med.-surg. U.S. Naval Hosp., Naples, Italy, 1967-69; pub. health nurse Dept. Human Resources, Washington, 1969-72; staff nurse, ob-gyn., nursery, recovery rm. Kapiolani Hosp., Honolulu, 1972-75; rsch. nurse U. Hawaii Newborn Psychology Rsch. Lab, Honolulu, 1974-75; staff nurse, med. and gynecol. oncology Naval Regional Med. Ctr., San Diego, 1975-78; staff nurse emergency rm. Naval Aerospace Reg. Med. Ctr., Pensacola, Fla., 1978-79; charge nurse, emergency rm. outpatient-inpatient care coord. U.S. Naval Hosp., Naples, Italy, 1979-83; charge nurse military med. dept., utilization rev., discharge planning Naval Hosp., Newport, R.I., 1983-86; head, Reg./Fleet Support, Naval Med. Command N.E. Region, Great Lakes, Ill., 1986-89; head health care plans spl. projects, head preventive med. health promotion br. Bur. Medicine and Surgery, Washington, 1989—92; exec. officer Naval Med. Clinic, Key West, Fla., 1993—. Asst. dir. nursing svcs. Naval Hosp., Jacksonville, Fla., 1992—95, exec. officer, Lemoore, Calif., 1995—98; comdg. officer U.S. Naval Med. Clins., U.K., 1998—2001; head clin. plans and mgmt., acting asst. dep. chief med. ops. support Bur. Medicine and Surgery, Washington, 2001—03; adminstrv. asst. to def. attaché office US Embassy, London, 2003—; adminstrv. asst. Def. Atache Office, Am. Embassy, London, 2003—. Contbr. articles to profl. jours. Lector, lay eucharistic minister, choir accompanist; vol. local sch.; vol. tchr. ESL; vol. women's homeless shelter. Capt., Nurse Corps, U.S. Navy, 1975-2003. Decorated Legion of Merit, Meritorious Svc. medal (5), Navy and Marine Corps Commendation medal (2), Nat. Def. medal (2), Vol. Svc. medal, Navy and Marine Corps Overseas Svc. Ribbon (7 stars);; recipient Clara Barton award, ARC, Naples, 1983, cert. of appreciation, Operation Desert Storm, Washington, 1991, Jane A. Delano award, ARC London, 2001, dir.'s award, Human Resources Svc. Ctr., Europe, 2001. Fellow Am. Coll. Healthcare Execs.; mem. ANA, APHA, Assn. Mil. Surgeons U.S. (life), Acad. Mgmt., Internat. Tng. in Comm., ARC (instr.), Navy Nurse Corps. Assn., Coll. Alumnae Assns., Sigma Theta Tau. Republican. Roman Catholic. Avocations: piano, theatre, art, travel, physical fitness. Home: 14 Bardsley Ln Greenwich London SE10 9RF England

DESBARATS, PETER HULLETT, journalist, academic administrator; b. Montreal, Que., Can., July 2, 1933; s. Hullett John and Margaret Ogston (Rettie) D. Student, Loyola Coll., Montreal, 1951. Feature writer The Gazette, Montreal, 1953-55; local reporter Reuters, London, 1955; feature writer The Winnipeg (Can.) Tribune, 1956, legis. reporter, 1957-60; polit. reporter, feature writer The Montreal Star, 1960-65; editor Parallel Mag., Montreal, 1965; host nightly news and pub. affairs show Sta. CBC-TV, Montreal, 1966-70; Ottawa editor Toronto Star, 1970-72; Ottawa bur. chief Global TV, 1973-80; sr. cons. Royal Commn. on Newspapers, Ottawa, 1980-81; dean Sch. Journalism U. Western Ont., London, 1981-96, assoc. prof. journalism, 1981-86, prof., 1986-96, dir. Univ. Club, 1987, also mem. various coms. MacLean Hunter chair comm. ethics U. Toronto, 2000—01; mem. comms. adv. com. Can. commn. UNESCO; cons. Task Force on Broadcasting Policy, 1985, Royal Commn. Electoral Reform, 1991, House of Commons Broadcasting com., Ottawa, 2002, others; mem. selection com. Can. News Hall of Fame, 1986—; spkr. on journalism and the role of the media numerous sites throughout the U.S., Can., overseas; mem. Ont. Task Force Cardiovasc. Scis., 1991, Can. Observers' Mission to Romania, 1992; commr. Commn. on Inquiry into Deployment of Can. Forces to Somalia, 1995—96; columnist The Globe and Mail, Toronto, 1997—2002, The Free Press, London, 1998—2002; former Can. corr. The Nat. Observer, Washington. Author: The State of Quebec, 1965, Gabrielle and Selena, 1966, René: A Canadian in Search of a Country, 1976; author: (book of poetry) The Night the City Sang, 1977; author: The Hecklers, 1979, Canada Lost/Canada Found: The Search for a New Nation, 1981, Colin and the Computer, 1985, Guide to Canadian News Media, 1990, rev. edit., 1996, Somalia Cover-up: A Commissioner's Journal, 1997, (plays) The Great White Computer, 1966, Her Worship, 2002; editor: What They Used to Tell About Indian Legends from Labrador, 1969, Freedom of Expression and New Communication Technologies, 1998; mem. editl. bd. Can. Jour. Comm., 1987—, co-host PBS series The Editors, 1987—91. Bd. dirs. Performing Arts Ctr. for Today, London, 1993-95, Orch. London, 1993-99; bd. dirs. London Mus. Archaeology, 1993—, v.p., 2001-2003, pres., 2003—. Recipient Best News Broadcaster award Assn. Can. TV and Radio Artists, 1977, Best TV Interviewer award Assn. Can. TV and Radio Artists, 1980, 125th Anniversary Confedn. Can. medal, 1992. Mem. Can. Assn. Journalists, Can. Civil Liberties Assn. (bd. dirs. 1998—), Can. Journalism Found. (bd. dirs. 1997—, chmn. rsch. com.). E-mail: desbarat@uwo.ca.

DESCH, THEODORE EDWARD, retired health insurance company executive, lawyer; b. Chgo., Oct. 1, 1931; s. Louis G. and Dorothy (Prieb) D.; m. Donna K. Thorsell, Feb. 3, 1951; children: Theodore M. (dec. 1968), Steven R., Katherine S. Collins, Gregory S. AB, U. Ill., 1952, LLB, 1954. Bar: Ill. 1954; cert. employee benefits specialist, CLU, ChFC. Asst. gen. atty. C.,R.I.&P. R.R., 1956-59, gen. atty., 1959-65, gen. counsel, 1965-68, v.p. and gen. counsel, 1968-70, vice chmn. bd., 1970-73, chmn. bd., 1973-74, chief exec. officer, 1970-74, dir., 1970-75; ptnr. Kirkland & Ellis, Chgo., 1975-77; sr. v.p. law and pub. affairs Health Care Svc. Corp., a Mut. Legal Res. Co., Blue Cross and Blue Shield Ill., Chgo., 1977-86, sr. v.p. law and corp. affairs, 1986-97; sr. v.p. govt. contracts Chgo., 1997-98; ret., 1998; acting deputy gen. counsel Blue Cross and Blue Shield Assoc., Chgo., 2001—02. Bd. dirs., chmn. Preferred Fin. Corp., Denver; bd. dirs. Walker Parking Cons., Inc., Elgin, Ill., Isaac Ray Ctr., Inc., Chgo., Colo. Bankers Life Ins. Co. Trustee North Cen. Coll., Naperville; bd. dirs., pres. Naperville Elderly Homes, Inc.; mem. adv. bd. dirs. Salvation Army, Chgo. 1st lt., inf. U.S. Army, 1954-56. Mem. ABA, Ill. Bar Assn., Chgo. Bar Assn., Union League, Sky-Line Club, Cress Creek Country Club, Delta Sigma Phi (found. bd. trustees), Phi Alpha Delta. Home: 129 Springwood Dr Naperville IL 60540-7331

DESCHAINE, BARBARA RALPH, retired real estate broker; b. Syracuse, N.Y., Feb. 16, 1930; d. George John and Dora Belle (Manchester) Ralph; children by previous marriage: Olav Bernt Kollevoll Jr., Kristan George Kollevoll, Eric John Kollevoll; m. Bernard Richard Deschaine May 23, 1981 (dec. 1994). BA, St. Lawrence U., 1952; postgrad., Pa. State U., 1969-72; grad., Pa. Realtors Inst., 1973; student, Realtors Nat. Mktg. Inst., 1974-75. Salesman Brose Realty, Easton, Pa., 1967-72, assoc. broker/mgr., 1973, broker, owner, 1974-85; broker, mgr. John W. Monaghan Corp. Realtors, 1985-91; assoc. broker The Prudential/Paul Ford Realtors, Easton, 1991-99. Mem. Pa. Real Estate Polit. Edn. Com. Bd. dirs. Easton Area C. of C., 1973-79, v.p. organizational improvement, 1975-76, v.p. econ. devel., 1976-77, pres., 1977-78; mem. Greater Easton Corp. Strategy Group, 1977-78; mem. Northampton County Revenue Appeals Bd., 1982-98, co-chmn., 1994-98; trustee Easton area YMCA, 1984-91; bd. dirs. State Theatre for the Arts, 1994-2002. Mem.: NAFE, Sales and Mktg. Execs. (bd. dirs. Easton area chpt. 1976—91, Disting. Sales award 1982), Homes for Living Network (state chmn. 1980), Ea. Northampton County Multiple Listing Svc. (bd. dirs. 1987—91, pres. 1986), Lehigh Valley Assn. Realtors (bd. dirs. 1973—87, sec. 1977, v.p. 1980—81, pres. 1972, Realtor of Yr. 1978), Pa. Assn. Realtors, Nat. Assn. Realtors, Phi Beta Kappa. Republican. Presbyterian. Address: 384 Hobson Place Blue Bell PA 19422

DESCHAMP, CLYDE, emergency medical technician; b. Memphis, Aug. 8, 1956; s. Hilbert Joseph and Edith Deschamp; m. Nancy Ann Deschamp; children: Christopher, David. BS, U. So. Miss., 1985, MEd, 1986. Ops. mgr. AAA Ambulance, Hattiesburg, Miss., 1985-90; dir. Ctrl. Miss. Emergency Med. Svcs. Dist., Jackson, 1993—; dir. helicopter transport SAA, Jackson, 1993—; chmn. EMTs U. Miss. Med. Ctr., Jackson, 1990—. Expert witness, bd. dirs. Trauma Sys. Ctrl. Region, Jackson, 1999—. Author: (with others) Financial Management in Public Organizations, 1995, Paramedic Emergency Care, 1998, Pediatric Prehospital Care, 1999. Mem. Am. Coll. Healthcare Execs., Alpha Eta. Home: 417 Millrun Rd Brandon MS 39047-9013 Office: U Miss Med Ctr 2500 N State St Jackson MS 39216-4500

DESCHAMPS, CLAUDE, thoracic surgeon; b. Montreal, Que., Can., Apr. 6, 1955; s. Julien Deschamps and Marcelle Despatis; m. Brigitte Barrette, July 27, 1991; children: Emilie, Brice. DEC, Rosemont Coll., Montreal, 1974; MD, U. Montreal, 1979. Gen. surgery resident U. Montreal Hosp.; thoracic surgery resident Mayo Clinic and Found.; asst. prof. surgery U. Montreal, 1989-91; cons. thoracic surgery Mayo Clin., Rochester, Minn., 1991—. Office: Mayo Clin 200 1st St SW Rochester MN 55905-0001

DESCHINNY, ISABEL, elementary school educator; b. Pine Springs, Ariz., Sept. 6, 1943; d. James Clah and Mabel Burnside Myers; m. Daniel Deschinny Sr., Aug. 28, 1965 (dec. Dec. 1997); children: Daniel Jr., Ronald Sr., Mark, Janet. BA, No. Ariz. U., 1986; BS in Elem. Edn., Prescott Coll., 1999. Cert. tchr. Ariz. Tchr. 2d grade, Window Rock, Ariz., 2002—03. Mem. Pine Springs Sch. Bd. (Navajo Nation), Pine Sprs. Houck, Ariz., 1986—92. Scholar, Navajo Tribal Edn. Com., Window Rock, 1963—86. Roman Catholic. Avocation: Navajo weaving. Home: PO Box 4677 Window Rock AZ 86515 Office: Window Rock Elem Sch Chee Dodge Dr Window Rock AZ 86515

DESCHNER, JANE WAGGONER, photo artist, public relations consultant; b. Bellefont, Pa., Feb. 9, 1948; d. George Ruble and Helen Louise (Talbert) Waggoner; m. William Henry Deschner, July 26, 1969 (div. Dec. 1987); children: John William, Elisabeth Anne. BA in Geography, U. Kans., 1969; BA in Art, Mont. State U., Billings, 1987; MFA in Visual Art, Vt. Coll., 2002. Economist Mid-Am. Regional Coun., Kansas City, Mo., 1970-73; ptnr., owner Castle Art Gallery, Billings, Mont., 1982-88; asst. dir. client svcs. Mont. Inst. of Arts Found., Billings, 1988-89; account exec., artist, writer Exclamation Point Advt., Billings, 1989-94; artist, project coord. Billings, 1981—; project coord., cons. pub. rels./graphic design, 1994—; curator Women's Ctrt. Gallery and D.A. Davidson & Co. Gallery, Billings, 2003—. Coord. Art in the Libr. program Rocky Mountain Coll., Billings. Exhibited at Nicolaysen Art Mus., Casper, Wyo., Toucan Gallery, Billings, U. Mont., Missoula, Mont., Art Mus. Missoula, Mont. State U., Billings, Holter Mus. Art, Helena, Mont., Broken Diamond Gallery, Billings, Mont. State U., Bozeman, Deering Galleries, Taos, N.Mex., Contemporary Art Mus., Sacramento, St. Vincent Healthcare, Billings, Mont. Art of Survival, Healing in Life, 2000-. Bd. dirs. Billings Mental Health Assn., 1988-92, v.p., 1989, 90; gallery dir., Bd. dirs. The Women's Ctr., St. Vincent Healthcare, Billings, 1991—; mem. Youth Ct. Conf. Com. 13th Jud. Dist. Mont., Billings, 1992—; Poets on the Prairie artist YMCA Writer's Voice; bd. dirs. InterMountain Planned Parenthood, 1998-2001. Recipient 1st pl. award in non-comml. art Billings Advt. and Mktg. Assn., 1992, 93; Sam and Alfreda Maloof scholar Anderson Ranch Arts Ctr., 1998-99; State of Mont. profl. devel. grantee, 1999. Mem. Yellowstone Print Club (bd. dirs., pres. acquisitions chair), Yellowstone Art Ctr. (Auction Artist 1989-2002), Soc. for the Arts in Healthcare (bd. dirs.). Unitarian Universalist. Avocations: travel, cooking, reading. Studio: 1313 Granite Ave Billings MT 59102-0869 E-mail: janed@wtp.net.

DESCHUYTNER, EDWARD ALPHONSE, biochemist, educator; b. Chelsea, Mass., Sept. 3, 1944; s. Alphonso and Josephine Elizabeth (Kiewlicz) D.; m. Carolyn Ann McGraw, Aug. 1, 1971; children: Brian Charles, Matthew Edward. BA, Northeastern U., 1967; PhD, Boston Coll., 1972. Asst. in floriculture Waltham Exptl. Field Sta. U. Mass., 1963-64; lab. technician Mass. Soldiers Home, Chelsea, 1964-65; rsch. asst. New Eng. Med. Ctr. Hosps., Boston, 1965-67; asst. Cancer Rsch. Inst., Boston Coll., 1967-71; from mem. faculty to prof. biology No. Essex C.C., Haverhill, Mass., 1971—2002, prof. biology, 2002—, chmn. dept. natural scis., 1988—95, asst. dean math., sci., and tech., 1995—98, assoc. dean math., sci., techs. and health professions, 1998—2002. Grant rev. panelist NSF, 1976-80; program coord. Eisenhower Title II Math. and Sci. Grant, 1989—; elected Region A dir. Nat. Sci. Edn. Leadership Assn., 1995-98; project dir. Bell Atlantic Ed Link, 1998-99, 2000-01; bd. dirs. Mass. Sci. Educators Hall of Fame, 2002--; project dir. Sci. Adventures for Everyone, 2000--. Author: (software) Biology in Action series, 1983, (with others) Principles of Biology, 2nd. ed., 1986, A Study and Laboratory Guide for Anatomy and Physiology, 2nd. ed., 1990. Recipient citation for Outstanding Performance, Commonwealth of Mass., 1991, Mass. Sci. Educator of Yr. for Essex County, 1996; Named Mass. Assn. Sci. Suprs. Outstanding Sci. Educator of Yr., 1998; Eisenhower Title II Math. and Sci. grantee, 1989-90, 91-92, 92-93, 93-94, 94-95, Nat. Edn. Act fellow Boston Coll., 1968-71, Sci. Educator of Yr. for Essex County, 1996, Outstanding Svc. and Leadership award Nat. Sci. Edn. Leadership Assn., 1998, 99, award for Excellence in Tchg. and Leadership, Nat. Inst. Staff and Orgnl. Devel., 2003; named to Mass. Sci. Educator's Hall of Fame, 2001. Mem. AAAS, Am. Soc. for Microbiology, N.Y. Acad. Scis., Mass. Assn. Sci. Tchrs., Mass. Assn. Sci. Suprs., Nat. Sci. Tchrs. Assn., North Shore Sci. Suprs. Assn. (pres. 1995-96, 96-97), Nat. Assn. Biology Tchrs. Office: No Essex Community Coll 100 Elliott St Haverhill MA 01830-2306 Business E-mail: edeschuytner@necc.mass.edu.

DESCOTEAUX, CAROL J. health facility administrator; b. Nashua, N.H., Apr. 5, 1948; d. Henry Louis and Therese (Arel) D. BA, Notre Dame Coll., 1970; MEd, Boston Coll., 1975; MA, U. Notre Dame, 1984, PhD, 1985. Jr. high sch. instr., dir. religious studies St. Joseph's Sch., North Grosvenordale, Conn., 1970-73; jr. high sch. tchr., dir. religious edn. Notre Dame Sch., North Adams, Mass., 1973-77, 1978—81; chairperson religious studies discipline Notre Dame Coll. Grad. Theol. Union, U. Notre Dame, Ind., 1982-83, 84-85; jr. high sch. instr. Sacred Heart Sch., Groton, Conn., 1977-78; pres. Notre Dame Coll., Manchester, NH, 1985—99; v.p. mission integration St. Joseph Hosp., Nashua, NH, 2000—. Trustee King's Coll., Wilkes-Barre, Pa., 1987-95; pres. Fedn. of Holy Cross Colls., 1985-96; mem. adv. bd. Manchester Christian Life Ctr., 1978-80; treas. N.H. Coll. and Univ. Council, Manchester, 1985-86; trustee N.H. Higher Edn. Assistance Found., 1986—. Mem. Manchester United Way campaign, 1985—; bd. incorporators, mem. ethics com., instl. research com. Cath. Med. Ctr., Manchester, 1986—99; mem. bd. trustees Dartmouth-Hitchcock Med. Ctr., Marguertie's Place, St. Joseph Cmty. Svcs., N.H. Partnership for End-of-Life Care, Stonehill Coll., Rivier Coll. Named Disting. Woman Leader of Yr., So. N.H. region YWCA, 1985, N.H. Disting. Woman Educator, 1994, Manchester Citizen of Yr., 1995, N.H. Boston Coll. Alumna of Yr., 1990, N.H. U. Notre Dame Alumna of Yr., 1992. Mem. Am. Acad. Religion, Coll. Theology Soc. Am., N.H. Women's Forum, Soc. Christian Ethics, Nat. Hospice and Palliative Care Assn., Cath. Hosp. Assn. Am. Democrat. Roman Catholic. Avocations: art, music, theater, fishing, bowling. Office: St Joseph Hosp 172 Kinsley St Nashua NH 03060-3688

DESCY, DON EDMOND, library media technology educator, writer, editor; b. Hartford, Conn., Jan. 11, 1944; s. Henry Julian and Lillian D.V. (Svenson) D. BS in Biology Edn., Ctrl. Conn. State U., 1967, MS in Biology Edn., 1970; cert. in instrnl. media, U. Conn., 1981, PhD in Media and Tech., 1987. Tchg. asst. Ctrl. Conn. State U., New Britain, 1967-68; rsch. asst. Coll. Edn. U. Conn., Storrs, 1985-87; asst. adminstrv. dir. Conn. State Bar Examining Com., Hartford, 1987-89; adj. prof. Ea. Conn. State U., Willimantic, 1987-89, Ctrl. Conn. State U., New Britain, 1988-89; prof. Minn. State U., Mankato, 1989—, tech. coord., 1994—, program dir., 1998—. Numerous presentations in field in 5 countries. Author: Computer as an Educational Tool; mem. editl. bd. Internat. Jour. Instrnl. Media, 1991—, Quar. Jour. Distance Edn., 1999—, Techtrends, 1994—; columnist, editor-in-chief Techtrends, 1993—; contbr. over 80 articles to profl. jours., 4 chpts. to books, 1 textbook. Scholar Conn. Ednl. Media Assn., 1984, rsch. scholar Japan, 1996. Mem. ALA, Internat. Soc. Tech. in Edn., Assn. Ednl. Comm. and Tech. (pres. Twin Cities chpt., Disting. Svc. award 2000), Am. Assn. Sch. Librs., Minn. Ednl. Media Orgn. Office: Minn State U Mankato 313 Armstrong Hall Mankato MN 56001-6042 E-mail: desc4@mnsu.edu.

DE SEAR, EDWARD MARSHALL, lawyer; b. Bradenton, Fla, Oct. 27, 1946; s. Robert Ashland and Shirley Ethelwyne (Griffin) De S.; m. Patricia Gail Healy, Aug. 8, 1970; children: Emily, Andrew. AB, Columbia Coll., 1968; JD, U. Va., 1973. Bar: NY 1974. Ptnr. Brown & Wood, NYC, 1973-82; v.p. Salomon Bros., Inc., NYC, 1982-88; ptnr. Milbank, Tweed Hadley & McCloy, NYC, 1988-93, Orrick, Herrington & Sutcliffe, LLP, NYC, 1993—2003, head structured fin. group, 1998—2003; ptnr. McKee Nelson LLP, NYC, 2003—. Mem. Alumni Recruiting Comm., Columbia U., NYC, 1984—. Mem. ABA, Phi Gamma Delta. Republican. Episcopalian. Office: McKee Nelson LLP 5 Times Square 35th Fl New York NY 10036

DE SELDING, EDWARD BERTRAND, retired banker; b. Summit, N.J., June 15, 1926; s. Edward Fitzgerald and Alene (Rockwell) deS.; m. Joan Bulkley, Oct. 21, 1950; children— Peter, Ann, Edward Bertrand. BA, Yale, 1950. With Spencer Trask & Co., Inc., N.Y.C., 1950-77, ptnr., 1962-68, sr. v.p., dir., 1968-77, Hornblower, Weeks, Noyes & Trask, Inc., N.Y.C., 1977-78; 1st v.p. Loeb Rhoades, Hornblower & Co., 1978-79; v.p. Bruns, Nordeman, Rea & Co., N.Y.C., 1979-81, Bache Halsey Stuart, Inc., 1981-82, Conn. Nat. Bank, 1982-91, ret. Served with USAAF, 1944-46. Mem.: NASD (chmn. dist. 12 com. 1971, gov. 1972), Tokeneke Club (pres. 1974—75), Sawgrass Country Club (gov., pres. 2001). Republican. Episcopalian (vestryman 1961-63, 67-69, 77-79, warden 1984-87). Home: 9003 Lake Kathryn Dr Ponte Vedra Beach FL 32082-2919

DESER, STANLEY, physicist, educator; b. Rovno, Poland, Mar. 19, 1931; BS summa cum laude, Bklyn. Coll., 1949; MA, Harvard U., 1950, PhD, 1953; DPhil (hon.), Stockholm U., 1978; DTech (hon.), Chalmers Tech. U., 2001. Mem. Inst. Advanced Study, Princeton, 1953-55, 93-94, Parker fellow, 1953-54; Jewett fellow Inst. for Advanced Study, Princeton, 1954-55; NSF postdoctoral fellow, mem. Inst. Theoretical Physics, Copenhagen, 1955-57; lectr. Harvard U., 1957-58; mem. faculty Brandeis U., Waltham, Mass., 1958—, prof. physics, 1965—, chmn. dept., 1969-71, 76-77, Ancell prof. physics, 1979—; E. Schrödinger prof. U. Vienna, 1996. Vis. scientist European Ctr. Nuclear Rsch., Geneva, 1962-63, 76, 80-81, 94; mem. physics adv. com. NSF, 1982-86; Fulbright and Guggenheim fellow, vis. prof. Sorbonne, Paris, 1966-67, 71-72; Loeb lectr. Harvard U., 1975; S.R.C. sr. fellow Imperial Coll., 1976; vis. prof. College de France, Paris, 1976, 84; vis. fellow All Souls' Coll., Oxford (Eng.) U., 1977; investigator titular ad honorem CIDA (Venezuela); Fulbright prof. U. of the Republic Montevideo Uruguay, 1970. Mem. editl. bd. Jour. Geometry and Physics, Jour. Math Physics, Jour. High Energy Physics, mem. sci. bd. I.H.E.S., France, 1991—97, Inst. Theoretical Physics, Santa Barbara, 1989—93, chmn. sci. bd., 1992—93. Recipient Dannie Heineman prize, Am. Inst. Physics, 1994. Fellow: NAS, Am. Acad. Arts and Scis., Am. Phys. Soc.; mem.: Turin (Italy) Acad. Sci. (hon.; fgn.). Office: Brandeis U Physics Dept MS057 Waltham MA 02454

DE SERRES, FREDERICK JOSEPH, genetic toxicologist; b. Dobbs Ferry, N.Y., Sept. 24, 1929; s. Frederick J. and Helen Marie (Henshaw) de S.; m. Christine Marie Covone, Sept. 18, 1954; children: Mark, John, Paul, David, Jonathan, Lianne. BS in Biology, Tufts U., Medford, Mass., 1951; MS in Botany, Yale U., 1953, PhD, 1955; Doctorate (honoris causa), Cath. U. of Louvain, 1987. Research assoc. biology div. Oak Ridge Nat. Lab., 1955-57, sr. staff biologist, 1957-72; experimenters rep. NASA biosatellite program, 1964-68; coord. environ. mutagenesis program Oak Ridge Nat. Lab., 1969-72; lectr. U. Tenn., 1971-73; adj. prof. dept. pathology U. N.C., Chapel Hill, 1973-90; chief environ. mutagenesis br. Nat. Inst. Environ. Health Scis., Research Triangle Park, N.C., 1972-76, assoc. dir. genetics, 1976-86, guest rschr., 1994-98; rsch. dir. Ctr. for Life Scis. and Toxicology Rsch. Triangle Inst., Research Triangle Park, N.C., 1986-93, prin. sci., 1993-94; guest rschr. Nat. Toxicology program Nat. Inst. Environ. Health Scis., Research Triangle Park, N.C., 1994—; sr. cons. Tech. Planning & Mgmt. Corp., 1996-97, program mgr., 1998. U.S. coord. biol. and genetic consequences project U.S.-USSR Environ. Protection Agreement, 1972-78; chmn. panel mutagenesis and carcinogenesis U.S.-Japan Coop. Med. Sci. Program, 1972-87; chmn. subcom. environ. mutagenesis, com. to coordinate toxicology and related programs Dept. Health and Human Svcs., 1972-85; mem. com. on assessment nitrate accumulation in environ., divsn. biology and agr. NAS/Nat. Rsch. Coun., 1970-72; mem. com. chem. toxicity and aging, commn. on life scis. Nat. Rsch. Coun., 1986-87; cons. in govt., chmn. workshops on environ. pollutants and mutagenesis, 1961-86; vis. prof. U. Zagazig, Egypt, Ain-Shams U., Cairo, 1982, Case We. Res. U., 1983. Mem. editl. bd. Radiation Botany, 1965-74, Mutation Rsch., 1969-72, Jour. Toxicology and Environ. Health, 1975-78, Carcinogenesis, 1979-85; editor Jour. Environ. and Exptl. Botany, 1975-77, Mutation Rsch., 1973-98; sect. editor: Jour. Environ. Pathology and Toxicology, 1979, Jour. Toxicology and Indsl. Health, 1984-88; co-editor: Chemical Mutagens, Vol. 5, 1978, Vol. 6, 1980, Vol. 7, 1982, editor Vol. 8, 1983, vol. 9, 1985, vol. 10, 1986; cons. editor: Environmental Research, 1981-86; contbg. editor: Environmental Mutagenesis, 1979-81; contbr. over 415 articles to profl. jours. Recipient Dir.'s award NIH, 1976; Univ. Scholar Yale U., 1951-52, Wadsworth fellow, 1954-55; Nat. Cancer Inst. predoctoral fellow, 1952-54. Mem. AAAS, Genetic Soc. Am. (rep. to NRC 1970-73), Internat. Assn. Environ. Mutagen Socs. (v.p. 1985-89), Radiation Rsch. Soc., Am. Soc. Cancer Rsch., Environ. Mutagen Soc. (coun. 1969-72, v.p., 1972-73, pres. 1973-76, editor newsletter 1969-72, ann. award 1979, contbg. editor jour. 1979), Internat. Commn. Protection Against Environ. Mutagens and Carcinogensis (vice-chmn. 1976-84, commn. 1985-89), Environ. Mutagen Soc. (pres. 1991-93), European Environ. Mutagen Soc., Japanese Environ. Mutagen Soc., Alpha-1 Nat. Assn. (bd. dirs. 1998-2000), Alpha One Found. (med. and sci. adv. com. 1999-2002, bd. dirs.). Home: 632 Rock Creek Rd Chapel Hill NC 27514-6716 Office: NIEHS Lab Toxicology MD 63-09 Research Triangle Park NC 27709 E-mail: deserres@niehs.nih.gov, deserres@bellsouth.net.

DESFORGES, JANE FAY, medical educator, physician; b. Melrose, Mass., Dec. 18, 1921; d. Joseph Henry and Alics Maher (Fay) Desforges; m. Gerard Desforges, Sept. 11, 1948; children: Gerard Joseph, Jane Alice. BA cum laude (Durant scholar), Wellesley Coll., 1942; MD cum laude, Tufts U., 1945; ScD (hon.), Holy Cross Coll., 1990. Diplomate Am. Bd. Internal Medicine, Am. Bd. Hematology. Intern in pathology Mt. Auburn Hosp., Cambridge, Mass., 1945—46; intern in medicine Boston City Hosp., 1946—47, resident in medicine, then chief resident, 1948—50; USPHS research fellow in hematology Salt Lake Gen. Hosp., Salt Lake City, 1946—47; research fellow in hematology

hosp. Thorndike Lab., 1950—52; physician-in-charge RH lab., 1952—53; mem. faculty Tufts U. Med. Sch., 1952—, prof. medicine, 1972—, disting. prof., 1992—, prof. emerita, 1994; asst. dir. Tufts Med. Svc., Boston City Hosp., 1952—67; assoc. dir. Tufts Med. Svc., 1967—68; acting dir., physician in charge, 1968—73; dir. Tufts Med. Svc., 1968—69; assoc. dir. Tufts hematology lab., 1954—67, asst. dir. hosp. labs., 1958—67, acting dir. labs., 1967—68. Sr. physician in hematology New Eng. Med. Ctr. Hosp., Boston, 1973—, rsch. assoc. blood resch. lab, 1973—92; attending physician VA Hosp., Jamaica Plain; cons. in hematology to various area hosps., 1955—72. Contbr. Bd. dirs. Med. Found., Inc., 1976—82; bd. trustees Boston Med. Libr., 1977—81; chmn. automation in med. lab. scis. rev. com. Nat. Inst. Gen. Med. Scis., 1974—76; chmn. consensus com. of infectious disease testing for blood transfusions NIH, 1995—96; mem. subcom. on hematology Am. Bd. Internal Medicine, 1976—82, bd. dirs., 1980—88, exec. com., 1984—88; chmn. blood diseases and resources adv. com. Nat. Heart, Lung and Blood Inst., 1978—81. Named to Internat. Women in Medicine Hall of Fame, Am. Med. Women's Assn., 2003; recipient Disting. Alumna award, Wellesley Coll., 1981; fellow NIH, 1955—88; grantee, 1955—88. Fellow: AAAS; mem.: Inst. Medicine, Am. Assn. Physicians, N.Y. Acad. Scis., Mass. Med. Soc. (mem. publs. com. 1995—99, Lifetime Achievement award 2001), Internat. Soc. Hematology, Am. Soc. Hematology (exec. com. 1975—78, adv. bd. 1980—82, v.p. 1982—83, pres. 1984—85), Am. Soc. Clin. Pathology, Am. Fedn. Clin. Rsch., ACP (chmn. med. knowledge self assessment program IX 1989—92, Master 1983, Disting. Tchr. award 1987), Alpha Omega Alpha (Outstanding Tchr. award 1994), Phi Beta Kappa. Home: 49 Lake Ave Melrose MA 02176-2701

DESHAZER, JAMES ARTHUR, biological engineer, educator, administrator; b. Washington, July 18, 1938; s. Grant Arthur and Velma DeShazer; m. Alice Marie DeShazer, Apr. 5, 1969; children: Jean Marie, David James. BS in Agriculture, U. Md., 1960, BSME, 1961; MS, Rutgers U., 1963; PhD, N.C. State U., 1967. Profl. engr., Idaho, Nebr. Assoc. prof. U. Nebr., Lincoln, 1967-75, prof., 1975-91, asst. dean, 1988-89; head agrl. engring. dept. U. Idaho, Moscow, 1991-95, head biol. and agrl. engring. dept., 1995—2001. Chair animal care and use com. U. Nebr., 1989—90; program coord. North Cen. Sustainable Agrl., Washington, 1988—89; nat. chair Modeling Responses of Swine CSRS, Washington, 1989-90, Sys. Approach to Poultry Prodn.-CSRS, Washington, 1990-91 ; dir. Idaho Rsch. Found., 1996—2001. Editor procs. Optics in Agr., 1990, Optics in Agr. & Forestry, 1992, Optics in Agr., Forestry & Biol. Processing, 1994, Optics in Agr., Forestry & Biol. Processing II, 1996, Precision Agriculture and Biological Quality, 1998, vol. II, 2000; contbr. chpt. in book. Trustee ASAE Found., 1996—2002; biol. and agr. engring. adv. bd. N.C. State U., 2002—. Recipient Livestock Svc. award Walnut Grove, Iowa, 1988. Fellow: Am. Soc. Agrl. Engrs. (chair 1984—94, nat. medal 1979); mem.: NSPE (chpt. chair 1986-87, 93-94, bd. dirs. 1994-2001, state pres. 1998-99, Young Engring. award 1974), NC State U. (BAE Adv. bd. 2002—04), Internat. Soc. Biometeorology, Am. Soc. Engring. Edn. (chair 1993—94), Lions (chpt. dir. 1995—97, 2002—), Alpha Gamma Rho (alumni bd. dirs. 1993—99). Home: 819 Nylarol St Moscow ID 83843-9313 Office: Biol & Agr Engring Dept Univ Idaho Moscow ID 83844-0904 E-mail: Jades@uidaho.edu.

DESHAZER, RUTH SHOMLER, health facility administrator, consultant; b. Glendale, Calif., July 17, 1954; d. Russell Paul and Pauline April (Lathrop) Shomler; 1 child, Michael Jr. BA magna cum laude, San Diego State U., 1982; AS, San Diego Mesa Coll., 1993. Registered health info. adminstr.; cert. profl. of healthcare quality; cert. med. staff coord. Med. records technician, coder Scripps Healthcare, La Jolla, Calif., 1993-94; cont. quality improvement coord. Adventist Health Systems, National City, Calif., 1994-96; applications specialist MED Data Systems Inc., San Diego, 1996-97; health info. mgmt. cons. Pyramid Healthcare Cons., L.A., 1997; health info. mgmt. sr. cons. Elacor Resources Group, L.A., 1997-98; health info. mgmt. dir. Brea (Calif.) Cmty. Hosp., Pacifica Hosp. of the Valley, Burbank, Calif., 1998-99; ind. cons. in healthcare quality, info. mgmt. and survey preparation, L.A. and Orange County, Calif., 1999—; med. staff coord. MemorialCare Health Systems, Orange County, Calif., 1999—. Med. staff coord. MemorialCare Health Sys., Orange County, Calif., 1999—. Contbr. articles to profl. jours. Mem. Calif. Assn. Quality Profls., San Diego Health Info. Assn. (various offices 1994-97), Greater Orange County Health Info. Assn. (pres.-elect 1998-99, pres. 1999-2000, past pres. 2000-01), Calif. Health Info. Assn. (nominating com. 1995-96, legis. com. 1996-97, convention com. 1997-98, chair convention com. 1998-99, membership com. 1998-99), Am. Health Info. Assn., Phi Beta Kappa, Phi Kappa Phi. Avocations: landscaping, floral design, swimming, travel. E-mail: cooknruth@aol.com.

DESHAZO, MARJORIE WHITE, occupational therapist; b. Syracuse, N.Y., Apr. 25, 1941; d. Rexford Everett and Joyce Winifred Ella (Brown) Young White; m. Del DeShazo, Dec. 22, 1966; stepchildren: Chad A., Karen A. Lynch. BS in Occupl. Therapy, U. Puget Sound, 1964. Lic. occupl. therapist, 1996. Occupl. therapist VA Med. Ctr., Roseburg, Oreg., 1965-70, Salisbury, N.C., 1970-78; occupl. therapist, co-chief VA Domiciliary, White City, Oreg., 1978-80; chief occupl. therapist VA Med. Ctr., Lexington, Ky., 1980-87; pvt. cons. occupl. therapy Camdenton, Mo., 1987—. Coord. TV21 Art Collections, Springfield, Mo. Inventor in field; exhibited at Lexington Art League, 1986-87, Laurie Fine Arts Show, 1993, Ozark Art and Palette, 1996, Artery Gallery, 1996, Lloyd's Art Ctr. & Gallery, 1996, Lisa Frick Gallery, 1996-98; co-artist Osage Beach City Hall Mural; permanent collection First Nat. Bank, Lake Ozark, Mo. Active Greater Lake Area Arts Coun., Osage Beach, Mo., 1987—. Kappa Kappa Gamma scholar U. Puget Sound. Mem. Ozark Art and Palette Club (treas. 1998-2000), Creative Artists Guild (coord. art hanging 1998—), Mo. Watercolor Soc. Democrat. Methodist. Avocations: sewing, art, gardening, gourmet cooking. Home: 12 Brookfield Ln Lake Ozark MO 65049-8673 E-mail: del@sockets.com.

DESHIELDS, ELIZABETH PEGGY BOWEN, artist, educator, poet; b. Ada, Okla., Nov. 11, 1928; d. Simuel Archie and Etta Berthel (Flowers) Bowen; m. Amos Jack DeShields, Sept. 19, 1947; children: Dennis Jack, Sheila Beth. BSBA and English Edn., East Ctrl. Okla. U., 1947, MEd in Counseling, 1977. Bus. tchr. Bearden (Okla.) H.S., 1947-48; confidential sec. to prodn. supt. Phillips Chem. Co., Borger, Tex., 1949-53; English tchr. Borger H.S., 1954-55; asst. prin., tchr. Ctrl. Oak Elem. Sch., Oklahoma City, 1955-68; tchr. Will Roger's Sch., Shawnee, Okla., 1968-70, Butner Pub. Schs., Cromwell, Okla., 1970-74, Castle (Okla.) Pub. Schs., 1976-79; counselor Okemah (Okla.) Pub. Schs., 1979-85; co-owner, bookkeeper DeShields' Energy, Cromwell, 1970—, Jack DeShields' Bldg. Stone, Cromwell, 1955—, Rainbow Hills Ranch, Cromwell, 1970—. Reporter Ada Times Democrat, 1947; news corr. Daily Oklahoman, Oklahoma City Times, 1947; abstracting asst. Pontotoc Co. Abstract Co., Ada, 1946; legal sec. C.F. Green Law Offices, Ada, 1944-46. Contbr. poems to profl. publs.; artist, illustrator for books. Mem. choir, Sunday sch. tchr. First Bapt. Ch., Cromwell, chmn. trustees, 1991; tchr. Cromwell Art Club. Named Ret. Tchr. of Yr., Okemah Alumni Assn., 2002; recipient Spl. Recognition Appreciation of Svc. award, Crooked Oak PTA, 1967, Yearbook Dedication, 1966, Svc. award, 1967, Leadership Svc. award, Girl Scouts U.S., 1968, Leadership Am. Secondary Edn., 1972, Yearbook award, 1971—73, Golden Eagle award for outstanding contbn. to journalism, 1973, Silver award, Columbia Scholastic Press Assn., numerous art awards, Okmulgee, Seminole and Hughes Counties, Okla., 1979—2003, Butner Yearbook Dedication, Appreciation Plaque, Cromwell Headstart, 1985, FFA, 1985, Plaque, First Bapt. Ch., 1991, Editor's Choice award, Nat. Libr. Poetry, 1996, Recognition award, Famous Poets Soc., 1999, 2000, 2001; scholar, Nat. Sch. Bus., 1944, East Ctrl. U., 1944. Mem. Okla. Ret. Tchrs., Okfuskee County Ret. Tchrs., Nat. Mus. Women in Arts (charter). Democrat. Avocations: painting, writing, gardening. Home: RR 2 Box 71 Okemah OK 74859-9623

DE SHIELDS-MINNIS, TARRA RAMIT, lawyer; b. Balt. d. Lawrence Franklin DeShields and Ramona Fleurette Brown. BA, U. Md., 1984; JD, U. Balt., 1987. Bar: Md. 1988, U.S. Dist. Ct. Md. 1990, U.S. Ct. Appeals (4th cir.), U.S. Supreme Ct. 1993. Jud. clk. Md. Ct. of Spl. Appeals, 1987-88; asst. state's atty. Office of the State's Atty., Montgomery County, 1988-90; asst. atty. gen. Office of the Atty. Gen., Balt., 1990-96; asst. U.S. atty. U.S. Atty.'s Office, Balt., 1996—. Recipient Am. Jurisprudence award Lawyer's Cooperative Pub. Co., 1988; Supreme Ct. fellow Nat. Assn. of Attys. Gens., 1993. Mem. Md. State Bar Assn., Nat. Bar Assn. Roman Catholic. Avocations: reading, antique shopping, racquetball. Office: US Attys Office 101 W Lombard St Baltimore MD 21201-2605

DESHPANDE, DEEPA SUHAS, research scientist; d. Suhas and Shobha Deshpande; m. Deepak Thakkar, May 19, 1994; 1 child, Ria Thakkar. PhD, W.Va. U., 1995. Sr. scientist GeneMedicine, Inc, The Woodlands, Tex., 1995—98, Aradigm Corp., Hayward, Calif., 1999—. Office: Aradigm Corporation 3929 Point Eden Way Hayward CA 94545 Home Fax: 510-265-0277; Office Fax: 510-265-0277. Personal E-mail: deshpanded@aradigm.com. E-mail: deshpanded@aradigm.com.

DESHPANDÉ, ROHIT, business educator; b. Bombay, Dec. 7, 1951; came to U.S., 1973; s. Prabhakar and Vimala (Waglé) D.; m. Rebecca Schorin, Dec. 29, 1979; children: Jay Alexander, Neil Benjamin. BSc, U. Bombay, 1971, MMS, 1973; MBA, Northwestern U., Evanston, 1975; PhD, U. Pitts., 1979; MA (hon.), Dartmouth Coll., 1993, Harvard U., 2000. Asst. and assoc. prof. mktg. U. Tex., Austin, 1979-87; assoc. prof. mktg. Dartmouth Coll., Hanover, 1987-89, prof., 1989-93, E.B. Osborn prof. mktg., 1993-97; prof. Harvard Bus. Sch., Cambridge, Mass., 1997-98, Sebastian S. Kresge prof. mktg., 1998—. Thomas Henry Carroll Ford Found. vis. prof. bus. adminstrn. Harvard Bus. Sch., 1993, chmn. strategic mktg. mgmt. program, 2001—; vis. scholar and vis. prof. Stanford Bus. Sch., 1994, 96; exec. dir. Mktg. Sci. Inst., 1997-99. Author/editor: Developing a Market Orientation, 1999, Using Market Knowledge, 2001; mem. editl. bd. Jour. Mktg., Jour. Mktg. Rsch., Jour. Bus. Rsch., Internat. Jour. Rsch. Mktg., Asian Jour. Mktg., Jour. Internat. Mktg., Internat. Jour. Rsch. in Mktg.; contbr. articles to profl. jours. Recipient Jack Taylor Teaching Excellence award. Fellow (consortium) Am. Mktg. Assn.; mem. Assn. for Consumer Rsch., Am. Sociol. Assn., Omicron Delta Kappa, Beta Alpha Phi. Office: Harvard Bus Sch Cambridge MA 02163

DESIATO, DONNA JEAN, school system administrator; b. Bridgeport, Conn., Nov. 28, 1949; d. William Joseph and Elvira Rosemarie (Cerreta) Gilberti; 1 child, Danielle DeSiato Creveling. BEd, U. Miami, 1971; MS in Edn., SUNY Cortland, 1977; cert. advanced study, SUNY Oswego, 1983; postgrad., Syracuse U. Cert. permanent tchr. cert. N.Y., 1976, sch. dist. adminstr. N.Y., 1983. Tchr. Syracuse (N.Y.) City Sch. Dist., 1974—79, instrl. specialist, 1979—83, vice prin., 1983—84, prin., 1984—94, dir. elem. edn., 1993—2000, asst. supt., 2000—. Mem. reading and lit. partnership N.Y. State Edn. Dept., Albany, 1999—; mem. lit. collaborative Success By Six, Syracuse, NY, 1999—; mem. edn. adv. bd. Syracuse Newspapers, 1990—95. Mem. Corinthian Club, Syracuse, 2000—. Recipient Outstanding Educator award, Supervisors and Adminstrs. Assn. N.Y. State, 1999, Adminstrs. Excellence award, Supervisors and Adminstrs. Assn. Syracuse, 1996, 1997, 1998, Leadership Recognition award, Commn. on Women in Leadership, 1995, Disting. Alumni award, Onadaga C.C., 2003. Mem.: N.Y. State Assn. Women in Adminstrn. (chair chpt.), Delta Kappa Gamma (Alpha Omega chpt.), Phi Delta Kappa. Office: Syracuse City Sch Dist 725 Harrison St Syracuse NY 13210

DESIDERIO, DOMINIC MORSE, JR., chemistry and neurochemistry educator; b. McKees Rocks, Pa., Jan. 11, 1941; s. Dominic Morse and Jewell Aline (Hull) D.; m. Julie Marie Thomas, Oct. 9, 1965; children— Annette Marie, Dominic Michael. BA, U. Pitts., 1961; MS, MIT, 1964, PhD, 1965. Organic control chemist Pitts. Coke and Chem. Co., 1958-60; research chemist U. Pitts., 1960-61; teaching asst. MIT, Cambridge, 1961-62, research asst., 1962-65; research chemist Am. Cyanamid Co., Stamford, Conn., 1966-67; asst. prof. chemistry Baylor Coll. Medicine, Houston, 1967-71, assoc. prof. chemistry and biochemistry, 1971-78; prof. neurology (chemistry) and molecular scis., dir. U. Tenn., Memphis, 1978—. Exch. student Internat. Assn. Exch. Students for Tech. Experience; polymer chemist Badische Anilin and Sodafabrik, Germany, summer 1962. Author and editor of books, chpts. in books and articles including Analysis of Neuropeptides by Liquid Chromatography and Mass Spectrometry, 1984, Mass Spectrometry of Peptides, 1990, Mass Spectrometry: Clinical and Biomedical Applications, vol. I, 1992, vol. II, 1994; co-editor (book series) Mass Spectrometry, 1997—; editor Mass. Spectrometry Rev., 1993—. Recipient 1st Ann. Internat. award Mass Spectrometry in Biochemistry and Medicine, Alghero, Italy, 1975; Intra-Sci. Research Found. fellow, 1971-75 Mem. Am. Soc. Biol. Chemistry, Am. Chem. Soc., Am. Soc. Mass Spectrometry, AAAS, Soc. for Neurosci., Memphis Neurosci. Soc. (pres. 1984-85), NIH (Metallobiochemistry study sect. 1985-89). Avocations: tennis, reading, ham radio, fishing, travel. Office: U Tenn Health Scis Ctr Stout Neurosci Mass Spectro Lab 847 Madison Ave Rm 117 Memphis TN 38163-0001 E-mail: ddesiderio@utmem.edu.

DESILVA, ALAN W. physics educator, researcher; b. L.A., Feb. 8, 1932; s. Woodruff and Dorothy Belle (Cole) DeS.; m. Mochiko Yokoyama, July 27, 1959; children: Audrey Hope, Eric Woodruff, Eliot Gen. MS, UCLA, 1954; PhD, U. Calif., Berkeley, 1961. NSF postdoctoral rsch. fellow The Culham Lab., Abingdon, Berkshire, Eng., 1962-64; asst. prof. physics U. Md., College Park, 1964-68, assoc. prof., 1968-74, prof., 1974-97, prof. emeritus, 1997—. Cons. Los Alamos Nat. Lab., 1963-81, U.S. Naval Rsch. Lab., Washington, 1973-90. Contbr. over 30 articles to sci. jours. With U.S. Army, 1954-56. Recipient sr. U.S. scientist award Alexander von Humboldt Found., Ruhr U., Bochum, Fed. Republic Germany, 1984-85. Fellow Am. Phys. Soc. Achievements include devel. of light scattering as a plasma diagnostic, light scattering observations of plasmas; rsch. on shock waves in plasmas and transport in strongly coupled plasmas. Office: U Md Inst Rsch Electronics/Applied Physics College Park MD 20742-0001

DESILVA, DAVID ARTHUR, theology studies educator; b. Summit, N.J., Apr. 15, 1967; s. John Arthur and Dorothy Alberta deSilva; m. Donna Jean Heitman, Aug. 4, 1990; children: James Adrian, John Austin, Justin Alexander. AB, Princeton U., 1987; MDiv, Princeton Theol. Sem., 1990; PhD, Emory U., 1995. Adj. faculty Candler Sch. Theology Emory U., Atlanta, 1993—95; prof. New Testament and Greek Ashland Theol. Sem., Ashland, Ohio, 1995—. Author: Introducing the Apocrypha: Its Content, Message, and Significance, 2002, New Testament Themes, 2001, Paul and the Macedonians, 2001, Praying with John Wesley, 2001, Honor, Patronage, Kinship, and Purity: Unlocking New Testament Culture, 2000, Perseverance in Gratitude: A Socio-Rhetorical Commentary on the Epistle to the Hebrews, 2000, The Hope of Glory: Honor Discourse and the New Testament, 1999, Bearing Christ's Reproach: The Challenge of Hebrews in an Honor Culture, 1999, 4 Maccabees, 1998, The Credentials of An Apostle: Paul's Gospel in 2 Corinthians 1 through 7, 1998; co-author (with Victor Matthews): Untold Stories of the Bible, 1998; author: Despising Shame: The Social Function of the Rhetoric of Honor and Dishonor in the Epistle to the Hebrews, 1995; contbr. Fellow: Soc. New Testament Studies; mem.: Soc. Bibl. Lit. Methodist. Office: Ashland Theol Sem 910 Center St Ashland OH 44805

DE SILVA, HANDUNNETTI SAKUNTALA V. physicist; b. Colombo, Sri Lanka, Oct. 11, 1960; s. Handunnetti Roland De S. and Phillippenge Tecla A. Jayasingha. BSc in Physics, U. Colombo, 1986; MS in Physics, U. Mo., Rolla, 1995. Demonstrator in physics U. Colombo, 1987-88, asst. lectr. in physics, 1989-92; tchg. asst. Northeastern U., Boston, 1992-93, U. Mo., Rolla, 1993-95, U. Nebr., Lincoln, 1996—2002. Mem.: Internat. Biog. Assn., Internat. Order of Merit. Buddhist. Avocation: reading. Home: 1429 N 34th St Apt 2 Lincoln NE 68503-2001

DE SILVA, JOHN ARTHUR F. pharmaceutical executive; b. Colombo, Sri Lanka, Sept. 23, 1933; s. Stephen Frederick and Mary Kathleen de S.; m. Dorothy Alberta Strout, Oct. 22, 1959; 1 child, David Arthur. BS, U. Ceylon, 1956; MS, Rutgers U., 1958, PhD, 1961. Sr. rsch. chemist Am. Cyanamid, Inc., Clarksville, N.J., 1961-63; group leader, sect. leader, asst. dir. Hoffmann-LaRoche, Inc., Nutley, 1963-85; dir., analytical R&D Zenith Lab., Northvale, N.J., 1985-87; editor Jour. Pharm. Sci. Am. Pharm. Assn., Washington, 1987-91; mgr. drug metabolism Schering-Plough Rsch. Inst., Kenilworth, 1991-96; assoc. dir. quality assurance DuPont Merck Pharma, Inc., Wilmington, Del., 1996-97; cons. R&D DorArtie Enterprises, North Port, Fla., 1997—. Contbr. 83 rsch. articles to numerous profl. jours. and publs.; contbr. chpts. to books in field. Vestryman St. Andrew Episc. Ch., South Orange, N.J., 1985-88, chmn. arsmusica, 1985-90; mem. Charlotte and Key Chorales. Fellow Am. Pharm. Assn., Am. Assn. Pharm. Scientists; mem. Am. Chem. Soc. Avocations: opera, choral singing, phys. fitness, golf, motor racing. Home: 5596 Sabal Trace Dr North Port FL 34287-3170 E-mail: jafdesilva@juno.com.

DESILVEY, DENNIS LEE, cardiologist, educator, university administrator; b. May 17, 1942; m. Kathleen Selkirk, Aug. 28, 1965; children: Ethan Selkirk, Caitlin O'Brian, Sarah Candace Shaw. BA in History and Religion magna cum laude, Yale U., 1964; MD, Columbia U., 1968. Lic. Vt., Va.; cert. Advanced Trauma Life Support instr. Intern medicine Cornell Med. Ctr., N.Y.C., 1968-69, resident medicine, 1969-71, resident medicine, cardiology, 1971; chief med. resident medicine North Shore U. Hosp., Manhasset, N.Y., 1972-73, instr. medicine, 1972-73; mem. staff Rancocas Valley Hosp., Willingboro, N.J., 1973-75; cardiologist Brachfeld Med. Assocs., Willingboro, N.J., 1974-75, Castleton (Vt.) Med. Assocs., 1975-77; attending physician Rutland Regional Med. Ctr., Rutland, Vt., 1975-92; pvt. practice Rutland, Vt., 1977-92; adj. asst. prof. clin. medicine Dartmouth Hitchcock Med. Ctr., Hanover, N.H., 1979-92; asst. prof. medicine U. Vt., Burlington, 1983-92; mem. staff Dwight David Eisenhower Med. Ctr., Ft. Gordon, Ga., 1991; dir. ambulatory cardiology, dir. cardiology consult svc., mem. clin. faculty cardiovascular divsn., dept. medicine Health Scis. Ctr. U. Va., Charlottesville, 1992—2001, assoc. prof. medicine Health Scis. Ctr., 1992—. Cons. Southwestern Vt. Med. Ctr., Bennington, 1986—, Keller U.S. Army Hosp., West Point, N.Y., 1985—, internal medicine Veteran Affairs Med. Ctr., Salem, Va., 1993—; mem. critical care com. Rutland Regional Med. Ctr., pharmacy and therapeutics com., investigational review bd., ethics com.; mem. pharmacy and therapeutics com. Health Scis. Ctr. U. Va., nutrition com., health care evaluation com., ambulatory policy com.; bd. dirs., mem. profl. affairs com., mem. bylaws com. Blue Cross/Blue Shield Vt.; bd. dirs., founding mem. Vt. Cardiac Network; presenter New Eng. regional meeting Am. Coll. Physicians, Hanover, N.H., 1976, Advanced Concepts Shock and Trauma, Woodstock (Vt.) Inn, 1982; dir. ACLS Tng. Ctr.; chmn/. Resolution Com. Contbr. articles to profl. jours. Med. advisor skiing svcs. Killington Ski Area, 1975-92, Smokey House Found., 1975-80, Farm and Wilderness Camps, 1975-85; mem. steering com. Vt. Med. Practice Variation Assessment Program, 1988; mem. cardiology study sect. Vt. Program Quality Care, 1988-92, Vt. Gov.'s Coun. Phys. Fitness, 1985-88; vestry Trinity Episcopal Ch., 1986-89; bd. dirs. Vermont Diabetes Assn., 1975-79, Rutland Mental Health Svc., 1975-82, Rutland Area Vis. Nurses Assn., 1975-77, chmn. profl. affairs com., mem. utilization review com.; bd. dirs. Barstow Sch., 1986-90; town health officer Wallingford, Vt., 1975-80. Maj. U.S. Army, 1973-75; col. USAR, 1985—. Decorated Nat. Def. Svc. medal, Reserve Achievement medal, Army Commendation medal; recipient Physician Recognition award Am. Med. Assn., Exceptional Svc. award, Spiritual Aims award Kiwanis Club Am., 1983, U. Va. Pres.'s Report award, 1992. Fellow Am. Coll. Physicians, Am. Coll. Cardiology, N.Am. Soc. Pacing and Electrophysiology; mem. Am. Heart Assn. (ACLS instr., BCLS instr., nat. faculty ACLS Vt., mem. mil. tng. network ACLS, Advanced Trauma Life Support; bd. dirs. 1978-80, bd. dirs., at large appointee 1988-93, agenda planning com. 1986-89, affiliate relations com. 1986-88, sci. pub. com. 1989-93, "heart and stroke" planning com. 1989-90, participant edn. and inf. group heart guide consumer health and info. program, 1989-91, chmn. task force mission to elderly 1989-90; v.p.-elect New Eng. region 1986-87, regional v.p. 1987-88, fellow coun. clin. cardiology, bd. dirs. Charlottesville divsn. 1992—, bd. dirs. Va. affiliate 1992—, bd. dirs. Rutland, Vt. divsn. 1986-92, program coun. 1986-92, bd. dirs. Vt. affiliate 1975-92, exec. com. 1978-92, pres.-elect 1982-83, pres. 1983-85, co-chair capital campaign 1988-90, nominating com. 1984-86, cardiac rehab. com. 1982-85, program coun. 1978-90, ACLS com. 1978-90, cardiac critical care com. 1978-82, hypertension com. 1975-82, chmn. emergency cardiac care com. region V 1976-80, bd. dirs. N.J. affiliate 1973-75, BCLS com. 1973-75, mem. greater N.Y. affiliate 1966-72, BCLS instr. 1968-72, del. N.E. regional heart com. 1985-91, reaffiliation com. 1987-89, nominating com. 1987-88, Pysician of Yr. award 1992), Am. Soc. Echocardiology, N.Y. Acad. Scis., Vt. Cardiac Network (vice chmn. 1982-86), Phi Beta Kappa. Avocations: cycling, running, cross country skiing, hiking, mountain climbing, theology. Home: 2712 Southern Hills Ct North Garden VA 22959 Office: Consultants in Cardiology 108 Houston St Ste B Lexington VA 24450 E-mail: dld3a@virginia.edu.

DE SIMONE, GIOVANNI, cardiologist, educator; b. Naples, Italy, Apr. 21, 1949; s. Luigi and Annamaria de Simone; m. Anna Venturini, Apr. 26, 1977; children: Sara, Sonia. MD, Federico II U., Naples, Italy, 1974. Diplomate Italian Fedn. of Physicians, 1974, Board in Cardiology, 1980. Investigator Federico II U. Hosp., Naples, 1980—2000, assoc. prof. of medicine, 2000—. Dir. Echocardiography Lab. Dept. Clin. and Exptl. Medicine Federico II U. Hosp., 1990—; adj. assoc. prof. Weill Med. Coll. of Cornell U., N.Y.C., 1994—. Contbr. articles to profl. jours. Coord., working group heart & hypertension Italian Soc. of Hypertension, Florence, Italy, 1997; mem. Italian Soc. of Cardiology, Naples, Italy, 2002. Lt. Italian Air Force, 1976—77. Fellow: Am. Heart Assn., Am. Coll. of Cardiology; mem.: Am. Soc. of Echocardiography, Italian Soc. of Hypertension (coord. working group heart and hypertension 1997), Italian Soc. of Cardiology. Avocations: music, history. Office: Federico II University Hospital Dprt Clin & Experim Med - vSPansini 5 Naples Naples 80131 Italy Office Fax: +1 815 346-8802. E-mail: simogi@unina.it.

DESIMONE, LIVIO DIEGO, retired diversified manufacturing company executive; b. Montreal, Que., Can., July 16, 1936; s. Joseph D. and Maria E. (Bergamin) De S.; m. Lise Marguerite Wong, 1957, children: Daniel J., Livia D., Mark A., Cynthia A. B.Chem. Engring., McGill U., Montreal, 957. Process engr. 3M Can., 1957-61; With 3M Co., St. Paul, 1961—; exec. v.p. life scis. sector 3M, St. Paul, 1981, exec. v.p. indsl. and consumer sector, 1984-86, exec. v.p. indsl. and consumer sector and pvt. svcs., 1986-89, exec. v.p. indsl. and electronic sector and corp. svcs., 1989-91, exec. v.p. info., imaging and electronic sector & pvt. svcs., 1991, exec. v.p., 1991, chmn. bd., CEO, 1991-2000; ret., 2001. Bd. dirs. NexiaBiotechnology, Montreal, Can., Am. Express Funds, Milliken & Co., Gen. Mills Inc., Vulcan Materials Co. Trustee U. Minn. Found. Mem. Bus. Roundtable. Office: 30 7th St E Ste 3050 Saint Paul MN 55101-4901

DESIMONE, ROBERT WALTER, medicinal chemist, educator; b. Stamford, Conn., Apr. 28, 1963; s. Robert Walter Sr. and Joyce Anne DeS.; m. Patricia Sue Buxton, Jan. 12, 1965; children: Gina, David. BS, Marist Coll., 1985; MS, Fairleigh Dickinson U., 1987; PhD, Wesleyan U., 1992. Postdoctoral assoc. Yale U., New Haven, 1992-93; sr. scientist I Neurogen Corp., Branford, Conn., 1993-97, sr. scientis II, 1997-99, mgr. high speed sythesis, 1999-2000, rsch. fellow, 2000—01; dir. chemistry Cellular Genomics, Inc., Branford, 2001—02, sr. dir. chemistry, 2002—. Vis. scholar Wesleyan U., Middletown, Conn., 1997-98, 98-99, 2000; tech. cons. Cantor Colburn LLP, Bloomfield, Conn., 2000. Contbr. numerous articles to profl. jours.; 20 patents in field. Pres. Wesleyan U. Grad. Student Assn., 1990-91, exec. com., 1991-92; mem. Durham Dem. Town Com., 1999; mem. Tax Stabilization Com., Durham, Conn., 2001. Mem. AAAS, Am. Chem. Soc. Office: Cellular Genomics Inc 36 E Industrial Rd Branford CT 06405 E-mail: robd@cellulargenomics.com.

DESIPIO, LOUIS, political science educator; b. Washington, Dec. 18, 1959; s. Jack Alexander and Martha Clark DeSipio; m. Janet DiVincenzo. AB, Columbia U., 1981; MA, U. Tex., 1984, PhD, 1993. Social sci. rsch. assoc. NALEO Ednl. Fund, Washington, 1985—88; vis. asst. prof. Wellesley (Mass.) Coll., 1993—94, Mt. Holyoke Coll., South Hadley, Mass., 1994—95; asst. prof. U. Ill., Urbana, 1995—2000, assoc. prof., 2000—02, U. Calif., Irvine, 2002—. Cons. Tomás Rivera Policy Inst., L.A., 1993—, NALEO Ednl. Fund, L.A., 1988-98. Author: (book) Latino Voices, 1992, Counting on the Latino Vote, 1996, Making Americans, Remaking America, 1998; editor: Awash in the Mainstream, 1999. Grantee Ford Found., 1992, Andrew W. Mellon Found., 1993. Office: Univ Calif Dept Polit Sci 3151 Social Science Plz Irvine CA 92697 E-mail: ldesipio@uci.edu.

DESISTO, ELIZABETH AGNES, medical records specialist; b. Medford, Mass., May 15, 1954; d. John Anthony and Josephine Loretta (Passero) DeS. AS cum laude, Mass. Bay Community Coll., 1974; BS magna cum laude, Northeastern U., 1979. Sr. med. record technician Children's Hosp. Med. Ctr., Boston, 1974-76; asst. dir. med. records dept. Glover Meml. Hosp., Needham, Mass., 1980-82, McLean Hosp., Belmont, Mass., 1982-83, acting dir. med. records dept., 1983-84, dir. med. records dept., 1984-91, New Eng. Meml. Hosp., Stoneham, Mass., 1991-95; project mgr. home health Vis. Nurse Assn., Inc., Haverhill and Andover, Mass., 1995-96; med. record coord. Harvard Pilgrim Health Care, Boston, 1996—97, cons., 1997—2001; med. record. dir. E. Boston Neighborhood Health Ctr., Boston, 2001—. Vol. Big Sister Assn. Greater Boston, 1985-87, Greater Boston Walk for Hunger, 1983-94, nat. and local congl. campaigns; bd. dirs. New Eng. Meml. Hosp. Aux., 1992-95. Mem.: Mass Health Info. Mgmt. Assn. (bd. dirs. 1985—96, sec. 1989—90, pres-elect 1996—97, pres. 1997—98), Am. Health Info.Mgmt. Assn. (registered health

info. adminstr., bd. dirs. mental health record sect. 1987—90, chmn. 1988—90). Democrat. Roman Catholic. Home: 235 Winthrop St Apt 7701 Medford MA 02155-3836 Office: EBNHC 10 Gove St Boston MA 02128

DESJARDINS, BENOIT, physician, researcher; b. Montreal, Jan. 22, 1963; came to U.S., 1990; s. Pierre and Michelyne (Varin) D.; m. Yolaine Côté, Aug. 20, 1988; children: Sarah Kimberley, David Alexandre. MD, U. Montreal, 1989; MS in Pure Math., Carnegie-Mellon U., 1995; PhD in Formal Philosophy, U. Pitts., 1995. Internal medicine intern Royal Victoria Hosp., Can., 1995-96; physician dept. radiology U. Pitts., 1997-2001, Harvard Med. Sch., Boston, 2001—02, U. Mich. Med. Ctr., Ann Arbor, 2002—. Can. Med. Rsch. Coun. fellow, 1991-95. Mem. Am. Math. Soc., Assn. for Symbolic Logic, Am. Assn. Artificial Intelligence, N.Am. Soc. Cardiac Imaging, Radiology Soc. N.Am., Can. Soc. Theoretical Biology (membership chair 1993), Am. Coll. Radiology, Prometheus Soc., Mega Soc. E-mail: benoitd@umich.edu.

DESJARDINS, CLAUDE, physiologist, dean; b. Fall River, Mass., June 13, 1938; s. Armand Louis and Marguerite Jean (Mercier) D.; m. Jane Elizabeth Campbell, June 30, 1962; children: Douglas, Mark, Anne. BS, U. R.I., 1960; MS, Mich. State U., 1964, PhD, 1967. Asst. prof. dept. physiology Okla. State U., Stillwater, 1968-69, assoc. prof., 1969-72; assoc. prof. physiology U. Tex., Austin, 1970-75; prof. physiology Inst. Reproductive Biology, Patterson Labs., 1975-86, U. Va. Med. Sch., Charlottesville, 1987-96, dir. Ctr. Rsch. Reprodn., 1990-96; prof. physiology & biophysics, sr. assoc. dean med. coll. U. Ill., Chgo., 1996—. Mem. Ctr. for Advanced Studies, 1986; cons. NIH, ASA, VA, FDA. Author: Cell and Molecular Biology of the Testis, 1993, Molecular Physiology of Testicular Cells, 1996; editor-in-chief Am. Jour. physiology: Endocrinology and Metabolism, 1991-95; editor-in-chief Jour. Andrology, 1989-91, Ency. of Reprodn., 1997-98; mem. editl. bd. Biology Reprodn., Endocrinology; contbr. articles to profl. jours.; patentee techs. for male contraception, mechanisms of peptide hormone transport in the microcirculation and ligand-dependent and ligand ind. action of steroid hormones in peripheral vasculature. Fellow The Jackson Lab., Bar Harbor, Maine, 1967, NIH Sr. fellow U. Va. Med. Sch., 1983-84, Danforth Found. fellow, 1960; C.F. Wilcox Found. scholar, 1958. Mem. Am. Physiol. Soc., Soc. Neurosci., Soc. Study Reprodn. (pres. 1982-83), Endocrine Soc., Am. Soc. Cell Biology, The Microcirculatory Soc. Office: U Ill at Chgo Office of Dean M/C 784 1853 W Polk St Chicago IL 60612-4316 E-mail: clauded@uic.edu.

DESJARDINS, DANIEL DEE, poet, composer, translator and playwright; b. Miami, Fla., May 27, 1954; s. Ulysses John-Joseph (Pete) and Regine Madelaine (Copus) D. BS in Chemistry, Fla. State U., 1977; BSEE, U. N.Mex., 1984; student, Am. Coll. Paris, 1973-74, Boston U., 1975-76; M in Playwriting, Queen Margaret U. Coll., 2001. Chemist Fla. Dept. Agr., Ft. Lauderdale, 1978; commd. 2nd lt. USAF, 1982, advanced through grades to capt., ret., 1992; maj. USAFR, 1996. Visual sys. project mgr. AFRL/HECV. Poet: Ode to Stoicism (World Poetry Golden Poet award 1992), Love's Tragedy (World Poetry Golden Poet award 1993), To Lord Acton and His Democratic Consorts, The Condensed Tale of Beowolf and Grendel in Modern English Prosody (semi finalist 1995, North Am. Open Poetry contest, Nat. Libr. Poetry), By The Wiskers of William Wallace (pub. in Best Poems of 1996, Nat. Libr. Poetry), To A Tender Gaoler (semi finalist 1996 N.Am. Open Poetry Contest, Nat. Libr. Poetry), The New India (semi-finalist 1998 N.Am. Open Poetry Contest, Nat. Libr. Poetry); composer: The Beacon of Havana, It's a Shame, The New Girl in Our Town, Allegretto (cert. of achievement Unisong Internat. Song Contest, 1997), Technical: Military Display Market: Third Comprehensive Edit., 2002, Oil-Seal Compatibilities, 2001, Military Display Market Segment: Wearable and Portable, 2003; translator: A View of Hitler and the 1935 Reichsparteitag by a Member of the Académie Française, 1992, The Notin Affair, 1996, A Few Reflections on the Abbé Pierre/Garaudy Affair, 1996, The Founding Myths of Israeli Politics, 1998; playwright: Der Anschluss, 1994, Young Man of Promise, 1995, Lazarro Spallanzani, 1998, Spectulations on the Nature of Heaven and Hell, 1999, rev. as 2-act play, 2002, A Few Greek Poets, 1999, The Sudeten Crisis, 2000, The Difference a Day Makes, 2002, Eye of the Needle, 2003, Athos' Wife, 2003. Mem. Internat. Soc. Optical Engring., Soc. for Info. Displays, Nat. Assn. Scholars, Phi Alpha Theta. Independent. Roman Catholic. Avocations: writing, jogging, collecting old records & books, scale model making.

DESJARDINS, RAOUL, medical association administrator, financial consultant; b. Montreal, Quebec, Can., Oct. 8, 1933; came to U.S., 1962; s. Elso and Blanche (Lemieux) D.; m. Regina Turgeon, Oct. 10, 1961; children: Bryan-Claude, John Andrew. BA, U. Montreal, 1953, MD, 1958; MS, Baylor U., 1964, PhD, 1966; MBA, Rutgers U., 1990. Diplomate Am. Bd. Medicine. Chief intern, resident St. Joan of Arc Hosp., Montreal, 1958-59; med. dir. Candiac (Can.) Med. Clinic, 1953-62, Ortho Research Found., Raritan, N.J., 1966-72; pres. Raoul Desjardins Assocs. Inc., Mendham, N.J., 1972-83, Research Cons. Inc., Mendham, 1983—, APG Internat., Inc., 1991—. Med. dirs. Iroquois Class Co., Candiac, 1959-62; asst. prof. Hahnemann Hosp. and U., Phila., 1976-80; bd. govs. Internat. Medicines Exch. and Devel., Georgetown, Ga., 1986—; chmn. bd. advisors Fed. Inst. Health, 1991—; chmn. bd. govs. Grand Masters Found., 1989—. Prodr. video: The Apgram: A New Tool to Measure Cardiovascular Performance, 1995. Recipient physician's recognition award AMA, 1969. Fellow: N.Y. Acad. Medicine, Am. Coll. Clin. Pharmacology, The Royal Soc. Health, Am. Coll. Angiology; mem.: Petroleum Club Houston, Doctors Club, Met. Club (membership com. 1991—), Med. Execs. Club, Beta Gamma Omega, Sigma Xi. Roman Catholic. Avocations: safaris, medieval history, economic theory, anti-aging. Office: Fed Inst Health 35 Stonecroft Pl The Woodlands TX 77381-5226 E-mail: doctord@candw.ky.

DESJARLAIS, GEORGIA KATHRINE, retired military officer; b. Chattanooga, Tenn., Oct. 31, 1958; d. Lowell and Lucy Caroline (Brown) Lawson; m. Daniel Eugene Desjarlais, Apr. 22, 1978 (div. May 1985). AA, Hawaii Pacific Coll., 1980, BS, 1982; MPA, Auburn U., Montgomery, 1999; student, Air U., 1999, Air Command and Staff Coll., 1998—99. Enlisted as E-1 USN, 1976, commd. as ensign, 1983, advanced through ranks to lt. comdr., 1994, ret., 2000; supply officer, food svc. officer NSGA Adak, Alaska, 1984—86; disbursing and stores officer USS Dixon (AS 37), San Diego, 1986—88; material officer COMNAVSUPPFORANTARCTICA, Oxnard, Calif., 1988—91; stock control and AOIC USNS Sirius (TAFS 8), Norfolk, Va., 1991—94; load mgr. COMNAVSURFLANT, Norfolk, 1994—96; asst. supply officer USS Emory S. Land (AS 39), Norfolk, 1996—98; logistics supr. Corning Inc., Oneonta, NY, 1999—2002. Mentor Ret. Officer's Assn., Washington, 1999—. Mem.: AAUW (sec. Oneonta br. 2001—02, membership chmn. Memphis br. 2002—). Methodist. Avocations: reading, history, wildlife. Home: 784 Canterbury Ln Oneonta NY 13820

DESKIN, WILLIAM C. healthcare educator; b. Des Moines, Iowa, Sept. 9, 1947; s. Jack L. and Iris E. Deskin; m. Patricia L. Snyder, Feb. 2, 1970; children: William C. Jr., Catherine D. Deskin-Constantine. BS in Health Planning, U. of Minn., 1976; MS in Health Svcs. Adminstrn., U. of St. Francis, Joliet, Ill, 1989; Exec. MBA, U. of Iowa, 1992; PhD, Walden U., Mpls., 2001. V.p. Ottumwa (Iowa) Regional Health Ctr., 1989—96; dir. quality mgmt., utilization and planning Bay Med. Ctr., Bay City, Mich., 1997—2001; educator Cen. Mich. U. Coll. of Extended Learning, Lansing, Mich., 1998—, Delta Coll., University Center, Mich., 1998—, Bay City, 1998—, Spring Arbor U., Flint, Mich., 2001—. Sculptures in stone and hard wood, various. Long range planning YMCA, Bay City, 1998—2002. Sgt. USMC, 1966—70. Fellow: Am. Coll. of Healthcare Execs. (profl. exam. com. 2000—); mem.: Nat. Coun. Quality Assurance (cert. profl. healthcare quality, cert. profl. in healthcare). Methodist. Avocations: racquetball, guitar, sculpting. Home: 2006-10th St Bay City MI 48708

DESLEY, JOHN WHITNEY, medical illustrator; b. Old Mystic, Conn., May 17, 1925; s. Clifford James and Hester (Walbridge) D.; m. Janice Reed, Dec. 22, 1951 (dec. Sept. 23, 1993); children: Christopher, Rebecca, Timothy, Rachel, Leah, Louisa; m. Margaret Wakeman, Aug. 31, 1996. BFA, Vesper George, Boston, 1950; M in Med. Illustration, Mass. Gen. Hosp., 1952; student, U. Conn., 1950. Asst. med. artist Mass. Gen. Hosp., Boston, 1951-52; chief med. artist VA Hosp., Birmingham, Ala., 1952-58; med. illustrator U. Minn., Mpls., 1958-63, Mayo Clinic, Rochester, Minn., 1963-90; freelance med. illustrator Rochester, 1990—. Illustrator for med. books, 1985—, (textbook) Cardiac Surgery, 1985; designer bicentennial medallion City of Rochester, 1976, bicentennial print design, 1977; author, illustrator: Persectives on Mayo (by John W. Desley), 1997; one man shows Salemtowne Galleries, Winston Salem, N.C., 2001, 2002-03. Chmn. sch. bd. Bamber Valley Sch., Rochester, Minn., 1973-75. With USN, 1943-46. Decorated Am. Theatre medal USN, African-European-Middle Eastern medal with 2 stars U.S. Army, Asiatic-Pacific medal with 1 star, Victory medal. Mem.: VFW, Assoc. Artists of Winston-Salem. Home: 609 Sumac Rd Lewisville NC 27023-9555 E-mail: desley@mindspring.com.

DESLOGE, CHRISTOPHER DAVIS, SR., real estate and merchant banking executive; b. St. Louis, July 23, 1958; s. William Livingston and Loriel Martens (Johnson) D.; m. Mary Roberta Dubuque, May 22, 1981; children: William Livingston II, Christopher Davis Jr., Raymond Amadee Dubuque. Student, Drake U., 1977-79, Maryville Coll., 1979-80. V.p. Follman Properties, St. Louis, 1982-85; leasing mgr. Paragon Group, St. Louis, 1985-86; pres. Desloge Co., St. Louis, 1986-90; v.p. Hilliker Corp., St. Louis, 1990-92; pres. Braeburn Ptnrs., St. Louis, 1992-96; account mgr. Maritz, Stamford, Conn., 1996-98; mng. dir. Baytree Investors, Merchant Banking, Inc., 1998-2001; owner Desloge Oak Tree Real Estate and Mcht. Banking, 2001—. Arbitrator BBB, St. Louis, 1991—. Author: Office Leasing: From the Tenants Point of View, 1995; contbg. editor St. Louis Bus. Jour., 1986-94. Mem. Real Estate Bd. Met. St. Louis, 1982-93; bd. dirs. St. Louis Psychoanalytic Inst., 1988-91, Internat. Tenant Representation Alliance, St. Louis, 1992-94, Ctr. Head Injury Svcs., 1994-96; co-chmn. disaster svcs. ARC-Bi State Chpt., St. Louis, 1992-94; pres. bd. dirs. Desloge Found., St. Louis and Conn., 1993—; bd. mem. Tax Assessment Appeals, Darien, Conn., 1999—. Recipient Recognition award for effort St. Louis Psychoanalytic Inst., 1992, Honor award for outstanding vol. ARC-Bi State Chpt., St. Louis, 1994. Mem. Nat. Coun. Consumer Arbitrators, Barnes Road Luncheon Group, Noonday Club, Veiled Prophet, St. Louis Country Club, Landmark Club, Darien Boat Club (bd. dirs., fin. sec. 1998—). Republican. Roman Catholic. Avocations: boating, shooting, golfing, tennis, automobiles. Home and Office: Sunny Hills Farm PO Box 127 Gray Summit MO 63039

DESLOGE, ROSEMARY BYRNE, otolaryngologist, educator; b. Tallahassee, Fla., Feb. 25, 1962; d. Edward Augustine and Moira Dunne Desloge. BS in Biology, U. Notre Dame, 1984; MD, U. Miami, 1989. Gen. surgery resident U. S.C., Columbia, 1989—91; internal medicine resident NYU/Bellevue Hosps., N.Y.C., 1992—93; ENT resident/fellow Manhattan Eye/Ear/Throat Hosp., N.Y.C., 1993—98; laryngology fellow Harvard U., Boston, 1993—99; asst. prof. dept. otorhinolaryngology Weill Med. Coll., Cornell U., N.Y.C., 1999—, Ann Belcher asst. professorship chair, 2001. Contbr. Fellow: ACS; mem.: AMA, Am. Bd. Otolaryngology (diplomate), Nat. Bd. Med. Examiners (diplomate), Am. Acad. Otolaryngology Head and Neck Surgery. Office: Dept Otorhinolaryngology Ste 541 520 E 70th St New York NY 10021

DESLONGCHAMPS, PIERRE, chemistry educator; b. St.-Lin, Que., Can., May 8, 1938; s. Rodolphe and Madeleine D.; 3d m. Marie-Marthe Leroux; children: Patrice, Ghyslain. BS., U. Montreal, Que., Can., 1959; PhD (hon.), U. Montreal, 1984; PhD, U. N.B., 1964, PhD (hon.), 1985, U. Pierre et Marie, 1983, Bishop's U., 1984, Laval U., 1984; DSc, U. Moncton, N.B., Can., 1995. Research fellow Harvard U., 1964, postdoctoral fellow, 1965; asst. prof. chemistry U. Montreal, 1966-67; asst. prof. U. Sherbrooke, Que., 1967-68, assoc. prof., 1968-72, prof., 1972—. Author: Stereoelectronic Effects in Organic Chemistry, 1983; contbr. over 215 articles to profl. jours.; holder 9 patents in field; inventor in field. Decorated Officer Order of Can., 1989; recipient E.W.R. Steacie prize Nat. Rsch. Coun. Can., 1974, Can. Gold medal for sci. and engring. Nat. Scis. and Engring. Rsch. Coun. Can., 1993, Sci. prize Province Que., 1971-72, Marie-Victorian prize, 1987, Alfred Bader award Can. Soc. Chemistry, 1991, R.U. Lemieux award Chem. Soc. of Chemistry, 1994; Shell Can. Co. fellow, 1963, A.P. Sloan fellow, 1970-72, E.W.R. Steacie fellow, 1971-74, John Simon Guggenheim Meml. Found. fellow, 1979; Can. Coun. Izaak Walton Killam scholar, 1976-77. Fellow AAAS, Chem. Inst. Can. (Merck, Sharp and Dohme Lectrs. award 1976), Royal Soc. Can., Royal Soc. London, World Innovation Found.; mem. Corp. Profl. Chemists Que., Am. Chem. Soc., New Swiss Chem. Soc., Assn. Harvard Chemists, Assn. Canadienne-Francaise pour l'Advancement des Sciences (medaille Vincent 1975, medaille Pariseau 1979), Assn. Advancement Scis. Can., Can. Com. Scientists and Scholars, Société Française de Chimie, Acad. des Scis. de Paris (foreign asst.). Address: Univ Sherbrooke Inst Pharm 3001 12 North Ave Sherbrooke Canada J1H 5N4 Home: 161 de Vimy Sherbrooke QC Canada J1J 3M6 E-mail: piere.deslongchamps@usherbrooke.com.

DESMARAIS, CHARLES JOSEPH, museum director, writer, editor; b. N.Y.C., Apr. 21, 1949; s. Charles Emil and Helen Barbara (Young) D.; m. Sharon McLeod, May 1, 1970; m. Patricia Jon Carroll, June 15, 1979; m. Katherine Ann Morgan, Dec. 31, 1985 Student, Western Conn. State Coll., Danbury, 1967-71; BS, SUNY-Rochester, 1975; M.F.A., SUNY-Buffalo, 1977. Curator Friends of Photography, Carmel, Calif., 1973-74; asst. editor Afterimage, Rochester, 1975-77; editor Exposure, Chgo., 1977-81; dir. Art Gallery, Columbia Coll., Chgo., 1977-79, Calif. Mus. Photography, U. Calif.-Riverside, 1981-88, Laguna Art Mus., Laguna Beach, Calif., 1988-94; Contemporary Arts Ctr., Cin., 1995—. Guest curator Mus. Contemporary Art, Chgo., 1980, L.A. Ctr. Photog. Studies, 1981; arts adv. com. Riverside County Bd. Suprs., 1981-86; chair Orange County Arts Coun., 1989-91; bd. mem. Regional Cultural Alliance, 2000—. Author, editor: Roger Mertin: Records 1976-1978, 1978, Michael Bishop, 1979, The Portrait Extended, 1980, Why I Got Into TV and Other Stories: The Art of Ilene Segalove, 1990, Proof: Los Angeles Art and the Photograph, 1960-1980, 1992, Humongolous: Sculpture and Other Works by Tim Hawkinson, 1996, Jim Dine Photographs, 1999, Stephan Balkenhol, 2000; arts columnist Riverside Press Enterprise, 1987-88. Art Critic's fellow Nat. Endowment Arts, 1979 Mem. Assn. Art Mus. Dirs., Soc. Photog. Edn. (dir. 1979-83), Am. Assn. Museums, Coll. Art Assn. Office: Contemporary Arts Ctr 115 E 5th St Cincinnati OH 45202-3998 E-mail: director@spiral.org.

DESMARAIS, PAUL, holding company executive; b. Sudbury, Ont., Can., Jan. 4, 1927; s. Jean-Noël and Lebea (Laforest) Desmarais; m. Jacqueline Maranger, Sept. 8, 1953; children: Paul, André, Louise, Sophie. BComm, U. Ottawa, Canada, 1949. Chmn. exec. com. Power Corp. Can., Montreal, 1968—, also. bd. dirs. Bd. dirs. Great-West Life Assurance Co., Great-West Lifeco Inc., Groupe Bruxelles Lambert S.A., Investors Group Inc., London Ins. Group, London Life Ins. Co., Power Fin. Corp., La Presse Ltée, Power Tex. Investment Corp., Les Journaux Trans-Can. Inc.; mem. internat. adv. com. Barrick Gold Corp. Can., Telegraph Group Ltd. (Eng.); chmn., mng. dir. Pargesa Holding S.A. Mem. Queen's Privy Coun., Canada. Decorated companion Order of Can., officer Nat. Order of Que., Legion of Honor France, Ordre de Léopold II Belgium. Office: Power Corp Can 751 Victoria Sq Montreal QC Canada H2Y 2J3

DES MARAIS, PIERRE, II, communications holding company executive; b. Montreal, Que., Can., June 2, 1934; s. Pierre and Rolande (Varin) Des M.; m. Lise Blanchard, Jan. 21, 1956; children: Suzanne, Lison, Pierre III, Jean, Danielle, Stéphane, Sophie, Philippe, Anik. BA, Coll. St. Marie, 1954; grad. graphics arts course, Toronto, 1954; HEC in Bus. Adminstrn., U. Montreal, 1958. Former pres., chief exec. officer Unimedia Inc., Montreal, 1987—2001. Former chmn. Carling O'Keefe Ltd., dept. chmn., 1987; former chmn. Canadair Ltd., 1986; bd. dirs. Imperial Oil Ltd., Rothman's Inc., Sleeman Breweries Ltd., Suzy Shier Ltd.; bd. dirs., chmn. Corp. de l'Hopital Maisonneuve-Rosemont. Former bd. dirs. Univ. de Montreal. Named hon. mem. Order of St. John, Que. Fellow Royal Geog. Soc.; mem. St. Denis Club, Mt. Royal Club, Forest and Stream Club. Avocation: skiing. Office: Gestion PDM Inc Office of the Pres 3781 Chemin Desjardins Saint-Faustin-Lac-Carre QC Canada J0T 1J2

DE SMET, LORRAINE MAY, artist; b. Passaic, N.J., May 5, 1928; d. Peter John and Mary (Lovas) Prevelige; m. Louis John de Smet, May 17, 1952; children: Mary Lizabeth, Jean Marie, Carolyn, Allise Marie. Student, Berkeley Sch., 1945, Art Students League, 1979-82. One woman show Pen and Brush Club, 1984 (Solo Show award). Bd. dirs. Art Ctr. of N.J., 1993—. Recipient 1st prize, Livingston (N.J.) Art Assn., 1987, 1988, Am. Artist award, Ridgewood Art Inst., 1998, Caldwell Progress award, 1998, 2003, LAA merit award, 1998, 1999, 2001, 2002, WEAA award, Caldwell Coll., 1999, merit award, 2000, Best of the Best exhbn., Trenton Mus., 2001, numerous other awards. Mem. U.S. Coast Guard Artists, Am. Artists Profl. League (Ann Waldron N.J. award 1998, N.J. Disting. Merit award 2002), Ringwood Manor Art Assn. (award 2000), Pen and Brush Club of N.Y. (bd. dirs. 1985-92, v.p. 1989-92, dir. brush divsn. 1987-89, mem. dir. 1990-92, co-chair brush sect. 1994-95, 97), Art Ctr. of N.J. (bd. dirs., sec., membership chair), West Essex Art Assn. (bd. dirs. 1992-98), Art Students League of N.Y. (life), Millburn-Short Hills Art Assn.(award of excellence 2001, 2002, Louise Melrose Gallery award 2002). Home: 33 Campbell Rd Fairfield NJ 07004-1735

DESMOND, JOHN JACOB, retired architect; b. Denver, Apr. 5, 1922; s. Timothy Desmond and Rose (Dvorak) D.; m. Blanche Russell, Sept. 29, 1951 (div.); children: John Michael, James Russell, Margaret; m. Nell Herring Lentz, Dec. 8, 1984. BArch, Tulane U., 1943; MArch., MIT, 1948. Archtl. draftsman Skidmore, Owings & Merrill, N.Y.C., 1947; archtl. designer, draftsman A. Hays Town, 1949-50, TVA, 1951-52; arch. Desmond & Davis, 1954-58, Desmond-Miremont-Burks, Baton Rouge, Hammond, La., 1958—2001; now pres. John Desmond & Assos., Baton Rouge.; ret., 2001. Author: Louisiana's Antebellum Architecture, 1970; contbr. articles to AIA Jour.; prin. works include Southeastern La. Coll. Cafeteria, Hammond (1st honor award Gulf States region, Nat. Merit award AIA), St. Thomas More Ch. and Sch, Baton Rouge (honor award Gulf States region AIA), Cath. Student Ctr., Southeastern La. Coll. (honor award Gulf States region AIA), La. State Libr., Baton Rouge (nat. AIA-ALA award, honor award Gulf States region AIA), Union Bldg, La. State U., Baton Rouge (1st honor award Gulf States region AIA), Cath. Life Ctr., Baton Rouge (honor award Gulf States region AIA); additions to Grace Meml. Episcopal Ch, Hammond (honor award Gulf States region AIA), D.C. Reeves Elem. Sch, Ponchatoula, La. (honor award Gulf States regional Nat. Honor award AIA), Tangipahoa Parish Courthouse, Amite, La. (honor award AIA and Office Civil Def., Gulf States Regional award 1997); design arch. Pennington Biomed. Rsch. Ctr. (regional AIA Honor award), Blue Bonnet Nature Ctr., Baton Rouge (regional AIA merit award), La. State Archives, U.S. Embassy, Monrovia, Liberia, Tulane U. Lindy Boggs Ctr., Baton Rouge Govtl. Ctr., Mobile County/City Courthouse Bldg. (honorable mention Nat. Archtl. Design Competition). Lt. USNR, 1943-46. Recipient Mayor Pres.'s medal for excellence in arts, 1994, award for hist. preservation of Warden's House Found. for Hist. La., Outstanding Alumnus award Tulane U. Sch. Architecture. Fellow AIA (planning and urban design com., mem. 14 regional urban design teams, U.S. Presdl. award for outstanding contbn. to design); mem. La. Archs. Assn., La. Landmarks Assn., Soc. Archtl. Historians, Nat. Trust for Hist. Preservation, Cosmos Club (Washington). Home: 1135 Carter Ave Baton Rouge LA 70806-7706

DESMOND, LEIF, writer; b. Inglewood, Calif., Mar. 2, 1920; s. Guy Marion and Elma Agusta (Miller) Smith; m. Soledad Saenz, July 9, 1945 (div. Apr. 1982); children: Judith, Virginia, Marilyn Susan, Theresa, Loretta, Lawrence, Glenn; m. Yolanda Elkins Rambo, June 21, 1982. Student, Iowa State Coll., 1939-40, 42, San Fernando State Coll., 1959-65, U. Calif. Ext., 1961; AA in Bus. Adminstrn., Ventura (Calif.) Coll., 1959. Author: In the June of Summer, 1986, The Sparrow Safari, 1995, In Old October, 1996. Avocations: creative landscaping, agriculture, animals, philosophy, nature. Home: 2113 S Javelina Ave Yuma AZ 85364-6171

DESMOND, NED, editor, writer; Student, Amherst Coll., 1980; MA, Tufts U.; Reuters fellow, Oxford U. Writer Fgn. Affairs, N.Y. Rev. Books; bur. chief New Delhi, 1988—91, Tokyo, 1992—96; sr. writer Fortune; v.p. ctrs. and content Infoseek; editor, pres. eCompany Now, 1999—2001, Bus. 2.0 mag., pres., 2001—02; exec. editor Time Inc. Interactive, 2002—. Office: American Online Inc 22000 Aol Way Dulles VA 20166-9032*

DESMOND, PATRICIA LORRAINE, psychotherapist, writer, publisher; b. Boston, June 25, 1946; d. Francis X. and Mary L. (Donohue) D.; children: June, Timothy. AB, Stonehill Coll., 1968; MEd, U. Mass., Boston, 1994. Reporter The Patriot Ledger, Quincy, Mass., 1968-81; publisher Hingham (Mass.) Mariner, 1981-83, The Women's Jour., Hingham, 1985, Milton (Mass.) Times, 1995—; assoc. editor The Hingham Jour., 1985-86; copy editor Boston Herald, 1987-89; columnist Hull (Mass.) Times, 1988-94; editor Mariner Newspapers, Marshfield, Mass., 1989-91; pvt. practice Milton, Mass., 1993—; pub. Milton (Mass.) Times, 1995—; outpatient therapist High Point, Plymouth, Mass., 1994-96; case mgr. Harbor Light Ctr., Boston, 1995. Columnist Tiny Town Gazette, Cohasset, Mass., 1993-96; publicist Share New Eng., Canton, Mass., 1993-95; therapist S. Bay Mental Health Ctr., Weymouth, 1995; relapse prevention counselor Nazareth Residence, Roxbury, 1995-96. Author: Cinnamon, 1988; co-author: How to Heal Your Heart, 1988; editor On the Edge, 1992-93; counselor/case mgr. St. Elizabeth's Comprehensive Alcoholism and Addictions Program, 1994-95. Chair Milton Bus. Coun., 2000—. Recipient Honorary Mention Mass. Womens Press Assn., 1971, New England Press Assn., 1983. Mem. NOW (state coord. 1973-74), ACA, Nat. Writers Union, Mass. Assn. Alcoholism and Drug Abuse Counselors, The Women's Poetry Collective, Kiwanis (Milton v.p. 2001), Rotary (Milton pres. 2001-02, chair Milton bus. coun. 2002—). Avocations: poet, novelist. Office: Milton Times 480 Adams St Milton MA 02186-4914 E-mail: miltonnews@aol.com.

DESMOND, SUSAN FAHEY, lawyer; b. Greenville, Miss., Feb. 24, 1961; d. Richard Paul and Bonnie Jean (Williams) Fahey; m. John Michael Desmond; May 28, 1994; children: Meghan, Kelsey. BA in English and History, U. Miss., 1982; JD, U. Tenn., 1985. Bar: Miss. 1985, Colo. 1996, La. 1998. Assoc. Robertshaw, Terney & Noble, Greenville, Miss., 1985-86, Miller, Milam & Moeller, Jackson, Miss., 1986-89, Phelps Dunbar, Jackson, Miss., 1989-92, ptnr., 1992-97, New Orleans, 1998—2003; shareholder Watkins, Ludlam, Winter and Stennis, P.A., Gulfport, Miss., 2003—. Author: Employment Issues for Hospital Supervisors, 1996; editor: Mississippi Pro Bono Material, 1989. Bd. dirs. Am. Cancer Soc. Hinds County Unit, Jackson, Miss., 1990-96, YMCA Greater New Orleans, 2002-03. Mem. Jackson Young Lawyers (dir. 1991-93, merit award 1988), Am. Bar Assn./Young Lawyers (labor com. chmn., Chgo., 1990-92), Miss. Bar Assn. (dir. 1990-92, Outstanding Young Lawyer 1997). Republican. Roman Catholic. Avocations: tennis, reading. Office: Watkins Ludlam Winter & Stennis PA 2510 14th St Ste 1010 Gulfport MS 39502 E-mail: sdesmond@watkinsludlam.com.

DESNICK, ROBERT JOHN, human geneticist; b. Mpls., July 12, 1943; s. Theodore David and Celia Janice (Marcus) D.; Julie E. Herzig, Oct. 23, 1988; 1 child, Jonathan Phillips. BA, U. Minn., 1965, PhD, 1970, MD, 1971. Diplomate Am. Bd. Med. Examiners, Am. Acad. Pediat., Am. Bd. Med. Genetics (bd. dirs. 1990-93, treas. 1991-93). Rsch. assoc. U. Minn., 1970-72, intern and resident dept. pediatrics, 1971-73; asst. prof. pediat. U. Minn. Dight Inst. Human Genetics, 1973-75; asst. prof. lab. medicine and pathology U. Minn., 1973-75; assoc. prof. genetics and cell biology U. Minn. Coll. Biol. Sci., 1975-77; assoc. prof. pediat. U. Minn. Dight Inst. Human Genetics, 1977. Arthur J. and Nellie Z. Cohen prof. pediat. and genetics, 1977—; chief divsn. med. and molecular genetics Mt. Sinai Sch. Medicine, N.Y.C., 1977—; med. adv. bd. Nat. Neurofibromatosis Found., 1978—81; dir. Mt. Sinai Ctr. Jewish Genetic Diseases, 1981—; chmn. med. adv. bd. Nat. Tay-Sachs and Allied Diseases Assn., 1975—; program dir. Mt. Sinai Gen. Clin. Rsch. Ctr., 1990—99; chair dept. Human Genetics Mt. Sinai Sch. Medicine, N.Y.C., 1993—; attending physician pediat. Mt. Sinai Hosp.; cons. physician pediat. Beth Israel Med. Ctr., N.Y.C., City Ctr. Hosp., Elmhurst, NY; med. adv. bd. Nat. Found. Jewish Genetic Diseases, 1981—2002; mem. N.Y. Gov.'s Adv. Com. on Genetics, 1982—; bd. dirs. Soc. Inherited Metabolic Diseases, 1983—92; med. adv. bd. Am. Porphyria Assn., 1984—, Mucolipidosis IV Found., 1984—, Nat. MPS Soc., 1987—; pres. Soc. Inherited Metabolic Diseases, 1989—91; sci. adv. bd. Dysautonomia Found., 1990—, Nat. Niemann-Pick Found., 1992—; med. adv. bd. Internat. Incontinenta Pigmenti Found., 1993—; mem. mental retardation study sect. NIH, 1995—98; sci. adv. bd. Ara Parshegian Med. Rsch. Found., 1995—2002, Bachman-Strauss Dystonia & Parkinson Found., 1997—; chmn. organizing com. Internat. Congresses Inherited Metabolic Diseases, 1990—; mem. NCRR adv. coun. NIH, 2000—; mem. adminstrv. bd., coun. acad. socs. Am. Assn. Med. Colls., 2001—; mem. exec. coun. Am. Assn. Med. Coll., 2003—. Editor: Enzyme Therapy in Genetic Diseases, 1973, Molecular Genetic Modification of Eucaryotes, 1978, Enzyme Therapy in Genetic Diseases, 1980, Gaucher Disease: A Century of Delineation and Research, 1982, Animal Models of Inherited Metabolic Disorders, 1982; mem. editl. bd. Clinica Chemica Acta, 1984—96; editor: Recent Advances in Inborn Errors of Metabolism, 1987, Treatment of Genetic Diseases, 1991; mem. editl. bd. Enzyme, 1979—98, Am. Jour. Human Genetics, 1980—84, Pediatrics, 1991—96, Human Mutation, 1991—, Biochem. Medicine and Metabolic

Biology, 1991—97, Jour. Clin. Investigation, 1992—97, Jour. Inherited Metabolic Disease, 1996—, Jour. Human Genetics, 1998—, Molecular Genetics and Metabolism, 1998—, Jour. Genomics; editor: Tay-Sachs Disease, 2001; mem. editl. bd. Molecular Medicine, 2002—; contbr. articles to profl. jours. Pres. fifth Internat. Congress of Inborn Errors of Metabolism, 1990. Recipient Ross award Soc. Pediat. Rsch., 1972, C.J. Watson award U. Minn. Med. Sch., 1973, NIH Rsch. Career Devel. award, 1975-80, E. Mead Johnson award Am. Acad. Pediatrics, 1981, Outstanding Faculty award Mt. Sinai Sch.of Medicine, 1991, NIH Merit award, 1992, J. Lester Gabrilove award for med. rsch., 2003; USPHS fellow, 1968-70. Mem. AAAS, Am. Soc. Human Genetics, Genetics Soc. Am., Am. Acad. Pediatrics, Minn. Human Genetics League dir. 1970-77, Soc. Complex Carbohydrates, Behavior Genetics Assn., Am. Fedn. Clin. Rsch., Am. Coll. Med. Genetics founding fellow, chair hon. membership com. 1990-98, chair biochem. and molecular resource com. 1993-2002, chmn. accreditation com. 1998-2000), Am. Coll. Med. Genetics Found. (bd. dirs. 1998—), Am. Soc. Biochemistry and Molecular Biology, Assn. Profs. Human/Med. Genetics pres-elect 1994, pres. 1996-98, Ea. Soc. Pediatric Rsch., Soc. Pediatric Rsch., Soc. Exptl. Biology and Medicine, Am. Soc. Exptl. Pathology, Cen. Soc. Clin. Rsch., Soc. Study Social Biology, Soc. Study Inborn Errors of Metabolism, N.Y. Acad. Sci., European Soc. Human Genetics, Harvey Soc. (sec. 1984-89), Soc. Inherited Metabolic Diseases (pres. 1989-90), Am. Pediatric Soc., Am. Soc. Microbiology, Am. Assn. Physicians, Am. Soc. Clin. Investigation, Assn. Patient-Oriented Rsch. (founding 1998—), Am. Soc. for Gene Therapy, Japanese Soc. Inherited Diseases (hon.), Società Italiana di Pediatrica (hon.), Peripatetic Club, Sigma Xi. Office: Mt Sinai Sch Medicine Dept Human Genetics 5th Ave & 100th St New York NY 10029 Business E-Mail: RJDESNICK@MSSM.EDU.

DESNOYERS, MEGAN FLOYD, archivist, educator; b. N.Y.C., Oct. 31, 1945; d. Lawrence Clifford and Frances Irene (Laffoon) Floyd; m. David George Desnoyers, Sept. 2, 1967; 1 child, Adam O'Neil. Postgrad., Am. U., 1972; AB, Vassar Coll., 1967; MLS, Rutgers U., 1968. Cert. archivist. Libr. John Jay H.S., Wappingers Falls, N.Y., 1968-69; archivist Franklin D. Roosevelt Libr., Hyde Park, N.Y., 1969; supervisory archivist John F. Kennedy Libr., Boston, 1970—, curator Ernest Hemingway Collection, 1987—96, 2000—01; instr. in archives adminstrn. Nat. Archives Modern Archives Inst., Washington, 1982-2000. Lectr. archives adminstrn. U. Mass., Boston, 1978-80; lectr. on Hemingway, 1992—; mem. Archives Adv. Commn., Boston, 1977-2000; archival advisor Girl Scouts U.S., N.Y.C., 1991—. Contbr. chpt. to book, articles to profl. jours. Mem. adv. bd., chmn. com. Voluntary Action Ctr., Mass. Bay United Way, Boston, 1974-80; mem., chair bd. trustees Randall Libr., Stow, Mass., 1976-80; mem. Mass. Hist. Records Adv. Bd., 1979-2000. Nat. Def. fellow, 1967-68. Fellow Soc. Am. Archivists; mem. New Eng. Archivists (sec. 1976-78), Soc. Am. Archivists (workshop instr.), Acad. Cert. Archivists (task force on recert. 1991-92), Beta Phi Mu. Democrat. Roman Catholic. Office: John F Kennedy Libr Columbia Point Boston MA 02125

DESO, ROBERT EDWARD, JR., lawyer; b. Albany, N.Y., Mar. 20, 1943; s. Robert Edward and Mary Audrey (Donahue) D.; m. Alice Rae Jones, Oct. 28, 1967; children: Robert, Susan, Karen, Kathleen. BSFS, Georgetown U., 1965; JD, U. Va., 1968. Bar: Va. 1968, D.C. 1973, U.S. Ct. Mil. Appeals 1968, U.S. Dist. Ct. D.C. 1977, U.S. Dist. Ct. (ea. dist.) Va. 1981, U.S. Ct. Claims 1975, U.S. Ct. Appeals (D.C. cir.) 1988, U.S. Ct. Appeals (4th cir.) 2003, U.S. Tax Ct. 2003. Spl. asst. to Judge Advocate Gen. U.S. Army-Pentagon, Washington, 1972-73; asst. gen. counsel Met. Police Dept., Washington, 1973-75, dep. gen. counsel, 1975-78; ptnr./prin. Deso & Greenberg, P.C., Washington, 1978-90; ptnr., prin. Deso, Thomas, Stien & Weitzman, Washington, 1990—2001. Rschr./author: Law at War, 1975. Scoutmaster Boy Scouts Am., Falls Church, Va., 1981-84; legis. chmn. PTA, McLean, Va., 1985-88. Capt. U.S. Army, 1968-73. Decorated Bronze Star medal. Mem. ABA, Va. Bar Assn., Bar Assn. of D.C. Lodges: Fraternal Order of Police. Roman Catholic. Office: Deso Thomas Buckley & Stien PC 1828 L St NW Ste 660 Washington DC 20036-5112 E-mail: redeso@dtswlaw.com.

DE SOFI, OLIVER JULIUS, data processing executive; b. Havana, Cuba, Dec. 26, 1929; came to U.S., 1956; s. Julius A. and Edith H. (Zsuffa) DeS.; m. Phyllis H. Dumich, Feb. 14, 1971; children: Richard D., Stephen R., Kerri L. BS in Math. and Physics, Ernst Lehman Coll., 1950; postgrad. in agronomy, U.Havana, 1952; BS in Aero. Engring., 1956. Dir. EDP tech. svcs. and planning Am. Airlines, N.Y.C., 1968-70; dir. Sabre II, Tulsa, 1970-72; v.p. data processinga nd comms. Nat. Bank N.Am., Huntington Sta., N.Y., 1972-76; sr. v.p. data processing and comms., 1976-78; sr. v.p. sys. and ops., 1978-79; sr. v.p. adminstrn., 1980-83; exec. v.p. adminstrn. group, 1980-83; exec. v.p. data processing methodologies adn arch. Anacomp, Inc., Ft. Lee, N.J., 1983-84; v.p. copr. devel. Computer Horizons Corp., N.Y.C., 1984-86; pres., CEO Coast to Coast Computers, Inc., Sarasota, Fla., 1986—; CEO, 1993-94. Chief data processing cons. Arab Nat. Bank, Riyadh, Kingdom of Saudi Arabia, 1991-92; CEO, ; bd. dirs. The Bentley Group, San Francisco, Innovative Mgmt. Systems, Inc., Sarasota, Doks Enterprises, Inc., Carson City, C.C. Lawn Care, Inc., Sarasota; lectr. program for women Adelphi Coll. Mem. AAAS, Am. Mgmt. Assn., NRA, Internat. Platform Assn., Data Processing Mgmt. Assn., Computer Exec. Round Table, Sales Execs. Club, Bank Adminstrn. Inst., Masons (Havana). E-mail: dsfi@aol.com.

DESOMBRE, NANCY COX, academic administrator, consultant; b. Lake City, Minn., Sept. 7, 1939; d. Ray Ronald and Marjorie Mae (Lipa) C.; m. Eugene DeSombre, Sept. 10, 1960; children: Elizabeth DeSombre, Michael DeSombre. BA, U. Chgo., 1961, MA, 1962. Prof. English dept. Wilbur Wright Coll., Chgo., 1962—, chair English dept., 1976—, dean vocat. program, 1981-82, dean of instrn., 1982-86, v.p. faculty, instr., 1987-94; pres. Harold Washington Coll., Chgo., 1994—. Cons. evaluator North Cen. Assn. of Coll./Schs., Chgo., 1987—; dir. LaSalle Bank, N.A., Chgo., 1994—; mem. bd. dirs. Greater State St. Coun., Chgo., 1995—, State Univ. Retirement System, Champaign, Ill., 1995—. Mem. bd. dirs. Frank Lloyd Wright Found., Oak Park, 1987—. Recipient Inst. Ednl. Mgmt. award Harvard U., 1990, Project Enhance award Wright Coll., 1991, Woman of the Yr. award Exec. Leadership Inst.-League for Innovation, 1993, 94. Avocation: gardening. Office: Harold Washington Coll 30 E Lake St Chicago IL 60601-2403

DE SOTO, ERNEST FRANK, artist, publisher; b. Tucson, Oct. 26, 1923; s. Robert Carlos and Artemisa Ortiz Soto; m. Rosalind Braun, Dec. 15, 1950 (div. June 1962); m. Josephine Mary Panyk, Aug. 6, 1962. Cert., Chouinard Art Sch., L.A., 1942-43, 46-48; BFA, U. Ill., 1961. Owner, dir. Ernest F. de Soto Workshop, San Francisco, 1978-93; master printer Edits. Press, San Francisco, 1972-76, Collectors Press, San Francisco, 1967-72. Pub.: (graphics) Limited Editions, 1978-93; book illustrator: Robin Crusoe, Folk Tales of Mexico, 1957-58. Bd. trustees Mex. Mus., San Francisco, 1987-93; art instr. Western Res. U., Cleve., 1952-53, U. Ill., Urbana, 1954-62. Sgt. USAF, 1943-46, PTO. Recipient Award of Honor, San Francisco Arts Commn., Bank of Am., 1982; rsch. tech. lithography grantee Ford Found., U. Ill., 1958, Master Printer Ford Found. grantee Tamarind Lithography Workshop, 1965-67. Avocations: art, painting, graphics. Home: 915 S La Huerta Green Valley AZ 85614-2120 E-mail: dsotowrkshopart@aol.com.

DESOTO, LEWIS DAMIEN, art educator; b. San Bernardino, Calif., Jan. 3, 1954; s. Lewis Dan and Albertina (Quiroz) DeS. BA, U. Calif., Riverside, 1978; MFA, Claremont Grad. Sch., 1981. Tchr. Otis Parsons, L.A., 1982-85; chmn. art dept. Cornish Coll. of Arts, Seattle, 1985-88; prof. art San Francisco State U., 1988—95; dir. grad. studies Calif. Coll. Arts and Crafts, Oakland, 1993-95; prof. art San Francisco State U., 1995—. Exhibitions include New Mus., N.Y.C., 1992, Centro Cultural De La Raza, San Diego, 1993, Moderna Museet, Stockholm, Sweden, 1993, Christopher Grimes Gallery, Santa Monica, Calif., 1994, Denver Art Mus., 1994, Columbus Mus. Art, 1994, Des Moines Art Ctr., 1995, Fundacao Serralves, Opporto, Portugal, 1995, MetronÓm, Barcelona, Spain, 1997, Public Art Commn., San Francisco Courthouse, 1998, San Francisco Internat. Airport, 2000, Public Commn., San Jose, Calif., 2002, U. Tex., San Antonio, 2001, Public Art Commn., List Visual Art Ctr., MIT, Cambridge, 1998, Bill Maynes Gallery, N.Y.C., 1999, 2000, Mus. of Contemporary Religious Art, St. Louis, 2000, Mus. Contemporary Art, San Diego, 2001, Worcester Art (Mass.) Mus., 2001, Bill Maynes Gallery, N.Y.C., 2002, Samek Art Ctr., Bucknell U., Lewisburg, Pa., 2002. Mem. photo coun. Seattle Art Mus., 1987-88, Eureka Fellowship, vis. arts, 1999. Recipient New Genres award Calif. Arts Coun., 1992, NEA fellow, 1996. Mem. L.A. Ctr. for Photographic Studies (bd. dirs. 1983-85), CameraWork (exec. bd. dirs. 1991-93), Ctr. for Arts (adv. bd. 1993-95), Friends of Photography (peer award bd. 1991-96). Office: San Francisco State U Art Dept 1600 Holloway Ave San Francisco CA 94132-1722 E-mail: Sotolux@sbcglobal.net.

DE SOTO, SIMON, mechanical engineer; b. N.Y.C., Jan. 8, 1925; s. Albert and Esther (Eskenazi) Soto; 1 dau., Linda Jane. B.M.E., CCNY, 1945; M.M.E., Syracuse U., 1950; PhD, UCLA, 1965. Lic. profl. engr., Calif., N.Y. Engr. Johns-Manville Corp., N.Y.C., 1946-48; instr. in engring. Syracuse U., 1948-50; research engr. Stratos-Fairchild Corp., Farmingdale, N.Y., 1950-54; research specialist Lockheed Missile Systems div. Lockheed Corp., Van Nuys, Calif., 1954-56; sr. tech. specialist Rocketdyne Rockwell Internat., Canoga Park, Calif., 1956-69; asso. prof. mech. engring. Calif. State U., Long Beach, 1969-72, prof., 1972—. Lectr. UCLA, 1954-70; cons. engr.; dir., sec.-treas. Am. Engring. Devel. Co.; mem. tech. planning com. Pub. Policy Conf.: The Energy Crisis, Its Effect on Local Govts., 1973; founding mem. Calif. State U. and Colls.; Statewide Energy Consortium and cons. tech. assistance program. Author: Thermostatics and Thermodynamics: An Instructor's Manual, 1963; author: research publs. in field. Served with U.S. Mcht. Marine, 1945-46. Mem. AAAS, SAG, Am. Soc. Engring. Edn. (prof. of recipients of Outstanding Design award 1990), Tau Beta Pi, Pi Tau Sigma. Avocation: acting on stage and film. Office: Calif State U Dept Mech Engring Long Beach CA 90840-0001

DE SOUSA, BYRON N.S. educator, physician, health and medical consultant; b. Goiania, Goias, Brazil, Jan. 15, 1949; came to the U.S., 1972; s. Lazaro Jose and Zarife (Chaul) de.; m. Ana Maria S., Nov. 15, 1991; stepchildren: Thiago M., Thais Martins; children: Daniela N., Elisabeth L. BS in Biology, U. Brasilia, Brazil, 1970, BS in Biology Edn., 1971, MD, 1973; PhD in Physiol. Chemistry, Ohio State U., 1976. Diplomate Am. Bd. Disability Analysis. Prin. CASEB & CSL biology tchr. Adult Sr. H.S., Brazil, 1969-71; instr. biochemistry U. Goias, Brazil, 1972; rsch. asst. prof. neurology UCLA-Wadsworth V.A. Med. Ctr., L.A., 1978-79; cons. physician Brentwood V.A. Med. Ctr., L.A., 1979-80; intern Wadsorth-Brentwood V.A. Med. Ctr., L.A., 1980-81; resident in Anesthesiology U. So. Calif. Med. Ctr., L.A., 1981-83; anesthesiologist Simi Valley Presbyn. Hosp., Calif., 1983-85, Simi Valley Community Hosp., Calif., 1983-85, Rio Hondo Meml. Hosp., L.A., 1983-85, Kaiser Permanente Med. Ctr., Orange County, Calif., 1983-84, Hollywood Presbyn. Med. Ctr., L.A., 1983-84, Pacoima Community Hosp., L.A., 1984; assoc. prof. biochemistry, pharmacology Fed. U. Goias, 1986-89; adj. prof. pharmacology U. North Tex. Health Sci. Ctr., Ft. Worth, 1993; anesthesiologist UTSMC affiliated hosps., Dallas, 1993; vis. prof. pharmacology, med. microbiology and immunology U. North Tex. Health Sci. Ctr., Ft. Worth. Cons. Alcon Labs., Inc., 1989-90; adj. prof. dept. pharmacology U. North Tex. Health Sci. Ctr., Ft. Worth; dir. continuing med. edn. Am. Coll. Internat. Physicians-U. Tex. Southwestern Med. Ctr., Dallas; exec. dir. Internat. Inst. Medicine; organizer numerous symposia and seminars, U.S.A., Africa, Asia, Europe, S.Am.; exec. dir. Internat. Inst. Medicine, Ft. Worth, 1996—; adj. prof. human anatomy and physiology Tex. C.C., 2000—; v.p. BDS Assocs. Worldwide Cons.-Pub. Health. Author, editor (book) Arts of Politics: Thoughts and Quotations, 1988; reviewer sci. and clin. jours.; contbr. over 60 articles to sci. jours. and other publs.; inventor in field. Bd. dirs., sec. Substance Abuse Inst. N. Tex., 1993—; bd. dirs. Harry Male Youth Found.; bd. dirs., mem. Longhorn coun. troop 17 Boy Scouts Am., Ft. Worth, 1995—, treas., 1995-97; commr. City of Ft. Worth Plan Commn., 1998—, chmn., 2001-. NIA postdoctoral fellow Med. Coll. Pa., 1976-77, postdoctoral fellow U. Wis., 1977-78, Internal Medicine fellow UCLA Med. Ctr., 1979-80. Fellow Am. Coll. Internat. Physicians (trustee 1994-2000, pres. Tex. chpt. 1994-99); mem. Am. Bd. and Coll. Disability Analysts, C.C. Tchrs. Assn., Am. Planning Assn. Avocations: biking, gemology, flying, sailing. Office: 2100 SE Pkwy Arlington TX 76018

DESPANZA-SPRENGER, LYNETTE CHARLIE, small business owner; b. New Orleans, June 7, 1948; d. Sylvester Issac and Yverdelle Ida Despanza; m. Charles Ricard II, May 1970 (div. May 18, 1978); m. Paul Henri Sprenger, Oct. 28 (div. June 2002); 1 child, Charles Ricard III. BSN, U. Hawaii, 1995; ASN, St. Pete Jr. Coll., 1988; student, Delgado Jr. Coll., 1972. Cert. respiratory therapist La.; RN La. Sedation rm. dir. King Khalid Eye Specialist Hosp., Riyadh, Saudi Arabia, edn. clin. instr. and stress mgmt. instr., 1989—98; ballroom dance and exercise instr. Inst. Royal Family and We. and European Families in Saudi Arabia, Saudi Arabia, 1990—98; clinic adminstr., dir. Columbia Gia Diah Internat., Vietnam; respiratory therapist Bay Front Hosp., St. Petersburg, Fla.; emergency nurse, ICU nurse Maxim Healthcare Agy. and Agy. Personnel, St. Petersburg, Fla., 1999—2000; owner, chef, operator Lagniappe Bistrot, St. Petersburg; co-operator Swiss Creole Connection, 2002—. Art restorer Leppa Rathner Mus., St. Petersburg. Vol. St. Petersburg Jr. Coll. N.O.L.A., Fla. Recipient pastels and oil painting award, Art Soc. of St. Petersburg, U. New Orleans. Roman Catholic. Avocations: jazz, tap, ballroom dancing, painting, fencing. Home: 732 17th Ave N Saint Petersburg FL 33704 E-mail: despanzalynette@hotmail.com.

DESPER, CLYDE RICHARD, retired polymer scientist; b. Greenwood, Ark., Dec. 14, 1937; s. John James and Eva May (Kiger) D.; m. Beatrice Smith, Aug. 17, 1963 (div. Dec. 1972); children: Elizabeth, John, Beatrice, Richard, Scott; m. Laura Taylor, Jan. 1, 1988. BSChemE, MIT, 1959, MSChemE, 1960; PhD in Chemistry, U. Mass., 1966. Rsch. asst. Fabric Rsch. Labs., Dedham, Mass., 1960-62; rsch. chemist U.S. Army Natick (Mass.) Labs., 1966-68, U.S. Army Rsch. Labs., Watertown, Mass., 1968-94; ret., 1994. Expert analyst Chemtracts: Macromolecular Chemistry, Phila., 1982-94. Author: (play) Star-Crossed Lovers, 1992 (Miller award Deep South Writers Conf. 1995); contbr. articles to Jour. Polymer Sci., Elizabeth Rev. Mem. Nat. Materials Adv. Bd. Com. on High Performance Fibers, Washington, 1987-92. Fellow Shakespeare fellow, De Vere Soc. Mem. Am. Chem. Soc., Am. Phys. Soc., Am. Crystallographical Assn., Materials Rsch. Soc., Sigma Xi. Achievements include research in macromolecules, question of Shakespeare authorship. Home: 55 Littleton Rd Apt 21E Ayer MA 01432-1760 E-mail: dickdesper@net1plus.com.

DESPOMMIER, DICKSON DONALD, microbiology educator, parasitologist, researcher; b. New Orleans, June 5, 1940; s. Roland Medd and Beverly (Wood) D.; children— Bruce, Bradley BS, Fairleigh Dickinson U., 1962; MS, Columbia U., 1964; PhD, U. Notre Dame, 1967. Postdoctoral fellow Rockefeller U., 1967-71; Asst. prof. pub. health Columbia U., N.Y.C., 1971-75, assoc. prof., 1975-77, prof. pub. health and microbiology, 1982—. Cons. NIH, 1980-84, Gen. Food Corp., 1976, Cordis Corp., 1973-74, Bionetics Rsch. Inc., 1986-89, Eco-Chem, Inc., 1993; Theobald Smith lectr. 1993; pres. Apple Trees Prodns., LLC, N.Y.C. Author: Parasitic Diseases, 4th edit., 2000, Parasite Life Cycles, 1988, West Nile Story, 2001. Bd. dirs., chmn. edn. com. Catskill Flyfishing Ctr. and Mus., 1994—, dir., 1994—. Named Tchr. of Yr. Columbia U., 1980, 81, 83, 84; recipient Career Devel. award Nat. Inst. A.I.D., 1971-75, Disting. Tchr. award Med. Coll. Ohio, 1980, Deans' Disting. Tchr. award Columbia U., 1989, Golden Apple Tchr. of Yr. award Am. Med. Students Assn., 2003. Mem. AAAS, Am. Soc. Parasitologists, Am. Soc. Tropical Medicine and Hygiene, Harvey Soc., N.Y. Soc. Tropical Medicine (pres. 1980), Internat. Commn. on Trichinellosis. Clubs: Trout Unltd. (bd. dirs. 1976-78) (Oradel, N.J.). Office: Room 124 Psychiat Inst Annex New York NY 10032 E-mail: ddd1@columbia.edu.

D'ESPOSITO, JULIAN C., JR., lawyer; b. N.Y.C., Aug. 6, 1944; BS, Loyola U., 1966; JD cum laude, Northwestern U., 1969. Bar: Ill. 1969, U.S. Dist. Ct. (no. dist.) 1969. Counsel to Gov. Ill., 1977-81; ptnr. in charge Chgo. office Mayer, Brown, Rowe & Maw. Chmn. Winnetka Plan Commn., 1985-89; mem. Ill. Med. Ctr. Commn., 1987-94; dir. Ill. Capitel Devel. Bd., 1994-95; chmn. Ill. State Toll Hwy. Authority, 1995-99. Co-editor-in-chief Jour. Criminal Law, Criminology & Police Sci., Northwestern U., 1968-69. Mem. ABA. Office: Mayer Brown Rowe & Maw 190 S La Salle St Ste 3100 Chicago IL 60603-3441

DESPOSITO, MARTHA SHEATS, artist, educator; b. Pensacola, Fla., Nov. 16, 1945; d. Carl William Sheats and Mina Jean (Glenn) Presley; m. Angelo John Desposito, Aug. 21, 1965; children: Angelo John III, Jean Paige. BFA in Fiber Design cum laude, U. Louisville, 1986; MFA in Painting, U. Ky., 1990. Adj. prof. U. Louisville, 1989, Ind. U. S.E., New Albany, 1990, Notre Dame Coll., Cleve., 1992-94, Lakeland C.C., Cleve., 1993-94, Ursuline Coll., Cleve., 1994—; art tchr. Sweetwater Ctr. for Arts, Sewickley, Pa., 1994-98, Pitts. Ctr. for Arts, 1997-98. Bd. dirs. art adv. bd. Notre Dame Coll., Cleve., 1992-96. One person shows include Spalding U. Gallery, Louisville, 1988, Colonial Gallery, Cleve., 1991, Kent (Ohio) State Student Ctr. Gallery, 1992, Notre Dame Coll. Gallery, Euclid, Ohio, 1992, Bolton Art Gallery, Cleve., 1993, Kimbo Art Gallery, Pitts., 1995, Art Inst. of Pitts., 1995, Sweetwater Ctr. for Arts, 1997, Glenville State Coll., 1998; exhibited in group shows including J. B. Speed Art Mus., Louisville, 1984, 88, Evansville (Ind.) Mus. of Arts and Scis., 1985, 87, Crescent Gallery, Louisville, 1986, 87, U. Wis., Green Bay, 1987, Owensboro (Ky.) Mus. Fine Art, 1988, Cen. Bank Gallery, Lexington, Ky., 1988, Western Ill. U., Macomb, 1989, Franklin St. Gallery, Chgo. 1990, Warehouse Dist., Cleve., 1990, Zephyr Gallery, Louisville, 1991, Trumbell Art Gallery, Warren, Ohio, 1991, Art at the Power House, Cleve., 1992, 93, Commonwealth Bank, Louisville, 1994, Mansfield (Ohio) Art Ctr., 1994, Bank 1 Gallery, Louisville, 1995, Gallery at Cedar Hollow, Malvern, Pa., 1995, Hoyt Inst. of Art nat. and regional shows, Pitts., 1996, Three Rivers Art Festival, Pitts., 1996, Artemesia Gallery, Chgo., 1997, Billingsley Gallery, Pensacola, 1997, Southern Allegheny Mus. Art, 1998-99, Pa. S.W. Regional, 1999, Agora Gallery, N.Y., 1999; regional artist for S. Allegheny's Mus. of Art, 1998-99; represented in corp. collections Nat. City Bank, Louisville, Sarnoff Deposition Svc., Inc., L.A., Western Ill. U., Macomb, PNC Bank, Louisville, Crown Equipment Corp., New Bremen, Ohio; works featured in publs. including Pensacola Magazine, Pitts. Mag., Fiber Arts Design Book IV, V and VI Cleve., Now Mag., Pensacola Magazine. Recipient 1st pl. award Commonwealth Bank, 1994, Merit award 1st Nat. Bank, 1990, Hon. Mention, Art Calendar Mag., 1997; Grad. Sch. grantee U. Ky., 1990; Allen R. Hite scholar U. Louisville, 1986. Mem. Nat. Mus. of Women in the Arts, Women's Caucus for Art, Coll. Art Assn. Home: 5460 N Shore Rd Pensacola FL 32507-9700

DESPRES, LEO ARTHUR, sociology and anthropology educator, academic administrator; b. Lebanon, N.H., Mar. 29, 1932; s. Leo Arthur and Madeline (Bedford) D.; m. Loretta A. LaBarre, Aug. 22, 1953; children— Christine, Michelle, Denise, Mary Louise, Renee. BA, U. Notre Dame, 1954, MA, 1956; PhD, Ohio State U., 1960. Research assoc. Columbia Psychiat. Inst. and Hosp., 1957-60; postdoctoral fellow Social Sci. Research Council, Guyana, 1960-61; asst. prof. Ohio Wesleyan U., 1961-63; faculty Case Western Res. U., Cleve., 1963-74, prof. anthropology, 1967-74, chmn. dept., 1968-74; prof. sociology, anthropology U. Notre Dame, Ind., 1974-97, chmn. dept., 1974-80, fellow Kellogg Inst. Internat. Studies, 1982—, prof. emeritus, 1997—. Cons. in field. Author: Cultural Pluralism and Nationalist Politics in British Guyana, 1968; editor: Ethnicity and Resource Competition in Plural Societies, 1975, Manaus: Social Life and Work in Brazil's Free Trade Zone, 1991. Fulbright scholar U. Guyana, 1970-71, Brazil, 1986; research grantee NSF, 1984. Mem. Am. Anthrop. Assn., Am. Ethnol. Soc., Latin Am. Studies Assn., Cen. States Anthrop. Soc. (pres. 1976-77), AAUP. Office: U Notre Dame Dept Anthropology Notre Dame IN 46556 Home: PO Box 6752 South Bend IN 46660-6752 E-mail: hdespres@nd.edu.

DESPRES, LEON MATHIS, lawyer, former city official; b. Chgo., Feb. 2, 1908; s. Samuel and Henrietta (Rubovits) D.; m. Marian Alschuler, Sept. 10, 1931; children— Linda Baskin, Robert Leon. PhB, U. Chgo., 1927, JD, 1929; DLitt, Columbia Coll., 1990, U. Ill., 2000. Bar: Ill. 1929. Ptnr. Despres, Schwartz and Geoghegan, Chgo.; trial examiner NLRB, Chgo., 1935-37; instr. U. Chgo., 1936, U. Wis., summers 1946-49; alderman 5th Ward Chgo. City Council, 1955-75, parliamentarian, 1979-87. Mem. Chgo. Plan Commn., 1979-89. Mem. Am., Ill., Chgo. bar. assns., Chgo. Council Lawyers, Order of Coif, Phi Beta Kappa. Home: 5830 S Stony Island Ave Apt 10A Chicago IL 60637-2024 Office: 77 W Washington St Chicago IL 60602-2801 E-mail: DSG777@aol.com.

DESPRES, PATRICK JOHN, artist, art educator; s. Louis and Marion Despres. BFA in Art Edn., U. Mass., N. Dartmouth, 1994; MFA in Sculpture, Wash. State U., 1998. Cert. tchr. art edn. grades 5-12 Mass. Instr. Brooks Coll., Long Beach, Calif., 1998—; designer online pilot art curriculum Prog. Learning, Santa Monica, Calif., 1998—2000. Exhibited in group shows at Spokane Art Gallery, 1996, U. Idaho, 1997, Wash. State U., 1998, El Camino C.C., 2003, one-man shows include U. Wash., 1997; artist (two man show) Dartmouth Art Gallery, U. Mass., 1993, U. Mass., Dartmouth, 1994, 1995. Business E-Mail: despres@brookscollege.edu.

DESPRIET, JOHN G. lawyer; b. Kortrijk, Belgium, Aug. 12, 1949; BS with honors, U. Fla., 1971, JD with honors, 1978; MBA, U. Utah, 1976. Bar: Ga. 1979, Fla. 1979. Mem. Smith, Gambrell & Russell, Atlanta. Sr. student editor U. Fla. Law Review, 1978. Capt. USAF, 1971-76. Mem. State Bar Ga., Fla. Bar. Office: Smith Gambrell & Russell 1230 Peachtree St NE Ste 3100 Atlanta GA 30309-3592

DES RIOUX, DEENA VICTORIA COTY, computer artist, digital graphics artist; b. Cambridge, Mass., Dec. 7, 1941; d. Sam and Sophina G. (Cohen) Coty; m. Philippe Roger Armand des Rioux de Messimy, Aug. 29, 1964. Student, RISD, 1959-62, Brown U., 1960-62, Sorbonne, Paris, 1961, 63-64. Package designer, illustrator, pvt. tchr., freelance artist, Boston, 1962-63, 64-70. Guest lectr. Mass. Coll. Art, Boston, 1975, Harvard Grad. Sch. Design, Lesley Coll., Cambridge, Mass., 1976, 77, UN Photography Soc., N.Y.C., 1993; juror Heritage Plantation Mus., Cape Cod, Mass., 1977, Digitalsplash at Artsplash for Rockaway Artists Alliance, Fort Tilden, N.Y., 2003; exhbns. coord. Women Exhibiting in Boston, Inc., 1973-75; founder, dir. 7 at Large (artists collective), Boston, 1975-78; exhbns. coord. Assn. Artist-Run Galleries, N.Y.C., 1980-82, pub. rels. dir., 1983-84; guest spkr. UN Photography Soc., N.Y., 1993, U. Wyo. Art Mus., Laramie, 1994, Nassau County Cmty. Coll. Firehouse Gallery, Garden City, N.Y., 1999, Rockaway Artists Alliance, Queens, N.Y., 1999, R.I. Coll. Bannister Gallery, Providence, 1999, Hockaday Mus. Art, Kalispell, Mont., 2000, Herkimer County Cmty. Coll., N.Y., 2001, Elmhurst Art Mus., Ill., 2001. Solo exhibns. Psychoanalytic Inst., Boston, 1974, Art Inst. Boston, 1975, Mus. Sci., Boston, 1978, Ward-Nasse Gallery, N.Y.C., 1978, Helander Gallery, Palm Beach, Fla., 1985, Columbia U., N.Y., 1992, U. Wyo. Art Mus., Laramie, 1994, Silicon Gallery, Phila., 1996, 2000, Bunkier Sztuki Art Ctr., Krakow, Poland, 1997, Mus. Gornoslaskie, Bytom, Poland, 1997, Northlight Gallery, Everett County C.C., Everett County, Wash., Northlight Gallery, 1998, 2000, Ctrl. Wash. U., Sarah Spurgeon Gallery, Ellensburg, 1998, Kans. State U. Gallery, Manhattan, 1998, Grants Pass Mus. Art, Grants Pass, Oreg., 1998, Nassau County C.C., Firehouse Gallery, Garden City, N.Y., 1999, R.I. Coll. Bannister Gallery, Providence, 1999, Hockaday Mus. Art, Kalispell, Mont., 2000, Wash. State U., Tricities, Richland, 2000, Columbia Basin Coll., Esvelt Gallery, Pasco, 2000, Herkimer County C.C., Cogar Gallery, N.Y., 2001, Elmhurst Art Mus., Ill., 2001, Schoolhouse History and Art Ctr., Colstrip, Mont., 2001, Mont. State U., Northcutt-Steele Gallery, Billings, 2001; group shows include Ward-Nasse Gallery, 1978-82, Helander Gallery, Palm Beach, 1984-87, Gallery Hirondelle, N.Y.C., 1985-87, Mokotoff Gallery, N.Y.C., 1986, Grace Harkin Gallery, N.Y.C., 1989, Warwick Mus., 1991, Downey Mus. Art, 1993, Alexandria Mus. Art, 1993, Latvia/Mus. Arsenāls, 1993, Mus. Art, RISD, 1994, Cartier/Fifth Ave., 1994, Fuller Mus. Art, 1995, S.I. Inst. Arts & Scis., 1995, Palm Springs Desert Mus., Calif., 1995, Japan/Tama Art Univ. Mus., Tokyo, 1995, Silicon Gallery, 1995, Nexus Found., Phila, 1996, Computer Art Invitational, Ea. Wash. U., Cheney, USA Mus. Tour, 1994-96, 96-98, 98-2000, Midwest Photography Invitational IX, X, XI, two-yr., ten-venue tours sponsored by U. Wis., Green Bay, 1996-98, 98-2000, 2000-02; represented in permanent collections Ctrl. Acad. Art, Kuala Lumpur, Malaysia, Hofstra U. Mus., Hempstead, N.Y., Internat. Ctr. Graphic Art, Ljubljana, Slovenia, So. Ill. U. Mus., Carbondale, Ind. U. Art Mus., Boise State U., Mus. Art at RISD, Austin, Mus. Art, Alexandria (La.) Mus. Art, Downey (Calif.) Mus. Art, Ea. Wash. U., Fuller Mus. Art, Brockton, Mass., Internat. Soc. Graphic Art, Krakow, Nat. Ctr. Fine Arts, Cairo, N.Y. Pub. Libr., Palm Springs Desert Mus., Tama Art U. Mus., Tokyo, U. Ala. at Birmingham, U. Pa., Phila., U. Wyo. Art Mus., Laramie, New Orleans Mus. Art, Elmhurst Art Mus., Elvehelm Mus. of Art, U. Wis.-Madison, Milw. Art Mus., Wis., Mont. State U., Northcutt-Steele Gallery, Billings; coord. exhibitor Art Inst. Boston, 1975 (grant), Mus. Sci. Boston 1977-78 (grant); cons. spl. exhibit Mus. City of N.Y., 1983-84; guest exhibitor Danvers Art and Hist. Soc., Attleboro Mus., Mass., Nashua Arts and Sci. Ctr., N.H.; competitive exhbns. include: 62d Newport Ann. Nat., 1973, 45th Ann. New Eng. Painting, Jordan Marsh, Boston, 1974, invited artist, Past/Post/Future, Robert Atkins, Pleiades Gallery, Soho, N.Y.C., 1985, Photo-Derived, Joel-Peter Witkin, Ind. U., 1989, At The Edge II, Wendy Weitman, Laguna Gloria Art Mus., Austin, Tex. tour, 1990-92, La Sierra U., Riverside, Calif., 1991, Seattle Ctr. Internat., 1991, Warwick Mus., R.I., 1991, Hill Country Arts Found. Nat., Ingram, Tex., 1991, Boise State U., Sun Valley Ctr.

for the Arts, Idaho, 1991, Adogi Barcelona, Tour, Cadaques, and Cities of Japan tour 1991-92, Juniper Gallery, Napa, Calif., 1991-92, Internat. Print Triennale, Krakow, Poland/Nuremberg, Germany, 1991-92, City Without Walls Gallery, Newark, 1992, L.A. Printmaking Soc. 12th Nat. Exhbn., UCLA, Palos Verdes Art Ctr., Calif., 1993, Boston Printmakers 44th N.Am. Exhbn., Roberta Waddell, Boston U. Gallery, Mass., 1993, Lubbock (Tex.) Fine Arts Ctr., James L. Enyeart, Illuminance '93, Alexandria Mus. Art 12th Ann. Sept., 1993, Soc. for Am. Graphic Artists 65th Nat. Print Exhbn., N.Y.C., 1993, Art Mus. Arsenals, 4th Internat. Miniprint Triennale, Riga, Latvia, 1993, Nat. Fine Arts Ctr./Giza, Egypt, guest/cultural ministry, 1st Egyptian Internat. PrintTriennale, 1994, 2d triennale 1997, 3d triennale, 2000, 4th Triennale, 2003, Fla. Ctr. Contemporary Art, Tampa, 1994, One West Art Ctr., Ft. Collins, Colo., 1994, Poland Internat. Trienniale of Graphic Arts '94, Nuremberg, Linz, Krakow, 1994, S.I. Inst. Arts and Scis., Biennial, 1995, Palm Springs Desert Mus., 26th Nat. Exhbn., Henry T. Hopkins, 1995, Franklin Inst., Phila., 1995, Tama Art U. Mus., Tokyo, 1995, Fine Arts Mus. L.I., Hempstead, N.Y., 1996, Silvermine Guild Galleries, Spectra '97, Robert Sobieszek, New Canaan, Conn., 1997, 26th Nat. Exhbn., juror R. John Bullard, Masur Mus. Art, Monroe, La., 1999, ANA 27, Holter Mus. Art juror Peter Frank, Helena, Mont., 1998, Internat. Ctr. Graphic Art, Ljubljana, Slovenia, Biennale 22, 1997, Ctrl. Acad. Art, Kuala Lumpur, Malaysia, 1997, Pitti Immagine srl., Stazione Leopolda, Florence, Italy, 1998, Polish Internat. Graphic Triennale, Krakow, 2000-02, Arena Gallery, Last of First, Chgo., 2001, Bklyn. Mus. Art, Digital: Printmaking Now, Marilyn S. Kushner, 2001, Museo Nacional de Bellas Arte, IV Salon and Colloquium of Digital Art, Havana, Cuba, 2002, 2003, Boston Printmakers 2003 N.Am. Print Biennial, Boston U. 808 Gallery, juror, Clifford S. Ackley, MFA Boston Print Curator, 2003. Hofstra U. Mus. Emily Lowe Gallery, Hempstead, 2003. Named one of N.Y. Outstanding Artists, Ethel Scull, N.Y.C., 1983; travel citation Mid-Am. Arts Alliance, 1990-92, recipient Juror/Roberta Waddell award Boston Printmakers, Mass., 1993; Grantee Duggal Color Projects, Inc., N.Y., 1992, Juror/Sachi Yanari award in Poly Grams, sponsored by Ind. U. Purdue U., Ft. Wayne, 1999. Mem. Boston Visual Artists Union (coord. 1973-75), Cambridge Art Assn. (juror 1973-74), RISD N.Y. Alumni Chpt., Art and Sci. Collaborations Inc., N.Y. Democrat. Jewish. Avocations: psychology, cinema, science fiction. Home: 251 W 19th St Apt 3B New York NY 10011-4039 E-mail: artpixel@hotmail.com.

DESROCHERS, ALAN ALFRED, electrical engineer; b. Northampton, Mass., June 1, 1950; s. Alfred George and Helen Mary (Punska) D. BSEE, U. Mass., Lowell, 1972; MSEE, Purdue U., 1973, PhD, 1977. Assoc. engr. Lockheed Missiles & Space Co., Sunnyvale, Calif., 1974-75; asst. prof. Boston U., 1977-80; asst. prof. elec., computer and systems engring. Rensselaer Poly. Inst., Troy, N.Y., 1980-86, assoc. prof., 1986-90, prof., 1990—. Summer faculty fellow USAF, Eglin AFB, Fla., 1978; cons. IBM, Cambridge, Mass., 1978-79, Alcoa, Pitts., 1983-85, Barron Assocs., Inc., Annandale, Va., 1985, Systolic Systems, Inc., San Jose, Calif., 1987, Kaiser Aluminum Co., Pleasanton, Calif., 1987, Law Offices of Frances E. Lehner, 1992—; vis. scientist Lab. for Info. and Decision Systems, MIT, 1987. Contbr. articles to profl. jours. Recipient V.L. Magoon Tchg. award Purdue U., 1977, LEAD award Soc. Mfg. Engrs., 1987; rsch. grantee NASA, Air Force Office Sci. Rsch., U.S. Army, IBM, Digital Equipment Corp., Alcoa, 1978-94. Fellow IEEE (sr., edn1. chmn. 1984-89); mem. Robotics and Automation Soc. of IEEE (elected officer 1989-95, editor Transactions on Robotics and Automation 1990-96), AAAS, N.Y. Acad. Scis., Sigma Xi, Eta Kappa Nu. Avocations: bicycling, sailing. Office: Rensselaer Poly Inst Elec Comp Sys Engring Dept 110 8th St JEC 6003 Troy NY 12180-3522 Business E-Mail: aad@ecse.rpi.edu.

DESROCHERS, GERARD CAMILLE, surgeon; b. Marlboro, Mass., June 8, 1922; s. Emery Hector and Eliane (Lemire) DesR.; m. Ellen Franklin, Sept. 27, 1958; children: Gerard, Emery, Lewis, Anthony. AB, Coll. of Holy Cross, 1944; MD, Tufts Coll., 1947. Diplomate Nat. Bd. Med. Examiners. Gen. rotating intern St. Mary's Hosp., Waterbury, Conn., 1947-48; teaching fellow in pathology Tufts Med. Sch., 1948-49; straight surg. intern Boston City Hosp., 1949-50, asst. resident surgeon, 1950-51; resident in surgery New Eng. Med. Center, Boston, 1955-57; practice medicine specializing in surgery, Manchester, N.H.; gen. surgeon staff Cath. Med. Center, Manchester; med. dir. Sea Supply Corp., Bangkok, Thailand, 1953-54; asst. chief surgery VA Hosp., Manchester, 1971-78. Contbr. articles to profl. jours. Incorporator Cath. Med. Ctr., Thomas More Found., Merrimack, N.H.; adv. bd. Lincoln Inst.; mem. N.H. Right to Life Com.; mem. bd. of policy Liberty Lobby. Served as 1st lt. M.C., U.S. Army, 1970. Named Disting. Physician Am., 1989. Mem. AAAS, Manchester Med. Soc., Hillsboro County Med. Soc., Am. Coll. Occupational and Environ. Medicine. Home: 402 Sagamore St Manchester NH 03104-3937 Office: 648 Belmont St Manchester NH 03104-5137

DESROSIERS, ANNE BOOKE, performing arts administrator, consultant; b. Bradford, Pa., Sept. 30, 1938; d. Benjamin and Twila Mae (Schwab) Booke; m. Roger Isadore DesRosiers, Dec. 27, 1960 (div. 1994); children Marc (dec.), Diana, Berinthia. BA in English, U. Fla., 1960. Tchr. Rantoul (Ill.) Elem. Sch., 1961-63, Oogontz Jr. H.S., Phila., 1969-73; dir. adult edn. Guadaloupe Ctr., Salt Lake City, 1974-77; dir. devel. Repertory Theater of St. Louis, 1977-85, St. Louis Zoo, 1985-88; pres. DesRosiers & Assocs., Cleve., 1988—; mng. dir. Great Lakes Theater Festival, Cleve., 1993-98; acting exec. dir. Cleve. Cultural Coalition, 1999-2000. Mem. Nat. Soc. Fund Raising Execs. (cert., Exec. Leadership Inst. 1990, Outstanding Fund Raising St. Louis chpt. 1988), Cleve. Cultural Coalition (vice chair 1995-98). Republican. Jewish. Avocations: golf, travel, sailing. Home and Office: 1 Bratenahl Pl Apt 1102 Bratenahl OH 44108-1155 Fax: 216-541-0344. E-mail: abdesr@megsinet.net.

DESROSIERS, APRYLLE LYNN, director, consultant; b. Cheverly, Md., Apr. 4, 1955; d. Arthur Herrmann and Marjorie de Cuba; m. Michael Wakefield, Oct. 16, 1976 (div. Sept. 1993); children: Travis Wakefield, Tucker B. Wakefield; m. Reed Barry Desrosiers, Feb. 19, 1995. AA in Chem. Dependency, BS in Health, Keene State Coll., 1983, MEd in Curriculum and Instrn., 1990, postgrad. Cert. health edn. N.H., trainer emergency mgmt. preparedness Fed. Emergency Mgmt. Agy., childbirth edn. Internat. Childbirth Edn. Assn. Health and substance abuse educator Greenfield (Mass.) Sch. Dist., 1987-92; substance abuse prevention educator Keene (N.H.) Sch. Dist., 1992-96; safe schs. coord. Manchester (N.H.) Sch. Dist., 1996—. Tng. family and peer mediation Franklin County Mediation Svcs., Greenfield; tng. advanced peer mediation and violence intervention program N.Mex. Inst. Dispute Resolution; tng. orgnl. conflict mgmt. Woodbury (Vt.) Inst. Dispute Resolution; tng. marital mediation Alternatives, Keene. Musician: (albums) Bits and Pieces, 1997, Into the Winter's Night, 1999, A Little Renaissance and Baroque and Romantic, 2003. Mem.: ASCD, N.H. Mediators Assn. (v.p. 1999—2000, pres. 2000—01, Exemplary Work in Conflict Resolution award 1997), Educators Social Responsibility. Democrat. Avocations: exercising, swimming, running, reading, weaving. Home: 64 Cove Woods Rd Munsonville NH 03457 Office: Manchester Pub Sch Dist 530 S Porter St Manchester NH 03103-3198 E-mail: aprylled@hotmail.com.

DESROSIERS, MURIEL C. music educator, retired nursing consultant; b. Woonsocket, R.I., Jan. 15, 1934; d. Rodolphe J. Desrosiers and Rhea M. Archambault; m. Albert A. Desrosiers; 6 stepchildren. BSN, Boston Coll., 1965; MSN, Boston U., 1967, cert. advanced grad. studies, 1975, EdD, 1977. Instr. St. Anselm's Coll. Sch. Nursing, Manchester, NH, 1968—74; cons. drug abuse prevention N.H. State Dept. Edn., Concord, 1974—75, sch. health cons., 1976—89; instr. piano performance, theory and technique. In-svc. educator N.H. Hosps., 1968—75; instr. leadership workshops, 1968—75; grant writer Sch. Nurse Achievement Program. Vol. Home for Little Wanderers; chair Am. Sch. Health Assn., 1984—87; pres. Nat. Assn. Sch. Health Consultants, 1984—87. Recipient Disting. Svc. award, Am. Sch. Health Assn., 1987, Sch. Nurse Achievement award, 1988. Mem.: N.H. Nurses Assn., Maine Nurses Assn., Maine Music Tchrs. Assn. (chair program 1990—95), Nat. Assn. Music Tchrs. (emeritus). Avocation: writing. Home: RR 4 Box 2350 Waterville ME 04901

DESSASO, DEBORAH ANN, freelance writer, online communications specialist, consultant; b. Washington, Feb. 6, 1952; d. Coleman and Virginia Beatrice (Taylor) D. AS in Bus. Adminstrn., Southeastern U., 1986, BSBA, 1988; MA in English Composition and Rhetoric, U. D.C., 1997. Clk.-stenographer FTC, Washington, 1969—70; sec. NEA, Washington, 1970—72, AARP, Washington, 1972—79, assoc. adminstrv. specialist, 1979—80, adminstrv. specialist, 1979—89, legis. comm. specialist, 1989—2000, mgr. issue response, 2000—01; cons., 2000—; adj. prof. English U. D.C., Washington, 2002—03, dir., The Writing Ctr., 2003—. Adj. prof. English, U. D.C.; founding mem., sec. Andrus Fed. Credit Union, 1980. Mem. Associated Writing Program. Home: 3042 Stanton Rd SE Washington DC 20020-7883 E-mail: dessaso749@earthlink.net .

DESSELLE, DEBRA DUKE, social worker; b. Manhasset, N.Y. d. George K. and Catherine D. Duke; m. Wayne J. Desselle, Aug. 20, 1988. BA, U. New Orleans, 1974, PhD, 1992; MSW, La. State U., 1977. Cert. social worker; bd. cert. diplomate. Counselor Dist. Atty.'s Office, New Orleans, 1978-82; social worker Orleans Parish Sch. Bd., New Orleans, 1982-95; pvt. practice Metairie, La., 1982-95; asst. prof. social work program dept. sociology/anthropology U. N.C., Wilmington, 1995-97; asst. prof. Sch. Social Work U. So. Miss., Hattiesburg, 1997-99; social worker Orleans Parish Sch. Bd., 1999—2001; pupil appraisal social worker St. Charles Parish Sch. Bd., 2001—. Mem. Am. Assn. Marriage & Family Therapy, Acad. Cert. Social Workers. Avocations: reading, movies, gardening, biking.

DESSEN, STANLEY BENJAMIN, lawyer, cosmetic company executive; b. N.Y.C., Mar. 25, 1938; s. Irving and Edith (Nelson) D.; m. Mimi Lynne; children: Eric, Cheryl. BS in Acctg., Bklyn. Coll., 1959; JD, NYU, 1962, LLM, 1969; LLM, Bklyn. Law Sch., 1967. Bar: N.Y. 1962, U.S. Tax Ct. 1965, U.S. Supreme Ct. 1968. Staff mem. Arthur Andersen & Co., N.Y.C., 1962-64; assoc. Melvin Semel, N.Y.C., 1964-66; dir. taxes Pfizer, Inc., N.Y.C., 1966-74; v.p. taxation Revlon, Inc., N.Y.C., 1974-90, sr. v.p. taxation, 1990—. Mem. ABA, N.Y. State Bar Assn., Pharm. Mfrs. Assn. (tax com.), Tax Execs. Inst., Cosmetic, Toiletry and Fragrance Assn. (chmn. tax com.). Republican. Jewish. Office: Revlon Inc 625 Madison Ave Fl 8 New York NY 10022-1894

DESSLER, ALEXANDER JACK, astrophysicist, educator; b. San Francisco, Oct. 21, 1928; s. David Alexander and Julia (Shapiro) D.; m. Lorraine Hudek, Apr. 18, 1952; children: Pauline Karen, David Alexander, Valerie Jan, Andrew Emory. BS, Calif. Inst. Tech., 1952; PhD, Duke, 1956. Sect. head Lockheed Missiles & Space Co., 1956-62; prof. Grad. Research Center, Dallas, 1962-63, prof. space physics and astronomy, 1963-82, 86-93; chmn. dept. Rice U., Houston, 1963-69, 79-82, 87-92, campus bus. mgr., 1974-76; dir. space sci. lab. MSFC NASA, Huntsville, Ala., 1982-86; sr. rsch. scientist Lunar and Planetary Lab. U. Ariz., Tucson, 1993—. Sci. adviser Nat Aeros. and Space Council, 1969-70; pres. Univs. Space Research Assn., 1975-81 Editor Jour. Geophys. Research, 1965-69, Revs. of Geophysics, 1969-74, The John Wiley Space Science Text Series, 1968-76, Geophys. Research Letters, 1986-89, Atmospheric and Space Science Series, 1986—; adv. bd.: Planetary and Space Sci., 1963-92; assoc. editor Space Solar Power Rev., 1980-85. Served with USN, 1946-48. Recipient Outstanding Young Scientist award Tex. Wing Air Force Assn., 1964, medal for contbns. to internat. geophysics Soviet Geophys. Com., 1984, Stellar award for acad. devel., Rotary Nat., 1988. Fellow AAAS, Am. Geophys. Union (Macelwane award 1963, John Adam Fleming medal 1993); mem. Am. Astron. Soc., Internat. Assn. Geomagnetism and Aeronomy (v.p. 1979-83), Royal Swedish Acad. Scis. (fgn. mem.), Cosmos Club (Washington). Home: 1434 E Seneca St Tucson AZ 85719-3645 Office: U Ariz Lunar Planetary Lab 901 Gould-Simpson Bldg Tucson AZ 85721-0001 E-mail: dessler@arizona.edu.

DESSYLAS, ANN ATSAVES, human resources and office management executive; b. Bklyn., Jan. 28, 1927; d. Charles and Agnes (Cocoros) Atsaves; m. George Dessylas, Dec. 28, 1969. BA, Bklyn. Coll., 1957; MA, NYU, 1961, MBA, 1977. Exec. asst. W.R. Grace & Co., N.Y.C., 1950-70; asst. sec. St. Joe Minerals Corp., N.Y.C., 1970-81, asst. v.p., 1981-85; cons. Cyprus Minerals, Denver, 1985-91; pres. AAD Enterprises, Forest Hills, N.Y., 1992—. Dir. Continental Owners Corp.; sec. Plato Malozemoff Found. Avocations: music, theater, golf, art, tennis. Home and Office: 70-20 108th St Ste 8-p Forest Hills NY 11375-4449

DESSYPRIS, EMMANUEL NICHOLAS, hematologist-oncologist; b. Athens, Nov. 10, 1946; m. Chryssie Maria Cassiotis, Sept. 6, 1973; children: Margaret, Nicholas. MD with highest honors, Athens U. Sch. Medicine, 1970. Diplomate Am. Bd. Internal Medicine, Am. Bd. Hematology, Am. Bd. Oncology. Resident PG I & II dept. medicine and divsn. rheumatology Athens Naval and Vets. Hosp., 1971-73; resident PG III, 1st med. divsn. U. Thesalonica Affiliated Svc., E. Venizelos Meml. Hosp., Crete, Greece, 1973-74; resident Dept. Medicine, Yale U. Affiliated Svcs. St. Mary's Hosp., Waterbury, Conn., 1975-77; fellow in hematology Vanderbilt U Hosp. and VA Med. Ctr., Nashville, 1977-79; NIH rsch. fellow divsn. hematology, clin. fellow Vanderbilt U., 1979-80, instr. of medicine, 1980-81, asst. prof. medicine to assoc. prof., 1981-92; assoc. investigator to rsch. assoc. VA Med Ctr., Nashville, 1980-85, staff physician sects. of oncology and hematology, 1985-88, clin. investigator sects. of hematology and oncology, 1988-92; prof. medicine Med. Coll. Va., Richmond, 1992—, acting chmn. hematology, oncology, 1997-99; chief hematology/oncology sect. McGuire Va. Med. Ctr., Richmond, 1992—2002, chief of medicine, 2002—. Adv. com. Clin. Rsch. Ctr., 1985-88; interviewer Admission com. Sch. of Medicine, 1985—; mem. grad. med. edn. com., 1986-88; adv. coun. Dean's Faculty, 1987-88; mem. health scis. sect. Univ. IRB/CPHS, 1987-88, chmn. 1988-91; cons. to rev. br. NIH, NHLBI, 1991, cons. to spl. com. for clin. trials and tng. rev. sect. 1990; ad hoc Hematology Merit Rev. Bd. VA Med. Rsch. Svc., 1990. Editl. reviewer New Eng. Jour. Medicine, Annals of Internal Medicine, Blood, British Jour. of Haematology, Exptl. Hematology, Cancer Rsch., Cancer Treatment Reports, Jour. Lab. and Clin. Medicine, So. Med. Jour., Am. Jour. Med. Scis., Kidney Internat.; author: Synopsis of Internal Medicine, 1970, Pure Red Cell Aplasia, 1989; contbr. chpts. to book and numerous articles to profl. jours. Grantee VA Career Devel. award, 1980-82, 82-85, 91-94, 88-93. Fellow ACP; mem. AAAS, Am. Soc. Hematology, Am. Soc. Clin. Oncology, Internat. Soc. Exptl. Hematology, Am. Fedn. for clin. Rsch., Soc. for Exptl. Biology and Medicine, So. Soc. for Clin. Investigation, N.Y. Acad. Scis., Hellenic Soc. of Hematology. Office: McGuire VA Med Ctr 1201 Broad Rock Blvd Richmond VA 23249-0001 E-mail: edessypr@hsc.vcu.edu.

DESTACHE, CHRISTOPHER J. education educator, researcher; b. St. Paul, Minn., Feb. 25, 1960; s. Karen Jean Destache; m. Densie Michelle Domet, May 10, 1985; children: Christopher J. Jr., Amanda Marie, Michele Kristine, Joseph Michael. PharmD, Creighton U., Omaha, Nebr., 1984. Lic. Pharmacist Dept. of Health and Human Svcs., Nebr., 1984. Asst. prof. pharmacy practice Creighton U., Omaha, 1985—93, assoc. prof. pharmacy practice, 1993—. Fellow: Am. Coll. of Clin. Pharmacy. Office: Creighton Univ Sch of Pharmacy 2500 California Plz Omaha NE 68178 Office Fax: 402-280-1268. E-mail: cdestach@creighton.edu.

DESTEFANO, L. TIMOTHY, music educator, conductor; b. Canton, Ohio, July 28, 1939; s. James John and Lucille Rita (Catalano) DeStefano; m. Elizabeth Anne French, July 19, 1974; children: Jennifer Leigh, Kathleen Elizabeth, Timothy James. BS in Pub. Sch. Music, Kent State U., 1961, MEd in Adminstrn., 1969. Cert. K-12 music educator Ohio. H.s. band dir., instrumental music grades 5-12 W. Br. Local, Beloit, Ohio, 1961—73, N.W. Local, Canal Fulton, Ohio, 1973—74, Jackson Local, Massillon, Ohio, 1974—95; asst. prof. music, band dir. Mt. Union Coll., Alliance, Ohio, 1995—. Dept. head music curriculum K-12 Jackson Local, Massillon, 1974—95, others, 1961—73; participant Internat. Jazz Festival, Montrex, Switzerland, 1972—73. Author: (textbooks) Fundamentals of Brass, Music Methods, Basic Rhythms from Scratch; contbr. articles to profl. jours. Mem. levy com. W. Br., Jackson, 1961—95. Mem.: Am. School Band Dirs. Assn. (state chmn., natl. dues chmn.), Ohio Music Educators (adjudicator 1973—98), Music Educators Nat. Assn., Kappa Kappa Psi (historian), Pi Kappa Lambda, Phi Beta Mu. Achievements include the distinction of being 1 of 4 high school bands in the world to perform in all national bowl parades and the International Jazz Festival in Switzerland. Avocations: yard work, civil war, old cars. Office: Mt Union Coll 1972 Clark Ave Alliance OH 44601 Office Fax: 330-823-2144.

DESTHIEUX, BERTRAND M. optical engineer, editor-in-chief; b. Limoges, Haute-Vienne, France, Mar. 19, 1966; arrived in US, 2000; s. Bernard Desthieux and Claude Nicard des Rieux; m. Celine M. E. Pollissard, Dec. 18, 1971; children: Charles R. M., Ambre M. S. Master Degree, Limoges U., 1988. Diplome d'Ingenieur, Ecole Superieure d'Optique, France, 1990. Rschr. Southampton (Eng.) U., 1990—92; vis. rschr. Fujitsu, Kawasaki, Japan, 1992—93; rsch. engr. Alcatel, Marcoussis, France, 1993—98, team leader Nozay, France, 1998—2000; mgr. Latus Lightworks, Richardson, Tex., 2000—01; sr. engr. Xtera Comm., Inc., Allen, Tex., 2001—. Editor-in-chief Elsevier Sci., Oxford, England, 2001—. Contbr. chapters to books, articles to profl. jours. Mem.: Optical Soc. Am. (tech. program com., topical meeting on optical amplifiers and their applications 1998—), Sons of the Am. Revolution (assoc.). Achievements include patents in field. Home: 7232 Hillwood Ln Dallas TX 75248 Office: Xtera Communications Inc 500 W Bethany Dr Allen TX 75013 Personal E-mail: bertrand_desthieux@hotmail.com. E-mail: bdesthieux@xtera.com.

DESTLER, WILLIAM W. academic administrator; BS, Stevens Inst. Tech., 1968; PhD, Cornell U., 1972. Former chair dept. elec. engring. U. Md., College Park, former dean sch. engring., former v.p. rsch., dean grad. sch., sr. v.p. acad. affairs, provost. Contbr. numerous articles to profl. jours. Recipient award for excellence in engring. edn. for Mid-Atlantic states, AT&T, 1989. Fellow: IEEE, Am. Phys. Soc. Office: U Md 119 Main Adminstrn Bldg College Park MD 20742-5031

DESUE, CHRISTINE L. lawyer; b. Pitts., Feb. 9, 1970; d. David Joseph and Linda Ann Desue; m. Scott Michael Verret, July 25, 1998. BA in Polit. Sci., Tulane U., 1992; JD in Civil and Common Law, Loyola U., New Orleans, 1995. Atty. Leger & Mestayer, New Orleans, 1994—. Mem., vol. The New Orleans Regional Chamber, 1999. Mem. ATLA, ABA, FBA, La. State Bar Assn., La. Trial Lawyers Assn., New Orleans Bar Assn. Avocations: reading, sports, working with special olympics. Office: Leger & Mestayer 9th Fl 600 Carondelet St Fl 9 New Orleans LA 70130-3511

DE TAKACSY, NICHOLAS BENEDICT, physicist, educator; b. Budapest, Hungary, Feb. 24, 1939; s. Constantin and Katalin (Jellenz) de T.; m. Mickey Mary Dawson, June 16, 1962; children: Victoria, Christine, Frederica. B.Sc., Loyola Coll., Montreal, Que., Can., 1959; M.Sc., U. Montreal, 1963; PhD, McGill U., 1966. Rsch. assoc. Calif. Inst. Tech., Pasadena, 1966-67; asst. prof. Loyola Coll., Montreal, Montreal, 1967-68; mem. faculty McGill U., Montreal, 1968—, prof. physics, 1978—, chmn. dept., 1979-82, assoc. dean of sci., 1993-94, 95-98, acting dean sci., 1994-95, assoc. vice prin. acad., 1998—. Mem.: Am. Phys. Soc., Can. Assn. Physicists. Roman Catholic. Office: 3600 University St Montreal QC Canada H3A 2T8 E-mail: nick@physics.mcgill.ca.

DETARY, TIMOTHY JAMES, banking and health care executive; b. Port Huron, MI, Jan. 27, 1954; s. Steven and Marilyn Joyce Detary; married; children: Jason G., April A. BA, Oakland U, Rochester, MI, 1981—83; MA, Central MI U, Pleasant, MI, 1983—86; ABD (DBA) candidate, U of Sarasota, Sarasota, Fl, 1997—2003. Bank officer Nat. Bank of Richmond, Richmond, Mich., 1979—88; VP HR Security Bank N.E., Richmond, Mich., 1988—91, First of Am. N.E., Richmond, Mich., 1991—92; hr con. Beverly Health Care, Fort Smith, Ark., 1993—98, div. dir., 1998—2001; VP HR Beverly Health care, Fort Smith, Ark., 2001—03. Petty officer USN, 1972—75, Fl. Mem.: Acad. of Mgmt., Soc. of HR. Office: Beverly Health Care 1000 Beverly Way Fort Smith AZ 72919-9008

DETELS, ROGER, epidemiologist, physician, former university dean; b. Bklyn., Oct. 14, 1936; s. Martin P. and Mary J. (Crooker) D.; m. Mary M. Doud, Sept. 14, 1963; children: Martin, Edward. BA, Harvard U., 1958; MD, NYU, 1962; MS in Preventive Medicine, U. Wash., 1966. Diplomate Am. Bd. Preventive Medicine. Intern U. Calif. Gen. Hosp., San Francisco, 1962-63; resident U. Wash., Seattle, 1963-66; med. officer, epidemiologist Nat. Inst. Neurol. Diseases, Bethesda, Md., 1969-71; assoc. prof. epidemiology Sch. Pub. Health UCLA, 1971-73, prof. Sch. Pub. Health, 1973—, dean, 1980-85, head div. epidemiology Sch. Pub. Health, 1972-80, chair, dept. epidemiology, 2001—. Guest lectr. various univs., profl. confs. and med. orgns., 1969—; sci. adv. com. Am. Found AIDS Rsch.; dir. UCLA/Fogarty AIDS Internat. Tng. & Rsch. Program, 1988—, Tng. Program in Epidemiology of HIV/AIDS, 1995—; cons. Ministries of Health, Thailand, Myanmar, The Philippines, 1989, Global Program on AIDS, 1995, Singapore, 1996, WHO, 1999, U.S. Agy. Internat. Devel., 1998, 99, 2000, 01, Cambodia, 1998, 99, 2000, 02, UN Devel. Program, 2001, St. Thomas Med. Sch., London, 1993-94, Myanmar, 1997, UN Devel. Program, Myanmar, 2001; mem. Nat. Adv. Environ. Health Scis. Coun., 1990-94; com. to study transmission of HIV through blood products Inst. Medicine, 1994-95. Editor: Oxford Textbook of Public Health, 1985, 2d edit. 1991, 4th edit., 2002; contbr. articles to profl. jours. Lt. comdr. M.C. USN, 1966-69. Grantee in field. Fellow AAAS, Am. Coll. Preventive Medicine, Am. Coll. Epidemiology (coun. 1987-89), Faculty Pub. Health Medicine Royal Coll. Physicians of U.K. (hon.); mem. Am. Epidemiol. Soc., Soc. Epidemiologic Rsch. (pres. 1977-78), Assn. Tchrs. Preventive Medicine (chmn. essay com. 1969-75), Am. Pub. Health Assn., Am. Assn. Cancer Edn. (membership com. 1978-85), Internat. Epidemiol. Assn. (exec. com. 1984-99, treas. 1984-90, pres. 1990-93), Assn. Schs. Pub. Health (sec.-treas. 1980-85), Sigma Xi, Delta Omega. Office: UCLA Dept Epidemiology Ctr for Health Scis Box 951772 Los Angeles CA 90095-1772 Fax: 310-206-6039. E-mail: detels@ucla.edu.

DETER, RUSSELL LEE, II, obstetrical ultrasonographer; b. Dallas, Jan. 14, 1936; s. Russell Lee and Virginia (Peden) D.; m. Susan Tipery, Dec. 14, 1981. BS, Baylor U., Waco, Tex., 1958; MS, MD, Baylor U., Houston, 1963. Postdoctoral fellow Rockefeller U., N.Y.C., 1964-66, U. Louvain, Belgium, 1966-67; asst. prof. anatomy Baylor Coll. Medicine, Houston, 1967-72, asst. prof. cell biology, 1973—, asst. prof. ob-gyn., 1975-80, dir. obstet. ultrasonography, 1977-95, assoc. prof. ob-gyn., 1981-84, prof., 1985—. Med. dir. outpatient ultrasound program Harris County Hosp. Dist., Houston, 1986—. Co-author: Quantitative Obstetrical Ultrasonography, 1986; editor-in-chief Jour. Clin. Ultrasound, 1982-96; contbr. articles to profl. jours., chpts. to books. Recipient rsch. grants Frankel Found., 1979-84, March of Dimes, 1979-83, 84-87, Joseph H. Holmes award Jour. Clin. Ultrasound, 1987. Mem. ACOG, Am. Inst. Ultrasound in Medicine (assoc.), Soc. Maternal-Fetal Medicine (assoc.), Internat. Soc. Ultrasound in Ob-Gyn. Home: 1721 Hawthorne St Houston TX 77098-1605 Office: Baylor Coll Medicine 1 Baylor Plz Houston TX 77030-3411 E-mail: russelld@bcm.tmc.edu.

DETERMAN, JOHN DAVID, lawyer; b. Mitchell, S.D., Feb. 18, 1933; s. Alred John and Olive Gertrude (Lovinger) D.; m. Gloria Esther Rivas, Nov. 15, 1980; children by previous marriage: James Taylor, Mark Sterling. B.Engring. in Elec. Engring. cum laude, U. So. Calif., 1955; LL.D. magna cum laude, UCLA, 1961. Electronics engr. Hughes Aircraft Co., L.A., 1955-60; sr. ptnr. Tuttle & Taylor, Inc., L.A., 1961-86; gen. counsel Provena Foods Inc., Chino, Calif., 1986-92, CEO, 1992-98, chmn. bd., 1992—, also bd. dirs. Founder Carl D. Spaeth Scholarship Fund, Stanford U. Law Sch., 1972; mem. nat. panel arbitrators Am. Arbitration Assn., L.A., 1962—, mem. adv. coun., 1982—, mem. nat. panel of mediators, 1986—, mem. large complex case panel of arbitrators, 1993—. Mem. Am. Coll. Constrn. Arbitrators (charter 1982—), Order of Coif, Eta Kappa Nu, Tau Beta Pi. Home: 25 S El Molino St Alhambra CA 91801-4102 Office: Provena Foods Inc 5010 Eucalyptus Ave Chino CA 91710-9216 *Tolerate even intolerance but never cruelty.*

DETERMAN, SARA-ANN, lawyer; b. Palmerton, Pa., Aug. 17, 1938; d. Albert H. and Evelyn (Tucker) Heimbach; m. Dean W. Determan, July 28, 1957 (div. Nov. 1981); children: Dann, David, Steven (dec.); m. Gary Sellers, May 21, 1988. Student, Conn. Coll., 1956-57, Stanford U., 1958; AB, U. Del., 1960; LLB, George Washington U., 1967. Bar: U.S. Dist. Ct. D.C. 1968. Law clk. to sr. judge U.S. Ct. Appeals (D.C. cir.), Edgerton, 1967-68; assoc. Hogan & Hartson, Washington, 1968-75, ptnr., 1975—. Trustee Lawyers Com. for Civil Rights Under Law, Washington, 1982-94, co-chmn., 1994—. Bd. dirs. Mex.-Am. Legal Def. and Ednl. Fund, 1983-88, Women's Legal Def. Fund, 1980-2002. Fellow Am. Bar Found.; mem. ABA (chmn. individual rights sect. 1985-86, commr. legal programs for elderly 1983-89, com. on delivery of legal svcs. 1989-93, mem. consortium on legal svcs.), ACLU (bd. dirs. 1975-92), D.C. Bar (pres. 1990-91). Democrat. Unitarian Universalist. Office: Hogan & Hartson Columbia Square 555 13th St NW Ste 800E Washington DC 20004-1161

DETERRA, SANDRA LEE SHIVERS, secondary school educator; b. Hattiesburg, Miss., Dec. 23, 1946; d. George Evan Shivers, Jr. and Zulma (Dubuisson) Shivers; m. Raymond James DeTerra, June 3, 1972; children: Andrea L., David J., Michael A. BS cum laude and spl. honors in Math., Miss. U. for Women, 1968; MA, La. State U., 1969. Secondary tchrs. lic. math. Alaska. Math. tchr. Natchez-Adams County H.S., Natchez, Miss., 1969—70, Gulfport (Miss.) Pub. Schs., 1974; math. instr. Miss. Gulf Coast C.C., Gulfport, 1970—71, 1974—78; adj. math. tchr. Ctrl. Tex. C.C., Ft. Richardson, Ark., 1978—84, Chapman Coll., Elmendorf AFB, Alaska, 1978—84, Panama City (Fla.) C.C., 1984—85, U. Alaska, Anchorage, 1978—84, 1986—; math. tchr. 9-12 Bartlett H.S., Anchorage, 2001—. Mem. St. Andrew Cath. Ch., Eagle River. Mem.: Anchorage Edn. Assn., Alaska Fedn. Tchrs., Nat. Coun. Tchrs. Math. Avocations: bowling, camping, church activities. Home: 9550 Dinaaka Dr Eagle River AK 99577 Office: Bartlett High Sch 25-500 N Muldoon Anchorage AK 99506

DETERS, THOMAS C. editor-in-chief, educator; BA in Sociology, U. Mich., 1982; degree with hons. in Human Biology, Nat. Coll. Chiropractic, 1986, DSc with hons. in Chiropractic, 1984. Assoc. pub. Men's Pub. Group of Weider Pubs., Inc., 1997, Flex; group publisher, editor-in-chief Muscle and Fitness mag., 2002—03; exec. v.p. Am. Media Inc., 2003—; pub. dir. WelderPubs. Enthusiast Group, Woodland Hills, Calif., 2003—. Cons. to many profl. athletes. Appeared numerous TV segments and videos; contbr. various articles; author: books; contbr. video cassettes. Dir. edn. Muscle and Fitness Tng. Camp, L.A. Mem.: Internat. Chiropractors Assn. (life Lifetime Achievement award, 1st ever lifetime membership award Coun. on Fitness and Sports Health Sci.). Office: Muscle and Fitness Mag 21100 Erwin St Woodland Hills CA 91367 also: Weider Publications Inc PO Box 864 Woodland Hills CA 91365-0864*

DETERT, MIRIAM ANNE, chemical analyst; b. San Diego, Calif., Sept. 16, 1925; d. George Bernard and Margaret Theresa Zita (Lohre) D. BS, Dominican Coll., San Rafael, Calif., 1947. Chem. analyst Shell Devel. Co., Emeryville, Calif., 1947-72, Houston, 1972-86. Photo participant Wax Rsch.: Quest, 1981; exhibited etchings Sight and Insight Art Studio, Mill Valley, Calif., 2002; contbr. poetry to books including The International Library of Poetry - Best Poems of the 90's, Spirit of the Age, The Nightfall of Diamonds, The Long and Winding Road, Through Oceans of Time. Vol. Falkirk Cultural Ctr., San Rafael, 1987-91, M.D. Anderson Tumor Inst., Houston, 1978-86, Rep. Party, San Rafael, 1990, 94; mem. Jewish Comm. Ctr. Recipient Disting. Alumni award Dominican Coll., 1994. Mem. Marin Geneal. Soc. Republican. Roman Catholic. Avocations: etching, oil painting, genealogy, swimming.

DETERT-MORIARTY, JUDITH ANNE, graphic artist, educator, civic activist; b. Portage, Wis., July 10, 1952; d. Duane Harlan and Anne Jane (Devine) Detert; m. Patrick Edward Moriarty, July 22, 1978; children: Colin Edward, Eleanor Grace, Dylan Joseph. BA, U. Wis., Madison, 1970-73, U. Wis., Green Bay, 1991. Cert. in no-fault grievance mediation, Minn. Legis sec., messenger State of Wis. Assembly, Madison, 1972, 74-76; casualty-property div. clk. Capitol Indemnity Corp., Madison, 1977-78; word processor consumer protection dvsn. Wis. Dept. Agr., Madison, 1978; graphic arts composing specialist Moraine Park Tech. Inst., Fond du Lac, Wis., 1978-79; freelance artist Picas, Pictures and Promotion (formerly Detert Graphics), 1978-90; prodn. asst. West Bend News, 1980-83; devel. asoc. Riveredge Nature Ctr., Inc., Newburg, Wis., 1983-84; exec. dir. Voluntary Action Ctr. Washington County, West Bend, 1984-86; instr. cmty. svcs. Austin (Minn.) C.C., 1988; art and promotional publs. dir. Michael G. and Co., Albert Lea, Minn., 1988-89; corp. art dir. Newco, Inc., Janesville, Wis., 1989-91; owner, artist Art Graphica, 1991-00. Substitute tchr. Janesville Sch. Dist., 1999—. Cartooning instr., contbg. artist Janesville Pub. Schs., 1989-93; contbr. articles to profl. jours.; contbg. artist Spotlight on Kids theatre, 1995-99, Rockport Peace Park Project, 1999-2002. Bd. mem. Montessori Children's House, West Bend, 1983—85; newsletter editor, artist Friends of Battered Women, West Bend, 1983—86; bd. pres. Wash. Co. Rep. Wis. State, 1984—85; bd. mem. Montessori Childrens House, West Bend, Wis., 1984—85; Wis. rep. Planned Parenthood of Wis. Bd., 1984—85; artist LWV Washington County, 1984—86; apptd. Austin Human Rights Commn., 1987—88; fundraiser Victims Crisis Ctr., 1987; cmty. contact, v.p. Caths. for Free Choice Wis., 1990—92; apptd. Janesville Hist. Commn., 1992—95; vol. bd. dirs., chmn. advt. com. Janesville Concert Assn., 1994—97; founder, pres. Parents' Assn., Montessori Childrens House, Janesville, Wis., 1994—97; sec. Janesville Hist. Commn., 1994—95; newsletter editor Roosevelt Elem. Sch. PTA, 1996—2002; vol. newsletter editor Badger coun. Girls Scouts, Inc., 1996—98; founder United Arts Alliance, 1996, pres., 1997—98, sec., 1998—2001, Roosevelt Elem. Sch. PTA, 1999—2001; founder, bd. mem., sec. Bower City Preservation Assn., 1999—; chpt. coord. Project Linus-Janesville, 2000—; editor ArtsRock, 2001—; founder, instr. after-school knitting clubs Roosevelt and Jefferson Elem. Schs. and Boys and Girls Club, Janesville, 2001—; organizer The Lysistrata Project, Janesville, 2003; vol. Austin Pub. Sch. Omnibus Program; newsletter editor, com. chmn. Montessori Childrens House, Janesville, Wis.; bd. mem. Montessori Children's Ho., Janesville, Wis.; student vol. McCarthy for Pres., U. Wis., Madison, 1968; coord. student residences McGovern for Pres., 1972; vol. Udall for Pres., 1976; Washington County Campaign coord. Nat. Unity Campaign for John Anderson for Pres., 1980; publicity coord. Wis. Intellectual Freedom Coalition, 1981; pres., founder People of Washington County United for Choice, 1981—83; bd. dirs., v.p. Wis. Pro-Choice Conf., 1981—82; Washington County ward coord. Earl for Gov., 1982, Mondale/Ferraro, 1984; Washington County campaign chmn. Peg Lautenschlager for Wis. state senate, 1984; sec., newsletter editor Dem. Party of Manitowoc County, Wis., 1986; precinct ofcr. and affirmative action ofcr. Dem. Party Mower County, Minn., 1986—88; local chair Women's Polit. Caucus1987, 1988; v.p. commn. officer Dem. Party Rock County, Wis., 1988—94, newsletter editor, 1988—; vol. coord. Rock County Dukakis for Pres., 1988; campaign chair Lew Mittness for Wis. State Assembly, 1990; newsletter editor Rock County Voice for Choice, 1990—94; founding exec. bd. dirs., newsletter editor Moral Alternatives, 1990—92; vol. Rock County Clinton for Pres., 1992, 1996; sec., v.p. commn. officer/newsletter editor Rock Co. Dem. Party, Wis., 1998—2001; 1st C.D. 4th vice chair Dem. Party of Wis., 1999—2001; mem. campaign coordinating com. Vote Graf, 2000; Rock County coord. Ralph Nader for Pres., 2000; mem. steering com., bd. mem. Rock County Citizens for Peace, 2001—; v.p. commn. officer Dem. Party Rock County, Wis., 2001—; newsletter editor, mem. coms. Planned Parenthood of Washington County, 1980—85, bd. dirs., 1984—85. Recipient award of Excellence Bd. Report Graphic Artists, 1994, 95, nominee UW-Green Bay Disting. Alumni, 1997, 2000, YWCA Women of Distinction, 1996-98, Governors award in support of the arts, 1997, Comm. Arts Devel. award, 1997. Mem. NOW (newsletter editor Dane County 1977-78, Wis. state 1994-99, coord. Wis. state reproductive rights task force 1982-84, coord. reproductive rights task force North Suburban chpt. 1981-84, Minn. pub. rels. coord. 1987-88), Forward Janesville (steering com. for Celebrate Janesville 1992, 93, 94). Mem. Soc. Of Friends. Avocations: reading, bicycling, gardening, knitting, world wide correspondence, antiques. Office: 23 S Atwood Ave Janesville WI 53545-4003 E-mail: proartist@aol.com.

DETHERO, J. HAMBRIGHT, banker; b. Chattanooga, Jan. 2, 1932; s. Jacob Hambright and Rosalie Frances (Gasser) D.; m. Charlotte Nixon Lee, Sept. 19, 1959; children: Dinah Lee, Charles Drew. BS in Bus. Adminstrn., U. Fla., 1953; BFT, Am. Grad. Sch. Internat. Mgmt., Phoenix, 1958. With Citibank, N.Y.C., P.R., Caracas, Venezuela, San Francisco, 1958-69; mgr. First Nat. City Bank (Internat.), San Francisco, until 1969; v.p. internat. div. Crocker Nat. Bank, San Francisco, 1969-75; sr. v.p. London, 1976-80, San Francisco, 1980-84, Bank America World Trade Corp., San Francisco, 1984-85; 1st v.p. Security Pacific Nat. Bank, Los Angeles, 1986-87; regional mgr. Calif. Export Fin. Office, Calif. State World Trade Commn., San Francisco, 1988-93; sr. v.p. Comml. Bank of San Francisco, 1994-98. Internat. bus. cons., instr., 1998—; adj. prof. Grad. Sch. Bus., St. Mary's Coll., Moraga, Calif., 1988—, John F. Kennedy U., Walnut Creek, Calif., 1997—. Author: Exporting Guide for California, 1993, 2d edit., 1999.. Bd. dirs. Calif. Coun. Internat. Trade, 1972-77, 82-98, pres., 1974-76; trustee World Affairs Coun. No. Calif., 1971-77, 88-93; chmn. dist. Export Coun. No. Calif., 1983-93; dir. Internat. Diplomacy Coun., San Francisco, 1995-2002, treas., 1997-2000, pres., 2000-01; mem. San Francisco Host Com., 2000-02. Recipient Export Citizen of the Year award No. Calif. Export Coun./San Francisco Bus. Times, 1996. Home and Office: 694 Old Jonas Hill Rd Lafayette CA 94549-5214 E-mail: hamdethero@aol.com.

DETHLOFF, HENRY CLAY, historian, educator; b. New Orleans, Aug. 10, 1934; s. Carl Curt and Camelia (Jordan) Dethloff; m. Myrtle Anne Elliott, Aug. 27, 1961; children: Clay, Carl. BA, U. Tex., Austin, 1956; MA, Northwestern State U., Natchitoches, La., 1960; PhD, U. Mo., Columbia, 1964. From instr. to assoc. prof. history U. So. La., 1962—66, assoc. prof., 1966—69; from mem. faculty to prof. emeritus Tex. A&M U., College Station, 1969—99, prof. emeritus history, 1999—. Pres. Intaglio, Inc. Author: (book) Our Louisiana Legacy, 1968, The Centennial History of Texas A&M University, 1976-1976, 1975, Americans and Free Enterprise, 1979, A History of the American Rice Industry 1685-1985, 1988, Suddenly, Tomorrow Came: A History of Johnson Space Center, 1993, The U.S. and the Global Economy, 1945-1995, 1997, A Bookmark: The Texas A&M University Press, 1999; co-author: A History of American Business, 1983, Timeless Heritage, A History of the Forest Service in the Southwest, 1988, Pattillo Higgins and the Search for Texas Oil, 1989, A Special Kind of Doctor: A History of Veterinary Medicine in Texas, 1991, Louisiana: A Study of Diveristy, 1998, Voyager's Grand Tour: To the Outer Planets and Beyond, 2003; co-editor: American Business History: Case Studies, 1987. Served to lt. (j.g.) USNR, 1956—58. Mem.: La. Hist. Assn., Tex. Hist. Assn., So. Hist. Assn., Econ. History Assn., Agrl. History Assn., Sigma Chi, Phi Alpha Theta, Phi Kappa Phi. Republican. Methodist. Home: 8709 Bent Tree Dr College Station TX 77845-5561

DETHOMAS, JOSEPH MICHAEL, ambassador; b. Easton, Pa., June 1951; BA, MA, Pa. State U.; MPA, Harvard U.; Disting. Grad., Nat. War coll. Former dir. Office of European Union and Regioanl Affairs and Bur. of Polit.-Mil. Affairs; former prin. dep. asst. sec. of state Bureau of Nonproliferation/Dept. of State; U.S. amb. to Estonia, 2001—. Recipient Meritorious Honor award for earthquake rescue work in Mexico, U.S. Dept. of State, numerous honor awards and citations. Office: DOS Amb 4530 Tallin Pl Washington DC 20521*

DETHOMASIS, CRAIG CONSTANTINE, lawyer, educator; b. Glen Cove, N.Y., Oct. 2, 1958; AA, U. Fla., 1978, BS, 1980, JD, 1983. Bar: Fla. 1983. Asst. pub. defender Pub. Defender's Office, Gainesville, Fla., 1983-87; atty. Silverman, Wilkov, DeThomasis & Buchanan, Gainesville, 1987-90, DeThomasis & Buchanan P.A., Gainesville, 1990—. Adj. prof. law U. Fla. Coll. Law, Gainesville, 1990—; chmn. grievance com. Fla. Bar 8th Jud. Cir., Gainesville, 1994-97. Bd. dirs. Children's Home Soc.-Mid. Fla. Divsn., Gainesville, 1994—; mem. Leadership Gainesville, Gainesville Co. of C., 1996. Mem. Fla. Assn. Criminal Def. Lawyers (treas., v.p., pres. 1994-96), Eighth Jud. Cir. Assn. Criminal Def. Lawyers, Eighth Jud. Cir. Bar Assn., J.C. Adkins Inn of Ct. (emeritus 1995—). Office: DeThomasis & Buchanan PA 1800 N Main St Gainesville FL 32609-8606

DE THOUARS, VICTOR IVAN CHARLES, professional martial artist, educator; b. Pare'/kediri, East Java, Indonesia, Sept. 25, 1941; s. Marquis Henry Alexandre and Susanna de Thouars; m. Jane Fischer, May 7, 1999; children: Valerie, Vincent, Marcus, Daniel. Grad. Mechanical Engineer, THS, Netherlands, 1960. Sr. mech. engr. Cooper Industries, Sumter, SC, 1998—2000; founder, chief instr. VDT Acad., Bellflower, Calif., 2000—. Dir. VDT Acad., Bellflower, Calif., 2000—; prodr. VDT Comm., 2000—; internat. dir. Internat. Silat Fedn., 2000—. Author: Personal Automation, 1995 (Automation award, 1995), The System of Serak, 2001, Serak the Tsunami, 2001, Sera the Last Butterfly, 2002, The Treshold of the Tsunami, 2002; composer: (Songs) Softwind, 1965; prodr.: (Video) The Edges of Sera, 2001, The Art of Serak, 2002, Kuntao Mang Po, 2002, Pentjak Silat Soempat, 2002. Conservative. Avocations: surfing, scuba diving, skiing, hunting. Home: PO Box 1663 Bellflower CA 90707-1663 Office: VDT Acad 17165 Bellflower Blvd Bellflower CA 90706 Office Fax: 562-920-1827. Personal E-mail: Lavaseur@aol.com. Business E-Mail: vdtacademy@aol.com.

DE TILLY, CHARLES-EDOUARD, sales professional; b. Versailles, France; s. Dominique de Tilly and Florence Brabant; m. Mélithe Dauger. Diploma, Ecole Sup. des Scis. Comml., Angers, France, 1995. With Sagem, Paris, 1996-98, 9 Telecom, Paris, 1998—. Lt. cav. French mil., 1995-96. Mem. Nat. Assn. Res. Officers. Office: 9 Telecom 38 Quai du Point du Jour 92100 Boulogne France

DETJEN, DAVID WHEELER, lawyer; b. St. Louis, Jan. 25, 1948; s. Don Wheeler and Shirley (Pence) Detjen; m. Barbara Louise Morgan, Jan. 6, 1973; children: Andrea Marlene, Erika Alexandra. AB magna cum laude, Washington U., 1970, JD with honors, 1973; postgrad., Eberhard-Karls-Universitaet, Tuebingen, Germany, 1969-70. Bar: Mo. 1973, U.s. Ct. Appeals (8th cir.) 1976, U.S. Supreme Ct. 1976, N.Y. 1981. Law clk. to chief judge U.S. Ct. Appeals (8th cir.), St. Louis, 1973-75; assoc. Lewis, Rice, Tucker, Allen & Chubb, St. Louis, 1975-80, Walter, Conston, Alexander & Green, P.C., NYC, 1980-83; ptnr. Walter, Conston, Alexander & Green, NYC, 1983-2000, Alston & Bird LLP, N.Y.C., 2001—, co-chmn. internat. practice group NYC, 2001—. Lectr. law Washington U., St. Louis, 1975—80; bd. dirs. Felix Schoeller Tech. Papers, Inc. Author: (book) Distributorship Agreements in the US, 1983, The Germans in Mo. 1900-1918: Prohibition, Neutrality and Assimilation, 1985, Licensing Tech. and Trademarks in the US, 1988, Establishing a US Joint Venture with a Fgn. Ptnr., 1988, 2d edit., 1989, 3d edit., 1993, 2d edit., 1997, US Joint Ventures with Internat. Partners, 2000. Sec. German Forum, N.Y.C., 1988—, bd. dirs., 1995—; co-pres. King-Merritt cmty. Assn., Greenwich, Conn., 1997—; mem. Am. Coun. Germany, N.Y.C., Atlantik-Bruecke, Berlin, St. Louis County Rep. Cen. Com., 1976—83, Rep. Town Meeting, Greenwich, 2000—, vice-chmn. labor contracts com., 2002—; mem. nat. coun. Washington U. Law Sch., St. Louis, 1989—; trustee Am. Inst. Contemporary German Studies, Johns Hopkins U., 1999—, corp. sec., 2000—. Recipient Disting. Alumnus award, Washington U. Law Sch., 1998. Mem.: ABA, Order of Coif, German Am. Law Assn., Assn. Bar City of NY, NY State Bar Assn. (exec. editor Interant. Law Practicum 1988—, mem. exec. com. internat. law and practice sect. 1999—), German-Am. C. of C. (bd. dirs. 2003—), William G. Eliot Soc. Washington U. (N.Y. chmn. 1993—), German Am. Round Table, Deutscher Verein Club NYC (bd. dirs. 1994—97, 1999—, v.p., sec. 2000—03), Delta Phi Delta. Presbyterian. Home: 35 Stonehedge Dr Greenwich CT 06831-3220 Office: Alston & Bird LLP 90 Park Ave Fl 14 New York NY 10016-1301 Fax: 212 210-9444. E-mail: ddetjen@alston.com.

DETLEFSEN, MICHAEL E. food products executive; Exec. v.p., vertical coord. Maple Leaf Foods Inc., Toronto. Office: Maple Leaf Foods Inc 30 St Clair Ave W Ste 1500 Toronto ON Canada M4V 3A2

DETMAR-PINES, GINA LOUISE, business strategy and policy educator; b. S.I., N.Y., May 3, 1949; d. Joseph and Grace Vivian (Brown) Sargente; m. Michael B. Pines, Sept. 11, 1988; 1 child, Drue Joseph Pines. BS in Edn., Wagner Coll., 1971, MS, 1972; MA in Urban Affairs and Policy Analysis, New Sch. for Social Rsch., 1987; MPhil, CUNY, 1995; PhD in Bus./Orgn. and Policy Studies, CUNY-Baruch Coll., 1996. Cert. adminstr. and supr., sch. dist. adminstr. Tchr. pub. schs., N.Y.C., 1971-82; coord. spl. projects, pub. affairs N.Y.C. Bd. Edn., 1982, spl. asst. to exec. dir. pupil svcs., 1983, asst. to chancellor, 1983-84, dir. Tchr. Summer Bus. Industry Program, 1984 93; prof. pub. adminstrn. and mgmt. John Jay Coll. Criminal Justice CUNY, 1992-93; prof. bus. Cen. Conn. State U., 2000—. Vis. prof. Rensselaer at Hartford, 1993—98, Fairfield U., 1998—2000; liaison for the Tech. Industry Program N.Y.C. Partnership, 1985—93. Mem. com. to re-elect Borough pres. Lamberti, S.I., 1985-86; chairperson Crystal Ball event Greater Hartford Easter Seals Rehab. Ctr., 1994, trustee, 1994—; bd. dirs. Hartford Symphony, com. mem. 50th Anniversary Gala, 1993. Mayor's scholar City of N.Y., 1984-96. Mem. ASPA, Fgn. Lang. Instrs. Assn., Strategic Mgmt. Soc., Acad. Mgmt., U.S. Seaplane Pilot's Assn., Internat. Orgn. for Lic. Women Pilots, Jr. League of Hartford, Hartford Task Force on Healthy Families, Chinese-Am. Soc., Am. Mgmt. Soc., Ea. Acad. Mgmt., Acad. of Internat. Bus., Cambridge Flying Group Club. Episcopalian. Avocations: flying, scuba diving, skiing. Office: Ctrl Conn State U 1615 Stanley St New Britain CT 06053-2439

DETMER, DON EUGENE, health management and policy researcher, medical educator, surgeon; b. Winfield, Kans., Feb. 3, 1939; s. Lawrence Oscar and Esther Beulah (McCormick) Detmer; m. Mary Helen McFerson, Aug. 26, 1961; children: Mary Catherine, Emily Anne. Student, U. Kans., 1957—59, U. Durham, 1959—60; MD, U. Kans., Kansas City, 1965; MA, U. Cambridge, 2002. Intern, then resident in surgery Johns Hopkins U., Balt., 1965—67; clin. assoc. surg. br. Nat. Heart Inst. NIH, Bethesda, Md., 1967—69; resident in surgery Duke U., Durham, NC, 1969—72; Global Cmty. Health fellow Dept. HEW, Inst. Medicine/NAS, Washington, 1972—73; prof. preventive medicine and surgery U. Wis., Madison, 1973—84; v.p. health scis., prof. surgery and med. info. U. Utah, Salt Lake City, 1984—88; univ. prof. health policy, prof. surgery and health evaluation scis. U. Va., Charlottesville, 1988—93, v.p., provost for health scis., 1988—96, sr. v.p., 1996—98, Louise Nurancy prof. health scis. policy, 1996—99, prof. emeritus, prof. med. edn., 1999—; Dennis Gillings prof. health mgmt. Cambridge U., 1999—2003; dir. Cambridge U. Health, 1999—2003. Cons. Hong Kong Hosp. Authority, Markle Found., N.Y.C., Japan, Australia, China, Australasian Coll. Surgeons, U. Algeria, Robert Wood Johnson Found., Princeton, NJ; bd. dirs. China Med. Bd. N.Y., Inc., NAS Inst. Medicine, Washington, chmn. bd. healthcare svcs., 1994—2000; chmn. nat. com. vital health stats. HHS, Washington, 1996—99; chmn. Blue Ridge Acad. Health Group, 1997—, co-chmn., 2002—; regent Nat. Libr. Medicine, NIH, Bethesda, Md., 1987—91; trustee Nuffield Trust, 2000—; bd. dirs., developer adminstrv. medicine U. Wis., Madison; membership com. chmn. sect. 12 NAS Inst. Medicine, Washington, 2002—; chair Nat. Libr. Medicine NIH, Bethesda, 1989—91; assoc. Nat. Acads., 2002. Mem. editl. bd.: Quality and Safety in Healthcare; contbr. Chmn. pub. svc. com. bd. dirs. United Way, Salt Lake City, 1986—88, Charlottesville, Va., 1992—97; with USPHS, 1967—69; pres. Peace Luth. Ch., 1996—99. Recipient Global Cmty. Health fellowship, HEW, 1972—73; fellow, Clare Hall, Cambridge U., 2000—. Fellow: ACS (vice chmn. com. allied health pers. 1989—90, chmn. 1990—94, internat. health com. 1996—2002), AAAS, Acad. Health, Am. Coll. Med. Info., Am. Coll. Sports Medicine; mem.: Royal Soc. Medicine, Soc. Med. Adminstrs. (treas. 1997—2000), Am. Acad. Physician Assts. (hon.), Am. Hosp. Assn. (chmn. coun. hosp. med. staffs 1984—87), Inst. of Medicine of NAS, Assn. Acad. Health Ctrs, (bd. dirs. 1996—98), Am. Med. Informatics Assn. (bd. dirs. 1996—98), Cosmos Club Washington, Alpha Omega Alpha. Lutheran. Avocations: fly fishing, painting, canoeing, horseback riding. Home: 5245 Browns Gap Tpke Crozet VA 22932-1613 Office: U Va Health Sys PO Box 800717 Charlottesville VA 22908 E-mail: detmer@virginia.edu.

DE TOLEDO, CATHERINE HOLT, medical writer; b. Columbus, Ohio, May 16, 1954; d. Golden Jr. and Petrea (Giles) Holt; m. Luiz Carlos de Toledo, Mar. 10, 1979; 1 child, Laura Holt. BS, Stanford U., 1976. Med. writer Alfred I. duPont Inst., Wilmington, Del., 1976-79; tchr. English Mich. Lang. Inst., Campinas, Brazil, 1980-81; propr. Belladerme Skin Care, Campinas, 1981-84; med. writer Louisville Hand Surgery, 1984-85; freelance med. writer Ft. Worth, 1985-98. Owner MedShare Office Concepts, 1998—. Asst. editor: Reconstruction of the Child's Hand, 1989; contbr. articles to various publs. Polit. Campaign Mgmt. Bd. dirs. North Tex. Planned Parenthood, 1992—, chmn. bd. 1998-2000. Mem. NAFE, Am. Med. Writers Assn., Soc. Profl. Journalists, Texpac Alliance (dist. chmn. 1989—, exec. com. 1990-2000), Tarrant County Med. Soc. Alliance (chmn. health fair 1988, v.p. publicity 1989, rep.-at-large 1990, pres.-elect 1992, pres. 1993), Tex. Med. Assn. Alliance (publ. editor 1990-92, legis. chmn. 1992, pres. 1993, v.p. legis. 1997), Women's Club Ft. Worth, Etta Newby Club. Avocations: running, sewing, biking, reading. Home and Office: 6651 Mike Lane Ct Fort Worth TX 76116-8112

DETOLLA, LOUIS JAMES, research scientist and veterinarian; b. Phila., Nov. 18, 1947; s. Louis James and Linda Liberatore DeTolla; m. Setsu Nakai, June 28, 1975; 1 child, Leonardo Nakai. BA, Temple U., 1970; MS, Rutgers U., 1974, PhD, 1978; VMD, U. Pa., 1982. Instr. biology Rutgers U., New Brunswick, N.J., 1975-78, tchg. asst. in immunology, endocrinology and genetics, 1973-78, postdoctoral fellow, 1978; NSF fellow U. Pa., Phila., 1979-82; rsch. veterinarian Sloan-Kettering Inst., N.Y.C., 1982-83; veterinarian Fox Chase Cancer Ctr., Phila., 1983-85; rsch. veterinarian Merck, Sharp & Dohme Labs., Rahway, N.J., 1985-88; dir. comparative medicine U. Md. Sch. Medicine, 1988—; vet. med. officer Balt. VA Med. Ctr., 1988—. Rsch. fellow Nat. Aquarium, Balt., mem. bd. govs., chmn. animal policy com., 1993—. Contbr. articles to profl. jours. Recipient Nat. Rsch. Svcs. award NIH, 1983; Nat. Needs Manpower fellow NSF, 1980; NIH fellow in immunobiology, 1982; grantee NIH, 1990—, Dept. Def., 1955—. Mem. AAAS, AVMA, Assn. Primate Veterinarians, Am. Soc. Lab. Animal Practitioners, Am. Soc. Zoologists, N.J. Acad. Scis., Am. Coll. Lab Animal Medicine (bd. cert.), Phi Zeta. Office: U Maryland MSTF Bldg Rm G-100 10 S Pine St Baltimore MD 21201-1116 E-mail: detolla@vetmed.umaryland.edu.

DE TONNANCOUR, PAUL ROGER GODEFROY, library administrator; b. Fall River, Mass., May 22, 1926; s. R. Godefroy and Emilie (St. Germain) de T.; m. Mary E. Fenno, Apr. 9, 1955; children— Paul Godefroy, Camille Marie. AB cum laude, Providence Coll., 1952; MS, Simmons Coll., 1953; postgrad., Western Res. U., U. So. Cal. Asst. librarian Enoch Pratt Library, Balt., 1953-54; chief librarian, tech. analyst Armco Steel Corp., Balt., 1954-56; dir. rsch. library Gen. Dynamics (Ft. Worth div.), 1956—, dir. tech. information programs, 1964-87, with Proposal Devel. Ctr., 1987—. Cons. MLA, U.S. Office Edn. on sci. info. pers.; John Cotton Dana lectr., 1966 Singer, Ft. Worth Opera Assn. Chorus; Author: The Exploitation of Technical Information, 1966; co-author: Science Information Personnel, 1963; Contbr. articles to profl. jours. Active United Fund and Community Council; mem. exec. com. Big Bros. Tarrant County.; Trustee Cosmopolitan Internat., 1961-63. Served with USNR, 1943-46. Named Boss of Year Am. Bus. Women's Assn., 1965 Mem. ALA, AAAS, Am., Nat. mgmt. assns., Ft. Worth Art Assn., Spl. Libraries Assn., Am. Soc. Information Sci., Delta Epsilon Sigma. Clubs: Mason, Fort Worth Boat. Episcopalian. Home: 6332 Genoa Rd Fort Worth TX 76116-2028 Office: PO Box 748 Fort Worth TX 76101-0748 *Above all, don't take yourself too seriously; Seek wisdom for itself and nurture a sense of humor. Together, they will serve you well.*

DE TORNYAY, RHEBA, nurse, former university dean, educator; b. Petaluma, Calif., Apr. 17, 1926; d. Bernard and Ella Fradkin; m. Rudy de Tornyay, June 4, 1954. Student, U. Calif., Berkeley, 1944-46; diploma, Mt. Zion Hosp. Sch. Nursing, 1949; AB, San Francisco State U., 1951, MA, 1954; Ed.D., Stanford U., 1967; Sc.D. (hon.), Ill. Wesleyan U., 1974; LHD (hon.), U. Portland, 1974, Georgetown U., 1994. Mem. faculty San Francisco State U., 1957-67, prof. nursing, 1966-67, chmn. dept., 1959-67; assoc. prof. U. Calif. Sch. Nursing, San Francisco, 1968-71, prof., 1971; dean, prof. Sch. Nursing UCLA, 1971-75; dean emeritus, prof. U. Wash., Seattle, 1986—. Author: Strategies for Teaching nursing, 1971, 3rd edit., 1987, Japanese transl., 1974, Spanish edit., 1986; co-author: (with Heather Young) Choices: Making a Good Move to a Retirement Community, 2001. Trustee emeritus Robert Wood Johnson Found. Mem. ANA, Am. Acad. Nursing (charter fellow, pres. 1973-75), Inst. Medicine (governing coun. 1979-81). Home: 4540 8th Ave NE Apt 1001 Seattle WA 98105-4795 E-mail: rheba@u.washington.edu.

DETRE, THOMAS, psychiatrist, educator; b. Budapest, Hungary, May 17, 1924; came to U.S., 1953, naturalized, 1958; m. Katherine Maria Drechsler, Sept. 15, 1956; children: John Allan, Antony James. BA, Gymnasium of Piarist Fathers, Kecskemet, Hungary, 1942; postgrad., Horthy Miklos U. and Pazmany Peter U., Hungary, 1945-47; MD, Rome U., 1952. Diplomate: Am. Bd. Psychiatry and Neurology (assoc. examiner). Intern Morrisania City Hosp., N.Y.C., 1953-54; resident in psychiatry Mt. Sinai Hosp., N.Y.C., 1954-55, Yale U., 1955-57, chief resident, instr., 1957-58, asst. prof., 1958-59, asst. prof., 1959-62; dir. psychiat. inpatient service Yale-New Haven Hosp., 1960-68, assoc. prof., 1962-70, asst. chief psychiatry div., 1965-68, psychiatrist in chief, 1968-73, prof., 1970-73; prof., chmn. dept. psychiatry U. Pitts., 1973-82, assoc. sr. vice chancellor, 1982-84, disting. svc. prof. health scis., 1982—, disting. prof. psychiatry and neurosci., 1993-98, sr. v.p. health scis., 1984-92, sr. vice chancellor for health scis., 1992-98, pres. med. and health care div., 1986-90, pres. med. ctr., 1990-92; dir. Western Psychiat. Inst. and Clin. Western Psychiat. Inst. and Clin., 1973-94; exec. v.p. internat. and acad. programs, dir. internat. med. affairs UPMC Health Sys., Pitts., 1998—. Mem. Nat. Adv. Mental Health Coun., NIH, 1994-97; mem. bd. regents Nat. Libr. Medicine. Author: (with H.G. Jarecki) Modern Psychiatric Treatment, 1971; contbr. chpts. to books. Fellow Am. Coll. Psychiatrists, Am. Coll. Neuropsychopharmacology (pres. 1994), Acad. Behavioral Medicine Rsch., Am. Psychiat. Assn. (life fellow); mem. AAAS, Inst. of Medicine, Collegium Internat. Neuropsychopharmacologicum, Pan Am. Med. Assn., Am. Soc. Clin. Pharmacology and Therapeutics, Phi Beta Kappa. Office: UPMC Health Sys 3811 Ohara St Pittsburgh PA 15213-2593

DETRICK, DONALD HOWARD, minister; b. Newberg, Oreg., Dec. 13, 1954; s. Howard Raymond and Madeline F. (Roth) D.; m. Jodi Lanette Dunlap, June 8, 1974; children: Kristina Lynne, Mark Andrew, Jana Kathleen. Student, Eugene Bible Coll., 1974-77; BA, Bapt. Christian Coll., 1985; MA in Counseling, Luther Rice Sem., 1990. Ordained to ministry Assemblies of God, 1980. Sr. pastor Dayton (Oreg.) Assembly of God, 1977-78; assoc. pastor First Assembly of God, Newberg, 1979-83; sr. pastor Abundant Life Ctr., Toledo, Oreg., 1983-91, Bethel Ch., Chehalis, Wash., 1991—. Presbyter Oreg. Coun. Assemblies of God, Salem, 1986-91, exec. presbyter, 1987-91; presbyter NW Dist. Assemblies of God, 1994-96, exec. presbyter, 1996—. Contbr. articles to religious publs. Mem. Am. Assn. Christian Counselors. Republican. Office: Bethel Ch 132 Kirkland Rd Chehalis WA 98532-8724 E-mail: bethel@bethel-church.com.

DETRO, JOHN FITZGERALD, military officer; b. Flint, Mich., Feb. 27, 1962; s. Jackie Lee and Irene (Schultz) D.; m. Moraima Acevedo, Aug. 11, 1992; children: Xaviera, Anthony, Jose. BS in Biology, Siena Heights Coll., 1985; BS in Physician's Asst. summa cum laude, U. Tex. Health Sci. Ctr., 1997; MS in Family Medicine, U. Nebr., 1998; grad. with disting. honor, U.S. Army Flight Surgeon course, 2000; grad., U.S. Army Jump Master course, 2001, U.S. Army Ranger Sch., 2000. Enlisted U.S. Army, 1987, advanced through grades to capt., medic, 1987-90; cytotechnology instr. Brooke Army Med. Ctr., Ft. Sam Houston, Tex., 1992-95, asst. resident orthop.; physicians asst. 2-69 Armor Batt., Ft. Benning, Ga., 1997—; physicians asst. 3d bn. 75th Ranger Regiment, Ft. Benning, Ga., 1999—. Vet., Operation Desert Shield/Storm, vet., Operation Enduring Freedom. Fellow Am. Acad. of Physicians Assts., Soc. of Army Physician Assts.; mem. Assn. of the U.S. Army, Columbus Track Club. Democrat. Avocations: running, armed force cross country team. Home: 1983 Oakwell Farms Pkwy # 1902 San Antonio TX 78218 Office: B Co Brooke Army Med Ctr San Antonio TX 78234 E-mail: rangerpa@earthlink.net.

DETSCHEL, FREDERICK WILLIAM, management consultant; b. Bklyn., Nov. 23, 1935; s. William Frederick and Johnann (Tighe) D.; m. Margaret Willette, (div. Nov. 1982); children: William, Kathy, Diana; m. Kathryn Ellen Rautio, Nov. 20, 1982. BS in Physics, CUNY, 1967; MS in Computer Info. Sci., Syracuse U., 1978. Tech. illustrator Volt Tech. Svcs., N.Y.C., 1959-63; devel. mgr. IBM Corp., Bethesda, Md., 1963-87; mgr. sys. programming Prodigy Svcs. Co., White Plains, N.Y., 1987-95; sr. cons., pres. FWD Enterprises Inc., Mashpee, Mass., 1995—. Adj. prof. Haskell Indian Jr. Coll., Lawrence, Kans., 1977-78, Dutchess County C.C., Poukeepsie, N.Y., 1981-82; sr. cons. IBM Global Svcs. Network, 1996-99, Purdue Pharma L.P., 2000-02; bd. dirs. Independence House, Hyannis, Mass., 2000—. Author, designer Nagano Olympic Web Site Architecture, 1998. Deacon, elder Hopewell Ref. Ch. Am., Hopewell Junction, N.Y., 1992-96; pres. Barclay Hts. Homeowners Civic Assn., Saugerties, N.Y., 1979-81, Holland Mill Estates Homeowners Assn., Mashpee, 2000—. Sgt. USAF, 1954-58. Recipient Casey Jones scholar Acad. Aeronautics, Astoria, N.Y., 1953; cert. appreciation contbns. to 1996 IBM Atlanta Olympic Web Site, 1996. Libr. Congress (assoc. mem.), mem. Appalachian Mountain Club (S.E. Mass. chpt.). Republican. Mem. United Ch. Christ. Avocations: woodworking, bicycling, gardening, racquetball, travel. Office: Continuity Concepts PMB281 39 Nathan Ellis Hwy Mashpee MA 02649-3267 E-mail: FWDinc@yahoo.

DETTBARN, WOLF-DIETRICH, neurochemist, pharmacologist, educator; b. Berlin, Jan. 30, 1928; came to U.S., 1958, naturalized, 1968; s. Erwin Bruno and MariaMagdalena (Conrady) D.; children: Donata-Andrea, Henning-Christian. MD, Dr.Med., D. Göttingen, 1953. Intern Univ. Clinic, Göttingen, 1953-54; research assoc. biol. dept. Ciba Co., Basel, 1954-55; research assoc. Physiol. Inst., U. Saarland, Homburg, Saar, 1955-58; research assoc. neurology Columbia U., N.Y.C., 1958-61, asst. prof., 1961-67, assoc. prof., 1967-68; prof. pharmacology Vanderbilt U., Nashville, 1968-96, prof. pharmacology emeritus, 1996—, prof. neurology, 1985—. Mem. com. on toxicology of anticholinesterase chems. NRC. 1981-83; cons. U.S. Army Med. R & D Command, 1981-82. Contbr. articles to profl. jours. Mem. internal rev. bd. Vanderbilt U., 1991-93. Recipient Career Devel. award, 1965; grantee NIH, 1958—. Mem. AAAS, Am. Physiol. Soc., Am. Soc. Pharmcology and Exptl. Therapeutics, Am. Soc. Neurochemistry, Soc. for Neurosci., Corp. Marine Biology Lab. (Woods Hole, Mass.). Home: 4422 Wayland Dr Nashville TN 37215-4024 Office: Emeritus Faculty 209 Oxford House Vanderbilt U Med Ctr Nashville TN 37232-4245 E-mail: wolf-d.dettbarn@vanderbilt.edu.

DETTERLINE, MILTON E., JR., minister; b. Bethlehem, Pa., Nov. 16, 1929; s. Milton Elmer Detterline, Sr. and Mary Elizabeth Detterline; m. Nancy Jane Day, June 26, 1954 (div. July 1976); children: James Lee, Jon Scott, Peter Kirk. BA, Moravian Coll., 1951; MDiv, Drew U., 1954. Ordained to ministry Evang. Congregational Ch., Pa. Conf., 1954. Pastor Pottsville (Pa.) Evang. Congregational Ch., 1954—57, St. John Evang. Congregational Ch., Allentown, Pa., 1957—61, St. John United Ch. of Christ, Tamaqua, Pa., 1961—69; pastoral fellow in ecumenics Yale U., New Haven, 1968; spl. asst. to pres., chaplain, alumni dir. Ursinus Coll., Collegeville, Pa., 1969—74; sr. pastor St. Peters United Ch. of Christ, St. Peters, Pa., 1972—. Dir. sch. methods Evang. Congregational denomina, bd. christian edn., various other offices. Contbr. articles to newspapers, reports and pubs. Past pres. Allentown Area Coun. Chs.; chmn. Lehigh County Child Care Commn., Schuylkill County Child Care Commn.; numerous other offices; moderator, co-founder Coventry-Warwick Ministerium; bd. Christian concern PSE Housing for Elderly, bd. Jefferson Apts.; pres., mem. bd. Orion Cmtys., Inc. Named Citizen of Yr., City of Tamaqua, Pa., 1968, Bldg. named in honor, St. Peter United Ch. Christ, 2001. Office: St Peter United Ch of Christ 1100 Mt Pleasant Rd Saint Peters PA 19470 Home: Box 156 Saint Peters PA 19470

DETTERMAN, ROBERT LINWOOD, financial planner; b. Norfolk, Va., May 1, 1931; s. George William and Jeanneille (Watson) D.; m. Virginia Armstrong; children: Janine, Patricia, William Arthur. BS in Engring., Va. Poly. Inst., 1953; PhD in Nuclear Engring., postgrad., Oak Ridge Sch. Reactor Tech., 1954; cert. in fin. planning, Coll. Fin. Planning, Denver, 1986. Registered investment advisor, Calif. Engring. test dir. Foster Wheeler Co., N.Y.C., 1954-59; sr. research engr. Atomics Internat. Co., Canoga Park, Calif., 1959-62; chief project engr. Rockwell Internat. Co., Canoga Park, Calif., 1962-68, dir. bus. devel., 1968-84, mgr. internat. program, 1984-87; pres. Bo-Gin Fin., Inc., Thousand Oaks, Calif., 1987—; owner Bo-Gin Arabians, Thousand Oaks, 1963—. Nuclear cons. Danish Govt., 1960, Lawrence Livermore Lab., Calif., 1959. Trustee, mem. exec. com. Morris Animal Found., Denver, 1984—, chmn., 1984-88, now trustee emeritus; mem. pres.' adv. com. Kellog Arabian Ranch, U. Calif. Poly., Pomona; treas., trustee Arabian Horse Trust, Denver, 1979-94, now trustee emeritus; chmn. Cal Bred Futurity. Named to Arabian Tent of Honor, Arabian Horse Trust, 1997. Mem. Nat. Assn. Personal Fin. Advisers, Fin. Planning Assn., Acad. Magical Arts, Am. Horse Shows Assn., Am. Horse Coun., Magic Castle Club, Internat. Arabian Horse Assn. Club, Tau Beta Phi, Eta Kappa Nu, Phi Kappa Phi. Republican. Avocations: collecting stamps, growing orchids. Office: 3609 E Thousand Oaks Blvd Ste 220 Westlake Village CA 91362-6941 E-mail: boginfin@aol.com.

DETTINGER, GARTH BRYANT, surgeon, physician, retired air force officer, county health officer; b. Syracuse, N.Y., Dec. 23, 1921; s. Maurice and Maxine Bryant (giddings) D.; m. Gladys Ruth Hickingbotham, Aug. 5, 1939 (dec. Aug. 1996); children: Holly Maxine Dettinger Dixon-Keane, Ronald Mark, Michael James; m. Jeffa Taylor, July 26, 1997. AB, Harvard U., 1948; MD, Columbia U., 1952; MS in Surgery, Baylor U., 1956. Diplomate: Am. Bd. Surgery. B-17 instr. pilot, B-29 aircraft comdr. U.S. Army Air Corps, 1941—45; Commd. officer U.S. Air Force, 1952, advanced through grades to maj. gen., 1977; intern Valley Forge Army Hosp., Phoenixville, Pa., 1952-53; resident in surgery Brooke Army Hosp., San Antonio, 1953-57; chief surgery MacDill Hosp., Tampa, Fla., 1957-59, Elmendorf Hosp., Alaska, 1959-62, Davis-Monthan Hosp., Tucson, 1962-64; hosp. comdr. Roswell, N.Mex., 1964-67; prime recovery helicopter surgeon Project Gemini, Cape Kennedy, Fla., 1964—67; chief profl. services Air Forces Europe, 1967-70; hosp. comdr. Vandenberg, Calif., 1970-72; surgeon Air Force Mil. Personnel Center, San Antonio, 1972-74; command surgeon Air Tng. Command, 1974-75; dir. plans and resources U.S. Air Force, Washington, 1975-77, dep. surgeon gen., 1977-80; asst. health dir. Fairfax County, Va., 1980—. Surg. cons. Surgeon Gen. U.S., CIA, 1978-99; clin. assoc. prof. Georgetown U. Med. Sch., 1983— Editor-in-chief: Surgeons Comments, 1967-70. Recipient Disting. Svc. medal, USAF, 1977. Fellow A.C.S. (bd. govs.); mem. Soc. Med. Cons. to Armed Services, Alpha Omega Alpha. Republican. Episcopalian. Home: #M-116 9120 Belvoir Woods Pkwy # M-116 Fort Belvoir VA 22060-2701 Office: Fairfax County Dept Health 10777 Main St Ste 203 Fairfax VA 22030-6900 *I've always tried to leave anyone, anything or anyplace a little better than before I had been there.*

DETTINGER, WARREN WALTER, lawyer; b. Toledo, Feb. 13, 1954; s. Walter Henry and Elizabeth Mae (Zoll) D.; m. Patricia Marie Kasper, June 21, 1975; children: John Robert, Laura Marie. BS cum laude, U. Toledo, 1977, JD magna cum laude, 1980. Bar: Ohio 1980, U.S. Dist. Ct. (no. dist.) Ohio 1980, U.S. Ct. Appeals (6th cir.) 1980, U.S. Tax Ct. 1981. Law clk. to presiding judge U.S. Ct. Appeals (6th cir.), Grand Rapids, Mich., 1980-81; assoc. Fuller & Henry, Toledo, 1981-84; atty. Sheller-Globe Corp., Toledo, 1984-87; v.p., gen. counsel Diebold, Inc., Canton, Ohio, 1987—. Mem. ABA, Ohio Bar Assn., Stark County Bar Assn., Am. Corp. Counsel Assn., Mfr.'s Alliance (law coun. II), Brookside Country Club, Phi Kappa Phi. Roman Catholic. Avocations: golf, travel, photography, tennis. Home: 5237 Birkdale St NW Canton OH 44708-1825 Office: Diebold Inc 5995 Mayfair Rd PO Box 3077 North Canton OH 44720-8077 E-mail: dettinw@diebold.com.

DETTKE, DIETER M. foundation executive; b. Brusendorf, Berlin, Germany, Jan. 15, 1941; s. Ferdinand and Marianne (Bartoschek) D.; m. Brigitte G. Ohm, June 27, 1969 (div.); 1 child, Nathalie; m. Gale A. Mattox, Aug. 20, 1983; 1 child, Elizabeth. Diplom-Politologe, Free U. Berlin, 1968, PhD, 1974. Rsch. assoc. German Soc. for Fgn. Affairs, Bonn, 1969-74; staff dir. German Fgn. Office, Bonn, 1982; fgn. policy advisor German Bundestag, Bonn, 1974-84; exec. dir. Friedrich-Ebert-Stiftung, Washington, 1984—. Author: Allianz im Wandel, 1976; editor book series International Political Currents, 1994. Expert transatlantic activities and German-Am. dialogue. Fulbright scholar, 1967-68. Mem. Am. Polit. Sci. Assn., Internat. Studies Assn., Cosmos Club. German Social Dem. Party. Lutheran. Avocations: tennis, skiing, swimming. Office: Friedrich-Ebert-Stiftung 1155 15th St NW Ste 1100 Washington DC 20005-2706 E-mail: fesdc@fesdc.org.

DETTLOFF, DONNA JEAN, psychiatric social worker; b. Detroit, Mar. 25, 1939; d. Donald Jesse and Mirabel (Hitchcock) Faragher; m. Dennis F. Dettloff (div. 1975); children: Denise Christine, Dennis Michael, Donald Joseph, David Allen. Diploma in practical nursing with honors, U. Hawaii, 1969, AA in Mental Health with honors, 1980; BS in Psychology with honors, Chaminade U., 1980. Lic. realtor, Hawaii. Practical nurse Hawaii State Hosp., Kaneohe, 1968-72, Kailua (Hawaii) Counseling Ctr., 1972-90, social worker, 1990-94, ret., 1994; mental health counselor Castle Med. Ctr., Kailua, 1983—2002; ret., 2002. Republican. Avocations: stamps, coins, travel, interior design, hawaiiana. Home: 501 Northwood Cir Cross Junction VA 22625-2537

DETTMANN, DAVID ALLEN, lawyer; b. Milw., Mar. 30, 1949; s. Karl F. and Beverly J. (Rusdal) D.; m. Jenee A. Nelson, June 26, 1971; children: Justin, Lisa, Jacob. BA in Acctg./Econs., Luther Coll., 1971; MBA, JD, Drake U., 1974. Bar: Iowa 1974, U.S. Dist. Ct. (so. dist.) Iowa 1974, U.S. Tax Ct. 1974, U.S. Ct. Appeals (8th cir.) 1989, Ill. 1993; CPA, Iowa; accredited estate planner, Am. Coll. Real Estate Lawyers, 1994. Ptnr. Lane & Waterman, Davenport, Iowa, 1974—. Former mem. and pres. ch. coun. Redeemer Luth. Ch.; trustee, vice chair, chair Miss. Valley Regional Blood Ctr., Davenport, 1984—; bd. dirs. Am. Inst. Commerce, Davenport, 1986—1998, Quad-City Estate Planning Coun., Quad Cities, Iowa, Ill., pres., 1990-91. Mem. ABA, AICPA, Am. Coll. Trust and Estate Counsel, Iowa Bar Assn. (title stds. com. 1985-94, real estate & title law sect. coun. 1993—96, 2001-, chair 1994—95, chmn. title guaranty subcom. 1990-94), Real Estate Modernization Com.(chmn. 2002-), Iowa Soc. CPAs, Scott County Bar Assn. (chmn. abstract/real estate com. 1985-95). Avocations: travel, photography, golf. Office: Lane & Waterman 600 Norwest Bank Bldg 220 N Main St Ste 600 Davenport IA 52801-1987

DETTMER, ROBERT GERHART, retired beverage company executive; b. Parsons, Kans., Sept. 11, 1931; s. Ira Gerhart and Dema (Hinze) D.; m. Patricia Isabel York, Aug. 20, 1955; children: Stephanie, Constance, Robert Brantley. Student, U.S. Naval Acad., 1949-52; B in Bus. and Engring. Adminstrn., MIT, 1955; MBA, Harvard U., 1957. Engr. Lincoln Electric Co., Cleve., 1957-60; assoc. Booz, Allen & Hamilton, Cleve., 1960-64; propr. Robert G. Dettmer, Investment Mgmt., Cleve., 1964-66; v.p. ops. Tasa Corp., Pitts., 1966-68; pres. Scott Aviation div. A-T-O, Lancaster, N.Y., 1968-70, George J. Meyer Mfg. div. A-T-O, Milw., 1970-72, N.Am. Van Lines subs. PepsiCo, Inc., Fort Wayne, Ind., 1973-76; v.p. fin. mgmt. and planning PepsiCo, Inc., Purchase, N.Y., 1976-79; pres. Pepsi Cola Bottling Group subs., Purchase, N.Y., 1979-86; exec. v.p., CFO PepsiCo., Purchase, N.Y., 1986-96. Bd. dirs. Valero Energy. Chmn. bd. Am. Movers Conf., 1974-76; trustee Miss Porter's Sch., 1978-84; trustee Manhattanville Coll., 1986-93, chmn. bd. trustees, 1988-92. Mem. Delta Tau Delta, Tau Beta Pi. Clubs: Harvard Bus. Sch. of Westchester-Fairfield County (chmn. bd. 1977-80), Harvard Bus. Sch. of Greater N.Y. (chmn. bd. 1982-83). Home: 80 Round Hill Rd Greenwich CT 06831-3743

DETTWILER, PEGGY DIANE, music educator; b. Freeport, Ill., Dec. 16, 1947; d. Frank F. and Isabel (Yarger) Ochsner; m. Robert Dettwiler, June 18, 1972 (div. 1985); m. Jürgen Thym, June 6, 1992. BS, U. Wis., Platteville, 1970; MusM, U. Wis., Madison, 1980, MusBM, 1982; MusM, U. Tex., San Antonio, 1985; DMA, Eastman Sch., 1991. Vocal music tchr. Mt. Horeb (Wis.) H.S., 1970-77; dir. music Christ Presbyn. Ch., Madison, 1979-84; dir. choral activities St. Mary's U., San Antonio, 1985-88, Mansfield (Pa.) U., 1990—. Guest condr. N.Y. State Sch. Music Assn., 1995, Pa. Music Edn. Assn., 1994, 96, 97, 98, 2000, 02, 03. Contbr. articles to profl. jours. Recipient Concert Choir Gold medal, Robert Schumann Internat. Choral Competition, 2002. Mem.: Music Educators Nat. Conf. (performance choral condr. nat. conv. 1994, guest clinician 1995, 1997, 2000, performance choral condr. nat. conv. 2001, 2003), Collegiate Choral Assn. (pres. 1993—95), Am. Choral Dirs. Assn. (performances at convs. 1999, pres.-elect Pa. chpt. 1999—2000, performances at convs. 2000—03, pres. Pa. chpt. 2001—03). Avocations: photography, horseback riding, travel. Home: 452 N Main St Mansfield PA 16933-1326 Office: Mansfield U Butler 105 Mansfield PA 16933 E-mail: pdettwil@epix.net.

DETWEILER, DAVID KENNETH, veterinary physiologist, educator; b. Phila., Oct. 23, 1919; s. David Rieser and Pearl Irene (Overholt) Detweiler; m. Inge E.A. Kludt, Feb. 2, 1965; children: Ellen, Diane, Judith, Inge, Kenneth, David. VMD, U. Pa., 1942, MS, 1949; ScD (hon.), Ohio State U., 1966; MVD (hon.), U. Vienna, Austria, 1968; DMV (hon.), U. Turin, Italy, 1969. Asst. instr. physiology and pharmacology Sch. Vet. Medicine, U. Pa., Phila., 1942—43, instr., 1943—45, assoc. in physiology, pharmacology, 1945—47, asst. prof., 1947—51, assoc. prof., 1951—62, Sch. Vet. Medicine, U. Pa. (Grad. Sch. Arts and Scis.); chmn. dept. vet. med. scis. Sch. Vet. Medicine, U. Pa. (Grad. Sch. Medicine), 1956—68, dir. comparative cardiovascular studies unit, 1960—90, prof., head lab. physiology and pharmacology, 1962—68, prof., head lab. physiology, 1968—90, prof. faculty arts and scis., 1968—90, chmn. grad. group comparative med. scis., 1971—87, prof. emeritus, 1990—. Mem. Inst. Medicine, NAS, 1974—; guest USSR Acad. Sci.; ; cons. cardiovascular toxicology, 1950—. Contbr. Recipient Disting. Veterinarian award, Pa. Vet. Med. Assn., 1989, Disting. Practitioner award, Nat. Acads. of Practice in Vet. Medicine, 1989, D.K. Detweiler prize in cardiology established in his honor, German Group of World Vet. Med. Assn., 1982, David K. Detweiler Conf. Rm. named in honor, Veterinary Sch. U. Pa., 1993, Centennial medal, Sch. Vet. Medicine, U. Pa., 1994, cert. appreciation, FDA, 1998; fellow Guggenheim Found. Fellow: AAAS; mem.: Vet. Med. Alumni Soc. (Merit award U. Pa. 1981), Am. Coll. Vet. Internal Medicine (diplomate, cardiology group), Acad. Vet. Cardiology (pres.), Am. Heart Assn., Coun. Basic Scis., Am. Vet. Med. Assn. (Gaines award and medal 1960, Honor Roll award 1990), N.Y. Acad. Scis., Am. Assn. Vet. Physiology and Pharmacology (pres.), Am. Physiol. Soc., Phi Zeta, Sigma Xi. Fax: 610-645-8719.

DETWEILER, GREG JEFFREY, music educator; b. Harrisburg, Pa., Dec. 31, 1951; s. Roderick Leon and Betty Mae Detweiler; m. Rebecca Ann Finley, Mar. 3, 1985 (div. Dec. 20, 1999); children: Jaron Matthew, Aaron Nathaniel. BS, Lebanon Valley Coll., Annville, Pa., 1973; MusM, U. Ill., 1978, DMA, 1985. Vocal music tchr. Susquehanna Twp. Mid. Sch., Harrisburg, Pa., 1973—74; vis. dir. choral-vocal studies Mercer U., Macon, Ga., 1980—81; dir. choral activities Idaho State U., Pocatello, 1982—86, Southeastern La. U., Hammond, 1986—88, Albertson Coll. Idaho, Caldwell, 1989—97, Morehead (Ky.) State U., 1998—. Condr., artistic dir. Boise (Idaho) Master Chorale, 1993—95; choral dir. 1st Bapt. Ch., Morehead, 1999—; prof., choral condr. Ky. Inst. for Internat. Studies, Salzburg, Austria, 2001; founder, dir. cmty. choir Idaho State Chorale, Pocatello, 1985—86, Albertson Coll. Choral Union, Caldwell, 1989—97. Specialist 6 U.S. Army, 1974—77. Named Outstanding Young Man of Am., 1983, Ky. Coll.-Univ. Tchr. of Yr., Ky. Music Educators Assn., 2002; recipient Outstanding Svc. award, Gen. Commn. Chaplains and Armed Forces Pers., 1977. Mem.: Nat. Assn. Tchrs. of Singing (Ky. Tchr. of Yr. 2002), Music Educators Nat. Conf., Am. Choral Dirs. Assn. (chair N.W. divsn. youth and student activities 1992—96), Phi Kappa Phi. Southern Baptist. Achievements include research in investigation of resonance source of the singer's formant; psychoacoustic ramifications of singer's formant; laryngeal configuration in pulse register phonation: MRI and stroboscopic data. Avocations: mountain biking, hiking, reading. Home: 45 Windy Cove Morehead KY 40351 Office: Morehead State U Dept Music Morehead KY 40351 E-mail: g.deweiler@moreheadstate.edu.

DETWEILER, NANCY LOGAN, social worker; b. Pitts, Mar. 13, 1947; d. Albert Asbury and Gertrude (Seibert) Logan; children: Catherine Seibert, David Logan. BA, Pa. State U., 1969; MA, U. Chgo., 1971. Lic. clin. social worker; lic. marriage and family therapist; NASW diplomate in clin. social work. Psychiat. social worker Lawndale Mental Health Ctr., Chgo., 1971-72, Pritzker Children's Hosp., Chgo., 1972-74; social work specialist Prince Georges County Dept. Edn., Upper Marlboro, Md., 1974-75; dir. partial hospitalization Prince Georges County Mental Health Dept., Capitol Heights, Md., 1975-76; cons. Middlesex Hosp. Psychiat. Clinic, Middletown, Conn., 1977-79; psychotherapist Ctr. for Study of Behavior, Hamden, Conn., 1979-82; asst. to dept. community health and family medicine U. Fla., Gainesville, 1984-87; pvt. practice clin. social work Gainesville, 1984—; dir. sch. based svcs. Mental Health Svcs. N.C., Gainesville, 1994-97; asst. in field instrn. Fla. State U. Sch. Social Work, 1998—. Co-founder Alachua County (Fla.) Health Coalition, 1984; mem. Alachua County Ad Hoc Health Needs Assessment Com., Gainesville, 1988; mem. Alachua County Health Bd., Gainesville, 1988-90; mem. Visions 2000, Alachua County, 1987—; mem. exec. com. Fla. Consumer Action Network, 1989-91; v.p. Fla. PACE, 1990-91, pres., 1991-93, mem. social workers' polit. action com.; v.p., bd. dirs. Acorn Clinic, 1990-92. Mem. NASW (health/mental health liaison Fla. chpt. 1990-92, sec. 1988-90, 98, Social Worker of Yr. State of Fla. 1998), Social Worker of Yr. Gainesville unit 1986, 90), Alachua County LWV (bd. dirs. 1988-89, Olive Christianson Outstanding LWV Mem. 1991-93), Alachua County Mental Health Assn. (v.p. 1990). Home: 3113 NW 24th Ave Gainesville FL 32605-2722

DETWEILER, RICHARD ALLEN, college president, psychology educator; b. L.A., Nov. 14, 1946; s. James Irvin and Dorothy Elizabeth D.; m. Carol Sue D., Aug. 26, 1967; children: Jerusha, Natasha, Carrick. BA, Calif. Western U., 1968; MA, Princeton U., 1972, PhD, 1973. Structural draftsman Young's Iron Works, Burbank, Calif., 1962-64; peace corps volunteer U.S. Peace Corps, Truk, Caroline Islands; prof. psychology Drew U., Madison, N.J., 1973-92, vice pres., 1985-92; pres. Hartwick Coll., Oneonta, N.Y., 1992—, prof. psychology. Vis. fellow Princeton (N.J.) U., 1973-74; internat. edn. cons. to various non-profit and govt. orgns., 1977—; vis. scholar U. Calif., Berkeley, Calif., 1980; profl. assoc. East West Ctr., Honolulu, HI, 1978. Contbr. numerous articles and speeches in the fields of psychology, edn. and info. tech. Recipient Outstanding Contbn. and Leadership award, Carnegie Mellon U., 1991; disting. scholar, Coun. on Libr. and Info. Resources, life fellow, Oxford U. Mem. Coun. Ind. Colls., Ind. Col. Fund., Am. Coun. on Edn. Office: PO Box 81 Cooperstown NY 13326

DETWILER, CHRISTINA LEFEVRE, elementary school educator; b. Richmond, Va., July 27, 1968; d. Michael Roy and Linda Harris LeFevre; m. Scott Douglas Detwiler, Aug. 1, 1998; 1 child, Sarah Catherine. Student, Longwood Coll., 1986—88, J. Sargeant Reynolds, Richmond, 1988—90, Va. Commonwealth U., 1990—91, BS in Psychology, MT in Elem. Edn., 1994. Postgrad. profl. lic. in early edn. NK-4. Kindergarten tchr. Elmont Elem., Ashland, Va., 1995—97, 1st grade loop tchr., 1997—98, 1st grade tchr., 1998—99, Acquinton Elem., King William, Va., 1999—2001. Active March of Dimes, Aylett, Va., 1998—, VFW, 1998—, Save the Mattaponi Orgn., King William, 1999—2002, Sept. 11 Fund, 2001. Mem.: NEA, Psi Chi, Sigma Kappa. Baptist.

DETWILER, CHRISTINE WENDLER, special education educator; b. Phila., Nov. 7, 1947; d. Frederick Lawrence Wendler Jr. and Eileen Casey Wendler; m. Barry Russell Detwiler, Dec. 9, 1967 (div. 1993); children: B.R. Brendan Jr., Benjamin Jonathan(dec.). AAS in Early Childhood Edn., Montgomery County C.C., Blue Bell, Pa., 1985; BS in Spl. Edn. cum laude, Gwynedd-Mercy Coll., Gwynedd Valley, Pa., 1990; Master's Equivalency Degree in Edn., U. Arts, Phila., 1994. Cert. tchr. for mentally or physically handicapped Pa. Instrnl. asst., spl. edn. North Penn Sch. Dist., Lansdale, 1983—90, spl. edn. tchr., all levels, 1990—99, program tchr., ann. young authors' conf., 1998—, learning support tchr., co-tchg. inclusion tchr., 1999—. Writer, implemented various ednl. programs; presenter in field. Contbr. articles to profl. jours. and newspapers. Tour guide narrator Independence Nat. Hist. Park, Phila., 1987—90. Scholar, Charlotte W. Newcombe Found., 1988, 1989, Lansdale Bus. and Profl. Women's Club, 1989, Primary-Aged, Student-Centered Reading Incentive Targeting Values-Centered Books grantee, North Penn Sch. Dist. Ednl. Found., 2001—02, 2002—03, 2003—. Avocations: travel, photography, writing for children, reading, antiques. Office: # 211 4275 County Line Rd Chalfont PA 18914

DETWILER, LARRY ALAN, music educator; b. Altoona, Pa., Feb. 7, 1966; s. Dick Herr and Billie Jane Detwiler; m. Kelly Ann Detwiler, June 30, 1990; children: Courtney Jennifer, Mackenzie Kathleen. BS, Pa. State U., 1990. Cert. in music edn. Band dir., music tchr. Bishop Guilfoyle H.S., Altoona, Pa., 1990-92, Glendale H.S., Flinton, Pa., 1992-93, Roosevelt Jr. H.S., Altoona, 1993-2000; band dir., music dept. chairperson Altoona Area H.S., 2000—. Mem. Music Educators Nat. Conf. Avocations: music, sports. Home: 203 Aldrich Ave Altoona PA 16602-3203 Office: Altoona Area HS 1415 6th Ave Altoona PA 16602 E-mail: larry@aasdcat.com.

DETWILER, PETER MURRAY, legislative staff member, educator; b. Visalia, Calif., Nov. 5, 1949; s. Donald M. and Mary Alice (Murray) D.; m. Caroline Margaret Cain, Sept. 2, 1972; children: Stephen C., Eric J. BA in Govt., St. Mary's Coll. Calif., 1971; MA in Pub. Policy and Adminstrn., U. Wis., 1972. Asst. exec. officer Local Agy. Formation Commn., San Diego, 1972-75; dir. local govt. unit Gov.'s Office Planning and Rsch., Sacramento, 1975-81; staff dir. Senate Local Govt. Com., Sacramento, 1982-95, 98—, Senate Housing and Land Use Com., Sacramento, 1995-98. Instr. Calif. State U., Sacramento, 1991—. Contbr. chpts. to books. Leader Boy Scouts Am., Sacramento, 1984—. Democrat. Roman Catholic. Avocations: sailing, cross-country skiing. Office: Senate Local Govt Com State Capitol Rm 410 Sacramento CA 95814-4906 E-mail: peter.detwiler@sen.ca.gov.

DEUBLE, JOHN L., JR., environmental science and engineering services consultant; b. N.Y.C., Oct. 2, 1932; s. John Lewis and Lucille (Klotzbach) D.; m. Thelma C. Honeychurch, Aug. 28, 1955; children: Deborah, Steven. AA, AS in Phys. Sci., Stockton Coll., 1957; BA, BS in Chemistry, U. Pacific, 1959. Cert. profl. chemist, profl. engr., environ. inspector; registered environ. profl., registered environ. assessor. Sr. chemist Aero-Gen Corp., Sacramento, Calif., 1959-67; asst. dir. rsch. Lockheed Propulsion Co., Redlands, Calif., 1968-73; asst. div. mgr. Systems, Sci. and Software, La Jolla, Calif., 1974-79; gen. mgr. Wright Energy Nev. Corp., Reno, Nev., 1980-81; v.p. Energy Resources Co., La Jolla, 1982-83; dir. hazardous waste Aerovironment Inc., Monrovia, Calif., 1984-85; sr. program mgr. Ogden Environ. and Energy Svcs., San Diego, 1989-96; environ. cons. Encinitas, Calif., 1986-88, 97—. Contbr. articles to profl. jours. With USAF, 1951-54. Recipient Tech. award Am. Ordnance Assn., 1969, Cert. of Achievement Am. Men and Women of Sci., 1986, Envrion. Registry, 1992. Fellow Am. Inst. Chemists; mem. ASTM, NSPE, Am. Chem. Soc., Am. Inst. Chem. Engrs., Am. Def. Inds. Assn., Air and Waste Mgmt. Assn., Calif. Inst. Chemists, N.Y. Acad. Scis., Environ. Assessors Assn. Republican. Lutheran. Achievements include development and pioneering use of chemical (non-radioactive) tracers--gaseous, aqueous, and particulate in environmental and energy applications. Home and Office: 2302 Calle De Rafael NE Albuquerque NM 87122

DEUBLE, LOTTIE EDWARDS, lay worker; b. Franklinton, N.C., July 2, 1922; d. Kenneth Kenzie and Lizzie Patty (Oakley) Edwards; m. Harold William Deuble, Sept. 2, 1943; children: Maria Elizabeth Deuble Pries, Harolyn Mae Deuble Scherry, Janet Susan Deuble Larry. Saleslady McClennan's, Petersburg, Va., 1939-40, F.W. Woolworth, Petersburg, Va., 1940-41; operator, supr., instr. Chesapeake & Potomac Telephone Co., Petersburg, Va., 1941-43; test operator Diamond State Telephone Co., Dover, Del., 1948-53; PBX operator Kent Gen. Hosp., Dover, Del., 1953-54; part-time saleslady J.C. Penney Co., Dover, Del., 1955, Pierce's Pharmacy, Dover, Del., 1955-56; sec. R.C. Nehi Co., Dover, Del., 1956-60; time computor Internat. Playtex, Dover, Del., 1970-72; receptionist Dr. William Flanagan and Dr. Terry Bryan, Dover, Del., 1975-76; missionary to Crow Indians Am. Bapt. Ch., Pryor, Mont., 1976-78, speaker, 1978—. Spkr., presenter Indian studies Endl. Resources Assn. Schs. Neighborhood chmn. Girl Scouts U.S., 1958; mem. Pryor Cmty. Planning Com., 1977; Sunday sch. tchr. So. Bapt. Ch., Cambridge, Md., 1946—88, Am. Bapt. Ch., Dover, 1946—88; v.p. programs, cir. leader, v.p. social concerns Am. Bapt. Women's Ministries, Dover, 1946—; bd. evangelism, prayer group leader 1st Bapt. Ch., Dover, 1957—, deaconess, 1970—, deacon emeritus, 1992, mem. 150th anniversary celebration com., 2000; active End-Time Handmaidens Missionary work, 1980—, Ch. Women United, 1959—66; leader, hostess 7 Holy Land tours; mem. steering com. Good Shepherd Bapt. Ch., 1990—91; convenor, mem. Order St. Luke the Physician, 1969—98. Mem.: DAR (chaplain 1992—95, 2001—, regent col. Haslet chpt. 1998—2001, state chaplain 2001—, voting del.), Christian Women's Club (various positions 1974—). Avocations: writing, art, photography, traveling. Home: 519 Wyoming Ave Dover DE 19904-4352

DEUKMEJIAN, GEORGE, lawyer, former governor; b. Albany, N.Y., June 6, 1928; s. C. George and Alice (Gairdan) D.; m. Gloria M. Saatjian, 1957; children: Leslie Ann, George Krikor, Andrea Diane. BA, Siena Coll., 1949; JD, St. John's U., 1952. Bar: N.Y. 1952, Calif. 1956, U.S. Supreme Ct. 1970. Mem. Calif. Assembly, 1963-67, Calif. Senate, 1967-79, minority leader; atty. gen. State of Calif., 1979-82, gov., 1983-91; former dep. county counsel Los Angeles County.; former ptnr. Sidley & Austin, 1991-2000. Served with U.S. Army, 1953-55. Republican. Episcopalian. Office: 5366 E Broadway Long Beach CA 90803-3549

DEUPREE, MARVIN MATTOX, accountant, business consultant; b. Woodbine, Iowa, Oct. 8, 1917; s. Archie Orin and Pearl (Mattox) D.; m. Katherine Anita Beard, Aug. 18, 1951; children: Marvin Mattox, Meredith Ann. BA with high distinction, State U. Iowa, 1941; MBA with distinction, U. Pa., 1948. C.P.A., N.Y., Ill., Mich., La., Iowa, Va., N.C. Instr. acctg. U. Pa., 1947-48; with Arthur Andersen & Co. (C.P.A.s), 1948-75, partner, 1960-75, mem. policy com. on acctg. and auditing, 1962-72; bus. cons., 1975—; pres. Emporium Specialties Co., Inc., 1977—. Adj. asso. prof. NYU Grad. Sch. Bus. Adminstrn., 1973-76 Contbr. articles to profl. jours. Served as officer USNR, 1943-46. Mem. AICPA, N.Y. State, Ill. Socs. CPA's, Nat. Assn. Accts., Am. Acctg. Assn., Execs. Club (Chgo.), Wharton Grad. Bus. Sch. Club (Chgo.), Univ. Club (Chgo.), Phi Beta Kappa. Episcopalian. Home: 5 Academy Rd Ho Ho Kus NJ 07423-1301

DE URIOSTE, GEORGE ADOLFO, software company executive; b. San Francisco, June 25, 1955; s. George Adolfo Sr. and Janet Germaine (Bruzzone) de U. BS, U. So. Calif., L.A., 1978; MBA, U. Calif., Berkeley, 1980. CPA, Calif. Auditor, cons. Deloitte Haskins & Sells, San Francisco, 1980-83; sr. fin. analyst Genstar Corp., San Francisco, 1983-85, Rolm Mil-Spec Computers, Inc., San Jose, Calif., 1986-88; mgr. fin. planning and analysis Ask Computer Systems, Inc., Mountain View, Calif., 1988-90; CFO TeamOne Systems, Inc., Sunnyvale, Calif., 1990-92; v.p. fin. and ops., CFO Remedy Corp., Mountain View, Calif., 1992-98; chmn., CEO Aeroprise, Inc., Mountain View, Calif., 2000—. Pres. U. So. Calif. Commerce Assocs., San Francisco, 1988-89; mem. area coun. Prison Fellowship Ministries. Mem. AICPA, Churchill Club (bd. dirs., vice chmn. Palo Alto, Calif. 1989-94), Fin. Execs. Internat. Avocations: tennis, hunting, fishing, skiing, mountain bike riding, antique auto restoration.

DEUTCH, JOHN M. former federal agency administrator, chemistry educator; b. Brussels, July 27, 1938; came to U.S., 1940, naturalized, 1946; s. Michael Joseph and Rachel Felicia (Fisher) D.; m. Pat Lyons; children: Philip, Paul, Zachary. BA, Amherst Coll., 1961, D.Sc. and Humane Letters (hon.), 1978; B. Chem. Engring, M.I.T., 1961, PhD in Phys. Chemistry, 1965; D.Litt. (hon.), U. Lowell, 1986. System analyst Office Sec. Def., 1961-65; fellow Nat. Acad. Scis./NRC, Nat. Bur. Standards, 1966-67; asst. prof. Princeton U., 1967-70; mem. faculty MIT, 1970—, prof. chemistry, 1971—, chmn. dept., 1976, dean sci., from 1982, provost, 1982-90, inst. prof., 1990—; under sec. for acquisition and technology Dept. of Defense, Washington, 1993-94, dep. sec.; dir. Central Intelligence, Washington, D.C., 1995-96; prof. MIT, 1996—. Chmn. adv. panel on chemistry NSF, 1974; mem. Def. Sci. Bd., 1977—, Pres.'s Nuclear Safety Oversight Com.; dir. Office Energy Rsch., U.S. Dept. Energy, Washington, 1977-79, acting asst. sec. for energy tech., 1979, under sec., 1979-80; mem. Army Sci. Adv. Panel, 1975-78, Pres.'s Commn. on Strategic Forces, 1983, The White House Sci. Coun., 1985-89; mem. Pres.'s Fgn. Intelligence Adv. Bd., 1990-94; chair Commn. on Nuclear Proliferation, 1998-99. Author research articles. Sloan fellow, 1969-71; Guggenheim fellow, 1974 Mem. Am. Phys. Soc., Am. Chem. Soc., Council Fgn. Relations, Am. Acad. Arts and Scis. Avocations: tennis, reading. Office: MIT Chemistry Dept 77 Massachusetts Ave Cambridge MA 02139-4307

DEUTSCH, ALINA, electrical engineer, researcher; b. Bucharest, Romania, June 6, 1949; came to U.S., 1969; m. Peter Deutsch, Apr. 21, 1974; 1 child, Simona. BSEE, Columbia U., 1971; MSEE, Syracuse U., 1976. Rshr. IBM Watson Rsch. Ctr., Yorktown Heights, N.Y., 1971—. Spkr. in field. Contbr. articles to profl. jours.; patentee in field. Fellow IEEE (bd. govs. 1999-2002, conf. chair 1995-98, workshop chair 1995-2002). Avocations: painting, book translator. Home: 5 Berol Close Chappaqua NY 10514 E-mail: deutsch@ieee.org.

DEUTSCH, BARRY JOSEPH, consulting and management development company executive; b. Gary, Ind., Aug. 10, 1941; s. Jack Elias and Helen Louise (La Rue) D. BS, U. So. Calif., 1969, MBA magna cum laude, 1970. Lectr. mgmt. U. So. Calif., L.A., 1967-70; pres., founder The Deutsch Group, Inc., L.A., 1970—; founder, CEO, chmn. bd., bd. dirs. Investment Planning Network, Inc., 1988—. Author: Leadership Techniques, 1969, Recruiting Techniques, 1970, The Art of Selling, 1973, Professional Real Estate Management, 1975, Strategic Planning, 1976, Employer/Employee: Making the Transition, 1979, Managing by Objectives, 1980, Conducting Effective Performance Appraisal, 1982, Advanced Supervisory Development, 1984, Managing a Successful Financial Planning Business, 1988, How to Franchise Your Business, 1991. Chmn. bd. govs. Am. Hist. Ctr., 1980—; mentor U. S.C. Career Advancement Program, 1999—. Mem. ASTD, Am. Mgmt. Assn., Am. Soc. Bus. and Mgmt. Cons., Internat. Mgmt. by Objectives Inst., Internat. Soc. for Performance Improvement, Organization Devel. Network, Planning Execs. Inst., Sponsors for Ednl. Advancement of Asians (bd. dirs.). Office: 1140 Highland Ave Ste 200 Manhattan Beach CA 90266-5335

DEUTSCH, DAVID M. lawyer; b. Dayton, Ohio, July 28, 1943; s. Jacob and Mary Deutsch; m. Joanne Deutsch. BS, Ohio State U., 1965; JD, Samford U., 1969. Bar: Ohio 1969, U.S. Ct. Appeals (4th, 6th cirs.) 1970, U.S. Ct. Appeals (11th cir.) 2000. Pvt. practice, Dayton, 1969—. Mem. head injury re-entry program adv. bd. Miami Valley Hosp., Dayton, 1991—. Chmn. Cmty. Rels. Coun., 1982-87, Supreme Ct. Ohio Commn. Continuing Legal Edn., 1994-99; bd. dirs. Greater Dayton Jewish Fedn., 1982-87; pres. govt. affairs com. Ohio Jewish Cmtys., 1986-88; bd. dirs., v.p. Temple Israel, Dayton, 1989-91. Mem. Ohio State Bar Assn. (sec. 1981-82), Ohio Acad. Trial Lawyers (governing trustee 1984-90), Dayton Bar Assn. Democrat. Avocations: skiing, jogging. Office: David M Deutsch Co LPA 208 W Monmument Ave Dayton OH 45402 E-mail: david@deutschatlaw.com.

DEUTSCH, DIDIER (DELAUNOY DEUTSCH), music producer, writer; b. Arcachon, France, Dec. 8, 1937; came to U.S., 1962; parents Ladislas Leopold and Simonne (Gruot) D. Baccalaureat, Michel Montaigne, Bordeaux, France, 1957. Dir. publicity CTI Records, 1973-77; publicity writer RCA Records, 1978-81; staff writer WEA Internat., 1983-86; record prodr. Columbia Records, N.Y.C., 1986—, Arista Records, 1997—, Rhino Records, 1995—, RCA Records, 1994-97, Time-Life Music, 1994-97. Drama critic musicals. Contbr. articles to Stereo Review, The New York Times, After Dark, Pulse! and other mags. and newspapers. Served with French Navy, 1957-60. Recipient nomination Grammy award for Frank Sinatra: The Columbia Years, 1995, Sony Music: Soundtrack for a Century, 2000. Mem. Nat. Acad. Rec. Arts and Scis., Am. Theatre Critics Assn.

DEUTSCH, DONNY, advertising executive; Grad., U. Pa. Chmn., CEO Deutsch, Inc., NYC, 1984—. Office: Deutsch Inc 111 8th Ave Fl 14 New York NY 10011-5295*

DEUTSCH, HARVEY ELLIOT, lawyer; b. Bklyn., Aug. 18, 1940; s. Harry Deutsch and Beulah (Deutsch) Koft; m. Paula Kantor, Nov. 26, 1964; children— Stacia Francine, Steven Harold, Karen Gail. B.A., So. Methodist U., 1962; LL.B., U. Tex., 1966. Bar: U.S. Dist. Ct. Colo. 1967, U.S. Ct. Appeals (10th cir.) 1967. Assoc., Holland & Hart, Denver, 1967-69; ptnr. Isaacson, Rosenbaum, Spiegleman & Friedman, Denver, 1970-82; v.p., gen. counsel Bill L. Walters Cos., Englewood, Colo., 1982-84; ptnr. Deutsch & Sheldon, Englewood, 1984—; lectr. in field. Contbr. chpts. to books. Bd. dirs. Anti-Defamation League of B'nai B'rith, Denver, 1976—; commr. Colo. Civil Rights Commn., 1972-80, chmn., 1976-78. Served with USNR, 1962-70. Mem. Tex. Bar Assn., Colo. Bar Assn. Office: Deutsch Spillane & Reutzel PC 7951 E Maplewood Ave Ste 329 Englewood CO 80111-4723 Home: 255 Cook St Denver CO 80206-5304

DEUTSCH, HERBERT ARNOLD, music educator; b. Baldwin, N.Y., Feb. 9, 1932; s. Barnet Baruch and Miriam (Meyersburg) D.; m. Margaret Ann Carbray, Oct. 10, 1955 (dec.); children: Lisbeth Ann, Edmund Barnet; m. Nancy DiNapoli Blau, Sept. 14, 1997. BS in Edn., Hofstra U., 1956; MusM, Manhattan Sch. Music, 1961; postgrad., NYU, 1973-75. Music faculty East Meadow (N.Y.) Pub. Schs., 1959-60; freelance musician N.Y.C. area, 1960-61; lectr. music Hofstra Univ., Hempstead, NY, 1961-63, instr., 1964-68, asst. prof., 1969-73, assoc. prof., 1974-79, prof., 1983—, dept. chair, 1995—2001, prof. emeritus, 2001—; dir. mktg. Moog Music div. Norlin Corp., Buffalo, 1980-81, dir. sales/mktg., 1981-83. Cons. Pulse Concepts, L.I., N.Y., 1971—, Jim Henson's Muppets, N.Y.C., 1983-86, Norlin Corp., Chgo., 1976-79; edn. cons. Music and Computer Educator, 1989-91. Author: Synthesis, 1975, 2d rev. edit., 1984, Electroacoustic Music: Its First Century, 1993; composer numerous mus. works; contbr. articles to profl. jours., 1972—, Am. Record Guide, 1987-93 Mem. Huntington (N.Y.) Spl. Edn. PTA, 1976-88; bd. dirs. Huntington Symphony, 1973-75, Suffolk County (N.Y.) Family Services, 1975-77. Served with U.S. Army, 1956-58. Recipient grad. assistantship, Manhattan Sch. Music, 1961, Estabrook Disting. Alumni award, Hofstra U., 1996, award for alumni achievment, 2001; grantee, Meet the Composer, 1976, 1986—88, 1990—98, 2000—03. Mem.: AAUP, ASCAP (awards 1992—), Music and Entertainment Industry Edn. Assn., Am. Fedn. Musicians, L.I. Composers Alliance (bd. dirs. 1972—91, v.p. 1991—95, pres. 1998—2000, archivist 2000—, founder, pres. 2003—).

DEUTSCH, JAMES BERNARD, lawyer; b. St. Louis, Aug. 24, 1948; s. William Joseph and Margaret (Klevorn) D.; m. Deborah Marie Hallenberg, June 26, 1976; children: Michael, Gabriel. BA, Southeast Mo. State U., 1974; JD, U. Mo., 1978. Bar: Mo. 1978, U.S. Dist. Ct. (we. dist.) Mo. 1978, U.S. Ct. Appeals (8th cir.), 1989, U.S. Supreme Ct., 1990. Assoc. Gt. Plains Legal Found., Kansas City, Mo., 1978-79; pvt. practice, Kansas City, 1979-81; gen. counsel Mo. Dept. Revenue, Jefferson City, Mo., 1981-83; commr. Mo. Adminstrv. Hearing Commn., Jefferson City, 1983-89; dep. atty.-gen State of Mo., Jefferson City, 1989-93; ptnr. Riezman & Blitz, P.C., Jefferson City, Mo., 1993-99; Ptnr. Blitz Bardgett & Deutsch LC, Jefferson City, 2000—. Served to lance cpl. USMC, 1968-70, Vietnam. Named one of Men of Yr. in Constrn. Industry, Engring. News, McGraw-Hill Pub., N.Y.C., 1985. Mem. ABA (jud. adminstrn. com.), ASCE (hon. fellow), Mo. Bar Assn. (council mem. taxation com. 1985—, adminstrn. law and jud. adminstrn. coms.), Mo. Inst. for Justice (bd. dirs. 1977—), VFW, Marine Corps League. Office: Blitz Bardgett & Deutsch LC 308 E High St Jefferson City MO 65101-3237 E-mail: jdeutsch@blitzbardgett.com.

DEUTSCH, JUDITH, clergywoman; b. N.Y.C., Apr. 18, 1929; d. Charles Shepard and Sadie (Freedman) Greene; m. Marshall E. Deutsch, June 27, 1947; children: Pamina Margret, Ethan Amadeus, Freeman Sarastro. BA, Hunter Coll., 1950; MA, New Sch. Social Rsch., 1965, Boston Coll., 1980. Ordained to ministry Unitarian-Universalist Ch., 1981. Dir. Hexiad, Cambridge, Mass., 1979-80; intern First Parish, Framingham, Mass., 1981; assoc. min. Unitarian-Universalist Soc., Hartford, Conn., 1982-85; interim min. First Parish Petersham, Mass., 1985-87, First Parish Sharon, Mass., 1988-90, Unitarian Universalist Ch., Worcester, Mass., 1990-91; min. Unitarian-Universalist Ch., Rockland, Mass., 1987-88, First Parish Medfield, Mass., 1991-2000, min. emerita, 2000—. Bd. dirs. Internat. League Religious Socialism, Stockholm; trustee Coop. Met. Ministries, 1999—; former chair religion and socialism commn. Dem. Socialists Am., 1989-95, bd. dirs.; chmn. Religious Coalition for Abortion Rights, Boston, 1987-90; acting pres. James Luther Adams Found., Newton, Mass., 1989-91, bd. dirs., sec., 1985—; former sr. co-chair Collegium, former chmn. ethics sect., co-chair faith-in-action com. First Parish. Producer, interviewer TV program Religous Issues in The News, 1994-95; author curriculum materials; contbr. articles to profl. publs. Co-chair Citizens for Kennedy and Johnson, Morris County, N.J., 1960; mem. Sudbury (Mass.) Dem. Town Com., 1985—; del. Mass. Dem. Conv., 1990, 94, 96, 2002, 03; lobbyist Coalition for Choice, Boston, 1988-92; mem. Medfield Alcohol and Other Drug Action Com., 1992-97; chair Religious Coalition for Reproductive Choice of Mass., 1996-97, mem. steering com.; candidate for state rep., 13th Middlesex dist., Mass., 2000; mem. Coun. on Aging, Sudbury, Mass., 2000—; mem. Mass. LWV Health Care Com.; chair Sudbury LWV Health Care Com. Hunter Coll. Hall of Fame inductee, 1999. Mem. Unitarian Universalist Ministers Assn., Liberal Religious Education Dirs. Assn., Mass. Bay Ministers Assn. Avocations: folk dancing, tai chi, cooking, reading, piano. Home and Office: 41 Concord Rd Sudbury MA 01776-2328 E-mail: revjd@aol.com.

DEUTSCH, LAWRENCE IRA, minister; b. Bklyn., June 17, 1939; s. Meyer Irving and Lillian (Ilkovitz) D.; m. Carolyn Ann Beaton, June 2, 1960 (div. Oct. 1986); children: Michael Keith, Eric Scott; m. Karol White, Dec. 31, 1987; stepchildren: Sharlette Lester, Jason Lester. AAS, Bklyn. Coll., 1961; BTh, Calvary Bible Coll., Lake Charles, La., 1990; MA, Cornerstone U., 1991; DRE, Moody Theol. Sem., 1992. Ordained to ministry Bapt. Ch., 1982. Pastor Congregation Beth Ha'Shem, Houston, 1988—. Chaplain T.D.C. & Houston Downtown Med. Ctr., 1981—; bd. dirs. Jesus the Messiah Sem., Beth Ha'Shem Christian Counseling Ctr. Author: Poetic Treasures-Past & Present, 1980, I Know a Place (Silver award), 1986, His Name is Peace (Golden award), 1987, Great Poems of Today, 1987 (Silver award), New American Poetry Anthology, 1988 (Golden award 1988, 89), Your Treasured Love (Golden award 1988, 89), 1988, A Moment Alone-A Collection of Poems, 1988, The Mystery of the Cloth, 1993, From Passover to the Lords Supper, 1993, Alternative to Assimilation, 1992, The Eight Great Covenants, 1993. Liaison officer to mayor Gulfport, Miss., 1968-69; founder Gulf Coast Acad. for the Performing and Visual Arts, 2000. With USMC, 1958-64. Recipient Silver award World of Poetry Press, 1986, Golden award, 1987-89. Mem. Internat. Writers Alive (v.p. 1990—). Republican. Mem. Messianic Ch. Home and Office: 3510 Greenwood Pl Deer Park TX 77536-5771 E-mail: larry_deutsch@mhhs.org. *LaChaim (To Life!). Life is very precious and very exciting. We need to make each day count to bring honor and glory to Yeshua Ha'Mashiach (Jesus the Messiah).*

DEUTSCH, MARSHALL E(MANUEL), medical products company executive, inventor; b. N.Y.C., Aug. 17, 1921; s. David and Madeline Lea (Roth) D.; m. Judith Greene, June 27, 1947; children: Pamina Margret, Ethan Amadeus, Freeman Sarastro. BS, CCNY, 1941; PhD, NYU, 1951. Tech. dir. NEN-Picker Radiopharms., Boston, 1966-68, Picker-Hoechst Inc., Bedford, Mass., 1968-70, Mead Diagnostics, Inc., Bedford, 1970-72, CIS Radiopharms., Bedford, 1972-74, Thyroid Diagnostics Inc., Bedford, 1972-85; chmn. Marshall Diagnostics Inc., Bedford, 1985-87; tech. adv. J&S Med. Assocs., Framingham, Mass., 1988—. Bd. dirs., corp. sec., v.p. Health Svcs. Internat., Washington, 1983-96; contractor Joint Publs. Rsch. Svc., Arlington, Va., 1984-92. Inventor self-contained technetium generator, 1971, various radiopharm. products, 1973, various clin. chem. test kits, devices, 1953-96; contbr. articles to mags. Cons. AID, Zaire, 1979, UN Capital Devel. Fund, Benin, 1977. 1st lt. A.C., U.S. Army, 1942-45, ETO. Fellow AAAS (life); mem. Am. Assn. Clin. Chemistry (emeritus, chmn. pub. rels. com. 1962), Am. Chem. Soc. (sr., emeritus), N.Y. Acad. Scis., Sci. Rsch. Soc. Am. Unitarian Universalist. Avocations: folk dancing, growing exotic mushrooms. Home: 41 Concord Rd Sudbury MA 01776-2328 Office: J&S Med Assocs Bldg 1 35 Tripp St Framingham MA 01702-8780 E-mail: med41@aol.com.

DEUTSCH, MARTIN BERNARD JOSEPH, editor, publisher; b. Karlsruhe, Fed. Republic of Germany, Apr. 7, 1931; came to U.S., 1939, naturalized, 1948; s. Benedikt and Margarethe (Zivi) D.; 1 son, Kenneth; m. Denise Elaine Brosius, Sept. 24, 1994; 1 adopted child, Ariel Jade YunXin. Student in history and journalism, CCNY, 1953; student in Eng. lit., Columbia U., summer 1955. CCNY coll. corr. N.Y. Times, 1951-53; mng. editor The Beachcomber, Long Beach Island, N.J., summers 1952, 53; reporter Southwest American, Ft. Smith, Ark., 1954-55; mng. editor Travel Courier and Travel Weekly, 1955-67; pres., editor, pub. travel mags. divsn. Ofcl. Airline Guides, N.Y.C., 1967-93; editor, pub. Reed Travel Mags., Secaucus, N.J., 1993-94; cons. travel industry shows (Cruise Tour World), Pleasanton, Calif., 2002—. CEO DB Prodns., Bedford, N.Y.; guest instr. U. Mass., 1975; cons., spkr. to travel and transp. industry. Monthly columnist: Up Front, Frequent Flyer mag., 1980-94; editor-at-large, monthly columnist Travel Agent mag., 1995-2001, pres. trade show divsn., 1995-99; pub. Selling North America, 1995-2000, CEO & columnist Travel Content on Demand, 2002—. Mem. Upper Manhattan Cmty. Planning Bd., 1965; mem. travel adv. bd. U.S. Dept. Commerce, U.S. Travel Svc., 1977-81; delegate White House Conf. on Travel and Tourism, 1995; officer Ctr. for Internat. Health and Coop., N.Y.C. With U.S. Army, 1953-55. Recipient various awards for travel journalism. Home and Office: 15 W 72nd St New York NY 10023-3402

DEUTSCH, NINA, musician, vocalist; b. San Antonio, Mar. 15; d. Irvin and Freda (Smukler) Deutsch. BS, Juilliard Sch. Music, 1964; MMA, Yale U., 1973. Concert pianist internat. and U.S. tours, 1965-82; entertainer, solo pianist Holland Am. Cruise Lines, 1987, 89-90; freelance pianist, lectr. music, 1990—. Exec. v.p. Internat. Symphony, N.Y.C., 1978—82. *Nina Deutsch achieved the first musical exchange on stage in the history of the People's Republic of China in 1982. As executive vice president of International Symphony for World Peace in 1982, she represented her organization in a series of concerts on that theme. ISWP had collected musical scores on the theme of Peace, Friendship, and Humanity. Her tour was endorsed by former U.S. President George Bush, and his brother Prescott Bush. Nina is also the first woman to have recorded the massive solo piano repertoire of Charles Ives. She presents lectures on leaders in American music and lectures with musical illustrations.* Musician (pianist): (albums) Charles Ives, 1976; author: (plays) Portrait of Clara Schumann, 1987, Portrait of Liberace, 1995; contbr. articles to mags. and newspapers. Bd. dirs. Metzner Found. Overseas Relief; Ft. Lee coord. Channel 13, 1974. Recipient award for Am. music, Nat. Fedn. Music Clubs, 1975; grantee, Philips Petroleum Found., 1982; scholar, Oberlin Coll.; Tanglewood fellow, Wulsin Fellowship, 1966. Mem.: Yale Alumni Assn. Bergen County. Avocations: swimming, hiking, baking. Home: PO Box 405 Leonia NJ 07605-0405 E-mail: ianist100@aol.com.

DEUTSCH, PETER R. congressman, lawyer; b. Bronx, NY, Apr. 1, 1957; m. Lori Ann Coffino; children: Jonathan Michael, Danielle Brooke. BA in Psychology, Swarthmore Coll., 1979; JD, Yale U., 1982. Atty., 1983—; mem. Fla. Ho. Reps., 1983—93, U.S. Congress 20th Fla. dist., 1993—; mem. energy and commerce com. Dir., founder Medicare Info. Program, Broward County, Fla., 1981-82. Recipient Humanitarian award Deborah Hosp., 1984, Torch of Liberty award Anti-Defamation League, 1985, Appreciation award Paralyzed Vets Assn., 1987, Scroll of Hon. Jewish Fedn., 1988; named Legislator of Yr. Broward County Chiropractic Soc., 1984, 85, Man of Yr. Lauderhill Regular Dem. Club, 1990, Alzheimer's Assn., 1990; Swarthmore Nat. scholar, 1975-79; J. Roland Pennock fellow, 1979. Mem. W. Broward Dem. Club, Broward Young Dems., Lauderhill Dem. Club, Pembrook Pines Dem. Club, Davie Dem. Club, United Dem. Club, Plantation Club, Sunrise C. of C., Tamarac C. of C., Margate Knights of Pythias, B'nai B'rith (Israeli award, Sunrise 1983), Jewish Fedn., Gold Key, Phi Beta Kappa. Democrat. Office: US Ho of Reps 2303 Rayburn Ho Office Bldg Washington DC 20515-0920*

DEUTSCH, ROBERT WILLIAM, physicist; b. Far Rockaway, N.Y., Mar. 21, 1924; s. Nathan and Lena (Berger) D.; m. Florence Kadish, Sept. 11, 1949; children: Jane Lisa, David Jeffrey. BS, MIT, 1948; PhD, U. Calif., 1953; LLD (hon.), U. Balt., 1999; LHD (hon.), Towson U., 1998; DSc (hon.), U. Md. Baltimore County, 2000. Registered profl. engr., Md., Mich. Physics cons. Martin-Marietta Corp., Balt., 1962-64; prof., chmn. dept. nuclear sci. and engring. Cath. U. Am., 1963-71; chmn. bd., CEO Gen. Physics Corp., Columbia, Md., 1966-87, RWD Tech. Inc., Columbia, 1988—. Contbr. articles to profl. jours.; author newspaper articles and pub. info. booklets on nuclear power. Bd. advisors U. Md. Tech. Advancement Program, 1988—; adv. bd. Johns Hopkins U., 1994—; bd. visitors U. Md. Baltimore County. Fellow Am. Nuclear Soc.; mem. NAE, AAAS, Am. Soc. Engring. Edn. Achievements include the founding of world class companies dedicated to improving human performance in high technology workplaces. Home: 8502 Arborwood Rd Baltimore MD 21208-1502 Office: RWD Tech Inc 5521 Research Park Dr Baltimore MD 21228 E-mail: rdeutsch@rwd.com.

DEUTSCH, SID, bioengineer, educator; b. N.Y.C., Sept. 19, 1918; s. Elias and Gussie (Hazen) D.; m. Ruth Appleman, Nov. 15, 1941 (div. June 1969), remarried, 1984; children: Alice, Phyllis, Naomi; m. Jane Arieti, Aug., 1969 (dec. Mar., 1978); m. Annette Page, Apr., 1979 (div. Dec., 1984). BEE, Cooper Union, 1941; MEE, Bklyn. Poly. Inst., 1947, PhD, 1955. Designer Fairchild Camera & Instrument Co., N.Y.C., 1943-44; instr. Madison Inst., Newark, 1946-50; engr. Poly. R & D Co., Bklyn., 1950-54; mem. faculty Bklyn. Poly. Inst., 1954-72, prof. elec. engring., 1962-72; prof. bioengring. Rutgers U. Med. Sch., Piscataway, N.J., 1972-79; vis. prof. U. S.Fla., Tampa, 1983-98. Vis. prof. Tel Aviv U., Israel, 1977, prof. bioengring, 1979-84; cons. Lewyt Mfg. Corp., 1958-60; affiliate Rockefeller Inst., 1961-64. Author: Theory and Design of TV Receivers, 1951, Models of the Nervous System, 1967, Return of the Ether: When Theory and Reality Collide, 1999; co-author: Biomedical Instruments: Theory and Design, 1976, 2d edit., 1992, Neuroelectric Systems, 1987, Understanding the Nervous System: An Engineering Perspective, 1993; assoc. editor: IEEE Transactions on Biomedical Engring., 1991-96; patentee pseudo-random dot scan for TV. Mem. adult edn. com. Roslyn (N.Y.) Pub. Schs., 1955-58. With USNR, 1944-46. Fellow IEEE, Soc. for Info. Display; mem. Sigma Xi, Tau Beta Pi, Eta Kappa Nu. Home: 3967 Oakhurst Blvd Sarasota FL 34233-1447 E-mail: deutsch@eng.usf.edu.

DEUTSCH, STANLEY, anesthesiologist, educator; b. N.Y.C., Apr. 4, 1930; s. Elias and Estelle (Press) D.; m. Margaret R. Zuanic, July 11, 1971; children: Susan, Ellen, Nina, Eva. BA, NYU, 1950; MA, Boston U., 1951, PhD, 1955, MD, 1957. Diplomate Am. Bd. Anesthesiology. Rsch. and teaching fellow in physiology Boston U. Sch. Medicine, 1951-55; intern U. Pa. Grad. Hosp., 1957-58; resident in anesthesiology Hosp. U. Pa., 1958-61; asst. prof. anesthesiology U. Pa., 1963-65; asst. prof. Harvard U., 1965-69; prof. U. Chgo., 1969-71; prof., head. dept. anesthesiology U. Okla. Health Scis. Center, 1971-82; prof. anesthesiology U. Tex. Med. Sch., Houston, 1982-89, George Washington Sch. Medicine, Washington, 1989-98, prof. emeritus, 1998—. Cons. VA Med. Center, Oklahoma City. Contbr. articles to profl. publs. Capt., M.C. USAR, 1961-63. Mem. AMA, Am. Soc. Anesthesiologists, D.C. Med. Assn., Sigma Xi, Alpha Omega Alpha. Home: 1508 Colonial Ct Arlington VA 22209-1439 Office: George Washington U Hosp 901 23rd St NW Washington DC 20037-2327

DEUTSCH, STANLEY, consulting company executive, behavioral scientist; b. Yonkers, N.Y. s. Benjamin Deutsch and Helene Klein; m. Thelma Fogel; children: Ellen, Robert, Paula. BA, Bklyn. Coll., 1948; MS, Purdue U., West Lafayette, Ind., 1951, PhD, 1957. Lic. psychologist Calif. Statistician Test & Advisement Unit Bklyn. Coll., 1948; rsch. psychologist Navy Electronic Lab, San Diego, 1948-57; human factors specialist Martin Co., Denver, 1957-58; chief human factors Douglas Aircraft Co., Santa Monica, Calif., 1958-62; dir. human factors programs HQ-NASA, Washington, D.C., 1962-80; cons. Home Factors/Ergonomics, 1980-84; study dir. human factors NRC/Nat. Acad. Sci., Washington, 1984-87; exec. dir. Inst. for Rsch. & Analysis, Bethesda, Md., 1987—. Cons. Inst. for Rsch & Analysis, Bethesda, 1980-84, 87—; exec. sec. Biotech & Human Rsch. Adv. Bd., HQ-NASA, Washington, 1962-66; space

biomedicine adv. bd. NASA, Washington, 1980-92. Editor, organizer: (symposium and proceedings) Human Factors in Automated & Robotic Space Systems, 1987; editor: (workshop report) Ergonomic Models, 1988. Mem. sch. adv. bd. Montgomery County Pub. Schs., 1963-68; judge science fairs Montgomery County, Bur. of Standards, Md., 1978-92; vol. tax counselor for the elderly IRS/AARP Montgomery County, Gaithersburg, Md., 1990-95. Technician U.S. Army, 1942-46. Recipient Meritorious Performance award U.S. Navy, San Diego, 1954, Superior Performance award NASA, Washington D.C., 1970. Fellow Washington Academy of Scis. (sec. 1985), Human Factors/Ergonomics Soc. (pres. 1972-73, exec. coun. 1968-78, founding pres., mem. exec. coun. Potomac chpt. 1967-89), Sigma Xi. Avocations: computer science, jewelry making, travel. Office: Inst for Rsch & Analysis 7109 Laverock Ln Bethesda MD 20817-4733 E-mail: stanthal@comcast.net.

DEUTSCH, STEPHEN B. lawyer; b. N.Y.C., Jan. 3, 1944; s. A. William and Rose (Berkowitz) D.; m. Jane M. Burnat, Nov. 23, 1986; children: Nancy, Jeffrey, Elizabeth. SB, MIT, 1965, PhD, 1969; JD, Harvard U., 1974. Bar: Mass. 1975, U.S. Dist. Mass., U.S. Ct. Appeals (1st cir.), U.S. Supreme Ct., U.S. Patent Office. Law clk. Supreme Judicial Ct. Mass., Boston, 1974-75; assoc. Foley, Hoag & Eliot, Boston, 1975-80, ptnr., 1981—. Mem. ABA, Mass. Bar Assn., Boston Bar Assn. Office: Foley Hoag LLP 155 Seaport Blvd Boston MA 02210

DEUTSCH, STUART LEWIS, law educator; b. Bronx, N.Y., Dec. 11, 1945; s. Abraham and Ruth (Zarkower) D.; m. Elizabeth A. Burki, Mar. 12, 1969 (div. 1985); 1 son, Michael J.; m. Holly W. Gauthier, May 17, 1986. BA, U. Mich., 1966; JD, Yale U., 1969; LLM, Harvard U., 1974. Bar: Calif. 1971, Ill. 1978, U.S. Dist. Ct. (no. dist.) Ill. 1978. Assoc. Olwine, Connolly, Chase, O'Donnell & Weyher, N.Y.C., 1969-70; assoc. prof. law U. Santa Clara, Calif., 1970-75; prof. law Chgo. Kent Coll. Law Ill. Inst. Tech., 1976-99, assoc. dean, 1987-90, 95-96, 1997-99, interim dean, 1996-97; dean, prof. of law Rutgers U., Newark, N.J., 1999—. Fellow in law and humanities Harvard Law Sch., Cambridge-,Mass., 1973-74; vis. assoc. prof. U. Ill. Coll. Law, Champaign, 1975-76; cons. various law firms and cmtys., Chgo., 1976—; mem. N.J. Commn. on Professionalism in the Law; bd. dirs. N.J. Inst. for Continuing Legal Edn., Pub. Interest Law Ctr. N.J. Author: Deutsch's Illinois Environmental Statutes Annotated, West, 1999, editor Land Use and Environment Law Rev., 1982-00; contbr. articles on land use and environment to profl. jours. Hearing officer Chgo. Commn. on Human Rels., 1992-98; chmn. bd. North Suburban Housing Ctr., Wilmette, Ill., 1983-87; chmn. adv. com., Eviction Ct., Chgo., 1986-89; chmn. interfaith Housing Devel. Corp., Wilmette, 1984-87; mem. atty. gen.'s Adv. Com. to Handicapped, Chgo., 1986-92; mem. attys.' revolving fund leadership coun. Met. Open Community Chgo., 1978-91. Named Outstanding Faculty Mem., Student Bar Assn., Ill. Inst. Tech., 1987, recipient Harold Washington Svc. award Black Students Assn., 1988, Distinguished Svc. award Chgo.-Kent Law Sch. Assn., 1998. Mem. ABA (diversity com., tech. com.), State Bar Ill., Internat. Council Environ. Law. Democrat. Jewish. Home: 224 Warwick Ave South Orange NJ 07079-2443 Office: Rutgers Univ Newark Sch of Law 123 Washington St Newark NJ 07102-3026 E-mail: sdeutsch@kinoy.rutgers.edu.

DEUTSCH, THOMAS ALAN, ophthalmologist, educator; b. Nagoya, Japan, Aug. 11, 1954; (parents U.S. citizens); William E. and Natasha S. (Sobotka) D.; m. Judith Silverman, Dec. 6, 1986. AB, Washington U., 1975; MD, Rush Med. Coll., Chgo., 1979. Diplomate Am. Bd. Ophthalmology. Intern Presbyn.-St. Luke's Hosp., Chgo., 1979-80; resident U. Ill. Eye and Ear Infirmary, Chgo., 1980-83; asst. prof. ophthalmology U. Ill., Chgo., 1983-84, Rush Med. Coll., Chgo., 1984-87, assoc. prof., 1987-94, prof., 1994—, chmn. ophthalmology, 1996—, assoc. dean grad. med. edn., 2000—, acting dean, 2002—. Lectr., U. Ill., Chgo., 1984-96; adj. asst. prof. biomed. engri., Northwestern U. Evanston, Ill., 1986-87, adj. assoc. prof., 1987-94, adj. prof., 1994-97. Assoc. editor Key Ophthalmology, 1986-88, Year Book Ophthalmology, 1986-88; author 6 books; contbr. articles to profl. jours. Recipient Chancellor's award Washington U., 1975, Henry Lyman award Rush Med. Coll, 1978, Mark Lepper tchg. award, 1994, Disting. Alumnus award Rush Med. Coll., 1998. Fellow: ACS, Am. Acad. Ophthalmology (sec. for instrn. 2001—02, sec. for new ophthalmic info. 2002—, Honor award 1990, Sr. Honor award 2003); mem.: Rush Alumni Assn. (pres. 1990—93, James A. Campbell award 1990), Chgo. Ophthalmol. Soc. (chmn. clin. conf. 1986, councillor 1988—89, sec.-treas. 1989—91, pres. 1994—95), Assn. Rsch. Vision Ophthalmology. Office: Rush Presbyn St Luke's Med Ctr 1725 W Harrison St Ste 918 Chicago IL 60612-3835

DEUTSCHE, KIRSTEN HANSEN, pharmaceutical company executive; b. Snartemo, Norway, June 2, 1949; came to U.S., 1952; d. Fridjof and Gerda Hansen; m. Donald Edgar Deutsche, Mar. 28, 1982 (div. Mar. 2000). BA, Central Coll., Pella, Iowa, 1971; MBA, NYU, 1998. Tchr. math. and sci. St. John's Sch., Dunellen, N.J., 1971-74; chemist BOC Inc., Murray Hill, N.J., 1974-82; regulatory affairs mgr. Anaquest/BOC Inc., Murray Hill, 1982-87, CIBA Geigy, Summit, N.J., 1987-88; regulatory affairs asst. dir. Organon/AKZO, West Orange, N.J., 1988-93; regulator affairs dir. Gynopharma, Somerville, N.J., 1993-95; pres., cons. Kearstin Pharm. Contracting, Summit, 1995—. Patentee in field. Active vol. Helpline, CASA, Supervised Visitation. Mem. Nat. Assn. Investors, Scandinavian House Assoc., Regulatory Affairs Profl. Soc., Am. Contract Bridge League (life master). Avocations: reading, travel, gardening, investing, exercise.

DEUTSCHMAN, LOUISE TOLLIVER, curator; b. Taylorville, Ill., Sept. 6, 1921; BA MacMurray Coll., 1937; postgrad., Northwestern U., U. Paris, 1950—66. Assoc. dir. Waddell Gallery, N.Y.C., 1966—74, Sidney Janis Gallery, N.Y.C., 1975—78; dir. Alex Rosenberg Gallery, N.Y.C., 1978—80; assoc. dir. Sidney Janis Gallery, N.Y.C., 1980—2000; curator Pace Wildenstein, N.Y.C., 2000—.

DEUTZ, NATALIE RUBINSTEIN, actress, consultant; b. Plymouth, Mass., Sept. 26; d. Louis and Lillian Rubinstein; m. Nov. 29, 1947 (dec.). Student, Simmons Coll., Modern Sch. Applied Art. Fashion buyer Wm. Filene's Sons Co., Boston, 1940-47; asst. to corp. pres. Columbia Textiles, Inc., N.Y.C., 1956-58; dir. John Robert Powers Sch., N.Y.C., 1968-72; v.p., nat. dir. fashion merchandising, dir. advt. workshop Barbizon Internat., Inc., N.Y.C., 1972-83. Cons., 1983— Films include Arthur on the Rocks, Crocodile Dundee, Moonstruck, Six Degrees of Separation; appeared on (TV) Sopranos; appeared in Super Elderly People for Japanese TV; commls. include Rogaine, Levis, Blockbuster. Mem.: AFTRA, SAG.

DEVAAN, JON, information technology executive; BS in Math. & Computer Sci., Oreg. State U. From mgr. to sr. v.p. Microsoft, Redmond, Wash., sr. v.p. TV divsn. Spkr. in field; panelist UN World TV Forum, 2000. Achievements include patents for simplifying user interface elements in PC applications. Office: One Microsoft Way Redmond WA 98052-6399

DEVALL, JAMES LEE, lawyer; b. Kansas City, Kans., Aug. 22, 1941; s. William Edward and Marie Etta (Culp) D.; m. Donna Jean Gould, Aug. 14, 1964; children: Carrie, David, John. BA, U. Kans., 1963; MA, Tufts U., 1964; JD, U. Calif., Berkeley, 1967. Bar: U.S. Dist. Ct. D.C. 1968, U.S. Ct. Appeals (D.C. and 9th cirs.) 1973, U.S. Supreme Ct. 1973. Legis. officer U.S. Bur. of the Budget, Washington, 1967-69; dir. legislation D.C. Govt., Washington, 1969-72; ptnr. Zuckert, Scoutt & Rasenberger, LLP, Washington; mem. CCH Aviation Law Coun., 1999—. Adj. prof. law Am. U., 1998— Mem. ABA, Fed. Bar Assn., Internat. Bar Assn., D.C. Bar Assn. Home: 6125 33d St NW Washington DC 20015-2403 Office: Zuckert Scoutt & Rasenberger 888 17th St NW Ste 600 Washington DC 20006-3309

DEVAN, DEBORAH HUNT, lawyer; b. Allentown, Pa., Jan. 22, 1950; d. Valerio R. and Audrey (Miller) H.; m. Mark S. Devan, May 30, 1981; children: Emily, David, Eric. BA in Econs. magna cum laude, U. Md., 1972, JD cum laude, 1975. Bar: Md. 1975, D.C. 1976, U.S. Dist. Ct. Md. 1976, U.S. Dist. Ct. D.C. 1987, U.S. Ct. Appeals (4th cir.) 1988, U.S. Ct. Appeals (2d cir.) 1991, U.S. Supreme Ct. 1980, Md. Ct. Appeals 1975, D.C. Ct. Appeals 1976. Ptnr. Weinberg and Green, Balt., 1974-94; prin. Neuberger, Quinn, Gielen, Rubin & Gibber, P.A., Balt., 1994—. Bd. dirs. Lutheran Hosp. Md., Inc., 1981-86, Cystic Fibrosis Found., 1983 (Community Svc. Gold award), Lutheran Health Care Corp., 1988-91, U. Md. Law Sch. Fund, 1991, Balt. Devel. Corp., 1999—, U. Md. Sch. Law Alumni Assn., 2000—; trustee Merry-Go-Round Enterprises, Inc. Fellow Am. Coll. Bankruptcy; mem. ABA (bus. bankruptcy com., subcommittee bankruptcy litigation, subcommittee claims and priorities), Am. Bankruptcy Inst., Turnaround Mgmt. Assn., Women's Bar Assn., Assn. Comml. Fin. Attys., Md. State Bar Assn., Inc. (subcommittee creditor's rights, bankruptcy and insolvency), Bankruptcy Bar Assn. Md. (corp. sec., bd. dirs., pres. 1996-97), Exec. and Profl. Women's Coun. Md. (1st v.p. 1984), Network 2000, Comml. Real Estate Women, Bar Assn. Balt. City (profl. ethics com. 1980, publicity com. 1981). Office: Neuberger Quinn Gielen Rubin & Gibber 1 South St Fl 27 Baltimore MD 21202-3282

DEVANE, DENIS JAMES, health care company executive; b. N.Y.C., Feb. 11, 1938; s. Eugene and Deborah (Courtney) D.; m. Margaret Mary Walsh, Oct. 14, 1961; children: Denise, Daniel, Deborah, Tara. BS, Fordham U., 1959. Asst. v.p. nat. sales mgr. C.I.T. Bldgs. Corp., N.Y.C., 1971-72, v.p., gen. mgr., 1973-74, pres., 1974-75; v.p. Lifemark Corp., Houston, 1975-80, sr. v.p., 1980-84; pres. Hosp. div. Health Group, Inc., Nashville, 1984; pres., chief operating officer Healthdyne, Inc., Marietta, Ga., 1985-86; pres., chief exec. officer Am. Rehab. Services Inc., Atlanta, 1987-88; chmn., CEO Rebound, Inc., Hendersonville, Tenn., 1989-92; exec. v.p. Healthsouth Corp., Birmingham, Ala., 1993-95; chmn. exec. com. Altria Healhcare Corp., Birmingham, 1997—, also bd. dirs. Bd. dirs. Shepherds Fold, Children's Village. Mem. Summit Club, Greystone Golf Club. Home: 1097 Greymoor Rd Birmingham AL 35242-7211

DEVANE, MINDY KLEIN, financial planner; b. Detroit, May 4, 1954; d. Myer and Maxine (Gold) Klein; m. Kenneth Manuel DeVane, Nov. 20, 1993. BS in Journalism, U. Fla., 1976, MBA in Fin., 1981. CFP. Mktg. rep. IBM, Tampa, 1981-85; account exec. Thomson McKinnon, Tampa, 1985-88, Smith Barney, Miami, 1988-89; underwriter Cigna, North Miami, Fla., 1989-92; sr. account exec. Cohig & Assocs., Tampa, 1992-93; v.p. Josephthal Lyon & Ross, Tampa, 1993-96; v.p. investments Raymond James, Tampa, 1996-99; fin. planner Griffith Bowles Fin. Mgmt. First Union Securities, Tampa, 1999—2001; proprietor DeVane Fin. Advisors, Tampa, 2001—. Allocations com. mem. United Way, Pinellas County, Fla., 1998, Hillsborough County, Fla., 1999; founder Hyde Park Exec. Women Leader Club, 1999-2002; bd. dirs. Vivo Fla. Orch. Guild, Sword of Hope; mem. ACS Guild. Recipient Outstanding Fin. Advisor award Asset Mgmt. Svcs. RJF, 1996-97. Mem. Fin. Planners Assn. (pres.-elect), Bus. and Profl. Women (editor 1986-88). Avocations: bicycling, swimming, collectibles. Home: 6308 Jacqueline Arbor Dr Temple Terrace FL 33617-3164 Office: PO Box 16626 Tampa FL 33687 E-mail: mdevane@tampabay.rr.com.

DEVANEY, CAROL SUSAN, management consultant; d. James H. DeVaney and Andrea Wong Mahoney; m. C. Eldon Taylor; 1 child, Taryne J. Taylor; 1 stepchild, Deborah A. Taylor (dec. 1997). BA, Cath. U., 1974, MSW, 1975. Nat. Acad. cert. social worker; lic. clin. social worker, Va. Cmty. educator Prince George Health Dept., Cheverly, Md., 1975-76; coord. social svcs. Detox Ctr., Cocoa, Fla., 1976-77; psychiat. social worker Brevard County Mental Health, Melbourne, Fla., 1977-79; sr. clin. social worker Chesterfield (Va.) Mental Health, 1979-81; coord. bus. programs Chesterfield County, Chesterfield, 1981-86; adminstr. orgnl. devel. and tng. Henrico County, Henrico, Va., 1986-90; owner, pres. DeVaney-Wong Internat., Fort Lauderdale, Fla., 1990—. Instr. Rollins Coll., Patrick AFB, Fla., 1977-79; cons. Coun. on Aging, Chesterfield, 1981-86; vol. Gilda's Club; adv. bd. Bermuda Run, Chesterfield, 1983-86. Contbg. author: Prevention in Community M.H. Practice, 1992; author: (manual) Stress Management, 1983; co-author: (book, manual, video) Let's Talk Diversity, 1992, Managing Diversity. Mem. Brind (Europe) Register Customer Recommended Cons., 1993-2001. Recipient program awards Nat. Assn. Counties, 1989-91. Mem. ASTD (v.p. comm. 1987-88, Richmond chpt. pres. 1989-90, founder/liaison nat. Ibero-Am. network 1990-97, D.C. met. v.p. programs 1997, v.p. programs Ft. Lauderdale chpt. 1998, internat. program conf. com. 2000-01, nat. advisor for chpts. 2001-03, program chair internat. conf. 2002, Nat. Torch award 1999, Citation award 2003), NASW, Soc. for Human Resource Mgmt., World Future Soc., Internat. Assn. Facilitators. Avocations: swimming, travel, ethnic cooking, languages, world philosophy.

DEVANEY, DENNIS MARTIN, lawyer, educator; b. Cheverly, Md., Feb. 25, 1946; s. Peter Paul and Alice Dorothy (Duffy) D.; m. Caryn Joanne; children: Jeanne Marie, Susan Theresa. BA in History, U. Md., 1968, MA in Govt. Politics, 1970; JD, Georgetown U., 1975. Bar: Md. 1976, D.C. 1976, Fla. 1977, Mich. 1999, U.S. Supreme Ct. 1980. Instr. European div. U. Md., Bremerhaven, Fed. Republic Germany, 1971-72; legis. asst. Md. Senate Jud. Commn., Annapolis, 1973-74; asst. gen. counsel U.S. Brewers Assn., Washington, 1975-77; counsel Food Mktg. Inst., Washington, 1977-79; ptnr. Randall, Bangert & Thelen, Washington, 1979-81; assoc. Tighe, Curhan & Piliero, Washington, 1981-82; mem. U.S. Merit System Protection Bd., Washington, 1982-88; gen. counsel Fed. Labor Relations Auth., Washington, 1988; mem. NLRB, 1988-94; commr. US Internat. Trade Commn., 2001; of counsel Winston & Strawn, 1995-97, Butzel Long, 1997—2001; ptnr. Williams, Mullen Clark and Dobbins, 2002—. Adj. prof. George Washington U., Washington, 1982—90, Boston U., 1992—94, 2002, Cornell U., 1995, Tulane U., 1995; assoc. prof. Wayne State U., 1995—2001. Served with USN, 1970-72, ETO. Mem. ABA, Md. Bar Assn., D.C. Bar Assn., Fla. Bar Assn., Mich. State Bar, Fed. Bar Assn., Phi Alpha Theta, Pi Sigma Alpha, Delta Theta Phi, Omicron Delta Kappa. Roman Catholic. Office: Williams Mullen 535 Griswold Fl 11 Buhl Bldg Detroit MI 48226 Home: 2661 Hidden Woods Dr Canton MI 48188-2477

DEVANEY, DONALD EVERETT, law enforcement official; b. Providence, Nov. 21, 1936; s. William Francis and Elizabeth Florence (Hill) D.; m. Tokiko Yoshida, May 19, 1960; 1 child, George Y. AA in Edn., El Paso Community Coll., 1973; BA, SUNY, Albany, 1979. Cert. healthcare protection adminstr. Internat. Healthcare Safety and Security Found. Sgt. maj. U.S. Army, 1954-83; customs inspector U.S. Customs Svc., Honolulu, 1983-84; provost marshal Tripler Army Med. Ctr., Honolulu, 1984—, regional chair Europe and Asia, 1989-93, 97—. Past dir. Kalihi-Palama Immigrant Svc. Ctr.; extraordinary min. of the eucharist Tripler Catholic Cmty.; sec. Friends Tripler Med. Ctr., Inc. Bd. dirs. Coalition for a Drug Free Hawaii, 1996—2000; sec. USO-Hawaii, 1998—2001; bd. dirs. U.S. Army Hawaii Housing Found., 2003—. Decorated Legion of Merit; recipient Disting Svc. award Hawaii Joint Police, 1977, 86, George Washington Honor medal Freedom's Found., 1973, Order Mil. Med. Merit, 1996, Elwood J. McGuire award Hawaii, 1997; elec. to Hawaii Jt. Police Assn. Hall of Fame, 1998, Nelson W. Aldrich H.S. Hall of Honor, 1998. Mem. Hawaii Joint Police Assn. (pres. 1985, 98, 99), CID Agt. Assn., Nat. Assn. for Uniformed Svcs. (v.p. Hawaii chpt., nat. bd. dirs. 1996-2000, 2002—, co-chmn. bd. nat. 2003—), U.S. Army Retiree Coun. (U.S. Army Hawaii vice chmn.), Internat. Assn. for Healthcare Security and Safety, Hawaii Coun. Police and Pvt. Security (bd. dirs. 1996—), Noncommd. Officer Assn. (life), Ret. Enlisted Assn. (life), DAV (life), Friend Med. Regt., Rotary (pres. Pearl Harbor chpt. 1991-92, dir. cmty. svc. dist. 5000, 1992-93), KC, Newtown Estate Cmty. Assn. (bd. dir.). Roman Catholic. Avocation: coin and stamp collecting. Home: 98-911 Ainanui Loop Aiea HI 96701-2766 Office: Office Provost Marshal Tripler Army Med Ctr Honolulu HI 96859-5000 Fax: (808) 433-4465. E-mail: donald.devaney@amedd.army.mil., ddevaney@hawaii.rr.com.

DEVANEY, DONNA BROOKES, lawyer; b. Orlando, Fla., Sept. 7, 1972; d. Edward Nolan and Carolyn (Jessen) B.; m. David Brooks DeVaney, Jr., May 24, 1997; children: Megan Kate, Sarah Grace. BS, Auburn U., 1993; JD cum laude, Stetson U., 1997. Bar: Fla. 1997, U.S. Dist. Ct. (mid. dist.) Fla. 1997, U.S. Dist. Ct. (so. and no. dists.) Fla. 1999, U.S. Ct. Appeals (11th cir.) 1999. Atty. Carlton Fields PA, Tampa, Fla., 1997—. Vol. Hillsborough Reads, Tampa, 1998-2000. Mem. ABA, Fed. Bar Assn., Fla. Bar Assn., Hillsborough County Bar Assn. (bd. dirs. young lawyers divsn.), Ferguson White Inn of Ct., Alpha House of Tampa, Inc. (bd. dirs.). Avocations: boating, swimming, running. Office: Carlton Fields One Harbour Pl Tampa FL 33602-5729 E-mail: ddevaney@carltonfields.com.

DEVANEY, EARL E. federal agency administrator; m. Judith Devaney; 2 children. BA in Govt., Franklin & Marshall Coll., 1970; grad. exec. devel. program, George Washington U., 1990. Joined Secret Svc., 1971, various positions including spl. agt., Chgo., spl. agt. in charge Office Investigations Washington, spl. agt. in charge Fraud Divsn.; dir. Office Criminal Enforcement, Forensics and Tng. EPA, 1991—99; inspector gen. U.S. Dept. Interior, Washington, 1999—. Office: US Dept Interior Inspector Gen 1849 C St NW Washington DC 20240

DEVANTIER, PAUL W. communications executive, broadcaster, administrator; b. Wausau, Wis., Mar. 25, 1946; w. Walter Herman and Ella Marie (Mundt) D.; m. Ellen Stapel, Aug. 2, 1970; children: Richard, John, Andrew, Katie, Susan. BA, Concordia Coll., 1968; M in Divinity, Concordia Seminary, 1972; M in Mass Comm., So. Ill. U., Edwardsville, 1993; LLD, Concordia U., 1998. Radio announcer Sta. WXCO, Wausau, 1965-68, Sta. KRCH, St. Louis, 1968-72; dir. devel. Sta. KFUO-AM-FM, St. Louis, 1972-74, gen. mgr., 1974-82; exec. dir. comms. Luth. Ch.-Mo. Synod, St. Louis, 1982-2000; chief comm. officer Bethesda Luth. Homes and Svcs., Watertown, Wis., 2000—02; nat. dir. Infant Adoption Awareness Tng. Program, Washington, 2002—. Speaker By the Way (internat. syndicated radio program) 1974—. Author: By the Way, 1993, By the Way, Encore, 1999; exec. prodr.: (religious documentary film) Hymn A Celebration of Change, 1984 (Angel award), (TV spl.) Easter Alive 'Round the World, 1993 (Emmy award nomination), (TV spl.) Not Without Hope, 1994 (Angel award), Martin Luther Promo, 1998 (Telley award), Message of Hope, 1998 (Angel award DeRose Hinkhouse award), Just in Time For Christmas, 1999 (Angel award De Rose Hinkhouse award), Message of Love, 2000 (Angel award); (radio) Lutheran School Spots, 1999 (Angel award), Classical Radio Station of the Year in America, 1999 (Marconi award), (video) Free to Voice the Gospel, 2000 (Angel award), By The Way, 2001 (Angel award), So Much Like Us, 2002 (Angel award, Wis. Coun. on Devel. Disabilities award); exec. dir. Lutheran Witness mag., 1999 (Associated Ch. Press Best of Class award). Trustee, pres. Luth. Film Assocs., N.Y.C., 1982-2000; bd. dirs. Excellence in Media, Hollywood, 2001—. Recipient Outstanding Parent award, Adoption and Foster Care Coalition, 2002. Office: Nat Coun for Adoption 225 N Washington St Alexandria VA 22314-2520 E-mail: pdevantier@infantadopt.org.

DEVANY, DONALD JOSEPH, II, music educator; b. Granite City, Ill., Nov. 27, 1974; s. Donald Joseph and Sondra Gay Devany; m. Melinda Samara Birger, July 7, 2001. B, Eastern Ill. U., 1998. Cert. tchr. Ill. State Bd. Edn. Band dir. Charleston H.S., 1998—99, Waubonsie Valley H.S., Aurora, 1999—2000, Glenbard Ea. H.S., Lombard, 2000—. Student adv. Glenbard Ea. H.S., 2001—; dir., jazz band Dist. 9 M.S., Ill. Music Educators Assn., 2002. Recipient Livinston C. Lord Scholar, Ea. Ill. U., 1996, Warner Presidl. Award, 1996—98. Methodist. Office: Glenbard East High School 1014 South Main st Lombard IL 60148

DEVARIS, JEANNETTE MARY, psychologist; b. Burbank, Calif., Jan. 7, 1947; d. Nicholas Propper Klein and Elizabeth (Von Lichtenberg) Schaeffer; m. Robert Lee Blake, May 20, 1967 (div. 1979); 1 child: Brendon; m. Panayotis Eric DeVaris, Dec. 5, 1988. BA, Adelphi U., 1968; MA, Fairleigh Dickinson U., 1977; PhD, Seton Hall U., 1987. Lic. psychologist, N.J. Caseworker N.Y.C. Welfare Dept., 1968-72; alcohol and drug rehab. counselor U.S. Army, Ft. Monmouth, N.J., 1972-76; psychol. intern N.J. State Intern Program, Trenton, 1977-78; psychologist Greystone Psychiat. Hosp., Greystone Park, N.J., 1979; sr. psychologist R. Hall Community Mental Health Ctr., Bridgewater, N.J., 1979-90; pvt. practice South Orange and Somerset, N.J., 1988—. Tng. supr. Grad. Sch. Applied and Profl. Psychology; adj. prof. Seton Hall U.; sponsor and participant in Cable TV program; mem. South Orange Critical Support Team Vol. Group of Psychologists. Contbr. articles to profl. jours. Mem. APA, Nat. Register Health Svc. Providers, N.J. Psychol. Assn. (bd. dirs., interprofl. rels. com.), Soc. Psychologists in Pvt. Practice (bd. dirs., spkrs. bur. com.). Avocations: travel, reading.

DEVARIS, PANAYOTIS ERIC, architect; b. Lefkas Island, Greece, Dec. 29, 1932; came to U.S., 1960; M.Arch, Ecole des Beaux Arts, Paris, 1960; grad. cert. in bus. adminstrn., L.I. U., 1981. Registered architect; cert. Nat. Council Archtl. Registration Bds.; cert. profl. planner. Sr. corp. architect AT&T, N.Y.C., 1972-90, PSE&G, N.J., 1990-93, cons., 1990-93; pres. DeVaris/Workspace Planning & Design, Inc., 1990-97. Prin. works include projects in N.Y.C.: World Trade Ctr., Park Lane Hotel, The Gershwin Theatre, The Sovereign Apts., The Uris Office Bldg.; in Conn.: Wesleyan U. Dormitories, 1960-72; for AT&T: Microelectronics Hdqs., Berkeley Heights, N.J., Network Software Ctr., Lisle, Ill., AT&T Corp. Ctr., Chgo., Materials Mgmt. Ctrs., Sacramento, Calif., Wichita, Kans., Ramapo, N.Y., AT&T Techs. Offices, Tokyo, 1972-90; author, internat. lectr. in field of work environments; juror furniture design competition Corp. Design mag., Annual Design Awards N.Y. State Assn. Architects; contbr. articles to trade mags. Mem. exec. com. Architects for Social Responsibility, 1988-90. Recipient tech. excellence award Western Electric Co., Inc., 1983. Fellow AIA (chmn. corp. architects com. N.Y. chpt. 1978, nat. chpt. 1986, N.J. chpt. 1992, mem. steering com. 1983-90, rep. to Internat. Union of Architects 1985-91). Home: 18 Harding Dr South Orange NJ 07079-1203

DE VARON, LORNA COOKE, choral conductor; b. Western Springs, Ill., Jan. 17, 1921; d. Vernon Walter and Hazel Mildred (Watts) Cooke; m. Jose de Varon, May 14, 1944; children: David, Joanna, Cristina, Alexander. BA, Wellesley Coll., 1942; MA, Radcliffe Coll., 1945; MusD honoris causa, New Eng. Conservatory, 1988. Asst. condr. Radcliffe Choral Soc., Radcliffe-Harvard Choir, 1942-44; condr. Bryn Mawr Coll. Choir, 1944-47; condr. chorus, chmn. choral dept. New Eng. Conservatory Music, Boston, 1947-88, condr. chorus for concerts with Boston Symphony Orch., 1952-86; concert performer New Eng. Conservatory Chorus, tours in U.S., Europe, Russia, Israel, China; condr. Israel Summer Festival, 1977-79; condr., tchr. choral conducting Tanglewood Festival Chorus, 1952-66; condr. New Eng. Conservatory Camerata, 1989—; prof. emerita New Eng. Conservatory; condr. Longy Chamber Chorus, 1989—. Guest condr. Cameron Singers, Israel, 1984, Radio Chorus Beijing, 1987; chmn. Choral Inst. of Composers Conf., 1983-85; mem. choral adv. panel Nat. Endowment for Arts; condr. New Eng. Conservatory Chamber Singers, summers 1982-87, Monadnock Music Festival. Editor, arranger choral works, E.C. Schirmer and Galaxy Pubs., Boston. Mem. Cambridge Arts Council. Recipient medal for Disting. Achievement City of Boston, 1967, medal for Disting. Achievement Radcliffe Grad. Soc., 1972, medal for Disting. Achievement Wellesley Coll., 1978, medal of Israel, 1977, Ludi award New Eng. Conservatory, 1983, Harvard Glee Club medal, 1987. Mem. Am. Choral Condrs. Assn., Pi Kappa Lambda. Home: 94 Lake View Ave Cambridge MA 02138-3326

DEVASSIE, TERRY LEE, publishing executive; b. Columbus, Ohio, Oct. 27, 1939; s. Robert William and Laura Belle (VanOrsdel) DeVassie; m. Lola Faye Sandifer, June 21, 1964; children: Trevor Lane, Thad Lamont. BA in Indsl. Design, Columbus Coll. Art & Design, 1964. Clk., sta. mgr. Columbus Dispatch, 1957-70, divsn. mgr., 1970-71, asst. to circulation dir., 1971-77, state circulation mgr., 1977-79, circulation mgr., 1979-81, asst. circulation dir., 1981—2001; ptnr. Preston-Strat Investments, 1993—; pres., CEO Creative Inserts Co., 1992—; mng. ptnr. WW Circulaton Cons. Group, 2002—. Owner, designer TLD Design, Columbus, 1964—69; arch.-designer Eagle Real Estate/Builders, Columbus, 1968—70; extrusion designer Plaskolite, Inc., Columbus, 1968—69; pub. spkr. newspaper circulation mgmt. and hosps. Designer drive-up newspaper rack, patentee graphic inserts for newspaper racks. Trustee Shriners Hosps. Children, 1996—; bd. govs., exec. com. Shriners Hosp. Burn Ctr., Cin., 1986—96; bd. govs. Lexington Unit of Shriners Hosp., 1991; endowment com. Simon Kenton Coun., Boy Scouts Am., 1998—2002; bd. dirs. St. Anthony Hosp., Columbus, 1987—91, Mercy Hosp., Columbus, 1987—91. Mem.: Press Club Ohio (pres. 1983, 1984), Circulation and Mktg. Fedn. Newspaper Assn. Am., Newspaper Assn. Am. (newspaper coun.), Internat. Circulation Mgrs. Assn. (chmn. Internat. Newspaper Carrier Day 1982—84), Ohio Newspaper Assn. (chmn. conv. 1983, Pres.'s award 1984), Ohio Circulation Mgrs. Assn. (sr. coord., instr. circulation mgmt. 1980—2000, pres. 1982, founder Pres.'s award 1982, Pres.'s award 1986), Charity Newsies, Shriners (Illustrious Potentate Aladdin Temple 1995, imperial pub. rels. com. 1995, chmn. edowment, wills and gifts for Shriners hosps. for children 1998—2000), Masons (33 degree). Republican. Methodist. Avocations: landscaping, architectural building and designing, coin collecting, golf. Home: 5808 La Paz Pl Westerville OH 43081-4112 E-mail: tdevassie@shrinenet.org.

DEVAUD, JUDITH ANNE See HALVORSON, JUDITH

DEVAUGHN, MICHAEL RICHARD, minister, administrator; b. Boston, July 6, 1959; s. Ludie David and Rose Anna Moore DeV.; 1 child, Terrance T. Moody. BA, Ind. U., 1984; MDiv, So. Meth. U., 1988; DDiv (hon.), Faith Inst. Christian Theology, 1994. Ordained elder, CME Ch. Sr. min. Antioch CME Ch., Abilene, Tex., 1988-89, St. Paul CME Ch., Midland, Tex., 1989-91; dean institutional advancement Tex. Coll., Tyler, 1991-93; sr. min. Starrville CME Ch., Tyler, Tex., 1991-93, Carter Chapel CME Ch., Amarillo, Tex., 1993—; exec. dir. Black Hist. Cultural Ctr., Amarillo, 1996—. Bd. dirs. Amarillo (Tex.) Opera, 1994—, United Way, Amarillo, 1994—, Salvation Army, 1994—; city councilman City of Midland, Tex., 1990. Mem. Nat. Soc. Fundraising Execs., Coalition of Black Men, Downtown Lions Club (planning chair), Tex. Lions Camp. Democrat. Methodist. Avocations: reading, gourmet cooking, writing, golfing, traveling. Home: 111 S Jackson St Amarillo TX 79101-1331 Office: Amarillo United Citizens Forum PO Box 2353 Amarillo TX 79105-2353 E-mail: michaeldevaughn@amaonline.com.

DEVAUL, DIANE D. policy director; b. Ames, Iowa, July 12, 1943; d. Wayne Allen DeVaul and Ruth Louise Dana; m. Thomas Andrew Twomey, June 6, 1965 (div. Oct. 1978); children: Heather B. Twomey, Antonio DeVaul; m. Hagos Alemayehu, Apr. 30, 1982; 1 chlid, Victor Hagos DeVaul. BA, U. Iowa, 1965; MA, U. Md., 1972, PhD, 1998. Instr. Am. U., George Mason U., U. Md., 1976-77; policy analyst N.E.-Midwest Inst., Washington, 1978-86, dir. policy, 1986—; cons. to asst. sec. U.S. Dept. HUD, Washington, 1979. Dir. N.E. Regional Resource Ctr. for Innovation, U.S. Dept. Energy, Washington, 1997-2002, mem. grant rev. panel, 1998-2001; presenter in field. Author poetry book, 1979; contbr. articles to profl. jours. Recipient Commendation, Gov. of N.H., 1998. Mem. Am. Studies Assn. Office: NE-Midwest Inst 218 D St SE Washington DC 20003 E-mail: ddevaul@nemw.org.

DEVAULT, JOHN LEE, oil company executive, geophysicist; b. Kansas City, Mo., Aug. 4, 1937; s. Isaac Henderson and Evelyn Margaret (Rowell) DeV.; m. Janet Ann Miller, Sept. 11, 1968; children: Bryan Charles, Chris Lee. B Chem. Engring., Case Inst. Tech., Cleve., 1959; BS, MacMurray Coll., Jacksonville, Ill., 1961; MS, U. Houston, 1975. Lic. geophysicist, Calif., Am. Assn. Petroleum Geologists, Am. Inst. Profl. Geologists, Soc. Ind. Profl. Earth Scientists. Geophysicist United Geophys., Europe, Africa, Middle East, Australia-Asia, Alaska and Houston, 1961-74; pres. Sercel Inc., Houston, 1974-88; chmn. Jade Corp., Houston, 1988—. Contbr. articles to Oil and Gas Jour. Dir. Jaycees, Springfield, Ill., 1960; downstate v.p. Young Rep. Club, Springfield, 1960; bd. dirs. Honors Coll., U. Houston, 1990—, MacMurray Coll.; trustee Culver Legion-Culver Academies. Mem. Geophys. Soc. Houston (hon. life, pres. 1987), Soc. Exploration Geophysics (1st v.p. 1993), Am. Inst. Profl. Geologists (pres. Tex. sect.), Culver Club of Greater Houston (pres.). Mem. Christian Ch. (Disciples Of Christ). Home: 703 Queensmill Ct Houston TX 77079-2411 Office: Jade Corp PO Box 218567 Houston TX 77218-8567

DE VEIRMAN, GEERT ADOLF, engineer; b. St. Amandsberg, Belgium, Nov. 20, 1961; came to U.S., 1984; s. Marcel M. De V. and Hilda Verschueren; m. Michele Y. Mage, Dec. 31, 1994. MSEE, Cath. U. Leuven, Belgium, 1984; PhD, U. Minn., 1988. Sr. design engr. I Silicon Systems, Tustin, Calif., 1988-90, sr. design engr. II, 1990-93, group leader, 1992-99, prin. engr., 1993-96, sr. prin. engr., 1996-99; tech. mgr. Tex. Instruments SPG, Tustin, Calif., 1999-2000; dir. analog IC devel. Agere Sys., Huntington Beach, Calif., 2001—. Contbr. articles to profl. jours. Fellow IEEE, IEEE CAS Soc. (v.p. 2000—), Eta Kappa Nu, Phi Kappa Phi. Home: 322 Orchid Ave Corona Del Mar CA 92625 Office: Agere Sys Ste 300 7777 Center Ave Huntington Beach CA 92647 E-mail: deveirman@agere.com.

DEVELLANO, JAMES CHARLES, professional hockey manager, baseball executive; b. Ont., Can., Jan. 18, 1943; came to U.S., 1979; s. James Joseph and Jean (Piter) D. Ont. scout St. Louis Blues NHL, Toronto, 1967-72; eastern Can. scout N.Y. Islanders, Toronto, 1972-74, dir. scouting, 1974-82; asst. gen. mgr. Islanders, L.I., N.Y., 1981-82; gen. mgr. Detroit Red Wings, 1982-90, sr. v.p., 1990—; v.p., gen. mgr. Indpls. Checkers, 1979-81; sr. v.p. Detroit Tigers, 2001—. Alternate gov. for Detroit Red Wings. Winner Stanley Cup with N.Y. Islanders, 1979-80, 80-81, 81-82, with Detroit Red Wings, 1996-97, 97-98, 2001-2002, Pres.'s Trophy with Detroit Red Wings, 1994-95, 95-96, 2001-2002. Mem. Nat. Hockey League (bd. govs.). Office: Detroit Red Wings Hockey Club Joe Louis Arena 600 Civic Center Dr Detroit MI 48226-4419

DEVENDORF, LOUISE MARIE, promoter, writer; b. LeRoy, Mich., Apr. 5, 1939; d. Louis George and Lucille Mariam (Dean) Hinkley; m. Richard George Devendorf, Aug. 10, 1974; 1 child, Laurie Anne Jarboe. Grad. high sch., 1957. Underwriter asst. Mich. Mut. Liability, Grand Rapids, 1957-63; dance instr. Arthur Murray Studio, Grand Rapids, 1959-61; insp. Wolverine Worldwide, Big Rapids, Mich., 1965-85; office mgr. Advt. Assocs., Grand Rapids, 1985-89; free-lance writer and promoter Reed City, Mich., 1989—. Author: Some Nostalgia Pertaining to Pearls, 1995, (poetry) War in Haiti, 1996. Mem. City Coun., Reed City, 1988—; mem. ex officio Libr. Bd., Reed City, 1992—; bd. dirs. Osceola Cares, Osceola County, 1993—, pres.; active Phone Tree, Reed City, 1995—; musician Furniture City Orch., 1957-59; pres. Sr. Adult Ministries Ch. of the Nazarene, 1999—. Recipient award Internat. Soc. Poets, 1996; elected to Internat. Poetry Hall of Fame, 1997. Avocations: reading, playing music, helping people. Home: 311 W Franklin PO Box 91 Reed City MI 49677-0091

DEVENIS, KEISTUTIS PETER, civil engineer, consultant; b. Waterbury, Conn., Mar. 25, 1928; s. Michael and Alena (Vileisis) D.; m. Luanna Ellis, June 6,1953 (div. 1982); children: Luanna Elena, Jonas Ellis; m. Inga Mary Percy, Apr. 9, 1985. BE, Yale U., 1948; MS, MIT, 1950, CE, 1956. Registered profl. engr., Mass. Engr. Maguire Group, Inc., Boston, 1950-80, sr. v.p., 1980-86, cons., 1986—. Adv. bd. So. Mass. U., Dartmouth, 1986—. Author: Ancient Lithuania and the History of Deltuva, 2002; contbr. articles to Boston Soc. Civil Engrs., Pub. Works Jour., Jour. New Eng. Water Pollution Control Assn., ASCE Jour. Pres. Nashawtuc Country Club, Concord, Mass., 1970. Cpl. U.S. Army, 1951-53. Recipient Presdl. award for design excellence, Charles River Project, 1986. Mem. ASCE, Boston Soc. Civil Engrs. (Desmond Fitzgerald medal 1965, 75), Water Pollution Control Fedn., Am. Water Works Assn. New Eng. Water Works Assn., New Eng. Water Pollution Assn. Republican. Home: 9 S Meadow Rdg Concord MA 01742-3000 Office: Maguire Group Inc 225 Foxborough Blvd Foxboro MA 02035-2885

DEVENNY, LILLIAN NICKELL, trophy company executive; b. Chesapeake, Ohio; d. Hayes Basil and Alice Irene (Noble) Nickell; m. John Paul DeVenny Jr., Dec. 31, 1955; children: Carrie DeVenny Paganini (dec.), John Hayes. Student, Covington Bus. Sch., 1954-55, Norfolk Coll., 1980-81. Office mgr., bookkeeper Nickell Electric Co., Covington, Va., 1950-55, exec., 1960-62; sec. 5th Naval Dist. Hdqtrs., Norfolk, Va., 1955-58, Profl. Realty, Virginia Beach, 1971; pub. rels. corp. sec. Hobby Industries, Virginia Beach, 1973-74; owner, sec.-treas. Deste Corp. t/a Hobby Assoc., Virginia Beach, 1974—. Singer, actress Tidewater Dinner Theater, Norfolk, 1971-75; mem. numerous continuing edn. units. Writer column on Va. travel, 1978-79; editor newsletter, 1972-73. Founding mem., chair bd. dirs. Va. Opposing Drunk Driving, 1981—, state v.p., 1981-86, state pres., 1986—; adv. bd. Va. Commn. on Alcohol Safety, 1987-91: participant Va. Assembly on Future of Va.'s Cts., U. Va., Commn. Pub. Svc., 1989; mem. spl. White House briefing on ways to combat tragedy of drunk driving, 1989; active Va. Civilian-Mil. Comty. Safety Com., 1988, Va. Alcohol Safety Action Program Commn., 1991—; co-chair Va. Coalition Against Drunk Driving, 1989—; contbr. passage Omnibus Alcohol Safety Act, Va. Gen. Assembly, 1994; legis. liaison for CCATS Transp. Safety Coalition, 1998-2003; apptd. mem. Gov.'s Task Force to Combat Drunk Driving, 2002. Recipient Cmty. Svc. award J.C. Penney Co., 1985, Hometown Hero, Sta. WVEC-TV, 1986, Gov.'s Transp. Safety award, 2000, Lifetime Achievement award Civilian/Mil. Workshop, 2002. Mem.: Internat. Ceramists Assn., Modern Woodmen Am. (regional sec. 1954). Episcopalian. Avocations: singing, costume design, reading, theatre, herb gardening. Office: Deste Corp t/a Hobby Assocs 5815 Hargrove St Norfolk VA 23502-4636

DEVENOT, DAVID CHARLES, human resource executive; b. Indpls., May 27, 1939; s. Charles Joseph and Pearl (Geodfry) D.; children: Daniel, Mark. BBA, U. Hawaii, 1962. Dir. indsl. rels. USP Corp subs. Consol. Foods, Sara Lee, San Jose, Calif., 1964-70; sr. human resource cons. Hawaii Employers Coun., Honolulu, 1970—. Bd. dirs. Hawn Humane Soc., Honolulu, 1975—, Am. Cancer Soc., 1989, pres. Pacific divsn. Mem. Santa Clara Valley Pers. Assn. (pres. 1968-69), Soc. Human Resource Mgmt., Indsl. Rels. Rsch. Assn. Avocations: travel, photography, watercolor painting, bicycling. Home: 2803 Puuhonua St Honolulu HI 96822-1765 Office: Hawaii Employers Coun 2682 Wai Wai Loop Honolulu HI 96819-1938

DEVENS, JOHN SEARLE, natural resources administrator; b. Shickshinny, Pa., Mar. 31, 1940; s. John Ezra and Laura (Bulkley) D.; m. Sharon I. Snyder (div. 1979); children: John, Jerilyn, James, Janis. BS, Belmont Coll., 1964; MEd, Emory U., 1966; PhD, Wichita State U., 1975. Dir. speech and hearing Columbia Coll., Columbia, SC, 1967—70; head dept. audiology Inst. Logopedics, Wichita, Kans., 1970—71; supr. audiology State of Alaska, Fairbanks, 1971—73; asst. prof. U. Houston, Victoria, Tex., 1975—77; pres. Prince William Sound C.C., Valdez, Alaska, 1977—92, Sterling Coll., Craftsbury Common, Vt., 1993—96; dir. Valdez Hearing and Speech Ctr.; exec. dir. Prince William Sound Regional Citizens' Adv. Coun., 1997—; prin., owner The Lake House a Country Inn, Valdez, 2000—. Owner, operator Valdez Hearing and Speech Ctr., 1977—92, Lake House Country Inn, 2000—. Prodr. films on hearing problems; contbr. articles to profl. jours. Mayor City of Valdez, 1985-89, mem. city coun., 1980-89; nat. chmn. adv. com. Horsemanship for Handicapped, 1964-67; mem. Alaska Gov.'s Coun. for Handicapped, 1980-82; pres. Valdez chpt. Alaska Visitors Assn., 1980; mem. small cities adv. coun. Nat. League Cities, 1983-87, mem. internat. econ. devel. task force; mem. Nat. Export Coun.; bd. dirs. Resource Devel. Coun.; Dem. nominee U.S. Ho. Reps., 1990, 92; hosted internat. conf. on oil spills for mayors; exec. dir. Prince William Sound Regional Citizens Adv. Coun., 1997—. Mem. Am. Speech-Lang. Hearing Assn. (cert. clin. competence in audiology and speech and lang. pathology), Am. C. of C. in Korea, Valdez C. of C., Alaska Mcpl. League (bd. dirs. 1984-89). Methodist. Avocation: charter boat operator. Home: PO Box 770 Valdez AK 99686-0770 Office: PO Box 3089 Valdez AK 99686-3089 E-mail: jhdvns@aol.com.

DEVENS, PAUL, lawyer; b. Gary, Ind., June 8, 1931; s. Zenove and Anna (Brilla) Dewenetz; m. Setsuko Sugihara, Aug. 14, 1955; children: Paula, Vladimir, Mignon. BA in Econs. cum laude, Ind. U., 1954; LLB, Columbia U., 1957. Bar: N.Y. 1958, U.S. Dist. Ct. Hawaii 1960, Hawaii 1961, U.S. Ct. Appeals (9th cir.) 1962, U.S. Ct. Internat. Trade 1963, U.S. Supreme Ct. 1970. Pvt. practice law, N.Y.C., 1958-60; ptnr. Lewis, Saunders & Key, Honolulu, 1960-69; corp. counsel City and County of Honolulu, 1969-72, mng. dir., 1973-75; ptnr. Devens, Nakano, Saito, Lee, Wong & Ching, Honolulu, 1975-94, of counsel, 1994—2002; ret., 2002. Judge Nuclear Claims Tribunal, Majuro, Republic of the Marshall Islands, 1988-90. Mem. Japan-Hawaii Econ. Coun., 1975-95, Honolulu Charter Reorgn. Com., 1979-80, Pacific and Asian Affairs Coun., 1983; trustee Japan-Am. Soc. Honolulu, 1981—, pres., 1987-89; chmn. bd. dirs. Nat. Assn. Japan-Am. Socs., 1989-91; mem. bd. govs. Japanese Cultural Ctr., Hawaii, 1989-94, mem. bd. dirs., v.p., 1994-96, chmn. bd. dirs., 1996-97. Decorated Imperial Order of the Sacred Treasure, Gold Rays with Neck ribbon Govt. of Japan, 1993. Mem.: Phi Beta Kappa. Democrat. Eastern Orthodox. Office: Devens Nakano Saito Lee Wong & Ching 220 S King St Ste 1600 Honolulu HI 96813-4597

DEVENS, RICHARD MATHER, publishing executive, economist; b. Boston, Aug. 15, 1950; s. Richard M. and Sylvia (Pearson) D.; m. Rita Sheehan, June 29, 1986; children: Richard M. III, Timothy Joseph. BA in Internat. Rels. and Econs., Am. U., 1976, MA in Econs., 1979. Economist Bur. of Labor Stats., Washington, 1976-80, sr. economist, 1983-94; internat. fellow Columbia U., N.Y.C., 1980-81; corp. rschr. Horizon House, Dedham, Mass., 1982; exec. editor Monthly Labor Rev., Washington, 1994—. Editl. dir.: Report on the American Workforce, 1994, 95, 97, 99, 01; contbr. articles to profl. jours. Issues analyst Sears for Gov., Boston, 1982; mem. bd. of friends Boston Renaissance Sch., 1996. Sgt. USMC, 1969-72. Recipient Sec. of Labor Exceptional Achievement award, 1992, 93, 95, 96, 01; Disting. Career Svc. award Dept. Labor, 1999, Exceptional Achievement award, 2000. 21st Century Workplace Award, 2002. Mem.: Am. Econ. Assn., Nat. Assn. Bus. Economists. Avocations: rugby, history. Office: Monthly Labor Review 2 Massachusetts Ave NE Washington DC 20212-0022

DEVENUTI, RICHARD R. information technology executive; BA in Acctg., U. Wash. Gen. mgr. sales ops. Microsoft, Redmond, Wash., dir. fin. analysis, U.S. contr., gen. mgr. N.Am. ops., v.p. worldwide ops., chief info. officer, v.p., chief info. officer Info. Tech. Group. Avocations: golf, skiing. Office: Microsoft One Microsoft Way Redmond WA 98052-6399

DEVER, DICK, state legislator; m. Pam Dever; 3 children. B, U. N.D. Owner DEVCO; mem. N.D. Senate from 32d dist., Bismark, 2001—. Elder Boy Scouts Am. With U.S. Army. Mem. VFW. Republican. Lutheran. Office: State Capitol 600 East Blvd Bismarck ND 58505 E-mail: ddever@state.nd.us.

DEVERA, GERTRUDE QUENANO, education educator; b. Malasiqui, Pangasinan, Philippines, Dec. 15, 1924; came to U.S., 1950; d. Paulino Castro and Filomena (del Rosario) Magsanoc; m. Perfecto Tamondong DeVera, June 23, 1946 (dec. Sept. 1976). BA, San Francisco State U., 1952; postgrad., U. Calif., Berkeley, 11952-54; MA in English Lit., San Francisco State U., 1956. Calif. tchrs. cert. and life diploma. Tchr. San Francisco Unified Sch. Dist., 1956-88, demonstration tchr., 1958-59; mem. aux. bd. trustees Don Adriano Geslani Montessori Sch., Malasiqui, Luzon, The Philippines, 1997—. Tchr. participant Project Read Behavioral Rsch. Labs., Palo Alto, Calif., 1967-68; cert. demonstrator Astra'a Magic Math-Alphaphonics, 1987-88; rschr. in preventive medicine, San Francisco, 1975—. Editing chmn.: Guidelines for Use of the Eudcational Facilities Planning model, 1968 (NDEA award 1968). Summer Inst. grantee NDEA, U. Wash., Seattle, 1968; recipient Hon. Svc. awards Calif. Congress Parents and Tchrs. Inc., Sacramento, 1975, San Francisco 2nd Dist., 1980. Mem. AAUW (legis. interview com. 1970's), Internat. Platform Assn., World Affairs Coun. No. Calif., Libr. of Congress. Democrat. Roman Catholic. Avocations: reading, creative writing, public speaking, attending lectures, various cultural pursuits.

DEVERE, RONALD, neurologist; b. Winnipeg, Can., Mar. 23, 1944; came to U.S., 1974; s. Leon and Sonya DeV.; divorced; children: Brent, Todd, Ross; m. Colleen Coleman, Sept. 2, 1995. MD, U. Manitoba, Can., 1968. Diplomate in neurology Am. Bd. Neurology and Psychiatry, cert. Am. Bd. Electrodiagnostic Medicine. Intern L.A. County-U. So. Calif. Med Ctr., 1968-69; resident in neurology U. Minn., Mpls., 1969-72; ptnr. Houston Neurology Assocs., Sugar Land, Tex., 1980-2000; pvt. practice Sugar Land, 2000—. Fellow Am. Acad. Neurology, Am. Acad. Disability Evaluating Physicians, Am. Acad Eletrodiagnostic Medicine. Office: Seton Lakeway 1602 Lohmans Crossing Austin TX 78734 E-mail: rdevere@austin.rr.com.

DEVEREUX, OWEN FRANCIS, metallurgy educator; b. Lexington, Mass., Aug. 23, 1937; s. George Francis and Mildred Anna (Gleeson) D.; m. Sally Williamson, June 15, 1957 (div. June 1969); children: Owen M., Amy L., Jonathan W., Nancy J.; m. Olivia Elaine Marin, June 13, 1969. BS, MIT, 1959, MS, 1960, PhD, 1962. Rsch. chemist Chevron Rsch. Co., La Habra, Calif., 1962-64, Corning (N.Y.) Glass Works, 1964-66, Chevron Oil Field Rsch. Co., La Habra, 1966-68; assoc. prof. metallurgy U. Conn., Storrs, 1968-76, prof., 1976-99, head dept., 1983-98. Author: Topics in Metallurgical Thermodynamics, 1983; contbr. articles to profl. jours. Rsch. grantee NSF, 1970-76, U.S. Dept. Energy, 1976-86, NSF Industry/Univ. Corp. Rsch. Ctr. for Grinding Rsch. and Devel., 1990-98. Mem. AIME, AAUP, Electrochem. Soc. (div. editor 1987-90), Nat. Assn. Corrosion Engrs. Avocations: quarter horses, carriage driving, saddle making, classical guitar. Home: 99 Summit Rd Storrs Mansfield CT 06268-1421

DEVEREUX, RICHARD BLYTON, internal medicine educator; b. Phila., Oct. 23, 1945; s. Robert T. and Dorothea A. (Kern) D.; m. Corinne Keating, Oct. 3, 1970; children: Jane Helena, Robert Jed. BA, Yale U., 1967; MD, U. Pa., 1971. Diplomate Am. Bd. Internal Medicine, Sub-bd. Cardiovascular Diseases. Intern, resident in internal medicine N.Y. Hosp., N.Y.C., 1971-74; fellow in caridology Hosp. of U. Pa., Phila., 1974-76; dir. echocardiography lab. N.Y. Hosp., N.Y.C., 1978—; asst. prof. medicine Cornell U. Med. Coll., N.Y.C., 1978-83, assoc. prof. medicine, 1983-92, prof. medicine, 1992—. Chmn. epidemiology study sect. NIH, Bethesda, Md., 1991-95, 97-99; chmn. professional adv. bd. Nat. Marfan Found., 1993-98. Mem. editl. bd.: Am. Jour. Cardiology, Am. Jour. Hypertension, Circulation; contbr. articles to profl. jours. Recipient Physician-Scientist award Andrew Mellon Found., 1980-82, rsch. award Nat. Marfan Found., 1987. Fellow: ACP; mem.: Assn. Univ. Cardiologists, Am. Soc. Hypertension (chair publs. com. 1994—97), Coun. on High Blood Pressure Rsch. Am. Heart Assn., Am. Coll. Cardiology (mem. editl. bd. jour.). Episcopalian. Avocations: movies, basketball, theatre. E-mail: rbdevere@med.cornell.edu.

DEVEREUX, TIMOTHY EDWARD, advertising executive; b. Chgo., Jan. 13, 1932; s. James Matthew and Nellie (Fitzmaurice) D.; m. Ann Sullivan, Apr. 2, 1956; children: Timothy Jr., Colette Marie, Jennifer Ann, Peter Gerard, Nora Marie, Matthew. BA in Communication Arts, U. Notre Dame, 1955. Copywriter Montgomery Ward & Co., Chgo., 1957-58; pub. relations dir. Victor Comptometer Corp., Chgo., 1958-60; sales promotion mgr. Bankers Life & Casualty Co., Chgo., 1960-61; dir. advt. and pub. relations Mid-America Foods, Inc., River Forest, Ill., 1961-62; mdse. mgr. Marshall John & Assos., Chgo. also Northbrook, 1962-65; acct. supr. Marshall John/Action Advt., Northbrook, Ill., 1965-70, exec. v.p., chief exec. officer, 1970-77, also dir.; pres. Devereux Direct, Ltd., 1977-79; v.p. direct response group Frankel & Co., Chgo., 1979-85; pres. Timothy E. Devereux & Assocs., Oak Park, Ill., 1985—. Served to 1st lt. USMCR, 1955—57. Home and Office: 1185 S Oak Park Ave Oak Park IL 60304-2048

DEVERS, GAIL, track and field athlete; b. Seattle, Nov. 19, 1966; BA in Sociology, UCLA, 1988. Gold medalist, 100m Track and Field Barcelona Olympic Games, 1992; Gold medalist 100m, 100m Hurdles World Track and Field Championships, Stuttgart, Germany, 1993; Gold medalist, 100m Track and Field Atlanta Olympic Games, 1996, Gold medalist 4x100m relay, 1996, World Championships, 1997. Named Nat. champion 100m hurdles, 1991, 1992, 1993, 1993, 1995, 1996, Nat. indoor champion 60m, 1993, World indoor champion 60m, 1993, World champion 100m, 1993, 1995, World champion 100m hurdles, 1993, Athlete of Yr., Women's Sports Found., 1997. Office: Elite Internat Sports and Mgmt 1034 S Brentwood Blvd Ste 1530 Saint Louis MO 63117-1215

DEVEY, RICHARD H. language educator; s. Samuel Richard Devey and Clara Catherine Kneip; m. Donna Jane Haggerty, June 19, 1982. BA, Thiel Coll., 1966; MA, U. Pitts., 1971, MAT, 1974. Cert. tchr. Spanish Pa., tchr. French Pa., tchr. English Pa. Tchr. Spanish, French and English Commodore Perry Sch., Hadley, Pa., 1978—93; lectr. Spanish Shenango campus Pa. State U., Sharon, 1993—. Deacon Emmanuel Christian Ch. Mem.: SPEBSQSA (Lawrence County chpt.). Office: Pa State U Shenango Campus 147 Shenango Ave Sharon PA 16146-1537

DEVGUN, DHARMINDER SINGH, lawyer; b. Dudley, U.K., Nov. 27, 1967; came to U.S., 1990; s. Mohan Singh and Kirpal Kaur Devgun; m. Amrit Bhooi, May 4, 1994; children: Kavya Devgun, Karishma Devgun. LLB with honors, U. Birmingham, 1990; JD with high distinction, U. Iowa, 1993. Bar: Minn. 1993, U.S. Ct. Internat. Trade 1997, Eng./Wales 2003. Assoc. Faegre & Benson, Mpls., 1993-96, Doherty, Rumble & Butler, St. Paul, 1996-98; sr. corp. counsel The St. Paul Cos., Inc., 1998-99; assoc. Dorsey & Whitney, Mpls., 1999—2003; ptnr. Lindquist & Vennum P.L.L.P., Mpls., 2003—. Lectr., adj. prof. William Mitchell Coll. of Law, St. Paul, 1994—. Author: Doing Business in the United Kingdom, 1998, Cooperatives, 2000; editor-in-chief Transnational Law and Contemporary Problems, 1992-93; contbr. articles to profl. jours. Mem. Minn. State Bar Assn., Order of Coif. Avocations: writing, computers. Office: Lindquist & Vennum PLLP 80 S 8th St Minneapolis MN 55402

DEVGUN, MOHAN S. manufacturing engineer, educator, metallurgical engineer, consultant; b. Shadur, India, July 4, 1942; arrived in U.S., 1986; m. Kirpal K. Devgun, Jan. 17, 1965; children: Dharminder, Surinder, Ravinder. BS, Punjab U., India, 1961; MS Aston U., Eng., 1970; PhD, Birminghan U., Eng., 1976; MBA, SUNY Buffalo, 2001. Cert. P.E., State of Iowa, registered prof. mfg. engr., State of Iowa, 1991. Mfg. engr., Wolverhampton, England, 1963—73; metall. engr. Birmingham, England, 1963—73; rsch. fellow Birmingham U., England, 1974—77; cons. nat. coun. rsch. Govt. of Venezuela, Caracas, 1977—83; prof. Iowa State, 1986—90, SUNY Buffalo, 1990—. Pres., owner MMQ Tech. Svcs., Williamsville, NY, 1991. Contbr. articles to profl. jours. Mem.: Soc. Materials, Soc. of Mfg. Engrs., Sikh Edn. and Cultural Soc. Sikh.

DEVI, TALLURI S. retired obstetrician/gynecologist; b. Sitaramapuram, India, Aug. 12, 1936; M.B.BS, Andhra Med. Coll., 1960. Diplomate Am. Bd. Obstetrics and Gynecology. Resident King George Hosp., Visakapatnam, 1960-62; intern Perth Amboy Gen. Hosp., 1970; resident Cleve. Met. Gen. Hosp., 1971-73; pvt. practice Casa Grande, Ariz.; attending ob-gyn. Casa Grande Regional Med. Ctr., Casa Grande, Ariz., 1995-2000; retired, 2000. Fellow: ACOG; mem.: So. Med. Assn. Home: PO Box 11332 Chandler AZ 85248-5433 E-mail: tsdevi812@hotmail.com.

DE VIDO, ALFREDO EDUARDO, architect; b. N.Y.C., Mar. 19, 1932; s. Eduardo and Maria (Zanucco) DeV.; m. Catherine Nelligan, 1962; children: Roberto, Antonio J. BArch, Carnegie Mellon U., 1954; MFA, Princeton U., 1956. Registered arch., N.J., N.Y., Conn., Mass., Pa. Arch. Archs. Collaborative, Rome, 1960-61, Marcel Breuer, N.Y.C., 1961-62, Ernest Kump, N.Y.C., 1963-67, McFadyen & Knowles, N.Y.C., 1967-69, DeVido Archs., N.Y.C., 1969—. Author: Designing Your Clients' House, 1983, Innovative Management Techniques for Architectural Design and Construction, 1984, House Design: Art and Practice, 1996, Master Architect III: Alfredo De Vido, 1999, Ten Houses/Alfredo De Vido, 1999. Recipient Solar award HUD, 1979, Bard award City Club N.Y., 1983, 89, award Am. Solar Energy Soc., 1982, Design award Interfaith Forum on Religion, Art and Arch., 1989, Design award Conn. Soc. Archs., 1991, Queens C. of C. award, 1993, Interior Design award Restaurants and Instns., 1997. Fellow AIA (honor award 1968, N.Y. chpt. design awards 1971, 77, 81, 94); mem. N.Y. State Assn. Archs. (design awards 1980, 81, 82, 86, 92, 95), Am. Inst. Steel Constrn. (award 1977), Am. Wood Coun. (award 1993). Office: Alfredo De Vido Architects 412 E 85th St New York NY 10028-6302 E-mail: adevido@devido-architects.com.

DEVIENCE, ALEX, JR., law educator; b. Chgo., Nov. 18, 1940; s. Alex and Charlotte (Patelski) D. B.A., U. Md., 1964; J.D., Loyola U., Chgo., 1967. Bar: Ill. 1968, U.S. Dist. Ct. (no. dist.) Ill. 1968, U.S. Tax Ct. 1968, U.S. Ct. Appeals (7th cir.) 1970, Supreme Ct. 1971, U.S. Ct. Internat. Trade 1984, U.S. Ct. Appeals (9th and fed. cir.) 1984. Sole practice, Chgo., 1967-71; prof. bus. law DePaul U., Chgo., 1975—. Author: Legal and Social Obligations of Business Managers, 1986; contbr. numerous articles to profl. jours. Apptd. by Gov. to Small Bus. Adv. Council, 1985; mem. Fed. and State Legis. Implementation Task Force, 1985. Mem. Am. Bus. Law Profs., Chgo. Bar Assn. Home: 630 Sylviawood Ave Park Ridge IL 60068-2246

DEVIGNE, KAREN COOKE, retired amateur athletics executive; b. Phila., July 31, 1943; d. Paul and Matilda (Rich) Cooke; m. Jules Lloyd Devigne, June 26, 1965; children: Jules Paul, Denise Paige, Paul Michael. AA, Centenary Coll., Hackettstown, 1963; student, Northwestern U., 1963-65; BA, Ramapo Coll., Mahwah, 1976; MA, Emory U., Atlanta, 1989. Founder GYMSET, Marietta, Ga., 1981—. Cons. Girls Club Am. Marietta, 1989; vol. Cobb County Gymnastic Ctr., Marietta, 1976-95, Ga. Youth Soccer Assn., Atlanta, 1976-95; fundraiser Scottish Rite Children's Hosp., Atlanta, 1989. Recipient recognition awards from various youth groups, Atlanta, 1976—; named Nominee Woman of Yr. ABC News, Atlanta, 1984. Avocations: skiing, tennis, bridge. Home: 3701 Clubland Dr Marietta GA 30068-4006 also: 445 White Cloud Breckenridge CO 80424

DEVILLE, DONALD CHARLES, accountant; b. New Roads, La., Sept. 18, 1953; s. Sterling Joseph and Barbara J. (Beaud) DeV.; m. Michelle L. Rinaudo, Apr. 14, 1984; children: Ariel Elizabeth, Stewart Charles, Olivia. BS in Acctg., La. State U., 1976. CPA, La. Auditor State of La., Baton Rouge, 1976-78; mgr. Hawthorn Waymouth & Carroll, Baton Rouge, 1978-89; pvt. practice Baton Rouge, 1989—. Pres. Baton Rouge Work Exch., 1988; publicity dir. Baton Rouge Opera, 1989-90, treas., 1991-95; liturg. min St. George Cath. Ch., Baton Rouge, 1987—; bd. dirs. Capital Area Safety Coun. La., treas., 1994-95; bd.

dirs. Baton Rouge Boys Club; chmn. fin. com. St. George Sch.; mem. Sisters of St. Joseph Congl. Devel. Coun. Recipient Freedom award La. Farm Bur. Mem. AICPA, La. Soc. CPAs, SAR (sec. 1990-93, pres. 1994, treas. La. 1998—, La. Meritorious Svc. award). Republican. Roman Catholic. Avocation: outdoor cooking. Home: 18002 Inverness Ave Baton Rouge LA 70810-5979

DEVILLION, KEVIN JOHN, computer systems administrator, consultant; b. St. Paul, Dec. 30, 1963; s. Lee Samuel and Freda Marcel (Loving) DeV.; m. Rosie L. Radin, June 28, 1996; children: Damien, Brandon, Nicholaus, Stepen. A in Computer Sci., Augsburg Coll., Mpls., 1983; B in Computer Sci., MIT, 1985; M in Computer Sci., U. Minn., 1987, PhD in Computer Sci. and Physics, 1989. Jr. analyst Oracle Corp., Redwood Shores, Calif., 1989-91; sr. analyst FTP Software Inc., Andover, Mass., 1991-92, Livermore Software Lab. Internat., Houston, 1993; sr. systems adminstr. On Tech. Corp., Cambridge, Mass., 1993-95, DeVillions Industries, Brainerd, Minn., 1995—. Maj. U.S. Army, 1979—. Republican. Avocations: bowling, painting, animation, native american pow-wows. Home: 1111 Highway 73 Moose Lake MN 55767-9452

DEVIN, CARL ERIC, artist; b. Pitts., Jan. 31, 1946; s. Carl and Elizabeth (Munson) D.; m. Robin Sue Block, Mar. 8, 1980; children: C. Eric, Darton B. BA in Environ. Design, Pt. Park Coll., 1970; tchg. cert., U. R.I., 1981. Asst. art dir. Reuter and Bragdon, Pitts., 1966-67, Krebs United Publs., Indiana, Pa., 1967; artist, gallery owner Rick Devin Ltd., Hope Valley, R.I., 1985—. Drawing instr. Ctr. for the Arts, Westerly, R.I., 1981-85, set designer, 1983-85; cons. regional art festivals, 1985-86. Artist (paintings) Butler Inst. Am. Art, 1989, (drawings) Foyer de Cultural Jeremie Haiti, 1993, (mural) Haitian Health Found., 1997; pub. book of drawings, 1980. Mem. Dem. Town Com., 1990—, Dem. Dist. Com., 1997—, treas., 2003, Chariho Regional Sch. Com., 1994-98; mem. Hopkinton Town Coun., 1988-93, Hopkinton Hist. Dist. Commn., 1999—, Hopkinton Charter Commn., 2001—, Hope Valley Revitalization Com., 2003; mem. strategic planning com. Chariho Regional Sch. Dist., 1999—2002, Chariho Cmty Ednl. Projects Rev. Com., 2003. Recipient 1st pl. award Newport Art Festival, 1985, Pawtucket Arts Coun., 1986, Glastonbury Art Guild, 1986. Mem. Wickford Art Assn. (Huzer award 1987, festival dir. 1984-88), Charlestown Artists Group, Fayerweather Craft Guild. Home and Office: PO Box 145 1054 Main St Hope Valley RI 02832-0145 E-mail: rickdevinltd@yahoo.com.

DEVIN, LEE (PHILIP LEE DEVIN), dramaturg, author; b. Glendale, Calif., Apr. 28, 1938; s. Philip Lee Sr. and Bernice Hermoine (Rogers) D.; m. Barbara Kathleen Norton, June 22, 1958 (div. 1986); children: Siobhan Kathleen, Sean Michael. AB, San Jose State Coll., 1958; MA, Ind. U., 1961, PhD, 1967. Lectr. Ind. U. extension, Indpls., 1960-62; instr., tech. dir. U. Va., Charlottesville, 1962-66; instr., assoc. dir. Exptl. Theatre Vassar Coll., Poughkeepsie, N.Y., 1966-67, asst. prof., assoc. dir., 1967-70; assoc. prof., dir. theatre Swarthmore (Pa.) Coll., 1970-79, prof., dir. theatre, 1979-98, prof., 1998—2003, sr. rsch. scholar, 2003—. Electrician, state mgr., prodn. stage mgr. Honey in the Rock, Beckley, W.Va., 1962-64; artist-in-residence Ball State U., Muncie, Ind., 1968, U. Calif. San Diego, La Jolla, 1973; assoc. artist People's Light and Theatre Co., Malvern, Pa., 1977—, dramaturg, 1985—. Author: (with Rob Austin) Artful Making: What Managers Need to Know About How Artists Work, 2003, (radio plays) Elegy for Irish Jack, 1973, When the Time Comes, 1978, Frankenstein, 1981 (WHA, Earplay Purchase awards); (with S. Hodkinson) (drama with music) Lament: for Guitar and Two Lovers, 1963; (active oratorio) Vox Populous, 1973; (opera) St. Carmen of the Main, 1987 actor various roles stage, film, TV; translator (with A. Adams) A Doll House, 1987, Oedipus, 1988. Recipient 1st prize WGBH Radio Drama, Boston, 1968, James S. Helms Playscript award, 1964, Calif. Olympiad of the Arts, 1965; librettist's grantee NEA, Washington, 1974, 75, 77; grantee Mellon Found., 1973, 77; Lang fellow 1990. Mem. Actors' Equity Assn., Assn. for Theatre in Higher Edn., Literary Mgrs. and Dramaturgs of the Ams. Avocation: fly fishing. Home: 603 Hillborn Ave Swarthmore PA 19081-1123 E-mail: ldevin1@swarthmore.edu.

DEVIN, RICHARD, casino gaming host; b. Rochester, N.Y., Oct. 30, 1963; s. Patsy and Antoinette (Perrone) LaFica. AA, Monroe Coll., Rochester, 1983; BA, Cornell U., 1986. Actor, N.Y.C., 1986-91; dir. project devel. Entertainment Mktg., Universal City, Calif., 1991-95; media advisor Simco & Assocs., L.A., 1995-96; exec. casting dir. Am. Film, L.A., 1996-98; exec. producer Devin Graham Entertainment, 1998—; negotiations leader Karrass Negotiations, 2000—. Producing dir. Light Opera of L.A., 1996-99. Author: Actors' resumes, 1994, Do You Want to be an Actor?, 1996; playwright: My Mother's Coming, 1990 (Gypsy award 1995), Deceptive Peace, 1990. Recipient Vital Arts award Found. for Vital Arts, 1990. Avocations: polo, champion equestrian. Office: Eclectic Mktg Inc 1377 Temporale Dr Henderson NV 89052 E-mail: eclecticmktginc@aol.com.

DEVIN, ROBIN B. librarian, anthropologist; b. Milw., May 9, 1948; d. John H. and Betty J. (Armour) Block; m. Carl E. Devin, Mar. 8, 1980; children: C. Eric, Darton B. BA, U. Wis., 1970, MLS, 1971; MA, U. R.I., 1984; PhD, U. Conn., 1995. Libr. Temple U. Librs., Phila., 1976-80, U. R.I. Libr., Kingston, 1980—. Bd. dirs. Wood River Health Svcs.; rschr. Haitian Health Found., Jeremie, Haiti, 1993, 97. Contbr. articles to profl. jours. Fellow Soc. for Applied Anthropology (Peter K. New award 2d place 1995); mem. AAUP (local newsletter editor 1995-2000), Am. Anthrop. Assn. (Beth Dillingham award 1990), Assn. of R.I. Health Scis. Librs. (instl. rep. 1994—, pres. 1999-2000), North Atlantic Health Scis. Librs., Med. Libr. Assn. (instnl. rep.), Beta Phi Mu, Phi Kappa Phi. Home: PO Box 145 Hope Valley RI 02832 Office: U RI Libr 15 Lippitt Rd Kingston RI 02881-2011 E-mail: rdevin@uri.edu.

DEVINATZ, ALLEN, mathematician, mathematics educator; b. Chgo., July 22, 1922; s. Victor and Kate (Bass) D.; m. Pearl Moskowitz, Sep. 16, 1956; children: Victor Gary, Ethan Sander. BS, Ill. Inst. Tech., 1944; A.M., Harvard U., 1947, PhD, 1950. Instr. Ill. Inst. Tech., 1950-52; NSF Postdoctoral fellow, 1952-53; fellow Inst. Advanced Study, Princeton, 1953-54; asst. prof. U. Conn., 1954-55; mem. faculty Washington U., St. Louis, 1955-67, prof. math., 1961-67, acting chmn. dept., 1963-64; prof. math. Northwestern U., Evanston, Ill., 1967-92, prof. emeritus, 1992—, asst. chmn. dept., 1968-70, acting chmn. dept., 1991. Vis. mem. Weizmann Inst., Israel, 1980, Inst. Hautes Etudes Sci., Paris, 1982, Inst. for Applications of Calculus-Mauro Picone, Rome, 1988; vis. scholar U. Calif., Berkeley, 1985; Disting. lectr. Hebrew U., Jerusalem, 1993. Contbr. articles profl. jours. Sr. NSF Postdoctoral fellow, 1960-61 Mem. Am. Math. Soc. (translation com. for Russian 1985-88), Sigma Xi, Tau Beta Pi. Office: Northwestern U Dept Math Lunt Bldg Evanston IL 60208-0001

DEVINATZ, VICTOR GARY, industrial relations educator; b. St. Louis, Oct. 19, 1957; s. Allen and Pearl (Moskowitz) D. BSE, Northwestern U., 1979, MA, 1980; MS, U. Mass., 1986; PhD, U. Minn., 1990. Lectr. U. Minn., Mpls., 1990-91; asst. prof. Ill. State U., Normal, 1991-94, assoc. prof., 1994-98, prof., 1998—. Contbr. articles to profl. jours. including Indsl. Relations Jour. Labor Rsch., Labor Studies Jour., Jour. Collective Negotiations in Pub. Sector, Labor Law Jour. Grantee, Henry J. Kaiser Family Found., Walter P. Reuther Libr., Wayne State U., 1989; Caterpillar scholar, 1999, Merl E. Reed fellow in so. labor history, 2003. Mem. Indsl. Rels. Rsch. Assn., United Assn. Labor Edn. Home: 102 S Oak St Apt 3 Normal IL 61761-3053 Office: Ill State U Dept Mgmt & Quant Methods Normal IL 61790-5580

DEVINE, BARBARA ARMSTRONG, risk manager; b. Lawrence, Kans., Mar. 2, 1965; BS in Microbiology, U. Ill., 1987; MBA, Lake Forest (Ill.) Grad. Sch., 1997; postgrad., George Washington U. Cert. purchasing mgr. R & D technician Abbott Labs., Abbott Park, Ill., 1987-90, asst. scientist, 1990-91, assoc. biochemist, 1991-93, purchasing agt., 1993-95, sr. purchasing agt., 1995-96, sect. head med. writing, 1996-97, sr. label editor, 1997-99, labeling group leader, 1999; chem. sales rep. AIC, Inc., Natick, Mass., 1999-2001; sr. purchasing agt. TAP Pharm. Products, Lake Forest, Ill., 2000—02, risk manager, 2002—. Patentee in field. Vol. Choices program Abbott Labs., 1994-99; bd. dirs. HIV Coalition, Wheeling, Ill., 1997. Named Outstanding Buyer, Chgo. Minority Bus. Devel. Coun., 1996. Mem. NAFE, AAUW, Risk and Ins. Mgmt. Soc., Inst. for Supply Mgmt., Project Mgmt. Inst. Achievements include patents in field. Home: 1903 S Warbler Ct Libertyville IL 60048-4612 E-mail: barbara.devine@tap.com.

DEVINE, BRIAN KIERNAN, pet food and supplies company executive; b. Washington, Mar. 1, 1942; s. William John and Rita Marie (Kiernan) D.; m. Silvija Viktorija Kutlets, June 13, 1964; children— Brian Jr., Brooke BA, Georgetown U., 1963; postgrad., Am. U., 1964-65, Yale U., 1965. Statis. adv. USPHS, Washington, 1963-70; with Toys "R" Us, 1970-88; gen. mgr. San Jose, Calif., 1970-75; regional gen. mgr. Chgo., 1975-77; v.p. Saddle Brook, N.J., 1977-82; sr. v.p. Rochelle Park, N.J., 1982-88; pres. of furniture mfr./retailer Krause's Sofa Factory, Fountain Valley, Calif., 1988-89; pres., CEO Petco, San Diego, 1990—, chmn., pres., CEO pet food and supplies, 1994—. Bd. dirs. Nat. Retail Fedn., Students in Free Enterprise, Wild Oats Markets, Inc.; mem. coll. bd. advisers Georgetown U. Contbr. articles to profl. publs. Mem. Internat. Mass Retail Assn. (bd. dirs.). Republican. Roman Catholic. Home: 6608 La Valle Plateada PO Box 1305 Rancho Santa Fe CA 92067-1305 Office: 9125 Rehco Rd San Diego CA 92121-2270

DEVINE, DONALD J. management and political consultant; b. Bronxville, N.Y., Apr. 14, 1937; s. John and Frances M. D.; m. Ann Delia Smith, Aug. 29, 1959; children: William, J. Michael, Patricia, Joseph. BBA, St. John's U., Jamaica, N.Y., 1959; MA, CUNY, 1965; PhD, Syracuse (N.Y.) U., 1967. Assoc. prof. govt. and politics U. Md., 1967-81; dir. U.S. Office Personnel Mgmt., 1981-85; pres. Donald Devine Co., 1985—. Columnist Washington Times; adj. scholar Heritage Found.; Grewcock chair Bellevue U., 2001—. Author: The Attentive Public, 1970, The Political Culture of the United States, 1972, Does Freedom Work? Liberty and Justice in America, 1978, Reagan Electionomics, 1983, Reagan's Terrible Swift Sword, 1991, Restoring the Tenth Amendment, 1996; editor Western Vision and American Values, 2002. Parliamentarian, mem. exec. com. Md. Rep. Com., 1974-79; Md. chmn. Reagan for Pres., 1976, 80; sr. cons. Dole for Pres., 1988, 96; cons. Steve Forbes for pres., 1999-2000; mem. rules com. Rep. Nat. Com., 1973-75, platform com., del., 1976-88, 96; vice chmn. Am. Conservative Union; Rep. nominee Md. State Comptroller, 1976, 5th Congl. Dist., 1994. With USAR, 1960-66. Mem. Am. Polit. Sci. Assn., Am. Assn. Public Opinion Research, Mt. Pelerin Soc., Phila. Soc. Roman Catholic. Office: 4805 Idlewilde Rd Shady Side MD 20764-9768

DEVINE, DONN, lawyer, genealogist, former city official; b. South Amboy, NJ, Mar. 30, 1929; s. Frank Edward and Emily Theresa (DeRevere) D. m. Elizabeth Cecilia Baldwin, Nov. 23, 1951; children: Edward (dec.), Mary Elizabeth, Martin Joseph. BS, U. Del., 1949; JD (hon.), Widener U., 1975. Bar: Del. 1975, US Dist. Ct. Del. 1976, US Supreme Ct. 1997; cert. genealogist and cert. genealogy instr. Bd. for Cert. Genealogists; cert. Am. Inst. Cert. Planners. Devel. chemist Allied Chem. Corp., Claymont, Del., 1950-52; newspaper writer, editor corp. publs. Atlas Powder Co., Wilmington, Del., 1952-60; mgmt. cons., 1960-68; dir. renewal planning City of Wilmington, 1968-79, dep. dir. planning, 1979-80, dir. planning, 1981-85; cons. Wilmington City Coun., 1985-01; pvt. practice, 1985-00; archival cons. Cath. Diocese Wilmington, 1989—; of counsel City of Wilmington Law Dept., 2001—. Spl. counsel Del. Div. Alcoholism, Drug Abuse and Mental Health, 1990-93; trustee Bd. for Cert. Genealogists, 1992—; mediator Del. Superior Ct., 1998—. Author: Delaware National Guard, A Historical Sketch, 1968, DeRevere Family of Peekskill, NY, 1982; editor Del. Geneal. Soc. Jour., 1980-81, Cultural Resources Survey of Wilmington, Del., 1982-84; assoc. editor Del. Jour. Corp. Law, 1974-75; assoc editor Professional Genealogy: A Manual for Researchers, Writers, Editors, Lecturers and Librarians, 2001. Past bd. dir. Wilmington Small Bus. Devel. Corp., Wilmington Econ. Devel. Corp.; past officer Delmarva Ecumenical Agy.; emeritus bd. dirs., past officer Generations Home Care (formerly Geriatric Svcs. Del.); past officer Christina Cultural Arts Ctr., Cath. Interracial Coun., Del. chpt. ACLU, Maplewood Housing for Elderly, St. Mary's-St. Patrick's Parish Coun. With USAR, 1950-54; brig. gen. Del. Army N.G., 1954-84, ret. Decorated Meritorious Svc. medal. Mem. Am. Planning Assn. (Peter Larson Achievement award 2002), Am. Chem. Soc., Del. Bar Assn., Del. Soc. SAR (past pres.), Nat. Geneal. Soc. (bd. dir. 1994-2002), Assn. Cath. Diocesan Archivists (bd. dir. 1993-95), Del. Geneal. Soc. (past pres.), Ft. Delaware Soc. (recognition award), Old Bohemia Hist. Soc. (bd. dirs. 1992—), Univ. and Whist Club, Chemists Club NYC, Ancient Order Hibernians, Phi Kappa Phi, Delta Theta Phi. Democrat. Home: 2004 Kentmere Pkwy Wilmington DE 19806-2014 E-mail: donndevine@aol.com.

DEVINE, EDMOND FRANCIS, lawyer; b. Ann Arbor, Mich., Aug. 9, 1916; s. Frank B. and Elizabeth Catherine (Doherty) DeV.; m. Elizabeth Palmer Ward, Sept. 17, 1955; children: Elizabeth Palmer, Stephen Ward, Michael Edmond, Suzanne Lee. AB, U. Mich., 1937, JD, 1940; LLM, Cath. U. Am., 1941. Bar: Mich. 1940, U.S. Dist. Ct. (ea. dist.) Mich. 1940, U.S. Ct. Appeals (6th cir) 1974, U.S. Supreme Ct. 1975. Spl. agt. FBI, 1941-43; chief asst. prosecutor Washtenaw County (Mich.), Ann Arbor, 1947-53, prosecuting atty., 1953-58; ptnr. DeVine & DeVine, Ann Arbor, 1958-74, DeVine, DeVine, Kantor & Serr, Ann Arbor, 1974-84; sr. ptnr. Miller, Canfield, Paddock & Stone, Ann Arbor, 1984-92, of counsel, 1992—. Asst. prof., adj. prof. U. Mich. Law Sch., 1949-79. Co-author: Criminal Procedure, 1960. Lt. USNR, 1943—46, PTO. Decorated Bronze Star with combat v. Fellow Am. Bar Found. Am. Coll. Trial Lawyers, Mich. Bar Found.; mem. ABA, State Bar Mich. (bd. commrs., chmn. judiciary com. 1976-85, mem. rep. assembly, chmn. rules and calendar com.1971-76, co-chair U.S. Cts. com. 1986-87), Internat. Assn. Def. Counsel, U.S. Supreme Ct. Hist. Soc., Ann Arbor C. of C. (chmn. bd. 1971), Detroit Athletic Club, Barton Hills Country Club, Pres.'s Club. U. Mich., Varsity M Club, Order of Coif, Barristers, Phi Delta Phi, Phi Kappa Psi. Republican. Roman Catholic. Avocations: golf, running, reading. Home: 101 Underdown Rd Ann Arbor MI 48105-1078 Office: Miller Canfield Paddock & Stone 101 N Main St Fl 7 Ann Arbor MI 48104-5507

DEVINE, HUGH JAMES, JR., marketing executive, consultant; b. Buffalo, N.Y., May 8, 1938; s. Hugh James Sr. and Ruth D. Devine; m. Bernice Riley Cushing, May 27, 1984; children: Hugh James III, Thomas C., Catherine D. Whitaker, Kent T., Diane C. Alleborn, Linda C. Hughes, Karen C. Krueger. AB in Econs., Bethany Coll., 1961; MBA, U. Bridgeport, 1971. Mgr. mktg. intelligence Winchester-Western Div. Olin Corp., New Haven, 1961-71; sr. v.p., dir. mktg. Rsch. Data Svcs., Inc., Princeton, NJ, 1971-75, exec. v.p., dir. mktg., 1975—93, dir., 1978-97, pres., 1993-96; COO Total Rsch. Corp., Princeton, N.J., 1996; mktg. cons.; pres. Hugh J. Devine & Assocs., 1997—. Speaker Am. Mgmt. Assn., N.Y.C., 1974-76, Assn. Nat. Advertisers, Washington, 1985, Fin. Independence Day, Princeton, 1986, U. N.C., Chapel Hill, 1989, 91, others. Author newsletter Strategic Goals Should Govern Mktg. Rsch. Budget, 1981; co-author newsletter The Value of Predictive Research, 1989; contbr. articles to mags. Sgt. USAR, 1961-67. Mem. Coun. Am. Survey Rsch. Orgn. (membership chmn. 1985, career planning chmn. 1986, survey quality com. 1990-91, 96), Am. Mktg. Assn., Inst. Mgmt. Consultants (v.p. membership 2000-02), SPEB-SQSA (mktg. task force 2002-03), Republican. Avocations: barbershop style singing, walking, reading. Home and Office: 49 Krebs Rd Plainsboro NJ 08536-1104 E-mail: HJDevine@aol.com.

DEVINE, NANCY, postmaster; b. Hyannis, Mass., Feb. 8, 1949; d. Joseph Peter and Rose (Almeida) Cabral; m. Michael G. Devine, Mar. 20, 1971 (div. 1975); 1 child, Paul. Student, U. Mass., 1967-70. Postal clk. U.S. Postal Svc., Centerville, Mass., 1977-80, postmaster West Hyannisport, Mass., 1980—. Affirmative Action planner U.S. Postal Svc., Brockton, Mass., 1979-80, prin. rep./exec. bd., Providence, 1993. Painter in acrylics. Art and Humanities grantee Barnstable Arts Coun., Mass. Art Coun., Nat. Endowment for the Arts. Mem. Nat. Assn. Women Artists, Cape Cod Art Assn., Smithsonian Instn. Home: PO Box 361 West Hyannisport MA 02672-0361 E-mail: ncdevine@mailcity.com.

DEVINE, OWEN JOHN, biostatician, public health service officer, researcher; b. Wilmington, Del., Nov. 5, 1957; s. Hugh Alexander and Margaret Mary Devine; m. Kathleen Dunn, Dec. 5, 1981; children: Connor Dunn, Brendan Dunn, Margaret Dunn. MS, The U. Gergia, 1982; PhD, Emory U., 1992. Math. statistician Ctrs. Disease Control and Prevention, Atlanta, 1986—2002, sr. rsch. scientist biostatistics, 2002—. Adjucnt faculty Emory U., Atlanta, 1994—2002. Contbr. articles to profl. jours. Mem.: Biometric Soc. (Travel Award 1992), Am. Statis. Soc. Avocation: irsih music. Office: Ctrs Disease Control and Preventi 1600 Clifton Rd Atlanta GA 30333

DEVINE, ROBERT JAMES, international affairs consultant; b. Benton Harbor, Mich., July 8, 1953; s. James Lincoln and Melitta Devine. BA, Tex. Christian U., 1974, MA, 1976; Dr. rer. Publ., U. St. Gallen, Switzerland, 1986. Spl. asst. fgn. affairs and def. com. German Bundestag, Bonn, Germany, 1977-78; cons. MS Mgmt. AG, St. Gallen, 1982-85; Robert Bosch Found. fellow German Fgn. Ministry, Bonn, 1986-87; spl. advisor Ministry of State, Baden-Wurttemberg, Stuttgart, Germany, 1987-88; pres. CEISA Rsch. Group, Ft. Worth, Tex., 1988—. Bd. dirs. World Affairs Coun. Greater Ft. Worth, 1994-2000. Named Knight Comdr., Equestrian Order of Holy Sepulchre of Jerusalem, 2001, Knight of Merit, Sacred Mil. Constantinian Order of St. George, 1997; recipient diploma Bene Merentium Proprium, Equestrian Order of Holy Sepulchre of Jerusalem, 1998; Paul Harris fellow Rotary Internat., 1995; Fulbright scholar. Mem. SAR (Maj. Van Zandt chpt.), Soc. Cath. Social Scis., Tex. Soc. Colonial Wars (gentleman of coun. 2000—, historian), Soc. Cin., Holland Soc., St. Andrews Soc. State of N.Y., Royal Soc. St. George, Sons of Am. Colonists, Sons of Union Vets. of Civil War, Mil. Order World Wars, Nat. Soc. Sons Colonial New Eng., Am. Coun. on Germany, Order Founders and Patriots of Am. (sec. Tex. Soc.), Tex. Soc. of War of 1812, Sons of the Revolution (Ill.), Mil. Order Loyal Legion (Tex. comdr.), Mil. Order Fgn. Wars, Vet. Corps of Arty. of State of N.Y., Sons and Daus. of Pilgrims, Naval Order the U.S., German Fgn. Policy Assn., Army & Navy Club, Ft. Worth Club, Aztec Club of 1847, Plimsoll Club, U. Club Chgo. Roman Catholic. Avocations: horticulture, medieval art, history, opera. Office: CEISA Rsch Group 100242 Trinity River Sta Fort Worth TX 76185

DEVINENI, MOHAN, pharmacist; b. Hyderabad, India, Aug. 15, 1957; arrived in U.S., 2001; s. Ranga Rao and Venkata Rathnam Devineni; m. Nirmala Devineni, May 21, 1983; children: Ramya, Abhilash. B Pharmacy, Coll. Pharmacy, Manipal, India, 1980; DPM, Indian Inst. Sci., Bangalore, 1984; MS in Pharmacy, Birla Inst. Tech., Pilani, India, 1989. Registered pharmacist India. Sr. chemist Kanpha Labs., Bangalore, 1982—88; dir. Strides Pharms., Bangalore, 1988—91; v.p. Strides Arcolab Ltd., Bangalore, 1991—96, sr. v.p., 1996—2000; dir. Murty Pharms., Inc., Lexington, Ky., 2001—02; v.p. Capricorn Pharma, Inc., Frederick, Md., 2002—. Bd. dirs. Pharmacon (India) Pvt., Ltd., Bangalore, Dry Cool (India) Pvt., Ltd., Bangalore; cons. in field. *Over 23 years of progressively responsible experience in pharmaceutical industry, with rich experience in product development, manufacturing, quality control, quality assurances, validations, facility designing etc. Played a key role in developing a small company to a world class, multinational pharmaceutical company. Designed and built several world-class pharmaceutical facilities. Built excellent teams with limited available resources. Experience in several dosage forms including tablets, capsules, soft gelatin capsules, liquid oral, ointments, liquid injections, sterile dry powder injections etc. A well respected consultant and handled several international projects. Member of Board of Directors in several companies.* Recipient Disting. Alumni award, Coll. Pharmacy, 2000. Mem.: Sci. Adv. Bd., Am. Assn. Pharm. Scientists, Indian Pharm. Assn. Achievements include design of several pharmaceuticals. Avocations: painting portraits and landscapes, cricket. Home: 6372 Lambert Ct Frederick MD 21703 Office: Capricorn Pharma Inc 6900 Unit A English Muffin Way Frederick MD 21703

DE VINK, LODEWIJK J. R. former consumer pharmaceutical products company executive; b. Amsterdam, Netherlands, Feb. 14, 1945; married; two sons. MBA, Am. U., Netherlands Sch. of Bus.; BBA, Washburn U. Pres. internat. ops. Schering-Plough Corp., 1969-88; v.p., pres. internat. ops. Warner-Lambert Co., Morris Plains, N.J., 1988-90, exec. v.p., pres. U.S. ops., 1990-91, pres., COO, 1991-2000. Bd. dirs. Meml. Hosp., Pharmacy Rsch. & Mfg. Assn., treas. Trustee Nat. Found. Infectious Diseases, 1992—; bd. dirs. Nat. Actors Theatre, N.Y.C., 1993—, Friends of Hassenfeld.

DEVINO, WILLIAM STANLEY, economist, educator; b. Burlington, Vt, Nov. 17, 1926; s. William Arthur and Elaine Anna (Blaise) D.; m. Raphaella Frances Gillespie, Aug. 27, 1949; children: Bonnie Ann, Denise Marie. BA, U. Vt., 1951; MA, U. Conn., 1953; PhD, Mich. State U., 1959. Instr. econs. Mich. State U., Mich., 1955-57, Ford Found. dissertation fellow econs., 1957-58; from rsch. assoc. to lectr. Mich. State U. Sch. Labor and Indsl. Rels., Mich., 1958-60; from faculty to prof. bus. and econs. U. Maine, Orono, Maine, 1960-96; dir. U. Maine Sch. Bus. Adminstrn., Orono, Maine, 1963-65; dean U. Maine Coll. Bus. Adminstrn., Orono, Maine, 1965-96, dean emeritus, 1997—. Cons. Mich. Senate Labor Com., 1955; mem. Gov. Mich. Task Force on Labor, 1959; mem. arbitration roster Fed. Mediation and Concilation Svc., 1962-97; mem. nat. labor panel Am. Arbitration Assn., 1962-97; mem. Gov. Maine Adv. Com. on Bus. Taxation, 1971-72; mem. fact finding panel Maine Labor Rels. Bd., 1973-1997. Author: Exhaustion of Unemployment Benefits During a Recession, 1960; co-author: A Study of Textile Mill Closings in Selected New England Communities, 1966. Served with AUS, World War II. Mem. Nat. Acad. Arbitrators. Home: 358 Howard St Bangor ME 04401-4152 Office: U Maine Coll Bus Adminstrn Orono ME 04469-0001

DEVINS, ROBERT SYLVESTER, retired lawyer; b. N.Y.C., Mar. 19, 1949; s. Arthur Sylvester and Judith Delores (Whelan) D. BA, Tulane U., 1971; JD, Emory U., 1978. Bar: Ga. 1978, Fla. 1981, U.S. Dist. Ct. (no. dist.) Ga. 1978, U.S. Tax Ct. 1978, U.S. Ct. Appeals (5th cir.) 1978, U.S. Supreme Ct. 1982, U.S. Dist. Ct. (mid. dist.) Ga. 1994. Pvt. practice, Atlanta, 1978-99; ret., 1999. Lt. USN, 1971-75. Mem. ABA, Internat. Bar Assn. (vice chmn. criminal law sect. 1985-87, chmn. 1987-89. rep. UN Conf. 1987, 89), Inter Am. Bar Assn., Nat. Assn. Criminal Def. Lawyers, Ga. Assn. Criminal Def. Lawyers, Assn. Trial Lawyers Am., Ga. Trial Lawyers Assn., Union International des Avocats. Avocation: reading. Home: Casa Ventosear 2335 S Ocean Blvd Palm Beach FL 33480-5368

DE VISSCHER, FRANCOIS MARIE, investment banker; b. Louvain, Belgium, Sept. 24, 1953; m. Maura Michaela Nicholson, Oct. 4, 1980; children: Patrick-Michel, Luke-Michel. BA in Applied Econs., U. Louvain, 1975; MBA, Rutgers U., 1977. CPA, N.Y. Staff asst. Coopers & Lybrand, Brussels, 1975-76, staff acct. N.Y.C., 1977-79, sr. acct., 1979-80, supr. audit, 1980; assoc. Smith Barney, Harris Upham & Co., Inc., N.Y.C., 1981-82, 2nd v.p., 1983-84, v.p., 1985-88, mng. dir., 1988-90; pres. de Visscher & Co., Greenwich, Conn., 1990-98; ptnr. de Visscher, Olson & Allen LLC, Greenwich, 1998—. Bd. dirs. Bekaert Corp. Pres. Family Firm Inst., Brookline, Mass.; chmn. European Family Office Conf., London. Mem. AICPA, Nat. Assn. Securities Dealers (registered rep.), N.Y. Soc. CPAs, Belgium Am. C. of C. (bd. dirs.), Bekaert N.V. Belgium (bd. dirs.), Larchmont (N.Y.) Yacht Club, Westchester Country Club (Rye, N.Y.), Pawling (N.Y.) Mt. Club. Avocations: sailing, shooting, fishing, golf. Office: de Visscher Olson & Allen 104 Field Point Rd Greenwich CT 06830-6481 E-mail: francois@devisscher.com.

DE VITA, MICHAEL RICHARD, obstetrician-gynecologist; b. Orange, N.J., 1928; BS in Biology, Georgetown Coll., 1950; MD, Georgetown U., 1954. Diplomate Am. Bd. Ob-gyn. Intern St. Michael's Hosp., Newark, 1954-55; resident Providence Hosp., Washington, 1957-60; with Pascack Valley Hosp., Westwood, N.J., ret., 1988. Min. Gospel of Jesus Christ. Fellow ACOG (life); mem. Am. Assn. Gynecol. Laparoscopists, Ams. Soc. for Reproductive Medicine, Am. Gynecol. Laser Soc., Gynecol. Laparascopy Soc., Internat. Soc. Microsurgery, Am. Soc. Cytology and Cervical Pathology. E-mail: soldocd@aol.com.

DEVITA, VINCENT THEODORE, JR., oncologist; b. Bronx, N.Y., Mar. 7, 1935; s. Vincent Theodore and Isabel DeVita; m. Mary Kay Bush, Aug. 3, 1957; children: Ted(dec.), Elizabeth. BS, Coll. William and Mary, 1957; MD, George Washington U., 1961; DSc (hon.), N.Y. Med. Coll., 1987, Georgetown U., 1989. Diplomate Nat. Bd. Med. Examiners, Am. Bd. Internal Medicine (subspecialty hematology, med. oncology). Intern U. Mich. Med. Center, Ann Arbor, 1961—62; resident in medicine George Washington U. Med. Service D.C. Gen. Hosp., 1962—63; clin. assoc. Lab. Chem. Pharmacology, Nat. Cancer Inst. NIH, Bethesda, Md., 1963—65; sr. resident in medicine Yale New Haven Med. Center, 1965—66; sr. investigator solid tumor service, medicine br. Nat. Cancer Inst. NIH, 1966—68, head solid tumor service, medicine br., 1968—71, chief med. br., 1971—74, dir. div. cancer treatment, 1974—80, clin. dir. inst., 1975—80; dir. Nat. Cancer Inst., Nat. Cancer Program, NIH, 1980—88; physician-in-chief Meml. Sloan-Kettering Cancer Ctr., N.Y.C., 1988—91, attending physician, mem., 1988—93, Benno C. Schmidt chair clin. oncology, 1988—93; prof. medicine Cornell U. Med. Coll., 1989—93; dir. Yale Cancer Ctr., New Haven, 1993—, med. dir. oncology, 2000—; prof. medicine Yale U. Sch. Medicine, New Haven, 1993—; attending physician Yale-New Haven Hosp., 1993—; prof. epidemiology and pub. health, dir. of Yale Cancer Ctr. Yale U. Sch. Medicine, New Haven, 1994—. Mem. editl. bd.: Cancer Rsch., 1981—91, Gynecologic Oncology, 1981—91, Hematol. Oncology, 1981—87,

Physicians' Drug Alert, 1982—, Jour. Clin. Oncology, 1983—87; co-editor: (textbooks) Cancer: Principles and Practice Oncology, edits. 1-6, Progress in Oncology, (jours.) The Cancer Jour., 1995—, Principles and Practice Oncology, 1987—; assoc. editor Online Jour. Current Clin. Trials, 1991—94; assoc. editor: Cancer Investigation, 1983—87, Am. Jour. Medicine, 1983—88, mem. extramural bd. assoc. editors: Physicians Desk Query (PDQ), Nat. Cancer Inst., 1989—, adv. bd.: Am. Health Mag., 1995—99, mem. editl. sci. bd.: Oncologia Clinica, 1996—, mem. editl. sci. bd.: Cancer Rsch., 1997, Current Oncology Reports, 1998—, Jour. Bone and Soft Tissue Sarcomas, 1999—, mem. editl. bd. or adv. editor: numerous other med. jours.; contbr. numerous articles to med. jours. Mem. awards assembly GM Cancer Rsch. Found., 1981—85, adv. coun., 1984—; chair med. adv. bd. CancerSource.com, 1999—; bd. advisors Breast Cancer Alliance, Inc., 1999—; mem. Armand Hammer Cancer Award Com., 1983—86. Served with USMC, 1955—61. Decorated Oren del Sol en el Grando de Official Govt. of Peru; named Stratton lectr., Am. Soc. Hematology, 1985, Leukemia Rsch. Fund lectr., London, 1985; named to, Conn. Acad. Sci. and Engring., 1994, Commendatore of Italian Rep. order of merit, Pres. Italy, 1998; recipient Albert and Mary Lasker Med. Rsch. award, 1972, Superior Svc. award, HEW, 1975, Esther Langer Found. award, 1976, Alumni medallion, Coll. William and Mary, 1976, Jeffrey Gottlieb award, 1976, Bronze medal, Am. Soc. Therapeutic Radiology, 1978, Karnofsky prize and lectr., 1979, Griffuel prize, Assn. for Devel. Rsch. on Cancer, 1980, James Ewing award, Soc. Surg. Oncology, 1982, Meml. Sloan-Kettering Cancer Ctr. award, 1972, Disting. Svc. medal, USPHS, 1983, Meyer and Anna Prentiss award, 1984, Second Emmanuel Cancer Found. award, 1984, Pierluigi Nervi award, Rome, 1985, Medal of Honor, Am. Cancer Soc., 1985, Barbara Bohen Pfeifer award, Am.-Italian Found. Cancer Rsch., 1985, Tenth Richard and Hilda Rosenthal Found. award, Am. Assn. Cancer Rsch., Inc., 1986, Stanley G. Kay Meml. award, D.C. Am. Cancer Soc., 1986, Sci. award, Brady Cancer Rsch. Inst., 1987, Prix Cino del Duca, Paris, 1988, Pezcoller award, European Soc. Oncology, Trento, Italy, 1988, Surgeon Gen.'s Exemplary Svc. medal, 1988, Armand Hammer Cancer prize, 1990, Outstanding Achievement in Clin. Rsch. award, Assn. Cmty. Cancer Ctrs., 1992, City of Medicine award, 1995, Presdl. award, New Eng. Cancer Soc., 1997, Key to Cure award, Cure for Lymphoma Found., 1997, Mary Waterman award, Breast Cancer Alliance, 1999, 50th Anniversary Leukemia Soc. Am., 1999, Saul Rosenberg Rsch. award, Lymphoma Rsch. Found. Am., 2000; fellow Tobacco Rsch. Industry fellow, 1959. Fellow: ACP, N.Y. Acad. Medicine; mem.: AMA, Assn. Am. Cancer Insts. (bd. dirs. 1999—, policy and planning com. 2000—), Internat. Coun. for Coordinating Cancer Rsch. (pres. Am. bd. 1989—92), Smith-Reed-Russel Med. Soc., Soc. Surg. Oncology, Assn. Am. Physicians, Am. Soc. Clin. Investigation, Am. Fedn. Clin. Rsch., Am. Assn. Cancer Rsch. (dir. 1976—79, Gertrude B. Elion cancer rsch. award com. 1999—2000), Am. Soc. Hematology, Am. Cancer Soc., Am. Soc. Clin. Oncology (chmn. program com. 1972, dir. 1973—76, pres. 1977—78), Alpha Omega Alpha. E-mail: vincent.devita@yale.edu.

DEVITIS, JOSEPH L. education educator; b. Balt. s. Joseph and Mary DeVitis; m. Mary Louise Gall, June 24, 1969 (div. Mar. 1980); m. Linda Anne Haren, June 4, 1988; 1 child, Leigh Garrett Irwin. BA, Johns Hopkins U., Balt., 1967; MEd, Johns Hopkins U., 1969; MA, Bowie State U., Md., 1982; PhD, U. Ill., 1972. Prof. edn. U. Tenn., Martin, 1972—88; prof. edn. and human devel. SUNY, Binghamton, 1988—2001; prof. edn. U. Louisville, 2001—. Co-author: To Serve and Learn, 1998, The Success Ethic, Education and the American Dream, 1996, Theories of Moral Development, 1994. Lector Centenary/Chenango St. United Meth. Ch., Binghamton, 1999—2001; bd. dirs. Citizens Action of N.Y., Binghamton, 1999—2001. Mem.: Coun. of Learned Socs. in Edn. (pres. 1994—97), Am. Ednl. Studies Assn. (pres. 1988—89), Soc. Profs. of Edn. (pres. 1995—98, Disting. Svc. award 2001). Democrat. Home: 1304 S 6th St Louisville KY 40208 Office: Univ of Louisville Coll of Edn and Human Devel 2301 S 3d St Louisville KY 40292-0001

DEVITO, DANNY MICHAEL, actor, director, producer; b. Neptune, N.J., Nov. 17, 1944; s. Daniel and Julia DeV.; m. Rhea Perlman, Jan. 8, 1982; children: Lucy Chet, Gracie, Daniel Jacob. Grad., Am. Acad. Dramatic Arts, 1966. Co-founder Jersey Films. Theater appearances include The Man With a Flower in His Mouth, Sheridan Sq. Playhouse, 1969, The Shrinking Bride, 1971, One Flew Over the Cuckoo's Nest, 1971, DuBarry Was a Lady, 1972, A Phantasmagoria Historia of D. Johann Fauster Magister, Ph.D, M.D., D.D., D.L., etc., 1973, The Many Wives of Windsor (N.Y. Shakespeare Festival), 1974, Where Do We Go From Here?, 1974; motion picture appearances include Lady Liberty, 1971, Hurry Up, or I'll Be 30, 1973, Scalawag, 1972, One Flew Over the Cuckoo's Nest, 1975, Car Wash, 1976, Hot Dogs for Gaugin, Goin' South, 1978, Swap Meet, 1979, Going Ape!, 1981, Terms of Endearment, 1983, Romancing the Stone, 1984, Johnny Dangerously, 1984, Jewel of the Nile, 1985, Wise Guys, 1986, My Little Pony (voice), 1986, Ruthless People, 1986, Tin Men, 1987, (dir. debut) Throw Momma from the Train, 1987, Twins, 1988, The War of the Roses (also dir.), 1989, Other People's Money, 1991, Batman Returns, 1992, Hoffa, (also producer, dir.) 1992, Jack the Bear, 1993, The Last Action Hero (voice), 1993, Renaissance Man, 1994, Junior, 1994, Get Shorty, (also prodr.), 1995, Matilda, (also dir.), 1996, Mars Attacks!, 1996, The Rainmaker, 1997, Hercules (voice), 1997; co-exec. prodr.: Reality Bites, 1994, Pulp Fiction, 1994; prodr.: Feeling Minnesota, 1996, Gattaca, 1997, Living Out Loud (also prodr.), 1998 The Virgin Suicides, 1999, The Big Kahuna, 1999, Man On the Moon, 1999 (also prodr.), Drowning Mona, 2000, Screwed, 2000, Erin Brokovich (prodr.), 2000, How High, 2001, Camp, 2003, Marx Brothers, 2003, What's the Worst That Could Happen, 2001, Heist, 2001, Death to Smoochy (also dir.), 2002, Anything Else, 2003; dir. only: Duplex, 2003; appeared in role of Louie in TV series Taxi, 1978-83; guest voice: The Simpsons, 1989; directed and appeared in cable TV movie The Ratings Game, 1984. Recipient Golden Globe award for TV series, Taxi, 1979; Emmy award 1981 Office: care Fred Specktor Creative Artists Agy Inc 9830 Wilshire Blvd Beverly Hills CA 90212-1804

DEVITO, MATHIAS JOSEPH, retired real estate executive; b. Trenton, N.J., Aug. 23, 1930; s. Charles P. and Margaret L. DeV.; m. Rosetta Kormuth, July 28, 1956; children: Ann DeVito Walker, Charles Michael. BA, U. Md., 1954, LLB with highest honors, 1956; L.H.D., Salisbury State Coll., 1984. Bar: Md. Asst. atty. gen. State of Md., 1963-64; ptnr. Piper & Marbury, Balt., 1965-70; sr. v.p., gen. counsel, then exec. v.p. Rouse Co., Columbia, Md., 1968-73, pres., CEO, bd. dirs., 1973-84, chmn. bd. dirs., pres., CEO, 1984-93, chmn. bd. dirs., CEO, 1993-95, chmn. bd. dirs., 1995-97, chmn. exec. com. bd., 1997-2001, chmn. emeritus, 2001—. Bd. dirs. Mars Supermarkets, Inc., Sitel Corp., Triton PSC; chmn. Greater Balt. Com., 1990—92. Editor Md. Law Rev., 1955-56. Chmn. bd. trustees Md. State Colls., 1970-73; trustee Johns Hopkins U., 1983-89, Md. Inst. Coll. Art, 1995—. Mem. Adirondack League, Elkridge Club, Order of Coif. Roman Catholic. Office: Ste 220 Village Sq II Baltimore MD 21210-1935

DEVITO, SHAWN JOSEPH, music educator; b. Lockport, N.Y., July 15, 1970; s. David Mark and Joan Catherine DeVito. Student, Fla. State U., 1993; MusB in Edn., SUNY, Fredonia, New York, 1993; MusM in Edn., Crane Sch. of Music, 1999. Cert. Tchr. N.Y. State, 1999. Music tchr. South Lewis Ctrl. Sch. Dist., Turin, NY, 1994—2000; mid. sch. music tchr. Watertown CSD-Case Mid. Sch., Watertown, NY, 2000—02; high sch. tchr. Gen. Brown Ctrl. Sch. Dist., 2002—. Music dir. Adams Village Baptist Ch., Adams, NY, 2000—. Singer: (plays) John Stainer's CRUCIFIXTION, 2002; music director : (plays) 1000 Islands Theatre Organization, 2002; singer: madrigal singing group for annual Garden Tour, 2002; actor: (plays) Jekyll and Hyde, 2002; singer: (plays) Richard Rodgers Musical Review, 2002, Legacy of Song, 2000, Gabriel Faure's REQUIEM, 1999. Third v.p. Watertown Musicales, Watertown, NY, 1997—2002; sec. South Lewis Shared Decision Making Com., Turin, NY, 1996—2000; prodr.-talent coach Miss Lewis County Scholarship Orgn., Turin, NY, 1996—2002. Recipient Prodn. of the Yr. Lewis County Scholarship Pageant award, Miss N.Y. State Scholarship Orgn., 1996. Mem.: Watertown Musicales (treas. 2000—01), Jefferson Lewis Counties Music Teachers Assn. (publicity dir. 1997—98), Music Educators Nat. Conf., N.Y. State Sch. Music Assn. (vocal adjudicator 2000—02, dir. Case Middle Sch. Chorus & Select Choir 2002, Gold Rating award 2002), Am. Choral Dir. Assn. Republican. Baptist. Avocations: travel, singing, conducting, acting. Home: 432 apt 1 College Heights Watertown NY 13601 Office: Gen Brown Ctrl Sch Dist 17643 Cemetery Rd Dexter NY 13634 Personal E-mail: sdevito@twcny.rr.com.

DEVITT, JOHN LAWRENCE, consulting engineer; b. Denver, Sept. 27, 1925; s. Oliver Hinkley and Ellen Elizabeth (McPherson) D.; children: Jane, David, Ellen. BSEE, U. Colo., 1945, MS, 1949. Registered profl. engr., Colo. Engr. U.S. Bureau of Reclamation, Denver, 1947-50; plant mgr. AMF Corp., Colorado Springs, Colo., 1951-55; v.p., gen. mgr. Whittaker Corp. Power Sources div., Denver, 1955-61; chief engr. Metron Instrument Co., Denver, 1962-65; mgr. of electrochemistry Gates Corp., Denver, 1965-71; pvt. practice as a consulting engr. Denver, 1971—. Profl. jazz musician (saxophone), Denver, 1946—. Co-inventor sealed lead-acid and lead-chloride batteries. Lt. USNR, 1943-54, PTO. Recipient Battery Research award, The Electrochem. Soc., 1986, Gaston Planté medal Bulgarian Acad. of Scis., 1999; named to Battcon hall of Fame, 2003. Mem. The Electrochem. Soc., Am. Chem. Soc., Inst. Elect. and Electronic Engrs., Colo. Mountain Club (pres. 1975), Am. Alpine Club, New York. Achievements include invention of first sealed lead-acid battery. Office: Consulting Engr 985 S Jersey St Denver CO 80224-1418

DEVITT-GRASSO, PAULINE VIRGINIA, civic volunteer, nurse; b. Salem, Mass., May 13, 1930; d. John M. and Mary Elizabeth (Cologey) Devitt; m. Frank Anthony Grasso, Oct. 26, 1968; 1 stepson, Christopher Anthony. BSN, Boston Coll., 1952; student, Boston U., 1954-55, Boston State Tchrs. Coll., 1953-54. RN. Staff nurse J.P. Kennedy Jr. Meml. Hosp., Brighton, Mass., 1952-53, head nurse, day supr., 1953-54, day supr., 1955, clin. instr., 1955-68, adminstrv. asst., 1968, dir. nursing edn., 1958-68. Vis. instr. Boston Coll., Mass. State Coll., Meml. Hosp. Sch. Nursing, Newton, Mass. Meml. Hosp. Sch. Nursing, 1955-68, CUA S of N, 1990. Pres. Project H.O.P.E., Manhattan Beach, Calif., 1982; pres. adv. coun. Meals on Wheels, Salvation Army, 1989, 90, 91, bd. dirs. Redondo Beach, 1992—, sec. bd. dirs., 1994; cons. Manhattan Beach Housing Found., 1986—, Manhattan Beach Case Mgr., 1982—; mem. adv. coun. South Bay Sr. Svcs., Torrance, Calif., 1986—, pres., 1995—, pres. adv. bd. 1985-2001; sr. advocate City of Manhattan Beach, 1982; bd. dirs. Ret. Sr. Vol. Program, Torrance, 1986-90; bd. dirs. Behavioral Health Svcs., 1992—, treas. 1996—, hosp. com., fin. com., exec. com., human resource com.; neighborhood chair Girl Scouts U.S.; mem. Beach City Coun. on Aging, 1983-91; mem. Salvation Army Ladies Aux.; mem. adv. bd. Salvation Army Corps, Redondo Beach. Recipient Cert. of Appreciation, County of L.A., 1988, South Bat Sr. Svcs., 1998 Vol. of the Yr. award City of Manhattan Beach, 1988, Award of Honor County of L.A., 1989, State of Calif. Senate Rules Com. Resolution Commendation, 1988; named Outstanding Vol. Cath. Daus. of Am., 1986, Vol. of Yr. City Manhattan Beach, 1986-87; Rose and Scroll award Manhattan Beach C. of C., 1989, Art Michel Meml. Community Svc. award Manhattan Beach Rotary Club, 1989, Cert. of Appreciation KC's Queen of Martyrs Coun., 1989, Redondo Beach Lila Bell award Salvation Army, 1989, others, Manhattan Beach Vol. Appreciation award, 1982, 83, 84, 85, 86, 88, 90, 91, 92, 93; nominated for Pres's. Vol. Action award Project H.O.P.E., 1987. Mem. AARP, South Bay Geneal. Soc., New Eng. Hist. and Geneal. Soc., Polish Genal. Soc. So. Calif., Am. Martyrs Altar Soc. (pres. 1983, coun. mem.-at-large 1992), Cath. U. Am. Nat. Alumni Assn. (hon.), Cath. U. Am. Sch. Nursing Alumni Assn. (hon.), Boston Coll. Alumni Assn. (Golden Eagle award 2002), Manhattan Beach Sr. Citizens Club (pres. 1985-86, 88-89), Lions (Citizen of Yr. award Manhattan Beach club 1986), DAV (comdr.'s club 1990, 91, 92), Lady in Equestrian Order of Holy Sepulchre of Jerusalem. Democrat. Roman Catholic. Avocations: gardening, needlecraft, genealogy, volunteerism. Home: 329 3rd St Manhattan Beach CA 90266-6410

DEVIVO, ANGE, former small business owner; b. Bay Shore, N.Y., Oct. 20, 1925; d. Romeo Zanetti and Karolina (Hodapp) King; m. John Michael DeVivo, Dec. 30, 1950; 1 child, Michael. Student, Washington Sch. for Secs., N.Y.C., 1945-46. Sec. Am. Airlines, N.Y.C., 1946-51; exec. sec. W.C. Holzhauer, N.Y.C., 1951-52; dist. sales mgr. Emmons Jewelers, Inc., Bound Brook, N.J., 1952-53; exec. sec. N.J. Rep. State Com., 1960-64; adminstrv. sec. Mercy Hosp., Charlotte, NC, 1973—81; pres. Secs., Plus, Convs., Plus, Charlotte, 1983—91; prin. Ange DeVivo & Assocs., Inc., Charlotte, 1991—92. Editor: The North Carolina Republican Woman, 2d edit., 1994, 3d edit., 1995; author Precinct Training Manual, 1971. Mem., Cardinal Bus. and profl. Women's Club, 1977-83, pres., 1979-81; mem.,Nat. Secretaries Assn., 1977-80; mem., Nat. Assn. of Female Executives, 1980-83; adminstrv. secretary, Nat. Broadcast Assn. for Cmty. Affairs, 1987-90; active in local politics in NJ, 1956-64, in Conn., 1964-68, in NC, 1968-96; mem. Human Svcs. Coun., Charlotte, 1984-88, conf. mgr., 8th Nat. Recycling Congress, 1989; mem. Emergency Med. Svc. Adv. Coun., Charlotte, 1981-92, chmn., 1988-90; mem. Charlotte Women's Polit. Caucus, 1972-96, Mecklenburg Evening Rep. Women's Club, Charlotte, 1970—, pres., 1973, 74, 1993, 94, Women's Roundtable, 1994, 95; mem. citizens adv. com. Conv. and Visitors Bur., 1986-90; coord. Women's Equality Day celebration Mecklenburg County Women's Commn., 1990, coord., fin. chair, 1991-92, co-chmn., fin. chair, 1993-96, mem. adv. bd. 1993-96, vice chair bd., 1995; fundraiser March of Dimes and Leukemia, Ala., 1999, 2002; mem. Rep. Women Today Ala., 1997-2001; participant many civic and polit. surveys, 2000—. Recipient Order of Long Leaf Pine award Gov. of N.C., 1974, Entrepreneur of Yr. award Women Bus. Owners, 1987, Spl. Recognition award for devotion, dedication and untiring efforts Mecklenburg County Women's Commn., 1996; honoree N.C. Fedn. Rep. Women, 1987; nominee for Cmty. Svc. award, 1994, nominee to the NC Rep. Party Hall of Fame representing Dist. 9, 1995. Mem. Rep. Women of the South, 2001-,(tel. com. 2002). Roman Catholic. Avocations: politics, community volunteer work. First woman elected chairperson Micklenburg County Republican Party, 1976. E-mail: jmdevivo531@cs.com.

DE VIVO, DARRYL CLAUDE, pediatric neurologist; b. Everett, Mass., Aug. 28, 1937; children: Cynthia, Jessica, Kristin. BA, Amherst Coll., 1959; MD, U. Va., 1964. Diplomate Am. Bd. Psychiatry and Neurology (dir. neurology 1991-99, pres. 1999). Intern Univ. Hosp., Boston, 1964—65; resident in pediat. and neurology Mass. Gen. Hosp., Boston, 1965—67; clin. assoc. NIH, 1967—69; fellow in pediatric neurology St. Louis Children's Hosp., 1969—70; mem. faculty Wash. U. Sch. Medicine, St. Louis, 1970—78, prof. pediat. and neurology, 1977—78; Sidney Carter prof. neurology and prof. pediatrics Coll. Physicians and Surgeons, Columbia U., N.Y.C., 1979—; dir. pediatric neurology Columbia-Presbyn. Med. Ctr., N.Y.C., 1979—2000, assoc. chmn. child neurology and devel. neurobiology, 1998—. Mem. coun. NANDS, 1997—2000. Assoc. editor Rudolph's Textbook of Pediatrics, 17th edit., 1982, 18th edit., 1987, 19th edit., 1990, 20th edit., 1996, 21st edit., 2000, Annals of Neurology, 1979—83, Advances in Pediatrics, 1989—; contbr. articles to profl. jours. With USPHS, 1967—69. Grantee NIH. Mem.: Soc. Neurosci., Internat. Child Neurology Assn., Am. Soc. Neurochemistry, Soc. Pediatric Rsch., Am. Pediatric Soc., Child Neurology Soc. (pres. 1989—91), Am. Acad. Neurology (sec. 1993—97, trustee Rsch. and Edn. Found. 1997—2001), Am. Neurol. Assn., Alpha Omega Alpha. Office: Presbyn Hosp Neurology Inst 710 W 168th St New York NY 10032-2603

DE VIVO, EDWARD CHARLES, lawyer, consultant; b. Newark, Dec. 10, 1953; s. Louis Joseph and Marian (Pistilli) DeVivo. BA cum laude, NYU, 1975, MA, 1982; JD, U. Norte Dame, 1978. Bar: NY 1979, US Dist. Ct. (so. dist.) NY, US Dist. Ct. (ea. dist.) NY. Assoc. Bigham Englar Jones & Houston, NYC, 1978—82, Condon & Forsyth, NYC, 1982—85, Catten, Muchin & Zavis, NYC, 1990—; cons. Contbr. articles. Recipient NYU Scholar, 1971—75. Mem.: Big Bros. Program, Pres. Reagan's Phys. Fitness Commn., United Way, Literacy Coun. Am., Bradford Pool and Raquet. Republican. Roman Catholic. Home: 10 Kips Rdg Verona NJ 07044-2929 Office: 40 Broad St New York NY 10004-2315

DEVLIN, FRANCIS JAMES, lawyer; b. N.Y.C., Apr. 12, 1943; s. Francis James and Marie A. D.; m. Patricia Ann Scheid; children: Christopher James, Kimberley Ann. BA magna cum laude, Providence Coll., 1964; JD, Fordham U., 1967. Bar: N.Y. 1968, Tex. 1979, U.S. Ct. Appeals (5th and 11th cirs.) 1981, U.S. Supreme Ct. 1993. Assoc. Rogers and Wells, N.Y.C., 1967-72; counsel Standard Oil Co. N.J., N.Y.C., 1972, Exxon Corp., N.Y.C., 1973-78, Exxon Co., U.S.A., Houston, 1978-90, sr. counsel, 1990-99, coord. gen. comml. practice group, 1996-99; sr. counsel Exxon Mobil Corp., Fuels Mktg. Co., 1999—2002, coord. mktg., 1999—2002; spl. counsel Duane Morris, LLP, Houston, 2003—. Articles editor Fordham Law Rev., 1966-67. Bd. dirs. Our Lady of Guadalupe Sch., Houston, 1994-2000, chmn., 1998-2000. Fellow Coll. State Bar Tex.; mem. ABA (vice-chmn. petroleum mktg. com., environment, energy and resources sect.), Tex. State Bar (Bar Jour. com. 1995-98, unauthorized practice of law com. 1989-92), Am. Petroleum Inst. (chmn. subcom. on mktg. law, gen. com. law, chmn. 1990-92, 97-98, vice-chmn. 1992-94, 98-99, emeritus mem.), Tex. Mid-Continent Oil and Gas Assn. (chmn. mktg. subcom. legal com. 1982-2000), Soc. Friendly Sons of St. Patrick in City N.Y. Republican. Roman Catholic. Home: Townhouse 112 12625 Memorial Dr Houston TX 77024-4889 Office: Duane Morris LLP 1 Greenway Plz Ste 500 Houston TX 77046 E-mail: fjdevlin@duanemorris.com.

DEVLIN, JAMES RICHARD, lawyer; b. Camden, N.J., July 7, 1950; s. Gerald William and Mary (Hand) D.; children: Grace, Jennifer, Kristen. BS in Indsl. Engring., N.J. Inst. Tech., 1972; JD, Fordham U., 1976. Bar: N.J. 1976, N.Y. 1977, Kans. 2002, U.S. Ct. Appeals (D.C. cir.) 1982. Various mgmt. positions in Long Lines Sect. AT&T, N.Y.C., 1972-76, counsel Long Lines Sect. Bedminster, N.J., 1976-82, counsel N.Y.C., 1982-83, gen. atty. comm. sect. Basking Ridge, N.J., 1983-86; v.p., gen. counsel telephone United Telecomm., Inc., Westwood, Kans., 1987-88; exec. v.p. gen. counsel and external affairs Sprint Corp., Westwood, 1989—. Past pres., bd. dirs. Ctr. for Mgmt. Assistance, Kansas City, Mo., 1993-96 Mem. ABA (past chmn. comm. com. pub. utility law sect.), Am. Arbitration Assn., Fed. Comm. Bar Assn. Home: 12300 Catalina St Leawood KS 66209-2220 Office: Sprint Corp Eisenhower A 6200 Sprint Pkwy Overland Park KS 66251

DEVLIN, JAMIE L. interior designer; b. Lebanon, Oreg., Feb. 9, 1952; d. Edward L. and Paula Y. Devlin; m. Thomas A. Sherwood. Grad., South Eugene (Oreg.) H.S., 1970. Staff designer, class instr. Ethan Allen, Portland, Oreg., 1980-85; owner Devlin Designed Interiors, Tigard, Oreg., 1985—. Recipient Golden Home award for best master suite Portland Home Bldrs. Assn., 1995, for best kitchen, 1995. Mem. Am. Soc. Interior Designers (co-chair Symphony Show House 1995). Office: Devlin Designed Interiors 12402 SW Chandler Dr Tigard OR 97224-2827

DEVLIN, JEAN THERESA, educator, storyteller; b. Jamaica, N.Y., Apr. 14, 1947; d. Edward Philip and Frances Margaret (Tillman) Creagh; children: Michael, Bernadette, Patrick. BA magna cum laude, Queens Coll., 1972, postgrad., 1994—; MA, St. John's U., Jamaica, 1987; PhD, So. Ill. U., 1991. Substitute tchr. Diocese of Bklyn., 1969-75; tchr. St. Gregory's Sch., Bellerose, N.Y., 1975-82; dist. mgr. Creative Expressions, Robesonia, Pa., 1980-83; asst. to dean, adj. instr. workshop supr. Spl. Univ. Program St. John's U., Jamaica, 1983-87, asst. prof. dept. English, 1992; asst. dean St. John's Coll. Liberal Arts, St. Johns U., 1993-94; owner Tara's Tees and Golden Hands Embroidery, 1984-87; from grad. asst. to doctoral fellow English dept. So. Ill. U., Carbondale, 1987-89, storytelling tchr. Continuing Edn., 1992; adj. asst. prof. St. John's U., Jamaica, 1992-94, Poly. U., N.Y., 1995-96, Bayside Acad., N.Y., 1995-97, St. Anthony's H.S., Huntington, N.Y., 1996-99; tchr. SCOPE (gifted and talented program) South Huntington Dist., N.Y., 1999-2000; tchr., asst. prin., tchr. Rambam Mesivta Maimonides H.S., Lawrence, NY, 1999—2001; tchr. Hicksville H.S., 2002, North Shore Hebrew Acad. H.S., 2002—; asst. prof. L.I. Conservatory, 2002—03. Cons. Family Lit. Project; supr. workshops Popular Culture, 1991-94, Children's Lit. Assn., 1990-92, Midwest Popular Culture, 1991, Wyo. Centennial, 1990; presenter poetry readings, dramatic interpretation, storytelling, including Internat. Rsch. Soc. in Children's Lit., Paris, 1991, Nat. Coun. Tchrs. English Conf., 1992, Ill. Assn. Tchrs. of English, 1990, 91, 92, South Atlantic MLA, 1992, Mid Atlantic Popular/Am. Culture, 1993; speaker Speak Easy Workshop, 1981; showcased Nat. Congress Storytelling, Children's Reading Roundtable, 1990; world-wide storyteller, 1991—; featured spkr. Puppet Guild of L.I., 1997; adj. asst. prof. So. Ill., St. John's U., Polytechnic U., Molloy Coll., 1998—. SUNY, Farmingdale, 2002—. Author: Gabby Diego, 1992, repub. 1994, Rainbows Stories and Customs from Around the World, 1996; contbr. articles to profl. jours. and children's mags.; contbg. photographer Eye of the Beholder, 2000; actress (videotape and audiocassette) Peter Kagan and the Wind, 1990, 91, played at White House, 1992, Sta. WKTS, 1992-94, Excerpts from Shakespeare, 1999, (videotape) Puppets from A to Z, 2000; performed as storyteller on 5 continents, 1991—;singer with North Shore Hebrew Acad. Choir, CD, Shiryla, 2003; mem. editl. bd. Habari Gari: A Newsletter for Catholics of African Ancestry, 1999-2000. Den leader Boy Scouts Am., Bayside, N.Y., 1975-80; troop leader Girl Scouts U.S.A., Flushing, N.Y., 1976-78; vol. Elderwise Day Care, Carbondale, Ill., 1992, Alice Wright Day Care Ctr., Carbondale, 1989-92, ABC Quilts (A Pediatric AIDS group), 1991-2000; mem. The Stage Co., Cill Cais Players. Honored for outstanding svc. Boy Scouts Am., 1978; recipient Outstanding Cmty. Svc. award, named Most Admired Woman of the Decade Sta. WPSD-TV, 1991, Internat. Women of Yr., 1993; grantee So. Ill. Art Coun., 1992; named Educator of Excellence, N.Y. State English Coun., 2000, L.I. Lang. Arts Coun., 2001. Mem.: AAUW, MLA, United Fedn. Tchrs., Am. Fedn. Tchrs., N.Y. State United Tchrs., United Univ. Profs., L.I. Lang. Arts Coun., NY State English Coun., Puppet Guild L.I., Nat. Theatre for Puppet Arts, Children's Lit. Assn., Nat. Assn. Preservation and Perpetuation of Storytelling, Nat. Coun. Tchrs. English, Phi Delta Kappa, Sigma Tau Delta, Alpha Sigma Lambda, Skull and Circle Honor Soc. (St. John's U.). Avocations: needlework, acting, puppetry. Home: 193 W 19th St Huntington Station NY 11746-2118

DEVLIN, JOHN GERARD, lawyer, author; b. Phila., Apr. 26, 1955; s. John and Catherine (Flannery) D.; m. Maureen Borneman, June 17, 1978; children: Caitlin, Colin, Courtenay, Conor. BA, Temple U., 1977, JD, 1980, LLM, 1996. Bar: Pa. 1980, N.J. 1992. Assoc. Spencer, Sherr & Moses, Norristown, Pa., 1980-82, Deasey, Scanlan & Bender, Phila., 1982-84; mng. atty. Devlin Assocs., P.A., Phila., 1984—. Author: Tort Liability for Bad Faith Claims, 1995. Mem. Union League Club, Phi Beta Kappa. Office: 1515 Market St Ste 2010 Philadelphia PA 19102-1920

DEVLIN, JOHN TOBEY, physician, educator; b. Allentown, Pa., May 22, 1951; s. John Joseph and Rosemary Ann (Kanehann) D.; m. Diane McCarthy, Dec. 18, 1976; children: Heather, Sean. BA, Lehigh U., 1973; MD, Cornell U., 1977. Resident in internal medicine Maine Med. Ctr., Portland, 1977-80; physician USPHS, Eastport, Maine, 1980-82; fellow in endocrine U. Vt., Burlington, 1982-85, asst. prof., 1985-90, assoc. prof., 1990—; assoc. dir. endocrinology Maine Med. Ctr., Portland, 1997, med. dir. Diabetes Ctr., 1991—. Co-dir. Maine Wound Ctr., 1999—. Editor: Diabetes Mellitus and Exercise, 1992, Health Professionals Guide to Diabetes and Exercise, 1995. Named Tchr. of Yr., U. Vt. Coll. Medicine, 1986. Fellow ACP, Am. Coll. Endocrinology; mem. Am. Diabetes Assn. (chmn. coun. on exercise 1993-95, Disting. Svc. award 1995). Avocations: sailing, hiking. Office: Maine Ctr Endo and Diabetes 100 US Route 1 Scarborough ME 04074-9308

DEVLIN, MARK A. pharmaceutical company executive; b. Bethlehem, Pa., July 3, 1964; s. Gerald Joseph and Carol Ann D.; m. Lynette Anne Devlin, Aug. 11, 1990; children: Thomas, Matthew, Sarah. BS, Fairleigh Dickinson U., 1986. Sales rep. Forest Labs. Inc., N.Y.C., 1986-88, divsn. sales mgr., 1988-93, regional sales dir., 1993-97, nat. dir. sales, 1997-2000, v.p. sales, 2000—. Mem. Corpus Christi Ch. Mem. Phi Sigma Kappa. Office: Forest Labs 909 3rd Ave New York NY 10022 E-mail: mark.devlin@FRX.com.

DEVLIN, MICHAEL COLES, bass-baritone; b. Chgo., Nov. 27, 1942; s. John Stott and Jane (Coles) D. MusB, La. State U., 1965. Debut, N.Y.C. Opera, 1966, appeared with, Santa Fe Opera, Houston Opera and Symphony, San Francisco Symphony, symphonies in Los Angeles, Phila., Boston, Chgo., New Orleans, Washington, N.Y. Philharm., opera cos. in, Boston, New Orleans, Washington, Ft. Worth, English debut, Glyndebourne Festival, 1974; appeared at, Covent Garden, 1975, 77, European debut, Holland Festival, 1977; appeared with, Frankfurt and Munich operas, 1977, Can. opera and symphony work in, Winnipeg, Toronto and Ottawa, debut, Met. Opera, 1978, San Francisco Opera, 1979, Hamburg and Paris operas, 1980, Miami and Monte Carlo operas, 1981, Dallas opera, 1983, Chgo. Opera, 1984, Los Angeles Opera, 1986.

DEVLIN, ROBERT MANNING, insurance company executive; b. Bklyn., Feb. 28, 1941; s. John Manning and Norma (Hall) D.; m. Katharine Bareis, Sept. 13, 1961; children: Michael Hall II, Matthew Bareis. BA in Econs., Tulane U., 1964. Various positions Mut. of N.Y., 1964-77; v.p., asst. to pres. Calif. Western States Life Ins. Co., Sacramento, 1977-80, sr. v.p., 1980; exec. v.p., dir. Am. Gen. Life and Accident Ins. Co., Nashville, 1980-85; exec. v.p. Am. Gen. Corp., Houston, 1986—; pres., CEO, dir. Am. Gen. Life Ins. Co. Tex., Houston, 1986-93; CEO, chmn. Am. Gen. Corp., Houston, 1997—; chmn. Curragh Capital Ptnrs. LLC. Vice chmn. Am. Gen. Corp., 1993—95, pres., CEO, 1995—97, chmn., bd. dirs., CEO, 1997; mem. Saratoga Reading Rms., Saratoga

Springs, NY; bd. dirs. Cooper Industries Inc., Phillips Petroleum Co.; mem. exec. com., bd. dirs. Internat. Ins. Soc. Inc. Nat. trustee Boys and Girls Club Am.; dir. Fin. Svcs. Roundtable; mem. Bus. Roundtable. Mem. Winged Foot Golf Club (N.Y.), Met. Club (N.Y.), Univ. Club (N.Y.C.), Caves Valely Golf Club (Owings Mill, Md.). Roman Catholic. Home: 11F 800 Fifth Ave New York NY 10021-7216 Office: Curragh Capital Ptnrs LLC 609 Fifth Ave 2d Fl New York NY 10017 also: 730 5th Ave Ste 2102 New York NY 10019

DEVLIN, THOMAS MCKEOWN, biochemist, educator; b. Phila., June 29, 1929; s. Frank and Ella Mae (McKeown) D.; m. Marjorie Adele Paynter, Aug. 15, 1953; children— Steven James, Mark Thomas. BA, U. Pa., 1953; PhD, Johns Hopkins U., 1957. Rsch. assoc. Merck Inst., Rahway, N.J., 1957-61, sect. head, 1961-66, dir. enzymology, 1966-67; prof., chmn. dept. biochemistry Hahnemann U. Sch. Medicine, 1967-94, prof., 1994-95; prof. emeritus, 1995—; acting dean, Sch. Allied Health Professions Hahnemann U., 1972-74, 80-81. Vis. scientist U. Brussels, 1964-65, Inst. Genetics, Naples, Italy, 1965; mem. NSF rev. panels, 1976-77; mem. coun. acad. soc. Assn. Am. Med. Colls., 1975-79; mem. com. on sci. and arts Franklin Inst., 1977-90; mem. test com. Nat. Bd. Med. Examiners, 1983-85; chair Med. Biochemistry Edn. Bd., 1986-93. Editor: (J. Wiley) Textbook of Biochemistry, 1982, 86, 92, 97, 2002; contbr. numerous articles to profl. jours. Mem. Commn. on Evaluation, Retention and Selection of Judges, Phila. Bar Assn., 1976-79, vice chmn., 1979; vis. com. Lehigh U., 1982-90; mem. selection panel for magistrate judges, 1993, 95; mem. tech. adv. com. Ben Franklin Tech. Ctr., 1991-2000. Mem. Am. Soc. for Biochemistry and Molecular Biology, Am. Assn. Cancer Research, Am. Soc. Cell Biology, Soc. Exptl. Biology and Medicine, Biophys. Soc., Biochem. Soc., Phi Beta Kappa, Sigma Xi. Clubs: Ocean City (N.J.) Yacht, Greate Bay Golf Club. Episcopalian. Home: 159 Greenville Ct Berwyn PA 19312-2071 Office: Drexel U Coll Medicine 159 Greenville Ct Berwyn PA 19312-2071 E-mail: tdevlin@drexel.edu.

DEVLIN, WILLIAM RUSSELL, newspaper owner; b. Northwood, N.D., Sept. 18, 1947; s. Russell T. and Marie E. Devlin; m. Marjorie Ann Offerdahl, Feb. 3, 1967; children: Russell, Patrick. Co-owner, co-pub. Steele County Press, Finley, N.D., 1970—. County Commr. Steele County, Finley, 1984-98; state rep. N.D., Bismarck, 1996—; mem. past pres. Finley Comm. Club. Named Legislator of Yr., ND Long-term Care Assn., 2001. Mem. N.D. Newspaper Assn. (bd. dirs. 1973-79, state pres. 1978-79), Eagles, Sigma Delta Chi (state pres. 1972-73). Office: Steele County Press Inc PO Box 475 Finley ND 58230-0475

DEVOE, DAVID, publishing executive; Dep. fin. dir. News Am. Holding Inc., N.Y.C., 1983—89; dep. CFO News Corp., N.Y.C., 1989—90, sr. exec. v.p., CFO, 1990—. Dir. William Collins Holdings, Harper Collins, British Sky Broadcasting Group, NDS Group, The News Corp. Office: News Corp Ste 300 1211 Avenue Of The Americas New York NY 10036-8795*

DEVOGT, JOHN FREDERICK, management science and business ethics educator, consultant; b. Detroit, Oct. 20, 1930; s. Leo Henry and Dorothy Helen (Gibbs) D.; m. Ann Marie Berby, Aug. 29, 1959; children— Joanne Elise, Linda Christine BS, U. N.C., 1957, PhD, 1966. Instr. Washington and Lee U., Lexington, Va., 1962-66, asst. prof., 1966-67, assoc. prof., 1967-70, prof., 1970-2000, head dept., 1968-90, prof. emeritus, 2000—; acad. dir. Washington and Lee Family Bus. Inst., 1987-89. State judge Blue Chip Enterprise Initiative, 1991-96; acad. Jonah A.Y. Goldratt Inst., 1991—; chmn. adv. bd. Lexington office CorEast Savs. Bank, Richmond, 1976-90. Chmn. Lexington City Sch. Bd., 1973; pres. Va. Sch. Bds. Assn., Charlottesville, 1974; v.p. Henry St. Playhouse, Lexington, 1985, Friends Rockbridge Choral Soc., 2000—. Served to staff sgt. USAF, 1951—55. Vis. fellow Univ. Coll., Oxford, Eng., 1983 Mem. So. Mgmt. Assn. (pres. 1975-76), Lexington Golf and Country Club (bd. dirs. 2003), Phi Beta Kappa, Phi Eta Sigma, Beta Gamma Sigma Presbyterian. Avocations: golf, amateur dramatics, singing. Home: 617 Stonewall St Lexington VA 24450-1947 Office: Washington and Lee Univ Lexington VA 24450 Personal E-mail: jdevogt@rockbridge.net. Business E-Mail: devogtj@wlu.edu.

DEVOL, GEORGE CHARLES, JR., manufacturing executive; b. Feb. 20, 1912; s. George C. and Elsa (Vance) D.; m. Evelyn R. Jahelka, Dec. 31, 1938; children: Christine, George C. III, Robert, Vance, Suzanne. PhD in Sci., U. Bridgeport, 1985. Pres. United Cinephone Corp., N.Y., 1933-39; project engr. Sperry Gyroscope Co., Garden City, N.Y., 1939-41; gen. mgr. Gen. Electronic Industries, Greenwich, Conn., 1941-45; pres. Devol Rsch. Co., Ft. Lauderdale, Fla., 1947—, Automatic Mfg. Sys., Inc., Ft. Lauderdale, 1984—. Patentee in field of indsl. robots (40 patents). Mem. Soc. Mfg. Engrs. (life), Ocean Reef Club, Key Largo Club, Lago Mar Club. Home and Office: 7460 NW 1st Pl Plantation FL 33317-2265 E-mail: georgedevol@hotmail.com.

DEVOL, LUANA, dramatic soprano, consultant, arts administrator; b. San Mateo, Calif., Nov. 30, 1942; AA, Coll. San Mateo, 1960; postgrad., San Francisco State U., 1962, U.S. Internat. U., San Diego, 1970. Asst. to bd. dirs. Spring Opera Theatre, San Francisco, 1972-75; asst. gen. mgr. Paramount Theatre, Oakland, Calif., 1975-84; soprano Mannheim Nat. Theater, Germany, 1987-91. Opera singer Bayreuth, Berlin, Hamburg, Munich, Dresden, Leipzig, San Francisco, Florence, La Scala, Vienna, Paris, Helsinki, others; pvt. voice cons.; guest lectr. U. Md., Mannheim, 1991, 94 Seminar, European Singing Career, 1987, master class U. Nev., Las Vegas, 1996, 98, N.Y., 1999; mem. editl. bd. The Oakland Paramount, 1988. Made European debut as Leonore in Fidelio, Württembergische Staatsoper, 1983; roles include Isolde, Senta, Elsa, Elisabeth, Brunnhilde, Elektra, Faerberin, Kaiserin, Ariadne, Norma, Aida, Amelia, Tosca, Donna Anna and Donna Elvira. Trustee Young Artists Festival, Bayreuth, Germany. U.S. Internat. U. scholar, 1971; named Singer of Yr. Opern Welt, 1997, 2000. Mem. Richard Wagner Soc. (hon.), Am. Guild Musical Artists, Am.-German C. of C. Home: 1908 Grey Eagle St Henderson NV 89074-0670

DEVONE, DENISE, artist, educator; BFA cum laude, Temple U., 1975; MFA, U. Hawaii, 1978. Instr. Newark Mus., 1990-97; art tchr. Holy Cross Sch., Harrison, N.J., 1995—. Adj. prof. County Coll. of Morris, Randolph, N.J., 1994—; cons. Donald B. Palmer Mus., Springfield, N.J., 1992-95. Executed murals Kaiser Hosp., Honolulu, 1985, Kaiser Pensacola Clinic, Honolulu, 1986, Distinctive Bodies Fitness, Warren, N.J., 1993, Ambulatory Pediatric Clinic, Overlook Hosp., Summit, N.J., 1994; one-woman shows include Contemporary Mus., Honolulu, 1992, ETS, Princeton, 1995, Montclair Kimberly Acad., N.J., 1995, 98, ADP Gallery, Roseland, N.J., 1997, Palmyra Gallery, Bound Brook, N.J., 1999; illustrator: Japanese Pilgramage, 1983, The Art of Featherwork in Old Hawaii, 1985. Recipient Purchase awards Hawaii State Found. on Culture and the Arts, 1976, 78, 80, 86, award of merit City and County of Honolulu, 1988; N.J. State Coun. on Arts/Dept. State fellow, 1994-95. Mem. Nat. Assn. Women Artists, Inc., Studio Montclair, Inc., City Without Walls, Artists Space. Avocation: piano. Home: 33 Kew Dr Springfield NJ 07081-2530

DEVONS, SAMUEL, educator, physicist; b. Bangor, N.Wales, U.K., Sept. 30, 1914; came to U.S., 1959; s. David Isaac and Edith (Edlestein) D.; m. Celia Ruth Toubkin, Sept. 7, 1938; children— Susan Danielle, Judith Rosalind, Amanda Jane, Cathryn Ann Julie. BA, Trinity Coll., Cambridge (Eng.) U., 1935, MA, PhD (Exhbn. 1851 scholar), 1939; M.Sc., Manchester (Eng.) U., 1959. Sr. sci. officer Air Ministry, Ministry Supply, U.K., 1939-45; fellow, dir. studies, lectr. physics Trinity Coll., 1946-49; prof. physics Imperial Coll., London, Eng., 1950-55; Langworthy prof. physics, dir. phys. labs. U. Manchester, 1955-60; prof. physics Columbia U., 1960-84, prof. emeritus, spl. rsch. scientist, 1985—, chmn. dept., 1963-67. Royal Soc.-Leverhulme vis. prof., Andhra, India, 1967-68; Racah vis. prof. physics Hebrew U., Jerusalem, 1973; Balfour vis. prof. history of sci. Weizmann Inst., Israel, 1974, bd. govs., 1971—; Royal Soc. Rutherford Meml. Lectr., Australia, 1989; mem. Tech. Assistance-UNESCO Team of UN to S. Am., 1957 Author: Excited States of Nuclei, 1949; Editor: Biology and the Physical Sciences, 1969, High Energy Physics and Nuclear Structure, 1970. Served with RAF, 1944-45. Recipient Rutherford medal and prize Inst. Physics, U.K., 1970 Fellow: Phi Beta Kappa, The Joseph Priestley Assn. (founder, convenor 1986—), N.Y. Acad. Scis., Am. Phys. Soc., Royal Soc. London. Home: 34 Lewis Rd Irvington NY 10533-2005 Office: Columbia U Nevis Lab PO Box 137 Irvington NY 10533-0137 E-mail: devons@nevis1.columbia.edu.

DEVONSHIRE, DAVID W. financial executive; BS in Acctg., Widener U.; MBA, Northwestern U. With Am. Hosp. Supply Corp., 1974—85; v.p. finance, controller Baxter Internat., 1985—87; corp. contr. Mead Corp., 1987—90; corp. v.p., controller Honeywell, 1990—92, v.p. finance, 1992—93; sr. v.p., CFO Owens Corning, Toledo, 1993-98; exec. v.p., CFO Ingersoll-Rand Co., 1998—2002, Motorola, 2002—. Office: Motorola Inc 1303 E Algonquin Rd Schaumburg IL 60196-1079

DEVORE, DALE PAUL, scientific research organization executive; b. Phillipsburg, N.J., Mar. 31, 1943; s. David Henry DeVore and Anna Elizabeth DeVore-Iskra; m. Sandra Bernice Grebowiec, Dec. 27, 1965; children: Mychelle Leigh, Braden Patrick. BS, Rutgers U., 1966, MS, 1972, PhD, 1973. Prin. biochemist Battelle Meml. Inst., Columbus, Ohio, 1972-79; sr. rsch. specialist 3M, St. Paul, 1979-85; v.p. sci. affairs MedChem Products, Woburn, Mass., 1985-88; chief sci. officer Autogenesis Tech., Inc., Acton, Mass., 1988-96; chief sci. officer, co-founder, sr. v.p. R&D, dir. Collagenesis, Inc., Beverly, Mass., 1996—. Cons. Auto Immune, Lexington, Mass., 1993-94; dir. biomaterials Organogenesis, Inc., Canton, Mass., 1994-95; chief tech. officer Keratoform, Inc., Westerly, R.I., 1994-98, Xium, Westerly, 1998—, Keracon Corp., 2000—; tech. advisor Pericor Sci., Inc., 1999—. Patentee 51 inventions; contbr. over 60 articles to profl. jours.; presenter in field. Mem. AAAS, Assn. Rsch. Vision Ophthalmology, Soc. Biomaterials, Am. Coll. Rheumatology, Am. Urol. Soc., Kiwanis (treas. 1978), Lions Club (v.p. 1984). Home: 3 Warwick Dr Chelmsford MA 01824-3769 Office: Collagenesis Inc 500 Cummings Ctr Beverly MA 01915-6142

DEVORE, KIMBERLY K. business executive; b. Louisville, June 19, 1947; d. Wendell O. and Shirley F. DeV. Student, Xavier U., 1972-76; AA, Coll. Mt. St. Joseph, 1979; BA, Internat. U. Metaphysics, 1999. Patient registration supr. St. Francis Hosp., Cin., 1974-76; cons., bus. mgr. Family Health Care Found., Cin., 1976-77; exec. dir. Hospice of Cin., Inc., 1977-80; pres. Micro Med, 1979-86; v.p. Sycamore Profl. Assn., 1979-86; ptnr. Enchanted House, 1979-86, sec., 1979-80, treas., 1980-83; dist. sales rep. Control-O-Fax, 1986; br. sales mgr., 1987; nat. dealer devel. rep., 1987; nat. computer field sales trainer, 1987-90; pres. U.S. Exec. Leasing and U.S. Med. Leasing, Inc., 1991—2001, Accu Svcs. Inc., 1993—, U.S. Med. Mgmt., Inc., 1994-98. Pres. U.S. Med. Mgmt. of Ga., Inc., 1996—. Pres. Saddle Creek Homeowners Assn., Inc., 1992-95, parliamentarian, 1995-96;; chairperson Citizen's Police Adv. Com. City of Roswell, 1997-99; chairperson found. grants Orch. Atlanta, 1998-99, pres., 1999—, vice-chmn., pres. & CEO, chaplin Unity N. Atlanta, 2000—; bd. dirs., membership chairperson Smith Plantation City of Roswell, 1996-97; pres. Roswell Citizen's Police Acad., Inc., 1994-95; mem. City of Roswell Med. Devel. Dist. Coun., 1995—; mem. North Fulton Civic League, Inc., 1995-96, 2001--; chaplin Unity N.Atlanta Ch.; bd. dirs. Nat. Hospice Orgn., 1979-82, chmn. long-term planning com., fin. com., ann. meeting com., 1979-82, sec., 1980-81, treas., 1981-82; bd. dirs. Hospice of Miami Valley, Inc., 1982-86, also chmn. pers. com., by-laws com.; bd. dirs. Orch. Atlanta, 1998—. Mem. Greater Clin. Soc. Fund Raisers, Better Housing League; mem. service and rehab. com. Hamilton County Unit, Am. Cancer Soc., 1977-78; chair road com. Saddle Creek Homeowners Assn., 1991-92. Mem. Ohio Hospice Assn. (co-founder, state chmn., pres., 1978-83), Nat. League for Nursing, Ohio Hosp. Assn., Nat. Fedn. Bus. and Profl. Women's Clubs, Ohio Fedn. Bus. and Profl. Women's Clubs, Cin. Bus. and Profl. Women's Clubs (pres. 1973-75).

DEVORE, PAUL CAMERON, lawyer; b. Great Falls, Mont., Apr. 25, 1932; s. Paul Theodore and Maxine (Cameron) DeV.; m. Roberta Humphrey, Feb. 3, 1962; children: Jennifer Ross, Andrew Cameron, Christopher Humphrey. BA, Yale U., 1954; MA, Cambridge U., 1956; JD, Harvard U., 1961. Bar: Wash. 1961. Assoc. Wright, Innis, Simon & Todd, Seattle, 1961-66; ptnr. Davis Wright Tremaine, Seattle, 1967—, chmn. exec. com., 1983-95. Mem. adv. bd. BNA Media Law Reporter, 1978—. Chmn. Seattle C.C., 1967-68, Bush Sch., Seattle, 1976-79, Virginia Mason Med. Found., 1984-85, Virginia Mason Rsch. Ctr., 1983-84, Seattle Found., 1985-87, Children's Hosp. Found., 1993-95; trustee Lakeside Sch., 1995—; chmn. bd. visitors U. Wash. Sch. Comm., 1989-98; pres. A Contemporary Theatre, Seattle, 1972-74; sec. Seattle Art Mus., 1973-2000. Mem. ABA (chmn. forum on comm. law 1981-84), Wash. State Bar Assn. (chmn. sect. corp. bus. and banking law 1981-82, bench, bar, press com. 1984-90), Seattle-King County Bar Assn. (trustee 1975-76), Seattle Tennis Club, Phi Beta Kappa, Beta Theta Phi. Home: 5740 27th Ave NE Seattle WA 98105-5512 Office: Davis Wright Tremaine 2600 Century Sq 1501 4th Ave Ste 2600 Seattle WA 98101-1688 E-mail: camdevore@dwt.com.

DE VORE, PAUL WARREN, technology educator; b. Parkersburg, W.Va., July 18, 1926; s. Harry and Eleanor Sarah (Dunn) De Vore; m. Eleanor Jean Condron, Apr. 7, 1952; children: Harry Edwin, Michelle Ann, Phillip Charles. BS, Ohio U., 1950; MA, Kent State U., 1954; EdD, Pa. State U., 1961; postgrad., Ohio State U., 1983. Postdoctoral fellow U. Md., 1965-66; instr. pub. schs. Chagrin Falls, Ohio, 1950-53; asst. prof. engring. Grove City Coll., 1953-56; asst. prof. SUNY-Oswego, 1956-60, dir. div. indsl. arts and tech., 1960-67; prof. tech. edn. W. Va. U., Morgantown, 1967-75, prof., chmn. tech. edn., 1975-85, prof., coord. rsch. project offices, dept. technology, 1985-92; dir. Appalachian Tech. Edn. Consortium, 1990-95; dir. div. edn. and tng. Nat. Tech. Transfer Ctr., 1992-93. Tech. cons., pres. PWD Assocs., Morgantown, W.Va., 1974—; cons. NSF, U.S. Dept. Edn., AID, pub. schs., colls., univs.; mem. com. technol. literacy Nat. Acad. Engring., 1999—; pres. Aviation Resources Inc., 1999—; pres. Hart Field Coalition, 1998-2003. Author: Technology: An Intellectual Discipline, 1964, Education in a Technological Society, 1971, Technology and the New Liberal Arts, 1976, Technology: An Introduction, 1980, Introduction to Transportation, 1983; cons. editor: Tech. Edn. Series, 1974-93. Mem. nat. commn. Tech. for All Ams., 1994—95; chmn. campaign United Fund, Oswego, 1962—63; mem. Monongalia County Devel. Authority, 2000—. Served with USN, 1944—46. Named Outstanding Tchr., W.Va. U., 1970-71, 89, W.Va. U. Coll. Resources and Edn., 1988; recipient Outstanding Rsch. award Phi Delta Kappa, 1978; recognized as one of individuals who has contbd. most to tech. edn., 1985, Internat. Tech. Edn. Assn. Acad. of Fellows, 1987. Mem. Coun. on Tech. Tchr. Edn. (life), Soc. History of Tech., Internat. Tech. Edn. Assn., Epsilon Pi Tau (Disting. Svc. award 1976, Paul T. Hiser Exemplary Publ. award 1988, 99, Bill Hart Aviation award 2001). Home: 668 Colonial Dr Morgantown WV 26505-2423 Office: W Va U Tech Edn Rsch Proj Offices Morgantown WV 26506-6680 *Seek quality in all you do and conduct your personal and civic affairs in a responsible and civil manner.*

DE VOS, GEORGE ALPHONSE, psychologist, anthropologist; b. Detroit, July 25, 1922; s. Medard Joseph and Marina Marie (Tack) De V.; m. Winifred Olsen, May 4, 1944 (div. 1974); m. Suzanne Lake, Nov. 18, 1974; children: Laurie, Susan, Eric, Michael. BA in Sociology, U. Chgo., 1946, MA in Anthropology, 1948, PhD in Psychology, 1951. Chief psychologist, dir. psychol. tng. Elgin (Ill.) State Hosp., 1951-53; asst. prof. psychology U. Mich., Ann Arbor, 1955-57; assoc. prof. social welfare U. Calif., Berkeley, 1957-63, prof. anthropology, 1963-91, prof. emeritus, 1991—. Vis. prof. U. Rome, 1975, U. Paris, 1979, Cath. U. Leuven, Belgium, 1986, U. Barcelona, 1992; exch. prof. U. Leningrad (now U. St. Petersburg), 1990; chmn. Ctr. for Japanese and Korean Studies U. Calif., 1965—91; cons. Family Planning Rsch., Korean Inst. Behavioral Scis., Seoul, Republic of Korea, 1970—71; rsch. assoc. Ecole des Hautes Etudes en Scis. Sociales, U. Paris, 1973—91; sr. cons. series prodn. The Japanese Film PBS, 1975; dir. NSF project The Korean Minority in Japan; cons. on Japanese culture Human Rels. Area File, New Haven, 1975—82; cons. Cultural Learning East-West Center, Hawaii, 1978—79. Author: 22 books, including Oasis and Casbah, 1960, Japan's Invisible Race, 1966, Socialization for Achievement, 1973, Ethnic Identity, 1975, 3d edit., 1995, Responses to Change, 1976, Koreans in Japan, 1981, Heritage of Endurance: Delinquency in Japan, 1984, Culture and Self, 1985, 1984, Religion and the Family in East Asia, 1986, Symbolic Analysis Cross Culturally: The Rorschach Test, 1989, Status Inequality, 1990, Social Cohesion and Alienation, 1992, Confucianism and The Family, 1998, Basic Dimensions in Conscious Thought, 2003, Narrative Research Crossing Cultural Boundaries, 2003. Fulbright fellow, Nagoya, Japan, 1953-55, NIMH fellow French Min. Justice, 1963, NSF fellow UN Social Def. Rsch. Inst., Rome, 1972-73; Fulbright Sr. Rsch. Sch. Cath. U. Rio Grande do Sul, Brazil, 1992. Mem. APA (pres. Soc. Sch. for Psychol. Anthropology 1984-85), Assn. Asian Studies, Am. Anthropology Assn. Home: 2835 Morley Dr Oakland CA 94611-2547 E-mail: devos@sscl-berkeley.edu.

DE VOS, PETER JON, ambassador; b. San Diego, Dec. 24, 1938; BA, Princeton U., 1960; MA, Johns Hopkins U., 1962. Consular officer Am. Consulate, Recife, Brazil, 1962-64; fgn. service officer for Brazil Dept. State, Washington, 1964-66; polit. officer Am. Consulate, Naples, 1966-68; dep. prin. officer Am. Embassy, Luanda, 1968-70; polit. officer Am. Consulate, Sao Paulo, 1970-71, Am. Embassy, Brasilia, 1971-73; spl. asst. Bur. Inter-Am. Affairs Dept. State, Washington, 1973-75; polit. officer Am. Embassy, Athens, 1975-78, Nat. War. Coll., 1978-79; dep. dir. So. African Affairs Dept. State, Washington, 1979-80; U.S. ambassador to Republic of Guinea-Bissau and to Republic of Cape Verde, 1980-83, Mozambique, Maputo, 1983-87; dep. asst. sec. of state U.S. Dept. State, Washington, 1987-89, prin. dep. asst. sec. state Bur. Oceans and Internat. Environ. and Sci. Affairsv, 1989-90, amb. to Republic of Liberia, 1990-92, appointed U.S. spl. envoy to Somalia, 1992, amb. to Republic of Tanzania, 1992-94, amb. to Republic of Costa Rica, 1994-97. Disting. guest lectr. U. Chgo., 1997—; Rivers chair prof. East Carolina U., 2000—. Home: 410 Point Of View Dr Merritt NC 28556-9624

DEVOS, RICHARD MARVIN, JR., (DICK DEVOS), retired direct sales company executive, sports team executive; b. Grand Rapids, Mich., Oct. 21, 1955; s. Richard Marvin and Helen June (Van Wesep) DeV.; m. Elisabeth Dee Prince, Feb. 24, 1979. BBA, Northwood U., 1981. Coordinator sales Amway Corp., Ada, Mich., 1973-75, coordinator meetings, 1975-77, mgmt. trainee, 1977-82, dir. spl. events, 1982-84, v.p. internat., 1984-89, pres., bd. dirs., 1993-00; ret.; pres., bd. dirs. Alticor, Inc., 2000—02. Bd. dirs. USA DSA, 1993-98, vice chmn. 1995-97, chmn. 1997, Old Kent Fin. Corp., 1994-01; bd. dirs. Fifth Third Bank W. Mich.; founder The Windquest Group, 1989—, pres., 1989-93. Author: Rediscovering American Values, 1992. Chmn. Kent Ottawa Muskegon Fgn. Trade Zone Bd., 1989-96, chmn. Coalition for Better Schs., 1993-94; bd. dirs. Mackinac Ctr., 1990-95, Kent Hosp. Fin. Authority, 1980-93, West Mich. Boy Scouts Am., 1985-93, chmn. Blodgett Health Care, Butterworth Found., 1994—; co-chmn. Grand Rapids Area Negro Coll. Fund, 1989-92; mem. by appointment of Pres. Bush Commn. on Presdl. Scholars, 1991-93; elected mem. Mich. State Bd. Edn., 1991-93; bd. trustees Davenport Coll. Bus., 1991-2000; apptd. mem. bd. of control Grand Valley State U., 1995-2000; bd. dirs., exec. com. Project Rehab, 1978-84; mem. bd. dirs. Bus. Industry Political Action Com., 1995—; co-chmn. Grand Action Com., 1992—; chmn. Edn. Freedom Fund, 1994—; bd. dirs. Willow Creek Assoc., 1997—; chmn. Restoring the Am. Dream, 1998—. Recipient Grand Rapids Jaycees Disting. Svc. award 1985, Disting. Svc. Citation Northwood U., 1991, Assn. Ind. Colls. and Univs. Mich. Disting. Svc. award, 1992. Mem. Nat. Assn. of Mfgs. (bd. dirs. 1994-2000. Lodges: Rotary. Avocations: sailing, skiing. Office: The Windquest Group 126 Ottawa NW Ste 400 Grand Rapids MI 49503 Home: 2003 Hillsboro Ave SE Grand Rapids MI 49546-9791*

DEVOY, STEPHEN DOUGLAS, marine engineer; b. Galveston, Tex., Dec. 23, 1950; s. Charles Stephen and Dee (Bryan) D.; m. Paula S. Devoy; children: Alicia, Erich Douglas. BS in Marine Engring., Tex. A&M U., 1973; MS in Ocean Engring., MIT, 1974; postgrad., U. Hawaii, 1975. Lic. adjuster, Tex. Bd. Ins.; lic. unltd. horsepower 1st. asst. engr. for any ocean, Tex. 1st asst. engr. Marine Engrs. Beneficial Assn., Houston, 1974-80; lectr. marine, elec. and indsl. engring., computer sci. Tex. A&M U., Galveston, 1981; marine engr., project mgr. ocean tows Matthews-Daniel Marine, Inc., Houston, 1981-83; v.p. J.F. Moore, Inc., Houston, 1983-84; sr. v.p., marine engr., project mgr. ocean tows Matthews-Daniel Co., Houston, 1984—, also bd. dirs. Contbr. articles to profl. publs. Mem. adv. bd. dirs. Offshore Energy Mus. Mem. Nat. Assn. Marine Surveyors (cert., regional v.p.), Soc. Naval Archs. and Marine Engrs., Marine Tech. Soc. (chmn. or co-chmn. program com. 1990-98), Marine Engrs. Beneficial Assn., Internat. Assn. Drilling Contractors (tech. sec. jack-up rig com.), Propeller Club U.S., Houston Mariners Club. Office: Matthews Daniel 4544 Post Oak Place Dr Houston TX 77027-3161

DE VRIES, BAREND ARIE, economist, educator; b. Utrecht, The Netherlands, Oct. 22, 1925; arrived in U.S., 1946; s. Jacob and Mettje (Verburg) De V.; m. Margaret Garritsen; children: Christine, Barton. BS, U. Utrecht, 1946; MA, U. Chgo., 1948; PhD in Econs., MIT, 1951. Economist Internat. Monetary Fund, Washington, 1949-55; div. chief Latin. Am., chief econs. Latin Am. and West Africa, dep. dir. econs. dept., dir. credit worthiness World Bank, 1955-84, cons., 1984—; prof. econs. Johns Hopkins U., Balt., 1966-67, George Washington U., Washington, 1969-72, Georgetown U., 1986-90. Guest scholar Brookings Inst., 1984-85. Author: The Export Experience of Developing Countries, 1967, The Debt Bearing Capacity of Developing Countries, 1971, Remaking The World Bank, 1987, Champions of the Poor, The Economic Consequences of Judeo-Christian Values, 1998. Grantee, Soc. Sci. Rsch. Coun., 1950—51. Mem.: Am. Econ. Assn., Assn. Christian Econs. Mem. United Ch. Of Christ. Home and Office: 10018 Woodhill Rd Bethesda MD 20817-1218

DEVRIES, DAVID JOHN, mathematician, educator; b. Grand Rapids, Mich., Sept. 22, 1942; s. John and Janet DeVries; m. Mary Elaine Vander Molen, Jan. 1, 1965. PhD, Penn State U., Univ. Pk., Pa. 1965—69; BA, Calvin Coll., Grand Rapids, Mich., 1962—65. Asst. prof. of math. Hobart & William Smith Colleges, Geneva, NY, 1969—71; assoc. prof. of math. Mars Hill Coll., Mars Hill, NC, 1971—83; prof. of math. Ga. Coll. & State U., Milledgeville, Ga., 1983—2003. Mem.: AAUP, Assn. of Rsch. in Undergraduate Math. Edn., Math. Assn. of Am. Office: Georgia College & State University Hancock Street Milledgeville GA 31061

DEVRIES, JAMES HOWARD, lawyer; b. Chgo., Mar. 17, 1932; s. James and Ruth Frances (Heuman) DeV.; m. Eleanor Newport Smith, Mar. 3, 1956; children: Sara, James, Peter, Adam, Mary. BS in Bus. Mgmt., U. Colo., 1954; JD with distinction, U. Mich., 1961. Bar: Ill. 1961. Assoc. Hopkins & Sutter, Chgo., 1961-62; ptnr. McBride & Baker, Chgo., 1963-82; chmn., chief exec. officer LaserVideo, Inc., Chgo., 1982-88; vice chmn. Disc Mfg. Inc., Chgo., 1991-97; exec. v.p., sec. Quixote Corp., Chgo., 1969-97, ret., 1997, also bd. dirs., 1969—; pres. Legal Techs. Inc., Chgo., 1993-96, also bd. dirs. Pres. Library Internat. Relations, Chgo., 1980-83; dir. Internat. Trade Club, Chgo., 1974-76, Chg. Commons, 1999—. Served to lt. USN, 1954-58. Mem. Univ. Club (Chgo.), Am. Corp. Counsel Assn., Michigan Shores Club (Wilmette, Ill.), Chgo. Literary Club. Avocations: photography, flying. Home: 467 Willow Rd Winnetka IL 60093-4140 Office: Quixote Corp 1 E Wacker Dr Chicago IL 60601-1802

DE VRIES, KENNETH LAWRENCE, mechanical engineer, educator; b. Ogden, Utah, Oct. 27, 1933; s. Sam and Fern (Slater) DeV.; m. Kay M. McGee, Mar. 1, 1959; children: Kenneth, Susan. AS in Civil Engring., Weber State Coll., 1953; BSME, U. Utah, 1959, PhD in Physics, Mech. Engring., 1962. Registered profl. engr., Utah. Rsch. engr. hydraulic group Convair Aircraft Corp., Fort Worth, 1957-58; prof. dept. mech. engring. U. Utah, Salt Lake City, 1969-75, 1976-91, disting. prof., 1991—, chmn. dept., 1970-81; sr. assoc. dean U. Utah Coll. Engring., Salt Lake City, 1983-97, acting dean, 1997-98. Program dir. div. materials rsch. NSF, Washington, 1975-76; materials cons. Browning, Morgan, Utah, 1972—; cons. 3M Co., Mpls., 1985—; tech. adv. bd. Emerson Electric, St. Louis, 1978-2002; mem. Utah Coun. Sci. and Tech., 1973-77; trustee Gordon Rsch. Conf., 1989-97, chair, 1992-93. Co-author: Analysis and Testing of Adhesive Bonds, 1978; contbr. chpts. to numerous books, articles and abstracts to profl. publs. Fellow ASME, Am. Phys. Soc.; mem. Am. Chem. Soc. (polymer div.), Soc. Engring. Scis. (nat. officer), Adhesion Soc. (nat. officer). Mem. Lds Ch. Office: U Utah Coll Engring 50 S Central Campus Dr Salt Lake City UT 84112-9249

DEVRIES, LINDA JANE, music educator; b. Conrad, Mont., May 1, 1937; d. Kenneth Paul and Leda Ruth Copley; m. Richard John DeVries, Sept. 11, 1959; children: Allan, Cheryl, Julie, Michelle. Bachelor of Music, U. Mont., 1959. Nat. cert. tchr. music. Tchr. piano pvt. practice, Malta, Mont., 1964—2003. Accompanist Malta Pub. Schs., 1974—2003. Mem.: Mont. State Music Tchrs. Assn. (student affiliate chair 1966—70, treas. 1970—82, cert. chair 1982—95, mem. cert. bd. 1995—2003).

DE VRIES, MARGARET GARRITSEN, economist; b. Detroit, Feb. 11, 1922; d. John Edward and Margaret Florence (Ruggles) Garritsen; m. Barend A. de Vries, Apr. 5, 1952; children: Christine, Barton. BA in Econs. with honors, U. Mich., 1943; PhD in Econs., MIT, 1946. With IMF, Washington, 1946-87, sr. economist, 1949-52, asst. chief multiple currency pratices div., 1953-57, chief Far Eastern Div., 1957-59, econ. cons., 1963-73, historian, 1973-87. Professo-

rial lectr. econs. George Washington U., 1946-49, 58-63 Author: The International Monetary Fund, 1966-71, The System Under Stress, 2 vols., 1977, The International Monetary Fund, 1972-78, Cooperation on Trial, 3 vols., 1985, The IMF in a Changing World, 1945-85, transl. into Chinese, 1986, Balance of Payments, Adjustment: The IMF Experience, 1945-86, transl. into Chinese, 1989, (with I.S. Friedman) Foreign Economic Policy of the United States in the Postwar, 1947, (with J.K. Horsefield) The International Monetary Fund, 1945 65, Twenty Years of International Monetary Cooperation, 3 vols., 1969; contbr. articles to profl. jours. Recipient Disting. Alumni award U. Mich., 1980, Cert. of Appreciation George Washington U., 1987, Outstanding Washington Woman Economist award, 1987; AAUW scholar, 1939-42; U. Mich. Univ. scholar, 1942; Phi Kappa Phi fellow, 1943; MIT fellow, 1943-46; Ford Found. grantee, 1959-62. Mem. Am. Econ. Assn. (CSWEP - Carolyn Shaw Bell award 2002), U. Mich. Alumni Assn., MIT Alumnae Assn., Phi Beta Kappa, Phi Kappa Phi. Mem. United Church of Christ. Home: 10018 Woodhill Rd Bethesda MD 20817-1218 *Probably the greatest factor in my life has been a sense of direction. Growing up in Detroit in the Great Depression of the 1930's, as a child I became aware of the problem of extensive unemployment. Then, as now, in times of recession, Detroit was one of the hardest hit cities. I knew I wanted to be an economist and to work in the public sector. Motivation, determination, a continuing interest in economics, and a feeling of the need for public service have carried me the rest of the way.*

DEVRIES, ROBERT ALLEN, foundation administrator; b. Chgo., May 12, 1936; s. Robert and Mildred (Burgess) DeV.; m. Eleanor Rose Siems, Aug. 16, 1958; children: Susan E., Robert S., Laura H., Steven P. BS in Physiology, U. Chgo., 1958, MBA in Hosp. Adminstrn., 1961. Adminstrv. resident, asst. Miami Valley Hosp., Dayton, Ohio, 1959-61, asst. dir., 1961-67; adminstr. McPherson Community Health Ctr., Howell, Mich., 1967-71; program dir. W.K. Kellogg Found., Battle Creek, Mich., 1971-88, program dir., dir. Kellogg Internat. Fellowship Programs, 1988-90, program dir., dir. Internat. Study Grants and Exchanges, 1990-97, mem. adminstrv. coun., 1995-97, program dir., mem. fellowship com., 1997-99; ret., 1999. Cons. on domestic and internat. programs W.K. Kellogg Found., 1999—; mem. com. vis. Sch. Nursing, U. Mich., 2000—; assisting min. St. Peter Luth. Ch.; chmn. quality com. bd. trustees Battle Creek Health Sys., 2001—; bd. dirs. Lifecare Ambulance, Mich. Health Coun.; v.p. Leila Arboretum Soc.; lectr. nursing orgn., adminstrn. Sch. Nursing Miami Valley Hosp., 1961-67, Grad. Sch. Pub. Health U. Mich., 1967—; adj. prof. Coll. Health and Human Svcs., Western Mich. U., 1986—; advisor Sch. Pub. Health Beijing Med. U., 1986—, Med. Coll. Health Staff, Shanghai, 1986—, 1st People's Hosp., Shanghai, 1986—; mem. nat. adv. com. on rural health U.S. Dept. Health and Human Svcs., Washington, 1988-92; mem. adv. panel acad. health scis. ctr. U.N.C., Chapel Hill, 1992-94; mem. policy coun. Nat. Inst. Rural Health Policy, 1987-90; mem. health planning and cert. of need workgroup Mich. Dept. Mgmt. & Budget, Mich. Dept. Pub. Health, 1986-87; vice chmn. adv. coun. Hosp. Rsch. & Ednl. Trust, Chgo., 1974-85; treas. coun. practice Am. Assn. Nurse Anesthetists, 1978-84; mem. Southwest Mich. Health Sys. Agy. Bd., 1980-83; guest lectr. King's Fund Coll., London, U. Leeds, Eng., French Nat. Sch. Pub. Health, Rennes, U. Toronto, Pan Am. Health Orgn., Washington and Brasilia, Brazil, Katholieke Universiteit Leuven, Belgium, Internat. Hosp. Fedn., London, Elton Mayo Sch. Mgmt., Adelaide, Australia, Ministry Pub. Health, Beijing, Indian Hosp. Assn., New Delhi. Editorial bds. Inquiry, Hosp. & Health Svcs.; contbr. articles to profl. jours., also book chpts. Counselor Baxter Am. Found. Prize in Health Svcs. Rsch., 1986—; assoc. trustee Florence Nightingale Mus. Trust, London; chair quality com. bd. trustees Battle Creek Health Sys., 2001—. Recipient Disting. Svc. award Am. Soc. Allied Health Professions, 1989, Med. Group Mgmt. Assn., Denver, 1990, Ohio State U. Alumni Assn., 1998; Monsignor Griffin award for disting. writing Ohio Hosp. Assn., 1965, Civic Achievement award Jr. C. of C., Chgo., 1955, recognition award for contbns. to svcs. to handicapped Commn. on Accreditation of Rehab. Facilities, 1976, Cmty. Health Leadership award Hosp. Rsch. and Ednl. Trust, 1994, Spl. Recognition award Mich. Health and Hosp. Assn., 1999; named Outstanding Young Men in Am. Howell, Mich. Area C. of C. and Jaycees, 1970; Nat. Health Svcs. rsch. fellow U. Mich., 1970-71. Fellow Am. Coll. Healthcare Execs.(life), U.S. China Ednl. Inst., Can. Sch. Mgmt. (hon.); mem. APHA, Am. Hosp. Assn. (hon. life, vice chair R&D coun. 1974-85, adv. panel multi-hosp. systems 1977-85, Living the Vision award 1999), Internat. Hosp. Fedn., Nat. Rural Health Assn., Mich. Hosp. Assn. (assn. governance and strategic planning com. 1986-89, pub. policy and govt. com. 1981-83), U. Chgo. Hosp. Adminstrn. Alumni Assn. (pres. 1982-83). Lutheran. Avocations: music, writing, travel, gardening.

DEVRIES, ROBERT CHARLES, scientist, researcher, consultant; b. Evansport, Ohio, Oct. 10, 1922; s. Charles and Rebecca (Goethe) DeV.; m. Ruth Elizabeth Wood, Oct. 30, 1943; children: David, Peter, Charles, Jonathan, Katherine. BA, DePauw U., 1948; PhD, Pa. State U., 1953. Topographer U.S. Geol. Survey, Washington, 1943-46; postdoctoral fellow Pa. State U., State College, 1953-54; staff scientist rsch. lab. GE, Schenectady, N.Y., 1954-61, staff scientist corp. R& D Ctr., 1965-88; assoc. prof. Rensselaer Poly. Inst., Troy, N.Y., 1961-65; cons. P-T-X, Burnt Hills, N.Y., 1988—. Adj. prof. Pa. State U., 1992-95; cultural exch. visitor, Japan, 1974; Coolidge fellow R&D Ctr. CE, 1981. Editor: The Reactivity of Solids, 1968, contbr. numerous articles to profl. jours.; patentee in field. With USAF, 1943. Rector scholar DePauw U., 1941; recipient Engring. Materials Achievement award Am. Soc. Metals, 1973. Fellow Am. Ceramic Soc., Am. Mineral Soc.; mem. AAAS, Am. Assn. Crystal Growth, Materials Rsch. Soc., Nat. Acad. Engring., Materials Rsch. Soc. (hon. Japan 1993), Mineral Soc. London, Sigma Xi. Avocations: gemmology, beekeeping, biking, reading, wood carving. Home and Office: P-T-X 17 Van Vorst Dr Burnt Hills NY 12027-9712 E-mail: rcdvriesptx@worldnet.att.net.

DE VRIES, ROBERT JOHN, investment banker; b. Pella, Iowa, Aug. 18, 1932; s. John G. and Anna (Kool) m. Patricia Lynn Jackson, Dec. 22, 1962 (dec.); children: Robert John Jr., Garrett Andrew. BBA, U. Tex., Austin, 1958; MBA, Harvard Grad. Sch. of Bus., Boston, 1960. Registered principal. Security analyst Cyrus J. Lawrence & Sons, N.Y.C., 1960-64, Jas. H. Oliphant and Co., N.Y.C., 1964-66; investment banker William D. Witter Inc., N.Y., 1966-68; v.p. Mgmt. Planning Inc., Princeton, N.J., 1968-73; pres. Cryomed Devices, Inc., Princeton, 1973-80; v.p. Smith Barney, Harris Upham, 1981-84; pres., dir., founder Robert J. De Vries and Co., Inc., Kansas City, 1984 2002; mng. dir. DeVries, Snedeker & Duncan, LLC, Overland Park, Kans., 2002—. Served with USAF, 1952-56. Inst. of Chartered Fin. Analyst, Harvard Club of N.Y., Beta Gamma Sigma. Republican. Presbyterian. Avocations: photography, marathon running. Home: 24185 W 190th St Gardner KS 66030 Office: De Vries Snedeker & Duncan LLC 10955 Lowell Ave Ste 1050 Overland Park KS 66210

DEVRIES, ROBERT K. religious book publisher; b. Sully, Iowa, July 6, 1932; s. Fred G. and Selena Irene (Willetts) DeV.; m. Carolyn Jo Schroeder, June 2, 1962 (div. 1978); children: Stephen Robert, Suzanne Mishael Dahill; m. Carolyn Gail Bergmans, May 26, 1979; children: Staci Ann McKellar, Keri Gail Bailey. AB, Wheaton Coll., 1954; ThM, Dallas Theol. Sem., 1958, ThD, 1969. Asst. registrar Dallas Theol. Sem., 1959-63; editor-in-chief Moody Press, Chgo., 1963-68; dir., v.p. pubs. Zondervan Pub. House, Grand Rapids, Mich., 1968-76, exec. v.p. book div., 1976-85; exec. v.p., publisher Zondervan Book Group, Zondervan Corp., Grand Rapids, Mich., 1985-86; pub., bd. dirs. Discovery House Pubs., Grand Rapids, 1987-2000, sr. publisher, bd. dirs., 2000—; cons., bd. dirs. Serendipity House, Littleton, Colo., 1990-99; bd. dirs. Serendipity House Found., Littleton, 1999—2003. Bd. dirs. Oswald Chambers Pub. Assn. Ltd., Eng. Bd. dirs. Ligonier Valley Study Ctr., Stahlstown, Pa., 1979-83, Bd. Publ., Evang. Covenant Ch. Am., Chgo., 1989-94, chmn., 1992-94; advisor Internat. Coun. Bibl. Inerrancy, Walnut Creek, Calif., 1978-87. Recipient Outstanding Young Men in Am. award Jaycees, 1965 Republican. Mem. Evangelical Covenant Ch. Avocation: model railroading. Home: 7554 Lime Hollow Dr SE Grand Rapids MI 49546-7439 Office: 3000 Kraft Ave SE Grand Rapids MI 49512-2024 E-mail: rdevries@rbc.org.

DEVRIES, WILLEM, philosophy educator; b. N.Y.C., Sept. 16, 1950; s. Willem Cornelis and Jenny (Broekman) deVries; m. Dianne Kaplan, Jan. 2, 1982; children: Hadriel, Jeremy. BA, Haverford Coll., 1972; MA, U. Pitts., 1975, PhD, 1981. Asst. prof. Amherst Coll., Mass., 1979-86; Mellon postdoctoral fellow Harvard U., Cambridge, Mass., 1986-87; vis. asst. prof. Tufts U., Medford, Mass., 1987-88; asst. prof. U. N.H., Durham, 1988-93, assoc. prof., 1993-98, chair philosophy dept., 1994-2000, prof., 1998—, dir. London Program, 2001—02. Project dir. Scientist as Humanist, Concord, N.H., 1991-93. Author: Hegel's Theory of Mental Activity, 1988; editor (book) Reality, Knowledge, and the Good Life, 1992; co-author: Knowledge, Mind and the Given: Reading Wilfrid Sellars Empiricism and the Philosophy of Mind, 2000; contbr. articles to profl. jours. Fulbright Doctoral fellow Fulbright Commn. Germany, 1976-77, sr. rsch. fellow 1982-83, NEH fellow, 1994-95. Mem. AAUP, Am. Philosoph. Assn., Soc. Philosophy and Psychology, N. Am. Kant Soc. Office: U NH Philosophy Dept Hamilton Smith Hall Durham NH 03824 Home: 397 Catamount Dr Northwood NH 03261- E-mail: Willem.devries@unh.edu.

DEW, CHARLES BURGESS, historian, educator; b. St. Petersburg, Fla., Jan. 5, 1937; s. Jack Carlos and Amy (Meek) D.; m. Robb Reavill Forman, Jan. 26, 1968. AB, Williams Coll., 1958; PhD, Johns Hopkins, 1964. Instr. Wayne State U., 1963-64, asst. prof., 1964-65, La. State U., 1965-68; assoc. prof. U. Mo., Columbia, 1968-72, prof., 1972-78; vis. assoc. prof. U. Va., 1970-71; vis. prof. history Williams Coll., Williamstown, Mass., 1977-78, prof. history, 1978-85, Class of 1956 prof. Am. Studies, 1985-96, chmn. dept. history, 1986-92, dir. Francis C. Oakley Ctr. for Humanities and Social Scis., 1994-97; prof. social scis. W. Van Alan Clark Third Century, 1996—2002, Charles R. Keller prof. history, 2002—03, Ephriam Williams prof. Am. history, 2003—. Author: Ironmaker to the Confederacy: Joseph R. Anderson and the Tredegar Iron Works, 1966, rev. edit., 1999, The Meanings of American History, 1972, Bond of Iron: Master and Slave at Buffalo Forge, 1994, Apostles of Disunion: Southern Secession Commissioners and the Causes of the Civil War, 2001; contbr. chpt. to Origins of the New South, 1877-1913 (C. Vann Woodward), rev. edit., 1972. Recipient Fletcher Pratt award, N.Y. Civil War Round Table, 1966, 2001, award of merit, Am. Assn. State and Local History, 1967, hon. mention Peter Seaborg award for Civil War scholarship, George Tyler Moore Ctr. for the Study of the Civil War, Shepherd Coll., Shepherdstown, W.Va., 2002. Mem. Am. Hist. Assn., Orgn. Am. Historians (Elliott Rudwick award 1995), Phi Beta Kappa, Delta Psi. Home: 218 Bulkley St Williamstown MA 01267-2023

DEW, JOAN KING, freelance/self-employed writer; b. Columbus, Ga., June 24, 1932; d. Henry Grady and Vivian Pauline (Cook) King; m. Clifford Dew (div.); children: Clifford L. Jr., Michael David; m. Albert Schmitt (div.); 1 child, Christopher Thomas. Student, Fla. State U., 1949—51. Reporter, feature writer Ft. Lauderdale (Fla.) Daily News, 1950—56; editor Nassau (Bahamas) Guardian, 1956—58; stringer UPI, 1956—58; copy chief Art and Publicity, Ltd., Kingston, Jamaica, 1958—60; feature writer, author column Male Call, Valley Times Today, North Hollywood, Calif., 1960—66; freelance writer Hollywood, Calif., 1966—77, Nashville, 1977—88; editor food and wine LA Herald Examiner, 1988—89; exec. editor Ctrl. Coast Adventures, Monterey Peninsula, Calif., 1992—2002; ret., 2002; with Peace Corps, 2003—. Author: Singers and Sweethearts: The Women in Country Music, 1977, Stand By Your Man: The Autobiography of Tammy Wynette, 1978, Minnie Pearl, The Autobiography of Minnie Pearl, 1980, 3 books on wine and food, 1984—88, Christmas, 1987; author: (with David Fox) Follow Your Heart, 1988; columnist Nashville Tennessean, 1988; contbr. numerous articles to nat. mags.

DEW, THOMAS EDWARD, lawyer; b. Detroit, Feb. 13, 1947; s. Albert Nelson and Irene Theresa (Morris) D.; m. Gail Ruth Tuesink, June 27, 1970. BA, U. Mich., 1969; JD, Detroit Coll. Law, 1974. Bar: Mich. 1974, U.S. Dist. Ct. (ea. dist.) Mich. 1974, U.S. Tax Ct. 1980. Agt. IRS, Detroit, 1969-74; trust officer Ann Arbor (Mich.) Trust Co., 1974-75, asst. v.p., 1975-78; ptnr. Conner, Harbour, Dew, Ann Arbor, 1978-83, Harris, Lax, Guenzel & Dew, Ann Arbor, 1983-87; private practice Thomas E. Dew Profl. Corp., Ann Arbor, 1987-88; prin. Dever and Dew Profl. Corp., Ann Arbor, 1988-99, Wise & Marsac, Detroit, 1999-2001, Berry Moorman, PC, Detroit, 2001—. Lectr. Am. Coll., Bryn Mawr, Pa., 1979-82, Am. Inst. Paralegal Studies, Detroit, 1982; adj. prof. Ave Marie Sch. Law, 2003—. Mem. Ann Harbor Housing Commn., 1979-81, pres. 1981; trustee Ann Arbor Area Cmty. Found. Named Law scholar, Sigma Nu Phi, 1974. Fellow Mich. State Bar Found.; mem. State Bar Mich., Washtenaw County Bar Assn., Washtenaw Estate Planning Coun. (pres. 1979-80), New Enterprise Forum. Republican. Presbyterian. Office: Berry Moorman PC 455 E Eisenhower Pky #210 Ann Arbor MI 48108 E-mail: tdew@berrymoorman.com.

DEWALD, BRIAN L, music educator; b. Parkston, Sd, Oct. 1, 1965; s. Maynard W and Adeline Dewald; m. Londa R Erck, July 22, 1989; children: Zachary J. children: Elizabeth J. Dr. of Musical Arts, U. of Iowa, Iowa City, Iowa, 1991—2001; MFA, U. of Iowa, Iowa City, IA, 1991—94, MA, 1991—93; MusB Edn., U. of SD, Vermillion, SD, 1983—87. K-12 Teaching Ill., 1994. Music dept. chair Glenbard South H.S., Glen Ellyn, Ill., 1994—; grad. tchg. asst. U. of Iowa Bands, Iowa City, Iowa, 1992—94; dir. of bands Fairmont H.S., Fairmont, Minn., 1988—91, Boyden-Hull H.S., Hull, Iowa, 1987—88. Adjudicator Various, Various, Ill., 1994—2002. Author: (article) ABA Journal of Band Research, Instrumentalist Magazine; musician: (video sountrack) Veggie Tales Video Series. Recipient Who's Who among America's Teachers, Who's Who, 2000, Citation of Excellence, Nat. Band Assn., 1997, 2000; grantee Grant Award, Partnership for Ednl. Progress, 1995, 1996, 1999, Glenbard Dist. 87 Tchr. Grant Program, 1999, 2001. Mem.: NEA, Coll. Band Directors Nat. Assn., Ill. Music Educators Assn., Mortar Bd., Omicron Delta Kappa. Achievements include research in Manuscript Band Works of the Goldman Band Library. Avocations: travel, minnesota twins baseball, golf, fishing. Home: 186 Woodlet Lane Bolingbrook IL 60490 Office: Glenbard South High School 23W200 Butterfield Road Glen Ellyn IL 60137 Office Fax: 630-469-6572. E-mail: brian_dewald@glenbard.org.

DEWALD, PAUL ADOLPH, psychiatrist, educator; b. N.Y.C., Mar. 12, 1920; s. Jacob Frederick and Elsie (Wurzburger) D.; m. Eleanor Whitman, Sept. 1, 1961; children: Jonathan S., Ellen F. BA, Swarthmore Coll., 1942; MD, U. Rochester, 1945; cert. psychoanalysis, SUNY, 1960. Intern, Strong Meml. Hosp., Rochester, N.Y., 1945-46, resident, 1948-52; instr. U. Rochester, 1952-57, asst. prof. psychiatry, 1957-61; pvt. practice psychoanalysis St. Louis, 1961-99; asst. clin. prof. psychiatry Washington U., St. Louis, 1961-65, 96—; asso. clin. prof. St. Louis U., 1965-69, clin. prof. psychiatry, 1969—. Dir. treatment svc. Psychoanalytic Found. St. Louis, 1961-72, med. dir., 1972-83 St. Louis Psychoanalytic Inst., 1973-83, supervising and tng. analyst, 1973—; mem. faculty Chgo. Inst. Psychoanlysis, 1961-75, supervising and tng. analyst, 1965 73; vis. prof. U. Cin., 1968-80; mem. Mo. State Mental Health Commn., 1978-83, chmn., 1981-83; asst. prof. clin. psychiatry Washington U., 1995—. Author: Psychotherapy: A Dynamic Approach, 1964, 2d edit., 1969, The Psychoanalytic Process, 1972, Learning Process in Psycho-analytic Supervision, 1987; co-editor: Ethics Case Book of the American Psychoanalytic Assn., 2001; contbr. articles to profl. jours. Served to capt. M.C., AUS, 1946-48. Fellow Am. Psychiat. Assn. (life); mem. Mo. Psychiat. Assn. (pres. 1970-71), Eastern Mo. Psychiat. Assn. (pres. 1969-70), Am. Psychoanalytic Assn. (life), St. Louis Psychoanalytic Soc. (pres. 1970-71, 86-88) Home: 60 Conway Ln Saint Louis MO 63124-1203 Office: 8820 Ladue Rd Saint Louis MO 63124 E-mail: padewald@mindspring.com. *I was encouraged by my parents to see my career as a potential source of creative enjoyment, fulfillment and self-esteem. I was fortunate to choose a field that encouraged those attitudes, and a wife who supported me in them. I have other interests and sources of fulfillment, but when there is nothing better or more enjoyable to do, I work.*

DEWALD, WILLIAM GUENTHNER, economist; b. Sioux City, Iowa, Nov. 9, 1928; s. William Frederick and Leah (Guenthner) D.; m. Ann Peterson, Mar. 6, 1952 (div. 1981); children: Jane Dewald Smirniotopoulos, Ruth Dewald Baginski, Charlotte Dewald O'Brien, Robin Dewald Yarinsky; m. Aileen Lee, Mar. 9, 1984 (div. 2003). BS, Northwestern U., Evanston, Ill., 1950; PhD, U. Minn., 1963. Assoc. economist Fed. Res. Bank, Mpls., 1957-60; assoc. prof. St. Olaf Coll., Northfield, Minn., 1960-62; asst. prof. U. Chgo., 1962-64; prof. Ohio State U., Columbus, 1964-85; sr. economist, dep. dir. planning and econ. analysis staff U.S. Dept. of State, Washington, 1985-92; sr. v.p., dir. rsch. Fed. Res. Bank of St. Louis, 1992-98; ret. Vis. scholar Res. Bank Australia, Sydney, NSW, 1966-67, Fed. Res. Bank, Kansas City, 1978-79, Fed. Res. Bank, San Francisco, 1981; vis. expert European Ctrl. Bank, Frankfurt, 2002-2003; dir. fgn. econ. rsch. U.S. Labor Dept., Washington, 1973-74; cons. IMF, 1984-85, Fed. Res. Bank of St. Louis, 1999; mem. adv. bd. Jour. Money, Credit and Banking, 1984—; exec. in residence No. Ariz. U., Flagstaff, 2001. Editor Jour. Money, Credit and Banking, 1975-83; contbr. articles to profl. jours. With U.S. Army, 1951-53. Recipient faculty fellowship Ford Found., 1969-70, Jour. Money, Credit and Banking grant NSF, 1983-84. Fax: 614-488-3855. E-mail: dewald@columbus.rr.com.

DEWALT, BILL, museum director; BA in Sociology and Anthropology, U. Conn., 1969, PhD in Anthropology, 1975. Dir. Carnegie Mus. Natural History, Pitts. Cons. World Wildlife Fund, World Bank, Inter-Am. Devel. Bank, Internat. Fin. Corp., U.S. Agy. for Internat. Devel., Latin Am. Scholarship Program in Am. Univs. Contbr. articles to profl. jours. Office: Carnegie Mus Natural History 4400 Forbes Ave Pittsburgh PA 15213

DE WAN-CARLSON, ANNA THERESA, artist; b. Syracuse, N.Y., Dec. 29, 1949; d. William Martin and Sarah Theresa (Kirchhof) De Wan; m. David G. Carlson, Aug. 8, 1971 (div. 1981); 1 child, Adam Edward. Student, Syracuse U., 1967, 68, 87; AAS in Design and Illustration, Art Inst. Pitts., 1971. Dir. 12rms-4 Gallery, Syracuse, N.Y., 1992-94; artistic dir. N.Y.C. Art Open, 1995—. Selected exhibits include The Space Group of Korea 6th Internat. Miniature Print Biennial, Seoul, Arts Ctr. of the Grand Prairie 5th Nat. Miniature Annual Art Exhibit, Stuttgart, Ark., Cooperstown Nat. Juried Art Exhibit, Cooperstown, N.Y., Munson-Williams-Proctor Inst. Artists of Cen. N.y. Annual Juried Exhibit, Utica, N.Y., San Bernadino County Mus., Redlands, Calif., Chapman Art Ctr. Gallery, Arena Internat. Art Exhibit, Binghamton, Print Club Albany, Print Club Rochester, Womanart Gallery, N.Y.C., Keane Mason Gallery, St. David's Invitational Celebration of Arts, Dewitt, N.Y., Sussex House Gallery, London, Cayuga C.C., Auburn, N.Y., Wilson Art Gallery, LeMoyne Coll., Syracuse, N.Y., Everson Mus. Art, Syracuse, Payne Hall, Mohawk Valley C.C., Utica, N.Y., Art Assn. Harrisburg (Pa.), Fingerlakes Exhbn. Meml. Art Gallery U. Rochester (N.Y.), Art Assn. Harrisburg, Pa., Pyramid Arts Ctr., Rochester, 12rms-4 Gallery, others; represented in collections Print Club of Albany, Onondaga Savs. Bank, Carrier Corp., Syracuse Savs. Bank, Dey Bros., Maria Regina Coll., Onondaga Hist. Assn., others; contbr. articles to profl. jours. Fundraiser March of Dimes, Jordan, N.Y., 1978-79; gallery fundraiser Everson Mus., S.W. Community Ctr., Vera House, Hospice Ctrl. N.Y., Onondaga County Pub. Libr., 1992—. Recipient 1st Prize Graphics award Allentown Festival Arts, Syracuse Arts and Crafts Festival, 2nd Prize award Art Ctr. of Grand Prairie, 2nd and 3rd prizes Syracuse Printmakers Ann. Mems. Exhibit, Merit award Ctrl. N.Y. Art Open Juried Exhibit, Best Shot Feature award Popular Photography mag., Best Graphics award Keane Mason Gallery. Mem. Print Club of Albany, Print Club Rochester, Print Club Phila., Everson Mus., Syracuse (N.Y.) Printmakers (pres. 1981, bd. dirs., collection curator, exhibits curator, publicist 1989-91), Ctrl. N.Y. Aquarium Soc. (publicist 1997-98, contbr. Jour. of the Print World, Fresh Water and Marine Aquarium mag.). Avocations: breeding Carassius Auratus, collecting Am. art pottery, photography, gardening. Home: 145 Avon Rd Syracuse NY 13206-3036

DEWANE, JOHN RICHARD, retired manufacturing company executive, consultant, business owner; b. Cooperstown, Wis., Mar. 4, 1934; s. Clarence John and Arvilla Anne (Gannon) D.; m. Judith Anne Arnold, Mar. 17, 1974; 1 child, Kelly Susanne. BSME, U. Wis., 1957; MBA, U. Minn., 1973. Lic. pvt. pilot. Dir. mktg. planning Honeywell, Inc., Washington, 1974-76, dir. mktg. Mpls., 1976-78, v.p. svc. engring., 1979-81, v.p. bus. devel., 1981-82, v.p., gen. mgr., 1982-87, group v.p., 1987-92, pres. space and aviation control Phoenix, 1992-97, pres. emeritus, 1997—. Mem. NASA Aeronautics Adv. Com.; adj. prof. strategt Ariz. State U. Vice chmn. Cmty. Long-Range Improvement Com., Maple Grove, Minn., 1980-81, chmn. Econ. Devel. Commn., 1982-86; mem. Polit. Action com. Honeywell, 1979-83; mem. alumni adv. coun. U. Wis., mem. dean's indsl. liaison coun., mem. capital com. Coll. Engring.; mem. tech. adv. com. on transp. equipment U.S. Dept. Commerce; bd. govs. Am. Def. Preparedness Assn., 1988-91; chmn. bd. dirs. Success By Six, 1989-98, Ariz. Cities in Schs. Inc., Honeywell Found.; nat. bd. advisor U. Ariz. Keller Bus. Sch., mem. dean's exec. com.; mem. deans 100 bd. Ariz. State U., bd. dirs., pres.'s club, chmn. undergrad. curriculum com.; chmn. indsl. liaison coun. Embry-Riddle Aero U.; mem. State of Ariz. Gov.'s Tech. Commn., State of Ariz. Smart Beginnings Com.; mem. strategy coun. United Way of Phoenix, chair dirs. coun. conf. bd., 1995-97; bd. dirs. Asia Pacific Econ. Coun.; mem. endowment com. Habitat for Humanity; mem. APEC Satellite and Comm. Com., Honeywell Execs. Cmty. Cons.; mem. hon. bd. Phoenix Found. for the Blind. With USN, 1957-60. Holder four world airplane speed records. Navy scholar, 1952-57. Mem. U.S. Navy League, Air Force Assn., Assn. U.S. Army, Am. Def. Preparedness Assn., Aircraft Owners and Pilots Assn., Gen. Aviation Mfrs. Assn. (dir. 1983-97, chmn. forecasting com., chmn. airport ops. com.), Mpls. C. of C. (aviation com. 1980-88), Provost Club Ariz. State U. West. Office: Honeywell Space and Aviation Control PO Box 21111 Phoenix AZ 85036-1111 Address: PO Box 42777 Phoenix AZ 85080

DEWAR, JAMES MCEWEN, marketing, aerospace and defense executive, developing nations consultant; b. Williamsport, Pa., Aug. 4, 1943; s. James Livingston and Margaret Ann (McEwen) D.; m. Margaret Cawley, Feb. 27, 1982; children: Alec, Porter, Leah. BS in Internat. Affairs, Trinity U., 1965, postgrad., 1965-66. Mgr. Dash brand Procter & Gamble Corp., Cin., 1969-71; CEO, DeLair & Dewar, Inc., Tucson and Washington, 1972—; chmn. bd. Cabot South Asia Inc. subs. Cabot Corp., 1982-87; pres., dir.-gen. ASI, Inc. subs. Boeing Co., 1987-97; CEO, J. Dewar Indochine, Ltd., Hanoi, Vietnam, 1993—. Pres., interim cons. CEO, N.Am. Automotive Project, Southfield, Mich., 1993-98; bd. dirs. Metz Constrn. Co., Marine Environ. Rsch. Corp., Computational Analysis Corp.; mem. Aerospace, Def. and Automotive Industry Devel. Commn., Detroit, 1994. Contbr. numerous articles to profl. publs. Bd. dirs. Casa de Los Ninos, Tucson, 1974—, Safari Club Internat., Tucson, 1974—, Internat. Marine Fisheries Corp.; founding mem. Dist. Atty.'s Victim/Witness Adv. Program; mem. White House Talent Pool, 1975-76, White House Nat. Cambodia Crisis Com., 1979-80, U.S. Aerospace Indsl. Reps. in Europe; adj. Mil. Order World Wars, Tucson, 1977-80, perpetual mem.; chmn. internat. bd. advs. Ariz.-Sonora Desert Mus.; bd. advs. guardian ad litem program Superior Ct. Ariz. Capt. USAF, 1966-70, Vietnam. Recipient Key to City of Seoul, 1973, citation Pres. of Korea, 1973, award for work with Mother Teresa, Cabot Found., 1982-87. Mem. Am. Soc. Agrl. Cons., Dirs. Guild Am., Assn. Old Crows, Australian/Asian Order Old Bastards (Sydney), John Carroll Soc., Mountain Oyster Club, Automobile Club France, Maxim's Bus. Club (Paris), St. James Club, Chambers Club (New Delhi), Univ. Club (Washington), Hanoi Club. Republican. Roman Catholic. Office: 8201 Greensboro Rd Ste 100 Mc Lean VA 22102

DEWAR, ROBERT EARL, JR., anthropologist, educator; b. Detroit, July 4, 1949; s. Robert Earl and Nancy (Miller) D.; m. Alison F. Richard, Aug. 21, 1976; children: Elizabeth Napier, Charlotte Mary. AB, Brown U., 1971; MPhil, Yale U., 1973, PhD, 1977. Instr. U. Conn., Storrs, 1975-77, asst. prof., 1977-82, assoc. prof., 1982—89, dept. head, 1986—96, prof., 1989—. Bd. dirs. Conn. State Mus. Natural History, Storrs, Liz Clairborne Art Ortenberg Found., N.Y. Editor: Connecticut Archaeology, 1981. Mem. Conn. State Hist. Preservation Rev. Bd., Hartford, 1987-97, Hist. Dist. Commn., Middle Haddam, Conn., 1986—. Recipient rsch. grants NSF, 1984, 86, 88, 92, Nat. Geographic Soc., 1978, 79, McArthur Found., 1998. Fellow Am. Anthropol. Assn.; mem. AAAS, Soc. for Am. Archaeology. Avocation: fly fishing. Home: PO Box 34 Middle Haddam CT 06456-0034 Office: Dept Anthropology Univ Connecticut Dept Anthropology # U-176 Storrs Mansfield CT 06269

DE WEERDT, MARK MURRAY, retired judge; b. Cologne, Germany, May 6, 1928; arrived in Can., 1949. s. Hendrik Eugen and Ina Dunbar (Murray) de W.; m. Linda Anne Alden Hadwen, Mar. 31, 1956; children: Simon André, Murray Hadwen, David Lockhart, Charles Dunbar. MA, Glasgow (Scotland) U., 1949; LLB, B.C. U., 1955. Cert. barrister and solicitor, B.C. 1956, N.W.T. 1958. Assoc. solicitor Cross & O'Grady, Victoria, B.C., 1956-57; adv. coun. Can. Dept. Justice, Ottawa, 1957-58; Crown Atty. Yellowknife, N.W.T., 1958-63; sr. counsel Can. Dept. Justice, Vancouver, 1976-79, gen. counsel and dir., 1979-81; sr. ptnr. deWeerdt, Searle, Finall et al., Yellowknife, N.W.T., 1958-71; magistrate and juvenile ct. judge N.W.T. Magistrate's Ct., Yellowknife, N.W.T., 1971-73; gen. solicitor Ins. Corp. B.C., Vancouver, 1974-76; justice N.W.T and Yukon Supreme Cts., Yellowknife & Whitehorse, 1981-96, Supreme Ct. of B.C., 1996-97, N.W.T and Yukon Cts. of Appeal, 1981-97, Ct. Martial Appeal Ct. of Can., 1995-97; ret., 1997; dep. judge Supreme Ct. N.W.T., 1996-97, 97—, Nunavut Supreme Ct., 1999—. Mem. Pension Appeals Bd. under Can. Pension Plan, 1999—; chair jud. coun. N.W.T., Yellowknife, 1981-96; dir. Canadian Judges' Conf., 1982-89; alternating mem. Can. Judicial Coun., 1985-7, 89-91, 93-95. Author profl. papers. Vice-chmn. Yellowknife Sch. Dist. #1, 1964-68. Apptd. Queen's Coun., Can., 1968; recipient Commr.'s award for pub. svc. at highest level, 1997. Mem. Can. Bar Assn., Can. Inst.

Administrn. Justice (life), N.W.T. Bar Assn. (pres. 1967-71), MacKenzie River and N.W.T. Progressive Conservative Assn. (pres. 1959-71). Avocations: reading, walking. Home: 5459 Crown St Vancouver BC Canada V6N 4K1

DEWEES, DONALD CHARLES, securities company executive; b. Phila., Sept. 7, 1931; s. John Coleman and Elva (Burke) DeW.; m. Martha V. Folk, July 31, 1954; children: Donald C., Suzanne C., Gretchen F. BS in Commerce and Finance, Bucknell U., 1953; MBA, U. Pa., 1954. Data processing rep. Nat. Cash Register Co., Wilmington, Del., 1954-62; account rep. Francis I. duPont Co., Investments, Wilmington, 1962-67, br. mgr. Balt., 1968, Butcher & Singer, Wilmington, 1969-71, v.p., 1971-76, 1st v.p., 1977, sr. v.p., 1978—, resident mgr., 1969-76, ltd. ptnr., 1976-87, exec. v.p., 1987, sr. exec. v.p., 1988—, mng. dir., 1988—, also bd. dirs. Mng. dir. Butcher & Singer, 1986-98, Wheat Securities, 1998-2000; dir. Mgmt. Scis. Inc., 1978-92, Bus. Trends Inc., 1977-91, Computer Terminals and Tapes Ltd., 1970-98, Wheat Securities, mng. dir. Wheat Securities Butcher & Singer, 1986-2000, Lloyds of London, 1985-2000, First Union Bank, 1998-2000; underwriting mem. Lloyds of London, 1985-02; cons. in field. Author sales tng. publs. Active Wilmington YMCA; bd. dirs. Delawre Ctr. of Contemporary Arts, 1992-94, Ingleside Nursing Home, 1989—, Ch. Home Found., 1986-92, Episcopal Hom of Del., 1983-90, Del. Symphony, 1995—, Del. Art Mus., 1996—, Kalmar Nyckle Found., 2001--; bd. dirs. Del Marva Boy Scouts of Am., 1989—, chmn. endowment com., 1993—2001; vice chmn. Nat. Assn. Christians and Jews, 1991-98; mem. allocation com. United Way, 1994; bd. dirs. Am. Cancer Soc., 1994—, Leukemia Soc., 1995—; chmn. Edgar A. Thronson Charitable Found., 1995—. Served with AUS, 1952-53, 58-59, Korea. Mem. Fin. Analysts Soc., Am. Philatelic Soc., Phi Kappa Psi, Univ. Club (Wilmington), Collectors Club (N.Y.), Rodney Square Club, Masons, Shriners, Greenville Country Club, Bonita Bay Country Club. Home: 4200 Pyles Ford Rd Wilmington DE 19807-1734 also: 25 Kelly Ln Bethany Beach DE 19930-9549 Office: Wheat Securities 3801 Kennett Pike Greenville DE 19807-2321

DEWEESE, BOB M. state representative; b. Nov. 8, 1934; MD, Univ. of Louisville; BS, Univ. of Ky. State Rep. House of Rep., Dist. 48, Ky., 1992—; Gen. surgeon. Vice chair Appropriations & Rev.; mem. Energy; vice chair Health & Welfare; mem. Sr., Mil. Affairs & Pub. Safety. Recipient Dr. Nathan Davis Award. Caucuses: House Minority Caucus Chair, 2002-present. Republican. Office: Capitol Capitol Annex, Rm 414 Frankfort KY 40601 also: Dist 6206 Glen Hill Rd Louisville KY 40222*

DEWEESE, ELDONNA ROSE, librarian, editor; b. Mo., Nov. 7, 1940; d. Osborne Kuhn and Helena Elizabeth DeWeese. MLS, Emporia State U., 1969; BS in Edn., Southwest Mo. State U., 1962; MA, Southwest Mo. State, 1984. Tchr. English, speech, libr. Pierce City (Mo.) H.S., 1962-68; ref. libr. Southwest Bapt. Coll., Bolivar, Mo., 1969-72, adminstrv. libr., 1972-82; grad. asst./ref. libr. Southwest Mo. State U., Springfield, 1982-85; computer software distbr. Micro Magic Systems, Bolivar, 1985-88; collection devel. libr. Southwest Bapt. U., Bolivar, 1991—2000, 2002—, interim dean univ. libr., 2000—02. Editor/prodn. mgr. So. Bapt. Periodical Index, 1987—. Mem. ALA, Am. Soc. Indexers, Mo. State Poetry Soc., Mo. Libr. Assn., So. Bapt. Libr. Assn. Baptist. Avocations: reading, poetry, writing, church choir. Office: Southwest Bapt Univ Libr 1600 University Ave Bolivar MO 65613-2578 E-mail: edeweese@sbuniv.edu.

DEWEESE, JAMES ARVILLE, surgeon, educator; b. Apr. 5, 1925; s. Arville Ottis and Vergie (Jenkins) DeW.; m. Margaret Brown, June 20, 1950 (dec. 1960); children: James Arville Jr., Margaret Ann, Elizabeth Lynn, Joanne Spencer; m. Patricia Bidwell, May 5, 1962; children; Robert Bidwell, Jamie Susan. Student, Harvard U., 1942-43, Kent State U., 1943-44; MD, U. Rochester, 1949. Diplomate Am. Bd. Surgery (bd. dirs. 1986-91), Am. Bd. Thoracic and Cardiovascular Surgery (bd. dirs. 1987-91); cert. spl. qualifications gen. vascular surgery. Intern Strong Meml. Hosp., Rochester, N.Y., 1949-50, resident, 1950-52, 54-56; instr. surgery U. Rochester (N.Y.) Sch. Medicine and Dentistry, 1955-58, asst. prof. surgery, 1958-63, assoc. prof. surgery, 1963-69, prof. surgery, 1969-74, prof. cardiothoracic surgery, 1975—, chmn. div. cardiothoracic surgery, 1977-91, assoc. chmn. dept. surgery, 1986-90, chief sect. vascular surgery, 1987-91. Bd. dirs. Jour. Vascular Surgery, 1983—; editor: Vascular Surgery, 1985; contbr. over 200 articles to sci. jours. and over 60 chpts. to books. Mem. bd. trustees Clifton Springs (N.Y.) Hosp., 1980—. Mem. Am. Heart Assn. (bd. dirs. 1982-86, chmn. coun. cardiovascular surgery 1982-84), Ea. Vascular Soc. (pres. 1988), Internat. Soc. Cardiovascular Surgery (pres. N.Am. chpt. 1984-85, sec.-gen. 1987-95, pres. 1995-97), Pan Pacific Surg. Assn. (pres. 1989-91), Soc. Vascular Surgery (pres. 1977-78), Am. Venous Forum (pres. 1993-94), Sr. Cardiovascular Surg. Soc. (pres. 1996), Oak Hill Country Club (bd. govs. 1978-81). Home: 601 Crittenden Blvd Rochester NY 14642-0001 Office: U Rochester Dept Surgery M&D Cardiothoracic Div 601 Elmwood Ave Rochester NY 14642-0001

DEWELL, JULIAN C. lawyer; b. San Antonio, Feb. 13, 1930; s. Julian and Hope (Correll) D.; m. Alice Jane Palmer, Aug. 28, 1954; children: Gwen A. Dewell Brown, Jane H., Laura M. BS, Trinity U., 1952; LLD, U. Wash., Seattle, 1957. Bar: Wash. 1957, Calif. 1958, U.S. Ct. of Appeals (9th cir.) 1958. Trial lawyer (anti trust) U.S. Dept. Justice, San Francisco, 1957-59; assoc. Howe, Davis, Riese & Jones, Seattle, 1959-63; ptnr. Anderson Hunter Law Firm, Everett, Wash., 1963-99, of counsel, 2000—. Freeholder City of Everett, Wash., 1966—67, mem. growth mgmt. com., 1982, mem.shoreline mgmt. rev. com., 1998—2000; bd. dirs. Everett Sch. Dist., 1966—71, U. Wash. Law Sch. Found., 1981—84, Snohomish County Land Trust, 1989—93; Law Fund, 1992—98, Sno-Isle Natural Foods Co-Op, 2000—02; Wash. Trails Assn., 2001—. Named to Law Sch. Honor Grad. Program, U.S. Dept. Justice, San Francisco, 1957. Fellow Am. Coll. Trial Lawyers; mem. ABA, Wash. Bar Assn. (disciplinary bd. 1974-77, bd. govs. 1980-83, advt. task force, 1985-86, access to justice bd. 1998—, professionalism award 1991, merit award 1998), Calif. Bar Assn. Democrat. Unitarian Universalist. Avocations: sailing, hiking, tennis. Home: 609 Maulsby Ln Everett WA 98201-1031 Office: Anderson Hunter Firm PO Box 5397 Everett WA 98206-5397

DEWERD, LARRY ALBERT, medical physicist, educator; b. Milw., July 18, 1941; s. Anthony Lawrence and Dorothy M. (Heling) DeW.; m. Vada Mary Anderson, Sept. 14, 1963; children: Scott, Mark, Eric. BS, U. Wis., Milw., 1963; MS, U. Wis., 1965, PhD, 1970. Rsch. assoc. U. Wash., Seattle, 1970-72, rsch. asst. prof., 1973-75; vis. asst. prof. U. Wis., Madison, 1975-76, clin. asst. prof., 1976-79, clin. assoc. prof., 1979-86, prof., 1990—. Mgr. product devel. Radiation Measurements, Middleton, Wis., 1986-90; dir. Radiation Calibration Lab., Madison, 1983-86, 90—; cons. Instrumentarium, Milw., 1990; v.p. Standard Imaging, Madison, 1990—; presenter in field; cons. IAEA. Contbg. author: Brachytherapy, Ionization Chambers and Dosimetry, Thermoluminescence and Mammography; also numerous articles. Science chmn. Am. Cancer Soc. State of Wis., 1986-90. Grantee Nat. Cancer Inst., 1979-86, 94-98. Fellow Am. Assn. Physicists in Medicine (pres. 1990-92), Health Physics Soc., Am. Phys. Soc., Coun. Ionizing Radiation Measurements and Standards (pres. 1995-98), Sigma Xi (bd. dirs. 1984-86). Avocations: golf, fishing, backpacking, hunting. Home: 13 Pilgrim Cir Madison WI 53711-4033 Office: U Wis 1530 Med Sci Ctr 1300 University Ave Madison WI 53706-1510

DEWERTH, GORDON HENRY, management consultant; b. Milw., Sept. 3, 1939; s. Henry Andrew and Elizabeth Barbara (Schlitt) DeWerth; m. Karen Lillian Overson, July 7, 1962 (div.); children: Julie, Christine, Amy. BBA, U. Wis., 1961; MBA, Bradley U., 1965. Asst. to treas. Jos. Schlitz Brewing Co., Milw., 1965—71; with ITT, N.Y.C., 1971—76; treas. Macmillan, Inc., N.Y.C., 1976—82; sr. v.p. fin. Cowles Media Co., Mpls., 1982—85; sr. v.p. fin., treas. U. Hartford, Conn., 1985—89; v.p., gen. mgr. Gestra Inc., West Caldwell, NJ, 1989—90; v.p. David Werner Internat. Corp., N.Y.C., 1990—94; mng. ptnr. Round Table Ptnrs. Cons. Group, Pawtucket, RI, 1994—. With U.S. Army, 1961-63. Mem. Assn. Corp. Growth, Turnaround Mgmt. Assn., Mensa. Office: Round Table Ptnrs Cons Group PMB 148 545 Newport Ave Pawtucket RI 02861-3239

DEWEY, ARTHUR EUGENE, federal agency administrator; b. Mainesburg, Pennsylvania, Feb. 18, 1933; s. Glenn Cecil and Florence (Tice) D.; m. Priscilla Ann (Parce), June 24, 1956; 1 child, Elisabeth Parce Ainsworth. BSE, U.S. Mil. Acad., 1956; MSE, Princeton U., 1961; post grad., Grad. Inst. Internat. Studies, Geneva, Switzerland, 1972-73. Officer U.S. Army, 1956; White House fellow Dept. State, Washington, 1968-69, dir. Pres. Commn. on White House Fellowships, 1971-72; advanced through grades to coll. U.S. Army, 1973, ret., 1981; dep. asst. sec. state, Bur. Refugee Program Dept. State, Washington, 1981-86; asst. sec. gen., dep. high commr. for refugees UN, Geneva, 1986-90; exec. dir. Congl. Hunger Ctr., 1993—97; asst. sec. for population, refugees, and migration Dept. State, Washington, 2002—. Decorated DFC, Legion of Merit with two oak leaf clusters, Air medal with nine oak leaf clusters, Army Commendation medal with three oak leaf clusters. Mem.: Cosmos Club, Army and Navy Club. Republican. Presbyterian. Home: 5219 Westbard Ave Bethesda MD 20816-1411 Office: US Dept State Bur Population Refugees and Migration 2201 C St NW Washington DC 20520

DEWEY, CLARENCE FORBES, JR., engineering educator; b. Pueblo, Colo., Mar. 27, 1935; s. Clarence F. and Elsie (Hafermalz) D.; m. Carolyn Miller, Aug. 3, 1963; 1 child, Devan Forbes. BE, Yale U., 1956; MS, Stanford U., 1957; PhD, Calif. Inst. Tech., 1963. Aero. rsch. scientist NASA-AMES, Moffet Field, Calif., summer 1956; tech. staff aeronutronic divsn. Ford, Newport Beach, 1957-59; rsch. asst. Calif. Inst. Tech., Pasadena, Calif., 1959-63; asst. prof. mech. engring. U. Colo., Boulder, 1963-68; assoc. prof. MIT, Cambridge, 1968-76, prof., 1976-98, prof. mech. engring. and bioengring., 1998—, heald fluid mechanics lab., 1975—83, head microfluids lab., 2001—03; assoc. in pathology Peter Brent Brigham Hosp., Boston, 1978-95. Vis. scientist Inst. Plasma Physics, Garching, Germany, 1966—67; vis. prof. Harvard U. Med. Sch., 1978—79, Hefei Poly. U., China, 1986, Imperial Coll. Ctr. Med. and Biol. Sys., London, 1992, London, 2001; biomed. engr. Mass. Gen. Hosp., Boston, 1975—76, cons. in medicine, 1976—80; founder Mass. Computer Corp., 1981; co-dir. Internat. Consortium for Med. Imaging Tech., 1992—; path. cons. Brigham and Women's Hosp., 1982—96. Patentee in field; contbr. articles to profl. jours. Chmn. MIT United Way, 1996—97; trustee Fidelity Non-Profit Mgmt. Found., 2001—. Grantee NIH, Bethesda, Md., 1971—, Office Naval Rsch., San Diego 1970-75, 1987-89, Air Force Office Sci. Rsch., Washington, 1976-79. Fellow Am. Inst. Med. Biol. Engring. (founding); mem. Am. Phys. Soc., Biomed. Engring. Soc. (sr.). Avocations: trout fishing, skiing. Office: 77 Massachusetts Ave Cambridge MA 02139-4301

DEWEY, COLIN DAVID, merchant seaman; b. Austin, Tex., Aug. 31, 1962; s. Desmond David and Maureen Katherine Dewey; 1 child, Desmond K. O'Connor. BA, U. Calif., Berkeley, 2003. Quartermaster USCG, 1982—86; able seaman Sailor's Union of the Pacific, San Francisco, 1986—92; boat capt. San Francisco Bar Pilots, San Francisco, 1992—2000. Del. Ctrl. Labor Coun., Oakland, Calif., 1998—. Mem.: Melville Soc., Modern Lang. Assn., Encinal Yacht Club, Phi Beta Kappa, Golden Key Honor Soc., Phi Theta Kappa. Avocations: yachting, motorcycling, travel.

DEWEY, CRAIG DOUGLAS, operations executive; b. Milw., Apr. 8, 1950; s. Ralph Earl and Suzanne Dewey; m. Madeline A. Reedy, Sept. 28, 1989. BSME, U. Wis., 1974. Registered profl. engr., Wis. Mgr. engring. Harnischfeger Corp., Milw., 1974-83, dir. engring., 1986-90; chief engr. Fairmont (Minn.) Rlwy. Motors, 1983-86; v.p. engring. Pemco, Inc., Sheboygan, Wis., 1990-91; dir. engring. Quad/Tech, Sussex, Wis., 1991-92, dir. ops., 1992-96; owner Toner Tech Cartridge Svc., Inc., Panama City, Fla., 1996—. Patentee in field. Mem.: Mensa. Avocations: personal computers, gardening. Home: 314 Massalina Dr Panama City FL 13240 Office: 2915 N East Ave Panama City FL 32405-6716 E-mail: cdeweypcb@att.net.

DEWEY, DENNIS JAMES, lawyer; b. Chgo., June 5, 1938; s. James Franklin and Dorothy Rose Dewey; m. Patricia Rees, Nov. 9, 1968; children: Joseph Arba, James Myron. BS, U. Evansville, 1963; LLB, Ind. U., 1966. Bar: Ind. 1966, U.S. Dist. Ct. (so. dist.) Ind. 1966, U.S. Ct. Appeals (7th cir.) 1968, U.S. Supreme Ct. 1976. Appellate staff mem. Ind. Atty. Gen's. Office, 1966-68; assoc. Early, Arnold & Ziemer, Evansville, Ind.; ptnr. Dewey & Feulner, Newburgh, Ind.; chief dep. prosecuting atty. 2d Jud. Cir.; bankruptcy trustee U.S. Dist. Ct. (so. dist.) Ind., Evansville; ptnr. Weyerbacher, Dewey, Neff & Weyerbacher, Newburgh, 1982-86, Weyerbacher, Dewey and Weyerbacher, Newburgh, 1986—. Chmn. 8th div. Rep. Young Lawyers,1969-70. Past pres. Southwestern Ind. Easter Seal Soc. and Rehab. Ctr., Inc.; past bd. dirs. United Way Southwestern Ind., Inc. Mem. ABA, Ind. Bar Assn., Warrick County Bar Assn. (past pres.), Evansville Bar Assn., Phi Delta Phi, Sigma Phi. Office: Weyerbacher Dewey & Weyerbacher 107 State St Newburgh IN 47630-1227

DEWEY, DONALD ODELL, dean, academic administrator; b. Portland, Oreg., July 9, 1930; s. Leslie Hamilton and Helen (Odell) D.; m. Charlotte Marion Neuber, Sept. 21, 1952; children: Leslie Helen, Catherine Dawn, Scott Hamilton. Student, Lewis and Clark Coll., 1948-49; BA, U. Oreg., 1952; MS, U. Utah, 1956; PhD, U. Chgo., 1960. Mng. editor Condon (Oreg.) Globe-Times, 1952-53; city editor Ashland (Oreg.) Daily Tidings, 1953-54; asst. editor, assoc. editor The Papers of James Madison, Chgo., 1957-62; instr. U. Chgo., 1960-62; from asst. prof. to prof. Calif. State U., L.A., 1962-96, dean Sch. Letters and Sci., 1970-84, dean Sch. Natural and Social Sci., 1984-96, dean emeritus, prof. emeritus, 1996—; v.p. acad. affairs Trinity Coll. Grad. Studies, Anaheim, Calif., 2000—. Author: The Continuing Dialogue, 2 vols., 1964, Union and Liberty: Documents in American Constitutionalism, 1969, Marshall versus Jefferson: The Political Background of Marbury v. Madison, 1970, Becoming Informed Citizens: Lessons on the Constitution for Junior High School Students, 1988, revised edit., 1995, Invitation to the Dance: An Introduction to Social Dance, 1991, Becoming Informed Citizens: The Bill of Rights and Limited Government, 1995, That's a Good One: Cal State L.A. at 50, 1997, The Federalist and Antifederalist Papers, 1998, Controversial Elections, 2001; contbr. chpts. to books. Recipient Outstanding Prof. award Calif. State U., 1976 Mem. Am. Hist. Assn. (exec. coun. Pacific Coast br. 1971-74), Orgn. Am. Historians, Am. Soc. Legal History (adv. bd. Pacific Coast br. 1972-75), Gold Key, Phi Alpha Theta, Pi Sigma Alpha, Phi Kappa Phi, Sigma Delta Chi. Office: Calif State U Dept History 5151 State University Dr Los Angeles CA 90032-4226 E-mail: ddewey@calstatela.edu.

DEWEY, DONALD WILLIAM, magazine publisher, editor, writer; b. Honolulu, Sept. 30, 1933; s. Donald William and Theckla Jean (Engeborg) D.; m. Sally Rae Ryan, Aug. 7, 1961; children: Michael Kevin, Wendy Ann. Student, Pomona Coll., 1953-55. With Pascoe Steel Corp., Pomona, Calif., 1955-56, div. Reynolds Aluminum Co., Los Angeles, 1956-58, Switzer Panel Corp., Pasadena, Calif., 1958-60; sales and gen. mgr. Western Pre-Cast Concrete Corp., Ontario, Calif., 1960-62; editor, pub. R/C Modeler Mag., Sierra Madre, Calif., 1963—, Freshwater and Marine Aquarium Mag., Sierra Madre, 1978—. Pres., chmn. bd. R/C Modeler Corp., Sierra Madre, 1963— Author: Radio Control From the Ground Up, 1970, Flight Training Course, 1973, For What It's Worth, Vol. 1, 1973, Vol. 2, 1975; contbr. articles to profl. jours. Sustaining mem. Rep. Nat. Com., 1981—; charter mem. Nat. Congl. Club, 1981—; mem. Rep. Presdl. Task Force, 1981—, U.S. Senatorial Club, 1983—, 1984 Presdl. Trust, Conservative Caucus, Nat. Tax Limitation Com., Nat. Conservative Polit. Action Com., Ronald Reagan Presdl. Libr. Served with Hosp. Corps, USN, 1951-55. Mem. Acad. Model Aeronautics, Nat. Aeronautic Assn., Republican. Lutheran. Home: Sierra Madre, Calif. Deceased.

DEWEY, JEFF D. music educator; b. Waukesha, Wis., Dec. 12, 1972; s. Daniel Charles and Lois Ann Dewey; m. Karen Lynn Rice; children: Laura Pearl children: William Jeffery. BM, U. of Wis. - Whitewater, Whitewater, Wisconsin, 1997. Cert. General and Instrumental Music Teaching Wis., 1997. Band dir. Antigo H.S., Antigo, Wis., 1999—, St. Joseph's Mid. Sch., Waukesha, Wis., 1998—99, St. Leonard's Sch., Muskego, Wis., 1997—99, St. James Sch., Muskego, Wis., 1997—99. Asst. dir. Antigo Area Cmty. Band, Antigo, Wis., 2000—; music coord. Ascension Luth. Ch., Antigo, Wis., 1999—. Coord. Brookfield Civic Band, Brookfield, Wis., 1992—93. Recipient Outstanding Young Music Educator, Wis. Music Educator's Assn., 2002. Mem.: Wisonsin Music Educator's Assn., Music Educator's Nat. Conf. Avocations: camping, boating, snowmobiling. Office: Antigo High School 1900 10th Avenue Antigo WI 54409 E-mail: jdewey@antigoschools.k12.wi.us.

DEWEY, RALPH JAY, school system administrator; b. N.Y.C., Feb. 8, 1944; s. Ralph Morris and Evelyn Elizabeth (Karle) D.; m. Vivian V. Barone Dewey, Dec. 20, 1970; children: Gabriella Maria, Meredith Elizabeth, Ralph Stephen. BS, Holy Cross Coll., Worcester, Mass., 1965; MAT, Brown U., Providence, 1968; EdS, Rutgers U., 1985. Teaching Cert., N.Y. Tchr. Moses Brown Sch., Providence, 1965-68; founding head of mid. sch. Portledge Sch., Locust Valley, N.Y., 1968-74; head of lower sch. Rutgers Preparatory Sch., Somerset, N.J., 1974-83; founding headmaster The Winston Sch., Summit, N.J., 1983-87; headmaster St. James Episc. Sch., Corpus Christi, 1987-95; headmaster, bd. dirs. Cape Fear Acad., Wilmington, NC, 1995—2001; dir. Schechter Regional H.S., Bergen County, NJ, 2002—. Regional coord. Southwestern Assn. Episcopal Schs., Corpus Christi, Tex., 1989-93, mem. stds. com. Southwestern Assn. Episcopal Schs., 1994-95, cons., Dallas, 1990-92; workshop presenter Nat. Assn. Ind. Sch., N.Y.C., 1991, Tex. Elem. Prins. and Suprs. Assn., 1991. Author, editor: Winston Newsletter, 1983-87, St. James Episcopal School Newsletter, 1987-95; author: Classical Vocabulary, 1990; contbr. articles to profl. jours. Treas. Coastal Bend Soc. Friends, 1988-95; sec., v.p. Harbor Playhouse, Corpus Christi, Tex., 1989-92; mem. Com. of 100, Wilmington, 1995; mem. exec. coun. Leadership Wilmington, 1996; bd. dirs. Ea. Plains Ind. Conf. Recipient U.S. Dept. Blue Ribbon Sch. Excellence award, Salute to Prins. award Nat. Assn. Elem. Sch. Prins. Mem. N.C. Assn. Ind. Schs. (bd. dirs. 1998-2002, membership chmn. 1998-2001), SAR, ASCD, Assn. Children with Learning Disabilities, Nat. Assn. for Edn. of Young Children, Nat. Coun. for Tchrs. English, Tex. ASCD, Network of Progressive Educators, Wilmington Rotary, Leadership Wilmington, Wilmington Execs. Club, City Club de Rossette. Mem. Soc. Friends. Avocations: russian literature, furniture building. Home: 1010 Primivera Ct Wilmington NC 28409-4869 Office: Solomon Schechter Regional H S 800 Broad St Teaneck NJ 07666

DEWEY, RICHARD B., JR., medical educator, administrator; b. Houston, Feb. 6, 1963; s. Richard Dewey Sr.; m. Deborah K. Dewey; children: Richard III, Campbell, Beall, Chad. BA in Zoology summa cum laude, Duke U., 1985; MD with high honors, Baylor U., 1989. Diplomate Am. Bd. Psychiatry and Neurology; lic. physician, Tex., Minn., Fla. Med. intern St. Joseph's Hosp., Houston, 1989-90; neurology resident Mayo Grad. Sch. Medicine, Rochester, Minn., 1990-93; movement disorders fellow Mayo Clinic, Rochester, 1993-94; assoc. prof. dept. neurology U. Tex. Southwestern Med. Ctr., Dallas, 1994—, dir. Clin. Ctr. for Movement Disorders, 1994—. Lectr. in field. Manuscript reviewer: Neurology, 1995—, Archives of Neurology, 1997—, The Med. Letter, 1997, Mayo Clinic Procs., 1998—; contbr. articles to med. jours., including Neurology, Clin. Neuropharmacology, Archives of Neurology, Movement Disorders. Pres.'s scholar Baylor Coll. Medicin, 1985. Mem. Am. Acad. Neurology, Tex. Med. Assn., Dallas County Med. Soc., Dallas Area Parkinson Soc. (med. adv. bd.), Movement Disorder Soc., Phi Beta Kappa, Alpha Omega Alpha. Home: 726 Bryson Way Southlake TX 76092-7708 Office: U Tex Southwestern Med Ctr Dept Neurology 5323 Harry Hines Blvd Dallas TX 75390-9036

DEWEY, THOMAS GREGORY, dean, physical chemist, educator; b. Pitts., June 2, 1952; s. Ralph Cooper and Frances Mary Dewey; m. Cynthia Elizabeth Miller, Aug. 4, 1957; children: Thomas Miller, John Stephen, Frances Elizabeth. BS, Carnegie-Mellon U., 1974; PhD, U. Rochester, 1979. Postdoctoral rsch. assoc. Cornell U., Ithaca, NY, 1979—81; faculty U. Denver, 1981—99, chair dept. chemistry, 1995—99; faculty Keck Grad. Inst., Claremont, Calif., 1999—2003, dean faculty, 2002—, Robert E. Finnigan chair applied life scis., 2002—. Author: (book) Fractal in Molecular Biophysics, 1998. Postdoctoral fellow, NIH, 1979—81, sr. fellow, 1986. Fellow: Am. Phys. Soc.; mem.: Am. Chem. Soc. Office: Keck Graduate Inst 535 Watson Dr Claremont CA 91711 Home Fax: 909-607-8598; Office Fax: 909-607-8598. Personal E-mail: greg_dewey@kgi.edu. E-mail: greg_dewey@kgi.edu.

DEWEY-BALZHISER, ANNE ELIZABETH MARIE, lawyer; b. Balt., Mar. 16, 1951; d. George Daniel and Elizabeth Patricia (Mohan) Dewey; m. Richard J. Balzhiser; children: Brendan M. Barnett, Andrew P. Barnett, Meghan E. Barnett. BA, Mich. State U., 1972; JD, U. Chgo., 1975; grad., Stonier Grad. Sch. Banking, East Brunswick, N.J., 1983. Bar: D.C. 1976. Legal clk. and atty. FTC, Washington, 1975-78; atty. and sr. atty. Comptr. of Currency, Dallas and Washington, 1978-86; assoc. gen. counsel, gen. counsel, spl. counsel Farm Credit Adminstrn., McLean, Va., 1986-92; counsel, closed bank litig. and policy sect. FDIC, Washington, 1993-94; gen. counsel, spl. advisor Office of Fed. Housing Enterprise Oversight, HUD, Washington, 1994—. Mem. D.C. study devel. coun. Mich. State U., 1999—. Mem.: FBA (bd. dirs. D.C. chpt. 1988—91, banking law com. exec. coun. 1995—2001), ABA (coun. 2002—, coun. mem. adminstrv. law and regulatory practice sect., coun. mem. govt. and pub. sect. law divsn., bus. law sect., banking law com.), D.C. Bar Assn., Women in Housing and Fin. (bd. dirs. 1982—83, gen. counsel 1991—93, co-chair, profl. devel. com. 2002—), Exchequer Club. Roman Catholic. Office: Office Fed Housing Enterprise Oversight 1700 G St NW Fl 4 Washington DC 20552-0003

DEWHIRST, JOHN WARD, lawyer; b. Richmond, Va., Aug. 12, 1937; s. Howard Homer and Edith Rowland (Ward) D.; m. Virginia Dell Pound, Dec. 1, 1958; children: Kathy Lynn Dewhirst Wincheski, Suzanne Ward, John Ward Jr., Matthew Lee, Jeffrey Christopher. B of Indsl. Engring., Ga. Inst. Tech., 1960; JD, George Washington U., 1965. Bar: Va. 1966, D.C. 1971, U.S. Ct. Appeals (fed. cir.) 1970, U.S. Supreme Ct. 1972. Patent examiner Patent and Trademark Office, U.S. Dept. Commerce, Washington, 1960-70, asst. solicitor, 1970-72, assoc. solicitor, 1972-92, retired, 1992; pvt. practice Fairfax, Va., 1992—2002; litig. cons. Williamsburg, Va., 2002—. Expert witness in field of patent law, practice and procedure. Pres. Country Club View Civic Assn., Fairfax, Va., 1968. Mem. Patent Lawyer's Club Washington, Fed. Cir. Bar Assn., Va. State Bar (intellectual property sect.). Episcopalian. Avocations: travel, cross-country skiing, camping, hiking, snorkeling. Home and Office: 2812 Strategy Ct Williamsburg VA 23185-3284

DEWHURST, CHARLES KURT, museum director, cultural administrator, curator, folklorist, English language educator; b. Passaic, N.J., Dec. 21, 1948; s. Charles Allaire and Minn Jule (Hanzl) D.; m. Marsha MacDowell, Dec. 15, 1972; 1 dau., Marit Charlene. BA, Mich. State U., 1970, MA, 1973, PhD, 1983. Editorial asst. Carlton Press, N.Y.C., 1967; computer operator IBM, N.Y.C., 1968; project dir. Mich. State U. Mus., 1975, curator, 1976-83, dir., 1982—. Guest curator Mus. Am. Folk Art, N.Y.C., 1978—83, Artrain, Detroit, 1980—83; dir. Festival of Mich. Folklife, 1987—95, Ctr. for Great Lakes Culture, 2000—. Author: Reflections of Faith, 1983, Artists in Aprons, 1979, Rainbows in the Sky, 1978, Michigan Folk Art, 1976 (Am. Assn. State and Local History award 1977), Art at Work: Folk Pottery of Grand Ledge, Michigan, 1986, Michigan Quilts, 1987, Michigan Folklife Reader, 1988, To Honor and Comfort: Native Quilting Traditions, 1998, MSU Campus: Buildings, Places and Spaces, 2002. Coord. South African-U.S. Partnership Project, 1967—; mem. and chair adv. com. Smithsonian Ctr. for Folklife and Cultural Heritage; vice chair Mich. Humanities Coun., 1995—; chairperson Mich. Coun. for Arts and Cultural Affairs; pres. bd. dirs. Fund for Folk Culture. Recipient Disting. Svc. and Humanities award, 1994. Mem. Am. Folkore Soc., Mich. Folklore Soc., Midwest Soc. Lit., Popular Culture Assn., Mich. Hist. Soc., Mich. Mus. Assn., Am. Assn. Mus., Internat. Coun. Mus. Home: 1804 Cricket Ln East Lansing MI 48823-1225 Office: Mich State U Mus W Circle Dr East Lansing MI 48824

DEWHURST, DAVID, lieutenant governor; b. Tex., Aug. 18, 1945; BA, U. Ariz. With CIA, U.S. State Dept.; founder Falcon Seaboard, 1981; ptnr. Falcon Seabord Diversified Energy and Investments Co.; commr. Tex. Gen. Land Office; lt. gov. State of Tex., 2003—. Chmn. Gov.'s Task Force on Homeland Security, 2001—03; mem. Gov.'s Bus. Coun., Pres.'s Commn. on Capabilities of U.S. Intelligence Cmty.; chmn. State Product Devel. Bd. Active civic and charitable bds., Houston. Officer USAF. Republican. Presbyterian. Office: Capitol Sta PO Box 12068 Austin TX 78711

DEWHURST, DAVID LITCHFIELD, university administrator; b. N.Y.C., Feb. 7, 1956; s. David Conrad and Eloise (Linscott) D.; 1 child, Lena. BA magna cum laude, Columbia U., 1994, MA, 1995. Adminstrv. officer Columbia U., N.Y.C., 1984-92, asst. mgr., 1990-92, mgr., 1992—. Mem. Columbia Cmty. Svc., N.Y.C., 1994—. Mem. Phi Beta Kappa. Democrat. Avocations: ancient political thought, british idealism, liberal political theory. Home: 140 Claremont Ave Apt 6D New York NY 10027-4657 Office: Columbia U 410 W 118th St # Mc3425 New York NY 10027-7213

DEWHURST, PETER, industrial engineer, educator; b. Great Harwood, Eng., Mar. 7, 1944; arrived in U.S., 1980; BSc, U. Manchester, Eng., 1970, MSc, 1971, PhD in Mech. Engring., 1973. With faculty mech. engring. U. Salford, 1973—80; vis. prof. mfg. group U. Mass., 1980—81, prof., 1980—85; prof. indsl. and mfg. engring. U. R.I., Kingston, 1985—, dir. grad. studies mfg.

engrng., 1985—. Referee: Internat. Jour. Applied Mechanics, Internat. Jour. Prodn. Rsch., Am. Soc. Mech. Engrs., assoc. editor: Mfg. Rev., Jour. Design and Mfg., Internat. Jour. Sys. Automation and Applications. Recipient Nat. medal Tech., U.S. Dept. Commerce Tech. Adminstrn., 1991. Mem.: Collegiate Internat. Pour Rsch. Prodn. (F.W. Taylor medal 1980), Soc. Mfg. Engrs. (sr.). Achievements include research in mechanics of metal forming; metal cutting; design of minimum-weight structures for manufacture and the application of robots in assembly procedures.

DE WILDE, CRAIG JAMES, music educator, researcher; b. Paterson, N.J., July 8, 1957; arrived in Australia, 1992; s. Ralph James and Jean Gorrie De Wilde; m. Karen Lynn Filippelli, June 25, 1983; children: Adam, Rhys. BA, Whittier Coll., 1979; MFA, U. Calif., Irvine, 1982; PhD, U. Calif., Santa Barbara, 1991. Lectr. City Colls. Chgo., Munich, 1987-89; assoc. dept. music U. Calif., Santa Barbara, 1989-91; sr. lectr., dep. head Sch. Music-Conservatorium Monash U., Clayton, Victoria, Australia, 1992—. Author: American Music and Popular Culture, 1993; contbr. articles to profl. jours. Com. mem. Monash Arts Coun., 1997-2001. music commentator, ABC Radio, Melbourne. Monash Arts Coun., 1997-02. Deutsche Akademische Austauschdienst fellow, 1986, 87. Mem. Musicol. Soc. Australia (nat. pres. 1998-2000), Am. Musicol. Soc., Internat. Assn. for the Study of Popular Music, Boobooks. Avocations: travel, sports, classic cars. Office: Monash U Sch Music Wellington Rd Clayton VIC 3800 Australia Office Fax: 61 3 9905 3241. E-mail: craig.dewilde@arts.monash.edu.au.

DEWILDE, DAVID MICHAEL, management consultant, former executive search consultant, financial services executive, lawyer; b. Bridgeton, N.J., Aug. 11, 1940; s. Louis and Dorothea (Donnelly) deW.; m. Katherine August, Dec. 30, 1984; children: Holland Stockdale, Christian DuCroix, Nicholas Alexander, Lucas Barrymore. AB, Dartmouth Coll., 1962; LLB, U. Va., 1967; MS in Mgmt., Stanford U., 1984. Bar: N.Y. 1968, D.C. 1972. Assoc. Curtis, Mallet-Prevost, Colt & Mosle, N.Y.C., 1967-69; assoc. gen. counsel HUD, Washington, 1969-72; investment banker Lehman Bros., Washington, 1972-74; dep. commr. FHA, Washington, 1974-76; pres. Govt. Nat. Mortgage Assn., Washington, 1976-77; mng. dir. Lepercq DeNeuflize & Co., N.Y.C., 1977-81; exec. v.p. policy and planning Fed. Nat. Mortgage Assn., Washington, 1981-82; pres. deWilde & Assocs., Washington, 1982-84; mng. dir., dir. fin. svcs. Boyden Internat., San Francisco, 1984-88; CEO Chartwell Ptnrs. Internat., San Francisco, 1989-97; mng. dir. LAI Worldwide, San Francisco, 1998-99; mng. ptnr. TMP Worldwide, San Francisco, 1999-2001; mgmt. cons., 2001—. Bd. dirs. Berkshire Realty Investment Trust, Fritzi of Calif., Silicon Valley Bankshares; bd. dirs. St. Luke's School, San Francisco, chair, 2001 03. Editor in chief Va. Jour. Internat. Law, 1966-67. Lt. USN, 1962-64. Mem. Pacific Union Club (San Francisco), Villa Taverna (San Francisco), Met. Club (Washington), Belvedere Tennis Club. Republican. E-mail: ddewilde@pacbell.net.

DEWIND, JOSH, social science researcher; b. Washington, Dec. 23, 1943; s. Adrian W. DeWind and Joan E. Mosenthal; m. Dona S. Ratterree, Nov. 28, 1985; children: A. Samuel R., William L.R. Student, Antioch Coll., 1963; BA, Columbia U., 1966, PhD, 1977. Rschr. N.Am. Congress on L.Am., N.Y.C., 1976—80; dir. Immigration Rsch. Program Ctr. for the Social Scis., Columbia U., 1981—89; dir. L.Am. and Caribbean Studies Program Hunter Coll., CUNY, 1989—2001, prof. dept. anthropology, 1989—2001, dir. Human Rights Program, 1990—2001; program dir. Internat. Migration Program Social Sci. Rsch. Coun., N.Y.C., 1994—. Cons. Rockefeller Found., N.Y.C., 1980—81; bd. chair Ctr. for Immigrants Rights, N.Y.C., 1981—89; bd. mem. Nat. Coalition for Haitian Rights, N.Y.C. Co-author: Aiding Migration, 1988 (Best Book of 1988 New Eng. Coun. on A.Am. and Caribbean Studies); co-editor: The Handbook of International Migration, 2000 (Best Book, Am. Sociol. Assn. Sect. on Internat. Migration). Grantee, Nat. Inst. for Child Health and Human Devel., 1984—87, Ford Found., 1985, 2001, N.Y. Cmty. Trust, 1987—89, Mellon Found., 1990—95, 1994—2003, Aaron Diamond Found. & Joyce-Mertz-Gilmore Found., 1991—96. Mem.: Am. Anthrop. Assn. Office: Social Sci Rsch Coun 810 Seventh Ave New York NY 10029

DEWINE, R. MICHAEL, senator, lawyer; b. Springfield, Ohio, Jan. 5, 1947; s. Richard and Jean DeWine; m. Frances Struewing, June 3, 1967; children: Patrick, Jill, Rebecca, John, Brian, Alice, Mark, Anna. BS in Edn., Miami U., Oxford, Ohio, 1969; JD, Ohio No. U., 1972. Bar: Ohio 1972, U.S. Supreme Ct. 1977. Asst. pros. atty. Greene County, Xenia, Ohio, 1973-75, pros. atty., 1977-81; mem. Ohio Senate, 1981-82, 98th, 99th, 100th, 101st Congress from 7th Ohio dist., Washington, 1983-90; lt. gov. State of Ohio, Columbus, Ohio, 1991-94; U.S. senator from Ohio, 1995—. Mem. judiciary com., labor and human resources com., intelligence com., Health Edn. Com., Labor and Pensions Com. Republican. Roman Catholic. Home: 2587 Conley Rd Cedarville OH 45314-9525 Office: US Senate 140 Russell Senate Bldg Washington DC 20510-0001

DEWING, HENRY WOODS, SR., telecommunications executive; b. Argentia, Nfld., Can., Dec. 11, 1962; s. Bruce Warren and Martha Woods (Potter) D.; m. Sarah Brett Hurley, Sept. 12, 1992; children: Sarah Cameron, Henry Woods Jr., Margaret Blair, John Brett. BS, Washington and Lee U., 1985; MBA, U. Va., Charlottesville, 1991. Supr. Bell Atlantic, Washington, 1985-89, mgr. Arlington, Va., 1991-94; cons. AT Kearney, Arlington, 1994-97; mgr. Compaq, Houston, 1997-2000; dir. Intel, 2000—; chmn. Enterprise Futures Working Group, Telecom. Industry Assn., 2000—. R.E. Lee scholar, 1983-85. Mem. Ky. Cols., Alumni Assn. of AOD of Chi Psi (v.p., pres., bd. dirs. 1985-93, Nelson T. Levings award 1985), Hunwick Racquet Club (v.p., membership dir. 2001—), Mantoloking Yacht Club (bd. govs. 2002—), Chi Psi Alumni Assn. of Nat. Capitol Area (pres. 1991-93). Episcopalian.

DEWITT, BARBARA JANE, journalist; b. Glendale, Calif., Aug. 5, 1947; d. Clarence James and Irene Brezina; m. Don DeWitt, Apr. 21, 1974; children: Lisa, Scarlett. BA in Journalism, Calif. State U., Northridge, 1971. Features editor The Daily Ind. Newspaper, Ridgecrest, Calif., 1971-84; fashion editor The Daily Breeze, Torrance, Calif., 1984-89; freelance fashion reporter The Seattle Times, 1990; fashion editor, columnist The Los Angeles Daily News, L.A., 1990—. Instr. fashion writing UCLA, 1988, Am. InterContinental U., L.A., 1996 . Dir. Miss Indian Wells Valley Scholarship Pageant, 1980-84. Recipient 1st Pl. Best Youth Page, Calif. Newspaper Pubs. Assn., 1980, 1st Pl. Best Fashion, Wash. Press Assn., 1989, The Internat. Aldo award for fashion journalism, 1995, 96. Republican. Lutheran. Avocations: antiques, reading, swimming. Office: The Daily News 21221 Oxnard St Woodland Hills CA 91367-5081

DEWITT, BRYDON MERRILL, development consultant; b. Westernport, Md., June 9, 1943; s. Brydon Owens and Helen Naomi (Fike) DeW.; m. Louise Muriel Wampler, May 22, 1965; 1 child, Brydon Mark. BA, Bridgewater Coll., 1965; MFA, Va. Commonwealth U., 1973. Tchr. English, history, speech Luray (Va.) H.S., 1965-66; tchr. English, speech Harrisonburg (Va.) H.S., 1966-67; dir. student activities Va. Commonwealth U., Richmond, 1968-70, Albion (Mich.) Coll., 1970-72; asst. dir. Kline Campus Ctr. Bridgewater (Va.) Coll., 1972-73, dir. ann. giving/alumni, 1973-75, dir. devel., 1975-90; assoc. Gonser Gerber Tinker Stuhr, Naperville, Ill., 1990-95; pres. DeWitt & Assocs. Inc., Richmond, 1995—. Author, pub. quar. newsletter The Development Companion. Mem. Va. Assn. Fund Raising Execs., Va. Planned Giving Study Group, Assn. Fund Raising Profls. Republican. Baptist. Avocations: reading, writing, sports. Home and Office: 12701 Crimson Ct Richmond VA 23233-7657 E-mail: brydon.dewitt@verizon.net.

DEWITT, CAROL A. publishing executive, writer; b. Indpls., Ind., Nov. 4, 1942; d. Robert William Kollmeyer; m. Robert Knox DeWitt, Oct. 27, 1983; m. Roy L. Bruner, Dec. 6, 1958 (div. May 0, 1973); 1 child, Robin Renee Chaffee. Associates, Applied Sci., Univ. Louisville, Louisville, KY, 1982. Sales rep. Br. Motor Freight, Louisville, 1975—77, Spector Freight Sys., Louisville, 1977—81; sales mgr. Atlantic Container Line, Jeffersonville, 1981—83; owner Land-Sea-Air, Louisville, 1983—85; sales exec. Ctrl. Transport, Inc., Louisville, 1985—87, Am. Pres. Dist., Louisville, 1987—89; writer StarPoint Pub., Sebring, 2001—02. Dir. nat. bd. Transp. Clubs Internat., Louisville, 1978—81, Kentuckiana World Commerce Coun., Louisville, 1977—80; pres. Women's Traffic Club, Louisville, 1981. Author: (book) God 101, composer christian music. Dir. St. Elizabeth's Home, New Albany, Ind., 1988—91, Indianapolis, Ind., 1991; mem. Louisville Forum, Louisville, Ky., 1986. Recipient Transp. Queen, Women's Traffic Club, Louisville, KY, 1976. Mem.: Ch. Women United, Span, Country Club of Sebring. United Church Of Christ. Avocations: golfing, painting, travel. Home: 2851 Briarwood Lane Sebring FL 33875 Office: Starpoint Publishing Co 2851 Briarwood Lane Sebring FL 33875

DEWITT, CHARLES BARBOUR, federal government official; b. L.A., Mar. 13, 1950; s. Homer Charles and Gwenyth Deakin (Barbour) DeW.; m. Bonnie St. Clair; 1 child, Anna. BA with univ. distinction and dept. honors, Stanford U., 1972; postgrad., Cambridge U., 1972-73. Dep. sheriff City of San Jose, Calif., 1973-74, specialist regional crime bd., 1974-78, dir. justice div., 1978-84; fellow U.S. Dept. of Justice, 1984-89; advisor White House, Washington, 1989-90; dir. Nat. Inst. Justice, 1990-93; ptnr. Lafayette Group, Inc., Vienna, Va., 1993—. Faculty Nat. Acad. Corrections, Boulder, Colo., 1986-90, Nat. Inst. Corrections, Washington, 1986-90; cons. Police Found., 1993-94. Author: National Directory of Corrections, 1986, 1988, Building on Experience, 1987, Prison Expansion, 1988. Adv. coun. The Ditchley Found. With USMCR, 1968-71. Recipient Atty. Gen's Achievement award, 1993, Dist. Attys. award, 1993, Am. Jails award, 1993. Mem. Am. Correctional Assn., Internat. Assn. Chiefs Police, Nat. Sheriffs Assn., Nat. Dist. Attys. Assn. Republican. Episcopalian. Avocations: jogging, skiing, tennis. Home: 5058 Sedgwick St NW Washington DC 20016 1940 Office: Lafayette Group Inc 8150 Leesburg Pike Ste 900 Vienna VA 22182-7749

DEWITT, CHARLES W. state legislator; b. Lecompte, La., Feb. 4, 1947; m. Patricia Riddick. Grad. h.s. Mem. for dist. 25 La. Ho. of Reps., Baton Rouge, 1980—, spk. of the ho. Chmn. legis. budgetary control coun.; mem. ho. exec. com., ho. legis. svcs. coun., state bond commn.; ex officio joint legis. com. on capital outlay, joint legis. com. on the budget. Mem. Belgian Am. Club, Rapides Parish Farm Bur., Amicus Club, Cattleman's Assn., Raides Parish C. of C., South Rapides Svc. Club. Office: PO Box 5526 Alexandria LA 71307-5526 E-mail: webreps@legis.state.la.us.*

DEWITT, DAWN E. medical educator, dean; arrived in Australi, 2003; m. Alan Talbot; 2 children. MD, Harvard U., 1990. Lic. internal medicine Am. Bd. of Internal Medicine. Assoc. prof., attending physician U. of Wash., Seattle, 2000—03; prof., dean Rural Clin. Sch., U. of Melbourne, Shepparton, Australia, 2003—. Dir. WWAMI regional cmty. based edn. in internal medicine U. of Wash., Seattle, 1998—2003. Editor, author: medi. knowledge self-assessment program MKSAP 13 for Primary Care. Chair Nat. Bd. of Med. Examiners, Phila., 2000—03. Fellow: ACP; mem.: Alpha Omega Alpha (hon.). Office: U Wash Med Ctr Roosevelt 354760 4245 Roosevelt Way NE Seattle WA 98105 Office Fax: 206-598-5952.

DEWITT, EDWARD FRANCIS, artist; b. Jersey City, Aug. 1, 1938; s. Elmer and Linda (Kroll) DeW.; m. Cora Finn, Nov. 11, 1959 (separated 1970); children: April, Lenneice, Edward, Linda; m. Mary Golazizian, Sept. 17, 1972. Artist cons. Bronx (N.Y.) Zoo, 1968-70, Aquarius Art Ltd., Fairview, N.J., 1971-73; artist, sculptor, v.p. Artistic Classics, Rutherford, N.J., 1974-77; artist, sculptor, Browns Mills, N.J., 1977-97. Artist 5-yr. silverplate series Anheuser Busch; commemorative works for Pub. Svc., Babe Ruth, Gen. Doolittle, Jim Thorpe PA; sculptures Ford Motor Co., GM Corp., Bicentennial Soc., Boy Scouts Am., Thomas Edison, NATO, Chesapeake Reproductions, Mappsville, Va.; award programs for Progresso Foods, Kentucky Fried Chicken; medallions John F. Kennedy, Dwight D. Eisenhower, Winston Churchill, Bobby Kennedy, Charles A. Lindbergh, Gerald Ford: President; artist prints-sculptures models and collector plates Abundant Ocean Treasures, Saddlebrook, N.J., Double Eagle Sculpture (ofcl. symbol for New Millenium chosen by U.S. Hist. Soc.); series of prints chosen for Zallies Shop-Rite chain; commd. to sculpt profiles of Am. Presidents Medallion Series, Chesapeake Reprodns., Mappsville, Va., 2003, Louis and Clark 200th anniversary sculpture, 2003; represented in numerous pvt. collections in U.S. and Europe; patentee on door striker plate. Double eagle sculpture chosen as official symbol by U.S. Hist. Soc., 2000. Avocations: the arts, music, guitar, fishing. Home: 411 N Carolina Trl Browns Mills NJ 08015-5405

DEWITT, EULA, accountant; b. Conway, S.C., Feb. 5, 1948; d. Joseph and Ethel Maude (Parmley) D.; m. John Ramos; children: Andre Carter, John Ramos III, David Carter. BS in Acctg., CUNY, 1981; cert., Bethlehem Missionary Bible Inst., 1990; ThM, Lighthouse Christian Coll., 1998, DDiv magna cum laude, 2000. Jr. acct. Kenneth Laventhol, CPA Firm, N.Y., 1981; agent IRS, N.Y., 1981—, staff pub. speakers bur., 1985—, instr. for revenue agents, 1986—. Author newsletter; contbr. numerous articles to profl. jours. Tutor York Coll. CUNY, Jamaica, 1991—; guest spkr. Hunter Coll. 6th Ann. Conv., 1991, Exploring Divsn. Greater N.Y., 1991, Cath. Charities Archdiocese, N.Y., 1991, First Corinthian Bap. Ch., Bklyn., 1996—, various Bapt. chs., 1996; Sunday Sch. tchr. Bethlehem Missionary Ch., 1979—, leader altar workers ministry, 1991—, missionary to Belize, 1991, to Eng., 1993, to Guyana, 1995, Kano State, Nigeria, 1997, Jos State, Nigeria, 1997, Benue State, Nigeria, 1997; mem. prison ministry team to Rikers island Bethlehem Misionary Ch., 1996—; missionary evangelist Wartburg Luth. Home for Srs., Bklyn., 1999—. Mem. Inst. Mgmt. Accts. (bd. dirs. 1982—, v.p. profl. edn. 1994-95, pres.-elect 1996-97, pres. 1997—), Toastmaster's 21 Club (v.p., past pres., Able Toastmaster ATM 1996), Inst. Mgmt. Accts. (bd. dirs., pres. 1997-98). Avocations: photography, reading. Office: IRS 110 W 44th St Fl 5 New York NY 10036-4049

DEWITT, MARY THERESE, forensic anthropologist, archaeologist; b. Chgo., Aug. 25, 1948; d. Robert Baldwin and Helen (Rossman) DeW. BA in Anthropology, U. Tex., Arlington, 1995, MA in Interdisciplinary Studies, 1997. Dir. mktg. Homart Devel. Co., Florence, Ky., 1975—76, Melvin Simon & Assocs., Inc., Hurst, Tex., 1976-79; pres. Mary DeWitt Co., Ft. Worth, 1979-85; v.p. mktg. Southmark Comml. Mgmt., Dallas, 1986-87; prin. DeWitt Group and subs. Cat's-Eye Intelligence Svc., Dallas and Ft. Worth, 1988-98; coord. program advisement U. N.Mex., Albuquerque, 1998—. Cons. logistics and documentation one team Internat. Group for Hist. Aircraft Recovery, The Phoenix Group South Pacific, 1989; mem. hist. survey and exhumation team Smithsonian and U. Tex., Giddings, Tex., 1998. Mem. Am. Coll. of Forensic Examiners, Archaeol. Inst. of Am., Internat. Assn. for Identification, Am. Assn. of Phys. Anthropologists, N.Mex. Academic Advising Assn., Lambda Alpha (v.p. 1994-97), Alpha Phi Omega (staff advisor). Home: 612 6th St SW Albuquerque NM 87102-3808 E-mail: mdewitt@unm.edu.

DEWITT, RALPH OGDEN, JR., military career history; b. Waynesville, Mo., June 30, 1942; m. Sheree Cully; children: Ogden, Ashley. DO, Kirksville Coll. Osteo., 1969. Diplomate Am. Bd. Family Practice. Pvt. practice; chief of staff Pulaski County Meml. Hosp., Waynesville; commd. officer U.S. Army, 1973, advanced through grades to brig. gen., 1996—; family practice residency faculty Tripler Army Med. Ctr., Hawaii; family practice dep. dir. Womack Army Cmty. Hosp., Ft. Bragg, N.C.; divsn. surgeon 82nd Airborne Divsn. U.S. Army, Ft. Bragg; ctr. surgeon JFK Spl. Warfare Ctr., Ft. Bragg; chief dept. family practice and family practice residency Tripler Army Med. Ctr., Hawaii; med. advisor to comdr. 14th Coast Guard Dist. U.S. Army, Hawaii; ambulatory care cons. to Army surgeon gen., commdr. Womack Army Hosp., Ft. Bragg; surgeon XVIII Airborne Corps U.S. Army, Ft. Bragg, surgeon Joint Task Force South; comdr. William Beaumont Army Med. Ctr.; asst. surgeon gen., dep. chief staff Office Surgeon Gen., U.S. Army Med. Command, Ft. Sam Houston, Tex., 1997—; comdr. Brook Army Med. Ctr., Great Plains Regional Med. Command. Decorated Legion of Merit with three oak leaf clusters, Bronze Star, Meritorious Svc. medal with three oak leaf clusters, Army Commendation medal, Army Achievement medal, Armed Forces Expeditionary medal. Office: US Army Med Command Fort Sam Houston TX 78234

DEWITT-MORETTE, CÉCILE, physicist; b. Paris, Dec. 21, 1922; came to U.S., 1948; d. André and Marie Louise (Ravaudet) Morette; m. Bryce S. DeWitt, Apr. 26, 1951; children: Nicolette, Jan, Chris, Abigail. BS, U. Caen, 1943; PhD, U. Paris, 1947. With Centre Nat. de la Recherche Sci., 1944-65, Maitre de Confs. prof., 1965-88. Mem. Inst. Advanced Studies, Dublin, 1946—47, Copenhagen, 1947—48, Princeton, 1948—50; lectr. U. Calif., Berkeley, 1952—55, U. N.C., Chapel Hill, 1956—71; prof. U. Tex., 1972—93, Jane and Roland Blumberg Centennial prof. physics, 1993—2000, prof. emeritus, 2000—; founder, dir. Ecole d'ete de Physique Theorique, Les Houches, France, 1951—72. Author: Particules Elementaires, 1951, (with Y. Choquet-Bruhat and M. Dillard-Bleick) Analysis, Manifolds and Physics, 1977, rev. edit., 1982, (with A. Maheshwari, B. Nelson) Path Integration in Non Relativistic Quantum Mechanics, 1979, (with Y. Choquet Bruhat) Analysis, Manifolds and Physics, Part II, 92 Applications, 1989, rev. edit., 2000, also articles. Decorated chevalier Ordre Nat. du Mérite, chevalier Ordre des Palmes Académiques; chevalier Ordre Nat. Legion d'Honneur; Rask-Oersted fellow, 1947-48, Prix des Sciences Physiques et Mathematiques (Comite du Rayonnement Français, 1992); recipient (with Bryce DeWitt) Marcel Grossman award, 2000. Fellow Am. Phys. Soc.; mem. Internat. Astron. Union, European Phys. Soc., Inst. Hautes Etudes Scientific (trustee), French Soc. Physics (hon.). Home: 2411 Vista Ln Austin TX 78703-2343 Office: U Tex Dept Physics Austin TX 78712 E-mail: cdewitt@physics.utexas.edu.

DEWLEN, ALTON LEROY (AL DEWLEN), writer; b. Memphis, Tex., Nov. 30, 1921; s. Aaron and Edna Louella (Sloan) D.; m. Jean Lamb, Sept. 9, 1942 (dec. 1990); 1 child, Michael Lee (dec.); m. Nella Faye Wood Watson, Jan. 24, 1991 (dec. 2002), m. Lucille Howard, July 22, 2003. Student, Hillsboro (Tex.) Coll., 1939-41, Baylor U., 1941-42, U. Okla., 1952-55. Reporter Amarillo (Tex.) Globe-News, 1946-47; city editor Amarillo Times, 1947-51; staffer/night editor UP, Dallas, Okla. City, 1951-54; free-lance mag. writer, 1954-56; novelist, 1956—. Polit., economic rschr. South Africa, 1972-75, Rhodesia, Namibia, South Africa, 1978-80, Kenya, 1982-86. Author: Night of the Tiger, 1956, The Bone Pickers, 1958, Twilight of Honor, 1961 (McGraw Hill Fiction award, 1962), Servants of Corruption, 1971, Next of Kin, 1977, The Session, 1981; editor: (Joe Wanjui) From Where I Sit, 1986; lectr. in fiction techniques. Active Baylor Bear Found. T/Sgt. USMC, 1942-45, PTO. Recipient Okla. Award for Literary Excellence U. Okla., 1970, Freedom Found. George Washington Medal for mag./newspaper article "Report to a Sleeping Son", 1969. Mem.: NRA (life). Mem. Christian Ch. Avocations: woodcraft, shooting sports, football recruiting. Home: 3024 Maple Hill Cir Waco TX 76708-1557

DE WOLF, DAVID ALTER, electrical engineer, educator; b. Dordrecht, The Netherlands, July 23, 1934; came to U.S., 1962; m. Peggy Louise Lumpkin; 1 dau., Sarah Eleonora; children by previous marriage: Naomi, Jiska. BS in Physics, U. Amsterdam, The Netherlands, 1955, MS in Physics, 1959; PhDEE, U. Eindhoven, The Netherlands, 1968. Rsch. scientist Edgewood (Md.) Arsenal U.S. Army Chem. Ctr., 1962; mem. tech. staff RCA Labs.-David Sarnoff Rsch. Ctr., Princeton, N.J., 1962-82; prof. elec. engrng. Va. Tech., Blacksburg, 1982—2003, prof. emeritus, 2003—. Commn. B and F U.S. Nat. Com. Internat. Union Radio Sci., sec. 1985-89. Author 2 books and contbr. numerous articles on wave propagation, electron optics to profl. jours. Fellow IEEE, Optical Soc. Am. (assoc. editor JOSA 1969-81); mem. Am. Assn. Physics Tchrs., Dutch Physics Soc., Electromagnetics Acad., Sigma Xi, Eta Kappa Nu. Avocations: music, piano, literature, tennis. Office: Va Tech Bradley Dept Elec and Computer Engring Blacksburg VA 24061-0111 E-mail: dadewolf@vt.edu.

DEWOLFE, JOHN CHAUNCEY, JR., lawyer; b. Chgo., June 9, 1913; s. John Chauncey and Mabel (Spafford) DeW.; m. Dorothy Fulton, May 9, 1942; children: John Chauncey, III, George F. BS, U. Ill.; JD, U. Wis., 1939. Bar: Wis. 1939, Ill. 1940. Ptnr. firm DeWolfe, Poynton & Stevens and predecessor firms, 1946 . Contbr. articles to profl. jours. Trustee Village of Riverside, Ill., 1963-70; Chmn. West Suburban Mass Transit Dist., 1974-76. Served from lt. to maj. AUS, 1942-45, 51-52; lt. col. USAR ret. Mem. Am., Ill., Wis. bar assns., Chgo. Bar Assn. (chmn. corp. law com. 1973-74), Bar Assn. 7th Fed. Circuit, Assn. Trial Lawyers Am., Sigma Phi Epsilon. Clubs: University (Chgo.). Republican. Episcopalian. Home: 1448 N Lake Shore Dr Chicago IL 60610-6655 Office: 135 S La Salle St Chicago IL 60603

DEWOLFE, RUTHANNE K.S. lawyer, psychologist, accountant; b. Milw., Aug. 14, 1933; d. Erich Max and Mary Elizabeth (Stork) Sobota; m. Alan S. Dewolfe Aug. 24, 1952 (div. July 1986); children: Kyle A., Hillary S., Elena M. BA, Heidelberg Coll., Tiffin, Ohio, 1954; PhD, Northwestern U., 1960; JD, DePaul U., Chgo., 1976; LLM, DePaul U., 1985. Bar: Ill. 1976, U.S. Dist. Ct. (no. dist.) Ill. 1976, U.S. Ct. Appeals (7th cir.) Ill. 1980, U.S. Supreme Ct. 1982; registered psychologist, Pa., Ill. Staff psychologist Hines VA Hosp., 1960-62; pvt. practice psychology Chgo., 1962—; staff atty. Legal Asst. Found., Chgo., 1975-77, supr. atty., 1980-97; regional atty. U.S. Civil Rights Commn., Chgo., 1977-80; pvt. practice, 1997—. Adj. faculty criminal justice dept. U. Ill., Chgo., 1980-86; lectr. in field. Contbr. numerous articles and papers to various publs. Mem. Evanston Symphony Orch. Mem. Internat. Fedn. Women Lawyers, John Howard Assn. (v.p. 1985-91), Sigma Xi. Home: 811 Colfax St Evanston IL 60201-2420

DE WOLFF, LOUIS, management consultant; b. N.Y.C., Dec. 21, 1929; s. Maurice and Minnie (Konrad) De W.; m. Grace Elise Sorrentino, Apr. 27, 1957 (dec. Dec. 2000); children: Douglas Louis, Cynthia Ann. AS, Bklyn. Coll., 1960; BS in Acctg., CCNY, 1962. Officer Lykes Bros. S.S. Co., New Orleans, 1950-57; export mgr. Cory Mann George Corp., N.Y.C., 1957-60; dist. supt. F&M Schaefer Brewing Co., N.Y.C., 1960-64; product and material mgr. Del Labs., Inc., Farmingdale, N.Y., 1965-69; exec. cons., exec. v.p. Pennington (N.J.) Industries, 1969-73; dir. ops. Alexander Proudfoot Co., Chgo., 1973-86; mgr. ops. Metra Proudfoot Ltd., Brussels, 1986-87; CEO, chmn. DeWolff Boberg & Assocs., Charleston, SC, 1987—. Lt. (j.g.) USMS and USNR, 1950-57, PTO, Mem.: U.S. Navy League, U.S. Naval Inst., Charleston Concert Assn. (bd. dirs.). Republican. Lutheran. Avocations: carpentry, sailing, gardening. Home: 53 Waterway Island Dr Isle Of Palms SC 29451 Office: DeWolff Boberg & Assocs PO Box 21989 Charleston SC 29413-1989

DEWOSKIN, ALAN ELLIS, lawyer; b. St. Louis, Sept. 10, 1940; s. Samuel S. and Lillian (Sachs) DeW.; m. Iris Lynn Shapiro, Aug. 15, 1942; children: Joseph, Henry, Franklin. BA, Washington U., St. Louis, 1962, JD, 1965; postgrad., U.S. Army Command & Gen. Staff Coll., 1978, U.S. Army War Coll., 1985. Bar: Mo. 1968, Ill. 1999, U.S. Dist. Ct. (ea. dist.) Mo. 1968, U.S. Ct. Appeals (8th cir.) 1969, U.S. Ct. Appeals (Armed Forces) 1976, U.S. Supreme Ct. 1990, U.S. Ct. Claims 1997. Pvt. practice, St. Louis, 1968-82; prin. Alan E. DeWoskin, PC, St. Louis, 1982—. Active Boy Scouts Am. Col. JAGC, USA Ret. Col. JAGC U.S. Army, ret. Recipient U.S. Legion of Merit, 1992. Fellow Am. Bar Found., Mo. Bar Found., St. Louis Bar Found. (disting.); mem. ABA (chmn., gen. practice sect. 1985-86, ho. of dels. 1986-87, assembly del., standing com. mil. law, standing com. assembly resolutions 1988-91, vice-chmn. task force solo and small firm practitioners), ATLA, Mo. Bar Assn. (chmn. gen. practice com. 1987-90, chmn. computer interest groups 1988-90), Bar Assn. Met. St. Louis (exec. com. 1993-94, bd. govs. 1994-95, chmn. solo and small firm sect. 1993-95), Mo. Assn. Trial Attys., Res. Officers Assn. (Mo. Dept. pres. 1979), Masons (past master, dir. 1972—), Am. Legion. Home: 14030 Deltona Dr Chesterfield MO 63017-3311 Office: 225 S Meramec Ave Ste 426 Saint Louis MO 63105-3511 E-mail: aedewoskin@cs.com.

DEWS, P(ETER) B(OOTH), medical scientist, educator; b. Ossett, Yorkshire, Eng., Sept. 11, 1922; s. G.A. and E. (Booth) D.; m. Grace Miller, Dec. 1949; children: Pamela, Kenneth, Alan, Michael. M.B.Ch.B., U. Leeds, Eng., 1944; PhD, MN, 1952; MA, Harvard U., 1959. House physician Grimsby Hosp., U.K., 1944-45; lectr. pharmacology U. Leeds, 1945-47; rsch. assoc. Wellcome Rsch. Labs., Tuckahoe, N.Y., 1948-49, Mayo Found., Rochester, Minn., 1950-52; from instr. to prof. Harvard Med. Sch., Boston, 1953-93, prof. emeritus, 1993—. Mem. Nat. Adv. Mental Health Coun., Washington, 1985-88, Nat. Adv. Space Coun., Washington, 1982-86; v.p. Internat. Life Scis. Inst., Washington, 1977-97. Mem. Inst. of Medicine. Office: Harvard Med Sch NEPRC PO Box 9102 Southborough MA 01772-9102 E-mail: peter_dews@hms.harvard.edu.

DEWSBURY, DONALD ALLEN, historian of psychology, comparative psychologist; b. Bklyn., Aug. 11, 1939; s. Edwin Leroy and Carol Wieler (Neil) D.; children: Bryan Bradley, Laura Alison. AB, Bucknell U., 1961; PhD, U. Mich., 1965. NSF postdoctoral fellow U. Calif., Berkeley, 1965-66; mem. faculty dept. psychology U. Fla., Gainesville, 1966—, prof., 1973—. Author: Comparative Animal Behavior, 1978, Comparative Psychology in the Twentieth Century, 1984; editor (with D. Rethlingshafer): Comparative Psychology: A Modern Survey, 1973; editor: (with T. McGill, B. Sachs) Sex and Behavior: Status and Prospectus, 1978; editor: Mammalian Sexual Behavior, 1981, Foundations of Comparative Psychology, 1984, Leaders in the Study of Animal Behavior, 1985, Studying Animal Behavior, 1989, Contemporary Issues in Comparative Psychology, 1990, Unification Through Division: Histories of the Divisions of the American Psychological Association, vol. 1, 1996, vol. 2, 1997,

vol. 3, 1998, vol. 4, 1999, vol. 5, 2000; editor: (with W. Pickren) Evolving Perspectives on the History of Psychology, 2002. Fellow APA (pres. divsn. 6 1992-93, pres. divsn. 26 1997-98), AAAS, Animal Behavior Soc. (pres. 1978-79); mem. Psychonomic Soc., History of Sci. Soc., Cheiron Soc., Phi Beta Kappa, Psi Chi. Home: 4004 NW 59th Ave Gainesville FL 32653-8358 Office: Univ Fla Dept Psychology Gainesville FL 32611-2250 E-mail: dewsbury@ufl.edu.

DEX, WALTER JOHN, radiologist; b. Allentown, Pa., July 15, 1930; s. John Theresa (Muhr) D.; m. Ruth G. Rojahn, May 19, 1956. BS in Biol. Sci., Rutgers U., 1952; MD, U. Pa., 1956. Diplomate Am. Bd. Radiology; lic. physician, Pa. Rotating intern Phila. Gen. Hosp., 1956-57, resident in radiology, 1957-60; staff Allentown Hosp., 1962-90, chief radiology, 1973-90; staff Lehigh Valley Hosp. Ctr., 1973-96, vice-chmn. dept. radiology, 1990-92; ret., 1996. Contbr. articles to profl. jours. Coun. mem. Christ Luth. Ch., Allentown; bd. dirs. Allentown Hosp., 1976-83, Lehigh Valley Hosp., 1991-93, HealthEast, 1984-91, sec. bd. dirs., 1991-93. Capt. U.S. Army, 1960-62. Fellow Am. Coll. Radiology; mem. AMA, Radiol. Soc. N.Am., Phila. Roentgen Ray.

DEXTER, DEIRDRE O'NEIL ELIZABETH, lawyer; b. Stillwater, Okla., Apr. 15, 1956; d. Robert N. and Paula E. (Robinson) Maddox; m. Terry E. Dexter, May 14, 1977; children: Daniel M. II, David Maddox. Student, Okla. State U., 1974-77; BS cum laude, Phillips U., 1981; JD with highest honors, U. Okla., 1984. Bar: Okla. 1984, U.S. Dist. Ct. (no. and ea. dists.) Okla. 1985, U.S. Dist. Ct. (we. dist.) Okla. 1987, U.S. Ct. Appeals (10th cir.) 1987; grad. Nat. Inst. Trial Advocacy Advanced Trial seminar. Jud. intern Supreme Ct. Okla., Oklahoma City, summer 1983; assoc. Conner & Winters, Tulsa, 1984-90, ptnr., 1991, shareholder, 1991-2000; assoc. dist. judge Tulsa County Dist. Ct., 2000—03; assoc. Frederic Dorwart, Lawyers, Tulsa, 2003—. Article editor Okla. U. Law Rev., 1982-84. U. Okla. scholar, 1983. Mem. Okla. Bar Assn. (advising atty. state champion H.S. mock trial team competition 1992), Tulsa County Bar Assn., mem. bd. dirs., Order of Barristers, Order of Coif, Am. Inns of Ct. (master), Delta Theta Phi. Republican. Baptist. Office: Old City Hall 124 E 4th St Tulsa OK 74103 E-mail: Ddexter@fdlaw.com.

DEXTER, DONALD HARVEY, surgeon, educator; b. Maywood, Ill., Apr. 8, 1920; s. Harry Malcolm and Theodora Jane (Trelawny) D.; m. Esther Ruth Reeve, May 16, 1953; children: Donald Harvey, Scott Reeve, Bryce Malcolm, Margaret Helen. BS, Tulane U., 1948; MD, Northwestern U., 1950; LHD (hon.), Western Ill. U., 1993. Diplomate: Am. Bd. Surgery. Intern Cook County Hosp., Chgo., 1950-51; resident in surgery Ill. Central Hosp., Chgo., 1951-52, Cook County Hosp., 1955-58; practice medicine specializing in surgery Macomb, Ill., 1958-89; ret.; prof. dept. health scis. Western Ill. U., 1975-89; ret.; physician surveyor Joint Commn. on Accreditation Healthcare Orgns., 1989-93; chief of staff Beu Health Ctr., Western Ill. U., 1993-2001, physician, 2001—. Sr. mem. Macomb Clinic; team physician; coroner McDonough County, Ill., 1964-76; mem. gov. bd., chmn. devel. coun. McDonough Dist. Hosp., 1995—. Mem. Western Ill. U. Found. Served with USNR, 1953-54. Named Outstanding Citizen of Macomb Jaycees, 1972, Outstanding Citizen of Macomb Macomb Area C. of C., 1973; recipient award of recognition Devel. Center of Western Ill. U. and Macomb Area C. of C., 1977; named to Hall of Fame Western Ill. U., 1991. Fellow ACS (pres. Ill. chpt. 1972, gov.-at-large Ill. chpt. 1983-88), state chmn. field liaison program commn. on cancer, 1983-89); mem. AMA, Ill. Med. Soc., (Outstanding Team Physician award 1985), Ill. Surg. Soc., M.W. Surg. Assn., Rotary (Paul Harris fellow 1987), Phi Beta Kappa. Republican. Episcopalian. Home: 1601 Tower Rd RR 1 Macomb IL 61455-9801

DEXTER, GREGORY WARREN, real estate and financial investor; b. White Plains, N.Y., Sept. 6, 1935; s. Gregory Mumford and Katie Wilhelmine (Jaecker) D. BA with high distinction, U. Mich., 1961. Computer programmer IBM, White Plains, 1963-67, sys. engr. N.Y.C., 1967-72, market rsch. analyst Armonk, N.Y., 1973-78, sys. engr. Norwalk, Conn., 1979-82; investor, 1983—. Author: The Search, 1986, The Baymen, 1987. Served with USCG, 1955-59. Mem. Bridgeport C. of C. Avocations: sailing, jogging, rowing, bike riding. Home: 128 Pierce Ave Bridgeport CT 06604-1607

DEXTER, ROBERT PAUL, lawyer; b. Halifax, N.S., Can., Dec. 11, 1951; s. Carl Edmund and Jean Rankin (Collins) D.; 1 child, Angela Elizabeth. BComm, Dalhousie U., 1973, LLB, 1976. With firm Stewart McKelvey Stirling Scales, Halifax, 1977—; CEO Maritime Travel, Halifax, Canada, 1978—. Vice chmn. N.S. Bus. Devel. Corp., 1992-94; bd. dirs. Empire Co. Ltd., Wajax Ltd., Sobeys Inc., High Liner Foods Inc., Maritime Life Assurance Co., Corpora Tel, Aliant Inc.; pres. Halifax Bd. Trade, 1993-94. Chmn. Metro United Way Campaign, 1997. I.W. Killam scholar, 1973, Sir James Dunn scholar, 1976. Mem. N.S. Barristers Soc., Can. Bar Assn., Young Pres. Orgn. Avocations: sailing, skiing, tennis. Home: 1028 Ridgewood Dr Halifax NS Canada B3H 3Y4 Office: Maritime Travel 2000 Barrington St Ste 202 Halifax NS Canada B3J 2X2

DEXTER, THEODORE HENRY, chemist; b. Preston, Cuba, June 1, 1923; parents Am. citizens; s. Harry Malcolm and Theodora Jane (Trelawny) D.; m. Marilyn Ann Cantara, July 26, 1952; children: Carol Dexter, Martha Dexter Rogala, John Dexter. BS, Tulane U., 1944; MS, 1947; PhD, U. Ill., 1950. Tchg. asst. chemistry Tulane U., New Orleans, 1943-44, 46-47; chemist E.I. du Pont de Nemours, Inc.; Okla. Ordnance Works, 1944-45; gen. aniline chem. rsch. asst. U. Ill., Urbana, 1947-49; group leader chem. rsch. Mathieson Chem. Corp., Niagara Falls, N.Y., 1949-55, sect. chief rsch., 1955-60; rsch. supr. Hooker Chem. Corp., Grand Island, N.Y., 1960-75; program leader, 1975-76; sr. rsch. chemist Hooker Indsl. and Splty. Chems div. Occidental Chem. Corp. Cons. Dexter Cons. Svcs., 1986—; lect., rsch. adv. Joe Berg Found., 1960-61; mem. photoreactivity task force Mfg. Chemists Assn., 1966-68; lectr. in field. Contbr. articles to profl. jours.; U.S., fgn. patentee inorganic chemistry and processes. Violinist Niagara Falls Philharm. Orch., 1950-72, Niagara Cmty. Orch., 1988-92, Niagara Symphony, 1992— 2001; group chmn. in-house steering com. United Givers Fund., 1970-73; mem. exec. com. Episc. Diocese We. N.Y., 1977-81, nursing home ministry, 1972—; lay reader, vestryman Episc. Ch., warden, 1967-68, 77-80, 92-94; vol. tax counselor AARP, 1998—. With USNR, 1945—46. Mem. Am. Chem. Soc. (chmn. Western N.Y. 1969-70, N.E. regional meeting divisional chm. 1971, founder Western N.Y. Inorganic Chemistry Group 1967, Schoellkopf Award jury chmn. 1970-72), Soap and Detergent Assn. (del. internat. conf. 1979, com. chmn.), Electrochem. Soc., Sigma Xi, Alpha Chi Sigma (Niagara Frontier pres. 1954), Phi Lambda Upsilon. Home and Office: 850 Hillside Dr Lewiston NY 14092-1828

DEY, CAROL RUTH, secondary education educator; b. N.Y., Mar. 9, 1943; d. Robert Lewis Adelson and Anne Millman Adelson Bedell; m. John Peter Dey, Feb. 9, 1968 (div. Feb. 1978). AA, San Bernardino Valley Coll., 1965; BA, Calif. State U., Sacramento, 1969; MBA, Calif. State U., San Bernardino, 1983, postgrad., 1994-95. Sec. U.S. Dept of Interior, USAF, Retail Industry, San Bernardino, Sacramento, Calif., 1960-80; logistics mgr. USAF, San Bernardino, 1980-94; substitute tchr. San Bernardino Unified Sch. Dist., 1994—, Inland Empire Job Corp. Ctr., 1997—. Dancer Coppélia, San Bernardino, Calif., 1984; mem. St. Anne's Ch., San Bernardino, 1978—. Mem. Am. Bus. Women's Assn. (Calif. State Coll. scholar), Smithsonian Inst., AF Assn., Alumni Assn. Calif. State U. San Bernardino. Republican. Roman Catholic. Avocations: ballet, piano, sewing, cooking, singing.

DEY, CHARLOTTE JANE, retired community health nurse; b. Benson, Minn., Dec. 14, 1927; d. Elmer Ellsworth and Charlotte Iona (Eastman) Bowers; m. Thomas A. Dey, June 25, 1948 (dec. Mar. 1973); children: Thomas A. Jr., Scott E. (dec.). Grad., St. Luke's Hosp. Sch. Nursing, 1948; student, Kansas City (Kans.) Jr. Coll., 1968; BS in Nursing with distinction, U. Kans., 1970; MPA, U. Mo., Kansas City, 1975. RN, Mo.; ordained deacon, Episcopal Ch., 1993. Head nurse communicable disease ward St. Luke's Children's Hosp., Kansas City, Mo., 1948-49; head nurse newborn nursery Providence Hosp., Kansas City, Kans., 1949-51; pub. health nurse Johnson County Health Dept., Olathe, Kans., 1951-52, 66-68, pub. health nurse, supr., 1970-72; evening supr. Olathe Community Hosp., 1953-55; office nurse B. Albert Lieberman, Jr., MD, Kansas City, Mo., 1960-66; coord. clin. confs. ANA, Kansas City, 1973-76; chief Bur. Community Health Nursing Mo. Dept. Health, Jefferson City, 1976-93; ret., 1993. Sem. expert panel to review and update criteria to estimate future requirements for nursing pers. div. nursing Dept. Health and Human Svcs., 1984, mem. nat. adv. coun. nursing edn. and practice div. nursing, 1998-2002; chair Mid-Am. Community Health Nursing Leadership Group. Recipient award of merit Assn. State and Territorial Dirs. Nursing, 1992. Mem. ANA (cert. nursing adminstrn. advanced, chairperson exec. com. coun. community health nursing 1989-92), APHA, Nat. League Nursing, Nat. Perinatal Assn., Am. Acad. Health Adminstrn. (pres. Mo. chpt. 1980-82), Mo. State Nurses Assn. (coun. nursing svc. facilitors exec. com. 1983-92), Mo. Pub. Health Assn., Mo. League Nursing, Mo. Perinatal Assn., Kans. State Nurses' Assn. (vice chairperson community health conf. group), Kans. Pub. Health Assn. (legislative com.), Sigma Theta Tau. Mem. Episcopal Ch. Home: G102 1310 Swifts Hwy Jefferson City MO 64109

DEY, PETER J. investment company executive; b. Mar. 3, 1941; m. Phyliss Ortved; 6 children. BS, Queen's U., 1963; B in Law, Dalhousie U., 1966; M of Law, Harvard U., 1967. Chmn. Ont. Securities Commn., Canada, 1983—85; former sr. ptnr. Osler, Hoskin & Harcourt; mng. dir. Morgan Stanley Can. Ltd., 1994; sr. advisor Morgan Stanley Dean Witter, Toronto, Canada; chmn. Morgan Stanley Can. Ltd., Toronto, Canada, 1994—. Chair Toronto Stock Exchg. Com. on Corp. Goverance, Canada, 1993—95. Fellow, Inst. Corp. Dirs., 2001. Office: Morgan Stanley Can Ltd Ste 3700 BCE Place 181 Bay St Toronto ON M5J 2T3 Canada Office Fax: 416-943-8444.

DEY, RADHESHYAM CHANDRA, cytologist; b. Calcutta, India, Jan. 30, 1950; came to U.S., 1978; s. Bhairab and Satyabala D.; m. Indrani Roy Chowdhury, July 5, 1981; children: Smita, Anita, Ishan. BSc, Bangabasi Coll., Calcutta, 1970; MSc, U. Calcutta, 1972, cert. in life sci., 1974; CT, Brooke Army Med. Ctr., San Antonio, 1983; cert. leaderhsip mgmt., ednl. devel., quality improvement and equal opportunity, Walter Reed Army Med. Ctr., 1989; postgrad., Laval U., Quebec City, Can., 1995, Albert Einstein Sch. Medicine, N.Y.C., 1997. Registered cytotechnologist, Am. Soc. Clin. Pathologists, Internat. Acad. Cytology, Calif., Md. Rsch. fellow U. Calcutta, 1975-77; with Anthropol. Survey of India, Indian Mus. Calcutta, 1977-78; biol. science asst. Army Inst. Rsch., Washington, 1980-83; cytology specialist U.S. Army Hosp., Ft. Campbell, Ky., 1983-85, SHAPE Med. Ctr., SHAPE/Mons, Belgium, 1985-87; cytotechnologist Nat. Health Lab., Vienna, Va., 1988; supervisory cytologist Walter Reed Army Med. Ctr., Washington, 1988—. Attended Indian Sci. Congress, U. New Delhi, Calcutta, Waltair, Gujarat, 1972—77; attended Internat. Congress of Cytology, Brussels, 1987, Internat. Cytology Tutorials, Vienna, 1986, Tokyo, 91, Harvard Med. Sch. Advances in Cytology, Boston, 1990, Coll. Am. Pathologists, Las Vegas, 1992, World Congress on Anthropol. and Ethnol. Scis., Mexico City, 1993, Williamsburg, Va., 98, Am. Soc. Clin. Pathologists and Cytopathology, Seattle, Risk Mgmt., ASCP, Hunt Valley, Md., 2000, Advanced Techniques in Human Identification, Armed Forces Inst. Pathology, Washington, 1994, Risk Mgmt. Pap Smears seminar, Armed Forces Inst. Pathology, Silver Spring, Md., 1987, Silver Spring, 2001, Palaeopathology, 1993, Forensic Anthropology, 1995, symposium USAF, Lackland AFB, Wilford Hall, Tex., 1999, Am. Soc. Cytopathology Symposium, Scottsdale, Ariz., 2001; participant Cytopathology Symposium, Washington Met. Assn. Cytology, 1999, 2000, 01, New Directions for Leaders Focus, 2000, Ft. Belvoir, Va., 1994, Immunol. Markers in Histopathology and Cytol Inst. Pathology, Ghent (Belgium) U. Hosp., 1987, numerous seminars; mem. symposium for suprs. and team bldg. dynamics for mgrs. U.S. Army Walter Reed Med. Ctr., Washington, 1995, Washington; 96; attended CAP/ASCP seminar, L.A., 1998, Balt., 2000, symposium on cytopathology, Met. Washington Assn. Cytology, 1999, Fine Needle Aspiration Cytology Meeting, Balt., 2000, risk mgmt. Am. Soc. Clin. Pathologists, Balt., 2000, Current Issues in Women's Health and Cytopathology, Am. Soc. for Clin. Pathology, New Orleans, 2003; vis. Indian Statis. Inst., Calcutta, 1999; participant Mastering the Challenges of Cytopathology The Johns Hopkins U. Sch. Medicine, Balt., 2002; participant Women's Health Risk Mgmt. in Gynecologic Cytology, HPV (DNA) testing NIH, Bethesda, Md., 2002, participant path to path sem. on molecular diagnostics in women's health-DNA HPV testing and breast cancer, 02. Contbr. articles to profl. jours. Decorated U.S. Army Commendation medal, 1985, Achievement medal, 1984, Good Conduct medals, 1982, 85; recipient Decree of Merit for outstanding contbn. to medicine and health care, 1995, Excellence in Tchg. award Nat. Capital Region Consortium Pathology Residency, 1997, Comdr.'s award for civilian svc. U.S. Army Walter Reed Med. Ctr., 1997. Mem.: AAAS, Md. Assn. Cytopathology, Washington Met. Assn. Cytology, Indian Anthropol. Soc., Ind. Sci. Congress, Md. Assn. Cytopathology, Belge de Cytologie Clinique (del. visit to People's Republic China 1987, internat. team cytologists exch. sci. knowledge with USSR 1990, del. visit to People's Republic China 1991), Soc. of Armed Forces Med. Lab. Scientists, N.Y. Acad. Scis., Am. Soc. for Cytotech., Am. Soc. Clin. Pathologists, Am. Soc. Cytopathology, Am. Anthropol. Assn., Internat. Acad. Cytology, Am. Legion. Avocations: soccer, swimming, running, traveling, theater. Home: 10110 Treble Ct Rockville MD 20850 Office: Walter Reed Army Med Ctr Dept Pathology Cytology Lab Washington DC 20307-0001 E-mail: dey_rad@hotmail.com.

DEYDE, VAROUGH MOHAMED, microbiologist, researcher; b. Kiffa, Mauritania, Dec. 31, 1972; s. Mohamed Deyde and Khadjettou Diallo. PhD, U. of Nev. Reno, 2003; M, U. of Medicine and Sci., Tunis, Tunisia, 2000; BS, U. of Nouakchott, Mauritania, 1994. Pres. African Students and Scholars Assn., Reno, 2002—, Assn. des Etudiants et Stagiaires Africans en Tunisie, Tunis, Tunisia, 1997—2000. Home: 1060 Nevada St Apt 2 Reno NV 89503 Office: Unr 1664 N Virginia St Reno NV 89557 Office Fax: 775-327-2332. Personal E-mail: mvarough@unr.med.edu. E-mail: mvarough@unr.med.edu.

DE YOE, DAVID P. lawyer; b. Muskegon, Mich., July 18, 1948; s. Frank A. and Mildred E. (Jensen) DeY.; m. Ilene L. Nevel, May 26, 1979; children: Andrew, Mary, Emily, Peter. BA in Econs., U. Mich., 1970; JD, Stanford U., 1973. Bar: Ill. 1973, U.S. Dist. Ct. (no. dist.) Ill. 1973, Cal. 1975. Assoc. McDermott, Will & Emery, Chgo., 1973-79, ptnr., 1979—. Contbr. articles to profl. jours. Office: McDermott Will & Emery 227 W Monroe St Ste 4700 Chicago IL 60606-5096

DEYOUNG, DAVID JEFFREY, state official; b. Hollywood, Calif., Sept. 30, 1954; s. David Henry and Lorraine DeY.; m. Susan Anne DeYoung, May 29, 1988 (dec. Oct. 1993); m. Kimberly Ann DeYoung, Sept. 5, 1999. BA in Psychology, U. Calif., Irvine, 1977, MA in Social Ecology, 1980. Rsch. analyst Orange County Probation, Orange, Calif., 1985-88; rsch. program specialist Calif. Dept. Motor Vehicles, Sacramento, 1988—2002, rsch. mgr. alcohol and drug projects sect., 2002—. Editl. bd. Jour. of Safety rsch., 1999—; contbr. articles to profl. jours. Pres. Davis (Calif.) Aquatic Masters, 2000-01. Mem. Am. Evaluation Assn., Am. Statis. Assn., Sacramento Statis. Assn. (v.p. 1995, pres. 1996). Avocations: running, hiking, skiing, travel, swimming. Office: California Dept Motor Vehicles 2415 1st Ave Sacramento CA 95818-2698

DE YOUNG, DAVID SPENCER, astrophysicist, educator; b. Colorado Springs, Colo., Nov. 29, 1940; s. Henry C. and Zona L. (Church) DeY.; m. Mary Ellen Haney. BA, U. Colo., 1962; PhD, Cornell U., 1967. Rsch. physicist Los Alamos Nat. Labs., Los Alamos, N. Mex., 1967-69; astronomer Nat. Radio Astronomy Obs., Charlottesville, Va., 1969-80, Kitt Peak Nat. Obs., Tucson, 1980—, assoc. dir., 1983-88, dir., 1988-94. Organizer numerous sci. confs.; mem. adv. bd. Aspen (Colo.) Ctr. Physics, 1977—, trustee, 1992—, pres., 2001—; mem. exec. com. steering com. San Diego Supercomputer Ctr., 1985-98, chmn., 1989-91; mem. steering com. Nat. Virtual Obs., 2000— (exec. com. 2001-), project scientist, 2001-, exec. com., 2001—; bd. dirs. WIYN Telescope Consortium, Tucson. Contbr. articles to profl. jours. NASA grantee. Mem. Am. Phys. Soc., Am. Astron. Soc., Astron. Soc. Pacific, Internat. Astron. Union, Internat. Union Radio Sci., Phi Beta Kappa. Office: Kitt Peak Nat Obs 950 N Cherry Ave Tucson AZ 85719-4933

DEYRUP, MARTA MESTROVIC, school librarian, writer; d. Mate Marko and Jane Esmay Mestrovic; m. Curtis Alden Deyrup, Aug. 18, 1984; children: Ivana Kestercanek, John Mestrovic. MA, Columbia U., 1995; MLS, Rutgers U., 1999. Freelance writer/editor, Glen Rock, NJ, 1985—95; asst. prof., libr. Seton Hall U., South Orange, NJ, 1999—. Assoc. editor: Libr. Adminstrn. and Mgmt.; contbr. articles. Named Fulbright Sr. Specialist, 2003; recipient Tech. Innovation in Libr. award, N.J. Libr. Assn., 2002. Mem.: ALA. Office: Seton Hall Univ Libr 400 S Orange Ave South Orange NJ 07079 Office Fax: 973-761-9432. Personal E-mail: curtdeyrup@aol.com. E-mail: deyrupma@shu.edu.

DEZII, CHRISTOPHER MICHAEL, medical researcher, organ transplant nurse; b. Philadelphia, Pa., Nov. 14, 1958; s. Randolph and Margherita Dezii; m. Karen Ann Charlton, July 25, 1987; children: Allyson Michelle, Alexis Nicole. MBA, La Salle U., Phila., 1994. RN Phila., 1981. Dir. of patient care svcs./clin. coord. Hahnemann U. Hosp., Phila., 1990—94; sr. mgr., outcomes rsch. Bristol-Myers Squibb Co., Plainsboro, NJ, 1997—2001, assoc. dir., sci. ops., 2001—. Contbr. articles to profl. jours. Recipient Pres.'s award, Bristol-Myers Squibb, 2001. Conservative. Avocation: music. Home: 36 Joanne Rd Holland PA 18966 Office: Bristol-Myers Squibb Co 777 Scudders Mill Road Plainsboro NJ 08536 Office Fax: 609-897-6068. E-mail: christopher.dezii@bms.com.

DEZURKO, EDWARD ROBERT, retired art educator; b. N.Y.C., Mar. 25, 1913; s. Edward and Hattie (Lehman) DeZ.; m. Madith Smith, July 30, 1938 (div. 1962); children: Robin Klein, Sandra Krchnak; m. Grace Crump, Sept. 5, 1964. BS in Edn., U. Ill., 1939, BS in Arch., 1940; MS in Arch., Columbia U., 1942; PhD, NYU, 1954. former registered arch. Tchr. Champaign (Ill.) H.S., 1941; tchr. arch. Kans. State Coll., Manhattan, 1942-47, Rice U., Houston, 1947-62; head dept. art Austin Coll., Sherman, Tex., 1962-66; prof. art, grad. coord. U. Ga., Athens, 1966-79, emeritus prof. art, 1979—. Draftsman, illustrator U.S. Naval Ordnance Lab., Washington, 1943-44. Author: Early Kansas Churches, 1949, Origins of Functionalist Theory, 1957, Vistas and Mazes, 1997, Through Cracks in the Wall, 2001; co-author: Man and the Cultural World, 1947; contbr. articles to profl. jours. Recipient Ga. Poet of Yr. award Nat. League Am. Pen Women, 1997, Internat. Order of Merit award. Mem. AIA, Ga. Poetry Soc., Author's Club Athens, Pi Delta Phi, Zeta Zeta. Avocations: poetry, gardening, travel. Home: 220 Meadowview Rd Athens GA 30606-4226 Office: Lamar Dodd Sch Art U Ga Athens GA 30602 Office Fax: 706-542-0226.

D'GABRIEL, CARLOS LEONARDO, retired travel executive; b. Havana, Cuba, Mar. 10, 1930; came to U.S., 1955; s. Zeidel and Hana (Schneider) D'G.; m. Judith Lobel, June 24, 1950 (div. 1971); children: Alexander P., Michelle E.; m. Prudence Saig, Dec. 4, 1971. Grad., Ga. Mil. Acad., 1946. Mgr. Shipairland Travel, Havana, 1946—50; corp. exec. Skycoach Internat. Airline, N.Y.C., 1950-55; mgr. Pan Am. World Airways, N.Y.C., 1955-62; v.p. Cophresi Travel Bur. Corp., N.Y.C., 1962-68; pres. Carber Travel Bur. Inc., N.Y.C., 1968-70, Superior Travel Bur., Inc., Miami Beach, Fla., 1970-95, regional v.p. Fla. Superior Travel, Castle Travel Group Co., Miami Beach, 1995-97. Recipient Shalom award Israel Ministry of Tourism, 1977, Willy Prestergard Meml. award Travel Industry Assn. Fla., 1980, Great Am. Traditions award B'nai B'rith Found. of U.S., 1993. Mem. Am. Soc. Travel Agts. (v.p. 1982), Inst. Cert. Travel Counselors, Assn. Retail Travel Agts. (bd. dirs. 1969), Turnberry Isle Resort and Club, Skal Club Internat., Calif. Golf Club, Presdl. Country Club. Republican. Jewish. Avocations: travel, tennis, golf. Home: Ste 2004 2800 Island Blvd Aventura FL 33160-4976 E-mail: cldg@usa.net.

DHALIWAL, HERB, Canadian government official; b. Punjab, India, Dec. 12, 1952; BA Commerce, U. B.C., 1971. Min. of nat. revenue Ho. of Commons, Ottawa, 1997-99, min. fisheries and oceans, 1999—. Office: Ho of Commons Rm 121 E Block Ottawa ON Canada K1A 0A6*

DHAMIJA, KAILASH RAJ, physician, consultant; b. India, Mar. 27, 1944; s. Mulkraj and Kaushalya R. (Bhusari) D.; m. Amarjeet Sachdeva, Mar. 17, 1971; children: Rajiv, Tina. BS, B.R. Coll., Agra, India, 1962; MBBS, S.N. Med. Coll., Agra, 1967; Diploma in Obstetrics, Royal Coll. Physicians Ireland, Dublin, 1978. Diplomate Am. Bd. Family Practice, Am. Bd. Forensic Medicine. Resident in medicine, surgery, ob-gun., others, India, 1967-69; resident in emergency medicine and orthopedics Manor Hosp., Nuneaton, Eng., 1971-72; resident in family medicine, orthopedics and obstetrics Royal Infirmary, Doncaster, Eng., 1972-75; resident in family medicine SUNY, Stony Brook, 1983-84, Southside Hosp./N.Y. Sate U., Bayshore, 1984-87; ind. family physician in pvt. practice, Long Beach and Artesia, Calif., 1987—. Mem. Am. Acad. Family Physicians, Am. Coll. Internat. Physicians, Am. Assn. Med. Rev. Officers, Am. Acad. Experts in Traumatic Stress. Avocations: physical fitness, music, travel. Office: 18326 Pioneer Blvd Artesia CA 90701-5533 also: Walk-In Med Care 3760 Atlantic Ave Long Beach CA 90807-3409

DHAND, RAJIV, physician; arrived in U.S., 1990; s. Arjan Dass and Krishna Dhand; m. Upinder Dhand, Dec. 28, 1977; children: Adarsh, Vivek. MBBS, Med. Coll., India, 1974; MD, Post Grad. Inst., India, 1978. Attending physician Post Grad. Inst. Med. Edn., Chandigarh, India, 1980—82, 1983—90; post doctoral fellow Va. Mason Rsch. Ctr., Seattle, 1982—83; staff physician Hines Va. Hosp., Ill., 1993—2001, Harry S. Truman Meml. Veterans Hosp., Columbia, Mo., 2002—; dir. divsn. pulmonary medicine U. Mo., Columbia, 2002—. Fellowship program dir. U. Mo., 2002—. Author numerous articles and abstracts in profl. jours.; co-author: (chpt. in book) Year Book of Pulmonary Disease, 1996, Oxford Textbook of Critical Care, 1999, Rehabilitation of the Patient with Respiratory Disease, 1999, Clinical Practice in Respiratory Care, 1999, Acute Respiratory Distress Syndrome: A Comprehensive Clinical Approach, 1999; editl. bd. Jour. Aerosol Medicine, 1999, CHEST India, 1999, CHEST, 2001—. Recipient numerous awards and distinctions, 1971—2002. Mem.: AAAS, Am. Soc. Respiratory Care, Int. Soc. Aerosols in Medicine, Soc. Critial Care Medicine, Am. Coll. Chest Physicians, Am. Thoracic Soc., Mo. Thoracic Soc. (v.p. 2002—). Achievements include research in (with Nirmal Charan) first electron microscopic demonstration of connections between bronchial circulation and pulmonary circulation; initial description of cellular composition of bronchoalveolar lavage fluid in patients with pulmonary tuberculosis; established sci. basis for use of metered-dose inhalers in mechanically-ventilated patients; co-investigator studying properties and mechanism of action of novel surfactant enzyme (surfactant convertase); first description of enantiospecific disposition after inhalation of racemic albuterol with MDI. Office: Univ Mo Columbia 1 Hosp Dr DC04300 Columbia MO 65212 Fax: 573-884-4892. E-mail: dhandr@health.missouri.edu.

DHANIREDDY, RAMASUBBAREDDY, neonatologist, researcher; b. Gunthachiyyapadu, India, July 8, 1951; s. Pedda Eswarareddy and Veeramma (Kasa) Dhanireddy; m. Brezeetha Peddireddy, Dec. 15, 1972; children: Shireesha, Kiran Kumar. MB, BS, Kurnool Med. Coll., 1974. Clin. asst. prof. pediatrics Georgetown U. Med. Ctr., Washington, 1982-84, asst. prof. pediatrics, 1984-91, dir. Term Newborn Nursery, 1987-92, co-dir. neonatal ICU, 1992-94; adj. scientist NIH, Bethesda, Md., 1984-99; med. dir. Neonatal Pulmonary Function Testing Lab. Georgetown U. Hosp., Washington, 1991-99, dir. nursery quality improvement, 1992-99, dir. neonatal ICU, 1994-99, assoc. prof. pediat., 1991-97, prof. pediat., 1998—, chief sect. neonatology, med. dir. neonatal ICU, 1999—; dir. neonatal-perinatal medicine fellowship program La. State U. Med. Ctr., Shreveport, 1999—. Contbr. Regional v.p. Telugu Assn. N.Am., Chgo., 1989—91; mem. D.C. Mayoral Com. to Promote Breast Feeding D.C. Mayor's Office, Washington. Lt. col. USAFR, 1993—97, col. USAFR, 1977—. Recipient Meritorious Svc. medal, USAF, 1993, 1998, 2001; grantee Surfactant Clin. Studies grant, Burroughs Wellcome Co., 1989—93. Fellow; Am. Coll. Nutrition, Am. Acad. Pediat.; mem.: Soc. Pediat. Rsch., So. Soc. Pediat. Rsch., Am. Fedn. Clin. Rsch. Democrat. Hindu. Avocations: travel, reading. Office: La State U Med Ctr Dept Pediats 1501 Kings Hwy Shreveport LA 71103-4228 E-mail: rdhani@lsuhsc.edu.

DHAR, JOSEPHINE PATRICIA, medical educator; BS in Biophysics, Wayne State U., 1978, MD, 1982. Bd. cert internal medicine Am. Bd. Internal Medicine, bd. cert. rheumatology Am. Bd. Internal Medicine. Intern internal medicine Wayne State U., Detroit, 1982—83, resident internal medicine, 1983—85, chief resident internal medicine, 1985—86, fellow in rheumatology, 1986—89, clin. instr., 1989—92, asst. prof. medicine, 1992—, assoc. dir. internal medicine residency program, dir. Lupus Clin. Program. Contbr. articles to profl. jours. Fellow: ACP, Am. Coll. Rheumatology; mem.: Phi Beta Kappa. Avocations: swimming, music, painting, hiking. Office: Wayne State Univ Univ Health Ctr 4201 St Antoine Detroit MI 48201

DHAR, PROMILA, researcher; b. Anantnag, Kashmir, India, Jan. 6, 1962; arrived in U.S., 1999; d. Triloki Nath and Shanta Raina; m. Soman Dhar, Oct. 5, 1990; children: Jyotsna, Archit. BSc in Biophysics with honors, Punjab U., Chandigarh, India, 1985, MSc in Biophysics with honors, 1987; PhD in Biomechanics, Indian Inst. Tech., New Delhi, 1996. Sr. rsch. asst. Indian Inst. Tech., New Delhi, 1988-93, sr. rsch. fellow, 1993-95; rsch. assoc. All India Inst.

Med. Scis., New Delhi, 1996-98, rsch. scientist Coun. for Sci. and Indsl. Rsch., 1998—2000. Contbr. articles to profl. jours. and procs. Mem. AAAS, Indian Biophys. Soc. (life), Assn. Physiologists and Pharmacologists India. Avocations: photography, gardening, reading. Home: #2107 1101 Iroquois Ave Naperville IL 60563 E-mail: promilaska@yahoo.com.

DHARA, VENKATA RAMANA, physician, educator; b. Gudivada, India, Nov. 14, 1953; came to U.S., 1985; s. Venkateswarlu and Sarojini Devi D.; m. Rosaline James Dodda, Feb. 16, 1979; children: Rahul, Vishal. MBBS, Armed Forces Med. Coll., 1976; MPH, U. Medicine Dentistry N.J., 1987; ScD, U. Mass., 2000. Diplomate Am. Bd. Preventive Medicine. Intern Sion Hosp., Bombay, 1976-77; med. dir. People's Clinic, Hyderabad, India, 1979-85; resident/fellow in occupl. and environ. medicine Robert Wood Johnson Med. Sch., Piscataway, N.J., 1985-89; cons. Envirotech Cons., New Delhi, 1990-92; med. officer Agy. Toxic Substances Disease Registry, Atlanta, 1992-96; dir. occupl. medicine Choice Care, Atlanta, 1997-2000; adj. clin. assoc. prof. Morehouse Sch. Medicine, Atlanta, 1998—; med. dir. Emory Eastside Med. Ctr., Snellville, Ga., 2000—; adj. clin. assoc. prof. Rollins Sch. Pub. Health, Emory U., 2000—. Cons. World Environment Ctr., N.Y.C., 1992—96, Internat. Labor Office, Geneva, 1992—; mem. Internat. Med. commn. Bhopal, Toronto, Canada, 1994—; cons. U.S. Dept. Energy, 2001—. Contbr. articles to profl. jours. Active Forum Protection Environment, Hyderabad, 1982-85. Recipient Disting. Svc. award Meridian Med. Group, 1997; grantee Nat. Inst. Environ. Health Scis., 1998-2000. Mem. Am. Coll. Occpl. Environ. Medicine. Avocations: writing, reading, snorkeling, yoga. Office: Emory Eastside Occupl Health Ctr 1700 Medical Way Snellville GA 30078-2195 E-mail: rdhara@aol.com.

DHARAMSI, SHAMEZ SHIRAZ, marketing professional, consultant; arrived in U.S., 1985; s. Shiraz Nazarali and Maherunissa Dharamsi. BS in Psychology and Sociology magna cum laude, Loyola U., Chgo., 1998; MA in Exptl. Psychology, DePaul U., 2000. Project mgr. FAA, Aurora, Ill., 1997—99; data mgr. Children's Meml. Hosp., Chgo., 1999—2000; rsch. analyst Leo Burnett, Chgo., 2000—01; project mgr. - e-commerce analytics Six Continents Hotels Inc., Atlanta, 2001—02; sr. analytical mktg. cons. Quaero Corp., Atlanta, 2002—. Cons. Quaero Corp., Atlanta, 2002—; database mktg. panel spkr. SAS Users Group, Atlanta, 2001—02. Project mgr. Aga Khan Youth and Sports Bd., Atlanta, 2001—02; camp evaluator Camp Mosaic, Chgo., 1997—98. Recipient Global Meeting of Generations Sponsorship, Aga Khan Found., 1999; grantee, DePaul U., 1998—2000; Loyola U. Presdl. scholar, Loyola U. Chgo., 1995—98. Mem.: Tech. Assn. Ga. (assoc.), Am. Statis. Assn. (assoc.), Am. Mktg. Assn. (assoc.). Muslim. Avocations: volunteerism, travel, photography.

D'HARNONCOURT, ANNE, museum director, executive; m. Joseph J. Rishel, June 19, 1971. BA, Radcliffe Coll., 1965; MA with distinction, Courtauld Inst. Art, U. London, 1967. Curatorial asst. Phila. Mus. Art, 1967-69; asst. curator 20th Century art Art Inst. Chgo., 1969-71; curator 20th Century art Phila. Mus. Art, 1971-82, the George D. Widener dir., 1982—. Mem. mus. panel NEA, 1976-78, mem. indemnity panel, 1985-88, mem. mus. program overview panel, 1986-87; mem. Indo-U.S. Subcommn. Edn. and Culture, 1983-87; bd. advs. Ctr. Advanced Study in the Visual Arts Nat. Gallery Art, 1987 89. Organizer: (with McShine) exhbn. Marcel Duchamp, 1973-74, (with others) Philadelphia: Three Centuries of American Art, 1976, Eight Artists, 1978, (with Percy) Violet Oakley, 1979, Futurism and the International Avant-Garde, 1980, (with Sims) John Cage: Scores and Prints, 1982; author: (with Walter Hopps) Etant Donnes. Reflections on a New Work by Marcel Duchamp, 1969, The Cubist Cockatoo: Preliminary Exploration of Joseph Cornell's Hommages to Juan Gris, 1978, John Cage: Paying Attention, 1993, also prefaces for various books. Mem. vis. com. J. Paul Getty Mus., Malibu, Calif.; bd. dirs. Henry Luce Found., Inc., N.Y.C.; trustee Fairmount Park Art Assn. Phila.; mem. adv. com. The Fabric Workshop, Phila.; trustee Georgia O'Keeffe Found.; bd. regents Smithsonian Instn. Fellow AAAS; mem. Am. Philos. Soc., Pa. Coun. Arts, 1992-99, Assn. Art Mus. Dirs. Office: Phila Mus Art Benjamin Franklin Pkwy PO Box 7646 Philadelphia PA 19101-7646

DHAWAN, ATAM PRAKASH, engineering educator, dean; b. Moradabad, India, Mar. 30, 1956; came to U.S., 1985; s. Chandar Bhan Dhawan and Shanti Devi Kapoor; m. Nilam Dhawan, Mar. 5, 1982; children: Anirudh, Akshay. B of Engring., U. Roorkee, India, 1977, M of Engring., 1979; PhD, U. Man., Winnipeg, Can., 1985. Asst. prof. elec. engring. U. Houston, 1985-88; from asst. prof. elec. and computer engring. to assoc. prof. U. Cin., 1988-95, prof. elec. engring., computer engring. and computer sci., 1995-96, dir. Ctr. Intelligence Vision Sys., 1994-96; prof./chmn. elec. engring. U. Tex., Arlington, 1996-97; adj. prof. radiol. scis. U. Tex. S.W., Dallas, 1996-98; prof. bioengring. U. Toledo, 1998-2000, asst. dean grad. studies/coll. engring., 1998-99, assoc. dean rsch. and grad. studies/coll. engring., 1998-2000; prof., chmn. elec. and computer engring. N.J. Inst. Tech., Newark, 2000—. Adj. assoc. prof. radiology U. Cin., 1990-95; mem. sci. adv. com. Life Spec Inc., Houston, 1997-99; mem. nat. adv. com. Rsch. Resource for Pharmacokinetic Studies, U. Wash., Seattle, 1999-2001; mem. external adv. com. Ohio Aerospace Inst., Cleve., 2000-01; dir. N.J. Ctr. for Multimedia Rsch., 2000-02; dir. NSF-NJ Inst. Tech. Industry Univ. Coop. Rsch. Ctr. Next Generation Video, 2000-02, N.J. Ctr. for Wireless Networking and Internet Security, 2002--. Author: (textbook) Medical Image Analysis, 2003; editor Internat. Jour. Computing Info. and Tech., 1997—; assoc. editor Internat. Jour. Pattern Recognition, 1999—. Recipient NIH F.I.R.S.T. award Nat. Cancer Inst., 1988-93, Martin N. Epstein award Student Paper Competition at Symposium of Computer Applications in Med. Care, 1984; Can. Commonwealth fellow U. Man., 1982-85; contbr. articles to profl. jours. Mem. IEEE (sr., assoc. editor Transactions on Biomed. Engring. 1996-2001, asst. editor Transactions on Rehab. Engring. 1994-2001, workshop chair 1996, 97, Engring. in Medicine and Biology Early Career Achievement award 1995), Engring. in Medicine and Biology Inst. of Elec. and Electronics Engrs. (chmn. emerging techs. com. 1998-2000, chair workshop on Intelligent Med. Image Analysis: Principles to Recent Advances, Cancun, Mex., 2003), World Congress on Med. Physics and Biomed. Engring. (chmn. New Frontier in Med. Physics and Biomed. Engring. Track 1999-2000), Eta Kappa Nu. Avocations: swimming, music, reading. Office: Chair ECE Dept NJ Inst Tech University Heights Newark NJ 07102 E-mail: dhawan@adm.njit.edu.

DHERE, NEELKANTH G, research scientist; s. Gurupad B and Parvati G Dhere; m. Sucharita Neelkanth Khare, May 19, 1970. BSc, U. of Poona, 1955—60, MSc, 1960—62, PhD, 1962—66. Program dir. Fla. Solar Energy Ctr., 1990—; sr. vis. rsch. scientist Solar Energy Rsch. Inst., Golden, Colo., 1986—90. Prof. Instituto Militar de Engenharia, Rio de Janeiro, 1971—86; rsch. fellow Comissão Nacional de Atividades Espaciais, São Paulo, Brazil, 1970—71; head, techniques lab. Phys. Rsch. Lab., India, 1966—70. Editor: (journal) Revista Brasileira de Aplicacoes de Vácuo. Founder and pres. Brazilian Vacuum Soc., Rio de Janeiro, 1978—80. Recipient Disting. Rschr. of the Yr. for Institutes and Centers, U. of Ctrl. Fla., 2002. Mem.: IEEE. Achievements include research in deleterious effects of impurities in photovoltaic modules. Office: Florida Solar Energy Ctr 1679 Clearlake Rd Cocoa FL 32922-5703

D'HEURLE, ADMA JEHA, psychology educator; b. Bishmizzine, Lebanon, June 24, 1924; d. Michael and Catherine (Jeha) Lebanon; m. Francois Max d'Heurle, May 6, 1950; children: Amal, David, Alain. BA, Am. U. Beirut, Lebanon, 1947; MA, Smith Coll., Northampton, Mass., 1948; PhD, U. Chgo., 1953. Asst. prof. psychology St. Xavier Coll., Chgo., 1954-58; prof. psychology Mercy Coll., Dobbs Ferry, NY, 1970—2001, Disting. prof., 2001—. Lectr. Stanford (Calif.) U., 1972-73; adj. prof. L.I. U., Dobbs Ferry, N.Y., 1975-80; Fulbright prof. U. Turku, Finland, 1987-88; vis. prof. U. Uppsala, Sweden, 1980 81. Editor jour. Cross Currents, New Rochelle, N.Y., 1978—; contbr. articles to profl. jours. Evaluator Mid. States Commn., 1973-84. Grantee Fulbright, 1978, Peace Inst. Finland, 1989. Mem. APA, AAUP, Ihsen Assn. Am., World Fedn. Mental Health, Soc. Cross Cultural Rsch., Soc. Advancement Scandinavian Studies.

D'HEURLE, FRANÇOIS MAX, research scientist, engineering educator; b. Paris, Nov. 23, 1925; came to U.S., 1946; s. Albert Emile and Odette (Valentini) d'H.; m. Adma Jeha, May 6, 1950; children: Amal, David, Alain. BSc Arts et Metiers, U. Paris, 1946; MS, Mich. Tech. U., 1948; PhD, Ill. Inst. Tech., 1958; D honoris causa, Royal Inst. Tech., Stockholm, 1995. Rsch. asst. U. Chgo., 1948-55; scientist IBM, Yorktown Heights, N.Y., 1958—. Prof. Royal Inst. Tech., Stockholm, 1995. Contbr. numerous articles to profl. jours.; holder 10 patents. Recipient award Am. Inst. Physics, 1991, Theory to Practice Prize Minerals, Metals and Materials Soc., 1998. Fellow IEEE (Cledo-Brunetti award 1989); Am. Vacuum Soc. (Gaede-Langmuir award 1990); mem. Minerals, Metals and Materials Soc., Materials Rsch. Soc. Home: Spring Valley Rd Ossining NY 10562 Office: IBM Rsch PO Box 218 Yorktown Heights NY 10598-0218 E-mail: dheurle@us.ibm.com.

DHIR, KRISHNA SWAROOP, business administration educator; b. Calcutta; s. Hari Das and Sushila Devi (Kochhar) D.; m. Shailaja Nair, July 3, 1983; children: Devika Dhir, Radhika Dhir. BTech, Indian Inst. of Tech., Bombay, 1966; MS, Mich. State U., 1967; MBA, U. Hawaii, 1968; PhD, U. Colo., 1975. Lectr. in bus. analysis U. Hawaii, Honolulu, 1967-69; devel. engr. Borg-Warner Corp., Parkersburg, W.Va., 1969-72; head dept. of bus. and industry W.Va. U., Parkersburg, 1969-72; asst. prof. mgmt. Clarkson U., Potsdam, N.Y., 1975-76; advisor Pharm. Divsn. Ciba-Geigy AG, Basle, Switzerland, 1976-82; assoc. prof. mgmt. sci. U. Colo., Boulder, 1979-82; v.p. strategic planning BioStar Med. Products, Inc., Boulder, 1984-86; dir. MIM degree program U. Denver, 1986-87; prof. health svcs. adminstrn. Med. U. S.C., Charleston, 1987-91; head, prof. dept. of bus. adminstrn. The Citadel, Charleston, 1987-91; dir., SBA prof. Sch. Bus. Adminstrn. Pa. State U., Harrisburg, 1991-96, prof. bus. adminstrn., 1991—2001; dean Campbell Sch. Bus., Berry Coll., Mt. Berry, Ga., 2001—. Assoc. prof. mgmt. U. Denver, 1982-87; vis. prof. mgmt. and stats., U. Bombay, 1985; vis. prof. bus. Swinburne U. Tech., Melbourne, Australia, 1997, 99; vis. faculty Econs. Inst., Boulder, Colo., 1973-75, 81-82, 99; vis. prof. bus. adminstrn. Coventry (U.K.) U., 2002—; track chmn. Western Decision Scis. Inst., Monterey, Calif., 1988-89, Maui, Hawaii, 1993-94, Vancouver, B.C., Can., 2000 01, San Francisco, 1994-95, The Big Island, Hawaii, 1996-97, Reno, Nev., 1997-98, S.E. Decision Scis. Inst., Washington, 1990-91, Nat. Decision Scis. Inst., Las Vegas, 1997-98, Internat. Decision Sci. Inst., Sydney, Australia, 1996-97, Athens, Greece, 1998-99; mem. adv. bd. Info. Resources Mgmt. Assn., 1988-93, chmn., 1990-91, others; v.p. Western Decision Scis. Inst., 1999-2002, program chair, 2001-2002, pres.-elect, 2002-03, pres., 2003—. Contbr. articles to profl. jours. Sen. Assn. of Students of U. of Colo., Boulder, 1973-74; pres. Internat. Club, Carnegie-Mellon U., Pitts., 1969. Lt. col. S.C. Militia, 1987-91. Recipient 1st prize in radio journalism, Art of Peace Competition, 1983, Merit scholarship, U.P. Bd. Edn., Allahabad, India, 1959, Gold medal, St. John's Ambulance Assn., India, 1956, Best Paper award, Western Decision Scis. Inst., 1994, 2001, Outstanding Achievement award, Decision Scis. Inst., 1993, Best Applications Paper award, Internat. Decision Scis. Inst., 1999, Excellence in Tchg. award, Pa. State U. at Harrisburg, 2000, James A. Jordan, Jr. Meml. award for tchg. excellence, 2001, Best Paper First Pl. award, Corp. Comms. Inst., 2003. Mem. Am. Soc. Quality Control (bd. dirs. Mid-Ohio Valley chpt. 1972-73, edn. chmn. 1972-73). Avocations: photography, travel, camping. Office: Campbell Sch Bus Berry Coll Mount Berry GA 30149 E-mail: kdhir@campbell.berry.edu.

DHONDT, STEVEN THOMAS, development officer; b. Xenia, Ohio, Aug. 4, 1944; s. Maurice Bernard and Madeline (Pierson) D.; m. Elizabeth Ann Emrick, June 11, 1966 (div. June 1972); 1 child, Jennifer Elizabeth; m. Patty Ruth Bayley, Jan. 9, 1982. BA, Adrian Coll., 1966; MA, Utah State U., 1967, PhD, Bowling Green State U., 1968, SUNY, Buffalo, 1971. Instr. English SUNY, Buffalo, 1968-74, assoc. dean of faculty, 1969-74; assoc. acad. dean Salem State Coll., Salem, Mass., 1974-77; dir. publishing Am.-Scandinavian Found., N.Y.C., 1977-79; prin. Dhondt Enterprises, N.Y.C., 1978-81; mgr. corp. communications Merck & Co., Inc., Rahway, N.J., 1981-83; sr. v.p., asst. dir. creative resources Shearson Lehman Bros. Inc., N.Y.C., 1983-93; sr. cons. Nagdeman & Co., Inc., N.Y.C., 1993-95; ind. mktg. cons., 1994-96; univ. dir. corp. and found. rels. L.I. U., Brookville, N.Y., 1996-99; dir. corp. and found. rels. NYU, N.Y.C., 1999—2002; dir. instl. giving Meml. Sloan-Kettering Cancer Ctr., 2002—. Trustee N.J. Coun. on Econ. Edn., Trenton, 1981-83, Borough of Manhattan Community Coll. Fund, Inc., N.Y.C., Poets House, N.Y.C., Ctr. Philanthropy and Fundraising, NYU; cons. Bayley, Leighton & Ryan, Inc., N.Y.C., 1988—. Author: First Reading, 1972, London Bridge, 1998, Yellow Monkey, 1999; mng. editor Coll. English Assn., Buffalo, 1972-74. Democrat. Methodist. Avocations: tennis, snorkeling, travel. Home: 175 W 93rd St Apt 14C New York NY 10025-9340 E-mail: dhondts@mskcc.org.

DHORE, PRASANNA G. mutual fund executive; b. Mysore, India, Apr. 28, 1961; s. D.K. and Chudamani Gopal; m. Indira Prasanna Dhore, Jan. 17, 1986; children: Karthik, Deepa. MS in Ops. Rsch. and Stats., NYU, 1994; MBA, Kans. State U., 1986. Asst. dir. database mktg. Time Warner Inc., N.Y.C., 1989—95; v.p. customer relationship mgmt. and market rsch. NatWest Bank, N.Y.C., 1995—96; exec. v.p. Dreyfus Svc. Corp, N.Y.C., 1996—. Office: Dreyfus Svc Corp 200 Park Ave New York NY 10166 Office Fax: 212-922-8175.

DIAISO, ROBERT JOSEPH, civil engineer; b. Jersey City, N.J., Jan. 3, 1940; s. Dominick A. and Marie M. (Sarno) DiA.; m. Elaine Ricca, June 8, 1963; 1 child, Michael. BS, U.S. Naval Acad., 1962; MCE, NYU, 1964; M in Urban and Regional Planning, U. Pitts., 1971; PhD, 1971, 1972; AA (hon.), Anne Arundel C.C., 1998. Engr. Clarke, Hartman & Dunn, 1955-57, 69; project dir. Inst. Urban Policy Analysis, 1970-71; assoc. partner Dewberry, Nealon & Davis, Annapolis, Md., 1971-81; sr. assoc. Dewberry & Davis, Annapolis, 1981-82; prin. Dewsberry & Davis, 1983-84; pres. Property Improvement Collaborative, Inc., 1984-90, LandScope, 1985—2000; dir. LandTech Corp., 1985-88, mng. dir., 1988-94; CEO, FM Tech Corp., 1991-94; pres., CEO The Tech Group, 1993—. Organizer, dir. Bay Nat. Bank; Land Tech. Corp., 1986—; bd. dirs. Scotts Seaboard Corp.; pres. Peacock Mgmt. Systems. Pres., Crofton Civic Assn., 1973, trustee emeritus, 1998; chmn. bd. trustees by 3 govs. Anne Arundel C.C., 1974-98, trustee emeritus, 1998; mem. County Zoning Adv. Task Force, 1983-84; mem. county coun. adv. com. on adequate facilities, 1977-78; bd. dirs. Anne Arundel Trade Coun.; chmn. Public Works Rev. Bd.; mem. Sewer Allocation Task Force; chmn. County Exec. Transition Task Force, 1982; mem. County Exec. Transition Team, 1991, County Exec. USN David Taylor Naval Facility Reuse Com., 1996; mem. Gov.'s com. on Affordable Housing, 1976-78; mem. adv. bd. Patuxent Water Reclamation Plant; mem. adv. com. Crofton on Municipal Incorp.; bldg. com. St. Elizabeth Ann Seton Ch. Served with USAF, 1962-69. Named Bus. Leader of Yr., Anne Arundel Trade Coun., 1982; HEW fellow, 1970-72. Mem. ASCE, Am. Planning Assn., Am. Inst. Certified Planners, Nat. Soc. Profl. Engrs., Assn. County Engrs. Roman Catholic. Office: 147 Old Solomons Island Rd Annapolis MD 21401-0903

DIAL, CARMEN MIRANDA, financial counselor, evangelist; b. Bessemer, Ala., May 12, 1950; d. Clifton and Idella A. Dial; 1 child, Clifton Millard Wright. BS, Ala. A&M U., 1972. Addressograph operator Fulton-Dekalb Hosp. Authority, Atlanta, 1972—77; fin. counselor Grady Health Sys., Atlanta, 1977—. Pres. Word of Knowledge, Atlanta, 1995. Author: Walking with Jesus, Crystal Fountain of Love, Jesus is The Light, Our Father, Rain Drops, To the Living God, I Give You Praise, To the Man of My Life. Mem. Chosen Vessel, Atlanta, 1992—; Bible tchr., chmn. Green Forest Cmty. Bapt., Decatur, Ga., 2001. Avocations: tennis, volleyball. Home: # D54 3000 Continental Colony Pky Atlanta GA 30331

DIAL, MARSHALL REECE, library director; b. Tiptonville, Tenn., Apr. 17, 1925; s. William Wright and Addie Elizabeth Nobles Dial; m. Mary Lynn Marr, Sept. 23, 1960; children: Thomas Wayne, Dorothy Elizabeth Dial Dodson. BA, Goddard Coll., 1971; postgrad., S.E. Mo. State U., 1975. Dir. county libr. system New Madrid County, Portageville, Mo., 1955-96. Cons. New Madrid County Libr., 1996-97. Author: Bootheel Swamp Struggle, 1961; editor: A Soldiers Life, 1963; contbr. articles to profl. jours. With U.S. Army, 1951-53. Democrat. Episcopalian. Avocations: coin collecting, civil war research, antiques. Home: 700 E 6th St Portageville MO 63873-1504

DIAMA, BENJAMIN, retired educator, artist, composer, writer; b. Hilo, Hawaii, Sept. 23, 1933; s. Agapito and Catalina (Buscas) D. BFA, Sch. Art Inst. Chgo., 1956. Cert. tchr., Hawaii. Tchr. art, basketball coach Waimea (Kauai, Hawaii) High Sch., 1963-67; tchr. music and art Campbell High Sch., Honolulu, 1967-68; tchr. math. and art Waipahu High Sch., Honolulu, 1968-69; tchr. art and music Palisades Elem. Sch., Honolulu, 1969-70; tchr. typing, history, art and music Honokaa (Hawaii) High Sch., 1970-73; tchr. music Kealakehe Sch., Kailua, 1973-74; ret., 1974. Author, writer, composer: Hawaii, 1983; author: Poems of Faith, 1983-88, School One vs. School Two On The Same School Campus, 1983, The Calendar-Clock Theory of the Universe with Faith-- Above and Beyond, 1984-90, Phonetic Sound-Musical Theory, 1990; contbg. author: Benjamin Diama--The Calendar Clock Theory of the Universe, 1991, 92, (poetry) Celebration of Poets, 1998, Poets Elite, Internat. Soc. of Poets, 2000; prodr., composer (Cassette) Hawaii I Love You, 1986; inventor universal clock, double floater boat, Gardener's Water Box, Full Court Half Court 6 vs. 6, 3 Offense-3 Defense Basketball Game. Recipient Achievement award Waimea Dept. Edn., 1964-67, Purchase award State Found. Arts on Culture and the Arts, 1984, State Found. Arts and Culture Acquisition Painting Art award State of Hawaii Govt. Art Collection. Mem. NEA, Hawaii Tchrs. Assn., Hawaii Edn. Assn., AAAS, Nat. Geog. Soc., Smithsonian Assocs., ASCAP, N.Y. Acad. Scis., Nat. Libr. Poetry (assoc.), Internat. Soc. Poets, Am. Geophysical Union. Mem. Salvation Army. Avocations: singing, writing science, coaching basketball. Home: PO Box 2997 Kailua Kona HI 96745-2997

DIAMANT, AVIVA F. lawyer; b. N.Y.C., Mar. 13, 1949; d. Herman and Anni (Silbermann) D.; m. Steven Kaufman, May 31, 1976; 2 children. BS cum laude, CCNY, 1969; JD, Columbia U., 1972. Bar: N.Y. 1973, U.S. Ct. Appeals (2d cir.) 1975, U.S. Dist. Ct. (so. dist.) 1976. Assoc. Fried, Frank, Harris, Shriver & Jacobson, N.Y.C., 1972-79, ptnr., 1979—. James Kent scholar, 1972. Mem. Assn. of Bar of City of N.Y. (com. on corps. 1982-85), Phi Beta Kappa. Jewish. Office: Fried Frank Harris Shriver & Jacobson 1 New York Plz Fl 22 New York NY 10004-1980

DIAMANT, JOEL CHARLES, internist; b. N.Y.C., Oct. 11, 1963; s. Bernard and Alice Susan (Ruskin) D.; m. Caroline Ruth Taliaferro, Oct. 9, 1994. AB, U. Calif., Berkeley, 1985; MD with honors, U. Ill., 1990. Diplomate Am. Bd. Internal Medicine. Intern Scripps Clinic/Green Hosp., 1990-91; resident in internal medicine Scripps Clinic, La Jolla, Calif., 1991-93, chief resident in internal medicine, 1993-94, staff physician, 1994—; assoc. dir. internal medicine residency Scripps Clinic/Green Hosp., 1996-98, dir. internal medicine residency, 1998—, head divsn. hosp. medicine. James scholar U. Ill. Coll. Medicine, 1990. Office: Scripps Clinic 10666 N Torrey Pines Rd La Jolla CA 92037-1092

DIAMANT, MICHAEL HARLAN, lawyer; b. Cleve., July 30, 1946; s. Eugene and Rita June (Hausman) D.; m. Amy Sarah Bresnick, Nov. 23, 1969; children: Aaron Jeremy, Ethan Ari. BS in Engring. with high honors, Case Western Res. U., 1968; JD cum laude, Harvard U., 1971. Bar: Ohio 1971, U.S. Dist. Ct. Ohio 1973, U.S. Ct. Appeals (6th cir.) 1977, U.S. Ct. Appeals (fed. cir.) 1982, U.S. Ct. Appeals (10th cir.) 1994, U.S. Ct. Appeals (11th cir.) 1995, U.S. Supreme Ct. 1977. Prin. Kahn Kleinman, Cleve., 1971-78, 1978—. Pres. Solomon Schecter Day Sch. Cleve., 1984-87; pres., Case Alumni Assn., 1995-96; mem. vis. com. undergrad. colls. Case Western Res. U., chmn. vis. com. Case Sch. Engring., 1993-99, mem., 1999--. Mem. ABA, Bar Assn. Greater Cleve. (chmn. computer law inst. 1983-85, chmn. jud. sel. com. 1985), Computer Law Assn., Case Alumni Assn. (pres. 1995-96). Democrat. Jewish. Office: Kahn Kleinman 2600 Tower at Erieview Cleveland OH 44114-1824

DIAMANT, WILLIAM, lawyer; b. May 30, 1928; s. James and Anna (Papanicholau) D.; m. Bertha Polydoros, Nov. 27, 1951; children: Anna Woods, Elaine Sikorski, Christine Kipp, James. BS, U. Pitts., 1952; JD, Naval Justice Sch., 1955; postgrad., Northwestern U., 1967, grad. in trust adminstrn. Bar: Pa. 1955, Ill. 1958, U.S. Dist. Ct. (no. dist.) Ill. 1984. Title legal officer Chgo. Title & Trust Co., 1957-62; v.p., gen. counsel Unibanctrust Co., Chgo., 1962-78; v.p., trust dept. head, counsel 1st Nat. Bank of Elgin, Ill., 1978-81; sr. v.p., gen. counsel, sec. bd. dirs. Elmhurst Nat. Bank, Ill., 1981-83; sole practice Hinsdale, Ill., 1983—. Tchr. Am. Inst. Banking, Chgo., 1972—. Sec. Sch. Bd. Unit Dist. 401, Elmwood Park, Ill., 1972-78. Served with USMC, 1955-57; capt. Res. (ret.), Recipient Meritorious Svc. award Sch. Bd. Unit Dist. 401, 1978, Disting. Svc. award Am. Inst. Banking, 1982. Mem. Ill. Bar Assn., Pa. Bar Assn., Chgo. Bar Assn., DuPage County Bar Assn. Club: Ahepa (Chgo.) (pres. 1060-62). Lodge: Elks. Office: 930 York Rd Ste 102 Hinsdale IL 60521-3541

DIAMANTOPOULOS, JOHN C.D. mathematician, educator; s. Maria Patricia and Demetrios Diamantopoulos; m. Karen Alisha Rydell, July 15, 2000. BA, Augustana Coll., 1991; MS, No. Ill. U., 1993, PhD, 1996. Asst. prof. math. and computer sci. Ouachita Bapt. U., Arkadelphia, Ark., 1996—2000; asst. prof. math. Monmouth Coll., Ill., 2000—01, Northeastern State U., Tahlequah, Okla., 2001—. Contbr. articles to profl. jours. Grantee, Ouachita Bapt. U., 1999, 1998, 1997. Mem.: Am. Math. Soc., Math. Assn. Am., Pi Mu Epsilon, Kappa Mu Epsilon, Phi Beta Kappa. Office: Northeastern State University 611 N Grand Tahlequah OK 74464 Office Fax: 918-458-2325. E-mail: diamantj@nsuok.edu.

DIAMOND, ANN CYNTHIA, lawyer; b. Hollywood, Calif., Apr. 7, 1947; d. I.A.L. and Barbara Ann (Bentley) D.; m. Robert Sidney Pynoos, Mar. 31, 1969 (div. June 1977). BA, Sarah Lawrence Coll., 1968; JD, NYU, 1978. Bar: N.Y. 1979, U.S. Dist. Ct. (so. dist.) N.Y. 1979, U.S. Dist. Ct. (ea. dist.) N.Y. 1979, U.S. Ct. Appeals (9th cir.) 1983, U.S. Ct. Appeals (2d cir.) 1984. Jr. editor McCall's Mag., N.Y.C., 1968-69; copy and features editor Bride's Mag., N.Y.C., 1969-73; copywriter Elizabeth Arden, Inc., N.Y.C., 1973-75; assoc. Proskauer Rose Goetz & Mendelsohn, N.Y.C., 1978-80, Finley, Kumble, Wanger, Heine, Underberg, Manley & Casey, N.Y.C., 1980-84, Bronstein, Van Veen & Bronstein, L.L.C., N.Y.C., 1985—2002; of counsel Sheresky Aronson & Mayefsky, LLP, N.Y.C., 2002—. Author: (with S.F. Enos) The Bride's Magazine Guide to the New Marriage, 1974; Bride's Book of Etiquette, 1972. Facilitator, presenter Parent Edn. and Custody Effectiveness Tng., 1999—2001; vol. counsel Assn. Bar City N.Y. Fund SHIELD Clinic; neutral evaluator Supreme Ct. State of N.Y., 1997—; arbitrator matrimonial fee disputes Supreme Ct. of the State of N.Y., 1994—, staff counsel Gov. Jud. Nominating Com., 1980-82; del. Dem. Jud. Nominating Convs. N.Y., 1974-78; adminstrv. dir. N.Y. State Hdqrs., McGovern for Pres., N.Y.C., 1972; pres. Cmty. Free Dems. 1974, v.p. 1975-77; sec. N.Y. New Dem. Coalition, 1976-77; mentor Network for Women's Svcs. (in Motion), 1996—. Mem. ABA, Assn. Bar City N.Y., NYU Pub. Interest Law Found. (founding), N.Y. County Lawyers Assn. Office: 750 Lexington Ave New York NY 10021-3310

DIAMOND, BERNARD ROBIN, lawyer; b. Bronx, N.Y., July 3, 1944; m. Elizabeth Heimbuch, Oct. 20, 1976; children: Jessica, Carey, Erin. BA, Rutgers U., 1966; JD, Bklyn. Law Sch., 1972. Bar: N.Y. 1973, U.S. Dist. Ct. (so. and ea. dists.) N.Y. 1973, U.S. Ct. Appeals (2d cir.) 1974. Gen. counsel The Trump Orgn., N.Y.C., 1995—. Mem. Assn. of the Bar of the City of N.Y. Office: Trump Orgn 725 5th Ave Fl 26 New York NY 10022-2520

DIAMOND, DANIEL LLOYD, surgeon; MD, Tulane U., 1970. Dipomate Am. Bd. Surgery (dir. 1995—). Intern U. Pitts. Health Ctr. Hosps., 1970-71, resident in surgery, 1971-76; dir. gen. surgery, divsn. surgery Allegheny Gen. Hosp., Pitts., 1976—95; prof. surgery Med. Coll. Pa., Pitts., 1992—95; chmn., prof. dept. surgery U. Tenn. Med. Ctr., Knoxville, 1995-98; pvt. practice, 1998—. Bd. dirs. Am. Bd. Surgery, 1994-2000. Mem. Assn. Program Dirs. (bd. dirs. 1994-2000). Office: 3075 Washington Rd Mc Murray PA 15317

DIAMOND, DAVID ARTHUR, law educator; b. N.Y.C., May 8, 1937; s. Samuel and Ann (Kottick) D.; m. Shelley Sherman, Aug. 7, 1977; 1 child, Daniel. A.B., Harvard U., 1959, LL.B., 1962; LL.M., NYU, 1963. Bar: N.Y. 1963, U.S. Ct. Appeals (2d cir.), U.S. Ct. Appeals (5th cir.), U.S. Dist. Ct. (so. dist.) N.Y., U.S. Dist. Ct. (ea. dist.) N.Y. Assoc. Hughes, Hubbard & Reed, N.Y.C., 1963-68; dir. law reform unit MFY Legal Services, N.Y.C., 1968-72, also dir.; law prof. Syracuse Law Sch., N.Y., 1972-75, Hofstra Law Sch., Hempstead, N.Y., 1975— ; co-dir. North East Regional Program Nat. Inst. Trial Advocacy. Mem. due process com. ACLU. Mem. Assn. Bar City of N.Y. (mem. spl. com. on law and edn.). Home: 43 Jayson Ave Great Neck NY 11021-4239 Office: Hofstra Law Sch Rm 214 Hempstead NY 11550

DIAMOND, DAVID LEO, composer; b. Rochester, N.Y., July 9, 1915; s. Osias and Anna (Schildhaus) Diamond. Student, Cleve. Inst. Music, 1927—29, Eastman Sch. Music, U. Rochester, 1930—34, Am. Conservatory, Fontainebleau, France, summers, 1937, student, 1938, New Music and Dalcroze Inst., N.Y.C., 1934—36; pvt. studies with Roger Sessions, N.Y.C.; pvt. studies with Nadia Boulanger, Paris; pvt. studies with Hermann Scherchen, Switzerland. Tchr. composition Met. Music Sch., N.Y.C., 1950; lectr. Am. music Seminar in Am. Studies Schloss Leopoldskron, Salzburg, Austria, 1949; Fulbright prof. U. Rome, 1951—52; Slee prof. music U. Buffalo, 1961, 1963; prof., chmn. dept.

composition Manhattan Sch. Music, N.Y.C., 1965—67; composer-in-residence Am. Acad. in Rome, 1971—72, Juilliard Sch. Music, 1973—97; Master Class Schola Cantorum, Paris, 1996, 1997. Vis. prof. U. Colo., Boulder, 1970, U. Denver, 1983, other univs.; composer-in-residence N;Y. Chamber Symphony, 1991—; hon. composer-in-residence Seattle Symphony, 1996. Contbr. ; compositions include 12 symphonies, concertos for violin, cello, piano and flute, 11 string quartets, various chamber music, 52 preludes and fugues for piano, miscellaneous choral music and songs, solo symphony for organ, scores for motion pictures, other forms of instrumental music, composer music for Columbia albums Fourth String Quartet, Romeo and Juliet, 4th Symphony (performed by Bernstein, N.Y. Philharm. Orch.), Quartet, Nonet, String Number 9, CRI Records, Two Sonatas for violin and piano, New World CD, Symphonies 1, 2, 3, 4, 8 and Concerto for small orch., Delos Records, Symphonies No. 5, New World Records, original score for Margaret Webster prodn. of The Tempest, 1944—45, incidental music for Cheryl Crawford prodn. of The Rose Tattoo, 1951, music for This Sacred Ground (Gettysburg Address, Delos Records), 1962; composer: (ballets) TOM Delos Records, 1936, The Dream of Audubon, 1941, Formal Dance for Martha Graham; commd. works include (Operas) The Noblest Game, Nat. Opera Inst., 1975, Mirandolina, The Golden Slippers, Secular Cantata, N.Y. State Arts Coun., cantata A Song for Hope, Elie Wiesel, Second Sonata for violin and piano, Libr. Congress McKim Fund, Second Sonata for cello and piano, Sonata for flute and piano, Trio for violin, clarinet and piano for Verdehr Trio, Libr. Congress, Kaddish for cello and orch., Yo-Yo Ma, Symphony for organ Leonard Raver, Ode for orch., Tokyo Bunkamura, Fantasy on Old 100th for organ and brass quintet, Princeton U., Concerto for string quartet and orch., Juilliard Sch., works performed by major orchs., other well-known music orgns. throughout U.S. and abroad. Named Elfrida Whiteman scholar, 1935, Guggenheim fellow, 1938, 1942, 1958; recipient numerous major awards and prizes, 1935—, including: Prix de Rome, Paderewski award, Juilliard Pub. award, Stravinsky award, ASCAP, Naumberg Rec. award for Nonet and String Quartet No. 9, William Schuman Lifetime Achievement award, 1986, Edward MacDowell Gold medal, 1991, Presdl. Medal of Honor, 1995, Nat. Medal of Arts, 1995; grantee, NEA, Rockefeller Found., 1983. Mem.: Am. Acad. (Gold medal for eminence 1991), Am. Acad. Arts and Letters (Gold medal 1991). Address: 249 Edgerton St Rochester NY 14607-3315

DIAMOND, DAVID ROGER, psychologist; b. Bridgeport, Conn., Dec. 7, 1942; s. Roger Merrill Diamond and Marion Evelyn Sprague; children: Daniel, Steven. BA, U. N.H., 1964; PhD, U. N.C., 1971. Lic. psychologist, N.H. Vol. U.S. Peace Corps, Kouve, Togo, 1964-66; psychologist Stafford Guidance Ctr., Dover, N.H., 1971-88; pvt. practice psychology Rochester, N.H., 1988-93; psychologist Salmon Falls Behavioral Health, Rochester, 1993—, pres., 1997-98. Chair steering com. N.H. Peace Action, Concord, 1996-98; originator Real Democracy Project, Dover, 1999. Mem. APA, N.H. Psychol. Assn., Phi Beta Kappa. Office: Salmon Falls Behavioral Health PC 1 Old Dover Rd Ste 1 Rochester NH 03867-3460 also: 660 Central Ave Ste 201 Dover NH 03820 Fax: 603-335-2226. E-mail: ddiam@ttlc.net.

DIAMOND, DIANA LOUISE, editor, graphic artist; b. Floral Park, NY, Feb. 4, 1937; d. Louis Bartholomew and Helen Stephanie (Strzelecki) Chmielewski; m. Horace Williams Diamond, Jr., June 29, 1958 (div. 1975); children: Bruce Williams, Scott Kenneth, Kent Christopher, Mark Patrick. BA in English, U. Mich., 1958. Reporter Lerner Newspapers, Highland Park, 1970-72, mng. editor, 1972-78, suburban coord., 1974-78; corr. (part-time) The N.Y. Times, 1975-78; prof. journalism fellow Stanford U., 1978-79, sr. writer, editor, spl. asst. to pres., 1983-88, exec. asst. to v.p. and dean Sch. of Medicine, 1988-89; writer, editl. bd. San Jose (Calif.) Mercury News, 1979—81; editor, sect., spl. projects editor Sunday Opinion, 1981; editor-in-chief Calif. Lawyer, 1981—83; spl. asst. to pres. Stanford U. Hosp., 1990-93, mgr. publs., 1993-94; pres. Diamond Comm. and Design, Palo Alto, Calif., 1994—. Columnist Palo Alto Daily News, 2001—. Bd. dirs. Midpeninsula Citizens for Fair Housing, pres., 1983-86; bd. dirs. New Forum, 1985-90, pres., 1987-89; bd. dirs. Pacific Art League, 1989-94; bd. dirs. Palo Alto Centennial '94, 1990-94; founder, chmn. bd. dirs. RotaCare Internat., 1992—; bd. dirs. Palo Alto chpt. ARC. Recipient Nat. Blue Ribbon Newspaper award, 1976-78; 3rd pl. Ill. Editor of Yr. contest, 1974; 1st pl. for best feature story, Ill. Press Assn., 1976, Suburban Newspapers Am., 1977; 2d pl. for best column Nat. Newspaper Assn., 1977, Maggie award We. Pubs. Assn., Silver Six award Internat. Bus. Comm., 1996, Crystal award Communicators Group, 1998, 1st pl. best column Pa. Press Assn., 2002. Mem. LWV, Rotary (pres. Palo Alto chpt. 1999-2000). Home: 2512 Cowper St Palo Alto CA 94301-4218 Office: Diamond Comm & Design 550 Hamilton Ave Ste 338 Palo Alto CA 94301-2031 E-mail: diana@dianadiamond.com.

DIAMOND, EUGENE CHRISTOPHER, lawyer, hospital administrator; b. Oceanside, Calif., Oct. 19, 1952; s. Eugene Francis and Rosemary (Wright) D.; m. Mary Theresa O'Donnell, Jan. 20, 1984; children: Eugene John, Kevin Seamus, Hannah Rosemary, Seamus Michael, Maeve Therese. BA, U. Notre Dame, 1974; MHA, St. Louis U., 1978, JD, 1979. Bar: Ill. 1979. Staff atty. AUL Legal Def. Fund, Chgo., 1979-80; adminstrv. asst. Holy Cross Hosp., Chgo., 1980-81, asst. adminstr., 1981-82, v.p., 1982-83, counsel to adminstr., 1980—, exec. v.p., 1983-91; exec. v.p., COO, St. Margaret Mercy Healthcare Ctrs., Hammond, Ind., 1991-93, pres., CEO, 1993—, regional COO, 2001—. Cons. Birthright of Chgo., 1979—, mem. benefit com., 1981—; bd. dirs. Hammond C. of C., 1993, North West Ind. Forum. Mem. Ill. State Bar Assn., Chgo. Bar Assn. Roman Catholic. Office: St Margaret Mercy Healthcare Ctrs 5454 Hohman Ave Hammond IN 46320-1999

DIAMOND, FRED I. electronic engineer; b. Bklyn., Dec. 13, 1925; s. Joseph and Celia (Just) D.; m. Edna R. Hutt, Sept. 2, 1956; children: Celia, Joel, Shari. S.B.E.E., MIT, 1950; M.E.E., Syracuse U., 1953, PhD, 1966. Electronic engr. Rome Air Devel. Center, Griffiss AFB, N.Y., 1950-51, sr. scientist, 1961-70, chief plans, 1970-73, tech. dir. communications and control div., 1973-81, chief scientist, 1981-91; dep. dir Rome Lab., 1991-94. Chmn. avionics panel NATO Adv. Group for Aerospace R & D, 1975-86; exec. chmn. communications subgroup Australian, Canadian, N.Z., U.K., U.S. Tech. Coordination Program; instr. dept. math. Utica Coll., 1957-59; lectr. dept. elec. engring. Syracuse U., 1959-61; mem. ednl. coun. MIT, 1968-92; bd. dirs. N.Y. State Photonics Devel. Corp. Contbr. articles to profl. jours. Bd. dirs. Rome Community Concert Assn., 1968-80, Cen. Assn. for Blind and Vision Impaired; trustee Jervis Pub. Libr., 1977-89, pres., 1980-83; mem. indsl. adv. com. U. Mass. Sch. Engring., Syracuse U. Sch. Engring.; mem. coun. SUNY Inst. Tech.; ad hoc visitor Accreditation Bd. for Engring. and Tech. With U.S. Army, 1944-46. Recipient Meritorious Civilian Svc. medal USAF, 1968, Exceptional Civilian Svc. award, 1978, 84, Outstanding Civilian Career Svc. award, 1994; 7 Outstanding Performance awards Sr. Exec. Svc., 1982-87, 89, 90, 92, 93, Presdl. rank award as disting. exec. Fellow IEEE (life), AAAS, AIAA (assoc.); mem. Acad. of Sr. Profls. of Eckerd Coll. E-mail: fdiamond.tampabay@r.r.com.

DIAMOND, GUSTAVE, federal judge; b. Burgettstown, Pa., Jan. 29, 1928; s. George and Margaret (Solinsky) D.; m. Emma L. Scarton, Dec. 28, 1974; 1 dau., Margaret Ann; 1 stepdau., Joanne Yoney. AB, Duke U., 1951; JD, Duquesne U., 1956. Bar: Pa. bar 1958, U.S. Ct. Appeals bar 1962. Law clk. to judge U.S. Dist. Ct., Pitts., 1955-61; 1st asst. U.S. atty. Western Dist. Pa., 1961-62, U.S. atty., 1963-69; partner firm Cooper, Schwartz, Diamond & Reich, Pitts., 1969-75; formerly individual practice law Washington, Pa.; former solicitor Washington County, Pa.; judge U.S. Dist. Ct. Western Dist. Pa.; chief judge U.S. Dist. Ct. (we. dist.) Pa., 1992-94, sr. judge, 1994—. Chmn. Jud. Conf. Com. on Defender Svcs. Mem. ABA, Fed. Bar Assn., Pa. Bar Assn., Allegheny County Bar Assn., Washington County Bar Assn. Office: US Dist Ct 821 US Courthouse 7th St Rm 2 Pittsburgh PA 15219

DIAMOND, HARRIS, corporate communications executive, lawyer; b. N.Y.C., Feb. 5, 1953; m. Amy Simon, Mar. 26, 1956. BA, Drew U., 1975; MBA, Fairleigh Dickinson U., 1978; JD, Bklyn. Law Sch., 1983. Bar: N.Y., 1984. Various mgmt. positions Prudential Ins. Co., Newark, 1975-80; confidential asst. to dist. atty. Office Kings County Dist. Atty., Bklyn., 1982-85; ptnr., chmn. mgmt. com. Sawyer Miller Group, N.Y.C., 1986-93; COO Robinson, Lerer, Sawyer & Miller, 1993-95; chmn. and CEO BSMG Worldwide, 1996—; dir. Bozell Jacobs Kenyon Eckert, 1996—; chmn. True North Diversified Cos., 1999—2001; CEO Weber Shandwick Worldwide, N.Y.C., 2001—. Polit. analyst for network and local TV; frequent speaker on crisis comm. for industry and co. forums; bd. dirs. Caremark. Mem. N.Y.C. Cmty. Bd., 1980-83; bd. visitors Drew U., Madison, N.J., 1991—. Mem. Rolling Hills Country Club (Wilton, Conn.; bd. dirs.). Office: Weber Shandwick Worldwide 640 Fifth Ave New York NY 10019-6102

DIAMOND, JARED MASON, biologist; b. Boston, Sept. 10, 1937; BA, Harvard U., 1958; PhD, Cambridge (Eng.) U., 1961. Jr. fellow Soc. Fellows Harvard U., 1962—65; assoc. in biophysics, 1965—66; asso. prof. physiology U. Calif. Med. Center, Los Angeles, 1966—68, prof., 1968—. Cons. in conservation and nat. park planning govts., Papua New Guinea, Solomon Islands, Indonesia. Author: Avifauna of the Eastern Highlands of New Guinea, 1972, Ecology and Evolution of Communities, 1975, Guns, Germs, and Steel (Pulitzer prize, 1998, Cosmos prize, 1998); contbr. Recipient Burr medal, Nat. Geog. Soc., 1979, Bowditch prize, Am. Physiol. Soc., 1976, Disting. Achievement award, Am. Gastroent. Assn., 1975, Nat. Medal Science, 1999. Fellow: MacArthur Found., Am. Acad. Arts and Scis.; mem.: NAS. Office: UCLA Med Ctr Dept of Physiology 10833 Le Conte Ave Los Angeles CA 90095-3075

DIAMOND, JESSICA, artist; b. Bronx, N.Y. BFA, Sch. Visual Arts, N.Y.C., 1979; MFA, Columbia U., N.Y.C., 1981. One-woman shows include Standard Graphic, Cologne, Germany, 1990, Jablonka Gallery, Cologne, 1991, Gallery Fahnemann, Berlin, 1991, Gallery Massimo DeCarlo, Milan, 1993, Ynglingagatan 1, Stockholm, 1994, Rix, Linköping, Sweden, 1996, Galerie Analix, Geneva, 1996, Deitch Projects, N.Y., 1996, le Consortium, Dijon, France, 1997, Vera Van Laer Gallery, Antwerp, Belgium, 1998, Ota Fine Arts, Tokyo, 1999, Mus. Het Domein, Sittard, The Netherlands, 1999, Birmingham (Ala.) Mus. of Art, 2000, Art Gallery-York U., Toronto, Ont., Can., 2001, Montreal (Can.) Mus. of Fine Arts, 2002; exhibited in group shows at Mus. van Hedendaagse Kunst Ghent, Belgium, 1993, Venice (Italy) Biennale, 1993, Vorarlberger Kunstverein, Bregenz, Austria, 1993, Corner House, Manchester, Eng., 1994, Deichtorhallen Hamburg, Germany, 1994, Mus. Contemporary Art, Sydney, Australia, 1994, Serpentine Gallery, London, 1994, Watari-um Mus., Tokyo, 1995, Kunsthalle Bern, Switzerland, 1995, Galerie Fahnemann, Berlin, 1996, Whitney Mus. Am. Art, N.Y.C., 1997, Stedelijk Mus. voor Actuele Kunst, Ghent, Belgium, 1999, Paula Cooper Gallery, N.Y.C., 1999, Tate Gallery Liverpool, Eng., 1999, Kunstmuseum Bonn, Germany, 1999, Kunstlerhaus Wien, Vienna, 2000, Sonsbeek 9, Arnhem, The Netherlands, 2001, The Tang Tchg. Mus. and Art Gallery, Skidmore Coll., Saratago Springs, N.Y., 2001, Casino Luxembourg, 2002, Neues Mus., Germany, 2002, MIT List Visual Arts Ctr., Cambridge, Mass., 2003. Recipient award Nat. Endowment for Arts, 1989; John Simon Guggenheim Meml. Found. fellow, 2000. Home: 549 83d St Brooklyn NY 11209-4503

DIAMOND, JOSEF, lawyer; b. L.A., Mar. 6, 1907; s. Michael and Ruby (Shifrin) D.; m. Violett Diamond, Apr. 2, 1933 (dec. 1979); children: Joel, Diane Foreman; m. Ann Dulien, Jan. 12, 1981 (dec. 1984); m. Muriel Bach, 1986. BBA, U. Wash., 1929, JD, 1931. Bar: Wash. 1931, U.S. Dist. Ct. (we. dist.) Wash. 1932, U.S. Ct. Appeals (9th cir.) 1934, U.S. Supreme Ct. 1944. Assoc. Caldwell & Lycette, Seattle, 1931-35; ptnr. Caldwell, Lycette & Diamond, Seattle, 1935-45, Lycette, Diamond & Sylvester, Seattle, 1945-80, Diamond & Sylvester, Seattle, 1980-82, of counsel, 1982-88, Short, Cressman & Burgess, Seattle, 1988—2002; pvt. practice Seattle, 2002—. Chmn. bd. Diamond Parking Inc., Seattle, 1945-70; cons. various businesses. Bd. dirs. Am. Heart Assn., 1960; chmn. Wash. Heart Assn., 1962. Col. JAGC, U.S. Army, WWII. Decorated Legion of Merit. Mem. Wash. Bar Assn., Assn. Trial Lawyers Wash., Seattle Bar Assn., Mil. Engrs. Soc., Wash. Athletic Club, Bellevue Athletic Club, Harbor Club. Office: Diamond Bldg Ste 200 3161 Elliott Ave Seattle WA 98121 Office Fax: 206-285-5598.

DIAMOND, LINDY S. financial executive; b. Vallejo, Calif., Nov. 17, 1958; s. Sam Binem and Donna Mae Diamond; m. Judy Ann Nakamura, June 30, 1990. BS, U. So. Calif., 1981; MBA, Loyola Marymount U., 1993. Registered investment advisor, CPA, Calif. Sr. auditor Coopers & Lybrand, L.A., 1981-83; sr. acct. Triton Group Ltd., Century City, Calif., 1984-86; sr. acct. mgr. Mann Theatres Corp., L.A., 1987; fin. analyst Hughes Space & Comms., L.A., 1988-92, fin. acctg. mgr., 1993-95, govt. acctg. liaison, 1996-2000; sr. fin. analyst Boeing Satellite Sys., L.A., 2000—01, bus. ops. mgr., 2001—; investment advisor, cons. Lindy S. Diamond Personal Fin. Svcs., L.A., 1997—. Adj. prof. acctg. Santa Monica (Calif.) C.C., 1985; adj. prof. Pepperdine U., 2003—. Avocations: thoroughbred horse racing, college football. Office: Lindy S Diamond Personal Fin Svcs 5611 S Holt Ave Los Angeles CA 90056-1314 E-mail: lindydiamond@comcast.net, lsdiamondpfs@comcast.net.

DIAMOND, M. JEROME, lawyer, former state official; b. Chgo., Mar. 16, 1942; s. Leo and Sonya (Pevsner) D.; m. Carol English Robinson; 8 children. AB, George Washington U., 1963; MA, U. Tenn., 1965, JD, 1968. Bar: Vt. 1968, U.S. Supreme Ct. 1975. Law clk. U.S. Dist. Judge Ernest Gibson, 1968-69; assoc. Kristensen, Cummings & Price, Brattleboro, Vt., 1969-70; state's atty. Windham County, Vt., 1970-74; atty. gen. State of Vt., 1975-81; atty., sr. ptnr. Diamond & Robinson, P.C., Montpelier, Vt., 1981—. Trustee Brooks Meml. Library, 1970-73; chmn. Putney Zoning Bd. Adjustment, 1971-74; mem. Vt. Criminal Justice Tng. Council, 1974-81, Vt. Commn. Adminstrn. of Justice, 1975-81; mem. Vt. Adv. Group, U.S. Civil Rights Commn.; gen. campaign chmn. United Way Washington County, 1986-87, 88-89; bd. dirs. Nat. Coun. on Aging, 1990-93, Vt. Bar Found., 1997—, Vt. State Employees Credit Union, 1997—; internat. commr. Anti-Defamation League, 1988-93. Mem. Vt. State's Attys. Assn. (past pres.), Vt. Bar Assn., Vt. Bar Found. (bd. dirs. 1997—), Washington County Bar Assn., Nat. Assn. Atty. Gens. (v.p. 1978-79, pres. 1980), Ea. Regional Conf. Attys. Gen. (chmn. 1975-76), B'nai B'rith (internat. commr. anti-defamation league 1988-93, internat. bd. govs. 1990-92), Jewish Inst. for Nat. Security Affairs (bd. dirs. 1993—), Am. Judicature Soc. (bd. dirs., Vt. rep. 1994-00), Vt. State Employees Credit Union, 1997 (bd. dirs., v.p. of bd. VSECU 2000—), Shriners, Masons, Montpelier Rotary Club (bd. dirs. 1998—, v.p. 2001-02, pres.-elect 2002-03, pres. 2003-04). Democrat. Jewish. Office: Diamond & Robinson PC PO Box 1460 Montpelier VT 05601

DIAMOND, MARIAN CLEEVES, anatomy educator; b. Glendale, Calif., Nov. 11, 1926; d. Montague and Rosa Marian (Wamphler) Cleeves; m. Richard M. Diamond, Dec. 20, 1950 (div.); m. Arnold B. Scheibel, Sept. 14, 1982; children: Catherine, Richard, Jeffrey, Ann. AB, U. Calif., Berkeley, 1948, MA, 1949, PhD, 1953. With Harvard U., Cambridge, 1952-54, Cornell U., Ithaca, N.Y., 1954-58, U. Calif., San Francisco, 1959—62, prof. anatomy Berkeley, 1962—. Asst. dean U. Calif., Berkeley, 1967-70, assoc. dean, 1970-73, dir. The Lawrence Hall of Sci., 1990-95, dir. emeritus, 1995—; vis. scholar Australian Nat. U., 1978, Fudan U., Shanghai, China, 1985, U. Nairobi, Kenya, 1988. Author: (with J. Hopson) Magic Trees of the Mind, 1998; author: Enriching Heredity, 1989; co-author: The Human Brain Coloring, 1985; editor: Contraceptive Hormones Estrogen and Human Welfare, 1978; contbr. over 155 articles to profl. jours. V.p. County Women Dems., Ithaca, 1957; bd. dirs. Unitarian Ch., Berkeley, 1969. Recipient Calif. Gifted award, 1989, C.A.S.E. Calif. Prof. of Yr. award, Nat. Gold medalist, 1990, Woman of Yr. award Zonta Internat., 1991, U. medal La. Universidad Del Zulia, Maricaibo, Venezuela, 1992, Alumna of the Yr. award U. Calif., Berkeley, 1995; Calif. Acad. Scis. fellow, 1991, Calif. Soc. Biomedical Rsch. Dist. Svc. award, 1998, Alumnae Resources-Women of Achievement Vision and Excellence award, 1999, Benjamin Ide Wheeler award 1999, Achievement award Calif. Child Devel. Adminstrs. Assn., 2001; named to Internat. Educators Hall of Fame, 1999. Fellow AAAS, AAUW (sr.; fellowship chair 1970-85, 1st Sr. Scholar award 1997); mem. Am. Assn. Anatomists, Soc. Neurosci., Philos. Soc. Washington, The Faculty Club (Berkeley, v.p. 1979-85, 90-95). Avocations: hiking, sports, painting. Home: 2583 Virginia St Berkeley CA 94709-1108 Office: U Calif Dept Integrative Biology 3060 Valley Life Sciences Bldg Berkeley CA 94720-3116 E-mail: diamond@socrates.berkeley.edu.

DIAMOND, MICHAEL SHAWN, science and math educator, computer consultant; b. St. Louis, Jan. 26, 1960; s. Robert Dale Diamond and Jean Marie (Reutner) White; m. Jennifer Atkins Albrighton, Jan. 1, 1999. BSChemE, U. Mo., 1982; MEd, Hyles-Anderson Coll., 1989. Cert. engr.-in-tng.; cert. tchr., S.C.; lic., ordained to ministry Baptist Ch., 1989; endorsed advanced placement calculus and stats. tchr., S.C., endorsed math. tchr. for techs. Nuclear engr. Charleston (S.C.) Naval Shipyard, Nuclear Engring. Dept., 1983-88, asst. shift test engr., 1983-85, asst. shift refueling engr., 1985-88; systems mgr. and sci. tchr. Faith Bapt. Ch. and Schs., Canoga Park, Calif., 1989-90, sci. tchr., 1989-92; programming asst., cons. Peterson Rsch., Costa Mesa, Calif., 1989-92; sci. dept. chmn. Gethsemane Bapt. Christian Sch., Long Beach, Calif., 1990-92; math. computer tchr. Pinewood Prep. Sch., Summerville, S.C., 1993-97, computer and tech. chair, 1994-97, 99; tng. splst. Software Tng. Ctr., North Charleston, S.C., 1997-98; quality assurance analyst in product devel. Blackbaud, Inc., Charleston, S.C., 1998; math. tchr. Ft. Dorchester H.S., 1999—; ednl. cons. Coll. Bd. AP Calculus Reader, 1999—. Adj. instr. transfer chemistry, math. and engring. Trident Tech. Coll., North Charleston, S.C., 1993-00; contract computer instr. Tng. Alliance, Charleston, 1993. Sunday sch. tchr. Gethsemane Bapt. Ch., Long Beach, 1990-92, Summerville (S.C.) Bapt. Ch., 1996-99; mem. choir Trident Bapt. Ch., Charleston, S.C., 1993-96, Grace Christian Fellowship, 2000-; singles Sun. sch. tchr. Summerville (S.C.) Bapt. Ch., 1996-99; head diving coach Coll. Charleston, SC, 2002-. Mem. NSPE, Am. Nuclear Soc., Nat. Sci. Tchrs. Assn., S.C. Sci. Coun., Nat. Coun. Tchrs. Math., S.C. Math. Tchrs. Assn., Low Country Math. Tchrs. Assn., S.C. Assn. Adv. Placement Math Tchrs., U.S. Judo Assn. (Winner's Cir. award 1987, 88, 89), Internat. Soc. of Tech. Educators, Pi Kappa Alpha. Republican. Avocations: reading, softball, personal computers, church work. Home: 107 Sawtooth Ln Summerville SC 29485-5807

DIAMOND, MURRAY J. lawyer; b. NYC, Dec. 25, 1923; s. Albert and Annie (Unger) D.; m. Beatrice Padwa, Apr. 4, 1955; children: Alyne, Lawrence. BA, Bklyn. Coll., 1947; JD, Bklyn. Law Sch., 1950, JSD, 1952. Bar: N.Y. 1950, U.S. Dist. Ct. (ea. and so. dists.) N.Y., U.S. Supreme Ct. 1956. Ptnr. firm Diamond & Dreifuss, N.Y.C., 1950-86; law lectr. N.Y.C. Tech. Coll., Bklyn., 1969-79; asst. prof. bus. law Hofstra U., Hempstead, N.Y., 1979-86; prof. St. Francis Coll., Bklyn., 1986-99, prof. emeritus, 1999—. Hearing officer N.Y. State Dept. Agr. and Markets; impartial hearing officer Bd. Edn., City of N.Y., Bd. Edn., State of N.Y. Co-author manual; contbr. articles to profl. jours. Served to maj. USAR, 1947-67. Mem. Am. Bus. Law Assn. Office: 267 Whitman Dr Brooklyn NY 11234-6934 E-mail: bdmjd@aol.com.

DIAMOND, RICHARD, retired secondary education educator; b. N.Y.C., June 23, 1936; s. Oscar and Frieda (Rosenfeld) D.; m. Donna Jean Berkshire Wilson, June 14, 1961 (div. June 1974); m. Betty Ruth Jane Foster, Nov. 17, 1975; children: Thomas, Laura, Rick, Jeff. BA, U. Calif., Berkeley, 1958. Cert. tchr., Calif. Tchr. Riverside (Calif.) Unified Schs., 1959-67, 73-99, coord. social studies, 1967-69, program dir. compensatory edn., 1969-72, attendance officer, 1972-73; project mgr. Biotech. Sch., 1999—2001. Author curriculum programs Afro-Am. history and Chicano studies, 1968; developer law and youth H.S. course, 1978, track coach, 1975-88. Contbr. articles and photographs to profl. jours. Co-creator nationally recognized h.s. vol. program, h.s. svc. learning coord., 1995—; mem. Riverside County Hist. Commn., 1997-2003; Dem. Party worker, 1964-72; Rep. Party worker, 1992—; historic commn. liaison Riverside County Archives Commn., 1998-2002; bd. dirs. Calif. Citrus Hist. State Park, 2000-2002, sec., 2000-2003; pres. Vail Ranch Restoration Assn., Inc., Temecula, Calif., 2000-2002. Named Social Studies Tchr. of Yr., Inland Empire Social Studies Assn., 1980, Tchr. of Yr., Arlington H.S., Riverside, 1992; recipient hon. svc. award Dist. Coun. PTA, Riverside, 1993, Johnny Harris Youth Action award City of Riverside,, 1998. Mem. NEA, Calif. Tchrs. Assn., Riverside County Tchrs. Assn. Presbyterian. Avocations: gardening, travel, reading, woodworking. E-mail: ddiamond@ix.netcom.com.

DIAMOND, RICHARD MARTIN, nuclear chemist; b. L.A., Jan. 7, 1924; divorced; 4 children. BS, UCLA, 1947; PhD in Nuclear Chemistry, U. Calif. Berkeley, 1951. Instr. chemistry Harvard U., 1951-54; asst. prof. Cornell U., 1954-58; mem. sr. staff Lawrence Berkeley Lab., U. Calif., 1958—, sr. scientist emeritus, 1995—. Mem. U.S. Physics del. to Russia, 1966, rev. com. physics divsn. Oak Ridge Lab., 1972-74, Dept. of Energy rev. com. Brookhaven (n, gamma) Facility and Isotope Separator, 1983, 8pi Gamma Spect. Com., Chalk River, Canada, 1983, adv. com. Ind. Cyclotron Facility, 1980-83, Tandem-Linac Facility Argonne Nat. Lab., 1983-86, Holifield Rsch. Facility, 1988-90, Holifield Radioactive Ion Beam Facility, 1994-97; chmn. Gordon Conf. on Nuclear Chemistry, 1965, Gordon Conf. on Ion Exch., 1969, rev. com. UNISOR, Oak Ridge Nat. Lab., 1974-75, subcom. high spin and nuclei far from stability Dept. Energy-NSF, 1983; vis. fellow Japan Soc. for Promotion of Sci., 1981; co-organizer Int. Conf. Nuclear Physics, 1980, workshop on nuclear str., 1986, workshop Nat. Gamma-Ray Facility, 1987. Guggenheim fellow, 1966-67, Fullbright fellow, 1977. Fellow AAAS, Am. Phys. Soc. (shared Tom W. Bonner award 1980); mem. Am. Chem. Soc. (award in nuclear chemistry 1993). Achievements include research in nuclear spectroscopy, coulomb excitation, high-spin nuclear structure. Home: 574 Santa Clara Ave Berkeley CA 94707-1647 Office: Lawrence Berkeley Nat Lab One Cyclotron Rd MS88R0192 Berkeley CA 94720-8101 E-mail: rmdiamond@lbl.gov.

DIAMOND, RICHARD S. lawyer; b. Newark, June 26, 1960; BA in Econs./Bus. Adminstrn., Rutgers U., 1981; JD, Seton Hall U., 1985. Bar: N.J. 1985, Fla. 1991, U.S. Dist. Ct. N.J. 1991; cert. matrimonial trial, Laywer by the N.J. Supreme Ct. cert. divorce mediator; ct. apptd. econ. mediator N.J. Supreme Ct. Law sec. to Hon. Burton J. Ironson State of N.J., Union County, N.J., 1985-86; assoc. Law Firm of Robert Diamond, Springfield, N.J.; ptnr. Diamond Hodes & Diamond, Springfield, Gourvitz, Diamond, Hodes, Braun & Diamond, Springfield, Diamond & Diamond P.A., Millburn, N.J. Spkr., guest lectr. TV and radio broadcasts. Contbr. articles to profl. jours. Mem. Union County Bar Assn.), Essex County Bar (matrimonial practice), N.J. Bar Assn. (lectr., speaker). Avocations: racquetball, running. Office: Diamond & Diamond PA 225 Millburn Ave Ste 208 Millburn NJ 07041-1712 Fax: 973-379-9210. E-mail: njdivorcelawyer@aol.com.

DIAMOND, ROBERT MACH, higher education administrator; b. Schenectady, N.Y., Mar. 5, 1930; s. Henry Gordon and Ruth Ada (Mach) D.; m. Dolores Lou Jacobs, Apr. 14, 1957; children: Harli Fait, H. Gordon. AB, Union Coll., Schenectady, 1951; MA, NYU, 1953, PhD, 1962. Secondary sch. tchr. math., TV tchr., TV project dir. Schenectady Pub. Schs., 1956-59; assoc. prof. edn., instructional TV prodn. supr. San Jose State U., 1959-63; dir. instructional rsch., vis. prof. U. Miami, Coral Gables, Fla., 1963-66; dir. instructional resources ctr., prof. edn. SUNY, Fredonia, 1966-71; asst. vice chancellor instrnl. devel., dir., prof. edn. Syracuse (N.Y.) U. Ctr. for Instructional Devel., 1971-97, rsch. prof., dir. Inst. Change in Higher Edn., 1998-99; rsch. prof. Syracuse U., 1999—; pres. Nat. Acad. Academic Leadership, St. Petersburg, Fla., 1999—. Nat. adv. bd. Bur. of Handicapped, Office of Edn.; dir. Focus in Tchg. Project, Fund for Improvement of Postsecondary Edn., Washington; Fulbright sr. lectr., 1976; dir. Nat. Project on Instnl. Priorities and Faculty Rewards, Lilly Endowment and Pew Charitable Trusts, Indpls., Phila., 1989-95; cons. NIH, NSF, Office of Edn., various colls., univs. and assns.; lectr. in field. Author: A Guide to Instructional Television, 1964, Designing and Improving Courses and Curricula in Higher Education, 1989, Serving on Promotion and Tenure Committees, A Faculty Guide, 1994, Preparing for Tenure and Promotion Review, 1995; co-author: Instructional Development for Individualized Learning in Higher Education, 1975, National Study of Teaching Assistants, 1987, A National Study of Research Universities on the Perceived Balance Between Research and Undergraduate Teacher, 1991; editor: Field Guide to Academic Leadership, 2002; co-editor: Recognizing Faculty Work: Reward Systems for the Year 2000, 1993, Preparing for Promotion & Tenure Review, 1995, Changing Priorities at Research Universities, 1997, Designing & Assessing Courses and Curriculum, 1998, Aligining Faculty Records With Institution Mission, 1999, The Disciples Speak, Vol. I, 1995, Vol. II, 2000; mem. editl bd. Jour. Higher Ednl. Rsch. and Devel., South African Jour. Edn.; contbr. chpts. to books and articles to profl. jours. Bd. dirs. Temple Adath, 1990-94, Jewish Family Svcs., Syracuse, 1975-83. With U.S. Army, 1973-75. Recipient award for Outstanding Practice in Instructional Devel., Assn. Ednl. Comm. and Tech., 1989. Mem. Am. Assn. Higher Edn. (cited for innovations in the improvement of higher edn. 1994). E-mail: r.m.diamond@worldnet.att.net.

DIAMOND, ROBERT MICHAEL, lawyer; b. N.Y.C., Dec. 23, 1948; s. Meyer and Libby (Leventhal) D.; m. Amy B. Pullman, July 5, 1987; children: Michael Israel, Philip Brenner, Julia Rose. AB, Colgate U., 1970; JD, Columbia U., 1974. Bar: D.C. 1974, Va. 1976, Md. 1982. Assoc. Fried, Frank, Harris, Shriver & Kampelman, Washington, 1974-75; from assoc. to ptnr. Reed Smith, LLP, Falls Church, Va., 1975—. Contbr. articles to profl. jours. and industry publications. Trustee Cmty. Assns. Inst., Alexandria, Va., sec., 1993, treas., 1994, pres.-elect, 1995, pres., 1996, liaison to Joint Editl. Bd. for Uniform Real

Estate Acts, 1997—; mem. condominium subcom. Va. Housing Study Commn., 1993, 96. Recipient various awards Cmty. Assns. Inst. including Outstanding Vol. 1989, Pres. Award for Outstanding Leadership, 1989-90. Mem. Coll. Cmty. Assn. Lawyers. Avocations: scuba diving, classic automobiles. Office: Reed Smith LLP 3110 Fairview Park Dr Ste 1400 Falls Church VA 22042-4503 E-mail: rdiamond@reedsmith.com.

DIAMOND, SEYMOUR, physician; b. Chgo., Apr. 15, 1925; s. Nathan Avruum and Rose (Roth) D.; m. Elaine June Flamm, June 20, 1948; children: Judi, Merle, Amy. Student, Loyola U., 1943-45; MB, Chgo. Med. Sch., 1948, MD, 1949. Intern White Cross Hosp., Columbus, Ohio, 1949-50; gen. practice medicine Chgo., 1950—; dir. Diamond Headache Clinic, Ltd., Chgo., 1970—; dir. inpatient headache unit St. Joseph Hosp., Chgo.; prof. neurology Finch U. Health Scis. Finch U. Health Scis., Chgo. Med. Sch., 1970-82, 85—, adj. prof. cellular and molecular pharmacology, 1985—, clin. professor family medicine, 1999—; clin. prof. dept. family medicine U. Medicine and Dentistry N.J. Sch. Osteo. Medicine, Stratford, N.J., 1994-98; cons. mem. FDA Orphan Products Devel. Initial Rev. Group. Lectr. dept. cmty. and family medicine Loyola U. Stritch Sch. Medicine, 1972-78; lectr. Falconbridge lecture series Laurentian U., Sudbury, Ont., Can., 1987; disting. lectr. neurology U. Tenn., 1992, AMA cons. on drug evaluation, 1993; mem. sci. com. neurology Internat. Jour. Pain Therapy, 1993; mem. panel Nat. Ctr. on Addiction and Substance Abuse, Columbia U., N.Y.C., 2003. Author: A Pain Specialist's Approach to the Headache Patient, 1994; (with Bill and Cynthia Still) The Hormone Headache, 1995; Diagnosing and Managing Headaches, 1994, 3d edit., 2001; (with Donald J. Dalessio) The Practicing Physician's Approach to Headache, 5th edit., 1992, More Than Two Aspirin: Help for Your Headache Problem, 1976, (with Judi Diamond-Falk) Advice from the Diamond Headache Clinic, 1982, (with Mary Franklin Epstein) Coping with Your Headaches, 1982, 2d edit., 1987, (with Arnold P. Friedman MD) Headache in Contemporary Patient Management series, 1983; (with Amy Diamond Vye) Headache and Diet, 1990; (with Michael Maliszewski) Sexual Aspects of Headaches, 1992; (with Mary A. Franklin) Conquering Your Migraine, 2001; (with Amy Diamond) Headache and Your Child, 2001; (with Merle L. Diamond) Contemporary Diagnosis and Management of Headache and Migraine, 2d edit., 2000; contbg. author: Wolff's Headache and Other Head Pain, 6th edit., 1993, Handbook of Pain Management, 2d edit., 1994, Nonsteroidal Anti-Inflammatory Drugs, 2d edit., 1994, Current Review of Pain, 1994, New Advances in Headache Research, 1994, Conn's Current Therapy, 1998, Advanced Therapy of Headache, 1999, Diamond and Dalessio's Practicing Physician's Approach to Headache, 6th edit., 1999; editor: Migraine Headache Prevention and Management; editor-in-chief Headache Quar., 1990-2002; editor-in-chief Headache and Pain, 2003—; mem. internat. editl. bd. Pediat. Drugs, 2001—; editl. cons. BIOSIS, 1986-90; contbr. numerous articles on headache and related fields to profl. jours. Bd. govs. Finch U. of Health/Chgo. Med. Sch. Recipient Disting. Alumni award Chgo. Med. Sch., 1977; Nat. Migraine Found. lectureship award, 1982, award Headache Consortium of New Eng., 1997, Cert. Appreciation, Chgo. Med. Soc., 1998, Presdl. award Alumni Assn. Chgo. Med. Sch., 2002; 1st recipient Migraine Trust lectureship, 1988; Brit. Migraine Trust 7th Internat. Migraine Symposium, London; Nat. Headache Found. Seymour Diamond fellow, 1993; Disting. lectr. in neurology U. Tenn., 1992. Fellow Royal Soc. Medicine; mem. AMA (Physicians Recognition awards 1970-73, 74, 77, 79, 82, 87, del. sect. clin. pharmacology and therapeutics 1987-89, mem. health policy agenda for Am. People, mem. Cost Effectiveness Conf., del. reference com. "C" on edn., reference com. C, 1988), mem. Bd. of Scientific and Policy Advs. for The Am. Council on Sci. and Health, So. Med. Assn., Am. Assn. Study of Headache (exec. dir. 1971-85, pres. 1972-74, #1 regent mem. 1984, svc. award 1971-85, Lifetime Achievement award 1999), Nat. Headache Found. (pres. 1971-77, exec. dir. 1977-95, exec. chmn. 1995—, 1st recipient cert. of added qualification in headache mgmt. Nat. Bd. Cert. in Headache Mgmt. 2001), World Fedn. Neurology (exec. officer 1980-95, research group on migraine and headache), Ill. Acad. Gen. Practice (chmn. mental health com. 1966-70), Ill. Med. Soc., Chgo. Med. Soc., Assn. for Applied Psychophisiology and Biofeedback, Internat. Assn. Study of Pain, Am. Soc. Clin. Pharmacology and Therapeutics (chmn. headache sect. 1982-89, mem. com. coordination sci. sects. 1983-89), Postgrad. Med. Assn. (pres. 1981). Office: 467 W Deming Pl Ste 500 Chicago IL 60614-1726 *I derive great satisfaction from helping a person who is totally disabled from pain to again lead a normal, functional life.*

DIAMOND, SHARI SEIDMAN, law and psychology educator, researcher; b. Chgo., Mar. 17, 1947; d. Leon Harry and Rita (Wolff) S.; m. Stewart Howard Diamond, Nov. 1, 1970; 1 child, Nicole. BA in Psychology, Sociology, U. Mich., 1968; MA in Psychology, Northwestern U., 1970, PhD in Social Psychology, 1972; JD with honors, U. Chgo., 1985. Bar: Ill. 1985. Rsch. assoc. Sch. Law U. Chgo., 1972-73; asst. prof. psychology and criminal justice U. Ill., Chgo., 1973-79, assoc. prof., 1979-90, prof., 1990-2000; assoc. Sidley & Austin, Chgo., 1985-87; sr. rsch. fellow ABF, Chgo., 1987—; lectr. U. Chgo. Law Sch., 1994-96; prof. law and psychology Northwestern U., 1999—, Stanton Clinton sr. rsch. prof., 2000-01, Howard J. Trienens prof. law, 2002—. Cons. govtl. and pub. interests groups including Rsch. Adv. Panel for U.S. Sentencing Commn., 1987-91; acad. visitor dept. law London Sch. Econs., 1981; hon. fellow Ctr. for Urban Affairs Northwestern U., Evanston, Ill., 1973-73; hon. rsch. assoc. U. London, 1970; speaker, lectr. in field; mem. NAS panel on sentencing rsch., 1981-83, panel on forensic DNA evidence, 1994-96. Editor Law and Soc. Rev., 1988-91; past mem. editorial bd. Law and Soc. Rev., 1983-88, Law and Human Behavior, Crime and Justice Annual, Evaluation Rev.; reviewer NSF; contbr. articles to profl. jours. Chair Coll. Edn. Policy Com., 1979-80; dir. tng. grant NIMH Crime and Delinquency, 1979-80. Fellow Northwestern U., 1968-69, NIMH, 1969-71; grantee Spencer Found., 1972-74, disting. scholar, grantee, U. Ill., 1995-98, Law Enforcement Assistance Adminstrn., 1974-76, Ctr. for Crime and Delinquency NIMH, 1976-81, NSF, 1980-83, 90-92, 99—; B. Kenneth West U. scholar, 1995-98. Fellow APA (Award for Disting. Contbns. to Rsch. in Pub. Policy 1991), Am. Psychol. Soc.; mem. ABA, Am. Psychology-Law Soc. (pres. 1987-88), Law and Soc. Assn. (trustee 1979-82). Office: Northwestern U Law Sch 357 E Chicago Ave Chicago IL 60611

DIAMOND, SIDNEY, chemist, educator; b. N.Y.C., Nov. 10, 1929; s. Julius and Ethel D.; m. Harriet Urish, May 2, 1953; children: Florence, Julia. BS, Syracuse U., 1950; M.F., Duke U., 1951, PhD, Purdue U., 1963. Research engr. U.S. Bur. Public Rds. (now Fed. Hwy. Adminstrn.), Washington, 1953-61, research chemist, 1961-65; assoc. prof. engring. materials Purdue U., 1965-69, prof., 1969—2002, prof. emeritus, 2002—; pres. Sidney Diamond and Assocs., Inc. Mem. Nat. Materials Adv. Bd. Com. on Status of Research in U.S. Cement and Concrete Industries; chmn. Internat. Symposium on Durability of Glass Fiber Reinforced Concrete, Chgo., 1985; mem. adv. com. NSF Ctr. for Advanced Cement-Based Materials, 1989—. Contbr. numerous articles on cement and concrete to profl. jours.; editor: Cement and Concrete Research. Served with U.S. Army, 1951-53. Fellow Am. Ceramic Soc. (past trustee, Copeland award), Am. Concrete Inst., Am. Concrete Inst. (anderson award 1993); mem. ASTM, Internat. Congress on Chemistry of Cement (pres. sect. 6 of 8th congress), Materials Rsch. Soc. Home: 819 Essex St West Lafayette IN 47906-1534 Office: Purdue U Sch Civil Engring West Lafayette IN 47907

DIAMOND, STANLEY JAY, lawyer; b. Los Angeles, Nov. 27, 1927; s. Philip Alfred and Florence (Fadem) D.; m. Lois Jane Broida, June 22, 1969; children: Caryn Elaine, Diana Beth. BA, UCLA, 1949; JD, U. So. Calif., 1952. Bar: Calif. 1953. Practiced law, Los Angeles, 1953—; dep. Office of Calif. Atty. Gen., Los Angeles, 1953; ptnr. Diamond & Tilem, Los Angeles, 1957-60, Diamond, Tilem & Colden, Los Angeles, 1960-79, Diamond & Wilson, Los Angeles, 1979—. Lectr. music and entertainment law UCLA; Mem. nat. panel arbitrators Am. Arbitration Assn. Bd. dirs. Los Angeles Suicide Prevention Center, 1971-76. Served with 349th Engr. Constrn. Bn. AUS, 1945-47. Mem. ABA, Calif. Bar Assn., Los Angeles County Bar Assn., Beverly Hills Bar Assn., Am. Judicature Soc., Calif. Copyright Conf., Nat. Acad. Rec. Arts and Scis., Zeta Beta Tau, Nu Beta Epsilon. Office: 12304 Santa Monica Blvd Fl 3D Los Angeles CA 90025-2551

DIAMOND, STUART, business executive, educator, lawyer, consultant; b. Camden, N.J., June 20, 1948; s. Irving H. and Ruth (Safran) D. BA in English, Rutgers U., 1970; JD, Harvard U., 1990; MBA, U. Pa., 1992. Bar: N.J. 1990, N.Y. 1991. Mcpl., investigative, polit., energy, tech. and fin. reporter Home News, New Brunswick, NJ, 1969—73, Newsday, L.I., NY, 1973—84, The N.Y. Times, N.Y.C., 1984—88; assoc. Morgan Stanley, N.Y.C., 1989, Sullivan & Cromwell, N.Y.C., 1989; assoc. dir. Harvard negotiation project, exec. dir. Conflict Mgmt. Group Harvard U. Sch. Law, Cambridge, Mass., 1990—92; CEO Global Strategy Group, L.I., L.A., Phila., NY, 1991—; prof. Wharton Sch. U. Pa., Phila., 1993—; chmn., CEO i-Luxury.com, 2000—01; chmn. High Speed Net Solutions, 2001. Lectr., TV commentator, 1978—, cons. U.N., 1991-97. Author: It's In Your Power, 1978, No-Cost, Low-Cost Energy Tips, 1980; contbg. editor: Omni mag., 1978-81; documentary films: The Energy War, 1980, The Future is Now, 1981; also nat. mag. cover stories. Recipient Amos Tuck award nat. econ. reporting, 1978, 80, 82, Polk award nat. reporting, 1980, Pulitzer Prize, 1987, Tchg. award Wharton, 1997, 98, 2001, 02; named Pietro & Elvira Giorgi lectr. in law, 2000. Mem. ABA, N.Y. Bar Assn., N.J. Bar Assn., Sigma Delta Chi.

DIAMOND, SUSAN ZEE, management consultant; b. Okla., Aug. 20, 1949; d. Louis Edward and Henrietta (Wood) Diamond; m. Allan T. Devitt, July 27, 1974. AB, U. Chgo., 1970; MBA, DePaul U., 1979. Dir. study guide prodn. Am. Sch. Co., Chgo., 1972—75; supr. publs. Allied Van Lines, Broadview, Ill., 1975—78, sr. account svcs. rep., 1978—79; pres. Diamond Assocs. Ltd., Bensenville, Ill., 1978—. Author: Records Management: A Practical Guide, 3d edit., 1995, Seventeen Steps to Slimness: A Sherlockian Guide to Dieting, 2002; editor: The Serpentine Muse, 1996—. Mem.: Assn. Record Mgrs. and Adminstrs., Inst. Mgmt. Accts., Baker St. Irregulars, Adventuresses of Sherlock Holmes.

DIAMOND, WENDI T. physician; b. Framingham, Mass., Mar. 6, 1964; d. Maurice and Anne (Berman) D.; m. Darrel P. Cohen, May 24, 1992; children: Marissa Diamond Cohen, Eric S. Cohen. AB, Harvard U., 1986; MD, Boston U., 1991. Diplomate Nat. Bd. Med. Examiners; diplomate in gen. psychiatry, child and adolescent psychiatry Am. Bd. Psychiatry and Neurology. Resident in psychiatry Walter Reed Army Med. Ctr., Washington, 1991-95; staff psychiatrist Ft. Bragg/Womack Army Med. Ctr., Fort Bragg, N.C., 1995-97, Duke U., Durham, N.C., 1997-98, fellow in child and adolescent psychiatry, 1998-2000. Mem. Am. Psychiat. Assn., Am. Acad. Child and Adolescent Psychiatry. Office: Integrated Behavioral Care 35 Beechwood Rd Ste 3A/B Summit NJ 07924

DIAMONDSTONE, LAWRENCE, retired paper company executive; b. N.Y.C., Mar. 27, 1928; s. Harry A. and Sally (Margulies) D.; m. Helen O'connor, Dec. 8, 1984 (div.); 1 child, Cynthia Ann. BS, U. Ill., 1950. Founder, pres., CEO, chmn. bd., officer Newbrook Paper Divsn., N.Y.C., 1958-99, Triangle Mktg. Corp., N.Y.C., 1975-99; ret., 1999. Home: 2 Beekman Pl New York NY 10022-8058

DIAMONSTEIN-SPIELVOGEL, BARBARALEE, writer, television interviewer/ producer; b. N.Y.C. d. Rubin Robert and Sally H. Simmons; m. Alan A. Diamonstein, July 22, 1956; m. Carl Spielvogel, Oct. 27, 1981. BA, BC, MA, Doctorate, NYU, 1963; DHL (hon.), Md. Inst. Coll. Art, 1990, Longwood U., 1995. Staff asst. The White House, 1963-66; 1st dir. Dept. Cultural Affairs City of New York, 1966-67; dir. of Forums McCall Corp., 1967-69; editor spl. supplements, columnist Harper's Bazaar, 1969-71; spl. project dir., guest editor Art News, 1971-93. Columnist Ladies Home Jour., 1979-84; contbr. to Saturday Rev., Vogue, Ms., Partisan Rev., N.Y. Times, Condé Nast, Traveller, House & Garden, others; mem. faculty Hunter Coll., CUNY, 1974-76, New Sch., 1976-84, Duke U. (Inst. Policy Scis.), 1978; arts cons. Sunday Morning CBS-TV, 1978-82; curator Buildings Reborn, Collaborations, Visions and Images, Remaking America, The Landmarks of N.Y. I, II & III (internat. travelling museum exhbns.), 1978—, and numerous others. TV interviewer, producer About the Arts, WNYC-TV, 1975—79, ABC-TV Arts, 1980—88, A&E Network, 1980—89; Leo Castelli Gallery, 1978, 1984, 1988, 1994; author: Open Secrets: 94 Women in Touch With Our Time, 1972, The World of Art, 1902-77, 75 Years of Art News, 1977, Buildings Reborn: New Uses, Old Places, 1978, Inside New York's Art World, 1979, Collaboration: Artists and Architects, 1981, Visions and Images: American Photographers on Photography, 1981, Interior Design: The New Freedom, 1982, Handmade in America, 1983, Fashion: The Inside Story, 1985, American Architecture Now, 1985, Remaking America, 1986, The Landmarks of New York, 1988, 18 Wonders of the New York World, 1992, The Landmarks of New York: Vol. II, 1993, Inside the Art World: Conversations with Barbaralee Diamonstein, 1994, Skills, Values, Dreams, 1995, Singular Voices: Americans Who Make a Difference, 1997, The Landmarks of New York: Vol. III, 1998, Barbaralee's Rules of the Road: 59 Simple Ways to Cope with a Complex World, 2001; editor: Our 200 Years: Tradition and Renewal, 1975, MOMA at 50, 1980. Commr. N.Y.C. Landmarks Preservation Commn., 1972—87, N.Y.C. Cultural Commn., 1975—86, N.Y.C. Arts Commn., 1991—94; vice-chmn. N.Y. Landmarks Conservancy, 1983—87; bd. advisors Film Anthology Archives, 1969—; chmn. N.Y. Landmarks Preservation Found., 1987—95; mem. Pres.' coun. Rockefeller U., 1987—; bd. visitors Pub. Policy Inst. Duke U., 1987—93; mem. meml. coun. U.S.Holocaust Mus., 1987—93; meml. coun. Holocaust Mus., 1987—93, chair Art Pub. Spaces com., 1987—96; bd. dirs. PEN Am. Ctr., 1980—96; chair Hist. Landmarks Preservation Ctr., 1995—; bd. trustees Mus. of Women, N.Y.C., 1999—; trustee N.Y. Hist. Soc., 1993—95, Central Park Conservancy, 1993—95; mem. drawing com. Met. Mus. Art, 1990—, Whitney Mus. Am. Art, 1995—98, bd. dirs., 1995—98, White House Endowment Fund, 1995—98; mem. U.S. Commn. Fine Arts, 1996—, vice-chmn., 2001—02; bd. dirs. Mcpl. Art Soc., 1973—83, Am. Coun. Arts, 1982—89, N.Y.C. Bicentennial Commn., 1973—77, Bklyn. Acad. Music, 1969—74, N.Y. Landmarks Conservancy, 1973—97, Fresh Air Fund, 1983—, Big Apple Circus, 1989—92, Corcoran Gallery Art, Washington, 1992—99, N.Y. State Hist. Archive's Trust, 1994—. Recipient Founder's Day award Pratt Inst., 1994, Outstanding Citizen award Citizen Ctrs., 1996, Heritage Trails award, 1998, Spirit of the City award Women's City Club, 1998, Manhattan award, 1999, New Millenium Humanitarian award HELP, 1999, Gen. Milan R. Stefanik award Slovak Am. Cultural Ctr., 2002, Aging in Am. Humanitarian award, 2003. Mem.: Assn. Culture Edn. and Comm. (co-chair 2001—). Home: 720 Park Ave New York NY 10021-4954

DIANA, JOSEPH A. retired foundation executive; b. New Castle, Pa., June 26, 1924; s. Joseph Anthony and Emma (Eardly) D.; m. Kathryn June Matthews, June 26, 1946; children: Mark Steven, Chris Joseph, Todd Francis, Paul Jeffrey. Student, Notre Dame U., 1942; BA, U. Mich., 1950, postgrad., 1950-51. Mem. adminstrv. staff U. Mich., 1950-56, sec. to faculty Med. Sch., 1956-69, asst. controller, 1969-70; v.p. fin. and mgmt. SUNY, Stony Brook, 1970-75; vice chancellor adminstrv. affairs, assoc. v.p. bus. affairs U. Ill., Champaign-Urbana, 1975-79; v.p., treas. emeritus John D. and Catherine T. MacArthur Found., Chgo.; pres. Dianaid Ltd., 1985-91. Interim pub. Harper's mag.; sec., treas. Harper's Mag. Found., 1980-82. Republican. Roman Catholic. Home: 2310 Saint Francis Dr Ann Arbor MI 48104-4807

DIANGELO, JOSEPH ANTHONY, JR., finance educator, dean; b. Phila., July 5, 1948; s. Joseph Anthony and Lucy (Lazzaro) Diangelo; m. Frances R. Marcelli, Mar. 18, 1972; children: Deana Diangelo, Kristen Diangelo, Joseph Anthony Diangelo III. BS, St. Joseph's U., 1970; MBA, Widener U., 1975; EdD, Temple U., 1985. Tchr. St. Thomas More HS, Phila., 1970-75; archbishop Carroll HS, Radnor, Pa., 1975-78; prof. mgmt. St. Joseph's U., Phila., 1978-80, dean Erivan K. Haub Sch. Bus., 2000—; prof., asst. dean Widener U., Chester, Pa., 1980-87, dean, 1985, asst. provost for grad. studies, 1986-88, dean Sch. mgmt., 1987-2000. Cons. Chespenn Health Svc., Chester, 1984. Contbr. articles to profl. jours. Pres., bd. dirs. Children's Clinic, Chester, 1983—86; gov.'s appointee Trial Ct. Nominating Com. Delaware County, Pa., 1987—; mem. pvt. industry coun. Delaware County, 1990—, workforce investment bd., 1999—; Delaware County Common Pleas Ct. appointee Sch. Dist. Bd. Control; chmn. edn. com., bd. dirs. Columbus Quincentennial Found., 1989—92; mem. Pa. Amb. Team, 1999—. With USNG, 1970—76. Mem.: ASTD, Am. Assn. Colls. Bus. Adminstrn. (bd. dirs. 2003—), Mid-Atlantic Assn. Colls. Bus. Adminstrn. (exec. com. 1994—98, 1st v.p. 1995, pres. 1996—97, sec. 2000—), Am. Arbitration Assn., Acad. Mgmt., Soc. Human Resource Mgmt., Soc. Advancement Mgmt. (Disting. Prof. award 1980—81), Assn. Adv. Coll. Bus. (bus. accreditation com. 1998—2001, bd. dirs. 2003—). Roman Catholic. Avocations: tennis, golf. Office: Widener U 14th Chestnut St Chester PA 19013

DIANTO, LINDA CHRISTINE, therapeutic activities coordinator, administrator; b. Bklyn., Dec. 11, 1949; d. Salvatore and Josephine (Battaglia) Lore; m. Nicholas L. Dianto, June 26, 1971. AA in Psychology, Staten Island C.C., 1969; BA, Richmond Coll., Staten Island, 1971, MS in Edn., 1974; 6th Yr. Cert., NYU, 1988, cert. in Philanthropy and Fundraising. Cert. tchr., N.Y.; cert. therapeutic recreation specialist; cert. recreation mgr.; lic. recreation adminstr. Tchr. St. Mary's Sch., Staten Island, 1971-74; staff Vacation Day Camp, N.Y.C. Bd. Edn., 1973-75; dir. activities and vols. Golden Gate Health Care Ctr., Staten Island, 1974-86; recreation cons. Princeton (N.J.) Nursing Home, 1980-81, Sheepshead Nursing Home, Bklyn., 1984-86; dir. Coler Goldwater Splty. Hosp., Roosevelt Island, NY, 1988—2002; coord. therapeutic activities St. Elizabeth Ann's Adult Day Care Ctr, S.I., 2002—. Lectr.; seminar presenter. Treas., Deborah Heart Found., Staten Island, 1985-85, v.p. membership com., 1986-88; scholarship chair Chiropractic Edn. Found., Inc., Albany, N.Y., 1985—; treas. Met. N.Y. Recreation and Parks Soc., 1995—, Grasmere Civic Assn., 2003. Recipient Worker's Pin, Deborah Hosp. Found., 1984, Disting. Svc. award N.Y. State Chiropractic Assn. Dist. 5, 1985; Tom and Ruth Rivers scholar, 1986. Mem. N.Y. State Parks and Recreation Soc. (Presdl. citation 1994), Nat. Recreation and Parks Assn., Nat. Therapeutic Recreation Soc., N.Y. State Therapeutic Recreation Assn. (founder), Women's Aux. N.Y. State Chiropractic Assn. (dist. pres. 1981-84, state treas. 1984-85, v.p. 1988-89), World Health and Leisure Assn., Chiropractic Edn. Found., Met. Recreation and Parks Soc. (pres.), Soroptimist Internat. of Manhattan. Roman Catholic. Avocations: travel, interior decorating, playing piano, sewing, antiquing.

DIANZANI, MARIO UMBERTO, pathology educator; b. Grosseto, Italy, June 13, 1925; s. Edgardo and Irma (Bocelli) D.; m. Maria Assunta Mor, Aug. 18, 1956; children: Irma, Chiara, Umberto, Paola. Degree in medicine, U. Siena, Italy, 1948, degree in pharmacy, 1950; hon. doctorate, Brunel U., London, 1978; hon. doctorate in chemistry, U. Genoa, Italy, 1995; hon. doctorate, U. Buenos Aires, 1996. Asst. in gen. pathology U. Siena, 1948-50, prof. gen. pathology, 1964-65; asst. in gen. pathology U. Genoa, Italy, 1950-58; prof. gen. pathology U. Cagliari, Italy, 1958-64, U. Turin, Italy, 1965-2000; ret., dean Faculty Medicine and Surgery, 1971-84, rector magnificus, 1984-96. Author textbook of gen. pathology, 1970. Recipient Premio Feltrinelli, Accademia del Lincei, Rome, 1979, Trevor Slater award, Internat. Free Radical Soc., 1994, Invernizzi prize, 1996, Esculapio prize, 2002. Roman Catholic. Avocations: archeology, fishing. Home: Corso D'Azeglio 118 10126 Turin Italy Office: U Torino Corso Raffaello 30 10125 Turin Italy

DIAS, KATHLEEN R. foreign language educator; b. Phila., Dec. 2, 1950; d. John Joseph and Dorothy; m. Lindolfo C. Dias; 3 children. BA, Immaculata Coll., 1977; cert. acad. excellence, Istituto Italiano di Cultura, Lima, Peru, 1980; MA, Marywood U., 1983; postgrad., Temple U., 1984, U. Pa., 1986-96; cert. proficiency, Berlitz Schs. Langs., 1983. Cert. Spanish K-12 tchr., elem. edn. tchr., 1984, elem./mid. and secondary sch. prin., Pa., 1996. Tchr., program dir. elem. edn., Phila., 1971-74, Chester County, Pa., 1976-78; tutor Fgn. Lang. Affairs, Delaware County, Pa., 1975-76; tchr., dir. Spanish elem. edn. Bucks County, Pa., 1978-79; tchr. ESL Lima, 1979-81; prof. Spanish Immaculata Coll., Pa., 1983, dir. L.Am. studies program, 1983-86; instr. fgn. lang. specialized tutoring program Delaware County, Pa., 1981—; vice-principal Drexel Hill Holy Child Acad., 1997-99, curriculum dir., 1997—. Chmn. VIP dept. U. Pa.; with Am. sect. Mus. Archaeology/Anthropology U. Pa., summers, 1986—, anthropology lab. analysis of Ctrl. and S.Am. artifacts; chmn., tchr. Latin, Spanish and English Holy Child Acad., Drexel Hill, adminstrv. asst., rep. various coms. bd. trustees, 1981-2001; coord. edn. dept. Mus. Anthropology and Archaeology, Univ. Pa., 1995-96, FLES program Haverford Sch. Dist., 2001—; lectr. U. Pa., 1996, Duke U. on Maya studies, 1999. Author 4-yr. lang. program Early Spanish learning for the Elementary School, 1982; Developing a Sensitivity to the Culture and History of Latin America, 1983, Mexico: Land, Culture and People, 1983, The Maya and Aztec Nations, 1984, The Inca Civilization: From Manco Capac to the Spanish Conquest, 1988, Manual for Teachers on Mesoamerican Cultures Grades 7-12, 1997; compilor, editor (study guide) for Hall of Ancient Mex. and Ctrl. Am. at Mus. of Natural History, N.Y.C., 1990; author, editor The Codex, PreColumbian Soc. Pub., 1994-96; contbr. articles to scholarly jours. Mem. citizen's bd. Am. Cancer Rsch.; site mgr./facilitator Maya Quest Interactive Expedition, 1994-95. Nominee Friedel and Otto Eberspacher award for Excellence in Tchg. of a Modern European Lang., Johns Hopkins U., 2001; recipient Disting. Leadership award, Comm. and Tech. award, Pa. State U., 1995; scholar Italian Cultural Attaché scholar, Peru, 1979—81. Mem. MLA, Nat. Coun. Tchrs. English, Assn. Tchrs. Spanish and Portuguese, L.Am. Studies Assn., Pa. Assn. Edn., Pre-Columbian Soc. (bd. dirs. 1993—), Mus. Archaeology and Anthropology of U. Pa.

DIAS, MARK STEVEN, neurosurgeon; b. Vallejo, Calif., Sept. 13, 1956; s. Caesar Joseph and Marian Alice (Angel) D.; m. Dana Beth Cohen, May 30, 1982 (wid. June 1988); 1 child, Erin Rebbeca; m. Anita Louise Grose, May 2, 1992; 1 child, Ethan Scott. BS, U. Calif., Davis, 1978; MD, Johns Hopkins U., 1982. Diplomate Am. Bd. Neurol. Surgery. Resident U. Pitts., 1982-89; fellow U. Utah, Salt Lake City, 1989-91; attending physician Northwestern U./Children's meml. Hosp., Chgo., 1991-93; assoc. prof. neurosurgery U. Buffalo, 1993-2001; chief of pediat. neurosurgery Children's Hosp. of Buffalo/U. Buffalo, N.Y., 1993-2001; assoc. prof. surgery (neurosurgery) Pa. State U. Milton S. Hershey Med. Ctr., Hershey, Pa., 2001—. Contbr. articles to profl. jours., chpts. to books. Profl. adv. coun. Spina Bifida Assn. Am., 1999-2004. Mem. Am. Assn. Neurol. Surgeons (Young Investigators award 1995), Congress of Neurol. Surgeons, Joint Sect. on Pediatrics, Am. Soc. Pediat. Neurosurgeons, Pediat. Oncology Group, Am. Acad. Pediatrics. Avocations: computers, bicyling. Office: Milton S Hershey Med Ctr 500 N Medical Dr Hershey PA 17033

DIASIO, ILSE WOLFARTSBERGER, volunteer; b. Linz, Austria, Nov. 12, 1946; came to U.S., 1967; d. D.I. Gottfried and Elfriede (Stuchlik) Wolfartsberger; m. Robert B. Diasio, July 4, 1970; children: Christoph, Thomas, Michael. Grad. in phys. therapy, U. Vienna, 1965-67. Phys. therapist Yale-New Haven Hosp., 1968-71, Vis. Nurse Assn., Rochester, N.Y., 1971-72; symposium coord. dept. pharmacology U. Ala., 1988. Vol. tchr. German, Pemberton Elem. Sch., Richmond, Va., 1980-84, Vestavia Hills Elem. and H.S., 1985-93; organizer student exch. program between Vestavia Hills H.S. and Seebacher Gymnasium, Graz, Austria, 1990, 91, 94; bd. dirs. World of Opportunity. Bd. dirs. Pemberton (Va.) Elem. Sch. PTA, 1979-84, pres., 1982-84, Va. Commonwealth U. Faculty Woman's Club, 1978-84, Greater Birmingham Ministries, 1998—, chmn. direct svcs. work group, 1999—02, Ala. chpt. Fulbright Assn., 1999—, LWV Greater Birmingham, 1999-2000, World of Opportunity, 2002—; pres. Childrens Svc. League, 1992-93, treas. 1991-92, asst. treas. 1990-91, 2d v.p., rec. sec., 1998-99; vol. Our Lady Queen of the Universe and Sacred Heart of Jesus Cath. Chs., 1988-90; St. Peter's rep. Alab. Arise, diocesan rep., rec. sec., 1988-94; mem. Peace and Justice Commn. of the Cath. Diocese of Birmingham, 1989-95, chair of commn., 1994-95; bd. dirs. Be an Apostle of Christ, 1988—; chair human concerns com. St. Peter's, 1988—; mem. Direct Svc. Network, 1989—; mem. Greater Birmingham Ministries program, 1989—; treas. Greater Birmingham UNA-USA chpt., 1992—, mem. coun. chpts. and divsns. steering com., 2001--; mem. COMPEER Bd., Birmingham, Ala., 1990-99; mem. WOC, Call to Action, Bread for the World, CALC, Pax Christi, Amnesty Internat., Nat. Conf. of Cmty. and Justice, Smithsonian Inst., UNICEF, Coalition Against Hate Crimes, 1997—, Birmingham Com. on Fgn. Rels., 1998—; organizer Christmas gift drive for needy families Angel Tree project St. Peter's Cath. Ch., 1988—; mem. steering com. UNA-USA CCD, 2001—; bd. dirs. The World of Opportunity, sec., 2002—; vol. tchr. for GED preparation. Recipient resolution City of Birmingham, 1999. Mem. AAUW, Nat. Mus. of Women in the Arts, U.S. Holocost Mus., Vereinigung Ehemaliger Körnerschülerinnen, LWV (bd. dirs. Greater Birmingham 1999-2000). Roman Catholic. Avocations: reading, music, skiing, cooking, travelling. Home: 1225 Branchwater Ln Birmingham AL 35216-2001 E-mail: idiasio@aol.com.

DIASIO, RICHARD LEONARD, power transmission executive, sports facility executive, race car manufacturer executive; b. Bridgeport, Conn., Nov. 25, 1937; s. Daniel Joseph and Rose Sarah (Agasi) D.; m. Julia Ann Krhla, Oct. 14, 1961; children: Richard J., Laura L., Christopher S. AS in Mech. Engring., Bridgeport Engring. Inst., 1965. Engr. U.S. Elec. Motors, Milford, Conn., 1962-64; sales prof. Reliance Electric, Hamden, Conn., 1964-66; sales mgr. Dynamatic div. Eaton Corp., Fairfield, N.J., 1966-72; mgr. regional sales Harnischfeger Corp., Woodbridge, N.J., 1972-74; mgr. nat. sales Kanematsu-Gosho, South Plainfield, N.J., 1974-77; dir. mktg. Ind. Gear Works, Indpls., 1977-78, gen. mgr., 1978-80; pres. Ind. Power Transmission Systems, Inc., Indpls, 1980—. Pres. Putnam Park Corp., Putnam County, Ind., 1990—, Diasio Car Co., 1999—. With USAF, 1955-59. Mem. Soc. Mfg. Engrs. (sr.), Dramatists

Guild, Authors League Am. Republican. Roman Catholic. Avocations: auto sports, writing. Achievements include designer Diasio D962 sports racer. Office: Ind Power Transmission Sys 470 Northfield Dr Brownsburg IN 46112-2113

DIAZ, ALAN, photojournalist; b. New York, 1947; Tchr., Univ. of Havana, Cuba, 1968. Photographer, Miami, Fla., 1978; tchr., 1978; freelance photographer AP Miami bur., Miami, Fla., 1994, staff photographer, 2000. The saga of the 6-yr. old Cuban boy gripped the nation for five mths., and Diaz's pictures were often on front pages. He was the only photographer to capture the pivotal moments inside the home in Miami's Little Havana section, and his dramatic pictures were immed. transmitted to AP mem. and subscribers around the world. I was just doing my job," he said afterwards, "I did what I always do - I shoot pictures.". Office: The Assoc Press Photo Dept AP 9100NW 36th St Miami FL 33178*

DIAZ, ALPHONSO VINCENT, aerospace executive; BS in Physics, St. Joseph U.; Ms in Physics, Old Dominion U.; MS in Mgmt., MIT. With NASA, 1964-88, dep. assoc. adminstr. for space sci., 1994-96; divsn. v.p. space and aeronautics svcs. GE Govt. Svcs. Divsn., Cherry Hill, N.J., 1988-89; dept. assoc. adminstr. Office of Space Sci. and Applications, 1989-93; dep. dir. Goddard Space Flight Ctr., Greenbelt, Md., 1996-98, dir., 1998—. Fellow AIAA (assoc.).

DIAZ, BENITO HUMBERTO, lawyer; b. Guines, Cuba, Dec. 6, 1950; came to U.S., 1962; s. Benito Marcos and Concepcion (Valdes) D.; m. Maria Adelaida Badenes, May 7, 1983; children: Ana Maria, Benito Ignacio, Patricia Maria. B.A., St. Peter's Coll., Jersey City, 1973; J.D., Duke U., 1976. Bar: Fla. 1976, U.S. Dist. Ct. (so. dist.) Fla. 1977, U.S. Ct. Appeals (5th cir.) 1977, U.S. Dist. Ct. (mid. dist.) Fla. 1979, U.S. Ct. Appeals (11th cir.) 1981. Assoc. Blackwell, Walker, Gray, Powers, Flick & Hoehl, Miami, Fla., 1976-82, Carroll & Halberg, Miami, 1982—. Vol. United Way of Dade County, Miami, 1982-83. Mem. ABA, Fla. Bar, Dade County Bar Assn., Cuban Am. Bar Assn. Roman Catholic. Office: Carroll & Halberg 2701 S Bayshore Dr Fl 5 Miami FL 33133-5337

DIAZ, CAMERON, actress; b. Long Beach, Calif., Aug. 30, 1972; Grad. high sch., Long Beach, Calif. Appeared in (films) The Mask, 1994, Feeling Minnesota, 1996, She's the One, 1996, The Last Supper, 1996, Keys to Tulsa, 1996, Head Above Water, 1996, My Best Friend's Wedding, 1997 (Blockbuster Entertainment award), a Life Less Ordinary, 1997, (television) Space Ghost Coast to Coast, 1994, Very Bad Things, 1998, Fear and Loathing in Las Vegas, 1998, There's Something About Mary, 1998 (N.Y. Film Critics Cir. award, MTV Movie award, Am. Comedy award), Invisible Circus, 1999, Being John Malkovich, 1999, Any Given Sunday, 1999, Charlie's Angels: The Movie, 2000, Things You Can Tell Just by Looking at Her, 2000, Shrek (voice), 2001, Vanilla Sky, 2001, The Sweetest Thing, 2002, Gangs of New York, 2002, Charlie's Angels: Full Throttle, 2003. Named Female Star of Tomorrow, Nat. Theatre Owners Assn., 1996, Boston Soc. of Film Critics best supporting actress award, 2001, Chicago Film Critics Award for best supporting actress, 2002. Address: c/o Nick Styne Creative Artist Agency 9830 Wilshire Blvd Beverly Hills CA 90212-1825*

DIAZ, ELENA R. community health nurse; b. Albuquerque; d. Maria E. Lopez. BSN, U. Ariz., 1975. RNC, ANA; cert. cmty. health nurse. Community health nurse Pima County Health Dept., Tucson, 1975—. Ad hoc com. for minority recruitment and retention Coll. Nursing U. Ariz. Tucson. Recipient St. Cyril's Clair Dunn/Judith Lovchik award Peace and Justice Com., 1987, La Esperanza award, 1987. Mem. Am. Assn. Hispanic Nurses (coun.), Nat. Alliance for Hispanic Health, Tucson Assn. Hispanic Nurses, Phi Beta Kappa. Office: Pima County Health Dept South Office 175 W Irvington Tucson AZ 85714

DIAZ, FERNANDO GUSTAVO, neurosurgeon; s. Fernando Diaz Calderon and Susana (Barriga) D.; children: Fernando Austin, David Frederick, Sean Christopher, Patrick Aaron. BS, Centro Universitario Mex., 1963; MD, Univ. de Mex., 1969; MA, U. Kans., Kansas City, 1973; PhD, U. Minn., 1979; MA in Bus., Cen. Mich. U., Mt. Pleasant, 1987; JD, Wayne State U., 1995. Diplomate Am. Bd. Neurological Surgery; lic. physician and surgeon Mex., Can., Ill., Mich., Fla.; mem. Michigan Bar, 1995. Intern Regina Gen. Hosp., Sask., Can., 1969-70, resident in anethesia, 1971; resident in gen. surgery U. Kans., Kansas City, 1971-73; resident in neurosurgery U. Minn. Hosps., Mpls., 1973-78; staff neurosurgeon Henry Ford Hosp., Detroit, 1978-87; chmn. Neurosci. Inst. Santa Fe, Gainesville, Fla., 1987-90; prof., chmn. dept. neurol. surgery Wayne State U., Detroit, 1990—; chief med. officer Detroit Med. Ctr., 2000—; cert. physician exec. ACPE, 2002. Neurosurg. nat. cons. to U.S. Surgeon Gen., USAF, 1991; coord. neurosurgery resident edn. Henry Ford Hosp., 1979—; clin. assoc. prof. surgery U. Mich., 1986—; mem. working group in neurosurgery WHO. Mem. editl. bd. Neurosurgery Jour.; contbr. articles to profl. jours. Lt. col. USAFR. Recipient awards Lily Pharms., Merck, Sharp & Dome Pharms., Organon Labs. Fellow Am. Chem. Soc., Interam. Coll. Physicians, Internat. Coll. Surgeons (vice regent U.S. sect. 1985); mem. AMA, Neurosurg. Soc. Am., Soc. Neurol. Surgeons, Mich. Med. Soc., Wayne County Med. Soc., Am. Assn. Neurol. Surgeons (cerebrovascular sect.), Congress of Neurol. Surgeons, Mich. Assn. Neurol. Surgeons (sec.-treas. 1984-86, v.p. 1986, pres. 1997-98), Detroit Neurosurg. Acad. (v.p. 1986-90), Soc. Critical Care Medicine, Mich. Heart Assn. (chmn. stroke com. 1984-86, cmty. site ad-hoc com. 1984, cmty. programs and edn. com. 1986), Mich. Assn. Neurosurgery (chmn. bd.), L.Am. Fedn. Neurosurgery (sec. gen., 1999-2002), Council State Neurological Soc.(vice chair) U. Minn. Alumni Assn. Roman Catholic. Office: Wayne State U Neurol Surg 4201 Saint Antoine St Detroit MI 48201-2153 E-mail: diaz@neurosurg.wayne.edu.

DIAZ, JUDY L. language educator; b. Manitowoc, Wis., Feb. 16, 1957; d. Patrick Daniel Kealey and Charlotte Mae (McCarthy) Kealey-Redding; m. Carlos Ricardo Diaz; children: Carlos Alejandro, David Ricardo. BA in English, U. West Fla., 1978, MA in Eng., 1984. Cert. pvt. pilot FAA. Tchr. ESL Instituto de Ingles, San Jose, Costa Rica, 1978; vol. U.S. Peace Corps, Mindanao, Philippines, 1979—81; EKG technician West Fla. Hosp., Pensacola, 1981—84; adj. English instr. Pensacola Jr. Coll., 1984—90; writing/reading lab. supr. Pensacola Jr. Coll., Warrington Campus, 1991—97, English instr., 1997—2000, asst. prof. English, 2000—02. Chmn. student excellence awards com. Pensacola Jr. Coll., 1998—2001, advisor faculty coun., 2000—02, rep. Faculty Assn., 2000—02; judge Health Occupations Students Assn., Pensacola, 1999—. Contbr. articles to mag. Mem.: Acad. Tchg. Excellence, Fla. Coll. English Assn., Fla. Assn. C.C.'s, Nat. Coun. Tchrs. English. Avocations: building bluebird houses, literature research, jogging, flying, riding Harley-Davidson. Office: Pensacola Jr Coll Warrington Campus Dept Arts & Scis 5555 W Hwy 98 Pensacola FL 32507

DIAZ, MANNY, state representative; m. Sandra Diaz; children: Marcos, Raquel, Lito. BS in Engring., Calif. State U., San Francisco. Housing devel. mgr. Mex. Am. Cmty. Svcs. Agy.; mgr. engring. Pacific Gas and Electric Co.; mem. Calif. Assembly, 2000—. Planning commn., San Jose, 1986—93; transp. bd. Santa Clara County Valley; councilmember San Jose City Coun., 1994—2000. Mem.: Soc. Hispanic Profl. Engrs. San Jose (co-founder). Democrat. Office: PO Box 942849 Rm 2136 Sacramento CA 94249 Address: 100 Paseo De San Antonio Ste 319 San Jose CA 95113*

DIAZ, MANUEL A. mayor; b. Havana, Cuba, Nov. 5, 1954; arrived in U.S., 1961; m. Robin Smith; children: Manny, Natlie, Bobby, Elisa. Grad. with high honors, Miami-Dade C.C., 1975, Fla. Internat. U., 1977; JD, U. Miami. Bar: Fla., U.S. Ct. Appeals (5th cir.), U.S. Dist. Ct. Appeals (11th cir.), U.S. Dist. Ct. (so. dist.) Fla., U.S. Supreme Ct. Founder, mng. ptnr. Berkowitz & Diaz; exec. v.p., gen. counsel Terremark Investment Svcs., Inc.; v.p., gen. counsel Monty's Restaurant Holdings; gen. counsel Fla. Worker's Compensation Ins. Guaranty Assn.; ptnr. Diaz & O'Naghten, L.L.P.; elected mayor City of Miami, 2001—. Founding bd. mem. State Bd. C.C.'s, Fla.; apptd. mem. Fla. Residential Property & Casualty JUA, chmn. investment com.; chmn. Dade County Com. for Fair Representation; bd. mem. numerous cmty. orgns.; founding mem. Little Havana Activities and Nutrition Ctr.; past mem. Little Havana Devel. Authority; founding mem. Coalition Hispanic Am. Women; past chmn. Spanish Am. League Against Discrimination; founding mem. Gtr. Miami United; co-chair Music Fest Miami; past bd. dirs. United Way Hispanic Leadership Devel. Program, Miami's for Me Com. of 100; Leadership Miami; City of Miami Bds. & Coms. Rev. Com.; City of Miami City Atty. Selection Com.; City of Miami Bond Underwriters Selection Com. Office: City Hall 3500 Pan American Dr Miami FL 33133*

DIAZ, MARIA E. director; b. Bloomington, Ill., Aug. 8, 1954; d. Roberto Bosquez and Adela Ramirez-Bosquez; m. Rigoberto Diaz, Mar. 6, 1974; children: Felipe, Andres. Student, Midstate Coll., 1987, Ill. Ctrl. Coll., 1996. Exec. asst. Peoria (Ill.) Friendship House, 1989—94; tchr. asst. Irving Middle Sch., Peoria, 1994—95; sys. operator, key club activities dir., advisor Woodruff H.S., Peoria, 1995—. Neighborhood activist Peoria Cmty.; bd. dirs. Cmty. Found., Peoria. Roman Catholic. Avocations: computers, bicycling, weightlifting. Office: Woodruff High 1800 NE Perry Peoria IL 61603

DIAZ, NELSON, lawyer; b. NYC, May 23, 1947; s. Luis Diaz and Maria (Cancel) Rodriguez; children: Vilmarie, Nelson M.V., Delia Lee. AAS, St. John's U., 1967, BS, 1969; JD, Temple U., 1972; LLD (hon.), LaSalle Coll., 1982, St. John's U., 1987, Temple U., 1990, Albright Coll., 1995, Lincoln U., 1996. Bar: Pa. 1972, D.C. 1978, U.S. Supreme Ct. 1978, N.Y. 1998. Legal intern Camden (N.J.) Regional Legal Svcs., 1970-71; asst. defender Defender Assn. Phila., 1972-73; asoc. counsel Temple U. Legal Aid Office, Phila., 1973-75; assoc. Fell, Spalding, Goff & Ruben, Phila., 1976-77; exec. dir. Spanish Mchts. Assn., Phila., 1973-77; White House fellow v.p. of U.S., 1977-78; assoc. Wolf, Block, Schorr & Solis-Cohen, Phila., 1978-81; adminstrv. judge Phila. Ct. of Common Pleas, 1981-93; gen. counsel HUD, Washington, 1993-97; ptnr. Blank, Rome, Comisky & McCauley, Phila., 1997—2001; city solicitor City of Philadelphia, Pa., 2001—. Lectr. Sch. Law Temple U., Phila., 1983—. Columnist Phila. Sun and Evening Bull., 1973-75; contbr. articles on Japanese, Peruvian legal system to various publs. Founder Phila. Leadership Prayer Breakfast, 1984-93; bd. dirs., com. chmn. Revitalized Neighborhood, 1983-87; participant, hon. chair Soviet Jewry Coun., 1985; com. mem. Charter Rev. Phila., 1986; chmn. Nat. Assn. Hispanic Elderly, L.A., 1978-93; trustee Young Life, 1989-93, Temple U., 1997—, Phila. Mus. Art; bd. govs. Temple Hosp., Phila., 1975-93; founder, bd. dirs. Nat. P.R. Coalition, 1978-86; co-chmn., bd. dirs. Urban Affairs Partnership, Phila., 1984-90; bd. dirs. USHLI, Chgo., 1982-93, 97—, World Affairs Coun., 1997—; chair Greater Phila. Billy Graham Crusade, active Found. Improvement Justice, 1992, Nat. Bar Assn. Jud. Coun., 1993, Frederick Douglass Soc. Found., 1995, Salvation Army, 1995, Boricua Coll., 1995. Recipient Life Achievement award Nat. Puerto Rican Coalition, Washington, 1988, Judge of the Yr. award Pa. Trial Lawyers Assn., 1989, Man of the Yr., NAACP, North Phila., 1990, Cesar Chavez award, 1995, Spirit of Excellence award ABA, 2001, William Hall award Barristers, 2003, Lifetime Achievement award Minority Bar, 2003, Learn Hand award Am. Jewish Com., 2003; named Grand Marshall, P.R. Milburne (Fla.) Parade; Japan Soc. fellow, Fulbright fellow, 1990. Mem. Pa. Bar Assn. (chair DNC Hispanic Caucus, exec. com., bylaws and rules com., Martin Luther King Barrister award 2003), Phila. Bar Assn., D.C. Bar Assn., Pa. Trial Lawyers Assn., State Conf. Trial Judges, Mayor's St. Police Discipline Task Force. Democrat. Avocation: sports. Office: City Solicitor One Parkway 1515 Arch St 17th Fl Philadelphia PA 19103 E-mail: nelson.a.diaz@phila.gov.

DIAZ, NILS JUAN, federal agency administrator; b. Moron, Cuba, Apr. 7, 1938; came to U.S., 1961; s. Rafael Octavio Diaz and Rosa Dalia (Rojas) Chao; m. Zenaida G. Gonzalez, Oct. 9, 1960; children: NIls, Ariadne, Allene. BSME, U. Villanova, Havana, 1960; MS in Nuclear Engring. Sci., U. Fla., 1964, PhD in Nuclear Engring. Sci., 1969. Rsch. assoc. nuclear engring. sci. U. Fla., Gainesville, 1965-69, asst. prof., reactor supr., 1969-74, assoc. prof., dir. nuclear facilities, 1974-79, prof., dir. nuclear facilities, 1979-84; assoc. dean for rsch. Sch. of Engring. Calif. State U., Long Beach, 1984-86; prof. nuclear engring. scis. U. Fla., Gainesville, 1986-96; dir. Innovative Nuclear Space Power and Propulsion Inst., Calif. and Fla., 1985-96; commr. U.S. Nuclear Regulatory Commn., Washington, 1996—, chmn., 2003—. Sr. cons. Exxon Nuclear, Fla. Power and Light-Fla. Power Corp., Bellevue, Wash. and Fla., 1974-79; pres., chief engr. Fla. Nuclear Assocs., Inc., Gainesville, 1976-96; prin. advisor Nuclear Safety Coun., Madrid, 1981-83; internat. energy cons., Argentina, Brazil, Mex., Santo Domingo, Spain; commr. U.S. Nuclear Regulatory Commn. Contbr. articles to profl. jours. Chmn. Minority Engr. Program Adv. Bd., Long Beach, 1984-86. Recipient Disting. Svc. Award Math. Engring. Sci. Achievements and Minority Engring. Program State of Calif., Long Beach, 1983; named Hispanic Engr. of Yr. for Outstanding Tech. Contbns., Hispanic Engr. Nat. Achievement Com., Houston, 1990. Fellow AAAS, ASME, Am. Nuclear Soc.; mem. Am. Soc. for Engring. Edn., Cuban-Am. Engring. Soc. (Engr. of Yr. 1993), Hispanic Assn. Profl. Engrs. Republican. Roman Catholic. Achievements include patents for heterogeneous gas core reactors, gamma ray flaw detection system; invention of vapor core nuclear rocket propulsion system. Office: US Nuclear Regulatory Commn Offices Of The Commr Washington DC 20555-0001 Office Fax: 202-415-1672.*

DIAZ, OLIVER E., JR., state supreme court justice; b. Biloxi, Miss., Dec. 16, 1959; s. Oliver E. Sr. and Sylvia (Fountain) D. AA, Miss. Gulf Coast Jr. Coll., 1979; BA, U. S. Ala., 1982; JD, U. Miss., 1985. Bar: Miss., U.S. Dist. Ct. (no. and so. dists.) Miss., U.S. Ct. Appeals (5th cir.). Assoc. Holkins Logan Vaughn & Anderson, Gulfport, Miss., 1985-86, Gerald R. Emil PA, Gulfport, 1986-88; ptnr. Diaz Davis & Emil, Gulfport, 1988—95; judge Miss. Ct. of Appeals, Jackson, 1995—2000; justice Miss. Supreme Court, Jackson, 2000—. Miss. state rep., 1988-94; mem. Harrison County Rep. exec. com., 1987—; treas. Miss. State Young Reps., 1987-88; pres. Miss. Gulf Coast Young Reps., Harrison County, 1987-88. Mem. Assn. Trial Lawyers Am., Miss. Trial Lawyers Assn., Am. Legis. Exchange Com., Jaycees. Office: Mississippi Supreme Ct Gartin Justice Bldg PO Box 249 Jackson MS 39205 also: PO Box 450 Jackson MS 39205*

DIAZ, OSCAR, JR., voice educator, music company executive; b. Havana, Cuba, Apr. 7, 1961; s. Oscar and Esther Diaz; life ptnr. Javier Julian Ferrer. Bachelors Degree, University of Texas at Arlington, Arlington, Texas, 1978—88. Voice instr. Performer's Music Inst., Miami, Fla., 1988—; voice instr. adj. faculty New World Sch. of Arts, Miami, 2000—; choir dir., cantor, music tchr. St. Maria Goretti Cath. Ch. and Sch., Arlington, Tex., 1983—87. Exec. dir. Performer's Music Inst., Miami, 1988—. Singer: (operas and mus.) Fla. Grand Opera, 1988—2001, Ft. Worth Opera, 1984—87, Dallas Symphony Chorus, 1984—87, (leading roles) U. Tex. Opera Theatre, Arlington Opera, Coral Gables Opera. Mem.: Nat. Guild Piano Tchrs., Nat. Assn. Tchrs. Singing, Miami Music Tchrs. Assn. (2d v.p. 1995—97). Office Fax: 305-757-7725. Personal E-mail: pmimusic@bellsouth.net. Business E-Mail: pmimusic@bellsouth.net.

DIAZ, SEBASTIAN R. education educator; arrived in U.S., 1996; s. Jose Bernardo Diaz and Lourdes M. Ruiz; m. Katty Garcia; children: Sebastian Raul, Andreina, Daniela. BBA, Simon Rodriguez U., Caracas, 1967, MA, 1978; PhD, Simon Ruiz U., Caracas, 1983; EdD, Eugenio Maria de Hostos, Santo Domingo, 1985. Dir. Simon Rodriguez U., 1978—98; v.p. Internat. Inst. Andragogy, Caracas, 1981—90, pres., 1991—98; provost U. Edn. Distancia, Panama, Panama, 1987—90; prof. Rutgers State U. NJ, New Brunswick, 2001, St. Peter's Coll., Jersey City, 2001, Yale U., New Haven, 2002—. Author: Aprendizaje del Adulto, 1985, Aprendizaje por Experiencia, 1988, Androgogia, 1990. Sec. Assn. Nac. de Educadores de Adultos, Venezuela, 1980, Fed. Interamericana Educadores de Adultos, Venezuela, CEO, 1990. Mem.: L.Am. Assn. Adult Edn., Internat. Fedn. Adult Edn. (mem. emeritus 1990), Internat. Coun. Adult Edn. (Robby Didd award 1996). Home: 143 Bertha Ct Paramus NJ 07652 Office: Yale U 82-90 Wall St New Haven CT 06520 E-mail: sebastian.diaz@yale.edu., sdiazrui@aol.com.

DIAZ, SHARON, education administrator; b. Bakersfield, Calif., July 29, 1946; d. Karl C. and Mildred (Lunn) Clark; m. Luis F. Diaz, Oct. 19, 1968; children: Daniel, David. BS, San Jose State U., 1969; MS, U. Calif., San Francisco, 1973; PhD (hon.), St. Mary's Coll. Calif., 1999. Nurse Kaiser Found. Hosp., Redwood City, Calif., 1969-73; lectr. San Jose (Calif.) State Coll., 1969-70; instr. St. Francis Meml. Hosp. Sch. Nursing, San Francisco, 1970—71; pub. health nurse San Mateo County, 1971—72; instr. Samuel Merritt Hosp. Sch. Nursing, Oakland, Calif., 1973—76; asst. dir. Samuel Merritt Hosp. Sch. of Nursing, Oakland, 1976—78, dir., 1978—84; founding pres. Samuel Merritt Coll., Oakland, 1984—; interim pres. Calif. Coll. Podiatric Medicine, 2001. V.p. East Bay Area Health Edn. Ctr., Oakland, 1980-87; mem. adv. com. Calif. Acad. Partnership Program, 1990-92; mem. nat. adv. com. Nursing Outcomes Project; bd. dirs. Calif. Workforce Initiative, U. Calif. San Francisco Ctr. for the Health Professions, 2000--. Bd. dirs. Head Royce Sch., 1990-98, vice chair, 1993-95, chair, 1995-97; bd. dirs. Ladies Home Soc., 1992—, sec. 1994-95, treas., CFO 1995-97, 2nd v.p. 1997-99; bd. dirs. George Mark Children's House, 2001--; mem. adv. bd. Ethnic Health Inst., 1997—; mem. com. minorities higher edn. Am. Coun. Edn., 1998—. Named Woman of Yr., Oakland YWCA, 1996. Mem. Am. Assn. of Pres. Ind. Colls. and Univs., Sigma Theta Tau (Leadership award Nu Xi chpt. 2001). Office: Samuel Merritt Coll 450 30th St Oakland CA 94609-3302 E-mail: sdiaz@samuelmerritt.edu.

DIAZ-ARCE, RAUL, professional soccer player; b. San Miguel, El Salvador, Feb. 1, 1970; Player New England Revolution, 1998—99, San Jose Clash, 1999, Tampa Bay Mutiny, 1999—2000, D.C. United, 1996—97, 2000—. Mem. El Salvadoran World Cup Nat. Team.

DIAZ-ARRASTIA, GEORGE RAVELO, lawyer; b. Havana, Cuba, Aug. 20, 1959; came to U.S., 1968; s. Ramon Fuentes and Elihut (Ravelo) D.-A.; m. Maria del Carmen Gomez, Aug. 6, 1983. BA in History, Rice U., 1980; JD, U. Chgo., 1983. Bar: Tex. 1983, U.S. Dist. Ct. (so. dist.) Tex. 1985, U.S. Ct. Appeals (5th and D.C. cirs.) 1985, U.S. Supreme Ct. 1992, U.S. Dist. Ct. (no., we. and ea. dists.) Tex. 1994. Assoc. Baker & Botts, Houston, 1983-88, Deaton & Briggs (formerly Deaton, Briggs & McCain), Houston, 1988-90; ptnr. Gilpin, Paxson & Bersch, LLP, Houston, 1991-98, Schirrmeister Ajamie LLP, Houston, 1998—. Fellow Tex. Bar Found., Houston Bar Found.; mem. ABA, Am. Judicature Soc., Am. Soc. Internat. Law, State Bar of Tex., Houston Bar Assn., Coll. of State Bar Tex. Republican. Roman Catholic. Home: 3794 Drake St Houston TX 77005-1118 Office: Schirrmeister Ajamie LLP 711 Louisiana St Ste 2150 Houston TX 77002-2720 E-mail: gdarrastia@salawfirm.com.

DIAZ-BALART, LINCOLN, congressman, lawyer; b. Havana, Cuba, Aug. 13, 1954; m. Cristina Fernandez; children: Lincoln Gabriel, Daniel. BA in Internat. Rels., New Coll. of U. So. Fla., 1976; diploma in Brit. Politics, Cambridge (Eng.) U.; JD, Case Western Res. U., 1979. Lawyer Legal Svcs. of Greater Miami, Fla.; asst. state atty. State of Fla.; mem. Fla. Ho. of Reps. from 110th Dist., 1986-89, Fla. State Senate from Dist. 34, 1989-92, U.S. Congress from 21st Fla. dist., 1993—; Select Com. on Homeland Security. Mem. rules com.; vice chmn. subcom. on rules of the house. Mem. exec. com. Congl. Human Rights Caucus; vice chmn. Nat. Rep. Congl. Com. Mem. ABA, Fla. Bar Assn., Dade County Bar Assn., Cuban-Am. Bar Assn., Rep. Nat. Lawyers Assn., Lions. Republican. Roman Catholic. Office: US Ho of Reps 2244 Rayburn Ho Office Bldg Washington DC 20515-0921*

DIAZ-BALART, MARIO, congressman; b. Ft. Lauderdale, Fla., Sept. 25, 1961; Student, U. South Fla. Pres. Gordeon, Sloan and Diaz-Balart; adminstrv. asst. to Mayor Xavier Suarez City of Miami, 1985-88; mem. Fla. Ho. of Reps., Tallahassee, 1988-92, 2000—02, Fla. State Senate, Tallahassee, 1992—2000, U.S. Ho. of Reps from 25th Fla. dist., 2003—. Vice chmn. Rules and Calendar Com.; chmn. Banking and Ins. Com.; mem. Subcom. E Fin. and Tax Ways and Means Com., Natural Resources Com., Edn. Com. Commerce and Econ. Opportunities Com. Mem. consultive com. Children's First; mem. Dade Ptnrs. for Safe Neighborhoods, Spanish-Am. League Against Discriminations; mem. Hispanic adv. bd. Rep. Nat. Com.; advisor nat. human rights commn. Municipios en el Exilio; bd. dirs. Fla. Entertainment Commn.; former mem. Fla. bd. dirs. Spl. Olympics Recipient award Fla. Assn. C.C.'s, award of honor, Pub. Svcs. award MADD, 1994, Furtherance of Justice award Fla. Attys. Assn., 1994, Govt. Recognition awrd Am. Assn. Poison Control Ctrs., 1996, Disting. Leadership award Police Benevolent Assn., 1996, Leadership award Fla. Assn. State Troopers, 1996, Resolution of Appreciation Fla. Conf. of Dist. Cts. of Appeal Judges, 1996. Mem. Nat. Assn. Latino Elected Officials, Asociacion Integral Mambisa, Westchester Lions Club. Democrat. Roman Catholic. Avocations: reading, biking, diving. Office: 313 Cannon Ho Office Bldg Washington DE 20515-0925*

DIAZ-ORTIZ, OSCAR A. education educator, researcher; b. Bogota, Colombia, May 15, 1962; s. José Diaz and Ody Ortiz; m. Irma del Pilar Gonzalez, Sept. 21, 1990; children: Oscar Steven Diaz, Paloma Laurich Diaz. PhD, Ariz. State U., 1997. Asst. prof. U. of Iowa, 1997—98; assoc. prof. Mid. Tenn. State U., Murfreesboro, 1998—. Dir. Latin Am. studies Mid. Tenn. State U., Murfreesboro, 1998—. Contbr. (Creative Rsch. Work, 2001). Office: Mid Tenn State U 1301 E Main St PO BOX 0079 Murfreesboro TN 37132

DIAZ-VERSON, SALVADOR, JR., investment advisor; b. Havana, Cuba, Dec. 31, 1951; s. Salvador and Metodia Diaz-V.; m. Patricia Dianne Floyd, Apr. 24, 1976; children: Salvador III, Patricia Elizabeth. BA in Fin., Fla. State U., Tallahassee, 1973. Chief investment officer Am. Family Life Assurance, Columbus, Ga., 1977-79; exec. v.p. Am. Family Corp., Columbus, 1980-83, pres., 1983-91, also dir.; pres. Diaz-Verson Capital Investment, 1991—. Bd. dirs. Regions Bank, Ga.; pres., CEO Diaz-Verson Capital Investment Inc., 1992. Trustee St. Francis Hosp.; chair United Americas Bank, 1999—; trustee United Way, Columbus, 1983—. Mem. Columbus C. of C. (bd. dirs. 1983—, chair 1989), Green Island Country Club, Country Club of Columbus. Roman Catholic. Office: Diaz-Verson Capital Investment 260 Brookstone Centre Pkwy Columbus GA 31904-2974

DIAZ-ZUBIETA, AGUSTIN, nuclear engineer, engineering executive; b. Madrid, Mar. 24, 1936; came to U.S., 1953; s. Emilio Diaz Cabeza and Maria Teresa Zubieta Atucha; m. Beth Lee Fortune, Sept. 6, 1958; children: Walter Agustin, Michael Joel, Anthony John. B, U. Madrid, 1953; BSc in Physics, U. Tenn., 1958; MSc in Mech. Engring., Duke U., 1960; PhD in Nuclear Engring., U. Md., 1981. Nuclear engr. Combustion Engring., Tenn., 1954-58; instr. engring. Duke U., Durham, N.C., 1958-60; nuclear physicist Allis Chalmers Co., Washington, 1960-64, country mgr. South Africa, 1964-66; mgr. internat. power generation projects GE, N.Y.C., 1966-69, mgr. Europe and Middle East strategic planning, 1969-71, dir. internat. constrn. planning Westport, Conn., 1971-75, dir. constrn., 1975-83; CEO GE Affiliate, Westport, 1983-87; v.p. internat. sales, devel. Internat. Tech. Corp., L.A., 1987-94. Mng. dir. IT Italia S.P.A., IT Spain, S.A. Author: Measurement of Subcriticality of Nuclear Reactors by Stocastic Processes, 1981. Pres. Fairfield (Conn.) Assn. Condo Owners, 1983-87. Named Astronomer of Yr. Barnard Astronomical Soc., Chattanooga, 1957; fgn. exchange scholar U.S. Govt., 1953-58; grantee, NSF, 1958-60, U.S. Office of Ordinance Rsch. U.S. Army, 1958-60. Mem. Am. Nuclear Soc., Am. Soc. Mech. Engrs., Am. Soc. Profl. Engrs., Sigma Xi. Republican. Roman Catholic. Avocations: golf, tennis, swimming, sailing, music. Home: 47 Country Meadow Rd Rolling Hills Estates CA 90274

DIAZ-ZUBIETA, ANA MARIA, social worker; b. Coral Gables, Fla., Jan. 11, 1972; d. Maribel Zubieta and Richard Diaz. BFA, NYU, 1991—94, MSW, 1996—97; MA, Fordham U., 2001, postgrad., 2003—. Certified Social Worker NY, 1997. Social worker Cath. Big Sisters, New York, 1997—98, Partnership With Children, Brooklyn, NY, 1998—99. Scholar Presdl. Scholarship, Fordham U., 1999-2003. Mem.: Sigma XI, The Sci. Rsch. Soc. (mem. 2002—), Phi Kappa Phi, Fordham U. Chpt. (mem. 2002—).

DIB, NABIL, cardiologist, researcher; b. Toumin, Syria, Nov. 24, 1961;, U.S. m. Cheryl A. Brandt, Apr. 12, 1996; children: Dib, Lauren. MD, U. Damascus, Syria, 1985; cardiologist, U. Wis., Milw., 1997; MSc, Harvard U., 1999. Lic. Mass., Wis., Ariz., diplomate Am. Bd. Internal Medicine, Am. Bd. Cardiovasc. Disease, Am. Bd. Interventional Cardiology. Dir. cardiovasc. rsch. Ariz. Heart Inst., Phoenix, 1998—; investigational interventional cardiology fellow Harvard Med. Sch., Boston, 1999. Spkr. in field; advisor Radi Med., 1995—, Possis Med., Minn., 1998—; cons. in field. Contbr. articles to profl. jours.; editl. cons.: Catheterization and Cardiovasc. Jour., 1996—. Recipient Med. Staff Sci. award, Tufts U., Boston, 1994; Med. scholar, Damascus U., 1985. Fellow: Am. Coll. Cardiology; mem.: ACP, Internat. Soc. Endovascular Interventionists. Avocations: swimming, fishing, travel. Office: Ariz Heart Inst 2632 N 20th St Phoenix AZ 85028

DIBACCO, T(HAD) JAY, financial services planner, career reserve officer; b. Casper, Wyo., June 8, 1954; s. Albert Joseph and Evelyn DeBacco; m. Nadine Louise Allen, June 1, 1976. MusB, cert. in edn., postgrad., U. Wyo., 1976;

diploma, F.A. Officer Basic & Cannon Battery Officer Course, Ft. Sill, Okla., 1979, F.A. Officer Advanced Course, Ft. Sill, 1989, U.S. Army Command & Gen. Staff, Ft. Leavenworth, Kans., 1994. Music tchr. St. Agnes Acad., Alliance, Nebr., 1976-77; instrumental music Gering (Nebr.) Pub. Schs., 1977-79; sales assoc. Panhandle Co-op, Scottsbluff, 1980-81; advanced underwriter Security Mut. Life Nebr., Scottsbluff, 1981-99; sr. assoc. Hi-Plains Fin. Svcs. Inc., Scottsbluff, 1985-99; owner, CEO DiBacco & Assoc.-WealthMaker$ Ltd., Scottsbluff, 1999—. Adj. faculty Western Nebr. C.C., Scottsbluff, 1989-90; agt. Security Mutual Life Nebr., 1981-99; registered rep. Nat. Assn. Securities Dealers, 1994—, Fin. Network Investment Corp., Lincoln, Nebr., 1994-99; gen. agt. Ohio Nat. Fin. Svcs., 2000—; reg. rep. O.N. Equity Sales Co., 1999—. Contbr. articles to profl. jours.; writer local newspaper column. Adv. bd. Regional West Med. Ctr. Found., Scottsbluff, 1989—; mem. MBA Catalyst Group, U. Nebr. Panhandle Sta., Scottsbluff, 1990-92; dist. commr. Longs Peak Coun. Boy Scouts Am., 1980-83; active emergency comms. Amateur Radio Emergency Svc., Scottsbluff, 1990—; founding pres., bd. dirs. Panhandle Estate Planning Coun., Scottsbluff, 1982-92. With Wyo. Army N.G., 1975-85, Nebr. Army N.G., 1985—, lt. col., 2001--. Decorated Army Commendation medal with oak leaf cluster; recipient Scouter Tng. award, Longs Peak Coun. Boy Scouts Am., 1977, Vigil Honor award, 1977, Assn. Achievement award, Nebr. Assn. Life Underwriters, 1988; fellow Life Underwriters Tng. Coun. fellow, Am. Coll., 1987. Mem. Fin. Planning Assn., Nat. Assn. Ins. and Fin. Advisors, N.G. Officers Assn. of U.S. (life mem., Nebr. del. 1990-92), Nebr. N.G. Officers Assn. (life), Soc. Fin. Svc. Profls., Gen. Agts. and Mgrs. Assn., Scottsbluff Gering United C. of C. (diplomate, founding chmn.), Soc. Creative Anachronism (regional safety officer 1995-99, Regional Svc. award 1995), Soc. Preservation and Encouragement Barbershop Quartet Singing in Am., Sugar Valley Singers (pres. 2002—, barbershopper of yr. 1997), Platte River Harmony, Scottsbluff Country Club, Am. Legion, Elks, Valley Vintners (pres. 2002—). Avocations: music, history, archery, travel, wine making. Home: PO Box 158 Gering NE 69341-0158 Office: PO Box 840 Scottsbluff NE 69363-0840 Fax: 308-220-3938. E-mail: info@wealth-makers.com.

DIBAIYAN, FATEMEH MARIAM, artist; b. Saveh, Iran, Sept. 21, 1937; d. Soltan Ali Dibaiyan and Mariam Vakili; widowed; children: Nasser, Danesh, Sadaf, Donna Rahimi. Student, U. Utah, 1993. Exhibited in group shows at Moon Flower Gallery, Salt Lake City, 1994, Phillips Gallery, Salt Lake City, 1994-95, Kimball Gallery, Park City, Utah, 1996, Amir Kabir Gallery, Tehran, Iran, 1994-96, Art of Utah, Salt Lake City, 1996—, Bellevue Art Mus., Wash., 1998; represented in permanent collections at U. Utah, Children's Mus., Salt Lake City, Kimball Gallery, Univ. Hosp., Tehran, Salt Lake C.C. Home: 408 S 1300 E #5 Salt Lake City UT 84102

DI BATTISTA, ANTHONY PAUL, secondary school educator; b. Newark, June 26, 1955; s. Ralph John Di Battista and Ida Maria Cattenari; m. Rosemary Genova Di Battista, Oct. 17, 1982; children: Anthony, Adam, John. BA, Rutgers Coll., 1977; PhD Rutgers U., 1995. Tchr. W.M. Regional H.S., Chester, NJ, 1978—95, dir. curriculum, 1995—. Vis. lectr. Rutgers U., New Brunswick, NJ, 1987—; project dir. US Dept. Edn., DC, 2000—. Fellow, NEH, 1986, 1991, Kezai Koho fellow, Govt. of Japan, 1999; Fulbright fellow, US Dept. Edn., 1983. Mem.: Orgn. Am. Historians, Am. Soc. Curriculum Devel. Democrat. Roman Catholic. Avocation: rock climbing. Home: 50 Farley Ave Fanwood NJ 07023 Office: West Morris Regional HS Dist Four Bridges Rd Chester NJ 07930

DIBATTISTE, CAROL A. lawyer; b. Phila., Dec. 28, 1951; d. Peter Martin DiBattiste and Hilda Yolanda (Battilana) Mignogna. BA magna cum laude, LaSalle U., 1976; JD, Temple U., 1981; LLM, Columbia U., 1986. Bar: Pa. 1982, U.S. Ct. Mil. Appeals 1982, U.S. Supreme Ct. 1985, N.Y. 1989, D.C. 1989, Fla. 1990, U.S. Dist. Ct. (so. dist.) Fla. 1991, U.S. Ct. Appeals (11th cir.) 1991. Commd. 2d lt. USAF, 1976, advanced through grades to maj., 1987, cir. trial counsel Pacific Region, 1982—85; mem. faculty USAF JAG Sch., Maxwell AFB, Ala., 1986—89; chief recruiting atty. Office of Judge Advocate Gen. USAF, Washington, 1989—91; asst. U.S. atty. So. Dist. Fla., Miami, 1991—92; dir. Office of Legal Edn. Dept. Justice, 1992—93; prin. dep. gen. coun. Dept. of Navy, 1993—94; dir. Exec. Office for U.S. Attys., Washington, 1994—98; dep. U.S. atty. So. Dist. Fla., Miami, 1998—99; undersec. USAF, Arlington, Va., 1999—2001; ptnr. Holland & Knight, LLP, 2001—03; chief of staff Transp. Security Adminstrn., 2003—. Adj. faculty U. Miami Sch. Law Trial Skills, 1998—99; bd. dirs. Holland & Knight Cons. Editor: The Reporter, 1986—87; mem. editl. bd.: Air Force Law Rev., 1984; contbr. articles to profl. jours. Mem. bd. visitors Temple U. Sch. Law, 1996-99; trustee USAF JAG Sch. Found., 1993-96. Mem. ABA (chmn. standing com. on mil. law 1989-91), Fed. Bar Assn. (Young Fed. Lawyer award 1985), Nat. Inst. for Trial Advocacy (faculty 1986-92), USAF Assn. Roman Catholic. Business E-Mail: carol.dibattiste@dhs.gov.

DIBB, DAVID WALTER, research association administrator; b. Draper, Utah, July 4, 1943; s. Walter and Mary (Lisinsky) D.; m. Vivian Berrett, Dec. 15, 1966; children: Stephanie, Gregory, Steven, Rebecca. BS, Brigham Young U., 1970; PhD, U. Ill., 1974. Cert. profl. agronomist, cert. profl. soil scientist. Rsch. asst. U. Ill., Urbana, 1970-74, tchg. asst., 1971-74; vis. asst. prof. N.C. State U., Raleigh, 1974-75; rsch. dir. Potash & Phosphate Inst., Atlanta, 1982-89, regional dir. Columbia, Mo., 1975-82, coord. Latin Am. Atlanta, 1982-85, v.p. North Am. West Lafayette, Ind., 1985-86, sr. v.p., 1987-88, pres. Atlanta, 1989—. Pres. Agronomic Sci. Found., Madison, Wis., 1983-85; mem. fertilizer industry adv. com. Food and Agrl. Orgn. of UN, Rome, 1988-94; exec. industry rev. group TVA, Muscle Shoals, Ala., 1989-94; adj. prof. Purdue U., West Lafayette, 1985-88; hon. prof. Chinese Acad. Agrl. Scis., 1996. Contbr. author: Potassium in Agriculture, 1985; editor: Fertilizer Research, 1989-90; contbr. articles to profl. jours. Instnl. rep. Boy Scouts Am., West Lafayette, 1982-85, asst. scoutmaster, Norcross, Ga., 1989-90; youth coach for basketball, baseball, and soccer, Mo., Ind., Ga., 1980-89; active PTA, Mo., Ind., Ga., 1978-96. Fellow AAAS, Am. Soc. Agronomy (chmn. budget and fin. com. 1988), Soil Sci. Soc. Am.; mem. Coun. for Agrl. Sci. and Tech., Internat. Soil Sci. Soc., Gamma Sigma Delta, Alpha Zeta. Office: Potash and Phosphate Inst 655 Engring Dr Ste 110 Norcross GA 30092 E-mail: ddibb@ppi-far.org.

DIBBLE, CAMERON SHAWN, music educator, concert pianist; b. Topeka, July 10, 1951; s. John Willis and Margaret (Griffeth) D. BMus, Oberlin Coll. Conservatory, 1974; MusM, U. Mo., 1981, D of Musical Arts, 1992. Teaching asst. Conservatory of Music, U. Mo., Kansas City, 1975—. Music dir. summer session Topeka (Kans.) Recreation Commn., 1970; adj. asst. prof. piano pedagogy U. Mo., Kansas City, 1997—. Pianist Heritage Chamber Ensemble, 1989-94; ch. organist, 1983—. Mem. Kansas City Music Tchrs. Assn. (v.p. achievement auditions 1996-98, v.p. master lessions 1998-2000, v.p. concerto competition/recital and concert 2001—), Mo. Music Tchrs. Assn. (exec. bd. 1989-92, pres.-elect 2002-03), Music Tchrs. Nat. Assn., Kansas City Mus. Club, Pi Kappa Lambda, Mu Phi Epsilon. Office: U Mo-Kans City Conservatory Music 4949 Cherry St Kansas City MO 64110-2229 Home: 8229 Belleview Ave Kansas City MO 64114-2109

DIBBLE, DAVID VAN VLACK, visually impaired educator, lawyer; b. San Francisco, Feb. 5, 1928; s. Oliver and Isabelle (Bishop) D.; m. Frances Bauer, May 3, 1984; 1 child, T.C. Clark. AA, San Mateo Jr. Coll., 1948; student, Mexico City Coll., 1950; BA, U. Calif., Berkeley, 1952; JD, U. Calif., San Francisco, 1962; grad. in Edn., Calif. State U., Hayward, 1969; MA, San Francisco State U., 1981. Bar: Calif., 1962; cert. elem. tchr., spl. edn. visually impaired, Calif. Tchr. Marine Corps Inst., Washington, 1953-54; purser Am. Pres. Lines, San Francisco, 1955, passenger agt. Honolulu, 1956-58, San Francisco, 1958-60; trial lawyer Barfield, Barfield & Dryden, San Francisco, 1963-65; ptnr. Thorpe & Dibble, Hayward, Calif., 1966-69; part time tchr. various Calif. sch. dist., 1970-74; lawyer and vision tchr. pvt. practice, San Francisco, 1974-82; sec., dir. Original Sixteen to One Mine, Inc., Alleghany, Calif., 1978-81; vision tchr. Oakland Pub. Sch., Calif., 1982-89; cons. vision edn. pvt. practice, Oakland, 1989—. Contbr. articles on Art of Seeing to various pubs. Pub. defender Legal Aid Soc., San Francisco, 1965-66; bd. dir. Healing Ctr., San Francisco, 1974-78; vol. Multiple Sclerosis Soc. No. Calif., Oakland, 1974-90; bd. dir., v.p. Calif. Heritage Coun., 1970—, Telegraph Hill Dwellers, 1979-88, pres., 1976, San Francisco; bd. dirs., v.p. Diamond Improvement Assn., Oakland, 1987-88; vestry and warden St. Paul's Episcopal Ch., Oakland, 1989-92; dir. In ernat. Maritime Ctr., Oakland, 1995—; docent Oakland Mus., 1992, presdl. yacht. U.S.S. Potomac, Jack London Mus.; dir. Fruitvale Cmty. Devel. Dist. Coun., Oakland, 1989-95, Hugenot Soc. Calif., Thomas Jefferson chpt. SAR. Recipient Cert. Appreciation, Calif. Heritage Coun., San Francisco, 1990. Mem. Bar Assn. Calif., Oakland Tchrs. Assn., Calif. Assn. Orientation and Mobility Specialists, Calif. Alumni Assn., Nat. Audubon Soc., Bay Area Assn. Disabled Sailors, San Francisco Bay Wildlife Soc., E.C.V. YB#1, History Soc., Sierra Club, Calif. Mus. History (docent coun.), Calif. Hist. Soc., Alameda County Hist. Soc., Bates-Corbett Tchr. Assn., Phi Gamma Delta. Republican. Episcopalian. Home: 2806 Bellaire Pl Oakland CA 94601-2010

DIBBLE, FRANCIS DANIEL, JR., lawyer; b. Holyoke, Mass., Mar. 1, 1947; s. Francis Daniel and Rita (Egan) D.; m. Mary Harris Dibble, June 26, 1971. AB, Amherst Coll., 1971; JD magna cum laude, Suffolk U., 1974. Bar: Mass. 1974, U.S. Dist. Ct. Mass. 1975, U.S. Dist. Ct. Conn. 1978, U.S. Dist. Ct. (ea. dist.) Mich. 1984, U.S. Ct. Appeals (1st cir.) 1987, U.S. Ct. Appeals (D.C. cir.) 1981, U.S. Supreme Ct. 1984. Law clk. to justice Supreme Jud. Ct. of Mass., Boston, 1974-75; from assoc. to mng. ptnr. Bulkley, Richardson and Gelinas, Springfield, Mass., 1975-94, chmn., exec. com., 1997—. Instr. Western New Eng. Law Sch., Springfield, 1979. Contbr. articles to profl. jours. Mem. civil justice adv. bd. U.S. Dist. Ct. Mass.; spl. counsel. Fellow Mass. Bar Found. (life); mem. ABA (antitrust law sect.), Mass. Bar Assn., Hampden County Bar, Boston Bar Assn., The Colony Club, Longmeadow Country Club, East Chop Assn., East Chop Yacht Club, East Chop Tennis Club. Home: 180 Eton Rd Longmeadow MA 01106-1516 Office: Bulkley Richardson and Gelinas LLP 1500 Main St Ste 2700 Springfield MA 01115-0001 E-mail: fdibble@bulkley.com.

DIBBLE, RICHARD EDWARD, academic administrator; b. Elmira, N.Y., Dec. 20, 1946; s. D. Charles and Bernice V. (Brasted) D.; m. Josephine Estrada, June 2, 1973; children: Cristina, Diana. BA in English, SUNY, Buffalo, 1971; MA in Polit. Sci., SUNY, Albany, 1973, PhD in Polit. Sci., 1977; MBA, N.Y. Inst. Technology, 1990. Cert. employment/tng. adminstr., sr. profl. human resources. Legis. intern N.Y. State Assembly, 1972; researcher to dir. rsch. Dept. Employment and Tng. Albany County, N.Y., 1977-80; rsch. and tng. dir. to dean, dir. Ctr. for Labor and Indsl. Rels., N.Y. Inst. Technology, 1980—, prof., 1994—. Labor arbitrator N.Y. State Employment Rels. Bd. panel, 1993—; presenter in field. Author publs./videos in field; editl. bd. mem. Jour. Individual Employee Rights, 1994; contbr. articles and book revs. to profl. jours. Bd. dirs., founding mem. L.I. Health Care Coalition, 1985-91; adv. bd. N.Y. Inst. Technology Transp., 1982-87; mem. task force on chem. dependency in the workplace, N.Y. State Div. Substance Abuse Svcs., 1983-84, N.Y. State Gov.'s Office for Voluntary Svcs., 1990, Addictions Adv. Bd. of L.I., 1993—, Ctr. for Labor and Indsl. Rels. Adv. Coun., 1982—, others; mem. pub. employment rels. bd., Suffolk County, N.Y., 1999—; chmn. youth coun. Town of Hempstead, 2001—. Recipient cert. merit for advancement of legal jurisprudence, Nassau County Acad. Law, 1990, 96, citation for contribution to edn. in dispute resolution, Suffolk County, N.Y., 1989, others; named Vol. of Yr. Adults and Children With Developmental Disabilities, Inc., 1996, MacGregor award L.I. IRRA, 1998. Mem. Am. Arbitration Assn. (comml. arbitrator 1988—), Indsl. Rels. Rsch. Assn. (various officers to pres. local chpt. 1993—, bd. dirs., Pres.'s Spl. Recognition award 1989, 95, MacGregor award 1998), Soc. for Human Resource Mgmt., Soc. Profls. in Dispute Resolution (various offices to pres. local chpt. 1992), Adults and Children with Learning and Devel. Disabilities (bd. dirs. to pres. 1991—, various coms., certs. of appreciation 1990, 91), Delta Mu Delta, also others. Avocation: travel. Office: Ctr Labor and Indsl Rels Rm 517 NY Inst Technology Old Westbury NY 11568

DIBBLE, SUZANNE LOUISE, nurse, researcher; b. Pittsburg, Calif., June 3, 1947; d. Charles Stanley and Evelyn Virginia (Hansen) D.; m. Myron Bottsford Palmer III, June 12, 1971 (div. July 1974); life ptnr. Jeanne Flyntz DeJoseph, 1984. BSN, U. Del., 1969; MSN, U. Calif., San Francisco, 1971, D Nursing Sci., 1986. RN, Del., Calif. Staff nurse emergency room Stanford (Calif.) U. Hosp., 1969-71, rschr. dept. nursing rsch., 1986-88; instr. med. and surg. nursing Stanford U., 1971-72, renal transplant nurse coord., 1972-73, nurse rschr. dept. diagnostic radiology, 1987-88; staff, charge, head nurse, then supr. Children's Hosp.-Stanford U., 1973-86; mem. faculty stats. dept. U. Phoenix, San Jose, Calif., 1985-92; pres. Data Mgmt. Assocs., San Carlos, Calif., 1985—2000; investigator U. Calif., 1988—; co-dir. Lesbian Health Rsch. Ctr., 1999—. Rsch. grant cons. NIH, Oakland, Calif., 1992-94, Loma Linda (Calif.) U., 1995—; co-dir. Lesbian Health Rsch. Ctr., U. Calif. San Francisco, 1999--; manuscript reviewer Oncology Nursing Forum, Pitts., 1993-96, Med.-Surg. Nursing, Pittmn, N.J., 1994 , Jour. of Gay and Lesbian Med. Assn. Editor: Culture and Nursing Care, 1996; contbr. articles to nursing jours. Chmn. task force, mem. NOW, Palo Alto, Calif., 1978—; mem., chmn. Maternal, Child and Adolescent Health Bd., San Mateo County, Calif., 1987-90; mem. strategic planning com. San Mateo County Health Bd., 1989-90. Rsch. grantee Nat. Cancer Inst., 1992-97, 2000—, Nat. Inst. for Nursing Rsch., 1994-99. Mem. ANA, Assn. for Care Children's Health (numerous offices), Oncology Nursing Soc. (numerous offices), Am. Statis. Assn., Sigma Theta Tau (pres. Alpha Eta chpt.). Democrat. Office: U Calif Box 0646 Inst Health & Aging San Francisco CA 94143-0646

DI BENEDETTO, ANN LOUISE, accounting administrator; b. Knoxville, Tenn., Jan. 26, 1954; d. William Brown and Louise (Emerson) Nixon; m. Raymond Peters, July 11, 1975 (dec.); m. Robert Di Benedetto, Sept. 22, 2002. BBA, Miami U., Oxford, Ohio, 1976; MBA, Xavier U., 1985. Cert. internal auditor. Acctg. officer Soc. Bank (formerly Citizens Bank), Hamilton, Ohio, 1977-85; internal auditor Procter & Gamble Co., Cin., 1985-86, audit sect. mgr., 1986-88, sr. cost analyst, beauty care, 1988-90; plant fin. mgr. Procter & Gamble Mfg. Co., Phoenix, 1990-92; sr. fin. analyst, beauty care Procter & Gamble Co., Cin., 1992-93, group mgr., gen. acctg., 1993-96, group mgr. R&D fin., 1996-99, group mgr., global fin., paper divsn., 1999—2002, group mgr. global fin. governance, 2002—03, group mgr., fin., global bus. svcs., 2003—. Mem. Inst. Internal Auditors, Inst. Mgmt. Accts. Republican. Congregationalist. Avocations: golf, swimming. Home: 7889 Ironwood Way West Chester OH 45069-1623 Office: Procter & Gamble Co PO Box 599 Cincinnati OH 45201-0599

DIBENEDETTO, ANTHONY THOMAS, engineering educator; b. N.Y.C., Oct. 27, 1933; s. Thomas and Mathilda DiB.; m. Rose Marie Lima, Feb. 12, 1955; children: Diane, Laura, Thomas, David, Stephen. B.Ch.E., CCNY, 1955; MS, U. Wis., 1956, PhD, 1960; Doctorate (hon.), Brno U. Tech., Czech Republic, 1999. Chem. engr. Union Carbide Corp., 1954-55; prof. chem. engring. U. Wis., 1960-67; prof., dir. materials research lab. Washington U., 1967-71; head dept. chem. engring. U. Conn., 1971-77, v.p. grad. edn. and research, 1979-81, v.p. acad. affairs, 1981-86, Univ. prof. chem. engring., 1986-97, prof. emeritus, 1997, dir. Inst. Materials Sci., 1991-95, univ. prof. chem. engring. emeritus, 1997—. Vis. prof. materials engring. and indsl. techs. U. Trento, Italy, 2002; cons. in field. Author: The Structure and Properties of Materials, 1967. Recipient Edni. Service award Plastics Inst. Am., 1973; NSF profl. devel. award, 1977-79; Disting. Service award U. Wis., 1981, Outstanding Leadership award U. Conn., 1992, Plueddemann award, 1996. Mem. AIChE, Sigma Xi, Tau Beta Pi. Home: 1 Brookside Ln Mansfield Center CT 06250-1109 Office: U Conn Inst Materials Sci # U136 Storrs Mansfield CT 06269

DI BENEDETTO, C. ANTHONY, marketing educator; b. Windsor, Ont., Can., June 23, 1957; arrived in U.S., 1984; s. Ray and Eileen Di Benedetto; m. Kimberly Gelbach, May 14, 1994; 1 child, Alessandra. BSc with great distinction, McGill U., Montreal, Que., Can., 1978, MBA, 1980, PhD, 1985. New product profl. cert. Asst. prof. U. Ky., Lexington, 1985-89, Temple U., Phila., 1990-91, assoc. prof., 1991-98, prof., 1998—. Co-author: (with R. Calantone) The Product Manager's Toolbox, 1993, (with M. Crawford) New Products Management, 2003; contbr. articles to profl. jours. Recipient Steven J. Shaw Best Paper award So. Mktg. Assn., 1992. Mem.: Product Devel. and Mgmt. Assn. (acad. news and book rev. editor Visions 1991—93, editor nat. newsletter Visions 1992—96, v.p. publs. 1994—95, abstracts editor Jour. Product Innovation Mgmt. 1996—2003, bd. dirs. 2001—), Am. Mktg. Assn. (treas. Phila. chpt. 1991—93, dir. Phila. chpt. 1993—95). Office: Temple U Fox Sch Bus and Mgmt 1810 N 13th St Philadelphia PA 19122-6012 E-mail: anthony.dibenedetto@temple.edu.

DIBENEDETTO, EMMANUELE, molecular physiology, biophysicist, writer; b. Lentini, Siracusa, Italy, Apr. 2, 1947; s. Nunzio and Elvira (Papalino) DiB.; m. Heidi Elisabeth Hamm, Dec. 25, 1975. Laurea, U. Florence, Italy, 1975; PhD, U. Tex., 1979. Vaclav Hlavaty prof. math. Ind. U., Bloomington, 1979-84; prof. Northwestern U., Evanston, Ill., 1984-2000, U. Rome, 1986-99; Centennial prof. math. Vanderbilt U., Nashville, 2000—, dir. Inst. for Briath., 2000—. Author: Degenerate Parabolic Equations, 1993, Partial Differential Equations, 1995, Appunti di Meccanica Razionale, 1997, Real Analysis, 2002; editor: Nonlinear Partial Differential Equations, 1999; editor-in-chief Soc. for Indsl. and Applied Math. Jour. on Math. Analysis, 1986-2000; mem. editl. bd. Electronic Jour. Differential Equations, 1992—, Differential and Integral Equations, 1992—, Advances in Differential Equations, 1992—, Comm. in Applied Analysis, 1992-2000, Revista Matematica Complutense, 1992-2000, Non-Linear Analysis TMA, 2002—, Internat. Jour. Pure and Applied Analysis, 2001—. Grantee NSF, 1983—, NATO, 1992-94, NIH, 2003—.

DIBENEDETTO, ROBERT LAWRENCE, retired obstetrician, gynecologist, insurance company executive; b. New Orleans, Apr. 14, 1928; s. Salvador and Eunice Madeline (Frisch) DiB.; m. Mary Nathalie Roeling, June 20, 1951; children: Madeline E., Robert R., Lawrence W. Student, Tulane U., 1945-47, BS, La. State U., 1948, MD, 1952. Diplomate Am. Bd. Ob-Gyn. Intern Mercy Hosp., New Orleans, 1952-53; resident in pathology La. State U. Med. Sch., 1955-56, clin. assoc. prof. ob-gyn., 1963; resident ob-gyn. Charity Hosp., New Orleans, 1956-59; practice medicine specializing in ob-gyn. Baton Rouge, 1959—94; pres., CEO La. Med. Mutual Ins. Co., New Orleans, 1994—99; ret., 2000. Founding chmn. Mid-La. Health Systems Agy., 1976-77; chmn. bd. dirs., med. dir. Woman's Hosp., Baton Rouge, 1999—; pres. Capitol Area Health Planning, 1975-76; mem. Perinatal Commn. La., Bd. Health, Edn. Authority La., State Health Coord. Council. Served with USPHS, 1953-55. Mem. AMA (past del.), ACOG (past chmn. La. sect.), South Ctrl. Ob-Gyn. Soc., La. Med. Soc. (co-chmn. polit. action com., past pres.), East Baton Rouge Parish Med. Soc. (past pres.), City Club (Baton Rouge), So. Yacht Club (New Orleans), Baton Rouge Country Club. Republican. Roman Catholic. Home: 6666 Pikes Ln Baton Rouge LA 70808-4272 E-mail: RLdiB@cox.com.

DIBERARDINIS, LOUIS JOSEPH, health and safety professional, industrial hygiene engineer, consultant, educator; b. Lawrence, Mass., July 2, 1947; s. Salvatore and Jane Marie (Lombari) DiB. BSChemE, Northeastern U., 1970; MS in Indsl. Hygiene, Harvard U., 1975. Diplomate Am. Acad. Indsl. Hygiene, Bd. Cert. Safety Profls. Rsch. asst. dept. environ. health scis. Harvard Sch. Pub. Health, Boston, 1966-68, staff indsl. hygienist, 1975-76, vis. lectr., 1986—, cons. dept. continuing edn., 1978—; asst. chemist div. occupational hygiene Mass. Dept. Labor and Industries, Boston, 1968-69; indsl. hygienist dept. environ. health and safety Harvard U. Health Svcs., Cambridge, Mass., 1976-86; indsl. hygiene engr. dept. health, safety-environ. affairs Polaroid Corp., Waltham, Mass., 1986-89; assoc. indsl. hygiene officer environ. med. svc. MIT, Cambridge, 1989-92, indsl. hygiene officer, 1992-97, assoc. dir., 1997-2000, dir. environ. health and safety, 2000—. Pres. DiBerardinis Assocs., Inc., Wellesley, Mass., 1980—; vice chair com. on safety codes for exhaust systems Am. Nat. Standards Inst., 1984—, also chmn. subcom. on lab. ventilation; cons. in field. Author: (with others) Guidelines for Laboratory Design: Health and Safety Considerations, 3d edit., 2001; editor: Handbook of Health and Safety, 1998, 2d edit.; mem. editl. bd. Chem. Health and Safety; contbr. articles to profl. jours., chpt. to books. Mem. sci. adv. com. City of Cambridge, 1984-86. Recipient Health and Safety Profl. of Year award Am. Chem. Soc., 1997. Fellow Am. Indsl. Hygiene Assn. (pres. New Eng. sect. 1985-86); mem. Am. Conf. Govtl. Indsl. Hygienists, Brit. Occupl. Hygiene Soc., Am. Soc. Safety Engrs., Am. Acad. Indsl. Hygiene (sec.-treas. 1983-88, pres. 1993), Harvard Club of Boston. Avocations: winemaking, basketball, racquetball. Home: 24 Twitchell St Wellesley MA 02482-6056 Office: 77 Massachusetts Ave Cambridge MA 02139-4301 E-mail: loudib@mit.edu.

DIBERARDINO, MARIE ANTOINETTE, developmental biologist, educator; b. Phila., May 2, 1926; d. Henry and Adelina (Belfi) DiB. BS in Biology, Chestnut Hill Coll., 1948, JD (hon.), 1990; PhD in Zoology, U. Pa., 1962. Rsch. asst. Fox Chase Cancer Ctr. (formerly Inst. Cancer Rsch.), 1948-58, rsch. assoc., 1960-64, asst. mem., 1964-67; assoc. prof. anatomy Drexel U. Coll. Medicine, Phila., 1967-71, prof. anatomy, 1971-81, prof. physiology, 1981-92, prof. biochemistry, 1992-96, prof. emerita, 1996—. Adv. bd. Internat. Rev. of Cytology, 1976-2000, Differentiation, 1981—, Series: Developmental Biology, A Comprehensive Synthesis, 1982-94; assoc. editor Jour. Exptl. Zoology, 1984-86; Contbr. articles on devel., genetics and cell biology to sci. jours.; contbr. book revs. in field. Mem. NIH Fogarty Internat. Fellowship Study Group, 1984. NSF grantee, NIH grantee; recipient Jean Brachet Meml. award. Fellow AAAS; mem. Am. Soc. Cell Biology (emerita), Soc. for Devel. Biologists (emerita, treas., trustee 1975-78), Internat. Soc. Devel. Biologists, Internat. Soc. of Differentiation (emerita, exec. com. 1978-85, 87-90, bd. dirs. 1980-94). Office: Drexel U Coll Medicine 2900 W Queen Ln Philadelphia PA 19129-1033 E-mail: mad26@drexel.edu.

DIBIAGGIO, JOHN A. university president; b. San Antonio, Sept. 11, 1932; s. Ciro and Acidalia DiBiaggio; married; children: David John, Dana Elizabeth, Deirdre Joan; m. Nancy Cronemiller, May 27, 1989. AB, Eastern Mich. U., 1954, D (hon.) of Edn., 1985; DDS, U. Detroit, 1958, LHD (hon.), 1985; MA, U. Mich., 1967; DSc (hon.), Fairleigh Dickinson U., 1981; LLD (hon.), Sacred Heart U., Bridgeport, Conn., 1984; LLD (hon.), U. Md., 1985; DHL (hon.), U. New Eng., 1987; DHL (hon.), Tokyo U. Agr., 1991; LLD (hon.), U. Nigeria, Nsukka, 1992; LHD (hon.), Fitchburg State Coll., 1994; LHD (hon.), Amer. Coll. Greece, 1998; LLD (hon.), Tufts U., 2002. Pvt. practice, New Baltimore, Mich., 1958—65; asst. prof., asst. to dean, dept. chmn. sch. dentistry U. Detroit, 1965—67; asst. dean student affairs U. Ky., Lexington, 1967—70; prof., dean sch. dentistry Va. Commonwealth U., Richmond, 1970—76; v.p. for health affairs, exec. dir. health ctr. U. Conn., Farmington, 1976—79, pres. Storrs, 1979—85, Mich. State U., East Lansing, 1985—92, Tufts U., Medford, Mass., 1992—2001, now pres. emeritus, 2001—. Bd. dirs. Kaman Corp.; mem. Knight Found. Commn. on Intercollegiate Athletics, 1990—2001, PEW Health Professions Commn., 1990—93; cons. in field. Author (with others): Applied Practice Management: A Strategy for Stress Control, 1979; contbr. articles to profl. jours. Bd. nominators Am. Inst. Pub. Svc., 1989—92; bd. dirs. Nat. Italian Am. Found., 1988—94; active Bus. Higher Edn. Forum, 1996—, WGBH Ednl. Found., 1992—, chmn. governance com., 1997—; trustee U. Detroit, 1979—86, Am. Film Inst., 1988—, Forsyth Dental Ctr., 1993—, Am. Cancer Soc. Found., 1993—, pres., 1999; trustee Oral Health Am., 1995—97; chmn. adv. com. dental scholars R.W. Johnson Found.; pres. com. Argonne Nat. Lab. 6, 1986—; coun. pres. Univs. Rsch. Assn., 1989—92; bd. dirs. Black Child and Family Inst., 1990, Coun. for Aid to Edn., 1994—96, Mass. Nat. and Cmty. Svc. Commn., 1994—97, Am. Coun. on Edn., 1995—, vice-chmn., 1998, chmn., 1999; exec. com. Mass. Campus Compact, 1995—, exec. dir. search com., 1996, chmn. devel. com., 1996—, governance com., 1996—98, chmn., 1998; bd. assocs. Whitehead Inst. for Biomed. Rsch., 1995—, chmn., 1998. Decorated Order of Merit Italy; named Disting. Profl. of Yr., Mich. Assn. Profls., 1985, Disting. Alumni, Ea. Mich. U., 1986, Man of Yr., City of Detroit, 1985; recipient Leadership award, Sacred Heart U., Pierre Fauchard Gold Medal award, 1989. Fellow: Internat. Coll. Dentists, Am. Coll. Dentist; mem.: NCAA (found. bd. dirs. 1988—2001, found. divsn. III pres.'s coun. 1997—2001), APHA, ADA, Nat. Assn. State Univs. and Land Grant Colls. (chmn. 1986—87), Internat. Assn. Dental Rsch., Am. Assn. Dental Schs., Mass. Automobile Assn. (bd. dirs. 1992—), Am. Automobile Assn. (bd. dirs. 1994—), Am. Film Inst., Golden Key, Alpha Lambda Delta, Alpha Sigma Chi, Alpha Omega Alpha (Achievement award 1993), Beta Gamma Sigma, Omicron Kappa Upsilon, Phi Kappa Phi. Avocations: golf, antique automobiles, skiing. E-mail: john.dibiaggio@tufts.edu.*

DI BISCEGLIE, LAUREEN GAIL, pianist, educator; b. Johannesburg, Gauteng, South Africa, Oct. 27, 1955; came to U.S., 1985; d. Peter Cyril and Mavis Gladys (Campbell) Pinn; m. Adrian Michael Di Bisceglie, Dec. 9, 1978; children: Michael James, Anne-Marie Hope. MMus cum laude, U. Witwatersrand, Johannesburg, 1987. Cert. tchr. music. Music tchr. Kingsmead Coll., Johannesburg, 1977-82, head dept. music, 1980-82; pvt. piano tchr. Washington, 1985-95; tchr. music, head music program Barrie Day Sch., Washington, 1987-90; accompanist Wilson Sch., St. Louis, 1987—; pvt. piano tchr. St. Louis, 1995—. Contbr. articles to profl. jours. Vol. music dept. Washington Nat. Cathedral, 1986-87; advisor search com. Christ Episc. Ch., Rockville, Md.,

1992-93, outreach com., 1991-92; bd. dirs. Woman's Club, SLU Sch. of Medicine, 1997, chmn. com., 1997—; mem. steering com. Parents Assn., 1997—; co-chair Wilson Sch.'s Thistle Auction, 1998-99, 99-2000; hon. mem. Liver Found.'s. Ann. Auction com.; mem. outreach com. Ch. of St. Michael and St. George Clayton, St. Louis. Anglo-Am. scholar, 1973-78; Royal Coll. of Ch. Music grantee, Croydon, Eng., 1985. Mem. Music Tchrs. Nat. Assn., St. Louis Area Music Tchrs. Assn. (chair dist. auditions 2002-03, bd. dirs.), Piano Tchrs. Round Table (, bd. dirs., v.p. programs), Suzuki Assn. Am., Fedn. Music Tchrs., Woman's Club (sec. 1998—). Episcopalian. Avocations: reading, travel, gardening, walking. Home: 5 Deer Creek Woods Saint Louis MO 63124-1411

DIBLASI, DIANNE CLARK, editor; b. Bklyn., May 3, 1960; d. Arthur J. and Constance C. (Clark) Mandick; m. Paul J. DiBlasi; 1 child, Bryan Gene. BA in Journalism, NYU, 1982. Asst. editor Random House/Fodor's Travel Guides, N.Y.C., 1983-85; writer, editor Constrn. Products Rev. Mag., Boston, 1986-88; prodn. editor Prentice Hall, Englewood Cliffs, N.J., 1988-91; owner, cons. D. DiBlasi Editl. Svcs., Allendale, NJ, 1991—. Copy editor: Take My Word For It, 1986; prodn. editor: Creativities! Elementary Curriculum Art Activities, 1991, Parenting Toward Solutions, 1997; editor, writer Constrn. Products Rev., 1986-88. Mem. Hillsdale Playground Assn., 1994-96, Hillsdale Centennial Com., 1996; mem., chair com. Meadowbrook Faculty and Family Assn., Hillsdale, 1996—; host Fresh Air Fund, 1997—; docent Wildlife Conservation Soc., Bronx Zoo. Mem.: Editl. Freelancer Assn., Brookside Music Assn. (chmn.). Avocations: animal wildlife outreach programs, fundraising. Home and Office: 222 E Crescent Ave Allendale NJ 07401

DIBLASI, GANDOLFO VINCENT, lawyer; b. Bklyn., July 7, 1953; s. Rudolph Francis and Theresa (Restivo) DiB.; m. Roberta Wilson, Sept. 13, 1980; children: Richard, William. BA, Yale Coll., 1975, JD, 1978. Bar: N.Y., 1979, U.S. Ct. Appeals (2d cir.), 1982, U.S. Ct. Appeals (4th cir.), 1991, U.S. Ct. Appeals (9th cir.), 1981, U.S. Supreme Ct., 1990, U.S. Dist. Ct. (so. dist.) N.Y., 1979, U.S. Dist. Ct. (ea. dist.) N.Y., 1982, U.S. Dist. Ct. (no. dist.) Calif., 1989. Assoc. Sullivan & Cromwell, N.Y.C., 1978-85, ptnr., 1985—. Home: 200 E End Ave Apt 15I New York NY 10128-7887 Office: Sullivan & Cromwell 125 Broad St Fl 28 New York NY 10004-2489

DIBLE, ROSE HARPE MCFEE, special education educator; b. Phoenix, Apr. 28, 1927; d. Ambrose Jefferson and Laurel Mabel (Harpe) McFee; m. James Henry Dible, June 23, 1951 (div. Jan. 1965); 1 child, Michael James. BA in Speech Edn., Ariz. State U., Tempe, 1949; MA in Speech and Drama, U. So. Calif., L.A., 1950; fellow, Calif. State U., Fullerton, 1967. Cert. secondary tchr., spl. edn. tchr. English and drama tchr. Lynwood (Calif.) Sr. High Sch., 1950-51, Montebello (Calif.) Sr. High Sch., 1952-58; tchr. English and Social Studies Pioneer High Sch., Whittier, Calif., 1964-65; spl. edn. tchr. Bell Gardens (Calif.) High Sch., 1967-85, spl. edn. cons., 1985-90. Mem. DAR, Daus. Am. Colonists, Whittier Christian Woman Assn., La Habra Womans Club, Eastern Star Lodge, Kappa Delts, Phi Delta Gamma. Republican. Presbyterian. Avocations: church choir, tap dancing, doll collecting, travel. Home: 1201 Russell St La Habra CA 90631-2530 Office: Montebello Unified Sch Dist 123 Montebello Blvd Montebello CA 90640

DIBNER, DAVID ROBERT, architect, writer; b. N.Y.C., May 29, 1926; s. Harry Jesse and Masha Leah (Goldberg) D.; m. Dorothy Joyce Siegel, June 22, 1947; children: Mark Douglas, Amy Lauren. B.Arch., U. Pa., 1949. Registered architect, N.Y., Md., Va., D.C. Ptnr. Fordyce & Hamby Assocs., N.Y.C., 1956-66, The Grad Ptnrship., Newark, 1966-77; pres. Grad-Hoffman, Inc., 1971-75; v.p. Walker-Grad, N.Y.C., 1972-77; exec. v.p. Grad Assocs. P.A., Newark, 1975-77; asst. commr. design and constrn. GSA, Washington, 1977-82; sr. v.p. Bernard Johnson Inc., Bethesda, Md., 1982-89; v.p. and prin. architect Sverdrup Corp., Arlington, Va., 1989-92. Adj. prof. Seton Hall U., South Orange, N.J., 1972-77; mem. Bldg. Rsch. Bd. of Nat. Acad. Sci., com. chmn., 1984-92. Author: Joint Ventures for Architects and Engineers, 1972, You and Your Architect, 1973, (with Amy Dibner-Dunlap) Building Additions Design, 1985; editor (with Andrew Lemer) The Role of Public Agencies in Fostering New Technology and Innovation in Building, 1992, Dreams and Schemes: Stories of People and Architecture, 2001; chmn. editorial bd. Architecture/N.J., 1968-71; contbr. articles to profl. jours. Mem. West Orange Bd. of Adjustment, N.J., 1970-77, Bldg. Rsch. Bd., 1984-90; Nat. Trust for Historic Preservation. Served with USN, 1944-46, PTO. Fellow AIA (Washington chpt.). E-mail: drdibs@cox.net.

DIBONA, CHARLES JOSEPH, retired trade association executive; b. Quincy, Mass., Feb. 26, 1932; s. Guido Ralph and Helen Elizabeth (Pangraze) DiB.; m. Evelyn Rauch, July 2, 1959; children: Caroline Anne, Charles J. BS, U.S. Naval Acad., 1956; MA (Rhodes scholar), Oxford U., Eng., 1962. Pres., chief exec. officer Center for Naval Analyses, 1967-73; spl. cons. to Pres. U.S., dep. dir.; White House Energy Policy Office, 1973-74; exec. v.p., chief oper. officer Am. Petroleum Inst., Washington, 1974-78, pres., chief exec. officer, 1979-98; ret., 1998. Mem. Fed. City Coun.; chmn. bd. dirs. Logistics Mgmt. Inst.; bd. dirs. Halliburton Co. Lt. comdr. USN, 1956-67. Mem. Cosmos Club, Met. Club, Chevy Chase Country Club. Roman Catholic. Home: 9306 Georgetown Pike Great Falls VA 22066-2725 Fax: 703-759-7369. E-mail: dibonac@erols.com.

DIBONAVENTURE, LORENZO, film company executive; Co-pres. Worldwide Theatrical Prodn. Warner Bros., Inc., Burbank, Calif. Office: Warner Bros Inc 4000 Warner Blvd Burbank CA 91522-0002

DICAMILLO, GARY THOMAS, manufacturing executive; b. Niagara Falls, N.Y., Dec. 10, 1950; s. Joseph John and Olga Marie (Parenti) DiC.; m. Susan Christine Whitaker, Sept. 13, 1975; children: David, John, Benjamin. BSChemE, Rensselaer Poly. Inst., 1973; MBA, Harvard U., 1975. Brand mgr. Procter & Gamble, Cin., 1975-80; mgr. Mckinsey & Co., Chgo., 1980-83; v.p., gen. mgr. Culligan Internat. Co., Northbrook, Ill., 1983-86; pres. Worldwide Power Tools Group Black & Decker Corp., Towson, Md., 1986-95; chmn., CEO Polaroid Corp., Cambridge, Mass., 1995—2002; pres., CEO TAC Worldwide Cos., 2002—. Bd. dirs. Whirlpool Corp., Pella Corp., Sheridan Group, 3Com Corp. Mem. bd. govs. New Eng. Aquarium, 1996-2003; commr. Md. Pub. Broadcasting Commn., 1988-93; trustee St. Paul's Sch., 1988-95, Greater Balt. Com., Md. Sci. Ctr.; bd. dirs. Leadership Balt., 1991-93; trustee Mus. of Sci., Boston, Rensselaer Poly. Inst.; mem. bd. trustees The Conf. Bd., 1999-2002. Recipient Albert Demers medal, Livingston Houston prize, Rensselaer Poly. Inst., 1973; Buffalo Alumni scholar Buffalo area Rensselaer Poly. Inst. Alumni, 1969; Chirurg Advt. fellow Harvard U. Bus. Sch., 1974; recipient Rensselaer Poly. Inst. Dirs. award, 1989. Mem. Water Quality Assn. (bd. dirs. 1985-86), Md. Acad. Scis. (bd. dirs. 1991-96), Rensselaer Poly. Inst. Club (bd. dirs. 1987-91, pres.), Rensselaer Alumni Assn. (bd. dirs. 1989-93, Alumni Key award 1990), Hardware Mktg. Coun., DIY Rsch. Inst. (bd. dirs. 1989-90), Skokie Country Club, Elkridge Club, Md. Club, L'Hirondelle Club, Willowbend Club, Wianno Club, Brae Burn Country Club, Harvard Club. Republican. Episcopalian. Avocations: golf, tennis, squash, antique furniture, italian cooking. Home: 113 Cliff Rd Wellesley MA 02481-3017 Office: TAC Worldwide Cos 888 Washington St Dedham MA 02026

DICAPRIO, LEONARDO, actor; b. Hollywood, Calif., Nov. 11, 1974; s. George and Irmelin DiC. Actor: (films) Critters III, 1991, This Boy's Life, 1993, What's Eating Gilbert Grape?, 1993 (Academy award nomination best supporting actor 1993), The Quick and the Dead, 1995, The Basketball Diaries, 1995, Total Eclipse, 1995, Romeo and Juliet, 1996, Marvin's Room, 1996, Titanic, 1997, The Man in the Iron Mask, 1998, Celebrity, 1998, The Beach, 2000, Dons Plum, 2001, Gangs of New York, 2002, Catch Me If You Can, 2002. (TV series) Parenthood, 1990, Growing Pains, 1991-92. Founder The Leondardo DiCaprio Charitable Found., 1998—. Recipient Green Cross Millenium award for Entertainment Ind. Environ., Global Green USA, 2003.

DI CARLI, MARCELO FERNANDO, cardiologist; arrived in US, 1991; s. Roman and Julieta Di Carli; m. Maria Elvira Landa, Sept. 19, 1987; children: Gilda, Milena. MD, U. Buenos Aires, 1984. Assoc. dir. PET Ctr. Children's Hosp. Mich., Detroit, 1994—2001; dir. nuc. cardiology Brigham and Women's Hosp., Boston, 2001—. Office: Brigham and Womens Hosp 75 Francis St Boston MA 02115 Office Fax: 617-582-6056. Personal E-mail: mdicarli@partners.org. E-mail: mdicarli@partners.org.

DICARLO, LAURETTE MARY, nurse; b. Cleve., Aug. 19, 1950; d. Amerigo and Helen (Senuta) DiC. LPN, Willoughby-Eastlake Sch., 1976; AS in Nursing, Santa Fe C.C., Gainesville, Fla., 1982; BSN magna cum laude, U. South Fla., 1991, MS in Nursing, 1997. RN, Fla., advanced registered nurse practitioner. Nurse Riverside Meth. Hosp., Columbus, Ohio, 1976-78, Lakeland (Fla.) Gen. Hosp., 1978-79, Alalhua Gen. Hosp., Gainesville, 1979-82; nurse mgr. progressive care Humana Northside Hosp., St. Petersburg, Fla., 1991-92; critical care nurse Columbia Largo (Fla.) Med. Ctr., 1982-91; med. supr. TGC Home Health, Clearwater, Fla., 1994-95; charge nurse cardiovascular intensive care, emergency nurse Columbia Largo Med. Ctr., 1992-98, nurse practitioner internal medicine and infectious disease, 1998—. Vol. Soc. for Prevention of Cruelty to Animals, Largo, 1991—. Santa Fe scholar, 1982, Joan K. Stout scholar Miami Heart Inst./U. South Fla., 1996-97. Mem. AACN, ANA, Am. Acad. Nurse Practitioners, Fla. Nurses Assn., Phi Kappa Phi, Sigma Theta Tau. Avocation: oil painting.

DICARLO, MICHAEL ALEXANDER, library director; b. Lake Charle, La., Feb. 9, 1953; s. Secondo Lawrence DiCarlo, Eugenia Bernadette DiCarlo; m. Rebecca Lynn McKillips; 1 child, Carrifrances. BA in History, Tulane U., 1975; MLS, La. State U., 0197. Info. svcs. libr. bus./social scis., instrnl. Northeast La. U., Monreo, 1978—81; head libr. automation La. Tech. U., Ruston, 1983—87, head reference & libr. automation, 1987—91, asst. dir. pub. svcs., 1991—96, interim dir. librs., 1996—97, assoc. dir. librs., 1997—. Recipient Certificate of Recognition, Sigma Xi, La. Tech.chpt., 1992. Mem.: La. Libr. Assn. (Anthony H. Benoit Mid-Career award, New Mem. Round Table 1995), Beta Phi Mu, Phi Alpha Theta. Roman Catholic. Office: La Tech Univ- Prescott Libr Everett St at The Columns Ruston LA 71272 Office Fax: 318-257-2579. Personal E-mail: miked@library.latech.edu. Business E-Mail: miked@library.latech.edu.

DICARLO, SUSANNE HELEN, financial analyst; b. Greensburg, Pa., Nov. 24, 1956; d. Wayne Larry and Clara Emogene (Weaver) Gower; m. John Joseph DiCarlo, June 21, 1980; children: Sarah Rose, Kristen Marie. BS in Acctg., Va. Tech., 1978. Auditor U.S. Army Audit Agy., Ft. Monroe, Va., 1978-79; acct. technician Fleet Combat Tng. Ctr., Virginia Beach, Va., 1980-82, supervisory auditor, 1982-83; fin. analyst Comml. Activity Mgmt. Team, Norfolk, Va., 1983—. Fed. women's program mgr. Fleet Combat Tng. Ctr., 1980—83. Creator newsletter: Fed. Women's Program Mgr., 1980—83. Mem.: Southeastern Assn. Trainers, Am. Soc. Mil. Comptrollers, Seaside Mountaineers Club (Virginia Beach) (treas. 1986—88). Home: 4013 Dillaway Ct Virginia Beach VA 23456-1257

DICE, BRUCE BURTON, exploration company executive; b. Grand Rapids, Mich., Dec. 24, 1926; s. William and Wilma (Rose) D.; children: Karen, Kevin, Kirk. BS in Geology, U. Mich., 1950; MS in Geology, Mich. State U., 1956. With El Paso Natural Gas, 1956—62, Drilling and Exploration Co., 1962—63, Ocean Drilling and Exploration, New Orleans, 1963—75; pres. Transco Exploration Co., Houston, 1975—82, Dice Exploration Co., Inc., Houston, 1982—95, Wadi Petroleum, Inc., Houston, 1996—. Cons. in field. Active Houston Symphony. Mem.: Shepherd Soc., Houston Geol. Soc., Am. Assn. Petroleum Geologists. Home: 1907 Grand Valley Dr Houston TX 77090-1052 Office: Wadi Petroleum Inc 14405 Walters Rd Houston TX 77014-1337 E-mail: sgc@wadipetroleum.com .

DICELLO, FRANCIS P. lawyer; b. Waukegan, Ill., May 5, 1941; s. Anthony M. and Mary Dicello; m. Mary Janice Dicello; children: Anthony, Andrew, Carlotta. BA, U. Notre Dame, 1963; JD, Fordham U., 1966. Bar: Conn. 1966, D.C. 1967, Md 1984, Va 1982. Trial atty. U.S. Dept. Justice, Washington, 1970-76; dep. asst., gen. counsel U.S. Railway Assn., Washington, 1976-78; asst., chief trial & settlement rev. sects. tax divsn. U.S. Dept. Justice, Washington, 1978-79; U.S. trustee ea. dist. Va. and D.C., 1979—82; ptnr., owner Hazel & Thomas, P.C., Washington, 1982-94; ptnr. Reed Smith, LLP, Washington, 1994—. Fellow Am. Coll. Bankruptcy; mem. Am. Bankruptcy Inst. Office: Reed Smith LLP 1301 K St NW Ste 1100E Washington DC 20005-3373 E-mail: fdicello@reedsmith.com.

DI CHIERA, DAVID, general director of opera company; b. McKeesport, Pa., Apr. 8, 1935; s. Cosimo and Maria (Pezzaniti) DiC.; m. Karen VanderKloot, July 20, 1965 (div. 1992); children: Lisa Maria, Cristina Maria. BA in Music summa cum laude, UCLA, 1956, MA in Composition (scholar), 1958, PhD in Musicology, 1962; certificate in composition and piano (Fulbright Research grantee), Naples Conservatory of Music, 1959; D (hon.), U. Mich., 1998. Instr. music U. Calif., Los Angeles, 1960-61; asst. prof. music, asst. dean Oakland U., Rochester, Mich., 1962-65, chmn. music dept., 1966-73; founding gen. dir. Mich. Opera Theatre, Detroit, 1971—; founding dir. Music Hall Center for the Performing Arts, Detroit, 1973—. Artistic dir. Dayton Opera Assn., 1981-92; founding gen. dir. Opera Pacific, Costa Mesa, Calif., 1985-97; trustee Nat. Opera Inst.; adj. prof. Oakland U., Wayne State U. Producer, dir.: Overture to Opera series for, Detroit Grand Opera series, 1963-71; Composer various works for piano, violin, orch., voice; author articles on Italian opera for various encyclopedias; contbr. revs. and articles to music jours. Mem. Arts Com. New Detroit, Inc.; trustee, mem. exec. com. Music Center for Performing Arts; mem. Arts Task Force City of Detroit. Recipient Atwater Kent award U. Calif., Los Angeles, 1961; Certificate of Appreciation City of Detroit, 1970; citation Mich. Legislature, 1976; Michaelangelo award Boys' Town of Italy, 1980; award Arts Found. of Mich., 1981; President's Cabinet award U. Detroit, 1982; George Gershwin fellow, 1958; named A Michiganian of Yr., 1980; cavaliere della Repubblica Italiana. Mem. Am. Arts Alliance (exec. com.), Nat. Opera Assn., Internat. Assn. Lyric Theatre (v.p.), Am. Symphony League, Am. Musicol. Soc., OPERA Am. (pres. 1979-83), AAUP, Phi Beta Kappa, Phi Mu Alpha Sinfonia. Clubs: Detroit Athletic. Office: Mich Opera Theatre 1526 Broadway St Detroit MI 48226-2115*

DICHTER, BARRY JOEL, lawyer; b. Brookline, Mass., Feb. 19, 1950; s. Irving Melvin and Arlene Dichter; m. Judith Rand, Oct. 22, 1972; children: Rebecca Lynn, Jason Benjamin. AB magna cum laude, Harvard U., 1972, JD cum laude, 1975. Bar: Mass. 1975, N.Y. 1976, U.S. Dist. Ct. (so. and ea. dists.) N.Y. 1976, D.C. 1980, U.S. Dist. Ct. D.C. 1980, U.S. Ct. Appeals (D.C. cir.) 1985. Assoc. Webster & Sheffield, N.Y.C., 1975-82, Cadwalader, Wickersham & Taft, N.Y.C., 1983-84, ptnr., 1984—. Lectr. in field. Contbg. editor: Collier on Bankruptcy, 15th edit., rev. Vice chmn. Harvard Law Sch. Fund, Cambridge, Mass., 1984-88, class agt., 1988-99; bd. dirs. Children's Corner, Inc., 1990-95, treas., 1992-95; mem. exec. com., bankruptcy and reorgn. group of lawyers divsn. N.Y. United Jewish Appeal. Mem. ABA (mem. task force on Sect. 110 1991-92, mem. task force on emerging issues in the transp. industry 1992-96, mem. task force on Article 9 securitization issues), Assn. of Bar of City of N.Y. (mem. bankruptcy com. 1986-89, 91-94). Office: Cadwalader Wickersham & Taft 100 Maiden Ln New York NY 10038-4818

DICHTER, MARK S. lawyer; b. Phila., Jan. 22, 1943; s. Harry B. and Mollie (Silverstein) D.; m. Tobey Gordon, Aug. 17, 1969; children: Aliza, Melissa. BSEE, Drexel U., 1966; JD magna cum laude, Villanova U., 1969. Bar: Pa. 1969, U.S. Ct. Appeals (3d cir.) 1969, U.S. Supreme Ct. 1979. Assoc. Morgan, Lewis & Bockius, LLP, Phila., 1969-76, ptnr., 1976—, chmn. labor and employment law practice group. Co-author: Employee Dismissal Law: Forms and Procedures, 1986-91; editor-in-chief Ann. Supplement Employment Discrimination Law, 1984-89; co-editor: Employment-at-will, 1985, 86, State-by-State Survey, 1984-89; adv. bd. Disability Law Reporter. Bd. dirs. Urban League Phila.; bd. dirs., chmn. Wilma Theater; bd. consultors Villanova U. Sch. Law; bd. dirs. Pub. Interest Law Ctr. Phila. Mem. ABA (labor and employment law sect., chmn. 2000-01, mem. governing coun. 1991-2000, co-chmn. equal opportunity com. 1986-89, employment law com. litigation sect.), FBA (vice chmn. equal employment com. 1983-86), Nat. Employment Law Inst. (adv. bd. 1984—), Am. Employment Law Counsel (bd. dirs.), Am. Coll. Employment Lawyers, Def. Rsch. Inst. (chmn. employment law com. 1989-93). Home: 1017 Clinton St Philadelphia PA 19107-6016 Office: Morgan Lewis & Bockius LLP 1701 Market St Philadelphia PA 19103-2903 Fax: 215-963-5001. E-mail: mdichter@morganlewis.com.

DI CICCO, JOSEPH NICHOLAS, JR., chemical engineer; b. Phila., Jan. 24, 1917; s. Joseph and Angela Theresa (Romani) DiC.; m. Laura Adolph Broadwater, Sept. 14, 1940; children: Dona Marie Kemling, Joseph III. Indsl. chem. cert., Camden County Vocat. Sch., 1937; petroleum engring. cert., Pa. State U., 1949. Registered profl. engr., N.J.; cert. profl. mgr. Rsch. chemist United Gas Improvement Co., Phila., 1937-40; devel. engr. Ugite Sales Corp., Chester, Pa., 1940-45; plant engr. Pa. Indsl. Chem. Corp., Chester, 1945-60, asst. mgr. engring., 1960-70, corp. chief engr. Clairton, 1970-73; mgr. engring. Hercules, Inc.-PICCO Resins Div., Clairton, 1973-82; pvt. practice cons. engr. Wilmington, NC, 1982—95. Bd. dirs. Century Adhesives Corp., Columbus, Ohio. Pres. bd. dirs. Gloucester County YMCA, Woodbury, N.J., 1965-70; v.p. bd. dirs. Gloucester County United Fund, Woodbury, 1967-70, Pitts. Met. YMCA, 1979-81; mem. internat. com. YMCA of USA, 1977-78; chmn. Delaware Valley Cluster of YMCA's, 1988-90; mem. East Field membership com. of YMCA's, 1988-90; bd. dirs. YMCA, Wilmington, N.C., 1992-2000, Cornelia Nixon Davis Health Care Ctr., 2003—; chmn. bd. trustees Found. for Geriatrics Independence, 1995—; pres. Kiwanis Club of Woodbury, 1988-89. Recipient Svc. to Youth award YMCA, 1965, Layperson of Yr. award Wilmington YMCA, 1994; named Alumnus of Yr., Camden County Vocat. Sch., 1975. Mem. Am. Inst. Chemical Engrs., NSPE, Inst. Cert. Profl. Mgrs., Internat. Mgmt. Coun. (nat. pres. 1969-70, dir., Disting. Svc. award 1976). Republican. Episcopalian. Avocations: golf, fishing, photography. E-mail: jdicicco124@cs.com.

DICICCO, TONY, soccer coach; b. Wethersfield, Conn., Aug. 5, 1948; m. Diane; children: Anthony, Andrew, Alex, Nicholas. Grad., Springfield Coll., 1970; M in Phys. Edn., Ctrl. Conn. State U.; advanced nat. diploma, Nat. Soccer Coaches Assn. Am. Lic. U.S. Soccer A. Profl. soccer player Conn. Wildcats, R.I. Oceaneers; asst. coach U.S. Women's Nat. Soccer Team, 1991-94, head coach, 1994-99; asst. women's coach Under 20 Men's Nat. Team, 1993. Founder Soccer Plus, Inc., Specialty Stores, 1981—, Soccer Plus Goalkeeper Schs., 1981—; region I boys goalkeeper dir.; goalkeeper specialist Nat. Soccer Coaches Assn. Am.; conductor U.S. Soccer and Nat. Soccer Coaches Assn. Am. nat. licensing camps. Recipient gold medal with team Olympics, Atlanta, 1996. Office: Soccer Plus Camps 20 Beaver Rd Ste 102 Wethersfield CT 06109-2201

DICK, BERTRAM GALE, JR., physics educator; b. Portland, Oreg., June 12, 1926; s. Bertram Gale and Helen (Meengs) D.; m. Ann Bradford Volkmann, June 23, 1956; children— Timothy Howe, Robin Louise, Stephen Gale. BA, Reed Coll., 1950; BA (Rhodes scholar), Wadham Coll., Oxford (Eng.) U., 1953, MA, 1958; PhD, Cornell U., 1958. Rsch. assoc. U. Ill., 1957-59; mem. faculty U. Utah, 1959-98, prof. physics, 1965-98, prof. emeritus, 1998—, Univ. prof., 1979-80, chmn. dept., 1964-67, dean grad. sch., 1987-93. Cons. Minn. Mining and Mfg. Co., 1960-67; vis. prof. Technische Hochschule, Munich, 1967-68; vis. scientist Max Planck Institut für Festkörperforschung, Stuttgart, Fed. Republic Germany, 1976-77; faculty Semester at Sea, fall 1983, 86. Mem. Alta Planning and Zoning Commn., 1972-76; pres. Chamber Music Salt Lake City, 1974-76; bd. trustees Citizen's Com. to Save Our Canyons, 1972—, Coalition for Utah's Future Project 2000, 1989-96. Served in USNR, 1944-46. Fellow Am. Phys. Soc.; mem. Am. Alpine Club, Phi Beta Kappa, Sigma Xi. Achievements include research in solid state theory. Home: 1377 Butler Ave Salt Lake City UT 84102-1803

DICK, DAVID E. construction company executive; b. Dec. 4, 1948; BS, Robert Morris Coll. With Dick Corp., Clairton, Pa., 1964—, now CEO. Officer Dick Enterprises, Inc., Clairton. Office: Dick Corp PO Box 10896 Pittsburgh PA 15236-0896

DICK, ERNST S. retired German language educator; b. Grabenhof, Germany, Apr. 7, 1929; s. Wilhelm and Berta Dick; m. Renate H. Jansen, July 28, 1961; children: Ina B., Arnolf W. PhD, Westphalian Wilhelms U., Muenster, Germany, 1961. Instr. German U. Mont., Missoula, 1961—62; assist. to assoc. prof. German U. Va., Charlottesville, 1962—67; prof. German U. Wis., Milw., 1967—68, U. Kans., Lawrence, 1968—2002, prof. emeritus, 2003—. Author (and editor): approximately 50 books and articles on German philology and lit. Recipient Festschrift prize, Winder McConnell, editor, 1989; grantee various rsch. grants, ACLS and others, 1962—; Exch. scholar, Johns Hopkins U., 1956—57, U. of Sheffield, Eng., 1953. Mem.: Am. Assn. Tchrs. of German, Wolfram von Eschenbach-Gesellschaft, Internat. Arthurian Soc., Internat. Assn. for German Studies, Medieval Acad. Am. Office: Dept German U Kansas Lawrence KS 66045

DICK, HAROLD LATHAM, manufacturing executive; b. Wichita, Kans., Oct. 24, 1943; s. Harold G. and Evelyn (Spines) D.; m. Jeanne Marie Luczai, Aug. 25, 1973; children: Harold Campbell, Edward Latham. BA, Washburn U., 1966; MBA, Harvard U., 1968. Exec. asst. to treas. Skelly Oil Co., Tulsa, 1968-70; mgmt. cons. McKinsey & Co. Inc., Chgo., Dallas, Houston, 1970-77; dir. planning Frito-Lay Inc., Dallas, 1977-80; v.p. Norton Simon Inc., N.Y.C., 1980-83; founder Summit Ptnrs., Wichita, Kans., 1983-85; pres., chief exec. officer Doskocil Cos. Inc., Hutchinson, Kans., 1985-88; founder, pres. The Summit Group, Hutchinson, 1988—. Adv. bd. dirs. Garvey Industries, Wichita, 1987-94, Petroleum Inc., Wichita, 1993—. Trustee Kanza coun. Boy Scouts Am., 1989-97, exec. bd., 1995-97, v.p. 1997—, exec. bd. dirs. Quivira coun., 1997—, v.p., 1997-98, coun. commr., 1998-2002, coun. pres., 2002-; Stephen minister, 1987-94; mem. bd. regents Washburn U., 1995—, chmn. bd. regents, 2001-02, chmn. fin. com., 1998-2001; trustee Washburn Endowment Assn., 1990-; mem. presdl. search com. Washburn U., 1987-88. Mem. Washburn Alumni Assn. (bd. dirs. 1986-89). Republican. Episcopalian. Office: The Summit Group PO Box 3216 Hutchinson KS 67504-3216

DICK, HENRY HENRY, minister; b. Russia, June 1, 1922; s. Henry Henry and Mary (Unger) D.; m. Erica Penner, May 25, 1946; children— Janet (Mrs. Arthur Enns), Judith (Mrs. Ron Brown), James, Henry. Th.B., Mennonite Brethren Bible Coll., 1950. Ordained to ministry Mennonite Brethren Ch., 1950; pastor in Orillia, Ont., Can., 1950-54, Lodi, Calif., 1954-57, Shafter, Calif., 1958-69; faculty Tabor Coll., 1954-55; gen. sec. Mennonite Brethren Conf. of U.S.A., 1969-72; pres. Mennonite Brethren Bibl. Sem., Fresno, Calif., 1972-76; vice moderator Gen Conf. Mennonite Brethren Ch., 1975-78, moderator, 1979-84; pastor Reedley Mennonite Brethren Ch., 1976-88; ret., 1989; dir. ch. and constituency relations Mennonite Brethren Biblical Sem., 1987-89; dist. min. emeritus Mennonites, 2002—. Moderator Pacific Dist. Conf., 1959-60, 61-63, 75-77; mem. exec. com. Mennonite Central Com. Internat., 1967-75, mem. bd. reference and counsel, 1966-69, 72-75, mem. bd. missions and services, 1969-72; exec. sec. Bd. Edn. Mennonite Brethren, 1969-72; chmn. Bd. Missions and Services, 1985-91; pastor emeritus Reedley Mennonite Brethren Ch., 1987. Columnist bi-weekly publ. Christian Leader, 1969-75. Bd. dirs. Bob Wilson Meml. Hosp., Ulysses, Kans., 1969-72; dist. minister Pacific Dist. Conf. Mennonite Brethren, 1989—. Recipient Humanitarian award Shafter C. of C., 1969, Citation bd. dirs. Bibl. Sem. Mem.: Kiwanis, Reedley Rotary. Mem. Mennonite Brethren Ch. Home: 783 W Carpenter Ave Reedley CA 93654-3903 Office: 1632 L St Reedley CA 93654-3340

DICK, HERBERT JAMES, music educator; b. Oneida, Ny, Aug. 27, 1957; s. Herbert James Dick Sr. and Verona R. Dick. BS, Mankato State U., Mankato, MN, 1976—80; MA, U. of Minn., Minneapolis, MN, 1991, ABD, 2002. Music educator Ind. Sch. Dist. 196, Rosemount, Minn., 1980—95; music curriculum specialist Minn. Ctr. for Arts Edn., Golden Valley, Minn., 1995—96; curriculum writer Am. Composers Forum, St. Paul, Minn., 1999—; music educator Ind. Sch. Dist. 196, Rosemount, Minn., 1996—. Mem. Ednl. Adv. Bd., Theater Live!, Minneapolis, Minn., 1999—2001; publ. cons. Music Educators Nat. Conf., Reston, Va., 1998—2001; cons. Minn. Dept. of Children, Familes and Learning, Roseville, Minn., 1998—2002. Named Minn. Music Educator of the Yr., Minn. Music Educators Assn., 1998. Mem.: Minn. Music Educators Assn., Music Educators Nat. Conf., Phi Kappa Phi. Avocations: music, racquetball, music composing, home improvement. Office: Rosemount Middle School 3135 143rd Street West Rosemount MN 55068 Personal E-mail: hjdick8@cs.com.

DICK, JAMES CORDELL, concert pianist; b. Hutchinson, Kans., June 29, 1940; s. George Gerhard and Dorothy Lois (Ulsh) D., 1958-63; studied with, Dalies Frantz; MusB with spl. honors, U. Tex., 1963; studied with Sir Clifford Curzon, 1963-65; postgrad., Royal Acad. Music, London, 1963-65. Concert pianist Sol Hurok Presents, N.Y.C., 1968-70, Shaw Concerts, N.Y.C., 1970-75, Columbia Artists, N.Y.C., 1975-89, A.G. Declert and Assocs., Round Top, Tex., 1989—. Founder, artistic dir. Internat. Festival-Inst., Round Top, 1971—; judge internat. recording competition Nat. Guild Piano Tchrs., 1970-71; nat. cons. music com. Inst. Internat. Edn., N.Y.C., 1971-72; mem. internat. jury Tschaikovsky Competition, Moscow, 1974, Van Cliburn Competition, Ft. Worth, 1975, 78; chmn. Fulbright Panel in Music, N.Y.C., 1978. Commd. (Am. piano

concerto) Shiva's Drum, (nominated Pulitzer Prize in music), 1994. Recipient First Prize award Shreveport Symphony Competition, 1958-60, San Angelo Symphony Competition, 1958-60, Dallas Symphony, 1961-62, Nat. Guild Piano Tchrs., 1961-62, Tschaikovsky Internat. Competition, 1965-66, Leventritt Piano Competition, 1965-66, Busoni Internat. Piano Competition, 1965-66, Citation cert. Tex. Ho. Reps., 1975, award Japan Soc. Houston, 1975, Presdl. citation Nat. Fedn. Music Clubs, 1979, Round Top award Gov. William. P. Clements, Tex., 1980, Headliner of Yr. award Headliners Club, 1983; honoree Pres. Lyndon B. Johnson, 1965-66; nominee Pulitzer Prize in Music, 1974; commd. Ambassador of Goodwill, State of Tex., 1978; named Hon. Texan, Gov. Dolph Briscoe, 1978, Chevalier des Arts et Lettres French Ministry Culture, 1994; Fulbright scholar, Tobias Matthay fellow, Royal Acad. Music, Hon assoc., 1969, recipient Merit cert., 1965, Beethoven prize, Recital medal, Chevalier des Arts et Lettres, French Ministry of Cult., 1994. Mem.: Tex. Lyceum Assn. (adv. dir. 1978—), Tex. Fedn. Music Clubs (hon. life), Philos. Soc. Tex. (treas. 1976—), English Speaking Union, Tex. State Musician, Bohemians Club (N.Y.C.), Tuesday Mus. Club (hon.), Rotary Internat. (hon. life), Sigma Alpha Iota (hon. nat. patron 2001, Tex. State Musician 2003). Avocations: architecture, landscaping, literature, poetry, woodworking. Fax: 979-249-5078. E-mail: jamesd@festivalhill.org.

DICK, JOHN STEWART, JR., rheologist, consultant; b. Hampton, Va., Dec. 26, 1945; s. John Stewart and Cecil Cooper Dick; m. Margaret Ashton Dick, Jan. 8, 1972; children: Ian Edwin, Norah Kate. BS in Chemistry, Va. Tech., Blacksburg, 1970; MA in Econs., U. Akron, Ohio, 1979. Cert. quality engr. Assoc. process engr. Sinclair Koppers Corp., Monaca, Pa., 1970; product engr., sect. mgr., devel. scientist B.F. Goodrich Corp., Akron, Ohio, 1971—91; mktg. tech., svc. specialist Monsanto Corp., 1991—. Rubber chemistry instr. U. Akron, 1988—, U. Wis., Milw., 1996—. Author: Compounding Materials for the Polymer Industries, 1987; editor: Rubber Technology, Compounding and Testing for Performance, 2001; contbr. Fellow: ASTM (subcom. chmn. 1982—90, Award of Merit 1990); mem.: Inst. Stds. Inst. (head US delegation to ISO for rubber), Am. Chem. Soc. (Rubber divsn. Best Paper award 1995). Achievements include invention of method to measure viscous heating. Avocations: amateur radio, photography. Office: Alpha Technologies 2689 Wingate Ave Akron OH 44314

DICK, PHILIP WIENS, county official; b. Glendive, Mont., Apr. 6, 1947; s. George G. and Helene (Wiens) Dick; m. Laura Roberts, Oct. 1, 1975; children: Kathryn, Joseph, Helen, Henry. BS, Ill. State U., 1986; postgrad., Fla. Atlantic U., 1986—87. Planner-intern City of Deerfield Beach, Fla., 1987-89; planner Palm Beach County, West Palm Beach, Fla., 1989-92, McLean County, Bloomington, Ill., 1993—2001, dir. Bldg. and Zoning Dept., 2001—. Mem.: Am. Inst. Cert. Planners (cert.). Home: 819 W Washington St Bloomington IL 61701 Office: McLean County Bldg and Zoning Dept PO Box 2400 Bloomington IL 61702

DICK, RAYMOND DALE, psychology educator; b. Toledo, Ohio, July 16, 1930; s. Floyd Edward and Clara Belle (Spilker) D.; m. Beverly Ann Sparks, June 18, 1955; children: Gregory Dale, Jeffrey Clayton. BS, Northwestern U., 1952; MA, U. Mo., 1955, PhD, 1958. Asst. prof. psychology Ft. Hays (Kans.) State Coll., 1958-62; assoc. prof. Fort Hayes (Kans.) State Coll., 1962-64, prof., 1964-66, acad. chmn. psychology dept., 1959-66; prof. psychology U. Wis., Eau Claire, 1966-98, dean Sch. Grad Studies, 1966-81, prof. emeritus, 1998—. Assoc. Danforth Found., 1962-84, also chmn. Upper Midwest selection com., 1969-72; mem. com. liberal arts edn. North Central Assn. Colls. and Secondary Schs., 1963-66, coordinator liberal arts com., 1965-68, cons-examiner, 1971—. Contbr. profl. jours. Mem. Am., Midwestern, Wis. Psychol. Assns., AAUP, AAAS. Home: 2823 Irene Dr Eau Claire WI 54701-6692

DICK, RICHARD IRWIN, environmental engineer, educator; b. Sanborn, Iowa, July 18, 1935; s. Laurence Irwin and Lillian Marie (Riesser) D.; m. Delores Kay Den Beste, Aug. 31, 1958; children: Natalie Ann, Kevin Irwin, Laura Lynn, Craig David. BS, Iowa State U., 1957; MS, State U. Iowa, 1958; PhD, U. Ill., 1965. Sanitary engr. USPHS, Kansas City, Mo., 1958-60; sanitary engr. Clark, Daily and Dietz (Cons. Engrs.), Urbana, Ill., 1960-62; instr. to prof. civil engring. U. Ill., 1962-72; prof. civil engring. U. Del., Newark, 1972-77; Joseph P. Ripley prof. engring. Cornell U., Ithaca, NY, 1977—2002, Joseph P. Ripley prof. emeritus, 2002—; Thomas R. Camp lectr. Boston Soc. Civil Engrs., 1981. Disting. vis. scientist U.S. EPA Water Engring. Rsch. Lab., Cin., 1986-89; vis. engr. Water Pollution Rsch. Lab., Stevenage, Eng., 1970-71; hon. rsch. fellow Univ. Coll. London, 1990; vis. prof. U. B.C., Vancouver, 1991, McGill U., Montreal, 1991. Contbr. over 200 articles to profl. jours. Served with USPHS, 1958-60. Recipient Disting. Alumnus award, U. Ill., 1996, Daniel M. Lazar '29 Excellence in Tchg. award, 1996, James M. and Martha D. McCormick award for excellence in advising, 1999. Mem.: ASCE (Rudolph Hering medal 1986), Charted Instn. Water and Environ. Mgmt., Am. Water Works Assn., Water Environment Fedn. (Harrison Prescott Eddy medal 1968), Internat. Water Assn. (past mem. exec. com., bd. govs.), Assn. Environ. Engring. Profs. (past pres., Disting. lectr. 1980, Outstanding Pub. award 1986, 1987, Founder's award 1998), Phi Kappa Phi, Chi Epsilon (U. Ill. Chpt. Honor mem. 1980, Cornell U. Prof. of Yr. 1995, 2002), Tau Beta Pi, Sigma Xi. Home: 115 W Upland Rd Ithaca NY 14850-1415 Office: Cornell U 105 Hollister Hall Ithaca NY 14853-3501

DICK, STEVEN JOSEPH, researcher, educator; b. Jasper, Ind., June 20, 1960; s. Thomas Phillip and JoAnn Dick; m. Hsiu-Yueh Hsu, Mar. 24, 1991; children: Joseph, LiAnne. BA, We. Ky. U., 1982; MA, So. Ill. U., 1986; PhD, Mich. State U., 1992. Asst. prof. McNeese State U., Lake Charles, La., 1991—97, So. Ill. U., Carbondale, 1997—. Creator, dir. Modern Media Barn, Carbondale, 1995—. Contbr. articles to profl. jours. Divsn. officer Broadcast Edn. Assn., 1999—2002, Assn. of Educators in Journalism and Mass Communication, 1996—98; officer Assn. for La. Media Edn., 1995—96. Mem.: Chinese Communication Assn. Independent. Roman Catholic. Avocation: parenting. Office: So Ill Univ Dept Radio-TV Carbondale IL 62901-6609 Personal E-mail: Dick@ModernMediaBarn.com.

DICK, SUSAN MARIE, English language educator; b. Battle Creek, Mich., Nov. 6, 1940; d. James Allen and Mildred Marie (Thomas) D. BA with honors, Western Mich. U., 1963; MA, Northwestern U., 1964, PhD, 1967. Prof. dept. English Queen's U., Kingston, Ont., 1967—. Editor: George Moore: Confessions of a Young Man, 1972, Virginia Woolf: Holograph of to the Lighthouse, 1982, Complete Shorter Fiction of V. Woolf, 1989, To the Lighthouse, 1992; co-editor: Essays for Richard Ellmann, 1989, Virginia Woolf: Between the Acts, 2002; author: Virginia Woolf, 1989; mem. editl. com. Virginia Woolf, 1989—.adr Fellow Royal Soc. Can. Avocations: reading, gardening. Home: 177 Churchill Crescent Kingston ON Canada K7L 4N3 E-mail: dicks@post.queensu.ca.

DICK, WILLIAM ALLEN, engineering educator; b. Belleville, Ill., June 7, 1956; s. William Allen and Ruth Anne (Racine) D.; children: Allen, Corinth, Barrett. B.Mech.Engring., U. Del., 1979; MBA, U. Ill., 1992. Composites engr. Ctr. Composite Materials, U. Del., 1979-82, dep. dir., 1982 86; asst. dir. engring. Coll. Engring., U. Ill., Urbana, 1986-90, dir. corp. programs, 1990-97, asst. dean, 1994-97, mng. dir., 1997—. Cons. Composites Tech. Assocs., Newark, 1979-86, Pi-d 2020, Champaign, 1999—; dir. Mfg. Extension Rsch. and Tech. Ctr., State of Ill., 1995—, dir. Ill. Ctr. for Indsl. Tech., 1987-92 Contbr. articles to profl. jours. Active Boy Scouts Am., Champaign, 1992—; audit dir. Empty Tomb Social Svcs., Champaign, 1989-93; deacon Windsor Rd. Christian Ch., Champaign, 1990-92. Exec. MBA scholar, 1990-92. Mem. AAAS, IEEE, AIAA, Am. Soc. Engring. Edn. (mem. coun., regional exec. com. 1996-97). Republican. Home: 706 Ashton Ln N Champaign IL 61820-7303 Office: Univ of Illinois 1304 W Springfield Ave Urbana IL 61801-2910 E-mail: wdick@uiuc.edu.

DICKARD-GREEN, ROXANNE LYNN, choreographer, dance educator; b. Galveston, Tex., Oct. 7, 1962; d. Ray Eugene and Ethel Mae (Caro) D.; m. Frank Joseph Green III, Oct. 29, 1988; children: Corinne, Brian. AAS in Mgmt., Galveston Coll., 1982; B of Performing Arts, Dance, Oklahoma City U., 1986. Mem. Am. Spirit Dance Co., 1984—86, The Comedy Zone troupe, 1985-86; musical comedy specialist Jewish Community Ctr., Houston, 1987; choreographer Welch Mid. Sch., Houston, 1987, Upper Deck Theatre, Galveston, 1987; choreographer, majorette instr. Ctrl. Sch., Galveston, 1980-84, 86-89; owner Dancemobile Classes & Choreography Svc., Galveston, 1991—. Performed in Maurice Hines Tap Show promo, 1990, Much Ado About Nothing with John Houseman's Actor's Theatre, 1987; mem. Discovery Dance Group, 1992; dance capt./dancer in Wildcat, Upper Deck Theatre, 1981, Annie in Chicago at 1894 Grand Opera House, 1982, Judy in A Chorus Line at Coll. of the Mainland Theatre, 1987; dancer/acrobat in Carnival, Coll. of the Mainland Theatre, 1984; dancer/chorus in How to Succeed in business Without Really Trying, 1894 Grand Opera House, 1986; played Reba in A Bad Year for Tomatoes, 1986, Shelby in Breakfast with Less & Bess, 1986. Choreographer (musical) Walk By Faith, 2001; actor: (TV films) Warning: Parental Advisory, 2002. Placed 16th in worldwide tap dance comp., 1990. Roman Catholic. Avocations: knitting, crocheting, bicycling, bowling, theater. Office: PO Box 57661 Webster TX 77598 E-mail: DANCEMOBILE@netscape.net.

DICKASON, JOHN HAMILTON, retired foundation executive; b. Wooster, Ohio, June 3, 1931; s. Donald Eugene and Martha Himes (Hamilton) D.; m. Barbara Helen Fee, June 20, 1953; children: John Harold, Kathryn Helen. AB, Dartmouth Coll., 1953, MBA, 1954; grad., Inst. Orgn. Mgmt., Mich. State U., 1965, Advanced Mgmt. Program, Harvard U., 1980. With Scott Paper Co., 1954-58; personnel technician Ill. Civil Service Commn., Springfield, 1958-60; bus. mgr., then asso. dir. Ill. Bar Assn., 1960 70, exec. dir., 1970-85, v.p. fin. and adminstrn. Markey Charitable Trust, Miami, Fla., 1985-97, v.p. disolution adminstrn., 1997-98; cons., 1999—. Pres. Springfield Mental Health Assn., 1965-66; sr. warden Christ Episc. Ch., Springfield, 1973-75, lic. lay reader, 1970-85, treas., 1966-69, 76-85; mem. fin. com. Diocese Springfield, 1975-77; treas. St. Philip's Episc. Ch., Coral Gables, Fla., 1986-93, sr. warden, 1988; chair St. Philips Found., 1998-2002; lic. eucharistic minister, 1997—; troop leader local Boy Scouts Am., 1966-85, mem. coun. exec. com., 1978-80; trustee Palmer Trinity Sch., 1999—. With AUS, 1954-56. Mem. ABA (assoc.), Ill. State Bar Assn. (hon.), Am. Soc. Assn. Execs. (life), Ill. Soc. Assn. Execs. (pres. 1972), Nat. Assn. Bar Execs. (pres. 1976-77, Man of Yr. 1983), Am. Judicature Soc., Found. Fin. Officers Group (steering com., editor newsletter), Coun. on Founds. (past chmn. legis. and regulations com., rsch. com.), Riviera Country Club (bd. govs. 1999-2002). Republican. Home: 751 Saldano Ave Miami FL 33143-6219

DICKAU, KEITH MICHAEL (MIKE DICKAU), artist, secondary school educator; b. Monterey Park, Calif., Apr. 20, 1944; s. Keith Robert and Beaula May (Chamness) D.; m. Ramona Sue Wilson, May 6, 1967; children: Robert Michael, Ian Christopher; m. Carolyn Gloria Isaak, Dec. 22, 1973. BA in Zoology, U. Calif., Davis, 1966. Cert. secondary tchr., Calif. Tchr. math. L.A. City Sch. Dist., 1967-70; tchr. sci. and math. Grant Joint Union H.S. Dist., Sacramento and Rio Linda, Calif., 1970-99. Exhibited in numerous shows including Le Sahuc, Sacramento, Candy Store Gallery, Folsom, Calif., A Gallery-Anna Gardner, Stinson Beach, Calif., Artists' Collaborative Gallery, Sacramento, Fla. State U., Tallahassee, Crocker Art Mus. Sculpture Park, Sacramento, Whittier (Calif.) Mus., Gallery 25, Fresno, Calif., L.A. Artist Equity Assn., Mercer Gallery, Rochester, N.Y., The Artery, Davis, Archivio Artistico, Ravenna, Italy, Antic Ajuntament, Terragona, Spain, Santa Barbara (Calif.) Mus., Ecole de Nuces, Valady, France, M.J.C., Saint-Cere, France, 1996, Seulement pour les Fous, Troyes, France, 1996, New Artworks Fine Arts Gallery, Fair Oaks, Calif., 1996, Bur. de Poste, Joigny, France, 1996, The Ink People Ctr. for the Arts, Eureka, Calif., 1996, Mercer Gallery, Monroe C.C., Rochester, N.Y., 1996, L'Inst. Superieur des Arts Appliques, Rennes, France, The Living Room, Santa Monica, Calif., 1997, Design Gallery, U. Calif., Davis, Kawaguchi-Shi, Japan, 1997, Solomon Dubnick Gallery, Sacramento, 1998, Mercer Gallery, Rochester, N.Y., East Sacramento Art Garage, 1999, Artworks/Bookworks, Santa Monica, Calif., Claudia Chapline Gallery, Stinson Beach, L'Ecume du Jour, Bouvais, France, 2000, 621 Gallery, Tallahassee, Fla., La Maison du Livre de L'Image, Villerbanne, France, 2000, Inst. Superiore, Spilimbergo, Italy, 2001, Southern Exposure Gallery, San Francisco, Calif., 2001, Internat. Mus. Postal Image, Ostrense, Italy, 2001, Todd Hughes Fine Art, South Pasadena, Calif., 2001, Shriner Hosps./No. Calif., Sacramento, 2002, Mayakovsky Mus., Moscow, Russia, 2003, others; contbr. poetry and art to mags. Recipient Hon. Sci. award Bausch and Lomb, 1962, Sculpture award Calif. Art League, 1987, Artist of Month award No. Calif. Artists, numerous other awards; NSF grantee, 1972. Mem. No. Calif. Artists, Inc. Democrat. Methodist. Avocations: music, travel. E-mail: mikedickau@aol.com.

DICKE, CANDICE EDWARDS, library educator; b. Elmhurst, Ill., Aug. 5, 1949; d. Frederick Francis and Bernice Pauline (Bartels) Cramer; m. Mark Edwin Edwards, June 19, 1971 (div. 1981); 1 child, Kristin Paige; m. Timothy Lee Dicke, Aug. 5, 1984; 1 child, Elizabeth Ann. BA, U. Iowa, 1971; MLS, George Peabody Coll. Tchrs., 1974. Media specialist, Ohio; cert. tchr., libr., tchr. educably mentally retarded Durant (Iowa) Cmty. Sch. Dist., 1971-72, Peabody Demonstration Sch., Nashville, 1972-75; reading tchr. Edgewood Ind. Sch. Dist., San Antonio, 1975-76; libr. Northside Ind. Sch. Dist., San Antonio, 1976-79; childrn's libr. DeKalb Libr. System, Decatur, Ga., 1979-80; media specialist DeKalb County Bd. Edn., Decatur, 1980-84, 86-88; libr. Elida (Ohio) Local Schs., 1988-91; tchr. 3rd grade Elida Elem. Sch., 1991-96, tchr. Title I reading and math., 1996—; pastor Botkins (Ohio) United Meth. Ch., 1997—2000; assoc. pastor Wayne St. United Meth. Ch., St. Mary's, Ohio, 2000—02; pastor family ministries Westside United Meth. Ch., Lima, Ohio, 2002—. Title 1/Hosts coord., 2003; adviser Elida H.S. Quiz Bowl, 1992-93; bookseller Back in Time, Inc. (formerly Everychild Bookstore), Duluth, Ga., 1984-86; treas. S.E. Advocates of Lit. for Young People, Athens, Ga., 1986-88. Author: The Reference Point, 1983. Sunday sch. tchr. mentally handicapped adults, 1989—, Chancel Choir; advisor Jr. High Youth Fellowship Wayne State United Meth. Ch., 1991-93, v.p. United Meth. Women, 1994-95, pres. 1996—; coord. Christian Personhood Lima Mission Dist., 1995-97, coord. Christian personhood Lima Dist., West Ohio Conf. United Meth. Ch.; leader Girl Scout Troop 3050, 1986-88. Mem. NEA, Ohio Edn. Assn., Elida Edn. Assn. Methodist. Office: Elida Elem Sch 300 Pioneer Rd Elida OH 45807 Home: 1815 Fenway Ct Saint Marys OH 45885-1366 Office: Westside United Meth Ch 604 Gloria Ave Lima OH 45805

DICKE, JAMES FREDERICK, II, manufacturing company executive; b. San Angelo, Tex., Nov. 9, 1945; s. James Frederick and Eilleen (Webster) D.; m. Janet St. Clair, July 6, 1968; children: James F. III, Jennifer S. BS, Trinity U., 1968. Intern U.S. Ho. of Reps., Washington, 1966; sales coord. Crown Controls Corp., New Bremen, Ohio, 1968-69, v.p. internat., 1970-78; exec. v.p. Crown Equipment Corp., New Bremen, Ohio, 1979-80, pres., CEO, 1980—2002, chmn., CEO, 2003—. Chmn. Crown Australia Pty. Ltd., Sydney, 1980—, Crown Ltd., Galway, Ireland, 1980—; bd. dirs. Dayton (Ohio) Power and Light Co. Chmn. bd. trustees Dayton (Ohio) Art Inst., 1998—; trustee, v.p., sec. Culver (Ind.) Ednl. Found., 1981-2001; Midwest dir. Boys and Girls Clubs Am., Chgo., 1987-2001; co-chmn. Ohio Rep. Fin. Com., 1995—. Recipient Disting. Svc. award Culver Acads., 1989, Disting. Alumnus award Trinity U., 1991; honoree Nat. Acad. Design, 1999. Mem. Young Pres.' Orgn. (bd. dirs. 1985-94, internat. pres. 1992-93), Cum Laude Soc. Culver Acads., Key Largo Angelers CLub (chmn. bd. dirs. 1999-2001). Mem. United Ch. of Christ. Office: Crown Equipment Corp PO Box 97 New Bremen OH 45869-0097

DICKEL, MICHAEL HUF, higher education administrator, writer; b. Elmhurst, Ill., Feb. 1, 1955; s. G. William Jr. and Pauline Jane Beach Dickel; m. Joanne Lillian Raymond, Apr. 29, 1955 (div. Sept. 2000); children: Julia, Rebecca. Bachelor's degree, U. Minn., 1979, MA in Creative Writing, 1990, PhD, 1999. Composition instr. U. Minn., Mpls., 1987-93, instr. Morris, 1994-95; cmty. faculty Met. State U., St. Paul, 1996-98; dir. Student Writing Ctr. U. Minn., Mpls., 1997-99; dir. Macalester Coll. Excellence Ctr., St. Paul, 1999—. Cons. Nat. Coun. Tchrs. English. Contbr.: (reference books) Identities and Issues in Literature, 1997, Masterpieces of Latino Literature, 1994, (anthologies) The Best of Northlight, 1990, O. Henry Festival Stories, 1987, Poems for a Livable Planet, 1994; co-creator: (audiocassette) 21st Century Beat, 1991; assoc. editor: (mag.) Journeymen, 1992-95; book rev. editor: (student newspaper) The Minn. Daily, 1989-91; mng. editor: (lit. mag.) Agassiz Rev., 1990; prodr.: (radio show) All the World's a Stage, 1986; contbr. to lit. jours. and mags. Mem. Parent Partnership Coun.-Mpls. Schs., 1995-96; sec. Clara Barton Open Sch. Leadership Coun., Mpls., 1993-94. Mem. MLA, Midwest MLA (chair creative writing sect. 1997-98, chair gender studies-male sect. 1999-2000), Midwest Writing Ctrs. Assn. (chair 1999-2001, assoc. chair 1998-2000), Conf. on Coll. Composition and Comm., The Loft. Jewish. Avocations: guitar, organic gardening. Office: Macalester Coll 1600 Grand Ave Saint Paul MN 55105

DICKENS, ALICE MCKNIGHT, minister; b. Edgecombe County, N.C., May 6, 1935; d. John and Candis Moore McKnight, m. Ernest Dickens, 1954; children: Ernest Douglas, Ronald, John, Larry, Candice, Mark. Degree in nursing, Edgecombe C.C., 1981. Lic. nurse, N.C. Founder, pastor Ch. of God of Deliverance, Rocky Mount, NC, 1971—; pres. N.C. Dist. Union Apostolic Faith Ch. of God, 1994—. Mem. pastoral staff Apostolic Faith Ch. of God, Franklin, Va., 1982—. Supporter Crisis Ministry/homeless shelter, Rocky Mount; bd. dirs. New Sources, Rocky Mount, NC, 2001—, Meals on Wheels, Rocky Mount, 1998—2000. Recipient hon. mention, Jefferson awards, WTVD-TV, Durham, N.C., 1995, tribute plaque, OIC HIV/AIDS Program, Rocky Mount, 1999. Home: 909 Columbia Ave Rocky Mount NC 27804 Office: Ch of God of Deliverance 900 Columbia Ave Rocky Mount NC 27804 Fax: 252-446-9186.

DICKENS, ALYCIA THOMPSON, nurse practitioner; b. Norfolk, Va., July 31, 1968; d. Freeman Robert and Doris Kennedy Thompson; m. Byron Patrick Dickens, Mar. 20, 1991; children: Schuyler Kennedy, Logan Alexandria. BSN, Hampton U., 1995, MS, 1997. RN, Va.; cert. family nurse practitioner. Nurse Ea. State Hosp., Williamsburg, Va., 1995-96, Med. Coll. Va. at Va. Commonwealth U., Richmond, 1996—; nurse bon secours Med. ICU, Depaul Med. Ctr., 1997-99; nurse practitioner infectious disease divsn. Ea. Va. Med. Sch., 1999—. Recipient grant Ea. State Hosp., 1994, 95, William Freeman scholarship Hampton U., 1995. Mem. ANA, Assn. Reproductive Health Profls., Va. Nurses Assn., Va. Coun. for Nurse Practitioners, Sigma Theta Tau, Alpha Kappa Alpha. Democrat. Baptist.

DICKENS, BERNARD MORRIS, law educator; b. London, Nov. 4, 1937; emigrated to Can., 1974; s. David and Rose (Jacobs) D.; m. Rebecca J. Cook, Apr., 1987. LL.B., King's Coll., U. London, 1961, LL.M., 1965, PhD, 1971; LL.D., U. London, 1978. Barrister, Inner Temple, 1963; barrister and solicitor, Law Soc. Upper Can. (Ont. bar), 1977. Tutorial student King's Coll., U. London, England, 1962-63; lectr. Coll. Law, London, 1964-68, sr. lectr., 1968-72, prin. lectr., 1972-74; rsch. prof. law U. Toronto, Canada, 1974-80, prof. law, 1980—; chair rsch. ethics bd. Health Can., 2001—. Cons. panel human rsch. WHO/Coun. Internat. Orgns. Med. Scis., Geneva, 1979-83, 91-93, prin. investigator epidemiol. rsch. and human organ transplantation, 1990-91; legal cons. reproduction law Commonwealth Secretariat, London, 1976—; project cons. Ont. Law Reform, Toronto, 1982-84; cons. mem. com. on ethics Can. Med. Assn., Ottawa, 1982-89; mem. rsch. ethics com. NRC Can., Ottawa, 1992-99, chair 1995-99; adj. faculty Ctr. for Population and Family Health, Faculty Medicine, Columbia U., 1987—; mem. WHO task force on organ transplantation, 1996-99. Author: Abortion and the Law, 1966, Medico-Legal Aspects of Family Law, 1979, (with R.J. Cook) Abortion Laws in Commonwealth Countries, 1979, Emerging Issues in Commonwealth Abortion Law, 1982, Medicine and the Law, 1993, (with D. Roy, J. Williams) Bioethics in Canada, 1993; (with R.J. Cook, M.F. Fathalla) Reproductive Health and Human Rights, 2003; mem. internat. editl. bd. Am. Jour. Law and Medicine; mem. editl. adv. bd. Bibliography of Bioethics, Kennedy Inst., 1978—; legal articles editor Jour. Law Medicine and Ethics, 1986—. Connaught grantee U. Toronto, 1974, 78; Julius Silver fellow Columbia Law Sch., 1987. Fellow Royal Soc. Medicine (London), Royal Soc. Can.; mem. Can. Bar Assn., Can. Assn. Law Tchrs., Am. Soc. Law, Medicine and Ethics (bd. dirs. 1986-92, sec. 1987-89, pres. 1990-91), World Assn. Med. Law (bd. dirs. 1994—, v.p. 1996—). Jewish. Home: 31 Walmer Rd #10 Toronto ON Canada M5R 2W7 Office: U Toronto Faculty of Law 84 Queen's Pk Toronto ON Canada M5S 2C5 E-mail: bernard.dickens@utoronto.ca.

DICKENS, CHARLES HENDERSON, retired social scientist, consultant; b. Thomasville, N.C., Nov. 22, 1934; s. Argie Marshall and Edna (Sullivan) D.; m. Jane McClung, Aug. 27, 1965; children: Martha Jane, Anne Elizabeth. BS, Duke U., 1957, MEd, 1964, ED, 1966. Asst. prof. Wake Forest U., Winston-Salem, N.C., 1965-67; planning specialist NSF, Washington, 1967-69, assoc. program dir. undergrad. instrnl. program, 1969-73, study dir. sci. edn. studies group, 1973-83, sect. head scientific and tech. pers. studies sect., 1983-86, sect. head surveys and analysis sect., 1986-90; sr. policy analyst Fed. Coordinating Coun. for Sci., Engring., and Tech., Washington, 1990-92, exec. sec., 1992-93, ret., 1993. Mem. adv. bd. Am. Men and Women of Sci., New Providence, N.J., 1991—. C.C. Cameron Applied Rsch. Ctr. U. N.C., Charlotte, 1994-99, Buncombe County Coun. on Aging, 2000—; cons. Stanford Rsch. Internat., 2002—. With U.S. Army, 1958-59. Recipient Angier B. Duke prize Duke U., 1953-57; Woodrow Wilson fellowship Woodrow Wilson Fellowship Found., 1963, James B. Duke fellowship Duke U., 1963, 64. Fellow: AAAS; mem.: Nat. Assn. Ret. Fed. Employees (v.p. chpt. 156 1995—96, pres. 1996—97, v.p. N.C. area I 1997—2001). Republican. Presbyterian. Avocations: computing, reading. Home: 4 Arrow Pl Asheville NC 28805-9748 E-mail: chd2002@bellsouth.net.

DICKENS, JOYCE REBECCA, addictions therapist, educator; b. Roanoke Rapids, N.C. d. Lydia Marie Dickens. M in Addiction Psychology with honors, Capella U., 2000, postgrad. in addiction psychology, 2000—. Cert. addiction profl. Adj. instr. Broward C.C., Ft. Lauderdale, Fla., 1991—; primary therapist addictions Treatment Works, Ft. Lauderdale, 2002—. Mem. AAUW, Phi Theta Kappa, Alpha Chi. Avocations: tennis, travel, public speaking. Office: House of Hope 908 SW 1st St Fort Lauderdale FL 33312 Fax: 954-467-8532.

DICKENS, JUSTIN KIRK, nuclear physicist; b. Syracuse, N.Y., Nov. 2, 1931; s. Milton Clifford and Jennette Martin (Holmes) D.; m. Marcay Cosette Jordan, Dec. 21, 1957; children: Alan Russell, Leonard Raymond, Steven Kenneth, Michael Loren. AB in Physics, U. So. Calif., L.A., 1955, PhD in Physics, 1962; MS in Physics, U. Chgo., 1956. Engring. assoc. Collins Radio Co., Burbank, Calif., 1955; electronic technician Enrico Fermi Inst. for Nuclear Studies, Chgo., 1956-57; grad. teaching asst. U. So. Calif., L.A., 1957-61, rsch. assoc., 1961-62; rsch. staff mem. Oak Ridge (Tenn.) Nat. Lab., 1962-78, sr. rsch. staff mem., 1978-94, cons., 2000—; private cons., 1995; rsch. prof. physics U. Tenn., Knoxville, 1996-99, 2001; cons. Oak Ridge Nat. Lab., 2000—. Gen. chmn. Internat. Conf. on Nuclear Data for Sci. and Tech., Gatlinburg, Tenn., 1994. Author: The Descendants of Ephraim Dickens (Jr.) and Thomas Dickens, 1992, rev. edit., vol. I, 1997, vol. II, 1998, Memoirs...and Memories, 2002; co-author (tech. standard) Am. Nat. Standard on Decay Heat; contbr. 200 articles to profl. jours. Bd. dirs. Oak Ridge Community Playhouse, 1972, 85. With U.S. Army, 1950-52. Recipient Lifetime Achievement award Oak Ridge Cmty. Playhouse, 1996, Lockheed Martin Energy Rsch. Tech. Achievement award, 1997. Mem. Am. Phys. Soc., Am. Nuclear Soc., Phi Beta Kappa, Sigma Xi. Office: Ctr of Excel Bldg 6010 Inst Heavy Ion Rsch MS 6354 Oak Ridge TN 37831-6354 E-mail: jkdickens@aol.com.

DICKERMAN, JOHN MELVIN, lawyer; b. Hope, Ark., Aug. 21, 1914; s. Charles and Dorothy W. (Schultz) D.; m. Serafina Peoria, Oct. 26, 1956; 1 child, Dorothea W. BA, U. Ill., 1938, JD, 1940. Bar: Ill. 1940, Ohio 1942, U.S. Supreme Ct. 1944, U.S. Dist. Ct. (D.C. dist.) 1964. Atty. Rep. Steel Corp., Massillon, Ohio, 1940-42, U.S. Alien Property Custodian, Chgo., 1942-43; atty., Washington rep. Airline Pilot's Assn., 1943-47; legis. dir. Nat. Assn. Home Builders, Washington, 1947-52, exec. v.p., 1952-64; pres. John Dickerman & Assocs., Washington, 1964—. Mem. Nat. Assn. Home Builders (life, bd. dirs. 1964, named to Hall of Fame 1980), Am. Soc. Assn. Execs., Chgo. Bar Assn., D.C. Bar Assn., Lambda Alpha. Republican.

DICKERSIN, KAY, researcher, educator; b. Phila., Nov. 10, 1951; d. George Richard and Barbara (Bray) D.; m. Robert Alan Van Wesep, June 30, 1973; children: Isaac, Edward. BA in Zoology, U. Calif., Berkeley, 1974, MA in Zoology, 1975; PhD in Epidemiology, Johns Hopkins U., 1989. Lectr. dept. epidemiology, faculty Ctr. for Clinical Trials, Johns Hopkins U., Balt., 1991—; asst. prof. U. Md. Sch. Medicine, Balt., 1989-96, assoc. prof., 1996-98, adj. assoc. prof., 1998—; assoc. prof. Brown U. Sch. Medicine, Providence, 1998—2002, prof., 2002—; dir. Balt. Cochrane Ctr., 1993-98; co-dir. New Eng. Cochrane Ctr., 1998—2002, US Cochrane Ctr., 2002—. Bd. dirs. Nat. Cancer Adv. Bd., 1994-2000. Recipient Ellen Barnett Meml. award Susan B. Komen Found. Race for the Cure, 1995; named to Women's Hall of Fame, Balt. City Commn. for Women, 1996; named one of Md.'s Top 100 Women, Md. Daily,

1998. Mem. Am. Epidemiol. Soc., Soc. for Clinical Trials. Home: 625 Angell St Providence RI 02906-5553 Office: New Eng Cochrane Brown Univ PO Box GS2 Providence RI 02912-0001 Fax: 401-863-9944. E-mail: kay_dickersin@brown.edu.

DICKERSON, ALLEN BRUCE, interior designer, consultant; b. St. Joseph, Mich., June 8, 1938; s. Harold Clyde and Lucille Anne (Thornton) D.; m. Arlene Virginia Bator, Mar. 26, 1965; children: Scott Denek, Maribeth Anne. BS in Indsl. Engring., U. Mich., 1961, MBA, 1962; Cert., N.Y. Sch. Interior Design, 1967. Sr. indsl. engr. Bohn Aluminum & Brass Co., Detroit, 1962-65, engring. ctr. adminstr., 1965-68, prodn. mgr., 1968-70, asst. plant mgr., 1970-72; plant mgr. DuWel Products Co., Bangor, Mich., 1972-74, corp. chief indsl. engr., 1974-75; contract and residential interior designer Klingman's, Grand Rapids, Mich., 1975—. Tchr. South Haven Cmty. Edn. Program, 1977, Western Mich. U., 1975, Am. Soc. Interior Designers, 1980-81. Author: Rental Condominiums--Interior Design for Fun and Profit, 1978, Vacation Home Furnishings, 1984, Decorating with Collectibles, 1990, Showcase of Interior Design--Midwest Edition, 1993, 97, Grand Rapids Home-Reality Renovation, 1998, Holiday Accents Decorating, 1998. Trustee First United Meth. Ch., South Haven, Mich.; bd. dir. Van Buren County (Mich.) ARC, 1965-68, Grand Rapids Symphony Designer Showhouse, 1993, 97; coord. Concord Coalition 6th Dist. Mem. Am. Inst. Indsl. Engrs., Am. Soc. Interior Designers, Nat. Coun. Interior Design Qualification, South Haven C. of C. (com. chmn.), Internat. Lightning Class Assn., South Haven Yacht Club, Shriners, Rotary. Republican. Home: 30 N Shore Dr N South Haven MI 49090-9169 Office: CenterPointe Mall 3665 28th St SE #1 Grand Rapids MI 49512-1603 E-mail: adickerson@cybersol.com.

DICKERSON, BRIAN, columnist; b. Rochester, N.Y., Dec. 25, 1956; s. Donald Thomas and Shirley Wright D.; m. Donna Pendergast; 1 child, Zachary. BA History, Princeton U., 1979. Editor, reporter Miami (Fla.) Herald, 1979-88; editor mag. Detroit Free Press, 1988-97, columnist, 1997—. Pres. Sunday Magazine Editors Assn., Phila., 1991-92. Office: Detroit Free Press 600 W Fort St Detroit MI 48226-2706 E-mail: dicker@freepress.com.

DICKERSON, CLAUDIA THOMPSON, psychologist; b. Greenville, SC, Aug. 11, 1953; d. Claude Vehorn and Bobbie (Swindell) Thompson. BA, Furman Univ., Greenville, SC, 1974; MA, Wake Forest Univ., Winston-Salem, NC, 1976; PhD, NC State Univ., Raleigh, NC, 1988. Sch. psychologist Gwinnett Co., Pub. Sch., Lawrenceville, Ga., 1982—, Wake County Pub. Sch. Sys., Raleigh, NC, 1980—82. Mem.: Am. Psychol. Soc., Nat. Assoc. of Sch. Psychol., Am. Psychol. Assoc. Baptist. Home: 2465 Sunset Dr Atlanta GA 30345 Office: Psychol Svc Gwinnett Co Sch PO Box 343 Lawrenceville GA 30046-0343

DICKERSON, COLLEEN BERNICE PATTON, artist, educator; b. Cleburne, Tex., Sept. 17, 1922; d. Jennings Bryan and Alma Bernice (Clark) Patton; m. Arthur F. Dickerson; children: Sherry M., Chrystal Charmine. BA, Calif. State U., Northridge, 1980; studied with John Pike. Presenter, instr. in field. One-woman shows include Morro Bay Cmty. Bldg., Amandas Interiors, Arroyo Grande, Calif., 1996, Gt. Western Savs., San Luis Obispo, Calif.; exhibited in group shows including Aquarius Show Ctrl. Coast Watercolor Soc., Calif., 2003; represented in permanent collections, including Polk Ins. Co., San Luis Obispo, Med. Ctr. MDM Ins. Co., L.A. Mem. Ctrl. Coast Watercolor Soc. (pres. 1986-87, Svc. award 1998), Art Ctr., Oil Acrylic Pastel Group (chmn., co-chmn. 1989-98, prize Brush Strokes show 1999), Morro Bay Art Assn. (scholarship judge 1998), San Luis Obispo Art Ctr., Valley Watercolor Soc. (co-founder). Avocations: egyptology, chinese painting, art history. Home: 245 Hacienda Ave San Luis Obispo CA 93401-7967

DICKERSON, DENNIS CLARK, history educator; b. McKeesport, Pa., Aug. 12, 1949; s. Carl O'Neal and Oswanna (Wheeler) D.; m. Mary Anne Eubanks, Aug. 6, 1977; children: Nicole Denise, Valerie Anne, Christina Marie, Dennis Clark Jr. BA, Lincoln U., 1971; MA, Washington (Mo.) U., 1974, PhD, 1978; LHD (hon.), Morris Brown Coll., 1990; postgrad., Hartford Sem. Instr. history Forest Park C.C., St. Louis, 1974, Pa. State U. Ogontz, Abington, 1975-76; from asst. to assoc. prof. history Williams Coll., Williamstown, Mass., 1976-85, assoc. prof., 1987-88, prof., 1988-99, Stanfield prof. history, 1992-99; assoc. prof. history Rhodes Coll., Memphis, 1985—87; prof. history and grad. dept. religion Vanderbilt U., Nashville, 1999—. Mem. com. examiners GRE History test Ednl. Testing Svc., Princeton, 1990-96; corporator Williamstown Savs. Bank, 1992-99; vis. prof. Payne Theol. Sem., Wilberforce, Ohio, 1992, 96, 98; vis. prof. Am. religious history Yale Div. Sch., 1995. Author: Out of the Crucible, 1986, Religion, Race and Region: Research Notes on A.M.E. Church History, 1995, Militant Mediator: Whitney M. Young, Jr., 1998; historiographer, exec. dir. rsch. and scholarship, editor A.M.E. Ch. Review; contbr. articles to profl. jours. Historiographer, African Meth. Episcopal Ch., 1988—, min. 1977—; trustee Mass. Coll. Liberal Arts, 1992-95. Rockefeller Found. fellow U. Va., 1987-88. Mem. Am. Bible Soc. (trustee), Am. Soc. Ch. History (pres.-elect 2003), Elks, Alpha Phi Alpha. Office: Vanderbilt U Dept History Nashville TN 37235-0001

DICKERSON, ERIC DEMETRIC, former professional football player; b. Sealy, Tex., Sept. 2, 1960; s. Helen Dickerson. Student, So. Meth. U. Running back Los Angeles Rams, 1983—87, Indianapolis Colts, 1987—91, L.A. Raiders, 1992, Atlanta Falcons, 1993—94. Author (with Richard Graham Walsh): Eric Dickerson's Secrets of Pro Power, 1989. Named All-Am. team, The Sporting News, 1982, NFL Player of Yr., 1983, Pro Football Writers Rookie of Yr., 1983, NFL All-Pro team, The Sporting News, 1983, 1984, 1986—88; named to Pro Football Hall of Fame, Canton, Ohio, 1999. Achievements include played in Pro Bowl, 1983-84, 86-89; set single season rushing yardage record, 1984; led NFL in rushing, 1983-84, 86; having the NFL record for most consecutive seasons with 1,000 or more rushing yards, 1983-89; NFL record for most yards rushing (2,105), 1984; most games with 100 or more yards rushing (12), 1984; shares NFL record for most seasons with 2,000 or more yards rushing and receiving combined.

DICKERSON, EUGENIE ANN (GENIE DICKERSON), writer, journalist; b. Chgo., Oct. 4, 1946; d. Hubert Eugene and Theresa Veronica (Tallarico) King; m. Brian W. Dickerson, Feb. 4, 1967. BA in History, U. Ill., 1968. Newsletter editor Sammamish Aero Modelers Soc., Redmond, Wash., 1976-79; freelance writer, 1977—; illustrator, 1981—; photographer, 1991—; speech writer, 1992—. Restaurant reviewer Seattle Times and others; columnist Bellevue (Wash.) Weekly News, 1990; book editor, cons. to various authors, 1988—. Co-author: (book) Developing Arguments, 1990, The Writer's Handbook, 1993, 1998, The Writer's Journal Guide to the Writing Life, 2000. Recipient 3d pl. for editl., Nat. Fedn. Press Women, 1989. Mem.: Soc. Profl. Journalists, Wash. Press Assn. (1st pl. for editl. 1989). Office: 1212 146th Ave SE Bellevue WA 98007-5651

DICKERSON, JOHN ROBERT, retired automotive engineer; b. Detroit, Oct. 8, 1030; s. James Eldridge and Edith Barrie Dickerson; m. Jacoueline Bowman, June 14, 1952 (div. Sept. 1967); children: Robert Floyd, Diane Lynn; m. Barbara Marie Gannon, Feb. 7, 1969; 1 child, Michael Edward Gannon. Cert., Wayne State U., Detroit, 1950; Cert. N.D. State U., 1951; Cert., Chrysler Inst. Engring., Highland Park, Mich., 1956, Chrysler Inst. Engring., 1964. Sr. designer Chrysler Corp., Highland Park, Mich., 1957—61, 1961—64, sr. designer, engr., 1964—69, product devel. engr., 1978—84, mgr. vehicle build ops., 1984—88; owner, CFO J. Robert Dickerson & Assocs., Detroit, 1969—72; fleet engring. supr. Am. Motors Corp., Detroit, 1972—78. Stylist designer cons. Creative Industries, Detroit, 1970—71; cons. Wayne State U. Consortium, Detroit, 1971—72; design cons. J. Robert Dickerson & Assocs., Detroit, 1969—73; chmn. adv. com. Tech. Comms., 2001—02. Author: (book) One Goal is Not Enough, 2001, (periodical) How to Build a 50 Foot Yacht, 1972. Charter mem. Rep. Nat. Com., Washington, 2000—; mem. Rep. Presdl. Task Force, Washington, 2000—. With USAF, 1950—52. Recipient Design award, GSA, 1980. Mem.: Am. Soc. Body Engring., NRA. Republican. Achievements include patents for in field; first to introduction and homologation of first pacer vehicle into Europe. Avocations: flying, boating, golf, travel, gardening.

DICKERSON, LON RICHARD, library administrator; b. Ypsilanti, Mich., Dec. 16, 1941; s. Lon E. and Maxine A. (Merryfield) D.; m. Anne Elizabeth Bryan, Aug. 24, 1968; children: Robert Lon, Sarah Elizabeth, Peter Bryan. AB, Albion Coll., 1964; MLS, U. Pitts., 1968. Dir. U. Liberia Librs., Monrovia, 1968-72, Lake Agassiz Regional Libr., Moorhead, Minn., 1972-85, Timberland Regional Libr., Olympia, Wash., 1985-92, Omaha Pub. Libr., 1993-96, Chatham-Effingham-Liberty Regional Libr., Savannah, Ga., 1996—. Pres. Adv. Coun. to State Libr., Minn., 1977-78, Minn. Regional Pub. Libr. Systems Adminstrs., 1980, No. Lights Libr. Network Adv. Coun., Minn., 1981-82; v.p. Ga. Coun. Pub. Librs., 1998-00, pres., 2000—. Contbr. articles to profl. jours. Libr. vol. Peace Corps Sierra Leone Libr. Bd., Freetown, 1964-67; mem. planning commn. City of Lacey, Wash.,1985-93; vice-chair planning commn. City of Lacey, 1991-93, mem. various sch. dist. coms.; bd. dirs. Clay-Wilkin Opportunity Coun., Moorhead, Minn., 1982-85; mem. steering com. Omaha 2000, 1993-96, Omaha Free-Net, 1994-96, United Way of the Midlands Com., Omaha, 1996. Mem. ALA (internat. rels. com. 1974-75), Wash. Libr. Assn. (co-chmn. legis. planning com. 1987-92, Pres.'s award 1988), Ga. Libr. Assn., Pub. Libr. Assn. (nominating com. 1989-90), Rotary, Tau Kappa Epsilon. Democrat. Congregationalist. Office: CEL Regional Libr 2002 Bull St Savannah GA 31401-8564

DICKERSON, MARTHA ANN, health facility administrator; b. Iowa City, Feb. 2, 1953; d. Wilbur R., Jr. and Phyllis (Schroeder) D. Diploma, Mass. Gen. Hosp. Sch. Nursing, Boston, 1975; BS, Iowa State U., 1978; MS, Rush U., 1983, postgrad. Head nurse, adminstrv. ednl. svcs. coord. Michael Reese Hosp. Med. Ctr., Chgo., 1978-87; clin. health edn. supr., corp. mgr., staff devel. Michael Reese Health Plan, Chgo., 1987-90; clin. svcs. mgr., nat. dir. nursing Buddy Systems, Inc., Chgo., 1990-92; corp. dir. clin. rsch. and spl. projects Cardiac Alliance, Inc., Chgo., 1992-95; mgr. cardiac care unit CareMed Chgo. (formerly Vis. Nurse Assn. Chgo.), 1995-98; adminstr./mgr. Coram Healthcare, Des Plaines, Ill., 1998—2001; care mgr. Northwestern Meml. Home Health Care, 2001—. Rsch. in field. Contbr. articles to profl. jours. Mem. AACN, Am. Soc. Health Edn. and Tng., Intravenous Nurses Soc., Am. Soc. Parenteral and Enteral Nutrition, Am. Heart Assn. (Chgo. divsn., chair CPR targeted activity group 1992-95, nat. CPR faculty 1992-95), Ill. Nurses Assn., Ill. League Nursing (pres. 1988-89), Sigma Theta Tau (eligibility com., by-laws com., rec. sec.). Home: 1522 W Thorndale Ave Chicago IL 60660-3311 Office: Northwestern Meml Home Health Care 680 N Lakeshore Dr # 920 Chicago IL 60611

DICKERSON, MONAR STEVE, city official; b. El Reno, Okla., Jan. 26, 1947; s. Monar Frank and Grace Elizabeth (Hooper) D.; m. Jean Rollins, May 16, 1969; 1 child, Kelli Leigh. Student, Oklahoma City U., 1965-69, Miss. Gulfcoast Jr. Coll., 1973-74; BS in Psychology, U. So. Miss., 1990. Cert. Meth. lay spkr. Asst. news dir. WVMI/WQID Radio, Biloxi, Miss., 1973-74, ops. mgr., 1974-75; news dir. WLOX-Radio, Biloxi, 1975-76; news anchor, reporter WLOX-TV, Biloxi, 1976-81; asst. to mayor City of Gulfport (Miss.), 1981-84; employee benefits specialist Stewart, Sneed, Hewes Inc., Gulfport, 1984-87; program specialist Area Agy. on Aging of So. Miss., Gulfport, 1987-90; bus. reporter Sun-Herald newspaper, Gulfport, 1990-93; asst. to mayor, pub. affairs mgr. City of Gulfport, 1993-97, bus. devel. coord., 1997—. Charter mem. strategic planning team Gulfport Sch. Dist., co-chair facilities planning com.; mem. devel. adv. com. U. So. Miss., Gulf Coast; past pres. adv. bd. Salvation Army; past pres. Miss. March of Dimes; lay leader 1st Meth. Ch. Gulfport; vol. Miss. Spl. Olympics. With USAF, 1969-73, mem. D.A.R.E. adv. bd., Annual Veteran's Day Parade Com. Mem. Miss. Tourism Assn., Pub. Rels. Assn. Miss., Miss. Econ. Devel. Coun., Internat. Coun. Shopping Ctrs., Internat. Trade Club Miss. (so. chpt.), Gulfport Downtown Assn., Gulfport Bus. Club. Avocations: sailing, horseback riding, bicycling, traveling. Home: 16 Independence Dr Gulfport MS 39507-1937 E-mail: stevedickerson@yahoo.com.

DICKERSON, ROLAND NELSON, pharmacy educator, clinical consultant; b. Plattsburgh, N.Y., June 26, 1956; s. Nelson Donald and Shirley Mae (LaPierre) D.; m. Erin Kristine Walker, July 19, 1980; children: Robert Nelson, Anne Louise, Gillian Rose. BS in Pharmacy, Temple U., 1979; Dr of Pharmacy, U. Tenn., Memphis, 1982. Diplomate Bd. Pharm. Specialties. Resident Thomas Jefferson U. Hosp., Phila., 1979-80; fellow U. N.C., Chapel Hill, 1982-83; clin. pharmacist in nutrition Hosp. U. Pa., Phila., 1983-88; asst. prof. pharmacy Phila. Coll. Pharm. Sci., 1988-92; prof. pharmacy U. Tenn., Memphis, 1992—. Mem. editl. adv. bd. Nutrition, 1989—; cons. editor Jour. Am. Coll. Nutrition, 1991-93; contbg. editor Hosp. Pharmacy, 1987—; mem. editl. bd. Nutrition in Clin. Practice, 1996—; contbr. more than 100 articles to profl. jours. Vol. Ronald McDonald House, Memphis, 1996-. Am. Soc. Hosp. Pharmacists Pharmacy Nutrition Support fellow, 1982; PHS grantee, 1992, others. Fellow Am. Coll. Nutrition; mem. Am. Soc. for Parenteral Enteral Nutrition (pharmacy com. 1989-91). Achievements include to demonstrate net protein anabolism with hypocaloric high protein parenteral nutrition in obese stressed patients. Office: U Tenn 26 S Dunlap St Memphis TN 38103-4909

DICKERSON, THOMAS PASQUALI, investment banker, lawyer; b. Mar. 8, 1950; s. John Osburn and Ina (de Pasquali) D.; m. Claire Anne Moore, May 22, 1976; children: Caroline, Susannah. AB in Econs., Harvard U., 1971, JD, 1974, MBA, 1979. Bar: N.Y. 1975, U.S. Dist. Ct. (ea. and so. dists.) N.Y. 1975, U.S. Ct. Appeals (2d cir.) 1975. Assoc. Coudert Bros., N.Y.C., 1974-77; asst. v.p. W.R. Grace & Co., N.Y.C., 1979-80; v.p. investment banking divsn. Lehman Bros. Kuhn Loeb, N.Y.C., 1981-85; 1st v.p. E.F. Hutton & Co., N.Y.C., 1985-87; gen. ptnr. Tullis-Dickerson Capital, Greenwich, Conn., 1988-90; pres. Tullis-Dickerson & Co., Inc., Greenwich, 1990-98, chmn., 1998—. Trustee U.S. Commn. for United World Coll. Schs., N.Y.C., 1969-74, chmn. 1974-80, vice chmn., 1980—; treas., bd. dirs. Alliance to Save Energy, Washington, 1982-92. Mem. Harvard Club N.Y.C. Roman Catholic. Office: Tullis-Dickerson & Co Inc One Greenwich Plz Greenwich CT 06830

DICKERT, LEWIS, JR. H. music educator, musician; b. Rock Hill, S.C., July 10, 1953; s. Lewis, Sr. H. and Lucille L. Dickert; children: Jessica Caitlin, Lewis H. III. PhD in Ethnomusicology, U. of Memphis, 1987—94. Asst. prof., dept. of music Winthrop U., Rock Hill, SC, 1991—. Musician, arranger, sideman, performer in music industry field. Mem.: Internat. Assn. of Jazz Educators, Phi Mu Alpha (faculty advisor 2001—03), Kappa Delta Pi, Phi Kappa Lambda, Phi Kappa Phi (chpt. pres. 2002—03). Avocations: golf, tennis, bicycling. Home: 520 - 201 Sumter Ave Rock Hill SC 29730 Office: Winthrop U Dept of Music Rock Hill SC 29733 E-mail: dickertl@winthrop.edu.

DICKERT, NEAL WORKMAN, lawyer; b. Newberry, S.C., July 28, 1946; s. Elbert Jackson and Mary Elizabeth (Layton) D.; m. Floride Cantey Clarkson, June 4, 1969; 1 child, Neal Workman. BA, Wofford Coll., 1968; MBA, U. S.C., 1969, JD, 1974. Bar: S.C. 1974, Ga. 1975, U.S. Dist. Ct. S.C. 1975, U.S. Dist. Ct. (so. dist. Ga.) 1975, U.S. Ct. Appeals (11th cir.) 1981. With Hull, Towill, Norman and Barrett, Augusta, Ga., 1974— . Chmn., Richmond County Bd. Elections, Augusta, 1980-89; bd. dirs. Episcopal Day Sch., 1982. With AUS, 1969-71. Decorated Bronze Star medal. Mem. Ga. Bar Assn. (bd. govs. 1986—), Ga. Def. Lawyers Assn., Def. Rsch. Inst., Nat. Assn. R.R. Trial Counsel, Augusta Bar Assn. (past chmn. Law Day, past mem. exec. bd.), Wofford Coll. Nat. Alumni Assn. (dir. 1981-84), Rotary (bd. govs. Augusta 1986—, sec. 1988—). Episcopalian (sr. warden 1984). Office: Hull Towill Norman & Barrett PO Box 1564 Augusta GA 30903-1564

DICKES, ROBERT, psychiatrist; b. N.Y.C., Apr. 15, 1912; s. Benjamin and Anna (Adler) D.; m. Bernice Livingston, June 12, 1938; children: Richard A., Susan R. Dickes Hubbard. BS, CCNY, 1933; MS, Emory U., 1934, MD, 1938. Diplomate: Am. Bd. Internal Medicine, Am. Bd. Psychiatry and Neurology. Intern L.I. Coll. Hosp., Bklyn., 1938-39, asst. resident in internal medicine, 1938-39, resident in medicine, 1939-41, dir. med. clinics, 1946-50; asso. in medicine L.I. Coll. Medicine, 1946, asst. prof. psychiatry, 1949; fellow in medicine Western Res. U.-Lakeside Hosp., 1941-42; fellow in psychiatry Kings County Hosp. Center-SUNY Bklyn., 1950-52, mem. staff, 1952—, pres. med. br., 1977-78. Clin. assoc. prof. psychiatry Downstate Med. Center SUNY, Bklyn., 1950-54, assoc. prof., 1954-56, clin. assoc. prof., 1956-61, assoc. prof., 1961-63, prof., 1963, 78-82, prof. emeritus, 1982—, tng. and supervising analyst, 1965—, acting chmn. dept. psychiatry, 1965-66, 71-72, dir. infant behavior study lab., 1973, dir. center human sexuality, 1973—, chmn. dept. psychiatry, 1975-78; clin. prof. psychiatry NYU Coll. Medicine, 1982—; cons. VA hosps., Bklyn., Northport, N.Y.; v.p. Am. Bd. Sexology, 1989—. Contbr. articles to profl. publs. Bd. govs., mem. acquisitions com. Bklyn. Museum. Maj. M.C. U.S. Army, 1942-46. Commonwealth fellow, 1941-42, 48-49 Fellow A.C.P., Am. Psychiat. Assn., Am. Coll. Psychiatry; mem. Am. Psychoanalytic Assn., Psychoanalytic Assn. N.Y. (treas. 1962-64), Bklyn. Psychiat. Soc. (pres. 1967), Kings County Med. Soc., Kings County Psychiat. Soc. (pres. 1967-68), Soc. Sex Therapy and Research (pres. 1979-81), Am. Bd. Sexology (v.p. 1989—).

DICKESON, ROBERT CELMER, retired university president, foundation executive, political science educator; b. Independence, Mo., June 28, 1940; s. James Houston and Sophie Stephanie (Celmer) D.; m. Ludmila Ann Weir, June 22, 1963; children: Elizabeth Ann, Cynthia Marie. AB, U. Mo., 1962, MA, 1963, PhD, 1968; postgrad., U. No. Colo., 1971, 72; postgrad. inst. ednl. mgmt., Harvard U., 1973. Adminstrv. asst. U. Mo., Columbia, 1962-64, dir. student activities, 1964-68, asst. dean students, 1968-69; dean student affairs No. Ariz. U., Flagstaff, 1969-70, assoc. prof. polit. sci., 1970-76, prof., 1976-81, on leave, 1979-81, v.p. student affairs, 1970-79, v.p., univ. relations, 1973-79; dir. Ariz. Dept. Adminstrn., Phoenix, 1979-81; pres. U. No. Colo., Greeley, 1981-91, prof. polit. sci., 1981-87, 88-91; chief of staff to gov., exec. dir. Office of State Planning and Budgeting State of Colo., 1987; pres. Noel/Levitz Ctrs. Inc., Iowa City, 1991-97; divsn. pres. USA Group Found. for Edn., Indpls., 1995-97. Sr. v.p. Lumina Found. for Edn., 1997—; adj. prof. U. Colo., Denver, 1987, Ariz. State U., Tempe, 1979-81; nat. vice-chmn. Cert. Public Mgr. Policy Bd., 1980-81; planning and mgmt. cons.; mem. univ. adv. council Am. Council on Life Ins.; dir. United Bank of Greeley; mem. Pres.' Commn. NCAA, 1989-91; mem. Nat. Commn. on Minorities in Higher Edn., 1989-91; nat. cons. Office of Women in Higher Edn., Am. Coun. on Edn., 1989-97. Author: Prioritizing Academic Programs and Services, 1999; contbr. articles to profl. jours. Active Boy Scouts Am., v.p. Grand Canyon council, Flagstaff, 1974-76, pres., 1976-79, mem. nat. council, 1976-81, T. Roosevelt council, 1979-81, v.p. Long's Peak Council, 1981-87; mem. state com. Ariz. Democratic Com., 1970-72; chmn. Gov.'s Commn. on Merit System Reform, 1979-80, Gov.'s Regulatory Rev. Council, 1980-81, Gov.'s Commn. Higher Edn., 1983-86; mem. Gov.'s Commn. Excellence in Edn., 1983-86, Gov.'s Coun. on Creative Schs., 1989-91; commr. from Colo. to Edn. Commn. of the States, 1987-91; internat. trustee Sigma Alpha Epsilon Found., 1993-97. Recipient Dist. award of Merit., 1973, Silver Beaver award, 1975, Disting. Service award Sigma Alpha Epsilon, 1969, Merit Key award 1997, Disting. Alumnus award U. Mo.-Columbia, 1988, Outstanding Pres. award Am. Assn. Colls. of Tchrs. Edn, 1991, Bus. Excellence award U. No. Colo., 1990, Faculty Alumni U. Mo. award, 1990, Disting. Svc award Am. Coun. Edn., 2000; named to N. Crtrl. Athletic Conf. Hall of Fame, 1991. Mem. Am. Polit. Sci. Assn., Am. Soc. Public Adminstrn. (Ariz. exec. bd., Superior Svc. award 1981), Am. Acad. Polit. and Social Sci., Coll. Student Pers. Inst. (acad. coun. 1969-73), Assn. Pub. Coll. and Univ. Pres. (pres. 1985-87), Assn. Pub. Coll. and Univ. Pres. (pres. 1985-87), Nat. Assn. Student Pers. Adminstrs. (regional coun. 1974-79), Am. Assn. State Colls. and Univs. (chmn. coun. on doctoral granting instns., Meritorious Svc. award 1991), Columbia Club (Indpls.), Newcomen Soc., Phi Kappa Phi. United Methodist (pres. bd. trustees 1974). Lodges: Kiwanis (pres. 1975-76); Rotary. E-mail: rdickeso@luminafoundation.org.

DICKEY, DAVID HERSCHEL, lawyer, accountant; b. Savannah, Ga., Dec. 31, 1951; s. Grady Lee and Sara (Leon) D.; children: David Bradford, Carolyn Amanda. BBA in Acctg. and Fin., Armstrong State Coll., 1974; M in Accountancy, JD, U. Ga., 1977. CPA; bar: Ga. 1978, U.S. Dist. Ct. (no. dist.) Ga. 1980, U.S. Ct. Claims 1978, U.S. Tax Ct. 1978, U.S. Ct. Appeals (5th and 11th cirs.) 1978, U.S. Supreme Ct. 1981. Assoc., acct. Thompson and Benken, Attys., Savannah, 1977-79; pub. acct. Arthur Andersen & Co., Atlanta, 1979-81; assoc. Oliver Maner & Gray, Attys. LLP, Savannah, 1981-82; ptnr. Oliver Maner & Gray, Attys., Savannah, 1982—. Pres. Savannah Estate Planning Coun., 1986-87, chmn. bd., 1987-88; bd. dirs. Chatham-Savannah Citizen's Advocacy; mem. legal adv. bd. Small Bus. Coun. Am., Inc., 1989—; pres. Seminar Group, Inc., 1989—, Hist. Investment Properties, Inc., 1991—. Pres. L'Alliance Francaise de Savannah, 2001—03; bd. dirs. Savannah Theatre Co., 1984, Savannah chpt. Am. Cancer Soc., 1986—91, Hist. Savannah Found., Inc., 1988—94, Chandler Hosp. Found., 2003; chmn., trustee Armstrong State Coll. Alumni Endowment Fund, Inc., 1991; chmn. lawyers divsn. Chatham County United Way, 1992; dir., v.p. Armstrong Atlantic State U. Found., 2001—03; bd. trustees The Candler Found., 2001—03. Recipient Outstanding Svc. award Am. Cancer Soc., 1987, Outstanding Alumni Svc. award Armstrong State Coll., 1992; named to Leadership Savannah, Savannah C. of C., 1984-86. Fellow: Am. Coll. Trust and Esttae Coun.; mem.: S.R. (pres. Ga. chpt. 2001—03), ABA (estate and give tax com. taxation sect. 1990—), AICPA, SAR (pres. Ga. 1999), Am. Assn. Atty.-CPAs, Ga. Soc. CPAs, Savannah Bar Assn., Ga. Bar Assn., St. Andrew's Soc., Soc. Colonial Wars, Sons Confederate Vets (commdr. Francis S. Bartow camp no. 93 1997—98), Chatham Club, First City Club (bd. dirs. Savannah 1987—90). Avocations: history, genealogy, music, computers, historic rehab. Home: 4 Springfield Pl Savannah GA 31411 Office: Oliver Maner & Gray 218 W State St Savannah GA 31401-3232

DICKEY, DENISE ANN, lawyer, arbitrator; b. L.A., Dec. 31, 1957; d. John W. and Virginia May (Giese) D. BA with high honors, U. Calif., Santa Barbara, 1979; JD, U. So. Calif., L.A., 1982. Bar: Calif. 1983, U.S. Dist. Ct. (ctrl. dist.) Calif. 1983, U.S. Ct. Appeals (9th cir.) 1983. Pvt. practice, L.A., 1983-84; dep. dist. atty. L.A. County Dist. Atty.'s Office, L.A., 1984-85; assoc. Shield & Smith, L.A., 1985-90, Tarkington, O'Connor and O'Neill, Ventura and L.A., 1990-91; pvt. practice Law Offices of Denise A. Dickey, Santa Barbara, Calif., 1991—. Arbitrator Ventura Superior Ct., Ventura Mcpl. Ct., Santa Barbara Superior Ct., 1991—; judge pro tem. Santa Barbara Mcpl. Ct., 1994—; cons. Inglewood (Calif.) Police Dept., 1986-92. Mem. Buy Santa Barbara Alliance, 1993-95. Mem. Santa Barbara Bar Assn. Episcopalian. Avocations: art, jewelry, photography, parrots, gardening. Office: 2022 Cliff Dr # 292 Santa Barbara CA 93109-1506

DICKEY, ELEANOR, humanities educator; b. New Haven, Apr. 9, 1967; d. Thomas Atherton and Barbara Dickey. BA, Bryn Mawr Coll., 1987, MA, 1989; MPhil, Balliol Coll., Oxford U., 1991; PhD, Merton Coll., Oxford U., 1994. Jr. rsch. fellow Merton Coll., Oxford, England, 1992—95; asst. prof. classics U. Ottawa, 1995—99, Columbia U., N.Y.C., 1999—. Mem. editl. bd. Bryn Mawr Classical Rev., 1998—. Author: Greek Forms of Address, 1996, Latin Forms of Address, 2002; co-author: New Selected Odes of Pindar, 1991. Mellon fellow, Inst. for Advanced Study, Princeton, NJ, 1998—99, jr. fellow, Ctr. for Hellenic Studies, Washington, 2002—03. Avocations: music, hiking, nature. Office: Columbia Univ Classics MC 2867 1130 Amsterdam Ave New York NY 10027

DICKEY, GARY ALAN, minister; b. Santa Monica, Calif., Jan. 25, 1946; s. Charles Harry and Audrey W. (White) D.; m. Tamara Jean Kimble, Jan. 11, 1976. BA, UCLA, 1968; MDiv, Fuller Theol. Sem., Pasadena, 1972; DMin, Sch. Theology, Claremont, Calif., 1974; PhD, Trinity Theol. Seminary, 1996; Advanced Diploma in Local History, Oxford U., 2002. Cert. genealogist Bd. Cert. Genealogists. Assoc. pastor Magnolia Pk. United Meth. Ch., Burbank, Calif., 1974-78; sr. pastor St. James United Meth. Ch., Pasadena, 1978-90, First United Meth. Ch. of Canoga Park, 1990—. Exec. com. mem. Calif.-Pacific Ann. Conf. Bd. of Ordained Ministry, 1980-88; chmn. Pasadena Dist. Com. on Ordained Ministry, 1978-90; supervising pastor Bd. Higher Edn., Nashville, 1978—. Recipient Polonia Restituta, 1990. Mem. Calif. State Soc. Colonial Wars (state gov. 1999-2000), Soc. War of 1812 (chaplian 1989—, Calif. state pres. 1997-98, v.p. gen. Calif. 1999), Soc. of Sons of Am. Revolution (chaplain 1988—, pres. 1994, 95, Outstanding Citizenship award 1990, Meritorious Svc. award 1995, Silver Good Citizenship award 1996, Patriot medal 1997), Soc. of Sons of the Revolution, Descendants of Soldiers of Valley Forge, Soc. Sons Am. Colonists, Soc. Sons. Vets. Civil War, Vet. Corps Artillery State N.Y., United Empire Loyalists Assn. (Can.), Royal Soc. St. George (Eng.), Rotary (pres. 1989-90, Paul Harris fellow 1986). Republican. Methodist. Avocations: photography, travel, genealogical research. Home: 22167 Bryant St Canoga Park CA 91304-2306 Office: First United Meth Ch 22700 Sherman Way Canoga Park CA 91307-2332

DICKEY, GLENN ERNEST, JR., sports columnist; b. Virginia, Minn., Feb. 16, 1936; s. Glenn Ernest and Madlyn Marie (Emmert) D.; m. Nancy Jo McDaniel, Feb. 25, 1967; 1 son, Kevin Scott. BA, U. Calif., Berkeley, 1958. Sports editor Watsonville (Calif.) Register-Pajoronian, 1958-63; sports writer San Francisco Chronicle, 1963-71, sports columnist, 1971—. Author: The Jock Empire, 1974, The Great No-Hitters, 1976, Champs and Chumps, 1976, The

History of National League Baseball, 1979, The History of American League Baseball, 1980, (with Dick Berg) Eavesdropping America, 1980, America Has a Better Team, 1982, The History of Professional Basketball, 1982, The History of the World Series, 1984, (with Jim Tunney) Impartial Judgment: The Dean of NFL Referees Calls Football As He Sees It, 1988, San Francisco Forty-Niners: The Super Year, 1989; (with Bill Walsh) Building a Champion, 1990; Just Win, Baby, Al Davis and His Raiders, 1991; Sports Hero Kevin Mitchell (juvenile), 1993, Sports Hero Jerry Rice (juvenile), 1993, San Francisco 49ers: 50 Years, 1995, San Francisco Giants: 40 Seasons, 1997, Glenn Dickey's 49ers, 2000; contbr. stories to Best Sports Stories, 1962, 68, 71, 75, 76. Home: 120 Florence Ave Oakland CA 94618-2249 Office: Chronicle Pub Co 901 Mission St San Francisco CA 94103-2905

DICKEY, JAY W., JR., former congressman, lawyer; b. Dec. 14, 1939; s. Jay W. and Margaret D.; divorced; children: John, Laura, Ted, Rachel. BA, U. Ark., 1961, JD, 1963. City atty., Pine Bluff, Ark., 1968-70; mem. U.S. Congress from 4th Ark. dist., 1993-2001. Bd. trustees Univ. Ark. Sys. Past pres. Pine Bluff Jaycees (Disting. Svc. award); huddle leader Pine Bluff High Sch. Fellowship of Christian Athletes (mem. state bd.); mem. Pillars Club United Way, Century Club Boy Scouts Am.; past mem. LifeSavers of Ark. Childrens' Hosp.; state chmn. Christian Legal Soc. Republican.

DICKEY, JEANNETTA BURKETT, social worker; b. Murphy, N.C., Oct. 19, 1928; d. Arthur Bascomb and Jenny Thelma (Mulcay) D.; m. John Arnette (div. 1967); children: John Arnette, Jeannetta Dickey Arnette, Claiborne Burkett Arnette, Benjamin Harrison Arnette. BA, Brenau Coll., 1949; MSW, U. N.C., 1969; postgrad., Duke U., 1970. Lic. clin. social worker, Calif.; cert. clin. social worker, N.C.; cert. Am. Assn. State Social Work Bds. Tchr. secondary edn., various locations, 1950-65; chief social worker, then sr. adminstr. Vance, Warren, Granville & Franklin CMHC, John Unstead Hosp., Henderson, N.C., 1969-72; chief social worker areas A, B, & C Mental Health Adminstrn., Washington, 1972-78; clin. social worker Met. State Hosp., Norwalk, Calif., 1981-88, Camarillo (Calif.) State Hosp., 1988-90; social worker Mental Health Adminstrn., Washington, 1990-92. Mem. exec. planning commn. Mental Health Adminstrn., Washington, 1974-78, mem. evaluation and cert. com., 1975-79; NIMH rsch. project for rural mental health, U. N.C., Chapel Hill, 1969-72. Author: The Multi Problem Family in Child Guidance, 1969; contbr. articles on rural mental health to profl. jours. Docent Nat. Gallery of Art, Washington, 1963, 64, 65; vol. family liaison Western Carolina Ctr., Black Mountain, N.C., 1980; vol. English as Second Lang., Washington, 1963-64; vol. United Fund-Meals on Wheels. Mem. AAUW (Cherokee County chpt.), DAR (various chpts.), Delta Delta Delta. Episcopalian. Home: 37 East Ave Murphy NC 28906-2967

DICKEY, JOHN HARWELL, lawyer; b. Huntsville, Ala., Feb. 22, 1944; s. Gilbert McClain and Marjorie Loucille (Harwell) D.; m. Nancy Margaret Eagar, Nov. 24, 1984; children: Marjorie Ruth, Gilbert Charles. BA, Samford U., 1966; JD, Cumberland Sch. of Law, 1969. Bar: Tenn. 1971, U.S. Dist. Ct. (ea. dist.) Tenn. 1972. Adminstrv. asst. Dist. Atty.'s Office, Huntsville, 1969-70; law clerk domestic and juvenille divsn. Cir. Ct., Huntsville, 1970-72; trial lawyer Legal Aid Soc., Chattanooga, 1972-75; pvt. practice Chattanooga, 1975-77, Fayetteville, Tenn., 1977-89; dist. pub. defender 17th jud. cir. State of Tenn., Fayetteville, 1989-98; pvt. practice, Fayetteville, Tenn., 1998—. Mem. continuing edn. com. Pub. Defenders Conf., Tenn., 1990-92, mem. long range planning com., 1991-93, mem. legis. com., 1990-93, mem. exec. com., Mid. Tenn. rep., 1993-94. Lectr. Fayetteville-Lincoln County Leadership Tng. Program, 1989—; mem. adv. bd. Community Correction South Ctrl. Tenn., Fayetteville, 1989—; mem. Bedford County Dem. Club, 1989—. Mem. Nat. Assn. Criminal Def. Lawyers, Tenn. Bar Assn., Tenn. Assn. Criminal Def. Lawyers (membership com. 1989—, juvenile law com. 1988—, Disting. Svc. award 1990, 91, 92), Marshall County Bar Assn., Fayetteville-Lincoln County Bar Assn. (treas. 1977, sec. 1978, v.p. 1979, pres. 1980), Fayetteville-Lincoln County C. of C., Elks, Masons (jr. steward 1991, sr. steward 1992, jr. deacon 1993, jr. warden 1994, sr. warden 1995, worshipful master 1996), York Rite Mason, Scottish Rite Mason (32d degree), Shriners (sgt.-at-arms 1993, v.p. 1994, dir. pub. rels. 1994, 96—, pres. 1995), Internat. Platform Assn., Order of Ea. Star (chaplain 1993-94), Tenn. 4-H Found., Gideons Internat. Democrat. Methodist. Avocations: hunting, fishing, canoeing, kayaking. Home: 122 Brookmeade Dr Fayetteville TN 37334-2046 Office: 105 Main Ave S Fayetteville TN 37334-3057

DICKEY, JOSEPH WILLIAM, utility executive, engineer; b. Decatur, Ill., Sept. 20, 1944; s. Lawrence Wayne and Helen Marie (Van Horn) D. BS in Chem. Engring., MIT, 1966, MS in Civil Engring., 1967; postgrad., U. Va., 1978. Registered profl. engr., Tenn., Fla. Plant mgr. Fla. Power & Light Co., Miami, 1973-76, mgmt. positions in nuclear energy and power resources, 1976-85, v.p. nuclear energy and nuclear ops., 1985-88, v.p. power resources, 1988-91; sr. v.p. fossil and hydro power TVA, Chattanooga, 1991-94, chief operating officer Knoxville, 1994-98; pres., CEO FGS & Assocs. LLC, 1999—. Mem. subcom., chmn., officer EEI Prime Movers Com., Washington, 1980-85; mem. subcom., officer S.E. Electric Exch., Atlanta, 1988-91; speaker in field. Contbr. numerous articles to jours. and trade mags. Chmn. for Broward County MIT Ednl. Coun., 1978-91; bd. govs. Dept. Energy Robotics Program, 1987-88; mem. industry adv. coun. U. Fla. Coll. Engring., Gainesville, 1987-91; trustee, chmn. FPL Polit. Action Com., 1981-85, 83-84. Recipient Ishikawa medal Am. Soc. Quality Control, 1996. Fellow Fla. Engring. Soc.; mem. NSPE, ASCE (br. pres. 1974-75).

DICKEY, ROBERT MARVIN (RICK DICKEY), property manager; b. Charleston, S.C., Dec. 3, 1950; s. John Lincoln II and Ruth (Marvin) D.; m. Teresa Ann Curry, Dec. 19, 1969 (div. 1979); 1 child, Gena Lynette; m. Martha Suzanne Coup, July 21, 1999; 1 child, Dylan Thomas. A of Computer Sci., USMC Degree Program, Washington, 1975. Cert. apt. property supr. Nat. Apt. Assn., Wash., occupancy specialist Nat. Ctr.for Housing Mgmt., Wash. Enlisted USMC, 1968, advanced through grades to staff sgt., 1968-78; shop mgr., bookkeeper Amalgamated Plant Co., Las Vegas, Nev., 1978-79; supr. constrn. Joseph Yousem Co., Las Vegas, 1979-80; apt. mgr. Robert A. McNeil Corp., Las Vegas, 1980, comml. bldg. mgr., leasing agt., 1980-82; asst. v.p., regional property mgr. Westminster Co., Las Vegas, 1982-87, Weyerhaeuser Mortgage Co., Las Vegas, 1988-89; pres., ptnr. Equinox Devel., Inc., Las Vegas, 1989-91; dir. residental properties R.W. Robideaux & Co., Spokane, Wash., 1992-97; mgr. residential divsn. G&B Real Estate Svcs., Spokane, 1997—. Contbr. articles to profl. jours. Mem. Nat. Assn. Realtors, Wash. Assn. Realtors, Spokane Assn. Realtors, Inst. Real Estate Mgmt. (accredited residential mgr., legis. chmn. 1987-88, Accredited Residential Mgr. award 1985, 86, 90), Nev. Apt. Assn. (v.p. 1985, pres. 1988—, bd. dirs.), So. Nev. Homebuilders Assn., Las Vegas Bd. Realtors (mgmt. legis. com. 1988).

DICKEY, SALLY ANN, retired cultural organization administrator; b. Indian Lake, Ohio, Jan. 5, 1937; d. Newton Melville and Martha Mae (Huston) Reiff; m. E. James Dickey, Aug. 17, 1958; children: Deborah Lynn, Douglas James, David Reiff, Derek Christopher. Student, Ohio Wesleyan U., Delaware, 1955-58; BS in Edn., Boston U., 1959; BA, Ohio Wesleyan U., 1959. Speech therapist Lynnfield (Mass.) Schs., 1959-60, Blanchester (Ohio) Schs., 1969-70; nursery sch. dir. Wilmington (Ohio) U. Meth. Ch., 1970-75; dir. cmty. involvement program U.A. City Schs., Columbus, Ohio, 1980-84; assoc. dir. ann. fund Ohio Wesleyan U., Delaware, 1984-85; dir. devel. Springfield (Ohio) Arts Coun., 1988-98; pvt. cons., 1998—. Mem. Clark County Mental Health Bd., Springfield; mem. bus. adv. com. Springfield City Schs., 1988-98; dir. devel. Landmark Preservation Inc., Bellefontaine, Ohio, 1999— Dir. religious dramas in local chs., 1963-97. Mem. adv. bd. Kappa Alpha Theta, Ohio Wesleyan U., 1986-89, mem. house corp., 1970-88; mem. ann. fund coun. Ohio Wesleyan U., 1986-99; mem. Ohio Weslay Assocs., 1999—; fundraising cons. Holland Theatre, Bellefontaine, Ohio. Recipient Upper Arlington Woman of Yr. award Rotary, 1985, Outstanding Alumni award Ohio Wesleyan U., 1985. Mem. Miami Valley Planning Giving Coun., Nat. Soc. Fund Raising Execs. (Miami Valley chpt.), Kiwanis Internat. (bd. dirs. 1994-95, chair cmty. svc. 1992-93, 96-97, chair fund raising 1997-98). Republican. United Methodist. Avocations: swimming, boating, reading.

DICKIE, GEORGE THOMAS, philosopher, educator; b. Palmetto, Fla., Aug. 12, 1926; s. George Harrison and Emily (Neal) Dickie; m. Ruth Joyce Petty, Aug. 5, 1950 (dec. Apr. 1975); children: Garrick George, Blake Allen; m. Suzanne Ruth Cunningham, June 25, 1977. BA, Fla. State U., 1949; PhD, UCLA, 1959. From instr. to assoc. prof. Wash. State U., Pullman, 1956—64; assoc. prof. U. Houston, 1964—65; assoc. prof. to prof. U. Ill. Chgo., 1965—95, prof. emeritus, 1995—. Pres. Ill. Philosophy Assn., 1990—91. Author: The Art Circle, 1984, The Century of Taste, 1996, Art and Value, 2001, Evaluating Art, 1988, Art and the Aesthetic, 1974, Introduction to Aesthetics, 1971. Pfc USMC, 1944—46. Fellow, NEH, 1971—72, 1989—90, Guggenheim Found., 1978—79. Mem.: Am. Soc. Philosophy, Am. Soc. Aesthetics (pres. 1993—94). Democrat. Home: 3110 43rd St W Bradenton FL 34209

DICKIE, ROBERT BENJAMIN, lawyer, consultant, educator; b. Glendale, Calif., Sept. 10, 1941; s. John A. and Dorothy C. Dickie; m. Susan J. Williams, Jan. 28, 1967 (div. 1987); children: Amy, John, Thomas. BA, Yale U., 1963; JD, U. Calif., Berkeley, 1967. Bar: Calif. 1967, N.Y. 1970, Mass. 1971. Assoc. Shearman & Sterling, N.Y.C., 1969-71, Sullivan & Worcester, Boston, 1971-77; asst. prof. mgmt. policy Boston U., 1977-83, tenured assoc. prof., 1983-94; prin The Dickie Group, 1994—. Cons. World Bank, Washington, Fortune 100 Cos., leading law firms in U.S., Europe and Asia. Author: Financial Statement Analysis and Business Valuation for the Practical Lawyer, ABA, 1999; contbr. numerous articles to Nat. Law Jour., Strategic Mgmt. Jour., Columbia Jour. World Bus., others. Mem.: Am. Bar Assn., Calif. Bar Assn., Boston Bar Assn., Longwood Cricket Club, Yale Club Boston. Office: The Dickie Group Reservoir Pl 1601 Trapelo Rd Waltham MA 02451

DICKIE, SHIRLEY DALME, vocational rehabilitation counselor and consultant; b. Natchitoches, La., July 8, 1946; d. Charles R. and Nell Dalme; m. Shelley Curran Dickie, Aug. 12, 1967; 1 child, Angela Rene. BS, Northwestern State U., Natchitoches, La., 1969; MEd, U. Tex., 1976. Cert. health, physical edn., spl. edn. tchr., reading specialist, La.; lic. vocat. rehab. counselor, profl. counselor, La.; cert. vocat. evaluator. Instr. swimming Northwestern State U., Natchitoches, 1964-67; tchr. St. Mary's H.S., Natchitoches, 1967-68, Natchitoches Parish Head Start, 1969, Ouachita Parish Sch. System, Monroe, La., 1972; instr. workshop State Com. for Head Start, Austin, Tex., 1973-76; coord. spl. edn. Mental Health Mental Retardation Regional Ctr. East Tex., Tyler, 1973-75; dir. rehab. svcs. Easter Seal Soc. Dade County, Miami, Fla., 1979-82; exec. dir. S.W. La. Rehab. Ctr., Lafayette, 1982-85; ind. vocat. rehab. counselor, Lafayette, 1985—; exec. dir. Rehab. Inst. of Acadiana, 1991-95; coord. regional vocat. svc. UpLIFTD, 1997-98, regional supr., 1998—. Cons. Nat. Easter Seal Soc., Chgo., 1980-82; vocat. expert Social Security Adminstrn., Washington, 1985—; cert. vocat. rehab. counselor U.S. Dept. Labor, Washington, 1983-95; lic. profl. counselor State of La., Baton Rouge, 1988—; instr. ARC, Natchitoches, Monroe, 1964-75, spl. edn. Tex. Ea. U., Tyler, 1976; bd. dirs. La. Rehab. Assn., others. Bd. dirs. Southwest La. Rehab. Ctr., Lafayette, 1985-91, Cmty. Habilitation Ctr.-Sheltered Workshop, Miami, 1978-82; bd. jurics dept. architecture U. S.W. La., Lafayette, 1983-85; bd. dirs., past pres. La. Com. for Comm. Disorders, New Orleans, 1983-95; adv. bd. Gulfcoast Teaching Families, Lafayette, 1987-91, Dept. Health and Human Resources/Office of Family Svcs. Medicaid Med. Adv. Bd., Baton Rouge, 1984-85, Cmty. Com. for Developmental Handicaps and Retardation, Miami, 1980-82; com. mem. Am. Heart Assn., Lafayette, 1984-86. Spl. Edn. Dept. grantee Northwestern State U., 1966-69. Mem. NAFE, Nat. Assn. Investment Clubs, Nat. Rehab. Assn., La. Rehab. Counselors, La. Assn. Rehab. Profls., La. Rehab. Assn. (bd. dirs. 1991—), Profitseekers Investment Club (treas. 1988, 93—, pres. 1989-90), Woodbriar Pub. Health Assn. (treas. 1984-86, pvt. industry coun. 1991-99), L.A. Vocat. Evaluation Work Adjustment Assn. (pres. 1996), S.W. Nat. Rehab. Assn. (pres. 1997—, past pres. 1998, Nat. Vewaa Mike Rubin award 1998, LeVewaa Julius Villemarette award 2002), Lafayette Parish JTPA (bd. dirs. 1991-99), Lafayette WIB (bd. dirs. 1999--). Republican. Roman Catholic. Avocations: horticulture, biking, snow skiing, gourmet cooking, decorating, reading. Home and Office: 126 Karolwood Dr Lafayette LA 70503-3505

DICKIESON, RICHARD MARK, travel company executive; b. July 23, 1951; BA, Mich. State U., 1973; MBA, DePaul U., 1979. Pres. McTravel/Pvt. Label Travel, Chgo., 1984-91, La Ola, Ltd., Park Ridge, Ill., 1991-95; v.p. operations DER Travel Svcs., Rosemont, Ill., 1995—2000; v.p. sys. devel. Classic Vacation Group, Downers Grove, Ill., 2001; pres. Pvt. Label Travel, Downers Grove, 2002—, pres., 2002—. Home: 840 Courtland Ave Park Ridge IL 60068-4834

DICKINSON, CAROL RITTGERS, arts administrator, writer, executive director; b. Des Moines, Apr. 16, 1933; d. Robert Johnson and Cecil Marjorie (Snyder) Rittgers; m. Donald Ira Dickinson, June 6, 1959; 1 child, Lauren Lucy. BA in English with honors, Drake U., 1954; MA in Art History, U. Hawaii, 1964. Lydia Roberts fellow Columbia U., N.Y.C., 1954-56; instr. Iowa State U., U. Hawaii, Colo Women's Coll., U. Petroleum and Minerals, Dhahran, Saudi Arabia, Colo. Sc. Mines, Golden, 1956-76; dir. pub. programs Denver Art Mus., 1980-83; dir. publicity and edn. Mus. Western Art, Denver, 1985-86; freelance writer, 1979—. Lectr., panelist numerous mus., univs. and profl. groups, Colo., 1980—. Co-editor, contbg. author: Colorado and the American Renaissance, 1980, Walking in Beauty, 1990; founding editor Denver Urban Design Forum Newsletter, 1984, 85; contbg. writer The Art of Dean Mitchell, 1999; contbr. more than 400 articles to nat. and regional newspapers and mags.; art critic Denver Rocky Mountain News, 1990-92. Exec. dir. Foothills Art Ctr., Golden, 1992-93. Recipient Denver Mayor's Award for Excellence in Arts, 2000, 1st Cultural award, Jefferson Symphony, 2000, medal, Colorado Sch. Mines, 2000. Mem. Colo. Press Women (first pl. award reviews features), Golden Fortnightly Club, Asian Art Assn. Democrat. Episcopalian. Avocations: Asian philosophies and history, Chinese brush painting, international hosting, films, felines.

DICKINSON, DONALD CHARLES, library science educator; b. Schenectady, N.Y., June 9, 1927; s. Charles William and Stella Barney (Sheldon) D.; m. Colleen Eleanor Schindler, Aug. 7, 1954; children: Ann, Jean, Ellen, Mary, Kathleen, Sheila. AB, SUNY, Albany, 1949; MLS, U. Ill., 1951; PhD, U. Mich., 1964. Ref. librarian Cen. Mo. State Coll., Warrensburg, 1951-53, Eastern Mich. U., Ypsilanti, 1953-56; asst. acquisitions U. Kans., Lawrence, 1956-58; head librarian Bemidji (Minn.) State Coll., 1958-66; dir. reader service U. Mo., Columbia, 1966-69; dir. grad. library sch. U. Ariz., Tucson, 1969-78, prof. grad. library sch., 1979-96, prof. emeritus, 1996—. Author: Bio-bibliography Langston Hughes, 1967, 2d edit., 1972, Hellmut Lehmann-Haupt, 1975, Dictionary of American Book Collectors, 1986, George Watson Cole, 1990, Henry E. Huntington's Library of Libraries, 1995, Dictionary of American Antiquarian Bookdealers, 1998. Am. Philos. Assn. grantee, 1969; Andrew W. Mellon fellow Henry E. Huntington Libr., 1989; Helm fellow Ind. U., 1999; C.P. Snow travel fellow U. Tex., 2000; Huntington/Brit. Acad. fellow, 2000. Mem. ALA (coun. 1972-73, travel grantee 1960), Bibliographic Soc. Am., Ariz. Libr. Assn. (pres. 1978-79), Grolier Club (N.Y.C.), Zamorano Club (L.A.). Democrat. E-mail: dickinsd@u.arizona.edu.

DICKINSON, ELEANOR CREEKMORE, artist, educator; b. Knoxville, Tenn., Feb. 7, 1931; d. Robert Elmond and Evelyn Louise (Van Gilder) C.; m. Ben Wade Oakes Dickinson, June 12, 1952; children: Mark Wade, Katherine Van Gilder, Peter Somers. BA, U. Tenn., 1952; postgrad., San Francisco Art Inst., 1961-63, Academié de la Grande Chaumière, Paris, 1971; M.F.A., Calif. Coll. Arts and Crafts, 1982, Golden Gate U., 1984. Escrow officer Security Nat. Bank, Santa Monica, Calif., 1953-54; mem. faculty Calif. Coll. Arts and Crafts, Oakland, Calif., 1971-2001, assoc. prof. art, 1974-84, prof., 1984-2001, prof. emerita, 2001—, dir. galleries, 1975-85. Artist-in-residence U. Tenn., 1969, Ark. State U., 1993, Fine Arts Mus. of San Francisco, 2000; faculty U. Calif. Ext., 1967-70; lectr. in field. Co-author, illustrator: Revival, 1974, That Old Time Religion, 1975; also mus. catalogs; illustrator: The Complete Fruit Cookbook, 1972, Human Sexuality: A Search for Understanding, 1984, Days Journey, 1985; commissions: University of San Francisco, 1990-2001; one-woman shows include Corcoran Gallery Art, Washington, 1970, 74, San Francisco Mus. Modern Art, 1965, 68, Fine Arts Mus. San Francisco, 1969, 75, Poindexter Gallery, N.Y., 1972, 74, Smithsonian Inst., 1975-81, U. Tenn., 1976, Galeria de Arte y Libros, Monterrey, Mex., 1978, Oakland Mus., 1979, Interart Ctr., N.Y., 1980, Tenn. State Mus., 1981-82, Hatley Martin Gallery, San Francisco, 1986, 89, Michael Himovitz Gallery, Sacramento, Calif., 1988-89, 91, 93, 97-98, Gallery 10, Washington, 1989, Diverse Works, Houston, 1990, Ewing Gallery, U. Tenn., 1991, G.T.U. Gallery, U. Calif., Berkeley, 1991, Mus. Contemporary Religious Art, St. Louis, 1995, Thacher Gallery, U. San Francisco, 2000; represented in permanent collections Nat. Collection Fine Arts, Corcoran Gallery Art, Libr. of Congress, Smithsonian Instn., San Francisco Mus. Modern Art, Butler Inst. Art, Oakland Mus., Santa Barbara Mus., Nat. Mus. Women in Arts, Washington; prodr. (TV) The Art of the Matter-Professional Practices in Fine Arts, 1986—. Bd. dirs. Calif. Confedn. of the Arts, 1983-88; bd. dirs., v.p. Calif. Lawyers for the Arts, 1986—; mem. coun. bd. San Francisco Art Inst., 1966-91, trustee, 1964-67; sec., bd. dirs. YWCA, 1955-62; treas., bd. Westminster Ctr., 1955-59; bd. dirs. Children's Theater Assn., 1958-60, 93-94, Internat. Child Art Ctr., 1958-68. Recipient Disting. Alumni award San Francisco Art Inst., 1983, Master Drawing award Nat. Soc. Arts and Letters, 1983, Cert. of Recognition, El Consejo Mundial de Artistas Plasticos, 1993, Pres.'s award Nat. Women's Caucus for Art, 1995, Lifetime Achivement award Nat. Women's Caucus for Art, 2003; grantee Zellerbach Family Fund, 1975, Calif. Coll. Arts and Crafts, 1994, NEH, 1978, 80, 82-85, Thomas F. Stanley Found., 1985, Bay Area Video Coalition, 1988-92, PAS Graphics, 1988, San Francisco Cmty. TV Corp., 1990, Skaggs Found., 1991. Mem. AAUP, Coalition Women's Art Orgns. (dir., v.p. 1978-80, 2000—), Coll. Art Assn. (Lifetime Achievement award 2003), Calif. Confederation of Arts (bd. dirs. 1983-89), Calif. Lawyers for Arts (v.p. 1986—), San Francisco Art Assn. (sec., dir. 1964-67), NOW, Artists Equity Assn. (nat. v.p., dir. 1978-92), Arts Advocates, Women's Caucus for Art (nat. Affirmative Action officer 1978-80, nat. bd. dirs. 2000—). Democrat. Episcopalian. Office: Calif Coll Arts and Crafts 1111 8th St San Francisco CA 94107-2247 E-mail: eleanordickinson@mac.com.

DICKINSON, GAIL KREPPS, educator; b. Lewistown, Pa., June 10, 1956; d. Harold and Esther (Bourdess) Krepps; m. Willis H. Dickinson, Dec. 22, 1979 (div. 1998); children: Margaret Lee, Elizabeth Ann. BS, Millersville U. Pa., 1977; MSLS, U. N.C., 1987; PhD, U. Va., 2000. Libr. Cape Charles (Va.) Pub. Sch., 1977-81, Broadwater Acad., Exmore, Va., 1981-85; instrnl. supervisor Union-Endicott Sch. Dist., Endicott, N.Y., 1987-96; asst. prof. U. N.C., Greensboro, 2000—. Adj. prof. James Madison U., Harrisonburg, Va., 1997-99. Mem. AAUW, ASCD, Am. Ednl. Rsch. Assn., Am. Assn. Sch. Librs. (bd. dirs. 1994-97), N.Y. Libr. Assn. (pres. sch. libr. media sect. 1994), Phi Delta Kappa. Avocations: reading, word and video games.

DICKINSON, JANE W. social services administrator; b. Sept. 27, 1919; d. Charles Herman and Rachel (Whaler) Wagner; m. E. F. Sherwood Dickinson, Oct. 23, 1943; children: Diane Jane Gray Clem, Carolyn Dickinson Vane. BA, Duke U., 1941; MEd, Goucher Coll., 1965. Exec. sec. Petroleum Industry Com., Balt., 1941-43, Sherwood Feed Mills Inc., Balt., 1943-79. Mem. exec. com. Children's Aid Md., 1960-61; mem. bd. women's aux. Balt. Symphony Orch., 1958-60; dist. chmn. Balt. Cancer Drive, 1957; co-chmn. Balt. United Appeal, 1968; bd. mgrs. Pickersgill Retirement Home. Mem. Three Arts Club (Balt., sec. 1958-60, bd. govs. 1960-64, 67-70, pres. 1970-72), Women's Club of Roland Park (bd. govs. 1960-64, 86-88, 92-94), Cliff Dwellers Garden Club, Alpha Delta Phi Home: Apt 609 1055 W Joppa Rd Baltimore MD 21204-3748

DICKINSON, JANET MAE WEBSTER, relocation consulting executive; b. Cleve., Oct. 2, 1929; d. Richard and Gizella (Keplinger) Fisher; m. Rodney Earl Dickinson, June 18, 1965 (div. 1976); 1 child, Kimberly Cae. Grad., Larson Coll. for Women, New Haven; student, Portland State Coll. Lic. broker, Oreg. Pub. rels./promotion dir. KPTV-Channel 27, Portland, Oreg., 1951-54; exec. dir. Exposition-Recreation Commn., Portland, 1954-58; v.p. Art Lutz & Co., Realtors, Portland, 1975-79, Lutz Relocation Mgmt., Portland, 1977-79; corp. relocation mgr. Ga. Pacific Corp., Portland, 1979-82; pres., broker Ga. Pacific Fin. Co., Portland, 1980-82; pres., chief exec. officer The Dickinson Cons. Group, Portland, 1982—; pres. Wheatherstone Press, Lake Oswego, Oreg., 1983—, The Relocation Ctr., Portland, 1984—. Cons. in field; lectr. in field; conductor workshops/seminars in field. Author: The Complete Guide to Family Relocation, The International Move, Building Your Dream House, Obtaining the Highest Price for Your Home, Have a Successful Garage Sale, Moving with Children, My Moving Coloring Book, The Group Move, Counseling the Transferee, Games to Play in the Car, Portland (Oreg.) Facts Book, Welcome to the United States, many others; contbr. articles to profl. jours. Mem. Pres.'s Com. to Employ Physically Handicapped, Oreg. Prison Assn.; established Women's Aux. for Waverly Baby Home; bd. dirs. Columbia River coun. Girl Scouts U.S.A., Salvation Army; active various polit. orgns.; chmn. ways and means com. Oreg. Symphony Soc., Portland Art Mus., Assistance League, Portland Jr. Symphony, March of Dimes, others. Mem.: Employee Relocation Coun., Internat. Platform Assn., Forbes CEO Network, Tualatin Valley Econ. Devel. Assn. (dir. 1988—), Multnomah Athletic Club, City Club. Republican. Episcopalian. Home: 6903 SE Riverside Dr # 16 Vancouver WA 98664-1672 Office: The Dickinson Cons Group Lincoln Ctr 10250 SW Greenburg Rd Ste 125 Portland OR 97223-5470 E-mail: jandickinson@attbi.com., relocntr@europa.com.

DICKINSON, JOSHUA CLIFTON, JR., museum director, educator; b. Tampa, Fla., Apr. 28, 1916; s. Joshua Clifton and Mary (Martin) D.; m. Lucy Jackson, Apr. 13, 1936 (wid. June 10, 1997); children: Joshua Clifton III, Martin Freeman, Susan Ellissa; m. Sarah Donnovin Hadley, Nov. 1, 1997. Student, U. Va., 1936-39, Cornell U., 1938; BS, U. Fla., 1940, MS, 1946, PhD, 1950. Faculty U. Fla., 1946—, asst. prof. biology, 1950-55, assoc. prof. biology, 1955, prof. zoology, 1973-79; curator Fla. State Mus. (name changed to Fla. Mus. of Natural History), 1952-79, chmn. natural scis., 1953-60, acting dir., 1959-61, dir., 1961-79, dir. emeritus, 1979—. Vis. investigator Woods Hole Oceanographic Inst., 1952; expdns. to, Honduras, 1946, Bahamas, 1958-62, 66-67, Jamaica, 1946, Baffin Island, 1955, Sombrero Island, 1964, Navassa Island, 1967, Turks and Caicos Islands, 1974. Contbr. articles to profl. jours. Chmn. Fla. Bd. Archives and History, 1967-69; mem. mus. adv. panel Nat. Endowment for Arts, 1970-72, co-chmn., 1972-74; panelist fellowship program NSF, 1966-68; mem. Nat. Council on Arts, 1976-82, also chmn. com. planning and policy; bd. dirs. Fla. Arts Celebration, 1984-92, vice chmn., 1985-86. Comdr. USCGR, 1942-46, ret. Grantee Nat. Park Service, 1954, NSF, 1955-57; Rsch. fellow Harvard U., 1951-52; recipient Disting. Alumnus award U. Fla., 1977, Presdl. Medallion U. Fla., 1979; Dickinson Hall named in his honor U. Fla. Mem. Am. Ornithologists Union, Am. Soc. Naturalists, Am. Assn. Museums (chmn. sci. mus. sect. 1961, mem. council 1964-70, sec. 1970), Am. Soc. Zoologists, Wilson Ornithol. Soc., Am. Assn. Sci. Mus. Dirs. (v.p. 1967-69), Assn. Systematic Collections (pres. 1972-75, bd. dir. 1974-76, chmn. membership com. 1976-79), Bahamas Nat. Trust, Assn. S.E. Biologists (sec. 1955-58), Fla. Acad. Scis. (chmn. biology sect. 1952, editor quar. jour. 1955-63), Conf. Dirs. Systematics Collections (pres. 1976-78), Fla. Audubon Soc. (bd. dir. 1958-64, 79-84), S.E. Museums Conf. (v.p. 1971-72, pres. 1972, James L. Shortt award 1987), Internat. Council Museums (exec. com. 1974-77), Am. Assn. Museums (vis. accreditation team 1973-75), Rotary (pres. Gainesville 1967-68), Sigma Xi, Phi Sigma, Alpha Tau Omega. Democrat. Presbyterian. Home: 9517 SW 40th Ln Gainesville FL 32608-4647 Office: U Fla Fla Mus Natural History Dickinson Hall Museum Rd Gainesville FL 32611

DICKINSON, LOIS JEAN BERWANGER, adult nurse practitioner, nurse staff officer; b. Covington, Ky., Dec. 13, 1953; d. Preston Gervase and Mary Ann Louise (Luken) Berwanger; m. Keith Allen Dickinson, Oct. 2, 1982; children: Justin Eugene, Laura Jean, Gerald Allen, Karen Marie. BS in Nursing, Coll. Mt. St. Joseph-on-Ohio, 1976; MS in Nursing, U. Tex. Health Sci. Ctr., Houston, 1985. RN and advanced practice nurse, Ohio; cert. adult nurse practitioner. Commd. lt. U.S. Army, 1974, advanced through grades to col.; asst. evenings/nights chief U.S. Army 121st Evacuation Hosp., Seoul, Korea, 1982-83; clin. head nurse med. surg. ward, emergency treatment ctr. Irwin Army Community Hosp., Fort Riley, Kans., 1985-88; clin. head nurse med./surg. ward Evans Army Community Hosp., Fort Carson, Colo., 1988-91, infection control practitioner, quality improvement coord., 1991-93; adult nurse practitioner Raymond W. Bliss Army Cmty. Hosp., Ft. Huachuca, Ariz., 1993-95, chief nurse, 1995-96; dir. adult primary care network clinic Brooke Army Med. Ctr., Ft. Sam Houston, Tex., 1996-97, chief ambulatory nursing svc., 1997-98; nurse staff officer U.S. Army Med. Command, Ft. Sam Houston, 1998—2002, St. Mary's Hosp., Blue Springs, Mo., 2002—. Decorated Legion of Merit, Meritorious Svc. medal, Order of Mil. Med. Merit. Mem. Am. Assn. Diabetes Educators, Am. Diabetes Assn., Am. Assn. Nurse Practitioners, Sigma Theta Tau, Kappa Gamma Pi. Home: 25805 S Harris Rd Greenwood MO 64034

DICKINSON, MICHAEL, physiologist; ScB, Brown U., 1984; PhD, U. Wash., 1989. Postdoctoral trainee Roche Inst. Molecular Biology, 1990—91; mem. faculty dept. organismal biology and anatomy U. Chgo., 1991—96; prof. integrative biology U. Calif., Berkeley, 1996—. Vis. scholar Max Planck Inst. Biol. Cybernetics, 1991, 93. Recipient Larry Sandler award, Genetic Soc. Am.,

1990, George Bartholomew award for physiology, Soc. Integrative and Comparative Biology, 1995; fellow, NSF, 1985, Packard Found., 1992. Office: U Calif Berkeley Valley Life Sci Bldg # 5054 and # 5056 Berkeley CA 92470

DICKINSON, RICHARD DONALD NYE, clergyman, educator, theological seminary administrator; b. Monson, Mass., Aug. 1, 1929; s. Richard Donald Nye and Phoebe Abigail (Naylor) D.; m. Nancy Leland Stone, Nov. 26, 1955; children: Elizabeth Stone, Richard Donald Nye III, Edward David McCrea. BA, Am. Internat. Coll., 1950, MA, 1951; STB, Boston U., 1954, PhD, 1959; cert., Institut Oecumenique, Geneva, 1955. Ordained to ministry United Ch. of Christ; chaplain, instr. Wheaton Coll., Norton, Mass., 1957-62; assoc. dir. Quaker Confs. in So. Asia, 1962-64; sr. research officer Inst. for Social Studies, The Hague, Netherlands, 1964-67; sec. for specialized assistance World Council Chs., 1967-68; now cons.; prof. Christian social ethics Christian Theol. Sem., Indpls., 1968-74, v.p., dean, 1974-86, acting pres., 1986-87, pres., 1987-97. Chmn. devel. commn. World Coun. Chs.; mem. edn. commn. Nat. Coun. Chs., 1972-74; mem. ch. world service com.; incorporating mem. Center for Exploration Values and Meaning.; bd. dirs. internat. affairs div. Am. Friends Service Com., div. overseas ministries of Christian Ch. Author: The Christian College and National Development, 1967, Line and Plummet, 1968, The Christian College in Developing India, 1969, To Set at Liberty the Oppressed, 1975, Poor, Yet Making Many Rich, 1983, Economic Globalization: Challenge for Christians. Bd. dirs. Ind. Opera Theatre, Internat. Ctr. Indpls., The Gemmer Found., Ind. Com. Econ. Edn., Martin Luther King Multiservice Ctr., Ind.-Ky. Conf. United Ch. of Christ, bd. dirs., chair fin. com.; mem. Greater Indpls. Progress Com.; moderator First Congl. Ch.; chmn. Ch. World Svc. Bd. Ind.-Ky. Mem. Am. Soc. for Christian Ethics, Soc. for Sci. Study Religion, Econs. Club of Indpls. (bd. dir.), Rotary. Mem. United Ch. Of Christ. Home: 5173 N Kenwood Ave Indianapolis IN 46208-2619 E-mail: rdndjnsd@aol.com.

DICKINSON, RICHARD HENRY, accountant; b. June 16, 1944; s. Everett I. and Gertrude T. (Frear) D.; m. Georgette M. Turner, Jan. 27, 1968 (dec. June 1998); children: Eric, Christine, Brent. BS, U. Wis.; BBA, Siena Coll., 1973; MBA, Dartmouth Coll., 1995. Assoc. acct. Alexander Varga, CPA, Catskill, N.Y., 1973; contr. Hocker Power Brake Co., Inc., Evansville, Ind., 1974; dep. contr. Watervliet (N.Y.) Arsenal, Dept. Def., 1975-76; auditor Melvin I. [illegible], CPA, Saratoga Springs N.Y. 1977; owner, prin. Richard H. Dickinson, CPA, Ballston Spa and Saratoga Springs, N.Y., 1978-83; owner Dickinson & Co., CPAs, Saratoga Spring, 1984—. Lectr. Siena Coll., Loudonville, N.Y., 1983-89, Skidmore Coll., 1990-96. With U.S. Army, 1967-70. Decorated Silver Star, Bronze Star. Mem. ABA (assoc.), Am. Inst. CPAs, N.Y. State Soc. CPAs, Inst. Mgmt. Accts., Masons, Rotary (pres. Ballston Spa chpt. 1979), Delta Epsilon Sigma, Alpha Kappa Alpha. Republican. Lutheran. Home: 4 Ritchie Pl Saratoga Springs NY 12866-2730 Office: 439 Maple Ave Saratoga Springs NY 12866-5503 also: 2 Washington Sq Greenwich NY 12834-1319 E-mail: rdcpa44@hotmail.com.

DICKINSON, RICHARD RAYMOND, retired oil company executive; b. Orange, Calif., Jan. 28, 1931; s. Raymond Russel and Florence Marie (Jacobson) D.; m. Barbara Jean Morrison, June 16, 1957; children: Roderick, Christine. BS, Calif. Inst. Tech., 1952; MS, U. So. Calif., 1960. Chem. engr. L.A. Refinery Texaco, 1952-68, gen. mgr. supply and distbn., 1968-76, plant mgr. Eagle Point plant Westville, N.J., 1976-79, gen. mgr. alternate energy group White Plains, N.Y., 1979, v.p. strategic planning, 1979-82; sr. v.p. U.S. refining, mktg., supply and transp. Texaco U.S.A., Houston, 1982-87; v.p. tech. Texaco, Inc., White Plains, N.Y., 1988-94. Served with USNR, 1955-58. Home: 944 Hills Creek Dr Mc Kinney TX 75070-5232

DICKINSON, ROBERT EARL, atmospheric scientist, educator; b. Millersburg, Ohio, Mar. 26, 1940; s. Leonard Earl and Carmen L. (Ostby) D.; m. Nancy Mary Mielinis, Jan. 5, 1974. AB in Chemistry and Physics, Harvard U., 1961; MS in Meteorology, MIT, 1962, PhD in Meteorology, 1966. Rsch. assoc. MIT, Cambridge, 1966-68; scientist Nat. Ctr. Atmospheric Rsch., Boulder, Colo., 1968-73, sr. scientist, 1973-90, head climate sect., 1975-81, dep. dir. A.A.P. div., 1981-86, acting dir., 1986-87; prof. atmospheric physics U. Ariz., 1990-93; regents prof., 1993-99; prof. earth and atmospheric scis. Ga. Inst. Tech., Atlanta, 1999—; chmn. Ga. Power/Ga. Rsch. Alliance. Mem. climate rsch. com. NRC, Washington, 1985-90, chmn., 1987-90, com. earth sci., 1985-88, global change com., 1985-92; mem. WCRP sci. steering group GEWEX, 1988-92; UNU steering com. Climatic, Biotic and Human Interactions in Humid Tropics, 1984-88, steering com. Internat. Satellite Land Surface Climatology project, 1984-89. Editor: The Geophysiology of Amazonia, 1986; contbr. articles to profl. jours. Recipient G. Unger Vetlesen prize, 1996. Fellow AAAS, Am. Meteorol. Soc. (chmn. com. biometeorol. and aerobiol. 1987-89, Meisinger award 1973, Editors award 1976, Jule Charney award 1989, Walter Orr Roberts lectr. in interdisciplinary sci. 1995, Carl-Gustaf Rossby award 1997), Am. Geophys. Union (atmospheric sci. sect. 1986-88, pres.-elect 1988-90, pres. 1990-92, pres.-elect 2000-02, pres. 2002-, Revelle medal 1996); mem. NAS, Nat. Acad. Engring. Democrat. Home: 1074 Peachtree Walk B311 Atlanta GA 30309 Office: Ga Inst Tech EAS 311 Ferst Dr Atlanta GA 30332-0340

DICKINSON, ROGER ALLYN, business administration educator; b. Bklyn., Sept. 8, 1929; s. Robert Albert and Esther (Odland) D.; m. Ruth Nordis, June 1, 1957; children: Robert Allyn, Roger Perry, Todd Charles, Bruce Gregory. AB, Williams Coll., 1951; MBA, UCLA, 1955; PhD, Columbia U., 1967. Lectr., asst. prof. bus. adminstrn. U. Calif., Berkeley, 1964-69; assoc. prof. Rutgers Grad. Sch. Bus., Newark, N.J., 1969-70, prof., 1970-75; prof. Coll. Bus. Adminstrn. U. Tex., Arlington, 1975-79, prof. mktg., 1979—; dean Coll. Bus. U. Tex., 1975-79. Author: Retail Management: A Channels Approach, 1974, (with others) A Basic Approach to Executive Decision Making, 1978, Retail Management, 1981; book note editor Jour. Retailing, 1970-92, Jour. Macromktg., 1992—; mem. editl. bd. Jour. Consumer Mktg., Jour. Macromktg.; contbr. chpts. to books and articles to profl. jours. Mem. Am. Collegiate Retailing Assn. (pres. 1980-82) Home: 2104 Tretorn Ct Arlington TX 76017-2763 Office: U Tex Coll Bus Arlington TX 76019-0001 E-mail: rogerd@uta.edu.

DICKINSON, VICTORIA ANN, visual arts administrator; b. Phila., Oct. 3, 1951; d. Eleanor Louisa Briscoe; divorced, Dec., 1990; 1 child, Geoffrey Lloyd McDonald. BA, U. Del., 1974; grad. Entrée Program, Katharine Gibbs Sch., Phila., 1983; MA, NYU, 1988; cert. in office asst., acctg. clk. and clerical, Portland (Maine) Adult Edn., 2001. Adminstrv. asst. Vitt Media Internat., NYC, 1973, RKO Gen., Inc., NYC, 1974, Can. Std. Broadcast Sales, NYC, 1975-76, Edward Durell Stone Assoc., PC, NYC, 1977-79, Del. Art Mus., Wilmington, Del., 1979-80, E.I. DuPont de Nemours & Co., Wilmington, Del., 1980-83, Gridley & Co., Wilmington, Del., 1983-84; bus. and arts mgmt. cons. Charles Colombo, painter, Wilmington, Del., 1984-86; bus. mgmt. cons. Susan Isaacs Gallery, Wilmington, Del., 1987-88, Sta. Gallery, Wilmington, Del., 1987, M. Knoedler & Co., NYC, 1987; bus. mgr., cons. Jean Davidson, painter, NYC, 1987-91; bus. mgmt. cons. Melita Westerlund, sculptor, Bar Harbor, 1988-91, Francis Hamabe, artist, Blue Hill, Maine, 1985-91, Joan Julien Grant, sculptor, LA, 1990; bus. mgr., cons. Arlene Waxman Sculptor, Malibu, Calif., 1990-92; bus. mgmt. cons. Victoria Fuller, Sculptor, Aspen, Colo., 1991-92; with Myrna Orsini, Sculptor, Tocoma, 1992. Adminstrv. asst. Vitt Media Internat., NYC, 1973, RKO Gen., Inc., NYC, 1974, Can. Standard Broadcast Sales, NYC, 1975-76, Edward Durell Stone Assocs., P.C., NYC, 1977-79, Del. Art Mus., Wilmington, 1979-80, E.I. DuPont de Nemours & Co., Wilmington, 1980-83, Gridley & Co., Wilmington, 1983-84. Contbr. to arts publs. Vol. various polit. activities including Maine State Dem. Com. and Portland Dem. City Com., 2000, Portland Waterfront Devel. Project, domestic violence, child abuse and custody issues, terrorism preparedness; chorus mem. Princess Ida, 1997-98; mem. ch. choir St. Saviour's Episc. Ch., Bar Harbor, 1997-98. Episcopalian. Avocation: collecting contemporary and avant garde regional art. E-mail: vad648@msn.com.

DICKINSON, WADE, physicist, oil and gas company executive, educator; b. Sharon, Pa., Oct. 29, 1926; s. Ben Wade Orr and Gladys Grace (Oakes) D.; m. Eleanor Creekmore, June 12, 1952; children: Mark, Katherine, Peter. Student, Carnegie Inst. Tech., 1944-45; BS, U.S. Mil. Acad., 1949; postgrad., Oak Ridge Sch. Reactor Tech., 1950-51. Commd. 2d lt. USAF, 1949, advanced through grades to capt., 1954, resigned, 1954; cons. physicist Rand Corp., Santa Monica, Calif., 1952-54; engring. cons. Bechtel Group, Inc., San Francisco, 1954-87; tech. advisor U.S. Congress, Washington, 1957-58; pres. Agrophysics, Inc., San Francisco, 1968—, Petrolphysics Inc., San Francisco, 1975—; ptnr. Radialphysics Ltd., San Francisco, 1980—, Robotphysics Ltd., San Francisco, 1983—; mng. mem. The Spark Group, 00—. Lectr. engring. and bus. U. Calif., Berkeley, 1984—; cardiology cons. Mt. Zion Med. Ctr., U. Calif., San Francisco, 1970-95; chmn. bd. Calif. Med. Clin. Psychotherapy. Contbr. articles to profl. jours; patentee in field. Trustee World Affair Coun., 1958-62; mem. San Francisco Com. Fgn. Rels., Young Republicans, Calif. Mem. Am. Phys. Soc., Am. Soc. Petroleum Engrs. Clubs: Bohemian (San Francisco). Lodges: Masons, Guardsmen. Episcopalian. Home: 2125 Broderick St San Francisco CA 94115-1627 Office: Petrolphysics Inc 1388 Sutter St Ste 603 San Francisco CA 94109-5452 E-mail: petrojet@ix.netcom.com.

DICKINSON, WILLIAM BOYD, JR., editorial consultant; b. Kansas City, Mo., Feb. 21, 1931; s. William Boyd and Aileen (Robinson) D.; m. Betty Ann Landree, Feb. 1, 1953; children: William Boyd IV, David Alan. AB, U. Kans., 1953; student, George Washington U. Law Sch., 1957-58. With U.P.I., 1955-59, mem. staff overnight desk, 1957-59; staff writer Editorial Research Reports, Washington, 1959-66, editor, 1966-73; editor, v.p. Congl. Quar., Inc., 1972-73; gen. mgr., editorial dir. Washington Post Writers Group, 1973-91; cons., 1991-96, Biocentric Inst., 1991—. Resident profl. Journalism Sch. U. Kans., 1993-99; manship chair Journalism Sch. La. State U., 1999-2003, disting. prof., 2003—; Winston Churchill Traveling fellow, summer 1968. Supervisory editor: Congl. Quar.'s Complete Guide to Congress. Served with AUS, 1953-55. Press fellowship Knight Internat., 1998. Mem. William Allen White Found. (trustee), Alpha Tau Omega, Omicron Delta Kappa. (Washington). Home and Office: 1617 Alvamar Dr Lawrence KS 66047-1715 also: LSU 221B Journalism Bldg Baton Rouge LA 70803-0001 E-mail: wdicki2@lsu.edu.

DICKINSON, WILLIAM RICHARD, retired geologist; b. Nashville, Oct. 26, 1931; s. Jacob McGavock and Margaret Adams (Smith) Dickinson; m. Margaret Anne Palmer, 1953 (div. 1968); children: Ben William, Edward Ross; m. Jacqueline Jane Klein, Feb. 20, 1970. BS in Petroleum Engring., Stanford U., 1952, MS in Geology, 1956, PhD in Geology, 1958. Prof. geology Stanford U., Palo Alto, Calif., 1958-79; prof. geoscis. U. Ariz., Tucson, 1979-91; retired, 1991. Contbr. articles to profl. jours.; editor: profl. jours. Lt. USAF, 1952—54. Guggenheim Meml. fellow, 1965. Fellow: Geol. Soc. Am. (Penrose medal 1991, Sloss award 1999); mem.: NAS, Soc. Sedimentary Geology (Twenhofel medal 2000), Am. Assn. Petroleum Geologists, Am. Geophys. Union. E-mail: wrdickin@geo.arizona.edu.

DICKINSON, WILLIAM TREVOR, hydrologist, educator; b. Toronto, Ont., Can., Aug. 30, 1939; s. Clarence Heber and Katie Isobel (Kneen) D.; m. Sharon Lucille Tutt, Aug. 24, 1963; children: Michael Trevor, Cathryn Ruth. BSA., U. Toronto, 1961, BASci., 1962, MSA., 1964; PhD, Colo. State U., 1967. Research assoc. Colo. State U., 1964-67; asst. prof. engring. U. Guelph, Ont., 1967-70, assoc. prof., 1970-78, prof., 1978-94, prof. emeritus, 1995—, coordinator instructional devel., 1979-82, 3M teaching fellow, coord. univ. teaching program, 1991-93; pvt. cons. water resources engring. Contbr. articles to profl. jours. Mem. Assn. Profl. Engrs. Ont., Can. Assn. Univ. Tchrs., Soil Conservation Soc. Am., Soc. Tchrs. Learning High Edn., Can. Water Resources Assn. Mem. United Ch. of Can. Home: 68 Pine Ridge Dr Guelph ON Canada N1L 1J1 Office: Univ Guelph Guelph ON Canada N1G 2W1 E-mail: wdickins@ucguelph.ca.

DICKISON, ALEXANDER KANE, physical science educator; b. Jamaica, N.Y., Oct. 16, 1943; s. William and Eileen S. (Kane) D.; m. Lois Jean Tansley, Mar. 21, 1967; children: Stephen William, Jonathan Harry. BS, Western Ill. U., 1965; MS, Mont. State U., 1968, EdD, 1972. Instr. U. Wis., Green Bay, 1969-72, Mont. State U., Bozeman, 1972-73, Seminole C.C., Sanford, Fla., 1973—, dept. chmn. phys. scis., 1986—. Adj. prof. U. Ctrl. Fla., Orlando, 1972-83; del. U.S.-Japan-China Confs. on Physics Tchg., 1989, 91, 93; mem. Fla. Statewide Com. on Common Course Numbering, 1981—; reader, table leader Advance Placement Test Readings, 1988-2001; mem. com. on career planning Am. Inst. Physics, 1991-95. Chair Seminole County Hist. Commn., Sanford, 1982—; mem. Citizen com., Expressway Authority, Seminole County, 1989-93; county liason St. John's Water Mgmt. Dist., Seminole County, 1981-91; energy com. East Fla. Regional Planning Com., Seminole county, 1976-82. Mem. NSTA, Am. Physics Soc., Am. Assn. Physics Tchrs. (exec. bd. 1991-95, treas. 1996-2002, Outstanding Physics Tchr. of Yr. award Fla. sect. 1990, Disting. Svc. award 2003), Fla. Assn. Physics Tchrs. (chmn. 1975-76), Fla. Acad. Scis. (exec. sec. 1986-91, Disting. Svc. award 1993), Fla. Assn. Sci. Tchrs., Sigma Pi Sigma. Avocations: history, outdoors, travel, reading, golf. Home: 4851 Hester Ave Sanford FL 32773-9402 Office: Seminole Community Coll 100 Weldon Blvd Sanford FL 32773-6132 E-mail: dickisoa@scc-fl.edu.

DICKISON, JOIE LEI, medical editor; b. Bloomington, Ind., Mar. 4, 1974; d. Stanley Eugene Dickison and Wendy Irene Arnold Rowe. BS, Ball State U., Muncie, IN, 1992—96. Temp. help Kelly Services, Indpls., 1996—97; tech. writer Howard W. Sams, 1997—98; editl. asst. Kelly Services, 1998—; assoc. med. editor Eli Lilly and Co., 1998—. Mem.: Am. Med. Writers (membership chair 1999—2002). Avocations: scrapbooking, scrapbooking, traveling.

DICKLER, HOWARD BYRON, biomedical administrator, research physician; b. Chgo., Jan. 2, 1942; s. Jerome Alvin and Josephine Rae (Sweet) D.; m. Ana Isabel Martinez, Sept. 20, 1986; children: Joanna, Carl. BA, Johns Hopkins U., 1964; MD with honors, George Washington U., 1968. Diplomate Am. Bd. Internal Medicine, Nat. Bd. Med. Examiners. Lt. comdr. USPHS, 1972, advanced through grades to capt., 1985; ret., 1999; intern N.Y. Hosp.-Cornell U. Med. Ctr., N.Y.C., 1968-69, resident in internal medicine, 1969-71; rsch. assoc. Rockefeller U., N.Y.C., 1971-72; clin. assoc. Nat. Cancer Inst., Bethesda, Md., 1972-74, sr. investigator, 1974-89, instnl. rev. bd., 1982-84; acting dep. divsn. dir. Nat. Inst. Allergy and Infectious Disease, Bethesda, 1990-91, chief clin. immunology br., 1989-99; assoc. dean rsch. and grad. studies U. Md. Sch. Medicine, Balt., 1999—. Leader trans-NIH initiative to develop hyper accelerated process to rev. and award grant applications; com. vice-chmn. WHO, Geneva, 1981-85; lectr., spkr. in field. Assoc. editor Jour. Immunology, 1976-79; contbr. articles to Jour. Exptl. Medicine, Advances in Immunology. Recipient Commendation medal USPHS, 1985, Outstanding Svc. medal, 1991. Mem. Am. Assn. Immunologists, Am. Soc. Clin. Investigation, Clin. Immunology Soc. (councilor 1991-94), Alpha Omega Alpha. Achievements include discovery of receptors for antibody on human cells, interactions between various immune cell receptors, and regulatory mechanisms which control antibody production; pioneering research on classification of human immune cell populations; leading major development of research infrastructure at U. Md. Sch. Medicine. Office: U Md Sch Medicine Rm 14-021 BRB 655 W Baltimore St Baltimore MD 21201-1509 E-mail: hdickler@som.umaryland.edu.

DICKMAN, CATHERINE CROWE, retired human services administrator; b. Talladega, AL, Jan. 27, 1931; d. William and Catherine Elizabeth (Graeber) Crowe; m. Frederick Norton Dickman Jr., May 19, 1956 (div. July 1975); children: Frederick Norton Dickman III, Catherine Dickman Taylor, Elizabeth Dickman Blank, Janet Dickman Elbetri; m. William Crutcher Ragland, Jan. 2, 2002. AB with honor, Agnes Scott Coll., 1952; MS, Cleve. State U. Coll. Urban Affairs, 1976. Pub. info. officer Cuyahoga County, Ohio, 1975-77; dir. Friends of Shaker Sq., Cleve., 1979-81; rsch. assoc. Frank Porter Graham Child Devel. Ctr., Chapel Hill, N.C., 1984; pres. Dickman Placement Svcs., Chapel Hill, N.C., 1988-91; dir. The Women's Ctr., Chapel Hill, N.C., 1991-96; ret. Author (newsletter) The Partnership Paper, 1986. Field dir. Girl Scout coun., Wilmington, N.C., 1952-53; dir. christian edn. St. Charles Ave. Presbyn. Ch., New Orleans, 1956-57; co-founder Fair Housing, Inc., 1966-80; mem. Jr. League of Cleve, Inc., 1957—; pres. 1966-68, chair Assn. 12 Largest Jr. Leagues, 1967-68, Assn. Cmty. Agys., Chapel Hill, 1991-96, bd. dirs., 1995-96; chair nominating com., trustee The City Club of Cleve., 1979-82; trustee Health Mus. and Edn. Ctr., 1957-63, Karamu House, Cleve., 1968-70, Fedn. for Cmty. Planning, Cleve., 1979-82; adv. com. Health Profession Schs. in Svc. to the Nation, Chapel Hill, 1996—; elder Fairmount Presbyn. Ch., Cleve., 1970-73, Univ. Presbyn. Ch., Chapel Hill, 1986-89. Women's Ctr. established Catherine C. Dickman Ednl. Fund in her honor, 1996. Mem. NOW (Chapel Hill chpt.), Nat. Audubon Soc., New Hope Audubon Soc. (bd. dirs. 1986-88), Chapel Hill Preservation Soc. (v.p., trustee 1989-90, sec. exec. com. 1997). Democrat. Avocations: bird watching, nature walks, writing. Home: 2003 Bay Gull Ct Wilmington NC 28405-4035

DICKMAN, FRANCOIS MOUSSIEGT, former foreign service officer, educator; b. Iowa City, Dec. 23, 1924; s. Adolphe Jacques and Henriette Louise (Moussiegt) D.; m. Margaret Hoy, June 3, 1947; children: Christine, Paul. BA, U. Wyo., 1947; MA, Fletcher Sch. Law & Diplomacy, 1948. Rsch. asst. Brookings Instn., Washington, 1950; with U.S. Fgn. Svc., 1951-84, consular/comml. officer, 1952-54, Arabic lang. trainee Beirut, 1955-57, econ./comml./consular officer Khartoum, Sudan, 1957-60; Egyptian-Syrian affairs desk officer Dept. State, 1961-65, econ. officer, 1965-68; student U.S. Army War Coll., Carlisle, Pa., 1968-69; econ. counselor Jidda, Saudi Arabia, 1969-72; dir. Arabian Peninsula affairs Dept. State, 1972-76, ambassador to United Arab Emirates, 1976-79, ambassador to Kuwait, 1979-83; diplomat in residence Marquette U., 1984; adj. prof. polit. sci. U. Wyo., Laramie, 1985—. Served with AUS, 1943-46, 50-51. Recipient Dept. State Meritorious Honor award, 1965, Disting. Alumni award U. Wyo., 1980, Exemplary Alumnus, 1993. Mem. VFW, U.S. Army War Coll. Alumni Assn., U. Wyo. Alumni Assn., Phi Beta Kappa, Phi Kappa Phi. Office: U Wyo Polit Sci Dept Laramie WY 82071-3197

DICKMAN, JAMES BRUCE, photojournalist; b. St. Louis, Mar. 25, 1949; s. Joseph Edward and Isabel Catherine (Brown) D.; m. Mary Kay Thomas, Sept. 23, 1968 (div.); children: Kristi Michele, Gavin Thomas; m. 2d Rebecca Lauren Skelton, Sept. 16, 1983; children: Matthew Benjamin, Margaret Catherine Anne. Student, U. Tex., 1967-69. Photographer McKinney Job Corps., Tex., 1969-70, Dallas Times Herald, 1970-86. Worked on photo projects Day in the Life of Can., Day in the Life of Am., Day in the Life of Spain, Day in the Life of the Soviet Union, Day in the Life of China; (book and CD-ROM) Passage to Vietnam, 1994, Day in the Life of Africa, 2002; contbg. editor Am. Way Mag. Recipient Pulitzer prize for photography Columbia U., 1983; recipient World Press Photo of Yr. award World Press Photo Orgn., Holland, Amsterdam, 1983, 89, awards Dallas Press Club, AP and UPI, Tex. Headliners, Damascus Syria, Internat. Orgn. of Photography, 1st place, Sigma Delta Chi Disting. Service award, Bronze Medallion, others Mem. Am. Soc. Mag. Photographers. E-mail: jaybec@att.net. *I've always felt that I've had a guardian angel pointing me in the correct directions. But it's always been up to me to do something with the opportunities once they're presented.*

DICKMAN, JAMES EARL, financial services executive; m. LaTricia P. Schendel, May 10, 1997. BS in Fin., Va. Tech., 1985. CFP. Agt., registered rep. Life of Va., Charlottesville, 1985-86; fin. cons. Merrill Lynch, Pierce Fenner and Smith, Roanoke, Va., 1986-90; v.p. Horton Fin. Svcs. Inc., Charlottesville, 1990—. Office Horton Fin. Svc. Inc., Charlottesville. Republican. Presbyterian. Avocations: photography, tennis.

DICKMAN, MARTIN J. federal agency administrator; b. Chgo. BS, U. Ill., 1966; JD, DePaul U., 1969. Asst. corp. counsel City of Chgo., 1970—72; counsel to minority leader Ill. Ho. Reps., 1972—73; mem. Bd. Trade, Chgo., 1972—91; asst. Peter Ftizpatrick and Assocs., 1973—89; hearings ref. Ill. Dept. Revenue, 1976—80; prosecutor Cook County Ill. State's Atty.'s Fin. and Govtl. Crimes Task Force, 1991—94; inspector gen. Railroad Retirement Bd., 1994—. Office: US Railroad Retirementt Bd 4th Fl 844 N Rush St Chicago IL 60611-2092

DICKMAN, ROBERT LAURENCE, physicist, researcher; b. N.Y.C., May 16, 1947; s. Sidney and Eva (Goldberg) D.; m. Albertina Catharina Otter, Sept. 18, 1975; children: Joshua, Ilana. AB, Columbia U., 1969, PhD, 1976. Postdoctoral rsch. assoc. Rensselaer Poly. Inst., Troy, N.Y., 1975-77; mem. tech. staff The Aerospace Corp., L.A., 1977-80; faculty rsch. assoc. U. Mass., Amherst, 1980-85, assoc. prof., staff assoc., 1985-92; program mgr. NSF, Washington, 1992—, unit coord., spl. assoc., 1999—. Editor: Molecular Clouds in the Milky Way and External Galaxies, 1988; contbr. 80 articles to profl. jours. Recipient Ernest Fullam award Dudley Obs., 1986. Mem. Am. Phys. Soc., Am. Astron. Soc., Internat. Astron. Union. Office: NSF Div Astronomical Scis 4201 Wilson Blvd Arlington VA 22230-0001 E-mail: rdickman@nsf.gov.

DICKMAN, ROBERT S. aerospace consultant, retired career officer; b. Brooklyn, N.Y. BS in Physics, Union Coll., 1966; MS in Space Physics, AF Inst. Tech.; MA in Mgmt., Salve Regina Coll.; grad. (dist.), Naval War Coll., 1983. 2nd. lt. USAF, 1966, advanced through grades to major gen., 1966-2000; prog. mgr. USAF Office Sci Rsch., Arlington, Va., 1968-72; prog. element monitor USAF Hdqs., Washington, D.C., 1972-73; terminal sys. mgr. USAF, Los Angeles AFB, Calif., 1973-75; operational mgr. USAF Hdqs., Washington, 1976-79; space Def. Opers. Ctr. Hdrs. Aerospace Def. Command, Cheyenne Mtn. AFB, Colo., 1979-82; dir. space sys., dep. chief staff ops. Hdqs. Air Force Space Command, Peterson AFB, Colo., 1983-84; chief comdr. group Hdqs. N. American Aerospace Def. Command, Space Command, Peterson AFB, Colo., 1984-85; vice comdr. 2d space wing Schriever AFB, Colo., 1985—86; asst. to dir. ops., then dir. missile warning Space Command, Colo., 1986-87; chief Space Sys. Divsn., Washington, 1987-89; dep. dir. space progams Office of Asst. Sec. USAF for Acquisition, Washington, 1987-92; dir. plans Hdqs. USAF Space Command, Peterson AFB, Colo., 1992-93; comdr. 45th Space Wing, Patrick AFB, Fla., 1993-95; dir. Eastern Range, Cape Canaveral Air Sta., Fla., 1993-95; dir. space programs Office Asst. Sec. USAF for Acquisition, Washington, 1995; space architect Dept. Def., Washington, 1995-98; dir. Office Plans and Analysis and Sys. of Sys. Architect Nat. Reconnaissance Office, Washington, 1998-2000, dir. corp. ops., chief info. officer, 2000; aerospace cons., 2001—01; dep. for military space, Office of Under-Sec., USAF, Washington, 2002—. Decorated Def. D.S.M., Air Force D.S.M., Def. Superior Svc. Medal, Legion of Merit; recipient Astronautics award Nat. Space Club, master space badge.

DICKOW, JAMES FRED, management consultant; b. Chgo., Mar. 27, 1943; s. Fred H. and Margaret I. (Arnold) D.; m. Yvonne A. Zabilka, Aug. 20, 1966; children: Michael J., Christine Y. BSME, Purdue U., 1965, MSME, 1967. Cert. mgmt. cons. Mech. engr. CPC Internat., Argo, Ill., 1965-66; engr. dynamics McDonnell-Douglas Corp., St. Louis, 1967-70; cons. Drake Sheahan/Steward Dougal, Chgo., 1970-71; dir. distbn. planning Will Ross Div. G.D. Searle, Milw., 1971-80; dir. distbn. Gentec Healthcare, Milw., 1980-82, R&J Med. Supply, Milw., 1982-83; exec. v.p., ptnr. Kowaski-Dickow Assoc. Inc., Mequon, Wis., 1983—. Mem. Coun. Logistics Mgmt. (pres. Milw. roundtable 1978-79), Phi Kappa Theta (bd. dirs., found. treas., nat. pres., pres. Ind. alumni 1980—). Home: 10011 N Miller Ct Thiensville WI 53092-6180

DICKS, NORMAN DE VALOIS, congressman; b. Bremerton, Wash., Dec. 16, 1940; s. Horace D. and Eileen Cora D.; m. Suzanne Callison, Aug. 25, 1967; children: David, Ryan. BA, U. Wash., 1963, JD, 1968; LLD (hon.), Gonzaga U., 1987. Bars: Wash. 1968, D.C., 1978. Salesman, Boise Cascade Corp., Seattle, 1963; labor negotiator Kaiser Gypsum Co., Seattle, 1964; legis. asst. to Senator Warren Magnuson of Wash., 1968-73, adminstrv. asst., 1973-76; mem. U.S. Congress from 6th Wash. Dist., Washington, 1977—; mem. appropriations com., homeland sec. com. Mem. U. Wash. Alumni Assn., Sigma Nu. Democrat. Lutheran. Office: US Ho Reps 2467 Rayburn Ho Office Bldg Washington DC 20515-0001*

DICKSON, BETSY G. social worker; b. Columbia, S.C., Apr. 18, 1944; d. Henry C. and Betty (Kabler) Garrett; m. Andrew L. Dickson, June 8, 1965; children: James, Marian. BA, U. S.C., 1965; MSW, U. So. Miss., 1977; MPH, U. Ala., Birmingham, 1987. Lic. cert. social worker Acad. Cert. Social Workers. Libr. Ark. River Valley Regional Libr., Russellville, Ark., 1965-67; art instr. Ark. Valley Cultural Enrichment Project, Russellville, 1967-68; br. libr. Okla. County Librs., Oklahoma City, 1968-70; advt. dir. Woolworth Store #253, Milledgeville, Ga., 1972-73; freelance comml. artist Hattiesburg, Miss., 1973-76; dist. social work supr. Miss. State Dept. Health, Hattiesburg, 1977-94; field instr. U. So. Miss., Hattiesburg, 1978—2001. Adj. prof. social work U. So. Miss., Hattiesburg, 1991—92; cons. social work Children's Med. Program, Miss. State Dept. Health, Jackson, 1994—99; area social work supt. Forrest Co. Dept. Human Svcs., Jackson, 1999—. Mem. Common Cause Miss., Hattiesburg, Miss., 1988—; mem. faculty Delta Reional AIDS Edn. Tng. Ctr., Jackson, 1994—96; mem. adv. bd. Children's Trust Fund, Miss., 1995—97; mem.outreach com. Trinity Episcopal Ch., Hattiesburg, 1988—90, 1997—; mem. Miss. Episcopal AIDS Commn., Jackson, 1994—96; bd. dirs. United Way

Emergency Welfare Fund, 1982—92. Mem.: NASW (local chair 1982—84, various coms.), Miss. Conf. Social Welfare, Aids Svcs. Coalition. Office: Miss State Dept Health Children's Med Program PO Box 1700 Jackson MS 39215-1700

DICKSON, BRENT E(LLIS), state supreme court justice; b. July 18, 1941; m. Jan Aikman, June 8, 1963; children: Andrew, Kyle, Reed. BA, Purdue U., 1964; JD, Ind. U., Indpls., 1968; LittD, Purdue U., 1996. Bar: Ind. 1968, U.S. Ct. Appeals (7th cir.) 1972, U.S. Supreme Ct. 1975; cert. civil trial adv., NBTA. Pvt. practice, Lafayette, Ind., 1968-85; sr. ptnr. Dickson, Reiling, Teder & Withered, 1977-85; assoc. justice Ind. Supreme Ct., Indpls., 1986—. Adj. prof. Sch. of Law Ind. U., 1992—. Past pres. Tippecanoe County Hist. Assn.; mem. dean's adv. coun. Sch. Liberal Arts Purdue U., 1990-94; mem. adv. bd. Heartland Film Festival, 1995-2000. Mem. Am. Inns Ct (founding pres. Sagamore chpt.), Am. Law Inst. Office: Ind Supreme Ct 306 Statehouse Indianapolis IN 46204-2213

DICKSON, DAVID WATSON DALY, retired college president; b. Portland, Maine, Feb. 16, 1919; s. David Augustus and Mary Margaret (Daly) D.; m. Vera Mae Allen, Aug. 5, 1951 (dec. July 1979); children: David Augustus II, Deborah Anne, Deirdre Elizabeth; m. Barbara Childs Mickey, Feb. 14, 1981; children: Robert Warren, Sharon Marlissa. AB, Bowdoin Coll., 1941, LHD (hon.), 1974; MA, Harvard U., 1942, PhD, 1949; LHD (hon.), Bloomfield Coll., 1983; DLitt (hon.), Montclair State Coll., 1989. Instr. to assoc. prof. English Mich. State U., 1948-63; prof., head English dept. No. Mich. U., Marquette, 1963-66; dean No. Mich. U. (Sch. Arts and Sci.), 1966-67, v.p. acad. affairs, 1967-68; provost, v.p. acad. affairs, prof. English Fed. City Coll., Washington, 1968-69; prof. English, asst. to pres. State U. N.Y. at Stony Brook, 1969-72, dean continuing and developing edn., prof. English, 1972-73; pres. Montclair State Coll., Upper Montclair, N.J., 1973-84, pres. emeritus, 1989, Disting. Service prof., 1984-88, prof. emeritus, 1989. Cons. Nat. Found. for Humanities, 1969-71, Mott Found., 1973-74; speaker in field. Author: An Isolate of Isolates, 1995; contbr. articles to profl. jours. Chmn. lt. com. Mich. Coun. Arts, 1963-68; bd. dirs. Nat. Com. on Future of State Colls. and Univs.; trustee Montclair Art Mus., North Essex Devel. and Action Coun., Bloomfield Coll., 1984-89; bd. overseers Bowdoin Coll., 1966-75, trustee, 1975-82; mem. policy bd. Project Change; mem. Bd. Commn. on Higher Edn. Mid. States Assn. Colls. and Secondary Schs., 1978-84; pres. Flagler County Auditorium, 1992-93. 1st lt. AUS, 1943-46. Recipient Disting. Teaching award Mich. State U., 1952; Disting. Educator award Bowdoin Coll., 1971; Austrian Cross of Honor for Letters and Arts; Rosenwald fellow, 1947-43; Smith Mundt fellow Syrian Nat. U. Damascus, 1958-59 Mem. MLA, Milton Soc., Am. Assn. State Colls. and Univs. (chmn. com. on undergrad. studies), Am. Assn. Colls. (commn. on liberal learning), Phi Beta Kappa, Omega Psi Phi, Sigma Psi Phi, Phi Kappa Phi, Rotary. Roman Catholic. Home: 125 Woodhaven Dr Palm Coast FL 32164-7979

DICKSON, EVA MAE, credit manager; b. Clarion, Iowa, Jan. 16, 1922; d. James and Ivah Blanche (Breckenridge) D. Grad. Interstate Bus. Coll., Klamath Falls, Oreg., 1943. Reporter, Mchts. Credit Service, Klamath Falls, 1941; credit dept. Montgomery Ward, Klamath Falls, 1941-42; bookkeeper Heilbronner Fuel Co., Klamath Falls, 1942; stenographer City of Klamath Falls, 1943, bookkeeper, office mgr., 1943-52; owner, operator All Star Bus. Service, Klamath Falls, 1953-58, Ace Mimeo Service, Klamath Falls, 1958-73; mgr. Mchts. Credit Service, 1973-87; customer service rep. CBI/Credit N.W., 1987-91. Bd. dirs. United Way, Klamath Falls, 1980-97; sec. Klamath Community Concert Assn., 1956-99; treas., memls. chmn. Klamath County chpt. Am. Cancer Soc.; bd. dirs., treas. Hope in Crisis; mem. Klamath County Centennial Com., 1982, Unification for Progress Joint Planning Com., 1985; mem. nursing adv. com. Oreg. Inst. Tech., 1982—; mem. Klamath Employment Tng. Adv. Com., 1983-86; bd. dirs., sec., treas. Klamath Consumer Council; sec. Unified City for Progress Task Force, 1983-84, Snowflake Winter Festival, 1984—; sec. First Presbyn. Ch., 1992—. Recipient Bronze Leadership award Assoc. Credit Burs., Inc., 1976. Mem. Daughters of Am. Colonists (past regent local chpt.), Consumer Credit Assn. Oreg. (pres. 1984-85), Credit Profl. Internat. (treas. dist. 10 1984-85, 2d v.p. dist. 10 1987-88, 1st v.p. 1988-89, pres. 1989-90, internat. bull. chmn. 1990-91, 92—), Assoc. Credit Bur. Pacific N.W. (pres. 1981-82), Assoc. Credit Bur. Oreg. (pres. 1978-80), Klamath Basin Credit Women Internat. (pres. 1976-78), Soc. Cert. Consumer Credit Exec., Internat. Consumer Credit Assn., Klamath County C. of C. (pres. 1979, ambs. com. 1980—, Nat. Fedn. Bus. and Profl. Women's Club (chmn. nat. fin. com. 1983-84, nat. fin. com. 1982-83), Oreg. Fedn. Bus. and Profl. Women's Club (state pres. 1971-72), Klamath Falls Bus. and Profl. Women's Club (pres. 1966-67, 76-77, 1996—). Republican. Presbyterian. Club: Quota (pres. 1958-59, dist. gov. 1969-70). Avocations: painting, traveling.

DICKSON, JAMES EDWARD, actor; b. Akron, Ohio, Jan. 5, 1949; s. George Leroy Dickson and Katherine Poland. Student, N.Y. Acad. Theatrical Arts, N.Y.C., 1970. Actor, writer: (films, videos) Luther T. Jones, 1991; prodr.: Luther Jones II, 1992; dir.: (plays) Road to Recovery, 2002; actor: (films) Big Daddy, Summer of Sam, Night Falls on Manhattan, Blue in the Face, (commercials) Wendy's, Nike, N.Y. Lottery, MCI, Conseco Ins., (music videos) Who You Wit, You Came Up, Remember We, Take the Train, others. Reader elem. schs. Book Pals, N.Y.C.; lectr. Boys Clubs, Cin. and N.Y.C. Recipient Talent Show winner, N.Y. Housing Projects, 1999, Citation of Dramatic Monologue for King Heroin, N.Y.C. Avocations: reading, watching documentaries, poetry. Office: Stanley Kaplan Agency Ste 503 139 Fulton St New York NY 10038

DICKSON, JAMES EDWIN, II, obstetrician, gynecologist; b. Pontiac, Mich., Feb. 18, 1943; s. James Edwin and Virginia (Farrar) D.; m. Joan Gayle Coonley, July 21, 1967; children: Alison, Andrew. BS, U. Mich., 1965; MD, Wayne State U., 1969. Diplomate Am. Bd. Ob-Gyn. Intern Harborview Med. Ctr., Seattle, 1969-70; resident U. Mich. Med. Ctr., 1972-75; pvt. practice Geneva, N.Y., 1975—; chief of med. staff Finger Lakes Health Sys. Capt. M.C., USAF, 1970-72. Fellow Am. Coll. Obstetricians and Gynecologists; mem. Soc. Am. Laparoscopists, Miller Ob-Gyn Soc., N.Y. State Med. Soc., Buffalo Ob-Gyn Soc., Rotary (pres. Geneva 1988). Avocation: astronomy. Home: 16 Maplewood Dr Geneva NY 14456-1420 Office: Finger Lakes Med Group 200 North St Geneva NY 14456-1502 E-mail: jedick2@lynnet.com.

DICKSON, JAMES FRANCIS, III, surgeon; b. Boston, May 4, 1924; s. James Francis Jr. and Mary Elizabeth (Rich) Dickson; m. Vivian Joan Franco, Dec. 23, 1977. AB, Dartmouth Coll., 1944; MD, Harvard Med. Sch., 1947. Diplomate Am. Bd. Surgery. Intern and resident Boston City Hosp., 1947—51; practice in thoracic and cardiovascular surgery Boston, 1951—61; NIH spl. fellow MIT, Cambridge, 1961—65; dir. engrng. in biology and medicine program NIH, Bethesda, Md., 1965—75; asst. surgeon gen. HHS, Washington, 1976—89. Sr. advisor to dean Harvard Med. Sch., 1992—2001, vis. com., 1992—2001; bd. overseers Dartmouth Med. Sch., 1990—, C. Everett Koop Inst., 1992—. Fellow: IEEE, ACS; mem.: Inst. Medicine of NAS.

DICKSON, KATHARINE HAYLAND, dance educator; b. East Hartford, Conn., Dec. 4, 1904; d. George Wentworth and Marguerite Moore (Stockman) D.; m. Harry Burton Ashenden, June 23, 1928 (dec. 1967); 1 child, David Dickson; m. Theodore Henry Brown, Oct. 26, 1968 (dec. 1973); m. Charles Thomas Alverson, Feb. 18, 1978 (dec. Mar. 1985). BEd, Boston U., 1948. Tchr. Ballroom dance Model Sch. of Modern Dance, Boston, 1923-26; tchr. ballroom, ballet, tap Hazel Boone Sch. Dancing, Boston, 1926-28; tchr. mus. comedy and tap Knickerbocker Sch., Boston, 1928-31; dir. Katharine Dickson Dance Studio, Cambridge, Mass., 1934-68; tchr. ballroom dance Boston Ctr. for Adult Edn., Boston, 1943-74; tchr. ballet and tap Newton Community Ctr., Mass., 1955-74, Hayden Recreation Ctr., Lexington, Mass., 1957-74; ballroom dance tchr. Englewood (Fla.) Recreation Ctr., 1975-88; tchr. ballroom dance Venice, Fla., 1989-94. Tchr. Ramblers Rest Resort, Venice. Author: Stockman-Gallison Ancestral Lines, 1984, Downeast Dicksons, 1987, Burton-Tyler, 1990, The Stockman Story, 1992, My Very Own 20th Century Rag, 1995, Ashenden, the English Background of Harry Burton Ashenden, 1997, A 1998 Sawyer Fickett Update to Downeast Dicksons of 1987; contbr. articles to profl. jours. Mem. Nat. Coun. Dance Tchr. Orgn. (early chmn.), Dance Tchrs. Club Boston (past pres., hon.), N.Y. Soc. Tchrs. Dancing. Unitarian. Avocations: swimming, gardening, growing wildflowers. Home (Winter): 2101 S Pine St Englewood FL 34224

DICKSON, PAUL WESLEY, JR., physicist; b. Sharon, Pa., Sept. 14, 1931; s. Paul Wesley and Elizabeth Ella (Trevethan) D.; m. Eleanor Ann Dunning, Nov. 17, 1952; children: Gretchen Ann, Heather Elizabeth, Paul Wesley. BS in Metall. Engring., MS, U. Ariz., 1954; PhD in Physics, N.C. State U., 1962. With Westinghouse Electric Corp., Large, Pa., 1963-84, mgr. weapon systems, 1965-68, mgr. advanced projects, 1969-72, mgr. reactor analysis and core design Madison, Pa., 1972-79, tech. dir. Oak Ridge, 1979-84; with EG & G Idaho, Idaho Falls, 1984-89, mgr. new tech. devel., 1984-87, mgr. reactor projects and programs, 1987-88; dir. Ctr. for Nuclear Engring. and Tech., 1988-89; tech. dir. reactor restart div. Westinghouse Savannah River Co., 1989-92; chief engr. nuclear materials processing div. Westinghouse, 1992-95; pvt. cons., 1995—. Mem. adv. com. on advanced propulsion systems NASA, Washington, 1970-72; mem. adv. com. reactor physics AEC/Dept. Energy, 1974-79; mem. rev. com. applied physics Argonne (Ill.) Nat. Lab., 1978-83, chmn., 1980; mem. rev. com. engring. physics Oak Ridge Nat. Lab., 1982-86, chmn., 1986; mem. fellow selection com. Dept. Energy, 1981-82; mem. rev. com. EBR II Argonne Nat. Lab., 1984, sci. and tech. adv. com., 1985-91. Contbr. numerous sci. articles to profl. publs. Capt. USAF, 1955-63. Fellow Am. Nuclear Soc.; mem. Am. Phys. Soc., N.Y. Acad. Scis., AIME, AAAS, Scabbord and Blade, Sigma Xi, Phi Kappa Phi, Tau Beta Pi, Phi Lambda Upsilon, Sigma Pi Sigma. Republican. Home: 4005 Woodvalley Dr Aiken SC 29803-8421 E-mail: pwdickson@scescape.net.

DICKSON, ROBERT JAY, lawyer; b. Waukegan, Ill., Sept. 20, 1947; s. Robert Jay and Suzanne Elizabeth (Smith) D.; m. J. Alyson Younghusband, June 21, 1969; children: Peter M., Joshua H., Theodore F., Ian A. BA, Northwestern U., 1969; JD, U. Ill., Champaign, 1972. Bar: Alaska 1972, U.S. Dist. Ct. Alaska 1972, U.S. Ct. Appeals (9th cir.) 1972, U.S. Supreme Ct. 1973. Assoc. Atkinson, Conway & Gagnon, Anchorage, 1972—, ptnr., 1974—. Mem. Forum Com. Constrn. Industry, 1978—. Co-author: AK Construct. Law, 1986, 6th rev. edit., 1998, Advanced Construct. Law in AK, 1999, State Pub. Construct. Law Source Book, 1997—. Mem. cmty. adv. bd. Providence Health Sys. Alaska, Anchorage; bd. dir. Alaskan Scottish Club, Alaska, 1973—88, Meier Lake Conf. Ctr., Wasilla, Alaska, 1979—88, Homer Soc. Natural History, Alaska, 1985—89, AK Ctr. for the Performing Arts, Alaska, 1990—91, Anchorage Sch. Bus. Partnerships, Alaska, 1995—, AK Support Industry Alliance, Alaska, 1997—, Gov.'s Prayer Breakfast, 1997—, Anchorage Symphony Orch., Alaska, 1987—, pres., 1989—91, 1999—2001; bd. dir., chmn. Russian AK Acad. Fine Arts, 1996—; chmn. bd. trustees Robert E. and Margaret E. Lyle Trust, 1996—. Mem. ABA, Alaska Bar Assn., Anchorage Bar Assn., Am. Acad. Healthcare Attys., Assoc. Gen. Contractors (legal affairs com. Alaska chpt.), Def. Rsch. Inst., Anchorage C. of C., Commonwealth North Club, Capt. Cook Athletic Club (Anchorage). Episcopalian. Avocations: piano, boating. Office: Atkinson Conway & Gagnon 420 L St Anchorage AK 99501-1937

DICKSON, ROBERT LEE, lawyer; b. Hot Springs, Ark., Sept. 3, 1932; s. Constantine John and Georgia Marie (Allen) D.; m. Christina Farrar, Oct. 29, 1978; children— Robert Lee, Geoffrey, Alexandra, Christopher, George, John. BBA, U. Tex., 1959, LLB, 1960. Bar: Tex. 1960, Calif. 1965, U.S. Dist. Ct. (no. dist.) Tex. 1960, U.S. Dist. Ct. (ea. dist.) Wis. 1979, U.S. Supreme Ct. 1980, U.S. Dist. Ct. (ea. dist.) Calif. 1983, U.S. Ct. Appeals (7th cir.) 1983, U.S. Dist. Ct. (no. and so. dists.) Calif. 1984, U.S. Ct. Appeals (9th cir.) 1987, U.S. Ct. Appeals (1st and 10th cirs.) 1989. Assoc. to ptnr. Eplen, Daniel & Dickson, Abilene, Tex., 1960-65; assoc. to sr. ptnr. Haight, Dickson, Brown & Bonesteel, Santa Monica, Calif., 1965-88; sr. ptnr. Dickson, Carlson & Campillo, Santa Monica, 1988-98; ptnr. Arter & Hadden, L.A., 1998—2001, Musick, Peeler & Garrett, 2001—. Contbr. articles to profl. jours. Fellow Am. Coll. Trial Lawyers; mem. Ind. Bar Com., Def. Rsch. Inst. (steering com. of drug and device litigation com.), Fedn. Ins. and Corp. Counsel (chmn. pharm. liability litigation sect. 1984-87, v.p. 1986-89, bd. dirs. 1989-95, sec.-treas. 1991-92, pres.-elect 1992-93, pres. 1993-94, chmn. 1994-95), Am. Bd. Trial Advocates, Assn. So. Calif. Def. Counsel (pres. 1976), Bel Air Country Club, Bel Air Bay Club (Pacific Palisades). Republican. Roman Catholic. Home: 14952 Alva Dr Pacific Palisades CA 90272-4401 E-mail: rdickson@mpglaw.com.

DICKSON, STANLEY, speech pathology/audiology services professional, educator; b. N.Y.C., N.Y., Sept. 3, 1927; s. Irving Richard and Beatrice Dickson; m. Marion Ruth Ernstorff, Nov. 20, 1950 (dec. Mar. 15, 1991); m. Ruth Marie Dickson, Oct. 9, 1999; children: Johanna M., Fran C., Neil H. BA, Bklyn. Coll., 1950, MA, 1954; EdD, U. Buffalo, 1960. Cert. clin. competence in speech pathology and audiology Am. Speech, Hearing and Lang. Assn. Speech and hearing therapist N.Y.C. Bd. Edn., N.Y.C., 1950—51, Rochester (N.Y.) Bd. Edn., 1951—52; exec. dir. Rochester Hearing and Speech Ctr., 1952—56; prof. speech pathology and audiology Buffalo (N.Y.) State Coll., 1956—92; audiological cons. Otolaryngologists, Buffalo, 1970—92; owner Wiliamvale Audiology Ctr., Buffalo, 1985—92; prof. emeritus SUNY, Buffalo, 1992—. Cons. editor: Jour. Speech Disorders, 1980—82, editor, author: book Communication Disorders, 2d edit., 1974; contbr. articles to profl. jours. Bd. dirs., chair com. on coll. and h.s. studies Bur. Jewish Edn., Buffalo, 1980—84; coord. adult edn. program Coun. Conservative Synagogues, 1972—74; bd. dirs. Kadmul Hebrew Day Sch., Buffalo, Temple Shaarey Zedek, Buffalo, 1970—72, 1994—96. Seaman U.S.C.G., 1944—46. Recipient Cleft Palate Study grant, Buffalo State Coll., 1984; scholar, United Cerebral Palsy Assn., Phila. County Med. Soc., 1950. Fellow: Am. Speech, Hearing and Lang. Assn. (chmn. membership com. 1982—84); mem.: Western Lang., Speech and Hearing Assn. (pres. 1965—67), N.Y. State Speech and Hearing Assn. (pres., v.p. 1984—86). Avocations: music, literature, sports, acting. Home: 34 Park Lane Ct Buffalo NY 14221 E-mail: stdickinson@adelphia.net.

DICKSON, TIM F. music educator; b. Covington, Ky., Apr. 1, 1952; s. Ray and Dorthea Dickson; m. Valerie McBeath, Nov. 29, 1986; 1 child, Melody. MusB in Edn., Morehead (Ky.) State U., 1974; MusM in Edn., Ea. Ky. U., 1980. Cert. tchr. Fla. Dept. of Edn. Band dir., chorus dir. Deming HS, Mount Olivet, Ky., 1977—79; grad. asst. Ea. Ky. U., Richmond, Ky., 1979—80; band dir., chorus dir. Ft. Campbell (Ky.) HS, 1980—88; band dir. Jefferson HS, Tampa, Fla., 1988—89, Chamberlain HS, Tampa, Fla., 1989—98, B. T. Wash. Magnet Mid. Sch., Tampa, Fla., 1998—2003, William Mid. Magnet Sch. for Internat. Studies, Tampa, 2003—. Sec., treas. Region IX Band Dirs. Assn., Ashland, Ky., 1977—78, pres., 1978—79. Mem.: Fla. Sch. Music Assn. (assoc.), Fla. Music Educators Assn. (assoc.), Music Educator's Nat. Conf. (assoc.), Fla. Bandmasters Assn. (assoc.). Home: 827 Birdie Way Apollo Beach FL 33572 Office: Williams Mid MagnetSchool 5020 N 47th St Tampa FL 33610 Fax: 813-744-8665.

DICKSON, VICTOR PAUL, lawyer; b. Pensacola, Fla., Aug. 20, 1950; s. Victor Lewis and Mary (Sasnette) D.; m. Paige Stenstrom, May 14, 1988. BA, U. West Fla., 1973; JD, Stetson U., 1976. Bar: Fla. 1976, Tex. 1979; bd. cert. criminal law splist. Tex. Bd. Legal Splization, 1988, bd. cert. Criminal Trial Adv. Nat. Bd. Trial Advocacy, 1992. Asst. pub. defender 20th Cir. Pub. Defenders Off., Naples, Fla., 1977—78; asst. city atty. City Atty.'s Office, Ft. Worth, 1979—84; asst. dist. atty. Tarrant County Criminal Dist. Atty.'s Off., Ft. Worth, 1984—94; pvt. practice Ft. Worth, 1994—. Office: PO Box 11611 Fort Worth TX 76110-0611

DICKSON, VIVIAN FRANCO, biomedical research consultant; b. Phila., June 2, 1937; d. Joseph Patrick and Vivian (Lange) Franco; m. James F. Dickson, III, Dec. 23, 1977. BA, U. Del., 1958; postgrad., Jefferson Med. Coll., 1959. Cert. med. technologist Am. Soc. Clin. Pathologists. Med. technologist NIH, Bethesa, Md., 1959-67, adminstr., 1968-74, 78-88; health policy analyst Office of Asst. Sec. Health, Dept. Health and Human Svcs., Washington, 1975-77; cons. in health care policy Mass., 1988—; cons. Hospice for Vis. Nurse Assn., Cape Cod, Mass., 1988-95; mem. hospice profl. adv. com. Vis. Nurse Assn., Cape Cod, 1991-95. Office: PO Box 343 Provincetown MA 02657-0343

DICKSTEIN, HARVEY LEONARD, pharmaceutical company executive; b. Springfield, Mass., Jan. 19, 1936; s. David and Ruth (Stein) D.; m. Judith Marie Barton, Mar. 26, 1966; children: Jason Adam, Debra Ann. BA in Biology, Am. Internat. Coll., 1957; MD, Tufts U., 1961. Diplomate Nat. Bd. Med. Examiners. Intern then resident Bronx Mcpl. Hosp. Ctr., 1961-63; surg. resident Springfield (Mass.) Hosp., 1963-64; surg. resident, then chief resident Boston U. Med. Ctr., 1964-66; med. monitor Baxter Labs., Morton Grove, Ill., 1968-69; assoc. dir. hosp. products div. Abbott Labs., North Chgo., Ill., 1969-72, assoc. dir. exptl. therapy, 1972-73; dir. clin. rsch. Johnson & Johnson, New Brunswick, N.J., 1973-83; group leader surg. anesthetic and dental products FDA, Rockville, Md., 1983-85; dir. regulatory med. affairs E.R. Squibb, New Brunswick, 1985-87; v.p. regulatory affairs Parke-Davis Div. of Warner-Lambert, Morris Plains, N.J., 1987-89, v.p. med. rsch., 1989-91, v.p. med. affairs, 1992-93, v.p. med. and regulatory affairs, consumer products R&D, 1993-96; v.p., med. dir. Metaworks, Inc., Boston, 1996-97; v.p. clin. rsch. Transcend Therapeutics, Inc., Cambridge, Mass., 1997-98. Pharm. cons., Cohasset, Mass., 1999—. Lt. comdr. USPHS, 1966-68. New England Arthritis and Rheumatism Found. summer scholar, 1959. Avocations: weight lifting, skiing, jogging. Home: 393 Beechwood St Cohasset MA 02025-1521 E-mail: Harveydickstein@aol.com.

DICKSTEIN, JACK, chemist; b. Phila., Dec. 14, 1925; s. Harry and Anna A. (Anselevitz) D.; m. Pauline M. Gotheif, Dec. 24, 1950; children: Jeffrey L., John F., Andrea E. BS in Biochemistry, Pa. State U., 1946; MA in Organic Chemistry, Temple U., 1951; PhD in Polymer Chemistry, Rutgers U., 1958. Rsch. assoc. E.R. Squibb & Sons, New Brunswick, N.J., 1951-56; lab. mgr. Borden Chem. Co., Phila., 1958-61, devel. mgr. thermoplastics divsn. Leominster, Mass., 1961-67, dir. R&D Phila., 1967-74; group mgr. R&D Haven Chem. Co., Phila., 1974-77; v.p., dir. R&D Seal Inc., Naugatuck, Conn., 1977-79; pres. Kibow Biotech Inc., Phila., 1977—, Monomer-Polymer & Dajac Labs., Inc., Feasterville, Pa., 1979—. Tech. cons. Avery Internat., Pasadena, Calif., 1978-81, Painesville, Ohio, 1981-83, Avmor Inc., Montreal, Can., 1982-84, Wesley Jessen, Chgo., Ill., 1980-90. Patentee in field; contbr. articles to profl. jours. 010Mem. AAAS, Am. Chem. Soc., Am. Inst. Chemists, N.Y. Acad. Scis., Franklin Inst., Sigma Xi, Sigma Phi, Lambda Upsilon, Phi Eta. Jewish. Avocations: sports statistics, photography. Home: 318 Keats Rd Huntingdon Valley PA 19006-3029 Office: Monomer-Polymer & Dajac Labs 1675 Bustleton Pike Feasterville PA 19053 E-mail: mpdajak@aol.com.

DICKSTEIN, JOAN BORTECK, arbitrator, conflict management consultant; b. Phila., June 20, 1919; d. Joseph and Mary (Leibovitz) Borteck; m. Benjamin Dickstein, Dec. 24, 1939; children: Howard, Kenneth, Mary. BA, Antioch Coll., 1974; MA in Sociology, U. Pa., 1978. Phila. coord. Gt. Books Found., Chgo., 1960-64; moderator, panelist Panel of Am. Women, Phila., 1964-73; trainer sensitivity courses Phila. Fellowship commn., 1966-69; rsch. assoc., cons. U. Pa. Human Resources Ctr., Phila., 1969-73; arbitrator comty. disputes Am. Arbitration Assn., Phila., 1969-82, Mcpl. Ct. of Phila., 1974-80, Commn. on Human Rels., Phila., 1979-82; facilitator interfaith dialogue Elkins Park (Pa.) Interfaith Dialogue, 1987—. Guest lectr. conflict mgmt. La Salle Coll., Phila., 1971-74; mem. adv. com. Episcopal Comty. Svcs., Phila., 1972-73; cons. staff devel. Covenant House Health Svc., Phila., 1979-80. V.p. Phila. chpt. Am. Jewish Com., Phila., 1970-73; study tour mem. Scandinavia, World Future Soc., Washington, 1974; study tour mem. Mid. East, United Presbyn. Ch., Roman Cath. Conf., Am. Jewish Com., N.Y.C., 1976; bd. dirs. Or Hadash Congregation, Ft. Washington, Pa., 1990-93; peer counselor Women's Ctr., Jenkintown, Pa., 1987—. Recipient Human Rights award City of Phila. Commn. on Human Rels., 1982. Democrat. Jewish. Avocations: great books discussion programs, interfaith dialogue, aerobics, crossword puzzles, volunteering at women's ctr. Home: 1250 Greenwood Ave Jenkintown PA 19046-2901

DICKSTEIN, SIDNEY, lawyer; b. Brooklyn, May 13, 1925; s. Charles and Pearl (Stahl) D.; m. Barbara H. (Duke), Sept. 20, 1953; children: Ellen Simeon, Matthew Howard, Nancy Joy. BA, Franklin and Marshall Coll., Lancaster, Pa., 1947; JD, Columbia U., 1949; LLD (hon.), Franklin and Marshall Coll., Lancaster, Pa., 2003. Bar: N.Y., 1949, D.C., 1959. Law clk. Joseph Richter, N.Y.C., 1949-50; assoc. law office Herman E. Cooper, 1950-53; founder Dickstein and Shapiro, N.Y.C., 1953; sr. ptnr. successor firm Dickstein, Shapiro, Morin, and Oshinsky, Washington, 1953-97, sr. counsel, 1998—. Mem. bd. advisors and article contbr., Jour. of Wealth Mgmt. Contbr. articles to profl. jours including Jour. Wealth Mgmt. Trustee Franklin and Marshall Coll., 1978—. Served with AUS, 1943-44; USNR, 1944-46. Mem.: Am. Jewish Com. (pres. Washington chpt., 1999-2001, mem. nat. bd. gov.), Bar Assn., D.C., ABA. Office: 9050 Bradgrove Dr Bethesda MD 20817-3003 also: Dickstein Shapiro Morin & Oshinsky 2101 L St NW Washington DC 20037-1526 E-mail: dicksteins@dsmo.com.

DICLAUDIO, JANET ALBERTA, health information administrator; b. Monroeville, Pa., June 17, 1940; d. Frank and Pearl Alberta (Wolfgang) DiC. Cert. in Med. Rsch. Libr. Sci., Luth Med. Ctr., 1962; BA, Thiel Coll., 1975; MS, SUNY, Buffalo, 1978. Registered record adminstr. Dir. med. records Bashline Hosp., Grove City, Pa., 1962, St. Clair Meml. Hosp., Pitts., 1963-73; asst. prof. Ill. State U., Normal, 1976-81; corp. dir. med. records Buffalo Gen. Hosp., 1981-85; dir. med. records Candler Hosp., Savannah, Ga., 1985-94, med. records analyst, 1994-98; pres. prn Assocs., Savannah, Ga., 1998—. Med. record cons. White Cliff Nursing Home, Greenville, Pa., 1973—75; mgmt. cons. Gifford W. Lorenz MD, Savannah, 1992—94; Medicare compliance officer and coder Health Claims, Inc., Savannah, 1999—2001; mgmt. cons. John D. Northup, Jr., MD, Savannah, 2001—. Contbr. articles to periodicals. Bd. dirs. Mid-Ill. Areawide Health Planning Corp., Normal, 1979-81. Mem. Am. Health Info. Mgmt. Assn., Ga. Health Info. Mgmt. Assn., S.E. Ga. Health Info. Mgmt. Assn. Avocations: painting, story telling, dancing, reading. Office: Ste 705 PMB 153 7400 Abercorn St Savannah GA 31406

DICLERICO, JOSEPH ANTHONY, JR., federal judge; b. Lynn, Mass., Jan. 30, 1941; s. Joseph Anthony and Ruth Adel (Cummings) DiC.; m. Laurie Breed Thomson, July 27, 1975; 1 child, Devon Thomson. BA, Williams Coll., Williamstown, Mass., 1963; LLB, Yale U., 1966. Bar: N.H. 1967, U.S. Dist. Ct. N.H. 1967, U.S. Ct. Appeals (1st cir.) 1973, U.S. Supreme Ct. 1975. Law clk. to presiding justice U.S. Dist. Ct. N.H., Concord, 1966-67, N.H. Supreme Ct., Concord, 1967-68; assoc. Cleveland Waters & Bass, Concord, 1968-70; asst. atty. gen. State of N.H., Concord, 1970-77; assoc. justice N.H. Superior Ct., Concord, 1977-91, chief justice, 1991-92; chief judge U.S. Dist. Ct. N.H., Concord, 1992-97. Chmn. Superior Ct. sentence rev. disvn., 1987-92. Fellow Am. Bar Found. (life), N.H. Bar Found. (jud.); mem. N.H. Bar Assn (nat. conf. state trial judges 1986-92, nat. conf. fed. trial judges, 1992-96, mem. com. on codes of conduct jud. conf. of U.S. 1994-2002, dist. judge rep. from 1st cir. to Jud. Conf. of U.S. 1997—), Phi Beta Kappa. Republican. Roman Catholic. Avocation: gardening. Office: 55 Pleasant St Concord NH 03301-3954

DICOLA, THEODORE, music educator; b. Vandergrift, Pa., Dec. 17, 1951; s. Sebastian and Ann Marie DiCola; m. Miriam Ruth Connell, Aug. 25, 1979; children: Theodore Brian, Daniel Addison, Allison Michelle. BS, Clarion U., Clarion, PA, 1969—73. Music educator Shikellamy Sch. Dist., Sunbury, Pa., 1973—. Marching band adjudicator Nat. Judges Assn., Pa. Mem.: NEA, Music Educators Nat. Conf., Internat. Assn. Jazz Edn., Pa. Music Educators Assn. D-Liberal. Roman Catholic. Avocation: music. Home: 14 Smokehouse Lane Selinsgrove PA 17870 Personal E-mail: tdicola@evenlink.com.

DICONTI, MICHAEL ANDREW, trade organization executive; b. Glendale, Calif., Aug. 19, 1958; s. Andrew Raphael Jr. and Diane Rose (Carlotti) DiC.; m. Veronica Donahue, Aug. 6, 1988; 1 child, Nolan James. AB in Psychology magna cum laude, Occidental Coll., 1980; MBA in Acctg./Fin., UCLA, 1983; MA in Polit. Sci., Johns Hopkins U., 1987, PhD in Polit. Sci., 1990. Tax advisor Arthur Young, L.A., 1983-85; instr. C.C. of Balt., 1985-90, Johns Hopkins U., Balt., 1987-90; exec. asst. to pres. The Bus. Roundtable, Washington, 1990-93, dir. adminstrn., 1993—. Author: Entrepreneurship in Training, 1992. Asst. treas. Ednl. Excellence Ptnrship., Washington, 1993—2001. Fellow Inst. for Study of World Politics, Washington, 1987-88. Mem. Phi Beta Kappa, Psi Chi (pres. Occidental Coll. chpt. 1979-80). Home: 3110 Pine Oaks Way Oak Hill VA 20171 Office: The Bus Roundtable 1615 L St NW Ste 1100 Washington DC 20036-5624 E-mail: mdiconti@brt.org.

DICORCIA, EDWARD THOMAS, retired oil industry executive; b. Richmond Hill, N.Y., Oct. 16, 1930; s. Domenick and Emma DiCorcia; m. Madelyn Faress. BA, Columbia Coll., 1951; BCE, Columbia U., 1955, MCE, 1956. Registered profl. engr., Tex. Plant mgr. Esso Std. Oil Co., Bayonne, N.J., 1965-67; mgr. employee rels. Humble Oil & Refining Co., Houston, 1969-70, refinery mgr. Baytown, Tex., 1970-73; exec. asst. to pres. Exxon Corp., N.Y.C., 1975-76, dep. mgr. corp. planning, 1976-79; v.p. supply Exxon Co. USA, Houston, 1979-81, v.p. refining, 1981-90; pres., CEO, The Uno-Ven Co.,

Arlington Heights, Ill., 1990-95; ret., 1995; gen. ptnr. Strategic Ptnrs., L.P., Houston, 1995—2003. Dir. Am. Petroleum Inst., Washington, 1987-89, Nat. Petroleum Coun., Washington, 1994-95. Lt. (j.g.) U.S. Navy, 1951-54. Pub. Affairs fellow Brookings Instn., 1966.

DI CORCIA, PHILIP-LORCA, artist, photographer; b. Hartford, Conn., 1953; Diploma, Sch. Mus. Fine Arts, Boston, 1975, postgrad. cert., 1976; MFA, Yale U., 1979. One-man shows include Zeus Arts, Milan, 1985, Photographer's Gallery, London, 1991, 1996, Galeria Palmira Suso, Lisbon, Portugal, 1993, Mus. Modern Art, N.Y.C., 1993, Ctr. Cultural Rocher, Lyon, France, 1993, Nikon Salon, Tokyo, 1994; actor: (Operas) Nikon Salon, 1994; one-man shows include Art and Pub., Geneva, 1995, Galerie Klemens Gasser, Cologne, Germany, 1995, 1996, 1998, Pace Wildenstein Macgill, N.Y.C., 1996, 1998, Theoretical Events, Naples, Italy, 1996, Pace Wildenstein, L.A., 1998, Mus. Nat. Ctr. Arts Reina Sofia, Madrid, 1998, Galerie Rodolphe Janssen, Brussels, 1998, Galerie Almine Rech, Paris, 1998, exhibited in group shows at Enjay Gallery Photography, Boston, 1977, Balt. Mus. Art, 1987, 1991, Mus. Modern Art, N.Y.C., 1987, 1991, Artists Space, N.Y.C., 1990, Art Gallery York U., Toronto, Ont., Can., 1991, Met. Mus. Art, N.Y.C., 1991, L.A. County Mus. Art, 1991, 1992, Galeria Tanjia Grunert, Cologna, 1992, Luhring Augustine Gallery, N.Y.C., 1993, San Francisco Mus. Modern Art, 1993, Robert Klein Gallery, Boston, 1994, Foto Manifestabe, Eindhoven, The Netherlands, 1994, Ansel Adams Ctr., San Francisco, 1995, Portland (Maine) Art Mus., 1995, 1997, Art and Pub., Geneva, 1995, Inst. Contemporary Art, Boston, 1995, Galerie Agnes B, Paris, 1996, Whitney Mus. Am. Art, 1997, Reykjavik (Iceland) Mcpl. Art Mus., 1997, Gemente Mus., Helmond, Germany, 1997, Mus. Contemporary Art, Chgo., 1997, Howard Greenberg Gallery, N.Y.C., 1998, Galerie Fotohof, Salzburg, Austria, Represented in permanent collections Boston Mus. Fin Arts, Chgo. Mus. Contemporary Photography, Dreyfus Corp., N.Y.C., L.A. County Mus. Art, Met. Mus. Art, Mus. Fine Art, Houston. Fellow Artist fellow, Nat. Endowment for the Arts, 1980, 1986, 1989; John Simon Guggenheim Meml. Found. fellow, 1987. Office: Pace/Wildnestein/MacGill 32 E 57th St New York NY 10022-2513

DI CORI, PAT MILLER, painter, sculptor; b. Cin., Nov. 15, 1929; d. Peter William and Ola (McCaffery) M.; m. Ferruccio di Cori, Nov. 18, 1963 (div. 1978). Studied with Robert Beverly Hale, 1960-61; Diploma, Inst. of Fin. N.Y.C., 1958. Tour guide, lectr. UN, N.Y.C., 1955-58; tour guide N.Y. Stock Exch., N.Y.C., 1958-60. Artist: (film documentary) Pat di Cori Reflections in the Mind's Eye, 1996; published in New York Art Review, 1988. Bd. dirs. Creative Arts Rehab. Ctr., N.Y.C., 1975-95, N.Y. Artists, Equity Assocs., Inc., 1991-95. Mem. Art Students League (life). Home and Office: APDO Postal 448 Patzcuaro CD61600 Mich Mexico E-mail: patdicori@yahoo.com.

DICOSIMO, PATRICIA SHIELDS, secondary school educator; b. Hartford, Conn., June 27, 1946; d. Richard Nichols and Rose Aimee (Roy) Shields; m. Joseph Anthony DiCosimo, Apr. 18, 1970. BFA in Art Edn. and Printmaking, U. Hartford, 1969; MS in Edn. and Art, Ctrl. Conn. State Coll., 1972; postgrad., Rochester Inst. Tech., 1986-87. Cert. tchr., Conn. Tchr. art Simsbury (Conn.) H.S., 1969—. Tchr. Farmington Valley Art Ctr., Avon, Conn., 1989-95; supr. Nat. Art Honors Soc., Simsbury, 1989—; mem. Conn. regional adv. bd. Scholastic Art Awards, 1991, 93—; mem. Conn. Scholastic Arts Awards Com., 1989—, co-chair exhibit, 1994—, prin.'s faculty adv. com., 1969—; guest lectr. secondary methods in art edn. Ctrl. Conn. State U., 1994; presenter in field; mem. Conn. Curriculum in Arts, 1995-96, writer, 1995. One-woman shows include Farmington Woods, 1972, Ellsworth Gallery Simsbury, 1974, Annhurst Coll., 1976, Canaan Nat. Bank, 1991, Terryvill Libr., 1994; exhibited in group shows at Ctrl. Conn. State Coll., 1969-72 (Best in Show award 1972), Bristol Chrysanthemum Festival Art Show, 1973-84 (Non-objective award 1973, Graphic award 1975, Mixed Media award 1977, Tracy Driscoll Co. Inc. award 1981, Plymouth Spring award 1983, Dick Blick award 1984), Hartford Ins. Co. Art Educators Exhibit, 1990, Simsbury Libr. Gallery Art Educators Exhibit, 1991, 92, 93, Henry James Meml. Gallery, 1992, Riverview Gallery, 1993, Simsbury Dinner Theater, 1994—, Canton Gallery on the Green, 1996, 98 (Best of Conn. Mural Contest 1996), Simsbury Mall Mural, 1999, End Meml. Hall, 2003; author: Design as a Catalyst for Learning, 1997. Sec. Greater Bristol (Conn.) Condo Alliance, 1990-95; mem. Family Life & Marriage Enrichment, New Britain, Conn., 1970-77; vol. painter Boundless Playground for Handicapped, Simsbury, Conn., 2002, W. Hartford Cow Parade, 2003. Named Conn. Art Tchr. of Yr., 1993, Patricia Shields DiCosimo Day in her honor, Town of Simsbury, 1993, Conn. Beginning Educator Support Tchr., Conn. Alliance for Arts Edn. Sch. Dist., 1995—96, Simsbury C. of C. Educator of Yr., 2000; recipient Book award, Hartford Art Sci., 1969, Recycling Cmty. Svc. award, Simsbury, 1999, K-12 Sculpture Tchr. 1st pl., Internat. Sculpture Com., 2001, hon. mention, 2000; grantee, Simsbury Edn. Enhancement Found., 1996—97. Mem. NEA, Nat. Art Edn. Assn., Nat. Art Honor Soc. (advisor 1983—), New Eng. Assn. Schs. and Colls. (evaluator 1998-99, 2001, 03), Conn. Art Edn. Assn. (H.S. rep. 1983-85, sec. 1985—, Conn. Art Educator 1993, Conn. Alliance for Arts Edn. award for Simsbury Art and Music 1995), Conn. Art Alliance Assn., Conn. Edn. Assn. (mem. 3-D curriculum project 1995-96, portfolio rev. com. 1999, Goals 2000 edn. project 1999—), Conn. Craftsman, Farmington Art Guild (tchr. 1992-95), U. Hartford Alumni Assn. Roman Catholic. Avocations: jewelry, painting, golf, travel. Home: 19 Hampton Ct Bristol CT 06010-4738 Office: Simsbury High Sch 34 Farms Village Rd Simsbury CT 06070-2399 E-mail: pat46art@aol.com.

DICPINIGAITIS, PAUL ANTHONY, orthopaedic surgeon; b. North Valley Stream, N.Y., July 1, 1969; s. Zigmas and Ausra Dicpinigaitis; m. Christine Baudin, Aug. 30, 1997. BS summa cum laude,Phi Beta Kappa, Dean's list, Yale U., 1991; MD with honors in Physiology and Neurosci., N.Y.U. Sch. Medicine, 1995. Flight surgeon U.S. Air Force, McGuire AFB, NJ, 1996—98; orthop. surgeon resident N.Y.U. Med. Ctr. Hosp. for Joint Diseases Orthop. Inst., N.Y.C., 1998—2002; chief orthopaedic surgery McGuire Health Care Ctr., 2002—. Contbr. articles to profl. jours. Maj. USAF, 1996—98, maj. USAF, 2002—. Recipient Air Force Commendation medal. Mem.: Phi Beta Kappa. Home: 378 Tavistock Dr Medford NJ 08055 Office: Orthop Clin McGuire AFB 305th MDDS/SGOSO 3458 Neely Rd NJ 08641 E-mail: cpo83097@aol.com.

DICROCE, DEBORAH MARIE, college president; b. Portsmouth, Va., Apr. 8, 1952; d. Quirino Gerry and Margaret (Yanalavage) DiC. BA, Old Dominion U., 1974, MA, 1975; EdD, Coll. William and Mary, 1984. Asst. editor Old Dominion U., Norfolk, Va., 1974—75; prof. English, Tidewater C.C., Portsmouth, Va., 1976—80, chmn. humanities div. Virginia Beach, Va., 1980—85, campus provost, 1985—89; pres. Piedmont Va. C.C., Charlottesville, 1989—98, Tidewater C.C., Norfolk, 1998—. Mem., chmn. numerous statewide coms. on edn., 1984—; adj. vis. prof. higher edn. Coll. William and Mary, Williamsburg, Va., 1985—, U. Va., Charlottesville, 1994—, Old Dominion U., Norfolk, 2000—; vis. coms. Commn. on Colls.; trustee Endowment Assn. of Coll. William and Mary, 1995-2000; bd. dirs. Hampton Roads Partnership, 1998—, Greater Norfolk Corp., 1998—, United Way Hampton Roads, bd. dirs., 1999-, gen. chmn., 2002, Forward Hampton Roads, bd. dirs., 2001-, bd. dirs. C.C., 1999-, mem., 2000-, vice chmn. reg. devel., 2002. Contbr. articles on higher edn. and lang. to profl. publs. Mem. Virginia Beach Arts and Humanities Commn., 1983-86, Portsmouth Partnership, 1985-89; bd. dirs. Friends of Women's Studies, Norfolk, 1985-89, Jr. Achievement Greater Hampton Rds., Norfolk, 1986-89; chmn. Virginia Beach Archtl. Design Awards Com., 1985, Portsmouth Vocat. Edn. Adv. Coun., 1988; chmn. cmty. campaign United Way, Portsmouth, 1988, Charlottesville, 1994; bd. dirs. Jefferson Area United Way, 1989-98, Thomas Jefferson chpt. Am. Heart Assn., 1990-92, Piedmont Coun. of the Arts, 1989-92, First Va. Bank Ctrl., 1990-94, Ash-Lawn Highland Adv. Bd., 1993-98; leadership coun. Martha Jefferson Hosp., 1991-96, Jefferson Nat. Bank, 1994-98. Mem. AAUW, Am. Assn. Higher Edn., Assn. for Study Higher Edn., So. Assn. Colls. and Schs. (vis. com. 1987—, commn. on colls. 1990-96, trustee 1996-98), Rotary (bd. dirs. Portsmouth 1988-89, Charlottesville 1994-96, Norfolk 2000—), Hampton Rd. C. of C., Hampton Rd. YMCA. Office: Tidewater CC 121 College Pl Norfolk VA 23510-1907

DIDDLE, ALBERT W. obstetrician, gynecologist; b. Hamilton, Mo., July 1, 1909; MD, Yale U., 1936. Diplomate Am. Bd. Ob-Gyn. Intern U. Iowa Hosp., 1936-37, resident in ob.-gyn., 1937-40; assoc. prof. ob.-gyn. Southwestern Med. Coll., Dallas, 1945-48; emeritus chmn. ob.-gyn. U. Tenn., Knoxville. Mem. ACOG, Am. Gynecol. and Obstetrics Soc., Continental Gynecology Soc., Ctrl. Assn. Ob.-Gyn., Tenn. Ob-Gyn. Soc., Sigma Xi.

DIDIK, FRANK X, writer; Author books on Eastern European econs. and bus. practices; designer developer solar/electric vehicles; developer Stereoscopic 3-D TV Sys.; founder NEWS1.net. Mem. Electric Car Owners Soc. (founder). Office: PO Box 7426 New York NY 10116-7426 E-mail: FDIDIK@DIDIK.COM.

DIDION, JOAN, writer; b. Sacramento, Calif., Dec. 5, 1934; d. Frank Reese and Eduene (Jerrett) D.; m. John Gregory Dunne, Jan. 30, 1964; 1 child, Quintana Roo. BA, U. Calif., Berkeley, 1956. Assoc. feature editor Vogue mag., 1956-63; former columnist Saturday Evening Post, Life, Esquire; now contbr. The N.Y. Rev. of Books, The New Yorker. Novels include Run River, 1963, Play It As It Lays, 1970, A Book of Common Prayer, 1977, Democracy, 1984, The Last Thing He Wanted, 1996; books of essays: Slouching Towards Bethlehem, 1968, The White Album, 1979, After Henry, 1992; nonfiction Salvador, 1983, Miami, 1987, Political Fictions, 2001; co-author: (with John Gregory Dunne) Screenplays for films The Panic in Needle Park, 1971, Play It As It Lays, 1972, A Star Is Born, 1976, True Confessions, 1981, Hills Like White Elephants, 1991, Broken Trust, 1995, Up Close and Personal, 1996 (screenplay), The Last Thing He Wanted, 1996, Political Fictions (Essays), 2001. Recipient 1st prize Vogue's Prix de Paris, 1956, Morton Dauwen Zabel prize AAAL, 1978, The Edward MacDowell medal, 1996, Columbia Journalism award, 1999. Mem. Am. Acad. Arts and Letters, Am. Acad. Arts and Scis., Coun. Fgn. Rels. Office: care Janklow & Nesbit 445 Park Ave New York NY 10022-2606*

DIDLO, LARRY L. writer, educator; b. Manitowoc, Wis., Sept. 19, 1940; s. John Harvey Sr. and Clara Myrtle (Wood) Didlo. BS, U. Wis., Oshkosh, 1963; MS in Edn., Ind. U., 1964. Founder St. Lawrence Consortium Ednl. Found., Oshkosh, Lawrence Hawthorne Photography. Docent Exptl. Aircraft Assn.; vol. driver Am. Legion, Oshkosh, Paine Art Ctr., Oshkosh; vol. YMCA, Oshkosh. Fellow James E. West fellow, Boy Scouts Am. Mem.: VFW (life), Nat. Eagle Scout Assn., Bay Lakes Heritage Soc., Overseas Am. Schs. Hist. Soc., Wis. State Reading Assn., U. Wis.-Oshkosh Nat. "O" Letterman Club, Elks, Am. Legion (life), Phi Delta Kappa. Republican. Presbyterian. Avocations: photography, swimming, golf.

DI DOMENICA, ROBERT ANTHONY, musician, composer; b. N.Y.C., Mar. 4, 1927; s. Angelo and Philomena (Mosca) DiD.; m. Leona Knopf, Feb. 6, 1951 (dec. 1998); children— David, Peter Josef, Claude Robert; m. Ellen Bender, Apr., 1999. BS, N.Y. U., 1951. Mem. theory-composition faculty New Eng. Conservatory, 1969-92, assoc. dean performing orgns., 1973-76, dean, 1976-78. Flutist, N.Y.C. Ctr. Opera, N.Y. Philharm., Symphony of Air, soloist, Composers Forum, 20th Century Innovations, rec. artist, RCA, Columbia, Colpix, MGM, Atlantic, Deutsche Grammophon records; recs. include Leona DiDomenica In Live First Performance of the Solo Piano Music of Robert DiDomenica, GM/200/CD; compositions include Symphony, 1961, Concerto for Violin and Chamber Orch., 1962, Quintet for Clarinet and String Quartet, 1965, Sonata for Violin and Piano, 1966; opera The Balcony, 1972, Black Poems (baritone, piano and tape), 1976, The Holy Colophon for Orch., Chorus, Soprano and Tenor, 1980, Piano Concerto No. 2, 1982, Dream Journeys for Orch., 1984, The Scarlet Letter (opera), 1986, Opera The Balcony given its world premier by The Opera Co. of Boston, 1990, performed at Moscow's Bolshoi Theater, 1991, (operatic trilogy) Francesco Cenci, 1996, Beatrice Cenci, 1993, The Cenci, 1995. Served with USNR, 1944-46. Guggenheim fellow, 1972-73; grantee Rockefeller Found., 1965; commd. by Goethe Inst., Boston, 1975 Mem. Broadcast Music Inc. Home: 159 Valley Rd Needham MA 02492-4724

DIDOMENICO, MAURO, JR., communication executive; b. Bronx, N.Y., Jan. 12, 1937; s. Mauro and Elizabeth DiD.; m. Angela M. Carracino, Aug. 29, 1964; children— Catherine Lee, David M. BS, Stanford U., 1958, MS, 1959, PhD, 1963. Mem. tech. staff Bell Labs., Murray Hill, N.J., 1962-66, supr., 1966-70, head optical device dept., 1970-80, dept. head integrated circuit customer service dept., 1980-82; divsn. mgr. strategic planning AT&T, Basking Ridge, N.J., 1982-84; divsn. mgr. applied rsch. BellCore, Morristown, NJ, 1984-85; exec. dir. tech. liaison office Bell Comms. Rsch., Morristown, N.J., 1985-92, ret., 1992; pres. CommTech Internat., Bernardsville, N.J., 1993-95; pres., founder FreeLinQ Comm., N.Y.C., 1995—99; founder, exec. v.p. eVideo Incorporated, 2000—; prin. UltraPro Internat., 2000—03. Contbr. numerous articles to profl. lit. Fellow IEEE, Am. Phys. Soc.; mem. N.Y. Acad. Scis., Sigma Xi, Tau Beta Pi. Roman Catholic.

DIDOMIZIO, ROBERT ANTHONY, JR., mechanical engineer; b. Ft. Worth, Aug. 3, 1955; s. Robert Anthony and Mary Rose (Bethell) D.; m. Diane Kathryn Sciacca, Mar. 17, 1979; children: Robert Anthony III, Gina Luisa, Nicolas Harry. AS in Tech. Engring., Montgomery County Community Coll., Blue Bell, Pa., 1975; BS in Mech. Engring., Drexel U., 1978, MS in Materials Engring., 1985. Registered profl. engr., Pa. Sr. design engr. Honeywell, Inc., Ft. Washington, Pa., 1978-81; supr. computer aided design SKF Bearing Industries, Inc., King of Prussia, Pa., 1981-87; pres. RAD Engring., Lansdale, Pa., 1987—. Cons. MRC Bearings, Jamestown, N.Y., 1987—, Precision Rebuilding Corp., Reading, Pa., 1985-91, SKF Bearings, King of Prussia, 1987—, Johnson & Johnson, 1991—, Bulova Techs., 1991—, Parker Hannifin Corp., 1991—, NUCOR Steel, Norfolk, Nebr., 1997—, Phila. Toboggan Coasters, Inc., Hatfield, Pa. Patentee in field. Mem. Montgomery County Republican Com., Lansdale, 1980-82; Webelos leader Cub Scouts, asst. scoutmaster, varsity team coach, merit badge counselor Boy Scouts Am.; Little League mgr. Towamencin Youth Assn.; soccer coach Montgomery Soccer Assn.; tribal chief Indian Guides YMCA. Mem. ASME, Soc. Carbide and Tool Engrs. (sec. 1987-88, vice chmn. 1988-89), Pa. Soc. Profl. Engrs. (bd. dirs. 1988—, pres. 1993-94, Young Engr. of Yr. 1990), North Pa. C. of C., Masons, Tau Beta Pi, Pi Tau Sigma. Republican. Lutheran. Avocations: hunting, fishing, carpentry, music. Home: 1804 Robin Dr Hatfield PA 19440-3754 Office: 1901 Gehman Rd Kulpsville PA 19443-1415

DIDZEREKIS, PAUL PATRICK, lawyer; b. Chgo., Mar. 17, 1939; s. Louis Joseph and Estelle (Traczyk) D.; m. Judith V. Wright, June 30, 1962 (div. 1968); children: Ann Frances, Paul Patrick; m. Heather Joy Izod, Aug. 1969 (dec. 1993); children: Alexandria, Alexis; m. Kathleen A. Breier, Mar. 31, 1994. BBA, Loyola U., Chgo., 1963; JD, Loyola U., 1964. Bar: Ill. 1964, U.S. Supreme Ct. 1971. Atty. govt. affairs law and tax depts. Sears, Roebuck & Co., 1960-65; mem. Ashcraft & Ashcraft, Chgo., 1965-72; sole practice Chgo., 1972-74; pres., ptnr. Didzerekis & Douglas Ltd., Chgo., 1972-74; sole practice Chgo., Wheaton, Ill., 1978—. Mem. paraprofl. adv. bd. Lewis U. Coll. Law, Glen Ellyn, Ill., 1975, adj. prof. legal ethics in action program, 1976-77; chmn. bd., pres. Real Estate Profls. Am. Inc., 1989—; bd. dirs., gen. counsel The Eleanor Assn., 1970-88, pres., 1983-84; commr. DuPage County Bd., 1998-2002. Pres. United Way, Wheaton, 1987-88; chmn. Milton Twp. Rep. Cen. Com., 1996-98; park dist. commr. Wheaton, 1991-98, pres., 1995-97; pub. adminstr. DuPage County, Ill., 01998—; commr. DuPage County Forest Preserve, 1998-2002. Recipient David. C. Hilliard award Chgo. Bar Assn., 1973-74. Fellow Am. Acad. Matrimonial Lawyers; mem. DuPage County Bar Assn., Kiwanis (dir. 1989-93, 2d v.p.). Home: 411 Hevern Dr Wheaton IL 60187-7395 Office: 610 W Roosevelt Rd Ste 2B Wheaton IL 60187-2303

DIEBEL, GARY R. architect; b. St. Paul; B in Architecture, U. Minn., 1983; M in Architecture, Cranbook Acad. Art, Bloomfield Hills, Mich., 1987. Architect DSPB, Inc., Virginia, Minn., 1983-85, Kodet Archl. Group, Ltd., Mpls., 1987-90, Diebel & Co., Burlingame, Calif., 1990—. Mem. AIA. Office: Diebel & Company PO Box 1044 Burlingame CA 94011-1044 E-mail: gdiebel@diebelstudio.com.

DIEBOLD, FRANCIS X. economist, educator; b. Nov. 12, 1959; m. Susan S. Diebold; 3 children. BS in Fin. and Econs., U. Pa., 1981, PhD in Econs., 1986. Rsch. economist, mem. bd. govs. FRS, 1986—89; asst. prof. econs., J.M. Cohen term chair U. Pa., 1989—92, assoc. prof., 1992—96, prof., 1996—99, prof. stats. Wharton Sch., 1996—, dir. Inst. Econ. Rsch., Lawrence R. Klein prof. econs., 1999—; faculty rsch. fellow Nat. Bur. Econ. Rsch., 1993—99, rsch. assoc., 1999—; prof. fin. Wharton Sch. U. Pa., 2001—, W.P. Carey prof. econs., 2000—, prof. fin., 2001—. Charter mem. Oliver Wyman Inst., 1996—; vis. prof. fin., econ., stats. Stern Sch. Bus., NYU, 1998-2000; vis. prof. Cambridge U., 1998, Princeton U., 1997, Johns Hopkins U., 1995, U. Chgo., 1993, London Sch. Econs., 1992, U. Minn., 1990; Benedum lectr. W.Va. U., 1992; mem. organizing com. Computational Fin., 1999—; mem. econs. panel NSF, 1998-2000, chmn. forecasting seminar, 1995—. Author: (with G. Rudebusch) Business Cycles: Durations, Dynamics and Forecasting, 1999, Elements of Forecasting, 1998, Empirical Modeling of Exchange Rate Dynamics, 1988; assoc. editor Rev. Econs. and Stats., 1993—, Jour. Bus. and Econ. Stats., 1993—, Jour. Forecasting, 1994—, Stata Tech. Bull., 1994—, Econometrica, 1994-97, Jour. Applied Econometrics, 1991-97, Jour. Empirical Fin., 1992-95, Econometric Revs., 1989-92; mem. adv. bd. Econ. Policy Rev., Fed. Res. Bank N.Y., 1997—, Macroecon. Dynamics, 1996—; co-editor Internat. Econ. Rev., 1993-99, Jour. Forecasting, 1990-94; contbr. articles to econ. and bus. jours.; spkr. at many profl. meetings and confs. Mem. bd. sr. scholars Nat. Ctr. for Ednl. Quality of Workforce, 1993-95. Fellow Wharton Fin. Instns. Ctr., 1997—; Alfred P. Sloan Found. rsch. fellow, 1992-94; grantee NSF, 1989-92, 92-94, 95-98, 98—, Pew Found., 1995-96, NSF and Cornell Super Computer Ctr., 1992-92. Fellow Econometric Soc. (program com. N.Am. winter mtg. 1999, program com. time-series econometrics 1993); mem. Am. Statis. Assn. (mem. editl. selection com. Jour. B sec., Econ. Stats., 1994, 2000, Zellner award selection com. 1995, sec./treas. bus. and econ. stats. sect. 1994, program chair 1991), Am. Econ. Assn., Am. Fin. Assn. Office: Dept Econs U Pa Dept Econs 3718 Locust Walk Philadelphia PA 19104-6297 E-mail: FDiebold@sas.upenn.edu.

DIEDE, NANCY, nursing educator; b. Dickinson, N.D. d. Lyle O. and Norma L. Vaagen; m. Quinn Diede. BSN, U. N.D., 1977, MS, 1984. RN, Okla.; bd. cert. clin. specialist in cmty. health nursing, AACN. Home health and maternal-child nurse Polk County Nursing Svc., Crookston, Minn., 1977-82; instr. nursing U. N.D., Grand Forks, 1984-88, asst. prof. nursing, 1988-91, Langston U., Tulsa, Okla., 1991-93; quality assurance provider specialist Health Cor, Inc., Tulsa, 1993-94; dir. nursing edn. Bacone Coll., Muskogee, Okla., 1994—, chair health sci. divsn., 2000—01, dean Sch. Health Scis., 2001—. Mem. ANA, Okla. Nurses Assn., Sigma Theta Tau. Office: Bacone Coll 2299 Old Bacone Rd Muskogee OK 74403 E-mail: dieden@bacone.edu.

DIEDERICH, J(OHN) WILLIAM, internet publisher; b. Ladysmith, Wis., Aug. 30, 1929; s. Joseph Charles and Alice Florence (Yost) D.; m. Mary Theresa Klein, Nov. 25, 1950; children: Mary Theresa Diederich Evans, Robert Douglas, Charles Stuart, Michael Mark, Patricia Anne Diederich Irelan, Donna Maureen (dec.), Denise Brendan, Carol Lynn Diederich Weaver, Barbara Gail, Brian Donald, Tracy Maureen Diederich Jorgensen, Theodora Bernadette Diederich Davidson, Tamara Alice Diederich Williams, Lorraine Angela. PhB, Marquette U., Milw., 1951; MBA with high distinction, Harvard U., 1955. With Landmark Comm., Inc., Norfolk, Va., 1955-90, v.p., treas., 1965-73, exec. v.p. fin., 1973-78, exec. v.p. community newspapers, 1978-82, exec. v.p., CFO, 1982-90, fin. cons., 1990—; internet pub. Wide World Web Internat., Incline Village, 1996—. Chmn. bd. dirs. Landmark Cmty. Newspapers, Inc., 1977-88; pres. Exec. Productivity Sys., Inc., 1982-88, LCI Credit Corp., 1991-93, Landmark TV Inc., 1991—, LTM Investments, Inc., 1991—; v.p., treas., KLAS, Inc., 1994-95; v.p. Internet Express, Inc., 1994-2000; pres., bd. dirs. Wide World Web Internat., 1995—, TWC Holdings, Inc., 1996—; instr. Boston U., 1954, Old Dominion U., 1955-59. Lt. col. USMC, 1951-53, USMCR, 1953-71. Baker scholar Harvard U., 1955. Mem. SAR, Nat. Assn. Accts., Am. Numismatic Assn., Nat. Geneal. Soc., Wis. Geneal. Soc., Pa. Geneal. Soc., Sigma Delta Chi. Roman Catholic. Home and Office: PO Box 7677 925 Jupiter Dr Incline Village NV 89451

DIEDERICH, MICHAEL DAVID, JR., lawyer; b. Bronxville, N.Y., June 14, 1954; s. Michael and Dorothy Elizabeth Diederich; m. Brigitte M. Gulliver, Sept. 24, 1988; children: M. Patrick, Victoria, Sean. BS, U. Vt., 1976; JD, Northwestern U., Portland, Oreg., 1980; LLM, Pace U., White Plains, N.Y., 1992. Bar: N.Y. 1981, Mass. 1981, U.S. Dist. Ct. (so. dist.) N.Y. 1982, U.S. Ct. Appeals (2d cir.) 1989, U.S. Supreme Ct. 1991. Pvt. practice, Stony Point, N.Y., 1981-84, 93—; assoc. Witte, Lestz & Hogan, P.C., Bronxville, N.Y., 1988-89; asst. county atty. Westchester and Rockland County Atty.'s Office, White Plains, New City, N.Y., 1989-93. Contbr. articles to profl. jours. Mem. Stony Point Planning Bd., 1994-95; mem., chmn. Rockland County Environ. Mgmt. Coun., New City, 1982-84. LTC. JAGC USAR, 1984—. Mem. ABA, Assn. Trial Lawyers Am., N.Y. State Bar Assn., Rockland County Bar Assn., Natl. Employment Lawyers Assn. Avocation: alpine ski racing. Office: 361 Rte 210 Stony Point NY 10980-3500

DIEDRICH, RICHARD JOSEPH, architect; b. South Bend, Ind., May 8, 1936; s. Arthur Joseph and Lucille D.; m. Francyne L. Diedrich (div. 1980); children: Dawn Marie, Lisa Lee, Andrea Lynn; m. Linda P. Diedrich. BArch, U. Ill., 1961, MArch, 1962. Archtl. designer Richardson Severns Scheeler & Assocs., Champaign, Ill., 1961-62; design critic U. Ill. Sch. Architecture, Champaign, 1961-62; archtl. designer Swensson & Kott, Nashville, 1963-64; architect, v.p. Miller Waltz Diedrich, Architects, Milw., 1965-77; pres. MWD Archs., Atlanta, 1978-80, Diedrich Archs., Atlanta, 1980-97; pres., exec. v.p. Diedrich/NBA, Atlanta, 1997—2002; pres. Diedrich LLC, Atlanta, 2002—. Instr. profl. devel. course Harvard Grad. Sch. Design, 1990—. Co-author: Golf Course Development and Real Estate; archtl. works include: Avondale Sta., Med. Ctr. Sta., Atlanta Rapid Transit, S. Miami Sta. of Miami Rapid Transit, Vt. Sunset Sta., L.A. Rapid Transit, Student Ctr., U. Ga., Bloomingdale's Stores, Boca Raton, Palm Beach Gardens, Mall of Am., Neiman Marcus Stores, Scottsdale, Ariz., Troy, Mich., Honolulu, Short Hills, N.J., King of Prussia, Pa., Paramus, N.J., Tampa, Fla., Coral Gables, Fla., Plano, Tex., Orlando, Fla., Grand Cypress Clubhouse, Orlando, English Turn Clubhouse, New Orelans, Golf Club Ga., Atlanta, Country Club North, Dayton, Old Overton Club House, Birmingham, Cherokee Country Club, Atlanta, Naples Nat. Golf Club, Sun City Hilton Head amenity facilities, Aerial Tram, Stone Mountain Park, Atlanta, Village Clubhouse, Kapaulua, Maui, Hawaii. Mem. Whitefish Bay Bd. Appeals, 1968-71; v.p. North Decatur Youth assn., 1975-76; bd. dirs. Lake Burton Civic Assn., 2002-03. Margaret T. Biddle scholar, 1960. Mem. AIA (past pres. Milw. chpt., six design awards, two S.E. regional awards, four Ga. AIA awards), Wis. Architect (past pres.). Home and Office: 8 Brookhaven Dr Atlanta GA 30319

DIEDRICH, WILLIAM FRANK, management consultant, speech professional; b. Detroit, Mich., June 21, 1949; s. Elmer H. and Esther E. Diedrich; m. Deborah J. Redmon, Aug. 4, 1970 (div. Jan. 1985); m. Peggy Ann Diedrich, July 14, 1994; 1 child, Melanie Rose Nadia. BA, Western Mich., 1971, MS in counseling and personnel, 1978. Tchr. Gibraltor (Mich.) Pub. Sch., 1972—74, Lawton (Mich.) Cmty. Sch., 1974—85; therapist Assoc. Therapy Cons., Paw Paw, Mich., 1984—85; cons. Meta Learning Sys., Paw Paw, 1986—87; facilitator Avis Enterprises, Ann Arbor, Mich., 1988—91; trainer U Mich., Ann Arbor, 1991; author,cons.,spkr. Transformative Leadership Sys., East Lansing, Mich., 1991—2003. Author: The Rd. Home: The Journey Beyond The Spiritual Journey, 2001; contbr. articles. Avocations: travel, running, music, spiritual growth. Office: Transformative Leadeship Sys 622 Hillcrest East Lansing MI 48823 Home: 622 Hillcrest East Lansing MI 48823

DIEDRICK, GERALDINE ROSE, retired nurse; b. Chgo., 1928; d. Milton Edward and Rose Agnes (Michalski) Goodman; divorced; 1 child, Scott Wesley (dec.). BS, Calif. State U., L.A., 1966; MS, UCLA, 1968. RN. Nurse State of Calif., 1960-83; dir. nursing Met. State Hosp., Norwalk, Calif., 1977-83; cons. in mental health, devel. disabilities. Recipient letter of commendation State of Calif., 1974-77. Mem. Am. Nurses Assn., Nat. League Nursing, Am. Assn. Devel. Disabilities, Calif. Nurses Assn. (svc. awards), Am. Hosp. Assn., World Future Soc., Town Hall Calif. Lutheran.

DIEDTRICH, ELMER, state legislator; b. Glenross, S.D., Mar. 31, 1927; m. Deloris Diedtrich; children: Dehain, Melanie. BS, No. State U., 1956. Territory sales Std. Oil Co. Ind., 1952-54; pres., owner ins. co./ins. brokerage, 1956-2000; mem. S.D. Ho. Reps., Pierre, 1989-2000, S.D. Senate from 3d dist., Pierre, 2001—. Petty officer USN, 1945-47. Mem. Eagles, Elks, Moose, Shriners. Republican. Lutheran. Office: 819 E Broadway Apt B2 Pierre SD 57501 E-mail: eandd@nvc.net.

DIEDWARDO, MARY ANN PASDA, artist, writer; b. Sept. 19, 1953; BA in Theatre Arts, Pa. State U., 1975; MA in English, Lehigh U., 1980; postgrad. in edn., Calif. Coast U. Originator theatre program for sr. citizens and youth Northampton C.C., 1977-79; artist-in-residence Pasda Studios Sch. of Art, Bethlehem, Pa., 1976—; dir. Mary Ann P. DiEdwardo Corr. Study, Bethlehem, 1994—; tchr. Pa. Homeschoolers HS diploma program AP English Online,

1999—2002; prin., owner Mary Ann P. DiEdwardo Pub.; lectr. De Sales U., 1979—2002, Allentown Coll., 1979—2002. Author: 79 books. Mem. Mortar Bd., Modern Lang. Assn., Phi Beta Kappa, Phi Kappa Phi, Sigma Tau Delta. E-mail: diedwardo7@enter.net.

DIEFENBACH, DALE ALAN, retired law librarian; b. Cleve., Aug. 14, 1933; s. Walter Ewald and Alice Naomi (Austin) D.; m. Olga Maspaitella, Jan. 20, 1973; 1 stepson, Andrew Ivan Ward. BA, Baldwin-Wallace Coll., 1955; MLS, U. Hawaii, 1970. Fgn. svc. officer U.S. Dept. State, 1961-68; reference libr. Cornell U. Law Libr., Ithaca, N.Y., 1970-87; sr. reference libr. Harvard U. Law Libr., Cambridge, Mass., 1987-97, ret., 1997; reference libr., adj. assoc. prof. law libr. Barry U. Sch. Law Euliano Law Libr., 1998—2003. Lt. (j.g.) USNR, 1956-60, Philippines. Recipient Ficken Meml. award Baldwin-Wallace Coll., Berea, Ohio, 1988. Mem. ALA, Am. Assn. Law Librs. Democrat. Home: 500 Windmeadows St Altamonte Springs FL 32701-3572 E-mail: deepbrook@earthlink.net.

DIEFENBACH, VIRON LEROY, dental, public health educator, university dean; b. Balt., Feb. 9, 1922; s. William Louis and Ardie Gertrude (Von Wachter) D.; m. Virginia Kent, Dec. 3, 1944 (div. Jan. 1956); children: Kathryn Louise, Arthur Karl; mem. Adele Larson Henderson, Apr. 18, 1956; children: William Henderson, Sue Henderson. Student, Western Md. Coll., 1940-42, Pratt Inst. Engring., 1943, Harvard U., 1944; DDS, U. Md., 1949; MPH, U. Pitts., 1954. Diplomate Am. Bd. Dental Pub. Health. Dental intern USPHS Hosp., Norfolk, Va., 1949-50, various clin. assignments, 1950-52, dental pub. health field tng., 1954-55; asst. regional dental cons. USPHS, Chgo., Office Personnel, Office Surgeon Gen., USPHS, Washington, 1955-56; information dir. USPHS Dental Public Health, 1957-59; regional dental cons. USPHS, Denver, 1959-61; dep. chief div. USPHS (Dental Health), Bethesda, Md., 1962-65, acting chief and dir., 1966; asst. surgeon gen. USPHS, 1966-70; asst. exec. dir. Am. Dental Assn., 1970-72; prof. health resources mgmt. Grad. Sch. Public Health, U. Ill., 1973-88, prof. emeritus, from 1988, assoc. dean, 1977, dean, 1978-83, dean emeritus, from 1988. With AUS, 1942-44; USPHS, 1949-70. Recipient Scholarship Gold medal U. Md., 1949, Meritorious Service medal USPHS, 1966; Disting. Dental Alumnus award Balt. Coll. Dental Surgery, U. Md., 1999. Fellow APHA (past sect. chmn., sec., John W. Knutson award 1999), AAAS, Am. Coll. Dentists; mem. Commd. Officers Assn. USPHS (mem. exec. bd., past chmn. bd.), ADA, Am. Assn. Pub. Health Dentists, Fedn. Dentaire Internationale. Achievements include early scientific studies on use of fluorides in preventive dentistry, innovations in dental education and feasibility of dental care insurance. Home: Silver Spring, Md. Deceased.

DIEFFENBACH, CHARLES MAXWELL, emeritus law educator, lawyer; b. Westfield, N.Y., July 9, 1909; s. Arthur Warren and Mary Bertha (Meyer) D.; m. Gladys Ethel Gray, June 29, 1935; children— Gretchen Dieffenbach Gehlbach, Roxann Huschard. B.S. in Civil Engring., U. Ala., 1934; postgrad. Bus. Sch., Harvard U., 1934-35; M.A. in Econs., U. Cin., 1948; J.D., Ohio No. U., 1957. Bar: Ohio 1957. Meat packing exec. H.H. Meyer Packaging Co., Cin., 1935-55; from asst. prof. to prof. law Chase Coll. Law, Cin., 1957-65; prof. bus. adminstrn. N.Mex. State U., Las Cruces, 1965-68; prof. law Chase Coll. Law, No. Ky. U., Highland Heights, 1968 79, prof. law emeritus, 1980— , vis. prof. law Detroit Coll. Law, 1979-80. Served to maj. U.S. Army, 1942-46, ETO. Republican. Episcopalian. Home: 7300 Dearwester Dr Apt 542 Cincinnati OH 45236-6127 Office: No Ky U Chase Coll Law 508 Nunn Hall Highland Heights KY 41076

DIEFFENBACH, OTTO WEAVER, III, real estate company executive; b. Key West, Fla., Aug. 4, 1953; s. Otto, Jr. and Alice Jean Thompson D.; m. Susan S., Jan. 16, 1982 (div. May 1997); children: Otto Weaver IV, Claire T., Bryan V.; m. Elisabeth I., June 12, 1997 (div. Sept. 2002). BSEM, USAF Acad., 1975; MBA, Golden Gate U., 1977; MS in Aeronautics, USAF Test Pilot Sch., 1978. With USAF, 1975-81, advanced through ranks to capt., 1979; flight test engr. Air Force Flight Test Ctr., Edwards AFB, Calif., 1975-78; sys. test engr. USAF Armament Divsn., Eglin AFB, Fla., 1979-81; sr. staff engr. Martin Marietta, Denver, 1981-83; regional ops. mgr. air traffic control divsn. Lockheed Martin, LA, 1984-93; mgr. bus. devel. Advanced Devel. Ops., San Diego, 1993-96; dir. bus. devel. L3 Comm., Anaheim, Calif., 1997-99; dir. mktg. Racal Comm., Bonn, Germany, 1999—2000; v.p. mktg. Spirent Comm., Calabasas, Calif., 2000—01; dir. Lockheed Martin, Lawndale, Calif., 2002—03; prtnr. Dieffenbach Real Estate, Rancho Santa Fe, Calif., 2003—. CEO Ariel Ltd., San diego, 1988-90. Developer autonomous precision approach and landing sys. (Best of Whats New award Popular Sci. 1997). Recipient Nat. Conservation award Dept. of Energy, 1980, Industry Leadership award Dubai-Partnership 21, 1995, Outstanding Tech. Paper award Air Traffic Control Assn., 1995, Aviation & Space award Popular Sci., 1996. Avocations: sailing, car restoration, water skiing. Home: PO Box 990 Rancho Santa Fe CA 92067 Office: Dieffenbach Real Estate 6013 La Granada Rancho Santa Fe CA 92067 E-mail: ottod@sbcglobal.net.

DIEHL, CAROL LOU, library director, retired, library consultant; b. Milw., Aug. 10, 1929; d. Gilbert Fred and Erna Lou (Braeger) Doepke; m. Russell Phillip Diehl, Aug. 8, 1953; children: Holly Lou Diehl Nelson, Jeffrey Phillip. BS, U. Wis., Madison, 1951; MA, U. Wis., Oshkosh, 1971. Tchr. English, libr. Port Washington (Wis.) High Sch., 1951-54, Minoqua (Wis.) High Sch., 1954-55; libr. Ozaukee High Sch., Fredonia, Wis., 1964-65, Vernon County Tchrs. Coll., Viroqua, Wis., 1965-67; libr. media coord. Manawa (Wis.) Sch. Dist., 1973-77; dir. libr. media svcs. Sch. Dist. of New London, Wis., 1977-95; ret., 1995; lectr. U. Wis., Oshkosh, 1993, 95—. V.p. Coun. on Libr. and Network Devel., Madison, 1979; pres. Lake Forest Bd. Dirs., Eagle River, Wis., 1987-89; libr. cons. Thern Design Ctrs. Inc., 1994. Author: (with others) School Library Media Annual, 1985-87; news corr. Appleton (Wis.) Post Crescent, 1971-81; contbr. articles to profl. jours. Past mem. Fox Valley Symphony League; mem. exec. com. Waupaca County Grand Ole Party, chair, 1994-97, vice chmn., 1991-94; del.-at-large White House Conf. Libr. and Info. Svcs., 1991; trustee Sturm Meml. Libr., 1996-2002, treas., 1998—; mem. bd. edn. Sch. Dist. of Manawa, 1997-2003; mem. Manawa City Appeals Bd., 1999-2002. Named Wis. Sch. Libr. Media Specialist of Yr. Assn. Ednl. Comm. and Tech., 1992. Mem. ALA (councilor-at-large 1998—, legis. com. 1986-91, ALA White House Conf. Libr. and Info. Svcs., 1995—, chair, 1992-95, legis. assembly chair 1989-90, membership com. 1995-99, ALTA legis. com. 1998-99, chair, 1999—, Outstanding Libr. Advocate of 20th Century 2000), AASL (legis. chmn. 1987-95, planning and implementation task force White House Conf. 1990-92, Disting. Sch. Adminstrs. chair 2001-02), Wis. Libr. Assn. (fed. rels. coord. 1990-91), Assn. Wis. Sch. Adminstr., Wis. Edn. Media Assn. (legis. com. 1986-93, Excellence award 1992), Futurae Club of Manawa, Manawa Federated Women's Club, Phi Delta Kappa. Republican. Lutheran. E-mail: diehl@netnet.net.

DIEHL, DEAN R. engineering company executive; b. Abbottstown, Pa., Oct. 28, 1934; s. Samuel J. and Bessie E. Diehl; m. Eileen Anna Diehl, Feb. 1, 1959; children: Michael P., Cathy D. Budd, Brian J. BS in Engring., Pa. State U., 1956. Sales engr. Jeffrey Mfg. Co., Columbus, Ohio, 1956-68; dist. mgr. Fairfield Engring. Co., Marion, Ohio, 1968-79; ENCO divsn. mgr. Derkin & Wise Inc., Toledo, 1979-86; pres. Diehl Innovative Conveyor Engring. Inc., Toledo, 1986—. With U.S. Army, 1957-64. Mem. Mensa Ltd. Office: Diehl Inc 6848 Woodmeadow Dr Toledo OH 43617

DIEHL, DEBORAH HILDA, lawyer; b. Troy, N.Y., Feb. 13, 1951; d. Warren S. and Norma K. (Apple) D.; 1 child, Alexandra Ellen. Student, U. de Rouen, France, 1971-72; BA, St. Lawrence U., 1973; JD, Syracuse U., 1976; postdoctoral, George Washington U., 1978-79. Bar: N.Y. 1977, D.C. 1981, Ohio 1982, Md. 1987. Atty. USDA, Washington, 1976-81; assoc. Thompson, Hine & Flory, Columbus, Ohio, 1981-87, Semmes, Bowen & Semmes, Balt., 1987-90, ptnr., 1990-95, Whiteford, Taylor & Preston, Balt., 1995—. Pres. Mt. Royal Improvement Assn., 1995—97; chair Midtown Cmty. Benefits Dist. Mgmt. Authority, 1998—2000, dir., 1995—2001, Midtown Devel. Corp., 2000—; participant Leadership Md., 1997; mem. U. Md. Balt. County Tech. Ctr. Adv. Bd., 2001—. Mem.: ABA, Bar Assn. City Balt., Md. State Bar Assn. (bus. law sect. coun. 1998—, chair 2002—03). Avocations: bicycling, travel, economic development.

DIEHL, DOLORES, communication arts director; b. Salina, Kans., Dec. 28, 1927; d. William Augustus and Martha (Frank) D. Student pub. schs., Kans., 1941-45. Bus. rep. Southwestern Bell Telephone Co., St. Louis and Kansas City, Mo., 1948-49, Mountain States Telephone Co., Denver, 1949-50; edn. coord. pub. rels. Pacific Telephone/AT&T, L.A. and San Diego, 1950-83; cons. Bus. Magnet High Sch., L.A. Unified Sch. Dist., 1977-79; pres. First Calif. Acad. Decathlon, 1979; owner Community Connection, L.A., 1983—; mgr., dir. DelMar Media Arts, Burbank, Calif., 1985-89; mgr. Susan Blu workshops Blupka Prodns., L.A., 1989—; ptnr., dir. animation and commls. voiceover workshops Elaine Craig Voicecasting, Hollywood, Calif., 1989—; freelance performer, voiceover L.A., 1990—; mgr. Sounds Great Film Looping Workshops, L.A., 1992-93; owner Voiceover Connection, L.A., 1994-95; pres. Voiceover Connection, Inc., L.A., 1995—. V.p. pub. rels. San Diego Inst. Creativity, 1965-67; exec. com. San Diego's 200th Anniversary Celebration, 1967; pub. rels. dir. Greater San Diego Sci. Fair, 1963-68. Mem. Better Bus. Bur. Recipient Dedication to Edn. award Industry Edn. Coun., Calif., 1964; named one of seven top voiceover trainers Animation Mag., 1999. Mem. L.A. Area C. of C. (bd. dirs. women's coun.), Calif. Magnet Sch. Consortium of Cities (chairperson), Industry Edn. Coun. Calif., L.A. and San Diego (past pres.), Bus. and Profl. Women's Club, Delta Kappa Gamma (hon.). Republican. Methodist. Home and Office: 691 Irolo St Apt 212 Los Angeles CA 90005-4110 E-mail: doloresdiehl@earthlink.net.

DIEHL, HARRY ALFRED, chemist, genealogist; b. York, Pa., Mar. 2, 1923; s. Ralph Eugene and Anna (Danner) D.; m. Margaret Marie Ehrhart, June 28, 1945; children: Rodney Eugene, Diane Susan Foster, Lori Elaine Vogan, Brian Eric. BA, Gettysburg Coll., 1948; MS, Pa. State U., 1951; MEd, U. Del., 1976. Tchr. chemistry William Penn Sr. High Sch., York, Pa., 1948-50; rsch. chemist E.I. DuPont, Wilmington, Del., 1951-83; genealogist pvt. practice, Wilmington, Del., 1977—. Author: Ancestors and Descendants of Francis & Lucinda Cornbower, 1982, Diehl-Deal-Dill-Dale Families of America, Vol. I, 1989. Cub Scout leader Boy Scouts Am., Wilmington, 1958-65, asst. scoutmaster, 1970-82; trustee, elder Presbyn. Ch., Wilmington, 1957-62, 95-2002. Sgt. USAF, 1941-46. Mem. Pa. Genealogy Soc. (bd. dirs. 1983-84), Del. Genealogy Soc. (bd. dirs., pres. 1981-82), Genealogy Soc. Sthn. Ctrl. Pa. (pres. 1992-93), Md. Genealogy Soc., Masons. Avocations: mineralogy, history.

DIEHL, JAMES HARVEY, church administrator; m. Dorothy Diehl; 4 children. BA, Olivet Nazarene U., 1959; DD, N.W. Nazarene U., 1990. Adminstr. MidAm. Nazarene U., 1973-76; dist. supt. Ch. of Nazarene, Nebr. and Colo., 1979-89; pastor Atlanta First Ch., 1976-79, Nazarene chs. in Iowa, Denver First Ch. of Nazarene, 1989-93; gen. supt. Ch. of the Nazarene, Kansas City, Mo., 1993—. Contbr. articles to Herald of Holiness, Preacher's Mag., Bread, World Mission, others; condr. daily radio program, weekly TV broadcast. Bd. trustees MidAm. Nazarene U., Nazarene Theol. Sem., Nazarene Bible Coll., N.W. Nazarene U.; chmn. bd. N.W. Nazarene U. Mem. Ch. Of Nazarene. Office: Ch of the Nazarene 6401 Paseo Blvd Kansas City MO 64131-1213

DIEHL, RICHARD KURTH, retail business consultant; b. Chgo., July 6, 1935; s. George Henry and Agnes Martha (Kurth) D.; m. Barbara Louise Clark, June 9, 1957; children— Clark Kurth, Scott Richard, Stacy Louise. BA, Beloit Coll., 1957; postgrad., Harvard U., 1957-58; MBA, U. Chgo., 1959. With brand mgmt. staff Procter & Gamble, Cin., 1959-62; v.p., account supr. Needham, Harper & Steers, Chgo., 1963-68; Dir. mktg. Kimberly-Clark Corp., Neenah, Wis., 1968-70; pres., chief exec. officer Purnell, Inc., Santa Monica, Calif., 1970-72; v.p., chief operating officer Theta Cable TV, Santa Monica, 1972-74; exec. v.p., chief savs. officer Western Fed. Savs. and Loan Assn., Los Angeles, 1974-80; exec. v.p., a founding officer Centurion Savs. and Loan Assn., Century City, Calif., 1980-8'; founder Diehl & Assocs., Los Angeles, 1983—; pres., CEO Stockwell and Binney/Royale, La Habra, Calif., 1992—. Mem. Citizens Adv. Council Los Angeles Schs., 1970-72. Woodrow Wilson fellow, 1957-58; Harvard Austin fellow, 1957-58; Sears Roebuck Found. fellow, 1958-59 Mem. Phi Beta Kappa, Sigma Alpha Epsilon. Clubs: Riviera Tennis, Santa Monica Tennis Patrons. Lodges: Rotary. Home: 17117 Ave Herradura Pacific Palisades CA 90272-2002

DIEHL, RICHARD PAUL, lawyer; b. Toledo, Dec. 25, 1940; s. Clair Bertrand and Josephine Frances (Kwiatkowski) D.; m. Laura Gean Carpenter, Mar. 26, 1966; children: Michelle, Michael. BSME, U. Mich., 1963; MBA, Tulane U., 1972; JD, U. Detroit, 1983. Bar: Mich. 1983, U.S. Dist. Ct. (ea. dist.) Mich. 1983, U.S. Supreme Ct. 1988, U.S. Ct. Fed. Claims 1990, U.S. Ct. Appeals (6th cir.) 1991, U.S. Ct. Appeals (fed., D.C. cirs.) 1992), U.S. Dist. Ct. (we. dist.) Mich. 1996. Commd. 2d lt. U.S. Army, 1963, advanced through grades to col., ret., 1986; pres. Diehl & Sobczak, PC, Troy, Mich., 1986-99; with Inst. for Def. Analyses, Alexandria, Va., 1999—. Adj. prof. bus. Am. Tech. U., Killeen, Tex., 1977-78; adj. prof. law U. Detroit, 1987-89. Contbr. articles to profl. jours. Decorated 2 Silver stars, five Bronze stars, 2 Purple Hearts, 2 Legions of Merit Meritorious Svc. medal, Army Commendation medal, 3 Air medals, Cross of Gallantry. Mem. Am. Def. Preparedness Assn., Assn. U.S. Army, U. Mich. Alumni Assn., Elks. Avocations: hunting, fishing, sports. Office: 1105 Kingsview Ave Rochester Hills MI 48309-2510 E-mail: rpdiehl@aol.com.

DIEHL, STEPHEN ANTHONY, human resources consultant; b. N.Y.C., Mar. 15, 1942; s. Anthony Stephen and Paula (Kula) D.; m. Barbara Lynn Marschman, Aug. 3, 1968. BS, L.I. U., 1963; postgrad. in bus., NYU, 1967-73. V.p. mktg. dir. Green Point Savs. Bank, Bklyn., 1969—77; sr. v.p., human resources dir. Green Point Bank, N.Y.C., 1977—95. Dir. Human Resources N.Y. Road Runners Club (N.Y. City Marathon), 1996-2001; officer, dir. Soc. for Human Resources Mgmt., N.Y. chpt., 1995-2001. Mem. Savs. Banks Mktg. Forum N.Y. State (chmn. 1973-74), N.Y.C. Mktg. Forum (chmn. 1975-76), Human Resources Officers Forum (chmn. 1980-81), Savs. Banks Officers Forum (pres. 1986-87). Avocations: photography, video, stereo. Fax: (919) 678-8558. E-mail: sadiehl@aol.com.

DIEHL, TIMOTHY JEREL, social services administrator; b. Kankakee, Ill., Mar. 6, 1949; s. Brice Gerald and June Iris (Ward) D.; m. Eva Marie Baker, June 23, 1971 (div. July 1979); children: Matthew Christian, Andrew Preston; m. Deborah Alexandra Charren, Sept. 7, 1980; children: Hannah Laurel, Zachary Ervin. Student, Olivet Nazarene Coll., 1967-70; MEd, Antioch U., 1979; cert. advanced grad. study, Boston U., 1989. Lic. cert. social worker, Mass. Ombudsman, asst. master Hampshire Coll., Amherst, Mass., 1973-79; dir. Agawam (Mass.) Youth Commn., 1979 81; exec. dir. Cmty. Multi-Svc. Agy., Northampton, Mass., 1981-86; program dir. Franklin County Mental Health Assn., Greenfield, Mass., 1986-88; dir. program devel. and planning Tri-County Youth Programs, Inc., Northampton, Mass., 1988-89; assoc. dir. Hampshire Cmty. Action Commn., Inc., Northampton, 1989—. Cons. Cmty. Multi-Svc. Agy., Northampton, Mass., 1986-87; bd. dirs. U. Mass./Five Coll. Fed. Credit Union. Founding mem. Dem. Town Com., Worthington, Mass., 1982; founder, mem. Cmty. of Reconciliation, Amherst, Mass., 1973; mgr., coach Little League Baseball, Worthington, 1983; pack leader Cub Scouts Am., Worthington, 1985; trustee Bd. Common Sch., Amherst. Recipient Helping Hands for Youth award Cmty. Multi-Service Agy., Northampton, 1988. Fellow Am. Orthopsychiatric Assn.; mem. Nat. Soc. Fundraising Execs. Democrat. Home: 155 South St Northampton MA 01060-4018 E-mail: timothy@diehl.net.

DIEHM, JAMES WARREN, lawyer, educator; b. Lancaster, Pa., Nov. 6, 1944; s. Warren G. and Verna M. (Hertzler) D.; m. Cathleen M. Hohmeier; children: Elizabeth Ann, Rebecca Jane. BA, Pa. State U., 1966; JD, Georgetown U., 1969. Bar: D.C. 1969, V.I. 1975, Pa. 1988. Asst. U.S. atty., Washington, 1970-74; asst. atty. gen. Atty. Gen.'s Office U.S. V.I., St. Croix, 1974-76; from assoc. to ptnr. Isherwood, Hunter & Diehm, St. Croix, 1976-83; U.S. atty. U.S. V.I., 1983-87; prof. law Widener U., 1987—. Bar examiner U.S. V.I. Bar, 1979-87. Mem. ABA. Republican. Lutheran. Office: Widener U Sch Law 3800 Vartan Way PO Box 69382 Harrisburg PA 17106-9382

DIEHR, DAVID BRUCE, retired social service administrator; b. Toledo, Ohio, June 4, 1939; s. Harlan E. and Lillis R. (Consaul) D.; m. Kathryn D. Welsh, Apr. 2, 1966; 1 child, Erik W. AB, Coll. William and Mary, 1961; postgrad., George Williams Coll., Chgo., 1961-63. Phys. dir. YMCA of Xenia-Greene County, Xenia, Ohio, 1964-68, YMCA of Joliet, Ill., 1968-74; exec. dir. N.W. YMCA of San Antonio, Tex., 1974-77; gen. dir. YMCA of Ctrl. Tex., Waco, 1977-86; group v.p. YMCA of Tucson, 1987-95; nat. field cons. YMCA of the USA-West, San Mateo, Calif., 1995-2001. Treas., bd. dirs. Calif. Collaboration for Youth, Sacramento, 1995-2000 Mem. Assn. Profl. Dirs. (chpt. prs. 1980-83, dist. v.p. 1983-86), U.S. Power Squadron, Omicron Delta Kappa. Republican. Presbyterian. Avocations: sailing, tractor restoration.

DIEKEMA, ANTHONY J. college president emeritus, educational consultant; b. Borculo, Mich., Dec. 3, 1933; m. Jeane Waanders, Dec. 20, 1957; children: Douglas, David, Daniel, Paul, Mark, Maria, Tanya. BA, Calvin Coll., Grand Rapids, Mich., 1956; MA in Sociology and Anthropology, Mich. State U., 1958, PhD in Sociology, 1965. Field interviewer Bur. Bus. Research Mich. State U., East Lansing, 1955-56, asst. dir. housing, 1957-59, instr., lectr. sociology and anthropology, 1959-64, admissions counselor, 1959-61, asst. dir. admissions and scholarships, 1961-62, asst. registrar, 1962-64; asst. dean admissions and records, research assoc. in med. edn. and asst. prof. sociology U. Ill. Med. Center, Chgo., 1964-66, dir. admissions and records, asst. prof. sociology and edn., 1966-70, asso. chancellor, asso. prof. med. edn., 1970-76; pres. Calvin Coll., 1976-96, pres. emeritus. Mem. adv. bd. NBD Grand Rapids, 1983-95 Trustee Blodgett Meml. Med. Center, Grand Rapids, 1979-91; bd. dirs. Met. YMCA, 1979-93, Project Rehab, 1978-84; treas. Back-to-God Hour Radio Com., 1970-76; chmn. Synodical Com. on Race Relations, 1973-75; pres. Strategic Christian Ministry Found., 1969-73; mem. bd. curators Trinity Christian Coll., 1969-73, chmn., 1972-73, mem. presdl. search com., 1972-73, NCAA coun. 1983-87, Pres'. commn. 1987-91. Mem. Am. Assn. Pres.'s Ind. Coll. and Univs. (bd. dirs. 1978-84, 88-91), Nat. Assn. Ind. Colls. and Univs. (bd. dirs. 1991-94), Assn. Ind. Colls. and Univs. Mich. (exec. com. 1979-84), Am. Assn. Higher Edn., Am. Sociol. Assn., Soc. Health and Human Values, Soc. Values in Higher Edn., Nat. League Nursing (accreditation com. 1974-79), Alpha Kappa Delta, Rotary. Office: Calvin Coll Grand Rapids MI 49546 E-mail: ajdiek@aol.com.

DIEKMAN, MARK A. animal science educator; b. Vincennes, Ind., Sept. 16, 1948; s. Earl William and Dorothy Marie Diekman; m. Patti L. O'Callaghan, Dec. 17, 1977; children: Casey, Brian. BS, Purdue U., 1970, MS, 1972; PhD, Colo. State U., Ft. Collins, 1978. Rsch. assoc. Iowa state U., Ames, 1978-79; asst. prof. animal sci. Purdue U., West Lafayette, Ind., 1979-84, assoc. prof. animal sci., 1984-89, prof. animal sci., 1989—. Contbr. articles to profl. jours.; mem. editl. bd., Jour. Animal Sci., 1998—. Coach, West Lafayette Youth Baseball, 1988-98, Athletic Amateur Basketball, 1992-96. Recipient Outstanding Faculty Alumni award, Vincennes U., 2000. Mem. AAAS, Am. Soc. Animal Scis., Biology of Reprodn. Assn. (reviewer 1994--), Alpha Zeta. Avocations: golf, softball, basketball, house repairs. Home: 927 N Salisbury St West Lafayette IN 47906 Office: Purdue U Dept Animal Scis West Lafayette IN 47907 E-mail: mdiekman@purdue.edu.

DIEKMANN, GILMORE FREDERICK, JR., lawyer; b. Evansville, Ind., Jan. 14, 1946; s. Gilmore Frederick Sr. and Mabel Pauline (Daniel) K.; children: Anne Westlake, Andrew Gilmore, Matthew Frederick. BSBA, Northwestern U., 1968, JD, 1971. Bar: Calif. 1972, U.S. Dist. Ct. Calif. (no., ea., cen. and so. dists.) Calif. 1972, U.S. Ct. Appeals (9th cir.) 1972, U.S. Supreme Ct. 1978. Assoc. Bronson, Bronson & McKinnon, San Francisco, 1971-78, ptnr. labor and employment law, 1979-99, chmn., mng. ptnr., 1991-93, chmn. labor, employment dept., 1993-99; ptnr. Seyfarth Shaw, San Francisco, 1999—, chmn. no. Calif. labor dept., 1999—. Author and speaker in field. Mem. ABA, Def. Rsch. Inst., Am. Employment Law Coun., Order of Coif. Republican. Lutheran. Home: 901 Powell St # 6 San Francisco CA 94108 Office: Seyfarth Shaw 101 California St Ste 2900 San Francisco CA 94111-5858 E-mail: gdiekmann@sf.seyfarth.com.

DIELMAN, RAY WALTER, radiologic scientist, natural hygienist, medical herbalist; b. Napoleon, Ohio, Dec. 25, 1938; s. Walter Carl and Gail Ann (Fenstermaker) D.; m. Diane Tahy, June 1961 (div. 1968); children: Joseph Scott, David Jon; m. Roberta Schreiber, June 1968 (div. 1980); m. Beverly Beavers Bryan, Oct. 16, 1994. Student, Defiance Coll., 1956-59; radiologic technologist diploma, St. Joseph Hosp. Sch., Ft. Wayne, Ind., 1962; nuclear medicine technologist cert., U. Mich., 1962; OPM, Harvard U., 1975; doctor of Naturopathy, Trinity Coll. Natural Health, 1997. Cert mgmt. cons., radiologic, nuclear medicine technologist. Supr. nuclear medicine U. Mich. Hosp., Ann Arbor, 1962-63; dir. nuclear medicine Mercy Hosp & Med. Ctr., Chgo., 1963-64; cons., nuclear medicine Picker Corp., White Plains, N.Y., 1964-67; pres. Dielman Cons., Inc., Chgo., 1967-88; dir. dept. of radiology Loyola U. Med. Ctr., Chgo., 1980-83; co-owner Island Cinema & Theatre, Sanibel Isle, Fla., 1983-87; mgr. Fla. Dept. Health Bur. Radiation Control, Tampa, 1988—. Assoc. mem., com. Conf. Radiation Control Progr m Dirs., Frankfort, Ky., 1989-96; vice chmn. Radiation Control Rsch. and E In. Found.; del. Internat. Com. of Radionuclide Metrology, London, 1976-85; chmn. Manatee County Health Care Adv. Bd., 1995—; mem. instnl. biosafety com. U. South Fla., 1999—, mem. instnl. rev. bd., 2002—. Co-editor/author: Essentials Nuclear Medicine Technology, 1970; contbr. articles to profl. jours. Recipient scholarship Am. Cancer Soc., 1962. Avocations: tennis, golf, sailing, skiing, travel. Home: Unit 208 2725 Terra Ceia Bay Blvd Palmetto FL 34221-5934

DIEM, RICHARD A. social studies educator, educational consultant; b. Kansas City, Mo., Dec. 13, 1945; s. William M. and Rose (Chawkin) D.; m. Roberta Ann Lewin, July 12, 1970; children: Joshua, Sarah. BS, Bradley U., 1967; MS, So. Ill. U., 1969; MA, Colo. State U., 1971; PhD, Northwestern U., 1975. Cert. tchr. Tex., Mo., Colo., Ill. Tchr. Maine North High Sch., Des Plaines, Ill., 1971-75; clin. prof. No. Ill. U., DeKalb, 1974-75; prof. U. Tex., San Antonio, 1975—, vice provost, dean honors coll. Contbr. articles to profl. jours.

DIEMER, EMMA LOU, composer, music educator; b. Kansas City, Mo., Nov. 24, 1927; d. George Willis and Myrtle (Casebolt) D. MusB, Yale U., 1949, MusM, 1950; PhD, Eastman Sch. Music, 1960; LHD (hon.), Ctrl. Mo. State U., 1999. Composer-in-residence Arlington (Va.) Schs., 1959-61; composer, cons. pub. schs., Arlington and Balt., 1964-65; prof. theory and composition U. Md., College Park, 1965-70, U. Calif., Santa Barbara, 1971-91. Organist Ch. of the Reformation, Washington, 1962—71, Ch. of Christ, Santa Barbara, 1973—84, 1st Presbyn. Ch., Santa Barbara, 1984—2001. Composer of over 100 choral and instrumental compositions including Music for Woodwind Quartet, 1976, Four Poems of Alice Meynell for Soprano and Chamber Ensemble, 1977, Symphony No. 2, 1980, Suite for Orchestra, 1981, Suite of Homages, 1985, Church Rock, 1986, Variations for Piano, 4 Hands, 1987, String Quartet No. 1, 1987, Serenade for String Orch., 1988, Concerto for Marimba, 1990, Concerto for Piano, 1991, Sextet, 1992, Four Biblical Settings for Organ, 1992, Fantasy for Piano, 1993, Kyrie for Mixed Chorus, Organ, and Piano - 4 Hands, 1993, Santa Barbara Overture, 1995, Gloria for Mixed Chorus, 2 Pianos and Percussion, 1996, Psalm 122 for Bass Trombone and Organ, Psalm 121 for Organ, Brass and Percussion, Psalms for Flute and Organ, Psalms for Trumpet and Organ, Psalms for Percussion and Organ, 1998, Latin Mass, 2000, Homage to Tschaikovsky, 2000, Piano Trio, 2000, Quartet for Piano and Brass, 2001, Songs for the Earth, 2002; composer-in-residence Santa Barbara Symphony, 1990-92. Fulbright scholar, 1952-53; grantee Ford Found. Young Composers, 1959-61, Kindler Found. Commn., 1963, Nat. Endowment Arts, 1980-81; Kennedy Ctr. Friedheim award, 1992. Mem. ASCAP (ann. awards 1962—), Am. Guild Organists (composer of yr. 1995), Internat. Alliance for Women in Music, Am. Music Ctr., Mu Phi Epsilon (award of merit 1995). Democrat. Presbyterian. Avocations: reading, electronic and computer music. E-mail: eldiemer@cox.net. *A composer who succeeds in some measure must have talent, encouragement, strong self-motivation, an almost obsessive need for self-expression through music, a belief in the importance of one's own contribution, the ability to appraise one's own work, the desire, at least part of the time, to communicate.*

DIENER, ANDREW M. educator; b. Tuscola, Ill. PhD, Tex. A&M, 1999. Lectr. Tex. A&M, College Station, 1999—2000. Vis. asst. prof. Rhodes Coll., Memphis, 2000—00. Fellow, State of Tex., 1991—92, 1992—93. Fellow: MAA (assoc.). Home: 36 S Merton Memphis TN 38112 Office: Christian Bros U 650 East Parkway Memphis TN 38112 Personal E-mail: adiener@cbu.edu.

DIENER, BETTY JANE, finance educator; b. Washington, Sept. 15, 1940; d. Edward George and Minnie (Feild) Diener; m. Robert D. Bell, 1987 (dec. 1993). AB, Wellesley Coll., 1962; MBA, Harvard U., 1964, DBA, 1974. Account exec. Young & Rubicam, Inc., N.Y.C., 1964-70; product mgr. Am. Cyanamid Co., Wayne, NJ, 1970-72; asst. dean Sch. Bus. Case Western Res. U., Cleve., 1974-79; dean Sch. Bus. Adminstrn. Old Dominion U., Norfolk, Va., 1986-87; provost, vice-chancellor acad. affairs U. Mass., Boston, 1987-88, prof. mktg., 1987—2002, spl. asst. to chancellor econ. devel., 1993-94. Pres. Environ. Bus. Coun. New Eng., Inc., 1995—97. Contbr. articles to profl. publs. Mem. Citizens Coun. Chesapeake Bay, 1986—87; adviser Jr. League, 1963—64, Plans for Progress, 1968—70, Leadership Met. Richmond,

1980—82; mem. Mass. Gov.'s Adv. Com. Sci. and Tech., 1988—90, Mayor's Task Force Empowerment Zones, 1994; mem. cmty. working group Mass. Mil. Reservation, 1997—2000; pres. Provincetown (Mass.) Repertory Theater, 2002, bd. dirs., 2001—; commr. Norfolk Indsl. Devel. Authority, 1979—82; bd. dirs. Norfolk Conv. and Visitors Bur., 1979—82, Norfolk C. of C., 1979—82, Greater Norfolk Corp., 1986—87, Va. Orch. Group, 1982—87, Va. Stage Co., 1986—87, Karamu Ho., 1975—79, Woodruff Hosp., 1975—79, Women's City Club Cleve., 1976—79; mem. adv. com. state and local govt. programs John F. Kennedy Sch. Govt., Harvard U., 1986—88. Named Outstanding Working Woman, Glamour Mag., 1979; named one of 10 Outstanding Career Women of Decade, 1984; recipient Honor award, Soil Conservation Soc., 1984; Fulbright scholar, 2001. Democrat. Home: 9304 NE 9th Pl Miami Shores FL 33138 Office: Barry Univ Andreas Sch of Business Miami Shores FL 33138 E-mail: bejade@aol.com.

DIENER, EDWARD FRANCIS, psychologist, researcher; b. Glendale, Calif., July 25, 1946; s. Frank C. and Mary Alice Diener; m. Carol I. Diener; children: Marissa, Mary Beth, Robert, Kia, Susan. BS, Calif. State U., Fresno, 1968; PhD, U. Wash., 1974. Prof. psychology U. Ill., Urbana, 1974—. Editor: Jour. Personality and Social Psychology, 1998-2003, Well-Being, 1999, Culture and Subjective Well-Being, 2000; contbr. over 150 articles to profl. jours. Recipient Distinguished Scientist Lectr. award, APA, 2001. Fellow APA, Am. Psychol. Soc., Soc. Personality and Social Psychology (pres. 2001), Internat. Soc. Quality of Life Studies (pres. 1997-98, Distinguished Scientist award 2000), Experimental Psychology; mem. Internat. Soc. Rsch. on Emotions. Office: U Ill Psychology Dept 603 E Daniel St Champaign IL 61820

DIENER, ERWIN, immunologist; b. Lucerne, Switzerland, Jan. 6, 1932; arrived in Can., 1970; s. Reinhold and Alice (Treichler) D.; m. Eva Schaufelberger, 1957. PhD, U. Zurich, 1963. Rsch. fellow Inst. for Radiobiology, Zurich, 1960-64; Roche fellow Walter and Eliza Hall Inst., Melbourne, Australia, 1964-67, rsch. fellow, 1967-70; prof. U. Alta., Edmonton, Can., 1970-73, prof., head dept. immunology, 1973-88, prof. emeritus, 1989—. Fellow Royal Soc. Can.

DIENER, ROYCE, corporate director, retired healthcare services company executive; b. Mar. 27, 1918; s. Louis and Lillian (Goodman) Diener; m. Jennifer S. Flinton; children: Robert, Joan, Michael, Dianne. BA, Harvard U.; LLD (hon.), Pepperdine U. Comml. lending officer, ivnestment banker, various locations, 1972; pres. Am. Med. Internat., Inc., Beverly Hills, Calif., 1972—75, pres., CEO, 1975—78, chmn., CEO, 1978—85, chmn. bd., chmn. exec. com., 1986—89. Bd. dirs. Calif. Econ. Devel. Corp., Acuson, Inc., Advanced Tech. Venture Funds, Am. Health Properties, AMI Health Svcs., plc., Constorium 2000. Author: Financing a Growing Business, 1966, 4th edit., 1995. Mem. bd. visitors Grad. Sch. Mgmt., UCLA Med. Ctr.; mem. vis. com. Med. Sch. and Sch. Dental Medicine, Harvard U.; bd. dirs. L.A. Philharm. Assn.; bd. dirs. L.A. chpt. ARC; bd. dirs. Heritage Sq. Mus., Santa Monica, Calif.; trustee Contemporary Mus., Honolulu; chmn. bd. UCLA Med. Ctr. Capt. USAF, 1942—46, PTO. Decorated D.F.C. with oak leaf cluster. Mem.: Calif. Bus. Round Table (bd. dirs.), Calif. C. of C. (bd. dirs.), L.A. C. of C. (bd. dirs.), Outrigger Canoe Club (Honolulu), Marks Club (London), Riviera Country Club (L.A.), Calif. Yacht Club, Regency Club, Harvard Club.

DIENER, THEODOR OTTO, plant pathologist, researcher; b. Zurich, Switzerland, Feb. 28, 1921; arrived in 1949, 1949, naturalized, 1955; s. Theodor Emanuel and Hedwig Rosa (Baumann) D.; m. Sybil Mary Fox, May 11, 1968; children from previous marriage: Theodor W., Robert A., Michael S. Diploma, Swiss Fed. Inst. Tech., 1946; DSc, Nat. Swiss Fed. Inst. Tech., 1948. Asst. Swiss Fed. Inst. Tech., Zurich, 1946—48; plant pathologist Swiss Fed. Exptl. Sta., Waedenswil, 1949—50; asst. prof. plant pathology R.I. State U., Kingston, 1950; asst. plant pathologist Wash. State U., Prosser, 1950—55, assoc. plant pathologist, 1955—59; rsch. plant pathologist agr. rsch. svc. USDA, Beltsville, Md., 1959—88, collaborator agr. rsch. svc., 1988—97; prof. botany, sr. staff sci. ctr. agr. biotech./dept. Botany U. Md., College Park, 1988—98, acting dir. Ctr. Agr. Biotech., 1991—92, Disting. Univ. prof., 1994—98; Disting. prof. U. Md. Biotech. Inst., 1998, Disting. univ. prof. emeritus, 1999—. Univ. lectr., rsch. instr.; Regent's lectr. U. Calif., Riverside, 1970; A.W. Dimock lectr. Cornell U., 1975, Andrew D. White prof.-at-large, 1979—81; James Law disting. lectr. N.Y. State Coll. Vet. Medicine, 1981; disting. lectr. Boyce Thomson Inst. for Plant Rsch., 1987, Hong Kong U. Sci. and Tech., 1992; Ernest Everett Just Meml. lectr. Howard U., Washington, 1990; disting. prof. U. Md., Coll. Park, 1994—98, Biotech Inst., 1998; guest lectr. Israel Soc. for Microbiology, Rehovot, 1994, Royal Swedish Acad. of Scis., Stockholm, 1997, Swedish Agrl. U., Uppsala, 1997, Royal Netherlands Acad. Arts and Scis., Amsterdam, 1998, Alexander von Humboldt Assn., Washington, 1999. Author: Viroids and Viroid Diseases, 1979; editor: The Viroids, 1987; assoc. editor: Virology, 1967—71, mem. editorial com.: Ann. Rev. Phytopathology, 1970—74, Annales de Virologie, 1980—88; contbr. articles to profl. jours. Named to USDA Sci. Hall of Fame, 1989; recipient Campbell award, Am. Inst. Biol. Scis., 1968, Superior Svc. award, USDA, 1969, Disting. Svc. award, 1975, Alexander von Humboldt award, 1975, Wolf prize in Agr., 1987, U.S. Nat. medal of Sci., 1987, Gov.'s citation, State of Md., 1988, E.C. Stakman award, U. Minn., 1988. Fellow: Am. Acad. Arts and Scis., N.Y. Acad. Scis., Am. Phytopath. Soc.; mem.: AAAS, NAS, German Acad. Natural Scientists, Leopoldina. Achievements include discovery of novel class of pathogens (viroids), 1971. Home: 11711 Battersea Dr PO Box 272 Beltsville MD 20704-0272 Office: U Md Ctr For Agrl Biotech College Park MD 20742-0001 E-mail: diener@umbi.umd.edu.

DIENHOFFER, MARGARET QUIGLEY, historian, educator; b. Auburn, N.Y., Mar. 16, 1956; d. John Vincent and Ethel Gwendolyn Quigley; m. Robert Ludwig Dienhoffer, Oct. 12, 1984; children: Robin Quigley, Daniel John. AA, Cayuga County C.C., 1976, AAS, 1977; BS, SUNY, Buffalo, 1979; MS, SUNY, Cortland, 2002. Tchr. h.s. social studies Summit Sch., Cayuga/Onondaga BOCES, Auburn, NY, 2000—02; tchr. world history I and II Moravia Ctrl. Sch., 2002—. Student coun. advisor Moravia Ctrl. Sch. Leader Girl Scouts USA, Moravia, NY, 1992—2002; asst. leader Cub Scouts USA, Moravia, NY, 2000—02; parish coun. rep. Good Shepherd Cath. Cmty., Moravia, NY, 1998—2000; mem. Masterworks Chorale, Skaneateles, NY, 1995—98. Mem.: Orgn. Am. Historians, N.Y. State Coun. for Social Studies, Phi Alpha Theta. Independent. Roman Catholic. Avocations: horseback riding, swimming, skiing. Office: Moravia Ctrl Sch PO Box 68 Moravia NY

DIENSTAG, CYNTHIA JILL, lawyer; b. N.Y.C., Apr. 17, 1962; d. Jack Jacob Helman and Roni Helene (Turk) Setti; div.; children: Marissa, Allison. AA, Fla. State U., 1981; BS, Fla. Internat. U., 1983; JD, U. Miami, 1988. Bar: Fla. 1989; cert. family law mediator, Fla. Judicial asst. Cir. Judge Frederick N. Barad, Miami, Fla., 1982-85; assoc. Brenner & Dienstag, P.A., Miami, Fla., 1988-90, Weissman & Greenblatt, Ft. Lauderdale, Fla., 1990-91, Elser, Greene & Hodor, Miami, 1991-93; pvt. practice Coconut Grove, Fla., 1993—. Active lectr., participant Schs.; mem. professionalism and ethics com., family law com., Dade County Bar, 1992-97; mem. support issues and gen. masters com. Fla. Bar. Mem. ABA (family law sect.), Fla. Assn. Women Lawyers. Office: Mellon Fin Ctr 1111 Brickell Ave Ste 2025 Miami FL 33133 Fax: 305-285-0688.

DIENSTAG, ELEANOR FOA, corporate communications consultant; b. Naples, Italy; d. Bruno Garibaldi and Lisa (Haimann) Foa; m. Jerome Dienstag (div. 1978); children: Joshua Foa, Jesse Paul. BA, Smith Coll., Northampton, Mass. Asst. editor Random House/Harper & Row, N.Y.C.; editor/writer Monocle Mag., N.Y.C.; cultural columnist Genesee Valley Newspapers, Rochester, N.Y.; sr. mgr., speechwriter Am. Express, N.Y.C., 1978-83. Freelance journalist, N.Y.C., 1983—; lit. resident Yaddo Y., Va. Ctr. for Creative Arts, 95; lectr., book pub. columnist and reviewer in field. Author: Whither Thou Goest, 1976, In Good Company: 125 Years at the Heinz Table, 1994; contbr. articles, essays and feature stories to N.Y. Times, Harper's, N.Y. Observer, McCalls; columnist New Choices Mag. Recipient Merit award for speechwriting Internat. Assn. Bus. Comm., N.Y., Merit award Am. Express Mgmt. Newsletter, Outstanding Mem. award Women in Comm. Mem. Am. Soc. Journalists and Authors (past pres.). Home and Office: Eleanor Foa Assocs 435 E 79th St New York NY 10021-1034 E-mail: efoa@compuserve.com.

DIENSTAG, JOSHUA FOA, political scientist, educator; b. NYC, May 23, 1965; PhD, Princeton U., 1993. Assoc. prof., assoc. chair U. Va., Charlottesville, 1992—. Author: Dancing in Chains: Narrative & Memory in Political Theory. Office: University of Virginia PO Box 400787 Charlottesville VA 22904-4787

DIENSTBIER, DAN, gas and oil company executive; b. 1940; Student, U. Nebr., Creighton U. Exec. v.p. Enron Corp., Houston, pres. gas ops.; also chmn., dir. Transwestern Pipeline Co. subs. Enron Corp., Houston. Office: Dynegy 1000 Louisiana Ste 5800 Houston TX 77002

DIEPHOUSE, DAVID JAMES, humanities educator, historian; b. Grand Haven, Mich., June 30, 1947; s. James and Jeannette D.; m. Evelyn De Jong, Aug. 12, 1970; children: Rachel, Amy, Miriam. AB, Calvin Coll., 1969; MA, Princeton U., 1971, PhD, 1974. Instr. Princeton (N.J.) U., 1973-74; asst. prof. Rutgers U., Newark, 1974-76, Calvin Coll., Grand Rapids, Mich., 1976-79, assoc. prof., 1979-84, prof., 1984—, chair dept. history, 1988-94, dean social scis., langs., literature and arts, 1997—2003. Author: Pastors and Pluralism in Wuerttemberg 1918-1933, 1987; translator: (books) The Natural History of the German People, 1990, Early American Railroads: Franz Anton Ritter von Gerstner's Die Innern Communicationen 1842-1843, 1997. Trustee Grand Rapids Christian Sch. Assn., 1987-90, Chamber Music Soc. Grand Rapids, 1988-99; bd. dirs. Interfaith Dialogue Assn., Grand Rapids, 1998; mem. spkrs. bur. Common Cause, Mich., 1977-78. Recipient Rsch. grant Nat. Endowment for the Humanities, fellowship Deutscher Akademischer Austauschdienst, 1982, 91, fellowship Inst. europaeische Geschichte, 1992, Rsch. grant Am. Philosophical Soc., 1992. Mem. Am. Hist. Assn., Am. Soc. Ch. History (mem. conf. onfaith and history, Latourette prize com. 1988-91), German Studies Assn., Conf. Group on Ctrl. European History. Avocations: music, running, hiking, reading, travel. Office: Calvin Coll 3201 Burton SE Grand Rapids MI 49546 E-mail: ddiephou@calvin.edu.

DIERCKS, CHESTER WILLIAM, JR., capital goods manufacturing company executive; b. Urbana, Ill., Oct. 15, 1926; s. Chester William and Anna (Gude) D.; children: Chester William, III, Lisa Beth; m. Elaine Hall, Oct. 3, 1992. BS in Gen. Engring., Iowa State U., Ames, 1950; MS in Indsl. Mgmt. (Sloan fellow), MIT, 1962. Gen. mgr. med. services, x-ray and splty. transformer div. Westinghouse Electric Co., Pitts., 1950-71; with Allis-Chalmers Corp. (and subs.), 1971-77, dir. Mgmt. Services, v.p., staff exec. Mgmt. Services, group exec., v.p. Indsl. Elec. Group, group exec., v.p. Elec. Products Group, sr. exec. v.p., chief fin. officer, 1976-77; pres., chief exec. officer Siemens-Allis, Inc., 1978-85, Utility Power Corp., Atlanta, 1978-89, ret., 1989. Mem. Industry Sector Adv. Com. to 1974 Trade Reform Act, 1976-77; mem. mgmt. adv. coun. Coll. Mgmt., Ga. Inst. Tech. Bd. dirs. Japan Am. Soc.; mem. bd. visitors Emory U.; trustee emeritus Berry Coll., Mt. Berry, Ga.; past bd. govs. Soc. Alfred P. Sloan Fellows, MIT; elder Peachtree Presbyn. Ch., Atlanta. Served to 1st lt. U.S. Army, 1945-47. Mem. Nat. Elec. Mfrs. Assn. (past bd. govs. mem. long range planning com., chmn. govt. & internat. policy com.), Machinery and Allied Products Inc., Atlanta C. of C. (past exec. com. mem., 1st v.p. bd. dirs.), Fla. Coun. 100, Fin. Execs. Inst., Capital City Club, Lexington Country Club. Home: 4000 Brookside Dr Roswell GA 30076-5558 E-mail: ce2642@aol.com.

DIERCKS, EILEEN KAY, educational media coordinator, elementary school educator; b. Lima, Ohio, Oct. 31, 1944; d. Robert Wehner and Florence (Huckemeyer) McCarty; m. Dwight Richard Diercks, Dec. 27, 1969; children: Roger, David, Laura. BS in Edn., Bluffton Coll., 1966; MS, U. Ill., 1968. Tchr. elem. grades Kettering City Schs., Ohio, 1966-67; children's libr. St. Charles County, Mo., 1968-69; libr. Rantoul (Ill.) H.S., 1970-71; elem. tchr. Elmhurst (Ill.) Sch. Dist., 1971-72; media coord. Plainfield (Ill.) Sch. Dist., 1980—2001, libr. media cons., 2001—03. Evaluator Rebecca Caudill Young Readers' Book Award, 1990-97; LTA adv. com. Joliet Jr. Coll., 2003. Founder, treas. FISH orgn., Plainfield, 1975-78; pres. Ch. Women United, 1974; sec. Plainfield Cmty. TV Access League, 1987-89; treas. Plainfield Congl. Ch., 1983-88; bd. dirs. Cub Scouts, 1983-86; leader, mem. Girl Scouts USA, Plainfield, 1985—; mem. Bolingbrook (Ill.) Cmty. Chorus, 1986-90, Plainfield Area Cmty. Chorus, 1999—. Mo. State Libr. scholar, 1967, Naperville chpt. Valparaiso U. Guild, treas., 1993-95. Mem.: ALA, Am. Assn. Sch. Librs., Ill. Sch. Libr. Media Assn. (membership chmn. 1992—93, mem. awards com. 1994—96, disaster relief chmn. 1996—97, treas. 2001—03), Plainfield Athletic Club (sec. 1984—86), Rotary (treas. 1994—95, bd. dirs. 1994—, v.p. 1995—96, pres.-elect 1996—97, pres. 1997—98, sec. Plainfield chpt. 2003—), Beta Phi Mu, Pi Delta, Delta Kappa Gamma (Beta Rho) (treas. 1993—97). Home: 13440 S Rivercrest Dr Plainfield IL 60544-8979

DIERCKS, ELIZABETH GORMAN, elementary education educator; b. Harrisburg, Pa., Aug. 12, 1944; d. Jerome Clement and Martha (Stoll) G.; m. Gregory Louis Diercks, July 24, 1982. BS, Pa. State U., University Park, 1966; MEd, U. Md., 1975. Advanced profl. cert. Tchr. Fairfax County (Va.) Pub. Schs., 1966-68, Prince George's County (Md.) Pub. Schs., 1968—, grade level chairperson, 1970-97. Early intervention coord. Ft. Washington Elem. Sch., Prince George's County, 1997—. Assoc. Nat. Trust for Historic Preservation, Washington; resident assoc. Smithsonian Assocs., Washington; sustainer The Kennedy Ctr., Washington. Mem. NEA, Md. State Edn. Assn., Prince George's County Edn. Assn., Nat. Mus. Women in the Arts (charter mem.), Nat. Mus. of the Am. Indian (charter mem.), Kappa Delta. Avocations: travel, hiking, swimming, fitness training. Office: Ft Washington Forest Elem Sch 1300 Fillmore Rd Fort Washington MD 20744-2935

DIERCKS, WALTER ELMER, lawyer; b. Irvington, N.J., July 6, 1945; s. Elmer Jules and Evelyn Sophie (Lauster) D.; m. Mary-Jane Atwater, Apr. 16, 1977; children: Emily Jane, Gillian Ruth. B.Chem. Engring., Rensselaer Poly. Inst., 1967; JD, U. Va., 1972. Bar: Va. 1972, D.C. 1973, U.S. Supreme Ct. 1984. Engr. Bethlehem Steel Corp., Balt., 1968-69; Devel. engr. Diamond Shamrock Corp., Balt., 1969-70; pub. Charlottesville (Va.) Consumer, 1970-72; atty. FTC, Washington, 1972-76; dep. asst. dir. compliance Bur. Consumer Protection, 1976-77; gen. counsel, sec. Washington Star Co., 1977-81; ptnr. Rubin, Winston, Diercks, Harris & Cooke, LLP, Washington, 1981—. Chmn. Alexandria (Va.) Landlord-Tenant Relations Bd., 1976; mem. Alexandria Charter Rev. Commn., 1980-81, Alexandria Democratic Com., 1979-81, 83-85. Recipient award excellence FTC, 1977 Mem. ABA Unitarian Universalist. Home: 304 Lamond Pl Alexandria VA 22314-4907 Office: 6th Fl 1155 Connecticut Ave NW Washington DC 20036-4306 E-mail: wdiercks@rwdhc.com.

DIERDORF, DANIEL LEE (DAN DIERDORF), sports commentator, football analyst, former professional football player; b. Canton, Ohio, June 29, 1949; m. Debbie D.; children: Dana, Kelly(dec.), Katherine;children: Dan, Kristen. Student, U. Mich. Football player St. Louis Cardinals, 1971—83; with Sta. KMOX, St. Louis, 1974—; sports dir. Sta. KMOV-TV, St. Louis, 1987—; football analyst CBS NFL broadcasts, 1985—87, ABC Monday Night Football broadcasts, 1987—99; NFL football analyst CBS Sports, 1999—. Named to NFL Pro-Bowl Team, 1974—78, 1980. Office: CBS Sports 51 W 52nd St New York NY 10019-6119

DIERKS, RICHARD ERNEST, veterinarian, educational administrator; b. Flandreau, SD, Mar. 11, 1934; s. Martin and Lillian Ester (Benedict) D.; m. Eveline Carol Amundson, July 20, 1956; children— Jeffrey Scott, Steven Eric, Joel Richard. Student, S.D. State U., 1952-55; BS, U. Minn., 1957, DVM, 1959, MPH, PhD, U. Minn., 1964; MBA, U. Ill., 1985. Diplomate Am. Coll. Vet. Microbiologists, Am. Coll. Vet. Preventive Medicine. Supervisory microbiologist Communicable Disease Ctr., Atlanta, 1964-68; prof. coll. veterinary medicine Iowa State U., Ames, 1968-74; head dept. veterinary sci. Mont. State U., Bozeman, 1974-76; dean Coll. Veterinary Medicine U. Ill., Urbana, 1976-89, prof., dean emeritus, 1989—; dean Coll. Veterinary Medicine U. Fla., Gainesville, 1989-97, prof., dean emeritus, 1997—. Mem. tng. grant rev. com. Nat. Inst. Allergy and Infectious Diseases, 1973-74 Contbr. articles on virology, immunology and epidemiology to profl. jours. Served with USPHS, 1964-67. Career Devel. awardee Nat. Inst. Allergy and Infectious Diseases, 1969-74, Nat. Acad. Practitioners, 1995. Mem. Am. Vet. Medicine Assn., Am. Soc. Virology, Am. Soc. Microbiologists, Am. Assn. Immunologists, Am. Assn. Vet. Lab. Diagnosis, Colo. Vet. Medicine Assn., Soc. Exptl. Biology and Medicine, Gamma Sigma Delta, Phi Kappa Phi, Phi Zeta. Clubs: Rotary. Republican. Lutheran. Office: 13651 N 115th St Longmont CO 80504-8017 E-mail: dierksrichardcar@msn.com.

DIERS, HANK H. drama educator, playwright, director; b. Dubuque, Iowa, Sept. 23, 1931; s. Hermann Henry and Elfriede Johanna (Langholz) D.; m. Doris Elaine Blumreich, Sept. 5, 1953; children: Daniel, Deborah, John, Alicia, David. BA, Wartburg Coll., 1953; postgrad., U. Dubuque, 1949, Loras Coll., 1953-54; MA, U. Ill., 1957, PhD, 1965; postgrad., Carnegie-Mellon U., 1987. Faculty drama dept. U. Miami, Coral Gables, Fla., 1960-86, chmn. dept. drama, 1967-83, prof., 1968-86, dir. univ. theatres, 1973-83; acting dir. theatre, guest cons. SUNY, Old Westbury, 1983-86; dean fine arts and communications Susquehanna U., Selinsgrove, Pa., 1986-98; dir. theatre Florida Gulf Coast U., 1998—. Exec. dir. So. Shakespeare Repertory Theatre, Coconut Grove Playhouse, 1961-68; exec. producer Ring Theatre Arts Festival Theatre, 1969— ; founder Fumpets Puppet Theatre, ASTA Fair, Amsterdam, Netherlands, 1970 Dir.: (plays) Hamlet, 1968, The Royal Hunt of the Sun, 1968, The Boy Friend, 1971 (winner Am. Coll. Theatre Festival 1972), The Apple Tree, 1970, Jacques Brel (winner Am. Coll. Theatre Festival 1973), Anastasia, Miami New World Festival of Arts, 1982, Glass Menagerie, Equity, L.I., 1986; original producer: plays including Miami; playwright: Doctor, Doctor, 1971, 307 Defense of Hermann Goering, 1972, Mine Eyes Have Seen the Glory, 1976; (playwright, producer) This Is The Lord's Doing, 1987; creator (one man show) Muhlenberg, Middletown and Trappe, 1989, (prodr. PBS Spl., Emmy award nomination) Christmas from Susquehanpa; originator Noel, Cole, Ira and George, Sugden Theatre, Naples, Fla., 1999; exec. dir. Ft. Myers Classical Repertory Theatre, 1999; adaptor Cher Chez The Doctor, Foulds Theatre, Ft. Myers, 1999. Mem. alumni bd. Wartburg Coll., 1968—, Omni Theatre.; Trustee 3rd Century Bicentennial. Served with AUS, 1954-56. Recipient Silver medal for Photography N.Y. World's Fair, 1964, Angel award for Theatre The Miami Herald, 1966, 67, Iron Arrow U. Miami, 1970; Pa. Playwright fellow, 1988-89; grantee Luth. Ch. Am., 1986-87. Mem. Am. Theatre in Higher Edn., Soc. Collegiate Journalism (Medal of Merit 1996), Speech Communications Assn., Southeastern Theatre Conf. (sec. 1962-64), Fla. Theatre Conf. (v.p.), Pa. Theatre Assn., Internat. Coun. Fine Arts Deans, Fla. Arts Congress (dir.), Soc. Collegiate Journalists, Alpha Psi Omega, Alpha Phi Gamma, Omicron Delta Kappa, Alpha Epsilon Rho. Lutheran (Dade County council 1969-72). Office: Florida Gulf Coast U Fort Myers FL 33965-0001

DIERSEN, DAVID JOHN, financial consultant; b. Chicago Heights, Ill., Sept. 29, 1948; s. John Robert and Esther Dorothy (Balgemann) D.; m. Karen Annette Gassner, Apr. 1, 1978. Student, U. Ill., Chgo., 1966-1968; BS in Mgmt., No. Ill. U., 1970; MBA, Loyola U., Chgo., 1976; MS in Acctg., De Paul U., 1980; MS in Fin. Markets and Trading, Ill. Inst. Tech., 1997. CPA, Ill. Mgr. retail sales Firestone Stores, Chicago Heights, 1970-71; revenue officer IRS, Chgo., 1971-76, spl. procedures staff adv., 1976-80; evaluator GAO, Chgo., 1980-86, sr. evaluator, 1986-97; cons. Wheaton, Ill., 1997—. Arbitrator Nat. Assn. Securities Dealers Regulation, Chgo., 1998—, Better Bus. Bur., 2001—; treas. Adversity.net, 1999—. Trustee Milton Twp. Cemeteries Authority, 2001—; webmster Milton Twp., 2001—; Rep. precinct committeeman, 1999—; Ill. editor GOPUSA.com, 2000—; webmaster Milton Twp. Rep. Ctrl. Com., 2000—; dir. Taproot Reps. Ill., 2002—; treas. Ill. Ctr. Right Coalition, 2003—. Mem.: ASPA, AICPA, Am. Assn. Polit. Cons. (bd. dirs. Midwest chpt. 2001—), Am. Bd. Forensic Accts. (cert.), Internat. Assn. Fin. Engrs., Nat. Assn. Fin. Svc. Auditors (cert.), Fed. Mgrs. Assn., Inst. Mgmt. Accts., Fed. Investigators Assn., Assn. Cert. Fraud Examiners (cert.), Ill. CPA Soc. (mem. membership com. 1989—97), Inst. Internal Auditors (cert.), Am. Arbitration Assn., Am. Acctg. Assn., Assn. Govt. Accts. (cert., bd. dirs. Chgo. chpt. 1983—96). Republican. Lutheran. Avocations: reading, bicycling, automobiles, travel. Home and Office: 915 Cove Ct Wheaton IL 60187-6326 E-mail: diersen@aol.com.

DIERSING, CAROLYN VIRGINIA, educational administrator; b. Rushville, Ohio, Sept. 13; d. Carl Emerson and Wilma Virginia (Neel) Deyo; m. Robert J. Diersing, Dec. 22, 1962; children: Robert, Timothy, Charles, Sheila, Christina. BA, Ohio State U., 1963; state cert., Ohio Dominican, 1985. Cert. tchr., Ohio. Libr. St. Mary's Sch., Delaware, Ohio, 1979-87; tech. svcs. asst. Beeghly Libr. Ohio Wesleyan U., Delaware, 1987-90, dir. curriculum resource dept. edn., 1990-96; libr. assoc. Westerville Pub. Libr., 1997—. Contbr. poetry to Voices. Mem. ALA, Del. Area Recovery Resources (bd. dirs. 1994-96, treas. 1995, sec. 1996), Ohio Libr. Coun. Office: Westerville Pub Libr Adult Svcs Dept 126 S State St Westerville OH 43081-2095 E-mail: cdiersin@wpl.lib.oh.us.

DIES, GEORGE A. lawyer; b. 1918; married. AB, Georgetown U., 1938; LLB, Columbia U., 1941. Assoc. counsel Gen. Dynamics Corp, 1959—71; gen. counsel Collins & Aikman Corp., 1971—79, v.p and gen. counsel, 1979—, sec. Lt. USNR, 1942—46. Office: Collins & Aikman Corp Office of the General Counsel 210 Madison Ave New York NY 10016

DIESCH, STANLEY LA VERNE, veterinarian, educator; b. Blooming Prairie, Minn., May 16, 1925; s. John Herman and Emma Lillian (Erickson) D.; m. Darlene Ardis Witty; July 22, 1956; children: Lauren, Stephanie. BS, U. Minn., 1951, DVM, 1956, MPH, 1963. Diplomate Am. Coll. Vet. Preventive Medicine and Epidemiology. Asst. prof. Coll. Vet. Med., U. Iowa, Iowa City, 1963-66; asst. prof. U. Minn. Coll. Vet. Medicine, St. Paul, 1966-69, assoc. prof., 1969-73, prof., 1973-95, prof. emeritus, 1995—, dir. internat. programs, 1985-98; prof. Sch. Pub. Health, U. Minn., Mpls., 1973-95. Advisor Pan Am. Health Orgn., Washington, 1971— Contbr. more than 100 articles to profl. jours., 4 chapters to books. Mem. East Buchanan County Sch. Bd., Winthrop, Iowa, 1960; Rep. del., Minn., 1970-85; co-chair nat. Outdoor Speedskating, St. Paul, 1973; dir. CENSHARE, Mpls., 1981-82; chmn. Veterinarians for Reelection of Durenberger, Minn., 1982, 88; bd. dirs. Minn.-Uruguay Ptnrs. Ams., 1981—, pres., 1990-94, chmn. bd., 1995-99; hon. consul of Uruguay in Minn., 1991-96. Recipient Am. Express award Nat. Assn. Ptnrs. Ams., 1984, Internat. Castricone U. Linkage award Nat. Assn. Ptnrs. Ams., 1998, Dummond Peck Hill Lifetime Achievement award Ptnrs. Ams., 2002; WHO travel fellow, 1974; grantee EPA, 1968-71, USDA, 1978. Mem. AVMA (Pub. Svc. award 1987, Internat. Vet. Congress award 1998), APHA (coun. 1971-84), U.S. Animal Health Assn. (com. chair, Appreciation award 1986), Internat. Soc. Animal Hygiene (exec. bd. 1988-2000, pres. 1991-94, Honor award 2000), Minn. Vet. Medicine Assn. (com. chair 1970-75, Disting. Svc. award 1996). Lutheran. Avocations: fishing, hunting, boating. Home and Office: 743 Heinel Dr Saint Paul MN 55113-2152 E-mail: diesc001@tc.umn.edu.

DIESEM, JOHN LAWRENCE, business executive; b. Albuquerque, July 16, 1941; s. Walter Franklin and Glen Ethel (Helpbringer) D.; m. Barbara Jane Willmarth, Feb. 25, 1967 (div. Oct. 10, 1976); m. Kathleen Terese Walsh, Feb. 2, 1979. BA with honors, George Washington U., 1964, MA, 1965; cert. in fin. mgmt., NYU, 1974; advanced profl. cert. in acctg., Pace U., 1992. CPA; cert. prodn. and inventory mgmt., mgmt. cons., mgmt. acct. Group mgr. Electronic Data Sys., N.Y.C., 1970-74; dep. commr. N.Y. State, 1974-75; sr. mgr. Arthur Andersen, N.Y.C., 1975-80; v.p. bus. sys. devel. McGraw-Hill, N.Y.C., 1980-84; sr. mgr. Touche Ross & Co., N.Y.C., 1984-86; dir. strategic sys. planning KPMG Peat Marwick & Co., 1986-89; sr. v.p. sys. tech. Am. Stock Exch., N.Y.C., 1989-92; group v.p. sys. and tech. Simon & Schuster, 1992-93; COO Beta Systems/Kemper Securities, Brookfield, Wis., 1993-95; COO, CFO Guy & O'Neill, Inc., Fredonia, Wis., 1996-99; mgmt. cons. Transitions Ptnr. Co., 1999—2001; mem. bd. govs. 32 deg. Masonic Learning Ctr. for Dyslexia, 2001—. Adj. prof. Bus. Sch., U. Mich., 1995-96, Cardinal Stritch U., Lakeland Coll., 1998—; dir. case study on microcomputer resource ctrs. Bus. Sch., Harvard U., 1981. Dir. George Washington U. dean's alumni adv. bd., 1981-83, mem. bd. vis. sch. bus. pub. mgmt., 1995—. Capt. USAF, 1965-69, Germany, Vietnam; to lt. col. USAFR ret.; grad. Nat. Def. U., Air War Coll., Air Command and Staff Coll., Indsl. Coll. Armed Forces. Decorated Bronze Star, Vietnamese Cross of Gallantry with Palm, Air Force Commendation medal; named Bus. Sch. Alumnus of Yr. George Washington U., N.Y.C., 1991. Mem. AICPA, Inst. Mgmt. Accts., Am. Prodn. and Inventory Control Soc., Royal Order of Jesters, Am. Arbitration Assn. (panel of arbitrators), N.Am. Coun. Info. Mgmt. Execs., Conf. Bd. (past chmn.), N.Y. Athletic Club, Army and Navy Club (Washington), Columbia Golf and Country Club, Cercle Sportif (Saigon, Vietnam), Nat. Assn. Eagle Scouts, Wis. Club, Nat. Sojourners (life, past pres.), Masons (life, past master), Grand Lodge Wis. (past dist. dep. grand master dist. 10), Scottish Rite,

Shriners, Omicron Delta Kappa, Sigma Chi (life), Phi Eta Sigma, Alpha Kappa Psi. Democrat. Episcopalian. Home: 11921 N Lantern Ln Mequon WI 53092-1567 also: Miller Rd Claverack NY 12513 Fax: 425-795-2348. E-mail: jdiesem@att.net.

DIESTE, TONY, marketing professional; b. Mex. married; children: Alejandro, Ashley. Founer Hawaiian Products, Inc., 1981—84; mgr. several key accts. and new bus. DDB Needham Worldwide Dallas Group; with BBDO; mng. ptnr., dir. devel. and execution of all client Hispanic mktg. activity O&A; pvt. practice as pres., founder, 2002—. Active mem. Hispanic cmty., several Hispanic coms., employee assns., and 2 bds. Named Ad Star of Yr., Am. Adv. Fed., 1993, one of 100 most influential Hispanics in USA, Hispanic Agy. Exec. of Yr., Assn. Hispanic Adv. Agys. ; named to Adv. Hall of Achievement, 1996. Mem.: Assn. Hispanic Adv. Agys. Office: 3102 Oaklawn Ste 109 Dallas TX 75219

DIETCH, HENRY XERXES, judge; b. Bklyn., Nov. 13, 1913; s. Isadore J. and Mary (Krieg) D.; m. Shirley Friedman, Jan. 11, 1941; children: William A., Nancie I., James T. AA, Crane Coll., 1933; JD, John Marshall Law Sch., 1937; grad., Nat. Jud. Coll. Bar: Ill. 1937. Ptnr. Davis, Dietch & Ryan, Chgo., 1954-77; assoc. judge Circuit Ct. Cook County, 1977-84; ret., 1984. Hearing officer Dept. of Labor, Chgo., 1937-46; v.p., dir. Unity Savs. of Park Forest, Ill. to 1977, arbitrator, mediator, 1987—. Columnist: Judiciously Speaking, 1979—; Contbr. articles to profl. jours. Mayor City of Park Forest, 1949-55, corp. counsel, 1958-77, vice chmn. Chgo. adv. bd., Salvation Army, 1969-89, hon. bd. dirs. 1989—. Lt. USAAC, 1942-45, ETO. Recipient Citation of Merit John Marshall Law Sch., 1972. Mem. ABA, Ill. Bar Assn., Chgo. Bar Assn., Am. Judicature Soc., Nat. Inst. Mcpl. Law Officers, Rotary, B'nai B'rith. Clubs: Rotary, B'nai B'rith. Office: 18161 Morris Ave Homewood IL 60430-2108 Fax: 708-799-8805.

DIETDERICH, SHIRLEY (JANE ROHLFING), interior decorator; b. San Dimas, Calif., Oct. 15, 1926; d. Rudolf Frederick Rohlfing and Helen Rebekah (Higgins) Stephenson; m. Rex Dietderich, Aug. 3, 1952; children: Frank, Jean. BA in Decorative Arts, U. Calif., Berkeley, 1950. Cert. interior designer, Calif. From decorator to head decorator Mauerhan's Decorating Studio, Berkeley, 1950-55; freelance interior decorator Shirley Dietderich Interiors, Berkeley, 1957—2002. Leader Campfire Girls, 1964-72; statistician Masters Age Records, 1983—. Named Sports Master of Yr., Bay Area Women's Sports Coun., 1994. Mem. Delta Zeta. Democrat. Presbyterian. Avocations: track and field (sprint, javelin, discus).

DIETEL, JAMES EDWIN, lawyer, consultant; b. Dallas, Sept. 14, 1941; s. Bernhard Herman and Gladys Ellen D.; m. Elizabeth Nathan, May 9, 1964; 1 child, Elizabeth Lindsay. BSME, So. Meth. U., 1964; JD, George Washington U., 1969; LLM in Internat. Trade, Georgetown U., 1977; MBA, U. Pa., 1992. Bar: D.C. 1971, U.S. Dist. Ct. D.C. 1971, U.S. Ct. Appeals (D.C. cir.) 1975, U.S. Supreme Ct. 1975, Va. 1990. Engr. CIA, Washington, 1964-70, program evaluation officer, 1970-73, assoc. gen. counsel, 1979-80, assoc. dep. gen. counsel, 1980—82, dep. gen. counsel, 1982—90, insp. and with office exec. dir., 1990—94, counsel for info. policy, 1994-95; pvt. practice, 1995—. Participant ann. jud. conf. U.S. Ct. Appeals (D.C. cir.), 1986; speaker, ltr. and presenter in field. Author: Leading a Law Practice to Excellence, 1992, Sustaining Law Practice Excellence, 1992, Designing Effective Records Retention Compliance Program, 1993, Leaders' Digest: A Review of the Best Books on Leadership, 1995; chmn. bd. Law Practice Quar.; contbr. articles to profl. jours. Mem. ABA (coun. mem. law practice mgmt. sect., chmn. govt. and pub. sector lawyers divsn.), Coll. Law Practice Mgmt., Cosmos Club, Pi Tau Sigma, Kappa Mu Epsilon, Kappa Alpha.

DIETEL, WILLIAM MOORE, former foundation executive; b. Islip, N.Y., Aug. 14, 1927; s. Frederick William and Zillah Yolanda (Vannuccini) D.; m. Linda Remington, June 16, 1951; children: Elizabeth Lynn, Cynthia Lyon, Lisa Remington, John Frederick, Victoria Moore. AB, Princeton U., 1950; MA, Yale U., 1952, PhD, 1959; postgrad., London U. Inst. Hist. Research, 1953-54. Instr. history U. Mass., Amherst, 1954-59; asst. dean of coll., asst. prof. humanities Amherst Coll., 1959-61; prin. Emma Willard Sch., Troy, N.Y., 1961-70; pres. Rockefeller Bros. Fund, N.Y.C., 1975-87. Chmn. F.B. Heron Found., N.Y. Pres. Pierson-Lovelace Found., chair. F. B. Heron Found., L.A., Brain Mapping Med. Rsch. Orgn., L.A.; trustee Guidestar Philanthropic Rsch. Inc, Williamsburg, Va., Winthrop Rockefeller Charitable Trust, Little Rock; mem. exec. com. Inst. for Philanthropy, London; co-chair pres.'s adv. coun. Am. Farmland Trust. Mem. Univ. Club (N.Y.C.), Cosmos Club (Washington). Office: PO Box 309 Flint Hill VA 22627-0309

DIETER, GEORGE ELWOOD, JR., university official; b. Phila., Dec. 5, 1928; m. Nancy Joan Russell, June 21, 1952; children: Carol Joan, Barbara June. BS in Metall. Engring, Drexel Inst. Tech., 1950; Sc.D., Carnegie Inst. Tech., 1953. Research engr. E.I. duPont Engring Research Lab., Wilmington, Del., 1955-59, research supr., 1959-62; prof., head dept. metall. engring. Drexel Inst. Tech., 1962-69; dean Coll. Engring. Drexel U., 1969-73; dir. Processing Research Inst., Carnegie-Mellon U., 1973-77; dean Coll. Engring. U. Md., College Park, 1977-94, dir. continuous quality improvement, 1994-2000, Glenn L. Martin prof. engring., 2000—. Cons. in field. Author: Mechanical Metallurgy, 1961, 3d edit., 1986, Engineering Design, 1983, 3d edit., 1999. Mem. 1953-55, AUS. Fellow AAAS, Am. Soc. Metals (A.E. White award 1986, Sauver award 1992), Am. Soc. Engring. Edn. (pres. 1993, Lamme award 1996), Minerals, Metals and Materials Soc. (educator award 1994); mem. NAE, AIME, Soc. Mfg. Engrs. (educator award 1987), Fedn. Materials Socs. (pres. 1990-92), Sigma Xi, Tau Beta Pi. Home: 1 Locksley Ct Silver Spring MD 20904-6321 Office: U Md Dept Mech Engring College Park MD 20742-0001 E-mail: gdieter@eng.umd.edu.

DIETER, MELVIN EASTERDAY, retired minister, educator; b. Cherryville, Pa., Oct. 12, 1924; s. Harold David Dieter and Laura Esther Easterday; m. Hallie Arline Kirtz, Dec. 27, 1945; 1 child, Judith Patrice. AB, Muhlenberg Coll., 1947; BTh summa cum laude, Ea. Pilgrim Coll., 1950; MA, Lehigh U., 1951; M Sacred Theology, Temple U., 1953; LLD, Houghton Coll., 1964; PhD, Temple U., 1973. Ordained to ministry Wesleyan Ch., 1952. From instr. to pres. Ea. Pilgrim Coll., Allentown, Pa., 1946-65; acad. dean Houghton (N.Y.) Coll., 1968; gen. sec. edn. The Wesleyan Ch., Marion, Ind., 1968-75; prof., provost, v.p. Asbury Theol. Sem., Wilmore, Ky., 1975-90. Dir. Wesleyan Holiness study project Asbury Theol. Sem., 1987-90; pres. William J. Harley Found., Allentown, 1961-85; chair Houghton Coll. Bd. Trustees, 1992-99. Author: The Holiness Revival of the Nineteenth Century, 1980, The 19th Century Holiness Movement, 1998; co-editor: God is Enough, 1986, The Church, 1984; contbr. articles to scholarly publs. Treas. Allentown Sch. Bd. Authority, 1963-65; pres. Lehigh Valley Pub. Rels. Club, 1965, Wesleyan Theol. Soc., 1977; pastor Chichester, Pa. Wesleyan Ch., 1965-67. Lt. (j.g.) USNR, 1942-46. Recipient Disting. Lifetime Svc. award Wesleyan Theol. Soc., 1996, Outstanding Alumnus award United Wesleyan Coll., 1976. Avocations: genealogy, gardening. Home: 400 Chinquapin Dr Lyndhurst VA 22952-2911

DIETER, RAYMOND ANDREW, JR., physician, thoracic and vascular surgeon; b. Chebanse, Ill., June 19, 1934; s. Raymond Augustus Sr. and Emma Rose Mayme (Witt) D.; m. Bette René Myers, Sept. 29, 1961; children: Raymond III, David, Lisa, Lynn, Deanna, Robert. Student, U. Ill., 1952-56, Olivet Nazarene Coll., 1954; MA in Physiology, U. Ill., Chicago, 1966; BS in Chemistry, U. Ill., Champaign, 1994; MD, Loyola U., 1960. Diplomate Am. Bd. Thoracic Surgery, Am. Bd. Surgery. Intern Cook County Hosp., Chgo., 1960-61; resident in gen. surgery VA Hosp., Hines, Ill., 1963-67, sr. resident in cardiopulmonary surgery, 1967-69; practice specializing in thoracic, cardiovascular surg. Glen Ellyn (Ill.) Clinic, 1969—, pres., 1982-85, also bd. dirs.; mem. staff Hines (Ill.) VA Hosp., 1963-74, Cen. DuPage Hosp., Winfield, Ill., 1969—, pres. staff, 1987-89; mem. staff Loyola U. Med. Ctr., Maywood, Ill., 1969-80, Meml. Hosp. DuPage County, Elmhurst, Ill., 1969—, Delnor Hosp., St. Charles, Ill., 1970-79, Community Hosp., Geneva, Ill., 1970—, Alexian Bros. Med. Ctr., Elk Grove Village, Ill., 1975-79, 93—, Good Samaritan Hosp., Downers Grove, Ill., 1976—, pres. staff, 1979; mem. staff Glendale Heights (Ill.) and Glen Oaks Cmty. Hosp., 1980—, St. Mary's Hosp., Streator, Ill., 1997—. Clin. instr. Stritch Sch. Medicine Loyola U., 1966-71, clin. asst. prof., 1971-80; trustee Ctr. Bank, Glen Ellyn, 1978-90, Lake Shore Bank, Glen Ellyn Found.; internat. lectr. on med. topics; chmn. Glen Ellyn Clinic Facilities, 1987-98, Physicians Benefit trust, 1988-92; pres., chmn. bd. No. Ill. Surg. Ctr., 1989—; pres. DuPage Doctors, Inc., Ctr. for Surgery; bd. dirs., co-founder Cmty. Bank of Wheaton, Glen Ellyn, 1993—, Cmty. Bank Wheaton-Glen Ellyn, 1998; co-founder, pres. Northeast DuPage Surgicenter, 1997—; chmn. bd. dirs., CEO, pres. Masterile, Inc., 1997-99; mem., chmn. negotiating com. Glen Ellyn Clinic, 1999. Author: (with B.R. Dieter and A.C. Mickelson) Mickelson and Peterson Family Sketch, 1970, (with M.C. Sorensen and E.R. Dieter) A Sorensen and Jensen Family Tree, 1975, (with B.R. Dieter, C. Myers, U. Myers, and D. Dieter) A Myers and Remley Family Tree, 1978, (with others) A Witt and (von) Ruehle Family Sketch, 1976, A Hofeling, Janssen, Lehnert, and Meier Family Sketch, 1979, A Dieter Family Tree: Sketches of German Families, 1981, Thoracoscopy for Surgeons, 1994; editor: Thoracoscopy for Surgeons-Diagnostic and Therapeutic, 1995; contbr. numerous articles to profl. jours. and chpts. in med. book. Mgr. Glen Ellyn baseball team, 1970, 71, 78-82; asst. leader 4-H Club, 1975-83; mem. Glenbard South High Sch. Boosters, World Fedn. Drs. Who Respect Human Life, 1980—; pres., bd. dirs. DuPage Med. Found.; pres. Econ. Devel. Coun. Glen Ellyn, 2003. Served with USPHS, 1961-63, with Res., 1982—. Fellow ACS, Internat. Coll. Angiology (editl. bd. 1995—), Internat. Coll. Surgeons (exec. com. 1991—, treas. 1993-94, pres. elect 1995-96, pres. 1997-98, U.S. sect., corp. sec. 1997-2000, pres.-elect 2001-02, pres. 2003—, World body); mem. AMA (Physician's Recognition awards, mem. ho. dels.), Internat. Mus. Surg. Sci. (chmn. bd. dirs. 1991—), Internat. Soc. Circumpolar Health, Internat. Soc. Outdoor Health, Am. Coll. Angiology, Am. Coll. Chest Physicians, Assn. Acad. Surgeons, Am. Soc. Circumpolar Health (charter), Assn. Mil. Surgeons, Assn. Res. Officers, Am. Heart Assn. (coun. 1974—), Nat. Assn. Interns and Residents, Soc. Med. Hist. Chgo., Soc. Critical Care Medicine, Soc. Thoracic Surgeons (membership com.), Ill. State Med. Soc. (trustee 1983-92, chmn. Ill. hosp. med. staff sect. 1985-87, pres., med. adminstrs. ctr. for surgery 1994—), Ill. Thoracic Surg. Soc. (sec. 1981-83, pres. 1984-85), DuPage County Med. Soc. (pres. 1977, mem. numerous coms.), Chgo. Med. Soc., Econ. Devel. Counc. of Glen Ellyn, Ill. (sec. 2000, v.p. 2001-02, pres. 2003), Charles B. Puestow Surg. Soc. (sec., treas. 1966-67, v.p. 1968), Good Samaritan Soc., Ala. Geographic Soc., Kankakee Valley Geneal. Soc., Ill. Geneal. Soc., U. Ill. Alumni Assn., Am. Rabbit Breeders Assn., Silver Marten Club. Clubs: Century (Elmhurst). Lodges: Chebanse Lions (charter), Resurrection Bay (Alaska) Lions. Republican. Roman Catholic. Avocations: alaska, large game animals, outdoor health, farming, fishing. Office: Glen Ellyn Clinic 454 Pennsylvania Ave Glen Ellyn IL 60137-4496 Fax: (630) 858-4575. E-mail: brdrad@aol.com.

DIETER, RICHARD CHARLES, marketing and management professional; b. Northampton, Pa., Feb. 13, 1952; s. Roland George and Martha (Bierman) D.; m. Ann Elaine Urwin, May 21, 1983; children: Amara Katherine, Cary Richard. BA, Valparaiso U., 1973; MDiv, Luth. Sch. Theology, Chgo., 1974. Exec. dir. Orgn. NorthEast, Chgo., 1976-84; dir. pub. rels. Green Mountain Coll., Poultney, Vt., 1986-87; pres., performing artist mgr. and rep. Dieter Assocs., Pitts., 1984—. Cons. on econ. devel. North Side Innovation Ctr., Pitts.; cons. bus. incubator Bus. Devel. Ctrs.; founder, dir. Horizon Inst.; ednl. reform and charter sch. cons. Bd. Dirs. Renewal Project; founder Ctr. Excellence; cons. Thurgood Marhsall Acad. Charter Sch., Cmty. Action Assn. Editor: Neighborhood Development, 1978. Bd. dirs. People's Music Sch., Chgo., 1980-83; founder Thurgood Marshal Acad. Charter Sch. Mem. South Ave. Assn. (mgr.), Phi Mu Alpha Sinfonia. Avocations: fishing, reading, travel, music. Home and Office: 289 W Prospect Ave Pittsburgh PA 15205-2027

DIETER, ROBERT SEAN, physician; b. Winfield, Ill., June 17, 1970; s. Raymond Andrew Jr. and Bette Renee (Myers) D.; m. Erin Leigh Dew, Dec. 6, 1997; 1 child, Robert Sean II. BS, Ill. Wesleyan U., 1991; MD, U. Ill., 1996. Lic. physician, Ill., WI., IN. Intern in surgery U. Tenn. Hosp., Knoxville, 1996; resident in internal medicine U. Ill. Hosp., 1997-99; fellow in cardiovasc. medicine U. Wis., Madison, 1999—, fellow in interventional cardiology and vascular medicine. Asst. editor Wisconsin Medical jour., 2001—, Internat. Jour. Angiology, 2002—. Tutor U. Ill. Coll. Medicine, Chgo., 1992-96, Urban Health Program, Chgo., 1993-95. Dunning scholar U. Ill. Coll. Medicine, 1993. Mem. AMA, ACP, NASPE, Am. Coll. Cardiology, Am. Coll. Chest Physicians, Internat. Coll. Surgeons, Wis. Med. Soc., Ill. State Med. Soc., Ill. State Acad. Sci., Chgo. Med. Soc. (adv. pub. health policy com. 1997-99, continuing med. edn. com. 1998-99), Alpha Omega Alpha. Lutheran. Avocations: hiking, fishing, hunting, reading, writing, traveling.

DIETERICH, DOUGLAS THOMAS, gastroenterologist, researcher; b. Queens, N.Y., Mar. 1, 1951; s. Albert Frederick and Florence Anna (Kilroy) D. BS, Yale U., 1973; M in Health Adminstrn., C.W. Post, 1974; MD, NYU, 1978. Diplomate Am. Bd. Internal Medicine and Gastroenterology. Intern, then resident Bellevue Hosp., N.Y.C., 1978-81, fellow gastroenterology, 1981-83; attending physician NYU Hosp., 1983; vice chair medicine Mt. Sinai Sch. Medicine, N.Y.C., 2002—, prof. medicine. Teaching asst. NYU, 1979-83, clin. instr. medicine, 1983-88, clin. asst. prof., 1988-93, clin. assoc. prof., 1993—; mem. AIDS Clin. Trials Group NIH, 1986-97, Internat. AIDS Soc. U.S.A.; pres. Liberty Med. LLP, N.Y.C., 1996-2002; chmn. HIV Ind. Physicians Assn. Contbr. articles to profl. jours. Bd. dirs. Cmty. Rsch. Initiative on AIDS, N.Y. chpt. Am. Liver Found. Fellow ACP, Am. Coll. Gastroenterology; mem. AMA, Am. Gastroent. Assn., Am. Soc. Gastrointestinal Endoscopy, Am. Soc. Internal Medicine, N.Y. County Med. Soc., N.Y. State Med. Soc., N.Y. Acad. Gastroenterology, Yale Club, Cherry Valley Club, Grand Harbor Club. Republican. Lutheran. Home: 62 Saint James St S Garden City NY 11530-6344 Office: Mt Sinai Sch Medicine One Gustav Levy Pl New York NY 10128 E-mail: douglas.dieterich@msnyuhealth.org.

DIETERT, RODNEY REYNOLDS, immunology and toxicology educator; b. Ft. Lee, Va., Dec. 6, 1951; s. Ralph O. and Beverly (Reynolds) D.; children: Grant C., Matthew W. BS, Duke U., 1974; PhD, U. Tex., 1977. Asst. prof. immunogenetics Cornell U., Ithaca, N.Y., 1977-83, assoc. prof., 1983-89, prof., 1989—, prof. immunotoxicology, 1997—; adj. prof. N.C. State U., 1992—; head grad. program in immunology Cornell U., Ithaca, N.Y., 1989-92, dir. Inst. for Comparative and Environ. Toxicology, 1992-97, prof. immunotoxicology, 1997—, dir. program on breast cancer and environ. risk factors, 2000—; sr. fellow Ctr. for the Environment, 1993-96. Cons. pesticide program EPA, Washington, 1984-86, Embrex, Inc., Research Triangle Park, N.C., 1991-95; panelist Nat. Inst. Environ. Health Scis. (AIDS Therapeutics), Research Triangle Park, 1988, mem. oxidative damage panel, 1997; USDA grant panel mgr., Washington, 1993-94; mem. Am. Inst. Biol. Scis.-Gulf War Illnesses panel Dept. Def., 1995, 97; invited testimony U.S. Congress Clean Water Act, 1995; spkr. at profl. confs. Jour. editor CRC Press, Inc., Boca Raton, Fla., 1986-90, editor book series, 1990—; editor jour. Elsevier Sci. Publs., Ltd., Oxford, U.K., 1990-95; contbr. to profl. pubs. Bd. dirs. Wesley Found., Ithaca, 1979-84; chmn. Minority Edn. Com., Ithaca, 1980; chmn. Environ. Com. on Native Americans, Ithaca, 1994-95. Mem. Am. Assn. Immunologists, Soc. Toxicology. Office: Cornell U Dept Microbiology/Immunol Coll Vet Med C5-135 UMC Ithaca NY 14853-5601

DIETHELM, ARNOLD GILLESPIE, surgeon; b. Balt., Jan. 13, 1932; s. Oskar Arnold and Grace (Gillespie) D.; m. Nancy Lee Lane, June 21, 1951; children: Nancy Elizabeth, Linda Lane, Eugene Arnold (dec.), Ellen Jeanette, Richard Gillespie. AB, Wash. State U., 1953; MD, Cornell U., 1958; DSc (hon.), U. Ala., 1993. Intern, then resident in surgery N.Y. Hosp., 1958-65; asst. in surgery, research fellow Peter Bent Brigham Hosp., Boston, 1965-66; research fellow surgery Harvard U. Med. Sch., 1966-67; instr. Cornell U. Med. Sch., 1964-65; mem. faculty U. Ala. Med. Center, Birmingham, 1967—, prof. surgery, 1973—, vice chmn. dept., 1973-82, chmn. dept. surgery, 1982-2000. Mem. residency rev. com. for surgery Accreditation Coun. for Grad. Med. Edn., 1994—, chmn., 1997-99. Contbr. articles med. jours. Mem. AAAS, ACS, AMA, Am. Soc. Nephrology, Am. Soc. Transplant Surgeons (pres. 1991-92), Am. Surg. Assn., Am. Bd. Surgery (dir. 1987-93), Assn. Acad. Surgery, Transplantation Soc., So. Surg. Assn. (pres. 1989). Home: 3248 Sterling Rd Birmingham AL 35213-3508 Office: U Ala Hosp Dept Surgery 619 19th St S Birmingham AL 35233-0001

DIETMEYER, DONALD LEO, retired electrical engineer, educator; b. Wausau, Wis., Nov. 20, 1932; s. Henry Joseph and Erna M. (Zastrow) D.; m. Carol White, Jan. 26, 1957; children: Karl Peter, Elizabeth Mary, Anne Katherine, Diana Lee. BSEE, U. Wis., Madison, 1954, MS, 1955, PhD, 1959. Mem. faculty U. Wis., Madison, 1958-63, 64-98, prof. elec. and computer engring., 1967-98, prof. emeritus, 1998—, assoc. dean Coll. Engring., 1983-95. Sr. engr. IBM Corp., Poughkeepsie, N.Y., 1964 Author: Logic Design of Digital Systems, 1978, 3rd rev. edit., 1988, Conlan Report, 1983. With AUS, 1957. Recipient Western Electric Fund award, 1972 Fellow IEEE; mem. Computer Soc., Assn. Computing Machinery, Sigma Xi. Home: 2211 Waunona Way Madison WI 53713-1619 Office: 1415 Engineering Dr Madison WI 53706-1607 E-mail: dld@engr.wisc.edu.

DIETRICH, BRUCE LEINBACH, planetarium and museum administrator, astronomer, educator; b. Reading, Pa., Oct. 10, 1937; s. Harold Richard and Emily Jeannette (Leinbach) D.; m. Renee Carol Long, Nov. 25, 1959; children: Dodson Bruce, Katie Ellen. BS, Kutztown U., 1960; MS, SUNY, Oswego, 1969. Tchr. Reading Pub. Schs., 1960-67; curator space sci. Reading Mus., 1967-69, dir. planetarium, 1969-92, dir., 1976-92, dir. emeritus, 1992—; instr. astronomy Reading Area Community Coll., 1972-75, asst. prof., 1975-82, prof., 1982—. Contbr. articles to profl. jours. Trustee Berks County Hist. Soc., 1994—, pres., 1996-98; sec. Interactive Video Sci. Consortium; sec. Reading Musical Found., 1980-88, trustee, 1989-98, hon. trustee, 1998—. Named Kellogg Mus. Profl., 1987; NSF grantee, 1965-67. Fellow: Internat. Planetarium Soc.; mem.: SAR, AAAS, Pa. Soc., Am. Assn. Mus., Mid-Atlantic Planetarium Soc., Can. Assn. Planetariums, Torch Club (Reading, pres. 1987). Home and Office: 1546 Dauphin Ave Reading PA 19610-2118

DIETRICH, DEAN FORBES, academic administrator; b. Davenport, Iowa, Jan. 10, 1966; s. Dean Willis and Carolyn (Brandhorst) Dietrich. AB summa cum laude, Dartmouth Coll., 1988; MA, U. Va., 1990, PhD, 1997. Viewer info., ednl. svcs. asst. C-SPAN, Washington, 1988, 89; grad. instr. U. Va., Charlottesville, 1990-97, computer, video cons. Law Sch., 1995-97; vis. asst. prof. English Hanover (Ind.) Coll., 1998-99; sr. rschr. advancement SUNY, Stony Brook, 2000—. Gov.'s fellow U. Va., 1990-91, 92-93. Mem. MLA, Assn. Profl. Rschrs. Advancement, Coun. Advancement and Support Edn., Greater N.Y. Assn. Profl. Rschrs. Advancement (sec. 2002-03), Phi Beta Kappa. Office: SUNY Stony Brook 330 Adminstration Stony Brook NY 11794-1601 Office Fax: 631-632-6321.

DIETRICH, DEAN RICHARD, lawyer; b. Milw., Sept. 22, 1952; s. Leon Martin and Enid Mary (Gamalski) D.; m. Cecelia Ann Frank, June 26, 1976; children; Sarah Elizabeth, Kathleen Ann, Michael Ryan. BS in Polit. Sci., Marquette U., 1974, JD, 1977. Bar: Wis., U.S. Dist. Ct. (ea. and we. dists.) Wis. Atty. Kramer, Nelson, Kussmaul, Hawley, Fennimore, Wis., 1977-79, Mulcahy & Wherry, S.C., Wausau, Wis., 1979-90, Ruder, Ware & Michler, S.C., Wausau, Wis., 1990—. Mem. Wausau Area Cath. Schs. Edn. Com.; interim pres. North Ctrl. Tech. Coll., 1994-95. Mem. ABA (labor and local govt. sect.), Wis. Bar Assn. (labor and local govt. sect., young lawyers divsn. 1984-90, pres. young lawyers divsn. 1988-89, bd. govs. 1994-98, 2001—, profl. ethics com. 1992—, chmn. 2000-2002, treas. 2001- chmn. fin. com. 2000—), Assn. Profl. Responsible Lawyers, Marathon County Bar Assn., Wausau C. of C. (pres. 2001, bd. dirs., chmn. legislature action). Lodges: Rotary (pres. 2001-02). Avocations: golf, ice hockey. Home: 3024 N 10th St Wausau WI 54403-3013 Office: Ruder Ware and Michler SC PO Box 8050 Wausau WI 54402-8050 Fax: 715-845-5987. E-mail: ddietrich@ruder.com.

DIETRICH, DENNIS WARD, neurologist; b. Chgo., Dec. 8, 1953; s. Jack and Sara Pope (Watkins) D.; m. Kimra Sue Johnston, June 18, 1976; children: Hunter, Alex, Marel. BS, Duke U., 1976; MD, Ind. U., 1980. Intern St. Vincent Hosp., Indpls., 1980-81; neurology resident U. Colo., Denver, 1981-85; pvt. practice Great Falls, Mont., 1985—. Mem.: Consortium of Multiple Sclerosis Ctrs., Mont. Med. Assn., Nat. Multiple Sclerosis Soc. (Mont. divsn. rsch. advocate), Nat. Stroke Assn., Am. Assn. Physicians and Surgeons, Christian Med. and Dental Soc., Am. Acad. Neurology. Home: 2312 47th Ave SW Great Falls MT 59404-4723 Office: Advanced Neurology Specialists 400 13th Ave S Ste 101 Great Falls MT 59405-4300

DIETRICH, JOSEPH JACOB, retired chemist, research executive; b. Bismark, N.D., Oct. 31, 1932; s. Jacob Peter and Elizabeth (Janzer) D.; m. Florence Kolodziejczak, June 27, 1959; children: Ann Marie, Michael, John, James. BA in Chemistry, St. John's U., Collegeville, Minn., 1953; PhD in Organic Chemistry, Iowa State U., 1957. Rsch. chemist PPG, Inc., Barberton, Ohio, 1957-59, Spencer Chem. Co., Kansas City, Kans., 1960-64; with Diamond-Shamrock Corp., Cleve., 1964-82, dir. rsch., 1973-78, dir. tech. devel., 1978-82; dir. tech. Eltech Systems Corp., Painesville, Ohio, 1982-85, dir. tech. and comml. devel./ Europe, Chardon, Ohio, 1986-90; pres. Eltech Internat. Corp., 1990-94, Elgard Corp., 1994; ret., 1994. Contbr. articles to profl. jours; patentee in field. Mem. Am. Chem. Soc., Soc. Plastic Engrs., Serra Club. Republican. Roman Catholic. Home: 6958 Pennywhistle Cir Painesville OH 44077-2141

DIETRICH, MELINDA, visual arts administrator; b. Bklyn., July 2, 1943; d. Charles Porter and Ethel Dietrich; children: Charles, Daniel, Vinton. Cert., Parsons Sch. Design, 1964; BFA, U. Hartford, 1968; MBA, Boston Coll., 1986. Art and graphics asst. J.B.W. Graphics, N.Y.C., 1968—69; art dir. Chiquita Brands Inc., Boston, 1970-75; designer James Perry Contractor, Lexington, Mass., 1977-83; cons. Small Bus. Devel. Ctr., Boston, 1986-87; co-founder, designer John Vinton Arch., Lexington, 1988-91; exec. dir. Arts Lexington, 1992-94, Munroe Ctr. Arts, Lexington, 1994—; founder Munroe Gallery, 2001; curator Spiritual Mosaic exhbn., 2002. Request for Proposal cons. Lexington Friends Arts, 1994; prof. devel. Mass. Cultural Coun., Lexington, 1993, curator Spiritual Mosaics exhbn., 2002. Exhibited in numerous exhbns., 1960—. Pub. rels. advisor Lexington Pub. Schs., 1988-91, elected Lexington Town Mtg. mem., 1988-2000; steward Lexington Conservation Com., 1996-99; mem. Lexington Town Meeting, 1988-2000. Recipient numerous awards and grants. Mem. Lexington C. of C., Art Ctrs. Consortium, Appalachian Mountain Club. Avocations: writing, poetry, bookmaking, gardening, painting. Office: Munroe Ctr Arts 1403 Mass Ave Lexington MA 02420-3804 E-mail: mcelticd@hotmail.com., munroe@ziplink.net.

DIETRICH, RENÉE LONG, fund raising executive; b. Emerald, Pa., Oct. 10, 1937; d. Emmett A. and Arlene I. (Fenstermaker) Long; m. Bruce L. Dietrich, Nov. 25, 1959; children: Dodson, Katie. BS, Kutztown (Pa.) U., 1959; MLS, Rutgers U., 1966. Cert. fund raising exec., ednl. specialist. Tchr. history Reading (Pa.) Pub. Schs., 1959-65, libr., 1965-69; coord. coop. ed. Reading Area C.C., 1978-81, program adminstr. title III grant, 1982-92, coord. cmty. and legis. rels., 1983-98, dir. instnl. advancement, 1991-98, exec. dir. Found. for Reading, 1986-98; dir. planned giving LUTHERCARE, Lititz, Pa., 1999—. Cons. U.S. Office of Edn., Washington, 1990—. Contbr. articles to profl. jours. Bd. dirs. Kutztown U. Found., 1981-90, LWV Pa., 1997-99, Great Valley Coun. Girl Scouts U.S., 1999—; chair bd. trustees Kutztown U., 1976-81; mem. Berks County Commn. for Women, 1993-96; pres. LWV Berks County, 1995-97. Recipient Disting. Alumni award, Kutztown U., 1981; named to Pa. Honor Roll of Women, 1996. Mem. Assn. Fundraising Professionals, Nat. Planned Giving Coun. Mem. United Ch. of Christ. Avocations: music, reading, politics. Home: 1546 Dauphin Ave Reading PA 19610-2118

DIETRICH, RICHARD VINCENT, geologist, educator; b. LaFargeville, N.Y., Feb. 7, 1924; s. Roy Eugene and Mida Amy (Vincent) D.; m. Frances Elizabeth Smith, Dec. 28, 1946; children: Richard Smith, Kurt Robert, Krista Gayle Brown. AB, Colgate U., 1947; MS, Yale U., 1950, PhD, 1951. Geologist Iowa Geol. Survey, 1947, N.Y. State Sci. Service, summers 1949-50; asst. prof. geology Va. Poly. Inst., Blacksburg, 1951, assoc. prof., 1952-56, prof., 1956-69, mineral technologist Va. Engring. Exp. Sta., 1951-58; fulbright rsch. prof. Oslo U., Norway, 1959-60; assoc. dean arts and scis. Va. Poly. Inst., 1966-69, dean, 1969; prof. geology Central Mich. U., Mt. Pleasant, 1969-86, prof. emeritus, 1986—, dean arts and scis., 1969-75. Dir. Econ. Geol. Pub. Co., 1966-72 Author or co-author over 20 sci. books and textbooks in field (transl. into German, Malaysian, Russian, and Japanese); also poems, haiku, essays, cartoons; editor Mineral Industries Jour., 1953-61; mng. editor Bull. Econ. Geology, 1966-73; exec. editor Rocks and Minerals, 1980-88, petrology adv. editor, 1988—; mem. editl. bd. Mineral Record, 1969-74; contbr. over 300 articles to profl. jours.; composer, performer music. Organizer N. Am. for Mineral. Abstracts, 1976-80. Served with U.S. Air Corps, 1943-46. Recipient Acad. Citation Mich. Acad. Sci., Arts and Letters, 1978, Children's Sci. Book award N.Y. Acad. Scis., 1981; Fulbright rsch. prof. U. Oslo, 1958-59; Pres.'s scholar, 1941-42, Austin Colgate scholar Colgate U., 1943, Newton Lloyd Andrews scholar, 1943, Colgate U. scholar, 1946; Edward S. Binney fellow, 1948-49, James Dwight Dana fellow Yale U., 1950-51. Fellow Am. Mineral. Soc. (assoc. life), Soc. Econ. Geol. (sr.);

mem. Norsk Geologisk Forening (life), Geol. Soc. Finland (life), Am. Geol. Inst. (gov. 1972-74), Assn. Earth Sci. Editors (pres. 1972-73), Phi Beta Kappa, Sigma Xi, Phi Kappa Phi, Sigma Gamma Epsilon. Presbyterian. Home: 1323 Center Dr Mount Pleasant MI 48858-4103 E-mail: dietr1rv@cmich.edu., r.v.dietrich@cmich.edu. *My parents were supportive although they had hoped for a different direction. Education, the work ethic, and retention of individualism and imagination were promoted.*

DIETRICH, ROBERT ANTHONY, pathologist, medical administrator, consultant; b. Buffalo, May 24, 1933; s. Charles Thomas and Mary Evelyn (Shoecraft) D.; m. Alison Elinor D'Arcy, June 13, 1959; children— Anne Marie, Alison D'Arcy, Karen Elizabeth, Kathleen Murray, Patricia Evelyn, Ellen Kiley BS, Canisius Coll., Buffalo, 1955; MD, Georgetown U., Washington, 1959; MS in Surg. Pathology, U. Minn., Mpls., 1964; JD, George Washington U., Washington, 1974. Diplomate Am. Bd. Pathology, Am. Bd. Nuclear Medicine. Intern D.C. Gen. Hosp., Washington, 1959-60; resident Mayo Clinic, Rochester, Minn., 1960-64; chief pathology svc. U.S. Army Hosp., Fort Gordon, Augusta, Ga., 1964-66; pathologist O.B. Hunter Meml. Lab., Washington, 1966-78; chmn. dept. pathology, chief div. nuclear medicine Montgomery Gen. Hosp., Olney, Md., 1972-78; vice chmn. dept. pathology, chief divsn. nuclear medicine Sibley Meml. Hosp., Washington, 1978-89; sec. Am. Soc. Clin. Pathologists, Chgo., 1981-88, exec. v.p./chief staff, 1982-92; cons., 1992—. Served to capt. U.S. Army, 1964-66. Noble Found. grantee Mayo Clinic, 1964 Fellow Am. Coll. Legal Medicine, Coll. Am. Path., Am. Soc. Clin. Path.; mem. Med. Soc. D.C. (sec. 1984-86, pres. 1988). Home and Office: 5506 Parkston Rd Bethesda MD 20816-3326

DIETRICH, SUZANNE CLAIRE, instructional designer, communications consultant; b. Granite City, Ill. d. Charles Daniel and Evelyn Blanche (Waters) D. BS in Speech, Northwestern U.; MS in Pub. Comm., Boston U., 1967; postgrad., So. Ill. U., 1973-83. Intern prodn. staff Sta. WGBH-TV, Boston, 1958-59; asst. dir., 1962-64; asst. dir. program invitation to art, 1958; cons. producer dir. dept. instructional tv radio Ill. Office Supt. Pub. Instrn., Springfield, 1969-70; dir. program prodn. and distbn., 1970-72; instr. faculty call staff, speech dept. Sch. Fine Arts So. Ill. U., Edwardsville, 1972-73; grad. asst. for doctoral program office of dean Sch. Edn., 1975-78; rsch. asst. Ill. pub. telecomms. study for Ill. Pub. Broadcasting Coun., 1979-80; cons. rsch. in comm., 1980—. Pub. advisor Bradly Pub., Inc., 1996. Exec. prodr., dir. tv programs Con-Con Countdown, 1970, The Flag Speaks, 1971. Mem. sch. bd. St. Mary's Cath. Sch., Edwardsville, 1991-92; cable tv adv. com. City of Edwardsville, 1994—, co-chair, 1996-98; bd. dirs. Goshen Preservation Alliance, Edwardsville, 1992-94, pres., 1995-97; dir. Madison County Hist. Mus. and Archival Libr., 1999—. Mem. Mdison County Hist. Soc. (bd. dirs. 1997-99). Roman Catholic. Home: 1011 Minnesota St Edwardsville IL 62025-1424 Office: 715 N Main St Edwardsville IL 62025-1111

DIETRICH, WILLIAM E. geophysicist, educator; BA, Occidental Coll., 1972; MS, U. Wash., 1975, PhD, 1982. Prof. U. Calif., Berkeley, 1981—. Crosby lectr. MIT, 1994; lectr. Istituto Veneto di Scienze, 1997. Co-recipient Wiley award, Brit. Geomorphological Rsch. Group, 1991; named Presdl. Young Investigator, NSF, 1985—90; recipient Gordon Warwick award, Brit. Geomorphological Rsch. Group, 1986; Milton fellow, U. Calif., 1998. Fellow: Geol. Soc. Am., Am. Geophys. Union (Horton award 1995); mem.: NAS. Office: Earth and Planetary Sci 313 McCone Berkeley CA 94720-4767 Business E-Mail: bill@geomorph.berkeley.edu.*

DIETRICH, WILLIAM GALE, lawyer, real estate developer, consultant; b. Kansas City, Mo., Mar. 6, 1925; s. Roy Kaiser and Gale (Gossett) D.; m. Marjorie Nell Reich, July 14, 1945; children: Meredith G. Dietrich Steinhaus, Ann. E. Dietrich Cooling, Walter R. AB with high honors, Yale U., 1948, LLB, 1951. Bar: Mo. 1951. Ptnr. Dietrich, Davis, Dicus, Rowlands, Schmitt & Gorman (and predecessors), 1953-73; project dir., gen. counsel Blue Ridge Shopping Ctr., Inc., Kansas City, 1955-73, pres., gen. mgr., 1964-73, Blue Ridge Tower, Inc., Kansas City, 1967-73; sec.-treas. A. Reich & Sons, Inc., Kansas City, 1973-88, chmn., 1988—; pvt. practice law Kansas City, 1973—; sec., treas. A. Reich & Sons Gardens, Inc., 1973-89; pres. J&D Devel., Inc., 1987—; gen. ptnr. J & D Enterprises, 1986—; gen. mgr. The Farm Shopping and Office Ctr., 1994-98; pres. BBJ Treats, L.L.C., 1994-98; mem. WGD Properties, LLC, 1999—. Sec., bd. dirs. Rsch. Med. Ctr., Kansas City, 1977, vice-chmn., 1980-83, chmn., 1983-87; bd. dirs. The Rsch. Found., 1980-91, vice-chmn., 1989-91; bd. dirs. Rsch. Health Svcs., 1980-81, vice chmn., 1983-87, chmn. 1987-89; bd. dirs. Mahana Condominium Assn., Maui, Hawaii, 1977-96, Blue Ridge Bank and Trust Co., Kansas City, 1982-94; vestry mem. Grace & Holy Trinity Cathedral, Kansas City, 1972-95, former treas. 1st lt. AUS, 1943-46, PTO. Recipient Army Commendation Ribbon, 1946. Mem. ABA, Mo. Bar Assn., Kansas City Bar Assn., Blue Ridge Mall Mchts. Assn. (dir. 1958-73), Internat. Coun. Shopping Ctrs. (past dir. for Mo., Kans, Iowa, cert. shopping ctr. mgr.), Lawyers Assn. Kansas City, Mission Hills Country Club, Yale Club, Kansas City (Mo.) Club, Rotary (bd. dirs., sec. found. Kansas City 1978—), Phi Beta Kappa (pres. Kansas City chpt. 1989-91), Phi Delta Phi. Home: 1000 Huntington Rd Kansas City MO 64113-1346 Office: 6155 Oak St Prof Bldg Ste A Kansas City MO 64113-2266 E-mail: wgdlo@aol.com.

DIETRICK, KEVIN M. military officer; b. Pitts. m. Aida Dietrick; children: Maria, Michael. BS in Physics, Indiana U. of Pa., 1979; MS in Physics, U. Va., 1990. Commd. 2d lt. U.S. Army Signal Corps, 1979, advanced through grades to col.; platoon leader, maint. officer and exec. officer 396th Signal Co., 193d Inf. Brigade, Panama; with U.S. Army Fgn. Sci. and Tech. Ctr., Charlottesville, Va., 1982—85; comdr. Hdqrs. and Hdqrs. Co. of 67th Signal Bn., Ft. Gordon, Ga., 1985; with Office of the TRADOC System Mgr. for Mobile Subscriber Equipment; faculty physics U.S. Mil. Acad., West Point; mgr. sml. bus. innovative rsch. tech. programs andn space applications tech. program for missile def. Army Space and Strategic Def. Command, Huntsville, Ala.; staff officer Office of Asst. Sec. of Army for Rsch., Devel. and Acquisition, Pentagon; product mgr. for manportable satellite systems Project Mgr. Milsatcom, 1997—2000; exec. sec. Army Sci. Bd., 2001—. Decorated Meritorious Svc. medal with 2 oak leaf clusters, Army Commendation medal, Army Achievement medal. Office: SAAL-Army Science Board 2511 Jefferson Davis Hwy #11500 Arlington VA 22202-3911

DIETZ, ARTHUR TOWNSEND, investment counseling company executive; b. Mt. Vernon, N.Y., Oct. 30, 1923; s. William Arthur and Adele Townsend (Dods) D.; m. Mary Archer, June 29, 1947 (dec. 1980); children; Adele Archer Dietz, Laura Townsend Burke, Amelia Edmunds Williams; m. Mary Laura Peavy, Sept. 16, 1982 (dec. 1992); m. Margie Nell Lee Baghose, Oct. 4, 1992. AB, Wesleyan U., Middletown, Conn., 1946; MA, Princeton U., 1948, PhD, 1953. Instr. Princeton U., 1948-49; asst. prof. Wesleyan U., 1949-54; Mills Bee Lane prof. fin. and banking, dir. MBA program Emory U., Atlanta, 1954—88; dir. Alpha Fund, Atlanta, 1972-85, Enterprise Funds, Atlanta, 1985—, Enterprise Accumulation Trust, 1995—, Car Trax Security Systems, 2000—. Pres. ATD Adv. Corp., 1996—, Strategic Portfolio Mgmt., 1988-95; trustee Emory U. Resolution in Honor, 1983, Amherst Coll., 1953-54; vis. prof. Internat. Inst. Mgmt. Devel., 1965-66; Robert Morris prof., Va., 1984-85. Author books; mem. editl. bd. Jour. of Mktg., 1950, Jour. of Pub. Law, 1950; contbr. articles to profl. jours. Pres. Fernbank PTA, DeKalb County, Ga., 1959-60; mem. DeKalb County Inflation com., 1974, DeKalb County Devel. Authority, 1980-84; Retirement Facility for Elderly Authority, DeKalb County, 1982-84. Sgt. AUS, 1942-45, ETO. Named one of Outstanding Educators of Am., 1972; recipient Emory Williams Disting. Tchg. award Emory U., 1983, Disting. Achievement award Emory Bus. Alumni Assn., 1985; Woodrow Wilson fellow, 1946. Fellow Fin. Analysts Soc.; mem. Phi Beta Kappa (pres. Gamma chpt. 1964-65). Methodist. Avocations: tennis, bridge. Office: ATD Adv 1917 Chamdun Way Atlanta GA 30341-1770 E-mail: atdadd@mindspring.com.

DIETZ, CHARLTON HENRY, lawyer; b. LeMars, Iowa, Jan. 8, 1931; s. Clifford Henry and Mildred Verna (Eggensperger) D.; m. Viola Ann Lange, Aug. 17, 1952; children: Susan (Mrs. Jay Kakuk), Robin (Mrs. Jack Mayfield), Craig. BA, Macalester Coll., 1953; JD, William Mitchell Coll. Law, 1957, LLD, 1993. Bar: Minn. 1957. Mem. pub. rels. staff 3M, St. Paul, 1952-58, atty., 1958-70, assoc. counsel, asst. sec., 1970-72, asst. gen. counsel, 1972-75, sec., 1972-76, gen. counsel, 1975-92, v.p. legal affairs, 1976-88, sr. v.p., 1988-93. Bd. dirs. Mairs & Power Mutual Funds; instr. William Mitchell Coll. Law, 1960-74, trustee, 1974-86, 87-96, pres., 1980-83. Bd. dirs. St. Paul Area YMCA, 1973-80, chmn. 1978-80, Minn. Citizens Coun. on Crime and Justice, 1976-88, 2002—, pres., 1982-84, St. Paul United Way, 1980-95, Ramsey County Hist. Soc., 1979-86, 2002—, St. Paul Lowertown Redevel. Corp., 1988-94, Minn. Hist. Soc., 1993-2002, Supreme Ct. Hist. Soc., 1991—, Children's Hosps. and Clinics, 1994-2002; trustee United Theol. Sem., 1976-82, Macalester Coll., 1983-89, Wilder Found., 1989-2003, chmn., 1996-2000; mem. Conferees of Minn. Citizens Conf. on Cts.; bd. dirs. Masonic Cancer Ctr. Fund, 1984—, pres. 1994-97; exec. bd. Indianhead Coun., Boy Scouts Am., 1986—, pres., 1992-93; bd. dirs. Historic St. Paul, 2002—. Fellow Am. Bar Found.; mem. ABA, Minn. Bar Assn., Ramsey County Bar Assn., Assn. Gen. Counsel, Am. Judicature Soc. (bd. dirs. 1989-95), Am. Law Inst., Masons, Shriners, Jesters. Republican. Mem. United Ch. of Christ. Home: 1 Birch Ln Saint Paul MN 55127-6402

DIETZ, DAVID WILLIAM, structural engineer; b. Rochester, N.Y., Sept. 4, 1968; s. Francis H. and Linda (Haacke) D.; m. Jennifer Montgomery. BSME, Northwestern U., Evanston, Ill., 1990. Registered profl. engr., Ohio. Structural engr. Stark Truss, Inc., Edgerton, Ohio, 1991-2000; engr. Cessna Aircraft Co., Wichita, Kans., 2000—. Mem. ASME, AIAA, NSPE. Avocations: theatrical performance, reading, biking. Home: 415 N Woodchuck Wichita KS 67212-3557 Office: 1 Cessna Blvd Wichita KS 67215 E-mail: dwdietz@cessna.textron.com.

DIETZ, JOHN RAPHAEL, consulting engineer executive; b. Carbondale, Pa., Jan. 31, 1912; s. John A. and Bridget (Barrett) D.; m. Elizabeth Harding Bezilla, Mar. 15, 1983; children by previous marriage: Robert J., Elizabeth Dietz Brown. BS in Civil Engring., Drexel U., Phila., 1934. Registered profl. engr., Pa. Contract estimator J.A. Dietz Co., 1934-35; designer Pa. Dept. Hwys., 1935-38; designer, resident engr. Pa. Turnpike Commn., 1938-40; san. engr. for J.E. Greiner Co., Camp Meade, Md., 1940; designer Caribbean Architect-Engrs., 1941-42; chief designer for Gannett Eastman & Fleming, Inc., Andrews Air Field, Washington, 1942-43; civilian with U.S. Engr. Corps on study Potomac River Basin flood control, 1943-44; with Gannett Fleming Corddry and Carpenter, Inc., cons. engrs., 1942—, dir. hwy. div., then pres., 1950-76, chmn. bd., 1970-83, chmn. emeritus, 1983—. Dir. CCNB Bank (N.A.) Trustee Drexel U. Bd.; dirs. Holy Spirit Hosp., Camp Hill, Pa., 1965—, pres., 1983; bd. dirs. Villa Teresa Nursing Home, Harrisburg, Pa., 1973—, pres., 1973-75. Recipient A.J. Drexel Paul award Drexel U., 1973; named Knight of St. Gregory, Pope John Paul II, 1983; selected in 100 Most Outstanding Men Drexel U. Alumni, 1992. Life fellow ASCE (past pres. Central Pa. chpt.); mem. Am. Council Cons. Engrs., Nat. Soc. Profl. Engrs., Am. Road and Transp. Builders Assn. (past dir.), Pa. Hwy. Info. Assn. (past pres.), Pa. Soc. Profl. Engrs. (Profl. Engrs. Disting. Service award Harrisburg chpt. 1965) Roman Catholic. Home: PO Box 485 Camp Hill PA 17001-0485 Office: PO Box 67100 Harrisburg PA 17106-7100

DIETZ, MARGARET JANE, retired public information director; b. Omaha, Apr. 15, 1924; d. Lawrence Louis and Jeanette Amalia (Meile) Neumann; m. Richard Henry Dietz, May 30, 1949 (dec. July 1971); children: Henry Louis, Frederick Richard, Susan Margaret, John Lawrence (dec.). BA, U. Nebr., 1946; MS, Columbia U., 1949. Wire editor Kearney (Nebr.) Daily Hub, 1946-47; state soc. editor Omaha World-Herald, 1947-48; libr. aide Akron (Ohio) Pub. Libr., 1963-66, publicity and display dir., 1966-74; editor Owlet, 1966-74; pub. info. officer Northeastern Ohio Univs. Coll. Medicine, Rootstown, 1974-85, dir. Office Commn., 1985-87, ret., 1987. Writer Ravenna (Ohio) Record-Courier, 1988-92; cons. Kent (Ohio) State U. Sch. Music, 1988-91. Author: Akron's Library: Commemorating Twenty Five Years on Main Street, Silver Reflections: A History of the Northeastern Ohio Universities College of Medicine, 1973-98. Mem. culture and entertainment com. Goals for Greater Akron, 1976; pres. bd. Weathervane Cmty. Playhouse, Akron, 1982-85, sec. to the bd., 1988-93, trustee, 1991-93, historian, 1993—, chair 60th anniversary season, 1994-95; trustee Family Svcs. Summit County, Ohio, 1980-84, dist. trustee, 1994—, Am. Heart Assn., Akron dist., 1986-91, Mobile Meals Found., Akron, 1988-91; v.p. Friends of Akron-Summit County Pub. Libr., 1988-94, pres., 1994-95; student tutor LEARN Literacy Coun., 1988-94, trustee, 1988-95. Recipient Trustee award Weathervane Cmty. Playhouse, 1985, Family Svcs. Bernard W. Frazier award, 1994, John S. Knight award Soc. Profl. Journalists, 1995. Mem. Women in Comm. (Mary Kerrigan O'Neill award 1995), LWV (edn. found. 1989-92, newsletter editor Akron 1957-60), Coll. Club, Press Club, Akron Women's City Club. Home: 887 Canyon Trl Akron OH 44303-2401 E-mail: mjd887@earthlink.net.

DIETZ, ROBERT BARRON, lawyer; b. San Diego, May 14, 1942; s. J. Thomas and Mary Agnes (Barron) D.; m. Grace Louise Purcell, Aug. 19, 1967; children: Thomas E., Michael B., Denis P., M. Alison. AB, Coll. Holy Cross, 1964; JD, Cornell U., 1968. Bar: N.Y. 1968, U.S. Dist. Ct. (no. dist.) N.Y. 1968, U.S. Dist. Ct. (so. and ea. dists.) N.Y. 1973, U.S. Supreme Ct. 1974. Asst. dist. atty. County of Dutchess, Poughkeepsie, N.Y., 1969-70, confidential law clk. to surrogate of Dutchess County, 1970-73; corp. counsel City of Poughkeepsie, 1973-75; assoc. Garrity & Dietz, Poughkeepsie, 1969-73, ptnr., 1973-75; assoc. Gellert & Cutler, P.C. and predecessor firms, Poughkeepsie, 1975-78, ptnr., 1978-86; pvt. practice law Poughkeepsie, 1986-94; ptnr. Dietz & Dietz LLP, Poughkeepsie, 1995—. Lectr. Dutchess C.C., Poughkeepsie, 1985-98, practical skills course N.Y. State Bar Assn. Bd. dirs. Mid Hudson Workshop for Disabled; former mem. Sports Mus. Dutchess County; chmn. Mid Hudson adv. bd. Salvation Army, 1998-2000; bd. trustees Vassar-Warner Home, 1997-2001; bd. counsellors The Children's Home of Poughkeepsie, Inc., 1997—; past bd. dirs. Dutchess County coun. Boy Scouts Am., 1997; former mem. City of Poughkeepsie Recreation Commn.; bd. dirs. Greystone Programs, Inc., 1999—; mem. Pastoral Coun. Ch. Holy Trinity, 1999-2001. Fellow Dist. 721 Rotary, Poughkeepsie, 1964-65. Mem. ABA, N.Y. State Bar Assn. (lectr. practical skills course, probate, elder), Dutchess County Bar Assn., Poughkeepsie C. of C., Kiwanis (pres. Poughkeepsie club 1974-75). Republican. Roman Catholic. Avocations: golf, tennis, reading, baseball card collecting. Office: 2 Cannon St Poughkeepsie NY 12601-3224 E-mail: rdietz@dietzllp.com.

DIETZ, THOMAS ANTHONY, curator, educator; b. Batesville, Ind., Sept. 13, 1948; s. Anthony Frederick and Agnes Mary (Weigel) Dietz; m. Sharon Lee Carlson, July 13, 1902. MA, Wayne State U., 1977. Curator edn. Detroit Hist. Mus., 1984—88, curator urban history, 1988—92; curator rsch. Kalamazoo (Mich.) Valley Mus., Kalamazoo, 1992—. Mem.: AAUP (pres. Mich. conf. 2001—), Orgn. Am. Historians, Am. Assn. for State & Local History, Am. Assn. Mus., Kalamazoo Valley C.C. Faculty Assn. (pres. 1999—2003). Office: Kalamazoo Valley Mus PO Box 4070 230 N Rose St Kalamazoo MI 49003-4070 Business E-Mail: tdietz@kvcc.edu.

DIETZ, WILLIAM RONALD, management executive; b. Seattle, Nov. 25, 1942; s. William Phillip and Helen Mae (Wilson) D.; m. Elizabeth R. Daoust; 1 child, David Phillip. BA, U. Wash., 1964; MBA, Stanford U., 1968. Fin. cons. 1st Nat. City Bank, N.Y.C., 1968-70; v.p., mgr. Citicorp Subs. Mgmt. Office, Citicorp, N.Y.C., 1971-74; chmn. Citicorp Factors, Inc., N.Y.C., 1974-75; v.p., mgr. N.Y., N.J. and Conn. comml. banking Citibank N.A., N.Y.C., 1976-78, sr. v.p., gen. mgr. Eastern region corp. banking, 1978-81, sr. v.p., head Caribbean Basin div., 1982-84; pres. Charter Assocs. Ltd., 1985-89; chmn. and chief exec. officer CorEast Savs. Bank, Richmond, Va., 1989-91; pres., CEO Am. Savs. Bank, White Plains, N.Y., 1991-92, Mo. Bridge Bank, Kansas City, 1992-93, Anthem Fin., Inc., Indpls., 1993-96; ptnr. Concord Ptnrs., 1997—; mng. ptnr. Customer Contact solutions, LLC, 1999—; pres. W.M. Putnam Co., 2001—. Bd. dirs. Capital One Fin. Corp., Stratis Corp., Baker Hill, W.M. Putnam Co.; mem. policy com. Bank Mgmt. Inst., SUNY-Buffalo. Contbg. author: Customer-Focused Marketing of Financial Services. Trustee Children's Mus. of Indpls.; bd. advisors Ind. U./Purdue U., Indpls.; bd. trustees Indpls.-Marion County Pub. Libr. Found. Lt. USNR, 1964-66. Mem. Univ. Club (N.Y.C.), Woodstock Country Club, Delta Tau Delta. Home: 2769 Woodwind Way Indianapolis IN 46268 Office: WM Putnam Co 1625 Commerce Pkwy Bloomington IL 61702 E-mail: rdietz@officeredi.com.

DIETZE, GOTTFRIED, political science educator; b. Kemberg, Germany, Nov. 11, 1922; came to U.S., 1949; s. Paul and Susanne (Pechstein) D. Dr.Jur., U. Heidelberg, Germany, 1949; PhD, Princeton U., 1952; S.J.D., U. Va., 1961. Instr. polit. sci. Dickinson Coll., 1952-54; mem. faculty Johns Hopkins, 1954—, prof. polit. sci., 1962—. Vis. prof. U. Heidelberg, 1956, 58-60, Brookings Instn., 1960-61, 67 Author: Ueber Formulierung der Menschenrechte, 1956, The Federalist, 1960, In Defense of Property, 1963, Magna Carta and Property, 1965, America's Political Dilemma, 1968, Youth, University and Democracy, 1970, Bedeutungswandel der Menschenrechte, 1971, Academic Truths and Frauds, 1972, Two Concepts of the Rule of Law, 1973, Deutschland-Wo Bist Du?, 1980, Kant und der Rechtsstaat, 1981, Kandidaten, 1982, El Gobierno Constitucional, 1983, Liberalism Proper and Proper Liberalism, 1984, Reiner Liberalismus, 1985, Konservativer Liberalismus in Amerika, 1987, Liberaler Kommentar zur Amerikanischen Verfassung, 1988, Amerikanische Demokratie, 1988, Politik-Wissenschaft, 1989, Der Hitler-Komplex, 1990, Liberale Demokratie, 1992, American Democracy, 1993, Problematik der Menschenrechte, 1995, Briefe aus Amerika, 1995, Begriff des Rechts, 1997, Deutschland, 1999, 1999, Deutschland: besser und schöner, 2001; editor: Essays on the American Constitution, 1964. Lutheran. Office: Johns Hopkins U Dept Polit Sci Baltimore MD 21218

DIETZE, JOACHIM, librarian; b. Dresden, Germany, Oct. 16, 1931; s. Richard and Meta (Reh) D. Diploma, U. Leipzig, Fed. Republic Germany, 1954, PhD, 1964, Dr. phil.habil., 1971. Cert. Slavistic diplomate, sci. libr. Jr. libr. Univ. Libr., Leipzig, 1954-55, German State Libr., Berlin, 1955-56; libr. Regional Libr. of Thuringia, Weimar, Fed. Republic Germany, 1956-59, Univ. Libr., Leipzig, 1959-65; chief libr. Univ. and State Libr. of Sachsen-Anhalt, Halle, 1965-96. Author: August Schleicher als Slawist, 1966, Die Sprache der 1. Novgoroder Chronik, 1975, Naukowa informacja i dokumentacja, 1977, Frequenzwörterbuch zur Synodalhandschrift der 1. Novgoroder Chronik, 1977, Frequenzwörterbuch zur jüngeren Redaktion der 1. Novgoroder Chronik, 1984, Frequenzwörterbuch zur 4. Novgoroder Chronik, 1984, Einführung in die Informationslinguistik, 1989, Texterschließung, 1994, Frequenzwörterbuch der russischen Schriftsprache des 18 Jh., 1997, B. Travens Wortschatz, 1998, Der Wortschatz Karl Mays, 1999; editor, translator: Die 1. Novgoroder Chronik (Synodalhandschrift), 1971. Avocation: sailing. E-mail: prof.dietze@12move.de.

DIETZEL, LOUISE ALVERTA, psychologist; b. Canton, Ohio, Nov. 18, 1937; d. Daniel Walter and Velma Irene Bender Miller; m. Cleason Samuel Dietzel, June 18, 1960; children: Laurie Christine, Rebecca Doreen, Beth Ann. BS, Goshen (Ind.) Coll., 1960; MS, St. Michaels Coll., 1976. Lic. Psychologist, lic. Clin. Mental Health Counselor, Vt. Dir. day care Mt. Pleasant, Mich., 1965-67, E. Lansing, Mich., 1967-71, Winooski, Vt., 1972-73; sch. cons. Essex Junction (Vt.) Schs., 1976-77; rsch. asst. U. Vt., Burlington, 1976-77; pvt. cons. practice Essex Junction, 1974—. Chair counselor Vt. Clin. Mental Health Counselors, Montpelier, 1989-95, elem. counselor Essex Junction Schs., 1977-94, cons. Head Start, Burlington, Vt., 1992-99; psychology instr. St. Michael's Coll., 1999—. Author: Parenting With Respect and Peacefulness, 1995. Mem. Am. Mental Health Counselors Assoc., Vt. Psychol. Assn., Am. and Vt. Counseling Assn. Avocations: cooking, furniture refinishing, camping, antiqueing. Home: 37 Prospect St Essex Junction VT 05452-3612 Office: Psychol Svcs 6 Hillcrest Rd Essex Junction VT 05452-3611

DIETZEN, CHRISTOPHER J. lawyer; b. Yakima, Wash., Mar. 8, 1947; s. John Frederick and Elizabeth P. (Schneider) D.; m. Peggy Marie Regan, Dec. 27, 1969; children: Stacey, Mark, Lisa, John. BS, Gonzaga U., 1969, JD, 1973. Bar: Wash. 1973, Minn. 1978. Assoc. Richter, Wimberley & Ericson, Spokane, Wash., 1973-78, Larkin, Hoffman, Daly & Lindgren, Mpls., 1978-81, ptnr., 1981—. Mem. Supreme Ct. Adv. Com. on Rules of Civil Procedure, 1998—; mem. Commn. on Jud. Selection, 2003—. Mem. Mpls. Reapportionment Commn., 1991-92; deanery rep. Ann. Cath. Appeal, 1991-94; chair outreach panel of fin. coun. Archdiocese St. Paul and Mpls., 1995—; bd. dirs. Tentmakers Youth Ministry, 1994-2001. Mem. Minn. State Bar Assn., Hennepin County Bar Assn. (rules of profl. conduct com. 1995—). Republican. Roman Catholic. Avocations: fishing, running, hiking. Home: 21 E 107th Street Cir # E Bloomington MN 55420-5311 Office: Larkin Hoffman Daly 7900 Xerxes Ave S Ste 1500 Minneapolis MN 55431-1128

DI EUGENIO, BARBARA, computer science educator; b. Turin, Italy, Mar. 5, 1961; d. Mario Di Eugenio and Adelaide Ricci; m. Milos Zefran, May 29, 1999. Laurea, U. Turin, Italy, 1985; MS in Engring., U. Pa., 1990, PhD, 1993. Spl. lectr. Carnegie Mellon U., Pitts.; rsch. assoc. U. Pitts., 1996-98; asst. prof. U. Ill., Chgo., 1999—. Guest editor spl. issue Computational Linguistics, 1998; contbr. articles to profl. jours. Vol. Recording for the Blind, Phila., 1991—93; leader Cath. Assn. Italian Girl and Boy Scouts, Turin, 1978—85. Grantee Fulbright fellow, 1987—88, rsch. grantee, NSF, 1998—, NATO Internat. Sci. Exch. Programmes, 1998—2000, Office Naval Rsch., 2000—. Mem.: Am. Assn. Artificial Intelligence, Assn. Computational Linguistics (sec. spl. interest group on discourse and dialogue 2000—01, area chair 1999, internat. conf. treas. N.Am. chpt. 2000—01). Office: U Ill-Chgo 1120 SEO (M/C 152) 851 S Morgan St Chicago IL 60607

DI FALCO, GERARD A. visual artist; b. Camden, N.J., Sept. 26, 1952; s. Horace Giovanni Robilotta-Di Falco and Marie Ann Mazur-Di Falco. BA in Visual Art, Rutgers U., 1974; MS in Arts Adminstrn., Drexel U., Phila., 1985. Teaching Certificate in Art Dept. of Edn., N.J., 1977. Visual artist DiFALCO Studios, Phila., 1978—; visual artist: juried into group Nexus Gallery/Found. for Today's Art, Phila., 1984—98; mus. curator The Port of History Mus., Phila., 1988—90; visual artist: juried into group Creative Artists Network, Phila., 1994—96; resident artist, delphi found. art futures project Phila. Mus. of Art, 2002—03. Ind. curator, 1973—; curator, chair, group and exch. show com. Nexus Gallery/Found. for Today's Art, Phila., 1984—90. One-man shows include The Midas Touch, The Spanish Paintings, Phila., The Madrid Paintings, Phila., The Spanish Paintings, Societal Genres, Art Golf Installation, Paintings and Installations by Di Falco, Paintings: A Thirteen Year Retrospective, U. of Pa., The Strega Dance, Davinci Art Alliance, Phila., exhibited in group shows at DiFalco, Reese-Horvitz & Wheeling, Phila., CAN Artists In Soho, Majority Rules, Scotland, Creative Artists Network Gallery, exhibited in group shows, Borowsky Gallery, Phila., exhibited in group shows, Across USA and Madrid, show of furniture, 10 Couturier, LA. Donating artist for ann. auction MANNA Met. AIDS Neighborhood Nutrition Alliance, Phila., 1994—2003; mem. Del. Valley Pagan Network, Phila., 2002—03; bd. mem. World AIDS Day/Day With(out) Art Com., Phila., 1995—2003. Grantee Individual Artist's Grant, Pa. Coun. on the Arts, 1992, Fellowship Grant, The Pollock-Krasner Found., Inc., N.Y.C., 2002; scholar Grad. Assistantship in Arts Adminstrn., Drexel U., 1984—85. Mem.: DaVinci Art Alliance, Nat. Italian Am. Found. Independent. Avocations: researching folklore, herbology, paranormal investigation, reading art history/literature, lecturing/workshop presentation. Home: 2201 Cherry St Philadelphia PA 19103 Personal E-mail: arthalloween@aol.com.

DIFEO, SAMUEL X. automotive executive; Exec. v.p. DiFeo Group United Auto Group, Inc., Detroit, 1992-98, pres., COO DiFeo Group, 1998—. Office: United Auto Group Inc Ste 36B 1340 Outer Dr West Detroit MI 48239-4001

DIFFRIENT, NIELS, industrial designer; b. Star, Miss., Sept. 6, 1928; s. Robert Ethan and Dovie Lee (Peacock) D.; m. Helena Hernmarck, May 29, 1976; children— (by previous marriage) Scott, Julie, Emily. Student, Wayne State U., 1951-52; B.F.A., Cranbrook Acad., 1954; hon. doctorate, Art Center Coll. of Design, 1975. Architect Eero Saarinen, Bloomfield Hills, Mich., 1948-53; with Walter B. Ford, Detroit, 1953-54, Marco Zanuso, Milan, Italy, 1954-55; gen. partner Henry Dreyfuss Assocs., N.Y.C., 1955-80; head ind. indsl. design studio Ridgefield, Conn., 1981—. Mem. faculty indsl. design UCLA, 1961-69; mem. faculty Yale U., 1990. Co-author: Humanscale, 3 vols., 1974, 80; mem. editorial bd.: Indsl. Design mag, 1976-89; contbr. articles to profl. jours.; inventor, designer human engineered comml. chairs for Knoll Internat., 1979, 80, for Sunar Co., 1981, table system for Home Furniture Co., 1988, 92, task seating and work lamp for Humanscale Corp., 2000. Mem. bd. govs. Cranbrook Acad., Bloomfield Hills, Mich. Recipient nat. design award U.S. Dept. Transp., 1981, awards Resource Coun., 1979, 81, gold medal Inst. Bus. Designers, 1979, 80, 92, 93, best of show award, 1984, ann. award Design and Environ. mag., 1975, (with Marco Zanuso) Compasso d'Oro, 1957, awards Indsl. Design mag., 1981, 82, 85, 89, gold medal AIA, 1989; gold medal IDEA Bus. Week mag., 1993; named hon. royal designer for industry Royal Soc. Arts, London, 1987, Best of Show NEOCON Furniture Exhbn., 1998; winner Nat. Design award Smithsonian Cooper Hewitt Nat. Design Mus., 2002, Nat. Design award Smithsonian Nat. Design Mus., 2002; Fulbright fellow, 1954-55; grantee Nat. Endowment for Arts, 1975-80. Fellow Indsl. Design Soc. Am. (Design

Excellence award 1980, Chrysler award for innovation 1996); mem. Internat. Design Conf. Aspen (bd. dirs. 1974-91), Internat. Design Edn. Found. (pres. 1976—), Am. Ctr. for Design (hon., bd. dirs.), Design Inst. New Zealand (hon.).

DIFLO, THOMAS, transplant surgeon; b. Oceanside, N.Y., Aug. 30, 1958; s. Robert Edward and Barbara Diflo; m. Amber Azniv Guth, Sept. 24, 1994; children: Elizabeth, Zoë, Benjamin. AB, Harvard U., 1980; MD, Boston U., 1984. Diplomate Am. Bd. Surgery with subspecialty in critical care. Resident in surgery Boston U., 1984-86, 88-91; transplant fellow Harvard U., Boston, 1986-88, 91-92; asst. prof. surgery NYU Med. Ctr., N.Y.C., 1992—, dir. renal transplantation, 1993—. Fellow ACS; mem. Am. Soc. Transplant Surgeons, Am. Soc. of Transplantation, The Transplantation Soc., Soc. for Critical Care Medicine. Office: New York Univ Med Ctr 403 E 34th St Fl 3D New York NY 10016-4972 E-mail: thomas.diflo@med.nyu.edu.

DIFORIO, ROBERT GEORGE, literary agent; b. Mamaroneck, N.Y., Mar. 19, 1940; s. Richard John and Mildred (Kuntz) Diforio; m. Birgit Rasmussen; children: Stephen Christopher, Danielle Alexandra. BA, Williams Coll., 1964. From book sales rep. to v.p. book sales Kable News Co., 1964-72; with New Am. Libr./E.P. Dutton, N.Y.C., 1972-89, exec. v.p., 1980-81, chmn., chief exec. officer, 1983-89; sr. v.p. book sales and mktg. Arcata Graphics Co., 1990-91; founder, prin. D4EO Lit. Agy., 1991—; sr. ptnr. D4EO Allen O'Shea. Served USCGR. Mem.: Conn. Golf Club. Home: 7 Indian Valley Rd Weston CT 06883-1018 E-mail: d4eo@optonline.net.

DIFRANCESCO, DONALD T. lawyer; b. Scotch Plains, N.J., Nov. 20, 1944; grad. Pa. State U., 1966; J.D., Seton Hall U., 1969; m. Diane Dragovic, June 17, 1967; children: Marie, Tracy, Marci. Bar: N.J. 1969. Practices in Warren, N.J.; ptnr. Bivona, Cohen, Kunzman, Coley, Yospin, Bernstein & DiFrancesco; mem. N.J. Assembly, 1976-79; mem. N.J. State Senate, 1979-2001, pres. State Senate, 1992-2001; acting gov., 2001; lawyer DiFrancesco, Bateman, Coley, Yospin, Kunzman, Davis & Lehrer, P.C., 2001-. Trustee N.J. Symphony; bd. dirs. Resolve Counseling Ctr., Children's Specialized Hosp., N.J.; mem. exec. com. Nat. Conf. State Legislators. Office: DiFrancesco, Bateman, Coley, Yospin, Kunzman, Davis & Lehrer 15 Mountain Blvd Warren NJ 07059-6327 Office Fax: 908-757-8039.

DIFRONZO, MICHAEL A. lawyer, accountant; b. Billings, Mont., Sept. 23, 1968; s. Michael J. and Ashlea C. DiFronzo. BS in Acctg., Mont. State U., 1991; JD, U. Mont., 1994; LLM in Tax, NYU, 1997. Mont. 1994, Nev. 1995, DC 1998, U.S. Ct. Appeals (fed. cir.) 1998, U.S. Tax Ct. 1998. Sr. tax cons. Deloitte & Touche, Reno, 1994-96, internat. tax mgr. Washington, 1997-99, internat. tax sr. mgr., 2000—; assoc. Weil Gotshal & Manges, Washington, 1999-2000. Contbr. articles to profl. jours. Mem. ABA, Mont. Bar Assn., Nev. Bar Assn., D.C. Bar Assn., Mont. Bd. CPAs.

DIFRUSCIA, ANTHONY R. lawyer, real estate executive; b. Lawrence, Mass., June 5, 1940; s. Carmine and Sebastina (Tine) DiF.; m. Kathleen Sullivan; children: Marc Anthony, Kara Ann, Tamra Lee, Daniel Anthony. B, Emerson Coll.; JD, New Eng. Sch. Law, 1966. Bar: Mass. 1967. Sr. ptnr., Lawrence, 1967—. Pres. A.D. Devel., Inc., Lawrence; pres., treas. A.D. Mgmt., Lawrence. Mem. Mass. Ho. of Reps., 1967-72; commerce com. N.H. Ho. of Reps., 1998—. Roman Catholic. Office: 302 Broadway Methuen MA 01844-1208

DIGAETANO, PAUL, state legislator; b. Passaic, N.J., Oct. 28, 1953; BS, U. Notre Dame. Mem. assembly dist. 36 N.J. State Assembly, 1986-87, 92—. Policy chmn. N.J. State Assembly, 1993; former city council, Passaic; pres. J. DiGaetano & Sons., Inc. Address: 71 Union Ave Rutherford NJ 07070-1272*

DIGANGI, FRANK EDWARD, academic administrator; b. West Rutland, Vt., Sept. 29, 1917; s. Leonard and Mary Grace (Zafonti) DiG.; m. Genevieve Frances Colignon, June 27, 1946; children— Ellen (Mrs. Philo David Hall), Janet (Mrs. W. Dale Greenwood). BS in Pharmacy, Rutgers U., 1940; MS, Western Res. U., 1942; PhD, U. Minn., 1948. Asst. prof. U. Minn. Coll. Pharmacy, 1948-52, asso. prof., 1952-57, prof. medicinal chemistry, 1957—, also asso. dean adminstrv. affairs. Author: Quantitative Pharmaceutical Analysis, 7th edit. 1977; Contbr. articles to pharm. jours. Served with USNR, 1943-46, PTO. Recipient Alumni Assn. Disting. Pharmacist award, 1977, Faculty Recognition award Coll. of Pharmacy Alumni Soc., 1981, Lawrence and Delores M. Weaver medal, 1997. Mem. Am. Pharm. Assn., Minn. Pharm. Assn. (pres. 1971, chmn. bd. 1972-73, Pharmacist of Yr. award 1972, Harold R. Popp Mcml. award 1979, hon. mem. 1994), Mpls. Soc. Profl. Pharmacists (hon.), AAUP, Am. Chem. Soc., Am. Assn. Colls. Pharmacy, Sigma Xi, Phi Beta Phi, Phi Lambda Upsilon Rho Chi. Clubs: University Campus (Mpls.), University Faculty Golf (Mpls.), Gown-in-Town (Mpls.). Home: 1666 Coffman St Apt 234 Saint Paul MN 55108-1343 Office: Univ Minn Coll of Pharmacy Minneapolis MN 55455

DIGGES, EDWARD S(IMMS), business management consultant; b. Pitts., June 30, 1946; AB, Princeton U., 1968; JD, U. Md., 1971. Bar: Md. 1972, U.S. Supreme Ct. 1975. With staff of gov. State of Md., Annapolis, 1973; ptnr. Piper & Marbury, Washington and Balt., 1977-84; founding ptnr. Digges, Wharton & Levin, Annapolis, 1984-89; corp. cons. various corps., Towson, Md., 1989—. Bd. dirs. Televest, LLC, Intervest, LLC, Corp. Comms. Mgmt. Group, LLC, Interlude, LLC, ITMG, LLC, DTC Telecom, LLC, Spindrift, LLC, Antiques News Group, LLC; instr. advanced bus. law Johns Hopkins U., 1975—78; lectr. civil procedure U. Balt. Law Sch., 1976—78; mem. govs. commn. to revise Md. code, 1978—90. Contbr. articles to profl. jours. Mem. Alumni Council Mercersburg Acad., 1982-88, pres. 1987-88; bd. advisors Indian Creek Sch., 1982-88, chmn. 1986-88; pres. Beacon Hill Community Assn., 1978-86. ROTC, U.S. Army, 1970-71. Mem. Md. State Bar Assn. (bd. govs. 1972-84), Am. Law Inst., Am. Bd. Trial Adv. (pres. Md. chpt. 1984-89), Inn XIII, Am. Inns of Ct. (Master of the Bench 1986-89), Scribes. Clubs: So. Md. Soc. (bd. govs., pres. 1988), Mid Ocean (Bermuda), Princeton Club of N.Y. Democrat. Roman Catholic. Home: PO Box 42737 Baltimore MD 21284-2737 E-mail: diggesy@aol.com.

DIGGINS, PETER SHEEHAN, arts administrator; b. Rochester, N.Y., June 23, 1938; s. Bartholomew A. and Mona (Sheehan) D. BA in English, Georgetown U., 1959. guest artist cons. San Francisco Opera, 1997. Staff reporter Washington Post, 1960-65; asst. artistic adminstr. Met. Opera, N.Y.C., 1965-72; dir. dance programs N.Y. State Coun. on the Arts, 1972-75; gen. adminstr. The Joffrey Ballet, N.Y.C., 1975-79; pres. Peter S. Diggins Assocs., 1979—; Am. entertainment coord. Winter Olympics, Nagano, Japan, 1998. Cons. in arts mgmt. dance and opera cos.; cons. for guest dancers San Francisco Opera, 1996; casting cons. Broadway and tour prodns. of Carousel, Titanic, Victor/Victoria, Cats, Red Shoes, Christmas Carol, 1993-98. Contbr. articles to Opera Mag. Recipient grant for European work-study tour Met. Opera, 1968 Home: 133 W 71st St New York NY 10023-3834 E-mail: Festspiel@AOL.com.

DIGGS, MATTHEW O'BRIEN, JR., air conditioning and refrigeration manufacturing executive; b. Louisville, Jan. 11, 1933; s. Matthew O'Brien and Dorothy (Leary) D.; m. Nancy Carolyn Brown, Nov. 5, 1955; children: Elizabeth, Joan, Judith, Matthew III. Student, Hanover Coll., 1950-52; BSME, Purdue U., 1955; MBA, Harvard U., 1961. With Lincoln Electric, Cleve., 1957-59, Toledo Scale Corp., 1961-63; cons., assoc., v.p., then v.p. and mng. officer East Cen. Region Booz, Allen & Hamilton, Inc., Cleve., 1963-72; v.p. mktg. Copeland Corp., Sidney, Ohio, 1972-74, exec. v.p., 1974, pres., chief exec. officer, 1975-87, vice chmn., 1987-90; CEO The Diggs Group McClintock Ind., Dayton, Ohio, 1990—. Bd. dirs. Ripplewood Holdings LLC, Price Bros. Cmty. bd. trustees Wright State U., 1995—; chmn. adv. bd. Herrick Labs. Perdue U., 1980—; former sr. warden St. Paul's Episcopal Ch. 1st lt. U.S. Army, 1955-57. Home: 1160 Lytle Ln Dayton OH 45409-2112 Office: 1515 Kettering Tower Dayton OH 45423-1005

DIGGS, WALTER WHITLEY, health science facility administrator; b. Memphis, Tenn., June 8, 1932; s. Lemuel Whitley and Beatrice (Moshier) D.; m. Ann C. Thobae, Nov. 29, 1958; children: Jennie, Thomas, Andrew. BS, Washington and Lee U., 1954; MHA, U. Minn., 1956. Adminstrv. resident Stormont-Vail Hosp., Topeka, 1955-56; asst. dir. The Johns Hopkins Hosp., Balt., 1959-66; adminstr. Med. Coll. Ga. Hosp., Augusta, 1966-70; asst. prof. Med. Coll. Ga., Augusta, 1970-71, U. Tenn. and U. Memphis, 1971-97; field rep. Joint Commn. Hosps., Chgo., 1981-88, 93—; supt. Memphis Mental Health Inst., 1987-93. Cons. Tenn. Dept. Mental Health, 1993-95. Pres. Delta Found., Miss., 1987—, Ballet South, Memphis Ballet, Augusta Civic Ballet. Lt. USNR, 1956-59. Recipient Peter Cooper award, Unitarian Ch., Memphis, 1975, Forrest Fletcher, Washington and Lee, Lexington, Va., 1954. Fellow Am. Coll. Healthcare Execs. (life). Avocation: seniors track and field. Home: 5282 Shady Grove Rd Memphis TN 38120-2404 E-mail: cordovawwd@aol.com.

DIGGS, YONNA DARLENE, civilian military employee; d. Hornell Russell and Essie Mae Floyd; m. Michael Wayne Diggs, Mar. 27, 1957; children: Alexia Shranique Olige, Talia Leniece Olice. BSW, U. West Fla., 1979. Cert. Level 2 Contract Specialist DAWIA, 1998, Myers Briggs Personality Indicator Indpls., 2001, Am. Job Search Trainers, 2003. Mgr. spouse employment assistance Fleet and Family Support Ctr., Pensacola, Fla., 1979—2003; procurement analyst Navy Pub. Works Ctr., Pensacola, 1995—99, Naval Air Sta., Fla., 1995—99; naval res. ombudsman-at-large Comdr. Naval Res. Forces, Arlington, Va., 1997—. Contbr. articles to profl. jours. Naval res. mil. family policy advisor Comdr. Naval Res. Forces, Washington, 1998—2003. Avocations: travel, public speaking, strategic planner, motivator, consultant. Home: 402 Brigadier Stl Pensacola FL 32507 Home Fax: 850-452-2868. Personal E-mail: yonna.diggs@cnet.navy.mil. E-mail: yonna.diggs@cnet.navy.mil.

DI GIACOMO, FRAN, artist; b. Miami, Ariz., Oct. 24, 1944; d. B.J. and LaVenia Marilyn (Beavers) Fain; m. Leonard May 9, 1970; children: Marc, Eric. Student, Scottsdale Artist's Sch., 1985—2000; studied, with David Leffel, with Joe Anna Arnette, with Greg Kreutz, with Howard Terpning. Artist, 1970—; represented by Gallerie Amsterdam, Carmel, Calif., Aspen Fine Art Gallery, Southwest Gallery, Dallas, Heritage Gallery, Scottsdale, Ariz. Commissions include portraits of Supreme Court Chief Justice Warren E. Burger, Dist. Atty., 1994, Henry Wade, 1995, Haggar Apparel, Dallas Cowboys' Emmitt Smith, 1993; subject of numerous articles. Recepient 2nd place, 1993, Hon. Mention, 1994, 1st place, 1996, Plano Art Assn.,1st place, 1994, Assoc. Creative Artists, Grumbacher Gold, 1997, 2nd place, 1994, Trinity Arts Guild, 1st place, 1998, 3rd place, 1999, Richardson Civic Art, 3rd place, 1995, Tex. and Neighbors 5 state. Mem. Oil Painters Am. (assoc., signature), Am. Soc. (assoc.), Classical Realism, Portrait Soc. Am., Assoc. Creative Artists (signature). Avocation: tennis.

DIGIACOMO, JODY CHRISTOPHER, physician; b. Detroit, Dec. 10, 1959; BA, U. Pa., Phila., 1982; MD, Temple U., Phila., 1986. Diplomate Am. Bd. Surgery, in gen. surgery and surg. critical care. Attending surgeon Brandywine Hosp., Coatesville, Pa., 1994-96; instr. surgery U. Pa., Phila., 1992-95, asst. prof. surgery, 1995-96; asst. dir. critical care, asst. dir. trauma Jersey Shore Med. Ctr., Neptune, N.J., 1996-97; attending physician dept. emergency medicine St. Mary Hosp., Passaic, N.J., 1997-98; assoc. dir. trauma dept. surgery Nassau County Med. Ctr., East Meadow, N.Y., 1998—; assoc. program dir. surg. residency Nassau U. Med. Ctr., East Meadow, NY, 2000

DIGILIO, JR. JOHN THOMAS, health care executive, consultant; b. Kew Gardens, N.Y., Oct. 18, 1944; s. John Thomas and Gloria Marie (Valenzio) D.; m. Dianne E. (Pilgrim), July 12, 1969; children: Susan Elizabeth, Sandra Marie, John Thomas III. Diploma, U.S. Army War Coll., 1966; BA, LaSalle Univ., 1967; MBA, Wagner Coll., 1969. Lic. nursing home adminstr., N.Y. Adminstr. VA Med. Ctr., Northport, N.Y., 1971-72; ambulatory care adminstr. Southside Hosp., Bay Shore, N.Y., 1972-75; rschr., faculty of med. Coll. Physicians and Surgeons, Columbia Univ., N.Y.C., 1975-76; hosp. adminstrn.. N.Y. Dept. of Health, 1976-81; adminstr. Brunswick Nursing Home, Amityville, N.Y., 1981-88, Luth. Ctr. for Aging, Smithtown, N.Y., 1988-92, Sunharbor Manor, Roslyn, N.Y., 1992-95; cons. Helme Assoc., Providence, 1995-99; adminstr. Patchogue Nursing Ctr., N.Y., 1999; exec. dir. John Foley SNF, Yapnank, N.Y., 1999—. Contbg. author: Organizing Health Care for Children, 1977. Chmn. bd. L.I. Arthritis Found., 1992. Brig. gen. U.S. Army-N.G., 1969-99. Decorated Legion of Merit, Bronze Star, Order of Mil. Med. Merit; recepient Joel T. Boone award, Assn. Mil. Surgeons U.S., 1997. Fellow Am. Coll. Health Care Adminstrs.; mem. Am. Legion Post 365 (trustee 1998—), La Société des Quarante Hommes Et Huit Chavaux (comdr. 1976—), Mil. and Hospitalier Order of St. Lazarus of Jerusalem (comdr. 2001—), Sovereign Mil. Order of the Temple of Jerusalem (knight comdr. 1998—). Home: 1430 Manor Ln Bay Shore NY 11706 Office: John J Foley SNF 14 Glover Dr Yaphank NY 11980 E-mail: johntd@aol.com.

DI GIOIA, ANTHONY MICHAEL, JR., civil engineer, business executive; b. Pitts., Aug. 24, 1934; s. Anthony Michael and Elvira (Luongo) Di G.; m. Carole V. Kerr, Sept. 1, 1956; children: Anthony Michael III, Christina, Stephen, Robert, Paula, David, Deanna, Matthew. BSCE, Carnegie-Mellon U., 1956, MS, 1957, PhD, 1960. V.p. E.D'Appolonia Assocs., Pitts., 1958-65; pres. Gen. Analytics, Inc., Pitts., 1965-74, GAI Cons., Inc., Monroeville, Pa., 1974—99, chmn. bd. dirs., 1966—. Asst. prof. civil engring. Carnegie-Mellon U., 1960-62, lectr., 1962-65. Contbr. articles to profl. jours. Mem. coun. St. Bartholomew's Ch., Pitts., 1962—. 1st lt. C.E., U.S. Army, 1961-62. Mem. (hon.) ASCE (pres. Pitts. sect. 1973, dist. 4 dir. 1974-77, Young Civil Engr. award 1970, Civil Engr. of Yr. award 1981), Soc. Am. Mil. Engrs. (pres. Pitts. post 1973-74, regional v.p. Ohio Valley 1974-76). Republican. Roman Catholic. Home: 11 Wisteria Dr Pittsburgh PA 15235-1968 Office: GAI Cons Inc 570 Beatty Rd Monroeville PA 15146-1334

DI GIOVANNI, ANTHONY, retired coal mining company executive; b. Phila., May 10, 1919; s. Charles and Josephine (Biacobbe) Di Giovanni; m. Rose Persichetti, July 28, 1946 (dec. Mar. 2003); children: Joanne, Diane, Rosemary, Charles. BS in Bus. Adminstrn, St. Joseph's U., 1940. CPA Pa. Acct. Service Supply Corp., Phila., 1940-42; account supr. Ernst & Ernst, 1942-51, mgr., 1952—65; former v.p., dir. United Eastern Coal Sales Corp.; exec. v.p. finance and adminstrn. Barnes & Tucker Co., Valley Forge, Pa., 1965-72, pres., 1972-84; group pres. resources div. Alco Standard Corp. (now Ikon Office Solutions, Inc.), 1973-85, v.p., 1976-85; pres. Alco Standard Canadian Coal Corp., 1976-85; v.p. Tri County bentures, Inc., Ebensburg, Pa., 1985—. Dir. Upshur Coals Corp. Bd. dirs. St. Joseph U., 1983—85. Mem.: AICPA, Pa. Inst. CPA (past bd. dirs., chmn. com.), Nat. Coal Assn. (bd. dirs. 1973—85, fin. com. 1978—83), Sons of Italy (treas., policy com. Commonwealth Lodge #1949 1989—91), Phoenixville Country Club. Roman Catholic.

DIGIOVANNI, CHRISTOPHER WILLIAM, orthopedic surgeon, orthopedist; b. Philip and Brenda DiGiovanni; m. Sudie DiGiovanni, Oct. 1, 1995; children: Nicholas, Cameron, Peter-Luca, William. BA Biochemistry, Dartmouth Coll., Hanover, NH, 1987; MD, Dartmouth-Brown Program, Hanover, NH, 1989—91; Orthop. Residency, Brown Univ. Sch. of Med., Providence, RI, 1996, fellow, orthop. Trauma, 1997; fellow, hip and knee reconstruction, Cornell Med. Sch., Hosp. for Spl. Surgery, NY, NY, 1998; fellow, foot and ankle reconstruction, Univ. of Wash. Sch. of Med., Harborview Med. Ctr., Seattle, Wash., 1999. Diplomate Nat. Bd. Med. Examiners 1992, cert. advanced Trauma Life Support 1992, fellow Am. Acad. of Orthop. Surgery, 2003, cert. Am. Bd. of Orthop. Surgery, 2002. Team phys. RI Stingrays (USL Affiliate of NE Revolution), RI, 2000—; asst. prof. Dept. Orthop. Surgery, Brown Univ. Sch. of Med., Providence, 1999—, dir., foot and ankle svc., 1999—; foot/ankle cons. Brown Univ. Athletic Teams, Providence, 1999—; cons. staff Providence VA Med. Ctr., Providence, 1999—; asst. team phys. Providence Bruins (AHL Affiliate of Boston Bruins), Providence, 1996—97. AO/ASIF Faculty AO No. Am., 1997—; mem. Am. Orthop. Foot & Ankle Soc., Seattle, 1998—; Surg. Adv. Bd. Kinetikos Med., Inc., San Diego, 2000—; assoc. editor Foot & Ankle Internat. (jour), Seattle, 2002—. Author: (book chapters, articles, rev. papers) in peer rev. lit. (approx. 40) on orthop. issues, (posters, presentations) various meetings (approx. 45) on orthop. issues. Eagle Scout Troop 11, Boy Scouts of Am., New Hempstead, NY, 1983, Asst. Scoutmaster, 1983; AMA Med. Student Sect. Del. State of NH, Hanover, NH, 1988. Recipient St. Joseph Medal, St. Joseph Regional HS/ Montvale, NJ, 1983, Valedictorian, 1983, Dartmouth Coll. Varsity Lightweight Team, Dartmouth Coll./Hanover, NH, 1983—86, Richter Trust Record Award for Biochemistry, 1985, Med. Student Rsch. Award, Am. Fed. for Clin. Rsch., 1991, Selected, "Best Doctors in RI", Better Living Mag., 2002. Fellow: Am. Acad. of Orthop. Surgeons; mem.: Outstanding Young Men of Am., Nat. Registry of Who's Who. Independent. Roman Catholic. Achievements include patents pending for working on various Patents for ankle replacement design & foot reconstruction; Rankedf amoungst top Med. Sch. Class, Brown-Dartmouth Program. Avocations: sailing, skiing, bicycling, rowing, chess. Home: Barrington RI 02806 Office: Univ Orthop Inc 1287 N Main St Providence RI 02904

DIGIOVANNI, ELEANOR ELMA, scaffold installation company executive; b. L.I., N.Y., May 14, 1944; d. Charles and Josephine (Laureni) DiGiovanni. Student, Queensboro Coll. Collector Atlas/Re/Sun Ins. Co., N.Y.C., 1965-69; instr. Oak Manor Equitation, Weyers Cave, Va., 1970-76; dispatcher, salesperson Safway Steel Products, L.I., N.Y., 1977-83; ops. mgr. York Scaffold, L.I., 1983—95; scaffold sales rep. Safway Steel Prod., Bklyn., 1977—83; ptnr. E-Z Scholarship Data Svs., 1992-94; scaffold sales rep. R&R Scaffolding, Moonachie, NJ, 2001—02, Highrise Hoisting and Scaffolding Inc., Long Island City, NY, 2002—. Mem.: NAFE, Women in Constrn., Mus. Natural History, Internat. Platform Assn. Democrat. Roman Catholic. Avocations: reading, horseback riding, needlepoint. Home: 14-34 30th Rd Astoria NY 11102-3640 Office: Highrise Hoisting and Scaffolding Inc 2800 Borden Ave Long Island City NY 11101 E-mail: ellie2002@aol.com.

DIGIOVANNI, LARRY JOSEPH, human resources executive, small business owner; b. Phila., Sept. 23, 1948; s. Salvatore and Viola (Lafen) DiG.; m. Susan Marie Pacelli, June 27, 1975. BBA, LaSalle U., Phila., 1970. Adminstrv. systems analyst Reliance Ins. Cos., Phila., 1971-74; salary analyst ICI Ams., Wilmington, Del., 1974-75; compensation and benefits specialist Mobil Chem. Co., Macedon, N.Y., 1975-77; compensation cons. NL Industries, Hightstown, N.J., 1977-79; mgr. compensation Hercules, Inc., Wilmington, 1979-82, dir. human resources, 1985-88, v.p. human resources aerospace div. Salt Lake City, 1982-85; v.p. human resources Hercules Aerospace Co., Wilmington, Del., 1988-95, Aerospace Sys. Group Alliant Techsystems, Inc., Hopkins, Minn., 1995—98, Conventional Munitions, 1997—98. Mem. adv. com. Del. Gov.'s Compensation Com., Wilmington, 1980-82. Mem. adv. group Nat. Alliance of Bus., Salt Lake City, 1984-85; bd. dirs. Utah Health Cost Mgmt. Found., Salt Lake City, 1983-85. Served with USN, 1971-73. Mem. Am. Compensation Assn., Aerospace Industries Assn. (human resources coun. 1987—). Republican. Roman Catholic. Avocations: reading, walking, boating, skiing. Office: Twin Cities Galleries LLC PO Box 390326 Edina MN 55439-0326 E-mail: ldigiovanni@mn.rr.com.

DIGIROLAMO, GLEN FRANCIS, actor; b. Paterson, N.J., Sept. 16, 1961; s. Frank and Phyllis (Vanecek) DiG. Pres., CEO, chmn. bd. Ultimate Assocs., Wayne, N.J.; pres., CEO Centillion Group Internat., Wayne; v.p., sec., treas. F. DiGirolamo & Son, Inc., Wayne. Actor TV comml., Aruba, W.I., 1989. Actor: (film) Gremlins II, 1989, Cadillac Man, 1989, Long Time Companions, 1989, Ambulance, 1989, Mo Better Blues, 1989, Godfather III, 1990, Other Peoples Money, 1990, Jersey Girls, 1991, The Sinatra Story, 1992, (infomercial) 1-800-uslawyer Infomercial, 2002. Elected candidate Dem. County Com., Bergen County, N.J., 1989, 90, 91, 92; legis. aide Assemblyman Thomas Duch, Bergen County, 1989. Mem. AFTRA, Harley Owners Group (charter mem., Bergen and Passaic county chpts.), Rolls Royce Owners Club. Roman Catholic. Avocations: guitar, photography, travel, billiards, motorcycles, boating.

DI GIROLAMO, ROSINA ELIZABETH, education educator; b. Monterey, Calif., Aug. 3, 1945; d. Anthony and Frances (Lucido) DiG. AA, Monterey Peninsula Coll., 1965; BA, Calif. State U., Hayward, 1967; MA, Calif. Polytech., San Luis Obispo, 1975. Tchr. Monterey (Calif.) Pub. Unified Sch. Dist., 1968—. Polit. action chairperson Monterey Bay Tchrs. Assn., 1993-94; mem. City's Youth Task Force, 1997. Recipient Outstanding Tchr. award Lori Flagg Found., Monterey, 2002, Outstanding Middle Sch. Tchr. of Yr. Rotary Club, 1998. Mem. Calif. Reading Assn., Calif. Tchrs. of English, Nat. Tchrs. of English, Calif. Leadership Team, Calif. Assn. Student Leaders (advisor). Democrat. Roman Catholic. Avocations: reading, com. work, travel. Home: 77 Via Chualar Monterey CA 93940-2528 Office: Walter Colton Mid Sch 100 Toda Vis Monterey CA 93940-4237

DI GIULIAN, BRUNO L. lawyer; b. West Palm Beach, Fla., Dec. 24, 1933; s. Angelo and Teresita Irma Di Giulian; m. Patsy R. Sammons, July 30, 1960; children: Teri, Bee Gee, Angelo. BA, Stetson U., 1954; JD, Yale U., 1957. Bar: Fla. 1957, U.S. Dist. Ct. (no. dist.) Fla. 1959, U.S. Dist. Ct. (so dist.) Fla. 1965, U.S. Ct. Appeals (11th cir.) 1981; cert. mediator. Assoc. Coe, Richardson & Broberg, Palm Beach, 1957-58; rsch. assoc. to chief justice Glenn Terrell Fla. Supreme Ct., Tallahassee, 1958-60; city atty. City of Pompano Beach, Fla., 1960-63; pvt. practice law Ft. Lauderdale, Fla., 1964-94; of counsel Ruden, McClosky, Smith, Schuster & Russell, P.A., Ft. Lauderdale, 1994—. Bd. dirs. BankAtlantic; chmn. 17th Cir. Trial Ct. Nominating Com., 1971-76. Trustee St. Thomas Aquinas Found., 1979-81; pres., bd. dirs. St. Thomas More Soc. South Fla. Recipient Young Man of the Yr. award Pompano Beach Jaycees, 1963. Mem. Fla. Bar (vice-chmn. com. on econs. 1966-71, chmn. group legal svc. com. 1975, real property and probate law sect. 1976-90, family law sect. 1978-94), Broward County Bar Assn. (chmn. 17th cir. grievance com. A 1969, treas. 1969-70, pres. 1971-72, Professionalism in Practice award 2000, Fla. bar grievance com. A 2000-2003, chmn. 2002), Phi Delta Phi. Roman Catholic. Avocations: travel, languages, computers. Home: 12045 NW 62d Ct Coral Springs FL 33076-1906 Office: Ruden McClosky Smith Schuster & Russell PA 200 E Broward Blvd Fort Lauderdale FL 33301-1963 E-mail: bld@ruden.com., bdigiulian@cs.com.

DIGIUSTINI, ANTONETTA ANNA, educational association administrator, educator; b. Boston, Mass., USA, July 10, 1961; d. Luigi and Elisa Carolina (Castrucci) DiGiustini. AB, Harvard U., 1997. Tchr., arts adminstr. Charles River Creative Arts Program, Dover, Mass., 1977—92; program asst. Nazzaro Cmty. Ctr., Boston, 1989—90; asst. dir. pub. programs and edn. Bostonian Soc., Boston, 1991—93; stewardship coord. Radcliffe Inst. for Advanced Study, Cambridge, Mass., 1995—; co-founder, dir., tchr. The Advent Sch.'s Learning-Boston, 1999—; tchr., mem. faculty The Saturday Course, Milton Acad., Milton, Mass., 2000—. Contbr. poetry to anthologies, 1976—. Recipient Am. Registry of Outstanding Profl., 2002—. Mem.: Assn. Fundraising Profls., Orgn. Am. Historians, Am. Hist. Assn. Avocations: writing poetry, photography, running, reading. Home: 107 Beacon St Apt 7 Boston MA 02116 Office: Radcliffe Inst Advanced Study 10 Garden St Cambridge MA 02138

DIGMAN, LESTER ALOYSIUS, management educator; b. Kieler, Wis., Nov. 22, 1938; s. Arthur Louis and Hilda Dorothy (Jansen) D.; m. Ellen Rhomberg Pfohl, Jan. 15, 1966; children: Stephanie, Sarah, Mark. BSME, U. Iowa, 1961, MSIE, 1962, PhD, 1970. Registered profl. engr., Mass. Mgmt. cons. U.S. Ameta, Rock Island, Ill., 1962-67; mgmt. instr. U. Iowa, Iowa City, 1967-69; head applied math. dept. U.S. Ameta, Rock Island, Ill., 1969-74, head managerial tng. dept., 1974-77; assoc. prof. mgt. U. Nebr., Lincoln, 1977-84, dir. grad. studies in mgmt., 1982—, prof. mgmt., 1984-87, Leonard E Whittaker Am. Charter disting. prof. mgmt., 1987-93, Met. Fed. Bank disting. prof. mgmt., 1993-95, First Bank disting. prof. mgmt., 1995-98, U.S. Bank disting. prof. mgmt., 1998—2002, Harold J. Laipply coll. prof., 2002—; dir. Ctr. for Tech. Mgmt. and Decision Scis., 1992-94; interim dir. Gallup Rsch. Ctr., 1994-95; mem. adv. bd. Ctr. for Albanian Studies, 1992—. Cons. various orgns., 1963-72; sec. treas. Mgmt. Svcs. Assocs. Ltd., Davenport, Iowa, 1972-77; owner L.A. Digman and Assocs., Lincoln, 1977—; gen. ptnr. Letna Properties, Madison, Wis., 1978—. Author: Strategic Management: Concepts, Decisions, Cases, 1986, 2d edit., 1990, Strategic Mangement: Concepts, Processes, Decisions, 1995, 3d edit., 1999, Strategic Management: Competing in the Global Information Age, 2004, Network Analysis for Management Decisions, 1982, Strategic Management: Cases for the Global Information Age, 2002, 2d edit., 2004; contbr. articles to profl. jours. Recipient Dist. award SBA, 1980, Certs. of Appreciation Dept. of Def., 1972. Fellow Decision Scis. Inst. (charter, program chmn. 1986, pres. 1987-88, coord. doctoral consortium 1989, strategy/policy track chmn. 1991, v.p. 1992-94, strategic mgmt. track chmn. internat. meeting 1993, chair long-range planning com. 1995-96, adv. com. for internat. meeting 1997, chair fellows com., 1999-2000), Pan Pacific Bus. Assn. (bd. adv. 1999—); mem. IEEE, Strategic Mgmt. Soc. (founding), Acad. of Mgmt., Strategic Leadership Forum, Inst. for Ops. Rsch. and Mgmt. Scis. (founding), MBA Roundtable (charter, steering com.), Nebr. Club, Firethorn Country Club, Confrerie de la Chaine Rotisseurs. Roman Catholic. Avocations: gardening, photography, wine tasting. Home: 7520 Lincolnshire Rd Lincoln NE 68506-1635 Office: U Nebr 277 CBA Lincoln NE 68588

DIGNAC, GENY (EUGENIA M. BERMUDEZ), sculptor; b. Buenos Aires, June 8, 1932; came to U.S., 1954; d. Jose Victor Marenco and Margarita Eugenia D.; m. Jose Y. Bermudez, Apr. 7, 1958; children—Alexander, Melanie. Ed., U. Buenos Aires, 1952-54. Lectr. in field. Exhibited in one-woman shows at Galeria 22, Caracas, Venezuela, 1967, Michael Berger Gallery, Pitts., 1969, Cinema 2, Caracas, 1971, Pyramid Gallery, Washington, 1971; exhibited in numerous group shows including Corcoran Gallery of Art, Washington, 1958, 59, Inst. Contemporary Arts, Washington, 1967, Bklyn. Mus., 1968, Mus. Modern Art, Buenos Aires, 1971, Mus. Fine Arts, Boston, 1971, Palais des Beaux Arts, Brussels, 1974, Inst. Contemporary Arts, London, 1974; represented in permanent collections including Fundacio Joan Miro, Barcelona, Spain, Palazzo Dei Diamanti, Ferrara, Italy, Museo La Tertulia, Cali, Colombia, Galeria del Banco Central, Guayaquil, Ecuador, The Latinoamerican Art Found., San Juan, P.R., and others in Argentina, Chile, Germany, Italy, Ireland, Spain, U.S. and Venezuela; works include 27 Fire Gestures-, 1970-2000; radio and TV interviews, U.S. and abroad; works with lights, fire and temperatures; subject of profl. articles, films. Recipient prize for light sculpture IX Festival of Art, 1969 Home: 4109 E Via Estrella Phoenix AZ 85028-4515 E-mail: gdignac@aol.com.

DIGNAM, WILLIAM JOSEPH, obstetrician, gynecologist, educator; b. Manchester, N.H., Aug. 11, 1920; s. Walter Joseph and Margaret Veronica (Lowe) D.; m. Winifred Kennedy, June 7, 1947; children— Mary Brett, Kevan Jean, Erin Margaret, Meighan Ann AB, Dartmouth Coll., 1941; MD, Harvard U., 1943. Intern Boston City Hosp., 1944; resident in ob-gyn U. Kans. Med. Ctr., Kansas City, 1947-50; from asst. prof. to prof. ob-gyn UCLA, 1951—. Affiliated with UCLA Med. Ctr., Cedars-Sinai Med. Ctr., Harbor-UCLA Med. Ctr. Roman Catholic. Home: 820 Alma Real Dr Pacific Palisades CA 90272-3704 Office: UCLA Sch Medicine Dept Ob-Gyn 10833 Le Conte Ave Los Angeles CA 90095-3075 E-mail: wdignam@mednet.ucla.edu.

DIGNAN, THOMAS GREGORY, JR., lawyer; b. Worcester, Mass., May 23, 1940; s. Thomas Gregory and Hester Clare (Sharkey) D.; m. Mary Anne Connor, Sept. 16, 1978; children: Kellyanne E., Maryclare E. BA, Yale U., 1961; JD, U. Mich., 1964. Bar: Mass. 1964, U.S. Supreme Ct. 1968. Assoc. firm Ropes & Gray, Boston, 1964-74, ptnr. firm, 1974-2000, of counsel, 2001—. Spl. asst. atty. gen. State of Mass., 1974-76; trustee NSTAR. Asst. editor: Mich. Law Rev., 1963-64; contbr. articles to profl. jours. Bd. dirs. Family Counseling and Guidance Ctrs., Inc., 1967-76, 78-94, v.p., 1983-87, pres., 1987-89; trustee Cath. Charitable Bur. of Boston, Inc., 1994-97, Dana Hall Sch., 1994—; bd. dirs. Gov.'s Mgmt. Task Force, 1979-81, Mass. Moderator's Assn., 1994-2000; mem. fin. com. Town of Sudbury, 1982-85, moderator, 1985—; bd. advisors Environ. Law Ctr., Vt. Law Sch., 1981—; mem. vis. com. U. Mich. Law Sch.; corporator Emerson Hosp., 1989—. Mem. Nashawtuc Country Club, Shadow Wood Country Club, Order of the Coif, Phi Delta Phi. Republican. Roman Catholic. Home: 9053 Windswept Dr Bonita Springs FL 34135 E-mail: Tdignanjr@aol.com.

DIIENNO, JOSEPH ANTHONY, psychiatrist; b. Phila., Feb. 23, 1941; s. Anthony Joseph and Mary (Cangemi) DiI.; m. Camille Giuffre, Apr. 10, 1965; children: Joy, Christopher, Stephanie, Jonathan. BS, St. Joseph's Coll., Phila., 1963; MD, Temple U., 1967. Diplomate Am. Bd. Psychiatry and Neurology. Intern, resident in psychiatry Albert Einstein Med. Ctr., Phila., 1967-71; asst. clin. prof. psychiatry U. Tex., San Antonio, 1972-73; asst. clin. prof. mental health Hahneman U., Phila., 1974—, dir. group sect., 1977-89; asst. dir. residency Phila. State Hosp., 1974-78; instr. group process Albert Einstein Med. Ctr., Phila., 1987—. Guest lectr. throughout Phila. area. Co-author: St. Paul Editions: Boston, Mass., 1979-89; author: (film) Pennsylvania Crime Commission; Harrisburg, Pennsylvania, 1971; contbr. articles to profl. jours. Maj. USAF, 1971-73. Fellow Am. Psychiat. Assn.; mem. Pa. Psychiat. Soc., Phila. Med. Soc. (ethics com. 1967-80). Roman Catholic. Avocations: philosophy, history, religion.

DIIPLA, JOYCE KATHERINE MARIE, physician; b. Oak Lawn, Ill., June 27, 1971; d. Jan Zdzistaw and Joyce Ida Diipla. BS, Univ. Ill., Chgo., 1994; MD, Karol Marcinkowski Univ. of Medicine, Poznan, Poland, 1999. Rsch. fellow Univ. Chgo., Ill., 2002—. Owner and pres. Diipla Enterprises, Chgo., 2002—. Contbr. scientific papers. Mem.: N.Y. Acad. of Sci. Roman Cath. Avocations: travel, music, gardening, culinary arts, linguistics.

DIKANOV, SERGEI A. physicist, researcher; b. Spokoiniy, Russia, Dec. 17, 1951; s. Alexei G. Dikanov and Tatyana M. Shileinkova; m. Irina P. Baladurina, June 6, 1980; 1 child, Dariia S. MS, Novosibirsk State U., Russia, 1968—73; PhD, Russian Acad. of Sci., Novosibirsk, 1973—78; DSc, Russian Acad. of Sci., Kazan, 1990. Sr. rsch. scientist Russian Acad. of Sci., Novosibirsk, 1978—92; a. von humboldt found. rsch. fellow Saarland U., Homburg, Germany, 1992—93; vis. scientist Pacific N.W. Nat. Lab., Richland, Wash., 1993—97; rsch. scientist SUNY, Binghamton, NY, 1998—99; rsch. asst. prof. U. of Ill., 1999—. Author: (book) Imidazoline Nitroxides, Electron Spin Echo Envelope Modulation (ESEEM) Spectroscopy. Recipient USSR State Prize, USSR Govt., 1988; fellow A. von Humboldt Rsch. Fellow, A. von Humboldt Found., Germany, 1992; grantee Collaborative Rsch. Grant, NATO, 2000, NSF, 2000-2004, Rsch. Grant, NIH, 2002-2007. Mem.: Internat. EPR Soc. Achievements include research in Pulsed Electron Paramagnetic Resonance Spectroscopy. Home: 3105 Weeping Cherry Dr Champaign IL 61822 Office: U of Ill 506 S Mathews Ave Urbana IL 61801-3618 E-mail: dikanov@uiuc.edu.

DIKE, MARGARET HOPCRAFT, retired education administrator; b. Prescott, Ariz., July 15, 1921; d. Walter Irving and Margaret Jennie (Lindsay) Hopcraft; m. Sheldon Holland Dike, Nov. 28, 1941 (div. 1971); children: Lawrence, Walter, Robert, Martin, Martha. BA, U. N.Mex., 1941, MA, 1975. Draftsman U. Calif., Los Alamos, N.Mex., 1943-45; coord. Albuquerque Pub. Schs., 1972-85; ret., 1985. Chair pub. adv. com. U. N.Mex., Albuquerque, 1973-74, chair search com. regional v.p., 1975. Co-editor: Bicentennial '76 - Albuquerque, 1977; editor booklet New Mexico Arts Resources Survey, 1957. Trustee Albuquerque Mus., 1969-81; chmn. Albuquerque R.R. Centennial, 1979-80, Keep Albuquerque Beautiful Edn., 1984—; pres. Albuquerque Sister Cities Found., 1985-87; Albuquerque Hist. Soc., 1971-78; N.Mex. Assn. for Cmty. Edn. Devel., 1980-82; chair Albuquerque Sister Cities Bd., 1988-91, 96—; life mem. N.Mex. PTA, pres., 1977-79, 92-95; sec. Edn. Forum N.Mex., 1988-89; chair, Ednl. Success Alliance, 1996-97. Recipient Lobo award U. N.Mex., 1968, Gov.'s award for outstanding N.Mex. women, Commn. on Status of Women, 1986, 90, 1st Lifetime Achievement award, 2002, N.Mex. Disting. Svc. award, 1996, Paragon award N.Mex. Assn. Ednl. Retirees, 2000, Cmty. Svc. award, AARP, 2001; named Woman on the Move for cmty. svc. YWCA, 1995, to Sr. Hall of Fame, 1995, Zia award U. N. Mex. Alumni Assn., 1999. Mem.: AAUW (pres. N.Mex. 1989—93, pres. Albuquerque br. 1968—70, 2000—01, Grace Barker Wilson award N.Mex. 2001), La Luz Am. Bus. Womens Assn., Albuquerque Assn. Ednl. Retirees (pres. 1998, 1999, 2002), Mortar Bd. (pres. alumni chpt. 1988—90, 1996—, Nat. Cmty. Svc. award 1993), Exec. Women Internat. (treas. 1983—85), Phi Kappa Phi, Phi Alpha Theta, Phi Delta Kappa. Methodist. Avocations: travel, reading, camping, sewing.

DIKSIC, MIRKO, research scientist, educator; b. Cvetković, Croatia, May 22, 1942; s. Mirko and Katarina (Boričević) D.; m. Ljubica Mlinarić, Apr. 30, 1968; children: Dubravka, Nikola. MSc, U. Zagreb, 1968, PhD, 1970. Rsch. assoc. U. Fla., Gainesville, 1973-74; postdoctoral fellow McGill U., Montreal, Can., 1971-73, rsch. assoc., 1974-79, asst. to assoc. prof., 1979-92, prof., 1992—; rsch. assoc. U. Fla., Gainesville, 1973-74; vis. scis. King Faisal Hosp and Rsch. Ctr., Riyadh, Saudi Arabia. Vis. prof. Nat. Tsing-Hua Univ., Hsinchu, Taiwan, 1990; dir. Radioch.-Cyclotron Unit, Montreal Neurol. Inst., Montreal, 1983—; mem. adv. bd. Croatian Brain Inst; vis. scientist King Faisal Hosp. and Rsch. Ctr., Riyadh, Saudi Arabia. Co-editor: Radiopharmaceuticals and Brain Pathology Studied with PET and SPECT, 1991; contbr. numerous articles to profl. jours. Operating grantee Med. Rsch. Coun., 1979—, NIH, 1984—, EJLB Found., 1990. Mem. AAAS, Soc. of Nuclear Medicine (bd. dirs. radiopharm. coun. 1990-92), Internat. Soc. of Cerb. Blood Flow and Metab. Avocations: soccer, chess, classical music, travelling. Home: 28 Viger Kirkland QC Canada H9J 2E5 Office: McGill Univ 3801 University St Montreal QC Canada H3A 2B4

DIKTAS, CHRISTOS JAMES, lawyer; b. June 17, 1955; s. Christos James and Elpiniki (Angelou) D. Student, U. Salonika, Greece, 1976, U. Copenhagen, Denmark, 1976; BA, Montclair State U., 1977; JD, Calif. Western Sch. Law, 1981; diplomate, Rutgers U., 1992. Bar: N.J. 1982, U.S. Dist. Ct. N.J. 1982, N.Y. 1989, U.S. Supreme Ct. 1989. Law sec. to Hon. James F. Madden Superior Ct., Hackensack, N.J., 1981-82; sr. assoc. Klinger, Nicolette, Mavroudis & Honig, Hackensack, 1982-85; ptnr. Montecallo & Diktas, Hackensack, 1985-86, Biagiotti, Marino, Montecallo & Diktas, Hackensack, 1986-89, Diktas & Habeeb, North Bergen, N.J., 1989-94, Diktas Gillen, 1995-99; pvt. practice Diktas Neiss, Cliffside Park, NJ, 2000—. Asst. counsel Bergen County, 1986-87; atty. zoning bd. adjustment Borough of Cliffside Park, 1986-94, borough atty., 1994—; planning bd. Borough of Ridgefield, N.J., 1987-99, 2001—, borough atty., 2000-01; borough atty., Bogota, N.J., 1989-91, Fairview, N.J., 1994-95; bd. edn. atty., Bogota, 1992-95; labor counsel Bergen County, N.J., 1990-2001; atty. planning bd. City of Garfield, N.J., 1994-2003; atty., sec. Garfield Redevel. Agy., 2002—; adj. prof. law Montclair (N.J.) State U., 1988—. Editor lead articles Calif. Western Internat. Law Jour., 1980-81. Campaign dir. Kingman for Senate Com., Bergen County, N.J., 1983; mcpl. coord. Kean for Gov. campaign, 1985; asst. treas. Arthur F. Jones for Congress, 9th Congl. Dist., 1986. Mem. ABA, N.J. Bar Assn., Bergen County Bar Assn., Order of Am. Hellenic Edn. Progressive Assn., Phi Alpha Delta (parliamentarian Campbell E. Beaumont chpt. 1978-81), Sons of Pericles (5th dist. gov. 1976-77, supreme gov. 1977-78). Greek Orthodox. Home: 445 Orcrest Ter Cliffside Park NJ 07010-2814 Office: Diktas Neiss 596 Anderson Ave Cliffside Park NJ 07010-1831 E-mail: diktasesqs@aol.com.

DILANDRO, ANTHONY CHARLES, science educator, funeral director; b. Flushing, N.Y., June 1, 1944; s. Antonio and Frances May DiLandro; m. Ana R. DiLandro, June 6, 1987; children: Donna, Adrienne, Andrew;1 child from previous marriage, Jeffrey. BA psychology, Coll. of New Rochelle, New Rochelle, N.Y., 1983; MEd, Fordam Univ., N.Y., 1984; EdD, City Univ. L.A., L.A., 1996. Lic. funeral dir. N.Y. State, 1966, Commonwealth of Pa., 1973. Funeral dir. and instr. Walter B. Cockor Inc., Bronx, NY, 1966—70; forensic asst. Nassau County Med. Examiner, Nassau County, NY, 1972—77; anatomy prosecutor and supr. Albert Einstein Coll. of Medicine, Bronx, NY, 1979—85; assoc. prof. N.Y. Coll. of Podiatric Medicine, N.Y., 1985—; med. prof. CUNY Med. Sch., N.Y., 2002—. Contbr. scientific papers to profl. jour., articles. Recipient Kappa Delta Pi, Tchr. Coll. Columbia Univ., 1987. Mem.: Internat. Assn. of Med. Sci. Educators. Office: N Y Coll of Podiatric Medicine Divsn Basic Sci 1800 Pk Ave New York NY 10035 Home: 133 S 66St Apt Howard Beach NY 11414

DILBECK, CHARLES STEVENS, JR., real estate company executive; b. Dallas, Dec. 2, 1944; s. Charles Stevens Sr. and Betty Doris (Owens) D.; 1 child, Stephen Douglas; m. Carolyn Jane DeBoer, Sept. 4, 1994. BS, Wichita State U., 1968; MS, Stanford U., 1969, postgrad., 1970-71. Engr. United Tech. Ctr., Sunnyvale, Calif., 1971-72; cons. Diversicom, Inc., Santa Clara, Calif., 1972-73; engr. Anamet Labs., San Carlos, Calif., 1973-75; cons. real estate investment Cert. Capital Corp., San Jose, Calif., 1975-82; pvt. practice in real estate, San Jose, 1981—; prin. Am. Equity Investments, San Jose, 1982—. Mem. Los Gatos (Calif.) Rent Adv. Com., 1988. Mem. Nat. Apt. Assn., San Jose Real Estate Bd., Tri-County Apt. Assn., Gold Key Club, Tau Beta Pi (pres. 1968), Sigma Gamma Tau. Republican. Avocation: ocean yacht racing. Office: Am Equity Investments 301 Alta Loma Ln Santa Cruz CA 95062-4620

DILCHER, DAVID LEONARD, paleobotany educator, research scholar; b. Cedar Falls, Iowa, July 10, 1936; m. Katherine Swanson, 1961; children: Peter, Ann BS in Natural History, U. Minn., 1958, MS in Botany, Geology and Zoology, 1960; postgrad., U. Ill., 1960-62; PhD in Biology, Geology, Yale U., 1964; participant OTS course field dendrology, Costa Rica, 1968. Teaching asst. U. Minn., Mpls., 1958-60, U. Ill., Urbana, 1960-62, Yale U., New Haven, Conn., 1962-63, Cullman-Univ. fellow, 1963-64, instr. biology, 1965-66; NSF postdoctoral fellow Senckenberg Mus., Frankfurt am Main, Fed. Republic of Germany, 1964-65; asst. prof. botany Ind. U., Bloomington, 1966-70, assoc. prof., 1970-76; Guggenheim fellow Imperial Coll., Univ. London, 1972-73; assoc. prof. geology Ind. U., Bloomington, 1975-77, prof. paleobotany, 1977-90, adj. prof. biology, adj. prof. geology, 1990—; grad. rsch. prof. Fla. Mus. Natural History, U. Fla., Gainesville, 1990—. Panel mem. for systematic biology program, NSF, 1977-79, panel mem. for selecting NATO postdoctoral fellow, 1982, mem. adv. com. Earth Sys. History, 1997-2000, bd. mem. on earth scis. and resources NRC, 2001—, minerals, 2001—; vis. lectr. to People's Republic of China Nat. Acad. Sci. com. on scholarly communications with China, 1986; corr. mem. Senckenberg Mus., Frankfurt, Fed. Republic Germany, 1989; hon. prof. Nanjing Inst. Geology and Paleontology, Acad. Sinica, China, 1998—, Jilin U., Changchau, China, 2001—; adj. prof. biology U. Tenn., Martin, 2000—; hon. prof., vice chmn. sci. com. rsch. ctr. paleontoloty and stratigraphy Jilin U., Changchun, China, 2001–; bd. dirs. Smithsonian Inst. Author: (with D. Redmon, M. Tansey and D. Whitehead) Plant Biology Laboratory Manual, 1973, 2d edit., 1975; editor: (with Tom Taylor and Theodore Delevoryas) Plant Reproduction in the Fossil Record, symposium vol., 1979; (with T. Taylor) Biostratigraphy of Fossil Plants: Successional and Paleoecological Analysis, 1980; (with William L. Crepet) Origin and Evolution of Flowering Plants, Symposium Volume, 1984; (with Michael S. Zavada) Phylogeny of the Hamamedidae, symposium vol., 1986; (with Patrick S. Herendeen) Advances in Legume Systematics Part 4, The Fossil Record, 1992; contbr. articles to profl. jours. Mem. utilities bd. City of Bloomington, 1974-76; ruling elder First Presbyn. Ch. Bloomington, 1975-77; bd. dirs. United Campus Ministries, 1971-72, Smithsonian Mus. Natural History, 1998—; mem. coun. Monroe County United Ministries, 1975-77. Dist. Vis. Rsch. scholar U. Adelaide, Australia, 1981, 88; Vis. Rsch. scholar Birbal Sahni Palaeonbot. Inst., Lucknow, India, 1992; grantee Sigma Xi, 1961-62, 66, Ind. U., 1967-68, Orgn. Tropical Studies, 1971, Travel grantee Ind. U., 1968, 71, 77, 80, Rsch. grantee NSF, 1966-89, 96—, Amax Coal Found., 1980-81, NATO Coop, 1991-93; Eaton-Hooker fellow, 1963, Cullman-Univ. fellow, 1963-64, Guggenheim fellow, Giessen, Fed. Republic of Germany, 1972-73, Ind. U., 1972-73, Brit. Mus. Natural History, London, 1988-89; recipient Tracey M. Sonneborn award for disting. rsch. and excellenc in tchg. Ind. U., 1978-88, Bot. Soc. Am. Merit award, 1991, Birbal Sahni Found. award, 1998. Fellow Ind. Acad. Sci.; mem. NAS, AAAS, Bot. Soc. Am. (chmn. paleobot. sect. 1974, sec.-treas. 1975-77, rep. to jour. editl. bd. 1978-79, jour. editl. bd. 1981-82, conservation com. 1978-81, chmn. conservation com. 1981, 82, program dir. 1982-84, exec. bd. 1982-91, sec. 1984-88, pres.-elect 1988-89, pres. 1989-90), Paleontol. Soc., Paleontol. Assn., Internat. Orgn. Paleobotany (N.Am. rep. 1975-81, v.p. 1987-93), Assn. Tropical Biology, Am. Inst. Biol. Scis., Am. Assn. Stratigraphic Palynologists, Internat. Assn. Angiosperm Paleobotany (pres. 1977-80), Geol. Soc. Am. (com. on collection and collecting 1978-85), Ky. Acad. Scis., Senckenberg Natur Mus. und Forschungsgeshellshaft Frankfurt am Main (corr. mem. 1990), Sigma Xi (pres.-elect Ind. chpt. 1985-86, pres. 1986-87). Office: U Fla Dept Natural Sci Fla Mus Natural History PO Box 117800 Gainesville FL 32611-7800 E-mail: dilcher@flmnh.ufl.edu.

DILDY, GARY ANDREW, III, maternal fetal medicine physician, educator; b. New Orleans, May 7, 1959; s. Gary Andrew Jr. and Barbara Mae (Barbier) D. BS, La. State U., 1981; MD, Tulane U., 1985. Diplomate Am. Bd. Ob-gyn, Am. Bd. Maternal-Fetal Medicine. Intern in ob/gyn Baylor Coll. Medicine, Houston, 1985-86, resident in ob/gyn, 1986-89, fellow, 1989-91; dir. Perinatal Ctr., Utah Valley Regional Med. Ctr., Provo, 1991-2000; asst. prof. U. Utah, 1991-97, assoc. prof., 1997-2000; prof. La. State U. Sch. Medicine, New Orleans, 2000—. Contbr. chapters to books, articles; editor: (jours.) editor Obstetrical Emergencies in Contemporary Ob-Gyn., 1993—95; editor-in-chief: textbook Critical Care Obstetrics, 4th edit. Mem. AMA, Soc. for Maternal-Fetal Medicine, Am. Coll. Ob-Gyn., Soc. Gynecologic Investigation. Achievements include orignal work in intrapartum fetal oxygen saturation monitoring. Office: La State U Sch Medicine 1542 Tulane Ave New Orleans LA 70112 E-mail: gdildy3@lsuhsc.edu.

DI LELLA, ALEXANDER ANTHONY, biblical studies educator; b. Paterson, N.J., Aug. 14, 1929; s. Alessandro and Adelaide (Grimaldi) Di L. BA, St. Bonaventure U., 1952; S.T.L., Cath. U. Am., 1959, PhD, 1962; S.S.L., Pontifical Bibl. Inst., Rome, 1964. Entered Franciscan Order, Roman Catholic Ch., 1949; ordained priest, 1955. Lectr. O.T. and bibl. Greek Holy Name Coll., Washington, 1964-67; asst. prof. Semitic lang. Cath. U. Am., 1966-68, assoc. prof., 1968-76, assoc. prof. Bibl. studies, 1976-77, prof., 1977-92, Andrews-Kelly-Ryan disting. prof. bib. studies, 1992—. Adj. prof. O.T., Washington Theol. Union, 1969-72; mem. Rev. Standard Version Bible Com., 1982—; chmn. bd. of control New Am. Bible, 1988—. Assoc. editor, translator New American Bible, 1965-87; editor New Revised Standard Version Bible Cath. Edit., 1993; author: The Hebrew Text of Sirach: A Text-Critical and Historical Study, 1966, The Book of Daniel, 1978, Proverbs in the Old Testament in Syriac According to the Peshitta Version, 1979, The Wisdom of Ben Sira, 1987, Il Libro di Daniele (1-6), 1995, (7-14), 1996, Daniel: A Book for Troubling Times, 1997, El libro de Daniel (1-6), 2000, (7-14), 2001; contbr. articles and revs. to scholarly and popular publs. Mem. instnl. rev. bd. Dubroff Eye Ctr., Silver Spring, Md., 1982-94; cancer care continuum group Washington Hosp. Ctr., 1995-96. Am. Sch. Oriental rsch. fellow, 1962-63; Guggenheim fellow, 1972-73. Mem. Soc. Bibl. Lit. (pres. Chesapeake Bay region 1972-73), Cath. Bibl. Assn. (pres. 1975-76, del. to Council on Study of Religion 1971-72) Home: Curley Hall Cath U Am Washington DC 20064-0001 Office: Cath U Am Rm 420 Caldwell Hall Washington DC 20064 E-mail: dilella@cua.edu. *Most of my adult life I have been a student of Biblical languages and literatures, interpretation and theology. Teaching, research and publications enable me to convey to others the value of the Bible as a primary document of Judaism and Christianity and as a significant factor in Western culture and civilization.*

DILEONE, CARMEL MONTANO, dental hygienist; b. New Haven, Aug. 24, 1926; d. Nicholas and Martha (Ercolano) M.; m. Eugene Francis Dileone, Jan. 28, 1948; children: Gina, Richard. Dental Hygienist, Temple U., 1945; AA, Albertus Magnus Coll., 1980; BS, U. Bridgeport, 1983; MS, So. Conn. State U., 1985. Registered dental hygienist. Dental hygiene practitioner George M. Montano, DDS, New Haven, 1946-50, George V. Montano, DDS, Orange, 1959-2000, Francis R. Mullen, DDS, West Haven, 1950-55; dental hygiene practioner Herbert Saunders, DDS, Orange, Conn., 1958-63, Children's Dental Assocs., Hamden, 2000—, Children's Dental Group, New Haven, 2000—; G. Instr. Huntington Inst., North Haven, Conn., 1983; adj. assoc. prof. U. Bridgeport, Conn., Fones Sch. Dental Hygiene, 1985-96; adj. faculty U. New Haven, 1994—. Dir., treas. Conn. Hygienists' Polit. Action Com., 1996—2002. Recipient Profl. Recognition award U. New Haven, 1999. Mem.: New Haven Dental Hygienists Assn. (pres. 1949, 1975), Conn. Dental Hygienists Assn. (treas. 1986—88, v.p. 1988—89, pres.-elect 1989—90, pres. 1991, Mabel C. McCarthy award 1983, Pres. award 1994), Am. Dental Hygienists Assn., Am. Soc. Dentistry for Children, Conn. Pub. Health Assn., Sigma Phi Alpha. Roman Catholic. Home: 348 Racebrook Rd Orange CT 06477-3109

DILFER, TRENT, professional football player; b. Santa Cruz, Ca, Mar. 13, 1972; m. Cassandra Dilfer; 1 child, Madeleine. Student, Fresno State U. Quarterback Tampa Bay Buccaneers, 1994—2000, Baltimore Ravens, 2000, Seattle Seahawks, 2001—. Active Fellowship Christian Athletes, Athletes in Action, United Way, Big Bros./Big Sisters, Police Athletic League, Hardy's Huddle. Achievements include broke Doug Williams 1982 record by throwing 138 consecutive passes without interception. Office: Seattle Seahawks 11220 NE 53rd St Kirkland WA 98033

DILG, JOSEPH CARL, lawyer; b. Dallas, Apr. 1, 1951; s. Millard John and Helen Mary (Gill) D.; m. Alexandra Gregg, Aug. 5, 1972; children: Helen Lane, Mary Saunders. BA, So. Meth. U., 1973; JD with high honors, U. Tex., 1976. Bar: Tex. 1976. Assoc. Vinson & Elkins, Houston, 1976-83, ptnr., 1983—. Editor U. Tex. Law Rev., 1976. Named Outstanding Editor U. Tex. Law Rev., 1976. Mem. ABA, Tex. Bar Assn., Houston Bar Assn., Chancellors, Order of Coif. Office: Vinson & Elkins 3401 First City Tower 1001 Fannin St Houston TX 77002-6760 E-mail: jdilg@velaw.com.

DILIBERTO, RICHARD ANTHONY, JR., lawyer; b. Hazleton, Pa., July 19, 1961; s. Richard A. Sr. and Marija (Vukcevich) D.; m. Faith Ann Petrovich, Sept. 4, 1982. BS in Edn. cum laude, Bloomsburg U. of Pa., 1982; JD cum laude, Widener U., Wilmington, Del., 1986. Bar: Del. 1986, Pa. 1987, N.J. 1987, U.S. Dist. Ct. Del. 1987. Law clk. Superior Ct. Del., Wilmington, 1986-87; ptnr. Young, Conaway, Stargatt & Taylor, Wilmington, 1987—. Adj. prof. paralegal program Widener U., 1987-90; rep. Del State House of Reps., 1992-2002. Contbr. articles to profl. jours. Coach basketball YMCA, softball, 1994—. Recipient Advocacy award ATLA, Outstanding Alumni Svc. award Widener U. Law Sch., 1999. Mem. ABA, Del. Bar Assn. (Disting. Legis. award 1999). Roman Catholic. Home: 311 Winterthur Ln Newark DE 19711-4136 Office: Young Conaway Stargatt & Taylor LLP PO Box 391 Wilmington DE 19899-0391 Fax: (302) 576-3290. E-mail: rdiliberto@ycst.com.

DILKS, PARK BANKERT, JR., lawyer; b. Phila., Mar. 25, 1928; s. Park Bankert and Gertrude Scott (Hilton) D.; children: Jonathan Park, Jennifer Robin. AB, U. Pa., 1948, JD, 1951. Bar: Pa. 1952, D.C. 1951, U.S. Supreme Ct. 1962. Asst. dist. atty., Phila., 1952; assoc. firm Souser & Schumacker, Phila., 1953-60, Morgan, Lewis & Bockius, Phila., 1961-63, ptnr., 1964-95, of counsel, 1996—. Chmn. bd. U.S. Investment Fund, 1973-2001. Served as 1st lt. USAR, 1952-58. Mem. ABA, Pa. Bar Assn., Phila. Bar Assn., D.C. Bar Assn., Fed. Bar Assn., Assn. Bar City N.Y., Union League, Phi Beta Kappa. Home: 140 Lakeside Ln Media PA 19063-2047 Office: 1701 Market St Philadelphia PA 19103-2903 E-mail: pbdilks@worldnet.att.net., pdilks@morganlewis.com.

DILL, CHARLES ANTHONY, manufacturing and computer company executive; b. Cleve., Nov. 29, 1939; s. Melville Reese and Gladys (Frode) D.; m. Louise T. Hall, Aug. 24, 1963 (dec. Sept. 28, 1983); children: Charles Anthony, Dudley Barnes; m. Mary M. Howell, Jan. 17, 1987. BSME, Yale U., 1961; MBA, Harvard U., 1963. With Emerson Electric Co., 1963-88, corp. v.p. internat., 1973-77; pres. A.B. Chance Co. subs. Emerson Electric Co., 1977-80; corp. group v.p. Emerson Electric Co., St. Louis, 1980-82, sr. v.p. office of chief exec., adv. dir., 1982-88; pres., COO, bd. dirs. AVX Corp., N.Y.C., 1988-90; pres., CEO, bd. dirs. Bridge Info. Systems, Inc., St. Louis, 1990-95; gen. ptnr. Gateway Equity Ptnrs. IV, St. Louis, 1995—. Bd. dirs. Maryville Technologies Inc., Neovision Hypersystems, V-Brick Inc., Digital Concepts of Mo., Zoltec Inc., Stifel Nicholaus Inc., Transact Techs., DT Industries, Potter Elec. Mem. St. Louis Country Club, Log Cabin Club. Republican. Home: 850 Beach Rd Apt 180 Vero Beach FL 32963 Office: Gateway Equity Partners 8000 Maryland Ave Ste 1190 Saint Louis MO 63105-3910 E-mail: cdill@gatewayventures.com.

DILL, ELLIS HAROLD, university dean; b. Pittsburg County, Okla., Dec. 31, 1932; s. Harold and Mayme Doris (Ellis) D.; m. Cleone June Granrud, Sept. 12, 1953; children: Michael Harold, Susan Marie. AA, Grant Tech. Jr. Coll., 1951; BS in Civil Engring, U. Calif. at Berkeley, 1954, MS in Civil Engring, 1955, PhD, 1957. Asst. prof. to prof. aeros. and astronautics U. Wash., 1956-77, chmn. dept. aeros. and astronautics, 1976-77; dean engring. Rutgers U., New Brunswick, N.J., 1977-98, univ. prof., 1998—. Mem. Soc. Natural Philosophy. Achievements include research, numerous publications on mechanics of solids. Home: 436 Brentwood Dr Piscataway NJ 08854-3608 Office: Rutgers U Coll Engring 98 Brett Rd Piscataway NJ 08854-8058

DILL, GARY A. academic administrator; Sr. v.p. Schreiner Coll., 1991—; pres. McPherson Coll., 2002—; pres. Coll. S.W., N.Mex., 2002—. Presbyn. miniter, former pastor Ch. Brethren; former chmn. Tex. Arts and Crafts Ednl. Found.; mem. bd. dirs. Ptnrs. in Parenting Edn. Bd.; dir. cmty. svc. Noon Rotary Club, Kerrville. Office: Coll SW 6610 Lovington Hwy Hobbs NM 88240

DILL, JOHN FRANCIS, retired publishing company executive; b. Hempstead, N.Y., May 3, 1934; s. Samuel Leland and Jeanne Marie (Dorsch) D.; m. Joan Eileen Shipps, Aug. 22, 1959 (div. 1973); m. Virginia Rae Dapson, Nov. 23, 1973; children: Patricia, Diane, Kevin, Catherine, Gina, BA, Oberlin Coll., 1957; MBA, NYU, 1963; LHD (hon.), Logan Coll., 1995, U. Mo., St. Louis, 1996. Mgmt. trainee Mut. Life Ins., N.Y.C., 1959-63; mgr. McGraw Hill Book Co., N.Y.C., 1963-68, dir. mktg., 1969-77, pub., gen. mgr., 1977-81; pres., CEO Year Book Med. Pubs., Chgo., 1981-89; pres., chief exec. officer CRC Press Inc., Boca Raton, Fla.; chmn., CEO, pres. Mosby Year Book, 1989-95, chmn. emeritus, 1995—. Bd. dirs. Copyright Clearance Ctr., 1989-95, Mathews Dickey Boy's Club, U. Mo., St. Louis, Chancellor's Coun., pres. 1994-95. Mem. Am. Med. Pubs. Assn. (pres. 1987-88), Am. Assn. Pubs. (chmn. profl. divsn. 1981, chmn. librs. com. 1979), Internat. Assn. Sci. Tech., Med. Pubs. of the World (bd. dirs., treas., chmn. 1994-96), Kensington Country Club. Home: 2988 Saint Barnabas Ct Naples FL 34105-5695

DILL, KENNETH AUSTIN, pharmaceutical chemistry educator; b. Oklahoma City, Dec. 11, 1947; s. Austin Glenn and Margaret (Blocker) D. SB, SM, MIT, 1971; PhD, U. Calif., San Diego, 1978. Fellow Damon Runyon-Walter Winchell Stanford (Calif.) U., 1978-81; asst. prof. chemistry U. Fla., Gainesville, 1981-82; asst. prof. pharm. chemistry and pharmacy U. Calif., San Francisco, 1982-85, assoc. prof., 1985-89, prof., 1989—, co-dir. program in quantitative biology, assoc. dean rsch. Sch. Pharmacy, 2001—. Adj. prof. pharmaceutics U. Utah, 1989—. Contbr. numerous sci. articles to profl. publs.; patentee in field. Recipient Hans Neurath award Protein Soc., 1998; PEW Found. scholar. Fellow AAAS, Am. Phys. Soc. (physics policy coun. 2002—), Biophys. Soc. (nat lectr. 1996, pres. 1998); mem. Am. Chem. Soc., Protein Soc. Office: Univ Calif Pharm Chemistry Dept San Francisco CA 94143-0001

DILL, LADDIE JOHN, artist; b. Long Beach, Calif., Sept. 14, 1943; s. James Melvin and Virginia (Crane) D.; children: Ariel, Jackson Caldwell. BFA, Chouinard Art Inst., 1968. Chmn. of visual arts The Studio Sch., Santa Monica, Calif. Lectr. painting and drawing UCLA, 1975-88. Exhibitions include San Francisco Mus. Modern Art, 1977—78, Albright Knox Mus., Buffalo, 1978—79, Charles Cowles Gallery, N.Y.C., 1983—85, Sonnabend Gallery, The First Show, L.A., Represented in permanent collections Mus. Modern Art, N.Y.C., Laguna Mus. Art, Los Angeles County Mus., Mus. Contemporary Art, L.A., Santa Barbara Mus., San Francisco Mus. Modern Art, Seattle Mus., Newport Harbor Art Mus., Oakland Mus., Smithsonian Instn., IBM, Nat. Mus., Seoul, Republic of Korea, San Diego Mus. Art, La. Mus., Denmark, Am. Embassy, Helsinki, Finland, Corcoran Gallery Art, Washington, Chgo. Art Inst., Greenville County (S.C.) Mus., Palm Springs Desert Mus., Phoenix Art Mus., William Rockhill Nelsen Mus., Kansas City, Phillips Collection. Nat. Endowment Arts grantee, 1975, 82; Guggenheim Found. fellow, 1979-80; Calif. Arts Council Commn. grantee, 1983-84

DILL, RICHARD EVERETT, software company development executive; b. Landstuhl, Fed. Republic of Germany, Mar. 12, 1952; came to U.S., 1956; s. Harlon Jewel and Marilyn Francis (Ritchie) D.; m. Nancy Ann McFarland, Jan. 10, 1981 (div. July 2001); children: Megan Elizabeth, Kimberly Ann; m. Kathleen Jewell, Mar. 29, 2003. BS in Computer Sci., Wash. State U., 1974. Resource mgr. Boeing Computer Services, Seattle, 1977-79; project lead Allied Stores Corp., Seattle, 1979-80; systems engr. Data Gen. Corp., Bellevue, Wash., 1980-82, systems engring. mgr. Denver, 1982-83; Original Equipment Mfr. support mgr. Microsoft Corp., Redmond, Wash., 1983-85, product mktg. group mgr., 1985-86, program mgr. Microsoft Windows, 1986-87, project mgr. Microsoft OS/2, 1987-91, network test group mgr. Microsoft Windows NT and OS/2, 1991—95; pres. New Techonology Cons. Corp., 1995—. Founder and pres. N.W. Pk. Found., 2002—. Editor: Windows Developers Seminar Notes, 1986, Windows Programming Secrets, 1987. Mem. Delta Tau Delta (treas. 1973-74). Avocations: sailing, skiing, woodworking. Home and Office: 22505 NE 99th Way Redmond WA 98053-1904 E-mail: rickd@exmsft.com.

DILL, WILLIAM ALLEN, lawyer; b. Sharon, Pa., May 18, 1918; s. Harry Armitage and Mary Rose (McCann) D.; m. Marjorie Croft, Sept. 3, 1946; children— Mary Alyson, Laurie Ann, Thomas Allen. B.S., U. Pitts., 1940, J.D., 1948. Bar: Pa. 1949. Pilot, Pan Am. Airways, North and South Atlantic, N.Y.C., 1941-42, Central and South Am., Miami, 1942-43; spl. lectr. U. Pitts. Sch. Transp., 1946-48; assoc. Fruit & Francis, Sharon, 1949-68; ptnr. Fruit Dill, Goodwin & Scholl, Sharon, 1968— ; asst. dist. atty., 1952-54; solicitor City of Sharon, 1958-68; spl. dep. atty. gen., 1966-71; lectr. Pa. Bar Inst., Def. Research Inst., Pa. Def. Inst., Am. Arbitration Assn. Rep. state committeeman, 1954-78. Served to capt. USNR, 1944-70, ret. Mem. Am. Jurisprudence Soc., Pa. Bar Assn., Mercer County Bar Assn. (pres. 1969). Home: 219 Case Ave Sharon PA 16146-3427 Office: 32 Shenango Ave Sharon PA 16146-1502

DILL, WILLIAM RANKIN, college president; b. Sewickley, Pa., Aug. 18, 1930; s. Frederick Hayes and Caroline (Rankin) D.; m. Jean McLeod, June 13, 1953; children: Jens McLeod, Holly Ruth, Harrison Rankin, Cynthia Wightman. AB, Bates Coll., 1951, LLD (hon.), 1987; MS, Carnegie Inst. Tech., 1953, PhD, 1956; postgrad., U. Oslo, 1953-54; LHD (hon.), Babson Coll., 1991. Faculty mem. Carnegie-Mellon U., Pitts., 1955-65; program dir. edn. R & D IBM, White Plains, N.Y., 1965-70; dean Grad. Sch. Bus. Adminstrn., NYU, N.Y.C., 1970-80, U.S.-Chinese Nat. Ctr. for Mgmt. Devel., Dalian, China, 1980-81; pres. Babson Coll., Wellesley, Mass., 1981-89; dir. Office of Global Enterprise U. So. Maine, Portland, 1989-91, cons., 1991-94; pres. Anna Maria Coll., 1995-96, Boston Arch. Ctr., 1996-97. Bd. dirs. Salomon Bros. Mut. Funds; trustee Maine Coll. of Art; chmn. overseers Boston Architectural Ctr. Author: The New Managers, 1962, The Carnegie Tech. Management Game, 1964, The Organizational World, 1973, Running the American Corporation, 1978, Planning in the US and USSR, 1978. Fulbright scholar, 1953-54; recipient Disting. Achievement award Carnegie-Mellon U., 1989. Fellow AAAS; mem. Phi Beta Kappa, Sigma Xi, Delta Sigma Rho, Beta Gamma Sigma. Unitarian Universalist. Home: 25 Birch Ln Cumberland Foreside ME 04110-1225 E-mail: wdill1@maine.rr.com.

DILLABER, PHILIP ARTHUR, budget and resource analyst, economist, consultant; b. Springfield, Mass., Aug. 24, 1922; s. Ralph E. and Grace (Holman) D.; m. Jacqueline M. Bertin, July 16, 1946; children: Anne Erline (Mrs. Donald Youngblood), Katherine Marie, John Philip, Patricia Elizabeth (dec.). BA with honors, Am. Internat. Coll., 1949; MBA, Ind. U., 1950; postgrad., U. Mich., Ind. U., 1950-54; PhD, Pacific Western U., 1985. Cert. govt. fin. mgr. Clk. rsch. and devel. div. Springfield Armory, 1946-47; rsch. asst. dept. econs. Ind. U., 1951, lectr. econs., 1955-57; orgn. and methods examiner USAF, Gulfport, Miss., 1952-53; mgmt. analyst 5th U.S. Army, Chgo., 1954-61; program progress and resources mgmt. analyst Continental Army Command, Ft. Monroe, Va., 1962-66; adminstrv. officer U.S. Army NIKE-X System Office, Alexandria, Va., 1967; program analyst Office Asst. Chief Staff Force Devel. Dept. Army, Washington, 1967-71, budget analyst Office Dep. Chief Staff Logistics, 1971-74; budget analyst Office Dep. Chief Staff Rsch., Devel. and Acquisition, Washington, 1974-80; sr. analyst Info. Spectrum, Inc., Arlington, Va., 1980-87; mem. Nat. Def. Exec. Reserve, Washington, 1985-97; cons. Profl. Group, Inc., 1992-99; del. Citizen Amb. Program Pub. Budgeting and Fin. Mgmt., People's Republic of China, 1995; mem. Nat. Exec. Svc. Corp., N.Y.C., 1997. Guest lectr. econs. Purdue U., 1959-61. Decorated Commendation medal Regional Coun., Normandy, France, 1994, Wall of Liberty Meml. Mus., Caen, France, 1994; mem. Exceptional WWII Fin. Unit displayed U.S. Army Fin. Corps Mus., Ft. Jackson, S.C. Mem. Am. Econ. Assn., Nat. Contract Mgmt. Assn., Nat. Def. Indsl. Assn., Am. Assn. Budget Program Analysis, Project Mgmt. Inst., Assn. Govt. Accts. (cert. govt. fin. mgr.), Am. Soc. Pub. Adminstrn., Sons. of Am. Revolution, Assn. Def. and Emergency Resources, Beta Gamma Sigma. Home: 3003 Arkendale St Woodbridge VA 22193-1223 E-mail: 103264.2265@compuserve.com.

DILLAHUNTY, GEORGE ROBERT, minister; b. Bklyn., Sept. 22, 1943; s. George Robert and Ruth Jean (Creighton) Bull; m. Mary Anna Cutler (div. Apr. 1996); children: Cheryl Ann, Pamela Jean, Kevin Michael; m. Alice Pearl Bender, Apr. 27, 1996; children: Earle Allen, Jeffrey Harold. AS, Mohegan C.C., 1977. Magistrate State Supreme Ct., Va.; ordained deacon AME Ch., 2002. Chief petty officer USN, 1961-85; bailiff Norfolk (Va.) Sheriff's Dept., 1985; magistrate Supreme Ct. of Va., Norfolk, 1985-94; rental mgr. Ford Rent-A-Car, Morehead City, NC, 1994—99; preacher Ame Zion Ch., 1999—2001; travelling min., 2001—; asst. pastor Morris Chapel Ame Zion Ch., Pollocksville, NC, 2001—02, Piney Grove AME Zion Ch., 2002—. Decorated Vietnam Combat Action Ribbon, Navy Achievement medal USN, 1982, Commendation medal, 85. Mem.: Assn. Naval Aviation, Masons. Democrat. Avocations: writing, bowling. Home: 230 Boone Rd Apt 2 Havelock NC 28532-8943 Office: 1430 Temples Point Rd Trenton NC 28532

DILLAHUNTY, WILBUR HARRIS, lawyer; b. Memphis, June 30, 1928; s. Joseph S. and Octavia M. (Jones) D.; 1 child, Sharon K. JD, U. Ark., 1954. Bar: Ark. 1954. City atty., West Memphis, Ark., 1968—79; U.S. atty. (ea. dist.) Little Rock, 1968-79; exec. asst. adminstr. SBA, Washington, 1979-80; prin. Dillahunty Law Firm, Little Rock, 1980—; chancery and probate judge 6th Jud. Dist., 6th Divsn., Little Rock, 1997—. Chmn. Ark. State Police Commn.; temp. assoc. justice Supreme Ct. Ark., 2000. Lt. U.S. Army, 1945-48, ETO. Mem. ABA, Pulaski Bar Assn., Nat. Assn. Former U.S. Attys. (pres. 1991X), Am. Inns of Ct. (pres. William R. Overton chpt. 1989-90). Home: 9710 Catskill Rd Little Rock AR 72227-5562

DILLARD, ANNIE, writer; b. Pitts., Apr. 30, 1945; d. Frank and Pam (Lambert) Doak; m. R.H.W. Dillard, 1965 (div.); m. Gary Clevidence, 1980 (div.); 1 child, Cody Rose; stepchildren: Carin, Shelly; m. Robert D. Richardson, Jr., 1988. BA, Hollins Coll., 1967, MA, 1968. Contbg. editor Harper's Mag., N.Y.C., 1974-81, 83-85; scholar-in-residence Western Wash. U., Bellingham, 1975-78; disting. vis. prof. Wesleyan U., 1979-83, adj. prof., 1983—, writer-in-residence, 1987—98, writer emeritus, 1998—, bd. dirs. Writers Conf., 1984—, chmn., 1991—. Fellow Calhoun Coll., Yale U., New Haven, Conn.; Phi Beta Kappa orator Harvard-Radcliffe U., 1983; mem. U.S. writers del. UCLA US.-Chinese Writers Conf., 1982; mem. U.S. cultural del. to China, 1982; bd. dirs. The New Press, Key West Writers Conf., Wesleyan Writers Conf., Key West Literary Seminars; mem. usage panel Am. Heritage Dictionary. Author: Tickets for a Prayer Wheel, 1974, 3d edit., 2002, Pilgrim at Tinker Creek, 1974 (Pulitzer prize for gen. non-fiction 1975, Best Fgn. Book Pub. in France 1990), Holy the Firm, 1978, Living by Fiction, 1982, Teaching a Stone to Talk, 1982, Encounters with Chinese Writers, 1984, An American Childhood, 1987 (Nat. Book Critics award finalist 1987), The Writing Life, 1989 (English-speaking union Amb. Book award 1990), The Living, 1992, The Annie Dillard Reader, 1994, Mornings Like This, 1995, For the Time Being, 1999 (Maurice Coindreau prize 2001); editor: (with Robert Atwan) Best Essays, 1988; (with Cort Conley) Modern American Memoirs, 1995. Mem. Nat. Com. on U.S.-China Rels., 1982—, St. Mary's Soup Kitchen, Key West, Fla.; bd. dirs. Milton Ctr., Authors League Fund, Key West Literary Seminars, Wesleyan Writers Conf. Recipient N.Y. Presswomen's award for excellence, 1975, Wash. Gov.'s award for contbn. to lit., 1978, Appalachian Gold medallion U. Charleston, 1989, Found. award St. Botolph's Club, 1989, History Maker award Hist. Soc. Western Pa., 1993, Conn. Gov.'s award in the arts, 1993, Milton Ctr. prize, 1994, Campion award Am. Mag., 1994, Am. Acad. Arts and Letters award in Lit., 1998; grantee NEA, 1980-81, Guggenheim Found., 1985-86. Mem. NAACP, Soc. Am. Historians, Authors Guild, Am. Acad. Arts and Letters, Key West Volleyball Assn.,Phi Beta Kappa. Democrat. Address: c/o Timothy Seldes Russell & Volkening 50 W 29th St New York NY 10001-4227*

DILLARD, DEAN INNES, English language educator, college official; b. Melvern, Kans., Aug. 13, 1947; s. Alva Everett and Dorothy Marie (Whitney) D. BS in Edn., Emporia (Kans.) State U., 1969, MA, 1975, postgrad., 1977, Ft. Hays State U., Hays, Kans., 1980. Tchr. English, Unified Sch. Dist. 379, Clay Center, Kans., 1969-70; tchr. English and social studies Unified Sch. Dist. 208, WaKeeney, Kans., 1972-84; instr. English, Neosho County C.C., Chanute, Kans., 1984—, chair divsn. liberal arts, 1996-99, interim v.p. acad. and student affairs, 1997-98, 99-00. Fine arts task force Neosho County C.C., Chanute, 1990-91. With U.S. Army, 1970-71. Mem.: MLA, VFW (life), Neosho County C.C. Educators Assn., Kans. Assn. Tchrs. English (exec. bd. 1981—84), Midwest Modern Lang. Assn., The Assn. Lit. Scholars and Critics (life), Nat. Coun. Tchrs. English, Kans. Assn. Scholars, Nat. Assn. Scholars, Assembly on Lit. for Adolescents (life), C.C. Humanities Assn., Am. Legion, Chanute Lions Club (zone chmn. 1988—90), Kappa Delta Pi. Republican. Home: 732 S Washington Ave Chanute KS 66720-2713 Office: Neosho County C C 800 W 14th St Chanute KS 66720-2639

DILLARD, JOHN MARTIN, lawyer, pilot; b. Long Beach, Calif., Dec. 25, 1945; s. John Warren and Clara Leora (Livermore) D.; m. Patricia Anne Yeager, Aug. 10, 1968; children: Jason Robert, Jennifer Lee. Student, U. Calif., Berkeley, 1963-67; BA, UCLA, 1968; JD, Pepperdine U., 1976. Bar: Calif. 1976. Instr. pilot, Norton AFB, Calif., 1973-77; assoc. Magana, Cathcart & McCarthy, L.A., 1977-80, Lord, Bissell & Book, L.A., 1980-85; of counsel Finley, Kumble, Wagner, 1985-86, Schell & Delamer, 1986-94, Law Offices of John M. Dillard, 1986—; v.p., gen. counsel, dir. Resort Aviation Svcs., Inc., Calif., 1988-93; mng. ptnr. Natkin & Weisbach, So. Calif., 1988-89; arbitrator Orange County Superior Ct. Atty. settlement officer U.S. Dist. Ct. Ctrl. Dist. Calif.; trained mediator Straus Inst. Active Am. Cancer Soc.; bd. dirs. Placentia-Yorba Linda Ednl. Found., Inc. Capt. USAF, 1968-73, Vietnam. Mem. ATLA (aviation litigation com.), Am. Bar Assn. (aviation com.), Orange County Bar Assn., Fed. Bar Assn., L.A. County Bar Assn. (aviation com.), Century City Bar Assn., Internat. Platform Assn., Res. Officers Assn., Orange County Com. of 100, Sigma Nu. Home: 19621 Verona Ln Yorba Linda CA 92886-2858 Office: 313 N Birch St Santa Ana CA 92701-5263

DILLARD, JOHN ROBERT, lawyer; b. Sylva, N.C., Mar. 14, 1955; s. George Washington and Ethel Thomasine (Freeman) Dillard; m. Olga M. Dillard, Feb. 3, 1998. BSBA cum laude, Western Carolina U., 1977; JD, Samford U., 1980; postgrad., Western Carolina U., 1986-88; PhD in Bus. Adminstr. with honors, S.W. U., 1989. Bar: N.C. 1980, U.S. Dist. Ct. (we. dist.) N.C. 1981. Sole practice, Cashiers, N.C., 1980-81; ptnr. Alley, Killian, Kersten & Dillard, Waynesville, N.C., 1981-85; sr. v.p., atty. Commonwealth Land Title Co., Asheville, N.C., 1985-93; pres., state mgr. Stewart Title of N.C., Asheville, 1993—. Legal counsel Woodmen of World Ins., Waynesville, 1982-85, bd. dirs.; sec. Beta-Zeta Ltd., Waynesville, 1982-84, bd. dirs.; cons. Nereus Inc., Greenville, Tenn., 1986-88; adj. faculty Asheville-Buncombe Tech. Coll., 1990-93, Mars Hill Coll., 1992; instr. Nat. Bus. Inst., 1996. Legal counsel, bd. dirs. Lambda Chi Alpha, Cullowhee, N.C., 1983-85; adv. Jr. Achievement, Clyde, N.C., 1984. Recipient Unsung Brother award, Lambda Chi Alpha, 1974. Mem.: ATLA, ABA (cert. arbitrator), N.C. Land Title Assn., N.C. Real Property Assn., Am. Land Title Assn., N.C. Coll. Advocacy, N.C. State Bar (mem. constl. law com. 1996—2000), N.C. Acad. Trial Lawyers, Woodsmen (trustee 1982—99), Masons. Democrat. Episcopalian. Home: 4 Wagner Branch Dr Asheville NC 28804-1000 Office: 53 Asheland Ave Ste 101 Asheville NC 28801-3522

DILLARD, KIRK WHITFIELD, state legislator, lawyer; b. Chgo., June 1, 1955; s. Edward Floyd and Martina Raye (Whitfield) D.; m. Carol E. Crumbaugh, Mar. 16, 1985. BA, Western Ill. U., 1977; JD, DePaul U., 1982. Bar: Ill. 1983, U.S. Dist Ct. (no. dist.) Ill. 1983, U.S. Dist Ct. (cen. dist.) Ill. 1984, U.S. Dist. Ct. (ea. dist.) Mich. 1988. Staff cons. Ill. State Senate, Springfield, 1977-81; atty., dir. legis. affairs Ill. Office Gov., civingfield, 1982-87, chief of staff Springfield, 1991-93; judge State of Ill. Ct. of Claims, Springfield, 1987-90; ptnr. Lord, Bissell & Brook, Chgo., 1987—; mem. Ill. Senate, 1993—. Legal writing and moot ct. tutor DePaul U. Coll. Laws, 1981-82; guest lectr. Loyola and DePaul U. Coll. Law, Chgo. Rep. precinct committeeman DuPage County, Wheaton, Ill., 1988; mem. Union League Chgo., Bi-State 3rd Airport for Chgo. Study Commn., Ill. Coalition. Named Legislator of the Yr. for Civil Justice, Am. Legis. Exch. Coun., 1995. Mem. ABA (Best performance in land use and local govt. law courses award Urban, State and Local Govt. sect. 1982), Ill. Assn. Def. Trial Counsel, Ill. State Bar Assn., Western Ill. U. Alumni Coun. (pres. 1989-92), Blue Key, Phi Alpha Delta. Methodist. Avocations: golf, tennis, travel, politics. Home: 120 Rosalie Ct Hinsdale IL 60521-3165 Office: Lord Bissell & Brook 115 S La Salle St Ste 3200 Chicago IL 60603-3902*

DILLARD, MARILYN DIANNE, property manager; b. Norfolk, Va., July 7, 1940; d. Thomas Ortman and Sally Ruth (Wallerich) D.; m. James Conner Coons, Nov. 6, 1965 (div. June 1988); 1 child, Adrienne Alexandra Dillard Coons (dec.). Studied with Russian prima ballerina, Alexandra Danilova, 1940's; student with honors at entrance, UCLA, 1958-59; BA in Bus. Adminstrn. with honors, U. Wash., 1962. Modeling-print work Harry Conover, N.Y.C., 1945; ballet instr. Ivan Novikoff Sch. Russian Ballet, 1955; model Elizabeth Leonard Agy., Seattle, 1955-68; mem. fashion bd., retail worker Frederick & Nelson, Seattle, 1962; retail worker I. Magnin & Co., Seattle, 1963-64; property mgr. Seattle, 1961—; antique and interior designer John J. Cunningham Antiques, Seattle, 1968-73; owner, interior designer Marilyn Dianne Dillard Interiors, 1973—. Rsch. bd. advisors Am. Biog. Inst., Inc., 1990—. Author: (poetry) Flutterby, 1951, Spring Flowers, 1951; contbr., asst. chmn. (with Jr. League of Seattle) Seattle Classic Cookbook, 1980-83. Charter mem., pres. Children's Med. Ctr., Maude Fox Guild, Seattle, 1965—, Jr. Women's Symphony Assn., 1967-73, Va. Mason Med. Ctr. Soc., 1990—, Nat. Mus. of Am. Indian, Smithsonian Instn., 1992—; mem. Seattle Jr. Club, 1962-65, 97—; mem. Friends of the Pike Place Market (saved the market from demolition), 1971; bd. dirs. Patrons N.W. Civic, Cultural and Charitable Orgns., chmn. various coms., Seattle, 1976—, prodn. chmn., 1977-78, 84-85, auction party chmn., 1983-84, v.p. party/prodn., 1984-85, exec. com., 1984-85, chmn. bd. vols., 1990-91, adv. coun., 1991—; mem. U. Wash. Arboretum Found. Unit, 1966-73, pres., 1969; bd. dirs. Coun. for Prevention Child Abuse-Neglect, Seattle, 1974-75; bd. dirs., v.p., mem. coms. Seattle Children's Theatre, 1984-90, asst. in lighting main stage plays, 1987-93, adv. coun., 1993—, asst. in lighting main stage plays Bathhouse Theatre, 1987-90; adv. bd. N.W. Asian Am. Theatre, 1987-2001, Co-Motion Dance Co., 1991—; organizer teen groups Episcopal Ch. of Epiphany, 1965-67; provisional class pres. Jr. League Seattle, 1971-72, next to new shop asst. chmn., 1972-73, bd. dirs., admissions chmn., 1976-77, exec. v.p., exec. com., bd. dirs. 1978-79, sustaining mem., 1984—; charter mem. Jr. Women's Symphony Assn., 1967-73; mem. Seattle Art Mus., 1975-90, Landmark, 1990—, Corp. Coun. for Arts, 1991—; founding dir. Adrienne Coons Meml. Fund, 1985, v.p. 1985-92, 95—, pres. 1992-95; mem. steering com. Heart Ball Am. Heart Assn., 1986, 87, auction chmn., 1986; mem. steering com. Bellevue Sch. Dist. Children's Theatre, 1983-85, pub. rels. chair, 1984, asst. stage mgr., 1985; mem. Hist. Seattle Preservation and Devel. Authority, 1997—; mem. Eastlake Cmty. Coun., 1997—; mem. Steamship Virginia V. Found., 1997—; mem. Floating Homes Assn., Seattle, 1999—; mem. Queen Anne Hist. Soc., 2000—; com. chmn. Rep. Precinct, 2000; mem. Kirkland Downtown on the Lake Orgn., 1999—; apptd. City of Kirkland Downtown Strategic Planning Action Com., 2001—; mem. City of Kirkland Transit Ctr. location com., 2001-03. Named Miss Greater Seattle, 1964; honored for leadership in the arts Jr. League of Seattle, 2002. Mem. U. Wash. Alumnae Assn. (life), Pacific N.W. Ballet Assn. (charter), Progressive Animal Welfare Soc., Associated Women (student coun. U. Wash. 1962), Profl. Rodeo Cowboys Assn. (assoc.), Seattle Tennis Club. Republican. Episcopalian. Avocations: needlepoint, horseback riding, theatre, travel, antique restoration. Home and Office: 2053 Minor Ave E Seattle WA 98102-3513

DILLARD, NANCY ROSE, naval officer; b. Rosebud, Tex., Oct. 31, 1950; d. Hilyard Blanchard and Rose Lee (Kuhn) D. BSEd, Ga So. Coll., 1973, MEd, 1974, EdS, 1978; MS, Naval Postgrad. Sch., 1990; MA, Naval War Coll., 1997. Ach. health admin. Public Schs., Savannah, Chatham Cty., 1974—79; field agt. N.Y. Life Ins. Co., Savannah, 1979—81; commd. ensign USN, 1982, advanced through grades to comdr., 1999; with U.S. Naval Comms. Sta., Nea Makri, Greece, 1982—85, Naval Telecomms. Command, Washington, 1985—88, Naval Comms. Detachment, Cheltenham, Md., 1990—92, Bur. Naval Pers., Washington, 1992—94, Naval Computer & Telecomms. Sta., New Orleans, 1994—96, U.S. Cen. Command, Tampa, Fla., 1997—2000, Naval Computer & Telecomms. Sta., Diego Garcia, 2000—02, U.S. Spl. Ops. Command, Tampa, Fla. Decorated Def. Meritorious Svc. medal, Meritorious Svc. medal, Navy Commendation medal with 3 gold stars, Joint Svc. Achievement medal, Navy Achievement medal with gold star. Mem. Armed Forces Comm. Electronics Assn., U.S. Naval Inst. Roman Catholic. Avocations: reading, golf, travel, jogging. Home: 3605 Elk Ridge Ln Valrico FL 33594

DILLARD, ROBERT PERKINS, pediatrician, educator; b. Ft. Benjamin Harrison, Ind., June 7, 1941; s. Harry Knight and Anna Frances (Perkins) D.; children: Robert Perkins, Ann Michelle, Christopher Stevens, Catherine Colleen; m. Roberta L. Schaffner, Oct. 20, 1991; 1 child, Preston Fielding. AB, Transylvania U., 1963; MD, U. Ky., Lexington, 1967. Diplomate Am. Bd. Pediat., Am. Bd. Pediat. Gastroenterology; lic. physician, Ky., Fla., N.C. Intern U. Okla. Med. Ctr., Oklahoma City, 1967-68; resident in pediat. Children's Meml. Hosp., U. Okla. Med. Ctr., Oklahoma City, 1968-71; fellow pediat. gastroenterology and nutrition Children's Hosp. Med. Ctr., Cin., 1989-90; clin. asst. prof. pediat. U. South Fla. Coll. Medicine, Tampa, 1975-77; asst. prof. pediat. medicine, assoc. dir. ambulatory pediat. East Carolina U., Greenville, N.C., 1977-83, dir. pediat. nutrition support svcs., 1981-83; assoc. prof. pediatrics U. Ky. Coll. Medicine, Lexington, 1983, dir. level I nursery, asst. dir. gen. pediatrics, 1983-89, assoc. prof., dir. pediatric gastroenterology and nutrition, 1990-94, assoc. prof. multidisciplinary PhD program, 1993-94; dir. pediatric gastroenterology and nutrition Sacred Heart Children's Hosp., 1994-97, Nemours Children's Clinic, 1997—. Sr. aviation med. examiner FAA, Lexington, 1983-94, Pensacola, 1994—. Author various handbooks, pamplets, manuals, and video; contbr. articles to profl. jours., chpts. to books. With USN, 1971-73, capt. Res., USN, 1973-2002 (ret.). Recipient various grants; named to Hon. Order Ky. Cols. Fellow Am. Acad. Pediat., N.Am. Soc. Pediat. Gastroenterology and Nutrition; mem. NRA, Sons Confederate Vets., Am. Gastroenterology Assn., Aerospace Med. Assn., Soc. USN Flight Surgeons, U. Ky. Coll. Medicine Alumni Assn., So. Pediat. Gut Club. Republican. Avocations: flying, shooting, sailing, scuba diving, drawing. Office: Nemours Childrens Clin 5153 N 9th Ave Pensacola FL 32504

DILLARD, RODNEY JEFFERSON, real estate executive; b. Short Hills, N.J., Jan. 1, 1939; s. Albert Jefferson and Anne E. (Willingham) D.; m. Anne Palfrey Lanston, June 10, 1961 (div.); children: Courtney Lanston, Carter Jefferson. BA, Rollins Coll., 1961. Account exec. A.M. Kidder Co., N.Y.C., 1961-62; v.p. Previews, Inc, Palm Beach, Fla., 1963-76; pres., chmn. bd. Illustrated Properties, Inc., Palm Beach, Fla., 1976-79; sr. v.p., bd. dirs. Sotheby's Internat. Realty Corp., Palm Beach, Fla., 1979-91; pres. John's Island Real Estate Co., Vero Beach, Fla., 1991-95, vice chmn., 1995-97; pres. The Dillard Investment Corp., Palm Beach, Fla., 1996, Illustrated Properties Internat. Inc., Palm Beach Gardens, 1998—. V.p. Christie's. Mem. Urban Land Inst., Bath and Tennis Club (Palm Beach), Spouting Rock Club (Newport, R.I.), The Travellers Club (Paris). Office: Illustrated Properties Internat Inc 249 Royal Palm Way Palm Beach FL 33480 E-mail: rodneyipi@aol.com.

DILLARD, RONDA LENSER, software engineer; b. Bartlesville, Okla. m. Scott S. Dillard, Aug. 21, 1982. BSChemE, Tex. A&M U., 1982; MS in Computer Sci., U. Tex., Dallas, 1985. Software engr. Tex. Instruments, Dallas, 1985-91; sr. software engr. E-Sys., Greenville, Tex., 1991-94; ind. software cons., 1994-95; sr. software engr. Raytheon, Garland, Tex., 1995—2002, L3Com, Greenville, 2002—. Appointee nat. membership com. U.S. Combined Tng. Assn., 1994—. Named Mem. of the Yr., Dallas Dressage Club, 1991. Mem. Assn. for Computing Machinery, U.S. Dressage Fedn., U.S. Eventing Assn. (bd. dirs. 2000-), North Tex. Eventing Assn. (Mem. of Yr. 2001), USA Equestrian, Alpha Gamma Delta. Avocations: equestrian activities, girl scouting, music. Home: PO Box 448 Nevada TX 75173-0448

DILLARD, STEPHEN C. lawyer; b. Tyler, Tex., Nov. 1, 1946; BA, Baylor U., 1968, JD, 1971. Bar: Tex. 1971. Mem. Fulbright & Jaworski L.L.P., Houston. Fellow: Am. Bd. Trial Advs., Internat. Assn. Def. Counsel, Am. Coll. Trial Lawyers (life), Tex. Bar Found. (life); mem.: ABA, Houston Bar Assn., Tex. Assn. Def. Counsel, State Bar Tex., Phi Alpha Delta (v.p. 1984—87). Office: Fulbright & Jaworski LLP 1301 Mckinney St Ste 5100 Houston TX 77010-3031

DILLARD, SUZANNE, interior designer; d. Jerome Wallace and Mary Mae (Price) Sorenson; m. Warren Marcus Dillard; 1 child, Jeremy Blake. Student, Tex. A&M U., 1961-64; BS, U. Tex., 1965; student, Pepperdine U., 1974, UCLA, 1977-78. Interior designer Pepperdine U., Malibu, Calif., 1982-95, exec. bd. dirs. Ctr. Arts, 1993—2002; cons., interior design Neptune and Thomas, Architects, Pasadena, Calif., 1979-80; pres. Suzanne Dillard Interiors, Pacific Palisades, Calif., 1974—. Prin. on camera designer TV pilot, Dream House, Forecast Group Prodns., 1983; speaker in field. Treas. Nat. Arts Assn., L.A., 1982—83, benefit chair, 2001; pres. Fine Arts aux. Assistance League So. Calif., L.A., 1984; patron, sponsor, prodn. chmn. The Footlighters, L.A., 1985—86, pres., 1992—93, League for Children, 1991—93, benefit chair, 2002; pres. Achievement Awards Coll. Scientists, 1994—96; benefit chair Freedoms Found., 1995—2002, 1st v.p., 1997—98, pres., 1997—99; bd. dirs. Ctr. for Arts, Pepperdine U. Mem.: NATAS (Acad. Emmy Blue Ribbon panel 2001—03), AFTRA, SAG (nominating com. Acad. awards 2003), Internat. Found. for Ednl. and Performing Arts (adv. bd.), Acad. TV Arts and Scis., Delta Delta Delta (pres. L.A. chpt. 1970—72, pres. sleighbell 1993—94). Republican. Mem. Ch. of Christ. Avocations: piano, voice, oil painting, reading, skiing. Office: 9620 Arby Dr Beverly Hills CA 90210-1202

DILLARD, TODD W. protective services official; b. Forest, Va., July 25, 1934; m. Audrey Virginia Robinson, Ayg. 16, 1958; 2 children. BS, Va. State Coll., 1957, MS, 1963; MBA, Cornell U., 1973. Asst. prin., tchr. G.W. Watkins High Sch., Va., 1959-64, prin., 1964-65; spl. agt. U.S. Secret Svc., 1965-90; U.S. marshal U.S. Marshals Svc., Washington, 1990—. 1st lt. U.S. Army Res., 1955-65. Mem. Assn. MBA Execs., Assn. Retired Police, D.C. Assn. Former Agts. U.S. Secret Svc., FOP. Office: H Carl Moultrie Crouthouse DC Superior Ct Rm C-250 500 Indiana Ave NW Washington DC 20001-2131

DILLARD, W. THOMAS, lawyer; b. Dothan, Ala., Nov. 28, 1941; s. William T. and Gladys (Harris) D.; m. Susan Jean Jakuboski, Oct. 26, 1974. BA, U. Tenn., 1963, JD, 1964. Bar: Tenn. 1965; cert. criminal trial specialist Nat. Bd. Trial Advocacy. Asst. U.S. atty. Dept. Justice, Knoxville, Tenn., 1967-76, chief asst. U.S. atty., 1978-83, U.S. atty., 1981, Tallahassee, 1983-86; ptnr. Ritchie, Fels, and Dillard, P.C., Knoxville, Tenn., 1987—; U.S. magistrate, 1976-78. Adj. prof. East Tenn. State U., Knoxville, 1979-80, U. Tenn. Coll. Law, 1993—; instr. Knoxville Police Acad., 1979-82, Nat. Inst. Trial Advocacy, Chapel Hill, N.C. and Boulder, Colo., 1985-2001, U. Tenn. Trial Advocacy Program, 1992-2001 mem. Tenn. Bar Profl. Stds. com.; pres. Fed. Def. Svcs., 2001. Deacon Presbyn. Ch., Knoxville, 1972-76, elder, 1978-82, 88-91, 95-98, 2000—; mem. Mayor's Commn. on Police; mem. Leadership Knoxville, 1998. Fellow Am. Coll. Trial Lawyers, Tenn. Bar Found.; mem. ABA, Am. Judicature Soc., Knoxville Young Lawyers (pres. 1972-73), Nat. Assn. Criminal Def. Lawyers, Tenn. Assn. Criminal Def. Lawyers (bd. dirs.), Nat. Assn. Former U.S. Attys. (bd. dirs.), Knoxville Bar Found. (bd. govs.). Avocations: reading, hiking, travel. Home: 8667 Ellijay Way Strawberry Plains TN 37871 Office: Ritchie Fels & Dillard 606 W Main St Knoxville TN 37902-2617 E-mail: dillard@rfdlaw.com.

DILLARD, WILLIAM, II, department store chain executive; b. 1945; married. Grad., U. Ark.; MBA, Harvard U. With Dillard Dept. Stores, Little Rock, 1967—, exec. v.p., 1973-77, pres. and chief oper. officer, 1977—, also dir., CEO. Office: Dillard Dept Stores Inc 1600 Cantrell Rd Little Rock AR 72201-1110

DILLE, JOHN ROBERT, physician; b. Waynesburg, Pa., Sept. 2, 1931; s. Charles Emanuel and Ruth Emma (South) D.; m. Joan Marie Sirtosky, Dec. 17, 1955 (wid. Mar. 1996); children: Paul Andrew, John Alan. BS, Waynesburg Coll., 1952; MD, U. Pitts., 1956; M in Indsl. Health, Harvard U., 1960. Diplomate Am. Bd. Preventive Medicine; cert. correctional health profl. Intern Akron City Hosp., 1956-57; resident in aerospace medicine USAF Sch. Aerospace Medicine, San Antonio, 1960-62; program adv. officer FAA Civil Aeromed. Rsch. Inst., Oklahoma City, 1961-64; western region flight surgeon FAA, L.A., 1965; chief FAA Civil Aeromed. Inst., U.S. Dept. Transp., Oklahoma City, 1966-87, ret., 1987; med. dir. Okla. Dept. Corrections, Oklahoma City, 1990-93. Assoc. prof. U. Okla., 1961-98, dir. tng. residency in aerospace medicine, 1967-72; state surgeon Okla. Army N.G., 1990-91; surveyor Nat. Commn. on Correctional Health Care. Assoc. editor: Ag Pilot Internat. mag., 1980-98, Conservation Aeronautics mag., 1989-92, Above All mag., 1992; mem. editorial bd. Aviation, Space and Environ. Medicine, 1987-94; contbr. chpts. to textbooks and articles to profl. jours. With USAF, 1957-59; col. M.C., U.S. Army N.G., 1976-91. Recipient Meritorious award William A. Jump Found., 1968; named Army N.G. Flight Surgeon of Yr. 1987, Master Flight Surgeon, 1987. Fellow: Am. Coll. Preventive Medicine (regent 1974—77), Aerospace Med. Assn. (mem. exec. coun. 1978—81, chmn. history and archives com. 1982—90, chmn. sci. program com. 1985, 1st v.p. 1990—91, pres. 1992—93, mem. exec. coun. 1993—98, chmn. nominating com. 1997—98, Theodore C. Lyster award 1978, Harry G. Moseley award 1987, Armstrong lectr. 1997); mem.: Acad. Correctional Health Profls., Soc. Correctional Physicians, Res. Officers Assn. (state surgeon Okla. dept. 2002—), Am. Air Mail Soc. (bd. dirs. 1990—92), Mil. and Hospitaller Order St. Lazarus of Jerusalem, Soc. U.S. Army Flight Surgeons (bd. govs. 1990—92, Order Aeromed. Merit), Internat. Acad. Aviation and Space Medicine, Nu Sigma Nu, Sigma Xi. Presbyterian. Home and Office: 335 Merkle Dr Norman OK 73069-6429 E-mail: jrobtdille@aol.com.

DILLE, ROLAND PAUL, college president; b. Dassel, Minn., Sept. 16, 1924; s. Oliver Valentine and Eleanor (Johnson) D.; m. Beth Hopeman, Sept. 4, 1948; children— Deborah, Martha, Sarah, Benjamin. BA summa cum laude, U. Minn., 1949, PhD, 1962, LHD (hon.), 1995. Instr. English U. Minn., 1953-56; asst. prof. St. Olaf Coll., Northfield, Minn., 1956-61; asst. prof. English Calif. Lutheran Coll., Thousand Oaks, Calif., 1961-63; mem. faculty Moorhead (Minn.) State U., 1964-94, pres., 1968-94; ret., 1994. Author: Four Romantic Poets, 1969; contbr. numerous articles and revs. to profl. jours. Treas. Am. Assn. State Colls. and Univs., 1977-78, bd. dirs., 1978-80, chmn., 1980-81; mem. Nat. Coun. for Humanities, 1980-86; vice-chair Commn. on Higher Edn., North Cen. Assn., 1989-91, chair, 1991-93. With inf. AUS, 1944-46. Disting. Svc. to Humanities award given by Minn. Humanities Commn. named in his honor; named one of 100 most effective Am. coll. pres., 1987. Mem. Phi Beta Kappa. Home: 516 9th St S Moorhead MN 56560-3519 Office: Minn State U Moorhead 11th St S Moorhead MN 56560-9980

DILLER, BARRY, interactive commerce company executive; b. San Francisco, Feb. 2, 1942; s. Michael and Reva (Addison) D. Vice pres. feature films and movies of week ABC, 1971-73, ABC (prime time TV ABC Entertainment), 1973-74; chmn. bd. Paramount Pictures Corp., 1974-84; pres. Gulf & Western Entertainment and Comm. Group, Simon and Schuster, Inc., Madison Sq. Garden Corp., SEGA Enterprises, Inc., 1983-84; chmn., CEO Twentieth Century Fox Film Corp., TCF Holdings, L.A., 1984-85, Fox, Inc., 1984-92, QVC Network, Inc., 1992-94; CEO, bd. chair, chmn. Silver King Comm., Inc., 1995-98; chmn. bd. dirs., CEO Home Shopping Network, Inc., 1996-98; chmn., CEO USA Interactive (formerly USA Networks, Inc.), N.Y.C., 1998—; co-CEO Vivendi Universal, 2002—03. Bd. dirs. News Corp Ltd., FCC Adv. Com. on Advanced TV Svcs., Mus. TV and Radio, Calif. Inst. Arts, Acad. Arts and Scis. Found., Ticketmaster Online-Citysearch, Inc., Seagram Co. Ltd., Channel 13/WNET, Washington Post., Sch. Cinema-TV U. So. Calif., bd. coun.; exec. bd. med. scis. UCLA; bd. trustees N.Y. U.; dean's coun. Tisch Sch. Art; mem. adv. bd. Ctr. Health Comm. Harvard U. Sch. Pub. Health. Mem. Pres. Export Coun.; bd. dirs. N.Y. Pub. Libr., Conservation Internat., Mus. TV and Radio. Office: US Interactive 152 W 57th St Fl 42 New York NY 10019-3310

DILLER, EDWARD DIETRICH, lawyer; b. Pandora, Ohio, Aug. 7, 1947; s. Hiram D. and Selma G. (Warkentin) D.; m. Karen Esmonde, June 1, 1968; children: Jason, Anna. BA, Bluffton Coll., 1969; postgrad., U. Oreg., 1969-70; JD cum laude, Harvard U., 1976. Assoc. Taft, Stettinius & Hollister, Cin., 1976-84, ptnr., 1984—, chmn. dept. bus. & fin., 1998—. Chmn. Gen. Conf. Coun. on Higher Edn., 1990-93, 96-2001, vice chmn., 1993-94; lectr. numerous seminars; mem. women's initiative adv. bd. Deloitte & Touche, Cin., 2000—. Tchr. Mennonite Ctrl. Com., Frankfield, Jamaica, 1970-73; chmn. edn. integration com. Mennonite Ch. USA, 1997-2001; trustee Mental Health Svcs. East, 1977-85, Bluffton Coll., 1979-2002, mem. exec. com., 1987-2002, chmn. bd., 1991-2002; mem. Family Svc. of Greater Cin. Area, 1989-96, chmn., 1992-95; trustee Habitat for Humanity (Southwestern Ohio and No. Ky. affiliate), 1995-2000; trustee Working in Neighborhoods, 1991-94, Dan Beard Coun. Boy Scouts of Am., 1996-, chmn. 2003-, Leadership Cin. Alumni Assn., 2001-02; mem. Leadership Cin. Class XVI; trustee Found. Family Svc., 1997-, chmn. 2002-. Mem. Ohio State Bar Assn., Cin. Bar Assn., Ohio Harvard Law Sch. Assn. Office: 1800 Firstar Tower 425 Walnut St Cincinnati OH 45202-3923 E-mail: diller@taftlaw.com.

DILLER, ELIZABETH E. artist, educator; BArch, The Cooper Union. Assoc. prof. arch. design Princeton (N.J.) U.; ptnr. Diller & Scofidio, N.Y.C. Co-pub. Back to the Front: Tourisms of War, Flesh: an anti-monograph, co-creator JETLAG, 1998. Office: Princeton U Sch Architecture 5116 Architecture Princeton NJ 08544-0001

DILLEY, CAROL, association administrator; b. Ft. Worth; Student, Ft. Worth Sch. Bus., Tarrant County Jr. Coll., Ft. Worth, Tex. Exec. dir. Tex. Longhorn Breeders Assn. Am., Ft. Worth. Office: Tex Longhorn Breeders Assn Am 2315 N Main St Ste 402 Fort Worth TX 76106-8581

DILLIARD, MAXINE K. retired school psychologist; b. Mpls., June 11, 1935; d. Gilbert Thomas and Florence Ingrid (Jensen) Kirst; m. Herman V. Dilliard, Aug. 4, 1955 (dec. June 1968); children: Alan Fredrick, Charles David. BA, U. Minn., 1965, MA, 1967, EdS, 1968. Lic. psychologist, Minn., sch. psychologist, Minn., Calif. Sr. acct. clk. U. Minn., Mpls., 1956-61; prin. survey interviewer U. Minn. Hosp., Mpls., 1961-65; sch. psychologist Robbinsdale (Minn.) Sch. Dist., 1967-86, Victor Elem. Sch. Dist., Victorville, Calif., 1989-2000; self-employed human svcs. cons. Mpls., 1986-89; ret., 2000. Mem. APA, Nat. Reading Assn., Assn. for Childhood Edn. Internat., Nat. Assn. Sch. Psychologists, Calif. Assn. Sch. Psychologists, Desert/Mountain Assn. Sch. Psychologists, Minn. Psychol. Assn., Phi Beta Kappa. Avocations: reading, travel, grandchildren. Home: 15252 Seneca Rd Spc 226 Victorville CA 92392-2271

DILLIN, JOHN WOODWARD, JR., retired newspaper editor, correspondent; b. Miami, Fla., July 6, 1936; s. John Woodward and Alberta (Thompson) D.; m. Gay Andrews, Oct. 1, 1966 (div. 1988); 1 child, Katherine. BSJ. with honors, U. Fla., 1958, postgrad. in U.S. history, 1961-63. Reporter St. Augustine Record, Fla., 1958, Tampa Tribune, Fla., 1960-61; with Christian Sci. Monitor, 1964—, reporter, 1964-66, corr. Saigon, Vietnam, 1966-67, city editor Boston, 1967-71, corr. Atlanta and Washington, 1971-79, mng. editor for news Boston, 1979-83, nat. polit. corr. Washington, 1983-94, mng. editor Boston, 1994-99, assoc. editor, Washington bur. chief Washington, 1999—, ret., 2001. Served with AUS, 1958-59. Recipient Sigma Delta Chi award for Washington Corr., 1993; named Alumnus of Distinction, Coll. Journalism and Comms., U. Fla., 2002. Christian Scientist. Home: 5525 15th St N Arlington VA 22205-2712 Office: 910 16th St NW Washington DC 20006-2903 E-mail: dillinj@csmonitor.com.

DILLIN, S. HUGH, federal judge; b. Petersburg, Ind., June 9, 1914; s. Samuel E. and Maude (Harrell) D.; m. Mary Eloise Humphreys, Nov. 24, 1940; 1 child, Patricia Wright. AB in Govt, Ind. U., 1936, LLB, 1938, LLD, 1992; D of Civil Law (hon.), Ind. State U., 1990. Bar: Ind. 1938. Ptnr. Dillin & Dillin, Petersburg, 1938-61; U.S. dist. judge So. Dist. Ind., 1961—, chief judge, 1982-84. Mem. Jud. Conf. U.S., 1979-82, mem. exec. com., 1980-82, mem. Jud. Conf. Com. on Ct. Adminstrn., 1983-89, chmn. subcom. on fed.-state rels., 1983-89; mem. Jud. Panel on Multidist. Litigation, 1983-92; sec. Pub. Svc. Commn. Ind., 1942; mem. Interstate Oil Compact Commn., 1949-52, 61. Mem. Ind. Ho. of Reps. from Pike and Knox Counties, 1937, 39, 41, 51, floor leader, 1951; mem. Ind. Senate from Pike and Gibson Counties, 1959-61, pres. pro tem, 1961. Capt. AUS, 1943-46. Recipient Disting. Alumnus award Ind. U. Coll. Arts and Scis., 1985, Ind. U. Sch. Law, 1987, 2001 Am. Inns of Ct. Professionalism award in the 7th Cir. Mem. Am. Bar Assn., Ind. State Bar Assn., Fed. Bar Assn., 7th Cir. Judges Assn. (pres. 1977-79), Am. Judicature Soc., Delta Tau Delta, Phi Delta Phi. Clubs: Indianapolis Athletic. Democrat. Presbyterian. Office: US Dist Ct 255 US Courthouse 46 E Ohio St Indianapolis IN 46204-1903

DILLING, KIRKPATRICK WALLWICK, lawyer; b. Evanston, Ill., Apr. 11, 1920; s. Albert W. and Elizabeth (Kirkpatrick) D.; m. Betty Ellen Bronson, June, 1942 (div. July 1944); m. Elizabeth Ely Tilden, Dec. 11, 1948; children: Diana Jean, Eloise Tilden, Victoria Walgreen, Albert Kirkpatrick (dec.). Student, Cornell U., 1939-40; BS in Law, Northwestern U., 1942; postgrad., DePaul U., 1946-47, L'Ecole Vaubier, Montreux, Switzerland; Degré Normal, Sorbonne U., Paris. Bar: Ill. 1947, U.S. Dist. Ct. (no. dist.) Ill., Ind., Mich., Md., La., Tex., Okla., Wis., Idaho, U.S. Ct. Appeals (2nd, 3rd, 5th, 7th, 8th, 9th, 10th, 11th, fed. and D.C. cirs.), U.S. Supreme Ct. Ptnr. Dilling and Dilling, 1948—. Counsel Cancer Control Soc., Nat. Coun. for Improved Health; bd. dirs. Nutradelle Labs., Ltd., V.E. Irons, Inc.; v.p. Midwest Medic-Aide, Inc.; spl. counsel Herbalife (U.K.) Ltd., Herbalife Australasia Pty., Ltd.; lectr. on pub. health law. Contbr. articles to pub. health publs. Bd. dirs. Adelle Davis Found., Liberty Lobby. 1st lt. AUS, 1943-46. Recipient Humanitarian award Nat. Health Fedn. Mem. ABA, Ill. Bar Assn., Chgo. Bar Assn., Assn. Trial Lawyers Am., Stalwart Cornell Soc. Engrs., Am. Legion, Air Force Assn., Pharm. Advt. Club, Rolls Royce Owners' Club, Tower Club, Cornell U., Chicago Club, Delta Upsilon. Republican. Episcopalian. Home: 1120 Lee Rd Northbrook IL 60062-3816 E-mail: dilling1@juno.com.

DILLING, RICHARD A. mathematician, educator; b. Everett, Pa., July 30, 1940; s. John Ealor and Janet Joanne Dilling; m. Linda Marlene Edmiston, Aug. 17, 1968; children: Dawn D., John Marvin, Richard A. Jr. BS in Edn., Shippensburg State U., 1962; MS in Physics and Math., Purdue U., 1968, PhD, 1975. Prof. Grace Coll., Math. Dept., Winona Lake, Idaho, 1966—. Chair of assessment Grace Coll., 1999—. Vice pres. Lake Land Art Assn., Warsaw, Ind., 2000—01. Mem.: Math. Assn. of Am., Nat. Sci. Tchrs. of Am., Am. Assn. for Higher Edn. Republican. Avocation: golf. Office: Grace Coll 200 Seminary Dr Winona Lake IN 46590 E-mail: dadillin@grace.edu.

DILLINGHAM, JOHN ALLEN, marketing professional; b. Kansas City, Mo., Jan. 9, 1939; s. Jay B. and Frances (Thompson) D.; m. Nancy Jane Abbott, Sept. 4, 1965; children: Allen Edwards, William Kemp. AS, Wentworth Mil. Acad., 1958; AB in Polit. Sci., U. Mo., 1961, MS in Pub. Adminstrn., 1962. Br. mgr. Rudy-Patrick divsn. W.R. Grace Co., Mt. Vernon, Ill., 1964-68; pres. Sho-Hawk Industries, Kansas City, Mo., 1968-72; v.p. comml. loans Traders Nat. Bank, Kansas City, 1972-79; sr. v.p. sales and mktg. Garney Constrn. Co., Kansas City, 1979-95; pres., bd. dirs. Jo Dill, Inc., 1985—, Dillingham Enterprises, 1997—. Bd. dirs. Weddell and Real Advisor Funds, Inc., Kansas City; chmn. Clay County Indsl. Devel. Authority, 1980—, Clay County EDC, 1972-74; adv. bd. for extension U. Mo., 1972-80; cons. CMSU Grad. Sch., Warrensberg, Mo., 1996-97; dir., cons. McDougal Constrn., Kansas City, 1996-97; adv. dir. Northland Bd. United Mo. Bank, 1998—, Synergy Svcs. Trustee Wentworth Mil. Acad., Lexington, 1978-80, 93-00; state chmn. Mo. 4H Found., Columbia, 1985-90; mem. ctrl. governing bd. Children's Mercy Hosp., Kansas City, 1987-92; bd. dirs. Kansas City Conv. and Vis. Bur., 1976-80, Northland Cmty. Fund, Kansas City, 1988-97, Kansas City Sports Commn., 1990-93; treas. Harry S. Truman Scholarship Nat. Alumni Assn., 1979-90; mem., v.p. Kansas City Bd. Police Commrs., 1990-95; chmn. Kansas City Mcpl. Asst. Corp., 1984—, Alex Doniphan Meml. Hwy. Naming, 1998; hon. co-chair St. Plus X H.S. Capital campaign, 1997-98; coordinating bd. task force on affordability of higher edn. State of Mo., 1999; mem. Nat. 4H Resource Devel. Com., 1990-92, Kansas City Mayor's Fast Forward Commn., 1996—; mem. exec. com. Metro C. C. Found., Kansas City, 1996—; exec. bd. Heart of Am. coun. Boy Scouts Am., 1993-01; 1st bd. dirs. alumni assn. U.S. Command and Gen. Staff Coll., Ft. Leavenworth, Kans., 1993—; dir. DARE of Greater Kansas City, 1995-98, CMSU Found. Warrensburg, 1995-97, Am. Royal, Kansas City, Mo., 1997-03; co-chmn. K.C. Storm runoff campaign, 1998. With U.S. Army, 1964. Recipient Faculty Alumni award U. Mo., Columbia, 1981, Silver Beaver award Boy Scouts Am. Heart Am. coun., 1992, Harry S. Truman Scholarship Appreciation plaque, 1993, Cmty. Svc. award Park Coll., 1993, Pub. Svc. award Ctrl. Mo. State Univ., 1994; named one of 100 Most Influential Kans. Citizens, Ingrams Mag., 1993, Spirit award Kansas City, 1999. Mem. SAR, VFW, Am. Legion, Sons of the Confederate Officers, Decendents of Magna Charta, Plantenegent Soc., Northland C. of C. (Quality of Life award 1990), KC Kings, Gold Coaters (pres. 1979-89), Mt. Vernon Ill. C. of C. (pres. 1968), Native Sons Kansas City (bd. dirs. 1991-92, 98—), Sigma Alpha Epsilon (KC Alumni Assn. pres. 1976, Honor Man 1988, trustee Nat. Found. 1987-93, Nat. Disting. Svc. award 1993). Democrat. Mem. Christian Ch. (Disciples Of Christ). Avocations: fishing, landscaping, family geneaology. Home: 4040 NW Claymont Dr Kansas City MO 64116-1751 Office: 924 Livestock Exch Bldg Kansas City MO 64102 Fax: 816-842-6803.

DILLINGHAM, WILLIAM BYRON, literature educator, author; b. Atlanta, Mar. 7, 1930; s. Cornelius Howard and Emerald (Storey) D.; m. Marion Elizabeth Joiner, July 3, 1952; children: Rebecca Lynn, Judith Ann, Paul Christopher. BA, Emory U., 1955, MA, 1956; PhD, U. Pa., 1961. Instr. Emory U., Atlanta, 1956-62, asst. prof., 1962-66, assoc. prof., 1966-68, prof., 1968-84, chair. dept. English, 1979-82, 85-86, 90-91, Charles Howard Candler prof. Am. lit., 1984-96; prof. emeritus, 1996—. Author: Frank Norris: Instinct and Art, 1969, An Artist in the Rigging, 1972, Melville's Short Fiction, 1977, Melville's Later Novels, 1986, Melville and His Circle: The Last Years, 1996; co-author: Humor of the Old Southwest, 1964, 2d edit., 1975, 3d edit., 1994, Practical English Handbook, 10th edit., 1996; mem. editl. bd. Nineteenth-Century Lit., 1990-97, South Atlantic Rev., 1986-89, Frank Norris Studies, 1986-94. Served with U.S. Army, 1950-52. Recipient Fulbright award U.S. Govt., 1964-65; Sr. fellow NEH, 1978-79, Guggenheim Found., 1982-83; Heilbrun Disting. Emeritus fellow, 2002-03. Mem. MLA (mem. adv. coun. Am. lit. sect. 1988-90), Nat. Assn. Scholars, Soc. Lit. Scholars and Critics, Frank Norris Soc., Melville Soc. (pres. 1987), Kipling Soc., Phi Beta Kappa, Omicron Delta Kappa. Home: 1416 Vista Leaf Dr Decatur GA 30033-2012 also: 3258 Esperanza Ave Daytona Beach FL 32118-6231

DILLMAN, DONALD ANDREW, sociologist, educator, survey methodologist; b. Chariton, Iowa, Oct. 24, 1941; BS, Iowa State U., 1964, MS, 1966, PhD, 1969. Rsch. assoc. Iowa State U., Ames, 1967-69; asst. prof. Wash. State U., Pullman, 1969-73, assoc. prof., dept. chair, 1973-81, prof., 1978—2003, dir. social and econ. scis. rsch. ctr., 1986-96, dep. dir. R&D Social Econ. Sci. Rsch. Ctr., 1996—, Thomas S. Foley disting. prof. govt. and pub. policy, 2000—, Regents prof., 2003. Guest prof. German Ctr. for Survey Methods Rsch., Mannheim, Fed. Republic of Germany, 1985, 87, 2000; sr. survey methodologist Office of Dir. US Bur. Census, 1991-95; sr. scientist Gallup Orgn., 1995—; cons. and lectr. in field. Author: Mail and Telephone Surveys, 1978, Mail and Internet Surveys, 2000; co-author 5 books; contbr. articles to profl. jour. Recipient Alumni Disting. Achievement citation Iowa State U., 2001, Lester F. Ward for Disting. Contbns. to Applied Sociology, Soc. for Applied Sociology, 2002; Kellogg fellow, 1981-83; grantee in field. Fellow AAAS, Am. Statis. Assn. (Roger Herriot award 2000); mem. Am. Sociol. Assn., Rural Sociol. Soc. Am. (pres. 1983-84, Outstanding Svc. award 1983, Excellence in Rsch. award 1998), Am. Assn. Pub. Opinion Rsch. (sec.-treas. 1995-97, councillor-at-large 1999, pres. 2001, AAPOR Award for Exceptionally Distinguished Achievement, 2003) Home: 705 SW Mies St Pullman WA 99163-2056 Office: Wash State U Wilson Hall 133 Pullman WA 99164-0001 E-mail: dillman@wsu.edu.

DILLMAN, KRISTIN WICKER, elementary and middle school educator, musician; b. Ft. Dodge, Iowa, Nov. 7, 1953; d. Winford Lee and Helen Caroline (Brown) Egli; m. Kirk Michael Wicker, Jan. 1, 1982 (dec. June 1982); m. David D. Dillman, Apr. 13, 1990; adopted children: Alek Joseph, Andrew Mikhail. AA, Iowa Cen. Coll., 1974; B in Music Edn., Morningside Coll., 1976; M in Mus., U. S.D., 1983. Cert. tchr., Iowa. Tchr. instrumental music Garrigan Affiliated Schs., Algona, Iowa, 1976-77, Sioux City (Iowa) Community Schs., 1977—. Sr. beauty cons. Mary Kay Cosmetics. Asst. prin. bassist Sioux City Symphony, 1974-93, 95—, prin. bassist, 1993-95; freelance bassist Sioux City, 1976—; pianist and accompanist, St. Mark Luth. ch., Sioux City. Named Tchr. of Yr. Sioux City Community Schs., 1988-89. Mem. NEA, Iowa Edn. Assn., Sioux city Edn. Assn., Iowa Bandmasters Assn., Sioux City Musicians Assn., Zeta Sigma, Mu Phi Epsilon. Republican. Lutheran. Avocations: golf, walking, gardening, skiing. Office: Bryant Elem Sch 821 30th St Sioux City IA 51104 E-mail: DunesDave@aol.com.

DILLMAN, ROBERT JOHN, academic administrator; b. Brooklyn, N.Y., June 30, 1941; s. George amd Emma (Drago) D.; m. Roseann Farley Morris; children: Deirdre, John, Siobhan, James. BS, SUNY, New Paltz, 1963; MS, Pa. State U., 1970; PhD, Clark U., 1976. Tchr. Connetquot High Sch., Bohemia, N.Y., 1963-64, 66-67; faculty mem. Bridgewater (Mass.) State Coll., 1967-78, chairperson, 1978-82, v.p. acad. affairs, 1982-87, acting pres., 1987-88; pres. Fairmont (W.Va.) State Coll., 1988-96, E. Stroudsburg (Pa.) U., 1996—. Bd. dirs. C.B. & T. Fin. Corp., Fairmont, W.Va. Bd. dirs. United Way, Fairmont, 1989. Nat. sci. faculty fellow NSF, Clark U., 1971-72. Mem. Am. Assn. Colls. and Univs., Am. Assn. Higher Edn., C. of C. Pocono Mountians (bd. dirs.). Office: E Stroudsburg U 200 Prospect St East Stroudsburg PA 18301-2999

DILLMORE, NILE, state representative; b. Neodesha, Kans., Sept. 4, 1947; m. Janet Miller; children: Jennifer, Alicia, Gabe. BBA, Wichita State U., 1981. Lender Mid Am. Credit Union; supr. specialized assets Empire Bank, 1981—; mem. Kans. Ho. of Reps., 2001—. Mem. nominating com. Wichita Mcpl. Judge, 1997; v.p. adv. bd. Wichita Alcohol Drug Abuse, 1998—2000; pres. Wichita Alternative Correctional Housing Bd., 1998—99; 6th dist. rep. Wichita Re-Districting Coun. Electors, 2002; pres., treas. Wichita Ind. Neighborhoods, 1999—2002; v.p. adv. bd. Wichita/Sedgwick County Alcohol and Drug Abuse; pres. Wichita/Sedgwick Alternative Correctional Housing. Democrat. Office: 278-W State Capitol 300 W 10th Ave Topeka KS 66612 Address: 1102 Jefferson Wichita KS 67203*

DILLOFF, NEIL JOEL, lawyer; b. Apr. 3, 1948; s. Marvin M. and Gertrude S. (Kraus) D.; m. Beverly A. Berd, June 6, 1971; children: Danielle, Shani, Scott. AB, U. N.C., 1970; JD, Georgetown U., 1973. Bar: Md. 1973, Pa. 1974, D.C. 1983, U.S. Dist. Ct. Md. 1977, U.S. Ct. Appeals (4th cir.) 1979, U.S. Supreme Ct. 1987. Assoc. Piper Rudnick, Balt., 1977-82, ptnr., 1982—. Head comml. lit. practice group, 1994-99, leader Balt. litigation group, 1999—; instr. Md. Inst. for Continuing Legal Edn., Balt., 1983—. Author: Civil Pretrial Practice - Maryland Institute for Continuing Education in the Law; contbr. articles to profl. jours. Served to lt. JAGC, USN, 1973-77. Mem. ABA (assoc. editor litigation news 1980-82), Md. Bar Assn., Balt. City Bar Assn., Phi Beta Kappa Democrat. Jewish. Office: Piper Rudnick 6225 Smith Ave Baltimore MD 21209-3600

DILLON, CLIFFORD BRIEN, retired lawyer; b. Amarillo, Tex., Oct. 25, 1921; s. Clifford Newton and Leone (Brien) D.; m. Audrey Catherine Johnson, Jan. 16, 1945; children: Audrey Catherine Dillon Peters (dec. Nov. 1997), Robert Brien, Douglas Johnson. BBA, U. Tex., 1943, LL.B. with honors, 1947. Bar: Tex. 1947. Practiced in, Houston, 1947—87; ptnr. Baker Botts LLP, 1957—87, ret. ptnr., 1987—. Mem. faculty Southwestern Legal Found., 1968-87. Author articles in field. Life mem., bd. dirs. U. Tex. Health Sci. Ctr., Houston; past mem. antitrust adv. bd. Bur. Nat. Affairs; past bd. dirs. Houston Vis. Nurses Assn.; bd. visitors, life mem. Mc Donald Obs. and Astronomy, 1986—. Fellow ABA (chmn. sect. antitrust law 1975-76, Ho. of Dels. 1974-75, 85-87, bd. govs. 1985-87), State Bar Tex., Am. Judicature Soc., Tex. Bar Found., Houston Bar Found.; mem. Houston Bar Assn., Houston C. of C., U.S. C. of C. (past mem. adv. coun. antitrust policy), Houston Country Club (Houston), Petroleum Club (Houston), Riverhill Country (Kerrville, Tex.), Old Baldy (Saratoga, Wyo.), Commanche Trace Country Club (Kerrville), Phi Kappa Psi, Phi Delta Phi. Presbyterian. E-mail: mardillon@compuserve.com.

DILLON, COREY, professional football player; b. Oct. 24, 1975; 1 child, Cameron. Student, U. Wash. Football player Cin. Bengals, 1997—. Office: Cin Bengals 1 Paul Brown Stadium Cincinnati OH 45202-3492

DILLON, DAVID ANTHONY, journalist, lecturer; b. Fitchburg, Mass., Aug. 24, 1947; s. John Joseph and Lauretta Irene (Morris) D.; m. Sally Ann Hall, June 5, 1971; children: Christopher, Catherine. BA, Boston Coll., 1963; MA, Harvard U., 1965, PhD, 1970. Asst. prof. So. Meth. U., Dallas, 1970-77; mag. editor D Mag., Dallas, 1978-81; archtl. editor Dallas Morning News, 1981—. Author: Experience and Expression, 1976, Dallas Architecture, 1986, Extending the Legacy: Planning America's Capital in the 21st Century, 1997, The Architecture of O'Neil Ford, 1999; contbg. editor Texas Architect, Landscape Architecture, 1990—, Archtl. Record, 1996—. Loeb fellow Harvard U., 1986-87; NEA Critic's grantee, 1980; recipient AP award for criticism, 1988, 90, 91, 2002. Democrat. Roman Catholic. Home: PO Box 3323 Amherst MA 01004-3323 Office: The Dallas Morning News 508 Young St Dallas TX 75202-4828

DILLON, DAVID BRIAN, retail grocery executive; b. Hutchinson, Kans., Mar. 30, 1951; s. Paul Wilson and Ruth (Muirhead) D.; m. Dee A. Ehling, July 29, 1973; children: Jefferson, Heather, Kathryn. BS, U. Kans., 1973; JD, So. Meth. U., 1976. V.p. Fry's Food Stores of Ariz. Inc. div. Dillon Cos. Inc., Phoenix, 1978-79, exec. v.p., 1979-83; v.p. Dillon Cos. Inc. (subs. of Kroger Co.), Hutchinson, 1983-86, pres., 1986-95; exec. v.p. Kroger Co., Cin., 1990-95; chmn. bd. Dillon Cos., Inc. (subs. Kroger Co.), Cin., 1993—95; pres., COO The Kroger Co., Cin., 1995—99, pres., 1999—2000, pres., COO, 2000—03, CEO, 2003—; also bd. dirs., 1995—. Bd. dirs. Convergys. Chmn. Leadership Hutchinson, 1986-87, Leadership Kans., 1988; bd. dirs. Bethesda Hosp., Cin., 1996—; bd. trustees U. Kans. Endowment Assn., 1993—, U. Cin. Found., 1997—, Den Beard Coun. of Boy Scouts Am., 1996—; bd. advisors U. Kans. Bus. Sch., 1990—. Recipient Brotherhood-Sisterhood award Kans. region NCCJ, 1992. Mem. U. Kans. Alumni Assn., Urban League of Greater Cin. (trustee 1998—), Order of Coif, Sigma Chi (Balfour award 1973). Republican. Presbyterian. Office: The Kroger Co 1014 Vine St Cincinnati OH 45202-1100

DILLON, DONALD WARD, management consultant; b. Wichita, Kans., Jan. 31, 1936; s. Maurice B. and Helen M. (Ward) D.; m. Jacquelyn A. Hicks, Dec. 28, 1958; m. Brenda Marie Rager, July 9, 1983. B.Music Edn., Wichita State U., 1959, M.Music Edn., 1961; D.Music. Edn., U. Okla., 1970. Tchr. music Derby (Kans.) public schs., 1959-66; mem. faculty Southeastern La. U., Hammond, 1968-69; exec. dir. Okla. Arts and Humanities Council, 1969-73; asst. dir. fed.-state partnership Nat. Endowment Arts, Washington, 1973-79, dir. grants office, 1979; exec. dir. Music Educators Nat. Conf., Reston, Va., 1979-83; pres.

Don Dillon Assocs. Inc., Dallas, 1983—. Exec. mgmt. cons., bd.dirs. Fund Advancement Music Edn., 1979— Exec. editor: Music Educators Jour, 1979—, Design for Arts Edn, 1980— ; Contbr. articles profl. jours. Bd. dirs. Nat. Com. Arts for Handicapped, 1980— . Mem. Am. Soc. Assn. Execs., Inst. Assn. Mgmt. Cos., Meeting Planners Internat. Methodist. Home: 6204 Trailwood Dr Plano TX 75024-6023 Office: 13140 Coit Rd Ste 320 LB120 Dallas TX 75240-5737 E-mail: don@dondillon.com.

DILLON, DORIS (DORIS DILLON KENOFER), artist, art historian; b. Kansas City, Mo., Dec. 1, 1929; d. Joseph Patrick and Geraldine Elizabeth (Galligan) D.; m. Calvin Louis Kenofer, Aug. 25, 1950; children: Wendy Annette Kenofer Barnes, Bruce Patrick Kenofer. BA in Art, U. Denver, 1950, MA in Art History, 1965. Stewardess United Air Lines, 1950-51; founder, chmn. fine arts dept. Regis Coll., Denver, 1970-74; cons. Sarkisian's Oriental Imports, Denver, 1975-93; mus. curator Van Vechten-Lineberry Taos Art, Taos, N.Mex., 1995. Coord. Inter-Relationship Between the Fine Arts and Science Seminars, 1970-74, Colo. Coun. on Arts & Humanities, Denver, 1980, adv. panel, 1981; consular rep. United Cultural Conv; dep dir. gen. Internat. Biog. Ctr., Eng., 1997; rsch. bd. advisors Am. Biog. Inst., 1997; lectr. in field. One-woman shows include El Pueblo Art Gallery/Mus., Pueblo, Colo., 1970, Heard Mus., Dallas, 1984, Nelson Rockefeller Collection, N.Y.C., 1984, Amparo Gallery, Denver, 1985, Veerhoff Gallery, Washington, 1986, Colo. Gallery the Arts Mus., Littleton, 1987, Highland Gallery, Atlanta, 1988, The Earth Sci. Mus., Asheville, N.C., 2003, exhibited in group shows at U. Denver, 1970, Denver Art Mus., 1970, Denver Mus. Natural History, 1976, U. Colo., 1986, Denver C. of C., 1987, Cadme Gallery, Phila., 1987, Internat. Platform Assn., Washington, 1998—2001, Nat. League Pen Arts Women, 1999, Lisbon, Portugal, 1999, 26th Congress on Arts and Humanities, Lisbon, Internat. Exhbn. Gallery, 2000, exhibitions include St. Johns Coll., Cambridge, Eng., 2001, Vancouver, Can., 2002, two-person shows, E Margo Gallery, Manhattan N.Y., 2003. Recipient 1st place drawing award, 4 States Conf. Ctr., Colo., 1960, Salute to Women award, AAUW, 1997, Key award, Excellence Arts, Rsch., Tchg., 1997, Best of Show award, Internat. Platform Assn., Washington, 2001, 2002. Mem.: Denver Art Mus., Asian Art assn. (bd. dirs. 1982—84, treas. 1985), Fine Arts Guild (v.p. 1982), Soc. for Arts, Religion and Contemporary Culture, Nat. Mus. for Women in the Arts (assoc.), Mensa (scholarship juror 1993—94). Avocations: piano, travel, bridge, swimming, hiking. Home and Office: 135 Delphia Dr Brevard NC 28712

DILLON, FRANCIS PATRICK, retired human resources executive, financial, insurance and tax consultant; b. Long Beach, Calif., Mar. 15, 1937; s. Wallace Myron and Mary Elizabeth (Land) D.; m. Vicki Lee Dillon, Oct. 1980; children: Cary Randolph, Francis Patrick Jr., Randee, Rick. BA, U. Va., 1959; MS, Def. Fgn. Affairs Sch., 1962; MBA, Pepperdine U., 1976. Traffic mgr., mgr. pers. svcs. Pacific Telephone Co., Sacramento and Lakeport, Calif., 1966-69; asst. mgr. manpower planning and devel. Pan-Am. World Airways, N.Y.C., 1969-71; mgr. pers. and orgn. devel. Continental Airlines, L.A., 1971-74; dir. human resources Bourns, Inc., Riverside, Calif., 1974-80; v.p. employee and cmty. rels. MSI Data Corp., 1980-83; pres. Pavi Enterprises, 1983—2003; ret., 2003. Cons. mgmt. Pers. Outplacement Counseling/Sales/Mgmt., fin. svcs., ins., tax oriented strategies, retirement planning for srs., and estate planning, 1983—; pres., CEO Pers. Products & Svcs., Inc., 1984-91; v.p. Exec. Horizons, Inc., 1988-94; sr. profl. svcs. cons. Right Assocs., 1994-97; pres. Meditrans Inc., 1977-80. Bd. dirs. Health Svcs. Maintenance Orgn., Inc., Youth Svcs. Ctr., Inc.; vol. precinct worker. Lt. comdr. USN, 1959-66; asst. naval attaché, Brazil, 1963-65. Recipient Disting. Svc. award Jaycees, 1969, Jack Cates Meml. Vol. of Year award Youth Svc. Ctr., 1977. Mem. ASTD, Assn. Internal Mgmt. Cons., Am. Soc. Pers. Adminstrn., Pers. Indsl. Rels. Assn., Am. Electronics Assn. (human resources com., chmn. human resources symposium), Lake Mission Viejo Assn. (sec., bd. dirs. 1990-94), Mission Viejo Sailing Club, YMCA Bike Club, Mission Viejo Ski Club, Caving Club, Toastmasters (pres. 1966-67), Have Dirt Will Travel, Capo Valley 4 Wheelers. Republican. Episcopalian. Office: Pavi Enterprises 27331 Via Amistoso Mission Viejo CA 92692-2410

DILLON, FRANCIS RICHARD, retired air force officer; b. Hartford, Conn., Nov. 3, 1939; s. Frank Clifford and Margaret Elizabeth (Drohan) D.; m. Judith Wheeler, June 15, 1963; children: Christopher R., Douglas C. BS in Mktg., U. Conn., 1962; MS in Polit. Sci., Troy (Ala.) State U., 1978. Commd. 2d lt. USAF, 1962, advanced through grades to brig. gen., 1988; various command and staff positions in U.S. and Europe; European area specialist responsible for counterintelligence and anti-terrorism for Air Force pers. in Europe, 1976-79; comdr. Air Force Office Spl. Investigations, Bolling AFB, D.C., 1988-93; retired, 1993; mng. dir. ops., COO MPC Telcom, LP, Annandale, Va., 1993-94; v.p. Background Rsch. Internat. L.L.C., Falls Church, Va., 1995-97; cons. DS/FX Internat., Falls Church, Va., 1997—. Bd. dirs. Bath Housing Authority, Mid Coast Ctr. for Higher Learning. Mem.: Am. Soc. Indsl. Security. Roman Catholic. Avocations: sailing, skiing, reading, tennis. Home: 47 W Chops Point Rd Bath ME 04530-4011

DILLON, HELEN KAYE, obstetrics staff nurse; b. Oakland, Nebr., Oct. 9, 1953; d. Jon Henry and Patricia Ann (Holman) Ferguson; m. Richard E. Setchell, Nov. 19, 1971 (div. Dec. 1977); 1 child, Shari Setchell; m. William E. Dillon, Jr., May 3, 1989 (div. May 2001). BA in Bus. Adminstrn., Bellevue Coll, 1986; BSN, Clarkson Coll., 1992. RN Nebr. Cmty. health nurse Carl T. Curtis Health Ctr., Omaha Indian Reservation, Macy, Nebr., 1993; obstetrics staff nurse Indian Health Svc., Belcourt, N.D., 1993-95, Gallup, N.Mex., 1995-97, Kaiser Permanente, San Diego, 1997—2001, Fairview/Univ. Med. Ctr., Mpls., 2001—. Office: Fairview Univ Riverside Campus 2450 Riverside Ave S Minneapolis MN 55454

DILLON, HERB LESTER, critical care and emergency room nurse; b. Duluth, Minn., June 7, 1948; m. Sharon Dillon, July 12, 1969; children: Herb T., Travis M. BA in Nursing, Coll. of St. Scholastica, Duluth, 1973. RN, Minn.; cert. in ACLS, BCLS; CEN; EMT, BCLS instr.; cert. trauma nursing critical care. Nurse emergency room, sppr. U.S. Army Hosp., Ft. Riley, Kans., 1973—76; staff nurse St. Mary's Med. Ctr., Duluth, 1973—, head nurse emergency rm., 1981—82, critical care transport nurse, 1984—85, EMT instr., 1985—99. Nurse dir. Grandma's Marathon, 1979—; Lt. col. USAR, 1971-94, ret. Mem.: Emergency Nurses Assn. (EMS Nurse of Yr. 1997). Home: 5127 Dodge St Duluth MN 55804-2436 E-mail: hdillon@chartermi.net.

DILLON, JAMES JOSEPH, lawyer; b. Rockville Ctr., N.Y., June 18, 1948; s. James Martin and Rosemary (Peter) D.; m. Martha Stone Wiske, Mar. 19, 1977; 1 child, Eleanor. BA, Fordham U., 1970, Oxford U., 1972; JD, Harvard U., 1975; MA, Oxford U., 1982. Bar: Mass. 1975, U.S. Dist. Ct. Mass. 1976, N.Y. 2000, U.S. Ct. Appeals (1st cir.) 1978, U.S. Ct. Appeals (5th cir.) 1986, U.S. Ct. Appeals (6th cir.) 1996, U.S. Ct. Appeals (11th cir.) 1995, U.S. Supreme Ct. 1990. Assoc. Goodwin Procter LLP, Boston, 1975-83, ptnr., 1983—2002, Foley Hong LLP. Dir. Beth Israel Deaconess Med. Ctr. Obstetrics and Gynecology Found., Inc.; trustee Huntington Theatre Co. Mem. ABA, Boston Bar Assn. Democrat. Office: Foley Hoag LLP 155 Seaport Blvd Boston MA 02210 E-mail: jjdillon@foleyhoag.com.

DILLON, JEAN KATHERINE, executive secretary, small business owner; b. Birmingham, Ala., May 18, 1925; d. Andrew Crawford and Nell (Cook) Dillon; m. Roy Lerone Morris, June 12, 1946 (div. May 1969); children: Norma Jean, Elizabeth Annell. BA in Bus. and Edn., Huntingdon Coll., 1950. Cert. tchr. secondary edn., Ala. Sec./bookkeeper H.T. Fitzpatrick CPA, Atty., Montgomery, Ala., 1948-50; sec., budget technician Dir. Budget, HQ Air Univ., Maxwell AFB, Ala., 1950-58; exec. sec., adminstrv. asst. Comptroller, HQ Air Univ., Maxwell AFB, Ala., 1958-86; adminstrv. asst. Family Violence Program, State Coalition, Montgomery, 1986; owner/operator The William Cook House, Nauvoo, Ala., 1989—. Pres. Nauvoo Hist. Soc., Inc., 1989—98, bd. dirs., 1998—2001; mem., patron Birmingham Hist. Soc., 1991—; mem. Nat. Hist. Preservation Forum, 1995—; mem.-at-large, bd. dirs. Jasper Scottish Heritage Soc., 1999—2001; planning com. Jasper Highland Games and Scots-Irish Festival, Jasper, Ala., 1999; sec., bd. dirs. Ofcl. State of Ala. Highland Games, Montgomery, 1992—2001; mem. Jasper Heritage Commn., 2000—; active Walker Celtic Festival, Oakman, Ala., 2002—; treas. Capital City Rep. Women, 1995—96, v.p., 1997—98, chmn. budget and fin. com., 1997—2003, mem. budget and fin. com., 2003—, Montgomery County Ala. Rep. Exec. Com., 2003—, active, 1998—; bd. dirs. St. Andrew's Soc., Montgomery, 1995—, Walker County Arts Coun., 1996—, Montgomery Landmarks Found., Nat. Trust for Hist. Preservation, Nat. Parks Svc. Mem. Huntingdon Coll. Alumni Assn. (life), Walker County C. of C. (sec.-treas., vice chair tourism task force 1990-98). Methodist. Avocations: travel, geneology, historical research, writing, heritage. Home and Office: 929 Parkwood Dr Montgomery AL 36109-1228

DILLON, JIMI, protective services official; b. Tototа, Monrovia, Bong Co., Liberia, Dec. 12, 1948; s. Jimmy Trybest and Vonnie Shebikollie Dillon; m. Pamela Denise Dillon, Oct. 12, 1985; children: Oleg, Jimmy Jr., Jerry, Paul Andrew; m. Bessie M. King, July 12, 1976 (div. Aug. 10, 1982); 1 child, Yeaetha Monete. Assoc. in Law Enforcement, Owens Tech. Coll., Oregon, Ohio, 1977. Police officer State Mental Health Bd., Toledo, Ohio, 1982—82; indsl. engr. Portside Assoc. Market Pl., Toledo, Ohio, 1984—86; corrections officer Harris County Juvenile Probation, Houston, Tex., 1994—. Counceling Harris County Juvenile Probation, Houston, 1994—. Author: (book) Calamity Of The Heathens. Scholar Ednl. Sholarship, Bapt. Gen. Conv., 2001. Democrat-Npl. Christian Baptist. Avocations: soccer, jogging, swimming. Home: 7630 Puerta Vallaea Drive Houston TX 77083 Office: Gateway International Christian Churdh 4270 SKirkwood Houston TX 77072 Personal E-mail: pdhcd@aol.com.

DILLON, JOHN T. paper company executive; b. Schroon Lake, N.Y., 1938; BA, U. of Hartford, 1965; M Bus., Columbia U., 1971. With Internat. Paper Co., Purchase, NY, 1965—, v.p. and group exec. for land and timber group, 1982—86, exec. v.p. packaging sector, 1987—95, pres., COO, 1995—96, chmn. bd., CEO, 1996—, dir., 1991—. Bd. dirs. Caterpiller, Inc. Trustee Nat. Coun. on Econ. Edn.; chmn. bd. govs. Nat. Coun. for Air and Stream Improvement; mem. Pres.'s Adv. Coun. on Trade Policy and Negotiations; mem. Bus. Coun.; chmn. bd. dirs. Nat. Coun. on Econ. Edn.; chmn. Bus. Roundtable Constrn. Task Force. Mem.: Am. Forest and Paper Assn. (vice chmn.). Office: Internat Paper Co 2 Manhattanville Rd Purchase NY 10577-2196

DILLON, JOSEPH FRANCIS, lawyer; b. Bklyn., Oct. 15, 1938; s. Joseph and Elizabeth (Sullivan) D.; m. Pamela Margaret Higbee, May 15, 1966 (div. Feb. 1972); children: Elizabeth Margaret, J. Alexander; m. Diane K. Long, Mar. 17, 1978. BBA, St. John's U., 1960; LLB, U. Va., 1963. Bar: Va. 1963, N.Y. 1964, U.S. Tax Ct. 1965, Mich. 1968, Ohio 1975, Fla. 1983. Tax trial atty. IRS, Washington and Detroit, 1963-68; mem. Raymond & Dillon, P.C., Detroit, 1969-93, Dykema Gossett PLC, Detroit, 1993-97, Cox, Hodgman & Giarmarco, P.C., Detroit, 1997—. Adj. prof. taxation U. Detroit Law Sch., 1977-87; spkr., planning chmn. Inst. CLE Programs; mem. magistrates merit selection panel and profl. assistance com. U.S. Dist. Ct. for Ea. Dist. Mich.; mem. U.S. Ct. Internat. Trade. Bd. dirs., exec. com. Met. Ctr. for High Tech., Detroit, 1993-96. Cpl. USAR, 1958-64. Fellow Mich. State Bar Found.; mem. ABA (taxation and internat. sects. 1963—), FBA (officer, pres. Detroit chpt. 1978-82), Mich. Bar Assn. 1988—, (taxation counsel 1979-82, internat. sec. 1990—), Detroit Bar Assn. (taxation com. 1973—), Ohio Bar Assn., Fla. Bar Assn., Am. Judicature Soc., Am. C. of C. in Japan, London Ct. of Internat. Arbitration, Inter-Pacific Bar Assn., Internat. Bar Assn., Greater Detroit-Windsor Japan Am. Soc. (bd. dirs. 1992—, exec. com. 1999—), Japanese Bus. Soc. Detroit Found. (v.p. 1992—), Detroit Regional Chamber (nominating com. for dirs.), French-Am. C. of C. of Detroit (bd. dirs. 1997-2000), Detroit Athletic Club, Lochmoor Club, Vineyards Country Club, World Trade Club, Econ. Club (Detroit). Republican. Roman Catholic. Avocations: golf, squash, skiing. Office: Cox Hodgman & Giarmarco PC 10th Fl Columbia Ctr 101 W Big Beaver Rd Troy MI 48084-5280 Fax: 248-457-7001. E-mail: jdillon@chglaw.com.

DILLON, MERTON LYNN, historian, educator; b. nr. Addison, Mich., Apr. 4, 1924; s. Henry J. and Cecil Edith (Sanford) D. BA, Mich. State Normal Coll., 1945; MA, U. Mich., 1948, PhD, 1951. Asst. prof. history N.Mex. Mil. Inst., Roswell, 1951-56; asst. prof. Tex. Tech. Coll., Lubbock, 1956-59, asso. prof., 1959-63, prof., 1963-65; asso. prof. Northern Ill. U., DeKalb, 1965-67; prof. Ohio State U., Columbus, 1967-91, prof. emeritus, 1991—. Author: Elijah P. Lovejoy, Abolitionist Editor, 1961, Benjamin Lundy and the Struggle for Negro Freedom, 1966, The Abolitionists, the Growth of a Dissenting Minority, 1974; Ulrich Bonnell Phillips, Historian of the Old South, 1985, Slavery Attacked: Southern Slaves and Their Allies, 1619-1865, 1990; contbr. articles to profl. jours. NEH fellow, 1973-74 Mem.Orgn. Am. Historians, So. Hist. Assn. (bd. editors 1959-63). Home: 10460 Addison Rd Jerome MI 49249-9723

DILLON, MICHAEL EARL, engineering executive, mechanical engineer, educator; b. Lynwood, Calif., Mar. 4, 1946; children: Bryan Douglas, Nicole Marie, Brendon McMichael. BA in Math., Calif. State U., Long Beach, 1978, postgrad. Registered profl. engr., Ala., Alaska, Ariz., Ark., Calif., Colo., Del., Fla., Ga., Hawaii, Idaho, Ill., Ind., Iowa, Ky., La., Mich., MInn., Mo., Mont., NC, Nebr., Nev., NJ, N.Mex., NY, Ohio, Okla., Oreg., Pa., Tenn., Tex., Utah, Wash., Wis., Wyo., Va.; chartered engr., U.K. Journeyman plumber Roy E. Dillon & Sons, Long Beach, 1967-69, ptnr., 1969-73; field supr. Dennis Mech., San Marino, 1973-74; chief mech. official City of Long Beach, 1974-79; mgr. engr. Southland Industries, Long Beach, 1979-83; v.p. Syska & Hennessy, L.A. and N.Y., 1983-87; prin. Robert M. Young & Assoc., Pasadena, Calif., 1987-89; pres. Dillon Cons. Engrs., Long Beach, 1989—. Mech. cons. in field; instr. in field; lectr. in field. Contbr. over 160 poems to various publs., contbr. articles to profl. jours. Former chair Mechanical, Plumbing. Elec. and Energy CodeAdv. Commn. of Calif. Bldg. Stds. Commn.; former vice chmn. bd. examiners Appeals and Condemnations, Long Beach; mem. adv. bd. City of LA; mem. bus. adv. bd. City of Long Beach. Recipient Environ. Ozone Protection award U.S. EPA, 1993, John Fies award Internat. Conf. Bldg. Ofcls., 1995. Fellow Chartered Inst. Bldg. Svc. Engrs. Gt. Britain and Ireland, Inst. Refrigeration, Heating, Air Conditioning Engrs. of New Zealand, Inst. Advancement Engring.; mem. ASCE, ASME, Internat. Soc. Fire Safety Sci., Nat. Inst. for Engring. Ethics, Nat. Fire Protection Assn., Internat. Assn. Bldg. Ofcls., Internat. Fire Code Inst., So. Bldg. Code Congress Internat., Bldg. Ofcls. and Code Adminstrn. Internat., Soc. Fire Protection Engrs., Tau Beta Pi, Pi Tau Sigma, Chi Epsilon, others. Avocation: poetry. Home: 669 Quincy Ave Long Beach CA 90814-1818 Office: Dillon Cons Engrs 671 Quincy Ave Long Beach CA 90814-1818 E-mail: medillon@dillon-consulting.com. *Rather I live and love in coventry than lust and rust in the public reign of insouciant sycophancy.*

DILLON, MILLICENT GERSON, writer; b. May 24, 1925; AB, Hunter Coll., 1944; MA, San Francisco State U., 1966. Author: Baby Perpetua and Other Stories, 1971, The One in the Back Is Medea, 1973, A Little Original Sin: The Life and Work of Jane Bowles, 1981, After Egypt, Isadora Duncan and Mary Cassatt, 1990, The Dance of the Mothers, 1991, You Are Not I: A Portrait of Paul Bowles, 1998, Harry Gold, 2000, A Version of Love, 2003. Home: 2571 Yarmouth Ln Tallahassee FL 32309 E-mail: millicentd@mindspring.com.

DILLON, PHILLIP MICHAEL, construction company executive; b. Ypsilanti, Mich., July 15, 1944; s. Robert Timothy and Maxine Helen (Elliott) Dillon; m. Phyllis Louise Brooks, Jan. 21, 1978; children: Richard, Debora, Michael, Robert, Karen. Student, Mich. State U., 1962-66. Lic. realtor Fla. . Store mgr. Morse Shoe, Inc., Detroit, 1964-68; asst. dir. store planning and constrn. Stride Rite Corp., Boston, 1972-74; sr. v.p. Capitol Cos., Inc., Arlington Heights, Ill., 1974-81; chmn. bd., chief exec. officer Std. Cos., Inc., Palatine, Ill., 1982-83; co-owner, sr. v.p. Eagle Constrn. Corp., 1983-88; chief exec. officer Dillon Enterprises, Ltd., Lamont, Ill., 1988-2000; also bd. dirs.; mem. Nationwide Constrn. Svcs. LLC, Ft. Walton Beach, Fla., 1999—2001; real estate agt. Keller Williams Realty, Clearwater, Fla., 2002—. Bd. dirs., sr. ptnr. Internat. Developers Partnership. Mem.: Inst. Store Planners. Roman Catholic. E-mail: dillonphil@aol.com.

DILLON, ROBERT SHERWOOD, retired government official; b. Chgo., Jan. 7, 1929; s. Dale Crowell and Viola May (Sherwood)D.; m. Caroline Sue Burch, June 16, 1951; children: Dale, Robert Jr., John, Elizabeth, Thomas. BA, Duke U., 1951; postgrad., Princeton U., 1958-59. Ops. officer CIA, 1951-56; fgn. svc. officer (including U.S. Amb. Lebanon, 1981-83) Dept. State, Washington, 1956-84; asst. sec. gen. UN, Vienna, Austria, 1984-88; pres. Am.-Mideast Ednl. & Tng. Svcs., Washington, 1988-95. UN spl. envoy for Rwanda and Burundi, 1994; advisor Dept. of State, 1995-96. Cpl. U.S. Army, 1947-48. Recipient Presdl. Honor award, White House, 1983.

DILLON, TERRI L. consulting firm executive; b. Winston-Salem, N.C., Sept. 12, 1962; d. Dallas Eugene and Opal Wall Shields; m. Victor Ray Dillon, Apr. 18, 1992; children: Mary Abigail, Leslie Gray, Summer Rae, Dalton Levi. Student, High Point U., 1984-88, Vanderbilt U., 1998, U. N.C., Greensboro, 1999. Proof operator, teller, customer svc. and consumer loan rep. Northwestern Bank (First Union Nat. Bank), Winston-Salem, N.C., 1979-86; adminstrv. asst., grant writer, sr. project mgr. Whitney jones, Inc., Winston-Salem, 1986-97, v.p. fin. and adminstrn., 1997-2001; v.p. adminstrn. Management Recruiters of Greensboro, 2001—. Mem. steering com., chair spkrs. bur. Leave A Legacy of the Triad, Winston-Salem, 1998-99; com. mem. Colfax (N.C.) Inc. Com., 1999; grad. Winston Class of Leadership, Winston-Salem, 2001. Mem. Nat. Ctr. for Non-Profit Bds., Nat. Soc. Fund Raising Execs. (cert., chair 1999 fund-raising day conf. 1999, charter N.C.-Triad chpt., treas. and 1st v.p. 1996-99, pres. 1999-2001), New Garden Moose Lodge, Jr. Achievement N.W. N.C., Inc. (bd. dirs. 1999-2000), Rotary Club of Winston-Salem (sec. 2001). Republican. Methodist. Office: Management Recruiters Greensboro 324 W Wendover Ave Ste 230 Greensboro NC 27408

DILLON, WILLIAM HENRY, retired secondary school educator; b. Pearisburg, Va., Nov. 4, 1941; s. Ernest Henry and Mary (Robertson) D.; m. Doris Jean Elliott, Jan. 3, 1964; 1 child, Mary Elliott. BA, Emory and Henry Coll., 1973; MS, Radford U., 1979. Cert. tchr., Va. English educator Castlewood (Va.) H.S., 1973—81, Riverheads H.S., Staunton, Va., 1981—2001. Adj. English instr. Blue Ridge C.C., Weyers Cave, Va., 1984-92. With USAR, 1966-72. Fellow Masons; mem. Schola Cantorum (pres. 1996-2000). Avocations: reading, herb and flower gardening. Home: 624 Rosser Ave Waynesboro VA 22980-3520

DILLON, WILLIAM PATRICK, neuroradiologist, radiologist; s. William P. and Mary Catherine Dillon; m. Irene Balcar Dillon, Jan. 25, 1986; children: Alexander Balcar, Andrea Balcar, Annelise Balcar. BS, U. Santa Clara, 1974; MD, U. Calif., L.A., 1978. Diplomate Am. Bd. of Radiology, 1982, cert. neuroradiology Am. Bd. of Radiology, 1996. Chief neuroradiology U. Calif., San Francisco, 1992—, vice-chair radiology, 1992—. Author: (book) Teaching Atlas of the Brain; contbr. articles. Bd. dir. Neuroradiology Rsch. and Edn. Found., Oak Brook, Ill., 2000—03. Mem.: Am. Soc. Head and Neck Radiology (pres. 1993—94), Am. Soc. Neuroradiology (pres. 2001—02). Office: UCSF Med Ctr 505 Parnassus Ave San Francisco CA 94143-0628

DILLON, WILTON STERLING, anthropologist, foundation administrator; b. Yale, Okla., July 13, 1923; s. Earl Henry and Edith Holland (Canfield) D.; m. Virginia Leigh Harris, Jan. 20, 1956; 1 child, James Harris. BA, U. Calif.-Berkeley, 1951; postgrad., Inst. Ethnology, U. Paris, U. Leyden, 1951-52; PhD, Columbia U., 1961. News reporter Holdenville (Okla.) Daily News, 1936-41; info. specialist, civilian mem. Civil Info. and Edn. Sect. SCAP, Tokyo, 1946-49; vis. lectr. sociology and anthropology Hobart and William Smith colls., Geneva, N.Y., 1953-54; staff anthropologist Japan Soc. N.Y.; also lectr. Japanese studies Fordham U., 1954; dir. Clearinghouse for Research in Human Orgn., Soc. Applied Anthropology, N.Y.C., 1954-56; exec. sec., dir. research Phelps-Stokes Fund N.Y.; including dir. research project on higher edn. and African nationhood U. Ghana, 1957-63; vis. lectr. Columbia U., New Sch. Social Research, 1957-63; staff dir. Nat. Acad. Scis., 1963-69; dir. symposia and seminars Smithsonian Instn., Washington, 1969-85, dir. interdisciplinary studies, 1986-90, sr. scholar, 1990—; sr. scholar emeritus. Dir. internat. commemoration of 250th anniversary of birth of Thomas Jefferson, 1992—; adj. prof. U. Ala., 1971—; chmn. Oxford U.-Smithsonian Seminars, 1985. Author: Gifts and Nations, 1968; editor: (with John F. Eisenberg) Man and Beast: Comparative Social Behavior, 1971, The Cultural Drama, 1974, (with Neil G. Kotler) The Statue of Liberty Revisited: Making a Universal Symbol, 1993; contbr. articles to profl. jours.; editl. bd. Ala. Heritage. Del. numerous internat. confs. including UNESCO, Pugwash; mem. adv. coun. on Africa Dept. State, 1964-68; hon. commr. Internat. Year of Child, 1979-80; pres. bd. dirs. Inst. Intercultural Studies, N.Y.C.; trustee emeritus Phelps-Stokes Fund, 1985—; sec.-treas., bd. dirs. Inst. Psychiatry and Fgn. Affairs; bd. visitors Wake Forest U., 1978-81; adv. com. Hubert Humphrey Inst. for Pub. Affairs, 1988-94; bd. dirs. Delta Rsch. and Ednl. Found., 1987-95; trustee Friends of Raoul Wallenberg Found., 1995-97, Lives and Legacies Inc., 1995—; advisor Nation's Capital Bicentennial Celebration 1999-2000, Margaret Mead Centenary 2001, Historic Mt. Vernon 1999, Benjamin Franklin Creativity Found., 2002. With USAAF, 1943-46. Decorated Chevalier de l'ordre des arts et lettres, 1983; Woodrow Wilson Internat. Center for Scholars guest scholar, 1970 Fellow Am. Anthrop. Assn., AAAS, Royal Soc. Arts; mem. Lit. Soc. Washington (pres. 1990), Anthrop. Soc. Washington. Episcopalian (lay reader N.Y. diocese 1958-60). Club: Cosmos (Washington). Home: 1446 Woodacre Dr Mc Lean VA 22101-2536 Office: Smithsonian Instn Nat Mus Natural History Rm 2205 MRC 124 PO Box 37012 Washington DC 20013-7012

DILLON-MCHUGH, CATHLEEN THERESA, librarian, consultant, editor; b. Newark, Jan. 31, 1951; d. William David and Rose (Baker) Dillon; m. Joseph F. McHugh, Apr. 16, 1988. BA cum laude, Bloomfield (N.J.) Coll., 1973; MLS, Rutgers U., 1976. Reference-cataloging libr. Neptune (N.J.) Pub. Libr., 1976-77; indexer Popular Periodical Index, Wayne, N.J., 1979-95; sch. libr. Hudson Cath. High Sch., Jersey City, 1980-81; govtl. reference libr. N.J. State Libr., Trenton, 1981-82, law reference libr., 1982-83, reference referral libr., 1983-87; tech. reference libr. Bell Communications Rsch., Red Bank, N.J., 1987; reference libr. Middletown Twp. Pub. Libr., N.J., 1988-89; libr./info. specialist, cons. various corps., N.J. and Maine, 1990-94; libr. Gov. Baxter Sch. for the Deaf, Falmouth, Maine, 1994-99; freelance writer, content developer, editor, 1999—; ref./children's libr. Scarborough (Maine) Pub. Library, 2000—02; asst. Vocat. Resources, Portland, Maine, 2002—. Cons. Quantum Enterprises, Inc., Middletown, 1985-86; dir. Edith Belle Libby Meml. Libr., Old Orchard Beach, Maine, 1991-94. Mem. Maine Libr. Assn. Avocations: needlework, ceili dancing, writing.

DILLS, JAMES ARLOF, retired publishing company executive; b. Guelph, Ont., Can., Aug. 11, 1930; s. George Arlof and Isma Marie (MacPherson) D.; m. Shirley Jean Elliott, Aug. 16, 1952; children— Steven George, James Mark, Paul David, Catherine Jane, Carolyn Shirley. Grad. in journalism, Ryerson Poly. Inst., 1951. Pub. The Can. Champion, Milton, Ont., 1966-78, The Georgetown (Ont.) Ind., 1973-78; sec.-treas. Dills Printing and Pub. Co. Ltd., Acton, Ont., 1954—; exec. dir. Can. Community Newspapers Assn., Toronto, Ont., 1979-87; mem. adv. com. journalism program Sheridan Coll., 1965-78; pres. Ont. Weekly Newspapers Assn., 1975-76; pub. County Chronicles Press, 1992—2003. Dir. Milton Evergreen Cemetery Co., 1997. Author: Moments in History, 1993; editor: Time Capsules from Milton's Past 1890-1894, 2002. Vice Chair, Mackenzie Heritage Printery, Queenston.,1998; pres. Milton Hist. Soc., 1977-80. Named Citizen of Yr., Milton, 1978; recipient Lifetime Achievement Cmty. award, Milton C. of C., 1999.

DILLY, BARBARA JANE, anthropologist, educator; b. Charles City, Iowa, July 30, 1949; d. Robert Carl and Maxine Lucille Dilly. BA, UCLA, 1988; PhD, U. Calif., Irvine, 1994. Asst. prof., anthropology Creighton U., Omaha, 2000—. Rep. City Coun., Shell Rock, Iowa, 2000—02. Fellow: Soc. for Applied Anthropology. Democrat. Lutheran. Avocation: classic automobiles collector. Home: 4906 Webster Omaha NE 68132 Office: Creighton Univ 2500 California Plaza Omaha NE 68178

DILLY, MARIAN JEANETTE, humanities educator; b. Vining, Minn., Nov. 7, 1921; d. John Fredolph and Mabel Josephine (Haagenson) Linder; m. Robert Lee Dily, June 22, 1946 (dec. Oct. 1987); children: Ronald Lee, Patricia Jeanette Dilly Vero. Studetn, U. Minn., 1944-45; grad., John R. Powers Finishing Sch., N.Y.C., 1957, Zell McC. Fashion Career Sch., Mpls., 1957, Estelle Compton Models Inst., 1966, Nancy Taylor Charm Sch., N.Y.C., 1967, Patricia Stevens Career Sch., Mpls., 1968; BS in English cum laude, Black Hills State U., Spearfish, S.D., 1975. Instr. Nat. Am. U., Rapid City, S.D., 1966-68; instr., dir. Nancy Taylor Charm Sch., 1966-68; hostess TV shows, 1966-74. Lectr. in personality devel., dir., prodr. beauty and talent pageants, freelance coord. in fashion shows, judge beauty and talent pageants of local, state and nat. levels, 1966—. Actress bit parts Nauman Films Inc., 1970. Active ARC; dir., 1st v.p. Black Hills Girl Scout Coun., 1967-72; chmn. bd. dirs., pres. Luth. Social Svc. Aux., Western S.D. and Eastern Wyo., 1960-65; chmn. women's events Dakota Days and Nat. Premiere, 1968; bd. dirs. YMCA, 1976-81; mem. Dallas Symphony Orch. League, 1987-90, Dallas Mus. of Art League, 1987-90,

Women's Club. Dallas County, Tex., Inc., 1987-90. Recipient award Rapid City C. of C., 1968, Fashion awards March of Dimes, 1967-72, Svc. award Black Hills Girl Scout Coun., award of appreciation Yellowstone Internat. Toastmistress Club. Mem. AAUW (sec., mem. exec.b d. 1988-90), Nu Tau Sigma (past advisor), Delta Tau Kappa, Singing Tribe of Wahoo. Avocations: golf, bridge, music, skiing. Address: 1607 Woodward St Erie CO 80516-7529

DILMORE, JOSEPH ERIC, carpenter, poet, writer; b. Meshoppen, Pa, June 7, 1964; s. James Roger Dilmore and Loretta Fanny (Parrish) Dilmore; m. Denine Marie Turner (div. June 28, 1998); children: Anthony Keegan James, Adam Keith Joseph; m. Victoria Regina Berghauer; 1 child, Dakota Nicole Tyler. Grad. HS, Tunkhannock Pa. Cert. phlebotomist N.Am. Biologicals Inc., autopheresis tech. N.Am. Biologicals Inc.; centrifuge tech. N.Am. Biologicals Inc., Baxter Auto-C field svc. tech. Sr. phlebotomist North Am. Biologicas, Inc.(NABI), Scranton, Pa., 1987—95; dancer The Horsemen, Scranton, 1992—96; pvt. practice carpenter Hawley, Pa., 1999—. Author poetry and short stories. With USN, 1982—83. Recipient Silver medal for prepared speech, Vocat. Indsl. Clubs Am., 1982. Avocations: comic book collecting, motorcycling, tattooes, collecting or creating edged weapons/or tools. Home: 1 Aspen Ridge Hawley PA 18428 Personal E-mail: jed197@ezaccess.net.

DI LORENZO, JOHN FLORIO, JR., retired lawyer (corporate); b. Paterson, N.J., May 18, 1940; s. John F. and Ida (Cona) Di L.; m. Ernestine R. De Rose, Nov. 15, 1969; children: Christina P., Roberta J. BA, Seton Hall U., 1962; LLB, MBA, Columbia U., 1966. Bar: N.J. 1967, N.Y. 1968, Ohio 1981. Assoc. Stryker, Tams & Dill, Esqs., Newark, 1966-68; atty. Am. Electric Power Svc. Corp., N.Y.C., 1968-79, asst. gen. counsel, asst. v.p., exec. asst. to pres., 1979-81, assoc. gen. counsel, v.p., sec. Columbus, Ohio, 1981-2001; ret., 2001. Sec. various Am. Electric Power Sys. cos., 1987-2001, asst. sec. 1979. Trustee Ballet Met. Columbus, 1981-87. Mem. ABA (chmn. subcom. on pub. utility holding co. act of fed. regulation of securities com. 1985-94), Knights of Malta, Knights of the Holy Sepulchre of Jerusalem, Scioto Country Club. Roman Catholic. Avocations: skiing, travel. Home: 2756 Elginfield Rd Columbus OH 43220-4248

DILORENZO, LOUIS PATRICK, lawyer; b. Waterloo, N.Y., Nov. 3, 1952; s. Luigi and Theresa Maria (Grieco) D.; m. Deborah Joan Boudreau, Aug. 18, 1973; children: Louis Patrick, Lisa Marie, Laura Gabriel. Student, U.S. Mil. Acad., West Point, 1970-72; BA, Syracuse U., 1973; JD, SUNY, Buffalo, 1976. Bar: N.Y. 1977, U.S. Dist. Ct. (no. dist.) N.Y. 1977, U.S. Supreme Ct. 1988. Assoc. Bond, Schoeneck & King, Syracuse, 1976-84, ptnr., 1985—, chair recruiting com., chair labor and employment law dept.; co-chair employment law litigation group, adj. prof. Syracuse U. Sch. Mgmt., 1988—. Participant NYU Ann. Conf. on Labor, 1989. Author: Syracuse Law Jour., 1978, Jour. of Coll. and U. Law Jour., 1980, N.Y. State Bar Jour., 1982; author: (with others) Corporate Counseling, 1988, Public Sector Labor Law, 1988, Duke Journal of Gender Law and Policy, 1999; mem. editl. bd. N.Y. State Bar Jour., 1998—; mem. editl. bd., N.Y. Civil Practice Before Trial, 2001. Bd. dirs. Syracuse Opera Co., 1986. Fellow Am. Coll. Employment and Labor Law Lawyers; mem. ABA, Nat. Assn. Coll. and Univ. Attys., Fedn. Def. and Corp. Counsel, N.Y. State Bar Assn. (mem. ho. of dels. 1984-90, 99—, chmn. young lawyers sect. 1987, chmn. labor rels. com. 1988, chmn. CLE com. 1990-93, chmn. labor and employment law sect. 1994). Republican. Roman Catholic. Avocations: golf, gardening, reading. Office: Bond Schoeneck & King 1 Lincoln Ctr Fl 18 Syracuse NY 13202-1324

DILS, ROBERT M. military officer; AS, BS, SUNY; postgrad., Ctrl. Mich. U. Commd. U.S. Army, advanced through grades to sgt. maj.; command sgt. maj. U.S. Army Maneuver Support Ctr., Ft. Leonard Wood, U.S. Army C.E., Washington. Decorated Legion of Merit with oak leaf cluster, Bronze Star medal, Meritorious Svc. medal with 2 oak leaf custers, Army Commendation medal with 4 oak leaf clusters, Army Achievement medal; recipient Silver de Fleury medal, Army Engr. Assn., Bronze Order of the Marechaussee medal, Army Mil. Police Regiment. Mem.: Sgt. Audie Murphy Club (hon.). Office: US Army Corps of Engrs 441 G St NW Washington DC 20314-1000

DILSIZIAN, VASKEN, cardiologist, nuclear medicine physician; b. Aug. 12, 1956; BSChemE magna cum laude, Tufts U., 1977, MSChemE, 1978, MD, 1982. Diplomate Nat. Bd. Med. Examiners, Am. Bd. Internal Medicine, Am. Bd. Cardiovascular Disease, Am. Bd. Nuclear Medicine; lic. physician Va., Md., Mass. Intern and resident in internal medicine Georgetown U. Hosp., Washington, 1982-85; fellow in cardiology Boston U. Med. Ctr./Boston City Hosp., 1985-87; fellow in cardiovascular and nuclear medicine Mass. Gen. Hosp./Harvard Med. Sch., Boston, 1987-88; sr. staff fellow cardiology br. Nat. Heart, Lung, and Blood Inst., Bethesda, Md., 1988-89, clin. investigator, 1989-92; resident in nuclear medicine NIH, Bethesda, Md., 1991-92, dir. nuclear cardiology, 1992—2001; dir. cardiovasc. nuc. medicine U. Md. Med. Ctr., 2001—, prof. medicine and radiology. Adj. prof. medicine Sch. Medicine George Washington U., 1994—; adj. prof. medicine and radiology Georgetown U. Sch. Medicine, 1999—; spkr., invited lectr. and presenter in field. Editorial cons. Circulation, Am. Jour. Cardiology, Jour. Am. Coll. Cardiology, Annals Internal Medicine, New England Jour. Medicine, Jour. Nuc. Cardiology; assoc. editor Jour. Nuc. Medicine, 1998-99; editor Myocardial Viability: A Clinical and Scientific Treatise, 2000, Atlas of Nuclear Cardiology, 2003; contbr. over 190 articles and abstracts to profl. jours., 15 chpts. to books. Fellow Am. Coll. Cardiology (editorial cons. jour., abstract reviewer), Am. Heart Assn. (coun. on clin. cardiology, com. on advanced cardiac imaging and tech. 1994-95, abstract reviewer); mem. Am. Soc. Nuclear Cardiology (founding, bd. dirs.), Soc. Nuclear Medicine (bd. dirs. cardiovascular coun. 1993—, abstract reviewer). Home: 7600 Dwight Drive Bethesda MD 20817 Office: U Md Med Ctr Gudelsky Bldg Rm N2W78 22 S Greene St Baltimore MD 21201-1595

DILTS, JON PAUL, law educator; b. Monterey, Ind., Sept. 7, 1945; s. Charles Albert and Janet Cecilia (Keitzer) D.; m. Anne Williams Avirett, Aug. 21, 1971; children: Christopher, Andrew. BA, Saint Meinrad Coll., 1967; MA, Ind. U., 1974; JD, Valparaiso U., 1981. Bar: Ind. 1981, U.S. Dist. Ct. (so. dist.) Ind. 1981, U.S. Supreme Ct. 2000. Reporter Peru (Ind.) Daily Tribune, 1972-73, wire editor, 1973-76, city editor, 1976-78; law clk. Ind. Ct. Appeals, Indpls., 1981-82; asst. prof. Ind. U., Bloomington, 1982-88, assoc. prof., 1988—, assoc. dean, 1985-2000. Author: The Magnificent 92 Indiana Courthouses, 1992; co-author: Media Law, 1994, 97; mem. editl. bd. Comms. Law & Policy, 1998—. Bd. overseers St. Meinrad Coll. Sch. Theology, 1992—, trustee 1996-98, 2003—, vice chmn., 2002—; exec. bd. dirs. Hoosier Trails coun. Boy Scouts Am., Bloomington, 1992-93. With U.S. Army, 1968-71. Nat. Press Club First Amendment fellow, 2002. Mem. Assn. for Edn. in Journalism and Mass Comm. (head law divsn. 1987-88), Internat. Comms. Assn., Soc. Profl. Journalists, AP Mng. Editors Assn., Rotary. Democrat. Roman Catholic. Avocations: skiing, hiking, backpacking, canoeing, sailing. Office: Ind U Sch Journalism 940 E 7th St Bloomington IN 47405-7108 E-mail: dilts@indiana.edu.

DILTZ, JERRY DWAINE, computer science educator, consultant; b. Bluefield, W.Va., Oct. 21, 1948; s. Eugene Gearheart and Mary Francis House; life ptnr. Thomas Michael Quealy, Mar. 27, 1985. Facilitator Convergys CMG TSS, Ft. Pierce, Fla., 1998—. Del. Volusia County Dem. Exec. Com., Daytona Beach, 1991-93. Mem. N.Y. Bd. of Scientists. Home: 389 N W Grandadeer St Port Saint Lucie FL 34983-8706 Office: Convergys CMG TSS Ste 400 4600 Montgomery Rd Cincinnati OH 45212

DILWORTH, ROBERT LEXOW, career military officer, educator; b. Chgo., Aug. 19, 1936; s. Robert Oliver and Linda Agnes (Lexow) D.; m. Doris Elthea Smith, Sept. 1, 1981; children by previous marriage: Alexa, Robert. BS in Advt., U. Fla., 1959; MS in Mil. Sci., U.S. Army Command and Gen. Staff Coll., 1971; MA in Pub. Adminstrn., U. Okla., 1975; MEd, EdD, Columbia U., 1993. Commd. 2nd lt. U.S. Army, 1959, advanced through grades to brig. gen., 1986, chief adminstrn. div. office chief of staff, 1968-70, chief mgmt. analysis br. office chief of staff, 1971-75, chief of staff 2nd infantry div., 1975-76, chief mgmt. div. adj. gen. ctr., 1976-77, chief compt. div. Nat. Guard Bur., 1978-81, dep. comdr. 1st pers. command Schwetzingen, Fed. Republic of Germany, 1981-84, dir. resource mgmt. U.S. Mil. Acad. West Point, N.Y., 1984-86, adjutant gen. army Alexandria, Va., 1986-88, dep. chief of staff base ops. support tng./doctrine command Ft. Monroe, Va., 1988-91; assoc. prof. adult edn., human resource devel. Va. Commonwealth U., Richmond, 1993—. Guest lectr. Hungarian Mil. Acad., 1989. Contbr. articles to profl. jours. Mem. ASPA (exec. com. mgmt. sci. and policy analysis sect. 1992-96), ASTD (chair nat. rsch. to practice com. 2000-2002), Acad. Human Resource Devel., Assn. U.S. Army, Mil. Officer Assn., Internat. Soc. Quality Govt. (nat. dir. 1992-93). Methodist. Avocation: writing for publication. Home: PO Box 29 Gum Spring VA 23065-0029 Office: Va Commonwealth U Sch Edn PO Box 842020 1015 W Main St Richmond VA 23284-9061

DIMACHKIE, MAZEN MOHAMMAD, health care educator; b. Beirut, Mar. 30, 1962; came to the US, 1988; s. Mohammad Cha'ban Dimachkie and Siham Ghalayini; m. Mary Frances Greenwell, Jan. 24, 1992; children: Mohamad Dave, Dena Catherine. BS in Chemistry with distinction, Am. U. Beirut, 1984, MD, 1988. Diplomate Am. Bd. Neurology and Psychiatry with added qualification in clin. neurophysiology. Intern internal medicine Stagnes Hosp., Balt., 1988-90; neurology resident U. Tex., Houston, 1990-93, neuromuscular fellow, 1993-94, instr., 1993-94; asst. prof. U. Okla. Health Sci. Ctr., Oklahoma City, 1994-95, U. Tex., Houston, 1995—2001, assoc. prof., 2001—, dir. neuromuscular disease program, 2000—. Cons. Med. Mktg. Conf., Livingston, NJ, 1998—, Vistalink Med. Cons., 1998—. Contbr. chpts. to books and articles to profl. jour. Recipient Spl. Action Svc. award VA Med. Ctr., Oklahoma City, 1995, Appreciation cert. Muscular Dystrophy Assn., Houston, 1996-98, Outstanding Achievement in Cmty. Svc. award 1999. Mem. AMA (Physician Recognition award 1997—), Am. Acad. Neurology, Am. Assn. for Electrodiagnostic Medicine, Am. Bd. Med. Specialties, Harris County Med. Soc. Avocations: fishing, movies. Office: Univ Tex 6431 Fannin St # 7044 Houston TX 77030-1501 E-mail: mdimachkie@dnamail.com.

DIMAGGIO, FRANK LOUIS, civil engineering educator; b. N.Y.C., Sept. 2, 1929; s. Serafino and Maria (Barbuto) DiM.; m. Irene C. Koehn, Dec. 15, 1963 (dec. June 1998); children: Samuel, Peter. BS, Columbia U., 1950, MS, 1951, PhD, 1954. Registered profl. engr., N.Y. Prof. civil engring. Columbia U., 1956—, chmn. dept., 1975-78, Carleton prof., 1978—. Cons. in field, 1956— Served with AUS, 1954-56. NSF sr. postdoctoral fellow, 1962-63; guest scholar Kyoto U., Japan, 1986. Fellow ASCE (chmn. exec. com. engring. mech. div. 1982-83, chmn. adv. bd. engring. mechanics div. 1985-86); mem. Sigma Xi. Home: 138 Van Orden Ave Leonia NJ 07605-1521 Office: Columbia Univ Dept Civil Engring and Engring Mechanics New York NY 10027 E-mail: dimaggio@civil.columbia.edu.

DI MAIO, VINCENT JOSEPH MARTIN, forensic pathologist; b. Bklyn., Mar. 22, 1941; s. Dominick J. and Violet (de Caprariis) Di M.; m. Theresa G. Richberg, Mar. 29, 1969; children: Dominick, Samantha. MD, SUNY, Bklyn., 1965. Diplomate Am. Bd. Pathology. Intern pathology Duke Hosp., Durham, N.C., 1965-66; resident pathology King's County Downstate Med. Ctr., Bklyn., 1966-69; fellow forensic pathology Office of Chief Med. Examiner, Balt., 1969-70; med. examiner Southwestern Inst. Forensic Scis., Dallas, 1972-81; chief med. examiner Bexar County Forensic Sci. Ctr., San Antonio, 1981—; prof. dept. pathology U. Tex. Health Sci. Ctr., San Antonio, 1987—. Author: Gunshot Wounds, 1985, 2nd edit., 1999, Forensic Pathology, 1989, 2nd edit., 2001, Handbook of Forensic Pathology, 1998; editor: Am. Jour. Forensic Medicien & Pathology, 1992—. Maj. U.S. Army, 1970-72. Recipient Commn. Continuing Edn. medal Am. Soc. Clin. Pthologists, Jean R. Oliver, MD Master Tchr. award SUNY Alumni Assn.-Downstate Med. Ctr., 1990. Fellow: Am. Acad. Forensic Scis.; mem.: Nat. Assn. Med. Examiners. Office: Bexar County Forensic Sci Ctr 7337 Louis Pasteur Dr San Antonio TX 78229-4565

DIMANCESCU, MIHAI D. neurosurgeon, researcher, educator; b. Maidenhead, Berkshire, Eng., Mar. 27, 1940; came to U.S., 1956, naturalized, 1963; s. Dimitri D. and Alexandra Irina (Radulescu) D.; m. Joan E. Brenner, Mar. 17, 1966; children: Stefan, Marc-Mihai. BA, Yale U., 1962; MD, U. Toulouse, France, 1968. Diplomate Am. Bd. Neurol. Surgery. Rotating intern Purpan Hosp., Toulouse, 1968-69; jr. resident in gen. surgery Hartford (Conn.) Hosp., 1969-70; jr. resident in neurosurgy Albert Einstein-Montefiore Hosp., Bronx, N.Y., 1970-72; rsch. fellow in spasticity and movement disorders U. Miami (Fla.)-VA Hosp., 1972-74; sr. resident in neurosurgery U. Miami, 1972-76, asst. instr. in neurol. surgery, 1975-76; pvt. practice in medicine specializing in neurosurgery Freeport and Garden City, N.Y., 1976—. Dir. Internat. Coma Recovery Inst., Garden City, 1977—; mem. faculty, dir. brain studies Internat. Sch. Evan Thomas Inst., Phila., 1980—; mem. staff, dir. dept. neurosurgery Franklin Hosp. Med. Ctr., Valley Stream, NY; mem. staff neurosurgery South Nassau Cmtys. Hosp., Oceanside, NY, Mercy Med. Ctr., Rockville Ctr., NY, St. Francis Hosp., Rockville Ctr., NY, Winthrop U. Hosp., Mineola, NY, North Shore U. Hosp., Manhasset, NY, continuing med. edn. lectr., 1977—; cons. neurosurgery Inst. for Achievement of Human Potential, Phila., 1977—; mem. surg. core faculty health Sci. Ctr., Sch. Medicine, SUNY-Stony Brook, 1980—; bd. dirs. South Nassau Cmty. Hosp.; mem. med. coun. L.I. Health Network; mem. bd. So. Nassau County Hosp. Contbr. articles to profl. jours. Bd. dirs. Inst. Achievement Human Potential, 1990—; bd. dirs. Princess Margarita Romania Found., chmn., 1998—. Recipient Golden medal World Orgn. Human Potential, 1978; VA grantee, 1972-74. Fellow ACS, Royal Soc. Arts; mem. AMA, Am. Assn. Neurol. Surgeons, Congress Neurol. Surgeons (Sci. Exhibit award 1974), Coma Recovery Assn. (chmn. bd. dirs. Garden City chpt. 1983), N.Y. State Neurosurg. Soc. (bd. dirs. 1983-88, pres.-elect 1986-87, pres. 1988), Med. Soc. State of N.Y. (neurosurg. del. interspltу. com. 1983-88), N.Y. State Head Injury Providers' Coun. (rotating chmn. 1986-87), World Med. Assn., Nassau County Med. Soc., Nassau Physicians' Rev. Orgn. Office: Neurol Surgery PC 88 S Bergen Pl Freeport NY 11520-3510 also: Neurol Surgery PC 520 Franklin Ave Garden City NY 11530-2906 E-mail: mihai.dimancescu@aol.com., neurofree@aol.com.

DIMANT, JACOB, internist; b. Rehovot, Israel, Apr. 27, 1947; came to U.S., 1972, naturalized, 1977; s. Simcha and Ita D.; m. Rose Bea Jearolmen, Sept. 11, 1974. MD, Hebrew U., Jerusalem, 1972. Diplomate Am. Bd. Internal Medicine and Rheumatology and Geriatric Medicine, Am. Bd. Quality Assurance and Utilization Rev. Physicians. Intern Maimonides Med. Ctr., Bklyn., 1972-73, resident in medicine, 1973-75, chief resident in medicine, 1975-76; fellow in rheumatology SUNY Downstate Med. Ctr., Bklyn., 1976-78; practice medicine specializing in internal medicine and rheumatology Bklyn., 1975—; dir. rheumatology Maimonides Med. Ctr., Bklyn., 1978-89, assoc. dir. med. edn., 1978-80; med. dir. Clove Lakes Nursing Home, S.I., N.Y., 1985-97; dir. divsn. of geriatrics Luth. Med. Ctr., Bklyn., 1998—. Med. dir. Prospect Park Nursing Home, Bklyn., 1977—87, Crown Nursing Home, Bklyn., 1983—2001, Hillside Manor Nursing Ctr., Queens, NY, 1993—98, Augustana Luth. Home, Bklyn., 1996—; pres. Crown Nursing Home Assocs., Inc., Bklyn., 1989—; asst. prof. medicine SUNY, Bklyn., 1978—. Contbr. articles to profl. jours. Named hon. police surgeon N.Y.C. Police Dept., 1982; fellow Arthritis Found. of N.Y., 1977-78. Fellow: ACP; mem.: N.Y. Med. Dirs. Assn. (bd. dirs. 1990—, pres. 1994—96), Am. Med. Dirs. Assn. (bd. dirs. 1995—97, treas. 1997—99, v.p. 2000—01, pres.-elect 2001—02, pres. 2002—03), Am. Geriatric Soc. Office: Crown Nursing Home 3457 Nostrand Ave Brooklyn NY 11229-5194

DI MARCO, BARBARANNE YANUS, special education educator; b. Jersey City, Nov. 16, 1946; d. Stanley Joseph and Anne Barbara (Dalack) Yanus; m. Charles Benjamin DiMarco, Mar. 15, 1986; 1 child, Charles Garrett. BA in Music Edn., Trenton State Coll., 1968; MA in Spl. Edn., Kean Coll., 1971, elem. edn. cert., 1974, adminstrv. cert., 1976. Cert. elem., music, adminstrn., spl. edn., N.J. Vocal music educator Roselle (N.J.) Bd. Edn., 1968-69, tchr. trainable mentally retarded, 1969-76, tchr. multiple handicapped, 1976—. Color guard instr. Roselle Bd. Edn., 1973-88, elem. tutor, 1976-92, adminstrv. asst. to supt., 1980-85; program dir., sec., Expanded Dimensions in Gifted Edn., Westfield, N.J., 1978—. Vestryperson St. Luke's Ch., Roselle, 1989-91. Recipient Govs. Tchr. Recognition award, Gov. Florio, N.J., Trenton, 1992-93. Mem. NEA, N.J. Edn. Assn., Roselle Edn. Assn., N.J. Assn. for Retarded Children, Eastern Star (25-yr award 1991), Delta Omicron. Republican. Episcopalian. Avocations: skiing, flying, oil painting, travel, swimming, music, golf. Home: 13 Gentore Ct Edison NJ 08820-1029 Office: Dr Charles C Polk Sch 1100 Warren St Roselle NJ 07203-2736

DIMARCO, BRIAN J. food and beverage consultant; b. Washington, July 25, 1966; s. Albert Jonathan DiMarco and Charlotte Ann DeAngelis. Degree, Kutztown (Pa.) U., 1991; diploma, French Culinary Inst., N.Y.C., 2002. Brand media mgr. Grey Worldwide, N.Y.C., 1992—95; sr. account exec. Anheuser-Busch, Inc., St. Louis, 1995—99; account dir. Darcy Massius Benton & Bowles, N.Y.C., 1999; group account dir. McCann Amsteryard, N.Y.C., 1999—2001; chef Food Network, N.Y.C., 2002; food and beverage cons. N.Y.C., 2002—. Author: Keeping the Feast, 2002. Served with USN, 1986—88. Mem.: N.Y. State Restaurant Assn., Slow Foods. Home: 101 W 80th St Apt 4B New York NY 10024

DIMARCO, DAVID, mathematician, educator; s. Jeanette Mary and Joseph Paul DiMarco. BS, Stevens Inst. of Tech., Hoboken, N.J., 1975—79; MS, Stevens Inst Tech., Hoboken, N.J., 1981, PhD, 1988; MS, Iona Coll., New Rochelle, N.Y., 1995—95. Instr. math. Various Colleges, 1983—; adj. asst. professor-math NYC Tech. Coll., Brooklyn, NY, 1994—2002; adj. instr. math Fairleigh Dickinson U., Teaneck, NJ, 1997—2002; asst. prof. math Neumann Coll., Aston, Pa., 2002—. Contbr. articles to profl. jours. Mem.: Am. Math. Soc. Avocations: chess, cross training, jogging. Office: Neumann Coll Div of Arts and Sci One Neumann Dr Aston PA 19014

DIMARCO, THOMAS WILLIAM, software engineer; b. Phila., Oct. 1, 1968; s. Salvatore Samuel and Susann Patricia (McAffe) DiM. BS in Computer Engring., Lehigh U., 1991; MSE in Computer and Info. Sci., U. Pa., Phila., 1994. Field design engr. Bell & Howell, Allentown, Pa., 1991-92, 93-94; assoc. software engr. ABB, Allentown, 1992; software developer Bellcore, Piscataway, N.J., 1995; analyst Andersen Cons., Phila., 1996—98. Mem. Assn. Computing Machinery. Republican. Avocations: chess, tennis, volleyball, bowling, softball. Home: 1430 W 3rd St Red Hill PA 18076-1444

DI MARINO, MICHAEL E. biostatistician; BA, Loyola Coll. in Md., 1991, MA, 1993; PhD, George Wash. U., 2003. Johns Hopkins behavioral rsch. unit Biostatistician, Baltimore, 1993—97; biostatistician Pinney Associates, Bethesda, Md., 1997—. Tchg. asst. George Wash. U., 2001—. Contbr. articles to profl. jours. Mem.: SCT, ASA, ISCB (assoc.). Office: Pinney Associates 4800 Montgomery Lane Ste 1000 Bethesda MD 20814-3472 E-mail: mdimarino@pinneyassociates.com.

DIMARTINO, CHRISTINA, writer; Student, Palm Beach Jr. Coll., Fla. Atlantic U. Owner Kornhauser of Palm Beach, Inc., 1976-92, Seminole Sandals, Inc., 1993; retail cons. Robert Bindschedler, Paris, 1994-95; creater TV programming, mktg. plan N.Am. Media Corp., 1994-95; author newsletter Glenn-Kelly Pub. Co., 1995—; writer Anderson Pub. Co., 1995—. Lectr. in field; writing lectr., tutor City of West Palm Beach. Contbr. numerous articles to profl. jours.; lead contbg. writer for 24 nat. mags.; author/collaborator 32 books. Exec. bd. Palm Beach Crime Watch; mem. Palm Beach Pub. Sch. PTA, past pres.; mem. Preservation Found. of Palm Beach County; active Cystic Fibrosis Found.; chmn. Kravis Ctr. Children's Com.; founder, pres. Royal Poinciana Bus. Assn.; mem., spl. events com. Palm Beach County Sch. Arts; coord. fgn. exch. students Interant. Edn. Forum. Named Mem. of the Yr. Palm Beach County Transp. Found., 1974; recipient Outstanding Mem. award Palm Beach Crime Watch, Inc., 1994, Appreciation award, 1989, Chmn. award Cystic Fibrosis Found., 1984, Adminstrv. Appreciation award Palm Beach Pub. Sch., 1989, Acknowledgement for authoring nat. award winning article Am. Bus. Press Assn., 1999, Jesse H. Neal Lit. Achievement award, 1999. Home: 292 18th St Fl 2 Brooklyn NY 11215

DIMARZIO, EDMUND ARMAND, physicist; b. Phila., Mar. 23, 1932; s. Antonio and Maria Christina (D'Allesandro) DiM.; m. Philomena Elizabeth Arrivello, Oct. 6, 1956; children: Maria Christina, John Anthony, Lisa Ann. BS in Physics, St. Joseph's Coll., Phila., 1954; MS in Physics, U. Pa., 1960; PhD in Physics, Cath. U. Am., 1967. Co-op student Philco Co., Phila., 1952-54; rsch. physicist Am. Viscose Co., Marcus Hook, Pa., 1956-62; vis. mem. tech. staff Bell Telephone Labs., Murray Hill, N.J., 1962-63; physicist Nat. Inst. Stds. and Tech., Gaithersburg, Md., 1963-98; adj. prof. U. Md., College Park, 1998—. Contbr. more than 120 articles to profl. jours. Recipient Stratton award Nat. Bur. Stds., 1971. Fellow Am. Phys. Soc. (High Polymer Physics prize 1967), Sigma Xi. Democrat. Roman Catholic. Achievements include research on understanding how phase transitions in polymers lead to biological self-assembly and concluding that evolved life-forms are necessarily polymeric. Home: 14205 Parkvale Rd Rockville MD 20853-2529 Office: Nat Inst Stds and Tech Poly A209 Gaithersburg MD 20899-8544 E-mail: dimarzio@nist.gov.

DIMARZIO, NICHOLAS ANTHONY, bishop; b. Newark, June 16, 1944; s. Nicholas Anthony and Grace (Grande) DiMarzio. BA, Seton Hall U., 1966; STB, Catholic U., 1970; MSW, Fordham U., 1980; PhD, Rutgers U., 1985. Ordained to ministry Roman Cath. Ch., 1970, ordained to bishop Roman Cath. Ch., 1996. Divsn. dir. spl. svcs. Cath. Cmty. Svcs., Newark, 1976-85, assoc. exec. dir., 1991-92, exec. dir., 1992-97, Migration & Refugee Svcs. U.S. Cath. Conf., Washington, 1985-91; bishop Camden, NJ, 1999—2003; pontifical coun. pastoral care of migrants and itinerant people, 1999—; bishop Brooklyn Diocese, 2003—. Cons. Carnegie Endowment, Washington, 1985—91, Ctr. Immigration, Georgetown U., Washington, 1985—91, Cath. U., Washington, 1985—91, Consejo Episcopal L.Am., Bogota, Colombia, 1987—91, Migration and Refugee Svcs., Washington, 1991—92, Migration Policy Inst., 2001—; vicar human svcs. Archdiocese of Newark, 1991—99. Co-author: (book) Profiling Unapprehended Undocumented Aliens in the New York Metropolitan Area: An Exploration into Their Social and Labor Market Incorporation, 1986; contbr. articles to profl. jours., mags., and newspapers. Chmn. bd. dirs. Nat. Immigration, Refugee and Citizenship Forum, Washington, 1986—89; bd. dirs. Ctr.. Migration Studies, Washington, 1988—93, Am. Com. Italian Migration, 1989—91; v.p. Internat. Cath. Migration Commn., 1989—92. Decorated Knight of the Italian Republic N.Y., Prelate of Honor Pope John Paul II, Vatican; recipient Spl. award, N.Y. Assn. New Ams. Mem.: NASW. Office: Brooklyn Diocese 75 Greene Ave PO Box C Brooklyn NY 11202 E-mail: dimarzio@camdendiocese.org.

DI MARZO, MARINO, engineering researcher, educator; b. Messina, Italy, Feb. 16, 1952; came to U.S., 1978; s. Guido and Maria Pia (Benini) diM.; m. Fulvia Veronese, June 11, 1986; children: Giulia Maria, Marina Antonia. Dr.Ing.Chem.Eng., U. Naples, Italy, 1976; PhD in Mech. Engring., Cath. U., 1982. Registered profl. engr., Italy. Project engr. CTIP, Rome, 1976-78; staff engr. Daedalean & Assocs., Inc., Woodbine, Md., 1978-81; lectr. U. Md., College Park, 1981-82, asst. prof. to assoc. prof., 1982-98, prof., assoc. chair, 1998-2001, prof., chair, 2001—. Vis. scientist Nat. Inst. Standards and Tech., Gaithersburg, Md., 1985-99; cons. U.S. Nuclear Regulatory Commn., 1995—; speaker in field; mem. adv. bd. ECO World, 1992. Contbr. numerous articles to profl. publs. Recipient Excellence in Mfg. award MIPS, 1992, U.S. NRC Spl. Act award, 1995; grantee NRC, 1982-97, U. Md., 1985-86, Nat. Bur. Standards, 1983-85, Md. Indsl. Partnerships, 1989-91, Nat. Inst. Standards and Tech., 1985-2000. Fellow ASME (mem. UIT coordinating com. 1990—, reviewer Jour. Heat Transfer, Nuc. Engring. and Design, others), Fellow AIChE (chmn. field 7a energy transport rsch. 1991-94, chmn. heat transfer and energy conversion divsn. 1996, mem. various coms., chair various conf. sessions, assoc. editor Heat and Tech.), mem. Internat. Assn. Fire Safety Sci., Soc. Fire Protection Engr., Unione Italiana di Termofluidodinamica. Roman Catholic. Achievements include spray cooling studies applied to fire safety, nuclear power plant behavior during accidents. Home: 8405 Burdette Rd Bethesda MD 20817-2816 also: MS T10G6 Us Nuclear Regulatory Commn Washington DC 20555-0001

DIMAS, MARILYN J. health resources executive; b. Portland, Oreg., Jan. 24, 1944; d. John Davidson Dow and Gladys Victoria (Lewis) Thompson;m. John F. Bass, m. George Dimas (div. 1981); children: Ron Farr, Kimberly Farr. BS, U. Oreg., 1967, MSN, 1970; MPA, NYU, 1978. Dir. Psychiat. Crisis Unit Med. Sch. U. Oreg., Portland, 1970-73; dir. Nat. Coun. on Alcoholism, N.Y.C., 1973-74; asst. dir. Am. Lung Assn., N.Y.C., 1974-76; exec. dir. Richmond Fellowship of N.Y., N.Y.C., 1978-84, Boley Manor, St. Petersburg, Fla., 1984-86; assoc. exec. dir. Woodhall Hosp., Bklyn., 1986-90; pres. Marilyn Dumas & Assocs., N.Y.C., 1978-88, Healthcare Quality Improvement Resources, Inc., N.Y.C., 1988—. Dir. Western Inst. Drug Problems Summer Sch., Portland, 1970-72; cons. Am. Lung Assn., N.Y.C., 1974, Nat. Health Coun., N.Y.C., 1975-76. Author: Standards for State Alcoholism Associations, 1971, Standards for Voluntary Health Organizations, 1976. Recipient Gold plaque Nat. Inst. on Alcoholism and Alcohol Abuse/NIAAA, 1974; named one of Outstanding Young Women of Am., 1980. Mem. Am. Hosp. Assn., Nat. Assn. Quality Assurance Profls., N.Y. State Quality Assurance Profls. Avocations:

swimming, horseback riding, jogging, cooking. Home: 1401 51st Ave NE Saint Petersburg FL 33703-3210 Office: Healthcare Quality Improvement Resources 1401 51st Ave NE Saint Petersburg FL 33703

DIMAS, TRENT, Olympic athlete, gymnast; b. Albuquerque, Nov. 10, 1970; Grad., Columbia U. Olympic gymnast, Barcelona, Spain, 1992. Recipient Men's Horizontal Bar Gold medal Olympics, Barcelona, 1992. Office: care USA Gymnastics Pan Am Plz 201 S Capitol Ave Ste 300 Indianapolis IN 46225-1058 Home: 554 W 114th St Apt 5F New York NY 10025-7842

DIMASCIO, JOHN PHILIP, lawyer; b. Bklyn., Feb. 4, 1944; s. Eugenio and Stella (Scheuermann) DiM.; m. Angela Piccininni, Apr. 2, 1967 (div. 1980); children: John Philip, Jr., Christine Pagano, Thomas; m. Linda Nick, Oct. 19, 1997. BA, C.W. Post Coll., 1975; MA, L.I. U., 1976; postgrad., NYU, 1976-79; JD, St. John's U., 1983. Bar: N.Y. 1984, U.S. Dist. Ct. (ea. and so. dists.) N.Y. 1984, U.S. Ct. Appeals (2d cir.) 1984, U.S. Supreme Ct. 1997, U.S. Ct. Appeals for Armed Forces 1997, U.S. Ct. of Fed. Claims, 1997, U.S. Ct. Appeals (fed. cir.) 1997. Sr. ct. officer N.Y. State Supreme Ct., Mineola, 1970-82; assoc. Joel R. Brandes, PC, Garden City, N.Y., 1984; pvt. practice N.Y., 1984-87; ptnr. Di Mascio, Meisner & Koopersmith, Carle Place, 1987-93; pvt. practice Garden City, 1993—. Lectr. Nassau Acad. Law. With USN, 1962—69. Recipient acad. awards. Mem.: ABA (family law sect.), Am. Inns of Ct. (N.Y. family law chpt.), Nassau County Bar Assn. (chmn. matrimonial com., ethics com., family ct. com. 1984—, editor Recent Decisions, contbg. author), N.Y. State Bar Assn. (family law com. 1982). Avocations: photography, boating. Office: 300 Garden City Plz Garden City NY 11530-3302 E-mail: jpdlawoff@msn.com.

DIMASI, LINDA GRACE, epidemiologist; b. Trenton, N.J., Feb. 7, 1949; d. Nick and Pearl LaVerne (White) D. BS in Biology, Alderson-Broaddus Coll., 1970; MPA, Rutgers U., 1992. Cert. pub. mgr. Field rep. N.J. State Dept. of Health, Trenton, 1971-85, epidemiologist, 1985—. Contbr. articles to profl. jours. Mem. ASPA, APHA, Phi Alpha Alpha. Avocations: flying, auto racing, traveling. Home: 35 Jennifer Ln Burlington NJ 08016-1144 Office: NJ State Dept of Health Divsn AIDS Prevention and Control PO Box 363 Trenton NJ 08625-0363

DI MASSA, ERNANI VINCENZO, JR., broadcast executive, television producer, writer; b. Phila., Sept. 12, 1947; s. Ernani Vincenzo and Rita C. (Iacovoni) Di M.; divorced; 1 child, Michael Colin. BS, La Salle Coll., 1970; MS, Temple U., 1972. Producer, writer Mike Douglas Show, Phila. and L.A., 1969-81, Regis Philbin Show, NBC-TV, 1981, Fantasy NBC-TV, L.A., 1981-83; exec. producer, writer Thicke of the Night, L.A., 1983-84, Tony Orlando Show, 1985-86; supervising producer Hollywood Squares, L.A., 1987-89; sr. v.p. programming and devel. King World Prodns., L.A., 1989-97; pres. DiMassa Prodns., 1998—. Supervising prodr. Candid Camera; exec. in charge prodn. Rolonda; exec. prodr. Terry Bradshaw-Fox TV; exec. in charge of programming and distbn. for The Oprah Winfrey Show, Wheel of Fortune, Jeopardy!, Inside Edition, Am. Jour., Instant Recall, The Arts and Entertainment Rev. Recipient Emmy award NATAS, 1982. Mem. Producers Guild Am., Writers Guild Am. Roman Catholic. Avocations: car collecting and restoring, photography. Office: Di Massa Prodns Inc RMB Studios Media Ctr 1600 Rosecrans Ave Manhattan Beach CA 90266 E-mail: ernani-d@usa.net.

DIMATTEO, RHONDA LYNN, speech-language pathologist, audiologist; b. Easton, Pa., Sept. 12, 1955; d. Michael John and Betty Lenora (O'Brien) DiM. Assoc. in Gen. Edn., Northampton County Area Community Coll., 1981; BS, Trenton State Coll., 1983; MA, Hahnemann U., 1985. Cert. clin. competence in speech-lang. pathology and audiology; registered therapy dogs trainer and handler Comfort Caring Canines. Lead tchr. The Nursery Sch. of Easton, Inc., 1974-83; speech-lang. pathologist, audiologist Warren Hills Regional Bd. Edn., Washington, N.J., 1985—, child study team mem., 1985—; speech-lang. pathologist, audiologist, lang. devel. tchr. Mountainview Youth Correctional Facility, Annandale, N.J., 1990—, theater instr., child study team mem., 1990—. Dir. speech and hearing screening ARC, Easton, 1982—; coach cross-country and track Warren Hills Regional Bd. Edn., Washington, N.J., 1987—. Author several poems; actress several theatre co.'s. Operation Search screening dir. ARC Hearing Screenings, Easton, 1982—; trainer dogs Northampton County Soc. for The Prevention of Cruelty to Animals, Easton, 1970—; mem. hearing ear dog program New Eng. Assistance Dog Svcs., West Boylston, Mass., 1985—; mem. adoption svc. Northampton County SPCA, Easton, 1970—. Recipient Proudly We Hail cmty. award Easton, Pa., 1993; named to Phillipsburg H.S. Wall of Fame, 2000. Mem. ASHA (cert., Project Enhance media campaign recruiter 1989), NEA (profl.), Pa. Speech-Lang.-Hearing Assn. (profl.), N.J. Speech-Lang.-Hearing Assn. (profl.), N.J. Edn. Assn. (profl.), N.J. Interscholastic Coaching Assn. (profl.), Nat. Coun. Tchrs. English (profl.), Nat. Student Speech-Lang.-Hearing Assn., Comm. Workers Am. (profl.), Warren County Edn. Assn., Warren Hills Edn. Assn., The Drama League. Lutheran. Avocations: dog shows, theatre, journalism, poetry, organized sports.

DIMBATH, MERLE F. economic consultant, business educator; b. Dayton, Ohio, Mar. 21, 1939; d. Merle S. and Zella (Shadowens) D.; children: Merle, Richard, Sesilie, Eric. BS in Commerce, U. Va., 1961; MA in Mktg., U. Fla., 1962, PhD in Econs. and Bus. Adminstrn., 1964. Qualified econ. expert witness state and fed. cts., Fla. Chmn. dept. econs. and bus. Fla. So. Coll., Lakeland, 1967-77; supt. pub. instrn. Polk County, Fla., 1968-69; exec. dir. Fla. Pub. Sch. Bd., Tallahassee, 1969; land developer, real estate and mortgage broker, investments Lakeland, 1971-80; pres. Dimbath Devel. Co., Lakeland, 1971-81, Dimbath & Assocs., Inc., Stuart, Fla., 1981—. Ec-n. rsch. and cons. Dimbath & Assocs., Stuart, Fla., 1980—; assoc. prof. Coll. Bus. and Pub. Adminstrn., Fla. Atlantic U., Boca Raton, 1981—98; money reporter sta. WPEC-TV, West Palm Beach, Fla., 1982-87; bd. dirs. Fla. State Bd. Ind. Postsec. Vocat., Tech., Trade and Bus. Schs., 1990, vice chmn., 1991-92. DuPont scholar, 1957-61; Ford Found. fellow, 1963-64. Mem. Am. Econ. Assn., Nat. Assn. Bus. Economists, Nat. Assn. Forensic Econs., So. Econ. Assn. Office: PO Box 2910 Stuart FL 34995-2910

DI MEDIO, GREGORY LAWRENCE, writer, information systems specialist; b. Columbus, Ohio, Nov. 17, 1963; s. Gabriel Silvio and Patricia Ann (Kennedy) Di M.; m. Rebecca Westmoreland Brown, Mar. 22, 1991. BA in English, U. Colo., 1987; MA in English, U. S.C., 1994. Tech. writer, editor Ctr. Rsch. in Human Devel. and Edn., Temple U., Phila., 1988-91; adj. faculty dept. arts and scis. Midlands Tech. Coll., Columbia, 1992-94, writing ctr. coord., 1993-94; prof. English dept. arts and scis. Denmark (S.C.) Tech. Coll., 1994-95; freelance tech. writer Pitts., 1995-97; writer, project mgr. Agnew Moyer Smith, Pitts., 1998-2000; project mgr. Blattner Brunner, Pitts., 2001—02; prin. Content Svcs. Group, Inc., Pitts., 2002—. Grants cons. WQED Pub. TV and Radio, Pitts., 1996; writing ctr. tutor U. S.C., Columbia, 1993. Contbr. articles to profl. jours. Mem. Soc. for Tech. Comm., Sierra Club (newsletter editor 1986-87, freelance editor 1989-91, lobbyist 1990-91), Trout Unltd., Sigma Tau Delta, Alpha Phi Gamma. Democrat. Avocations: nature walks and writing, fly fishing, live jazz, internet. Home: 14 4th St Pittsburgh PA 15215-2914 Office: Content Svcs Group Inc 1382 Old Freeport Rd 2B Pittsburgh PA 15238 E-mail: csgconnect@yahoo.com.

DIMEGLIO, NICOLAS JOSEPH, real estate broker, small business owner; m. Robin White. AS in Paralegal Scis., Mercer County C.C., Trenton, N.J., 1981; Real Estate Sales Qualification course, Mercer County C.C., 1988; BS in Polit Sci., Trenton State Coll., 1984; Broker Qualification course, Real Estate Sch., Princeton, N.J., 1991. Accreditd buyer rep. real estate buyers agt. Sr. paralegal McCarthy & Schatzman P.A., Princeton, N.J., 1982-88; sales rep. Century 21, Robert M. Goldberg Realtors, North Brunswick, N.J., 1988-89, Fox & Lazo Realtors, Jack Burke Real Estate, Inc., North Brunswick, N.J., 1989-91; broker, assoc. Gloria Zastko Realtors, North Brunswick, N.J., 1991-94; pres., broker Prudential DiMeglio Realtors, Somerset, N.J., 1994-97; pres. DiMeglio Realty Group, Somerset, N.J., 1997—. Corp. sponsor Heritage Day Com., No. Brunswick, 1996, 97, 98, Toys for Tots Drive, 1996, 97, 98. Recipient cert. of commendation Mercer County Vol. Lawyers Project, 1987, cert. of merit Nat. Paralegal Assn., 1988; named to NJAR Million Dollar Club, 1990, 91, 92, 93, 94, N.J. Bd. Realtors, Silver level 92, 94, gold level 93. Mem. Soc. Hill of Somerset (pres.), MIddlesex-Somerset Realtors Assn., Nat. Assn. Realtors (real estate buyer's accreditation). Home: 18 Nepote Pl Somerset NJ 08873 Office: DiMeglio Realty Group 1711 Rte 27 Somerset NJ 08873

DIMENGO, JOSEPHINE, medical/surgical nurse; b. Cleve., Jan. 9, 1954; d. Joseph and Mary (Rihtar) Staric; m. Mark Dimengo, May 25, 1979; children: Cristina, Nicholas, Alexa. Diploma, St. Vincent Charity Hosp., Cleve., 1975; MSN, Frances Payne Bolton Sch., Cleve., 1990. Clinical dir. heart failure Am. Heathways, 2002—. Recipient Helen Lathrope Bunge award. Mem. AACN, Heart Failure Soc. Am., Am. Heart Assn., Sigma Theta Tau.

DI MEO, DOMINICK, artist, sculptor, painter; b. Niagara Falls, N.Y., Feb. 1, 1927; s. Antonio and Michelina (Sandonato) Di M.; m. Judith S. Cousins, Dec. 26, 1963. B.F.A., Sch. Art Inst., Chgo., 1952; M.F.A., State U. Iowa, 1953. Vis. artist Sch. of Art Inst. Chgo., 1977; instr. Chgo. Acad. Fine Arts, 1967-69 One man shows include Lake Forest (Ill.) Coll., 1955, Bemidji (Minn.) Coll., 1963, Fairweather-Hardin Gallery, Chgo., 1964, 68, 71, Barat Coll., Lake Forest, 1966, Chgo. Public Library, 1966, Kendall Coll., Evanston, Ill., 1967, Westbroadway Gallery, N.Y.C., 1973, 75, 76, Project Studios One, Long Island City, N.Y., 1982, group exhbns. include, Albright-Knox Art Gallery, Buffalo, 1953, 54, Art Inst. Chgo, 1959, 60, 61, 63, 65, 66, 67, 68, 71, 76, 79, 89-90, Ann. Exhbn. of Contemporary Am. Painting, Whitney Mus. of Am. Art, N.Y., 1967-68, Mus. Contemporary Art, Chgo., 1969, Joan Miro Internat. Drawing Prize Competition, Barcelona, Spain, 1977, 78, 79, 80, Centro Cultural/Arte Contemporaneo, Mexico City, Nov. 1986-Jan. 1987, Art Inst. Chgo., 1989-90; represented in permanent collections, Art Inst. Chgo., Whitney Mus. Am. Art, N.Y.C., U. Mass., Amherst, Nat. Collection Fine Arts, Smithsonian Instn., Elmhurst (Ill.) Coll. Fellow Guggenheim Found., 1972, sculpture fellow Nat. Endowment for Arts, 1983. Mem. Momentum (founding mem.), Participating Artists Chgo.), Artists Collaborative. Address: 429 Broome St New York NY 10013-2686

DIMES, EDWIN KINSLEY, lawyer; b. Hartford, Conn., Apr. 13, 1923; s. Alfred Eustace and Charlotte (Miller) D.; m. Edwina May Adams, Feb. 3, 1945 (div. 1981); children: Martha, Deborah, Kimberley; m. S. Antoinette Morton, Dec. 29, 1990. BA, Conn. Wesleyan U., Middletown, 1947; JD, Yale U., 1950. Bar: Conn. 1950, U.S. Tax Ct. 1960, U.S. Supreme Ct. 1960. From assoc. to ptnr. Wake, See, Dimes and Bryniczka, Westport, Conn., 1950—. State trial referee State of Conn., 1985—. Chmn. bd. fin. City of Westport, 1979-97. 2d lt. USAF, 1943-45. Mem. ABA, Westport Bar Assn., Conn. Bar Assn. (bd. govs.). Republican. Congregationalist. Avocations: boating, tennis. Home: 70 Morningside Dr S Westport CT 06880-5415 Office: Wake See Dimes and Brynicza 27 Imperial Ave Westport CT 06880-4303 E-mail: edimes@wsdb.com.

DIMICCO, DANIEL R. manufacturing executive; BS in Engring., Metallurgy and Materials Sci., Brown U., 1972; MS in Metallurgy and Materials Sci., U. Pa., 1975. Rsch. metallurgist, project leader Republic Steel, Cleve., 1975—82; plant metallurgist, mgr. quality control Nucor Steel, Plymouth, Utah, 1982—88, mgr. melting and casting Utah divsn., 1988—91; gen. mgr. Nucor-Yamato, Blytheville, Ark., 1991—92, v.p., 1992—99, exec. v.p., 1999—2000; pres., CEO Nucor Corp., 2000—, vice chmn., 2001—. Office: 2100 Rexford Rd Charlotte NC 28211*

DIMICELI, VINCENT EDWARD, mathematician, educator; b. Port Arthur, Tex., Aug. 18, 1962; s. Vito Emanuel and Betty Lee Dimiceli; m. Linda Marie Kleihege, Aug. 11, 1990; 1 child, Peter Vincent Emanuel. BS, Lamar U., Beaumont, Tex., 1986; MS, Tex. A&M U., 1989, PhD, 1999. Math. tchr. asst. Tex. A&M U., College Station, 1987—89, math. lectr., 1989—96; math. tchr. Bryan (Tex.) H.S., 1996—97; asst. prof. of math. Oral Roberts U., Tulsa, 1997—. Faculty advisor for Okla.-Delta chpt. of Kappa Mu Epsilon Oral Roberts U., Tulsa, 1997—, treas. of arts and scis. faculty senate, 2000—02, advisor for Coll. Reps., 2002—, v.p., pres.-elect of arts and scis. faculty senate, 2002—03, pres. of arts scis. faculty senate, 2003—. Treas. for campaign for Michael Bates for city coun. Rep. Party, Tulsa, 2001—02, del. to county conv., 2000, del. to state conv., 2000, vice-chmn. precinct 50, 2000—03; exec. com. Tulsa County Reps., 2003—; bd. dirs. Mt. Horeb Ch., Bryan, 1995—97; dir. Brazos Valley Mar. for Jesus, Bryan and College Station, 1996—97; worship leader for Sunday sch. class Victory Christian Ctr., Tulsa, 1999—2003, actor in Christmas and Easter dramas, 2001—02; voice-over for character in outdoor theater Impact Prodns., Tulsa, 2002. Recipient undergrad. rsch. fellowship, U.S. Govt., 1987. Mem.: Nat. Coun. of Tchrs. of Math., Math. Assn. of Am., Phi Kappa Phi, Kappa Mu Epsilon (corr. sec. Okla.-Delta chpt. 1997—), Alpha Phi Omega (life). Conservative. Charismatic Christian. Achievements include first to First teacher at Texas A&M University to develop a college algebra course utilizing calculator graphing technology to teach concepts in algebra; In the group of teachers to first implement computer laboratories for calculus at Texas A&M University; First to develop and implement computer laboratories for calculus at Oral Roberts University. Avocations: photography, reading, singing, acting. Office: Oral Roberts U 7777 S Lewis Ave Tulsa OK 74171 Office Fax: 918-495-6660. Personal E-mail: dimiceli@oru.edu. E-mail: dimiceli@oru.edu.

DIMICHELE, DONNA, medical educator, researcher; MD, McGill U., 1978. Cert. Am. Bd. Pediat., 1985, Am. Bd. Pediatric Hematology/Oncology, 1987. Instr. pediatrics U. Colo. Med. Sch., Denver, 1982—83, Tufts U. Sch. Medicine, Boston, 1988—90; asst. prof. pediatrics Northwestern U. Med. Sch., Chgo., 1990—95, Weill Med. Coll. Cornell U., N.Y.C., 1995—2000, assoc. prof. clin. pediatrics, 2001—. Attending pediatiatrician Children's Meml. Hosp., Chgo., 1990—95, N.Y. Presbyn. Hosp., N.Y.C., 1995—; asst. attending pediatrician Hosp. Spl. Surgery, 1999—. Co-author: Thrombosis and Hemorrhage, Anticoagulants: Physiologic, Pathologic and Pharmacologic, Pediatric Clinics of North America, Thrombosis and Hemorrhage, Hematology/Oncology Clinics of North America, Disorders of Hemostasis and Thrombosis, Inhibitors in Patients with Haemophilia, Thrombosis and Hemorrhage. Recipient David W. Smith Pediat. Trainee Rsch. award, Western Soc. Pediatric Rsch., 1987; grantee Altered Coagulation Pediatric Stem Cell Patients, Am. Cancer Soc., 1998—2000. Mem.: Nat. Hemophilia Found. (med. and sci. adv. coun. 2002—), Internat. Soc. Thrombosis and Haemostasis (subcom. chair 2000), World Fedn. of Hemophilia (med. specialist adv. 2000). Office: NY Presbyn Hosp 525 East 68th St Payson 695 New York NY 10021

DI MINO, ANDRÉ ANTHONY, manufacturing executive, consultant; b. Bklyn., Aug. 24, 1955; s. Alfonso and Nancy (Zarbo) DiM.; m. Jenny DiCapua, May 30, 1981. BS in Indsl. Engring., Fairleigh Dickinson U., 1978, MBA in Fin., 1981. Engr. ADMTronics Inc., Emerson, NJ, 1977—79, dir. tech., 1979—82, sec./treas. Northvale, NJ, 1982—86, exec. v.p. and dir., 1986—2001; pres. ADMTronics, Northvale, NJ, 2002—; founder, dir. Enviro-Pack Devel. Corp., Northvale, 1991—2003. Ptnr., cons. Tech. Mgmt. Cons., Woodcliff Lake, N.J., 1978-94; v.p., dir. Pegasus Labs., Inc., Northvale, N.J., 1989—, Sonotron Med. Sys., Inc., Northvale, 1988—, VET-Sonotron Sys., Inc., Northvale, 1988-2003; pres. AANorthvale Med. Assocs., Inc., 1998—. Inventor in field. Mem. coun. Borough of Woodcliff Lake, 1984-97, pres., 1987-93, 97, mem. cable adv. com., 1999-; corr. sec. Office N.E. Rep. Orgn. (NERO), 1989-93, treas., 1992-93, vice chmn., 1993; co-chmn. privatization subcom. Bergen County Cost Containment Rev. Team, 1991; mem. open space com. Bergen County, 1997, 98; fundraising dir. Our Lady Mother of the Ch., Woodcliff Lake, 1990-99; founding mem., 1st v.p. Woodcliff chpt. Unico Nat. Svcs. Orgn., 1990-92, pres., 1992-94, 97-00; dep. dist. gov., 1993-94, dist. gov., 1994-96, nat. treas., 2002—; founder, pres. Cmty. Access TV studio WCL-TV, 1990—; pres. Woodcliff Lake Rep. Club, 1994-96; devel. chmn. NW Bergen chpt. Am. Heart Assn. (vice chmn. 1995-96), 1994; founder, chmn. Woodcliff Lake Sr. Assn., 1989-99; trustee Pascack Hist. Soc., 1995-99; vice chmn. Pascack Valley Region Cmty. Devel. com., 1997; mem. computer sci. adv. bd. Fairleigh Dickinson U., Madison, N.J., 2000-; chmn. Marconi Sci. Award Com., 2000—. Named Vol. of Yr. Bergen County, N.J., 1991, 93, Citizen of Yr. Pascack Valley C. of C., 1993. Mem. Woodcliff Lake Vol. Fire Assn. (hon.). Republican. Roman Catholic. Avocations: classic cars, antiques, video and photography. Office: ADMTronics Inc 224S Pegasus Ave Northvale NJ 07647-1904 E-mail: andre@adtronics.com.

DIMINO, SYLVIA THERESA, elementary and secondary educator; b. N.Y.C., June 6, 1955; d. John Anthony and Elena (Berardesca) D. BA, St. John's U., 1977; MPA, NYU, 1980, MA in Elem. and Secondary Edn., 1982, cert. advance studies in edn1. adminstrn., 1986, cert. in advanced studies in mgmt., 1992; MA in Tchg. ESL, Adelphi U., 1984; MA in Libr. Sci., Pratt Inst., 1998; chef, Nat. Gourmet Cooking Sch., 1999. Cert. elem. and secondary tchr., sch. adminstr., in mgmt. practices, social studies, math., N.Y. Traffic coord. Creamer Inc., N.Y.C., 1977-79; tchr. St. Patrick's Sch., N.Y.C., 1979-82, IS 131, Manhattan, N.Y.C., 1984-90, adminstr., coord., 1985-90, asst. prin., 1990-99; tchr. high sch. ESL, N.Y.C. Bd. Edn., 1995-99, libr. sci. tchr., 1999—; chef Natural Gourmet Cookery Sch., 1999—; City Harvest chef for children's programs, 2000—; tchr. Hatha Yoga for Kids, 2000—. Prana yoga tchr., 1998; Thai yoga body massage therapist, 1998. Named to 2000 Most Notable Women. Mem. NAFE, AAUW, Nat. Orgn. Women in Adminstrn., Bus. Cir. N.Y., Nat. Coun. Adminstrv. Women in Edn., Nat. Orgn. Italian-Am. Women (mentoring dir.), Yoga Tchrs. Assn. Roman Catholic. Avocations: walking, hiking, yoga. Address: FH LaGuardia HS Music Arts Performing Arts 100 Amsterdam Ave New York NY 10023-6406

DIMITRAKOPOULOS, CHRISTOS DIMITRIOS, materials scientist; b. Athens, Greece; arrived in U.S., 1987; BS, Nat. Tech. U., Athens, Greece, 1986; MS, Columbia U., 1989, MPhil, PhD, Columbia U., 1993. Tchg. asst., grad. rsch. asst. Columbia U., N.Y.C., 1987—90; co-op rschr. T.J. Watson Rsch. Ctr. IBM, Yorktown Heights, NY, 1989—92; postdoctoral fellow Philips Rsch. Lab., Eindhoven, Netherlands, 1993—95; mem. rsch. staff T.J. Watson Rsch. Ctr. IBM, Yorktown Heights, 1995—. Contbr. With Greek Army, 1998. Recipient Outstanding Innovation awrd, IBM, 2000, EDS Paul Rappaport awrd, IEEE, 2002, Francis Rhodes prize, Columbia U., 1989. Mem.: Materials Rsch. Soc. Achievements include patents for in field. Office: IBM TJ Watson Rsch Ctr PO Box 218 Rte 134 Yorktown Heights NY 10598

DIMITRIOU, DOLORES ENNIS, computer consultant; b. Phila., Apr. 7, 1932; d. Charles Adair and Rubye Stanton (Greene) Ennis; m. John Alexander Dimitriou, Sept. 25, 1954 (div. Aug. 1983); 1 child, Sandra Irene Dimitriou Falor. BS in Math., U. Miami, 1954; MA in Linguistics, U. Tex., 1994. Jet engine supr. GE, Evendale, Ohio, 1954-58; rsch. aide Marine Lab. U. Miami, Coral Gables, 1959-65; supr. tests Weathering Rsch. Svc., Princeton, Fla., 1959-87; income tax preparer H&R Block, Homestead, Fla., 1981-83; small bus. cons., pres., co-founder Facts & Figures Svcs., Homestead, 1983-87; computer cons., trainer Wycliffe Bible Translators, Orlando, Fla., 1987-97, Sec., treas., co-founder Weather Rsch. Svcs., Perrine, Fla., 1959-95; treas. GILLBT, Ghana, 1994-96. Mem. ch. rels. Wycliffe Bible Translators, 1998—; bd. dirs.,Ch. Women United, 1999—; ombudsman long-term care, 1998—; tax aide Am. Assn. Ret. Persons, 1998—. Named Outstanding Woman in Religion YWCA, U. Miami, 1953-54. Mem.: Cutler Ridge Woman's Club, Mortar Board, Phi Mu Epsilon. Democrat. Avocations: computers, travel, reading, crafts. Home and Office: 10381 SW 209 Ln Miami FL 33189-3612 E-mail: dolores_dimitriou@sil.org.

DIMITROULEAS, WILLIAM PETER, judge; b. Lynn, Mass., Mar. 28, 1951; s. Leo Peter and Mary (Kakatolis) Dimitrouleas; m. Linda Ruth Loughlin, Feb. 25, 1982 (div. Sept. 1982); m. Natalie Laine Barone, Mar. 26, 1985; 1 child, Scott. BA, Furman U., 1973; JD, U. Fla., 1975. Bar: Fla. 1976, U.S. Dist. Ct. (so. dist.) Fla. 1976. Asst. pub. defender Office Pub. Defender, Ft. Lauderdale, Fla., 1976-77; asst. state's atty. State Atty.'s Office, Ft. Lauderdale, 1977-89; judge Circ. Ct., Ft. Lauderdale, 1989-98, U.S. Dist. Ct., Fort Lauderdale, 1998—. Mem. Broward County (Fla.) Criminal Justice Planning Coun., 1983-89. Author: Sentencing Guidelines, 1987. Mem. Fla. Bar Assn. (criminal rules com., criminal cert. com., chmn. grievance com. 1987-88). Republican. Greek Orthodox. Avocation: track and field. Office: 299 E Broward Blvd # 203F Fort Lauderdale FL 33301-1944

DIMITROV, IVAN KOLEV, education educator, researcher; b. Yambol, Yambol, Bulgaria, Apr. 2, 1968; s. Kolyo Dimitrov Kolev and Yanka Ivanova Koleva; m. Nadia Peneva Nedeltcheva, Aug. 21, 1993. PhD, U. of Calif., Riverside, 1994—98. Herdick asst. prof. UCLA, 1998—2001; fellow Max-Plack Intitute for Math., Bonn, 1999—99; lectr. Yale U., 2001—01, 2002—; postdoc MSRI, Berkeley, Calif., 2002—02. Author: (rsch. papers in math.) Am. Jour. of Math., Transactions of AMS, Internat. Math. Rsch. Notices, etc. Grantee AMS Centennial Fellowship, Am. Math. Soc., 2001. Mem.: Am. Math. Soc. Achievements include research in Representations of finite and infinite dimensional Lie algebras and Lie superalgebras. Office: Dept of Math Yale University 10 Hillhouse Ave PO Box 208283 New Haven CT 06520 Office Fax: 203-432-7316. E-mail: dimitrov@math.yale.edu.

DIMITRY, THEODORE GEORGE, retired lawyer; b. New Orleans, Jan. 15, 1937; s. Theodore Joseph and Ouida Marion (Seiler) D.; m. S. Elizabeth Warren; children: Mary Elizabeth Hyry, Theodore Warren. BS, Tulane U., 1958, JD, 1960. Bar: La. 1960, Tex. 1964. Assoc. firm Phelps, Dunbar, Marks, Claverie & Sims, New Orleans, 1965-69, ptnr., 1969-75; ptnr. firm Vinson & Elkins, Houston, 1975-98; ret., 1998; pvt. arbitrator and mediator, 1999—. Rsch. fellow Southwestern Legal Found., Dallas, 1973-98; spkr. on maritime law, offshore contracting, ins. and resource devel. at profl. seminars, 1975—. Contbr. articles to profl. jours. Mem. permanent adv. bd. Tulane U. Admiralty Law Inst., 1985—2000. Served with USN, 1960—64. Mem.: Maritime Law Assn. U.S. Fax: 713-467-7153. E-mail: dimitry@net1.net.

DIMLER, G(EORGE) RICHARD, German language educator, editor; b. Balt., Oct. 21, 1931; s. George Herbert and Gertrude Helena (Kelly) D. BS, Fordham U., 1960, MA, 1962, cert. computer programming, 1985; S.T.L., Woodstock Coll., 1964; MA, Middlebury Coll., 1966; Ph.D., UCLA, 1970; MA in Edn1. Computing Iona, 1989. Asst. prof. German, Loyola Coll., Balt., 1970-72; assoc. prof. Fordham U., Bronx, 1972-82, prof., 1982—, dir. honors program, 1977-92, editor-in-chief Thought mag., 1979-92; rsch. prof. Jesuit Emblem studies, 1999—. Author books, including Friedrich Spee's Trutznachtigall, 1975; translator: Personal Faith (Carlos Cirne-Lima), 1964; co-translator: A Theology of Proclamation (Hugo Rahner), 1965, Friedrich Spee: Eine Beschreibende Bibliographi, 1987, Johann Kreihing's Emblemata Socio-Politica, The Jesuit Series, 4 vols.; also more than 30 articles on Jesuit emblematics, books revs.; spkr. in field. Grantee Fordham U. Office Research Services, 1973, 76, 77, NEH, 1974, Am. Coun. Learned Socs., 1975, Jesuit Writers Fund, 1975, German Acad. Exch. Service, 1976, 77. Herzog August Bibliothek Zu Wolfenbuettel Gaststipendium, 1979, Title III-Mellon Found., 1983-84, Perkins Found. Mem. Editors Learned Jours., Am. Assn. tchrs. German, Soc. German Renaissance and Baroque Lit., Renaissance Soc. Am., MLA, Catholic Press Assn., Soc. Scholarly Publ., German Soc. Md., Soc. Emblem Studies, Alpha Mu Gamma (hon.). Roman Catholic. Home: Fordham U Bronx NY 10458 Office: Fordham U Faber Hall Bronx NY 10458 E-mail: dimler@fordham.edu., emblem98@aol.com.

DIMLING, JOHN ARTHUR, marketing executive; b. Pitts., Apr. 9, 1938; s. John Arthur and Elizabeth (Powell) D.; m. Marilyn Jean O'Connor; children: Courtney O'Connor, Meredith O'Connor. AB, Dartmouth Coll., 1960; MS, Carnegie Mellon U., 1962; JD, George Washington U., 1977. Bar: Md. 1977, D.C. 1978. Group mgr. Spindletop Rsch. Corp., Lexington, Ky., 1965-69; v.p. rsch. analysis Nat. Assn. Broadcasters, Washington, 1969-79; v.p. rsch., planning and analysis Arbitron Co., 1979; dir. planning & policy Corp. Pub. Broadcasting, Washington, 1979-82; exec. dir., chief exec. officer Electronic Media Rating Council, N.Y.C., 1982-85; sr. v.p. A.C. Nielsen Co., N.Y.C., 1985-88, exec. v.p., 1988-93, pres., 1993—2001, chmn., 2001—. Chmn. Coltram, N.Y.C., 1969-79; asst. treas. Broadcasting Rating Coun., N.Y.C., 1971-79; cons. Western Broadcasting Corp., Missoula, Mont., 1981; sec., treas. Electronic Media Rating Coun., N.Y.C., 1970-72; bd. dirs. Advt. Rsch. Found., 1989-95, sec., 1992, chmn., 1993-94; mem. exec. com. Market Rsch. Coun., 1995-96; chmn. bd. dirs. NetRatings, Inc.; bd. dirs., Coun. for Value-Based Leadership. Author: (with others) The Role of Analysis in Regulatory Decision Making-- The Case of Cable Television, 1973; contbr. articles to profl. jours., book. Bd. dirs. Ctr. for Comm., 1994—; trustee Masters Sch., 2000—. 1st lt. U.S. Army, 1963-65. Mem. ABA, Radio-TV Rsch. Coun., Ardsley Country (bd. govs. 1987-94), Dartmouth (N.Y.). Avocation: tennis. Home: 198 Judson Ave Dobbs Ferry NY 10522-3028 Office: Nielsen Media Rsch 770 Broadway New York NY 10003 Business E-mail: dimling@tvratings.com.

DIMMA, WILLIAM ANDREW, real estate executive; b. Montreal, Que., Can., Aug. 13, 1928; s. William Roy and Lillian Norine (Miller) D.; m. Katherine Louise Vacy Ash, May 13, 1961; children: Suzanne Elizabeth Irene, Katherine Lillian Louise. BA in Sci., U. Toronto, Can., 1948; postgrad., Harvard U., 1956, DBA, 1973; MBA, York U., Toronto, 1969; LLD (hon.), York U., 1998; D of Commerce (hon.), St. Mary's U., 1991. Registered profl. engr., Ont. With Union Carbide Can Ltd., 1948-70, exec. v.p., bd. dirs., 1967-70; prof., dean faculty adminstrv. studies York U., 1974-76; pres., bd. dirs. Torstar Corp.,

Toronto Star Newspapers Ltd., Toronto, 1976-78; pres. A.E. LePage Ltd., Toronto, 1979-84; pres., CEO Royal LePage Ltd., Toronto, 1984-86, dep. chmn., 1986-93. Bd. dirs. Trilon Fin. Corp., Minacs Worldwide Inc., Magellan Aerospace Corp.; chmn. bd. dirs. Home Capital Group, Malibu Engring. and Software Ltd., Royal Le Page Comml.; dir. York U. Devel. Corp. Author: Canada Development Corporation: Diffident Experiment on a Large Scale, Excellence in the Boardroom, 2002, John Wiley & Sons, 2002. Hon. dir. Niagara Inst., chmn. 1983-86; hon. gov. York U., chmn., 1992-97; hon. trustee Hosp. for Sick Children; gov. Jr. Achievement of Met. Toronto, chmn., 1992-93; gov. Can. Journalism Found. Decorated knight comdr. Order of St. Lazarus of Jerusalem, 1984; Elmslie Meml. scholar, 1944; Stevens gold medal Harvard Bus. Sch., 1971; Can. Coun. fellow, 1970-73; apptd. to Order of Can., 1996; recipient York Univ. award Outstanding Corp. Leadership, 2001, Schulich Sch. Bus. Outstanding Leadership award, 1992, Queen's Golden Jubilee medal, 2002. Fellow Inst. Corp. Dirs. (bd. dirs.); mem. Order of Ont., Toronto Club, Toronto Golf Club, York Club, Howard Club Toronto, Beta Theta Pi. Avocations: swimming, cycling, writing. Home: Apt 302 407 Walmer Rd Toronto ON Canada M5R 3N2 E-mail: wdimma@sympatico.ca., ewilliams@brascancorp.com.

DIMMICH, JEFFREY ROBERT, lawyer; b. Bethlehem, Pa., Mar. 13, 1948; s. Robert Carl and Barbara Sylvia (Worth) D.; m. Kathleen B. Brobst, Aug. 21, 1971. BA, Lehigh U., 1970; JD, Dickinson Sch. Law, 1973. Bar: Pa. 1973, U.S. Dist. Ct. (ea. dist.) Pa. 1974, U.S. Dist. Ct. (mid. dist.) Pa. 1974, U.S. Ct. Appeals (3d cir.) 1974. Assoc. Worth Law Offices, Allentown, Pa., 1973-78; sole practice Allentown, 1978-83; ptnr. Snyder & Dimmich, Allentown, 1983-86, Snyder, Dimmich & Guldin, Allentown, 1986-97, Dimmich, Guldin, Dinkelacker & Brieza, P.C., Orefield, Pa., 1997—. Instr. Lehigh County C.C., Schnecksville, Pa., 1974-76; solicitor Borough of Catasauqua, Pa., 1977—, Upper Saucon Twp. Mcpl. Authority, 1991—, Salisbury Twp. Civil Svc. Commn., 1994—; solicitor Borough of Emmays Civil Svc. Commn., 1996—, Upper Saucon Twp., 2002-; asst. solicitor County of Lehigh, Pa., 1978-86. Republican. Office: Dimmich Guldin Dinkelacker & Brieza PC 2970 Corporate Ct Ste 1 Orefield PA 18069-3158 E-mail: dgdb.jeff@erols.com.

DIMMICK, CAROLYN REABER, federal judge; b. Seattle, Oct. 24, 1929; d. Maurice C. and Margaret T. (Taylor) Reaber; m. Cyrus Allen Dimmick, Sept. 10, 1953; children: Taylor, Dana. BA, U. Wash., 1951; JD, 1953; LLD, Gonzaga U., 1982, CUNY, 1987. Bar: Wash. 1953. Asst. atty. gen. State of Wash., Seattle, 1953-55; pros. atty. King County, Wash., 1955-59, 60-62; sole practice Seattle, 1959-60, 62-65; judge N.E. Dist. Ct. Wash., 1965-75, King County Superior Ct., 1976-80; justice Wash. Supreme Ct., 1981-85; judge U.S. Dist. Ct. (we. dist.) Wash., Seattle, 1985-94, chief judge, 1994-97, sr. judge, 1997—. Chmn. Jud. Resources Com., 1991-94, active, 1987-94. Recipient Matrix Table award, 1981, World Plan Execs. Council award, 1981, Vanguard Honor award King County of Washington Women Lawyers, 1996, Disting. Alumni award U. Wash. Law Sch., 1997, Outstanding Jurist award King County Bar Assn., 2003. Mem. ABA, Am. Judges Assn. (gov.), Nat. Assn. Women Judges, World Assn. Judges, Wash. Bar Assn., Am. Judicature Soc., Order of Coif (Wash. chpt.). Office: US Dist Ct 407 US Courthouse 1010 5th Ave Seattle WA 98104-1189 E-mail: carolyn_dimmick@wawd.uscourts.gov.

DIMMICK, CHARLES WILLIAM, geology educator; b. Elizabeth, N.J., Feb. 16, 1940; s. Byron Orme and Claire Louise (Pilger) D.; m. Charleen Fristoe, Aug. 30, 1963; children: Byron Wesley, Edward Arthur. Geol. Engr., Colo. Sch. Mines, 1962; MS in Geology, U. Fla., 1964; PhD, Tulane U., 1969. Lic. geologist, N.C. Asst. prof. geology Stephen F. Austin State U., Nacogdoches, Tex., 1967-70, Austin Peay State U., Clarksville, Tenn., 1970-72; prof. geology Cen. Conn. State U., New Britain, 1972—. Cons. and assoc. dir. Environ. Mgmt. Corp., Kensington, Conn., 1974-94. Contbr. articles to profl. jours. Vice chmn. Cheshire Inland Wetlands Commn., Conn., 1974—; pres. Cheshire Fair Assn., 1984-87, pres., Conn. Agrl. Fair, 1994-97. NSF fellow, 1963-64, 66-67. Mem. Am. Inst. Profl. Geologists (hon. mem., cert., pres. N.E. sect. 1988-90, del. nat. adv. bd. 1990-92, nat. editor 1993-94), Paleontologic Rsch. Inst., Soc. Econ. Paleontologists and Mineralogists, Assn. Conn. Fairs, Patrons of Husbandry, Sigma Xi. Episcopalian. Home: 60 Broadview Rd Cheshire CT 06410-4202 Office: Cen Conn State U Dept Physics And Earth Scis New Britain CT 06050

DIMMICK, KRIS DOUGLAS, civil engineer; b. North Tonawanda, N.Y., Mar. 7, 1963; s. Calvin A. and Judith G. (Baker) D. AAS, Paul Smith's (N.Y.) Coll., 1983; BS in Forest Engring., SUNY, Syracuse, 1985, MS in Environ. Engring., 1991. Registered profl. engr., N.Y. Forest technician Superior Forestry Svc., Leslie, Ark., 1983; constrn. inspector N.Y. State Dept. Transp., Binghamton, 1984-85; intern engr. Clough Harbour & Assocs., Albany, N.Y., 1985-86; project engr. John S. MacNeill, Jr., PC, Homer, N.Y., 1986-91; ptnr. Bernier, Carr & Assocs. PC, Watertown, N.Y., 1991—. Mem. ASCE (Key Alert mem. 1989-91, chmn. membership com. 1990-91), N.Y. State Soc. Profl. Engrs., Am. Motorcyclist Assn., Am. Pub. Wks. Assn. (exec. com. 1990-91). Office: Bernier Carr & Assocs PC 172 Clinton St Watertown NY 13601-3602

DIMMITT, LAWRENCE ANDREW, retired lawyer, law educator; b. Kansas City, Kans., July 20, 1941; s. Herbert Andrew and Mary (Duncan) Dimmitt; m. Lois Kinney, Dec. 23, 1962; children: Cynthia Susan, Lawrence Michael. BA, Kans. State U., 1963, MA, 1967; JD, Washburn U., 1968. Bar: Kans. 1968, U.S. Dist. Ct. Kans. 1968, U.S. Ct. Appeals (10th cir.) 1969, Mo. 1973, N.Y. 1975, U.S. Supreme Ct. 1986. Atty. Southwestern Bell Tel. Co., Topeka, 1968-73, gen. atty. Kans., 1979-94, atty. St. Louis, 1973-74, gen. atty. regulation, 1979; atty. AT&T, N.Y.C., 1974-79; ret., 1994. Adj. prof. telecom. law Washburn U. Sch. Law, 1996—; mem. polit. sci. adv. coun. Kans State U., 2003—. Mem. master planning com. Hist. Ward-Meade Pk., 1998—; bd. dirs. 1st United Meth. Ch., Topeka, 1979—84, mem. nominating com., 1985—87; bd. dirs. Sunflower Music Festival, 1993—94. Recipient commendation, Legal Aid Soc. Topeka, 1986, 1990, 1993. Mem.: Topeka Bar Assn., Kans. Bar Assn. (pres. adminstrv. law sect. 1985—86, bd. editors newsletter), Jayhawk Lit. Club, Rotary (bd. dirs., 1st v.p. 2000, pres. 2001, asst. gov. 2003—), Phi Alpha Delta (alumni bd. 1986—88, 1993—97). Home: 3123 SW 15th St Topeka KS 66604-2515 E-mail: LLDimmitt@aol.com.

DIMMOCK, JOHN OLIVER, university research center director; b. Mineola, N.Y., Nov. 24, 1936; s. Clarence Oliver and Eleanor Stevens (Waste) D.; m. Barbara Welch Clark, June 21, 1958 (div. Nov. 1973); children: Leanne, Cynthia, John; m. Cynthia Kalliope Vouros, May 12, 1974 (div. 2000); children: Jonathan, Justin, James; m. Linda R. Leslie, June 30, 2001. BS in Physics, Yale U., 1958, PhD in Physics, 1962. Mem. staff rsch. div. Raytheon, Waltham, Mass., 1962-63, MIT Lincoln Lab., Lexington, 1963-66, leader applied physics group, 1966-71, leader applied optics group, 1971-74; dir. electronics and solid state scis. Office Naval Rsch., Arlington, Va., 1974-81, dep. dir., dir. tech. programs, 1981-84; tech. dir. Air Force Office Sci. Rsch., Washington, 1984-89; staff v.p. for rsch. McDonnell Douglas Corp., St. Louis, 1989-92; tech. dir. strategic technologies McDonnell Douglas Corp., St. Louis, 1992-93; dir. ctr. applied optics U. Ala., Huntsville, 1993—. Author: Properties of the Thirty-Two Point Groups, 1963; contbr. over 60 articles to sci. jours.; patentee in field. Recipient Superior Civilian Svc. award USN, 1984. Fellow AIAA (assoc.), Am. Phys. Soc.; mem. IEEE (sr.), AAAS, Sigma Xi. Office: U Ala Huntsville Ctr Applied Optics Huntsville AL 35899-0001

DIMON, JAMES, bank executive; b. N.Y.C., Mar. 13, 1956; s. Theodore and Themis Dimon; m. Judith Kent, May 21, 1983; children: Julia, Laura, Kara. BA, Tufts U., 1978; MBA, Harvard U., 1982. V.p., asst. to pres. Am. Express Co., N.Y.C., 1982-85; sr. v.p., CFO Comml. Credit Co., Balt., 1986-88; exec. v.p., CFO Primerica Corp., N.Y.C., 1989—90, pres., 1990—93; pres., COO Travelers Inc.; pres., COO, CFO The Travelers Inc, 1993—98; pres. Citigroup Inc, 1998; chmn. & CEO Bank One Corp., Chicago, 2000—.

DIMOND, EDMUNDS GREY, medical educator; b. St. Louis, Dec. 8, 1918; s. Edmunds Grey and Gertrude Ruth (Schmidt) D.; m. Mary Dwight Clark, Nov. 28, 1968 (dec. June 1983); children: Sherri Grey Byrer, Lea Grey, Lark Grey Dimond-Cates. Student, Purdue U., 1938-39; BS, Ind. U., 1942, MD, 1944. Mem. faculty Med. Ctr., U. Kans., Kansas City, 1950-60, prof., chmn. dept. medicine, 1953-60, dir. cardiovascular lab., 1950-60; mem., dir. Inst. for Cardiopulmonary Diseases, Scripps Clinic and Rsch. Found., 1960-67; rsch. assoc. physiology Scripps Inst. Oceanography, La Jolla, Calif., 1960-68; prof. in residence Sch. Medicine, U. Calif., San Diego, 1967-68; scholar in residence Nat. Libr. Medicine, 1967; spl. asst. to asst. sec. HEW, Washington, 1968; Disting. univ. prof. medicine U. Mo., Kansas City, 1968-98, provost for health scis., 1968-79. Fulbright prof., The Netherlands, 1956; vis. prof., Israel, 1978; scholar in residence Rockefeller Found. Study Ctr., Bellagio, Italy, 1978; chmn. overseas edn. team Dept. State, 1962, 64-66, 73; guest lectr. Chinese Med. Assn., 1971-73, 76-80, 82-92; pres. Edgar Snow Fund, Inc., Diastole-Hospital Hill, Inc. Author: Electrocardiography, 1952, rev. edits., 1955, 60, 64, Digitalis, 1957, Exercise Electrocardiograms, 1961, More Than Herbs and Acupuncture, 1975, Inside China Today, 1981, Take Wing, 1991, Dr. Horse of China, 1992, Reverend Whitehead, Mississippi Pioneer, 1987, Letters from Forest Place, 1993, Essays By An Unfinished Physician, 1995, Milepost Eighty, 2000; editor: Diastole on Hospital Hill Audiotape, 1980-86; editor-in-chief Accel, 1968-77; contbr. articles to profl. jours. Bd. dirs. Truman Med. Ctr., Kansas City, Mo., Eye Found., Kansas City, Sci. Edn. Partnership, Kansas City. With M.C., AUS, 1945-47. Paul Dudley White Traveling scholar, 1956-57. Master Am. Coll. Cardiology (pres. 1962, Disting. Svc. award 1969). Home and Office: 2501 Holmes St Kansas City MO 64108-2742 E-mail: gdimond@planetkc.com.

DIMOND, ROBERT EDWARD, publisher; b. Washington, Dec. 12, 1936; s. James Robert and Helen Marie (Murphy) D.; m. Patricia Berger (div.); children: Mark Edward, Michele Lynn Keating, Melinda Ann. BA in Journalism, George Washington U., 1961. Mng. editor Nat. Automobile Dealers Assn. Mag., Washington, 1955-63; editor, pub. Bus. Products Mag., Washington, 1963-69; v.p. Hitchcock Pub. Co.; pub. Infosystems Mag., Office Products Mag., Wheaton, Ill., 1969-81; pres. R.E. Dimond & Assocs., Hinsdale, Ill., 1981-83; pub. Networking Mgmt. Mag., Westford, Mass., 1983-89, Home Improvement Ctr. Mag., Lincolnshire, Ill., 1989-90; v.p., pub. dir. mining and constrn. group Intertec; pub. Coal, Rock Products, Internat. Construction, Concrete Products, Engring. and Mining Jour., C&D Materials Recycling and Keystone Directory, 1990-96; group v.p. Intertec Pub. Co., 1996-99; pres. R.E. Dimond & Assocs., 1999—. Keynote spkr. COMDEX, 1979. Served with USAF, 1961-62. Democrat. Roman Catholic. Home and Office: 400 Bentley Pl Buffalo Grove IL 60089-2500 E-mail: dimondre@attbi.com. *Never lose your sense of humor.Everyone has been helped in life somewhere along the way by an unselfish act; don't forget this when you have the opportunity to extend a hand.*

DIMOND, THOMAS, investment advisory company executive; b. Scarsdale, N.Y., Jan. 24, 1916; s. George A. and Jessie (Kennedy) D. BA magna cum laude, Princeton U., 1939; MBA, Harvard U., 1941. Mem. faculty Wharton Sch. Fin., U. Pa., 1948; economist, account mgr. Lionel D. Edie & Co., 1948-50; economist, mgr. comml. rsch. Youngstown Sheet & Tube Co., Ohio, 1951-56; sr. account mgr., security analyst deVegh & Co., N.Y.C., 1956-60; pres. Humes-Schmidlapp Assocs., N.Y.C., 1960—. Bd. dirs. Mercer Mgmt. Corp., co-mgr. Mercer Fund, 1963-67; bd. dirs. Scudder Spl. Fund, 1967-72, Scudder Duv-Vest, 1968-71; gen. ptnr. HS Spl. Fund. Contbr. articles to profl. publs. Trustee, Humes Found., 1963—. Capt. USAAF, 1941-46. Mem. N.Y. Soc. Security Analysts, Racquet & Tennis Club, Down Town Assn. (N.Y.C.). Episcopalian. Home: 200 E 66th St Apt C1703 New York NY 10021-9187 Office: Humes-Schmidlapp Assoc 375 Park Ave Ste 3505 New York NY 10152-0002

DI MUCCIO, MARY-JO, retired librarian; b. Hanford, Calif., June 16, 1930; d. Vincent and Theresa (Yovino) DiMuccio. BA, Immaculate Heart Coll., 1953, MA, 1960; PhD, U.S. Internat. U., 1970. Tchr. parochial schs., Los Angeles, 1949-54, San Francisco, 1954-58; tchr. Govt. of Can., Victoria, B.C., 1959-60; asst. libr. Immaculate Heart Coll. Libr., Los Angeles, 1960-62, head libr. City of Sunnyvale, 1962-72; adminstrv. libr. City of Sunnyvale, Calif., 1972-88; ret., 1988. Instr. Foothill C.C., Los Altos, 1977—95. Exec. bd., past pres. Sunnyvale Community Services. Mem. ICF (past pres.), Cath. Libr. Assn. (past pres.), Sunnyvale Bus. and Profl. Women, Peninsula Dist. Bus. and Profl. Women (pres.). Home: 736 Muir Dr Mountain View CA 94041-2509 E-mail: MJ736@aol.com. *My goal has been to become a universal person, and that is my responsibility as a professional person-to see that the society we are building for tomorrow is appropriate to the needs of the people we serve.*

DIMURO, BERNARD JOSEPH, lawyer; b. Boston, Mar. 3, 1954; s. Bernard P. and Katherine (Deuce) D. BA, Northwestern U., 1976; JD, George Washington U., 1979. Bar: Va. 1979, U.S. Dist. Ct. (ea. dist.) Va. 1979, U.S. Ct. Appeals (4th cir.) 1979, Ill. 1980, D.C. 1985, U.S. Ct. Appeals (9th cir.) 1986, U.S. Ct. Appeals (8th cir.) 1987. Ptnr. Hirschkop, DiMuro & Mook, Alexandria, Va., 1979—89; found. ptnr. Dimuro, Ginsberg & Mook PC, Alexandria, Va., 1990—. Founder, pres. The Civil Workplace, 1996—. Mem. ABA, Va. State Bar Assn. (mem. com. to implement pro bono report, chmn. 8th dist. grievance com., disciplinary bd. 1988-95, chair 1993-95, exec. com. 1995-97, 2000-, chair task force on public access to the disciplinary system, mem. task force on corp. counsel 2001-, Va. model rules com. 1995-99, lawyers serving as fiduciaries com. 1993-94, vice chair publications/public info. com. 1996-2001, faculty for the professsionalism course 1995-98, pres. 2002-03), Ill. State Bar Assn., D.C. Bar, Va. Trial Lawyers Assn. (bd. govs. 1997-2000), Assn. Trial Lawyers Am.; fellow Va. Law Found. 1995, ABA 1998 Roman Catholic. Home: 7705 Northdown Rd Alexandria VA 22308-1333 Office: DiMuro Ginsberg & Mook PC 908 King St Ste 200 Alexandria VA 22314-3018

DINAN, DONALD ROBERT, lawyer; b. Nashua, N.H., Aug. 28, 1949; s. Robert J. and Jeanette F. (Farland) D.; m. Amy Littlepage, June 24, 1978; 1 child: Emma. BS in Econs., U. Pa., 1971; JD, Georgetown U., 1974; LLM, London Sch. Econs., 1975. Bar: Mass. 1976, D.C. 1977, N.Y. 1986, U.S. Ct. Appeals (1st, 2d, D.C. and fed. cirs.), U.S. Supreme Ct. 1979, U.S. Ct. Internat. Trade 1982. Atty. advisor U.S. Internat. Trade Commn., Washington, 1976-81, chief patent br., 1981-82, chief unfair imports investigation div., 1981-82; ptnr. Adduci Dinan & Mastriani, Washington, 1982-88, Fitzpatrick, Cella, Harper & Scinto, Washington, 1988-90, O'Connor & Hannan, Washington, 1990-98, Hall Estill, 1998—. Prof. internat. trade Georgetown U., Wharton Econs. Soc.; prin. Coun. for Excellence in Govt. Mem. Mayor's Internat. Adv. Coun., Washington, D.C. Regulatory Reform Com.; mem. Washington Dem. State Com., gen. counsel, 1988-92, 94-2000; chmn. D.C. Affirmative Action Com. for Dem. Conv. 2004; chmn. D.C. Dem. Campaign Victory Fund, 2004. Mem. ABA, Fed. Bar Assn., ITC Trial Laywers Assn., Am. Intellectual Property Law Assn. (chmn. internat. trade com., export lic. com.). Democrat. Roman Catholic. Home: 221 9th St SE Washington DC 20003-2112 Office: Hall Estill Hardwick Gable Goldin & Nelson 1120 20th St NW Ste 700N Washington DC 20036-3485

DINAN, ROBERT MICHAEL, lawyer; b. Quebec City, Que., Can., Aug. 12, 1956; s. John H.T. and Lorraine (Matte) D.; m. Alicia Soldevila, June 11, 1983; children: Karina, Philippe, John. LLB, U. Laval, Que., 1978. Bar: Que., 1980. Assoc. Pothier Begin et al, Quebec City, 1980-87, ptnr., 1987-94, Lepage Dinan, Quebec City, 1994—2002; chmn. bd. TeleFilm Can., Montreal, 1993-98; ptnr. O'Brien, Avocats, Quebec City, 2003—. Mem. exec. com., v.p., pres. Jeffery Hales Hosp., Quebec City, 1992-95, bd. dirs., 1992—, chmn. bd. dirs., 1996—; bd. dirs. Duke of Edinburgh's award, bd. dirs. Voice of English Que., 1992-98, mem. exec. com., 1995-98, v.p., 1997-98; v.p. St. Brigid's Home, 1985-89, pres., 2002—; v.p. Danse Partout, 1989-91; v.p. Morrin Coll. Found., 1997-2000, fin. com. 1997-2000, bldg. com. 1997-2000; mem. Centre Aide Que., 1985—, Assemblée Regie Régional Santé et Svcs. Sociaux, 1992-97, appt. Queen's Coun., 1992; bd. dirs. Can. TV and Cable Prodn. Fund, 1996-98. Recipient Bursery award Minister of Justice, Can., 1978. Mem. Can. Bar Assn., Que. Bar Assn. (external rels. com. 1993-96, libr. com. 1986-88), Que. C. of C. Avocations: gardening, oil painting, skiing, cycling. Home: 2391 Marie-Victorin Sillery QC Canada G1T 1K2

DINANZIO, PHILIP JOSEPH, city official; b. Yonkers, N.Y., Jan. 6, 1947; s. Philip Joseph and Santina (Gentile) D.; m. Marie Palazzo, Mar. 23, 1980; children: Christopher, Joseph, Dianna. BA, CCNY, 1969. Supr. stats. unit N.Y.C. Housing Police, 1981-93; asst. chief employment and pers. N.Y.C. Housing Authority, 1969-81, chief applications modernization div., 1993—. Mem. working group on incident-based crime stats. N.Y. State Div. Criminal Justice Svcs., Albany, 1988-93. Contbr. articles to The Housing Authority Jour.; assoc. editor Axis Europa Mag., 1995—. Mem. Mt. Carmel Mens Cath. Club (pres. 1999—). Republican. Avocations: collecting military memorabilia, martial arts. Home: 34 Lefferts Rd Yonkers NY 10705-1636

DINARDO-EKERY, DOROTHY MARIA, retired internist, cardiologist, educator; b. Jersey City, Oct. 29, 1938; d. Alfred and Angela Adrianna (Bancora) DiN.; m. Fred Nicholas Ekery, June 5, 1965; children: Deborah Ekery-Dorris, Rachel Ekery-Kley, Laura Ekery. BA, NYU, 1959, MD, 1963. Diplomate Am. Bd. Internal Medicine in Cardiovasc. Diseases. Resident in internal medicine Bellevue Hosp., N.Y.C., 1963-65, Dallas VA Med. Ctr., 1965-66; fellow in cardiology Parkland Hosp., Dallas, 1966-67; cons. Bluff Hosp., Yokohama, Japan, 1967-69; staff physician Thomason Gen. Hosp., El Paso, Tex., 1969-74; prof. internal medicine Tex. Tech. U. Health Scis. Ctr., El Paso, 1974-96; med. dir. Alliance Care of Tex., El Paso, 1992-99; ret., 1999. Bd. dirs. El Paso C.C., 1975, Tex. Med. Assn. Found., Austin, 1995-96; vol. tchr. Therapeutic Horsemanship, El Paso, 1997. Named Woman of Yr. in Medicine, El Paso Women's Polit. Caucus, 1975; recipient YWCA Reach award, El Paso, 1989. Fellow Am. Coll. Cardiology; mem. Am. Heart Assn. (fellow coun. on clin. cardiology; pres. El Paso chpt., v.p. West Tex. coun., Disting. Svc. award 1990), NYU Sch. Medicine Alumni Assn. (regional mem. at large 2002—). Republican. Roman Catholic. Avocations: scuba diving, horseback riding, reading, travel. Home: 4256 Park Hill Dr El Paso TX 79902-1356

DI NATALE, MARISA LYN, economist; b. Boston, Aug. 8, 1977; d. Vincent and Linda Joyce Di Natale. BA in Internat. Rels., Boston U., 1999. Economist Bur. Labor Stats., Washington, 1999—. Contbr. chapters to books, articles.

DINCECCO, JENNIE ELIZABETH WILLIAMS, healthcare administrator, mentor, volunteer; b. Atlanta, Aug. 5, 1932; d. Chester Arthur and Cleo Annie Williams; m. Richard Edward Swanson, Apr. 24, 1954 (div. 1994); children: Laurel Dee Swanson, Jeffrey Richard Swanson, Scott Edward Swanson; m. Thomas M. Dincecco, Aug. 26, 2000. BS, Northwestern U., 1954; MS, No. Ill. U., 1972, EdD, 1976. Pub. sch. tchr., 1954-69; psycho-ednl. diagnostician, 1969-72; faculty Loyola U., Chgo., 1976-82, asst. prof. ob-gyn and pediat., 1979-82; dir. pre-start project depts. ob-gyn and pediat. Stritch Sch. Medicine, 1978-82; dir. spl. svcs. Cmty. Unit Sch. Dist. 220, 1982-92. Hospice bereavement vol., 1997—; coun. mem., mentor Cong. Unitarian Ch.; antique dealer; mem. Gov. Ill. Com. Preventive Svcs., 1979-80; chair B-3 subcom. First Chance Consortium, 1978-80; chair INTER-ACT, 1979-80; cons. in field. Author: (with others) Partners in Child Development, 1978. Grantee HEW, 1973-76, 78-82. Mem.: Ret. Tchrs. McHenry County, Nat. Assn. Edn. Young Child, Nat. Acad. Neuropsychology, Nat. Perinatal Assn., Assn. Maternal and Child Health, Coun. Exceptional Children, Woodstock Opera House Commn. (chairperson, chmn.), Northwestern U. Alumni Assn., Nu Alumni Club, Delta Kappa Gamma (scholar 1974), Delta Delta Delta. Unitarian Universalist.

DINCULEANU, NICOLAE, mathematician, educator; b. Padea, Romania, Feb. 26, 1925; came to U.S., 1976. s. Nicolae and Frusina (Lusca) Dobrescu; m. Elena Constantinescu, Feb. 9, 1959. Engr., Poly. Inst., Bucharest, 1950; licencie math., U. Bucharest, 1951; PhD in Math, U. Bucarest, 1957; Doctor honoris causa, U. Craiova, 1995, U. Bucharest, 2001. Prof. math. U. Bucharest, 1950-77; vis. prof. Queen's U., Kingston, Ont., Can., 1966-67, U. Rennes, France, U. Erlangen, Germany, 1970; Disting. vis. prof. U. Pitts., 1970-71; vis. research prof. U. Fla., Gainesville, 1972-77, prof. math., 1977—. Author: Vector Measures, 1967, Integration on Locally Compact Spaces, 1974, Textbook of Mathematical Analysis, 2 vols, 1962, Vector Integration and Stochastic Integration in Banach Spaces, 2000; also articles. Recipient Stoilov prize Romanian Acad., 1964 Mem. Am. Math. Soc., Romanian Acad. (hon.). Mem. Romanian Orthodox Ch. Club: Torch. Office: U Fla Math Dept Little Hall # 450A Gainesville FL 32611-2082 E-mail: nd@math.ufl.edu.

DINCULESCU, ANTONIE, chemical engineer, scientist; b. Bucharest, Romania, Mar. 29, 1941; came to U.S., 1991; s. Antonie and Maria (Negruse) D.; m. Elefteria Arnautu, Dec. 15, 1965; 1 child, Astra. MSChemE, Polytech. U., Bucharest, 1965, PhD in Organic Chemistry, 1980. Registered chemical engr., Bucharest. From rsch. scientist to dept. head Chem. Pharm. Rsch. Inst., Bucharest, 1965-91; sci. advisor Ortho-Cycle Co., Hollywood, Fla., 1991-92; sr. rsch. scientist, group leader Pharmos Corp., Alachua, Fla., 1992-97; sr. process chemist Cedar Chem. Corp., Helena, Ark., 1998—2002; sr. rsch. investigator, group leader Esperion Therapeutics, Ann Arbor, Mich., 2002—. Author: Pyrylium Salts, 1982, Solar Energy Storage, 1991; contbr. articles to Jour. Chem. Rsch., Jour. Pharm. Sci., Il Nuovo Cimento, Romanian Jour. Physics, Talanta, Tetrahedron, Heterocycles, Chemica Scripta. Mem. AAAS, Am. Chem. Soc., N.Y. Acad. Sci. Achievements include patents for new compounds or methods of preparation, the field of solar energy or energy conversion, vacuum pumps, installation for catalytic hydrogenation at atmospheric pressure, the first industrial method for the synthesis of trimethylpyrylium salts. Office: Esperion Therapeutics Western Mich U 5110 McCracken Hall Kalamazoo MI 49008 E-mail: tonyd@esperion.com.

DINEEN, JOHN K. lawyer; b. Gardiner, Maine, Jan. 21, 1928; s. James J. and Eleanor (Kelley) D.; m. Carolyn Foley Reardon (dec. 1982); children: Jane, Martha, Louisa, Jessica, John; m. Susan Lowell Wales, Aug. 15, 1986; children: Theodore, Ralph, Andrew. BA, U. Maine, 1951; JD, Boston U., 1954; DHL (hon.) (hon.), Cambridge Coll., 2001. Bar: Maine 1954, Mass. 1954. Ptnr. Weston, Patrick & Stevens, Boston, 1954-67, Gaston & Snow, Boston, 1970-91, Peabody & Arnold, Boston, 1967—70, ptnr., 1991—2000, counsel, 2000—02; sr. counsel Nutter McClennen & Fish, 2002—. Spl. asst. atty. gen. Commonwealth of Mass., Boston, 1965-67; dir. Dingle Am. Properties Ltd., Dingle, County Kerry, Ireland, 1973—; pres., trustee Boston Local Devel. Corp., 1982—. Trustee emeritus Waring Sch., Beverley, Mass., 1981—, Cambridge (Mass.) Coll.; life trustee U.S.S. Constn. Mus., 1993—; trustee, chmn. Nahant (Mass.) Pub. Libr., 1996—; former trustee Boston U. Med. Ctr., Winsor Sch. Emmanuel Coll., Boston, Hebron Acad., Maine; trustee Boston Aid to the Blind, 1994—. With U.S. Army, 1946-48. Mem. Boston Bar Assn., Mass. Bar Assn., Boston Law Sch. Alumni Assn. (exec. com. 1989-91), Marshall Street Hist. Soc., Tavern Club, Union Club, Cary Street Club, Apollo Club, Norway Weary Club. Republican. Roman Catholic. Home: 40 Pleasant St Nahant MA 01908-1632 Office: Nutter McClennen & Fish LLP World Trade Ctr West 155 Seaport Blvd Boston MA 02110-2604

DINEEN, JOSEPH LAWRENCE, legal compliance professional, consultant; b. Jersey City, Sept. 25, 1942; s. Cornelius P. and Dolores (Fitzsimmons) D.; m. Andrea J. Manzone, Nov. 20, 1965; children: Jacqueline, Kimberley A. BA in Polit. Sci., Fordham U., 1964; MBA in Human Resources, St. John's U., Springfield, La., 1984, PhD in Indsl. Psychology, 1988. Tchr. Xavier H.S., N.Y.C., 1964-67; adminstrv. mgr. Royal Globe Ins., N.Y.C., 1967-72; pers. mgr. U. Ga., Athens, 1972-74; v.p., dir. Fowler Products Co., Athens, 1974-85; sr. v.p. Scovill, Inc., Clarksville, Ga., 1985-88; dir. human resources Charter Med. Corp., Macon, Ga., 1988-93, G&O Mfg. Co., Jackson, Miss., 1993-96; chief compliance officer Union (S.C.) Hosp. Dist., 1996-2000, Spartanburg (S.C.) Regional Healthcare Sys., 2000—. Dir., chmn. bd. N.E. Ga. Employee Assistance Program, Athens, 1974-85, Employer Assistance Group-Dept. of Labor, Athens, 1988-93; mem., cert. tchr. Dept. Labor, 1986—; budget dir. United Way of N.E. Ga., Athens, 1985-88; cons. Gov.'s Com., Jackson, 1995-96. Author: Management in 21st Century, 1995, Management in the Twenty First Century - A Primer. Dir. United Way, Athens and Jackson, 1974-93, Employee Assistance Program, Athens, 1974-85; mem. Pres. Carter's Roundtable of Businessmen, Dept. of Commerce, 1978. Mem. Soc. Human Resource Mgmt. Avocations: teaching seminars, racquetball, tennis, reading. Home: 102 Rockport Way Pacolet SC 29372-3443

DINEL, RICHARD HENRY, lawyer; b. L.A., Sept. 16, 1942; s. Edward Price and Edith Elizabeth (Rheinstein) D.; m. Joyce Ann Korsmeyer, Dec. 26, 1970; children: Edward, Alison. BA, Pomona Coll., 1964; JD, Stanford U., 1967. Bar: Calif. Owner Richard H. Dinel, Profl. Law Corp., L.A., 1971-79; ptnr. Richards, Watson & Gershon, L.A., 1979-92, of counsel, 1992-93; pres. R.H. Dinel Investment Counsel, Inc., L.A., 1992—. Chmn. bd. Pomona Coll. Assocs., 1987-89; ex-officio trustee Pomona Coll., 1987-89; arbitrator Chgo. Bd. Options Exch., 1978—, Pacific Stock Exch., 1979—; bd. govs. Western Los Angeles County coun. Boys Scouts Am., 1993—. Mem. Securities Ind. Assn. (speaker compliance and legal div. 1978-92), Pomona Coll. Alumni Assn. (chmn. alumni fund and continuing edn. com. 1972-73), Nat. Assn. Securities Dealers (mem. nat. bd. arbitrators 1978-90). Office: 11661 San Vicente Blvd Ste 400 Los Angeles CA 90049-5112

DINER, STEVEN JAY, history educator; b. N.Y.C., Dec. 14, 1944; s. Dave and Helen (Fenster) D.; m. Hasia R. Schwartzman), July 12, 1970; children: Shira Miriam, Eli Moshe, Matan David. BA, SUNY, Binghamton, 1966, MA, 1968; PhD, U. Chgo., 1972. Asst. prof. urban studies U. D.C., Washington, 1972-76, assoc. prof., 1976-81, prof., 1981-85, chair dept. urban studies, 1978-83, dir. Ctr. for Applied Rsch. and Urban Policy, 1984-85; prof. history George Mason U., Fairfax, Va., 1985-98, vice provost, 1985-89, assoc. sr. v.p., 1990-94; prof. history, dean faculty arts & scis. Rutgers U., Newark, 1998—2002, provost, 2002—. Chair Edn. Licensure Commn. D.C., Washington, 1988-93. Author: A City and Its Universities, 1980, Housing Washington's People, 1983, A Very Different Age, 1998; mem. editl. bd. Washington History, 1993-99. Bd. dirs. D.C. Cmty. Humanities Coun., Washington, 1983—87, Regional Bus. Partnership, 2002—, Sci. Pk., Newark, 2002—. Mem. Am. Hist. Assn., Orgn. Am. Historians, Hist. Soc. Washington. Democrat. Jewish. Office: Rutgers U Office of the Provost Newark NJ 07102-1801

DINERMAN, MIRIAM, social work educator; b. N.Y.C., Apr. 13, 1925; d. Abraham J. and Frances (Shostac) Goldforb; m. Harold Dinerman, June 12, 1951 (dec. June 1976); children: David, Ellen, Ruth. BA with honors, Swarthmore Coll., 1945; MSW, Columbia U., 1949, D Social Work, 1972. Youth dir. Jewish Assn. for Neighborhood Ctrs., N.Y.C., 1949-50, program dir., 1951-54; various social work partime positions, 1955-60; asst. prof. Rutgers U. Grad. Sch. Social Work, New Brunswick, N.J., 1961-72, assoc. prof., 1972-76, prof., 1976-99, asst. dean for acad. planning, 1973-75, assoc. dean, 1975-81, acting dean, 1978, chmn. health care sequence, mem. New Brunswick faculty coun., 1989-93, chair, 1991-92; dir. PhD program Rutgers U. Sch. Social Work, New Brunswick, N.J., 1992-97, emerita, 1999—. Mem. grants rev. panel Office Human Devel. Svcs., HHS, 1986 90; cons. on health and social svcs. N.J. Legis. Task Force on 21st Century; mem. task force on std. of need N.J. Divsn. Econ. Assistance, 1989—91; manuscript rev. editor Longman's Press, Methuen Press; dir. Ctr. for Internat. and Comparative Social Work, 1977—99; adj. prof. Yeshiva U. Sch. Social Work, 1999—. Editor: Social Work Futures, 1983; mem. editl. bd. Affilia: Jour. Women and Social Work, 1985-94, 95—, book rev. editor., 1995-00, editor-in-chief, 2000—; contbr. articles to profl. jours., chpts. to books. Bd. dirs. Def. for Children Internat., 1980—88. Grantee NIMH, 1966-67, Rutgers U. Rsch. Coun. and Samuel Silberman Fund, 1979-80. Mem.: AAUP (N.J. task force on health care policy), NASW (chpt. pres. 1984—86, nat. com. on nominations and leadership identification 1988—97, editl. com. 1991—95, steering com. polit. action for candidate election 1996—2001, bd. dirs. N.Y.C. chpt. 1999—2001), Group for Advancement of Doctoral Edn. (sec. steering com. 1990—96), Coun. on Social Work Edn. (program planning com. 1984—89, ednl. policy and planning commn. 1989—94), Internat. Assn. Schs. Social Work (agt. 1988—95, bd. dirs.), Acad. Cert. Social Workers. Home: 353 W 29th St New York NY 10001-4784 E-mail: dinerma@ymail.yu.edu.

DINERSTEIN, ROBERT DAVID, lawyer; b. N.Y.C., May 3, 1953; s. Irving and Helen (Risch) D.; m. Joan Patricia Fread, June 4, 1983; children: Michael Fread, Jonathan Fread. AB in History magna cum laude, Cornell U., 1974; JD, Yale U., 1977. Bar: N.Y. 1978, D.C. 1983, Md. 1984, U.S. Dist. Ct. D.C. 1984, U.S. Dist. Ct. Md. 1985, U.S. Supreme Ct. 1988. Trial atty. U.S. Dept. Justice, Washington, 1977-82; from clin. lectr., supervising atty. to prof. Am. U., Washington, 1983—90, prof., 1990—, assoc. dean for acad. affairs, 1997—. Bd. dirs. D.C. Law Students in Ct., Washington, 1983-96, chmn., 1995-96; bd. dirs. Evros; Fair Employment Coun. Greater Washington, 1993-99; appted. mem. President's Com. on Mental Retardation, 1994-2001, civil rights cluster Dept. Justice Clinton Transition Team, 1992, hearing officer Va. Dept. Edn. v. Riley, 1994-95; mem. bd. govs. D.C. Bar, 2002. Author: (with others) Report on the Chilean Electoral Process, 1987, (with others) A Guide to Consent, 1998; contbr. chpts. to books, articles to profl. jours.; mem. bd. editors, co-founder Clinical Law Rev., 1992-99. Bd. dirs. Mental Disability Rights Internat., 1997—, chair, 1997-2002; bd. dirs. Equal Rights Ctr., 1999—; pres. bd. dirs. Quality Trust for Individuals with Disabilities, Inc., 2001—. Recipient Spl. Commendation award U.S. Dept. Justice, 1979, 80, Meritorious Service award U.S. Dept. Justice, 1981, Outstanding Performance Ratings 1978-82, Pro Bono Service award Internat. Human Rights Law Group, Washington, 1988, bd. mem. svc. award Md. Disability Law Ctr., 1997. Mem. ABA (skills tng. com., sect. on legal edn. and admissions to the bar 1991-94, mem. stds. rev. com. 2002—), Assn. Am. Law Schs. (mem. exec. com. sect. on clin. legal edn. 1987-88, chair sect. clin. legal edn. 1992, membership rev. com. 2000—02, chair award for contributions sect. clin. legal edn. 1994, com. on clin. legal edn. 1996), Clin. Tchr. Conf. (planning com. 1988, 90, 95), Washington Legal Clin. for the Homeless (bd. dirs. 1988—) Legal Coun. for the Elderly (bd. dirs. 1990-92), Am. Assn. Mental Retardation (pres. legal process and adv. div. 1990-91, legis. and social issues com. 1992-95), Soc. Am. Law Tchrs. (bd. govs. 2001—), DC Bar (bd. govs. 2002). Democrat. Jewish. Avocations: piano, sports, reading, politics. Home: 5909 Cranston Rd Bethesda MD 20816-1115 Office: Am U Washington Coll of Law Ste 366 4801 Massachusetts Ave NW Washington DC 20016-1955 E-mail: rdiners@wcl.american.edu.

DING, AI-YUE, conductor, music educator; b. Beijing, Dec. 17, 1942; arrived in U.S., 1990; d. Depan Ting and Susan Cheng; m. Chenghua Sun Ding, Jan. 17, 1968; children: Tian, Sun. B in Conducting, Conservatory of Music, Shanghai, 1966; M in Sacred Music, So. Meth. U., 1993; postgrad., U. North Tex., 1993—96. Prin. condr. Hunan Symphony Orch., Chang Sha, China, 1967—83, Jiangsu Symphony Orch., Nanjing, China, 1983—90; finding condr. 100 Voice Choir of Ambassadors for Christ, Dallas, 1993—94, Chinese Youth Orch., Dallas, 1995—99, Great Land Choral Soc., Dallas, 1995—. Guest condr. Broadcast Symphony Orch., Shanghai, 1996, Symphony Orch of Shanghai Conservatory of Music, Shanghai, 1997; condr. North Tex. Philharm. Orch., Tex., 1997; guest condr. Voice of Change Inc., Dallas, 1998; condr. United Choir, Dallas, 2000. Named one of Ten Top-Ranked Women Condrs., People's Music Jour., Beijing, 1980; recipient Grand Prize for Condr., 1st Music and Dance Festival, Jiangsu, China, 1987. Mem.: Chinese Musicians Assn., Tex. Music Tchrs. Assn., Music Tchrs. Nat. Assn. Avocations: sports, dancing.

DING, JIANCHI, embryologist, researcher; b. Jiangyin, Jiangsu, Peoples Republic of China, Oct. 24, 1957; came to U.S., 1996; s. Xufu and Xiujin (Gao) D.; m. Mingxian Shen, Nov. 15, 1983; children: Helen Guangning, Jennifer Guangting. BSc, Jiangsu Agrl. Coll., Yangzhou, 1982, MSc, 1985; PhD, U. Alta., Edmonton, Can., 1993. Cert. high complexity lab. dir. Am. Bd. Bioanalysis . Instr. Jiangsu Agrl. Coll., Yangzhou, 1985-87; Natural Sci. and Engring. Rsch. Coun. postdoctoral fellow U. Guelph, Guelph, Ont., Can., 1993-95, rsch. assoc., 1993-96; sr. rschr. Inst. for the Study and Treatment of Endometriosis, Oak Brook, Ill., 1996—; lab. dir. Oak Brook Fertility Ctr., 1996—. Contbr. articles to profl. jours. including Biology of Reprodn., Molecular Reprodn. Devel., and Human Reprodn.; assoc. editor: New Technics to Animal and Poultry Production. Recipient scholarship Jiangsu Edn. Com., China, 1987-88. Mem. Am. Assn. Bioanalysts, Am. Soc. for Reproductive Medicine, Am. Soc. Andrology, Soc. for Study Reprodn., Coll. Reproductive Biology. Home: 117 Hawkins Cir Wheaton IL 60187-8564 Office: Oak Brook Fertility Ctr 2425 W 22nd St Ste 102 Oak Brook IL 60523-4643

DING, JINWEN, biomedical researcher; MD, Tongji Med. U., Wuhan, China, 1983; PhD, Lund U., Sweden, 1993. Rsch. scientist U. of Toronto, Canada, 1993—99; asst. prof. Loyola U. Med. Ctr., Maywood, Ill., 1999—. Recipient Rsch. award, Ill. Transplant Soc., 2002, Basic Rsch. award, Can. Assn. of Gastroenterology, 1997, Sheila Sherlock Basic Rsch. award, The U. of Toronto, 1997. Mem.: World Assn. of HPB Surgery, Am. Gastroent. Assn. Achievements include research in immunological and molecular mechanisms of liver injury. Office Fax: 708-327-2813.

DING, MICHAEL S. physical scientist; b. Shanghai, May 11, 1959; s. Zhiguang Ding, Xiufang Chen. M in Engring., Shanghai Inst. Ceramics, Academia Sinica, 1986; PhD, Ariz. State U., 1993. Rsch. fellow Ariz. State U., Tempe, 1994—95; rsch. assoc. Northwestern U., Evanston, Ill., 1995—96; phys. scientist U.S. Army Rsch. Lab., Adelphi, Md., 1996—. Contbr. articles to profl. jours. Recipient R&D Achievement award, Dept. of the Army, 1999, 2002. Mem.: Electrochem. Soc. Avocations: swimming, jogging, hiking, reading, music.

DING, SHUSEN, mathematics educator; arrived in U.S., 1990; s. Baoshan Ding and Wanrong Zhang; m. Qiumin Yang, July 21, 1985; 1 child, Yuhao. BS in Applied Math., Harbin Inst. of Tech., 1981, MS in Math., 1996; PhD in Math., Fla. State U., 1996. Asst. prof. U. of Minn., Duluth, 1996—99, Seattle U., 1999—. Reviewer: math. rsch. profl. jours.; contbr. articles to profl. jours. Mem.: Am. Math. Soc. (reviewer math. revs. 1993). Home: 24302 SE 3d Pl Sammamish WA 98074

DINGELL, JOHN DAVID, congressman; b. Colorado Springs, Colo., July 8, 1926; s. John D. and Grace (Bigler) D.m. Deborah Insley; 4 children. BS in Chemistry, Georgetown U., 1949, JD, 1952. Bar: D.C. 1952, Mich. 1953. Pk. ranger U.S. Dept. Interior, 1948-52; asst. pros. atty. Wayne County, Mich., 1953-55; mem. U.S. Ho. of Reps. from 15th Mich. dist., 1955-65, 2003—, U.S. Ho. of Reps. from 16th Mich. dist., 1965—2002. Mem. migratory bird conservation commn.; ranking mem. energy and commerce com. 2nd lt. inf. AUS, 1945-46. Democrat. Office: US Ho of Reps 2328 Rayburn Bldg Washington DC 20515-2216 also: 19855 W Outer Dr Ste 103-E Dearborn MI 48124*

DINGES, RICHARD ALLEN, entrepreneur; b. Englewood, N.J., June 17, 1945; m. Kathie A. Headley; children: Kelly, Courtney, Daniel. Grad., Jersey City State Coll., 1967; MEd, U. Hawaii, 1972; postgrad., William Peterson Coll., 1974-79. Cert. sch. adminstr.; cert. sch. spl. services dir., N.J., Ariz., Hawaii. Pres. Def. Industry Assocs., Sierra Vista, Ariz., 1979—. Fed. Career Cons., Sierra Vista, Ariz., 1985; dir. Nat. Scholarship Locators, Sierra Vista, 1985—. Spl. needs counselor Pinelands Regional Sch. Dist. Editor: Guide to U.S. Defense Contractors, 1985, 87, 10 Step Guide to College Selection, Salary Negotiations for Military, How to Survive the Job Interview. Vice prin. Little Egg Harbor Primary Sch.; founder Families in Touch, 1992. Mem. Cochise County Merit Commn. (vice-chmn.), Platform Soc. Speakers' Assn. Office: 12 Cohanzick Ct Little Egg Harbor Township NJ 08087-3019 E-mail: Richard_Dinges@hotmail.com.

DINGLE, ALBERT NELSON, meteorology educator; b. Bismarck, N.D., May 22, 1916; s. Victor Stanley and Nanna Bergetha (Nelson) D.; m. Eleanor Amelia Nelson, Nov. 20, 1941 (dec. Dec. 1994); children: Karen Louise, Timothy Nelson; m. Florence Ellen Altenbernt Miller, Oct. 15, 1996. BS in Agrl. Engring., U. Minn., 1939; MS in Agrl. Engring., Iowa State Coll., 1940; SM in Meteorology, MIT, 1945, ScD, 1947. Asst. prof. physics Hampton (Va.) Inst., 1941-43; rsch. assoc. meteorology MIT, Cambridge, 1943-47; asst. prof. physics Ohio State U., Columbus, 1947-54; rsch. assoc. meteorology U. Mich., Ann Arbor, 1954-55, assoc. prof. meteorology, 1955-63, prof. atmospheric sci., 1963-81, prof. emeritus, 1981—. Cons. Pres. Adv. Com. Weather Control, Washington, 1951 55; lectr. Am. Meteorol. Soc., 1952-56; mem. NCAR Aviation Adv. Com., Boulder, Colo., 1965-78; pres. Air Surround, Inc., Dexter, Mich., 1968-83; rschr. in field. Co-author: (with Charles Young) Computer Applications in the Atmospheric Sciences, 1965; inventor optical raindrop-size spectrometer. Active various bds., coms. Zion Luth. Ch., Ann Arbor, 1954-96; councilman City Coun. Ann Arbor, 1958-60; bd. dirs. Luth. Social Svcs. Mich., Detroit, 1983-92. NSF grantee, 1952. Fellow AAAS; mem. Sigma Xi. Democrat. Avocations: golf, skiing, bridge, handcrafts. Home: 728 W Union Bell Dr Green Valley AZ 85614-5926 E-mail: n.dingle@worldnet.att.net.

DINGLE, CAROL A. state agency administrator, writer; b. Winchester, Mass., May 12, 1943; d. Leon B. and Lillian Dingle; m. Melvin Green (dec. Mar. 1989). BA, Merrimack Coll., N. Andover, Mass., 1965. English tchr. Springbrook H.S., Silver Spring, Md., 1965—67; program dir. USO, Okinawa, Japan, 1967—69, dir. vols. Frankfurt, Germany, 1970—72, dir. fleet canteens Athens, Greece, 1973—74; bus. owner D&D Advertising, Arlington, Mass., 1975—92; grant administr. Commonwealth of Mass., Boston, 1992—2003. Editor: (book) Memorable Quotations: Philosophers of Western Civilization, 2000, Memorable Quotations: English Writers of the Past, 2000, Memorable Quotations: French Writers of the Past, 2000, Memorable Quotations: Irish Writers of the Past, 2001, Memorable Quotations: Massachusetts Writers of the Past, 2001, Memorable Quotations: Jewish Writers of the Past, 2003.

DINGLE, PATRICIA A. education educator, artist; b. Washington, Apr. 19, 1954; d. Asbery and Loretha (Bryant) D. BA, Conn. Coll., 1976; MA in Tchg., RISD, 1977; PhD in Curriculum and Instrn., U. Md., 1996. Cert. art and dance tchr., Md.; ordained to ministry Bapt. Ch., 1998. Instr. dance RISD, Providence, 1976-77; visual artist, dancer R.I. Coun. on Arts, Providence, 1977-78; tchr. art Ctrl. H.S., East Providence, R.I., 1978-79, Friendly H.S., Prince Georges County, Md., 1979-82, Prince George's County Pub. Schs., Upper Marlboro, Md., 1987—; chair dept. fine arts High Point H.S., 2000—02; asst. prof. dept. edn. Clarion U. of Pa., 2002—. Dir. summer playground Md. Nt. Capital Park and Planning Commn., Prince Georges County, 1999; adj. prof. Western Md. Coll., Westminster, 1999; propr. Ding La Gift Studio, Bowie, Md., 1994—; presenter Md. Art Edn. Assn., Towson, 1997, 98, Nat. Coun. Tchrs. Math., Springfield and Phila., Success 2002 Conf., U. Md.; mem. discussion panel Conn. Coll., New London, 1998; vis. minority scholar/artist U. Wis., Eau Claire, 2000; lectr. Cath. U. Am., summer 2000; asst. min. Amazing Grace Bapt. Ch., 1998-2002; youth min. Village Bapt. Ch., 2002; presenter in field. Exhibited in solo shows at Office of Cmty. Affairs, New London, Conn., 1973, Parkview Bapt. Ch., Landover, Md., 1975, First Bapt. Ch. in Am., Providence, 1978, others; group shows include Marlborough (Conn.) Arts Festival, 1974, Cummings Art Ctr., New London, 1976, Woods-Gerry Gallery, Providence, 1977, Marlboro Gallery/Prince George's C.C., 1981, Montpelier Mansion, Laurel, Md., 1998, Bowie Arts Expo, Allen Pond, 1999, Electronic Exhibit, N.Y., 2001, NAEA Women's Caucus Womens Artwork, N.Y., 2001, Art Celebrating Women, PA-SSHE Conf., 2002; works represented in permanent collections Carlson Libr. Clarion U.; dir. Young Designers Am. program Ashton-Drake Gallery, 2000. Facilitator youth study circle Prince Georges County Human Rels. Commn., Landover, 1998; mem. grants in comtys. adv. panel Md. State Arts Coun., 2000-01; active In Touch Ministries, 1998—; mem. mission trip Appalachian Outreach Ctr., Jefferson City, Tenn., 2003 Sgt. U.S. Army, 1983-87. Recipient Anna Lord Strauss award for cmty. svc., 1976, awards for art; grad. fellow U. Md., 1989; Md. Tech. fellow, 2000; NEH summer seminar faculty profl. devel. project grantee, 2001, 03; faculty profl. devel. grantee, 2003. Mem.: Nat. Art Edn. Assn. (book reviewer 2002—03). Avocations: research, writing, piano playing, painting. Office: Clarion Univ of Pa Dept of Education Clarion PA 16214

DINGLER, MAURICE EUGENE, civil engineer; b. Salina, Kans., Mar. 29, 1952; s. Herman Ludwig and Helen Josephine (Craig) D.; m. Shirley Jean Barnthson, Aug. 24, 1974; children: Eugene Edward, April Nicole. BS, Kans. State U., 1974. Registered profl. engr., Kans., Okla. Cons. engr. Reiss and Goodness Engrs., Wichita, Kans., 1974-83; sr. engr. Kans. Gas and Electric, Wichita, 1983-84, tech. staff engr., 1984-85; lead engr. Wolf Creek Nuclear Oper. Corp., Wichita, 1985-86, mgr. facilities engring. and analysis Burlington, Kans., 1986-90, mgr. nuclear plant engring. systems, 1990-92; mgr. nuclear plant engring. support, 1992-93; project coord. materials mgmt. and paperless processing Wolf Creek Nuclear Op. Corp., 1995-97, sr. engr., 1997—. Chmn. sys. and equipment subcom. Westinghouse Owners Group; mem. nuclear energy task forces. Mem. ASCE (v.p, Wichita br. 1979-80, pres. 1980-81), Am. Nuclear Soc., Chi Epsilon. Office: Wolf Creek Nuclear Op Corp PO Box 411 Burlington KS 66839-0411

DINGMAN, MICHAEL DAVID, industrial company executive, international investor; b. New Haven, Sept. 29, 1931; s. James Everett and Amelia (Williamson) D.; children from 1st marriage: Michael David, Linda Channing (Mrs. Michael S. Cady), James Clifford; m. 2d, Elizabeth G. Tharp; children: James Tharp, David Ross, Patrick Michael. student, DSc Bus. Mgmt. (hon.), U. Md. Various mgmt. positions Sigma Instruments, Inc., Braintree, Mass., 1954-64; gen. and ltd. ptnr. Burnham & Co., N.Y.C., 1964-70; pres., CEO, bd. dirs. Wheelabrator-Frye Inc., Hampton, N.H., 1970-83, chmn. bd., 1977-83; pres., bd. dirs. The Signal Cos., Inc., La Jolla, Calif., 1983-85, AlliedSignal, Morristown, N.J., 1985-86; chmn. bd., CEO The Henley Group, Inc. and affiliates, Hampton, N.H., 1986-92; chmn. bd. Fisher Sci. Internat. Inc., Hampton, 1991-98; chmn. bd., CEO Abex Inc., Hampton, 1992-95; pres., CEO Shipston Group Ltd., Nassau, Bahamas, 1994—. Bd. dirs. Ford Motor Co., Fisher Sci. Internat. Inc. Trustee The John A. Hartford Found. Mem. IEEE (adv. bd.). Clubs: Links, Yacht (N.Y.C.); Union (Boston); Cruising of Am. (Conn.); Bohemian (San Francisco); Lyford Cay (Nassau); La Jolla Country, San Diego Yacht. Office: Shipston Group Ltd Lyford Cay PO Box N7776 Nassau The Bahamas

DINH, ANTHONY TUNG, internist; b. Jan. 1, 1938; s. Hoan B. and Phieu T. (Nguyen) D.; m. Lisa L. Tran, Jan. 8, 1971; children: Andrew A., Thomas A. BS, U. Saigon, Vietnam, 1959, MD, 1967. Diplomate Am. Bd. Internal Medicine, Am. Bd. Infectious Disease, Am. Bd. Med. Microbiology. Intern in internal medicine Phila. Gen. Hosp., 1976-77; resident in internal medicine Wayne State U., 1977-79; fellow in infectious diseases U. Pa., 1979-81; asst. prof. U. Saigon, 1970-75; chief infectious disease VA Med. Ctr., Beckley, W.Va., 1981-82, chief med. svc., 1982-85, chief staff, 1985—. Adj. clin. prof. medicine W.Va. Sch. Osteopathic Medicine, Lewisburg, 1987—; cons. in infectius disease. Contbr. articles to profl. jours. Mem. ACP, N.Y. Acad. Scis., Am. Soc. Microbiology, Raleigh County Med. Soc. (chmn. continuing med. edn. 1987—), W.Va. State Med. Assn. Office: Beckley Med Arts 2401 S Kanawha St Beckley WV 25801-6905

DINH, VIET D. law educator; b. Saigon, Vietnam, Feb. 22, 1968; came to U.S., 1978; s. Phong Hong Dinh and Thanga Thi Nguyen. AB, Harvard U., 1990, JD, 1993. Legal methods instr. Harvard Law Sch., Cambridge, Mass., 1991-93; law clk. U.S. Ct. Appeals, Washington, 1993-94, U.S. Supreme Ct., Washington, 1994-95; assoc. spl. counsel U.S. Senate, Washington, 1995-96; prof. law Georgetown U., Washington, 1996—; asst. atty. gen. legal policy U.S. Dept. Justice, Washington, 2001—03. Pres. Viet D. Dinh, LLC, Alexandria, Va., 1996—. Contbr. articles, essay to profl. publs. Dep. issues dir. legal policy Wilson for Pres., 1996; mem. Dole/Kemp Econ. Policy Adv. Com., 1996. Republican. Roman Catholic. Avocations: tennis, golf, chess. Office: Georgetown U Law Ctr 600 New Jersey Ave NW Washington DC 20001-2075 E-mail: dinhv@law.georgetown.edu.

DINI, JOSEPH EDWARD, JR., state legislator; b. Yerington, Nev., Mar. 28, 1929; s. Giuseppe and Elvira (Castellani) D.; m. Mouryne Landing; children: Joseph, George, David, Michael. BSBA, U. Nev., Reno, 1951. Mem. Nev. State Assembly, Carson City, 1967—, majority leader, 1975, speaker, 1977, 87, 89, 91, 93, 97, 99, minority leader, 1985, interim fin. com. mem., 1985-01, speaker pro tem, 1973, co-spkr., 1995, chmn. water policy com. Western Legis. Conf., 1993-94, 96-00, speaker emeritus, 2001; pres. Dini's Lucky Club Casino, Yerington, Nev., 1972—. Mem. legis. com. Nev. State Assembly, 1971-77, 91, 93, 95, 97, vice chmn., 1981-82, 96-97, chmn., 1982-83, 93-94. Mem. Yerington Vol. Fire Dept.; mem. Lyon County Dem. Ctrl. Com., Nev. Am. Revolution Bicentennial Commn.; past dist. gov., active mem. 20-30 Club. Recipient Outstanding Citizen award Nev. Edn. Assn., 1973, Friend of Edn. award Nev. State Edn. Assn., 1986, Citizen of Yr. award Nev. Judges Assn., 1987, Dedicated and Valued Leadership award Nat. Conf. State Legislatures, 1989, Excellence in Pub. Svc. award Nev. Trial Lawyers Assn., 1990, Silver Plow award Nev. Farm Bur., 1991, Skill, Integrith, Responsibility award Assoc. Gen. Contractors, 1994, Guardian of Small Bus. award Nat. Fedn. Ind. Bus., 1996, Spl. Recognition award Nev. State Firefighters Assn., 1998, Appreciation award Nev. Emergency Preparedness Assn., 1998, Friendship Medal of Diplomacy, Taiwan, 2000; named Conservation Legislator of Yr. Nev. Wildlife Fedn., 1991, Alumni of Yr., U. Nev. Alumni Assn., 1997, Legislator of Yr., Nev. Rural Water Assn., 1999, Italian American of Yr. Augustus Soc. Las Vegas, 2001, Arts Advocate Nev. Arts Advocates, 2002. Mem. Mason Valley C. of C. (pres.), Rotary (pres. Yerington 1989), Lions (pres. Yerington chpt. 1975), Masons, Shriners, York Rite, Scottish Rite, Order Ea. Star, Gamma Sigma Delta, Phi Sigma Kappa (Disting. Alumna award 1993). Home: 104 N Mountain View St Yerington NV 89447-2239 Office: Dini's Lucky Club Inc 45 N Main St Yerington NV 89447-2230

DINIACO, GUS G. real estate appraiser; b. Steubenville, Ohio, Sept. 1, 1927; s. George J. and Siestine D.; m. Penny S. Stakias, Sept. 7, 1952; children: Chrys Ann, Tina C. Gaston. Diploma, Weaver Sch. Real Estate, Kansas City, Mo., 1951; student, Syracuse U., Purdue U. Cert. rev. appraiser, gen. real estate appraiser, residential evaluation specialist. Realtor appraiser, Weirton, W.Va., 1952-56; supr. of appraisers W.Va. Tax Dept., Charleston, 1956-61, dist. appraiser, 1961-89; gen. appraiser Weirton, 1959—. Past pres. Weirton Bd. Realtors; past chmn. Weirton Zoning Bd.; lectr. Home Builders Assn., Steubenville, Am. Inst. of Banking, Wheeling, W.Va., W.Va. Assessors, Charleston. Past chmn. sub-com. State Geographic Info. System, 1999; mem. Property Valuation Tng. and Procedures Commn., Charleston, 1993—. With USMC, 1944-45. Mem. Rotary (Svc. award, Paul Harris fellow, pres. Weirton club 1974-75, dist. gov. 1992-93), W.Va. Assessors Assn. (hon.), Weirton C. of C. Greek Orthodox. Office: 4021 Palisades Dr Weirton WV 26062-4364

DINICOLA, ROBERT, consumer products company executive; With Macy's Dept. Store, N.Y.C., 1973-89, Federated Stores, N.Y.C., 1989-91; chmn. bd., ceo Bon, Seattle, 1991-94; chmn. Zale Del. Inc., 1994—. Office: Zale Inc 901 W Walnut Hill Ln Irving TX 75038-1003

DI NICOLO, ROBERTO, allergist; b. Trieste, Italy, Mar. 29, 1958; s. Michele and Maria (Universo) Di N.; m. Lisa Joy Goetz, Sept. 1, 1984; 1 child, Calvin Alexander. Grad., Superior Sch. Sci., Trieste, Italy, 1977; MD, U. Trieste, 1985. Diplomate Am. Bd. Pediats., Am. Bd. Internal Medicine, Am. Bd. Allergy and Immunology. Intern SUNY, Winthrop Univ. Hosp., Stony Brook, N.Y., 1986-87; resident dept. pediats. All Children's Hosp., U. South Fla., 1987-89; clin. fellow adult and pediat. allergy and immunology U. South Fla. Tchg. Hosps., St. Petersburg and Tampa, Fla., 1989-91; pvt. practice allergy and immunology Volusia Asthma and Allergy Specialists, Ormond Beach, Fla., 1991-93, The Asthma, Allergy and Sinus Clinic, Daytona Beach, Fla., 1993—. Part-time emergency room physician Bayfront Med. Ctr., St. Petersburg, Fla., 1990-91; part-time pvt. practice allergy and immunology Drs. W. Schmid and R. Doyle, St. Petersburg, 1990-91. Med. columnist Daytona Beach (Fla.) News Jour., 1992—. Recipient McCarthy award Halifax Med. Ctr., 1991. Fellow Am. Acad. Pediats.; mem. Am. Coll. Allergy and Immunology, Fla. Med. Assn. (Physician Communicator of Yr. 1994), Volusia County Med. Soc. Office: The Asthma Allergy & Sinus Clinic 353 N Clyde Morris Blvd Ste 1 Daytona Beach FL 32114-2732

DINITZ, JEFFREY H. mathematics educator; b. N.Y.C., Aug. 25, 1952; s. Simon and Mildred Dinitz; m. Susan Dinitz, Aug. 3, 1980; children: Michael, Amy, Thomas. BS, Carnegie-Mellon U., 1974; MS, Ohio State U., 1976, PhD, 1980. Prof. dept. math. U. Vt., Burlington, 1980—, dept. chair, 1998—. Cons. XFL Football League, Stamford, Conn., 2000—; found. fellow Inst. for Combinatorics and Its Applications, exec. bd., 1993-98. Author: (books) Contemporary Design Theory, 1992, CRC Handbook of Combinatorial Designs, 1996; mng. editor-in-chief: Jour. Combinatorial Designs, 1998—. Recipient Apple award for Vol. of Yr., Hinesburg Elem. Sch., 1997. Mem. Am. Math. Soc. Avocations: skiing, sailing, running. Office: U Vt Dept Maths and Stats 16 Colchester Ave Burlington VT 05401

DINIZ-PIRAINO, SIGLIA LEITE, cardiologist; b. Rio de Janeiro, June 9, 1963; d. Jose and Fatima Leite Diniz; m. Joseph Piraino; 1 child, Mariana Diniz. MD, Universidade de Brasilia, Brazil, 1987; MPH, Harvard U., Boston, 1999. Tchg. asst. Universidade de Brasilia, Brasilia, Brazil, 1982—86, rschr., scholar of Sci. of Scientific Initiation of the Nat. Coun. of Rschrs., 1984—85; internal medicine specialist/resident in internal medicine Hosp. das Forcas Armadas, Brasilia, Brazil, 1988—90; resident in cardiology Hosp. de Base, Brasilia, Brazil, 1990—93; cardiologist Hospital das Forcas Armadas, Brasilia, Brazil, 1993—97; assoc. med. rsch. dir. San Diego, 2000—; pvt. practice cardiology Prontonorte Clinic, Brasilia, Brazil, 1995—97; researcher Baystate Medical Center-Dept of cardiology, Springfield, MA, 1998—98; clinical research assistant-consultant Brigham&Women's Hospital-Dept of Tropical Medicine, Boston, 1998—98; rschr. tropical medicine and epidemiology Universidade de Brasilia & Universidade de Minas Gerais, Brasilia & Uberaba, Brazil, 1985—90. Cons. at a Women's Protective Service SMOC (a coun. related to the Dept. Pub. Health), Framingham, Mass., 1998—99; cons. Golden Cross Ins., Brasilia, Distrito Federal, Brazil, 1996—97; adminstr. Golden Garden Hosp., Brasilia, Distrito Federal, Brazil, 1996; vol. Brazilian Woman's Assn., Framingham, 1998—99; vol. Latino Rsch. Assn. San Diego State U., 1999; vol. genetics dept. Harvard Med. Sch., Boston, 1997; rschr. dept. cardiology Baystate Med. Ctr., Springfield, 1998. Founder, collaborator Brazilian Woman Soc., Framingham, 1998—99; collaborator Brazilian Assn. of Harvard U., Boston, 1997—99. Mem.: APHA, Med. Assn. of Brasilia, Brazil, Brazilian Soc. of Cardiology, Am. Acad. Pharm. Physicians, Internat. Assn. Physicians in AIDS Care, Harvard Sch. Pub. Health Alumni Assn. (life), Harvard Club of San Diego. Avocations: music, travel, hiking, gardening. Personal E-mail: sigliadiniz@yahoo.com.

DINKEL, JOHN GEORGE, automotive executive, consultant; b. Bklyn., Aug. 1, 1944; s. Charles Ernest and Loretta Gertrude D.; m. Leslie Hawkins, Oct. 25, 1969; children: Meredith Anne, Kevin Carter. BS in Mech. Engring, U. Mich., 1967, MS in Mech. Engring, 1969. Staff engr. Chrysler Corp., Highland Park, Mich., 1967-69; engring. editor Car Life Mag., Newport Beach, Calif., 1969-70, Road & Track Mag., Newport Beach, 1972-79, editor, 1979-88, editor in chief, 1988-91, editor at large, 1991-92; dir. product communications Hill-Holliday, 1991-92; pres. John Dinkel & Assocs., 1991—; editor-at-large Sports Car Internat., 1992—; v.p. editl. ops. Calcar, 1995-97; group mgr. member info. and comm. svcs. Automobile Club So. Calif., Costa Mesa, 1998-2000; pub. Westways, 1998-2000; v.p. pub. Driving Media, Inc./Driving.com, 2000—02; asst. pub. relations dir. Pirelli Tire and Saleen, Inc., 2002—. Commencement spkr. U. Mich., Dearborn, 1987; hon. judge Meadow Brook Hall Concourse D'Elegance, 1985-86, Hillsborough Concourse D'Elegance, 1989, Palo Alto Concours D'Elegance, 1990; spkr. Direct Mktg. Club So. Calif., 1992; SCCA competition driving instr., 2000—. Author: Road & Track Auto Dictionary, 1977, Road & Track Illustrated Auto Dictionary, 2000; co-author: RX-7: Mazda's Legendary Sports Car, 1991, Mazda MX-5 Miata, 1998, The Mazda RX-8: World's First 4-Door, 4-Seat Sports Car, 2003; co-host daily radio show Auto Report, 1986-88; host weekly radio show Drive Time, 1996—; contbr. articles to profl. jours.; patentee method and sys. for adjusting settings of vehicle functions, 2000. Nat. chmn. U. Mich. Ann. Fund, 1988—; commr. Irvine (Calif.) Baseball Assn.; sec. Irvine Pony Baseball-Softball, 1995—; organizer clothing drive victims of Armenia earthquake, 1988; soccer coach AYSO, 1984-90, Irvine Soccer Club, 1991—; baseball coach Northwood Little League, 1994—; basketball coach Irvine Boys and Girls Club, 1993—; vol. mem. corp. alliance com. Orange County chpt. Nat. Multiple Sclerosis Soc., 2002. Honored by Colden Ctr. for the Performing Arts, Queens Coll., N.Y.C., 1990. Mem. SAE (panelist conf. on impacts of intelligent vehicle hwy. systems 1990, organizer, chmn. sessions on fuel economy and small cars 1978-79, chmn. pub. affairs Future Transp. Conf. 1997), Am. Racing Press Assn., Internat. Motor Press Assn., Sports Car Club Am., Internat. Motor Sports Assn., Motor Press Guild (pres. 1991), Pi Tau Sigma. Achievements include being the Four-time winner of SCCA Nelson Ledges 24-hour endurance auto race.

DINKES, WILLIAM, lawyer; b. N.Y.C., Apr. 24, 1942; s. Nathan and Estelle (Ludwig) D.; m. Linda Joan Plofsky, Aug. 15, 1965; children— Jill Ann, Jodi Allison, Jamie Alyse. J.D., Bklyn. Law Sch., 1965. Bar: N.Y. 1965, Ill. 1966, U.S. Dist. Ct. (so. and ea. dists.) N.Y. 1971; U.S. Ct. Appeals (2d cir.) 1981. Ptnr. Dinks Mandel & Dinkes, 1966-80, Dinkes Soll & Dinkes, Chgo., 1966—, Dinkes Mandel Dinkes & Morelli, N.Y.C., 1981— . Mem. N.Y. State Trial Lawyers Assn. (bd. dirs.), N.Y. State Bar Assn., Assn. Trial Lawyers N.Y.C., Met. Women's Bar Assn. Lodge: B'nai Brith (bd. dirs., past pres., Person of Yr. award 1982). Office: Dinkes Soll & Dinkes 179 W Washington St Chicago IL 60602-2305

DINKINS, CAROL EGGERT, lawyer; b. Corpus Christi, Tex., Nov. 9, 1945; d. Edgar H. Jr. and Evelyn S. (Scheel) Eggert; m. Bob Brown; children: Anne, Amy. BS, U. Tex., 1968; JD, U. Houston, 1971. Bar: Tex. 1971. Prin. assoc. Tex. Law Inst. Coastal and Marine Resources, Coll. Law U. Houston, Tex., 1971-73; assoc., ptnr. Vinson & Elkins, Houston, 1973-81, 83-84, 85—, mem. mgmt. com., 1991-96; asst. atty. gen. environ. and natural resources Dept. Justice, 1981-83, U.S. dep. atty. gen., 1984-85. Chmn. Pres.'s Task Force on Legal Equity for Women, 1981-83; mem. Hawaiian Native Study Commn., 1981-83; dir. Nat. Consumer Coop. Banks Bd., 1981 Contbr. articles to profl. jours. Chmn. Gov.'s Conservation Task Force, 2000, Tex. Gov.'s Flood Control Action Group 1980-81; commr. Tex. Parks and Wildlife Dept., 1997-2001; bd. govs. The Nature Conservancy, 1996—, vice chmn. 2002-2004, Oryx Energy Co., 1990-95, (dir.) U. Houston Law Ctr. Found., 1985-89, 96-98, Environ. and Energy Study Inst., 1986-98, Houston Mus. Natural Sci., 1986-98, 2000—, Tex. Nature Conservancy, 1985—, chmn., 1996-99., chair com. on fed. judiciary, 2002-03. Mem. ABA (ho. of dels., past chmn. state and local govt. sect., past chair sect. nat. resources, energy, and environ. law, standing com. on Fed. Judges 1997-98, bd. editors ABA Jour.), Fed. Bar Assn. (bd. dirs. Houston chpt. 1986), State Bar Tex., Houston Bar Assn., Tex. Water Conservation Assn., Houston Law Rev. Assn. (bd. dirs. 1978). Republican. Lutheran. Office: Vinson & Elkins 2300 First City Tower 1001 Fannin St Houston TX 77002-6706

DINKINS, TYRONE MORRIS, music educator, conductor; b. Phila., Jan. 15, 1975; s. Tyrone Morris Dinkins, Sr.; m. Nicole Marie Beane, Feb. 15, 1976; 1 child, Moira Leigh. MusM in Conducting, Western Wash. U., Bellingham, 2001. Cert. tchr. Pa., N.J. Performing arts dir. Wilmington Friends Sch., Del., 1997—99, interim head performing arts dept., 1999—2000; dir. choral activities Centennial Sch. Dist., Warminster, Pa., 2001—. Choral dir. Am. Music Abroad, Haddonfield, NJ, 1998—. Dir.: (play) Much Ado About Nothin, 1998, (musical) Oliver, 2000, Bye Bye Birdie, 1999, (music director) A Funny Thing Happened on the Way to the Forum, 2002; prodr.: (CD) Cloudburst, 2002. Recipient Nat. Collegiate Edn. award, 2002. Mem.: Bucks County Music Educators Assn., Coll. Music Soc., Am. Choral Dir. Assn., Music Educators Nat. Conf. Republican. Office: Centennial Sch Dist 333 Centennial Rd Warminster PA 18974 E-mail: dinkty@centennialsd.org.

DINMAN, BERTRAM DAVID, retired metal products executive, health educator; b. Phila., Aug. 9, 1925; s. Meyer and Minnie (Kaufman) D.; m. Gabrielle Stamm, June 11, 1950; children: Stefanie, Jonathan David, Emily, Joshua. Student, Temple U., 1944, 46-51, MD, 1951; ScD, U. Cin., 1957. Asst. prof. to prof. Ohio State U. Coll. Medicine, 1957-65; prof., dir. Inst. Indsl. Health, U. Mich. Sch. Pub. Health, 1965-73; corp. med. dir. Aluminum Co. Am., Pitts., 1973-78, v.p. health and safety, 1978-87; clin. prof. dept. environ. and occupational health U. Pitts., 1987—2002; ret. Trustee Am. Bd. Preventive Medicine, vice chmn., 1976-85; cons. U.S. Army, USN, WHO; mem. U.S. del. ILO, 1980-81, 84-85; vis. fellow Green Coll. U. Oxford, 1986-92. Served with C.E. U.S. Army, 1944-46. Fellow Am. Coll. Occupl. and Environ. Medicine (A.G. Kammer Merit in authorship award 1972, S. Knudsen award 1988, Health Achievement in Occupl. Medicine award 1992); mem. Permanent Commn. and Internat. Assn. Occupational Health (dir., emeritus), Am. Acad. Occupational Medicine (pres. 1973-74, Kehoe award, G. H. Gehrmann Lectr. 1982). Home: 4710 Bayard St Pittsburgh PA 15213-1708 E-mail: dinman@pitt.edu.

DINNAGE, JAMES DAVID, lawyer; b. Eastbourne, England, Sept. 2, 1950; s. Norman and Peggy Kathleen Belle (Martin) D.; m. Karen Lynn Frick, Oct. 10, 1974; 1 child, Russell James. BA, Cambridge (Eng.) U., 1972, MA, 1976; licence spl. en droit Européen, Inst. d'Etudes Européennes, Brussels, 1974. Lectr. in law Southampton (Eng.) U., 1977-79; legal adviser Du Pont Ltd., Stevenage, U.K., 1979-84; asst. co-sec., sr. counsel E.I. du Pont de Nemours & Co., Wilmington, Del., 1985-93; sr. legal adviser Conoco (U.K.) Ltd., London, 1993-97; ptnr. Arnold & Porter, London, 1997-2000; corp. counsel E.I. du Pont de Nemours, Wilmington, Del., 2000—02; gen. counsel DuPont Textiles and Interiors, Inc., 2003—. Lectr. law Villanova (Pa.) U., 1988-93. Co-author: EEC Law, 2d edit., 1981, The Constitutional Law of the European Union, 1996. Dep. chmn. St. Annes Luth. Ch., London, 1994—02. Mem. Inner Temple. Lutheran. Avocation: tennis. Office: E I du Pont de Nemours & Co 1007 E Market St Wilmington DE 19890-0001

DINNEEN, GERALD PAUL, electrical engineer, former government official; b. Elmhurst, N.Y., Oct. 23, 1924; s. Walter James and Anna Constance (Costello) D.; m. Mary Purington, June 28, 1947; children: Patricia Dinneen Mooney, Barbara Dinneen Sehr, Michael. BS, Queens Coll., 1947; MS, U. Wis., 1948, PHD, 1952. Teaching asst. U. Wis., 1947-51; sr. devel. engr. Goodyear Aircraft, 1951-53; with MIT, Lexington, 1953-77, prof. elec. engring., dir. Lincoln Lab.; asst. sec. of def., 1977-81; corp. v.p. sci. and tech. Honeywell Inc., Mpls., 1981-89; fgn. sec. NAE, Washington, 1988-95; chair policy and global affairs divsn. Nat. Rsch. Coun., Washington, 1997—. Cons. Def. Dept. NASA, USN, USAF. Served with AC, AUS, 1943-46. Recipient Disting. Pub. Service award Dept. Def., 1981. Mem. NAE, Engring. Acad. Japan, Swiss Acad. of Engring. Scis., Royal Acad. of Engring. (U.K.), Am. Math. Soc., Math. Assn. Am., Cosmos Club (Washington), Sigma Xi, Phi Beta Kappa. Home: 1010 Waltham St #C460 Lexington MA 02421 Office: Nat Rsch Coun 500 5th St Washington DC 20001 E-mail: gdinneen@nas.edu.

DINNER, JANICE MARIE, lawyer; b. San Francisco, Sept. 21, 1957; d. Fredrick Cohn and Sondra (Rosenthal) Cohn Eastham; m. Dean M. Dinner, May 25, 1986; children: Scott Michael, Brett Alan, Bryan Jeffrey. Student, L'Inst. de Sci. Politique, Paris, 1978; BA, Stanford U., 1979; JD, U. Mich., 1982. Bar: Colo. 1982, Ariz. 1985. Assoc. Holland & Hart, Denver, 1982-85; assoc. gen. counsel Banner Health Sys. (f/k/a Samaritan Health Sys.), Phoenix, 1985—. Bd. dirs. Contact Inc., 1989-92. Bd. dirs. Samaritan Fed. Credit Union, 1996-99, Temple Chai, 2002—. Mem. Am. Health Lawyers Assn., Ariz. Bar Assn., Maricopa Bar Assn. (vol. instr. young lawyers sect. 1988-89), Ariz. Assn. Health Care Lawyers (pres. 1991-92, exec. com. 1991—), Stanford Club of Phoenix (bd. dirs. 1989-91). Office: Banner Health 1441 N 12th St Phoenix AZ 85006-2837

DINNERSTEIN, HARVEY, artist; b. N.Y.C., Apr. 3, 1928; s. Louis and Sarah (Kobilansky) D.; m. Lois Behrke, May 25, 1951; children: Rachel, Michael. Student of, Moses Soyer, 1944-46; student, Art Students League, 1946-47, Tyler Art Sch., Temple U., 1950; D (hon.), Lyme Acad. Fine Arts, 1998. Instr. drawing and painting Sch. Visual Arts, N.Y.C., 1963-80, N.A.D., 1974-92, Art Students League, 1980—. One-man shows include Davis Galleries, N.Y.C., 1955, 60-61, 63, Kenmore Galleries, Phila., 1964, 66, 69-70, F.A.R. Galleries, N.Y.C., 1972, 79, Sindin Galleries, 1983, Deutsch Galleries, 1989, Capricorn Galleries, 1990, Butler Inst. Am. Art, Youngstown, Ohio, 1994, Gerold Wunderlich Galleries, 1997, Frey Norris Gallery, San Francisco, 2003; exhibited in group shows at Whitney Mus. Am. Art, N.Y.C., 1955, New Britain (Conn.) Mus. Am. Art, 1964, Am. Acad. and Inst. Arts and Letters, N.Y.C., 1974, Pa. State U. Mus. Art, 1974, others; works represented in collections Met. Mus. Art, Lehman Coll., Whitney Mus. Am. Art, Martin Luther King Labor Ctr., N.Y.C., New Britain Mus. Art, Fleming Mus. at U. Vt., Burlington: author: A Portfolio of Drawings, 1968, Harvey Dinnerstein-Artist at Work, 1978. Served with U.S. Army, 1951-53. Recipient Temple Gold medal Pa. Acad. Fine Art, 1950; Allied Artist Gold medal, 1977; President's award Audubon Artists, 1978; Arthur Ross award Classical Am., 1983; others; Tiffany Found. grantee, 1948, 61 Mem. N.A.D. (Samuel F.B. Morse medal 2003). Home: 933 President St Brooklyn NY 11215-1603

DINNERSTEIN, LEONARD, historian, educator; b. N.Y.C., May 5, 1934; s. Abraham and Lillian (Kubrik) D.; m. Myra Anne Rosenberg, Aug. 20, 1961; children: Andrew, Julie. B of Social Scis., CCNY, 1955, MA, Columbia U., 1960, PhD, 1966. Instr. N.Y. Inst. Tech., N.Y.C., 1960-65; asst. prof. Fairleigh Dickinson U., Teaneck, N.J., 1967-70; prof. Am. history U. Ariz., Tucson, 1970—, dir. Judaic studies, 1993-2000. Adj. prof. Columbia U., summers 1969, 72, 74, 81, 87, 89, NYU, summers 1969-70, 82, 86. Author: The Leo Frank Case, 1968 (Anisfield-Wolf award 1969), America and the Survivors of the Holocaust, 1982, Uneasy at Home, 1987; (with David M. Reimers) Ethnic Americans: A History of Immigration and Assimilation, 1987, 4th edit., 1999; (with R.L. Nichols, D.M. Reimers) Natives and Strangers, 1996, 4th edit., 2003, Antisemitism in America, 1994 (Nat. Jewish Book prize 1994); contbr. articles to profl. jours.; editor: (with Fred Jaher) The Aliens, 1970; (with Kenneth T. Jackson) American Vistas, 1971, 7th edit., 1995; (with Mary Dale Palsson) Jews in the South, 1973; (with Jean Christie) Decisions and Revisions: Interpretations of 20th Century American History, 1975, America Since World War II, 1976. Mem. Orgn. Am. Historians, Am. Hist. Assn., Am. Jewish Hist. Assn. Democrat. Jewish. Home: 1981 E Miraval Cuarto Tucson AZ 85718-3032 Office: U Ariz Dept History Tucson AZ 85721-0027 E-mail: dinnerst@u.arizona.edu.

DINNERSTEIN, SIMON ABRAHAM, artist, educator; b. Bklyn., Feb. 16, 1943; s. Louis and Sarah (Kobilansky) D.; m. Renée Sudler, Aug. 28, 1965; 1 child, Simone. BA, CCNY, 1965; postgrad., Bklyn. Mus. Art Sch., 1964-67, Hochschule für Bildende Kunst, Kassel, Fed. Republic Germany, 1970-71. Instr. in fine arts New Sch. Social Rsch., Parsons Sch. of Design, N.Y.C., 1975—. Adj. lectr. N.Y.C. Tech. Coll., Bklyn., 1979—88; vis. prof. Pratt Inst., Bklyn., 1986—87; vis. artist Calhoun Sch., NY, 1988—89; lectr. Am. Acad. Rome, 1977—78, USIS, Barcelona and Madrid, Spain, 1979, Pa. State U., 1984, Pt. Washington Pub. Libr., 1990, St. Paul's Sch., Concord, N.H., 1991, Nassau County C.C., 1994, NAD, 2000, Walton Arts Ctr., Fayetteville, Ark., 1999, U. Richmond, Va., 2000. One-man shows include Staempfli Gallery, N.Y.C., 1975, 1979, 1988, Inst. Internat. Edn., 1976—77, 1979, Am. Acad. Rome, 1977, Pratt Inst., 1987, New Sch. Social Rsch., 1981, 1993, Martin Luther King, Jr., Labor Ctr., N.Y.C., 1985, St. Paul's Sch., Concord, 1991, N.J. Ctr. for Visual Art, Summit, 1994, ACA Galleries, N.Y., Bread and Roses Gallery, N.Y. and St. Peter's Church, N.Y., 1999, Walton Arts Ctr., Fayetteville, Texarkana Regional Arts Ctr., Tex./Ark., Marsh Art Gallery, U. Richmond, 2000, Arnot Art Mus., 2003; subject of books: The Art of Simon Dinnerstein, 1991, Simon Dinnerstein: Paintings and Drawings, 2000; included in anthology Drawing from Life, 1992, Drawing from Life (Clint Brown), 1997, Centennial Directory, Am. Acad. Rome, 1995, Hooked on Drawing: Illustrated Lessons and Exercises for Grades 4 and up, 1996, Community of Creativity, A Century of MacDowell Colony Artists, 1996, Drawing Dimensions, 1999, Ont. Rev., 1998, St. Ann's Rev., 2000, Rattapallax Jour., 2000, Bklyn. Jews, 2001, Great Am. Writers, 2001, City Secrets, Rome, 2000, City Secrets, Florence, Venice and the Towns of Italy, 2001, City Secrets, New York, 2002, Hanging Loose, 2003; represented, ACA Galleries, N.Y.C. Recipient Rome prize Am. Acad. in Rome, 1976-78, Ingram Merrill Found. award for painting, 1978-79, Cannon prize NAD, 1988, Ralph Fabri prize NAD, 1997, Bertelsen award NAD, 1998; Childe Hassam purchase award Am. Acad. Arts and Letters, 1976-78; fellow Fulbright Found., Germany, 1970-71, Louis Comfort Tiffany Found., 1976, MacDowell Colony, 1969, 79, N.Y. Found. for Arts, 1987; E.D. Found. grantee, 1977-78, 78-79. Mem. NAD, Soc. Fellows Am. Acad. Rome. Democrat. Jewish. Avocations: reading, film, walking, travel, dreaming. Home: 415 1st St Brooklyn NY 11215-2507

DINNIMAN, ANDREW ERIC, county commissioner, history educator, academic program director, international studies educator; b. New Haven, Oct. 10, 1944; s. Harold and Edith (Stephson) D.; m. Margo Portnoy, June 8, 1969; 1 dau., Alexis. BA, U. Conn., 1966; MA, U. Md., 1969; EdD, Pa. State U., 1978. Student pers. worker U. Md., 1969-71, U. Denver, 1971-72; prof. West Chester (Pa.) State U., 1972—, dir. Ctr. for Internat. Programs, 1986-2001; commissioner Chester County, 1992—. Author: Book of Human Relations Readings, 1980, Education for International Competence in Pennsylvania, 1988; contbr. articles to profl. jours. Chmn. Chester County Dem. Com., 1979-85; mem. Pa. Dem. State Com., 1982-89, mem. exec. com., 1984-89; chmn. Eastern Pa. Dem. County Chmn. Assn., 1982-85; mem. Dem. Nat. Com., 1984-89; del. Dem. Nat. Conv., 1984, 88, 92, 96; pres. Pa. Coun. on Internat. Edn., 1989-91; v.p. Downingtown Area (Pa.) Sch. Bd., 1975-79; mem. Ctrl. Chester County Vocat.-Tech. Sch. Bd., 1978-79; mem. Chester County Conservation Dist., 1992—; mem. Pa. State Transp. Adv. Com., 1992-95, mem. Chester County Econ. Devel. Bd., 1992-96; mem. Nat. Assn. Counties Com. on Globalization, 1997-98, Chester County Internat. Trade Coun., 1999—. Recipient Bicentennial award Pa. Sch. Bds. Assn., 1976, Outstanding Acad. Svc. award Commonwealth Pa., 1977, Human Rights award W. Chester State U. chpt. NAACP, 1980, Cmty. Svc. award Coatesville NAACP, 1997, Mil. Order of Purple Heart Nat. citation for outstanding svc., 1998, Excellence in Local Govt. award Commonwealth of Pa., 1998, Grange award for pub. svc., 1999, Regional Leadership award Exton Regional C. of C., 1999, Leadership award Chester County Water Resources Authority, 2003. Mem. Chester County Hist. Soc., Pa. Soc. Jewish. Home: 471 Spruce Dr Exton PA 19341-2025 Office: Courthouse 2 N High St West Chester PA 19380-3025 E-mail: adinniman@chesco.org.

DINNING, WOODFORD WYNDHAM, JR., lawyer; b. Demopolis, Ala., Aug. 15, 1954; s. Woodford W. and Gladys (Brown) D.; m. Tammy E. Cannon, May 27, 1994. AS, U. Ala., 1976, JD, 1979. Bar: Ala. 1979, U.S. Dist. Ct. (so. dist.) Ala. 1980. Mcpl. judge City of Demopolis, 1980-93, 98—; ptnr. Lloyd & Dinning, LLC, Demopolis, 1979—; mcpl. judge City of Linden, Ala., 1997—. Pres. and bd. dirs. Tenn. Tom Motel, Inc.; atty. Marengo County Commn. and City of Linden, Ala. Mem. U. Ala. Alumni Assn. (chmn. 1985-86). Avocations: water skiing, marathon running. Office: Lloyd & Dinning LLC PO Drawer Z Demopolis AL 36732

DINOS, NICHOLAS, engineering educator, administrator; b. Tamaqua, Pa., Jan. 15, 1934; s. Christophoros and Calliope (Haralambos) D.; m. Lillian Gravell, June 18, 1955; children: Gwen Elizabeth, Christopher Nicholas, Janet Kay. BS, Pa. State U., 1955; MS, Lehigh U., 1966, PhD., 1967. Engr. E.I. duPont Co., Terre Haute, Ind., 1955-57, rsch. engr. Augusta, Ga., 1957-64; assoc. prof. Ohio U., Athens, 1967-72, prof., 1972—, chmn., 1976-89. Vis. prof. Chubu U., Nagoya, Japan, 1976. Contbr. articles to profl. jours. Elder Presbyn. Ch., Athens, 1967—; Danforth Found. assoc., Ohio U., 1978—. NASA fellow Lehigh U., Stanford U., 1966, 72, 74, U.S. Steel fellow Lehigh U., 1965. Mem. AIChE, Am. Soc. Engring. Edn., Sigma Xi, Phi Kappa Phi, Tau Beta Pi. Democrat. Avocations: reading, music, outdoors, travel. Home: 29 Briarwood Dr Athens OH 45701-1302 Office: Ohio U Dept Chem Engring Athens OH 45701 E-mail: dinos@ohio.edu.

DINOSO, VICENTE PESCADOR, JR., physician, educator; b. San Marcelino, Philippines, Oct. 17, 1936; came to U.S., 1961, naturalized, 1973; s. Vicente Dinoso and Eugenia Corpus (Pescador) D.; m. Alice M. Dinoso, June 19, 1965; children— Vincent, David. BS, U. Philippines, 1955, MD, 1960. Intern Mt. Sinai Hosp., Hartford, Conn., 1961-62; resident St. Mary's Hosp., Waterbury, Conn., 1962-64, Lahey Clinic Found., Boston, 1964-65; research fellow Temple U. Sch. Medicine, Phila., 1965-66, 68-69, instr. medicine, 1969-72, asst. prof., 1972-74; assoc. prof. medicine Hahnemann U. Sch. Medicine, Phila., 1974-78, prof. medicine, assoc. prof. physiology, 1978—. Practice medicine specializing in gastroenterology, 1969— Co-editor: Gastrointestinal Emergencies, 1976; contbr. articles to med. jours. Mem. Am. Gastroenterol. Assn., Am. Physiol. Soc., Am. Fedn. for Clin. Research, AAAS, Sigma Xi. Republican. Home: 1421 Granary Rd Blue Bell PA 19422-2124 Office: Hahnemann U Hosp Broad and Vine St Philadelphia PA 19102-5087

DINSE, JOHN MERRELL, lawyer; b. Rochester, N.Y., June 26, 1925; s. Frank John and Lois Vanlora (Merrell) D.; m. Ann Thompson (Goodenough), Dec. 27, 1948; children— Jeffrey P., Pamela D. Johnston AB, U. Rochester, 1947; LL.B., Cornell U., 1950. Bar: N.Y. 1950, Vt. 1951, U.S. Dist. Ct. Vt. 1952, U.S. Ct. Appeals (2d cir.) 1957. Assoc. firm Austin & Edmunds, Burlington, Vt., 1950-57; ptnr. Dinse, Erdmann, & Clapp (and predecessor firms), Burlington, 1957-90; of counsel Dinse, Knapp, & McAndrew (and predecessor firms), Burlington, 1990—. Mem. Med. Ctr.Hosp. Assocs.; dir. Vt. Mcpl. Bond Bank, 1980—83; past trustee Burlington (Vt.) YWCA; past bd. govs. Med. Ctr. Hosp. Vt.; past bd. dirs. Vt. Diabetes Assn., Arthritis Found.; bd. dirs. Vt. Symphony Orch., v.p., 1995—2001, chmn. bd., 2001—; mem. Vt. Waterways Commn., 1962—63; chmn. Jud. Nominating Bd., 1967—77; campaign chmn. Gov. Deane C. Davis, 1968, 1970; mem. Waterways Commn. on Champlain Basin. With USAR, 1943—46. Decorated Bronze Star U.S. Army. Fellow Am. Coll. Trial Lawyers, Am. Bar Found., Am. Coll. Trust and Estate Counsel; mem. ABA, New Eng. Bar Assn. (bd. dirs. 1977-80), Chittenden County Bar Assn., Vt. Bar Assn. (bd. mgrs. 1974—, pres. 1978-79), Am. Bd. Trial Advs. (bd. dirs. 1990-92), Am. Judicature Soc. (dir. 1975-79), Am. Acad. Hosp. Attys., No. New Eng. Def. Counsel Assn. (pres. 1971-72), Assn. Def. Attys., Internat. Assn. Def. Counsel, Def. Research Inst. (dir. 1975-81, pres. 1980, chmn. bd. 1981), Am. Law Inst., Nat. Assn. Coll. and Univ. Attys. Clubs: Lake Champlain Yacht (commodore 1961-62); Malletts Bay Boat (master 1957-58). Home: Harbor Rd Shelburne VT 05482 Office: Dinse Knapp & McAndrew PO Box 988 209 Battery St Burlington VT 05402

DINSMOOR, JAMES ARTHUR, psychology educator; b. Woburn, Mass., Oct. 4, 1921; s. Daniel Stark and Jean Erskine (Masson) D.; m. Anne Darrow Berninger, July 17, 1943 (div. Mar. 1953); 1 son, Daniel Stark; m. Marise Kay Sawyer, Jan. 1, 1956; children: Mara Jean, Robert Scott. BA, Dartmouth Coll., 1943; MA, Columbia U., 1945, PhD, 1949. Instr. Newark Colls., Rutgers U., 1945-46; lectr. Columbia U., N.Y.C., 1946-51; asst. prof. Ind. U., Bloomington, 1951-58, assoc. prof., 1958-63, prof. psychology, 1963-86, prof. emeritus psychology, 1987—. Author: Operant Conditioning: An Experimental Analysis of Behavior, 1970. Mem. nat. bd. Nat. Com. for a Sane Nuclear Policy, Washington, 1966-68. Fellow APA (divsn. v.p. 1977-80, divsn. pres. 1992-93); mem. Soc. Exptl. Analysis of Behavior (pres. 1979-81), Midwestern Psychol. Assn. (coun. 1973-82, pres. 1980-81), Assn. for Behavior Analysis (orgnl. com. 1974-76). Home: 1511 E Maxwell Ln Bloomington IN 47401-5144 Office: Ind U Dept Psychology 1101 E 10th St Bloomington IN 47405-7007 E-mail: dinsmoor@indiana.edu.

DINSMOOR, MARA JEAN, obstetrician-gynecologist, educator; b. Indpls., June 30, 1956; d. James Arthur and Marise Kay (Sawyer) D. AB, Dartmouth Coll., 1978; MD, Ind. U., 1982; MPH, Va. Commonwealth U., 2002. Diplomate Am. Bd. Ob-Gyn., Am. Bd. Maternal and Fetal Medicine. Intern ob-gyn. U. Vt., 1982-83, resident, 1983-86; instr., maternal-fetal medicine fellow U. Tex. Health Sci. Ctr., San Antonio, 1986-88, asst. prof., 1988-89, Med. Coll. Va., Richmond, 1989-94, assoc. prof., 1994—2000, Feinberg Sch. Medicine, Northwestern U., Evanston, Ill., 2000—. Contbr. articles to profl. jours., chpts. to books. Fellow Am. Coll. Ob-Gyn.; mem. Soc. for Maternal-Fetal Medicine, Infectious Disease Soc. for Ob-Gyn., Am. Soc. Microbiology.

DINSMOOR, ROBERT DAVIDSON, lawyer, judge; b. El Paso, Tex., May 19, 1955; s. William Bell Jr. and Mary (Higgins) D. BA in Polit. Sci., Brigham Young U., 1979, JD, 1982. Bar: Tex. 1983, U.S. Dist. Ct. (we. dist.) Tex. 1985, U.S. Ct. Appeals (5th cir.) 1986, U.S. Supreme Ct. 1987. Rsch. assoc. J. Reuben Clark Law Sch., Brigham Young U., Provo, Utah, 1981-82; asst. dist. atty. El Paso (Tex.) Dist. Atty., 1983-90; dist. ct. judge State of Tex., El Paso, 1991—2002; ptnr. Ray, Valdez, Mc Christian, Jeans, 2003—. Spkr. in field; co-founder El Paso Criminal Law Study Group. Contbr. articles to profl. jours. Bd. dirs. S.W. Repertory Orgn., El Paso, 1994-95; Sunday Sch. pres. Latter Day Saints Ch., 5th ward, El Paso, 1993-95; exec. sec. to bishop, 1995-2001, mem. high coun., 2001—. Recipient Outstanding Achievement award El Paso Young Lawyers Assn., 1990, Outstanding Jurist award, 1999, 2001. Mem.: El Paso Mex.-Am. Bar Assn. (bd. dirs. 2001—), El Paso Bar Assn. (bd. dirs. 1993—96, sec. 1996—97, others 1996—, treas. 1997—98, v.p. 1998—99, pres.-elect 1999—2000, pres. 2000—01, mem. Law Day com., libr. com., criminal law com., Professionalism award 2002), State Bar Tex. (victim/witness com. 1992—95, mem. indigent representation com. 1994—98, victim/witness com. 1997—98, chmn. victim/witness com. 1999—2000, mem. indigent representation com. 1999—2001, victim/witness com. 1999—2001). Democrat. Avocations: playing piano, writing music, bicycle riding, basketball, accordion playing. Office: 5822 Cromo Dr El Paso TX 79912

DINSMORE, JENNIFER J. student affairs professional; b. Bethesda, Md., Nov. 8, 1975; d. David A. and Sharon Faulconer Dinsmore. BA mass comm., U. of NC, 1997; MEd Student Pers. Adminstrn., Western Wash. U., 1998. Residential life HS coord. N.C. Sch. of the Arts, Winston-Salem, 1998—2000; asst. dir. student activities Loyola U. New Orleans, 2000—02, assoc. dir. student activities, 2002—. Web site mgmt. project team leader Assn. of Coll. Unions Internat.; ctrl. region comm. coord. Nat. Assn. for Campus Activities, 2003—. Liberal. Avocations: travel, reading, singing, designing webpages. Office: Loyola U New Orleans 1707 Second St Apt #3 New Orleans LA 70113 Home Fax: 504-865-3612. Personal E-mail: jendin@yahoo.com. E-mail: jjdinsmo@loyno.edu.

DINSMORE, ROBERTA JOAN MAIER, library director; b. Phila., Sept. 30, 1934; d. Bert Faust and Emma Baker (Keen) Maier; m. Ray W. Dinsmore, Sr., Oct. 20, 1956; children: Ray Wilson Jr., Jeffrey Maier, Debra Joan, Matthew Bert. BA, Pa. State U., 1956; MLS, Clarion U. Pa., 1990. Proofreader Aluminum Co. Am., Pitts., 1957-60; office mgr. Dinsmore, Lithographer, Punxsutawney, Pa., 1969—; dir. Punxsutawney Meml. Libr., 1978—. Freelance writer Greenburg (Pa.) Tribune Rev., 1980—81; adult edn. tchr. Jeff Tech., Reynoldsville, Pa., 1981—82. Mem. Jefferson County Constrn. Com., Jefferson County Heritage Com.; mem. sch. dist. strategic planning com.; chair, sec. Civil Svc. Commn., Punxsutawney; exec. bd. Theatre Arts; accreditation team Clarion Univ. of Pa.; ch. libr. Punxsutawney Presbyn. Ch., 1985—; elder Presbyn. Ch.; mem. com. on ministry Kiskiminetas Presbytery; mem. exec. bd. Punxsutawney Area Arts Coun.; head hostess Welcome Wagon Internat., Memphis, 1976—80; mem. libr. sci. accreditation team Clarion U., Pa.; v.p., treas. Punxsutawney Area Arts Coun.; hospice vol.; tchr. adult discussion class; coun. mem. R.S.V.P., chair; chairperson numerous orgns. Mem.: AAUW (Woman of the Yr. 1987), RSVP (mem. coun., chair), ALA, Goschenhoppen Historians, Bus. and Profl. Women, Punxsutawney Area Hist. and Geneol. Soc. (sec. bd. dirs., charter), Clarion Dist. Libr. Assn. (pres. 1984—86), Pa. Libr. Assn. (past chair pub. libr. divsn.), Punxsutawney Hosp. Aux., Pa. Citizens for Better Librs., Friends of Libr., Irving Club (past pres.), Garden Club (past pres. Punxsutawney chpt.), PEO. Republican. Avocations: reading, making and

selling crafts in small, self-owned business, genealogy. Home: 808 E Mahoning St Punxsutawney PA 15767-2320 Office: Punxsutawney Meml Libr 301 E Mahoning St Punxsutawney PA 15767-2142

DINTENFASS, MARK, writer, English educator; b. Bklyn., Nov. 15, 1941; s. Sidney Dintenfass and Gerri Berger; m. Phyllis Schulman; children: David, Nathan, Mark. BA, Columbia U., 1963, MA, 1964; MFA, U. Iowa, 1968. Prof. English Lawrence U., Appleton, 1968-99. Author: Make Yourself An Earthquake, 1969, Montgomery Street, 1978, Old World, New World, 1982, A Loving Place, 1986. Recipient Disting. Achievement award Wis. Libr. Assn., 1987; named Notable Wis. Writer, Wis. Libr. Assn., 1986. Mem. PEN, Author's Guild. Avocations: music, computing. Office: Lawrence Univ Main Hall Appleton WI 54911 E-mail: mdintenfass@new.rr.com., dintenfm@lawrence.edu.

DINTRONE, CHARLES VINCENT, librarian; b. NYC, May 16, 1942; s. Vincent Charles and Harriet Marie Dintrone; m. Antonia Rowena Fleck, Sept. 25, 1977 (div. Aug. 1980); m. Patricia Nancy Langer, July 24, 1982. BA in History, UCLA, 1964, MA in History, 1966; MLS, U. Calif., Berkeley, 1968. Asst. head govt. publs. Fresno (Calif.) State U., 1968-72; head govt. pubs. San Diego State U., 1972-89, instrn. coord., 1989-92, reference libr., 1992-99, head gen. reference divsn., 1999—2002, head reference svcs., 2002—. Author: Television Program Master Index, 1996, 2d edit., 2003; co-author: How to Use the Library. Active Big Bros., San Diego, 1981-90. Mem.: ALA (LIRT publicity coord. 1988—94), Ref. and User Svcs. Assn. Democrat. Avocations: travel, spectator sports, reading. Office: San Diego State U Libr 5500 Campanile Dr San Diego CA 92182-8050 E-mail: dintrone@mail.sdsu.edu.

DI NUNZIO, DOMINICK, educational administrator; b. Bristol, Pa., Mar. 7, 1931; s. Anthony and Mary (Minni) Di N.; m. Helen Mae Appleton, Dec. 29, 1953; children: Dominick, Mark, Douglas, Celeste. BS, Millersville (Pa.) U., 1953; MEd, Rutgers U., 1960, postgrad., 1960-63, U. Pa., 1965-68, Temple U., 1969-71, Lehigh U., 1983; PhD, Walden U., 1972. Tchr., basketball coach Bristol H.S., 1955-61; vice prin. Pemberton Twp. (N.J.) H.S., 1961-65, prin., 1965-73, Pemberton Twp. H.S. No. 2, 1973-76, Pemberton Twp. Elem. Schs., 1976-84, Mid. Schs., 1984-91, asst. supt., 1991—. Mem. acad. policy bd. Walden U., 1978-83. With U.S. Army, 1953-55. Recipient Legion of Honor, Chapel of Four Chaplains, 1982, Disting. Alumnus award Walden U., 1982; named Secondary Educator of Am., 1973. Mem. ASCD, NEA, N.J. Edn. Assn., Nat. Assn. Secondary Sch. Prins., N.J. Assn. Secondary Sch. Prins., Am. Assn. Sch. Adminstrs., Nat. Doctorate Assn., N.J. Schoolmasters Club, South Jersey Schoolmens Club, Coun. for Basic Edn., Nat. Soc. for Study Edn., Millersville U. Alumni Assn. (exec. com. 1972—, v.p. 1978-80, pres. 1980-82, Disting. Svc. award 1987, Outstanding Svc. award 1987, Disting. Alumni award 2003), Walden U. Alumni Assn. (pres. 1978-84), Walden U. Mid. States Regional Assn. (pres. 1983-85), Order Sons of Italy in Am., Pemberton Rotary (pres. 1976-77, Paul Harris fellow 1996), Masons (worshipful master 1987, dist. G chmn. Masonic edn. 1988-91, facilitator dist. C Hiram Leadership program 1990—, chmn. dist. C membership devel. and retention 1992—), Phi Delta Kappa. Presbyterian. Home: 37 Underwood Rd Levittown PA 19056 2601 Office: PO Box 98 Browns Mills NJ 08015-0098

DINWIDDIE, BRUCE WAYLAND, lawyer; b. New Orleans, Aug. 24, 1943; s. George Summey and Augusta Rosser (Benners) D.; m. Judith Zatarain, May 7, 1966 (div. 1971); 1 child, Patrick; m. Kate Marie Crawford, Aug. 2, 1972 (div. 1987); children: Kate, Bruce, Wayland; Anita Rhea Cleaver, Dec. 5, 1987. B.S., Centenary Coll. of La., 1965; J.D., Tulane U., 1968. Bar: La. 1968, U.S. Dist. Ct. (ea. dist.) La. 1968, U.S. Dist. Ct. (we. dist.) La. 1978, U.S. Dist. Ct. (mid. dist.) La. 1970, U.S. Ct. Appeals (5th cir.) 1969, U.S. Supreme Ct. 1975. Law clk. to dist. atty. Orleans Parish, 1967-68; assoc. Terriberry, Carroll, Yancey & Farrell, New Orleans, 1968-72; ptnr. Ungar, Dulitz, Jacobs & Manuel, New Orleans, 1972-76; sole practice, Metairie, La., 1977-80; ptnr. Dinwiddie & Brandao, Metairie, 1981— . Mem. ABA, La. State Bar Assn., Assn. Trial Lawyers Am., La. Trial Lawyers Assn., Tulane Maritime Law Soc. (adv. editor 1976—). Republican. Methodist. Office: Dinwiddie & Brandao 2313 N Hullen St Metairie LA 70001-6910

DIODATO, LUIS HECTOR, physician, researcher; s. Luis Hector Diodato and Amanda Angela Bellezze; m. Maria Cecilia Bahit, June 6, 1997; 1 child, Martina. MD, U. of Buenos Aires, 1983—88. Specialist in cardiovascular surgery CACCV, 1997. Residency in gen. surgery and cardiovasc. surgery Italian Hosp. of Buenos Aires, 1989—97; jr. faculty Italian Hosp. of Buenos Aires, Divsn. of Cardiovasc. surgery., 1997—99; rsch. fellow in cardiothoracic surgery Duke U. Med. Ctr., Durham, NC, 1999—2001; clin. fellow in cardiovasc. and thoracic surgery Brown U., RI Hosp., 2001—02; ho. staff Duke U. Med. Ctr., Durham, NC, 2002—. Achievements include contribution to develop the program in Robotics surgery at Duke University Medical Center.

DIODOSIO, CHARLES JOSEPH, lawyer; b. Pueblo, Colo., Apr. 27, 1951; s. Warren Joseph and Lucille Julia Diodosio. BSChemE, U. Colo., 1973; JD, Northwestern U., 1976. Assoc. McDermott, Will & Emery, Chgo., 1976-80; internat. counsel Beatrice Co., Chgo., 1980-84, v.p. Asia devel., 1984-88; chmn. TMGC Ltd., Chgo., 1988—, Meadow Gold Investment Holding Co., Beijing, 1993—; chmn. L&D International Corp., Beijing, 1993—. Chmn. L&D Internat. Corp., Beijing, China, 1993—. Mem. ABA, Ill. Bar. Home: 1387 Calle de Maria Palm Springs CA 92264-8503 Fax: 760-327-1200. E-mail: meadgo@aol.com.

DION, CELINE, musician; b. Charlemagne, Quebec, Can., Mar. 30, 1970; Singer: (albums) Unison, 1990 (album of the year, 1990), Celine Dion, 1992, Colour of My Love, 1993 (multi-platinum, 1994), Premieres Anees, 1994, Dion Chante Plamondon, 1994, Des Mots Qui Sonnent, 1995, Power of Love, 1995, French Album, 1995, Live A Paris, 1996, Falling Into You, 1997 (Grammy award, 1997), C'est Pour Vivre, 1997, The Collection, 1982—88, 1997, Let's Talk About Love, 1997 (Best Album by a Female Artist Billboard Music award), S'il suffisait d'aimer, 1998, These are Special Times, 1998 (Grammy & Juno awds., 1999), All The Way, 1999; apperances include Real Love, 1979, Beauty & the Beast, 1991 (Grammy award, 1992, best selling single, 1992, Acad. award, 1992), Sleepless in Seattle, 1993, Through the Fire, 1994, My Heart Will Go On (Record of Yr, Best Female Pop Vocal Performance Grammy awards), Titanic, 1999 (Best Soundtrack Single Billboard Music award). Recipient Favorite Female Pop/Rock Artist award, Music awards, 1999, Favorite Adult Contemporary Artist award, Am. Music awards, 1999, Album of Yr. for Titanic, Billboard Music awards, 1999, Album Artist, Billboard Music award, 1999, Adult Contemporary Artist Billboard Music award, 1999. Office: Sony Music 550 Madison Ave New York NY 10022-3211

DION, CHARLES J. statistician; b. Chicopee Falls, Mass., Apr. 8, 1961; s. Normand C. and Patricia A. Dion; m. Brenda G. Dion, July 25, 1987; children: Matthew, Christine, Kimberly. BA in Math., U. South Fla., 1986, MA in Math., 1995. Statistician Fla. Med. Quality Assurance, Tampa, 1994-96, lead statistician, 1996-99, dir. analytic svcs., 1999—. Mem. AAAS, Am. Statis. Assn., Pi Mu Epsilon. Office: Fla Med Quality Assurance 4350 W Cypress St Ste 900 Tampa FL 33607-4181

DION, JACQUES EDGAR, physician, neuroradiologist; b. Quebec City, Que., Can., Oct. 27, 1954; came to U.S., 1987; s. Raymond Marie and Yvonne Dion. BA, Ottawa (Ont.) U., 1974, MD, 1978. Diplomate in radiology and neuroradiology Am. Bd. Radiology. Asst. prof. Hopital Saint-Luc, Montreal, 1985-87, UCLA Med. Ctr., 1987-91; prof. U. Va. Med. Ctr., Charlottesville, 1991-98, Emory U. Hosp., Atlanta, 1998—. Author, editor: Interventional Neuroradiology, 1991; contbr. articles to profl. jours. Mem. Am. Soc. Therapeutic and Interventional Neuroradiology (v.p.), Am. Soc. Neuroradiology, Radiol. Soc. N.Am., Am. Roentgen Ray Soc., World Fedn. Therapeutic and Interventional Neuroradiology. Roman Catholic. Avocations: golf, skiing, reading, computing, music. Office: Emory U Hosp Radiology Dept 1364 Clifton Rd NE Atlanta GA 30322-1061 E-mail: jacques_dion@emoryhealthcare.org.

DION, MARC MUNROE, newspaper columnist; b. Fall River, Mass., May 10, 1957; s. Eugene Wilfred and Margaret Munroe Dion. BA in English, U. Mo., 1980. Newsman AP, Kansas City, Mo., 1983-89; book reviewer Kansas City Star, 1992—; columnist Fall River Herald News, 1992—. Author: To Veronicas New Lover, 1984. Bd. dirs. Arts Unltd., 1995. Recipient 1st Pl. Humor Column award New England Press Assn., 1995, 99, 2d Pl. Serious Column award, 1999, Editorials award New England Associated Press News Execs. Assn., 1997, 3d Place award 2002; winner 3d pl. for 9/11 column New Eng. AP, 2001. Mem. Nat. Soc. Newspaper Columnists (v.p.), Vets. Assn. of Bristol (bd. dirs. 1997—), Boxing Writers Assn. of Am. Roman Catholic. Avocation: boxing. Home: 631 Walnut St Fall River MA 02720 5236 Office: Herald News 207 Pocasset St Fall River MA 02721-1532 E-mail: dionmarc@hotmail.com.

DION, STÉPHANE, federal official; b. 1955; married; 1 daughter. BA in Polit. Sci., U. Laval, 1977, MA in Polit. Sci., 1979; D in Sociology, Inst. Polit. Paris. Prof. polit. sci. U. Moncton, Can., 1984, U. Montréal, Can., 1984-96; pres. Privy Coun., Can., 1996—; min. Intergovernmental Affairs, Canada, 1996—2002; min. Natural Resources of Canada, 2002—. Vis. prof. Lab. Econ. Pub., Paris; sr. rsch. fellow Brookings Inst., Washington; rsch. fellow Can. Ctr. Mgmt. Devel. Co-dir. Can. Jour. Polit. Sci.; contbr. articles to profl. jours. Office: Min of Natural Resources Herb Dhaliwal 580 Booth St K1A 3E4 Ottawa ON Canada E-mail: dions@parl.gc.ca.*

DION, SUSAN FRANCES, historian, poet, writer; b. Manchester, Conn., July 6, 1953; d. Antoinette Frances and Norman Eugene Dion; m. H. Thomas Francis, July 2, 1989; children: Brett Thomas, Raena Patience Iocona. BA, U. of Conn., 1977; MA, Marquette U., Milw., 1980; PhD, Marquette U., 1991. Tchg. asst. Marquette U., Milw., 1978—80; history faculty Nicolet Coll., Rhinelander, Wis., 1980—87, dir., women's resource bur., 1981—87; adj. history faculty LaSalle U., Phila., 1987—88, Widener U., Chester, Pa., 1988—93; founder, dir. Write Now, Penns Grove, NJ, 1991—; tchr./tutor New Concept For Self Devel., Milw., 1979—79. Pubs. adv. com. CFIDS Assn. of Am., Charlotte, NC, 1995—; lectr. and presenter in field, 1980—; adv. com. mem. Coun. on Quality and Leadership for Persons with Disabilities, Towson, Md., 1998—99. Author: (book) WRITE NOW: Maintaining a Creative Spirit While Homebound and Ill (4 editions, 1993, 1994, 1997, 2000), (poem) Joey and the Black Boots (Hon. Mention, 2002); contbr. ; guest editor Skywriters No. VII and VIII, 1997. Mem. NJ CFS Assn., Chatham, NJ, 2001—03. Fellow Smith Family fellow, Marquette U., 1988—89; grantee Puffin Found. Ltd. grantee, 1991, 1994, 1997, 2000, Nat. Assn. for Poetry Therapy grantee, 2000, NJ CFS Assn. grantee, 2000. Mem.: AAUW (v.p. for programs 1989—91), Orgn. of Am. Historians, Phi Beta Kappa. Avocations: travel, reading, shipspotting on the Delaware River, photography. Office: Write Now PO Box 341 Penns Grove NJ 08069-0341

DIONG, BILLY MING, energy control engineering researcher; b. Singapore, Oct. 22, 1962; came to U.S., 1983; s. Woong-Siew and Soo-Eng (Ting) D.; m. Temmy King, July 22, 1989; 1 child, Stephanie. BS with honors, U. Ill., 1986, MS, 1988, PhD, 1992. Engr. Automation Applications Ctr., Singapore, 1988; rsch. asst. dept. gen. engring. U. Ill., Urbana, 1988-91, rsch. asst. coord. sci. lab., 1991-92; rschr. Sundstrand Aerospace, Rockford, Ill., 1992-95; asst. prof. elec. engring. U. Tex.-Pan Am., Edinburg, 1995-99, U. Tex., El Paso, 1999—, Lewis Endowed prof. elec. engring., 2000-02. Contbr. articles to profl. jours. Engring. scholar Sundstrand Corp., 1983-87; Conf. Travel grant U. Ill., 1991, Faculty Rsch. Coun. grant U. Tex.-Pan Am., 1995, 96, NSF grant, 1997, 99, Grants Program grant Hewlett-Packard Found., 1999, Univ. Rsch. Initiative grant U. Tex., El Paso, 1999; Air Force Office of Sci. Rsch. summer fellow, 1997; grantee Agilent Found., 2000, Ballistic Missile Def. Orgn., 2001, USAF, 2003, Tex. Tobacco Settlement Funds, 2003. Mem. IEEE (sr.), Am. Soc. Engring. Edn., Tau Beta Pi (hon.), Eta Kappa Nu (hon., Dean Eugene Thomas award for outstanding faculty 1999), Phi Eta Sigma (hon.). Avocations: computers, music, chess, swimming. Home: 1305 Desert Canyon Dr El Paso TX 79912-7689 Office: U Tex-El Paso Elec and Computer Engring 500 W University Ave El Paso TX 79902-5816 E-mail: bdiong@utep.edu.

DIONNE, AUBRIE ANNE, music educator; b. Manchester, N.H., Nov. 14, 1978; d. Andy William Dionne and Joanne Lillian Dionne; m. Christopher Lee Gantner, Aug. 10, 2002. MusB in Performance, U. of N.H., 2000; student in Performance, Longy Sch. of Music, 2000—. Flute tchr. The Bell Ctr. for Music and the Arts, Dover, NH, 1996—, Manchester (N.H.) Cmty. Music Sch., 1998—; adj. lectr. of flute Plymouth (N.H.) State Coll., 2001—. Substitute principle flute N.H. Philharm. Orch., Manchester, NH, 2000—; condr. and clinician N.H. All State Chamber Music Festival, Bow, NH, 2003—03; condr. Manchester (N.H.) Cmty. Music Sch. Flute Choir, 1999—, Bell Ctr. Flute Choir, Dover, NH, 1998—, Plymouth (N.H.) State Coll. Flute Choir, 2001—. Author: Adventures in Flute Playing, 2002; composer: (songs) Fantasies for Flute Choir, 2003. Recipient 1st Pl. award Wind Symphony Symphony Concerto Competitions, U. of N.H. Music Dept., 1999, 2000; grantee, Fredrick Symth Inst., 2000; scholar Emerson scholarship, Interlochen Arts Camp, 1994, U. of N.H., 1996, Longy Sch. of Music, 2000—02. Mem.: N.H. Music Educators Assn. (music festival adjucator), Manchester Chamber Players (flute performer 2000—03), Music Tchrs. Nat. Assn. (mem. flute tchr. 2000—03, music festival adjucator N.H. chpt. 2002—03, Student of the Yr. award 2000, 1st Pl. award artist performace competition 1996, 1997, 1998, 1999). Achievements include 1996 Soloist Debut with New Hampshire Symphony. Avocations: composing, music arranging for flute choir, travel. Home: 195 Rhode Island Ave Manchester NH 03104-5444 Office: Plymouth State College Music Department 17 High Street Plymouth NH 03264-1595 Personal E-mail: aubriedionne@yahoo.com.

DIONNE, GERALD FRANCIS, research physicist, educator, consultant; b. Montreal, Feb. 5, 1935; came to U.S., 1964, naturalized, 1980; s. Louis Philip and Clare Isabel (Flood) D.; m. Claudette Leblanc, June 29, 1963; 1 child, Stephen. BS summa cum laude, Loyola Coll., U. Montreal, 1956; B of Engring. magna cum laude, McGill U., Montreal, 1958, PhD in Physics, 1964; MS, Carnegie-Mellon U., 1959. Jr. engr. IBM Corp., Poughkeepsie, N.Y., 1959-60; sr. engr. Sylvania Electric Products, Woburn, Mass., 1960-61; rsch. asst., lectr. McGill U., 1964; sr. rsch. assoc. Pratt & Whitney Aircraft, North Haven, Conn., 1964-66; mem. rsch. staff Lincoln Lab., MIT, Lexington, Mass., 1966-96, expert svcs. pers., 1996—. Grad student rsch. advisor, sci. and tech. advisor to industry and govt. Contbr. articles to sci. jours. NRC of Can. fellow. Fellow IEEE; mem. Am. Phys. Soc., Corp. Profl. Engrs. Que., Sigma Xi. Achievements include numerous research advances in magnetism and magnetic materials; research in magnetoelastic and magneto-optic phenomena; magnetic spin transport; magnetoresistance; superconductivity theory and devices; microwave and submillimeter-wave physics and instrumentation; physics of electron emission; patents for microwave, superconducting, and magnetic devices. Home: 182 High St Winchester MA 01890-3366 Office: 244 Wood St Lexington MA 02421-6426

DIONYSIOU, DIONYSIOS DEMETRIOU, adult education educator, researcher; s. Demetris Dionysiou and Kyriaki Christoforou; m. Polymnia Ioannou Antoniou; children: Marianna children: Stella. BS in Chem. Engring., Nat. Tech. U., Athens, Greece, 1991; MS in Chem. Engring., Nat.Tech. U., Athens, Greece, 1991, Tufts U., 1992—95; PhD in Environ. Engring., U. of Cin., 1995—2001. Rsch. engr. W. R. Grace, Cambridge, Mass., 1994—95; asst. prof., environ. engring. U. of Cin., 2000—. Author: (ph.d. dissertation) Engineered Process for the Photocatalytic Oxidation of Hazardous and Toxic Organic Contaminants in Water (Am. Water Works Association's First Pl. 2002 Academic Achievement Award for Best Dissertation, 2002); contbr. numerous articles to profl. jours. Mem., internat. organizing com. Internat. Conferences on TiO_2 Photocatalysis, 2001—02; mem., adv. com. Cin. Water Works, 2000; mem., young professionals com. Ohio Am. Water Works Assn. (OAWWA), Ohio Water Environment Assn. (OWEA), 2001. Recipient Recognition as a Mem. of Good Standing by ACS Pres., Am. Chem. Soc., 2001, Grad. Student Rsch. Paper Award for Excellence in Rsch. and Presentation in Environ. Sci., Divsn. of Environ. Chemistry, Am. Chem. Soc., 2001, Grad. Student Award for Excellence in Grad. Studies in Environ. Sci., 2001, First Pl. Student Rsch. Paper Award and Presentation, [00b7] Ohio Water Environment Assn. (OWEA), 2001, [00b7] Dr. Pasquale V. and Flora Jean Scarpino and Family Award for The Best PhD Dissertation, Environ. Engring. Divsn., U. of Cin., 2001; grantee Gerondelis Found. Fellowship, Gerondelis Found. Inc., 1992-1994, Rsch. on Ionic Liquids, NSF, 2000-2002, Rsch. on MTBE, EPA, 2001, Rsch. on Mercury Pollution in Aquatic Systems, 2000-2001, Rsch. on Pollution Treatment in Estuarine Systems, The Coop. Inst. for Coastal and Estuarine Environ. Tech. (CICEET), 2002; scholar Tuition/Rsch., U. of Cin., 1995-2000, Tufts U., 1992-1994, Hellenic Nat. Scholarship Found. (I.K.Y.) Fellowship, Hellenic Nat. Scholarship Found. (I.K.Y.), Greece, 1986-1991, Hellenic Nat. Scholarship Found. (I.K.Y.) Award for Excellent Performance, 1998-1991. Mem.: Water Environment Fedn., Tri-State Catalysis Soc., North Am. Catalyst Soc., Internat. Ultraviolet Assn., Fed. Water Quality Assn., Assn. of Environ. Engring. and Sci. Professors, Am. Water Works Assn., ASEE, AIChE, ACS (recognition as member of good standing by ACS pres. 2001), Sigma Xi. Achievements include development of Novel Photocatalytic Reactors; research in Transition Metal Chemical Oxidation; Membrane Biofouling; Novel Properties of Ionic Liquids in Environmental Engineering; development of Efficient Photocatalytic Reactors; New Green Processes for Treating Water; research in Advanced Oxidation Technologies; Novel Methods for Treating Drinking Water; development of Advanced Water Treatment Systems; discovery of Novel Photochemical Reactions in Ionic Liquids; research in Mercury Pollution in Aquatic Systems. Avocations: swimming, fishing, dancing. Home: 1122 Scarborough Way Cincinnati OH 45215 Office: University of Cincinnati 765 Baldwin Hall CEE Department Cincinnati OH 45221-0071 Office Fax: 513-556-2599. E-mail: dionysios.d.dionysiou@uc.edu.

DIOP, SAMBA, language educator; b. Dakar, Senegal, June 13, 1957; s. Mapate Diop and Aida Niang. BA, U. of Mass., 1989; MA, U. Calif., Berkeley, 1991, PhD, 1993. Vis. asst. prof. U. Calif., Los Angeles, 1993—94; asst. prof. SUNY, Buffalo, 1994—97, Harvard U., French Dept., Cambridge, Mass., 1997—. Author: The Oral History and Literature of the World, 1995, Discours nationaliste et identite ethinque, 1999, The Epic of El HADJ UMAR, 2000. Mem.: Phi Beta Kapp. Office: Harvard U RLL 507 Boylston Cambridge MA 02138

DIORIO, ROBERT MICHAEL, lawyer, public official; b. Phila., Aug. 5, 1947; s. Carl and Yolanda D. (DiJohn) DiO.; m. Bianka M. Chojnacki; children: Danielle, Stephanie Lauren. BA in Polit. Sci., Pa. State U., 1969; JD, Temple U., 1973. Cert. elem. tchr., Pa. Pvt. practice, Media, Pa., 1973—; asst. pub. defender Delaware County, Media, 1974-76, asst. dist. atty., 1976-79, support master, 1980, custody conciliator, 1980-97, solicitor, controller, 1985-90; ptnr. DiOrio & Sereni LLP, Media, Pa., 1989—. Spl. solicitor City of Springfield, Pa., Upper Darby Sch. Dist., Marple-Netown Sch. Dist., Penn-Delco Sch. Dist.; solicitor County Svcs. for Aging, Delaware County Bd. Prison Insps., S.E. Delco Sch. Dist. Commr. Springfield Twp. Bd. of Commrs., 1977-87, pres. 1981-87; bd. dirs. Deaf Hearing Comm. Ctr., Springfield, Immaculata (Pa.) Coll. Pres. Council, Met. Hosp., Phila., Delaware County Regional Water Quality Control Authority, 1987-89; mem. Delaware County Leadership Adv. Bd., Delaware County Bur. Elections; mem. liberal arts coun. Pa. State U. Mem. ATLA, Pa. Bar Assn., Pa. Assn. Trial Lawyers, Delaware County Bar Assn (sect. dir. 1976, 93-95), Delaware County C. of C. (chmn. family bus. com.), Pa. State U. Alumni Assn. (pres.), Lions. Republican. Roman Catholic. Avocations: golf, skiing. Home: 3 Springton Pointe Dr Newtown Square PA 19073-3931 Office: DiOrio & Sereni LLP Front and Plum Sts Media PA 19063 Fax: (610) 891-0652. E-mail: rdiorio@diorioisereni.com.

DIOSEGY, ARLENE JAYNE, lawyer, consultant; b. Pitts., Sept. 13, 1949; d. William Cornelius and Rosemarie Arlene (Voivoda) D.; 1 child, Corey Redling. BA, Allegheny Coll., 1971; JD, Temple U., 1974. Bar: Pa. 1974, U.S. Dist. Ct. (mid. and ea. dists.) Pa. 1974, U.S. Supreme Ct. 1980, Colo. 1981, U.S. Dist. Ct. (ea. dist.) Colo. 1981, N.C. 1987, U.S. Cir. Ct. (4th cir.) 1987. Assoc. Smith & Roberts, Harrisburg, Pa., 1974-75; asst. atty. gen. Dept. of Edn., Harrisburg, 1975-77; chief counsel Gov.'s Coun. on Drug and Alcohol Abuse, Harrisburg, 1977-80; dir. legal affairs and risk mgmt. U. Colo. Health Scis. Ctr., Denver, 1980-81; asst. univ. counsel Duke U. Med. Ctr., Durham, N.C., 1981-85, adj. asst. prof. grad. dept. health adminstrn., 1983-87; v.p. legal svcs. Coastal Group Inc., Durham, 1985-87; assoc. Faison and Brown, Durham, 1987-90; gen. counsel N.C. Med. Soc., Raleigh, 1990-91; shareholder Maupin Taylor, P.A., Raleigh, 1992—. Cons. Colo. Dept. Health, Denver, 1980-81. Author, editor: Body Medical/Body Legal, A Look at Health Law in North Carolina, 1989—. Bd. dirs. Durham Health Ptnrs., Durham County Advs. for the Mentally Ill, Inc., 1988-90; mem. Durham County Area Mental Health Authority, 1989-91. Mem. ABA, Am. Acad. Hosp. Attys., Nat. Health Lawyers Assn., N.C. Bar Assn. (sec. health law program com. 1983-84, vice chmn. 1984-85, chmn. 1985-86, 86-87, long range planning com., bd. govs. 1989-92, trustee health benefit trust 1991-94), Wake and Durham County Bar Assns., N.C. Soc. Health Care Attys. (legis. com. 1983, program chmn. 1983, bd. dirs. 1985). Republican. Methodist. Avocations: fishing, reading, badminton. Office: Maupin Taylor PA PO Box 13646 Research Triangle Park NC 27709 E-mail: adiosegy@maupintaylor.com.

DIPACE, STEVEN B. lawyer; b. Leominster, Mass., July 17, 1948; s. B. Vincent and Lucille C. (Boucher) DiP.; m. Gail S. Moskowitz, May 29, 1971; children: Angela Val, Michael Steven. BA, Brandeis U., 1970; JD, Suffolk U., 1974. Bar: Mass. 1974, U.S. Dist. Ct. Mass. 1974. Pvt. practice, Fitchburg, Mass., 1974—. Counsel North Ctrl. Mass. Bd. Realtors, Fitchburg, 1987—. Mem. Montachusett Regional Planning Commn., Fitchburg, 1980, Leominster Planning Bd., 1980-81; chmn. Leominster Zoning and Appeals Bd., 1981-87. Mem. Mass. Bar Assn., No. Worcester County Bar Assn. (exec. bd. 1989-92), Mass. Conveyancers Assn. Avocation: coaching youth sports. Home: 40 Wilder Ln Leominster MA 01453-6640 Office: 18 Hartwell St Fitchburg MA 01420-3237 E-mail: DiPaceEsq.@aol.com.

DIPADOVA, REGINA MARIA, counselor; b. Flushing, N.Y., Oct. 24, 1959; d. Anthony and Carmela DiPadova. BA, U. So. Colo., 1984; AA, Pikes Peak C.C., 1982. Cert. addiction counselor, Colo., therapeutic recreation specialist. Counselor Emily Griffith Ctr., Colorado Springs, 1984-87, Cmty. Learning Ctr., Colorado Springs, 1987-90; program dir., founder Inside/Out, Colorado Springs, 1990-99; adolescent counselor El Paso Health Dept., Colorado Springs, 1990—; recreation dir. Comcor Inc., Colorado Springs, 1999—. Founder, dir. Learning Through Challenges, Colorado Springs, 1990—; HIV outreach dir. Inside/Out, Colorado Springs, 1998—; presenter in field; trainer, educator on gay issues, 1990—. Editor, writer New Phazes Mag., 1988-96; contbr. poetry to anthologies. Bd. dirs. Pikes Peak Gay Cmty., 1999-2000, Urban Peak, 2000-2001. Recipient Equality Pride award Equality Colo., 1998, Paul Hunter award Human Rights Campaign, 1999. Democrat. Buddhist. Avocations: rock climbing, triathlons, racquetball, hiking, reading. Office: 301 S Union Blvd Colorado Springs CO 80910-3123 E-mail: reginadipadova@elpasoco.com.

DI PALMA, JOSEPH ALPHONSE, investment company executive, lawyer; b. N.Y.C., Jan. 17, 1931; s. Gaetano and Michela May (Ambrosio) Di P.; m. Joycelyn Ann Engle, Apr. 18, 1970; children: Joycelyn Joan, Julianne Michelle. BA, Columbia U., 1952; JD, Fordham U., 1958; LLM in Taxation, NYU, 1959. Bar: N.Y. 1959. Tax atty. CBS, N.Y.C., 1960-64; v.p. tax dept. TWA, N.Y.C., 1964-74; pvt. practice law N.Y.C., 1974-87; investor, exec. dir. Di Palma Family Holdings, Las Vegas and N.Y.C., 1987—. Cons. in field; head study group Comprehensive Gaming Study, N.Y.C. and Washington, 1990—; think tank exec. dir. Di Palma Position Papers; founder Di Palma Forum, U. Nev., Las Vegas; established The Di Palma Ctr. for Study of Jewelry and Precious Metals at Cooper-Hewitt, Nat. Design Mus., Smithsonian Instn., N.Y.C. Contbr. articles to profl. jours.; author: Di Palma Position Papers. Bd. dirs. Friends of the Henry St. Settlement, N.Y.C., 1961 63, Outdoor Cleanliness Assn., N.Y.C., 1961-65; chmn. Air Transport Assn. Taxation Com., 1974. With U.S. Army, 1953-54. Recipient Disting. Svc. and Valuable Counsel commendation award, Air Transport Assn., 1974, spl. commendation, NYC mayor Rudolph Giuliani, 1997, U. Nev., Las Vegas, 1999, Tiffany Smithsonian Benefactors Circle award, 2001, WNET/Thirteen Pub. Spirit award, 2002. Mem. Internat. Platform Assn., N.Y. State Bar Assn., N.Y. Athletic Club. Roman Catholic. Home: 3111 Bel Air Dr Apt 21B Las Vegas NV 89109-1506 Office: PO Box 72158 Las Vegas NV 89170-2158 also: 930 5th Ave # 4 J&H New York NY 10021-2651

DIPALMA, JOSEPH RUPERT, pharmacology educator; b. N.Y.C., Mar. 21, 1916; s. Frank and Anna (Attanasio) DiP.; m. Mary Solowey, June 26, 1948; children: Maria, Dorothea, Joan, Yvonne, Mary-Jo. BS, Columbia U., 1936; MD, SUNY, Bklyn., 1941; DSc (hon.), Hahnemann U., 1980. Intern, resident in internal medicine Kings County Hosp., Bklyn., 1942-44; asst. prof. medicine and pharmacology State U. N.Y. Downstate Med. Sch., 1946; prof. pharmacology, chmn. dept. Hahnemann Med. Coll. and Hosp., Phila., 1951-67, dean, 1967-82, v.p., 1971-82, sr. v.p., 1972-82, prof. pharmacology and medicine, 1982-86, emeritus prof. pharmacology and medicine, 1986—, emeritus dean, 1986—. Mem. bd. Regional Med. Program Southeastern Pa., 1967-75, Health Systems Agy., 1977-82, Hahnemann Hosp., 2000-, St. Davids Instnl. Rev.,

1975-. Editor: Pharmacology in Medicine, 1971, Basic Pharmacology in Medicine, 1976, 4th edit., 1994; contbr. med. jours. Bd. dirs. Hahnemann U. Hosp., 2000—. Recipient Alumni medallion SUNY, Downstate Med. Sch., 1966, Corp. medal Hahnemann U., 1990 Mem. Coll. Physicians Phila. (council 1969-78), AMA, Pa., Phila. County Med. socs., Am. Physiol. Soc., Am. Soc. Pharmacology and Exptl. Therapeutics, Am. Soc. Clin. Investigation, Am. Soc. Clin. Pharmacology, Alpha Omega Alpha. Home: 100 Pembroke Ave Wayne PA 19087-4819 Office: 235 N 15th St Philadelphia PA 19102-1101 E-mail: josephdipalma@yahoo.com. *The creation of new ideas and approaches is always the ultimate goal.*

DI PAOLO, MARIA GRAZIA, language educator, writer; d. Alfredo and Giosina (Di Cicco) Di P.; m. Gianroberto Sarolli; 1 child, Giandomenico Sarolli. BA, Hunter Coll., 1969; MA, Columbia U., 1972, PhD, 1977. Instr. Columbia U., N.Y.C., 1973-77; asst. prof. Vassar Coll., Poughkeepsie, N.Y., 1977-85, CUNY, N.Y.C., 1985-90, assoc. prof., 1990-94, prof., 1994—, chair dept. langs. & lit. Lehman Coll., 2001—. Mem. pers. & budget com. Lehman Coll., CUNY, 1986—; chair Italian Rev. Panel CUNY Rsch. Found., 1988-89, 90-91, 96-97; mem. editl. bd. Can. Jour. Italian Studies, 1988—; pres. Italian Culture Soc. Lehman Coll., 1996-98. Author: B. Fenoglio, 1988; translator: Fenoglio's a Private Matter, 1988; editor: D'Annunzio's Correspondence with Son Veniero, 1994; contbr. articles to various publs. Recipient Faculty fellowship Columbia U., 1970-75, Sabbatical grant Vassar Coll., 1982-83, PSC-CUNY Rsch. award, 1988-89, 90-91, 2001—. Mem. MLA, Am. Assn. Tchrs. Italian. Roman Cath. Avocations: tennis, reading club, opera going. E-mail: mgdipaolo@cuny.edu.

DI PASQUALE, EMANUEL PAUL, poet, English language and literature educator; b. Sicily, Ragusa, Italy, Jan. 25, 1943; came to U.S., 1957; s. Serafino and Giuseppa (Scannavino) Di P.; children: Paul, Laura, Elizabeth. BA, Adelphi U., 1965; MA, NYU, 1966. Instr. Elizabeth (N.C.) City State U., 1966-68; asst. prof. English Middlesex County Coll., Edison, N.J., 1968—. Author: The Dynamics of Student Writing, 1984, Genesis, 1989, The Silver Lake Love Poems, 2000, Escapes the Night, 2001. Recipient Chelsea Poetry Prize, Chelsea Mag., 2002; fellow Raiziss/de Palchi Fellowship, Acad. of Am. Poets, 2002. Buddhist. Avocations: swimming, opera singing, swimming, walking. Office: Middlesex County Coll Edison NJ 08818

DIPENTIMA, RENATO ANTHONY, systems executive; b. Jan. 17, 1941; s. Victor and Mary (Cadolino) DiP.; m. Patricia Ellen Gillespie, July 24, 1965; children: Margaret Ellen, Katherine Alice. BA, NYU, 1963; MA, George Washington U., 1979; PhD, U. Md., 1984. With Social Security Adminstrn., N.Y.C., 1963, 68-69, ops. analyst Balt., 1969-70; sr. planning specialist Pres.'s Welfare Reform Task Force, HEW, Washington, 1970-72; chief mgmt. info. Bur. of Supplement Security Income Social Security Adminstrn., Balt., 1972-73, dir. sys., 1973-75, mem. strike force, 1975, dir. control and coord. Office of Advanced Sys., 1975-79, dir. assistance payments Office of Policy, 1979-82, exec. officer Nat. Commn. Social Security Reform, 1982, dep. assoc. commr. for sys. requirements, 1982-84, dep. assoc. commr. for sys. integration, 1984-88, assoc. commr. for sys. design and devel., 1988-90, dep. commr. for sys., 1990-95; v.p., chief info. officer Sys. Rsch. and Applications Corp., Arlington, Va., 1995-97; pres. SRA Fed. Sys., 1997-98, SRA Govt. Sector, 1999—2000, SRA Cons. and Sys. Integration, 2001—. Adj. faculty mem. U. Md., 1981-95, Loyola Coll., 1991-95; mem. adv. bd. Entrust, Inc. Mem. Coun. on Excellence, vice-chmn. industry adv. coun., 2002—. Recipient Under Sec.'s Spl. citation HEW, 1972, Sec.'s citation, 1974, Commr.'s citation Social Security Adminstrn., 1974, Dir.'s citation, 1979, Dep. Commr.'s citation, 1984, Commr.'s citation, 1991, Sec.'s Exec. Mgmt. citation Health and Human Svcs., 1987, Presdl. Meritorious Rank award, 1989, Presdl. Disting. Rank award, 1990. Mem. Nat. Acad. of Soc. Ins. Home: 4 Weems Creek Dr Annapolis MD 21401-

DIPERNA, FRANK PAUL, photographer, educator; b. Pitts., Feb. 4, 1947; s. Frank Paul and Virginia Carmella (DeRenna) DiP. BS in Mech. Engring., Va.Polytech. Inst., 1970; student, Visual Studies Workshop, 1971-72; MA in Photography, Goddard Coll., 1977. Assoc. prof. art and photography Corcoran Coll. Art and Design, Washington, 1974-94, prof., 1994—, chmn. photography dept., 1978—81, 1984—87, 1999—2002. Instr. photography No. Va. C.C., Alexandria, 1973-78, George Washington U., Washington, summer 1974; lectrs. and workshops Smithsonian Inst., 1976, Maine Photog. Inst. Rockport, 1977, Am. U., Washington, 1977, 78, 79, Internat. Ctr. Photography, N.Y.C., 1979, U. Del., 1981, James Madison U., Harrisonburg, Va., 1982, Rice U., Houston, No. Va. C.C., Sterling, 1991; resident Vt. Studio Ctr., Johnson, Vt., 1993, 2002. Solo exhbns. include Kathleen Ewing Gallery, Washington, 1982, 84, 89, 95, 98, 2000, Diane Brown Gallery, Washington, 1977, 78, 80, Bird in Hand Gallery, Alexandria, 1973, Corcoran Gallery Art, 1974, 77, Recontres Internationales de la Photographie, Arles, France, 1981, Rice Univ., Houston, 1986; group exhbns. include Athenaeum Mus., Alexandria, 1972, Photo Impressions Gallery, Washington, 1974, Va. Mus. Fine Arts, Richmond, 1973, 75, 80, The Franklin Inst., Phila., 1978, Susan Spiritus Gallery, Newport Beach, Calif., 1979, Mus. Fine Arts, Houston, 1979, Decordova Mus., Lincoln, Mass., 1979, Mpls. Inst. Arts, 1979, L.A. Inst. Contemporary Art, 1979, Denver Art Mus., 1979, Art Inst. Chgo., 1979, Phila. Coll. Art, 1980, Brown U., Providence, R.I., 1980, Arlington (Va.) Arts Ctr., 1981, Everson Mus. Art, Syracuse, N.Y., 1985, Comfort Gallery Haverford (Pa.) Coll., 1986, Washington Ctr. Photography, 1992, Nat. Mus. Am. Art, 1992, Smithsonian Inst., 1992, Carnegie Mus. Art, 1992, New Orleans Mus. Art, 1992, Corcoran Gallery of Art, 1994, 96, 98, Virginia's Photographers, Longwood Ctr. for the Visual Arts, Farmville, Va., 1997, Kathleen Ewing Gallery, Washington, 1999, Art Mus. Western Va., Roanoke, 2002, Smithsonian AM. Art Mus., 2003, 1708 Gallery, Richmond, Va., 2003, many others; represented in permanent collections Chrysler Mus., Norfolk, Va., Recontres Internationale de la Photographie, Arles, France, Bibliotheque Nationale, Paris, Libr. Cong., Washington, Polaroid (Euopa) Amsterdam, The Netherlands, Corcoran Gallery of Art, Va. Mus. Fine Arts, Smithsonian Inst., Balt. Mus. Art, Nat. Mus. Am. Art, Washington, Met. Mus. Art, N.Y., Ctr. for Creative Photography, U. Ariz. Artist-in-Residence Lightwork, Syracuse, N.Y., 1982, Camargo Found., Cassis, France, 1980, Vt. Studio Ctr., Johnson, 1992; Graduate fellow Va. Mus. Fine Arts, 1975. Avocations: tennis, fishing, playing guitar, birdwatching, furniture making. Office: Corcoran Coll Art & Design 500 17th St NW Washington DC 20006-4804

DIPIAZZA, MICHAEL CHARLES, insurance company executive; b. N.Y.C., Aug. 22, 1953; s. Carmelo and Grace (Vassallo) DiP.; m. Lillian Dugan, Dec. 21, 1979. CLU. Asst. v.p. sales Nat. Benefit Life Ins. Co., N.Y.C., 1975-79, asst. v.p. product devel., 1979-81; pres. Wm. B. Smith Agy., N.Y.C., 1979; cons. Ins. Sales Support Systems, Piscataway, N.J., 1981-82; asst. v.p. merchandising MONY, N.Y.C., 1982-86; v.p. merchandising Home Life Ins. Co., N.Y.C., 1986-92; asst. v.p. product devel. and mktg. MetLife, Bridgewater, N.J., 1992-97; v.p. mktg. MONY, N.Y.C., 1998—. Mem. Nat. Assn. Life Underwriters, Am. Soc. CLU's. Avocations: music, model railroading, wood working, Am. history.

DIPIAZZA, SAMUEL, JR., marketing professional; Degree acctg./econs., U. Ala.; MS Tax Acctg., U. Houston. Ptnr. Coopers & Lybrand, 1979, mem. firm coun., 1986, midwest regional mng. ptnr., 1992, regional mng. ptnr., client svc. vice chmn. N.Y. metro region, 1994, leader Ams. tax and legal svs., 1998—2000, mem. internat. tax bd., global tax and legal svc. exec., Pwc consulting global bd.; chmn, sr. ptnr. U.S. firm Pricewaterhouse Coopers, 2000—02, mem. global leadership team, CEO, 2002—. Trustee Fin. Acctg. Found. Mem. exec. coun. Inner City Sholarship Fund; mem. exec. com. Nat. Corp. Theatre Fund; pres. Big Bros./Sisters, N.Y.C.; mem. internat. adv. bd. Jr. Achievement; mem. bd. dirs. N.Y.C. Ballet. Named Acct. of Yr., Beta Alpha Psi Soc. ; recipient Ellis Island medal of honor, INROADS Leadership award. Mem.: Mergers and Acquistions Group (Frankfurt). Office: Pricewaterhouse Coopers 1301 Ave of Ams New York NY 10036*

DIPIETRO, JOSEPH A. dean, educator; DVM, U. Ill., 1976, Master's degree, 1980. Asst. prof., assoc. prof. vet. clin. medicine and vet. pathobiology U. Ill., 1980—90, acting assoc. dean, asst. dean for rsch., 1990—; acting and asst. dir. Agr. Experiment Sta. U. Ill. Coll. Agr.; assoc. dean rsch., 1994—; dean, prof. vet. parasitology U. Fla. Coll. Vet. Medicine, 1997—. Office: U Fla Coll Vet Medicine 2015 SW 16th Ave Gainesville FL 32610

DIPIETRO, RALPH ANTHONY, marketing and management consultant, educator; b. N.Y.C., Oct. 27, 1942; s. Joseph and Marie (Borelli) DiP. BBA, CUNY, 1964, MBA, 1966; PhD, NYU, 1972. Chmn., prof. mktg. and internat. bus. dept. Sch. Bus. Montclair State U., Upper Montclair, N.J., 1972—. Adj. prof. mgmt. NYU, 1976-97, mgmt. tng. dir. Inst. Retail Mgmt., 1976-86; cons. Mfrs. Hanover Trust, N.Y.C., 1979-85, Sharp Electronics, N.Y.C., 1980-94, Battus Corp., N.Y.C., 1982-85, AT&T Bell Labs., 1989-91; program dir. Bally of Switzerland, N.Y.C., 1981-93, Fortunoff's, N.Y.C., 1984-86. Author: Managerial Effectiveness: A Review and an Empirical Testing of a Model, 1973; contbr. articles to profl. jours. Mem. Am. Mktg. Assn., Acad. Mktg. Scis., Internat. Assn. Applied Psychology, Omicron Delta Epsilon. Avocations: tennis, swimming, opera. Home: 12 Manor Dr Warren NJ 07059

DIPKO, THOMAS EARL, retired minister, national church executive; b. St. Michael, Pa., June 26, 1936; s. John and Sarah Jane (Gittins) D.; m. Sandra Jane Faust, Nov. 19, 1960; children: Lisa Renee, Sarah Marie. BA, Otterbein Coll., 1958; MDiv, United Theol. Sem., 1961; PhD in Ecumenical Theology, Boston U., 1969; LLD (hon.), Heidelberg Coll., 1987; DD (hon.), United Theol. Sem. of the Twin Cities, 1992; LHD (hon.), The Defiance Coll., 1992; DD (hon.), Elmhurst Coll., 1993, Ursinus Coll., 1994. ordained min. Youth min. First United Methodist Ch., Dayton, Ohio, 1958-61; ecumenical intern social action office Ch. Rhineland-Westphalia, Germany, 1962; asst. pastor First Ch. Congregational, Swampscott, Mass., 1963-64; pastor First United Methodist Ch., East Conemaugh, Pa., 1964-66; asst. pastor South Ch. Congregational, Andover, Mass., 1966-68; sr. pastor Christ Ch. United in Lowell, Mass., 1969-77, Grace Congregational Ch., Framingham, Mass., 1977-84; conf. min. and exec. Ohio conf. United Ch. of Christ, Columbus, 1984-92; exec. v.p. United Ch. Bd. for Homeland Ministries, Cleve., 1992-2000. Mem. bd. trustees The Defiance Coll., 1985—; mem. exec. com. Consultation on Church Union, 1989—2002; del. Seventh Assembly World Coun. Churches, Canberra, Australia, 1991; mem. bd. dirs. Ryder Meml. Hosp., Humacao, Puerto Rico, 1993-96. Author: (first draft, book) United Church of Christ Book of Worship, 1986; contbr. chpts. to books, articles to profl. jours. Chmn. Lowell Drug Action Com., 1971-74; mem. bd. dirs. Internat. Inst., 1971-77. Samaritans (suicide intervention), 1983-84; del. gen. coun. World Alliance Reformed Chs., Debrecen, Hungary, 1997; bd. trustees LeMoyne-Owen Coll. Fellow Coll. Preachers, 1983. Mem. N.Am. Acad. Ecumenists (mem. exec. com. 1981-83), Christians Associated for Rels. in Eastern Europe, Consultation on Common Texts. Avocations: swimming, perennial gardening, canoeing.

DI PRIMA, STEPHANIE MARIE, educational administrator; b. Chgo., Aug. 29, 1952; d. Joseph and Ann Marie (Albate) Di P. BA in English, Rosary Coll., 1974; MEd in Adminstrn. and Supervision, Loyola U., Chgo., 1979. Tchr. St. Vincent Ferrer Sch., River Forest, Ill., 1974-78; prin. Our Lady of Hope Sch., Rosemont, Ill., 1978-81, Sacred Heart Sch., Winnetka, Ill., 1981-84, St. Monica Sch., Chgo., 1984-91, St. Martha Sch., Morton Grove, Ill., 1991-97; asst. prin. for student svcs. St. Viator H.S., Arlington Heights, Ill., 1997-2000; prin. Queen of All Saints Sch., Chgo., 2000—. Instr. Rosary Coll., River Forest, Ill., Dominican U., River Forest, Ill., 1988—. Mem. ASCD, Nat. Cath. Ednl. Assn., Ill. Prins. Assn., Ill. Assn. Supervision and Curriculum Devel., Women in Mgmt., Nat. Assn. Elem. Sch. Principals. Avocations: piano, reading, theatre and fine arts, needlecrafts, travel. Office: Queen of All Sts Sch 6230 N Lemont Ave Chicago IL 60646-4910

DIR, DAVE, professional soccer coach; b. June 23, 1959; Student, Western Ill. U. Profl. soccer player Chgo. Sting, 1980-84; soccer coach Trinity Prep Luth. Sch., Orlando, Fla., 1984-90; coach Regis U., Denver, 1990-92; head coach Colo. Foxes, 1992-93; dir. player devel. Major League Soccer, 1993-95; head coach Dallas Burn, 1995—. Goalkeeper coach U.S. Youth Soccer Assn. Region IV Olympic Devel. Program. Named Coach of the Yr., Colo. Athletic Conf., 1991. Office: c/o Dallas Burn 2602 Mckinney Ave Ste 200 Dallas TX 75204-8543

DIRCKS, PHYLLIS TOAL, English language educator; b. N.Y.C., Jan. 8, 1935; d. John Joseph and Catherine Henderson (Whyte) T.; m. Richard Joseph Dircks, Aug. 17, 1963; children: Cathy, Laurie, Deirdre, Richard, Joseph, Gillian. BA summa cum laude, St. John's U., N.Y.C., 1957; MA, Brown U., 1960; PhD, N.Y. U., 1967. Instr. Coll. New Rochelle, N.Y., 1958-61, St. John's U., 1961-63; instr. to prof. Long Island U., Brookville, N.Y., 1963—. Exec. sec Long Island British Studies Group, 1974-80. Author: David Garrick, 1985, Two Burlettas of Kane O'Hara, 1987, The Eighteenth Century English Burletta, 1999; editor: American Puppetry; contbr. numerous articles to profl. jours. Assoc. Danforth Found., 1986-92. Grantee Danforth Found., 1965, 66, 67; NEH, 1993, 94; fellow Am. Coun. Learned Societies, 1972, Nat. Woodrow Wilson Fellowship Found., 1957. Mem. MLA, Am. Soc. Theatre Rsch. (exec. com. 1973—, editor newsletter 1973-94, archivist 1978-2002), Soc. Theatre Rsch., Am. Soc. 18th Century Studies. Home: 5 Edwin Ln Huntington NY 11743-2332 Office: Long Island Univ CW Post Campus Greenvale NY 11548 E-mail: dircks@liu.edu.

DIRCKS, RICHARD JOSEPH, English language educator, writer; b. N.Y.C., May 22, 1926; s. Curt and Georgette Elizabeth (Middleton) D; m. Phyllis Ann Toal, Aug. 17, 1963; children: Cathy, Laurie, Deirdre, Richard, Gillian, Joseph. BA, Fordham U., 1949, MA, 1950, PhD, 1961. Asst. prof. Seton Hall U., South Orange, N.J., 1950-56; from asst. prof. to prof. English, St. John's U., Jamaica, N.Y., 1956—, chmn. dept., 1964-67, 94-95, assoc. dean grad. sch., 1973-75, dir. humanities rsch. ctr., 1975-77. Departmental rep., St. John's Coll., 1962-64; lectr. in writing Fordham Sch. Adult Edn., 1963-69; cons. on writing Union Carbide Corp., N.Y.C., 1968-69. Author: Richard Cumberland, 1976, Henry Fielding, 1983; co-author: Functional English, 1959; editor: Letters of Richard Cumberland, 1988, The Unpublished Plays of Richard Cumberland, 2 vols., 1991-92, The Memoirs of Richard Cumberland, 2001; contbr. numerous articles to profl. jours. With U.S. Army, 1944-45. Shell Rsch. Grantee, 1967; assoc. Danforth Found., 1978-86. Mem. MLA, Am. Soc. 18th-Century Studies, Am. Soc. For Theatre Rsch. Avocations: sailing, photography. Home and Office: 5 Edwin Ln Huntington NY 11743-2332

DIRECTOR, STEPHEN WILLIAM, electrical and computer engineering educator, academic administrator; b. Bklyn., June 28, 1943; s. Murray and Lillian (Brody) D.; m. Lorraine Schwartz, June 20, 1965; children: Joshua, Kimberly, Cynthia, Deborah. BS, SUNY, Stony Brook, 1965; MS, U. Calif., Berkeley, 1967, PhD, 1968. Prof. elec. engring. U. Fla., Gainesville, 1968-77; vis. scientist IBM Rsch. Labs., Yorktown Heights, N.Y., 1974-75; prof. elec. and computer engring. Carnegie-Mellon U., Pitts., 1977-96, U.A. and Helen Whitaker Univ. prof. electrical and computer engring., 1980-96, prof. computer sci., 1981-96, head dept. elec. and computer engring., 1982-91; univ. prof., 1992-93; dean Carnegie Inst. Tech. Carnegie-Mellon U., Pitts., 1991-96; Robert J. Vlasic Dean of Engring. U. Mich., Ann Arbor, 1996—, prof. elec. engring. and computer science, 1996—. Advisor info. and comm. tech. Techno Venture Mgmt., 1999—2002; sr. rsch. fellow IC2 Inst., 1996—; sr. cons. editor McGraw-Hill Book Co., N.Y.C., 1976—; dir. Rsch. Ctr. Computer-Aided Design, Pitts., 1982—89; mem. tech. adv. bd. Nextwave, Inc., 1990—95, CAD Framework Initiative, 1991—93, Aspect Devel. Corp., 1991—92, JW2 Inc., 1991—94, LSI Logic, 1994, Autogate Logic, 1994—96, EDF Ventures, 1999—; bd. dirs. Job Gravity, 1999—; mem. adv. coun. Lutron Electronics Inc., 1999—; cons. in field. Author: Introduction to System Theory, 1972, Circuit Theory, 1975, VLSI Design for Manufacturing: Yield Enhancement, 1989, Principles of VLSI System Planning: A Framework for Conceptual Design, 1991; editor: Computer-Aided Design, 1974; co-editor: Advances in Computer-Aided Design for VLSI: vol. 8, Statistical Approach to VLSI, 1994. Chair bd. dirs. Am. Soc. Engring. Edn., Engring. Deans Coun., 1999-2001. Recipient Frederick Emmons Terman award Am. Soc. Engring. Edn., 1976; named Distinguished Alumnus, SUNY, Stony Brook, 1984; Aristotle Award Semiconductor Rsch. Corp., 1996, Outstanding Alumnus award in Elec. Engring. U. Calif., Berkeley, 1996, Berkeley Disting. Engring. Alumnus award, U. Calif., 1999; named Hon. Prof. of Shanghai Jiao Tong U., 2002. Fellow IEEE (W.R.G. Baker prize 1979, Edn. Soc. Outstanding Achievement award 1995, Edn. medal 1998, Millennium medal 2000); mem. NAE (chair com. on engring. edn.), IEEE Cirs. and Sys. Soc. (pres. 1981, assoc. editor jour. 1973-75, best paper award 1970, 85, 89, 92, Centennial medal 1984, soc. award 1992, Golden Jubilee medal 1999). Office: Univ Michigan Coll Engring Robert H Lurie Engring Ctr Ann Arbor MI 48109 E-mail: director@umich.edu.

DIRENZO, GORDON JAMES, sociologist, psychologist, educator; b. North Attleboro, Mass., July 19, 1934; s. Santo and Giulia (Petti) DiR.; m. Mary Kathleen Ryan, July 6, 1968; children: Maria Giulia, Chiara Veronica, Marco Santo. BA, U. Notre Dame, 1956, MA, 1957, PhD, 1963; postgrad., Harvard U., 1959, Columbia U., 1963-65, U. Colo., 1964. Lic. psychologist, Del.; cert. social psychologist. Instr. Coll. of St. Rose, Albany, N.Y., 1957-59; Instr. U. Portland, Oreg., 1961-62; asst. prof. Fairfield (Conn.) U., 1962-66; asso. prof. Ind. U., South Bend, 1966-70; prof. sociology U. Del., Newark, 1970—; mem. faculty Siena Coll., Albany (N.Y.) Med. Center, 1958-59, U. Notre Dame, 1960-61, Coll. White Plains, 1963-65, Bklyn. Coll., 1965, Western Conn. State U., 1964, SUNY, Stony Brook, 1980, Cortland, 1966; affiliate mem. med. and dental staff Med. Center Del., Wilmington, 1976-80, St. Francis Hosp., Wilmington, 1980—, Northeastern Hosp., Phila., 1982-85, Rockford Ctr., Wilmington, 1995—. Pres. Behavior Cons., Newark, Del., 1975—; dir. Sociol. Cons. Group, North Attleboro, Mass., 1963-75; Fulbright-Hays prof. U. Rome, 1968-69, U. Bologna, Italy, 1980-81; mem., exec. sec., bd. examiners psychologists State of Del., 1991-99, 2003—. Author: Concepts, Theory and Explanation in the Behavioral Sciences, 1966, Personality, Power and Politics, 1967, Personality and Politics, 1974, We, the People: American Character and Social Change, 1977, Sociological Perspectives, 1987, Human Social Behavior, 1990, Personality and Society, 2001, The Social Individual, 2002, Individuo e Società, 2003; contbr. articles to profl. jours. Recipient Disting. Svc. award Am. Assn. Family Practice, 1980, 82, 84, Excellence in Teaching award U. Del., 1991; fellow U. Notre Dame, 1959-60, Italian Ministry Edn., 1960, NSF, 1964; grantee Ford Found., 1960, NEH, 1975, Del. Inst. Med. Edn. and Rsch., 1975. Fellow Am. Sociol. Assn. (diplomate); mem. APA, AAUP, AAAS, Assn. Behavioral Scis. in Med. Edn., Soc. Personality and Social Psychology, Soc. for Advancement Social Psychology (bd. dirs. 1988-94), Am.-Italian Hist. Assn. (nat. exec. council 1977-80), Fulbright Alumni Assn., Internat. Sociol. Assn., Clin. Sociology Assn., Internat. Soc. Polit. Psychology (charter), Soc. Psychologists in Medicine, Internat. Polit. Sci. Assn., Soc. for Study Social Problems, Soc. Psychol. Study Social Issues, Eastern Sociol. Soc., Am. Sociol. Assn., Nat. Assn. Scholars, Alpha Kappa Delta. Home: 28 Deer Run Little Baltimore Farms Newark DE 19711 Office: U Del Dept Sociology Newark DE 19716 E-mail: gdirenzo@udel.edu.

DIRETTE, DIANE KAY, occupational therapist, educator; d. Lewis Eugene Powers and Janice Marie Hilliker; m. Floyd Leonard Dirette, July 26, 1986; children: Madeleine Kay, Claire Marie. BS, Ea. Mich. U., 1985; MA, PhD, NYU, 1997. Cert. occupl. therapist Mich., 1985. Occupl. therapist Kessler Inst. for Rehab., East Orange, NJ, 1986—96; prof. Ea. Mich. U., Ypsilanti, 1996—99, Western Mich. U., Kalamazoo, 1999—. Recipient Rsch. Devel. award, Western Mich. U., 2001. Mem.: Am. Occupl. Therapy Assn. Avocations: tennis, rollerblading, swimming, bicycling. Office: Western Mich Univ 1903 WMichigan Ave Kalamazoo MI 49008 Office Fax: 269-387-7262. Personal E-mail: diane.dirette@wmich.edu. E-mail: diane.dirette@wmich.edu.

DIRIENZO, MARGARET HELEN, nursing administrator; b. Tampa, Fla., May 17, 1962; d. Raymond Thomas and Helen Irene (onnors; m. James Basilio Dirienzo, Sept. 21, 1984; children: James, Kaitlyn. AAS, Pace U., 1982, BSN, 1985. RN, cert. emergency nurse, ACLS, PALS. From staff nurse to asst. mgr. emergency dept. Danbury (Conn.) Hosp., 1982-92; patient care mgr. asst. ER Geisinger Med. Ctr., Danville, Pa., 1992-94; sr. mgr. customer access svcs. Geisinger Health Sys., Danville, 1994-99; dir. patient care svcs. Call Ctr. Seton Med. Ctr., Austin, Tex., 1999-2000; dir. critical care svcs. North Austin Med. Ctr., Austin, 2000—. Acting trauma coord. Danbury Hosp., 1991-92. Mem. Emergency Nurses Assn. Democrat. Roman Catholic. Avocations: cross stitch, travel, craft making. Home: 1553 Jerusalem Dr Round Rock TX 78664-8618 Office: North Austin Med Ctr Austin TX 78708 E-mail: marge.dirienzo@stdavids.com.

DIRKS, KENNETH RAY, pathologist, medical educator, army officer; b. Newton, Kans., Feb. 11, 1925; s. Jacob Kenneth and Ruth Viola (Penner) D.; m. Betty Jean Worsham, June 9, 1946; children: Susan Jan, Jeffrey Mark, Deborah Anne, Timothy David, Melissa Jane. MD, Washington U., St. Louis, 1947. Diplomate: Am. Bd. Pathology. Rotating intern St. Louis City Hosp., 1948, asst. resident in gen. surgery, 1948-49; resident in pathology VA Hosp., Jefferson Barracks, Mo., 1951-53, resident in pathology, asst. chief lab. service Indpls., 1953-54; resident in pathology Letterman Army Hosp., San Francisco, 1956-57; fellow in tropical medicine and parasitology La. State U., Central Am., 1958; asst. in pathology Washington U. Sch. Medicine, 1952-53; asst. chief lab. service VA Hosp., Jefferson Barracks, 1953; instr. pathology U. Ind. Med. Center, Indpls., 1953-54; commd. capt. M.C. U.S. Army, 1954, advanced through grades to maj. gen., 1976; dir. research Med. Research and Devel. Command, Washington, 1968-69, dep. comdr., 1969-71, comdr., 1973-76; asst. surgeon gen., research and devel. U.S. Army, 1973-76; dep. comdr., comdr. Med. Research Inst. Infectious Diseases, Ft. Detrick, Frederick, Md., 1972-73; comdr. Fitzsimons Army Med. Center, Denver, 1976-77; supt. Acad. Health Scis., Ft. Sam Houston, Tex., 1977-80; assoc. prof. to prof. pathology and lab. medicine Coll. Med. Tex. A&M U., College Station, 1980-95; interim head dept. Coll. Medicine, Tex. A&M U., College Station, 1990-91; prof. emeritus pathology, 1995—; asst. dean coll. Coll. Medicine, Tex. A&M U., College Station, 1985-88; dir. dept. student health svcs. and A.P. Beutel Health Ctr. Tex. A&M U., College Station, 1989-95; dir. student health svcs. emeritus, 1995—. Contbr. articles to med. jours. Decorated D.S.M., Legion of Merit with oak leaf cluster, Meritorious Service medal, Army Commendation medal with oak leaf cluster. Fellow Coll. Am. Pathologists, Internat. Acad. Pathology. Address: 2513 Oak Cir Bryan TX 77802-2009 E-mail: kdemeritus@aol.com. *1) Know your job and work hard. 2) Respect all persons. 3) Be candid and honest always. 4)Persevere in the face of adversity. 5) Love God, country, and other people. 6) Help others.*

DIRKS, LEE EDWARD, newspaper executive; b. Indpls., Aug. 4, 1935; s. Raymond Louis and Virginia Belle (Wagner) Dirks; m. Barbara Dee Nutt, June 16, 1956 (div. Jan. 1985); children: Stephen Merle, Deborah Virginia, David Louis; m. Judith Ann Putman, Dec. 28, 2001. BA, DePauw U., 1956; MA, Fletcher Sch. Law and Diplomacy, 1957. Reporter Boston Globe, 1957, Nat. Observer, Washington, 1962-65, news editor, 1966-68; securities analyst specializing in newspaper stocks Dirks Bros., Ltd., Washington, 1969-71, Delafield, Childs, Inc., Washington, 1971-75, C.S. McKee & Co., Washington, 1975-76; asst. to pres. Detroit Free Press, 1976-77, v.p., gen. mgr., 1977-80; chmn. Dirks, Van Essen & Murray, Santa Fe, N.Mex., 1980—. Author: Religion in Action, 1965; pub. Newspaper Newsletter, 1970-76. Bd. dirs. Nat. Ghost Ranch Found., Santa Fe, 1973-97, Santa Fe Opera, 1998—; pres. Georgia O'Keeffe Mus., Santa Fe, 2000—. Capt. USAF, 1957-61. Named Religion Writer of Yr. Religious Newswriters Assn., 1964 Fellow Religious Pub. Relations Council; mem. Phi Beta Kappa, Lambda Chi Alpha. Clubs: Nat. Press (Washington); Oakland Hills (Detroit); Las Campanas (Santa Fe). Presbyterian. Home: 11 E Arrowhead Cir Santa Fe NM 87506-8248 Office: 119 E Marcy St Ste 100 Santa Fe NM 87501-2046 E-mail: info@dirksvanessen.com.

DIRKS, LESLIE CHANT, communications and electronics company executive; b. New Ulm, Minn., Mar. 7, 1936; s. Emerald Francis and Eva Gay (Fabianke) D.; m. Janet Church; children: Anthony, Jason, Elizabeth. BS in Physics, MIT, 1958; BS, Oxford (Eng.) U., 1960. Registered elec. engr., Calif. Instr. physics Philips Acad., Andover, Mass., 1960-61; with office directorate of Sci. & Tech. U.S. Govt., Washington, 1961-71, dir. Office of Spl. Projects., 1971-76, dep. dir. Sci. and Tech., 1976-82; corp. v.p. of research and devel. Raytheon Corp., Lexington, Mass., 1982-84; v.p. Space and Communications group Hughes Aircraft Co., El Segundo, Calif., 1984-90, ret., 1990. Recipient Nat. Security Metal Pres. U.S., 1978. Mem. Nat. Acad. Engring., Nat. Research Council (mem. Army-Space com. 1986—). Unitarian Universalist. Avocations: hiking, bicycling. Home: Torrance, Calif. Died Aug. 2001.

DIROLL, DAVID JOHN, lawyer; b. Youngstown, Ohio, June 2, 1951; s. Robert Joseph and Catherine Lucia (Petergal) D.; m. Linda Beals; children: Benjamin, Caroline, William. BA, Youngstown State U., 1974; JD, Ohio State U., 1977. Bar: Ohio 1977. Staff atty. Ohio Legis. Svc. Commn., Columbus, 1977-85; policy chief Gov.'s Office Criminal Justice Svcs., Columbus, 1985-91; dir. Ohio Criminal Sentencing Commn., 1991—. Dir. Gov.'s Com. on Prison and Jail Crowding, Columbus, 1985-90; mem. faculty Ohio Jud. Coll., 1992, 95-2003, Nat. Conf. State Legislators, 1992, Ohio State U. Learning Guild, 1990, Ohio CLE Inst., 1995-98, 2001; mem. Lt. Gov.'s Work Group on Prison

Crowding, 1992, Lt. Gov.'s Task Force on Parole, 1992-94, Gov.'s/Chief Justice's Task Force on Pre-Sentence Investigations, 1995, Gov.'s task force on impaired driving, 2003; registered lobbyist Ohio Gen. Assembly, 1998-2003; mem. steering com. Ohio Ctr. Law-Related Edn., Columbus, 1990, Ohio Risk Think Tank, 1992-95; judge Ohio Mock Trial, 1990, 91, 92, 93, 99, 2000; chmn. legis. work group Dept. Alcohol and Drugs, Columbus, 1990. Author, editor: Victorian Village Architectural Guidelines, 1988, Ohio Felony Sentencing Manual, 1996, 2002, Ohio Juvenile Sentencing Manual, 2001, 2002, Ohio Traffic Law Primer, 2003; contbr. articles to publs. Mem. City Coun. Appeals Task Force, Columbus, 1988, Downtown Housing Task Force, Columbus, 1988, Victorian Village Traffic Com., 1994-95; chmn. Victorian Village Commn., Columbus, 1987-96; com. chair Victorian Village Tour of Homes, Columbus, 1986-94; youth soccer coach, 1994-98, youth baseball coach, 1996-99. Recipient Cert. of Appreciation, Columbus City Coun., 1987, 88, Recognition award Crime Victims Assistance Program, Akron, 1989, Pub. Policy Leadership award Ohio Ct. of Claims Victims Program, 1996; named one of Outstanding Young Men Am., 1987. Mem. Nat. Assn. Sentencing Commns., Victorian Village Soc. (trustee 1987-89, tour com. 1986-90, program chair 1984-85), Actors' Theatre Co. Avocations: music, history, sports, architecture. Home: 6741 Lower Brook Way New Albany OH 43054-9366 Office: Ohio Criminal Sentencing Co 513 E Rich St Ste 100 Columbus OH 43215-5376 E-mail: dirolld@sconet.state.oh.us.

DIROSA, STEVEN JOSEPH, primary and secondary school educator; b. Phila. s. Joseph and Patricia (Bealer) D. BS, Temple U., 1989; MS in Ednl. Technologies, Rosemont Coll., 1996. Cert. elem., secondary tchr., Pa. Tchr., dept. head Chester-Upland (Pa.) Sch. Dist., 1989-2000; spl. assignmnet middle sch. tchr. Penn-Delco Sch. Dist., 2000—. Tech. dir. STEP Summer Student Prog., Chester, Pa., 1990-95; intramural sports asst. dir. Chester-Upland Sch. Dist., 1993-96. Author: Travel Tales (Billy the Shoe), 1989 (best children's short story award Pa. Tchr. Pages 1990). Recipient Pres.' award Pres.' Acad. Excellence Com., Rosemont, Pa., 1992, outstanding svc. award S.E. Pa. STEP Prog., Chester, Pa., 1994. Fellow Smithsonian Instn.; mem. World Wildlife Fund, Nat. Coun. Tchrs. Math., Sierra Club, Audubon Soc. Home: 232 Talbot Dr Broomall PA 19008-3729 Office: STS 849 Providence Rd Media PA 19063

DIRUSCIO, LAWRENCE WILLIAM, advertising executive; b. Buffalo, Jan. 2, 1941; s. Guido Carmen and Mabel Ella (Bach) DiR.; m. Gloria J. Edney, Aug. 19, 1972; children: Lawrence M., Lorie P., Darryl C., Teresa M., Jack D. With various broadcast stas. and instr., adminstr. Bill Wade Sch. Radio and TV, San Diego, San Francisco, Los Angeles, 1961-69; account exec. Sta. KGB Radio, San Diego, 1969, gen. sales mgr., 1970-72; pres. Free Apple Advt., San Diego, 1972-94, Fin. Mgmt. Assocs., Inc., San Diego, 1979-84, Self-Pub. Ptnrs., San Diego, 1981—, Media Mix Assocs. Enterprises, Inc., 1984-86; pres. Press-Courier Pub. Co., Inc., 1985-86; pres. Media Mix Advt. and Pub. Relations, 1985—, Taking Care of Bus. Pub. Co., 1990—; pres. Formula Mktg. Co., 1993. Chmn. bd. Quicksilver Enterprises, Inc., A Public Corp., 1992-93; lectr., writer on problems of small bus. survival. Served with USN, 1958-60. Five Emmy nominations for T.V. commercial writing and prodn. Mem. Nat. Acad. TV Arts and Scis. Democrat. Roman Catholic. Office: Media Mix Advt and Pub Rels 726 W Kalmia St San Diego CA 92101-1311

DI RUSSO, TERRY, communications educator, writer; b. Trenton, N.J., Nov. 1, 1947; d. Joy (Urban) Rooy; m. Dennis John, June 23, 1973 (div. July 1985); 1 child, Elaine Marie; m. Robert L. DiRusso, Aug. 17, 2002. BS in Comm., Psychology, Edn., Murray State U., 1970, MS in Comm., 1971; postgrad., Cen. Conn. State U., New Britain, 1972. Tchr., teaching asst. Murray (Ky.) State U., Murray, Ky., 1970-71; instr. adult edn. Wincester Bd. of Edn., Winsted, Conn., 1973-76; special lectr. Central Conn. State U., New Britain, Conn., 1975-85; lectr. comm. dept. Tunxis C.C., Farmington, Conn., 1986—; comm. lectr. U. Conn., Waterbury, 1986, Torrington, 1986—; English educator Wincester Bd. of Edn., Conn., 1971—. Cons., lectr. Vets. Hosp. Nursing Staff, Meridan, 1981, Bus. and Profl. Women, 1982; faculty cons. Conn. State Conf. Emergency Med. Techs., Hartford, 1988-96; cons. Pvt. Individuals Pub. Speaking Coach, 1976—; comms. lectr. gender comms. and sexual harassment United Techs., E. Hartford, Conn., 1995; presenter in field. Author: (mystery novel, as Terry Finello) Absolute Vengeance, 1999; mem. editl. bd. Elements of Speech Comm., 3rd edit., 1995. Mem. AAUP, NEA, Conn. Edn. Assn., Winsted Edn. Assn., Nat. Coun. Tchrs. English, New Eng. League Mid. Schs., Litchfield County Women's Network, Conn. Assn. Pubs. and Authors. Avocations: tennis, writing. Home: 126 Winterbourne Ln Canton CT 06019 Office: Univ of Conn University Dr Torrington CT 06790 E-mail: tdirusso@snet.net.

DIRVIN, GERALD VINCENT, retired consumer products company executive; b. Phila., Mar. 28, 1937; s. Vincent A. and Mary (Fitch) D.; m. Polly Burnett, June 27, 1959; children: John, David, Barbara. BA, Hamilton Coll., Clinton, N.Y., 1959. With Procter & Gamble Co., 1959-94, sales mgt., then v.p. coffee divsn., 1975-80, group v.p., 1980-89, exec. v.p., 1990-94, dir., 1981-94. Bd. dirs. Cintas Corp. Bd. trustees Hamilton Coll. Mem. Comml. Club, Plantation Golf Club, Commonwealth Club, Camargo Club, Pine Valley Golf Club, Double Eagle Golf Club, Confrerei des Chevaliers du Tastevin, Pablo Creek Golf Club, Kingsley Golf Club, Ponte Vedra Club. Republican. Roman Catholic. E-mail: 9dirvin@aol.com.

DISA, JOSEPH JAMES, plastic surgeon; s. Rose and Ralph Disa; m. Julie Lynn Stebbins, Oct. 2, 1961. MD, U. of Mass., Worcester, MA, 1984—88. American Board of Plastic Surgery Am. Bd. of Med. Specialties, 1999, American Board of Surgery Am. Bd. of Med. Specialties, 1995. Attending surgeon Meml. Sloan-Kettering Cancer Ctr., New York, NY, 1997—; asst. prof. of plastic surgery Cornell Weill Sch. of Medicine, New York, NY, 1997—2003. Fellow: ACS; mem.: Am. Soc. of Reconstructive Microsurgery, Am. Soc. of Plastic Surgeons. Achievements include research in Microsurgical Reconstruction. Office: Memorial Sloan-Kettering Cancer Center 1275 York Avenue New York NY 10021 Office Fax: 212-717-3677.

DISALLE, MICHAEL DANNY, secondary education educator; b. Denver, May 16, 1945; s. Michael and Agnes Marie (Kulik) DiS.; m. Marikaye Lucas, June 22, 1968; children: Katharine Marie, Kristin Jean, Michael Charles, Matthew Gregory. BA, Regis Coll., 1967; MEd, Lesley Coll., 1992. Cert. tchr., Colo. Tchr. Assumption Sch., Welby, Colo., 1968-74, Cherry Creek High Sch., Englewood, Colo., 1974-95; poet, writer, 1995—. Author: (computer program/tchr.'s guide) Adventures of Tom Sawyer, 1983, One Day in the Life of Ivan Denisovich, 1984. Asst. den leader Boy Scouts Am., Aurora, Colo., 1988-89. Avocations: fly fishing, gardening, cooking, fly tying.

DI SALVO, NICHOLAS ARMAND, dental educator, orthodontist; b. N.Y.C., Nov. 2, 1920; s. Frank and Mary (Ruberto) DiS.; m. Pauline Rose Pluta, June 2, 1945; children— Allan, Donald BS, CCNY, 1942; D.D.S., Columbia U., 1945, PhD in Physiology, 1952, cert. in orthodontics, 1957. Diplomate Am. Bd. Orthodontics. Fellow Inst. Dental Research, Columbia U., 1950-52; instr. physiology Coll. Physicians and Surgeons, Columbia U., 1948-51, asst. prof. physiology, 1952-57, assoc., 1957-58, prof. dentistry, 1958-87, dir. orthodontics, 1957-87, prof. emeritus dentistry, 1987—; attending dentist Presbyterian Hosp., N.Y.C., 1975-87, cons. emeritus dentistry, 1987—. Cons. N.Y. State Dept. Health, 1970—, VA, N.Y.C., 1975, Project/HOPE/Egypt, Alexandria and Cairo, 1976, Nat. Def. Med. Ctr., Taipei, Taiwan, 1982 Contbg. editor book chpts. Contbr. articles to profl. jours. Pres., Hartsdale-Fels Civic Assn., 1960-66. Served to lt. USNR, 1945-50 Recipient Disting. Service award Orthodontic Alumni Soc. Columbia U., 1973; fellow 8th Inst. Advanced Edn. in Dental Research Mem. Am. Assn. Orthodontists (del. 1970-76), Northeastern Soc. Orthodontists (pres. 1974-75, Disting. Svc. award 1995), Angle Soc. of Orthodontists (pres. 1977-79), Internat. Soc. Craniofacial Biology (pres. 1965-66). Republican. Roman Catholic. Home: 145 Princeton Dr Hartsdale NY 10530-2010 Office: Columbia U Dental Sch 630 W 168th St New York NY 10032-3702

DISANTO, CAROL L. (CAROL LA CHIUSA), artist; b. Cleve., July 26, 1930; d. Theodore Christian Jenks and Evelyn Mildred Bushnell; m. Salvatore A. Lachiusa, Sept. 14, 1950 (dec. Feb. 1991); children: Drew, Cyd Marie, Dean, Dane; m. Paris Di Santo, June 28, 1992. Student, Cleve. Inst. Art, 1948-50, U. Mexico, Puebla, 1992. Art instr. Grosse Pointe (Mich.) War Meml., 1969-99; watercolor instr. The Art Ctr., Mt. Clemens, Mich., 1988-99, instr., 1988—2002. Host watercolor workshop program Grosse Pointe Cable TV-Comcast, 1986—2002; workshop lectr. Crooked Tree Art Assn., Petoskey, Mich., 1986—87; exhbn. lectr. Kettering U., Flint, Mich., 1999; lectr. various art assns., Mich., 1981—99; artist-in-residence Grosse Pointe War Meml., 1996—98. One-woman shows include Troy Art Gallery, Royal Oak, Mich., 1979, 1984, 1991, 1994, Venice, Italy, 2001, Mich. Women's Hist. Ctr. and Hall of Fame, Lansing, 2002, Remember Mama, 2002, The Art Ctr., Mt. Clemens, Mich., 2003, Grosse Artists Ctr., Mich., 2003, prin. works include Rockport Best of Watercolor, 1997, Encyclopedia of Living Artists, 11th edit., 1998, Am. Artist Mag., 1999, Grace Mag., 1999, Encyclopedia of Living Artists, 12th edit., Grosse Pointe News, 1995—97, exhibited in group shows at Gallery Bai, N.Y., N.Y., 1998, Mich. Watercolor Travelling Show, 2001, Women's Show, Plymouth, Mich., 2003 (1st prize, 03), Great Lakes Juried Show, 2003 (3d prize, 03), Detroit (Mich.) Women Painters and Sculptors, 2003 (1st prize, 03). Co-founder Grosse Pointe Arts Coun., 1993, pres., 1995-97. Mem.: Mich. Coun. Arts and Cultural Affairs, Grosse Pointe Artists Assn. (v.p. 1988—90), Detroit Soc. Women Painters and Sculptors (pres. 1998—2000), Mich. Watercolor Soc., Mich. Assn. Cmty. Arts Agys., Grosse Pointe United Ch. Womens Assn. (bd. 1999—, pres. 2001—). Home: 418 Barclay Rd Grosse Pointe MI 48236-2814

DISBERGER, DENNIS JAY, manufacturing executive; b. Syracuse, Kans., Sept. 9, 1958; s. Jay M. and Vina E. Disberger; m. Martha Ann Kater, June 6, 1981; children: Joel, Kara, Monica. BSME, Kans. State U., 1981, MBA, 1984. Cert. engr. Mgr. Disberger Harvesting, Hutchinson, Kans., 1976-81; quality supr. Caterpillar Tractor Co., Peoria, Ill., 1982, devel. engr., 1984-86, svc. mgr. Hartford, Conn., 1986-90, quality mgr. Caterpillar Inc., Aurora, Ill., 1991-93, mktg. cons., 1993-95; program mgr. combines, new product introduction mgr. Caterpillar Claas Am., Omaha, 1996—2001, mktg. mgr. combines, 2001—. Asst. editor Farming on Track, 1996—. Mem.: Am. Soc. Agrl. Engrs., Optimist Club (pres.), Omaha Suburban Rotary (bd. dirs.). Republican. Roman Catholic. Avocations: travel, horticulture. Home: 21 Emerald Ct Morton IL 61550 Office: Caterpillar OEM Sales 100 NE Adams St Peoria IL 61629-9540 E-mail: powercat@insightbb.com.

DISBROW, LYNN MARIE, communication educator; b. Chgo., Sept. 2, 1961; d. Ervin John and Patricia Ann (Grabarek) Lodyga; m. Michael Ray Disbrow, July 14, 1984; children: Matthew Ray, Nicole Marie. BA, Ind. U., South Bend, 1982; MA with distinction, Emerson Coll., Boston, 1986; PhD, Wayne State U., Detroit, 1989. High sch. program mgr. Jr. Achievement of Michiana, Inc., South Bend, 1982-84; account exec. AM The WNDU Stas., South Bend, 1984; instr. Emerson Coll., Boston, 1985-86, Wayne State U., Detroit, 1986-87, grad. teaching asst., 1987; lectr. Ind. U., South Bend, 1988; lectr. I Sinclair C.C., Dayton, Ohio, 1989-90, asst. prof., 1993-97, assoc. prof., 1997—2002, prof., 2002—; vis. asst. prof. comm. U. Dayton, 1990-92. Author conv. papers Mass. Comm. Assn., 1985, Nat. Comm. Assn., 1986-91, 94, 96-98, 99-2002, Ctrl. State Comm. Assn., 1989, 91-92, 94-2002, others; mem. editl. bd. Ohio Speech Jour., 1993, 2000-03, Basic Course Annual, 2000-02, N.D. Jour. Speech and Theatre, 1992-2000, Comm. Rsch.eports, 1999, 2000, Ky. Jour. Comm., 1998-2000. Rumble fellow, 1986-87; recipient award for innovative excellence Nat. Ctr. for Tchg., Learning and Tech., 1997, outstanding award Nat. Assn. C.C., 1999, 2000, Disting. Alumni award Ind. U. at South Bend; named Tchr. of Yr., Ohio Assn. 2-Yr. Colls. Mem. Nat. Comm. Assn., Ctrl. States Comm. Assn., Speech Comm. Assn. Ohio (exec. bd. 1995-98). Republican. Roman Catholic.

DISBROW, MICHAEL RAY, aerospace supplier company executive; b. Highland Park, Mich., June 12, 1959; s. Arthur Ray and Vivian (Childress) D.; m. Lynn Marie Lodyga, July 14, 1984; children: Matthew Ray, Nicole Marie. BSME, Purdue U., 1981; MBA, Harvard U., 1986. Co-op. assoc. BFGoodrich Co., Akron, Ohio, 1978-81; axle engr. Bendix Automotive Brake Sys. divsn. Allied Signal, Inc., South Bend, Ind., 1982-83, R & D engr., 1983-84, disc brake engr., 1984, mgr. strategic planning, 1986-87, mgr. Far East bus. planning, 1987-88, mgr. N.Am. joint venture programs, 1988; internal cons. Fram divsn. Allied Signal, Inc., East Providence, R.I., 1985; dir. svc. ctr. Hartzell Propeller, Inc., Piqua, Ohio, 1988-94, v.p. Dornier 328 program, 1994-95, v.p. product support, 1995-97, v.p. mktg. and customer support, 1997-2000, sr. v.p. mktg., applications and customer support, 2000—. Mem. indsl. adv. com., dept. aviation tech. Purdue U., 1996—. Prodn. advisor Jr. Achievment of Michiana, South Bend, 1982-83, exec. advisor, 1983-84; mem. bus. adv. bd. Oakwood (Ohio) City Bd. Edn., 1996—, chmn., 1999-2000; bd. dirs. Miami County YMCA, 1997-2003, Jr. Achievement of Dayton, 1998—. Named Prodn. Advisor of Yr., Jr. Achievment of Michiana, 1983; fellow The Little Family Found., 1984, 85, Allied Signal Inc., 1984-86. Mem. Regional Airline Assn. (assoc. mem. coun. 1996-99), Tau Beta Pi. Republican. Methodist. Home: 820 Shafor Blvd Dayton OH 45419-3450 Office: Hartzell Propeller Inc One Propeller Pl Piqua OH 45356

DISBROW, SIDNEY ARDEN, JR., chiropractor; b. Ann Arbor, Mich., Sept. 22, 1946; s. Sidney Arden Sr. and Leona Irene (Reinhart) D.; m. Marilyn Ann Musson, Dec. 28, 1968 (div.); 1 child, Mary Elizabeth; m. Kathleen Riemesma, Oct. 3, 1998. BA, Hope Coll., 1968; MA, U. Mich., 1971; DC, Nat. Coll. of Chiropractic, 1975. Diplomate Am. Bd. Chiropractic Examiners. Tchr. Plymouth (Mich.) Community Schs., 1968-72; psychotherapist Milan (Mich.) Fed. Correctional Instn., 1970-72; pvt. practice Plymouth, 1975—99, Grand Haven, 1998—. Lectr. continuing edn. program U. Mich. Med. Sch., Ann Arbor, 1980; adv. cont. Muskegon Community Coll. Massage Therapy Prog. Pres. Plymouth Rotary Found., 1990; chair fundraising com. United Way, Plymouth, 1990—, pres., 1996, campaign chmn. Tri-Cities United Way. Recipient Night of 100 Stars, 2002, Dabridge Community Service award, 2003. Mem. Am. Chiropractic Assn., Internat. Coll. Applied Kinesiology, Mich. Chiropractic Assn., Coun. on Diagnostic Imaging, Alumni Assn. Nat. Coll. Chiropractors, U. Mich. Alumni Assn., Masons, Rotary (pres. 1997), Rotary Club Grand Haven (dist. conf. chmn. Rotery Dist. 9290, 2003-), Delta Tau Alpha. Presbyterian. Avocations: running, painting, skiing, sailing, trumpet. Office: 518 S Beacon Blvd Grand Haven MI 49417-1954 also: 518 S Beacon Blvd Grand Haven MI 49417-1954

DISCH, THOMAS M(ICHAEL), author; b. Des Moines, Iowa, Feb. 2, 1940; s. Felix H. and Helen Margaret (Gilbertson) D. Student, NYU, 1959-62. Drama critic The Nation, N.Y.C., 1987-91, N.Y. Daily News, 1992-93; artist-in-residence Coll. of William and Mary, 1996. Author: The Genocides, 1965, Mankind Under the Leash, 1966, The House That Fear Built, 1966, Echo Round His Bones, 1967, Black Alice, 1968, Camp Concentration, 1968, The Prisoner, 1969, 334, 1974, Clara Reeve, 1975, Getting Into Death and Other Stories, 1976 (O'Henry prize 1975), On Wings of Song, 1979 (John W. Campbell Meml. award 1980), Xmas, 1979 (O'Henry prize 1979), Neighboring Lives, 1981, The Businessman: A Tale of Terror, 1984, Amnesia, 1985, The M.D.: A Horror Story, 1991, The Priest: A Gothic Romance, 1994, The Dreams Our Stuff is Made of; How Science Fiction Conquered the World, 1998, The Sub; A Study in Witchcraft, 1999, (juvenile) A Tale of Dan de Lioni, 1986, The Brave Little Toaster: A Bedtime Story For Small Appliances, 1986 (Brit. Sci. Fiction award 1981), The Brave Little Toaster Goes to Mars, 1988, (poetry) The Right Way To Figure Plumbing, 1972, ABCDEFG HIJKLM NOPQRST UVWXYZ, 1981, Orders of the Retina, 1982, Burn This, 1972, Here I Am, There You Are, Where Were We, 1984, Yes Let's: New and Selected Poems, 1989, Dark Verses and Light, 1991 (story collections) One Hundred and Two H-Bombs and Other Science Fiction Stories, 1966, Under Compulsion, 1968, Getting Into Death: The Best Short Story or Thomas M. Disch, 1973, The Early Science Fiction Stories of Thomas M. Disch, 1977, Fundamental Disch, 1980, The Man Who Had No Idea, 1982, (short stories) Ringtime, 1983, Torturing Mr. Amberwell, 1985, (lit. criticism) The Castle of Indolence, 1995, The Dreams Our Stuff Is Made Of (Hugo award), 1998, The Castle of Perseverance, 2002; scriptwriter: (TV episode) Miami Vice, 1987; editor: The Ruins of the Earth: An Anthology of Stories of the Immediate Future, Bad Moon Rising: An Anthology of Political Foreboding, 1975, New Constellations: An Anthology of Tomorrow's Mythologies, 1976, Strangeness: A Collection of Curious Tales, 1977; contbr.: numerous poems and articles, lit. criticism to publs. including Poetry; libretto opera The Fall of the House of Usher, Frankenstein; dramatic adaptation Ben Hur, 1989, The Cardinal Detoxes, 1990. Recipient Michael J. Braude award Am. Acad. Arts and Letters, 1999. Mem. PEN, Writer's Guild East.

DISCH, WILLIAM BURTON, psychologist, researcher; Rsch. scientist, exptl. psychologist, Alaska.

DISCIULLO, ALAN MICHAEL, lawyer; b. Long Branch, N.J., Mar. 18, 1950; s. Peter Michael and Marion (Kaney) DiS.; m. Mary Jo Coppola, Oct. 13, 1979; children: Megan Eileen, Corinne Leigh. AB cum laude, Georgetown U., 1972, JD, 1977; MBA, NYU, 1986; M in Corp. Real Estate with honors, NACORE Inst., 1997. Bar: N.J. 1977; U.S. Dist. Ct. N.J. 1977, D.C. 1980, N.Y. 1980. Law clk. to presiding justice U.S. Tax Ct., Washington, 1975-76; assoc. Shanley & Fisher, Newark, 1977-78; asst. v.p. Paine Webber Jackson, N.Y.C., 1978-83; v.p., 1st v.p. Morgan Stanley Dean Witter Co., N.Y.C., 1983—. V.p., dir. Wall St. Realty, N.Y.C., 1981—83; bd. dirs., gen. counsel, sec. Dean Witter polit. action com., N.Y.C., 1986—91; prof. masters real estate program NYU, 1991—; v.p. North Brunswick (N.J.) Tenants Assn., 1979—81; mem. task force Pres.'s Pvt. Sector Survey on Cost Control, Grace Commn., Washington, 1982—83; mem. land use adv. com. 12th Congl. Dist. N.J., 1999—; elected mem. Am. Coll. of Real Estate Lawyers, 2003—; spkr., panelist comml. real estate & planning issues; lectr. Practicing Law Inst., 1996—, Strategic Rsch. Inst., 1996—98, NACORE Inst. for Corp. Real Estate, Corenet Global, 2002—; mem. Corenet Learning Adv. Bd., 2002—; vice chmn. Negotiating Comml. Leases Panel, 2000—. Co-author: (treatise) Negotiating and Drafting Office Leases, 1995; co-editor: Met. Corp. Counsel Real Estate Corner column, corp. counsel adv. com., 1997—99; bd. editors: Jour. of Corp. Real Estate Mgmt., 1998—, exec. mem.:, 2003—, mem. edtl. bd.: Comml. Leasing Law and Strategy, 1999—, Comml. Tenant's Lease Insider, 2003—; contbr. articles to profl. jours., book chpt. Treas., dir., coach West Windsor Plainsboro Soccer Assn., 1990—97; mgr. West Windsor Little League, 1993—2000; coach West Windsor Wildcats Traveling ASA Team, 1998—2001; dir. Princeton Soccer Assn., 2001—02; lectr. Sobelsohn Sch.; advisor site plan rev. com. West Windsor Twp., 1987—88, mem. growth mgmt. planning com., 1988—90, mem. growth mgmt. adv. com., 1991—93, zoning bd., 1997—98; chmn. West Windsor Planning Bd., 1993—97; co-chair Mayor's Bus. Task Force, 2003—; mem. West Windsor Plainsboro sch. redistricting com., 1995; trustee West Windsor Plainsboro Sch. Dist. Edn. Found., Inc., 1996—2002, v.p., 1999—2001; mem. Mayor's (N.Y.C.) Bldg. Industry Adv. Com., 2003; dir. N.J. Planning Ofcls., 1997—. Recipient O'Connor award for disting. legal writing, 1987, 89, 91, Individual Achievement in Planning award N.J. Planning Ofcls., 1996, Outstanding Svc. award NYU, 1998, Outstanding Tchr. award NYU, 2002. Fellow: Am. Bar Assn. Found.; mem.: ABA (chmn. young lawyers divsn. 1985—86, vice chair office lease sect. 1994—98, chmn. task force bldg. safety 1995—, chair 1998—, v.p. securities law divsn., corp. banking and bus. law sect., comml. leasing subcom., exec. com. mem., chmn.coms. on tenant equity participation, subrogation, idemnification), Georgetown U. Wall Street Alliance (mem. adv. bd.), Practising Law Inst. (real estate adv. bd. mem. 1996—), N.Y. County Lawyers Assn. (exec. com. corp. law sect. 1994—95, co-chair 1996—98), Internat. Assn. Attys. in Corp. Real Estate, NACORE Internat. (dir. N.Y. chpt. 1996, pres. N.Y.C. chpt. 1997—98, internat. bd. dirs. 1997—2002, dir. NACORE Inst. 1999—2002, pres.-elect 2001—02, pres. 2002), Young Lawyers of N.Y.C. (treas. 1982—83, chmn. 1983—85), Mensa, Carnegie Lake Rowing Club, Princeton (N.J.) Athletic Rugby Club, Gavel Club, Pi Sigma Alpha. Democrat. Roman Catholic. Avocations: athletics, photography, reading. Home: 19 Taunton Ct Princeton Junction NJ 08550-2164 E-mail: Adisciu9@aol.com, alan.disciullo@morganstanley.com.

DISENHAUS, HELEN ELIZABETH, lawyer; b. Washington, Nov. 2, 1948; d. Nathan and Henrietta (Weiss) D.; m. Brian Girard Driscoll, Sept. 11, 1977; children: Daniel Benjamin Driscoll, David Michael Driscoll. AB, Mt. Holyoke Coll., 1970; MAT, Wesleyan U., Conn., 1972; JD, Yale U., 1977. Bar: D.C. 1977. Tchr. English Glastonbury (Conn.) H.S., 1971-74; atty. Dow, Lohnes & Albertson, Washington, 1977-87; of counsel Swidler & Berlin, Washington, 1987-94, counsel, 1994, mem., 1995-98, Swidler, Berlin, Shereff, Friedmen LLP, Washington, 1998—. Pres. D.C. chpt. Am. Women in Radio and TV, 1982-83, bd. dirs., 1983-84, nat. v.p. govt. industry affairs, 1984-86, nat. sec.-treas., 1986-88. Sarah Williston scholar, 1968; recipient Leadership award Am. Women in Radio and TV, 1995. Mem. ABA, D.C. Bar Assn., Womens Bar Assn. D.C., Fed. Comm. Bar Assn. (chair continuing legal edn. com. 1991-93, transactional practice com. 1994-96), Yale Law Sch. Assn. (pres. D.C. 1982-83, exec. com. 1983-84), Mt. Holyoke Club, Phi Beta Kappa. Jewish. Office: Swidler, Berlin Shereff Friedman LLP 3000 K St NW Ste 300 Washington DC 20007-5116 E-mail: hedisenhaus@swidlaw.com.

DISERIO, FRANK JOSEPH, pharmaceutical company executive, consultant; b. N.Y.C., Oct. 3, 1931; s. Anthony and Catherine (Solimando) DiS.; m. Lauretta Brunck, 1954 (div. May 1984); children: Anthony Mark, Francis Joseph, Paul James; m. Marjatta Niemioja, Oct. 19, 1985). BS, NYU, 1963; MBA, Fairleigh Dickinson U., 1970; PhD, Union Inst., 1979. Ptnr. Foam Age Lounge, Inc. and Dawn W.W. Co., N.Y.C., 1956-59; from sales rep. to clin. rsch. dir. Sandoz Pharmaceuticals, Inc., East Hanover, N.J., 1959-80; dir. CNS Med Rsch., 1985-90; exec. dir. CNS clin. rsch., head OTC/analgesia clin. rsch. dept. Sandoz Rsch. Inst., East Hanover, 1988-95; pharm. devel. cons. Morristown, N.J., 1995—; assoc. prof. dept. family practice U. Medicine & Dentistry N.J. Sch. Osteo. Medicine, Stafford, 1998—. Contbr. articles to profl. jours. Capt. USAF, 1952-56. Mem. Internat. Headache Soc., Am. Headache Soc., Am. Acad. Neurology, Am. Soc. Clin. Pharmacology and Therapeutics, Nat. Bd. for Cert. in Headache Mgmt., N.Y. Acad. Scis., Rock Spring Club. Republican. Roman Catholic. Avocations: golf, travel, arts. Home: 24 Pippins Way Morristown NJ 07960-6971 E-mail: pharmdevco@aol.com.

DISHAROON, LESLIE BENJAMIN, retired insurance executive; b. Phila., Aug. 6, 1932; s. Theodore Lee and Sally (Oglesby) D.; m. Ann Merriwether, June 26, 1954; children: Lee Ann Disharoon Tolzmann, Beth Disharoon Wilgis, Martha Disharoon Wright, Carrie Disharoon Souter. BA, Brown U., 1954; MBA, Columbia U., 1956. C.L.U. With Conn. Gen. Life Ins. Co., 1956-60, Conn. Mut. Life Ins. Co., Hartford, Conn., 1960-77; chmn. bd. Monumental Life Ins. Co., Balt., 1977-83; pres., dir. Monumental Corp., 1978-89, chmn. bd., 1979-89, MSD&T Funds Inc., Travelers Property & Casualty Co., Aegon, USA, Inc. Mem. Farmington Country Club (Charlottesville, Va.), Green Spring Valley Hunt Club (Garrison, Md.), Swan Island Club (Curituck, N.C.), Caves Valley Golf Club, Beta Gamma Sigma. Address: care Caves Valley Golf Club 2910 Blendon Rd Owings Mills MD 21117-2360

DISHER, DAVID ALAN, lawyer, consultant; b. Chgo., Apr. 15, 1944; s. Hugh George and Beatrice Rose (Selmanovitz) D.; children: Karl Theodore, Carol Ann, Kathy; m. Clara Hoffman, Sept. 17, 1991. BS in Elec. Engring., MIT, 1965, MS in Elec. Engring., 1966; JD, U. Houston, 1983. Bar: Tex. 1984, U.S. Ct. Appeals (5th cir.) 1984, U.S. Tax Ct. 1984, U.S. Dist. Ct. (so. dist.) 1986, U.S. Supreme Ct. 1987. Mathematician Shell Devel., Houston, 1966-68; sr. engr. Tex. Instruments, Stafford, 1968; dir. rsch. GEOCOM, New Orleans, 1969-70; cons., inventor Disher Consulting Svc., Houston, 1970-73; pres., chmn. bd. Seismic Programming Internat., 1973-84, 1974-84; pvt. practice law LaMarque, Tex., 1984-99; pvt. practice Houston, 1999—. Ind. geophys. rsch. cons. Contbr. articles to Geophysics. Mem. crime control com. Houston C. of C., 1974—76. Mem. ACLU, Coll. State Bar Tex., Tex. Criminal Def. Lawyers Assn., Galveston County Bar Assn., Harris County Bar Assn., Harris County Criminal Lawyers Assn., Houston Geophys. Soc., Houston Bar Assn. Office: 3318 Mercer St Houston TX 77027-6020 Fax: 713-961-9402. E-mail: disherdave@aol.com.

DISHEROON, FRED RUSSELL, lawyer; b. Hot Springs, Ark., Nov. 21, 1931; s. Andrew Russell and Ruth Fayrene (Bearden) D.;children: Terri Suzanne, John Frederick; m. Diane L. Donley, Apr. 8, 1989; 1 child, Travis William. AB, Hendrix Coll., 1953; JD, So. Meth. U., 1956; LLM in Environ. Law, George Washington U., 1976. Bar: Tex. 1956, U.S. Ct. Appeals (1st, 5th, 6th, 8th, 9th, 10th, 11th D.C. and fed. cirs.), U.S. Supreme Ct. 1964, Va. 1974. Atty. Superior Ins. Co., Dallas, 1960-64; claims atty. Sentry Ins. Co., Dallas, 1964-67; litigation counsel Stigall, Maxfield & Collier, Dallas, 1967-69; sole practice Dallas, 1969-70; asst. gen. counsel for litigation C.E. U.S. Army, Washington, 1970-75; spl. litigation counsel Dept. Justice, Washington, 1975—. Instr. environ. law U. Ala.-Huntsville, 1979-82; lectr. law George Washington U., 1981-86; vis. rsch. specialist U. Calif., Davis, 1990. Co-author: Sustainable Environmental Law, 1993, Water Law, Trends, Policies and Practice, 1995; editor Southwestern Law Jour., 1955-56. Col. JAGC, USAR. Recipient numerous outstanding performance awrds U.S. Army, Dept. Justice, Sr. Exec. Svc. meritorious award Dept. Justice, 1984, Outstanding Civilian Svc. medal Dept.

Army. Mem. Sr. Execs. Assn. Home: 3508 Riverwood Rd Alexandria VA 22309-2720 Office: Dept Justice Environ & Natural Resources Divsn 601 D St NW Washington DC 20004 E-mail: fred.disheroon@usdoj.gov.

DISHMAN, BOB N. pharmacist; b. Gainesville, Tex., Sept. 11, 1936; s. William Odus and Mildred Christine (Clark) Dishman; m. Ruth A. Haight, Aug. 1, 1958; 1 child, Karen Christine Dishman Walters. BS in Pharmacy, Southwestern Okla. State U., 1959. Staff pharmacist Ray's Pharmacy, Lawton, Okla., 1959—66; owner, pharmacist Dishman's Pharmacy, Lawton, 1966—. Pres. Hospice, Lawton area, 1990; affil. instr. in pharmacy practice S.W. Okla. Sch. of Pharmacy; pres. Okla. Pharmacy Heritage Found., 1991. Sgt. Nat. Guard, 1959—65. Named Hall of Fame, Okla. Pharmacy Heritage Found., 1992; recipient Disting. Alumnus award, SW Okla. Sch. Pharmacy, 1998, Bowl of Hygeia Pharmacy award, Okla. Pharmacists Assn./Wyet Labs, 2003. Mem.: Comanche County Bd. Health, Pharmacy Providers Okla., Okla. Pharmacists Assn. (pres. 1997—98, Pharmacy Leadership award 1998), Nat. Cmty. Pharmacists Assn. (Pharmacy Leadership award 1997), Am. Pharma. Assn., Lawton C. of C. Democrat. Methodist. Home: 735 NW Heinzwood Cir Lawton OK 73505 Office: Dishman's Pharmacy 1310 SW Lee Blvd Lawton OK 73501

DISHMAN, RODNEY KING, physical education educator; b. Springfield, Mo., Feb. 2, 1951; s. Willard King and Virginia Lanette Dishman; m. Sharon Emily Alter, Aug. 17, 1974; children: Jessica, Corinne, Adrienne. PhD, U. Wis., 1978. Asst. rsch. prof. U. Calif., Davis, 1983-85; prof. exercise sci. U. Ga., Athens, 1985—, dir. Exercise Psychology Lab., 1987—. Cons. various internat. govt. agencies. Author 5 books; contbr. over 70 articles to profl. jours. Fellow Am. Coll. Sports Medicine, Am. Acad. Kinesiology and Phys. Edn., Am. Psychol. Assn., Am. Psychol. Soc.; mem. Acad. Sports Scis. (founding). Office: U Ga 300 River Rd Athens GA 30602-6554

DISHON, CRAMER STEVEN, sales executive; b. Craven County, N.C., June 21, 1953; s. Harley Cramer and Sylvia Elaine (McCroskey) D.; m. Patricia Jenkins, June 25, 1977; children: Sarah Marie, Elizabeth Dawn. Student, Dundalk Cmty. Coll., 1972-73, Va. Western Cmty. Coll., 1985. Bonded weighmaster Am. Smelting and Refining, Balt., 1972-73; time keeper Bethlehem Erection, Balt., 1973-74; permit ironworker Ironworks Local 16, Balt. 1974-75; sanitary op. technician Back River WWTP, Balt., 1975-77; svc. technician Fairbanks Weighting Divsn., Balt., 1977-79; sales engr. Security Scale Svc., Roanoke, Va., 1979-90; sales mgr. Am. Scale and Equipment, Balt., 1990—; agt.-ins. Primercia Fin. Svcs., Balt., 1993—. Bd. dirs. Vinton Dem. Com., Roanoke, 1988-90, Highshire Cmty. Orgn., Dundalk, Md., 1990-93; pres. Dunshire Cmty. Orgn., 2002-; chmn. CBMC, Rosedale, Md., 1993-95, 2003-; chmn. deacons North Point Bapt., Balt., 1993-96; various positions Vinton Bapt. Ch., Roanoke, 1980-90; Sunday sch. dir. Woolford Meml. Bapt. Ch., Dundalk, 1990, ch. coun., budget com., chmn. fin. com., 2002-, Sunday sch. tchr., 2002-, deacon, 2003; Sunday sch. dir. North Point Bapt. Ch., Dundalk, 1991-96, ch. coun., fin., budget chmn., chmn. fin. com., Sunday sch. tchr., deacon, 2003; pres. East County Rep. Club; bd. mem. Greater Dundalk Alliance, 2002-. Mem. Internat. Soc. of Weighing and Measurement (sgt.-at-arms, lt. gov. 1996-2000, chmn. Potomac divsn. 1993-95, vice chmn. Potomac divsn. 1991-93, 2003-Svc. award 1995, cert. weighing salesperson, cert. weighing technician, cert. weighing profl.), Gideons Internat. (v.p., treas. S.E. Balt. camp), Christian Bus. Mens Caleb Group. Baptist. Avocations: softball player, baseball fan, church service, walking, baseball collectibles. Home: PO Box 4044 117 Highshire Ct Baltimore MD 21222-3054 Office: Am Scale & Equipment Co Inc 8839 Kelso Dr Baltimore MD 21221-3141

DISHONG, MORRIS WILLIAM, forensic investigator, nurse; b. Canton, Ohio, Aug. 13, 1953; s. Morris W. and Vera M. Dishong; 1 child, Jeffery. Cert. death investigator, St. Louis U., 1997. Firefighter Plain Twp. Fire Dept., North Canton, Ohio, 1975-85; staff nurse emergency rm. Massillon (Ohio) Cmty. Hosp., 1986—; forensic investigator Stark County Coroner, Massillon, 1997—. Mem. Am. Assn. Critical Care Nurses. Republican. Avocations: travel, land exploration. Office: Stark County Coroner 400 Austrin Ave NW Massillon OH 44646 Office Fax: 330-837-3380. E-mail: headtotoe@raex.com.

DISHY, BOB, actor; b. Bklyn. s. Nathan and Amy (Barazani) D.; m. Judy Graubart; 1 child, Samuel Nathan. Ed. in drama, Syracuse U. Appeared in Broadway plays Damn Yankees, 1955, From A to Z, Flora The Red Menace, The Unknown Soldier and His Wife, Something Different, The Goodbye People, A Way of Life, The Creation of the World and Other Business, An American Millionaire, Sly Fox, Murder at the Howard Johnsons, Grown Ups, Cafe Crown, The Tenth Man, The Price, Morning's at Seven; off-Broadway plays Chic, There Is A Play Tonight, Can-Can, By Jupiter, The Shawl; actor, dir. N.Y. Second City Co.; also appeared in various regional theaters, Stratford Shakespeare Festival, Mark Taper Forum, Am. Repertory Theatre, The Public Theatre, Berkshire Theatre Festival, Williamson Theatre Festival, Westport Country Playhouse; appeared in films including The Tiger Makes Out, Lovers and Others Strangers, The Big Bus, Last Married Couple in America, First Family, Author, Author, Brighton Beach Memoirs, Critical Condition, Stay Tuned, Used People, My Boyfriend's Back, Don Juan DeMarco and the Centerfold, Jungle 2 Jungle, The Fish in the Bathtub, Judy Berlin, Labor Pains, The Untitled Hamburg Project; numerous network and PBS shows including Frasier, Columbo, Law and Order, All in the Family, Mary Tyler Moore, Barney Miller, The Good Doctor, The Cafeteria; mem. TV series co. That Was The Week That Was; actor, dir. TV series Story Theatre. Served with U.S. Army 1957-59. Winner All-Army Entertainment Contest; Tony award nomination; recipient Drama Desk award, Chancellor's medal for disting. achievement Syracuse U., Outer Critics Cir. award. Mem. Acad. Motion Picture Arts and Scis.

DI SIMONE, ROBERT NICHOLAS, radiologist, educator; b. Canton, Ohio, Nov. 15, 1937; s. Nicholas Joseph and Margaret Elizabeth (Karas) DiS.; m. Patricia Anne Zwigard, June 22, 1963; children: Christopher, Angela, Elizabeth. BSc summa cum laude, Ohio State U., 1959, MSc, MD cum laude, Ohio State U., 1963. Diplomate Am. Bd. Radiology, Am. Bd. Nuclear Medicine. Intern, fellow Johns Hopkins U. Hosp., Balt., 1963-64, asst. resident, fellow in internal medicine, 1964-65, asst. resident, fellow in radiology, 1967-70, instr., radiologist, 1970-71; dir. nuclear medicine Aultman Hosp., Canton, 1971-95, pres., med. staff, 1986-87, vice-chmn. dept. radiology, 1988-96, sec.-treas. med. staff, 1977-79; chmn. nuclear medicine sect. Northeastern Ohio Univs. Coll. Medicine, Rootstown, 1979-97; chmn. dept. radiology Northeastern Ohio Univs. Coll. of Medicine (NEOUCOM), Rootstown, 1992-93; diagnostic radiologist Aultman Health Found., Canton, Ohio, 1971-2000; radiology cons. North Canton, Ohio, 2000—. Author: Imaging of the Endocrine System in Organ System Radiology, 1984; contbr. articles to profl. jours. Fellow Am. Coll. Radiology; mem. AMA, Soc. Nuclear Medicine, Ohio State Med. Soc. (del. 1983-95), Radiol. Soc. N.Am., Stark County Med. Soc. (trustee 1979-95, chmn. bd. censors 1980-82, pres. 1993), Unique Club Stark County, Phi Beta Kappa, Sigma Xi, Alpha Omega Alpha, Phi Lambda Upsilon. Avocations: playing bluegrass guitar music, collecting antique old trains, traveling, hiking. Home and Office: 2465 Oakway St N North Canton OH 44720-5886 E-mail: rnd@neoucom.edu.

DISINGER, JOHN FRANKLIN, natural resources educator; b. Lockport, N.Y., July 7, 1930; s. Allan Eugene and Grace (Meeks) D.; m. Norma Jean Vescovi, June 25, 1960; children: David C., Douglas A. BS, SUNY, Brockport, 1952; MEd, U. Rochester, 1960; PhD, Ohio State U., 1971. Lic. sci. tchr., N.Y. Tchr., chmn. mid. sch. sci. dept. West Irondequoit Cen. Sch. Dist., Rochester, N.Y., 1955-70; prof. Sch. Natural Resources Ohio State U., Columbus, 1971-95, prof. emeritus, 1995—, acting dir., 1988-89; faculty Ohio State U. Coll. Edn., Columbus, 1971-95. Assoc. dir. Ednl. Resources Info. Ctr. Clearinghouse for Sci., Math, Environ. Edn., Columbus, 1971-91; cons. TVA, Knoxville, 1985-88, N. Am. Assn. Environ. Edn., 1993. Mem. editl. bd. The Environmentalist, 1984-03; book rev. editor Jour. Environ. Edn., 1999—; contbr. articles to profl. jours. Mem. Environ. Lit. Coun., 1996—; treas. Korean War Vets Ednl. Grant Corp., 2002—. Recipient Pres.' award Ohio Alliance for Environ., 1984, Alumni award for disting tchg. Ohio State U., 1995. Fellow Ohio Acad. Sci.; mem. N.Am. Assn. Environ. Edn. (pres. 1985-86, Walter Jeske award 1984, Pres. award, 1991). Presbyterian. Office: Ohio State Univ Sch Natural Resources 2021 Coffey Rd Columbus OH 43210-1044 E-mail: disinger.1@osu.edu.

DISIPIO, ROCCO THOMAS, writer; b. Phila., Dec. 17, 1949; s. Rocco Benjamin and Rita Elizabeth Bilotti. BS in Police Adminstrn., Mich. State U., 1971. Chief tour guide Mich. State U., 1970-71; probation, parole officer Pa. Ct. Common Pleas, 1971-79; gen. mgr. Poniard Books, Inc., Broomall, Pa., 1980-82; ops. mgr. Myles Med. Equip., Ardmore, Pa., 1982-85; editor-in-chief Merit Industries, Bensalem, Pa., 1985-87; freelance writer, 1987—. Prodr. Fgn. Films Enterprises, L.A., 1995—. Author: (world's 1st internet novel) Arcadia Ego, 1996 (USA Today award), (novel) Darkness. Paradise. 1997. Avocation: target shooting. Office: PO Box 405 New Kingstown PA 17072-0405

DISKANT, GREGORY L. lawyer; b. Phila., June 7, 1948; s. Robert and Eda (Grunberg) D.; m. Sandra S. Baron, Feb. 29, 1980; children: Edward, Benjamin. AB, Princeton U., 1970; JD, Columbia U., 1974. Bar: N.Y. 1975. Law clk. to Hon. J. Skelly Wright, U.S. Ct. Appeals for D.C. Cir., Washington, 1974-75; law clk. to Hon. Thurgood Marshall, U.S. Supreme Ct., Washington, 1975-76; asst. U.S. atty. for so. dist. N.Y., Dept. Justice, N.Y.C., 1976-80, chief appellate atty., 1980; assoc. Patterson, Belknap, Webb & Tyler, N.Y.C., 1981—82, ptnr., 1982—, co-chmn., 1997—2002, chmn., 2003—. Editor-in-chief Columbia Law Rev., 1973-74. Kent scholar, 1972, Stone scholar, 1973, 74. Fellow Am. Coll. Trial Lawyers; mem. ABA, N.Y. State Bar Assn., Assn. Bar of City of N.Y. Office: Patterson Belknap Webb & Tyler Rm 2400 1133 Avenue Of The Americas Fl 22 New York NY 10036-6731

DISKIN, MICHAEL EDWARD, plastics industry executive, food service executive; b. Dallas, Aug. 8, 1946; s. William Michael and Edna Patricia (Loughran) D.; m. Mary Jean Fraser, Oct. 8, 1972; children: Robyn Kristine, Karyn Marie, Michael Alexander, Stephen James, Alisyn Krystal. BS in Bus. Adminstrn & Econs., No. Mich. U., 1971. Sales rep. Lincoln Nat. Life, Fort Wayne, Ind., 1971-73, Durkee Foods, Dayton, Ohio, 1973-75, sales mgr. Cleve., 1975-78, from product mgr. asst. to sr. mktg. mgr. Westlake, Ohio, 1978-87; bus. mgr. Engelhard Corp., Cleve., 1987-88; dir. mktg. Master Builders Technologies, Cleve., 1988-92; exec. v.p. Specrete-Ip, Inc., Cleve., 1992-98; pres., owner Four Seasons Industries, Garretsville, Ohio, 1998—. V.p. Put-in-Bay (Ohio) Property Owners Assn.; cpl. USMC, 1966-68. Mem. Lake Erie Islands Hist. Soc., Put-in-Bay Yacht Club, Crews Nest Club. Republican. Roman Catholic. Avocations: trap and target shooting, boating, fishing, travel. Home: 1745 Halls Carriage Path Westlake OH 44145-2030 Office: Diskin Enterprises Inc Four Seasons Industries 10420 Industrial Dr Garrettsville OH 44231-9764 E-mail: mediskin@fourseas.net.

DISMUKES, ROBERT KEY, medical scientist; b. Dahlonega, Ga., June 21, 1943; s. Camillus Jackson and Marion (Mullen) D.; children: Antony, William, Renee. BS, North Ga. Coll., Dahlonega, 1964; MA, Vanderbilt U., 1966; PhD, Pa. State U., 1971. Staff fellow NIH, Bethesda, Md., 1973-75; staff scientist neurosciences rsch. program MIT, Brookline, Mass., 1977-79; dir. study com. vision Nat. Acad. Scis., 1979-83; dir. life scis. Air Force Office Sci. Rsch., Bolling AFB, 1983-89; chief rsch. divsn. aerospace human factors NASA, Moffett Field, Calif., 1989-91, chief scientist aerospace human factors, 1991—. Vis. faculty mem. Free Univ., Amsterdam, 1975-76; with interagy. com. low vision Nat. Inst. Handicapped Rsch. Washingotn, 1981-84; with forum on rsch. mgmt. Fedn. Behavioral, Psychol. and Cognitive Scis., 1983-89. Editor: (with Robert Sekuler, Donald Kline) Aging and Human Visual Function, 1982, (with Guy Smith) Facilitaiton and Debriefing in Aviation Training and Operations, 2000; contbr. articles to profl. jours. Vol. pilot, Lighthawk, San Francisco, 1994—. With U.S. Army, 1966-68. Fellow Nat. Endowment for Humanities, NSF, Inst. Society, Ethics and Life Scis., 1976-77. Home: 1357 Harrison St Santa Clara CA 95050 Office: NASA Ames Rsch Ctr Mailstop 262-4 Moffett Field CA 94035 E-mail: kdismukes@mail.arc.nasa.gov.

DISMUKES, VALENA GRACE BROUSSARD, photographer, former physical education educator; b. St. Louis, Feb. 22, 1938; d. Clobert Bernard and Mary Henrietta (Jones) Broussard; m. Martin Ramon Dismukes, June 26, 1965; 1 child, Michael Ramon. AA in Edn., Harris Tchrs. Coll., 1956; BS in Phys. Edn., Washington U., St. Louis, 1958; MA in Phys. Edn., Calif. State U., L.A., 1972; BA in TV and Film, Calif. State U., Northridge, 1981. Cert. phys. edn. tchr., standard svc. supr. Phys. edn. tchr., coach St. Louis Pub. Sch., 1958-60, L.A. Unified Sch. Dist., 1960-84; health and sci. tchr., mentor tchr. LA Unified Sch. Dist., 1984-93; coord. gifted and talented program 32d St./U. So. Calif. Magnet Sch., 1993-95, magnet coord., 1995; adminstrv. asst. Ednl. Consortium of Ctrl. LA, Calif., 1993-95; free-lance photographer, 1970—; owner, bus. cons. Grace Enterprises, 1994-95; owner World Class Images, 1997—. Coord. Chpt. I, 1989—93; mem. sch. based mgmt. team, 1990—93; lectr. in field. Author: (photography book) As Seen, 1995; editor: parent newsletter, 1975—80; one-woman shows include The Olympic Spirit, 1984, LA-The Ethnic Pl., 1986, Native Am.: Red Black Connection, 1999, Tibet-Photos from the Roof of the World, 2000, Chocolate Women, 2001, The Tarahamara of Copper Canyon, 2001; photographer (photo montage) Homeless on the Street, 2002, Views from Ghana, 2003; contbr. Mem. adv. coun. Visual Comm., LA, 1980; mem. Cmty. Consortium, LA, 1986—87; mem. adv. com. LA Edn. Partnership, 1986—87; mem. adv. bd. Espo Sports Club, LA, 1994; co-founder Alliance of Native Am. of So. Calif. (ANASCA), 1999; v.p. Alliance of Native Am. of So. Calif., 1999—2003; mem. adv. coun. Ne'ayah, 2001—03; bd. dir. NACHES Found., Inc., LA, 1985—86. Marine Educators fellow, 1992; photography grantee LA Olympic Organizing Com., 1984, See's Candies, 2000, Long Beach Fine Arts, 2001, Teaching grantee L.A. Edn. Partnership, 1987-89; recipient Honor award LA-Calif. Assn. Health, Phys. Edn. and Recreation, 1971. Mem. ACLU, NAACP, Urban League, Sierra Club treepeople. Avocations: travel, collecting dolls and baskets, ethnic art. Home: 3800 Stocker St Apt 1 Los Angeles CA 90008-5119 E-mail: vdismukes@netzero.net.

DISNEY, ANTHEA, publishing executive; b. Dunstable, Eng., Oct. 13, 1946;, naturalized, U.S., 1973; d. Alfred Leslie and Elsie (Wale) Disney; m. Peter Robert Howe, Jan. 28, 1984. Ed., Queen's Coll., Eng. Fgn. corr. London Daily Mail, N.Y.C., 1973-75, features editor London, 1975-77, bur. chief N.Y.C., 1977-79; columnist London Daily Express, N.Y.C., 1979-84; dep. mng. editor N.Y. Daily News, N.Y.C., 1984-87; editor Sunday Daily News, 1984-87, US Mag., 1987-88; editor-in-chief Self mag., 1988-89; mag. developer Murdoch Mags., 1989-90; exec. producer Fox TV's A Current Affair, 1990-91; editor-in-chief TV Guide mag., N.Y.C., 1991-95; editorial dir. Murdoch Mags., 1993-95; editor-in-chief I-Guide, Newscorp's Internet Svc., 1995-96; pres., CEO Harper Collins Publishers, 1996-97; chmn., CEO News Am. Pub. Group, N.Y.C., 1997—, TV Guide, Inc., 1999; exec. v.p. content News Corp., N.Y.C., 1999—. Office: News Corp Ste 300 1211 Avenue Of The Americas New York NY 10036-8795*

DISNEY, RALPH L(YNDE), retired industrial engineering educator; b. Balt., Feb. 27, 1928; BE, Johns Hopkins U., 1952, MSE, 1955, DEng., 1964. Engr. Industrial Diecraft Inc., 1953-55, rsch. analyst Ops. Rsch. Office, 1955-56; asst. prof. Lamar State Coll., Beaumont, 1956-59; assoc. prof. U. Buffalo, 1959-63; vis. assoc. prof. U. Mich., Ann Arbor, 1963-64, assoc. prof., 1964-68, prof. indsl. engring., 1968-77; Charles O. Gordon prof. indsl. engring. Va. Polytech Inst. & State U., Blacksburg, 1977-87; prof. indsl. engring. dept. Tex. A&M U., College Station, 1988-96; ret., 1996. OAS vis. prof. Inst. Aeron. Tech., Brazil, 1970-71; disting. vis. prof. Grad. Sch. Ohio State U., Columbus, 1974-75; vis. prof. dept. math. and stats. U. São Paulo, Brazil. Author 2 books; editor sects. in books; contbr. more than 70 articles to profl. jours. Erskine fellow Canterbury U., Christchurch, New Zealand, 1995. Fellow Am. Inst. Indsl. Engrs. (A.G. Holzman award 1986, David Baker award 1972, Frank and Lillian Gilbreth Indsl. Engring. award 1993); mem. ORSA (mem. coun. 1978-82), INFORMS (founder sect. on applied probabilities, sect. pres. 1979), NAE. Home: 1395 Locust Ave Blacksburg VA 24060 also: 8445 Charter Club Cir # 5 Fort Myers FL 33919 E-mail: rdisneyva@adelphia.net.

DI SPIGNO, GUY JOSEPH, international management consultant, industrial psychologist; b. Bklyn., Mar. 6, 1948; s. Joseph Vincent and Jeanne Nina (Renna) DiS.; m. Gisela Riba, May 23, 1979; children: Michael Paul, Abie Francis. BS, Carroll Coll., 1969; MA (fellow), No. Ill. U., 1972; MEd, Loyola U., 1974; PhD, Northwestern U., 1977. Instr. No. Ill. U., DeKalb, 1969-70; chmn. humanities dept. Quincy (Ill.) Boys' High Sch., 1970-71; dir. religious edn. St. Mary's Ch., DeKalb, 1971-72; dir. edn. Immaculate Conception Parish, Highland Park, Ill., 1972-77; dir. human resources Am. Valuation Cons., Des Plaines, Ill., 1977-79; psychologist Hay Assocs., Chgo., 1979-80; v.p. mktg. Exec. Assets Corp., Chgo., 1980-82; dir. mgmt. devel. and personnel svcs. Borg-Warner Corp., Chgo., 1982-84; ptnr., cons. psychologist Medina & Thompson, Chgo., 1984-91; pres. Exec. Synergies, Inc., Northbrook, Ill., 1991—. Contbr. articles to profl. jours. Mem. Highland Park Human Relations Commn., 1975-77, Home Owners and Businessmen's Assn., Highland Park, 1976-77; mem. legis. com. Vernon Hills (Ill.) Sch. Bd., alumni coun. Carroll Coll., 1981-83; soccer coach, Am. Youth Soccer Orgn., Glenview, Ill.; chmn.'s cabinet Ill. Dem. Party, 1988-92; benefactor Jesuit Partnership, Chgo. province, 1995—. Clifford B. Scott scholar, 1967; named to Order Ky. Cols. Mem. APA, Community Religious Edn. Dirs. (nat. vice chmn. 1971-73), Ill. Psychol. Assn., Nat. Registry Health Svc. Providers in Psychology, Am. Personnel and Guidance Assn., Soc. Indsl. and Orgnl. Psychology, Carroll Coll. Alumni Counsel, Phi Alpha Theta, Sigma Phi Epsilon. Home: 2330 Greenview Rd Northbrook IL 60062-6633 Office: 555 Skokie Blvd Ste 260 Northbrook IL 60062-2889 E-mail: guyd@executivesynergies.com.

DISPIRITO, ROCCO, restaurant owner, chef; Degree, Culinary Inst. Am., 1986; student, Jardin de Cygne, Paris; BA, Boston U., 1990. Chef de partie Lespinasse, N.Y.C.; chef under Jean-Michel Diot and Jacques Chibois Adrienne, N.Y.C.; worked with chef Mark Baker Aujourd'hui, Boston; exec. chef Dava Restaurant, 1995, Union Pacific, N.Y.C., 1997—; founder, exec. chef Rocco's, N.Y.C., NY, 2003—. Stagiere with Dominique Cecillon, with David Bouley, with Charles Palmer, with Gilbert Le Coze, with Gray Kunz. Named Best New Chef, Food and Wine, 1999; recipient 3-star rev., N.Y. Times, favorable cooking revs., N.Y. Mag., Crain's N.Y. Bus., N.Y. Observer, Food Arts. Avocations: guitar, mountain biking, collecting wine and cookbooks. Office: Rocco's 12 East 22nd St New York NY 10010*

DISSEN, JAMES HARDIMAN, lawyer; b. Pitts., Jan. 26, 1942; s. William Paul and Kathryn Grace (Reilly) D.; m. Shirley Ann Stark, Dec. 17, 1976; children: Elizabeth Ann, William Stark, Anna Kathryn. BS, Wheeling (W.Va.) Jesuit U., 1963; MBA, Xavier U., Cin., 1966; JD, Duquesne U., Pitts., 1972. Bar: Pa. 1972, U.S. Dist. Ct. (we. dist.) Pa. 1972, W.Va. 1973, U.S. Dist. Ct. (so. dist.) W.Va. 1973, U.S. Supreme Ct. 1976. Spl. agent Counter Intelligence U.S. Army Intelligence Corps, 1963-66; personnel mgr. Columbia Gas of Pa., Inc., Uniontown, 1969-73; dir. labor rels. Columbia Gas Transmission Corp., Charleston, W.Va., 1973-84, dir. personnel and labor rels., 1984-87, dir. employee rels., 1987-96, v.p. Columbia Nat. Resources, Charleston, W.Va., 1996-2001; v.p., ptnr. Triana Energy, Charleston, W.Va., 2001—. Bd. dirs. Fourth Venture Investment Group, Inc.; adj. prof. W.Va. Grad. Coll., 1996-97, Wheeling Jesuit U., 1997, U. Charleston, 1998; chmn., exec. com., bd. dirs. Star U.S.A. Fed. Credit Union. V.p., bd. trustees Highland Hosp., 1991—; chmn. bd. dirs. Inroads/W.Va., 1995-2001, Christmas in April, 2000-01. Mem. ABA, W.Va. State Bar, Soc. Human Resource Mgmt., W.Va. C. of C. (chmn. human resource com., bd. dirs.), St. Thomas Moore Soc., Berry Hills Country Club. Republican. Roman Catholic. Avocation: golf. Home: 1501 Brentwood Rd Charleston WV 25314-2307 Office: Triana Energy 300 Summers St Ste 300 BB&T Bldg Charleston WV 25301 E-mail: jdissen@trianaenergy.com.

DISSEN, WALTER CHARLES, lawyer; b. Garrison, N.D., Nov. 20, 1931; s. Victor H. and Lydia A. Dissen. BS in bus. adminstrn. cum laude, Kent State U., 1958; JD, U. Akron, 1962. Bar: Ohio 1962, Mo. 1979. Atty. N.Y. Chgo. and St. Louis R.R. Co., Cleve., 1962—64; solicitor, asst. gen. atty., gen. atty. Norfolk and Western Rlwy. Co., St. Louis, 1964—84; sr. gen. atty. Norfolk So. Corp., Atlanta, 1984—. Bd. regents Concordia Sem., St. Louis, 1971—; mem. commn. on appeals Luth. Ch. Mo. Synod, 1984—. Served with U.S. Army. Recipient Christus Vivit, faculty, Concordia Sem., 1984. Mem.: ABA, ICC Practitioners Assn., Mo. Bar Assn, Ohio Bar Assn. Republican.

DISSETTE, ALYCE MARIE, television multimedia and theatrical producer, non-profit foundation executive; b. Flint, Mich., Mar. 16, 1952; d. Leland Richard and Carol A.R. (Scott) D. Student, U. Mich., Flint, 1972-73, U. Wis., 1975-76. Personal asst. Gilbert V. Helmsly Jr., Madison, Wis., 1975-78; adminstrv. asst. Presentations, Met. Opera, N.Y.C., 1977-79; exec. dir. ODC/Dance, San Francisco, 1983-86; producer, exec. dir. David Gordon/Pick Up Co., N.Y.C., 1986-89; dir. media mktg. and tech. Performance Space 122, N.Y.C., 2000-01. Dir. computer art competitition New Voices, New Visions, 1994. Exec. prodr.: (TV series) Alive TV/Alive from Off-Center, 1991—93, Cable Ace Award ALIVE/MTV Co-prodn., 1994; prodr.: Art Spiegelman's Drawn to Death, A Three Panel Opera, 1997—2001, John Kelly & Co., 2000—, David Gordon & Ain Gordon, 2002—. Office: 520 8th Ave New York NY 10018 E-mail: alyce@thorn.net.

DI STEFANO, JULIA MARY, communications educator; b. N.Y.C. d. Francesco and Emanuela Di Stefano; widow; children: Julie, Valerie, Nicholas. BA cum laude, Queens Coll., 1957; MA in English and Edn., Hunter Coll., CUNY, 1963; MA in English and Liberal Studies, SUNY, Stony Brook, l97l, PhD in English, l977. Tchr. H.S. N.Y.C. Bd. Edn., 1957-6l; adj. prof. humanities Suffolk C.C., Selden, NY, l976-80; asst. to dean Sch. Allied Health Professions SUNY Health Scis. Ctr., Stony Brook, 1977-78; prof. communication So. N.H. U., Manchester, 1980—. Humanist N.H. Humanities Coun. Editor N.H. Coll. Jour.; mem. editl. bd. N.E. Assn. Tchrs.; contbr. articles and book revs. to profl. jours. Cons. on conflict resolution Episcopal Diocese N.H. Recipient faculty excellence in teaching award N.H. Coll., l982; rsch. grantee Am. Coun. Learned Socs., l978, N.H. Coll., l98l, 83, 89, Dartmouth Coll. Mem. AAAS, Internat. System Dynamics Soc. (charter; policy coun. 1989-93), Nat. Coun. Tchrs. English, N.H. Mediators Assn. Avocations: photography, fly fishing. Office: NH Coll 2500 N River Rd Hooksett NH 03106-1067

DISTELHORST, GARIS FRED, trade association executive; b. Columbus, Ohio, Jan. 21, 1942; s. Harold Theodore and Ruth (Haywood) D.; m. Helen Cecilla Gillen, Oct. 28, 1972; children: Garen, Kristen, Alison. BSc, Ohio State U., 1965. V.p. Smith, Bucklin & Assocs., Washington, 1969-80; chief staff exec., CEO, pres. Nat. Assn. Coll. Stores, Oberlin, Ohio, 1980-98; pres. Assn. Initiatives, Inc., Westlake, Ohio, 1998—2002; pres., CEO Conv. Industry Coun., 1999—2001, Marble Inst. Am., 2002—. Mem. book and libr. adv. com. USIA, 1990-93; bd. dirs. FirstMerit Bank, N.A., Holcombs, Inc. Pres. Oberlin Cmty. Improvement Corp., 1985-88; bd. dirs. Leadership Lorain County, 1988-89, Access Program, 1994-97, Conv. and Visitors Bur. Greater Cleve., 1994-2003, Lorain County C.C. Found., Lorain County United Way, 1991-97, v.p., 1993-94, pres., 1994-96, campaign chmn., 1993. Decorated USN Achievement medal, 1969 Mem. Inst. Assn. Mgmt. Soc. (treas. 1979-80, award of merit), Am. Soc. Assn. Execs. (bd. dirs. 1981-84, vice chmn. 1985, chmn.-elect 1994, chmn. 1995-96, bd. dirs. found. 1990-94, vice chmn. found. 1991-92, chmn. found. 1992-93, Key award 1984, chmn. Assn. Advance Am. 1993-94), Oberlin Area C. of C. (pres. 1987-90, bd. dirs. 1987-90), Greater Cleve. Soc. Assn. Execs. Republican. Roman Catholic. Office: Marble Inst Am 28901 Clemens Rd Ste 100 Cleveland OH 44145 E-mail: gdistelhorst@attbi.com. *Leadership isn't about having followers, but rather about providing an inspiring vision of a better future for your associates & colleagues.*

DISTER, JOHN E. religious organization administrator; b. Cleveland, Ohio, Mar. 18, 1931; s. Arthur C. Dister and Geraldine M. Riehl. MA, Loyola U., 1959; STL, U. Innsbruck, Austria, 1963; PhD, U. Bristol, Eng., 1969. Cath. chaplain, lectr. in religion Case Western Res. U., Cleve., 1972—77; dir. Colombiere Retreat and Conf. Ctr., Clarkston, Mich., 1979—84; asst. v.p. for univ. mission John Carroll U., Cleve., 1991—96; provincial asst. for social and retreat ministries Detroit Province of the Jesuits, 1996—. Editor, contbr.: book A New Introduction to the Spiritual Exercises of St. Ignatius, 1993. Mem. Interfaith Ctr. for Corp. Responsibility, N.Y.C., NY, 1996—2002. Mem.: Cath. Theol. Soc. of Am. Roman Catholic. Office: Detroit Province of the Soc of Jesus 7303 W Seven Mile Rd Detroit MI 48221-2121 Personal E-mail: jedister@jesuits.net. Business E-Mail: jedister@jesuits.net.

DISTLER, MEGAN J. economist; b. Lehigh Valley, Pa., June 6, 1975; d. Henry A. and Jane A. Distler. BA in Comm. Studies, Cedar Crest Coll., 1997; MBA, DeSales U., 2003. Mgr. bus. devel. Adams Outdoor, Lehigh Valley, Pa., 1997—99; mktg. cons. Tu Way Wireless, 2002—03; v.p. mktg. and pub. rels. Lehigh Valley Econ. Devel., 1999—. Home: 1144 Morris Ln Slatington PA 18080 Office: Lehigh Valley Econ Devel 2158 Ave C Bethlehem PA 18017

DI SUVERO, MARK, sculptor; b. Shanghai, Sept. 18, 1933; s. Vittorio and Matilde (Millo) Di Suvero. BA, U. Calif., Berkeley, 1957. Co-founder Park Place Gallery, N.Y.C., 1963. Founder Socrates Sculpture Pk., N.Y.C., 1986; one-person shows include Green Gallery, N.Y., 1960, Park Place Gallery, N.Y., 1966, Van Abbemuseum, Eindhoven, Netherlands, 1972, City of Chalon-sur-Saone, France, 1974, Jardin des Tuileries, Paris, 1975, Whitney Mus., N.Y.C., 1975, Oil and Steel Gallery, N.Y.C., 1983, Storm King Art Ctr., 1985, 95, 96, Wurttembergischer Kunstverein, Stuttgart, 1988, City of Valence, France, 1990, Musee d'Art Moderne et d'Art Contemporain de Nice, France, 1991, City of Chalon/Saône, France, 1992, IVAM Centre Julio Gonzalez, Valencia, Spain, 1994, XLVI Venice Biennial, 1995, City of Paris, 1997, Hiroshima Mus. Contemporary Art, 1998, Gagosian Gallery, N.Y.C., 2001, others; represented in permanent collections, Art Inst. Chgo., Whitney Mus., N.Y.C., Museum of Modern Art, N.Y.C., Nat. Gallery Art, Washington, Hirshhorn Mus. and Sculpture Garden, Washington, Mus. of Contemporary Art, L.A., others. Grantee Longview Found., Walter K. Gutman Found.; recipient Art Inst. Chgo. award, 1963, Creative Arts award Brandeis U., 1969, Skowhegan Sch. award, 1974. Business E-Mail: disuvero@spacetimecc.com.

DITKA, MICHAEL KELLER, former professional football coach; b. Carnegie, Pa., Oct. 18, 1939; s. Mike and Charlotte (Keller) D.; m. Margery Ditka, Jan. 21, 1961 (div. 1973); children: Michael, Mark, Megan, Matthew; m. Diana S. Ditka, July 8, 1977. Student, U. Pitts. Profl. football player Chgo. Bears, 1961-66, Phila. Eagles, 1967-68, Dallas Cowboys, 1969-72, asst. coach, 1973-81; head coach Chgo. Bears, 1982-93; coach Chgo. Bears Superbowl Championship Team, 1985; owner Ditka's Restaurant, Chgo., 1986—; head coach New Orleans Saints, 1997-99. Named Rookie of Yr., NFL, 1961; named to Pro Bowl, 1962-66; inducted into Hall of Fame, 1988; named coach of the year, NFL, 1988. Roman Catholic.

DITKOFF, EDWARD CHARLES, reproductive endocrinologist; b. N.Y.C., Jan. 12, 1960; s. Jerome Lionel and Adele Helen (Liebermann) D.; m. Patricia Marie Hansen, May 1, 1988; children: Rebecca, Erica. BS in Biology, Emory U., 1981; MD, Chgo. Med. Sch., 1985. Intern. ObGyn. Brookdale Med. Ctr., Bklyn., 1985-86; resident ObGyn. Albany Med. Ctr., N.Y.C., 1986-87; resident Washington Med. Ctr., 1987-90; fellow reproductive endocrinology U. So. Calif., L.A., 1990-92; asst. prof., med. dir. divsn. asst. reproduction Columbia U., N.Y.C., 1992-98; physician Advanced Fertility Svcs., N.Y.C., 1998—. Asst. instr. George Washington Med. Sch., 1987-90. Contbr. articles to profl. jours. Fellow Am. Coll. ObGyn.; mem. Am. Soc. Reproductive Medicine, Soc. Laproscopic Surgeons, Endocrine Soc. Office: 1625 Third Ave New York NY 10128 also: 30 Davis Ave White Plains NY 10605 E-mail: reproed@aol.com.

DITKOWSKY, KENNETH K. lawyer; b. Chgo., July 12, 1936; s. Samuel J. and Lillian (Plavnik) D.; m. Judith Goodman, Aug. 9, 1959; children— Naomi, Deborah, R. Benjamin. B.S., U. Chgo.; J.D., Loyola U., Chgo. Bar: Ill. 1961, U.S. Dist. Ct. (no. dist.) Ill. 1962, U.S. Ct. Apls. (7th cir.) 1973, U.S. Tax Ct. 1973, U.S. Sup. Ct. 1975. Ptnr., Ditkowsky & Contorer, Chgo., 1961— . Mem. Ill. Bar Assn. Office: Ditkowsky & Contorer 2626 W Touhy Ave Chicago IL 60645-3110 E-mail: kenditkowsky@yahoo.com.

DITMORE, HARRY B. surgeon; b. Ft. Sam Houston, Tex., July 25, 1930; s. Harry Boaz and Pauline Ramsey Ditmore; m. Rosanne Young Ha Roh, Jan. 18, 1960; 1 child, John. Student Vanderbilt U., 1946—49; MD, Harvard U., 1953. Diplomate Am. Bd. Gen. Surgery, Am. Bd. Thoracic and Cardiovascular Surgery. Intern Mass. Gen. Hosp., 1953—54; gen. and cardiovascular surgeon Good Samaritan Hosp., Portland, Oreg., 1963-75; resident Mass. Gen. Hosp., 1954—58; resident Children's Meml. Hosp., 1952—53; capt. surgeon U.S. Coast Guard, New London, Conn., 1977-82; gen. surgeon Cassie Meml. Hosp., Burley, Idaho, Minidoka Meml. Hosp., Rupert, Idaho. Capt. USCG, 1977-82. Fellow: ACS; mem.: Minico Med. Assn., Idaho Med. Assn., Am. Statis. Soc. Methodist. Avocations: tree farming, alfalfa farming, mathematical statistics. Office: 1218 9th St Ste 9 Rupert ID 83350 E-mail: harrydit@pmt.org.

DITO, WILLIAM ROBERT, pathology educator; b. Alameda, Calif., Aug. 8, 1929; s. Salvatore Mario and Mary Josephine (Silvestri) D.; m. Bridget Claire O'Rourke, Sept. 25, 1954; children: Robert W., David M., Matthew T., Mark A., William K. BS, U. San Francisco, 1950; MD, Loyola U., Chgo., 1954. Diplomate Am. Bd. Pathology; Clin. and Anatomical Pathology Radioisotopic Pathology. Commd. capt. U.S. Army, 1955; advanced through grades to major, 1961; chief lab. service U.S. Army Hosp., Nuremberg, Fed. Republic Germany, 1961-64; resigned U.S. Army, 1965; chief clin. lab. Letterman Gen. Hosp., San Francisco, 1964-65; dir. labs., dir. Sch. Med. Tech. Pontiac (Mich.) Gen. Hosp., 1965-73; assoc. prof. pathology U. Ariz., Tucson, 1973-76; med. dir. Sch. Med. Tech. Ariz. Med. Ctr., Tucson, 1974-76; head div. lab. medicine Scripps Clinic and Research Found., La Jolla, Calif., 1978-94; regional commr. lab. accreditation program Coll. Am. Pathologists, San Diego, 1994—98. Adj. instr. Wayne State U., Detroit, 1970-73; adj. assoc. prof. pathology, U. Calif.-San Diego, La Jolla, 1977-86, assoc. clin. prof., 1986-98; chief of labs. VA Hosp., Tucson, 1973-74. Co-editor: (with Nakamura and Tucker) Immunologic Analysis—Recent Progress in Diagnostic Laboratory Immunology, 1982; editor: (jour.) Informatics in Pathology, 1985-88; mem. editorial bd. Lab. Medicine, 1978-85; contbr. articles to profl. jours. Fellow. Coll. Am. Pathologists (bd. govs. 1998--), Am. Soc. Clin. Pathologists (mem. editl. bd. 1979-82, Disting. Service award 1980, 98), Internat. Acad. Pathology, La Jolla Profl. Mens Club. Republican. Roman Catholic. Avocations: golf, photography, computers.

D'ITRI, FRANK MICHAEL, environmental research chemist; b. Flint, Mich., Apr. 25, 1933; s. Dominic and Angelina D'Itri; m. Patricia Ann Ward, Sept. 10, 1955; children: Michael Payne, Angela Kathryn, Patricia Ann, Julie Lynn. BS in Zoology, Mich. State U., 1955, MS in Analytical Chemistry, 1966, PhD, 1968. Lab. technician Dow Industry Service Labs., Midland, Mich., 1960-62; research asst. dept. chemistry Mich. State U., East Lansing, 1963-68, asst. prof. dept. fisheries and wildlife, 1968-72, assoc. prof. dept. fisheries and wildlife, 1973-76, prof. dept. fisheries and wildlife, 1977—; assoc. dir. Inst. Water Rsch., 1987—; asst. dir. Mich. Agrl. Exptl. Sta., 1996—. Cons. U.S. Dept. Energy, Washington, 1983-85, FFC, UN, Geneva, 1982—; vis. prof. U. Dahia, Brazil, 1978, Tokyo U. Agr., 1980, 84-85, 87, 94, 2000, 01; mem. adv. bd. Lewis Pubs., Inc., Springer-Verlag. Author: The Environmental Mercury Problem, 1972, (with P.A. D'Itri) Mercury Contamination: A Human Tragedy, 1977, (with A.W. Andren, R.A. Doherty, J.M. Wood), Assessment of Mercury in the Environment, 1978, Acid Precipitation, 1982, Artificial Reefs, 1985; editor (with J. Aguirre M., M. Athie L.), Municipal Wastewater in Agriculture, 1981, Land Treatment of Municipal Wastewater: Vegetation Selection and Management, 1982, Acid Precipitation: Effects on Ecological Systems, 1982, (with M.A. Kamrin) PCBs: Human and Environmental Hazards, 1983, Artificial Reefs: Marine and Freshwater Applications, 1985, A System Approach to Conservation Tillage, 1985, (with H.H. Prince) Coastal Wetlands, 1985; (with L.G. Wolfson) Rural Groundwater Contamination, 1987, Chemical Deicers And The Environment, 1992, (with H.W. Belcher) Subirrigation and Controlled Drainage, 1995, Zebra Mussels and Aquatic Nuisance Species, 1997, (with Y. Itakura) Integrated Environmental Management, 1999; contbr. numerous articles to profl. jours. Mem. critical materials adv. subcom. Mich. Water Resources Commns. Mich. Dept. Natural Resources, 1971-79, mem. solid waste com., 1971-79; mem. subcom. Mich. State U. Waste Control Authority Chem. Waste, 1971—; mem. tech. adv. com. Great Lakes Protection fund tech. adv. com., 1990-93; mem. Great Lakes Commn., 1992—; mem. subirrigation steering com. Mich. Soil Conservation Svc., 1986—; mem. fluctuating lake levels com. Internat. Joint Commn., 1992-93; mem. internat. rsch. group mercury pollution in Amazon, Brazil, 1992—. NIH summer fellow, 1964 67, Socony-Mobil fellow Mich. State U., 1967-68, Japan Soc. Promotion Sci. fellow, 1980; Rockefeller Found. Bellagio Resident scholar, 1972, 75. Mem. Am. Chem. Soc., Am. Soc. Limnology and Oceanography, Assn. Analytical Chemists, Water Pollution Research Soc., Midwest Univs. Analytical Chemists Conf., Mich. Acad. Sci., Arts and Letters, Sigma Xi, Setac. Home: 4395 Elmwood Dr Okemos MI 48864-3034 Office: Mich State U 115 Manly Miles 1405 S Harrison Rd East Lansing MI 48823-5289 E-mail: ditri@msu.edu.

DITTENHAFER, BRIAN DOUGLAS, banker, economist; b. York, Pa., Aug. 15, 1942; s. Nathaniel Webster and Evelyn Romaine (Myers) D.; m. Miriam Marcy, Aug. 22, 1964; 1 child BA, Ursinus Coll., 1964; MA, Temple U., 1966, postgrad., 1967-71. Personnel asst. Philco Corp., Phila., 1965-66; teaching asst. Temple U., Phila., 1966-67, research asso., 1968-69; bus. economist Fed. Res. Bank of Atlanta, 1971-76; v.p., chief economist Fed. Home Loan Bank of N.Y., N.Y.C., 1976-79, sr. v.p., chief fin. officer, 1979-80, exec. v.p., 1980-85, pres., 1985-92, Collective Fed. Savs. Bank, 1992-94, Collective Bancorp, 1992-94; chmn. MBD Mgmt. Co., 1994—. Vice chmn. Fin. Instns. Thrift Plan, 1991-92, chmn., 1992; trustee Fin. Instns. Retirement Fund, 1985-92, vice chmn., 1991, chmn., 1992; bd. dirs. Investors Savs. Bank, 1997—. Bd. dirs. Social Compact, 1990-99, sec., 1995-99; mem. FNMA Found. Adv. Group, 1994; deacon Ctrl. Presbyn. Ch., 1981-84; bd. dirs. N.Y. Coun. Econ. Edn., 1983-89; chmn. Resolution Funding Corp., 1989-92. Temple U. fellow, G.E. Found. fellow Temple U. Mem. Nat. Assn. Bus. Economists, Am. Econ. Assn., Forecaster's Club N.Y. (sec.-treas. 1982-84), Suntree Country Club (dir., treas. 2000-2003), Omicron Delta Epsilon.

DITTES, JAMES EDWARD, psychology of religion educator; b. Cleve., Dec. 26, 1926; s. Mercein Edward and Mary (Freeman) D.; children: Lawrence William (dec.), Nancy Eleanor, Carolyn Ann, Joanne Frances; m. Anne Hebert Smith, Nov. 27, 1987. AB, Oberlin Coll., 1949; B.D., Yale U., 1954, MS, 1955, PhD, 1958. Instr. Am. Sch., Talas, Turkey, 1950-52; ordained to ministry United Ch. Christ, 1954; mem. faculty Yale U., 1955—2002, prof. psychology of religion, 1967-84, prof. pastoral theology and psychology, 1984-2001, chmn. dept. religious studies, 1975-82, Squire prof. pastoral counseling, 2001—02. Chmn. Council on Grad. Studies in Religion in U.S. and Can., 1970-71 Author: The Church in the Way, 1967, Minister on the Spot, 1970, Bias and the Pious, 1973, When the People Say No, 1979, The Male Predicament, 1985, When Work Goes Sour, 1987, Men at Work, 1996, Driven by Hope, 1996, Pastoral Counseling, 1999, Re-Calling Ministry, 1999, (with Robert Menges) Psychological Studies of Clergymen, 1965, (with Donald Capps) The Hunger of the Heart, 1990. Served with USNR, 1945-46. Guggenheim fellow, 1965-66; Fulbright Research fellow Rome, 1965-66; sr. fellow NEH, 1972-73 Mem. Soc. Sci. Study of Religion (exec. sec. 1959-63, editor jour. 1966-71, pres. 1971-73) Home and Office: 1157 Whitney Ave Hamden CT 06517-3434

DITTMAN, DUANE SCOTT, registrar; b. Summit, N.J., Oct. 4, 1953; s. Duane A. and Virginia (Scott) D.; m. Susan Humphreys, Mar. 25, 1978; children: Sarah Anne, Griffin Hope, Douglas Clay. AB, Colgate U., 1975; postgrad., Western Ill. U., 1980, Trinity Internat. Univ., 1995-96. Devel. researcher Colgate U., Hamilton, N.Y., 1976-77; asst. dir. admissions Muskingum Coll., New Concord, Ohio, 1977-82, registrar, 1982-85; univ. registrar Washington & Lee U., Lexington, Va., 1985—, dir. instl. rsch., 2002—, ind. cons., 1995—. Assoc. editor AACRAO Netnews, 1999-2001; contbg. editor AACRAO Transcript, 2001—. Vol. ARC Blood Drives, Ohio, Va. and N.Y., 1971—; sec. Rockbridge Christian Action Coun., Lexington, 1987-92; mem. Rockbridge Young Life Com., 1989-2001, treas., 1994-98. Mem. Am. Assn. Collegiate Registrars and Admissions Officers, So. Assn. Collegiate Registrars and Admissions Officers (bd. jour. editors 1989-93, exec. com. 1993-94, nom. & elections com. 1997-98, 2001—, chair 2002—), Va. Assn. Collegiate Registrars and Admissions Officers (exec. com. 1987-89, 90-93, sec. 1990-93, Disting. Svc. awards 1991, 95, chair tech. and data com. 1995-97, chair leg. and inter assn. issues com. 1996-98), Konosioni Soc., Alpha Phi Omega, Beta Theta Pi, Omicron Delta Kappa. Avocations: bible study, sports, trombone, vocal music. E-mail: sdittman@wlu.edu.

DITTMANN, MELISSA ANN, journalist; b. St. Joseph, Mich., Apr. 18, 1979; d. John Paul and Brenda Arlene Dittman. BS in Commn., Grand Valley State U., 2000. Corr. writer Herald Palladium, St. Joseph, 1997—98; intern CNBC-Chgo., 1999; editor in chief The GVSU Lanthorn, Allendale, Mich., 1999—2000; reporter Chronicle-Telegram, Elysia, Ohio, 2000—. Recipient 2 Hon. Mention News and Feature awards, Cordelia Robbins Awards, 2000; scholar, Mich. Press Assn., 2000. Mem.: Am. Screenwriters Assn., Soc. Profl. Journalists.

DITTMER, JOHN AVERY, history educator; b. Seymour, Ind., Oct. 30, 1939; s. J. Avery and Melba Roberta (Ahlbrand) D.; m. Ellen Ann Tobey, June 3, 1961; children: Julia Susan, John David. BS in Edn., Ind. U., 1961, MA in History, 1964, PhD in History, 1971. Asst. prof. Tougaloo (Miss.) Coll., 1967-68, acad. dean, 1968-70, assoc. prof., 1971-79; assoc. prof. history DePauw U., Greencastle, Ind., 1985-92, prof., 1993—. Vis. assoc. prof. Brown U., Providence, R.I., 1979-80, 81-82, 83-84, MIT, Cambridge, 1982-84; cons. NEH, Washington, 1980-83, PBS Series, Eyes on the Prize, Boston, 1986. Author: Black Georgia in the Progressive Era, 1900-1920, 1977, Local People: The Struggle for Civil Rights in Mississippi, 1994 (Lillian Smith book award, 1994, Bancroft prize Columbia Univ. 1995); contbr. articles to profl. jours. Younger Humanist fellow NEH, 1973-74, fellowship-in-residence NEH, Vanderbilt U., 1976-77, Rockefeller Found., 1980-81, Am. Coun. Learned Socs., 1983-84, Ctr. for Study of Civil Rights, U. Va., 1988-89, NEH, 2000-01, Nat. Humanities Ctr., 2001-01. Mem. Orgn. of Am. Historians (Frederick Jackson Turner award finalist 1972), So. Hist. Assn., Am. Hist. Assn. Avocations: tennis, golf, jazz music. Home: 230 Westwood Rd Fillmore IN 46128-9621 Office: DePauw U Dept History Greencastle IN 46135 E-mail: rip@depauw.edu.

DITTMER, LUTHER ALBERT, publisher, educator; b. Bklyn., Apr. 8, 1927; s. Clarence Christian and Marie Edith Alberta (Hachtmann), June 15, 1921; m. Anna Klara Ingeborg Poser, Dec. 27, 1951; children: Kâlogréant Sigurd Dittmer, Christopher-Günter Dittmer. AB, Columbia U., N.Y.C., 1947, AM, 1949; PhD, U. Basel, Switzerland, 1952. Instr. Wagner Coll., N.Y.C., 1953-54, Adelphi Coll., Garden City, N.Y., 1954-59, Manhattan Sch. Music, N.Y.C., 1955-58; assoc. prof. Bklyn. Coll., 1959-76; prof. titulaire Université d'Ottawa, Ottawa, 1976-80; dir. Institut für Mittelalterliche Musikforschung, N.Y.C., 1957—. Author: The Worcester Music Fragments, 1957, Eine Zentrale Quelle der Notre Dame- Mehrstimmigkeit, 1958. Dir. Deutsche Schule der Zionskirche, N.Y.C., 1959-60. Served with USNR, 1945-46. Freisinnige Partei der Schweiz. Lutheran. Home: Melchtalstrasse 11 CH-4102 Binningen Switzerland Office: PO Box 295 Henryville PA 18332-0295 E-mail: InstitutMe@cs.com.

DITTMER, SYLVESTER STEPHEN WESS, retired nursing administrator; b. Herman, Pa., Apr. 27, 1949; s. Joseph Robert and Mary-Elizabeth (Raith) D. BS in Bus. Adminstrn., Gannon U., 1971; ADN, Butler County C.C., Butler, Pa., 1991. RN, Pa., N.Y., Ohio. Mgr. Morgan Restaurant, Butler, 1976-77, Dunhams Sporting Goods, Pitts., 1995-96; nurse Olsten Health Care, Pitts., 1978-94, Presbyn. Med. Ctr., Oakmont, Pa., 1996-97; nursing supr. St. Francis Health Sys., Pitts., 1994-95, ret., 1995—. Pres. Herman Area Safety Coun., 1999—. Capt. U.S. Army, 1972-79. Mem. Am. Assembly Men in Nursing, Am. Legion, Inst. German-Am. Rels., German Beneficial Union, Teutonia Mannerchor, Scabbard and Blade Mil. Fraternity. Roman Catholic. Avocations: military history, politics, current events. Home: Box 107 Dittmer Rd Herman PA 16039-0107

DITTNER, DEBORAH MARIE, nurse practitioner in family health; b. Apr. 7, 1954; BSN, Western Conn. State U., 1976; student, Albany Med. Coll., 1980; postgrad., Clayton Coll. Natural Health; coaching cert., Adirondack C.C., 1994. RN, N.Y.; cert. primary care nurse practitioner; cert. Reiki. Pvt. practice family nurse practitioner, Saratoga Springs, N.Y., 1981-90; employee health nurse practitioner Samaritan Hosp., Troy, N.Y., 1990-92; pvt. practice ob-gyn. nurse practitioner, Clifton Park, N.Y., 1995-96; pvt. practice family nurse practitioner Bellevue Hosp. Women, Niskayuna, 1996 2001; dir. Wellness Ctr./Health Svcs., Russell Sage Coll., Troy, 1996—; dir. Wellness Ctr./Health Svcs. Sage Coll. of Albany, 2001—; pvt. practice family nurse practitioner Seton Health Sys., Troy, 1997-2000. Reiki master tchr. practitioner Reiki Rm., Saratoga Springs, NY, 2002—. Founder, dir., author, editor newsletter The Baby Umbrella Newsletter, 1987-90. N.Y. state coord. Melpomene Inst. for Women's Health Rsch., St. Paul, 1981-2000; prs. Girls Basketball Booster Club, Saratoga Springs H.S., 1995-98. Mem.: N.Y. State Coll. Health Assn., N.Y. State Coalition of Nurse Practitioners (treas. 1997—99), Am. Coll. Health Assn., Hist. Soc. for the Preservation of the Underground Railroad (treas. 2000—01, v.p. 2001—), Greenfield Hist. Soc. (life; treas. 2000—01, v.p. 2001—), Zonta Club Saratoga County (pub. rels. chair 1985—87). Address: 3149 Route 9N Greenfield Center NY 12833-1713 E-mail: dittnd@sage.edu., dmd7@netzero.net.

DITTO, EDWARD WILSON, III, retired family physician; b. Hagerstown, Md., July 24, 1924; s. Edward Wilson Jr. and Neva Beryl (Nihiser) D.; m. Glenice Ardell Allen (dec. Mar. 1999); children: Allen Wilson, David Curtis, Betsey Page Lillard. BS, Franklin and Marshall Coll., 1947; postgrad., U. Md., 1947-48; MD, Jefferson Med. Coll., 1952. Diplomate Am. Bd. Family Practice. Intern Allegheny Gen. Hosp., Pitts., 1952-54; pvt. practice, Hagerstown, Md.; dep. med. examiner Washington County, Hagerstown, 1959—; mem. staff (hon.) Washington County Hosp. Bd. dirs. Cmty. Rescue Svc., 1969—80. With M.C. USN, 1944—45, lt. comdr. M.C. USNR, 1964—. Mem.: MAFC, AAFP, AMA, SMA, Washington County Med. Soc. (2-time past pres.), Med.-Chirug. Soc. Md., Am. Legion, Fountain Head Country Club, Rotary (del., Paul Harris fellow), Elks. Republican. Avocations: travel, stamp collecting, swimming, hiking.

DI TURI, CHRISTOPHER, dentist, maxillofacial prosthodontist, educator, researcher; b. N.Y.C., Dec. 21, 1961; s. Dominic and C. Paula (DiRaffaele) Di T. BS in Biochemistry, SUNY, Stony Brook, 1983; DDS, NYU, 1987; MS in Combined Prosthodontics, N.J. Dental Sch., 1990. Resident Richmond Meml. Hosp., S.I., 1987-88; prof. prosthodontics and biomaterial sci., rschr. U. Medicine Dentistry of N.J., Newark, 1990—; pvt. practice Fair Haven, N.J., 1994—; dir. implant residency Monmouth Med. Ctr. Bd. dirs. Columbus Hosp., 2000-. Editor: Introduction to the Dental Industry, 1992; contbr. articles to profl. jours. Recipient scholarship Richmond County Dental Soc., NYU, 1983-84. Mem. ADA, Am. Coll. Prosthodontics (bd. dirs., pres. N.J. sect. 1997-), Acad. Osseointegration, Northeast Gnathological Soc., N.J. Acad. Medicine, Boys Town Italy (N.Y.C.), Columbus Citizens Found., Theatre Devel. Found., Nat. Italian Am. Found., Coalition Italo-Am. Orgns., Italian Welfare League Republican. Roman Catholic. Home: 133 Hooper Ave Staten Island NY 10306-3752 Office: 600 River Rd Fair Haven NJ 07704-3221

DIUGUID, LEWIS WALTER, newspaper executive, columnist; b. St. Louis, July 17, 1955; s. Lincoln Isaiah and Nancy Ruth (Greenlee) D.; m. Valerie Gale Words, Oct. 25, 1977; children: Adrianne, Leslie Ellen. BJ, U. Mo., 1977. Reporter, photographer, copy and automotive editor Kansas City Times, Mo., 1977-85; asst. minority recruiting coord. Kansas City Times and Star, 1985—; asst. bur. chief Johnson County office The Kansas City Star, 1985-87, bur. chief Southland bur., 1987-92, columnist, 1987—, asst. city editor Southland bur., 1992-94, diversity trainer, 1993—, assoc. editor, met. columnist, 1994-99; v.p. cmty. resources, editl. bd. mem., columnist, diversity co-chair The Star Co., 1995—. Recipient Media award Ark of Friends of Greater Kansas City, 1990, 91, 92, 93, 94, 95, Black Achievers award, 1997, Mental Health award, 1991, Rsch. Mental Health Media award, 1992, Difference Maker award Urban League Greater Kansas City, 1992, Mo. C.C. Assn. Media award, 1993, Mental Health Awareness award Mental Health Kansas City, 1993, Pub. Affairs/Social Issues Unity award, 1993, 1st Place Kansas City Press Club award, 1993, Comprehensive Mental Media award State Mo., 1995, Project HEART award Swinney and Red Bridge Schs., 1995, Evelyn Wasserstrom award So. Christian Leadership Conf., 1996, Black Achievers award, 1997, James K. Batten Knight Ridder Excellence award for Cmty. Svc., 1998, Mo. Honor medal for disting. svc. in journalism U. Mo.-Columbia Sch. Journalism, 2000, Millennium award NAACP Br. 4071, 2000, Freedom Fighter award, 2002, HIV/AIDS Edn. award SCLC Greater Kansas City and Good Samaritan Project, 2001, Charles E. Bebb Peace Merit award for Outstanding Svc. in Cause of Peace PeaceWorks Kansas City, 2002, Kansas City Interfaith Peace award, 2002, Beacon award in Media Rels. Kansas City Human Rights Commn., 2002, Media award Kansas Correctional Assn., 2002, Gail & Irv Achtenberg Civil Libertarian award ACLU of Kans. and We. Mo., 2002, Crescent Peace Soc. Journalism award, 2002; named one of 100 Most Influential African Ams. in Greater Kansas City, 1992, 93, 94, 95, 96, 97; Inst. for Journalism Edn. fellow U. Ariz., Tucson, 1984. Mem. Nat. Assn. Black Journalists, Kansas City Assn. Black Journalists (pres. 1986, sec. 1987, v.p. 1993, treas. 1994-96), Nat. Soc. Newspaper Columnists, Monroe Trotter Group of Black Voices in Commentary. Roman Catholic. Avocations: jogging, weight lifting, bike riding, woodworking. Office: Kansas City Star 1729 Grand Ave Kansas City MO 64108-1413 E-mail: Ldiuguid@Kcstar.com.

DIVAKARAN, AJAY, electrical engineer, research and development company executive; b. Vellore, Tamil Nadu, India, Feb. 25, 1964; s. Subbanarasu and Bharathi Divakaran; m. Padma Akella, Sept. 6, 1989; 1 child, Swathi Chandrika. PhD Elec. Engring., Rensselaer Poly. Inst., 1993. Sr. prin. mem. of tech. staff Mitsubishi Electric Rsch. Laboratories, Murray Hill, NJ, 2002—, prin. mem. of tech. staff, 1998—2002. Author: (technical papers in journals) IEEE and SPIE journals on Video and Image related topics. Mem.: IEEE (sr.). Achievements include patents for One patent awarded several pending/allowed. Office: Mitsubishi Electric Rsch Labs 558 Central Ave Murray Hill NJ 07834 Office Fax: 908-363-0550. Personal E-mail: ajayd@merl.com.

DIVALE, WILLIAM T. s. Joseph Divale and Josephine Viola Crocco, Josephine Viola Crocco; m. Maria Victoria Cardona, May 10, 1999. AA in Social Sciences, Pasadena (Calif.) City Coll., 1966; BA in History, UCLA, 1969; MA in Anthropology, Calif. State U., L.A., 1971; PhD in Anthropology, SUNY, Buffalo, 1973. Prof. of anthropology York Coll., CUNY, N.Y.C., 1973—. Author (researcher): (books, articles) Matrilocal Residence in Primitive Society, 1983 (C.S. Ford Cross-Cultural Rsch. award, 1973, 1974); author: (bibliography) I Lived Inside the Campus Revolution, 1969; editor-in-chief: World Cultures. MARC Tng. grantee for minority students, Nat. Istitute of Gen. Med. Sciences, 1994—. Fellow: Am. Anthrop. Assn.; mem.: Northeastern Anthrop. Assn. (program chmn. 1999—2000), Am. Assn. for Pub. Opinion Rsch., Internat. Soc. for Cross-Cultural Psychology, Soc. for Cross-Cultural Rsch. (pres. 2000—). Roman Catholic. Home: 27 Canopus Hollow Rd Putnam Valley NY 10579 Office: York College CUNY 94-20 Guy R Brewer Blvd Jamaica NY 11451 Office Fax: 718-262-3790. E-mail: divale@york.cuny.edu., divalebill@aol.com.

DIVARIS, MICHAEL B. real estate development company; B in Bus. Adminstrn., U. Natal, 1972. Personal asst. to chmn. Anglo Am. Property Co., 1972-74; co-founder Divaris Real Estate Co., Cape Town, South Africa, 1974-87, pres. Virginia Beach, 1987—. Past pres Va. Stage Co. Office: Divaris Real Estate One Columbus Ctr Ste 700 Virginia Beach VA 23462

DIVENERE, ANTHONY JOSEPH, lawyer; b. Bari, Italy, June 20, 1941; s. Joseph and Donna (Montini) DiV.; m. Sylvia Kathleen Scarnati, June 19, 1965; children: Anthony, Diana, John. AB, John Carroll U., 1964; JD, Ohio State U., 1967. BAr: Ohio 1967. Atty. in charge Cleve. Legal Aid Soc., 1967-70; prin., v.p. Burke Haber & Berick Co., L.P.A., Cleve., 1971; shareholder McDonald, Hopkins, Burke & Haber. Recipient Claude E. Clark award Cleve. Legal Aid. Soc., 1968, Cmty. Svc. aard North Olmsted Jaycees, 1972. Mem. ABA, Ohio Bar Assn., Cleve. Bar Assn. (Appreciation award 1979-80), Cleve. Assn. Trial Attys. (pres. 1979-80), Def. Rsch. Inst., Vermilion Yacht Club. Avocations: sailing, marathon running, squash, opera. Home: 310 Rye Gate St Cleveland OH 44140-1272 Office: McDonald Hopkins Burke & Haber 2100 Bank One Center Cleveland OH 44114 E-mail: ajd@mhbh.com.

DIVER, COLIN S. academic administrator, educator; b. 1943; BA, Amherst Coll., 1965; LLB, Harvard U., 1968; MA, U. Pa., 1989; LLD, Amherst Coll., 1990. Bar: Mass. 1968. Spl. counsel Office of The Mayor, Boston, 1968-71; asst. sec. consumer affairs Exec. Office Consumer Affairs, Boston, 1971-72; under-sec. adminstrn. Exec. Office Adminstrn. and Fin., Boston, 1972-74; assoc. prof. Boston U., 1975-81, prof., 1981-89, from assoc. dean to dean, 1985-89; dean, Bernard G. Segal prof. U. Pa., Phila., 1989—99, Charles A. Heimbold, Jr., prof., 1999—2002; pres. Reed Coll., Portland, Oreg., 2002—. Cons. Adminstrv. Conf. of U.S., 1980-88. Chmn. Mass. State Ethics Com., 1983-89; mem. adv. com. on enforcement policy NRC, 1984-85. Office: Reed Coll 3203 SE Woodstock Blvd Portland OR 97202

DIVINE, ROBERT ALEXANDER, history educator; b. Bklyn., May 10, 1929; s. Walter E. and Emily (Mable) D.; m. Barbara C. Renick, Aug. 6, 1955 (dec.); children: J. Douglas, Elisabeth T., Richard L., Kirk M.; m. Darlene S. Harris, June 1, 1996 (dec.). BA, Yale U., 1951, MA, 1952, PhD, 1954. Instr. U. Tex., Austin, 1954-57, asst. prof., 1957-61, assoc. prof., 1961-63, prof. history, 1963-96, chmn. dept. history, 1963-68, Piper prof., 1972, George W. Littlefield prof. Am. history, 1981-96, prof. emeritus, 1996—. Fellow Center for Advanced Study in Behavioral Scis. Stanford, Calif., 1962-63; Albert Shaw lectr. in

diplomatic history, Johns Hopkins, 1968 Author: American Immigration Policy, 1924-52, 1957, The Illusion of Neutrality, 1962, The Reluctant Belligerent, 1965, Second Chance, 1967, Roosevelt and World War II, 1969, Foreign Policy and U.S. Presidential Elections, 1940-60, 2 vols., 1974, Since 1945: Politics and Diplomacy in Recent American History, 1975, Blowing on the Wind, 1978, Eisenhower and the Cold War, 1981, The Sputnik Challenge, 1993, Perpetual War for Perpetual Peace, 2000; co-author: America Past and Present, 1984, 6th edit., 2002. Mem. Orgn. Am. Historians, Soc. for Historians of Am. Fgn. Rels. Methodist. Home: 10617 Sans Souci Pl Austin TX 78759-6185 E-mail: rdivine@austin.rr.com.

DI VIRGILIO, NICHOLAS, voice music educator; b. North Tonawanda, N.Y. BM, Eastman Sch. Music, 1958. Prof. voice, opera U. Ill. Sch. Music, Urbana, 1975—. Leading tenor, Met. Opera, N.Y.C., 1970-73, N.Y.C Opera, 1966-74. With U.S. Army, 1952-54. Home: 1901A E Amber Ln Urbana IL 61802-6922 Office: U Ill Sch Music 1114 W Nevada St Urbana IL 61801-3859

DI VITTORIO, SALVATORE, music educator, composer, conductor; b. Palermo, Italy, Oct. 22, 1967; s. Giuseppe Di Vittorio and Caterina Chiello Di Vittorio. MusB, Manhattan Sch. of Music, 1997; MA, Columbia U., 2000. Instr. of music Di Vittorio Music Studio, N.Y.C., 1997—2002; dir. of music dept. Loyola Sch., N.Y.C., 2002—. Rep. Am. Guild Musical Artists, N.Y.C., 1997—2002; composer-in-residence Internat. Chamber Ensemble of Rome, 2001—, Florence (Italy) Symphonietta, 2001—, Accademia Musicale Siciliana, Palermo, Italy, 2001—; judge Ibla Festival Grand Prize in Music Composition, Ragusa, Italy, 2002—03; conducting apprenticeship Rome Conservatory of Music, 2003. Composer (and librettist): (opera) Romeo E Giulietta; composer: Sinfonia No.2 Lost Innocence, Sinfonia No.1 Isolation; performer (premier): N.Y. Symphony, 1997, 2003, Rome Symphony, 2003, Florence Symphony, 2002, 2003, San Jose Symphony, 2003, Perugia Symphony, 2002, Venice Symphony, 2001, Palermo Symphony, 1998, 1999, 2000, Orvieto Symphony, 1997. Grantee, Italy Am. C. of C. of Washington, 1998, Italian Inst. of Culture of N.Y., 2002. Mem.: ASCAP (assoc. Std. awards 1999—2002), Am. Music Ctr., Am. Soc. Aesthetics (assoc.), Am. Symphony Orch. League (assoc.), Condrs. Guild (assoc.). Roman Catholic. Office: Loyola Sch 980 Park Ave New York NY 11105 Personal E-mail: sdvittorio@aol.com.

DIVONE, LOUIS VINCENT, aerospace engineer, educator, federal official, author; b. NYC, July 24, 1934; s. Dominic and Christina Agnes (Cassa) D.; m. Judene Frances Smith, Aug. 10, 1968. B in Aero. Engring., Poly. Inst. Bklyn., 1955; MS, MIT, 1956. Mem. tech. staff Jet Propulsion Lab., Calif. Inst. Tech., 1956-67, 69-72; program mgr. NASA, 1962-63; cons. Dept. Transp., 1968-69; dir. wind energy systems NSF, 1973-74; dir. Wind Energy Tech. Divsn. Dept. Energy, Washington, 1977-83, dir. Office Solar Elec. Techs., 1982-84, 86-90, assoc. dep. asst. sec. Transp. Tech., 1990-91, assoc. dep. asst. sec. for Bldgs. Tech., 1992-94, acting dep. asst. sec. bldg. techs., 1994-95, acting dep. asst. sec. bldg. tech., state and cmty. programs, 1996, assoc. dep. asst. sec. for indsl. techs., 1997-99; pvt. cons. Washington, 2000—. Spl. asst. to dir. market planning and rsch. Grumman Aerospace Corp., 1984-85; professorial lectr. George Washington U., 1976-84; cons. Wind Energy Working Group, UN, 1979-81; chmn. wind energy exec. com. Internat. Energy Agy., 1978-82. Co-editor Energy series Inst. Elec. Engrs., 1990-2000; contbr. papers to profl. symposia; patentee variable area rocket nozzle, self-attaching fluid coupling. Recipient Apollo Achievment award NASA, 1970, Spl. Achievement award ERDA, 1976, Pres.'s Exec. Exch. Program appointment, 1984-85, Disting. Career Svc. award DOE, 1999. Fellow: AAAS, AIAA (assoc.); mem.: Sr. Exec. Assn., Seaplane Pilots Assn., Va. Aero. Hist. Soc., Smithsonian Assn., Antique Airplane Assn., Cessna 180 Owners Club, Tau Beta Pi, Sigma Xi. Home: 2530 Leeds Rd Oakton VA 22124-1406 E-mail: ldivone@aol.com.

DIWAKAR, DEEPTI, architect, dancer; b. Bangalore, Karnataka, India, Oct. 31, 1958; came to the U.S., 1995; d. Anant Ranganath and Shanta (Acharya) D. BArch, U. Coll. Engring., Bangalore, 1984; MA in Broadcast and Electronic Comm., San Francisco State U., 2001. Pvt. practice performer, tchr., choreographer, various locations, 1991-96. TV and radio announcer All India Radio and All India TV, Bangalore, 1986-91; prin. arch. Adithya Archs., Bangalore, 1990-91. Author: The Tree of Verse, 2000; author of science fiction stories and poems; contbg. journalist The Times of India, 2001—. Joint sec. exec. com. Soc. for Prevention of Cruelty to Animals, Bangalore, 1983-86; exec. com. mem. World Conf. on Religions for Peace, New Delhi, 1984-87; active Gandhi Peace Found., Bangalore, 1995—; bd. dirs. Cultural Integration Fellowship, San Francisco, 2001—. Recipient The Great Diamond of Indian Classical Dance, World Devel. Parliament, West Bengal, India, 1989, Pres.' award for Literary Excellence, Iliad Press, Mich., 1995, 97;, Bronze medal Juphilex Philatelic Exhbn., Berne, 1977, Holland, 1979; named Miss India for Miss World, Femina Mag., Bombay, 1981. Hindu. Avocations: painting, traveling, social work, reading, yoga. Home: 950 Cabrillo St Apt 11 San Francisco CA 94118 also: 233/1 Palace Upper Orchards Sadashivanagar 560080 Bangalore India E-mail: deeptidiwakar@hotmail.com.

DIX, GARY ERROL, engineering executive; b. Bieber, Calif., Jan. 10, 1942; s. Errol Alvin and Evelyn Nadine (Miller) D.; m. Lanaya Diane Easley, Jan. 4, 1964. BS in Mech. Engring., U. Calif., Berkeley, 1963, MS in Mech. Engring., 1965, PhD in Mech. Engring., 1971. Engr. Gen. Electric Nuclear, San Jose, Calif., 1965-71, mgr. thermal devel., 1971-75, mgr. safety and hydraulics, 1975-82, mgr. core methods, 1982-85, mgr. automation sys., 1985-89, mgr. quality assurance and automation, 1989-94, mgr. devel. programs, 1994-97. Code rev. group cons. Nuclear Regulatory Commn., Washington, 1976-85; cons. in field, 1997—. Contbr. articles to profl. jours.; patentee in field. Fellow Am. Nuclear Soc. (exec. com. Thermal Hydraulics divsn. 1981-91, chmn. 1986-87). Avocations: computers, wine, motorcycles, basketball, movies.

DIX, ROLLIN C(UMMING), mechanical engineering educator, consultant; b. NYC, Feb. 8, 1936; s. Omer Houston and Ona Mae (Cumming) D.; m. Elaine B. VanNest, June 18, 1960; children: Gregory, Elisabeth, Karen. BSME, Purdue U., 1957, MSME, 1958, PhD, 1963, Registered profl. engr., Ill. Asst. prof. mech. engring. Ill. Inst. Tech., Chgo., 1964-69, assoc. prof., 1969-80, prof., 1980—, assoc. dean for computing, 1980-96; pres. Patpending Mktg., Inc., 1996—. Bd. dirs. USI Romania, Reformteh, Inc., Romania. Patentee road repair vehicle, method for vestibular test. Chmn. bd. dirs. Pilsen affiliate Habitat for Humanity, Chgo. 1st lt. U.S. Army, 1960—61. Fellow: ASME. Home: 10154 S Seeley Ave Chicago IL 60643-2037 Office: Ill Inst Tech 10 W 32d St Chicago IL 60616-3729 Business E-Mail: dix@iit.edu.

DIX, SAMUEL MORMAN, industrial engineer, physical economist, appraiser; b. Grand Rapids, Mich., Nov. 20, 1916; s. Horace Philip and Helen (Morman) D., m. Dorothy Swanson, Jan. 1951 (dec. 1981); children: Stephen, Peter, Pamela. BA, Dartmouth, 1939, MCS, 1940; postgrad., Univ. Calif., 1941-42. Plant industrial engr. Am. Box Board Co., Buffalo, N.Y., 1940-41; staff engr. Albert Ramond & Assocs., 1946-48; asst. to chief industrial engr. Gen. Foods Corp., N.Y., Can., 1948-52; ceo S.M. Dix & Assocs., Grand Rapids, 1952-86; farmer, mfg. and mktg. cons., Belmont, Mich., 1988—. Author: Energy: A Critical Decision for the United State Economy, 1977, The Cost of Future Freedom, 1982. Energy adv. to Pres. Ford, 1974-76, Congress Subcom. Energy and Power, 1976-78. With USNR, 1941-46. Mem. N.Y. Acad. Scis., Nat. Assn. Accts. (officer 1954-56), Am. Mktg. Assn., Am. Soc. Appraisers, Indsl. Mgmt. Soc. (founder West Mich. chpt.), World Future Soc. (contbr.). Avocations: tennis, golf, camping, music, farming.

DIXIT, BALWANT NARAYAN, pharmacology and toxicology educator; b. Kerawade, India, Jan. 7, 1933; came to U.S., 1962; s. Narayan V. and Janakibai N. (Gokhale) D.; m. Vidya B. Ghanekar, Dec. 26, 1969; children: Sunil, Sanjay. BS in Chemistry and Biology, Fergusson Coll., Poona, India, 1954; BS in Chemistry with honors, U. Poona, 1955; MS in Biochemistry with honors, U.Poona, 1956; MS in Pharmacology with honors, U. Baroda, India, 1962; PhD, U. Pitts., 1965, MBA, 2001. Sr. research fellow Baroda U., 1960-61; asst. prof. pharmacology U. Pitts., 1965-68; assoc. prof., 1968-74; prof., 1974—; asst. chmn., 1969-74; acting dean, 1976-78; chmn., 1974-87; assoc. dean, 1974-84; dir. Ctr. for the Performing Arts of India, 1992—. Recipient Disting. Alumnus award U. Pitts. Sch. Pharmacy, 1982; fellow Internat. Union Physiological Scis., 1962 Mem. Am. Soc. Pharmacology and Explt. Therapeutics, Soc. Neurosci., Internat. Soc. Xenobiotic Metabolism Home: 608 Ravencrest Rd Pittsburgh PA 15215-1120 Office: U Pitts 559 Salk Hall Pittsburgh PA 15261-1905 Fax: (412) 648-8475. E-mail: bdixit@pitt.edu.

DIXIT, VIVEK, biomedical scientist, medical educator; b. Mumbai, India, Nov. 7, 1954; came to US, 1988; s. Mahesh Chandra and Kaushal (Tiwari) Dikshit; m. Neeta Awasthi, Dec. 27, 1987; children: Vineet Aditya, Ram Anand. BSc in Biology magna cum laude, Concordia U., Montreal, Que., Can., 1978; MSc in Physiology, McGill U., Montreal, 1980, PhD in Physiology, 1986. Postdoctoral fellow Sunnybrook Med. Ctr./U. Toronto, Can., 1986-88; vis. asst. rschr. UCLA, 1988-91, asst. rschr., 1991-93, assoc. prof. medicine, 1993—2002, prof. medicine, 2002—. Mem. steering com. liver diseases program Sunnybrook Med. Ctr., Toronto, 1986—87; dir. rsch. bio-support hepatitis rsch. lab., 1990—; co-dir. basic sic. tng. program divsn. digestive diseases, 1993—95; mem. sci. program com. 3rd Internet World Congress on Biomed. Sci., Symposium on Tissue Engring. and Bioartificial Organs, 1996; co-chmn. symposium on artificial organs 3rd World Internet for Biomed. Sci., 2000; lectr. and presenter in field; webmaster divsn. digestive diseases dept. medicine UCLA, 2000—; prin. invest. HepaHope Bioartificial Liver Evaluation, 2002; mem. Internat. Sci. Program Comm., Ankara Univ., Turkey, 2002; Study sect. mem. Nat. Sci. Found., Biomaterials, 2003. Manuscript reviewer: Artificial Orgnas ASAIO Jour., Cell Transplantation, Digestive Disease and Sci., Jour. Infectious Diseases, Gastroenterology, Hepatology, Jour. Artificial Cells, Blood Substitutes and Immobilization Biotech., Jour. Biomaterial Sci., Jour. Hepatology and Liver Transpantation and Surgery, Med. Principles and Practices. Fellow McGill U. fellow, 1981, 1985, Min. Edn. Quebec, 1981—83, Sunnybrook Fund fellow, U.Toronto, 1987; grantee, Physicians Svcs. Inc. Found., 1987—89, United Liver Assn., 1988, 1990—92, 1995, UCLA, 1994, 1996, Oppenheimer Found., 1995, 1998, Stein-Oppenheimer Found., 2002. Mem. Internat. Soc. Artificial Organs, Internat. Soc. for Artificial Cells, Blood Substitutes and Immobilization Biotech. (mem. internat. program com., editl. bd. jour.), Internat. Assn. Study of Liver, Am. Soc. for Artifical Internal Organs (mem. sci. program com., editl. bd. jour.), Cell Transplant Soc. (editl. bd. jour.), Gastroenterology Rsch. Group, Am. Gastroenterol. Assn., Am. Assn. for Study Liver Diseases. Hindu. Achievements include pioneer investigator in hybrid bio-artificial liver support systems, cell microencapsulation and transplantation, tissue engineering. Home: 5522 Babcock Ave North Hollywood CA 91607-1531 Office: UCLA Sch Medicine 675 Circle Dr S # 1240 Los Angeles CA 90095-8348 E-mail: vdixit@mednet.ucla.edu.

DIXON, ANDREW DERART, retired academic administrator; b. Belfast, No. Ireland, Oct. 27, 1925; arrived in came to U.S., 1963, naturalized; s. Andrew and Martha (Stewart) Dixon; m. Mary Elizabeth Hernderson, Oct. 14, 1948; children: Penelope Jane, Melinda Sara, Alison Mary. Licentiate in Dental Surgery, Queens U., Belfast, 1948, B in Dental Surgery, 1949, M.Dental Surgery, 1953, BS (Nuffield Found. dental fellow), 1954, D.Sc., 1965; PhD, U. Manchester, 1958. Asst. lectr. anatomy U. Manchester, 1954—56, lectr., 1956—62, sr. lectr., 1962—63; 1vis. assoc. prof. anatomy U. Iowa, 1959—61; prof. dental sci. U. N.C., Chapel Hill, 1963—65, prof. dental sci., anatomy, 1965—69, prof. oral biology and anatomy, 1969—73, asst. dean, coordinator research Sch. Dentistry, 1966—69, dir. Dental Research Ctr., 1967—73, assoc. dean research, 1969—73; prof., dean UCLA, 1973—80, assoc. dean for faculty affairs, 1985—92, assoc. dean adminstrn., 1989—92; prof. emeritus, 1993—. Chmn. dental tng. com. Nat. Inst. Dental Rsch., 1972—73; mem. No. Ireland Partnership. Author sci. texts; contbr. articles; Studies on early devel. and growth of the jaws, sex chromatin in oral smears as a diagnostic tool, nerve supply to oral mucous membrane, facial tissues and temporomandibular joint, craniofacial skeletal growth, trigeminal pathway. Grantee Fulbright Sr. Fellow award, 1959—61, Commonwealth Fund Travel fellow, 1961. Fellow: AAAS, Internat. Coll. Dentists, Am. Coll. Dentists; mem.: Pierre Fauchard Acad., Internat. Soc. Craniofacial Biology, N.Y. Acad. Sci., Am. Soc. Cell Biology, AAAS, Internat. Assn. Dental Rsch., Am. Assn. Anatomists, Anat. Soc. Gt. Britain and Ireland (sr.), Western Conf. Dental Examiners and Dental Deans, Pacific Coast Soc. Orthodontists (hon.), Inst. of Medicine, ADA, Psi Omega, Omicron Kappa Upsilon, Sigma Xi. Home: 2213 Quail Point Terr Medford OR 97504 E-mail: addixRVM@charter.net.

DIXON, ANN RENEE, writer; b. Richland, Wash., Feb. 26, 1954; d. David Sherman and Barbara Mae (Cook) Dixon; m. Walter Raymond Pudwill, May 30, 1982; children: Linnea Clare, Noranna Noel. BA in Swedish Lang. and Lit., U. Wash., 1976. Libr. Willow (Alaska) Pub. Libr., 1987-97. Author: (children's books) How Raven Brought Light to People, 1991, The Sleeping Lady, 1994, Merry Birthday, Nora Noel, 1996, Trick-or-Treat!, 1998, The Blueberry Shoe, 1999, Waiting for Noel: An Advent Story, 2000, (with Pam Flowers) Alone Across the Arctic: One Woman's Epic Journey by Dog Team, 2001, Winter Is, 2002, Big-Enough Anna: The Little Sled Dog Who Braved The Arctic, 2003. Recipient Contbn. to Literacy in Alaska award, 2000, Nat. Outdoor Book award, 2000. Mem. Author's Guild, Soc. Children's Book Writers and Illustrators, Alaska Libr. Assn., Alaska Ctr. for the Book. Avocations: gardening, cross country skiing, swimming, walking, reading.

DIXON, ARMENDIA PIERCE, school program administrator; b. Laurel, Miss., July 15, 1937; d. L.E. and Denothras (Pickens) Pierce; m. Harrison D. Dixon Jr., Aug. 28, 1971; 1 child, Harrison D. III BS in Edn., Jackson (Miss.) State U., 1960; postgrad., No. Ill. State U., 1965-66; MEd, Edinboro (Pa.) U., 1978; PhD, PhD, Kent State U., 1994. Cert. English and secondary edn., Miss. Tchr. English, libr. Laurel City Schs., 1962-67; tchr. English, dir. summer pre-sch. Erie (Pa.) Pub. Schs., 1967-72; tchr. English, drama, journalism, forensic coach Crawford Cen. Schs., Meadville, Pa., 1972-85, asst. prin., facilitator sch. improvement coun., 1985-89, coord. successful student partnership, 1988—; prin. Meadville Area Sr. High, 1993. Exec. dir. Meadville Latch-Key Program, 1985—; coord. Urban Tchrs. Project, Kent State U., adj. asst. prof., 1989—, dir. Prospective Tchrs. Program for Phi Delta Kappa; charter mem. Results chpt., Kent State U., 1990; dir. high sch. edn. Sch. dist. City of Erie, 1993-2001; instr. English Edinboro U. Pa.; dir. of high sch. edn., The Sch. Dist. of the City of Erie, Pa., 1993—. Fundraiser Cystic Fibrosis Found., Pitts., 1976. 79, 81, Sickle Cell Anemia, Erie, 1978-83; pres. Martin Luther King Jr. Scholarship Fund, Inc., 1979-89; bd. dirs. ARC, Erie, 1996—, Villa Marie Coll., Erie, 1995—, Internat. Inst., 1994—; mem. adv. bd. Am. Enterprise, Erie, 1993—; mem. alumni bd. dirs. Edinboro U. Alumni, 1997—. Mem. NAACP (pres. Meadville chpt. 1984—), Nat. Assn. Secondary Sch. Prins., Pa. Assn. Secondary Sch. Prins., Order Eastern Star (worthy matron), Navy Mothers, Rainbow Ill, Burres, Phi Delta Kappa, Alpha Kappa Alpha. Methodist. Avocations: collecting dolls, writing, gardening. Home: PO Box 561 Meadville PA 16335-0561 Office: Crawford Ctrl Schs 847 N Main St Meadville PA 16335-2655 E-mail: armendia@alltel.net.

DIXON, BARBARA BRUINEKOOL, provost; b. Sparta, Wis., June 14, 1943; MusB magna cum laude in Applied Piano, Mich. State U., 1966, MusM, 1969; MusD, U. Colo., 1991. Instr. vocal music K-12 Capac (Mich.) Cmty. Schs., 1970-71; tchr. dept. music Ctrl. Mich. U., Mt. Pleasant, 1971-89, assoc. dean coll. arts and scis., 1989-95, interim dean coll. arts and scis., 1995-97; provost, v.p. acad. affairs SUNY, Geneseo, 1997—2003; pres. Truman St. U., Kirksville, Mo., 2003—. Rep. acad. senate exec. bd., acad. senate liaison com., univ. acad. planning coun. Ctrl. Mich. U., 1986-89; dir. tchr. edn. search com., 1990, 95; chair faculty load equity study com., 1988-89, undergrad. curriculum com., 1992-93, formal hearing com. for grievance under senate rules, 1988-89; mem. profl. edn. coun., 1990-95, honors coun., 1989-94, task force on distance learning, 1992-93, piano search com., 1989, 90, 92, 95, music awards policy com., 1980-81, numerous others. One-woman performances include Kirtland C.C., Roscommon, Mich., 1986, Lansing (Mich.) C.C. Artist Series, 1987, Wurlitzer Hdqs., Holly Springs, Miss., 1989, Benefit for Cmty. Arts Coun., Pigeon, Mich., 1991, Beethoven Festival, Lansing, 1993, and others; accompanying performances include Backstage Recital Series, Jasper, Ind., 1984, Bridgeport (Mich.) Voice Symposium, 1986, Manistee (Mich.) Opera House, 1986, Saginaw (Mich.) Choral Soc., 1987, Alma (Mich.) Coll. Faculty, 1995, Black Forest Music Festival (Broadway rev.), Harbor Springs, Mich., 1995, and others. Active Art Reach Mid-Mich. (gallery com. 1995-96, chamber music com. 1995-97, fund drive com. 1996-97, bd. dirs. 1995-97, treas. 1996-97), Lions Club (chair spl. events com., bd. dirs. 1995-97), United Way (liaison to campus campaign); vol. Mich. Spl. Olympics. Mem. Mich. Music Tchrs. Assn. (bd. of certification 1976-79, 84-90, 95-97, chair 1996-97, pres. local chpt. 1991-92; chmn. collegiate activities 1979-81; mem. spkrs. bur. 1974-97, adjudicators bur. 1975-97, exec. bd. 1979-81, 96; rep. Mich. Youth Arts Festival bd. 1976-81, Mich. Alliance for Arts in Edn. 1988-89), Dalcroze Soc. Am., Delta Omicron, AAUW, Am. Assn. Higher Edn., Phi Beta Delta, Pi Kappa Lambda, Phi Kappa Phi Mortar Bd. Office: Truman St U 100 E Normal St MC200 Kirksville MO 63501 E-mail: dixon@truman.edu.

DIXON, BILLY GENE, academic administrator, educator; b. Benton, Ill., Oct. 25, 1935; s. John and Stella (Prowell) D.; m. Judith R. McCommons, June 7, 1957; children: Valerie J., Clark A. BS, So. Ill. U., 1957, PhD, 1967; MS, Ill. Wesleyan U., 1961. Tchr. math., chmn. dept. Cahokia (Ill.) High Sch., 1960-61; tchr. Univ. Sch., So. Ill. U., Carbondale, 1961-67, chmn. dept. math., 1963-67; dir. rsch. and evaluation ESEA Title II Project Uplift, Mt. Vernon, Ill., 1967-69; coordinator profl. edn. experiences Coll. Edn. So. Ill. U., Carbondale, 1968-75, mem. faculty, coord. grad. program in secondary edn., 1975-78, departmental exec. officer curriculum and instrn., 1978—2001, asst. to dept. exec. officer for spl. projects, 2001—. Pres. Benton Cmty. Pk. Dist., 1974—95; bd. dirs. The Holmes Partnership, 2000—. Named Citizen of Yr., Benton C. of C., 1982; recipient Liberty Bell award, 1995. Mem. Ill. Assn. Tchr. Educators (pres. 1973, exec. coun. 1976-79, Disting. mem. 1984), Assn. Tchr. Educators (chmn. nat. rev. panel Disting. Program in Tchr. Edn. 1976-86, exec. bd. 1983-86, pres. 1988-89, Pres.'s award 1983, 84, 95, 99, Disting. mem. 1992), Pi Mu Epsilon, Phi Kappa Phi, Phi Delta Kappa, Kappa Delta Pi. Democrat. Methodist. Home: 9793 Stuyvesant St Benton IL 62812-5916 Office: So Ill U Coll Edn Human Svcs Carbondale IL 62901-4624

DIXON, CHARLES SIM, urban planner; b. Chattanooga, Tenn., Dec. 6, 1962; s. Charles Earl and Jacqueline June D.; m. Phyllis Arlene Mincy, Dec. 17, 1988; children: Jacqueline, Caroline. BS cum laude, U. Tenn., 1985, MS in Planning, 1989. Planning cons. Heniger & Ray Engring. Assocs., Crystal River, Fla., 1989-91; cmty. devel. dir. Citrus County Govt., Inverness, Fla., 1991—. Methodist. Office: Citrus County Govt Ste 140 3600 W Sovereign Path Lecanto FL 34461 E-mail: rockytop@atlantic.net., charles.dixon@bocc.citrus.fl.us.

DIXON, CORBIN, retired electrical engineer, conservationist; b. N.Y.C., Sept. 25, 1918; s. Harvey John Dixon and Genevieve Veronica Dvorshak; m. Mary Hammer; stepchildren: Laura Plecker, Carla Tinsley. BEE, NYU, 1941. Registered profl. engr. NY, Va.; lic. realtor Va. Engr., engring. supr. GE, 1942—80. Engring. instr. Blue Ridge CC, 1957; edn. chmn. scholarship com. NYU, Albany, 1950—54, mem. bd. admissions S. Ctrl. Region, 1970—. Host (environ. radio show) Sta. WSVA, Harrisonburg, Va.; author: (columns) News Virginian; contbr. articles to profl. jours. Bd. dirs. Friends of Rivers of Va., 1996—. Named Conservationist of Yr., Izaak Walton League and Float Fisherman of Va., 1996. Mem.: Va. Outdoors Writers Assn. (S.E. regional v.p. Trout Unlimited nat., past bd. dirs.). Achievements include 7 patents. Avocations: fishing, hunting, whitewater canoeing, sailing, designing and building furniture. Home and Office: 651 Barrenridge Rd Staunton VA 24401

DIXON, DENISE, psychologist, educator; b. Rockville Center, N.Y., Aug. 14, 1964; d. Stephen C. and Aileen B. (O'Campo) D.; m. John Richard Lanza, Mar. 9, 2002. AB, Smith Coll., 1986; MA in Psychology, Yeshiva U., 1995, PhD in Clin. Health Psychology, 1997. Psychology intern Jackson Meml. Hosp., U. Miami (Fla.) Sch. Medicine, 1996-97; postdoctoral assoc. U. Miami, 1997-98; sr. rsch. assoc. U. Miami Behavioral Medicine Rsch. Ctr., 1998-2000; asst. prof. psychiatry U. Medicine and Dentistry of N.J./N.J. Med. Sch., 2000—. Scientist mentor Sci.-By-Mail, Boston, 1999; presenter in field. Contbr. numerous articles to profl. jours. Recipient Nat. Rsch. Svc. award NIMH, 1997-98; Acad. scholar Smith Coll., Northampton, Mass., 1982-86, Yeshiva U., Bronx, 1992-94, Rukin scholar Yeshiva U., Bronx, 1994-95; grantee NIH-LRP, 2002—. Mem. AAAS, APA, Psychoneuroimmunology Rsch. Soc. (Trainee award 1998), Soc. Pediat. Psychology, Soc. Health Psychology, European Health Psychology Soc., Soc. Exercise and Sports Psychology. Avocations: tennis, running, photography. E-mail: dixonda@umdnj.edu.

DIXON, E. A., JR., lawyer; b. Bryn Mawr, Pa., Dec. 12, 1939; m. Margaret Kennedy Cortright; children: Thomas W.W., Abigail C., Marion W., Meghan. AB, Princeton U., 1962; JD with honors, George Washington U., 1967. Bar: Pa. 1968, U.S. Dist. Ct. (ea. dist.) 1968. Assoc. Montgomery, McCracken, Walker & Rhoads, Phila., 1967-69; assoc. resident counsel Industrial Valley Bank, Phila., 1970-73; ptnr. Hepburn, Ross, Wilcox & Putnam, Phila., 1974-78; owner wholesale nursery business, 1979-85; atty. Monumental Title Corp., Severna Park, Md., 1985-86; mgr. comml. divsn. The Sentinel Title Corp., Balt., 1987-89; regional underwriting counsel Nations Title Ins. (formerly Nat. Attys and TRW Title), Trevose, Pa., 1989-96; sr. title counsel Lawyers Title Ins. Corp., Phila., 1996, N.J. area counsel Iselin, 1997; counsel Stewart Title Guaranty Co., Wayne, Pa., 1998—. Seminar spkr. Nat. Bus. Inst., N.J., 1995-96, Title Acad. N.J., 1995—. Contbr. articles to co. publs., 1990—. 2d lt. USAF, 1963—64. Mem. Pa. Land Title Assn. (exec. com. 1993-96), Pa. Bar Assn., The Phila. Club, Rittenhouse Club, St. Andrew's Soc. (Phila.), Montrose Club. Libertarian. Episcopalian. Avocations: horticulture, sailing, fly fishing, tennis. Office: 900 W Valley Rd Wayne PA 19087-1830

DIXON, FRANK JAMES, medical scientist, educator; b. St. Paul, Mar. 9, 1920; s. Frank James and Rose Augusta (Kuhfeld) D.; m. Marion Edwards, Mar. 14, 1946; children: Janet Wynne, Frank, Michael. BS, U. Minn., 1941, MB, 1943, MD, 1944; DS (hon.), Med. Coll. Ohio, 1983; DSc (hon.), Washington U., 1992. Diplomate: Am. Bd. Pathology. Intern U.S. Naval Hosp., Great Lakes, Ill., 1943-44; research asst. dept. pathology Harvard, 1946-48; instr. dept. pathology Washington U., 1948-50, asst. prof., 1950-51; prof., chmn. dept. pathology U. Pitts. Med. Sch., 1951-60; chmn. dept. exptl. pathology Scripps Clinic and Research Found., La Jolla, Calif., 1961-74, chmn. biomed. research depts., 1970-74, dir. research inst., 1974-86, dir. emeritus, 1987—. Rsch. assoc. dept. biology U. Calif., San Diego, 1961-64, prof. in residence dept. biology, 1965-68, adj. prof. dept. pathology, 1968-96; sci. advisor NIH, Nat. Found., Helen Hay Whitney Found., St. Jude's Med. Ctr., Christ Hosp. Inst., Cin.; mem. expert adv. panel on immunology WHO; sci. adv. bd. Nat. Kidney Found.; Pahlavi lectr. Ministry of Sci. and Higher Tech., Iran, 1976: mem. adv. com. Lupus Rsch. Inst., Nat. Multiple Sclerosis Soc., Harold C. Simmons Arthritis Rsch. Ctr., Irvington House Inst. Editor: Advances in Immunology; mem. editorial bd. Excerpta Medica, Jour. Exptl. Medicine, Am. Jour. Pathology, Cellular Immunology, Kidney Hosp. Practice, Perspectives in Biology and Medicine, Jour. Exptl. Clin. Cancer Rsch., Springer Seminars in Immunopathology, Immunological Revs.; contbr. articles to profl. jours. Served with M.C. USNR, 1943-46. Recipient Theobald Smith award, 1952, Parke-Davis award in exptl. pathology, 1957, Disting. Achievement award Modern Medicine, 1961, Martin E. Rehfuss award in internal medicine, 1966, Von Pirquet medal Ann. Forum on Allergy, 1967, Bunim medal Am. Rheumatism Assn., 1968, Internat. award Gairdner Found., 1969, Mayo Soley award Western Soc. Clin. Research, 1969, Albert Lasker Basic Med. Research award, 1975, Dickson prize U. Pitts., 1975, Homer Smith award N.Y. Heart Assn., 1976, Rous-Whipple award Am. Assn. Pathologists, 1979, So. Calif. Permanente Med. Group Immunology award, 1979, Regents award U. Minn., 1985, H.P. Smith award Am. Soc. Clin. Pathologists, 1985, Gold-Headed Cane award, 1987, Distinguished Service award Lupus Found. Am., 1987, 88; Flame of Hope award Terri Gotthelf Rsch. Inst., 1987, Paul Klemperer award N.Y. Acad. Medicine, 1989, Jean Hamburger award Internat. Soc. Nephrology, 1990. Fellow Am. Coll. Allergists, Am. Acad. Allergy, Royal Coll. Pathologists (hon.); mem. NAS, N.Y. Acad. Scis. Western Assn. Physicians, Western Soc. Clin. Research, Soc. Exptl. Biology and Medicine, Transplantation Soc., AAAS, Am. Soc. Clin. Investigation, Am. Acad. Allergists, Interurban Path. Soc., Harvey Soc. (lectr. 1962), Am. Soc. Exptl. Pathology (pres. 1966), Am. Assn. Immunologists (pres. 1972), Am. Assn. for Cancer Research, Assn. Am. Physicians, Am. Acad. Arts and Scis., Am. Heart Assn., Coun. on the Kidney in Cardiovascular Disease, Fedn. Am. Scientists, Internat. Acad. Pathology, U.S. Acad. Pathologists, Can. Acad. Pathologists, Scandinavian Soc. for Immunology (hon.), Japanese Nephrology Soc. (hon.), Sigma Xi, Nu Sigma Nu, Alpha Omega Alpha. Office: Scripps Rsch Inst 10550 N Torrey Pines Rd La Jolla CA 92037-1000

DIXON, FRED, retired literature educator; b. Cookville, Tenn., Apr. 1, 1934; s. Cordell Henry and Dora Hunter (Grimes) Dixon; m. Linda Calahan Smithers, Aug. 8, 1954 (div. Jan. 1, 1963); m. Barbara Bridgeman Dixon, Jan. 24, 1964; 1 child, Fredrick Marcus stepchildren: Sandra Jean Myers Smith, Robert Louis Myers. BA, Memphis State Univ., Memphis, Tenn., 1961; MA, Memphis State Univ., Memphis, Tenn., 1962. Instr. of English So. State Coll., Magnolia, Ga.,

1962—66, Univ. Ga., Athens, Ga., 1966—67; assoc. prof. English East Stroudsburg Univ., East Stroudsburg, Pa., 1967—95. Field testing Ea. Testing Svc., Princeton, NJ. Author short stories. Planning commn. Borough of Delaware Water Gap, Delaware Water Gap, Pa., 1975—80, borough coun., 1980—84. A/1C USAF, 1954—58, Korea, Japan, Nebr. Independent. Avocations: tennis, golf. Home: 716 Westchester Fairfield Glade TN 38558

DIXON, FREDERICK DAIL, architect; b. Raleigh, N.C., Dec. 18, 1942; s. Frederick Dail (dec.) and Mary Isabel (Richbourg)(dec.) D.; m. Artemis Markatos, July 7, 1968; children: Frederick Markatos. BArch, Clemson (S.C.) U., 1966; MFA in Sculpture, U. N.C., 1970. Intern Leslie Boney, Architects, Wilmington, NC, 1966—68; arch. John D. Latimer & Assocs. Durham, NC, 1968—72, Cogswell/Hausler Assocs., Chapel Hill, NC, 1972—74; founding ptnr. Designworks, Carrboro, NC, 1974—82; dir. Dixon Weinstein Architects, PA, Chapel Hill, 1982—. Instr. Boston Archtl. Ctr., 1970-71; vis. prof. arch. N.C. State U. Coll. Design, Raleigh, 1983-2003. HUD grantee. Fellow AIA, South Atlantic Region AIA (award for Excellence in Arch. 1991, 92, Merit award 1998), N.C. AIA (Merit award 1991, 92, 95, 98, Honor award 2002, Outstanding Firm award 2003). Democrat. Office: Dixon Weinstein Architects PA #25 The Courtyard 431 W Franklin St Chapel Hill NC 27516-2319 E-mail: dail@dixonweinstein.com.

DIXON, GEORGE DAVID, radiologist; b. Valley City, N.D., Mar. 27, 1936; s. George Sherman and Isabel Ruth (Eaton) Dixon; m. Carol Marie Vannerstrom, Feb. 28, 1958; children: Barbara Sarah, George David Dixon Jr. Student, Willamette U., 1954-55; BA, U. N.D., 1959; MD, Tulane U., 1961. Diplomate with added qualifications in vascular and interventional radiology Am. Bd. Radiology. Intern St. Luke's Hosp., Duluth, Minn., 1961-62; gen. practice Lenont-Peterson Clinic, Cook, Minn., 1962-64; resident in radiology Mayo Clinic, Rochester, Minn., 1964-66, 68-70; radiologist St. Luke's Hosp. Radiol. Group, Inc., Kansas City, Mo., 1970—, sec., 1971-98; clin. prof. radiology U. Mo. Sch. of Medicine, Kansas City, 1985—, acad. chair radiology residency, 2002. Mem.editl. adv. bd. Diagnostic Imaging, 1979—; contbr. articles to med. jours. Pres. Interdenominational Christian Youth Coun., Fargo, ND, 1953—54; lay leader Indian Heights United Meth. Ch., Overland Park, Kans., 1977—79. Capt. U.S. Army, 1966—68, Vietnam. Fellow: Soc. Interventional Radiology, Am. Heart Assn., Am. Coll. Radiology (councilor Mo.); mem.: AMA, Greater Kansas City Radiol. Soc. (treas. 1977—78, sec. 1978—79, pres.), Met. Med. Soc., Mo. Radiol. Soc. (councilor), Mo. State Med. Soc., Am. Roentgen Ray Soc., Radiol. Soc. N.Am. (counselor We. Mo. dist. 1988—92, 1998—2002), New Eng. Hist. Geneal. Soc., Masons, Wally Byan Caravan Club Kansas City, Phi Beta Pi, Beta Theta Pi, Phi Beta Kappa. Republican. Avocations: genealogy, traveling by trailer. Home: 10416 Mohawk Ln Shawnee Mission KS 66206-2551 Office: St Lukes Hosp Dept Radiology PO Box 119000 Kansas City MO 64171-9000 E-mail: ddixon@saint-lukes.org. *Personal philosophy: Words by which I have come to live by - "All I really need to know I learned in kindergarten and Sunday School.".*

DIXON, GORDON HENRY, biochemist, educator; b. Durban, South Africa, Mar. 25, 1930;, naturalized, Can. s. Walter James and Ruth (Nightingale) Dixon; m. Sylvia W. Gillen, Nov. 20, 1954; children: Frances Anne, Walter Timothy, Christopher James, Robin Jonathan. MA with honors, U. Cambridge, Eng., 1951; PhD, U. Toronto, 1956. Rsch. assoc. U. Wash., 1954-58, U. Oxford, Eng., 1958-59; asst. prof. biochemistry U. Toronto, 1959-61, assoc. prof., 1961-63; prof. U. B.C., 1963-72; prof., chmn. dept. biochemistry U. Sussex, Eng., 1972-74; prof. med. biochemistry U. Calgary, Alta., Can., 1974-94; emeritus, 1994—; chmn. U. Calgary, Alta., Can., 1983-88. Contbr. articles to prof. jours. Decorated officer Order of Can.; recipient Steacie prize, Steacie Found., 1966, Killam Meml. prize, Can. Coun., 1991, Queens Golden Jubilee medal, 2002. Fellow: Royal Soc. Can. (Flavelle medal 1980), Royal Soc. London; mem.: Internat. Union Biochemistry (mem. exec. coun. 1988—94), Pan-Am. Assn. Biochem. Socs. (v.p. 1984—87, pres. 1987—90), Can. Biochem. Soc. (pres. 1982—83, Ayerst award 1966).

DIXON, JACK EDWARD, biological chemistry educator, consultant; b. June 16, 1943; BA, UCLA, 1966; PhD, U. Calif., Santa Barbara, 1971. NSF Found. postdoctoral rsch. fellow U. Calif., San Diego, 1971—73; from asst. prof. to assoc. prof. biochemistry Purdue U., West Lafayette, Ind., 1973—82, prof. biochemistry, 1982—86, Harvey W. Wiley disting. prof. biochemistry, 1986—91; Minor J. Coon prof. biol. chemistry, chmn. dept. U. Mich., Ann Arbor, 1991—. Adj. asst. prof. biochemistry Ind. U. Sch. Medicine, 1976—78, assoc. prof. biochemistry, 1978—91, adj. prof. biochemistry, 1983—91, part-time prof. medicine, 1985—91; vis. lectr. Wash. State U., 1985; cons. Wyeth-Ayrst Co., Phila., 1985—, Monsanto Chem. Co., St. Louis, 1985—, Mitotix Inc., Cambridge, Mass., 1993—98, Ceptyr, 1997—; P.T. Varandani Meml. lectr. Wright State U., Dayton, Ohio, 1987; chmn. rsch. rev. com. Ind. affiliate Am. Heart Assn., 1983; spl. reviewer alcohol study NIH, 1983, 84, endocrine study sect., 1985—90; Nathan O. Kaplan lectr. U. Calif., San Diego, 1991; Vestling lectr. U. Iowa, 1991; Edmund Fischer lectr. U. Wash., Seattle, 1993; Årets Novo Nordisk lectr. U. Copenhagen, 1994; presenter in field. Recipient Rsch. award, Ind. affiliate Am. Diabetes Assn., 1985—86, Merit award, NIH, 1987, 1996, Lions award for cancer rsch., 1990. Fellow: Am. Acad. Arts and Sci., Mich. Soc. Fellows U. Mich. (sr.); mem.: Am. Soc. Neurosci., Am. Soc. Cell Biology, Am. Soc. Biochemistry and Molecular Biology (program chmn. 1994—, pres. 1996—97), Am. Physiol. Soc., Am. Chem. Soc., NAS (elected mem. Inst. Medicine 1993), AAAS, Phi Kappa Phi, Sigma Xi. Office: U Mich Biochem Dept M5416 Med Sci 1 0606 Ann Arbor MI 48109-0606

DIXON, JO-ANN CONTE, management consultant; b. Orange, N.J., Aug. 5, 1942; d. Rocco Louis and Antoinette (DeRosa) Conte; m. Michael Eugene Dixon, July 26, 1964; children: Christopher Michael, Peter Eugene. Student, Paterson State Coll., 1960-63; AA, Thomas A. Edison Coll., 1976, BA, 1978; MA, Depeuw U., 1985. Tchr. St. Raphael's Sch., Livingston, NJ, 1963-68; owner Orgn. Unltd., Glen Ridge, NJ, 1972-76; market rsch. analyst Harkness & Assoc., San Francisco, 1976-78; adminstr. corp. tng. dept. Rapidata, Inc., Fairfield, NJ, 1978—79, mgr. corp. tng. dept., 1979—80, dir., 1980—81; pres., prin. cons. Q, Inc., Essex Fells, 1980-89; pres. MatchPlay Internat., Inc., 1989—96; regional dir. Am. Mgmt. Assoc., 1996—. Trustee Mt. St. Dominic Acad., 1989-95; dir. alumni rels. N.J. Inst. Tech., Newark, 1981-83, West Essex Cmty. Health Svcs., devel. chair, 1988-93, pres. 1993-95; dir. mgmt. devel. Rutgers U. Grad. Sch. Mgmt., 1983-84; bd. dir. alumni affairs/devel. officer Seton Hall Law Sch., Newark, 1984-85; chmn. bd. trustees Nat. Inst. for Orgnl. and Mgmt. Rsch., Essex Fells, N.J., 1987-92. Chmn. bd. Passaic River Coalition, Basking Ridge, N.J., 1976-83, vice chmn. bd., 1983-88, regional coord., 1971-76; chmn. mayor's com. on environ., Glen Ridge, 1974-75; mem. N.J. Gov.'s Task Force for Passaic River, 1976-78; mem., pres. Home and Sch. Bd., Glen Ridge, 1978-79. Recipient citation Borough of Glen Ridge; Charles T. Morgan award for excellence in tng. and devel., 1989; Nat. Trust Hist. Preservation scholar, 1977. Mem.: ASTD (v.p. comms. profl. excellence award), LWV, Exec. Women of N.J. (strategic planning chair 1996—99, pres.-elect 1999—2002, pres. 2002—), West Essex C. of C. (bd. dirs. 1988—89, v.p. 1990—91, pres. 1991—92, Bus. Person/Cmty. Leader of Yr. 2001), Exec. Women's Golf Assn. of No. N.J. (founder, comms. chair 1997—98, v.p. 1999—2000, sectional dir. Metro N.E. 2001—02, founder), Glen Ridge Hist. Soc. (founder), Kiwanis (N.J. found. bd. trustees 1990—92, sec. bd. dirs. 1990—93, v.p. Caldwell/West Essex chpt. 1996—97, sec. 1996—98, pres. elect 1997—98, pres. 1998—99, chair pediat. trauma program N.J. dist. 1999—2001, lt. gov. divsn. 12 2002—, Hixson fellow 2001), Knights of Malta-Order St. John of Jerusalem (Dame of Malta 1986). Home and Office: 97 Lane Ave West Caldwell NJ 07006-7426

DIXON, JOHN EMIT, health physics specialist; b. Sparks, Nev., June 30, 1959; s. John Lee and Phylis Mae Dixon; m. Paula Ann Parsons, Feb. 20, 1981; children: Matthew Ryan, Shannon Renne', Connor John, Grace Catherine. BS, Thomas Edison State Coll., Trenton, N.J.; Assoc. in Sci., Excelsior Coll., Albany, N.Y. Leading engring. lab. technician USN, Portsmouth, NH, 1981—88; sr. health physics technician Gen. Tech. Svcs., Shippingport, Pa., 1989; health physics coord. MK Ferguson of Oak Ridge, Oak Ridge, 1991—93; radiation protection technologist, sr. DOE RCT U. Tenn.-Battelle, Oak Ridge, 1993—2002; health physics specialist Safety and Ecology Corp., Knoxville, Tenn., 2002—. Author: (novels) Interlude: Common Thread Series, Book One. Registered bone marrow donor Red Cross, Knoxville, 2000. With USN, 1980—88. Recipient Freshman scholarship, U. of the Pacific, Stockton CA, 1977—78. Mem.: Nat. Registry of Radiation Protection Technologists (registered radiation protection technologist, Don Marshal scholarship 1995), Health Physics Soc. (East Tenn. chpt.). Avocations: astronomy, guitar, hiking. Home: 1231 Saybrook Ln Knoxville TN 37923 Office: Safety and Ecology Corp 2800 Solway Rd Knoxville TN 37931 Personal E-mail: jdixon@sec-tn.com. E-mail: jdixon@sec-tn.com.

DIXON, JOHN FULTON, village manager; b. Bellingham, Wash., Dec. 17, 1946; s. Fulton Albert and Patricia (Broderick) D.; m. Karen Elizabeth Creagh, May 19, 1973; children: Neil, Craig. BS, Bradley U., 1971; M in Mgmt., Vanderbilt U., 1973. Asst. village mgr. Village of Hoffman Estates, Ill., 1974-76, village mgr., 1980-86; dir. village svcs. Village of Roselle, Ill., 1976-79; asst. village mgr. Village of Schaumburg, Ill., 1979-80; village adminstr. Village of Lake Zurich, Ill., 1986-87; village mgr. Village of Mt. Prospect, Ill., 1987-92; village adminstr. Village of Lake Zurich, 1992—. Mem. exec. bd dirs. N.W. Suburban Mcpl. Joint Action Water Agy., Hoffman Estates, 198)-92; mem. exec. bd. dirs. N.W. Cen. Dispatch, Arlington Heights, Ill., 1987-92. Troop com. chmn. Boy Scouts Am., 1989-93; bd. dirs. Marklund Chilren's Home, 1999—, treas. 2001-. Recipient Chief Scout's award Gov. Gen. of Jamaica, Kingston, 1970; Adminstrv. fellow Woodrow Wilson Found., 1973 74, Houston fellow Vanderbilt U., 1972-73; Baker scholar Vanderbilt U., 1971-73. Mem. Met. Chgo. City Mgrs. Assn. (bd. dirs., pres. 1986-87), Ill. City Mgmt. Assn. (bd. dirs., pres. 1990-91), Rotary (bd. dirs. 1989—, pres. Lake Zurich chpt. 1997-98). Roman Catholic. Avocations: golf, travel. Home: 248 Sebby Ln Lake Zurich IL 60047-1358 Office: Village of Lake Zurich 70 E Main St Lake Zurich IL 60047-2416

DIXON, JOHN MORRIS, magazine editor; b. Long Branch, N.J., June 22, 1933; s. Abram C. and Emily (Minton) D.; m. Carol Ruth Nipomnich, Dec. 27, 1959; children: Peter, Susannah. B.Arch., MIT, 1955. From asst. editor to sr. editor Progressive Architecture, 1960-65, editor, 1971-96; assoc. editor Archtl. Rsch. Quar., 1999—2002. Sr. editor Archtl. Forum, 1965-71 Author: Architectural Design Preview, U.S.A, 1962, (with N. White and E. Willensky) A.I.A. Guide to New York City, 1967, Urban Spaces, 1999, Urban Spaces No. 2, 2001, The World Bank, 2002. Served to 1st lt. AUS, 1955-57. Fellow A.I.A. (chmn. exhibits com. N.Y. chpt. 1964-65, co-chmn. visitors com. N.Y. chpt. 1965-66, chmn. pub. relations com. N.Y. chpt. 1970-71, mem. design com. 1978—, chmn. 1983) Home: 382 Sound Beach Ave Old Greenwich CT 06870-2223 E-mail: jmdixon@snet.net.

DIXON, JOHN MORRIS, JR., lawyer; b. Cadia, Ky., Apr. 3, 1940; s. John Morris Sr. and Margaret (Herndon) D.; children: John M. III, Kathryn D. BS, U. Ky., 1962, JD, 1965. Bar: Ky. 1965, Ark. 1968. Assoc. Bridges, Young, Matthews & Davis, Pine Bluff, Ark., 1968-70; ptnr. Turner & Dixon, Hopkinsville, 1970-75, Turner, Dixon, Kemp & Fletcher, Hopkinsville, 1975-77, Turner, Dixon & Kemp, Hopkinsville, 1977-89; prin. John M. Dixon Jr., Atty., Hopkinsville, 1989; ptnr. Dixon & Kemp, Hopkinsville, 1989-91; U.S. magistrate judge Bowling Green, Ky., 1971-91; of counsel Fletcher, Cutthoxx & Willen, Hopkinsville, 1999—, Natural Resslute Systems, Inc., 1998—. Capt. U.S. Army, 1965-68. Mem. ABA, Ky. Bar Assn.

DIXON, JOHN SPENCER, international executive; b. London, Apr. 23, 1957; s. Richard Kennedy and Elizabeth Ann (Flaxman) D.; m. Karen Beth Swanson, Aug. 18, 1984; children: Katherine Elizabeth, John Spencer Jr. BA with honors, Oxford U., 1979, MA, 1985; MBA, Harvard U., 1982. Supply exec. Hi-Tec Sports Ltd., Essex, England, 1982-86; pres. Hi-Tec Internat. Ltd., Taichung, Taiwan, 1983-84; founder, ptnr. Transatlantic Mktg. Co., Essex, England, 1985-2000; exec. v.p. Decipher, Inc., Norfolk, Va., 1988-90; pres. Waller Whittemore & Co., Virginia Beach, Va., 1992—, PH Internat., Virginia Beach, Va., 1997—2001; organist, composer-in-residence Providence Presbyn. Ch., Virginia Beach, Va., 1998—. Mem.: Am. Guild Organists. Presbyterian. Avocations: music, sports. Home: 4829 Berrywood Rd Virginia Beach VA 23464-5874 Office: 5497 Providence Rd Virginia Beach VA 23464

DIXON, JOHN WESLEY, JR., retired religion and art educator; b. Richmond, Va., Aug. 18, 1919; s. John Wesley and Margaret (Denny) D.; m. Vivian Ardelia Slagle, Jan. 9, 1943; children: Susan Raglan, Judith Ann, Miriam Elizabeth. BA, Emory & Henry Coll., 1941; PhD, U. Chgo., 1953. Instr. Mich. State U., East Lansing, 1950-52; asst. prof. Emory U., Atlanta, 1952-57; exec. dir. Faculty Christian Fellowship, N.Y.C., 1955-57; assoc. prof. Dickinson Coll., Carlisle, Pa., 1957-60; prof. Fla. Presbyn. Coll., St. Petersburg, 1960-63; prof. religion and art U. N.C., Chapel Hill, 1963-87, prof. emeritus, 1987—. Author: Nature and Grace in Art, 1964, Art and the Theological Imagination, 1978, The Physiology of Faith, 1979, The Christ of Michelangelo, 1994, Images of Truth, 1996. Served to 1st lt. U.S. Army, 1941-45. Recipient Tanner Teaching award, 1967. Democrat. Episcopalian. Home: 216 Glenhill Ln Chapel Hill NC 27514-5916 Office: U NC Dept Religion Chapel Hill NC 27514 E-mail: jwdixon@email.unc.edu.

DIXON, LARRY DEAN, state legislator; b. Aug. 31, 1942; s. Chesley Lafayette and Charlene (Walker) D.; m. Gaynell Kimbrough, Dec. 23, 1967; children: Katherine Dixon Hert, Elizabeth Walker. AAS, Columbia Basin Jr. Coll., 1966; BS in Police Sci., Wash. State U., 1968, MA in History, 1970. Cons. Ala. State Dept. Edn., 1970-72; dir. dept. edn. Med. Assn. State of Ala., Montgomery, 1972-76; dir. Montgomery Family Practice Residency Program, 1976-78, Jackson Hosp. Found., Montgomery, 1978-81; exec. dir. Ala. Bd. Med. Examiners, Montgomery, 1981—. Mem. Montgomery City Coun., 1975-78, Ala. Ho. of Reps., 1978-82, Ala. Senate, 1982—; past mem. steering com. Nat. Clearinghouse on Licensure, Enforcement and Regulation; past bd. dirs. Fedn. State Med. Bds.; presdl. appointee Intergovt. Agy. Coun. on Edn., 1986-90, 90-94; mem. legis. adv. bd. So. Regional Edn. Bd., 1986-90; mem. Med. Scholarship Bd., State of Ala., 1988-98; past trustee Tuskegee U.; commr. So. Assn. Colls. and Schs., 1998-2001. With U.S. Army, 1961-64. Mem. Nat. Conf. State Legislatures, Adminstrs. in Medicine Soc. (pres. 1984-85), Edn. Commn. of the States, Ala. Ex POWs (hon.), Blue Gray Assn., Lions. Republican. Methodist. Home and Office: 820 E Fairview Ave Montgomery AL 36106-1818 also: PO Box 946 Montgomery AL 36101-0946

DIXON, MARC ALAN, numismatist, consultant, illustrator; b. Arkansas City, Kans., Sept. 17, 1962; s. Lonnie D. Dixon and Peggy A. Admire. AA in Data Processing, Cowley County C.C., 1987. Prin., owner Numismatics Unlimited, Ark. City, Kans., 1985—87; numismatist Heritage Capital Corp., Dallas, 1987—89; mng. gen. ptnr. Q-Cards Assoc., Dallas, 1988—90; prin., owner Hindsight Fin., Dallas, 1990—92, Ark. City, 1990—92, M.A. Dixon Fine Art & Illustration, Ark. City, 1992—. Cons. in field, 1995—. Author: Success Habits From A to Z, 1994, Art & Science of Day Trading Antiques & Collectibles, 2002, Targets of Opportunity: The Ten Most Exciting Profit Strategies in Rare Coins Today, 2003, Ravings of a Lunatic: The Suicidal Poetic Meanderings of a Tortured Soul, 2003, 9 additonal books; editor and pub.: The Classic Fishing Tackle Mkt. Informer, 1997—2000; contbg. editor: Red Book & Blue Book of U.S. Coin Values, 1989—93, Old Fishing Lures And Tackle, 6th edit., 2002; prodr.: (audio tape) The Customer Substitute Sales Trainer, 1988. With USN, 1980—85. Mem.: Nat. Fishing Lure Collectors Club. Avocations: reading, health & fitness, securities analysis, real estate, gemology.

DIXON, MICHAEL WAYNE, designer, writer, researcher; b. Honolulu, Hawaii, May 3, 1942; s. Gordon Alvin and Terry (Mendes) Dixon; m. Janis Marie Travis, Jan. 4, 1963 (div. Jan. 1977); children: Kimberlee Ann, Gregory Page, Morgan Ashley; m. Harlene Miller, Dec. 15, 1997. Tech. illustrator Rockwell Internat., Anaheim, Calif., 1962-66, Western Gear Corp., Lynwood, Calif., 1966-69; ind. biochem. rschr., 1968—; owner Unisex Clothing Store, Norwalk, Calif., 1969-71; mgr. Am. Health Industries, Downey, Calif., 1971-72; police officer Vernon Police Dept., LA Police Dept., 1972-81; designer, pres. Dornaus and Dixon Enterprises, Inc., Huntington Beach, Calif., 1979-88; freelance writer Huntington Beach, 1986—; founder, pres., CEO Gusty Winds Corp., 1991—, Maxcelint Labs. Inc., 2000—, Maxcelint Health Inc., 2000—, Maxcelint Internat., 2000—; founder, dir. The Health Ctr., 2001—. Founder, dir. The Rsch. Lab, 1991—, The Health Ctr., 2001—. Author: Bren Ten Owner's Manual, 1982, BodyShaping, 1985, BodyQuest, 1993, BodyLanguage, 1993, Courtroom Rapport, 1993, Naked Truth, 1995, There is a Magic Bullet After All, 1996, Cardiovasc. Disease, Potent. Magnesium and the True Fountain of Youth, 1999, pMg and Heart Wellness, 2000, Potentiated Magnesium--The Super Mineral for Super Good Health, 2001, Nature's Magic Bullet, 2001, The Finest Handgun Ever Made, 2002. Founder, dir. Street Smart Pepper Spray Hdqs. of Calif. With USN, 1959—62. Mem.: Rsch. Coun. Scripps Clinic and Rsch. Found., Am. Film Inst., NY Acad. Sci., Linus Pauling Inst. Sci. and Medicine, LA County Mus. Art, Smithsonian Instn. Achievements include invention of firearm safety devices; 10mm auto cartridge; Just'n Case police holster; MAWB cutter police bullet; BodyHugger holsters and ammunition holders; piper nigrum and acetic acid lachrymator; nutritional supplement formula that prevents atherosclerosis; potentiated magnesium; patents for first double ligand compounded coordination complex; potentiated calcium; holds 48 U.S. and internat. patents.

DIXON, MICHEL L. educational administrator; b. Norman, Okla., Oct. 2, 1945; s. Gerald R. and Erma M. (Fischer) D.; m. Mary Dee Brown, July 12, 1970 (div. 1995); children: Terri, Kelly, Kristi, Johanna. BA, Athens Coll., 1968, BE, 1972; MEd, U. Ala., 1976. Ins. adjustor Gen. Adjustment Bur., Birmingham, Ala., 1968-71; tchr. Adamsburg Sch., DeKalb County, Ala., 1971-72, Decatur (Ala.) City Schs., 1972-80; pubs. rep. Economy Pub. Co., Oklahoma City, 1980-82, Jostens Printing & Pub. Div., Mpls., 1982-84; course dir. AS100 Air Force ROTC, Maxwell AFB, Ala., 1984-85; pub. Civil Air Patrol News Aux. USAF, Maxwell AFB, 1985-86; tng. specialist, course mgr. Corps Engrs. Tng. div. U.S. Army, Huntsville, Ala., 1986-89; adminstr. Lawrence County High Sch., Moulton, Ala., 1989-90, Dept. Defense Dependent Sch., Nuernburg, Fed. Repub. Germany, 1990-91; dir. edn. programs in all western states U.S. Army 6th Recruiting BDE, Ft. Baker, Calif., 1991-94; prin. Round Valley H.S., Covelo, Calif., 1994-95; asst. prin. Calexico (Calif.) H.S., 1996-97, Capistrano Adult Sch., 1997-98; dir. cmty. edu. Mt. Brook (Ala.) Schs., Ala., 1998-1999; instrnl. sys. specialist in tech. specialized tng. program Pension Benefit Guaraty Corp., 1999—. With Pension Benefit Guaranty Corp., Washington, 1999—. Author: textbook AS 100, 1984; editor The Air Force Today, 1985; author, editor 3 slide briefings Aircraft and Weapons of AF, Vietnam, Korea, 1984-85; pub. Civil Air Patrol News, 1985-86. Test proctor Am. Mensa Soc. Presbyterian. Avocations: photography, electronics, country dancing, woodworking, bicycling. Home: 631 N Ripley St Alexandria VA 22304-2715 Office: Pension Benefit Guaranty Corp 1200 K St NW Fl 4 Washington DC 20005-4026 E-mail: dixon.mike@pbgc.gov.

DIXON, PAUL EDWARD, lawyer, metal products and manufacturing company executive; b. Bklyn., Aug. 27, 1944; s. Paul Stewart and Bernice (Mathisen) D.; m. Kathleen Constance Kayser, Sept. 23, 1967; children: Jennifer Pyne, Paul Kayser, Meredith Stewart. BA, Villanova U., 1966; JD, St. Johns U., 1972. Bar: N.Y. 1972, U.S. Supreme Ct. 1976. Assoc. mem. firm Rogers & Wells, N.Y.C., 1972-77; sec., asst. gen. counsel Volvo of Am. Corp., Rockleigh, N.J., 1977-79, v.p., gen. counsel, 1979-81; v.p., gen. counsel, sec. Reichhold Chems. Inc., 1981-88; sr. v.p., gen. counsel, sec. The Warnaco Group Inc., 1988-91; v.p., gen. counsel, sec. Handy & Harman, Rye, N.Y., 1992-97, sr. v.p., gen. counsel, sec., 1997—. Chmn. Teeches Ltd., Bermuda. Mem. ABA, Assn. Bar City N.Y., N.Y. State Bar Assn., U.S. Supreme Ct. Hist. Soc., Am. Corp. Counsel Assn., Bedford Golf and Tennis Club. Office: Handy & Harman 555 Theodore Fremd Ave Rye NY 10580-1451

DIXON, PAUL WILLIAM, psychology educator; b. N.Y.C., Aug. 1, 1936; s. Edward Everet and Esther (McCracken) D.; children: Michael H., Theodore K., Eleanor T., Aaron T. BA in English, Blackburn Coll., 1960; MA in Gen. Exptl. Psychology, U. Hawaii, 1963, PhD in Gen. Exptl. Psychology, 1966. Cert. tchr., Ill. Prof. psychology Coll. Arts and Scis. U. Hawaii, Hilo, 1965—, chmn. dept. liberal studies Coll. Arts and Scis., 1972-82, chmn. dept. psychology Coll. Arts and Scis., 1972-75. Vis. assoc. prof. psychology internat. divsn. Sophia U., Tokyo, 1971-72; vis. prof. dept. microbiology and immunology, UCLA, 1978-79; all-campus faculty pers. com. U. Hilo, 1967-68, pers. com. social scis. and edn. divsn., 1968-69, faculty senate, 1970-71, libr. com., 1970-71, acad. freedom, privilege and tenure com., 1973-74, dissertation com. dept. polit. sci., 1974-78, Rsch. Coun., 1977-78, chmn. all-coll. faculty pers. com., 1970, libr. com., 1973-74, liberal studies com., 1973-82. Contbr. numerous articles to psychol. and ednl. jours. Presenter, demonstrator Frequency Transfer Hearing Aid to Action Group for the Hearing Impaired, Honolulu, 1980, also to State Hearing and Visual Handicapped Svc., Hilo, Hawaii, 1980; chmn. commn. on anthropology of math. Internat. Union Anthrop. and Ethnol. Scis. Nominee Nobel prize in physics, 1986, 95, 98; NDEA fellow, 1963-66; aid grantee U. Hwaii Rsch. Coun., 1965-70, U. Hawaii Hilo Fund, 1970. Fellow Am. Anthrop. Assn., Soc. for Applied Anthropology; mem. AAAS, APA (travel grantee 1972), Internat. Congress of Anthrop. and Ethnographic Scis. Achievements include pioneering immunotherapy of cancer with levamisole, cancer vaccine, and pyrogen; life extension with immortalized autograft; generation of supernovae via high-energy physics experimentation; solution to Last Theorm of Fermat and Continuum Hypothesis of Gregor Cantor; research in linguistry. Home: PO Box 244 Volcano HI 96785-0244 Office: U Hawaii Coll Arts and Scis 200 W Kawili St Hilo HI 96720-4075

DIXON, RICHARD DEAN, lawyer, educator; b. Columbus, Ohio, Nov. 6, 1944; s. Dean A. and Katherine L. (Currier) D.; m. Kathleen A. Manfrass, June 17, 1967; children: Jennifer, Lindsay. BSEE, Ohio State U., 1967, MSEE, 1968; MBA, Fla. State U., 1972, JD, 1974. Bar: Fla. 1975, Colo. 1985, Mich. 1992, U.S. Dist. Ct. (mid. dist.) Fla., U.S. Dist. Ct. Colo. 1985, U.S. Patent and Trademanrk Office 1975. Telemetry sys. engr. Pan Am. World Airways, Patrick AFB, Fla., 1968-72; sole practice Melbourne and Orlando, Fla., 1975-80; sr. counsel Harris Corp., Melbourne, 1980-85; corp. counsel, dir. strategic and bus. planning Ford Microelectronics, Inc., Colorado Springs, Colo., 1985-89; mgr. strategic alliances electronics divsn. Ford Motor Co., Dearborn, Mich., 1989-90, assoc. counsel intellectual property, 1991-93, dep. chief patent counsel, 1994—2000; with Dixon Mediation Svcs., 2001—. Adj. prof. bus. law U. Cen. Fla., Cocoa, 1977, Fla. Inst. Tech., Melbourne, 1980-84. Cooper Industries Engring. scholar Ohio State U., 1964-67. Mem. ABA, Licensing Execs. Soc., Am. Intellectual Property Law Assn., Am. Corp. Counsel Assn., Sigma Iota Epsilon, Eta Kappa Nu, Phi Eta Sigma. Home and Office: 8162 Old Tramway Dr Melbourne FL 32940-2183

DIXON, RICHARD WAYNE, retired communications company executive; b. Hubbard, Oreg., Sept. 25, 1936; s. Harlow C. and Mabel (Nilsson) D.; m. Rosina O. Berry, July 4, 1970; children: Erica, Douglas, Andrew. BA summa cum laude, Harvard U., 1958, MA, 1960, PhD, 1964. Tech. staff mem. AT&T Bell Labs., Murray Hill, N.J., 1965, supr. lightwave lasers group, 1968-79, head optoelectronics devices dept., 1979-83, dir. lightwave devices lab., 1983-90, dir. platforms and new products labs., 1991-93; now expert witness and tech. cons., Bernardsville, N.J. Contbr. articles to various publs. Nat. scholar Harvard U., 1955-58; NSF fellow, 1959-63. Fellow IEEE (editor Electronic Device Letters 1980-90, Medal of Engring. Excellence 1993); mem. AAAS, Am. Phys. Soc. Home: 43 Old Wood Rd Bernardsville NJ 07924-1416 E-mail: rdixon@worldnet.att.net.

DIXON, ROBERT CLYDE, systems engineer, consultant; b. Greensboro, N.C., Jan. 8, 1932; s. Earnest Patrick and Alma Leona (Moore) D.; m. Nancy Tom Zurborg, July 9, 1955; children: David Thomas, Theresa Anne, Robert Weldon. BSEE, Pacific States U., 1961; MS in Sys. Engring., West Coast U., 1968. Registered profl. engr., Calif.; cert. bus. for tech. pers. UCLA, 1971, profl. designation in bus. UCLA, 1972. Sr. engr. Magnavox Rsch. Labs., Torrance, Calif., 1959-68; staff engr. TRW, Redondo Beach, Calif., 1968-71; sr. rsch. engr. Northrop Corp., Palos Verdes, Calif., 1971-74; sr. tech. staff asst. Hughes Aircraft Co., Fullerton, Calif., 1974-75, chief scientist Irvine, Calif., 1982-84; pres. Spectrack Sys. Inc., Cypress, Calif., 1975-82; cons. R.C. Dixon & Assocs., Cypress, 1975-85, Palmer Lake, Colo., 1985—; chief scientist Spread Spectrum Scis., Palmer Lake, 1981-89, Omnipoint Data Co. Inc., 1989-91, Omnipoint Corp., 1991-96. Lectr. UCLA, Westwood, 1975-95, George Washington U., 1976—; chmn. bd. Ditrans Corp., 1999—; adv. com. Pinpoint Corp., 1997—; bd. dirs. Sunwest Corp., Ditrans Corp., Vari-L Co. Inc. Author: Spread Spectrum Systems, 1976, 84, 96, Radio Receiver Design, 1998; editor: Spread Spectrum Techniques, 1976, Spread Spectrum Signals and Systems, 1985; contbr. articles to profl. jours. Elder's pres. Ch. of Jesus Christ of Latter Day Saints, Cypress, 1975, mem. High Coun., 1977-83; bd. dirs. Robert and Nancy Dixon scholarship, 1994—. With USN, 1951-55. Fellow IEEE (co-editor spl. issue comms. transactions 1978, mem. procs. editl. bd.). Mem. Lds Ch. Office: RC Dixon & Assoc PO Box 100 Palmer Lake CO 80133-0100

DIXON, ROBERT GENE, retired manufacturing engineering educator, retired mechanical engineering company executive; b. Clatskanie, Oreg., Feb. 15, 1934; s. Hobart Jay and Doris Marie D.; m. Janice Lee Taylor, Sept. 19, 1954; children: Linda Dixon Johnson, Jeffrey, David. AS in Indsl. Tech., Chemeketa C.C., 1978, related spl. courses, 1978-80. Cert. welder, Oreg. Journeyman machinist to asst. mgr. AB McLauchlan Co., Inc., 1956-69; supt. design, rsch., devel. engrng. and prodn. Stevens Equipment Co., 1969-70; co-owner, operator Pioneer Machinery, 1970-72; supt. constrn. and repair Stayton Canning Co., 1972-73; mgr. Machinery div. Power Transmission, 1973-75; owner, operator Dixon Engrng., Salem, Oreg., 1975-96, ret., 1996; instr., program chair mfg. engrng. tech. Chemeketa C.C., 1975-92, tech. project coord. Oreg. Advanced Tech. Ctr., 1992-95; apptd. tech. project coord. Oreg. Advanced Tech. Consortium., 1995-96. With U.S. Navy, 1952-56. Named Tchr. of Yr., Chemeketa Deaf Program, 1978, Outstanding Instr. of Yr., Am. Tech. Edn. Assn., 1983. Mem. ASTD, Am. Prodn. and Inventory Control Soc., Am. Vocat. Assn. (Outstanding Tchr. award 1981), Oreg. Vocat. Assn. (Instr. of Yr. 1980; pres. 1984), Oreg. Vocat. Trade Tech. Assn. (Instr. of Yr. 1979; pres. 1981; Pres.'s Plaque 1982), Soc. Mfg. Engrs. (cert., sr., chmn. Oreg. sect. 1988—, internat. dir. nominating com, 1992, 95, Outstanding Internat. Faculty adv., 1989, 91), Am. Welding Soc., Am. Soc. Metals, Chemeketa Edn. Assn. (pres. 1979), Am Soc. Quality Control, Computer Automated Systems Assn., Phi Theta Kappa. Author: Benchwork, 1980, Procedure Manual for Team Approach for Vocational Education Special Needs Students, 1980, Smart Cam CNC/CAM Curriculum for Point Control Company; tech. reviewer textbook pubs., 1978—; designer, patentee fruit and berry stem remover. Home: 4242 Indigo St NE Salem OR 97305-2134

DIXON, ROBERT JAMES, aerospace consultant, former air force officer, former aerospace company executive; b. N.Y.C., Apr. 9, 1920; s. William H. and Mary A. (Smith) D.; m. Elizabeth Harriman (dec.); m. Lamana M. Kelly, July 19, 1958; children: Kelly Lee, Thomas Fries, Roland Cahill, Mary Lucinda. Grad., Collegiate Sch., N.Y.C., 1937; AB, Dartmouth Coll., 1941; grad., Air War Coll., 1959. Enlisted RCAF, 1941; trans. USAAF, 1943; advanced through grades to gen. USAF, 1973; served as pilot ETO, World War II; vice comdr. 7th Air Force, Vietnam, 1969-70; dep. chief staff personnel Hdqrs. USAF, Washington, 1970-73; comdr. TAC Air Command, Langley, Va., 1973-78; ret., 1978; pres. Fairchild Republic Co., Farmingdale, N.Y., 1978-81, chmn., 1982, ret. 1982. Decorated D.S.C., D.S.M. (4), Legion of Merit (2) U.S.; D.F.C. (2) U.S. and U.K.; Legion of Honor France; recipient Collier trophy, 1978 Died Apr. 10, 2003.

DIXON, ROSINA BERRY, physician, pharmaceutical development consultant; b. Columbus, Ohio, Dec. 3, 1942; d. Loren C. and Florence H. (Bateson) Berry; m. Richard W. Dixon, July 4, 1970; children: Erica H., Douglas R., Andrew D. BA in Chemistry, Radcliffe Coll., 1964; MD, Columbia U., 1968. Diplomate Am. Bd. Internal Medicine. Intern, resident, and chief med. resident Roosevelt Hosp., N.Y.C., 1968-72; from sr. assoc. to exec. dir. Ciba-Geigy, Summit, N.J., 1972-81; med. dir. Schering Labs., Kenilworth, N.J., 1981-84; v.p. Med. Market Spltys., Boonton, N.J., 1985-86; cons. pharm. devel. Bernardsville, N.J., 1986—. Bd. dirs. Cambrex Corp., East Rutherford, N.J., Enzon Pharms., Inc., Piscataway, N.J., Church & Dwight Co., Inc., Princeton, N.J.; instr. medicine Coll. Phys. and Surg., Columbia U., 1972-99; preceptor in family practice Overlook Hosp., Summit, 1979—; mem. governing bd. Daytop at Mendham, N.J., 1991—; trustee Bonnie Brae, N.J., 1992. Mem. Am. Coll. Clin. Pharmacology, Am. Soc. Clin. Pharmacology and Therapeutics, Nat. Assn. Corp. Dirs. (dir.). Home and Office: 43 Old Wood Rd Bernardsville NJ 07924-1416

DIXON, SAMUEL B, retired comedian, film director, film producer; s. Paul Dixon and Thomas G Elzie; m. Rita F Lusk, June 1, 1991; children: Smauel Jr., Karla, Cedrick, Derrick children: Renetta F Lesure, Sherita L Peterson, Charles R Peterson. BAAS, Stephen F. Austin State U., 1976—80. Electronic Technician Lee Coll. Tex., 1978. Author (actor, dir., prodr.): (movie script) Hanging With the Big Boys; dir.(prodr.): (movie dir.) Hanging With The Big Boys; composer (poet): (poetry) Wake Up Am. (Nat. Mag. Publ., 2002); composer: (country western music selection) Lost Respect For Love (Nat. Mag. Publ., 2002), (r.&.b musical selection) Gotta Go On (Nat. Mag. Publ., 2002). Newsletter pub. Lion's Club Internat., Plano, Tex., 1994—96; mem. Leadership Memphis, Tenn., 1990—2003. With U.S. Army, 1967—71. Named to Internat. Hole-In-One Hall-of-Fame. Mem.: US Golf Assn. Home: 109 N Main Apt #1701 Memphis TN 38103 Office: Center Stage Productions 109 North Main Ste 1701 Memphis TN 38103

DIXON, SHIRLEY JUANITA, retired restaurant owner; b. Canton, N.C., June 29, 1935; d. Willard Luther and Bessie Eugenia (Scroggs) Clark; m. Clinton Matthew Dixon, Jan. 3, 1953; children: Elizabeth Swanger, Hugh Monroe III, Cynthia Owen, Sharon Henson. BS, Wayne State U., 1956; postgrad., Mary Baldwin Coll., 1958, U. N.C., 1977. Acct. Standard Oil Co., Detroit, 1955-57; asst. dining room mgr. Statler Hilton, Detroit, 1958-60; bookkeeper Osborne Lumber Co., Canton, N.C., 1960-61; bus. owner, pres. Dixon's Restaurant, Canton, 1961-99; ret. Judge N.C. Assn. Distributive Edn. Assn., state and dist., 1982—; owner Halbert's Family Heritage Ctr., Canton; dir. rep. Avon. Past Pres. Haywood County Assn. Retarded Citizens Bd., 1985-94, past v.p., chmn. bd. dirs.; bd. commrs. Haywood Vocats. Opportunities, 1985-94, treas. bd. dirs.; Haywood Sr. Leadership Council; dist. dir. 11th Congl. Dist. Dem. Women, 1982-85; state Teen-Dem. advisor State Dem. party, 1985-90; del. 1988 Dem. Nat. Conv., Atlanta; alderwoman Town of Canton, N.C.; vice-chair Gov.'s. Adv. Coun. on Aging, State N.C., 1982-89; 1st v.p. crime prevention Community Watch Bd., State N.C., 1985, 86; mem. Criminal Justice Bd., N.C. Assembly on Women and the Economy; chair Western N.C. Epilepsy Assn., Haywood County N.C. Mus. History, 1987—; bd. dirs. W.N.C. Women's Coalition, 1999-2000; co-chair Haywood County Commn. on the Bi-Centennial of Constn., 1987-92; Haywood County Econ. Strategy Commn.; v.p., bd. dirs. Haywood County Retirement Coun., Region A Coun. on Aging; bd. dirs. Haywood County Sr. Housing, C.B.C. United Way (mem. chair); chair bd. Canton Sr. Citizen's Ctr.; mem. Haywood County Ease Retirement Com.; pres., chairwoman bd. Haywood County Assn. Retarded Citizens; bd. dirs. W.N.C Womens Coalition, 1999; pres. N.C. coun. Alzheimer's Disease and Related Disorders Assn.; bd. dirs. Canton Recreation Dept., Western N.C. Alzheimer's Disease and Related Disorders Assn., 1987-91, v.p., C.B; bd. dirs. Haywood Literary Coun., Haywood Sr. Leadership Coun., W.N.C. Econ. Devel. Com., United Way, 1991—, drive chmn.; mem. legis. subcom. Alzheimer's-State of N.C.; bd. dirs. N.C. Conf. for Social Svcs., 1987-91; v.p. bd. Western N.C. Alzheimer's Assn., 1987-91; pres. State Coun. on Alzheimer's; apptd. mem. Legis. Study Com. on Alzheimer's; apptd. mem. State of N.C. Adv. Bd. on Community Care and Health; mem. Habitat for Humanity Haywood County; bd. chair Pigeon Valley Optimist Club; apptd. by Senate Western N.C. Econ. Devel. Commn.; appointee Haywood County Econ. Devel. Commn., Canton Hist. Commn.; judge U.S. Olympic Torch Bearers. Recipient Outstanding Svc. award Crime Prevention from Gov., 1982, Gov.'s Spl. Vol. award, 1983, Outstanding Svc. award N.C. Cmty. Watch Assn., 1984, Cmty. Svc. award to Handicapped, 1983-84, Outstanding Svc. award ARC, 1988; named Employer of Yr. for Hiring Handicapped N.C. Assn. for Retarded Citizens, 1985, Cmty. Person of Yr. Kiwanis Club, 1991, Citizen of Yr. in Western N.C., 1995, Rec. Outstanding award Haywood Co. Sr. Games, 1992, Roy A. Taylor award for disting. svc., 1999; inducted into N.C. Softball Hall of Fame, 1997. Mem. AAUW, NAFE, Women's Polit. Caucus (So. Women's Leadership award 1998), Internat. Platform Assn., Women's Forum N.C., Nat. Bd. Alzheimers Assn. (regional del.), Canton Bus. and Profl. Assn. (pres. 1974-79, Woman of Yr. 1984), Altrusa (Woman of Yr. in N.C. 1989). Democrat. Episcopalian. Avocation: softball club. Home: 104 Skyland Ter Canton NC 28716-3718 Office: Dixons Restaurant 30 N Main St Canton NC 28716-3805 E-mail: sjdixon28716@yahoo.com.

DIXON, SHIRLEY LEE, emergency physician; b. NYC, Dec. 10, 1947; d. Henry Ester and Ethel Mae (Samuels) D. BS in Biology, CCNY, 1969; MD, Howard U., 1976; MPH, Columbia U., 1983. Intern Harlem Hosp. Ctr., NYC, 1976-77, resident in internal medicine, 1979-81, attending physician dept. ambulatory care, 1981-83; attending physician La Guardia Med. Group PC, 1983-85; emergency rm. attending Interfaith Med. Ctr., 1985-87; med. dir. Triboro Divsn. US Postal Svc., Flushing, NY, 1986-93, med. officer, 1993-96; attending emergency room VA Hosp., Bronx, 1993-96. Mem. cmty. adv. bd. Harlem Hosp., 1981—83; attending physician night screening clinic Lincoln Hosp., 1989—91. Active People to People Citizen Amb. Program, Spokane, Wash., 1991; mem. People to People Internat. Commd. officer USPHS, 1977-79. Health Professions scholar, USHPS scholar; Nat. Med. fellow. Fellow: Fgn. Policy Rsch. Assn., Am. Bd. Forensic Examiners (life; diplomate); mem.: APHA, Assn. Clinicians for Underserved (charter), NY Acad. Sci., Am. Profl. Practice Assn. (life), Am. Bd. Disability Analysts (life; diplomate, sr. analyst), Am. Acad. Experts in Traumatic Stress (cert. illness trauma 2001, cert. disability trauma 2001, cert. stress mgmt. 2001, diplomate). Home: 752 West End Ave New York NY 10025-6230 E-mail: vze34pbn@verizon.net.

DIXON, STEVEN BEDFORD, lawyer; b. San Bernardino, Calif., Dec. 25, 1945; s. Harold James Dixon and Jane Anna (Bedford) Kennedy; m. Lucy Pearson Dixon; children: Melanie Anne, Zachary David; stepchildren: Michael, Katherine. BA, U. Hawaii-Hilo, 1975; JD, Calif. Western Sch. Law, 1978; postgrad. Chaminade U. of Hawaii, Hawaii Tax Inst., 1978-82. Bar: Hawaii, U.S. Dist Ct. Hawaii, U.S. Tax Ct.; cert. continuing real estate edn. instr., Hawaii. Trial counsel, U. S. Army, 1969-70, Law clk. Linley, McDougal, Meloche & Murphy, El Cajon, Calif., 1976, D. Stephen Boner, San Diego, 1977, Tyson & Churchill, San Diego, 1977; law intern Legal Aid Soc. of Hawaii, 1978; law clk., investigator Stephen Christensen, Hawaii, 1978; gen. ptnr. Altman, Dicker & Dixon, tax attys., Hilo, 1978-79, Altman Dixon & Assocs., tax attys., Hilo, 1979-81; pvt. practice, Hilo, 1981-82; gen. ptnr. Dixon & Okura, Hilo, 1982-90; pvt. practice, 1990—; corp. counsel, broker Internat. Realty Corp., emphasizing Japan trade; arbitrator State of Hawaii Ct.; tchr. Hawaii Assn. Realtors, Grad. Realtor Inst., past Vitosek Real Estate Sch.; speaker, news columnist in field; writer; instr. bus. law U. Hawaii-Hilo, 1979-80 ; past bd. dirs. Elec. Co-operative Hawaii Inc. Columnist Money, Real Estate and You; radio show 50 Minutes with Steve Dixon. Past v.p. Hawaii Concert Soc.; counsel discharge Vets. Outreach, San Diego, 1976; bd. dirs. Big Island Substance Abuse Council; active community svcs. Served to 1st lt. 1967-70, Vietnam. Decorated Bronze Star. U. Hawaii-Hilo scholar, 1973. Mem. Hawaii County Bar Assn., Rotary.

DIXON, STEWART STRAWN, lawyer, consultant; b. Chgo., Nov. 5, 1930; s. Wesley M. and Katherine (Strawn) D.; m. Romayne Wilson, June 24, 1961 (dec. July 1993); children: Stewart S. Jr., John W., Romayne W. Thompson; m. Ann Wilson Grozier, Sept. 15, 1997. BA, Yale U., 1952; JD, U. Mich., 1955. Bar: Ill. 1957, U.S. Dist. Ct. 1957, U.S. Ct. Appeals 1974, U.S. Supreme Ct. 1974. Ptnr. Kirkland & Ellis, Chgo., 1957-67, Wildman, Harrold, Allen & Dixon, Chgo., 1967—. Dir. Lord, Abbett & Co. Managed Mut. Funds, N.Y.C., 1976-2002, ret. Dec. 31, 2002; dir. Otho Sprague Inst., Chgo. Trustee, past chmn. Chgo. Hist. Soc., 1982-87. 1st lt. U.S. Army, 1955-60. Mem. Am. Bar Assn., Am. Law Inst., Ill. Bar Assn., Chgo. Bar Assn. Clubs: Chgo., Commonwealth, Commercial, Met., Univ., Old Elm, Onwentsia, Rolling Rock. Republican. Episcopalian. Office: Wildman Harrold Allen & Dixon 225 W Wacker Dr Chicago IL 60606-1224

DIXON, TAMECKA, professional basketball player; b. Dec. 14, 1975; Grad., Kans. State U., 1997. Basketball player Los Angeles Sparks Women's NBA, Inglewood, Calif., 1997—. Mem. Olympic Festival Team South, 1995. Avocations: dancing, shopping. Office: Los Angeles Sparks Gt Western Forum 3900 W Manchester Blvd Inglewood CA 90305-2200

DIXON, THELMA DUNNEBACKE, research scientist; b. Nashville, Dec. 23, 1925; d. Frederick Charles and Thelma Hudson Dunnebacke; m. Jonathan S. Dixon, June 9, 1954; children: James Dunnebacke, Lindsay Ann, Frederick Charles. AB, Washington U., St. Louis, 1947, MA, 1949, PhD, 1954. Rsch. scientist virus lab. U. Calif., Berkeley, 1954-76; rsch. scientist Viral and Rickettsial Disease Lab. Calif. Dept. Health Svcs., Berkeley, 1976—. Grantee NSF, NIH. Mem. AAAS, Am. Soc. Cell Biology, Soc. Protozoologists, Soc. Tissue Culture, N.Y. Acad. Sci., Electron Microscope Soc. Home: 2326 Russell St Berkeley CA 94705-1926 Office: Calif Dept Health Svcs Viral and Rickettsial Disease 850 Marina Bay Pky Richmond CA 94804

DIXON, WARREN EVERETT, robotics engineer; b. York, Pa., June 15, 1972; s. Dwight Mercer Dixon, Belinda Lee Dixon; m. Lisa Ross Dixon; 1 child, Ethan. BS, Clemson U., 1994, PhD, 2000; M in Engring., U. S.C., 1997. Tchg. asst. U. S.C., Columbia, 1995—97; rsch. asst. Clemson (S.C.) U., 1997—2000, grad. tchr. record, 2000; staff scientist Oak Ridge (S.C.) Nat. Lab., 2000—. Author: (book) Nonlinear Control of Wheeled Mobile Robots, 2001 (Oak Ridge National Laboratory Early Career Award for Engineering Achievement, 2002); contbr. articles to profl. jours.; author: (book) Nonlinear Control of Engineering Systems: A Lyapunov-based Approach, 2003. Fellow Eugene P. Wigner, Oak Ridge Nat. Lab., 2000-2002. Mem.: IEEE Control Sys. Soc., IEEE Robotics and Automation Soc., Alpha Epsilon Lambda (life; pres. 1998—99), Omicron Delta Kappa (life), Sigma Xi, Eta Kappa Nu (life). Presbyterian. Office: Oak Ridge Nat Lab PO Box 2008-6305 1 Bethel Valley Rd Oak Ridge TN 37831 Office Fax: 865-574-4624. Business E-Mail: dixonwe@ornl.gov.

DIXON, WHEELER WINSTON, film and video studies educator, writer; b. New Brunswick, N.J., Mar. 12, 1950; s. Percival Vincent and Hilda-Barr (Wheeler) D.; m. Gwendolyn Audrey Foster, Dec. 23, 1985. AB, Livingston Coll., 1972; MA, MPhil, Rutgers U., 1980, PhD, 1982. Instr. English Rutgers U., New Brunswick, 1974-84; lectr. film studies The New Sch. for Social Rsch., 1983, 97, 98; asst. prof. English and art U. Nebr., Lincoln, 1984-88; assoc. prof. English SUNY Press, 1988—92; chmn. film studies program U. Nebr., Lincoln, 1988—2003, prof. English, 1992—2002; series editor Cultural Studies in Cinema Video Series SUNY Press, 1995—, endowed chair, Ryan prof. of film studies, 2000—. Guest programmer, lectr. Nat. Film Theatre of Brit. Film Inst. and Mus. of Moving Image, London, 1991; guest programmer Nat. Film Theatre of Brit. Film Inst., London, 1992; mem. ad hoc curriculum rev. com. dept. English, U. Nebr., Lincoln, 1992, mem. faculty devel. fellowship com., 1992-95, chmn. Robinson Prize com., spring 1994, chmn. faculty devel. fellowship com., 1994, mem. various MA thesis and PhD coms.; panelist NEH, 1993—; presenter papers in field; lectr. Lincoln Ctr., Mus. Modern Art, N.Y.C., New Sch. Univ., N.Y.C., 1997; guest lectr. on digital prodn., U. Amsterdam, 1999. Author: The "B" Directors: A Bibliographical Directory, 1985, The Cinematic Vision of F. Scott Fitzgerald, 1986, The Films of Freddie Francis, 1991, The Charm of Evil: The Films of Terence Fisher, 1991, The Films of Reginald Le Borg: Interviews, Essays and Filmography, 1992, The Early Film Criticism of François Truffaut, 1993, Re-Viewing British Cinema 1900-1992: Essays and Interviews, 1994, It Looks at You: The Returned Gaze of Cinema, 1995, The Films of Jean-Luc Godard, 1997, The Exploding Eye: A Re-visionary History of 1960s Experimental Cinema, 1997, The Transparency of Spectacle, 1998, Disaster and Memory, 1999, The Second Century of Cinema, 2000, Film Genre 2000, 2000, Collected Interviews: Voices from 20th Century Cinema, 2001, Experimental Cinema: The Film Reader, 2002, Straight: Constructions of Heterosexuality in the Cinema, 2003, Visions of the Apocalypse: Spectacles of Destruction in the American Cinema, 2003; editor-in-chief Quarterly Review of Film and Video, 1999—; guest editor Film Criticism, Fall-Winter 1991-92, mem. editl. bd., 1991—, article reviewer, 1991—; article reviewer Jour. of History of Sexuality, 1991-93, Cinema Jour., 1993—; mem. adv. bd. Jour. Popular Brit. Cinema; manuscript reviewer SUNY Press, 1993—; contbr. articles and revs. to profl. jours. and essays to various publs., including Film Criticism, Films in Rev., Cineaste, Interview, others; writer, dir., prodr. Coming Attractions: A History of the Motion Picture Trailer, 1986-88, (feature film) What Can I Do?, 1993 (Layman Fund award 1993-94); co-prodr., co-dir., co-writer: Women Who Made The Movies, 1988-90; dir./prodr.: (feature film) Squatters, 1994; exhibited in group shows at U. Nebr.-Lincoln, 1985-86, 87-88, 89-90, Syracuse U., 1986, W.Va. U., 1986, Lincolnshire Coll. Art, Lincoln, Eng., 1988-89; performances include That's Different: Tales of Nebraska, 1987; exhibitions of films include Whitney Mus. Am. Art, 1972, Mus. Modern Art, 1994, Mus. Moving Image, London, 1994, Millennium Film Workshop, 1997, Mus. Modern Art, 2003; complete films archived exclusively at Mus. of Modern Art, 2003, Career Retrospective, 2003. Grantee Royal Film Archive of Belgium, 1974, N.J. State Arts Coun., 1972, Rsch. Coun., U. Nebr., 1984-85, Ind. Filmmaker, S.W. Alt. Media Project, 1985, Interdisciplinary Arts Fellowship Program, Rockefeller Found. and NEA, 1987, Rsch. Coun., 1987, 89, S.W. Alt. Media Project Ind. Prodn. Fund, 1993; George Holmes Faculty fellow, 1989. Office: U Nebraska Dept English 202 Andrews Hall Lincoln NE 68588-0333 E-mail: wdixon@unlserve.unl.edu.

DIXON, WILLIAM ROBERT, musician, composer, educator; b. Nantucket, Mass., Oct. 5, 1925; s. William Robert and Louise Ann (Wade) D.; children: William, Claudia Gayle, William. Diploma, Hartnette Conservatory Music, 1951. Clk., internat. civil servant UN Secretariat, N.Y.C., 1956-62; free lance musician, composer N.Y.C., 1962-67; mem. faculty Columbia U. Tchrs. Coll., 1967-70; composer-in-residence George Washington U., Washington, 1967; dir. Conservatory of Univ. of the Streets, N.Y.C., 1967-68; guest artist in residence Ohio State U., 1967; mem. faculty dept. dance Bennington (Vt.) Coll., 1968-95, chmn. dept. black music, 1973-86. Vis. prof. U. Wis., Madison, 1971-72; lectr. painting and music Mus. Modern Art, Verona, Italy, 1982, Palast, Nuremberg, Fed. Republic Germany, 1990; lectr. workshop on contemporary music Pori, Finland, 1991, Jerusalem, Tel Aviv, Israel, 1990; lectr. in Black Art Music Maison du Livre et du Son, Villeurbanne, France, 1994; tchr. Master Classes in Improvisation Ecole Nationale de Musique, Villeurbanne, France, 1994, Master Class Composition and Performance NYU, 1996. Recs. include Archie Shepp-Bill Dixon Quartet, 1962, Bill Dixon 7-Tette, 1963, Intents and Purposes: The Bill Dixon Orchestra, 1967, For Franz, 1976, New Music, Second Wave, 1979, Bill Dixon in Italy, 2 vols., 1980, considerations 1 and 2 Bill Dixon, 1980, 82, November: 1981, 1982, Bill Dixon in the Labyrinth, 1983, Collection, 1985, Thoughts, 1986, Son of Sisyphus, 1990, Bill Dixon: Vade Mecum, 1994, Vade Mecum II, 1996, (6-CD set) Bill Dixon: Solo Trumpet, 1998, PAPYRUS vol. 1 and 2, compositions for trumpet, percussion & piano, 1999, Berlin Abbozzi, 2000; retrospective of music compositions 1963-91 by Radio Sta. WKCR, Columbia U., 1991-92; trumpet soloist Celebration Orchestra, Berlin, Germany, 1994; concert performance of original compositions Espace Tonkin, Villeurbanne, France, 1994, Teatro Colosseo, Rome, Italy, 1996, Nickelsdorf, Austria, 1997; composed orch. piece Cologne (Germany) Radio Sta., 1998; paintings exhibited, Ferrari Gallery, Verona, Italy, 1982, Multimedia Contemporary Art Gallery, Brescia, Italy, 1982, Uferpalast, Nuremberg, Germany, 1990, Cite de la Musique, Paris, 2002; exhibited lithographs Villeurbanne, France, 1994, Chittenden Bank, Bennington, Vt., 1994-95, Skoto Gallery, N.Y.C., 1996; retrospective of paintings 1968-91, So. Vt. Coll., 1991; author: L'Opera, (biodiscography by Ben Young) Dixonia, 1998; prodr. lithographs Union Regionale pour le Devel. de la Lithographie d'Art, Lyon, France, 1994; orchestral work Index, 2000; artist album cover, 2002. Mem. adv. com. New Eng. Found. of the Arts. Served with U.S. Army, 1944-46. Recipient Disting. Visitor in the Arts Middlebury Coll., 1986. Fellow Vt. Acad. Arts and Scis.; mem. Am. Fedn. Musicians, Duke Ellington Jazz Soc. (hon.) *Were it possible to live for three thousand years, one could lay around the house and do nothing for the first five hundred years, go to school for the next five hundred and then have two thousand years left to find a way to do work, etc., of substance. Since that is NOT the case (and even if one crosses with the green and not in between and manages to live to be one hundred--in cosmic or universal time akin to attempting to spit in the Atlantic Ocean from a height of 50,000 feet and expecting a ripple to follow) there is another reality extant. And from the time THAT reality dawned on me, I have endeavoured (albeit not always with success) to do everything one hundred percent. Those things I felt I COULDN'T (for whatever reason) expend that kind of energy upon, I have left alone.*

DIXON, W(ILLIAM) ROBERT, retired educational psychology educator; b. Hudson, Pa., Sept. 16, 1917; s. William Robert and Mary (George) D.; m. Carol Everson Lewis, Dec. 20, 1940; children: William R., Barbara Ann. AB, Syracuse U., 1938, MA, 1939; PhD (Horace H. Rackham fellow 1947-48, Burke Aaron Hinsdale scholar 1948), U. Mich., 1948. Tchr., prin. W. Canada Valley Central Schs., Middleville, N.Y., 1940-42; asst. prof. U. Ill., 1948-49, U. Mich., 1949-52, asso. prof., 1952-56, prof. ednl. psychology, 1956-86, ret., 1986. Vis. prof. edn. U. Bombay, India, 1964-65 Contbr. articles to profl. jours. Dir. Mich. Interdisciplinary Research Tng. Program, 1967-72. Served with USAAF, 1942-45. Decorated Air Medal with 10 oak leaf clusters, D.F.C. Fellow Am. Psychol. Assn., AAAS; mem. Am. Ednl. Research Assn. Achievements include being nationally ranked tennis player Men's Singles, 1945, Vets. Singles, 1962. Home: 2793 W Fairway Loop Dunnellon FL 34434-4829

DIXON, WRIGHT TRACY, JR., retired lawyer; b. Raleigh, N.C., Oct. 7, 1921; s. Wright T. and Marion Jefferson (Homes) D.; m. Elizabeth Prince Nufer, June 3, 1950; children: Wright III, William N., Elizabeth Prince. AB, Duke U., 1947; LLB, U. N.C., 1951. Bar: N.C. 1951, U.S. Dsit. Ct. (ea., mid. and we. dists.), N.C. 1951, U.S. Ct. Appeals (4th cir.) 1956. Ptnr. Bailey & Dixon, Raleigh, N.C., 1956-99; ret. Mem. Bd. of Adjustments, Raleigh, 1960-74, chmn., 1969-74. Jr. warden, sr. warden, mem. vestry St. Michael's Episcopal Ch., Raleigh; trustee So. Sem. Va., 1961-81, N.C. Client Security Fund, 1986-91. With USMC, 1943-59. Fellow Am. Bar Found.; mem. ABA (del. 1984-88), N.C. State Bar (counselor 1979-86, pres. 1985-86, Gen. Practice Hall of Fame 1997), Wake County Bar Assn. (pres. 1976, mem. N.C. commn. on code recodification 1979-81, hon. bd. mem. 1995, Joseph Branch professionalism award 1996), Raleigh Kiwanis Club (pres.), Sphinx Club (pres.), Carolina Country Club, Capital City Club. Avocations: golf, woodworking, genealogy, tennis, reading. Home: 414 Marlowe Rd Raleigh NC 27609-7018 Office: Bailey & Dixon PO Box 1351 2 Hannover Sq Raleigh NC 27602 E-mail: WDixon@BDixon.com.

DIXSON, DIANE ELIZABETH, acquisitions librarian, tax preparation business owner; b. Washington, Sept. 26, 1943; d. Charles Hanan and Doris (Cover) D. BA in English and German, George Mason U., 1978; grad., Fin. Mgmt. Sch., 2002. Bibliographic technician Libr. Congress, Washington, 1966-68, preliminary cataloger, 1968-72, sr. acquisitions tech., 1973—, sr. acquisitions specialist, 1997—, bd. dirs., 1998—. Chair supervisory com. Libr. Congress Fed. Credit Union, 1982—90, bd. dirs., 1991—94, 2001—, chmn. credit. com., 1994—. Recipient Edward A. Filene award Credit Union Nat. Assn., 1992, Vol. Assistance Program award, 1994, numerous credit union svc. awards, 1982-2002. Roman Catholic. Avocations: travel, classical music, beach, tennis, financial planning. Office: Libr Congress 1st & Independence Ave SE Washington DC 20540-4183 E-mail: ddix@loc.gov.

DIXSON, J. B. communications executive; b. Norwich, N.Y., Oct. 19, 1941; d. William Joseph and Ann Wanda (Teale) Barrett. BS, Syracuse U., 1963; postgrad. in bus. adminstrn., Wayne State U., 1979-81; MBA, Ctrl. Mich. U., 1984. Pub. rels. editl. asst. Am. Mus. Natural History, N.Y.C., 1963-64; writer, prodr. Norman, Navan, Moore & Baird Advt., Grand Rapids, Mich., 1964-67; prin. J.B. Dixson Comm. Cons., Detroit, 1967-74; dir. Pub. Info. Svcs. divsn. Mich. Employment Security Commn., Detroit, 1974-82; news rels. mgr. Burroughs Corp., 1982-83, dir. creative svcs., 1983-85, dir. pub. rels., 1985-86; prin. Dixson Comm., Detroit, 1986-93, Durocher Dixson Werba, LLC, Detroit, 1994—. Lectr., spkr. in field at colls., univs., cmty. orgns. Author: Guidelines for Non-Sexist Verbal and Written Communication, 1976, Sexual Harassment on The Job, 1979, The TV Interview: Good News or Bad?, 1981. Mem. Detroit Mayor's Transition Com. of 100, 1972; mem. bd. mgmt. Detroit YWCA, 1974; chmn. Detroit Women's Equality Day Com., 1975; bd. dirs., founding mem. Feminist Fed. Credit Union, Detroit, 1976; centennial chair Indian Village Assn., 1993-95; founding mem. Mich. Women's Campaign Fund, 1980; active Mich. Task Force on Sexual Harassment in Workplace, Mich. Women's Com. of 100, Mich. Women's Polit. Caucus, Mich. Women's Found. Named Outstanding Sr. Woman in Radio and TV, Syracuse U., 1963; recipient Five Watch award Am. Women in Radio and TV, Mich., 1969, 75, Outstanding Women in Comm. Women's Advt. Club, 1998, cert. of recognition Detroit City Coun., 1976, Feminist of Yr. award NOW, 1977, City of Detroit Human Rights Commn., 1988, Design in Mich. award Mich. Coun. of Arts/Gov. William G. Milliken, 1977, Achievement award U.S. Dept. Labor, 1979, Spirit of Detroit award Detroit City Coun., 1980, PR Casebook, 1983, PR News Case Study, 1986, Pinnacle award Mich. Hosp. Pub. Rels. Assn., 1987, award Nat. Sch. Pub. Rels. Assn., 1992, 21st Century award Corp. Detroit Mag., 1995, Creativity in Advt. award Detroit Newspapers Assn., 2000; subject of Mich. Senate Resolution 412, 1979. Fellow Pub. Rels. Soc. Am. (accredited, pres. chpt. 1983-84, Dist. award and citation 1984, 86, 87, 93, exec. com. corp. sect. 1996-2001, Disting. Svc. award 1999), Internat. Assn. Bus. Communicators (Silver Quill award chpt. 1987, 88, 91, 93, dist. 1987, Renaissance award 1988, 91, Mercury award 1987), Nat. Assn. Govt. Communicators (Blue Pencil award 1977, Gold Screen award 1980), Automotive Press Assn., Women's Advt. Club (Top 75 Women in Comm. 1999), Econ. Club Detroit, Maple Grove Gun Club, Detroit Athletic Club. Office: Durocher Dixson Werba LLC 16th Fl Buhl Bldg 535 Griswold St Detroit MI 48226-3604 E-mail: dixson@ddwpr.com.

DI XX MIGLIA, GABRIELLA, artist, conservationist; b. Genoa, Italy, June 10, 1949; d. Walter and Maria Giovanna (Lupo) Repetto Carboneschi di Ventimiglia; m. Fredi Chiappelli Zdekauer, June 10, 1980 (dec. Mar. 1990). Student, Acad. Ligustica of Art, Genoa, 1970, student, 1974-77; degree in painting conservation, Lab. di Restauro, 1977; M in Fashion, Fashion Inst. Design Merchandising, LA, 2003. Owner G. Di XX Miglia Painting, L.A., 1980—. Conservationist/restorationist paintings L.A., 1979-85, China, 1985-91; cons. in art conservation, 1990—. One woman shows include La Piccola Gallery, Esther Robles Gallery, L.A., City art Mus., Florence, UCLA Faculty Ctr.; group shows include L.A. Art Orgn., 1990-93, 2003, What's Women Got to do With It, SCLA, 1993, Gallery 825, West Hollywood, Calif., 1996, World Contemporary Art, L.A. Conv. Ctr., 1998, Galerie Internat., Palo Alto, 1998, Galerie Everart, Paris, 1999, 2000, Harwest Festival Silk Show, Long Beach, Calif., 2001, Lawrence Gallery, Beverly Hills, Calif., 1999. Active LACMA Costume Coun., 1989—, Hammer Mus., L.A., 1995-99. Recipient Gold medal for best drawing Genoa, 1972, Cert. of Commendation County of L.A. Bd. Suprs., 1991, arts award UCLA, 1995. Mem. Westwood Art Assn. (bd. dirs. 1983-84), AFEA (bd. dirs. 1983-86), L.A. Art Assn. Galleries (bd. dirs. 1990-2000), Am. Portrait Assn., UCLA Medieval and Renaissance Ctr. (hon.), Spin, Calif. Silk Group, Surface Design Assn. Roman Catholic. Avocations: gardening, tennis, interior decorating, jewelry design, ballroom dancing. Office: 600 N Kenter Ave Los Angeles CA 90049-1918 E-mail: g.dixxmiglia@verizon.net.

DIZARD, WILSON PAUL, JR., international affairs consultant, educator; b. N.Y.C., Mar. 6, 1922; s. Wilson Paul and Helen Marie (Oliver) D.; m. Lynn Margaret Wood, Mar. 11, 1944; children: John William, Stephen Wood, Wilson Paul III, Mark Christopher. BS, Fordham Coll., 1947; postgrad., Columbia U., 1947-49. Writer, editor Time Inc., N.Y.C., 1947-51; with Dept. State and USIA, 1951-80; vice consul Istanbul, Turkey, 1951-53; chief Greece-Turkey-Iran br., 1953-55; info. officer Am. embassy, Athens, Greece, 1955-60; pub. affairs officer consulate-gen. Dacca, Pakistan, 1960-62; spl. asst. dep. dir., 1964-65; asst. dep. dir., 1966-67; 1st sec. Am. Embassy, Warsaw, 1968-70; asst. dir. Pub. Affairs Office, Saigon, Vietnam, 1970; spl. adviser polit. sect. U.S. Embassy, Saigon, 1971; comm. adviser to dir. USIA, Washington, 1971-73, chief plans and program policy, 1973-77; vice-chmn. U.S. del. to 1979 World Adminstrv. Radio Conf. Dept. State, Washington, 1978-79; v.p. Kalba-Bowen Assocs., Cambridge, Mass., 1980-86; adj. prof. internat. affairs Georgetown U., 1975-95, sr. fellow, 1983-89; sr. assoc. Ctr. for Strategic and Internat. Studies, 1989-2001; cons. comm. policy U.S. Dept. State, 1984-88. Mem. U.S. del. and exec. asst. to conf. dir. Internat. Telecom. Satellite Conf., Washington, 1968-69; rsch. assoc. Ctr. Internat. Studies, MIT, 1962-63; vis. lectr. polit. sci. dept. MIT, 1981. Author: The Strategy of Truth, 1961, Television-A World View, 1966, The Coming Information Age, 1981, Mikhail Gorvachev's Information Revolution, 1987, Old Media, New Media, 1994, Meganet: Building the Global Information Highway, 1997, Digital Diplomacy, 2001; contbr. articles to profl. jours. Cons. Carnegie Found. Commn. on Endl. TV; mem. adv. bd. Pacific Telecom. Coun., 1990-91; bd. dirs. Pub. Diplomacy Found., 2000—. With AUS, 1943-46. Rsch. fellow Assn. Diplomatic Studies and Tng., 1997—. Mem.: Washington Inst. Fgn. Affairs, Am. Fgn. Svc. Assn., Soc. Historians Am. Fgn. Rels., Assn. Diplomatic Studies and Tng., Am. Polit. Sci. Assn., Internet Soc., Cosmos Club (Washington), Diplomatic and Consular Officers Ret. Club. Home: 3050 Military Road NW Apt 536 Washington DC 20015 E-mail: wilsond106@aol.com.

DIZER, JOHN T., JR., engineering educator; b. Norwood, Mass., Nov. 7, 1921; s. John Thomas Dizer and Eunice Haven Homer; m. Virginia Marie Leerkamp, Dec. 25, 1947 (dec. Dec. 1993); 5 children. BS in Engring., Northeastern U., 1943; MS in Engring., Purdue U., 1947, PhD in Engring., 1969. Registered mfg. engr., N.Y. Various positions to engr./supr. Cummins Engine Co., Columbus, Ind., 1952—59; prof. Mohawk Valley C.C., Utica, NY, 1959—67, head, mech. engring. tech. dept., 1967—81, prof., dean engring. tech. and bus., 1981—85, prof., dean emeritus, 1985—. Cons. in field. Author: (book) Tom Swift and Company, 1982, Tom Swift and the Bobbsey Twins, 1997; contbr. articles. Exec. bd. land of the Oneidas Coun. Boy Scouts Am., Utica, 1985—; trustee, v.p. Oneida County Hist. Soc., Utica, 1964—79. Fellow: ASME; mem.: Soc. of Mfg. Engrs.

DJEDDAH, RICHARD NISSIM, investment banker; s. Joseph N. and Nelly (Serper) D.; m. Rachel Ruth Baron; 1 child, Esteevered. BS in Physics, CCNY, 1971; MBA, CUNY, 1986, PhD in Fin., 1990. Notary pub., N.Y. Prin., pres. Richard N. Djeddah & Assocs., N.Y.C., 1976—. Author: The Impact of Advertising on Security Prices, 1990. Mem. N.Y. Acad. Scis., Alliance Francaise, Baron Rothchild Gulf and Country Club (Caesaria). Republican. Avocations: skiing, golf, chess, collecting ancient coins and art. Home: 346 Heathcote Rd Scarsdale NY 10583-7132 Office: RN Djeddah & Assocs 4 Park Ave New York NY 10016-5339

DJERASSI, CARL, writer, retired chemistry educator; b. Vienna, Oct. 29, 1923; s. Samuel and Alice (Friedmann) Djerassi; m. Virginia Jeremiah (div. 1950); m. Norma Lundholm (div. 1976); children: Dale, Pamela(dec.); m. Diane W. Middlebrook, 1985. AB summa cum laude, Kenyon Coll., 1942, DSc (hon.), 1995; PhD, U. Wis., 1945; DSc (hon.), Nat. U. Mex., 1953, Fed. U., Rio de Janeiro, 1969, Worcester Poly. Inst., 1972, Wayne State U., 1974, Columbia U., 1975, Uppsala U., 1977, Coe Coll., 1978, U. Geneva, 1978, U. Ghent, 1985, U. Man., 1985, Adelphi U., 1993, U. S.C., 1995, Swiss Fed. Inst. Tech., 1995, U. Md.- Balt. County, 1997, Bulgarian Acad. Scis., 1998, U. Aberdeen, 2000, Polytechnic U., 2001. Rsch. chemist Ciba Pharm. Products, Inc., Summit, NJ, 1942—43, 1945—49; assoc. dir. rsch. Syntex, Mexico City, 1949—52, rsch. v.p., 1957—60; v.p. Syntex Labs., Palo Alto, Calif., 1960—62, Syntex Rsch., 1962—68, pres., 1968—72, Zoecon Corp., 1968—83, chmn. bd. dirs., 1968—86; prof. chemistry Wayne State U., 1952—59, Stanford (Calif.) U., 1959—2002. Founder Djerassi Resident Artists Program, Woodside, Calif. Author: The Futurist and Other Stories, 1988; author: (novels) Cantor's Dilemma, 1989, The Bourbaki Gambit, 1994, Marx Deceased, 1996, Menachem's Seed, 1997, NO, 1998; author: (poetry) The Clock Runs Backward, 1991; author: (drama) An Immaculate Misconception, 1998, BBC World Svc. Play of Week, 2000; author: (with Roald Hoffmann) (drama) Oxygen, 2001; author: (drama) BBC World Svc. Play of Week, 2001; author: (drama) Calculus, 2002, ICSI--a pedagogic wordplay for 2 voices, 2002; author: (drama) Ego, 2003; author: (with Pierre Laszlo) NO--a pedagogic wordplay for 3 voices, 2003; author: (autobiography) The Pill, Pygmy Chimps and Degas' Horse, 1992; author: (memoir) This Man's Pill, 2001; author: 9 other books; mem. editl. bd. Jour. Organic Chemistry, 1955—59, Tetrahedron, 1958—92, Steroids, 1963—2001, Procs. NAS, 1964—70, Jour. Am. Chem. Soc., 1966—75, Organic Mass Spectrometry, 1968—91, contbr. numerous articles to profl. jours., poems, memoirs and short stories to lit. publs. Named to Nat. Inventors Hall of Fame; recipient Intrasci. Rsch. Found. award, 1969, Freedman Patent award, Am. Inst. chemists, 1970, Chem. Pioneer award, 1973, Nat. medal of Sci. for first synthesis of oral contraceptive, 1973, Wolf prize in Chemistry, 1978, John and Samuel Bard award in Sci. and Medicine, 1983, Roussel prize, Paris, 1988, Discovers award, Pharm. Mfg. Assn., 1988, Nat. medal Tech. for new approaches to insect control, 1991, Nev. medal, 1992, Thomson medal, Internat. Soc. Mass Spectroscopy, 1994, Prince Mahidol award, Thailand, 1995, Sovereign Fund award, 1996, Austrian Cross of Honor First Class, 1999, Othmer Gold medal, Chem. Heritage Found., 2000, Author's prize, German Chem. Soc., 2001, Erasmus medal, Acad. Euopeae, 2003. Mem.: NAS (Indsl. Application of Sci. award 1990), Bulgarian Acad. Scis. (fgn. mem.), Mex. Acad. Scis., Brazilian Acad. Scis., Royal Swedish Acad. Engring. (fgn. mem.), Royal Swedish Acad. Scis. (fgn. mem.), German Acad. Leopoldina, Am. Acad. Arts and Scis., Royal Soc. Chemistry (hon. fellow, Centenary lectr. 1964), Am. Chem. Soc. (award pure chemistry 1958, Baekeland medal 1959, Fritzsche award 1960, award for creative invention 1973, award in chemistry of contemporary tech. problems 1983, Esselen award 1989, Priestley medal 1992, Gibbs medal 1997), NAS Inst. Medicine, Am. Acad. Pharm. Scis. (hon.), Sigma Xi (Proctor prize for sci. achievement 1998), Phi Beta Kappa, Phi Lambda Upsilon (hon.). Office: Stanford U Dept Chemistry Stanford CA 94305-5080 E-mail: djerassi@stanford.edu.

DJERASSI, ISAAC, physician, medical researcher; b. Sofia, Bulgaria, July 27, 1925; came to U.S., 1954, naturalized, 1962; s. Rahamim and Adela (Tadjer) D.; m. Nira Eskenazy, Jan. 31, 1954; children— Ram Isaac, Ady Lynn. Student, Sofia U. Med. Sch., 1944-49; MD, Hebrew U., Jerusalem, 1952; DH (hon.), Villanova U., 1977. Intern Hadassah Hosp., Tel Aviv, 1951-52, resident, 1953-54; rsch. assoc. Med. Sch. Harvard U., Boston, 1955-60; asst. prof. pediats. U. Pa., Phila., 1960-69; dir. rsch. oncology-hematology Mercy Cath. Med. Ctr., Phila., 1969-98. Prof. oncology Med. Sch. U. Tel Aviv, Israel, 1986, dir. Djerassi-Elias Oncology Inst., 1987. Contbr. articles to profl. jours. Mem. med. advisory bd. Nat. Hemophilia Found., Phila., 1964-75 ; mem. med. advisory bd. Leukemia Soc., 1970-75. Recipient Albert Lasker Found. award, 1972, E. Cohn-De Laval award, 1990. Mem. Am. Soc. Cancer Rsch., Am. Soc. Clin. Oncology, Am. Assn. Blood Banks. Inventor filtration leukopheresis system and machine for white blood cell transfusions, 1970; discoverer high methotrexate-citrovorum rescue chemotherapy of cancer, 1964-77; developer platelet and white cells transfusions and supportive care, 1955-71; developed curative treatments for acute childhood leukemia, non-Hodgkin lymphoma, 1964-68, osteogenic sarcoma, 1971, effective brain gliomas, 1983-99. Home: 1820 Rittenhouse Sq Philadelphia PA 19103 Office: Mercy Cath Med Ctr PO Box 19709 Philadelphia PA 19143-0709

DJEREJIAN, EDWARD PETER, institute administrator, former diplomat; b. N.Y.C., Mar. 6, 1939; s. Peter Minas and Mary (Yazudjian) D.; m. Francoise Andrée Haelters, July 31, 1971; children: Gregory, Francesca. BS in Fgn. Svc., Georgetown U., 1960, hon. doctorate, 1992. Staff asst. to sec. of state U.S. Dept. of State, 1963-64; Political officer Am. Embassy, Beirut, Lebanon, 1965-69; political/labor officer Am. Consulate Gen., Casablanca, Morocco, 1969-72; spl. asst. Under Sec. of State, Washington, 1973-75; prin. officer Am. Consulate Gen., Bordeaux, France, 1975-77; political counselor Am. Embassy, Moscow, USSR, 1979-81, dep. chief of mission Amman, Jordan, 1981-84; dep. spokesman & dep. asst. sec. Dept. of State, Washington, 1984-85; spl. asst. to the pres., dep. press sec. The White House, 1985-86; prin. dep. asst. sec. for Near East/South Asia, 1987-88; Am. ambassador Am. Embassy, Damascus, Syria, 1988-91; asst. sec. Near Eastern and South Asian Affairs bur. Dept. State, Washington, 1991-93; amb. to Israel Tel Aviv, 1993-94; dir. James A. Baker III Inst. for Pub. Policy Rice U., Houston, 1994—. Bd. dirs. Occidental Petroleum Corp., Global Industries, Ltd., Baker Hughes. 1st Lt. U.S. Army, 1961-62 (Korea). Recipient Presdl. award, Presdl. Meritorious Svc. award, 1988, Superior Honor award Dept. State, 1984, Disting. Honor award, 1993, Presdl. Disting. Svc. award, 1994, Ellis Island medal of honor, Moral Statesman award ADL, 1994. Mem. Coun. on Fgn. Rels. Armenian Apostolic. Avocations: writing, skiing. Office: Baker Inst Pub Policy Rice Univ 6100 Main St Houston TX 77005-1827

DJEREJIAN, ROBERT ASBED, architect; b. N.Y.C., July 6, 1931; s. Peter Minas Djerejian and Mary Yazudjian; children: Linda, Madeline, Pier; m. Marian Patrice Lair, Sept. 14, 1997. B in Architecture, Pratt Inst., 1955. Registered arch., N.Y., planner, N.J. Plans and project officer U.S. Army Corp. Engrs., 1955-57; dir. design Haines Lundberg Waehler, N.Y.C., 1965-75, ptnr., 1976, mng. ptnr., 1977—82; sr. mng. ptnr. HLW Internat., N.Y.C., 1983—95, sr. cons., 1996—. Bd. adv. Pa. State U., 1982—; trustee Pratt Inst., 1992—, bd. dirs. Delaware Coll. Arts & Design. Bd. dir. Fonar Corp., Chmn. bd. of zoning and appeals, Yonkers, N.Y., 1972. Recipient Excellence in Design Nat. Honor award Nat. Endowment of the Arts, 1989; named Architect of Yr. N.J. Contractors Assn., 1986 Mem. AIA (emeritus, chmn. com. natural environment 1974, N.Y. State AIA chpt. excellence in design award 1992), Am. Arbitration Assn., Union League Club. Avocations: mountain climbing, skiing, vintage auto racing. Home: 37 Dewitt Ave Bronxville NY 10708-5635 Office: HLW International 115 5th Ave New York NY 10003-1004 E-mail: rdjerejian@hlw.com.

DJORDJEVIC, BOZIDAR, radiation biologist; b. Belgrade, Serbia, Yugoslavia, Jan. 5, 1929; s. Petar Djordjevic and Mileva Bailoni; m. Radmila Stambolovic, Nov. 20, 1955; 1 child, Gordana Harris. Degree in Agrl. Engring., U. Belgrade, 1952; PhD in Microbiology, Rutgers U., 1960. Rsch. asst. Inst. Nuclear Scis., Vincha, Belgrade, Yugoslavia, 1954-60, rsch. assoc., 1960-66, Meml. Sloan-Kettering, N.Y.C., 1966-68, assoc., 1968-78, Mount Sinai Med. Ctr., N.Y.C., 1978-80, Downstate Med. Ctr. SUNY, Bklyn., 1980-87, rsch. assoc. prof., 1982-01, rsch. prof., 2001—. Patentee in field. Recipient Eminent Scientist of the Decade 1990-99, Internat. Rsch. Promotion Coun., 1999. Mem. Radiation Rsch. Soc. Democrat. Serbian Orthodox. Avocation: horticulture. Home: 30-60 Crescent St Apt 5M Astoria NY 11102 Office: SUNY Health Sci Ctr 450 Clarkson Ave Brooklyn NY 11203-2056

DJORDJEVIC, DIMITRIJE, historian, educator; b. Belgrad, Yugoslavia, Feb. 27, 1922; came to U.S., 1970, naturalized, 1977; s. Vladimir and Jelena (Rasic) D.; m. Nan Fletcher, June 1981; 1 child, Jelena Grad., U. Beograd, 1954, PhD, 1962. Sr. staff mem. Inst. History, Serbian Acad. Scis. and Arts, 1958-69, Inst. Balkan Studies, 1969-70; prof. U. Calif., Santa Barbara, 1970-91, prof. emeritus, 1991—, chmn. Russian area studies, 1976-82. Mem. Nat. Com. to Promote History of Habsburg Monarchy, 1973-79 Author: Austro-Serbian Customs War 1906-1911, in Serbian, 1962, Revolutions nationales des peuples balkaniques, 1804-1914, 1965, Scars and Memory, 1997; co-author: The Balkan Revolutionary Tradition, 1981, also papers, essays, revs.; editor: The Creation of Yugoslavia, 1914-1918, 1980; editorial bd. profl. jours. Mem. Am. Hist. Assn., Am. Assn. Advancement Slavic Studies, Conf. Slavic and East European History (pres. 1984), Serbian Acad. Scis., N. Am. Assn. Serbiam Studies (pres. 1986-88). Serbian Orthodox. E-mail: vmarkovic@msn.com.

DJORDJEVICH, MIROSLAV-MICHAEL, bank executive; b. Belgrade, Yugoslavia, 1936; arrived in U.S., 1956; s. Dragoslav and Ruzica Georgevich; m. Marie Louise Hohman, 1963; children: Marie, Alexander, Michelle. BS, U. Calif., Berkeley, 1960; MBA, San Francisco State U., 1963; cert. advanced fin., U. Stanford. Fin. analyst Fireman's Fund Ins. Co., San Francisco, 1962-68, asst. v.p. investments, 1972-76, v.p. investments, 1976-78, v.p., treas., 1978-84; pres., CEO U.S. Fidelity and Guaranty Fin. Co., San Francisco, 1985-86; chmn., pres., CEO Capital Guaranty Ins. Co., San Francisco, 1986-94; pres., CEO Monad Fin., San Rafael, Calif., 1994-97, Bank S.E. Europe Internat., San Juan, P.R., 1997—. Author: About Happy Living, 1985. State pres. Calif. Young Reps., 1965-66; commr. Statue of Liberty Ellis Island Centennial Commn., 1986; pres. Serbian Unity Congress, 1990-93, Coun. for Dem. Changes, 1998-01, Studenica Found., 1995-; dir. World Affairs Coun. of Am., 2002—. Pvt. U.S. Army, 1961-63. Recipient Excellence award Am. Security Coun., 1967, Americanism medal Nat. Soc. DAR, 1969. Mem.: First Serbian Benevolent Soc. (treas. 1978—82). Avocations: reading, tennis, politics. Office: Bank SE Europe Internat 535 4th St Ste 203 San Rafael CA 94901-3314 E-mail: monadf@ix.netcom.com.

DLAB, VLASTIMIL, mathematics educator, researcher; b. Bzi, Czech Republic, Aug. 5, 1932; came to Can., 1968; s. Vlastimil Dlab and Anna (Stuchlikova) Dlabova; m. Zdenka Dvorakova, Apr. 27, 1959 (div.); children— Dagmar, Daniel Jan; m. Helena Briestenska, Dec. 18, 1985; children: Philip Adam, David Michael. R.N.Dr., Charles U., Prague, Czech Republic, 1956, C.Sc., 1959, Habilitation, 1962, DSc, 1966; PhD, U. Khartoum, Sudan, 1962. Rsch. fellow Czechoslovak Acad. Sci., Prague, 1956-57; lectr., sr. lectr. Charles U., Prague, 1957-59, reader, 1964-65; lectr., sr. lectr. U. Khartoum, Sudan, 1959-64; rsch. fellow, sr. rsch. fellow Inst. Advanced Studies, Australian Nat. U., Canberra, 1965-68; prof. math. Carleton U., Ottawa, Ont., Can., 1968-98; dir. Grad. Inst. Charles U., 1992-94; chmn. dept. Carleton U., Ottawa, Ont., Can., 1971-74, 94-97, disting. rsch. prof., 1998—, prof. emeritus; professorem hospitem Charles U., 1995—. Vis. prof. U. Paris VI, Brandeis U., U. Bonn, Monash U., U. Tsukuba, U. Sao Paulo, U. Stuttgart, U. Poitiers, Nat. U. Mex., U. Essen, U. Bielefeld, Hungarian Acad. Sci., Budapest, U. Warsaw, U. Normal Beijing, U. Vienna, UCLA, U. Va., Czechoslovak Acad. Sci., U. Trondheim, U. Paderborn, U. St. Petersburg, U. Reims, U. Sao Paulo, Osaka U., Yamaneashi U., Shinshu U., Eotvos U., Budapest, Charles U., Prague, U. Murcia, Spain, Erdos Rsch. Ctr., Budapest, Australian Nat. Univ., Canberra, Gadjah Mada U., Jogjakarta; presenter in field. Editor: procs. internat. confs., 1974, 1979; author: Representations of Valued Graphs, 1980, An Introduction to Diagrammatical Methods, 1981; editor: procs. internat. confs., 1984, 1987, 1990, 1992, 1993, 1994; author: Quasi-hereditary Algebras, 1994; editor: procs. internat. confs., 1996, Algebra and Representation Theory, 1998—, procs. internat. confs., 2002; contbr. numerous articles to profl. jours.; editor: Algebra and Discrete Mathematics, 2002—. Recipient Diploma of Honour Union Czechoslovak Mathematicians, 1962; Can. Council fellow, 1974; Japan Soc. Promotion of Sci. sr. rsch. fellow, 1981; sci. exchange grantee Nat. Sci. and Engring. Rsch. Coun. Can., 1978, 81, 83, 85, 88, 91. Fellow Royal Soc. Can. (convenor 1977-78, 80-81, coun. mem. 1980-81, editor-in-chief Comptes rendus mathematiques-Math. Reports 1997—); mem. Am. Math. Soc., Math. Assn. Am., Can. Math. Soc. (coun., chmn. rsch. com. 1973-77, editor Can. Jour. Math. 1988-93), European Math. Soc., London Math. Soc., Czech Math. Union. Roman Catholic. Avocations: sports, music. Home: 277 Sherwood Dr Ottawa ON Canada K1Y 3W3 Office: Carleton U Sch Math & Stat Math Dept Ottawa ON Canada K1S 5B6 E-mail: vdlab@math.carleton.ca.

DLOTT, SUSAN JUDY, judge, lawyer; b. Dayton, Ohio, Sept. 11, 1949; d. Herman and Mildred (Zemboch) D.; m. Austin E. Knowlton, July 11, 1986 (div. 1988); m. Stanley M. Chesley, Dec. 7, 1991. BA, U. Pa., 1971; JD, Boston U., 1973. Bar: Ohio 1973, U.S. Dist. Ct. (so. dist.) Ohio 1975, U.S. Ct. Appeals (6th cir.) 1976, U.S. Supreme Ct. 1980, U.S. Dist. Ct. (ea. dist.) Ky. 1984, U.S. dist. Ct. (no. dist.) Ohio 1989, Ky. 1990. Law clk. Ohio Ct. of Appeals, Cleve., 1973-74; asst. U.S. atty. U.S. Dist. Ct. (so. dist.) Ohio, Dayton, 1975-79; ptnr. Graydon, Head & Ritchey, Cin., 1979-95; dist. judge U.S. Dist. Ct. for So. Dist. Ohio, Cin., 1995—. Legal reporter Multimedia Program Prodn., Inc., 1982-84. Mem. Ohio Bldg. Authority, 1988-93, vice chmn., 1990-93, Jewish Fedn. Cin., trustee and mem. com. 1979-93, Jewish Cmty. Rels. Coun. Cin., 1980-90, Hamilton County Park Dist. Vol. in Parks, 1983-86; mem. Dress for Success Bd., Fine Arts Fund Bd. Recipient U.S. Postal Serv. Commendation, 1977, Service award Dayton Bar Assn., 1975-76. Mem. ABA, FBA (asst. treas. 1981-82, treas. 1982-83, sec. 1983-84, v.p. 1984-86), Ohio Bar Assn., Ky. Bar Assn., Dayton Bar Assn., Dayton Women's Bar Assn., Cin. Bar Assn., Leadership Cin. Alumni Assn., Queen City Dog Tng. Club, 6th Cir. Jud. Conf. (life), NAACP (life), Hadassah (life). Jewish. Office: 100 E 5th St Cincinnati OH 45202-3927

DLUGIE, PAUL DAVID, physician; b. Chgo., June 17, 1940; s. Samuel R. and Ruth M. (Mesirow)D.; m. Lida Pira, July 23, 1965. BA, Johns Hopkins U., 1961; MD, Chgo. Med. Sch., 1965. Diplomate, Nat. Bd. Med. Examiners; bd. cert. Am. Bd. Quality Assurance and Utilization Physicians, Am. Acad. of Experts in Traumatic Stress. Rotating intern Louis A. Weiss Meml. Hosp., Chgo., 1965-66; dir. emergency room USAF Hosp., Mt. Clemens, Mich., 1966-68; pvt. practice Palm Desert, Calif., 1968—. Dir., Indio (Calif.) Cmty. Hosp., 1975-80, chmn. bd. dirs., 1978-80, pres. bd. dirs., 1980-85; bd. dirs. Lentz Inst., Indio, United Stroke Found., L.A., Columbia Savs. and Loan, Beverly Hills, Calif.; mem. adv. bd. S.W. Pain Control and Sports Therapy Ctr., Palm Desert, Calif., 1991—; mem. insl. rev. and sci. adv. bd. Darr Eye Clinic, Palm Desert, 1988-99. Host, The Medicine Show, KMIR TV, Palm Springs, Calif., 1983-95. Capt. USAF, 1966-68. Fellow Am. Acad. Family Physicians; mem. AMA, Calif. Med. Assn., Maricopa County Med. Soc., World Orgn. Family Drs. Office: Ste 5 12002 E Shea Blvd Scottsdale AZ 85259-4161

DLUGOFF, MARC ALAN, lawyer; b. N.Y.C., Oct. 6, 1955; s. Arnold M. and Ruth B. (Schnall) D. AB, Colgate U., 1976; JD, Hofstra U., 1980; LLM in Taxation, NYU, 1981. Bar: N.Y. 1981, D.C. 1985, Calif. 1988. Law clk. to presiding justice U.S. Tax Ct., Washington, 1981-83; assoc. Mudge, Rose, Guthrie, Alexander & Ferdon, N.Y.C., 1983-85, Milbank, Tweed, Hadley & McCloy, N.Y.C., 1985-89, ptnr., 1989—92; counsel Roberts & Holland, N.Y.C., 1993-94; pres., CEO, Atlantic Adv. Corp., N.Y.C., 1995—. Fundraiser lawyers divsn. United Jewish Appeal, N.Y.C. chpt., 1986-90. Charles Dana scholar Colgate U., 1976. Mem. ABA, N.Y. State Bar Assn., Assn. Bar City N.Y., State Bar Calif., Phi Beta Kappa. Jewish. Home and Office: 130 Water St Ste 5-G New York NY 10005-1625 E-mail: marcnyc130@hotmail.com.

DLUGOSZEWSKI, LUCIA, artistic director; b. Detroit, June 16, 1934; Student, Wayne State U.; studied with, Carl Beutel, Edward Bredshall, Ktja Andy, Grete Sultan, Felix Salzer, Edgard Varese. Composer: (structure for the Poetry) Everyday Sound, 1949, Archaic Timbre Piano Music, 1958, Space Is a Diamond, 1970, Tender Theatre Flight Nageire, Densities, Nova, Corona, Clear Core, Amos Elusive Empty August, Strange Tenderness of naked Leaping, (commd. by Mikhail Baryshnikov), Disparate Stairway Radical other Quartet, 1994, Radical Quidditas Dew Tear Duende; artist dir. Erik Hawkins Dance Co., 1998—; recording artists: various labels. Named Musician of Yr. Musical Am., Village Voice, 1975; recipient Recipient Koussevitzky Internat. Recording award, 1979, Phoebe Kechum Thorne award, others; Guggenheim fellow. Office: Erick Hawkins Sch Dance PO Box 1117 New York NY 10013-0866

DLUHY, DEBORAH HAIGH, college dean; b. Summit, N.J., Mar. 4, 1940; d. Richard Hartman Haigh and Elin Frederika Anderson Neumann; m. Robert George Dluhy, June 11, 1962; 1 child, Leonore Alexandra. BA, Wheaton Coll., 1962; postgrad., Boston U., 1962-63, U. Heidelberg, Germany, 1963-65; PhD, Harvard U., 1976. Instr. fine arts Wheaton Coll., Norton, Mass., 1975—76, Radcliffe Coll., Cambridge, Mass., 1977, Boston Coll., Newton, Mass., 1976—78; devel. officer Mus. Fine Arts, Boston, 1978—84, asst. dir. devel., 1984—86; assoc. dean adminstrn. Sch. Mus. Fine Arts, Boston, 1986—87, dean acad. programs and adminstrn., 1987—93, dean, 1993—; dep. dir. Mus. Fine Arts, Boston, 1999—. Trustee Wheaton Coll., Norton, Mass., 1988—, pres. Alumni Assn., 1994—2000; trustee Cultural Edn. Collaborative Boston, 1987—90; visitor Walnut Hill Sch., Natick, Mass., 1996—; pres. Pro Arts Consortium, 1999—2000; mem. exec. com., vice chair fin. and facilities, mem. governance bd.affairs Wheaton Coll., Norton, Mass.; bd. dirs. Boston Arts Acad., 1999—. Woodrow Wilson fellow, 1963. Mem.: Assn. Ind. Coll. Art and Design (program com. 1995—2001, bd. dirs., exec. com., chair), Copley Soc. Boston (hon. trustee 1997—), Nat. Assn. Schs. Art and Design (rsch. com. 1990—96, evaluator 1996—, bd. dirs. 1996—, sec. bd. dirs. 2001—, exec. com. 2001—). Home: 104 Fletcher Rd Belmont MA 02478-2018 Office: Sch Mus of Fine Arts 230 Fenway Boston MA 02115-5534 E-mail: ddluhy@mfa.org., ddluhy@earthlink.net.

D'LUHY, JOHN JAMES, investment banker; b. Passaic, NJ, Sept. 18, 1933; s. John George and Leonara (Fila) D'L.; m. Gale Rainsford, Dec. 7, 1968; children: Amanda, Pamela. AB, Trinity Coll., 1955; MBA, U. Pa., 1959. Lic. amateur radio operator K2EXI, comml. pilot (instrument-rated). Jr. exec. trainee Merrill Lynch, N.Y.C., 1956-58, with over-the-counter research dept., 1959-60; assoc. syndicate dept., investment mgmt., investment banking Lazard Freres & Co., N.Y.C., 1960-68; sr. v.p., ptnr., dir. money mgmt. and venture capital divs. R.W. Pressprich & Co., N.Y.C., 1968-72; dir. money mgmt. and pvt. placements Wood Walker & Co., N.Y.C., 1972-73; pres. U.S. Oil Co., 1973-83, founder, pres., 1983-84; pvt. investor Dominick & Dominick, N.Y.C., 1983-86; fin. advisor Robert Thomas Securities divsn. Raymond James Assocs., NYC, 1990—2002; pvt. investor Spring Lake, NJ, 2002—. Trustee Collier Svcs. Found., Marlboro, N.J., 1986-92, USN War Coll. Found., Newport, R.I., 2001— ; bus. coun. Monmouth Univ., West Long Branch, N.J., 1994-98. Hon. usher St. Patrick's Cath., N.Y.C., 1969—, chief hon. usher, 1975-76; founding mem. U.S. Naval War Coll. Found., 1969, Newport, R.I., trustee, 2001—, fin. com. 2002—; co-chmn. Spring Lake Centennial Com., 1990-92; pres. Spring Lake Chorus, 1990-92; mem. Bond Club N.Y., 1963-91, Thursday Evening Club, 1981-87, Chorus of Atlantic, 2000—, barbershop chorus; 1st pilot, aux. air arm, U.S. Coast Guard Aux., flotilla air officer, 2001—, vice comdr., 2003—. Served with USNR, 1955. Mem. Investment Assn. N.Y. (bd. dirs. 1967, chmn. capital and money mktgs. com.), Assn. Investment Mgmt. and Rsch., N.Y. Soc. Security Analysts (sr. analyst, mem. high net worth investors com. 2000-02, mem. career devel. com. 2000-02), Am. Radio Relay League, Aircraft Owners and Pilots Assn., Univ. Club N.Y.C. (coun. 1977-83, exec. com., treas. 1979-83), Spring Lake (N.J.) Bath and Tennis Club, Jersey Aero Club (chmn. rules com. 1992), Blue Hill (N.Y.C.) Troupe, Penn Club of N.Y., Clayton (N.Y.) Yacht Club. Roman Catholic. Home: 115 Ludlow Ave Spring Lake NJ 07762-1547 Home (Summer): Club Island Clayton NY 13624 E-mail: johngale@worldnet.att.net.

DLUHY, ROBERT GEORGE, physician; b. Montclair, N.J., Jan. 23, 1937; s. John George and Leona (Fila) D.; m. Deborah Haigh; 1 child, Leonore Alexandra. AB magna cum laude, Princeton U., 1958; MD, Harvard Med. Sch., 1962. Intern/resident Peter Bent Brigham Hosp., Boston, 1962, 65-67, endocrine fellow, 1967-69; instr. med. Harvard Med. Sch., Boston, 1969-74, asst. prof. med., 1974-80, assoc. prof. med., 1980-98, prof. med., 1998—. Assoc. editor New Eng. Jour. Medicine. Capt. med. corp. U.S. Army, 1964-66, Germany. Fellow: Endocrine Soc., Hypertension Coun. AHA; mem.: Phi Beta Kappa. Office: Endocrine Hypertension Divs 221 Longwood Ave # Rfb2 Boston MA 02115-5804 E-mail: rdluhy@partners.org.

DMITROVSKY, ETHAN, dean, cancer physician, medical educator, researcher, oncologist; Resident internal medicine, N.Y. Hosp.-meml. Sloan Kettering Cancer Ctr.; tng. med. and molecular oncology, Nat. Cancer Inst.; grad. biochemical scis. magna cum laude, Harvard Coll., 1976; grad., Cornell U. Med. Coll., 1980. Assoc. prof. Cornell U. Med. Coll.; head lab. molecular medicine Meml. Sloan-Kettering Cancer Ctr., 1987, assoc. mem. medicine; assoc. mem. molecular pharmacology and therapeutics program Sloan-Kettering Inst.; chmn. dept. pharmacology and toxicology Dartmouth Med. Sch., co-chmn. search com., Andrew G. Wallace prof. pharmacology, toxicology and toxicology, 1998, acting dean, 2002—. Tchr., mentor undergrad. and grad. students, postdoctoral fellows and faculty; dir. clin. and molecular oncology tng. rsch. program NIH; mem. Am. Soc. Clin. Investigation; invited spkr. in field. Contbr. articles to profl. jours., more than 100 pubs. ; mem. editl. bds. (major oncology jours.) Jour. Nat. Cancer Inst., Cancer Rsch., Clin. Cancer Rsch., Jour. Clin. Oncology, Molecular Cancer Therapeutics ; assoc. editor; Encyclopedia of Cancer. Recipient Young Investigator award, Am. Soc. Clin. Oncology, Meml. Sloan-Kettering Ctr. Mem.: Am. Soc. Clin. Oncology (mem. peer rev. com.), Am. Assn. Cancer Rsch. (mem. peer rev. com.), Am. Cancer Soc. (mem. peer rev. com.), Nat. Cancer Inst. (mem. peer rev. com.), Strang Cancer Prevention Ctr. (mem. sci. adv. bd.), Abbott Labs. (mem. sci. adv. bd.), Lance Armstrong Found. (mem. sci. adv. bd.), Am. Health Found. (mem. sci. adv. bd.). Achievements include research on mechanisms of human tumor cell growth and differentiation helping to advance cancer therapy and prevention; helped clone the abnormal retinoid receptor found in acute promyelocytic leukemia and led the team that developed the molecular test used to diagnose this disease. Office: Dartmouth Med Sch 1 Rope Ferry Rd Hanover NH 03755-1404 Office Fax: 603-650-1202.

DMOWSKI, W. PAUL, obstetrician, gynecologist, educator, endocrinologist, researcher; b. Lodz, Poland, May 17, 1937; came to U.S., 1964; naturalized 1988; s. Thaddeus and Mirona D.; m. May 20, 1967 (div. 1975); 1 child Andrzej. T. MD, The Warsaw (Poland) Med. Acad., 1962; PhD in Endocrinology, Med. Coll. Ga., 1971. Diplomate Am. Bd. Ob. and Gyn., Reproductive Endocrinology/Infertility. Intern Warsaw U. Hosps., 1961-62; resident dept. ob-gyn Ottawa (Can.) Gen. Hosp., 1962-64, Beth Israel Med. Ctr., N.Y.C., 1964-67; Population Coun. rsch. fellow in gynecologic endocrinology Med. Coll. Ga., Augusta, 1967-69; asst. prof. dept. ob-gyn Pritzker Sch. Medicine, U. Chgo., 1971-74, assoc. prof. dept. ob-gyn Pritzker Sch. Medicine, 1974-79; prof. U. Ark. for Med. Scis., Little Rock, 1979-81, Rush Med. Coll., Chgo., 1981—; assoc. attending physician dept. ob-gyn Michael Reese Hosp. and Med. Ctr., Chgo., 1971-76, attending physician, 1976-79, U. Ark. for Med. Scis., 1979-81; sr. attending physician Rush-Presbyn.-St. Lukes Med. Ctr., Chgo., 1981—; attending physician Grant Hosp., Chgo., 1982—. Mem. cons. staff dept. ob-gyn. Christ Hosp., Oak Lawn, Ill., 1982—; mem. courtesy staff MacNeal Hosp., Berwyn, Ill., 1989—; cons. staff dept. ob/gyn Elmhurst (Ill.) Hosp., 1994—; assoc. dept. ob-gyn. Good Samaritan Hosp., Downers Grove, Ill., 1999—; founder, dir. fertility unit Michael Reese Med. Ctr., 1973-79, co-dir. sect. reproductive endocrinology and infertility, 1976-79; dir. div. reproductive endocrinology and infertility U. Ark. for Med. Scis., 1979-81; founder, dir. fellowship tng. program in reproductive endocrinology and infertility Rush Med. Coll., 1982-88, dir. sect. reproductive endocrinology and infertility, 1981-88; founder, dir. in vitro fertilization and embryo transfer program Rush-Presbyn. St. Luke's Med. Ctr., 1983-88; founder, dir. family fertility ctr. Grant Hosp., 1988-95, Inst. for Study and Treatment Endometriosis, 1988—, Oak Brook Fertility Ctr., 1990—; presenter in field. Contbr. over 300 articles to profl. jours., 40 chapts. to books; numerous invited articles, letters to editor in field. Recipient Cert. Appreciation ACS, 1979; grantee, clin. investigator Winthrop Rsch. Inst., 1967—88, Ill. Inst. Tech., 1971-72Program Applied Rsch. on Fertility Regulation, 1973-75, Nat. Ist. Child Health and Human Devel., 1973-75, Carnrick Labs., 1975-79, Organon Internat., 1979-82, Abbott Labs., 1984—, Hoechst-Roussel Pharm., 1985-90, ICI Pharm., 1988-92, Syntex Labs., 1992-94, Ostex Internat., 1993-95, Serono Labs., 1998—, Praecis Pharms., 1998—, Femme Pharma, 2001—. Fellow Am. Coll. Ob-Gyn. (Prize award 1975, 76, Coll. award 1977); mem. AMA (Cert. Merit 1969, 76, 78), Am. Assn. Gynecologic Laparoscopists, Am. Assn. Tissue Banks, Am. Soc. Reproductive Medicine (Cert. award 1977, Ortho Symposium Award 1980, Poster award 1992), Am. Soc. for Immunology of Reprodn., Ark. Med. Soc., Assn. Profs. Gynecology and Obstetrics, Chgo. Assn. Reproductive Endocrinologists, Chgo. Gynecol. Soc., Chgo. Med. Soc., Endocrine Soc., Ill. State Med. Soc., Little Rock Gynecol. Soc., N.Y. Acad. Scis., Soc. for Advancement Contraception, Soc. for Gynecologic Investigation, Soc. Reproductive Endocrinologists, Soc. Reproductive Surgeons, Soc. for Study Reprodn., Soc. for Assisted Reproductive Tech. Office: 2425 W 22nd St Ste 102 Oak Brook IL 60523-4643 also: Ste 102 2425 W 22nd St Oak Brook IL 60523-4643 E-mail: wpdmowski@oakbrookfertility.com.

DMYTRYK, EUGENE THOMAS, retired surgeon; b. Yonkers, N.Y., 1917; MD, St. Louis U., 1941, MS in Surgery, 1947. Diplomate Am. Bd. Surgery. Intern St. John's Hosp., St. Louis, 1942; resident surgery St. Mary's Group Hosp., St. Louis, 1943-44, 45-46; pvt. practice, 1947-85; ret., 1985; pro record rev. med.- legal cons., 1985-97.

DMYTRYSHYN, BASIL, historian, educator; b. Poland, Jan. 14, 1925; came to U.S., 1947, naturalized, 1951; s. Frank and Euphrosinia (Senchak) Dmytryshyn; m. Virginia Roehl, July 16, 1949; children: Sonia, Tania. BA, U. Ark., 1950; MA, U. Ark. 1951; PhD, U. Calif.-Berkeley, 1955; hon. diploma, U. Kiev-Mohyla Acad., 1993. Asst. prof. history Portland State U., Oreg., 1956-59, assoc. prof., 1959-64, prof., 1964-89, prof. emeritus, 1989—, assoc. dir. Internat. Trade and Commerce Inst., 1984-89. Vis. prof. U. Ill., 1964-65, Harvard U., 1971, U. Hawaii, 1976, Hokkaido U., Sapporo, Japan, 1978-79; adviser U. Kiev-Mohyla Acad., 1993. Author books including: Moscow and the Ukraine, 1918-1953, 1956, Medieval Russia, 900-1700, 4th edit., 2000, Imperial Russia, 1700-1917, 4th edit., 1999, Modernization of Russia Under Peter I and Catherine II, 1974, Colonial Russian America 1817-1832, 1976, A History of Russia, 1977, U.S.S.R.: A Concise History, 4th edit., 1984, The End of Russian America, 1979, Civil and Savage Encounters, 1983, Russian Statecraft, 1985, Russian Conquest of Siberia 1558-1700, 1985, Russian Penetration of the North Pacific Archipelago, 1700-1799, 1987, The Soviet Union and the Middle East, 1917-1985, 1987, Russia's Colonies in North America, 1799-1867, 1988, The Soviet Union and the Arab World of the Fertile Crescent, 1918-1985, 1994, Imperial Russia, 1700-1917, 1999, Medieval Russia, 850-1700, 2000; contbr. articles to profl. jours. U.S., Can., Yugoslavia, Italy, South Korea, Fed. Republic Germany, France, Eng., Japan, Russia, Ukraine. State bd. dirs. PTA, Oreg., 1963-64; mem. World Affairs Council, 1965-92. Named Hon. Rsch. Prof. Emeritus, Kyungnam U., 1989—; Fulbright-Hays fellow W. Germany, 1967-68; fellow Kennan Inst. Advanced Russian Studies, Washington, 1978; recipient John Mosser award Oreg. State Bd. Higher Edn., 1966, 67; Branford P. Millar award for faculty excellence Portland State U., 1985, Outstanding Retired Faculty award, 1994; Hillard scholar in the humanities U. Nev., Reno, 1992. Mem. Am. Assn. Advancement Slavic Studies (dir. 1972-75), Am. Hist. Assn., Western Slavic Assn. (pres. 1990-92), Can. Assn. Slavists, Oreg. Hist. Soc. (hon. mem. coun.), Nat. Geog. Soc., Conf. Slavic and East European History (nat. sec. 1972-75), Am. Assn. for Ukrainian Studies (pres. 1991-93), Ctr. Study of Russian Am. (hon.), Assn. Study Nationalities (bd. mem.-at-large USSR and Ea. Europe 1993—), Czechoslovak Soc. Arts and Scis., Soc. Jewish-Ukraine Contacts, Assn. Home: 5291 Woodscape Dr SE Salem OR 97306

DOAN, DANIEL R, electrical engineer, consultant; m. Barbara L Long. BSEE, MIT, 1976—80, MSEE, 1980—81. Profl. Engr., Commonwealth of Pa., 1991. Design engr. ITS, Newton, Mass., 1981—83; project engr. DuPont, Towanda, Pa., 1983—97; cons. DuPont Engring., Wilmington, Del., 1997—. Author: (tech. paper) Design and Protection of Captive Motor-Transformers (IEEE Transactions on Industry Applications, 2000), Improvements in Modeling and Evaluation of Electrical Power Sys. Reliability (IEEE Transactions on Industry Applications, 2001), Integrating Networks in Motor Control Systems (Prize Paper Award, IEEE/IAS/PCIC, 2002), A Summary of Arc Flash Energy Calculations (IEEE/PCIC Conf. Procs., 2002). Youth coun. chair Quarryville UMC Youth Coun., 1999—2002. Mem.: IEEE (sr.; papers rev. chair - ias/pcic 2000—02). Office: DuPont Engineering PO Box 80840 Wilmington DE 19880-0840 E-mail: doan@ieee.org.

DOAN, GERALD XUYEN VAN, lawyer; b. Hadong, Vietnam, Apr. 1, 1949; came to U.S., 1975; s. Quyet V. Doan and Binh T. Kieu; m. Binh Thanh Tran, 1980; children: Quy-Bao, Ky-Nam. Licence en droit, U. Saigon Law Sch., Vietnam, 1971; MBA, U. Ark., 1977; JD, U. Calif., Hastings, 1982. Bar: Saigon 1972, Calif. 1982. Sole practice, Costa Mesa and San Jose, Calif., 1982-84; ptnr. Doan & Vu, San Jose, 1984-90; prin. Law Offices of Xuyen V. Doan, 1990-95; ptnr. Doan & Tran, San Jose, 1995—2003; prin. Law Offices of Xuyen V. Doan, San Jose, 2003—. Author: Of the Seas and Men, 1985, other publs. in English and Vietnamese. Named Ark. Traveler Ambassador of Good Will, State of Ark., 1975. Office: 945 McLaughlin Ave San Jose CA 95122 E-mail: jd@vietlawyers.com.

DOAN, MARY FRANCES, advertising executive; b. Vallejo, Calif., Apr. 16, 1954; d. Larry E. and Dudley (Harbison) D.; m. Timothy Warren Hesselgren, Mar. 19, 1988; children: Edward Latimer, Clinton Robert. BA in Linguistics, U. Calif., Berkeley, 1976; M in Internat. Mgmt., Am. Grad. Sch. Internat. Mgmt., 1980. Trading asst. The Capital Group, L.A., 1980-81; fin. analyst Litton Industries, Beverly Hills, 1981-82; account exec. Grey Advt., San Francisco, L.A., 1982-84, J. Walter Thompson, San Francisco, 1984-85, Lowe Marshalk, 1985-86; account supr. Young & Rubicam, 1986-89; acct. mgr. Saatchi & Saatchi, 1989—95, CEO, pres., 1995—96, worldwide dir. client svc. applications, 1997—98; cons., 1999; v.p. mktg. Roundl, San Francisco, 1999-2000; cons., 2001—02; dir. advt. Good Guys, Alameda, Calif., 2002—03, v.p. mktg. and advt., 2003—. E-mail: mfdoan@hotmail.com.

DOAN, MICHAEL FREDERICK, editor; b. Oakland, Calif., Feb. 5, 1942; s. Philip Melville and Agnes Blair (Gee) Doan; m. Mary Pickett Craddock, May 11, 1985; 1 child, Sara. BA in Journalism, U. Calif., Berkeley, 1963. Corr. AP, Las Vegas, 1968-69, econs. corr. Washington, 1970-79; assoc. editor U.S. News and World Report, Washington, 1979-87; editor Satellite Orbit mag., Vienna, Va., 1987-92; sr. assoc. editor Kiplinger Washington Editors, 1992-99; editor Kiplinger Calif. Letter, 2000—. Treas. United Meth. Ch., Washington. With USAR, 1964—70. Mem.: Washington Press Club (chmn. membership, sec. 1980—87). Methodist. Avocations: skiing, biking, jazz piano. Home: 3316 21st Ave N Arlington VA 22207-3821 Office: Kiplinger Washington Editors 1729 H St NW Washington DC 20006-3925

DOAN, TAI DANH, social worker, director; b. Thuy Loi, Vietnam, July 14, 1936; arrived in U.S., 1975; s. Cuc Danh Doan and Bong Thi Chu; m. Thu Minh Thi Nguyen, 1962; children: Trinh Thuy, Trang Thuy, Hoai Thu, Minh Danh. Grad., Vietnamese Naval Acad., 1957; MS in Mgmt., US Naval Acad., 1974. Skipper Navy ships Vietnamese Navy Fleet, 1962—68; chief bur. naval ops. Vietnamese Navy Hdqrs., Saigon, 1968—72, chief bur. naval personnel, 1974—75; project dir. title XX Vol. Agys. Employment Svc. Consortium, San Diego, 1979—81; social work supr. Health & Human Svcs. Agy., San Diego, 1981—. Adj. faculty Mesa Coll., San Diego, 1997—. Commr. Equal Opportunity Commn., San Diego, 1987—91; employment equal opportunity com. Dept. Social Svcs., San Diego, cultural awareness com.; chair San Diego Refugee Coalition; vice chair adv. bd. Pan Asian Parents Edn. Project; adv. bd. Indochinese bilingual edn. program San Diego City Schs.; adv. bd. ESSA; adv. bd. family planning project Linda Vista Health Ctr.; adv. bd. Indochinese Continuing Edn. Project San Diego C.C., San Diego; adv. bd. tchr. corps. Coll. Edn., San Diego State U.; adv. bd. nat. project Indochinese document evaluation Calif. State U., Long Beach; adv. bd. Indochinese needs assessment survey project Social Sci. Rsch. Lab., San Diego State U.; bd. dirs. Bayside Settlement Ho. Home: 14335 Bourgeouis Way San Diego CA 92129 Office: HHSAA 4370 54th St San Diego CA 92115

DOANE, CHRISTOPHER PHILIP, music educator; s. Philip Earl and Gladys Irene Doane; m. Sue Ellen Warner, June 20, 1982; 1 child, Emily Sue. B Music Edn., Ohio State U., 1974, PhD, 1981; MMusic, U. Akron, 1980. Prof. music, dir. bands Case Western Res. U., Cleve., 1981—82; prof. music U. South Fla., Tampa, 1982—2002, dir. prof., 1995—2002; dean, prof. U. Louisville, 2002—. Contbr. articles to prof. jours. Office: U Louisville School Music Louisville KY 40292 Office Fax: 502-852-0520.

DOARN, CHARLES R. medical educator; b. Toledo, Ohio, Nov. 15, 1957; s. Charles Raymond and Dorothy Elizabeth Doarn; m. Terri J. Banford, Jan. 6, 1990; children: Michael Charles, Christopher Glenn, Katelin Elizabeth. BS, Ohio State U., 1980; MBA, U. Dayton, 1988. Chemist Ohio Dept. Liquor Control, Columbus, Ohio, 1980—83; sr. technician Batelle Meml. Inst., Columbus, 1983—85; rsch. assoc. Hazleton Labs. Am., Rockville, Md., 1985—86; scientist NSI Tech. Svcs. Corp., Dayton, Ohio, 1986—89; environ. scientist Krug Life Scis., Houston, 1990, sect. supr., 1990—92; mgr. and prin. scientist Lockheed Engring. and Scis. Corp., Washington, 1992—94; lectr. Wright State U., Dayton, Ohio, 1994—; program exec. for aerospace medicine and telemedicine NASA Hdqs., Washington, 1995—99; lectr. Yale U. Sch. of Medicine, New Haven, 1998—2000, exec. dir. Med. Informatics and Tech. Applications Consortium, 1999, Va. Commonwealth U., Richmond, 1999—, asst. prof., 1999—2003, assoc. prof., 2003—. Pres., CEO, OrbitalMed, LLC, Richmond, 2000—; cons. MDirect, Tel Aviv, 1999—2000, Expert Medic, Montreal, Que., Canada, 2000, Medivision, Houston, 2000—01, Advanced Tech. Inst., Charleston, SC, 2000—; advisor Russian Telemedicine Found., Moscow, 2001—. Mem. editl. bd.: Telemedicine Jour., E-Health; contbr. articles to profl. publs. Recipient Silver Snoopy award, NASA Human Space Flight, 1997, Space Flight Awarness award, 1997; grantee, NASA, 1999, 2001, 2002, Va. Ctr. Innovative Tech., 2002, Internet Tech. Innovation Ctr., George Mason U., 2002. Fellow: Aerospace Med. Assn. (assoc.); mem.: Internat. Soc. Telemedicine, Am. Telemedicine Assn. (treas. and sec. 2001—), Nat. Eagle Scout Assn., Phi Beta Delta. Conservative. Roman Catholic. Achievements include patents pending for VitalPoll. Avocations: running, travel, reading, Ohio State U. football. Office: Va Commonwealth U MITAC 1101 E Marshall St Richmond VA 23298-0480 Office Fax: 804-827-1029. E-mail: crdoarn@hsc.vcu.edu.

DOBAY, SUSAN VILMA, artist; b. Budapest, Hungary, May 12, 1937; arrived in U.S., 1957; d. Otto and Lenke Stiasny Heltai; m. Endre Imre Dobay, Oct. 16, 1954; children: Vivian, Andrew. Diploma, Famous Artists Sch., Westport, Conn., 1963. One-woman shows include featured artist Vasarely Mus., Budapest, Hungary, 1993, Joslyn Arts Ctr., Torrance, Calif., 1994, Deri Mus., Hungary, 1999, BGH the Loft Gallery, Santa Monica, Calif., 2001, Lurdy House Gallery, Budapest, 2001, Hungarian Consulate, N.Y.C., 2001, one-woman shows include Mystic Sisters Gallery 2, Monrovia, Calif., 2002, 2003, exhibited in group shows at Calif. Mus. Sci. and Industry, L.A., 1967, 1975, UN Woman Conf., Nairobi, Kenya, 1985, Jillian Coldirow Fine Art, South Pasadena, Calif., 1993—, Hungarian Consulate, N.Y.C., 1996—, Kortars Galleria, Budapest, 1996—, Mus. Downtown L.A., 1998—, Hungarian House, San Diego, 2003, illustrator, Lloyd's Advt., L.A., 1963—64, fashion illustrator, Pasadena Star News, 1985. Mem. World Fedn. Hungarian Artists, N.Y. Artists Equity, L.A. Artists Equity. Avocations: reading, travel, theater, movies, classical music. Home: 125 W Scenic Dr Monrovia CA 91016-1610 E-mail: altrionet@sedobay.com.

DOBB, LINDA SUE, university official, librarian; b. Reading, Pa., Aug. 6, 1952; d. Rhea Beverly Blachman; m. Arthur Michael Small, Aug. 14, 1985; 1 child, Lorelei Small. AB, U. Calif., Berkeley, 1973; MLS, Simmons Coll., 1974; JD, Hastings Coll., 1983. Cataloging libr., instr. libr. sci. City Coll. San Francisco, 1974-83; processing libr. Libr. Congress, Washington, 1984-85; chief bibliographic control sect. Govt. Printing Office, Washington, 1985-87; asst. univ. libr. San Francisco State U., 1990-95; dean librs. Bowling Green (Ohio) State U., 1995-99, exec. v.p., 2000—. Fellow Coro Found-City Focus Program, San Francisco, 1993-94; adv. bd. Kent (Ohio) State Sch. Libr. and Info. Sci., 1997—; reviewer NSF and Inst. for Mus. and Libr. Svcs., Washington, 1998-2000. Bd. dirs. Calif. Libr. Authority for Sys. and Svcs., San Jose, Calif., 1990-95, OhioNet, Columbus, 1996-2000, Horizon Youth Theatre, Bowling Green, 1999-2001. Mem. ALA, AFTRA, Libr. Adminstrn. and Mgmt. Assn. (v.p./pres.-elect 2001—), Kiwanis. Avocation: acting. Office: Bowling Green State U McFAll Ctr 220 Bowling Green OH 43403 Home: PO Box 743 Bowling Green OH 43402-0743 Fax: 419-372-7723. E-mail: ldobb@bgnet.bgsu.edu., bgsulib@wcnet.org.

DOBBEL, RODGER FRANCIS, interior designer; b. Hayward, Calif., Mar. 11, 1934; s. John Leo and Edna Frances (Young) D.; m. Joyce Elaine Schnoor, Aug. 1, 1959; 1 child, Carrie Lynn. Student, San Jose State U., 1952-55, Chouinard Art Inst., L.A., 1955-57. Asst. designer Monroe Interiors, Oakland, Calif., 1957-66; owner, designer Rodger Dobbel Interiors, Piedmont, Calif., 1966—. Pub. in Showcase of Interior Design, Pacific edit., 1992, 100 Designers' Favorite Rooms, 1993, 2d edit., 1994; contbr. articles to mags. and newspapers. Decorations chmn. Trans Pacific Ctr. Bldg. Opening, benefit Oakland Ballet, various other benefits and openings, 1982—; chmn. Symphonic Magic, Lake Marritt Plaza, Opening of Oakland Symphony Orch. Season and various others, 1985—; cons. An Evening of Magic, Oakland Hilton Hotel, benefit Providence Hosp. Found., bd. dirs., 1991; auction chmn. County Meals on Wheels, 1994, 95; prodn. chmn. Nutcracker Ball, benefit Oakland Ballet, 1995; mem. bd. regents Holy Names Coll., 1997—; prodr., chmn. Modern Pentathlon World Championship Evening of Celebration, Runneymede Farms, 2002. Recipient Cert. of Svc., Nat. Soc. Interior Designers, 1972, 74; recipient Outstanding Contbn. award, Oakland Symphony, 1986, Nat. Philanthropy Day Disting. Vol. award, 1991. Mem. Nat. Soc. Interior Designers (profl. mem. 1960-75, v.p. Calif. chpt. 1965, edn. found. mem. 1966—, nat. conf. chmn. 1966), Am. Soc. Interior Designers, Claremont Country, Diabetic Youth Found. Democrat. Roman Catholic. Avocations: travel, gardening.

DOBBERT, DANIEL JOSEPH, data analyst, researcher, educator; b. Chgo., Feb. 2, 1946; s. Daniel Benjamin and Mary Jane (Miller) D.; m. Marion Lynne Lundy, Dec. 21, 1969 (div. Mar. 1993); 1 child, Joan Ellen; m. Valerie M. Parker, Dec. 28, 1996. BA, Aurora (Ill.) U., 1967; MEd, No. Ill. U., 1970, EdD, 1975. Cert. elem. tchr., secondary tchr., spl. edn. tchr., Ill. 1st to 6th grade tchr., middle sch. tchr. Media Generalist (Minn.) schs.; from research assoc. to asst. prof. U. Minn., Mpls., 1973-85; gen. mng. ptnr. Old Highland Restoration and Old Highland Ltd., Mpls., 1981—2002; data/research analyst Met. Mosquito Control Dist., St. Paul, 1986-95; sr. cons. Cons. Svcs., P.A., St. Paul, 1990-94; data/rsch. analyst Accugran, Mpls., 1991-92; chief mgr. ADA Svcs., LLC, 1995-96; pres. Biota Environ. Svcs. Internat., Inc., 1996—. Apptd. to Minn. Pesticide Mgmt. Com., 1996—2000; pres. B & D Environ. Svcs., Inc., 1997—; chmn., co-mng. dir. TekHelp, Ltd., 1998—2001; cons. in field; bd. dir. Travel Evolution. Contbr. chpts. to books, articles to profl. jours. Mem. Will County First Aid and Safety Com., Joliet, Ill., 1967-69; bd. dirs. Northside Residents Redevel. Coun., Mpls., 1974-77, Pilot City Regional Ctr., Mpls., 1976; first aid and CPR instr. ARC, 1969, 89—. Mem. NEA (life), Am. Mosquito Control Assn. (life), Am. Evalution Assn. (charter), Phi Delta Kappa (life). Mem. Democratic-Farmer-Labor Party. Mem. Soc. Friends. Lodge: Masons. Avocations: camping, canoeing, travel, photography. Office: 2029 NW 16th Terr New Brighton MN 55112-5560 E-mail: ddobbert@tekhelp.f9.co.uk.

DOBBIN, EDMUND J. university administrator; b. Bklyn., 1935; BA in Philosophy. Villanova U., 1958; MA, Augustinian Coll., 1962; SDT, U. Louvain, Belgium, 1971. ordained priest Roman Cath. Ch., 1962. Tchr. math. and religion, prefect of students Malvern Prep. Sch., 1962-67; tchr. systematic theology Washington Theol. Union, 1971-87, asst. prof., assoc. prof.; assoc. prof. Villanova (Pa.) U., 1987—, pres., 1988—. Trustee Villanova U., 1979-87, Merrimack Coll., North Andover, Mass., 1971-89, chmn. bd., 1986-89; mem. provincial coun. Augustinian Province of St. Thomas of Villanova, 1982-89. Mem. Am. Acad. Religion, Cath. Theol. Soc. Am. Office: Villanova U Office of the President 800 E Lancaster Ave Villanova PA 19085-1603*

DOBBINS, CARYL DEAN, lawyer; b. Indpls., July 3, 1947; s. Caryl L. and Janet (Matlock) D.; m. Amanda M. Cline, Nov. 22, 1972 (div. Jan. 1977); 1 child, Heather Lynn; m. Barbara J. Perry, Nov. 10, 1977; 1 child, Jason Dean. BS, Purdue U., 1969; postgrad., Valparaiso (Ind.) U., 1969-70; spl. med. student, Ind. U. Med. Sch., 1970-72; JD, Ind. U., Indpls., 1972; postgrad., Oxford (Eng.) U. and Brunel U., 1971. Bar: Ind. 1972, U.S. Dist. Ct. (so. dist.) Ind. 1972, U.S. Ct. Appeals (7th cir.) 1973, U.S. Supreme Ct. 1987. Chief law clk. to chief judge U.S. Dist. Ct. for So. Dist. Ind., Indpls., 1972-74; pros. atty. 18th jud. cir. State of Ind., 1975-78, dir. child support, 1979; pvt. practice, Greenfield, Ind., 1979—. Dir. Ind. Law Enforcement Asst. Adminstrn., 1976-78; bd. dirs. Ind. Pros. Atty. Coun., 1976-78. Recipient Am. Farmer degree Future Farmers Am., 1967, Preservation award Greenfield Hist. Landmarks, 1984. Mem. ABA (gen. practice link bar leader award 1997), Ind. Bar Assn. (del. 1988-98, 2001—, bd. govs. 2002—, chair gen. practice, solo and small firm sect. 1996-97, chair, law practice mgmt. 1998-2001, bd. govs. 2002—, Gen. Practice Hall of Fame 2003), Ind. Bar Found. (master fellow), Hancock County Bar Assn. (pres. 1999-2000), C. of C. Greater Hancock County and Greenfield (bd. dirs. 2d v.p. 1990, 1st v.p. 1991, pres. 1992, chmn. bd. dirs. 1993), Rotary (bd. dirs. 1991-94, 99-2003, v.p. 1999-2000, pres. elect 2000-01, pres. 2001-02, chmn. bd. 2002-03, Paul Harris fellow), Sertoma (treas. Greenfield 1982-84, sec. 1984-85, pres. 1985-86, chmn. bd. dirs. 1986-87, internat. del. 1983-86, Cmty. Achievement award 1986), Farm House, Phi Alpha Delta. Avocations: gardening, travel. Home: 4392 E 100 S Greenfield IN 46140-9758 Office: 19 W Main St Greenfield IN 46140-2340 Office Fax: 317-462-4903.

DOBBINS, FREDA J. librarian; b. Hutchinson, Kans., June 1, 1940; d. Mahlon F. and Verna (Detter) Stauffer; m. James R. Dobbins, Aug. 3, 1968; children: Jared S., Janelle K. BA, Southwestern Coll., 1962; MA, U. Denver, 1963. Head adult svcs. Hutchinson Pub. Libr., 1964-67; sys. cons. S. Ctrl. Kans. Libr. Sys., Hutchinson, 1967-68; reference libr. Main Post Libr., Fort Knox, Ky., 1968-69; from dir. ext. to legis. reference libr. Kans. State Libr., Topeka, 1970-78; dir. Pottawatomie Wabaunsee Regional Libr., St. Marys, Kans., 1985—. Bd. dirs. Friendly Acres Retirement Ctr., Newton, Kans. Mem. ALA, Kans. Libr. Assn. (legis. com. 1993—). Methodist. Avocation: reading. Home: RR 2 Box 105 Goff KS 66428-9647 Office: Pottawatomie Wabaunsee Regional Libr 306 N 5th St Saint Marys KS 66536-1404

DOBBINS, JAMES TALMAGE, JR., analytical chemist, researcher; b. Chapel Hill, N.C., June 13, 1926; s. James Talmage and Lila (Shore) D.; m. Jacqueleene Bowen, Dec. 22, 1951; children: James Talmage III, Steven Earl. BS in Chemistry, U. N.C., 1947, PhD in Analytical Chemistry, 1958. Chief indsl. hygiene sect. Med. Gen. Lab., Tokyo, 1953-55, head dept. chemistry, 1955-6; rsch. chemist II R.J. Reynolds Tobacco Co., Winston-Salem, N.C., 1958-65, rsch. sect. head II, 1965-72; mgr. analytical rsch. div. R.J. Reynolds Industries, Winston-Salem, 1972-75; master scientist RJR Nabisco, Winston-Salem, 1975-83; master chemist Bowman Gray Tech. Ctr., Winston-Salem, 1983-89; retired, 1989. Contbr. articles to Jour. Assn. Official Agrl. Chemists, Jour. Assn. Official Analytical Chemists, Spectroscopy, Encyclopedia Ind. Chem. Analysis. Fellow Am. Inst. Chemists; mem. AAAS, Soc. for Applied Spectroscopy, N.Y. Acad. Sci., N.C. Acad. Sci., Am. Chem. Soc. (sec., chmn. elect and chmn. ctrl. N.C. sect. 1964, 65, 66), Sigma Xi (sec. Wake Forest chpt. 1986-90). Democrat. Baptist. Achievements include conception of column-elutive sample prep for plant matter analysis; design of clean room facilities for ICP spectrometry of trace inorganics, and of first-of-its-kind computer intelligent auto-dilution by flow injection/ICP analysis. Home: 2838 Bartram Rd Winston Salem NC 27106-5105

DOBBINS, MAGGIE SONNE, real estate investment company executive; b. Pasadena, Calif., July 14, 1958; d. Roscoe Newbold Jr. and Ann Miriam (Vierhus) S.; m. Donald Alan Blackburn, Sept. 8, 1979 (div. 1983); m. Paul Dobbins, June 7, 1997. AS, Oreg. Inst. Tech., 1981, BS, 1983. Sales trainee NCR Corp., Dayton, Ohio, 1983-84, sales rep. Portland, Oreg., 1984-86, account mgr. Seattle, 1986-87, sr. account mgr. Portland, 1987-88; sr. account rep. Wang Labs., Portland, 1988-91; account exec. Tandem Computers, Portland, 1991-94; sr. acct. exec. Fin. Svcs., L.A., 1994-96; pres. Trofast Investments, Altadena, Calif., 1998—. Active Emily's List, Project Vote Smart, Habitat for Humanity, Rebuilding Together, Pasadena Heritage. Avocations: bicycling, golf, gardening, walking. Home: 1242 E Altadena Dr Altadena CA 91001-2004 E-mail: maggie@trofast.net.

DOBBINS, RICHARD ANDREW, engineering educator, researcher; b. Burlington, Mass., July 15, 1925; s. William John and Catherine (Porter) Dobbins; m. Iona Mae Blake, Nov. 28, 1953; children: Deborah Ann, Catherine Blake Ryan. BS, Harvard U., 1948; MS, Northeastern U., 1958; PhD, Princeton U., 1961. Inspection engr. Ea. Inspection Bur., Boston, 1948—50; rsch. engr. Arthur D. Little Inc., Cambridge, Mass., 1950—53; sr. engr. Sylvania Electric Products, Waltham, Mass., 1953—56; asst. prof. engring. Brown U., Provi-

dence, 1960—64, assoc. prof. engring., 1964—67, prof. engring., 1968—93, prof. engring. (rsch.), 1993—. Vis. prof. Calif. Inst. Tech., Pasadena, 1967—68, Abadan (Iran) Inst. Tech., 1975; vis. scientist Nat. Inst. Stds. and Tech., Gaithersburg, Md., 1981—82, Gaithersburg, 1988—89; divsn. chmn. Divsn. Engring., Providence, 1983—88. Author: Atmospheric Motion and Air Pollution, 1979. Ensign USNR, 1943—46. Fellow: ASME; mem.: Soc. Automotive Engrs., Am. Assn. for Aerosol Rsch. (bd. dirs. 1986—91, David Sinclair award 2001), Combustion Inst. Achievements include co-inventor thermophoretic sampling of particles in flames; discovery of liquid precursor particles in flames; patents for minimizing combustion instability. Avocations: sailing, skiing. Home: 11 President Ave Providence RI 02906 Office: Divsn Engring Brown Univ Providence RI 02912

DOBBS, C. EDWARD, lawyer, educator; b. Richmond, Virginia, July 15, 1949; s. Glenn Wellington and Sarah Catherine (Judy) D.; m. J. Elisabeth (Kuypers), Aug. 29, 1981; children: Elisabeth Peyten, Edward Palmer, Virginia Whitney. BA, Davidson Coll., 1971; JD, Vanderbilt U., 1974. Bar: Ga., 1974, U.S. Dist. Ct. (no., mid. dists.) Ga., 1974, U.S. Ct. Appeals (11th cir. and 5th cir.), 1974, U.S. Supreme Ct., 2001. Ptnr. Kutak Rock, Atlanta, 1974-83, Parker, Hudson, Rainer & Dobbs, LLP, Atlanta, 1983—. Adj. prof., Emory Law Sch., Atlanta, 1987-92; mem. adv. bd., Atlanta Legal Aid Soc., 1980-82. Author: Reorganization Under Chapter 11 of the Bankruptcy Code, 1979, Enforcement of Security Interests in Personal Property, 1978. Bd. dir., trustee Trinity Sch., Inc., Atlanta, 1992-96; chmn. Ga. Fin. Lawyers Conf., 1995—; bd. dir. Comm. Fin. Assn. Edn. Found., 1996—. Fellow Am. Coll. Bankruptcy, Ga. Bar Found., Am. Coll. Comml. Fin. Laws (bd. regents 1990—, pres. 1996-98); mem. ABA (chmn. young lawyers divsn. 1981-82), Am. Arbitration Assn., Southeastern Bankruptcy Law Inst. (bd. dirs., chmn. 1992-93), Order of Coif, Omicron Delta Kappa, Alpha Psi Omega. Presbyterian. Avocations: golf, tennis, fishing, trees. Office: Parker Hudson Rainer and Dobbs LLP 1500 Marquis Two Tower 285 Peachtree Center Ave NE Atlanta GA 30303-1229 E-mail: edobbs@phrd.com.

DOBBS, CARNEY H. retired lawyer, retired insurance company executive; b. Birmingham, Ala., Oct. 26, 1924; s. John Hoyt and Gertrude (Compton) D.; m. Josephine Philips, Aug. 18, 1956; children: John C., Philip G. JD, U. ala., 1949. Bar: Ala. 1949, U.S. Dist. Ct. (no. dist.) Ala. 1950; CPCU. Ptnr. Dobbs & Faulkner, Birmingham, 1949-51; asst. city atty. City of Birmingham, 1951-52; spl. agt., atty. U.S. Govt., Birmingham, 1952-53; atty., claim rep. State Farm Ins., Birmingham, 1954-60, claim supt., 1960-66, divsnl. claim supt., 1966—; ret., 1989. Arbitrator, mediator; expert witness. Contbr. articles to profl. jours. Chmn., Spl. Arbitration com., Birmingham, 1965-74, Ala. Arson Prevention Task Force, 1979-83; mem. adv. com., Ala. State Fire Coll., 1979—; active Boy Scouts Am. Mem. ABA, Ala. Bar Assn. (task force on cmty. edn. 1985, 86—), Birmingham Bar Assn., Ala. Claims Assn. (pres. 1963), Internat. Assn. Arson Investigators (Carney Dobbs award for disting. svc. 1982), Mountain Brook Swim and Tennis Club, Downtown Club, Sigma Chi (Outstanding Alumnus U. Ala. 1981). Republican. Methodist. Home and Office: 4009 Little Branch Rd Birmingham AL 35243-5815 E-mail: carneydobbs@webtv.net.

DOBBS, DAN BYRON, lawyer, educator; b. Ft. Smith, Ark., Nov. 8, 1932; s. George Byron and Gladys Pauline (Stone) D.; m. Betty Jo Teeter, May 31, 1953 (div. 1978); children: Katherine, George, Rebecca, Jean. BA, LL.B., U. Ark., 1956; LL.M., U. Ill., 1961, J.S.D., 1966. Bar: Ark. 1956. Partner firm Dobbs, Pryor & Dobbs, Ft. Smith, 1956-60; asst. prof. law U. N.C., Chapel Hill, 1961-63, assoc. prof., 1963-66, prof., 1967, Aubrey L. Brooks prof. law, 1975-77; Rosenstiel prof. law U. Ariz., 1978—, Regents prof., 1992—. Vis. asst. prof. U. Tex., summer 1961; vis. prof. U. Minn., 1966-67, Cornell Law Sch., 1968-69, U. Va. Law Sch., 1974, U. Ariz. Law Sch., 1977-78 Author: Handbook on the Law of Remedies, Damages, Equity, Restitution, 1973, Problems in Remedies, 1974, The Law of Remedies, 3 vols., 2d edit., 1993, The Law of Torts, 2000; co-author: Prosser and Keeton on Torts, 5th edit., 1984, Torts and Compensation, 1985, 4th edit., 2001, (with Paul Hayden), 1997; contbr. articles to legal jours. Office: U Ariz Law Coll Tucson AZ 85721-0001

DOBBS, GEORGE ALBERT, funeral director, embalmer; b. Atlanta, Oct. 16, 1943; s. Albert F. and Ruby Lee (Haynes) D. Student, Fla. Bapt. Theol. Coll., 1963-67; BA, Cornell U., 1974; AA in Mortuary Sci. and Adminstrn., John A. Gupton Coll., 1990. Cert. funeral svc. practitioner. Retail store mgr. Alterman Foods, Atlanta, 1962-74; ind. mng. agt. George A. Dobbs & Assocs., Decatur, Ga., 1974-78, motivational spkr., Hermitage, Tenn., 1992—; retail mgr. K-Mart Corp., Decatur, 1978-91; funeral dir., embalmer SCI Nashville Group, 1991-97, coord. svc. ctr. Nashville Family Funeral Homes, 1997—2001; funeral dir., embalmer Stewart Enterprises, Nashville, 2001—; wedding and funeral celebrant, 2003—. Named Small Bus. Man of Yr., Dekalb Businessman's Assn., 1974, 76. Mem. Capital City Club, Order Ky. Cols., Masons (past master Ga. and Tenn.), Shriners, Philalethes Soc., York Rite, Scottish Rite (32d degree), Tex, Lodge of Rsch., N.Am. Soc. Pipe Collectors, Universal Coterie of Pipe Smokers, Soc. of Pipe Collectors, Pipe Club London, Ky. Bourbon Cir., Khorasoan MOUPER (Tex., Calif. and Mo. grand lodges), Internat. Optimist Club, J. Barleyconn Club, Knights of Mecca, Tenn. Yellow Dogs (life), Quatuor Coronati Lodge. Baptist. Republican. Address: PO Box 290275 Nashville TN 37229-0275

DOBBS, GREGORY ALLAN, journalist; b. San Francisco, Oct. 9, 1946; s. Harold Stanley and Annette Rae (Lehrer) D.; m. Carol Lynn Walker, Nov. 25, 1973; children: Jason Walker, Alexander Adair. BA, U. Calif., Berkeley, 1968; MSJ, Northwestern U., 1969. Assignment editor, reporter Sta. KGO-TV, San Francisco, 1966-68; news dir. San Francisco Tourist Info. Program Service, 1968; editor ABC Radio, Chgo., 1969-71; prodr. ABC News, Chgo., 1971-73, corr., 1973-77, 1977-82, Paris, 1982-86, Denver, 1986-92; host The Greg Dobbs Show/Sta. KOA Radio, 1992—98; host The Greg Dobbs Morning Show KNRC Radio, Denver, 2002—; host Colo. State of Mind Rocky Mt. PBS, 2003—. Adj. prof. Northwestern U. Sch. Journalism, 1975, 76; prof. U. Colo. Sch. Journalism, 1996—. Columnist The Denver Post, 1996—2001, Rocky Mountain News, 2001—, nationally syndicated columnist Scripps Howard, 2001—. Recipient Sigma Delta Chi Disting. Svc. award for TV reporting Soc. Profl. Journalists, 1980, Emmy award for outstanding documentary, 1989, award of excellence Colo. Broadcasters Assn., 1993, 94, award for best talk show Colo. Soc. Profl. Journalists, 1994; Lippmann fellow Ford Found., 1975; named Best Talk Show Host in Denver, Westword Mag., 2002. Office: 1153 Bergen Pkwy Ste M150 Evergreen CO 80439-9501

DOBBS, HERBERT HOTALING, automotive executive, consultant, engineer, scientist, retired army officer; b. Mpls., July 5, 1931; s. Willis Clark and Mary Evalyn (Hotaling) D.; m. Joyce Belle Roberts, Mar. 20, 1954; children: Herbert H., Jr., Douglas Edwin, Graeme Clark. BSME, U. Minn., 1954; MSME, U. Mich., 1961, PhD in Mech. Engring., 1972; grad., U.S. Army Command and Gen., 1972, U.S. Army War Coll., 1977. Registered profl. engr., Mich. Commd. 2d. lt. U.S. Army, 1954, advanced through grades to col., 1977, assigned to Italy, 1955-57, assigned to Vietnam, 1966—67, assigned to Taiwan, 1975—76, ret., 1983; tech. dir. U.S. Army Tank-Automotive Command, 1983-85; chmn. Torvec, Inc., Pittsford, NY, 1998—2002. Design engr. Aerojet Gen. Corp., Sacramento, 1957; mem indsl. adv. bd. mech. engring. dept. Wayne State U., 1986—, Oakland U.; cons. Dobbs Assocs., Rochester Hills, Mich., 1986—; cons. Office Naval Rsch. USN, 1997; mem. or cons. U.S. Army Sci. Bd., 1994—; various govt. adv. bds., 1986—; mem. adv. bd. Nat. Jr. Sci. and Humanities Symposium, 1995—. Contbr. articles to profl. jours.; patentee for turbulent flow research work and military research and development work. State chmn. MSPE Mathcounts, 1986—. Mem. AIAA, ASME, AAAS, NSPE, Mich. Soc. Profl. Engrs., Soc. Automotive Engrs., Soc. Mfg. Engrs., Assn. Unmanned Vehicle Systems Internat., Res. Officers Assn., Assn. U.S. Army, Detroit chpt., exec. bd. 1985-99, chmn. jr. sci. and humanities seminar 1988-99, Armor Assn., Nat. Def. Indsl. Assn. Avocations: reading, mathematics, woodworking, opera. Home: 448 Maryknoll Rd Rochester Hills MI 48309 Office: Torvec Inc 11 Pondview Dr Pittsford NY 14534-9501 E-mail: dr.hh.dobbs@earthlink.net.

DOBBS, JOHN BARNES, artist, educator; b. Nutley, N.J., Aug. 2, 1931; s. John Montgomery and Catherine (Barnes) D.; m. Anne Baudement, 1959; children: Nicolas, Michel. Student, R.I. Sch. Design, 1949, Bklyn. Mus. Art Sch., 1950-52, Skowhegan Sch., 1952. Prof. studio art John Jay Coll. CUNY, N.Y.C., 1974-96. Twenty-seven one-man shows in U.S. and France; group exhbns. include Am. Acad. Arts and Letters (Childe Hassam purchase prize 1972, Art award 1994), Whitney Mus., Nat. Acad. Design (Ranger Fund purchase prize 1966, 90, Benjamin Altman prize 1980, Edwin Palmer prize 1991, Obrig prize 2003), Mus. Modern Art, Butler Inst. Am. Art, Salon des Independents. Cpl. U.S. Army, 1952-54, ETO. Louis Comfort Tiffany grantee, 1967 Mem. NAD (academician), Century Club. Home: 463 West St Apt B339 New York NY 10014-2032

DOBBS, STANLEY, military officer, information quality engineer; s. Nancy Mae Miles; m. Cecily A. Williams, Mar. 13, 1993 (div. Aug. 1, 2001); children: Nia, Naomi, Niles Stanley, Fentrice A. Assoc. in Sci. Nuclear Engring. Tech.(hon.), Naval Nuclear Power Sch., Orlando, Fla., 1986; BSEE, U. of Memphis, 1991; MBA, Fla. Inst. of Tech., Melbourne, 1999; MS in Ops. Rsch. Engring., Naval Postgrad. Sch., Monterey, Calif., 2001. Cert. nuclear quality assurance, Chief Naval Edn. and Tng., data quality engring., MIT, info. tech. program mgmt., George Wash. U. Instr. Naval Nuclear Power Program, Ballston Spa, NY, 1984—86; officer candidate Broadened Opportunity for Officer Selection and Tng., San Diego, 1986—87; profl. naval instr. Naval Air Sta. Millington, Tenn., 1987—91; logistics quality assurance officer USS Holland (AS 32), Agana, 1992—94; chief logistics officer USS Sunfish (SSN 649), Norfolk, Va., 1994—97; fed. contracts negotiator/ officer Naval Sea Sys. Command, Washington, 1997—99; ops. rsch. engr. Naval Postgrad. Sch., Monterey, Calif., 1999—2001; dep. dir. ops. rsch. Naval Inventory Control Point, Phila., 2001—02; dir. Data Integrity Mgmt. Ctr., Phila., 2002—. Dir. Data Integrity Mgmt. Ctr., Pa., 2001—; program mgr. Info. Quality Support Engring., Phila., 2001—03. Author (presenter): (quality engring. support sys.) Information Quality: When Profit is NOT the Bottomline; author: (edn. cons.) Re-engineering the Forecasting Enrollment Management System for the MPUSD (Superior Svc. award, 2001). Distinguished chpt. mem. Alpha Phi Alpha, Memphis, Tenn., 1989—91. Lt. comdr. US Navy, 1983, Naval Inventory Control Point. Recipient Superior Svc. Bronze award, Fed. Exec. Bd., 2001, Superior Svc. Silver award, 2001, EEO/Diversity award, Phila. Area Human Resource, 2003. Master: Student Govt. Assn. (assoc.; v.p. student govt. 1989—90, Man of the Yr. 1989); mem.: Toastmasters Internat. (assoc.; club founder 2001—02), Alpha Phi Alpha (life; dean of pledges 1989—90, Brother of the Yr. 1990). Achievements include first to Information Centric Quality Management Methodology; Information Quality Support Management Circles of Excellence. Avocations: golf, youth development, computers, motivational speaking. Home: Ste N20 9601 Ashton Rd Philadelphia PA 19114 Office: Naval Inventory Control Point 700 Robbins Ave Philadelphia PA 19111 Home Fax: 603-699-7761; Office Fax: 603-699-7761. Personal E-mail: stan_dobbs@yahoo.com. E-mail: stan_dobbs@yahoo.com.

DOBECK, ROBERT BRADLEY, lawyer; b. Socorro, N.Mex., Feb. 27, 1954; s. R. J. and D. E. (Dickenson) D.; m. J. Weili Cheng, Sept. 15, 1979; 1 child, Stephen Cheng. BS, U. Conn., 1976; JD, MS in Foreign Svc., Georgetown U., 1981, LLM, 1988. Bar: Hawaii 1981, D.C. 1983, N.Y. 1989. Assoc. Cades, Schutte, Fleming & Wright, Honolulu, 1981-82; staff Mondale for Pres. Campaign, Washington, 1983; fed. contracts negotiator IBM Corp., Bethesda, Md., 1984-87, atty. fed. sector divsn., 1987-92, arbitrator, 1992-96; prelaw advisor Georgetown U., Washington, 1996-2000; gen. counsel Faith and Action, Washington, 2000—; pres. PrelawAdvisor.com, 2000—. Contbr. book Legal Environment for Foreign Direct Investment in the United States, 1981. Mem. admissions com. Georgetown U. MS in Foreign Svc. program, Washington, 1983-89, grad. advisor Law and Policy in Internat. Bus., 1987-88. Mem. ABA, Christian Legal Soc., Republican. Avocations: bicycling, running. Home: 4751 34th Rd N Arlington VA 22207-4209 E-mail: BradDobeck@aol.com.

DOBELIS, MIERVALDIS CHRISTIAN, systems designer; b. Riga, Latvia, Mar. 19, 1929; arrived in U.S., 1949, naturalized, 1955; s. Arthur and Emily Pauline Dobelis; m. Inge H. Nachman, May 4, 1969; 1 child, Arthur Nachman. BBA cum laude, CCNY, 1957; postgrad., NYU, 1957—58. With Guardian Life Ins. Co. Am., N.Y.C., 1950—71, mgr. corp. planning, dir. sys., lead sys. analyst, 1971—82, EDP auditor, 1982—. Instr. NYU, 1972—77. Author (monographs): The Three-Day Week, 1976, Bridging the Gap Between Computer Technicians and Users, 1977; contbr. Pres. Friends of Librs. U.S.A., 1975—; vol. coord. Homeless Program, 1982—; dir., officer Park Towers Corp., 1985—2000; chmn. Save the Police Acad., 1986—; mem. exec. bd. Murray Hill Dem. Club, 1969—74; mem. N.Y. County Dem. County Com., 1969—74, 1987—. Recipient Journalist of Yr. award, Concerned Citizens Speak, 1995. Mem.: Assn. Sys. Mgmt. (Merit award 1975), Stuyvesant Park Neighborhood Assn., Am. Latvian Assn., Beta Gamma Sigma. Lutheran. Home: 201 E 17th St New York NY 10003-3607 Office: 7 Hanover Sq 21 B New York NY 10004-2616 Business E-Mail: inged@ix.netcom.com.

DOBELL, BYRON MAXWELL, magazine consultant; b. Bronx, N.Y., May 30, 1927; s. Jacob and Marie (Schaeffer) D.; m. Edith Spielberg, 1952 (div. 1957); m. Ande Rubin, 1958 (dec. 1967); 1 dau., Elizabeth; m. Elizabeth Rodgers Dempster, 1969 (dec. 1992); m. Alexandra Mayes Birnbaum, 1999. AB, Columbia U., 1947. Picture editor U.S. Camera, 1952-55; asso. editor Popular Photography, 1956-57; feature editor Pageant, 1957-58, This Week, 1958-60; sr. editor Time-Life Books, 1960-62, asso. dir. editorial planning, 1971-72; mng. editor Esquire mag., N.Y.C., 1962-67, 79-82, editor-in-chief, 1977, Book World (weekly lit. supplement Chgo. Tribune and Washington Post), 1967-69; editor-in-chief book div. McCall Pub. Co., 1969-71; editorial dir. New York mag., 1972-77; sr. editor Life mag., N.Y.C., 1978-79; editor-in-chief Am. Heritage mag., 1982-90, Am. Heritage of Invention & Tech. mag., 1984-90; mag. cons. N.Y.C., 1990—. Bd. dirs. Am. Soc. Mag. Editors, 1987-91. Editor: Life Guide to Paris, A Sense of History. Served with AUS, 1946-47. Named to Am. Soc. of Mag. Editor's Hall of Fame, 1998. Mem. PEN (N.Y.C.), Century Assn. Home and Office: 145 E 76th St New York NY 10021-2843

DOBELLE, EVAN SAMUEL, academic administrator; b. Washington, Apr. 22, 1945; s. Martin and Lillian (Mendelsohn) Dobelle; m. Edith Huntington Kit, June 7, 1970; 1 child, Harry Huntington. BA, U. Mass., 1983, MEd, 1970, EdD, 1987; MPA, Harvard U., 1984. Exec. asst. U.S. Senator Edward Brooke, Boston, 1971—73; mayor City of Pittsfield, 1973—76; commr. environ. mgmt. State of Mass., Boston, 1976—77; chief protocol U.S., Washington, 1977—78; treas. Dem. Nat. Com., 1978—79, dep. chair, 1980—81; chairman Carter-Mondale Presdl. Com., 1979—80; v.p. Bear Stearns and Co., N.Y.C., 1984—87; pres. Middlesex Cmty. Coll., Mass., 1987—90; chancellor City Coll. San Francisco, 1991—; pres. Trinity College, Hartford, Conn., 1995—2001, U. Hawaii, Honolulu, 2002—. Bd. dirs. Jacobs Pillow Dance Festival, Conn. Pub. TV; bd. govs. Jewish Fedn., Hartford, Conn. Jewish. Avocations: golf, swimming, reading, travel, history. Office: Univ Hawaii Office of the President 2444 Dule St Bachman Hall 202 Honolulu HI 96822*

DOBER, RICHARD PATRICK, campus and facility planner, writer; b. Phila., Mar. 30, 1928; s. Lawrence Joseph and Veronica (Brake) D.; m. Betty Edwards, Dec. 28, 1957 (Sept. 1958); m. Eleanor Lee Lyman, Sept. 23, 1961; children: Patrick Lee, Claire Brake Danaher. BA in Design, Bklyn. Coll., 1953; M of City Planning, Harvard U., 1957. Cert. planner. Frederick C. Sheldon Travelling fellow, 1958; exec. dir. Sasaki, Walker and Assocs., Watertown, Mass., 1958-62; sr. cons. Dober and Assocs., Inc., Cambridge, Mass., 1962-92, Dober, Lidsky, Craig and Assocs., 1992—; Frederick C. Sheldon travelling fellowship Harvard U., 1958. Cons. Bush Found., World Bank, U.S. Dept. of Edn., UNESCO, Ford Found., others; v.p. Boston Architectural Ctr., 1969-72; lectr. Grad. Program Urban Design, MIT, 1972; vis. critic Beijing U., 1985, MIT, 1980, Coll. of Design, Iowa State U., 1979, U. Ill., 1974, Harvard U., 1963-65; faculty Inst. of Ednl. Mgmt. Harvard Grad. Sch. Edn., 1991-92. Author: Campus Planning, 1964, Campus Design, 1992, Campus Architecture, 1996, Campus Landscape, 2000; contbr. numerous articles to profl. jours. With U.S. Army, 1953-55. Recipient Award of Merit Am. Assn. of Jr. Colls., 1968, 1st Prize Coun. for Advancement and Support of Edn., 1983, Disting. Alumnus award Bklyn. Coll., 1992, Founder's award for Disting. Achievement and Exceptional Contbns. to Higher Edn. Planning Soc. for Colls. and Univs. Planning, 1992. Mem. Am. Inst. of Cert. Planners, Soc. for Coll. and Univ. Planning (founding mem., bd. dirs. 1969-72), The Renaissance Soc. of Am., Assn. of Collegiate Schs. of Architecture, Internat. Coun. of Mus., Can. Arts Coun. (cons. 1972). Avocations: travel, opera, books on Georgian architecture. Office: Dober Lidsky Craig and Assocs Inc 385 Concord Ave Belmont MA 02478-3083 E-mail: rpd@dlca.com.

DOBERENZ, ALEXANDER R. nutrition educator, chemist; b. Newark, Aug. 17, 1936; s. Alexander J. and Marie (Zink) D.; m. Angela Rajoppi, June 7, 1958; children: Annamarie Wexler, Judith Lynn, Hoke Jr. BS in Chemistry, Tusculum Coll., 1958; MS, U. Ariz., 1960, PhD in Biochemistry and Nutrition, 1963. Research assoc. dept. physics U. Ariz., Tucson, 1963-69; vis. assoc. prof. nutrition U. Hawaii, 1969; assoc. prof. nutritional scis. U. Wis., Green Bay, 1969-71, prof., 1971-76, assoc. dean Coll. and Sch. Profl. Studies, 1969-76, prof. growth and devel., 1975-76; prof. food sci. and human nutrition U. Del., Newark, 1976-97, dean Coll. Human Resources, 1976-93, coord. home econs. rsch., 1978-93, spl. asst. to the pres., 1993, interim v.p. for student life, 1994-95, prof. nutritional scis., Coll. of Health and Nursing Scis., 1997-99, prof. emerita, 1999—. Cons. food industry, 1976-93; mem. nat. steering com. new initiatives for home econs. U.S. Dept. Agr., 1979-81, USDA Planning com. Workshops on Improving Health Maintenance, 1984-87. Contbr. numerous articles on food chemistry and nutrition to profl. publs. Head underwater recovery unit Pima County Sheriff's Dept., 1966-68; warrant officer CAP, 1965-69; mem. Brown County Comprehensive Health Planning Council, 1973-76; bd. dirs. Pima County Sheriff's Search and Rescue, 1968. Recipient Research Career Devel. award NIH, 1966-69, Outstanding Educator Am., 1971, 72. Fellow Am. Inst. Chemists; mem. Am. Chem. Soc., Am. Home Econs. Soc., Am. Inst. Nutrition (Mead Johnson award nominating com. 1973-76), Nutrition Soc. Today, Soc. for Nutrition Edn., Nutrition Soc. London Soc. Exptl. Biology and Medicine, Am. Soc. Clin. Nutrition, AAAS, Assn. Adminstrs. of Home Econs., Del. Gerontol. Soc. (exec. com. 1978), Nat. Council Adminstrs. Home Econs. (exec. bd. 1982-83), Am. Pub. Health Assn., Del.-Panama Ptnrs. of Ams., Assn. for Devel. Computer Based Instruction, Del. Acad. Sci., Sigma Xi, Phi Lambda Upsilon., Phi Kappa Phi Clubs: University and Whist. Roman Catholic. Office: U Del 222 Alison Hall Newark DE 19716 E-mail: ard@udel.edu.

DOBES, WILLIAM LAMAR, JR., dermatologist, educator; b. Atlanta, Apr. 16, 1943; s. William Lamar and Sara (Wilson) Dobes; m. Martha Husmann, June 16, 1966; children: Margaret Alison Key, William Shane. BA, Emory U., 1965, MD, 1969. Diplomate Am. Bd. Dermatology. Intern Grady Meml. Hosp., Atlanta, 1969-70; fellow in dermatology Mayo Clinic, 1970-71; fellow U. Miami, 1971-73; clin. instr. Emory U. Sch. Medicine, Atlanta, 1973-77, asst. prof. dermatology, 1977-83, assoc. prof., 1983—. Dir. immunofluorescense lab., 1978-85; mem. staff Crawford Long, Grady Meml., Piedmont hosps., Atlanta; dir. Skin Cancer Project, Emory U., 1981-89; chmn. profl. edn. unit Atlanta chpt. Am. Cancer Soc., 1980-86, also bd. dirs., pres., 1986-87, chmn. bd. dirs., 1987-88; pres. Carter's Atlanta, project chmn. Physicians Com., 1992-95. Contbr. articles to profl. jours. and texts. Chmn. Ga. med. bd. Lupus Found., 1988, bd. dirs. Whitney Rsch. Lab., U. Fla., 1998-2002. Dermatology Found. Rsch. award, 1979. Fellow Am. Dermatol. Assn.; mem. AMA, ACP, Am. Soc. Cosmetic and Aesthetic Surgery, Am. soc. Cosmetic Dermatolgie and Asthetic Surgery, Soc. Investigative Dermatology, Am. Acad. Dermatology (chmn. com. quality assurance 1982-84, adv. coun. 1985-95, ad coun. exec. com. 1991-95, com. on stds. of care 1987-91, chmn. CLIA task force 1993-97), So. Med. Assn. (vice chmn. 1983), Pan Am. Med. Assn., Am. Soc. Dermatologic Surgery, Ga. Dermatol. Assn. (pres. 1986-87), Atlanta Dermatol. Assn. (pres. 1979), N.Am. Clin. Dermatologic Soc., Soc. Tropical Dermatology, Med. Assn. Atlanta (bd. dirs. 1985-92, chmn. comm. com. 1985-90, sec. 1988-89, pres.-elect 1989-90, pres. 1990-91), Med. Assn. Ga. (Interspity. Coun. 1984-97, com. on cancer 1988-93, pub. rels. com. 1988-94, del. to Ga. Med. Assn. 1985—, Outstanding Svc. award 1993), Atlanta Clin. Soc., Atlanta Olympic Med. Com. (chmn. dermatology sect. 1996), Emory U. Med. Alumni Assn. (pres. 1980, 86, exec. com. 1992-97), Phi Delta Theta (past pres.), Phi Chi (past pres.), Cherokee Town & Country Club (Atlanta). Home: 2807 Osborne Dr Atlanta GA 30319 Office: 2045 Peachtree St NE Ste 525 Atlanta GA 30309-1414 also: Emory U Sch Medicine Dept Dermatology Atlanta GA 30308

DOBEY, JAMES KENNETH, banker; b. Vallejo, Calif., June 20, 1919; s. Austin E. and Margaret (Hansen) D.; m. Jean Smith, Apr. 18, 1942; children: James A., Peter M. AB, U. Calif., Berkeley, 1940; postgrad., Rutgers U., 1956. With Shell Oil Co., Comml. Credit Corp., 1940-42, Wells Fargo Bank, San Francisco, 1946-72, exec. v.p., 1965-72, vice chmn. bd., 1973, chmn. bd., 1977-80, ret. Capt. airborne inf. AUS, 1942-46. Mem. Delta Chi. Mailing: Carmel Valley Manor 8545 Carmel Valley Rd Carmel CA 93923-9556

DOBIE, JEANNE H. artist; b. Phila., June 1, 1930; d. Aubin Joseph Dobie and Helen F. Kelleher; m. Theodore Andrew Klaus, Dec. 26, 1951; children: Jeanine Marie, Cherie Louise, Michelle Rene, Theodore Andrew, Monique Suzanne. Student, Phila. Mus. Sch. of Art, 1948-51. Faculty Rangemark Masterclass Program, Birch Harbor, Maine, 1973-77, Moore Coll. of Art, Phila., 1979-81; instr. watercolor seminars throughout U.S., Can., Europe, 1977-98; juror of selection Am. Watercolor Soc., N.Y.C., 1986, 2001, juror of awards, 1995; juror selection/awards Frye Mus., Seattle, 1990. Artist adv. bd. Winsor & Newton Art Materials, Piscataway, N.J., 1993-95; juror for nat., regional and state watercolor socs., 1977—. Author/artist: (book) Making Color Sing, 1986; contbr. articles to profl. jours. Named to Pa. Honor Roll of Women, State of Pa., Capitol, Harrisburg, 1996, Achievement in the Arts award Phila. Water Color Club, 1996. Mem. Am. Watercolor Soc. (High Winds medal 1980, Mary S. Litt medal 1985), Nat. Watercolor Soc. (juror of selection, L.A. 1997, Arches award 1981, Daler-Rowney award 1999, award Phila. chpt. exhbn., 2002), Midwest Watercolor Soc. (Am. Acad. of Art award 1985, Dupage Art award 1987, Edgar A. Whitney award 1989, Door County Art award 1992), Phila. Water Color Soc. (pres. Charles Taylor award 1976, Best of Show 1988, Grumbacher Gold medallions 1992, 95), Pa. Watercolor Soc. (Watson-Guptill award). Avocations: travel, designing houses. Home: 160 Hunt Valley Cir Berwyn PA 19312-2302

DOBIE, ROBERT ALAN, otologist; b. Annapolis, Md., July 26, 1945; AB in Biology with great distinction, Stanford U., 1967, MD, 1971. Intern Stanford (Calif.) U. Sch. Medicine, 1971, resident in otolaryngology, 1971-75; asst. prof. dept. otolaryngology-head and neck surgery U. Wash., Seattle, 1975-80, assoc. prof., 1980-85, prof., 1985-90; rsch. fellow in auditory physiology Kresge Hearing Rsch. Lab. La. State U. Med. Ctr., New Orleans, 1977-78; T.W. Folbre prof., chmn. dept. otolaryngology U. Tex. Health Sci. Ctr., San Antonio, 1990-99; dir. divsn. extramural rsch. Nat. Inst. on Deafness and Other Comm. Disorders, NIH, Bethesda, 1999—2002; clin. prof. otolaryngology U. Calif. Davis, Sacramento, 2003—. Vis. prof. otolaryngology Johns Hopkins U., 2000—; attending otolaryngologist Med. Ctr. Hosp. (name now Univ. Hosp.), Audie L. Murphy Meml. Vets. Hosp., San Antonio, 1990-99, NIH Clin. Ctr., 1999-2002, Vets. Affairs Med. Ctr., Washington, 2000-02; dir. Virginia Merrill Bloedel Hearing Rsch. Ctr. U. Wash., 1988-90; rsch. affiliate Child Devel. & Mental Retardation Ctr., 1988-90; cons. in otology Madigan Army Med. Ctr., Tacoma, Wash., 1987-90, Kaiser Aluminum and Chem. Corp., Oakland, Calif., 1976-86; chief otolaryngology svc. VA Med. Ctr., Seattle, 1978-83, 75-77; clin. fellow in otoneurosurgery Univ. Hosp., Zurich, 1983-84; mem. Coun. for Accreditation in Occupl. Hearing Conservation, 1990-99; mem. program adv. com. Nat. Inst. on Deafness and Other Communicative Disorders, 1996-98; bd. dirs. Deafness Rsch. Found., 1991—. Author: Medical-Legal Evaluation of Hearing Loss, 1993, 2d edit., 2001, (with others) Guide for the Evaluation of Hearing Handicap, 1981, Guide for Conservation of Hearing in Noise, 1982; editor: Approach to Swallowing Disorders, 1984; mem. editl. bds. Am. Jour. Otology, Laryngoscope, Otolaryngology-Head and Neck Surgery, Noise and Health; contbr. articles to profl. jours. and chpts. to books. Mem. ACS, AMA, Am. Acad. Otolaryngology-Head and Neck Surgery (chair noise subcom. 1981-87, 95-98), Am. Laryngological, Rhinological and Otological Soc., Am. Otological Soc., Am. Neurotology Soc., Am. Auditory Soc., Collegium Oto-Rhino-Laryngologicum Amicitiae sacrum, Politizer Soc., Assn. for Rsch. in Otolaryngology (pres. 1993-94), Am. Coll. Occupational Medicine, So. Med. Assn. Office: Dept Otolaryngology UC-Davis Ste 7200 2521 Stockton Blvd Sacramento CA 95817 Office Fax: 916-456-7509. E-mail: radobie@ucdavis.edu.

DOBIN, EDWARD I. lawyer; b. Binghamton, N.Y., Jan. 30, 1936; s. David I. and Frances (Lieber) D.; m. Gloria Schreiber, Aug. 16, 1959; children: Marc S., Nanette, Andrea. Student, Cornell U., 1953-54; BS, Franklin & Marshall Coll., 1957; LLB, U. Pa., 1960. Bar: Pa. 1961, U.S. Dist. Ct. (ea. dist.) Pa. 1961, U.S. Ct. Appeals (3d cir.) 1973, U.S. Supreme Ct. 1974. Assoc. Curtin & Heefner LLP, Morrisville, Pa., 1961-66, ptnr., 1967—87, mng. ptnr., 1988-94, ptnr., 1995—2001, of counsel, 2002—. Trustee Adath Israel Congregation, Trenton, N.J., 1972-81; chmn. Mid Atlantic Ter. ARC, Phila., 1988-92, bd. dirs. Lower Bucks chpt., Langhorne, Pa., 1978-2000, pres., 1983-84; bd. dirs. Abrams

Hebrew Acad., Yardley, Pa., 1975—, pres., 1980-84; chmn. Jewish Fedn. of Phila.-Buck Co. div., 1991-93, bd. dirs., 1994—; bd. dirs. Phila. Geriatric Ctr., 1999-2001; trustee Jewish Fedn. Phila., 2001-03. Fellow Am. Bar Found. (life), Pa. Bar Found.; mem. ABA, Pa. Bar Assn., Bucks County Bar Assn. (bd. dirs. 1971-72, treas. 1973-74, pres. 1981-82); mem. Nat. Assn. Bond Lawyers, Pa. Assn. Bond Lawyers (founder, bd. dirs. 1988-93, pres. 1990-91). Jewish. Home: 250 Woodhill Rd Newtown PA 18940-2514 Office: Curtin & Heefner LLP 250 N Pennsylvania Ave Morrisville PA 19067-1104 E-mail: eid@curtinheefner.com., eidd@att.net.

DOBIS, JOAN PAULINE, education administrator; b. S.I., N.Y., Sept. 11, 1944; d. Victor Raymond and Rosanna Elizabeth (Dandignac) Mazza; m. Robert Joseph Dobis, Dec. 21, 1968. BA in History, Notre Dame Coll., S.I., 1966; MS in Advanced Secondary Edn. and Social Studies, Wagner Coll., 1968; profl. diploma in ednl. adminstrn. supervision, Fordham U., 1979, postgrad. Cert. adminstr. and supr. K-12, social studies and math. tchr. K-12, elem., intermediate and jr. high sch. asst. prin., elem., intermediate and junior high sch. prin., N.Y. Tchr. Prall Intermediate Sch., Staten Island, 1966-98, administrv. asst., 1977-82; coord. social studies Dist. 31, Staten Island, NY, 1998—2003; ret., 2003. Mem. S.I. Hist. Soc., 1968-78, Friends of Down's Syndrome Found., S.I., 1978—, Sister Helen Flynn Scholarship Com., S.I., 1981—, Friends Seaview Hosp. and Home, S.I., 1984—, Friends S.I. Coll., 1979—. Recipient St. John's U. Pietas medal, 1991; scholar N.Y. State Bd. Regents, 1962, Can. Consulate St. Lawrence U., 1987, Internat. Brotherhood Teamsters U. Calif., 1988, Nat. Geog. Soc. Geography Edn. Program SUNY, Binghamton, 1989, Women in History Program, N.Y. State Coun. for the Humanities, Albany, 1992, Immigration Program, Bard Coll., 1999; Impact II grantee N.Y.C. Bd. Edn., 1992, 98. Mem. ASCD, Nat. Coun. Social Studies, N.Y. State Coun. Social Studies, N.Y.C. Coun. Social Studies, S.I. Coun. Social Studies, United Fedn. Tchrs., Am. Fedn. Tchrs., N.Y. State Hist. Soc., Notre Dame Coll. Alumnae Assn. (regent 1978-80, pres. 1982-84), St. John's U. Alumni Fedn. (del. 1980-88, sec. exec. bd. 1988-90, chmn. bd. 1990-94), Phi Delta Kappa (co-founder S.I. chpt., pres. 1985-87, other offices, Tchr. of Yr. award Fordham U. 1993, named Disting. Kappan 1994, Tchr. of Yr. award S.I. chpt. 1998, Kappan of Decade, 1999). Republican. Roman Catholic. Home: 174 Bertha Pl Staten Island NY 10301-3807

DOBKIN, ERIC DAVID, critical care surgeon, educator; b. Phila., Dec. 31, 1951; s. Franklin and Ray (Decovny) D.; m. Ceil K. Goldfield, June 7, 1981; children: Michael, Emily, David. BA, Pa. State U., 1973; MD, U. Pa., 1981. Diplomate Am. Bd. Surgery with added qualifications in surg. critical care. Surg. intern, resident U. Tex. Med. Br., Galveston, 1981-85; resident, chief resident in gen. surgery Tex. Tech. U., El Paso, 1985-88; fellow in critical care medicine Hartford (Conn.) Hosp., 1989, dir. surg. ICU, 1998—; dir. surg. critical care Mt. Sinai Hosp., Hartford, 1989-91, St. Francis Hosp. and Med. Ctr., Hartford, Conn., 1991-97; asst. prof. surgery U. Conn., Farmington, 1989-96, assoc. prof., 1996—, assoc. program dir. surg. residency. Fellow: ACS; mem.: ACS Execs., Ea. Assn. Sco. for Trauma, N.Eng. Surg. Soc., Soc. Critical Care Medicine, Assn. Surg. Educators. Office: Hartford Hospital Surg Critical Care 80 Seymour St Hartford CT 06102-8000 E-mail: edobkin@harthosp.org.

DOBLER, DONALD WILLIAM, retired college dean, consultant, corporate executive; b. Rocky Ford, Colo., Apr. 18, 1927; s. William L. and Anna (Nelson) D.; m. Elaine Carlson, Dec. 27, 1951; children: Kathleen, David, Daniel. BS in Engring., Colo State U., 1946-50; MBA, Stanford U., 1958, PhD, 1960. Application and sales engr. Westinghouse Elec. Corp., Pitts. and Phila., 1950-53; mgr. purchasing and materials FMC Corp., Green River, Wyo., 1953-57; guest lectr. Stanford Sch. Bus., 1960; asst. prof. mgmt. State U. Utah, Logan, 1960-63, assoc. prof., 1964-66, head dept. bus. adminstrn., 1964-66; vis. prof. mgmt. Dartmouth Coll., 1963-64; dean Coll. Bus., Colo. State U., Ft. Collins, 1966-86; ind. mgmt. cons. Ft. Collins, 1986-91; corp. v.p. for cert. and program devel. Nat. Assn. Purchasing Mgmt., Tempe, Ariz., 1990-94. Past bd. dirs. U. Nat. Bank, Home Fed. Savs. Bank; pres. Parklane Arms, Inc., 1967-77; part-time mgmt. cons., 1960-86; cons. European Logistics Mgmt. Program, 1970, 72, 77, European Fedn. Purchasing, 1970; faculty Mgmt. Center Netherlands, 1972; dean's adv. coun. logistics mgmt. program Ariz. State U., 1991-94; mem. adv. bd. Mgmt. Inst. U. Wis., 1992-97. Sr. author: Purchasing and Supply Management, 1965, 6th edit., 1996; co-author: The Purchasing Handbook, 1993; mem. editl. bd. European Jour. Purchasing and Supply Mgmt., 1993—; contbr. articles on mgmt. to profl. jours., chpts. to books. Mem. Colo. Gov.'s Adv. Com., 1968-77, Ft. Collins Mayor's Budget Com., 1968-71; dist. chmn. Boy Scouts Am., 1974-77; mem. adv. council Colo. Region, SBA, 1973-79, No. Region, Colo. Div. Employment, 1975-77; bd. dirs., div. chmn. Ft. Collins United Way, 1973-80, pres., 1977; bd. dirs. Ft. Collins Jr. Achievement, 1973-87; bd. dirs. Colo. Assn. Commerce and Industry Ednl. Found., 1988-91. Served with USNR, 1945-46. Mem. Acad. Mgmt., Nat. Assn. Purchasing Mgmt. (Shipman Medalist 1987, chmn. nat. acad. plan com. 1976-81, mem. profl. cert. bd. 1981-86, chmn. 1985-86, assoc. editor Internat. Jour. Purchasing and Materials Mgmt. 1975-80, editor 1980-97), Denver Purchasing Mgmt. Assn. (dir. 1975-83, v.p. 1977, pres. 1979), Am. Prodn. and Inventory Control Soc., Green River Jr. C. of C. (pres. 1955), Am. Assn. Collegiate Schs. Bus. (nat. com. continuing accreditation 1972-78, nat. standards commn. 1978-81, dir. 1980-83, chmn. fin. and audit com. 1983), Sigma Tau, Phi Kappa Phi (editorial cons. Nat. Forum, 1988-94), Rotary, Beta Gamma Sigma (nat. gov. 1975-78) Methodist.

DOBLER, JANIS DOLORES, small business owner; b. Dearborn, Mich., June 7, 1946; d. Ralph Orville and DeLoris (Fredrick) Yager; m. Gordon John Dobler, June 24, 1977; children Curtis John, Kristin Marie. BS, Wayne State U., 1966. Cert. tchr., Mich. Owner, mgr. Mark Travel, Portage, Mich., 1982—. Grad. asst. Dale Carnegie, Kalamazoo, 1982-84. Bd. dirs. Davenport Coll., Kalamazoo, 1985-87. Named tchr. yr. State of Mich, 1965. Mem. Assn. Retail Travel Agts., Airlines Reporting Corp., Internat. Assn. Travel Agts., Cruise Lines Internat. Assn., Travel Savers, Portage C. of C., Nat. Fedn. Indt. Bus., Better Bus. Bur., Jr. Achievement (bd. dirs. 1985-87). Republican. Roman Catholic. Avocations: knitting, reading, watersports, travel, genealogy. Office: The Mark of Travel 1595 West Center Suite 105 Portage MI 49024-3542

DOBOS, ERZSEBET, language educator; b. Budapest, Hungary, Aug. 27, 1951; arrived in U.S., 2001; d. Gyula Dobos and Erzsebet Nemes; m. Istvan Kazsmer, Feb. 27, 1983 (div. Mar. 19, 1999); children: Laura Kazsmer, Fanni Kazsmer. MA in Spanish and Russian Lang. and Lit., U. Elte, Budapest, 1975, PhD in Spanish Lang. and Lit., 1979, MA in Portuguese Lang. and Lit., 1988, PhD in Romance Philology, 1997. Tchr. Hungarian lang. Embassy of Spain, Budapest, 1993—96; instr. Spanish lang. Internat. Bus. Sch., Budapest, 1999, U. Elte, 1999—2000; prof. Budapest Coll. Econs., 1976—2001; lectr. dept. Spanish and Portuguese UCLA, 2001—. Recipient scholarship, Ministry of Edn. Hungary, 1980, 1991, Ministry of Fgn. Affairs of Spain, 1993. Mem.: MLA, Am. Fedn. Tchrs., European Assn. Tchrs. of Spanish, Assn. Modern Philology. Avocations: literature, cinematography, classical music. Office: UCLA Dept Spanish and Portuguese 405 Hilgard Ave Los Angeles CA 90024

DOBOSZ, MARK JOSEPH, fundraiser; b. Detroit, Nov. 23, 1960; s. Richard J. and Aurelia M. (Maciejewski) D.; m. Stephany A. Czech, June 10, 1983; children: Peter, Katie, Tim. BA, St. Mary's Coll., Orchard Lake, Mich., 1982. V.p. Easter Seals S.W. Fla. Mem. Assn. Fundraising Profls. Democrat. Roman Catholic. Avocations: home remodeling, theatrical lights. Home and Office: 4135 Center Gate Blvd Sarasota FL 34233-1520

DOBRANSKI, BERNARD, law educator; b. Sept. 3, 1939; s. Walter John and Helen Dolores (Rudnick) Dobranski; m. Caroll Sue Wood, Aug. 31, 1963; children: Stephanie, Andrea, Christopher. BBA in Fin., U. Notre Dame, 1961; JD, U. Va., 1964. Bar: Va. 64, U.S. Supreme Ct. 68, U.S. Ct. Appeals (DC cir.) 71. Legal advisor to bd. Nat. Labor Rels. Bd., 1964—67; profl. staff mem. Pres.'s Adv. Commn. on Civil Disorders, 1967—68; adminstrv. asst. U.S. Ho. of Reps., 1968—71; gen. counsel Washington Met. Area Transit Commn., 1971—72; mem. faculty Creighton U. Sch. of Law, Omaha, 1972—77, U. Notre Dame, 1977—83; prof., dean U. Detroit Sch. of Law, 1983—95; dean Cath. U. Am. Sch. of Law, 1995—99; pres., dean Ave Maria Sch. of Law, Ann Arbor, Mich., 1999—. Labor arbitrator Fed. Mediation and Conciliation Svc.; active Mich. Commn. on Death and Dying. Contbr. articles to profl. jours. Mem.: ABA, Am. Law Inst., Am. Arbitration Assn., Detroit Athletic Club, Hurlingham Club, Frank Murphy Honor Soc. Roman Catholic. Office: Ave Maria Sch of Law 3475 Plymouth Rd Ann Arbor MI 48105 E-mail: bdobranski@avemarialaw.edu.

DOBRANSKI, STEPHEN BITONTI, literature educator; b. Abington, Pa., Apr. 12, 1966; s. Stephen and Irene Dobranski; m. Shannon Prosser, Mar. 21, 1998. BA with high honors in English Lit., U. Va., 1988; MA in English Lit., U. Tex., 1991, PhD in English Lit., 1996. Asst. prof. Ga. State U., Atlanta, 1996—2002, assoc. prof. dept. English Lit., 2002—. Contbg. editor: Variorum Commentary on the Poems of John Milton, 2000—; author: Milton, Authorship and the Book Trade, 1999—; co-editor: Milton and Heresy, 1998—; co-author: Student Guide to First-Year Writing, 1994—; contbr. Rotary Internat. fellow, 1988—89. Mem.: MLA, Malone Soc., Milton Soc. Am. (exec. com. 2002—, Irene Samuel Meml. award 1999). Office: Georgia State Univ Dept English Atlanta GA 30303

DOBRAY, ALAN MICHAEL, theoretical physicist, research scientist; b. Waukegan, Ill., Aug. 25, 1954; s. Michael Dobray and Ann Davis Ziezel; 1 son, Shane Alan. Mech. engr. Texaco Oil, Lake Forest, Ill., 1975-79; fabricating engr. Connor Gear Machine and Transmission Svcs., Highland Park, Ill., 1983-84; elec. engr. Inland Marine, Waukegan, 1985; theoretical physicist N.Y. Acad. Scis., N.Y.C., 1996—; rsch. scientist AAAS, Washington, 1998—. Mem. Nat. Space Soc., 1996. Co-author: (textbook) Gang Delinquency in an American Suburb, 1983; inventor in field of ice boats. Active Duff Olympics, 1982-83, Silver Moon Blues Oasis, 1995—. Recipient Hon. Mem., MIT Alumni Assn., 1996; scholar Milw. Sch. Engring., 1970. Mem. Union of Concerned Scientists, Planetary Soc., Wilderness Soc., Libr. of Congress. Democrat. Roman Catholic. Achievements include helping solve the telemetry problem for NASA and having name engraved on computer chip used on Cassini space probe to Saturn and all subsequent missions leaving earth's orbit. Avocations: ice sailing, planting trees, playing horse-shoes, drums. Home: N 3325 Jute Rd Lake Geneva WI 53147

DOBREV, STANISLAV, finance educator, researcher; b. Burgas, Bulgaria, Sept. 28, 1968; arrived in U.S., 1991, permanent resident; s. Dimitar D. Dobrev and Velitchka S. Dobreva. BA, SUNY, 1993; MA, Stanford U., Calif., 1995; PhD, Stanford U., 1997. Rsch. fellow Stanford (Calif.) U. Grad. Sch. Bus., 1997—98; asst. prof. Tulane Bus. Sch., New Orleans, 1998—2000; asst. prof. U. Chgo. Grad. Sch. Bus., 2000—. Cpl. Bulgarian Army, 1987—89. Named Jr. scholar, EGOS, 1998. Mem.: Acad. Mgmt., Am. Sociol. Soc. Avocations: music, rollerblading, skiing, theater. Office: Univ Chgo Grad Sch Bus 1101 E 58th St Chicago IL 60637

DOBRIANSKY, LEV EUGENE, economist, educator, diplomat; b. N.Y.C., Nov. 9, 1918; s. John and Eugenia (Greshchuk) D.; m. Julia Kusy, June 29, 1946; children: Larisa Eugenia, Paula Jon. BS (Charles Hayden Meml. scholar), NYU, 1941, MA, 1943, Hirshland polit. sci. fellow, 1943-44, PhD, 1951; LLD, Free Ukrainian U. at U. Munich, Germany, 1952. Faculty NYU, 1942-48; from asst. prof. econs. to prof. Georgetown U., 1948-86; prof. emeritus, 1986—; chmn. dept. Georgetown U., 1953-54; exec. mem. Inst. Ethnic Studies, 1957-65; dir. Inst. Comparative Econ. and Polit. Systems, 1970-86; grad. faculty Nat. War Coll., 1957-58; U.S. ambassador to Bahamas, 1982-86; pres. Global Economic Action Inst., 1987-92; chmn. Victims of Communism Meml. Found., Inc., 1994—. Lectr. on Soviet Union, Communism, U.S. Fgn. Policy; chmn. Nat. Captive Nations Com., Inc., 1959—; pres. Ukrainian Congress Com. Am., 1949-82, Am. Coun. for World Freedom, 1976-79; mem. Economists Nat. Com. on Monetary Policy; strategy staff Am. Security Coun., 1962-70; econs. editor Washington Report; mem. Pres.'s Commn. on Population, 1974-75; cons. Corpus Instrumentation, Kreber Found., Dept. State, 1971-75, USIA, 1971-74; mem. Am. Com. to Aid Katanga Freedom Fighters, Emergency Com. Chinese Refugees; Internat. mem. Pacific Rim Cmty. Inst., 1992-96; hon. pres. Ukrainian Congress com. Am., 1992—. Author: A Philosophico-Economic Critique of Thorstein Veblen, 1943, The Social Philosophical System of Thorstein Veblen, 1950, Free Trade Ideal, 1954, Communist Takeover of Non-Russian Nations in USSR, 1954, Veblenism: A New Critique, 1957, Captive Nations Week Resolution, 1959, Shevchenko Statue Resolution, 1960, Vulnerabilities of USSR, 1963, The Vulnerable Russians, 1967, U.S.A. and the Soviet Myth, 1971; co-author: The Great Pretense, 1956, The Crimes of Khrushchev, 1959, Decisions for a Better America, 1960, Nations, Peoples, and Countries in the USSR, 1964; pub.: Revista Americana, 1977; editor: Europe's Freedom Fighter: Taras Shevchenko, 1960, Tenth Anniversary of the Captive Nations Week Resolution, 1969, The Bicentennial Salute to the Captive Nations, 1977, Twentieth Observance and Anniversary of Captive Nations Week, 1980; assoc. editor: (1946-62) Ukrainian Quar., chmn. editorial bd., 1962-94; contbr.: Peace and Freedom Through Cold War Victory, 1964, Nationalism in the USSR and Eastern Europe, 1977, Ukraine in a Changing World, 1978; contbr. articles to profl. jours. Planning mem. Freedom Studies Center, Boston; asst. sec. Republican Nat. Conv., 1952; adviser Rep. Nat. Com., 1956; mem. Com. on Program and Progress of Rep. Party, 1959; asst. to chmn. Rep. Nat. Conv., 1964; vice chmn. nationalities div. Rep. Nat. Com., 1964; sr. adviser United Citizens for Nixon-Agnew, 1968; exec. mem. ethnic div. Com. to Reelect the Pres., 1972; advisor to Gov. Reagan, 1980; issues dir. Republican Nat. Com., 1980; chmn. Ukrainian Catholic Studies Found., 1970-73; bd. govs. Charles Edison Youth Fund, 1976-87; mem. expert adv. bd. NBC, Washington, 1977-80. chmn. Victims of Communism Meml. Found. Inc. Lt. col. (res.) 352d Mil. Govt. Civil Affairs 1958; col. U.S. Army Res., 1966. Recipient Freedoms Found. award, 1961, 73; Shevchenko Freedom award Shevchenko Meml. Com., 1964; Shevchenko Sci. Soc. medal, 1965; Hungarian Freedom Fighters' Freedom award, 1965; Latvian Pro Merito medal, 1968; Freedom Acad. award Korea, 1969; Wisdom award of honor Calif., 1970; named Outstanding Am. Educator, 1973; decorated M.S.M., 1973; Georgetown U. Centennial medal of honor, 1982; Ellis Island medal of honor, 1986; Thomas C. Corcoran award, 1987. Mem. Free World Forum (exec. com.), Citizens for Democracy, Acad. Polit. Sci., Nat. Acad. Econs. and Polit. Sci., AAUP, Am. Acad. Polit. and Social Sci., Am., Cath. econ. assns., Am. Finance Assn., Nat. Soc. Study Edn., Shevchenko Sci. Soc., U.S. Global Strategy Council, Social List of Washington, Council Am. Ambassadors, NYU Alumni Assn., Georgetown U. Alumni Assn. (hon.), Reagan Alumni Assn., Internat. Cultural Soc. Korea (hon.), Am. Legion, Res. Officers Assn., Nat. War Coll. Alumni Assn., University Club of Washington (hon.), Capitol Hill Club, Internat. Club, Gold Key Soc., Beta Gamma Sigma, Delta Sigma Pi.

DOBRIANSKY, PAULA JON, federal agency administrator; b. Sept. 14; d. Lev Eugene and Julia Kusy Dobriansky. BS summa cum laude, Georgetown U., 1977; MA, Harvard U., 1980, PhD, 1991; LHD, LLD, Flagler Coll., 2003. Adminstrv. aide Dept. Army, Washington, 1973-76; staff asst. Am. Embassy, Rome, 1976; rsch. asst. joint econ. com. U.S. Congress, Washington, 1977-78; NATO analyst Bur. Intelligence and Rsch. Dept. State, Washington, 1979; staff mem. NSC, White House, Washington, 1980-83, dep. dir. European and Soviet affairs, 1983-84, dir. European and Soviet affairs, 1984-87; dep. asst. sec. of state Human Rights and Humanitarian Affairs, 1987-90; dep. head U.S. Del. to Conf. on Security and Cooperation in Europe, Copenhagen, 1990; assoc. dir. for policy and programs U.S. Info. Agy., 1990-93; co-chair internat. TV coun. Corp. Pub. Broadcasting, 1993-94; sr. internat. affairs and trade advisor Hunton and Williams, Washington, 1994-97; sr. v.p., dir. Washington Office Coun. on Fgn. Rels., 1997—2001; under sec. of state for global affairs U.S. State Dept., Washington, 2001—. Commr. U.S. Adv. Commn. on Pub. Diplomacy, 1997-2001; adj. fellow Hudson Inst., 1993-2001. Host: Freedom's Challenge, Nat. Empowerment Television, 1994-96; co-host: Worldwise, 1997. Bd. dirs. Congl. Human Rights Found., 1994-95, Freedom House, 1999-2001, Western NIS Enterprise Fund, 1994-2001, Am. Com. for Aid to Poland, 1994-95, ABA Ctrl./East European Law Initiative, 1994-99; mem. bd. visitors George Mason U., 1994-98; mem. adv. bd. Horton Internat. Inc., 1998-99. Named Ethnic Woman of Yr., 1990; named one of 10 Most Outstanding Young Women in Am., 1982, 10 Outstanding Working Women of 1990; recipient Georgetown U. Alumni Achievement award, 1986, State Dept. Superior Honor award, 1990, Poland's Highest medal of Merit, 1998, Democracy Svc. medal, Nat. Endowment Democracy, 2002, Dialogue on Diversity Internat. award, 2001, Grand Cross of Comdr., Order of Lithuanian Grand Duke Gediminas, 2003; fellow, Rotary Found., 1979, Ford Found., 1980; scholar Fulbright-Hays scholar, 1978. Mem. Internat. Inst. Strategic Studies, Coun. Fgn. Rels., Am. Polit. Sci. Assn., Fulbright Assn., Nat. Endowment for Democracy (bd. dirs. 1993-2001, vice-chmn. 1995-2001), Am. Coun. on Young Polit. Leaders (trustee 1993-2001), U.S. Environ. Tng. Inst. (bd. adv. 1992-93), Harvard Club (bd. dirs. 1982-85), Univ. Club, Phi Beta Kappa, Phi Alpha Theta, Pi Sigma Alpha. Office: US State Dept Washington DC 20520

DOBRICK, JO-ANNE, retail executive, environmentalist, consultant; b. Sept. 19, 1945; d. Nathan Shaye and Lillian (Davis) Shaye-Hirsch; 1 child, Rebecca. Student, Ohio State U., Art Inst. Chgo.; BA, Roosevelt U., 1972. Dir. Dobrick Gallery, Chgo., 1974-84; exec. search, 1984-86; cons. Laventhol & Horwath, Chgo., 1986-90; sales and mktg. Splty. Advt., 1992-97; cons. EPA and SCAA, Washington, 1997-98; CEO Basket Classics, Chgo., 1997—; pres. Comfort Kollection, 1999—. V.p. Indsl. Water, Waste and Sewage Group, Chgo., 1988—90; assoc. bd. dirs. Film Festival, Chgo.; spl. edn. tchr. F.A.C.E. program Chgo. Pub. Sch., 2003. Bd. dirs. Steppenwolf Theatre, Chgo., 1986—91; chair auction Sta. WTTW, Chgo., 1976. Home: 2128 N Bissell St Chicago IL 60614-4202 E-mail: Jodo19@RCN.com.

DOBRIN, SHELDON L. architect; b. Chgo., June 2, 1945; s. Max and Sophie (Schuman) D.; m. Marlene K. Smith, Jan. 26, 1969; children: Stefanie, Jonathan. BArch, Ill. Inst. Tech., 1969, BS, 1970. Registered architect, Ill., Ind., Mich., Wis., Mo., Pa. Architect Form Assocs., Chgo., 1969; tchr. Chgo. Bd. Edn., 1969-72; architect Robert L. Friedman & Assocs., Ltd., Chgo., 1972-78; v.p. Robert L. Friedman, Chgo., 1978-84; prin. Friedman, Dobrin and Assocs., Northbrook, Ill., 1984-90; pres. Dobrin Assocs., Ltd., Lincolnshire, Ill., 1991—. Contbr. articles to profl. jours. Docent Chgo. Archtl. Found., 1971-78; caucus bd. Highland Park Sch. Dist., 1988; mem. Highland Park Historic Preservation Commn., 1988-96; active Highland Park Design Rev. Com., 1999—, vice-chmn., 2000, chmn., 2001-03. Recipient Spl. Recognition for Archtl. Design awards, 1985, 1988, 1989, 2001. Mem. AIA (Chgo. chpt. voting del. convs. 1985, 88, 89, com. chair 1993 conv.), Bldg. Ofcls. and Code Adminstrs. Internat., Nat. Coun. Archtl. Registration Bds. (cert.), Art Inst. Chgo., Alpha Epsilon Pi. Avocations: bicycling, travel. Office: Dobrin Assocs Ltd Ste 140 75 Tri-State Internat Lincolnshire IL 60069 E-mail: sdobrin@dobrin.com.

DOBRINSKY, HERBERT COLMAN, university administrator; b. Montreal, Quebec, Can., Apr. 6, 1933; came to U.S., 1962; s. Victor and Lillian D.; m. Dina Loebenberg, Dec., 1954; children— Deborah Kramer, Tova Cohen, Aaron David. B.A., Yeshiva U., 1954, M.S. in Edn., 1959, D. in Edn., 1980; Semikha (rabbinic ordination), Rabbi Isaac Elchanan Theological Sem., Yeshiva U., 1957. Rabbi, Beth Israel Synagogue, Halifax, N.S., Can., 1958-62; assoc dir. div. communal services Yeshiva U., N.Y.C., 1962-73, dir. rabbinic placement, 1964-73, dir. Sephardic community activities program div. of communal service, 1964-80, exec. asst. to pres., 1973-80, v.p. univ. affairs, 1980— . Author: A Treasury of Sephardic Laws and Customs, 1986. Office: Yeshiva U Univ Affairs 500 W 185th St New York NY 10033-3299

DOBRINSKY, SUSAN ELIZABETH, human resources director; b. Warren, N.J., Sept. 25, 1943; d. Samuel Henry Jr. and Janet Adeline (Ryder) Christie; m. Stanley Dobrinsky, Feb. 12, 1972; children: David Stanley, Mark Alan. BA, Lycoming Coll., 1965. Cert. for Sr. Execs., John F. Kennedy Sch. of Govt. of Harvard U., 1994, PHR Cert. by SHRM, Profl. in Human Resources, 1997-2003. Pers. asst. County of Somerset, Somerville, N.J., 1970-74, pers. mgr., 1974-82, pers. dir., 1982-90, dir. adminstrn., 1991-95, dir. human resources, 1995—. Gov. apptd. Pub. Employees Occupl. Safety and Health Adv. Bd., Dept. of Labor, Trenton, N.J., 1984—; bd. trustees, treas. N.J. Pub. Employer Labor Rels. Assn., Somerville, N.J., 1993—; mem. Soc. Human Resource Mgmt. Cen. Jersey, Somerset, 1978—; pres. Comty. Indsl. Rels. Orgn., Somerset, 1990-92; apptd. senate pres., mem. Pension Commn., Trenton, 1992-2001. Mem., dep. mayor Green Brook Twp. Commn., 1987-88, mayor, 1989-92; v.p. Somerset County Governing Offcls., 1990, pres., 1991; mem. Somerset County Mcpl. Com., 1999-01, 2002—; sec. Rep. Club, Green Brook, 1977; mem. staff parish com. Meth. Ch. Recipient N.J. Alumni award 4-H Youth Devel. Program, 1992. Mem. Nat. Pub. Employer's Labor Rels. Assn., N.J. Pub. Employer Labor Rels. Assn. (bd. trustees, treas. 1993—), Soc. Human Resource Mgmt., Ctrl. N.J. Soc. Human Resource Mgmt., Internat. Personnel Mgmt. Assn., N.J. Pension and Health Commn., Cmty. Indsl. Rels. Orgn. (treas. 1988-90, pres. 1990-92), Pub. Pers. Orgn. (pres. 1990—), DAR (Elizabeth Snyder chpt. regent 1998-99, 2001-2003), County Com. Republican. Methodist. Avocations: skiing, genealogy, reading, crafts. Home: 11 Glenn Ave Green Brook NJ 08812-2431 Office: County of Somerset 20 Grove St Somerville NJ 08876-2306

DOBRITT, DENNIS WILLIAM, physician, researcher, pain management specialist; b. Detroit, July 13, 1953; s. Walter Peter and Catherine Janet (Aiuto) D.; m. Kitty Louise Burros, June 21, 1980; children: Carol Ann, Julie Marie, Diane Elizabeth. BS magna cum laude, Western Mich. U., 1975; DO, Phila. Coll. Osteo. Medicine, 1981. Diplomate Nat. Bd. Osteo. Examiners, in anesthesiology and in pain mgmt. Am. Bd. Anesthesiology, Am. Bd. Pain Medicine. Intern Garden City (Mich.) Hosp., 1981-82, emergency physician, 1982-83, McPherson Hosp., Howell, Mich., 1983-84; resident physician Providence Hosp., Southfield, Mich., 1983-85, fellow, 1985-86, chief resident, 1985, attending physician, 1986—, Botsford Hosp., Farmington Hills, Mich., 1986-87; asst. clin. prof. coll. osteopathic medicine Mich. State U., East Lansing, 1987—. Dir. Botsford Ctr. for Pain Control, Farmington Hills, 1986—87, Farmbrook Pain Control Ctr., Southfield, 1987—96; chief pain medicine Providence Hosp., 1994—98; dir. pain mgmt. ctr., 1996—2001. Editor newsletter Osteo. Pain Mgmt. News, 1987-88; guest editor Mich. Osteo. Jour., 1987-88; contbr. articles to profl. jours. Mem. adv. com. on pain and symptom mgmt. State of Mich., chmn. subcom. on profl. stds. for pain and symptom mgmt. Mem.: AMA, Internat. Soc. Study of Pain, Am. Pain Soc., Internat. Anesthesiology Rsch. Soc., Mich. Soc. Interventional Pain Physicians (exec. dir.), Am. Soc. Anesthesiology, Am. Osteo. Assn. Roman Catholic. Avocations: computers, reading, basketball, waterskiing, softball. Office: Tri-County Pain Cons PC 30055 Northwestern Hwy Ste L-50 Farmington Hills MI 48334

DOBROW, ROBERT PAUL, statistician, educator; b. Boston, Mass., Dec. 13, 1952; s. George and Dorothy Dobrow; m. Angela Lynn Parker, June 28, 1984; children: Joseph Benjamin Parker, Daniel Alexander, Thomas Michael. PhD, Johns Hopkins U., 1994. APL computer cons., New York City, NY, 1980—90; rsch. fellow NIST, Gaithersburg, Md., 1994—95; asst. prof. Truman State U., Kirksville, Mo., 1995—99, Clarkson U., Potsdam, NY, 1999—2001, Carleton Coll., Northfield, Minn., 2001—. Consulting Rider, Bennett, Egan and Arundel, LLP, Mpls., 2002; cons. Round Table Group, Inc., Chgo., 2002. Contbr. articles to profl. jours. Mem.: Math. Assn. Am., Inst. Math. Stats., Am. Statis. Assn. Office: Carleton College 1 North College St Northfield MN 55057 Office Fax: 507-646-4312. E-mail: rdobrow@carleton.edu.

DOBRZANSKI, SLAWOMIR, music educator; arrived in U.S., 1992; s. Joseph and Ewa Dobrzanski; 1 child, Angelina Sophie Dominici. MusM, Chopin Acad. Music, Warsaw, 1991; D in Musical Arts, U. Conn., 2001. Asst. prof. piano Concordia Coll., Moorhead, Minn., 2002—. Vis. artist Nat. Conservatory Music, Lima, Peru, 2000. Mem.: Polish Inst. Arts and Scis. Am., Music Tchrs. Nat. Assn., Coll. Music Soc., Chopin Soc. Conn. (pres. 1998—2001). Avocations: travel, languages, enviroment.

DOBRZYN, JANET ELAINE, quality management professional; b. Allentown, Pa., Oct. 9, 1956; d. Frank John and Doris (Ross) D. Diploma, Pottsville Hosp. Sch. Nursing, 1977; AA, L.A. Valley Coll., 1984; BSN, Calif. State Coll., Long Beach, 1985; MSN, Azusa (Calif.) Pacific U., 1991. RN, Calif., Okla., Pa., Ky., Ga.; cert. profl. healthcare quality. Charge nurse evenings Allentown (Pa.) Osteo. hosp., 1977-80; charge nurse relief Encino (Calif.) Hosp., 1980-81; registry nurse Profl. Staffing, Northridge, Calif., 1981-82; clin. nurse II pediatric ICU Childrens Hosp. of L.A., 1982-86, clin. info. specialist, 1986-89; quality mgmt. specialist PacifiCare of Calif., Cypress, 1989-91, quality mgmt. spl. projects coord., 1991-92; mgr. quality mgmt. PacifiCare of Okla., Tulsa, 1992-93, sr. project specialist quality mgmt., 1993-95; accreditation facilitator Humana, Louisville, 1995-96; mgr. quality mgmt. Healthwise of Ky., Lexington, 1996-97; mgr. nat. Medicare med. svcs. Prudential Healthcare, Atlanta, 1997-2000; med. affairs assoc. UCB Pharma, Smyrna, Ga., 2000—02; dir. Ctr. for Quality Cobb and Douglas Bds. of Health, 2002—. Adj. faculty Sch. Nursing U. Louisville; guest lectr. Spaulding U.; cons., reviewer of prototype pub. Commerce Clearing House, Inc., Riverwoods, Ill., 1993; mem. ANA/GHAA task force to develop nursing curriculum in managed care for nursing students, 1994; speaker in field. Camp nurse vol. Forest Home Conf.

Ctr., San Bernardino, Calif., 1988; mem. orch. Johnson Ferry Bapt. Ch. Mem. Am. Assn. Managed Care Nurses, Nat. Assn. for Healthcare Quality, Nat. Assn., Prolife Nurses Assn., Sigma Theta Tau (newsletter editor). Republican. Avocations: reading, travel, walking, swimming, videos. Home: 889 Lake Hollow Blvd SW Marietta GA 30064 E-mail: jedobrzyn@gdph.state.ga.us, changeagent1@juno.com.

DOBRZYNSKI, JUDITH HELEN, journalist, commentator; b. Rochester, N.Y., Mar. 8, 1949; d. Francis Anthony and Theresa (Contino) Dobrzynski. BS cum laude, Syracuse U., 1971. Corr. McGraw-Hill, San Francisco and N.Y.C., 1971—75, Bus. Week, Washington, 1976—79, London, 1979—83, corp. strategies editor, assoc. editor N.Y.C., 1983—88, sr. writer, 1988—91, sr. editor, 1991—94; bus. reporter N.Y. Times, N.Y.C., 1995—97, culture reporter, 1997—2000, dep. bus. editor and editor Sunday Money and Bus. sect., 2000—03; mng. editor CNBC, Ft. Lee, NY, 2003—. Adj. instr. Columbia U. Sch. Journalism, 2002; mem. New Founds. Corp. Governance Group Harvard U., Boston, 1992—95; adv. panel Corp. Investment Project U.S. Coun. on Competitiveness, Washington, 1990—92. Contbr. Trustee CEC Internat. Ptnrs., N.Y.C., 1993—96; bd. dirs. City Lights Youth Theatre, N.Y.C., 1994—96. Named Knight Found. fellow, Salzburg Seminar, 2002. Mem.: Syracuse U. Newhouse Sch. Alumni Assn. (bd. dirs. 1991—94, pres. 1992—93), Century Assn. Office: CNBC 2200 Fletcher Ave Fort Lee NJ 07024

DOBSON, BRIDGET MCCOLL HURSLEY, television executive and writer; b. Milw., Sept. 1, 1938; d. Franklin McColl and Doris (Berger) Hursley; m. Jerome John Dobson, June 16, 1961; children: Mary McColl, Andrew Carmichael. BA, Stanford U., 1960, MA, 1964; CBA, Harvard U., 1961. Assoc. writer General Hospital ABC-TV, 1965-73, head writer General Hospital, 1973-75; producer Friendly Road Sta. KIXE-TV, Redding, Calif., 1972; head writer Guiding Light CBS-TV, 1975-80, head writer As the World Turns, 1980-83; creator, co-owner Santa Barbara NBC-TV, 1983—, head writer Santa Barbara, 1983-86, 91, exec. producer Santa Barbara, 1986-87, 91, creative prodn. exec. Santa Barbara, 1990-91; pres. Dobson Global Entertainment, L.A., 1994—. Bd. dirs. Emory U. Carlos Mus.; bd. advisors Atlanta Internat. Sch., 1997-2000. Author, co-lyricist: Slings and Eros, 1993; prodr. Confessions of a Nightingale, 1994; exhibited in gallery show acrylic paintings Swan Coach House, Atlanta, 1997, exhibited oil paintings Raymond Lawrence Gallery, Atlanta, 1999, Fay Gold Gallery, Atlanta, 1999, Tippy Stern Fine Art, Charleston, S.C., 2002; one-woman shows include Mus. S.W., Midland, Tex., 2001, Midwest Mus. Am. Art, Elkhart, Ind., 2001, Charles Allis Art Mus., Milw., 2001, Albrecht-Kemper Mus. Art, St. Joseph, Mo., 2001, Walter Wickiser Gallery, N.Y.C., 2001, Danville (Va.) Mus. Fine Art, 2002, Burroughs-Chapin Art Mus., Myrtle Beach, S.C., 2002, Tippy Stern Fine Art, 2002, Anderson (Ind.) Fine Art Ctr., 2002, Ella Sharp Mus., Jackson, Miss., 2002. Bd. dirs. Carlos Mus., 1998-2001. Walter Wickiser Gallery, N.Y.C., 2003. Recipient Emmy award, 1988. Mem. Nat. Acad. TV Arts and Scis. (com. on substance abuse 1986-88), Writers Guild Am. (award for Guiding Light 1977, for Santa Barbara 1991), Am. Film Inst. (mem. TV com. 1986-88). Office: PO Box 52813 Atlanta GA 30355-0813

DOBSON, CARL WILHELM, education educator; b. Nuremburg, Germany, Jan. 6, 1958; arrived in U.S., 1959; s. Charles William and Stella Flora (Smith) Dobson. BS in Polit. Sci., Charleston So. U., 1981; postgrad., U. N.C., MA in History, 1986; AAS in Paralegal Studies, Cecils Coll., 1989; MDiv, Erskine Sem., 2001; postgrad., U. N.C., 2001—. Instr. Cecils Jr. Coll., Asheville, NC, 1990—98, Shaw U., 2003. Author of poems. Republican. Presbyterian. Home: 16 Graystone Rd Asheville NC 28804-1320 Office: Shaw U 31 Coll Pl Asheville NC 28801

DOBSON, CHRISTOPHER CALVIN, physicist; b. Johnson City, Tenn., Aug. 19, 1955; s. Wayne Wilson and Annette Maude (Shepard) D.; m. Teresa Gaye Lee, 1978 (div. Aug. 1980). BS in Physics, East Tenn. State U., 1983; MS in Physics, U. Tenn., 1987; PhD in Physics, U. Ala., 1998. Musician, Ind. and Tenn., 1977-83; rsch. asst. Space Inst. U. Tenn., Tullahoma, 1984-87, physicist, 1988, NASA/Marshall Space Flight Ctr., Huntsville, Ala., 1989—. Contbr. articles to profl. jours. including Jour. Optical Soc. Am., Phys. Rev. A., Applied Optics. Vol. Big Bros./Big Sisters Ala., Huntsville, 1998—. Mem. AAAS, Nat. Space Soc. Avocations: music, tennis, reading, movies. Home: 29919 Orville Smith Rd Harvest AL 35749-6807 Office: NASA Marshall Space Flight Ctr Mail Stop TD40A Huntsville AL 35812

DOBSON, DONALD ALFRED, retired electrical engineer; b. Evanston, Ill., Feb. 19, 1928; s. Alfred Topping and Agnes Lucille (Park) D. BSEE, Northwestern U., 1950, PhD, 1955; MSEE, MIT, 1951. Research assoc. Northwestern U., Evanston, 1951-54; engr. Indsl. Research Products, Franklin Park, Ill., 1952; sr. engr. Sperry Gyroscope Co., Great Neck, N.Y., 1954-59; sr. tech. specialist N.Am. Aviation, Columbus, Ohio, 1959-63; research staff mem. Inst. for Def. Analyses, Arlington, Va., 1963-90, adj. staff mem., 1990-98, ret., 1998. Instr. physics Adelphi Coll., Garden City, N.Y., 1956 Mem. IEEE, Sigma Xi, Tau Beta Pi, Eta Kappa Mu, Pi Mu Epsilon Home: 6800 Fleetwood Rd Apt 420 Mc Lean VA 22101-3607

DOBSON, EDWARD TAUSCHER, mathematician; b. Athens, Ga., Aug. 20, 1965; s. Gerard Ramsden and Kay Ann Tauscher Dobson; m. Susan Deborah Cook, July 16, 1994; children: Beatrice Rose Cook children: Magdalen Ruth Cook. BS, U. North Tex., 1983, MA, 1989; PhD, La. State U., Baton Rouge, 1995. Vis. scholar U. Cambridge, England, 1991—94; instr. La. State U., Baton Rouge, 1995—97; vis. asst. prof. Okla. State U., Stillwater, 1997—98; assoc. prof. Miss. State U., Mississippi State, 1998—. Contbr. articles to profl. jours. Home: 2009 Buckner St Starkville MS 39759 Office: Dept Math and Stats Miss State U Mississippi State MS 39762 Office Fax: 662-325-0005. E-mail: dobson@math.msstate.edu.

DOBSON, F. STEPHEN, ecologist; b. Oakland, Calif., Aug. 21, 1949; s. Stuart Cromar and Beverly (Richardson) D.; m. Julia Dee Kjelgaard, Feb. 14, 1982. AB in Biology, U. Calif., Berkeley, 1975; MA in Biology, U. Calif., Santa Barbara, 1978; PhD in Biology, U. Mich., 1984. NATO postdoctoral fellow U. Alberta, Edmonton, Can., 1984-85; rsch. assoc. U. Lethbridge, Alta., 1986; vis. curator U. Mich., Ann Arbor, 1987-88; asst. prof. Auburn U., Ala., 1988-94, assoc. prof., 1994—99, prof., 1999—. Prof. invité U. Paris, 1995, 2000-02, chevalier dans l'Order des Palmes Academiques, 2002—. Contbr. articles to profl. jours. Oak Ridge Inst. for Sci. and Edn. fellow, 1995; NSF Rsch. grantee, 1990-92, 2001-, Nat. Geographic Soc. rsch. grantee, 1992, The Ctr. for Field Rsch. rsch. grantee, 1990; recipient Post Rouge award Ctr. Nat. Rsch. Sci., France, 1997, 2001. Mem. Am. Soc. Naturalists, Animal Behavior Soc., Ecological Soc. Am. (bd. editors 2002—), Soc. for the Study Evolution. Home: 612 Samford Ave Auburn AL 36830-7410 Office: Auburn U Dept Biol Scis Auburn AL 36349

DOBSON, JOHN, finance educator; b. Whitstable, Eng., Dec. 9, 1957; arrived in U.S.A., 1979; s. Peter and Nancy Straker Dobson; m. Sharon Lynn Stalcup, Aug. 2, 1987. BA in Econs., Lancaster U., 1979; MA in Econs., U. S.C., 1981, PhD, 1988. Asst. prof. U. Miss., 1988—90; assoc. prof. Calif. Poly., San Luis Obispo, 1990—. Author: (book) Finance Ethics, 1997, The Art of Management, 1999. Mem.: Soc. Bus. Ethics, Fin. Mgmt. Assn. Office: Coll of Bus Calif Poly State Univ San Luis Obispo CA 93407 E-mail: jdobson@calpoly.edu.

DOBSON, RICHARD LAWRENCE, dermatologist, educator; b. Boston, Apr. 12, 1928; s. Joseph William and Celia Beatrice (Siegler) D.; m. Marie C. Mollomo, Aug. 19, 1950; children: Richard Lawrence, Pamela Blair, Lisa Marie. MD, U. Chgo., 1953; BS, U. N.H., 1981. Diplomate Am. Bd. Dermatology (v.p. 1987-88, pres. 1988-89). Intern Cin. Gen. Hosp., 1953-54; resident Hitchcock Clinic, Hanover, N.H., 1954-57; asst. prof. dermatology U. N.C., Chapel Hill, 1957-61; prof. U. Oreg., Portland, 1961-72, SUNY-Buffalo, 1972-79, Med. U. S.C., Charleston, 1980-98, acting dean, 1985-86, chmn. dept. anatomy and cell biology, 1991-92, prof. emeritus, 1998—. Vis. prof. U. Nijmegen, The Netherlands, 1969-70; hon. prof. Shanghai 2d Med. U.; hon. cons. Royal Prince Alfred Hosp., Sydney, Australia. Editor: Year Book of Dermatology, 1979-82, Clinical Dermatology, 1972-82, Contemporary Review, 1973-87; asst. editor: Jour. Am. Acad. Dermatology, 1979-87, editor, 1988-98; mng. editor Arch. Dermatol. Research, 1982-87 . Served with USN, 1946-47. Fellow ACP, Am. Acad. Dermatology (pres. 1983-84); mem. Am. Dermatologic Assn. (treas. 1977-82), Soc. Investigative Dermatology (pres. 1975-76), Oreg. Dermatol. Soc. (pres. 1971-72); hon. mem. Brit. Assn. Dermatology, Spanish Assn. Dermatology, French Dermatology Soc., Polish Dermatology Soc., Finnish Dermatology Soc., Dutch Dermatology Soc., German Dermatology Soc., N.Am. Dermatology Soc., Ga. Dermatology Soc., Iowa Dermatology Soc., Snee Farm Club. Republican. Roman Catholic. Home: 1429 Wittenberg Dr Mount Pleasant SC 29464 Office: Med U SC 171 Ashley Ave Charleston SC 29425-0001

DOBSON, ROBERT ALBERTUS, III, lawyer, executive, volunteer; b. Greenville, S.C., Nov. 27, 1938; s. Robert A. Jr. and Dorothy (Leonard) D.; m. Linda Josephine Bryant, Nov. 18, 1956; children: Robert, William, Michael, Daniel, Jonathan, Laura (dec.); m. Catherine Elizabeth Cornmesser, Sept. 17, 1983; children: Andrew, Thomas, Juana. BS in Acctg. summa cum laude, U. S.C., 1960, JD magna cum laude, 1962; DPS, Limestone Coll., 2002. Asst. dean of students U. S.C., 1960-62; pvt. practice pub. acctg. Greenville, 1962-64; ptnr. Dobson & Dobson, Greenville, 1964-93. Chmn., bd. trustees Limestone Coll., 1987-89, founder Christian edn. and leadership program; trustee The King's Coll., 2003—. Contbr. articles on tax and acctg. to profl. jours. Lay minister St. Francis Episcopal Ch., Greenville; chmn. bd. Dobson Tape Ministry, Homeless Children Internat., Inc.; bd. dirs. A Child's Haven, Inc.; v. chmn. Walker Found. for the S.C. Sch. for the Multihandicapped, Deaf and Blind, Spartanburg, S.C.; mem. adv. bd. Salvation Army, Greenville; chmn. bd. Sch. Ministries, Inc.; mem. History's Handful Campus Crusade for Christ; founder Dobson Vol. Svc. Program, U. S.C. Mem. ABA, S.C. Bar Assn., AICPAs, Am. Assn. Attys. and CPAs, S.C. Assn. Pub. Accts., Block C Assn. The Group, U. S.C. Alumni Assn. (cir. v.p.), Kappa Sigma (chmn. legal com. 1989-93, dist. grand master 1971—, Nat. Dist. Grand Master of the Yr. 1986, John G. Tower Disting. Alumni award 1997, Stephen Alonzo Jackson award 1998), Phi Beta Kappa. Lodges: Sertoma Internat. (dist. treas.), Sertoma Sunrisers (pres. Greenville club). Episcopalian. Home: 1207 Pelham Rd Greenville SC 29615-3643 Office: 1306 S Church St Greenville SC 29605-3814

DOBSON, WENDY KATHLEEN, economics educator; BSN, U. B.C., 1963; MPA, Harvard U., 1971, SM, 1972; PhD in Econs., Princeton U., 1979. Pres. C.D. Howe Inst., Toronto, 1981-87; assoc. dep. minister Dept. Fin., Govt. of Can., Ottawa, Ont., 1987-89; prof., dir. Inst. for Internat. Bus. Rotman Sch. Mgmt., U. Toronto, 1993—. Bd. dirs. Toronto-Dominion Bank, TransCan. Pipelines, MDS Inc., DuPont Can. Inc., Can. Pub. Accountability Bd.; steering com. Pacific Trade Devel. Network; adv. com. Inst. Internat. Econs., Washington; mem. Trilateral Commn. Author: Shaping the Future of North American Economic Space: A Framework for Action, 2002, Japan in East Asia: Trade and Investment Strategies, 1993, Multinationals and East Asian Integration, 1997 (Ohira prize 1998), Financial Services Liberalization in the WTO, 1998, (chpts.) Bretton Woods: Looking to the Future, 1994, A Part of the Peace, 1994, Trade Technology and Economics: Essays in Honour of Richard G. Lipsey, 1997, Fifty Years After Bretton Woods: The Future of the IMF and the World Bank, 1995, The Growing Importance of the Asia Pacific Region in the World Economy: Implications for Canada, 1997, Trade Technology and Economics, 1997, Whither APEC?, 1997, Prisoners of the Past: Canada's Policy Framework for the Financial Services Sector, 1999; co-editor: Shaping Comparative Advantage, 1987, East Asian Capitalism: Diversity and Dynamism, 1996, Managing U.S. Japanese Trade Disputes, 1996, The People Link, 1997, Fiscal Framework and Financial Systems in East Asia, 1998, East Asia in Transition, 1999; contbr. articles to profl. jours. Office: Rotman Sch Mgmt U Toronto 105 St George St Toronto ON M5S 3E6 Canada Business E-Mail: dobson@rotman.utoronto.ca.

DOBY, JOHN THOMAS, social psychologist; b. Gray, Ky., May 29, 1920; s. Daniel W. and Minnie (Farris) D.; m. Rose Catherine Hopper Doby, Dec. 21, 1942; children: Mary Catherine, Nancy H. AB cum laude, Union Coll., Barbourville, Ky., 1946; MS, U. Wis., 1950; PhD, 1956. Assoc. prof., prof. Sociology and Anthropology Wofford Coll., Spartanburg, S.C., 1950-57; assoc. prof. Sociology and Anthropology Emory U., Atlanta, 1958-63, prof., 1963-85, chmn. Dept. Sociology and Anthropology, 1960-69, chmn. Dept. Sociology, 1980-85, prof. emeritus of Sociology, 1985; cons. Engring. Ga. Inst. Tech., Atlanta, 1960-62; cons. Ednl. Testing Svc., Princeton, N.J., 1969; mem. faculty Grad. Sch. Consumer Banking U. Va., summer 1972-75. Vis. scientist lectr. NSF Am. Sociological Assn., 1965-66; chair Tech. Scientific Adv. Com. on Mental Retardation, Ga. Dept. Health, 1965-66; dir. NSF Summer Inst. for Coll. Tchrs. of Sociology, Emory U., 1965-66; mem. NSF fellowship panel Nat. Acad. Sci., adv. com. Divsn. Mental health, Ga. Dept. Health, 1966-72, Sci. faculty Panel Am. Coun. Learned Soc., Nat. Sci. Postdoctoral Panel, 1976-77; pres. So. Sociological Soc., 1969-70; chair Com. on Undergraduate Curriculum and teaching, Am. Sociological Assn., 1968-70; dir. Nat. Sci. Found. Emory U., 1970-71, program on skill conversion tng. of aerospace engrs., 1970-71. Author: Introduction to Social Research, 1954, Introduction to Social Psychology, 1966, Introduction to Social Research, 1967; editor, author: Sociology: A Study of Man in Adaptation, 1973; contbr. articles to profl. jours., chpt. to Science, Mind, and Psychology, 1989. Maj. USAF, 1941-46. Grantee NIMH, 1960, NSF, 1964, 65, 71, Office of Econ. Opportunity, 1966-67, Nat. Inst. Child Health and Human Devel., 1979-80. Methodist. Home: 473 Ky-1629 Corbin KY 40701-9469

DOBY, MARGARET GAIL, interior designer; b. Iowa City, Aug. 15, 1955; d. George William and Gertrude Estelle (Hiser) Smiley; m. Harry Glore Doby, May 4, 1991. BSBA in Fin. and Mktg., U. Ark., 1977; postgrad., U. Houston 1980-81; AAS in Interior Design, Arapahoe C.C., Denver, 1994. Mktg. rep. Armstrong World Industries, Oklahoma City, 1977-79, sr. mktg. rep. Houston, 1979-83; comml. mgr. Adleta Corp., Dallas, 1983-87; pres., prin. designer Network Design, Dallas, 1987-89; dir. mktg. Coral Pacific, Denver, 1989-92; pres., prin. designer Renaissance Design, Inc., Denver, 1992—. Contbr. Bd. dirs. Children's Diabetes Found., 1996—99; v.p. devel. Families First, Inc., Denver, 1996—97, co-chair fall fundraiser, 1997, pres.-elect, 1998—99, pres., 1999—2000; mem. Gathering Pl., 1995—2000, Vols. Am. Named Outstanding Friend New Vol., Families First, Inc., 1996; recipient Friend of the Children award, Families First, 2003. Mem.: Home Builders Assn. (profl. remodelers coun.), Nat. Assn. Remodeling Inst. (1st pl. Specialty Remodel 1997, Spl. Recognition Kitchen Remodel 1997), Nat. Kitchen and Bath Assn. (Friend of the Children award 2003), Denver Ctr. of Performing Arts, Daughters of Denver, Ballet Guild (life), Gathering Place, Met. Club, Cancer League, Phi Theta Kappa. Republican. Presbyterian. Avocations: travel, bicycling, reading, entertaining.

DOBYNS, BROWN MCILVAINE, surgeon, educator; b. Jacksonville, Ill., May 14, 1913; s. Henry D. and Leah (McIlvaine) D.; married; children— Mary Meredith, Courtney Sara, Brown McIlvaine. BA, Ill. Coll., 1935; MD, Johns Hopkins, 1939; MS, U. Minn., 1944, PhD, 1946. Diplomate: Am. Bd. Surgery. Intern surgery Johns Hopkins Hosp., 1939-40; fellow surgery Mayo Found., 1940-43; resident surgery Kahler Hosp., Mayo Clinic, 1943-45, 1st asst. surgery, 1945-46, asst. surg. staff, 1946; research fellow surgery, med. sch. Harvard, 1946-48, asst. prof. surgery, 1948-51; grad. asst. surgery Mass. Gen. Hosp., 1946-48, asst. surgery, 1946-51; assoc. prof. surgery Case Western Res. U. Med. Sch., 1951-58, prof. surgery, 1958—88, prof. emeritus, 1984—88. Asst. chief surg. service Cleve. Met. Gen. Hosp., 1951-88, assoc. chief surg. service, 1967-88; asst. surgeon Univ. Hosp., Cleve., 1951-88; Fulbright lectr., Australia, 1966. Mem. fellowship subcom. Com. on Growth NRC, 1950-54; mem. fellowship com. NSF, 1954-61, chmn., 1955-61; adv. screening com. med. scis. Fulbright, 1955-58; adv. com. research on etiology cancer Am. Cancer Soc., 1956-59, chmn. adv. com. on instnl. grants, 1963-65; mem. Dernham Scholarship com. Calif. Cancer Soc., 1964-74; cons. Markle Found. Selection Com., 1961-62. Recipient Van Meter prize, 1946, award of merit, 1954, Disting. Service award, 1978; all Am. Thyroid Assn.; citation for disting. public service Ill. Coll.; elected to Cleve. Med. Hall of Fame, 1997. Fellow ACS; mem. AAAS, Soc. Univ. Surgeons, Am. Soc. Clin. Investigation, Am. Surg. Assn., Ctrl. Surg. Assn., Am. Thyroid Assn. (pres. 1956-57), Cleve. Surg. Soc. (pres. 1966-67), Halstead Soc., Société Internationale de Chirurgie, Endocrine Soc., Sigma Xi. Home: 9930 Kirtland Rd Chardon OH 44024-9746 *Try to have a new experience every day.*

DOBYNS, WILLIAM B. human geneticist, pediatrician, neurologist; b. Columbus, Ohio, June 9, 1952; BS with distinction, U. Mich., 1974; MD, Mayo Med. Sch., 1978. Resident in pediatrics Gundersen Clinic and Luth. Hosp., LaCrosse, Wis., 1978-80; fellow in pediatric neurology Baylor Coll.Medicine, Houston, 1980-83; fellow in med. genetics Mayo Grad. Sch. Medicine, Rochester, Minn., 1983-85; asst. prof. neurology and pediatrics Med. Coll. Wis., Milw., 1985-89; assoc. prof. neurology Ind. U. Sch. Medicine, Indpls., 1989-92, assoc. prof. med. genetics, 1989-92; asoc. prof. neurology U. Minn. Med. Sch., 1992-93, assoc. prof. neurology and pediatrics, 1993-99; prof. human genetics, neurology and pediatrics U. Chgo., 1999—. Office: U Chgo Dept Human Genetics CLSC 319C 920 E 58th St Chicago IL 60637-1474 E-mail: wbd@genetics.bsd.uchicago.edu.

DOCARMO, JERRY SOARES, academic administrator; b. Sao Paulo, Sao Paulo, Brazil, Aug. 15, 1967; s. Benedito Do Carmo, Marina Soares Docarmo; m. Ana Oliveira Docarmo; children: Andrew children: Kevin. BA in Mgmt., Hamilton U., 2000, M in Mgmt., 2002. Dir. internat. fair preparation The Chinese Porcelain Co., N.Y.C., 1995—96; travel dir. Ark Travel Corp, Parsippany, NJ, 1996—98; v.p. Am. English Ctr., Newark, 1997—99; pres., CEO Harvest Inst., Newark, 1999—. Cons. Welb Franshising, Sao Jose dos Campos, Sao Paulo, Brazil, 1999—. Contbr. Recipient Outstanding Svc. to Cmty. award, Civil Svc. Leader Newspaper, 1999, 2000, 2001, 2002. Avocations: travel, reading. Office: Harvest Inst 128 Wilson Ave Newark NJ 07105 Office Fax: 973-274-0339. Business E-Mail: harvest@harvestinstitute.net.

DOCKENDORFF, ROBERT LAWRENCE, computer graphics designer; b. Bronx, N.Y., May 19, 1930; s. Lawrence Christian and Madeline (Krollmann) D.; m. Geraldine Neyens, Oct. 10, 1954 (div. Aug. 1978); m. Kathleen Rose McGlynn, July 27, 1980. Student, Pratt Inst., Bklyn., 1949-51, Cornell U., 1955-56. Tech. illustrator GE Advanced Electronics Ctr., Ithaca, N.Y., 1956-65; indsl.-graphics designer Electronics Lab. GE, Syracuse, N.Y., 1965-69; human factors designer GE Genigraphics, Syracuse, 1969-77, cons. trainer, 1975-79; pres., cons. DK: Assocs., Syracuse, 1979, Basking Ridge, N.J., 1979-80, Sparta, N.J., 1980-85; pres., chief exec. officer Computer Arts, Inc., Sparta, 1985-1992. Cons. Aetna Ins. Co., Hartford, Conn., 1979-85; cons., trainer Digital Equipment Corp., Bedford, Mass., 1979-85, Exxon Rsch., Houston, 1979-85, Nat. Security Agy., Ft. Meade, Md., 1979-84. Author, designer: (trade periodical) Police Vehicle Concept, 1969; author: (tng. course) Genigraphics System, 1971-74, (trade periodical) History-Genigraphics Devel., 1987. Chmn. publicity com. United Fund, Ithaca, 1963-65. Staff sgt. USAF, 1951-55, Korea.Chmn. local road commn., 1993-1996. Local v.p. mktg. and comm. Am. Cancer Soc., 1993-1995. Dir./Advisor Morongo Basin Shack Attack program, 1996—. Advisor Homestead Valley Pk. & Recreation, 1997—; dir. Basin Wide Found., 2001—. Recipient Computer Graphics Pioneer award Computer Graphics Pioneers, Chatsworth, Calif., 1988. Mem.: Homestead Valley Cmty. Coun. (pres. 1997—2002). Republican. Avocations: camping, marksmanship, motorcycling, woodworking. Home: 159 Geronimo Trl Yucca Valley CA 92284-1491

DOCKERY, J. LEE, retired medical school administrator; b. Amity, Ark., 1932; MD, U. Ark., 1957. Rotating intern Jackson Meml. Hosp., Miami, Fla., 1957—58, active attending staff, 1963—75; resident in ob-gyn. U. Miami, 1958—61; active staff Doctor's Hosp. Miami, 1963—75; active staff, chmn. dept. ob-gyn. Bapt. Hosp. Miami, 1972—73; staff Shands Hosp., Gainesville, Fla., 1975—91; prof. ob-gyn. U. Fla., Gainesville, 1980—92, assoc. dean, 1980—86, exec. assoc. dean, 1986—88, interim dean, assoc. v.p. clin. affairs, 1988—91; exec. v.p. Am. Bd. Med. Specialties, 1991—97. Clin. adj. prof. dept. ob-gyn. Northwestern U. Med. Sch., 1992—; clin. prof. dept. ob-gyn. U. Fla. Coll. Medicine, 1992—2000, prof. emeritus, 2000—; mem. Accreditation Coun. for Grad. Med. Edn., 1984—89, Liaison Com. for Med. Edn., 1989—91, Fla. Bd. Medicine, 1988—92; mem. exam. bd. Fed. State Med. Bds., 1991—94; mem. U.S. Med. Licensing Exam. Composite Com., 1996—2002, Nat. Com. on Fgn. Med. Edn. and Accreditation, 2001—. Mem.: AMA (mem. coun. med. edn. 1983—92, chmn. 1987—88), Fla. Med. Assn. (pres. 1983—84), So. Med. Assn. (pres. 1987—88), Alpha Omega Alpha.

DOCKERY-SCHILLIG, LINDA, writer; b. Louisville, Sept. 23, 1952; d. Willie Dockery and Minnie Cotton; m. Roger Lee Schillig. Freelance consulting tchr., Louisville, 1975—2002. Author: Distant Drums, 1997 (Can.n Fiction award, 1997), Three Little Words, 2002 (Adcott Publishing award Fiction, 2002), Anna Claus (The Woman Behind the Legend), 2003, Cowgirl UP, 2003, An Angel for Christmas, 2003, North Pole Kitchen, 2003, (screenplays) My Special Angel, 1977, Wilderness Love, 1976 (Lippincott award for most promising new screenplay, 1976), Inherit the Devil, 1978 (Sun Burst award Best Screenplay, 1978), Rain Softly Till Then, 1984, (TV series) A Time for Love, 1981, singer country music. Recipient Faith and Love award Best Christian Short Story, 1980, Golden pen, 1991, Marshal award Poetry, 1992. Mem.: American Film Inst., Ind. Film Inst., Nat. Hist. Soc., Women Writing the West, Women's Writers Guild. Home and Office: 11117 E Old 56 Scottsburg IN 47170 Personal E-mail: dockery002@aol.com.

DOCKHAM-LEONG, SONDRA MARGUERITE, social worker; b. Paris, Tex., Nov. 28, 1942; d. George Frederick and Marguerite Agnes (Ingalls) Cuthrell; m. Rodney Koon Ho Leong, July 4, 1990; children: Gregory Kent Dockham, Glen Charles Dockham. BA, Tex. Christian U., 1965; MSW, U. Hawaii, 1974. Cert. clin. social worker. Social worker Dept. Social Svcs. of Hawaii, Honolulu, 1975-78, Residential Treatment for Youth, Honolulu, 1978-79; coord. Victim Witness Prosecutor's Office, Honolulu, 1980-82; psychiat. social worker Kalihi Palama Mental Health, Honolulu, 1982-87; pvt. practice clin. social work, 1983—2001; acting head Children's Team Diamond Head Mental Health, Honolulu, 1989, clin. social worker, 1986-89, Family Advocacy Tripler Army Med. Ctr., Honolulu, 1989-90; clin. supr. Fleet & Family Support Ctr. Pearl Harbor, Honolulu, 1990—. Instr. MSW program social work U. Hawaii, 1996—2002. Columnist: The Honolulu Advertiser, 1995—2000. Bd. dirs. Neighborhood Bd. 5, Diamond Head area, Honolulu, 1989-91; bd. dirs. Diamond Head Area Bd. Mental Health, 1988-89. Mem. NASW (v.p. Hawaii chpt. 1973—), Alumnae and Friends Sch. Social Workers (bd. dirs. 1973—). Home: 3772 Diamond Head Cir Honolulu HI 96815-4424 E-mail: sondra.dockham-leong@navy.mil.

DOCKHORN, ROBERT JOHN, physician, educator; b. Goodland, Kans., Oct. 9, 1934; s. Charles George and Dorotha Mae (Horton) D.; m. Beverly Ann Wilke, June 15, 1957; children: David, Douglas, Deborah. AB, U. Kans., 1956, MD, 1960. Diplomate Am. Bd. Pediat. Intern Naval Hosp., San Diego, 1960-61, resident in pediat. Oakland, Calif., 1963-65; resident in pediat. allergy and immunology U. Kans. Med. Ctr., 1967-69, adj. asst. prof. pediat., 1969—; resident in pediat. allergy and immunology Children's Mercy Hosp., Kansas City, Mo., 1967-69, chief divsn., 1969-83, practice medicine specializing in allergy and immunology Prairie Village, Kans., 1969-94, U. Mo. Med. Sch., Prairie Village, Kans., 1969-94; pres. Internat. Med. Tech. Cons., Inc., Kansas City, 1979—; with D&B Med. Consulting, LLC, Overland Park, Kans., 1999—. Pres. I.M.T.C.I. (Internat. Med. Tech. Cons., Inc.), Kansas City, 1979-99; founder, CEO Internat. Med. Tech. Cons., Inc., Lenexa, Kans., subs. Immuno-Allergy Tech. Cons., Inc., Clin. Rsch. Cons., Inc. Contbr. articles to med. jours.; co-editor: Allergy and Immunology in Children, 1973. Fellow Am. Acad. Pediatrics, Am. Coll. Allergists (bd. regents 1976—, v.p. 1978-79, pres. 1981-82), Am. Assn. Cert. Allergists (pres. 1991—), Am. Acad. Allergy; mem. AMA, Kans. Med. Soc., Johnson County Med. Soc., Kans. Allergy Soc. (pres. 1976-77), Mo. Allergy Soc. (sec. 1975-76), Joint Coun. Socio-Econs. of Allergy (bd. dirs. 1976—, pres. 1978-79). Home: 8510 Delmar Ln Shawnee Mission KS 66207-1926 Office: D&B Med Consulting LLC 8220 Travis St Ste 101 Overland Park KS 66204-3963 Fax: 913-649-0464.

DOCKING, THOMAS ROBERT, lawyer, former state lieutenant governor; b. Lawrence, Kans., Aug. 10, 1954; s. Robert Blackwell and Meredith (Gear) D.; m. Jill Sadowsky, June 18, 1977; children: Brian Thomas, Margery Meredith BS, U. Kans., 1976, MBA, JD, 1980. Bar: Kans. 1980. Assoc. Regan & McGannon, Wichita, Kans., 1980-82, ptnr., 1983-90, Ayesh, Docking, Herd & Theis, Wichita, 1990, Morris, Laing, Evans, Brock & Kennedy, Wichita, 1990—; lt. gov. State of Kans., Topeka, 1983-87. Dem. nominee for Gov. of Kans., 1986; chmn. adv. bd. Docking Inst. Pub. Affairs, Ft. Hays State U. Mem. steering com. Campaign Kans.; chmn. campaign com. Coll. Liberal Arts and Sci., 1988-91; bd. dirs. Kans. Easter Seals-Goodwill Industries, 1987-93, chmn. 1989 Telethon, vice-chair, 1991-93; bd. dirs. Wichita Conv. and Visitors Bur., 1988-2002; chmn., bd. dirs. St. Francis Found., 1988-94; trustee Emporia State U. Sch. Bus.; chmn. Wichita Water Conservation Task Force, 1991—; mem. Wichita/Brookes Water Task Force, 1997; chmn. allocation com. United Way of

the Plains, 2003; mem. bd. govs. U. Kans. Sch. Law, 1998—2000; bd. dirs. Wichita Downtown Devel. Corp., 2001—, bd. Fin. Fitness Found., 1999—. Recipient Bob Brock award, Kansas City Dem. Party, 2003. Mem. ABA, Kans. Bar Assn., Pi Sigma Alpha, Beta Gamma Sigma, Beta Theta Pi. Presbyterian. Home: 125 S Crestway St Wichita KS 67218-1309 Office: Morris Laing Evans Brock & Kennedy 200 W Douglas Ave Fl 4 Wichita KS 67202-3013

DOCKINS, GEORGE JOEL, retired insurance and securities company executive; b. Jefferson County, Ala., May 21, 1920; s. Daniel C. Davenport and Maggie Ophelia (McCay) D.; m. Sarah Marise Nelson, July 4, 1942; children: Linda Kay, Sandra Elizabeth, Deborah Marise. Student, Jacksonville State Tchrs. Coll, 1938-40. Instrumentman E.I. duPont de Nemours & Co., Childersburg, Ala., 1941-43; inspector Bell Aircraft Corp., Marietta, Ga., 1943-45; party chief Merrit & Welker Engring. Co., Marietta, 1945-46; vets. coord. Birmingham (Ala.) Bd. Edn., 1946-47; salesman Mut. Benefit Life Ins. Co., Birmingham, 1947-52; brokerage mgr., mgr. Occidental Life Ins. Co., Birmingham, 1952-57; co. officer, supt. agys. State Mut. Life Ins. Co., Worcester, Mass., 1957-74, gen. agt. Mobile, Ala., 1975-80; owner The Dockins Agy., Mobile, 1981-98; ret., 1998. Mem. Brandywine Condo. Assn. (bd. dirs. 2000, 01—). Democrat. Methodist. Avocations: bridge, tennis, physical workouts. Home: 1215 Medinah Dr Fort Myers FL 33919-7310 E-mail: iam81goingon29@msn.com.

DOCKSEY, JOHN ROSS, lawyer; b. Milw., Sept. 4, 1951; s. John Warren and Marilyn Ruth (Skinner) D.; m. D. Christine Bjorum, May 21, 1988; children: John Thomas, Adam Christopher. BS, U.S. Mil. Acad., 1973; JD, U. Minn., 1981. Bar: Ill. 1981, U.S. Dist. Ct. (no. dist.) Ill. 1981. Assoc. Sonnenschein Nath & Rosenthal, Chgo., 1981-88, ptnr., 1988—, chmn. corp. practice group, 1998—2002; chmn. tech. and outsourcing group Lex Mundi internat. assn. law firms. Bd. dirs. Daubert Industries, Oak Brook, Ill., Gullikson Found., Chgo., United Svcs. Orgn. of Ill., Chgo.; chmn. tech. and outsourcing group Lex Mundi, 2003—. Contbr. articles to profl. jours. Capt. U.S. Army, 1973-78. Mem. Met. Club, West Point Soc. Chgo. (v.p. 1984-86), Royal Melbourne Country Club, Human Resoures Outsourcing Assn. Avocations: skiing, family, golf. Office: Sonnenschein Nath & Rosenthal 8000 Sears Tower Chicago IL 60606 E-mail: jdocksey@sonnenschein.com.

DOCKSTADER, EMMETT STANLEY, engineer, construction executive; b. Elmira, N.Y., Nov. 7, 1923; s. Roy S. and Gertrude (Everts) D.; m. Ruth Norma Emery, May 11, 1946 (dec.); children: Deborah Ruth, David Stanley; m. Muriel Thomas Fearnot, Oct. 31, 1999. BCE cum laude, Syracuse U., 1947. Registered profl. engr. R.I., Pa., W.Va., Ga., N.C. Engr. Am. Bridge Co., Elmira, 1948-50; field engr. Sessinghaus & Ostergaard, Inc., Erie, Pa., 1950-53; project mgr., 1953-58; v.p., 1958-69; sr. v.p., sec., 1972-79; pres., 1984-86; gen. mgr. constrn. divsn. H.H. Roberston Co., Ambridge, 1969-71; constrn. exec. Gilbane Bldg. Co., Providence, R.I., 1979-84; pres. Dockstader Constrn. Assocs., 1986—. Dir. Erie Constrn. Coun.; mem. Erie Port Commn., 1967—69; chmn. N.W. Pa. Rail Authority; mem. Erie City Wter Authority. Dir. Erie Civic Music Assn.; trustee Ch. of the Covenant. Inductee Hall of Achievement, Thomas A. Edison H.S. Alumni Assn., 2000. Mem. Nat. Soc. Profl. Engrs. (life), Am. Arbitration Assn. (arbitrator), Soc. Profls. in Dispute Resolution, Nat. Railway Hist. Soc. (bd. dirs. Lakeshore chpt.), Erie Mannerchor (life), SAR, The Pa. Soc., Masons (32nd degree), Rotary (Paul Harris fellow), Erie Yacht Club, Y Mens Club (past pres.), Tau Beta Pi. Office: 125 Lincoln Ave Erie PA 16505-2441

DOCKSTADER, JACK LEE, retired electronics executive; b. LA, Dec. 14, 1936; s. George Earl and Grace Orine (Travers) D.; m. Kerry Jo King, Oct. 24, 1987; children: Travis Adam King, Bridget Olivia Mayer. Student, UCLA, 1960-70. Rate analyst Rate Bur. So. Pacific Co., L.A., 1954-57; traffic analyst traffic dept. Hughes Aircraft Co., Fullerton, Calif., 1957-58, Culver City, Calif., 1958-59; traffic mgr. Hughes Rsch. Labs., Malibu, Calif., 1959-70, material mgr., 1970-75, Hughes Aircraft Co., Culver City, 1975-80; prodn. material mgr. Electro-Optical and Data Sys. Group, El Segundo, Calif., 1980-84, mgr. material total quality, 1984-85, mgr. cen. material ops. and property mgmt., 1987-88, mgr. group property mgmt., 1988-93, mgr. electro optical sys., property mgmt., aerospace/def., 1993, ret., 1993. Adv. coun. transp. mgmt. profl. designation program UCLA, 1966-80, mem. Design for Sharing Com., 1977-82; adv. com. transp. program LA Trade Tech. Coll., 1970-80; vol. USN Ret. Activities Office, Seal Beach, Calif., 1995—; mem. Friends of Phineas Banning Mus., Wilmington, Calif., 1996-2002; apptd. sec. Navy's Retiree Coun., 2000-02. With USNR, 1954-96, ret., 1996. Mem. Nat. Property Mgmt. Assn. (pres. LA chpt. 1992-93), UCLA Alumni Assn., Nat. Contracts Mgmt. Assn., Naval Enlisted Res. Assn., Hughes Aircraft Co. Mgmt. Club, Hughes Aircraft Retirees Assn., Sec. of the Navy's Retiree Coun., Delta Nu Alpha (pres. San Fernando Valley chpt. 1965-66, v.p. Pacific S.W. region 1969-71, regional man of yr. 1971). Presbyterian. Home: PO Box 3156 Redondo Beach CA 90277-1156 E-mail: jkdocks@gte.net.

DOCKSTEADER, KAREN KEMP, marketing professional; b. Salisbury, Md., Feb. 11, 1953; d. Robert George and Laverne (Briggs) Kemp; m. Gerald Hugh Docksteader, Apr. 3, 1997; children from previous marriage: Daniel Richard Arrington IV, James William Arrington. BS, Iowa State U., 1975; MEd, Salisbury U., 1979. Dir. horticultural project Chesapeake Rehab. Ctr., Easton, Md., 1975-76; mgr. greenhouses Bountiful Ridge Nurseries, Inc., Princess Anne, Md., 1976-77; instr. horticulture Dorchester Bd. Edn., Cambridge, Md., 1978-80, Fredrick (Md.) Bd. Edn., 1980-87; instr. agronomy Frederick C.C., 1985; treas. Kemp's Ltd., Inc., Martinsburg, W.Va., 1985-87, pres. Frederick, 1987—2001; mgr. U.S. retail sales Kord Products, Ltd., Brampton, 1995-98; sales and mktg. dir. Angelica Nurseries, Inc., Kennedyville, Md., 2001—. Keynote spkr. Vocat. Counseling Orgn., Md., 1980—88; cons. retail and comml. mktg. groups, 1977—91; dir. Russian-Georgian Rose Project, Tblissi, Georgia, 1993. Editor: (newsletter) The Spreader, 1990; featured narrator : (documentaries) Our Land, Our Future, 1980; exhibitor Assn. Nurserymen, Balt. and King of Prussia, Pa., 1986—2003. Coach 4-H, FFA, NJHA, and other youth orgns., 1977—98; state chair Soil Conservation Poster Competition, Md., 1990—91; judge horticulture county fairs, state and nat. 4-H and FFA activities, 1977—91; co-founder Windows of Oppotunity Found., 2000—. Named Conservation Tchr. of the Yr., State Soil and Water Conservation Svc., 1984. Mem.: DAR, Somerset Pa. Hist. Soc., Hackers Creek Hist. Soc., Md. Hist. Soc., New Market Grange, Md. Greenhouse Growers Assn. Avocations: geneaology and historical research, writing, needlepoint, gardening. Office: Kemp's Ltd Inc 26875 Mallard Rd Chestertown MD 21620 E-mail: dock5153@earthlink.net., kkemp@angelica.psemail.com.

DOCKTERMAN, MICHAEL, lawyer; b. Davenport, Iowa, Dec. 14, 1954; s. Jerome and Elaine (Epstein) D.; m. Laura Di Giantonio, Sept. 25, 1983; 1 child, Eliana. BA, Yale U., 1975; JD, Duke U., 1978. Bar: Ill. 1978, US Dist. Ct. (no. dist.) Ill. 1978, US Dist. Ct. (ea. dist.) Mich. 1986, US Dist. Ct. (ctrl. dist.) Ill. 1988, US Dist. Ct. (so. dist.) Ill. 1991, US Dist Ct. (we. dist.) Mich. 1995, US Dist. Ct. (ea. dist.) Mo. 1996, US Ct. Appeals (7th cir.) 1978, US Ct. Appeals (4th, 6th and fed. cir.) 1990, US Ct. Appeals (2d cir.) 1993, US Supreme Ct. 1992. Ptnr. Wildman, Harrold, Allen and Dixon, Chgo., 1978—. Co-author: IICLE Class Actions, 1986, 92, 2000; contbg. author: ABA Criminal Antitrust Litigation Manual; contbr. articles to profl. jours. Active Chgo. Vol. Legal Svc., 1983—, The Chgo. Com., Chgo. Coun. on Fgn. Rels., Am. Refugee Com.; adult bd. dir. Greater Midwest region B'nai B'rith Youth Orgn., 1985—; bd. dir. KAM Isaiah Israel Congregation, 1993-96, 2002—; bd. dir. Duke Law Alumni Assn., 1994-2003, pres., 2000-02; bd. of visitors, 2003-; trustee Max and Gretel Janowski Fund, Chgo., 1992-99. Recipient Award for Advocacy Internat. Acad. Trial Lawyers, Charles A. Dukes award for vol. svc., Leadership Devel. award B'nai B'rith Youth Orgn., Fellow Pvt. Adjudication Found., Am. Bar Found.; mem. ABA (chair corp. governance subcom. Corp. Counsel com. Bus. Law Sect.), Chgo. Bar Assn., Lawyers Club Chgo., B'nai B'rith Justice Lodge. Office: Wildman Harrold Allen Dixon 225 W Wacker Dr Chicago IL 60606-1229 E-mail: dockterm@wildmanharrold.com.

DOCTER, CHARLES ALFRED, lawyer, former state legislator; b. Hamburg, Germany, Aug. 5, 1931; s. Alfred Joseph and Annie Beatrice D.; m. Marcia Kaplan, Nov. 27, 1958; children: Henry David Will, Michael Warren, Adina Jo. BA magna cum laude, Kenyon Coll., 1953; JD, U. Chgo., 1956. Bar: D.C. 1959, Md. 1962, U.S. Supreme Ct. 1959. Former aide to late Sen. Paul H. Douglas, U.S. Senate, Washington; practice law, specializing in bankruptcy and reorgn., Washington, 1959—; sr. ptnr. Docter, Docter, Lynn, P.C., Washington, 1967—. Presdl. appointee to bd. Pa. Ave. Devel. Corp., 1995-96; pres. Montgomery County (Md.) Com. for Fair Representation, 1962-65. Pres. Western Suburban Democratic Club, 1965-66; mem. Md. Ho. of Dels., 1967-78; serving variously as chmn. Montgomery and Prince George's counties Bi-County Dels.; bd. dirs. Met. Washington Coun. Govts., 1970, Downtown D.C. Bus. Improvement Dist., 1997—; chmn. Downtown Housing Now Com., 1997—; D.C. adv. neighborhood commr. for Dist. 6C 09, 2003—. Lt. USNR, 1956-59. Fellow Am. Coll. Bankruptcy, Walter Chandler Am. Inn of Ct. (master emeritus). Achievements include sponsoring Md. tenants' rights laws, Md. Pub. campaign financing law, Md. revolving credit law and other consumer measures. Home: 1101 Market Sq W 801 Pennsylvania Ave NW Washington DC 20004-2615 Office: Docter Docter & Lynn PC 666 11th St NW Ste 1010 Washington DC 20001-4525 E-mail: ddl@bankruptcy-docter.com.

DOCTOR, KENNETH JAY, publishing executive; b. L.A., Jan. 5, 1950; s. Joseph and Ruth (Kazdoy) D.; m. Katherine Conant Francis, June 14, 1971; children: Jenika, Joseph, Katy. BA in Sociology, U. Calif., Santa Cruz, 1971; MS in Journalism, U. Oreg., 1979. Editor, pub. Willamette Valley Observer, Eugene, Oreg., 1975-82; mng. editor Oreg. Mag., Portland, 1982-84; mng. editor, features Boulder (Colo.) Daily Camera, 1984-86; assoc. editor, features St. Paul Pioneer Press, 1986-90, mng. editor, features, 1990-94, mng. editor, 1994-97; v.p. editl. Knight Ridder New Media, San Jose, Calif., 1997-99; v.p. strategy Knight-Ridder.com., 1999-2001; v.p. content svcs. Knight-Ridder Digital, 2001—. Chair Knight-Ridder Task Force on Family Readers, Miami, Fla., 1991, Knight-Ridder mgmt. devel. program, Harvard U., 1993. Exec. v.p. Alumni Assn. U. Calif., Santa Cruz. Recipient Achievement award Oreg. Civil Liberties Union, Eugene, 1982. Mem. Soc. Newspaper Design, Am. Soc. Newspaper Editors. Avocations: baseball, travel. Office: Knight Ridder Digital 35 S Market St San Jose CA 95113 E-mail: kdoctor@pacbell.net.

DODD, CHRISTOPHER J. senator; b. Willimantic, Conn., May 27, 1944; s. Thomas J. and Grace (Murphy) D. BA in English Lit., Providence Coll., 1966; JD, U. Louisville, 1972. Bar: Conn. 1973. Vol. Peace Corps, Dominican Republic, 1966-68; atty. Suisman, Shapiro, Wool & Brennan, New London, Conn., 1973-74; mem. 94th-96th Congresses from 2d Conn. Dist., 1975-80; sen. from Conn. U.S. Senate, Washington, 1980—, mem. fgn. rels., banking, housing & urban affairs coms., rules com., 1981—, mem. subcom. edn., arts & humanities, founder & co-chmn. Senate Children's Caucus, 1983—, ranking mem. Western Hemisphere subcom., mem. subcom. children & families, labor com., randing mem. subcom. securities, banking com. Chmn. Dem. Nat. Com.; mem. Whitewater com. Served with AUS, 1969-75. Recipient Hubert H. Humphrey Pub. Svc. award, Outstanding U.S. Senator award, Nathan Davis award AMA, Head Start Senator of Decade award. Democrat. Roman Catholic. Office: US Senate 448 Russell Senate Bldg Washington DC 20510-0001*

DODD, DARLENE MAE, nurse, retired air force officer; b. Dowagiac, Mich., Oct. 11, 1935; d. Charles B. and Lila H. Dodd. Diploma in nursing, Borgess Hosp. Sch. Nursing, Kalamazoo, 1957; grad., USAF Flight Nurse Course, 1959, USAF Squadron Officers Sch., 1963, Air Command and Staff Coll., 1973; BS in Psychology and Gen. Studies, postgrad., So. Oreg. State Coll., 1987. Commd. 2d lt. USAF, 1959, advanced through grades to lt. col., 1975, staff nurse, 1959-60, Ladd AFB, Alaska, 1960-62, Selfridge AFB, Mich., 1962-63, Cam Rahn Bay Air Base, Vietnam, 1966-67, Seymour Johnson AFB, N.C., 1967-69, USAF Acad., Colorado Springs, Colo., 1971-72; flight nurse 22d Aeromed. Evacuation, Tenn., 1963-66; chief nure USAF, Danang Air Base, Vietnam, 1968, flight nurse Yokota AFB, Japan, 1969-71, clin. coord. ob-gyn., flight nurse Elmendorf AFB, Alaska, 1973-76; clin. nurse coord. ob-gyn. and pediatric svcs. USAF Med. Ctr., Keesler AFB, Miss., 1976-79; ret., 1979; with Bear Creek Corp., Medford, Oreg. Decorated Bronze Star. Mem. DAV, VFW, Am. Legion (life), Soc. Ret. Air Force Nurses, Ret. Officers Assn., Vietnam Vets. Am., Uniformed Svcs. Disabled Retirees, Air Force Assn., Women of Moose, Psi Chi, Phi Kappa Phi. Home: 712 1st St Phoenix OR 97535-9787

DODD, JACK GORDON, JR., physicist, educator; b. Spokane, Wash., June 19, 1926; s. Jack Gordon and Mary Ida (Stuart) D.; m. Mary Ann Howell, June 11, 1951; children— Jeffrey John, Laura Jean. Student, State Coll. Wash., 1946-48; BS in Physics, Ill. Inst. Tech., 1951; MS in Physics, U. Ark , 1957, PhD in Physics, 1965. With Argonne (Ill.) Nat. Lab., 1951-53; tchr. Fourche Valley High Sch., 1953-55, 56-57; asst. prof. Drury Coll., 1957-60; assoc. prof. Ark. Poly. Coll., 1960-65, U. Tenn., Knoxville, 1965-69; Charles A. Dana prof. physics and astronomy Colgate U., Hamilton, N.Y., 1969-87, ret., 1988; v.p. Spectrum Sq., Ithaca, N.Y., 1987—; bd. trustees McCrone Rsch. Inst., Chgo., 1999—. Cons. on phys. optics, microscopy, detonation theory, spectral and image data processing Served with USN, 1944-46. Mem. Am. Assn. Physics Tchrs., Am. Phys. Soc., Am. Astron. Soc., Optical Soc. Am., Sigma Xi. Office: 213 Sears Pond Rd Sherburne NY 13460-5018 E-mail: jackdodd@clarityconnect.com.

DODD, JAMES B. internet executive; BA in Econs., Stanford U.; MBA, Harvard U. CPA. With Sprint; pres., CEO Nat. Info. Consortium Inc., Overland Park, Kans. Office: National Info Consortium Inc 12 Corporate Woods 10975 Benson St Ste 390 Overland Park KS 66210-2120

DODD, JERRY LEE, lawyer; b. Bakersfield, Calif., Nov. 16, 1953; s. James Luther and Juanita Louise (Holmes) D.; m. Phena Fite, Jan. 9, 1972; children: Jody, Kimberly, Kristy, Julie, Timothy, Andrew, Matthew, Lindsey, Allison, Daniel. BS magna cum laude, U. Ark., 1975; MBA, Monmouth Coll., 1978; JD, Rutgers U., 1979. Bar: N.J. 1979, Pa. 1983, Minn. 1988; CPA. Commd. 2d. lt. USAF, 1975, advanced through grades to capt., auditor A.F. Audit Agy., 1975-78, base counsel Alexandria, La., 1979-81, def. counsel, 1981-82, contract trial atty. A.F. Contract Law Ctr. Dayton, Ohio, 1982-86, ret., 1986; govt. contracts counsel U.S. Army 7th Signal Command, Ft. Richie, Md., 1986-87; group counsel Honeywell, Mpls., 1987-90; divsn. counsel Harsco-BMY Wheeled Vehicles Divsn., Marysville, Ohio, 1990—. Mem.: ABA (com. mem.), Ark. Soc. CPAs, Ohio Bar Assn. (com. mem.), Assn. Corp. Counsels Am. (bd. dirs.). Home: 700 Kirkpatrick Rd Malvern AR 72104 Office: Harsco BMY Wheeled Vehicles 700 Kirkpatrick Rd Malvern AR 72104 E-mail: jerryleedodd@yahoo.com.

DODD, JOE DAVID, safety engineer, consultant, administrator; b. Walnut Grove, Mo., Jan. 22, 1920; s. Marshall Hill and Pearl (Combs) D.; m. Nona Bell Junkins, Sept. 17, 1919; 1 child, Linda Kay Dodd Craig. Student, S.W. Mo. State U., 1937-39, Washington U., St. Louis, 1947-55. Cert. profl. safety engr., Calif. Office asst. retail credit co., Kansas City, Mo., 1939-42; bus driver City of Springfield, Mo., 1945-47; varous ops., engring. and pers. positions Shell Oil Co., Wood River (Ill.) Refiney, 1947-66; mgr. health and safety dept. Martinez (Calif.) Mfg. Complex, 1966-83; ret., 1983. Exec. dir. Fire Protection Tng. Acad., U. Nev., Reno; rep. Shell Oil Co., Western Oil and Gas Assn., 1970-81. Mem. Rep. Presdl. Task Force. With USMC, 1942-45. Mem. Western Oil and Gas Assn. (Hose Handler award 1972-81, Outstanding Mem. award), Am. Soc. Safety Engrs., Vets. Safety, State and County Fire Chiefs Assn., Peace Officers Assn., Natr. Fire Protection Assn. Presbyterian (elder). Established Fire Protection Tnng. Acad., Stead Campus, U. Nev., Reno.

DODD, JOHN ROBERT, non-profit organization administrator; b. Dallas, Oct. 15, 1951; s. Carlos Lestor and Betty (Ayers) D.; m. Mary Teresa Parsons, Nov. 12, 1983; children: Katherine Howard, Mary Alexandra. BA, Coll. William and Mary, 1975; MA, U. N.C., 1980. Tchr. Cinnaminson (N.J.) H.S., 1975-78; grad. asst. U. N.C., Chapel Hill, 1978-80; PAC coord. Nat. Congl. Club, Raleigh, N.C., 1981-82; v.p. Coalition for Freedom, Raleigh, 1982-85; pres. J & T Dodd Assocs., Fairfax, Va., 1985-94, Jesse Helms Ctr, Wingate, N.C., 1994—. Cons. to various mems. of Congress. Bd. dirs. Fellowship of Christian Athletes, Washington, 1991-94; head Lacrosse coach Wingate U.; del. Rep. Nat. Conv., 2000. Named Deep South Conf. Coach of Yr., 2001, coach North-South Coll. All-Star Game, 2001. Mem. Nat. Soc. Fund Raising Execs. (D.C. chpt. membership com. 1985-89). Republican. Office: Jesse Helms Ctr PO Box 247 Wingate NC 28174-0247

DODD, LOIS, artist, art educator; b. Montclair, N.J., Apr. 22, 1927; d. Lawrence Dodd and Margaret Vanderhoff; m. William Dickey King (div.); 1 child, Eli Benjamin. Student, Cooper Union, 1945-48. Tchr. art Bklyn. Coll., 1971-92. One-woman shows include Tanager Gallery, N.Y.C., 1954—62, Green Mountain Gallery, 1969—76, Fischbach Gallery, 1978—2002, Washington (Conn.) Art Assn., 1977, Cape Split Pl., Maine, 1977—83, N.J. State Mus., Trenton, 1981, Lyman Allyn Mus., Conn., 1980, La. State U., Baton Rouge, 1984, Anne Weber Gallery, Maine, 1987, Caldbeck Gallery, 1990, 1995, 1998, 2001, Dartmouth (N.H.) Coll., 1990, Rider (N.J.) U., 1993, Montclair Art Mus., N.J., 1996, Farnsworth Art Mus., Rockland, Maine, 1996, Trenton City Mus., Alexandre Gallery, 2002—, Represented in permanent collections Colby Coll. Mus., Cooper Hewitt Mus., Farnsworth Mus., Kalamazoo Art Ctr., Montclair Art Mus., NAD, AT&T, Chase Manhattan Bank, Commerce Bancshares Inc., Met. Life Ins. Co., Readers Digest, R.V. Reynolds Security, Pacific Nat. Bank, First Nat. City Bank. Bd. govs. Skowhegan Sch. of Painting and Sculptures, 1980—. Recipient award Am. Acad. Arts and Letters, 1986, Disting. Alumni citation Cooper Union, 1987; Ingram Merrill Found. grantee, 1971. Mem. NAD, Am. Acad. Arts and Letters. Home: 30 E 2d St New York NY 10003-8906

DODD, MARY ANN, organist, educator; b. Pullman, Wash., Sept. 6, 1931; d. Elmo Raymond and Mary Alice (Sexton) Howell; m. Jack Gordon Dodd, June 11, 1951; children: Jeffrey John, Laura Jean. MusB, U. Ark., 1956; MusM, U. Tenn., 1971. Music tchr., choral dir. Fourche Valley Sch., Briggsville, Ark., 1953-55; piano instr. Drury Coll., Springfield, Mo., 1957-60; organist, choirmaster Tenn. Valley Unitarian Ch., Knoxville, Tenn., 1968-69; organist First Baptist Ch., Hamilton, N.Y., 1972-73; univ. organist Colgate U., Hamilton, 1973-93, spl. instr., 1973-93. Adj. lectr. SUNY, Binghamton, 1987-90, vis. Link prof. organ, 1989; lectr. and workshops on organ repertoire and contemporary organ music, 1973—. Co-author (with Jayson Engquist) Gardner Read: A Bio-Bibliography, 1996; contbr. numerous revs. and articles to profl. jours. Mem. Am. Guild of Organists (regional councillor, mem. nat. coun. 1988-92, state chmn. 1982-87, nat. com. on new music 1986-93, nat. com. AGO improvisation competition 1988-89), N.Y. State Music Tchrs. Assn. (state chmn. for organ/harpsichord 1984-86), Music Tchrs. Nat. Assn., Organ. Hist. Soc., Coll. Music Soc. Democrat. United Ch. of Christ. Office: 213 Sears Pond Rd Sherburne NY 13460-5018 E-mail: madodd@norwich.net.

DODD, ROGER J. lawyer; b. Sewickley, Pa., Sept. 15, 1951; s. Carl Roger and Dorothy Maude (Barley) Dodd; m. Marcia J. Dodd; children: Matthew A., Andrew J., Kristin. BA in Econs., Bucknell U., 1973; JD, U. Pitts., 1976, Ga., 1976, Fla., 1977. Ptnr. Blackburn, Bright, Edwards Dodd & Joseph, Valdosta, Ga., 1976-87; prin. Roger J. Dodd Lawyers, P.C., Valdosta, 1987—; spl. asst. atty. gen. State of Ga., 1979-85; mem. faculty Ga. Inst. Trial Advocacy, 1986—92, chmn. of bd., 1988—91; mem. faculty Nat. Coll. Criminal Def., 1986—. Mem. faculty Nat. Coll. Criminal Def., 1986—, Advance Cross Exam., Advance Trial Inst.; adj. prof. Valdosta State Coll.; guest lectr. sch. law Mercer U. Ga. State U.; mem. family law sect. exec. com., 1985-88, criminal law sect., mem. family law sect., exec. com. 1985-88; mem. ABA family law sect., criminal law sect. exec. coms., 1992—; internat. lectr. in field. Co-author: Cross Examination: Science and Techniques, 1993; guest commentator on Court TV; peer rev. lawyer Trial Mag., 1991—; contbr. articles to profl. jours., newspapers; videos: Killer Cross-Examination (6 hrs. of audio & video tapes) The Art and Science of Cross Examination, 2 parts, 1990, How to Dominate a Courtroom on Cross Examination, 4 parts, 1994. Bd. dirs. Lowndes Country Assn. Retarded Citizens, Valdosta, 1977, Valwood Sch., Valdosta, 1984-86, Nat. Bd. Trial Advocacy, 1989, civil trial specialist, criminal trial specialist, 1990; peer rev. lawyer Trial Mag., 1991; mem. Boy Scouts Am., sustaining mem. Alapaha Coun. Mem.: Am. Acad. Matrimonial Lawyers, Internat. Acad. Matrimonial Lawyers. Libertarian. Presbyterian. Home: 5634 Danieli Dr N Lake Park GA 31636 Office: PO Box 1066 613 N Patterson St Valdosta GA 31601-4609 E-mail: doddlaw@doddlaw.com.

DODD, STEVEN LOUIS, systems engineer; b. Gainesville, Ga., Aug. 19, 1953; s. Oscar Louis and Vivian Irene (King) D.; m. Laureen Tyler, Apr. 8, 1989; children: Kevin Forrest, Emma Catherine. BS in Math., Davidson (N.C.) Coll., 1975; MS in Applied Math., N.C. State U., 1977, PhD in Ops. Rsch., 1982. Cons. EPA, Research Triangle Park, N.C., 1976-77; systems engr. AT&T Bell Labs., Holmdel, N.J., 1982-86, supr., systems engr. and developer, 1986-90; dist. mgr., tech. mktg. AT&T Bus. Communications Svcs., Bridgewater, N.J., 1990-91; dir. strategic planning Cin. Bell Info. Systems, Fairfax, Va., 1991-92, dir. platform mgmt., 1992, dir. gas and electric group, 1993, dir. comm. solutions group, 1993-96; v.p. Win Star Telecomm., Tysons Corner, Va., 1996-99, sr. v.p., 1999-2000; COO CityNet Telecom, 2000—01; CEO Ring Tech. Enterprises Inc., 2001—. Contbr. articles to profl. jours. Mem. Phi Beta Kappa, Omicron Delta Kappa, Omega Ro, Upsilon Pi Epsilon, Pi Mu Epsilon. Achievements include research in performance evaluation review, IEEE computer graphics and applications and numerische mathematik.

DODD, SYLVIA BLISS, special education educator; b. Ft. Worth, July 21, 1939; d. William Solomon and Sylvia Bliss (Means) Fisher; m. Melvin Joe Dodd, Sept. 4, 1959 (div. 1967); children: Lisa Dawn, Marcus Jay, Chadwick Scott. BA, Tex. Wesleyan Coll., Ft. Worth, 1960; MEd, Tex. Christian U., Ft. Worth, 1976. Tchr. Castleberry Ind. Sch. Dist., Ft. Worth, 1960-62, Hurst-Euless-Bedford (Tex.) Ind. Sch. Dist., 1967-69, dir. spl. edn., 1969-94. Instr. Tex. Wesleyan U., Ft. Worth, 1978, Ft. Worth, 1994—, coord. tchr. cert., 1996—2001; instr. Tex. Christian U., Ft. Worth, 1980. Mem. adminstrv. bd. 1st United Meth. Ch., Ft. Worth, 1990—93, 1995—; lay leader West Ft. Worth Dist. United Meth. Ch., 1992—96, Ctrl. Tex. Conf., United Meth. Ch., 2000—; bd. dirs. Mental Health Assn., Ft. Worth, 1983—88, 1991—95, March of Dimes, Mid Cities, Tex., 1990, United Cmty. Ctrs., 1989—97, pres., 1994—95; bd. dirs. So. Meth. U. Campus Ministry, 1992—97, Tex. Meth. Found., 2000—, Bedford Hist. Found., 2002—. Named Conf. Chairperson of Yr. Nat. Health and Welfare Ministries, 1981; recipient Outstanding Woman award Tex. Wesleyan U., 1991, Disting. Educator award, 1991, Key City, Ft. Worth, 1998. Mem. AAUP, Mental Health Assn. (pres. 1979-80), Nat. Coun. Exceptional Children, Tex. Coun. Adminstrs. Spl. Edn. (Hall of Honor award 1991, pres. 1975-76). Democrat. Methodist. Avocations: music, art, drama, Tex. history, walking. Home: 829 Timberhill Dr Hurst TX 76053-4240

DODD, WAYNE D. poet, editor; b. Clarita, Okla., Sept. 23, 1930; s. Homer Dewey and Maggie Mathilda Dodd; m. Betty Coshow, June 7, 1958 (div. Nov. 1980); children: Elizabeth Caroline, Hudson Callahan; m. Joyce Barlow, June 27, 1981. BA with distinction, U. Okla., 1955, MA, 1957, PhD, 1963. Asst. prof. U. Colo., Boulder, 1960-68; asst. editor Abstracts of English Studies, Boulder, 1961-68; prof. English Ohio U., Athens, 1968-94, disting. prof., 1994—; editor Ohio Rev., Athens, 1971—2001. Mem. adv. bd. Coordinating Coun. Lit. Mags., N.Y.C., 1975-77. Author: We Will Wear White Roses, 1974, Made in America, 1975, A Time of Hunting, 1975, The Names You Gave It, 1980, The General Mule Poems, 1981, Sometimes Music Rises, 1986, Echoes of the Unspoken, 1990, Toward the End of the Century, 1993, Of Desire & Disorder, 1994, The Blue Salvages, 1998, IS, 2003. Mem. adv. bd. Ohio Arts Coun., Columbus, 1970-79. With USN, 1948-52. Recipient Krout award Ohioana Found., 1991, Ohio Gov.'s award Ohio Arts Coun., 2001; Poetry fellow Nat. Endowment Arts, 1982, Artist's fellow Ohio Arts Coun., Isabella Gardner Poetry award, 2003, Residency fellow Rockefeller Found., 1995. Mem. Phi Beta Kappa. Democrat. Home: 11292 Peach Ridge Rd Athens OH 45701 E-mail: doddw@ohiou.edu.

DODD, WILLIAM HORACE, lawyer; b. Richmond, Va., Jan. 8, 1934; s. William Horace and Myrtle Ann (Clark) Dodd; m. Carol Santoki, Dec. 20, 1961; children: Michael William, Anna Laura. AB, Coll. William and Mary, 1959; post grad., U. Va., 1959—60; LLB, George Washington U., 1962. Bar: Va. 1962, Hawaii 1963, U.S. Ct. Appeals (9th cir.) 1963. Ptnr. Fong, Miho, Choy & Robinson, Honolulu, 1962—69, Chun, Kerr & Dodd, Honolulu, 1970—. Bd. dirs. Big Brothers Am., Boys Club, Honolulu, sec.; pres. Big Brothers Hawaii. With USAF, 1952—56. Mem.: ABA, Trial Lawyers Am., Nat. Conf. Bar Pres.'s Assn., Hawaii Bar Assn., Va. Bar Assn., Am. Judicature Soc., Adventures (Honolulu), Pacific Club, Wakiki Yacht Club, Honolulu Club. Office: 14th Floor 700 Bishop St Fl 14 Honolulu HI 96813-4124

DODDI, SESHAGIRI RAO, psychiatrist; b. Guntur, India, July 2, 1949; came to U.S., 1976; s. Nageswara Rao and Rajya Lakshmi D.; m. Vijaya Lakshmi Mullapudi, Dec. 18, 1974; children: Anita, Kishore. MBBS, Guntur Med. Coll., 1973. Diplomate Am. Bd. Psychiatry and Neurology; lic. psychiatrist, N.Y. Intern SUNY, Stony Brook, 1977-78; resident in psychiatry Mt. Sinai Svcs./City Hosp. Ctr., Elmhurst, N.Y., 1978-81, psychiatrist, 1982-88, G.W. Bryan Psychiat. Ctr., Columbia, S.C., 1981-82; chief residency tng. unit dept.

psychiatry Queens Hosp. Ctr., Jamaica, N.Y., 1989-90; chief inpatient psychiatry Our Lady Mercy Med. Ctr., Bronx, N.Y., 1991-94, assoc. dir., dir. edn. psychiatry dept., 1995—99, dir. psychiatry, 1999—2002; chief geriatric svcs. St. Vincent's Hosp., Westchester, 2002—. Instr. Mt. Sinai Sch. Medicine, N.Y.C., 1982-87, asst. clin. prof., 1987-88; asst. prof. Albert Ainstein Coll. Medicine, Bronx, 1989-91; clin. assoc. prof. N.Y. Med. Coll., Valhalla, 1992—. Contbr. articles to profl. jours. Active Bronx Mental Health Coalition, 1994-97. Fellow Am. Psychiat. Assn. (treas. Bronx dist. br. 1997-2000, pres. elect 2000-2002, pres. 2002—); mem. Nat. Alliance for Menta Ily Ill, Telugu Assn. No. Am. (life), Am. Assn. Physicians Indian Origin, Am. Telugu Assn. Avocations: skiing, jogging, reading, classical music southern india. Office: Our Lady Mercy Med Ctr 600 E 233rd St Bronx NY 10466-2697 E-mail: sdoddi@pol.net.

DODDS, BRENDA KAY, nurse; b. Wheeling, W.Va., July 14, 1961; d. Ray Charles and Kathryn June (Ries) D. BS, Graceland Coll., 1983; A in Child Devel., 1990; MS, Graceland U., 2002. Cert. Advanced Practice RN. Staff nurse Resthaven Retirement Home, Independence, Mo., 1983-84; staff nurse telemetry unit Independence Regional Health Ctr., 1983—; camp nurse Mo-Kan Salvation Army Camp, Kansas City, Mo., 1984; dental asst. Ronald E. Jennings, DDS P.C., Independence, 1985-87; sch. nurse Noland Child Devel. Ctr., Independence Pub. Sch. Dist., 1988-96, head tchr., 1990-96, morning supr., 1993-96. Staff Independence Head Start program Independence Sch. Dist., 1997-2000. Vol. ARC, Independence, 1983—, Voluntary Action Ctr., 1987-95; vocalist Independence Messiah/Festival Choir, 1983—; musician Independence Symphony Band, 1988— Mem. Am. Assn. Nurse Practitioners, Mo. Nurses Assn., Mensa, Sigma Theta Tau Internat. Avocations: hand crafts, gardening, spinning, weaving.

DODDS, LAWRENCE DONALD, lawyer; b. Ogdensburg, N.Y., Mar. 31, 1967; s. Donald Wilbur and Virginia Ann (Moore) D.; m. Amy Elizabeth Haugh, June 17, 1995. AB, Hamilton Coll., 1989; MA, Hahnemann U., 1997, PhD, 1999; JD, Villanova U., 1997. Clin. counselor Wediko Children's Svcs., Hillsboro, N.H., 1989-90, clin. coord., 1990-91; legal intern Defender Assn. Phila., 1993-94, Schnader Harrison Segal & Lewis, Phila., 1996; psychology intern Settlement Music Sch., Phila., 1993-94, Hahnemann Univ., Phila., 1994-95, The Devereux Found., 1997-98; atty. Schnader Harrison Segal & Lewis, LLP, Phila., 1998—; adj. asst. prof. psychiatry MCP-Hahnemann U., 2000—. Bd. dirs. Meth. Svcs. Child and Family. Mem. ABA, APA, Am. Psychology Law Soc., Order of Coif, Phi Beta Kappa, Phi Kappa Phi. E-mail: ldodds@schnader.com.

DODDS, LINDA CAROL, special education educator; b. Tucson, June 2, 1957; d. George A. and Bette R. (Bell) D. AA, U. Md., 1979; BA, Tex. Tech U., 1982; MBA, Our Lady of the Lake U., 1986, MEd, 2001. Svc. rep. USAA, San Antonio, 1982-84; portfolio asst. USAA-IMCO, San Antonio, 1984-85; sr. rep. USAA, San Antonio, 1985-86, asst. area mgr. Tampa, Fla., 1986-88, area mgr., 1988-92, dist. mgr., 1992-97, San Antonio, 1997-98; reading resource tchr. Boerne (Tex.) Ind. Sch. Dist., 1999—, head spl. edn. dept., 2000—02; resource tchr. N.E. Ind. Sch. Dist., San Antonio, 2002—. Treas. Forest Hills Homeowners Assn., Tampa, 1992-93; mem. Tex. Fedn. Rep. Women, San Antonio, 1985; co-chair United Way, 1995-96; active USAA Vol. Corp., Tampa, 1989—. Mem. Soc. CPCU, Delta Mu Delta, Sigma Iota Epsilon. E-mail: doddsl@boerne-isd.net.

DODDS, ROBERT JAMES, III, lawyer; b. San Antonio, Sept. 19, 1943; s. Robert James Jr. and Kathryn (Bechman) D.; m. Deborah N. Detchon, June 25, 1966 (div. Mar. 1989); children: Zachary Bechman, Seth Detchon; m. D.J. Knowles, Dec. 27, 1990. BA, Yale U., 1965; LLB, U. Pa., 1969. Assoc. Reed Smith Shaw & McClay, Pitts., 1969-77, ptnr., 1978-91; ptrn. Davenport & Dodds, LLP, Santa Fe, 1992—; of counsel Strassburger, McKenna, Gutnick & Potter, Pitts., 1991—. Bd. dirs. ATP Inc., Davison Sand & Gravel Co., Pitts.; pres. Homewood Cemetery, Pitts., 1980-91, bd. dirs. Trustee Mus. Art, Carnegie Inst, 1974-84, Westmoreland Mus. Art, Greensburg, Pa., YMCA of Pitts., Carnegie-Mellon U.; dir., pres. Pitts. Plan for Art, 1981-85; dir., chmn. West Pa. Hosp. Found., Carnegie Mellon Art Gallery; bd. dirs. Western Pa. Hosp., Western Pa. Healthcare Systems Inc., Pitts. Athletic Assn., Inst. Am. Indian Arts Found., Santa Fe; mus. panel Pa. Coun. on the Arts. Mem.: Rolling Rock Club (Ligonier, Pa.), Duquesne Club (Pitts.). Democrat. Episcopalian. Home: 3101 Old Pecos Trl Unit 687 Santa Fe NM 87505-9547 Office: Davenport & Dodds LLP 721 Don Diego Ave Santa Fe NM 87505

DODERER, MINNETTE FRERICHS, retired state legislator; b. Holland, Iowa, May 16, 1923; d. John A. and Sophie S. Frerichs; m. Fred H. Doderer, Aug. 5, 1944 (dec. 1991); children: Dennis, Kay Lynn. BA, U. Iowa, 1948. Chair standing com. public health Iowa Ho. of Reps., 1965-66, mem., 1964-69, 81-01, minority whip, 1967-68, chairperson ways and means com., 1983-88, chair small bus. and commerce com., 1989-90, chair small bus., econ. devel. and trade com., 1991-92; mem. Iowa Senate, 1968-78, pres. pro tem, 1975-76; ret., 2001. Vis. prof. Stephens Coll., Iowa State Univ. (both 1979); vice-chairwoman Iowa Interstate Cooperation Commn., 1965-66; vice-chairwoman Democratic Party Johnson County, 1957-60; vice chairperson com. on budget and taxation Nat. Conf. State Legislatures, 1989-90; mem. Dem. Nat. Com., 1968-70, Dem. Nat. Policy Council Elected Ofcls., 1973-76; chairwoman Iowa del. Internat. Women's Yr. Del. Bd. fellows Iowa Sch. Religion; Senate activities: chair subcom. Election Law Revision, 1975-76, Legislative Census Liaison Commn., Legislative Interim Study of Juvenile Justice, Senate State Govt. Standing com., 1977-78; vice chair Legislative Coun.; mem. Departmental Rules Review com., 1975-76, Interim Study com. on Prison Reform, Child Abuse Coun. Recipient Disting. Legis. Svc. award Iowa State Edn. Assn., 1969, Iowa Fedn. Bus. & Profl. Women's Clubs recognition, 1972, Iowa Civil Liberties award, 1978, Special award Midwest Race and Sex Desegregation Fed. Assistance Ctrs., 1979, Good Citizenship medal Sons of Am. Revolution, Friend of Edn. award Iowa City, 1986, Christine Wilson award for Equality and Justice Commn. on Status of Women, 1989, Gold Seal award Iowa Coalition Against Domestic Violence, 1995, Friend of Nursing award, 1996, citation Am. Acad. Pediat., 1996, Feminist of Yr. award, 1996, Friend of Nursing award, 1996, Woman of Achievement award Bus. and Profl. Women, 1997, Reproductive Rights Advocate award, 1998, medal of honor Vet. Feminists Am., 1999; named to Iowa Women's Hall of Fame, 1978, Woman of Yr. Iowa City Sr. Ctr., 1995. Mem. LWV, Pioneer Lawnmakers (pres. 1993-95), Delta Kappa Gamma (hon.). Democrat. Methodist.

DODGE, CALVERT RENAUL, education and training executive, author, educator; b. Chgo., Apr. 15, 1921; s. Lawrence Frank and Anna Rose (Manke) D.; m. Mary Irene Dodge, Apr. 2, 1951; children: Lawrence Wesley, Laura Irene, Valarie Le, James Calvert. BS in Agrl. Sci., U. Wyo., 1947, MA in Sociology, 1957; cert., Air U., Montgomery Ala., 1968; PhD in Speech Comm., U. Denver, 1971; BA in Video and Film Prodn., U. Md., 1998. Cert. supr. edn., Calif.; masters lic. 25 ton ships USCG; cert. USAF Parachute Jump Sch., 1969. Dir. youth, ednl. activities Standard Oil Ind. AMOCO, Chgo., 1948-51, dir. employee, pub. rels., 1951-55; pres. Western Concrete Products Inc., Laramie, Wyo., 1955-64; dir. state tng. ctr. State of Colo. Youth Svcs., Denver, 1964-71; dir. rsch. Ky. Manpower Devel. Commn., Louisville, 1971-76; instr. U. Ky., 1974-75; assoc. prof. U. D.C., Washington, 1979-82; instr. in Japan, Korea, Turkey, Germany, Spain and U.K. U. Md., 1976-82; exec. v.p. Human Equations, Inc., Balt., 1982-87; pres. Dodge-Marck Assocs., Balt., 1991—. Pres. Seminars at Sea, Balt., 1983-97; dir. pub. affairs Md. Motorcycle Safety Program, Balt., 1990-92, asst. chief tng. and employee devel., dir. videography Md. Transp. Authority, 1992-96. Author: Power Machinery Maintenance, 1955, A World Without Prisons, 1979, Executive Communication Development, 1986, Profit Recovery Management, 1986, Strategic Sales Development System, 1986; editor: A Nation Without Prisons, 1975, New Mind Power, Increasing Your Brain Powers for Lifetime Change with Malcolm E. Bernstein, 1999; producer videos. Sponsors com. Nat. 4H, Nat. FFA, Nat. Jr. Achievement. Grantee U.S. Dept. Justice, 1966, 69; recipient Outstanding Cmty. Svc. award, Am. Assn. Cmty. Resource Devel., 1990, Cmty. Svc. award USAFR, 1968. Mem. ASTD (v.p. 1969-71), Md. Assn. Adult Edn., Inter-Am. Assn., Dodge Family Assn., Annapolis Naval Sailing Assn., Am. Soc. Group Psychotherapy and Psychodrama, Internat. TV Assn., Masons, Alpha Zeta, Omicron Delta Kappa, Tau Kappa Epsilon. Buddhist. Avocations: teaching sailing, oil painting, video and film production. Home: 8 S Broadway Baltimore MD 21231-1713 Office: Dodge-Marck Assocs Baltimore MD 21222 E-mail: granitewyo@aol.com.

DODGE, CLEVELAND EARL, JR., manufacturing executive, director; b. N.Y.C., Mar. 7, 1922; s. Cleveland Earl and Pauline (Morgan) D.; m. Phyllis Boushall, Dec. 19, 1942; children: Alice Berkeley, Sally Mole, Cleveland Earl III. BS in Mech. Engring., Princeton U., 1943; D Humanics, Springfield Coll., 1996. With DeLaval Steam Turbine Co., 1942, Gen. Electric Co., 1946-51; v.p., dir. Warren Wire Co., Pownal, Vt., 1951-55; pres., dir. Dodge Industries, Inc., Hoosick Falls, N.Y., 1955-67; v.p., dir. Engineered Yarns, Inc., 1962-68; pres., dir. Circuit Materials Corp., 1962-68; pres., treas., dir. Internat. Dodge, Inc., 1968—; pres., dir. Dodge Machine Co., 1968—; pres., bd. dirs. Alta Energy Corp., 1980-89, Amex Plastics Inc., 1972-74, Amm. Hydride Corp., 1991—. Bd. dirs. Display Sys., Inc., Imetrix Corp.; bd. dirs. Internat. Dodge, Inc., Cleeland Corp., Am. Hydride Corp., Dodge Machine Co., Inc., Wild Goose Island Corp., Imetrix, Inc.; bd. dirs. emeritus Phelps Dodge Corp., Atlantic Mutual Ins., Key Bank. Patentee in field. Chmn., bd. dirs. Cleveland H. Dodge Found.; vice chmn. emeritus YMCA Retirement Fund; bd. dirs. emeritus Springfield Coll., Bennington Mus., Antique Boat Mus., Brisbee Coun. on Arts and Humanities, Silver City Mus., YMCA Retirement Fund. Lt. USNR, 1943-45. Mem. Princeton Engring. Assn., Princeton Rowing Assn., Laurentian Lodge (Shawbridge, Que., Can.), Taconic Golf Club (Williamstown, Mass.), Kiwanis. Congregationalist. Avocations: skiing, golf, travel. Office: Internat Dodge Inc PO Box 178 Hoosick Falls NY 12090-0178

DODGE, CLIFFORD HOWLE, geologist; b. Lancaster, Pa., Aug. 20, 1950; s. Richard Keller and Nancy Howle D.; m. Christine Miles, Apr. 4, 1981 (div. Aug. 1995). BA, Lehigh U., Bethlehem. Pa., 1972; MS, Northwestern U., Evanston, Ill., 1976. Registered profl. geologist, Pa.; cert. profl. geologist Am. Inst. Profl. Geologists. Hydrologist/geologist U.S. Geol. Survey/Water Resources Divsn., Harrisburg and Meadville, Pa., 1976-79; geologist Pa. Geol. Survey/Dept. Conservation and Natural Resources, Harrisburg, 1979—. Expert witness Pa. Dept. Environ. Resources, Harrisburg, 1991, Carbon/Graphite Group, Inc., Saint Marys, Pa., 1991. Contbr. numerous articles to profl. jours. and publs. Mem. Friends of the Lancaster Cemetery. Mem. Geol. Soc. Am., SEPM Soc. for Sedimentary Geology, History of Earth Sci. Soc., Harrisburg Area Geol. Soc., Demuth Found., Nat. Geog. Soc., Pa. Soc. Sons of the Revolution, Lancaster County Hist. Soc., Elk County Hist. Soc., Elk County Fisherman Watershed and Habitat Group, Beverly Hist. Soc., Wyoming Hist. and Geol. Soc., Friends of the R.R. Mus. Pa., Sigma Xi, Theta Chi. Episcopalian. Home: 145 Primrose Dr Hershey PA 17033-2638 Office: 3240 Schoolhouse Rd Middletown PA 17057-3534 E-mail: cdodge@state.pa.us.

DODGE, DAVID A. lawyer; b. Grand Rapids, Mich., Mar. 3, 1946; s. Richard C. and Lorraine G. Dodge; m. Carol Ruth Longstreet, Apr. 27, 1968; children: David II, Brian, Julia, Mark, Emily. BA, U. Mich., 1968; JD, Ind. U., 1970. Bar: Ind., Mich., U.S. Dist. Ct. (we. dist.) Mich., U.S. Ct. Appeals (6th cir.), U.S. Supreme Ct. Asst. atty. Kent Prosecutor Office, Grand Rapids, 1973-74; ptnr. Dodge & Dodge, P.C., Grand Rapids, 1974-88; pvt. practice Grand Rapids, 1988—. Served to capt. (judge advocate) USMC, 1970-73. Mem. Mich. Bar Assn. (chmn. prisons and corrections com. 1983-86), Grand Rapids Bar Assn. (trustee 1982-84). Clubs: Peninsular, Spring Lake Country Club. Roman Catholic. Office: 200 N Division Ave Grand Rapids MI 49503-2535

DODGE, EDWARD JOHN, retired insurance executive; b. Malone, N.Y., Mar. 28, 1935; s. Harry Gilman and Marjorie Dietz (Wright) D.; m. Ann Louise Cupps, Aug. 21, 1932. Grad., Phoenix Union H.S., 1953. Map clk. N.Y. Underwriters, San Francisco, 1956-57; underwriter Reliance Ins., San Francisco, 1957-58; agt. Am. Hardware Mut., San Francisco, 1958; investigator Retail Credit Co., 1963-68; claims adjuster Allstate Ins., Arlington Heights, Ill., 1968-70, Epiic Ins., Phoenix, 1974; claims examiner GEICO, Chgo., 1970-73; multi-line adjuster Ariz. Adjustment, Phoenix, 1973-74; investigator Equifax, Chgo., 1974-78; sales br. mgr. Hooper Holmes, Chgo. and Springfield, Ill., 1978-80; multi-line agt. Met. Ins., Springfield, 1980-81; subrogation examiner Horace Mann Ins., Springfield, 1982-97; ret., 1997. Author: Relief is Greatly Wanted, The Battle of Fort William Henry, 1998; contbr. articles to hist. publs. Commr. Boy Scouts Am., Arlington Heights, Ill., 1971-78, Springfield, 1981-92, Phoenix, 1983-84, vice chmn. scouting, Arlinton Heights, 1977-79, vice chmn. exploring, 1988-90. Sgt. USMC, 1952-56, USAF, 1958-62. Recipient Dist. Commrs. award Boy Scouts Am., 1978, Bronze Big Horn award Boy Scouts Am., 1989, Scouter of Month award Boy Scouts Am., 1978. Mem. Masons, The Queen's Regimental Assn. (hon. life mem.), The Princess of Wale's Royal Regimental Assn. (hon. life mem.). Republican. Methodist. Avocations: historical research, historical writing. Home: 1223 N Rutledge St Springfield IL 62702-2524

DODGE, JUDITH C. musician; b. Florence, Ariz., Mar. 15, 1940; d. Natt Noyes and Mildred (Johnson) Dodge; m. David Worthy Breneman, June 10, 1962 (div. Dec. 1992); children: Erica Vernice Breneman, Carleton David Dodge Breneman. BME, U. Colo., 1962; MA, San Francisco State U., 1970. Asst. dir. San Francisco Boys Chorus, 1967-70; dir. music, organist St. Columba's Episcopal Ch., Washington, 1972-83; organist, choirmaster St. Lukes Episcopal Ch., Kalamazoo, 1987-889; adj. lectr. music Kalamazoo Coll., 1983-89; music dir., condr. Bach Festival Soc. Kalamazoo, 1985-89; dir. music, organist St. Philips in the Hills Ch., Tucson, 1989-93, St. Columba's Episcopal Ch., Washington, 1993—. Chair music and program bd. Cathedral Choral Soc., Washington, 1996-2003; mem. adv. bd., sacred circles Nat. Cathedral, Washington, 1998—; mem. standing commn. liturgy and music Nat. Epis. Ch., 2000—. Mem. editl. bd. Jour. Assn. Anglican Music; contbr. articles to profl. jours. Mem. task force Kalamazoo Pub. Schs., 1983-84; mem. selection com. New Yrs. Fest, Kalamazoo, 1986; mem. artistic adv. bd., trustee emeritus Gilmore Internat. Keyboard Festival, 1989-94. Named to Outstanding Young Women of Am., 1965. Mem. Am. Choral Dirs. Assn., Am. Guild Organists, Assn. Anglican Musicians (sec., pres., v.p. 1992-95), Royal Sch. Ch. Music, Am. Guild English Handbell Ringers, Kappa Delta Pi, Pi Kappa Lambda, Sigma Alpha Iota. Democrat. Avocations: tennis, opera, golf, travel, theatre. Office: St Columba's Episcopal Ch 4201 Albemarle St NW Washington DC 20016-2009

DODGE, PETER, retired sociology educator; b. N.Y.C., Nov. 12, 1926; s. Martin Dodge and D'Etta (Brown) Dodge Green; m. Renata de Kanicky, Sept. 6, 1952 (dec. Oct 1990); children: Timothy, Christopher; m. Pat Moreinis, Oct. 23, 1994. BA, Swarthmore Coll., 1948; AM, Harvard U., 1950, PhD, 1961. Prof. Harper Coll., SUNY Binghamton, 1958-64; prof. sociology U. N.H., Durham, 1964-96, ret., 1996. Author: Beyond Marxism: The Faith and Works of Hendrik de Man, 1966; editor, translator: A Documentary Study of Hendrik de Man, 1979. Cpl. USAF, 1945-46. Fulbright scholar, 1955, 56; named disting. scholar Rockefeller Found., 1965-66. Democrat. Home: 14 Runnymede Dr North Hampton NH 03862

DODGE, PHILIP ROGERS, physician, educator; b. Beverly, Mass., Mar. 16, 1923; s. Israel R. and Anna (McCarthy) D.; children: Susan, Judith. Student, U. N.H., 1941-43, Yale, 1943; MD, U. Rochester, 1948. Diplomate: Am. Bd. Psychiatry and Neurology. Intern Strong Meml. Hosp., 1948-49; asst. resident neurology Boston City Hosp., 1949-50, resident, 1950, sr. resident, 1951-52; practice medicine, specializing in child neurology Boston, 1956-67, St. Louis, 1967—; teaching fellow neurology Harvard Med. Sch., 1950, 51-53, instr. neurology, 1956-58, assoc. in neurology, 1958-61, asst. prof., 1962-67; asst. neurologist Mass. Gen. Hosp., 1956-59, dir. pediatric neurology program, 1958-67, assoc. neurologist, 1959-63, neurologist, 1963-67, assoc. pediatrician, 1961-62, pediatrician, 1962-67; investigator Joseph P. Kennedy, Jr. Meml. Labs. for Study Mental Retardation, 1962-67; pediatric neurologist Boston Lying-In Hosp., 1961-67; cons. in neurology Walter E. Fernald State Sch. for Retarded Children, 1963-67; med. dir. St. Louis Children's Hosp., 1967-84, pediatrician-in-chief, 1967-86; assoc. neurologist Barnes Hosp., 1967—; chmn. Mallinckrodt Dept. Pediatrics, Washington U. Sch. Medicine, 1967-86, prof. pediatrics and neurology, 1967-93; prof. emeritus pediatrics and neurology Washington U. Sch. Medicine, 1993—; lectr. in pediatrics, 1993-99. Vis. scientist Clin. Research Center, U. P.R., 1965-66, hon. vis. prof. physiology, 1967; cons. collaborative project on cerebral palsy Nat. Inst. Neurol. Diseases and Blindness, 1958; bd. dirs., chmn. research adv. com. Mass. Soc. for Prevention Cruelty to Children, 1961-67; mem. sci. research adv. bd. Nat. Assn. for Retarded Children, 1963-67; bd. dirs. Central Midwestern Regional Lab., Inc., 1968-70; mem. gen. clin. research centers adv. com. USPHS, 1971-74; mem. Mo. Gov.'s Council on Developmental Disabilities, 1971-74; chmn. Mo. Mental Health Commn., 1974-78; mem. nat. adv. child health and human devel. council NIH, 1974-77; chmn. panel on neurol. disorders, developmental, long range program strategies NINCDS, 1977-79; panel chmn., consensus devel. conf. on diagnosis and treatment of Reye's Syndrome, 1981; vis. prof. pediatrics and adolescent medicine, Royal Postgrad. Med. Sch., U. London, 1986—; hon. vis. fellow dept. pathology U. Western Australia, Nedlands, Australia, 1986-87; vis. prof. neurology Columbia U. Coll. Physicians and Surgeons, N.Y.C., 1987-88; spl. asst. to dir. for mental retardation Nat. Inst. Child Health and Human Devel., NIH, Washington, 1987-88. Author: (with others) Nutrition and the Developing Nervous System, 1975; Editorial bd.: (with others) Jour. Developmental Medicine and Child Neurology, 1965—, Jour. Pediatrics, 1970-80, Pediatric Research, 1970-78, Current Problems in Pediatrics, 1969-84, Neurology, 1973-76; Contbr. (with others) articles to profl. jours. Served from 1st lt. to maj. M.C. U.S. Army, 1950-56. Mem. Am. Pediatric Soc. (coun. 1972-78, chmn. coun. 1978-79), Am. Acad. Neurology (past com. chmn.), Am. Neurol. Assn., Child Neurology Soc., Assn. for Rsch. in Nervous and Mental Disease, Soc. Pediatric Rsch., Soc. Biol. Psychiatry, St. Louis Soc. Neurol. Scis., Assn. Med. Sch. Pediatric Dept. Chmn. (pres. 1975-77), Alpha Omega Alpha. Home: 410 N Newstead Ave Saint Louis MO 63108-2654 Office: 1 Childrens Pl Saint Louis MO 63110-1002

DODGE, R(ALPH) EDWARD, JR., physician; b. Salamanca, NY, Jan. 14, 1936; s. Ralph Edward and Eunice Elvira (Davis) D.; m. Nancy Lou De Lay, Aug. 14, 1957 (dec. 1999); children: Randall, Jeffrey, Amy; m. Carol Marie Fitzgerald, Dec. 17, 1999. BA, Taylor U., 1958; MD, Ind. U., 1962; MPH, Johns Hopkins U., 1967. Diplomate Am. Bd. Preventive Medicine, Am. Bd. Family Practice. Rotating intern L.A. County Gen. Hosp., 1962-63; resident gen. preventive medicine sch. hygiene & pub. health Johns Hopkins U., 1966-69; asst. prof. pub. health Haile Sellassie U., Gondar, Ethiopia, 1967-69; staff physician Frontier Nursing Svc., Hyden, Ky., 1970-71; med. dir. Citrus-Levy County Health Dept., Inverness, Fla., 1971-74; physician emergency dept. Waterman Meml. Hosp., Eustis, Fla., 1974-75; pvt. practice Inverness, 1975-96; med. dir. Citrus Primary Care Network, 1994-96. Clin. asst. prof. U. Fla., 1994-98. Contbr. articles to med. jours.; editor Fla. Family Physician, 1991-95, 97-99; newspaper columnist: Health Simplicity, 1988-90, Life and Health, 1990-2000. Bd. dirs. Marion-Citrus Mental Health Ctrs., Ocala, Fla., 1972—74, North Ctrl. Fla. Health Planning Commn., Gainesville, 1979—80, Fla. divsn. Am. Cancer Soc., 1988—90, Citrus Meml. Health Found., Inverness, 1988—94, Citrus County Edn. Found., 1998—2002, Citrus County Assn. for Retarded Citizens, 1998—, v.p., 1999—; trustee Old Courthouse Heritage Mus., 1999—2000; active Citrus County Hist. Soc.; trustee Unity Ch. of Citrus County, 2000—03, pres., 2001—03. Lt comdr. USPHS, 1964—66. Recipient Disting. Svc. award Fla. Assn. Emergency Med. Technicians, 1976, Community Svc. award Seventh Day Adventist Ch., Inverness, 1978, Citizen of Yr. award Citrus County Chronicle, 1987, Svc. Above Self award Rotary Club Inverness, 1998. Mem. AMA, Am. Coll. Preventive Medicine, Am. Acad. Family Physicians, Fla. Acad. Family Physicians (bd. dirs. 1994-96), Fla. Med. Assn., Citrus County Med. Soc. (pres. 1977, sec.-treas. 1981-86). Democrat. Avocations: tennis, chess, gardening. E-mail: edodge@atlantic.net.

DODGE, TIMOTHY DE K. college librarian; b. Boston, Mass., Apr. 15, 1957; s. Peter and Renata de Kanicky Dodge. BA, Swarthmore Coll., Swarthmore, Pa., 1979; MS, Columbia Univ., N.Y., 1980; MA, Univ. N.H., Durham, N.H., PhD, 1992. Cemetery maintenance man Town of Lee, Lee, NH, 1971—77, 1981—83, 1988; gen. asst. Butler Libr., Columbia Univ., N.Y., 1979—80; spl.collections libr. Dimond Libr., Univ. N.H., Durham, NH, 1982—84; serials and reference libr. Barry Univ. Libr., Miami Shores, Fla., 1984—87; spl. collections libr. Dimond Libr., Univ. N.H., Durham, NH, 1987—92; reference libr. Draughon Libr., Auburn Univ., Auburn, Ala., 1992—. Author: Crime & Punishment in N.H. 1812-1914, 1995, Poor Relief in Durham, Lee & Madbury N.H., 1995; contbr. articles to profl. jour. Mem.: Ala. Libr. Assn. (sec. 2000—01), Ala. Assn. of Coll. & Rsch. Libr. (pres. 2000—01, pres.-elect 2003—). Democrat. Congregationalist. Avocation: radion broadcaster. Office: Ralph Brown Draughon Libr Auburn Univ 231 Mell St Auburn University AL 36849-5606

DODGE, WILLIAM DOUGLAS, insurance company consultant; b. Savannah, Ga., Sept. 26, 1937; s. Kenneth Douglas and Bettie Wilbur (Sadler) D.; m. Susan Penny, Dec. 27, 1958 (div. 1976); children: Gregory D., Phillip C., Warren D., Andrew L.; m. Marian Elizabeth Monroe, Apr. 2, 1983. BS, Ga. Inst. Tech., 1959; MBA, Ga. State U., 1966. CPCU, ARM. Underwriter Liberty Mutual Ins. Co., Atlanta, 1960-66; ins. adminstr. Lockheed Corp., Marietta, Ga., 1966-78; risk mgr. Schlumberger Ltd., Atlanta, 1978-79; v.p. ins. Fuqua Industries, Inc., Atlanta, 1979-90, v.p. ins. and benefits, 1991-92; pres. Fuqua Ins. Co. Ltd., Hamilton, Bermuda, 1978-92, Fuqua Risk Retention Group, Atlanta, 1989-92; ind. risk mgmt. cons. Atlanta, 1992-95. Adv. bd. Risk Mgmt. Inc., N.Y.C., 1978-92; chmn. bd., mem. investment com. J&H WF Syndicate B., N.Y. Ins. Exch., N.Y.C., 1984-88. Co-author: The Hold Harmless Agreement, 1968. Mem. Exec. Com. Reorgn. and Mgmt. Improvement State of Ga., 1971, Agts. Licensing Exam. Revision Bd. State Ga., 1970; bd. dirs. Ga. State U. Ednl. Found., 1980-88; lt. comdr. USPS/Tybee Light Power Squadron, 1999, comdr., 2000—. Republican. Methodist. Avocations: gardening, boating. Office: Mickey Dodge & Assocs Inc 12 Pipers Pond Ln Savannah GA 31404-1122 E-mail: savdodges@aol.com.

DODGEN, JOHN N. manufacturing executive; b. Sapulpa, Okla., June 22, 1926; s. Claude W. and Pearl M. (Glass) D.; m. Wanda Lou Edwards; children: James, Mary Lou, John C.T., Lori. BA, Ottawa U., 1956; PMD, Harvard U., 1961. V.p. distbn. farm equipment Dodgen & Co., Fort Dodge, Iowa, 1947-56; v.p. mfg. and distbn. farm equipment Dodgen Associated Mfrs., Sioux City, Iowa, 1956-58; pres. mfg. and distbn. farm equipment Silbaugh Mfg., Humboldt, Iowa, 1958-61; pres. mfg. farm and indsl. equipment Dodgen Industries, Inc., Humboldt, 1961—. Pres., founder John N. Dodgen Found., 1960—; pres. Dodgen Leasing Corp., Humboldt, 1964—, Born Free, Inc., Humboldt, 1969—, Fiberglass Fabricators, Inc., Humboldt, 1984—, Dodgen Mobile Technologies, Humboldt, 1990—, Custom Cabinets, Humboldt, Born Free Fla., 1998—, Born Free Nev., 1999—; bd. trustees Ottawa (Kans.) U., 1964-99; bd. dirs. Iowa Assn. Bus. and Industry. Licensed Bapt. lay min., 1954—; trustee Ctrl. Bapt. Sem., 1963-73; chmn. campaign Humboldt Area Family Aquatic Ctr; pres. Humboldt County Taxpayers Assn., 2002. Mem.Rotary. Avocations: hunting pheasants, geese and ducks, golf, fishing, public speaking. Office: Dodgen Industries Inc Hwy 169 N Humboldt IA 50548

DODGEN, LARRY J. career officer; b. June 12, 1949; Commd. U.S. Army, advanced through grades to maj. gen., 1999; dir. Joint Theater Air Missile Def. Orgn., Washington, 1998—. Office: Joint Theater Air Missile Def Orgn 8000 Joint Staff Pentagon Washington DC 20318-8000

DODGE ROBBINS, DOROTHY ELLIN, English educator; b. Aug. 16, 1958; MA, U. S.D., 1991; PhD, U. Nebr., 2000. Lectr. Tex. A&M, College Station, 1987-88; asst. prof. English Dakota Wesleyan U., Mitchell, S.D., 1995-99; instr. speech comms. La. Tech. U., Ruston, 1999-2000, asst. prof. English, 2000—. Office: PO Box 3162 Ruston LA 71272-0001 E-mail: drobbins@garts.latech.edu.

DODOHARA, JEAN NOTON, music educator; b. Monroe, Wis., Feb. 21, 1934; d. Albert Henry and Eunice Elizabeth (Edgerton) Noton; BA, Monmouth (Ill.) Coll., 1955; MS, U. Ill., 1975, adminstrv. cert., 1980, EdD, 1985; m. Laurence G. Landers, June 7, 1955 (div.); children: Theodore Scott, Thomas Warren, Philip John; m. Edward R. Harris, Nov. 27, 1981 (dec.); stepchildren: Adrianne, Erica; m. Takashi Dodohara, Aug. 7, 1988; 1 stepchild, Eve D. Dodohara. Tchr. music schs. in Ill. and Fla., 1955-76; tchr. ch. music for children, 1957-72; tchr. music Dist. 54, Schaumburg, Ill., 1976-93; teaching asst. U. Ill., 1979. Named Outstanding Young Woman of Yr., Jaycee Wives, St. Charles, Mo., 1968; charter mem. Nat. Mus. Women in Arts. Mem. NEA (life), AAUW, Music Educators Nat. Conf. (life), Ill. Educators Assn. (life), Elgin Area Ret. Tchrs. Assn., U. Ill. Alumni Assn. (life), Mortar Bd., Mensa, Delta Kappa Pi. Mem. United Ch. of Christ. Home: 1068 Hampshire Ln Elgin IL 60120-4905

DODSON, CARL EDWARD, nuclear engineer, real estate agent, executive, minister, assistant superintendent; b. Chgo., July 8, 1956; s. John Eddie and Birdie (Dodson) Allen; m. Peggy E. Dodson; children: LaTreesa, Letiticia, LaTonya, Carl Jr., Barry. A in Engring., State Tech. Inst. at Memphis, 1980. Cert. plant engr.; lic. FCC 3d class, lic. Tenn. Bd. Realtors; ordained elder. Engring. aide Spl. Design, Knoxville, Tenn., 1980-82, Sequoyah Nuclear Plant, Knoxville, Tenn., 1982-84, design engr. Soddy, Tenn., 1985-88; real estate agt. Holmes Real Estate Co., Knoxville, Tenn., 1989-91; pres., chief exec. officer Ezra Inc., Knoxville, 1990-91; sr. technician, analyst Weston Gulf Coast, University Park, Ill., 1992-94; pharm. technician Centeon, Kankakee, Ill., 1994-96; assoc. pastor (ordained) Shiloh Full Gospel Bapt. Ch., Kankakee; asst. supt. pub. works City of Kankakee, 1996—2002, mgr. bldg. maintenance, 2002—. Author (software): New Student, 1980. Mem. Nat. Inst. Certification in Engring. Technologies, Jaycees (Chattanooga). Mem. Cert. in Plant Engring.. Avocations: chess, reading, computer programming, bowling, photography. Home: 354 S 5th Ave Kankakee IL 60901-3647 Personal E-mail: carled@prodigy.net.

DODSON, CARR GLOVER, lawyer, director; b. Americus, Ga., Aug. 29, 1937; s. William A. Dodson Jr. and Mary (Crisp) Dodson Glover; m. Edith Katherine Pilcher; children: Mary Christine, Katherine, Carr Glover, Will. BA, U. Ga., 1959, JD, 1961. Bar: Ga. 1961, U.S. Dist. Ct. (mid. dist.) Ga. 1964, U.S. Ct. Appeals (11th cir.) 1984. Ptnr. Jones, Cork & Miller, Macon, Ga., 1966—. Dir. Glover Wholesale Co., Americus. Active Ga. Ho. of Reps., 1966-71, minority leader, 1968-71; chmn. Macon United Way, 1981—. Capt. USAF, 1961-64. Fellow Am. Coll. Trial Lawyers; mem. State Bar Ga. (sect. chmn. 1976-78), Bacon Bar Assn. (pres. 1976), Macon C. of C. (bd. dirs. 1976—), Macon Civic Club (bd. dirs.), Idle Hour Country Club (pres. 1980). Republican. Presbyterian. Home: 1168 Jackson Springs Rd Macon GA 31211-1435 Office: Jones Cork & Miller 500 Trust Co Bank Bldg Macon GA 31298

DODSON, DANIEL, SR., advertising executive; Exec. Barton Brands, Chgo., Joseph Schlitz Brewing Co., Milw.; sr. v.p., gen. mgr. McCann Spectrum Mktg.; founder, chmn., CEO Mastermind Mktg., Atlanta. Office: Mastermind Mktg 3405 Piedmont Rd NE Ste 550 Atlanta GA 30305-1797

DODSON, DANIEL, JR., advertising executive; Staff acct.; jr. acct. exec. Mastermind Mktg., Atlanta, 1983, now pres., COO. Office: Mastermind Mktg 3405 Piedmont Rd NE Ste 550 Atlanta GA 30305-1797

DODSON, DANITA JOAN, secondary school educator, consultant; b. Morristown, Tenn., Feb. 16, 1964; d. Alfred Clarence and Joyce Ann D. BA in English, Lincoln Meml. U., 1985; MA in English, East Tenn. State U., 1986; PhD in English, U. So. Miss., 1994. Profl. tchg. cert. social studies, Spanish, English. Tchr. English, dept. chair Hancock County High Sch., Sneedville, Tenn., 1986—; prof. English, dept. chair Lat. Am. campus U. Mobile, San Marcos, Carazo, Nicaragua, 1995-96. Adj. prof. English Walters State C. C., Morristown, Tenn., 1986—; review panelist for grant proposals 2001 summer insts. and seminars NEH, Washington, 2000. Contbr. articles to profl. jours. Bd. dirs. Clinch-Powell Enterprise Cmty., Rutledge, Tenn., 1998-2001; co-dir. Sneedville/Hancock Cmty. Ptnrs. for Econ. Devel. and Civic Improvement, Sneedville, 1996-99. Fellow in native Am. lit. NEH, 1997. Mem. Nat. Coun. Tchrs. English, NEA (pres. local chpt. 1988-90), Nat. Women's Studies Assn., MLA, Soc. Utopian Studies, Sneedville Woman's Club (pres. Gen. Fedn. Women's Clubs/Tenn. Fedn. Women's Clubs 1996-98), Delta Kappa Gamma. Avocations: travel, writing poetry, hiking, collecting art. Home: 5444 Tazewell Hwy Sneedville TN 37869 Office: Hancock County High Sch Harrison st Sneedville TN 37869 E-mail: danita@naxs.net.

DODSON, DARYL THEODORE, ballet administrator, arts consultant; b. Warrensburg, Mo., Oct. 9, 1934; s. Theodore and Ada Marie (Ayres) D. BS, Ctrl. Mo. State U., 1956. Mem. Gov. S.C.'s Coun. of the Arts, 1974; mem. adv. panel Vt. Coun. on Arts, 1978; mgr. Am. tour 1st cultural exch., People's Republic of China and U.S., 1978, Nat. Ballet Cuba, 1979, Royal Ballet Eng., 1981; pres. Pine Cone Enterprises, Ltd., 1977-81; propr. Pine Cone Inn, Haverhill, N.H., 1978-81; mgr. Opera House, John F. Kennedy Ctr., Washington, 1981; mgr. U.S. and Can. tour Sweeney Todd, 1982; mgr. U.S. tours Amadeus, 1982-83, The Wiz, 1983-84, Les Miserables, 1988-92, Phantom of the Opera, 1992-2003; mgr. N.Y. engagement The Golden Land, 1985; mgr. Porgy and Bess, 1986-87, La Cage Aux Folles, 1987, N.Y. and U.S. tour Paris Opera Ballet, 1988; gen. mgr. John Curry Skating Co., 1984. Asst. dir. The Mikado, N.Y.C. Opera, 1959; regisseur Chgo. Opera Ballet, 1960, asst. stage mgr. Am. Ballet Theatre, N.Y.C., 1960, stage mgr., 1961, prodn. stage mgr., 1961, prodn. mgr., 1963, gen. mgr., 1968-77. Served with U.S. Army, 1957-59. Recipient Nat. Touring Broadway Achievement award, 2003. Mem. Theta Chi, Theta Alpha Phi. Episcopalian. Home: On The Commons Haverhill NH 03765 Office: 1650 Broadway Ste 800 New York NY 10019-6833

DODSON, DONALD MILLS, retired restaurant executive; b. Shamrock, Tex., Nov. 2, 1937; s. Freeman Mills and Marvie Hazel (Rives) D.; m. Sharon Jane Webb, Feb. 6, 1961; children— Randal, Stephanie, Kendal. Student, Tex. Tech. Trainee Furrs Bishops Cafeteria, Odessa, Tex., 1958, asst. mgr., 1958-59; mgr. Furrs Cafeteria, Odessa, Lubbock, Tucson, Denver, 1959-68, dist. mgr. Lubbock, Tex., 1968-75, v.p. region, 1975-77, v.p. personnel devel., 1977-82, exec. v.p. ops., 1982—, sr. exec. v.p. ops., chief oper. officer support depts., 1987-90, regional v.p. West Tex. and Ea. New Mex., 1990—, sr. v.p. food and beverage, 1990—, divisional v.p., 1991-92, v.p. ops. Richardson, Tex., 1993—2002, v.p. product and new bus. devel., 2002; cafeteria cons., 2002—. Mem. Nat. Restaurant Assn., Tex. Restaurant Assn. E-mail: ddodson@furrs.net.

DODSON, GEORGE WAYNE, computer company executive, consultant; b. Danville, Ill., Jan. 21, 1937; s. Maurice Keith and Marjorie Ruth (Ingalsbe) D.; m. Evandra May Mendenhall, Aug. 4, 1957; children: Michael, Curtis, Janet. BS in Math., U. Ill., 1966; MS in Ops. Rsch., Union Coll., 1970. Statis. mgr. U. Ill., Urbana, 1960-66; sr. performance anayst IBM Corp., Poughkeepsie, N.Y., 1966-70, performance mgr., 1970-79, lab. performance mgr. Tucson, 1979-85, program mgr. Roanoke, Tex., 1987-91, prin. info. systems mgmt. cons., 1991-93, IBM Consulting Group, Dallas, 1994-96; dir. tech. svcs. Morino Assocs., Vienna, Va., 1985-86; dir. performance products UCCEL Corp., Dallas, 1986-87; prin. IBM Global Svcs., 1996-97; dir. info. tech. mgmt. consulting Candle Corp., Dallas, 1997—2001; pres. IT Mgmt. Cons., Colleyville, Tex., 2001—03; dir. performance engring. HyPerformix, Dallas, 2003—. Mem. Computer Measurement Group (chmn. 1983, 89, pres. 1983-85, bd. dirs. 1985-89, 99—, treas. 1990-95, A.A. Michelson award lifetime achievement 1997). Avocations: softball, music, photography. Office: 7309 Balmoral Dr Colleyville TX 76034 E-mail: gdodson@hyperformix.com., gwdodson@flash.net.

DODSON, HELEN ZRAKE, television news producer; b. Bklyn., Nov. 20, 1954; d. Elias Najeeb Zrake and Evelyn (Saydah) Deschner; m. Robert Andrew Dodson, May 9, 1987; children: Richard Elias, Jana Elizabeth. BS, Northwestern U., 1975. Freelance writer, producer, N.Y.C. and Los Angeles, 1975-77; prodn. asst. United Way of Am., Alexandria, Va., 1977; audio-visual producer Am. Soc. for Microbiology, Washington, 1978; producer AVMD Med. Mktg., N.Y.C., 1979; news writer Sta. WNEW-TV, N.Y.C., 1979-82, Sta. WCBS-TV, N.Y.C., 1982-86, news producer, 1986-96; sr. producer The News With Brian Williams, MSNBC, NBC News, 1996-97; prodr. Dateline NBC, NBC News, N.Y.C., 1997—2002; writer NBC Nightly News, 2002—. Mem. Writers Guild Am., Nat. Assn. Broadcast Employees and Technicians. Avocations: reading, piano, tennis, watching football. Home: 40 Woodbine Ln Fairfield CT 06825-1441 Office: NBC 30 Rockefeller Plz Fl 2 New York NY 10112-0044

DODSON, SAMUEL ROBINETTE, III, investment banker; b. Nashville, Feb. 24, 1943; s. Samuel Robinette and Helen Elizabeth (Maiden) D.; m. Marsha Robertson Moody, Aug. 2, 1969; children— Bradley John, Andrew Caldwell. Student, Yale U., 1961-63; BS, Vanderbilt U., 1966; MBA, U. Chgo., 1968; MS, London Sch. Econs., 1968. Various fin. and planning positions Exxon Corp. and Affiliates, Houston, 1968-81; v.p. First Boston Corp., 1981-84, mng. dir., 1984-93, Merrill Lynch, Houston, 1993—. Served to 1st lt. U.S. Army, 1963-64 E-mail: sam_dodson@ml.com.

DODSON, VERNON NATHAN, physician, educator; b. Benton Harbor, Mich., Feb. 19, 1923; m. Shirley Jane Wheelihan: children: Martha Ione, Kathryn Anne, Christine Louise, John Nathan, Elizabeth Marie. Student, Mich. State Coll., 1941-43, 46, Northwestern U., summer 1942, Compton (Calif.) Coll., 1943, U. Oreg., 1943-44, Corpus Christi Coll., U. Oxford, Eng., 1945, U. Mich., 1946-47, 48, 51-52, BS, 1952; MD, Marquette U., 1951. Intern in surgery Henry Ford Hosp., Detroit, 1952-53; asst. in pathology Johns Hopkins U. Hosp., Balt., 1953-54, asst. pathologist, 1953-54; resident in internal medicine Univ. Hosp., Ann Arbor, Mich., 1954-57; rsch. assoc. U. Mich. Med. Sch., Ann Arbor, 1957-60, 60-71, lectr., 1959, from jr. clin. instr. to assoc. prof., 1956-64, assoc. prof. Dept. Indsl. Health, Sch. Pub. Health, 1965-71; attending physician U.S. VA Hosp., Ann Arbor, 1961-70; mem. med. staff Milw. County Gen. Hosp., 1971-72; rsch. assoc. U.S. VA Ctr., Wood, Wis., 1971-72; prof. medicine and environ. medicine Med. Coll. Wis., Milw., 1971-72; vis. prof. dept. preventive medicine U. Wis. Med. Sch., Madison, 1973-74, prof. medicine, sect. internal medicine, and preventive medicine, 1977-94, prof. emeritus medicine and preventive medicine, 1994—, prof. emeritus dept. population and health scis., 1994—. Lectr. Sch. Dentistry, U. Mich., Ann Arbor, 1957-58, Sch. Nursing, U. Mich., 1958-60, Coll. Lit., Sci. and Arts, Inst. Social Work, U. Mich., 1957-58; cons. staff physician Rochester, Minn. Meth. Hosp., 1974-77; dir. Univ. Employee Health Svc., U. Wis., Madison, 1977-80, mem. staff Ctr. Health Sci., 1978-95, hon. staff, 1995—; physician cons. VA Hosp., Madison, 1978-95; mem. interdepartmental program in toxicology, U. Mich., 1965-71, vice chair, 1969-71; mem. Environ. Toxicology Ctr., Divsn. Health Scis., U. Wis., Madison, 1972-74, 77-94, acting dir., 1974-76, 78-79, assoc. dir. Sch. Biotron., 1979-84; vis. prof. U. Tex. Health Sci. Ctr., Sch. Pub. Health, Houston, 1986, So. Occupational Health Ctr., U. Calif., Irvine, 1986; mem. com. on edn. and libr., Trinity Meml. Hosp., Cudahy, Wis., 1971-71, assoc. med. staff, 1972-73; mem. assoc. med. staff St. Lukes Hosp., Milw., 1972-73; cons. Joint Commn. on Hosp. Accreditation, Chgo., 1974-76; cons. in preventive medicine and internal medicine, Mayo Clinic, Mayo Found., Rochester, 1974-77; cons. GM, Warren, Mich., 1963-65, 72-84, med. dir. GM, Oak Creek, Wis., 1971-72; cons. Oscar Mayer Co., 1973-74; cons. plant physician, IBM, Rochester, 1976-77; cons. med. dir. George A. Hormel co., Austin, Minn., 1977; mem. occupational health adv. bd. GM, UAW, 1982-85; cons. Owens-Corning Fiberglas, Toledo, 1968—, Gen. Mills, Mpls., 1980—; bd. dirs. Nat. Biogerontology Inst., 1984—; cons. USPHS, Dept. Natural Resources, Wis., Dept. Health and Social Svcs., Wis., U.S. Dept. Agr., OSHA, Wis., Nat. Inst. Occupational Safety and Health, Ctr. for Disease Control, Dept. Industry, Labor and Human Rels., Wis.; mem. Gov.'s Task Force on Occupational Health and Safety, State of Wis., Extramural Ctr. Adv. Rev. Panel, Nat. Inst. for Occupational Health and Safety, Sentinel Event Notification System for Occupational Risks, Divsn. Health, State Dept. Health and Social Svc., Madison, Wis.; vice chair Residency Rev. Com. for Preventive Medicine, Coun. Health & The Pub., Accreditation Coun. for Gen. Med. Edn., State of Wis. Occupl. Disease and Illness Ctr. Edn. cons. editor Am. Jour. Occupational Medicine, 1979-89; assoc. editor Am. Jour. Indsl. Medicine, 1986-80; author 5 books, 17 book chpts., 44 sci. rsch. papers, 119 abstracts and presentations, 4 TV programs; co-editor 1 book. Mem. spl. citizen's adv. com. on safety Ann Arbor Bd. Edn., 1969, gov.'s com. on crime detection and law enforcement, ad hoc com. on lab. svcs., State of Mich., 1969; chmn., mem. com. on sch. safety, King Sch., Ann Arbor, 1969-70; mem. Kettle Moraine High Sch. Band Parents, Wales, Wis., 1972-74, v.p., 1973-74, citizen's com. on drug abuse, Waukesha County, Wis., 1973-74. With U.S. Army, 1942-45, ETO. Recipient Disting. Svc. award, Occupational Health award UAW, GM, 1988. Fellow ACP, Am. Coll. Occupl. Medicine (bd. dirs. 1987—, award 1988), Am. Coll. Medicine, Am. Occupl. Medicine Assn. (bd. govs. 1985, award 1988), Am. Coll. Occupl. and Environ. Medicine, Am. Coll. Preventive Medicine, Soc. Occupl. and Environ. Health; mem. AAAS, AMA (rep. residency rev. com., vice chair accreditation coun. for gen. med. edn., Physician's Recognition award 1981-2002), Am. Fedn. for Clin. Rsch., The Biochem. Soc. (London), Wis. State Med. Soc. (environ./occupl. health commn., legis. affairs commn., continuing med. edn. commn. coun. on health of the pub., coun. on med. edn., coun. on the health and the pub., 1999—, Meritorious Svc. award 1991, 96), Ctrl. States Occupl. Medicine Assn. (bd. govs.), Dane County Med. Soc., Am. Pub. Health Assn., Wis. Pub. Health Assn., Am. Cancer Soc. (award 1987), Internat. Commn. for Occupl. Health (Geneva), alumnae orgns. Mich. State U., U. Mich., Marquette U., Johns Hopkins U., Mayo Clinic, Med. Coll. Wis., U. Wis., Henry Ford Hosp., VFW, 11th Armored Divsn. Assn., Friends of WHA-TV, Smithsonian Instn., Nat. Geog. Soc., World Wildlife Fund, Sierra Club, Natural Resource Def. Coun., Sigma Xi. Office: MD FACP Dept Med Wis U J5 220 CSC 2454 600 Highland Madison WI 53705-2335

DODSON, W(ILLIAM) EDWIN, child neurology educator; b. Durham, N.C., Dec. 23, 1941; s. Howard William and Mildred (Sorrell) D.; m. Doreen Carol Davis, June 4, 1964 (div. May 1976); children: Anna Elizabeth, William Edwin Jr., Jason David; m. Sandra Schorr (div. Mar. 1993); children: Steven Gage, Matthew Sorrell; m. Karen Leigh Pursel. AB, Duke U., 1963, MD, 1967. Intern Children's Hosp., Boston, 1967-68, resident in pediat., 1970-71; resident, fellow in child neurology Barnes Hosp. and St. Louis Children's Hosp., 1971-75; asst. prof. child neurology Washington U., St. Louis, 1975-80, resident in pediat., 1970-71, assoc. prof., 1980-86, prof. child neurology, 1986—; assoc. dean admissions and fin. aid Washington U. Sch. Medicine, St. Louis, 1990—. Assoc. vice-chancellor for continuing edn., admissions and fin. aid Washington U. Sch. Medicine, St. Louis, 1997—; bd. dirs. Family Resource Ctr., St. Louis, Physicians Corp., Washington U. Alliance Corp., First Tier Health Corp., Grace Hill Health Ctr., Nat. Com. to Prevent Child Abuse, Mo.; pres. bd. dirs. St. Louis Child Abuse Network, v.p. Family Support Network. Mem. editl. bd. Annals of Neurology and Clinical Neuropharmacology; contbr. articles to profl. jours. Bd. dirs. City St. Louis Bd. Children's Welfare, 1984-86; mem. profl. adv. bd. Epilepsy Found. Am., 1987-94, chmn.-elect, 1991-93, pres.-elect, 1993-95, pres. 1995-97, chmn. bd., 1997-98; co-chmn. Blue Ribbon Commn. on Future Svcs. to Children & Families, Mo., 1987-88; chmn. Children's Trust Fund Mo., 1989-91, bd. dirs., 1985-91; bd. dirs. Epilepsy Found. St. Louis, 2000--. Recipient Spl. Recognition award State of Md., 1971, Career Acad. Devel. award NIH, 1975, Disting. Social Svcs. award Mo. Dept. Social Svcs., 1988, Child Adv. award St. Louis Child Abuse Network, 1990, Child Adv. award Family Resource Ctr., 1991, 29th Ann. honoree, 1999; Spl. Recognition award Epilepsy Fedn. St. Louis, 1992, Guardian Angel award St. Louis Family Support Network, 1999, Samuel Clemmens award Epilepsy Found., St. Louis, 1999. Fellow Am. Acad. Neurology, Am. Acad. Pediat.; mem. Child Neurology Soc. (bd. dirs. 1985-87), Am. Neurol. Assn., Soc. Pediat. Rsch., Cen. Soc. Neurol. Rsch. (sec., treas. 1985, pres. 1989), Alpha Omega Alpha. Avocations: fly fishing, water sports, photography. Office: St Louis Childrens Hosp One Childrens Pl Saint Louis MO 63110-1014 E-mail: dodsone@msnotes.wustl.edu.

DODSWORTH, ROY W. pharmaceutical company executive; b. Norwood, Mass., Sept. 6, 1948; s. James W. and Beulah G. Dodsworth; m. Genevieve Dodsworth, June 26, 1971; children: Dawn Terri, Roger H. Whitford Jr. BA, Drew U., 1970. Asst. dir. Ayerst Labs. Inc., N.Y.C., 1983-86; dir., N.Am. head regulatory affairs Organon, Inc., West Orange, NJ, 1986-94; sr. assoc. dir. Sandoz, East Hanover, N.J., 1995-97, dir. N.Am. head, Regulatory CMC, 1995-97; dir., regional area head-asthma, hormone replacement therapy, bone Novartis Pharm. Co., East Hanover, 1997, exec. dir., worldwide therapeutics area head, 1997-98, exec. dir., worldwide therapeutics area head ctrl. nervous sys., 1998—. Contbr. numerous tech. publs. Active Budd Lake Rescue Squad, 1992-93; adv. com. Mt. Olive Township Multiple Family Dwelling, Budd Lane, 1980-83. Fellow Am. Inst. Chemists; mem. Regulatory Affairs Profl. Soc., Am. Chem. Soc., Drug Info. Assn., Parenteral Drug Assn. Republican. Methodist. Avocations: raquetball, basketball, football, softball, fishing. Home: 10 Crossing Dr Flanders NJ 07836-4709 Office: Novartis Pharm Co 1 Health Plz East Hanover NJ 07936

DOE, PATRICIA LOUISE, information technology executive; b. Hazelton, Pa., Mar. 8, 1948; d. Thomas Victor and Dorothy Eleanor (Kimmel) McLaughlin; m. Lawrence Whittier Doe, Dec. 27, 1969; children: Lawrence Whittier Jr., Christopher Thomas. BA in Math., Newark State Coll., 1970; MS in Indsl. Engring., Lehigh U., 1987. Sr. tech. analyst Bell Telephone Labs, N. Andover, Mass., 1970-72; math tchr. St. Maria Goretti High Sch., Hagerstown, Md., 1976-77, 80-81; programmer analyst Air Products & Chems., Inc., Allentown, Pa., 1981—83, sr. programmer analyst, 1983-84, tech. support analyst, 1984-85, sr. tech. support analyst, 1985-88, prin. tech. analyst, 1988-91, prin. tech. assessment analyst, 1991-92, prin. info. tech. analyst applied tech., 1992-94; mgr. client/server tech. svcs. The Vanguard Group, Valley Forge, Pa., 1994-95; prin. Laredo Assocs., Boca Raton, Fla., 1995—; dir. ops. Alliance Entertainment Corp., Coral Springs, Fla., 1996-97; sr. prin. RMS Info. Systems, Inc., Lanham, Md., 1998—2000; mgr. Delivery Mgrs. US Internetworking, Annapolis, Md., 2000—02; v.p. info. tech. Andrews Fed. Credit Union, Suitland, Md., 2002—. Asst. treas. Washington County (Md.) PTA, 1980-81; fin. sec. Faith Presbyn. Ch., Emmaus, Pa., 1982-84; dir. bell choir St. Andrews Presbyn. Ch., Williamsport, Md., 1978-81. Mem.: Kappa Delta Pi. Republican. Avocations: reading, needlework. Home: 1310 Salem Run Crownsville MD 21032-2229 Office: Andrews Fed Credit Union 5711 Allentown Rd Suitland MD 20746

DOEBLER, BETTIE ANNE, language educator, researcher, writer; b. Atlantic City; d. Willoughby Foster and Ann (Ratledge) Young; m. John W. Doebler, Sept. 1, 1954 (dec. Aug. 26, 1994); 1 child, Mark B. BA, Duke U., 1953, MA, 1955; PhD, U. Wis., 1961. From instr. to assoc. prof. Dickinson Coll., Carlisle, Pa., 1961-70; assoc. prof. Ariz. State U., Tempe, 1971, prof., 1975, prof. emeritus, 1994—, dir. interdisciplinary humanities program, 1989-94. Contbr. articles to profl. jour.; author: The Quickening Seed: Death in the Sermons of John Donne, 1974; contbr. poetry to Passages North, The Awakenings Rev., South: An Anthology of the Southern Counties, Eng., 2002, articles; co-editor: Funeral Sermons Publ. for Women (1600-1630), 5 vols., 1993—2001; author: Rooted Sorrow: Dying in Early Modern Eng., 1994; co-author: Book of the Mermaid: Poems by Doebler, Slotten, Thiem, 2001; co-editor: Nine Waves: Poems by Doebler, Slotten, Thiem, 2003. Angier B. Duke Grad. fellow Duke U., 1954; recipient Faculty Rsch. award Ariz. State U., 1984. Episcopalian. E-mail: bettieadoebler@aol.com.

DOEDE, JOHN HENRY, investment company executive; b. Chgo., Sept. 29, 1937; s. Clinton Milford and Dorothy Ruth (Hagemeyer) D.; m. Jean Anne Dabbs, May 6, 1983; children: Danna, Tina, Timothy. AB in Chemistry, Harvard U., 1959; MS in Phys. Chemistry, U. Chgo., 1962, PhD in Phys. Chemistry, Physics, 1963. Physicist Argonne (Ill.) Nat. Lab., 1963-65; mgr. EMR computer div. (electro magnetic rsch). Schlumberger Corp., Mpls., 1965-67; pres. Data Internat. Inc., Mpls., 1967-70; v.p. Heizer Corp., Chgo., 1970-72; v.p., dir. 1st Chgo. Investment Corp., 1972-83; pres. The Polaris Capital Group, San Diego, 1983-88; chmn. JDJD, Inc., Palm Beach, Fla., 1992-97, Blue Eagle Golf Ctrs., Inc., Wayne, Pa., 1996-98, AIG Silk Road Fund, N.Y.C., 1997—, Am. European Industries, Inc., 1999—, The Answer System, Inc., 1999. Republican. Home: 8480 N Canta Bello Paradise Valley AZ 85253 E-mail: fordoede@ix.netcom.com.

DOEDÉE, MARIJO, chemist; b. Albany, N.Y., Apr. 30, 1966; d. Robert Johann and Joanne Van Beusichem; m. Gerardus Johannes Petrus Doedée, May 15, 1992; children: Janneke, Sabine. BS in Pharmacy, Albany (N.Y.) Coll. Pharmacy, 1989; PhD in Chemistry, U. Vt., 1994. Pharmacist Knightes' Pharmacy, St. Albans, Vt., 1990—94; sr. scientist Wyeth-Ayerst Rsch., Rouses Point, NY, 1994—97, sr. rsch. scientist i Pearl River, NY, 1998—99, sr. scientist I, 1998—99, sr. scientist II, 2000—01; sect. head Wyeth Rsch., Pearl River, NY, 2001—03, assoc. dir., 2003—. Invited spkr., workshops in field. Contbr. articles to profl. jours. Mem.: Dissolution Discussion Group, Am. Assn. Pharm. Scientists, Germania Almrausch Schuplattler Verein (trachtenmutter 2002—03), Rho Chi. Roman Catholic. Avocations: German folk dancing (schuplattling), cake decorating. Home: 21 Woodfield Dr Washingtonville NY 10992 Office: Wyeth Rsch 401 N Middletown Rd Pearl River NY 10992

DOENECKE, JUSTUS DREW, history educator; b. Bklyn., Mar. 5, 1938; BA magna cum laude, Colgate U., 1960; MA, Princeton U., 1962, PhD, 1966. Instr. history Colgate U., Hamilton, NY, 1963—64, Ohio Wesleyan U., Delaware, 1965—66, asst. prof. history, 1966—69, New Coll., Sarasota, Fla., 1969-71, assoc. prof. history, 1971-75, New Coll. Univ. South Fla., Sarasota, 1975-77, prof. history, 1977—2000, New Coll. Fla., Sarasota, 2000—. Author: Not to the Swift: The Old Isolationists in the Cold War Era, 1979, The Diplomacy of Frustration: The Manchurian Crisis of 1931-1933 as Revealed in the Papers of Stanley K. Hornbeck, 1981, The Presidencies of James A. Garfield and Chester A. Arthur, 1981, When the Wicked Rise: American Opinion-Makers and the Manchurian Crisis of 1931-33, 1984, Anti-Intervention: A Bibliographical Introduction to Isolationism and Pacifism from World War I to the Early Cold War, 1987, In Danger Undaunted: The Anti-Interventionist Movement of 1940-41 as Revealed in the Papers of the America First Committee, 1990, (with J. Wilz) From Isolation to War, 1931-1941, 2003 (3rd edit.), The Battle Against Intervention, 1939-41, 1997, Storm on the Horizon: The Challenge to American Intervention, 1939-1941, 2000, The New Deal, 2003; contbr. articles to profl. jours. Recipient Herbert Hoover Book award Herbert Hoover Presdl. Libr. Assn., 2001, Woodrow Wilson Nat. fellow, 1960, Danforth fellow, 1960, Non-resident summer fellow Inst. for Humane Studies, 1970, 71, resident summer fellow Inst. for Humane Studies, 1975, 76, 78, 81, sr. rsch. fellow acad. yr. Inst. for Humane Studies, 1977-78, summer fellow NEH, 1971, fellow John Anton Kittridge Ednl. Fund, 1973, 80, Harry S. Truman Libr., 1973, Earhart Found., 1995, vis. fellow New Coll., Oxford, 1991. Mem. Soc. for Historians Am. Fgn. Rels. (Arthur S. Link prize for documentary editing 1991), Am. Hist. Assn., Am. Soc. Ch. History, Orgn. Am. Historians, Hist. Soc. Episcopal Ch., Hist. Soc., Peace History Soc. (coun. 1996—), Phi Beta Kappa. Episcopalian. Office: New Coll of Fla Sarasota FL 34243-2197 Fax: 941-359-4475. E-mail: doenecke@ncf.edu.

DOENGES, BYRON FREDERICK, economist, educator, former government official; b. Ft. Wayne, Ind., June 18, 1922; s. Arthur Philip and Elsie (Mesing) D.; m. Elaine Aiken, June 15, 1947. Diploma, Internat. Bus. Coll., 1941; student, DePauw U., 1943-44; AB, Franklin (Ind.) Coll., 1946; MBA, Ind. U., 1948, PhD, 1962; DLtrs (hon.), Franklin Coll. of Ind., 1985. Instr., headmaster boarding dept. Punahou Sr. Acad., Honolulu, 1948-50; dir. scholarships and loans Ind. U., Bloomington, 1951-56, asst. dean Coll. Arts and Scis., 1955-65; prof. econs., dean Coll. Liberal Arts Willamette U., 1965-71; econ. cons. Gov. Oreg., 1971-72; dep. asst. dir. ACDA, Washington, 1972-73, chief econs. and spl. studies div., 1973-76; sr. econs. advisor U.S. Arms Control and Disarmament Agy., 1976-93; ind. writer and internat. econ. cons., 1993—. Program devel. head Title II NDEA, U.S. Office Edn., Washington, 1958-59; assoc. dir. Salzburg (Austria) Seminar Am. Studies, 1962-64; mem. Higher Commn. N.W. Assn. Secondary and Higher Schs., 1968-71; mem. exec. bd. N.W. Assn. Pvt. Colls. and Univs., 1969-70; chmn. planning com. Navy V-12 Nat. Colloquium, 1989; conduct spl. rsch. on internat. capital movements, econs. higher edn., econs. arms control, Soviet and successor states to former Soviet Union economies, econ. impact of def. spending. Editor: Accountability, 1973, World Military Expenditures and Arms Transfers, 1981-84, Arms Control Ann. Report, 1981-91, Arms Control Impact Statement for the Congress, 1991; contbr. articles to profl. jours. Lt. comdr. USNR, 1943-46, PTO. Recipient alumni citation Franklin Coll., 1977. Mem. Am. Econ. Assn., Cosmos Club (Washington), Lambda Chi Alpha (mem. nat. fellowship bd. 1965-2000, Meritorious Svc. award 1984), Pi Gamma Mu, Omicron Delta Kappa. Home: 1002 Fearrington Post Pittsboro NC 27312-5503 Office: 4 E Madison Pittsboro NC 27312 E-mail: byron-doenges@mindspring.com.

DOENGES, RUDOLPH CONRAD, finance educator; b. Tonkawa, Okla., Dec. 7, 1930; s. Rudolph Soland and Helen Elizabeth (Lower) D.; m. Ellen Ione Gummere, Oct. 5, 1963; children: Rudolph Conrad, John Soland, William Gummere. AB magna cum laude (scholar 1948-54), Harvard U., 1952, MBA, 1954; D.BA (Ford Found. fellow 1963-64), U. Colo., Boulder, 1965. Mktg. analyst Ford Motor Co., Dearborn, Mich., 1954; gen. mgr. Doenges-Long Motors and Western Auto Rentals, Colorado Springs, 1958-61; mem. faculty U. Tex., Austin, 1964-2000, prof. fin., 1974-2000, Arthur Andersen & Co. prof. fin., 1983-2000, assoc. dean Grad. Sch. Bus., 1972-76, chmn. dept. fin., 1976-80, assoc. dean Coll. Bus. Adminstrn., 1987-97. Author: (with E. W. Walker) Case Problems in Financial Management, 1968, Consumer Credit in Texas, 1970; editor: Readings in Money and Banking, 1968, (with H. A. Wolf) Corporate Planning Models, 1971; contbr. articles in field to profl. jours. Gen. Bd. Pensions United Meth. Ch., 1988-96; trustee Iliff Sch. Theology, 1992-96. Served with USN, 1955-58. Mem. Austin C. of C., Fin. Mgmt. Assn. (dir. 1980-82), Southwestern Fin. Assn. (pres. 1973-74), Southwestern Fedn. Administrv. Disciplines (pres. 1975-76), Austin Soc. Fin. Analysts, El Paso Club (Colorado Springs), Austin Club, Garden of the Gods Club. Republican. Methodist. Home: 3500 Hillbrook Cir Austin TX 78731-4036 Office: U Tex Dept Finance Austin TX 78712

DOEPKE, KATHERINE LOUISE GULDBERG, retired music educator; b. Suttons Bay, Mich., Dec. 18, 1921; d. Gottfried Johannes and Aasta Agnethe (Kalstad) Guldberg; m. Henry August Doepke, Aug. 13, 1944; children: Karen Sernett, Chris, Bruce, Barabara Potuck. BS, U. Minn., 1944, MA, 1967, postgrad. Tchr. music Mpls. Pub. Schs., 1963-83; ret., 1983. Cons./mentor Mpls. Pub. Schs., 1984—87; vol. tchr. Elder Learning Inst. Contbr. articles to profl. jours. Vol. Courage Ctr., Mpls., 1983—86, Food Your Door, 1984—88; dir. Gray Aires Chorus, Mpls., 1986—95; bd. dirs., publicity chair, mem. various coms. Thursday Musical, 1984—, pres., 1998—2000; choral dir. Trinity First Luth. Ch., Mpls., 1953—92. Named composer in residence, Mpls. Pub. Schs., 1985. Mem.: AAUW (prodr. anniversary video 1997, v.p. programs 2000—02, chair coms., v.p. mktg. 2003—), Music Educators Nat. Conf. (clinician 1976, 1978, 1980), Am. Choral Dirs. Assn. (state sec.-treas., historian, sec. F.M. Christiansen Endowment Fund com., F. Melius Christiansen Meml. award 2001), Mu Phi Epsilon (internat. pres. 1992—95). Avocations: walking, reading. Home: 8300 Golden Valley Rd Apt 329 Minneapolis MN 55427-4456 E-mail: katdoepke@usfamily.net.

DOERFLER, LEO G. audiology educator; b. N.Y.C., June 25, 1919; s. Gustav S. and Anna (Steiner) D.; m. Alice Laura Turechek, Dec. 19, 1943; children—Dennis Lee, Donald Lee, David Lee, Ann Laura. AB, N.Y.U., 1939; MS, Washington U., St. Louis, 1941; PhD, Northwestern U., 1948. Tchr.-psychologist Iowa Sch. Deaf, Council Bluffs, 1941-43; instr. audiology Northwestern U., 1946-48; chief dept. audiology-speech pathology Latrobe Area Hosp., 1976—; prof. audiology emeritus (Sch. Medicine); dir. doctoral program bioacoustics U. Pitts., 1948-76; dir. dept. audiology Eye and Ear Hosp., Pitts., 1948-76; pres. Westmoreland Hearing Assocs.; chmn. bd. Audiology Coop. Cons. in field, 1946—, Nat. Inst. Neurol. and Communicative Diseases and Stroke. Contbr. articles to profl. jours. Bd. dirs. Cerebral Palsy Assn. Pitts., 1958— . Served with AUS, World War II. C.C. Bunch fellow Northwestern U., 1946-47 Fellow AAAS, Am. Speech and Hearing Assn. (pres. 1967); mem. Am. Indsl. Hygiene Assn. (com. on noise), Indsl. Med. Assn. (com. on noise), Am. Acad. Ophthalmology and Otolaryngology (com. on hearing and equilibrium), Am. Bd. Examiners in Speech Pathology and Audiology (pres. 1960), Acad. Dispensing Audiologists (pres. 1978-79), Sigma Xi. Inventor D-S test for psychogenic deafness. Home: 245 Foxhunt Crescent Syosset NY 11791

DOERING, CHARLES HENRY, research scientist, educator, editor, publisher; b. Munich, Jan. 7, 1935; came to U.S., 1950; s. Heinrich and Marianne (Fleischmann) D.; m. Panayiota Maria Thliveris, June 17, 1961; children: Andreanna, Erika, Stefan, Anselm. BS in Chemistry, U. San Francisco, 1956; MS in Organic Chemistry, U. Munich, 1959; PhD in Biochemistry, U. Calif., San Francisco, 1964. Postdoctoral fellow Harvard Med. Sch., Boston, 1964-67; rsch. scientist Stanford (Calif.) U. Sch. Medicine, 1967-76; rsch. assoc. prof. SUNY, Stony Brook, 1976-86; editor Springer Verlag Publs., N.Y.C., 1986-90, Oxford Univ. Press, N.Y.C., 1990-91; exec. editor VCH Publs., Inc., N.Y.C., 1991-94; sr. editor, mgr. conf. proceedings program Am. Inst. Physics Press, Melville, NY, 1994—. Contbr. over 30 articles to profl. jours. Mem. AAAS, Am. Chem. Soc., Soc. Scholarly Pub. Home: 21 Dyke Rd Setauket NY 11733-3014 Office: Am Inst Physics 2 Huntington Quadrangle Melville NY 11747-4502

DOERING, PAUL LOUIS, pharmacist, educator; b. Miami, Feb. 25, 1949; s. Juanita Brown and Ernest Doering; m. Cheryl Rainey, Aug. 22, 1970; children: Christopher, Tracy, Jennifer. BS in Pharmacy, U. Fla., 1972, MS in Pharmacy, 1975. Asst. prof. pharmacy practice U. Fla., Gainesville, 1976—81, assoc. prof. pharmacy practice, 1981—88, prof. pharmacy practice, 1988—95, disting. svc. prof. pharmacy practice, 1995—2002. Co-dir. Drug Info. and Pharmacy Resource Ctr., Gainesville, 1988—2002. Contbr. articles to profl. jours. Lectr.-drug abuse prevention Various, Various, Fla., 1976—2002. Mem.: Fla. Pharmacy Assn., Am. Coll. Clin. Pharmacists, Am. Assn. Colls. Pharmacy, Am. Soc. Health Sys. Pharmacists, Am. Pharm. Assn. Democrat. Methodist. Office: U Fla Coll Pharmacy Box 100486 Gainesville FL 32610 Home Fax: (352)-338-9860; Office Fax: 352-338-9860. Personal E-mail: doering@shands.ufl.edu. E-mail: doering@shands.ufl.edu.

DOERINGER, FRANKLIN M. historian, educator; b. Cleve., Oct. 2, 1940; s. Frank J. and Bertha Ann (Warek) D.; m. Frederica Cagan, Dec. 28, 1975; children: Adam Henry, Andrea Cagan. BA, Columbia Coll., 1962; PhD, Columbia U., 1971. Asst. prof. Chinese Columbia U., N.Y.C., 1970-71; Nathan M. Pusey prof. history and East Asian studies Lawrence U., Appleton, Wis., 1972—, chair East Asian langs. and cultures, 1989-96, chair dept. history, 1997—2000. Author: Discovering the Global Past, 1995; contbr. articles to profl. jours. Curriculum rev. com. mem. Appleton Bd. Edn., 1991—; v.p. bd. dirs. Outagamie County Hist. Soc., 2002—. Grantee 3M Found., 1990, Chiang Ching Kuo Found., 1993, Freeman Found., 2000. Mem. Internat. Soc. Chinese Philosophy, Am. Hist. Assn. Office: Lawrence Univ Dept History Appleton WI 54915

DOERNBERG, DONALD LANE, law educator; b. Chgo., May 21, 1945; s. Dudley David and Nanette (Lowenstern) D.; m. Cynthia A. Pope, July 31, 1983. B.A., Yale U., 1966; J.D., Columbia U., 1969. Bar: N.Y. 1969, U.S. Ct. Appeals (2d cir.) 1970, U.S. Ct. Appeals (3d cir.) 1971, U.S. Dist. Ct. (ea. and so. dists.) N.Y. 1971, U.S. Dist. Ct. (no. dist.) N.Y. 1972, U.S. Ct. Appeals (5th and 10th cirs.) 1972, U.S. Ct. Appeals (D.C. cir.) 1973, U.S. Dist. Ct. (we. dist.) 1973, U.S. Supreme Ct. 1974, U.S. Ct. Appeals (8th cir.) 1975, U.S. Ct. Appeals (9th cir.) 1984, Calif. 1985, U.S. Dist. Ct. (no. dist.) Calif. 1985. Tchr. League Sch. for Seriously Disturbed Children, Bklyn., 1969-70; assoc. Levy, Gutman et al, N.Y.C., 1970-74; Hofheimeret al, N.Y.C., 1974-75; staff atty. spl. litigation Legal Aid Soc., N.Y.C., 1975-78, dir. spl. litigation, 1978; prof. law Pace U., 1979— ; vis. prof. law Hastings Coll. Law, San Francisco, 1984-85, Santa Clara (Calif.) Sch. of Law, 1985-86. Contbr. articles to law revs. Mem. Westchester Civil Liberties Union (legal dir. 1978-84, vice chmn., 1974-77, 80-81, chmn. 1978-80). Office: Pace Univ Sch Law 78 N Broadway White Plains NY 10603-3710

DOERPER, JOHN ERWIN, journal editor, publishing executive; b. Wuerzburg, Germany, Sept. 17, 1943; came to U.S., 1963, naturalized resident, 1973; s. Werner and Theresia (Wolf) D.; m. Victoria McCulloch, Dec. 2, 1970. BA, Calif. State U., Fullerton, 1968; postgrad., U. Calif., Davis, 1972. Writer/author, Seattle, 1984—; food columnist Washington, Seattle, 1985-88, Seattle Times, 1985-88; food editor Wash.-The Evergreen State Mag., Seattle, 1989-94, Pacific Northwest mag., 1989-94, Seattle Home and Garden, 1989-91; pub., editor, founder Pacific Epicure, Quarterly Jour. Gastronomy, Bellingham, Wash., 1988—. Dir. Annual N.W. Invitational Chef's Symposium. Author: Eating Well: A Guide to Foods of the Pacific Northwest, 1984, The Eating Well Cookbook, 1984, Shellfish Cookery: Absolutely Delicious Recipes from the West Coast, 1985, Pacific Northwest Wine Country, 2001; author, illustrator: The Blue Carp, 1994, Wine Country: California's Napa and Sonoma Valleys, 1996, Pacific Northwest, 1997, Coastal California, 1998 (Lowell Thomas Travel Journalism Competition Gold medal 1999); contbr. articles to profl. jours., intro. and chpts. to books; co-author: Washington: A Compass Guide, 2002, Fodor's Pacific Northwest, 2002, Fodor's Seattle, 2000. Recipient Silver medal, White award for city and regional mags. William Allen White Sch. Journalism, U. Kans., Lowell Thomas award Gold medal for best guide book, 1999. Mem. Oxford Symposium Food and Cookery (speaker 26th Ann. Pacific N.W. Writer's Conf. 1982, 92). Avocations: food, wine, travel, painting, printmaking. E-mail: pacificepicure@att.net.

DOERR, JOHN MAXWELL, lawyer; b. Pontiac, Mich., Oct. 3, 1939; s. Maxwell Hilberg and Jane (Park) D.; m. Eleanor Kilmon, Feb. 11, 1967 (div. Jan. 1989); children: Jennifer Anne, Julie Kristin. B.A., Coll. Wooster, 1961; postgrad., Johns Hopkins U., 1962 64; J.D., U. Md., 1973. Bar: Md. 1973, Pa. 1974, U.S. Dist. Ct. (ea. dist.) Pa. 1974. Various positions Acme Markets, Inc., Balt., 1961-73, dir. real estate, Phila., 1973-80, asst. sec., 1973—, counsel, 1980— . Del., Delaware County Bus. Task Force, Bryn Mawr, Pa., 1976-77. Recipient Freidlander award Coll. Wooster, 1961. Mem. ABA, Phila. Bar Assn. Republican. Presbyterian. Office: Acme Markets Inc 75 Valley Stream Pkwy Malvern PA 19355-1406

DOERR, PATRICIA MARIAN, elementary and special education educator; b. Rochford, Essex, Eng., Mar. 14, 1947; came to U.S., 1976; d. Edward Earnest and Winifred May (Daniels) Earl; m. Hans Joachim Doerr, Dec. 17, 1983; children: Daniel, Nicholas, Carla. Cert. of Edn., Sussex U., 1968; Diploma in Edn. of Handicapped, London U., 1974; MS, Calif. Luth. U., 1986. Tchr. Long Road Jr. Sch., Canvey Island, Eng., 1968-70; tchr. scale 1 Belvedere (Kent, Eng.) Jr. Sch., 1970-71; tchr. scale 2 Bostal (Kent, Eng.) Manor Jr. Sch., 1971-73; tchr. scale 3, head remedial Warren Wood Boys Comprehensive Sch., Rochester, Kent, 1974-76; ednl. therapist Westvalley Ctr. for Ednl. Therapy, Canoga Park, Calif., 1977-79; tchr. K-2 Sundance Sch., Simi Valley, Calif., 1977-78; spl. tchr. Conejo Valley Unified Sch. Dist., Thousand Oaks, Calif., 1979-94; elem. tchr. Meadows Elem. Sch., Thousand Oaks, Calif., 1994—98; tchr. on leave (lang. arts specialist) Ventura County, 1998—. Ednl. cons., Ventura County, 1998-; mem. London Panel of Art Tutors, ILEA Evening Inst., 1969-73; mentor spl. edn. and lang. arts Conejo Valley Unified Sch. Dist., 1988-95. Recipient Award of Tchr. Excellence, AMGEN, 1996; Scwrip fellow Santa Barbara U., 1988. Mem. Calif. Assn. Mediated Learning (bd. dirs. 1991-95). Episcopalian. Home: 1933 Tamarack St Westlake Village CA 91361-1841 E-mail: tdoer@vcss.k12.ca.us.

DOERRIE, BOBETTE, secondary education educator; b. Albuquerque, June 22, 1944; d. Neill and Dorothy Madelyn (Jones) Patterson; m. Edward Lewis Horton, Aug. 21, 1966 (div. 1990); children: Leah, James, Carol, Neill; m. Jerome Lee Doerrie, July 28, 1991; children: Jennifer, Elena. BA, McMurry Coll., 1966; MEd, DePaul U., 1977. Cert. sec. broadfield sci. Tchr. physics and phys. sci. G/T coord. Perryton (Tex.) H.S.; tchr. Summit Sch., Dundee, Ill., 1974-77, Lamesa Middle Sch., 1980-85, Lamesa H.S., 1968-69, 85-91, Perryton High Sch., 1991—. Co-dir. Dawson County Sci. Fair, 1981-91; coach Odyssey of the Mind, 1988-91; mem. McMurry U. Ednl. Adv. Bd., 1991-97, engring. team faculty advisor, 1993—, sci. olympiad coach, 1998-2000, sci. bowl advisor, 2001—; mem. Mus. Bd. Dawson County, 1983-90; mem. Libr. Bd. Ochiltree County, 1993-95, v.p., 1994-95. Recipient Excellence in Teaching award Tex. State Assn. for Physics Tchrs., 1992, Tchr. of Yr., Region XVI Gifted and Talented Tchrs., 1994, Nat. Tchg. award RadioShack, 2001; NSF/Tex. Edn. Assn. Christa McAuliffe grantee, 1993, Outstanding Sci. Educator, Tex. Acad. Sci., 2002, Nat. Tchg. award Health Physics Soc., 2002. Mem.: Sci. Tchrs. of Tex. (treas. 1998—2001, Sci. Bowl Sponsor 2001—03), South Plains Sci. Soc. (pres. 1988, Sharon Christa McAuliffe Tchr. of Yr. 1987), Delta Kamma Gamma (pres.). Avocations: amateur radio, painting, archaeology, reading, writing. Home: 13925 CR B Booker TX 79005-9713 Office: Perryton High Sch 1200 S Jefferson St Perryton TX 79070-3700 E-mail: bdoerrie@yahoo.com.

DOERRIES, REINHARD RENÉ, modern history educator; b. Berlin, Sept. 25, 1934; came to U.S., 1954; s. Hermann and Annemarie (Kochendoerffer) D.; m. Elaine Sulli, Jan. 20, 1963; 1 child, Chantal-Aimée. BA, Concordia Coll., 1958; MFA, Ohio U., 1960; MA, Yale U., 1962; MBA, Inst. Européen d'Adminstrn. des Affaires, Fontainbleau, France, 1965; PhD, Bochum U., 1971; habilitation, U. Hamburg, 1982. With internat. divsn. 1st Nat. Bank of Boston, 1962-64; internat. mgmt. cons. Booz Allen & Hamilton Internat., Zurich, Switzerland, 1965-68; asst. prof. modern history Hamburg U., Germany, 1970-73, 75-83, prof., 1983-86, U. Kassel, Germany, 1986-88, U. Erlangen-Nuremberg, Germany, 1988—. Guest prof. U. Southampton, Eng., 1986; internat. fellow Am. Council Learned Socs., N.Y.C., 1973-75; lectr. in field. Author: Washington-Berlin 1908/1917, 1975, Iren und Deutsche in der Neuen Welt, 1985, Imperial Challenge, 1989, Prelude to the Easter Rising, 2000, Hitler's Last Chief of Foreign Intelligence, 2003; editor: Memoirs of Erika von Watzdorf-Bachoff, 1997, Diplomaten und Agenten, 2001; co-editor: Amerikastudien, 1990—, American Studies Book Series, 1990—; adv. editor: Perspectives in Intelligence History, 1991—95; contbr. articles. Bd. dirs. Internat. Sch., Hamburg, 1979-80; bd. dirs. Am. House Nuremberg, 1995—, vice chmn., 1996—. Danforth Found. fellow Yale U., 1962. Mem. German Soc. for Am. Studies (dir. 1976-84, pres. 1987-90, dir. 1990—), Am. Hist. Assn., German Soc. for Can. Studies, Immigration History Soc., Intelligence History Study Group (dir. 1993-2000), Soc. for Historians of Am. Fgn. Rels., German Hist. Assn., Group 65 Club (founder), Yale Club. Avocation: painting. Office: U Erlangen-Nuremberg Findelgasse 9 90402 Nuremberg Germany

DOERSAM, CHARLES HENRY, JR., engineer, educator, entrepreneur; b. NYC, Nov. 1, 1921; s. Charles Henry, Sr. and Mary Emily (Davenport) D.; m. Cynthia Ann Wick, Dec. 7, 1954 (div. dec. 1980); children: Charles Henry III, Donna Davenport, Dean Robert. BS in Engr., Columbia U., 1942, MSME, 1944; post grad., MIT, U. Mich., N.Y.U. Registered profl. engr., N.Y. Indsl. engr. Pratt & Whitney, East Hartford, Conn., 1941-42; mem. tech. staff Bell Telephone Labs, N.Y.C., 1942-44; sr. project engr Specl. Devices Ctr., Sands Pt., N.Y., 1946-53; project mgr. Sperry Gyroscope Co., Lake Success, N.Y., 1953-60; new product planning mgr. Potter Instrument Co., Plainview, N.Y., 1960-62; dir. mktg. chief engr. Instruments for Industry, Hicksville, N.Y., 1962-64; prof. Polytech. Instit. of Bklyn., 1964-69; pres. Com Comp Inc, Hauppauge, N.Y., 1969-71; chmn., CEO Fiber Optic Sensors, Inc., Old Lyme, Conn., 1983—. Pres. DOERCO Cons., CUB Computer Co., NUTEK Corp., Princeton Automated Labs., Pedagogy Rsch. Inst.; nat. chmn. IRE Profl. Group on Space Electronics, 1950. Pantentee in field; contbr. articles to profl. jours. Bd. Advisors Waldorf Sch., Garden City, N.Y., 1964-68, Portledge Sch., Locust Valley, N.Y., 1977. Lt. (j.g.) USNR, 1944-46. Mem. North Shore Yacht Club (commn. 1968-69), Point O'Woods Club. Republican. Congregationalist. Avocations: tennis, sailing, woodworking, gardening, construction. Home and Office: 67 Shore Rd PO Box 927 Old Lyme CT 06371-0927 E-mail: fosi1@juno.com.

DOERSHUK, CARL FREDERICK, physician, pediatrics educator; b. Warren, Ohio, Dec. 24, 1930; s. Carl Frederick and Eula Blanche (Mahan) D.; m. Emma Lou Plummer, Aug. 21, 1954; children: Rebecca Lee, John Frederick, David Plummer. BA, Oberlin Coll., 1952; MD, Case Western Res. U., 1956. Intern U.S. Naval Hosp., Camp Pendleton, Ohio, 1956-57; resident in pediat. Cleve. Met. Gen. Hosp. and Babies and Children's Hosp., Cleve., 1959-61; postdoctoral pulmonary fellow Babies and Children's Hosp. USPHS, Cleve., 1961-63; sr. instr. to prof. pediatrics specializing in academic pediatric pulmonary medicine Case Western Res. U., Cleve., 1963-98, emeritus prof., 1998—. Co-editor Pediatric Respiratory Therapy, 1974, 3d edit., 1986; contbr. articles to profl. jours. Chmn. med. adv. coun. Cystic Fibrosis Found., Washington, 1966-72, bd. trustees, 1969-81, exec. com., 1969-74, v.p. med. affairs Cleve. chpt., 1965-90. Lt. M.C., USN, 1957-59. Named Young Man Yr. Cystic Fibrosis Found., 1970; recipient Richard C. Talamo Clinician Scientist award Cystic Fibrosis Found., 1997. Mem. Am. Pediatric Soc., Soc. Pediatric Research, Am. Acad. Pediatrics (exec. com. chest sect.), Am. Thoracic Soc. (chmn. pediatric pulmonary sect. 1971), No. Ohio Pediatric Soc., Acad. Medicine. Avocations: sailing, raising dahlias. Office: Rainbow Babies and Childrens Hosp 11100 Euclid Ave Cleveland OH 44106

DOESBURG, JOHN C. military career officer; b. Milw., May 15, 1947; m. Denise Doesburg; children: Sean, Russell. Grad., U. Okla., 1970, Command & Gen. Staff Coll., Army War Coll. Commd. officer U.S. Army, 1970, advanced through grades to maj. gen., battery exec. officer A Battery, 1st Battalion, 10th Field, brigade chem. officer 2nd Brigade, 82nd Airborne Divsn., comdr. hdqrs. co., 2nd Brigade, 82nd Airborne Divsn.; comdr. 21st Chem. Co., 82nd Airborne Divsn.; career program mgr. MILPERCEN; mem. U.S. Negotiations Team for a Chem. Weapons Treaty U.S. Arms Control and Disarmament Agy.; exec. officer U.S. Army Chem. Activity Western Command U.S. Army, divsn. chem. officer 25th Infantry Divsn., comdr. 84th Chem. Battalion, comdr. U.S. Army Chem. Activity Pacific, chief chem. and NBC def. divsn., Office Dep. Chif Staff Ops., dir. Joint Program Office for Biol. Def.; commanding gen. U.S. Army Soldier and Biol. Chem. Command, Aberdeen Proving Ground, Md., 1998—. Decorated Def. Superior Svc. medal, Legion of Merit, Def. Meritorious Svc. medal, Army Meritorious Svc. medal with five oak leaf clusters, Army Commendation medal with one oak leaf cluster. Office: US Army Soldier & Biol Chem Command Aberdeen Proving Ground MD 21010-5424

DOESCHER, WILLIAM FREDERICK, communications executive; b. Utica, N.Y., Dec. 9, 1937; s. Frederick William and Katherine Ann (Kipp) D.; m. Linda Blair, Nov. 25, 1977; children: Michelle Blair, Douglas C., Marc H. Blair, Cinda L. BA in Econs., Colgate U., 1959; MS in Journalism, Syracuse (N.Y.) U., 1961; postgrad. in advanced mgmt., Columbia U., 1973. Pub. rels. assoc., editor Chase Manhattan News Chase Manhattan Bank, N.Y.C., 1961-65; mgr. press rels. Inmont Corp., 1965-66; asst. corp. rels. mgr. U.S. Plywood Corp., 1966-67; pub. affairs mgr. ea. region Champion Internat. Corp., 1967-69, mgr. advt. svcs., then dir. corp. advt., 1969-71; v.p. pub. rels. and advt. Drexel Heritage Furnishings, Inc., 1971-78; v.p. comms. Dun & Bradstreet, Inc., 1978-83, v.p. pub. rels. and advt., 1983-96, sr. v.p. global comm., 1992—; sr. v.p., chief comm. officer Dun & Bradstreet Corp., 1996—; also pub. D&B Reports mag., N.Y.C., 1978-94. Author numerous articles in mags., periodicals. Bd. dirs. Direct Mktg. Assn., Jackie Robinson Found., BBBonline, PRSA Found.; mem., adv. com. S.I. Newhouse Sch. Pub. Comm. and its Distant Learning Program at Syracuse U.; bd. govs. Scarsdale (N.Y.) Golf Club; bd. dirs. N.Y.C. divsn. N.Y. Easter Seal Soc.; past pres. Nat. Combined Health Appeal; past pres. Scarsdale, N.Y. Civic Club; past bd. dirs. Colgate Alumni Corp., Nat. Easter Seal Soc., N.Y. Easter Seal Soc., N.Y.C. divsn. Am. Cancer Soc. With USAR, 1959-65. Mem. Pub. Rels. Seminar, Arthur Page Soc., Pub. Rels. Soc. Am., Wisemen. Office: 1 Diamond Hill Rd New Providence NJ 07974-1200

DOETSCH, VIRGINIA LAMB, former advertising executive, writer; b. NYC, Oct. 12, 1920; d. Andrew Thomas and Cameola Weeden (Burns) Lamb; m. Gunter H. Doetsch, Oct. 12, 1953 (div. Feb. 1972); 1 child, Hugo. BS, Northwestern U., 1941; postgrad., Columbia U., 1943—44, postgrad., 1946—47. Writer, dir. pub. rels. J. Walter Thompson, Frankfurt, Germany, 1953 56; v.p., creative group head Tatham-Laird & Kudner (now Euro RSCG Tatham Ptnrs.), Chgo., 1959—76, Needham Harper & Steers (now DDB Chgo.), Chgo., 1976-83; free-lance advt. writer and prodr. Chgo., 1983—; writer, rschr. OmniTech Cons. Group now Diamond Tech. Ptnrs., Chgo., 1992-99. Bd. dirs Chgo. Symphony Orch. Women's Assn., 2002—; bd. dirs. Better Bus. Bur., Chgo., 1973—76, Jr. Achievement, Chgo., 1973, Women's Assn., Chgo. Symphony Orch., 2002—. With ARC, 1944—46, China, Burma, India. Decorated Bronze Star; named Woman of Yr., Am. Advt. Fedn., 1973. Mem. Women's Advt. Club Chgo. (Woman of Yr. award 1973), Chgo. Advt. Club (bd. dirs. 1973-76). Home: 400 E Randolph St Apt 828 Chicago IL 60601-7309

DOFT, BERNARD HARVEY, ophthalmologist; b. N.Y.C., Aug. 13, 1946; children: Michelle, Amy, Jennifer. Student, Cornell U., 1964—67; MD, NYU, 1971. Diplomate Am. Bd. Internal Medicine, Am. Bd. Ophthalmology. Intern, asst. resident in internal medicine Barnes Hosp., Washington U. Sch. of Medicine, St. Louis, 1971—73; rsch. assoc. NIH, Nat. Heart & Lung Inst. and Bur. of Biologics, Bethesda, Md., 1973—75; resident in ophthalmology Bascom Palmer Eye Inst., U. Miami Sch. Medicine, 1975—78, fellowship in diseases and surgery of retina and vitreous, 1978—79; asst. prof. ophthalmology U. Pitts. Sch. Medicine, 1979—84, clin. assoc. prof. ophthalmology, 1984—99, clin. assoc. prof. epidemiology, 1989—, clin. prof. ophthalmology, 1999—; pvt. practice Retina Vitreous Cons, Pitts., 1984—. Cons. vision rsch. rev. com. NIH Nat. Eye Inst., 1985, protocol rev. com, 2003; apptd. ophthalmic steering com., diabetic control and complications trial NIH, 1983; quality assurance com. Bascom Palmer Eye Inst., Ann Bates Leach Eye Hosp., U. Miami Sch. Medicine, 1977—78; co-dir., retina svc. Eye and Ear Hosp., U. Pitts., 1979—84, operating rm. com., 1982—87, chmn. com. on lasers, 1982—85; clinic coord. com. Eye and Ear Hosp., Pitts., 1982—85, ad hoc. com. for adminstrn./staff rels., 1983—85, chmn. oversight com. outpatient testing and laser ctr., 1983—85, med. staff nursing oversight com., 1983—98; study chair the endophthalmitis vitrectomy study Nat. Eye Inst., Bethesda, 1989—96; SurgiCenter task force U. Pitts. Med. Ctr., 1995, ophthalmology search com. dept. of ophthalmology chmn., 95; network cons. Diabetic Retinopathy Clin. Rsch. Network, 2003. Vitreoretinal Surgery and Technology, 1989—99; contbr. articles. Parent coun. Emory U., Atlanta, 1998—2002. With USPHS, 1973—75. Grantee in field. Fellow: ACS, Am. Acad. Ophthalmology; mem.: AMA, Pa. Acad. Ophthalmology (coun. mem. 1990—91), Retina Soc., Vitreous Soc., Macula Soc., Allegheny County Med. Soc., Pa. Med. Soc., Pitts. Ophthalmology Soc. (exec. com. 1980—91, program co-chmn. 1982—83, program chmn. 1983—87, v.p., pres.-elect 1987—88, pres. 1989—91, chmn. nominating com. 1991—93), Bascom Palmer Eye Inst. Alumni Assn., Alpha Omega Alpha. Avocation: tennis. Home: 123 South Dr Pittsburgh PA 15238-2313 Office: Retina-Vitreous Cons Ste 500 3501 Forbes Ave Pittsburgh PA 15213-3317 E-mail: doft@pitt.edu.

DOGANAY, KAZIM LEVENT, physician; b. Canton, Ohio, Apr. 26, 1959; s. Sacit and Fahamet Doganay; m. Guldeniz Cicek, Oct. 13, 1988; children: Bora, Melodi. MD, U. Istanbul, Turkey, 1984. Diplomate Am. Bd. Surgery, Am. Bd. Colon and Rectal Surgery. Intern SUNY Downstate, 1988-89; resident in surgery Bronx-Lebanon Hosp., N.Y., 1989-94; fellow in colon rectal surgery Beaumont Hosp., Royal Oak, Mich., 1994-95; attending physician Bronx-Lebanon Hosp., 1995-97; pvt. practice West Islip, N.Y., 1997— . Office: 1249 Montauk Hwy West Islip NY 11795-4916

DOGANÇAY, BURHAN C. artist, photographer, sculptor; b. Istanbul, Turkey, Sept. 11, 1929; s. Adil and Hediye Dogançay; m. Angela Hausmann, Dec. 11, 1978. Student, Acad. de la Grande Chaumière, 1955; PhD in Econs., U. Paris, 1956. Dir. dept. tourism Govt. of Turkey, Ankara, 1959-62, dir. Turk Info. N.Y.C., 1962-64; artist N.Y.C., 1964—. Author: Dogancay, 1986, Dessine-Moi L'Amour, 1992, Bride of Dreams, 1999, Dogancay: A Retrospective, 2001, Dogancay: Works on Paper, 2003, Walls of the World, 2003, Blue Walls of New York, 2003; exhibitions include Ctr. Georges Pompidou, Paris, 1982, Mus. St.-Georges, Liége, Belgium, 1982, Mus. Art Contemporain, Montreal, 1983, Seibu Mus. Art, Tokyo, 1989, State Russian Mus., Leningrad, 1992, Artists' Union, Moscow, 1992, JFK Internat. Airport, 1998—, Aubusson tapestry, —. Recipient Cert. of Appreciation, City of N.Y., 1964, medal of appreciaiton Ministry of Culture Russia, 1992, Nat. Medal of Arts for Lifetime Achievement and Cultural Contbn., Pres. of Turkey, 1995; fellow Tamarind Lithography Workshop, 1969; design selected for UNICEF cards, 1974, 96 *Mostly unshattered self-confidence, hard work and the willingness to meet new challenges are the basis of my success and happiness.*

DOGGETT, AUBREY CLAYTON, JR., real estate executive, consultant; b. Greensboro, N.C., Nov. 8, 1928; s. Aubrey Clayton and Ann (Blevins) D.; m. Judy Perier, July 26, 1952; children: Aubrey Clayton III, Kathryn Ann, Russell Lee, Robert Keith, Karen Michelle. BS, U. N.C., 1950, grad. exec. program, 1960. Salesman Richardson Realty, Inc., Greensboro, 1950, 52-53; reviewing appraiser Prudential Ins. Co. Am., Greensboro, 1953-58; exec. v.p., dir., mem. exec. com. Kavanagh-Smith and Co., Greensboro, 1958-63; v.p. mortgage loan dept. Wachovia Bank & Trust Co., Winston-Salem, N.C., 1963-66, sr. v.p., 1966-70; pres., founder Wachovia Mortgage Co., 1970-71; pres., trustee, founder Wachovia Realty Investments, 1970-71; pres., dir. Wingreen Corp., Winston-Salem, 1971—; sr. v.p., bd. dirs. AMIC Corp. (now G.E. Mortgage Ins. Co.), 1981-83. Mem. Gov. N.C. Com. Low Income Housing, 1964-68; chmn. ad hoc com. Winston-Salem Model Cities Commn., 1969; bd. dirs., mem. investment com. Richardson Corp., 1989-93; past mem., past chmn. N.C. Housing Adv. Coun.; past adv. asset mgr. Mo. Savs. Assn., Preferred Savs. Bank. Past mem. bd. dirs. Winston-Salem Housing Found. Exec. Bd., Granville Place Inc., Koerner Place, Inc., East Salem Homes, Inc. (housing for elderly); chmn. Greater Greensboro Open Golf Tournament, 1960. Lt. Col. USMCR, 1950-52; lt. col. Res. ret. Decorated Purple Heart. Mem. Mortgage Bankers Assn. Am. (hon., gov. at large 1971-82, legis. exec. com., income property com., chmn. mortgage bankers polit. action com.), Mortgage Bankers Assn. Carolinas (pres. 1970, bd. dirs. 1966-71), Western Piedmont Bd. Realtors (life), SAR, Sigma Chi. Episcopalian. Home: 382 Hanover Arms Ct Apt C Winston Salem NC 27104-4154 Office: PO Box 21523 Winston Salem NC 27120-1523

DOGGETT, LLOYD, congressman, former state supreme court justice; b. Austin, Tex., Oct. 6, 1946; s. Lloyd A. and Alyce (Freydenfeldt) D.; m. Elizabeth Belk, 1969; children: Lisa, Cathrine. BBA in Bus., U. Tex., 1967, JD with honors, 1970. Bar: Tex. 1971, U.S. Ct. Appeals (5th cir.) 1972, U.S. Dist. Ct. (we. dist.) Tex. 1972. Mem. Tex. State Senate, Dist. 14, 1973-85; ptnr. Doggett and Jacks, Austin, 1975-88; justice Tex. Supreme Ct., Austin, 1989-94; mem. U.S. Congresses from 10th Tex. dist., Washington, 1995—; mem. ways and means com. Adj. prof. U. Tex. Sch. of Law, 1989-94; chair Supreme Ct. Task Force on Jud. Ethics, 1992-94; co-founder Info. Tech. Working Group; mem. Congl. Task Force on Tobacco and Health. Named one of Five Outstanding Young Texans Tex. Jaycees, 1977, Outstanding Young Lawyer of Austin, 1978, one of Best Legislators, Tex. Monthly, 1979, 81, Outstanding State Senator, Common Cause, 1980, Disting. Alumnus, Bus. Adminstrn. Honors program U. Tex., 1989, Outstanding Jurist in Tex., Mex. Am. Bar Assn., 1993; recipient James Madison award Freedom of Info. Found. Tex., 1990, First Amendment award Nat. Soc. Profl. Journalists, 1990, Arthur B. DeWitty award

for outstanding achievement in human rights Austin NAACP, others. Mem. Consumers Union U.S. (bd. dirs. 1976-79, 80-81, 86-89), Tex. Consumer Assn. (pres. 1973). Democrat. Methodist. Office: US House Reps 201 Cannon Ho Office Bldg Washington DC 20515-4310*

DOGLIONE, ARTHUR GEORGE, data processing executive; b. Bklyn., May 24, 1938; s. Francis and Georgia (Smith) D.; m. Maryann Laurette Bonfanti, Sept. 3, 1960; children: Dana Ann, Arthur Todd, Lora Michele. AA, Scottsdale (Ariz.) Community, 1978; AAS, Maricopa Tech. Coll., Phoenix, 1984; BS, Ariz. State U., 1985. Salesman Columbus Realty Co., Trenton, N.J., 1962-65; appraiser J.H. Martin Appraisal Co., Trenton, 1965-68; office mgr. Mcpl. Revaluations, Avon-by-the-Sea, N.J., 1968-69; pres., broker Area Real Estate Agy., Wall, N.J., 1969-76; property appraiser Ariz. Dept. Revenue, Phoenix, 1976-78; investment appraiser Continental Bank, Phoenix, 1978-79; appraisal systems specialist Ariz. Dept. Revenue, Phoenix, 1979-80; project dir. Ariz. Dept. Adminstrn., 1980-83; pres. Logical Models, Scottsdale, Ariz., 1983-95; founder GENUS Technology, Scottsdale, 1989—. Tax assessor Upper Freehold Twp., N.J., 1974-75, Borough of Bradley Beach, N.J., 1975; lectr. in field. Author various software; pantentee infield. Counselor SCORE, SBA, Mesa, Ariz., 1986-90. Mem. Phi Theta Kappa. Republican. Roman Catholic. Achievements include patents for system and method for defining and creating surrogate addresses for township and range quarter sections. Office: GENUS Technology PO Box 725 Scottsdale AZ 85252-0725

DOGOLOFF, LEE ISRAEL, clinical social worker, psychotherapist, consultant; b. Balt., Oct. 19, 1939; s. Mark and Minnie Lottie (Gresser) D.; m. Jane Roberta Greenberg, June 17, 1962 (div. 1973); children: Jody, Ilene; m. Mary Louise Gumpper, Feb. 3, 1974; 1 child, Kathryn Ann. BA in Sociology, U. Md., 1961; MSW, Howard U., 1964. Lic. social worker, Md., Del.; bd. cert. diplomate in Clin. Social Work, 1990—. Dep. adminstr. Narcotics Treatment Adminstrn., Washington, 1970-72; dir., govt. asst. Spl. Action Office on Drug Abuse Prevention, Washington, 1972-73; dir. div. community assistance Nat. Inst. Drug Abuse, Rockville, Md., 1974-75; dep. fed. drug mgmt. program Office Mgmt. and Budget, Washington, 1975-76; assoc. dir. White House Domestic Policy, Washington, 1977-80; exec. dir. Am. Coun. Drug Edn., Rockville, 1981-92; pres. Employee Health Programs, Inc., Bethesda, Md., 1992-93; psychotherapist, pvt. practice, 1980—. Ind. counselor drug abuse treatment; field instr. Sch. Social Work, U. Md., 1986-92; moderator edn. sect. White House Conf. for Drug Free Am., 1987-88; Presdl. appointee Pres.'s Drug Adv. Coun., 1989-94. Contbr. numerous articles to profl. publs. Mem. Nat. Assn. Social Workers. E-mail: lidog@mchsi.com.

DOGRA, SUNIL, anesthesiology educator; b. Meerut, India, Aug. 28, 1955; parents Jatinder Nath and Raj Dogra; m. Ranju Kapila, Feb. 20, 1982; children: Kamna, Shibani. MB BChir, Armed Forces Med. Coll., Pune, India, 1979. Cert. anesthesiology and pain mgmt. Am. Bd. Anesthersiology. Assoc. prof. dept. anesthesiology U. N.C., Chapel Hill, 1991—, dir. pain fellowship program, 2001—. Capt. M.C., Indian Army, 1979-84. Fellow Royal Coll. Surgeons in Ireland, Royal Coll. Anesthetists London (diplomate); mem. Internat. Anesthesia Rsch. Soc., Internat. Assn. for Study of Pain, Am. Pain Soc., So. Pain Soc., Am. Soc. Anesthesiologists, N.C. Soc. Anesthesiologists, Am. Soc. Regional Anesthesia, Sigma Xi. Office: U NC Hosps Dept Anesthesiology CB 7010 N2201 Chapel Hill NC 27599-7010 E-mail: sdogra@aims.unc.edu.

DOGRA, VIJAY KUMAR, physician; b. Pachmarhi, India, Jan. 13, 1961; came to U.S., 1991; s. Prem and Thakuri (Devi) Singh; m. Narinder Kaur, Feb. 19, 1992. MB BS, I.G. Med. Coll., Shimla, India, 1984. Diplomate Am. Bd. Internal Medicine. Med. officer State Health Svcs., India, 1986-91; resident physician Raritan Bay Med. Ctr., Perth Amboy, N.J., 1993-96, emergency rm. attending physician, 1997—; emergency rm. physician Bucktail Med. Ctr., Renovo, Pa., 1996-97. Mem. ACP, AMA. Avocation: travel. Home: 50 Proctor St Edison NJ 08817-5330

DOHANIAN, DIRAN KAVORK, art historian, educator; b. Somerville, Mass., Mar. 26, 1931; s. Hagop Mardiros and Esther (Babigian) D. B.F.A., Mass. Sch. Art, 1952; A.M. in Teaching, Harvard, 1953, MA, 1955, PhD, 1964. Instr. art Eastern Nazarene Coll., Wollaston, Mass., 1952—55; reader in fine arts Harvard U., Cambridge, Mass., 1954—57, teaching fellow fine arts, 1955—57; vis. asst. prof. history art U. Ala., 1957—58; vis. asst. prof. history Oriental art U. Hawaii, 1959—60; asst. prof. fine arts, dir. course in Oriental humanities U. Rochester, NY, 1960—65, assoc. prof. fine arts, 1965—71, prof., 1971—87, prof. art history, 1988—2001, acting chmn. dept. fine arts, 1977—78, chmn. dept. fine arts, 1980—83, mem. faculty coun. Coll. Arts and Sci., 1991—94, sec. faculty coun., 1992—94, prof. art history emeritus, 2002—. Cons., curator Oriental art The Meml. Art Gallery, Rochester, 1976—88, bd. mgrs., 1977—78, 1980—83; Cooke-Daniels Meml. lectr. Cooke-Daniels Found. and Denver Art Mus., 1965; Louise Weiser lectr. Mt. Holyoke Coll., 1983; cons. in field. Author: The Mahayana Buddhist Sculpture of Ceylon, 1977, also articles in profl. jours. C.R.B. fellow Belgian Art Seminar, Brussels and Antwerp, 1956, Fulbright fellow India, 1958-59, sr. research fellow Am. Inst. Ceylonese Studies, Colombo, 1968, Am. Council Learned Socs. fellow India, 1973; fine arts rsch. scholar, 2002—. Fellow Am. Philos. Soc.; mem. Am. Inst. Indian Studies (trustee 1964-65), Am. Com. for History South Asian Art (dir. 1969-71). Home: 269 Payson Rd Belmont MA 02478-3406

DOHERTY, BRIAN GERARD, alderman; b. Chgo., Oct. 25, 1957; s. Daniel Joseph and Kathleen (McDonagh) D.; m. Rose Mary Gillespie, 1986; children: Kathleen Marie, Kevin Michael. BA, U. N.E. Ill., 1984. Alderman 41st Ward, Chgo., 1991—. Boxing champ Chgo. Pk. Dist., 1972, 73, Chgo. Golden Gloves champion Tribune Charities, 1973. Mem. Alpha Chi Honor Soc. Roman Catholic. Home: 7805 W Catalpa Ave Chicago IL 60656-1640 Office: 6650 N Northwest Hwy Chicago IL 60631-1307

DOHERTY, BRIAN JAMES, musicologist; b. Elizabeth, N.J., Feb. 9, 1962; s. Francis Vincent Doherty and Elizabeth Joan Nestor; m. Xia Zhang. MusB, Westminster Choir Coll., 1984; MA, MLS, Rutgers U., 1990; PhD, U. Kans. Head Music Libr. Harid Conservatory, Boca Raton, Fla., 1991—94, Stetson U., Deland, Fla., 1994—98, Southwest Mo. State U., Springfield, 1998—2002, Ariz. State U., Tempe, 2002—. Mem.: Am. Musicol. Soc., Soc. Am. Music, Music Libr. Assn. Office: Arizona State Univ Music Libr Box 870505 Tempe AZ 85287

DOHERTY, CHARLES VINCENT, investment counsel executive; b. Pitts., Dec. 17, 1933; s. Charles V. and Emma (Lager) D.; m. Marilyn Bongiorno, Oct. 17, 1964; children: Charles, Michelle, Kristen. BS, U. Notre Dame, 1955; MBA, U. Chgo., 1967. CPA, Ill. Tax specialist Haskins & Sells, CPA, Chgo., 1960-67; ptnr. Lamson Bros. & Co., Chgo., 1968-73; pres. Doherty Zable & Co., Chgo., 1974-85, Chgo. Stock Exch., Inc., 1986-92; mng. dir. Madison Adv. Group, Chgo., 1993—. Bd. dirs. Lakeside Bank, Howe Barnes Securities, Inc., Banc of Am. Fin. Products, Brauvin Capital Corp., Knight Trading Group, Inc; trustee Wayne Hummer Investment Trust, CCM Advisors Funds. E-mail: cdoherty@ameritech.net.

DOHERTY, DANIEL JOSEPH, III, lawyer; b. Washington, May 14, 1964; s. Daniel Joseph Doherty Jr. and Gail (Howard) Doherty. BA, Wake Forest U., 1986; JD, W.Va. U., 1989. Bar: W.Va. 1990, D.C. 1991, U.S. Supreme Ct. 1994, Md. 1997. Assoc. atty. John P. Ball Law Offices, Morgantown, W.Va., 1991-95; assoc. investigator D.J. Doherty & Assocs., Davidsonville, Md., 1995-96; rsch. assoc. Callahan & Callahan, Crofton, Md., 1996-98, assoc. atty., 1998—. Legal counsel Annapolis Jaycees, Md., 1998—2002. Mem.: Prince George's County Bar Assn., Anne Arundel County Bar Assn., D.C. Bar Assn., Md. Bar Assn. Independent. Roman Catholic. Avocation: coaching collegiate ice hockey. Office: Callahan & Callahan 2133 Defense Hwy Crofton MD 21114-2436 E-mail: attyirish@aol.com.

DOHERTY, EDMOND JOHN, retired librarian; b. N.Y.C., Dec. 9, 1933; s. George and Marie Eloise (Ducote) D.; m. Frances Jeffreys, Aug. 1, 1959; children: Jon, Elizabeth, Margaret, Katharine. BA, St. Martin's Coll., Lacey, Wash., 1955; MLS, Rutgers U., 1960. Adult svcs. libr. East Orange (N.J.) Pub. Libr., 1958-61; br. libr. Free Libr. of Phila., 1961-66; libr. dir. Reading (Pa.) Pub. Libr., 1966-90; libr. Reading Alloys, Inc., Robesonia, Pa., 1990-98. Contbr. articles to profl. jours. Chmn. planning com. United Way of Berks County, Reading, 1972-74, active mem., 1968-90; pres. Fellowship House of Reading, 1978—, LWV of Berks County, 1992-93; pres., founder Friends Hopewell Furnace Nat. Historic Site, 1995-98, treas. 1999—; mem. ethics bd. City of Reading, 1996-2000, chair, 1997-00. Recipient Doran award United Way of Berks County, 1979. Mem. Middle Atlantic Regional Libr. Fedn. (pres. 1977-79), Pa. Libr. Assn. (treas. 1973-75), Interlibr. Delivery Svc. of Pa. (treas. 1980-82). Avocations: travel, hosting cable tv programs. Home: 855 N Park Rd Apt BB103 Wyomissing PA 19610-3405

DOHERTY, EVELYN MARIE, data processing consultant; b. Phila., Sept. 26, 1941; d. James Robert and Virginia. Diploma, RCA Tech. Inst., Cherry Hill, N.J., 1968. Freelance data processing programmer, NJ, 1978-81; data processing cons., 1981—. Cons. collection agy., brokerage, banking, med., edn., transp., pub., food wholesaleing, utility systems, mfg.; reseller of PC's and software; lectr., mgr. data processing Camden County (N.J.) Coll. Contbr. articles to profl. jours.; author poems. Chair Collingswood (N.J.) Dems.; founder Babe Didrikson Collingswood Softball Team for Women; organizer Erlton South Town Watch (pub. cmty. notebook); mem. budget com. Cherry Hill Sch. Dist.; mem. Year 2000 Cherry Hill Schs. Technology Design Com.; adv. for vol. firefighters; vol. tech. lab learning ctr. Cherry Twp. Libr., vol. Cherry Hill Schs. Classroom Computer Learning Ctr. Mem.: Data Processing Mgmt. Assn. (chmn., mem. ednl. com.). Roman Catholic. Avocations: tennis, bridge, chess, charitable activites.

DOHERTY, GLEN PATRICK, lawyer; b. Toledo, Ohio, Jan. 3, 1963; s. Daniel Owen and Elaine (May) D.; m. Rhonda Jo Hugick, Nov. 14, 1998. BS, Cornell U., 1986; D in Law, Cornell Law Sch., 1989. Bar: Bar: N.Y. 1990, U.S. Dist. Ct. (no. dist.) N.Y. 1990, U.S. Dist. Ct. (so. and ea. dists.) N.Y., 1991. Assoc. Bond, Schoeneck & King, Syracuse, N.Y., 1989-91, Degraff, Foy, Holt-Harris & Kunz, LLP, Albany, 1991-96, ptnr., 1996—2003, McNamee Lochner, 2003—. Author: Employment and Labor Law Review; co-editor N.Y. Employment Law, 1997—; contbr. articles to profl. jours. Committeeman N.Y. State Reps., Colonie, 1991; designer Albany County Flag, 1979; bd. dirs. Albany Symphony Orch., 1999—, St. Peters Hosp. Found. Mem. Lake George Club, Cornell Club of N.Y., Fort Orange Club, Phi Kappa Phi. Republican. Roman Catholic. Avocations: sailing, squash. Office: McNamee Lochner 75 State St Albany NY 12201 Fax: 518-436-0210. E-mail: doherty@mltw.com

DOHERTY, JOHN FRANCIS, criminal justice educator; b. N.Y.C., July 2, 1947; s. John Joseph and Mary Cecilia (Delaney) D.; m. Kathleen Marie Hogan, Aug. 30, 1975; children: Matthew, Kathleen Margaret. BA in History, Marist Coll., 1969, MPA, 1988; MPS in Criminal Justice, L.I. U., 1978; PhD, Walden U., 1996. Police officer City of Poughkeepsie (N.Y.) Police Dept., 1970-77, watch comdr., st. supr., 1977-83, commanding officer of detective bur., 1983-90; asst. prof. criminal justice Marist Coll., Poughkeepsie, 1990—, chmn. dept. criminal justice, 1998—. Adj. prof. Marist Coll., Poughkeepsie, 1990. Mem. AAUP, ASPA, Am. Soc. Criminology, Am. Correctional Assn., Internat. Ass. Chiefs of Police, Acad. Criminal Justice Scis., Dutchess County Detectives Assn., Police Conf. N.Y., Criminal Justice Educators of N.Y., N.E. Assn. Criminal Justice Sci., Police Exec. Rsch. Forum, Fraternal Order of Police. Roman Catholic. Avocations: golf, education. Home: 30 Kingston Ave Poughkeepsie NY 12603-3419 Office: Marist Coll Dept Criminal Justice Poughkeepsie NY 12601 E-mail: John.Doherty@Marist.edu.

DOHERTY, KAREN ANN, import company executive; b. Elizabeth, NJ, July 6, 1952; d. Eugene Nason Godfrey and Helen L. (Andersen) D.; m. Jonathan Kent Tillinghast, June 17, 1972 (div. Oct. 1978); 1 child, Robert. Account exec. John O'Donnell Co., N.Y.C., 1979-80; nat. conservation rep. Sierra Club, N.Y.C., 1980-81; dir. membership and top mgmt. programs Am. Mgmt. Assn., N.Y.C., 1981-97; program mgr. Am. Mgmt. Assn. Pres. Assn., N.Y.C., 1998-99; v.p. mktg. Internat. Inst. Learning, Inc., N.Y.C., 1999, Exaclair Inc., N.Y.C., 1999—. Bd. dirs. Old Mill Landowners Assn., 1994-98, Coop. Jamestown Tenants Assn., 1990-99. Mem. Trinity Coll. Alumnae Assn. (bd. dirs. Com. N.Y.C. group 1979-82), Women in Need (corp. adv. coun.). Democrat. Roman Catholic. Home: 138 71st St Apt F1 Brooklyn NY 11209-1141 Office: Exaclair Inc 143 W 29th St Ste 1000 New York NY 10001 Personal E-mail: karenadoherty@yahoo.com. Business E-Mail: kad@exaclair.com.

DOHERTY, KATHERINE MANN, librarian, writer; b. N.Y.C., July 11, 1951; d. Jack Howard Mann and Glenn (Ellis) Andrews; m. Craig A. Doherty, June 16, 1973; 1 child, Meghan Corinne. BA, U. N.Mex., 1973; MSLS, Simmons Coll., 1976. Cataloger Mass. Hist. Soc., Boston, 1976-79; libr. media specialist Zuni (N.Mex.) Pub. Sch.s, 1982-86; libr. dist. Zuni Pub. Schs., 1985-86; unified media specialist Nantucket (Mass.) Elem. Sch., 1986-87; dir. learning resources Fortier Libr., N.H. Cmty. Tech. Coll., Berlin, 1987—. Author: (children's books) Apaches and Navajos, 1989, Iroquois, 1989, (young adult books) Benazir Bhutto, 1990, The Zunis, 1993, Arnold Schwarzenegger, 1993, The Huron, 1994, The Narragansett, 1994, The Chickasaw, 1994, The Ute, 1994, The Chuilla, 1994, The Sioux, 1994, The Golden Gate Bridge, 1995, Hoover Dam, 1995, Mount Rushmore, 1995, Washington Monument, 1995, Gateway Arch, 1995, The Wampanoag, 1995, The Penobscot, 1995, The Astrodome, 1996, The Erie Canal, 1996, the Empire State Building, 1997, The Alaska Pipeline, 1997, Richard I and the Crusades, 2002; pub. Field Trial Mag. Office: NH Com Tech Coll Coll Libr 2020 Riverside Dr Berlin NH 03570-3717 E-mail: kdoherty@tec.nh.us.

DOHERTY, PATRICIA ANN, computer systems analyst; b. Perth Amboy, N.J., Jan. 21, 1959; d. William Urban and Marion Ann (Mazola) O'Brien; m. Stephen Joseph Doherty, Feb. 12, 1983; children: Kathleen Elizabeth, Brian Stephen. BA summa cum laude, Rutgers U., 1981, MS in Math., 1987. Cert. tchr. math., N.J. Bank teller Nat. State Bank, Elizabeth, NJ, 1979; intern Merck & Co., Inc., Rahway, NJ, summer 1980, programmer technician, 1981-82, from programmer to sr. systems assoc./program mgr., 1982—. Math. workshop tutor, Rutgers U., New Brunswick, 1978-81. Advisor St. James Youth Group, St. James Ch., Woodbridge, N.J., 1985-86; computer advisor Rutgers U., pres., 1979-80; leader North Edison coun. Girls Scouts U.S., 1992—; treas. pack 77 Boy Scouts Am., North Edison, 1999-2000. Recipient award for excellence Merck & Co., Inc., 1990, 95, 99, 2000; named Leader of Yr. N. Edison Girl Scouts U.S., 1995-96. Mem. Am. Math. Soc., Phi Beta Kappa, Pi Mu Epsilon (sec. 1980-81, Jr. award in Math. 1980), Kappa Delta Pi (v.p. 1980-81). Roman Catholic. Avocations: oil painting, skiing, crafts, decorating. Home: 7 Old Hickory Ln Edison NJ 08820-1124

DOHERTY, PATRICIA ANNE, psychologist; b. Ottumwa, Iowa, May 25, 1947; d. Russell S. and Dorotha L. (Moehle) Cadwallader; m. Michael Doherty, Sept.6, 1969; 1 child, David M. BA in History, U. Iowa, 1969, MA, 1974, PhD in Counselor Edn., 1979. Lic. prof. counselor, Wis.; nat. cert. counselor. Grad. asst. U. Iowa, Iowa City, 1974-78; counseling intern Colo. State U., Ft. Collins, 1978-79; sr. psychologist U. Wis., Stevens Point, 1979—. Co-author: Women, Power and Relationships; contbr. articles to profl. jour. Mem. Wausau (Wis.) Lyric Choir, 1995—, bd. dir., 1999-2003; ofcl. Wis. Spl. Olympics, Stevens Point, 1989—. Mem. ACA, Am. Coll. Pers. Assn., Silvan Tomkins Inst., Nature Conservancy, Phi Delta Kappa, Phi Kappa Phi (exec.com. 2001--), Pi Lambda Theta. Avocations: singing, tennis, swimming, running, skiing. Office: U Wis Stevens Point Counseling Ctr 317 Delzell Hall Stevens Point WI 54481 Home: 9411 Woodland Cir Amherst Junction WI 54407-9169

DOHERTY, PATRICK WILLIAM, municipal official; b. Amityville, N.Y., May 24, 1951; s. Patrick John and Catherine Anne (Lydon) D. BA, Hofstra U., Hempstead, N.Y., 1976; JD, Hofstra Law Sch., Hempstead, N.Y., 1983; MIA, Columbia U. Sch. Internat. and Public Affairs, N.Y.C., 1984. Bar: N.Y. 1985. Editor, writer N.Y.S. Assembly, Albany, 1976, regional coord., 1977-80; adminstrv. assoc. N.Y.C. Comptroller's Office, 1984-88, dir. investment responsibility, 1988—. Assoc. editor Hofstra Law Review, Hempstead, N.Y., 1982-83. Recipient Atty. of the Yr. award Kings County Dist. Atty's. Office, 1994, Sean MacBride Human Rights award City of N.Y., 1994, Irish Am. Top 100 award Irish Am. Mag., 1994. Mem. bd. advisors Britain and Ireland Human Rights Ctr., London. Mem. Coun. Instnl. Investors, Social Investment Forum, Brehon Law Soc. Democrat. Avocation: antiquarian books and coins. Home: 43 Simon St Babylon NY 11702-2325 Office: Office Comptroller City NY 1 Centre St Rm 729 New York NY 10007-1602

DOHERTY, PETER CHARLES, immunologist; b. Brisbane, Australia, Oct. 15, 1940; s. Eric C. and Linda Doherty; m. Penelope Stephens, 1965; children: James, Michael. B.V.Sc. U. Queensland, Australia, 1963, MVSc, 1966; PhD, U. Edinburgh, Scotland, 1970; hon. doctorates from, 16 univs. Vet. officer Animal Rsch. Inst., Brisbane, Australia, 1963—67; sci. officer Moredun Rsch. Inst., Edinburgh, 1967—71; postdoctoral fellow John Curtin Sch. Med. Rsch., Canberra, Australia, 1972—75, prof., head dept. exptl. pathology, 1982—88; from assoc. prof. to prof. The Wistar Inst., Phila., 1975—82; mem., chmn. dept. immunology St. Jude Children's Rsch. Hosp., Memphis, 1988—2001; laureate prof. dept. microbiology and immunology U. Melbourne, Australia, 2002—. Bd. dirs. Internat. Lab. Animal Diseases, Nairobi, 1986—92; mem. exptl. virology study sect. NIH, 1982—83, 1990—. Contbr. chapters to books, articles. Co-recipient Nobel Prize for medicine, 1996; recipient Paul Ehrlich prize, Fed. Republic Germany, 1983, Gairdner Internat. award for med. sci., Can., 1986, Lasker award for Basic Med. Rsch., 1995. Fellow: Australian Acad. Sci., Royal Soc. London. Avocations: walking, reading. Office Fax: 61-3-8344-7990. E-mail: peter.doherty@stjude.org., pcd@unimelb.edu.au.

DOHERTY, ROBERT CHRISTOPHER, lawyer; b. Elizabeth, N.J., Sept. 3, 1943; s. Christopher Joseph and Marie Veronica (McLaughlin) D.; m. Sarajane Frances Doherty, June 12, 1965; children: Dennis Michael, Amy Elizabeth, Tracey Carolan. AB, St. Peter's Coll., 1965; JD, Seton Hall U., 1970. Bar: N.J. 1970, U.S. Ct. Appeals (3d cir.) 1982, U.S. Supreme Ct. 1977. Asst. prosecutor Union County, Elizabeth, 1971-72; mem. firm Schumann, Hession, Kennelly & Dorment, Jersey City, 1972-73, Robert D. Younghans, Westfield, N.J., 1973-76; ptnr. Doherty & Kopnicki, Westfield, 9176-87; county counsel, Union County, 1981-88; assoc. Nelinson, Roche & Carter, East Orange, N.J., 1988-92, Stanley Marcus, Newark, 1992-98, Weiner Lesniak, Parsippany, N.J., 1998-2000; dep. atty. gen. N.J. Divsn. Law, Trenton, 2000—. Mem. ABA, N.J. Bar Assn., Union County Bar Assn., N.J. Assn. County Counsels. Republican. Roman Catholic. Home: 771 Fairacres Ave Westfield NJ 07090-2027 Office: RJ Hughes Justice Complex PO Box 112 Trenton NJ 08625-0112

DOHERTY, ROBERT FRANCIS, JR., aerospace and defense industry professional; b. North Quincy, Mass., Aug. 7, 1954; s. Robert Francis and Rose Virginia (Wheeler) D. BS in Mgmt., U. Mass., Dartmouth, 1977. Sales mgr. Jordan Marsh Co., Boston, 1977-78; ops. mgr. Cramer Electronics, Newton, Mass., 1978-79; from d/e supr. to sect. mgr. nat. accts. Data Gen. Corp., Westboro, Mass., 1979-84, sales ops. mgr. Printronix, Inc., Malden, Mass., 1984-87; sales-contracts adminstrn. mgr. M/A-COM, Inc., Burlington, Mass., 1987-89, mktg. mgr. Chelmsford, Mass., 1989-92, mgr. customer satisfaction Lowell, Mass., 1992-94, internal cons. sys. applications products, 1994-95, program mgr., 1995—99; dir. program mgmt. M/A-COM divsn. Tyco Internat., Lowell, Mass., 1999—. Newspaper corr., chmn. restructuring coms.; cons. internal reengring. Active human rights groups, health founds. Mem. Nat. Contract Mgmt. Assn., Assn. of Old Crows, M/A-COM Mgmt. Club, Nat. Def. Indsl. Assn., Air Force Assn., Algonquin Club (sr.). Roman Catholic. Avocations: jogging, swimming, skiing, antiques, travel. Home: 84 Berkeley St Ste 1 Boston MA 02116-6262 E-mail: dohertyb@tycoelectronics.com.

DOHERTY, ROGER DAVIDGE, adult education educator, consultant; b. London, Middlesex, United Kingdom, June 15, 1939; s. Albert Henry and Edna May Doherty; m. Judith Ellen Thornton, Oct. 17, 1964; children: Steven James, Clare Gillian Luzuriaga-Doherty, Jane Edna. MA, Oxford U., Eng., 1957, PhD, 1963. Rsch. scientist Tube Investments Co., Saffron Walden, England, 1963—65; lectr. in materials sci. U. of Sussex, England, 1965—82; vis. scientist Brazilian Aerospace Ctr., Sao Jose dod Campos, Brazil, 1975—76; prof., materials engring. Drexel U., 1982—. Guest prof. of metallurgy Delft U. of Tech., Netherlands, 1978—79. Co-author: (research monograph) Stability of Microstructure in Metallic systems; co-editor: Aluminum Alloys Contemparary Rsch. and Applications; contbr. over 170 rsch. pubs. and reviews. D-Liberal. Achievements include patents for 6 US Patents on Metallurgical Processing. Avocations: hiking, planting trees, travel, discussing politics. Office: Drexel U 32 & Market Sts Philadelphia PA 19104 Office Fax: 215-895-6760. E-mail: dohertrd@drexel.edu.

DOHERTY, STEVE, lawyer, former state legislator; b. Great Falls, Mont., May 5, 1952; s. Arthur Frederick and Myra M. Doherty. BA, U. Pa., 1975; JD, Lewis & Clark Law Sch., 1984. Assoc. Spears, Lubersky, Campbell, Bledsoe, Anderson & Young, Portland, 1984-86; from assoc. to ptnr. Graybill, Ostrem, Warner & Crotty, Great Falls, Mont., 1986-92; assoc. Smith & Guenther, Great Falls, Mont., 1992-97; mem. Mont. Senate, Dist. 24, Great Falls, 1991—2003; majority whip, chmn. jud. com. Mont. Senate, Great Falls, Mont., 1993-94, mem. taxation and nat. resources com., 1991-94, mem. environ. quality coun. com., 1991-94, mem. edn. com., 1995, mem. fish and game and ethics com., 1997, minority leader, 1999-2001, mem. rules com., 1999—; ptnr. Smith & Doherty, Great Falls, 1998—2002, Smith, Doherty & Belcourt, P.C., Great Falls, 2003—. Mem. legis. del. to Taiwan, 2000, Mont. del. to Mnsfield Ctr. Conf. on Environment, Kumamoto, Japan, 2000; bd. dirs. Rural Employment Opportunities, Helena, 1990—92. Recipient Conservation Eagle award, N.W. Energy Coalition, 1999, Pub. Svc. award, Mont. Trial Lawyers Assn., 2001; Flemming fellow, Ctr. for Policy Alts., 1998, Eleanor Roosevelt Global fellow, Chile, 2001. Mem. Great Falls Pub. Radio Assn. (bd. dirs. 1986-91). Democrat. Avocations: hunting, fishing, hiking, skiing, western history. Office: Smith Doherty & Belcourt PC 410 Central Ave Ste 522 Great Falls MT 59401-3128 Fax: (406) 452-9787.

DOHERTY, THOMAS, publisher; b. Hartford, Conn., Apr. 23, 1935; Thomas and Elizabeth (Story) D.; m. Barbara Slocum, Feb. 14, 1958 (dec.); children: Thomas, Kathleen, Linda; m. Tatiana Pachina, July 19, 1991; 1 stepchild, Elena. Student, Trinity Coll., 1953-57. From salesman to divsn. sales mgr. Pocket Books, 1958—68; nat. sales mgr. Simon & Schuster, 1968—70; pub. Tempo Books, 1971-75; pub., gen. mgr. Ace and Tempo divsns. Grossett & Dunlap Inc., 1976-80; founder, pres. Tom Doherty Assocs., Inc., N.Y.C., 1980-87; pres., pub. Tor & Forge Imprints of Tom Doherty Assocs. LLC, A Holtzbrinck Co., N.Y.C., 1987—. Tor and Forge Books. Winner Skylark award, Locus award for best pub. sci. and fantasy, annually, 1987—. Mem. World Sci. Fiction Assn. (charter), Nat. Space Inst. Roman Catholic. Home: 280 Park Ave S Apt 15A New York NY 10010-6131 Address: 23 Terry's Trl East Hampton NY 11937 Office: Tor Books 175 Fifth Ave New York NY 10010-7703 E-mail: Tom.Doherty@tor.com.

DOHERTY, THOMAS JOSEPH, financial services industry consultant; b. Cambridge, Mass., Oct. 20, 1933; s. Thomas Joseph and Margaret Cecelia (O'Connell) D.; m. Carol Anne Conroy, Jan. 5, 1957; children: William, John, Robert, Susan. AB cum laude, Suffolk U., Boston, 1961. With Merrill Lynch & Co., Inc., N.Y.C., 1958-90; v.p. Merrill Lynch, Pierce, Fenner & Smith Inc., 1978-90; mng. dir. Merrill Lynch White Weld Capital Markets Group, 1979-83, Merrill Lynch Capital Markets, 1989-90; pres., chief exec. officer Merrill Lynch Specialists, Inc., 1985-90. Trustee Cin. Stock Exch., 1979-83; past mem. Am. Stock Exch., N.Y. Stock Exch.; bd. govs Pacific Stock Exch., 1984-90. Served with AUS, 1953-55. Mem. Security Traders Assn. N.Y., Nat. Security Traders Assn. (chmn. exchange liaison com. 1986-87), Gen. Alumni Assn. Suffolk U. (bd. dirs. 1976-77). Republican. Roman Catholic.

DOHERTY, WILLIAM THOMAS, JR., historian, retired educator; b. Cape Girardeau, Mo., Mar. 30, 1923; s. William Thomas and Kittie (Baird) D.; m. Dorothy Ashley Huff Zienowicz, Aug. 13, 1947; children: Victor Sargent, Dorothy Ashley, Catherine Baird, Julia Holbrook, William Thomas III. AB, BS, S.E. Mo. State U., 1943; MA, Am. U., 1950; PhD, U. Mo., 1951. Instr. history Westminster Coll., Fulton, Mo., 1947-48, Christian Coll., 1949-50, U. Mo., 1948-49, 50-51; asst. prof. history U. Miss., 1951-53, assoc. prof. history, 1956-58, prof., chmn. dept. history, 1958-61; asst. prof., then assoc. prof. history U. Ark., 1953-56; prof. history, dir. Ford Found. 3 yr. Master's program Kan. State U., Manhattan, 1961-63; prof. history, chmn. dept. W.Va. U., Morgantown, 1963-79, univ. historian, 1979-88, prof. emeritus, 1988—. Author: Louis Houck: Missouri Historian and Entrepreneur, 1960, Berkeley, U.S.A.: A Bicentennial History of a Virginia and West Virginia County 1772-1972, 1972, West Virginia History, 1974, West Virginia University: Symbol of Unity in a Sectionalized State, 1982, West Virginia Studies, 1984, West Virginia: Our Land, Our People, 1990; editor: Minerals, Vol. IV in Conservation History of the United States, 1971; editor in chief West Virginia History Jour., 1979-88; contbr. numerous articles to profl. jours. Served with

AUS, 1943-46. Decorated Bronze star medal, 1946. Mem. Am. Hist. Assn., So. Hist. Assn., Orgn. Am. Historians, AAUP, Kappa Delta Pi, Sigma Tau Delta, Phi Alpha Theta. Democrat. Home: 15115 Interlachen Dr Apt 214 Silver Spring MD 20906-5638

DOHMEN, FREDERICK HOEGER, retired wholesale drug company executive; b. Milw., May 12, 1917; s. Fred William and Viola (Gutsch) D.; m. Gladys Elizabeth Dite, Dec. 23, 1939 (dec. 1963); children: William Francis, Robert Charles; m. Mary Alexander Holgate, June 27, 1964. BA in Commerce, U. Wis., 1939. With F. Dohmen Co., Milw., 1939-82, successively warehouse employee, sec., v.p., 1944-52, pres., 1952-82, dir., 1947—, chmn. bd., 1952-82. Travel lectr. various orgns., 1980—. Bd. dirs. St. Luke's Hosp. Ednl. Found., Milw., 1965-83, pres., 1969-72, chmn. bd., 1972-73; bd. dirs. U. Wis. Milw. Found., 1976-79, bd. visitors, 1978-88, emeritus mem., 1988—; assoc. chmn. Nat. Bible Week, Laymen's Nat. Bible Com., N.Y.C., 1968-82, mem. coun. of advisors, 1983—; elder Presbyn. Ch.; bd. dirs. Riveredge Nature Ctr., Newburg, Wis., 1993-94. Mem. Nat. Wholesale Druggists Assn. (chmn. mfr. rels. com. 1962, resolutions com. 1963, bd. control 1963-66), Nat. Assn. Wholesalers (trustee 1966-75), Druggists Svc. Coun. (dir. 1967-71), Wis. Pharm. Assn., Miss. Valley Drug Club, Univ. Club Town Club (Milw.), Beta Gamma Sigma, Phi Eta Sigma, Delta Kappa Epsilon. Home: 3903 W Mequon Rd Mequon WI 53092-2727

DOHMEN, MARY HOLGATE, retired primary school educator; b. Gary, Ind., July 28, 1918; d. Clarence Gibson and Margaret Alexander (Kinnear) Holgate; m. Frederick Hoeger Dohmen, June 27, 1964; children: William Francis, Robert Charles. BS, Milw. State Tchrs. Coll., 1940; M of Philosophy, U. Wis., 1945. Cert. tchr., Wis. Tchr. primary grades Baraboo (Wis.) Pub. Schs., 1940-43, Whitefish Bay (Wis.) Pub. Schs., 1943-64. Contbr. articles, story, poems to various pubs. Bd. dirs. Homestead H.S. chpt. Am. Field Svc., Mequon, Wis., 1970-80; mem. Milw. Aux. VNA, 1975—, 2d v.p., 1983-85, Milw. Pub. Mus. Enrichment Club, 1975—, Boys and Girls Club of Greater Milw., 1986—; vol. Reading is Fun program, 1987—, Milw. Symphony Orch. League, 1960—, Ptnrs. in Conservation, World Wildlife Fund, Washington, 1991—, Milw. Art Mus. Garden Club, 1979—, com. chmn., 1981-86; mem. Chancellor's Soc. U. Wis.-Milw., 1991—; travel lectr. various orgns., 1980—. Mem. AAUW, Milw. Coll. Endowment Assn. (v.p. 1987-90, pres. 1991-93), Bascom Hill Soc. (U. Wis.), Woman's Club Wis., Alpha Phi (pres. Milw. alumnae 1962-64), Pi Lambda Theta (pres. Milw. alumnae 1962-64), Delta Kappa Gamma. Republican. Presbyterian. Avocations: writing, travel, nature. Home: 3903 W Mequon Rd Mequon WI 53092-2727

DOHNAL, WILLIAM EDWARD, retired steel company executive, consultant, accountant; b. Cleve., May 25, 1912; s. Frank and Anna (Florian) D.; children: David, Dennis. Student Western Res. U., 1940. CPA, Ohio. Auditor, Lybrand, Ross Bros. and Montgomery, 1942-45; acting auditor Cleveland-Cliffs Iron Co., Cleve., 1946-47, auditor, 1947-53, asst. treas., 1953-58, compt., 1958-63, v.p., compt., 1963-64, v.p. internat., 1964-73, sr. v.p., from 1973, now ret.; internat. bus. cons. Mem. Coun. World Affairs. Mem. Am. Soc. CPA's, Ohio Soc. CPA's, Weld Club (Perth, Australia). Address: 1710 Lake Cypress Dr Safety Harbor FL 34695-4503

DOHNANYI, CHRISTOPH VON, musician, conductor; b. Berlin, Sept. 8, 1929; s. Hans and Christine (Bonhoeffer) Von Dohnányi. Student, U. Munich, Hochschule fuer Musik, Munich, Fla. State U., Berkshire Music Ctr.; doctorate (hon.), Oberlin Coll., Cleve. Inst. Music, Kent State U., Case Western Res. U., Eastman Sch. Music, 1998. Coach, condr., asst. to Sir George Solti Frankfurt (Germany) Opera, 1952-57, gen. music dir., artistic dir., 1968-77; gen. music dir. Lubeck, Germany, 1957-63, Kassel, Germany, 1963-66; chief conductor West German Radio Symphony Orch., Cologne, 1964-70; artistic dir., chief condr., intendant Hamburg (Germany) State Opera, 1977-84; music dir. designate Cleve. Orch., 1982-84, music dir., 1984—2002; prin . guest conductor Philharmonia Orch., London, 1995—97, prin. condr., 1997—. Guest conductor Salzburg Festival, Chatelet Paris, Zurich Opera House, Israel Philharm., Orchestre de Paris, Vienna Philharm., Berlin Philharm. Recordings with Vienna Philharmonia include opera Wozzeck, Lulu, Fidelio, Flying Dutchman, Salome, 5 Mendelssohn symphonies, works by Stravinsky, Tschaikovsky, Glass, Schnittke, recordings with Cleve. orch. include symphonies of Beethoven, Brahms, Schumann, Bruckner, Dvorak, Mahler, Mozart, Schubert, orchestral works by Bartok, Lutoslawski, R. Strauss, Webern, Ives, Ruggles, Birtwistle, opera Rheingold, Walkure. Recipient Scopus award, Am. Friends of Hebrew U. in Jerusalem, 1996, Scroll of Remembrance for Von Dohnányi and Bonhoeffer Families in German resistance U.S. Holocaust Mus., Washington, 1995, Condr. of Yr. award Musical Am., 1992, Comdr.'s Cross Republic of Austria, 1992, Comdr. de L'Ordre des Arts et des Lettres, France, Cross Order of Merit, Cross Order of Merit, Germany, Bartok prize, Hungary, 1982, Goethe medal City of Frankfurt, 1979, Richard Straus prize Munich, 1951, Torch of Liberty award Anti Defamation League, 2001. Address: Colbert Artists Mgmt 111 W 57th St Ste 1416 New York NY 10019-2211 Office: Philharmonia Orch 125 High Holborn 1 FL London WCIV6QA England

DOHR, JOHN MICHAEL, JR., banker; b. St. Louis, Dec. 13, 1952; s. John Michael and Frances Christine Dohr; m. Mary Sue Palmer, June 19, 1976; 1 child, Christine Ann. BSBA, U. Mo., St. Louis, 1974, MBA, 1982. Methods analyst Merc. Bank St. Louis N.A., 1975-77, asst. mgr., 1977-78, asst. ops. officer, 1978-81, banking officer, 1981-83, asst. v.p., 1983-87, v.p., 1987-96, group mgr., 1989-90, 91-92, 93-95; pres. Dohr Consulting Svcs., Inc., St. Louis, 1996-2000; v.p. Jefferson Bank and Trust Co., St. Louis, 1997-98, South Side Nat. Bank, St. Louis, 1998—2001; sr. v.p. Midwest BankCentre, St. Louis, 2001—03. Bd. dirs. Am. Lung Assn. Ea. Mo., St. Louis, 1981-87, asst. treas., 1981-86, treas., 1986-87; mem. adv. bd. dirs. Mo. Small Bus. Devel. Ctr., 1994-99. Mem. U. Mo. St. Louis Alumni Assn. (coll. bus. chpt.), South Side Optimist Club. Home: 10695 Hackamore Ln Saint Louis MO 63128-1200

DOHRENWEND, BRUCE PHILIP, psychiatric epidemiologist, social psychologist, educator; b. N.Y.C., July 26, 1927; s. Gustav John and Gertrude Elise (Funke) D.; m. Barbara Anne Snell, Sept. 21, 1951 (dec. June 1982); m. Catherine J. Douglass, June 1, 1985 BA, Columbia U., 1950, MA, 1952; PhD, Cornell U., 1955. Cert. psychologist, N.Y. Research assoc. Cornell U., Ithaca, N.Y., 1954-58; research assoc. Columbia U., N.Y.C., 1958-63, asst. prof., 1963-67, assoc. prof., 1967-70, prof., 1970—; chief of rsch. dept. social psychiatry N.Y. State Psychiat. Inst., N.Y.C., 1979—. Mem. task panel on problems, scope and boundaries Presl. Commn. on Mental Health, Washington, 1977-78; head task group on behavioral effects Presl. Commn. on Accident at Three Mile Island, Washington, 1979; mem. tech. evaluation bd. Vietnam Era Veterans study, VA, Washington, 1983-89. Author: (with others) Social Status and Psychological Disorder, 1969, Mental Illness in the United States, 1980, (with others) Socioeconomic Status and Psychiatric Disorders, 1992; editor: (with others) Stressful Life Events, 1974, Stressful Life Events and Their Contexts, 1981 Served with USNR, 1945-46 Recipient Research Scientist award NIMH, 1971, 76, 81, 86, 91, Emily Mumford award Columbia U., 1992; NIMH grantee, 1964-82, 77—. Fellow AAAS (co-recipient prize for behavioral rsch. 1990), APA (co-recipient disting. contbns. div. community psychology award 1980), Am. Psychopathol. Assn. (Hamilton award 1994); mem. Am. Pub. Health Assn. (co-recipient Rema Lapouse Mental Health Epidemiology award 1981), Am. Sociol. Assn. (Leo G. Reeder award for disting. contbn. med. sociology sect. 1999), Soc. for Study of Social Problems (Disting. Contbrs. award divsn. psychiat. sociology 1994). Home: 1056 5th Ave New York NY 10028-0112 Office: NY State Psychiat Inst 1051 Riverside Dr Unit 8 New York NY 10032-1013

DOHRMANN, RUSSELL WILLIAM, manufacturing company executive; b. Clinton, Iowa, June 29, 1942; s. Russell Wilbert and Anita Doris (Miller) D.; m. Rita Marie Meade, Dec. 26, 1964 (dec. Feb. 1978); m. M. Jean Stapleton, Aug. 18, 1979. BS, Upper Iowa U., 1965; MBA, Drake U., 1971. Acct. Chamberlain Mfg. Corp., Clinton, 1965-66, plant controller Derry, Pa., 1967-68; fin. analyst Frye Copysystems Inc., Des Moines, 1968-71, v.p., controller, 1971-77, pres., 1980-97, also bd. dirs.; internat. controller Wheelabrator-Frye, N.Y.C., 1977-78; pres. FryeTech, Inc., Des Moines, 1997-98; group controller Wheelabrator-Frye, Des Moines, 1978-80; cons., 1998—. Mem. Nat. Assn. Accts., Des Moines C. of C. Republican. Methodist. E-mail: rwdohrmann@robsoncom.net.

DOI, DOROTHY MITSUE YANO, educator, consultant; b. Honolulu, Feb. 21, 1934; d. Tokuju Yano and Hisayo Kashiwabara; children: Ken Kenichi, Claire Emiko, Garret Seitoku. BS in Edn., Phillips U., Enid, Okla., 1956; postgrad., UCLA, 1958, U. Hawaii, Honolulu, 1966-67, 72-74, Chaminade Coll. Honolulu, 1972-74, 77, LaVerne (Calif.) Coll., 1970-71. Cert. tchr., Hawaii. Tchr. L.A. City Schs., 1957-58, Hawaii, 1956-57, 65, 70-71; account exec. Catering, ind. contractor, Honolulu; skin care, health and beauty cons. Honolulu; travel agt., ind. contractor, dba Triple C Svcs., Honolulu, 1983—. Rschr. Manoa ethnic studies program U. Hawaii; account exec., cons. Royal Banquet, 1988-89. Active Kamuki Y-Teens, 1947-52; fund-raising co-chair Kaimuki HS, Hui O'Hauolani Y-Teens Jesters Ball, 1952; mem. World Wildlife Fund, 1991—, Hawaii Theatre Ctr., 1990—; vol. ARC, 1944-49, Salvation Army, 1945-50, bell ringer, 1989-98; translator Jal Honolulu Marathon Info. Booth Svc., 1995—. Mem. VFW Ladies Aux. (life), Am. Biograph. Rsch. Assn. (rschr., dep. gov.), NAFE, Nature Conservancy Local, Nat., Hawaii Fukuoka Kenjin Kai (gen. chair 35th anniversary and award ceremony 1992, com. chair, editor commemorative booklet, sec. 1988-91, 2d v.p. 1992-93, 1st v.p. 1993-95, pres. 1996, immediate past pres. 1997, vol. mayors and chamber pres. conf. Honolulu 1997, translation svc. registration desk rep. Hawaii Fukuoka Kenjn Kai), Smithsonian Instn., Kaimuki HS Alumni Assn. (charter, bd. dirs. 1988-2001, pub. rels. chair 1988 90, writer, rschr., editor, mng. editor Bulldogrowl newsletter), Okla. Sooners Club (Hon. Citizen of Okla. 1985), Japanese Cultural Ctr. Hawaii (hon. lifetime charter), Future Tchrs. Am. (treas. 1955-56), United Japanese Soc. Hawaii (sec. 1991-95, youth com. chair 1992—, gen. chair youth com. picnic Bunka Pikunikku 1994, culture day Bunka-no-Hi 1995, co-chair fundraising com. 1992-93, 95-96, mcee New Year luncheon 1993, 2d v.p. 1994-95, registration, score card analyzer Ganbare Golf Classics 1994-98, Mulligan sales co-chair 1995-97, program com. chair, lei com. chair Japan Festival 1996, chair welfare com. 1999-2001), Internat. Platform Assn., Honolulu Japanese C. of C. (ann. art exhbn. 1997-2000, ann. fundraising 1996-99). Avocations: commemorative postal stamp collecting, spectator sports, cooking and baking. Home: 1628 Kalakaua Ave #405 Honolulu HI 96826-2421

DOI, TAKAO, astronaut; b. Minamitama, Tokyo, Sept. 18, 1954; m. Abe Hitomi. B in Engring., U. Tokyo, 1978, M in Engring., 1980, D in Aerospace Engring., 1983. Rsch. student Inst. of Space & Astronautical Sci., Japan, 1983—85; with nat. space devel. agy. NASA, Houston, 1985—. Rschr. U. Colo., 1987—88; vis. scientist Nat. Aerospace Lab., Japan, 1989; backup payload specialist Spacelab Japan mission, 1992; project scientist Internat. Microgravity Lab. 2 mission, 1994; astronaut U.S. Microgravity Payload flight. Contbr. articles over 40 to profl. jours. Recipient Commendation award, Min. of State for Sci. & Tech., Spl. citation, Sci. Coun. Japan, Outstanding Svc. award, Nat. Space Devel. Agy. of Japan, 1992. Mem.: AIAA, Japan Soc. Aeronautical & Space Sci., Japan Soc. Microgravity Application. Avocations: flying, soaring, tennis, jogging, soccer. Office: Astronaut Office CB NASA Johnson Space Center Houston TX 77058

DOI, YUTAKA, electrical engineer; b. Osaka, Japan, Nov. 26, 1936; came to U.S., 1967; s. Hiroshi and Hiroko (Tsuyama) D.; m. Michiko Doi, Nov. 26, 1972; children: Masao, Mary. BA in Econs., Keio U., Tokyo, 1960; BS in Physics, Osaka U., 1967; MS in Physics, San Francisco State U., 1970; PhD in Mech. Engring., U. Miami, 1988; postgrad., Johns Hopkins U., 2002—. Registered profl. engr., Fla., Ariz. Banker Mitsui Bank, Osaka, 1960-62; tchg. asst. San Francisco State U., 1967-68, U. Calif., Berkeley, 1969-71; elec. engr. Yokogawa Hewlett Packard, Tokyo, 1972-74; rsch. asst. U. Miami, Coral Gables, Fla., 1974-79; prin. staff engr. Motorola, Tempe, Ariz., 1979-98; elec. engr. Honeywell, St. Louis Park, Minn., 1998—2002. Chmn. elec. simulation divsn. Internat. Electronic Mfg. Tech., Tokyo, 1991-92. Contbr. articles to profl. jours. Coun. mem. Keio U. Athletic Club, Tokyo, 1960. Mem. NSPE. Achievements include computer simulation of nuclear energy using nuclear optical model; flowmetry using nuclear magnetic resonance; three dimensional electric and magnetic fields simulation using finite element, optical wave-guide. Home: 10350 Swift Stream Pl Apt 206 Columbia MD 21044 E-mail: ydoi@comcast.net.

DOIG, BEVERLY IRENE, retired systems specialist; b. Bozeman, Mont., Oct. 21, 1936; d. James Stuart Doig and Elsie Florence (Andes) Doig Townsend. AA, Graceland Coll., 1956; BA, U. Kans., 1958; MS, U. Wis., 1970; cert. in Interior Design, UCLA, 1993, tng. classes Windows NT oper. sys., 1996, tng. classes in AUTOCAD, 1st level cert. AUTOCAD, 1998. Cert. NCIDQ 2001, lic. interior designer N.Mex., 2002. Aerodynamic technician II Ames Labs.-NACA, Moffett Field, Calif., 1957; real time systems specialist Dept. of Army, White Sands Missile Range, N.Mex., 1958-66; large systems specialist computing ctr. U. Wis., Madison, 1966-70; sr. systems analyst Burroughs, Ltd., Canberra, Australia, 1970-72; systems specialist Tech. Info. Office Burroughs Corp., Detroit, 1973-78; sr. systems specialist Burroughs Gmbh, Munich, 1978-79, Burroughs AB, Stockholm, 1979-80; networking cons. Midland Bank, Ltd., Sheffield, Eng., 1980-83; networking specialist Burroughs Corp. (now UNISYS), Mission Viejo, Calif., 1983-98; ret. Tchg. asst. Canberra (Australia) Coll., 1972; tchr. Wayne State U. Ext., Detroit, 1976-77; freelance interior designer, 1992-98; with Homeworks Decorating Showroom, Farmington, N.Mex., 1998—; part-time tchr. computer application San Juan Coll., Farmington, 1998—. Vol. youth groups and camps Reorganized LDS Ch., N.Mex., Wis., Australia, Mich., Calif., Germany, U.K.; inner youth worker, Detroit; mentor Saddleback H.S., Santa Ana, Calif. Scholar Mitchell Math., 1956-58, Watkins Residential, 1956-58. Mem. Assn. Computing Machinery (local chpt. chmn. membership 1969), Lambda Delta Sigma. Republican. Avocations: working with junior high, doing craft projects, designing. Office: c/o Homeworks 115 W Main St Farmington NM 87401-6242

DOIG, JAMESON WALLACE, political science educator; b. Oakland, Calif., June 12, 1933; s. James Rufus and Mary (Jameson) D.; m. Joan Nishimoto, Oct. 8, 1955; children: Rachel, Stephen, Sean. AB, Dartmouth Coll., 1954; M.P.A., Princeton U., 1958, MA, 1959, PhD, 1961. Research asst. N.J. Republican Com., 1957; staff mem. Brookings Instn., 1959-61; from asst. prof. to prof. politics and pub. affairs Princeton U., 1961—; assoc. dean Woodrow Wilson Sch., Princeton U., 1972-73, dir. univ. research program in criminal justice, 1973-93. Dir. grad.studies dept. polit. sci. Princeton U., 1988—90, chair undergrad. studies, 1991—94, chair dept. polit. sci., 1997—2000; dir. Mamdouha S. Bobst Ctr. for Peace and Justice, 2000—, chair Can. studies, 2002—; cons. Fels Fund, 1966—68, Daniel and Florence Guggenheim Found., 1970—, Nat. Prison Overcrowding Project, 1983, Lavenburg Found., 1983—90; vis. prof. John Jay Coll. Criminal Justice, 1967—68, 1970—72; mem. adv. com. Gov. N.J., 1965—71, Vera Inst. Justice, 1986—92; mem. NRC/Trans. Rsch. Bd., 1990—92; mem. adv. coun. N.J. Dept. Corrections, 1974—82, vice-chmn., 1980—82, cons. on parole to gov. of N.J., 1975—78; dir. Guggenheim Summer Intern. Program, 1997—. Author: Metropolitan Transportation Politics and the New York Region, 1966, (with D.E. Mann) The Assistant Secretaries, 1965, (with D.T. Stanley and D.E. Mann) Men Who Govern, 1967, (with M. Danielson) New York: The Politics of Urban Regional Development, 1982, Empire on the Hudson, 2001; co-author, editor: Criminal Corrections. Ideals and Realities, 1983, Leadership and Innovation, 1987, 90, Combating Corruption/Encouraging Ethics, 1990; contbr. Governing the States and Localities, 1969, Agenda for a City, 1970, Metropolitan Politics, 1971, Urban Politics and Policy-Making, 1973, Crime and Criminal Justice, 1975, Public Administration of Law Enforcement Policies, 1979, Politics of Urban Development, 1987, Public Authorities and Public Policy, 1991, Landscape of Modernity, 1992, Studies in American Political Development, 1993, Technology and Culture, 1994, Building the Public City, 1995, Seaport, 2001, Innovation, 2002. Served to lt. (j.g.) USNR, 1954-56. Recipient Herbert Kaufman award, 1989, A.P. Usher prize, 1995, A. Wildavsky award, 1997, Abel Wolman award, 2001, Humanities Honor award, 2002. Mem. Am. Correctional Assn., Am. Polit. Sci. Assn., Am. Soc. Pub. Adminstrn., Law and Soc. Assn., Soc. History of Technology, Policy Studies Orgn., Can. Studies Assn., Phi Beta Kappa. Office: Princeton U Corwin Hall Robertson Hl Princeton NJ 08544-0001

DOKE, DAVID REED, music educator, musician; b. Springfield, Mo., Oct. 1, 1964; s. Elah Reed and Sharon Kay Doke; m. Allison Jane Graham, Nov. 25, 1989; 1 child, Eleanor Kay. MusB, U. Mo., Kansas City, 1991; MusM, DePaul U., 1993. Cert. tchr. Ga. Violinist La Orquesta Sinfonica del Estado de Mex., Toluca, 1987—88, Am. Inst. Musical Studies, Graz, Austria, 1988, Chgo. Chamber Orch., 1991—93; dir. orchs., instr. advanced placement theory North Cobb H.S., Kennesaw, Ga., 1994—. Violinist Acworth (Ga.) United Meth. Ch., 1994—2003; musician Burnt Hickory Bapt. Ch., Kennesaw, 1994—2003. Mem.: Nat. Sch. Orch. Assn., Am. String Teachers Assn., Music Educators Nat. Conf., Ga. Music Educators Assn. (clinician and adjudicator 1994—, dir. symphony orch. performance state conf.), Phi Mu Alpha. Home: 3900 Stoney Creek Ct Marietta GA 30067 Office: North Cobb HS 3400 Hwy 293 N Kennesaw GA 30144 Office Fax: 770-975-4242. Personal E-mail: davidrdoke@earthlink.com. E-mail: davidrdoke@cobbk12.org.

DOKE, MARSHALL J., JR., lawyer; b. Wichita Falls, Tex., June 9, 1934; s. Marshall J. and Mary Jane (Johnson) D.; m. Betty Marie Orsini, June 2, 1956; children: Gregory J., Michael J., Laetitia Marie. BA magna cum laude, Hardin-Simmons U., 1956; LLB magna cum laude, So. Meth. U., 1959. Bar: Tex. 1959. Founding ptnr. Rain Harrell Emery Young & Doke, Dallas, 1965-87; assoc. Thompson, Knight, Wright & Simmons, Dallas, 1959, 62-65; founding ptnr. Doke & Riley, Dallas, 1987-92; ptnr. McKenna & Cuneo, 1993-96, Gardere Wynne Sewell L.L.P., Dallas, 1996—. Gen. counsel Tex. Rep. Party, 1976-77; mem. adv. coun. U.S. Ct. Fed. Claims, 1982—. Author: Ann. Procurement Rev., Govt. Contractor Briefing Papers, Contract Changes, Fed. Contract Mgmt., 1982—, also articles; editor-in-chief: Southwestern Law Jour., 1958-59. Pres. Hope Cottage-Children's Bur., Inc., 1969-70, Hope Cottage Found., 1997-2002, pres., 1998-2002; bd. visitors Law Sch., So. Meth. U., 1966-69, McDonald Obs., U. Tex., 1990—; dir. Tex. Hist. Found., 1993—, v.p., 1996-98, pres. 2000—; law com., bd. trustees So. Meth. U., 1977-78; bd. dirs., pres. World Trade Assn., Dallas-Ft. Worth, 1979-80; chmn. bd. dirs. Internat. Trade Assn. Dallas/Ft. Worth, 1993-94; bd. dirs., sec. Theater Trustees Am., 1983-93; chmn. Mayor's Internat. Com., City of Dallas, 1984-87, mem. Judicial Nominating Commn., Dallas, 1997—, vice chair, 1998-2000, chair, 2000—. 1st lt. JAGC, U.S. Army, 1959-62. Fellow Am. Bar Found., Tex. Bar Found.; mem. ABA (chmn. sect. pub. contract law 1969-70, ho. of dels. 1970-72, 74-2003, bd. govs. 1980-82, nominating com. 1988-91, 2000-2003, chmn. conf. sect. dels. 1991—), Tex. Bar Assn., U.S. Ct. of Fed. Claims Bar Assn. (bd. govs. 1987-2001, pres. 1996), Bd. of Contract Appeals Bar Assn. (pres. 1988-90, bd. govs. 1988—), Am. Bar Retirement Assn. (bd. dirs., trustee 1980-84, pres 1982-84), Nat. Conf. Lawyers and CPAs (co-chmn. 1983-85), Nat. Contract Mgmt. Assn. (nat. bd. advisors 1983—), Dallas C. of C. (chmn. internat. com. 1979-83). Home: 6910 Dartbrook Dr Dallas TX 75254-7926 Office: Gardere Wynne Sewell LLP Thanksgiving Tower Ste 3000 Dallas TX 75201-7254 E-mail: mdoke@gardere.com.

DOKHOLYAN, NIKOLAY VASILYEVICH, physicist; b. Tbilisi, Republic of Georgia, July 7, 1971; came to U.S., 1994; s. Vasily Victorovich and Lyubov Grigoryevna Dokholyan; m. Rachel S. Dokholyan, Aug. 17, 1996; children: Katherine Nicole, Sophia Elizabeth. BS, Moscow Inst. Physics and Tech., 1992, MS, 1994; MS, PhD, Boston U., 1999. Rsch. assoc. Harvard U., Cambridge, Mass., 1999—, Boston U., 1999; asst. prof. biochemistry and biophysics U. N.C., Chapel Hill, 1999—. Cons. Brit. Petroleum, Boston, 1997—. Contbr. articles to profl. jours.; referee papers Phys. Rev. Letters, 1998—, Physica A, Jour. of Chem. Physics, others. Recipient Student award NSF, 1995, 98, NSF Travel award, 2001; grantee Brit. Petroleum/Brit. Petroleum Amoco, 1998, 99; predoctoral fellow NIH, 1998-88, postdoctoral fellow, 1999-02. Mem. AAAS, Am. Phys. Soc. Office: UNC-Chapel Hill Dept Biochemistry & Biophysics Sch Medicine Campus Box 7260 Chapel Hill NC 27599 E-mail: dokh@unc.edu.

DOKURNO, ANTHONY DAVID, lawyer; b. Gardner, Mass., Mar. 14, 1957; s. Anthony Chester and Damcy Anteena (Aleson) D. BA, Holy Cross Coll., 1979; JD, Vt. Law Sch., 1982; postgrad., Johns Hopkins U., 1993-94. Bar: Mass. 1982, U.S. Ct. Appeals for the Armed Forces 1986, U.S. Supreme Ct. 1987. Pvt. practice, Fitchburg, Mass., 1982-86; appellate counsel Navy-Marine Corps Appellate Rev. Activity, Navy JAG, Washington, 1986-88; atty. admiralty law divsn. Navy JAG, Washington, 1988-90, atty. ops. and mgmt., 1991-93. Assoc. counsel, bd. vets. appeals Dept. Vets. Affairs, 1994-96; analyst Dept. of Def., 1996—. Comdr. USNR, 1998—. Mem.: Nat. Cryptologic History Found., Maritime Law Assn., Mensa, Naval Res. Assn., Amnesty Internat., Navy League, Am. Legion, Phi Beta Kappa.

DOLACK, PETER CHARLES, editor, writer; b. Paterson, N.J., Feb. 20, 1961; s. Robert John Dolack and Denise Ann (Gallo) Shortway. BA, William Paterson U., Wayne, N.J., 1983. Staff writer The Hudson Dispatch, Union City, N.J., 1982-87; sports editor Suburban Trends, Butler, N.J., 1988-92, news editor, 1992-93, mng. editor, 1993-94; editor-in-chief The Highlands Times, West Milford, N.J., 1994; aromatic organics editor Schnell Publishing Co., N.Y., 1995-96; nat. copy reader Dow Jones News Svc., Jersey City, N.J., 1996-98; self-employed writer, editor, rschr., 1998—2001; copy desk chief Nat. Law Jour., NY, 2001—. Freelance writer, editor Pete Dolack: Writer/Editor For Hire, Garfield, N.J., 1992-95. Contbr. poems to numerous publs., including Will Work for Peace anthology. Coord. Bergen County group Amnesty Internat., Teaneck, N.J., 1991-94; organizer, speaker Emergency Women's Action Com., N.Y., 1995-96; steering com. mem. Artists Against the Contract on Am., N.Y., 1995; organizer, speaker Nat. People's Campaign, N.Y., 1995-97, N.Y. Workers Against Fascism, 1997-98, Bklyn. Greens/Green Party, N.Y., 1999-2003, co-editor G, N.Y. Green Party newspaper, 2001-03; mem. exec. com., organizer, speaker NoSpray Coalition, N.Y., 1999—. Recipient Responsible Journalism-Enterprise award N.J. Press Assn., 1992, Column Writing award N.J. Press Assn., 1993; nominated Pushcart Prize, 2000. Mem. Soc. Profl. Journalists (Newspaper Series award 1992, Health and Sci. Reporting award 1993). Avocations: hiking, poetry/performance, theatre, astronomy. Home: 147 Franklin St Brooklyn NY 11222-1689 Office: Nat Law Jour 105 Madison Ave New York NY 10016-7418

DOLAN, ANDREW KEVIN, lawyer; b. Chgo., Dec. 7, 1945; s. Andrew O. and Elsie Dolan; children: Andrew, Francesca, Melinda. BA, U. Ill., Chgo., 1967; JD, Columbia U., 1970, MPH, 1976, DPH, 1980. Bar: Wash. 1980. Asst. prof. law Rutgers-Camden Law Sch., N.J., 1970-72; assoc. prof. law U. So. Calif., L.A., 1972-75; assoc. prof. pub. health U. Wash., Seattle, 1977-81; ptnr. Bogle & Gates, Seattle, 1988-93; pvt. practice law, 1993—. Commr. Civil Svc. Commn., Lake Forest Park, Wash., 1981; mcpl. judge City of Lake Forest Park, 1982-98. Russell Sage fellow, 1975. Mem. Order of Coif, Washington Athletic Club. Avocation: book collecting. Office: 5800 Columbia Ctr 701 5th Ave Seattle WA 98104-7097

DOLAN, BRIAN THOMAS, lawyer; b. Springfield, Ill., Dec. 27, 1940; s. William Stanley and Dorotha Caroline (Battles) D.; m. Kathleen Lois Smith, Sept. 14, 1963; children: Elizabeth Beaumont, Leslie Caroline. AB, Stanford U., 1963, JD, 1965. Bar: Calif. 1966, Colo. 1966, D.C. 1980. Capt. USAF, 1966-70; ptnr. Davis, Graham & Stubbs LLP, Denver, 1970—2001; prin. Resource Capital Funds, Denver, 2000—. Office: Resource Capital Funds 1400 16th St Ste 200 Denver CO 80202 E-mail: btd@rcflp.com.

DOLAN, CHARLES FRANCIS, media, entertainment company executive; b. Oct. 16, 1926; m. Helen Burgess; children: Patrick, Tom, James, MariAnne, Kathleen, Deborah. Student, John Carroll U. Founder Sterling Manhattan Cable, 1961, Teleguide, Inc., HBO, 1971, Cablevision, Sterling Manhattan Cable, 1973; mng. gen. ptnr. Cablevision and predecessor firms, 1973—85; chmn. Cablevision Systems Corp., Woodbury, NY, 1985—. Mng. dir. Met. Opera, N.Y.C.; majority owner Madison Square Garden Properties, 1995—, also bd. dirs. Bd. dirs., bd. govs. St. Francis Hosp., L.I., NY; bd. dirs. Cold Spring Harbor Lab.; trustee Fairfield (Conn.) U. Avocation: sailing. Office: Cablevision Systems Corp 1111 Stewart Ave Bethpage NY 11714-3581

DOLAN, DENNIS JOSEPH, airline pilot, lawyer; b. St. Louis, Mar. 19, 1946; s. Robert Glennon and Lucille Anne (Stanley) D.; m. Aura Maritza Vargas, June 8, 1974; children: Dennis J. Jr., Rebecca and Robert (twins). BSC, Spring Hill Coll., Mobile, Ala., 1967; JD cum laude, St. Louis U., 1985. Bar: Mo., 1985, U.S. Dist. Ct. (ea. dist.) Mo. 1987. Commd. 2nd lt. USMC, 1967, advanced through grades to capt., 1970, resigned, 1976; served to maj. USMCR; flew in numerous combat missions, 2 combat tours Vietnam; airline pilot Western Air Lines, L.A., 1976-87, Delta Air Lines, Inc., Atlanta, 1987—; pvt. practice law Clayton, Mo., 1985-88. Mem. ABA, Assn. Trial Lawyers Am., Air Line Pilots Assn. (bd. dirs. 1992-94, exec. v.p. 1994-96, chmn. Delta Master exec. coun. 1996-98, 1st v.p. 1999—), Internat. Fedn. Airline Pilot Assns. (prin. v.p. profl. affairs 2000-2003, pres., 2003—). Roman Catholic. Avocations: skiing, woodworking. Home: PO Box 906 Roswell GA 30077-0906

DOLAN, EDWARD FRANCIS, writer; b. Oakland, Calif., Feb. 10, 1924; s. Edward Francis Sr. and Zelda Olympia (Vieira) D.; m. Rose Esther Puddefoot, Nov. 17, 1945 (dec.); children: Timothy L. (dec.), Wendy Anne Irving. Student, U. So. Calif., L.A., 1942-43, U. San Francisco, 1958-59. Free-lance writer KRON-TV, Bay Area Pub. Schs. TV Coun., Pub. Svc. telecasts for Archdiocese, San Francisco, 1949-53; instr. dept. speech and drama Monticello Coll., Alton, Ill., 1953-56; writer, 1957—. Author: Pasteur and the Invisible Giants, 1958, White Battleground: The Conquest of the Arctic, 1961, Disaster 1906: The San Francisco Earthquake and Fire, 1967, Legal Action: A Layman's Guide, 1972; A Lion in the Sun: The Rise and Fall of the British Empire, 1973, Amnesty: The American Puzzle, 1976, Gun Control: A Decision for Americans, 1978, Child Abuse, 1980, revised edit., 1992, Adolf Hitler: A Portrait in Tyranny, 1981, History of the Movies, 1983, The Simon & Schuster Sports Question and Answer Book, 1984, Hollywood Goes to War, 1985, Drugs in Sports, 1986, revised edit., 1992, The Old Farmer's Almanac Book of Weather Lore, 1988, MIA: Missing in Action, 1989, America after Vietnam: Legacies of a Hated War, 1989, (with M.M. Scariano) Nuclear Waste: The 10,000-Year Challenge, 1990, Our Poisoned Sky, 1991, America in World War II: 1941, 1991, America in World War II: 1942, 1992, America in World War II: 1943, 1992, Animal Folklore: From Black Cats to White Horses, 1992, The American Wilderness and Its Future, 1992, America in World War II, 1944, 1993, Folk Medicine: Cures and Curiosities, 1993, America in World War II: 1945, 1994, Your Privacy: Protecting It in a Nosy World, 1994, Teenagers and Compulsive Gambling, 1994, (with M.M. Scariano) Illiteracy in America, 1995, The American Revolution: How We Fought the War of Independence, 1995, America in World War I, 1996, (with M.M. Scariano) Shaping U.S. Foreign Policy, 1996, In Sports, Money Talks, 1996, Our Poisoned Waters, 1997, The Civil War: A House Divided, 1997, America in the Korean War, 1998, Beyond the Frontier: the Story of the Trails West, 1999, The Spanish-American War, 2001, The Irish Potato Famine, 2003, The American Indian Wars, 2003, 113 non-fiction titles. With U.S. Army, 1943-45, ETO. Mem. Calif. Writers Club (pres. Redwood br. 1976-77, 83-84). Avocation: golf.

DOLAN, JAMES, communications executive; m. Kristin Dolan; 5 children. Past advt. sales v.p. Cablevision Sys. Corp., past advt. corp. dir. Rainbow Advt. Sales Corp., past CEO Rainbow Programming Holdings, Inc., CEO, pres., 1995—, also bd. dirs.; creator Rainbow Advt. Sales Corp. Chmn. Madison Sq. Garden; creator Sta. WKNR-AM, Cleve. Chmn. capital campaign com. Friends Acad.; trustee WNET; bd. dirs. Lustgarten Found. for Pancreatic Rsch. Avocations: music, sailing. Office: Cablevision Sys Corp 1111 Stewart Ave Bethpage NY 11714-5310

DOLAN, JAMES VINCENT, lawyer; b. Washington, Nov. 11, 1938; s. John Vincent and Philomena Theresa (Vance) D.; m. Anne McSherry Reilly, June 18, 1960; children: Caroline McSherry, James Reilly. AB, Georgetown U., 1960, LLB, 1963. Bar: U.S. Dist. Ct. 1963, U.S. Ct. Appeals (D.C.) cir. 1964, U.S. Ct. Appeals (4th cir.) 1976. Law clk. U.S. Ct. Appeals D.C., 1963-64; assoc. Steptoe & Johnson, Washington, 1964-71, ptnr., 1971-82; mem. Steptoe & Johnson Chartered, Washington, 1982-83; v.p. law Union Pacific R.R., Omaha, 1983—2002, vice chmn., 2002—. Co-author: Construction Contract Law, 1981; contbr. articles to legal jours.; editor-in-chief: Georgetown Law Jour., 1962-63. Mem.: ABA, Barristers, D.C. Bar Assn., Nebr. Bar Assn., Omaha Country Club, Congl. Country Club (v.p. 1982, pres. 1983). Republican. Roman Catholic. Home: 1909 County Road 8 Yutan NE 68073-5013 Office: Union Pacific RR 1416 Dodge St Omaha NE 68179

DOLAN, JAN CLARK, former state legislator; b. Akron, Ohio, Jan. 15, 1927; d. Herbert Spencer and Jean Risk Clark; m. Walter John Dolan, Apr. 22, 1950 (dec. July 1986); children: Mark Raymond, Scott Spencer, Gary Clark, Todd Alvin. BA, U. Akron, 1949. Home svc. rep. East Ohio Gas Co., Akron, 1949-50; dietitian Akron City Hosp., 1950-51; tchr. Brecksville (Ohio) Sch. Dist., 1962-66; adminstr. Orchard Hills Adult Day Ctr., West Bloomfield, Mich., 1978-83; mem. Farmington Hills (Mich.) City Coun., 1975-88, Mich. Ho. of Reps., Lansing, 1989-96. Mayor City of Farmington Hills, 1978, 85; elder Presbyn. Ch. Republican. Home: 22587 Gill Rd Farmington Hills MI 48335-4037

DOLAN, JOHN E. consultant, retired utility executive; b. N.Y.C., May 9, 1923; s. John A. and Marie C. (Comiskey) D.; m. Anne Dolan, Feb. 16, 1952; children— John E., Bryan, Vincent, Robert, Raymond, Philip, Lawrence, Paul. Student, Rensselaer Poly. Inst., 1946-47; BSM.E., Columbia U., 1950. With Am. Electric Power Service Corp., Columbus, Ohio, 1950-88, chief mech. engr., 1966, chief engr., 1967, sr. exec. v.p. engring., 1975-79, vice chmn. engring. and constrn., 1979-88; ret.; bd. dir., v.p. subs. cos. and Am. Electric Power Service Corp.; cons., 1988—. Bd. dirs. Dravo Corp. Served to 1st lt. USAAF, 1942-46. Decorated Air medal (4). Fellow ASME (James N. Landis medal 1990); mem. NAE, Tau Beta Pi. Roman Catholic. Home: 14448 Mark Dr Largo FL 33774-5102

DOLAN, JOHN F. lawyer; b. Cleve., Oct. 19, 1925; s. John Francis and Lillian Marie (Courtad) D.; m. Rose M. Fitzsimmons, June 13, 1953 (dec.); children: Patricia Ann, John Patrick, Mary Bridget, Margaret Mary, Ann Marie, Kathleen Marie, Michael Anthony, Daniel Joseph. AB, Harvard U., 1947; JD, LLB, Western Res. U., 1949. Asst. dir. law City of Cleve., 1951-56, chief of litigation, 1955-56; dir. law City of Shaker Heights, Ohio, 1956-57; asst. gen. atty. N.Y.C., Penn Cen. Conrail, Cleve., 1957-78; sole practice Cleve., 1978—. Served to lt. (j.g.) USN, 1943-46. Mem. Ohio State Bar Assn., Cleve. Bar Assn. Democrat. Roman Catholic.

DOLAN, JOHN RALPH, retired corporation executive; b. Peabody, Mass., Apr. 20, 1926; s. John L. and Ethel M. D.; m. Lois M. Burkhart, Jan. 24, 1948 (dec.); children: Mary Ellen, Geraldine, Dorothy, John, Peter; m. Barbara C. Gleason, Dec. 22, 1995; stepchildren: Janet Rogers, Barry, David, Julie Doyle. Student, Boston Coll., 1943, Bryant and Stratton Coll., 1945-46, Bentley Coll., 1948-50. Passenger accountant Cunard Steamship Co., 1947-50; office mgr. Dolan Tanning Co., 1950-56; gen. mgr. Flash Sportswear, 1957-59; budget mgr. CBS Electronics Co., 1959-62; controller/treas. Am. Polymer & Chem. Co., 1962-63; dir. financial planning E.G. & G., Inc., Bedford, Mass., 1963-71, controller, 1971-86; sr. v.p., chief fin. officer EG&G Inc., Wellesley, Mass., 1986-91. Mem. Town Meeting, Danvers, Mass., 1964-70, Sch. Bldg. Com., Danvers, 1966-69. Served with USNR, 1943-45. Mem. Financial Execs. Inst. Home: 56 Summer St Danvers MA 01923-1549

DOLAN, MICHAEL WILLIAM, lawyer; b. Kansas City, Mo., Dec. 13, 1942; s. William Michael and Vivian (Bush) D.; m. Laurel C. Cummings, June 13, 1964 (div. 1984); children: Matthew, Abigail. BA, U. Kans., 1964; JD with honors, George Washington U., 1969; LLM, Georgetown U., 1981. Bar: Va. 1969, D.C. 1970, U.S. Ct. Claims 1981, U.S. Tax Ct. 1981, U.S. Supreme Ct. 1973. Atty. Dept. Justice, Washington, 1971-73, dep. legis. counsel, 1973-79, dep. asst. atty. gen., 1979-85; with Fed Exec. Devel. Program, 1978-79; assoc. Winthrop, Stimson, Putnam & Roberts, Washington, 1985-94; chief Article III Judges divsn. Adminstrv. Office of U.S. Ct., Washington, 1994—2002; atty. Michael W. Dolan, PLLC, 2003—. Contbr. numerous articles to profl. jours. 1st lt. U.S. Army, 1964-66. Recipient John Marshall award Dept. Justice, 1978 Democrat. Office: 2021 L St NW 2d Fl Washington DC 20036 E-mail: mwdolan@att.net.

DOLAN, PETER BROWN, lawyer; b. Bklyn., Mar. 25, 1939; s. Daniel Arthur and Eileen Margaret (Brown) D.; m. Jacqueline Elizabeth Gruning, Sept. 9, 1961; children: Kerry Anne, Peter Brown Jr. BS, U.S. Naval Acad., 1960; JD, U. So. Calif., 1967. Bar: Calif. 1967, U.S. Ct. Appeals (9th cir.) 1968, U.S. Dist. Ct. (no. and ctrl. dists.) Calif. 1967, U.S. Dist. Ct. (ea. dist.) Calif. 1972, U.S. Dist. Ct. (so. dist.) Calif. 1973, U.S. Claims Ct. 1982, U.S. Supreme Ct. 1986. Dep. L.A. County counsel, 1967-69; assoc. Macdonald, Halsted & Laybourne, L.A., 1969-71, ptnr., 1972-77, Overton, Lyman & Prince, L.A., 1977-87, Morrison & Foerster, L.A., 1987-93, Morgan, Lewis & Bockius LLP, L.A., 1993-99; prin. The Dolan Law Firm, L.A., 1999—. Active Pasadena (Calif.) Tournament of Roses Assn., 1973—; pres. West Pasadena Residents Assn., 1979-81. Served to lt. USN, 1960-64, comdr. USNR, 1964-86. Mem.: ABA, L.A. County Bar Assn., Assn. Bus. Trial Lawyers, State Bar Calif., Chancery (LA), Bel-Air Bay Club, Phi Delta Phi. Roman Catholic. Fax: 213-680-9889. E-mail: dolanlaw@earthlink.net., jacquiedol@aol.com.

DOLAN, PETER J. corporate financial consultant; b. N.Y.C., July 22, 1927; s. Peter Dolan and Mary Fitzpatrick; m. Ruth E. Bachop, Aug. 26, 1950; children: Robert, Kevin, Paul, James, William, Eileen, Elizabeth, Mary. MS, Columbia U., 1954; BBA, Manhattan Coll., 1949. CPA, N.Y. Ptnr., nat. dir. Ernst & Young, N.Y.C., 1954-83; vice-chmn., dir. Universal Matchbox Ltd., Hong Kong, 1985-89; prin. P. J. Dolan Assocs., Algonquin Assocs., Fla., 1985—. Dir. Springer-Verlag USA, N.Y., 1983-88, Hodder Assocs. LLC, N.Y., 1998—. Chmn. fin. com., dir. Marymount Manhattan Coll., 1988-92; mem. fin. com., dir. Calvary Hosp., N.Y., 1985-94; dir., pres. S.E. Yonkers Comty. Assn., N.Y., 1968-70; dir. Armonk (N.Y.) Pub. Schs., 1971-75. With U.S. Army, 1946—47, Japan, with U.S. Army, 1950, Korea. Recipient Ann. Outstanding award Campfire Girls, N.Y., 1970-72; decorated 2 Bronze Stars U.S. Army, Merit Unit Commendation award U.S. Army.

DOLAN, PETER ROBERT, pharmaceutical executive; b. Salem, Mass., Jan. 6, 1956; s. John Ralph and Lois D. (Burkhart); m. Katherine Helen Lange, Sept. 12, 1981; children: Christopher Lange, Timothy Lange. B, Tufts U., 1978; MBA, Amos Tuck Sch. Bus. Dartmouth Coll., 1980. Asst. product mgr. Gen. Foods Corp., White Plains, N.Y., 1980-81, assoc. product mgr., 1982-83, product mgr., 1983-84, sr. product mgr., 1985, group product mgr., 1986-87, category mgr., 1987-88; v.p. mktg. Bristol-Myers Co., N.Y.C., 1988-90, sr. v.p. mktg. & sales, 1990-91, sr. v.p. mktg., sales & ops., 1991-92, exec. v.p., 1992, pres., 1993-94, Mead Johnson Nutritional Group, Evansville, Ind., 1995-96; group pres. nutritionals and med. devices Bristol-Myers Squibb Co., 1997—98, pres. Europe, Worldwide medicines, 1998, pres., 2000, sr. v.p. strategy, 1998—2000, CEO, chmn., 2001—. Bd. dirs. Old Nat. Bank; bd. overseers Tufts Medical Sch. Bd. Co-author: Insider's Guide to the Top Ten Business Schools, 1982. Mem.: Young Pres. Orgn., Non-Prescription Drug Mfrs. Assn. (bd. dirs. 1993). Avocations: triathlons, tennis, scuba diving. Office: Brystol Meyers Squibb 345 Park Ave New York NY 10154

DOLAN, RAYMOND BERNARD, insurance executive; b. Chgo., Feb. 13, 1923; s. Christopher P. and Florence M. (Taylor) D.; m. Theresa, May 25, 1946; children— Paul, Ronald, Donald, Sharon. Student, No. Mich. U., 1942; D.Arts and Scis. (hon.), Mt. Marty Coll., Yankton, S.D., 1980. With Equitable Life Assurance Soc. U.S., 1946—, v.p., chief line ops., 1971-74, sr. v.p. corp. communications, 1974-79, exec. v.p., chief agy. officer, 1979—; chmn. bd. Equitable of Del., 1985—. Inst. Life Ins. prof. in residence, econs. dept. St. Olaf Coll., 1975; dir. Equitable Variable Life Ins. Co., Equitable Capitol Mgmt. Corp., Equitable Life Leasing Corp., Equico Securities Corp., Donaldson, Lufkin & Jennette Inc., U.S. Marshalls Found. Vice chmn. Holy Spirit Ch. Parish Council, Stamford, Conn., 1968-71; chmn. Stamford dist. Boy Scouts Am., 1970-73; past trustee, vice chmn. bd. dirs. Teledaga Coll., Ala.; chmn. bd. dirs. Nat. Council Better Bus. Burs. Served to lt. col. USAF, 1942-45, 51-52, 61-62. Decorated D.F.C., Air medal with 4 oak leaf clusters. Mem. Nat. Assn. Life Underwriters, C.L.U.'s N.Y., Nat. Guard Assn. (life), Consumer Council, Am. Council Life Ins., Res. Officers Assn., Conf. Bd., Pub. Affairs Research Council. Clubs: K.C. (4th deg.). Republican. Roman Catholic. Home: 5 Kings Grant 377 Main St New Canaan CT 06840-5941 Office: Equitable Life Assurance Soc US 787 7th Ave Fl 38 New York NY 10019-6018

DOLAN, TERESA A. dean, educator, researcher; MPH, UCLA; BA Zoology, Rutgers U., 1979; DDS, U. Tex., 1983; cert. gen. practice, L.I. Jewish Med. Ctr., 1985; cert. geriatric dentistry, Vets. Adminstrn., 1989; cert. dental pub. health, U. Fla., 1991; grad., Pub. Health Leadership Inst. Fla., 1998; grad. cert., U. Fla., 2001. Diplomate Am. Bd. Dental Pub. Health, 1994. Resident in gen. dentistry dept. dentistry L.I. Jewish Med. Ctr., 1983—84, chief resident in gen. dentistry dept. dentistry, 1984—85; fellow geriatric dentistry Vets. Adminstrn. Med. Ctr., Sepulveda, Calif., 1987—89; asst. prof. U. Fla. Coll. Dentistry, 1989—93, assoc. prof. with tenure, 1993—98, acting assoc. dean acad. affairs, 1996—97, assoc. dean acad. affairs, 1997—2001, prof. with tenure, 1998—, assoc. dean edn., 2001—, interim dean, 2002—. Rschr., tchr., spkr. in field, lectr. various seminars; vis. asst. prof. U. Calif., 1985—87, adj. asst. prof., 1987—89; faculty discipline com. Fla. Dept. Edn., Statewide Course Numbering Sys., 1998—; reviewer grants in field; participant NIH Summer Inst. Rsh. on Minority Aging, 1991. Contbr. articles to profl. jours. ; exec. prodr.: (ednl. satellite videoconf.) Dental Care for the Developmentally Disabled Patient, 1991, Challenges in Geriatrics: Moving on- Rehabilitation After Stroke, 1991, How Much is Enough? Dental Tretament Decisions for Older Adults, 1992; author (dir.): Five Steps to Improving the Oral Health of Your Older Patients: A Guide for Non-dental Health Professionals, 1994. Adv., treating dentist cmty. nursing homes, 1989—96; dentist to low income elderly participants U. Fla. Geriatric Dental Demonstration Project, Jacksonville, 1990—92; dir. dental svcs. to older and medically compromised patients U. Fla. Geriatric Dental Group, 1990—95. Named honorable mention AARP Healthy Order Adults, 2000 Recognition Programs Exemplary Contbns. to Healthy Aging, 1992; recipient numerous grants and awards; fellow Vets. Adminstrn. Geriatric Dentistry; scholar Rsch., Robert Wood Johnson Found. Dental Health Svcs., 1985—87, L.I. U., 1984—85. Mem.: APHA, Am. Coll. Dentists, Phi Beta Kappa, Am. Soc. Geriatric Dentistry (ad hoc reviewer Spl. Care in Dentistry 1992—93, judge Saul Kamen Sci. Report award competition 1993—, chmn. ann. sci. session 1996), Fla. Coun. Aging, Fla. Pub. Health Assn., Am. Assn. Pub. Health Dentistry (abstract reviewer 1987, co-chmn. local arrangements ann. meeting 1992, ad hoc reviewer Jour. Pub. Health Dentistry 1994, session co-chmn. ann. meeting 1996, judge grad. student merit award projects 1997, mem. at large exec. coun. 1997—2000, mem. awards and nominations com. 2000, Pres.'s award 1999), Am. Dental Assn. (com. G Coun. Dental Edn. and Licensure 1999—, Geriatric Dental Care award 1991), Internat. Assn. Dental Rsch. (v.p. abstract reviewer geriat. oral rsch. sect. 1992—93, dir. behavioral sci. and health svcs. rsch. sect. 1992—95, pres.-elect program chmn. geriat. oral rsch. sect. 1993—94, pres. symposium organizer geriat. oral rsch. sect. 1994—95), Am. Assn. Women Dentists (chmn. com. student and component chpts. 1986—88, trustee dist. XIII Calif. 1986—89, contbg. editor Chronicle 1986—91), Acorn Clinic (v.p., acting pres. 1996—97, pres. 1997—99, past pres. 1999—2000), Fla. Coun. Aging (bd. trustees 1993—95)), U. Health Sci. Ctr., Edn. Task Force, U. Curriculum Com., Geriatric Rsch., Edn. and Clin. Ctr., ACORN Clinic, Internat. Assn. Dental Rsch. (session co-chmn., abstract reviewer geriat. oral rsch. sect. 1991—92, immediate past-pres., chmn. nominations com. geriat. oral rsch. sect. 1995—96, mem. awards com. geriat. oral rsch. sect. 1996—97, constn. and bylaws com. 1996—), Am. Bd. Dental Pub. Health (dir.-elect 2000—01), Am. Dental Edn. Assn. (chair-elect spl. interest group in geriatric dentistry 1991—92, editl. rev. bd. Jour. Dental Edn. 1991—94, chmn. spl. intertest group in geriatric dentistry 1992—93, immediate past chmn. sect. on gerontology and geriat. edn. 1993—94, abstract reviewer ann. session 1998—2000, ann. session planning com. 2002—), Beta Beta Beta, Omicron Kappa Upsilon (Xi Omicron chpt. 1998), Phi Beta Kappa. Office: U Fla Coll Dentistry 1600 SW Archer Rd D Box 100405 JHMH Gainesville FL 32610-0405 Office Fax: 352-392-3070.

DOLAN, THOMAS CHRISTOPHER, professional society administrator; b. Chgo., Dec. 31, 1947; s. Thomas Christopher and Bernice Mary (Doyle) D.; m. Georgia Ann Siebke, Feb. 14, 1983; children: William, Barbara, Lauren. BBA, Loyola U., Chgo., 1969; PhD, U. Iowa, 1977. Instr. U. Iowa, Iowa City, 1971-72; vis. fellow U. Wash., Seattle, 1973-74; asst. prof. U. Mo., Columbia, 1974-79; assoc. prof., dir. St. Louis U., 1979-86; v.p. Am. Coll. Healthcare Execs., Chgo., 1986-87, exec. v.p., 1987-91, pres., 1991—. Mem. Accrediting Commn. on Edn. for Health Svcs. Adminstrn., Washington, 1985-86; chmn. Assn. Univ. Programs in Health Adminstrn., Washington, 1983-84; cons. HEW, Kansas City, Mo., 1974-79, State of Mo., Jefferson City, 1974-79. Author: Systems for Health Care Administration: A Model for the Education of Health Manpower, 1975; contbr. articles to profl. jours. Pres. Mental Health Assn. Boone County, Columbia, Mo., 1977-78, Mental Health Assn. Mo., Jefferson City, 1980-82; bd. dirs. Alexian Bros. Hosp., St. Louis, 1980-86; chair Inst. for Diversity in Health Mgmt., 1994—, chair, Assn. Forum, 1999-2000, Am. Soc. Assn. Execs. Found., Washington, 1999-2000. Fellow Am. Coll. Healthcare Execs., Am. Soc. Assn. Execs. (cert. assn. exec.; bd. dirs.); mem. APHA. Roman Catholic. Avocations: golf, motorcycling, reading. Office: Am Coll Healthcare Execs 1 N Franklin St Ste 1700 Chicago IL 60606-4425

DOLAN, THOMAS JOSEPH, judge; b. Bronx, N.Y., Oct. 24, 1943; s. Joseph William and Helen Winnifred (Hannigan) D.; m. Barbara Louise Nuesell, Apr. 6, 1968; children: Claire Jean, Claudia Barbara. BS, Fordham U., 1965; JD, St. John's U., 1968. Bar: N.Y. 1968, U.S. Ct. Mil. Appeals 1969, U.S. Dist. Ct. (so. and ea. dists.) N.Y. 1975, U.S. Supreme Ct. 1980. Asst. dist. atty. Office of Dist. Atty., Dutchess County, Poughkeepsie, N.Y., 1973-92; county ct. judge Dutchess County, 1993—; acting judge N.Y. State Supreme Ct., 2001—. Served to capt. JAGC, U.S. Army, 1968-73. Decorated Bronze Star (2), Army Commendation medal (2). Mem. N.Y. State Bar Assn., Dutchess County Bar Assn. Clubs: So. Dutchess Exchange (Fishkill, N.Y.). Republican. Home: Neville Rd Wappingers Falls NY 12590 Office: County Court 10 Market St Ste 7 Poughkeepsie NY 12601-3233 E-mail: BTDolan@aol.com., tdolan@courts.state.ny.us., tdolan@courts.state.nyus.

DOLAN, TOM, Olympic athlete; b. Arlington, Va., Sept. 15, 1975; Grad., U. Mich., 1998. Swimmer; gold medalist 400m individual medley Olympic Summer Games, 1994, 98; 14-time U.S. nat. champion; sponsor Carl-Burke Swim Club; 4 nat. titles, 1994, 98; gold medalist 400m Individual Medley Olympic Summer Games, Sydney, 2000. Spokesperson Am. Lung Assn. Achievements include the World record-holder 400m individual medley, Am. record-holder 500y, 1650 freestyle and 400y individual medley. Office: c/o USA Swimming 1 Olympic Plz Colorado Springs CO 80909-5746

DOLAN, WILLIAM J. media executive; b. Portland, Oreg., Feb. 8, 1959; s. John Lee and Dolores Maureen Dolan; m. Camilla Anne Derby, Aug. 1, 1981; children: Heather, Brittain, Courtney, William, Keenan. Student, Mt. Hood Coll., 1977-79, Portland State U., 1979—80. CFP. Dir. KATU-TV, Portland, 1979-92; pres., creative dir. Spirit Media, Portland. Prodr. (TV documentary) Foundations of Freedom, 1999 (The Vision award 2000), (TV spl.) Luis Palau Festival, 1999 (Emmy nomination 2000). Speech scholar Mt. Hood Coll., 1977. Mem.: Media Comm. Assn. Internat. (bd. dirs.), Oreg. Media Prodn. Assn., Nat. Religious Broadcasters. Office: Spirit Media #700F 10117 SE Sunnyside Rd Portland OR 97015 Office Fax: 503-698-8408. E-mail: bill@spiritmedia.com.

DOLAS, EVELYN ANN, poet, musician; b. Chicago, Ill., Oct. 2, 1960; d. George Evangelos and Clara Dolas. English Composition, City Colleges Chgo., Chicago, IL; Cert. Graduation, Automation Acad., 1982. Author: (book of poetry) America at the Millennium: The Best Poems and Poets of the 20th Century, Poetry's Elite: The Best Poems of 2000, Echoes of Yesteryear, Rainstorms and Rainbows, Nature's Echoes, By the Light of the Moon, Mythology of the Heart, A Secret Language. Recipient Achievement award, Chgo. Pk. Dist. Dept. Recreation, 1973, Cert. Achievement, Chgo. Pub. Schools, Cert., Curie Concert Chorus, 1973-1977, Cert. Excellence, Curie Chamber Chorus, 1977, seven Editor's Choice awards, 2000—02, Internat. Poet of Merit award, 2002. Mem.: Internat. Soc. Poets. Home: PO Box 4763 Hailey ID 83333

DOLBERG, DAVID SPENCER, business executive, marketing professional, lawyer, scientist, molecular biologist; b. L.A., Nov. 28, 1945; s. Samuel and Kitty (Snyder) D.; m. Katherine Blumberg, Feb. 22, 1974 (div. 1979); 1 child, Max; m. Sarah Carnochan, May 23, 1992 (div. 1995); m. Elana Mann, June 15, 1997; children: Kayla, Sophia. BA in Biology with honors, U. Calif., Berkeley, 1974; PhD in Molecular Biology, U. Calif., San Diego, 1980; JD, U. Calif., Berkeley, 1989. Bar: Calif. 1989, U.S. Dist. Ct. (no. dist.) Calif. 1989, U.S. Patent and Trademark Office, 1990. Staff biologist, postdoctoral fellow Lawrence Berkeley Lab. U. Calif., 1980-85; assoc. Irell & Manella, Menlo Park, Calif., 1989-91; v.p. EROX Corp., Menlo Park, Calif., 1991-92; v.p. sci. and patents Pherin Corp., Menlo Park, Calif., 1992-94; pvt. practice Berkeley, 1994-98, N.Y.C., 1996-97, Richmond, Calif., 1998—. Speaker in field. Contbr. articles to Jour. Gen. Virology, Jour. Virology, Nature, Science, Psychoneuroendocrinology. Address: 37 Terrace Ave Richmond CA 94801-3937 E-mail: dsdol@pacbell.net.

DOLBY, RAY MILTON, engineering company executive, electrical engineer; b. Portland, Oreg., Jan. 18, 1933; s. Earl Milton and Esther Eufemia (Strand) Dolby; m. Dagmar Baumert, Aug. 19, 1966; 1 child, Thomas Eric;1 child, David Earl. Student, San Jose State Coll., 1951-52, 55, Washington U., St. Louis, 1953—54; BSEE, Stanford U., 1957; PhD in Physics (Marshall scholar 1957-60, Draper's studentship 1959-61, NSF fellow 1960-61), Cambridge (Eng.) U., 1961, ScD (hon.), 1997; Doctor of the U. (hon.), U. York. Lic. Comml. pilot instrument rating FAA. Electronic technician/jr. engr. Ampex Corp., Redwood City, Calif., 1949—53, engr., 1955—57, sr. engr., 1957; PhD research student in physics Cavendish Lab., Cambridge U., 1957—61, research in long wavelength x-rays, 1957—63; fellow Pembroke Coll., 1961—63; cons. U.K. Atomic Energy Authority, 1962—63; UNESCO adviser Central Sci. Instruments Orgn., Chandigarh, Punjab, India, 1963—65; owner, chmn., CEO Dolby Labs. Inc., San Francisco and Wootton Bassett, U.K., 1965—. Mem. Marshall Scholarship selection com., 1979—85; Trustee Univ. High Sch., San Francisco, 1978—84; bd. dirs. San Francisco Opera; bd. govs. San Francisco Symphony. Served with U.S. Army, 1953—54. Decorated officer Most Excellent Order of Brit. Empire; named Man of Yr., Internat. Tape Assn., 1987; recipient Beech-Thompson award, Stanford U., 1956, Emmy award, 1957, 1989, Trendsetter award, Billboard, 1971, Top 200 Execs. Bi-Centennial award, 1976, Lyre award, Inst. High Fidelity, 1972, Emile Berliner Maker of the microphone award, Emile Berliner Assn., 1972, Sci. and Engring. award, Acad. Motion Picture Arts and Scis., 1979, Oscar award, 1989, Pioneer award, Internat. Teleprodn. Soc., 1988, Edward Rhein Ring award, Edward Rhein Found., 1988, Life Achievement award, Cinema Audio Soc., 1989, Grammy award, NARAS, 1995, Nat. medal Tech., U.S. Dept. Commerce, 1997, medal of Achievement, Am. Electronics Assn., 1997; fellow Pembroke Coll., Cambridge U., 1983. Fellow: Inst. Broadcast Sound, Soc. Motion Picture and TV Engrs. (Samuel L. Warner award 1979, Alexander M. Poniatoff Gold medal 1982, Progress award 1983), Sound and TV Soc. (outstanding tech. and sci. award 1995), Audio Engring. Soc. (bd. govs. 1972-74 1979—84, Silver medal 1971, Gold medal 1992), Brit. kenematograph; mem.: IEEE (Ibuka award 1997), Pacific Union Club, St. Francis Yacht Club, Tau Beta Pi. Achievements include research in Achievements include inventions, rsch., publs. in video tape recording, x-ray microanalysis, noise reduction and quality improvements in audio and video systems; holder 50 U.S. patents. Office: Dolby Labs 100 Potrero Ave San Francisco CA 94103-4886

DOLCE, CARL JOHN, education administration educator; b. New Orleans, June 3, 1928; s. John and Nina (Puglia) D.; m. Nancy Lockwood, July 27, 1955; children: Carla, John. BA, Tulane U., 1947; MEd, Loyola U., New Orleans, 1955; EdD, Harvard U., 1963. Elem. sch. tchr. New Orleans Pub. Schs., 1948-54, secondary sch. tchr., 1954-55, jr. high sch. prin., 1955-63, supt. schs., 1965-69; rsch. assoc., lectr. Harvard Grad. Sch. Edn., Cambridge, Mass., 1963-65; dean Coll. Edn. and Psychology, N.C. State U., Raleigh, 1969-88, dean emeritus, prof. edn. adminstrn., 1989—. Chair adv. com. aesthetic edn. Cen. Midwest Regulatory Lab., St. Louis, 1968-71; chair exptl. schs. selection com. Office Edn., Washington, 1971-72; pres. Coun. Basic Edn., Washington, 1972-79; vice chmn. nat. assn. Elem. and Secondary Edn. Act Title IV state adv. councs., 1978-79 Editorial bd. Ednl. Forum, 1988; author book chpts., monographs, articles. Chmn. Wake County (N.C.) Sch. Study Com., Raleigh, 1978-79; chmn. tech. advisors Durham City/County Merger Task Force, 1988. Sgt. U.S. Army, 1950-52. U.S Office Edn. grantee, 1971-78, 81-82, 86-87. Mem. Raleigh Chamber Music Guild (pres. 1978-1980, Phi Kappa Phi (pres. N.C. State U. chpt. 1982-83). Avocations: gardening, reading, mysteries, puzzles. Home: 801 Macon Pl Raleigh NC 27609-5552

DOLCE, JULIA WAGNER, lawyer; b. West Palm Beach, Fla., Aug. 13, 1959; d. Arthur Ward and Ruth Alice (Shingler) W. BSBA, So. Meth. U., 1980; JD, Marquette U., 1985. Bar: Wis. 1985, U.S. Dist. Ct. (ea. and we. dists.) Wis. 1985, Fla. 1989, U.S. Dist. Ct. (so. and mid. dists.) Fla. 1990, U.S. Supreme Ct. 1993. Atty. Marcus Corp., Milw., 1986-88; judicial asst. Fla. State Ct. Appeals (4th dist.), West Palm Beach, Fla., 1989; ptnr. Wagner, Nugent, Johnson & McAfee, West Palm Beach, 1990-95; atty. pvt. practice, West Palm Beach, 1995—2003; assoc. Michael Walsh, P.A., West Palm Beach, 2003—. Bd. dirs. Hope House of the Palm Beaches, West Palm Beach, 1993-97. Avocation: reading.

DOLD, ROBERT BRUCE, journalist; b. Newark, Mar. 9, 1955; s. Robert Bruce and Margaret (Noll) Dold; m. Eileen Claire Norris, July 10, 1982; children: Megan, Kristen. BS in Journalism, Northwestern U., 1977, MS in Journalism, 1978. Reporter Suburban Tribune, Hinsdale, Ill., 1978—83, Chgo. Tribune, 1983—90, mem. editl. bd., 1990—95, dep. editl. page editor, columnist, 1995—2000, editl. page editor, 2000—. Pulitzer Prize juror, 1997—98;

columnist Chgo. Enterprise, 1991—95; critic Downbeat Mag., 1980—84; commentator Chgo. Week in Rev., 1987—. Bd. dirs. Jazz Inst. Chgo., 1980—83. Recipient Peter Lisagor award, Sigma Delta Chi, 1988, Pulitzer Prize for editl. writing, 1994, Scripps Howard Found. Nat. award for commentary, 1999. Mem.: Am. Soc. Newspaper Editors. Roman Catholic. Avocations: golf, basketball, jazz. Home: 501 N Park Rd La Grange Park IL 60526-5516 Office: Chgo Tribune 435 N Michigan Ave Chicago IL 60611-4066 E-mail: bdold@tribune.com.

DOLE, ARTHUR ALEXANDER, psychology educator; b. San Francisco, Oct. 25, 1917; s. Arthur Alexander and Ella Elizabeth (Duncan) D.; m. Marjorie Elizabeth Welsh, Mar. 19, 1949; children: Peter, Steven, Barbara. BA, Antioch Coll., 1946; MA, Ohio State U., 1949, PhD, 1951; MA (hon.), U. Pa., 1973. Diplomate Am. Bd. Examiners in Profl. Psychology. Asst. psychology and edn. Antioch Coll., 1946-48; counselor Ohio State U., 1948-51; dir. Bur. Testing and Guidance, U. Hawaii, 1951-60, from asst. prof. to prof. psychology, 1951-67; prof. psychology in edn. U. Pa., 1967-88, chmn. dept., 1967-88, prof. emeritus, 1988—. Mem. internat. adv. bd. Univ MSG, Romero, El Salvador. Author articles in field.; cons. editor profl. jours. Bd. dirs. Am. Family Found., PEACE, Internat. Fellow APA, AAUP, ACA, Am. Ednl. Rsch. Assn., Internat. Coun. Psychologists, Internat. Assn. Applied Psychology, Nat. Rehab. Assn. E-mail: aadole@acadia.net.

DOLE, ELIZABETH HANFORD, senator, former charitable organization administrator, former federal official; b. Salisbury, N.C., July 29, 1936; d. John Van and Mary Ella (Cathey) Hanford; m. Robert Joseph Dole (former U.S. Senator from Kans.), Dec. 6, 1975. BA with honors in Polit. Sci., Duke U., 1958; postgrad., Oxford (Eng.) U., summer 1959; MA in Edn. and Govt., Harvard U., 1960, JD, 1965. Bar: D.C. 1966. Staff asst. to asst. sec. for edn. HEW, Washington, 1966-67; practiced law Washington, 1967-68; assoc. dir. legis. affairs, then exec. dir. Pres.'s Com. for Consumer Interests, Washington, 1968-71; dep. asst. to Pres. The White House, Washington, 1971-73; commr. FTC, Washington, 1973-79; chmn. Voters for Reagan-Bush, 1980; dir. Human Services Group, Office of Exec. Br. Mgmt., Office of Pres.-Elect, 1980; asst. to Pres. for pub. liaison, 1981-83; sec. U.S. Dept. Transp., 1983-87; with Robert Dole Presdl. Campaign, 1987-88; participant 1988 Presdl. and Congl. campaigns; sec. U.S. Dept. Labor, 1989-90; pres. ARC, 1991-99; U.S. senator from N.C., 2003—; mem. armed services, agr., banking and aging coms., 2003—. Mem. nominating com. Am. Stock Exch., 1972, N.C. Consumer Coun., 1972. Trustee Duke U., 1974-88; mem. coun. Harvard Law Sch. Assocs., mem. vis. com. Harvard Sch. Pub. Health, 1992-95; mem. bd. overseers Harvard U., 1989-95. Recipient Arthur S. Flemming award U.S. Govt., 1972, Humanitarian award Nat. Commn. Against Drunk Driving, 1988, Disting. Alumni award Duke U., 1988, N.C. award, 1991, Lifetime Achievement award (Breaking The Glass Ceiling) Women Execs. in State Govt., 1993, North Carolinian of the Yr. award N.C. Press Assn., 1993, Radcliffe medal, 1993, Leadership award LWV, 1994, Maxwell Finland award Nat. Found. Infectious Diseases, 1994, Disting. Svc. award Nat. Safety Coun., 1989, Raoul Wallenberg award for Humanitarian Svc., 1995, Christian Woman of Yr. award, 1996; named one of Am.'s 200 Young Leaders, Time mag., 1974, one of World's 10 Most Admired Women, Gallup Poll, 1988, one of 10 most fascinating people 1996 Barbara Walter's Spl., most inspiring polit. figure 1996 MSNBC, 3d most admired woman in Am. Good Housekeeping, 1996, 98; selected for Safety and Health Hall of Fame Internat., 1993; inducted into Nat. Women's Hall of Fame, 1995. Mem. Phi Beta Kappa, Pi Lambda Theta, Pi Sigma Alpha. Office: Dirksen Sen Off Bldg Rm 34 Washington DC 20510*

DOLE, JANICE GAIL ARNOLD, literacy educator; b. Boston, Jan. 31, 1947; d. Walter Francis and Jenny Clare (Sapuppo) Arnold; m. Patrick John Brennan, Dec. 30, 1992; 1 child, Melissa Erin. BA, U. Mass., Boston, 1969; MA, U. Colo., 1974, PhD, 1977. Cert. elem. tchr., Mass., Calif. Elem. tchr. Medford (Mass.) Sch. Sys., 1969-70, Ridgecrest (Calif.) Sch. Dist., 1970-73; rsch./tchg. asst. U. Colo., Boulder, 1974-77; asst. prof. U. Denver, 1978-84; asst. vis. prof. Ctr. for Study of Reading U. Ill., 1984-86; asst. prof. Mich. State U., East Lansing, 1986-88, U. Utah, Salt Lake City, 1988—. Adv. bd. Reading Rsch. Quarterly, Contemporary Edn. Psychology, Jour. Lit. Rsch.; mem. devel. panel Nat. Assessment Ednl. Progress, Princeton, N.J., 1992—; co-dir. Utah Reading Excellence Act, 1999-2001; mem. Rand Panel Reading, 2000—, cons. to numerous sch. dists. Author: Elementary Language Arts, 1984; contbr. articles to profl. publs. Mem. Am. Edn. Rsch. Assn., Nat. Reading Conf., Internat. Reading Assn., Soc. for Sci. Study of Reading. Avocations: skiing, hiking, reading, running. Office: U Utah 1705 E Central Campus #120 Salt Lake City UT 84112-1169 E-mail: dole@ed.utah.edu.

DOLE, ROBERT J. lawyer, former senator; b. Russell, Kans., July 22, 1923; s. Doran R. and Bina Dole; m. Elizabeth Hanford, Dec. 1975. Student, U. Kans., 1941—43, U. Ariz.; AB, LLB, Washburn Mcpl. U., Topeka, 1952; LLD (hon.), Washburn U., Topeka, 1969. Bar: Kans. 1952. Mem. Kans. Ho. of Reps., 1951—53; sole practice Russell, Kans., 1953—61; Russell County atty., 1953—61; mem. 87th Congress from 6th Dist. Kans., 1961—63, 88th-90th Congresses from 1st Dist. Kans., 1963—69; U.S. senator from Kans., 1969—96; Senate majority leader, 1985—87, 1995—96; Senate minority leader, 1987—95; chmn. Rep. Nat. Com., 1971—73; of counsel Verner, Liipfert, Bernhard, McPherson & Hand, 1999—, Alston & Bird, 2003—. Rep. vice-presdl. candidate, 1976; Rep. presdl. candidate, 96. Author: Great Political Wit, Great Presidential Wits. Chmn. Int.. Commn. on Missing Persons, Nat. WWII Meml., Dole Found. Served with U.S. Army, WW II. Decorated Purple Heart (2), Bronze Star with 2 clusters; recipient Horatio Alger award, Horatio Alger Assn. Disting. Ams., 1988, Presdl. medal of Freedom. Mem.: DAV, VFW, 4-H Fair Assn., Am. Legion, Kiwanis, Elks, Shriners, Masons, Kappa Sigma. Methodist. Office: Office of Sen Dole c/o Alston & Bird 601 Pennsylvania Ave NW Washington DC 20004

DOLE, VINCENT PAUL, medical research executive, educator; b. Chgo., May 8, 1913; s. Vincent Paul and Anne (Dowling) Dole; m. Elizabeth Ann Strange, May 23, 1942 (div. 1965); children: Vincent Paul III, Susan, Bruce; m. Marie Nyswander, 1965 (dec. 1986); m. Margaret E. Cool, 1992. AB, Stanford U., 1934; MD, Harvard U., 1939. Intern Mass. Gen. Hosp., Boston, 1940—41; mem. staff Rockefeller U., N.Y.C., 1941—, prof., 1951—. Developer methadone maintenance treatment program for heroin addiction. Office: Rockefeller U PO Box 308 1230 York Ave New York NY 10021-6399*

DOLE, VINCENT PAUL, III, food products executive; b. N.Y.C., May 30, 1944; s. Vincent Paul Dole and Elizabeth (Strange) Paine; m. Genevieve de la Pieuse, Jan. 17, 1945; 1 child, Alexandre Paul. BA, U. Pa., 1966; MBA, NYU, 1971. Chmn. Dolefam Corp., Washington, 1979—. Bd. dirs. JMC Investment Co., Washington, North Fork Group, St. Louis; bd. dirs. Cardel Hotel Corp., Miami, Fla. Mem. Bus. Promotion Coun., U.S. Dept. Commerce, Washington, 1988—; bd. dirs. Hosp. Relief Fund, Washington; trustees Nat. Archives of the U.S., Washington. Mem. U. Club (N.Y.C.), Club des Alpes (Nice, France).

DOLEAC, CHARLES BARTHOLOMEW, lawyer; b. New Orleans, Sept. 20, 1947; s. Cyril Bartholomew and Emma Elizabeth (St. Clair) D.; m. Denise Kilfoyle, Feb. 2, 1972; children: Keith Gabriel, Jessa Lee. BS cum laude, U. N.H., 1968; JD, NYU, 1971. Bar: Mass. 1972, N.H. 1972, Maine 1973. Law clk. to Justice Grimes N.H. Supreme Ct., Concord, 1972-73; assoc. Boynton, Waldron, Dill & Aeschliman, Portsmouth, N.H., 1973-76; ptnr. Boynton, Waldron, Doleac, Woodman & Scott, Portsmouth, 1977—. Apptd. mediator N.H. Superior Ct., 1992—; del. to tour Chinese legal system Chinese Ministry Justice, 1982; del. to People's Republic of China/U.S. joint session on trade investment and econ. law Chinese Ministry Justice/U.S. Dept. Justice, Beijing, 1987; propr. Portsmouth Athenaeum; moderator seminars on ethics for Leaders & Comparative Cultures and Values/East & West and Exec. Seminar Aspen Inst., 1990-95; moderator exec. sem. Aspen Inst., 1997-2000; mem. faculty Southwestern Legal Found. Internat. & Comparative Law Ctr., 1997—; ofcl. guest Fgn. Ministry Japan, Tokyo, 1998; developed Asian Seminar, Aspen Inst., 2000; spkr. ethics Ann. Nat. Conf. Appellate Ct. Clks., 1999-2000. Contbr. articles to profl. jours. Mem. citizens adv. coun. Portsmouth Cmty. Devel. Program, 1976-77; incorporator N.H. Charitable Found.; pres., bd. dirs. Seacoast United Way; chmn. Portsmouth Bd. Bldg. Appeals, 1976-77; chmn. stewardship com. Soc. Preservation New Eng. Antiquities, 1980-84, also trustee; pres. bd. trustees Strawbery Banke Mus., 1985-88; founder Daniel Webster Inn of Ct., 1993, Charles C. Doe Inn of Ct., 1994, Portsmouth Peace Treaty Forums I-IV, 1994-2000; founder, pres. Japan-Am. Soc. N.H., 1988; develop Asian seminar, Aspen Inst., 2000. Named Citizen of Yr., Portsmouth, N.H., 1991; recipient John E. Thayer III award, Japan Soc. Boston, Inc., 2001. Fellow N.H. Bar Found; mem. ATLA, Mass. Bar Assn., Maine Bar Assn., N.H. Bar Assn., N.H. Trial Lawyers Assn., Maine Trial Lawyers Assn. Avocation: masters swimming. Home: Little Harbor Rd Portsmouth NH 03801 Office: Boynton Waldron Doleac Woodman & Scott PA 82 Court St Portsmouth NH 03801-4414 E-mail: cdoleac@nhlawfirm.com.

DOLEN, WILLIAM KENNEDY, allergist, immunologist, pediatrician, educator; b. Memphis, Oct. 16, 1952; s. William Smith and Dorothy DeWitt (Kennedy) D.; m. Carolyn Canon, Dec. 21, 1974; children: John William, Susan Elizabeth. BS in Biology with distinction and honors, Rhodes Coll., 1974; MD, U. Tenn., 1977. Cert. Nat. Bd. Med. Examiners, Am. Bd. Pediatrics, Am. Bd. Allergy and Immunology. Commd. 2d lt. U.S. Army, 1974, advanced through grades to maj., 1982; intern in pediatrics U. Tenn. Hosp., Knoxville, 1977-78; med. officer SHAPE Med. Ctr., Belgium, 1978-79; comdr. U.S. Army NATO Health Clinic, Belgium, 1979-80; resident in pediatrics Letterman Army Med. Ctr., San Francisco, 1980-82; pediatrician Bassett Army Community Hosp., Ft. Wainwright, Alaska, 1982-84; fellow allergy and clin. immunology Fitzsimons Army Med. Ctr., Aurora, Colo., 1984-86; allergist, immunologist Ochsner Clinic, New Orleans, 1988-89, Allergy Respiratory Inst. Colo., Denver, 1989-92; chief pediatric allergy sect. allergy-immunology svc. Fitzsimons Army Med. Ctr., Aurora, Colo., 1986-88; clin. assoc. prof. medicine Ctr. for Health Scis. U. Colo., Denver, 1990-92; assoc. prof. pediatrics and medicine Med. Coll. Ga., Augusta, 1992-98, prof., 1998—. Presenter in field. Author: (with others) Rhinolaryngoscopy, 2d edit., 1989;; mem. editl. bd. Annals of Allergy, 1993-99; contbr. articles to profl. jours., chpts. to books. Assoc. dir. Augusta Choral Soc. Fellow Am. Coll. Allergy, Asthma and Immunology (bd. regents, 1993-96, exec. com. 1995-96, chair comm. coun. 1993-96, chair workshop com. 1990-97, mem. ann. program com. 1986-87, 90—, CME com. 1988-94, chair Rhinitis com. 1988-93, workshop com. 1989-90, disting. fellow), Am. Acad. Allergy and Immunology (com. computers and tech. 1994-97, workshop com. 1993-96), Am. Acad. Pediats.; mem. AMA, Allergy, Asthma and Immunology Soc. of Ga. (pres. 2001—), Southeastern Allergy, Asthma and Immunology Soc. (pres. 2002-03), European Acad. Allergology and Clin. Immunology, Am. Guild of Organists. Episcopalian. Office: Sect Allergy Immunology Med Coll GA Augusta GA 30912

DOLEV, JACQUELINE, physician, researcher; b. Feb. 25, 1975; d. Sharon and Mark Dolev. BA, U. Calif, Berkeley, 1997; MD, Yale U. Sch. Medicine, 2001. Lic. Calif., 2002. Internal medicine resident Stanford U. Hosp., Clinics, Stanford, Calif., 2001—03; dermatology fellow UCSF, San Francisco. Dir. Looking with Care; med. observational skills curriculum, Stanford Med. Sch., The Cantor Center for Visual Arts, Calif.; healthcare fellow U.S Senate, Washington, 1998; co-founder Med. observational skills curriculum, Yale Ctr. for Brit. Art, New Haven, 1998—2001. Contbr. articles various profl. jours., chapters to books; author: (resolution) AMA Policy Compendium; author: (illustrator) (children's book) Around the World. Mem.: AMA (pres., med. student chpt..Yale U. 1997—99), Calif. Med. Assn., Psi Chi Nat. Honor Soc. in Psychology (life). Personal E-mail: dolevjc@aya.yale.edu.

DOLEZAL, DALE FRANCIS, truck manufacturing company executive; b. Ronan, Mont., Apr. 9, 1936; s. Henry Lewis and Regina Marie (Nedjelski) D.; m. Patricia Louise Johnson, Aug. 27, 1960 (div. Dec. 1980); children: Craig, Kelly, Kathleen, Kari. BS in Indsl. Engring., Mont. State U., 1961; student Exec. Program for Mgmt. Devel., Bus. Sch., Harvard U., 1974. Registered profl. engr., Oreg. Indsl. and methods engr. Westinghouse Electric Corp., Sunnyvale, Calif., 1962—63; chief indsl. engr. Clarke Equipment Corp., Spokane, Wash., 1963—65; mgr. materials Freightliner Corp., Portland, Oreg., 1965—67; dir. purchasing and inventory mgmt. Internat. Harvester Co., Chgo., 1977—80, dir. materials and ops. planning, 1980—81; gen. mgr. parts and retail Indsl. Trucks div. Eaton Corp., Phila., 1981—84; pres. Modern Group, Phila., 1984—86; group v.p., gen. mgr. Holland Atlantic Hitch. Co. of Denmark, Whitehouse Sta., NJ, 1986—2001; COO Holland U.S.A., 2001—. Pres. Positive Prints, Inc.; dir. Real Am. Corp.; mem. bd. bus. and indsl. advisers U. Wis., Madison; bd. dirs. Ops. Tng. Inst., Ea. Leadership Mgmt., Inc. Contbr. articles to trade jours. Mem. parents adv. bd. Naperville (Ill.) Central High Sch., 1977—; mem. adv. bd. Sch. Dist. 203, Naperville, 1978—; mem. New Hope (Pa.) Solebury Sch. Bd., 1982-87. Served with USMC, 1954-57. Mem. Am. Inst. Indsl. Engrs., Am. Prodn. and Inventory Control. Soc. (pres. 1968-74), Am. Soc. Indsl. Engrs., Rotary (Paul Harris fellow 1992, bd. dirs. 1988—, pres. 1989-90), K.C. (pres.), Harvard Club. Republican. Avocations: golfing, hunting, fishing. Home: 3149 Landing Way NE Orangeburg SC 29118-1803 Office: Holland Group 31 Holland St Denmark SC 29042 E-mail: jmartin512@aol.com.

DOLEZAL, VACLAV JAN, retired mathematician, educator; b. Ceska Trebova, Czech Republic, May 21, 1927; arrived in U.S., 1968; s. Vaclav Dolezal and Marie Dolezalova; m. Stana Kabickova, Feb. 22, 1963; children: Tomas, Peter, Zuzana. MEE, Tech. U., Prague, Czech Republic, 1949; CSc in Applied Math., Czech Acad. Sci., Prague, Czech Republic, 1956, DrSc in Applied Math., 1967. Rschr. Rsch. Labs., Prague, 1949—51, Czech Acad. Sci., Prague, 1951—65, 1966—68; vis. prof. SUNY, Stony Brook, 1965—66, prof., 1968—97; ret., 1997. Author: Dynamics of Linear Systems, 1967, Nonlinear Networks, 1977, Monotone Operators, 1979. Grantee, NSF. Office: SUNY @ Stony Brook Dept Applied Math & Stats Stony Brook NY 11794

DOLGAN, ROBERT JOSEPH, journalist; b. Cleve, Nov. 11, 1932; s. Joseph and Pauline Dolgan; m. Cecilia Jo Valencic, Aug. 4, 1973; children: Robert, Ann. BS in English, John Carroll U., 1955. Sportswriter Plain Dealer, Cleve., 1957—63, 1967—72, 1977—, news columnist, 1972—77; publicist Thistledown Racetrack, Cleve., 1964; news editor Valley Morning Star, Harlingen, Tex., 1965; copy editor Detroit News, 1965—67. Author: The Polka King, 1977, Heroes, Scamps, Good Guys, 2003. Named Column of Yr., U.S. Football Writers Assn., 1987. Mem.: Press Club Cleve. (Top Sport Column 1968—69, Journalism Hall of Fame 1999). Avocations: theater, music, golf, hiking. Home: 2892 Istra Ln Willoughby Hills OH 44092 Office: The Plain Dealer 1801 Superior Ave Cleveland OH 44114 Fax: 216-999-6276. E-mail: bdolgan@plaind.com.

DOLGEN, JONATHAN L. motion picture company executive; b. N.Y.C., Apr. 27, 1945; Ed., Cornell U., grad., 1966; JD, N.Y.U. Law Sch., 1969. Lawyer Fried, Frank, Harris, Shriver & Jacobson, N.Y.C, 1969-76; asst. gen. counsel, deputy gen. counsel Columbia Pictures Industries, 1976-85, sr. v.p. Worldwide Bus. Affairs, 1979, exec. v.p., 1980; sr. exec., v.p. Fox Inc., 1985-90, sr. exec. v.p. telecommunications, 1985-88, pres., 1988-91, Columbia Pictures, 1990-94; pres. TV div. 20th Century-Fox Film Corp., Beverly Hills, Calif.; pres. motion picture group Columbia Pictures, Culver City, Calif., 1991—; chmn., CEO Viacom Entertainment Group, N.Y.C., 1994—. Bd. fellows Claremont U. Ctr. and Grad. Sch.; founder Friends of the Cornell U. Theater Arts Ctr.; mem. Alumni Coun. N.Y.U. Law Sch.; founding mem. Edn. First; adv. Calif. State Summer Sch. for the Arts.; pres. Columbia's Pay Cable & Home Entertainment Group, 1983; chmn. Twentieth TV, 1988-90; mem. bd. dirs. Sony Pictures. Office: Viacom Entertainment Group 1515 Broadway New York NY 10036-8901

DOLGIN, MARTIN, cardiologist, educator; b. N.Y.C., Apr. 12, 1919; s. Samuel and Bertha (Brodsky) D.; m. Jeanne Rydell, Feb. 12, 1950; children: Barbara, Deborah, Stuart. AB, NYU, 1939, MD, 1943. Diplomate: Am. Bd. Internal Medicine; cert. cardivascular disease. Intern, resident in medicine Lincoln Hosp., N.Y.C., 1943, 44; fellow in internal medicine Lahey Clinic, Boston, 1945, 46; fellow in cardiovasc. disease rsch. Michael Reese Hosp., Chgo., 1947; instr. to assoc. prof. medicine NYU, N.Y.C., 1948-73, prof. clin. medicine, 1973—; attending physician Bellevue Hosp. and Tisch Univ. Hosp., N.Y.C., 1973—; adj. attending physician Montefiore Hosp., N.Y.C., 1948-68; cons. in cardiology Will Rogers Hosp., Saranac Lake, N.Y., Columbus Hosp., N.Y.C., 1960-70; chief cardiology sect. N.Y. VA Hosp., 1955-89, cons. cardiology, 1989—. Editorial bd.: Jour. Electrocardiology; contbr. articles in electrocardiography to publs. Served with M.D. U.S. Army, 1952-54. Fellow ACP, Am. Coll. Cardiology, N.Y. Acad. Sci.; mem. Am. Fedn. Clin. Research, Am. Heart Assn., AAAS, Alpha Omega Alpha Home: 32 Mountainview Ave Ardsley NY 10502-2010 Office: NY VA Hospital 423 E 23rd St New York NY 10011-1401

DOLGOW, ALLAN BENTLEY, management consultant; b. N.Y.C., Dec. 14, 1933; children from previous marriage: Nicole, Marc, Ginger, Kimbie. B in Indsl. Engring., NYU, 1959, MBA, 1972; postgrad., Hunter Coll., 1976, U. Calif., 1991. With Republic Aviation Corp., Farmingdale, NY, 1959-60, Internat. Paper Co., N.Y.C., 1960-73, J. C. Penney Co., Inc., N.Y.C., 1973-76, Morse Electro Products, N.Y.C., 1976-77, Morse Electrophonic Ltd., Hong Kong, 1976-77, Revlon, Inc., Edison, NJ, 1977-79, SRI Internat., Menlo Park, Calif., 1979-96, Dolgow Cons., Stockton, Calif., 1996—. With U.S. Army, 1954—56. E-mail: allandolgow@aol.com.

DOLHANCYK, DIANA See PAMIN, DIANA DOLHANCYK

DOLIBER, DARREL LEE, retired engineering consultant, hotel executive; b. Mpls., June 19, 1940; s. Russell Clifford Doliber and Helen Carol (Homa) Price; m. Ethel Lorraine Dzivi, June 17, 1962; children: Wendy Lorraine, Heather Leigh; m. Helga Renate Miggo, Oct. 31, 1986. AA, Palomar Coll., 1973. Prodn. engr. Hughes Aircraft Co., Carlsbad, Calif., 1969-74; sr. engr. I.T.T., Roanoke, Va., 1974-77; dir. mfg. Gainsboro Elec. Mfg. Co., Inc., Roanoke, Va., 1977-78; mfg. engr. Litton Industries, Tempe, Ariz., 1978-82; sr. engr. Datagraphix, Inc., San Diego, 1982-84; lab. mgr. S.A.I.C., San Diego, 1984-98; cons. in photon counting detectors, UHV sys. Cleanroom Design, Med. Devices, Alpine, Calif., 1996—2002. Proprietor Victoria Rock Bed and Breakfast, 1995—. Contbr. articles in field; patentee in field. Mem. Soc. Photo-Optical and Instrumentation Engrs. Roman Catholic. Avocations: art, soaring. Home and Office: 2952 N Victoria Dr Alpine CA 91901-3673

DOLIBOIS, ROBERT JOSEPH, trade association administrator; b. Hamilton, Ohio, Aug. 26, 1947; s. John E. and Winifred E. (Englehart) D.; m. Susan K. Lallathin, June 16, 1973; children: Ryan, Sara. BA, Miami U., Ohio, 1969. Lt. USN, 1969-74; v.p. Nat. Assn. Life Underwriters, Washington, 1974-88; pres. Assn. Mgmt. Group, 1988-91; exec. v.p. Am. Nursery and Landscape Assn., 1991—. Chmn. bd. dirs. Am. Soc. Assn. Execs., Washington, 1992-99. Elder McLean (Va.) Presbyn. Ch., 1990-93. Lt. USN, 1969-74. Named Cert. Assn. Exec. Am. Soc. of Assn. Execs., Washington, 1979. Mem. Am. Soc. Assn. Execs. Presbyterian. Home: 2709 N Brandywine St Arlington VA 22207-2722 Office: Am Nursery & Landscape Assn 1000 Vermont Ave NW Ste 300 Washington DC 20005-3922

DOLICE, JOSEPH LEO, art publisher, exhibition director; b. Newark, Oct. 12, 1941; s. Leon Louis and Mary Sabina (Lewandowski) D. BA, Iona Coll., 1963; MA, Hunter Coll., 1978. Dir., stage designer F. Richard Love Theatrical Prodns., White Plains, N.Y., 1969; stage designer various theater companies, N.Y., 1969-73; exhbn. dir. New Rochelle (N.Y.) Coun. on the Arts, 1977—; art dir. Stan Rose Assocs., N.Y.C., 1980-90; exhbn. dir. Fulton Gallery, N.Y.C., 1980-92; theater mgr. Village Gate, N.Y.C., 1987-92; art dir. Dezer Enterprises, N.Y.C., 1987-89; exhbn. dir. Janapa Gallery, N.Y.C., 1990; prodn. dir. Ruff Theatrical, Bklyn., 1991-95; publisher Dolice Graphics, N.Y.C., 1980—. A/v corporate and events tech. mgmt., various companies in N.Y.C. and Calif., 1994—. Author: Old New York Remembered, 1982; author, pub. Demo Directory, 1994-95, Free Computer Media, 1996, Vintage New York, 1998; exec. editor N.Y. Downtown News, 1987-89; contbr. articles to various pubs. Publicity dir. Putnam County Bicentennial Commn., Carmel, N.Y., 1976; exhbn. dir. Danbury (Conn.) State Arts & Crafts Fair, 1979-83; dir. Putnam Arts Coun. ann. profl. art exhibit, 1976; advt. dir. TheARTgallery Mag., 1974-76; exhbn. dir. New Rochelle Coun. on Arts. With U.S. Army, 1964-66, U.S., Korea. Mem. Internat. Assn. Fine Art Digital Printmakers, Entertainment Svcs. and Tech. Assn., Mus. Store Assn. Affiliate, Montauk Artists Assn., Ctr. Book Arts N.Y.C., Internat. Assn. of Fine Art Digital Printmakers. Avocations: writing, theatrical and performance work. Office: Dolice Graphics 163 3d Ave Ste 321 New York NY 10003-2523 Fax: 212-260-9217. E-mail: joe@dolice.com.

DOLICH, ANDREW BRUCE, sports marketing executive; b. Bklyn, NY, Feb. 18, 1947; s. Mac and Yetta (Weiselter) D.; m. Ellen Andrea Fass, June 11, 1972; children: Lindsey, Caryn, Cory. BA, Am. U., 1969; MEd, Ohio U., 1971. Adminstrv. asst. to gen. mgr. Phila. 76ers, NBA, Pa., 1971-74; v.p. Md. Arrows Lacrosse, Landover, Md., 1974-76; mktg. dir. Washington Capitals, NHL, Landover, Md., 1976-78; exec. v.p., gen. mgr. Washington Diplomats Soccer, 1978-80; v.p. bus. ops. Oakland A's Baseball, Calif., 1980-92, exec. v.p., 1993-95; pres., COO Golden State Warriors NBA, Oakland, Calif., 1995-98; pres. Dolich & Assoc. Sports Mktg., Alameda, Calif., 1996—; exec. v.p. Tickets.com, 1998—; pres. Memphis Grizzlies, 2000—. Nat. fundraising chmn. sports adminstrs. program Ohio U., Athens, dir., 1978-82; lectr. sports mktg. U. Calif. Ext. Bd. dir. Bay Area Sports Hall of Fame, 1982—, Internat. Sports Mktg. Coun., Oakland Zoo Adv. Coun.; bd. dir. Grizzlies Found, Sports Exec. Leadership Coun., 2000-2003. Recipient Alumni of Yr. award Ohio U. Sports Adminstrs. Program, Athens, 1982; recipient Clio award Am. Advt. Fedn., 1982 E-mail: adolich@grizzlies.com.

D'OLIMPIO, JAMES THOMAS, oncologist; b. Quincy, Mass., June 3, 1950; s. Orlando James D'Olimpio and Marie Johanna Ricciuti; m. Louise Mary Simon, May 30, 1980 (div. Apr. 1994); children: Matthew, Christopher; m. Mary Suzanne Clifford, Dec. 30, 1995; 1 child, John. BA, Boston U., 1972; MD, U. Guadalajara, 1978. Diplomate Am. Bd. Internal Medicine and Med. Oncology, and Hospice/Palliative Medicine. Intern, resident Mt. Sinai Hosp., N.Y.C., 1979—82; resident Oncology, fellow Montefiore Med. Ctr., Bronx, NY, 1982—84; rsch. fellow Albert Einstein Coll. Medicine, Bronx, 1984—85; dir. Hospice Care Network North Shore L.I. Jewish Health Sys., Westbury, NY, 1992—97, dir. Supportive Oncology and Palliative Medicine Program Manhasset, NY, 1997—. Asst. prof. medicine NYU Sch. Medicine. Contbr. Grantee, United Hosp. Fund, 2000—02. Mem.: Cancer and Leukemia Group B, Multinat. Assn. Supportive Care in Cancer, Am. Acad. Hospice and Palliative Medicine (cert. 1997), Am. Pain Soc., Am. Soc. Clin. Oncology. Avocations: jazz, painting, golf. Office: North Shore Univ Hosp 300 Community Dr Manhasset NY 11030

DOLIN, LONNY H. lawyer; b. Youngstown, Ohio, Jan. 24, 1954; d. Lawrence Joseph and Sonya (Sacks) Heselov; m. Gordon S. Black, Aug. 20, 1988; children: Nathaniel, Brooke, Aaron, Benjamin, Lindsay. AB, Georgetown U., 1976; JD, Cath. U., 1979. Bar: Vt. 1980, N.Y. State Bar 1984, U.S. Dist. Ct. (we. dist.) N.Y. 1984. Assoc. Downs, Rachlin & Martin, Burlington, Vt., 1979-81; pvt. practice Burlington, 1981-84; assoc., then ptnr. Harris, Beach, Wilcox, Rubin & Levey, Rochester, N.Y., 1984-90; ptnr. Harris, Beach & Wilcox, Rochester, N.Y., 1990-93; former of counsel to U.S. Congressman Fred J. Eckert, N.Y.; ptnr. Lonny H. Dolin and Assocs., Rochester, 1993—. Bd. dirs. Monroe County Legal Services Corp.; faculty mem. Nat. Adv. Inst.; co-chair 2d and 3d Ann. Nat. Inst. on Sexual Harassment; spkr. in field. Asst. editor ABA's Sect. of Labor and Employment Law Newsletter; contbr. chpts. and articles to profl. jours. Mem. Pittsford Town and County Com., N.Y., 1983—, Town of Pittsford Bd. of Zoning Appeals, N.Y., 1984—, vice chair 1990; chmn. Monroe County Comparable Worth Task Force, Rochester, 1985—, Fred J. Eckert Women's Adv. Council, Rochester, 1985—; del. The Jud. Dist. N.Y., Rochester, 1985—, chair 1990; bd. dirs. Nat. Council Jewish Women. Recipient Corpus Juris Secundum award West Pub. co., 1979. Fellow Coll. Labor and Employment Lawyers; mem. ABA (plaintiff's chair labor and employment law sect., co-chair nat. CLE/Inst. and Meetings Com., nat. co-chair employee's rights and responsibilities ethics subcom., nat. vice chair tort and ins. practice sect., spkr. ann. meetings), Nat. Employment Law Assn. (co-chair disabilities rights com.), Vt. Bar Assn., N.Y. Bar Assn., Monroe County Bar Assn. (mem. practice and perf. com.), Greater Rochester Women's Bar Assn. (treas. 1986), Assn. Trial Lawyers Am., N.Y. State Trial Lawyers Assn., Genesee Valley Trial Lawyers Assn. (treas. 1990). Republican. Avocations: golf, skiing, tennis. Home: 9 Hidden Springs Dr Pittsford NY 14534-2897 Office: Ste 130 135 Corporate Wood St Rochester NY 14623 Fax: 716-272-0574. E-mail: ldolin@dts.esg.com.

DOLIN, RAPHAEL, medical educator; b. Kaunas, Lithuania, Aug. 31, 1941; came to the U.S., 1950; s. Simon and Sara (Zolkov) D.; m. Kelly Millar, June 17, 1989; children: Eric, Nathaniel, Brooke, Allison. BS, Harvard U., 1963, MD, 1967. Resident Boston City Hosp., 1967-69; rsch. assoc. NIAID, 1969-72, fellow in infectious disease, 1972-73; head med. virology sect. NIAID, NIH, Bethesda, Md., 1972-78; prof. medicine U. Vt., Burlington, 1978-82; prof. medicine, head infectious disease unit U. Rochester, N.Y., 1982-91, prof. microbiology and immunology, 1982-98, Charles A. Dewey prof., chair dept.

medicine, 1991-98; Maxwll Finland prof. medicine; prof. medicine Harvard Med. Sch., 1998—, dean for clin. programs, 1998—, dean for acad. and clin. programs, 2003. Editor: Principles and Practice of Infectious Disease, 1995, AIDS Therapy, 1999. Fellow Infectious Disease Soc. Am.; mem. Am. Soc. for Clin. Investigation, Assn. Am. Physicians. Office: Harvard Med Sch 25 Shattuck St Rm 101 Boston MA 02115-6027

DOLINER, NATHANIEL LEE, lawyer; b. Daytona Beach, Fla., June 28, 1949; s. Joseph and Asia (Shaffer) D.; m. Debra Lynn Simon, June 5, 1983. BA, George Washington U., 1970; JD, Vanderbilt U., 1973; LLM in Taxation, U. Fla., 1977. Bar: Fla. 1973. Assoc. Smalbein, Eubank, Johnson, Rosier & Bussey, PA, Daytona Beach, Fla., 1973-76; vis. asst. prof. law U. Fla. Law Sch., Gainesville, 1977-78; assoc. Carlton, Fields, Ward, Emmanuel, Smith & Cutler, PA, Tampa, Fla., 1978-82; shareholder Carlton Fields, PA, Tampa, 1982—, chair bus. transactions practice group, 1998—. Adv. bd. Mergers and Acquisitions Law Report, pub. Bur. Nat. Affairs. Dist. commr. Gulf Ridge coun. Boy Scouts Am., 1983—84; bd. dirs. Kol Ami Synagogue, Tampa, 2003—, Big Bros./Big Sisters Greater Tampa, Inc., 1980—82, Child Abuse Coun., Inc., 1986—95, asst. treas., 1987—88, treas., 1988—89, pres.-elect, 1989—90, pres., 1990—91; bd. dirs. Tampa Jewish Fedn. Bd., 1988—91, Mus. Sci. and Industry, Tampa, 1994—, exec. com., 1994—, sec., 1995—97, first vice-chmn., 1997—99, chair, 1999—2001; mem. alumni bd. Vanderbilt Law Sch., 1999—2000; bd. dirs., exec. com. Hillel Sch., Tampa, 1998—, first v.p., 1999—2000, pres., 2001—03. Fellow: Am. Coll. Tax Counsel, Am. Bar Found.; mem.: ABA (vice-chmn. cont. legal edn. com. 1986—88, chmn. 1988—90, chmn. task force preliminary and ancillary agreements 1992—95, acquisition rev. task force 1992—95, chmn. 1993, chmn. programs subcom. 1995—98, vice-chmn. 1997—98, chmn. 1998—2002, com. negotiated acquisitions bus. law sect.), Tampa C. of C. (chmn. Ambassadors Target Task Force of Com. of 100 1984—85, 1987—88, vice-chmn. govt. fin. and taxation coun. 1987—88, chmn. 1988—89, chair geographic task force 1989—90, bd. govs. 1991—93, exec. com. 1992, chmn. govtl. affairs com. 1992), Fla. Bar Assn. (exec. coun. tax sect. 1980—82, tax cert. com. 1987—88, vice-chmn. 1988—89, chmn. 1989—90), Am. Law Inst., Anti-Defamation League (regional bd. dirs. 1986—90, exec. com. 1987—90), Tampa Club (sec. 1987—89, bd. dirs. 1987—92, pres. 1990—91). Home: 13341 Golf Crest Cir Tampa FL 33624-4648 Office: Carlton Fields Ward Emmanuel Smith & Cutler PA Ste 500 777 S Harbour Island Blvd Tampa FL 33602-5729

DOLIS, JOHN, English educator; b. St. Louis, Apr. 25, 1945; s. John J. Sr. and Anna Marie (Bonelle) D. BA, St. Louis U., 1967; MA, Loyola U., 1969, PhD, 1978. Teaching asst. Loyola U., Chgo., 1967-69, 70-73; instr. Notre Dame High Sch., Chgo., 1969-70; lectr. Loyola U., Chgo., 1974-75, 78-80; instr. Northeastern Ill. U., 1978-80; Fulbright lectr. U. Turin, Italy, 1980-81; instr. U. Kansas, 1981-85; assoc. prof. Pa. State U., Scranton, 1990-92; sr. Fulbright lectr. U. Bucharest, Romania, 1989-90. Instr. Columbia Coll., Chgo., 1970-71. Author: The Style of Hawthorne's Gaze: Regarding Subjectivity, 1993, Bl( )nk Space, 1993, Time Flies: Butterflies, 1999; editor: Nat. Assn. Remedial/Devel. Studies in Post-Secondary Edn. newsletter, 1979-80, Loyola U. Info. Systems newsletter, 1972; mem. editl. bd. Franciscan Sesquicentennial Poetry Contest, 1974, Ill. English Bull., 1970, 71, Nat. Hawthorne Rev., 1993—, Antemnae, 2002—, Ariz. Quar., 2002—; copywriter, music writer Neil Stewart and Assocs., Chgo., 1973-74; interviewer U.S. Info. Agy.; contbr. articles to profl. jours. Mem. Am. Philos. Assn., Internat. Assn. for Fantastic in Arts, Internat. Assn. Philosophy and Lit., Internat. Husserl and Phenomenological Rsch. Soc., Internat. Imagery Assn., Internat. Soc. for Phenomenology and Human Scis., Internat. Soc. for Phenomenology and Lit., Assn. for Applied Psychoanalysis, Ctr. for Psychoanalytic Studies, Fulbright Assn., Modern Lang. Assn., Nathaniel Hawthorne Soc., Northeast Modern Lang. Assn., North East Popular Culture Assn., Soc. for Advancement of Am. Philosophy, Soc. for Phenomenology and Existential Philosphy, Soc. for Phenomenology and Psychiatry, Thoreau Soc., World Phenomenology Inst. Home: 711 Summit Pt Scranton PA 18508-1057 E-mail: jjd3@psu.edu.

DOLL, LINDA A. artist, educator; b. Bklyn., May 5, 1942; d. William James Harrington and Ann B. (Casey) Cook; m. William John Doll, Feb. 4, 1962; children: Patricia, William Jr. AA, Palomar Coll., 1974; BA, San Diego State U., 1976. Chairperson Arts Adv. Com. to Congressman Jim Bates, 1983-84; U.S. Coast Guard Artist, 1985—. Exhibited in group shows with Am. Watercolor Soc., 1985-91 (selected for one yr. nat. travel show, Elsie and David Ject-key award 1988) N.Y.C., 1986, 87, 88, Canton, Ohio, 1985, Nat. Watercolor Soc., Brea, Calif., 1984-89, Watercolor West Annual, Riverside, Calif., 1982, 84-88 (E. Gene Crain Purchase Selection award 1985, Second Place Jurors award 1982), Rocky Mountain Nat., Golden, Colo., 1984-85, Midwest Annual, Davenport, Iowa, 1983, 85, Nat. Watercolor Soc., Riverside, 1985 (selected for one yr. nat. travel show) 88, Canton Ohio, 1985, Watercolor Internat., San Diego, 1978-79, 82-88 (selected for one yr. nat. travel show 1983-84), Watercolor Okla., 1982-84 (Harry Hulett Jr. award 1984), Pa. Soc. Watercolor Painters, Harrisburg, 1988, 1982 (hon. mention); represented in permanent collections including E. Gene Crain Collection, Laguna Beach, Calif., Scripps Hosp., La Jolla, Calif., Redlands Community Hosp., Riverside, Calif., Campbell River Community Art Council, Can., Simpact Assocs. Inc., San Diego. Mem. San Diego Watercolor Soc. (past pres., life), Nat. Watercolor Soc. (past pres., life), Am. Watercolors Soc. (bd. dirs., treas., past juror). Office: 17490 Matinal Dr San Diego CA 92127-1238 E-mail: lindadoll@san.rr.com.

DOLL, LYNNE MARIE, public relations agency executive; b. Glendale, Calif., Aug. 27, 1961; d. George William and Carol Ann (Kennedy) D.; m. David Jay Lans, Oct. 11, 1986. BA in Journalism, Calif. State U., Northridge, 1983. Freelance writer Austin Pub. Rels. Systems, Glendale, 1978-82; asst. account exec. Berkhemer & Kline, L.A., 1982-83; pres. Rogers & Assocs., L.A., 1983—. Exec. dir. Suzuki Automotive Found. for Life, Brea, Calif., 1986-91; mem. strategic planning com. Gateway to Indian Am. Corp. for Am. Indian Devel., San Francisco, 1988-90. Pub. rels. cons., Rape Treatment Ctr., L.A., 1986—. Mem. Ad Club L.A. (bd. dirs., pres. 1994-95), Pub. Rels. Soc. Am. (L.A. chpt. Outstanding Profl. 1999), So. Calif. Assn. Philanthropy, Coun. on Founds., Internat. Motor Press Assn., Nat. Conf. for Cmty. and Justice (L.A. region bd. dirs. 1996—, nat. bd. dirs. 2002—). Democrat. Office: Rogers & Assocs 1875 Century Park E Ste 300 Los Angeles CA 90067-2504

DOLL, PATRICIA MARIE, marketing and public relations advertising consultant; b. Bryn Mawr, Pa., Apr. 13, 1960; d. Otello Louis (dec.) and Eleanor Caroline (De Pasquale) De Grandis; m. John Russell Doll, Oct. 5, 1985. BS in Speech Comms., Millersville (Pa.) U., 1982. Lic. radio operator. News reporter, dj, writer, promotions coord. WIXQ and WLAN Radio, Lancaster, Pa., 1978-82; prodr., writer, rschr. WGAL-TV, Lancaster, Pa., 1982; copywriter, advtsg.-mktg. coord. Strawbridge & Clothier, Phila., 1982-87; freelance writer, 1984—; mktg. dir. Rouse & Assocs., Internat. Developer, Phila., Pa., 1987-90; owner Publicity Works, Bowmansville, Pa., 1990—. Contbr. articles to newspapers and trade mags.; producer TV documentary, 1982. Mem. chambers, trade, local orgns.; registered alumni mentor Millersville U. Named Internat. ATHENA Small Bus. Woman of Yr. award Berks County C. of C., 1996; recipient numerous regional and nat. awards for mktg. and cmty. work, SBA's Women's Bus. Advocate of Yr. award for Ea. Pa., 1997, MS Corp. Achievers award Nat. Multiple Sclerosis Soc., 1999; named 1 of Top 40 Under 40 Profls. in Ctrl. Pa., 1996, 1 of the Best 50 Women in Bus., Pa., Gov. of Pa., 1997, 2 awards for outstanding fundraising Am. Heart Assn., 1987. Mem. Kappa Delta Phi. Roman Catholic. Avocations: writing, dancing, professional violinist, modeling, community service. E-mail: pworx@epix.net.

DOLLENS, RONALD W. pharmaceuticals company executive; b. Ind., Dec. 17, 1946; s. William Franklin and Louise Anna (Davis) D.; m. Susan Stanley, Aug. 30, 1969; children: Stephanie, Grant. BS, Purdue U., 1970; MBA, Ind. U., 1972. From sales rep. to dir. bus. devel. Eli Lilly & Co., Indpls., 1972-85; sr. v.p. Advanced Cardiovasc. Sys., Santa Clara, 1985—88, pres., CEO Santa Clara, 1988—94; pres. med. devices divsn. Eli Lilly & Co., 1991-94; pres., CEO Guidant Corp., Indpls., 1994—. Mem., Adv. Com. on Regulatory Health US Dept. Health and Human Svcs., 2002—. Mem.: AdvaMed, Alliance for Aging Rsch., Healthcare Leadership Coun. Office: Guidant Corp PO Box 44906 Indianapolis IN 46244-0906

DOLMAN, JOHN PHILLIPS, JR., (TIM DOLMAN), communications company executive; b. Phila., May 22, 1944; s. John Phillips and Dodie Lewis (Porter) D.; m. Rebecca Critchlow, Oct. 29, 1977; children— John P. III, Timothy Chadwick (dec.). AB in History, Wagner Coll., 1966; MBA. in Internat. Bus, U. Pa., 1971. Asst. account exec. Benton & Bowles Inc., N.Y.C., 1971-72, account exec., 1972-73, account dir Amsterdam and London, 1973-75, v.p., account supr., 1975-78; pub. Motor Boating & Sailing mag., 1978-80; gen. mgr. mag. devel. Hearst Mags., N.Y.C., 1980-82; v.p., asst. pub. Pub. div. Playboy Enterprises, Inc., Chgo., 1983-84, sr. v.p., 1984-88; pres. Dolman & Co., New Canaan, Conn., 1988-92; sr. v.p. mktg. Championship Auto Racing Teams, Inc. dba IndyCar, 1992-94; v.p. mktg. and bus. devel. OCC Sports Inc. subs. ESPN, Inc. subs. ABC, Inc. subs. Walt Disney Co., 1994-99; v.p. dir., bus. ops. ESPN, ABC Sports Mktg. and Sales, 1999—. Contbr.: Marine Bus. mag, 1977-78. 1st lt. U.S. Army, 1966-69, Vietnam; lic. capt. USCG, 1988. Decorated Bronze Star. Mem. VFW, N.Y. Yacht Club. Republican. Episcopalian. E-mail: TDolman@aol.com.

DOLMATCH, THEODORE BIELEY, management consultant; b. N.Y.C., Apr. 22, 1924; s. Aaron and Diana (Bieley) D.; m. Blanche Ormont, Dec. 28, 1948; children: Karen Ann, Stephen Joseph. BA, NYU, 1947, MA, 1948; student, Columbia U., N.Y.C., 1948-50. Tchr. Queens Coll., 1948-50; asst. supr. Sch. Gen. Studies, Bklyn. Coll., 1950-55; publs. bus. mgr. Am. Mgmt. Assn., 1955-62; pres. Pitman Pub. Corp., N.Y.C., 1962-71, Intext Publishers Group, N.Y.C., also Intext Ednl. Devel. Group, N.Y.C., 1971-75, Info. Please Pub., Inc., N.Y.C., 1976-80, Dolmatch Publs., Inc., N.Y.C., 1979-85; cons. to govt. agys. and corps., 1981—; chmn. ISD/Shaw, Inc., Washington, 1986-2000. Author (sometimes under pseudonym Stephen Josephs) books and articles. Home: 15 Pond View Ln Ossining NY 10562 E-mail: t.dolmatch@verizon.net.

DOLPH, WILBERT EMERY, lawyer; b. Palatka, Fla., Dec. 29, 1923; s. Wilbert Emery and Ophelia (Reynolds) D.; m. Roberta Hundley; children: Wilbert Emery III, Kenneth Alan, Scott Marshall, Cheryl Karlsson. Student, U. Ariz., 1941-42, LL.B., 1949. Bar: Ariz. 1949. Asst. city atty., Tucson, 1949-50; asst. atty. gen., 1950-51; pvt. practice, 1951—93; counsel. jud. com. Ariz. Senate, 1952; shareholder Bilby & Shoenhair, P.C., 1953-89; ptnr. Snell & Wilmer, Tucson, 1989-93, of counsel, 1993-93; ret. 1993. Pres. Pima County Young Dems., 1952-53; v.p. Ariz. Young Dems., 1952-53; trustee Tucson Med. Ctr., pres., 1973-75; mem. U. Ariz. Found., U. Ariz. Pres.'s Club; past chmn. bd. dirs. Friends of Libr., U. Ariz., 1995-97; past bd. visitors U. Ariz. Law Coll.; past bd. dirs. Ariz. Sonora Desert Mus., Ariz. Heart Assn., So. Ariz. Heart Assn., Tucson Festival Soc., Ariz. Children's Home Assn., Tucson YMCA, Ariz. Coun. Econ. Edn.; past vestryman, parish warden St. Phlips in the Hills Episcopal Ch., 1974-76. With USNR, 1942-44, to capt. USMCR, 1944-46. Decorated Air medal. Mem. ABA, Ariz. Bar Assn., Pima County Bar Assn. (exec. com., pres. 1974-75), Phi Delta Phi, Sigma Chi, Coronado Yacht Club.

DOLSEN, DAVID HORTON, mortician; b. Durango, Colo., Feb. 27, 1940; s. Donald B. and Florence I. (Maxey) D.; m. Jo Patricia Johnson, Dec. 23, 1962; children: Wendy, Douglas. BA, Southwestern Coll., 1962; Mortuary Sci. degree, Dallas-Jones Coll Mortuary Sci, 1963. Apprentice Davis Mortuary, Pueblo, Colo., 1963-64; bus. mgr. George F. McCarty Funeral Home, Pueblo, 1964-65; owner Dolsen Mortuary, Lamar, Colo., 1965-72; pres., gen. mgr., dir. Almont, Inc., Pueblo, 1972-92; sec. Dolsen, Inc., 1967—; pres. Wilson Funeral Dirs. Inc., 1972-92, Carlson Travel Network/Let's Talk Travel, Inc., Pueblo/Denver. Bd. dirs. Afrin U., 1989—; spl. asst. to pres. Southwestern Coll., 1997; dir. adminstrv. svcs. Mt. conf. United Meth. Ch., Denver, 1995-98, mem. coun. on adminstrv. ministries Kans. West conf., 2001—. Mem Am. Soc. Travel Assn. Execs., Nat. Funeral Dirs. Assn., Nat. Selected Morticians, Cremation Assn. Am., Monument Builders N.Am., Colo. Funeral Dirs. Assn., Internat. Assn. Travel Agts., Nat. Assn. Coll. and Univ. Bus. Officers, Nat. Assn. Univ. Buyers, Assn. Higher Edn. Facilities Officers, Ctrl. Assn. Coll. and Univ. Bus. Adminstrs., Ctrl. Assn. of Coll. and Univ. Bus. Mgrs., Masons, Shriners, Elks, Rotary (bd. dirs., pres. 1965—, Paul Harris fellow), Pi Sigma Eta, Pi Kappa Delta, Pi Gamma Mu. Home: 1315 Plum St Winfield KS 67156-4619 Office: 100 College St Winfield KS 67156-2443

DOLSON, EDWARD M. lawyer; b. Kansas City, Mo., Sept. 21, 1939; s. Ralph H. and Elinor M. Dolson; m. Kay M. Clancy, Aug. 10, 1963; children: Michael, Patricia, Jennifer. BSBA, U. Kans., 1960; JD, U. Mich., 1963. Bar: N.Y. 1963, N.Y. Dist. Ct. (so. dist.) N.Y., Mo. 1966, U.S. Dist. Ct. (we. dist.) Mo., U.S. Dist. Ct. (ctrl. dist.) Wis., U.S. Ct. Claims, U.S. Ct. Appeals (7th, 8th and 10th cirs.). Assoc. Reid & Priest, N.Y.C., 1963-66; ptnr. Dietrich, Davis et al, Kansas City, Mo., 1966-90, Armstrong, Teasdale et al, Kansas City, 1990-92, Smith, Gill et al, Kansas City, 1992-95, Swanson Midgley LLC, Kansas City, 1995—. Co-author: Missouri Corporate Forms Practice, 1981; contbg. author: Missouri Bar Supplement, 1981, Speaker ABA Forum on Franchising, 1988. Chmn. Alliance for Safer Met. Kansas City, 1971-73; fin. chmn. Visitation Ch., Kansas City, 1993; mem. fin. com., bd. dirs. St. Joseph Health Ctr., Kansas City, 1989-92; tutor Laubach Lit. Soc., Kansas City, 1998. Mem. Lawyers Assn. Kansas City (pres. 1991), mem. Found. (pres. 1992), Kansas City Met. Bar Assn. (chmn. franchise law com. 1983-87), Heartland Franchise Assn. (founder, bd. dirs. 1989—), U. Mich. Club Kansas City (pres. 1974-77). Office: Swanson Midgley LLC 2420 Pershing Rd Ste 400 Kansas City MO 64108-2505

DOLTER, GERALD THOMAS, voice educator; b. Dubuque, Iowa, Apr. 18, 1955; s. Gerald Thomas Dolter, Sr. and Clara G. Dolter; m. Karen T. Crowley, Aug. 17, 1984; children: Lydia Christine, Corey Thomas. MA in Arts Adminstrn., Ind. U., 1980. Pub. rels. dir. Richmond (Va.) Symphony, 1981—82; pub. rels. mgr. Phoenix (Ariz.) Symphony Orch., 1982—85; leading baritone Theatre der Freienhansestadt Bremen, Germany, 1985—91; prof. of vocal music Southwestern U., Georgetown, Tex., 1991—95, Tex. Tech Sch. of Music, Lubbock, Tex., 1995—, dir. music theatre, 1998—. Finalist, Met. Opera, 1984. Mem.: Nat. Ass. Tchrs. Singing, Rotary Club. Avocation: travel. Office: Texas Tech University School of Music 18th and Boston Lubbock TX 79409 Fax: 806-742-2294.

DOLUISIO, JAMES THOMAS, pharmacy educator; b. Bethlehem, Pa., Sept. 28, 1935; s. Dominic and Sue (Powell) D.; m. Phyllis M. Sabolski, June 20, 1959; children— Thomas, James, Rebecca. BS in Pharmacy, Temple U., 1957, MS, 1959; PhD, Purdue U., 1962; DSc, Phila. Coll. Pharmacy and Sci., 1983; DSc (hon.), Purdue U., 1995, Wilkes U., 2000. From asst. prof. to assoc. prof. pharmacy Phila. Coll. Pharmacy and Sci., 1961-67, also assoc. dir. dept., 1965-67; prof., chmn. dept. pharmacy U. Ky., Lexington, 1967-73; prof., dean U. Tex., Austin, 1973-98. Bd. dirs. Eckerd Corp., 1986-96, COR Therapeutics, 1994-02; cons. Smith Kline & French Labs., Phila., 1962-67, McNeil Labs., Ft. Washington, Pa., 1967-72, Hoechst Labs., Somerville, N.J., 1973-93, Nat. Inst. Drug Abuse, 1976-78, HEW, U.S. Surgeon Gen., 1975-83; cons. Merck-Medco, Franklin Lakes, N.J., 2000-2001. Contbr. to profl. and sci. jours. Active Pharmacists Against Drug Abuse Found, 1984; chmn. U.S. Pharmacopeial Conv., Inc., 1990-95; v.p. Fedn. Internat. Pharmaceutique, 1994-98. NSF fellow, 1959-61; Am. Found. Pharm. Edn. fellow, 1957-59 Mem. Am. Pharm. Assn. (Remington Honor medal 1995), Am. Assn. Colls. Pharmacy, Am. Soc. Hosp. Pharmacy, Am. Assn. Pharm. Scientists, Fed. Internat. Pharmacists (Lifetime Achievement award 2000), Rho Chi. Office: U Texas College of Pharmacy Austin TX 78712 E-mail: doluisio.jt@mail.utexas.edu.

DOMAHIDY, MARY RODGERS, public policy educator; b. Ft. Eustis, Va., Sept. 14, 1945; d. James Maxey and Adelaide Louise (Cox) Rodgers; m. Steve E., July 28, 1973. BA, Vanderbilt U., 1967; MA, St. Louis U., 1978, PhD, 1990. Cert. secondary social studies tchr., Mo. Dir. spl. programs YWCA, Greenville, S.C., 1967-69, program coord., 1974-76; tchr. social studies, dept. chmn. Greenville County Schs., 1969-74; planner St. Louis County Govt., 1980-84; rsch. asst. St. Louis U., 1977-80, asst. prof. dept. pub. policy studies, 1990-98, assoc. prof., 1998—, dept. chmn., 1996—. Exec. bd. St. Louis-Jefferson Solid Waste Dist., St. Louis, 1993-2000 Contbr. articles to profl. jours. Mem. Planning Commn., Chesterfield, Mo., 1988-95, chair 1991-93; bd. dirs. Mo. Goodwill Industries, St. Louis, 1991—; bd. dirs., exec. bd. Focus - St. Louis, 1996-2002, Leadership St. Louis 2000. Recipient Gov.'s award for Excellence in Tchg., Mo. Coord. Bd. for Higher Edn., 1996, YWCA Leadership award St. Louis U., 2001. Office: Dept Pub Policy Studies 3663 Lindell Blvd Ste 180 Saint Louis MO 63108-3342 E-mail: domastm@msn.com.

DOMAN, MARGARET HORN, government policy and process consultant, civic official; b. Portland, Oreg., July 28, 1946; d. Richard Carl and Dorothy May (Teepe) Horn; m. Steve Hamilton Doman, July 12, 1969; children: Jennifer, Kristina, Kathryn. BA, Willamette U., 1968; postgrad., U. Wash., 1968-69, 72. Cert. tchr. Tchr. jr. high Bellevue (Wash.) Sch. Dist., 1969-70, subs. tchr., 1990-91; tchr. jr. high University City (Mo.) Sch. Dist., 1970-71; employment counselor Wash. State Dept. Employment Security, Seattle, 1971; planning commn. mem. City of Redmond, Wash., 1980-83, chmn., 1982-83, city coun. mem., 1983-91, pres., 1990-91; exec. dir. Eastside Human Svcs. Coun., Redmond, Wash., 1992; employment specialist Wash. State Dept. Employment Security, 1993; cons. land use planning & govt. process Redmond, 1993—. Redmond rep. Puget Sound. Coun. of Govt., Seattle, 1984-91, vice chmn., 1988, 90, chmn. transp., 1986-88, exec. bd., 1987, mem. standing com. on transp., 1986-91; bd. dirs., pres. Eastside Human Svcs. Coun., Bellevue, 1983-91, pres., 1990. Mem. state exec. com. Nat. History Day, Olympia, Wash., 1986; vol. Bellevue Sch. Dist., 1977—96; bd. dirs. Redmond YMCA, 1985—86, Youth Eastside Svcs., 1998—2001; bd. dirs. Eastside br. Camp Fire, Bellevue, 1992—94, Redmond Hist. Soc., 1999—2001. Mem. Redmond C. of C. (land use and transp. com. 1994-98), Bellevue Rotary (bd. mem. 2001—). Republican. Unitarian Universalist. Avocations: skiing, hiking, sailing, world travel. Home: 2104 180th Ct NE Redmond WA 98052-6032 E-mail: domanms@comcast.net.

DOMANSKIS, ALEXANDER RIMAS, lawyer; b. Chgo., June 3, 1952; s. Van and Alina Alexandra (Tamasauskas) Domanskis; m. Frances Laucka, May 6, 1978; children: Maria Laucka, John Joseph Laucka. AB, U. Mich, 1973; JD, U. Mich., 1977. Bar: Ill. 1977, U.S. Dist. Ct. (no. dist.) Ill. 1977, U.S. Ct. Appeals (7th cir.) 1978, U.S. Supreme Ct. 1985. Law clk. U.S. Dist. Ct. (no. dist.) Ill., Chgo., 1977—79; assoc. Ross & Hardies, Chgo., 1979—84, ptnr., 1985—87, 1993—94, of counsel, 1987—92; ptnr. Shaw, Gussis, Domanskis, Fishman & Glantz, 1994—2002, Boodell & Domanskis, LLC, 2002—. Assoc. gen. counsel and v.p. Intercounty Title Co. of Ill., 1987—91, bd. dir., 1990—91. Editor (adminstrv.): (jour.) U. Mich Jour. Law Reform, 1976—77. Pres. Lithuanian World Ctr., 1988—92, bd. dir., 1988—95, chmn. bd., 1994—95; bd. dir. Intercounty Credit Corp., Chgo., 1988—91, Lithuanian Montessori Soc., Chgo., 1987—90. Mem.: Lithuanian Roman Cath. Fedn. Am. (bd. dir. Chgo. 1980—87), Lithuanian Am. Coun. (bd. dir. Chgo. 1981—88), Chgo. Bar Assn., ABA. Home: 4236 Hampton Ave Western Springs IL 60558-1310 Office: Boodell & Domanskis LLC 205 N Michigan #4307 Chicago IL 60601 Fax: 312-540-1162.

DOMAR, ALICE DIANE, psychologist, educator; b. Balt., MD, May 1, 1958; d. Evsey David and Carola Rosenthal Domar; m. David Allen Ostrow, Aug. 26, 1990; children: Sarah Domar Ostrow, Katherine Domar Ostrow. BA, Colby Coll., Waterville, Maine, 1980; MA, Yeshiva U., N.Y., 1984, PhD, 1986. lic. psychologist, Mass. Staff psychologist Deaconess Hosp., Boston, 1988-96; sr. scientist Mind/Body Med. Inst., Boston, 1994—2002, dir. ctr. women's health, 1994—2002; dir. Mind/Body Ctr. Women's Health, Boston IVF, 2002—. Asst. prof. Harvard Med. Sch., Boston, 1994—. Author: (book) Healing Mind, Healthy Woman, 1996, Self-Nurture, 2000, Conquering Infertility, 2002; co-author: Six Steps to Increased Fertility, 2000; adv. bd.: Parent's Mag., columnist: Health Mag. Recipient Young Investigators award, Mass. Dept. Pub. Health, 1993; grant Nat. Inst. Mental Health, 1990, 94. Mem. Mental Health Profl. Group (chair), 1997-98. Avocations: travel, cooking, reading. Office: 40 Second Ave Ste 300 Waltham MA 02451 Office Fax: 781-890-9599. E-mail: alice.domar@bostonivf.com.

DOMAR, CAROLA ROSENTHAL, social worker; b. Franfurt, Fed. Republic of Germany, Dec. 17, 1919; arrived in U.S., 1940; d. Siegfried and Betty (Warschauer) Rosenthal; m. Evsey David Domar, Apr. 16, 1946; children: Erica Domar Banderob, Alice Domar. BS, Carnegie Inst. Tech., 1947; MSW, Simmons Sch. Social Work, 1968. Cert. social worker; bd. cert. diplomate; lic. social worker, Mass. Social worker Burlington (Mass.) Pub. Sch. System, 1968-73; clin. social worker, dir. retardation svc. Eliot Community Mental Health Clinic, Concord, Mass., 1974-80; pvt. practice Concord, Mass., 1980—. Cons. Acton (Mass.) Pub. Health Nursing Svc., 1981-90, 97—, Nashoba Nursing Svc., Harvard, Mass., 1990-97. Pres. bd. Coun. for Children, Acton, 1975-78; v.p. bd. Dept. Mental Health and Retardation, Concord, Mass., 1985-88; bd. dirs. Dept. Mental Health, Arlington, Mass., 1988-91, Dept. Retardation, Arlington, 1988-95; mem. Acton Family Self-Sufficiency Com., 1997—; Coun. on Aging liaison to Affordable Housing Bd., 1997—. Recipient Cert. of Recognition, Gov. M. Dukakais, Boston, 1983, Cert. of Recognition, Office for Children, Boston, 1985; Ofcl. Citation, Ho. of Reps., Boston, 1983. Mem. NASW, Mass. Assn. Gerontology, Concord Mental Health Assn. (bd. dirs. 1988-89). Home and Office: 264 Heaths Bridge Rd Concord MA 01742-4921 E-mail: carola@ourconcord.net.

DOMBALIS, CONSTANTINE NICHOLAS, minister, writer; b. Norfolk, Va., July 29, 1925; s. Nicholas John and Helen Constantine (Matinos) D.; m. Mary Christine Fourgis, June 6, 1954; children: Nicholas, Christopher. BTh, Hellenic Coll., 1947; BD, Holy Cross Sem., 1949; STB, Gen. Theol. Sch., 1951; DD (hon.), U. Richmond, 1988; DHL (hon.), Randolph Macon Coll., 1996. Ordained to ministry Greek Orthodox Ch., 1954. Pastor Greek Orthodox Ch., Richmond, Va., 1954—71; dean Greek Orthodox Cathedral, Richmond, 1971—96, dean emeritus, 1996—; vicar Archdiocese of Va., Richmond, 1976—96. Exec. com. Va. Coun. Chs., Richmond, 1978—96; mem. U.S. Holocaust Meml. Coun., 1980—86; U.S. amb. to UN 38th Gen. Assembly, 1983; mem. coun. religious leaders U.S. Holocaust Meml., Washington, 1989—94; exec. bd. dirs. Sts. Cosma and Damianos Sr. Residence, Richmond, 1988—; established Richmond Internat. Airport Interfaith Chapel, 1996. Contbr. articles to profl. jours. Chmn. Va. Dept. of Rehab., 1979-83; mem. First Union Bank Bd., 1988-94; chmn. religious com. Va. Statute for Religious Freedom, 1989-; mem. bd. visitors Va. Commonwealth U., 1991-96; founder Richmond Internat. Airport Interfaith Chapel, 1996; mem. Ctr. for Study of Religious Freedom, Va. Weslyan Coll., 1995. Recipient DAR award, 1968, NCCJ award 1974, B'nai Brith Torch of Liberty award 1976, 2000 1st Freedom award Coun. for Am.'s 1st Freedom, Faith award Va. Coun. of Chs., 2002; named one of 100 Most Influential Richmonders 1986, one of 100 Power Players of Richmond, 1998. Mem. UNESCO (bd. dirs. 1980-82), Holy Cross Theol. Sch. Alumni Assn. (pres. 1978-82). Home: 304 Sandalwood Dr Richmond VA 23229-7637 E-mail: cdomba1821@msn.com.

DOMBECK, HAROLD ARTHUR, insurance company executive; b. Bronx, N.Y., Mar. 23, 1941; s. Max J. and Rose R. (Schefren) D.; m. Cynthia E. Kofoed, May 14, 1983; children: Mark J., Glenn D., David S. B of Civil Engring., NYU, 1962, M of Civil Engring., 1963. Profl. engr., N.Y., N.J., Conn., Ga. Instr. San Antonio Coll., San Antonio, Tex., 1964-65, SUNY, Farmingdale, 1965-68; project mgr. H2M Group, Melville, N.Y., 1965-74, dir. environ. engring., 1971-81, dir. mktg., 1982-85, exec. v.p., 1986-88, pres., 1989-91, pres., chief exec. officer, chmn., 1991-94; CEO Dombeck Assocs. Inc., Duluth, Ga., 1995—. Chmn., CEO Archs. and Engrs. Ins. Co., Hockessin, Del., 1987—; v.p., CFO, Dod/Pritchard Comms. Inc., Norcross, Ga., 1998-2001; dir., Perceptive Solutions, Inc., Norcross, 2001-03; chmn. bd. dirs. Am. Cons. Engrs. Pension Trust, St. Louis, 1991-94; chmn. ACEC Bus. Inst. Trust, St. Louis, 1994-96. Pres. High Woods Civic Assn., St. James, N.Y., 1971-73, River Plantation Homeowners Assn., 1999-2001. 1st lt. USAF, 1963-65. Fellow ASCE, Am. Cons. Engrs. Coun. (pres. L.I. 1982-84); mem. Am. Acad. Environ. Engrs. (diplomate), NSPE (dir. 1982-85), N.Y. State Water Pollution Control Assn. (dir. 1980-83), N.Y. State Soc. Profl. Engrs. (pres. 1983-84, pres. Suff County chpt. 1978-80, Engr. of Yr. 1989, 90, Outstanding Svc. awards 1988, 89). Avocations: reading, golf, history. Office: AEIC 720 Yorklyn Rd Ste 40 Hockessin DE 19707 E-mail: had@dombeck.net.

DOMBROW, ANTHONY ERIC, lawyer; b. N.Y.C., Apr. 6, 1945; s. Oscar and Nettie (Maslow) D.; m. Penny McClurg, July 21, 1978; children: Joshua Alan, Ashley Smith. B.A., U. Wis., 1966, J.D., 1969. Bar: Wis. 1969, Ill. 1973, U.S. Ct. Apls. (8th cir.) 1974, U.S. Ct. Apls. (7th cir.) 1975, U.S. Sup. Ct. 1976, U.S. Ct. Appeals (9th cir.) 1987. Atty., Nat. Labor Relations Bd., Chgo., 1969-72; ptnr. Laner, Muchin, Dombrow & Becker Ltd., Chgo., 1972— . Office: Laner Muchin Dombrow & Becker Ltd 350 S Clark St Chicago IL 60604-3504

DOMBROWSKI, ANNE WESSELING, retired microbiologist, researcher; b. Cin., Jan. 26, 1948; m. Allan Wayne Dombrowski, Apr. 17, 1982; children: Amy, Alicia. BA summa cum laude, Xavier U., 1970; MS, U. Cin., 1972, PhD, 1974. Fellow Scripps Clinic & Rsch. Found., La Jolla, Calif., 1974-76; sr. rsch. microbiologist Merck & Co., Inc., Rahway, N.J., 1976-87, rsch. fellow, 1987-96, sr. rsch. fellow, 1996—2003, ret., 2003. Contbr. articles to profl. jours. Mem.: AAAS, Mycol. Soc., Am. Soc. Microbiology, Soc. Indsl. Microbiology (sec. 1982—85, dir. 1998—2001). Achievements include patents in field. Avocations: reading, gardening. Home: 51 Landsdowne Rd East Brunswick NJ 08816-4156 E-mail: annewd@aol.com.

DOMBROWSKI, BOB, artist, publisher; b. Buffalo, Feb. 16, 1944; s. Edward A. and Mary Ann Dombrowski. BS, SUNY, Buffalo, 1965; postgrad., Cornish Inst., Seattle, 1975-76. Artist, N.Y.C., 1976—; owner, mgr. GB Art Co., N.Y.C., 1994—. Cons. Cementex Corp., N.Y.C., 1989—. Creator, prodr. Ode to Birth of Shiva, 1987, Elegy for the Republic, 1991, Hwy. 17, 1993, On Thinking Thoughts, 1997; author: Theme Show, 2002, A Delicate Membrane, 2002; contbr. to poetry anthology Emerson of Harvard: Anthology, 2003; exhibited in group shows at Albright-Knox Art Mus., Buffalo, 1980, Ashford Hollow (N.Y.) Found., 1980, Storefront for Art and Architecture, N.Y.C., 1985, Franklin Furnace, N.Y.C., 1986, Nelson-Atkins Mus., Kansas City, 1989, Shedhalle (Rote Fabrik), Zurich, 1989, Barking Legs Dance Theater, Chattanooga, 1995 (Daimler-Chrysler Spirit of the Word award 1999), Mus. of New Art in Detroit; represented in permanent collections including N.Y.C. Cmty. Bd. #3, Nico Smith Gallery, N.Y.C., Mus. Modern Art Libr., N.Y.C., Bettina Riedel Ltd., Phila., Pernod Corp., N.Y.C., La Perla Garden, N.Y.C., Francis Pratt Usui, Nicholson, Pa., Dorah Rosen Birmingham, Ala., Cleve. Art Inst.; contbr. publ. Help Yourself. Bd. dirs. La Perla Cmty. Garden, N.Y.C. Mem. Internat. Sculpture Ctr., N.Y. Artists Equity (bd. dirs. 1989-90), The Unbearables Poet Group. Avocations: photography, walking. Home and Office: 805 6th Ave New York NY 10001-6301 E-mail: d.p.productions@earthlink.net., dombrowski@webbittown.net.

DOMBROWSKI, FRANK PAUL, JR., pharmacist; b. Nashua, N.H., May 10, 1943; s. Frank Paul and Yvonne Joan (Paris) D.; m. Eleanor Cassady, June 15, 1968; children: Michael, Peter, Laura, Cheryl, Douglas. BS, Mass. Coll. Pharmacy, 1965, MS, 1967; MBA, U. Phoenix, 2002. Pharmacist Androscoggin Valley Hosp., Berlin, N.H., 1974-75, Eastern Maine Med. Ctr., 1975-77; dir. pharm. svcs. and ctrl. supply Concord Hosp., N.H., 1977-82; founder, pres. Hosp. Home Health Care of N.H., 1982-92, Hosp. Home Health Care of Maine, 1986-92, Weare Family Pharmacy, 1992-96; asst. pharmacy mgr. Del Sol Med. Ctr., El Paso, Tex., 1998—2001; dir. pharm. svcs. Southwestern Gen. Hosp., El Paso, Tex., 2001—. Commr. N.H. Bd. Registration of Pharmacy; cons. nurse anesthetist sch. Concord Hosp. Served with U.S. Army, 1968-74. Decorated Combat Inf. badge, Bronze Star medal, Army Commendation medal. Fellow Am. Acad. Med. Adminstrs., Am. Coll. Apothecaries; mem. Am. Pharm. Assn., Am. Soc. Hosp. Pharmacists, Tex. Soc. Hosp. Pharmacists, El Paso Soc. Hosp. Pharmacists, Lions (chpt. pres). Home: 1212 Wind Ridge Dr El Paso TX 79912-7348 E-mail: frankd@schwendt.com.

DOMBROWSKI, MITCHELL PAUL, physician, inventor, researcher; b. Detroit, Apr. 24, 1953; s. Mitchell Stanley and Dorothy Julia (Silarski) D.; m. Jocelyn McKinley, Mar. 7, 1981; children: Michael, Jacqueline, David, Elizabeth. BS, U. Mich., 1975; MD, Wayne State U., 1979. Diplomate Am. Bd. OB-Gyn, Am. Bd. Perinatology. Resident in obstetrics and gynecology, Detroit, 1979-84; fellow in perinatology, 1984-86; from asst. to assoc. prof. Wayne State U. Sch. Medicine, Detroit, 1986-98, prof., 1998, chmn., chief, 1996-98; chief St. John Hosp., 2002. Prin. investigator maternal fetal medicine network units Nat. Inst. Child Health and Human Devel., 1996. Contbr. articles to med. publs.; patentee fetal blood sampling device, reagent test strip, digital medication device, self-capping needle assemblies, amnicentesis needle. Recipient Research award Nat Insts Hlth. Recipient Nat. Inst. Alcohol Abuse and Alcoholism award, AMA; grantee Nat. Heart, Lung and Blood Inst./NICHD, 1994; fellow Am. Coll. Obstetrics and Gynecologists, Soc. Perinatal Obstetricians; Diabetes Rsch. Office: St John Hosp & Med Ctr 22151 Moross Rd Detroit MI 48236-2114

DOMBROWSKI, ROBERT THEODORE, materials scientist and information architect; b. New Brunswick, N.J., Jan. 8, 1956; s. Theodore Frank and Grace (Keri) D.; m. Karen Marie Thornton. BS in Biol. Scis., Rutgers U., 1979, MS in Materials Sci., 1988. Jr. rsch. scientist Carter Wallace, Cranbury, N.J., 1979-84; scientist, rsch. scientist Colgate Palmolive, Piscataway, N.J., 1984-91; rsch. assoc., microscopy lab. mgr. Novon Products divsn. Warner Lambert, Morris Plains, N.J., 1991-93; pres., prin. scientist Microview Consultancy, Inc., Mendham, N.J., 1993—; adminstr. Rutgers Internet Inst., Piscataway, NJ, 1999; dir. ops. N.J. Ctr. for Biomaterials, Piscataway, 2000; chief web officer The Pharma Network, Woodcliff Lake, NJ, 2001. Mem. characterization sub-team Biodegradable Packaging and Materials Consortium, Natick, Mass., 1991-93; instr., creator tng. course Microscopy for the New Millennium, 1999. Pub., webmaster Bobby D's Mysterious Sci., 1998. Recipient Colgate Palmolive Chmns. You Can Make a Difference award, Baxter Edu Net & Critical Mass award, 1999, Wisdom award, The Blue Ribbon award, Golden Web Awards, 2000-01; nominee Pirelli INTERNETional award 2001. Mem. Microscopy Soc. Am., Am. Chem. Soc., N.Y. Microscopical Soc., Biogradable Polymer Soc., HTML Writers Guild, Internat. Assn. Web Masters and Designers. Achievements include development of state-of-the-art materials characterization methods using optical analytical microscopy, chemical microscopy, video microscopy, image analysis, SEM, TEM, AFM, EDS and CLSM to determine the microstructure of starch based biodegradable polymers; first to use automated image analysis to determine the degree of starch destructurization in biodegradable materials; development of unique iodine based staining method to observe the ultrastructural elements of destructured starch used in combination with TEM; determination of the precise phase morphology of starch/synthetic biodegradable polymer blends using micro-milling, epi-DIC and FESEM. Office: Microview Consultancy Inc PO Box 148 Mendham NJ 07945-0148 Personal E-mail: gammux@yahoo.com. Business E-Mail: principal@microviewconsult.com.

DOMEN, RONALD EUGENE, physician; b. Dennison, Ohio, Apr. 22, 1950; s. George and F. Jean (Berkshire) D.; m. Kathryn Heske, Aug. 30, 1991; children: Michael E., Erika M., Laura K. AB, Youngstown (Ohio) State U., 1972; MD, U. Autonoma de Guadalajara, Guadalajara, Mex., 1975. Bd. cert. internal medicine, clin. pathology, blood banking, transfusion medicine. Intern, resident internal medicine St. Luke's Hosp., Cleve., 1976-79; fellow in hematology-med. oncology Ohio State U., Columbus, 1979-80, resident clin. pathology, 1980-82, asst. prof. pathology, 1982-84, assoc. prof. pathology, 1995-99; asst. prof. pathology U. South Fla., Tampa, 1984-88; med. dir. Miller Meml. Blood Ctr., Bethlehem, Pa., 1988-93; staff physician Cleve. Clinic, 1993-99; assoc. prof. pathology Ohio State U., 1995-99; med. dir. transfusion medicine, assoc. prof. pathology Milton S. Hershey Med. Ctr. Pa. State U. Coll. Medicine, 1999—2002, prof. pathology, medicine, humanities, 2002—. Contbr. articles to profl. jours. Bd. dirs. Pa. Assn. Blood Banks, 1990-93, Ohio Assn. Blood Banks, 1995-97. Fellow Coll. Am. Pathologists; mem. Am. Soc. Hematology, Am. Assn. Blood Banks, Internat. Soc. Blood Transfusion. Office: Pa State Milton S Hershey Med Ctr HG160 PO Box 850 500 University Dr Hershey PA 17033 E-mail: rdomen@psu.edu.

DOMENICI, PETE V. (VICHI DOMENICI), senator; b. Albuquerque, May 7, 1932; s. Cherubino and Alda (Vichi) D.; m. Nancy Burk, Jan. 15, 1958; children: Lisa, Peter, Nella, Clare, David, Nanette, Helen, Paula. Student, U. Albuquerque, 1950-52; BS, U. N.Mex., 1954, LLD (hon.); LLB, Denver U., 1958; LLD (hon.), Georgetown U. Sch. Medicine; HHD (hon.), N.Mex. State U. Bar: N.Mex. 1958. Tchr. math. pub. schs., Albuquerque, 1954-55; ptnr. firm Domenici & Bonham, Albuquerque, 1958-72; chmn., ex-officio mayor Albuquerque, 1967; city commr., 1966-68; U.S. senator from N.Mex., 1972—. Mem. appropriations com., energy and natural resources com., chmn. subcom. on energy rsch. and devel.; mem. com. on environ. and pub. works, mem. govtl. affairs com.; chmn. budget com., com. on Indian affairs; mem. Presl. Adv. Com. on Federalism; senate Rep. policy com. Mem. Gov.'s Policy Bd. for Law Enforcement, 1967-68; chmn. Model Cities Joint Adv. Com., 1967-68. Recipient Nat. League of Cities award Outstanding Performance in Congress; Disting. Svc. award Tax Found., 1986, Legislator of Yr. award Nat. Mental Health Assn., 1987, public sector leadership award, 1996. Mem. Nat. League Cities, Middle Rio Grande Council Govts. Republican. Office: US Senate 328 Hart Senate Office Bldg Washington DC 20510-0001*

DOMENICO, ANTHONY WAYNE, music educator; b. Martinsburg, W.Va., June 26, 1971; s. Anthony Wayne Domenico, Sr. and Diane Marie Domenico. BA in Music Edn., Shepherd Coll., 1994; MusM Edn., Shenendoah U., 2003. Cert. Tchg. Md., 1994. Band dir. South Hagerstown H.S., Hagerstown, Md., 1996—. Musician: (freelance trumpet) Big Band and classical work. Mem.: Md. Band Dir. Assn. (western md. regional rep. 2001—02), Internat. Trumpet Guild, Phi Mu Alpha (pres., v.p. 1993—94, Outstanding Brother 1993). Office: South Hagerstown High School 1101 S Potomac St Hagerstown MD 21740 E-mail: domenton@wcboe.k12.md.us.

DOMENICO, ROY PALMER, history educator; b. New Orleans, Feb. 9, 1954; s. Palmer Roy and Barbara Ann Domenico; m. Robin Domenico, May 28, 1988; children: Catherine, John, Matthew, Clare. BA in Internat. Rels., U. Wis., Milw., 1977; MA in History, U. Conn., 1979; PhD in History, Rutgers U., 1987. Asst. prof. Upsala Coll., East Orange, NJ, 1987—92, Truman State U., Kirksville, Mo., 1992—97; assoc. prof. U. Scranton, Pa., 1997—. Author: (book) Italian Fascists on Trial, 1991 (Howard and Helen Marraro prize, 1992), The Regions of Italy, 2002, Remaking Italy in the Twentieth Century, 2002. Mem.: Am. Cath. Hist. Assn., Soc. Italian Hist. Studies. Office: U Scranton History Dept Scranton PA 18510 Office Fax: 570-941-5843. E-mail: domenicor2@scranton.edu.

DOMENICONI, RETO, business executive; b. Zurich, Switzerland, Oct. 7, 1936; diploma in mech. engring., Doctorate in Tech. Scis., Fed. Inst. Tech., Zurich. With Arthur D. Little, Inc., 1964-68, Heberlein Group, Wattwil, Switzerland, 1968-75, Züllig Group, Rapperswil, Switzerland, 1976-82; with fin., control and administrn. Nestlé, S.A., Vevey, Switzerland, 1983—, exec. v.p.; pres. adminstrv. bd. Coutts & Co., Zürich, 1991—. Bd. dirs. Nestlé, S.A., Switzerland, Sulzer Medica, Bobst Group; supervisory bd. mem. Suez Lyonnaise. Office: BOBST SA Route des Flumeaux 50 1008 Prilly Switzerland

DOMERACKI, FRANK ROBERT, physician; b. Chester County, Pa., June 28, 1960; s. Frank James and Frances Mary (Parr) D. BA in Psychology, Temple U., 1983, MD, 1987. Physician Abington (Pa.) Meml. Hosp., Temple U. Hosp., Phila., 1990—. Mem. ACP, AMA, Pa. Med. Assn., Am. Coll. Radiology, Alpha Omega Alpha.

DOMESHEK, SOL, aeronautical engineer; b. N.Y.C., 1920; m. Florence Schnepf, 1942; 2 children. BS, CCNY, 1940; B in Mech. Engring., NYU, 1956. Lic. profl. engr. N.Y., N.J. Photo-mapper U.S. Geol. Survey, Washington, 1942-44; various engring. mgmt. assignments U.S. Naval Tng. Device Ctr., Port Washington, N.Y., 1946-66; dir. display and navigation devel. divsn. U.S. Army Avionics Lab., Fort Monmouth, N.J., 1966-86; pvt. practice Scotch Plains, N.J., 1986—. Mem. U.S. Civil Svc. Bd. Engring. Examiners, N.Y., 1956-64; chmn. symposium on cockpit environment NATO, 1968; co-sponsor Internat. Symposium on Geographic Orientation in Flight, 1969; presenter sch. workshops engring. in cmty. life, 1990—. Lt. (j.g.) USN, PTO, 1944-46; with U.S. Navy Rsch. Reserve, 1946-52. Mem. NSPE, Am. Soc. Photogrammetry, Optical Soc. Am., Army Aviation Assn. Am. Achievements include 17 patents in areas of photo-mapping, projection systems for training, terrain modeling, day/night map displays for drivers and pilots. Office: 2320 Edgewood Ter Scotch Plains NJ 07076-2107

DOMINA, DAVID ALAN, lawyer; b. Laurel, Nebr., Nov. 27, 1950; s. Marvin Everett and Jacqueline Mae (Hansen) D.; children from previous marriage: Thurston A., Salesia. J.D. with distinction, U. Nebr., 1972. Bar: Nebr. 1973, Mo. 1973, U.S. Tax Ct. 1973, U.S. Ct. Appeals (8th cir.) 1973. Assoc., Shook, Hardy & Bacon, Kansas City, Mo., 1973-74; ptnr. Jewell, Gatz & Domina, Norfolk, Nebr., 1974-82, Domina & Gerrard, P.C., Norfolk, 1982— ; gen. counsel Affiliated Foods Coop., Norfolk, 1982— ; dir. Farmers State Bank, Carroll, Nebr. Mem. state central com. Nebr. Democratic party, 1976-78; commr. Nebr. Econ. Devel. Commn., 1986— ; trustee Nebr. Bd. Edn. Lands and Funds, Lincoln, 1983— ; spl. atty. gen. Nebr. Dept. Justice, Lincoln, 1983-84; counsel Nebr. Dept. Banking, Lincoln, 1983-84. Mem. ABA, Mo. Bar Assn., Nebr. Bar Assn. (vice chmn. young lawyers sect. 1982, chmn. corrections com. 1983), Assn. Trial Lawyers Am., U. Nebr. Coll. Law Alumni Assn. (bd. dirs.), Norfolk C. of C., Order of Coif, Order of Barristers. Lutheran. Office: Domina & Gerrard PC 2425 Taylor Ave Norfolk NE 68701-4511

DOMINGO, ESTHER, music educator; b. Havana, Cuba, July 13, 1954; d. Silverio and Esther (Benitez) D. MusB in Music Edn., MusB in Piano Performance, Mercer U., Atlanta, 1978; MusM in Piano Pedagogy, Ga. State U., 1985. Cert. Yamaha music edn. sys.; cert. Music in Edn. Nat. Tchr. Inst.; cert. ESOL; cert. tchr. grades K-12, Ga. Sec., Spanish/ESOL tchrs. asst. Atlanta Pub. Schs., 1978-81; pvt. piano and Yamah music edn. tchr. Atlanta Music Ctr., 1983-89; piano and music theory tchr. Mercer U., Atlanta, 1980-91; piano and group music classes tchr. The Children's Sch., Atlanta, 1989-92; ESL tchr. Internat. Edn. Ctr., Atlanta, 1991-92; piano, theory and group classes tchr. pvt. home music studio, Atlanta, 1976—; pvt. piano and music theory tchr. Ga. Acad. Music, Atlanta, 1992—; gen. music, choral tchr. Atlanta Pub. Schs., 1992—. Pianist Spanish Mission, Second-Ponce de Leon Bapt. Ch., Atlanta, 1970—; panelist Fulton County Art Coun., 1999; adjudicator for various music festivals in the state. Neighborhood rep. Hispanic cmty. Ga. Power Co., Atlanta, 1978-79; young artist performer DeKalb Coun. for the Arts; panelist Fulton County Arts Coun., 1999; pianist, handbell soloist; mem. handbell choir Second Ponce deLeon Bapt. Ch., 1985—. Recipient Excellence in Edn. award, BellSouth/Braves, 2002; Fine Arts grantee, Atlanta Pub. Schs., 1998. Mem. Music Tchrs. Nat. Assn. (cert.), Atlanta Music Tchrs. Assn. (cert., program chmn. 1990-91, membership chmn. 1991-92, v.p. 1992-93, pres. 1993-94), Ga. Music Tchrs. Assn. (cert.). Baptist. Avocations: handbell performer/choir, swimming, travel. Office: Morningside Elem Sch 1053 E Rock Springs Rd NE Atlanta GA 30306-3099 E-mail: estherdomingo@hotmail.com.

DOMINGO, ORVILLE HAROLD, surgeon; b. Mangalore, India, Feb. 13, 1947; came to U.S., 1972; MD, Bangalore U., 1971. Diplomate Am. Bd. Surgery. Intern Tata Main Hosp., 1971-72; resident in surgery Mercy Cath. Med. Ctr., Darby, Pa., 1973-77; fellow in surgery Mt. Sinai Hosp., Hartford, Conn., 1977-78; mem. staff Mercy Cath. Med. Ctr., Darby, Pa., 1978—, Del. County Meml. Hosp., Drexel Hill, Pa., 1979—; pvt. practice. Fellow ACS; mem. Delaware County Med. Soc., Metro. Chpt. Am. Coll. Surgeons, Pa. Med. Soc. Office: Lansdowne Towers Bldg B 772 E Providence Rd Clifton Heights PA 19018-4321

DOMINGO, PLACIDO, tenor; b. Madrid, Jan. 21, 1941; s. Placido and Pepita (Embil) Domingo; m. Marta Ornelas; children: Jose, Placido, Alvaro Maurizio. Student, Conservatory in Mexico City; hon. degree, Royal Coll. Music, 1982, Complutense de Madrid, 1989. Artistic dir. Washington Opera, 1994—, L.A. Opera, 2000—. Singer: (Operas) made operatic debut in La Traviata, 1961, debut Met. Opera, 1968, (star tenor with opera cos. including) La Scala, Covent Garden, Hamburg State Opera, Vienna State Opera, N.Y.C. Opera, San Francisco Opera, Nat. Hebrew Opera in Tel-Aviv, (leading roles 116 opera including) Don Rodrigo, Ofello, Walkure, Tosca, Andrea Chenier, Don Carlo, Carmen, La Boheme, Errani, Parsifal, Idomeneo, (films) Traviata, 1983, Carmen, 1984, Otello, 1986, (made more than 100 recs. including 93 full-length opera) BMG (formerly RCA), DGG, Sony, Decca/London, Philips, Time Warner, EMI (Angel), made more than 50 videos, (performed in concert) PBS TV spl. (with José Carreras & Luciano Pavorotti) The Three Tenors, 1994; condr. numerous performances at major opera houses including: Met. Opera, London's Covent Garden, Vienna State Opera, music dir.: Seville World's Fair, active: Operalia internat. vocal competition. Performed concerts to benefit victims of 1985 Mexican earthquake. Named Kennedy Ctr. honoree, 2000; recipient 9 Grammy awards, 2 Latin Grammy awards, Legion of Honor, France, 2002, Medal of Freedom, U.S., 2002, Gran Cruz de la Orden del Merito Civil, 2002, Knight Comdr. of the Brit. Empire, 2002. Address: care Vincent & Farrell Assocs 481 8th Ave Ste 740 New York NY 10001 Mailing: The Washington Opera 2600 Virginia Ave NW Ste 104 Washington DC 20037 : Los Angeles Opera 135 North Grand Ave Los Angeles CA 90012

DOMINGUE, EMERY, consulting engineering company executive, retired; b. Scott, La., Jan. 9, 1926; s. Lucien and Mathilde (Hebert) D.; m. Beatrice Broussard, Dec. 30, 1950; children: Dave, Cal James, Kevin Drew. BS, U. Southwestern La., 1949; MS, U. Ill., 1955. Engr. La. Dept. Hwys., 1949-50, East Tex. Constrn. Co., 1950-51; tchr. civil engring. U. Southwestern La., 1951-61; prin. Domingue, Szabo & Assocs., Inc., Lafayette, La., 1957-96, ret., 1996. Mem. Lafayette Parish Planning Commn.; pres. La. Intracoastal Seaway Assn. With U.S. Army, 1944-46, ETO. Fellow ASCE (pres., cert. of appreciation Baton Rouge br.), Am. Cons. Engrs. Coun.; mem. Am. Soc. Profl. Engrs., Profl. Engrs. Pvt. Practice, Am. Concrete Inst., Am. Congress Surveying and Mapping, Am. Pub. Works Assn., Am. Ry. Engring. Assn., Cons. Engrs. Coun. La. (A.E. Wilder award), C. of C. (exec. com., dir.), Kiwanis (Lafayette) (pres.), Ragin Cajun Club. Republican. Roman Catholic. Home: 203 Beverly Dr Lafayette LA 70503-3107 Office: 400 E Kaliste Saloom Rd Lafayette LA 70508-8508

DOMINGUE, GERALD JAMES, medical scientist, microbiology, immunology and urology educator, researcher, clinical bacteriologist; b. Lafayette, La., Mar. 2, 1937; s. Edgar Paul and Sarah Ann (Prejean) D.; m. Marie H. Dugas, Aug. 30, 1958 (div. 1980); children: Andrea, Yvonne, Michelle, Gerald Jr., Marcel; m. Kathryn H. Colbert, June 20, 1981 (div. 1985). BS in Bacteriology, U. La., Lafayette, 1959; PhD in Med. Microbiol. and Immunology, Tulane U., 1964. Post-doctoral research fellow Children's Hosp., asst. research instr. pediatrics SUNY, Buffalo, 1965-66; dir. microbiol. Snodgras Lab. of Pathology and Bacteriology, St. Louis, 1966-67; instr. microbiology St. Louis U., 1966-67; asst. prof. microbiology, immunology and urology Tulane U., New Orleans, 1967-70, assoc. prof. microbiology, immunology and urology, 1970-74, prof. microbiology, immunology and urology, 1974-97, prof. emeritus, 1997—. Lectr. microbiology sch. dentistry Washington U., St. Louis, 1966-67; vis. prof., lectr. Peruvian Urol. Assn., Lima, 1973, First Internat. Congress Bacteriology, Jerusalem, 1973, Internat. Convocation Immunology, Buffalo, 1974, World Health Orgn. Conf. on Sperm Immunology, Aarhus, Denmark, 1974, European Soc. Exptl. Urol. Research, Wurzburg, Fed. Republic Germany, 1976, Internat. Seminar L-Forms, Montpellier, France, 1976, U. Melbourne, Royal Melbourne Hosp., Australia, 1978, XII Internat. Congress Microbiology, Munich, 1978, Internat. Symposium Vaccines and Vaccinations, Institut Pasteur, Paris, 1985; speaker U. Montpellier Sch. Medicine, 1985, 4th Internat. Congress on Pyelonephritis, Goteborg, Sweden, 1986, Orion Diagnostica, Helsinki, Finland, 1986, Nat. Inst. Hygiene, Warsaw, Poland, 1986, Symposium on Molecular Biology and Infectious Diseases, Institut Pasteur, 1987; mem. com. for infection control So. Bapt. Hosp., 1971-75, Charity Hosp. La., 1977—, Tulane U. Hosp., 1977—; mem. infectious disease com. St. Louis City Hosp., 1966-67; mem., reviewer, visitor project sites NIH Grant Review Study Sects., 1967-97, NSF, Kaiser Rsch. Found., Kidney Found. of Can.; cons. bacteriology So. Bapt. Hosp., New Orleans, 1968-84, Tulane U. Hosp., 1978-83, Med. Tech. Corp., Somerset, N.J., 1983—; research cons. VA Hosp., New Orleans, 1970-78; cons., mem. tech. adv. bd. Analytab Products, Inc., N.Y.C., 1972-77; expert witness to subcom. on dept. investigation oversight and research for Animal Cancer Research Act, U.S. Ho. of Reps., 1980. Author, editor: Cell Wall-Deficient Bacteria, 1962; editorial bd. cons. numerous jours.; contbr. over 160 articles to profl. jours. and chpts. to books. Pres. France-Louisiane de la Nouvelle Orleans, 1985—, pres. fondateur, 1988; apptd. mem. Gov.'s Council for Devel. of French Lang. in La., 1985, 88; mem. Met. Area Com., New Orleans, 1987, Bur. Govtl. Research, New Orleans, 1987; mem. Mayor's Com. New Orleans-Paris Cultural Exchange, 1988; chmn. scholar's com. La. Com. on French Revolution, 1988; mem. Alliance for Good Govt., 1980-84; mem. Greater New Orleans French Bd., 1987—; rep. Coun. for Devel. French and France Louisiane for celebration of French Bicentennial, 1989. Served with La. N.G., USAR, 1955-63. Guaranty scholar U. Southwestern La., 1958; grantee NIH, 1970-97, Schlieder Found., Armour Pharm. House, VA, Cadwallader Family Found., Med. Tech. Corp., Orion Diagnostica; decorated chevalier Order of Palmes Academiques (France); recipient French Medal, 1996. Fellow Am. Acad. Microbiology, Infectious Disease Soc. Am.; mem. Am. Soc. Microbiology (divisional lectr. 1978, found. lectr. 1979-80, symposium lectr. 1994), Soc. Basic Urologic Rsch. (state of art lectr. 1994), Soc. for Exptl. Biology and Medicine, AAAS, Am. Assn. Univ. Profs., Fedn. Am. Scientists, Southwestern Assn. Clin. Microbiology (editor newsletter 1983-85, pres. 1985-86), N.Y. Acad. Scis., Am. Assn. Lab. Animal Sci., Soc. Basic Urological Research (nominating com. 1988), Am. Urological Assn. (affiliate mem.), French-Am. Bus. Assn., 1988, Sigma Xi. Republican. Roman Catholic. Avocations: painting, writing. Home: PO Box 51999 New Orleans LA 70151-1999 Office: Tulane U Sch Medicine 1430 Tulane Ave New Orleans LA 70112-2699

DOMINGUE, MICHAEL W. community developer; b. New Orleans, Nov. 26, 1955; s. Darden Daniel Domingue and Jacquie Massicot Moscona; m. Mary Carr Domingue, Jan. 4, 1980; children: Aimee Lee, Patrick Darden, James Michael, Katie Noel. BA in Polit. Sci., U. New Orleans, 1979. Apptd. mem. La. Housing Fin. Agy., Baton Rouge, 1996; elected mem. St. Mary Parish Coun., Franklin, La., 1999. Democrat. Home: 619 Second St Franklin LA 70538 Office: City of Franklin 300 Iberia St Franklin LA 70538

DOMINGUEZ, DANIEL R. judge; b. 1945; BA, Boston U., 1967; LLB cum laude, U. P.R., 1970. Bar: P.R. Atty. Hector M. Laffitte Law Offices, 1970—72; ptnr. Laffitte, Dominguez & Totti, 1973—84, Dominguez & Totti, 1983—94; judge U.S. Dist. Ct. P.R., San Juan, 1994—. Gov. Adv. Com. on Labor Policy, 1984; mem. bd. fed. Bar Examiners U.S. Dist. Ct. P.R., 1989—94; mem. Civil Justice Reform Act Adv. Group, 1991—94; mem. merit selection com. Appointment of U.S. Magistrate Judge, 1993; mem. com. for jud. reform Gov. P.R., 1993—94. Mem.: Hyatt Dorado Beach Country Club, Berwind Country Club. Office: US Dist Ct PR US Courthouse CH-129 150 Ave Carlos Chardon San Juan PR 00918-1703

DOMINGUEZ, EDDIE, artist; b. Tucumcari, N.Mex., Oct. 17, 1957; BFA, Cleve. Inst. Art, 1981; MFA, Alfred U., 1983. Grad. asst., ceramics and visual design courses Alfred (N.Y.) U., 1981-83; artist-in-residence, lectr. Ohio State U., Columbus, 1984; artist-in-edn. N.Mex. Arts Divsn., Santa Fe, 1985-86; artist-in-residence Cleve. Inst. Art, 1986; artist-in-residence, lectr. U. Mont., Missoula, 1988; asst. prof. art U. Nebr., Lincoln, 1998—. Lectr., presenter workshops, mem. panels Ill. Arts Coun., Chgo., 1994, NEA, Washington, 1994, Ariz. Commn. on the Arts, 1994, Concordia U., Montreal, Que., Can., 1994, Mass. Coll. Art, Boston, 1994, Bennington (Vt.) Coll., 1994, 95, 96, Peters Valley, Layton, N.J., 1994, Firehouse Art Ctr., Norman, Okla., 1994, Haystack Mountain Sch. Arts & Crafts, Deer Isle, Maine, 1994, Ghost Ranch, Abiquiu, N.Mex., 1995, We. States Arts Fedn., Santa Fe, 1995, Colo. Coun. on the Arts, Boulder, 1995, Durango (Colo.) Art Ctr., 1995, Tamarind Inst., Albuquerque, 1995, 96, Kansas City (Mo.) Ar Inst., 1995, Hallmark Cards, Kansas City, 1996, Wichita (Kans.) Ctr. Arts, 1996, La. State U., Baton Rouge, 1996, Idaho State Arts Coun. Grants, Boise, 1996, Mattie Rhodes Counseling and Art Ctr., Kansas City, 1996, Southwest Ctr. Crafts, San Antonio, 1997, Very Spl. Arts, Albuquerque, 197, Topeka (Kans.) and Shawnee County Pub. Libr., 1997, U. Alaska, Anchorage, 2000, Craft Guild of Tex., Dallas, RISD, 2001, S.W. Ctr. for Crafts, San Antonio, 2002, numerous others; mem. fellowship panelist Colo. Coun. on the Arts, Denver, Penland Sch. of Crafts, N.C., 2001. Solo exhbns. include Pro Art Gallery, St. Louis, 1990, Mobilia Gallery, Cambridge, Mass., 1990, Munson Gallery, Santa Fe, 1990, 92, 94, 95, 97, 99, 2001, Mariposa Gallery, Albuquerque, 1990, Joanne Rapp Gallery, Scottsdale, Ariz., 1991, 93, 95, Felicita Found., Escondido, Calif., 1991, Tucumcari (N.Mex.) Area Vocat. Sch., 1992, Manchester Art Ctr., Pitts., 1993, Wetsman Collection, Detroit, 1993, Clovis (N.Mex.) C.C., 1993, Firehouse Art Ctr., 1994, Kavesh Gallery, Sun Valley, Idaho, 1995, Jan Weiner Gallery, Kansas City, 1995, 96, 2000, Jan Weiner Gallery, 2000, Gallerymateria, Scotsdale, Ariz., 2001, Munson Gallery, Santa Fe, 2001, Univ. Tulsa, Okla., 2001, Roswell (N.Mex.) Mus. and Art Ctr., 2002, numerous others; group exhbns. include Fred Jones Mus. Art, U. Okla., Norman, 1995, Roswell (N.Mex.) Mus. & Art Ctr., 1995, Nancy Margolis Gallery, N.Y.C., 1995, Sharadin Art Gallery, Kutztown (Pa.) U., 1995, Richard Kavesh Gallery, 1995, Jan Weiner Gallery, 1995, Ariz. State U. Art Mus., Tempe, 1995, Islip (N.Y.) Mus., 1995, Bruce Kapson Gallery, Santa Monica, Calif., 1996, Site Sante Fe Gallery, 1996, Johnston County C.C., Overland Parks, Kans., 1996, Jane Haslem Gallery, Washington, 1996, Karen Ruhlen Gallery, Santa Fe, 1996, Margo Jacobson Gallery, Portland, Oreg., 1996, Very Spl. Arts Gallery, Albuquerque, 1997, Joanne Rapp Gallery, 1997, Munson Gallery, 1999, numerous others; pub. art project include, among others, murals at Great Brook Valley Health Ctr., Worcester, Mass., 1994, Mass. Gen. Hosp., 1996, (mural) Island Nursing Home, Deer Isle, 2000, (mural) Big Red, Lincoln, Nebr., 2000,

Washington Park, Albuquerque, 2002; represented in many permanent collections, including Cooper-Hewitt, N.Y.C., Mus. Fine Arts, Santa Fe, Cleve. Inst. Art, Fed. Reserve Bank, Dallas, Roswell Mus. and Art Ctr., Albuquerque Mus. Fine Arts, City of Tucson (Ariz.), Phoenix Airport, Renwick Gallery Nat. Mus. Am. Art Smithsonian Inst., Washington, Detroit Inst. Art, Hallmark Cards Corp., Kansas City, State Capitol Art Collection, Santa Fe, pvt. collections. Recipient numerous grants, including NEA fellowships, 1986, 88, Kohler Arts-in-Industry grant, Sheboygan, Wis., 1988, 2000, Percent for Art Project grant, Phoenix Arts Coun., 1990, 1992, artist-in-residence grantee Roswell (N.Mex.) Mus. and Art Found., 1986, 2001.

DOMINGUEZ, JORGE IGNACIO, government educator; b. Havana, Cuba, June 2, 1945; came to U.S., 1960; s. Jorge Jose and Lilia Rosa (de la Carrera) D.; m. Mary Alice Kmietek, Dec. 16, 1967; children: Lara Lisa, Leslie Karen. AB, Yale U., 1967; AM, Harvard U., 1968, PhD, 1972. From asst. prof. to prof. govt. Harvard U., Cambridge, Mass., 1972—93, Frank G. Thomson prof. govt., 1993—96, chmn. Latin Am. and Iberian studies, 1979—83, 1990—93, acting dir. ctr. for internat. affairs, 1995, Clarence Dillon prof. internat. affairs, 1996—, dir. Weatherhead Ctr. for Internat. Affairs, 1996—, Harvard Coll. prof., 1998—2003. Active Coun. on Fgn. Rels., Inter-Am. Dialogue, 1982—, sr. fellow, 1993-94, assoc. fellow, 1995—. Author: Cuba: Order and Revolution, 1978, Insurrection or Loyalty, 1980, To Make the World Safe for Revolution: Cuba's Foreign Policy, 1989, Democratic Politics in Latin America and the Caribbean, 1998, Democracy in the Caribbean, 1993, Technopols: Freeing Politics and Markets in Latin America in the 1990s, 1997, Democratic Transitions in Central America, 1997, Toward Mexico's Democratization: Parties, Campaigns, Elections, and Public Opinion, 1999, The Future of Inter-American Relations, 2000, Mexico, Central and South America: New Perceptions, 5 vols., 2001, Constructing Democratic Governance in Latin America, 2003; co-author: Democratizing Mexico: Public Opinion and Electoral Choices, 1996, The United States and Mexico: Between Partnership and Conflict, 2001; mem. editl. bd. Am. Polit. Sci. Rev., 1979—81, Foreign Affairs en español, Polit. Sci. Quar., 1984—, Cuban Studies, 1991—, Latin Am. Rsch. Rev., 2003—, series editor Crisis in Central America: A Four-Part Special Report, Frontline, PBS (Peabody award), 1985—, chief editl. adv. 3-part spl. report Mexico, 1988. Chmn. bd. trustees Latin Am. Scholarship Program of Am Univs., Cambridge, Mass., 1981-82. Recipient Joseph Levenson Meml. Teaching award Harvard U., 1991; mem. Antilles Rsch. Program Yale U., New Haven, 1974-75; jr. fellow Harvard U., 1969-72, Fulbright-Hays fellow, 1983, 88. Mem. Latin Am. Studies Assn. (pres. 1982-83), New Eng. Coun. Latin Am. Studies (pres. 1980), Inst. Cuban Studies (pres. 1990-94). Clubs: Elihu (New Haven). Office: Harvard U Ctr Weatherband Internat Affairs 1033 Mass Ave Cambridge MA 02138-3016

DOMINGUEZ, KATHRYN MARY, educator; b. Santa Monica, Calif., Nov. 26, 1960; d. Frederick A. and Margaret M. (McGauren) D. AB, Vassar Coll., 1982; MA, Yale U., 1984, M in Philosophy, 1985, PhD, 1987. Researcher Congl. Budget Office, Washington, summer 1984; rsch. scholar bd. of govs. FRS, Washington, 1985-86; asst. prof. pub. policy Kennedy Sch. Govt. Harvard U., Cambridge, Mass., 1987-91, assoc. prof. pub. policy, 1991-97; assoc. prof. pub. policy and econs. U. Mich., Ann Arbor, 1997—. Rsch. cons IMF, Washington, 1989; vis. asst. prof., asst. dir. internat. fin. sect. dept. econs. Princeton U., 1990-91; Nat. Bur. Econs. Rsch. Olin fellow, 1991-92. Author: (monograph) Oil and Money, 1989; Exchange Rate Efficiency and the Behavior of International Asset Markets, 1992; (with Jeff Frankel) Does Foreign Exchange Intervention Work?, 1993. Mem. Nat. Bur. Econ. Rsch. (rsch. assoc. 2000—), Am. Econ. Assn., Am. Fin. Assn., Phi Beta Kappa. Democrat. Office: U Mich Sch Pub Policy Lorch Hall 611 Tappan Ave Ann Arbor MI 48109-1220

DOMINGUEZ, MICHAEL L. federal agency administrator; BS, U.S. Mil. Acad., West Point, N.Y., 1975; MBA, Stanford U., 1983; program for sr. ofcls. in nat. security, Harvard U., 1989. Commd. 2d lt. U.S. Army, 1975; program analyst for program analysis and evaluation Office of Sec. Def., Washington, 1983—88; exec. asst. for program analysis and evaluation Asst. Sec. Def., Washington, 1988—91; dir. for planning and analytical support for program analysis and evaluation Office of Asst. Sec. Def., Washington, 1991—94; assoc. dir. for programming Office of Chief of Naval Ops., Washington, 1994—97; gen. mgr. Tech 2000 Inc., Herndon, Va., 1997—99; rsch. project dir. Ctr. for Naval Analyses, Alexandria, Va., 1999—2001; asst. dir. for space, info. warfare, and command and control Office of Chief Naval Ops., Washington, 2001; asst. sec. Manpower and Res. Affairs USAF, Dept. Def., Washington, 2001—. Decorated Def. Meritorious Civilian Svc. medal. Office: Dept Def Manpower and Res Affairs 1660 Air Force Pentagon Washington DC 20330-1660

DOMINGUEZ, RAMON EMILIO, composer, visual artist; b. Camagüey, Cuba, Apr. 1, 1960; s. Ramon Emilio Dominguez and Bertha Rosa Roque. MusB, U. of Miami, 1975. MTNA Fla. State Music Tchrs., 1991. Artistic cons. Civic Chorale Greater Miami, Coral Gables, Fla., 2000—; rec. artist Musicality Studios, Coconut Grove, Fla., 2002—. Honors recital chmn. Miami Music Tchrs. Assn., Miami, 2002—. Composer: (opera) BERNADETTE (Archdiocese Commn., 2002). Publicity chmn. Miami Music Tchrs., Miami, 2003. Recipient Honoris Causa, Cuban Lyceum of Geater Miami, 2003. Mem.: Phi Mu Alpha (assoc.; pianist 1978—80). Achievements include research in The Music of Cuban composer Sindo Garay. Avocations: marathon running, chinese calligraphy, vocal performance, foreign language, jazz. Home: 2119 Tigertail Ave Coconut Grove FL 33133-3243 Home Fax: 305-858-7442. Personal E-mail: tiger9@bellsouth.net.

DOMINIAK, GERALDINE FLORENCE, accounting educator, retired; b. Detroit, Sept. 28, 1934; d. Benjamin Vincent (dec.) and Geraldine Esther (Davey) D. BS, U. Detroit, 1954, MBA, 1956; PhD, Mich. State U., 1966. CPA, Mich. Audit supr. Coopers & Lybrand, 1958-63; asst. prof. U. Detroit, 1965-68; assoc. prof. Mich. State U., 1968-69; prof. acctg. Tex. Christian U., Ft. Worth, 1969-97, chmn. dept. acctg., 1974-83; Arthur Young prof. acctg. Fla. A&M U., 1977. Author: (with J. Edwards and T. Hedges) Interim Financial Reporting, 1972; (with J. Louderback) Managerial Accounting, 1975, 9th edit., 2000. Ford Found. fellow, 1964-65. Mem. AICPA, Am. Acctg. Assn., Inst. Mgmt. Accts., Am. Woman's Soc. CPAs, Tex. Soc. CPAs, AAUP, ACLU, Beta Alpha Psi, Beta Gamma Sigma. Roman Catholic. Home: 4401 Cardiff Ave Fort Worth TX 76133-3513 *To teach is to learn.*

DOMINICK, CHARLES ALVA, college official; b. Canton, Ohio, Mar. 31, 1943; s. Joseph and Dorthy (Hawkins) D.; m. Nancy Unkefer, July 26, 1969; 1 child, Timothy Joseph. BA, Coll. of Wooster, 1965; MA, Ohio State U., 1968; PhD, U. Mich., 1987; postgrad., Harvard U., 1988. Admissions counselor Davis and Elkins (W.Va.) Coll., 1965-67, Mt. Union Coll., Alliance, Ohio, 1967-68; admissions asst. U. Mich., Ann Arbor, 1977-78, rsch. assoc. Project Choice, 1978-79; asst. dean admissions Wittenberg U., Springfield, Ohio, 1972-77, assoc. dir. for univ. advancement, 1979-80, asst. to pres., 1980-85, v.p. for instnl. rels., 1985—. Contbg. author: Managing Change in Higher Education, 1990, Student Recruitment, 1991. Mem. Com. Housing Resources Bd., Springfield, 1986—92; bd. dirs. Clark County Labor-Mgmt. Rels. Com., Springfield, Ohio, 1987—90, Jr. Achievement, 1990—95, Aid for Coll. Opportunities; trustee Oakwood Village, Springfield, 1988—96, Clark County Hist. Soc., 1986—94, 2001—, pres., 1989—92; bd. dirs. Cmty. Hosp. Found., 1996—, Cmty. Hosp., 2000—. Mem.: Springfield Country Club, Springfield Polo Club (pres. 1999—2001), Springfield Univ. Club (v.p. 1991—92, pres. 2002—03), Rotary. Home: 829 Linmuth Ct S Springfield OH 45503-1903 Office: Wittenberg U PO Box 720 U Ward St at N Wittenberg Springfield OH 45501

DOMINICK, KATHLEEN MARILYN, small business owner, consultant; d. Albert and Mary Masurat. BS, Phila. (Pa.) U., 1985; MBA, Phila.(Pa.) U., 1988; DBA, Nova S.E. U., 2000. Mgr. bus. planning Bell Atlantic, Phila., 1986—88, mgr. product mgmt., 1988—90, dir. pub. affairs, 1990—95; cir. external affairs AT&T Wireless Svcs., Bensalem, Pa., 1996—2000; COO County of Bucks, Doylestown, Pa., 2000—03; pres. DCS Group, Bayville, NJ, 1994—. Dispute conflict adminstr. De mars & Assocs., Milw., 2000—; adj. faculty Bucks County C.C., Newtown, Pa., 1989—, Del. Valley Coll., Doylestown, 1996—; asst. prof. Rider U., Lawrenceville, NJ, 2002—. Mem. exec. com. Bucks County Econ. Devel. Corp., 1992—; bd. dirs. Federal Lands Reuse Authority, Doylestown, 1994—, Bucks County Econ. Devel. Corp., Doylestown, 1992—. Recipient Theodore L. Mitchell award, Lower Bucks County C. of C., 1999, Clara Barton award, Am. Red Cross, 2000. Mem.: Bucks County Hist. Soc. (bd. dirs. 1996—2003), Doylestown (Pa.) Country Club. Avocations: sailing, piano, art.

DOMINICK, PETER HOYT, JR., architect; b. N.Y.C., June 9, 1941; s. Peter Hoyt and Nancy Parks D.; m. Philae M. Carver, Dec. 9, 1978; children: Philae M., James W. BA, Yale U., 1963; MArch, U. Pa., 1967. Registered architect, Colo. Project designer John R. Wild, Pty., Ltd., Papau, New Guinea, 1968-69, Spence Robinson, Hong Kong, 1969-71, W.C. Muchow & Ptnrs., Denver, 1971-74; pres. Wazee Design/Devel., Denver, 1973-75; prin. Dominick Architects, Denver, 1975-88; sr. prin. Urban Design Group, Inc., Denver, 1988—. Pres., chmn. bd. Urban Design Group, Inc., 2001—. Trustee Downtown Denver, Inc., Civic Ventures, 1984-94, Met. Denver Arts Alliance, 1983-84; active Mayor's Commn. on the Arts, 1983; juror Gov.'s awards, Denver, 1982; nat. com., exec. com. Whitney Mus. Am. Art.; bd. trustees Denver Art Mus., 2002. Fellow AIA (nat. com. on design, bd. dirs.); mem. Colo. Soc. Architects, Cactus Club, Arapahoe Tennis Club. Republican. Episcopalian. Office: Urban Design Group Inc 1621 18th St Ste 200 Denver CO 80202-1267 E-mail: pdominick@urbandesigngroup.com.

DOMINIK, JACK EDWARD, lawyer; b. Chgo., July 9, 1924; s. Ewald Arthur and Gertrude Alene (Crotzer) D.; children: Paul, David, Georgia Lee, Elizabeth, Sarah, Clare. BSME with distinction, Purdue U., 1947; JD, Northwestern U., 1950. Bar: Ill. 1950, U.S. Patent Office 1953, Wis. 1959, Fla. 1964, U.S. Dist. Ct. (ea. dist.) Wis. 1959, U.S. Supreme Ct. 1965, U.S. Dist. Ct. (no. dist.) Ohio 1962, U.S. Dist. Ct. (so. dist.) Ill. 1965, U.S. Ct. Appeals (7th and 9th cirs.) 1965, U.S. Ct. Appeals (4th cir.) 1973, U.S. Dist. Ct. (so. dist.) Fla. 1974, U.S. Ct. Appeals (5th cir.) 1977, U.S. Dist. Ct. (mid. dist.) Fla. 1979, U.S. Ct. Appeals (fed. cir.) 1983, U.S. Ct. Appeals (11th cir.) 1984, U.S. Ct. Appeals (2d cir.) 1987. Assoc. Carlson, Pitzner, Hubbard & Wolfe, Chgo., 1950—54; ptnr. Ooms and Dominik, Chgo., 1954—59, White & Hirshboeck, Milw., 1959—62, Dominik, Knechtel, DeMeur & Samlan, Chgo., 1962—78, Dominik & Assocs., Miami, Fla., 1978—. Served to 1st lt., C.E. AUS, 1943-46, ETO. Mil. govt. judge, 1945-46. Mem. ABA, Wis. Bar Assn., Fla. Bar Assn., Chgo. Bar Assn., Am. Patent Law Assn., Chgo. Patent Law Assn. (chmn. taxation com. 1966, 69-70), Milw. Patent Law Assn., Patent Law Assn. So. Fla. (founder, dir. 1982—, past pres.), Chgo. Yacht Club, Union League Club, Tau Beta Pi, Pi Tau Sigma, Tau Kappa Alpha. Avocation: flying. Home: 14751 Lewis Rd Miami Lakes FL 33014-2731 Office: 6175 NW 153rd St Miami Lakes FL 33014-2435

DOMINIK, JOHN JULIUS, retired advertising company executive; b. St. Cloud, Minn., Oct. 9, 1922; s. John and Mary (Appert) D.; m. Shirley Ann Moline, Sept. 3, 1962; five children. BA, St. John's U., 1946. Reporter, photographer St. Cloud Sentinel, 1947-49; acct. exec. The Stockinger Co., St. Cloud, 1949-61; advt. mgr. The Liturgical Press, Collegeville, Minn., 1962-92; wrote continuity for comic strip Sunday Museum, St. Paul Sunday Pioneer Press, 1972. Author: Cold Spring Granite, Three Towns into One City, 1976, St. Cloud: The Triplet City, 1980, That You May Find Healing, 1982, The Legendary Sam Pandolfo, 2003. Home: 2298 Rodeo Rd Sartell MN 56377-2368 E-mail: jjdominik@yahoo.com.

DOMINIK, WILLIAM JOHN, classicist, educator; b. Cleve., Dec. 29, 1953; arrived in New Zealand, 2002; s. William Carl and Shirley Anne (Crisman) Dominik. BA, U. of the Pacific, Stockton, Calif., 1975; MA, Tex. Tech U., 1982; PhD, Monash U., Melbourne, Australia, 1989. Cert. tchr., Calif. Student tchr. Am. Sch. Found., Mexico, 1975; tchr., adminstr. Ministry of Edn., Melbourne, 1976-90; teaching and rsch. asst. Tex. Tech U., Lubbock, 1981-82, asst. prof., 1990-91; tutor, rsch. asst. Monash U., 1985—88; lectr. U. Natal, Durban, South Africa, 1991—94, assoc. prof. classics, 1994—97, 1998—2000, prof., chair classics, 2001; prof. classics U. Leeds, England, 1997—98; prof., chair classics U. Otago, New Zealand, 2002—. Rsch. and tchg. fellow Clare Hall, U. Cambridge, England, 2000—01; tutor Coun. Adult Edn., Victoria, Australia, 1989; life mem. Clare Hall, U. Cambridge, England, 2001—. Author: The Mythic Voice of Statius, 1994, Speech and Rhetoric in Statius' Thebaid, 1994; editor: Roman Eloquence, 1997; co-editor: Concordantia in Sidonii Apollinaris Epistulas, 1997; editor Scholia, 1991—; asst. editor: Concordantia in Claudianum, 1988; co-author: Roman Verse Satire, 1997; co-editor: Flavian Rome, 2003; editor: Words and Ideas, 2002; co-editor: Literature, Art, History, 2003, Concordantia Anthologiam Latinam, 2002; author, editor over 140 publs. Recipient over 125 grants and awards, Commonwealth Rsch. award, Australia, 1987—88; fellow Commonwealth, 1997—98; Rsch. grantee, U. Natal, 1992—2001, Rsch. and Conf. grantee, Ctr. Sci. Devel., 1993—2001, Rsch. grantee, U. Otago, 2002—03. Mem. Am. Philological Assn., Classical Assn. South Africa, Australian Soc. Classical Studies, New Zealand Assn. Classical Tchrs., Classical Assn. Otago. Office: U Otago Dept Classics PO Box 56 Dunedin 9015 New Zealand E-mail: william.dominik@stonebow.otago.ac.nz.

DOMINIQUEZ, CARI M. federal agency administrator; BA, MA, Am. U. Ptnr. Heidrick & Struggles, Washington; dir. Spenser Stuart, San Francisco; prion. Diminiguez & Assocs., Md., 1999—2001; chair Equal Opportunity Commn., Washington, 2001—. Mem. leadership found. bd. Internat. Womens Forum, Hispanic Bus. Roundtable; bd. dirs. Holy Names Coll., Oakland, Calif., Human Resources Planning Soc. Fellow advanced study program pub. mgmt., MIT. Office: EEOC 1801 L St NW Washington DC 20507

DOMINO, CONSTANCE MAE, genetics researcher; b. Winnebego, Minn., Mar. 12, 1950; d. Virgil Dean Domino and Loretta Antonette Zahorski; 1 child, Kirk. AA, North Hennepin Cmty. Coll., 1976, MPls. Cmty. Coll., 1981; BS, U. Minn., 2002. RN Minn., 1981. Surgical nurse U. Minn. Hosp., Mpls., 1981—82; med-surg nurse Fairview Hosp., Mpls., 1982—85; float pool nurse Staff Builders, Mpls., 1985—90; triage nurse Group Health, Mpls., 1990—92; rschr. Ind., Mpls., 1982—; sales assoc. Target Corp., Mpls., 1997—. Sperzem scholarship, U. Minn. Nursing Sch., 1994. Mem.: NY Acad. of Scis., AAAS. Democrat. Roman Catholic. Achievements include discovery of use of bone marrow transplants for genetic diseases, 1985. Home: 727 15th Ave SE Minneapolis MN 55414

DOMINO, FATS (ANTOINE DOMINO), pianist, singer, songwriter; b. New Orleans, Feb. 26, 1928; Pianist since youth; performer: with groups in clubs, for dances, in theaters, composer (blues) ; recording artist (albums) Here Comes Fats Domino, 1963, Fats on Fire, 1965, Fats '65, Getaway With Fats Domino, Fats Domino, 1966, Stompin' Fats Domino, 1967, Trouble in Mind, Fats is Back, 1968, Live in Montreux, 1973, Sleeping on the Job, 1978, The Best of Fats, 1990, All Time Greatest Hits, Fats Domino, 1991, Best of Fats Domino Live, Antoine "Fats" Domino, 1992, The Fat Man, 1995, Live in Concert, Early Imperial singles 1950-52, 1996, Fabulous Mr. D./Swings, 1998, Here Stands/this is, vol. 3 Imperial Singles, 1998, Live at Gilleys, 1999, Collector's Edition, 2000, toured Britain, 1967, appeared (films) Shake, Rattle & Rock, Disc Jockey Jamboree, The Big Beat, The Girl Can't Help It, Any Which Way You Can, appeared on TV spl (TV films) Fats Domino & Friends, 1987. Named to Rock and Roll Hall of Fame, 1986; recipient Nat. Medal Arts, 1998, Grammy Lifetime Achievement award, 1987. Office: care Atlantic Records 1290 Ave of the Ams New York NY 10104-0101 also: SMS Records 14134 NE Airport Way Portland OR 97230-3443

DOMINO, KAREN BARBARA, anesthesiology educator; b. Chgo., Oct. 21, 1951; d. Edward F. and Antoinette (Kaczorowski) D.; m. Gene L. Brenowitz, June 7, 1975; children: Willa Domino Brenowitz, Noah Domino Brenowitz. BA, Vassar Coll., 1973; MA in Psychology, U. N.Mex., 1974; MD, U. Mich., 1978; MPH, U. Wash., 1998. Diplomate Am. Bd. Anesthesiology. Asst. prof. anesthesiology U. Pa., Phila., 1982-83, U. Pitts., 1983-86, U. Wash., Seattle, 1986-91, assoc. prof. anesthesiology, 1991-98, prof. anesthesiology, 1998—. Adj. assoc. prof. neurologic surgery U. Wash., Seattle, 1991-98, adj. prof.neurologic surgery, 1998—; assoc. examiner Am. Bd. Anesthesiology, 1995—. Contbr. articles to med. jours.; editl. bd. Jour. Cardiothoracic Vascular Anesthesiology, 1995—. Recipient B.B. Sankey Anesthesia Advancement award, 1990, Clin. Investigator award Nat. Heart, Lung, and Blood Inst., 1990-95. Mem.: Am. Soc. Anesthesiologists (chair com. on profl. liability, mem. com. occupl. health operating room pers.), Assn. Univ. Anesthesiologists, Soc. Neurosurg. Anesthesia and Critical Care (v.p. for edn. rsch.), Internat. Anesthesia Rsch. Soc., Phi Beta Kappa, Alpha Omega Alpha. Avocations: cooking, hiking, camping. Office: Univ of Wash Sch of Medicine PO Box 356540 Seattle WA 98195-6540 E-mail: kdomino@u.washington.edu.

DOMINOWSKI, ROGER L. psychologist, educator; b. Chgo., Feb. 21, 1939; s. Frank Dominowski and Annette Dalton; m. Nancy Ricketts, May 27, 1961 (div. Mar. 1976); children: Barbara, Andrew, Tracy Richards, Matthew; m. Carol Jean DeBoth, Sept. 19, 1984. BA, DePaul U., 1960, MA, 1962; PhD, Northwestern U., Evanston, Ill., 1965. Adminstrv. asst. to dean DePaul U., Chgo., 1961-62, instr., 1962-65, asst. prof., 1965-66; from asst. prof. to assoc. prof. U. Ill., Chgo., 1966-73, prof., 1973-2000, ret., 2000. Postdoctoral rsch. fellow U. Aberdeen, Scotland, 1972-73. Consulting editor Jour. Exptl. Psychology, 1970-84, Memory and Cognition, 1974-81; author: Cognitive Process, 2d edit., 1986, Teaching Undergraduates, 2001. Mem. Com. Civil Rights, Oak Park, Ill., 1970-72. Mem.: APA, Brit. Psychol. Soc., Sigma Xi. Avocations: travel, soccer, golf. E-mail: rdomin@uic.edu.

DOMIT, JOHN, surgeon; b. Mexico City, Oct. 9, 1960; MD, U. Anahuac, Mex., 1985. Diplomate Am. Bd. Surgery. Intern McKeesport Hosp., 1986-87, resident in surgery, 1986-91; staff Frick Hosp., Mt. Pleasant, Pa., 1991—, pvt. practice in gen. surgery, 1991—. Fellow Am. Coll. Surgeons; mem. Pa. Med. Soc., Westmoreland County Med. Soc. Office: John Domit Surg Assocs PC Exec Bldg Ste 202 220 Bessemer Rd Mount Pleasant PA 15666

DOMJAN, JOSEPH, artist; b. Budapest, Hungary, Mar. 15, 1907; s. Paul and Maria (Lika) D.; m. Evelyn A. Domjan, Mar. 13, 1944; children— Alma Domjan Melbourne, Michael P., Daniel G. BA, Hungarian Royal Acad. Fine Arts, 1940, MA, 1942. Founder Domjan Mus., Sarospatek, Hungary, 1977. Exhibited in over 550 one-man shows including Ernst Mus., Budapest, 1955, Mus. Art and History, Geneva, 1975, Cin. Art Mus., 1958, 74, N.J. State Mus., Trenton, 1966, 73, Dallas Pub. Libr., 1964, 77, Mueso della Bellas Artes, Mexico City, 1966, Cuyuga Mus., Auburn, N.Y., 1975; represented in numerous permanent collections including Met. Mus., Victoria and Albert Mus., Tate Gallery, London, Mus. Modern Art, Paris, Albertina Graphische Sammlung, Vienna, Nat. Gallery Fine Arts, Libr. of Congress, Washington, Nat. Mus., Stockholm, Mus. Modern Art, Tokyo; author, illustrator 24 books; author: The Proud Peacock, 1966, The Little Cock, 1966, The Artist and the Legend, 1975, Bellringer, 1975, Wing Beat, 1976, Edge of Paradise, 1979. Rockefeller Found. grantee, 1958; Recipient numerous prizes Soc. Illustrators, numerous prizes Am. Inst. Graphic Arts, numerous prizes Print Club of Albany, numerous prizes Am. Color Print Soc. Mem. Nat. Acad. Design, Soc. Am. Graphic Artists, Soc. Illustrators, Print Council Am., Silvermine Guild, Internat. Platform Assn. Address: West Lake Rd Tuxedo Park NY 10987

DOMJAN, LASZLO KAROLY, newspaper editor; b. Kormend, Hungary, Apr. 19, 1947; arrived in U.S., 1956; s. Frank and Violet Domjan; m. Louise Replogle, June 6, 1969; children: Andrew P., Eric S. BJ, U. Mo., 1969. Copy editor St. Louis Globe-Democrat, 1969; reporter, bureau chief UPI, St. Louis, 1969-81; reporter, night city editor St. Louis Post-Dispatch, 1981-87, exec. city editor, 1987-96, projects editor, 1996-97, asst. mng. editor, 1997-99, sr. editor, 1999—. Author, editor: Dioxin: Quandary for the 80s, 1983 (numerous awards); author: (reporter series) Hungary: Thirty Years After, 1986; editor: (series) Prosecutorial Corruption (1993 Pulitzer prize finalist). Active Leadership St. Louis. Recipient Herb Trask award Sigma Delta Chi, St. Louis, 1968. Mem. Press Club of Met. St. Louis, Investigative Reporters and Editors. Roman Catholic. Avocations: reading, freelance writing, music. Office: St Louis Post-Dispatch 900 N Tucker Blvd Saint Louis MO 63101-1099 E-mail: ldomjan@post-dispatch.com. *Always do right. Always do your best. Always make time for romance.*

DOMMEN, ARTHUR JOHN, agricultural economist, historian; b. Mexico City, Mex., June 24, 1934; came to U.S., 1940, naturalized, 1958; s. John Henry and Sarah (Hall) D.; m. Phan Thi Hong Loan. B.Sc., Cornell U., 1955; PhD, U. Md., 1975. Mem. staff UPI, 1957-63, bur. chief, 1959-61, 1961-63; mem. staff Los Angeles Times, 1965-71; bur. chief Japan, 1965—66, Los Angeles Times, New Delhi, 1966-68, Saigon, Vietnam, 1968-71; agrl. economist Intech, Inc., Silver Spring, Md., 1975-77; mem. AID mission to Tunisia, 1977-79; with USDA, Washington, 1980-96; affiliate prof. Indochina Inst., George Mason U., Fairfax, Va., 1996-98; ind. rschr., 1998—. Author: Conflict in Laos, The Politics of Neutralization, 1964, Laos: Keystone of Indochina, 1985, The Indochinese Experience of the French and the Americans, 2001. Served with AUS, 1955-57. Press fellow N.Y. Council Fgn. Relations, 1963-64 Home and Office: 7716 Radnor Rd Bethesda MD 20817-6282

DOMMERMUTH, WILLIAM PETER, marketing consultant, educator; b. Chgo. s. Peter R. and Gertrude Dommermuth; m. H. Joan Hasty, June 6, 1959; children: Karin, Margaret, Jean. BA, U. Iowa; PhD, Northwestern U., 1964. Advt. copywriter Sears, Roebuck & Co., Chgo., sales promotion mgr.; asst., then asso. prof. mktg. U. Tex., Austin, 1961-67; asso. prof. U. Iowa, Iowa City, 1967-68; prof. So. Ill. U., Carbondale, 1968-86, U. Mo., St. Louis, 1986—; CEO Optiphonics, Inc. Cons. in field. Author (with Kernan and Sommers): Promotion: An Introductory Analysis, 1970, (with Andersen) Distribution Systems, 1972, (with Marcus and others) Modern Marketing, 1975, Modern Marketing Management, 1980, Promotion: Analysis, Creativity and Strategy, 1984, 2d edit., 1989; contbr. articles to profl. jours. Mem. Am. Mktg. Assn., Am. Psychol. Assn., So. Mktg. Assn., Midwest Mktg. Assn., Phi Beta Kappa, Beta Gamma Sigma, Theta Xi, Delta Sigma Pi. Home: 11 Paris Ct Lake Saint Louis MO 63367-1506 E-mail: optomizer@consultant.com.

DOMNING, DARYL PAUL, paleontologist, educator; b. Biloxi, Miss., Mar. 14, 1947; s. Emile Frederick and Maud Louise (Mugnier) D.; m. Katherine Hubbell, July 10, 1987; 1 child, Charlotte Roxanna. BS, Tulane U., 1968; MA, U. Calif. Berkeley, 1970, PhD, 1975. Rsch. biologist Inst. Nacional de Pesquisas da Amazonia, Manaus, Brazil, 1976-78; asst. prof., assoc. prof. Howard U., Washington, 1978-92, prof., 1992—. Mem. sci. advisors com. U.S. Marine Mammal Commn., Washington, 1982-85, 93-97; mem. manatee tech. adv. coun. Fla. Fish & Wildlife Conservation Commn., Tallahassee, 1981—; mem. sci. adv. com. Save the Manatee Club, Maitland, Fla., 1986—, bd. dirs. 2000—. Editor: Sirenews, 1984—. Fellow Linnean Soc. London; mem. Am. Soc. Mammalogists, Soc. Marine Mammalogy, Soc. Systematic Zoology, Soc. Vertebrate Paleontology, Fla. Paleontol. Soc. Democrat. Roman Catholic. Home: 9211 Wendell St Silver Spring MD 20901-3533 Office: Howard Univ Dept Anatomy 520 W St NW Washington DC 20059-0001 E-mail: ddomning@fac.howard.edu.

DOMOWITZ, IAN, economics educator; b. N.Y.C., Nov. 29, 1951; s. Jacob and Marilyn (Raffer) D.; m. Marguerite Morton, Sept. 25, 1984. BA, U. Conn., 1977; PhD, U. Calif., San Diego, 1982. Asst. prof., assoc. prof., prof. econs. Northwestern U., Evanston, Ill., 1982-98, mem. rsch. faculty Inst. for Policy Rsch., 1987-98; Mary Jean and Frank P. Smeal chaired prof. fin. Pa. State U., University Park, 1998—; mng. dir. product mgmt. ITG, Inc., 2001—. Rsch. dir. K2 Capital Mgmt., 1992-94; cons. IMF, 1992, World Bank, 1993-96, 98-99, to various internat. fin. markets with respect to automated exch. structures, 1991-97; cons. U.S. Commodity Futures Trading Commn., 1991, 95-96; mem. sci. adv. bd. ITG, Inc., 1997-. Contbr. over 75 articles to profl. jours., chpts. to books. Sgt. U.S. Army, 1972-75, Germany. NSF grantee, 1984, 85, 87, 90. Mem. Am. Fin. Assn., Fin. Mgmt. Assn., Nat. Assn. Securities Dealers (econ. adv. bd. 1998-2000, chair 1998-2000, bond market transparency com. 1998-99), Econometric Soc. Home: Frnt 27 Mercer St New York NY 10013-2517 E-mail: idomowitz@itginc.com.

DOMPKE, NORBERT FRANK, retired photography studio executive; b. Chgo., Oct. 16, 1920; s. Frank and Mary (Manley) D.; m. Marjorie Gies, Dec. 12, 1964; children: Scott, Pamela. Grad., Wright Jr. Coll., 1939-40; student, Northwestern U., 1946-49, CPA, Ill. Cost comptr., budget dir. Scott Radio Corp., 1947; pres. TV Forecast, Inc., 1948-52; editor Chgo. edit. TV Guide, 1953, mgr. Wis. edit., 1954; pres. Root Photographers, Inc., Chgo., 1955-91; also chmn. bd. dirs.; bd. dirs. Root Studio, Inc., 1991-96, ret., 1996. Adv. com. photography & audiovisual tech., So. Ill. U., 1980-81; adv. bd. Gordon Tech. High Sch., 1979-86; co-founder TV Guide, 1947. With USAAC, 1943-47. Mem. NEA, Nat. Sch. Press Assn., Nat. Collegiate Sch. Press Assn., United Photographers Orgn. (pres. 1970-71), Profl. Photographers Am., Profl. Sch. Photographers Am. (v.p. 1966-67, 87-88, sec.-treas. 1967-69, pres. 1969-70, dir. 1971-78, treas. 1985-86, sec. 1986-87, pres. 1988-89), Photo Mktg. Assn. (Disting. Svc. award 1992), Photographic Art and Sci. Found. (Hall of Fame elector 1969-96), Ill. Small Bus. Men's Assn. (dir. 1970-73), Chgo. Assn.

Commerce and Industry (edn. com. 1966-94), Ill. H.S. Press Assn., North Cen. Assn. (visitation com. 1986), Chgo. Bible Soc. (bd. advisors), Ill. C. of C., Internat. Club. Home: 918 Cornwallis Ln Munster IN 46321-2877

DOMZELLA, JANET, retired library director; b. Marquette, Mich., Mar. 22, 1935; d. Jack Carl and Alice Margaret (Blom) Messenger; m. Theodore S. Wodzinski (div. 1974); children: Christopher, Joseph, Daniel; m. Perry Landon Domzella, July 15, 1977; stepchildren: Perry, Pamela. BS, No. Mich. U., 1973; MLS, U. Buffalo, 1979. Sch. libr. media specialist Niagara Falls (N.Y.) Bd. Edn., 1974-75, Iroquois Ctrl. Sch., Elma, N.Y., 1975-77; dir. Lewiston (N.Y.) Pub. Libr., 1977-2000, libr. emeritus, 2001—; ret., 2000. Mgr. LaSalle br. Niagara Falls Pub. Libr., NY, 2002. Co-author: Lewiston: Self Guided Tour, 1986. Vol. firefighter Upper Mountain Vol. Fire Co., Lewiston, 1980—90, treas., 1984—90; mem. Town of Lewiston Bur. Fire Prevention, 1988—90; mem. adv. bd. Documentary Heritage Program, 1991—93; mem. pub. libr. program Coll. of Charleston (S.C.) Conf., 1998, 2000, 2001. Democrat. Roman Catholic. Avocations: rosemaling, watercolor.

DONABEDIAN, AVEDIS, physician, educator; b. Beirut, Jan. 7, 1919; arrived in U.S., 1955, naturalized, 1960; s. Samuel and Maritza (Der Hagopian) Donabedian; m. Dorothy Salibian, Sept. 15, 1945; children: Haig, Bairj, Armen. BA, Am. U., Beirut, 1940, MD, 1944; MPH, Harvard U., 1955. Physician, acting supt. English Mission Hosp., Jerusalem, 1945—47; instr. physiology, clin. asst. dermatology and venereology Am. U. Med. Sch., 1948—51, univ. physician, dir. univ. health service, 1949—54; med. assoc. United Community Services Met. Boston, 1955—57; asst. prof., then assoc. prof. preventive medicine N.Y. Med. Coll., 1957—61; mem. faculty U. Mich. Sch. Pub. Health, Ann Arbor, 1961—, prof. med. care orgn., 1964—79, Nathan Sinai disting. prof. public health, 1979—89, emeritus. Author: A Guide to Medical Care Administration: Medical Care Appraisal--Quality and Utilization, 1969, Aspects of Medical Care Administration, 1973, Benefits in Medical Care Programs, 1976, The Definition of Quality and Approaches to Its Assessment, 1980, Medical Care Chartbook, 1986, The Criteria and Standards of Quality, 1982, Methods and Findings of Quality Assessment and Monitoring, 1985; co-author: Striving for Quality in Health Care: An Inquiry into Policy and Practice, 1991. Recipient Dean Conley award, Am. Coll. Hosp. Adminstrs., 1969, Norman A. Welch award, Nat. Assn. Blue Shield Plans, 1976, Elizur Wright award, Am. Risk and Ins. Assn., 1978, Nat. Merit award, Delta Omega, 1978, Richard B. Tobias award, Am. Coll. Utilization Rev. Physicians, 1984, Outstanding Contbns. in Health Svcs. Rsch. award, Assn. Health Svcs. Rsch., 1985, Baxter Am. Found. Health Svcs. Rsch. prize, 1986, Gold medal award, Med. Alumni Assn., Am. U. Beirut, 1986, The Ernest A. Codman award, Joint Commn. on Accreditation of Healthcare Orgns., 1997. Fellow: APHA (Sedgewick Meml. medal 1999), Am. Coll. Med. Quality, Am. Coll. Healthcare Execs. (hon.), Am. Coll. Utilization Rev. Physicians (hon.), Royal Coll. Gen. Practitioners (hon.); mem.: Inst. Medicine NAS, Internat. Soc. Quality Assurance in Health Care (hon.), Nat. Acad. Medicine of Mex. (hon.), Avedis Donabedian Found. (Barcelona, hon. pres. 1990—, Buenos Aires, hon. pres. 1994—). Home: 1739 Ivywood Dr Ann Arbor MI 48103-4523 Office: HMP-SPH II 109 Observatory St Ann Arbor MI 48109-2029*

DONAGHAY, MARIE MARTENIS, historian, educator; b. Wilmington, Del., Jan. 10, 1943; d. Edwin W. and Marie (Martenis) D. BA, U. Del., 1965, U. Va., 1967, PhD, 1970. Assoc. prof. history Radford (Va.) Coll., 1970-74; adj. prof. history Villanova (Pa.) U., 1983-89, asst. prof. history, 1989-92; adj. prof. history Phila. Textile, 1986-89; assoc. prof. history East Stroudsburg (Pa.) U., 1992—. Contbr. articles to profl. jours. Commentator, sessions chair Consortium on Revolutionary Europe, 1981, 89, 95, 99. Dissertation fellow Woodrow Wilson Found., 1968. Mem. Am. Hist. Assn., World History Assn. (treas. 1992-2000, sec. 2000-02), Soc. French Hist. Studies, So. Hist. Assn. Avocations: travel, photography, research. Office: History Dept East Stroudsburg U 200 Prospect St East Stroudsburg PA 18301

DONAGHY, DANIEL DELET, literature educator, poet; b. Bristol, Pa., Oct. 8, 1970; s. Daniel Delet and Anna Marie (Lewandowski) Donaghy; m. Karen Elizabeth Schneller, Aug. 24, 1996; 1 child, Abigail Lauren. BA in English, Kutztown U., 1993; MA in English, Hollins Coll., 1994; MFA in Creative Writing, Cornell U., 1997; postgrad., U. Rochester, 2000—. Lectr. Cornell U., Ithaca, NY, 1996—98; poet-in-residence Allendale Columbia Sch., Rochester, NY, 1999—. Lectr. in field. Author: (poetry collection) Kensington Avenue, 1997 (Cornell Coun. for the Arts Grant, 1997), Stadium Traffic, 2003, numerous poems. Recipient Poetry prize, Two Rivers Rev., 1999; Hollins Coll. Tuition fellow, 1993—94, Cornell U. Creative Writing fellow, 1994—96, NEH Summer Seminar fellow, 2001, Cornell Coun. for the Arts Writing grantee, 1996, Cornell Coun. for the Arts Project grantee, 1997, Cmty. Arts Partnership grantee, Tompkins County Arts Coun., 1998, Constance Saltonstall Found. for the Arts Poetry grantee, 2002. Mem.: N.Y. Coll. English Assn. Office: Univ Rochester 404 Morey Hall River Campus Rochester NY 14627 Personal E-mail: daniel_donaghy@hotmail.com.

DONAHER, JOSEPH G, speech pathology/audiology services professional, director; b. Lansdowne, Pa., Feb. 25, 1970; s. Thomas and Elizabeth Donaher; m. Kristine Lynne Donaher, Oct. 4, 1997; 1 child, Erin. M, Temple U., 1995—97. Coord. of stuttering program Ctr. for Childhood Communication at the Children's Hosp. of Phila., 1997—. Mem.: Am. Speech-Lang. Hearing Assn. Office: Children's Hospital of Phila 3405 Civic Ctr Blvd Philadelphia PA 19104-4388

DONAHO, JOHN ALBERT, consultant; b. Chgo., Sept. 9, 1917; s. John and Pauline (Langdon) D.; m. Patricia A. Maguire, Sept. 23, 1961. BA, Ctrl. YMCA Coll., 1941; cert. pub. adminstrn., MA, U. Chgo. Asst. to contr. Commonwealth Edison Co., Chgo., 1935-42; asst. dir. work simplification and measurement U.S. Bur. Budget, Exec. Office of the Pres., Washington, 1943-47; v.p. devel. Roosevelt U., Chgo., 1947-48; budget dir., city mgr. City of Richmond, Va., 1948-52; pres. John A. Donaho & Assocs. Inc., Reisterstown, Md., 1953—. Cons. to Mayor of Balt. and Gov. of Md., 1952-54, 74-87, 88-89; chmn. Md. Local Govt. Ins. Trust, 1987-88; ins. commr. State of Md., 1989-93; lectr., mem. faculty Am. U., Washington, Washington (D.C.) U., Goucher Coll., Balt., Johns Hopkins U., Balt., U. Balt., Fgn. Svc. Inst., Va. Commonwealth U., Roosevelt U., Chgo.; chmn. Va. State Commn. on Uniform Fin. Reporting. Contbr. articles to profl. jours. Pres., dir. Univ. Club, Balt.; dir. United Reisterstown Residents; pres. Lakeview Club, Inc., Reisterstown, Civitan Club Balt., Md., Civitan Club Richmond, Va.; mem., sec. Balt. (Md.) City Com. on Workers' Compensation, Balt. (Md.) City Com. on Ins. and Risk Mgmt.; mem. Md. Gov.'s Task Force on Liability Ins., Md. Gov.'s Blue Ribbon Task Force on Self-Ins., Gov.'s Blue Ribbon Commn. on Ins., Gov.'s Prescription Drug Commn.; chmn. Ad Hoc Com. on Liability Ins. for Md.; mem. Balt. County Restructuring Commn.; trustee Balt. Internat. Culinary Coll., Balt. Street Car Mus.; mem. Baltimore County Redistricting Commn. Fellow Soc. for Advancement Mgmt. (pres. Balt. regional chpt., v.p. Richmond chpt., chmn. round table on work simplification D.C. chpt.), Am. Soc. Pub. Adminstrn. (sr. mem., pres. Md. chpt., dir. Olympia chpt.); mem. Nat. Assn. Ins. Commrs. Office: 120 Cockeysville Rd # S100 Cockeysville Hunt Valley MD 21030 E-mail: donassoc@bellatlantic.net.

DONAHOE, DAVID LAWRENCE, state and city official; b. Pitts., June 5, 1949; s. Thomas Kernan and Anna Mae (Lawrence) D.; m. Judith DiNardo, June 5, 1971; children: Jennifer, Jeffrey. BA in Secondary Edn., U. Pitts., 1971; MA in Pub. Adminstrn., U. Pitts, 1978. Asst. dir., adminstr. Allegheny County, Pitts., 1974-76, dep. controller, 1976-77, county clk., 1977-78, dir. aviation, 1980-83; sch. treas. City of Pitts., 1978-80, exec. sec. to Mayor, 1986-88; exec. dir. Urban Redevel. Authority of Pitts., 1988-89; sec. of revenue State of Pa., 1989-91; exec. dir. Pitts. Schs., 1991-95, Allegheny Regional Asset Dist., 1995—. Sec. bd. Port Authority Allegheny County, 1975-80; teaching asst. U. Pitts, 1976, instr., 1985. Exec. dir. Pa. Econ. League, Pitts., 1983-85; bd. dir. Community Coll. Allegheny County, 1988. Mem. ASPA, Mcpl. Fin. Officers Am. (debt. com. 1979), Airport Operators Council Internat., League Municipalites (bd. dirs. Pitts. 1975-76) Democrat. Roman Catholic. Office: 1 Smithfield St Pittsburgh PA 15222-2221

DONAHOE, MAUREEN ALICE, accounting consultant; b. N.Y.C., June 9, 1959; d. William A. and Alice P. (O'Connor) D. BA in Acctg., Belmont Abbey Coll., 1982; MBA in Fin., Fordham U., 1992. CPA, N.Y.; cert. insolvency and reorgn. advisor. Staff acct. Bankers Trust Co., N.Y.C., 1982-85; sr. auditor Feldman Radin and Co., 1985—87; valuation svcs. mgr. Ernst & Young, 1987-91; sr. mng. dir. FTI Cons., Inc., 1991—2003; founder, ptnr. CCV Restructuring, Hackensack, NJ, 2003—. Dir. 417 E. 90th St. Corp., N.Y.C., 1995—. Mem. alumni bd. Belmont Abbey Coll., 1994—. Mem. AICPA, Assn. Insolvency Accts., N.Y. State Soc. CPAs (mem. insolvency and reorgn. com. 1993-94). Republican. Roman Catholic. Avocation: golf. Home: 12 Upper Mountain Ave Montclair NJ 07042-1814 Office: CCV Restructuring 411 Hackensack Ave 9th Fl Hackensack NJ 07601

DONAHOE, PETER ALOYSIUS, lawyer; BA in Polit. Sci., U. Wash., Seattle, 1957; JD, Harvard U., 1960. Bar: Hawaii 1961. Assoc. Carlsmith, Carlsmith, Wichman & Case, Hilo, Hawaii, 1960-63; staff Senate Majority Hawaii State Senate, Honolulu, 1963; dep. Atty. Gen. anti-trust divsn. State of Hawaii, Honolulu, 1963-65; asst. U.S. Atty. U.S. Dept. Justice, Honolulu, 1965-67; ptnr. Robertson, Castle & Anthony, Honolulu, 1967-71; pvt. practice Honolulu, 1973-91; dir. Atty.'s and Judge's Assistance Program Supreme Ct. for State of Hawaii, Honolulu, 1993—. Vis. prof. polit. sci. Am. Coll. Switzerland, Leysan, 1971-73; chmn. liquor commn., City and County of Honolulu, 1969; lectr. Hawaii Inst. CLE. Contbr. articles to profl. jours. Mem. Hawaii State Bar Assn. Home: 47-516 Hui Iwa St Kaneohe HI 96744-4615

DONAHOO, JAMES SAUNDERS, cardiothoracic surgeon; b. Jackson, Tenn., Sept. 30, 1937; s. Henry Amos and Ruby Burt (Welch) D.; m. Rose Carol Manasco, June 24, 1961; children: Paige, James. AB, Birmingham So. Coll., 1959; MD, Med. Coll. Ala., 1963. Chief resident surgeon Vanderbilt U. Hosp., Nashville, 1969; chief resident cardiac surgery Johns Hopkins U., Balt., 1971; asst. prof. surgery Johns Hopkins U. Sch. of Medicine, Balt., 1971-75; assoc. prof. surgery Johns Hopkins U., Balt., 1975-82, Jefferson Med. Coll., Phila., 1983-89; prof. cardiothoracic surgery Univ. Medicine Dentistry N.J., Newark, 1989—. Chief thoracic surgery East Orange (N.J.) VA Hosp., 1989—; chief divsn. cardiothoracic surgery N.J. Med. Sch., 1999-02. Editor: Practical Reviews in Surgery, 1975-82; contbr. articles to profl. jours. Col. USAR, 1964-92, Op. Desert Storm, 1991. Decorated Army Def. Svc. medal, Army Achievement medal; recipient Gold Medal Paper award S.E. Surg. Conv., 1967. Fellow ACS; mem. Am. Assn. Thoracic Surgery, So. Surg. Assn., So. Thoracic Surg. Assn. (coun. mem., Osler Abbott award 1982), N.Y. Soc. Thoracic Surgery, N.J. Soc. Thoracic Surgeons (pres. 1994), Elkridge Harford Hunt Club (exec. com. 1980), Merion Cricket Club, Baltusrol Golf Club, Alpha Omega Alpha. Episcopalian. Avocations: polo, fox-hunting, opera, oriental carpets, 19th century paintings. Home: 71 Hillcrest Ave Summit NJ 07901-2012 Office: Univ Medicine and Dentistry NJ 150 Bergen St Ste F-102 Newark NJ 07103-2714 E-mail: JamDonahoo@netscape.net.

DONAHOO, LEONARD E. retired engineer; b. Feb. 4, 1954; BS, USMA, 1976. Water treatment sales Nalco Chem., Cleve., 1981-84; auto coating sales BASF Corp., Atlanta, Ga., 1981-89. Pres. Ballard Assn. Choral Harmonics, 1999—. Home: 5615 Wolf Pen Trce Prospect KY 40059-9630

DONAHOO, WILLIAM PATRICK, science administrator, consultant, science administrator, educator; b. Van Buren, Ark., July 22, 1928; s. Clifford Stuart and Mathilda Augusta Feldman D.; m. Vada Ann Hadfield, Aug. 16, 1949 (div. 1963); 1 child, Carol Anne; m. Dorothy Ann Rosko, Dec. 30, 1965; 1 child, Frank. BS, Hendrix Coll., 1950; MS, Okla. State U., 1952, PhD, 1956. Rsch. chemist Monsanto, St. Louis, 1954-61; lab. mgmt. Griffith Labs., Chgo., 1961-71; dir. retail rsch. Anderson Clayton Foods, Dallas, 1971-77; v.p. rsch. and quality assurance Rich Seapak, St. Simons Island, Ga., 1977-91; pres. Quality Assocs., St. Simons Island, Ga., 1991—99. Adj. prof. chemistry Coastal Ga. C.C., 1999—. Contbr. articles to profl. jours. Mem. Rotary Internat. (club pres. 1985-86, dist. gov. 1994-95, citation for meritorious svc. 1998). Avocations: travel, birding, playing in concert and dance bands. Home: 113 Augusta Saint Simons GA 31522-2438

DONAHUE, ARTHUR THOMAS, television producer; b. Adams, Mass., Nov. 30, 1954; s. Arthur William and Jeanne Claire (Roulier) D.; m. Mary Virginia Lawson, Sept. 9, 1978; children: Erin Marion, Sean Lawson. BA in Comm. Studies, U. Mass., 1976. Lic. 1st class radiotelephone operator FCC, 1979. Photographer, editor Sta. WWLP-TV, Springfield, Mass., 1972-77, Sta. WBZ-TV, Boston, 1977-80; prodr., photographer Sta. WFSB-TV, Hartford, Conn., 1980-86; prodr. Sta. WCVB-TV, Boston, 1987—. Cons. TV news, 1986—. Prodr.(writer, photographer): 87 "Chronicle" news mag. programs, 1989—2003, : HDTV Videography, 2000 (Emmy award, 2001); (documentaries) New England Portrait, 1995 (Emmy award, 1996), Mill River Disaster, 1993 (Telly award, 1994). Named New Eng. TV News Photographer Yr. Boston Press Photographers Assn., 1977-85. Mem. NATAS (Emmy awards 1980-96), Nat. Press Photographers Assn. (TV documentary Greetings From the Grange 1993, Nat. TV News Photographer Yr. 1985). Office: Sta WCVB-TV 5 Television Pl Needham MA 02494-2302

DONAHUE, CHARLES BERTRAND, II, lawyer; b. Hampton, Iowa; s. Charles B. and Alta M. (Sykes) D.; m. Brenda K. Kumpf (div. Dec. 1980); children: Kaylie Elizabeth, Megan E. (dec.); m. Kathleen L. Komnenovich, June 27, 1987. AB, Harvard U., 1959; JD cum laude, Cleve. State U., 1967. Bar: Ohio 1967, Fla. 1970. Commd. 2d lt. USAF, 1959, advanced through grades to capt., 1962, res., 1969, contracting officer, 1959-62; subcontract adminstr. Westinghouse, Pitts., 1962-63; contract adminstr. TRW, Inc., Cleve., 1963-67; atty., ptnr. Calfee Halter & Griswold, Cleve., 1967-79; founder, ptnr. Donahue & Scanlon, Cleve., 1979-99. Trustee Cleve. Artists Found., 1999; civil svc. commn. City Westlake, Ohio, 1995-96. Avocations: cooking, reading, travel. Home and Office: 827 Brick Mill Run Westlake OH 44145-1602 E-mail: cbdonahue@prodigy.net.

DONAHUE, CHARLES LEE, JR., health network executive; b. Norwood, Mass., Mar. 31, 1943; s. Charles and Katherine (Gallagher) D.; m. Nancy Turner, Aug. 15, 1971; children: Jessica, Charles, Morgan, Caroline, Matthew. AB, Brown U., 1965; MA, Cornell U., 1973. Vol. U.S. Peace Corps, Trengganu, Malaysia, 1967-68, project co-dir. Mass. Health Rsch. Inst., Boston, 1973-75; health planning analyst Boston U., Boston, 1976-80; regional program analyst U.S. Pub. Health Svc., Boston, 1980-81; exec. dir. Health Planning Coun., Boston, 1981-89; pres. Healthcare VALUE Mgmt., Norwood, Mass., 1990—. Pres. Mass. Health Coun., 1990-91; adj. asst. prof. Pub. Health Boston U., 1990—. Contbr. articles to profl. jours. Bd. dirs. New England Employee Benefit Coun., 2000—. Recipient Schlesinger award Am. Pub. Health Assn. and Am. Health Plan Assn., 1987. Avocations: coaching youth hockey, golf, fatherhood. Home: 407 Gay St Westwood MA 02090-1729 E-mail: cdona@aol.com.

DONAHUE, CHARLOTTE MARY, lawyer; b. Columbus, Ohio, Sept. 29, 1954; d. Patrick Henry and Helen Dillon (Meany) D. AB, Holy Cross Coll., 1976; JD, U. Toledo, 1983. Bar: Pa. 1984, D.C. 1985, U.S. Dist. Ct. (ea. dist.) Pa. 1985, U.S. Ct. Appeals 3d cir.) 1985, U.S. Supreme Ct. 1990, Mass. 1992. Jud. clk. to presiding justice Commonwealth Ct. Pa., Phila., 1983-84; spl. asst. U.S. atty. U.S. Dist. Ct. (ea. dist.) Pa., Phila., 1987-90; atty. HUD, Phila., 1984-93, Boston, 1993—. Mem. Fed. Bar Assn., Pa. Bar Assn., Mass. Bar Assn., D.C. Bar Assn., Order of Barristers, Internat. Platform Assn., Supreme Ct. Hist. Soc. Home: 40 Meredith Cir Milton MA 02186-3916 Office: HUD Thomas P O'Neill Jr Fed Bldg 10 Causeway St Boston MA 02222-1092

DONAHUE, CONRAD JAMES, career naval officer, educator; b. Patuxent River, Md., Apr. 12, 1951; s. Conrad and Regina D.; m. Karen Ann Donahue, Feb. 26, 1977; children: Melissa, Michael, Monica, Megan. BS in Oceanography, U.S. Naval Acad., 1973; MA in Internat. Security Affairs, Naval War Coll., 2000. Commd. USN, 1973, advanced through grades to capt., 1993; commdg. officer USS Simon Bolivar U.S. Submarine Force Atlantic, Charleston, S.C., 1989-92; commdg. officer USS Henry M. Jackson U.S. Submarine Force Pacific, Bangor, Wash., 1995-98; head submarine acquisition and modernization br. USN, Washington, 1998-99; prof. naval sci. MIT, Boston U., 2000-01. Mem. KC (Family of Month 1990, Knight of Month 1991). Roman Catholic. Avocations: running, biking, kayaking, singing, reading. Home: 224 Rhode Island Blvd Portsmouth RI 02871 Office: Boston NROTC Consortium 116 Bay State Rd Boston MA 02215 E-mail: cdonahue@bu.edu.

DONAHUE, JEFFREY DAVID, music educator; b. Circleville, Ohio, 1976; s. David Jay and Sandra Sue Donahue. Bachelor o f Music, Ohio U., Athens, Ohio, 1995—99. Music dir. Santa Cruz Christian Learning Ctr., Santa Cruz, Bolivia, 1999—2000; asst. band dir. Waverly City Sch., Waverly, Ohio, 2000—02. Mem.: Music Educators Nat. Conf. (assoc.). Independent-Republican. Churches Of Christ In Christian Union. Avocations: running, woodworking, reading, movies, swimming. Home: 1355 Western Avenue Apt 115 Chillicothe OH 45601

DONAHUE, JOHN DAVID, public official, educator; b. Alexandria, Ind., June 17, 1956; s. Thomas Edward and Judith Ann (Wheatley) D.; m. Margaret Ann Pax, Aug. 23, 1986; children: Kathleen, Benedict. BA, Ind. U., 1979; M in Pub. Policy, Harvard U., 1982, PhD, 1987. From asst. prof. to assoc. prof. Harvard U., Cambridge, Mass., 1987-93; asst. sec. U.S. Dept. Labor, Washington, 1993-94, counselor to sec., 1994-95; assoc. prof. pub. policy Harvard University, Cambridge, Mass., 1995-99, Raymond Vernon lectr. in pub. policy, 1999—. Cons. econ., Cambridge, 1985-2002; adv. com. on shareholder responsibiity Harvard U., 1998—. Author: The Privatization Decision, 1989, Disunited States, 1997, Hazardous Crosscurrents, 1998; co-author: New Deals: The Chrysler Revival, 1985; editor: Cost-Benefit Analysis and Project Design, 1980, Making Washington Work: Tales of Innovation in the Federal Government, 1999; co-editor: Governance in a Globalizing World, 2000, Governance Amid Bigger, Better Markets, 2001, Market-Based Government Supply Side, Demand Side, Upside and Downside, 2002, For the People, 2003; book rev. editor Jour. Policy Analysis and Mgmt., 2002—. Advisor Clinton Presdl. Transition, Washington, 1993. Doctoral fellow NSF, 1980, fellow Dively Found., 1984. Office: Harvard University 79 JFK St Cambridge MA 02138-5801

DONAHUE, JOHN EDWARD, lawyer; b. Milw., Aug. 22, 1950; s. Joseph Robert and Helen Ann (Kelly) D.; m. Maureen Dolores Hart, Sept. 20, 1974; children: Timothy Robert Hart, Michael John Hart. BA with honors, Marquette U., 1972; JD, U. Wis., Madison, 1975. Bar: Wis. 1975, U.S. Dist. Ct. (we. and ea. dists.) Wis. 1975. Assoc. Weiss, Steuer, Berzowski and Kriger, Milw., 1975-80; ptnr. Weiss, Berzowski, Brady & Donahue LLP, Milw., 1981-2001; shareholder Godfrey & Kahn, S.C., Milw., 2001—. Guest lectr. Marquette U. Law Sch., Milw., 1976-90; presenter programs Wis. Inst. CPAs, 1984—, Minn. Soc. CPAs, 1992-97; expert witness.. Past chmn. bd. trustees, past chmn. bd. dirs., past chmn. bd. govs., trustee, exec. com., com. chmn. Mt. Mary Coll., Milw., 1984-2001, past pres., bd. dirs. com. chmn. Met. Milw. Civic Alliance, 1980—, Children's Hosp. Found., Milw., 1984—; mem. steering com. Greater Milw. Initiative, 1989-92; v.p., bd. dirs. Future Milw., 1984-88; v.p., bd. dirs., com. chmn., scoutmaster Boy Scouts Am., 1990—. Recipient citation Milw. County Bd. Suprs., 1990, spl. svc. award Met. Milw. Civil Alliance, 1990, silver beaver award Boy Scouts Am., 1995; named outstanding instr. AICPA, 1991. Mem. ABA, Wis. Bar Assn., Milw. Bar Assn. (program chmn. employee benefits sect.), Wis. Retirement Plan Profls., Greater Milw. Employee Benefits Coun., Kiwanis Club (pres. Milw. unit 1989-90, Outstanding Kiwanian 1989-97, Kiwanian of Yr. 1993). Office: Godfrey & Kahn SC 780 N Water St Milwaukee WI 53202-3590 Business E-Mail: jdonahue@gklaw.com.

DONAHUE, JOHN EDWARD, physician; b. Revere, Mass., Apr. 27, 1966; s. Edward Francis and Camille (Santoro) D. BS summa cum laude, Tufts U., 1988, MD, 1992. Diplomate Am. Bd. Psychiatry and Neurology, Am. Bd. Pathology, Nat. Bd. Med. Examiners. Intern St. Elizabeth's Med. Ctr., Boston, 1992-93; resident New Eng. Med. Ctr., Boston, 1993-96; fellow R.I. Hosp., Providence, 1996-99; dir. neuropathology NJ Neuroscience Inst., Edison, 1999—2003; asst. prof. neuroscience Sch. Grad. Med. Edn. Seton Hall U., Orange, 2000—03; asst program dir. neurology residency program NJ Neuroscience Inst., 2001—03; attending neuropathologist RI Hosp., 2003—. Asst. prof. pathology Brown U. Sch. Medicine, 2003—. Contbr. articles to profl. jours. Recipient David L. Kasdon prize Tufts U. Sch. Medicine, 1992, Second Place award Gustaf Retzius Neuroanatomy Competition, 1997, 98, champion 1999. Mem.: Neuroplex, Inc./N.Y. Soc. Neuropathologists, Soc. Neurosci., Coll. Am. Pathologists, Am. Assn. Neuropathologists, Am. Acad. Neurology, Mass. Med. Soc., Phi Beta Kappa. Avocations: swimming, computers. Office: RI Hosp Dept Pathology 593 Eddy St Providence RI 02903 E-mail: jdonahue@massmed.org.

DONAHUE, JOHN FRANCIS, investment company executive; b. Pitts., 1924; Grad., U.S. Mil. Acad., 1946. Chmn. Federated Investors, Inc., Pitts. Office: Federated Investors Federated Investors Tower 1001 Liberty Ave Pittsburgh PA 15222-3779

DONAHUE, JOHN JOSEPH, park and recreation director; b. Bklyn., Nov. 20, 1952; s. John and Anna Donahue; m. Sarah Grassi, July 2, 1977; 1 child, John Vincent. Degree in natural resource mgmt., Calif. State U., Sonoma, 1986. Instr. Bklyn. Bot. Garden, 1977-78; supr. N.Y.C. Parks Dept., 1978-79; gardener Cape Cod Nat. Seashore, 1980-83, John Muir Nat. Hist. Site, 1983-86; specialist nat. resource mgmt. Morristown (N.J.) Nat. Hist. Park, 1986-89; specialist environ. protection Nat. Park Svc., Washington, 1989-94; supt. Thomas Stone Nat. Hist. Site, Charles County, Md., 1994—, George Washington Birthplace Nat. Monument, Washington's Birthplace, Va., 1994—. Adv. bd. mem. Olmsted Ctr. Landscape Preservation, Valley Forge Archeol. Ctr.; bd. dirs., treas. George Wright Soc.; chief visitor protection and resource mgmt. Cape Cod Nat. Seashore, 1993. Spkr. in field; contbr. articles to profl. jours. Office: George Washington Birthplace Nat Monument RR 1 Box 717 Washingtons Birthplace VA 22443-9801 Fax: 804-224-2142.

DONAHUE, MARTHA, librarian, educator, retired; b. Danville, Ky., Jan. 5, 1936; d. Thomas E. and Mary Louise (Craig) D. BA, Centre Coll., 1958; MA, Ind. U., 1961; 6th Yr. Specialist's Cert., U. Wis., 1971. Tchr. Pompano Beach (Fla.) Jr. H.S., 1958-60; post libr. U.S. Army, Europe, Bad Tölz, Germany, 1961-65; instr. library Centre Coll., Danville, Ky., 1966-67, U. Wis., Whitewater, 1967-70; assoc. prof. library Mansfield (Pa.) U., 1971-93. Bd. dirs. Mansfield Free Pub. Libr., 1995-97, vol., 1998 ; vol. Area Agy. on Aging, Towanda, Pa., 1993—, Sr. Citizen Meals Delivery, 1993—; mem. Parish Coun., Mansfield, 1994-97; bd. dirs. Ctr. Coll. Alumni Bd., 1996-98. Recipient Higher Edn. Act fellowship U. Wis., 1960. Mem. ALA, Pa. Libr. Assn. (chair various coms. 1971—), Friday Club of Wellsboro, Mansfield Garden Club, Columbia Lit. Exchange, The Book Group, Tioga County Hist. Soc., 1901 Soc. (pres. 2001-02). Roman Catholic. Avocations: reading, gardening, travel, cross-country skiing, bicycling. Home: 146 S Main St Mansfield PA 16933-1522

DONAHUE, MICHAEL CHRISTOPHER, lawyer; b. Norwood, Mass., Apr. 20, 1946; s. Michael Christopher and Helen (Joyce) D.; m. Erna Joyce Carrigan, Apr. 20, 1968; children: Kirsten, Michael, Brendan, Brian. AB, Boston Coll., 1968; JD, Boston U., 1972. Bar: Mass. 1972. Assoc., Klainer & Kappel, Boston, 1972-73, Sheridan, Garrahan & Lander, Framingham, Mass., 1981-88; asst. atty. gen. Mass. Atty. Gen., 1973-79; gen. counsel Mass. Dept. of Corrections, Boston, 1979-81; mem. Gov.'s Adv. Com. on Corrections, 1988—; spl. asst. atty. gen. Mass., Boston, 1979—; lectr. grad. criminal justice program Anna Maria Coll., Paxton, Mass., 1981-86. Contbr. articles to law review jours. Me.m Gov.'s Adv. Com. on Corrections, 1989. With USAR, 1968-72. Mem. ABA, Assn. Trial Lawyers Am., Mass. Bar Assn., Mass. Acad. Trial Attys. (author, editor), South Middlesex Bar Assn. Democrat. Roman Catholic. Home: 167 Depot St South Easton MA 02375-1537 Office: Gelerman and Cashman 270 Bridge St Ste 204 Dedham MA 02026-1798

DONAHUE, MICHAEL JOSEPH, lawyer; b. Manchester, N.H., Dec. 28, 1947; s. Francis Lawler and Laura (Veroneau) D.; m. Diane Landry, May 26, 1973; children: Sarah, Kerry. AB, Holy Cross Coll., Worcester, Mass., 1970; JD, U. Pa., Phila., 1973. Bar: N.H. 1973, U.S. Dist. Ct. N.H. 1977, U.S. Ct. Appeals (1st cir.) 1982, U.S. Ct. Mil. Appeals 1991. Ptnr. Kearns, Colliander, Donahue & Tucker, P.A., Exeter, N.H., 1977-85, Donahue, Tucker & Ciandella, Exeter, 1985—. Bd. dirs. Greater Seacoast United Way, 1985-92; v.p., sec., bd. trustees Strawbery Banke Mus., 1992-98. Capt. JAGC, USNR, 1970-98. Mem. ABA, N.H. Bar Assn. (bd. dirs. mcpl. law sect. 1984-86). Roman Catholic. Home: 8 Old Locke Rd North Hampton NH 03862-2236 Office: Donahue Tucker & Ciandella PO Box 630 Exeter NH 03833-0630 E-mail: donahue.m.j@comcast.com., MDonahue@DTCLAWYERS.com.

DONAHUE, PATRICIA TOOTHAKER, retired social worker, administrator; b. Alamo, Tex., Sept. 6, 1922; d. Henry Tull and Minnie Elizabeth (Scott) Toothaker; m. Hayden Hackney Donahue, Feb. 22, 1947; children: Erin Kathleen, Kerry Shannon, Patricia Marie. BA, U. Okla., 1977, MSW, 1978. Lic. social worker with specialty in clin. social work, Okla. Clin. social worker Cen. Okla. Community Mental Health Ctr., Norman, 1979-91. Participant VII World Congress Mental Health, Vienna, Austria, 1983; adj. asst. prof. U. Okla. Sch. Social Work, Norman, 1989—. Vol. counselor Woman's Resource Ctr., Norman, 1978-79; active Cleve. County Aging Svcs. Adv. Coun., 1988-91. Mem. Cleve. County Med. Aux. (pres. 1970-71), Reviewers Club Norman (pres. 1970).

DONAHUE, RAFE MICHAEL, statistician; b. Milwaukee, Wis., Jan. 8, 1965; s. Parnell Melvin and Mary Ann Donahue; m. Michelle Marie Hitchens, May 11, 1991; children: Harrison Moriarity, Zachary Mathias, Olivia Maryrose. BS, U. of Dayton, 1983—87; PhD, Colo. State U., 1987—92. Statistician Hoescht Marion Roussel, Kansas City, 1992—96; statistician / data miner Glaxo SmithKline, NC, 1996—. Grand knight KC, Raleigh, 1999—2000.

DONAHUE, RICHARD JAMES, secondary school educator; b. New Rochelle, N.Y., Dec. 11, 1950; s. Raymond Douglas and Helen Andrea (Garibaldi) Silva. BS in Math., SUNY, Oneonta, 1972; MS (spl.), Coll. New Rochelle, 1977; MS in Ednl. Computing, Iona Coll., 1986. Cert. spl. edn. tchr., N.Y., tchr. secondary math., N.Y. Tchr. spl. edn. Adams Sch., N.Y.C., 1973-75, curriculum coord., 1976-77; tchr. math. and computer literacy Eastchester (N.Y.) Jr. H.S., 1975-76, 77—; tchr. math. SAT preparation New Rochelle H.S., 1981-83, tchr. Gen. Ednl. Devel. math., 1981—. Tchr. computers Coll. New Rochelle, 1988, adj. asst. prof., 1988-92; tchr. computers Manhattanville Coll., Purchase, N.Y., 1983-85; mem. challenge gifted and talented program Concordia Coll., Bronxville, N.Y., 1988-89; tchr. tng. courses in computer applications Eastchester Union Free Sch. Dist., 1993-94; tchr. mentor on use of telecom. Am. Online's Scholastic Network, 1994; adv. bd. world wide web Scholastic Network; participant Waikoloa Sci. Project, Hawaii, 1997; ednl. cons. and web designer Nat. Optical Astronomy Observatories and Kitt Peak Nat. Observatory, 1999. Author: BASIC Number Theory Programs, 1985-86, PASCAL Number Theory Programs, 1987, also computer software series in math. edn., 1982-83; also articles and internet column. Recipient N.Y. State Model Schs. Tchr. Integration award Madison-Oneida Bd. Coop. Edn. Svcs., 1998, N.Y. Wired Applied Tech. award The N.Y. Jour. News, 1999; NSF Math. Devel. Program grantee, 1981, NEWMAST grantee Ednl. Workshop NASA, 1994, Tchr. Resource Agt. grantee Am. Astron. Soc., 1996, Reader's Digest Found. Interdisciplinary Learning Project grantee, 1998, BEPT mini grantee, 1998, Impact II grantee BOCES N.Y. State Edn. Dept., Westcherter/Rockland Impact II Developer award, So. Westchester BOCES, 1999, N.Y. Wired Applied Tech. award, N.Y. Jour. News, 1999. Mem. Nat. Coun. Tchr. Math. (reviewer and referee for Math. Tchr. publ.), Assn. Math. Tchrs. N.Y. State, Math. Assn. Am., Eastchester Tchrs. Assn. (treas. 1983-97), N.Y. State Congress of Parents and Tchrs. (life, Jenkins award 1994), Eastchester Tchrs. Inst. (treas. 1983-85), Nat. Sci. Tchrs. Assn., N.Y. State Assn. for Computers and Tech. in Edn., N.Y. State Tech. Edn. Assn., Film Soc. Lincoln Ctr., Am. Film Inst., Bronxville, Eastchester, Pelham and Tuckahoe Consortium, Westchester Amateur Astronomers, Internat. Tech. Edn. Assn. Home: 60 Locust Ave Apt A201 New Rochelle NY 10801-7360

DONAHUE, SHIRLEY OHNSTAD, elementary education educator; b. Darlington, Wis., Aug. 29, 1937; d. Joseph and Edna L. (Peterson) Ohnstad; m. John V. Donahue, Aug. 20, 1960; children: Roger K., Jeffrey J. BS, U. Wis., Platteville, 1959; MS, No. Ill. U., 1978. Cert. tchr., Ill. Tchr. Freeport (Ill.) Sch. Sys., 1959-62, Belvidere (Ill.) Sch. Sys., 1962-64, Pecatonica (Ill.) Sch. Sys., 1964-66, Orangeville (Ill.) Sch. Sys., 1966-67, Rock Falls (Ill.) Sch. Sys., 1967-93; ret. Rock Falls (Ill.) Sch. System, 1993. Co-author gifted student curriculum materials. Mem. Liturgical com. St. Mary's Ch., Sterling, Ill., 1980-84, aux. min., 1980-94; mem. Friends of Sterling Pub. Libr., v.p. 1990-93, 96, pres. 1995; bd. dirs. YWCA, sec. bd. dirs., 1994-95, pres. bd. dirs. 1997-99; mem. Cmty. Gen. Hosp. Med. Ctr. Aux., 1993—, co-chair sr. health ins. program, 1994-2000, pres. 1995-99, v.p. ways and means, 1999—; pres. YWCA, 1997-99; bd. dirs. ARC, Lincolnland chpt., 1996-99. Recipient Western Ill. Master Tchr. award, 1991. Mem. NEA, Rock Falls Elem. Edn. Assn. (chmn. polit. action com. for edn. 1985-87), Ill. Edn. Assn. Roman Catholic. Avocation: bicycling. Home: 1720 Avenue E Sterling IL 61081-1124

DONAHUE, THOMAS MICHAEL, physics educator; b. Healdton, Okla., May 23, 1921; s. Robert Emmett and Mary (Lyndon) D.; m. Esther Marie McPherson, Jan. 1, 1950; children: Brian M., Kevin E., Neil M. AB, Rockhurst Coll., 1942, DSc (hon.), 1981; PhD, Johns Hopkins U., 1947. Rsch. assoc., asst. prof. Johns Hopkins U., 1947-51; asst. prof. U. Pitts., 1951-53, assoc. prof., 1953-57, prof., 1957-74, dir. Lab. Atmospheric and Space Sci., 1966-74, dir. Space Rsch. Coordination Ctr., 1966-74; chmn. dept. atmospheric and oceanic sci. and Space Physics Rsch. Lab., U. Mich., Ann Arbor, 1974-81, prof., 1981-87, Edward H. White II disting. univ. prof. planetary sci. dept. atmospheric oceanic and space scis., dept. physics, 1987-94; disting. univ. prof. emeritus, 1994—; dir. ctr. for integrated study global change U. Mich., 1990-93. Mem. phys. scis. com. NASA, 1972-77, adv. coun., 1982-88, solar system exploration com., 1981-82; mem. Arecibo adv. bd. Cornell U., 1971-76, 86-89, chmn. 1989; mem. Space Telescope Sci. Inst. Adv. Com., 1986-89, chmn., 1987-89; chmn. solar terrestrial rels. com. NAS, mem. atmospheric scis. com., mem. geophysics rsch. bd., mem. climate bd., chmn. space sci. bd. 1982-88, mem. nominating com., 1987-88; chmn. space sci. in the 21st Century study NAS, 1984-87, com. for U.S.-USSR workshop on planetary scis., 1988-91, com. on planetary and lunar exploration, 1992-93; chmn. sci. steering groups Pioneer Venus multi-probe and orbital missions to Venus, 1974-93, chmn., pub. affairs com. Am. Geog. Union; trustee-at-large Upper Atmosphere Rsch. Corp., 1975-87; vice-chmn. exec. com., trustee Univ. Corp. for Atmospheric Rsch., 1978-85; chmn. bd. trustees Univs. Space Rsch. Assn., 1978-82; mem. vis. com. Max Planck Gesellschaft fur Aeronomie, 1989-96; mem. nat. tech. adv. com. Nat. Inst. for Global Environ. Change, 1992; chmn. vis. com. Dept. Earth and Planetary Scis. Harvard U., 1996-2001; Marcel Nicolet lectr. Am. Geophys. Union, 1993; NAS liaison to NRC in Geophysics, 1997-2001; chmn. sec. geophys. NAS, 2002-. Editor: Space Research X, 1969; assoc. editor numerous publs., particularly specializing in atomic physics and properties of planetary atmospheres; editor: Venus, 1983; assoc. editor: Planetary and Space Sci. With U.S. Army, 1944—46. Guggenheim fellow, Paris, 1960; recipient Public Svc. award NASA, 1977, 88, 8, achievement awards Disting. Public Svc. medal, 1980, Wellock Disting. Rsch. Accomplishments award U. Mich., 1981, Stephen S. Attwood award Excellence in Engring., U. Mich., 1994; Arctowski medal Nat. Acad. Sci., 1981, Fleming medal Am. Geophys. Union, 1981; Rsch. Excellence award Coll. Engring., 1981; Henry Russel lectr. U. Mich., 1987; Space Sci. award AIAA, 1988; 1st Space Sci. medalist Nat. Space Club, 1989. Fellow AAAS, Am. Phys. Soc., Am. Geophys. Union (pres. solar-planetary rels. 1972-75, v.p. 1969-72, chmn. pub. policies com. 1990-93, Marcel Nicolet lectr. 1993), Mich. Soc. Fellows; mem. NAS (chmn. geophys. sect. 2001—), Internat. Acad. Astronautics. Achievements include participation in Voyager mission to outer planets, Galileo mission to Jupiter, Cassini Mission to Saturn, Planet B Mission to Mars, Spacelab 1, Apollo 17, Apollo-Soyuz, chmn. sci. steering group Pioneer Venus multiprobe/orbiter missions. Home: 1781 Arlington Blvd Ann Arbor MI 48104-4105

DONAHUE, THOMAS REILLY, trade union official; b. N.Y.C., Sept. 4, 1928; s. Thomas Reilly and Mary E. (Purcell) D.; children: Nancy Angela, Thomas Reilly III. BA, Manhattan Coll., 1949; JD, Fordham U., 1956; LLD (hon.), U. Notre Dame, 1980, Loyola U., Chgo., 1984, SUNY, 1988, Manhattan Coll., 1988, U. Mass., 1990, Nat. Labor Coll., 2001. Dir. edn., bus. agt. local 32B Bldg. Svc. Employees Internat. Union, AFL-CIO, 1949-52, dir. contract dept., 1952-57; European labor program coord. Free Europe Com., Paris, 1957-60; asst. to pres. Bldg. Svc. Employees Internat. Union, AFL-CIO, 1960-67; asst. sect. for labor-mgmt. rels. U.S. Dept. Labor, 1967-69; exec. sec. Svc. Employees Internat. Union, 1969-71, v.p., 1971-73; exec. asst. to pres. AFL-CIO, 1973-79, sec.-treas., 1979-95, pres., 1995. Chmn. adv. com. to Sec. of State and Pres. on Labor Diplomacy, 1999—; co-chmn. Found. for Prevention and Early Resolution of Conflict, 1996-97; vice-chmn. Nat. Endowment for Democracy, 1999—. Former mem., bd. dirs. U.S. Cath. Conf. Com. on Social Devel., Coun. on Fgn. Rels., Carnegie Corp., Nat. Urban League, Brookings Instn., Muscular Dystrophy Assn., African Am. Inst.; bd. dirs. Work in Am. Inst., Nat. Planning Assn., Inst. Multi-Track Diplomacy. With USNR, 1945-46. Sr. fellow Work in Am. Inst., 1997—. Democrat. Home: 613 G St SW Washington DC 20024-2439 Office: AFL-CIO 1717 K St NW Ste 707 Washington DC 20036-5331

DONAHUE, TIMOTHY M. communications executive; Pres. McCaw Cellular Comm., 1986-91; pres., gen. mgr. AT&T Wireless of N.Y. and N.J., 1991-96; pres. Nextel Comms. Inc., Reston, Va., 1996-99, pres., CEO, 1999—. Office: Nextel Comm Inc 2001 Edmund Halley Dr Reston VA 20191-3421

DONAHUE, TIMOTHY PATRICK, lawyer; b. Phila., Sept. 7, 1955; s. Joseph Thomas and Margaret Teresa (Golden) D.; m. Diane Gilbert, June 26, 1982; children: Timothy Patrick Jr., Elizabeth O'Reilly. BA, U. Ala., 1977, JD, 1981. Bar: Ala. 1982. Assoc., then ptnr. Clark & Scott, P.A., Birmingham, Ala., 1982-87; assoc. then ptnr. Edmond & Vines, Birmingham, 1987-91; ptnr. Clark & Scott P.C., Birmingham, 1991—; shareholder Bradford & Donahue P.C., 1995—2001, Donahue & Assocs. LLC, 2002—. Mem. Ala. Bar Assn., Ala. Trial Lawyers Assn., Birmingham Bar Assn. (exec. com. young lawyers sect. 1986-89). Roman Catholic. Home: 2044 Magnolia Rdg Birmingham AL 35243-2018

DONALD, AIDA DIPACE, retired publishing executive; d. Victor E. and Bessie DiPace; m. David Herbert Donald; 1 child, Bruce Randall. AB cum laude, Barnard Coll.; MA, Columbia U.; PhD, U. Rochester. Instr. history dept. Columbia U., N.Y.C.; cons. and series editor Hill and Wang Pubs., N.Y.C.; editor Mass. Hist. Soc., Boston, 1960-64, Johns Hopkins U. Press, Balt., 1972-73; social sci. editor Harvard U. Press, Cambridge, Mass., 1973-79, exec. editor, 1979-89, editor in chief, 1989—2000, asst. dir., 1990—2000; ret., 2000. Editor: John F. Kennedy and the New Frontier, 1966, (with David Herbert Donald) Charles Frances Adams Diary, 2 vols., 1965. Columbia U. Dibblee fellow, 1952-53, U. Rochester fellow, 1953-55, 56-57, Oxford U. Fulbright fellow, 1959-60. Fellow AAUW; mem. Am. Hist. Assn., Orgn. Am. Historians. Avocations: writing, tennis, first editions, antique silver, coins.

DONALD, ALEXANDER GRANT, psychiatrist, educator; b. Darlington, S.C., Jan. 24, 1920; s. Raymond George and Chesnut Evans (McIntosh) D.; m. Emma Louise Coggeshall, Oct. 25, 1958; children: Sandy, Mary Chesnut, Marion Lide. BS, Davidson Coll., 1948; MD, Med. U. S.C., 1952. Diplomate: Am. Bd. Psychiatry and Neurology. Intern Jefferson Med. Coll., 1952-53; resident in psychiatry Walter Reed Hosp., 1956-59; dir. Mental Health Clinic, Florence, S.C., 1962-66; dept. commr. S.C. Dept. Mental Health, 1966-67; dir. William S Hall Psychiat. Inst., Columbia, 1967-90; prof., chmn. dept. neuropsychiatry and behavioral scis. Sch. Medicine, U. S.C., Columbia, 1975-90, Disting. prof. neuropsychiatry, assoc. dean ednl. planning, 1990-91, Disting. prof. emeritus, 1991—. Bd. dirs. Health Resource Found. Trustee Richland Meml. Hosp., 1993—2002, vice-chmn., 1997, chmn., 1999; bd. dirs. S.C. Inst. Med. Edn. and Rsch., pres., 1992—96; trustee Palmetto Health Alliance, 1999—, vice-chmn., 2003. Fellow Am. Coll. Psychiatrists, Am. Psychiat. Assn. (pres. S.C. chpt. 1967), So. Psychiat. Assn. (v.p.); mem. AMA, Columbia Med. Soc. (v.p. 1981, del. 1981, pres. 1989-90), Evening Music Club (pres. 1989-90), Alpha Omega Alpha. Presbyterian. Office: U SC Sch Medicine 3555 Harden Street Ext Ste 104 Columbia SC 29203-6894 E-mail: grantd@aol.com. *Accepting responsibility for ones' actions - using one's mind to understand one's self is the highest function of mankind.*

DONALD, ARNOLD W. company executive; m. Hazel Donald; children: Radiah, Alicia, Zachary. BA, Carleton Coll.; BSME, Washington U., St. Louis. Indsl. chem. sales Monsanto Co., St. Louis, 1977—98, sr. v.p., 1998-99; chmn., CEO Merisant Co., 2000—. Home: 1 N Brentwood Saint Louis MO 63105

DONALD, DAVID HERBERT, author, history educator; b. Goodman, Miss., Oct. 1, 1920; s. Ira Unger and Sue Ella (Belford) D.; m. Aida DiPace, 1955; 1 son, Bruce Randall. Student, Holmes Jr. Coll., 1937-39; AB, Millsaps Coll., 1941, LHD, 1976; AM, U. Ill., 1942, PhD, 1946, LHD (hon.), 1992; MA (hon.), U. Oxford, 1959, Harvard U., 1973; LittD (hon.), Coll. Charleston, 1985; D in History, Lincoln U., 1996; LHD, U. Calgary, 2000; LLD, Ill. Coll., 2002; LittD, Middlebury Coll., 2003. Teaching fellow U. N.C., 1942; research asst. history U. Ill., 1943-45, research assoc., 1946-47; fellow Social Sci. Research Council, 1945-46; instr. history Columbia U., 1947-49; assoc. prof. history Smith Coll., 1949-51; asst. prof. history Columbia U. Grad. Faculty, 1951-52, assoc. prof., 1952-57, prof. history, 1957-59, Princeton U., 1959-62; prof. Am. history Johns Hopkins U., Balt., 1962-73, Harry C. Black prof., 1963-73, dir. Inst. So. History, 1966-72; Charles Warren prof. Am. history and prof. Am. civilization Harvard U., 1973-91, prof. emeritus, 1991—, chmn. grad. program in Am. civilization, 1979-85. Vis. assoc. prof. Amherst Coll., 1950; Fulbright lectr. Am. history U. Coll. North Wales, 1953-54; mem. Inst. Advanced Study, 1957-58; Harmsworth prof. Am. history Oxford U., 1959-60; John P. Young lectr. Memphis State U., 1963; Walter Lynwood Fleming lectr. La. State U., 1965; Benjamin Rush lectr. Am. Psychiat. Assn., 1972; Commonwealth lectr. Univ. Coll., London, 1975; Samuel Paley lectr. Hebrew Univ. of Jerusalem, 1991. Author: Lincoln's Herndon, 1948, Divided We Fought, A Pictorial History of the War, 1861-65, 1952, Inside Lincoln's Cabinet: The Civil War Diaries of Salmon P. Chase, 1954, Lincoln Reconsidered: Essays on the Civil War Era, 1956, rev. 3d edit., 2001, A Rebel's Recollections, (G.C. Eggleston), 1959, Charles Sumner and the Coming of the Civil War, 1960 (Pulitzer prize in biography), Why the North Won the Civil War, 1960, rev. edit., 1996, (with J.G. Randall) The Civil War and Reconstruction, 2d edit., 1961, rev., enlarged edit., 1969, (with Jean H. Baker and Michael F. Holt) rev. edit., 2001, The Divided Union, 1961, The Politics of Reconstruction, 1863-67, 1965, The Nation in Crisis, 1861-1877, 1969, Charles Sumner and the Rights of Man, 1970, (with Sidney Andrews) The South Since the War, 1970, Gone for a Soldier, 1975, (with others) The Great Republic, 1977, rev. edit., 1981, 3rd edit., 1985, 4th edit., 1992, Liberty and Union, 1978, Look Homeward: A Life of Thomas Wolfe, 1987 (Pulitzer prize 1988), Lincoln, 1995 rev. edit., 1996, Charles Sumner, 1997, Lincoln at Home: Two Glimpses of Abraham Lincoln's Domestic Life, 1999, We Are Lincoln Men: Abraham Lincoln and His Friends, 2003; editor: War Diary and Letters of Stephen Minot Weld, 1979; gen. editor: Documentary History of American Life, The Making of America Series, 6 vols.; co-editor: (with wife) Diary of Charles Francis Adams, 2 vols., 1964; contbr. articles to periodicals. Recipient Abraham Lincoln Lit. award Union League Club N.Y.C., 1977, C. Hugh Holman prize MLA, 1988, Benjamin L.C. Wailes award Miss. Hist. Soc., 1994, Barondess-Lincoln prize, 1996, Christopher award, 1996, Lincoln prize Gettysburg Coll., 1996, Jefferson Davis award Mus. of Confederacy, 1996, Nevins/Freeman award Chgo. Civil War Round Table, 1999, Joseph R. Levenson award Harvard U. 1993; Guggenheim fellow, 1964-65, 85-86, fellow Am. Coun. Learned Socs., 1969-70, Ctr. for Advanced Study Behavioral Scis., 1969-70, George A. and Eliza G. Howard fellow, 1957-58, sr. fellow NEH, 1971-72. Fellow Am. Acad. Arts and Scis.; mem. Orgn. Am. Historians, Am. Hist. Assn., So. Hist. Assn. (v.p. 1968, pres. 1969), Soc. Am. Historians, Mass. Hist. Soc., Am. Antiquarian Soc., Phi Beta Kappa, Phi Kappa Phi, Pi Kappa Delta, Pi Kappa Alpha, Omicron Delta Kappa. Clubs: Harvard (N.Y.C.); Cosmos, Signet, Fox. Episcopalian. Home: 41 Lincoln Rd PO Box 6158 Lincoln MA 01773-6158 E-mail: donald@fas.harvard.edu.

DONALD, HELEN LOUISE, software engineer; b. Cliftonville, Miss., Mar. 20, 1946; d. James and Aretha (Hall) Stewart; m. Lee Edward Donald, June 14, 1973 (div. Nov. 1985); children: Christopher Edward, Chinue Efia. BS in Math., Tuskegee Inst., 1967; MS in Computer Sci., Newark Coll. Engring., 1972. Dir. Gavin Child Devel. Ctr., Bigbee Valley, Miss., 1967-68; programmer IBM, Morris Plains, N.J., 1968-71; mem. rsch. staff Xerox Palo Alto (Calif.) Rsch. Ctr., 1974-77; dir. computer ctr. Mary Holmes Coll., West Point, Miss., 1977-81; comm. sys. rep. South Ctrl. Bell, Jackson, Miss., 1981-83; asst. prof. Jackson State U., 1982-84; software engr. Hewlett Packard, Cupertino, Calif., 1984-90; ind. contractor Hewlett Packard Applied Materials, Calif., 1991—; bus. owner ComEdDa Computer Svcs., Campbell, Calif., 1991—. Commr. Commn. for Status of Women, Santa Clara County, 1996—2000; bd. dirs. Santa Clara County coun. Girl Scouts U.S., 2001—; youth advisor St. James African Meth. Episcopal Ch. Mem. NAACP (life), NAFE, AAUW Nat. Assn. Univ. Women (founder Silicon Valley br., pres. 2002-), Nat. Assn. Black Telecom. Profls., Nat. Coun. Negro Women (life; publicity chair 1990-92), Black C. of C. (bd. dirs. 1994-98), Met. C. of C., Rotary Internat. San Jose-Willow Glen (bd. dirs., dir. youth and vocat. svcs. 1992-93, 96, Rotarian of the Yr. 1992, pres. 1998-2000). Democrat. Methodist. Avocations: reading, traveling, sewing. Home: 1928 Dandini Cir San Jose CA 95128-3614 Office: ComEdDa Computer Svcs 1928 Dandini Cir San Jose CA 95128-3614

DONALD, JACK C. corporate executive; b. Edmonton, Alta., Can., Nov. 29, 1934; s. Archibald Scott and Margaret Catherine (Cameron) D.; m. Joan M. Schultz, Oct. 29, 1955. Student, Southern Alberta Inst. Tech., 1959. Owner, operator Parkdale Auto Svc., Edmonton, 1957-60; sales mgr. Sanford Oil Ltd., Edmonton, 1960-63, Pacific Petroleums, Edmonton, 1963-64; pres., gen. mgr. Parkland Oil Products, Red Deer, Alta., 1964-71; v.p. mktg. Turbo Resources, Calgary, Alta., 1971-76; pres., chief exec. officer Parkland Industries Ltd., Red Deer, 1977—2001, founder, chmn. bd. dirs., 2001—. Chmn., bd. dirs. Can. Western Bank, Edmonton, Can. Western Trust; v.p., bd. dirs. Deermart Equipment Sales Ltd., Red. Deer, Brandt Industries Ltd., Regina, 1984—; bd. dirs. TransAlta Corp., Ensign Resources Svc. Group Inc., past coun. Inst. Chartered Accts. Alta. Alderman City of Red Deer, 1971-77. Mem.: Rotary. Office: Parkland Properties Ltd 5102 58th St #110 Red Deer AB Canada T4N 2L8 E-mail: jackdonald@telus.net.

DONALD, JAMES, food service executive; Trainee Publix Super Mkts., Inc., 1971-76; mgmt. exec. Fla., Ala. and Tex. divsns. Albertson's, 1976-91; exec. Wal-Mart, 1991-94; sr. v.p., mgr. 130 store ea. divsns. Safeway, Inc., 1994-96; CEO, pres., chmn. Pathmark Stores, Inc., Carteret, NJ, 1996—2002, also chmn. bd. dirs.; pres, North Am. div. Starbucks Corp., Seattle, 2002—. Office: Starbucks Corp 2401 Utah Ave S Seattle WA 98134*

DONALD, JAMES E. career officer; b. Jackson, Miss., Apr. 20, 1949; m. August S. Green; children: Jeff, Cheryl. BA in Polit. Sci. and History, U. Miss., 1970; MPA, U. Mo., 1983; grad., Command Gen. Staff Coll., Nat. War Coll. Commd. 2nd lt. U.S. Army Inf., 1970, advanced through grades to maj. gen., bn. adj./comdr. C Co. 1st Bn., 87th Inf. Regiment, inf. advisor Readiness Group Stewart, inspector gen., inspection team chief 101st Airborne Divsn., bn. exec. officer 2d Bn., 502d Inf. Regiment, bn. comdr. 1st Bn., 502d Inf. Regiment, chief forces team War Plans divsn., Office Dep. Chief Staff, comdr. 1st Brigade, 101st Airborne divsn., chief mil. support divsn., dep. dir. ops./JE U.S. Pacific Command, asst. divsn. comdr. ops. 25th Inf. Divsn. Schofield Barracks, Hawaii-; dep. commdg. gen. U.S. Army Pacific, Ft. Shafter, 1998—. Decorated Def. Superior Svc. medal, Legion of Merit with oak leaf cluster, Bronze Star, Meritorious Svc. medal with four oak leaf clusters, Army Commendation medal with oak leaf cluster, Nat. Def. Svc. medal with svc. star, Armed Forces Expeditionary medal, Kuwait Liberation medal, S.W. Asia Svc. ribbon.

DONALD, JAMES ROBERT, federal agency official, economist, outdoors writer; b. Omega, Ga., Dec. 31, 1933; s. Clinton Ernest and Lorena (Branan) D.; m. Nancy Ripple, Sept. 16, 1961; children: James Gordon, Mary Carol. Cert., Abraham Baldwin Agrl. Coll., 1952; BS, U. Ga., 1954; MS, N.C. State U., 1956; cert. in govt. tng., Mich. State U., 1975. Economist Econ. Rsch. Svc., USDA, Washington, 1957-76, outlook officer World Agrl. Outlook Bd., 1977-81; retired, 1994; chairperson USDA, Washington, 1982-94. Freelance writer on fishing affairs, 1972—. With U.S. Army, 1957-63. Recipient Superior Svc. award USDA, 1968, Presdl. rank award, 1989. Mem. Am. Agrl. Econs. Assn. (Best Info. Bull. award 1976), Bass Angler's Soc. Am. Home: 584 Laurelwood Dr Mineral VA 23117-4734 E-mail: nrd33@ns.gemlink.com.

DONALD, NORMAN HENDERSON, III, lawyer; b. Denver, Nov. 1, 1937; s. Norman Henderson Jr. and Angelene (Pell) D.; m. Alice Allen, Oct. 31, 1970 (div. Aug. 1980); children: Norman H. IV (dec.), Helen P.; m. Kathryn Akers, Sept. 26, 1981 (div. Jan. 1998). AB, Princeton U., 1959; LLB, Harvard U., 1962. Bar: N.Y. 1962. Assoc. Davis, Polk & Wardwell, N.Y.C., 1962-67, Skadden, Arps, Slate, Meagher & Flom, N.Y.C., 1967-68, ptnr., 1968-94. Chmn. bd. dirs. Norwil Holdings, Inc., N.Y.C., Atlanta and Sarasota. Mem. Assn. of Bar of City of N.Y., Practising Law Inst. (editor Reit Restructuring 1977—), St. Paul's Sch. Alumni Assn. (v.p., bd. dirs. 1984-86), Union Club (N.Y.C.), Rotary, Gold Creek Club (Dawsonville, Ga.). Republican. Episcopalian. Home: Mistral Farms 1544 Bailey Waters Rd Dawsonville GA 30534-1807 Office: care Brock & Silverstein 800 3d Ave New York NY 10022 Fax: 706-265-2810. E-mail: mistral@syclone.net.

DONALD, ROBERT GRAHAM, human resources executive; b. Vancouver, B.C., Can., May 22, 1943; came to U.S., 1946; s. H. Graham and Marion O. (Benoit) D.; m. Patricia K. Shea, Oct. 17, 1970; children: Linda M., Lisa A. Student Delaware Valley Coll., Doyleston, Pa., 1961-63; BS, Iowa State U., 1965; grad. exec. program food industry mgmt., Cornell U., 1972. With Grand Union Co., Wayne, NJ, 1968—2000, labor relations asst. Elmwood Park, N.J., 1974-75, dist. sales mgr., 1976-78, dir. personnel, 1978-81, v.p.-personnel and adminstrv. services, 1981-86, v.p. compensation and benefits, 1986-2000; v.p. human resources Prodn. Resource Group LLC, New Windsor, NY, 2000—. Served in U.S. Army, 1966-68. Mem. Soc. for Human Resources Mgmt., Internat. Found. of Employee Benefits, Am. Compensation Assn., Food Mktg. Inst. Benefits Coun., Health Care Equity Action League, Health Care Payor's Coalition N.J., Vt. Employer's Health Alliance. Office: The Grand Union Co 201 Willowbrook Blvd Fl 1 Wayne NJ 07470-7010 E-mail: rdonald@prg.com.

DONALDSON, COLEMAN DUPONT, aeronautical engineer, consultant, aerospace engineer, consultant; b. Phila., Sept. 22, 1922; s. John W. and Renee (duPont) Donaldson; m. Barbara Goldsmith, Jan. 17, 1945; children: B. Beirne, Coleman duPont, Evan F., Alexander M., William M. BS in Aero. Engring., Rensselaer Poly. Inst., 1943; MA, Princeton U., 1954, PhD, 1957. Staff, NACA, Langley Field, Va., 1943-44, head aerophysics sect., 1946-52; gen. aerodynamics USAC, Wright Field, Ohio, 1945-46; aerodynamic evaluation Bell Aircraft, Niagara Falls, N.Y., 1946; sr. cons., pres. Aero Research Assos. of Princeton, N.J., 1954-79, chmn. bd., 1979-86; group gen. mgr. Aero Research Assocs. Princeton Inc., 1986-87; v.p. Titan Systems, Inc., 1986-87; ret., 1987. Cons. missile guidance and control Gen. Precision Equipment Corp., 1957—68; cons. magnetohydro-dynamics Thompson Ramo Woolridge, Inc., 1958—61; cons. aerodynamic heating, gen. aerodynamics Martin Marietta Corp., 1955—72, adv. devel. and tech. ops., 1989—96; gen. editor Princeton series on high speed aerodynamics and jet propulsion, 1955—64; cons. boundary layer stability, aerodynamic heating, missile and ordnance sys. dept. GE, 1956—72; cons. Grumman Aerospace Corp., 1959—72; Robert H. Goddard vis. lectr. with rank of prof. Princeton (N.J.) U., 1970—71, chmn. adv. coun. dept. aerospace and mech. scis., 1973—78; mem. rsch. tech. adv. coun. panel rsch. NASA, 1969—76, hypersonic tech. com., 1986—90; mem. indsl. profl. adv. com. Pa. State U.; mem. Pres.' Air Quality Adv. Bd., 1973—74; chmn. lab. adv. bd. for air warfare Naval Rsch. Adv. Com., 1986—89, DARPA Tech. Adv. Panel on Hydrodynamics and Acoustics, 1991—94; cons. Ctr. Naval Analysis, 1990—98; mem. adv. panel NASA Ctr. Turbulence Rsch., 1993—95. Contbr. articles to profl. jours. Recipient Meritorious Pub. Svc. award, Chief Naval Rsch., 1990. Fellow: AIAA (gen. chmn. 13th aerospace scis. meeting 1975, Dryden Rsch. lectr. award 1971); mem.: Am. Phys. Soc., Nat. Acad. Engring., Delta Phi, Sigma Xi. Home: 7 Merry Point Ter Newport News VA 23606-2824

DONALDSON, EDWARD MOSSOP, research scientist, aquaculture consultant; b. Whitehaven, Cumbria, England, June 25, 1939; arrived in Can., 1961; s. Edward and Margaret Elizabeth (Mossop) D.; m. Judith Denise Selwood, Aug. 8, 1964; 1 child, Heather Jean. BSc with honors, Sheffield (Eng.) U., 1961, DSc, 1975; PhD, U. B.C., Vancouver, Can., 1964. Rsch. scientist Dept. Fisheries and Oceans, West Vancouver, B.C., 1965-97, sect. head fish culture rsch., 1981-89, sect. head biotech., genetics and nutrition, 1989-97, head Ctr. of Disciplinary Excellence for Biotech. and Genetics in Aquaculture, 1987-97, scientist emeritus, 1997—; cons. in aquaculture and the environment, 1997—; dir. Ed Donaldson & Assocs. Ltd. Aquaculture and Fisheries Cons., 2001—. Hon. rsch. assoc. U. B.C., 1979-88, adj. prof., 1988—; cons. finfish aquaculture FAO, UN Devel. Program, Can. Internat. Devel. Agy., Internat. Devel. Rsch. Ctrs., U.S. AID, Office of Tech. assessment of the U.S. Congress, Can. Exec. Svc. Overseas, Sci. Com. on Problems of Environment, WHO, U.S. Seagrant, Portugese Min. of Sci. & Tech., 2002-; mem. Nat. Scis. and Engring. Rsch. Coun. Can., mem. strategic grant selection com. for food agriculture and aquaculture, 1988-93; mem., active in strategic planning for applied rsch. and knowledge com. biotech. B.C. Sci. Coun. Mem. editl. bd. Gen. and Comparative Endocrinology, 1971-78, Can. Jour. Fisheries and Aquatic Sci., 1985-88, Aquaculture, 1983—, sect. editor, 1999—; mem. editl. bd. Can. Jour. Zoology, 1986-91, Revista Italiana de Acquacoltura, 1991-96; contbr. over 400 articles to

sci. jours. and conf. procs.; contbr. to books on endocrinology, biotech. and aquaculture; patentee in field. Recipient award for best publs. in Transactions of Am. Fisheries Soc., 1977, Ministerial Merit award Min. of Fisheries and Oceans, 1989, B.C. Sci. Coun. Gold medal, 1992, Ministries Commendation award, 1997; B.C. Sugar Co. scholar, 1961; NIH fellow, 1964-65; recipient Thomas W. Eadie medal Royal Soc. Can., 1995 Fellow Acad. Sci. of Royal Soc. Can. (mem. Rowmanoswky medal com. 1994, Thomas W. Eadie medal com. 1995-96, life sci. fellowship selection com., 2001-); mem. Can. Soc. Zoologists (councilor 1980-83), World Aquaculture Soc., Aquaculture Assn. Can. Office: Dept Fisheries & Oceans 4160 Marine Dr West Vancouver BC Canada V7V 1N6 E-mail: donaldso@direct.ca.

DONALDSON, JAMES NEILL, banker; b. Washington County, Pa., Mar. 25, 1940; s. James Reed and Mary Alice (Neill) D. BA in Polit. Sci., Westminster Coll., 1962; MEd, U. Pitts., 1965, postgrad. in law, 1962-64. cert. trust and fin. advisor; accredited estate planner. Trust adminstr. Bankers Trust Co., N.Y.C., 1967-70, asst. trust officer, 1970-73, trust officer White Plains, N.Y., 1973-76, officer-in-charge Trust Adminstrv. Unit, 1976, v.p., 1976-78, head trust office, 1978-82, with Trust Adminstrn. Unit, 1982-83; head new bus. devel., trust and estates group Chem. Bank, N.Y.C., 1983-88, head trust and estates adminstrn. mgmt., 1989-90; sect. head mgr. trust and estates adminstrn. Chase Manhattan Bank, N.Y.C., 1990-2001, personal trust sales Global Trust and Fiduciary Unit, 1996-2000; wealth transfer and succession planning J.P. Morgan Chase & Co., N.Y.C., 2001; sr. v.p. regional mgr. wealth mgmt. Hudson United Bank, 2002—. Chase rep. to Corp. Fiduciaries Assn. of N.Y.C.; editl. mini-adv. bd. Trusts & Estates Mag., 1997-2002; lectr. Bank Mktg. Assn. Conf., 1995, 99; mem. Estate Planning Coun. Westchester County (N.Y.), 1975—, bd. dirs., 1980-85, treas. 1986-87, v.p., 1988-89, pres. 1989; mem. Estate Planning Coun. Rockland County (N.Y.), 1973—, pres., 1984-85; mem. Estate Planning Coun. N.Y.C., 1983—, bd. dirs., 1988-91, 97-2000, sec., 2001-02, treas., 2002-03, v.p., 2003—, estate adminstrn. Trust Div., N.Y. State Bankers Assn., 1975, 90, 93, 96, mem. estate planning com., 1980-83, mem. mktg. com., 1984—, chmn. 1989-94. Contbr. articles to profl. publs. Mem. Planned Giving Com., U. Pitts.; mem. planned giving com. N.Y. chpt. Arthritis Found. Mem. Am. Bankers Assn. (adv. com. for trust, asset mgmt. and mktg. conf. 2001—), Phi Kappa Tau. Office: Hudson United Bank Wealth Management 90 Post Road East Westport CT 06880

DONALDSON, JAMES OSWELL, III, neurology educator; b. Butler, Pa., July 19, 1942; s. James Oswell Jr. and Estelle Mathilda (Unverzagt) D.; m. Mary Hoopingarner, Aug. 23, 1969 (div. Dec. 1983); 1 child, Andrew Robert; m. Susan McKernin, Nov. 3, 1984; stepchildren: Brendan McDonald, Ian McDonald. BS, Haverford Coll., 1964; MD, U. Pa., 1968. Diplomate Am. Bd. Psychiatry and Neurology, Am. Bd. Internal Medicine. Intern in medicine Hosp. of U. Pa., Phila., 1968-69, resident, 1969-70, resident in neurology, 1974-76; hon. house physician Nat. Hosp. for Nervous Diseases, London, 1973-74, sr. vis. fellow, 1991; asst. prof. neurology U. Conn. Sch. Medicine, Farmington, 1977-82, assoc. prof., 1982-88, prof., 1988—. Author: Neurology of Pregnancy, 1978, 2nd edit., 1989. Maj. M.C., U.S. Army, 1970-73. Fellow ACP, Am. Acad. Neurology; mem. Am. Neurol. Assn. Office: U Conn Health Ctr 263 Farmington Ave Farmington CT 06030-1840

DONALDSON, JOHN CECIL, JR., consumer products company executive; b. Bklyn., Dec. 8, 1933; s. John Cecil and Josephine (Greason) D.; m. Marilyn J. Smith, Aug. 29, 1959; children: Susan, John III. AB, Brown U., 1956; MBA, U. Pa., 1959; postgrad., Bentley Sch. Acctg., 1957, LaSalle Law Sch., 1959. Various positions Gen. Motors Corp., Flint, Mich., 1960-71, zone mgr. Buffalo, 1971-76, Newark, 1976-77, mgr. forward product planning, 1977-78; from dir. sales and mktg. to v.p. Corbin Ltd., 1979-85; exec. v.p. and gen. mgr. TMG Corp., N.Y.C., 1986—. Pres. Gen. Motors Exec. Club, Newark, N.J., 1977-78. Mem. Am. Mktg. Assn. Republican. Avocations: ice skating, tennis, golf. Home: 36 Nottingham Way Millington NJ 07946-1917 Office: TMG Corp 1290 Avenue Of The Americas New York NY 10104-0101 Address: 101 Baxters Neck Rd Marstons Mills MA 02648

DONALDSON, JOHN WEBER, lawyer; b. Lebanon, Ind., Oct. 13, 1926; s. Fred R. and Esther Ann (Coombs) D.; m. Sara Jane Rudolph, Nov. 22, 1953; children: Carmen Donaldson Cumbee, Catherine Donaldson Buckallew, J. Bradford. AB, DePauw U., 1951; JD, Ind. U., 1954. Bar: Ind. 1954, U.S. Dist. Ind. 1954, U.S. Supreme Ct. 1973. Sole practice law, Lebanon, Ind., 1958-76; ptnr. Hutchinson & Donaldson, Lebanon, 1954-58, Donaldson & Andreoli, Lebanon, 1976-81, Donaldson, Andreoli & Truitt, Lebanon, 1982—. City atty. City of Lebanon, 1965-66; mem. Ind. Gen. Assembly, 1956-58, 60-92, criminal law study commn., 1969-89, commn. on trial cts., 1987-90; chmn. Gov.'s Task Force on Drunk Driving, 1982-88. Served with USN, 1944-49; ATO. Recipient Disting. Svc. award Jaycees, 1958, Boone County Citizen of Yr. award, 1992. Mem. ABA, Ind. Bar Assn., Boone County Bar Assn., Ind. Criminal Law Study Commn., Lebanon Jaycees, Ind. Def. Lawyers Assn., DAV, Am. Legion, Elks, Kiwanis (pres. 1964). Republican. Presbyterian. Avocation: tennis. Address: 129 N Meridian St Lebanon IN 46052-2263

DONALDSON, LEIGH, writer, editor; b. N.Y.C., Mar. 27, 1956; d. Lee Sr. and Geraldine (Rolle) D. BA with honors, U. Mich., 1977; postgrad., U. So. Maine. Editl. asst. Unitarian Universalist Svc. Com., Boston, 1985-87; permissions editor Houghton Mifflin Pub. Co., Boston, 1987-89; reporter Portsmouth Press, N.H., 1989-93; editl./rsch. asst. Ctr. for Humanities U. N.H., Durham, 1996-97; freelance writer, editor; columnist Portland Press Herald. Featured poet Harvard Divinity Sch., Cambridge, Mass., 1985, Stone Soup Poets Series, Boston, 1989, 1st Night Literary Program, Portsmouth, N.H., 1992, Boston Pub. Libr. Reading Series, 1993, U. N.H., Durham, 1993, Critic's Choice, Voice of Am./USIA, 1994, Kittery Art Assn., 1997; panelist I'll Make Me a World: A Century of African American Arts, Portsmouth Music Hall, 1999; leader poetry workshops and readings. Contbr. poetry to Manhattan Poetry Rev., Internat. Poetry Rev., Art Times, Care Rev., Animus, Shooting Star Rev., Catalyst Mag., Hawaii Rev., others. Recipient Abraham Woursell award U. Vienna, 1985, Nat. Press Found. award, 1987, Goldstein Rsch. award John F. Kennedy Sch. Govt., Harvard U., 1994; Martin Dibner Meml. fellow Maine Cmty. Found., 1999. Mem. Maine Writers and Pubs. Alliance, Portland Arts & Cultural Alliance, Sierra Club (Maine chpt.), Maine Hist. Soc., Kittery Adult Edn. Program. Home: PO Box 4363 Portland ME 04101 E-mail: leighd@mailcity.com.

DONALDSON, LISA MILLER, city administration; b. Tallahassee, Fla., Aug. 8, 1963; d. Charles D. and Virginia Reynolds Miller; m. Gary E. Donaldson, July 24, 1993; 1 child, Haley. AA, Fla. State U., 1984; BA, Fla. Atlantic U., 1996. Asst. to CAO Cen. Corp., Ft. Lauderdale, Fla., 1987-88; planner Broward County Govt., Ft. Lauderdale, 1988-91, equal opportunity compliance analyst, 1991-94; cons. The Donaldson Group, Plantation, Fla., 1996-99, pres., 1999—; spl. projects coord. City of Oakland Park, Fla., 1999-2001; commn. adminstr. Ft. Lauderdale City Commn., 2001—. Chair Census 2000 adv. bd. City of Plantation, 1999. Bd. dirs. 1st United Meth. Ch. Adminstrv. Bd., Ft. Lauderdale, 1999; v.p. El Dorado Homeowners Assn., Plantation, 1998—; mem. fin. bd., bd. dirs. Oakland Park Main St. Orgn.; bd. dirs. Downtown Ft. Lauderdale TMA; trustee 1st United Meth. Ch. Mem. Am. Planning Assn., Am. Polit. Sci. Assn., LEAD Alumni (pres. 1993 94), Plantation Jr. Women's Club, Pi Sigma Alpha. Democrat. Methodist. Avocations: gardening, travel, history. Home: 7400 SW 5th St Plantation FL 33317-3805 Office: City Ft Lauderdale 100 N Andrews Ave Fort Lauderdale FL 33301 Fax: (954) 581-6374. E-mail: Donaldsongroup@aol.com.

DONALDSON, LORAINE, economics educator; b. Clearwater, Fla. d. Lonnie Milton and Lois Lorene (Young) D. BSBA, U. Fla., 1960, MA, 1961; D in Bus. Adminstrn., Ind. U., 1965. Asst. prof. Ga. State U., Atlanta, 1964-66, assoc. prof., 1966-70, prof. econs., 1970—94, prof. emeritus, 1994—. Cons. econs., 1964—. Author: Development Planning Ireland, 1966, Economic Development, 1984, Fertility Transition, 1991; contbr. numerous articles to profl. jours. Mem. Am. Econ. Assn., Soc. Internat. Devel., Am. Assn. U. Profs. Democrat.

DONALDSON, LORETTA MARIE, retired librarian; b. Butler, Pa., Jan. 2, 1943; d. Harry Vernon and Anna Agnes (Lehnerd) Kidd; m. Raymond Benjamin Snyder Jr., June 6, 1964 (dec. Dec. 1985); children: Kenneth Scott Snyder, Timothy Patrick Snyder; m. Wilbert James Donaldson, Jr., Oct. 31, 1992 (dec. Dec. 1997). BS in Edn., Clarion U., 1964; MA in English, Slippery Rock (Pa.) U., 1989. Cert. tchr., Pa. Libr. Keystone Oaks High Sch., Dormont, Pa., 1964-66, Butler (Pa.) Area Sr. High Sch., 1966-67, Butler County C.C., 1967—68, English instr., 1988—2001; substitute tchr. Butler Area Sch. Dist., 1971-83; English tchr. Moniteau Jr./Sr. HS, West Sunbury, Pa., 1983—89, libr., 1989—2003; ret., 2003. Advisor Moniteau chpt. Nat. Honor Soc., West Sunbury, 1988-95; libr. specialist Mid. States Evaluation Com., Punxsutawney, Pa., 1987. Editor (newsletter) The Good News, 1987-93. Pub. rels. LWV, Butler, 1989—; personnel mgr. Butler County Symphony, 1994—. Grantee NEH, Ind. U. of Pa., 1986. Mem. NEA, Butler AAUW Investors (pres. Butler chpt. 1990-92, v.p. 1988-90, treas. 1992—), Moniteau Edn. Assn. (negotiation team 1989), Pa. State Edn. Assn. Republican. Methodist. Avocation: world wide travel. Home: 104 Wildwood Dr Butler PA 16002-3906

DONALDSON, MARCIA JEAN, lay worker; b. Wilmington, Del., June 20, 1925; C. Aubrey Smith and Marcia Allen (Hall) Whitman; m. Robert Donald Donaldson, Jan. 8, 1944; children: Robert Gary, Pamela Lynn, David Keith. Student pub. schs., Wilmington. Sunday Sch. tchr., Del., N.J., 1943-70; tchr. Child Evangelism Fellowship, Wilmington, 1943-55, tchr., bd. dirs., 1955-64, dir., 1964-73; pres., exec. dir. Christian Children's Assocs., Toms River, N.J., 1973—. Writer radio and TV syndicated programs worldwide for children; author: (booklet) A 30 Year Adventure; producer, hostess radio and TV program Adventure Pals. Mem. Nat. Religious Broadcasters Assn., Gideons Aux. Office: Christian Children's Assn Inc PO Box 446 Toms River NJ 08754-0446 E-mail: adventurepals@juno.com. *Of all the important achievements one can accomplish in this life I believe the most rewarding is to be able to introduce another person to the one true and living God, who alone can give us real joy and hope and peace.*

DONALDSON, MICHAEL CLEAVES, lawyer; b. Montclair, N.J., Oct. 13, 1939; s. Wyman C. and Ernestine (Greenwood) D.; m. Diana D., Sept. 12, 1969 (div. 1979); children: Michelle, Amy, Wendy. BS, U. Fla., 1961; JD, U. Calif., Berkeley, 1967. Bar: Calif. 1967, U.S. Dist. Ct. (cen. dist.) Calif. 1967, U.S. Ct. Appeals (9th cir.) 1967. Assoc. Harris & Hollingsworth, L.A., 1969-72; ptnr. McCabe & Donaldson, L.A., 1972-79; pvt. practice Law Office of M.C. Donaldson, L.A., 1979-90; ptnr. Dern & Donaldson, L.A., 1990-94, Donaldson & Hart (formerly Berton & Donaldson), Beverly Hills, Calif., 1994—. Lectr. in field; judge, preliminary and finalist judge Internat. Emmys; preliminary judge Night Time Emmys; gen. counsel Ind. Feature Project West, Writers Guild Found.; pres. Internat. Documentary Assn. Author: EZ Legal Guide to Copyright and Trademark, 1995, (booklet) A Funny Thing Happened on the Way to Dinner, 1976; contg. author: Conversations with Michael Landon, 1992, Negotiating for Dummies, 1996, Clearance & Copyright What the Independent Filmmaker Needs to Know, 1997, 2d edit., 2003, Film Secrets, 2003. Bd. dirs. Calif. Theatre Coun., L.A. 1st lt. USMC, 1961-64. Mem. ABA (entertainment and sports sect.), NATAS, Nat. Acad. Cable Broadcasting, Beverly Hills Bar Assn. (chmn. entertainment sect.), L.A. Copyright Soc., pres. Internat. Documentary Assoc. Republican. Avocations: photography, writing, gardening, hiking, skiing. Home: 1057 20th St Santa Monica CA 90403 Office: Donaldson & Hart 9220 W Sunset Blvd Ste 224 Los Angeles CA 90069-3501 E-mail: mcd@donaldsonhart.com.

DONALDSON, MYRTLE NORMA, music educator, musician; b. Priddy, Tex., Feb. 9, 1923; d. Emil Otto and Brunhilda Eleanore (Riewe) Schneider; m. Fletcher William Donaldson, Feb. 12, 1943; children: Patricia Annette, Rebecca Joyce. BA, U. Ariz., 1970; MA, Middle Tenn. State U., 1982. Cert. profl. piano tchr. Tenn. Music Tchrs. Assn., profl. piano tchr.'s cert. Nat. Music Tchrs.' Assn. Organist Luth. chs., Aleman and Austin, Tex., 1937-42, 43-50, Kinston, N.C., 1943, Los Alamos, N.Mex., 1951-53; Ft. Worth, 1954-56; organist Tullahoma, Tenn., 1969-81; piano tchr., 1972-2001. Composer: sonata, 1981, theme and variations, 1980. Mem. Cmty. Concert Bd., Tullahoma, 1973-99; mem. Cmty. Concert Membership Ch., 1974-78, pres., 1978-80, 89-93. Mem. Music Tchrs. Nat. Assn. (coms. 1983-99, cert. 1991), Mid. Tenn. Music Tchrs. Assn. (sec. Murfreesboro chpt. 1975-77, chair membership state 1977-78, pres. Mid. Tenn. chpt. 1979-81, 87-89), Delta Phi Alpha. Republican. Lutheran. Avocations: knitting, sewing, creative memories album, national background of grandparents.

DONALDSON, REBECCA S. elementary education educator, reading specialist; b. Price, Utah, Feb. 8, 1955; d. Joseph Fazzio and Martha Beatrice Cook; m. Brady Evan Donaldson, Jan. 14, 1978; children: Megan, Brady Christopher, Alyssa Nichole. BS, Brigham Young U., 1977; MEd, Utah State U., 1993. Cert. elem. tchr., Utah, reading endorsement; cert. collaborative literacy intervention program early intervention specialist, advanced reading specialist and gifted/talented endorsements. Educator Carbon Sch. Dist., Price, 1979-96; reading specialist S.E. Edn. Svc. Ctr., Price, 1996—2000, staff developer Reading Excellence Act project, 2000—03; Reading First dir. Utah State Office Edn., Salt Lake City, 2003—. State sec. Utah Coun. Internat. Reading Assn., Salt Lake City, 1996-99. Mem. ASCD, Internat. Reading Assn., Assn. Edn. Young Children. Avocations: reading, writing, baking, gardening, home decorating, music. Office: Utah State Office of Edn 250 E 500 S PO Box 144200 Salt Lake City UT 84114-4200 E-mail: rdonalds@usoe.k12.ut.us.

DONALDSON, ROBERT HERSCHEL, university administrator, educator; b. Houston, June 14, 1943; s. Herschel Arthur and Vera Edith (True) D.; m. Judy Carol Johnston, June 27, 1964 (div. Apr. 30, 1984); children: Jennifer Gwynne, John Andrew; m. Sally S. Abravanel, Mar. 31, 1985; children: Mark Elliot, Ryan Scott. AB, Harvard U., 1964, A.M., 1966, PhD, 1969. Prof. polit. sci. Vanderbilt U., 1968-81, assoc. dean Coll. Arts and Sci., 1975-81; provost, v.p. acad. affairs, prof. polit. sci. Herbert H. Lehman Coll. CUNY, 1981-84; pres. Fairleigh Dickinson U., Rutherford, N.J., 1984-90, U. Tulsa, 1990-96, trustees prof. polit. sci., 1996—. Vis. research prof. U.S. Army War Coll., 1978-79; pres. Am. coms. fgn. rels., 2002-. Author: Stasis and Change in Revolutionary Elites, 1971, Soviet Policy toward India, 1974, The Soviet-Indian Alliance: Quest for Influence, 1979, The Soviet Union in the Third World: Successes and Failures, 1981, Soviet Foreign Policy since World War II, 1981, 85, 88, 92, The Foreign Policy of Russia: Changing Systems, Enduring Interests, 1998, 2002. Council Fgn. Relations fellow, 1973-74 Mem. Coun. on Fgn. Rels., Phi Beta Kappa. Republican. Methodist. Home: 6449 S Richmond Ave Tulsa OK 74136-1669 Office: Univ Tulsa 600 S College Ave Tulsa OK 74104-3126 E-mail: robert-donaldson@utulsa.edu.

DONALDSON, SAMUEL ANDREW, journalist; b. El Paso, Tex., Mar. 11, 1934; s. Samuel Andrew and Chloe (Hampson) Donaldson; m. Billie Kay Butler, Nov. 30, 1963 (div.); children: Samuel, Jennifer, Thomas, Robert; m. Janice Claire Smith, Apr. 16, 1983. BA, U. Tex., El Paso, 1955; postgrad., U. So. Calif., 1955—56. Radio/TV news reporter/anchorman WTOP, Washington, 1961—67; Capitol Hill corr. ABC News, Washington, 1967—77, White House corr., 1977—89; panelist This Week With David Brinkley, 1981—96; co-anchor This Week With Sam Donaldson and Cokie Roberts, 1996—2002, Prime Time Live, ABC, 1989—98; chief White House corrs. ABC News, 1998—99; co-anchor 20/20 ABC, 1998—99; anchor SamDonaldson@abcnews.com, 1999—2002, The Sam Donaldson Show, ABC Radio Network, 2001—. Author: (book) Hold On Mr. President, 1987. Capt. U.S. Army, 1956—59. Named Best TV White House Corr. in Bus., The Washington Journalism Rev., 1985, Best TV Corr. in Bus., 1986; recipient Broadcaster of Yr. award, Nat. Press Found., 1998, Best TV Corr. in Bus., 1987, 1988, 1989, 4 Emmy awards, 2 George Foster Peabody awards, others. Mem.: AFTRA (past pres. Washington-Balt. chpt.), Nat. Acad. of Achievement. Office: ABC 1717 Desales St NW Washington DC 20036*

DONALDSON, SARAH SUSAN, radiologist; b. Portland, Oreg., Apr. 20, 1939; BS, RN, U. Oreg., 1961; MD, Harvard U., 1968. Intern U. Wash., 1968—69; resident in radiol. therapy Stanford (Calif.) Med. Ctr., 1969—72; fellow in pediatric oncology Inst. Gustave-Roussy, 1972—73; prof. radiol. oncology Stanford U. Sch. Medicine., 1973—. Office: Stanford U Med Ctr Dept Radio/Oncology 300 Pasteur Dr Stanford CA 94305-5302

DONALDSON, SCOTT, English language educator, writer; b. Mpls., Nov. 11, 1928; s. Frank Arthur and Ruth Evelyn (Chase) D.; m. Janet Kay Mikelson, Apr. 12, 1957 (div.); children— Matthew Chase, Stephen Scott, Andrew Wilson; m. Vivian Lee Baker, Mar. 5, 1982; stepchildren— Janet Breckenridge, Britton Donaldson. BA in English, Yale U., 1951; MA in English, U. Minn., 1952, PhD in Am. Studies, 1966. Reporter Mpls. Star, 1956-58; editor, pub. Bloomington Sun, Minn., 1958-61; exec. editor Sun Newspapers, Twin City suburbs, Minn., 1961-64; asst. prof. English Coll. William and Mary, Williamsburg, Va., 1966-69, assoc. prof., 1969-74, prof., 1974—, Louise G.T. Cooley prof. English, 1984-92. Author: The Suburban Myth, 1969, Poet in America: Winfield Townley Scott, 1972, By Force of Will: The Life and Art of Ernest Hemingway, 1977, (with Ann Massa) American Literature: Nineteenth and Early Twentieth Centuries, 1978, Fool for Love, F. Scott Fitzgerald, 1983, John Cheever: A Biography, 1988, Archibald MacLeish: An American Life, 1992 (Ambassador Book award), Hemingway vs. Fitzgerald, 1999; editor: On the Road, 1979, Critical Essays on F. Scott Fitzgerald's The Great Gatsby, 1984, Conversations with John Cheever, 1987, New Essays on a Farewell to Arms, 1990, Cambridge Companion to Hemingway, 1996; also numerous revs. and articles on Am. lit. and Am. culture. Served with U.S. Army, 1953-56 Recipient Mid Am. award, Soc. for Study of Midwestern Lit., 1996, Monroe K. Spears award, 1999, Robert B. Heilman prize, 2001, Fulbright Sr. lectureship, 1970—71, 1979—80; fellow, Bruern Found., 1972—73, MacDowell Colony, 1980—81, Rockefeller Found., 1982, NEH, 1984—85, 1990—. Mem. MLA, Am. Studies Assn., Fulbright Alumni Assn. (bd. dirs. 1977-80), Authors Guild, Fitzgerald Jurist (hon.) Hemingway Soc. (treas. 1999—, pres. 2000-2002), PEN, Nat. Book Critics Cir., Mpls. Club, Minikahda Club (Mpls.), Cosmos Club (Washington), Phi Beta Kappa. Avocations: tennis, golf, duplicate bridge. Home and Office: Desert Highlands 303 10040 E Happy Valley Rd Scottsdale AZ 85255-2395 E-mail: scottd10@mac.com.

DONALDSON, STEPHEN REEDER, author; b. Cleve., May 13, 1947; s. James R. and Mary Ruth (Reeder) D. BA, Coll. of Wooster, 1968; MA, Kent State U., 1971; LittD (hon.), Coll. of Wooster, 1993. Asst. dispatcher Akron City Hosp., 1968-70; tchg. fellow Kent State U., 1971; acquisitions editor Tapp-Gentz Assos., West Chester, Pa., 1973-74; instr. Ghost Ranch Writers Workshops, N.Mex., 1973-77. Author: Lord Foul's Bane, 1977, The Illearth War, 1977, The Power That Preserves, 1977, The Wounded Land, 1980, The One Tree, 1982, White Gold Wielder, 1983, Daughter of Regals, 1984, The Mirror of Her Dreams, 1986, A Man Rides Through, 1987, The Real Story, 1991, Forbidden Knowledge, 1991, A Dark and Hungry God Arises, 1992, Chaos and Order, 1994, This Day All Gods Die, 1996, Reave The Just, 1999, The Man Who Fought Alone, 2001, (as Reed Stephens) The Man Who Killed His Brother, 1980, The Man Who Risked His Partner, 1984, The Man Who Tried to Get Away, 1990; editor: Strange Dreams, 1993. Recipient John W. Campbell award best new writer World Sci. Fiction Conv., 1979, Best Novel award Brit. Fantasy Soc., 1979, Balrog award for best novel, 1981, 83, for best collection, 1985, Saturn award for best fantasy novel, 1983, Book ofYr. award Sci. Fiction Book Club, 1987, 88, World Fantasy award, Best Collection,2000. Mem. Am. Contract Bridge League, Internat. Assn. for the Fantastic in the Arts, N.M. Shotokan, Life - Dance Kajukenbo. Office: care Howard Morhaim Rm 604 11 John St Ste 407 New York NY 10038

DONALDSON, SUE KAREN, nursing educator, researcher; b. Detroit, Sept. 16, 1943; BSN, Wayne State U., 1965, MSN, 1966; PhD, U. Wash., 1973. Asst. assoc. prof. physiology and nursing U. Wash., Seattle, 1973-78; assoc. prof. physiology and nursing Rush U., Ill., 1978-84, dir. clin. nursing rsch. program, 1980-84; prof. physiology/nursing, former assoc. dean rsch. Sch. Nursing, U. Minn., Mpls., 1984—94; dean Sch. Nursing, Johns Hopkins U., Balt., 1994—2001, prof. physiology and nursing. Grantee, Wash. State Heart Assn., 1973—74, NIH, 1973—96, USPHS, 1980—, Muscular Dystrophy Assn., 1981—. Mem. ANA, AAN, IOM, NAS, Am. Heart Assn., APS, Biophysical Soc. Office: Johns Hopkins U Sch Nursing 525 N Wolfe St Baltimore MD 21205-2110

DONALDSON, THOMAS, ethicist, educator; b. Wichita, Kans., July 23, 1945; s. Paul J. and Louisene (Sadler) D.; m. Sally Leisure, May, 1970 (div. 1973); m. Jean Shephard, Sept. 3, 1977; children: Paul, Keith, Paige. Student, U.S. Naval Acad., 1963-65; BS, U. Kans., 1967, PhD, 1976. Asst. prof. Loyola U., Chgo., 1976-81, assoc. prof., 1981-84, Henry J. Wirtenberger prof. ethics, 1984-88; C. Stewart Sheppard vis. prof. bus. adminstrn. U. Va., Charlottesville, 1988-89; John Carroll prof. bus. ethics Georgetown U., Washington, 1989-92, John F. Connelly prof. bus. ethics, 1992-96; Mark O. Winkelman endowed prof. Wharton Sch., U. Pa., Phila., 1996—. Testified in U.S. Congress (Senate Judiciary Com.) on Sarbanes-Oxley legis., 2002; participant World Econ. Forum, Davos, Switzerland, 2003. Editor: Issues in Moral Philosophy, 1986, Case Studies in Business Ethics, 1987,Ethical Issues in Business, 1979, 83, 87, 92; author: The Ethics of International Business, 1989, Corporations and Morality, 1982, (with Thomas W. Dunfee) Ties That Bind: A Social Contracts Approach to Business Ethics, 1999; assoc. editor Acad. of Mgmt. Rev., 2002—, mem. editl. bd., 1996-2002; contbr. articles to profl. jours.; mem. editl. bd. Bus. Ethics Quar., 1990—. Mem. Haverford Friends Meeting, 1998—. With USN, 1963-65. Fellow Bus. Enterprise Trust; mem. Ctr. for Advanced Study Ethics (coun. scholars 1990—), Phila. Country Club. Avocations: music, skiing. Home: 214 N Roberts Rd Bryn Mawr PA 19010-2818 Office: U Pa Wharton Sch Philadelphia PA 19104

DONALDSON, WILLIAM HENRY, financial executive, insurance company executive; b. Buffalo, June 2, 1931; s. Eames and Guida (Marx) D.; m. Sept. 17, 1960; children: Adam, Kimberly, Matthew. BA, Yale U., 1953, MA (hon.), 1970; MBA with distinction, Harvard U., 1958; LLD (hon.), Webster U., 1992; DPhil (hon.), St. Lawrence U., 1995; DHL (hon.), Alfred U., 1995. Chmn., chief exec. Donaldson, Lufkin & Jenrette, Inc., N.Y.C., 1959-73; undersec. of state U.S. Dept. State, Washington, 1973—75; spl. cons. to v.p. of U.S. Washington, 1975; dean, Beinecke prof. mgmt. Yale Grad. Mgmt. Sch., New Haven, 1975-80; chmn., CEO Donaldson Enterprises, Inc., N.Y.C., 1980-90; chmn., chief exec. N.Y. Stock Exch., N.Y.C., 1990-95; founder, sr. advisor Donaldson, Lufkin and Jenrette, Inc., 1996-2000; chair., pres., CEO Aetna Inc., Hartford, 2000—02; former chair., CEO Donaldson Enterprises, 2001—; chmn. SEC, 2003—. Bd. dirs. Aetna Life & Casualty, Honeywell Inc., Bright Horizons Family Solutions, Inc., Mail.com Inc. Trustee, chmn. fin. com. Ford Found., N.Y.C., 1968-80; trustee Yale U., New Haven, 1970-75; ptnr. N.Y.C. Partnership; bd. dirs. Bus. Coun. of State of N.Y., 1990-96, Lincoln Ctr. for Performing Arts, N.Y.C.; trustee N.Y. Police Found., Marine Corps Univ. Found., Aspen Inst.; gov. Fgn. Policy Assn.; chmn. Carnegie Endowment for Internat. Peace, 1999-2003. 1st lt. USMC, 1953 55. Recipient Pres.'s Disting. Svc. award SUNY, 1976; named Businessman of Yr., AP, 1969. Mem. Inst. CFAs, Yale Mgmt. Sch. (chmn. bd. advisors 1995-2003), Coun. on Fgn. Rels. Office: SEC Headquarters 450 Fifth St NW Washington DC 20549 E-mail: chairmanoffice@sec.gov.*

DONALDSON, WILMA CRANKSHAW, elementary education educator; b. Havre de Grace, Md., Aug. 28, 1942; d. John Hamilton and Wilma Chaffee (Thurlow) Crankshaw; m. James Neill Donaldson, Aug. 5, 1967. BA in Edn. cum laude, Westminster Coll., 1964; MA in Edn., Fairfield U., 1976. Educator Hurlbutt Elem. Sch., Weston, Conn., 1964-78, 92—, Weston Mid. Sch., 1979-91; tchr. Greek Mythology Elem. Sch., 1999—. Team leader Hurlbutt Elem. Sch., 1967—68, 1976—78, sci. rep., 1992—99, developer of curriculum; judge Odyssey of the Mind, Conn., 1995—2001; tchr. photography and Greek myth courses elem. sch., 2002—; tchr. pvt. student art courses; tchr. Music/Lit./Theater Workshop, 1997—; presenter in field. Author: (filmstrip script) Science Series, 1972, Metric Math Series, 1973. Chairperson fine arts New England Sch. Accreditation Com., Weston, 1990-91; trainer Project CHEM, Exxon Corp., 1991—; state planning com., program/site chmn. Conn. Elem. Sci. Day Conf., 1994—; organizer, advisor Student Elem. Sch. Environ. Orgn., 1992—; co-organizer, co-founder Elem. Family Sci. Night, Weston, 2000; dir./tchr. Camp Invention, Weston, 2002—. Recipient Faculty Mem. Presdl. Recognition Sch. award U.S. Dept. Edn., 1987-88, Celebration of Excellence award State of Conn., 1989, 92, 95, 98. Mem. NEA, Nat. Sci. Tchrs. Assn. (workshop presenter Moscow 1991, NASA-NEWEST awardee 1997), ASCD, Conn. Edn. Assn., Conn. Alliance Arts Edn. (Weston Tchr. of Yr. 1994-95, Conn. Alliance for Art Edn. Disting. Tchr. of Yr. 1995), Coun. Elem. Sci. Internat. (com. chmn. 1991-98), Delta Zeta. Avocations: art, theater, photography, travel.

DONALSON, MALCOLM DREW, classics educator; b. Albany, Ga., July 24, 1951; s. William Levon Donalson and Julia Janet King; m. Deborah Ellen Hoffman, June 25, 1988; children: Christopher Damian, Sabina Anuradha, Zoë Simone, Simon Zachary. BA in Latin and History, Fla. State U., 1974, MA in Classics, 1985, PhD in Humanities, 1991. Ordained clergy F.O.I., 2000; cert. tchr. Latin and history Fla. Tchr. Latin, Greek, and history Marianna (Fla.) H.S.,

1974-84; tchg. asst. dept. classics Fla. State U., Tallahassee, 1984-89; tchr. Latin, Episcopal H.S., Baton Rouge, 1989-90, McKinley Mid. Magnet Sch., Baton Rouge, 1990-91, Istrouma Med. Magnet Sch., Baton Rouge, 1990-91; prof. fgn. langs. Ala. Sch. Math. and Sci., Mobile, 1991—. Author: St. Jerome's Chronicon, 1996, The Domestic Cat in Roman Civilization, 1999, The Cult of Isis in the Roman Empire. Isis Invicta, 2003; contbr. articles. Mem. Am. Classical League, Classical Assn. Midwest and South, Classical Assn. Ala., Women's Classical Caucus. Hindu. Avocation: classical coinage. Office: Ala Sch Math & Sci 1255 Dauphin St Mobile AL 36604-2519 E-mail: malcolmdonalson@aol.com.

DONATELLI, DANIEL DOMINIC, JR., medical/surgical and oncological nurse; b. Youngstown, Ohio; s. Daniel D. Sr. and Nerina J. Donatelli; m. Deborah I. Pihonsky, May 17, 1986; children: Danamarie, Danielle, Deborah. BS in Zoology and Biology, Ohio U., 1981; BSN, Kent (Ohio) State U., 1986; MBA, Youngstown State U., 1999. RN, Ohio; cert. med./surg. nurse, clin. nurse II, oncology nurse. Resident dir. Bromly Corp., Athens, Ohio; asst. mgr. Tel Star Restaurant, Youngstown, 1991-96; asst. clin. nurse mgr. oncology unit Western Res. Care System, Youngstown, Ohio, 1996-2000, nurse clinician dept. quality mgmt., decision support coord., clin. integrations, 2000—. Vol. Athens Mental Health Ctr., 1977-81. Named Nurse of Hope for Mahoning County, Am. Cancer Soc., 1992-94. Mem. ANA, Ohio Nurses Assn. (dist. 3), Sigma Theta Tau. Home: 8499 Ivy Hill Dr Poland OH 44514-5209

DONATH, FRED ARTHUR, geologist, geophysicist; b. St. Cloud, Minn., July 11, 1931; s. Arnold C. and Elizabeth (Crary) D.; m. Mavis Eleanor Hagen, July 19, 1952; children: Robert William, Deborah Ann. BA, U. Minn., 1954; MS, Stanford U., 1956, PhD, 1958. Mem. faculty San Jose (Calif.) State Coll., 1957-58; mem. faculty Columbia U., N.Y.C., 1958-67, prof. geology, 1966-67, U. Ill., Urbana, 1967-80, head dept. geology, 1967-77; cons. U.S. Nuclear Regulatory Commn., 1977-80; pres. CGS, Inc., Urbana, 1980-83; dir., prin. geoscientist The Earth Tech. Corp., Long Beach, Calif., 1983-85, v.p. geoscis., dir. research, 1985-86, v.p. R&D, 1987-88, sr. cons., 1988-90; exec. dir. Inst. for Environ. Edn., Geol. Soc. Am., 1990-94. Advisor Office Sci. and Tech. Policy, 1978-79; mem. U.S. Nat. Com. Rock Mechanics, 1978-81; mem. environ. mgmt. adv. bd. U.S. Dept. Energy, 1992-94, rsch. in exptl. high pressure geophysics, dynamic structural geology, deep geol. disposal of nuclear waste. Editor: Ann. Rev. Earth and Planetary Scis., 1970-80; assoc. editor: Geol. Soc. Am., 1963-73; acting editor, 1964; mem. editl. bd. Engring. Geology, 1964-83, Tectonophysics, 1964-77; contbr. numerous articles on geology and geophysics to sci. jours. Trustee Geol. Soc. Am. Found., 1988-95. Recipient Semicentennial Medallion, Rice U., 1962, Outstanding Contbn. award Am. Geol. Inst., 1994, Outstanding Achievement award U. Minn., 1996; hon. trustee Geol. Soc. Am. Found., 1996—. Fellow Geol. Soc. Am., Geol. Soc. London, AAAS; mem. Am. Geophys. Union (sec. tectonophysics sect. 1964-68, vis. lectr. 1967-72), Am. Assn. Petroleum Geologists (lectr. continuing edn. program 1965-78), Phi Beta Kappa, Sigma Xi. E-mail: donath@uneedspeed.net.

DONATH, JOSEPH, physician; b. Budapest, Oct. 24, 1947; s. Istvan and Margit (Schein) D.; m. Judith Vago Donath, July 4, 1971; children: John, Esther, Aliza. MD, Semmelweis U. Med. Sch., Budapest, 1972. Asst. physician Emil Weil Hosp., Budapest, 1972-76; intern/resident Bronx VAMC, N.Y., 1977-80; fellow in pulmonary medicine Mt. Sinai Med. Ctr., N.Y.C., 1980-82; staff physician Queens Hosp. Ctr., Jamaica, N.Y., 1982-88; chief pulmonary divsn. and dir. MICU St. John's Queens Hosp., Elmhurst, N.Y., 1988—. Contbr. articles to profl. jours. Fellow Am. Coll. Chest Physicians, Am. Coll. Physicians; mem. AMA, Am. Thoracic Soc., Mem. Soc. of the State of N.Y., Med. Soc. of County of Queens. Jewish. Office: 11241 Queens Blvd Forest Hills NY 11375-5564

DONATH, THERESE, artist, author; b. Hammond, Ind., Dec. 14, 1928; Student, Monticello Coll., 1946-47; BFA, St. Joseph' Coll., 1975; additional study, Oxbow Summer Sch. Painting. Radio/TV personality, 1978-92; interviewer, prodr. Viewpoint Sta. WLNR-FM, Lansing, Ill., 1963-64; reporter, columnist N.W. Ind. Sentinel, 1965; freelance writer Monterey Peninsula Herald, 1981-85; contbg. author Monterey Life mag., 1981-85; asst. dir. Michael Karolyi Found., Vence, France, 1979. Creative cons. Aslan Tours and Travel, 1983-85; instr., lectr. Penland, N.C., 1970, Haystack Mountain Sch., Deer Isle, Maine, 1974, Sheffield Poly., Eng., 1978; bd. dirs., sec. Mental Health Soc. Greater Chgo., 1963-64; exec. dir. Lansing (Ill.) Mental Health Soc., 1963-64. One-woman shows include: Palos Verdes (Calif.) Mus., 1974, L.A. Inst. Contemporary Art, 1978, Mus. Contemporary Art, Chgo., 1975, Calif. State U., Fullerton, 1973, No. Ill. U., DeKalb, 1971, Bellevue (Wash.) Mus. Art, 1986-87; represented in permanent collections including Kennedy Gallery, N.Y.C., also pvt. collections; represented in the Mirror Book, 1978; author: Screams and Laughter, 1992; author, illustrator: Before I Die, A Creative Legacy, 1989; contbr. articles to profl. jours., newspapers; illustrator: Run Computer Run. Recipient awards No. Ind. Art Mus., 1966, 70, 71, 73; grantee Ragdale Found., Lake Forest, Ill. 1982. *Settle into old age like a thumb in the mouth. Comfort, not conformity, loom like figures on tapestry. I read my life between the lines.*

DONATICH, JOHN E, publishing executive, writer; b. May 23, 1960; s. Ernest and Mary Donatich; m. Elizabeth S Lerner, Apr. 5, 1982; 1 child, Raffaella. BA, NY U., 1978—82, MA, 1982—84. Dir. nat. accounts Putnam Pub. Group, NYC, 1989—92, Harper Collins, 1992—93, v.p., dir. of product & mktg. dev., 1995—96; v.p., pub. Basic Books, New York, NY, 1996—2003; dir. Yale U. Press, New Haven, 2003—. Recipient GSAS fellowship Scholarship and Stipend, Bush Baer Meml. award for Excellence in the Study of English Lit., Forensic Award in Poetry, Founder's Day award. Mem.: Yale Club. Office: Yale University Press 302 Temple St New Haven CT 06511 Office Fax: 203-432-0948. E-mail: john.donatich@yale.edu.

DONAWAY, CARL D. messenger service executive; Pres. & CEO ABX Air Inc., 1992—2000; pres. & COO Airborne Express, 2000—02; CEO & chmn. Airborne Inc., 2002—. Office: PO Box 662 Seattle WA 98111-0662*

DONBAVAND, JAMES JOSEPH, JR., medical facility administrator; b. Brooklyn, May 28, 1947; s. James Joseph and Gloria Frances D.; m. Nancy Jean Bermingham, Feb. 13, 1971; children: Lisa, James, Thomas, Peter. BBA, Fla. Internat. U., 1974; MBA, Nova U., 1989. Cost acct. Harris Corp., Ft. Lauderdale, Fla., 1974-78; budget analyst Hartford (Conn.) Hosp., 1978-80; budget mgr. Baystate Med. Ctr., Springfield, Mass., 1980-84; mgr. info. analysis and planning Meth. Hosp., Houston, 1984-94; dir. fin. planning Christus Santa Rosa Health Care, San Antonio, 1999-2000; budget and fin. analysis Duke U. Med. Ctr., Durham, NC, 2000—01; sr. corp. analyst Clark Am., 2001—03; mgr. decision support Hillcrest Health Sys., Waco, Tex., 2003—. Bd. dirs., treas. Gandara Mental Health Ctr., Springfield, 1982-84, Housing Cmty. Svcs., Inc., San Antonio, 2002; treas. Boy Scouts Am., Houston, 1985-89. With USN, 1968-72. Republican. Roman Catholic. Home: 31468 Longhorn Trl Bulverde TX 78163-2458

DONDANVILLE, JOHN WALLACE, lawyer; b. Moline, Ill., Nov. 29, 1937; s. Laurence A. and Eva C. D.; m. Maureen C. Ryan, Apr. 16, 1966; children: Edward John, Julie Ann. AB in History, Holy Cross Coll., 1959; JD, Northwestern U., 1962. Bar: Ill. 1962. Ptnr. Baker & McKenzie, Chgo., 1965-97; ret., 1997. Author: Product Liability Trends & Implications, 1970. Mem.: Ill. Bar Assn. Avocation: hiking.

DONDERS, JOSEPH GERARD, priest; b. Tilburg, N. Brabant, The Netherlands, Mar. 11, 1929; came to U.S., 1984; s. Jan P.J. and Riet L. (Panhuijsen) D. BA, Gregorian U., Rome, 1958, MA, 1960, PhD, 1962. Ordained priest, Roman Cath. Ch., 1957. Lectr. Tilburg U., Holland, 1962-68; vis. reader Nairobi Univ., Kenya, 1968-74, prof., chmn. dept. philosophy and religious studies, 1974-84; exec. dir. Africa Faith and Justice Network, Washington, 1984-87; prof. Mission and Cross-cultural Studies Washington Theol. Union, Washington, 1987—. Author: Non Bourgeois Theology, 1986, Jesus the Stranger, 1971 (Nat. Religious Book award 1979), Praying and Preaching the Sunday gospel, 1990 (Cath. Book Club selection 1991), over forty other books in several langs. Mem. U.S. Cath. Mission Assn. (bd. dirs. 1990—), Philos. Assn. of Kenya (founder 1972), Thomistische Vereniging, Teilhard de Chardin Assn. Roman Catholic. Avocations: writing, lectr. tours, travel. Home: 1624 21st St NW Washington DC 20009-1003 Office: Washington Theol Union 6896 Laurel St NW Washington DC 20012-2016 E-mail: donders@wtu.edu.

DONDYSH, VICTORIA, pianist; b. Moscow, July 8, 1963; arrived in U.S., 1976; d. Leon Michael Dondysh and Zhanna N. Stepanitskaya-Dondysh; m. Gary Katz, June 28, 1991; children: Samuel Katz, Elizabeth Katz. Prep. divsn., Julliard Sch. of Music, NYC, 1976—78, Mannes Coll. of Music, 1979—81; MusB, Manhattan Sch. of Music, NYC, 1986, MusM, 1988. Performer: (concerts) Ctrl. Hall Arts, 1975, 2000, Hubbard Hall, 1986, Paul Hall, 1976—78, Soesterberg Music Festival, 2001, Free Libr. of Westhampton, 2001, Clayton - Liberatore Gallery, 2002, Fairleigh Dickenson U., 2002, Roger Meml. Libr., 2003; author: Children's Art Composer edit., 1992; appearances: on radio and TV; performer: (albums) Victoria Dondysh Piano Recital. Recipient Young Artists Competition, Hoppauge, NY, 1978; grantee scholarship, Julliard Sch. of Music, 1976—79, Mannes Sch. of Music, 1979—81. Mem.: MTNA, Piano Tchr. Congress. Achievements include featured artist at mp3.com. Home: 141 Oakdene Ave Leonia NJ 07605

DONE, ROBERT STACY, educator, consultant; b. Tucson, Apr. 7, 1965; s. Richard Avon Done and Nancy Jane (Meeks) Burks; m. Michele Renae Barwick, May 17, 1987 (div. Mar. 1990); m. Elizabeth Evans Robinson, Feb. 20, 1993; children: Rachel Evans, Ethan James. AS in Law Enforcement, BS in Criminal Justice Adminstrn., Mo. So. State Coll., 1987; MPA, U. Ariz., 1992, MS in Mgmt., 1998, PhD in Mgmt., 2000. Criminal investigator Pima County, Tucson, 1988-99; asst. rsch. prof. U. Ariz., 2000—02. Pres. Data Methods Corp., Tucson, 1984—. Contbr. articles to profl. jours. Mem. APA, Acad. Mgmt., Soc. Human Resource Mgmt. Home: 805 N Camino Miramonte Tucson AZ 85716-4623

DONEGAN, CHARLES EDWARD, lawyer, educator; b. Chgo., Apr. 10, 1933; s. Arthur C. and Odessa (Arnold) D.; m. Patty Lou Harris, June 15, 1963; 1 son, Carter Edward. BSC., Roosevelt U., 1954; MS, Loyola U., 1959; JD, Howard U., 1967; LL.M., Columbia, 1970. Bar: N.Y. 1968, D.C. 1968, Ill. 1979. Pub. sch. tchr., Chgo., 1956-59; with Office Internal Revenue, Chgo., 1959-62; labor economist U.S. Dept. Labor, Washington, 1962-65; legal intern U.S. Commn. Civil Rights, Washington, summer 1966; asst. counsel NAACP Legal Def. Fund, N.Y.C., 1967-69; lectr. law Baruch Coll., N.Y.C., 1969-70; asst. prof. law State U. N.Y. at Buffalo, 1970-73; assoc. prof. law Howard U., 1973-77; vis. assoc. prof. Ohio State U., Columbus, 1977-78; asst. regional counsel U.S. EPA, 1978-80; prof. law So. U., Baton Rouge, 1980—; sole practice law Chgo. and Washington, 1984—. Arbitrator steel industry, 1972, U.S. Postal Svc., New Orleans, D.C. Superior Ct., 1987—, Fed. Mediation and Conciliation Svc., 1985—, N.Y. Stock Exch.; vis. prof. law La. State U., 1981, N.C. Cen. U., Durham, 1988—, So. U., Baton Rouge, spring 1992; real estate broker; mem. bd. consumer claims Dist. D.C., 1988—; mem. Mayor's Transition Task Force, Washington, 1995; moot ct. judge Georgetown U. Law Sch., Washington, 1987—, Howard U. Law Sch., Washington, 1987—, Balsa, 1987—; spkr. in field. Author: Discrimination in Public Employment, 1975; contbr. articles to profl. jours. Active Ams. for Dem. Action; me. adv. com. D.C. Bd. of Edn. Named one of Top 42 Lawyers in Washington Area, Washington Afro-Am. Newspaper, 1993, 94, 95, 96' Ford Found. scholar, 1965-67, Columbia U., 1972-73, NEH Postdoctoral fellow in Afro-Am. studies Yale U., 1972-73. Mem. ABA (vice-chmn. edn. and curriculum com. local govt. law sect. 1972-80, pub. edn. com. sect. local govt. 1974-84, chmn. liaison com. AALS, 1984, chair arbitration sect.), Nat. Bar Assn. (labor and employment law sect., steering com., editor arbitration sect. newsletter 1997—), D.C. Bar Assn., Washington Bar Assn. (chmn. legal edn. com.), Chgo. Bar Assn., Fed. Bar Assn., Cook County Bar Assn., Am. Arbitration Assn. (arbitrator), D.C. Fee Arbitration Bd. (bd. govs. 1990—), Nat. Conf. Black Lawyers (bd. organizers), Nat. Futures Assn. (arbitrator), Nat. Assn. Securities Dealers (arbitrator), Assn. Henri Capitant, Roosevelt U. Alumni Assn. (rep. at George Washington U. 175th anniversary charter day convocation 1996), Loyola U. Alumni Assn. (v.p. Washington), Howard U. Alumni Assn. (rep. at Hunter Coll. Centennial 1970), Columbia U. Alumni Assn. (v.p. law Washington), Alpha Phi Alpha, Phi Alpha Kappa, Phi Alpha Delta. Home: 4315 Argyle Ter NW Washington DC 20011-4243 Office: 601 Pennsylvania Ave NW Ste 900 Washington DC 20004-3615 also: 311 S Wacker Dr Ste 4550 Chicago IL 60606-6622 *I have always tried to do my best and never give in to obstacles. I have also been blessed with wonderful parents, relatives, friends, teachers and mentors who had confidence in me.*

DONEGAN, CHERYL, artist; b. New Haven, 1962; BFA in Painting, R.I. Sch. Design, 1984; MFA, Hunter Coll., 1990. Artist-in-residence Banff Ctr. Fine Arts, Alta., Canada, 1985. One-woman shows include Elizabeth Koury Gallery, N.Y.C., 1993, Studio Guenzani, Milan, Italy, 1994, All Girls, Berlin, 1994, Galerie Rizzo, Paris, 1994, Nice Fine Arts, France, 1994, Basilico Fine Arts, N.Y.C., 1996—97, Baumgartner Galleries, Washington, 1997, Lotta Hammer, London, 1998, exhibited in group shows at The Walter Philips Gallery, Banff, 1985, Jon Gerstadt Gallery, N.Y.C., 1986, P.S. 122, 1987, Althea Viafora Gallery, 1990, Simon Watson Gallery, 1990—91, 522 Lafayette St. Space, 1991, Dooley Le Cappelaine Gallery, N.Y.C., 1991, Kim Light Gallery, L.A., 1993, Mus. Contemporary Art, Chgo., 1994, Whitney Mus. Am. Art, 1995, Trans Hudson Gallery, Jersey City, N.J., 1996, 1998, Mus. Modern Art, N.Y.C., 1997, ACC Galerie Wiemar, 1998, Bard Ctr. Curatorial Studies, N.Y., 1999, numerous others; author: The Power of Feminist Art, 1994; contbr. Recipient Grand Prix, 7th Internat. Festival of Saint-Gervais, Geneva, 1997. Office: DIA Ctr for the Arts 542 W 22nd St New York NY 10011-1108 Fax: 212-334-5187.

DONEHEY, MARILYN MOSS, social services executive; b. Malad City, Idaho, Sept. 5, 1946; d. Ray Wesley and LaRue Camp Jones; m. Robert David Donehey, Apr. 15, 1966 (div. June 1989); children: Troy Robert, David Ray, Calli-Anne, Suzanne, Erin. AA, Elgin Cmty. Coll., 1987; BA, Judson Coll., 1992. Sec., receptionist Fox Valley Ctr. for Ind. Livng, Elgin, Ill., 1987-88, devel. dir., 1990-91; cmty. outreach specialist Tri-County Ind. Living Ctr., Akron, Ohio, 1993-94; program dir. Soc. of the Blind, Akron, 1997—2002. Subs. tchr. dispatcher, Ill. Sch. Dist. 300, Carpentersville, 1972-81. Precinct com. person Rep. Cen. Com., Kane County, Ill., 1977-90; pres. Consumer Advocacy coun., Akron, 2000-2002.; participant blindness adjustment program La. Ctr. Blind. Mem. Nat. Fedn. of the Blind (vice chair 1997-2001, sec. 2001-2002, scholar 1987). Republican. Mem. Lds Ch. Avocations: music, writing. Office: Soc of the Blind 325 E Market Akron OH 44304 E-mail: mmoss325@aol.com., Lynssom@aol.com.

DONEHOWER, JOHN W. retired paper company executive; b. Pitts., 1946; m. Elizabeth Donehower; 2 children. BS in Indsl. Engring., Va. Poly. Inst.; M Indsl. Adminstrn., Carnegie-Mellon U. Sr. fin. analyst Kimberly-Clark Corp., Neenah, Wis., from 1974, varous fin. and planning positions in U.S., fin. dir. for Europe, v.p. mktg. and sales for nonwoven products, 1981-82, v.p. splty. papers, 1982; mng. dir. Kimberly-Clark Australia, 1982-85; v.p. prof. health care, med. and nonwoven fabrics Kimberly-Clark Corp., Neenah, 1985-87, pres. splty. products, 1987-90, pres. world support group, 1990-93, sr. v.p., CFO Dallas, 1993—2003; ret., 2003. Bd. dirs. Allendale Mut. Ins. Co., Eastman Chem. Co. Officer USAR ret. Office: Kimberly-Clark Corp 351 Phelps Dr Irving TX 75038

DONEHUE, JOHN DOUGLAS, interdenominational ministries executive; b. Cramerton, N.C., July 9, 1928; s. John Sidney and Annie (Shepherd) D.; m. Mary Phelps, Jan. 9, 1952 (dec. 1964); children: Teresa Jean, Marilyn Phelps; m. Sylvia Louise McKenzie, Feb. 11, 1966 (dec. Nov. 1971); children: Hayden Shepherd, John Douglas; m. Virginia Kirkland, June 28, 1975; children: Anne Mikell, Robertson Carr. Student, Am. Press Inst., Columbia U., 1965, 71-73; LHD (hon.), Charleston So. U., 1985. Sports editor Orangeburg (S.C.) Times and Dem., 1948-50; polit reporter Montgomery (Ala.) Advertiser, 1954-55; sports editor Charleston (S.C.) News and Courier, 1956, copy editor, 1958, state editor, 1959-62, city editor, 1962-68, mng. editor, 1968-71, promotion dir., 1971-75, v.p. for corp. pub. rels., 1975-96; v.p. corp. comm., adminstr. The Post and Courier Found., 1996—; bd. dirs. Star Gospel Mission, Charleston, 1962-80, chmn. bd. dirs., 1980-96, exec. dir., 1996—. Faculty advisor Student Newspaoer, Charleston So. U.; lectr.; spl. adviser comdt. 7th USCG dist. for establishment of dist.-wide pub. info. program, 1960-61; journalism lectr. Charleston So. U.; sec. 1st bd. founders, 1969. Author: Charleston on the Air, A History of Radio Broadcasting in Charleston, 2000; compiler: News and Courier Style Books, 1969; guest commentator Nat. Pub. Radio. Chmn. adv. bd. Salvation Army; chmn. regional adv. coun. S.C. Dept. Youth Svc.; chmn. planning bd. United Way; pres. Palmetto Safety Coun.; chmn. bd. Charleston County Libr. Found.; lay reader, vestryman, sr. warden Episc. Ch.; bd. dirs. Charleston Mus., S.C. Tricentennial Parade Com., 1972, S.C. Humanities Coun. Served with S.C., N.G., 1948—50 USAF, 1950—54 USMCR, 1955—56 USAR, 1956—59 USCGR, 1959—66, served with USNR, 1966—75. Recipient Freedoms Found. award, 1969, S.C. Family of Yr. award, Am. Advt. Fedn., Silver Medal award, 1987, VA citation for meritorious svc., 1971, La Societe Francaise de Bienfaisance Humanitati medal of Honor, 2001. Mem. John Ancrum Soc. of Soc. Prevention Cruelty to Animals, Carolina Art Assn., Internat. Newspaper Promotion Assn., S.C. Press Assn. (pres. 1985), Air Force Assn. (dir. Charleston coun.), Naval Civilian Mgrs. Assn., Navy league (v.p. Charleston coun.), Charleston Trident C. of C. (pres. 1983), Toastmasters Internat. (charter mem. Okinawa club), Okinawa Soc., Downtown Athletic Club, Pacific Stars and Stripes Alumni Assn. (bd. dirs.), Rotary Charleston (pres. 1974-75). Achievements include first to only person who has served in all 5 branches of armed forces per Def. Dept. records. Home: 66 Bull St Charleston SC 29401-1303 Office: Star Gospel Mission PO Box 20235 474 Meeting St Charleston SC 29403-4831 E-mail: ddonehue@charleston.net.

DONELAN, PETER ANDREW, dermatologist; b. Memphis, Nov. 13, 1953; s. Richard T. and Irene M. (Jacobson) D. BA in Chemistry, Wake Forest U., 1975; MD, U. South Fla., 1978. Diplomate, Am. Bd. Dermatology. Intern U. South Fla., Tampa, Fla., 1978-79, resident in internal medicine, 1979-80, resident in dermatology, 1980-83, assoc. clin. prof. medicine, 1984—; instr. dermatologic surgery VA Hosp., 1993—; pvt. practice, Tampa, 1983—. Chief dermatology Tampa Gen. Hosp., 1987-88, U. Conn. Hosp., 1993—. Mem. editorial bd. Bull. Hillsboro County Med. Soc., 1987—. Named to Best Doctors in Am., 1996—. Fellow Am. Acad. Dermatology, Am. Soc. Dermatol. Surgery; mem. Fla. Dermatol. Soc., Leaders Soc. of Dermatology Found., Fla. Med. Soc., Green Jacket Club, Pres.'s Coun. Avocations: golf, skiing. Office: 3000 E Fletcher Ave Ste 200 Tampa FL 33613-4644

DONELIAN, ARMEN, pianist, composer, author; b. N.Y.C., Dec. 1, 1950; s. Khatchik Ohannes and Lillian (Sarkisian) D. Artists cert., Westchester Conservatory Music, 1968; BA in Music, Columbia U., 1972; studies with, Carl Bamberger, Ludmila Ulehla, Harold Seletsky, Richard Beirach. Jazz pianist, composer, 1972—; pvt. tchr. piano and theory, 1965—. Instr. piano Westchester Conservatory Music, White Plains, N.Y., 1972-75, 83-87, instr. theory, 1974-75; instr. piano, ear tng., jazz ensemble New Sch. Jazz Program, N.Y.C., 1986—, William Paterson U., N.J., 1993—; founder Jazz in Armenia Project in cooperation with Yerevan State Cons., 1998—. Composer: (albums) Wave, Mystic Heights, The Wayfarer, Stargazer, Secrets, Trio 87, Sofrito, A Reverie, Hurricane, Positively Armenian 2, others; (film) Passion City (Best Film Score, 1988, Tisch Sch. of Arts, N.Y.U.); performer numerous worldwide tours, TV, radio and film appearances, 1976—; pianist with many jazz artists including Sonny Rollins, Mongo Santamaria, Billy Harper, Lionel Hampton, Chet Baker, Dave Liebman, Paquito D'Rivera, Anne-Marie Moss, Night Ark; author: Training the Ear: For the Improvising Musician, 1992; contbr. articles to Jazz World mag. and Op mag., Downbeat mag., Keyboard mag., Rutgers Ann. Rev. of Jazz Studies. Recipient Cert. of Appreciation, New Sch. U., 1998, Internat. Ptnr./Artslink Collaborative award, CEC, 1999, Fulbright Sr. Specialist award, 2003; fellow Nat. Endowment for Arts Jazz Performance, 1983, 1994, 1996, in composition N.J. State Coun. on Arts, 2000; grantee Meet the Composer, 1979, 1983, 1987, 1999, 2000, Faculty Devel. at New Sch., 1995, Nat. Endowment for Arts Jazz Performance, 1986, 1990, 1992; scholar Fulbright Scholar award, 2002. Mem. Am. Fedn. Musicians (local 802), Steinway Affiliated Artist. Office: New Sch Jazz Program 55 W 13th St Fl 5 New York NY 10011-7958 E-mail: info@armenjazz.com.

DONELSON, JOHN EVERETT, biochemistry educator, molecular biologist; b. Ogden, Iowa, May 23, 1943; s. Mervin E. and Christine (James) D.; m. Linda Meyers, Sept. 16, 1966; children: Christina, Loren, Lyn, Emory. BS, Iowa State U., 1965; PhD, Cornell U., 1971. Postdoctoral fellow MRC Lab. Molecular biology, Cambridge, Eng., 1971-74, Stanford (Calif.) U., 1974; from asst. prof., assoc. prof. to prof. biochemistry U. Iowa, Iowa City, 1975-89, Disting. prof. biochemistry, 1989—, chmn. dept. biochemistry, 1998—; investigator Howard Hughes Med. Ctr. Howard Hughes Med. Inst., Iowa City, 1989-97. Contbr. numerous articles to profl. jours., sci. mags. Vol. Am. Peace Corps, Dormaa, Ghana, 1965-67. Recipient Molecular Parasitology award Burroughs-Wellcome Found., N.C., 1983, Medal of Sci. Achievement award Iowa Gov., 1990. Office: U Iowa Dept Biochemistry Iowa City IA 52242

DONELY, GEORGE ANTHONY THOMAS, III, economist, consultant; b. New Orleans, Aug. 14, 1934; s. George A.T. and Valerie Clare (Burmaster) D.; m. Lisa Suzanne Young, June 30, 1963; 1 child, Valerie Jennie Young. AB in Econs. cum laude, Williams Coll., 1956; MA in Econs., Columbia U., 1958; PhD, U. Mashad, Iran, 1967. Economist Lionel D. Edie & Co., N.Y.C., 1959-60; instr. La. State U., New Orleans, 1960-61; joined Fgn. Service, Dept. State, 1961-69; economist IMF, Washington, 1969-91; mng. dir. sr. vol. program St. Mary's County, Md., 2000—. Cons. Miss Lisa's Sugarless Foods, Inc., Washington, 1985-92. Contbr. articles to profl. jours. Mem. steering com. Friends of Music at Smithsonian, Washington, 1972—; vol. Md. Hist. Trust, Annapolis, 1982—85; mem. restoration adv. bd. Patuxent River NAS; bd. dirs., treas. Chamber Orch. So. Med., 1998—2000; bd. dirs. St. Mary's County Arts Coun., 2002—. Ford Found. fellow Columbia U., 1958. Mem. Am. Econ. Assn., Econ. History Assn., Round Table, St. Mary's River Yacht Club, Met. Club, Williams Club, Rotary (Paul Harris fellow). Home: St Richard's Manor 22880 Old Manor Ln Lexington Park MD 20653-2146

DONENFELD, ALICE R. GREENBAUM, producer, broadcast executive; b. N.Y.C., Oct. 25, 1938; d. Lawrence Samuel and Gladys Ann (Tompkins) Greenbaum; m. Irwin Donenfeld, Apr., 1963 (div. Sept. 1970); children: Mimi Rachel Donenfeld Foss, Harry Lawrence. LLB, N.Y. Law Sch., 1965; LLM, NYU, 1969. Bar: N.Y., 1965. Assoc. Greenbaum, Wolf & Ernst, N.Y.C., 1963-67, Colton, Fembach, Weissberg, N.Y.C., 1968-70; asst. legal counsel Time Inc., N.Y.C., 1970-71; assoc. Harris & Fredericks, N.Y.C., 1973-77; v.p. Marvel Comics Group, N.Y.C., 1977-82; exec. v.p. Filmation Studios, Woodland Hills, Calif., 1982-89; pres. Alice Entertainment, Inc., L.A., 1989—2000, Alice4tv.com, 2000—. Distbr. TV programs to over 100 countries worldwide. Contbr. articles to Copyright Soc.; prodr. (tv series) Internat. Outdoorsman, 1989, (tv series) The Gamesman, 1989, (tv series) Bingo & Molly (Cine Golden Eagle 1998), 1997, UFOs and Aliens: Search for the Truth, 2000, (tv miniseries) Oracles of the Future, 2001, (tv series) World of Dogs Biography, 2002. Spkr. NOW, River Head, N.Y., 1971-72; dir. Coop. Extension, River Head, 1971-72. Mem. Nat. Assn. TV Prodrs. and Execs., Acad. of TV Arts and Scis. Office: PO Box 2087 Thousand Oaks CA 91358-2087

DONENFELD, KENNETH JAY, management consultant; b. Nov. 2, 1946; s. Israel James and Anne (Puretz) D.; m. Sharon Etta Kamer, June 23, 1968; children: Elissa Meredith, Jonathan Lloyd. BA, CUNY, 1967; MA, Syracuse U., 1968; postgrad., N.Y. Inst. Fin., 1971. Mgmt. cons. Georgeson & Co., N.Y.C., 1969-79; exec. v.p., dir. investor rels. divsn. Robert Marston and Assocs., N.Y.C., 1979-89; pres. Robert Marston Investor Rels., Inc., N.Y.C., 1988; exec. v.p. D.F. King and Co., Inc., N.Y.C., 1989-91; pres. The Donenfeld Group, Inc., N.Y.C., 1991—, DGI Investor Rels., Inc., N.Y.C., 1996—. N.Y. State Regents scholar, 1963-67. Merm. Nat. Investor Rels. Inst. (adv. bd. IR mag.), N.Y. Assn. for Internat. Investment, Swedish C. of C., N.Y. Soc. Security Analysts, The Bd. Rm. Club, Media Club. Republican. Home: 15 Maplewood Dr Northport NY 11768-3431 E-mail: donfgroup@aol.com.

DONER, GARY WILLIAM, lawyer; b. Louisville, Nov. 3, 1951; s. Charles and Billie (Miller) D.; m. Cynthia Ann Herman, July 7, 1973; 1 child, Laura. BS, Wright State U., 1974; JD cum laude, U. Toledo, 1990. CPA, Ohio. Tax analyst NCR Corp., Dayton, Ohio, 1975-80; tax mgr. Dayco Corp., Dayton, 1980-85; tax dir. Cooper Tire & Rubber Co., Findlay, Ohio, 1985-99; mgr. fed. taxes Dana Corp., Toledo, Ohio, 1999—. Part-time instr. Owens Coll., Toledo, 1985-86, acctg. adv. com., 1985—; officer Tax Execs. Inst.; pres. Tax Forum, Toledo, 1993. Named Ky. Col. Mem. AICPA, Ohio Soc. CPAs, Tax Execs. Inst., Ohio Bar Assn., Ohio C. of C. (tax com., adv. on taxes). Roman Catholic. Avocations: tennis, weightlifting. Home: 26065 Edinborough Cir Perrysburg OH 43551-9545 Office: DANA Corp PO Box 1000 Toledo OH 43697-1000

DONEY, WILLIS FREDERICK, philosophy educator; b. Pitts., Aug. 19, 1925; s. Willis Frederick and Ora (Powell) D. BA, Princeton, 1946, MA, PhD, 1949; MA, Dartmouth, 1966. Instr. Cornell U., Ithaca, N.Y., 1949-52; vis. lectr. U. Mich., Ann Arbor, 1952; asst. prof. Ohio State U., Columbus, 1953-56, 57-58; George Santayana fellow Harvard U., Cambridge, Mass., 1956-57, vis. lectr., 1963; mem. faculty Dartmouth Coll., Hanover, N.H., 1958—, prof. philosophy, 1966—. Mem. Inst. for Advanced Study, Princeton, N.J., 1972-73; vis. lectr. Harvard, 1963; vis. prof. Edinburgh U., 1980 Author articles on 17th Century philosophy.; Editor: Descartes: A Collection of Critical Studies, 1967, Malebranche: Entretiens sur la Métaphysique, 1980, (with Vere Chappell) Twenty Five Years of Descartes Scholarship 1960-1984: A Bibliography, 1987, Eternal Truths and the Cartesian Circle, 1987, Berkeley on Abstraction and Abstract Ideas, 1989. Ford-Dartmouth fellow, 1970; Camargo Found. fellow, 1978-79 Home: 6 Union Village Rd Norwich VT 05055-9643 also: 3 Rue du Pas de la Mule 75004 Paris France Office: Philosophy Dept Dartmouth Coll Hanover NH 03755 E-mail: willis.f.doney@dartmouth.edu., d2980@aol.com.

DONFRIED, KARL PAUL, minister, theology educator; b. NYC, Apr. 6, 1940; s. Paul and Else (Schmuck) D.; m. Katharine E. Krayer, Sept. 10, 1960; children: Paul Andrew, Karen Erika, Mark Christopher. AB, Columbia U., 1960; BD, Harvard U., 1963; STM, Union Theol. Sem., 1965; ThD, U. Heidelberg, Germany, 1968. Ordained to ministry Lutheran Ch. in Am., 1963; named ecumenical canon Christ Ch. Cathedral, Springfield, Mass., 1977. Assoc. pastor ch., N.Y.C., 1963-64; acting Luth. chaplain (Columbia U.), 1963-64; faculty Smith Coll., Northampton, Mass., 1968—, prof. N.T. and early Christianity, 1968-2000, Elizabeth A. Woodson prof. religion and bibl. lit., 2000—, chmn. dept. religion, 1980-83, 97-00, N.T. panel Nat. Luth.-Roman Cath. dialogue, 1971-73, 75-78, dir. ancient studies, 1994-95. Vis. prof. Assumption Coll., Worcester, Mass., 1975, Amherst Coll., 1976, 78, 85, 2002, St. Hyacinth Coll. and Sem., Granby, Mass., 1976, Brown U., 1979, Mt. Holyoke Coll., 1983, U. Hamburg, 1985, Yale U. Div. Sch., New Haven, 1993, U. Geneva, 2001; Fulbright vis. prof. Hebrew U., Jerusalem, 1997; vis. chaplain Ho. of Reps., 1999; ofcl. rep. Evang. Luth. Ch. in Am. to Signing of Joint Declaration on Justification between Luth. World Fedn. and the Vatican, Augsburg, Germany, 1999. Author: (with R.E. Brown, J. Reumann) Peter in the New Testament, 1973, The Setting of Second Clement in Early Christianity, 1974, (with others) Mary in the New Testament, 1978, The Dynamic Word, 1981; editor: The Romans Debate, 1977, The Romans Debate: New and Expanded Edition, 1991, (with I.H. Marshall) The Shorter Pauline Epistles, 1993, (with Peter Richardson) Judaism and Christianity in First-Century Rome, 1998, (with Johannes Beutler) The Thessalonians Debate: Methodological Discord or Methodological Synthesis?, 2000, Paul, Thessalnica and Early Christianity, 2002; mem. editl. bd. Jour. Bibl. Lit., 1975-81. Mem. Am. Acad. Religion (dir. 1972-73, pres. New Eng. region 1971-72), Studiorum Novi Testamenti Societas (chmn. Paul seminar 1975-78, exec. com. 1979-83, chmn. New Testament Texts in Their Cultural Environment seminar 1990-94, chmn. Thessalonian Correspondence seminar 1995-2000), Soc. Bibl. Lit. (pres. New Eng. region 1975-76), Cath. Bibl. Assn. (participant internat. congresses scholars in Aberdeen, Basel, Bern, Bielefeld, Bonn, Cambridge, Canterbury, Copenhagen, Edinburgh, Einhoven, Göttingen, Heidelberg, Frankfurt, Jerusalem, Louvain, Milan, Montreal, Newcastle, Oxford, Prague, Rome, Sigtuna, Strasbourg, Toronto, Tubingen). Office: Smith Coll Dept Religion Northampton MA 01063-0001 E-mail: kdonfrie@smith.edu. *As the son of immigrant parents, I learned early the value of hard and honest work, the necessity for integrity in all human relations and the blessings of generosity to those less fortunate. These values, together with my commitment to Christianity, have shaped, and continue to shape, my life.*

DONG, HANMIN, forest products executive; b. Hebei, China, Nov. 11, 1960; s. Hongsen Dong and Dabiao Zhang; m. Jun Wen, Dec. 18, 1989; children: Michael, James. Bachelor's degree, Cen. China Agrl. U., Wuhan, 1981; M. Forestry, U. B.C., Vancouver, Can., 1986; PhD, Tex. A&M U., 1990. Project leader Internat. Paper, Bainbridge, 1990-95, China resource mgr. Shanghai, 1995-97; chief rep. Internat. Paper (Asia) Ltd., Shanghai, 1997-2000; gen. mgr. Shanghai Internat. Paper Trading Co., Ltd., Shanghai, 1999-2000; mgr. bus. analysis and planning Masonite Corp., Chgo., 2001; mgr. internat. sales CraftMaster Mfg., Inc., Chgo., 2002—, dir. internat. sales, 2002—. Mem. Soc. of Am. Foresters. Avocation: badminton. Home: 838 N Kenilworth Oak Park IL 60302

DONG, KUI, music educator, composer; d. Naixing Dong and Jiaxin Sun; m. Duo Huang, June 1990. BA, Ctrl. Conservatory of Music, Beijing, China, 1983—87; MA, Ctrl. Conservatory of Music, 1988—89; MusD, Stanford U., 1991—97. Prof. of music Dartmouth Coll., Hanover, NH, 1997—. Composer: The Blue Melody (1st prize Alea III Internat. Composition Competition for Chamber Music, 1994), (3-act ballet) Imperial Concubine Young (Commd. by Ctrl. Ballet Group of China, 1988), Flying Apples (Hon. mention, Prix Ars Electronica Internat. competitions for Computer Music and Art, Linz, Austria, 1996), Pangu's Song (League of Composers/Internat. Soc. of Contemporary Music Internat. composition competition, 2001), Three Voices (Internat. Music Competitions of the Val Tidone, Italy, 1999), Shui Tiao Ge To (Dale Warland Singers New Chorus Music Competition, 2000), Four Image Songs (The Nat. Ann. Collegiate Art Song Competition, first prize, Beijing, China, 1990), Three Piano Pieces (3d prize 1st Nat. Piano Works Competition, 84), Zhan Jing Tang (The Third Nat. Dance & Music Competition, First Music award, Beijing, China, 1989). Recipient Commissioning Award, Koussevitsky Music Found. & Libr. of Congress, 2001, Commissioning award, Mary Cary Flagler Trust Fund, 1999, Commissioning Program Award, Meet The Composer/USA, 1997, ASCAP Award for Young Composers, the Am. Soc. of Composers, Authors and Publishers., 1995; fellow Fellowship for Composers, Santa Clara Art Coun., 1995, Composer Resident Program, Djaressi Found., Bellagio Artist Residency Program, Rockefeller Found., 2000, Gerald Oshita Stipend Fellowship, Djaressi Found., 1995; grantee Rsch. Grant, Asia-Pacific Ednl. Rsch. Grant, Md., ME, 1993, Dickey Ctr. for Internat. Understanding, Dartmouth Coll., Dickey Fundation, 1998, Short-term Travel grant, Internat. Rsch. & Exch. Bd., 2000. Office: Music Dept Dartmouth Coll 6187 Hopkins Ctr Hanover NH 03755 Office Fax: 603-646-2551. E-mail: kui.dong@dartmouth.edu.

DONG, QUAN, ecologist, educator; b. Beijing, July 18, 1954; came to U.S., 1986; s. Chung Cai and Duan Fang (Jiang) D. MS, Duke U., 1992; PhD, Vanderbilt U., 1994. Rsch. asst. Inst. Zoology, Chinese Acad. Scis., Beijing, 1974—77, rsch. fellow, 1982—85; vis. scholar Can. Wildlife Svc., Edmonton, Canada, 1985—86; rsch. asst., teaching asst. Sch. of the Environment, Duke U., Durham, NC, 1986—89; hon. fellow U. Wis., Madison, 1991; fellow Electric Power Rsch. Inst., 1991—93; teaching asst. Vanderbilt U., Nashville, 1993—95; rsch. assoc. U. Miami, Fla., 1995—96, sr. scientific assoc., 1996; environtl. scientist South Fla. Water Mgmt. Dist., 1997—98; rsch. scientist Fla. Internat. U., 1998—2001; ecologist U.S. Nat. Park Svc., Homestead, Fla., 2002—. Sci. advisor U.S.-China Found., 1999—. Writer TV sci. documentary Ctrl. TV Sta. of China, 1983 (Milky Way award 1984); editor Chinese Jour. Applied Ecology, 1996—; author one book; editor Acta Ecologia Sinica; contbr. chpts. to books, articles to profl. jours. Gen. sec., chief editor newsletter Sino-Eco Club, 1994, pres., 1995. Recipient Tng. award World Univ. Svc. of Can., 1985-86. Mem. AAAS, Ecol. Soc. Am., Ecol. Soc. China (coun. mem. 1995), Sigma Xi. Avocations: travel, photography, reading, music, sports. Office: SFNRC/ENP 40001 S R 9339 Homestead FL 33035

DONG, XUZHU, information technology manager; s. Xinyou Dong and Yun Peng; m. Haili Xue; 1 child, Wendy. PhD, Va.Tech., 2002, Tsinghua U., Beijing, 1998. Rsch. scientist Va. Tech., Blacksburg, 1998—2000; project mgr. Eprisolutions, Palo Alto, Calif., 2002—. Office: EPRIsolutions 3412 Hillview Ave Palo Alto CA 94304

DONG, ZHONG, biomedical scientist; b. Guizhou, China, July 10, 1957; m. Misa Mi, Aug. 9, 1988; 1 child, Peter. MS, Guiyang (China) Med. Coll., 1988, MD, 1985; PhD, Wayne State U., 1999. Rsch. asst. Guiyang Trad. Chinese Med. Coll., 1979-80; pathologist Guiyang Med. Coll., 1988-92; grad. tchg. asst. Wayne State U. Sch. Medicine, Detroit, 1995-97, grad. rsch. asst., 1997-99, rsch. assoc., 1999—. Contbr. articles to profl. jours. Recipient Third prize Advancement of Sci. & Tech. Min. Health, China, 1991, Second prize Advancement Sci. & Tech. Gov. of Guizhou Provice, 1990; grant for Young Scientists and Rschrs. Min. of Health, 1990. Avocations: playing violin, collecting stamps, photography. Office: Wayne State U Sch Medicine 9105 Scott Hall 540 E Canfield St Detroit MI 48201-1928 Fax: 313-844-1603. E-mail: zdong@med.wayne.edu.

DONGARRA, JACK, mathematician, educator; b. Chgo., July 18, 1950; s. Joseph and Anne (Danca) D.; m. Susan Sauer, Oct. 4, 1980; children: Nicholas, Benjamin, Katherine. BS in Math., Chgo. State U., 1972; MS in Computer Sci., Ill. Inst. Tech., 1973; PhD in Applied Math., U. N.Mex., 1980. Undergrad. honors participant Argonne Nat. Lab., 1973, resident student assoc., 1973, rsch. assoc., 1974, asst. computer scientist, 1975-80, sr. computer scientist, 1980-89, scientific dir. advanced computing rsch. facility, 1985-89; cons. Los Alamos Scientific Lab., 1978; rsch. asst. U. N.Mex., 1978; disting. scientist U. Tenn., Knoxville, 1989—, Oak Ridge (Tenn.) Nat. Lab., 1989—. Vis. scientist Los Alamos Scientific Lab., 1977, IBM T.J. Watson Rsch. Ctr., 1981; vis. scholar Stanford U., 1979; vis. Ctr. for Supercomputer Rsch. and Devel., U. Ill., Urbana/Champaign, 1985-87; adj. prof. Rice U., 1988—, No. Ill. U., 1988-90; mem. office of advanced scientific computering adv. com. NSF, 1987-90. Mem. editorial bd. Parallel Computing, Jour. Distributed and Parallel Computing, Jour. Supercomputing, Rsch. Monographs on Parallel and Distributed Computing, IMPACT of Computing in Sci. Applications; editor-in-chief Internat. Jour. Supercomputer Application; contbr. articles to profl. jours. Grantee NSF, 1985-88, 87, 87-90, 88 (2), 89—, 90-93, USAF, 1984-87, Advanced Rsch. Projects Agy., 1992—; recipient 4 R & D 100 awards. Fellow IEEE, AAAS, Assn. Computing Machinery (editorial bd. Comm., mem. SIGNUM bd. dirs. 1985-89); mem. NAE, Soc. Indsl. and Applied Math. (coun. mem. 1985—, chmn. supercomputing 1985-88, referee Jour. Numerical Analysis, Jour. Statis. and Sci. Computing, Jour. Discreat Methods). Office: Univ Tenn Dept Computer Sci Knoxville TN 37996-0001

DONGOSKI, CRAIG R. art educator; BFA, Millikin U., 1988; MFA, U. S.D., 1991. Instr. Art Founds. for Tchrs. Elem. Edn. U. S.D., Vermillion, 1988—91; faculty, area chair printmaking Sch. Mus. Fine Arts, Boston, 1991—99; vis. lectr. Sch. Art & Design Ga. State U., Atlanta, 1999—2001, asst. prof. art, 2001—; curator Nat. Screenprint Invitational Sch. Mus. Fine Arts, Boston, 1993. Juror Concord (Mass.) Art Assn. Ann. Juried Exhbn., 1994; vis. artist U. St. Marie, Antwerp, Belgium, 1995, Charles U., Prague, Czech Republic, 1995, U. Windsor, Ont., Canada, 1997; co-curator Volatile Alliances First Africus-Johannesburg Biennale, Johannesburg, 1995; founder, dir. Shifting Grounds: The New Terrain of Printmaking Boston Print Symposium, 1996—97; organizer pilot program Contemporary Art Ctr., North Adams, Mass., 1997; artist resident Franz Mascreel Ctr., Kasterlee, Belgium, 1999; curator Random Channels EYEDRUM Space, Atlanta, 2001; vis. lcctr. Cortona program U. Ga. Studies Abroad, Corona, Italy, 2001; vis. lectr. Kinki U., Osaka, Japan, 2002—; curator That Smell of Beauty The Consulate of the Bolivarian Republic Venezuela Gallery, N.Y.C., 2002; curator, organizer Pulse Field Ga. State U. Galleries, Atlanta, 2003; vis. artist and lectr. in field. Exhibitions include Warren Lee Ctr. for Fine Arts, Vermillion, S.D., 2001, TUBE Space, Atlanta, 2001, Ga. Coll. State U., Milledgeville, 2001, Swan Coach House, Atlanta, 2001, Boston U. Gallery 808, Boston, 2001, Raymond Lawrence Gallery, Atlanta, 2001, Cortona Internat. Symposium, 2001, EYEDRUM Gallery, Altanta, 2001, Savannah (Ga.) Coll. Art and Design Artist Gallery, 2002, Lunar Landing Gallery, Bklyn., 2002, Gusto House Gallery, Kobe, Japan, 2002, Galerie Entropia, Wroclaw, Poland, 2003, Scaldis Room, KBC Tower, Antwerp, Belgium, 2002—03, many others, Represented in permanent collections Antwerpen Mus. Art, The N.Y. Pub. Libr., N.Y.C., The Fogg Mus., Cambridge, Mass., Butler Mus. Am. Art, Stubenville, Ohio, Trenton (N.J.) State Coll., Mus. Fine Arts, Boston, First Am. Bank, Peoria, Ill., U. S.D., Vermilion, Bradley U., Peoria, Ill. Home: 1090 Standard Dr NE Atlanta GA 30319

DONICA, CHERYL MARIE, elementary education educator; b. Greensburg, Ind., Aug. 26, 1953; d. Thurman Lloyd and Kathryn Lucille (Chadwell) D. BS in Edn., Ind. U., 1975, MS in Edn., 1979. Tchr. Decatur County Schs., Greensburg, Ind., 1975-81, Escola Americana de Brasilia, Brazil, 1981-85, Fontana (Calif.) Unified Schs., 1986—. Mentor tchr. Fontana Unified Schs., 1989-92, 93-94, program specialist, 1990-92, 96-99, reading recovery tchr., 1993-98. Reading and Literacy Merit award Arrowhead Reading Coun., San Bernardino, Calif., 1989. Mem. NEA, Calif. Tchrs. Assn., Internat. Reading Assn., Assn. Childhood Edn. Internat. Calif. Kindergarten Assn., Nat. Assn. Edn. of Young Children. Republican. Methodist. Avocations: reading, travel. Home: 1823 Brookstone St Redlands CA 92374-1770 Office: Oak Park Elem 14200 Live Oak Ave Fontana CA 92337-8389 E-mail: cmdca@msn.com.

DONIGER, JAY, health information executive; b. Bklyn., Mar. 22, 1944; s. Irving and Ann Doniger; m. Marcia Sherman, Jan. 26, 1967; children: Elizabeth Einsenberg, Jeremy. PhD, Purdue U., 1972. Asst. biologist Brookhaven Nat. Lab., Upton, NY, 1975—77; sr. staff fellow Nat. Cancer Inst., Bethesda, Md., 1978—89; assoc. prof. Georgetown U. Med. Ctr., Washington, 1989—99; cons. BIO/Info Tech. Link, Bethesda, 1999—2002; pres. BIO Info. Tech. Strategies, Bethesda, 2002—. Mem. of the nat. program com. Biophysical Soc., Washington, 1982; reviewer rsch. grants VA, Washington, 1986; mem. Nat. Ctr. Biotech. Info. Visitor Program Rev. Com., Bethesda, 1990—94, NIH Spl. Rev. Com., Bethesda, Md., 1990; founder, chief sci. officer Am. Med. Records, Washington, 2001. Contbr. chapters to books, articles; mem. editl. bd.: Biophysical Jour., 1983—86. V.p. Ayrlawn Elem. Sch. PTA, Bethesda, 1981—82; mem. biomed. tech. com. No. Va. Tech. Coun., Herdon, 2001—. Recipient predoctoral fellowship, NIH, 1966—72, NIH postdoctoral fellowship, Brandeis U., 1972—75; scholar Reagents scholar, N.Y. State, 1961—65. Mem.: AAAS, Am. Assn. Cancer Rsch., Am. Soc. Photobiology, Biophysical Soc., Genetics Soc. Am.

DONIGER, WENDY, history of religions educator; b. N.Y.C., Nov. 20, 1940; d. Lester L. and Rita (Roth) Doniger; m. Dennis M. O'Flaherty, Mar. 31, 1964; 1 child, Michael Lester O'Flaherty. BA summa cum laude, Radcliffe Coll., 1962; PhD, Harvard U., 1968. Lectr. U. London Sch. Oriental and African Studies, 1968-75; vis. lectr. U. Calif., Berkeley, 1975-77; prof. history of religions Div. Sch., dept. South Asian langs., com. on social thought U. Chgo., 1978-85, Mircea Eliade prof., 1986—. Author: (under name of Wendy Doniger O'Flaherty) Asceticism and Eroticism in the Mythology of Siva, 1973, Hindu Myths, 1975, The Origins of Evil in Hindu Mythology, 1976, Women, Androgynes and Other Mythical Beasts, 1980, The Rig Veda: An Anthology, 1981, Karma and Rebirth in Classical Indian Traditions, 1980, Dreams, Illusion and Other Realities, 1984, Other Peoples' Myths, 1988, (under name of Wendy Doniger), The Laws of Manu, 1991, Mythologies, 1991, Purana Perennis, 1993, The Implied Spider, 1998, Splitting the Difference, 1999, The Bedtrick, 2000, The Kamasutra, 2002; editor Jour. Am. Acad. Religion, 1977-80, History of Religions, 1979—; mem. editl. bd. Ency. Britannica, 1987-98, Daedalus, 1990—. Recipient Lucy Allen Paton prize, 1961, Phi Beta Kappa prize, 1962; Jonathan Fay Fund scholar, 1962, Am. Inst. Indian Studies fellow, 1963-64, NEH summer stipend, 1980, Guggenheim fellow, 1980-81. Fellow: Am. Acad. Arts and Scis., Am. Philos. Soc.; mem.: Assn. Asian Studies (pres. 1998), Am. Acad. Religion (pres. 1984), Phi Beta Kappa. Home: 1319 E 55th St Chicago IL 60615-5301 Office: U Chgo Div Sch 1025 E 58th St Chicago IL 60637-1509

DONKERVOET, RICHARD CORNELIUS, architect; b. Detroit, Oct. 8, 1930; s. Cornelius and Anna Eva Hendrika (Boer) D.; m. Carolyn Eugenia Moore, May 4, 1957; children: Carolyn Daralice Donkervoet Boles, Sharon Elisabeth Donkervoet Credit, John Cornelius. BArch, U. Mich., 1952; MArch, MIT, 1953. Fulbright fellow Tech. U., Delft, Holland, 1954-55; arch. Cochran, Stephenson & Wing, Balt., 1957-63; ptnr. Cochran, Stephenson & Donkervoet, Inc., Balt., 1963-68, exec. v.p., 1968-83, pres., 1983-96, chmn., 1996—. Trustee Roland Park Country Sch., Balt., 1968-75, Balt. Mus. Art, 1970—; pres. bd. trustees Westminster House, Balt., 1975—; pres. bd. dirs. Citizens League Balt., 1980-82. With U.S. Army, 1956-58. Fellow AIA (pres. Balt. chpt., treas. 1966, bd. dirs. 1973, Disting. Svc. awards 1977, 99); mem. Md. Club, Hamilton St. Club (mem. steering com. 1983-88). Avocations: reading, travel, tennis. Home: 13801 York Rd Unit M-12 Cockeysville Hunt Valley MD 21030- Office: C S & D Inc 323 W Camden St Ste 700 Baltimore MD 21201-8601 E-mail: csd@csdarch.com.

DONLAN, THOMAS GARRETT, journalist; b. N.Y.C., Mar. 31, 1945; s. Thomas Garrett and Elizabeth May (Beard) D.; m. Carol Knopes Donlan, Feb. 5, 1972; children: Nicholas G., Alice E. AB, Hamilton Coll., 1967; MA, Ind. U., 1968. Reporter The Record, Hackensack, N.J., 1969-74; newsman AP, Trenton, N.J., 1974-79; assoc. editor Barron's Mag., N.Y.C., 1979-81, Washington editor Washington, 1981-91, editor editorial page, 1992—. Author: Supertech: How America Can Win the Technology Race, 1991, Don't Count On It: Why Your Pension May Be In Jeopardy and How to Protect Yourself, 1994. Mem. Nat. Press Club, Severn Sailing Assn., Sailing Club of the Chesapeake, Annapolis Yacht Club. Avocations: sailing, squash. Home: 6516 Jay Miller Dr Falls Church VA 22041-1135 Office: Barron's Mag 1025 Connecticut Ave NW Ste 800 Washington DC 20036-5419 E-mail: tg.donlan@barrons.com.

DONLE, HAROLD P. director, advocate; b. Meriden, Conn., Nov. 3, 1948; s. Harold P. Donle and Antoinette S. Silvestre. BA in Comm., Ctrl. Conn. State U., 1993; MA in Comm., Purdue U., 2000. Pres., organizer Vietnam Veterans Am. Chpt. 120, Hartford, Conn., 1983—84; pres. Donle Enterprises, Conn., 1985—92; exec. dir. Veterans Ednl. Resources Agy., Hartford, 1992—; lectr. Ind.-Purdue U., Indpls., 2001—; comm. dir. Concerned Citizens Ind., Indpls., 2002—. Actor(director, writer): (plays) Who By Fire. Mem. Indpls. Peace and Justice Ctr., 2002; Conn. spokesperson Clinton/Gore 92 Veterans Rapid Response Team, Hartford, 1992—92; founding mem. Hartford County Green Party, 1995—99. Pvt. first class USMC, 1966—69. Decorated Purple Heart with star USMC. Mem.: Nat. Comm. Assn. Green Party. Avocations: politics, veterans issues, social justice, travel. Office: Indiana-Purdue Univ Indpls 425 University Blvd Indianapolis IN 46205 Personal E-mail: hpdonle@comcast.net. E-mail: hdonle@iupui.edu.

DONLEAVY, JAMES PATRICK, writer, artist; b. Bklyn., Apr. 23, 1926; m. Valerie Heron (div.); children: Philip, Karen; m. Mary Wilson Price (div.); children: Rebecca, Rory. Student, Trinity Coll., Dublin, Ireland. Author: novel, later adapted as play The Ginger Man, 1955; drama Fairy Tales of New York, 1960; A Singular Man novel, later adapted as play, 1963, Meet My Maker the Mad Molecule, short stories, sketches, 1964, The Saddest Summer of Samuel S, novella, later adapted as play, 1966, The Beastly Beatitudes of Balthazar B, novel, later adapted as play, 1968, The Onion Eaters, 1971, The Plays of J.P. Donleavy, 1972; novel A Fairy Tale of New York, 1973; The Unexpurgated Code, A Complete Manual of Survival and Manners, 1975, The Destinies of Darcy Dancer, Gentleman, 1977; novel Schultz, 1979, Leila, 1983, Are You Listening Rabbi Löw, 1987; De Alfonce Tennis, The Superlative Game of Eccentric Champions. Its History, Accoutrements, Rules, Conduct and Regimen, 1984, J.P. Donleavy's Ireland. In All Her Sins and in Some of Her Graces, 1986 (Gold award Worldfest Houston 1993, Cine Golden Eagle award), A Singular Country, 1989, That Darcy, That Dancer, That Gentleman, 1990, The History of the Ginger Man, 1994, Wrong Information is Being Given Out at Pinceton, 1998, (novella) The Lady Who Liked Clean Rest Rooms, 1996, An Author and His Image, 1997; contbr. to numerous mags. and jours. including Times of London, N.Y. Times, Washington Post, Atlantic Monthly, The Daily Telegraph, The New Yorker, Rolling Stone, others; art exhbns.: Painter's Gallery, St. Stephen's Green, Dublin, 1950, 51, Bronxville, N.Y., 1959, Langton Galleries, London, 1975, Godolphin Gallery, Dublin, 1986, Caldwell Galleries, Belfast, 1987, Anna Mei Chadwick Gallery, London, 1989, 91, 94, Alba Fine Art Gallery, London, 1991, Front Lounge Gallery, 1995, Walton Gallery, London, 2002. Served with USNR, World War II. Recipient Creative Arts award Brandeis U., 1961-62; AAAL grantee, 1975 Home: Levington Park Mullingar County Westmeath Ireland

DONLEVY, JOHN DEARDEN, lawyer; b. Chgo., May 29, 1933; s. Frank and Alice Genevieve (O'Connor) D.; m. Kristin Bach Minnick, Apr. 20, 1963 (div. Sept. 1985); 1 son, John Dearden. Student, Stanford U., 1950-52; BS, Northwestern U., 1954; JD, U. Chgo., 1957; postgrad., Northwestern U., 1958. Bar: Ill. 1957, U.S. Dist. Ct. (no. dist.) 1957, U.S. Ct. Appeals (7th cir.) 1969, U.S. Supreme Ct. 1972. Asst. state's atty. Cook County Criminal Divsn., Chgo., 1958-61; city prosecutor City of Evanston, Ill., 1961; assoc. Mayer, Brown & Platt, Chgo., 1962-73, ptnr., 1973-90; pvt. practice law Chgo., 1990—. Participant Hinton Moot Ct. Competition U. Chgo., 1955-56, judge, 1972. Bd. dirs. English-Speaking Union, Chgo., 1964-65; active Rep. Orgn., 1958-60. Recipient Disting. Legal award Am. Legion, Chgo., 1960; named spl. prosecutor-labor racketeering Cook County State's Atty., Chgo., 1959-61; profiled in Lindberg "Summerdale--35 Year Anniversary", 1995. Mem. ABA, Ill. Bar Assn., Chgo. Bar Assn. (criminal law com., chair def. of prisoners com., criminal law and in-court criminal def. panels), Chgo. Athletic Assn. Office: Ste 2040 30 N La Salle St Chicago IL 60602-2506 *I always try to examine problems carefully to obtain a good understanding of them, as with understanding, nothing in life need be feared.*

DONLEY, DEEDRA ANN, medical educator; b. Jacksonville, N.C., Aug. 1966; d. E. Alexander and Martha A. (Turner) Donley. BS in Adminstrn. of Criminal Justice, BA in Psychology, U. N.C., 1988; MS in Orgn. Mgmt., Pfeiffer U., 2001; MEd in Adult Edn., Pa. State U.; PhD in Bus. and Tech., North Ctrl. U., Ariz. Cert. in tng. and devel./adult edn. N.C. State U., notary pub. N.C. AHEC coord. U. N.C. Sch. Medicine, Chapel Hill, 1994—95, registrar, 1995—96, program coord., 1997—98, ops. mgr., 1999—2000, assoc. dir., 2001—. Mem. employee forum U. N.C., Chapel Hill, 1996—2000; pres. Legion Rd. Homeowners Assn., Chapel Hill, 2001—. N.C. scholar, State of N.C., 1984. Mem.: N.C. Substance Abuse Profls., Alliance for Continuing Med. Edn., Am. Coll. Healthcare Execs. Avocations: entertaining, refinishing furniture, reading, travel, dachshunds. E-mail: deedradon@intrex.net.

DONLEY, DENNIS LEE, school librarian; b. Port Hueneme, Calif., July 19, 1950; s. Mickey Holt and Joan Elizabeth (Smith) D.; m. Ruth Ann Shank, June 10, 1972; children: Eric Holt, Evan Scott. AA, Ventura Coll., 1970; BA with honors, U. Calif., Santa Barbara, 1973; MLS, San Jose State U., 1976. Cert. secondary tchr., Calif. Libr. media tchr. San Diego Unified Sch. Dist., 1975—. Lectr. Calif. State U., L.A., 1987-89; libr. cons. San Diego C.C. Dist., 1990; chmn. sch. adv. com. Point Loma H.S., San Diego, 1986-87; coop. book rev. bd. San Diego County, 1984-86; creator adult sch. curriculum, 1984-86; contbr. Deadbase X, Deadbase 94, The Deadhead's Taping Compendium, Vols. 1-3, The Deadhead's Taping Addendum. Mem. ALA, Calif. Libr. Media Educators Assn. Avocations: reading, music, fitness. Office: Hoover HS 4474 El Cajon Blvd San Diego CA 92115-4312 E-mail: ddonley@mail.sandi.net.

DONLEY, JAMES WALTON, management consultant; b. Cleve., June 27, 1934; s. Howard Russell and Mary Louise (Mullikin) D.; m. Frances Elizabeth Jordan, July 5, 1963 (div. Oct. 1983); children: Dana, Elizabeth; m. Mary Todd Mann Goodspeed, May 25, 1985; children: Bennett, Mary Todd, Emily, Jonathan Goodspeed. BA, Denison U., 1958; MBA, U. Pa., 1960. Asst. to pub. Time Mag., N.Y.C., 1960-67; sr. v.p. Thomas J. Deegan Co., N.Y.C., 1967-71; asst. commr. N.Y.C. Dept. Commerce, 1971-72; asst. sec. U.S. Dept. Treasury, Wash., 1972-74; chmn. Donley Comm., N.Y.C., 1974—; country dir. Bulgaria Internat. Exec. Svc. Corps, Sofia, 1995—2003; v.p. Donley Farm Co., Boston Mills, Ohio, 1998—. Bd. dirs. Technoserve, Inc. Mem. bd. visitors Western Res. Acad., Hudson, Ohio, mem. bd. advisors Internat. Exec. Svc. Corps, Stamford, Conn.; bd. dirs. Greenwich C. of C., 1999—. With U.S. Army, 1954-56, Germany. Mem. Round Hill Club, Belle Haven Club. Republican. Congregationalist. Home: 28 Wooddale Rd Greenwich CT 06830-3824

DONLEY, JERRY ALAN, lawyer; b. Denver, Feb. 17, 1930; s. Richard O. and Mildred K. (Bailey) D.; m. Dorothy Jean Mayhew, Sept. 5, 1953; children— Charles Alan, Jack Edward, David William. B.A., Beloit Coll., 1951; LL.B., U. Mich., 1954. Bar: Colo. 1954, U.S. Dist. Ct. Colo. 1954, U.S. Supreme Ct. 1977. Atty. Legal Aid Soc., Colorado Springs, Colo., 1957; dep. dist. atty. 4th Jud. Dist., Colorado Springs, 1957-60; sole practice, Colorado Springs, 1960-64; ptnr. Rector, Kane & Donley, 1964-68, Rector, Kane, Donley & Wills, 1968-71, Kane, Donley & Wills, 1971-83, Kane & Donley, 1983-90, Kane, Donley & Shaffer, 1990—. Active 1st Presbyterian Ch. of Colorado Springs; bd. dirs. Boys Club Colorado Springs and Vicinity, Colorado Springs Charter Assn., Pikes Peak Road Runners; mem. track and field com Colo. Assn. of Athletic Congress; chmn. masters track and field com. Athletics Congress U.S.A., 1984-85. Served to cpl. U.S. Army, 1954-56. Mem. Colorado Springs Estate Planning Council (sec. 1979), Colorado Springs Jaycees (bd. dirs.), El Paso County Bar Assn. Lodge: Kiwanis. Home: 2354 Wood Ave Colorado Springs CO 80907-6775

DONLEY, RUSSELL LEE, III, former state legislator; b. Salt Lake City, Feb. 3, 1939; s. Lee and Leona (Sherwood) Donley; m. Karen Kocherhans, June 4, 1960; children: Tammera Sue, Tonya Kay, Christina Lynn. BSCE with honors, U. Wyo., 1961; MS in Engring., U. Fla., 1962. From mem. to spkr. of house Wyo. Ho. of Reps., 1969-84; chmn. bd. Nat. Ctr. Constl. Studies, Wyo. region, 1983-87; CEO Constitution Schs. Inc., Casper, 1987—; owner Russell L. Donley & Assocs., 1988—. Chmn. appropriations com. Wyo. Ho. of Reps., 1975—78, chmn. legis. mgmt. coun., 1983—84. Pres. bd. dirs. YMCA, Casper, 1976—77; chmn. western region Coun. State Govts., 1982—83; Rep. candidate for Gov. Wyo., 1986; precinct committeeman Rep. Ctrl. Com., 1987—96; chmn. Wyo. Young Reps., 1968; fin. chmn. Natrona County Rep. Ctrl. Com., 1970; state chmn. Initiative 3 dr. Invest in Wyo. not Wall St., 1994. Named Wyo. Outstanding Young Engr., Sigma Tau, 1974, Disting. Wyo. Engr., Tau Beta Pi, 1976; recipient award for engring. excellence, Am. Cons. Engrs. Coun., Legislator of the Yr. award, Nat. Rep. Legislators Assn., 1981. Republican. Mem. Lds Ch. Home: 1140 Ivy Ln Casper WY 82609-2702 Office: 240 S Wolcott St Ste 234 Casper WY 82601-2552 Business E-Mail: russ.rlda@bresnan.net.

DONLON, JOSEPHINE A. diagnostic and evaluation counseling therapist, educator; b. N.Y.C., Apr. 3, 1921; d. Henry R. and Josephine V. (Klarer) Janssen; m. William James Donlon; children: William James, Gregory A., Michele L., DruAnn. R.N., Englewood (N.J.) Hosp., 1941; BA in Psychology, Colo. Coll., Colorado Springs, 1945; MEd, Nat. Coll. Edn., Evanston, Ill., 1975. Cert. in nursing, spl. edn., Ill., Colo.; specialist in social maladjusted, learning disabled, educable mentally handicapped. Pediatric psychiat. nurse N.Y. State Psychiat. Inst., N.Y.C., 1941-42; supr. psychiat. nursing Colo. U. Psychiat. Inst., 1945-47; pub. health nurse Denver Sch., 1947-48; diagnostic educator Schaumburg (Ill.) Sch. Dist. 54, 1969-78; pvt. practice diagnostic evaluation and counseling Brookeville, Md., 1979-87, Pineland, Fla., 1987—. Leader Girl Scouts U.S.A., 1958-62; previously active PTAs in Colo. and Ill. Mem. Council Exceptional Children, Council for Children with Behavioral Disorders, Council for Ednl. Diagnostic Services. Research in genetic endocrine diseases of pancreas and thyroid and relation to learning and behavior. Home: PO Box 2212 Pineland FL 33945-2212

DONLON, WILLIAM JAMES, retired lawyer; b. Colorado Springs, Colo., Apr. 22, 1924; s. John Andrew and Kathleen M. D; m. Josephine A. Janssen, July 19, 1946; children: William James, Gregory A., Michele, Dru Ann Gazelle. Student, Colo. Coll., 1941-43; BS, U. Denver, 1949, JD, 1950. Bar: Colo. 1950, Ohio 1964, Ill. 1969, U.S. Dist. Ct. Colo. 1956, U.S. Dist. Ct. (no. dist.) Ill. 1974, U.S. Ct. Appeals (10th cir.) 1957, U.S. Ct. Appeals (5th cir.) 1970, U.S. Ct. Appeals (7th cir.) 1974, U.S. Ct. Appeals D.C. 1979, U.S. Supreme Ct. 1965. Dep. clk. Dist. Ct., Denver, 1949-50; pvt. practice Denver, 1953-63; gen. counsel Brotherhood Ry. Airline & S.S. Clks., Freight Handlers, Express & Sta. Empl., Rosemont, Ill., 1963-84, Rockville, Md., 1963-86; ret., 1985. Instr. labor U. Ill., 1972-78. With USAAF, 1942-45. Decorated Air medal with 2 oak leaf clusters; named Ky. Col. Mem. ABA (coun. sect. labor and employment law 1977-86), Ill. Bar Assn., D.C. Bar Assn., Am. Legion, VFW, KC (Grand Knight coun. 10329 1991-93), 34th Bomb Group Assn., Phi Alpha Delta, Phi Delta Theta. Democrat. Roman Catholic. Office: PO Box 2212 Pineland FL 33945-2212

DONMA, HATICE, artist; b. Adana, Turkey, 1931; d. Mehmet Huseyin and Esma Pismis; m. Mustafa Sadik Donma, June 6, 1953; children: Orkide, M. Metin. Diploma, Ministry of Nat. Edn., Turkey. Juror painting contest for 75th anniversary of Republic of Turkey, Ministry of Environment, Dept. Environ. Edn. and Press Office, Istanbul, 1998, Little Picasso Painting Contest, Pfizer, Istanbul, 1998; honored guest Gen. Assembly Meeting, Istanbul Governorship, Istanbul Environ. Coun., 1999; organizer, contbr. tng. of presch. children affected by earthquake disaster; spkr. in field. One-woman shows include U. York, Eng., 1990, Aegean U., Izmir, Turkey, 1991, Conf. Environ. Problems in Developing Countries, Internat. C. of C., 1991 (plaque and cert. acknowledgement 1991), Ministry of Culture, Beyoglu State Gallery Fine Arts, Istanbul, Turkey, 1995, World Trade Ctr., Istanbul, 1997, 19 May U., Samsun, 1997, 99, Gulhane Mil. Med. Acad., Ankara, Turkey, 1998, Bakirkoy Municipality Culture and Art Ctr., 1998, U. Istanbul, 2000, Ministry of Environment, Istanbul Governorship, City Environment Dept., Istanbul, 2000; exhibited in group shows Art in Our Region, Turkish Radio-TV, Mersin, 1990, 1993, From Istanbul, Turkish Radio-TV Internat., Istanbul, 1995, Art and Cinema, Turkish Radio, TV, Antalya, 1998, Green Corner, 1998; artist cover page Exhbns. in World Environment Weeks, A Cross Sectional View from Contemporary Turkish Art by Turkish Profl. Union of the Fine Artistic Work Owners, 1999. Recipient plaque Adana Met. Municipality and Golden Cotton Culture and Art Festival Com., 1993, Habitat II City Summit, Istanbul Carousel Activity Ctr., 1996, Antalya Met. Municipality and Antalya Golden Orange Culture and Art Found., 1998, Ministry of Nat. Edn., 2000, Istanbul (Turkey) Beyogtu Municipality, 2003; recipient Cert. Commendation Istanbul Governorship, City Nat. Edn. Dept., City Environ. and Forestry Dept., 2003. Mem. Painting and Sculpture Museums Assn., Turkish Profl. Union Fine Artistic Work Owners, Soc. Européenne de Culture. Avocations: walking, tracking, instrumental music, floriculture, pets. Office: 9-10 Kisim A-5 A Block # 40 34750 Atakoy Istanbul Turkey Fax: 00-90-212-5608898.

DONNALLY, PATRICIA BRODERICK, writer; b. Cheverly, Md., Mar. 11, 1955; d. James Duane and Olga Frances (Duenas) Broderick; m. Robert Andrew Donnally, Dec. 30, 1977; 1 child, Danielle Christine. BS, U. Md., 1977. Fashion editor The Washington Times, 1983-85, The San Francisco Chronicle, 1985-2000; sr. fashion and beauty editor eLuxury.com, 2000; mng. editor PaperCity mag., 2002—. Recipient Atrium award U. Ga., 1984, 87-89, 90, 94-98, 99, Lulu award U. Ga., 1985, 87, award Am. Cancer Soc., 1991, Aldo award, U. Ga., 1994, George A. Hough III award, U. Ga., 1999. Avocation: travel. E-mail: trish@papercitymag.com.

DONNALLY, ROBERT ANDREW, lawyer; b. Washington, July 10, 1953; s. Reaumur Stearnes and Katherine Ann (Sutliff) D.; m. Patricia Kane Broderick, Dec. 30, 1977; 1 child, Danielle Christine. BA in Psychology, U. Md., 1976; JD, U. Balt., 1980; cert. in bus., Stanford U., 1996. Bar: Md. 1980, Calif. 1986. Pvt. practice, Oxen Hill, Md., 1980-81; rsch. contract staff officer Dept. Def., Ft. Meade, Md., 1981-85; with legal and contractual ops. ARGOSystems, Inc., Sunnyvale, Calif., 1985-90; asst. dir. Inst. Def. Analyses, San Diego, 1990-91; dep. chief counsel ARGOSystems, Inc., 1991-93, chief counsel, corp. sec., 1993-98; chief counsel comms. and infomanagement divsn. Boeing Co., 1997-98; gen. counsel, mng. ptnr. BT Comml. Real Estate, Palo Alto, Calif., 1998-99; assoc. gen. counsel Inhale Therapeutic Sys. Inc., San Carlos, Calif., 1999—. Editor-in-chief The Forum, 1979-80. Active The Pillars Soc./United Way, 1991-98. Waxter Legal scholar U. Baltimore, 1978. Mem. Am. Corp. Counsel, Nat. Contract Mgmt. Assn., Md. Bar Assn., Calif. Bar Assn., Assn. of Silicon Valley Brokers, Tae Kwon Do Assn. (Black Belt), Black Belt, Kukkiwon World Tae Kwon Do Assn. Avocations: martial arts, marathons and triathlons, hiking, travel, reading. E-mail: robertdonnally@hotmail.com.

DONNELL, BRIAN JAMES, lawyer; b. Glen Cove, N.Y., Oct. 27, 1955; s. John Francis and Margaret (Grosek) D.; m. Karen Wachtell, June 20, 1981. BA in Polit. Sci. & Econs, Trinity Coll., 1977; JD cum laude, Boston Coll., 1980. Bar: Conn. 1980, U.S. Dist. Ct. Conn. 1981, U.S. Supreme Ct. 1991, U.S. Ct. Appeals (2nd cir.) 1994. From assoc. to ptnr. Halloran & Sage LLP, Hartford, Conn., 1980—. Editor-in-chief Boston Coll. Law Sch., 1979, Uniform Comml. Code Reporter-Digest, 1980. Mem. U. Hartford Constrn. Inst., 1987—. Mem. ABA, Conn. Bar Assn. (sects. on antitrust, constrn. law exec. com., comml. and bankruptcy law), Hartford County Bar Assn., Am. Arbitration Assn. (panel arbitrators constrn. industry), Pi Gamma Mu. Republican. Office: Halloran & Sage LLP 1 Goodwin Sq Hartford CT 06103-4300 E-mail: donnell@halloran-sage.com.

DONNELL, HAROLD EUGENE, JR., professional society administrator; b. Balt., Mar. 12, 1935; s. Harold Eugene and Ruth Elizabeth (Meeth) D.; m. Rosemary Gatch, Apr. 25, 1959; children— David Crawford, Laurette Butler. BA, Amherst Coll., 1957. Field asst., agt. Equitable Life Assurance Soc., Balt., 1958-61; salesman Eastern Products Corp., Balt., 1961-64, asst. nat. sales mgr., 1964-66; exec. dir. Md. State Dental Assn., Towson, 1966-74, Acad. Gen. Dentistry, Chgo., 1974—. Trustee Am. Fund for Dental Health, 1976-84. Served with U.S. Army, 1957-58. Recipient Disting. Service award N.C. Acad. Gen. Dentistry, 1980; ann. Walter E. Levine Meritorious Service award Alpha Omega, 1970 Fellow Acad. Gen. Denistry (hon.); mem. ADA, Am. Soc. Assn. Execs. (cert. assn. exec.), Assn. Forum, Acad. Gen. Dentistry. Republican. Lutheran. Office: Academy of General Dentistry 211 E Chicago Ave Chicago IL 60611-2637 E-mail: haroldd@agd.org. *Any degree of success I have achieved in this life is a result of dedicatedly applying the talents I have been given or acquired with single minded drive to accomplish specific goals.*

DONNELL, JOHN RANDOLPH, retired petroleum executive; b. Findlay, Ohio, June 22, 1912; s. Otto Dewey and Glenn (McClelland) D.; m. Margaret Louise Watt, Feb. 1, 1939 (dec.); children: John Randolph, Ann (Mrs. R. Kennedy Davis), William Watt, Thomas Blakeman, Richard Holmes; m. Maureen Nahas, July 31, 1981. BS, Case Inst. Tech., 1934. Spl. rep. Marathon Oil Co., Findlay, 1938, asst. to mgr. prodn., 1944-50, treas., 1950-54, v.p. supply and transp., 1954-61, dir., 1954-73, v.p. charge internat. activities, 1961-65, sr. v.p. internat., 1965-67, sr. v.p. corporate planning, 1967-69, sr. v.p. finance and planning, 1969-73; pres. Marathon Internat. Oil Co., 1961-67. Dir. First Nat. Bank Findlay, 1939-83, chmn. bd., 1947-83; dir. Toledo Trust Co., 1958-80, Toledo Trustcorp., Inc., 1970-80 Pres. Bd. Edn. Findlay, 1944-54; Trustee Case Western Res. U., Cleve.; Regional chmn. Boy Scouts Am., 1953-56, mem. nat. exec. bd., 1953-83; bd. dirs. World Scout Found., 1980-88. Mem. Findlay Country Club, Toledo Club, Belmont Country Club (Toledo), The Country Club, Union Club (Cleve.), Rolling Rock Club (Ligonier, Pa.), Bath and Tennis club, Beach Club, Everglades Club (Palm Beach, Fla.), Bailey's Beach Club, Country Club, Chagrin Valley Hunt Club (Cleveland, OH.), Newport (R.I.) Sigma Xi, Tau Beta Pi. Presbyterian. Home: 300 Parc Monceau Palm Beach FL 33480-5113

DONNELL, WILLIAM RAY, small business owner, communications executive; b. Lewiston, Maine, Oct. 3, 1931; s. William Thomas and Gladys Mae (Spinney) D.; m. Mayra Cintia Colon, June 16, 1962 (div. Jan., 1996); children: William Thomas, Jose Ismael, Ariadne Elizabeth. BA, U. Maine, 1959. Comml. capt.'s lic. 1954. Comml. fisherman, Maine, 1948-52, 55-60; tchr. Bath (Maine) Jr. H.S., 1962, substitute tchr., 1963; tchr. Deer Isle (Maine) H.S., 1965, 71, tchr. adult edn., 1976; tchr. St. Jude Integrated H.S., St. Finians, Nfld., Can., 1972, Stonington (Maine) Elem. Sch., 1973; v.p., bd. dirs. Fisheries Comm., Inc., 1977—; owner, operator Donnell's Clapboard Mill, Sedgwick, Maine, 1983—. Recreational dir. City of Bath, 1963, capt. prin comml. passenger schooner 1965-71; remedial instr. Harpwell Islands Sch., Maine, 1965; farmer Deer Isle, 1968-71, 72-78, Highlands, NFld. 1971-72, Sedgwick, 1978—; lectr. in field, guest speaker TV Can.-U.S. offshore boundary issue. Contbg. editor Comml. Fisheries News, 1981-83; editor Maine Comml. Fisheries, 1979-80, Fisheries Fed. Register Rev., 1981-82; author numerous poems. Mem. Gov.'s Lobster Adv. Coun., Maine, 1980-85; candidate state legislature from Bath Area, Sagadahoc County, Maine, 1969; charter mem., bd. dirs. Maine Fisherman's Forum, Inc., 1985; lectr. discussion team Theleme's Laguna Beach, Calif., 1985; co-chmn. Hancock County 4-H Citizenshp Com., 1987-88; mem. exec. com. Hancock County Extension, 1988—; mem. Downeast Resource Conservation & Devel. Coun., 1994—; moderator Sedgwick Town Meeting, 1993-94, 2002—; mem. Sedgwick Budget Com., 1995—; v.p. Brooklin Sedgwick Hist. Soc., 2000-2002. Sgt. U.S. Army, 1952-54, Korea. Decorated Bronze Star, Korean Svc. medal with 2 bronze stars, Combat Infantryman's badge; recipient Poetry award Nfld. and Labrador Arts and Letters Contest, 1972. Mem. Sigma Chi (pres.). Avocations: antique vehicles, vessels and machinery. Home and Office: Donnells Clapboard Mill County Rd Sedgwick ME 04676

DONNELLA, MICHAEL ANDRE, lawyer, pharmaceutical company executive; b. Great Lakes, Ill., Oct. 16, 1954; s. Joseph Anthony and Jacqueline (Reddick) D. BA in Mathematics, Wesleyan U., Middletown, Conn., 1976; JD, U.Chgo., 1979. Bar: Ga. 1979, U.S. Ct. Appeals (D.C. and 11th cirs.) 1980, N.J. 1987. Assoc. Troutman, Sanders et al, Atlanta, 1979-83; atty. AT&T So. Region, Atlanta, 1983-86; sr. atty. AT&T Internat., Basking Ridge, N.J., 1986-95; asst. gen. counsel Am. Home Products Corp., St. Davids, PA, 1995—; v.p., counsel Wyeth-Ayerst Pharmaceuticals, 2000—01; v.p., dep. chief counsel Wyeth Pharms., 2001—. Vis. prof. Nat. Urban League Black Exec. Exchange Program, 1986, Huston-Tillotson Coll., Austin, Tex. Interviewer Wesleyan Schs. Com., Middletown, 1976—; counsel Ga. Legis. Black Caucus, Atlanta, 1982-86; mem. visitors com. U. Chgo. Law Sch., 1989-92. Named to 100 Black Men of N.J., Inc. Black Elected Ofcls. Found. Roman Catholic. Avocations: jazz, sports. Office: Wyeth Pharms 170 N Radnor Chester Rd Saint Davids PA 19087-5221

DONNELLEY, JAMES RUSSELL, printing company executive; b. Chgo., June 18, 1935; s. Elliott and Ann (Steinwedell) D.; m. Nina Louis Herrmann, Apr. 11, 1980; children: Niel J., Nicole C. BA, Dartmouth Coll., 1957; MBA, U. Chgo., 1962. With R.R. Donnelley & Sons Co., Chgo., 1962-2000, v.p., 1974-75, group pres. fin. svcs. group, 1985-87, group pres. corp. devel., 1987-90, vice chmn. bd., 1990-2000, also bd. dirs. Bd. dirs. Sierra Pacific Resources, PMP Inc., Melbourne, Australia. Office: Stet & Query LTD Partnership Ste 1009 360 N Michigan Ave Chicago IL 60601-3803

DONNELLY, BARBARA SCHETTLER, retired medical technologist; b. Sweetwater, Tenn., Dec. 2, 1933; d. Clarence G. and Irene Elizabeth (Brown) Schettler; children: Linda Ann, Richard Michael. AA, Tenn. Wesleyan Coll., 1952; BS, U. Tenn., 1954; cert. med. tech., Erlanger Hosp. Sch. Med. Tech., 1954; postgrad., So. Meth. U., 1980-81. Med. technologist Erlanger Hosp., Chattanooga, 1953-57, St. Luke's Episcopal Hosp., Tex. Med. Ctr., Houston, 1957-58, 62; engring. R&D SCI Systems, Inc., Huntsville, Ala., 1974-76; cons. hematology systems Abbott Labs., Dallas, 1976-77; hematology specialist Dallas, Irving, Tex., 1977-81; tech. specialist microbiology systems Irving, Tex., 1981-83; coord. tech. svc. clin. chemistry systems, 1983-84; coord. customer tng. clin. chemistry systems, 1984-87; supr. clin. chemistry tech. svcs., 1987-88; supr. clin. chemistry customer support ctr., 1988-93; supr. clin. chemistry and x-systems customer support ctr., 1993-97; ret., 1997. Contbr. articles on cytology to profl. jours. Mem. Am. Soc. Clin. Pathologists (cert. med. technologist), Am. Soc. Microbiology, Nat. Assn. Female Execs., U. Tenn. Alumni Assn., Chi Omega. Republican. Methodist. Home: 204 Greenbriar Ln Colleyville TX 76034-8616

DONNELLY, GERARD KEVIN, marketing and retail executive; b. N.Y.C., July 2, 1933; s. Joseph R. and Margaret M. (Siefert) D.; m. Maria McAllister, Aug. 29, 1964; children: Gerard K., Peter F., Deirdre A., Patrick J., James V. BBA in Acctg., Pace U., 1957; cert. in indsl. rels., Colgate U., 1966. Asst. contr. Allied Stores Corp., N.Y.C., 1957-65; gen. auditor Lone Star Industries, N.Y.C., 1965-67; contr., asst. sec. Computer Applications Inc., N.Y.C., 1967-70; pres. Rhodes S.W., Phoenix, 1970-75; sr. v.p. Hart Schaffner & Marx, Chgo., 1975-81; CEO, chmn. bd. dirs. Hughes & Hatcher Inc., Phila., 1981-83; sr. v.p., dir. Macys-N.E. Inc., N.Y.C., 1983-90; pres., CEO H.C. Prange Co., Green Bay, Wis., 1990-94. Mng. cons. Houlihan, Lokey, Howard & Zukin, N.Y.C., 1994-99; mng. dir. GeKayDee Assocs., 1994—; bd. dirs. Frederick Atkins, Inc., N.Y.C., Younkers Inc., Des Moines, Mottahedeh & Co., N.Y.C., H.C. Prange Co., Green Bay, Saks, Inc., Birmingham, Ala. Mem. County Com., Queens County, N.Y., 1955-64; commr. pks. and recreation, Manalapan Twp., N.J., 1967-68; bd. dirs. Ctrl. Bus. Dist. Assn., Detroit, 1981-83, U. Wis. Green Bay Founders Assn., 1991-94. With USN, 1951-53. Mem.: Menswear Retailers Am., Internat. Coun. Shopping Ctrs., Am. Mgmt. Assn., Nat. Retail Fedn., Due Process Golf Club, Celtic Soc. Football (referee), N.Y. Athletic Club, U.S. Power Squadron, Cherry Valley Country Club, KC (4th degree). Roman Catholic. Home: 160 Spring Hill Rd Skillman NJ 08558-1418 Office: 2490 Pennington Rd Ste 201 Pennington NJ 08534

DONNELLY, JAMES CORCORAN, JR., lawyer; b. Newton, Mass., June 10, 1946; s. James C. and Margery J. (MacNeil) D.; m. Carol R. Burns, June 28, 1968; children: James C. IV, Sarah Y. BA, Dartmouth Coll., 1968; JD, Boston Coll., 1973. Bar: Mass. 1973, U.S. Dist. Ct. Mass. 1974, U.S. Ct. Appeals (7th cir.) 1979, U.S. Ct. Appeals (1st cir.) 1983, U.S. Tax Ct. 1988, U.S. Dist. Ct. (no. dist.) Ohio 1991, U.S. Ct. Appeals (2d cir) 1994, U.S. Ct. Appeals (3d cir.) 1999. From assoc. to ptnr. Hale & Dorr, Boston, 1973-84; sr. ptnr. Mirick, O'Connell, DeMallie & Lougee, Worcester, Mass., 1985—, chmn. litigation dept., 1993-97. Editor-in-chief 1972 Annual Survey of Mass. Law. Corporator Greater Worcester Cmty. Found., 1986—, mem. monitoring and evaluation com., 1997—; trustee Higgins Armory Mus., Worcester, 1985—, pres. 1994-97; corporator Worcester Art Mus., 1986—, pres., mem. coun., 1987-88; councilor Am. Antiquarian Soc., 1996—, treas., 1997—; mem. club officers exec. com. Dartmouth Coll., 1997—, pres., 1999-2002, mem. alumni coun., 2000—, mem. com. on alumni orgns., 2000-2003, exec. com., 2002-03, chmn., 2003-03, coll. rels. group, 2002—, com. on alumni orgn., 2000—, chmn. 2002-03. Lt. U.S. Army, 1968-70. Decorated Army Commendation medal for meritorious svc., 1970. Fellow Mass. Bar Found. (life); mem. ABA (appellate bench bar com. 1994-1995, bus. law sect. coun. 2003—), Mass. Bar Assn. (bus. law sect. coun. 2003—), Worcester County Bar Assn. (co-chmn. fed. ct. com. 1995-98), Dartmouth Lawyers Assn., Worcester Club (bd. dirs. 1995-98), Worcester Fire Soc., Dartmouth Club Ctrl. Mass. (exec. com. 1996—, pres. 1997-2002), Shakespeare Club of Worcester. Avocations: sailing, bicycling, hiking, history. Home: 285 Salisbury St Worcester MA 01609-1661 Office: Mirick O'Connell 100 Front St Worcester MA 01608-1425

DONNELLY, JOHN JAMES, III, immunologist; b. Phila., June 26, 1954; s. John James Jr. and Erma Marie (Cocci) D.; m. Betsy Ann Burkhardt, Dec. 30, 1976; children: Ann Marie, James Arthur. BA, U. Pa., Phila., 1975, PhD, 1979. Fellow U. Cambridge, U.K., 1979-81, Johns Hopkins U., Balt., 1982-83; asst. prof. U. Pa., Phila., 1983-88; rsch. fellow Merck & Co., Inc., West Point, Pa., 1988-94; assoc. dir. immunology and vaccine rsch. Merck & Co. Inc., West Point, Pa., 1994-98; dir. vaccine adjuvant rsch. Chiron Corp., Emeryville, Calif., 1998-2000, sr. dir. vaccine rsch., 2000—. Adj. asst. prof. U. Pa., Phila., 1988-98; cons. WHO, Geneva, 1983—, U.S. Agy. for Internat. Devel., Washington DC, 1988—, USPHS, NIH, Nat. Int. for Allergy and Infectious Diseases, Washington DC, 1999—. Contbr. chpt. to book, articles to profl. jours. Dir. Blood Donor Program, 79th U.S. Army Res. Command, Pa., 1987-90. Col. USAR, 1984—. Decorated Bronze Star; NIH fellow, 1975, Fight for Sight, Inc. fellow, 1980, NIH fellow, 1982. Fellow Royal Soc. Tropical Medicine and Hygiene; mem. Am. Assn. Immunologists, Assn. for Rsch. in Vision and Ophthalmology, British Soc. for Immunology. Achievements include patent for novel carrier protein for use in vaccines; rsch. in antigen processing, regulation of transplantation antigen expression, transplantation and tumor immunity, polynucleotide vaccines. Office: Chiron Corp M/S 4 3156 4560 Horton St Emeryville CA 94608-2900 E-mail: john_donnelly@chiron.com.

DONNELLY, MICHAEL JOSEPH, management consultant; b. Montreal, Quebec, Can., Dec. 28, 1951; m. Barbara Lynne Webb. BA in Commerce, Simon Fraser U., 1976. Chartered acct. Acct. Campbell, Sharp, Chartered Accts. Victoria, B.C., Can., 1973-76, KPMG, Victoria, 1976-79; controller Park Pacific Group of Cos., Victoria, 1979-80, gen. mgr. Indsl. Plastics (A subs. of the Park Pacific Group of Cos.), Victoria, 1980-83; chief fin. officer Action Group of Cos., Ft. Lauderdale, 1984-85; pres. Beacon Mgmt. Group, Inc., Pompano Beach, Fla., 1985—. Trustee, mem. bd. trade PAC Inc., 1990-95; dir. Enterprise Amb. Program, 1991-98, chmn. adv. bd., 1995-98; dir. NatBank, 1996-97. Contbr. articles to profl. jours. Chmn. adv. bd. Fla. Atlantic U. Small Bus. Devel. Ctr., 1993-96; exec. adv. bd. Fla. Atlantic U. Coll. Bus., 1996-98; bd. dirs. Broward Alliance, 2001-02. Mem. Nat. Assn. Accts. (bd. dirs. Ft. Lauderdale chpt. 1988-90), Inst. Chartered Accts. B.C., Can. Am. C. of C. (pres. 1989-95, dir. 1989—), Assn. for Corp. Growth (bd. dirs. South Fla. chpt. 1998—), Fla. Small Bus. Devel. Ctr. Network (adv. bd. 1990—, chmn. 1995—), Turnaround Mgmt. Assn., Assn. Insolvency Accts., Uptown Bus. Assn. (pres. 1989-90, chmn. CEO adv. coun. 1991-94, chmn. Uptown Bus. Coun. 1996), Greater Ft. Lauderdale C. of C. (bd. govs. 1995-96, 98—, bd. dirs. 1996, 99—, chair 2001, vice-chmn. govt. affairs, 1999-2000), Gold Coast Venture Capital Club (bd. dirs. 1986—, pres. 1989-91). Avocations: bicycling, walking, golf, running, rollerblading. Office: Beacon Mgmt Group Inc 1000 W McNab Rd Pompano Beach FL 33069-4719 E-mail: md@beaconmgmt.com.

DONNELLY, PAJA LEE, nursing educator and nurse practitioner; b. Kyangnam, Republic of Korea, Nov. 9, 1939; arrived in U.S., 1967; d. Pansool Lee and Tae-Soon Kim; m. Paul Donnelly (div. 1975). BSN, L.I. U., 1977; MSN, Adelphi U., Garden City, N.Y., 1985, PhD in Nursing, 1998, Nurse Practitioner in Psychiatric Nursing, 1999. RN N.Y., cert. nurse practitioner mental health nursing, N.Y. State Edn., clin. nurse specialist in adult psychiatric mental health nursing, ANCC. Asst. prof. N.Y. Inst. Tech., Old Wesbury, NY, 1978—79; cmty. nurse Steinway Mental Health Clinic CPC, Astoria, NY, 1979—89; asst. dir. nursing cmty. svcs. Creedmoor Psychiatric Ctr., Queens, NY, 1989—98; asst. prof. nursing St. Peter's Coll., Jersey City, 1998—99, N.Y. Inst. Tech., Old Wesbury, 1999—. Family partnership coord. Steinway Mental Health Clinic, Astoria, 1988—89; counseling and consultation L.I. Psychotherapy Assn., 2001—; cons., family edn. Asian Mental Health Clinic, 1996—. Contbr. articles to profl. jours. Mem.: ANA, N.Y. Korean Nurses Assn. (pres. 1991—93), N.Y. Nurses Assn., Korean Am. Behavioral Health Assn. (v.p. 2002—03, founder), Internat. Transcultural Nursing Assn. (mem. at large), Sigma Theta Tau. E-mail: pdonnell@nyit.edu.

DONNELLY, PHILLIP JOHNATHAN, literature educator; b. Nanaimo B.C., Dec. 22, 1969; s. Gordon Arthur and Patricia Anne Donnelly; m. Nicole Marie Siska, May 6, 1995; children: Ruth A., Rachel M.E., Joseph P.J. BA, U B.C., 1992; MA, U. Ottawa, 1995, PhD, 2001. Asst. prof. 17th century lit. Tex Tech. U., Lubbock, 2001—02; asst.. prof. lit. Baylor U., Waco, Tex., 2002— Author: Rhetorical Faith, 2000. Doctoral fellow, Social Sci. Human Rsch Coun. of Can., 1997—2000, Postdoctoral fellow, 2001—03. Mem.: MLA Renaissance Soc. Am., Milton Soc. Am. Office: Baylor Univ PO Box 9714 Waco TX 76798-7144

DONNELLY, RICHARD E. physician assistant, educator; b. Winslow, Ariz. May 18, 1948; s. Vernon Roy and Vera Mae (Barnes) D.; m. Kathryn K Donnelly, Mar. 2, 1968; children: Michael, David, Aaron, Michelle, Daniel Christine. BS, Ariz. State U., 1975, U. Tex. Med. Br., Galveston, 1979; MS in Physician Asst. Studies, U. Neb., 1999. Cert. med. technologist; lic. physician asst., Ariz. Med. technologist Desert Samaritan Hosp., Mesa, Ariz., 1975-76, U Tex. Med. Br., Galveston, 1976-79; physician asst. Steven Davis, MD, Pampa Tex., 1979-80, Phoenix Bapt. Hosp., Gila Bend, Ariz., 1980-83, Safford, Ariz. 1983-87, Mayo Clinic, Scottsdale, Ariz., 1987—. Adj. faculty Midwestern Osteopath Sch. Medicine, Glendale, Ariz., 1997—; presenter in field. Author editor: Surgical handbook for Physician Assistant, 1997; editor family medicine Jour. Am. Acad. P.A. Recipient Disting. Allied Health Educator of Yr. award Mayo Clinic, 2002. Fellow Am. Acad. Physician Assts. (clin. and sci. affairs coun. 1996-2001), Physician Asst. in Orthopaedic Surgery (past v.p., pres.) mem. Am. Soc. Clin. Pathologists as Med. Technologist, Ariz. State Acad Physician Assts., Alpha Epsilon Delta, New England Pain Assn. (pres. 1999 2001). Office: Mayo Clinic 13400 E Shea Blvd Scottsdale AZ 85259-549 E-mail: pared@cox.net.

DONNELLY, ROBERT L. lawyer, corporation executive; b. 1925; married BA, U. Conn., 1951, JD, 1955. CPA Conn.; bar: Conn. Adminstrv. asst Armstrong Rubber Co., New Haven, 1959—64, corp. atty., 1964—66, sec corp. atty, 1966—. Office: Armstrong Rubber Co 500 Sargent Dr New Haven CT 06511-6109

DONNELLY, RUSSELL JAMES, physicist, educator; b. Hamilton, Ont Can., Apr. 16, 1930; naturalized 2000; s. Clifford Ernest and Bessie (Harrison D.; m. Marian Card, Jan. 21, 1956 (dec. 1999); 1 son, James. BSc, McMaster U., 1951, MSc, 1952, LLD, 1999; MS, Yale U., 1953, PhD, 1956. Faculty U Chgo., 1956-66, prof. physics, 1965-66, U. Oreg., Eugene, 1966—, chmn. dept 1966-72, 82-83; vis. prof. Niels Bohr Inst., Copenhagen, Denmark, 1972 co-founder Pine Mountain Obs., 1967. Cons. GM Co. Rsch. Labs., 1958—68 NSF, 1968—76, mem. adv. panel for physics, 1970—73, chmn,., 1971—72 mem. adv. coms. on materials rsch., 1979—84; mem. task force on fundamental physics and chemistry in space, space sci. bd. NRC; cons. Jet Propulsion Lab Calif. Inst. Tech., Pasadena, 1973—82; chmn. Sci. Adv. Com. Low Temp Facilities in Space, 1990—91; mem. fluid dynamics discipline working group NASA, 1992—95; gen. chmn. 20th Internat. Conf. on Low Temp. Physics 1993; Chia-Shun lectr. U. Mich., 1995; Fritz London meml. lectr. Duke U 1996, 2002; Howard Vollum award Reed Coll., 1997. Author: (with Parks Glaberson) Experimental Superfluidity, 1967, (with Francis) Cryogenic Science and Technology: Contributions of Leo Dana, 1985, Quantized Vortices in Helium II, 1991; editor: (with Herman, Prigogine) Non-Equilibrium Thermodynamics Variational Techniques and Stability, 1966, High Reynolds Number Flows Using Liquid and Gaseous Helium, 1991, Procs. 20th Internat. Con Low Temperature Physics, Physica B, 1994; editor: (with Sreenivasan) Flow at Ultra-High Reynolds and Rayleigh Numbers, (with Barenghi and Vinen) Quantized Vortex Dynamic and Superfluid Turbulence; mem. editl. bd. Physic

of Fluids, 1966-68, Phys. Rev. E, 1978-84, assoc. editor, 1987-93; mem. editl. bd. Jour. Phys. and Chem. Ref. Data, 1989-92, Handbook of Chemistry and Physics, 1989-98; contbr. articles to profl. jours. Bd. dirs. U. Oreg. Found., 1970-72, 88-91, investment com., 1990-91; bd. dirs. Oreg. Mus. Park Commn., 1975-87, chmn., 1975-82; bd. dirs. Oreg. Bach Festival, 1975-87, Oreg. Mozart Players, 1990-93. Recipient Disting. Alumnus award, McMaster U., 1992, Lars Onsager medal, Norwegian U. Sci. and Tech., 1996, Fritz London prize, Internat. Union Pure and Applied Physics, 2002; Alfred P. Sloan fellow, 1959—63, sr. vis. fellow, Sci. Rsch. Coun., Eng., 1978. Fellow: AAAS, Inst. of Physics (London), Am. Phys. Soc. (exec. com. divsn. fluid dynamics 1966—72, 1980—84, 1988—91, sec.-treas. 1967—70, 1988—91, chmn. 1971—72, 1983—83, Otto Laporte award 1974), Am. Acad. Arts and Scis.; mem.: Soc. Archtl. Historians, Nat. Trust for Scotland, Cosmos Club. Episcopalian. Achievements include research on physics of fluids, especially hydrodynamic stability, turbulence and superfluidity. Home: 2175 Olive St Eugene OR 97405-2837 Office: Univ Oreg Dept Physics Eugene OR 97403-1274 E-mail: russ@vortex.uoregon.edu.

DONNELLY, SHARLOTTE K. B. NEELY, anthropology educator, author; b. Savannah, Ga., Aug. 13, 1948; d. Joseph Bowden and Kathleen Bell Neely; m. Thomas Christian C. Donnelly, June 21, 1980; 1 child, Bridgette. BA, Ga. State U., 1970; MA, U. NC, 1971, PhD, 1976. Prof. of anthropology No. Ky. U., Highland Heights, 1974—, anthropology coord., 1992—2000. Author: (book) Snowbird Cherokees, 1991; co-author: This Land Was Theirs, 1996, 1999; contbr. articles to profl. jours., chpts. to books. Pres. League for Animal Welfare, Cincinnati, Ohio, 1984—85. Recipient Strongest Influence Award, No. Ky. U. Alumni Assn., 1996. Fellow: Am. Anthrop. Assn.; mem.: Anthropologists and Sociologists of Ky. (pres. 1979—80). Democrat-Npl. Roman Catholic. Avocations: writing, travel. Office: No Ky U Nunn Dr Highland Heights KY 41099 Personal E-mail: donnelly@one.net. E-mail: neelys@nku.edu.

DONNELLY, SHAUN EDWARD, government agency administrator; b. Culver, Ind. m. Susan Buesing; children: Alex, Eric. BA in Econs., Lawrence U., Appleton, Wis., 1968; MA in Econs., Northwestern U., 1971. With U.S. Fgn. Svc., 1972—, econ./comml. officer, fin. economist Office of Devel. Fin.; dep. asst. sec. for energy and econ. sanctions State Dept. Bur. of Econ. and Bus. Affairs, Washington, 1994—95, dep. asst. sec. for trade policy, 1996—97; amb. to Sri Lanka and Republic of Maldives U.S. Dept. State, Colombo, 1997—2000, prin. dep. asst. sec. for econ. and bus. affairs Washington, 2001—. Office: Economic and Business Bureau Room 6828 US Department of State Washington DC 20520 E-mail: donnellyse@state.gov.

DONNELLY, THOMAS JOSEPH, lawyer, director; b. Pitts., Mar. 4, 1925; s. Thomas E. and Ruth L. (Beitzer) D.; m. Marilyn A. Pfohl, Apr. 16, 1955; children: Thomas C., Elizabeth A., Daria, Heather, Michael, Marilyn, Peter. Student, MIT, 1943-44; BS in Engring., U. Mich., 1946, JD, 1950. Bar: Pa. 1951. Student engr. Westinghouse Electric Corp., 1946-47; since practiced in Pitts. Trustee Carlow Coll., Pitts.; bd. dirs. Weston Jesuit Sch. Theology, Cambridge, Mass.; mem. adv. bd. Pitts. Symphony Soc. With USNR, 1943-46. Mem. Barristers Soc., Am., Pa., Allegheny County Bar assns., Tau Beta Pi. Clubs: Knight of Malta, Toastmasters U. Mich. Lawyers (Ann Arbor); University, Duquesne, Chatham (Mass.) Yacht. Roman Catholic. Home: 1085 Shady Ave Pittsburgh PA 15232-2912 Office: 650 Smithfield St Ste 1810 Pittsburgh PA 15222-3907

DONNELLY, TIMOTHY B. editor, writer; b. Providence, June 3, 1969; s. Donald Anthony and Annette Leonore (Lemoi) Donnelly; m. Lynn Melnick, Dec. 16, 2002. BA, Johns Hopkins U., 1991; MFA, Columbia U., 1998. Poetry editor Boston Rev., Cambridge, Mass., 1996—. Author: Twenty-Seven Props For A Production of Eine Lebenszeit, 2003. Recipient Bernard F. Conners prize, The Paris Rev., 2003; Master Writer fellow, N.Y. State Writers Inst., 2001. Democrat. Roman Catholic. Home: Apt 3 357 A Clinton St Brooklyn NY 11231

DONNELLY, WILLIAM HENRY, pathology educator; b. Jersey City, N.J., Sept. 4, 1936, s. William Henry and Florence (Kelly) D.; m. Michelle Marie Emond, July 18, 1964; children: Carolyn, Christopher. AB, Coll. of Holy Cross, 1958; MD, U. Ottawa, Ont., Can., 1963. Diplomate Am. Bd. Pathology, Am. Bd. Anatomic Pathology, Am. Bd. Pediatric Pathology. Asst. prof. pathology and pediatrics Coll. Medicine, U. Fla., Gainesville, 1971-76, assoc. prof., 1977-83, prof., 1984—. Lt. USN, 1963—66. Fellow: Coll. Am. Pathologists; mem.: Am. Acad. Pediat., Soc. Pediat. Pathology (pres. 1991—92). Democrat. Roman Catholic. Office: U Fla Coll Medicine Dept Pathology Gainesville FL 32610

DONNELLY-KEMPF, MOIRA ANN, nursing administrator; b. Toledo, June 11, 1963; d. Gerald M. and Ruth Ann (Crawford) Donnelly; m. Ronald W. Kempf, Aug. 31, 1985. Diploma, Mercy Sch. Nursing, Toledo, 1983; student, Eastern Mich. U., St. Joseph's Coll., 1992. RN, Clin. rehab. nurse Meml. Hosp., South Bend, Ind., 1983-84, U. Mich. Med. Ctr., Ann Arbor, 1985-87; med. claims nurse analyst Kapner Wolfberg & Assocs., Van Nuys, Calif., 1988-89; sr. auditing specialist Intracorp, Southfield, Mich., 1989-94, sr. early intervention specialist, 1994-97; mktg. assoc. The Lakeland Ctr, Southfield, 1997—. Mem. Mercy Sch. Nursing Alumnae Assn.

DONNEM, ROLAND WILLIAM, retired lawyer, real estate owner, developer; b. Seattle, Nov. 8, 1929; s. William Roland and Mary Louise (Hughes) D.; m. Sarah Brandon Lund, Feb. 18, 1961; children: Elizabeth Donnem Sigety, Sarah Madison. BA, Yale U., 1952; JD magna cum laude, Harvard U., 1957. Bar: N.Y. 1958, U.S. Dist. Ct. (ea. and so. dists.) N.Y. 1959, U.S. Ct. Appeals (2d cir.) 1959, U.S. Ct. Claims 1960, U.S. Tax Ct. 1960, U.S. Supreme Ct. 1963, U.S. Ct. Appeals (3d cir.) 1969, D.C. 1970, U.S. Ct. Appeals (D.C. cir.) 1970, Ohio 1976, U.S. Dist. Ct. (no. dist.) Ohio 1980, U.S. Ct. Appeals (7th cir.) 1980, U.S. Ct. Appeals (6th cir.) 1984. With Davis Polk & Wardwell, N.Y.C., 1957-63, 64-69; law sec. appellate divsn. N.Y. Supreme Ct., N.Y.C., 1963-64; dir. policy planning antitrust divsn. Justice Dept., Washington, 1969-71; v.p., sec., gen. counsel Standard Brands Inc., N.Y.C., 1971-76; from v.p. law to sr. v.p. law and casualty prevention Chessie System, Cleve., 1976-86; ptnr. Meta Ptnrs., real estate devel., 1984—2002, mng. ptnr., 1989—2002, registered security rep., 1985-90; bd. dirs., gen. counsel Acorn Properties, Inc., Cleve., 1985—2002, pres., 1989—2002; bd. dirs., gen. counsel Meta Devel. Corp., Cleve., 1985—2002, pres., 1989—2002; bd. dirs., gen. counsel Meta Properties, Inc., Cleve., 1988—2002, pres., 1989—2002. Founding mem., bd. dirs. Assn. Sheraton Franchisees N.Am., 1997—2002. Mem. editl. bd. Harvard Law Rev., 1955-57. Bd. dirs., fin. v.p. Presbyn. Home for Aged Women, N.Y.C., 1972-76; bd. dirs., treas. James Lenox Ho., Inc., 1972-76; trustee Food and Drug Law Inst., 1974-76; trustee, sec. Brick Presbyn. Ch., N.Y.C., 1974-76; sec. class of 1952, Yale U., 1992-97; bd. dirs. Yale Alumni Fund, 1990-95; chmn. Cleve. Area Yale Campaign, 1991-97. Lt. (j.g.) USNR, 1952-54. Fellow Timothy Dwight Coll., Yale U., 1987—. Mem. Am. Law Inst. (life), Am. Arbitration Assn. (nat. panel arbitrators), Def. Orientation Conf. Assn. (bd. dirs. 1996-99), Yale U. Alumni Assn. Cleve. (treas. 1982-84, del. 1984-87, trustee 1984-93, adv. coun. 1993—), Yale U. Alumni Assn. (bd. govs. 1987-90), Union Club (N.Y.C. and Cleve.), Capitol Hill Club (Washington), Washington Chevy Chase Club, Cleve. Racquet Club, Kirtland Club (Cleve.), Met. Club (Washington), Mory's Assn. (New Haven), Phi Beta Kappa. Republican. Presbyterian. Home: 2945 Fontenay Rd Shaker Heights OH 44120-1726 Home (Winter): Ft Sumter Ho 1 King St Apt 307 Charleston SC 29401

DONNEM, SARAH LUND, financial analyst, non-profit and political organization consultant; b. St. Louis, Apr. 10, 1936; d. Joel Y. and Erle Hall (Harsh) Lund; m. Roland W. Donnem, Feb. 18, 1961; children: Elizabeth Prince Donnem Sigety, Sarah Madison. BA, Vassar Coll., 1958. Tech. aide, computer programmer Bell Labs, Whippany, N.J., 1959-60; chmn. placement vol. opportunities N.Y. Jr. League, 1972-73, asst. treas., 1974-75, chmn. urban problems relating to mental health, 1967-69, mem. project rsch. com., 1967-70, chmn., 1973-74, mem. bd. mgrs., 1973-74. Chmn. cmty. rsch. Washington Jr. League, 1970-71, mem. bd. mgrs., 1970-71; mem. Stratford Hall (N.Y.) Com., 1970—; bd. dirs. East Side Settlement House, Bronx, N.Y., 1972—, v.p., 1975-76, chmn. Nat. Horse Show Benefit, 1976, winter antiques show com., 1994—, co-chmn. adv. com., 1991-94, chmn. VIP Day, 1999—, mem. nominating com., 1990—, mem. investment com., 1993—; bd. dirs. Stanley M. Isaacs Neighborhood Ctr., N.Y.C., 1973-76, v.p., 1975-76; bd. dirs. Presbyn. Home for Aged Women, N.Y.C., 1974-76, v.p., 1976; mem. exec. bd. N.Y. Aux. of Blue Ridge Sch., 1971-75, sec. 1965-67, pres., 1973-75; budget and benevolence com. Brick Presbyn. Ch., N.Y.C., 1973-76, mem. social svc. com., 1973-74, chmn. fgn. students com., 1963-64; bd. dirs. Search and Care, N.Y.C., 1973-76, Project LEARN, cleve., 1990-96, 2000—; chmn. Literacy Fund, 1991-95, mem., 1995—; mem. Friends of Project LEARN, 1986—, mem. Fedn. Cmty. Planning, Cleve., coun. on Older Persons, 1978-82, mem. future Planning task Force, 1980-81, commn. on social concerns, 1982-84; trustee Golden Age Ctrs. Greatr cleve., 1979-92, investment com., 1993, 1st v.p., 1980-81, pres. 1981-85, chmn. Western Res. Antiques show, 1979, 80; chmn. cleve. antiques Show Silver Anniv., 2000; mem. women's adv. coun. Westrn Res. Hist. Soc., 1977—, coord. sec., 1978; mem. women's com. Cleve. Orch., 1979-85, Vassar Coll. cleve. sec. 1980-82, v.p., 1983, pres. 1984-86; mem. AAVC Club Liaison com., 1986-89, chmn. regional program com., 1987-89; bd. dirs. Cleve. Ballet, 1980-2001, exec. com. 1981, fin. com. 1982-88, 95-98, nominating com., 1988-90, 95-2000, co-chmn. 1997-99; co-chmn. Yale Ball, 1983; bd. advisors Ret. Sr. Vol. Program, 1982, trustee, 1983-90, chmn. long range planning comm., 1986, sec. 1987-89; mem. Family Friends Adv. Coun., 1987-89; trustee Fairmount Presbyn. Ch., 1985-88; mem. long range planning com. United Way, Cleve., 1985-87; coord. Friends of Voinovich, 1987-89; womens adv. com. Voinovich for Governor, 1990, Voinovich for Senate, 1997-98, chmn. Voinovich Task Force on Aging, 1990-91, Ohio Adv. Coun. on Aging, 1991-2002, legis. com., 1994-2000; chmn.legis. com. Cuyahoga County Republican Party, 1994-2000, mem. policy com., mem. fin. com., 1999—, Plain Dealer adv. counsel for elderly coverage, 1991-93; chmn. Johns Hopkins Parents Fund, 1986-88, Project LEARN 15th Anniversary celebration (with Barbara Bush, hon. chmn.), 1989-90; coord. Decorative Arts Trust Cleve. Symposium, 1996; mem. Leadership Cleve. Class 1992; del. White House Conf. on Aging, 1995. Named Vol. of Yr. N.Y. Jr. League, 1975; recipient Sustainer Svc. award Jr. League Cleve., 1990. Mem. Nat. Inst. Social Scis. (membership com. 1972-92, trustee 1984-96), Nat. Soc. Colonial Dames, Colony Club (N.Y.C.), Chevy Chase Club (Washington), Intown club, Vassar Club, Kirtland Club (Cleve.). Address: 2945 Fontenay Rd Shaker Heights OH 44120 Home (Winter): 1 King St Apt 305 Charleston SC 29401

DONNENFELD, ERIC DAVID, ophthalmologist; b. Sangley Naval Base, Philippines, July 18, 1955; s. Robert Seymour Donnenfeld and Phyllis Levine; m. Marleen Brajer, Apr. 20, 1983; children: Ashley, Robert. AB, Dartmouth Coll., Hanover, N.H., 1977; MD, Dartmouth Med. Sch., Hanover, N.H., 1980. Cert. Am. Acad. of ophthalmology, 1985. Instr. Manhattan Eye and Ear, N.Y.C., 1985—87; program dir. North Shore Hosp., NY, 1992—95; med. dir. TLC Laser Ctr., N.Y., 1995—. Residency Manhattan Eye and Ear, N.Y.C., 1984; fellowship Wills Eye Hosp., Phlia., 1985; adv. bd. Allergan Pharm., Irving, Calif., 1997—2003; pres. Microbiology Group, N.Y., 2001—02. Contbr. chapters to books, articles over 100 to prol. jour. Surgical dir. Lions Eye Bank, NY, 1993—; v.p. Sid JCC, East Hills, NY, 1997—. Recipient Honor award, Am. Acad. of, 1973, Physician of Yr., Sons of Italy, 1999, Man of the Yr., Lions Club, 1999. Fellow: Cornia Soc. (bd. dir. 1998—2002), Nalian Surgical Soc. (pres. 1994—95). Independent. Jewish. Avocations: tennis, golf, skiing. Home: 5 Verity Ln Roslyn NY 11576 Office: OCLI 2000 N Village Ave Rockville Centre NY 11570

DONNER, HENRY JAY, lawyer; b. Atlantic City, N.J., Sept. 1, 1944; s. Harry and Sylvia (Payes) D.; m. Katherine Weiner, Dec. 20, 1969; children: Benjamin James, Melissa Faith. BA, Am. U., 1966; JD, Villanova U., 1969. Bar: Pa. 1969, U.S. Dist. Ct. (ea. dist.) Pa. 1969, U.S. Ct. Appeals (3d cir.) 1983. Staff mem. U.S. Senator Joseph A. Clark, Washington, 1965-68; assoc. Dilworth, Paxson, Kalish and Levy, Phila., 1969-74; ptnr. Jacoby, Donner & Jacoby, Phila., 1974-82; sr. mem. Jacoby Donner, P.C., Phila., 1982—. Lectr. Nat. Home Builders Assn., Pa. State U., State Coll., 1989-90. Author: West Legal Forms: Specialized Forms, Vol. 27, Chpt. 8, Building Agreements. Mem. sch. com. Germantown Friends Sch., 1993—; bd. dirs. Germantown Jewish Ctr., 1989-91. Mem. ABA, Phila. Bar Assn. (exec. com. real property sect. 1987-96, chmn. constrn. law com., real property sect. 1986-89, chmn. real property sect. 1993, bd. govs. 1993), Constrn. Fin. Mgmt. Assn. (bd. dirs. Phila. chpt. 1990-95), Union League Phila., Germantown Cricket Club. Office: Jacoby Donner PC 1515 Market St Ste 2000 Philadelphia PA 19102-1920 E-mail: hdonner@jacobydonner.com.

DONNER, RICHARD, film director, producer; b. N.Y.C., Apr. 24, 1930; Dir.: X-15, 1961, Salt and Pepper, 1968, The Omen, 1976, Superman, 1978, Inside Moves, 1981, Radio Flyer, 1991; exec. prodr.: The Final Conflict, The Lost Boys, 1991, Delirious, 1991, Free Willy, 1993, Free Will2, Free Willy 3; dir., exec. prodr.: The Toy, 1982; dir., prodr.: Ladyhawke, 1985, Goonies, 1985, Lethal Weapon, 1987, Scrooged, 1988, Lethal Weapon 2, 1989, Lethal Weapon 3, (MTV movie award, best action sequence) 1992, Maverick, 1994, Assassins, 1995, Lethal Weapon 4, 1998; prodr.: Blackheart, 1999, The Final Conflict, 1981 (exec.), 1981, The Lost Boys (exec.), 1987, Delirious (exec.) 1991, Demon Knight, 1995, Double Tap, 1997, Ritual, 2001 (TV); dir., prodr.: Made Men, 1999, W.E.I.R.D. World, (exec.) 1995, Perversions of Science, 1997, Matthew Blackheart: Monster Smasher, 2001; dir. (TV episodes) Wanted: Dead or Alive, 1958, Sam Benedict, 1962, The Nurses, 1962, Combat, 1962, The Fugitive, 1963, The Wild Wild West, 1965, The Trials of O'Brien, 1965, Get Smart, 1965, The FBI, 1965, Its About Time, 1966, Felony Squad, 1966, Cannon, 1971, Cade's County, 1971, The Six Sense, 1972, Ghost Story, 1972, The Streets of San Francisco, 1972, The Six Million Dollar Man, 1974, Petrocelli, 1974, Twilight Zone, Have Gun Will Travel, Perry Mason, Cannon, Get Smart, The Fugitive, Kojak, 1973, Bronk, 1975, Lucas Tanner, Gilligan's Island, Man From U.N.C.L.E., Twilight Zone, The Banana Splits, 1968, Combat, Tales from the Crypt, 1989-91, Two Fisted Tales, 1991, Conspiracy Theory, 1997; (TV movies) Portrait of a Teenage Alcoholic, 1975, Senior Year, A Shadow in the Streets, 1975, A Very Special Place, 1977, Senior Year, 1974, Twinky, 1969, Lola, 1972, London Affair, 1972, Statutory Affair, 1969; prodr.: Any Given Sunday, 1999; exec. prodr.: X-Men, 2000. Office: Richard Donner Prodns 4000 Warner Blvd Bldg 102 Burbank CA 91522-0001 also: Creative Artists Agy 9830 Wilshire Blvd Beverly Hills CA 90212-1804*

DONNER, TED A. lawyer, b. N.Y.C., Nov. 22, 1960; s. Robert A. and Barbara (Wood) D.; m. Leslie Lynn Wasserman, Sept. 16, 1990; children: Alexandra Sofia, Samuel Joseph. BA, Roosevelt U., 1987; JD, Loyola U., 1990. Bar: U.S. Dist. Ct. Ill. 1990. Assoc. Rock, Fusco, Reynolds & Garvey, Chgo., 1990-94; of counsel Altheimer & Gray, Chgo., 1994-2000; ptnr. Bischoff Ptnrs. LLC, Chgo., 2000—02; mgr. Donner & Co. Law Offices LLC, 2002—. Instr. Loyola U. Chgo. Sch. Law, 1990—96, lectr., 1996—. Author: Attorney's Practice Guide to Negotiations, 2d edit., 1995-2003, Jury Selection Strategy & Science, 3d edit., 2000-03, Jury Selection Handbook, 1999. Mem. ATLA, ABA, Am. Soc. Trial Consultants, Am. Soc. Legal Writers, Internat. Platform Assn., DuPage County Bar Assn., Chgo. Bar Assn., Alpha Sigma Nu. Office: 203 N LaSalle St # 2100 Chicago IL 60601 also: 1131 Wheaton Oaks Ct Wheaton IL 60187 E-mail: email@donnerco.com.

DONNESON, SEENA SAND, artist; b. NYC; d. Max and Ann (Silber) S.; m. Sam Gershwin (dec.); children: Erika Donneson, Lisa Donneson. Attended, Pratt Inst., Art Students League. Art staff NYU, Nassau County Office Cultural Devel., New Sch. for Social Rsch., N.H. Coll.; guest artist Tamarind Lithography Workshop; vis. artist Clayworks, N.Y.C. One-woman shows include Lauren Rogers Mus. Art, Laurel, Miss., Greenville (N.C.) Mus. Art, Galerie #836, Sante Fe, N.Mex., Lehigh U., Princeton U., Portland (Maine) Mus. Art, Piertrantonio Gallery, N.Y.C., U. Calif., L.I. U., George Washington U., Danville (Va.) Mus. Fine Arts and History, others; exhibited in group shows at SUNY, N.Y.C., Quietude Sculpture Garden, N.J., Sculpture in Color, N.Y.C., Ft. Lauderdale (Fla.) Mus., Norfolk Mus. Arts and Scis., Bklyn. Mus., San Francisco Mus. Art, DeCordova Mus., Alternate Spac Mod Art Foundry, N.Y.C., fgn. traveling exhbns., USIS, Mcpl. Art Mus., Tokyo, also on tour throughout Japan, Musseo de Belles Artes, Buenos Aires, Argentina, Scotland, Eng.; represented in permanent collections Va. Mus. Fine Art, Bklyn. Mus., Doris Freidman Sculpture garden, Albright U., Reading, Pa., Norfolk Mus., USIA Art in Embassies, L.A. County Mus. Art, Mus. Modern Art, N.Y.C., Smithsonian Mus., Ft. Lauderdale Mus. Fine Art, Snug Harbor Cultural Ctr., N.Y.C., N.Y. Pub. Libr., Cornell Med. Sch., N.Y.C., others; also pvt. collections; revs. Newsday, The N.Y. Times, The N.Y. Post, Art News, Conran Octopus Ltd., others. Recipient numerous art awards; fellow Edward MacDowell Found., guest artist Tamarind Lithography Workshop, Creative Artists Pub. Svc. grant N.Y. State Coun. on Arts, 1983-84; grantee Mcpl. Art Soc., N.Y. Art in Park, 1974, Queens Coun. on Arts, 1992. Mem. Artists Equity, Nat. Assn. Women Artists (bd. dirs.), L.I.C. Artists (bd. dirs.). Studio: 43-49 10th St Long Island City NY 11101-6923 Fax: (718) 706-1342. E-mail: elaici@aol.com.

D'ONOFRIO, MARY ANN, medical transcription company executive; b. Detroit, Jan. 24, 1933; d. Charles Henry and Cecilia Rose (Levan) Clifford; m. Dominic Armando D'Onofrio, Apr. 19, 1958; children: Margaret Clement, Anthony, Elizabeth, Maria Spurgeon. BA, Marygrove Coll., 1954; MLS, U. Mich., 1955. Cert. med. transcriptionist. Reader's advisor Detroit Pub. Libr., 1955-58; cataloger Willow Run (Mich.) Pub. Libr., 1959-61, St. Thomas Grade and High Sch., Ann Arbor, Mich., 1968-72; med. record analyst Chelsea (Mich.) Community Hosp., 1972-79; pres. Meditranscript Svc., Ann Arbor, 1979-81; asst. office mgr. Dr. Maxfield, D.O., Tucson, 1981-82; quality assurance analyst, utilization rev. Tucson (Ariz.) Gen. Hosp., 1983-86; exec. asst. Dr. McEldoon M.D., Tucson, 1986-88; pres. Meditranscript Svc., Tucson, 1986-88; co-owner Med-Comm Assocs., Tucson, 1989—. Co-owner, assoc. designer EMA of Tucson custom apparel and jewelry design co. Co-author: Psychiatric Words & Phrases, 1998, 2d edit., 1998; contbr. articles to profl. jours. Block leader Am. Heart Assn., 1994, Am. Cancer Soc., 1992, 1996, 2001; Leukemia Soc. Am., 1997, 1998, 1999, 2000, 2001; block leader Infantile Paralysis Assn., Ann Arbor, 1975—2001, Easter Seal Assn., Tucson, 1983—86. Mem.: Fdnl. Honor Soc., Pi Lambda Theta (life). Avocations: desert gardening, sunset/landscape photography, reading. E-mail: mcamad@hotmail.com.

DONOFRIO, PETER DANIEL, neurology educator; b. Syracuse, N.Y., June 5, 1950; s. Carmin Peter and Donna Marie (Powers) D.; m. Kathleen Ann Fitzgerald, May 29, 1976; children: Molly, Emily, Julie. BS, U. Notre Dame, 1972; MD, Ohio State U., 1975. Diplomate Am. Bd. Internal Medicine, Am. Bd. Neurology, Am. Bd. Emergency Medicine. Resident internal medicine Good Samaritan Hosp., Cin., 1978; resident neurology U. Mich. Med. Ctr., Ann Arbor, 1981, instr., 1982-84, V.A. Hosp., Ann Arbor, 1982-84, asst. prof., 1984-85, U. Mich. Med. Ctr., Ann Arbor, 1984-85; asst. prof. neurology Wake Forest U. Sch. Medicine, Winston-Salem, N.C., 1986-89, assoc. prof., 1989-97, prof., 1997—, vice chmn. dept., 1993—. Cons. in neurology, Winston-Salem, 1984—. Contr. articles to profl. jours. Dept. rep. United Way, Winston-Salem, N.C., 1989—. Scholar U. Notre Dame U., 1968. Fellow Am. Acad. Neurology; mem. Am. Assn. Electrodiagnostic Medicine, Am. Neurological Assn. Roman Catholic. Avocations: woodworking, piano, hi-fidelity, landscaping. Home: 3509 Donegal Dr Clemmons NC 27012-8678 Office: Wake Forest Univ Medical Center Blvd Winston Salem NC 27157-0001

D'ONOFRIO, PETER JOSEPH, protective services official, educator; b. Bronx, N.Y., Sept. 20, 1947; s. Elia Danato and Chella Concetta (Diorio) D'O.; m. Sharon Warner, Oct. 17, 1971 (div. 1976); m. Barbara Ann Jefferson, Dec. 10, 1977; children: Randyll Thomas, Robyn Margaret Smith. AAS, Sinclair C.C., Dayton, Ohio, 1973; BSBA, U. Dayton, 1974, MBA, BS in Edn., 1975; AAS in Fire Sci., Columbus State C.C., 1988; grad. exec. fire officer program, Nat. Fire Acad., Emmitsburg, Md., 1993; PhD in Am. History, LaSalle U., 1998. Registered paramedic, fire, EMS instr., fire safety inspector, Ohio. Fire tng. officer, emergency med. svcs. tng. coord. Ohio Fire Acad., Reynoldsburg, 1984—. Mem. faculty paramedic edn. Grant Med. Ctr., Columbus, 1987—; mem. adj. faculty Nat. Fire Acad., 1989—; firefighter, paramedic, insp., investigator Miami Twp. Fire Divsn., Miamisburg, Ohio, 1980-84; emergency rm. technician Kettering (Ohio) Med. Ctr., 1978-79; firefighter, paramedic Huber Heights (Ohio) Fire Divsn., 1976-78; instr. Sinclair C.C., 1977-84; lectr. Bowling Green (Ohio) Fire Sch., Ohio State Firefighters Conf., Am. Med. Writers Assn., Fire Dept. Instrs. Conf., others. Editor, pub. newsletter North South Med. Times, 1984-96; editor, pub. Jour. of Civil War Medicine, 1996—. Vol. firefighter Kettering Fire Dept., 1974-80; vol. paramedic Minerva park (Ohio) Fire Dept., 1992-95, Truro Twp. (Ohio) Fire Dept., 1995-97. Mem. Internat. Rescue and Emergency Care Assn. (conf. lectr.), Internat. Assn. Fire Fighters (charter, hon.), Nat. Registry EMT's, Ohio Soc. Fire Svc. Instrs. (bd. dirs. 1985-87), Ohio EMT Instrs. Assn., Mil. Order Loyal Legion of U.S., Hon. Order Ky. Cols., VFW (Meritorious Svc. award 1977), Soc. Civil War Surgeons (pres., CEO 1988—). Avocations: civil war medical reenactments, fire and ems patch collecting, stamp collecting. Home: 539 Bristol Dr SW Reynoldsburg OH 43068 Office: Ohio Fire Acad 8895 E Main St Reynoldsburg OH 43068-3340

DONOGHUE, EILEEN M. former mayor; BA, U. Mass., 1976; JD, Suffolk U., 1979. Atty.; mayor City of Lowell, Mass., 1998—2001; city councilor Lowell, Mass., 2001—. Office: Office of the Mayor City Hall 375 Merrimack St Lowell MA 01852

DONOGHUE, JOHN CHARLES, software management consultant; b. Oswego, N.Y., Sept. 19, 1950; s. James Charles and Marion Louise (Farrell) D.; m. Ann Marie Perry, Dec. 20, 1969; children: John Charles II, Kelly Anne. BS in Electronic Tech., Chapman Coll., 1981; student, U. Calif., Irvine, 1981-82; MA, U. Redlands, 1987; postgrad., Western State U. Coll., 1988-89, Azusa Pacific U., 1991-93. Enlisted USAF, 1969, advanced through grades to staff sgt., 1977, resigned, 1979; mgr. Lockheed Aircraft, Ontario, Calif., 1979-85; project engr. Northrop Corp., Pico Rivera, Calif., 1985-99; sr. prin. software engr. Raytheon Missile Syss., Tucson, 1999—; Raytheon cert. Six Sigma expert, 2001—; with Tucson Software Process Improvement Network, 2000—. Cons., Fontana, Calif., 1981-2001; mem. software coun. Northrop Corp., Hawthorne, Calif., 1987-97, software improvement network U. Calif., Irvine, 1988-2000, capability maturity model corr. group Software Engring. Inst., Pitts., 1993-2002, L.A. software improvement network U. So. Calif., 1994-2000; charter mem. Software Inspection and Rev. Orgn., Sunnyvale, Calif., 1981—. Vol. cons. S.W. Anthropol. Assn. Calif. State U., L.A., 1996-97, Resource Conservation Dist., Rancho Cucamonga, Calif., 1996-99, Southwest Mus., L.A., 1997-2000. Mem. IEEE, N.Y. Acad. Scis., Nat. Space Soc. Avocations: motorcycling, snorkeling. Office: Raytheon Corp Mil Aircraft Sys Divsn Bldg M03 PO Box 11337 Tucson AZ 85734-1337

DONOGHUE, JOHN FRANCIS, archbishop; b. Washington, D.C., Aug. 9, 1928; Student, St. Mary's Sem., Cath. U. Ordained priest Roman Cath. Ch., 1955. Chancellor and vicar gen. Washington Archdiocese, Washington, 1973—84; bishop Charlotte, NC, 1984—93; archbishop archdiocese of Atlanta, 1993—. Home: 136 W Wesley Rd NW Atlanta GA 30305-3523 Office: Archdiocese of Atlanta Chancery Office 680 W Peachtree St NW Atlanta GA 30308-1931*

DONOGHUE, MILDRED RANSDORF, education educator; b. Cleve. d. James and Caroline (Sychra) Ransdorf; m. Charles K. Donoghue (dec. 1982); children: Kathleen, James. EdD, UCLA, 1962; JD, Western State U., 1979. Asst. prof. edn. and reading Calif. State U., Fullerton, 1962-66, assoc. prof., 1966-71, prof., 1971—. Founder, dir. Donoghue Children's Lit. Ctr., Calif. State U., Fullerton, Calif., 2001—. Author: Foreign Languages and the Schools, 1967, Foreign Languages and the Elementary School Child, 1968, The Child and the English Language Arts, 1971, 75, 79, 85, 90, Using Literature Activities to Teach Content Areas to Emergent Readers, 2001; co-author: Second Languages in Primary Education, 1979; contbr. articles to profl. jours. and Ednl. Resources Info. Ctr. U.S. Dept. Edn. Mem. AAUP, AAUW, Nat. Network for Early Lang. Learning, Nat. Coun. Tchrs. English, Nat. Coun. Tchrs. Math., Nat. Coun. Social Studies, Nat. Sci. Tchrs. Assn., Am. Ednl. Rsch. Assn., Nat. Soc. for Study of Edn., Am. Assn. Tchrs. Spanish and Portuguese, Internat. Reading Assn., Nat. Assn. Edn. Young Children, Orange County Med. Assn. Women's Aux., Assn. for Childhood Edn. Internat., Phi Beta Kappa, Phi Kappa Phi, Pi Lambda Theta, Alpha Upsilon Alpha. Address: 800 State College Blvd Fullerton CA 92831

DONOHEW, ROBERT LEWIS, SR., communications educator; b. Owingsville, Ky., May 9, 1929; s. Butler Ford and Ethel (Couchman) D.; m. Ethel Cox, Sept. 6, 1950 (div. Oct. 1974); children: Robert L. Jr., Susan Kerry Donohew Schneider, John Patrick. AA, Cumberland Coll., 1949; AB, U. Ky., 1951, MA, 1961; PhD, U. Iowa, 1965. Editor Pikeville (Ky.) Daily News, 1951-52; city editor Owensboro (Ky.) Messenger & Inquirer, 1954-57; pub. info. officer U. Ky., Lexington, 1957-61, from instr. to prof. journalism, 1962-70, prof. comm., 1970—, dir. Sch. Comm., assoc. dean Coll. Arts and Scis., 1971-73. John F. Murray vis. prof. U. Iowa, Iowa City, 1979-80; pres. Bloomsbury Consulting and Rsch., Lexington, 1988—, Media Rsch. Assocs., Inc., Lexington, 1991-95. Editor: Communication, Social Cognition and Affect, 1988, Persuasive Communication and Drug Abuse Prevention, 1990; contbr. more than 80 articles to

1952-54. Rsch. grantee Nat. Inst. Drug Abuse, 1985—, Prevention, 1991-95, Nat. Inst. on Alcohol Abuse and ... recipient Health Commn. Scholar of Yr., Nat. Commn. Assn., 2001, others; scholar Old Gold. Mem. Nat. Comm. Assn., Internat. Comm. Assn. Democrat. Avocations: writing, traveling, farming. Office: Dept Comm Univ Ky Lexington KY 40506-0001 E-mail: Donohew@uky.edu.

DONOHO, TIM MARK, charity founder and executive, entrepreneur; b. St. Louis, Sept. 25, 1955; s. James O. and Jean (Dace) D.; m. Deborah Ann Peeples, Feb. 27, 1981; children: Drew Morgan, Jourdan Alexis. BABA, Columbia Coll., 1979. Editor U.S. Army, Okinawa, Japan, 1973-77; sales mgr. Unival Investments, Okinawa, 1975-77; nat. dir. mktg. Pyramid Life Ins. Co., Springfield, Mo., 1978-82; chmn., owner Ins. Mktg. Group, Springfield, 1982-90; pres., owner Am. Dental Program, Inc., Ft. Lauderdale, Fla., 1984-97, Donoho Gruppe Cos., Ft. Lauderdale, 1985—; owner Advantage Dental Health Plans, Ft. Lauderdale, Fla., 1984-97; pub., editor, owner Prime Years News Mag., Ft. Lauderdale, 1985-92; chmn., owner Bus. Healthcare Coalition Inc., 1995-98; chmn. Express Bakery, 1998—. Bd. dirs. So. Fla. chpt. Nat. Multiple Sclerosis Soc., 1996-97; founder, chmn. bd. dirs. Pastors Closet, 2000—, chmn., founder, Film the Bible, Inc., 1996—; bd. govs. Graves Archael. Mus., 1998-2000. With U.S. Army, 1973-77. Mem. Nat. Assn. Dental Plans (chmn. bd. dirs. 1996-97). Republican. Baptist. Avocations: tennis, golf, loudspeaker design. Home: 1075 Hillsboro Mile Hillsboro Beach FL 33062

DONOHOE, CATHRYN MURRAY, journalist; b. Bronx, N.Y. d. Harry and Helen (Crowley) Murray; m. Thomas W. Donohoe, Dec. 1, 1962. BA cum laude in Am. Lit., Middlebury Coll., 1958; student in Russian lit., Columbia U., 1958—60; student in journalism, American U., 1983—84; cert. in Russian Lang. and Culture, Gornyi Inst., St. Petersburg, Russia, 1993. Rsch. and policy coord. Radio Liberty, N.Y.C., 1963—74; freelance journalist, 1977—84; reporter Potomac Almanac, Potomac, Md., 1985, Washington Times, Washington, 1985—94, deputy editor, features, 1994—. Recipient Nat. Mag. award for pub. svc., 1985. Office: Washington Times 3600 New York Ave NE Washington DC 20002-1996

DONOHOE, CHARLES RICHARD, general patent counsel; b. Iowa City, Apr. 29, 1941; s. Charles Joseph and Sarah Henrietta D.; m. Kathryn Ann Lyons, Apr. 20, 1968; children: Kelly, Patrick, Mark, Charles Jr. BSEE, Ohio State U., 1964, MSEE, 1965; JD, George Washington U., 1970. Bar: Md. 1970, D.C. 1973. Engr. GM, Milford, Mich., 1965-68; patent engr. Burroughs Corp., Washington, 1968-70; assoc. atty. Pennie & Edmonds, N.Y.C., 1970-73; ptnr. Cushman, Darby & Cushman, Washington, 1973-89; gen. patent consul, sr. v.p. Samsung Electronics Co. Ltd., Washington and Seoul, 1989—. Lectr. Patent Resources Group, Washington, 1977-88, Kyoto U. Comparative Law Conv., Tokyo, 1984. Co-author: Advanced Patent Prosecution, 1977; patentee in field. Mem. adv. bd. G.W. Law Sch. Recipient Caldwell scholarship Ohio State U., 1964. Mem. ABA, Am. Intellectual Property Assn., Md. Bar Assn., Customs and Internat. Trade Bar Assn., Seoul Club, Am. C. of C., Manor Country Club. Democrat. Roman Catholic. Avocations: golf, tennis. Home: 15309 Basswood Ct Rockville MD 20853-1801 Office: Samsung Electronics 2445 M St NW Washington DC 20037-1435 also: Samsung Main Bldg 10th Fl 250 Taepyung-Ro, Chung-Ku Seoul Republic of Korea

DONOHOE, JAMES DAY, lawyer; b. Rochester, N.Y., Aug. 10, 1943; s. James Vincent and Constance Traganza (Day) D.; m. Laurel Andrews, Aug. 8, 1987; children by previous marriage: J. Douglas, Jeffrey, Cynthia. BS, Cornell U., 1965; JD, Cath. U. Am., 1969; MBA, Case Western Res. U., 1979. Bar: N.Y. 1970, Ohio 1974, Pa. 1988., S.C. 2002. Assoc. Pennie & Edmonds, N.Y.C., 1967-73; house counsel Republic Steel Corp., Cleve., 1973-84, LTV Corp., Dallas, 1984-89, Republic Engineered Steels Inc., Massillon, Ohio, 1989-98; atty. Squire, Sanders & Dempsey, Cleve., 1998-99, Legal Affairs Adminstrn. LLC, Massillon, 1999—2003, The Bullard Law Firm, Hilton Head, SC, 2003—. Mem.: ABA, S.C. Bar Assn. Home: 1587 Breining St Pittsburgh PA 15226-1940 Office: 8 Lafayette Pl Hilton Head Island SC 29925

DONOHOE, JEROME FRANCIS, lawyer; b. Yankton, S.D., Mar. 17, 1939; s. Francis A. and Ruth D. Donohoe; m. Elaine Bush, Jan. 27, 1968; 1 child, Nicole Elaine. BA, St. John's U., 1961; JD cum laude, U. Minn., 1964. Bar: Ill. 1964, S.D. 1964. Atty. Atchison, Topeka & Santa Fe Ry. Co., Chgo., 1967-73, gen. atty., 1973-78; gen. counsel corp. affairs Santa Fe Industries Inc., Chgo., 1978-84; v.p. law Santa Fe Industries, Inc., Chgo., 1984-90, Santa Fe Pacific Corp., Chgo., 1984-94; ptnr. Mayer, Brown, Rowe & Maw, Chgo., 1990-99, sr. counsel, 1999—. Bd. dirs. Evanston Cmty. Found., 2000—. Capt. JAGC U.S. Army, 1964—67. Fellow: Ill. Bar Found.; mem.: ABA (sect. officer, pub. utility, comm. and transp. law sect.), Northwestern U. Assocs., Mich. Shores Club (Wilmette, Ill.), Chgo. Athletic Assn., Chgo. Club. Office: Mayer Brown Rowe & Maw 190 S La Salle St Ste 3100 Chicago IL 60603-3441 E-mail: jdonohoe@mayerbrown.com.

DONOHUE, CRAIG S. trade association administrator; married; 3 children. BA, Drake U.; LLM in Fin. Svcs. Regulation, Ill. Inst. Tech., Chgo.; JD, John Marshall Law Sch.; M in Mgmt., Northwestern U. Bar: Ill. Assoc. McBride, Baker & Coles, Chgo.; corp. atty. Chgo. Mercantile Exch., Inc., 1989—95, v.p., assoc. gen. counsel, 1995—97, v.p. market regulation, 1997—98, sr. v.p., gen. counsel, 1998—2000, mng. dir., bus. devel. and corp./legal affairs, 2000—01, mng. dir., chief adminstrv. officer, 2001—02; exec. v.p., chief adminstrv. officer, Office of the CEO Chgo. Mercantile Exch. Holdings Inc. and Chgo. Mercantile Exch. Inc., 2002—. Office: CME 30 S Wacker Dr Chicago IL 60606*

DONOHUE, DAVID PATRICK, engineering executive, retired navy rear admiral; b. N.Y.C., May 7, 1931; s. Patrick Joseph and Beatrice Anna (Bligh) D.; m. Dolores Theresa Bowen, Nov. 24, 1956; children: Christine, David, Steven, Joanne, Denise. AB, Holy Cross Coll., 1953; MSEE, U.S. Naval Postgrad. Sch., 1961; postgrad., Harvard Bus. Sch., 1969, Kennedy Sch. Nat. Security, 1986. Design advisor Vietnam Naval Shipyard, Saigon, Vietnam, 1965-66; plan/estimating supt. Puget Sound Naval Shipyard, Bremerton, Wash., 1966-69; ship projects officer, supr. shipbuilding USN, Seattle, 1969-71; ship systems engr. Staff Naval Air Forces Pacific, San Diego, 1971-75; exec. dir. surface platforms Naval Sea Systems Command, Washington, 1975-77; prodn., planning officer Pearl Harbor (Hawaii) Naval Shipyard, 1977-80; shipyard commdr. Norfolk Naval Shipyard, Portsmouth, Va., 1980-83; rear adm., dir. maintenance U.S. Atlantic Fleet USN, Norfolk, Va., 1983-89; gen. mgr. The Jonathan Corp., Norfolk, 1989-91, program mgr., 1991-93, v.p., gen. mgr. shipyard, 1993-95; corp. tech. dir. Integrated Sys. Analysts, Inc., Chesapeake, Va., 1995—2002; chmn. bd. dirs. Cen. Mgmt. Sys., 2000—01; corp. tech. dir. Thermal Spray & Machine, Inc., Norfolk, 2002—. Exec. adv. coun. Old Dominion U. Coll. Bus. and Pub. Adminstrn., 1996-99; bd. dirs. Unitech Corp., Hampton. Va. Pres. Portsmouth Area United Way, 1981-82, com. mem. South Hampton Roads chpt., Norfolk, 1983-88; chmn. Portsmouth Armed Svcs. YMCA, 1981-82. Mem. Am. Soc. for Quality Control (vice-chmn. Tidewater, Va. sect. 1995-97, chmn. 1997-98, sec. 1998-2000), Am. Soc. Naval Engrs. (councillor Tidewater sect. 1981-84, vice chmn. Tiewater sect. 2003—, ret. nat. councillor 1990-93, 2002—), Soc. Naval Architects and Marine engrs. (Hampton Rds. sect. chmn. 1985-86, chmn. ship prodn. com. nat. shipbuilding rsch. program 1990-95, Va. gov.'s commn. on base retention 1995), Norfolk Naval Shipyard Portsmouth Assn. (pres. 1998-2000), Town Point Club (bd. govs. 1994-2002). Republican. Roman Catholic. Home: 216 Brackenridge Ave Norfolk VA 23505-4322 Office: Integrated Sys Analysts Inc 2400 Hampton Blvd Norfolk VA 23517-1004 E-mail: donohued6@cox.net., dave.donohue@tsmnorfolk.com.

DONOHUE, EDITH M. human resources specialist, educator; b. Nov. 10, 1938; d. Edward Anthony and Beatrice (Jones) McParland; m. Salvatore R. Donohue, Aug. 23, 1960; children: Kathleen, Deborah. BA, Coll. Notre Dame, Balt., 1960; MS, Johns Hopkins U., 1981; postgrad., CASE (cert. of adv. study in edn.), 1985; PhD in Human Resources, CASE, 1990. Cert. counselor, national, sr. profl. human resources. Dir. pub. rels. Coll. Notre Dame, Balt., 1970—71, dir. continuing edn., 1981—86; program coord. bus. and industry Catonsville C.C., Balt. County, Md., 1986—88; mgr. tng. and devel. Sheppard Pratt Hosp., Balt., 1988—90; assoc. prof., Sch. Edn. Barry U., 1993—98; cons. in human resources Stuart, Fla., 1985—. Adj. faculty Loyola Coll. Grad. Studies Program, Fla. Inst. Tech., Indian River C. of C. Co-author: Communicate Like a Manager, 1989, Life After Layoff, 2003; contbg. author career devel. workshop manual, 1985; contbr. articles to profl. jours. Pres. Cathedral Sch. Parents Assn., 1972-74; asst. treas., treas. Md. Gen. Hosp. Aux., 1975-78; dir. sect. Exec. Women's Network, Balt., 1983-85; adv. bd. Mayor's Commn. on Aging, 1981-86; dir. Md. Assn. Higher Edn., 1985-88; vol. trainer United Way Martin County, co-chair campaign, 1994—, strategic planning com., 1998—; mem. steering com. Chautauqua South. Recipient Mayor's Citation, City of Balt. Council, 1985, Woman of Distinction, Martin County, 1999. Mem. AAUW (dir., v.p. 1980-83),, Am. Assn. Tng. and Devel. (bd. dirs.), Am. Counseling Assn., Soc. Human Resources Mgmt., Martin County Personnel Mgt. Assn. (edn. chmn. 1991-94), Martin County Libr. Assn. Inc. (pres. 2001-2003), Martin County C. of C. (edn. com. 1991-94), Friends of Lyric (bd. dirs. chmn., strategic planning, pres.), Soroptimist Internat. of Stuart, Chi Sigma Iota (pres.), Phi Delta Kappa. Republican. Roman Cath. Avocations: tennis, performing arts, reading, wellness. Home: Apt 3103 144 NE Edgewater Dr Stuart FL 34996-4477 E-mail: edonohue@gate.net.

DONOHUE, GEORGE L. mechanical engineer, educator; b. Wichita, Kans., July 8, 1944; s. George Edward and Dorothy Mae (Cunningham) Custer; m. Andreana Grillis, June 7, 1969; children: Carmen, Kathleen, Georgiana, Caroline. Student, Ga. Inst. Tech., Atlanta, 1962-64; BSME, U. Houston, 1967; MS, Okla. State U., 1968, PhD, 1972. Coop student NASA, Clear Lake, Tex., 1963-67; postdoctoral fellow Naval Undersea Ctr., Pasadena, Calif., 1972-73; br. head Naval Ocean Sys. Ctr., San Diego, 1973-76, divsn. head, 1977-79; prog. mgr. Def. Adv. Rsch. Project Agy., Arlington, Va., 1976-77, office dir., 1988-89; v.p. Dynamics Tech. Inc., Torrance, Calif., 1979-84; prog. mgr. Rand Corp., Santa Monica, Calif., 1984-88, v.p., 1989-94; assoc. adminstr. rsch. and acquisition FAA, Washington, 1994-98; prof. George Mason U., Fairfax, Va., 2000—. Vis. prof. air transp. tech. and policy Sch. IT & Engring. George Mason U., Fairfax, 1998—2000, prof. sys. engring., 2000—. Author: book on air transp. sys. engring., 2001; contbr. articles to profl. jours. Treas. YMCA Girls Gymnastics Team, San Pedro, Calif., 1983; adult advisor Girl Scouts U.S., Torrance, 1987—88. Recipient Merit Civil Svc. medal, Dept. of Def., 1977; NDEA fellow, 1967, NRC fellow, 1972. Fellow: AIAA (mem. policy com. 1990—94); mem.: Air Traffic Control Assn., Exptl. Aircraft Assn., Aircraft Owners & Pilots Assn., Elks, Sigma Xi, Pi Tau Sigma, Omicron Delta Kappa, Tau Beta Pi. Roman Catholic. Avocations: flying, skiing, sailing, backpacking.

DONOHUE, JAMES J. lawyer; b. N.Y.C., Dec. 3, 1947; s. Joseph P. and Constance (Anderson) D.; m. Carol A. Mager, July 29, 1973; children: Jay Mager, Megan Constance. AB, Dartmouth Coll., 1969; JD, U. Pa., 1972. Atty. Fed. Defender Phila., 1972-76; ptnr. White and Williams, Phila., 1976—. Mem. ABA (chair trial evidence com., litigation sect. 1995-99, judiciary task force 2000—), Phila Bar Found. (trustee 1992-97), Phila. Racquet Club, Phila. Cricket Club, Rotary Club Phila. (bd. dirs. 1993-95), WYCK (bd. dirs. 1996—, treas. 1998—). Avocations: skiing, golf. Office: White and Williams 1800 One Liberty Pl 1650 Market St Philadelphia PA 19103-7395 E-mail: donohuej@whiteandwilliams.com.

DONOHUE, JOHN JOSEPH, law educator; b. Alexandria, Va., Jan. 30, 1953; s. Mildred (Sileo) Donohue; m. Marijke Rijsberman, Dec. 27, 1986 (div.); 1 child, Lauren Elizabeth; m. Maureen O'Kicki, Oct. 25, 1995; children: Aidan John, Patrick John. BA, Hamilton Coll., 1974; JD, Harvard U., 1977; PhD, Yale U., 1986. Bar: Conn. 1977, D.C. 1978. Assoc. Covington & Burling, Washington, 1978-81; fellow Civil Liability Program, Law Sch. Yale U., New Haven, 1985-86; rsch. fellow Am. Bar Found., Chgo., 1986-95; Class of 1967 James B. Haddad prof. law Northwestern U., Chgo., 1994-95; prof. Stanford (Calif.) Law Sch., 1995—, William H. Neukom prof. law, 2002—. Vis. prof. Harvard Law Sch., 2003. Contbr. articles to profl. jours. Mem. ABA, Am. Econ. Assn., Phi Beta Kappa. Office: Stanford Law Sch Crown Quad Stanford CA 94305 E-mail: jjd@stanford.edu.

DONOHUE, JOHN PATRICK, lawyer; b. N.Y.C., Sept. 16, 1944; s. Joseph Francis and Catherine Elizabeth (Feeney) D.; m. Patricia Ann Holly, June 11, 1977; children: Eileen Mary, Anne Catherine. BA, Providence Coll., 1966; JD, Catholic U. Am., 1969. Bar: N.Y. 1973, U.S. Ct. Appeals (2d cir.) 1973, U.S. Ct. Appeals (fed. cir.) 1974, N.J. 1975, U.S. Dist. Ct. N.J. 1975, U.S. Dist. Ct. (so., ea. dists.) N.Y. 1975, U.S. Supreme Ct. 1978, D.C. 1981, Pa. 1986. Spl. agt. FBI, Washington, 1969-71; assoc. Donohue & Donohue, N.Y.C., 1971-74, ptnr., 1974—. Adj. prof. law internat. bus. transactions Seton Hall U. Sch. Law, Newark, 1986-94, 2002—. Author book sect. Customs Fraud Section on Business Crimes, 1982; co-author: The Prevention and Prosecution of Computer and High Technology Crime. Bd. dirs. Maritime Exch. Delaware River and Bay, 1989—; mem. bd. regents Cath. U. Am., 1990-2000, chmn., 1997-2000; trustee Rosemont (Pa.) Sch., 1995—, chmn., 1996-2001; mem. bd. visitors Cath. U. Sch. Law, 1998—; mem. Congress of Fellows, Ctr. for Internat. Legal Studies, Salzburg, Austria. Named Man of Yr., Phila. Customs, Brokers and Forwarders Assn., 1984. Mem. Customs and Internat. Trade Bar Assn., Pa. State Bar Assn., Republican. Roman Catholic. Office: Donohue & Donohue 232 S 4th St Philadelphia PA 19106-3704 E-mail: jdonohue@donohueanddonohue.com.

DONOHUE, JOYCE MORRISSEY, biochemist, toxicologist, nutritionist, educator; b. Holyoke, Mass., Jan. 27, 1940; d. Richard Charles and Anna Elizabeth (Joyce) Morrissey; m. John Thomas Donohue, Jan. 27, 1973; children: Maura Joyce, John Thomas, Sean Richard, Eric Patrick. BS, Framingham (Mass.) State Coll., 1961; MS, U. Mass., 1964; PhD, U. N.H., 1972. Cert. secondary sch. tchr., Mass. ; registered dietitian. Tchr. West Springfield (Mass.) H.S., 1962-66; instr. Framingham State Coll., 1966-68, asst. prof. biochemistry and nutrition, 1971-72, assoc. prof., 1972-73; adj. prof. No. Va. C.C., Annandale, 1974—, Va. Poly. Inst. and State U., Falls Church, 1979-97; health scientist VJ Cicconi & Assocs., Woodbridge, Va., 1981-89; toxicology svc. mgr. Law Environ. Washington Svc. Ctr., Woodbridge, Va., 1989-90; program mgr., prin. scientist ICAIR/Life Sys. Inc., Arlington, Va., 1990-94; mgr. toxicology NSF Internat., Washington, 1994-96; program mgr., sr. toxicologist Office Water U.S. EPA, Washington, 1996—. Mem. Prince William County Wetlands Bd., 1989—; mem. dietetics program adv. com. James Madison U., Va., 1997—. Recipient Alumni Achievement award Framingham State Coll., 1986. Mem. AAAS, Am. Dietetic Assn. (cert.), No. Va. Dietetic Assn., Sigma Xi. Home: 11979 William And Mary Cir Woodbridge VA 22192-1314 Office: USEPA 1200 Pennsylvania Ave NW Mail Code 4304T Washington DC 20460

DONOHUE, KENNETH M. federal agency administrator; m. Kathleen Donohue; children: Kenneth Martin, Timothy Patrick, Brian Richard. Sect. chief Office Investigations Resolution Trust Corp., asst. dir.; fed. law enforcement staff U.S. Secret Svc.; mem. nat. bank fraud working group Fed. Deposit Ins. Corp., 1996; inspector gen. Dept. HUD, Washington. Office: Dept HUD Inspector Gen 451 7th St SW Washington DC 20410-9000

DONOHUE, MARC DAVID, chemical engineering educator; b. Watertown, N.Y., Sept. 10, 1951; s. Paul Francis and Beverly Gertrude (Hodge) D.; m. Mary Ann Chamberlain, July 20, 1974; children: Paul, Megan, Ian. BS, Clarkson Coll. Tech., 1973; PhD, U. Calif., Berkeley, 1977. Asst. prof. chem. engring. Clarkson Coll. Tech., Potsdam, N.Y., 1977-79; asst. prof. Johns Hopkins U., Balt., 1979-83, assoc. prof., 1983-87, prof., 1987—, chmn. dept., 1984-95, assoc. dean, 1999—. Recipient Adminstr.'s Pollution Prevention award for Region III, U.S. EPA, 1992, Md. sect. Outstanding Engring. Achievement award NSPE, 1989. Mem. Am. Inst. Chem. Engrs., Am. Chem. Soc. (Md. chemist 1999), Am. Soc. Engring. Edn. (Outstanding Young Engr. award 1984), Tau Beta Pi. E-mail: mdd@jhu.edu.

DONOHUE, MARGARET ANNE, retail company executive; b. Bronxville, N.Y., Aug. 13, 1953; d. James Patrick and Marie Elizabeth (Strack) D. AAS in Merchandising, Fashion Inst. Tech., N.Y.C., 1973, AAS in Textile Tech., 1976; BS in Mktg., SUNY, 1978. Asst. buyer Sears, Roebuck & Co., N.Y.C., 1973—79; asst. to pres., gen. mgr. Lonia Designs, Inc., N.Y.C., 1979—87; buyer ladies' dept. Bancroft Haberdashers, Ltd., N.Y.C., 1987—90; COO Beaucamp Pl., Greenwich, Conn., 1990; buyer, mgr. Accessoires, N.Y.C., 1990—91; sales assoc. Galeries Lafayette, N.Y.C., 1991—94; costume designer Dicapo Opera Theatre, Inc., 1994—97; evening, weekend and holiday mgr. Lori's Hallmark, Inc., 1997—2001. Vol. Women's Aux. Hosp. for Joint Diseases, 1996—. Home: 285 Avenue C Apt 8E New York NY 10009-2328 Office: 310 E 17th St New York NY 10003

DONOHUE, MARY, lieutenant governor; b. Rensselaer County, N.Y. children: Sara, Justin. B.Edn., Coll. New Rochelle, 1968; MS in Edn., Russell Sage Coll., Troy, N.Y., 1973; JD, Union U., 1983. Bar: N.Y. 1983. Tchr. elem., jr. h.s. Rensselaer and Albany County (N.Y.) sch. dists., Albany, 1969-78; law clk., intern U.S. Atty.'s Office, Albany, 1980-83; assoc. O'Connell & Aronowitz, Albany, 1983-88; pvt. practice Troy, 1988-92; asst. county atty. Rensselaer County, 1990-92, dist. atty., 1992-96; justice N.Y. Supreme Ct., 3rd Jud. Dist., 1996-98; lt. gov. State of N.Y., Albany, 1998—. Chair Capital Dist. Women's Adv. Coun., 1996; mem. Gov.-elect Pataki's Transition Team for Criminal Justice, 1994-96. Republican. Office: Office of Lt Governor State Capitol Rm 246 Albany NY 12224*

DONOHUE, PATRICIA CAROL, academic administrator; b. St. Louis, Jan. 11, 1946; d. Carroll and Juanita Donohue; m. James H. Stevens Jr., Aug. 27, 1966 (div. Mar. 1984); children: James H. Stevens III, Carol Janet Stevens. AB, Duke U., 1966; MA, U. Mo., 1974, PhD, 1982. Tchr. math. in secondary schs., Balt., St. Louis and Shawnee Mission, Kans., 1966-71; lectr. U. Mo., Kansas City, 1975-76, rsch. asst. affirmative action, 1976-79, coord. affirmative action, 1979-82, instl. rsch. assoc., 1982-84, acting dir. affirmative action and acad. pers., 1984; dir. instl. rsch. Lakeland C.C., 1984-86; asst. dean acad. affairs, math., engring. and tech. Harrisburg Area C.C., 1986-89, dean sch. bus., engring., and tech., 1989-93, dean Lebanon campus, v.p. cmty. devel. and external affairs, 1993; vice chancellor edn. St. Louis C.C., 1993—2002, acting pres. Florissant Valley campus, 1998-99; pres. Luzerne County C.C., 2002—. Active Pa. Coun. on Vocat. Edn., 1989—93; v.p. St. Louis Sch. to Work, Inc., 1994—96, pres., 1996—2002; chairperson Pa. Occupl. Deans, 1988—93; bd. dirs., chmn. edn. com. Humane Soc. Mo., 1997—2002; cons. evaluator North Ctrl. Assn., 2000—; bd. dirs. Diamond City Partnership. Leader Hemlock coun. Girl Scouts U.S.A.; Bd. dirs., v.p. Am. Cancer Soc. Jackson County, 1975—84; mem. adv. coun. Ben Franklin Partnership, 1988—93; sec. Cen. Pa. Tech. Coun., 1992—93; mem. steering com. New Baldwin Corridor Coalition, 1991—93, chair edn. task force, 1992—93; mem. Leadership St. Louis, 1996—97; bd. dirs. Hemlock coun. Girl Scouts U.S.A., 1986—93, PTA, 1975—77, Cmty. Lebanon Assocs., Cen. Pa. Tech. Coun., 1989—93, Mantec, 1988—93, Delta Gamma Ctr. for Children with Visual Impairments, 2001—02, Diamond City Partnership, 2003—. Recipient Outstanding Service and Achievement award U. Mo. Kansas City, 1976, Outstanding Svc. award Ctrl. Pa. Tech. Coun., 1993; Jack C. Coffey grantee, 1978; named Outstanding Woman AAUW, 1989, one of Outstanding Leaders Nat. Inst. Leadership Devel., 1986, Exec. Leadership Inst., 1990. Mem.: Assn. Inst. Rsch., Women's Network, Nat. Assn. Student Pers. Adminstrs., Women's Equity Project, Soc. Mfg. Engrs. (chmn. 1989—90), Am. Assn. Women in Cmty. and Jr. Colls. (Pa. state coord. 1988, bd. dirs. Region 3 1989—91), Nat. Coun. for Occupl. Edn. (chairperson diversity task force 1991, chairperson job tng. 2000 task force 1992, v.p. programs 1992—93, bd. dirs. 1992—2000, v.p. membership 1993—94, pres. 1995—96, past pres. 1996—97), Am. Assn. Cmty. Colls. (coun. affiliated chairpersons 1994—2000, commn. on cmty. and workforce devel. 1995—97, chairperson coun. 1996—2000, commn. on cmty. and workforce devel. 1998—2001), Am. Vocat. Assn., Math. Assn. Am., Nat. Coun. Tchrs. of Math., ASCD, Delta Gamma (v.p., del. nat. conv. 1988, pres. 1989-91, bd. dirs. Delta Gamma Ctr. for Children with Visual Impairment 2001-) (del. nat. conv. 1988, pres. 1989—91, v.p., Cream Rose Outstanding Svc. award 1970), Pi Lambda Theta, Phi Kappa Phi, Phi Delta Kappa (pres. 1975, Read fellow 1989). Home: 40 Elmcrest Dr Dallas PA 18612 Office: Luzerne County C C 1333 S Prospect St Nanticoke PA 18634

DONOHUE, STACEY LEE, English language and literature educator; b. East Patchogue, NY, Dec. 1, 1963; BA in English, SUNY, Binghamton, 1985; PhD in English, CUNY, 1995. Instr. English, Borough of Manhattan C.C., CUNY, 1988-95; assoc. prof. English, Ctrl. Oreg. C.C., Bend, 1995—; acting chair Fine Arts Dept., 2003—04. Adj. instr. NYU, 1990-93; adj. instr. English Ea. Oreg. U., 1996—, Oreg. State U. Cascades Campus, 1996—. Editor: Cmty. Coll. Humanist, 2002—. Bd. dirs. Human Dignity Coalition, Bend, 1998-2002. Mem. MLA, chair MLA Com. on Com. Coll., Pamla MLA, Multi Ethnic Lit. of U.S. Avocations: hiking, movies. Office: Ctrl Oreg CC Humanities Dept 2600 NW College Way Bend OR 97701-5933 E-mail: sdonohue@cocc.edu.

DONOHUE, THOMAS JOSEPH, transportation association executive; b. N.Y.C., Aug. 12, 1938; s. Thomas Joseph Sr. and Ruth (Ahern) D.; m. Elizabeth Schulz, June 29, 1963; children: Thomas, Keith, John. BA, St. John's U., 1963, PhD (hon.), 1985; MBA, Adelphi U., 1965; PhD (hon.), Marymount U., 1991. V.p. Fairfield (Conn.) U., 1967-69; dep. asst. postmaster gen. U.S. Postal Svc., Washington, 1969-71, asst. regional postmaster gen. San Francisco, 1971-73, dist. mgr. N.Y.C., 1973-75; asst. regional postmaster gen. U.S. Postal Service, N.Y.C., 1975-76; group v.p. U.S.A. C. of C., Washington, 1976-84; pres., CEO Am. Trucking Assns., Alexandria, Va., 1985—; pres. and CEO US Chamber of Commerce, Wash., DC, 1997—. Bd. dirs. Sunrise Assisted Living, Fairfax, Va., Internat. Planning and Analysis Ctr., Arlington, Va., Newmyer Assn., Marymount U., Hwy. Users Fedn., Washington, Hudson Inst., Indpls.; mem. Nat. Commn. on Intermodal Transp., Transp. Rsch. Bd.; mem. adv. com. transp. Northwestern U. Bd. dirs. Marymount U. Office: US Chamber of Commerce 1615 H St NW Washington DC 20062-0001

DONOHUGH, DONALD LEE, physician; b. LA, Apr. 12, 1924; s. William Noble and Florence Virginia (Shelton) D.; m. Virginia Eskew McGregor, Sept. 12, 1950 (div. 1971); children: Ruth, Laurel, Marilee, Carol, Greg; m. Beatrice Ivany Redick, Dec. 3, 1976; stepchildren: Leslie Ann, Andrea Jean. BS, US Naval Acad., 1946; MD, U. Calif., San Francisco, 1956; MPH and Tropical Medicine, Tulane U., 1961. Diplomate Am. Bd. Internal Medicine. Intern U. Hosp., San Diego, 1956-57; resident Monterey County Hosp., 1957-58; dir. med. svc. US Dept. Interior, Am. Samoa, 1958-60; instr. Tulane U. Med. Sch., New Orleans, 1960-63; resident Tulane Svc. VA and Charity Hosp., New Orleans, 1961-63; cons. Internat. Ctr. for Rsch and Tng., Costa Rica, 1961-63; asst. prof. medicine and preventive medicine La. State U. Sch. Medicine, 1962-63, assoc. prof., 1963-65; vis. prof. U. Costa Rica, 1963-65; faculty advisor, head of AID program U. Costa Rica Med. Sch., 1965-67; dir. med. svcs. Med. Ctr. U. Calif. (formerly Orange County Hosp.), Irvine, 1967-69; assoc. clin. prof. U. Calif., Irvine, 1967-79, clin. prof., 1980-85; pvt. practice Tustin, Calif., 1970-80; with Joint Commn. on Accreditation of Hosp., 1981; cons. Kauai, Hawaii, 1981—. Author: The Middle Years, 1981, Practice Management, 1986, Kauai, 1988, 4th edit., 1992, Our Ancestors, 1995, The Story of Koloa, 2001, (second edition, 2002); co-translator; Rashomon (Ryonosuke Akutagawa), 1950; also numerous articles. Lt. USN, 1946-52, capt. USNR, 1966-84. Fellow Am. Coll. Physicians (life); mem. Delta Omega. Republican. Episcopalian. Home: 4890 Lawai Beach Rd Koloa HI 96756-9675 E-mail: dld@aloha.net.

DONOIAN, GEORGE, education executive; b. Detroit, Apr. 12, 1931; s. John H. and Irma Helen (Mekhitarian) D.; m. Eleanor Amanda Hall, July 29, 1961 (div. Feb. 1986); 1 child, John Hayden. BA, Wayne State U., 1954, MEd, 1955, EdD, 1963, postgrad., 1965. Cert. tchr. elem. and secondary edn., Mich. Elem. tchr. Detroit Pub. schs., 1954-65, reading coord., 1965-66, adminstr. h.s., 1966-67, program devel. adminstrn., 1967-71, bus. adminstr. schs., 1971-86; faculty Wayne County C.C., Detroit, 1970-71, prof. dept. psychology, 1971-72; prof. psychology and sociology St. Mary's Coll., Orchard Lake, Mich., 1991-94. Prof. psychology/edn. No. Mich. U., Marquette, 1965 Contbr. articles to profl. jours. Field rep. Am. Diabetes Assn., Dearborn Heights, Mich., 1991—. Sgt. U.S. Army, 1951-59. Recipient Anthony Wayne award Wayne State U., 1983. Mem. APA (emeritus mem.), Soc. for Armenian Studies, Armenian Numismatic Soc., Ret. Orgn. for Suprs. and Adminstrs., Wayne County Sch. Bus. Ofcls. (pres. 1982), Knights of Vartan (comdr. 1991-92). Republican. Presbyterian. Avocations: collecting miniature books, pocket knives and coins, travel, photography, jewelry making. Home: 26005 Joy Rd Dearborn Heights MI 48127-1100

DONOVAN, AGNES M. nun; b. Binghamton, N.Y., Sept. 23, 1949; BA in Psychology, U. Pitts., 1971; MS, SUNY, Oswego, 1979; PhD, U. N.C., 1985, Franciscan U. of Steubenville, Ohio, 2000. Counselor, instr. Cortland C.C., Dryden, NY, 1979—80; sch. psychologist The Spl. Children's Ctr., Ithaca, NY, 1980—81; dir. of cons. dept. Cortland C.C., Dryden, 1980—81; sch. psychologist Durham (Va.) City Schs., 1984—85; asst. prof. psychology The Coll. of William and Mary, Williamsburg, Va., 1985—99, Columbia U., N.Y.C.,

1989—91; mother gen. Sister of Life, N.Y.C., 1993—. Cons. Montessori Ctr. for Tchr. Edn., Scarsdale, NY, 1976—91. Mem.: Nat. Assn. Sch. Psychologists, Am. Psychol. Assn. Roman Catholic. Office: Sisters of Life 586 McLean Ave Yonkers NY 10705

DONOVAN, ANDREW JOSEPH, financial consultant; b. N.Y.C., Nov. 22, 1952; s. Andrew Joseph and Marion (Cooley) D.; m. Margaret Mary Dowd, June 17, 1984; children: Andrew, John, Daniel. BA, Fordham U., 1974, MA, 1976, PhD, 1983; grad., Coll. Fin. Planning, 1996, Naval War Coll., 2000. Adj. instr. Fordham U., Bronx, N.Y., 1976-78; ops. mgr. Merrill Lynch, Pierce, Fenner & Smith, N.Y.C., 1978-79, stockbroker Mt. Kisco, N.Y., 1984-88, Kidder Peabody, White Plains, N.Y., 1988-89; dir. devel. N.Y. Med. Coll., Valhalla, 1989-93, U.S. Merchant Marine Acad. Found., Inc., Kings Point, N.Y., 1993-96; fin. cons. Chase Investment Svcs. Corp., 1996-2001, Donovan Fin., 2001—. Chmn. N.Y. State 4-H Found., Inc., 1990-92. Author: The Political Clock, 1983. Councilman Town of Yorktown, N.Y., 1990-93; legislator Westchester County, N.Y., 1994-97. Lt. cmdr. USNR, 1979—. Fellow H.B. Earhart Found., 1976. Republican. Roman Catholic. Avocation: collecting books. Home: 3195 Radcliffe Dr Yorktown Heights NY 10598 2520

DONOVAN, ANN BURCHAM, medical office administrator; m. Gary Leonard Donovan, (div. June 1988); children: Leonard Matthew, William Marshall. Student, Baker U., 1970-71; Cert., Kansas City Sch. Med. Assts., 1973. Cert. med. practice exec. Med. asst. Penn Valley Med. Group, Kansas City, Mo., 1973-76, supr. accounts receivable, 1976-82; office adminstr. Heartland Hematology-Oncology Assn., Inc., Kansas City, Mo., 1982—. Cons. on cancer and AIDS patients for med. offices, Kansas City, Mo., 1982—. Contbr. articles to profl. jours. Mem. NAFE, Northland Med. Mgrs. Assn., Med. Group Mgrs. Assn., Adminstrs. of Oncology-Hematology Assn., Greater Kansas City Med. Mgrs. Assn. (recognition com.), Kansas City Sci. Fiction and Fantasy Soc. Avocations: painting, horseback riding, fishing, traveling. Office: Heartland Hematology Oncology Assn Inc 2000 NE Vivion Rd Kansas City MO 64118-6127

DONOVAN, BILLY, university basketball coach; b. May 30, 1965; m. Christine D'Auria; children: William, Hasbrouck, Bryan. BA, Providence Coll., 1987. Profl. basketball player N.Y. Knicks, NBA, 1987-88; grad. asst. coach U. Ky., Lexington, 1989-90, asst. coach, 1990-93, assoc. coach, 1993-94; head coach Marshall U., 1994-96, U. Fla., Gainesville, 1996—. Named Nat. Rookie Coach of Yr., Basketball Times, 1994, W.Va. Coll. Coach of Yr., 1994, So. Conf. Coach of Yr., 1994. Office: U Fla Basketball Office PO Box 14485 Gainesville FL 32604-2485

DONOVAN, BRIAN, freelance journalist; b. Syracuse, N.Y., Mar. 11, 1941; children: Gregg, Becky. BA, Syracuse U., 1963. With Dem. and Chronicle, Rochester, NY, 1964—67; investigative reporter Newsday, Melville, NY, 1967—2001. Recipient Pulitzer Prize for investigative reporting, 1995, George Polk award for Nat. Reporting, 1980, John Hancock award for Fin. Reporting, 1985, others. E-mail: briandonovan26@hotmail.com.

DONOVAN, BRIAN JOSEPH, lawyer; b. Paterson, N.J., Feb. 12, 1953; s. John Harold and Helen (Cheevers) D.; m. Rachael Cecile Couvillon, Jan. 16, 1982; children: Meaghan Marie, Michael John. Student, Villanova U., 1970-71; BS in Marine and Nuclear Engring., U.S. Merchant Marine Acad., 1975; JD, Syracuse U., 1997. Lic. chief engr. USCG. Marine engr. J. Ray McDermott, U.K., 1975-77; sr. project mgr. Offshore Logistics, Inc., various fgn. cities, 1977-82; prin. B. Donovan and Assocs., Inc., Lafayette, La., and Riyadh, Saudi Arabia, 1982—; chmn., chief exec. officer Internat. Drilling and Exploration, Inc., Lafayette, Montevideo, Uruguay, 1987—. Del. U.S.-China Joint Session on Industry, Trade, and Econ. Devel., China, 1988; founder The Mercosur Group, Buenos Aires, 1992. Author: Vessel Preservation, 1986; patentee oil and gas well blowout suppression system. Mem. ABA, Fla. Bar, Internat. Bar Assn., Inter-Am. Bar Assn., Am. Soc. Naval Architects and Marine Engrs., U.S. Mcht. Marine Acad. Alumni Assn. Roman Catholic. Avocations: golf, skiing, Karate, world travel. Office: PO Box 13272 Tampa FL 33681-7455 Home: 3221 Oakellar Ave Tampa FL 33611 E-mail: donovanb@gte.net.

DONOVAN, BRUCE ELLIOT, classics educator, university dean; b. Lawrence, Mass., Mar. 8, 1937; s. Harry Albert and Ruth Hannah (Kent) D.; m. Doris Louise Stearn, Sept. 7, 1959; children: Gregory Stearn, Erika Ruth. AB, Brown U., 1959; postgrad., U. Bristol, Eng., 1959-60; MA, Yale U., 1961, PhD, 1965; postgrad., Rutgers Center for Alcohol Studies, 1976. Instr. Yale U., 1962-65; from instr. to prof. classics Brown U., Providence, 1965—, assoc. dean for chem. dependency, 1977—, dean freshmen and sophomores, 1981-87, assoc. dean coll., 1977—. Instr. summer sch. alcohol studies Rutgers U.; cons. on collegiate alcoholism and other drug abuse. Author: Euripides Papyri from Oxyrhynchus, 1969; author articles and revs. on ancient Greek lit. and alcohol and other drug issues. Bd. dirs. Vols. in Action, 1975-90, R.I. Coun. on Alcoholism and Other Drug Dependence, 1973-94, New Eng. Inst. Alcohol Studies, 1978-91; founding mem. New Eng. Coll. Alcohol Network, Academics Recovering Together; steering com. Network Colls. and Univs. Committed to the Elimination of Substance Abuse, 1988-93. Fulbright fellow, 1959-60; Woodrow Wilson fellow, 1960-61; fellow Center for Hellenic Studies, Washington, 1971-72 Mem. Am. Philol. Assn., Employee Assistance Profl. Assn. Home: 261 President Ave Providence RI 02906-5537 Office: Brown U PO Box 1865 Providence RI 02912-1865

DONOVAN, CHARLES STEPHEN, lawyer; b. Boston, Feb. 28, 1951; s. Alfred Michael and Maureen (Murphy) D.; m. Lisa Marie Dicharry, Apr. 21, 1979; children: Yvette, Martine, Neal. BA, Haverford Coll., 1974; JD, Cornell U., 1977. Bar: Mass. 1977, La. 1977, Calif. 1982, U.S. Supreme Ct. 1988. Atty. Phelps, Dunbar, Marks, Claverie & Sims, New Orleans, 1977-81, Dorr, Cooper & Hays, San Francisco, 1981-84, Walsh, Donovan & Keech LLP, San Francisco, 1984-2000, Schnader Harrison Segal & Lewis, LLP, San Francisco, 2000—03, co-chmn. internat. practice group, 2002—03, Sheppard Mullin Richter & Hampton LLP, San Francisco, 2003—. Instr. maritime law Calif. Maritime Acad., Vallejo, 1982 ; spl. advisor U.S. State Dept., 1993-96. Contbr. numerous articles to profl. jours. Recipient Gustavus H. Robinson prize Cornell Law Sch., 1977. Mem.: ABA (chmn. admiralty and maritime law com. Chgo. 1989—90), Marine Exch. (bd. dirs. San Francisco Bay region 1993—96), Tulane Admiralty Inst. (permanent adv. bd.), Maritime Law Assn. U.S. (chmn. com. on maritime criminal law 1998—2001, chmn. subcom. on maritime liens and mortgages 1994—2001), Internat. Bar Assn. Avocations: skiing, hiking, mandolin, guitar, soccer. Office: Sheppard Mullin Richte & Hampton LLP 17th Fl 4 Embarcadero Center 17th Fl San Francisco CA 94111 E-mail: cdonovan@sheppardmullin.com.

DONOVAN, CRAIG POULENEZ, public administration educator; b. Calif; married; 3 children. BA, U. Calif., 1979, 80; MA, San Francisco State U., 1985; PhD, U. Wash., 1994. Mem. faculty various coll., Calif., Wash., and, NJ, 1983-94; sr. cons., mgr. Parallel Lines/Quantum Svc., San Francisco, 1984-89; assoc. prof., dir. BA/MPA honors program Kean U., Union, NJ, 1994—. V.p. policy and rsch. Pub. Policy Ctr. of NJ, 2000—. Co-author: Psychologically Speaking: A Self-Assessment, 1996; editor: A Guide to Graduate Education in Public Affairs and Public Administration, 1997; creator, prodr. : (TV series) The Reinvention Machine, Part of the Communicating Committment: The Public Service Excellence and Leadership Program, 1997—99; author: Director of Journals in Public Affairs, Public Administration and Political Science, 1999; contbr. articles to profl. jours.; author: Internships for Dummies, 2001, NJ Mcpl. Almanac, 2003, (almanac), 2003. Recipient Rsch. award Wash. Dept. of Transp., 1993, 94. Mem. Am. Soc. Pub. Adminstrn. (nat., NJ chpt.), Nat. Assn. Sch. Pub. Affairs and Adminstrn. (spl. projects editor), NJ Rsch. Consortium (exec. coun.), Acad. Mgmt. Office: Kean U Coll Bus and Pub Administration 1000 Morris Ave Union NJ 07083-7131

DONOVAN, DENNIS DALE, priest; b. Nyack, N.Y., Feb. 26, 1954; s. Thomas A. and Helen I. (Rudolph) D. BA in Philosophy, Don Bosco Coll., 1977; MA in Theology, MDiv in Theology, Pontifical Coll. Josephinum, 1983. Joined Soc. St. Francis de Sales, Roman Cath. Ch., 1973, ordained priest, 1983; cert. tchr. N.Y., N.J. Asst. adminstr. Salesian Sch., Goshen, N.Y., 1983-85; adminstr. Salesian Ctr., Columbus, Ohio, 1985-94, vicar, 1998—; dir. devel. Salesians of Don Bosco Province of St. Philip the Apostle, New Rochelle, N.Y., 1994-98; assoc. pastor St. Anthony Ch., Nanuet, N.Y., 1994-98; vicar Salesian Provincial House, New Rochelle, N.Y., 1994-98, Salesian Ctr., Columbus, Ohio, 1998—; assoc. pastor St. Joseph Cathedral, Columbus, Ohio, 1998—, St. Catherine Ch., Bexley, Ohio, 2002—. Assoc., youth min. St. Andrew Parish, Upper Arlington, Ohio, 1985-94; mem. Nat. Cath. Devel. Conf., 1995—; chmn. Ea. province Salesian Centennial Com., 1995-98. Chaplain Ohio Senate, Columbus, 1987-94, 2002—, Don Bosco Ladies Guild, Larchmont, N.Y., 1994—; trustee Salesian Boys and Girls Club Columbus, 1993—; mem. Juvenile Delinquency Task Force, Franklin County, 1988-90; mem. Westchester chpt. Crohn's and Colitis Found. Am., 1980—, Ctrl. Ohio chpt., 2000-; exec. dir. Salesian Boys and Girls Club, Columbus, Ohio, 1998—; mem. Profl. Adv. Coun. United Way Franklin County, Columbus, 1998—, Ohio Alliance of Boys & Girls Clubs, 1998—; mem. growth and measurement best practices task force Boys & Girls Clubs Am., Atlanta, 2002—; bd. trustees Discovery Dist. Devel. Corp., Columbus, 1998—; mem. race rels. vision coun. United Way Franklin County, 1999-2002, Columbus Met. Area Ch. Coun., 1999—; mem. Columbus Truancy Task Force, 2000-02; mem. adv. bd. City of Columbus Youth Commn., 2001—; mem. youth adv. commn. Cath. Diocese Columbus, 2003— ; mem. blue ribbon panel Jefferson Awards, Columbus, 2003. Recipient Senate Resolution award Ohio Senate, 1988. Mem. Acad. Boys & Girls Club Profls., Nat. Soc. Fundraising Execs., Am. Guild Organists (bd. dirs., chaplain 1986—), KC (chaplain 1987—), Assn. Boys and Girls Clubs Profls.; mem. cmty. adv. bd. Jr. League of Columbus, 2001—. Home: 80 S 6th St Columbus OH 43215-4726 E-mail: d.donovan@sbgcc.org.

DONOVAN, DENNIS FRANCIS, lawyer; b. Duluth, Minn., Jan. 29, 1925; s. Dennis Francis and Gertrude (Flaherty) D.; m. Lila Lindeman Munyon, Aug. 12, 1950; children: Kathleen Donovan Walsh, Theresa Donovan Brown, Dorothy Donovan; m. Marie Kendrick, Oct. 9, 1983. B.A., U. Minn., 1948, 1952, J.D., 1952. Bar: Minn. 1952, Calif. 1962. Ptnr. McCabe, VanEvera, et al, Duluth, 1952-61; assoc. U.S. atty. U.S. Dept. Justice, Los Angeles, 1961-64; assoc. Gendel, Raskoff, et al, Los Angeles, 1964-67; ptnr. Donovan & Somers, Los Angeles, 1967-82; v.p., sr. counsel Union Bank, Los Angeles, 1982; v.p., asst. gen. counsel Mitsui Mfrs. Bank, Los Angeles, 1983—; judge pro-tem Los Angeles Mcpl. Court, 1972-84; mem. exec. com. trial lawyer's sect. Los Angeles County Bar, 1977-80; dir. Legal Aid Soc., Duluth, 1957-59. Editor, contbr. to legal jours. Bd. dirs. Duluth Jr. C. of C., 1958, Duluth Playhouse, 1958; chmn. Duluth Port Authority Com., 1959. Served with USN, 1944-46, PTO. Mem. ABA, Los Angeles County Bar Assn. (exec. com. 1977 80), State Bar of Calif. (conf. of dels. 1977-78), U. Minn. Alumni Assn. (chmn. Los Angeles chpt. 1970). Club: Los Angeles Athletic. Home: 4047 Pala Mesa Oaks Dr Fallbrook CA 92028-8939 Office: 840 Union Bank Towers Torrance CA 90503

DONOVAN, DENNIS JOSEPH, addictionologist; b. Bklyn., Dec. 3, 1946; s. Denis Joseph and Mary Rita Donovan. BA, CCNY, 1970; MA, New Sch. for Social Rsch., 1973; MPS, L.I. U., 1991; PsyD, Newport (Calif.) U., 1996; PhD, Internat. U., 2001. Cert. practitioner energy diagnostic and treatment methods, master addiction counselor NAADAC. Tchr., adminstr. Nazareth Regional H.S., Bklyn., 1967-91; substance abuse psychotherapist Seafield, L.I., N.Y., 1991-92; addictionologist Interfaith Hosp., Bklyn., 1992—. Fellow: Nat. Assn. Forensic Counselors (diplomate), Nat. Assn. Cognitive/Behavioral Therapy (diplomate), Internat. Acad. Behavioral Medicine (diplomate), Am. Bd. Med. Psychotherapists (diplomate). Home: 3218 Fillmore Ave Brooklyn NY 11234-4837

DONOVAN, DONNA MAE, newspaper publisher; b. Jersey City, Mar. 14, 1952; d. William Clayton and Elizabeth Dorothy (Hanley) Hagemann; m. Jerome Francis Donovan, Nov. 6, 1982; children: Matthew James, Andrew William, Erin Elizabeth. BA in Journalism, Syracuse U., 1974. Pub. Burlington (Vt.) Free Press, 1986-91, Utica (N.Y.) Observer-Dispatch, 1991—; v.p. East region Gannett Co., 1986-88. Bd. dirs. Chittenden County United Way, 1987-91, also chmn. cmty. svc. div.; bd. dirs. Leadership Champlain, 1987-91; bd. dirs. Leadership Mohawk Valley, 1992-98, pres., 1995-96, sec., 1997-98; bd. dirs. Ctrl. N.Y. Cmty. Arts Coun., 1994—, Downtown Utica Devel. Assn., 1992-98, sec., 1996-98; bd. dirs. Oneida County Indsl. Devel. Corp., 1993-97; bd. dirs. Oneida County EDGE, 1998—, Mohawk Valley C.C. Found., 1997—; mem. nat. adv. bd. Syracuse U. Sch. Journalism; mem. Our Lady of Lourdes Parents Adv. Bd., 1992-98; bd. dirs. Sch. & Bus. Alliance Oneida-Madison Boces, 2000 . Mem. Newspaper Assn. Am., N.Y. Newspaper Pubs. Assn. (bd. dirs. 1993-96, 2001—), Mohawk Valley C. of C. (bd. dirs. 1999-2000), United Way of Greater Utica (bd. dirs. 1999-00, 99—). Roman Catholic. Office: Observer-Dispatch 221 Oriskany Plz Utica NY 13501-1201 E-mail: ddonovan@utica.gannett.com.

DONOVAN, DOROTHY DIANE, adult nurse practitioner; b. Red Bank, N.J., Apr. 26, 1961; d. John J. and Elsie H. (Carey) D. BSN, Seton Hall U., 1986, MSN, 1995. RN, N.J.; ANP, N.J.; cert. adult nurse practitioner. Adult nurse practitioner HIP Healthplan of N.J., Edison, N.J.; nurse dept. emergency Riverview Med. Ctr., Red Bank, NJ, 1999—2001, nurse mgr. emergency dept., 1999—2001; nurse Rheumatology Clin. Specialists, Amgen, Inc., 2001—. Mem. ANA, Am. Acad. Nurse Practitioners, N.J. Nurses Assn., Sigma Theta Tau.

DONOVAN, ELAINE F. social worker; b. Worcester, Mass., Nov. 17, 1938; d. Joseph James Donovan and Jeanette Josephina Kallery. BS, St. Joseph's Coll., Phila., 1977; MS, Springfield (Mass.) Coll., 1994. Cert. med. lab. tech. Carnegie Inst.; lic. social worker. Biochem. rsch. asst. Tuft's Med./Dental Sch., Boston, 1960-69; social worker Pernet Family Health Svc., Mass., N.Y., Ky., N.C., 1969-86; pastoral assoc. St. Mary's Parish, Lynn, Mass., 1986-91; aftercare coord. Solimine & Rhodes Funeral Home, Lynn, 1991-93; substance abuse clinician CAB Health and Recovery Svcs., Lynn, 1994—2001; cons. Project Cope, Lynn, Mass., 1997—2001, substance abuse and bereavement therapist, 2001—. Cons. Project Cope, Lynn, 1997—; dir. program devel. Renew Life Program, Lynn, 1993—, Puritan Lawn Meml. Park, Peabody, Mass.;, 1993-2000; mem. adv. bd. St. Mary's Parish, 1986-91; cons. Conway Funeral Home, Peabody, 1993-2000; social worker, substance abuse clinician New Eng. Shelter for Homeless Vets.-Vietnam Vets. Workshop, 1997-99. Contbr. articles to profl. jours.; program developer grief and substance abuse curriculum. Polit. campaigner Dem. Youth Com., Mass., 1965-69; advocate for hungry Bread for the World, Phila., 1974-77. Recipient Laudable Lynner award Dept. Environ. Mgmt., Boston, 1991, Live Wires award Classical H.S., Lynn, 1991, Youth Commn. award Lynn Youth Commn., 1958; grantee Campaign for Human Devel., Lynn, 1990. Mem. Am. Counseling Assn., Polish Legion of Am. Vets. Aux. (state sec. 1992-94), Assn. for Death, Edn., and Counseling. Democrat. Roman Catholic. Avocations: music, seaside walking, photography, reading. Home: 731 Boston St Lynn MA 01905-1539 Office: 100 Munroe St Lynn MA 01901-1520

DONOVAN, GEORGE JOSEPH, industry executive, consultant; b. Jersey City, Apr. 15, 1935; s. Matthew T. and Jean (Wilson) D.; m. Susan M. Tamborini; children— Marybeth, George Joseph Jr., Amy BS in Chemistry, St. Peter's Coll., Jersey City; postgrad. in organic chemistry, Seaton Hall U.; postgrad. in fin. and mktg., NYU; postgrad. in internat. relations, U. Pa. Research chemist Reaction Motors, Inc., Denville, N.J., 1956-58; research and devel. tech. rep. Thiokol Corp., Washington, 1961-63, asst. mgr. midwest regional office, 1963-65, mgr., dir. aerospace mktg., 1965-74, asst. to pres., 1974-75, corp. dir. mktg., 1975-77, v.p., 1977-82; dep. asst. sec. for systems Office of Asst. Sec. Air Force for Research Devel. and Logistics, Washington, 1983-85, prin. dep. asst. sec., 1985-86; pres. Prime Resources, 1986-87; v.p. Washington ops. Tex. Instruments Inc., 1988-91; v.p. govtl. rels. Smiths Industries, 1991—2003; also bd. dirs. Smiths Aerospace, Inc., 1991—; v.p. govtl. rels. Prime Resources, 2003—. Cons. to industry and govt., Def. Sci. Bd.; mem. Naval Rsch. Adv. Com.; bd. dirs. USO Capital. Patentee liquid and solid propellant ingredients and formulations (13); contbr. articles to profl. jours. Recipient Exceptional Civilian Svc. award USAF. Mem. AIAA, Navy League, Air Force Assn. (bd. dirs.), Navy League (exec. com.), Assn. U.S. Army, Navy League (bd. dirs.), Nat. Def. Indsl. Assn. (bd. dirs., chmn. pub. policy com.), Congression Country Club. Clubs: Congression Country. Avocations: hunting, fishing, golf, boating, reading. Home: 4632 Charleston Ter NW Washington DC 20007-1900

DONOVAN, GERALD ALTON, retired academic administrator, former university dean; b. Hartford, Conn., Feb. 10, 1925; s. Gerald Joseph and Alice Gertrude (Gleason) D.; m. Barbara Ann Hue, Feb. 1, 1948; children: Deborah E. (Mrs. Alan Abare), Clayton H., Bruce G. BA, U. Conn., 1950, MS, 1952; PhD, Iowa State U., 1955. Poultry nutritionist Charles Pfizer & Co., Inc., Terre Haute, Ind., 1955-60; prof., chmn. poultry sci. dept. U. Vt., 1960-66; asso. dir. U. Vt. (Vt. Agrl. Expt. Sta.); asso. dean Coll. Agr. and Home Econs., U. Vt., 1966-73; dean Coll. Resource Devel., U. R.I., Kingston, 1973-89, dir. Internat. Ctr. Marine Resource Devel., 1975-89, ret., 1989—; exec. dir. Northeastern Region Aquaculture Ctr., Southeastern Mass. U., 1988-90, ret., 1990. Mem. U.S. AID/BIFAD Joint Research Council, 1979-83. Contbr. articles to profl. jours. Bd. dirs. Vt. C.C., 1970-73, Operation Clean Govt., 1997—; tech. specialist AARP-Tax Aide Program, 1993-2001; chairperson Narragansett Rep. Com., 1991-93; vol. tax cons. to the elderly. With USN, 1943-46. Mem. Am. Inst. Nutrition, Agrl. Research Inst., Assn. Agrl. Expt. Sta. Dirs., Sigma Xi, Alpha Zeta, Alpha Gamma Rho. Home: 65 Wyndcliff Dr Saunderstown RI 02874 2408

DONOVAN, GREGORY STEARN, human services administrator; b. Sept. 11, 1962; BA, Grinnell Coll., 1984; MPA, U. Mo., 1990. Clin. counselor Youth Opportunities Upheld, Worcester, Mass., 1985-87; dir. agy. rels. Heart of Am. United Way, Kansas City, Mo., 1987-94; budget analyst Nebr. Unicameral Legis., Lincoln, Nebr., 1994-97; dir. spl. initiatives Lincoln Action Program, 1997—. Office: Lincoln Action Program Inc 210 O St Lincoln NE 68508-2322

DONOVAN, HELEN W. newspaper editor; Graduated from, Mount Holyoke Coll., 1969. Exec. editor Boston Globe, 1993—. Adv. bd., Nat. Arts Journalism Program. Office: Boston Globe Newspapers PO Box 2378 Boston MA 02107-2378*

DONOVAN, JAMES M. librarian, anthropologist; b. Chattanooga, Ten.., June 6, 1959; s. Dennis Howard Donovan and Yvonne Marie Fine; life ptnr. Gary Simmons. BA, U. Tenn., Chattanooga, 1981; M of Libr. Info. Scis., La. State U., 1989; PhD U., Tulane U., 1994; JD, Loyola University, New Orleans, LA, 2000—03; MA, La. State U., 2000. Libr. asst. Chattanooga-Hamilton County Bicentennial Libr., Chattanooga, 1978—84; libr. Tulane Law Libr., New Orleans, 1985—96; libr. Law Library U. Ga., 2003—. Contbr. Chair Mayor's Adv. Com. for Lesbian, Gay, Bisexual and Transgender Issues, New Orleans, 1998—99; bd. dirs. AIDSLaw of La., New Orleans, 2001—03. Mem.: Am. Assn. Law Librs., Am. Anthropol. Assn., Pi Kappa Alpha. None. Home: 2360 W Broad St Apt R1 Athens GA 30606 Office: U Ga Law Libr Athens GA 30602 Personal E-mail: JamesMDonovan@aol.com.

DONOVAN, JOHN VINCENT, consulting company executive; b. Chgo., May 13, 1924; s. Timothy Vincent and Mabel (Hederman) D.; m. Patricia Hasselhorn, Dec. 29, 1950; children: James, Timothy, Walter. AB, DePauw U., 1947, postgrad. in law, 1947-48; postgrad. in bus., Northwestern U., 1949-54. Mem. adminstrv. staff Swift-Brazil, 1947-50; asst. treas. Mid State Corp. Mobil Homes, Union City, Mich., 1951-55; gen. mgr. Bailey Corp., cosmetics, Chgo., 1955-58; sales mgr. Dole Corp., Honolulu, Ill., 1961-63; chmn. Intercon Rsch. Assocs. Ltd., Lincolnwood, Ill., 1963—. Past bd. dirs. Ind. Voters Ill., Chgo. Lt. (j.g.) USNR, 1942-45, PTO. Mem. AAAS, Licensing Execs. Soc., Assn. Corp. Growth, World Future Soc., Chgo. Athletic Assn., Mich. Shores Club. Home: 431 Laurel Ave Wilmette IL 60091-2809 Office: Intercon Rsch Assocs Ltd 6865 N Lincoln Ave Lincolnwood IL 60712-4612 Address: 770 Frontage Rd Ste 124 Winnetka IL 60093-1275 Fax: 847-446-5551.

DONOVAN, LESLIE D., SR., state legislator; m. Mary (Sissy) Donovan. Kans. state rep. Dist. 94, 1993—; auto dealer, investor. Home: 314 N Rainbow Lake Rd Wichita KS 67235-8533*

DONOVAN, MARIE PHILLIPS, television executive; b. Detroit; m. Tom Donovan; children: Kathleen Marie, Kevin Thomas. Student, Wayne U., U. Mich. Profl. actress Actors Equity Assn., N.Y.C., AFTRA, N.Y.C.; bus. mgr. Dirs. Service Inc., N.Y.C., exec. v.p., treas. Mem. NAFE, Young Men's Philanthropic League, Am. Contract Bridge League (life master), Am. Bridge Tchr.'s Assn. (accredited tchr.), Cavendish Club.

DONOVAN, MARION CONRAN, school social worker; b. Quincy, Mass., Oct. 11, 1926; d. Joseph and Ellen Conran; m. Francis Joseph Donovan, Nov. 22, 1952; children: Jeanne Francis Jr., Darilyn, Judith, Kenneth, Brian, David. AB, Emmanuel Coll., 1948; MSW, Boston Coll., 1950. Lic. social worker. Family caseworker Newark Family Svc., 1953; family svc. worker Boston Family Svc., 1950-52, 54; sch. social worker Plainville (Mass.) Pub. Sch. System, 1977-78, Needham (Mass.) Pub. Schs., 1978-91, ret., 1991. Chmn. child abuse study LWV, 1989-90; founding pres. St. Elizabeth's Hosp. Aux., Brighton, Mass., 1969—; bd. dirs. Tufts Med. Sch. Faculty Wives, 1968-75, Mass. Hosp. Assn. Aux., 1970-73. Mem. NEA, LWV, Nat. Assn. Social Workers, Mass. Tchrs. Assn. Roman Catholic. Avocations: reading, water activities, genealogy, digital photography, watercolor painting. E-mail: marioncdonovan@yahoo.com.

DONOVAN, MAUREEN DRISCOLL, lawyer; b. N.Y.C., Dec. 2, 1940; d. Bartholomew Driscoll and Josephine (Keohane) Driscoll. AB, Coll. of New Rochelle, 1962; LLB with honors, Fordham U., 1966. Bar: N.Y. 1966, U.S. Supreme Ct. 1971, U.S. Ct. Appeals (2d cir.) 1975, U.S. Dist. Ct. (so. dist.) N.Y. 1976. Assoc. White & Case LLP, N.Y.C., 1966-75, ptnr., 1975—. Trustee St. Barnabas Hosp., Bronx, N.Y., 1992—, chair fin. com. 1997—, vice chair bd., 1998—; trustee N.Y. Urban Coalition, N.Y.C., 1990-94. Mem. ABA, Princeton Club (N.Y.), Coral Beach Club (Paget, Bermuda), Englewood (N.J.) Field Club. Office: White & Case LLP 1155 Avenue of the Americas New York NY 10036-2787

DONOVAN, R. MICHAEL, management consultant, b. Worcester, Mass., Aug. 30, 1943; s. George F. and Ethel May (Dowell) D.; m. Sarah Jean Lawrence, Dec. 19, 1992; children: James M., Thomas M., Kandace H., R. Michael II. BSBA, Northeastern U., Boston, 1965; MBA, Calif. Western. U., 1978. Exec. v.p. Donovan, Zappala Assocs., Inc., N. Andover, Mass., 1970-74; v.p. ops. SW Industries, Providence, R.I., 1974-77; dir. Touche Ross & Co., Boston, 1977-79; sr. mgr. Peat, Marwick, Mitchell & Co., Boston, 1979-83; pres. R. Michael Donovan, Inc., Framingham, Mass., 1983—. Bd. dirs. Am. Inst. Mfg., Boston. Author: Planning and Controlling Manufacturing Resources, 1978, Time-Based Manufacturing Performance: Guidelines for Quick Response, 1993, Reengineering the Manufacturing Enterprise, 1994, Supply Chain Management: Strengthening Manufacturing's Weak Links, 1996, Demand-Based Flow Manufacturing to Achieve Quick Reponse, 1997, Cycle Time Reduction: Faster Is Better, 1998, Lean Supply Chain Management, 2003. Dir. Contact-Boston, 1987-88; pres. Natick Baseball League, 1979-85. Mem. Am. Prodn. & Inventory Control Soc., Soc. Mfg. Engrs., Inst. Industrial Engrs. Office: R Michael Donovan Inc 945 Concord St Framingham MA 01701-4613

DONOVAN, RITA R. nurse anesthetist, trauma and critical care nurse, educator; b. Bklyn., May 19, 1957; d. Joseph and Antoinette (Burdo) Nigro. Student, Bklyn. Coll., 1975-77; BSN, SUNY, Bklyn., 1979. RN, N.Y. Sr. staff nurse med. surg. unit Maimonides Med. Ctr., Bklyn., 1979—81, staff nurse med. ICU, 1981—84, asst. head nurse pulmonary ICU, 1985—86; grad. nurse anesthetist Kings County Hosp., Bklyn., 1988—89, clin. and acad. instr., 1989—90; clin. specialist surg. ICU Maimonides Med. Ctr., Bklyn., 1990—91; performance improvement coord. dept. anesthesia Kings County Hosp., Bklyn., 1991—, clin., acad. instr., 1991—. Contbr. rsch. articles to profl. jours. and texts. Anesthetist, ICU Desert Storm Task Force, 1991; mem. Healing the Children, Tunja, Columbia, 1998. Recipient 5-Yr. Outstanding award Maimonides Med. Ctr., 1985, Agatha Hodgins Meml. award Outstanding Nurse Anesthetist, 1988, Cert. award Cardiac Anesthesia, Kings County Hosp., 1988, others; named Best All Around Student, 1988. Mem. ACN, Am. Assn. Nurse Anesthetists, Soc. Critical Care Medicine, Soc. Trauma Nurses. Office: Kings County Hosp Ctr Dept Anesthesia 451 Clarkson Ave Rm B2175 Brooklyn NY 11203-2097

DONOVAN, ROBERT ALAN, English educator; b. Chgo., Sept. 27, 1921; s. John Elmer and Dorothy (Dickey) D.; m. Hope Elaine Taussig, Sept. 15, 1942; children: Faith, Peter Alan, Brian Roger. PhB, U. Chgo., 1948, MA, 1950; PhD,

Washington U., St. Louis, 1953. Instr. English Cornell U., Ithaca, N.Y., 1953-56, asst. prof., 1956-62; prof. English SUNY, Albany, 1962-91, prof. emeritus, 1991—, chmn. dept. English, 1981-84. Author: The Shaping Vision: Imagination in the English Novel from Defoe to Dickens, 1966; contbr. articles to profl. jours. Sgt. U.S. Army, 1942-46, ETO. Mem. MLA, Phi Beta Kappa. Home: 5945 State Farm Rd Guilderland NY 12084-9531 Office: SUNY Dept English Albany NY 12222-0001 E-mail: rhdonovan@aol.com.

DONOVAN, SEAN WILLIAM, small business owner, writer; b. Upper Darby, Pa., Feb. 20, 1975; s. David William and Jeanne Louise Donovan. BA in Biology, Temple U., 1997. Bus driver West Gate Pub., Havertown, 1989—91; grill cook Allegro, Havertown, 1999—2001; lighting tech. Explosion Lighting Inc., Gladwyne, 1994—98; writer, pres., CEO A.E.G., Havertown, 1998—. Author: The Poets Tree, 1997. Mem.: SGA, Dortington Biol. Soc., Theta Chi. Republican. Lutheran. Achievements include patents for Recycler 2000; invention of new telephone area code system. Avocations: skiing, bicycling, chess, black jack. Home: 71 Jennifer Dr Chester Springs PA 19425

DONOVAN, SHARON ANN, educator; b. Balt., Feb. 17, 1944; d. Jesse F. and Ruth Elizabeth (Keller) D. BA, U. Md., Balt., 1969. Cert. profl. tchr. Assoc. Coppin-Hopkins Humanities Program, Balt., 1986-91; asst. dean arts and humanities UMBC, Catonsville, Md., 1973-76; asst. to dean fine arts Towson (Md.) State U., 1977-85; tchr. Balt. City Schs., 1986—. Contbr. articles to publs.; founding mem., bd. dirs. The Feminist Press; founder "Herstory" MS Mag., 1976. Grantee Fund for Endl. Excellence. Mem. NCTE, MCTELA, Md. State Conf. on Women's Studies (chairperson, Tchr. of Yr. 1994, 95). Home: 2039 E Lombard St Baltimore MD 21231-1924 Office: 2555 Harford Rd Baltimore MD 21218-4837

DONOVAN, THOMAS B. judge; b. Oakland, Calif., 1935; m. Shirley Ann Rapaport; children: Brian, Robin. BA, U. Calif., Berkeley, 1957, JD, 1962. Bar: Calif., D.C., U.S. Dist. Ct. (no. and ea. dists.) Calif., U.S. Dist. Ct. D.C., U.S. Ct. Appeals (9th and D.C. cirs.), U.S. Supreme Ct. Assoc. Covington & Burling Washington, 1962-63; assoc., then ptnr. Dinkelspiel & Dinkelspiel, San Francisco, 1964-69; ptnr., mng. ptnr Dinkelspiel, Donovan & Reder, San Francisco, 1969-93; judge U.S. Bankruptcy Ct., L.A., 1994—. Judge pro tem Mcpl. Ct. and Superior Ct., San Francisco, Oakland and Berkeley, Calif., 1979-93; bd. dirs. L.A. Bankruptcy Forum, 1994—. Author, editor Calif. Law Rev., 1960-62. Bd. dirs. Berkeley Repertory Theatre, 1977-87, Drama Studio London, Berkeley, 1982-84, Aurora Theatre Co., 1992-94, Women Empowering Women, 1987-94, Entrade, 1991-94, Barlow Group (Barlow Respiratory Hosp.), L.A., 1999—; mem. Fair Campaign Practices Commn., Berkeley, 1977-79, Fin. Lawyers Conf., 1994—. Fellow: Am. Coll. Bankruptcy. Office: US Bankruptcy Ct 255 E Temple St Ste 1352 Los Angeles CA 90012-3332

DONOVAN, WILLARD PATRICK, retired elementary education educator; b. Grand Rapids, Mich., Sept. 1, 1930; s. Willard Andrew and Thelma Alfreda (Davis) D.; m. Dorothy Jane Nester, Nov. 27, 1954 (dec. May 1981); children: Cindy Jane, Kimberly Sue. BS, Ea. Mich. U., 1965, MA, 1969. Cert. grades K-8, Mich. Enlisted U.S. Army, 1947, advanced through grades to master sgt., 1953; platoon sgt. U.S. Army of Occupation, Korea, 1947-48, 1948-50, U.S. Army Korean War Svc., 1950-51; ret. U.S. Army, 1964; pharm. sales Nat. Drug Co., Detroit, 1964-66; tchr. Cromie Elem. Sch. Warren (Mich.) Consol. Schs., 1966—, ret., 1995. Reading textbook and curriculum devel. com. Warren (Mich.) Consol. Schs., 1969-73, sci. com., 1970-95; curriculum and textbook com. Macomb County Christian Schs., Warren, 1982-95. Decorated Combat Infantry badge U.S. Army, Korea, 1947-50, Purple heart with three clusters, Korea-Japan Svc. medal, 1951, Presdl. citation, 1951, Korean medal with three campaign clusters, 1951, Nat. Def. Svc. medal, 1951, Bronze star, Silver star; Chosin few Army and Marines Assn. 31st Inf. Assn. Mem. NRA, Am. Quarterhouse Assn., Assn. U.S. Army, Detroit Area Coun. Tchrs. Math., Met. Detroit Sci. Tchrs. Assn., The Chosin Few (U.S. Army), Nat. Edn. Assn., Mich. Edn. Assn., Warren (Mich.) Edn. Assn., U.S. Army Assn. Avocations: theatre, arts, horsemanship, traveling, pistol shooting. Home: PO Box 563 8440 Mission Hills Arizona City AZ 85223

DONOVAN, WILLIAM ALAN, retired librarian; b. Rochester, N.Y., Jan. 29, 1937; s. Joseph Leo and Wilhelmina (Fawcett) D. BA, St. John Fisher Coll., Rochester, 1958; MA, U. South Fla., 1981. Libr. Chgo. Pub. Libr., 1961—93. Cartoon gagwriter; contbr. articles and book revs. to profl. jours. With U.S. Army, 1958-61. Mem. ALA, Phi Kappa Phi, Beta Phi Mu. Roman Catholic. Home: 2233 Ednor St Port Charlotte FL 33952-4314

DONZE, JERRY LYNN, electrical engineer; b. Wauneta, Nebr., June 12, 1943; s. John Henry and Virgina May (Francis) D.; m. Marilyn Grace Bascue, Feb. 22, 1964 (div. May. 1980); children: Scott L., Michele A.; m. Sandra Kay Morris, July 25, 1981. Cert. technician, Denver Inst. Tech., 1964; BSEE, U. Colo., 1972; postgrad., Advanced Metaphysics Inst. Religios Sci., 1986. Electronic technician A.B.M. Co., Lakewood, Colo., 1964-71; computer programmer Nat. Bur. Standards, Boulder, Colo., 1971-72; electronic engr. Autometrics Co., Boulder, Colo., 1972-76, Gates Research and Devel., Denver, 1976-77; devel. engr. Emerson Electric Co., Lakewood, 1977; engring. mgr. Storage Tech., Louisville, Colo., 1977—. Cons. Sun Co., Arvada, Colo., 1974-75. Patentee in field. Mem. IEEE Student Soc. (treas. 1971-72), Eta Kappa Nu. Republican. Religious Scientist. Avocation: giving workshops and presentations. Home: 12021 W 54th Ave Arvada CO 80002-1907 Office: Storage Tech 2270 S 88th St Louisville CO 80028-0002

DOOB, JOSEPH LEO, mathematician, educator; b. Cin., Feb. 27, 1910; s. Leo and Mollie (Doerfler) Doob; m. Elsie Haviland Field, June 26, 1931 (dec. Jan. 1991); children: Stephen, Peter, Deborah. BA, Harvard U., 1930, MA, 1931, PhD, 1932; DSc (hon.), U. Ill., 1981. Faculty U. Ill., Urbana, 1935—, successively assoc., asst. prof., assoc. prof., 1935—45, prof. math., 1945—, now emeritus prof. Recipient Nat. medal of sci., 1979. Mem.: NAS, Acad. Scis. (Paris) (fgn., assoc.), Am. Acad. Arts and Scis. Home: 101 W Windsor Rd # 1104 Urbana IL 61802-6663

DOODY, BARBARA PETTETT, computer specialist; b. Cin., Sept. 18, 1938; d. Philip Wayne and Virginia Bird (Handley) P.; 1 child, Daniel Frederick Reasor Jr. Attended Sinclair Coll., Tulane U., 1973-74. Owner, mgr. Honeysuckle Pet Shop, Tipp City, Ohio, 1970-76; office mgr. Doody & Doody, CPAs, New Orleans, 1976-77, computer ops. mgr., 1979—; office mgr. San Diego Yacht Club, 1977-79. Owner Hope Chest Linens, Ltd., 1994—2002. Mem. DAR, UDC, Jamestown Soc., Magna Charta, So. Dames, Colonial Dames of 17th Century, Nat. Soc. Daus. of 1812, Daus. Am. Colonists, Dames Ct. Honor, Colonial Order of the Crown, Societe Huguenot Nouvelle-Orleans, Huguenot Soc. Manakin, Soc. Knights of the Garter, Americans of Royal Descent, Plantaget Soc. Republican. Lutheran. Home: 36 Cypress Rd Covington LA 70433-4306 Office: 2525 Lakeway III 3838 N Causeway Blvd Metairie LA 70002-1767 E-mail: bdoody@bellsouth.net.

DOODY, DANIEL PATRICK, pediatric surgeon; b. Evergreen Park, Ill., July 19, 1952; s. Francis Xavier and Mary Therese (Neylon) D.; m. Scarlet Beverly Artruc, Nov. 28, 1981; children: Colin James, Shaylyn Claire, Evan Patrick. BS, U. Ill., Urbana, 1973; MD, U. Ill., Chgo., 1977. Intern surgery U. Ill., Chgo., 1977-78, resident surgery, 1978-79; rsch. fellow Mass. Gen. Hosp., Boston, 1979-81; resident surgery U. Ill./Cook County Hosps., Chgo., 1981-83, chief resident surgery, 1983-84; rsch. fellow Mass. Gen. Hosp., Boston, 1984-85, pediatric surgeon, 1987—; resident pediatric surgery Montreal (Que., Can.) Children's Hosp., 1985-87. Instr. advanced trauma life support, Boston, 1988—, pediatric ALS, Boston, 1990—; asst. prof. surgery Harvard Med. Sch., 1990, assoc. prof. surgery, 1998. Contbr. articles on basic sci., pediatric and pediatric surgery to profl. jours., chpts. to books. Recipient Golden Apple award U. Ill. Sch. Medicine, Chgo., 1984. Fellow ACS, Am. Acad. Pediatrics; mem. Am. Pediatric Surg. Assn., New Eng. Pediatric Surg. Soc., Warren Cole Soc., Karl Meyer Soc., Pediatric Oncology Group, Soc. Critical Care Medicine. Avocations: pencil and ink sketching, photography, oenology, physical fitness. Home: 2 Fletcher Rd Lynnfield MA 01940-2224 Office: Mass Gen Hosp Fruit St Boston MA 02114

DOODY, LOUIS CLARENCE, JR., accountant; b. New Orleans, Feb. 5, 1940; s. Louis Clarence and Elsie Clair (Connors) D.; m. Barbara Virginia Pettett, Oct. 9, 1982; children by previous marriage: Dana Lori, Mary Lyn, Kathleen Louise. BCS, Tulane U., 1963. CPA, La., Tex., Miss. Acct. Louis C. Doody, C.P.A., 1963-68; ptnr. Doody and Doody, C.P.A.'s, Metairie, La., 1969—. Mem. AICPA, La. Soc. CPA's. Home: 36 Cypress Rd Covington LA 70433-4306 Office: 3838 N Causeway Blvd Ste 2525 Metairie LA 70002-8317

DOODY, MARGARET ANNE, English language educator; b. St. John, N.B., Can., Sept. 21, 1939; came to U.S., 1976; d. Hubert and Anne Ruth (Cornwall) D. BA, Dalhousie U., Can., 1960; BA with 1st class hons., Lady Margaret Hall-Oxford U., Eng., 1962, MA, 1965, D.Phil., 1968; LLD (hon.), Dalhousie U., 1985. Instr. English U. Victoria (B.C., Can.), 1962-64, asst. prof. English, 1968-69; lectr. Univ. Coll. Swansea, Wales, 1969-76; assoc. prof. English U. Calif.-Berkeley, 1976-80; prof. English dept. Princeton U., N.J., 1980-89; Andrew W. Mellon prof. humanities, prof. English Vanderbilt U., Nashville, 1989-99, dir. comparative lit. program, 1992-99; John and Barbara Glyn Family prof. lit. U. Notre Dame, 2000—, dir. PhD in Lit. program, 2001—. Author: (non-fiction) A Natural Passion: A Study of the Novels of Samuel Richardson, 1974, The Daring Muse: Augustan Poetry Reconsidered, 1985, Frances Burney: The Life in the Works, 1988, The True Story of the Novel, 1996, (novels) Aristotle Detective, 1978, The Alchemists, 1980, Aristotle e la giustizia poetica, 2000, Aristotle and Poetic Justice, 2002; author: (with F. Stuber) (play) Clarissa, 1984; editor (with Peter Sabor): Samuel Richardson Tercentenary Essays, 1989; co-editor (with Douglas Murray): Catharine and Other Writings by Jane Austen, 1993; co-editor: (with Wendy Barry and Mary Doody Jones) Anne of Green Gables, 1997; author: (novels) Aristotle and the Secrets of Life, 2003. Guggenheim postdoctoral fellow, 1979; recipient Rose Mary Crawshay award Brit. Acad., 1986. Episcopalian. Office: U Notre Dame PhD in Literature Program Notre Dame IN 46556 E-mail: mdoody@nd.edu.

DOOGE, JAMES CLEMENT IGNATIUS, civil engineer, hydrologist, former senator; b. Birkenhead, Eng., July 30, 1922; s. Denis Patrick and Veronica Catherine (Carroll) D.; m. Roni O'Doherty, Nov. 25, 1946 (dec. Nov. 1991); children: Colm, Diarmuid, Cliona, Dara, Meliosa (dec. Feb. 2000). CBS, Dun Laoghaire; BE, BSc., Univ. Coll., Dublin, 1942, ME, 1952; MS, U. Iowa 1956; DrAgrSci (hon.), U. Wageningen, 1978, DrTech (hon.), 1980; DSc (hon.), U. Birmingham, Eng., 1985, U. Dublin, 1988; D Engring. (hon.), Heriot-Watt U., 2000; Dr. (hon.), Cracow Tech. U., 2000; DSc (hon.), Nat. U., Ireland, 2001, Madrid, 2001. Jr. civil engr. Irish Office Pub. Works, 1943-46; design engr. E.S.B., 1946-58; prof. civil engring. Univ. Coll., Cork, Ireland, 1958-70, Dublin, 1970-81, 82-84; minister for fgn. affairs Ireland, 1981-82; leader Irish Senate, 1983-87; mem. Coun. of State, 1973-77. Recipient Horton award Am. Geophys. Union, 1959, Bowie medal, 1986, Ven Te Chow award ASCE, 1993, John Dalton medal European Geophys. Soc., 1998, Internat. Meteorology prize WMO, 1999. Mem. Instn. Civil Engrs. Ireland (pres. 1968-69, Kettle Premium and Plaque awards 1948, Mullins medal 1951, 62), Royal Irish Acad. (pres. 1987-90), Polish Acad. Sci. (fgn.), Russian Acad. Scis. (fgn.), Spanish Acad. Sci. (fgn.), Internat. Assn. Hydrological Scis. (pres. 1975-79), Internat. Coun. Sci. Unions (pres. 1993-96), Royal Acad. Engring. (fgn.). Roman Catholic. Home: 2 Belgrave Rd Monkstown County Dublin Ireland Office: U Coll Earlsfort Terr Dublin 2 Ireland

DOOLEY, ANN ELIZABETH, freelance writers cooperative executive, editor; b. Mpls., Feb. 19, 1952; d. Merlyn James and Susan Marie (Hinze) Dooley; m. John M. Dodge, May 8, 1983; children: Christopher Dooley Dodge, Kathryn Dooley Dodge. BA in Journalism, U. Wis., 1974. Free-lance journalist, 1974-75; photo editor C.W. Communications, Newton, Mass., 1975-77, writer, photographer, 1977-79; editor Computerworld O A, Framingham, Mass., 1979-83; editorial dir. Computerworld Focus, Framingham, 1983-92; pres. freelance writers coop. Dooley & Assocs., West Newbury, Mass., 1992—. Speaker, chmn. mem. editorial adv. bd. various computer confs. Mem. Pub. Relations Soc. Am., Women in Communications (sec. 1982-84). Democrat. Home and Office: 1 Old Parish Way West Newbury MA 01985-1222

DOOLEY, BETTY PARSONS, educational association administrator; Student, Tex. Inst. Tech., Tex. U. Lobbyist, Austin, Tex., 1969-70; dir. regional orgns. Health Security Action Coun., 1971-77; exec. dir. Congl. Caucus Women's Issues, 1977-79; pres. Women's Rsch Edn. Inst., Washington, 1979—. Mem. women's health adv. bd. Duke Med. Sch.; mem. adv. com. employment tng. Vets. Sec. Labor; mem. outreach com. Ctr. Cross Cultural Rsch. on Women, Oxford, Eng. Washington corr. Tex. Monthly Mag., 1974-75. Candidate Tex. State Legis., 1970, U.S. Congress, 1964. Mem. Nat. Coun. Rsch. Women (charter). Office: Womens Rsch Edn Inst 1750 New York Ave NW Ste 350 Washington DC 20006-5309

DOOLEY, CALVIN MILLARD, congressman; b. Visalia, Calif., Jan. 11, 1954; BS, U. Calif., Davis, 1977; MA, Stanford U., 1987. Mem. U.S. Congresses from 17th Calif. dist., 1991-93, U.S. Congresses from 20th Calif. dist., 1993—; mem. agriculture com.; mem. natural resources com. Democrat. Methodist. Office: Ho of Reps 1201 Longworth Bldg Washington DC 20515-0520*

DOOLEY, DAVID INSKEEP, artist, educator; b. Olney, Ill., Jan. 15, 1940; s. David Earl and Virginia Mae Dooley; m. Debra Ann Edwards, Dec. 20, 1970; children: David E., Dara L. BS in Edn., Ea. Ill. U., Charleston, 1968, MS in Edn., 1972; postgrad., U. Ill., 1979. Tchr. art Arcola (Ill.) Sch. Dist., 1968-69; art supr. Unit 20 Sch. Dist., Lawrenceville, Ill., 1970-82; prof. art Vincennes (Ind.) U., 1982-2000. Spkr. Nat. Art Materials Trade Assn., Clifton, N.J., 1992-94; instr. art workshop Discover Art, San Diego, 1992-99. One-man shows Bicentennial Art Ctr. and Mus., Paris, Ill., 1995, Shircliff Gallery Art, Vincennes, 1996; exhibited in group shows Mitchell Mus., Mt. Vernon, Ill., 1982, Tarble Art Ctr., Ea. Ill. U., Charleston, 1983, Sheldon Swope Art Mus., Terre Haute, Ind., 1984-91, Evansville (Ind.) Mus. Arts and Scis., 1984-92, Massey Fine Arts, Santa Teresa, N.Mex., 1993, New Harvony (Ind.) Gallery Contemporary Art, 1994, Campbell-Thiebaud Gallery, San Francisco, 1994; author: Isolated in the Absurd, 1969; contbg. author: Colored Pencil Basics: A Walter Foster Book, 1994; artist video Reflections of Excellence, 1994. Elder White House Christian Ch., Bridgeport, Ill., 1997—. With U.S. Army, 1961063. Recipient People's Choice award Massey Fine Arts, 1993, purchase awards Evansville (Ind.) Mus. Arts and Sci., 1984-92, Austin Peay U., 1993. Avocation: travel. Home: RR 3 Box 384 Lawrenceville IL 62439 E-mail: ddooley@midwest.net.

DOOLEY, DONALD JOHN, retired publishing executive; b. Des Moines, Aug. 16, 1921; s. Martin and Anne Marguerite (Barger) D.; m. Beverly Frederick, Dec. 21, 1955 (div. 1977); children: Nancy Elizabeth, Katherine Anne(dec.), Mary Bridget, Robert Frederick; m. Patricia Connell, Dec. 28, 1996. BA, U. Iowa, 1947; postgrad., Drake U., 1949-50. Gen. Promotion and pub. relations mgr. Meredith Corp., Des Moines, 1953-59, dir. pub. relations, 1960-65; art and editorial dir. Better Homes & Gardens Books & Spl. Interest Publs., Des Moines, 1965-77; dir. editorial planning and devel. Better Homes and Gardens Books (Meredith Corp.), Des Moines, 1977-84; cons., 1985. Chmn. bd. adv. com. Sch. Vol. Program, Des Moines; steering com. Intercultural Affairs program to Desegregate Dist. Schs., 1975-77; treas. Iowa U. Parents Assn., 1977-79; bd. dirs. Iowa Cystic Fibrosis Found., 1979-87, v.p., 1981-85; trustee Citizens Scholarship Found. Am., 1976-85, Iowa Freedom of Info. Council, 1977-87; adv. bd. Adult and Community Edn., Des Moines Pub. Sch., 1982—99; cons. White House Conf. on Families, 1981. Officer USAAF, 1942-46. Decorated 2 battle stars; recipient Dorothy Dawe award Home Furnishings Industry, 1973. Mem. Pub. Rels. Soc. Am. (accredited, pres. chpt. 1969, dir. chpt. 1965-76), ACLU, Beyond War (co-dir. Iowa office 1987-88), Friendship Force, Ams. for Dem. Action, Sigma Nu (comdr. chpt. 1946-47), Found. for Global Community, 1991—. Clubs: Echo Valley Country. Democrat. Home and Office: 3711 Oak Creek Pl West Des Moines IA 50265-7968

DOOLEY, J. GORDON, food scientist; b. Nevada, Mo., Nov. 15, 1935; s. Howard Eugene and Wilma June (Vanderford) D. BS in Biology with honors, Drury Coll., Springfield, Mo., 1958; postgrad., U. Mo., Rolla, 1961, Kirksville (Mo.) State Coll., 1959; MS in Biology, Brown U., 1966; postgrad. in bus mgmt., Alexander Hamilton Inst., 1973-75, No. Ill. U., 1964. Tchr. sci. Morton West H.S., Berwyn, Ill., 1963-64; dairy technologist Borden Co., Elgin, Ill., 1964-65; project leader Cheese Products Lab., Kraft Corp., Glenview, Ill., 1965-73; sr. food scientist Wallerstein Co. div. Travenol Labs., Inc., Morton Grove, Ill., 1973-77; mgr. food sci. GB Fermentation Industries, Inc., Des Plaines, Ill., 1977-79, mgr. product devel., 1979-82; group leader Food Ingredients divsn. Stauffer Chem. Co., Clawson, Mich., 1982-84; sr. rsch. scientist Schreiber Foods, Inc., Green Bay, Wis., 1984-87, DMV/Ridgeview, LaCrosse, Wis., 1987-92; mgr. regulatory affairs, info. svcs. DMV USA, LaCrosse, 1992-95; rsch. scientist AMPC Inc., Ames, Iowa, 1996-98; regulatory compliance officer Colo. Biolabs, Inc., Aurora, Colo., 1999—. Sci. lectr. seminars, Mex., 1975; assoc. mem. Ad Hoc Enzyme Tech. Com., 1978—; dairy rsch. adv. bd. Utah State U.; del. in field. Patentee in food and enzyme tech.; contbr. sci. articles to profl. jours. Recipient Spoke award Nevada (Mo.) Jr. C. of C., 1960; NSF grantee. Mem. Am. Dairy Sci. Assn., Inst. Food Technologists, Am. Chem. Soc., Cousteau Soc., Am. Inst. Biol. Scis., Nat. Sci. Tchrs. Assn., Whey Products Inst., Toastmasters Internat. (pres. club 1976-77), Brown U. Club (Chgo.), Beta Beta Beta, Phi Eta Sigma. Republican. Presbyterian. Home: 4208 30th St Greeley CO 80634-8738 Office: Colo Biolabs Inc PO Box 6296 Aurora CO 80045-0296

DOOLEY, JAMES C. newspaper editor, director of photography; m. Susan Levy; children: David, Marc, Steven, Thomas. From reporter to state editor The Ariz. Republic, 1966-78; photo assignment editor, dep. dir. photography L.A. Times, 1978-86; dir. photography Newsday, N.Y.C., 1986—. Office: Newsday Inc 235 Pinelawn Rd Melville NY 11747-4250

DOOLEY, JO ANN CATHERINE, retired publishing company executive; b. Cin., Nov. 24, 1930; d. Joseph Frank and Margaret Mary (Flynn) Dooley. Ed, U. Cin., 1966. Clk. Castellini Co., Cin., 1949-52; IBM operator Kroger Co., Cin., 1952; asst. acct. Gardner Publs., Inc., Cin., 1953-67, treas., sec., 1967-95, bd. dirs., 1983-99, v.p. fin., 1986-95, ret., 1995. Mem.: Am. Soc. Women Accts. (advt. mgr. Woman CPA 1979—81, nat. pres. 1982—83, exec. com., Achievement award), Mercy Franciscan Western Hills Aux. (treas. 2003—), Deaconess Hosp. Aux. (pres. 2003—). Roman Catholic.

DOOLEY, JOHN AUGUSTINE, III, state supreme court justice; b. Nashua, N.H., Apr. 10, 1944; s. John A. and Edna Elizabeth (Elwell) D.; m. Sandra C. Sapp, Dec. 19, 1970. BS, Union Coll., 1965; LLB, Boston Coll., 1968. Bar: Vt. 1968. Law clk. to presiding judge U.S. Dist. Ct. Vt., 1968-69; asst. dir. Vt. Legal Aid, 1969-72, dir., 1972-78; legal counsel to gov. of Vt., 1985; sec. of adminstrn. State of Vt., 1985-87; assoc. justice Vt. Supreme Ct., 1987—. Part-time U.S. magistrate for Vt., from 1971. Co-author: Cases and Materials on Urban Poverty Law, 1974. Mem. Vt. Bar Assn. Office: Vt Supreme Ct 109 State St Montpelier VT 05609-0001*

DOOLEY, LENA ROSE (NELSON), writer, editor; b. Hot Springs, Ark., Nov. 13, 1942; d. Bennel Alden and Frances Arabella (Brians) Nelson; m. James Allan Dooley, Nov. 7, 1964; children: Marilyn Van Zant, Jennifer Waldron. BA in Speech and Drama, Howard Payne Coll., Brownwood, Tex., 1964; student, Ouachita Bapt. Coll., Arkadelphia, Ark., 1960-62, Abilene Christian U., 1970-71. Cert. tchr., Tex. Tchr. Schleicher County Ind. Sch. Dist., El Dorado, Tex., 1964-65; aux. rural mail carrier U.S. Postal Svc., Colleyville, Tex., 1982-84; mng. editor The Christian Informer, Dallas, 1991; video script writer Accelerated Christian Edn., Lewisville, Tex., 1991-93; instr. Fine Arts Acad., Bedford, Tex., 1996—2003; adminstrv. editor curriculum divsn. Paradigm Alternative Ctrs., Dublin, Tex., 1996-97; project coord., adminstrv. editor F.L.A.M.E.S. curriculum 1st United Meth. Ch., Bedford, Tex., 1998—2003, pastoral adminstrv. asst., 2000—03. Freelance writer/editor, Hurst, Tex., 1985—; clown Granny Pockets, Hurst, 1989—; seminar spkr. Am. Christian Romance Writers. Author: Home to Her Heart, 1993, The Other Brother, 2002; asst. movie prodr., dir. To Love Enough, 1990, Christmas with Lena Nelson Dooley, 2000; playwright, dir. Sleeping Beauty, 1986. Developer Write Right seminar, Hurst, 1996; dir. Bedford Players, 1st United Meth. Ch., 1982-2003; leader writer's group AAUW, Abilene, 1970-72; chmn. book sale Friends of Hurst Libr., 1985-88, chmn. craft sale, 1987-88. Mem. Am. Christian Romance Writers, North Tex. Romance Writers Am. (membership chmn. 1998), Gospel Artists and Musicians Assn. (bd. dirs. 1990-92), Mid-Cities Christian Writers (coord. 1997), Christians in Theatre Arts, Trinity Valley Christian Writers (coord. seminars 1984-87). Republican. Methodist. Avocations: travel, needlework, volunteering with children, reading. Home and Office: PO Box 54614 Hurst TX 76054-3138 E-mail: safe-idwrites@flash.net.

DOOLEY, MICHAEL P. law educator; b. 1939; BA, U. Iowa, 1960, JD, 1963. Bar: Iowa 1963, N.Y. 1964, Ill. 1971, Va. 1979. Assoc. Dewey, Ballantine, Bushby, Palmer & Wood, 1963-68; assoc. prof. U. Ill., 1968-71, prof., 1971-72; vis. prof. U. Va., 1971-72, prof., 1972-80, Doherty prof., 1980-90, William S. Potter prof. and dir. grad. studies, 1990—. Mem. Saltzburg Seminar in Am. Studies, 1986; mem. legal adv. com. N.Y. Stock Exch. Mem. ABA (com. on corp. laws 1983-91, 96—, corp. practice com. 1995—), Am. Law Inst. (reporter Model Bus. Corp. Act 1996—). Office: U Va Sch Law 580 Massie Rd Charlottesville VA 22903-1738 E-mail: mpd@virginia.edu.

DOOLEY, PATRICK JOHN, graphic designer, design educator; b. Cleve., May 29, 1950; s. John William and Edna Ann (Mellick) D.; m. Mary Leah Spicer, Apr. 3, 1982; children: Claire Adele, Grace Ellen, James Joseph. BFA, U. Iowa, 1975, MA, 1977, MFA, 1978. Designer J. Paul Getty Mus., L.A., 1980-89; design mgr. J. Paul Getty Mus., J. Paul Getty Trust, L.A., 1987-89; designer, owner Patrick Dooley Design, Santa Monica, Calif., 1989-93, Lawrence, Kans., 1993—; mem. faculty Otis Parsons Sch. Art and Design, L.A., 1988-93; assoc. prof. dept. design Sch. Fine Art U. Kans., Lawrence, 1993—, Gretchen Van Bloom Budig tchg. prof., 1997. Freelance graphic designer, L.A., 1978-80, designer, cons. Walt Disney Co., Burbank, Calif., 1989-93, Lannan Lit. Found., L.A., 1991—, The Lapis Press, Venice, Calif., 1989-93, Nelson-Atkins Mus., Kansas City, Mo., 1995-96; spkr. Assn. Am. U. Presses ann. conf., 1994, Art Dirs. Club Tulsa, 1996; judge 42nd Art Dirs. Club L.A. Show, 1988 Designer: (poster) Illuminated Manuscripts, 1984 (N.Y. Type Dirs. Club award of excellence 1985), (books) Whisper of the Muse, 1986 (N.Y. Art Dirs. Club award of merit 1987), Pierre Dubreuil, 1988 (Am. Inst. Graphic Arts Book Show cert. of excellence 1989), The Surrealists Look at Art, 1990 (N.Y. Art Dirs. Club award of merit 1991), Explorations, 1992 (Am. Inst. Graphic Arts 50 Books of 1992), Pacific Wall, 1992 (Am. Inst. Graphic Arts Cover Show 1994), Walter Evans: The Getty Museum Collection, 1996 (Assn. Am. Univ. Presses cert. of excellence 1996). Recipient over 60 awards from Comm. Arts Mag., Print Mag., Am. Assn. Museums, Art Mus. Assn. Am., Am. Fedn. Arts, Univ. and Coll. Designer's Assn., others; Fulbright sr. scholar Fachhochschule, Trier, Germany, 2002. Mem.: Am. Inst. Graphic Arts. Avocation: gardening. Office: U Kans Dept Design 300 Art And Design Bldg Lawrence KS 66045-0001

DOOLEY, ROBERT S. finance educator; b. Athens, Tenn., Aug. 21, 1961; s. Thomas S. Dooley and Nancy W. Burn; m. Kimberly D. Pate, Dec. 7, 1985. PhD, U. Tenn., 1996. Assoc. prof. dept. mgmt. Okla. State U., Stillwater, 1996—. Mem.: Acad. of Mgmt. Democrat. Home: 701 W Harned Ave Stillwater OK 74075 Office: Okla State U Dept Mgmt Stillwater OK 74078 Business E-Mail: rdooley@okstate.edu. E-mail: rdooley@okstate.edu.

DOOLEY, SUSAN MARGARET, writer; b. Chgo., July 17, 1940; d. Roland John and Mary (Raab) D.; m. George G. Carey, 1995. Grad., Maine Twp. High Sch., Park Ridge, Ill., 1958. Reporter Chgo. Sun-Times, 1961-66; editor Vol. in Svc. to Am. mag., Washington, 1966-70; assoc. editor Sunday mag. Washington Post, 1972-76, columnist, 1980-90; book reviewer Newhouse News Svc., Washington, 1986-92; columnist Self Mag., N.Y.C., 1990-92; contbr. Book World Washington Post, 1980—. Author: The World of Garden Design, 2000; contbg. author: Slow Hand, 1992, Fever, 1994; contbg. editor Garden Design Mag., 2000—02. Mem. Nat. Book Critic's Circle.

DOOLITTLE, JESSE WILLIAM, JR., lawyer; b. Wheaton, Ill., May 19, 1929; s. Jesse William and Selma Caroline (Schacht) D.; m. Annette Danforth Bush, May 5, 1962; children: Danforth Bush, Alice Walters. AB, DePauw U., 1951; LLB magna cum laude, Harvard, 1954. Bar: D.C. 1954. Law clk. to U.S. Supreme Ct. Justice Felix Frankfurter, 1957-58; assoc. firm Covington & Burling, Washington, 1958-61; asst. to solicitor gen. of U.S. Dept. Justice, Washington, 1961-63, 1st asst. civil div., 1963-66; gen. counsel Dept. Air Force, Washington, 1966-68, asst. sec. for manpower and res. affairs, 1968-69; partner

firm Prather Seeger Doolittle & Farmer, Washington, 1969-94. Editl. cons. Lexis-Nexis, 1995-98; comml.arbitrator, 1992-. Mem.: Harvard Law Rev, 1952-54. Pres. bd. trustees Nat. Child Rsch. Ctr., Washington, 1972-74; mem. bd. overseers com. to visit ROTC programs Harvard, 1967-69; com. to visit Law Sch., 1969-75; mem. governing bd. Nat. Cathedral Sch. for Girls, Washington, 1979-85, vice-chmn., 1981-82, chmn., 1982-85; mem. chpt. Washington Nat. Cathedral, 1982-85; mem. policy bd. Legal Counsel for the Elderly, Washington, 1992-97; bd. dirs. Westchester Corp., Washington, 2000-2003. 1st lt. AUS, 1954-57. Recipient Career Service award Nat. Civil Service League, 1968, Exceptional Civilian Service award Dept. Air Force, 1969 Mem. Am. Law Inst., Harvard Law Sch. Assn. (coun. 1964-68), Harvard Law Rev. Assn. (bd. overseers 1967-72, 92-98), Phi Beta Kappa, Delta Chi. Democrat. Episcopalian (sr. warden 1973-75, past vestryman). Clubs: Metropolitan, Chevy Chase. Home: 4000 Cathedral Ave NW Apt 444B Washington DC 20016-5282

DOOLITTLE, JOHN TAYLOR, congressman; b. Glendale, Calif., Oct. 30, 1950; s. Merrill T. and Dorothy Doolittle; m. Julia Harlow Doolittle, Feb. 17, 1979; children: John Taylor, Jr., Courtney A. BA with hons. in History, U. Calif., Santa Cruz, 1972; JD, U. Pacific, 1978. Mem. Calif. State Senate, 1980 90; mem. 4th Calif. Dist. U.S. Congress, 1991—. Mem. agr. com. U.S. Congress, mem. resource com., chmn. water and power resources subcom. Republican. Mem. Lds Ch. Office: Ho of Reps 2410 Rayburn Ho Office Bldg Washington DC 20515-0504*

DOOLITTLE, WARREN T. retired federal official; b. Webster City, Iowa, July 24, 1921; s. Edward and Rhoda Leone (McGuire) D.; m. Jane Anne Beddow, Dec. 29, 1942; children: Linda Jane, Randolph James, Steven Eric. BS in Forestry, Iowa State U., 1946; MS in Forestry, Duke U., 1950; PhD in Forestery, Yale U., 1955. Enlisted USAF, 1943, advanced through grades to lt. col., 1969, navigator, 1943-45, 1951-52; rsch. scientist USDA Forest Svc., Asheville, N.C., 1946-57, Washington, 1957-59, from asst. dir. to dir. Upper Darby, Pa., 1959-74, assoc. dep. chief Washington, 1974-80, ret., 1980. Contbr. articles to profl. jours. Moderator Congrl. Ch., Asheville, N.C., 1956-57. Lt. col. USAF, 1943-69. Decorated DFC. Fellow Soc. Am. Foresters (pres. 1986, John Beale Meml. award 1983); mem. Am. Forests (B.E. Fernow award 1993), Internat. Soc. Tropical Foresters (pres. 1984—), Res. Officers Assn. Republican. Avocations: golfing, skiing. Home: 16112 Berkeley Dr Haymarket VA 20169-1824 E-mail: wdoolittle@msn.com.

DOONER, JOHN JOSEPH, JR., advertising executive; b. Mt. Vernon, NY, Aug. 3, 1948; s. John Joseph and Elizabeth Ann (Forrest) D.; m. Cynthia Ann Stewart, Aug. 16, 1975; children: Miriam, Jaclyn. BA, St. Thomas Villanova U., Miami, Fla.; postgrad., Iona Coll. Advt. media supr. Grey Advt., N.Y.C., 1970-73; assoc. media dir. The Marschalk Co., N.Y.C., 1973-74, account mgr., 1974-84; exec. v.p. McCann-Erickson, N.Y.C., 1984—, gen. mgr. N.Y. office, 1984-88, pres. N.Am. region, 1988-94; pres., COO McCann-Erickson Worldwide, N.Y.C., 1992-94; chmn., CEO McCann-Erickson WorldGroup, N.Y.C., 1995—2000, 2003—. Bd. dirs. The Interpublic Group. Bd. trustees Sound Shore Med. Ctr., 1993—, Coll. New Rochelle; bd. dirs. Nat. Multiple Sclerosis Soc., 1998—. Mem. Pelham Country Club, Lago Mar Club (Ft. Lauderdale, Fla.). Avocations: tennis, boating. Office: McCann-Erickson Worldwide 622 3rd Ave New York NY 10017-2798*

DOORENBOS, JUDY TUCKER, cardiology critical care nurse; b. Birmingham, Ala., Oct. 6, 1954; d. James Melvin and Clytee (Whitman) Tucker; divorced. Lic. practical nurse, Itawamba Jr. Coll., Tupelo, Miss., 1974, ADN, 1982; BSN, Miss. U. for Women, Tupelo, Miss., 1994. RN, Miss.; cert. in ACLS. Physician's asst. in cardiology Internal Medicine Assocs. Ltd., Tupelo; critical care nurse North Miss. Med. Ctr., Tupelo, staff nurse cardiac catheterization lab., noninvasive cardiol supr. Mem. AACN, Miss. Nursing Assn., Sigma Theta Tau.

DOORISH, JOHN FRANCIS, physicist, mathematician, educator; b. Bklyn., Jan. 13, 1957; s. Thomas Joseph Anthony and Annunciata Ann (Longobardi) D. BS in Physics, St. John's U., 1980; MS in Applied Physics, Columbia U., 1985, EdD in Math. and Astrophysics, 1988. Rsch. physicist N.Y.C. Bur. Noise Abatement Dept. Environ. Protection, 1981; adj. asst. prof. Boro. Manhattan Community Coll., N.Y.C., 1991-94; assoc. prof. physics Wagner Coll., S.I., N.Y., 1994-96; rsch. scientist eye radiation and environ. rsch. lab. Columbia U. Coll. Physician and Surgeons, N.Y.C., 1996-99; prin. investigator Artificial Retina Package Project, Eye Radiation Lab., Columbia U., 1996-99; pres., founder Second Sight of N.Y., Inc., 1999—. Assoc. rsch. scientist Princeton (N.J.) U., 1992-93; pres. Second Sight N.Y. Inc. Contbr. articles to profl. jours. and internat. sci. confs. Mem. ASCPA, N.Y.C., Internat. Fund Animal Welfare, Boston. St. John's scholar. Mem. AAAS, Am. Astron. Soc., Am. Phys. Soc., Assn. Rsch. in Vision and Ophthalmology, N.Y. Acad. Scis., Planetary Soc. Republican. Roman Catholic. Fax: 718-336-5187. E-mail: jfdoorish@worldnet.att.net.

DOORLEY, JOHN, marketing professional, educator; b. Uniontown, Pa., May 25, 1942; s. John T. Doorley, Sr. and Mary Grasinger; m. Carole Tierney Doorley, Aug. 27, 1972; children: Nanci, Jonathan. BS in Biology, St. Vincent Coll., 1964; MA in Journalism, NYU, 1980; degree in Exec. Mgmt. Program, Harvard U., 1999. Social worker Pa. Dept. Pub. Assistance, Uniontown, 1964—66; with sales and mktg. Sterling Drug Inc., N.Y.C., 1966—81; dir. corp. comm. Hoffmann-LaRoche, Nutley, NJ, 1981—87; exec. dir. corp. comm. Merck & Co., Inc., Whitehouse Station, NJ, 1987—2000; freelance developer comprehensive reputation mgmt., 2003—. Instr. Rutgers U., New Brunswick, NJ, 2001—; chmn. N.J. Health Products Com., Union, 1988; dir. ann. summer inst. pub. rels. NYU, N.Y.C., 2001—. Bd. dirs. Emmanuel Cancer Found., Summit, NJ, 1983—93, Little League Baseball, Mountainside, NJ, 1994—98; pub. rels. advisor Elizabethport Presbyn. Ctr., Elizabeth, NJ, 1998—. Mem.: AAUP, Nat. Comm. Assn. Roman Catholic. Avocations: running, golf. Office: Rutgers U 4 Huntington St New Brunswick NJ 08901-1071

DOPF, GLENN WILLIAM, lawyer; b. N.Y.C., June 6, 1953; s. William Bernard and Doris Virginia (Roxby) D. BS cum laude, Fordham Coll., 1975; JD, Fordham U., 1979; LLM, NYU, 1983. Bar: N.J. 1979, U.S. Dist. Ct. N.J. 1979, N.Y. 1980, U.S. Dist. Ct. (so. and ea. dists.) N.Y. 1980, U.S. Ct. Appeals (2d cir.) 1980, U.S. Ct. Internat. Trade 1981, U.S. Supreme Ct. 1983. Assoc. Martin, Clearwater & Bell, N.Y.C., 1980-81; ptnr. Kopff, Nardelli & Dopf LLP, N.Y.C., 1982—. Mem. ABA, Assn. Bar City N.Y. Office: Kopff Nardelli & Dopf LLP 440 9th Ave Fl 15 New York NY 10001-1688

DOPKIN, MARK DREGANT, lawyer; b. Balt., Jan. 14, 1943; s. Wilford and Beverly (Dregant) D.; m. Ilene Kleinman, Mar. 21, 1967 (div.); children: Rebecca, Peter; m. Deborah Cohn, May 28, 1984. BA, Union Coll., Schenectady, 1964; JD, U. Md., 1967. Bar: Md. 1967, U.S. Dist. Ct. Md. 1968, U.S. Supreme Ct. 1974. Assoc. Blades & Rosenfeld, Balt., 1968-71, Kaplan, Heyman, Greenberg, Engelman & Belgrd, P.A., Balt., 1971-76, ptnr., 1977-98, Tydings & Rosenberg LLP, Balt., 1998—. Mem. Real Property Records Improvement Fund Oversight Com., 1995—. Mem. Gov.'s Salary Rev. Com., Md., 1980-85, Balt. County Charter Rev. Com., 1977-79; treas. Congressman Benjamin L. Cardin, Balt., 1985—; 1st v.p. Har Sinai Cong., Balt., 1987-89, pres., 1989-91, trustee, 1973-75, 77-80, 86—; active various charitable orgns. With U.S. Army, 1967-73. Fellow Md. Bar Found.; mem. ABA, Bar Assn. Balt. City, Md. Bar Assn. (chair real property sect. 2000-01). Democrat. Jewish. Office: Tydings & Rosenberg LLP 100 E Pratt St Fl 26 Baltimore MD 21202-1009 E-mail: mdopkin@tydingslaw.com.

DOPP, BONNIE JO, musicologist, school librarian; b. Milwaukee, Wis., Mar. 30, 1942; BA, Am. U, 1963; MLS, U of Maryalnd, 1971; MM, U of Md., 1993. Peace corps vol. tchr. Mid. Sch., Njombe, Tanzania, 1963—65, Pub. Schools, Ok-Cheon, Korea (South), 1966—68; reference libr. San Francisco Pub. Libr., 1974—79; cheif, biography divsn. and music libr. DC Pub. Libr., Washington, 1979—92; curator, spl. collections in performing arts U of Md., 1996—. Musicologist Theater Chamber Players, Washington, 1992—. Recipient Pauline Alderman award from Internat. Alliance for Women in Music, 1995. Avocation: choral singing. Home: 7508 Citadel Dr College Park MD 20740

DOR, CAPLYN, artist; b. Buffalo, Nov. 13, 1952; d. Triest Joseph and Josephine Lenore (Condello) Cappello; m. Kenneth James Doerfler, Nov. 17, 1979; 1 child, Daniel Allen Sheehy. Guest spkr. Hallwall's Performing and Contemporary Art Ctr., Buffalo, 2000. One-woman shows include J.C. Mazur Gallery, Buffalo, 1989, Hilbert Coll., Hamburg, N.Y., 1990, Arts Coun. Buffalo and Erie County, 1991, Castellani Art Mus., Niagara U., Niagara Falls, N.Y., 1992, Waligui-Doering Gallery, Hamburg, N.Y., 1997; featured artist Clary-Miner Gallery, Buffalo, 1991, Albright-Knox Art Gallery/Mus., Buffalo, 1992, 94, Del Bello Gallery, Toronto, 1995-96; exhibited in group shows Ariel Gallery, N.Y.C., 1990 (award), 92 (award), Trans-Hudson Gallery, N.Y.C., 1998, Abraham Lubelski Gallery, N.Y.C., 1998, Hallwalls Performing and Contemporary Art Ctr., Buffalo, 2000, Cork Gallery Avery Fisher Hall Lincoln Ctr., N.Y.C. (first digital graphic advanced tech. show), (digital graphic presentation) Harappa Art Festival, Tokyo, 2000, XI Biennial Internat. Art Exhbn. Vila Nova de Cerviera, Portugal, 2001, Albright Knox Art Gallery/Mus., Buffalo, N.Y., 2003-04; internat. R2001 group and individual presentation of paintings, graphics, mail art, web page for show entitled: "Exhibition 1999 zero and One", Keio U., Shounan Fujisawa campus, Japan; artist (cover) Salamander Rev. Mag., 2003. Active Arts Coun. Buffalo and Erie County, 1988—, Castellani Art Mus., 1992—. Recipient Hon. Mention Art Calendar's Crabbie Awards, 1997, Internat. "Gold" Computer, Animation, Photography, Illustration award, 1998, Artistic Excellence Achievement award TINT mag., 1998, Best of Show award Artistic Impressions Spring Art Competition, 1998, Judges Choice award Art Career, 1999, 2nd prize, hon. mention MOCA Digital Art Contest, 2001, others; Creative arts fellow N.Y. State Coun. Arts, 1992. Mem. Internat. Registry Artists and Artwork, Renaissance 2001, Western N.Y. Artists Group. Avocations: computers, reading, photography, travel, cooking. Home: 4246 Mistymeadow Ln Hamburg NY 14075-1336

DOR, YORAM, accountant; b. Tel Aviv, Apr. 17, 1945; arrived in U.S., 1974; s. Simon and Shulamit (Remple) Dor; m. Ofra Lipshitz, Apr. 9, 1967; children: Gil, Ron. Diploma in Acctg., Hebrew U., Jerusalem, 1969; BA in Econs., Tel Aviv (Israel) U., 1971; MBA, UCLA, 1977. CPA Calif. Sr. auditor Somekh Chaikin, CPA, Tel Aviv, 1969—72; CFO East African Hotels, Dar-es-Salaam, Tanzania, 1972—74; staff acct. Hyatt Med. Enterprises, Inc. (name now Nu Med., Inc.), Encino, Calif., 1974—75, asst. contr., 1975—77, corp. contr., 1977—79, v.p. fin., 1979—82, sr. v.p. fin., CFO, 1982—87, exec. v.p. fin., CFO, 1987—95; ptnr. Sloman and Dor, Encino, 1995—, also bd. dirs. Mem.: AICPA, Calif. Soc. CPA's. Office: Sloman & Dor 16633 Ventura Blvd Ste 913 Encino CA 91436-1849 Business E-Mail: yoramdor@slomananddor.com.

DORADO, MARIANNE GAERTNER, lawyer; d. Wolfgang Wilhelm and Marianne L. Gaertner; m. Richard Manuel Dorado, Oct. 1, 1982; children: Marianne Christine, Kathleen Gina. BA, Yale U., 1978; JD, U. Mich., 1981. Bar: N.Y. 1982, U.S. Supreme Ct. 1993. Ptnr. The Dorado Law Group, LLC, N.Y.C., 1998—. Contbr. Extern office legal advisor U.S. Dept. State, Washington, 1980. Republican. Roman Catholic. Office: The Dorado Law Group LLC 74 Trinity Pl Ste 1204 New York NY 10006 E-mail: mdorado@doradolaw.com.

DORAISWAMY, P. MURALI, physician; Author: Therapies for Alzheimer's Disease (Paul Beeson award, 1996); contbr. articles and monographs to profl. publs. Achievements include research in Research into causes, treatment and prevention of Alzheimer's disease and brain aging.

DORAISWAMY, P(UDUGRAMAM) MURALI, psychiatrist, educator, researcher, neuroscientist; MBBS, U. of Madras, 1981—86. Dir., psychiatry clin. trials Duke U., Durham, NC, 1996—2001; chief, divsn. of biol. psychiatry, dept. of psychiatry Duke U. Med. Ctr., Durham, NC, 2000—. Sr. fellow, ctr. for the study of aging and human devel. Duke U., Durham, NC, 1996—; presenter in field. Editor: (textbook) Brain Imaging in Clinical Psychiatry; contbr. articles to over 100 scientific publs. Recipient Paul Beeson Faculty Physician in Aging Rsch. award, Am. Fedn. for Aging Rsch., 1996, Standing Resident award, NIMH, 1994. Achievements include one of leaders in field of mental fitness, psychopharmacology and brain aging.

DORAN, CHARLES EDWARD, textile manufacturing executive; b. Hartford, Conn., Mar. 31, 1928; s. Charles Edward and Josephine Catherine (Maher) D.; m. Anne Marie McGovern, May 18, 1957; children: Charles Francis, John Francis, Pamela Anne. BA, Hamilton Coll., 1951; MA, Yale U., 1952. Trainee Gen. Elec. Co., 1953-56, financial mgmt. positions, 1956-65; asst. treas. Collins & Aikman Corp., N.Y.C., 1965-71, treas., 1971-88. Mem. adv. bd. Arkwright-Boston Ins. Co., 1981-87. Served with USNR, 1946-48. Mem. Fin. Execs. Inst., Nat. Assn. Corp. Treasurers, Yale Club, Union League Club (N.Y.C.), Phi Beta Kappa, Chi Psi. Republican. Roman Catholic.

DORAN, DORIS JEANNE, librarian; b. Chambersburg, Pa., July 19, 1932; d. John Franklin and Kathleen Elmira (Cooke) Fraker; m. Francis Joseph Doran, Feb. 5, 1955 (div. Sept. 1991); children: Brenda Lou, Polly Ann. BS, Wilson Coll., 1954; MS, U. Md., 1970, postgrad., 1976-77. Asst. buyer Joseph Horne Co., Pitts., 1955-56; dir. research library Sears Roebuck & Co., Chgo., 1956-58; project officer contracts John I. Thompson Co., Washington, 1967-69, staff asst. to v.p. info. sci. div., 1969-70; program officer grants div. Nat. Library of Medicine, Bethesda, Md., 1970-79, program analyst Office of Dir., 1980-82; project dir. Nat. Med. Audiovisual Center, 1979; asst. for network devel. VA, Washington, 1982-84; co-owner, treas., gen. mgr. Gilran Lighting Products, Springfield, Va., 1970-90; project mgr. Preservation Microfilm Project, REMAC Info. Corp., 1987-88, Nat. Library Medicine; acquisitions specialist Nat. Tech. Info. Service, 1988—. Mem. Am. Library Assn., Med. Library Assn. Home: Unit # 410 8340 Greensboro Dr Apt 410 Mc Lean VA 22102-3544 Office: 5285 Port Royal Rd Springfield VA 22161-0001 Business E-Mail: ddoran@ntis.gov.

DORAN, JAMES MARTIN, retired food products company executive; b. Toronto, Ohio, Apr. 21, 1933; s. Hugh John and Mary Agnes (Murray) D.; m. Peggotty Hanks Namm, Dec. 9, 1967 (dec. Dec. 1978); children— Beth Doran Putnam, Wendy Harrison BS in Bus. Adminstrn., John Carroll Univ., 1955. C.P.A., Pa., Ohio. Sr. acct. Deloitte, Haskins & Sells, Pitts., 1956-60, sr. corp. acct. Revere Copper & Brass, Rome, N.Y., 1960-64; contr. A.C. Gilbert Co., New Haven, 1964-67, Heublein Spirits & Wine, Farmington, Conn, 1967-83; sr. v.p. fin. Heublein, Inc., Farmington, 1983-89, ret. V.p., trustee Namm Found., N.Y.C., 1970—; mem. Leadership Greater Hartford, 1977— ; trustee, Julie Edn. Ctr., 1996—; pres., trustee The Dornam Found. Mem. AICPA. Roman Catholic. Avocations: investing, platform tennis, tennis, golf. Home: 83 Rumford St West Hartford CT 06107-3754

DORAN, KATHLEEN BREWER, dean, consultant; b. Glen Ridge, N.J., Mar. 5, 1955; d. Ambrose Benedict and Marjorie Westgate Doran. AB, Dartmouth Coll., 1976; MBA, U. of Va., 1978; PhD, McGill U., Montreal, Que., Can., 2000. Sr. sales rep. Internat. Paper Co., Chgo., 1978—80, sr. fin. analyst Dallas, 1980—81, strategic planning specialist, 1981—82; sr. assoc. Harbidge House, Denver, 1982; owner Eagle Valley Aviation, Vail, Colo., 1982—86, Condor Aviation, Oceano, Calif., 1986—90; lectr. Calif. Poly. State U., San Luis Obispo, 1986—90, McGill U., Montreal, 1991—95; asst. prof. Babson Coll., Wellesley, Mass., 1995—2000; dean Sch. Bus. and Info. Sci. Lasell Coll., Newton, Mass., 2000—. Instr. Tsinghua U., Beijing, 2001—02; prin. Narod Enterprises Consulting, Vail, 1982—86. Contbr. articles to profl. jours. Named Outstanding Scholar in Chinese Mktg., Soc. for Mktg. Advances, Chinese Golden Tripod Com., 2002; recipient Sr. fellowship, Dartmouth Coll., 1975—76, Rsch. fellowship, U. of Nairobi, Inst. of African Studies, 1975—76, Rsch. scholarship, McGill U., 1990—91, Rsch. fellowship, McGill and Renmin Univs., 1994—95, Babson Coll., 1997—99, Sr. Specialist grant, Fulbright Fgn. Scholarship Bd., 2003. Mem.: Assn. for Consumer Rsch., Acad. of Internat. Bus. Liberal. Episcopalian. Avocations: travel, skiing, cooking. Home: 241 Captain Eames Cir Ashland MA 01721 Office: Lasell Coll 1844 Commonwealth Ave Auburndale MA 02466 Office Fax: 617-796-4054. E-mail: bdoran@lasell.edu.

DORAN, KENNETH JOHN, lawyer; b. Janesville, Wis., Feb. 10, 1950; s. Henry James and Alice Elizabeth (Fanning) D.; m. Dianne Marie Carlson, Feb. 28, 1987; children: Taylor, Olivia. BA, U. Wis., 1974, JD, 1977. Atty. The Legal Clinic, Madison, Wis., 1978-79, Doran Law Offices, Madison, 1980-84, Smoler & Albert, S.C., Madison, 1984-88, Kassner Law Offices, Middleton, Wis., 1988-92, Doran Law Offices, 1993—. Author: Personal Bankruptcy and Debt Adjustment, 1991, 2d edit., 1996. Bd. dirs. Wis. Madison chpt. Civil Liberties Union, Wis., 1983-85. Mem. Dane County Bar Assn., Western Dist. Wis. Bankrutpcy Bar Assn. (pres. 2000-01). Democrat. Home: 2101 Fox Ave Madison WI 53711-1920 E-mail: kendoran@execpc.com.

DORAN, MARK RICHARD, real estate financial executive; b. Chgo., June 17, 1954; s. Paul George and Mae (Olson) D.; m. Wendy Carole Beckham, Dec. 17, 1977; children: Blake, Barrett, Hayley. BBA in Acctg., Baylor U., 1975, MBA, 1976. From asst. acct. to supr. Peat, Marwick, Mitchell & Co., Dallas, 1977-81; sr. v.p. fin. Lincoln Property Co., Dallas, 1982-89; exec. v.p., CFO Prentiss Properties Trust, Dallas, 1990-98, Transwestern Comml. Svcs., 1999—2002, COO, 2002—. Deacon Park Cities Bapt. Ch., Dallas, 1988—. Mem. Nat. Assn. Real Estate Investment Trusts, Nat. Assn. Indsl. and Office Pks., The Urban Land Inst., The Real Estate Coun., Baylor U. Alumni Assn. Avocations: basketball, golf, snow skiing. Office: Transwestern Comml Svcs 5001 Spring Valley Ste 600W Dallas TX 75244

DORAN, ROBERT STUART, mathematician, educator; b. Winthrop, Iowa, Dec. 21, 1937; s. Carl Arthur D. and Imogene (Ownby) Doran Nodurft; m. Shirley Ann Lange, June 27, 1959; children: Bruce Robert, Brad Christopher. BA with hons., U. Iowa, 1962, MA, 1964; MS, U. Washington, 1967, PhD, 1968. Instr. U. Wash., 1968; asst. prof. U. No. Iowa, Cedar Falls, 1968-69; asst. to prof. math. Tex. Christian U., Ft. Worth, 1969—, chmn. dept. math., 1990—, John William and Helen Stubbs Potter prof. math., 1995—. Vis. prof. U. Tex., Austin, 1979; cons. in field. Author: Approximate Identities and Factorization in Banach Modules, 1979, Characterizations of C*-Algebras: The Gelfand-Naimark Theorems, 1986, Representations of Locally Compact Groups and Banach *-Algebraic Bundles, 1988; editor: Selfadjoint and Nonselfadjoint Operator Algebras and Operator Theory, 1991, C*-Algebras: A Fifty Year Celebration, 1994, Automorphic Forms, Automorphic Representations and Arithmetic, 1999, The Mathematical Legacy of Harish-Chandra, 2000; editor Cambridge U. Press, 1987; contbr. articles to profl. jours. Chmn. bd. deacons Birchman Bapt. Ch., Ft. Worth, 1987; vol. Van Cliburn Internat. Piano Competition, 1984—, Am. Cancer Soc., 1987—. Recipient Burlington No. award for Disting. Teaching, 1988, Top Ten Prof. award Ho. of Reps., 1986, 87, 91, Mortar Bd. Preferred Prof. award, 1983, 87, 91, 93, 95, Gold medal for Prof. of Yr. Coun. for Advancement and Support of Edn., 1989, Honors Prof. of Yr. award, 1993; vis. scholar MIT, 1981, Oxford U., 1988; Minnie Stevens Piper prof., 1989. Mem. Inst. Advanced Study (chmn. we. U.S. 1984—), Assn. Mems. Inst. for Advanced Study (pres. bd. trustees 1990-99), Am. Math. Soc., Math. Assn. Am. (vis. lectr. 1990—, Beckenbach Book award prize com. 1990-94), Phi Beta Kappa, Sigma Xi, Pi Mu Epsilon. Republican. Avocations: chess, running, swimming. Home: 4204 Ridglea Country Club Dr Fort Worth TX 76126-2224 Office: Tex Christian U Dept Math Fort Worth TX 76129-0001

DORAN, THOMAS GEORGE, bishop; b. Rockford, Ill., Feb. 20, 1936; Licentiate in Sacred Theology, Pontifical Gregorian U., Rome, 1962, PhD in Canon Law, 1978. Ordained priest Roman Cath. Ch. 1961, bishop 1994. Asst. pastor St. Joseph Parish, Elgin, Ill., St. Peter Parish, South Beloit; various admin. duties Diocese of Rockford, Ill., rector diocesan cathedral; prelate auditor Roman Rota, 1986—94; bishop Rockford, 1994—. Mem. Supreme Tribunal of the Apostolic Signatura, 2000. Mem.: Congregation for the Clergy. Roman Catholic. Office: Diocese of Rockford PO Box 7044 Rockford IL 61125-7044

DORAN, TIMOTHY PATRICK, educational administrator; b. N.Y.C., July 1, 1949; s. Joseph Anthony and Claire (Griffin) D.; m. Kathleen Matava, Aug. 1, 1981; children: Claire Marie, Bridget Anne. BA in Econs., Le Moyne Coll., 1971; MA in Tchg., U. Alaska, Fairbanks, 1984; Edn. Specialist, U. Alaska, 1990. Cert. type A secondary, econs., type B K-12 prin., supt. Svc. rep. Emigrant Savings Bank, N.Y.C., 1971-72; exec., dir. Project Equality Northwest, Seattle, 1972-73, Jesuit Vol. Corps., Portland, Oreg., 1973-75, adminstv. advisor Kaltag City (Alaska) coun., 1975-77; program developer Diocese Fairbanks, Alaska, 1978-81, adminstr., supt. St. Mary's Cath. High Sch., 1981-83; prin. intern U. Alaska, Fairbanks, 1984, vis. instr., 1990-94; tchr. Anthony A. Andrews Sch., St. Michael, Alaska, 1984-86; prin., tchr. James C. Isabell Sch, Teller, Alaska, 1986-88; prin. Unalakleet (Alaska) Schs., 1988-90, Denali Elem. Sch., Fairbanks, 1992—. Acad. coord. U. Alaska summers, Fairbanks, 1984—86; instr. Elderhostel, 1991—; docent U. Alaska Mus., 1991—; sch. edn. adv. bd. U. Alaska, 1998—, adj. instr., Anchorage, 2001—. Active nat. com. Campaign for Human Devel., 1980-83; mem. manpower planning coun. Tanana Chiefs Conf., 1976-77, parish coun. Sacred Heart Cathedral, 1979-81; Sunday Sch. tchr. St. Mark's Univ. Parish, 1990-97, adv. coun., 1998-2001; mem. com. chair Fairbanks Arts and Culture in Edn., 1995—; bd. dirs., v.p., pres. Literacy Coun. Alaska, 1997-2002. Recipient Merit awards Alaska Dept. Edn., 1986-90; named Alaska Disting. Prin., 1998, Fairbanks Elem. Prin. of Yr., 2003. Mem. ASCD, Nat. Assn. Elem. Sch. Prins., Alaska Assn. Elem. Sch. Prins. (v.p., pres.-elect, pres. 2000-2002, past pres.), Fairbanks Prins. Assn. (v.p., pres. 1999-2000), Alaska Math. Consortium (bd. dirs. 1992-99). Home: 512 Windsor Dr Fairbanks AK 99709-3439 Office: Denali Elem Sch 1042 Lathrop St Fairbanks AK 99701-4124 E-mail: tdoran@northstar.k12,ak.us.

DORAN, VINCENT FRANCIS, economic development executive; b. Pitts., Oct. 25, 1950; s. Gerald Aloysius and Alice Elizabeth (Wright) D.; m. Lynn Lanz, July 16, 1977; children— Kelly Maureen, Sean Michael. B.A., Mercyhurst Coll., 1972; postgrad. Cambridge U., Eng., 1973, U. Pitts., 1977, 85; MBA Duquesne U., 1989. Eastern regional program dir. Teledyne Corp., Los Angeles, 1979-83, dir. Teledyne Job Corps Ctr., Grafton, Mass., 1983, Pitts., 1984-91; v.p. Teledyne Econ. Devel., 1991-95, pres., 1995-97, pres. ResCare, Divsn. Tng. Svs., Louisville, 1997—. Writer manuals, mag. articles in job tng. field. Republican. Roman Catholic. Club: Rotary (exec. bd. 1984—) (Oakland, Pa.). Avocations: reading, travel, tennis, racquetball. Home: 6838 Melrose Dr Mc Lean VA 22101-2807 Office: ResCare 10140 Linn Station Rd Louisville KY 40223-3813 E-mail: vdoran@rescare.com.

DORAN, WILLIAM MICHAEL, lawyer; b. Albany, N.Y., May 26, 1940; s. James R. and Lorene Tinsley (Nees) D.; m. Susan Coryell Lloyd; children: Melissa, Heather, Leigh. BS in Journalism, Northwestern U., 1962; LLB, U. Pa., 1966. Assoc. Morgan, Lewis & Bockius, Phila., 1967-76, ptnr., 1976—. Dir. SEI Investments Co.; trustee SEI Liquid Asset Trust, SEI Daily Income Trust, SEI Tax Exempt Trust, SEI Instl. Managed Trust, SEI Index Funds, SEI Internat. Trust, The Advisors Inner Cir. Fund, The Arbor Fund, Inventor Funds, Incs.; chmns. adv. coun. Eisenhower Exchange Fellowships, Phila. Vice chmn. World Affairs Coun. Phila. Mem. ABA, Pa. Bar Assn., Phila. Bar Assn. Home: 27 Druim Moir Ln Philadelphia PA 19118-4134 Office: Morgan Lewis & Bockius LLP 1701 Market St Philadelphia PA 19103-2903 E-mail: wdoran@morganlewis.com.

DORATO, PETER, electrical and computer engineering educator; b. N.Y.C., Dec. 17, 1932; s. Fioretto and Rosina (Lachello) D.; m. Marie Madeleine Turlan, June 2, 1956; children: Christopher, Alexander, Sylvia, Veronica. BEE, CCNY, 1955; MSEE, Columbia U., 1956; DEE, Poly. Inst. N.Y., 1961. Registered profl. engr., Colo. Lectr. elec. engring. dept. CCNY, 1956-57; instr. elec. engring. Poly. Inst. N.Y., Bklyn., 1957-61, prof., 1961-72; prof. elec. engring., dir. Resource System Analysis U. Colo., Colorado Springs, 1972-76; Gardner-Zemke prof. elec. and computer engring. U. N.Mex., Albuquerque, 1984—, chmn. dept., 1976-84. Hon. chaired prof. Nanjing Aero. Inst., 1989; vis. prof. Politecnico di Torino, Italy, 1991-92l dir. Ctr. for Intelligent Systems Engring. U. N.Mex., 2001. Author: Analytic Feedback Systems Design, 2000; co-author Linear Quadratic Control, 1995, Robust Control for Unstructured Perturbations, 1992, Robust Control-System Design, 1996, Italian Culture—A View from America, 2001; editor: Robust Control, Recent Results in Robust Control and Advances in Adaptive Control, reprint vols., 1987, 90, 91, IEEE Press Reprint Vol. Series, 1989-90; assoc. editor Automatica Jour., 1969-83, 89-92, editor rapid publs., 1994-98; assoc. editor IEEE Trans on Edn., 1989-91; contbr. articles on control systems theory to profl. jours. Recipient John R. Ragazzini edn. award Am. Automatic Control Coun., 1998 Fellow IEEE (3rd Millenium medal); mem. IEEE Control Systems Soc. (Disting. Mem. award).,

World Automation Congress (Life Achievement award 2002). Democrat. Home: 1514 Roma Ave NE Albuquerque NM 87106-4513 Office: U NMex Dept Elec Computer Eng Albuquerque NM 87131-1356 E-mail: peter@eece.unm.edu.

D'ORBAN, PAUL THEODORE, psychiatrist; b. London, May 26, 1930; s. Charles and Constance Emily (Hill) D'O.; m. Jocelyn Laura Ho-a-Shu, Oct. 15, 1955; children: Charles Mark, Andrea Nora. MB ChB, Aberdeen U., 1956; diploma psychol. medicine, Royal Coll. Physicians, 1961, Royal Coll. Surgeons Eng., 1961. Med. officer, Georgetown, Guyana, 1956-59; registrar Friern Hosp., London, 1960-62; cons. psychiatrist Kingston, Jamaica, 1962-65; med. officer Home Office, London, 1966-73; cons. psychiatrist St. George's Hosp., London, 1974-77; hon. sr. lectr. St. George's Hosp. Med. Sch./U. London, 1974-77; cons. forensic psychiatrist Home Office and Royal Free Hosp., 1977-87; hon. sr. lectr. U. London-Royal Free Hosp. Sch. Medicine, 1977-90; cons. forensic psychiatrist Royal Free Hosp., 1987-90. Mem. working party on evaluation of treatment of drug dependence Med. Rsch. Coun., 1968-70; mem. panel of examiners Gen. Med. Coun. London, 1982-90; hon. cons. WHO, Iran, 1974, Egypt, 1978, Iraq, 1979. Author: (with others) Principles and Practice of Forensic Psychiatry, 1990, International Handbook of Addiction Behaviour, 1991, Forensic Psychiatry, 1993; contbr. numerous articles to profl. jours. Fellow Royal Coll. of Psychiatrists, Royal Soc. Medicine; mem. Brit. Acad. of Forensic Scis. Avocations: bridge, chess, fine arts. Home: 5555 Kiowa Rd Victoria BC V9E 1J9 Canada E-mail: jocelyndo@shaw.ca.

DORCHAK, THOMAS J. lawyer; b. Cleve., Aug. 31, 1940; s. Joseph J. and Julia H. D.; m. Eileen C. Coakley, June 27, 1964; children: Joshua, Andrew, Claire Marie, Sarah T. BA with honors, Xavier U., 1962; JD, Boston Coll., 1965. Bar: Ohio 1966, U.S. Dist. Ct. (no. dist.) Ohio 1970, U.S. Ct. Appeals (6th cir.) 1981. In house def. atty. Allstate Ins. Co., Cleve., 1969-73; assoc. Bertsch Edelman & Fludine, Cleve., 1973-76; pvt. practice Cleve., 1976-92; assoc. The Crombie Law Firm, North Olmsted, Ohio, 1993—. Actor cmty. theater. Office: The Crombie Law Firm 4615 Great Northern Blvd North Olmsted OH 44070-3426

DORDEK, ALAN EUGENE, marketing executive; b. Chgo., Dec. 22, 1939; s. Jules E. and Agnes (Mirsky) D.; m. Nina Fisher D., June 21, 1964; children: Amy, Eileen, Andrew. BS, Se Paul U., 1961. Acct. exec. Bronner and Haas Advt., Chgo., 1962-64; asst. rsch. dir. Makemont Corp., Chgo., 1964-65; sr. rsch. analyst Automatic Electric Co., Northlake, Ill., 1965-67; v.p. syndicated svcs. Market Rsch. Corp. of Am., Chgo., 1967-74; chgo. area mgmt. Maritz Market Rsch. Svcs., Chgo., 1974-77; v.p. dir. rsch. planning Jack Levy and Assoc., Ill., 1977-83; v.p. market rsch. mgr. Talman Home Federal S and L, Chgo., 1983-86; dir. mktg. Interim Systems Corp., Northbrook, 1986—90, Sorkinenenstein Rsch. Svc., 1990—2000, D'Ancona & Pflaum LLC, 2000—. Mem. Newtrier Township High Sch. Caucus, Winnetka, 1983-85, Avoca Sch. Dist. Caucus, 1986-88. Sgt. U.S. Army, 1961-67. Mem. Am. Mktg. Assn. Jewish. Avocations: sports, participation and coaching. Home: 606 Lawler Ave Wilmette IL 60091-2032 Office: Interim Systems Corp 500 Skokie Blvd Northbrook IL 60062-2856

DORDELMAN, WILLIAM FORSYTH, food company executive; b. Glen Ridge, N.J., Oct. 18, 1940; s. Wilbert E. and Dorothy F. (Forsyth) D.; m. Barbara Ann Gaddis, Sept. 16, 1959; children: Dorothy Ann, William Edward, Patricia Lynne, Lauren Forsyth. BA in Econs, U. Va., 1962; MBA, Harvard U., 1964. With Gen. Foods Corp., White Plains, N.Y., 1965—, advt. and merchandising mgr. Birdseye divsn., 1972-73, gen. mgr. main meal strategic bus. unit, 1973-77, v.p. corp., pres. food products divsn., 1977-80, corp. group v.p., 1980-86; pres. Fairfield Capital, Rowayton, Conn., 1986-92; co-CEO B. Manischewitz Co., 1992-93; chmn., CEO Colo. Prime Foods, 1993-98; prin. Kohlberg & Co., Mcht. Bankers, 1998—. Bd. dirs. Bailey & Alling Lumber Co., Oscar Mayer, Entemanns, B. Manischewitz Co., Color Spot Nursery, United Signature Foods, Colo. Prime Food, S.W. Supermarket, Urgrocer.com.; chmn. Am. Homecare Supply, Orion Food Supply. Innotek Inc.; bd. dirs. Internat. Cancer Screening Lab. Bd. dirs. Mid-Fairfield Youth Hockey Assn., 1973-77, St. Vincent's Hosp. Mem. Am. Mgmt. Assn., Am. Mktg. Assn., Young Pres. Orgn. (bd. dirs. N.Y. chpt. 1982), Weeburn Country Club, Ocean Reef Club, Westchester/Fairfield County Club, Harvard Bus. Sch. Club (dir. 1978—), Zeta Psi. Episcopalian. Home: 9 Woodley Rd Darien CT 06820-2622

DORE, ANITA WILKES, English language educator; b. N.Y.C., Dec. 16, 1914; d. Abraham P. and Rose (Hirsch) Wilkes; m. Robert M. Dore, June 26, 1938; children: Marjorie Dore Allen, Elizabeth. BA, Vassar Coll., 1935; MA with honors, Columbia U., 1937. Cert. English tchr., N.Y. Tchr. H.S. English, Bd. Edn., N.Y.C., 1937-41, 56-59, TV broadcaster, producer, 1961-65, coordinator English jr. high sch. div., 1959-61, chair English dept., 1965-67, asst. dir. English, 1967-73, dir. English, N.Y.C. schs., 1973-83, cons., 1983—; cons. Young Playwrights Dramatists Guild, N.Y.C., 1983-87. Author: Premier Book of Major Poets, 1970, Emerging Woman, 1974; co-author: Distrust of Authority, 1981; also articles. Pres., bd. dirs. Sch. Settlement House, Bklyn., 1951-53; mem. edn. com. NOW, N.Y.C., 1972-75; chair Child Study Children's Book Com. Bank St. Coll., 1983-98; sec., bd. dirs. Westport-Westport Arts Ctr., Conn., 1983-93; trustee Westport Libr., Conn.; 1985-92; chair adv. com. young poets and playwrights festivals of Conn. Westport Arts Ctr., 1983—. Recipient Elizabeth Dana prize in English, Vassar Coll., 1934; named Honoree Salute to Women YWCA, 1991. Fellow N.Y. State English Council (v.p. 1970-75); mem. Nat. Council Tchrs. English Lit. Commn., N.Y.C. Assn. Tchrs. English (v.p. 1962-70), Alumnae Assn. Vassar (class 1935 pres. 1996—). Democrat. Avocations: theatre, traveling, politics. Home: 36 E 36th St New York NY 10016-3463

DORE, STEPHEN EDWARD, JR., retired civil engineer; b. Providence, Apr. 1, 1918; s. Stephen Edward and Anna Caroline (Chace) D.; m. Evelyn Mae Andrews, Mar. 14, 1942 (dec. Jan. 1995); children: Linda Jane, Jeffrey Stephen, Sherrill Ann. BS in Engring, Brown U., 1940. Registered profl. engr., Conn., Maine, Mass., N.H., R.I. registered land surveyor, Maine. Surveyor Met. Dist. Hartford County, Conn., 1940; engring. draftsman design dept. U.S. Navy, Quonset Point, R.I., 1940-42; draftsman R.I. Dept. Pub. Works, Providence, 1946; hydraulic engr. C.E., Providence, 1946; structural designer E.B. Badger Co., Boston, 1946-47; with Coffin & Richardson Inc. (Cons. Engrs.), Boston, 1947-83, sr. project engr., 1958-62, v.p., chief engr., 1962-73, exec. v.p., 1973-79, pres., 1979-83, also bd. dirs.; ret., 1983. Treas. Cedarcrest Civic Assn., Canton, Mass., 1952-55. Served to capt. C.E. U.S. Army, 1942-46. Fellow ASCE, Cons. Engrs. Council; mem. Am., New Eng. water works assns., Soc. Mil. Engrs., Boston Soc. Civil Engrs. Unitarian Universalist. Home: 1438 W Schwartz Blvd Lady Lake FL 32159-6115

DOREIAN, PATRICK, sociologist, educator; b. Cambridge, Eng., Oct. 1, 1942; arrived in U.S., 1971; s. Harold Doreian and Tove Jensen; m. Esther Sales, May 24, 1981; children: Leeza, Brian Sales, Francis. BSc in Math., U. Leicester, Eng., 1964; MA in Sociology, U. Essex, Colchester, Eng., 1966. Lectr. U. Essex, 1967—71; vis. assoc. prof. U. Pitts., 1971—72, assoc. prof., 1972—81, prof., 1981—. Gast prof. Inst. Advanced Studies, Vienna, 1974; vis. prof. U. Calif., Irvine, 1980; chair dept. sociology U. Pitts., 1999—; keynote spkr. Internat. Social Networks Conf., London, 1995; Centennial prof. London Sch. Econs., 2002. Author, editor: books and monographs; contbr. articles to profl. jours., chapters to books; editor: Jour. Math. Sociology, 1982—. Mem.: Internat. Network of Social Network Analysts (bd. dirs. 1996—, editl. bd.), Am. Sociol. Assn. (chair math. sociology sect. 2001—02). Avocations: movies, travel, wine. Office: Dept Sociology U Pitts Pittsburgh PA 15260 E-mail: pitpat@pitt.edu.

DOREMUS, OGDEN, lawyer; b. Atlanta, Apr. 23, 1921; s. C. Estes and Mary (McAdory) D.; m. Carolyn Wooten Greene, Aug. 30, 1947 (dec. Aug. 1989); children: Celia Jane, Frank O., Dale Marie Doremus; m. Linda Parker, Dec. 4, 1992. BA, Emory U., 1946, JD, 1949. Bar: Ga. 1947; cert. U.S. postal mediator, 1999. Asst. solicitor gen., Atlanta, 1947-49; ptnr. firm Smith Field Doremus & Ringel, Atlanta, 1949-60, Falligant, Doremus and Karsman, Savannah, Ga., 1960-72, Doremus, Jones & Smith, P.C., Metter, Ga., 1972-94; of counsel Karsman, Brooks & Callaway, 1994—2000. Prof. Woodrow Wilson Sch. Law, Atlanta, 1948-50; judge State Ct. Candler County, Ga., 1985—, chair uniform rules com. Coun. State Cts., 1990—; pres. Ga. Coun. State Ct. Judges, 1990-91, chair legis. com., 1997-99; mem. Jud. Coun. State of Ga., 1989-91, Unified Trial Ct. Commn., 1997; mem. ct. futures com. State Bar Ga., 1996—; bd. dirs. Ctr. for Law in the Pub. Interest, 1996—; judge Mcpl. Ct., Metter, Ga., 1997-2001; mem. commn. on judiciary Supreme Ct. Ga., 1999—. Mem. editl. adv. bd. Environ. Law, Reporter, 1969-80. Scoutmaster Boy Scouts Am., Atlanta, 1951-60, commn., 1961-70; chmn. Ga. Day and Savannah Arts Festival, 1968-72; mem. Atlanta City Coun., 1950-53; mem. Savannah Govtl. Reorgn. Commn., 1960-61, Ga. Ct. Futures Commn., 1991-93, 97—; adv. com. Nat. Coastal Zone Mgmt. Coun., 1978-86; trustee Ga. Conservancy; bd. dirs. Legal Environ. Assistance Found., 1983-86, Ga. Hazardous Waste Authority, 1989—, Chatham Environ. Forum, 1990-93; mem. strategic planning com. Coun. State Cts. Ga., 1996—; bd. dirs. Coastal Environ. Orgn. Ga., 1998—, Cancochee Riverkeeper. Served with USAAC, 1942-46, ETO. Named Young Man of Yr. Atlanta, 1951; recipient Thomas H. gignilliat award Cultural Progress of Savannah, 1969, Tradition of Excellence award Ga. State Bar, 1988, 1st Ann. Coun. of State Cts. award named Ogden Doremus in his honor, 1993. Mem.: ABA (chmn. environ law com., gen. practice 1976—77), Atlanta Soc., Ga. Inst. Trial Advocacy (chmn. 1984—89), Savannah Bar Assn., State Bar Ga. (chmn. ins. law sect. 1963—67, 1977—83, mediator for U.S. Postal Svc. 1999—, cert. mediator Ga. commn. on dispute resolution), Izaak Walton League (founder Ga. chpt. 1950), Willow Lake Country Club, Chatham Tennis Club, Chatham Club, Sierra Club (exec. com. Chattahoochee chpt. 1965—75, chair legal com. Ga. chpt. 1997—2001, Lifetime Achievement Ga. environ. coun. Citizenship award 1997, 1999, Conservation Leadership award Ga. chpt. 1999, Common Cause Citizenship award 1998). Home: RR 2 Box 188A Metter GA 30439-9570 Office: Doremus and Assocs Courthouse Sq PO Box 702 Metter GA 30439-0702 E-mail: odoremus@excite.com. *It has been my experience that a love for this earth and all that it has is the most precious of our possessions. My hope is that love and kindness become universal.*

DOREMUS, ROBERT HEWARD, glass and ceramics processing educator; b. Denver, Sept. 16, 1928; s. Francis Heward and Elsie Marion (Segelke) D.; m. Germaine Briancon, Mar. 19, 1956; children: Marc Francis, Elaine, Carol, Natalie. BS, U. Colo., 1950; MS, U. Ill., 1951, PhD, 1953; PhD (Fulbright fellow), U. Cambridge, Eng., 1956. Phys. chemist Gen. Electric Research and Devel. Ctr., Schenectady, 1956-71; N.Y. State prof. glass and ceramics Rensselaer Poly. Inst., Troy, N.Y., 1971—, chair materials engring. dept., 1986-95. Cons. in field. Author: Glass Science, 1973, 94, Rates of Phase Transformations, 1985, Diffusion of Reactive Molecules in Solids and Melts, 2001; co-editor: Growth and Perfection of Crystals, 1958; contbr. articles to profl. jours. Bd. dirs. Phila. Luth. Sem., 1967-76. Fellow Am. Ceramic Soc.; mem. AAAS, Sigma Xi, Sigma Tau, Tau Beta Pi. Lutheran. Office: Materials Dept Rensselaer Poly Instit Troy NY 12181 E-mail: doremr@rpi.edu.

DOREN, BONNIE E. special education educator, researcher; b. Tampa, Fla., July 19, 1960; d. Anthony John and Kay Freer Doren. BA, SUNY, Binghamton, 1982; PhD, Temple U., 1987. Asst. prof., rsch. assoc. U. Oreg., Eugene, 1988—. Contbr. articles to profl. jours.; mem. editl. bd. Career Devel. of Exceptional Children, 1998—2002. Grantee, Office of Spl. Edn. Programs. Mem.: Coun. for Exceptional Children (rsch. com. divsn. career devel. and transition 2002—). Avocations: yoga, hiking, wine tasting, movies.

DORENFELD, ALAN STEVEN, fundraising executive; b. Balt., Nov. 30, 1945; s. Sylvan and Edith (Rosenberg) D.; m. Sharon Roslyn Heyman, July 3, 1966; children: Melissa Pam, Amy Lynn, David Jonathan. BS, U. Md., 1967; MS, George Washington U., 1971. Registered profl. engr., Md. Design engr. U.S. Coast Guard, Washington, 1966-71; project engr. Century Engring., Balt., 1971-77; exec. Monumental Paper Co., Balt., 1977-93; exec. v.p. Kayboys Empire Paper Co., Balt., 1993-96; v.p. Systematic Way, Inc., Balt., 1996-99; dir. devel. Beth El Congregation, Balt., 1999—. Pres. Md. Paper Trade Assn., Balt., 1986-88; adv. coun. Ga.-Pacific Corp., Atlanta, 1990-93. Pres. WGN Cmty. Swim Club, Balt., 1986-88; pres. Beth El Congregation, Balt., 1995-97. Lt. (j.g.) USCG, 1968-71. Recipient Disting. Svc. award United Cerebral Palsy, 1985. Mem. ASCE, Tau Beta Pi, Chi Epsilon Civil Engr. Soc. Jewish. Home: 4706 Hawksbury Rd Baltimore MD 21208 E-mail: w-aland@bethelbalto.com.

DOREY, LOUIS J. gas industry executive, lawyer; BBA, U. Okla.; JD, U. Tex. Sch. Law. Lawyer, Houston; pres. Dynegy Wholesale Energy Network; mgr. bus. devel. Destec Energy (formerly known as Dynegy), 1991, mgr., dir. and v.p. mergers and acquisitions; v.p. fin. and planning Dynegy, 1997, CFO, exec. v.p. fin., 2002—. Office: Dynegy 1000 Louisiana Ste 5800 Houston TX 77002

DORF, EVE BUCKLE, artist; b. Oakland, Calif., July 31, 1946; d. John Franklin and Ruth Eva (Kratzer) Buckle; m. Frank Holman, mar. 22, 1970; children: John Buckle Dorf, Frank Lester Dorf. BA, Westminster Coll., 1968; 2d BA, Calif. State U., Sacramento, 1990. Cert. tchr., Calif. Tchr. 2nd grade San Juan Unified Sch. Dist., Carmichael, Calif., 1968-72; docent and internship Crocker Art Mus., Sacramento, 1980-86; children's art instr. Folsom (Calif.) Parks and Recreation, 1987-98. Artist-in-schs. Sacramento Met. Arts Commn., Calif. Artist: Art Auction for Pub. TV, Calif. Juried Shows, 1995-97, Roseville Art Ctr. Juried Shows, 1983-89, 33 group and solo artshows, 1983-98, travelling exhibit Strength from Unity: Expressions from the Island of Ireland and the United States, 2000, Hospice Mask Project, 2002; represented in pub. collections. Vol. art docent Roseville Art Ctr., Calif., 1980-89; juror children's art Folsom Sch. Dist., 1994-98; insp. for voting poll place Sacramento County Voter Registration, 1980-98. Recipient Witt Meml. fellowship 1990. Mem. Crocker Art Mus., AAUW (br. photographer 1974-80). Democrat. Episcopalian. Avocations: gardening, cooking, hiking, snowshoeing, picnics. Home: 4400 La Mirada Cir Fair Oaks CA 95628-6664 E-mail: buckledorf@sbcglobal.net.

DORF, RICHARD CARL, electrical engineering and management educator; b. N.Y.C., Dec. 27, 1933; s. William Carl and Marion (Fraser) D.; m. Joy H. MacDonald, June 15, 1957; children: Christine, Renée. BS, Clarkson U., 1955; MS, U. Colo., 1957; PhD, U.S. Naval Postgrad. Sch., 1961. Registered profl. engr., Calif. Instr. Clarkson U., Potsdam, N.Y., 1956-58; instr., asst. prof. U.S. Naval Postgrad. Sch., Monterey, Calif., 1958-63; prof., chmn. U. Santa Clara, Calif., 1963-69; v.p. Ohio U., Athens, 1969-72; dean of extended learning U. Calif., Davis, 1972-81, prof. in mgmt. and elec. engring., 1972—. Lectr. U. Edinburgh, Scotland, 1961-62; cons. Lawrence Livermore (Calif.) Nat. Lab., 1981—; chmn. Sacramento Valley Venture Capital Forum, 1985-90. Author: The Mutual Fund Portfolio Planner, 1988, The New Mutual Fund Advisor, 1988, Electric Circuits, 5d edit., 2000, Modern Control Systems, 9th edit., 2000; editor: Ency. of Robotics, 1987, Circuits, Devices and Systems, 1991, Handbook of Electrical Engineering, 2d edit., 1997, Handbook of Manufacturing and Automation, 1994, Handbook of Technology Management, 1999, Technology, Humans and Society, 2001. Bd. dirs. Sta. KVIE, PBS, Sacramento, 1976-79; ruling elder Davis Cmty. Ch., 1973-76, 1999—; chmn. Sonoma Valley Econ. Devel. Assn., 1993-2000; mem. City Coun., City of Sonoma, 1994-98; vice mayor City of Sonoma, 1994, 98, mayor, 1996; chmn. Davis Open Space Commn., 2000—. With U.S. Army, 1956. Recipient Alumni award Clarkson U., 1979, Disting. Alumni award Colo. U., 1998. Fellow IEEE; mem. Am. Soc. Engring. Edn. (sr., chmn. div. 1980—), University Club (bd. dirs. 1988-91), Rotary (bd. dirs. 1978-80). Presbyterian. Office: U Calif Elec Engring Dept Davis CA 95616 E-mail: rcdorf@ucdavis.edu.

DORF, ROBERT CLAY, lawyer, broadcaster; b. N.Y.C., Apr. 4, 1943; s. Irving and Jeanne (Hayflick) D.; m. Wendy Rappaport, Nov. 27, 1968; children— Andrew R., Jessica L. B.A. in History, U. Fla., 1964; student Alliance Francise, Paris, 1967; J.D., Bklyn. Law Sch., 1972. Bar: N.Y. 1973, U.S. Dist. Ct. (ea. and so. dists.) N.Y. 1974, U.S. Ct. Appeals (2d cir.) 1980. Announcer Sta. WIVI, V.I., 1964-65; office clk. Reuters News Service, Paris, 1967; film editor sta. WMAL-TV, Washington, 1968; asst. dist. atty. Bronx Dist. Atty.'s Office, 1972-76; practice law, N.Y.C., 1976-94; ptnr. law firm Dorf & Perlmutter, N.Y.C., 1984-94; prin. law clk. to Hon. James G. Starkey, Supreme Ct. State of N.Y., Kings County, 1995—; arbitrator U.S. Dist. Ct. (ea. dist.) N.Y., 1990-94; hearing officer Environ. Control Bd., N.Y.C., 1976-77; arbitrator N.Y. County Civil Ct., N.Y.C., 1981— ; adj. prof. geog. law Hunter Coll./CUNY, 1997. Methadone counselor Beth Israel Hosp., 1969. Served with U.S. Army, 1965-67. Mem. Bklyn. Bar Assn. Democrat. Jewish. Home: 101 Clark St Brooklyn NY 11201-2746

DORFF, STEPHEN, actor; b. Atlanta, July 29, 1973; Actor: (TV series) In Love and War, 1987, The Absent-Minded Professor, 1988; (TV films) Quiet Victory: The Charlie Wedemeyer Story, 1988, I Know My First Name is Steven, 1998, Do You Know the Muffin Man?, 1998; (TV series) What A Dummy, 1990; (TV films) A Son's Promise, 1999; (films) The Gate, 1987, The Power of One, 1992, Judgment Night, 1993, Rescue Me, 1993, Backbeat, 1993, S.F.W., 1994, Les Cent et une nuits, 1995, Halcyon Days, 1995, Reckless, 1995, I Shot Andy Warhol, 1996, The Audition, 1996, Space Truckers, 1997, Blood and Wine, 1997, City of Industry, 1997, Blade, 1998, Entropy, 1999, Cecil B. DeMented, 2000, Zoolander, 2001, The Last Minute, 2001, All for Nothin', 2002, Riders, 2002, FearDotCom, 2002, Den of Lions, 2002, numerous appearances on TV series. Mailing: 9350 Wilshire Blvd # 4 Beverly Hills CA 90212

DORFMAN, ALLEN BERNARD, international management consultant; b. N.Y.C., Mar. 30, 1930; s. Harry and Jean (Schreiber) D.; m. Elaine Turbé, Jan. 9, 1955; children: Nancy Ann, Jeffrey David. BBA summa cum laude, 1952; postgrad. mgmt. studies, Harvard Bus. Sch. From mem. exec. tng. squad to sr. mgmt. R.H. Macy's, N.Y.C., 1954-67; asst. gen. mdse. mgr., v.p., mem. mgmt. com. N.Y. div. Allied Stores Corp., N.Y.C., 1967-69; v.p., gen. mdse. mgr. hard and soft goods, mem. exec. com. Town & Country Full Line Discount Stores div. Lane Bryant Corp., N.Y.C., 1969-71; pres., dir. Nat. Bellas Hess Inc., Kansas City, Mo., 1971-73; corp. sr. v.p. and pres., CEO retail div. Jewelcor, Inc., N.Y.C., 1973-77; corp. sr. v.p., dir. corp. ops., mem. exec. com. Vornado, Inc., Garfield, N.J., 1977-78; chmn. bd. dirs., CEO Allen B. Dorfman, Mgmt. Consulting Co., 1978—. Prof. Grad. Sch., L.I. U., evenings. Bd. dirs., exec. v.p. Am. Cancer Soc.; bd. dirs. Kings Point Civic Assn. With AUS, 1952-54. Recipient award Advt. Club N.Y., Torch of Liberty award Nat. Anti-Defamation League. Mem. Mass. Retailing Inst., Nat. Retail Mchts. Assn., Nat. Assn. Catalog Showroom Merchandisers, Inc., Adelphi Coll. Found., Boy Scouts Am., Boys Club, Philhamonics Assn., Police Athletic League, Polo Club (mem. adv. bd. govs.-exec. com., chmn. coun. pres., chmn. emeritus coun. of pres.), Wildwood Country Club (pres., bd. dirs., Kings Point, N.Y.), Beta Gamma Sigma, Eta Mu Pi, Sigma Alpha. Achievements include patents pending for zippered ice and roller skates. Office: Allen B Dorfman Mgmt Consulting Co Polo Club-Penthouse Villa 17588 Ashbourne Ln Ste C Boca Raton FL 33496-4434

DORFMAN, BENJAMIN FRIDEL, physicist; b. St. Petersburg/Leningrad, Russia, Apr. 10, 1939; s. Fridel Khaim Dorfman, Rachel Benjaminovna Ravikovich; m. Nina Artemievna Lazareva; children: Igor, Ilya, Lena Lazareva. M. Phys. Chemistry, Moscow Inst. of Steel, Russia, 1961; PhD in Phys. Chemistry, Moscow Inst.of Fine Chemistry, 1966; ScD in Physics, Inst. Semiconductors Physics & Inst. of Electronic Controlling Mashines, Russia, 1974; ScD in Microelectronics, Moscow Inst. of Electronic Technique, 1977. Cert. sr. scientist in Microelectronics by Supreme Attest Commi.USSR 1971. Scientist Inst. of Electronic Controlling Mashines, Moscow, 1961—66, head Lab. for Solid State Physics and Techn. for new Computer Generations, 1966—90; head of lab. Moltech Corp., Stony Brook, NY, 1991; sr. scientist Advanced Refractory Tech., Buffalo, 1992—93; chief scientist and CEO Atomic-Scale Design, San Francisco, 1994—. Vis. scientist Brookhaven Nat. Lab., Brookhaven, NY, 1992—97; adj. prof. SUNY, Stony Brook, 1991—; prof. for rsch. Polytechnic U., N.Y.C., 1992—97, SUNY, Farmingdale, 1992—97. Author: At the Border of Millenniums (in Russian), 1982 (Best Scientific-Popular Book of the USSR, 1983), (chpt.) Stabilized sp3/sp2 Carbon and Metal-Carbon Composites of Atomic Scale as Interface and Surface Controlling Dielectric and Conducting Materials, 2001 (distinguished as Excellent, Outstanding Chapter, 2001), Computer and its Elements: Development and Optimization (in Russian), 1988, Synthesis of Solid State Structures (in Russian), 1986, Micrometalurgy in Microelectronics, 1978, Wings of Creative Fantasy, 2000, Thought Settled in Crystal, 1988, Evolution of Technologies or New History of the Time, 1990, Evolution of Technology of Microelectronics and Micromechanics, 1995. Founder, organizer USA-Russian Seminar for Sci., Tech. and Defence Conversion, A Premier Forum for Govt. Ofcls., Corp. Tech. Officers, CEO's of High Tech. Tocs., Academicians, Students, and Venture Capitalists, Stony Brook-Brookhaven-Farmingdale, NY, 1994; mem. Coun. for Microelectronics of the USSR, Moscow, 1966—91; apptd. chmn. of Periodic Sci. Commns. for Complex Projects Devices Bldg. Industry of the USSR, Moscow, 1967—89; founder, chmn. Inter-disciplinary Seminar for Adv. Technologies, Moscow, 1978—90. Recipient Gold Medal for Disting. Labor, Govt. of the USSR, 1970, Grand prize, First Internat. Nanotech. Contest, Japan, 2003, Gold medal for best tech. achievement of USSR, 1989; grantee 12 SBIR and ATP grants for Stabilized Diamondlike Carbon R&D and applications, Fed. Agencies of the USA and NIST, 1991—98. Mem.: N.Y. Acad. Sci. (New York 1994—97), Internat. Acad. of Authors of Sci. Discoveries and Inventions (life; Moscow 2000, Hon. Medal 2000). Achievements include patents for in field. Avocations: architecture, wild travels. Business E-Mail: bfd137@pacbell.net.

DORFMAN, HOWARD DAVID, pathologist, educator; b. N.Y., July 20, 1928; s. Louis and Helen (Weingarten) D.; m. Esther Novick, June 21, 1952; children: Richard H., Peter W., Leslie Jane. BA, NYU, 1947; MD, SUNY, Bklyn., 1951. Resident in pathology Mt. Sinai Hosp., N.Y., 1952-54, Columbia Presby. Medical Ctr., N.Y., 1954-58; dir. pathology Sharon (Conn.) Hosp., 1958-60; assoc. pathologist Sinai Hosp. Balt., Baltimore, Md., 1960-64; dir. pathology Hosp. Joint Diseases, N.Y., 1964-74; pathologist-in-chief Sinai Hosp. Balt., 1974-85; prof. orthopedic pathology Johns Hopkins Sch. of Medicine, Balt., 1985; prof. pathology, radiology and orthopaedic surgery Albert Einstein Coll. Medicine, Bronx, N.Y., 1985—. Walter Putschar lectr. Mass. Gen. Hosp. Harvard Med. Sch., 1983; vis. prof. Wayne State U. Sch. Medicine, 1984, Baylor Coll. Medicine, Houston, 1984, Cleve. Clinic, 1984, SUNY, Stonybrook, 1994, Johns Hopkins U. Sch. Medicine, 1995, U. Mich. Sch. Medicine, 1997, Cornell U. Sch. Medicine, Meml.-Sloan Kettering Cancer Ctr., 1998, U. Pitts. Sch. Medicine, 1998, Brigham and Women's Hosp., Harvard Med. Sch., 1998, Yale U. Sch. of Medicine, 2003. Author: Bone Tumors, 1998; co-author: Tumors of Bone and Cartilage, 1971. Recipient Henry Jaffe award Hosp. Joint Diseases, 1984. Mem. N.Y. Pathological Soc. (pres. 1989-91), Internat. Skeletal Soc. (pres. 1986-88). Home: 201 E 79th St Apt 10G New York NY 10021-0836

DORFMAN, JEFFREY H. economist, educator; b. Evanston, Ill., Jan. 14, 1965; BSc, U. Calif., Davis, 1987, PhD, 1989. Prof. U. Ga., Athens, 1989—, coord. Ctr. for Agribusiness, 1997—2000. Cons. Sprint, Pennington Seed, American Farmland Trust, Turner Found. Treas. Ctrl. Presbyn. Ch., Athens, 1999—2002. Mem.: Internat. Soc. for Bayesian Analysis (newsletter editor 1994—96), Am. Statis. Assn., Am. Econs. Assn., Am. Agrl. Econs. Assn. Office: Univ Ga 315 Conner Hall Athens GA 30606-7509 Office Fax: 706-542-0739. Business E-Mail: jdorfman@agecon.uga.edu.

DORFMAN, JOHN CHARLES, lawyer; b. Wilkinsburg, Pa., Feb. 3, 1925; s. Leo O. Dorfman; m. Ruth B. Davison; children: Beverly Dorfman Lenci, Laura Carolyn, Bradley. BEE, Yale U., 1945; JD, Cornell U., 1949. Bar: N.Y. 1949, U.S. Patent & Trademark Office 1949, Conn. 1950, Pa. 1956, U.S. Dist. Ct. (ea. dist.) Pa. 1957, U.S. Ct. Appeals (3d cir.) 1957, U.S. Supreme Ct. 1959, U.S. Ct. Appeals (fed. cir.) 1982. Patent counsel Machlett Labs. Inc., Springdale, Conn., 1950-54; assoc. Pennie & Edmonds, N.Y.C., 1949-55, Howson & Howson, Phila., 1955-59, ptnr., 1960-73; ptnr., chmn. Dann, Dorfman, Herrell & Skillman, Phila., 1974—. Elder Wayne Prebyn. Ch. Served to lt. (j.g.) USNR, 1943—46. Mem.: ABA (chmn. sect. patent, trademakr and copyright law 1984—85, hon. mem. coun.), Nat. Inventors Hall of Fame Found. (pres. 1977—78, bd. dirs. 1979—99, hon. mem. coun. 1999—, mem. joint bd. NIHF and Inveture Pl. 1997—2000), Phila. Patent Law Assn. (pres. 1974—76), Am. Intellectual Property Law Assn. (bd. dirs. 1973—76), Nat. Coun. Patent Law Assn. (chmn. 1978—79), Yale Club (Phila.), Union League Club (Phila.), St. David's Golf Club (Wayne), Delta Tau Delta (bd. dirs. Cornell U. ho. corp. 1969—), Tau Beta Pi. Republican. Avocations: skiing, golf, travel. Home: 215 Midland Ave Wayne PA 19087-4108 Office: Dann Dorfman Herrell & Skillman 1601 Market St Ste 720 Philadelphia PA 19103-2307 E-mail: jdorfman@ddhs.com.

DORGAN, BYRON LESLIE, senator; b. Dickinson, N.D., May 14, 1942; s. Emmett P. and Dorothy (Bach) D.; m. Kimberly Olson Dorgan; children: Scott, Shelly (dec.), Brendon, Haley. BBA, U. N.D., 1965; MBA, U. Denver, 1966. Exec. devel. trainee Martin Marietta Corp., Denver, 1966-67; dep. tax commr., then tax commr. State of N.D., 1967-80; mem. 97th-102nd congresses from N.D., Washington, 1981-92, U.S. Senate from N.D., Washington, 1992—; asst. Dem. floor leader U.S. Senate, Washington, 1996—. Mem. commerce, sci. and transp. com., select com. on Indian affairs, appropriations com., energy and natural resource com., chmn. Dem. policy com., 1992-, instr. econs. Bismarck (N.D.) Jr. Coll., 1969-71. Contbr. articles to profl. jours. Recipient Nat.

Leadership award Office Gov. N.D., 1972 Mem. Nat. Assn. Tax Adminstrs. (exec. com. 1972-75) Democrat. Office: US Senate 713 Hart Senate Off Bldg Washington DC 20510-0001 E-mail: senator@dorgan.senate.gov.

DORIA, ANTHONY NOTARNICOLA, college dean, educator; b. Savona, Italy, June 2, 1927; s. Vito Sante and Jolanda (Giampaolo) Notarnicola. MBA, Wharton Sch., U. Pa., 1953; LL.M. (equivalent), U. Paris, 1960; D.Jr., U. Rome, 1962. Prof. history, bus. and internat. law Community Coll. at Suffolk County, Selden, N.Y., 1960-65, L.I. U., Southampton, N.Y., 1964-65; founder, pres. Royalton Coll. Sch. Internat. Affairs, S. Royalton, Vt., 1965-72; founder, dean Vt. Law Sch., 1972-74; dean Royalton Coll. Sch. Internat. Affairs (Royalton Coll. Law Study Center), 1974-92; prof. internat. law U. China, Beijing, 1992—; dir. grad. sch. program Internat. Bus. and Law - Hong Kong Ctr. Dir. grad. sch. program internat. bus. and law Hong Kong Ctr.; cons. internat. law and orgns.; panelist Am. Arbitration Assn.; mem. Vt. Gov.'s Commn. on Student Affairs, 1972-75 Author: Italy and the Free World, 1945, The Conquest of the Congo, 1947, Influences in the Making of Foreign Policy in the United States of America, Great Britain and France, 1953, Introduction to the Study of International Law, 1990. Candidate for U.S. Senate, 1986. Served with underground resistance movement World War II. Recipient Merit cert. UN; citation Boy Scouts Am., 1965 Mem. Am. Judicature Soc., Internat. Bar Assn., Internat. Law Assn., Am. Soc. Internat. Law, AAUP, Acad. Polit. Sci., Noble Assn. Chevaliers Pontificaux (life), Elysee (Paris), Penn and Pencil, Rotary (pres. 1990-91). Home: The Royalton Inn South Royalton VT 05068 Office: Royalton Coll Law Study Ctr South Royalton VT 05068

DORIA, CATALDO, transplant surgeon; b. Apr. 1, 1965; Degree in medicine and surgery, U. Perugia, Italy, 1990. Diplomate European Bd. Gen. Surgery. Fellow in transplantation surgery U. Pitts., 1997, 1997; asst. prof. surgery Presbyn. U. Hosp., Pitts., 1997—, Children's Hosp., Pitts., 1998—, VA Hosp., Pitts., Italy, 1998; clin. dir. transplant divsn. U. Pitts. Med. Ctr., Palermo, Italy, 1999—. Developer, implementer transplantation facility in So. Europe, U. Pitts. Med. Ctr., Palermo, Italy, 1998-99. Contbr. articles to profl jours. Grantee U. Perugia, 1991-92, 94, 95, Pfizer, Inc., 1997-98, U. Pitts., 1998. Office: Univ Surg 3601 Fifth Ave 4W Falk Clinic Pittsburgh PA 15213-3403

DORIA, JOSEPH V., JR., state legislator; b. June 28, 1946; m. Maribeth Keselica. AB, St. Peter's Coll., 1968; MA, Boston Coll., 1969; postgrad., Columbia Tchrs. Coll. Assembly mem. dist. 31 N.J. State Assembly. Speaker N.J. State Assembly, 1990-91, chmn. higher edn. & regulated professions com. Past pres. Bayonne Bd. Edn.; dir. edn. svc. St. Peter's Coll.; vol. Bayonne coun. Boy Scouts Am., Urban League. Mem. Rotary. Office: 595 Broadway Bayonne NJ 07002-3818

DORIAN, PATRICK CHARLES, music educator; b. Montreal, Can., Mar. 22, 1956; arrived in U.S., 1958; s. Charles P. and Marian Dorian; m. Mary Ann Ridlon, Apr. 8, 1982. BMus in Performance and Edn., Ithaca Coll., 1978; MMus, Northwestern U., 1980. Music educator East Stroudsburg (Pa.) Area Schs., 1980—89, Pocono Mountain Area Schs., Swiftwater, Pa., 1989—94; jazz ensemble dir. Wilkes U., Wilkes-Barre, Pa., 1982; adj. prof. music Moravian Coll., Bethlehem, Pa., 1986—87; assoc. prof. music East Stroudsburg U. of Pa., 1987—. Profl. trumpeter Phil Woods Big Band, 1996—, David Leibman Big Band, 2000—. Author: CD insert booklets; contbr. articles and papers to profl. publs.; musician: (CD) Celebration! (Grammy award nomination, 98). Vol. Meals on Wheels, 1996—; pres. Celebration of Arts, Delaware Water Gap, Pa., 1991—92, 1994—95, 1997—98. Recipient Fred Waring award, Celebration of Arts, 1990, Outstanding Advisor, Omicron Delta Kappa, 1996. Mem.: Internat. Assn. Jazz Edn. (mem. resource team 1992—), Mensa. Avocations: travel, film music, humor, television. Home: 1253 Kroucher Rd Stroudsburg PA 18360-8856 Office: East Stroudsburg U Music Dept 200 Prospect St East Stroudsburg PA 18301-2999 Fax: 570-422-3008. E-mail: pdorian@po-box.esu.edu.

DORIGHI, NANCY S. computer engineer; BS in Math., U. San Francisco; MSEE, Stanford U. Mgr. future flight ctrl. Ames Rsch. Ctr. NASA, Moffett Field, Calif., mgr. air traffic control tower simulator Future Flight Ctrl. Fellow: AIAA (assoc.; assoc.); mem.: ASME (assoc. editor ASME jour.). Avocations: hiking, skiing, gardening.

DORINSKY, PAUL MICHAEL, physician, researcher, educator; b. Columbus, Ohio, July 2, 1953; s. Albert Paul and Anna Marie Dorinsky; m. Nancy Lynn Dorinsky; children: Kathryn, Matthew, William. BS in Math. summa cum laude, Ohio State U., 1974, MD cum laude, 1978. Diplomate Am. Bd. Internal Medicine, Am. Bd. Pulmonary Medicine, Am. Bd. Critical Care. Intern Ohio State U., 1978-79, resident in internal medicine, 1979-81, fellow in pulmonary and critical care medicine, 1981-83, asst. prof. medicine, 1983-89, assoc. prof. medicine, 1989-97; assoc. dir. Boehringer Ingelheim, Ridgefield, Conn., 1997—98, prin. clin. rsch. physician Glaxo Wellcome, Research Triangle Park, NC, 1999—2000; sr. dir. R&D GlaxoSmithKline, 2001—. Clin. assoc. prof. U. N.C., Chapel Hill, 1999—. Guest editor: Medical Clinics of North America, 1996; contbr. articles to profl. jours. Trustee Am. Lung Assn. Ohio, Columbus, 1996-97, Pregnancy Distress Ctr., Columbus, 1994-97, Hopeline, Danbury, Conn., 1998. Fellow Parker B. Francis Found., 1980-81, Edward Livingston Trudeau fellow Am. Lung Assn., 1985-87; recipient award NIH, 1991-97; rsch. grantee Ohio Lung Assn., 1989-97. Fellow Am. Coll. Chest Physicians; mem. Am. Thoracic Soc. (critical care assembly chair 1992-94), Am. Assn. Pharm. Physicians, Ohio Thoracic Soc. (pres. 1995-97). Republican. Avocations: tennis, jogging, golf. Office: GlaxoSmithKline 5 Moore Dr Research Triangle Park NC 27709

DORIO, MARTIN MATTHEW, JR., real estate company executive, investor; b. Bklyn., Nov. 12, 1945; s. Martin M. and Josephine V. (Marsala) D.; m. Gayle M. Morris, June 16, 1968; children: Paul, Jay. BS, SUNY, Stony Brook, 1967; PhD, U. Mass., 1975. Rsch. chemist Diamond Shamrock Corp., Painesville, Ohio, 1975-76, group leader, 1977-79; venture mgr. Gen. Electric Lighting Bus., Cleve., 1979-81, quality and mfg. tech. mgr., 1981-87; dir. quality and productivity FMC Corp., Chgo., 1987-90; v.p. worldwide product mgmt. and market strategy Case Corp., Racine, Wis., 1990-91; v.p. corp. planning and devel. J.I. Case Corp., Racine, Wis., 1992-95; pres., CEO, dir. CLARK Material Handling Co., Lexington, Ky., 1995-99, chmn., CEO, dir., 1999—2001; prin. ARGENT Internat., Inc., 2001—. Mem. adv. com. Dept. Energy, Washington, 1977-79, Am. Productivity and Quality Ctr., Houston, 1988-90; mem. adv. com. on quality Ency. Brittanica, 1988-90; mem. bd. examiners Malcolm Baldrige Nat. Quality Award, 1988-90; mem. adv. bd. Bioblend Lubricants Internat., Inc.; counselor Sr. Corps of Ret. Execs., 2002—. Author: Multiple Electron Resonance Spectroscopy, 1979; contbr. articles to profl. jours.; patentee in field. Adv. bd. dirs. Mus. Culture and Diversity, 1997-99, chmn. elect; bd. dirs. Lexington Arts & Cultural Coun., 1996-99; co-chair advanced divsn. Lexington: Strides Ahead, 1998-99. Capt. USAF, 1968-71. Recipient Nat. Svc. award Nat. Inst. Sci. and Tech., 1988-90. Mem. Am. Soc. Quality Control (exec. com. 1984-85), Am. Mgmt. Assn. Avocations: tennis, raquetball, photography, reading, writing. Home and Office: ARGENT Internat LLC 1472 Pal ma Blanca Ct Naples FL 34119-3368 E-mail: marty@martydorio.com.

DORION, ROBERT CHARLES, entrepreneur, investor; b. N.Y.C., Dec. 28, 1926; s. William J. and Adelaide (Bacardi) D.; m. Ana Maria Ferber, Nov. 26, 1954; children: Robert Patrick, Marianne Michelle, Nicholas Christian, Kristel Alexia. Student, Columbia U., 1943-44; B of Naval Scis., Dartmouth Coll., 1946. Buyer Balfour, Guthrie and Co. Ltd., 1948-49; capt. M/V Assault Shark Industries div. Borden & Co., 1950-51; pres. Dorion, Rubio and Cia, 1952-57; mgr., ins., mining and chem. dept. Grace & Co., 1954-59; sales mgr. Gen. Tires, Guatemala, 1960-61; chmn. El Salto, S.A., 1962-78; pres. Tecnicos En Seguros, S.A., 1974—, Marcas Mundiales, S.A., 1978-99. Dir. emeritus Bacardi Ltd., Bermuda; pres. Marcas Mundiales S.A.; dir. Industrias Rio Dulce S.A.; pres. Fancap Found. of Inst. Nutricion de Centroamerica y Panama. Contbr. articles to profl. jours. Friend Am. Mus. of Nat. History, N.Y.C.; field assoc. Fla. Mus., Gainesville, Mote Marine Lab., Sarasota, Fla., Interamer. Scout Found. Fellow Internat. Oceanographic Found. (life); mem. Rotary (Paul Harris fellow), World Scout Orgn. (Baden-Powell fellow), Interam. Scout Found. (dir.), U.S. Navy Meml. Found. (dir.), U.S. Naval Inst. (life), Audubon Soc. (life), Internat. Wildlife Soc., Order of The Bronze Wolf. Avocations: pre-columbian archaeology, cryptozoolical studies, shark research, deep sea fishing. Office: Sect 2870 PO Box 02-5339 Miami FL 33102-5339 also: Kristel SA Apt 195A Guatemala City Guatemala

DORIS, ALAN S(ANFORD), lawyer; b. Cleve., June 18, 1947; s. Sam E. and Rebecca (Sunshine) D.; m. Nancy Rose Spitzer, Jan. 10, 1976; children: Matthew, Lisa. AB and BS in Bus. cum laude, Miami U., Oxford U., 1969; JD cum laude, Harvard U., 1972. Bar: Ohio 1972, U.S. Dist. Ct. (no. dist.) Ohio 1972, U.S. Tax Ct. 1972, U.S. Ct. Appeals (6th cir.) 1972. Assoc. Stotter, Familo, Cavitch, Elden & Durkin, Cleve., 1972-77; ptnr. Elden & Ford, Cleve., 1978-79, Benesch, Friedlander, Coplan & Aronoff, Cleve., 1980-2000, Squire, Sanders & Dempsey, 2000—. Editor: Ohio Transaction Guide. Treas. Hawthorne Valley Country Club, Cleve., 1984-85; chmn. Cleve. Tax Inst., 1994. Mem. ABA (chmn. capital recovery com. taxation sect. 1994-96). Avocation: golf. Office: Squire Sanders & Dempsey LLP 4900 Key Tower Cleveland OH 44114

DORKEY, CHARLES E., III, lawyer; b. Phila., June 23, 1948; s. Charles Edward and Peggy O'Neal D.; children: Charles Edward IV, John Hilliard, Marjorie Lyddon. AB cum laude, Dartmouth Coll., 1970; JD, Univ. Pa., 1973. Bar: Pa. 1974, N.Y. 1975, D.C. 1977. Law clk. to hon. Samuel J. Roberts Supreme Ct. of Pa., 1973-74; assoc. Sullivan & Cromwell, N.Y.C., 1975-81, ptnr. Reboul, MacMurray, Hewitt, Maynard & Kristol, N.Y.C., 1981-84, Richards & O'Neil, N.Y.C., 1984-91, Haythe & Curley, N.Y.C., 1992-99, Torys LLP, N.Y.C., 1999—. Approved mediator U.S. Dist. Ct. (so. dist.), N.Y. Panel Disting. Neutrals for Ctr. for Pub. Resources; mediator Supreme Ct., N.Y. County, Banking Dept., Jud. Hearing Office, State of N.Y.; chair Hudson River Park Trust. Trustee Citizens Budget Commn., 1993—98, N.Y. Hist. Soc., 1998—; mem. mayor's adv. com., housing ct. adv. coun. 1st Dept. Jud. Screening Com., 1995—99; mem. State Ct. of Claims Jud. Screening Com., 1995—99; mem. Departmental Disciplinary Com. 1st Jud. Dept.; trustee N.Y. Interest Lawyers Acct. Fund; overseer U. Pa. Law Sch., 1993—99; nat. chmn. Law Annual Giving, 1991—93; trustee Hist. Hudson Valley; chair Hudson River Park Trust; bd. dirs. Empire State Devel. Corp., N.Y.C. Water Fin. Authority, N.Y. State Job Devel. Authority, Harlem Cmty. Devel. Corp., 42d St. Devel. Project, N.Y. State Mortgage Loan Enforcement and Adminstrn. Corp., N.Y. Parks and Conservation Assn., Liberty Devel. Corp.; mem. alumni coun. Dartmouth Coll., 1990—93, pres. class 1970, 1991—95. Mem. ABA, N.Y. State Bar Assn. (exec. com. comml. and fed. litigation sect. 1986—, fed. judiciary com. 1989—, internat. law and practice sect., com. internat. dispute resolution 1987—) Assn. of Bar of City of N.Y. (products liability com. 1983-86. fed. legis. com. 1990-93, state cts. of superior jurisdiction 1993-96, coun. jud. adminstrn. 1996-99, fed. judiciary 2000—), N.Y. Athletic Club. Republican. Congregationalist. Home: 205 E 69th St Apt 6C New York NY 10021-5431 also: 74 Pascal Ave Rockport ME 04856 5919 Office: Torys LLP 237 Park Ave Fl 20 New York NY 10017-3161 E-mail: cdorkey@torys.com.

DORKIN, FREDERIC EUGENE, lawyer; b. Bridgeport, Conn., Feb. 1, 1932; s. William and Selma (Kraus) D.; m. Harriette A. Garfinkel, June 14, 1959; children: Rosalyn Gail, David Ira, Deborah Ruth. AB, Dartmouth Coll., 1953; LLB, Duke U., 1956; LLM, George Washington U., 1968. Bar: Conn. 1956, D.C. 1968, Wash. 1979. Atty. SEC, Washington, 1956-57; pvt. practice Bridgeport, 1960-61; asst. sec. CT Corp. Sys., N.Y.C., Washington, 1961-68; assoc. counsel, asst. sec. Susquehanna Corp., Alexandria, Va., 1968-69; sec., counsel Microdot Inc., Greenwich, Conn., 1969-72; gen. counsel Boeing Computer Svcs., Inc., Morristown, N.J., 1972-78; corp. counsel Boeing Co., Seattle, 1978-82, sr. corp. counsel, 1982-83, asst. gen. counsel, 1984-85; divsn. chief counsel Boeing Electronics Co., 1985-90; sr. counsel Boeing Def. & Space Group, Seattle, 1991-93, ret., 1993; legal cons., arbitrator-mediator Seattle, 1993—. With JAGC, U.S. Army, 1957-60. Mem. Phi Delta Phi, Tau Epsilon Phi. Home: 501 Kirkland Ave Apt 207 Kirkland WA 98033-6248

DORLAND, BYRL BROWN, retired civic worker; b. Apr. 25, 1915; d. David Alma and Ethel Myrle (Petersen) Brown; m. Jack Albert Dorland, June 11, 1944; children: Lynn Dorland Ballinger, Lee Allison. *In 1620, ancestor Edward Fuller, with wife, Ann, and son, Samuel, sailed from England to America on the Mayflower. Shortly after docking, both parents died, leaving twelve-year-old Samuel to fend for himself. Samuel's progeny, George Austin Brown, migrated to Utah after marrying Rachel Savage. This couple (paternal grandparents) and Frands Peter and Ingerkjatena Petersen (maternal grandparents) were the first Caucasians to penetrate Utah's mid-Rocky Mountains--Ute territory. On this frigid, hostile mountaintop, these pioneers founded a settlement called "Koosharem." In or near this Historic Pioneer Landmark, Mrs. Dorland's father, mother and their nine children grew up. Among Samuel Fuller's latest descendants are Byrl's grandchildren: Dawn Carolyn, Mitzi Mary, Chance Charles, Shenandoah See.* Cert. AA, Snow Jr. Coll., Ephraim, Utah, 1936; tchg. cert., Brigham Young U., 1937; BA, Utah State Coll., Logan, 1940; BS, Family Inst. Vassar Coll., Poughkeepsie, N.Y., 1978; grad., John Robert Powers, Sch. Profl. Women, N.Y.C., 1980. Sch. tchr., Utah, 1937-39, 40-42. Restored Washington Irving's graveplot in Sleepy Hollow (N.Y.) Cemetery (named Nat. Hist. Landmark 1972); nat. dir. Washington Irving Graveplot Restoration Program, 1968—, designer landmark plaque for grave; mem. Nat. Coun. State Garden Clubs,1959—; pres. Potpourri Garden Club, Westchester, N.Y., 1966—; nat. chmn. for graveplot programs Washington Irving Bicentennial, 1983-84; dir. Dorland Family Graveyard Restoration, N.J. Hist. Landmark, 1983—. Named Miss Congeniality, World's Fair Golden Gate Internat. Exposition, Treasure Island, Calif., 1939—40; recipient May Duff Walters trophy, Nat. Coun. State Garden Clubs, 1974, Nat. Trophy, Nat. Historic Landmark Com., 1974, citation, Keep Am. Beautiful, 1974, Disting. Alumni award for Cmty. Svc. Snow Coll., 1989. Mem. Nat. Trust for Historic Preservation (assoc., Pres.'s award 1977), Nat. Historic Soc. Am., Gen. Soc. Mayflower Desc., Am. Mus. Natural History (hon.), Internat. Washington Irving Soc. (founder, pres. 1981-), Nat. Assn. for Gravestone Studies (hon.), Herb Soc. Am., DAR, Internat. Platform Assn., Old Dutch Churchyard Restoration Assn., Am. Mus. Natural History (hon.), Nature Conservancy (hon.), Girls and Boys Town (hon.). Home: 20802 N Cave Creek Rd Apt 60 Phoenix AZ 85024-4438

DORLAND, ELIZABETH M. chemistry educator; b. Humboldt, Nebr., Nov. 17, 1948; d. Warren Bruce Dorland and Ruth Ann Lange; m. Robert E. Blankenship, June 26, 1971; children: Larissa Blankenship, Sam Blankenship BS, Kans. State U., Manhattan, 1970; MS, U. Calif., Berkeley, 1971. Educator Diablo Valley Coll., Pleasant Hill, Calif., 1972-75, Seattle Cen. C.C., 1975-76, Shoreline C.C., Seattle, 1976-79, Am. Internat. Coll., Springfield, Mass., 1979-85, Glendale (Ariz.) C.C., 1985-94, Mesa (Ariz.) C.C., 1994—; chemistry program dir. NSF Divsn. Undergrad. Edn., 2003—. Mem. Am. Chem. Soc. (mem. com. on computers in chem. edn. divsn. chem. edn. 2000-03). Democrat. Avocations: travel, hiking, reading, cooking, tennis. Office: Mesa C C 1833 W Southern Ave Mesa AZ 85202-4822 E-mail: liz.dorland@mcmail.maricopa.edu.

DORMAN, ALBERT A. consulting engineer executive, architect; b. Phila., Apr. 30, 1926; s. William and Edith (Kleiman) D.; m. Joan Bettie Heiten, July 29, 1950; children: Laura Jane, Kenneth Joseph, Richard Coleman. BS, Newark Coll. Engring., 1945; MS, U. So. Calif., 1962; ScD (hon.), N.J. Inst. Tech., 1999. Registered profl. engr., Calif., N.Y., Ill., Oreg., Ariz., Pa., Nev., registered architect, Calif., Oreg. Owner firm Albert A. Dorman, Hanford, Calif., 1954-66; v.p. Daniel, Mann, Johnson & Mendenhall, Los Angeles, 1967-73, pres., chief oper. officer, 1974-77, pres., chief exec. officer, 1977-84, chmn., chief exec. officer, 1984-91, chmn., 1991-99; chmn., chief exec. officer AECOM Tech. Corp., L.A., 1984-91, chmn., 1991-92; founding chmn. AECOM Tech Corp., L.A., 1992—; chmn. Holmes & Narver, Inc., Orange, Calif., 1991-97, Frederic R. Harris, Inc., N.Y.C., 1988-91, Consoer, Townsend and Assocs., Inc., Chgo., 1988-91. Pres., chmn. bd. dirs. Hanford Savs. & Loan Assn., 1963-72. Contbr. articles to profl. jours. Pres. Cmty. Concerts Assn., 1962-64; past mem. bd. councilors Sch. Urban and Regional Planning, U. So. Calif.; trustee Harvey Mudd Coll., J. David Gladstone Found., 1988—, Nat. Found. Advancement in Arts, 1988-99; bd. overseers N.J. Inst. Tech., 1989—; vice chmn. Los Angeles County Earthquake Fact-Finding Commn., 1980. With U.S. Army, 1945-47. Recipient Civil Engring. Alumnus award U. So. Calif., 1976, Edward F. Weston medal N.J. Inst. Tech., 1986, Golden Beaver Engring. award, 1991, Eponym, Albert Dorman Honors Coll., N.J. Inst. Tech., 1993, Disting. Award of Merit, ACEC, 1996, Medal, U. Calif., San Francisco, 1996. Fellow AIA, Am. Cons. Engrs. Coun. (life); mem. ASCE (hon. mem., Harland Bartholomew award 1976, Opal Outstanding Lifetime Achievement award 2000), NAE (elected mem.), Parcel-Sverdrup Civil Engring. Mgmt. award 1987, pres. L.A. sect. 1984-85), Real Estate Constrn. Industries (Humanitarian award 1986), Am. Pub. Works Assn. (life), Cons. Engrs. Assn. Calif. (bd. dirs. 1982-88, pres. 1985-86), Am. Water Works Assn. (life), Water Pollution Control Fedn. (life), Calif. C. of C. (bd. dirs. 1986-94), L.A. Area C. of C. (bd. dirs. 1983-88, exec. com. 1985-87), Calif. Club, Met. Club, Kiwanis (pres. 1962), Tau Beta Pi, Chi Epsilon. Office: AECOM Tech Corp Ste 3700 555 S Flower St Los Angeles CA 90071-2300 Office Fax: 213-593-8184.

DORMAN, CRAIG EMERY, oceanographer, academic administrator; b. Cambridge, Mass., Aug. 27, 1940; s. Carlton Earl and Sarah Elizabeth (Emery) D.; m. Cynthia Eileen Larson, Aug. 25, 1962; children: Clifford Ellery, Clark Evans, Curt Emerson. BA, Dartmouth Coll., 1962; MS, Navy Post Grad. Sch., 1969; PhD, MIT/WHOI Joint Prog. Oceanog., 1972. Commd. ensign USN, 1962, advanced through grades to rear adm., 1987, ret., 1989; CEO Woods Hole (Mass.) Oceanographic Instn., 1989-93; dep. dir. Def. Rsch. and Engring. for Lab. mgmt., Washington, 1993-95; sr. scientist Applied Rsch. Lab. Pa. State U., 1995—2002; chief scientist, tech. dir. internat. field office Office Naval Rsch., 1995-98, ONROID, 1998-99; chief scientist ONR, 1999—2001; govt. coord., GSC chair Medea, 2000—02; chief scientist CH Internat. Assts., 2001—; v.p. rsch U. AUSEA, 2002—. Dir. Maritrans, Tampa; vis. prof. Imperial Coll., London, 1996-97. Corp. mem. WHOI, Bermuda Biol. Sta. for Rsch.; trustee Naval Undersea Mus. Found. Decorated Legion of Merit (2). Mem. Russian Acad. Natural Sci. Home: 4107 27th Rd N Arlington VA 22207-5116 Office: 800 N Quincy St Arlington VA 22217-0001 E-mail: dormanc@onr.navy.mil.

DORMAN, DAVID W. telecommunications industry executive; B in Indsl. Mgmt., Ga. Inst. Tech. With Sprint; pres. Sprint Bus., 1990—94; pres., chmn. bd. dirs., CEO Pacific Bell, 1994—97; exec. v.p. SBC Comm., 1997; chmn., pres., CEO PointCast, 1997—98; CEO Concert, 1998—2000; pres. AT&T Corp., 2000—02, chmn. bd. dirs., CEO, 2002. Bd. dirs. AT&T, Sci. Applications Internat. Corp. Bd. dirs. Episcopal H.S., Alexandria, Va.; Ga. Tech. Found. Office: AT&T Corp One AT&T Way Bedminster NJ 07921

DORMAN, JOHN FREDERICK, genealogist; b. Louisville, July 25, 1928; s. John Frederick and Sue Carpenter (Miller) D. BA, U. Louisville, 1950; MA, Emory U., 1955. Asst. archivist Coll. William and Mary, 1953-55; genealogist, 1955—; editor The Virginia Genealogist, 1957—; lectr. Nat. Inst. Geneal. Research, 1963-74, 77-93, Inst. Geneal. and Hist. Research Samford U., 1977-88. Trustee Bd. for Cert. of Genealogists, 1964-84, pres., 1979-82, exec. dir., 1983-96. Fellow Am. Soc. Genealogists (treas. 1959-66, pres. 1982-85), Va. Geneal. Soc.; mem. Soc. Cincinnati, Soc. Colonial Wars (dep. registrar gen. 1969-81, D.C. gov. 1980-82), SR (gen. registrar 1976-85, pres. D.C. chpt. 1982-84), SAR (D.C. pres. 1967-68), Nat. Geneal. Soc. (v.p. 1958-59, 68-70, libr. 1959-60), Children Am. Revolution (sr. nat. registrar 1960-62, sr. nat. treas. 1962-64, 66-68, sr. nat. 2d v.p. 1968-70), Descs. Colonial Govs. (gov. gen. 1973-76), Descs. Lords Md. Manors (pres. 1985-89), Sovereign Mil. Order Temple Jerusalem. Clubs: Cosmos (Washington). Republican. Episcopalian. Home: 175 Hulls Chapel Rd Fredericksburg VA 22406-5218

DORMAN, LINNEAUS CUTHBERT, retired chemist; b. Orangeburg, S.C., June 28, 1935; s. John Albert and Georgia D.; m. Phae Louise Hubble, June 21, 1958; children: Evelyn Suzanne, John Albert III. BS, Bradley U., 1956; PhD, Ind. U., 1961; DSc(hon.), Saginaw Valley State U., 1988. Chemist No. Regional Lab., U.S. Dept. Agr., Peoria, Ill., summers 1956-59; research chemist Dow Chem. Co., Midland, Mich., 1960-68, research specialist, 1968-76, research assoc., 1976-83, assoc. scientist, 1983-93, sr. assoc. scientist, 1993-94; ret., 1994. Lawrence lectr. Bradley U., 1990, mem. adv. bd., 1994; active Centurion Soc., 1993, Burgess award selection com., 1996-2000, chemistry dept. adv. bd.; cmty. adv. panel Dow Corning Midland Plant. Contbr. articles to profl. jours.; patentee in field. Mem. NAACP, Midland Commn. on Cmty. Rels., 1963-73, vice-chmn., 1967; mem. Black Exec. Exch. Program, Urban League, 1971, 75; trustee Midland Found., 1980-90, v.p., 1987-90; dir.-at-large Midland Ctr. for the Arts, 1984, 85; bd. fellows Saginaw Valley State Coll., 1975-87, emeritus mem., 1987, v.p., 1981-83, pres., 1983-85, ann. fund drive, 1985-95, presdl. search com., 1989; chmn. Cen. Rsch. and Devel. Scientists Orgn., 1992; mem. exec. coun. Ind. Univ. Alumni Assn., 2002—. Paul Harris fellow Rotary, 1989; co-recipient Bond award Am. Oil Chemists Soc., 1960; recipient Cen. Rsch. Inventor of Yr. award Dow Chem. Co., 1982. Mem. AAAS, Nat. Orgn. Black Chemists and Chem. Engrs. (Percy L. Julian award 1999), Am. Chem. Soc. (sect. treas. 1966, sec. 1967, dir. 1968-70, councilor 1971-76, 80 81, 84-92), Midland Rotary (sec. 1980-81, v.p. 1981-82, pres. 1982-83), Saginaw Valley Torch Club, Midland County Hist. Soc. (bd. mgrs. 2002), Little Forks Conservancy, Sigma Xi (chpt. treas. 1969, sec. 1970, pres. 1975), Phi Lambda Upsilon, Pi Kappa Delta, Omega Psi Phi. Mem. United Ch. of Christ. Home: PO Box 1732 Midland MI 48641-1732

DORMAN, PATRICIA M. sociologist, educator; b. Salt Lake City; d. Charles C. McLain and Phyllis C. (Rees) DeBois; m. Lynn C. Dorman, May 4, 1963; 1 child, Terrance Lynn. BS, U. Utah, 1960, MS, 1961, PhD, 1971. Project dir. Idaho Office on Aging, Boise, 1969-70; co-dir. Idaho State Exec. Inst., Boise, 1978-82; rsch. analyst Idaho Dept. Health, Boise, 1961-64, asst. project dir., 1965-67; prof. sociology Boise State U., 1967—2002, sociology dept. chair, 1972-77, 86-90, 1998—2002, dir. women's studies, 1997—2002, ret., prof. emeritus, 2002—. Bd. dirs. Instnl. Rev., Boise; cons./trainer U.S. Soil Conservation Svc., Northwest Region, Calif., 1975-86; faculty senate Boise State U., 1988-92; reviewer for several pubs. of sociology texts, 1990—. Assoc. editor: Social Sci. jour., 1993—; contbr. articles to profl. jours. Pres. bd. dirs. Idaho Lung Assn., Boise, 1975-76, mem., 1970-77; chair Ada County Democrats, 1976-78. Grantee Idaho State Bd. Edn, 1993, 97, GTE, NSF, U.S. Soil Conservation Svc., 1980s. Mem.: AAUP, AAUW, NOW, Am. Soc. Pub. Adminstrs., We. Social Sci. Assn. (exec. coun. 1995—98, v.p. 2001—02). Democrat. Avocations: golf, bowling, gardening, reading.

DORMAN, RICHARD FREDERICK, JR., association executive, consultant; b. Peoria, Ill., June 3, 1944; s. Richard Frederick and Pauline Elizabeth (Dryfus) D.; children: Richard F., Kevin M.; m. Anne Marie Carlton, May 28, 1976. Student, Franklin U., Columbus, Ohio, 1963-65, 68-69, New Sch. Social Reform, N.Y.C., 1979-80, U. Md., 1982. Field rep. Ohio Civil Service Employees Assn., Columbus, 1972-75; regional dir. St. Jude Children's Research Hosp., N.Y.C., 1975-80; exec. dir. Assembly Govtl. Employees, Washington, 1980-85; with Quality Mgmt. Inst., Washington, 1985-86; exec. dir. Am. Congress on Surveying and Mapping, Falls Church, Va., 1986-90, Ohio Coun. for Home Care, 1991-93; exec. v.p., COO Assn. for Profls. in Infection Control and Epidemiology Inc., Washington, 1993-95; v.p. Assn. Mgmt. Group, Arlington, Va., 1995-96. Ptnr. McIntoch & Dorman, Washington, 1982-86; pres. Catalyst Group, Alexandria, 1996—. Founder, pres. Columbus Ind. Jr. High Football League, Ohio, 1970. Recipient Recognition for Contbn. to Women's Sports Ohio Ho. of Reps., 1975, 76 Mem. Am. Soc. Assn. Execs. (cert. assn. exec., fellow 1988), Greater Washington Soc. Assn. Execs., Alexandria C. of C. (bd. dirs.). Republican. Presbyterian. E-mail: rfdorman@aol.com.

DORMAN, THOMAS ALFRED, internist, orthopaedist; b. Nairobi, Kenya, Nov. 16, 1936; came to U.S., 1977; s. Charles and Elizabeth D.; m. Allison Margaret Millar, Oct. 24, 1970; children: Jill, Michael, Andrew, Erin. Student, Liverpool U., 1959-62; MB, BChir, Edinburgh U., 1965. Diplomate Am. Bd. Internal Medicine. Staff gen. surgery Leith Hosp., Edinburgh, 1965-66; staff gen. medicine Western Gen. Hosp., Edinburgh, 1966; staff Elsie Inglis Maternity Hosp., Edinburgh, 1966-67, Norway House Hosp., Northern Manitoba, 1967; resident in medicine Union Meml. Hosp., Balt., 1967; staff anaesthetics dept. Sir Patrick Duns Hosp., Dublin, 1967-68; staff gen. surgery Naas Hosp., Ireland, 1968; staff pediat. neurology Royal Hosp. Sick Children, Edinburgh, 1969-69; registrar cardiology, gen. medicine Western Gen. Hosp., Edinburgh, 1969-71; staff internal medicine and cardiology Ft. Frances Clinic, Ontario, 1971-77; resident in internal medicine Winnipeg Gen. Hosp./U. Manitoba, 1972-73; pvt. practice San Luis Obispo, Calif., 1977—. Staff Sierra Vista Hosp., San Luis Obispo, French Hosp., San Luis Obispo Gen. Hosp. Editor, columnist Jour. Orthop. Medicine; contbr. articles to profl. jours. Fellow Royal Coll. Physicians; mem. Assn. Am. Physicians and Surgeons, Am. Back Soc. (bd. dirs.), British Med. Assn., British Inst. Manual Medicine, Am. Assn. Orthop. Medicine (charter mem., bd. dirs., chmn. rsch. com., newsletter editor), Cyriax Found., N.Am. Spine Soc., Assn. Musculoskeletal Medicine, Coll. Physicians and Surgeons Ontario, Calif. Med. Assn., San Luis Obispo County Med. Soc. Office: # 100 2505 S 320th St Federal Way WA 98003-3700 Fax: (253) 529-3104. E-mail: td@parcelsusclinic.com.

DORMANS, JOHN PAUL, surgeon, educator; b. Ft. Wayne, Ind., Jan. 13, 1957; s. Paul M. and Viginia Ann Dormans; m. Nanette J. Dormans; children: Nicholas, Andrea, Laura, Kath. BA magna cum laude, Ind. U., 1979, MD, 1983. Diplomate Am. Bd. Orthopedic Surgery. Resident in orthop. surgery Mich. State U., Grand Rapids, 1988; pediatric orthop. fellow Hosp. Sick Children, Toronto, Ont., Can., 1989; orthop. surgeon Children's Hosp. Phila., 1989—96, chief orthop. surgery, 1996—, pres. med. staff, 1999-2001, also trustee; from asst. prof. to assoc. prof. orthop. surgery U. Pa., 1991—2000; prof. orthop. surgery Sch. Medicine U. Pa., Phila., 2000—. Pres. Surg. Assoc. Rsch. and Edn. Found., 1997-98; dir. pediatric orthop. fellowship Children's Hosp. Phila. Editor: Caring for the Child with Cerebral Palsy, 1998; section editor: The Cervical Spine, 2000; assoc. editor Jour. Bone and Joint Surgery, 2000—; contbr. articles to profl. jours. Travelling fellow Am. Orthop. Assn. and Am. Acad. Orthop. Surgeons, 1996. Fellow ACS, Am. Acad. Orthop. Surgeons, Sooliosis Rsch. Soc.; mem. Am. Orthop. Assn., Pediatric Orthop. Soc. N.Am., Musculoskeletal Tumor Soc., Phi Beta Kappa. Lutheran. Avocations: fly fishing, painting, reading, history of medicine. Office: Childrens Hosp Phila Wood Bldg, 2d Fl 34th and Civic Center Blvd Philadelphia PA 19104-4399 E-mail: dormans@email.chop.edu.

DORMEYER, LAVON, school counselor; b. Salt Lake City, Sept. 17, 1949; d. George William and Adelia Pippy; m. Michael J. Dormeyer, July 31, 1971; children: Michael George, Piers Ian. BA, U. Utah, 1971; MA, Murray State U., 1986. Cert. tchr., Fla., guidance counselor, cert. family mediator, Fla. Supreme Ct. Tchr. Pre-discharge Edn. Program, Bad Kissingen, Germany, 1972-75, U.S. Army Edn. Ctr., West Berlin, Germany, 1976-79, St. Theresa Sch., Parkville, Mo., 1982-84; guidance counselor Cypress Elem. Sch., New Port Richey, Fla., 1987—. Mem. Guidance Adv. Coun., Pasco Dist. Schs., Land O'Lakes, Fla., 1992-93, 93-94; mem. athletic adv. bd., Gaither H.S., 1990-91. Author: How I Weathered the Storm of Divorce, 1998; contbr. Classroom Guidance Activities Sourcebook for Elementary Counselors, 1997. Docent Lowry Park Zoo, Tampa, 1989-95; lectr., rehabilitator Fla. Bat Ctr., Punta Gorda, Fla., 1994—. Named Tchr. of Yr., Dist. Sch. Bd. Pasco County, 1995, 96. Mem. Pasco Counseling Assn. (Counselor of Yr. 1994-95), Tampa Rep. Women Federated (publicity chairperson 1997-98). Roman Catholic. Avocations: wildlife education and conservation, gardening, floral work, writing, reading. Office: Cypress Elem Sch 10055 Sweet Bay Ct New Port Richey FL 34654-5799 E-mail: stadelia@aol.com.

DORMINEY, HENRY CLAYTON, JR., allergist; b. Tifton, Ga., May 15, 1949; s. Henry Clayton and Virgina (Petty) D. BS, Davidson Coll., 1971; MD, U. Iowa, 1975. Diplomate Am. Bd. Internal Medicine, Am. Bd. Allergy and Immunology; lic. physician, Ga. Med. intern U. Iowa Hosps. and Clinics, Iowa City, 1975-76, med. resident, 1976-78, allergy and immunology fellow, 1978-80; practice medicine specializing allergy and clin. immunology Allergy, Asthma and Sinus Clinic of Tifton, Ga., 1981—. Mem. staff Tift Regional Med. Ctr.; bd. dirs. Brumby's Crossing, Dorminey Enterprises; chmn. and founder Tifton Mus. Arts and Heritage, 1991; mem. Allergy, Asthma & Sinus Clinic of Tifton. Assoc. editor, contbg. author Vital Signs, 1969-71. Bd. dirs. Tift County Found. Ednl. Excellence, 1996—, chmn. investment com., 1998—; bd. dirs. Tifton Heritage Found., 1992; bd. dirs. Tifton Mus. Arts and Heritage, 1991—. Recipient Physician's Recognition award AMA, 1979, 85, Lee Willingham III trophy Davidson Coll., 1987, Tifton Main Street Program award, 1989, Best Adaptive Re-Use Project, Tifton Historic District, The Coca Cola Bldg., 1993; grantee Am. Coll. Allergy, 1980. Mem. Am. Acad. Allergy (travel grantee 1980), Tift County Med. Soc. (sec., treas. 1983-84, v.p., 1984-85, pres. 1985-86), Med. Assn. Ga., Am. Numismatic Soc., Forward Tifton, Tifton C. of C. Lodges: Rotary (Spl. Merit award, founder Tifton Directory, bd. dirs. 1988-93, pres.-elect 1989-90, pres. 1990-91, Paul Harris fellow 1993). Democrat. Home: 21 Duck Dr Tifton GA 31794-3953 Office: 820 Love Ave Tifton GA 31794-4071 E-mail: dorminey@friendlycity.net.

DORMISH, JEFFREY FRANK, chemist; b. Cleve., Feb. 25, 1954; s. Frank C. Dormish and Beverly Jane Blum; m. Nancy Leathers; children: Robert Brian, Philip Edward. BS in Chemistry, U. Dayton, 1975; PhD in Chemistry, Pa. State U., 1980. Sr. rsch. chemist Mobay Chem. Corp., Pitts., 1980-85; rsch. chemist Bayer AG, Dormagen, Germay, 1985-87; project leader structural adhesives Mobay Corp., Pitts., 1987-90, group leader adhesive raw materials, 1990-91; mgr. applications devel. Miles Inc./Bayer Corp., Akron, Ohio, 1991-98; mgr. tech. Bayer Corp., Pitts., 1999—2000, prin. scientist, 2001—. Tech. seminars com. chmn., Adhesive & Sealant Coun., Washington, 1995-97, vice chair, 1993-95, mem. Waterborne com., 1995—, ASC Conv. internet session chair, 1995, 97, manufactured housing session chair, 1995, reactive hotmelt session chair, 1994. Contbr. articles to profl. jours.; patentee in field. Nation Chief YMCA Indian Guides, Hudson, Ohio, 1997-99, coach youth basketball, 1998; coach youth soccer, Upper St. Clair (Pa.) Athletic Assn., 1999; mem. St. Mary's Ch. Men's Club, Hudson, 1994-98. Mem. SAE, Am. Chem. Soc. Roman Catholic. Avocations: golf, travel. Home: 1308 Wellington Dr Upper Saint Clair PA 15241 Office: Bayer Corp 100 Bayer Rd Pittsburgh PA 15205

DORN, ALFRED, poet, retired English educator; b. N.Y.C., Dec. 9, 1929; s. Frederick and Julia (Memminger) D.; m. Anita Lorenz Paslack, Sept. 11, 1971. BS, NYU, 1953, MA, 1956, PhD, 1966. Grad. asst. NYU, N.Y.C., 1956-60; English prof. Rider Coll., Trenton, N.J., 1963-64, Queensborough C.C., Bayside, N.Y., 1966-92; ret. Chmn. World Order Narrative and Formalist Poets, Flushing, N.Y. Author: Claire and the Christmas Village, 2002; co-editor: New Orlando Poetry Anthologies, 1958, 1963, 1968; author: (poetry) From Cells to Mindspace, 1997, Voices From Rooms, 1997, Claire and Christmas Village, 2002. Penfield fellow NYU, N.Y.C., 1957. Mem. Poetry Soc. Am. (bd. mem. 1963-66, v.p. 1969-72, conf. fellow 1966), Nat. Trust for Hist. Preservation. Avocations: art history, writing art and literary criticism, antiques, psychic research, cats. Office: World Order Narrative & Formalist Poets Sta A PO Box 580174 Flushing NY 11358-0174

DORN, CHARLES MEEKER, art education educator; b. Mpls., Jan. 17, 1927; s. Melville Wilkinson and Margaret (Meeker) D.; m. Virginia Josephine Coble, July 11, 1947; children: Mary Jan, Charles Meeker. BA, MA, George Peabody Coll. Tchrs., 1950; Ed.D., U. Tex., 1959. Asst. prof. art Union U., Jackson, Tenn., 1950-54; instr. art and edn. Memphis State U., 1954-57; lectr. edn. U. Tex., 1957-59; head art dept. Nat. Coll. Edn., Evanston, Ill., 1959-61; assoc. prof. art No. Ill. State U., 1961-62; exec. sec. Nat. Art Edn. Assn., Washington, 1962-70; prof., chmn. dept. art Calif. State U., Northridge, 1970-72; prof. creative arts Purdue U., Lafayette, Ind., 1972-86, head dept., 1972-76; prof., dir. Ctr. for Arts Adminstrn. Fla. State U., Tallahassee, 1986—, chmn. dept. art edn., 1986-90. Served with AUS, 1945-46. Recipient 25th Anniversary award for disting. service Nat. Gallery Art, 1966. Mem.: Internat. Soc. Edn. Through Art, Nat Art Edn. Assn. (pres. 1975—77, Disting. Svc. award 1979, Disting. fellow 1982, Southeastern Higher Edn. Art Educator award 1990, Higher Edn. award 1990, 1999, Nat. Art Educator of the Yr. 2003), Fla. Art Edn. Assn., Kappa Phi Kappa, Phi Delta Kappa. Home: 377 Castleton Cir Tallahassee FL 32312 Office: Fla State U Dept Art Edn Tallahassee FL 32306 E-mail: dornetal@aol.com., cdorm@mailer.fsu.edu.

DORN, GORDON JOSEPH, artist, art educator; b. Sheboygan, Wis., Dec. 5, 1943; s. Frank and Olive G. (Rollman) D. BA in Edn., Wis. State U., 1966; MFA in Painting, U. Wis., 1969. Prof. art No. Ill. U., Dekalb, 1969-2000; prof. emeritus, 2000—. State v.p. AAUP of Ill., 1990-92, state pres., 1992-96. One-man shows include Roy Boyd Gallery, Chgo., 1977, 79, 82, 85, 88, 91, 95, 97, 98, 2000; group exhbns. include Art Inst. Chgo., 1977, 79, Chgo. Internat. Art Exposition, 1997, 98, 99; patentee in field. Recipient prize Art Inst. Chgo., 1977; exhbns. reviewed in Chgo. Tribune, 1991, 95, 98, Chgo. Sun Times, 1982, 84. Avocations: writing education materials, inventing. Home: 9-B Regency Tower 5838 Collins Ave Miami FL 33140-2226

DORN, JAMES ANDREW, editor; b. Buffalo, Aug. 26, 1945; s. Andrew William and Mary Carol (Gannon) D.; m. Carol Evans Cronmiller, Sept. 5, 1970; children: Andrea Yvonne, Heather Katherine. BS in Econs., Canisius Coll., 1967; MA in Econs., U. Va., 1969, PhD, 1976. Prof. Towson U., Md., 1973—, 1989—; editor Cato Jour. Cato Inst., Washington, 1982—, v.p. for acad. affairs, 1989—; rsch. fellow Inst. Humane Studies George Mason U., Fairfax, Va., 1986-95. Editor: The Future of Money in the Information Age, 1997, China in the New Millennium, 1998; co-editor: (with Henry G. Manne) Economic Liberties and the Judiciary, 1987, (with Anna J. Schwartz) The Search for Stable Money, 1987, (with William A. Niskanen) Dollars, Deficits and Trade, 1989, (with Wang Xi) Economic Reform in China, 1990, (with Roberto Salinas-León) Money and Markets in the Americas, 1996, (with Steve Hanke and Alan Walters) The Revolution in Development Economics, 1998, (with T.G. Carpenter) China's Future, 2000; contbr. articles to profl. jours. Mem. White House Commn. on Presdl. Scholars, Washington, 1984-90. Recipient Regent's Faculty Award for Excellence in Rsch./Scholarship Univ. Sys. Md., 1998; Hayek Fund grantee Inst. for Humane Studies, 1986-87, Earhart grantee 1969-70, 81; Thomas Jefferson Ctr. fellow U. Va., 1969-70. Mem. Am. Econ. Assn., Mont Pelerin Soc., West Side Rowing Club (Buffalo). Avocations: alpine hiking, photography, geology, jogging. Office: Cato Inst 1000 Massachusetts Ave NW Washington DC 20001-5400 E-mail: jdorn@cato.org.

DORN, JENNIFER L. federal agency administrator; 2 children. Degree, Oreg. State U.; MPA, U. Conn. Dir. Office of Comml. Space Transp., 1983—85; assoc. dep. sec. transp. U.S. Dept. Transp., 1985—87; sr. v.p. Am. Nat. Red Cross, 1991—98; asst. sec. for policy U.S. Dept. Labor; adminstr. fed. transit adminstn. U.S. Dept. Transp., Washington, 2001—. Pres. Nat. Health Mus., 1998—2001. Office: US Dept Transp Fed Transit Adminstrn 400 7th St SW Washington DC 20590-0001 Office Fax: 202-366-9854.

DORN, LOUIS OTTO, retired minister, consultant; b. Detroit, July 1, 1928; s. Theodore Herman and Thekla Maria (Frederking) D.; m. Erna Ruth Koessel, June 14, 1953; children: Margaret Ligaya Dorn White, Peter Bayani, Martin Louis, Judith Anne Dorn. BA, Concordia Theol. Sem., St. Louis, 1951, BD, 1962; MA in Linguistics, Ateneo de Manila U., Quezon City, The Philippines, 1974; PhD, Luth. Sch. Theology, Chgo., 1980. Ordained to ministry Luth. Ch.-Mo. Synod, 1953. Missionary Luth. Ch. in The Philippines, Manila, 1953-74; candidate Ohio dist. Luth. Ch. -Mo. Synod, 1975-80; candidate N.J. dist. Luth. Ch.-Mo. Synod, 1980-99; transls. rsch. assoc. Am. Bible Soc., N.Y.C., 1979-90; transl. cons. United Bible Socs., N.Y.C., 1990-99. Chmn. Luth. Philippine Mission, Manila, 1962-63, 71-72; sec. Luth. Ch. in The Philippines, Manila, 1962-63, commn. for ecumenical affairs. 1964-74, dir. transls. dept., 1966-74; hon. transls. advisor Philippine Bible Soc., Manila, 1968-74; bd. dirs. Interchurch Lang. Sch., Quezon City, 1964-74, chmn. bd., 1967-74. Contbr. articles and revs. to religious publs. Grantee Cen. dist. Luth. Ch.-Mo. Synod, 1944-53; scholarship grantee Luth. Sch. Theology, Chgo., 1974-78. Mem. Soc. Bibl. Lit. Home: 1414 N Gregson St Durham NC 27701-1110 *People often don't know how to live under God's grace because they can't forgive themselves and know only God's law. To accept God's grace, to be willing to be forgiven, results in an amazing life of freedom that honors the Savior.*

DORN, MARK S. music educator, musician; b. Milwaukee, Wis, Aug. 5, 1957; s. Thomas John and Barbara Irene Dorn; children: Nathan, Emily, Nicole, Christopher. MusB in Edn., Ind. U., 1979, MusM in Trumpet Performance, 1981; MA in Biblical Counseling, Colo. Christian U., 1994. Assoc. prof. Colo. Christian U., Lakewood, 1995—. Free lance trumpet artist, Denver, 1993—. Prodr.: Kids From Wisconsin, 1996—. Mem.: Internat. Trumpet Guild, Internat. Assoc. of Jazz Ed., Music Ed. Nat. Conf. Avocations: racquetball, travel, reading, bicycling, hiking. Home: 11726 W Radcliff Ave Morrison CO 80465

DORN, MARY ANN, retired auditor; b. Overland, Mo., May 1, 1933; d. Bernard J. and Marie (Kunkler) Engler; children: Glennon (dec.), Pat Michael, Michelle; m. Donald Patrick Dorn, June 3, 2002. Student, Fontbonne Coll., 1951-52; AA, Sacramento City Coll., 1975; BS in Bus., Calif. State U., 1981. CPA, Calif.; cert. fraud examiner; cert. govt. fin. mgr. From asst. to acct. Mo. Rsch. Labs., Inc., St. Louis, 1953-55, adminstrv. asst., 1955-60; sec. western region fin. office Gen. Electric Co., St. Louis, 1960-62; credit analyst Crocker Nat. Bank, Sacramento, 1962-72; student tchr. Sacramento County Dept. Edn., 1979-81; acctg. technician East Yolo Community Services Dist., 1983; mgmt. specialist USAF Logistics Command, 1984; auditor Office Insp. Gen. U.S. Dept. Transp., 1984-92; auditor-in-charge Adminstrn. for Children and Families U.S. Dept. Health and Human Svcs., 1992—. Mem. Sacramento Community Commn. for Women, 1978-81, bd. dirs., 1980—; planning bd. Golden Empire Health Systems Agy. Mem. AARP (tax counselor), AAUW (fin. officer 1983—), AICPA, Nat. Assn. Accts. (dir., newsletter editor), Fontbonne Coll. Alumni Assn., Calif. State Alumni Assn., Assn. Govt. Accts. (chpt. officer), Calif. Soc. CPAs, German Geneological Soc. (bd. dirs. 1990—, publicity dir. 1994—), Sun City Lincoln Hills Assn., Beta Gamma Sigma, Beta Alpha Psi. Roman Catholic. Home: 815 Magnolia Ln Lincoln CA 95648-8429

DORN, NATALIE REID, consultant; b. N.Y.C. d. John A. and Marianna (Tresenberg) Borokhovitch; m. Ed Reid, July 3l, l938 (div. Apr. l963); children: Michael John, Douglas Paul; m. Robert M. Dorn, Nov. 28, l964. Student, Bklyn. Coll., 1937-40, Pepperdine Coll., l969-70. Model Conover Agy., N.Y.C., 1940-54; columnist Westchester (N.Y.) Recorder, l954-59; ptnr. Dateline, Las Vegas, Nev., 1957-61; mgr., buyer Joseph Magnin, Las Vegas, Nev., l961-62; ptnr., cons. Personnel Placement Employment Agy. and Conv. Coords., Las Vegas, l961-63; account exec. John A. Tetley Co., L.A., l963-65; cons. Sport Ct. Am., Salt Lake City, l975-. Realtor, Va., Calif., l974-. Exec. v.p. Clark County Mental Health Assn., 1961-63; ednl. chmn. Hollywood Wing, Greek Theatre Assn., 1965, mem. hospitality com. LWV, 1969; co-founder Child Abuse Listening Line, 1973—; sponsor Ashland (Oreg.) Sheakesperean Festival, 1984; concertmaster Sacramento Opera; patron, Davis Art Ctr.; docent Internat. House, Davis, 1987—; bd. dirs. El Macero Niners, Davis Art Ctr. Guild. Mem.: AMA Aux., Crocker Soc., Crocker Art Mus., Nat. Mus., L.A. County Med. Assn. Aux., Nat. Trust for Historic Preservation, Women in Arts, El Macero Country Club. Avocations: painting, writing.

DORN, NORMAN PHILIP, management consulting firm executive; b. Ithaca, NY, Jan. 29, 1945; s. Saul James and Pearl Dorn; m. Evelyn Mary Samonas, July 3, 1966; children: Paul, Ian, Nathan, Mark. BS, Carnegie-Mellon U., 1966; MS, U. Pitts., 1969. Engr. Westinghouse Electric, Pitts., 1969-78; sr. engr. GPU Svc. Corp., Forked River, NJ, 1978-79; mng. dir. Accountable Systems Co. Internat. Inc., Toms River, NJ, 1979—. Mem. Inst. Mgmt. Cons., Telephone Pioneers, Masons, Toastmasters. Achievements include inventions, quality improvements, requirements process engrng., process controls devel. instruction, system stability analysis procedures, telecommunications tech., systems (applications) architecture and mfg. mgmt. E-mail: norman@askee.org.

DORN, SAMUEL O. endodontist; b. N.Y.C., Jan. 1, 1946; s. Benjamin and Mae (Baylin) Dorn; m. Linda Frances Neuger, Dec. 23, 1984; children: Lanelle, Brian, Adam, Dawn. BA, Queens Coll., 1966; DDS, Fairleigh Dickinson U., 1970; cert., Nassau County Med. Ctr., 1976. Diplomate Am. Bd. Endodontics. Capt. USAF, Washington, 1970-72; pvt. practice Forest Hills, N.Y., 1972-76, Ft. Lauderdale, Fla., 1976—; prof. Nova Southeastern U., Ft. Lauderdale. Clin. instr. fairleigh Dickinson U. Dental Sch., Hackensack, NJ, 1973—74; cons. in field; chmn. advanced endodontics Dade County Dental Rsch. Clinic, Miami, 1977—93; clin. assoc. prof. U. Fla. Sch. Dentistry; clin. asst. prof. U. Miami Sch. Medicine, 1977—93; dir., treas. Am. Bd. Endodontics, 1991—98; prof., dir. postgrad. endodontics Nova Southeastern U. Sch. Dental Medicine; lectr. in field. Trustee Endowment & Meml. Found., Chgo, 1987—88. Named Dentist of Yr., East Coast Dental Soc., 1987. Fellow: Internat. Coll. Dentists, Am. Coll. Dentists; mem.: Am. Assn. Dental Rsch., East Coast Dist. Dental Soc. (pres. 1996—97), South Fla. Endodontic Soc. (pres. 1982—83), Greater Hollywood Dental Soc. (pres. 1988—89), Fla. Assn. Endodontists (pres. 1990—92), Am. Assn. Endodontists (bd. dirs. 1988—91, pres. 2002—). Jewish. Avocation: Avocations: tennis, travel, cycling. Home: 1031 SW 91st Ave Fort Lauderdale FL 33324-3817 Office: 8200 W Sunrise Blvd Fort Lauderdale FL 33322-5426 also: Nova Southeastern U Coll Dental Medicine 3200 S University Dr Fort Lauderdale FL 33328-2018 E-mail: sdorn@nova.edu.

DORN, SUE BRICKER, consultant, retired hospital administrator; b. Seattle, Apr. 1, 1934; d. Barney and Frances B. (Schnitzer) Bricker; m. Philip Henry Dorn, Dec. 31, 1955 (dec.); children: Charles, Martha Dorn. BA, Stanford U., Palo Alto, 1955; MA, Bank St. Coll., 1973. Cert. tchr., N.Y. Dir. promotion exec. compensation svc. Am. Mgmt. Assn., N.Y.C., 1956-58; tchr. spl. edn. N.Y.C. Bd. of Edn., 1969-77; assoc. dir. Yale U., New Haven, 1977-79; v.p. Bank St. Coll. of Edn., N.Y.C., 1979-81, Aspen Inst. for Humanistic Studies, N.Y.C., 1981-82; assoc. v.p. Yale U., New Haven, 1982-87; dep. dir. devel. and pub. affairs Mus. of Modern Art, N.Y.C., 1987-94; v.p., vice provost for devel. The N.Y. Hosp.-Cornell Med. Ctr., 1994—98. Mem. maj. gifts com. Stanford U.; cons. in field; bd. dirs. First Citicorp Life Ins. Co. Pres. LWV, Warren, Mich., 1962-65, Stanford Alumni Club of N.Y., N.J. and Conn., N.Y.C., 1968-70, 25 East 86th St. Corp., N.Y.C., 1989-93, 95—; mem. dirs. adv. bd. Yale Comprehensive Cancer Ctr., Yale U., 1990-94. Named Citizen of the Yr., Warren C. of C., 1962; recipient Citation, City of Warren, 1963, Gold Spike award and Cert. of Outstanding Achievement, Stanford U., 1976. Mem. Stanford Assocs., Univ. Club. Home: 25 E 86th St New York NY 10028-0553 E-mail: sdorn@nyc.rr.com.

DORN, VIRGINIA ALICE, artist, art gallery director; b. Mpls., June 22, 1916; d. Raymond Edwin and Ruth Virginia (Nylander) Henneman; m. John Emil Dorn, Feb. 22, 1937 (dec. Sept. 1971); children: John Robert, Michael Raymond. BS, U. Minn., 1937. Mgr. med. lab., Orinda, Calif., 1955-61; instr. art Orinda Civic Ctr., 1980-81; mgr., tchr. San Francisco Women Artists Gallery, 1984—. One woman shows include Lucien LaBaudt Gallery, San Francisco, 1975, St. Paul's Towers, Oakland, Calif., 1976, Contemporary Arts, Berkeley, Calif., 1977, 80, Trinity Gallery, Berkeley, 1982, Valley Arts Gallery, Walnut Creek, Calif., 1982, Univ. Club, San Francisco, 1983, Holy Names Coll. Gallery, Oakland, 1987, Wellness Cmty. Gallery, Walnut Creek, 1991, Vincent's Ear Gallery, Orinda, Calif., 1994, also many juried and invitational shows in Calif.; represented by San Francisco Women Artists Gallery and East Bay Royal Ground Gallery, Oakland, Calif. Recipient Lifetime Achievement award Women's Caucus for Art, 1996. Mem. San Francisco Women Artists (bd. dirs., fund raiser, mgr., instr., coord.), Oakland Art Assn., Valley Art Assn., Berkeley Art Ctr., East Bay Women Artists. Avocations: travel, music. Home: 95 Evergreen Dr Orinda CA 94563-3114

DORNAN, DONALD C., JR., lawyer; b. Columbus, Miss., Oct. 26, 1952; s. Donald C. and Virginia (Shelley) D.; children: Gloria Diana, Donald Patrick. BA, Miss. State U., 1974; JD, U. Miss., 1976. Bar: Miss. 1977, U.S. Dist. Ct. (no. and so. dists.) Miss. 1977, U.S. Ct. Appeals (5th and 11th cirs.) 1981, cert. civil trial advocate Nat. Bd. of Trial Advocacy. Atty. Page, Mannino & Peresich, Biloxi, Miss., 1976-80; ptnr. Dornan Law Office, Biloxi, 1980-87; sole practice Biloxi, 1987—; asst. city prosecutor City of Biloxi, 1977-80, city judge pro tem, 1982—; bd. dirs. Gulf Law Inst., 1981—. Mem. ABA, Fed. Bar Assn., Miss. Bar Assn. (pres. elect 2001, pres. 2002-03), Harrison County Bar Assn., Harrison County Young Lawyers (treas. 1980-81, v.p. 1981-82, pres. 1982-83), Miss. Trial Lawyers Assn., Assn. Trial Lawyers Am., Southeastern Admiralty Law Inst., Phi Delta Phi. Methodist. Office: PO Box 154 771 Water St Biloxi MS 39530-4219

DORNAN, JOHN NEILL, public policy center professional; b. Canonsburg, Pa., July 20, 1944; s. Carl Edward and Kathryn (Neill) D.; m. Jacquelin Riggs (div. 1971); children: Jodie Lynn, John Neill; m. Carol Michaels (div. 1976); m. Anne Marie Deegan (div. 1993). BA, Indiana U. of Pa., 1966; postgrad., U. Pitts., 1966-68. English tchr. Moon Twp., Coraopolis, Pa., 1966-69; field rep. NEA, Harrisburg, Pa., 1969-70, media rep. San Francisco, 1970-71; asst. exec. dir. Ill. Edn. Assn., Springfield, Ill., 1970-74; asst. to pres. AFSCME, Washington, 1974-75; assoc. exec. dir. Coalition of Am. Pub. Employees, Washington, 1975-76, N.Y. Edn. Assn., Albany, 1976-82; exec. sec. N.C. Assn. Educators, Raleigh, 1982-86; pres. Pub. Sch. Forum, Raleigh, 1986—. Cons. in field; adj. faculty Cornell U., Albany, 1981-82, Appalachian U., Boone, N.C., 1987-88, N.C. Prin's. Exec. Program, 1986-90. Contbr. numerous articles to profl. jours. Nat. bd. dirs. Parents for Pub. Schs., The Columbia Group; bd. dirs. N.C. Ctr. Internat. Inderstanding, Wake Edn. Ptnrship; treas. S.E. Ctr. Tchg. Quality Found. Mem.: Raleigh C. of C. Democrat. Presbyterian. Avocations: reading, collecting antique posters. Home: 1409 Granada Dr Raleigh NC 27612-5109 Office: Koger Ctr Cumberland Bldg 3739 National Dr Ste 210 Raleigh NC 27612-4844

DORNAN, READE WHITING, literature educator, writer; b. Denver, Dec. 7, 1940; d. William Foster and Lila Louise Day; m. David Benton Dornan, Mar. 7, 1964; children: Wythe Whiting, Ellen Kathlean. BA, U. Colo., 1963; MA, Mich. State U., 1980, PhD, 1988. Cert. tchr. Colo., 1963. Tchr. Hinckley H.S., Aurora, Colo., 1963—65; H.S. tchr., dept. head Fleur du Lac Sch., Homewood, Calif., 1965—66, The Garden Sch., Kuala Lumpur, Malaysia, 1972—74; prof. U. Mich., Flint, 1985—95, Purdue U., West Lafayette, Ind., 1995—96, Mich. State U., East Lansing, 1996—98, Ctrl. Mich. U., Mt. Pleasant, 1998—. Author: Arnold Wesker Revisited, 1995; co-author (with Lois Rosen and Marilyn Wilson): Multiple Voices, Multiple Texts: Reading in the Content Areas, 1997; co-author: (with Lois M. Rosen and Marilyn Wilson) Within and Beyond the Writing Process in the Secondary English Classroom, 2002; editor: Preserving the Game: Gambling, Mining, Hunting and Conservation in the Vanishing West, 1989, Arnold Wesker: A Casebook, 1998. Deutscher Akademischer Austauschdienst grantee, Heidelberg, Germany, 2001. Mem.: Ctr. for the Expansion of Lang. and Tchg., Soc. for Values in Higher Edn., Nat. Coun. Tchrs. English, Phi Kappa Phi. Mem. Soc. Of Friends. Avocation: weaving.

DORNAN, ROBERT KENNETH, former congressman; b. N.Y.C., Apr. 3, 1933; s. Harry Joseph and Gertrude Consuelo (McFadden) D.; m. Sallie Hansen, Apr. 16, 1955; children: Robin Marie, Robert Kenneth II, Theresa Ann, Mark Douglas, Kathleen Regina. Student, Loyola U., Westchester, Calif., 1950-53. Nat. spokesman Citizens for Decency Through Law, 1973-76; mem. 95th-97th Congresses from 27th Calif. dist., 1977-83, 99th-103rd Congresses from 38th Calif. dist., 1985-93, 103rd Congress and 104th Congress from 46th Calif. dist., 1993-96. Chmn. Nat. Sec. Subcom. on Military Personnel, chmn. Tech. and Tactical Intelligence. Host TV polit. talk shows in Los Angeles, 1965-73; host, producer: Robert K. Dornan Show, Los Angeles, 1970-73; combat photographer/broadcast journalist assigned 8 times to Laos-Cambodia-Vietnam, 1965-74; originator POW/MIA bracelet. Served to capt., fighter pilot USAF, 1953-58, fighter pilot, amphibian rescue pilot and intelligence officer USAFR, 1958-75. Mem. Am. Legion, Navy League, Air Force Assn., Res. Officers Assn., AMVET, Assn. Former Intelligence Officers, Am. Helicopter Soc. Special Forces Assn., AFTRA. Lodges: K.C. Republican. Roman Catholic. also: Dornan For Congress PO Box 3260 Garden Grove CA 92842-3260

DORNBUSCH, ARTHUR A., II, lawyer; b. Peru, Ill., Nov. 8, 1943; s. Arthur A. Sr. and Genevieve C. (Knudtson) D.; children: Kimberly, Brendan, Courtney, Eric; m. Jacqueline Bahrs Montanus, Feb. 10, 1996. BA, Yale U., 1966; LLB, U. Pa., 1969. Bar: N.Y. 1970, U.S. Ct. Appeals. (2d cir.) 1971, U.S. Dist. Ct. (so. and ea. dists.) N.Y. 1971. Assoc. Dewey, Ballantine, Bushby, Palmer & Wood, N.Y.C., 1969-72; asst. gen. counsel Boise Cascade Corp., N.Y.C., 1972-75; asst. gen counsel Teleprompter Corp., N.Y.C., 1975-76; asst. gen. counsel Engelhard Industries div. Engelhard Minerals and Chem. Corp., Edison, N.J., 1976-80; v.p., gen. counsel minerals and chems. divsn. Engelhard Corp., Edison, 1980—84, v.p., gen. counsel, sec. Iselin, NJ, 1984—. Mem. Pelham (N.Y.) Union Free Sch. Bd., 1979-82. Mem. ABA, N.Y. State Bar Assn., Assn. Bar City N.Y., Am. Corp. Counsel Assn., Am. Intellectual Property Law Assn., Am. Soc. Corp. Secs., Mfrs. Alliance for Productivity and Innovation. Office: Engelhard Corp PO Box 770 101 Wood Ave S Iselin NJ 08830-0770 E-mail: arthur.dornbusch@engelhard.com.

DORNBUSH, K. TERRY, former ambassador, consulting company executive, educator; b. Atlanta, Oct. 31, 1933; m. Marilyn Pierce; 3 children. BA magna cum laude, Vanderbilt U.; postgrad., Emory U., N.Y. Inst. Fin. Former CEO, Hipolex Corp.; former pres. DOAG USA Inc.; former vice chmn. Am. Western Corp.; former ptnr. Courts & Co. & Investment Bankers; amb. to The Netherlands, Am. Embassy, The Hague, 1994-98; CEO, Nalim Holdings BV, cons., Amsterdam, The Netherlands, 1998—; mem. adv. bd. Rand Europe, Leiden, The Netherlands. Former prof. Nijenrode U., The Netherlands. Office: Rand Europe Newtonweg 1 2333 CP Leiden Netherlands

DORNE, DAVID J. lawyer; b. Chgo., Dec. 9, 1946; BS magna cum laude, U. Ill., 1969; MSc, London Sch. Econs., 1970; JD cum laude, Boston U., 1973. Bar: N.Y. 1973, U.S. Ct. Appeals (2d cir.) 1973, U.S. Tax Ct. 1973, U.S. Dist. Ct. (so. dist.) N.Y. 1975, Calif. 1978. Mem. Seltzer Caplan McMahon Vitek P.C., San Diego. Mem. City of San Diego Charter Rev. Commn., 1989—. Mem. ABA (taxation sect., corp., banking and bus. law sect.), State Bar Calif. (taxation sect., real property law sect., chmn. personal income tax subcom. 1982-84), San Diego County Bar Assn., Assn. of Bar of City of N.Y. (taxation sect.), Beta Gamma Sigma. Office: Seltzer Caplan McMahon Vitek PC 2100 Symphony Tower 750 B St San Diego CA 92101-8114

DORNER, PETER PAUL, retired economist, educator; b. Luxemburg, Wis., Jan. 13, 1925; s. Peter and Monica (Altmann) Dorner; m. Lois Cathryn Hartnig, Dec. 26, 1950. BS, U. Wis.-Madison, 1951; MS, U. Tenn., Knoxville, 1953; PhD, Harvard U., 1959. Asst. prof. agrl. econs. U. Tenn., 1953-54; asst. prof. U. Wis.-Madison, 1954-56, assoc. prof., 1959-62, prof., 1962-89, dir. Land Tenure Center, 1965-66, 68-71, chmn. dept. agrl. econs., 1972-76, dean internat. studies and programs, 1980-89, prof., dean emeritus, 1989—. Prof. U. Chile, Santiago, 1963—65; sr. staff economist Pres.'s Coun. Econ. Advisors, Washington, 1967—68; cons. UN, UN Food, Agrl. Orgn., World Bank, U.S. Govt., State Govtl. Agys., InterAm. Devel. Bank. Author: Land Reform and Economic Development, 1972, Latin American Land Reforms in Theory and Practice: a Retrospective Analysis, 1992; editor: Cooperative and Commune: Group Framing in the Economic Development of Agriculture, 1977, Resources and Development: Natural Resource Policies and Economic Development in an Interdependent World, 1980; contbr. Inf. U.S. Army, 1944—46. Mem.: AARP. Home: 3111 Pheasant Branch Rd #109A Middleton WI 53562 E-mail: ppdorner@facstaff.wisc.edu.

DORNETTE, RALPH MEREDITH, religious organization administrator, educator, minister; b. Cin., Aug. 31, 1927; s. Paul A. and Lillian (Bauer) D.; m. Betty Jean Pierce, May 11, 1948; 1 child, Cynthia Anne Dornette Orndorff. AB, Cin. Bible Coll., 1948; DD (hon.), Pacific Christian Coll., 1994; D.D., Pacific Christian Coll., Fullerton, Calif., 1974. Ordained to ministry Christian Ch., 1947. Min. Indian Creek Christian Ch., Cynthiana, Ky., 1946-51; assoc. prof. Cin. Bible Coll., 1948-51; sr. min. First Christian Ch., Muskogee, Okla., 1951-57; founding min. Bellaire Christian Ch., Tulsa, 1957-59; exec. dir. So. Calif. Evangelistic Assn., Torrance, Calif., 1959-62, 68-77; sr. min. Eastside Christian Ch., Fullerton, Calif., 1962-68; dir. devel., prof. ministries Cin. Bible Coll. & Sem., 1977-79; exec. dir. Ch. Devel. Fund, Inc., Fullerton, 1968-77, CEO, 1979-94; sr. preaching minister 1st Christian Ch., Downey, Calif., 1971, 91; preaching minister Hemet (Calif.) Valley Christian Ch., 1992-98; ret., 1998. Pres. So. Calif. Christian Mins. Assn., Fullerton, 1975. Author: Bible Answers to Popular Questions, 1954, Walking With Our Wonderful Lord, 1955, Bible Answers to Popular Questions II, 1964. Pres. Homeowners Assn., Anaheim, Calif., 1980-81. Named Churchman of Yr. Pacific Christian Coll., Fullerton, 1973; recipient Disting. Alumni award Cin. Bible Coll. and Seminary, 1994. Mem. N.Am. Christian Conv. (conv. com. Cin. chpt. 1963, chair nat. registration 1963, v.p. 1972, exec. com. 1963, 70-72, 80-82). E-mail: rmdorn@aol.com.

DORNETTE, W(ILLIAM) STUART, lawyer, educator; b. Washington, Mar. 2, 1951; s. William Henry Lueders and Frances Roberta (Hester) D.; m. Martha Louise Mehl, Nov. 19, 1983; children: Marjorie Frances, Anna Christine, David Paul. AB, Williams Coll., 1972; JD, U. Va., 1975. Bar: Va. 1975, Ohio 1975, U.S. Dist. Ct. (so. dist.) Ohio 1975, D.C. 1976, U.S. Ct. Appeals (6th cir.) 1977, U.S. Supreme Ct. 1980. Assoc. Taft, Stettinius & Hollister, Cin., 1975-83, ptnr., 1983—. Instr. law U. Cin., 1980-87, adj. prof., 1988-91. Co-author: Federal Judiciary Almanac, 1984-87. Mem. Ohio Bd. Bar Examiners, 1991-93, Hamilton County Rep. Exec. Com., 1982—; bd. dirs. Zool. Soc. Cin., 1983-94, Cin. Parks Found., 1995—; bd. visitors U. Cin. Law Sch., 2002—. Mem. FBA, Ohio State Bar Assn., Cin. Bar Assn., Am. Phys. Soc., Nat. Assn. Coll. and Univ. Attys. Methodist. Home: 329 Bishopsbridge Dr Cincinnati OH 45255-3948 Office: 1800 US Bank Tower 425 Walnut St Cincinnati OH 45202-3923 E-mail: dornette@taftlaw.com.

DORNFELD, DAVID ALAN, engineering educator; b. Horicon, Wis., Aug. 3, 1949; s. Harlan Edgar and Cleopatra D.; Barbara Ruth Dornfeld, Sept. 18, 1976. BS in Mech. Engring. with honors, U. Wis., 1972, MS in Mech. Engring., 1973, PhD in Mech. Engring., 1976. Asst. prof. dept. sys. design U. Wis., Milw., 1976-77; asst. prof. mfg. engring. U. Calif., Berkeley, 1977-83, assoc. prof. mfg. engring., 1983-89, vice-chmn. instrn. dept. mech. engring., 1987-88, dir. Engring. Sys. Rsch. Ctr., 1989-98, prof. mfg. engring., 1989—, Will C. Hall Family prof. engring., 1999—, assoc. dean interdisciplinary studies Coll. Engring., 2001—; assoc. dir. rsch. Ecole Nationale Superieure des Mines de Paris, Berkeley, 1983-84. Invited prof. Ecole Nationale Superieure D'Arts et Metiers, Paris, 1992-93; cons., expert witness for intellectual property issues, sensor systems, mfg. automation. Contbr. articles to profl. jours., chpts. in books; presenter numerous seminars, confs.; patentee in field. Recipient Dist. Svc. citation U. Wis. Coll. Engring, Madison, 2000. Fellow ASME (past editor, mem. editl. bd. Mfg. Rev. Jour., pres advisory com., Blackall Machine Tool and Gage Award 1990), Soc. Mfg. Engrs. (fellow editl. bd. Jour. Mfg. Systems, Outstanding Young Engr. award 1982); mem. Am. Soc. Precision Engring., Acoustic Emission Working Group, N.Am. Mfg. Rsch. Inst. (past pres., scientific com.), Japan Soc. Precision Engring., Coll. Internat. pour l'Etude Scientifique des Techniques de Production Mechanique (CIRP). Avocations: hiking, travelling, reading. Office: U Calif Dept Mech Engring Berkeley CA 94720-1740 E-mail: dornfeld@me.berkeley.edu.

DORNFEST, BURTON SAUL, anatomy educator; b. N.Y.C., Oct. 31, 1930; s. Irving and Yetta (Rosengarten) D.; m. Eveline Drucker, June 13, 1954; children: Michael Barry. BA, NYU, 1952, MS, 1954, PhD, 1960. Rsch. asst. dept. biostats. Sloan-Kettering Inst. and Meml. Hosp., N.Y.C., 1952-53; rsch. asst. dept. biology NYU, 1953-54, 56-58, instr. gen. sci., 1958-63; instr. anatomy N.Y. Med. Coll., 1963-64, SUNY Health Sci. Ctr., Bklyn., 1964-67, asst. prof., 1967-73, assoc. prof., 1973-91; cons. study sect. Nat. Heart and Lung Inst., 1975; adj. prof. Med. Sch. CUNY, 1974-97; adj. prof. hematology sch. health scis. Hunter Coll., 1978-82, 90-91; adj. prof. anatomy Inst. Continuing Biomed. Edn., 1979-86, N.Y. Med. Coll., 1982-85, 91-96, Touro Coll. Ctr. Biomed. Edn., 1983-88, Einstein Coll. Medicine, 1991-99. Contbr. articles to profl. jours. Served with U.S. Army, 1954-56. NIH fellow, 1958-60, 61-63; Leukemia Soc., 1960-61; Nat. Inst. Arthritis and Metabolic Diseases grantee, 1964-71; Nat. Cancer Inst. grantee, 1973-75; Mildred Werner League for Cancer Research grantee, 1976-77; co-prin. investigator NIH Heart, Blood and Lung Inst., 1982-85. Mem. AAAS, N.Y. Acad. Scis., Am. Soc. Hematology, Am. Assn. Clin. Anatomists, Sigma Xi. Jewish. Home and Office: 96 Everett Rd Demarest NJ 07627-1225 E-mail: bureve35@aol.com.

DORNHECKER, SANDRA LEE, human resources executive, consultant; b. Chgo., Mar. 15, 1958; d. Robert Joseph and Joan Edith (Bechtel) Dagenais; m. James J. Kukuczka, Sept. 5, 1981 (div. June, 1988); m. Mark S. Dornhecker, Aug. 4, 1992. BA, Nat. Coll Edn., 1986; postgrad. studies, DePaul U., 1987-88, Gov.'s State U., 1991—. Correspondent N. Am. Life Ins., Chgo., 1975-76; paralegal James Wilton, Atty., Chgo., 1977-78; word processing mgr. Pullman Trailmobile, Chgo., 1978-80; human resource mgr. Ill. Cancer Coun., Chgo., 1980-86, human resources dir., 1986-92, Brookfield (Ill.) Zoo, 1992—. Owner, mgr. Resumes, Inc., Frankfort, Ill, 1989—; cons. The Mgmt. Team, Highland Park, Ill., 1989-93. Mem. Soc. Human Resource Mgmt., Soc. Human Resource Profls. Lutheran. Office: Chgo Zoological Soc 3300 Golf Rd Brookfield IL 60513-1060

DORNHOFFER, JOHN LOUIS, neurologist; b. Estherville, Iowa, Aug. 14, 1962; m. Mary Scherrer, June 13, 1962. MD, U. Kans., 1988. Cert. Otolaryngology Bd., 1994. Asst. prof. U. of Ark. for Med. Sciences, 1994—99, assoc. prof., 1999—. Exec. dir. Prosper Meniere Soc., Little Rock, 1999—. Achievements include invention of Dornhoffer Ossicular Replacement Prostheses.

DORNIN, CATHARINE QUILLEN, music educator, concert pianist; b. Louisville, Apr. 19, 1946; d. Rodney White and Carmel (Jett) Quillen; m. Christopher Laird Dornin; children: Sarah, Christopher, Laird, Rebecca, Rachel. BA in Music, Oberlin Conservatory, 1968. Piano instr. Pittsfield (Mass.) Cmty. Music Sch., 1968-69, Hochstein Music Sch., Rochester, N.Y., 1969-71, St. Paul's Sch., Concord, N.H., 1981—. Piano instr. Concord Cmty. Music Sch., 1984—, Notre Dame Coll. Cmty. Music Sch., Manchester, N.H., 1986—, Greater Manchester Ctr. for Arts and Music, 1991-92, St. Paul's Sch.; pianist Pemigewasset Choral Soc., 1973-78; piano accompanist Philomel Camerata, Concord, 1982—, Pemigewasset Choral Soc., Plymouth, N.H., 1973-78, Plymouth State Coll., 1976-77; staff accompanist Plymouth State Coll., 2000—; performances at Williams Coll., Harvard U., Tufts, U., New Eng. Coll., Plymouth State Coll., 1983—, Arlington Street Ch., Boston, 2001—, N.H. Composer's Conf. at River Coll., 2000; solo concert dedicating new piano at Hunt Meml. Bldg., Nashua, N.H.; featured on Concord N.H. Pub. TV in a First Night/New Year's Eve solo performance, 2000; concert perfromances Bach's Lunch Series at Nashua Pub. Libr., 2000-01; several performances St. John The Evangelist Ch., Concord, N.H., 2000-01. Soloist with Louisville Symphony Orch., 1964, Lakes Region Symphony Orch., 1989, N.H. Philharm. Orch., 1991; debut as piano soloist Boston Ch., 1986, Carnegie Hall, N.Y.C., 1990; 18 guest appearances on St. Paul's Sch. Keiser Concert Series, 1981—; performer Musicians of Wall St. Concert Series, Concord, 1993, Omni Concert Series, Cleve., 1993, Oberlin Coll., 2003; made CD with soprano Holly Outwin-Tepe, Music Sweet as Love, 1994; solo piano concert 1st Bapt. Ch., Concord, N.H., 1996, pianist, 1994; performer Bach's Lunch Concert Series, Concord Cmty. Music Sch.; pianist Concord Covenant Ch., 1996—, featured solo pianist in prodn. celebrating and explaining MacDowell Colony, 1996, PBS, 1996; featured in Am. Music Tchr. mag., 1997; pianist Benjamin Britten's Let's Make An Opera, N.H. State Wide Arts in Edn. Conf., 1998, 2003; concert tour Concord Cmty. Music Sch., 2000, Steinert's on the Boston Common, 2000; taped Hermit Thrush at Morn (Amy Beach) for MacDowell Colony, Mus. N.H. History; featured in spl. program honoring 100 most important people of 20th Century, N.H.; performed with Gov. Jean Shaheen and poet Donald Hall; 2 concerts, Shaker Village, Canterbury, N.H., 2001; pianist, organizer concert St. Paul's Sch., 2002—, Concord Cmty. Prodn. The Messiah, 2002, McGill U., Montreal, Can., 2002, Concord Cmty. Chorus, 2002; musician (album) Music of 5 Centuries: Back to Ziffrin, 2002, Opera, 2002, St. Paul's School Piano Faculty, 2002. Organist, choir dir. St. James Episc. Ch., Laconia, N.H., 1981-90; active prison ministry N.H. State Prison, Concord, 1988, Neighbors in Need Program, Laconia, 1988. Winner Louisville Symphony Concerto competition, 1964; recipient Spl. award Belknap Mill Soc., 1989, Tchr. of Excellence, Gov. N.H., 1996; recognized by Concord Comty. Music Sch. as tchr. of students winning most certs. of achievement; honored by being listed on a permanent plaque in Concord Comty. Music Sch's. new bldg. as one of its founding tchrs.. Mem. N.H. Music Tchrs. Assn. (v.p. 1983-87, 89-91, pres.-elect 1991-93, pres. 1993-95, immediate past pres. 1995-97, organized 4-state conv. 1993, spkr. Eastern divsn. meeting 1994, Sister Anita Marchessault Tchr./Mem. of Yr. award 1996), Piano Guild, New Eng. Piano Tchrs. Assn., N.H. State Coun. on Arts Touring Artists Roster. E-mail: mcqdornin@aol.com.

DORNING, JOHN JOSEPH, nuclear engineering, engineering physics and applied mathematics educator; b. Bronx, N.Y., Apr. 17, 1938; s. John Joseph and Sarrah Cathrine (McCormack) D.; m. Helen Marie Driscoll, July 27, 1963; children: Michael, James, Denise. BS in Marine Engring., U.S. Mcht. Marine Acad., 1959; MS (AEC fellow), Columbia U., 1963, PhD (AEC fellow), 1967. Marine engr. U.S. Mcht. Marine, 1960-62; asst. physicist Brookhaven Nat. Lab., Upton, N.Y., 1967-69, assoc. physicist, group leader, 1969-70; assoc. prof. nuclear engring. U. Ill., Urbana, 1970-75, prof., 1975-84; Whitney Stone prof. nuclear engring., engring. physics and applied math. U. Va., Charlottesville, 1984—. NRC vis. prof. math. physics U. Bologna, Italy, 1975-76, 81, 85, 87; internat. prof. nuclear engring. Italian Ministry of Edn., 1983, 84, 86; physicist plasma theory group, div. magnetic fusion energy Lawrence Livermore (Calif.) Nat. Lab., 1977-78; cons. to U.S. nat. labs. and indsl. research labs., 1970—. Contbr. articles to various publs. Served as ensign USN, 1959-60. Recipient Ernest O. Lawrence award U.S. Dept. Energy, 1990. Fellow AAAS, Am. Phys. Soc., Am. Nuclear Soc. (Mark Mills award 1967, Arthur Holly Compton award 1998, Eugene P. Wigner award 1999, Glenn T. Seaborg medal 2002); mem. Am. Soc. for Engring. Edn., (Glenn Murphy award 1988), Soc. Indsl. and Applied Math., N.Y. Acad. Scis., Sigma Xi.

DOROCKE, LAWRENCE FRANCIS, lawyer; b. Chgo., Oct. 4, 1946; s. Walter P. and Effie M. (Gillis) D.; m. Diane L. Roberts, June 22, 1968; children: Todd D., Rob L., Jill A. BS in Econs., Purdue U., 1968, MS in Indsl. Relations, 1970; JD magna cum laude, Ind. U., 1973. Bar: Ind. 1973, U.S. Dist. Ct. (so. dist.) Ind. 1973, Iowa 1974, U.S. Ct. Appeals (7th cir.). Asst. mgr. personnel Comml. Solvents Corp., Terre Haute, Ind., 1970-71; law clk. to chief justice U.S. Dist. Ct. (so. dist.) Iowa, Des Moines, 1973-75; ptnr. Dann, Pecar, Newman & Kleiman P.C., Indpls., 1975—. Mem. ABA, Ind. Bar Assn., Indpls. Bar Assn. Roman Catholic. Office: Dann Pecar Newman & Kleiman PO Box 82008 Indianapolis IN 46282-2008 E-mail: ldorocke@dannpecar.com.

DOROJEVETS, MIKHAIL, application developer, educator; b. Debin, Russia, May 10, 1958; arrived in U.S., 1996; s. Nikolai Fedorovich and Olga (Makarovna) Dorojevets. BS in Physics, Inst. Physics and Tech., Moscow, 1980, MS in Physics and Electronic Engring., 1982; PhD in Computer Engring., USSR Acad. Sci., Novosibirsk, Russia, 1988. Leading designer Next-Generation Computers project USSR Acad. Scis., Novosibirsk, Russia, 1982—90; dir. parallel sys. divsn. Inst. Informatics Sys. Russian Acad. Sci., Novosibirsk, Russia, 1990—96; asst. prof. SUNY, Stony Brook, NY, 1996—2000, assoc. prof., 2000—. Cons. SONY US Rsch. Labs, San Jose, 1997. Inventor MARS-M; co-author: Future Trends in Microelectronics: The Road Ahead, 1999, Frontiers in Electronics: From Materials to Systems, 2000; contbr. articles to profl. jours. Sr. lt. Russian mil., 1981. Grantee Multithreaded Arch. and Design of High-Speed Processors for HTMT Computers grant, Jet Propulsion Lab. NASA, 1999—2001. Mem.: IEEE. Avocations: guitar, singing, digital photography, travel. Office: SUNY Dept Electrical and Computer Eng Stony Brook NY 11794-2350 Office Fax: 631-632-8494. Business E-Mail: midor@ece.sunysb.edu.

DOROSCHAK, JOHN Z. dentist; b. Zolochiv, Ukraine, Feb. 11, 1928; s. William and Anna (Stroczan) D.; came to U.S., 1950, naturalized, 1954; student U. Minn., 1955-57, BS, 1959, DDS, 1961; m. Nadia Zahorodny, June 30, 1962; children: Andrew, Michael, Natalie, Maria. Pvt. practice dentistry, Mpls., 1961—. Cons., St. Joseph's Home for Aged, Mpls., 1974-77, Holy Family Residence, St. Paul, 1977-84. Mem. steering com. St. Anthony West Neighborhood, Mpls., 1971-72, bd. dirs. 1988-89; chmn. Mpls. dentists com. Little Sisters of the Poor Devel. Program, 1975; Webelos leader troop 50, Boy Scouts Am., 1975-76; pres. N.E. Regional Sch. Assn. Parents and Tchrs., 1978-79; bd. dirs. East Side Neighborhood Svc., 1972; treas. Plast Inc., Ukrainian youth orgn., Mpls., 1979-83; mem. Sr. Citizen Centers Health Adv. Com., Mpls., 1979-83; chmn. aquatenial health fair Mpls. Dist. Dental Soc., 1985, mem. exec. coun., 1990-93, mem. constn. and by-laws com., 1987-88; mem. com. Dental Health Edn., 1989-90. Served with AUS, 1953-55. Fellow Am. Soc. Geriatric Dentistry; mem. Am. Dental Assn., Minn. Dental Assn. (com. on dental care access 1980-83, ascending alt. del. to Ho. of Dels. 1989, del. 1990, 91, 92), Minn. Soc. Preventive Dentistry (dir. 1977-83, treas. 1979-83), Am. Soc. Dentistry for Children, Mpls. Dist. Dental Soc. (nursing home com. 1974—, chmn. 1979-82, 84-87, emergency care com. 1983-84), Ukrainian Med. Assn. (sec.-treas. Minn. chpt. 1971-75), Ukrainian Profl. Club, Univ. Minn. Alumni Club (charter mem.), KC (4th degree), Psi Omega. Mem. Ukrainian Catholic Ch. (new ch. campaign chmn. 1966-80, mem. ch. com. 1965—). Home: 7254 Stage Coach Trl Lino Lakes MN 55014-1988 Office: Broadway and Univ Profl Bldg 230 Broadway St NE Minneapolis MN 55413-1902

DOROSLOVACKI, MILOS, engineering educator, consultant; b. Belgrade, Yugoslavia, July 1, 1955; arrived in U.S., 1988; s. Ivan and Bosiljka Doroslovacki; m. Svetlana Vukasinović Doroslovacki, Oct. 11, 1979; 1 child, Pavle. BSEE, U. Belgrade, 1979, MSEE, 1984; PhD, U. Cin., 1994. Rsch. engr. Inst. Nuclear Scis., Belgrade, 1980—88; rsch. asst. U. Cin., 1988—94; rsch. engr. Compunetix, Monroeville, Pa., 1994—95; asst. prof. George Washington U., Washington, 1995—2001, assoc. prof., 2001—. Cons. Telogy Networks, Germantown, Md., 1998—2001. Contbr. articles to profl. jours. Mem.: IEEE, European Assn. for Signal Processing. Office: George Washington Univ 801 22d St NW Washington DC 20052 E-mail: doroslov@seas.gwu.edu.

DORPAT, THEODORE LORENZ, psychoanalyst; b. Miles City, Mont., Mar. 25, 1925; s. Theodore Ertman and Eda (Christiansen) D.; married; 1 child, Joanne Katherine. BS, Whitworth Coll., 1948; MD, U. Wash., 1952; grad., Seattle Psychoanalytic Inst., 1964. Resident in psychiatry Seattle VA Hosp., 1953-55, Cin. Gen. Hosp., 1955-56; instr. in psychiatry U. Wash., 1956-58, asst. prof. psychiatry, 1958-59, asso. prof., 1969-75, prof., 1976—; practice medicine specializing in psychiatry Seattle, 1958-64; practice psychoanalysis, 1964; instr. Seattle Psychoanalytic Inst., 1966-71, tng. psychoanalyt, 1971—, dir., 1984. Chmn. Wash. Gov.'s Task Force for Commitment Law Reform; trustee Seattle Community Psychiat. Clinic; pres., trustee Seattle Psychoanalytic Inst. Contbr. numerous articles, books, revs. to profl. jours. Served to ensign USNR, 1943-46. Fellow Am. Psychiat. Assn.; mem. Am. Psychoanalytic Assn., AMA, Seattle Psychoanalytic Soc. (sec.-treas. 1965-67, pres. 1972-73), AAAS, Alpha Omega Alpha, Sigma Xi. Home: 7700 E Green Lake Dr N Seattle WA 98103-4971 Office: Blakely Bldg 2271 NE 51st St Seattle WA 98105-5713

DORR, ANN PIERCE, science educator; b. Tulsa, Aug. 11, 1918; d. Oscar Charles Pierce and Grace Esther Myers; m. John Van Nostrand Dorr II, Feb. 5, 1946; children: John Van Nostrand Dorr III, Charles Pierce Dorr, Katherine Grace Dorr. BA, U. Kansas City, 1939; MEd, Am. U., 1968. Geol. asst. Ark. Geol. Survey, Little Rock, 1942-43; asst. rsch. analyst Petroleum Adminstrv. for War, Washington, 1943-44; geol. asst. Great Lakes Carbon Corp., Wichita, Kans., 1943-46; earth sci. tchr. Fairfax County Pub. Schs., Va., 1964-75; co-instr. course for earth sci. tchrs. U. Va. Sch. of Continuing Edn., Fairfax County, 1974-76; cons. crustal evolution Nat. Assn. Geology Tchrs., Washington, 1977; author course guide and faculty materials Internat. Univ. Consortium, Md., 1982-83. Mem. coms. in field, including Nat. Sci. Resources Ctr.-Smithsonian Instn.-Nat. Acad. Sci. adv. com. for Middle Sch. Project "Catastrophic Events", 1997-2000. Author: Minerals: Foundations of Society, 3d edit., 2002, numerous other publs. in field. Mem. natural resources com. LWV, Mongtomery County, Md., 1974—, chair 1974-78; cons. editor: Science Activities, 1982-85; bd. dirs. Mineral Info. Inst., 1984-98, v.p. Southeastern Region, MII, 1984-89; mem. energy and environ. task force Woman's Nat. Dem. Club, 1986—, chair 1992-96, co-chair 1987-92, 92-97, others. Recipient numerous awards in field, including Outstanding Earth Sci. Tchr. of Va., Nat. Assn. Geology Tchrs., 1974, Outstanding Earth Sci. Tchr. in S.E. U.S., Nat. Assn. Geology Tchrs. Mem. Women in Mining, Assn. Women Geoscientists, Am. Inst. Mining, Metallurgy, Petroleum Engrs., Population Ref. Bur. Democrat. Avocations: writing, backcountry travel, music. Home: 9707 Old Georgetown Rd Apt 2514 Bethesda MD 20814-1761

DORR, DANIEL ALAN, personal and professional development facilitator; b. Cherokee, Iowa, Oct. 4, 1946; s. Ronald Dorr and Dora Dean (McManus) Kahl; children: Molly, Gabriel. Student, U. No. Iowa, 1965-69, Rudolf Steiner Coll., Sacramento, 1980-82, Calif. Coast U., 1993—. Cert. PSI World facilitator. Divsn. gen. mgr. U.S. Solar Corp. West, Sacramento, 1980-81; sales and mktg. dir. precious metals and jewelry mfg. co. Sausalito, Calif., 1981-83; lead instr. PSI World Seminars, San Rafael, Calif., 1983-90; owner, CEO Ptnrs. in Excellence seminars, 1990-94; pres. Mastering Peak Performance series seminars, 1994—. Personal and profl. devel. exec. coach; designer, facilitator numerous profl. and personal performance seminars and workshops including Creating Abundance in All Areas of Your Life, The Vision-Mission Workshop, Ptnrs. in Excellence, Mastering Peak Performance: The Personal Leadership Programme. Contbr. articles to profl. publs. Bd. dirs. Marin Waldorf Sch., San Rafael, 1977-80. Recipient Award of Acknowledgement and Appreciation, Gov. of Guam, 1993, Award of Appreciation, Portuguese-Am. Conf., 1990, Award of Appreciation, Manitoba (Can.) Sales Assn., 1989, Award of Appreciation, Dr. John Hall, The Options for Youth Orgn., 1988. Mem. ASTD, Am. Soc. for Transpersonal Psychology, Assn. Transpersonal Psychology, Nat. Assn. for Self-Employed, Inst. Noetic Scis., C. of C. Avocations: musician, listening to music, reading, hiking, jewelry design. Office: Dan Dorr Assocs Inc 836 Mcfarlane Ave Sebastopol CA 95472-4418 E-mail: dandorr7@cs.com.

DORR, ROBERT CHARLES, lawyer; b. Denver, Jan. 7, 1946; s. Owen and Rose Esther (Tudek) D.; m. Sandra Leah Gehlsen, Feb. 26, 1972; children: Bryan, Aric. BSEE, Wichita State U., 1968; MSEE, Northwestern U., 1970; JD, U. Denver, 1975. Bar: Colo. 1975, U.S. Dist. Ct. Colo. 1975, U.S. Patent Office 1975. Mem. tech. staff Bell Labs, Naperville, Ill., 1968-72, mem. patent staff Denver, 1975-76; ptnr. Dorr, Carson, Sloan & Birney, P.C., Denver, 1976-86, sr. ptnr., 1986—. Ptnr. Internat. Practicum Inst., Denver, 1979—; seminar speaker various profl. orgns. Mem. IEEE, AAAS, Sigma Xi. Roman Catholic. Home: 6101 Muddy Creek Rd Pueblo CO 81004-9747 Office: Dorr Carson Sloan & Birney PC 3010 E 6th Ave Denver CO 80206-4328 E-mail: bobdorr@patnet.com.

DORR, RODERICK A. lawyer; b. Oklahoma City, Aug. 10, 1937; s. Clyde H. and Mary A. D. BS in Aero. Engring., U. Okla., 1961, JD, 1975. Bar: Okla., 1975, N.Mex., 1975, Calif., 1983, U.S. Dist. Ct. N.Mex. 1975, U.S. Dist. Ct. (no., ctrl., ea., so. dists.) Calif. 1983, U.S. Ct. Appeals (9th cir.) 1988, U.S. Ct. Appeals (10th cir.) 1977, U.S. Supreme Ct. 1982. Fighter pilot USAF, 1961-67, USAR, Dallas, 1967-72; comml. airline pilot Braniff Airways, Dallas, 1967-72; assoc. Civerolo, Hansen & Wolf, Albuquerque, 1975-77; asst. atty. gen. State of N.Mex., Santa Fe, 1977-78; ptnr. Terrazaz & Dorr, P.A., Santa Fe, 1978-81, asst. dist. atty. 1st Jud. Dist., Santa Fe, 1981-83; assoc. Thomas H. Lambert, P.C., San Diego, 1983, Pothier, Moore & Hinricks, Santa Ana, Calif., 1983, Magana, Cathcart et. al., L.A., 1984-93; pvt. practice Albuquerque, 1995, 96—; assoc. John A. Budagher & Assocs., Albuquerque, 1993-95; ptnr. Moore, Brewer & Burbott, La Jolla, Calif., 1995-96. Capt. USAF; LCDR USNR. Mem. N.Mex. Trial Lawyers Assn., Lawyer Pilots Bar Assn., Albuquerque Bar Assn. Office: 4163 Montgomery Blvd NE Albuquerque NM 87109-6755

DORR, STEPHANIE TILDEN, psychotherapist; b. Orlando, Fla., Sept. 21, 1950; d. Luther Willis Tilden II and Lillian Murfee (Grace) Owen; m. Darwin Dorr, May 21, 1986. AA, El Camino Coll., 1975; BA, U. N.C., 1985; MA, Western Carolina U., 1991. Cons. psychologist Sylva (N.C.) Psychol. Assocs., 1991-92; staff psychologist Park Ridge Hosp., Naples, N.C., 1992, Blue Ridge Ctr., Asheville, N.C., 1991-93; pvt. practice psychology Asheville, 1991-93; project mgr. Sedgwick County Dept. Mental Health, Wichita, Kans., 1993-95; pvt. practice psychotherapy and psychol. assessment Counseling and Mediation Ctr., Wichita, Kans., 1995-98; therapist United Meth. Youthville Clinic, Wichita, 1998—2001; clin. therapist Wichita (Kans.) Pub. Schs. Greiffenstein Spl. Edn. Ctr., 2002—. Adj. faculty Kans. Newman Coll., Wichita, 1995—, Butler County (Kans.) Cmty. Coll., 1996-97; Assertive Cmty. Treatment (ACT) team clinician United Meth. Youthville, Wichita, 1997-98; presenter in field. Contbr. articles to profl. publs. Recipient Excellence in Tchg. award Butler County C.C., 1997, Outstanding Faculty Mem. award Butler County C.C., 1998. Mem. Soc. for Personality Assessment, Psychoanalytic Study Group (sec. 1989-93, award 1993), Wichita N.C. Psychol. Assn. (mem.-at-large 1985-93, pres.-elect 1993), Psi Chi, Pi Gamma Mu. Episcopalian. Avocations: sewing, rock collecting, gardening. Office: Wichita Pub Schs Greiffenstein Spl Edn Ctr 1221 E Galena Wichita KS 67216 E-mail: sdorr@usd259.net., stdorr@cox.net.

DORRILL, WILLIAM FRANKLIN, political scientist, educator; b. Dallas, July 25, 1931; s. William Cumbie and Ruth (Esther Webb) D.; m. Martha Jeanne Brawley, Mar. 3, 1951; children: Jennifer Ruth, William Sidney, Rebecca Jeanne, Lisa Kathryn. BA, Baylor U., 1952; MA, U. Va., 1954; postgrad., Australian Nat. U., Canberra, 1954; PhD, Harvard U., 1972. Fgn. affairs analyst U.S. Govt., Washington, 1961-63; polit. scientist RAND Corp., Santa Monica, Calif., 1963-67; project chmn., sr. staff mem. Rsch. Analysis Corp., McLean, Va., 1967-68; dir. Asian Studies Ctr., assoc. prof. polit. sci. U. Pitts., 1969-77, chmn. dept. East Asian langs. and lits., 1972-77; dean Coll. Arts and Sci., prof. polit. sci. Ohio U., Athens, 1977-84; provost, prof. polit. sci. U. Louisville, 1984-88; pres. Longwood Coll., Farmville, Va., 1988-96, pres. emeritus, 1996—, prof. polit. sci. and history, 1988-96, bd. visitors, disting. prof., 1996—. Vis. lectr. Fgn. Svc. Inst., U.S. Dept. State, Washington, 1962—80, cons., 1999—2001; mem. faculty coll. mgmt. program Carnegie-Mellon U. and Nat. Ctr. for Higher Edn. Mgmt. Systems, summer, 1980; vis. lectr. univ. adminstrn. Chinese univs., 1980, 84, 85, 87, 89; program cons. La. Bd. Regents, Baton Rouge, 1982—83, U. Tenn., Knoxville, 1988, Odessa (Ukraine) State U., 1998, U. Va., 1999, James Madison U., 1999, Warsaw (Poland) Sch. Econs., 1999, Mary Washington Coll., 2003; mem. com. on internat. edn. Am. Coun. on Edn., 1990, U.S. AID Univ. Ctr. Program Adv. Group, 1991; cons. TV History Channel, 1999. Contbr. articles on East Asian politics and internat. relations to profl. jours., chpts. on Chinese politics and history to scholarly books. Mem. Athens County Bd. Mental Retardation and Devel. Disabilities, Ohio, 1982-84; chmn. bd. dirs. Kentuckiana Metroversity, 1986-88. Recipient Disting. Achievement medal Baylor U., 1980; Fulbright scholar, 1954; Soc. for Values in Higher Edn. Kent fellow, 1957-58; Ford Found. fgn. area fellow Taiwan, Hong Kong, 1959-61 Fellow: Soc. for Values in Higher Edn.; mem.: Coun. on Postsecondary Edn. Environ. Task Force, Coun. for Internat. Exch. of Scholars (bd. dirs. 1992—96), Gov.'s Bus. Edn. Commn., Nat. Assn. State Univs. and Land Grant Colls. (acad. coun., exec. com. 1987—88), Southside Va. Bus. and Edn. Com. (exec. coun. 1992—2000), So. Assn. Colls. and Schs. (commn. on colls. 1986—88, 1991—96, chair vis. coms. 1990—), Am. Assn. State Colls. and Univs. (com. on accreditation and instl. assessment 1989—96, chmn. 1990—96, nominating com. 1993—94, gov.'s commn. econ. devel. in Southside Region Commonwealth Va. 1990—96), Nat. Com. on U.S.-China Rels., Asia Soc. (adv. com. performing arts 1977—85), Assn. Asian Studies, Am. Conf. Acad. Deans (vice chmn. 1981—82, chmn. 1982—83, bd. dirs.

1980—84), Va. C. of C. (Va. emissary 1993—96), Rotary Internat. (gov.-elect dist. 7600 2002—03, gov. 2003—). Democrat. Presbyterian. Home: 1007 Fayette St Farmville VA 23901-2029 Office: Longwood Coll Dept History & Polit Sci Farmville VA 23909-0001 E-mail: wdorrill@ntelos.net.

DORRIS, GEORGE EDWARD, historian, educator, editor, author; b. Eugene, Oreg., Aug. 3, 1930; s. Benjamin Fultz and Klysta (Cornet) D. BA, U. Oreg., 1952; MA, Northwestern U., 1953, PhD, 1962. Instr. Duke U., Durham, N.C., 1957-60, Rutgers U., New Brunswick, N.J., 1960-62, Queen's Coll., CUNY, N.Y.C., 1964-67; from asst. prof. to assoc. prof. York Coll., CUNY, N.Y.C., 1967-98. Author: Paolo Rolli and the Italian Circle in London 1715-1744, 1967; editor: The Royal Swedish Ballet 1773-1998, 1999; co-editor, co-founder Dance Chronicle, 1977—; music editor Ballet Rev., 1967-77; record reviewer, Ballet Rev., 1993-; assoc. editor Internat. Ency. of Dance, 1981-98; sr. rschr. the Popular Balanchine Project of the Balanchine Found., 1999-2002. Sec. bd. dirs. Dance Perspectives Found., 1975—81. Mem. Dance Critics Assn. (bd. dirs. 1980-83, 96-99), Soc. Dance History Scholars (bd. dirs. 1979-82, 90-93, editl. bd. 2001—), World Dance Alliance Ams. (bd. dirs. 1994—). Home: 40 E 10th St New York NY 10003-6221

DORSCH, JEFFREY PETER, journalist; b. Rockville Ctr., N.Y., July 12, 1956; s. Frederick John and Elinor (Eilhardt) D.; m. Vicki Lynne Rice, Jan. 16, 1993; 1 child, Cali Sierra. BA, Fordham Coll., The Bronx, N.Y., 1978. Staff reporter Bay City News Svc., San Francisco, 1979, Healdsburg (Calif.) Tribune, 1979-82; correspondent Electronic News, San Francisco/Palo Alto, Calif., 1982-86, sr. editor N.Y.C., 1986-90, mng. editor N.Y.C. and Mountain View, Calif., 1991-95, editor-in-chief Mountain View, 1995—, editor-at-large Cedar Park, Tex., 1998-99; sr. editor Semiconbay, Cedar Park, 1999—2001; city reporter Williamson County Sun, 2001—02; industry editor Hoover's Inc., 2003—. Avocations: reading, travel, family. Home: 5800 Brodie Ln # 315 Austin TX 78745

DORSCHNER, JON PETER, education educator, diplomat; b. Wuerzburg, Germany, Dec. 5, 1952; s. Harold William and Elizabeth Dorschner; m. Nilu Anjali Dayal, Dec. 27, 1979; children: Kristl Vidya, Kristian Anand. PhD, U. of Ariz., 1981. Diplomat Dept. of State, Washington, 1983—2002; prof. US Mil. Acad., West Point, NY, 2001—. Author (book) Alcohol Consumption in a Village in North India. Office: Dept of Social Sciences US Military Academy West Point NY 10996

DORSEN, DAVID M(ILTON), lawyer; b. N.Y.C., Oct. 10, 1935; s. Arthur and Tanya (Stone) D.; m. Margaret L. Stern, Mar. 5, 1969 (div. Feb. 1976); m. Kenna D. Peusner, Jan. 24, 1997. AB, Harvard U., 1956, JD, 1959. Bar: N.Y. 1960, D.C. 1960, U.S. Supreme Ct. 1977. Assoc. Kaye, Scholer, Fierman, Hays & Handler, N.Y.C., 1960-64; asst. U.S. atty. U.S. Dist. Ct. (so. dist.) N.Y., 1964-69; dep. commr. and 1st dep. commr. N.Y.C. Dept. Investigation, 1969-73; asst. chief counsel Senate Watergate Com., Washington, 1973-74; ptnr. Sachs, Greenebaum & Tayler, Washington, 1974-91; of counsel Hughes Hubbard & Reed, Washington, 1991-94; pvt. practice Washington, 1994-98; of counsel Wallace King Marraro & Branson PLLC, Washington, 1998—. Vis. lectr. pub. policy studies Terry Sanford Inst. Pub. Policy, Duke U., Durham, N.C., 1995—; adj. prof. Georgetown U. Law Ctr., Washington, 2000—. Contbg. editor, wine and food editor The Washingtonian Mag., 1982—; assoc. prodr. Tolstoy, 1996; columnist The Hill, Washington, 1998-2000. Mem. D.C. Bar Assn. (chmn. arbitration bd. 1982-84), Internat. Club of Washington (chief counsel 1981-89). Home: 3501 Davis St NW Washington DC 20007-1426

DORSEN, NORMAN, lawyer, educator; b. N.Y.C., Sept. 4, 1930; s. Arthur and Tanya (Stone) D.; m. Harriette Koffler, Nov. 25, 1965; children: Jennifer, Caroline Gail, Anne. BA, Columbia U., 1950; LLB magna cum laude, Harvard U., 1953; postgrad., London Sch. Econs., 1955-56; LLD (hon.), Ripon Coll., 1981, John Jay Coll. Criminal Justice, 1992. Bar: D.C. 1953, N.Y. 1954. Law clk. to chief judge Calvert Magruder U.S. Ct. Appeals, Boston, 1956-57; law clk. to Justice John Marshall Harlan U.S. Supreme Ct., Washington, 1957-58; assoc. Dewey, Ballantine, Bushby, Palmer & Wood, N.Y.C., 1958-60; prof. law NYU Sch. Law, N.Y.C., 1961-81, Stokes prof., 1981—, dir. Hays civil liberties program, 1961—, dir. global law sch. program, 1994-96, chmn., 1996—2002; counselor to pres. NYU, 2002—. Vis. prof. law London Sch. Econs., 1968, U. Calif., Berkeley, 1974-75, Harvard U., 1980, 83, 84; cons. U.S. Commn. on Violence, 1968-69, Random House, 1969-73, B.B.C., 1969-73, U.S. Commn. on Social Security, 1979-80, Native Am. Rights Fund, 1978-89; exec. dir. spl. com. on courtroom conduct Assn. Bar N.Y.C., 1970-73; chmn. Com. for Pub. Justice, 1972-74; vice chmn. HEW sec.'s rev. panel on new drug regulation, 1975-76, chmn., 1976-77; mem. N.Y.C. Commn. on Status of Women, 1978-80; chmn. Sec. of Treasury's Citizen Rev. Panel on Good O' Boy Round-up, 1995-96. Author (with others): Political and Civil Rights in U.S., 3rd edit., 1967, Political and Civil Rights in U.S., 4th edit., Vol. I, 1976, Political and Civil Rights in U.S., 4th edit., Vol. II, 1979, Frontiers of Civil Liberties, 1968, Discrimination and Civil Rights, 1969, Comparative Constitution, 2003; author: (with L. Friedman) Disorder in the Court, 1973; author: (with S. Gillers) Regulation of Lawyers, 1985, Regulation of Lawyers, 2d edit., 1989; editor: The Rights of Americans, 1971; editor: (with S. Gillers) None of Your Business, 1974; editor: Our Endangered Rights, 1984, The Evolving Constitution, 1987; editor: (with others) Human Rights in Northern Ireland, 1991, The Unpredictable Constitution, 2001, with P. Gifford: Democracy and the Rule of Law, 2001; ; editor: (with others) Constitutionalism Cases and Materials, 2003; editl. dir. Internat. Jour. Constl. Law, 2002—. 1st lt. JAGC, U.S. Army, 1953-55. Recipient medal French Minister of Justice, 1983, Eleanor Roosevelt Human Rights award 2000; Fulbright Disting. Prof., Argentina, 1987, 88. Fellow Am. Acad. Arts and Scis.; mem. ABA (chmn. com. free speech and press 1968-70), ACLU (gen. counsel 1969-76, pres. 1976-91), Am. Law Inst., Coun. on Fgn. Rels., Lawyers Com. Human Rights (chmn. bd. dirs. 1995-2000), Lawyer Com. Civil Rights, Internat. Assn. Constnl. Law (exec. com.), U.S. Assn. Constnl. Law (pres. 1996—), Soc. Am. Law Tchrs. (pres. 1972-74, Tchg. award 1997), Thomas Jefferson Ctr. for Free Expression (trustee). Home: 146 Central Park W New York NY 10023-2005 Office: NYU Sch Law 40 Washington Sq S New York NY 10012-1005 E-mail: norman.dorsen@nyu.edu.

DORSET, PHYLLIS FLANDERS, technical writer, editor; b. Tacoma, Sept. 10, 1924; d. William Winchell and Rhea Louise (MacDougall) Flanders; m. Donald Edward Dorset, Apr. 20, 1963. BA, U. Wash., 1948, MA, 1949; postgrad., U. N.Mex., 1949-50. Tech. writer Sandia Corp., Albuquerque, 1952-56; tech. writer/editor SRI Internat. (formerly Stanford Rsch. Inst.), Menlo Park, Calif., 1956—. Author: Historic Ships Afloat, 1967, The New Eldorado, 1970; (with Stephen W. Miller) A Finite Difference, History of SRI's Physics Division, 2003; contbr. articles to profl. jours. Mem. Arts Commn., Menlo Park, 1970-73. Mem. Authors Guild. Home: 460 Sherwood Way Menlo Park CA 94025-3716 E-mail: phyllis.dorset@sri.com.

DORSETT, BURT, investment company executive; b. Chgo., Nov. 8, 1930; s. Burton and Della (Reader) D.; m. Judith Martin, Dec. 14, 1952 (div.); children: Mark, Deborah, Jeffrey, Cindy (dec.); m. Trixie Landsberger, Mar. 1, 1981. BA, Dartmouth Coll., 1953; MBA, Harvard U., 1959. Indsl. engr. E.I. duPont de Nemours, Seaford, Del., 1953-57; cons. Booz-Allen & Hamilton, N.Y.C., 1959-62; v.p. U. Rochester, 1962-70; exec. v.p., trustee Coll. Retirement Equities Fund, N.Y.C., 1970-79; chmn., pres. Westinghouse Pension Investment Corp., N.Y.C., 1979-86, Dorsett-McCabe Capital Mgmt. Inc., 1987—. Chief investment officer Money Growth Inst., 1999-2002; bd. dirs. Smith Barney Funds, N.Y.C. Author: (with others) Epoxy Resins, Market Survey and Users Reference, 1959. Budget com. Cmty. Chest, Rochester, 1967-70; trustee Convalescent Hosp. for Children, Rochester, 1967-70, Hillside Children's Home, Rochester, 1968-70, Keuka Coll., N.Y., 1968-71; mem. com. Boys Club of N.Y.C.; investment com. Am. Psychol. Assn., 1969-87. William J. Cook scholar, 1953. Mem. Dartmouth Club, Harvard Bus. Sch. Club, WeeBurn Country Club (Darrien, Conn.). Office: Ste 5700 500 5th Ave New York NY 10110-3199

DORSEY, DAVID BYARD, non-profit executive; b. Oak Park, Ill., Mar. 7, 1939; s. Clifford J. and Frances B. Dorsey; m. F. Wendy Dorsey, Oct. 13, 1984; children: Viviane, Eliana, Paulo, Reuben Patterson. BS in Math., U. Mich., 1962; MBA, Harvard Bus. Sch., 1966. Spl. asst. deputy commr. FDA, Rockville, Md., 1970-71, chief evaluation staff, 1971-72; mgmt. cons. World Bank, AID, others, Washington, 1972-79; asst. exec. dir. D.C. Bar Assn., Washington, 1979-86; exec. dir. Nat. Assn. Criminal Def. Lawyers, Washington, 1986-89; dir. adminstrn. Manna Inc., Washington, 1989-95, CFO, 1996—. Treas. St. Stephen's Episcopal Ch., Washington, 1997-98; pres. Arts in Action, Washington, 1991-99. Mem. Soc. Human Resource Mgmt. Democrat. Avocations: running, hiking, camping. Office: Manna Inc 828 Evarts St NE Washington DC 20018-1722

DORSEY, DOLORES FLORENCE, retired corporate treasurer, business executive; b. Buffalo, May 26, 1928; d. William G. and Florence R. D. BS, Coll. St. Elizabeth, 1950. With Aerojet-Gen. Corp., 1953—, asst. to treas., 1972-74, asst. treas., 1974-79, treas., 1979—2001. Mem. Cash Mgmt. Group San Diego (past pres.), Nat. Assn. Corp. Treas., Fin. Execs. Inst. (v.p.). Republican. Roman Catholic. Office: 10300 N Torrey Pines Rd La Jolla CA 92037-1020

DORSEY, EUGENE CARROLL, former foundation and communications executive; b. Springfield, Ill., Feb. 7, 1927; s. Prentiss Eugene and Reta Mae (Bennett) D.; m. Rita LaVerne Sutzer, June 18, 1949; children— David Eugene, Philip Alan BS in Journalism, U. Ill., 1949; hon. doctorate, Coll. of Idaho, 1987, Keuka Coll., 1990. Program dir. Sta. WSOY, Decatur, Ill., 1953-57; sta. mgr. Sta. WVLN, Olney, Ill., 1957-59; gen. mgr. Metro-East Jour., East St. Louis, Ill., 1959-63, Idaho Statesman, Boise, 1963-65, pub., 1965-71, State Jour., Lansing, Mich., 1971; dir. Federated Publs., Inc., Battle Creek, Mich., 1966-71, v.p., 1969-71; gen. mgr. Gannett Rochester Newspapers, N.Y., 1971, pub., 1972-79; v.p. spl. divs. Gannett Co., 1978-79; pres. Gannett N.W. div. pub. Idaho Statesman, 1979-81; mem. adv. bd. UPI, 1979; pres., chief exec. officer, trustee The Freedom Forum, Rochester, 1981-89; ret.; chmn. Ind. Sector, Washington, 1989-92. Bd. dirs. Prudential Mut. Funds, 1987-02. Trustee emeritus Coll. Idaho; hon. bd. dirs. Meml. Art Gallery, Internat. Mus. of Photography at George Eastman House; past pres. Rochester Grantmakers Forum; past chmn. Am. Coun. for Arts, Ind. Sector's Give Five campaign to encourage donation of 5%income and 5 hrs. vol. work; past dirs. Family Svc. Am. With USNR, 1945-46. Named Outstanding Young Man of Ill., Ill. Jr. C. of C., 1961; recipient Honor medal Freedom Found., 1968 Mem. Country Club Rochester, Longboat Key Club. Home: 2010 Harbourside Dr Unit 2003 Longboat Key FL 34228-4236 also: 68 Winding Creek Ln Rochester NY 14625-2175

DORSEY, J KEVIN, dean; MD, So. Ill. U.; PhD in physiologic chemistry, U. Wis., Madison; postgrad., The Johns Hopkins U. Diplomate Am. Bd. Internal Medicine, of rheumatology subspecialty Am. Bd. Internal Medicine. Resident in internal medicine U. Iowa, Iowa City, fellow in rheumatology; asst. prof. So. Ill. U., Carbondale; med. dir. So. Ill. Arthritis Found.; attending rheumatologist Carbondale (Ill.) Clinic; consulting rheumatologist V.A. Hosp., Marion, Ill.; prof. internal medicine So. Ill. U. Sch. Medicine, interim dean and provost, dean and provost, 2002—. Mem. Nuc. Magnetic Resonance Mgmt. Com. So. Ill. U., mem. Molecular Biology, Microbiology and Biochemistry com. Co-host (edn. television program) Medically Speaking, reviewer Developmental Biology, Ill. Med. Jour., Tchg. and Learning in Medicine, Acad. Medicine; contbr. articles to profl. jours. Office: So Ill Univ Sch Medicine 801 N Rutledge St Springfield IL 62794-9620

DORSEY, JAMES FRANCIS, JR., naval officer; b. Balt., May 28, 1934; s. James Francis Sr. and Elizabeth Rosalee (MacNamara) D.; m. Jeanne Lynch Hobbs, Aug. 16, 1958; children: James Francis III, Timothy Walker. Grad. in naval aviation, USN, Pensacola, Fla., 1956; degree in Polit. Sci., Naval Postgrad. Sch., Monterey, Calif., 1967. Commd. ensign USN, 1956, advanced through grades to VADM, 1991, comdg. officer 3 fighter squadrons, 1971-76, exec. officer USS Midway, 1976-78, comdg. officer USS Caloosehatchee, 1978-80, comdg. officer USS America, 1981-82, dir. joint program office, undersec. def. policy, dep. dir. def. mobilization systems planning activity, 1982-84, comdr. carrier group FOUR, and NATO comdr. carrier striking force Atlantic, 1984-85, dir. ops. U.S. European Command, 1985-87, dep. asst. chief naval ops. for plans, policy and ops., dep. ops. dep. for joint chief staff matters, 1987-89, comdr. 3d Fleet, 1989-91, ret., 1991; CEO Flag Ltd., Alexandria, Va., 1991—. Mem. Assn. Naval Aviation, U.S. Naval Inst., Chesapeake Bay Soc., Harbor Pt. Hoa (v.p.), Golden Eagle--The Early Pioneer Naval Aviators Assn. Office: PO Box 1119 Solomons MD 20688-1119 E-mail: j.dorsey@starpower.net.

DORSEY, JEREMIAH EDMUND, pharmaceutical company executive; b. Worcester, Mass., Oct. 15, 1944; s. Jeremiah Edmund and Mary Theresa D.; m. Nadia S. Vidach, Dec. 6, 1970; children: Todd Edmud, Jaime Erin, Megan Elizabeth, Kelly Ann. AB, Assumption Coll., 1966; MBA, Farleigh Dickinson U., 1978. With Johnson & Johnson, New Brunswick, N.J., 1969-88, nat. indsl. engring. mgr., 1975-76, supt. ops. and maintenance, 1976-88, dir. ops. mem. mgmt. bd., 1976-88; v.p. mktg., ops., gen. mgr. sales Johnson & Johnson Dental Products Co., New Brunswick, 1976-88; exec. v.p. The Kaelin Group, Bridgeton, N.J., 1988; pres. Towle Housewares Co., Newburyport, Mass., 1988-90; pres., CEO Foster Med. Supply, Inc., Dedham, Mass., 1990-92; group pres. Carvel Hall Corp., Crisfield, Md., 1990—; pres., COO West Pharm. Svcs. Inc., Lionville, Pa., 1992—. Corp. officer J.E. Dorsey Co., Carvel Hall Corp., Crisfield, Md.; bd. dirs. West Co. de Mex., Daikyo Seiko, Tokyo, Schubert Seals, Horsens, Denmark, DanBioSyst, Nottingham, Eng., Geschaftsfuherer West Co., Europe. Editor: Spl. Forces Assn. News. Active N.J. Commn. for Discharge Upgrade, Appalachian Trail Conf.; mem. alumni bd. dirs. Assumption Coll., adv. com. U. P.R. Sch. of Pharmacy; mem. mil. acad. selection com. U.S. Senate; vice chmn. N.J. Vietnam Vets Leadership Program; mem.Mercer County Pvt. Industry Coun. (N.J.), N.J. SR-92 Coalition. With U.S. Army, 1966-69, Vietnam. Decorated Silver Star, Bronze Star, 2 oak leaf clusters, Purple Heart, 4 oak leaf clusters, Army Commendation medal, Air medal with oak leaf cluster, Medal of Honor., Gallantry Cross, Vietnam; recipient Corp. Affirmative Action award 1981. Mem. DAV, KC, Sierra Club, Spl. Forces Assn., Smithsonian Assocs., Soc. First Divsn., Tiger Karate Soc., (Black Belt), Johnson & Johnson Mgmt. Club, Delta Epsilon Sigma. Roman Catholic. Office: 101 Gordon Dr Exton PA 19341-1320 Home: PO Box 910 Quechee VT 05059-0910

DORSEY, JOHN RUSSELL, journalist; b. Balt., Dec. 17, 1938; s. Charles Howard and Emma (Deputy) D. AB, Harvard U., 1961. Mem. staff Balt. Sun, 1962-81, 83-99, Sunday Sun book rev. editor, 1967-69, Sunday Sun restaurant critic, 1971-81, 84-86, Sun art critic, 1983-84, 86-99. Author: (with James D. Dilts) A Guide to Baltimore Architecture, 1973; Mount Vernon Place, 1983; editor: On Mencken, 1980. Mem. Md. Club, 14 West Hamilton Street Club, Harvard-Radcliffe Club. Home: 600 Edgevale Rd Baltimore MD 21210-1904

DORSEY, JOHN WESLEY, JR., university administrator, economist; b. Hagerstown, Md., June 13, 1936; s. John Wesley and Abbie Virginia (Wy) D.; m. Jeanne Ascosi; 1 child, Rachel Lynette. BS, U. Md., 1958; cert., London Sch. Econs., 1959; MA, Harvard U., 1962, PhD, 1964. Teaching fellow Harvard U., 1961, 62-63; asst. prof. econs. U. Md., 1963-66; asso. prof., dir. U. Md. (Bur. Bus. and Econ. Research), 1966-70; vice chancellor for adminstrv. affairs U. Md., College Park, 1970-77, acting chancellor, 1974-75, prof. econs., 1976-2001, prof. emeritus, 2001—; chancellor U. Md. Baltimore County, 1977-86; asst. to pres. U. Md. System, 1986-89. Cons. to govt. Md. Employees Credit Union Bd., 1975—. Rotary Found. scholar, 1958-59; Brookings research fellow, 1961-63 Mem. Phi Beta Kappa, Phi Kappa Phi, Omicron Delta Kappa. Home: 8234 Bubbling Spg Laurel MD 20723-1079 E-mail: john1@erols.com.

DORSEY, MARY ELIZABETH, lawyer; b. Florissant, Mo., July 4, 1962; d. Richard Peter Jr. and Dolores Irene (McNamara) D. BA in Acctg., Benedictine Coll., 1984; JD, St. Louis U., 1987. Bar: Mo. 1989, U.S. Dist. Ct. (we. dist.) Mo. 1989, U.S. Dist. Ct. (ea. dist.) Mo. 1990, U.S. Supreme Ct. 1994, U.S. Ct. Appeals (8th cir.) 1997. Rschr. Ind. Legal Rsch., Florissant, 1987-89; atty. assoc. Deeba Sauter Herd, St. Louis, 1989-98; ptnr. Ahlheim & Dorsey, LLC, St. Charles, 1998—. Bd. dirs. North County, Inc. Merit badge counselor St. Louis Area coun. Boy Scouts Am., 1988—, mem. com. Troop 748, mem. Order of the Arrow, 1992, Brotherhood, 1994; corr. sec. Florissant Twp. Open Dem. Club, 1989-91, sgt. at arms, 1991-2000; treas. Friends of Rick Dorsey, St. Louis, 1988, 90, 92, 96; mem. Dem. Com., Florissant Twp., 1996—. Mem.: ATLA, ABA, St. Charles County Bar Assn., Bar Assn. Met. St. Louis (lectr. law related edn. com. 1988—96), Mo. Assn. Trial Attys., Mo. Jaycees (state legal counsel 1997—99, dist. dir. 1998—99, region dir. 2000, membership v.p. 2001, state legal counsel 2002—03), Florissant Valley Jaycees (dir. 1993—94, treas. 1994—95, state dir. 1995—97, v.p. 1997—98), U.S.Jaycees (regional coord. 2002, Nat. Resource Team 2003). Democrat. Roman Catholic. Avocations: golf, camping, theatre. Office: Ahlheim & Dorsey LLC 2209 1st Capitol Dr Saint Charles MO 63301-5809 E-mail: med@ahlheimdorsey.com.

DORSEY, RICHARD PETER, III, lawyer, former state legislator; b. St. Louis, Sept. 7, 1959; s. Richard P. and Dolores (McNamara) D.; m. Elaine F. Dochnal; 1 child, Catherine Lian. BSBA, St. Louis U., 1981, MBA, JD, St. Louis U., 1984. Bar: Mo. 1985, U.S. Dist. Ct. (ea. and we. dists.) Mo. 1985, U.S. Supreme Ct. 1991, U.S. Ct. Appeals (8th cir.) 1996. Assoc. Niedner, Niedner, Ahlheim and Bodeux, St. Charles, Mo., 1985-90; ptnr. Niedner, Ahlheim, Bodeux and Dorsey, St. Charles, 1990-95; mem. Ahlheim & Dorsey LLC, St. Charles, Mo., 1995—, Mo. Ho. of Reps., 1991-93; spl. counsel Ohio Atty. Gen., 1999—2002. Bd. dirs. St. Charles County ARC, 1985-91, Eagle Scout Assn., St. Louis, 1987-93, 94-2000, Florissant Twp. Dem. Party, 1987—2003, Ferguson Twp. Dem. Club, 1994—2003, Florissant Valley Jaycees, 1990-95, 96-99, pres., 1995-96, life mem.; bd. dirs. Florissant Valley Shelter Workshop, 1990-2000, pres. 2000-02; bd. dirs. St. Louis High Alumni, 1994-2002, Ctr. for Pastoral and Profl. Svcs., 1994-2002, Florissant Rotary Club, 1997-98, St. Louis U. Sch. Bus. Adminstrn., 1995-2000, North County, Inc., 2001—; commr. Boy Scouts Am., St. Louis, 1984-92; mem. Cath. Commn. on Scouting, St. Louis, 1984—. Recipient Polaris award St. Louis Area coun. Boy Scouts Am., 1986, St. George award Boy Scouts Am., 1987; named One of Ten Outstanding Young Missourians, Mo. Jaycees, 1992. Mem. Bar Assn. Met. St. Louis, Mo. Bar Assn., St. Charles County Bar Assn., Assn. Trial Lawyers Am., Mo. Assn. Trial Attys., U.S. Jr. C. of C. (ambassador award 1998). Democrat. Roman Catholic. Home: 16 Harneywold Dr Saint Louis MO 63136-2402 Office: Ahlheim & Dorsey LLC 2209 1st Capitol Dr Saint Charles MO 63301-5809 E-mail: rpd@ahlheimdorsey.com.

DORSEY, WILLIAM WALTER, aerospace engineer, engineering executive; b. Long Branch, N.J., Dec. 23, 1934; s. Walter Gorman and Esther (Smith) D.; m. Lorraine Shirley Sanders, June 26, 1962; children: William W., Suzanne E. BSME, George Washington U., 1958, MS in Engring., 1965. Aerospace engr. Nat. Bur. Standards, Washington, 1960-65; sr. engr. Fairchild Hiller Corp., Germantown, Md., 1965-69; spacecraft mgr. European Space Agy., Noordwijk ann Zee, Holland, 1970-76; prin. engr. Fairchild Industries, Germantown, 1977-79; mem. tech. staff INTELSAT, Washington, 1979-85; dir. engring. Fairchild Space & Def. Co., Germantown, 1985-94; mech. systems mgr. Lockheed Martin Svcs., Lanham, Md., 1995; v.p. engring. Astral Inc., Rockville, Md., 1995-97; v.p. Kris Engring., North Potomac, Md., 1997-99; cons., 1999—2000; pres. D-Tech, 2001—. Contbr. articles to sci. jours.; patentee in field. Capt. USAF, 1958-60. Mem. AIAA, ASME. Achievements include development of unique design for the deployment control of the GEOS spacecraft 20 meter cable boom, of an analytical approach to the station keeping problem of colocating communication satellites in the same orbital location; design of numerous spacecraft thermal control subsystems including ATS-F, SERT-II, NIMBUS-D, and IMP-I using large computer programs; management of design, development and manufacture of instrument module for TOPEX Scientific Spacecraft.systems engineer for the first Hubble Telescope Repair Mission. Home and Office: 47740 My Way Saint Inigoes MD 20684-3000 E-mail: wwdsr@aol.com.

DORSHOW-GORDON, ELLEN, epidemiologist; b. St. Paul, Minn., May 16, 1946; d. Bennie and Goldie (Salita) Dorshow; m. Charles Gordon, May 15, 1977; 1 child, Gayle. BS in Med. Tech., U. Minn., 1968, MPH, 1983; postgrad., Western Mich. U., 2002—. Infection control coord. Samaritan Health Ctr., Detroit, 1980-83; cons Infection Control Resource Ctr., 1983-84; grad. rsch. asst. Rehab. Inst. Detroit, 1984-85; health and safety/mental health/nutrition coord. Renaissance Head Start, Detroit, 1984-86; infection control market specialist Calgon Vestal Labs., 1986-90; infection control coord. Sinai Hosp., Detroit, 1990-94; dir. quality svcs./infection control Great Lakes Rehab. Hosp., Southfield, Mich., 1994-95; epidemiologist Oakland County Health Divsn. Dept. Human Svcs., Pontiac, Mich., 1995-2000, Kalamazoo County Human Svcs. Dept., 2000—03, Jackson County Health Dept., Independence, 2003—. Mem. Nat. Sanitation Found. Task Group, 1997-99; mem. S.E. Mich. Epidemiology Com., Coun. of State and Territorial Epidemiologists; mem. 5th Dist. Med. Response Coalition; presenter in field. Contbr. articles to profl. jours. Vol. B'nai Brith Women Twin Cities Coun., 1973-80, Hadassah, Am. Arab and Jewish Friends. Recipient U. Minn. Alumnae Freshman scholarship, 1964, Calgon Exec. Dir's. award, 1986, Calgon Vestal Lab. Pacesetter award, 1987. Fellow Mich. Pub. Health Leadership Inst.; mem. NOW, ACLU, AARP, NAFE, Minn. Soc. Med. Tech. (bd. dirs.1972-75), Minn. Alumnae Assn., Assn. Practitioners Infection Control and Epidemiology (edn. com. chair 1983-85), Mich. Soc. Infection Control, Women and AIDS com., Am. Pub. Health Assn., Mich. Pub. Health Assn. Avocations: reading, net surfing, volunteering. Office: 313 S Liberty Independence MO 64055

DORSI, STEPHEN NATHAN, lawyer; b. Bklyn., June 2, 1947; s. Stephen Nathan and Fannie (Christopher) D.; m. Phyllis Elizabeth Blastervold, Aug. 12, 1976; 1 child, Michael. AA, Pasadena City Coll., 1968; BA, Calif. State U., L.A., 1970; JD, Golden Gate U., 1973. Bar: Calif. 1973, U.S. Dist. Ct. (no. dist.) Calif. 1973, U.S. Dist. Ct. (cen. dist.) Calif. 1974, U.S. Ct. Appeals (9th cir.) 1973. Sole practitioner, San Luis Obispo, Calif., 1974—. Bd. dirs. Sta. KCBX Pub. Radio, San Luis Obispo. Author: Horse Trader's Guide, 1987. Bd. bldg. trustee San Luis Obispo Art Ctr., 1976—; bd. dirs. KCBXNET (formerly SLONET), non-profit ISP, 1997. Avocations: mock trial coach, speech and debate judge. Home: PO Box 1253 San Luis Obispo CA 93406-1253 Office: Ste 6 1026 Chorro St San Luis Obispo CA 93401-3230 E-mail: trusts@DorsiLaw.com., trademark@DorsiLaw.com., RealProperty@DorsiLaw.com.

DORSKY, NATHANIEL, filmmaker; b. N.Y.C. Student, Antioch Coll., 1961, NYU, 1962. Instr. U. Calif., Berkeley, Stanford U. Filmmaker : Bend in the River, 1955; Ingreen, 1964; A Fall Trip Home, 1965; Summerwind, 1965; Hours for Jerome, 1966—82; Gaugerion in Tahiti, 1968 (Emmy award); Pneuma, 1976—83; Ariel, 1983; 17 Reasons Why, 1985—87; Alaya, 1976—87; Triste, 1974—96; What Happened to Kerouac?, 1985 (Emmy award); Vacations, 1992—98; Night Waltz: The Music of Paul Bowles, 1999 (Emmy award). Fellow Guggenheim fellow, 1997; grantee, NEA, Calif. Arts Coun.

DORSMAN, JERRY, addictions therapist, writer; b. St. Petersburg, Fla., Apr. 6, 1947; s. Henri Versigny Dorsman and Ruth Mae Haddick; m. Kathy Cunningham, Sept. 27, 1954; children: Molly Serena, Benjamin Theo. BA in Econs., U. Del., 1969, BA in Psychology, 1971. Baccalaurate Addictions Counselor, Nat. Bd. Addiction Examiners. Addictions therapist Upper Bay Counseling and Support Svcs., Elkton, Md., 1988—; mental health counselor, dir. drug and alcohol counseling ctr., 1971-79; various jobs in mktg., advt. and publicity, 1979-88. Freelance writer New Dawn Pub., Elk Mills, Md., 1992—. Author: How to Quit Drinking Without AA, 1991, How to Quit Drugs for Good, 1998; co-author: You Can Achieve Peace of Mind, 1994; contbr. articles to profl. jours. Avocations: hiking, dancing, yoga. Office: New Dawn Pub Box 71 Elk Mills MD 21920 E-mail: jdorsman@iximd.com.

DORTON, LOUISE, library director; b. Oklahoma City, Mar. 6, 1936; d. Charles William Blatt and Beula O. (Williams) Nelson; m. Jack M. Dorton, Sept. 30, 1956 (div. 1985); children: Brenda, Kenneth, Janet, Dana. BA, Douglass Coll., 1973; MLS, Rutgers U., 1974. Dir. Pemberton (N.J.) Community Libr., 1974-79, Johnson City (Tenn.) Pub. Libr., 1979-89; br. dir. Chattanooga Libr.-Northgate, 1989-90; owner, mgr. Spoken Word Book Shop, Knoxville, Tenn., 1990-93; dir. Darlington County Libr., Darlington, S.C., 1991-96, Granville County Library System, Oxford, N.C., 1996—. Mem. North Johnson City Bus. Club, 1985-89; bd. dirs. Johnson City Girls' Club, 1986-89, pres., 1987-88. Grantee N.J. State Libr., 1975, 76, 77, N.J. Labor Dept., 1976, Tenn. State Libr., 1986, 87, U.S. Dept. Edn., 1987. Mem. ALA, AAUW (pres. 1984-85), Oxford C. of C. (Leadership 2000 1986-87), Rotary. Office: Granville County Library System PO Box 339 210 Main St Oxford NC 27565-3321

DORTON, TRUDA LOU, medical, surgical and geriatrics nurse; b. Elkhorn Creek, Ky., Aug. 26, 1949; d. Clair Otis Parsons and Joyce Kidd; m. Eugene Anderson, Nov. 26, 1966 (dec. Apr. 1971); children: Gena Lynn, Richard Eugene; m. Leon Dorton, Dec. 15, 1972; children: Leondra Michelle, Jerald Thomas, Jonathan Layne. AS, student, Pikeville Coll., 1993. RN, Ky.; cert.

ACLS, PALS. Instr. computer usage Lookout (Ky.) Elem. Sch., 1983; water/sewage technician McCoy & McCoy Environ. Cons., Pikeville, Ky., 1984; owner Signs of the Times, Elkhorn City, Ky., 1979-89; sec.'s asst. humanities and social scis. divsns. Pikeville Coll., 1989-92; nurse aide Mud Creek Clinic, Grethel, Ky., 1992-93; charge nurse Jenkins (Ky.) Cmty. Hosp., 1993-94; case mix coord. Parkview Manor Nursing Home, 1994-95, minimum data set and nursing care plan coord., 1995; acute care nurse Harrison Meml. Hosp., Cynthiana, Ky., 1996—2002; dir. nursing Robertson County Health Care Facility, Mt. Olivet, Ky.; long-term care charge nurse Trilogy Health Ctr. at Harrison Meml. Hosp., Cynthiana; med. inpatient svcs. Floyd Meml. Hosp., New Albany, Ind. Vol. nurse aide Mud Creek Clinic, Grethel, 1989-92. Founder free blood pressure clinic H.E.L.P.S. Community Action Program, Hellier, Ky., 1983; co-founder H.E.L.P.S. Community Action Group, Hellier, 1983; mem. Ellis Island Centennial Commn., N.Y., 1986. Appalachian Honors scholar Pikeville Coll., 1989-92. Mem. Nat. Geog. Soc., Ky. Nursing Assn., Order Ky. Cols. (Honorable Ky. Col. 1989), Smithsonian Inst., Nat. Trust Hist. Preservation, World Wildlife Fund, Pikeville Coll. Alumni Assn. Democrat. Mem. Worldwide Ch. of God. Avocations: creating indian jewelry and wall hangings, classical music. Home: RR 1 Box 80 Mount Olivet KY 41064

DORWARD, JUDITH A. business ordering customer service representative; b. Hazleton, Pa., Apr. 16, 1941; d. Eugene Joseph and Dorothy Cecelia (Shields) McNertney; m. Douglas Dean Owens, Apr. 15, 1961 (div. 1968); children: Kevin Patrick Owens, Kelly Shawn Owens. AA, Lehigh County Community Coll., 1979; BA, Muhlenberg Coll., 1984; grad. in statis. process control, Process Mgmt. Inst., Inc., Mpls., 1986. Customer svc. clk. Pa. Power & Light Co., Allentown, 1959-61; mgr. Merle Norman Cosmetic Studios, Allentown and Bethlehem, Pa., 1968-70; adminstrv. clk. Pillsbury Co., East Greenville, Pa., 1970-85, ops. prodn. mgr., 1985-87, mgr. distbn. and prodn. control, 1987-93, chair labor rels. com., 1987-91, customer svc., vender liaison mgr., 1993-94; Pillsbury customer svc. rep. Americold Corp., Fogelsville, Pa., 1994-95; exec. field rep. Better Bus. Bureau Ea. Pa., 1996—2001; nat. bus. ordering customer svc. rep. West Corp., Reno, 2001—. Held various offices Gen. Fedn. Women's Clubs; former voting machine operator Lehigh County, Slatington, Pa. Mem.: Exec. Women Internat. (dir. publs. 1991, dir. membership 1992—93, v.p., pres.-elect 1994, pres. 1995), Phi Beta Kappa. Democrat. Roman Catholic. Avocation: foreign travel. Home: Apt 306 650 Record St Reno NV 89512 E-mail: JudyAD@aol.com.

DORWART, BRIAN CURTIS, geotechnical engineer, consultant; b. Corning, N.Y., June 9, 1949; s. Robert Morris and Nancy (Anderson) D.;m. Dana Joy Wallace, Dec. 8, 1979; children: Kelsey, Casey, Keeley, MacKenzie. BA in Geology, U. Rochester, 1972; MSCE, U. Mass., 1979. Registered profl. engr., Mass., N.H., Maine, Conn., Wash., N.Y., N.J.; registered profl. geologist engr., N.H. Field technician, driller Rochester (N.Y.) Drilling Co., 1972-75; engr., sr. project mgr. GZA GeoEnviron. Inc., Newton, Mass., 1979-87, sr. project mgr. Manchester, N.H., 1987-91; assoc. Shannon & Wilson, Inc., Seattle, 1991-94, sr. assoc., 1995—2003; v.p. Haley & Aldrich, Inc., Manchester. Republican. Home: 206 Joe English Rd New Boston NH 03070-3820 Office: Haley & Aldrich Inc 340 Granite St Manchester NH 03102

DORWART, DONALD BRUCE, lawyer; b. Zanesville, Ohio, Dec. 12, 1949; s. Walter G. and Katherine (Kachmar) D.; children: Claire Lauren, Hillary Beth. BA, Vanderbilt U., 1971; JD, Washington U., St. Louis, 1974. Bar: Mo. 1974, U.S. Dist. Ct. (ea. dist.) Mo. 1974. Assoc. Thompson Coburn LLP, St. Louis, 1974-79, ptnr., 1980—; dir. New Energy Corp. Ind., 1992-95. Contbr. articles to profl. jours. Mem.: ABA, FOCUS St. Louis (mem. selection com. 1990—91, mem. fin. com. 1990—2002, mem. cmty. policy com. 2000—02, bd. dirs. 2000—, treas. 2001—02, pres. 2002—), Bar Assn. Met. St. Louis (chair securities regulation com. 1979), Maritime Law Assn. U.S. (mem. maritime fin. com. 1980—, proctor), Noonday Club. Office: Thompson Coburn LLP One US Bank Plz Ste 3300 Saint Louis MO 63101-1643 E-mail: ddorwart@thompsoncoburn.com.

DORWART, ROGER WILSON, retired civil engineer; b. Pitts., Sept. 22, 1936; s. Harold Laird and Carolyn (Yeisley) D.; m. Elita Lucy Pols, July 3, 1965; children: Richard W., Jonathan A. BS, Trinity Coll., Hartford, Conn., 1959; BCE, Rensselaer, Troy, N.Y., 1960, MCE, 1963. Registered profl. engr., Vt., N.Y. Engr. in tng. Soil Testing Svcs., Inc., Chgo., 1960-61; grad. teaching asst. Rensselaer, Troy, N.Y., 1961-63; instr. U. Vt., Burlington, 1963-64; engr., pres. Knight Consulting Engrs., Inc., Williston, Vt., 1964-98; ret., 1998. Contbr. articles to New Eng. Builder and Jour. of Light Constrn. Mem. ASCE, Vt. Soc. Engrs. Home: 14 Sunset Cliff Rd Burlington VT 05401-1325

DOS, SERGE JACQUES, surgeon, physiology researcher; b. Paris, Jan. 24, 1934; came to U.S., 1957; s. Octave Pierre Marie and Fernande Lucienne (Daire) D.; m. Rasma Kupers, Aug. 19, 1966; children: Soshana, Yasmin, Maiya. M.D., U. Paris, 1964; Ph.D. in Physiology, U. Minn., 1965. Diplomate Am. Bd. Surgery. Lab. instr. physiology U. Minn., Mpls., 1962-65; instr. in surgery Cornell U., N.Y.C., 1971-73; asst. prof. surgery SUNY-Stony Brook, 1973, asst. prof. clin. physiology, 1973-76; surgeon St. John's Episcopal Hosp., Smithtown, N.Y., 1978-89; Mercy Hosp., Rockville Centre, N.Y., 1989-91, Beth Israel Med. Ctr., N.Y.C., 1991—; research com. VA Hosp., Northport, N.Y., 1974-76. Contbr. chpt. to book. USPHS trainee., 1962-65; various research grants NIH; various research grants Am. Heart Assn.; various research grants pvt. labs.; Laureate (Silver Medal) Faculty of Medicine U. Paris, 1966. Fellow ACS, N.Y. Acad. Scis.; mem. Am. Fedn. Clin. Research, AAAS, Am. Physiol. Soc., Assn. Acad. Surgery. Current Work: Physiology, history. Subspecialties: Surgery; Cardiac surgery. E-mail: sergedos@aol.com.

DOSANJH, DARSHAN S(INGH), aeronautical engineer, educator; b. Sultanwind, Punjab, India, Feb. 21, 1921; came to U.S., 1946, naturalized, 1965; s. S. Arur and Inder (Hundal) D.; m. Harwant K. Gill, Mar. 18, 1957; childen: Amrita K., Kiren K., Rajit S. BSC with honours in Physics, Punjab U., 1944, MS, 1945; MS in Aero. Engring., U. Mich., 1948; PhD in Aeros., Johns Hopkins U., 1953. Rsch. assoc. U. Md. Inst. Fluid Dynamics and Applied Math., 1955-56; assoc. prof. mech. and aerospace engring. Syracuse (N.Y.) U., 1956-62, prof., 1962-91, prof. emeritus, 1992—. Vis. prof. Coll. Aeros., Cranfield, Eng., 1961-62; Fulbright-Hayes sr. faculty research fellow and vis. prof. Southampton (Eng.) U., 1971-72. Editor: Modern Optical Methods in Gas Dynamics Research, 1971, Effects of Noise on Hearing, 1976; contbr. numerous articles to sci. jours. NATO fellow, 1967. Assoc. Fellow AIAA mem. Aeroacoustics Tech. Com. AIAA. mem. ASME, AAUP, Acoustical Soc. Am., Am. Physics Soc., Am. Soc. Engring. Edn. Home: 5176 Brockway Ln Fayetteville NY 13066-1704 E-mail: profdsd@aol.com.

DOSCHER, RICHARD JOHN, protective services official; b. Livermore, Calif., Aug. 31, 1952; s. Henry John and Violet Mary (Sutton) D.; m. Kathryn Laura Vierria, May 5, 1979; children: Cameron, Shannon. AS in Adminstrn. Justice, Yuba C.C., Maryville, Calif., 1987; BPA, U. San Francisco, 1991, MPA, 1993. From police officer to sgt. Yuba City (Calif.) Police Dept., 1977-85, sgt., watch commander, 1985-86, lt., divsn. commdr., 1986-89, lt., divsn. cmmdr. tech. svcs. and support, 1989-91, capt., divsn. cmmdr. field ops, 2d in command agy., 1991-93, capt., divsn. cmmdr. investigation, 2d in commd. agy., chief of police, 1995—. Adj. prof. ethics and professionalism/history Yuba C.C., 1997—. Bd. dirs. Yuba/Sutter Easter Seal Soc., 1988-96; vol. Calif Prune Festival, 1988—, Spl. Olympics, 1987—, Bok Kai Chinese Cultural Festival, 1993—, Yuba City Cmty. Theater, 1992—; adv. com. Adminstrn. of Justice Yuba Coll., 1993—; eucharistic min. St. Isidore's Cath. Ch., 1984—; hon. squadron comdr. security forces Beale AFB, 1998--. With USAF, 1972-76. Mem. Am. Soc. for Pub. Adminstrn., Calif. Assn. Police Tng. Officers, Calif. Police Chiefs Assn. (bd. dirs. 1998—), Calif. Peace Officers Assn., Peace Officers' Rsch. Assn. Calif., Yuba City Police Officers Assn. (past officer 1978-80), League of Calif. Cities (pub. safety com. 1996--), Kiwanis Club (bd. dirs., 2d v.p. Yuba City), Yuba City Health and Racquet Club. Avocation: astronomy. Office: Yuba City Police Dept 1545 Poole Blvd Yuba City CA 95993-2615

DOSÉ, FREDERICK PHILIP, JR., art historian, art and antiques appraiser, consultant, liquidator; b. Chgo., Sept. 9, 1946; s. Frederick P. and Alfa Elaine (Bahr) D.; m. Dee Hampton Keehn, June 8, 1985. BA, Northwestern U., 1968, MA, 1981. Faculty, art historian Northeastern Ill. U., Chgo., 1974-75, Colgate U., Hamilton, N.Y., 1976-80, Ray Coll., Chgo., 1984-97; fine arts & antiques appraiser for ins., probate, donation, estate, 1980—; art critic Chgo. Journal, 1982-85. Curator, dir. Chgo. br. Daniel B. Grossman Gallery, 1983; agt., broker Charles Lipson Antiquities, Jamaica Plain, Mass., 1985-98; ct. apptd. liquidator, 1987—; adv. bd. GotoSell.com., 1999—; appraiser Eppraisals.com., 1999-2001; expert, witness in field. Co-author: (with Dennis Minichello) Appraisal and Insurance of Fine Art and Antiques, 1997; author (catalogue) Wilson Irvine, 1984; contbr. articles to profl. jours. Judge furniture, painting, original comic art and antiquities Old Town Art Fair, Chgo., 1991. Mem. Coll. Art Assn., Internat. Soc. Appraisers (contbg. editor bull. 1981—), Newberry Libr. Assocs., Friends of Victoria & Albert Mus., Furniture History Soc. London, Soc. for Ancient Numismatics, Am. Numismatics Soc., Archaeol. Inst. Am., Napoleonic Soc. Am. E-mail: fdoseappraisals@comcast.net.

DOSHI, PARUL D. research scientist; b. Bombay, Sept. 23, 1960; arrived in U.S., 1983; d. Dhirajlal and Lata Doshi. CBSc in life sci. and biochemistry, Bombay U.; PhD, Rutgers U., 1988. Instr. Wash. U., St. Louis, 1994—96; prin. rsch. scientist Pharmacia Corp., St. Louis, 1996—. Recipient Ms. Oomen's prize for chemistry, Sophia Coll., 1979; fellow Gujarati Mandal fellow, 1979, postdoctoral fellow, Alfred P. Sloan Found., 1989—90; scholar Royal Western India Tennis Club Scholarship for Acad. Excellence, Sophia Coll., Bombay, 1980. Mem.: Am. Soc. Clin. Oncology, Am. Soc. Hematology. Office: Pfizer Corp 700 Chesterfield Pkwy W Chesterfield MO 63198 Office Fax: 636-737-6136. Business E-Mail: parul.doshi@pfizer.com.

DOSIK, GARY M. internist, oncologist, hematologist, educator; BS, U. Ill., Chgo., 1968, MD, 1971. Diplomate Am. Bd. Internal Medicine, Am. Bd. Med. Oncology, Am. Bd. Hematology. Internal medicine intern Rush-Presbyn.-St. Luke's Med. Ctr., 1971—72, resident in internal medicine, 1972—74; fellow in medical oncology, faculty assoc. M.D. Anderson Hosp. and Tumor Inst./U. Tex., 1976—78; pvt. practice, Encino, Calif., 1979—. Asst. clin. prof. medicine UCLA, 1981-84; assoc. clin. prof. medicine U. So. Calif., L.A., 1984—; chief staff Encino Tarzana Regional Med. Ctr., 1996-2000. Maj. USAF, 1994-96. Fellow ACP, Am. Soc. Hematology. Office: Hematology-Oncology Med Group 16133 Ventura Blvd Ste 470 Encino CA 91436 Fax: 818-784-3106. E-mail: gdosik@socal.rr.com.

DOSS, MARION KENNETH, lawyer; b. Wildwood, Fla., Sept. 25, 1939; s. Marion D. and Clide (Maxwell) D.; m. Addren Taylor, July 8, 1977; children—M. Kenneth Jr., Lisa Marie. B.S., Ga. Inst. Tech., 1961; LL.B., U. Ga., 1963. Bar: Ga. 1965, N.C. 1979, U.S. Dist. Ct. (no. dist.) Ga. 1977, U.S. Ct. Apls. (5th cir.) 1976, U.S. Sup. Ct. 1978. Ptnr., Northcutt, Edwards & Doss, Atlanta, 1963-71; v.p., gen. counsel Roy D. Warren, Atlanta, 1971-73; ptnr. Doss & Sturgeon, Atlanta, 1973-75; atty. Rollins, Inc., Atlanta, 1975-78; assoc. gen. counsel, asst. sec. Fieldcrest Mills, Inc., Eden, N.C., 1978-86; gen. counsel, sec., 1986—. Past pres., bd. dirs. Eden YMCA; past pres., bd. dirs. Rockingham County Arts Council. Mem. Assn. Trial Lawyers Am., Def. Research Inst., Ga. Assn. Plaintiffs Trial Attys., Corp. Counsel Assn. Greater Atlanta, Atlanta Bar Assn., N.C. Trial Lawyers Assn., ABA (corp. counsel com.), N.C. State Bar, Ga. Bar Assn., Rockingham County Bar Assn., Internat. Assn. of Ins. Counsel, Am. Textile Mfrs. Assn., N.C. C. of C. (past dir.). Democrat. Club: Meadow Greens Country. Office: Fieldcrest Mills Inc 326 E Stadium Dr Eden NC 27288-3523

DOS SANTOS, CARLOS, ambassador; Rep. to UN Republic of Mozambique Office: Permanent Mission Republic Mozambique 420 E 50th St New York NY 10022-8002

DOSSENA, TIZIANO THOMAS, environmental scientist; b. Milano, Italy, Sept. 19, 1952; arrived in U.S.A., 1968; s. Emilio Guiseppe Dossena and Cornelia Ginevra Zacchetti; m. Nicoletta Mita Dossena, July 28, 1979; children: William, Samantha. AS in Math., Kinsborough Coll., 1974; BA in Italian Studies, Queen's Coll., 1976; BS in Liberal Studies, Regents Coll., 1979; AAS in Environ. Control, N.Y.C. (N.Y.) Tech. Coll., 1995; BA in Environ. Sci., SUNY, 1998. Bldg. engr. Prentiss Properties, White Plains, NY. Editl. dir.: L'Idea Mag., 1989— (Journalism Premio Emigrazione award, 2000); contbr. articles to profl. jours. Mem. coun. Italian Govt., N.Y.C., 1997—. Recipient 1st prize, Assn. Culturale, 1980, Acad. Citta Dimodica, 2000. Mem.: N.Y. Acad. Scis., Am. Soc. Heating, Refrigeration, Air Conditioning Engrs. (Ashrae Student award 1995), Refrigeration Svc. Engrs. Soc.

DOSSIN, ERNEST JOSEPH, III, credit consulting company executive; b. Detroit, May 24, 1941; s. Ernest Joseph and Jean (Dickson) D.; m. Mary Jane Mortimore, July 24, 1965; children: Ernest Joseph IV, Tobias Alfred. BA in Bus., Valparaiso U., 1963; MBA in Fin., Fairleigh Dickinson U., 1978; postgrad., Walden U., 1995-98. Asst. store mgr. W.T. Grant, Norfolk, Va., 1967-68; dir. acctg. Am. Express, Trenton, N.J., 1968-69; asst. to chmn. Americana Hotels, N.Y.C., 1969, dir. casinos, 1970-72, corp. dir. credit, 1972-79; v.p. Myers Group, Rouses Point, N.Y., 1979-92; exec. v.p. Global Collections Inc., Plattsburgh, N.Y., 1985-93; pres. Dossin's Consulting Assocs., Plattsburg, N.Y., 1993—. Guest lectr. Plattsburgh State U., 1995; leader seminars in improving credit practices, 1985-91; adj. faculty SUNY, Plattsburgh, 1993—, C.C. of Vt., 1993—. Author: Strictly Business, 1991. Corp. bd. mem. Champlaine Valley Physicians Hosp., 1998—; treas. New Eng. Synod Evang. Luth. Ch. Am., 1997—; congl. pres. Redeemer Luth. Ch., Plattsburh, 1985-8 9, congl. v.p., 1990-93; bd. dirs. Oratorio Soc., pres. 1996-98; bd. dirs. Plat tsburgh, 1986-90; treas. Luth. Coll., Teaneck, N.J., 1975-79; mem. exec. com. Boy Scouts Am., Clinton County, 1994—. Mem. Nat. Assn. Credit Mgrs. (cited 1984, 85), Internat. Credit Assn. (exec.), Soc. Cert. Consumer Credit Execs. (cert. exec.), Plattsburgh C. of C., Soc. for Preservation Barbershop Quartet Singing (v.p. 1990-93), Mgmt. Club Plattsburgh (bd. dirs. 1987-91). Republican. Lutheran. Avocations: boating, barbershop quartet singing, football. Home: 1318 Lake Shore Rd Chazy NY 12921-1912 Office: Dossin's Consulting Assocs Plattsburgh NY 12901 E-mail: ernieD3@aol.com.

DOST, MARK W. lawyer; b. Attleboro, Mass., May 22, 1955; s. Raymond and A. Louise (Fraser) D.; m. Karen M. Sullivan, Aug. 1976; children: Christopher, Stephen, Gregory, Isaac. AB summa cum laude, U. Mass., 1978; JD cum laude, Boston Coll., 1981. Bar: Conn. 1981, U.S. Dist. Ct. Conn. 1986, U.S. Tax Ct. 1985. Atty. Gager & Henry, Waterbury, Conn., 1981-95; ptnr. Tinley, Nastri, Renehan & Dost, Waterbury, 1995—. Author: (with John V. Galiette) Planning for Retirement Benefit Distributions, 1995, 2d revised edit., 1999. Fellow Am. Coll. Trust and Estate Counsel; mem. ABA, Conn. Bar Assn. (exec. com., elder law sect. 1991—, exec. com., estates and probate sect. 1991—, chair elder law sect. 1994-96, chair publs. com. 1997-2000), Nat. Acad. Elder Law Attys. Office: Tinley Nastri Renehan Dost 60 N Main St Waterbury CT 06702-1403

DOSTART, PAUL JOSEPH, lawyer, investor and director; b. Iowa, Nov. 12, 1951; s. Leonard A. and Lois M. Dostart; m. Joyce A. Dostart; children: Zachariah Paul, Samuel Paul. BS, Iowa State U., 1973; JD, U. Houston, 1977; LLM in Taxation, NYU, 1978. Bar: Tex, 1977, Calif. 1978; CPA, Ill. Mng. ptr. Dostart, Clapp & Coveney LLP. Adj. prof. U. San Diego, 1986—90; bd. dirs. Q3DM Inc. Editor Houston Law Rev. Founder U. Houston Tax Law Soc.; bd. dirs. Neuroscis. Rsch. Found. Lasker scholar, NYU, Nat. Merit scholar. Fellow Am. Bar Found. (life), Am. Coll. Tax Counsel; mem. ABA (chmn. various subcoms. sect. taxation 1982—, exempt orgns. com. 1977—), Calif. Bar Assn. (tax and bus. sects.), San Diego County Bar Assn. (chmn. tax sect. 1989), San Diego Tax Practitioners Group, Am. Electronics Assn. (San Diego coun. exec. com. 1993-95), World Trade Assn. (bd. dirs.). Presbyterian. Office: Dostart Clapp & Coveney LLP Ste 970 4370 La Jolla Village Dr San Diego CA 92122-1249 E-mail: pdostart@sdlaw.com.

DOSTER, DANIEL HARRIS, retired counselor, minister; b. Moultrie, Ga., Dec. 15, 1934; s. Percy James and Juanita (Huff) D.; m. Robin Baker, Mar. 29, 1964; children: Christopher Robin Eagy, Sally Sheppard Powell. BA, Fla. State U., 1961; MS, Ft. Valley State U., 1984. Ordained minister, 1980; cert. criminal justice specialist with master addiction cert.; ordained deacon Episcopal Ch., 1980, ordained priest Episcopal Ch., 1997. Min., deacon Christ Episcopal Ch., Dublin, Ga., 1980-97, min., 1997—; counselor Dodge Correctional Instn. (now Dodge State Prison), Chester, Ga., 1984-87, Community Mental Health Ctr. Mid. Ga., Dublin, 1987-96. Pres. Ga. Retail Bakers Assn., Atlanta, 1964-65; chaplain Parkside Lodge Dublin, 1984-92, Al Sihah Shrine Temple, Macon, 1991-97. Pres. Cmty. Concert Assn., Dublin, 1985, 86, 87, bd. dirs., 1984-92; membership chmn. Al Sihah Shrine Temple, 1993-95, chaplain, 1992-97; wildlife habitat steward, 2000—. Mem. Kiwanis (pres. Dublin-Shamrock Club 1981, Kiwanian of Yr. 1981), Masons, Shriners, Laurens Shrine Club (Dublin, Ga., sec. 1992-93), Fla. State U. Mid. Ga. Seminole Club (bd. dirs. 1993, v.p. acad. affairs 1994, pres. 1998-99, master gardener), Kappa Alpha. Republican. Avocations: music, cookbook collecting, cooking, gardening. Home: 724 Victoria Cir Dublin GA 31021-5542 Fax: (478) 275-1499. E-mail: ddoster13@hotmail.com.

DOSTER, ROSE ELEANOR WILHELM, artist; b. Balt., May 11, 1938; d. Lewis Milford and Leeanora A. (Naylore) Wilhelm; m. Jesse Alfred Doster, Feb. 22, 1958; children: Jeffrey Allen, Roxane Elana. Cert. illustration and design, Art Instrn. Sch. Mpls., 1956; cert. design and painting, Md. Inst. Coll. Art., 1960, postgrad., 1960-62. Tchr. drawing, painting and ceramics, 1968—; craft supt. Carroll County 4H Fair, 1982, 83, 84, 85. Exhibited in one-woman shows: Hampstead Library Gallery, 1969, 70, Aurora Fed. Gallery, Balt., 1969, Goodman Gallery, Ellicott City, Md., 1971, Central Savs. Gallery, Towson, Md., 1971, Parkville (Md.) Library Gallery, 1972, Equitable Trust Bank Reisterstown Gallery, Balt., 1973, Hanover Art Guild, 1981, Md. Ctr. Pub. Broadcasting, 1982, Kent Island Fedn. of Art Gallery, 1990, Heron Point Gallery, 2003, others; exhibited in group shows: St. John's Coll., Johns Hopkins, Goodman Gallery, Slayton House, Columbia, Md., Paynter Gallery, Rehoboth, Del., Hilltop House, Harpers Ferry, W.Va., 1974-86, Balt. Mus. Art Downtown Gallery, 1976, Towsontowne Arts Festival, 1977-79, 82, 84, McDonough Sch.'s Cleve. Gallery, 1978, Unicorn Gallery, 1979, Canon Bldg. U.S. Ho. of Reps., Washington, 1981-82, Md. State NLAPW, Art Exhibit, Balt., 1983, Annapolis, 1985, Md. chpt. Nat. League Am. Penwomen, 1983, Easton Art Acad., 1987, 88, 89, 90, 91, 92, 93, 94, 95, 96, 97, International Craft Show, Cordova, 1988, Dorchester County Art Showcase, 1989, 90, 91, 92, 93, 94, 95, 96, 97, Salisbury-Wicomico Arts Festival, 1993, St. Michaels Maritime Mus. Show, 1992-93, 94, 95, Chesapeake Coll. Art Show, 1987, 88, 89, 90, 91, 92, 93, 94, 95, Dorchester Educators Art Show, 1990, 91, 92, 94, 95, 96, 97, Working Artists Forum juried show, 1995, 96, 97, 98, 99. Active Boy Scouts Am., Girl Scouts U.S.; leader Shiloh Clovers 4-H Club, 1983-84; trustee Balt. Mus. Art; pres. Carroll County Arts Coun., 1975-76, 94; v.p. Caroline County Arts Coun., 1993, pres., 1994; judge Montgomery Cunty Fair, 1984, 86, 87, Howard County Fair, 1985, Balt. County 4-H Fair, Frederick County Fair, 1988, Caroline County Fair, 1989, 90, Easton Art Acad. Children's Exhibit, 1994, Federation Women's Club of Denton Children's Competition, 1992-93, 94, Md. State fair, 1993, 94, 95; mem. bd. Carroll County Farmers Market—crafts; elected mem. Working Artists Forum, 1987-88, 89, 90, 91, 97, 93—, sec., 1992-93, treas., 1993-94, 95, 96, 97, 98, 99. Recipient numerous awards including George Peabody award, 1960, Judges Choice award Dorchester Educators Art Show, 1990, Best of Painters award Artisan's Fair Queen Anne Rotary Club, 1992, Nat. Potpourri Contest winner Floral and Nature Crafts Mags., 1995, 96, medal from Gov. and First Lady of Md., 1998, 2nd price Wash. Coll. Juried Art Show, 2000. Mem. Nat. League Am. Pen Women (bd. art chmn. 1970-72, 1st v.p. 1972-74, pres. Carroll br. 1974-76, br. historian 1976-88, 89, 90, 91-94, 95-, 96, branch achievement chmn. 1988-90, 92-94, br. newsletter editor 1992-93, 94, state historian 1982-84, 88-90, 93, chmn. tri-state miniature art show 1993, chmn. 50th anniversary Show 1995), Working Artist Forum (treas. 1994, 95, 96, 97, 98, 99, 2000, chmn. miniature painting show 1997), Kent Island Fedn. of Art, Chestertown Art League, Rehoboth Art League, Md. Inst. Art Alumni Assns., Balt. Watercolor soc. (assoc.), Carroll County Hist. Soc. (bd. dirs. 1986—), Caroline County Hist. soc., Portrait Soc. Am., Betsy Patterson Doll Club, Lady Baltimore Doll Club, Miss Carroll's Doll Study Club (founder, pres.), Ea. Shore Miniature Enthusiasts Club (founder, pres.), Ea. Shore Doll Study Club (histroian 1993, libr. 1995, 96), Oil Painters Am. Home: 9472 Quail Run Rd Denton MD 21629-1731

DOSWALD, HERMAN KENNETH, German language educator, academic administrator; b. Oakland, Calif., Mar. 24, 1932; s. Herman and Caroline Josephine (Mello) D.; m. Ruth Eugenie Hannes, Dec. 21, 1956; children: Caroline Susan, Stephanie Ann. AA, U. Calif., Berkeley, 1952, BA, 1955; MA, U. Wash., 1959, PhD, 1965. Instr., dept. German and Russian Oberlin (Ohio) Coll., 1959-60; instr., dept. German U. Wash., Seattle, 1960-61; instr., dept. fgn. langs. Seattle U., 1961-62; asst. prof. German U. Kans., Lawrence, 1964-67; asst., then assoc. prof., dept. fgn. langs. Fresno (Calif.) State U., 1967-72; prof., chmn. dept. German and Russian Kent (Ohio) State U., 1972-79; head dept. fgn. langs. Va. Poly. Inst. and State U., Blacksburg, 1979-84, assoc. dean adminstrn., Coll. Arts & Scis., 1984-86, interim dean Coll. Arts & Scis., 1986-87, dean, 1987-93, prof. German, 1993-96, prof. German, dean Coll. Arts & Scis. emeritus, 1996—. Contbr. articles to profl. jours. Served to 1st lt. U.S. Army, 1962-64. Adenauer scholar, Munich, Fed. Republic Germany, 1953-54; Fulbright fellow, Vienna, Austria, 1958-59. Mem. Phi Beta Kappa, Phi Kappa Phi, Omicron Delta Kappa. Home: 4592 Preston Forest Dr Blacksburg VA 24060-8660 E-mail: doswald@vt.edu.

DOTAN, Z. medical researcher, urologist; b. Tel-Aviv, Israel, Dec. 28, 1964; s. Uri and Aviva Dotan; m. Sigal Dotan, Sept. 11, 1991; children: Arad, Inbar, Shaked, Avishag. MD, Sackler Sch of Medicine, Israel, 1994; PhD, Sackler Sch. of Medicine, 2003. Resident Te-Hashomer Hosp., Ramat-Gar, Israel, 1996—2000, physican, 2001—02; fellow in urology MSKCC, NYC, 2002—. Gene Chromosome and Cancer, 2000. Recipient 1st Cap-Cure at the annual meeting of the Am. Urological Assn., Soc. of Urol-oncology, 2003, ASCO Merit award, Am. Assn. of Clin. Oncology, 2003. Avocations: sailing, fishing. Home: 1233 York Ave Apt 17N New York NY 10021 Office: Meml Sloan-Kettering Cancer Ctr 353 E 68th St 6th Fl New York NY 10021

DOTI, FRANK JOHN, law educator, consultant; b. Chgo., May 24, 1943; s. Roy and Carmelina Doti; m. Margaret Ann Elliott, Dec. 21, 1973; children: Matthew, Emily, Jillian. BS in Accountancy, U. Ill., Urbana, 1966; JD, Ill. Inst. Tech., 1969. Bar: Ill. 1969, U.S. Dist. Ct. (no. dist.) Ill. 1969, Calif. 1985, U.S. Tax Ct. 1987, Colo. 1992; cert. tax law specialist, Calif. Bd. Specialization; CPA, Ill. Assoc. McDermott, Will & Emory, Chgo., 1969-74; tax dir. CF Industries, Inc., Long Grove, Ill., 1974-77; v.p., tax dir. Leo Burnett Co., Inc., Chgo., 1977-82; prof. law Western State Law Sch., Fullerton, Calif., 1982-96, Chapman U. Sch. Law, Orange, Calif., 1996—, William P. Foley, II chair in corp. and tax law, 2002. Contbr. articles to law revs. and legal jours. and mags. Bd. dirs., Ill. Inst. Tech.-Chgo. Kent Alumni Assn., 1979-83. Recipient 1st place award Moot Ct. Chgo.-Kent Law Sch., 1967, Corpus Juris award, 1969. Mem. ABA (com. on tchg. taxation), Calif. Bar Assn. Home: 7431 E Mill Stream Cir Anaheim CA 92808-1320 Office: Chapman U Sch Law Orange CA 92866

DOTO, IRENE LOUISE, statistician; b. Wilmington, Del., May 7, 1922; d. Antonio and Teresa (Tabasso) D. BA, U. Pa., 1943; MA, Temple U., 1948, Columbia U., 1954; M of Quantitative Sys., Ariz. State U., 1986. Engring. asst. RCA-Victor, 1943-44; rsch. asst. U. Pa., 1944; actuarial clk. Penn Mut. Life Ins. Co., 1944-46; instr. math. Temple U., 1946-53; commd. lt. health svcs. officer USPHS, 1954, advanced through grades to capt., 1963; statistician Communicable Disease Ctr., Atlanta, 1954-55, Kansas City, Kans., 1955-67; chief statis. and publ. svcs., ecol. investigations program Ctr. for Disease Control, Kansas City, 1967-73, chief statis. svcs., divsn. hepatitis and viral enteritis Phoenix, 1973-83; statis. cons., 1984—. Mem. adj. faculty Phoenix Ctr., Ottawa U., 1982-98. Mem. APHA, Am. Statis. Assn., Ariz. Pub. Health Assn., Ariz. Coun. Engring. and Sci. Assn. (officer 1982-90, pres. 1988-89), Primate Found. Ariz. (mem. animal care and use com. 1986—), Bus. and Profl. Women's Club Phoenix, Mil. Officers Assn. Am. (state sec.-treas. 1995-96), Ariz. SPCA (bd. dirs. 2000-01), Sigma Xi, Pi Mu Epsilon. Office: PO Box 22197 Phoenix AZ 85028-0197

DOTRICE, ROY LOUIS, actor; b. Guernsey Channel Isles, U.K., May 26, 1929; came to U.S., 1967; s. Louis and Neva (Wilton) D.; m. Kay Newman, May 8, 1947; children: Michele, Karen, Yvette. Student, Elizabeth Coll., Guernsey Channel Isles. Actor in leading roles Royal Shakespeare Co., Eng., 9 yrs.; actor 12 West End, London and Broadway prodns. including A Life (Tony award nomination), Moon for the Misbegotten (Tony, Critics Circle, Drama Desk, Jefferson awards), others; actor: (TV series) Beauty and the Beast, Going to Extremes, Picket Fences, Mr. and Mrs. Smith, Sliders, Madigan Men. With RAF, 1940-45, ETO. Recipient award Guiness Book of World Records for World's Longest Running One-Person Show "Brief Lives", Best Actor award "B.A.F.T.A.", 1969, Emmy award "Caretaker", 1966. Mem. Garrick Club (London). Avocations: fishing, riding. Office: Award Assocs 9720 Wilshire Blvd Beverly Hills CA 90212-2021 E-mail: RoyDotrice@aol.com.

DOTSON, DONALD L. lawyer; b. Rutherford County, N.C., Oct. 8, 1938; s. Herman A. and Lottie E. (Hardin) D. AB, U. N.C., 1960; JD, Wake Forest U., 1968. Bar: N.C., Pa., D.C., U.S. Supreme Ct. Atty. NLRB, 1968-73, chmn., 1983-87; labor counsel Westinghouse Electric Corp., 1973-75; labor atty. Western Electric Co., 1975-76; chief labor counsel Wheeling-Pitts. Steel Corp., 1976-81; asst. sec. labor, 1981-83, 2001—; pvt. practice law, 1987-91; sr. v.p. Beverly Enterprises, 1991—2001; pvt. practice, 2001—. Served with USN, 1960-65. Republican. Episcopalian. Home: RD Louisa VA Office: 6914 W Grace St Richmond VA 23226

DOTSON, GEORGE STEPHEN, drilling company executive; b. Okemah, Okla., Dec. 25, 1940; s. Hilmer C. and Alma Lucille (McGee) D.; m. Phyllis A. Nickerson, Aug. 17, 1963; children: Sarah, Grant. BS, M.I.T., 1963; MBA, Harvard U., 1970. Asst. to pres. Helmerich & Payne, Inc., Tulsa, 1970-73; v.p. Helmerich & Payne (Peru) Drilling Co., 1974-75, Helmerich & Payne Internat. Drilling Co., 1976-77, pres., chief operating officer, 1977—; v.p. drilling Helmerich & Payne, Inc., 1977—, also bd. dirs. Bd. dirs. Atwood Oceanics, Inc., Varco Internat., Inc.; chmn. Internat. Assn. Drilling Contractors, 1995. Served to capt. U.S. Army, 1964-68. Decorated Bronze Star. Office: Helmerich Payne Internat Drilling Co 1579 E 21st St Tulsa OK 74114-1398

DOTSON, JOHN LOUIS, JR., former newspaper publisher; b. Paterson, N.J., Feb. 5, 1937; s. John Louis and Evelyn Elizabeth (Nelson) D.; m. Peggy Elaine Burnett, Apr. 4, 1959; children: John, Damon, Christopher, Brandon, Leslie. BS, Temple U., 1958, Doctor of Journalism (hon.), 1981. Reporter Newark News, 1959-64; gen. assignment reporter Detroit Free Press, 1965; with Newsweek Mag., 1965-83; corr. Detroit, 1965-69, L.A., 1969-70; bur. chief, 1970-75; news editor N.Y.C., 1976-77; sr. editor, 1977-83; asst. to exec. editor Phila. Inquirer, 1983-84; exec. asst. to pres. Phila. Newspapers, Inc., 1984-85, dir. night ops., 1986-87; pres., pub. Daily Camera, Boulder, Colo., 1987-92; pub. Akron Beacon Journal, Akron, Ohio, 1992—2001. Bd. dirs. Robert C. Maynard Inst. Journalism Edn., 1974—, treas., 1974-78, chmn., 1980-84, 93-99; mem. Pulitzer Prize Bd., 1991-2000; mem. nat. adv. bd. Poynter Inst. for Media Studies, 1994-2000; bd. dirs. Nat. Conf. for Cmty. Justice, Mus. Arts Assn. Mem. bd. visitors John S. Knight Fellowships, Stanford U., 1983—, Sch. Journalism, U. N.C., Chapel Hill, 1987—; mem. adv. bd. Sch. Journalism and Mass Comms., U. Colo., Boulder, 1988—; trustee Akron Cmty. Found., 1993-2000, chmn., 1995-96; mem. exec. com. Akron Regional Devel. Bd.; mem. governing bd. Summit Edn. Initiative.

DOTSON, ROBERT CHARLES, news correspondent; b. St. Louis, Oct. 3, 1946; s. William Henry and Dorothy Mae (Bailey) D.; m. Linda Gay Puckett, July 1, 1972; 1 child, Amy Michelle. BS in Journalism and Polit. Sci., Kans. U., 1968; MS in TV, Syracuse U., 1969. News dir. Sta. KANU-FM, Lawrence, Kans., 1966-68; reporter, photographer, documentary producer KMBC-TV, Kansas City, Mo., 1968; dir. spl. projects WKY-TV, Oklahoma City, 1969-75; corr. WKYC-TV, Cleve., 1975-77; network corr. NBC News, Dallas, 1977-79; corr. Prime Time Saturday Atlanta, 1979-80; corr. Today Show, 1980-85; nat. corr. NBC Nightly News, Atlanta, 1985-2000, Dateline NBC, 1985—; spl. nat. corr. NBC News Today Show, N.Y.C., 2000—. Vis. prof. journalism U. Okla., 1969-73; faculty affiliate Colo. State U., Ft. Collins; writer, host Bob Dotson's Am., travel channel and NBC Superchannel, 1996-98. Author: ...in Pursuit of the American Dream, 1985 (George Washington Honor medal Freedom Found. 1985), Make it Memorable, 2000; documentaries include Through the Looking Glass Darkly, 1974 (Emmy award, RFK award), The Urban Reservation, 1975 (RFK award DuPont-Columbia Journalism award), Still Got Life to Go, 1972, (Emmy nomination), Smoke and Steel, 1973 (Emmy nomination), The Sunshine Child, 1983 (Emmy nomination), People Who Make a Difference, 1987 (Emmy nomination), Bob Dotson's NBC Nightly News Stories, 1987 (Gabriel award 1987), Bob Dotson, 1987 (Media Acess award 1987), Assignment Am., 1989 (Nat. Headliners award 1990, Emmy nomination, 1989, Ohio State award 1989), El Capitan's Courageous Climbers, 1990 (Cine Golden Eale, Italian Film Festival grand prize, Union of Mountain Climbers grand prize, Wilbur award U.S. Film Festival 1990, 91, Cine Grand Prize Best Am. Non-Fiction Film, 1991, Bombay, India Internat. Film Festival Grand Prize, 1991, Japan, Spain Internat. Sprots Film Fest. Grand Prize, 1991, Juan Antonio Samaranch Spl. Citation, 1991), The River's Edge, Dateline NBC, 1994 (Emmy award), Susan Smith Coverage, 1994 (Clarion award), Bob Dotson's America Closeup, 1994 (Clarion award), The River's Edge, 1994 (Emmy award), Bob Dotson's Am., 1996. Recipient numerous awards including Elec. Media Grand Prize Nat. Assn. Yr. Round Edn., 1993, Gabriel Grand Prize Bob Dotson's Am. Diary, 1992, TV of Merit award DAR, 1985, Gabriel award Nat. Cath. Assn. Broadcasters, 1984, Clarion award Women in Communications, 1983, Epilepsy Found. Am. award, 1977, Silver medal Internat. Film and TV Festival of N.Y., 1976, Nat. Headliner award, NBC Today Show, 2001, Edward R. Murrow award for best network news writing Radio and TV News Dirs. Assn., 1999, for best reporting, 2001, 03, Diversity award, Columbia U., 2001, Emmy award for best story in regularly scheduled broadcast, 2003. Mem. Nat. Acad. TV Arts and Scis., Nat. Press Photographers Assn. (The Sprague Meml. award 1989), Writers Guild Am., Internat. Platform Assn., Radio and TV News Dirs., Explorers Club (N.Y.C.), Sigma Delta Chi. Avocation: writing. Office: NBC News-Today Show Ste 1028W 30 Rockefeller Plz New York NY 10112-0002 E-mail: dotson@nbc.com.

DOTT, ROBERT HENRY, JR., geologist, educator; b. Tulsa, June 2, 1929; s. Robert Henry and Esther Edgerton (Reed) Dott; m. Nancy Maud Robertson, Feb. 1, 1951; children: James, Karen, Eric, Cynthia, Brian. Student, U. Okla., 1946-48; BS, U. Mich., 1950, MS, 1951; PhD, Columbia U., 1956. Exploration geologist Humble Oil & Refining Co., Ariz., Oreg., Wash., 1954-56, 1958; mem. faculty U. Wis.-Madison, 1958-94, prof. geology, 1966-84, Stanley A. Tyler Disting. prof., 1984—, chmn. dept. geology and geophysics, 1974-77, emeritus prof., 1994—. Vis. prof. U. Calif., Berkeley, 1969; Cabot disting. vis. prof. U. Houston, 1986—87; NSF sci. faculty fellow Stanford U. and U.S. Geol. Survey, 1978, U. Colo., 1979; acad. visitor Imperial Coll., Oxford U., London, 1985—86, Adelaide U., Australia, 1992; cons. Roan Selection Trust, Ltd., Zambia, 1967, Atlantic-Richfield Co., 1983—85, Hubbard Map Co., 1984—86; lectr. Bur. Petroleum and Marine Geology, China, 1986; Erskine fellow, vis. prof. Canterbury U., New Zealand, 1987; Woodford-Ellis lectr. Pomona Coll., 1994. Co-author: Evolution of the Earth, 7th edit., 2003; contbr. articles to profl. jours. 1st lt. USAF, 1956—57. Recipient Outstanding Tchr. award, Wis. Student Assn., 1969, Ben. H. Parker award, Am. Inst. Profl. Geologists, 1992; fellow AEC, Columbia U., 1956. Fellow: Edinburgh Geol. Soc. (hon. corr. 1997), Geol. Soc. Am. (chmn. history of geology divsn. 1990, councilor 1992—94, History of Geology award 1995, L.L. Sloss award 2001); mem.: AAAS, History of Earth Sci. Soc. (pres. 1990), Internat. Assn. Sedimentologists, Soc. Econ. Paleontologists and Mineralogists (sec.-treas. 1968—70, v.p. 1972—73, pres. 1981—82, hon., William H. Twenhofel medal 1993), Am. Assn. Petroleum Geologists (Pres.'s award 1956, Disting. Svc. award 1984, Disting. lectr. 1985), Sigma Xi (Disting. lectr. 1988—89). Unitarian Universalist. Office: U Wis Dept Geology and Geophysics 1215 W Dayton St Madison WI 53706-1600 E-mail: rdott@geology.wisc.edu. *To understand the earth's past, which no human could witness, has long seemed to me the most exciting challenge imaginable. It is like a great Sherlock Holmes mystery story.*

DOTTEN, MICHAEL CHESTER, lawyer; b. Marathon, Ont., Can., Feb. 23, 1952; came to U.S., 1957; s. William James and Ona Adelaide (Sheppard) D.; m. Kathleen Curtis, Aug. 17, 1974 (div. July 1991); children: Matthew Curtis, Tyler Ryan; m. Cheryl Calvin, Apr. 16, 1994. BS in Polit. Sci., U. Oreg., 1974, JD, 1977. Bar: Idaho 1977, Oreg. 1978, U.S. Dist. Ct. Idaho 1977, U.S. Dist. Ct. Oreg. 1978, U.S. Ct. Appeals (9th cir.), U.S. Ct. Appeals (D.C. cir.) 1987, U.S. Ct. Claims 1986, U.S. Supreme Ct. 1996. Staff asst. to Senator Bob Packwood, U.S. Senate, Washington, 1973-74; asst. atty. gen. State of Idaho, Boise, Idaho, 1977 78; chief rate counsel Bonneville Power Adminstrn., Portland, Oreg., 1978-83; spl. counsel Heller, Ehrman, White & McAuliffe, Portland, 1983-84, ptnr., 1985-98, 99—; gen. counsel PG&E Gas Transmission, N.W. Corp., Portland, 1998-99; co-chair Energy Nat. Practice Group, 2003—. Utility com. mem. Ctr. for Pub. Resources, N.Y.C., 1992—. Coun. Emanual Hosp. Assocs., Portland, 1988-92; bd. dirs. William Temple House, 1995-99, chmn. devel. com., 1996-98, v.p., 1997-98, pres., 1998-99; active Portland Interneighborhood Trans. Rev. Commn., 1986-88; vestryman Christ Episcopal Ch., Lake Oswego, Oreg., 1999-2003, sr. warden, 2001-03. Hunter Leadership scholar U. Oreg., 1973, Oreg. scholar, 1970. Mem. ABA (chmn. electric power com. sect. natural resources 1985-88, coun. liaison energy com. 1990-93, coordinating group on energy law 1992-96), Fed. Bar Assn. (pres. Oreg. chpt. 1989-90, Chpt. Activity award 1990, Pres. award 1988-89), Oreg. State Bar (chmn. dispute resolution com. 1986-87), U. Oreg. Law Sch. Alumni Assn. (pres. 1989-92), Arlington Club, Multnomah Athletic Club. Democrat. Episcopalian. Avocations: snow skiing, golf, hiking, travel, racquetball. Office: Heller Ehrman White & McAuliffe 200 SW Market St Ste 1750 Portland OR 97201-5722

DOTTIN, ROBERT P. biologist, educator; b. Trinidad, West Indies, May 23, 1943; BS in Microbiology (with hons.), U. Toronto, 1968, MS in Med. Biophysics, Med. Cell Biology, 1970, PhD in Med. Genetics, 1974. Asst. prof. biology Johns Hopkins U., 1976—82, assoc. prof. biology, 1982—87; prof. biology CUNY, 1986—, program coord. ctr. study gene structure and function, 1988—98, program dir., 1998—. Presenter in field; adv. coun. Nat. Inst. Gen. Med. Sci., 1991—92; vis. prof. U. Copenhagen, 1975. Contbr. articles to profl. jours. Named Disting. Scientist, U. Calif. Berkeley, 1996, Howard U., 1997; recipient Fogarty Internat. Sr. Collaboration award, 1992—95; fellow Centennial fellow, Med. Rsch. Coun. Can., 1974—76, Postdoc. fellow, MIT, 1974—76, Fogarty Sr. Internat. fellow, 1991—92; grantee, March of Dimes, 1980—82, Am. Heart Assn., 1982—83, NSF, 1977—79, NIH, 1979—, NSF, 1983—84, NSF1984, 1987, NSF, 1991—94, Travel grantee, NATO, 1991—94. Mem.: AAAS, Am. Soc. Human Genetics, Am. Soc. Cell Biology, Am. Soc. Biochemistry Molecular Biology (membership com.), Coalition Advancement Blacks Biomed. Sci. (founding, editor, pub. resource dir.), Sigma Xi (exec. com.). Office: Dept Biol Sci Hunter Coll CUNY 695 Park Ave New York NY 10021

DOTTO, PETER ATTILIUS, retired marine corps officer, defense consultant; b. Milan, June 30, 1949; s. Gianni Abraham and Renata Carla (Zagni) D.; m. July 15, 1978 (div. May 1994); children: John, Nicole, Regina, Anthony, Donna, Joseph; m. Marilyn Anne Capotosto, Sept. 12, 1999. BS in Biology, U. Dayton, 1971; MS in Govt., Campbell U., 1984; MA in Nat. Security-Strategic Studies, Naval War Coll., Newport, R.I., 1991. Commd. 2d lt. USMC, 1971, advanced through grades to col., 1992; dir. future ops. Unified Task Force, Somalia, 1992-93; comdr. Hdqs. Bn., 1st Marine Divsn., Camp Pendleton, Calif., 1993-94; vice dir. strategy, plans and policy U.S. So. Command, Panama, 1994-95; asst. chief staff for spl. ops. tng., exercises-simulations I Marine Expeditionary Force, Camp Pendleton, 1996-98, chief staff, 1998; ret., 1998; sr. exec. officer Avatar Sentry, Ltd., Hollywood, Fla., 1998; program dir. M2 Techs., Inc., West Hyannisport, Mass., 1999—. Adj. prof. Marine Corps U., San Diego, 1999—; cons. Naval Sea Sys. Command, Corona, Calif., 1999, Sierra Cybernetics, Yorba Linda, Calif., 1999. Contbr. articles to profl. jours. Decorated Def. Superior Svc. medal; recipient merit award U.S. Dept. State, 1993. Mem. DVA (life), Ret. Officers Assn., 1st Marine Divsn. Assn. (legal officer 1999-2000), Am. Legion, Marine Corps Assn. Republican. Roman Catholic. Avocations: hiking, travel. Office: M2 Techs Inc 1444 Eagle Glen Escondido CA 92029 Fax: 760-781-5539. E-mail: dottop@cox.net.

DOTY, DALE VANCE, educator, psychotherapist, hypnotherapist; b. Rochester, N.Y., Apr. 11, 1954; s. Charles F. and E. Alta (Smith) D.; m. Kristine R. Krystan, Aug. 19, 1989; children: Bryce, Kimberly, David. BS, U. Rochester, 1974, MA, 1976; PhD, City U., 1990. Registered hypnotist. Tchr. N.Y. State Edn. Dept., Albany, N.Y., 1974—; psychotherapist Confidential Interpersonal Counseling, Hemlock, N.Y. Prof. psychology Monroe C.C., Rochester, St. John Fisher Coll., Rochester Inst. Tech., SUNY, Geneseo; coord./cons. AKSED Rehab.; cons. Highland Hosp.; drug edn. coord. Marketview Heights Assn.; speaker weekly radio program, 1990. Contbr. articles to profl. jours.; author ednl. progs. in field. EMT Henrietta (N.Y.) Vol. Ambulance, 1975-90, Honeoye Falls (N.Y.) Vol. Ambulance, 1979-85; counseling specialist Chances and Changes/Domestic Violence, Geneseo, N.Y., 1990-98; instr. Nat. Red Cross. Mem. Am. Assn. Counseling (assoc.), Am. Mental Health Counselors, Am. Coll. Pers. Assn., Am. Psychol. Practitioners Assn., Internat. Counselors and Therapists ASsn., Nat. Headache Found. Avocations: fishing, hunting, camping, music. Home: 5310 Curtis Rd Hemlock NY 14466-9619 Office: Confidential Interpersonal Counseling 5310 Curtis Rd Hemlock NY 14466-9619 E-mail: ddoty@monroecc.edu.

DOTY, DAVID SINGLETON, federal judge; b. Anoka, Minn., June 30, 1929; BA, JD, U. Minn., 1961; LLD (hon.), William Mitchell Coll. Law. Bar: Minn. 1961, U.S. Ct. Appeals (8th and 9th cirs.) 1976, U.S. Supreme Ct. 1982. V.p., dir. Popham, Haik, Schnobrich, Kaufman & Doty, Mpls., 1962-87, pres., 1977-79; instr. William Mitchell Coll. Law, Mpls., 1963-64; judge U.S. Dist. Ct. for Minn., Mpls., 1987—. Mem. Adv. Com. on Civil Rules, 1992-98, Adv. Com. on Evidence Rules, 1994-98; trustee Mpls. Libr. Bd., 1969-79, Mpls. Found., 1976-83. Fellow ABA Found.; mem. ABA, Minn. Bar Assn. (gov. 1976-87, sec. 1980-83, pres. 1984-85), Hennepin County Bar Assn. (pres. 1975-76), Am. Judicature Soc., Am. Law Inst. Home: 23 Greenway Gables Minneapolis MN 55403-2145 Office: US Dist Ct 14 W US Courthouse 300 S 4th St Minneapolis MN 55415-1320 E-mail: dsdoty@mnd.uscourts.gov.

DOTY, DELLA CORRINE, organization administrator; b. Marshalltown, Iowa, Mar. 12, 1945; d. Edwin Francis and Della Edna (Keller) Mack; m. Philip Edward Doty, Dec. 23, 1967; children: Sarah Corrine, Anne Elizabeth. BSBA in Acctg., Drake U., 1967. CPA, Colo. Audit staff mem. Alexander Grant & Co. CPAs, Denver, 1967-71; controller Valley View Hosp. and Med. Ctr., Denver, 1971-75; rate rev. specialist Colo. Hosp. Assn., Denver, 1975-79; dir. Colo. Medicare Group Appeal Program, Littleton, 1979-91; assoc. dir. Comms. Inst., 1992-94; alumni coord. Colo. Children's Chorale, 2003—. Lectr. in field. Contbr. articles to profl. jours. Bd. dirs., asst. treas. YWCA of Metro Denver, 1972-74; bd. dirs. Colo. Heart Assn., 1974-82, Calvary Bapist Ch. Denver, 1998-01, chair, 2000-01; dir. Families First, Inc., 1987-89, chmn., bd. dirs., 1988-89; trustee Colo. Children's Chorale, 1988-94, 95-01, chmn., 1992-94; pres. Denver Symphony Debs, 1996, Alpha Phi Nat. Housing Corp., 1999-01; mem. Jr. League of Denver, 1979—, v.p. mktg., 1985-86; sec. Littleton Pub. Schs. Bldg. Authority, 1983-86; active various charitable orgns.; v.p. fin. and housing Alpha Phi Internat., 1974-78, trustee, 1980-86; dir., treas. Alpha Phi Found., 1978-86; trustee Ursa Major award, 1980. Recipient Founders Merit award Healthcare Fin. Mgmt. Assn., 1976, 83, Ursa Major award, 1980, Outstanding Vol. award Jr. League of Denver, 1984, Sustainer Cmty. Svc. award, 1994, Pub. Svc. award Colo. Soc. CPA's, 2001. Republican. Baptist. Address: 5981 S Coventry Ln W Littleton CO 80123-6706

DOTY, DONALD D. retired banker; b. Independence, Kans., June 30, 1928; s. Laton L. and Dorothy (Russell) D.; m. Cheri F. Montgomery, June 14, 1952; children: John Scott, Susan Dorothy, Mark Montgomery. BS, Okla. State U., 1950; postgrad., U. Wis. Grad. Sch. Banking, 1963. Rancher, nr. Bartlesville, Okla., 1950-94; asst. cashier First Nat. Bank, Bartlesville, 1956-58, asst. v.p., 1958-60, v.p., 1964-69, exec. v.p., 1969-74; pres. WestStar Bank, n.a. (formerly First Nat. Bank), Bartlesville, 1974-93; also bd. dirs.; retired, 1993. Pres. First Bancshares, Inc., Bartlesville, 1974-93, bd. dirs.; chmn. S.W. Cattlemen's Credit Corp., 1979-90; pres. Bartlesville Credit Bur., 1972—; pres. Bartlesville-Area Indsl. Devel. Co., 1970—; chmn. First Okla. Life Ins. Co., Oklahoma City, 1990-95; chmn. Coll. Bus. Assocs., Okla. State U., 1991-92. Chmn, trustees Jane Phillips Episcopal Meml. Med. Ctr., 1970—; trustee Washington County Indsl. Devel. Trust Authority, 1973-80; chmn. Frank Phillips Found., bartlesville, 1975—; bd. trustees St. John Hosp., Tulsa. Capt. USAF, 1953-55. Named to Okla. State U., Coll. of Bus. Hall of Fame, 1994; recipient Disting. S c. award Bartlesville, 1957, Disting. Alumni award Okla. State U., 2000. Mem. Am. Bankers Assn., Okla. Bankers Assn. (pres. 1984-85), Bartlesville C. of C. (v.p., bd. dirs. 1965-81, pres. 1981-82), Jaycees (Outstanding Young Man Bartlesville 1957, Okla. 1958), Masons, Shriners, Rotary, Sigma Alpha Epsilon. Republican. Episcopalian. Avocations: skiing, hunting, golf. Home: 2407 Kyle Ct Bartlesville OK 74006-6340 E-mail: dandcdoty@aol.com.

DOTY, DUANE HAROLD, business educator; b. Wichita, Kans., July 5, 1960; s. David H. and Martha (Parker) D.; m. Susan Michal Smith, Dec. 30, 1991; children: Lindsey, Michala, Zachary, David. BA with honors, S.W. Tex. State U., San Marcos, Tex., 1982; MBA, U. Tex., Austin, 1986, PhD, 1990. Asst. prof. U. Ark., Fayetteville, 1990—95; chair dept. strategy and human resources Syracuse U. Sch. Mgmt., 1995. Contbr. articles. Mem.: Acad. Mgmt. (mem. editl. bd. Acad. Mgmt. Jour., Best Article award 1993, Scholarly Achievement award human resouces divsn. 1997). Avocations: family, hunting, fishing, horses. Office: Syracuse U Sch Mgmt Syracuse NY 13244 Office Fax: 314.443.5457. Business E-Mail: hdoty@som.syr.edu.

DOTY, GRESDNA ANN, theatre historian, educator; b. Oelwein, Iowa, Feb. 22, 1931; d. James William and Gresdna (Wood) D.; m. James G. Traynham, Nov. 28, 1980. AA, Monticello Coll., Alton, Ill., 1951; BA, U. No. Iowa, 1953; MA, U. Fla., 1957; PhD, Ind. U., 1967. Instr. S.W. Tex. State U., San Marcos, 1957—61, asst. prof., 1964—65, La. State U., Baton Rouge, 1967-73, assoc. prof., 1973-79, dir. theatre, 1973-77, 81-91, prof., 1979-84, alumni prof., 1984—, alumni prof. emeritus, 1996—, chair dept. theatre, 1991-93. Author: Anne Brunton Merry in the American Theatre, 1971; co-editor: (with Billy J. Harbin) Inside the Royal Court Theatre, 1956-81: Artists Talk, 1990; contbr. articles to profl. jours. Bd. dirs. Arts Coun. Greater Baton Rouge, 1987-92, pres., 1990-91; mem. exec. com. Swine Palace Prodns. Rsch. grantee Nat. Endowment Humanities, 1981, Exxon Edn. Found., 1981. Fellow S.W. Theatre Assn.; mem. Am. Theatre Assn. (bd. dirs. 1977-80), Am. Coll. Theatre Festival (nat. chmn. 1976-79), Am. Soc. Theatre Rsch. (mem. exec. com. 1988-91, v.p. 1994-97), Nat. Theatre Conf. (sec. 1999-02), Coll. of Fellows of Am. Theatre (dean-elect 2003-04). Home: 122 Highland Trace Baton Rouge LA 70810-5061

DOTY, JAMES EDWARD, pastor, psychologist; b. Lakewood, Ohio, May 8, 1922; s. Ordello Luce and Margaret (McCurdy) D.; m. Mary Merciel Smith, Sept. 8, 1943; children: Mark Allen, David Wesley, Martha Suzanne. AB, Mt. Union Coll., Alliance, Ohio, 1944, DD (hon.), 1965; MDiv cum laude, Boston U., 1947, PhD, 1959; postgrad., Harvard U., Oxford U.; DD (hon.), DePauw U., 1966. Ordained to ministry Meth. Ch., 1945. Pastor in, Salem, Mass., 1947-51, Lynn, Mass., 1951-57; founder, dir. Greater Lynn Pastoral Care and Counselling Ctr., 1954-57; dir. pastoral care and counselling Ind. Area Meth. Ch., 1957-66; pres. Baker U., 1966-73; pvt. practice pastoral psychology Corpus Christi, Tex., 1973—2000; exec. dir. Corpus Christi Pastoral Counselling Ctr., 1973-84; interim sr. pastor First United Methodist Ch., Corpus Christi, 1988-89; interim pastor 1st Presbyn. Ch., Portland, Tex., 1991-98; pastor New Franklin (Ohio) United Meth. Ch., 2000—01; interim pastor Sebring (Ohio) Presbyn. Ch., 2001—03. Mem. staff Boston Ctr. Adult Edn., 1949—53; spl. lectr. Union Theol. Sem., Buenos Aires, 1962, Meth. Theol. Sem., Sao Paulo, Brazil, 1962, Epworth Theol. Sem., Salisbury, Rhodesia, 1963, Meth. Theol. Sem., Mulungwishi, Congo, 1964, Trinity Theol. Coll., Singapore, 1967, Union Theol. Sem., Manila, 1967, Cbanga Meth. Theol. Sem., Monrovia, Liberia, 1975, Meth. Theol. Sem., Suva, Fiji, 1986; mem. First Student Christian Movement Conf. in postwar Germany Heidelberg U., 1947; del. World Family Life Consultation, Birmingham, England, 1966; chmn. World Family Life, 1981—86; mem. World Meth Coun., London, 1966, Denver, 71, Dublin, 76, Honolulu, 81, del., Nairobi, Kenya, 86, Singapore, 1991—2001; chmn. exec. com., chmn. bd. visitors Sch. Theology Boston U. Author: The Pastor as Agape Counselor, 1964, Postmark Lambarene: A Visit with Albert Schweitzer, 1965; editor: Authentic Man Encounters God's World, 1967, Students Search for Meaning, 1971, (with Merciel S. Doty) For Heaven's Sake, 1993, Albert Schweitzer: Reverence for Life, 1993, With Schweitzer in Africa, 1994; producer, moderator weekly program Focus, Sta. KEDT-TV, 1984-95. V.p. Pike Twp. Sch. Bd., Marion County, Ind., 1960-66. Recipient Alumni of Yr. award, Mt. Union Coll., 1963, Alumni award of merit, Boston U., 1969. Mem. APA, S.W. Conf. United Meth. Ch., Tex. Bd. Profl. Counselors, Am. Bd. Sexology (diplomate), Am. Assn. Pastoral Counselors (diplomate, bd. dirs.), Am. Assn. Marriage and Family Therapy, Rotary, Sigma Alpha Epsilon, Zeta Chi. Home: 800 S 15th St Sebring OH 44672-2050 E-mail: drjedoty@juno.com.

DOTY, JEFFREY EDWARD, surgeon; b. Stamford, Conn., Mar. 28, 1952; s. Roy Edward and Louise Fitch (Hall) D.; m. Elvira Lanani Muller, Mar. 15, 1986; children: Michael Lawrence, Rachel Marie. MD, Washington U., St. Louis, 1978. Intern UCLA, 1978-79, resident, 1979-84, fellow, 1984-85; chmn. divsn. gen. surgery Good Samaritan Hosp., San Jose, Calif.; clin. assoc. prof. Stanford Univ. Sch. Medicine. Mem. ACS (gov. 2001—, chmn. com. on oper. environ. 2000-02, councillor No. Calif. Chpt. 1996-98, pres. No. Calif. chpt. 1999), Am. Gastroenterol. Assn., Am. Soc. Gastrointestinal Endoscopy, Soc. Am. Gastrointestinal Endoscopic Surgeons, Soc. Surgery Alimentary Tract, Pacific Coast Surg. Assn. Office: 2450 Samaritan Dr San Jose CA 95124-3912

DOTY, LEILANI, geriatric neuropsychologist, administrator; b. Everett, Mass., July 28, 1942; BA, U. Fla., 1976, PhD in Counselor Edn., 1986. RN, MGH, Mass.; nat. cert. counselor Am. Assn. Counseling and Devel.; cert. gerontology Ctr. for Gerontol. Studies, U. Fla. Adminstr. Alzheimer's Disease Initiative U. Fla. Memory Disorder Clinic, Gainesville, 1987—, mem. faculty dept. neurology Coll. Medicine, 1988—. Cons. Ctr. for Rsch. on Telehealth & Healthcare Comms. U. Fla., 2000—. Author: Basic Communication Skills and Assertiveness Training for Older Persons, 1982, Advanced Communication Skills and Selective Assertiveness Training for Older Persons, 1982, Life Satisfaction Determinants in Older Persons, 1986, Communication and Assertion for Older Persons, 1987, (with others) Helping People with Progressive Memory Disorders: A Guidebook for You and Your Family, 2d edit., 1998 (Nat. Health Info. Bronze award 1997); guest editor: (with N. S. Hardt) spl. issues Jour. Fla. Med. Assn., 1996, 97; contbr. chpts. to books, articles to profl. jours. Women's liason officer, U. Fla., 1995-2002; co-founder, 1st chair Cmty. Ptnrs., 1997; chair Nat. Women's Health Rsch. Conf., 1996-98; co-founder, bd. dirs. U. Fla. Inst. Women's Health. Recipient Pres. award Mental Health Assn. Alachua County, Fla., 1982, U. Fla. Women of Achievement award, 1998; postdoctoral fellow Geriat. Soc. Am., 1989, PhD Cmty. Svc. award, 2001. Office: Dept Neurology Box 100236 U Fla Brain Inst Gainesville FL 32610-0236 Fax: (352) 392-6893. E-mail: dotyl@neurology.ufl.edu.

DOTY, PHILIP EDWARD, accountant; b. Red Oak, Iowa, Dec. 9, 1943; s. Wade Bryan and Vera Mae D.; m. Della Corrine Mack, Dec. 23, 1967; children: Sarah, Anne. BSBA, Drake U., 1967. CPA, Colo. Ret. ptnr. Arthur Andersen LLP, Denver, 1967-2000, dir. oil and gas practice and tng., 1987-2000; ptnr. Ehrhard Keefe Steiner & Hottman, 2002—. Mem. Colo. State Bd. Accountancy, 2000—. Treas. Mile High United Way, Denver, 1984-88, 2000-02, bd. dirs., 1998-2002; treas. Mile High br. Girl Scouts U.S.A., 1987-92; bd. dirs. Leadership Denver Assn., 1987-89, Artreach, Inc., 1986-89, Colo. Ballet, 1992-98; mem. exec. bd. Denver Area Coun. Boy Scouts Am., 1998—; treas. Denver Ballet Guild Endowment Trust, 2000—. With USAR, 1967-73. Mem. AICPA (nat. coun. 1994-97), Petroleum Accts. Soc. (pres. 1989), Ind. Petroleum Assn. Mountain States (bd. dirs. 1987-97, treas. 1991-92), Colo. Soc. CPA's (pres. 1994, Pub. Svc. award 2001), Denver Petroleum Club (sec.-treas. 1988-91, Man of Yr. award 1993, bd. dirs. 1997-99), Classic Car Club Am. (dir. Colo. region 1996-98, treas. 1999—), Beta Gamma Sigma. Republican. Baptist. Avocations: classic cars, skiing, hunting.

DOTY, RALPH EDWARD, classics educator; b. Sapulpa, Okla., May 22, 1945; s. Ralph E. and Willa H. (Dutcher) D.; m. Debra Ramirez, June 7, 1976 (div. 1981); m. Jeanette L. Hobbs, June 3, 1983. BA, U. Okla., 1967; MA in Philosophy, Columbia U., 1969, PhD in Philosophy, 1973. Preceptor Columbia U., N.Y.C., 1972-73; instr. East Los Angeles Coll., Monterey Park, Calif., 1977-79, George Lynn Cross Acad., Norman, Okla., 1979-82; asst. prof. U. Okla., Norman, 1984-91, assoc. prof., 1991—2002, prof., 2002—. Author: The Criterion of Truth, 1992, Xenophon on Hunting, 2001, Hiero, A New Translation, 2003, Poroi, A New Translation, 2003; contbr. articles to profl. jours. Mem. Am. Philos. Assn., Classical Assn. of Midwest and South, Phi Beta Kappa. Office: U Okla Dept Of Classics Norman OK 73019-0001 Home: 509 W Symmes Norman OK 73069

DOTY, RICHARD L. medical researcher; b. Boulder, Colo., Oct. 14, 1944; s. George David and Frances Amelia (Bradley) D. BS, Colo. State U., 1966; MA, Calif. State U., 1968; PhD, Mich. State U., 1971; postgrad., U. Calif., Berkeley, 1973. Instr. dept. psychology Calif. State U., San Francisco, 1971-72, U. San Francisco, 1971-72; asst. mem. Monell Chem. Senses Ctr., Phila., 1974-76, assoc. mem., head human olfaction sect., 1976-78; dir. smell and taste ctr. Hosp. U. Pa., Phila., 1979—, Sch. Medicine, U. Pa., Phila., 1980—, asst. prof. dept. otorhinolaryngology, human communication, 1983-89, assoc. prof., 1989-93; prof. dept. otorhinolaryngology U. Pa., Phila., 1994—. Cons. in field; lectr. in field; editorial cons. for numerous profl. jours.; external adv. bd. Taste and Smell Ctr. U. Conn./Yale U., 1982-84, Rocky Mountain Taste and Smell Ctr., U. Colo. Sch. Medicine, 1985, Mayo Found. Project, 1989; internat. adv. bd. 1st Internat. Congress on Food and Health, Salsomaggiore Terme, Italy, 1985. Author: The Smell Identification Test (TM) Administration Manual, 1983, 2d edit., 1989, 3d edit., 1995; editor: Mammalian Olfaction, Reproductive Processes and Behavior, 1976, Handbook of Olfaction and Gustation, 1995, 2d edit., 2003; co-editor:

(with T.V. Getchell, E.P. Koster) Chemical Senses, spl. edit., 1981, (with D.G. Laing, W. Breopohl) Human Olfaction, 1990, (with L.M. Bartoshuk, T.V. Getchell and J.B. Snow) Smell and Taste in Health Disease, 1991, (with D. Muller-Schwartze) Chemical Signals in Vertebrates VI, 1992. NIH postdoctoral rsch. fellow, 1973-75; grantee Nat. Inst. on Aging, 1989-91, Nat. Inst. Deafness and Other Comm. Disorders, 1980—. Mem. European Chemoreception Rsch. Orgn. (mem. organizational com. 1981), Assn. for Chemoreception Scis. (mem. program com. 1985, 87, mem. elections com. 1987), AAAS, N.Y. Acad. Scis., Assn. for Rsch. in Otolaryngology, Am. Acad. Otolaryngology (head and neck surgery), Am. Psychol. Assn., Internat. Soc. for Chem. Ecology, Phila. Coll. Physicians (mem. adv. com., sect. on geriatrics and gerontology). Home: 125 White Horse Pike Haddon Heights NJ 08035-1909 Office: U Pa Smell & Taste Ctr 5 Ravdin Bldg 3400 Spruce St Philadelphia PA 19104-4206 E-mail: doty@mail.med.upenn.edu.

DOTY, ROBERT DOUGLAS, SR., retired surgeon; b. Rogersville, Tenn., 1919; MD, Johns Hopkins U., 1943. Diplomate Am. Bd. Surgery. Intern Church Home-Hosp., Balt., 1944-45, resident in surgery, 1945-46, Mt. Alto Hosp., Washington, 1948-50; staff surgeon VA Hosp., Salem, Va., 1950-52; mem. surg. staff Holston Valley Gen. Hosp., Kingsport, Tenn., 1952-87, Hawkins County Meml. Hosp., Rogersville, Tenn., 1953-87; ret., 1987. Fellow ACS. Home: 1401 Crescent Dr Kingsport TN 37664-2035

DOTY, ROBERT WALTER, lawyer; b. Aliquippa, Pa., Sept. 19, 1942; s. David Lucien and Iona (Fox) D.; m. Joyce Marie Shaffalo, Sept. 10, 1961; children: Genie, Merrie Beth. BA cum laude, Wheaton Coll., 1963; JD, Vanderbilt U., 1966. Bar: Pa. 1966, U.S. Supreme Ct. 1982. Assoc. Eckert Seamans Cherin & Mellot, Pitts., 1966-74, ptnr., 1975-91; dir. Cohen & Grigsby, P.C., Pitts., 1991—. Solicitor Crescent Township, Allegheny County, Pa., 1969—; arbitrator Am. Arbitration Assn., nat. panel, 1978—, speaker at seminars; lectr. Westinghouse Internat. Sch. Environ. Mgmt., Ft. Collins, Colo., 1980-82. Mem. nat. com. on wills and trusts centennial campaign Vanderbilt U., 1977-81. Recipient Archie B. Martin Meml. scholarship medal Vanderbilt U., 1964, Robert F. Jackson Meml. scholarship prize, 1965, Founder's medal, 1966; 3 Am. Jurisprudence awards in contracts, civil procedure and criminal law The Lawyers Co-operative Pub. Co., Rochester, N.Y., 1964, 65; Mark Woodworth Walton scholar Vanderbilt U., 1965. Mem. Pa. Bar Assn., Allegheny County Bar Assn. (governing coun. civil litigation sect.), Wheaton Club (past pres.), Fox Chapel Racquet Club, Breckenridge Golf and Tennis Club, Vines Country Club, Racquet Club Memphis, Order of Coif, Phi Kappa Delta, Phi Alpha Delta. Avocations: swimming, tennis. Office: 11 Stanwix St 15th Floor Pittsburgh PA 15222

DOTY, ROBERT WILLIAM, neurophysiologist, educator; b. New Rochelle, N.Y., Jan. 10, 1920; s. Earle Birdsell and Ethel Laurette (Mack) D.; m. Elizabeth Natalie Jusewich, Aug. 30, 1941; children— Robert William, Mary E., Cheryl A., Richard M. BS, U. Chgo., 1948, MS, 1949, PhD, 1950. Postdoctoral fellow U. Ill., Chgo., 1950-51; asst. prof. U. Utah, Salt Lake City, 1951-56; from asst. to assoc. prof. U. Mich., Ann Arbor, 1956-61; prof. U. Rochester, N.Y., 1961—. Vis. prof. U. Mex., 1975, U. Osaka, Japan, 1981; sci. adviser NIMH, Bethesda, Md., 1975-79, Yerkes Inst., Atlanta, 1975-78 Assoc. editor: Acta Neurobiologiae, Warsaw, 1971—, Behavioral Brain Research, 1981 ; contbr. articles to profl. jours. Served to capt. U.S. Army, 1942-46 Recipient Javits award, Nat. Inst. Neurol. and Communicative Disorders and Stroke., NIH, 1986. Fellow AAAS; mem. Am. Psychol. Soc. (pres. div. 6, 1984), Internat. Brain Research Orgn., Current Anthropology (assoc.), Soc. for Neurosci. (pres. 1975-76, councilor 1970-74) Avocations: photography, history, langs. Office: Box 603 U Rochester Med Ctr Neurobiology And Anatomy Ctr Rochester NY 14642-0001

DOTY, SHAYNE TAYLOR, organist; b. Memphis, Aug. 19, 1961; s. Robert Allen and Janice Moffet Doty. BA, Duke U., 1983; diploma, Conservatoire Nat. Superieur Musique Lyon, 1986; MM, So. Meth. U., 1991. Rsch. assoc. Capital Campaign for Arts and Scis., Duke U., 1983-84; organist, choirmaster St. Paul's Episcopal Ch., Washington, 1991-98; organist Am. Cath., Paris, 1995-96; asst. dir. corp. and found. rels. U. Md., College Park, 1997-98; sr. major gift officer Met. Opera Assn., N.Y.C., 1998—. Organ recitalist including St. Denis, Paris, St. Paul's, Toronto, Nat. Cathedral, Washington. Mary Duke Biddle scholarship Duke U., 1979-83; Frank Huntington Beebe fellow, 1984-86. Mem. Am. Guild of Organists. Episcopalian. Office: Met Opera Assn Lincoln Ctr New York NY 10023

DOUB, WILLIAM OFFUTT, lawyer; b. Cumberland, Md., Sept. 3, 1931; s. Albert A. and Fannabelle (Offutt) D.; m. Mary Graham Boggs, Sept. 12, 1959; children: Joseph Peyton, Albert A., II. AB, Washington and Jefferson Coll., 1953; LLB, U. Md., 1956. Bar: Md. 1956, D.C. 1974. With law dept. B. & O. R.R., 1955-57; assoc. Bartlett Poe & Claggett, Balt., 1957-61; ptnr. Niles Barton & Wilmer, Balt., 1961-71; commr. AEC, 1971-74; ptnr. LeBoeuf, Lamb, Leiby & MacRae, Washington, 1974-77, Doub, Muntzing and Glasgow, Washington, 1977-91, Newman & Holtzinger, P.C., Washington, 1991-94, Morgan Lewis & Bockius, Washington, 1995-2000. Chmn. Minimum Wage Commn., Balt., 1964-66; peoples' counsel Md. Pub. Service Commn., 1967-68, chmn., 1968-71; vice chmn. Washington Met. Area Transit Commn., 1968-71; mem. President's Air Quality Adv. Bd., 1970-71; mem. exec. adv. com. FPC, 1969-71, Nat. Gas Survey, 1975-78; pres. Great Lakes Conf. Pub. Utility Commrs., 1971; mem. nat. adv. bd. Am. Nat. Standards Inst., 1975-80; mem. Md. Adv. Com. Retardation, 1969-71 Mem. Adminstrv. Conf., U.S., 1973-75; chmn. U.S. Energy Assn., Inc., World Energy Conf., 1978-80, U.S. del., 1974, 77, 80, 83, 86, 89, 92, 95, 98; vice chmn. World Energy Conf., 1986-88, hon. vice chmn., 1988—; mem. adv. groups Nat. Acad. Pub. Adminstrn., NSF; presdl. appointee as rep. to So. States Energy Bd., 1983-90; bd. govs. Md. East Inst. of U.S., 1982-86, 88-94, 95-2000; mem. exec. com. Thomas Alva Edison Found., 1983-90, 85-90; presdl. appointee 33d Ann. Conf. of Internat. Atomic Energy Agy., 1989. Recipient Nat. Energy award U.S. Energy Assn., 1998. Mem. Met. Club. Home (Summer): 512 Neapolitan Lane Naples FL 34103 E-mail: fudoub@aol.com.

DOUBLEDAY, NELSON, former professional baseball team executive; Grad., Princeton, 1954. With Doubleday & Co. Inc., N.Y.C., 1954—56, former pres., chief exec. officer, chmn. bd. dirs.; chmn. bd., majority owner N.Y. Mets Baseball Team, 1980—2002. Served with USAF, 1956-59.

DOUCET, HOSEA JOSEPH, III, pediatrician; b. Opelousas, La., Mar. 13, 1950; s. Hosea Joseph Jr. Doucet and Marian Antoinette Marmande. BS, U. Southwestern La., 1975; MD, La. State U., 1976; MPH, Tulane Sch. Pub. Health, 1993. Diplomate Am. Bd. Pediatrics. Intern, resident Charity Hosp. of New Orleans-La. State U. divsn.; instr. Tulane Med. Sch., New Orleans, 1979-80, asst. prof., 1980-86, assoc. prof., 1986-99, dir. residency program, 1990—, prof. pediatrics, 1999—; adj. assoc. prof. Tulane Sch. of Pub. Health, New Orleans, 1997—; clin. assoc. prof. La. State U. Sch. Medicine, New Orleans, 1991—. Pres. med. staff Med. Ctr. La.-New Orleans, 2000-02, chmn. exec. com., 2000-02; perinatal task force Office of Pub. Health, New Orleans, 1994-96. Contbr. articles to profl. publs. Pres. Friends of Saint Alphonsus, New Orleans, 1995-97; del. La. State Med. Soc. Ho. of Dels., 1988-91; med. dir. Covenant House, New Orleans, 1987-91; mem. Mayor's Task Force on Nutrition, New Orleans, 1984-85; adv. coun. New Orleans/AIDS task force, 1994-96. Recipient Tchg. Excellence award Tulane Owl Club, 1991-92, 97-98, Outstanding Tchr., 1993-94. Mem. Am. Acad. of Pediatrics (pediatrics adv. com. La. chpt. 1998—), Assn. of Pediatric Program Dirs., La. State Med. Soc. (com. on pediatric health 1988—), Greater New Orleans Pediatric Soc. (exec. com. 1997—), Ambulatory Pediatric Soc., So. Soc. for Pediatric Rsch. Roman Catholic. Avocations: historical renovations, restorations. Office: Tulane Med Sch 1430 Tulane Ave New Orleans LA 70112-2699

DOUCETTE, BETTY, public and community health and geriatrics nurse; b. Mosinee, Wis., Jan. 29, 1924; d. Wenzel and Margretta (Brietenstein) Vavra; m. Nieland R. Doucette, Nov. 12, 1949; children: Tom, Bob, Dan, John, Carol, Bill, Jeanne, Sue, Judy. Diploma, St. Marys Hosp. Sch. Nursing, Wausau, Wis., 1945; student, Nicolet Coll. and Tech. Inst., Rhinelander, Wis., 1971-81, Viterbo Coll., LaCrosse, Wis., 1982. Cert. pub. health nurse. Supr. med. ward St. Marys Hosp., Wausau, 1945-49; indsl. nurse Owens-Ill. Mill, Tomahawk, 1964-69; nurse supr. Golden Age Nursing Home, Tomahawk, Wis., 1969-78; home care nurse Lincoln County Nursing Svcs., Merrill, Wis., 1978-91; RN Lincoln County Health Bd., 1994—; parish nurse, 2000—.

DOUCETTE, DAVID ROBERT, computer systems company executive; b. Pitts., Feb. 2, 1946; s. Adrian Robert and Mary Alyce (Newland) D. BSEE cum laude, Poly. Inst. Bklyn., 1968, MSEE, 1970, PhD, 1974. Asst. prof. electrical engring. Poly. Inst. N.Y. (now Poly. U.), 1973-74, assoc. prof. computer sci., 1975-82, prof., 1982—, dir., 1994—2002, assoc. dean, 1997—2002; sr. staff specialist advanced planning Gruman Data Sys. Corp., Bethpage, N.Y., 1979-80, program mgr., 1979-80, mgr. graphics sys., 1980-84, from asst. dir. to dir. interactive sys. support, 1984-86; dir. interactive sys. Gruman Data Sys., Corp., Bethpage, N.Y., 1986-94; pres., CEO D3Software Corp., 1994—. Active Nassau County Hist. Soc., Garden City Hist. Soc Recipient Achievement award Engrs. Joint Coun. L.I., 1999. Mem. IEEE (past sect. chmn., Centennial medal, Third Millennium medal), Assn. Computing Machinery (past chpt. chmn.), Nat. Space Soc., Planetary Soc., Nat. Eagle Scout Assn., Sigma Xi, Tau Beta Pi, Eta Kappa Nu, L.I. Early Fliers Club. Office: Poly U Dept Computer/Info Sci 6 Metrotech Ctr Brooklyn NY 11201

DOUCETTE, JODI LEAZOTT, lawyer; b. Eau Claire, Wis., June 5, 1962; d. Lawrence George and Sylvia Elaine Leazott; m. Dennis Joseph Doucette, March 26, 1988; children: Lauren E., Chanelle N., Lucas L. Cert. interpreter, U. Sampere, Madrid, 1983; BA, Pepperdine U., 1984; postgrad., Oxford U., 1985; JD, U. San Diego, 1987. Bar: Calif., U.S. Dist. Ct. (so. dist.) Calif. Dep. county counsel County San Diego, 1988-93; dep. city atty. City of Oceanside (Calif.), 1993—. Author: (model ordinance) League of California Cities Sign Ordinance, 1999; contbr. to handbook. Big sister Vol. in Parole, San Diego, 1988—93; chair, mem. Commn. Children and Youth, San Diego County, 1989—93; bd. dirs., treas. Hanna Fenichel Pre-Sch., 1994—; bd. mem., com. chair U. San Diego Law Sch., 1995—99; bd. dirs., v.p., sec. Lawyers Club, 1994—97; classroom vol. Del Mar (Calif.) Heights Elem. Sch., 1995—; Sunday sch. tchr. St. James Ch., Solana Beach, Calif., 1995—97; mem. bd. dirs., chmn. project rev. Torrey Pines Planning, 2001—. Mem. Bar Assn. No. San Diego (bd. dirs., com. chair, v.p., sec.). Roman Catholic. Avocations: running, skiing, reading, crafts. Office: City Attys Office 300 N Coast Hwy Oceanside CA 92054-2824

DOUCETTE, MARY-ALYCE, computer company executive; b. Pitts., Feb. 12, 1924; d. Andrew George and Alice Jane (Sloan) Newland; m. Adrian Robert Doucette, Feb. 6, 1945 (dec. June 1983); children: David Robert, Regis Robert. BS cum laude, U. Pitts., 1945. Mgr. Newland Bros., Millvale, Pa., 1946-53; gen. mgr. Newland-Ludlo, Pitts., 1953-72; mgmt. cons. D3 Software, Garden City, N.Y., 1972-80, sec., corp. officer, 1980—. Fin. sec. Cerebral Palsy Assn., Garden City, Helen Keller Svcs. for Blind, Garden City; mem. Winthrop-U. Hosp. Aux., Mercy League, Friends of Adelphi Univ. Libr., Friends of Hist. St. George Ch. of Hempstead, N.Y., Adv. Coun. for Continuing Edn., Garden City Sch. Dist., 1988—. Mem. AAUW, L.I. Panhellenic, Univ. Club, Nassau County Hist. Soc. (life), Garden City Hist. Soc., Community Club Garden City-Hempstead, Woman's Club Garden City, Alpha Delta Pi, Pi Lambda Theta. Home: 146 Washington Ave Garden City NY 11530-3013 Office: D3 Software PO Box 8051 Garden City NY 11530-8051

DOUD, WALLACE C. retired information systems executive; b. Bellingham, Wash., Feb. 25, 1925; s. Forrest Roy and Florence (Pollock) D.; m. Marjorie K. Fenton, Oct. 25, 1949 (dec. 1962); children: Forrest J., Mary, Margaret, Barbara, Melissa; m. Janice F. Freudenberg, June 15, 1963 (dec. 1978); children: Michael, Karen; m. Jean A. Kennedy, Oct. 13, 1979. BBA, U. Wis., 1948; DHL (hon.), Mercy Coll., 1983. Salesman IBM Corp., Milw., St. Paul, Detroit, dir. patent relations Armonk, N.Y., 1960-71, v.p. services staff, 1971-77, v.p. comml. and industry rels., 1977-85. Chmn. Bd. Parks and Recreation White Plains, N.Y., 1983-84; chmn., pres. United Way, White Plains, 1975-80. Recipient Youth Services award B'nai B'rith, 1972, Medallion Westchester Community Coll., 1980. Mem.: St. Andrews Club, Rockland Golf Club, Meguniticook Golf Club, Little Club, Country Club of Fla. Republican. Presbyterian.

DOUDS, VIRGINIA LEE, elementary education educator; b. Pitts., Jan. 17, 1943; d. Leland Ray and Virginia Helen (Dodds) Frazier; m. William Wallace Douds, June 20, 1964; children: William Stewart Douds, Michael Leland Douds. BA in Elem. Edn., Westminster Coll., New Wilmington, Pa., 1964; MA (Master's Equivalency), Dept. Edn., State of Pa., 1990. Cert. elem. tchr., Pa. Elem. tchr./non-graded Good Hope Elem. Sch., Glendale-Riverhills, Wis., 1964-65; elem. tchr./1st grade Carlisle Elem. Sch., Delaware, Ohio, 1965-66; elem. tchr./3rd grade Meml. Elem. Sch., Bethel Park, Pa., 1973-74; elem. tchr./1st and 3rd grades Logan Elem. Sch., Bethel Park, Pa., 1974-91; elem. tchr./3rd grade Neil Armstrong Elem. Sch., Bethel Park, 1991-99, Ben Franklin Elem. Sch., Bethel Park, 1999—. Software cons. Coal Kids, U.S. Dept. Mines, 1993; mem. lang. arts, reading com. Bethel Park Schs., 1989-92, cooperating tchr., 1986—, mentor tchr. 1992-93, 95—, mem. instrnl. support team, 1988-91, integrated lang. arts com., 1999-2000; judge Ben Franklin Scholarship Comm., 2001-03; mem. Mid. States Accreditation com., 1993-94, strategic planning com., 1994-95; SIP scholarship com. Bethel Park Fedn. Tchrs., 1973—. Mem. alumni coun. exec. bd. Westminster Coll., 1979-83; mem. exec. bd. Parents Assn., 1985-89. Recipient mini grant/writing, publishing ctr. Bethel Park Schs., 1989, Gift of Time tribute Am. Family Inst., 1990, 91, All Star Educator award U. Pitts./Pitts. Post Gazette, 1996. Mem. Nat. Coun. Tchrs. of English (lang. arts/reading com. 2000-01), Bethel Park Fedn. Tchrs., PTO. Republican. Presbyterian. Avocations: reading, gardening, golf. Home: 2679 Burnsdale Dr Bethel Park PA 15102-2005

DOUGAL, ARWIN ADELBERT, electrical engineer, educator; b. Dunlap, Iowa, Nov. 22, 1926; s. Adelbert Isaac and Goldya (White) D.; m. Margaret Jane McLennan, Sept. 3, 1951; children: Catherine Ann, Roger Adelbert, Leonard Harley, Laura Beth. BS, Iowa State U., 1952; MS, U. Ill., 1955, PhD, 1957. Registered profl. engr., Tex. Radio engr. Collins Radio Co., Cedar Rapids, Iowa, 1952; research asst., research asso., asst. prof., asso. prof. U. Ill., Urbana, 1952-61; prof., mem. grad. faculty, dir. labs. for electronics and related sci. research U. Tex., Austin, 1961-67, prof., 1969—91; dir. Electronics Research Center, 1971-77, sec. grad. assembly, 1972-74; dir. Austron, Inc., 1977-82; prof. emeritus U. Tex., 1992—. Asst. dir. def. research and engring. for research Office Sec. Def., Washington, 1967-69; cons. Tex. Instruments, Inc., Dallas, Gen. Dynamics Corp., Ft. Worth, U. Calif. Los Alamos Sci. Lab. Contbr. articles to profl. jours. Faculty sponsor U. Tex. Conservative Democrats Club, 1966-67; sr. mem. CAP, 1984—; elder local Presbyn. Ch. With USAF, 1946-49. Recipient Teaching Excellence awards U. Tex. Students Assn., 1962, 63, Spl. award for outstanding service as program chmn. S.W. IEEE Conf. and Exhbn., 1967; Outstanding Grad. Adviser award Grad. Engring. Council, U. Tex., 1971; Disting. Advisor award Grad. Engring. Council, U. Tex., 1977, 84; Teaching Achievement award Grad. Engring. Council, U. Tex., 1977; Profl. Achievement citation in engring. Iowa State U. Alumni Assn., 1975 Fellow Am. Phys. Soc., IEEE (dir. 1980-81, Centennial medal 1984, Student Br. citation 1988, Outstanding Br. Counselor award, 1991, chmn. ctrl. Tex. sect. 1993-94); mem. Am. Soc. Engring. Edn., Rockport Yacht Club, Sigma Xi, Phi Kappa Phi, Tau Beta Pi, Eta Kappa Nu, Pi Mu Epsilon, Phi Eta Sigma. Home: 6115 Rickey Dr Austin TX 78757-4437 E-mail: aadougal@att.net.

DOUGALL-SIDES, LESLIE K. lawyer; b. Washington, Sept. 5, 1953; d. George Malcolm Richardson and Kathleen (Cahill) Dougall; m. Kenneth Jacob Sides, Feb. 19, 1994. BA, New Coll., Sarasota, Fla., 1975; JD cum laude, Florida State U., Tallahassee, 1978. Bar: Fla. 1981, DC 1981, Oreg. 1986, cert.: in city, county and local govt. law 1996, cert. profl. human resources 2001, bar: U.S. Dis. Ct. (middle and southern dist.) Fla., U.S. ct. appeals (11th cir.). Staff atty. Ctrl. Fla. Legal Svcs., Cocoa, 1982—85, dir. atty. Handicapped Law Ctr., 1985—87; asst. city atty., acting city atty. City of Key West (Fla.), 1987—95; asst. city atty. City of Clearwater (Fla.), 1995—; bd. dirs. IRRA, 2000—02; sec. West Ctrl. Fla. Chpt., Indsl. Rels. Rsch. Assn., 2003. Mem.: Indsl. Rels. Rsch. Assn. (sec. West Ctrl. Fla. chpt. 2003, bd. dirs. 2000—02), Soc. Human Resources, Clearwater Bar Assn., ABA. Avocation: sailing. Office: City of Clearwater City Atty's Office PO Box 4748 Clearwater FL 33758 Office Fax: 727-562-4021. E-mail: lsides@clearwater-fl.com.

DOUGAN, DEBORAH RAE, neuropsychology professional; b. Urbana, Ill., Jan. 22, 1952; d. Francis William and Barbara Belle (Ash) D. BA in Psychology, U. Ill., 1973; MA in Counseling, Gov.'s State U., 1978; PhD in Neuropsychology, Oreg. State U., 1982. Lic. psychol. assoc., Tex. Staff therapist Ozark Community Mental Health, Joplin, Mo., 1982-85; neuropsychol. cons. Tex. Commn. for Blind, Austin, 1985-87; psychol. assoc. Warm Springs Rehab. Hosp., Gonzales, Tex., 1987-88, Rehab. Hosp. South Tex., Corpus Christi, 1988-89; psychosocial dir. New Medico Rehab. Ctr., Lindale, Tex., 1989-90; clin. coord. Rainbow Rehab. Ctrs., Ft. Worth, 1991-93; neuropsychology profl. Cypress Creek Rehab. Ctr., Houston, 1993-95; coord. Strategic Stress Mgmt. Seminars, Houston, 1996—; with info. dept. McGregor Med. Assn., 1996—. Predoctoral intern State Hosp., Vinita, Okla., 1981-82. Mem. APA, Tex. Head Injury Assn. (North Ctrl. chpt. bd. dirs., survivors coun. liaision 1991-93, survivors group leader Corpus Christi head injury chpt. 1988-89, Tyler (Tex.) head injury chpt. 1989-90, survivors group leader Ft. Worth head injury chpt. 1991-93, vice chair chpt. rels. state orgn. 1994-96, bd. dirs., sec. Houston chpt. 1995-96), Toastmasters Internat. Avocations: jazzercise, computer, house plants. Home and Office: 10909 Fawnlily St The Woodlands TX 77380-4003

DOUGAN, JOHN, music educator; b. Worcester, Mass., Dec. 23, 1954; s. Richard Kenneth Dougan and Virginia Concetta Faugno; m. Carol Smith, Aug. 31, 1985; 1 child, Eamon Smith. PhD, MA, Coll. William & Mary, 2001; BA, Westfield (Mass.) State Coll., 1994. Instr. Coll. William & Mary, Williamsburg, 1998—2000; adj. asst. prof. Thomas Nelson C.C., Hampton, Va., 2000—01; asst. prof. Mid. Tenn. State U., Murfreesboro, 2001—. Adj. asst. prof. Vanderbilt U., Nashville, 2003—. Author: (essay) American Music; contbr. music criticism, reviews to popular and profl. publs. Grantee John Seigenthaler grantee, Mid. Tenn. State U., 2001, Faculty Rsch. and Creative Activity grantee, 2003. Mem.: Soc. Am. Music (assoc.), Am. Studies Assn. (assoc.; exec. dir. Ky., Tenn.), Internat. Assn. Study Popular Music (assoc.). Democrat. Avocation: travel. Office: Middle Tenn State Univ 1301 E Main St Box 21 Murfreesboro TN 37127 E-mail: jdougan@mtsu.edu.

DOUGHERTY, ALFRED FRANKLIN, JR., lawyer; b. Helena, Mont., July 5, 1941; BS, U.S. Naval Acad., 1963; JD, George Washington U., 1970. Bar: D.C. 1970, Mo. 1982. Assoc. Hogan & Hartson, Washington, 1970—74; asst. to dir. Bur. Competition FTC, 1974—75, asst. dir. gen. litigation, 1975, dep. dir., 1975—76, dir., 1977—80; ptnr. Hogan & Hartson, Washington, 1977; exec. v.p., gen. counsel May Dept Stores Co., St. Louis, 1981—. Contbr. With USN, 1963—67. Fellow, Commn. of European Communities and Brookings Instn., 1980. Mem.: ABA, Bar D.C. Office: May Dept Stores Co 6th & Olive Sts Suite 1750 Saint Louis MO 63101

DOUGHERTY, CHARLES HAMILTON, pediatrician; b. St. Louis, June 1, 1947; s. Charles Joseph and Suzanne Louise (Hamilton) D.; m. Mary Laverty Peckham, July 7, 1972; children: Bridget, Matthew, Erin, Kelly. BA in Biology, Coll. of the Holy Cross, 1969; MD, U. Rochester Sch. of Medicine, N.Y., 1973. Pediatric resident St. Louis Children's Hosp., 1973-76; pvt. practice pediatrics Primary Pediatric Care Group, St. Louis, 1976-86, Esse Health, St. Louis, 1986—. Fellow Am. Acad. Pediatrics. Roman Catholic. Avocations: marathon running, adventure vacations, computers, water sports, powered parachute pilot. Office: Esse Health 13303 Tesson Ferry Rd Saint Louis MO 63128-4062 E-mail: cdougher@essehealth.com., cdoughe103@aol.com.

DOUGHERTY, CHARLES JOHN, university administrator, philosophy and medical ethics educator; b. N.Y.C., June 28, 1949; s. Charles Aloysius and Mary Elizabeth (Quinn) D.; m. Sandra Lee Drabik; children: Constance Marie, Justin Charles. BA, St. Bonaventure U., 1971; MA, U. Notre Dame, 1973, PhD in Philosophy, 1975. Prof. philosophy Creighton U., Omaha, 1975-88, dir., Ctr. for Health Policy and Ethics, 1988-95, v.p. acad. affairs, 1995-2001; pres. Duquesne U., Pitts., 2001—. Author: Ideal, Fact, and Medicine, 1985, (with R.P. Heaney) Research for Health Professionals, 1988, American Health Care: Realities, Rights and Reforms, 1988, (with Jerry Cederblom) Ethics at Work, 1990, (with A. Haddad and B. Edwards) Ethical Dilemmas in Perioperative Nursing, 1990, Back to Reform, 1996; contbr. articles to profl. jours.; mem. bd. editors Health Progress, 1989—. Chmn. Nebr. Com. for the Humanities, Lincoln, 1987-88; bd. dirs. Fedn. of State Humanities Couns., 1986-89; mem. disciplinary rev. bd. Nebr. Supreme Ct., 1988—, Nebr. Accountability and Disclosure Commn., 1991—; bd. dirs. Sisters of Charity Health Sys. of Cin., 1994-96; bd. trustees Cath. Health Assn., 1995—. Mem. Am. Philos. Assn., Am. Catholic Philos. Assn. (exec. council mem. 1987-90), Alpha Sigma Nu. Democrat. Roman Catholic. Office: Duquesne Univ 600 Forbes Ave Pittsburgh PA 15282

DOUGHERTY, CHARLOTTE ANNE, financial planner, insurance and securities representative; b. Canton, Ohio, Nov. 9, 1947; d. Myron Martin and Wilma Rose Brown; m. John Edwin Dougherty, Jr., Feb. 14, 1976; 1 child, John Edwin. BA, Miami U., Oxford, Ohio, 1969; powtgrad., Kent State U., 1971-73. Cert. fin. planner. Social worker Summit County Welfare, Akron, Ohio, 1971-73; rsch. coord. Tufts U., Medford, Mass., 1973-74; corp. recruiter Lincoln Nat. Sales Corp., Ft. Wayne, Ind., 1976-79; registered rep. Lincoln Nat. Life, Cin., 1980—, Lincoln Fin. Advisors, Cin., 1989—. Contbr. articles to profl. jours. Mem. Inst. Cert. Fin. Planners, Internat. Assn. Fin. Planners (v.p. Cin. chpt. 1990—), Internat. Assn. for Fin. Planning (pres.-elect Cin. chpt. 1991, pres. 1992-93), Nat. Assn. Life Underwriters, Cin. Assn. Life Underwriters. Office: Dougherty & Assocs 8044 Montgomery Rd Ste 400W Cincinnati OH 45236-2923

DOUGHERTY, DANA DEAN LESLEY, television producer, educator; b. Birmingham, Ala. d. Paul Russell and Daisy Dean (Dunham) Lesley; m. Floyd Wallace Dougherty; 1 child, Lesley Dean. BS in Secondary and Bus. Edn., Speech Therapy, Drama, Auburn U., 1968. Cert. secondary edn. tchr. Ala. Tchr. speech, drama, computer typing, shorthand, acctg., bus. law Jefferson State Jr. Coll., Birmingham, 1968-73; office mgr. Baker, McDaniel & Hall, Birmingham, 1973-78; tchr. Mountain Brook Bd. Edn., Birmingham, 1979—; prodr., dir. variety and music TV show Dean and Company, Time/Warner Cable, 1980—; corp. sec. F.W. Dougherty Engrs. and Assocs. Inc., 1987—. Composer various songs. Mem. Arlington Hist. Soc.; mem. women's com. Ala. Ballet, Salvation Army Women's Aux. Recipient numerous awards Birmingham Cable TV, 1981-89, Cable TV Vulcan award, 1989-90, 90-91, World Poetry Golden Poet award, 1990, 91, Silver poet award, 1991. Mem. ALA, Poetry Soc., Actors and Theatre Guild, So. Bus. Edn. Assn., Ala. Assn. Legal Secs., Ala. Theater Orgn. Soc., Ala. Cable Network Affiliates, Nat. Theater Orgn. Soc., Jr. Women's C. of C., Thalian Lit. Club (Woman of Yr. award 1994—, Millennium 1st Pl. Poetry award, 1st Place Poetry award), Arlington Hist. Soc., Nat. Bus. Edn. Assn., Quill Club (libr. award, libr. writing award), Beta Sigma Phi. Baptist. Avocations: children's puppet workshops, crocheting, costuming puppets, piano and organ music, singing. Office: Dean and Co 2441 Old Springville Rd Birmingham AL 35215-4081

DOUGHERTY, ELMER LLOYD, JR., retired chemical engineering educator, consultant; b. Dorrance, Kans., Feb. 7, 1930; s. Elmer Lloyd and Nettie Linda (Anspaugh) Dougherty; m. Joan Victoria Benton, Nov. 25, 1952 (div. June 1963); children: Sharon, Victoria, Timothy, Michael(dec.); m. Ann Marie Da Silva (dec.). Student, Ft. Hays State Coll., 1946-48; BS in Chem. Engring., U. Kans., 1950; MS in Chem. Engring., U. Ill., 1952, PhD in Chem. Engring., 1955. Chem. engr. Esso Standard Oil Co., Baton Rouge, 1951-52; chem. engr. Dow Chem. Co., Freeport, Tex., 1955-58; research engr. Standard Oil of Calif., San Francisco, 1958-65; mgr. mgmt. sci. Union Carbide Corp., N.Y.C., 1965-68; cons. chem. engring. Stamford, Conn. and Denver, 1968-71; founder and owner Maraco, Inc., Monarch Beach, Calif., 1980—; prof. chem. engring. U. So. Calif., L.A., 1971-95, prof. emeritus, 1995—. Cons. OPEC, Vienna Austria, 1978-82, SANTOS, Ltd., Adelaide, Australia, 1980—, Kuwait Oil Co., 1995—. Contbr. numerous articles to profl. jours. Mem. Soc. Petroleum Engrs. (Disting. mem., chmn. Los Angeles Basin sect. 1984-85, Ferguson medal 1964, J.J. Arps award 1989), Am. Inst. Chem. Engrs., Internat. Assn. Energy Economists, Inst. Mgmt. Sci. Clubs: El Niguel Country (bd. dirs. 1976-78) (Laguna Niguel, Calif.). Republican. Avocation: golf. Home and Office: Maraco Inc 33531 Marlinspike Dr Monarch Beach CA 92629-4426 E-mail: eld@maraco.com.

DOUGHERTY, FLOYD WALLACE, design engineer; b. Birmingham, Ala., Oct. 25, 1942; s. Floyd Patrick and Mary Josephine (Wallace) D.; m. Dana Dean Lesley, Sept. 2; 1 child, Lesley Dean. BS, Auburn U., 1966; BSCE, U. Ala., 1970. Registered prof. engr., Ala., Miss., Ga. Design engr. Paul B. Krebs & Assocs., Birmingham, Ala., 1967-87; pres., owner F.W. Dougherty Engring. & Assocs., Birmingham, Ala., 1987—. Dir. Dean & Co. Variety TV Show, Birmingham, 1980—. Sgt. U.S. Army Corp Engrs. U.S. Army. Recipient EPA Nat. award Excellence Waste Water/Bio-Solids Engring., 2000. Mem. ASCE,

Am. Water Works Assn., Ala. Water & Pollution Control Assn., Water Environment Fedn. (George W. White award 1996), Ctrl. Ala. Am. Concrete Inst. (Outstanding Achievement award 1999), Assoc. Gen. Contrs. Am. (Engr. of the Yr. 2001). Republican. Baptist. Avocations: fishing, skiing, model plane building and flying.

DOUGHERTY, F(RANCIS) KELLY, data processing executive; b. Lubbock, Tex., May 15, 1953; s. Francis Kelly and Mary Ann (Odell) D.; m. Bonnie Lee Burch, June 14, 1975; children: Anne Katherine, Margaret Erin, Mary Bridget, Kerry Meaghan, Frances Cara. BA in Math. and Physics summa cum laude, U. Dallas, 1975; MS in Computer Sci., U. Tex., Dallas, 1998; cert. assoc. customer svc., Life Office Mgmt. Inst., 1992. CLU; cert. computing profl.; chartered fin. cons.; Microsoft cert. programmer. Actuarial trainee Ranger Nat. Life Ins., Houston, 1975-77; mgr. time sharing svcs. Phila. Life Ins. Co., Houston, 1977-81; sys. engr. Electronic Data Sys., Dallas, 1981-85; IT analyst AEGON Direct Mktg. Svcs., Inc., Plano, Tex., 1985—. Pres. St. Elizabeth Seton Parish Bd. Edn., 1989-92. U. Dallas scholar, 1971-75; Rice U. fellow, 1975-76. Fellow Life Mgmt. Inst. (master); mem. IEEE, Assn. for Computing Machinery, K.C. Republican. Roman Catholic. Home: 2713 S Cypress Cir Plano TX 75075-3154 Office: AEGON Direct Mktg Svcs Inc 2700 W Plano Pky Plano TX 75075-8200 E-mail: fdougher@AegonUSA.com.

DOUGHERTY, JAMES, orthopedic surgeon, educator, author; b. Lawrence, Mass., July 31, 1926; s. James A. and Maude D. (Dillard) D.; m. Marilyn Hays (dec.); m. Rita Buchman; children: James (dec.), Charles, Janice, Jonathan, Christopher. *Wife, Rita Buchman Dougherty. Pioneer woman home builder. Property manager and real estate broker. Winner "People's Choice" National Needlepoint Guild Convention, 1991. Former President ANG Southwestern chpt. Daugher Janice B.S., MPT is a physical therapist and hospital rehabiltation director, Son Thomas is steel industry consultant, Son Jonathan BA, MS is executive Vice President of Albany (N.Y.) County Medical Society, Christopher a Fire Fighter paramedic and a Maratime historian, Charles is an F.B.I. Supervisor.* BS, Trinity Coll., Hartford, Conn., 1950; MD, Albany Med. Coll., N.Y., 1951. Diplomate, examiner and monitor Am. Bd. Orthopaedic Surgery, 1965-82; diplomate Am. Bd. Forensic Examiners, Am. Bd. Forensic Medicine. Intern U. Chgo. Clinics, 1951-52, resident, 1951-56, instr., 1955-56; chmn. divsn. orthop. surgery SUNY, Syracuse, 1958-60; prof. clin. surgery Albany Med. Coll., 1960-96, attending surgeon, 1961-94, chief of staff, 1987-89, prof. emeritus, 1996—. Trustee Albany Med. Ctr., 1993-95; cons. Subacute Care Alternative Project, Washington. Author: Ponies in The Window, 1998, (hymns) Life's Narrow Pathways, A Babe Was Born; mem. editl. bd.: Techniques in Orthops.; proponent and architect Fla. state program for pro-bono volunteerism of ret. physicians for medically disadvantaged, 2001; contbr. articles to profl. jours. and Ency. Brittanica. Mem. bd. edn. Ravena-Coeymans-Selkirk Ctrl. Schs., Ravena, NY, 1960—75; med. dir. N.Y. Sr. Games, 1986—89, Catskill Children's Orthop. Clinic, 1960—95; trustee Schaeffer Meml. Libr., 1990—92, Albany Med. Ctr., 1993—95; vol. coord. We Care Program, Lee County, Fla.; bd. dirs. Inst. for Study of Aging, 1990—95. Served with U.S. Army, 1944—46. Recipient Alumni medal Albany Med. Coll., 1951. Fellow: Am. Acad. Orthopaedic Surgeons; mem.: Sr. and Ret. Physicians' Assn. of Lee County Fla. (founder, pres. 1997—98), Albany Med. Coll. Alumni Assn. (trustee 1990—99, pres. 1994—96, Meritorious Svc. award 1996), Northeastern Regional Assn. Sports Medicine (chmn. 1984—89), Asean Orthop. Soc. (hon.), We. Orthop. Soc. (hon. honored guest, Scottsdale, Ariz. 2000), U. Chgo. Surg. Soc., Crawford Campbell Soc. (founder, pres. 1978—88), Sigma Nu, Sigma Psi, Alpha Omega Alpha. Presbyterian. Home: 3510 Pine Fern Ln Bonita Springs FL 34134-1918 *As an orthopaedic surgeon I have sometimes been tempted to exaggerate my role and massage my ego. But then I am reminded that I merely treated. The surgeon operates... God heals ... and the patient makes it work.*

DOUGHERTY, JOCELYN, retired neurologist; b. Topeka, Kans., Oct. 10, 1934; d. Arthur McIntyre and Helen Marie (Olson) Dougherty; m. Fred Herzig. BS in Edn., U. Kans., 1956, MD, 1967. Diplomate Am. Bd. Quality Assurance. Intern Presbyn. Hosp., San Francisco, 1967—68, resident, 1968—70, U. Calif., Davis, Calif., 1970—71, fellow, 1971; fellow in neuro-ophthalmology Columbia Presbyn. Hosp., NY, 1972; neurologist Bronx VA Hosp., Bronx, NY, 1972; cons. Sydenham Hosp., NY, 1973—74, Fairview State Hosp., Calif., 1975—2000; ret., 2000. Cons. St. Barnebes Hosp., Bronx, 1972, Columbia-Presbyn. Harlem Divsn., 1974. Contbr. articles to profl. jours. Mem.: Am. Acad. Neurology. Home: 700 Malabar Dr Corona Del Mar CA 92625-1839

DOUGHERTY, JOHN MARTIN, bishop; b. Scranton, Pa., Apr. 29, 1932; Student, St. Charles Coll., Cantonsville, Md., 1951, St. Mary's Sem., Balt., 1957, U. Notre Dame, 1956; LLD, U. Scranton. Ordained priest Roman Cath. Ch. 1957. Titular bishop Diocese of Sufetula, 1995—; auxiliary bishop Diocese of Scranton, 1995—. Office: Chancery Office 300 Wyoming Ave Scranton PA 18503-1285*

DOUGHERTY, JOHN CHRYSOSTOM, III, retired lawyer; b. Beeville, Tex., May 3, 1915; s. John Chrysostom and Mary V. (Henderson) D.; m. Mary Ireland Graves, Apr. 18, 1942 (dec. July 1977); children: Mary Ireland, John Chrysostom IV; m. Bea Ann Smith, June 1978 (div. 1981); m. Sarah B. Randle, 1981 (dec. June 1997). BA, U. Tex., 1937; LLB, Harvard U., 1940; diploma, Inter-Am. Acad. Internat. and Comparative Law, Havana, Cuba, 1948. Bar: Tex. 1940. Atty. Hewit & Dougherty, Beeville, 1940-41; ptnr. Graves & Dougherty, Austin, Tex., 1946-50, Graves, Dougherty & Greenhill, Austin, 1950-57, Graves, Dougherty & Gee, Austin, 1957-60, Graves, Dougherty, Gee & Hearon, Austin, 1961-66, Graves, Dougherty, Gee, Hearon, Moody & Garwood, Austin, 1966-73, Graves, Dougherty, Hearon, Moody & Garwood, Austin, 1973-79, Graves, Dougherty, Hearon & Moody, Austin, 1979-93, sr. counsel, 1993—; ret., 1997. Spl. asst. atty. gen., 1949-50; Hon. French Consul, Austin, 1971-86; lectr. on tax, estate planning, probate code, community property problems; mem. Tex. Submerged Lands Adv. Com., 1963-72, Tex. Bus. and Commerce Code Adv. Com., 1964-66, Gov.'s Com. on Marine Resources, 1970-71, Gov.'s Planning Com. on Colorado River Basin Water Quality Mgmt. Study, 1972-73, Tex. Legis. Property Tax Com., 1973-75; adv. com. Mex. Ctr. Inst. of Latin-Am. Studies U. Tex., 1997—. Co-editor: Texas Appellate Practice, 1964, 2d edit., 1977; contbr. Bowe, Estate Planning and Taxation, 1957, 65; Texas Lawyers Practice Guide, 1967, 71, How to Live and Die with Texas Probate, 1968, 7th edit., 1995, Texas Estate Administration, 1975, 78; mem. bd. editors: Appellate Procedure in Tex., 1964, 2d edit., 1982; contbr. articles to profl. jours. Bd. dirs. Tex. Beta Students Aid Fund, 1949-84, Grenville Clark Fund at Dartmouth Coll., 1976-90, Umlauf Sculpture Garden, Inc., 1990-91, New Life Inst., 1993-2001; past bd. dirs. Advanced Religious Study Found., Holy Cross Hosp., Sea Arama, Inc., Nat. Pollution Control Found., Austin Nat. Bank; trustee St. Stephen's Episcopal Sch., Austin, 1969-83, Tex. Equal Access to Justice Found., 1986-90, U. Tex. Law Sch. Found., 1974-2002; mem. adv. com. Legal Assts. Tng. Inst., U. Tex., 1990-98; mem. vis. com. Harvard Law Sch., 1983-87. Capt. C.I.C., AUS, 1941-44, JAGC, 1944-46, maj. USAR. Decorated Medaille Française, France, Medaille d'honneur en Argent des Affairs Etrangeres, France, chevalier l'Ordre Nat. du Merite; recipient Wm. Reece Smith Spl. Svcs. to Pro Bono award Nat. Assn. of Pro Bono Coords., 2000. Fellow Am. Bar Found., Tex. Bar Found., Am. Coll. Trust and Estate Counsel, Am. Coll. Tax Counsel; mem. ABA (ho. of dels. 1982-88, standing com. on lawyers pub. responsibility 1983-85, spl. com. on delivery legal svcs. 1987-91, com. legal problems of the elderly 1997-2000, Sr. Lawyers divsn. Pro Bono Lawyer of 1999), Am. Arbitration Assn. (nat. panel arbitrators 1958-90), Travis County Bar Assn. (pres. 1979-80), Internat. Acad. Estate and Trust Law (exec. coun. 1988-90), State Bar Tex. (chmn. sect. taxation 1965-66, pres. 1979-80, com. legal svcs. to the poor 1986-94), Am. Judicature Soc. (bd. dirs. 1985-87), Am. Law Inst. (adv. com. project law governing lawyers 1990-97), Tex. Supreme Ct. Hist. Soc. (trustee 1997—, chmn. 1999-2002), Philos. Soc. Tex. (pres. 1989, bd. dirs. 1989—), Harvard Law Sch. Assn. (com. on pub. svc. law 1990-95, chmn. 1990-95, coun. 1991-95, exec. com. 1992-95), Tex. Appleseed, Inc. (bd. dirs. 1996—), The Austin Project (bd. dirs. 1999—), Rotary. Presbyterian. Home: 1801 Lavaca St Apt 5J Austin TX 78701 Office: Bank of America Center 515 Congress Ave Ste 2300 Austin TX 78701-3508 also: PO Box 98 Austin TX 78767-0098 Home Fax: 512-476-8186. E-mail: cdougherty@gdhm.com.

DOUGHERTY, JUDE PATRICK, philosophy educator, dean; b. Chgo., July 21, 1930; s. Edward Timothy and Cecilia Anastasia (Loew) D.; m. Patricia Ann Regan, Dec. 28, 1957; children: Thomas, Michael, John, Paul. BA, Cath. U. Am., 1954, MA, 1955, PhD, 1960; LHD (hon.), Thomas More Coll., 1995, Cath. U. Lublin, Poland, 2000. Instr. Marquette U., 1957-58; instr. Bellarmine Coll., 1958-60, asst. prof., 1960-63, assoc. prof., 1963-66, Cath. U. Am., 1966-76, prof., 1976—; dean Cath. U. Am. (Sch. Philosophy), 1967-99. Vis. assoc. prof. Georgetown U., summer, 1965; vis. prof. Katholieke Universiteit te Leuven, Belgium, 1974-75 Author: Recent American Naturalism, 1960, Western Creed; Western Identity, 2000, The Logic of Religion, 2002, Jacques Maritain: An Intellectual Profile, 2003, Religion-Gesellschaft-Demokratie, 2003; co-author: Approaches to Morality, 1966; editor: (books) Theological Directions of the Ecumenical Movement, 1964, The Impact of Vatican II, 1966, The Good Life and Its Pursuit, 1985; editor Rev. of Metaphysics, 1971—; gen. editor: Studies in Philosophy and the History of Philosophy, 1978— . Mem. bd. advisors Franklin J. Matchette Found., 1971—; trustee Bellarmine Coll., 1972-75, U. Bridgeport, 1995-99; mem. Pontifical Acad., St. Thomas, Rome, 1981—; mem. Academia Scientiarum et Artium Europae, Salzburg, 1991—. Decorated Knight of St. Gregory the Great, Pope John Paul II, 1999. Mem. Am. Philos. Assn. (program chmn. ea. divsn. 1988, exec. com. ea. divsn. 1989-93), Am. Cath. Philos. Assn. (pres. 1974-75, Aquinas medal 1994), Washington Philosophy Club (pres. 1968-69), Soc. for Philosophy Religion (pres. 1978-79), Metaphys. Soc. Am. (pres. 1983-84), Fellowship Cath. Scholars (exec. sec. 1994-97, treas. 1994-97, Cardinal Wright award 1994), Am. Maritain Assn. (scholarly achievement award 2000). Home: 9036 Rouen Ln Potomac MD 20854-3130 Office: Cath U Am Sch Philosophy 620 Michigan Ave NE Washington DC 20064-0001 E-mail: judeandpat@aol.com., dougherj@cua.edu.

DOUGHERTY, JUNE EILEEN, librarian; b. Union City, N.J., Mar. 27, 1929; d. Robert John and Jane Veronica (Smith) Beyrer; m. Donald E. Dougherty, Dec. 2, 1946; 1 child, Glen Allan. BA in Edn., Peterson State Coll., 1967; postgrad., Rutgers U. Sch. Libr. Sci., 1959-69. With A. B. Dumont, Paterson, N.J., 1950-54; sch. libr. St. Paul's Elem. Sch., Prospect Park, N.J., 1957—. Dir. North Haledon (N.J.) Free Pub. Libr., 1957—92; sec.-treas. Dougherty & Dougherty, Inc., North Haledon, 1968—73. Den mother Boy Scouts Am., 1954-57, 92; mem. Gov. N.J.'s Tercentenary Com., 1962-64. Mem. Am. Libr. Assn., N.J. Libr. Assn., North Haledon Libr. Assn., Cath. Libr. Assn., N.J. Librs. Roundtable, Bergen Passaic Libr. Club, Friends N. Haledon Publ. Libr., St. Paul's Social Club. Roman Catholic. Home: 155 Westervelt Ave Haledon NJ 07508-3074 Office: 129 Overlook Ave North Haledon NJ 07508-2570

DOUGHERTY, MARK RICHARD, university administrator; b. Brookville, Pa., May 15, 1977; s. Richard Glenn and Jonni Leah Dougherty; m. Amanda Ivey Houston, July 14, 2001. BS, Gardner-Webb U., Boiling Springs, N.C., 1999. Math. tchr. Kings Mountain Mid. Sch., Kings Mountain, NC, 2000; grad. resident dir. Gardner-Webb U., Boiling Springs, NC, 2000—01, northside area dir., 2002, coord. of jud. affairs, 2002—03, asst. dir. residence life, 2003—. Residence hall assn. advisor Gardner-Webb U., Boiling Springs, NC, 2002—. Mem.: Internat. Assn. for Coll. and U. Housing Officers, Southeastern Assn. Univ. Housing Officers, Assn. for Student Jud. Affairs, Southeastern Assn. Univ. Housing Officers, NC Housing Officers (assoc.). R-Liberal. Avocation: reading. Office: Gardner-Webb U GWU Box 7267 Boiling Springs NC 28017 E-mail: mdougherty@gardner-webb.edu.

DOUGHERTY, MOLLY IRELAND, organization executive; b. Austin, Tex., Oct. 3, 1949; d. John Chrysostom and Mary Ireland (Graves) D.; m. Richard Pells, Oct. 2, 1999. Student, Stanford U., 1968-71, Grad. Theol. Union, Berkeley, 1976; BA, Antioch U., 1980. Tchr., fundraiser Oakland Cmty. Sch., Calif., 1973-77; assoc. prodr., asst. editor film Nicaragua: These Same Hands, Palo Alto, Calif., 1980; freelance journalist, translator Nicaragua, 1981; assoc. prodr. film Short Circuit: Inside the Death Squads; exec. dir. Vecinos, Austin, 1984—; cons. Magee & Magee Assocs., 1991—93; English, French and Spanish lang. tutor St. Stephen's Episcopal Sch., Austin, 2003—. Spanish lang. tutor St. Stephen's Episcopal Sch., Austin, 1988-89. Bd. dirs. Nat. Immigration Refugee and Citizenship Forum, Washington, 1985-88; spkr., fundraiser Salvadoran Assn. for Rural Health, 1986—; lectr. St. Stephen's Episcopal Ch., 1989. Home: 1100 Claire Ave Austin TX 78703-2502 Office: Vecinos Inter-Am Initiative PO Box 4562 Austin TX 78765-4562

DOUGHERTY, NEIL JOSEPH, physical education educator, safety consultant; b. Elizabeth, N.J., Apr. 7, 1943; s. Neil Joseph and Doris Burnett (Lindsay) D.; m. Margaret Ruth Quaranta, July 17, 1965; 1 child, Margaret Elizabeth. BS, Rutgers U., 1964, EdM, 1965; EdD, Temple U., 1970. Tchr. phys. edn. St. Joseph's Sch., Bound Brook, N.J., 1964-65; teaching assoc. Temple U., Phila., 1967-70; prof. Rutgers U., New Brunswick, N.J., 1970—. Mem. adv. bd. Youth Sports Rsch. Coun., New Brunswick, 1987—; nat. faculty mem. U.S. Sports Acad., 1988—. Co-author: Understanding and Assessing Human Movement, 1980, Management Principles in Sport and Leisure Sciences, 1985, Contemporary Approaches to the Teaching of Physical Education, 1979, 87, Sport, Physical Activity and the Law, 1993, 2002; editor: Physical Education and Sport for Secondary School Students, 1983, 93, 2002, Principles of Safety in Physical Education and Sport, 1987, 93, 2002, Outdoor Recreation Safety, 1998, (jour.) The Reporter, 1977-81, (monograph series) Briefings, 1974-75; mem. editl. bd. Leisure Times Focus, 1984-88, Jour. of Tchg. in Phys. Edn., 1981-85, Safety Notebook, 1998—; contbr. to profl. jours. 1st lt. U.S. Army, 1965-67. Recipient Merit award Ea. Assn. for Health, Phys. Edn., Recreation and Dance, 1980, Honor award, 1982, Honor award Soc. for Study of Legal Aspects of Sport and Phys. Activity, 1998. Fellow N.Am. Soc. Health Edn., Phys. Edn, Recreation, Sport and Dance (charter); mem. Am. Assn. Active Lifestyles and Fitness (pres. 2001—03), Nat. Assn. Phys. Edn. Higher Edn. (pres. 1984-86), Sch. and Cmty. Safety Soc. Am. (pres. 1996-98, Profl. Svc. award 1991, 97, Scholar award 1994), N.J. Assn. of Dirs. of Health, Phys. Edn. and Recreation (pres. 1976-78), N.J. Assn. for Health, Phys. Edn., Recreation and Dance (pres. 1979-80, Honor fellow award 1983, Disting. Leadership award 1982), Coll. and Univ. Phys. Edn. Coun. (chmn. 1985-88). Avocations: fishing, water sports, golf. Home: 1655 East Dr Point Pleasant NJ 08742-5117 Office: Rutgers U Dept Exercise Sci/Sport Stu New Brunswick NJ 08903 E-mail: njd@rci.rutgers.edu.

DOUGHERTY, PERCY H. geographer, educator, politician, planner; b. Kennett Square, Pa., Feb. 20, 1943; s. Percy H. Sr. and Anna (Cloud) D.; m. Anne Barbara Zinn, July 9, 1966; children: Thomas P., Robert J. BS in Geography, Biology, West Chester U., 1967, MEd in Phys. Geography, 1968; PhD in Phys. Geography, Geology, Boston U., 1980. Tchr. geography and earth sci. Plymouth Meeting (Pa.) Jr. H.S., 1967-68; asst. prof. West Chester (Pa.) U., 1968-70, Trenton (N.J.) State Coll., 1972-77, CUNY, 1977-78, U. Cin., 1978-83; vis. prof. Ohio U., Athens, 1983-84; vis. asst. prof. U. Ky., Lexington, 1984-85; assoc. prof. Kutztown (Pa.) U., 1985-90, prof. geography, 1990—. Editor of 2 books on karst; editor GEO2, 1980-88, Bulletin of the Nat. Speliological Soc., 1984-85; contbr. articles to profl. jours. Chmn. Lower Macungie Twp. Planning Commn., 1991-92; bd. dirs. Sloans Valley Conservation Task Force, Lexington, Ky., Allentown (Pa.) Art Mus., Allentown Symphony, Lehigh Valley Arts Coun., Wildlands Conservancy; past chmn. comprehensive planning com., bd. dirs. Lehigh Valley Planning Commn. Lehigh and Northampton Counties, Pa., 1990-95, past chmn. bd. dirs. 1995-97; Rep. committeeman Lower Macungie Twp. Dist. 2, 1990-96; elected mem. Lehigh County Commn., 1994—, chmn., 2000-03; bd. dirs. County Commn. Assn. Pa., 1998-2000, 02—, chair energy, environ. and land use com., 1998-2000. NSF fellow, 1971, 80, 92, NASA fellow, 1981, NOAA fellow, 1982. Fellow Nat. Speleol. Soc. (life), Miami Valley Grotto (hon. life), Ctrl. Jersey Grotto (hon. life); mem. Assn. Am. Geographers (life, mem. com. c.c.'s 2000-01, nat. councillor 2000-03, past pres., sec., treas., editor, bd. dirs.), Delaware Valley Geog. Assn. (past pres., bd. dirs.), Nat. Coun. Geog. Edn. (life), Am. Water Resources Assn., Am. Soc. Photogrammetry and Remote Sensing, Conf. Latin Am. Geography, Pa. Geog. Soc. (past v.p., bd. dirs.), Am. Wine Soc. (cert. wine judge). Achievements include research on remote sensing, air photo, geomorphology, karst, climatic geomorphology, groundwater diffusion, water resources, geographic education, planning. Office: Kutztown Univ Dept Geography 115 Grim Hall Kutztown PA 19530-9621 also: Lehigh County Courthouse PO Box 1548 Allentown PA 18105-1548 E-mail: percydougherty@lehighcounty.org., doughert@kutztown.edu.

DOUGHERTY, RALEIGH GORDON, manufacturer representative; b. Saginaw, Mich., Aug. 19, 1928; s. Raleigh Gordon and Helen Jean (McCrum) D.; 1 child, Karen Kealani. Salesman H.D. Hudson Mfg. Co., Chgo., 1946-48; field sales rep. Jensen Mfg. Co., Chgo., 1948-50; field sales mgr. Regency Idea, Indpls., 1950-54; mgr. Brenna & Browne, Honolulu, 1954-56; owner, pres. Dougherty Enterprises, Honolulu, 1956—. With U.S. Army, 1950-52. Mem. Internat. Exec. Housekeepers Assn., Hawaii Hotel Assn., Internat. Home Furnishings Reps. Assn., Air Force Assn., DAV (life), Navy League U.S., Am. Legion, Korean Vet., Elks (past trustee Hawaii). Republican. Methodist. Home and Office: 1326 Lunalilo Home Rd Honolulu HI 96825-3216

DOUGHERTY, RICHARD MARTIN, library and information science educator; b. East Chicago, Ind., Jan. 17, 1935; s. Floyd C. and Harriet E. (Martin) D.; m. Ann Prescott, Mar. 24, 1974; children— Kathryn E., Emily E.; children by previous marriage— Jill Ann, Jacquelyn A., Douglas M. BS, Purdue U., 1959, LHD honoris causa, 1991; M.L.S., Rutgers U., 1961, PhD, 1963; LHD honoris causa, U. Stellenbosch, South Africa, 1995. Head acquisitions dept. Univ. Library, U. N.C., Chapel Hill, 1963-66; assoc. dir. libraries U. Colo., Boulder, 1966-70; prof. library sci. Syracuse U., N.Y., 1970-72; univ. librarian U. Calif-Berkeley, 1972-78; dir. univ. library U. Mich., Ann Arbor, 1978-88, acting dean. Sch. Library Sci., 1984-85, prof. sch. info., 1978-98, prof. emeritus, 1999—; pres. Dougherty & Assocs., 1994—. Cons., change mgmt. libs.; founder, pres. Mountainside Pub. Corp., 1974—. Author: Scientific Management of Library Organizations, 2d edit., 1982; co-author: Preferred Futures for Libraries II, 1993; editor Coll. and Research Libraries jour., 1969-74, Jour. Acad. Librarianship, 1975-94, Library Issues, 1981—. Trustee Ann Arbor Dist. Libr., 1995—2002, pres. bd. trustees, 1998—2000. Recipient Esther Piercy award, 1968, Disting. Alumnus award Rutgers U., 1980, Acad. Librarian Yr., Assn. Coll. and Research Libraries, 1983, ALA Hugh C. Atkinson Meml. award, 1988, Blackwell Scholarship award, 1992, Joseph Lippincott medal, 1997; fellow Council on Library Resources. Mem. ALA (coun. 1969-76, 89-92, exec. bd. 1972-76, 89-92, endowment trustee 1986-89, pres. 1990-91), Assn. Rsch. Librs. (bd. dirs. 1977-80), Rsch. Librs. Group, Inc. (exec. com. 1984-88, chmn. bd. govs. 1986-87), Soc. Scholarly Pub. (bd. dirs. 1990-92, exec. com. 1991-92), Internat. Fedn. Libr. Assns. (round table of editors of library jours. 1985-87, standing com. univ. libr. sect. 1981-87). Home: 6 Northwick Ct Ann Arbor MI 48105-1408 Office: Dougherty & Assoc PO Box 8330 Ann Arbor MI 48107-8330 E-mail: rmdoughe@umich.edu.

DOUGHERTY, ROBERT ANTHONY, retired manufacturing company executive; b. St. Louis, May 3, 1928; s. Joseph A. and Venita E. (Gretline) D.; m. Rosemary Schmertmann, Jan. 29, 1955; children: Kevin, Patrick, Michael, Mary Ann, Timothy. BS in Mech. Engring, U. Notre Dame, 1952. Registered profl. engr., Calif. cert. mfg. engr. Sales engr. Robert R. Stephens Machinery Co., St. Louis, 1952-60, dist. mgr., 1961-72; pres. Dougherty & Assos., Prairie Village, Kans., 1972-99, ret., chmn. bd. dirs. Bd. dirs. Tech-Industry Cons., Lenexa, Kans.; exec. com. Kans. Industry/Univ./Govt. Engring. Edn. Consortium. Mem. adv. com. Pittsburg, Kans. Sch. Sci. and Tech., 1987—; coord. cons. Kans. U. Ctrs. Excellence for Kans. Tech. Enterprise Corp., 1991—. Served with U.S. Army, 1946-48. Recipient Productivity award Coll. and Univ. Mfg. Edn. Council, 1979, Soc. Mfg. Engrs. Joseph A. Siegel Meml. honor award, 1992; Outstanding Engring. Achievements award San Fernando Valley Engrs. Council, 1980. Fellow Instn. Prodn. Engrs. Gt. Britain (life); mem. ASME (state legis. fellow), Am. Soc. for Metals, Soc. Mfg. Engrs. (pres. 1980-81, dir. 1971-82, Region 5 award of merit 1969), Serra Club of Kansas City Kans. (pres. 2003—), Round Hill Bath and Tennis Club (pres. 1971), Hillcrest Country Club (v.p. 1982, pres. 1983—). Roman Catholic.

DOUGHTEN, MARY KATHERINE (MOLLY DOUGHTEN), retired secondary education educator; b. Belvidere, Ill., Apr. 26, 1923; d. Edwin Albert and Theora Teresa (Tefft) Loop; m. Philip Tedford Doughten, Oct. 15, 1947; children: Deborah Doughten Hellriegel, Susan Doughten Myers, Ann Doughten Fickenscher, Philip Tedford Jr., David, Sarah Doughten Wiggins. BA, DePauw U., 1945; MS, Western Res. U., 1947. Social worker Children's Svcs., Cleve., 1947, San Antonio, 1948-49; tchr. English Indian Valley High Schs., Gradenhutten, Ohio, 1962-66; tchr. English and sociology New Philadelphia (Ohio) High Sch., 1966-86. Mem. Tuscarawas County Juvenile Judges Citizen's Rev. Bd., 1980—2003, United Way, 1960—67, ARC, PTA, 1955—58, coun. pres., 1960—62, mental health chmn. state bd., 1963—65, libr. chmn., 1966—68; mem. Hospice, 1987—; founding cm. Kent State U. Tuscarawas campus, 1961—62; v.p. Tuscarawas County U. Found., 1996—98, pres., 1998—2000; leader Girl Scouts, 1959—68; bd. mem. Tuscarawas County U. Found., 2000—; vol. Ohio Reads, 2000—; vol. reach for recovery Am. Cancer Soc., 2002—; mem. arts coun. Tuscarawas Philharmonic League; vol. Tuscarawas County Work and Family Svcs., 2003—; mem. Dem. Women, 1986—; bd. dir. Tuscarawas Valley Guidance Ctr., 1950—62, Cmty Mental Health Care, Inc., 1974—82, 1984—92, pres., 1979—81; bd. dir. Alcohol, Drug and Mental Health Svcs. bd., Tuscarawas-Carroll County, 1992—2001, v.p., 1996—98; bd. mem. State CC, 1965—68; founder, bd. dir. Ohio Cmty. Mental Health Svcs., Columbus, Ohio, 1970—80; bd. dir. Mobile Meals, 1992—. Recipient Mental Health award Community and Profl. Svcs., 1978; Martha Holden Jennings scholar, 1975-76; named WJER Woman of the Yr., 2002. Mem. AAUW (sec. 1962, v.p. 1996-98), Ohio Ret. Tchrs. (sec. 1987-89), New Philadelphia Edn. Assn., Friends of Libr., Chestnut Soc. (bd. dirs. 1987-89, 2001—), Tuscarawas County Med. Aux. (pres. 1959-60, 86-87, state bd. 1960-64), Union Hosp. Aux. (bd. dirs. 1986-98, editor 1986-98), DAR, Tuscawaras County Ret. Tchrs. Assn. (bd. dirs. 1999—), Coll. Club (scholarship chair 1989-91, 99-2001), Union Country Club, Atwood Yacht Club, Lady Elks, Mortar Bd., Phi Beta Kappa, Alpha Chi Omega, Theta Sigma Phi. Democrat. Presbyterian. Avocations: travel, golf, sailing, reading, photography. Home: 204 Gooding Ave NW New Philadelphia OH 44663-1727 E-mail: philmoll@tusco.net.

DOUGHTY, A. GLENN, minister; b. Somers Point, N.J., Aug. 30, 1942; s. Alfred and Irene Dorothy (Colhouer) D.; m. Carole True, June 17, 1967; children: Matthew Glenn, Lynn Carole. BS in Bible Studies, Phila. Coll. of Bible, 1965; MDiv, Faith Theol. Sem., 1968. Ordained to ministry Fellowship Fundamental Bible Chs., 1970. Pastor Community Bible Ch., Barrington, N.J., 1968-70, The Bible Ch. of Westville, N.J., 1970—. Chmn. Bible Protestant Ch. Ext., 1970-73; sec. Fellowship of Fundamental Bible Chs., 1976-95, 2001—, mem. ministerial qualifications com., 1980-95, Fundamental Bible Inst., 2001. Chmn. Cmty. Dispute Resolution Com., Westville, 1986—. Named Outstanding Vol. of Yr., Gloucester Co. Mem. Am. Coun. Christian Chs. (mem. exec. com. 1990—), Fellowship of Fundamental Bible Chs. (trustee 1985-95, pres. trustees 1985-91, chmn. trustees 1993-95, sec. Fundamental Bible Missions 1996-98, pres. 1998—2002). Home and Office: 134 Delsea Dr Westville NJ 08093-1159 E-mail: gcdoughty@quadnet.net.

DOUGHTY, GEORGE FRANKLIN, airport administrator; b. Wheeling, W.Va., Mar. 11, 1946; s. Ernest Heyward and Elizabeth Gertrude (Dei) D.; m. Jennifer L. Tyma; children: Susan Elizabeth, Jennifer Anne, Patrick George, Shannon Marie. BS in Aerospace Engring., W.Va. U., 1968. Asst. mgr. Cedar Rapids Mcpl. Airport, Iowa, 1975-78; dep. dir. Balt.-Washington Internat. Airport State of Md., 1978-80; dir. port control City of Cleve., Ohio, 1980-84; dir. aviation Stapleton Internat. Airport City and County of Denver, 1981-92; exec. dir. Lehigh-Northampton Airport Authority, Allentown, Pa., 1992—. Recipient Laurels award Aviation Week and Space Tech., 1988. Mem. Am. Assn. Airport Execs. (dir. 1980), Airports Coun. Internat. N.Am. (chmn. govtl. affairs com. 1985-86, bd. dirs. 1986-89, 1st vice chmn. 1992, chmn. 1993). Home: 2131 Stonewall Dr Macungie PA 18062-9064 Office: Lehigh Valley Intl Airport 3311 Airport Rd Ste 4 Allentown PA 18109-3040

DOUGHTY, MICHAEL DEAN, insurance agent; b. Oklahoma City, Nov. 7, 1947; s. Charles Dean and Francis Jean (Schumpert) D.; m. Sherrie Lynn Perkins, May 30, 1970; children: Steven Kyle, Brian Edward. BS in Edn., Okla. State U., 1971; postgrad., Command Sgts. Maj. Acad.; Assoc. in Risk Mgmt., Ins. Inst. Am., 1993. Cert. ins. counselor; cert. profl. ins. agt., Cert. Profl. Ins. Agts. Soc.; EIS Designation; accredited adviser in ins. Ins. Inst. Am. Tchr., coach Perry (Okla.) Pub. Schs., 1971-80; asst. v.p., field agt. Coaches Ins. Assn. Am., Memphis, 1980-84; v.p., officer mgr. Albright Ins. Agy., Inc., Perry, Okla., 1984-88; prodr. Holt Ins. Agy., Perry, 1988—, co-owner, 1992—. Instr. Indian-Meridian Voc. Tech., Stillwater, Okla., 1985, new ins. edn. program Excellence in Svc., Ava, Moa., 1996-98, bus. adv. com., 2000, 2001; faculty instr. Cert. Ins. Svcs. Rep. Program, Soc. Cert. Ins. Couns., 1992—, Excellence in Svc. Comml. Ins. courses, 1996-98. Bd. dirs. United Fund Perry, 1983-86, 94-96, 97-99, 2003-06; youth sports cons. Noble County Family YMCA, Perry, 1985; vocat. bus. adv. bd. Perry H.S., 1990-95; mem. fin. adv. com. on taxes Noble County, 1993; mem. bus. devel. com. Perry Devel. Coalition, 1994-96; trustee First Bapt. Ch., 1997-99, chmn. 1999. Command sgt. maj. Okla. Army

N.G., 1970-96, ret. 1996. Mem.: Inst. Inst. Am. (assoc. risk mgmt.), Ind. Ins. Agts. Am., Okla. Assn. Ins. Agts. (discussion leader 1988, mem. pub. rels. com. 1988—91, chmn. 1990—91, rural and small agts. com. 1992—93), Profl. Ins. Agts. Okla. (bd. dirs. 1998—, v.p. 1999—, pres.-elect 2000—, pres. 2001—02, Agent of Yr. 2000—01), N.G. Assn. Okla. (life), Perry Diamond Club (v.p. 1990—91), Perry Quarterback Club (pres. 1990—92, 1991—92), Am. Legion (adjutant 1998—2000, 2003—), Perry C. of C. (v.p. 1993—94, bd. dirs. 1993—96, v.p. 1994, pres. 1994—96, 1995—96, named Citizen of Yr. 2000), Jaycees (chpt. pres. 1976—77, 1992—93), Elks (chmn. Americanism 1989—94). Democrat. Avocations: golf, volleyball, hunting, fishing. Home: 915 Jackson St Perry OK 73077-3012 Office: Holt Ins Agy 402 N 7th St Perry OK 73077-6425

DOUGLAS, ANDREW, retired state supreme court justice; b. Toledo, July 5, 1932; 4 children JD, U. Toledo, 1959. Bar: Ohio 1960, U.S. Dist. Ct. (no. dist.) Ohio 1960. Former ptnr. Winchester & Douglas; judge Ohio 6th Dist. Ct. Appeals, 1981-84; ret. justice Ohio Supreme Ct., 1985—2002. Mem. nat. adv. bd. Ctr. for Informatics Law John Marshall Law Sch., Chgo.; former spl. counsel Atty. Gen. of Ohio; former instr. law Ohio Dominican Coll. Served with U.S. Army, 1952-54 Recipient award Maumee Valley council Girl Scouts U.S., 1976, Outstanding Service award Toledo Police Command Officers Assn., 1980, Toledo Soc. for Autistic Children and Adults, 1983, Extra-Spl. Person award Central Catholic High Sch., 1981, Disting. Service award Toledo Police Patrolman's Assn., 1982, award Ohio Hispanic Inst. Opportunity, 1985, Disting. Merit award Alpha Sigma Phi, 1988, Gold "T" award U. Toledo, First Amendment award Cen. Ohio Chpt. Soc. Profl. Journalists Sigma Delta Chi, 1989; named to Woodward High Sch. Hall of Fame. Mem. Toledo Bar Assn., Lucas County Bar Assn., Ohio Bar Assn., Toledo U. Alumni Assn., U. Toledo Coll. Law Alumni Assn. (Disting. Alumnus award 1991), Internat. Inst., North Toledo Old Timers Assn., Old Newsboys Goodfellow Assn., Pi Sigma Alpha, Delta Theta Phi. Office: Ohio Supreme Ct 30 E Broad St Fl 3 Columbus OH 43215

DOUGLAS, BRUCE LEE, oral and maxillofacial surgeon, public health educator, gerontology and workplace health consultant; b. N.Y.C., July 14, 1925; s. William and Carrie (Basescu) D.; m. Janet Ramsden; children: Clifford, Steven, Jennifer, Sarah, Sandra. AB, Princeton U., 1947; D.D.S., NYU, 1948; postgrad. in oral surgery, Columbia U., 1949-51, MA in Edn, 1955, diploma in higher edn, 1957; M.P.H., U. Calif. at Berkeley, 1962. Diplomate Am. Bd. Oral and Maxillofacial Surgery. Prof. oral medicine and community dentistry Coll. Dentistry U. Ill., 1962-72, prof. preventive medicine Coll. Medicine, 1962-72; prof. health adminstrn. Sch. Pub. Health, 1972-98; prof. dental and oral surgery Rush Med. Coll., 1970-76; clin. prof. environ. and occupl. medicine Sch. Pub. Health, U. Ill. at Chgo., 1998—, health policy rsch., 2001—. Chief dentistry and oral surgery Rush-Presbyn.-St. Luke's Med. Ctr., Chgo., 1968-75; chief divsn. dental health, Ill. Dept. Pub. Health, 1976-78; chief sect. dentistry and oral surgery Lincoln Park Hosp. Chgo. (formerly Grant Hosp.), 1980-90, attending oral and maxillofacial surgeon, 1967—; Fulbright prof. oral surgery and anesthesiology Okayama (Japan) U. and Tokyo Med.-Dental U., 1959-61; WHO cons. to U. Antioquia, Colombia, Nat. U. and U. Zulia, Venezuela, 1964-69, Mahidol U., Bangkok, Thailand, 1973, Nat. Health Svc., Gt. Britain, 1977. Mem. Ill. Ho. of Reps., 11th Dist., 1971-72, 12th Dist., 1973-74; chmn. Ill. Coalition Against Tobacco, 1991-93. With USNR, 1943-53, lt. Dental Corps, 1951-53, Korea. Fellow Chgo. Inst. Medicine (bd. dirs. 1970-80), Am. Dental Soc. Anesthesiology (past pres.); mem. Am. Assn. Hosp. Dentists (past pres.), Fulbright Assn. (pres. Chgo. chpt. 1990-92). Address: 2401 Duffy Ln Riverwoods IL 60015 E-mail: douglasclan@comcast.net. *A health professional career can be the portal through which an educated person can pass to a fuller and richer life. My health professional, education, and public health degrees have made it possible for me to broaden my involvement in the affairs of my community, my nation, my world, and now the world of business, and to serve individuals in need as well.*

DOUGLAS, CAROLE NELSON, writer; b. Everett, Wash., Nov. 5, 1944; m. Sam Scott Douglas, Nov. 25, 1967. BA, Coll. of St. Catherine, 1966. Reporter St. Paul Pioneer Press, 1967—83, columnist, 1968—77, home interiors writer, 1977—80, copy layout editor, 1980—84, opinion page copy and layout editor, 1983—84, freelance fiction writer, 1984—. Mem., editl. bd. St. Paul Pioneer Press, 1983—84; mem. of bd. Newspaper Guild of Twin Cities, 1970—72; chair Gridiron Show, 1971, Page One Awards, 1972. Author: (novels) Femme Fatale, 2003, (Midnight Louie Mystery) Cat in a Neon Nightmare, 2003, Another Scandal in Bohemia, 2003, Castle Rouge, 2002, White House Pet Detectives, 2002, (Midnight Louie Mystery) Cat in a Midnight Choir, 2002, Cat in a Leopard Spot, 2000, Cat in a Kiwi Con, 2000, (Midnight Louie Quartet) The Cat and the Jill of Diamonds, 2000, (Midnight Louie Quartet) The Cat and the Queen of Hearts, 1999, (Midnight Louie Mystery) Cat in a Jeweled Jumpsuit, 1999, (Midnight Louie Quartet) The Cat and the King of Clubs, 1999, (Midnight Louie Mystery) Cat in an Indigo Mood, 1999, Cat on a Hyacinth Hunt, 1998, Midnight Louie's Pet Detectives, 1998, (Midnight Louie Mystery) Cat in a Golden Garland, 1997, Cat in a Flamingo Fedora, 1997, Cat with an Emerald Eye, 1996, Cat in a Diamond Dazzle, 1996, Cat in a Crimson Haze, 1995 (Best Novel award, 1995), Cat on a Blue Monday, 1994, Pussyfoot, 1993, Catnap, 1992, (Midnight Louis Quartet) The Cat and the Jack of Spades, 2000, Irene's Last Waltz, 1994, Irene at Large, 1992, Good Morning, Irene, 1992, Good Night, Mr. Holmes, 1990 (Best Novel award, 1990), (short stories) Magic and Murder, 2003, Much Ado About Murder, 2002, White House Pet Detectives, 2002, Present Lives, Past Tense, 1999, Fathers & Daughters, 1999, Cat Crimes Through Time, 1999, Best Cat Mysteries of the 20th Century, 1998, Roger Caras's New Treasury of Cat Stories, 1998, A Treasury of Cat Mysteries, 1998, Deadly Women, 1997, Cat Crimes for the Holidays, 1997, Marilyn: Shades of Blonde, 1997, First Cases II, 1997, Wild Women, 1997, Rivals of Dracula, 1996, Holmes for the Holidays, 1996, Great Writers & Kids Write Mystery Storie, 1996, Celebrity Vampires, 1995, Malice Domestic 4, 1995, The Mysterious West, 1995, Malice Domestic 2, 1993, Cat Crimes II, 1992, The Fine Art of Murder, 1993, Danger in D.C. Cat Crimes IV, 1993, The World's Finest Crime & Mystery Stories 2000, 2001—03, The Year's 25 Finest Crime & Mystery Stories, 1993, 1994, 1995, 1996, 1998, 2000, (Taliswoman series) Cup of Clay, 1991, Seed Upon the Wind, 1992, Counterprobe, 1988, Probe, 1985, (Sword & Circlet series) Six of Swords, 1982, Exiles of the Rynth, 1984, Keepers of Edanvant, 1987, Heir of Rengarth, 1988, Seven of Swords, 1989, Fair Wind, Fiery Star, 1981 (Porgie award, silver medal, 1982), Amberleigh, 1980, Lady Rogue, 1983, Angel Christmas, 1995, A Dreamspun Christmas, 1994, Azure Days, Quicksilver Nights, 1985, Crystal Days and Crystal Nights, 1990, In Her Prime, 1982, Her Own Person, 1982, The Best Man, 1983, The Exclusive, 1986, (various articles) profl. books and magazines, 1983—97. Recipient First Pres. citation, Am. Soc. Interior Designers, Minn. Chtr., 1980, Newswriting award, 2nd place, childfree couple series, Minn. AP, 1975, numerous awards, Newspaper Guild of Twin Cities, 1966—84, mag. awards, Romantic Times. Mem.: Sisters in Crime, Sci. Fiction and Fantasy Writers of Am., Romance Writers of Am. (Career Achievement award 1997, Lifetime Achievement award 1991, Popular Fiction award 1987, Sci. Fiction Fantasy award 1984), Novelists, Inc., Cat Writers' Assoc., Am. Crime Writers League. Avocations: dancing, collecting homeless cats, vintage clothing. Office: P O Box 331555 Fort Worth TX 76163 E-mail: cdouglas@catwriter.com.

DOUGLAS, CINDY HOLLOWAY, consultant; b. Queens, N.Y., Aug. 8, 1960; d. Richard Stephen and Beverly Bunny (Harris) Tannenbaum; m. David Milton Holloway (div. Mar. 1986); 1 child, Benjamin Jerome; m. Michael William Douglas, Mar. 21, 1998. BA, Calif. State U., Fullerton, 1981. Lic. real estate broker. Waitress Bob's Big Boy, San Bernardino, Calif., 1984-85; receptionist RNG Mortgage Co., San Bernardino, 1985; loan processor Quality Mortgage Co., Colton, Calif., 1985-88, loan officer, 1988-91, RNG Mortgage, 1991-92; v.p., br. mgr. Mountain West Fin., 1992-97; prodn. and mktg. mgr. South Pacific Fin., 1997-97; real estate loan mgr. Arrowhead Credit Union, 1998-2000; cons. mortgage banking, brokerages and credit unions, 2000—. Mem. San Bernardino Bd. Realtors (spl. events com. 1988—, comm. com. 1990—), Nat. Trust for Hist. Preservation, San Bernardino Execs. Assn., Assn. Profl. Mortgage Women (bd. dirs. 1989-90, v.p. 1992-93, Affiliate of Yr. award 1990), San Bernardino Execs. Group (bd. dirs. 1994—). Home: PO Box 3187 Crestline CA 92325-3187 E-mail: cindyd@cindydouglas.com.

DOUGLAS, FRANCES SONIA, minister; b. Stanaford, W.Va., May 12, 1931; d. Frank Gordon and Mary Celia Bradley; m. Paul Alexander Douglas, Jan. 6, 1949 (dec. Mar. 1993); children: Paul Jr., Sonia Paulette, Norton James, Mary Louise, Elizabeth Maria, Naomi Denise, Regina Michele, André(dec.). Doctorate(hon.), Christian Fellowship Ednl. Bible Coll., 1999. Housekeeper, 1955—70; sales rep. Amway Products, Niagara Falls, NY, 1970, Stuart McGuire Shoes, Niagara Falls, 1970, Finelle Products, Niagara Falls, 1980; founder, pastor True Deliverance Temple, Niagara Falls, 1974—. Chmn. Cleve. Ave. Sch. Parent Group, Niagara Falls, Harriet F. Abate Sch. Parent Group, Niagara Falls; vice chmn. Niagara Falls Faith Based Collaboration, 2000—01; former treas. Niagara Falls Ministerial Coun.; founder Emmanuel Temple No. 2 Ch., 1952; bd. dirs. Niagara Falls Faith Based Collaboration, 2001—. Recipient Cert. of Appreciation for Outstanding Cmty. Svc., Rainbow Sr. Citizens Inc., 1986. Avocations: embroidery, crocheting, sewing, travel. Office: True Deliverance Temple 1318 Niagara St Niagara Falls NY 14303

DOUGLAS, FRED ROBERT, cost engineering consultant; b. Newark, N.J., Apr. 25, 1924; s. Nathan and Sara (Schneider) D.; m. Lenore Berger, Mar. 20, 1954; children: Neil Richard, David Nathaniel. BSChemE, N.J. Inst. Tech., 1945; MSChemE, Poly. Inst. N.Y., 1949. Asst. to prodn. mgr. Bristol-Myers Corp., N.Y.C., 1948-52; chem. engr. Jefferson Chem. Co. Inc., N.Y.C., 1952 53; technologist Texaco Inc., Beacon, N.Y., 1953-88; pvt. practice cons., 1988—. Lectr. in cost engring. Contbr. articles to profl. jours. Pres. Hudson Valley Community Concerts Assn., 1968-69. With U.S. Army, 1945-47. Named Engr. of Distinction, Engrs. Joint Coun., 1970. Fellow Am. Assn. Cost Engrs. Internat. (sec. 1968-69, bd. dirs. 1983-84, v.p. 1985-89); mem. Rsch. Soc. Am. (treas. 1958-59). Home: PO Box 193 Glenham NY 12527-0193

DOUGLAS, GEORGE HALSEY, writer, educator; b. East Orange, N.J., Jan. 9, 1934; s. Halsey M. and Harriet Elizabeth (Goldbach) D.; m. Rosalind Braun, June 19, 1961; 1 son, Philip. AB with honors in Philosophy, Lafayette Coll., 1956; MA, Columbia U., 1966; PhD, U. Ill., 1968. Tech. editor Bell Tel. Labs., Whippany, N.J., 1958-59; editor Agrl. Expt. Sta., U. Ill., Urbana, 1961-66, instr. dept. English, 1966-68, asst. prof. English, 1968-77, assoc. prof. English, 1977-88, prof. English, 1988—. Author: H.L. Mencken Critic of American Life, 1978, The Teaching of Business Communication, 1978, Rail City: Chicago and Its Railroads, 1981, Edmund Wilson's America, 1983, Women of the Twenties, 1986, The Early Days of Radio Broadcasting, 1987, The Smart Magazines, 1991, All Aboard: The Railroad in American Life, 1992, Education Without Impact: How Our Universities Fail the Young, 1992, Skyscraper: A Social History of the Tall Building in America, 1996, Postwar America, 1998, The Golden Age of the Newspaper, 1999; editor numerous books; contbr. articles to profl. jours., reference books, television documentaries. Mem. MLA, Am. Studies Assn., Am. Bus. Comm. Assn. (editor jour. bus. comm. 1968-80). Home: 809 Mendota Dr Champaign IL 61820-7566

DOUGLAS, HOPE M. psychotherapist, forensic hypnotist; b. Marblehead, Mass., Jan. 14, 1947; d. W.I. and Beatrice B. Kenerson. BA in Psychology, Mich. State U., 1969, MA in Rehab. Counseling, 1970. Cert. mental health counselor, Fla.; cert. Ericksonian hypnotist. With Bur. Narcotics and Dangerous Drugs, U.S. Dept. Justice, Denver, 1971; with narcotics investigation, officer Glendale Police Dept., Denver, 1971-74; exec. dir., dir. edn., nat. speaker Child and Family Agy. of S.E. Conn., 1974 84; evidence technician, instr. homicide investigation Naples (Fla.) Police Dept., 1984-90; founder, pres. wildlife rehab. svcs. and edn. Wind Over Wings, Inc., Clinton, Conn., 1990—. Instr. wildlife rehab. Conn. Dept. Environ. Protection, 1991-92, 95, 96, 98-2002, 2003; adj. faculty Conn. Coll., Mitchell Coll., 1974-84; mem. Yale U. wildlife conservation internat. program India, Peru, 1993-2003. Contbr. articles to profl. jours. Mem. adv. bd. Child Welfare League Am.; bd. dirs. Branford River Raptor Ctr. Recipient J. Edgar Hoover award for excellence, 1985. Mem. Conn. Wildlife Rehab. Assn. (pres. 1992, bd. dirs. 1996-2000), Internat. Wildlife Rehab. Coun. (v.p. 1993-94, 97, acting exec. dir. 1995, bd. dirs. 1995-96, illustrator rehab. book series and disability book series 1995, 96), Wildlife Rehab. Eagles. Home: 22 Old Rd Clinton CT 06413-1855 E-mail: wings@snet.net.

DOUGLAS, JAMES, construction engineering educator; b. Uvalde, Tex., Oct. 1, 1914; s. Raymond C. and Mae (Savage) D.; m. Sarah Maria Bisset, July 22, 1941; children— Sarah A., Susan E., Bonnie B., James A. BS, U.S. Naval Acad., 1938; B.C.E., Rensselaer Poly. Inst., 1942; M.C.E., 1943; PhD, Stanford U., 1963. Registered profl. engr., D.C., Calif. Commd. ensign U.S. Navy, 1938, advanced through grades to capt., 1956; in charge constrn. (Cubi Point Naval Air Sta.), Philippines, 1951-54; dir. Seabee div. U.S. Navy, 1954-58; in charge constrn. (Antarctic bases Internat. Geophys. Yr.), 1956-58; prof. constrn. engring. Stanford, 1963—. Cons. constrn. engring. Stanford Research Inst., various corps., U.S. and fgn. govts., 1963— ; chmn. com. constrn. mgmt. Transp. Research Bd., NRC, 1969-76 Author: Construction Equipment Policy, 1975, also numerous tech. articles. Active Boy Scouts Am., 1946— . Served with Armed Forces, World War II. Decorated Bronze Star; recipient Thomas Fitch Rowland prize ASCE, 1969, Constrn. Mgmt. award, 1975 Fellow ASCE (chmn. constrn. equipment com. 1960-65); mem. Tau Beta Pi, Sigma Xi, Chi Epsilon, Chi Phi. Republican. Episcopalian. Home: 100 Thorndale Dr Apt 272 San Rafael CA 94903-4567 *In retrospect I realize that the most important things in life are your friends and your relations with other people. Regardless of wealth or status, life cannot be wholly satisfactory without agreeable human relations, and these are not dependent on race, creed, color, age or sex but on the quality of the individuals.*

DOUGLAS, JAMES (BUSTER), boxer; b. Columbus, Ohio; s. Billy and Lula Douglas; children: Lamar, Cardaé. Profl. boxer 1981—; defeated Mike Tyson, Feb. 1990 to become undisputed heavyweight champion. Office: Attn Lawrence Nallie 465 Waterbury Ct Ste A Gahanna OH 43230-5312

DOUGLAS, JAMES HOLLEY, governor; b. Springfield, Mass., June 21, 1951; s. Robert James and Cora Elizabeth (Holley) D.; m. Dorothy Foster, May 24, 1975; children: Matthew James, Andrew Foster. AB, Middlebury Coll., 1972. Gen. mgr. Credit Bur. of Middlebury, Vt., 1972-76; exec. dir. United Way of Addison County, 1976-79; exec. asst. to Gov. of Vt., 1979-80; sec. of state State of Vt., Montpelier, 1981-93, treas., 1994—2002, gov., 2003—. Mem. Vt. Ho. of Reps., 1973-79, majority leader, 1975-77, 77-79 Mem. Nat. Assn. Secs. State (pres.). Lodges: Masons. Republican. Congregationalist. Office: Office of the Governor Pavilion, 109 State St Montpelier VT 05609*

DOUGLAS, JAMES M. university president; BA in Math., Tex. So. U., 1966, JD, 1970; JSM, Stanford U., 1971. Programmer analyst Singer Gen. Precision, Houston, 1971—72; asst. prof. law Thurgood Marshall Sch. Law, Tex. So. U., 1972—74, Cleve.-Marshall Coll. Law, Cleve. State U., 1974—75, asst. prof. law, asst. dean for student affairs, 1974—75; assoc. prof. law, assoc. dean Syracuse U. Coll. Law, 1975—80; prof. law Northeastern U. Sch. Law, Boston, 1980—81; dean, prof. law Tex. So. U., 1981—95, interim provost, sr. v.p. for acad. affairs, 1995, interim pres., 1995, pres., 1995—99, disting. prof. law, 1999—. Contbr. articles. Mem. steering com. Houston Campaign for Homeless, 1988—89; Bd. dirs. Sickle Cell Found. Tex., 1988—94, pres., 1990—91; bd. dirs. Boy Scouts Am., 1993—, Greater Houston Partnership, 1996—99. Mem.: Houston C. of C., Nat. Bar Assn., Houston Bar Assn. (chair law practice mgmt. sect. 1995—), Tex. Supreme Ct. Hist. Soc. (trustee 1990—), State Bar Tex., ABA. Office: Tex So U 3100 Cleburne St Houston TX 77004-4501

DOUGLAS, J(OCELYN) FIELDING, toxicologist, consultant; b. Delta, Utah, Jan. 25, 1927; s. Benjamin and Amelia (Fielding) D.; m. Rose Mary Terrazzino, Sept. 16, 1951; children: David Benjamin, Pamela Susan, Jason Terrell. BS with high honors, U. Ill., 1948; MA, Columbia U., 1950, PhD, 1953. Project leader Johnson & Johnson, New Brunswick, N.J., 1952-58; dir. biochemistry Carter-Wallace, Cranbury, N.J., 1958-74; dep. dir. carcinogenesis testing program Nat. Cancer Inst., Bethesda, Md., 1976-80; chief ops. Nat. Toxicology Program, Bethesda, 1980-84; pres. Sci. Svcs., Inc., Front Royal, Va., 1984—. Expert cons. NIH, Bethesda, 1976-81; cons. in field; pres. High Knob Owners Assn. Inc., 1999—; bd. dirs. High Knob Utilities Inc., Front Royal, Va. Author, editor: Carcinogenesis and Mutagenesis Testing, 1984; contbr. numerous articles to profl. jours. Pvt. U.S. Army, 1944-46. Recipient Richard Neff award Richard Neff Soc., 1966, Dir. award Nat. Cancer Inst., 1979; USPHS fellow, 1950-52. Fellow AAAS; mem. Soc. Toxicology, Am. Soc. Pharmacology and Exptl. Therapeutics, Am. Chem. Soc. (chmn. biochem. sect. 1954). Avocations: gardening, reading, meditation. Home and Office: Sci Svcs Inc PO Box 533 Front Royal VA 22630-0533

DOUGLAS, JOHN PAUL, lawyer; b. Louisville, Jan. 6, 1939; s. John Samuel and Margaret Mary (Wagner) D.; m. Laura Christine Welborn, Feb. 17, 1968; children: Constance, John, Robert, D. Bear. AB, Regis U., Denver, 1968; JD, No. Ky. U., 1976. Bar: Ohio 1976, Tex. 1981, U.S. Supreme Ct. 1982. Program officer Cath. Relief Svcs., India, 1968-70; adminstr. Hamilton County, Cin., 1970-76, trial atty., 1976-80; gen. counsel Gen. Exploration Co., Dallas, 1980-86; pvt. practice Douglas & Assocs., Dallas, 1989-90, 92-99, 1990—92, 1999 . Adj. prof. law U. Dallas, Dallas, 1989—91. Contbr. articles to various publs. Pres. Maria Kannon Zen Ctr., Dallas, 1996. With USN, 1958-62, 90-92, capt. USNR, 1973-99, ret. Mem. Am. Arbitration Assn. (arbitrator 1990—), Camaldolese Oblate. Roman Catholic. Avocations: backpacking, arctophie. Home: PO Box 851521 Richardson TX 75085-1521 Office: 1750 N Collins Blvd Ste 200F Richardson TX 75080

DOUGLAS, JOHN WOOLMAN, lawyer; b. Phila., Aug. 15, 1921; s. Paul H. and Dorothy S. (Wolff) D.; m. Mary Evans St. John, July 14, 1945; children: Katherine D. Torrey, Peter R. AB, Princeton U., 1943; LLB, Yale U., 1948; DPhil, Oxford U., 1950. Bar: N.Y. 1948, D.C. 1953. Law clk. to justice Harold H. Burton U.S. Supreme Ct., 1951—52; asst. atty. gen. U.S. Dept. Justice, 1963—66; lawyer Covington & Burling, Washington, 1950—51, 1952—63, ptnr., 1966—. Chmn. Carnegie Endowment for Internat. Peace, 1978-86. Served to lt. (j.g.) USNR, 1943-46, MTO, PTO. Trustee Deerfield Acad., 1972-77; co-chair Citizens for McGovern com., 1972; chmn. Robert F. Kennedy Meml. Found., 1980-83. Rhodes scholar, 1948-50. Fellow Am. Coll. Trial Lawyers; mem. ABA, D.C. Bar Assn. (pres. 1974-75), Nat. Lawyers Com. for Civil Rights Under Law (co. chmn. 1969-71), Nat. Legal Aid and Defender Assn. (pres. 1970-71), Yale Law Sch. Assn. (pres. 1975-77). Democrat. Presbyterian. Home: 5700 Kirkside Dr Bethesda MD 20815-7116 Office: Covington & Burling 1201 Pennsylvania Ave NW PO Box 7566 Washington DC 20044-7566

DOUGLAS, JON DAVID See OETJEN, DAVID

DOUGLAS, KARIN NADJA, engineer; b. Berlin, Sept. 2, 1931; came to U.S., 1963; d. Fritz and Irma (Rutke) Kruse; m. Karl Vonmoos, May 21, 1955 (div. Dec. 1961); m. Robert P. Douglas, Dec. 13, 1969. AS in Legal Adminstrn. magna cum laude, Sacred Heart U., Fairfield, Conn., 1984. Apprentice in tech. drafting and design Hasler AG., Bern, Switzerland, 1961-63; elec. designer UOP Air Correction Divsn., Norwalk, Conn., 1968-83; engring. cons. various engring. corps., Fairfield County, Conn., 1983-87; agy. compliance coord. ITT Flygt Corp., Trumbull, Conn., 1987—. Mem. univ. coll. coun. Sacred Heart U., 2000—. Sec. Friends of Boothe Park, Inc., mus. and rose garden, Stratford, Conn., 1985—; bd. dirs. Nat. Lympedema Network, Oakland, Calif., 1997—2002; creator Evelyn Conley scholarship for Sacred Heart U., 1988; also patient adv./activist, 1996—97; creator Dr. M. Palliser Endowment for Phys. Therapy for Sacred Heart U., 2001. Named Woman of Substance, Conn. Post, 1997; recipient D-Day award, Nat. Lymphedema Network, 1996, Disting. Alumni award, Sacred Heart U., 2002, Harold S. Geneen Cmty. Svc. award, ITT Industries, 2002. Achievements include invention of pink wristband for hospitals; lymphedema alert bracelet; design of lymphedema Awareness pin with turquoise ribbon. Avocations: sailing, fishing, cooking.

DOUGLAS, KATHLEEN MARY HARRIGAN, retired psychotherapist, educator; b. Boston, Apr. 24, 1950; d. John Joseph and Kathleen Margaret (Connolly) Harrigan; m. Dr. Robert E. Douglas, Feb. 24, 1977; children: David, Pamela, Elizabeth. Student, Uxbridge, England; BA in Psychology, Sophia U., Tokyo, 1972; MA in Counseling Psychology, Chapman U., Orange, Calif., 1983; PhD in Counselor Edn., U. Fla., 1990. Elem tchr. Marymount Prep Sch., Palos Verdes, Calif., 1973-99; pvt. practice Orlando, Fla., 1985-95; psychology prof. Valencia C.C., Orlando, Fla., 1989-93; prof. Fla. Inst. Tech., 1990-94; asst. prof., grad. acad. advisors, clin. internship supr. Troy State U., Orlando, Fla., 1993-97; software developer of clinically oriented software, 1994—; assoc. prof. Barry U., Orlando, 1999—2002; ret., 2002. Drug/alcohol counselor, Ft. Belvoir, Va., 1981—82; counselor Orange County Mental Health Ctr., Winter Park, Fla., 1982—83, victims of child abuse therapist Thee Door, Orlando, 1983—84; presenter in field. Author: The Therapeutic Superhighway, 1995. Counselor Winter Park Towers Nursing Home, 1985; vol. group counselor Hillcrest Halfway House, Orlando, 1985. 1st Lt. U.S. Army, 1976-80. Recipient Marion medal Cath. Ch., Boston, 1966, Civic award Spouse Abuse, Inc., Orlando, 1984. Mem.: Fla. Assn. Mental Health Counselors (elected counselor edn.), Am. Assn. for Counseling and Devel., Chi Sigma Iota, Pi Lambda Theta, Kappa Delta Phi. Roman Catholic. Home: 1781 Lake Berry Dr Winter Park FL 32789-5911 E-mail: drkathyd@msn.com.

DOUGLAS, KENNETH DALE, artist; b. Fulton, Mo., Mar. 29, 1943; s. G. Louis and Lois Dean (Self) D.; m. Ruby Mae Bushnell, May 30, 1971; children: Kimberly Marie, Joanna Leigh. BA, U. Mo., 1971, MA, 1973. Artist, engraver Silver Products, Memphis, Tenn., 1974-75; freelance artist, engraver Olive Branch, Miss., 1975—. Mem.: Fedn. Internat. Médaille, Am. Medallic Sculpture Assn. (bd. dirs. 2001—, 2nd v.p. 2003—). Home: 8940 Deer Creek Ln Olive Branch MS 38654-5985 E-mail: dieman@midsouth.rr.com.

DOUGLAS, KENNETH JAY, food products executive; b. Harbor Beach, Mich., Sept. 4, 1922; s. Harry Douglas and Xenia (Williamson) D.; m. Elizabeth Ann Schweizer, Aug. 17, 1946; children: Connie Ann, Andrew Jay. Student, U. Ill., 1940-41, 46-47; JD, Chgo. Kent Coll. Law, 1950; grad., Advanced Mgmt. Program, Harvard, 1962. Bar: Ill. 1950, Ind. 1952. Spl. agt. FBI, 1950-54; dir. indsl. relations Dean Foods Co., Franklin Park, Ill., 1954-64, v.p. fin. and adminstrn., 1964-70, chmn. bd., chief exec. officer, 1970-87, chmn. bd., 1987-89, vice-chmn., 1989-92. Bd. dirs. Andrew Corp. Mem. Chgo. Com. With USNR, 1944-46. Mem. Chgo. Club, Econ. Club, Execs. Club, Comml. Club (Chgo.), Oak Park Country Club, River Forest Tennis Club, Old Baldy Country Club (Wyo.). Republican. Office: 1440 W North Ave Ste 207 Melrose Park IL 60160-1425 E-mail: kenmilk@aol.com.

DOUGLAS, KIRK (ISSUR DANIELOVITCH), actor, motion picture producer; b. Amsterdam, NY, Dec. 9, 1916; s. Harry and Bryna (Sanglel) Danielovitch; m. Diana Dill (div. Feb. 1950); children: Michael, Joel; m. Anne Buydens, May 29, 1954; children: Peter, Eric Anthony. AB, St. Lawrence U., 1938, D.F.A. (hon.), 1958; student, Am. Acad. Dramatic Arts, 1939-41. Appeared on Broadway in Spring Again, Three Sisters, Kiss and Tell, Wind is Ninety, Alice in Arms, Man Bites Dog; producer, star Broadway play One Flew over the Cuckoo's Nest; appeared in films: The Strange Love of Martha Ivers, 1946, Morning Becomes Electra, 1947, I Walk Alone, 1947, Out of the Past, 1947, Walls of Jericho, 1948, My Dear Secretary, 1948, A Letter to Three Wives, 1948, Champion, 1949, Young Man with a Horn, 1950, The Glass Menagerie, Ace in the Hole, Along the Great Divide, Detective Story, 1951, The Big Sky, 1951, The Big Trees, The Bad and the Beautiful, 1952, Equilibrium, 1952, The Story of Three Loves, The Juggler, 1953, Act of Love, Ulysses, 20,000 Leagues Under the Sea, 1954, Man Without a Star, The Racers, 1954, Lust for Life, 1956, Top Secret Affair, Gunfight at O.K. Corral, Paths of Glory, 1957, Last Train for Gunhill, 1958, Strangers When We Meet, 1958, The Devil's Disciple, 1959, Town Without Pity, The Last Sunset, 1961, Two Weeks in Another Town, 1962, The List of Adrian Messenger, For Love or Money, The Hook, 1963, In Harm's Way, Heroes of Telemark, 1965, Cast a Giant Shadow, Is Paris Burning?, 1966, War Wagon, The Way West, 1967, A Lovely Way to Die, 1968, The Arrangement, 1969, There Was a Crooked Man, 1970, The Light at the Edge of the World, Catch Me A Spy, 1971, A Man To Respect, 1972, Master Touch, 1972, Scalawag, 1973, Jekyl & Hyde, 1973, Posse, 1975, Once is Not Enough, 1975, Holocaust 2000, 1977, The Fury, 1978, The Villain, Saturn 3, Home Movies, 1979, The Man from Snowy River, 1982, Eddie Macon's Run, 1983, Tough Guys, 1986, Oscar, 1991, Greedy, 1994, Welcome to Veraz, 1990, A Song for David, 1996; producer, dir. films Scalawag, 1973, Posse, 1975; pres. Bryna Co.; producer, actor films: The Final Countdown, Indian Fighter, 1955, Vikings, 1964, Spartacus, 1960, The Last Sunset, 1961, Lonely are the Brave, 1962, Summertree, 1963, Seven Days in May, 1964, The Brotherhood, 1968, A Gunfight, 1971, Oscar, 1991, The Secret, 1991, Take Me Home Again, 1994, Diamonds, 1999, It Runs in the Family, 2003; co-producer film One Flew Over the Cuckoo's Nest, 1975, The Final Countdown, 1979; TV

miniseries appearance: Queenie, 1987; TV film appearance: Mousy (also dir.), 1973, The Money Changers, Victory at Entebbe, 1976, Remembrance of Love, 1982, Draw!, 1984, Amos, 1985, Inherit the Wind, 1988, Touched by An Angel, 2000; author: (autobiography) The Ragman's Son, 1988, Climbing the Mountain, 1997, My Stroke of Luck, 2002; (novels) Dance with the Devil, 1990, The Gift, 1992, Last Tango in Brooklyn, 1994, The Broken Mirror, 1997, (juvenile) Young Heroes of the Bible, 1999. Nominated for Acad. Award, 1949, 52, 56; nominated for Emmy, 1985, 98, 2000; recipient N.Y. Film Critics award, 1956, Hollywood Fgn. Press award, 1956, Heart and Torch award Am. Heart Assn., 1956, Splendid Am. award of merit George Washington Carver Meml. Found., 1957, cited in Congl. Record for service as goodwill ambassador, 1964, Cecil B. DeMille award for contbns. in entertainment field, 1967, Presdl. Medal of Freedom, 1981, elected to Cowboy Hall of Fame, 1984, Lifetime Achievement award Am. Film Inst., 1991; decorated Legion of Honor (France), 1985, Chevalier de la Legion d'Honneur, 1985, Officer de la Legion d'Honneur, 1990; Kennedy Center Honor, 1994; Honorary Oscar, Lifetime Achievement, 1996, Meltzer award for breaking blacklist Writers Guild Am., 1999, Lifetime Achievement SAG, 1999, Golden Boot award, 1999, Spencer Tracy award Outstanding Achievement in Drama, 1999, Lifetime Achievement Jerusalem Film Festival, 2000, Golden Bear award Berlin Film Festival, 2001, Nat. medal of Arts, 2002. Mem. UN Assn. (dir. Los Angeles chpt.) Achievements include making State Dept.-USIA tours around world. Office: Warren Cowan Assoc Ste 919 8899 Beverly Blvd Los Angeles CA 90048-2427 E-mail: mnewberger@warrencowan.com.

DOUGLAS, LESLIE, investment banker; b. Enon Valley, Pa., Mar. 14, 1914; s. Robert R. and Margaret M. (Mc Anlis) D.; m. Jean Wallace, Oct. 12, 1946; children— David, Ann and Joan (twins). BS, Geneva Coll., Beaver Falls, Pa., 1935; MBA, Harvard U., 1937. Investment mgr. Royal Liverpool Group, N.Y.C., 1937-41; investment banker Folger Nolan Fleming Douglas, Inc., Washington, 1946—, v.p., 1955—; bd. govs. Assn. Stock Exchange Firms, 1969-72, Securities Industry Assn., 1972-75. Trustee Holton Arms Sch., Washington, Landon Sch., Vis. Nurses Assn., Washington. Served to lt. comdr. USN, 1941-46. Mem.: Chevy Chase; Met. (Washington), Met. Club. Republican. Presbyterian. Home: 4733 Woodway Ln NW Washington DC 20016-3240 Office: 725 15th St NW Washington DC 20005-2109

DOUGLAS, MARY YOUNGE RILEY, secondary education educator; b. St Louis, Dec. 4, 1930; d. Walter Archibald and Jerdie Lee (Bibb) Younge; m. John Samuel Riley Jr., Apr. 17, 1954 (dec. July 1973); children: John Samuel Riley III, Jerda Marie Riley, Joel Younge Riley; m. Walter Wadsworth Douglas, Jan. 14, 1989. Student, Fisk U., 1947-49; BS, Fontbonne Coll., 1951; Masters, U. Ill., 1953. Tchr. Sumner High Sch., St. Louis, 1953-55, Hadley Tech. Sch., St. Louis, 1956-57; subs. tchr. St. Louis C.C., 1975; tchr. Soldan High Sch., St. Louis, 1975-90, Roosevelt High Sch., St. Louis, 1990-93, Soldan-Internat. High Sch., 1993—2001. Past bd. dirs. Nursery Found., St. Louis, Met. YWCA, St. Louis, Mo. Assn. Social Welfare.

DOUGLAS, MAURICE LAJOHN, private school educator, music educator; b. Rock Hill, S.C., Aug. 8, 1970; s. John Daniel and Mildred Barber Douglas; m. Marlene Spencer, Apr. 12, 2002; 1 child, Damani. BA in Music, Charleston (S.C.) So. U., 1993; MEd, Cambridge (Mass.) U., 1999; degree in Music Edn., Winthrop U., 2001; student in Edn. Adminstrn., U. S.C., 2001—. Cert. tchr. Choral dir. and chmn. Music Dept. East Sch., Monroe, NC, 1994—97; dir. student affairs Clinton Jr. Coll., Rock Hill, SC, 1997—99; choral dir. Charlotte (N.C.) Christian Sch., 1999—2001; dir. guidance and fine arts Montrose Christian Sch., Rockville, Md., 2001—. Pvt. vocal coach, 1987—. Singer: summers at Walt Disney World, 1989—2000, TRUTH, 1993—94. Named Show Designer of Yr., Show Choir Internat., 1999. Mem.: Kappa Alpha Psi.

DOUGLAS, P C, producer, director, reporter, editor; b. Houston; s. Hilda Florence Carrithers. BA in Broadcast Journalism, Tex. Tech. U., 1994. Reporter/photographer KCBD-TV, Lubbock, Tex., 1992-93; copy editor La Ventana, Tex. Tech. U., Lubbock, 1993-94; reporter The Independent, Gallup, N.Mex., 1994; radio announcer KDLK/KLKE, Del Rio, Tex., 1994; reporter Del Rio News-Herald, 1994; reporter/photographer KOSA-TV, Odessa, Tex., 1994-96; radio announcer KQRX-FM, Odessa, 1996; flight attendant Southwest Airlines, Dallas, 1996-97; polit./govtl. reporter Houston News Today Online, 1997—98; media coord. Motivators, Inc., Houston, 1998-99; prodr., dir., reporter, editor, anchorperson Houston Internat. Bus. Ch., 1999—2000; video editor KTRK-TV ABC, Houston, 2000; prodr. TV Guide Channel, Tulsa, 2000—02; freelance journalist Houston Chronicle, 2002—; account coord. L'Oréal U.S.A., Houston, 2002—. Co-prodr.: (TV documentary) Lubbock Hispanic Women Leaders, 1993 (1st place award 1993). Media vol. Make-A-Wish Found. West Tex., Odessa, 1994-96. Recipient 1st Pl. award, Soc. Profl. Journalists, 1993. Avocations: Hawaiian culture and history research, travel, stamp collecting, running, cycling. Home and Office: L'Oréal USA 1205 Banks Houston TX 77006 E-mail: pcloreal@aol.com.

DOUGLAS, PAUL WOLFF, retired mining executive; b. Springfield, Mass., Sept. 12, 1926; s. Paul Howard and Dorothy (Wolff) Douglas; children: Philip LeBreton, Carolyn Jory Jacobs, Christine Sanders Tansey, Paul Harding(dec.). AB, Princeton U., 1948; student, Leeds (Eng.) U., 1948. Dir. internal finance sect. ECA Mission to France, 1948-52; with Freeport Minerals Co., 1952—, exec., v.p., dir., 1970-75, pres., chmn. exec. com., 1975—; pres., CEO Freeport-McMoran Inc., 1981-83; chmn., CEO Pittston Co., 1984-91; ret., 1991. Chmn. Cmty. Planning Bd. #2, N.Y.C., 1966—68. With USNR, 1944—46. Mem.: Phi Beta Kappa. Home: 45 E 62nd St New York NY 10021-8025 Office: Rm 4600 60 E 42nd St Ste 4600 New York NY 10165-0006

DOUGLAS, PHILIP A. writer; b. Urbana, Ill., Aug. 19, 1966; s. George H. and Rosalind M. Douglas. BA, U. Ill.; M, Purdue U., 1996, PhD, 2003. Grad. tchg. asst. Purdue U., West Lafayette, Ind., 1995—2001; english lit. exam reader Daytona Beach, Fla., 2003—. Internat. English exam reader Trinity U. Coll. Bd., San Antonio, 2001—02; presenter in field. Com. chair for rev. of composition readers Purdue U., 1997—98, lit. awards judge, 2000. Grantee, Purdue U. Rsch. Found., 1999—2000. Mem.: MLA, Soc. Study Midwestern Lit., Nat. Assn. of African-Am. Studies, Am. Lit. Assn. Achievements include development of Literature Class Syllabi and Lectures. Avocation: environmentalism and animal rights. Personal E-mail: dougphi@purdue.edu.

DOUGLAS, PHILIP LE BRETON, lawyer; b. Paris, Apr. 18, 1950; s. Paul Wolff and Colette Marie Louise (Smith) Douglas; m. Elizabeth Kean, June 18, 1983; children: Eliza Shaw, Samuel Garrison, Henry Hamilton Paul. AB, Princeton U., 1972; JD, NYU, 1975. Bar: NY 76, DC 80, U.S. Dist. Ct. (so. and ea. dists.) NY 77, U.S. Ct. Appeals (2d cir.) 81, U.S. Ct. Appeals (8th cir.) 87, U.S. Ct. Appeals (9th cir.) 00, U.S. Ct. Appeals (DC cir.) 02, U.S. Supreme Ct. 91. Law clk. to Hon. Robert A. Ainsworth U.S. Ct. Appeals (5th cir.), New Orleans, 1975—76; assoc. Davis Polk & Wardell, N.Y.C., NY, 1977—79; asst. U.S. atty. U.S. Dist. Ct. (so. dist.) NY, 1979—84; ptnr. Hale Russell & Gray, N.Y.C., 1984—85, Pillsbury Winthrop LLP (and predecessor firm), N.Y.C., 1985—. Articles editor: NYU Law Rev., 1974—75. Trustee Grace Ch. Sch., N.Y.C., 1986—92. Root-Tilden scholar, NYU Law Sch., 1972—75. Mem.: ABA, Inst. Dispute Resolution (energy and utilities panel neutral arbitrator), Fed. Bar Coun., Assn. Bar City NY. Home: 76 MacDougal St New York NY 10012-2505 Office: Pillsbury Winthrop LLP 1 Battery Park Plz Fl 31 New York NY 10004-1490 Business E-Mail: pdouglas@pillsburywinthrop.com.

DOUGLAS, ROBERT GORDON, JR., physician; b. N.Y.C., Apr. 17, 1934; s. Robert Gordon and Alice (Lewis) D.; m. Ann Castle Moses, Dec. 22, 1956; children: Robert Gordon, 3d, Timothy Stuart, Catherine Lewis. AB, Princeton U., 1955; MD, Cornell U., 1959. Diplomate Am. Bd. Internal Medicine. Successively intern, asst. resident in internal medicine, resident N.Y. Hosp., 1959-61, 62-63; asst. resident Johns Hopkins Hosp., 1961-62; USPHS clin. assoc., clin. investigator Nat. Inst. Allergy and Infectious Disease, 1963-66; asst. prof. microbiology and medicine Baylor Coll. Medicine, Houston, 1966-70; mem. faculty Sch. Medicine and Dentistry U. Rochester, N.Y., 1970-82, prof. medicine and microbiology Sch. Medicine and Dentistry, 1974-82, head infectious disease unit Sch. Medicine and Dentistry, 1970-82, sr. assoc. dean edn. Sch. Medicine and Dentistry, 1979-82; prof., chmn. dept. medicine Med. Coll. Cornell U., 1982-90; physician in chief N.Y. Hosp., 1982-90; sr. v.p. medi. and sci. affairs Merck Sharp & Dohme Internat., 1990-91; pres. Merck Vaccines, 1991-99; chmn. bd. dirs. Vical Inc., 1999—. Bd. dirs. Elusys Inc., Advancis Pharm. Corp.; cons. in field; adj. prof. medicine Cornell U. Med. Coll., 1990—; hon. attending physician N.Y. Hosp., 1990—; bd. dirs. Interant. AIDS Vaccine Inst., 1997—; chmn. Sequella Global Tb Found., 2001—. Editor: Principles and Practices of Infectious Diseases, 1979, 2d edit., 1985, 3d edit., 1990; contbr. articles to profl. jours. Recipient Hawkins award Assn. Am. Pubs., 1980. Fellow ACP, Infectious Diseases Soc. Am. (pres. 1991-92, Feldman award); mem. Inst. Medicine, Am. Soc. Clin. Investigation, Assn. Am. Physicians, Am. Clin. Climatol. Assn. (pres. 1999-2000), Nat. Found. for Infectious Disease (Maxwell Finland award 2000). Home and Office: 84 Old Black oint Rd Niantic CT 06357

DOUGLAS, ROXANNE GRACE, secondary school educator; b. Orange, N.J., Dec. 17, 1951; d. Joseph Samuel and Mary (Ferro) Battista; m. Richard Joseph Douglas, June 26, 1982; 1 child, Regina Grace. BA cum laude, Montclair State Coll., 1973; student, Sorbonne U., Paris. Cert. French, social studies and elem. sch. tchr., N.J. Tchr. social studies West Orange (N.J.) Bd. Edn., 1973-74, Orange (N.J.) Bd. Edn., 1974-75; substitute tchr. various schs. N.J., 1975-76; supplemental tchr. Irvington (N.J.) Bd. Edn., 1976-80, tchr. govtl. programs, 1980—. Advisor 7th dist. NJSFWC-JM State Bd., 1991-93, 2002-04, membership chmn., 1994-96, 98—, pub. affairs chmn., 1996—, state membership task force, 1999—, edn. chmn., 2000-01, dist. asst., 2001—, 7th dist. v.p., 2002—. InSchool System, James Caldwell High Sch. Scholarship Fund. 2nd v.p., James Caldwell High Sch. HSA Corresponding sec. West Caldwell town columnist for local newspaper. Mem. West Caldwell Centennial Com., 2002—; cultural arts chmn. Caldwell/West Caldwell HSA League. Recipient Creative Writing awards NJSFWC-JM, Citizenship award Am. Legion. Mem. Victorian Soc., N.J. Edn. Assn., Nat. French Hon. Soc., Nat. Edn. Hon. Soc., Jr. Women's Club of West Essex (co-pres., liaison internat. affairs chmn., pub. affairs chmn.), Coll. Club Orange-Short Hills, West Essex Women's Club (liaison to jr. woman's club, chmn. internat. affairs and pub. affairs dept. 1st night com. mem., pres., parent adv. coun.-bd. edn., pres., 1994—, internat. affairs chmn., centennial chmn., comm. chmn., performing arts chmn. 1996—), Verona Women's Club (membership chmn., v.p. 1998—, recording sec. 2000—, twp. centennial com. mem., first v.p. 2003-04), Willing Hearts and Cultural Arts (chmn.), Caldwell West Caldwell HSA League, NJJFWC (state bd. 2002-04), West Essex League Hist. Soc. (Seventh Dist. v.p., corrs. sec.), JCHSS (v.p. scholarship com. 2003-04), James Caldwell H.S. HSA (corrs. sec. 2003-04). Roman Catholic. Avocations: reading, antiques, walking, writing, travel.

DOUGLAS, SAMUEL OSLER, musician, educator; b. Mansfield, La., Mar. 31, 1943; s. Edward Osler and Minnie Flanders Douglas; m. Judith Lorraine Rose, Aug. 15, 1966; children: Samuel Sean, Sarah Shanno0n, Amanda Christina. B in Music Edn., McNeese State U., 1966; MMus, La. Sate U., 1968; D in Musical Arts, La. State U., 1972. Prof. music U. SC, Columbia, 1973—2003. Double bassist SC Philharm., Columbia, 1973—; jazz bassist Billie Mustin Trio, Columbia, 1974—99. Fellow NDEA fellow, La. State U., 1969—71. Mem.: ASCAP (awards 1990—). Avocation: fishing. Office: U SC Sch Music Columbia SC 29208

DOUGLAS, SHIRLEY LORENE, small business owner, councilwoman; b. Kansas City, Kans., Apr. 12, 1944; d. Roy W. Ellifrits and Nellie Heathman; m. Fred L. Douglas, Apr. 13, 1963; children: Michael W., Brett A. Grad. H.S., Kansas City. Teller Brotherhood State Bank, Kansas City, 1962-68; bookkeeper, owner Douglas Pump Svc., Inc., Overland Park, Kans., 1973—; councilwoman City of Shawnee, Kans., 1991—2000, pres., 1993—94. Mem. exec. bd. Ednl. Com. for Excellence, Shawnee Mission, Kans., 1985-88, Johnson County Commn. on Aging, 1994—, vice-chair, 1996—; mem. exec. bd. Met. Coun. of Couns., Mo. and Kans., 1996—. Pres. Shawnee Mission PTA; dep. chmn. Shawnee Dept. Fin. and Adminstrn. and Pub. Works, 1994, 97, chmn., 1998. Recipient Golden Rule award J.C. Penney, 1989; named Friend of Edn., Pub. Edn. Task Force for State of Kans., 1989-90, life mem. PTA Kans. Mem. C. of C. (Citizen of the Yr. 1995), Rotary (charter). Avocations: rose gardening, collectibles, traveling. Office: Douglas Pump Svc Inc 4719 Merriam Dr Overland Park KS 66203-1399

DOUGLAS, STEPHEN LANE, academic administrator; b. Clarksburg, W.Va., Oct. 6, 1952; s. Charles Hugh and Lucille (Dyer) D.; m. Sandra Jean Auvil, Aug. 7, 1977; children: Ashley Tara, Clark Stephen. BS, W.Va. U., 1974, MS, 1979. Dir. pub. info. Alderson-Broaddus Coll., Philippi, W.Va., 1977-81; dir. coll. relations W.Va. Wesleyan Coll., Buckhannon, 1981-82; assoc. dir. W.Va. Alumni Assn., Morgantown, 1982-88, editor newsletter, mag., 1982-88, exec. dir., 1988-90; exec. v.p., 1990—. Advisor Student Alumni Assn., Morgantown, 1982-88; exec. sec. Loyalty Permanent Endowment Fund. Editor A-B Alumni Magazine, 1977-81. Pres. Mountaineer Country Travel Council, Morgantown, 1980-83; mem. adminstrv. bd. Wesley United Meth. Ch., Morgantown, 1985-86, chpt. advisor Sigma Chi, 1985-87. Named Disting. West Virginian W.Va. Regional Travel Councils, Morgantown, 1983, Practitioner of Yr. Pub. Relations Student Soc. W.Va. U., 1984. Mem. Coun. Advancement and Support Edn., Coun. Alumni Assn. Execs., W.Va. Alumni Dirs. Assn., W.Va. Press Assn. Assocs. (pres. 1981-82, Outstanding Publ. 1984), Morgantown Rotary. Democrat. Kiwanis (lt. gov. Philippi club 1981-82). Home: 20 Heather Dr Morgantown WV 26505-3668 Office: WVa U Alumni Assn Erickson Alumni Ctr Morgantown WV 26506

DOUGLAS, SUSAN, data processing specialist, consultant; b. Chgo., Oct. 29, 1946; d. Lawrence and Phoebe Fern (Sibbald) D.; m. John D. Hauenstein, Dec. 21, 1972 (div. June 1975). BA, U. Iowa, 1972; postgrad., U. Wis., Whitewater, 1985, U. Wis., Madison, 1991—. Project coord. Westinghouse Learning Corp., Iowa City, Iowa, 1967-75; echocardiology technician Chgo. Osteo. Hosp., 1975-78; sys. programmer, analyst Household Fin. Corp., Prospect Heights, Ill., 1978-81; applications analyst Burdick Corp., Milton, Wis., 1981-84; cons. Edgerton, Wis., 1984—. Mem. Data Processing Mgmt. Assn. Episcopalian. Avocations: crafts, tree farming, skiing, sailing, hiking. Home and Office: 8203 County H Edgerton WI 53534-8887

DOUGLAS, VICTORIA JEAN, marketing professional, communications executive, consultant; b. Wilmington, Del., Sept. 1, 1972; d. Richard Otto and Genevieve Douglas. Student, U. Caen, France, 1993, Oxford (Eng.) U., 1995, NYU Paris, 1996; BA in English/French, U. Del., 1996, MA in French Lit., 1999. Dir. comm. Mayor's Office, Wilmington, 1993—2001; mktg. and comm. chief cons. Met. Wilmington Urban League, 2001—; CEO Barracuda Comm., Wilmington. Founder, chair Fgn. Lang. and Lit. Assn. Grad. Students, Newark, 1996—97; mem. mktg. com. Dept. Youth and Families, Wilmington, 1999—2000; supporting mem. Del. Ctr. for Contemporary Arts, Wilmington, 2001—; bd. mem. Kuumba Acad., Wilmington, 2001—; curriculum devel. staff, instr. English U. Caen Sch. Law, France, 1997—98; account supr. Saatchi and Saatchi, Rowland, NY, 2001. *Victoria's accomplished public relations and communications career spans municipal government, private industry, the non-profit sector, and two continents:Victoria served as the Director of Communications in Municipal Government, where she developed successful strategies for crisis communication management in addition to authoring several notable speeches by Wilmington's first African American Mayor.James H.Sills,Jr.As Editor of three business and economic texts, educator, and communications professional, Victoria was invited to implement curriculum and teach English at the University level in France.Today, Victoria heads a dynamic team of marketing and communications professionals who are client team builders and results focused.* Organizer Nat. Night Out, Wilmington, 1993—95, Mayor's Breast Cancer Awareness Campaign, Wilmington, 2001; mem. ball com. Am. Diabetes Assn., 2002, mem. leadership coun., 2002—; v.p. sales Wilmington Drama League. Recipient Tomorrow's Leaders Today award, Pub. Allies, 1994, proclamation, City of Wilimington, 2000, Apex Award for Excellence in Mktg. and Pub. Rels. Brochures, 2002. Mem.: AAUW, Pub. Rels. Soc. Am., Met. Wilmington Urban League, Am. Kiteflyers Assn., Pi Delta Phi, Golden Key Nat. Honor Soc., Phi Sigma Tau, Sigma Tau Delta. Office: Hagley Bldg Ste 104 3411 Silverside Rd Wilmington DE 19810 Business E-Mail: vdouglas@barracudacommunications.net.

DOUGLAS, WILLIAM ERNEST, retired government official; b. Charleston, South Carolina, Nov. 26, 1930; s. William Ernest and Helen A. (Fortune) D.; m. Nancy Anne (Gibson), July 18, 1980. BA cum laude(hon.), The Citadel, 1956; post grad., U. S.C., 1956-59. With IRS, 1959—80, divsn. chief Newark dist., 1970—72, asst. dir. Jackson (Miss.) dist., 1972-73, asst. dir. Atlanta dist., 1973-74, asst. commr. S.E. region, 1974-78, dir. Regional Svc. Ctr. S.E. region, 1978-80; commr. fin. mgmt. svc. U.S. Treasury Dept., Washington, 1980-91. Served in U.S. Army, 1948-52, Korean War, 1950-51. Recipient Exec. Excellence award Fed. Interagency Com. on Info. Resources Mgmt., 1985; Exec. Achievement award Sr. Exec. Svc., 1985; Am. Univ. Roger W. Jones Fed. Exec. Leadership award, 1986; Sec. of Treasury's Disting. Svc. award, 1991; Presdl. Exec. Disting. award, 1991. Home: 205 Settlers Rd Saint Simons GA 31522

DOUGLAS, WILLIAM W. physician, consultant; b. Medford, Oreg., Dec. 2, 1934; s. Wallace S. and Jane (Phyfer) Douglas; m. Nancy Georgetta Classon; children: William S., Cathryn J., Nancy M. BS pre-med, Univ. Idaho, Moscow, Idaho, 1956; MD, Northwestern Univ. med. Sch., Chgo., 1960. Cons. in pulmonary and critical care medicine Mayo Clin., Rocheshter, Minn., 1967—. Contbr. articles to profl. jour. Capt. USAF, 1961—63. Mem.: Am. Theracic Soc. Achievements include research in orignal on treatment of idiopathic pulmonary fibrosis, early work establishing critical care medicine at Mayo Clin. Avocations: photography, travel, fly fishing, orchids. Home: 1005 7th St S W Rochester MN 55902 Office: Mayo Clin Rochester 200 First St S W Rochester MN 55905

DOUGLASS, BETTY JEAN, retired executive secretary; b. Oil City, Pa., June 5, 1928; d. Nelson Earl and Hazel Vesta (Graham) Stover; m. Paul James Douglass, Jan. 15, 1946; children: Paul James Jr., Linda Jean Wolfe, Timothy Earl, Gary Arthur. Student, Diablo Valley Coll., Pleasant Hill, Calif., 1973-74, Cerritos (Calif.) Coll., 1975-76; AS, L.A. Harbor Coll., 1982. Auditor Gen. Dynamics/Astro., Kearney Mesa, Calif., 1958-60; sec. Gen. Dynamics, Topeka, 1960-62; co-owner 7-11 Southland, Del Mar, Calif., 1965-69; pers. U. S.C., Charleston, 1969-71; bookkeeper Breuner's, Concord, Calif., 1972-75; office adminstr. 4 Seasons Cabinet, Vancouver, Wash., 1976-79, Nat. Nursing, Inc., Carson, Calif., 1979-81, Quality Mgmt. Cons., Ormond Beach, Fla., 1987—; now ret. Contbr. poems to anthologies. Vol. Long Beach (Calif.) Rape Crisis Ctr., 1985-86; treas. Bapt. Ch., Walnut, Calif., 1972; mem. visitation com. Tomoka Christian Ch., Ormond Beach, 1997. Mem. Internat. Poetry Soc., Alpha Gamma Sigma. Republican. Avocations: oil painting, computers, bicycling.

DOUGLASS, BRUCE E. physician; b. Berwyn, Ill., Sept. 26, 1917; s. Frank Lionel and Helen Mary (Eccles) D.; m. Charlotte Maurer Natwick, Oct. 14, 1942; children: Jean N., Bruce G., John F. BA, U. Wis., 1938, MD, 1942; MS in Medicine, U. Minn., 1949. Intern Med. Coll. of Va., Richmond, 1942-43; resident in internal medicine Mayo Clinic, Rochester, Minn, 1947-50, mem. staff, 1949—, chmn. div. preventive medicine, 1962—; dir. Mayo Clinic (Mayo sect. of Patient and Health Edn.), 1976—. Dir. Occupational Health Inst., Chgo., 1968— Author: Anatomy of the Portal Vein and Its Tributaries, 1949, The Problem of Benign Bronchial Obstruction, 1954, Predicting Disease: Is It Possible? 1971, Health Problems of Hospital Employees, 1971, Examining Healthy Persons: How and How Often? 1980. Chmn. Rochester Music Bd., 1960-70; v.p. Minn. Zool. Soc., 1974-77. Served to capt. M.C. AUS, 1944-47. Fellow Am. Acad. Occupational Medicine (Keogh award 1981), Am. Occupational Med. Assn. (pres. 1977-78, Meritorious Service award 1979); mem. AMA (Physician's Recognition award 1974-77, chmn. sect. council on preventive medicine 1978-80, del. for occupational med. to ho. of dels. 1978-85), Minn. Med. Assn. (chmn. com. on public health edn. 1979), Ramazzini Soc., Assn. Tchrs. Preventive Medicine, Am. Coll. Preventive Medicine, Minn. Zool. Soc., Sigma Xi, Phi Kappa Phi, Sigma Phi, Nu Sigma Nu. Office: Mayo Clinic Rochester MN 55905-0001 Home: Charter House 211 2d St NW Rochester MN 55901

DOUGLASS, DONALD ROBERT, banker; b. Evanston, Ill., Oct. 7, 1934; s. Robert William and Dorothy (Gibson) D.; m. Susan Douglass. BBA, U. N.Mex., 1959, MBA, 1966. With Security Pacific Nat. Bank, L.A., 1961—, mgmt. trainee, 1962-63, asst. mgr. Vernon, Calif., 1963-64, Whittier, Calif., 1964, asst. v.p., 1965, asst. v.p., credit officer regional adminstrn. L.A., 1966-69, v.p. San Francisco, 1969-74; mgr. corp. accts. credit adminstrn. No. Calif. Corp. Banking, 1974-77; group v.p. Annco Properties, Burlingame, Calif., 1977-79; v.p., sr. loan officer Borel Bank and Trust Co., San Mateo, Calif., 1979-83, sr. v.p., 1983-84, exec. v.p. mortgage banking divsn. comml. property sales Los Altos, Calif., 1984-87. Ptnr. Key Equities, Inc., San Mateo, 1987—; ptnr., broker Centre Fin. Group, Inc., San Mateo, 1987-96, Centre Fin. Group South Inc., Menlo Park, 1987-96; pres. ServiCtr. Mortgage, Inc., 1996—, Sage Fin., Inc., 1999—; instr. Am. Inst. Banking, 1963, Coll. San Mateo, 1982—; nat. adv. bd. Anderson Schs. Mgmt. U. N.Mex. With AUS, 1954-56. Mem. U. N.Mex. Alumni Assn., Sigma Alpha Epsilon, Delta Sigma Phi. Republican. Presbyterian. Home: 745 Celestial Ln San Mateo CA 94404-2771 E-mail: ddougl2@aol.com.

DOUGLASS, ENID HART, educational program director; b. L.A., Oct. 23, 1926; d. Frank Roland and Enid Yandell (Lewis) Hart; m. Malcolm P. Douglass, Aug. 28, 1948; children: Malcolm Paul Jr., John Aubrey, Susan Enid. BA, Pomona Coll., 1948; MA, Claremont (Calif.) Grad. Sch., 1959. Research asst. World Book Ency., Palo Alto, Calif., 1953-54; exec. sec., asst. dir. oral history program Claremont Grad. U., 1963-71, dir. oral history program, 1971—, lectr. history, 1977—. Mem. Calif. Heritage Preservation Commn., 1977-85, chmn. 1983-85. Contbr. articles to hist. jours. Mayor pro tem City of Claremont, 1980-82, mayor, 1982-86; mem. planning and rsch. adv. coun. State of Calif.; mem. city coun. City of Claremont, 1978-86; founder Claremont Heritage, Inc., 1977-80; bd. dirs., 1986-95; bd. dirs. Pilgrim Pla., Claremont; founder, steering com., founding bd. Claremont Cmty. Found., 1989-95, pres., 1990-94. Mem. Oral History Assn. (pres. 1979-80), Southwest Oral History Assn. (founding steering com. 1981, J.V. Mink award 1984), Nat. Coun. Pub. History (founding com. 1980), LWV (bd. dirs. 1957-59, Outstanding Svc. to Cmty. award 1986). Democrat. Home: 1195 N Berkeley Ave Claremont CA 91711-3842 Office: Claremont Grad U Oral History Program 710 N College Ave Claremont CA 91711-3921 E-mail: enid.douglass@cgu.edu.

DOUGLASS, FRANK RUSSELL, lawyer; b. Dallas, May 29, 1933; s. Claire Allen and Caroline (Score) D.; m. Carita Calkins, Feb. 5, 1955 (div. 1983); children: Russell, Tom, Andrew, Cathy; m. Betty Elwanda Richards, Dec. 31, 1983. BBA, Southwestern U., 1953; LLB, U. Tex., 1958. Bar: Tex. 1957, U.S. Dist. Ct. (we. dist.) Tex. 1960, U.S. Dist. Ct. (so. dist.) Tex. 1981, U.S. Dist. Ct. (no. dist.) Tex. 1985, U.S. Dist. Ct. (ea. dist.) Tex. 1987, U.S. Supreme Ct. 1964, U.S. Ct. Appeals (5th cir.) 1985; cert. in civil trial law, and oil, gas and energy law. Various positions to ptnr. McGinnis, Lochridge & Kilgore, Austin, Tex., 1957-76; sr. ptnr. Scott, Douglass & McConnico, Austin, 1976—. Bd. dirs. Pierce Energy Corp., Amarillo, Tex.; trustee Southwestern U., Georgetown, Tex. Contbr. articles to profl. jours. City atty., Westlake Hills, Tex., 1968. Served as airman USAF, 1953-55. Named Dist. Alumus Southwestern U., 1999. Fellow Am. Coll. Trial Lawyers; mem. ABA (natural resources law sect., coun. 1987-90, Am. Bar Found.), Am. Inns of Ct., State Bar of Tex., Tex. Bar Found., The Tex. Ctr. for Legal Ethics and Professionalism (founding), Dallas Bar Assn., The Littlefield Soc. U. Tex. (charter). Home and Office: 10424 Woodford Dr Dallas TX 75229-6317 Fax: 214-352-4588.

DOUGLASS, GUS RUBEN, state agency administrator; b. Leon, W.Va., Feb. 22, 1927; s. Gus Rodney and Fannie Elizabeth (Grimm) D.; m. Anna Lee Roush, Oct. 23, 1947; children: Steve, Thomas, Mary Lee, Cynthia. BA, W.Va. U., 1985; LLD (hon.), W.Va. State Coll., 1999, W.Va. U., 2001. Asst. commr. agr. W.Va. Dept. Agr., 1957, commr. agr., 1964-88, 92—. Bd. dirs. Peoples Bank Point Pleasant; trustee Pleasant Valley Hosp.; trustee, adminstr. W. Va. Rural Rehab. Loan Fund; chmn. so. regional com. Food and Agr. under Pres. Jimmy Carter; past pres. So. U.S. Trade Assn.; mem. adv. com. fgn. animal and poultry diseases U.S. Sec.; mem., past chmn. W.Va. Rural Devel. Coun.; chmn. State Soil Conservation Com.; past chmn. W.Va. Air Pollution Control Commn., State Forestry Commn.; mem. W.Va. Housing Devel. Fund; co-operator 400 acre beef and grain farm. Gubernatorial candidate W.Va., 1988; bd. dirs. State Farm Mus., State Fair W.Va.; mem. Leon Bapt. Ch. Recipient Disting. Svc. award Gamma Sigma Delta, Man of Yr. award Progressive Farmer Mag., Adminstr.'s award for Animal Health USDA-APHIS, 2002; named to Agriculture and Forestry Hall of Fame, 1990. Mem. Future Farmers Am. (state and nat. pres.), Nat. Future Farmers Am. Alumni Assn. (past pres.), Nat. Assn. State Depts. Agriculture (past. pres.), So. Assn. State Depts. Agriculture (past pres.), Farm Bureau (county pres.), Poultry Assn., Livestock Assn., Masons, Shriners. Democrat. Avocations: carpentry, gardening, hunting, fishing, reading. Office: WVa Dept Agriculture Rm E-28 State Capitol Charleston WV 25305 E-mail: douglass@ag.state.wv.us.

DOUGLASS, JAMES FREDERICK, business administration educator; b. Detroit, Sept. 17, 1934; s. Samuel Henry and Edith Rachel (Day) D.; m. Dorrine Marie Harma; children: James Lloyd, Marie Rachel. BA in Social Scis., Mich. State U., 1957; MBA, U. Ala., 1973; advanced cert., Coll. William and Mary, 1977, postgrad. in higher edn. Enlisted man U.S. Army, 1957-59; new bus. rep. Consumer's Power Co., Jackson, Mich., 1959-63; commd. 2d lt. USAF, 1963, advanced through grades to lt. col., 1967; sr. Air Force advisor 6146th Adv. Group, Camp Humphrys, Republic of Korea, 1969-70; assigned to Hdqrs. Tactical Communications Div., Langley AFB, Va., 1971-75; ret. USAFR, 1991; adminstr. Fla. Inst. Tech., Melbourne, 1975-79; assoc. prof. grad. bus. adminstrn., acad. advisor Embry Riddle Aero U., Langley AFB, 1979—. Edn. specialist Dept. Army, Ft. Eustis, Va., 1979-88. Chpt. pres. Protestant Men of Chapel, Fed. Repulic Germany and Japan, 1958-65; deacon Presbyn. Ch., Detroit, 1961-63. Mem. ASTD (editor Southeastern Va. chpt. jour. 1983-84), Armed Forces Communications and Electronics Assn., Ret. Officers Assn. (pres. Ft. Eustis chpt. 1980). Democrat. Avocations: travel, golf, study, reading. Home: 22 Bayview Dr Poquoson VA 23662-1034 Office: Embry-Riddle Aero U PO Box 816 Hampton VA 23665-0816

DOUGLASS, JANE DEMPSEY, theology educator; b. Wilmington, Del., Mar. 22, 1933; d. Hazell Brownlie and Ethel Katherine (Smith) Dempsey; m. Gordon Klene Douglass, Aug. 23, 1964; children: Alan Bruce, Anne Lorine, John Gordon. AB, Syracuse U., 1954; postgrad., U. Geneva, Switzerland, 1954-55; AM, Radcliffe Coll., 1961; PhD, Harvard U., 1963; ThD (hon.), U. Geneva, 1994; LHD (hon.), Franklin and Marshall Coll., 1992; DD (hon.), U. St. Andrews, Scotland, 1992; STD (hon.), MacMurray Coll., 2000. Assoc. dir. Presbyn. Student Ctr., Columbia, Mo., 1955-58; teaching fellow Harvard Divinity Sch., Cambridge, Mass., 1959-62; from instr. to prof. Sch. of Theology at Claremont and Claremont Grad. Sch., Claremont, Ca., 1963-85; Hazel Thompson McCord prof. hist. theology Princeton (N.J.) Theol. Sem., 1985-98, emerita, 1998—. Pres. Am. Soc. Ch. History, 1983; v.p. World Alliance of Reformed Chs., 1989-90, pres. 1990-97, hon. mem. exec. com., 1997—. Author: Justification in Late Medieval Preaching: A Study of John Geiler of Keisersberg, 1966, 2d edit., 1989, Women, Freedom and Calvin, 1985; editor: (with Jack L. Stotts) To Confess the Faith Today, 1990, (with James F. Kay) Women, Gender and Christian Community, 1997, (with Páraic Réamonn) Partnership in God's Mission in the Middle East, 1998; contbr. articles to profl. jours. Presbyterian. E-mail: jgdouglass@aol.com.

DOUGLASS, JOHN W. commissioner; BS, U. Fla.; MS, Tex. Tech. U., Fairleigh Dickinson U.; postgrad., Cornell U. Dir. nat. security programs The White House; spl. asst. Office of the Undersec. of Def. for Acquisition; dir. plans and policy, dir. sci. and tech. Office of Sec. of Air Force; dep. U.S. mil. rep. NATO; asst. sec. Navy for Rsch., Devel. and Acquisition; pres., CEO Aerospace Industries Assn., 1998—; commr. Commn. on the Future of the U.S. Aerospace Industry. Brigadier gen. USAF, ret. Office: Aerospace Commn Crystal Gateway One 1235 Jefferson Davis Hwy Ste 940 Arlington VA 22202-3283

DOUGLASS, MARY CLEMENT, curator, small business owner; b. McAlester, Okla., Dec. 5, 1944; d. Albert Bittick and Mary Agnes (Hamilton) Clement; m. Errol Dwight Douglass, June 24, 1966; children: John Vodette, Aran Bittick. Student, East Ctrl. State U., 1963-66; BA in Edn., Ctrl. State U., 1967; postgrad., Kans. State U., 1988, U. Tex., 1990. Cert. geneal. records specialist. Social studies tchr. Ell-Saline H.S., Brookville, Kans., 1967-69; archtl. historian City of Salina (Kans.) Heritage Commn., 1984-88; registrar Smoky Hill Mus., Salina, 1986-88, curator of collections, 1989-97; ret.; proprietor Hist. Matters, 1997—. Dist. 1 rep. Kans. Mus. Assn., Topeka, 1991-92, v.p., program chair, 1993-94; mem. Landon grants com. Kans. State Hist. Soc., Topeka, 1992-93, mem. deaccession rev., 1993-97; mem. program com. Mountain-Plains Mus. Assn., 1992-93. Author: Clement Chronicles, 1982, Salina Kansas Historical Resources, 1984 (also video); editor Tree Climber, 1982-87. Grad. Leadership Salina C. of C., 1987; bd. mem., pers. com. Salina Rescue Mission, 1992-93, vol. GED tutor, 2000, City of Salina Heritage Commrs., 1998—, chmn., 2000—2003. Recipient medal of appreciation Kans. Soc. SAR, Salina, 1988, Martha Washington medal Kans. Soc. SAR, Salina, 1989, Seaton award for Prose, Kans. Quarterly, 1989, award for Outstanding Quarterly, Kans. Coun. Geneal. Socs., 1988, Mus. accreditation Am. Assn. Mus., Washington, 1997, grantee Salina Arts and Humanities, 1986, 87, Tlhen grantee Kans. State Hist. Soc., 2000. Mem. DAR (regent Mary Wade Strother chpt. 1985-86, registrar 2001—), United Daus. of the Confederacy, Assn. Profl. Genealogists (publs. adv. com., organizer, sec.-treas. Heartland chpt. 2002—), Geneal. Spkrs. Guild (bd. dirs.), Inst. Mus. Svcs. (surveyor MAP program 1992—), Christian Motorcyclists Assn. (sec. chpt. 363 1997-99, 2001—), Smoky Valley Geneal. Soc. (bd. dirs. 1983-2000, v.p. 1995-99, archivist 1999-2000), Salina Heights Christian Ch. (libr. 1997-99). Republican. Avocations: family history research, needle arts, motorcycle touring, painting, ministry. Home: 259 N Kansas Ave Salina KS 67401-8515 E-mail: mdoughm@swbell.net.

DOUGLASS, MELVIN ISADORE, middle school administrator, educator, clergyman; b. N.Y.C., July 21, 1948; s. Isadore Douglass and Esther L. Tripp. AS in Early Childhood Edn., Vincennes U., 1970; BS in Early Childhood and Elem. Edn., Tuskegee Inst., 1973; MS in Urban Elem. Edn., Morgan State U., 1975; MA in Orgn. Adminstrn. Supervision, NYU, 1977; MEd in Curriculum and Teaching, Columbia U., 1978, DEd, 1981; Cert. in Urban Sch. Leadership, Harvard U., 2003. Cert. social studies tchr., N.Y.; cert. sch. dist. adminstr. and supr., N.Y.; cert. elem. tchr., N.Y.; ordained to ministry Bapt. Ch., 1987. Tchr., dean students Bronx Pub. Sch., N.Y., 1973-75; sch. age program dir. Amistad Child Day Care Ctr., Jamaica, N.Y., 1976-77; adminstrv. dir. Beck Meml. Day Care Ctr., Bronx, 1983-84; primary sch. dept. chair City of N.Y. Dept. Juvenile Justice, 1984-85, ombudsman, 1985-88; chmn. depts. English, reading and social studies Stimson Jr. High Sch., Huntington Station, N.Y., 1988—. Adj. instr. sociology and African Am. studies Coll. of New Rochelle, N.Y., 1992—, adj. asst. prof. Bklyn. Coll. Grad. Sch. of Edn., N.Y., 2000—, adj. prof. Metropolitan Coll of N.Y., 1999—; coord. various edn. confs., 1986—; CEO Minority Educators' Network, N.Y., 1999—, mem. community adv. bd. City of N.Y. Dept. of Correction, Queens House of Detention for Men, 1991-95; edn. liaison N.Y. State Senator Alton R. Waldon, Jr., 1991—. Author: Black Winners: A History of Spingarn Medalists, 1915-1983, 1984, Carter G. Woodson: A Biography, 1987; contbr. articles to profl. jours. Assisting minister Calvary Bapt. Ch., 1987-91; co-chairperson edn. com. N.Y.C. Black Leadership Council, 1987-88, N.Y. State Conf. NAACP, 1986-89; chmn. anti-drug com. Met. Council NAACP Brs., 1986-89; cons. Jamaica East/West Adolescent Pregnancy Consortium, 1986-89; mem. area policy bd. #12 subunit 2, 1987—; mem. Queens adv. bd. N.Y. Urban League, 1988-93, adv. bd. Gerlad W. Deas Professorship U. N.Y. Downstate Med. Ctr., 2002— pres. bd. dirs. N.Y.C. Transit br. NAACP, 1984-89; bd. dirs. Queens Council on Arts, 1983-86, Black Exptl. Theatre, 1982—, United Black Men Queens County Inc., 1986-90, Dance Explosion, 1987-89; mem. community adv. bd. Pub. Sch. 40, Queens, 1992-95. Recipient citation for community svc. N.Y. State Gov. Mario Cuomo, 1986, citation award N.Y.C. Mayor Edward Koch, 1986, citation of honor Queens Borough Pres. Claire Shulman, 1986, Svc. award N.Y.C. Transit br. NAACP, 1986, Jefferson award Am. Inst. for Pub. Svc. and WNYW-Fox TV, 1987, Civil Rights award N.Y.C. Transit br. NAACP, 1988, citation N.Y.C. Coun., 1988, Alumni Faculty citation Vincennes U., 1991, resolution Senator A.R. Waldon, Jr., 1991; named Nu Omicron chpt. Omega Man of Yr., 1987. Mem. Nat. Black Child Devel. Inst., NEA, St. Albans C. of C., Am. Fedn. Sch. Adminstrs., Coun. Adminstrs. and Suprs., South Huntington Chairmen's Assn., L.I. Tuskegee Alumni Assn. (v.p. bd. dirs. 1987-89), Jamaica Track Club (pres., founder 1973—), Masons, Shriners, Kappa Delta Pi, Omega Psi Phi (basileus Nu Omicron chpt. 1986-89, bd. dirs. Nu Omicron chpt. Day Care Ctr. 1984—), Phi Delta Kappa, Sigma Pi Phi, One Hundred Black Men. Address: 395 Stuyvesant Ave Brooklyn NY 11233

DOUGLASS, ROBERT JOSEPH, JR., computer scientist; b. Moline, Ill., June 8, 1951; s. Robert Joseph and Hattie Jane (Holmes) Douglass; m. Barbara Walker Mahan, June 3, 1973 (div. Aug. 1981); m. Cyndi Louise Wagner, Dec. 1, 1990. BEE magna cum laude, Princeton U., 1973; MS in Computer Scis., U. Wis., 1974, PhD in Computer Scis., 1978. Postdoctoral rschr. dept. physics and astronomy U. London, 1978; asst. prof. computer sci. U. Va., Charlottesville, 1978-81; assoc. group leader for rsch. Los Alamos (N.Mex.) Nat. Lab., 1981-85; machine intelligence unit head Martin Marietta, Denver, 1985, program mgr. Autonomous Land Vehicle, 1987-89, program mgr., 1989, program mgr. Automatic Radar Air-to-Ground Target Acquisition, 1990-93; co-founder, CEO DiamondBack Vision, Washington and Denver, 1998—; asst. dir. info. sys. Def. Adv. Rsch. Projects Agy., U.S. Dept. Def., Arlington, Va., 1995—98; co-founder, chief tech. officer SET Assocs., Inc., 2002—. Mem. panel Computer Architecture Pres.'s Sci. Adv. Nat. Acad. Sci., Washington, 1984. Editor: Characteristic of Parallel Algorithms, 1987; assoc. editor: Jour. Parallel and Distributed Processing, 1984—89; contbr. Mem.: AAAS, IEEE, Assn. Computing Machinery. Achievements include patents for virtual reality interface to human-body, Salt Lake City, 93-95. Avocations: paleontology, alpine skiing, boxing, soccer. Office: 11600 Sunrise Valley Dr Ste 290 Herndon VA 20191-1410

DOUGLASS, ROBERT ROYAL, banker, lawyer; b. Binghamton, N.Y., Oct. 16, 1931; s. Robert R. and Frances (Behan) D.; m. Linda Ann Luria, June 2, 1962; children: Robert Royal, Alexandra Brooke, Andrew. BA with distinction, Dartmouth Coll., 1953; LL.B., Cornell U., 1959. Bar: N.Y. Asso. Hinman, Howard & Kattell, 1959-64; 1st asst. counsel to Gov. N.Y. State, Albany, 1964-65, counsel to gov., 1965-70, sec. to gov., 1971-72; partner Milbank, Tweed, Hadley & McCloy, 1972-76; exec. v.p., gen. counsel Chase Manhattan Bank, N.Y.C., 1976-83, exec. v.p., 1983-85, vice chmn., 1985-93; of counsel Milbank Tweed Hadley & McCloy, N.Y.C., 1994—. Dir. Rockefeller Ctr., Inc., 1976-82, Urstadt Biddle Properties, 1990—, Gryphon Holdings, 1993-95, Home Ins. Co., 1993-96; chmn. Cedel Internat., 1994—, Alliance for Downtown N.Y., 1995—, Clearstream Internat., 2000—; chmn. Nelson Rockefeller's Campaign for Rep. Presdl. Nomination, 1958; commr. Port Authority of N.Y. State and N.J., 1972-76; trustee N.Y.C. Pub. Libr., 1972-86; bd. dirs., chmn. exec. com. Downtown-Lower Manhattan Assn., N.Y.C., 1973-91, chmn., 1991—; mem. vis. com. John F. Kennedy Sch. Govt., Harvard U., 1974-79; mem. N.Y. Landmarks Conservancy, 1977-80. Trustee Dartmouth Coll., 1983-93, Mus. of Modern Art, 1989-94. Served with M.C., U.S. Army, 1954-56. Recipient Wallace award Am.-Scottish Found., 1974 Mem. ABA, N.Y. State Bar Assn., Coun. Fgn. Rels. Clubs: Century Assn, Downtown Assn., Round Hill, Seal Harbor, Blind Brook. Roman Catholic. Office: Milbank Tweed Hadley & Mc Cloy 1 Chase Manhattan Plz Fl 47 New York NY 10005-1413

DOUGLASS, SUSAN DANIEL, retired consultant; b. South Charleston, W.Va., Sept. 17, 1959; d. Charles David and Juliet Sue (Summers) Daniel; m. Michael Watson Douglass, Apr. 5, 1992. BS in Electrical and Electronic Engring., Calif. State U., Sacramento, 1985; MBA, Embry-Riddle Aero. U., 1989; Grad., squadron officer sch., 1988. Radio systems technician USAF, George AFB, Calif., 1978-80, radio systems instr. Keesler AFB, Miss., 1980-82, commd. 2d lt., 1985; advanced through grades to capt., 1989; program mgr. USAF, McClellan AFB, Calif., 1985-86, project engr., 1986-89, project mgr. L.A. AFB, 1989-91, exec. officer, 1991-92; program mgr. Scientific-Atlanta, 1993. Report survey officer Sacramento Air Logistics Ctr., 1985—87; cons., 1993—95; report survey officer Sacramento Air Logistics Ctr., 1985—87; cons., 1993—95. V.p. Bush Hill Elem. PTA, 2001—01; mem. Va. Run Elem. PTA; co-chmn. Canterbury Neighborhood Adv. Bd., 1996—98; math and English tutor Dyer-Kelly Elem. Sch., Sacramento, 1985—87. Capt. USAF, 1989. Mem.: Co. Grade Officers Coun. (Officer of Quarter award 1987), Armed Forces Comms. and Electronics Assn., Air Force Assn. Republican. Avocations: dancing, golf, horseback riding.

DOUMANI, GEORGE ALEXANDER, earth and environmental scientist; b. Acre, Palestine, Apr. 16, 1929; s. Alexander A. and Victoria (Issa) D.; m. Anne R. Davenport, June 14, 1985. BA in Geol. Scis., U. Calif., Berkeley, 1956, MA in Paleontology, 1957; PhD in Environ. Scis., Pacific Western U., 1985. Geologist Glaciologist Arctic Inst., Byrd Station, Antarctica, 1958-60; rsch. assoc. Inst. Polar Studies Ohio State U., Columbus, 1960-63; head, Cold Regions Bibliog. Sect. Sci. and Tech. divsn. Libr. of Congress, Washington, 1963-66, sci. adviser to U.S. Congress, Sci. Policy Rsch. divsn., 1966-75; pres. Adar Corp., Washington, Beirut, 1975-77, Tech. Transfer Internat. Corp., Washington, 1977-79; v.p. tech. transfer Human Resources Mgmt., Inc., Washington, 1979-85; dir. Peace Corps, Yemen, 1985-88; dir. office tech. policy Dept. of Energy, Washington, 1988-90; dir. earth and environ. scis. program Directorate for Edn. and Human Resources, NSF, Washington, 1990-91. Environ. protection specialist EPA, Washington, 1995—; cons. and lectr. in field. Editorial adv. bd. Sci. Digest, 1970-81; author numerous books, papers, reports and articles; appeared on numerous radio broadcasts, domestic and overseas including UN radio, BBC, and Voice of Am.; several TV appearances, domestic and fgn. Recipient Antarctic Svc. medal Def. Dept., 1961; decorated Knight of Nat. Order of Cedars, Lebanese Republic, 1961; W.W. Van Arsdale meml. scholar, 1954-55; U.S. Bd. on Geographic Names named Doumani Peak 1962 and Mount Doumani in Antarctica, 1967. Fellow Geol. Soc. Am. (sr., com. on geology and pub. policy), Nat. Explorers Club; mem. Am. Assn. Petroleum Geologists, Am. Polar Soc., Antarctican Soc. (pres. 1970-71), Geol. Soc. Washington, Cosmos Club, Internat. Freelance Photographers Orgn. (life), Old Antarctic Explorers Assn. (life), Sigma Xi (life). E-mail: gad_taico@yahoo.com., doumani.george@epa.gov.

DOUMANIAN, HERATCH OHANNES, radiology; b. Beirut, Feb. 11, 1934; s. Ohannes Toros Doumanian and Hripsime Kupelian; m. Sonya L. Dermenjian, Mar. 17, 1967; children: Greta, John, Leo. MD, Am. U. Beirut, Lebanon, 1957. Diplomate Am. Bd. Radiology. Resident in radiology U. Chgo. Hosp., Chgo., 1962-65; fellow in cardiovascular radiology U. Minn. Hosp., Mpls., 1965-66; dir. radiology St. Mary Med. Ctr., Hobart, Ind., 1967-92. Capt. M.C., U.S. Army, 1960-62, Germany. Mem. AMA, Radiol. Soc. N.Am., Am. Coll. Radiology, Innsbrook Country Club. Armenian Orthodox. Home: 6451 Arthur St Merrillville IN 46410-3122 Fax: 219 980-0945.

DOUMATO, LAMIA, librarian, art historian; b. Aug. 26, 1947; d. A.G. and Victoria (Peters) D. BA, R.I. Coll., 1969; MA, Pa. State U., 1971; MLS, Simmons Coll., 1974; student, Columbia U., 1976-78. Intern Providence Pub. Library, 1970-71; reference asst. Boston U. Libraries, 1971-74; reference librarian Mus. of Modern Art, N.Y.C., 1974-78; from asst. prof. to dir. art and architecture U. Colo. Library, Boulder, 1978-81; reference librarian Nat. Gallery of Art, Washington, 1981-88, head rsch. svcs., 1988—. Cons. George Sand Festival, Boulder, 1980, Nat. Mus. Women in the Arts, Washington, 1982; project reviewer Nat. Endowment for Humanities, Washington, 1987—. Author: American Drawings, 1979, Women and American Architecture, 1988, History of American Architecture, 1988, Artist's Book Librarians, 1990, The Art of Bishop Dioscorus Theodorus, 1999, England Collection of Artists Books, 2000, Opening the Door to Paradise, 2000, Michael the Great: Iconoclast or Art Patron, 2002, Pontifical of Ignatius II, 2003; contbr. Architecture: A Place for Women, 1989, Graphic Studio, 1991. Mus. Modern Art grantee, 1977-78, Coun. on Rsch. grantee U. Colo., 1979; recipient Performance award Nat. Gallery Art, 1989, Wilson award ARHS, NA, 2001; Robert H. Smith fellow 1997-98, 98-99, Bibliographical Soc. Am. fellow, 1999-2000, Ailsa Mellow Bruce fellow CASVA, 2001-02, Worldwide art fellow, 2002, Oxford rsch. fellow, 2002. Mem. ALA (serials adv. com. 1980, N. Am. chpt. pubs. com. 1996-97, rsch. com. 1999 2000), Art Librarians, Assn. Archtl. Librarians (chair 1988, adv. com. 1988-91), Art and Architecture Thesaurus (adv. com. 1982-84). Home: 3001 Veazey Ter NW Washington DC 20008-5454 Office: Nat Gallery of Art 6th And Constitution Ave Washington DC 20565-0001 E-mail: l-doumato@nga.gov.

DOUSKEY, THERESA KATHRYN, health facility administrator; b. New Haven, Conn., Nov. 30, 1938; d. Stanley Anthony and Wadia (Mekdeci) D. RN, Grace New Haven Sch. Nursing, 1959; BS in Nursing, So. Conn. State U., 1962; MPA in Health Care, U. New Haven, 1979. Various positions Yale New Haven Hosp., 1959-80; asst. dir. nursing Meriden (Conn.) Wallingford Hosp., 1980-81; nurse Regional Visiting Nurse Agy., North Haven, Conn., 1983-87; home care coord. Milford (Conn.) Hosp., 1990-93; case mgr., nurse Cmty. Care, Inc., New Haven, 1988-90, 93-97; nurse cons. Anthem Blue Cross/Blue Shield, North Haven, Conn., 1997-98; nurse case mgr. home care program for elderly South Ctrl. Area Aging, New Haven, Conn., 1998—. Mem. ANA, Conn. Nurses Assn. (nominating com. 1972-74, profl. adv. com. 2000—), Conn. Assn. Continuity of Care, Orange Vis. Nurse Assn., Sigma Theta Tau. Republican. Avocations: needle crafts, gardening, working with animal humane groups, established social ministries outreach program at local church. Home: 412 Narrow Ln Orange CT 06477-3315

DOUTY, LUCY EVELYN, sales and marketing executive; b. Boston, Sept. 22, 1951; d. Michael H. and Irma O. (Fusco) Gionfriddo; m. George E. Douty Jr., May 20, 1972. AS in Bus. Adminstrn., Northeastern U., 1988; postgrad., Simmons Coll., 1991-93. Mktg. mgr. Dynamics Rsch. Corp., Wilmington, Mass., 1974-85; natl. sales mgr. U.S. Law News, San Juan, Calif., 1986; client svcs. mgr. Price Waterhouse, Waltham, Mass., 1987-91; dir. mktg. Macdonald, Levin, Jenkin & Co., 1991-93. Total quality mgmt. seminar developer, presenter. Author: CNC Operating Manual, 1984, Sales Training Manual, 1986. Mem. vol. staff Nat. Multiple Sclerosis Soc. Mem. Boat U.S. Club. Roman Catholic. Avocations: sailing, skiing, reading, travel, golf.

DOVE, DONALD AUGUSTINE, city planner, educator; b. Waco, Tex., Aug. 7, 1930; s. Sebert Constantine and Amy Delmena (Stern) Dove; m. Cecelia Mae White, Feb. 9, 1957; children: Angela, Donald, Monica Gilstrap, Celine, Cathlyn, Dianna, Jennifer. BA, Calif. State U., L.A., 1951; MA in Pub. Adminstrn., U. So. Calif., 1966. Planning & devel. cons. D. Dove Assocs., L.A., 1959-60, supr. demographic rsch. Calif. Dept. Pub. Works, L.A., 1960-66; dir. transp. employment project State of Calif., L.A., 1966-71, chief L.A. Region transp. study, 1973-84; chief environ. planning Calif. Dept. Transp., L.A., 1972-75; dir. U. So. Calif., L.A., 1984-87; panelist, advisor Pres. Conf. Aging, Washington, 1970—; environ. coord. Calif. Dept. Pub. Works, Sacramento, 1971-75; panelist, advisor Internat. Conf. Energy Use Mgmt., 1981. Guest lectr. univs. We. U.S., 1969—. Author: Preserving Urban Environment, 1976, Small Area Population Forecasts, 1966. Chmn. Lynwood City Planning Commn., Calif., 1982—; pres. Area Pastoral Coun., L.A., 1982—83; mem., del. Archdiocesan Pastoral Coun., L.A., 1979—86, Compton Cmty. Devel. Bd., Calif., 1967—71; pres. Neighborhood Esteem/Enrichment Techniques Inst., 1992—93. With U.S. Army, 1952—54. Mem.: Assn. Environ. Profls. (cofounder 1973), Am. Inst. Cert. Planners, Calif. Assn. Mgmt. (pres. 1987—88), Am. Inst. Planners (transp. chmn. 1972—73), Am. Planning Assn., Optimists Club (sec. 1978—79). Democrat. Roman Catholic. Home and Office: 11356 Ernestine Ave Lynwood CA 90262-3711 E-mail: dondve@aol.com.

DOVE, JEFFREY AUSTIN, lawyer; b. Syracuse, N.Y., Sept. 21, 1959; s. Austin and Jane (Mooney) D.; m. Cathy Stein, Oct. 12, 1985. BA cum laude, Middlebury Coll., 1981; JD, Syracuse U., 1984. Bar: N.Y. 1985, U.S. Dist. Ct. (no. and we. dists.) N.Y. 1985, U.S. Dist. Ct. (we. dist.) Wis. 1994. Ptnr. Menter, Rudin & Trivelpiece, P.C., Syracuse, 1984—. Lectr., author N.Y. State Bar Assn., Nat. Bus. Inst. Mem. ABA, N.Y. Bar Assn., Onondaga County Bar Assn., Ctrl. N.Y. Bankruptcy Bar Assn. (pres. 1997, founding mem., dir.), Capitol Region Bankruptcy Bar Assn. Office: Menter Rudin & Trivelpiece 500 S Salina St Ste 500 Syracuse NY 13202-3300 E-mail: jdove@menterlaw.com.

DOVE, LORRAINE FAYE, gerontology nurse; b. West Reading, Pa., Feb. 20, 1960; d. Blaine Hoye Sr. and Faye Louise (Heisey) D. Diploma, Reading Hosp. Sch. of Nursing, 1982. RN, Fla., Pa.; cert. gerontol. nurse, PICC lines, CDONA LTC, chemotherapy. Asst. dir. nursing Leader Nursing and Rehab. Ctr., Lebanon, Pa., 1983-84; dir. nursing Sunrise Manor, Ft. Pierce, Fla., 1986-88, Vero Beach (Fla.) Care Ctr., 1988-92, Okeechobee (Fla.) Health Care Facility, 1992-94; regional nurse cons. Patient Care Pharmacy, Pompano Beach, Fla., 1994-95; CQI/RA coord. Colonial Palms East, Pompano Beach, 1995; dir. nursing Atlantis, Lantana, Fla., 1995-96, Springtree, Sunrise, Fla., 1996-97; quality assurance coord./corp. clin. svcs. dir./educator Premiere/Integrated Health Svcs., Pembroke Pines, Fla., 1997-99; dir. nursing North Miami Rehab, 1999-2000; mobile dir. nursing, dir. nursing HCR Manor Care, Toledo, 2000—. Past mem. FHCA AIDS task force, Health and Human Svcs. Bd., Aging and Adult Com., AIDS Consortium of the Treasure Coast. Mem. Nat. Assn. Dirs. Nursing Adminstrn., Pa. Assn. Dirs. Nursing Adminstrn. E-mail: LD38@webtv.net.

DOVE, RITA FRANCES, poet, English language educator; b. Akron, Ohio, Aug. 28, 1952; d. Ray A. and Elvira E. (Hord) D.; m. Fred Viebahn, Mar. 23, 1979; 1 child, Aviva Chantal Tamu Dove-Viebahn. BA summa cum laude, Miami U., Oxford, Ohio, 1973; postgrad., Universität Tübingen, Fed. Republic Germany, 1974-75; MFA, U. Iowa, 1977; LLD (hon.), Miami U., Oxford, Ohio, 1988, Knox Coll., 1989, Tuskegee U., 1994, U. Miami, Fla., 1994, Washington U., St. Louis, 1994, Case Western Res. U., 1994, U. Akron, 1994, Ariz. State U., 1995, Boston Coll., 1995, Dartmouth Coll., 1995, Spelman Coll., 1996, U. Pa., 1996, U. N.C., 1997, U. Notre Dame, 1997, Northeastern U., 1997, Columbia U., 1998, Washington & Lee U., 1999, SUNY, Brockport, 1999, Pratt Inst., 2001, Howard U., 2001. Asst. prof. English Ariz. State U., Tempe, 1981-84, assoc. prof., 1984-87, prof., 1987-89, U. Va., Charlottesville, 1989-93, Commonwealth prof. English, 1993—; U.S. poet laureate, cons. in poetry Libr. of Congress, Washington, 1993-95, spl. cons. in poetry, 1999-2000; columnist Washington Post, 2000—02. Writer-in-residence Tuskegee (Ala.) Inst., 1982; lit. panelist Nat. Endowment for Arts, Washington, 1984-86, chmn. poetry grants panel, 1985; judge Walt Whitman award Acad. Am. Poets, 1990, Pulitzer prize in poetry, 1991, Ruth Lilly prize 1991, Nat. Book award in poetry 1991, 98, Anisfield-Wolf Book awards, 1992—, Shelley Meml. award, 1997, Amy Lowell fellowship, 1997; poetry panel chmn. Pulitzer prize, 1997; final judge Brittingham and Pollack prizes, 1997; juror Christopher Columbus Fellowship Found., 1998—, Duke Ellington awards, 1999. Author: (poetry) Ten Poems, 1977, The Only Dark Spot in the Sky, 1980, The Yellow House on the Corner, 1980, Mandolin, 1982, Museum, 1983, Thomas and Beulah, 1986 (Pulitzer Prize in poetry 1987), The Other Side of the House, 1988, Grace Notes, 1989 (Ohioana award 1990), Selected Poems, 1993 (Ohioana award 1994), Lady Freedom Among Us, 1994, Mother Love, 1995, Evening Primrose, 1998, On the Bus with Rosa Parks, 1999 (Ohioana award 2000); (verse drama) The Darker Face of the Earth, 1994 (W. Alton Jones Found. grant 1994, Kennedy Ctr. Fund for New Am. Plays award 1995, Geraldine Dodge Found. grant, 1997), completely rev. 2d edit., 1996 (first performance Oreg. Shakespeare Festival 1996); (novel) Through the Ivory Gate, 1992 (Va. Coll. Stores Book award 1993); (short stories) Fifth Sunday, 1985 (Callaloo award 1986); (essays) The Poet's World, 1995, (song cycle) Seven for Luck (music by John Williams), 1st performance Boston Symphony Orch., Tanglewood, 1998; mem. editl. bd. Nat. Forum, 1984-89, Iris, 1989—; mem. adv. bd. Ploughshares, 1992—, N.C. Writers Network, 1992-99, Civilization, 1994-97; assoc. editor Callaloo, 1986-98; adv. and contbg. editor Gettysburg Rev., 1987—, TriQuarterly, 1988—, Ga. Review, 1994—, Bellingham Rev., 1996—, Internat. Quarterly, 1997—, Callaloo, 1998—, Mid-Am. Rev., 1998—; editor Best Am. Poetry, 2000. Commr. The Schomburg Ctr. for Rsch. in Black Culture, N.Y. Pub. Libr., 1987—; mem. Renaissance Forum Folger Shakespeare Libr., 1993-95, Coun. of Scholars Libr. of Congress, 1994—; mem. nat. launch com. AmeriCorps, 1994; mem. awards coun. Am. Acad. Achievement, 1994—; mem. adv. bd. Thomas Jefferson Ctr. Freedom of Expression, 1994—, U.S. Civil War Ctr., 1995-99, Va. Ctr. Creative Arts, 1995—; The Poets Corner elector Cathedral Ch. St. John the Divine, N.Y.C., 1991—; bd. govs. Humanities Rsch. Inst. U. Calif., 1996-99. Presdl. scholar, 1970, Nat. Achievement scholar, 1970-73; Fulbright/Hays fellow, 1974-75, rsch. fellow U. Iowa, 1975, teaching/writing fellow U. Iowa, 1976-77, Guggenheim Found. fellow, 1983-84, Mellon sr. fellow Nat. Humanities Ctr., 1988-89, fellow Ctr. for Advanced Studies, U. Va., 1989-92, fellow Shannon Ctr. for Advanced Studies, U. Va., 1995—; grantee NEA, 1977, 89; recipient Lavan Younger Poet award Acad. Am. Poets, 1986, GE Found. award, 1987, Bellagio (Italy) residency Rockefeller Found., 1988, Ohio Gov.'s award 1988, Literary Lion citation N.Y. Pub. Libr., 1991, Women of Yr. award Glamour Mag., 1993, NAACP Great Am. Artist award, 1993, Golden Plate award Am. Acad. Achievement, 1994, Disting. Achievement medal Miami U. Alumni Assn., 1994, Renaissance Forum award for leadership in the literary arts Folger Shakespeare Libr., 1994, Carl Sandburg award Internat. Platform Assn., 1994, Heinz award in arts and humanities, 1996, Charles Frankel prize/Nat. Humanities medal Pres. of U.S. and NEH, 1996; inducted Ohio Women's Hall of Fame, 1991, Nat. Assn. of Women in Edn. Disting. Woman award, 1997, Sara Lee Frontrunner award, 1997, Barnes & Noble Writers for Writers award, 1997, Levinson prize Poetry mag., 1998, John Frederick Nims Translation prize, 1999, Libr. Lion award N.Y. Pub. Libr., 2000, Duke Ellington Lifetime Achievement award, 2001, Emily Couric Women's Leadership award, 2003; named Phi Beta Kappa poet Harvard U., 1993. Mem. PEN, ASCAP, Am. Philos. Soc., Poetry Soc. Am., Associated Writing Programs (bd. dirs. 1985-88, pres. 1986-87), Am. Acad. Achievement (mem. golden plate awards coun. 1994—), Phi Beta Kappa (senator 1994-2000), Phi Kappa Phi. Office: U Va Dept English 219 Bryan Hall PO Box 400121 Charlottesville VA 22904-4121

DOVEL-CASH, MICHELLE, engineer; b. Annapolis, Md., Feb. 24, 1962; d. William Lawrence and Jean Ann (Hughes) D. BS in Computer Engring., Tulane U., 1984; MBA, Fla. Inst. Technology, 1987-91; MS in Computer Sci., Webster's U., 1998. Customer service Software Solutions, Metairie and Baton Rouge, La., 1984-85; software engr. Lockheed Martin (formerly Martin Marietta), Orlando, Fla., 1985—2000; software process improvement mgr. Veridian, 2000—. Longaberger cons. Mem. NAFE, Tulane U. Engrs. Avocations: long distance running, hand crafts. Home: 709 Hallowell Cir Orlando FL 32828-8663

DOVENBARGER, BARBARA, accountant; b. California, June 9, 1953; m. Larry Dovenbarger; 1 child, Kyle. B, Pepperdine U., 1976; M, U. of Redlands, 1986; grad., U.S. Dept. Commerce Export Lic. Program, Hughes Aircraft Mgmt. Devel. Program, Covey Inst.: Seven Habits Highly Successful Leaders, Stanford Exec. Leadership Inst. Asst. mgr. Hughes Aircraft Co., Indsl. Products Divsn., Carlsbad, Calif., 1973—92, mgr., internat. adminstrn., customer svc., mgr. of fin. ops., continuous measurable improvement coord.; dir. of fiscal ops. Calif. State U., 1992—98, contr., 1998—2002, dir. of internal audit, 2002—. Exec. coun. Hughes Aircraft Mgmt. Club, Carlsbad, Calif., 1989—92, Fin. Officers Assn. of the Calif. state U. sys., 1995—2002. Mentor Women's Leadership Conf., San Marcos, Calif., 2002. Mem.: Western Assn. of Coll. and U. Bus. Officers, Assn. of the U. Auditors. Luth. Avocations: piano, movies, dogs. Office: Calif State U at San Marcos San Marcos CA 92096 Business E-Mail: dove@csusm.edu.

DOVER, SIR KENNETH JAMES, retired Greek scholar; b. Croydon, Eng., Mar. 11, 1920; s. Percy Henry and Dorothy Valerie (Healey) D.; student Balliol Coll., Oxford (Eng.) U., 1938-40, 45-47, MA, 1946, DLitt, 1974, student Merton Coll., 1948, hon. fellow; LLD, Birmingham U., St. Andrews U.; DLitt, U. Bristol, U. Liverpool, U. London, St. Andrews U., U. Durham; DHL, Oglethorpe U.; m. Audrey Ruth Latimer, Mar. 17, 1947; children: Alan Hugh, Catherine Ruth. Fellow, tutor Balliol Coll., Oxford (Eng.) U., 1948-55, hon. fellow, pres. Corpus Christi Coll., 1976-86, hon. fellow; prof. of Greek, St. Andrews U., 1955-76; chancellor St. Andrews U., 1981—; prof.-at-large Cornell U., 1983-89; vis. lectr. Harvard U., 1960; Sather vis. prof. U. Calif., 1967; prof. Stanford U., winter quarter, 1987-92. Served with artillery Brit. Army, 1940-45; mentioned in dispatches. Created Knight, 1977. Fellow Brit. Acad. (pres., 1978-81, Kenyon medal 1993); mem. Hellenic Soc. (pres., 1971-74), Classical Assn. (pres., 1975), Am. Acad. Arts and Scis., Netherlands Acad. Arts and Scis. Author: Greek Word Order, 1960; Lysias and the Corpus Lysiacum, 1968; Aristophanic Comedy, 1972; Greek Popular Morality in the Time of Plato and Aristotle, 1974; Greek Homosexuality, 1978; The Greeks, 1980; Greek and the Greeks (Collected Papers I), 1987; The Greeks and Their Legacy (Collected Papers II), 1988, Marginal Comment (memoirs), 1994, The Evolution of Greek Prose Style, 1997; contbr. to other books and articles; editor: Aristophanes' Clouds, 1968; Theocritus, 1971; Plato, Symposium, 1980, Perceptions of the Ancient Greeks, 1992, Aristophanes' Frogs, 1993. Home: 49 Hepburn Gardens Saint Andrews KY16 9LS Scotland

DOVEY, BRIAN HUGH, health care products company executive, venture capitalist; b. Cleve., Nov. 12, 1941; s. Hugh Albert and Dorothy (Garde) D.; m. Elizabeth Barrett Hartzell, Aug. 17, 1963; children— Laurel, Kimberly, Christine AB, Colgate U., 1963; MBA, Harvard U., 1967. Sales mgr. N.Y. Telephone, N.Y.C., 1963-69; dir. planning Howmet Corp., N.Y.C., 1969-70; dir. ops. Howmedica, Inc., Cheshire, Conn., 1970-71; v.p. ops. Survival Tech., Bethesda, Md., 1971-75, pres., 1975-83; pres. surg. products div. Rorer Group Inc., Fort Washington, Pa., 1983-86, exec. v.p., 1985-86, pres., 1986-88; gen. ptnr. Domain Assocs., 1988—. Former dir. Origin Medsys., Inc., Brit. Biotech. Group plc, Health Industry Mfrs. Assn., Washington, Non-Prescription Drug Mfrs. Assn., Virna Pharm., Inc.; former chmn. Athena Neuroscis., ReSound Corp.; bd. dirs. Polar Materials, NABI., Advanced Corneal Systems, Cadent Med. Corp., Vivus, Inc., Trimeris Co., Connetics Corp., Microsurge, Inc., Geron Corp.; pres., bd. dirs. Nat. Venture Capital Assn.; chmn. bd. dirs. Creative BioMolecules; trustee Coriell Inst. for Med. Rsch., 1995—. Inventor syringe assembly. Trustee Germantown Acad., Fort Washington, 1983-88, v.p. 1987—; overseer U. Pa. Sch. Nursing, Phila., 1985-88; bd. dirs. Huntington's Disease Soc., 1986-89, chmn. 1988-89, Greater Phila. Economic Devel. Council, 1987-88. Mem. Phila. Pres.'s Orgn., Proprietary Assn. (bd. dirs. 1987-88), Nat. Venture Capital Assn. (pres. and chmn. 1997-98), Phila. Cricket Club, Penllyn Club. Office: Domain Assocs 1 Palmer Sq Princeton NJ 08542-3718

DOVIAK, INGRID ELLINGER, elementary school educator; b. New Britain, Conn., Feb. 10, 1971; d. John Leonard and Marjorie Chain Ellinger; m. Stephen Michael Doviak, June 8, 1996. BS, MA, So. Conn. State U., 1993. Tchr. head dept. enrichment grades k-8 Wntergreen Interdist. Magnet Sch., Hamden, Conn., 1998—. Adj. instr. deptl edn. Sacred Heart U., Fairfield, Conn., 2000—; adj. instr. So. Conn. State U., New Haven, 1998—; presenter Atomic Math Conf., 2001, 02, Conn. Assn. Math. Precocious Youth, 2000, 01, 02, Conn. Assn. Schs.

DOVRING, KARIN ELSA INGEBORG, writer, poet, playwright, communication analyst; b. Stenstorp, Sweden, Dec. 5, 1919; arrived in US, 1953, naturalized, 1968; m. Folke Dovring, May 30, 1943. Grad., Coll. Commerce, Gothenburg, Sweden, 1936; MA, Lund (Sweden) U., 1943, PhD, 1951; Phil. Licentiate, Gothenburg U., 1947. Journalist several Swedish daily newspapers and weekly mags., 1940-60; tchr. Swedish colls.; rsch. assoc. of Harold Lasswell Yale U., New Haven, 1953-78; fgn. corr. Swedish newspapers, Italy, Switzerland, France and Germany, 1956-60; freelance writer, journalist, 1960—; rsch. prof. comms. and media studies U. Ill., Urbana, 2002. Vis. prof. Internat. U., The Vatican, Rome, 1958-60, Gottingen (W.Ger.) U., 1962; lectr. U.S. Army, Peace Corps, Yale U., U. Wis., McGill U., U. Iowa; rsch. assoc. U. Ill., Urbana, 1968-69, guest lectr., 2001-02; invited contbr. Social Sci. Rsch. Coun., 1988; speaker Conf. Law and Policy, Yale U. Law Sch., 1992-93, 99—; hon. mem. Profl. Women's Adv. Bd. Am. Biograph. Inst., Raleigh, N.C., 2003; adv. coun. Internat. Biographical Ctr., Cambridge, Eng.; interviewee radio and TV programs; writer Ill. Alliance to Prevent Nuclear War, radio, theater; hon. rsch. prof. comm. and media studies U. Ill. Coll. Comm., 2002—; songwriter Hollywood and Nashville; plays for TV movies. Author: Songs of Zion, 1951, Land Reform as a Propaganda Theme, 3d edit., 1965, Road of Propaganda, 1959, Optional Society, 1972, Frontiers of Communication, 1975, English as Lingua Franca: Double Talk in Global Persuasion, 1997, (short stories) No Parking This Side of Heaven, 1982, Harold D. Lasswell: His Communication with a Future, 1987, 2d edit., 1988; (novel) Heart in Escrow, 1990; (poems) Faces in a Mirror, 1995, Changing Scenery, 2002, In the Service of Persuasion: English as Lingua Franca Across the Globe, 2001; contbr. articles to mags.; represented in several poetry anthologies. Recipient Swedish Nat. award for short stories Bonniers Pub. House Stockholm, 1951, Internat. Poet of Merit award Internat. Soc. Poets, 2002; named to Internat. Poetry Hall of Fame, 1996, Poet of Yr., 2000, 01, 02. Mem. Soc. Jean Jacques Rousseau of Geneva (hon. life), Acad. Am. Poets. Democrat. Address: 613 W Vermont Ave Urbana IL 61801-4824

DOW, DAVID SONTAG, retired ophthalmologist; b. Ann Arbor, Mich., Feb. 15, 1934; s. William Gould and Edna Lois (Sontag) D.; m. Gail Anita Bade, Feb. 11, 1961 (dec. Feb. 2000); children: Steven Michael, Bonnie Jean, William Herbert, James Patrick; m. Figes Flaherty, March, 17, 2001. BS with distinction, U. Mich., 1956, MD, 1958, MS in Ophthalmology, 1964. Diplomate Am. Bd. Ophthalmology. Intern Denver Gen. Comm. Hosp., 1958-59; psychiatrist USAF Med. Svc., Wichita Falls, Tex., 1959-61; resident in ophthalmology U. Mich. Med. Ctr., Ann Arbor, 1961-64; pvt. practice ophthalmology Scruggs, Dow, and Kannwischer ptnr., Waco, Tex., 1964-88, Cen. Tex. Eye Clinic, Waco, 1988-97; ret., 1997. Contbg. editor Waco Tribune Herald, 1983—; author pamphlets in field. City coun. mem., mayor Waco City Con., 1977—81; mem. Woodway City Coun., 1997—2001; bd. dir. Waco Symphony Assn., 1970—89, 1994—2001, pres., 1982—83; bd. dir. Tex. Med. Polit. Action Com., Austin, 1973—82; founding bd. dirs., chmn. Greater Waco Arts Coun., 1986—, chmn., 1992, 1994—2000. Capt. USAF, 1959—61. Mem. Am. Acad. Ophthalmology, Tex. Med. Assn., Waco Striders Club, Ridgewood Country Club, Rotary. Episcopalian. Avocations: politics, musical theater, yard/garden construction, singing. Home: 400 Ivy Ann Ct Waco TX 76712-3629

DOW, GARNETT MCCORMICK, geoscientist; b. Biddeford, Maine, Aug. 5, 1934; s. Derry Walter Fogg and Charlotte Adelade (Cousens) D.; m. Sigrid Irene Dow, May 26, 1972; children: Michael Eric, Tod McCormick, Erin Renee. BA, U. Maine, 1959; MS, U. Ill., 1962, PhD, 1965. Geophysicist, geologist Amoco, Oklahoma City, 1964-67; sr. rsch. scientist Amoco Rsch. Ctr., Tulsa, 1967-73; geol. supr. Amoco Internat., Chgo., 1973-76; regional chief geologist Amoco Europe, London, 1976-80; exploration mgr. Amoco Indonesia, Jakarta, 1980-83; sr. geol. assoc. Amoco, Houston, 1983-92; exploration cons. Noble Energy, Inc., Houston, 1995—. Cons. in field. Sustaining mem. Repu. Nat. Com., 1990's. With U.S. Army, 1954-56. Mem. Am. Assn. Petroleum Geologists, Am. Geophys. Union, Assn. Internat. Petroleum Negotiators, Houston Geol. Soc., Planetary Soc. Avocations: sailing, photography, amateur astronomy.

DOW, PETER ANTHONY, advertising agency executive; b. Detroit, Oct. 7, 1933; s. Douglas and Mary Louise (Murray) D.; m. Jane Ann Ottaway, Mar. 21, 1959; children— Jennifer Dow Murphy, Peter Kinnersley, Thomas Anthony BA, U. Mich., 1955. Account exec. Campbell-Ewald Co., Detroit, 1958-66, exec. v.p., 1979-82, pres., 1982-93, vice chmn., 1993-95, ret., 1995; account supr. Young & Rubicam, Detroit, 1966-68; advt. dir. Chrysler Corp., Detroit, 1968-77, dir. mktg., 1977-79. Bd. dirs. Techno Brands, Inc., The Stroh Cos., Inc., Nasco Corp. Trustee emeritus Lawrenceville Sch., N.J. Served to lt. (j.g.) USNR, 1955-58. Mem. Mich. Advt. Industry Alliance (past pres.), Grosse Pointe Club, Detroit Athletic Club, Adcraft Club (past pres.), Country Club Detroit, Old Club. Republican. Presbyterian.

DOW, SIMON, artistic director; b. Australia; Diploma, Australian Ballet Sch. Joined Australian Ballet, Stuttgart (Germany) Ballet; joined, prin. dancer Wash. Ballet, 1979; prin. dancer Australan Ballet, 1982-85, San Francisco Ballet, 1985-88, Boston Ballet, 1988-90; freelance guest artist and master tchr., 1990; assoc. artistic dir. Wash. Ballet, 1992-93, 96-97; art dir. Milw. Ballet Co., 1999—2002; artistic dir. West Australian Ballet, Perth, Australia, 2003—. Master tchr. Australian Ballet, Australian Ballet Sch., Sydney Dance Co., NSW Coll. Dance, Am. Ballet Theatre, Boston Ballet, Met. Opera Ballet, Feld Ballet, Milw. Ballet, Internat. Tanz Wochen, Vienna, Austria, Frankfurt Ballet, Germany, Les Grands Ballet Cans.; tchr. Wash. Sch. Ballet, David Howard Sch. Dance, NY. Guest appearances include Mann Performing Arts Ctr., Phila., Spoleto Festival, Wolf Trap Farm park, Jacob's Pillow Dance Festival, Pendleton Music Festival, Detroit Symphony; choreographer (ballets) Wash. Ballet, N.Y. Festival Ballet, Boston Ballet, Theater Artaud, San Francisco, Cin. Dance Pl. Recipient Cecchetti Jr. medal. Office: West Australian Ballet PO Box 7228 Cloisters Sq Perth 6850 Australia*

DOW, STEVEN BENJAMIN, social studies educator; b. Washington, 1951; s. Thomas W. and Priscilla M. Dow; m. Linda Lee Dow; children: T. Adam, Eric. BA, Bowling Green State U., 1973; JD, Ohio State U., 1978; MA, U. Mich., 1989, PhD, 1999. Bar: Ohio 1979. Counsel DeSelm, DeSelm & Baker, Cambridge, Ohio, 1979; lectr. Sch. Bus. Mich. State U., East Lansing, 1979—80, asst. prof. Sch. Bus., 1980—85, assoc. prof. Sch. Bus., 1985—98, assoc. prof. Sch. Criminal Justice, 1998—. Vis. assoc. prof. Bus. Sch. U. Mich., Ann Arbor, 1996—97, vis. prof. polit. sci. dept., 2000—03. Editor: Am. Bus. Law Jour., 1989—90; contbr. Mem.: Am. Sociol. Assn., Midwest Polit. Sci. Assn., Tri-State Acad. Legal Studies in Bus., Acad. Legal Studies in Bus., Am. Soc. Criminology, Acad. Criminal Justice Scis., Am. Polit. Sci. Assn., Law & Soc. Assn., Phi Kappa Phi. Avocations: music, bicycling, cooking. Office: Mich State Univ Sch Criminal Justice 532 Baker Hall East Lansing MI 48824

DOW, WILLIAM FRENCH, III, lawyer; b. New Haven, Dec. 7, 1941; s. William French and Mary Carolyn (Grandel) D.; m. Diane Ruth McClure, July 15, 1967; children: Brian, Nancy, Tony, Andy, Tina, Mary, Becky. BA, Yale U., 1963; LLB, U. Pa., 1968. Bar: Fla. 1968, Conn. 1969, D.C. 1969, U.S. Dist. Ct. D.C. 1969, U.S. Dist. Ct. (mid. dist.) Fla. 1969, U.S. Ct. Appeals (D.C. cir.) 1970, U.S. Dist. Ct. Conn. 1974, U.S. Ct. Appeals (2d cir.) 1975, U.S. Ct. Appeals (3d cir.) 1977, U.S. Supreme Ct. 1981, U.S. Dist. Ct. Vt. 1995. Staff atty. Fla. Migrant Legal Svcs., 1968-69, Neighborhood Legal Svcs. Program, Washington, 1969-70, Pub. Defender Svc., Washington, 1970-74; asst. U.S. atty. U.S. Atty. for Dist. of Conn., New Haven, 1974-76; ptnr. Jacobs, Grudberg, Belt & Dow, New Haven, 1976—. Campaign mgr. Einhorn for Mayor, New Haven, 1992; trustee Hopkins Sch., New Haven, 1988-98; bd. edn. St. Aedans, New Haven, 1981-82. Recpient Commendation Dept. Justice, 1976. Mem. Conn. Criminal Def. Lawyers Assn. (pres. 1991-92, Pres.'s Commendation 1991), Conn. Bar Assn. (chmn. exec. for criminal justice 1991-94), New Haven County Bar Assn., Assn. Trial Lawyers Am., Conn. Trial Lawyers Assn. Democrat. Roman Catholic. Avocations: tennis, little league.

DOWBEN, CARLA LURIE, lawyer, educator; b. Chgo., Jan. 22, 1932; d. Harold H. and Gertrude Lurie; m. Robert Dowben, June 20, 1950; children: Peter Arnold, Jonathan Stuart, Susan Laurie. AB, U. Chgo., 1950; JD, Temple U., 1955. Bar: Ill. 1957, Mass. 1963, Tex. 1974, U.S. Surpeme Ct. 1974. Assoc. Conrad and Verges, Chgo., 1957-62; exec. officer MIT, Cambridge, Mass., 1963-64; legal planner Mass. Health Planning Project, Boston, 1964-69; assoc. prof. Life Scis. Inst. Brown U., Providence, 1970-72; asst. prof. health law U. Tex. Health Sci. Ctr., Dallas, 1973-78, assoc. prof., 1978-93; ptnr. Choate & Lilly, Dallas, 1989-92; head health law sect. Looper, Reed, Mark & McGraw, Dallas, 1992-95, of counsel, 1995-99. Adj. assoc. prof. health law U. Tex., 1993-95; cons. to bd. dirs. Mental Health Assn., 1958-86, Ft. Worth Assn. Retarded Citizens, 1980-90, Advocacy, Inc., 1981-85; dir. Nova Health Systems, 1975—, Tockwotton Home, 1994-98. Contbr. articles to profl. jours. Active in drafting health and mental health legis., agy. regulation in several states and local govts. Mem. ABA, Tex. Bar Assn., Dallas Bar Assn., Am. Health Lawyers Assn., Hastings Inst. Ethics, Tex. Family Planning Assn. Mem. Soc. Of Friends.

DOWBEN, ROBERT MORRIS, physician, scientist; b. Phila., Apr. 18, 1927; m. Carla Lurie, June 20, 1950; children: Peter Arnold, Jonathan Stuart, Susan Laurie. AB, Haverford Coll., 1946; MS, U. Chgo., 1947, MD, 1949. Intern U. Chgo. Clinics, 1949-50; research fellow U. Oslo, 1950-51; fellow Johns Hopkins Hosp., 1951-52; resident in medicine U. Pa. Hosp., 1952-53; instr. medicine U. Pa. and dir. radiosotope unit VA Hosp., Phila., 1953-55; asst. prof. medicine Northwestern U. Med. Sch., 1957-62; asso. prof. biology M.I.T., 1962-68; lectr. medicine Harvard U. Med. Sch., 1962-68; prof. med. sci. Brown U., 1968-72; prof. biochemistry U. Bergen, Norway, 1972; prof. physiology and neurology, dir. grad. program in biophysics U. Tex. Health Sci. Center, Dallas, 1972-88; prof. neurology U. Tex. Health Sci. Ctr., Dallas, 1988-93; dir. Med. Cell Biology Lab. Baylor Rsch. Inst., Dallas, 1987-93; prof. physiology Brown U., Providence, R.I., 1993—. Cons. neurologist Children's Hosp., Scottish Rite Hosp., Presbyn. Hosp., Baylor Hosp, all Dallas, 1972-93; mem. corp. Haverford (Pa.) Coll., 1979-01, Marine Biol. Lab., Woods Hole, Mass., 1964-79; trustee Mt. Desert Island Biol. Lab., 1994-98; ; adv. com. to the pres., Haverford Coll., 1997-01; bd. dirs. Greenhill Sch., Dallas, 1974-77. Author: Biol. Membranes, 1969, General Physiology, 1971, Cell Biology, 1972, also numerous articles; editor: Cell and Muscle Motility. Served to capt. M.C. USAF, 1955-57. Lalor fellow; recipient Disting. Service award Assn. Neuromuscular Diseases, 1964, Disting. Service award Alumni Assn. U. Chgo., 1980 Mem. Am. Physiol. Soc., Am. Soc. Biol. Chemists, Am. Chem. Soc., Soc. Exptl. Biology and Medicine, Biophys. Soc., Soc. Clin. Investigation, Central Soc. Clin. Research, Mass. Med. Soc., So. Med. Soc., Dallas County Med. Soc., Tex. Med. Assn., Biochem. Soc. London, Faraday Soc. (London), Phi Beta Kappa, Sigma Xi. Mem. Soc. Of Friends. Office: Brown U Physiology Dept PO Box G-B3 Providence RI 02912-9107

DOWD, ANDREW JOSEPH, lawyer, utility company executive; b. Boston, Nov. 17, 1929; s. Andrew Joseph and Mary Ellen (Higgins) Dowd; m. Teresa Anne Mack, June 30, 1956; children: Michael, Joseph, William(dec.), Timothy. AB magna cum laude, Harvard U., 1951, LLB magna cum laude, 1957. Bar: N.Y. 1958, U.S. Supreme Ct. 1968. Assoc. Dorr, Hand, Wittaker & Peet, N.Y.C., 1957—62; with Am. Electric Power Svc. Corp., N.Y.C., 1962—81, Columbus, Ohio, 1981—, sr. v.p. and gen. counsel, 1974—, corp. sec., 1975—. Bd. dirs. Am. Electric Power Co., Inc., Am. Electric Power Svc. Corp., Appalacian Power Co., Columbus So. Power Co., Ohio Power Co., Ky. Power Co., Wheeling Electric Co., Kingsport Power Co., Am. Electric Power Generating Co., Associated Electric and Gas Ins. Svcs. Ltd. Bd. dirs. Nat. Hemophelia Found., 1980—83, Cen. Ohio Lung Assn. With U.S. Army, 1952—54. Mem.: ABA, Phi Beta Kappa. Office: Am Electric Power 1 Riverside Plz Columbus OH 43215-2355

DOWD, CAROLYN LAY, social worker; b. Hagerstown, Md., May 1, 1940; d. James S. Jr. and Emily Graham (Miller) Lay; m. William J. Dowd, Sept. 1, 1962 (dec.); children: William J. Jr., James P. AB, Meredith Coll., 1962; MSW, Catholic U., 1987. Cert. social worker, clin. social worker. Social work cons. Bethesda (Md.) Fellowship House, 1987-89; social worker Family Svcs. Agy., Gaithersburg, Md., 1987-98, dir. svcs. for srs., 1991-98, clin. dir., 1996-98; pvt. practice Gaithersburg, 1991-98; clin. care mgr. Falls Church, Va., 1998—. Presenter in field. Past mem. bd. dirs. Alzheimer's Assn. of Greater Wash. Mem. NASW (register of clin. social work, diplomate), Acad. Cert. Social Workers. Home: 21913 Foxlair Rd Gaithersburg MD 20882-1306 Address: 12369 C Sunrise Valley Dr Reston VA 20191 E-mail: cdowd@erols.com.

DOWD, DAVID JOSEPH, banker, builder; b. Long Island City, N.Y., June 6, 1924; s. David Joseph and Elsie (Schaeffler) B.; children— Laury, David, Patrick, Carol. BS in Bus. Adminstrn, NYU, 1949. Asst. v.p. Irving Trust Co., N.Y.C., 1952-64; v.p. Franklin Nat. Bank, N.Y.C., 1964-66; sr. v.p. Security Nat. Bank, Huntington, N.Y., 1966-72; pres. Nassau Trust Co., Glen Cove, N.Y., 1972-75, Bankers Service Co., 1975—; pub. Long Island Financial Newsletter, 1976-82; pres. Victorian Homes, Inc., 1980-97. Pres. Suffolk County council Boy Scouts Am., 1969-70; chmn. Suffolk Community Devel. Corp., 1973-74; Trustee Stony Brook Found., State U. N.Y., 1972. Served with USMCR, 1942-45, 51-52. Mem. N.Y. State Bankers Assn. (chmn. group VII 1972-75), L.I. Bankers Assn. (dir. 1969-74), Suffolk County Bankers Assn. (pres. 1971-72), Empire State C. of C. (dir. 1969-75) Address: PO Box 1057 Shelter Island NY 11964

DOWD, EDWARD L., JR., lawyer, former prosecutor; s. Edward L. Dowd; m. Jill Goessling; 3 children. JD with distinction, St. Mary's Univ. With Dowd, Dowd & Dowd; from asst. U.S. atty. to chief narcotics sect., regional dir. south cen. region Pres.'s Organized Crime Drug Enforcement Task Force U.S. Atty.'s Office, 1979-84; pvt. practice, 1984-93; U.S. atty. ea. dist. of Mo. U.S. Dept. Justice, St. Louis, 1993-99; dep. spl. counsel to John C. Danforth Spl. Counsel Waco Investigation, 1999; ptnr. Bryan Cave, LLP, St. Louis, 1999—. Office: Bryan Cave LLP One Metropolitan Square 211 N Broadway Ste 3600 Saint Louis MO 63102-2733 Office Fax: 314-259-2020. E-mail: eldowd@bryancave.com.

DOWD, FRANCES CONNELLY, retired librarian; b. Newburyport, Mass., Dec. 9, 1918; d. Martin Francis and Nelle Magdalen (Quinn) Connelly; m. James Reynolds Dowd, June 7, 1941 (dec. June 1944); children: James Reynolds Jr., Thomas Henry III. AB, Wellesley Coll., 1941; MLS, Columbia U., 1955. Cataloger Phillips Acad. Libr., Andover, Mass., 1955-57; asst. libr. Wheelock Coll. Libr., Boston, 1957-59; head of circulation U. R.I., Kingston, 1959-62; head libr. Ins. Libr., Boston, 1962-66; head bus. & sci. dept. Providence (R.I.) Pub. Libr., 1966-70; reference libr. Boston U. Libr., 1970-74; head libr. Mass. Horticulture Soc., Boston, 1974-79; reference libr. Haverhill (Mass.) Pub. Libr., 1979-89, Endicott Coll. Libr., Beverly, Mass., 1989—2001; ret., 2001. Lifelong learning instr. No. Essex C.C., 1997—. Editor: Whittier, 1992. Pres. Whittier Home Assn., Amesbury, Mass., 1989-96; treas. Macy-Colby House, 1979—; sec. Amesbury Carriage Mus., 1982—; reunion chmn. Wellesley Coll., 1971, 86. Mem. ALA, Abenaqui Country Club, Wellesley Coll. Club. Republican. Avocations: historic houses and gardens, travel, golf, gardening. Home: 3 Hillside Ave Amesbury MA 01913-2213

DOWD, IRENE, dance educator, choreographer; b. San Francisco, Sept. 29, 1946; d. David Lloyd and Lyla (Bylinkin) D.; m. Charles Stokes, Aug. 12, 1993. BA in Philosophy, Vassar Coll., 1968. Faculty program in dance Tchrs. Coll., Columbia U., N.Y.C., 1977-95, Juilliard Sch., 1995—; faculty GLSP Wesleyan U., Middleton, Conn., 1985-93. Faculty Nat. Ballet Sch. Can., Toronto, Ont., 1991—. Author: Taking Root to Fly: Articles on Functional Anatomy, 3d edit., 1995. Rsch. grantee Ctr. for Nursing Rsch., U. Pa., 1984-85, Divsn. Nursing Dept. Health & Human Svcs., 1985-86. Office: 14 E 4th St Ste 606 New York NY 10012-1141

DOWD, JANICE LEE, foreign language educator; b. N.Y.C., Jan. 6, 1948; d. Edward H. and Mary A. (Vanek) D. BA, Marietta (Ohio) Coll., 1969; MA, Columbia U., 1971, MEd, 1979, EdD, 1984. Tchr. Teaneck (N.J.) Bd. Edn., 1970-99, supr. world langs., 1999—. Adj. asst. prof. Queens Coll., CUNY, 1984-94, Columbia U., N.Y.C., spring 1988, 93—; N.J. alternate route prof., 1990—; asst. prof. MA TESOL program in China, Changsha, 1986, Shanghai, 1987; SAT program adminstr. Teaneck H.S., 1978-83, yearbook sponsor, 1975-79, newspaper sponsor, 1984-92, co-chair Global/Multicultural Mgmt. Team, 1992-95. Contbr. articles to profl. jours. Mem. program com. PEO, Teaneck, 1966—. Fellow Rockefeller Found., 1988. Mem. Am. Assn. Tchrs. of French, Tchrs. English to Speakers Other Langs., N.Y. State Tchrs. English to Speakers Other Langs., N.J. Tchrs. English to Speakers Other Langs., Am. Assn. Applied Linguists, Am. Coun. Tchrs. Fgn. Langs., Fgn. Lang. Educators N.J., Nat. Assn. of Dept. Heads and Suprs. of Fgn. Langs. Home: 56 Boulevard New Milford NJ 07646-1602 Office: Teaneck High Sch 100 Elizabeth Ave Teaneck NJ 07666-4798

DOWD, JOHN PETER, physics educator; b. New Bedford, Mass., Feb. 1, 1938; s. John Henry and Estelle (Fournier) D.; m. Mary Beth Vancini, Feb. 12, 1960; children: Michael, Paul. BS, MIT, 1959, PhD, 1966. Vis. rschr. German Electron Synchrotron, Hamburg, W.Ger., 1966-67; asst. prof. physics U. Mass., Dartmouth, 1967-72, assoc. prof., 1972-77, prof., 1978-95, chancellor prof., 1995-99, chancellor prof. emeritus, 1999—, dept. chairperson, 1985-86. Exec. com. U. Mass. Faculty Fedn., 1991—; faculty senator U. Mass., 1991-93; guest rschr. Cambridge Electron Accelerator, Mass., 1967-72, Brookhaven Nat. Lab., Upton, N.Y., 1972—; guest scientist U. Bonn., W.Ger., 1978-79; external rev. com. Ctr. for Marine Sci. and Tech., 1997—; mem. New Bedford Airport Commn., 2000—. NSF grantee. Mem. AAAS, Am. Phys. Soc., Am. Assn. Physics Tchrs., So. Mass. MIT Club (pres. 1992-93), Sigma Xi. Home: 134 Orchard St New Bedford MA 02740-3626 Office: U Mass Dept Physics 285 Old Westport Rd North Dartmouth MA 02747-2300 E-mail: jdowd@umassd.edu.

DOWD, MAUREEN, columnist; b. Washington, Jan. 14, 1952; BA in English, Catholic U., 1973. From editl. asst. to feature writer The Washington Star, 1974-81; from corr. to writer Time mag., 1981-83; metro reporter N.Y. Times, 1983-86, D.C. reporter, 1986-95, opinion-editl. columnist, 1995—. Recipient Pulitzer Prize for commentary, 1999. Office: care NY Times 1627 I St NW Washington DC 20006-4007

DOWD, MORGAN DANIEL, political science educator; b. Boston, Feb. 21, 1933; s. Joseph Francis and Marion Caroline (Calcari) D.; m. Dianne May Robichaud, Aug. 29, 1959; children: Megan Eileen, Sean Morgan, Colin Martin, Blaine Christopher, Roarke Terence. BA cum laude, St. Michael's Coll., 1955; JD, Catholic U. Am., 1958; MA, U. Mass., 1962, PhD, 1964. Instr. U. Maine, 1959-60, U. Mass., 1960-61; asst. prof. polit. sci. SUNY-Fredonia, 1963-67, assoc. prof., 1967-76, prof., 1976—, dean grad. studies and research, 1969-78, dean faculty for natural and social scis., 1978-84, joint prof. bus. and polit. sci., 1984-99, dist. svc. prof., 1995-99, ret., 1999. Cons. Mid. States Assn. Colls. and Univs., 1977—; project dir. USIA grant, Albania, 1992-94, 95-96. Contbr. articles to law jours., 1956-78; co-editor: World Dictionary of Environmental Research Centers, 2d edit., 1974. Bd. dirs. com. Health Systems Agy. Western N.Y., 1986-87, mem. exec. com.; regional member N.Y. state commn. Bicentennial of Constn., 1987; convocation speaker West Chester U. Pa., 1991. Recipient Pres.'s Medallion award, West Chester U. Pa., 1991, Extraordinary Svc. to Commn. on Higher Edn. U. Rochester, 1994. Mem. Columbia U. Seminar on History of Legal and Polit. Theory, Torch Club, Delta Epsilon Sigma, Pi Sigma Alpha, Delta Theta Phi, Phi Eta Sigma Democrat. Roman Catholic.

DOWD, PETER JEROME, public relations executive; b. Bklyn., Oct. 5, 1942; s. Jerome Ambrose and Mary Agnes (Young) D.; m. Brenda Badura, Nov. 25, 1972; 1 child, Kelly Ann. AB, Fordham U., 1964. Reporter UPI, N.Y.C., 1964-66; account exec. Hill and Knowlton, N.Y.C., 1966-71, v.p., 1971-74; sr.

v.p., mgr. Hill and Knowlton (Los Angeles office), 1974-78, mng. dir. Western region, 1978-80, exec. v.p., 1980; ptnr. Haley, Kiss & Dowd, Inc., Los Angeles, 1980-83; group v.p. Am. Med. Internat., 1983-88; v.p. pub. rels. Texaco Inc., White Plains, N.Y., 1989-96; sr. v.p. corp. affairs Fidelity Investments, Boston, 1996-99; pub. affairs cons., 1999—. Instr. U. So. Calif., Calif. State U., Fullerton. Bd. dirs. Cath. Big Bros., Nature Conservancy (Lower Hudson chpt.). Mem. Pub. Rels. Soc. Am., Alan Page Soc., Town Hall West (v.p., dir.), Westchester County Assn. (bd. dirs.), Nature Conservancy (bd. dirs. Lower Hudson chpt.), U.S. Mil. Acad. Pub. Affairs (adv. com.). Republican. Roman Catholic. Office: Fidelity Investments 82 Devonshire St Boston MA 02109-3605

DOWDA, WILLIAM F. internist; b. Cobb County, Ga. MD, Emory U., 1949. Intern Peter Bent Brigham Hosp., Boston, 1949—50; resident Barnes Hosp., 1950—51, resident, 1952—54; staff Piedmont Hosp., 1953—76; clin. assoc. prof. medicine Emory U., 1962—76; pvt. practice internal medicine, 1976 —. Pathology fellow, mem. staff Grady Meml. Hosp. Lt. med. corps USNR, 1950—52. Mem.: Inst. Medicine-NAS, AMA, ACP, Soc. Med. Adminstrs. Address: 490 Peachtree St NE Ste 129B Atlanta GA 30308-3136

DOWDALL, GEORGE WILLIAM, sociology educator; b. N.Y.C., May 18, 1943; s. George W. and Monica K. (McGovern) Dowdall; m. Jean A. Amatneek, Dec. 20, 1970; 1 child, Nina Greeley. AB, Holy Cross Coll., Worcester, Mass., 1965; AM, Brown U., Providence, 1969; PhD, Brown U., 1972. Asst. prof. Ind. U., Bloomington, 1970—73; assoc. prof. SUNY, Buffalo, 1973—82; dir. program evaluation Buffalo Psychiat. Ctr., NY, 1980—82; prof., chmn. St. Joseph's U., Phila., 1982—. Vis. prof. Brown U. Sch. Medicine, Providence, 1993—96. Contbr. NDEA fellow, NIMH fellow, USPHS fellow, NEH fellow. Mem.: APHA, Eastern Sociol. Soc., Soc. for Study of Social Problems, Am. Sociol. Assn., Phila. Area Computing Soc. (sec. 1985—87). Avocation: running. Home: 241 S 6th St Apt 1705 Philadelphia PA 19106-3733 Office: Saint Joseph's Univ Dept Sociology Philadelphia PA 19131

DOWDELL, MICHAEL FRANCIS, critical care nurse, forensic and anesthesia nurse practitioner; b. Cleve., June 5, 1949; s. Harry William and Dorothy May (McGivney) Dowdell; 1 child, Michael Patrick. BSN, Ohio State U., 1975; MA in Counseling, Nat. U., San Diego, 1981; MSN, Calif. State U., Long Beach, 1991; diploma in nursing anesthesia, Kaiser Sch. Anesthesia, L.A., 1991; postgrad., Case Western Res. U., 1996—. Diplomate Am. Bd. Forensic Nursing, Am. Bd. Forensic Examiners; CRNA, ARNP, critical care nurse specialist, cert. ACLS instr.; c.c. instr. Calif. Enlisted USN, 1968, commd. ensign, 1974, advanced through grades to lt. comdr., 1984, ret., 1988; resident nurse anesthesist Kaiser Sch. Anesthesia for Nurses, 1989-91; staff nurse anesthetist Kaiser Hosp., Panorama City, Calif., 1991-92, HCA Med. Ctr., Largo, Fla., 1992-93, Meml. Mission Hosp., Asheville, N.C., 1993-97; owner Anesthesia Nursing Svcs. P.A., 1998—. Vis. lectr. dept. anesthesia Makerere U., Kampala, Uganda, 1995. Mem.: VFW, NRA, AACN, Nat. Muzzle-Loading Rifle Assn., Fleet Res. Assn., Assn. Mil. Surgeons U.S., Am. Assn. Nurse Anesthetists, North-South Skirmish Assn., Ret. Officers Assn., Am. Legion, Sigma Theta Tau. Republican. Avocations: fishing, shooting sports, travel. Home and Office: 136 N Tiree Way Inverness FL 34450-1713

DOWDEN, MARK VINCENT, editor, publishing company executive; b. Louisville, Sept. 18, 1962; s. Carroll Vincent and Eleanor Therese (Dion) D.; m. Kathy Olwen Lee, Oct. 7, 1989; children: Henry Nathaniel, Griffith Charles. AB, Princeton U., 1984; MPhil, U. St. Andrews, Scotland, 1987. Med. projects editor Bozell, Jacobs, Kenyon & Eckhardt Healthcare, N.Y.C., 1984-86; assoc. prodr. Med. Pub. Enterprises, Fair Lawn, N.J., 1987-88; sec.-treas. Dowden Pub. Co. (name changed to Dowden Health Media 2000), Montvale, N.J., 1988—, sr. editor, 1988-91, exec. editor, 1991-93, editor, 1993-2000, pub. consumer newsletter divsn., 1995—2002, v.p. consumer health, 1997—2000, sr. v.p., 2000—02, pres., 2002—, also bd. dirs. Freelance writer and editor, 1987-88; trustee The Princeton (N.J.) Tiger, Inc., 1992—. Home: 21 White Rock Ln Warwick NY 10990-2342 Office: Dowden Health Media 110 Summit Ave Montvale NJ 07645-1712

DOWDLE, JEFF, real estate broker; b. Salt Lake City, Utah, Jan. 10, 1973; s. Lynn and Linda Dowdle; m. Brandy Ellsworth, Aug. 26, 1995. BS, Brigham Young U., 1999. Lic. real estate broker Tex. Comml. real estate broker Marcus & Millichap, Dallas, 1999—. Youth group leader LDS Ch., Sachse, Tex., 2001—02. Republican. Home: 7114 Park Hill Tr Sachse TX 75048 Office: Marcus & Millichap 14185 North Dallas Pkwy Suite 980 Dallas TX 75254 Personal E-mail: jeffdowdle@byu.edu. E-mail: jdowdle@marcusmillichap.com.

DOWDLE, PATRICK DENNIS, lawyer; b. Denver, Dec. 8, 1948; s. William Robert and Helen (Schraeder) D.; m. Eleanor Pryor, Mar. 8, 1975; children: Jeffery William, Andrew Peter. BA, Cornell Coll., Mt. Vernon, Iowa, 1971; JD, Boston U., 1975. Bar: Colo. 1975, U.S. Dist. Ct. Colo. 1975, U.S. Ct. Appeals (10th cir.) 1976, U.S. Supreme Ct. 1978. Acad. dir. in Japan Sch. Internat. Tng., Putney, Vt., 1974; assoc. Decker & Miller, Denver, 1975-77; ptnr. Miller, Makkai & Dowdle, Denver, 1977—. Designated counsel criminal appeals Colo. Atty. Gens. Office, Denver, 1980-81; guardian ad litem Adams County Dist. Ct., Brighton, Colo., 1980-83; affiliated counsel ACLU, Denver, 1980—. Mem. Colo. Bar Assn., Denver Bar Assn. (various coms.), Porsche Club of Am. Avocations: scuba diving, photography, wine making, travel, skiing. Home: 3254 Tabor Ct Wheat Ridge CO 80033-5367 Office: Miller Makkai & Dowdle 2325 W 72nd Ave Denver CO 80221-3101 E-mail: pdowdle@rm.ince.net.

DOWDY, EUGENE BROWN, music educator; b. Kingsville, Tex., Sept. 14, 1960; s. Warren Coburn and Hazel Marie Dowdy; m. Stacy Schneider, Aug. 13, 1983; children: Jessica Marie, Rachel Anne. DMA, U. Iowa, 1995; MusM, U. Tex., San Antonio, 1990; MusB, U. Tex., 1983. Cert. life tchg. cert. music Tex. Sch. orch. dir. N.E. Ind. Sch. Dist., San Antonio, 1983—92; assoc. prof. music, chair dept. music U. Tex., San Antonio, 1996—. Resident condr. Youth Orchs. San Antonio, 1985—; orch. condr., faculty Interlochen (Mich.) Arts Camp, 1988—96; concertmaster S.E. Iowa Symphony Orch., Washington, 1993—95. Recipient Disting. Tchg. Finalist, U. Tex.-San Antonio Alumni Assn., 2001; grantee $15,000 grant to start U. Tex.-San Antonio String Project, Am. String Teachers Assn./NSOA/FIPSE, 2002—04. Mem.: Am. Fedn. of Musicians, Am. String Teachers Assn./NSOA, Tex. Music Educators Assn., Music Educators Nat. Conf., Tex. Orch. Dirs. Assn. (pres. 2003). Avocations: family time, outdoor activities, reading. Home: 4603 Tex Woods San Antonio TX 78249 Office: U Tex-San Antonio 6900 N Loop 1604 W San Antonio TX 78249 Personal E-mail: edowdy@satx.rr.com.

DOWDY, JOHN VERNARD, JR., lawyer, educator, arbitrator, mediator; b. Malakoff, Tex., July 3, 1942; s. John Vernard Sr. and Johnnie Dena (Riley) D.; m. Sarah Ellen Chambers, June 13, 1964; children: Rebekah Anne, Susannah Lynn. BSc in Phys. Edn., Baylor U., 1966, JD, 1968. Bar: Tex. 1968, U.S. Dist. Ct. (no. dist.) Tex. 1972, U.S. Dist. Ct. (ea. dist.) Tex. 1980. Assoc. Warwick, Jenkins Law Firm, Waxahachie, Tex., 1968-69, Atkins, Carpenter & Dowdy, Arlington, Tex., 1969-72, Duke, Rosenberry & Dowdy, Arlington, 1972-74; pvt. practice law Arlington, 1974—; lectr. bus. law U. Tex., Arlington, 1974—. Mem. ptnrs. in search of ednl. excellence Arlington Ind. Sch. Dist., 1989-90; pres., bd. dirs. AWARE Found., Inc., Arlington, 1989-90, 92. Mem. ABA, Assn. Atty.-Mediators (bd. dirs. 2002-03, pres.-elect 2003—), Christian Legal Soc., State Bar Tex., Arlington Bar Assn., Tarrant County Bar Assn., Tarrant County Probate Bar Assn. (bd. dirs. 2001-2003). Baptist. Avocations: scuba diving, backpacking, running, physical fitness, handball. Home: 3706 Shadycreek Dr N Arlington TX 76013-1017 Office: Ste A 2400 Garden Park Ct Arlington TX 76013-1339 Fax: 917-460-8366. E-mail: jdowdy1@mindspring.com.

DOWDY, WILLIAM CLARENCE, JR., retired lawyer; b. McKinney, Tex., Feb. 27, 1925; s. William C. and Emily Harryette (Gilson) D.; m. Ann Atkinson, Aug. 31, 1947; children: William Clarence III, Jill Ann, Daniel Andrew. Student, North Tex. Agrl. Coll., Arlington, 1942-43; BBA, U. Tex., Austin, 1949, JD, 1951. Bar: Tex. 1951, U.S. Supreme Ct. 1957, U.S. Dist. Ct. (no. dist.) Tex. 1960, U.S. Ct. Appeals (5th cir.) 1974. Asst. dist. atty. Dallas County, 1951-54; atty. Tex. & Pacific Ry. Co., Dallas, 1954-59; gen. atty. Tex. & Pacific Ry. Co./Mo. Pacific R.R. Co., Dallas, 1959-82; gen. solicitor Mo. Pacific R.R. Co./Union Pacific R.R. Co., Dallas, 1982-86, sr. counsel, 1986-87; ret., 1987. Dir. Great S.W. R.R.; v.p., asst. sec., dir. Weatherford, Mineral Wells & Northwestern R.R. Elder, trustee Presbyn. Ch. With field arty., 24th divsn. AUS, 1943-46; PTO. Mem. Tex. Bar Assn., Dallas Bar Assn., Collin County Bar Assn., Nat. Assn. R.R. Trial Counsel (exec. com., regional v.p.), Tower Club (Dallas), Eldorado Club (McKinney, Tex.), Phi Alpha Delta, Kappa Sigma. Home: 510 Tucker St Mc Kinney TX 75069-2714

DOWDY, WILLIAM LOUIS, consulting and engineering company executive; b. San Antonio, Dec. 3, 1937; s. Eugene Joseph and Estelle Helen (Schmid) Dowdy; m. Diane Marie Erickson, Nov. 9, 1996; children from previous marriage: Mark Allen, John Joseph, Daniel Patrick. BS in Physics, St. Mary's U., San Antonio, 1959; M in Nuclear Engring., Tex. A&M U., 1964. Registered profl. engr., Calif.; registered environ. assessor, Calif. Mgr. advanced programs Rockwell Internat., N. Am., Downey, Calif., 1964-73; gen. mgr. Air Monitoring Ctr., Rockwell Internat., Newbury Park, Calif., 1973-77; mgr. program devel. Electric Power Rsch. Inst., Palo Alto, Calif., 1977-78; dir. new product devel. BSP divsn. Envirotech Corp., Belmont, Calif., 1978-80; dir. feasibility evaluation Lurgi Corp., Belmont, 1980-83; dir. tech. and innovation mgmt. SRI Internat., Menlo Park, Calif., 1983-88; v.p. PA Consulting Group, Princeton, N.J., 1988-90; gen. mgr. MSE Environ., Camarillo, Calif., 1990-93, also bd. dirs.; pres., chmn., CEO TRAK Environ. Group, Inc., Ventura, Calif., 1993—98; CEO Captran Group, Inc., Temple, Tex., 1998—. Pvt. cons., Thousand Oaks, Calif., 1976-77. Contbr. numerous articles on tech. and mgmt. to profl. jours. Bd. dirs. March of Dimes, San Mateo, Calif., 1980—83, Forum on Entrepreneurship, San Antonio, 1998—. Recipient Tech. Utilization award NASA, 1968, Apollo Achievement award NASA, 1969. Mem. NSPE, Calif. Soc. Profl. Engrs. (v.p.). Home: 2512 Canyon Creek Dr Temple TX 76502-3105 Office: Captran Group Inc 2512 Canyon Creek Dr Temple TX 26502

DOWELL, EARL HUGH, university dean, aerospace and mechanical engineering educator; b. Macomb, Ill., Nov. 16, 1937; s. Earl S. and Edna Bernice (Dean) D.; m. Lynn Cowell; children: Marla Lorraine, Janice Lynelle, Michael Hugh. BS, U. Ill., 1959; S.M., Mass. Inst. Tech., 1961, Sc.D., 1964. Rsch. engr. Boeing Co., 1962-63; rsch. asst. MIT, 1963-64, rsch. engr., 1964, asst. prof., 1964-65; asst. prof. aerospace and mech. engring. Princeton U., 1964-68, assoc. prof., 1968-72, prof., 1972-83, assoc. chmn., 1975-77, acting chmn., 1979; prof. Sch. Engring. Duke U., Durham, NC, 1983—, dean, 1983-99. Cons. to industry and govt.; mem. sci. adv. bd. USAF; mem. bd. visitors Office of Naval Rsch. Author: Aeroelasticity of Plates and Shells, 1974, A Modern Course in Aeroelasticity, 1978, 3rd edit., 1995, Nonlinear Studies in Aeroelasticity, 1988; assoc. editor: AIAA Jour., 1969-72, Jour. Sound and Vibration, 1988—, Jour. Fluids and Structures, 1987—, Jour. Nonlinear Dynamics, 1990—; contbr. articles to profl. jours. Chmn. N.J. Noise Control Council, 1972-76. Named outstanding young alumnus U. Ill. Sch. Aero. and Astronautical Engring., 1973, disting. alumnus, 1975; recipient Alumni Honor award Coll. Engring. U. Ill. Fellow: ASME, AIAA (v.p. publs. 1981—83, Structures, Structural Dynamics and Material award 1980, Theodore Von Karman lectr. 2002), Am. Acad. Mechs. (pres. 1991, Disting. Svc. award 1994); mem.: Nat. Acad. Engring., Acoustical Soc. Am., Am. Helicopter Soc. Home: 847 Inglenook Rd Durham NC 27707-3961 Office: Duke U Sch Engring Durham NC 27708

DOWELL, JAMES DALE, lawyer; b. Goose Creek, Tex., July 17, 1932; s. James Dale and Margaret (King) D.; m. Patricia Jo Skaggs, Feb. 2, 1957; children: Terry Dowell Owens, James Dale III. BA, Tex. A&M U, 1954; LLB, U. Tex., 1957. Bar: Tex. 1956, U.S. Dist. Ct. (ea. dist.) Tex. 1958, U.S Ct. Appeals (5th cir.) 1964, U.S. Supreme Ct. 1969. Assoc. King, Sharfstein & Rienstra, Beaumont, Tex., 1957-63, ptnr., 1963-68, Rienstra, Rienstra & Dowell, Beaumont, 1968-85, Rienstra, Dowell & Flatten, Beaumont, 1985—. Mem. Tex. Dem. Exec. Com., 1966-68, del. Nat. Conv., 1976—. Mem. ABA, State Bar Tex., Tex. Bar Found., Jefferson County Bar Assn. (pres. 1978-79, Blackstone award 2000), Def. Rsch. Inst., Tex. Assn. Def. Counsel, Beaumont Country Club, Beaumont Club (bd. dirs. 1975-77), Rotary (Paul Harris fellow 2000), Phi Gamma Delta. Methodist. Avocation: reading. Home: 6275 Wilchester Ln Beaumont TX 77706-4328 Office: 595 Orleans St Beaumont TX 77701-3214

DOWELL, JENNIFER ANN, mechanical engineer; b. Frankfort, Ill., July 24, 1969; d. Albert Frank and Janice Ruth Lewis; m. Christopher Lee Dowell, Sept. 17, 1994; children: Christopher Landon, Megan Kelley. BSME, U. of Ky., Paducah, 2002. Cert. drafter, Am. Design Drafting Assn., 1998. Drafter Panduit, Tinley Park, Ill., 1990—93; scuba instr., mgr. Aaron's Dive Shop, Kailua / Camp Smith, Hawaii, 1993—96; drafter North Star Steel Ky., Calvert City, Ky., 1997—2000; engring. intern TVA, West Paducah, Ky., 2001—02, systems engr., 2002—. Team capt. March of Dimes, Calvert City, Ky., 1998—2000. Scholar Helen Murphy scholar, Dr. William Murphy, 2000—01; NSF grantee, 2001—02. Mem.: AIAA (assoc.), ASME (assoc.; chair student sect. 2001—02). Avocations: martial arts, scuba diving. Office: Tennessee Valley Authority 7900 Metropolis Lake Rd West Paducah KY 42086 E-mail: jadowell@tva.gov.

DOWELL, MICHAEL BRENDAN, chemist; b. N.Y.C., Nov. 18, 1942; s. William Henry and Anne Susan (Cannon) D.; m. Gail Elizabeth Renton, Mar. 16, 1968; children: Rebecca, Margaret. BS, Fordham U., 1963; PhD, Pa. State U., 1967. Physicist U.S. Army Frankford Arsenal, Phila., 1967-69; rsch. scientist Parma (Ohio) Tech. Ctr., Union Carbide Corp., 1969-74, devel. mgr. carbon fiber applications, 1974-76, group leader metals and ceramics rsch., 1976-80, sr. group leader process rsch., 1980-82, mgr. market devel., 1982-92, Praxair Advanced Ceramics Inc. (formerly Union Carbide Corp), Ohio, 1992-93, Advanced Ceramics Corp., Cleve., 1993—, v.p. tech., 1999—2002; v.p. 5iTech, LLC, Cleve., 2003—. Mem. materials tech. adv. com. U.S. Dept. Commerce, 1994—2001; lectr. ops. mgmt. Case Western Res. U. Contbr. articles to profl. jours. Capt. ordnance AUS, 1967—69. Mem. Am. Chem. Soc., Am. Phys. Soc., U.S. Advanced Ceramics An. (bd. dirs. 1988-96), Am. Soc. Metals Internat. (govt. and pub. affairs com. 1989—), Soc. Prof. Fellows Case Western Res. U., Phi Lambda Upsilon. Roman Catholic. Home: 368 N Main St Hudson OH 44236-2246 Office: 5iTech LLC 1768 E 25th St Cleveland OH 44114

DOWELL, RICHARD PATRICK, technology company executive; b. Washington, Apr. 21, 1934; s. Cassius McClellan and Mary Barbara (McHenry) D.; m. Eleanor Craddock Halley, Dec. 23, 1957 (div. Sept. 1973); children: Richard Patrick Jr., Robert Paul, Christopher Lee; m. Sandra Susan Humm, June 16, 1974; children: Ethan Leslie Smith, Allison Smith Temple. BS, U.S. Mil. Acad., 1956; MA, Stanford U., 1961, postgrad., 1962, The Am. U., 1971-80; grad., The Nat. War Coll., 1975. Commd. 2d lt. USAF, 1956, advanced through grades to lt. col., 1974, ret., 1976; mgr. The BDM Corp., Fairfax, Va., 1977-79; sr. analyst ANSER Inc., Arlington, Va., 1979-81, div. mgr., 1981-84, v.p., 1984-91, cons., 1991; sr. staff MITRE Corp., Arlington, 1991-92; program dir. The Orkand Corp., Silver Spring, Md., 1992-93; pres., CEO Software Valley Corp., Morgantown, W.Va., 1993-97; chmn., pres. Software Valley Found., 1993-97; pres., CEO Tech. Bus. Svcs., Inc., 1997—. Exec. dir., bd. dirs. W.Va. Statewide Health Info. Network, 1995-97; bd. dirs. Charleston Coun., Navy League of U.S. Contbr. articles to profl. jours. Pres. Alexandria (Va.) Taxpayer's Alliance, 1983. Decorated Bronze star, Air medal with 13 oak leaf clusters, D.F.C. with one oak leaf cluster. Mem. Nat. War Coll. Alumni Assn., Navy League, Air Force Assn. Republican. Episcopalian. Avocations: running, swimming, squash, bridge. Home and Office: 41 Hasell St Charleston SC 29401-1604 E-mail: rdowell@tecserve.com.

DOWER GOLD, CATHERINE ANNE, music history educator; b. South Hadley, Mass., May 19, 1924; d. Lawrence Frederick Dower and Marie (Barbieri) Barber; m. Arthur Gold, Mar. 24, 1994 (dec. Oct. 1998). AB, Hamline U., 1945; MA, Smith Coll., 1948; B in Liturgical Music, U. Mont., Gregorian Inst. Am., 1949; PhD, The Cath. U. Am., 1968. New England rep. Gregorian Inst. Am., Toledo, 1948-49; tchr. music, organist St. Rose Sch., Meriden, Conn., 1949-53; supr. music Holyoke (Mass.) Pub. Schs., 1953-55; instr. music U. Mass., Amherst, 1955-56; prof. music Westfield (Mass.) State Coll., 1956-90, prof. emerita, 1991—; columnist and freelance writer Holyoke Transcript Telegram, 1991-93. Organist St. Theresa's Ch., South Hadley, 1937-41, St. Michael's Ch., N.Y., 1945-46; concert series presenter Westfield State Coll., 1987-91, rschr. tchr.; vis. scholar U. So. Calif., 1969; vis. assoc. prof. music Herbert Lehman Coll. CUNY, 1970-71. Author: Puerto Rican Music Following the Spanish American War, 1898-1910, 1983; (monograph) Yella Pessl, 1986, Alfred Einstein on Music, 1991, Yella Pessl: First Lady of the Harpsichord, 1992, Fifty Years of Marching Together, 2001; editor: (newsletter) Westfield State Coll., 2000—; presenter Irish Concert Springfield Symphony Orch., 1981 (plaque 1982); author numerous poems. Pres. Coun. for Human Understanding Holyoke, 1981-83, Friends of Holyoke Pub. Libr., 1990-91; bd. dirs., chmn. nominating com. Holyoke Pub. Libr., 1987-89; bd. dirs. Holyoke Pub. Libr. Corp., 1991-94, Springfield Symphony Orch., 1992—; bd. dirs. Fla. Philharm. Orch., 2000-03, trustee, 2002-03; presiding officer inauguration Dr. Irving Buchman pres. of Westfield State Coll.; ethics com. Holyoke Hosp., 1988-94; sec. Haiti Mission, 1982-94; bd. overseers Mullen U., 1993; hon. mem. bd. Coun. Human Understanding, 1994-; hon. mem. WSC Found., 1994-; co-chair United Jewish Appeal/Jewish Fedn. Boca Lago Women's Divsn., South Palm Beach County, 1996-97; 1st. v.p. fin. and adminstrn. Temple Beth El Women in Reformed Judaism, Boca Raton, 1997-99; active St. Patrick's Com., 1991—; bd. dirs. Friends of Music of Lynn U. Conservatory Music, 2003—. Recipient citation Academia InterAmericana de P.R., 1978, plaque Mass. Tchrs. Assn., Boston, 1984, medal Equestrian Order Holy Sepulchre of Jerusalem, Papal Knighthood Soc., Boston, 1984, Performance award Gov. Dukakis, Mass., 1988, award from Puerto Rican Jour. Al. Margens, 1992, Human Rels. award Coun. for Human Understanding, Holyoke, 1994; named Lady Comdr., Equestrian Order of the Holy Sepulche of Jerusalem, 1987, with star, 1990, Career Woman of Yr., Quota Internat. Holyoke, Mass., 1988; Westfield State U. concert series named Catherine A. Dower Performing Arts Series in her honor, 1991; recipient 1st prize in Raddock Eminent Scholar Chair Essay Contest, Fla. Atlantic U., 1996, Internat. Poet of Merit Silver Bowl award Internat. Libr. Poetry, 2002, First prize Essay Contest on World Peace by Broherly Love Press, Mass. 2002, Outstanding Achievement in Poetry award Internat. Sox. Poets, 2003. Mem. Nat. Soc. Arts and Letters, Am. Musicol. Soc., Coll. Mus. Soc., Ch. Music Assn. Am. (journalist), Acad. Arts and Scis. P.R. (medal 1977), Internat. Platform Assn., Friends of the Holyoke Pub. Libr. (pres. 1990-91), Irish Am. Cultural Inst. (chmn. bd. 1981-89), Holyoke Quota (v.p. 1976-79, pres. 1979-81, 90-92, chmn. speech and hearing com. 1987-94), B'nai B'rith of Boca Lago (sec. bd. dirs. 1994-1999, newsletter editor 1999-2000), Lifelong Learning Soc. Fla. Atlantic U. (life, sec. 1994-97, bd. dirs. 2003—), Westfield State Coll. Found., Women's Symphony League (life), Philharm. Assn. Boca (pres. 2002-03), Univ. Club Fla. Atlantic U. (parliamentarian 2003—), Nat. Soc. Art Letters, Phi Beta Kappa. Democrat. Home: 8559 Casa Del Lago Boca Raton FL 33433-2107 E-mail: cathig@juno.com.

DOWIE, IAN JAMES, management consultant; b. London, Mar. 3, 1938; came to U.S., 1980; s. James George and Ethel (Watker) D.; m. Barbara Eva Page, Jan. 9, 1960 (div. 1991); children: Paul James, David Ian; m. Nancy M. Pollard, 1993. BSEE, A.City & Guilds Inst., U. London, 1958. Registered profl. engr., Ont., Can. Seismic engr. Seismograph Svcs. Ltd., Eng., 1958-61; design engr. GE, Toronto, Ont., 1961-62; v.p., div. dir. IBM Can., Toronto, 1962-80; v.p. field ops. Exxon Office Systems, Stamford, Conn., 1980-82; pres. Aregon Internat. Inc., Stamford, 1983-84, Benchmark East, Westport, Conn., 1985-96, Park City, Utah, 1993-97, Benchmark Pub. Inc., Park City, Utah; developer Goshawk Ranch, Park City, Utah, 1997—, The Overlook, Park City, Utah, 2000—02. Pres. Benchmark-Goshawk, Inc., Park City, Utah; v.p. bus. develop. Interloci Inc., 2002—03. Pub. Once A Londoner, 1989, What's Love Got To Do With It?, 1993, From Womb to Tomb, 1994, Remuda Dust, 1994. Chmn. Credit Valley Assn. for Handicapped Children, Toronto, 1972-79. Mem. Shore and Country Club (Norwalk, Conn.), Jeremy Ranch Golf Club (Park City, Utah). Avocations: tennis, travel, skiing, golf. E-mail: ian@benchmarkventures.com.

DOWIS, LENORE, lawyer; b. N.Y., Nov. 7, 1934; d. Thomas and Julianna (Csitkovits) Esteves; children: Daniel, Lenore, Denise, Jonathan. AAS, Suffolk County Community Coll., 1981; BA, SUNY, Stony Brook, 1983; JD, Touro Coll., 1987. Bar: N.Y. 1988, N.J. 1988, U.S. Dist. Ct. N.J. 1988, U.S. Dist. Ct. (so. and ea. dists.) N.Y. 1992, U.S. Ct. Mil. Appeals 1993, U.S. Ct. Claims 1993, U.S. Ct. Appeals (fed. cir.) 1993, U.S. Supreme Ct. 1993. Tel. operator N.Y. Tel. Co., L.I., 1951-58; real estate sales agt. Gen. Devel. Corp., Hauppauge, N.Y, 1974-75; student law clk. to assoc. judge appellate div. U.S. Supreme Ct. N.Y., Bklyn., 1986; staff atty. Nassau/Suffolk Law Svcs., Bay Shore, N.Y., 1988; pvt. practice, Smithtown, N.Y., 1988 —. Mem. ABA, Suffolk County Bar Assn., N.Y. State Bar Assn., Phi Theta Kappa, Alpha Beta Gamma. Republican. Home and Office: 33 Beverly Rd Smithtown NY 11787-5324

DOWLEY, JOEL EDWARD, manufacturing executive, lawyer; b. Jackson, Mich., Apr. 27, 1952; s. William J. and Beth E. (Morell) D.; m. Janelle Smith, Nov. 12, 1983; children: Kara Marie, Alayna Kristine. BA, Spring Arbor Coll., 1974; JD, U. Notre Dame, 1977. Bar: Mich. 1977. Atty. Fraser, Trebilcock, Davis and Foster, P.C., Lansing, Mich., 1977-83; exec. v.p., gen. counsel Dowley Mfg. Inc., Spring Arbor, Mich., 1983-87, chmn., CEO, 1987—. Pub. mem. Mich. Bd. Psychology, 1978-82, vice chmn., 1980, chmn., 1981-82; pub. mem. ethics com. Am. Assn. Marriage and Family Therapy, 1980; mem. Ingham County Rep. Exec. Com., Mich., 1978-84, 3d Dist. Rep. Exec. Com., 1983-85; Rep. candidate for Ingham County commr., 1978, 82; trustee Highfield's, Inc., 1983-89, youth opportunity camp, Onondaga, Mich., 1983-89, sec., 1984-85, pres., 1986-87; trustee BoarsHead Theater, Lansing, 1982-92, treas., 1985-87, vice-chmn., 1987-89, Okemos Edn. Found., 1988-90, treas., 1989-90, Handicapped Children and Adults Found., trustee, 1994-2000, v.p., 1995-96, pres., 1996-97, treas., 1998-99; mem. elected ofcls. compensation commn. Meridian Twp., Mich., 1989—, elected chmn., 1993—. Mem. Mich. Bar Assn., Spring Arbor Coll. Alumni Assn. (trustee 1979-82, pres. 1981-82, Young Leader award 1983), Hand Tools Inst. (bd. dirs. 1986-89, 90-2001, sec., treas. 1993-95, v.p. 1995-97, pres. 1997-99). Home: 1864 Cimarron Dr Okemos MI 48864-3810

DOWLEY, JOSEPH KYRAN, lawyer, member congressional staff; b. L.A., Apr. 23, 1946; s. Michael F. and Charlotte (Moore) D.; m. Carol Walsh, Jan. 22, 1972; children: Kristin, Michael, Patricia. BA, Georgetown U., Washington, 1968, JD, 1976. Bar: Va. 1976, D.C. 1980. Adminstrv. asst. to Honorable Dan Rostenkowski U.S. Ho. of Reps., Washington, 1977-81, asst. chief counsel Com. on Ways and Means, 1981-84, chief counsel Com. on Ways and Means, 1985-87; ptnr. Dewey Ballantine, 1987—. 1st lt. U.S. Army, 1969-71. Mem. Bar Assn. Va., Bar Assn. D.C., Georgetown Univ. Alumni Club (pres. 1984-85). Roman Catholic. Office: Dewey Ballantine 1775 Pennsylvania Ave NW Washington DC 20006-4672

DOWLING, DORIS ANDERSON, business owner, educator, consultant; b. Clover Valley, Minn., Sept. 24, 1917; d. Gustaf Axel and Amanda Sophia (Karlsson) Anderson; m. John Joseph Dowling, Jan. 8, 1943 (dec. Feb. 1953); 1 child, Mary Kathryn. Home econs. degree, U. Minn., Virginia, 1937. Fashion coord., lectr. Fair Store/Montgomery Ward, Chgo., 1939-65, Marshall Field's, Chgo., 1967-82; founder, owner Doris Anderson Sewing Schs., 1948—. Cons. colls., textile industry, retail stores, 1948—; lectr. retail stores, 1954-94. Author: Simplified Systems of Sewing and Styling, 1948. Career counselor, trainer, Chgo., 1948-82. Recipient Future Farmers Am. award Duluth C. of C. Coun. Agr., 1934. Mem. Nat. Needlework Assn., Fashion Group Internat. Inc., Assn. Crafts & Creative Industries, Chgo. Apparel Ctr., Merchandise Mart. Avocations: designing, gardening, writing, research. Home and Office: Doris Anderson Sewing Schs 222 E Pearson St Apt 1108 Chicago IL 60611-7356

DOWLING, EDWARD THOMAS, economics educator; b. N.Y.C., Oct. 22, 1938; s. Edward Thomas and Mary Helen (Finegan) D. BA, Berchmans Coll., Philippines, 1962, MA in Philosophy, 1963; M.Div., Woodstock Coll., Md., 1969; PhD, Cornell U., Ithaca, N.Y., 1973. Asst. prof. econs. Fordham U., Bronx, 1973-79, assoc. prof., 1979-85, prof., 1985—, dean, 1982-86, chmn. dept., 1979-82, 88-94. Author: Development Economics, 1977, Mathematics for Economists, 1980, Calculus for Business, Economics, and the Social Sciences, 1990, Introduction to Mathematical Economics, 1992, 3d edit., 2000, Mathematical Methods for Business and Economics, 1993, Intermediate Statistics for Business and the Social Sciences, 2000. Mem. Am. Econ. Assn. Office: Fordham U Loyola Hall New York NY 10458-5198

DOWLING, JOAN E. lawyer; b. N.Y.C., July 11, 1953; d. James J. and Natalie E. Dowling. BA, Marywood U., 1975; cert. attendance, Temple U., 1978, Athens (Greece) U., 1978; JD, Seton Hall U., 1979. Bar: N.J. 1980, U.S. Dist. Ct. N.J. 1980, U.S. Supreme Ct. 1985; cert. mediator N.J., 2001. Pvt. practice law, Plainfield, NJ, 1981—2000, North Plainfield, NJ, 2001—. Counsel Zoning Bd. Adjustment, Middlesex Borough, NJ, 1989—. Trustee Union County Legal Svcs., Elizabeth, NJ, 1986—91; bd. dirs. Rolling Hills Coun. Girls Scouts U.S.,

North Branch, NJ, 1988—94, v.p. Rolling Hills Coun., 1995—2001; pres. Middlesex Borough Sr. Citizen Housing Corp., NJ, 1994—2000. Recipient Outstanding Citizen award, Middlesex Borough Coun., 1985, Outstanding Cmty. Svc. Resolution, Union County Bd. Freeholders, 1986, Honor award, Rolling Hills Girl Scout Coun., 1995, Thanks award, 1997. Mem.: Women Lawyers in Union County (treas. 1992—93, v.p. 1994—96, pres. 1996—98). Democrat. Roman Catholic. Avocation: canoeing. Address: PO Box 5616 Plainfield NJ 07061 Office: 948 US Hwy 22 East North Plainfield NJ 07060

DOWLING, JOHN CLARKSON, language educator; b. Strawn, Tex., Nov. 14, 1920; s. Albert Clarkson and Georgia Ann (Turrill) Dowling; m. Constance Guinevere Ford, Dec. 26, 1949; 1 child, Robert Clarkson. BA, U. Colo., 1941; MA, U. Wis., 1942, PhD, 1950. Instr. Spanish U. Wis., Madison, 1951-53; prof., head fgn. langs. Tex. Tech. U., Lubbock, 1953-63; prof., chmn. Spanish & Portuguese Ind. U., Bloomington, 1963-72; prof., head romance langs. U. Ga., Athens, 1973-79, dean grad. sch., 1979-89, prof. alumni found., 1980-91, prof. emeritus alumni found., 1992—. Vis. prof. romance langs. U. Tex., Austin, 1957; vis. prof. Spanish U. Iowa, Iowa City, 1993; interim dean arts & humanities Fla. Atlantic U., Boca Raton, 1995. Author: (book) Saavedra Fajardo, 1957, Saavedra Fajardo, 2d edit., 1977, Moratin, 1971, Jose Melchor Gomis, 1974; contbr. articles to profl. jours. Mem. exec. com. grad. deans African-Am. Inst., N.Y.C., 1985—92. Lt. (j.g.) USNR, 1942—46, lt. comdr. USNR, 1946—66. A. C. Markham Travel fellow, U. Wis., 1950—51, J. S. Guggenheim fellow, 1959—60, Rsch. grantee, Am. Philos. Soc., 1971, 1974. Mem.: Critica Hispanica Diechiocho, Am. Assn. Tchrs. Spanish & Portuguese, Hispanic Soc. Am. (corr.). Episcopalian. Home: 7101 Patriots Colony Drive Williamsburg VA 23188-0131

DOWLING, JOHN ELLIOTT, biology educator; b. Pawtucket, R.I., Aug. 31, 1935; s. Joseph Leo and Ruth W. (Tappan) D.; children by previous marriage: Christopher, Nicholas.; m. Judith Falco, Oct. 18, 1975; 1 dau., Alexandra. AB, Harvard U., 1957, PhD, 1961; MD (hon.), U. Lund (Sweden), Sweden, 1982. Asst. prof. biology Harvard U., Cambridge, 1961—64, prof., 1971—87, Maria Moors Cabot prof. natural sci., 1987—2001, Llura and Gordon Gund prof. neurosci., 2001—; assoc. prof. Johns Hopkins Sch. Medicine, 1964—71. Pres. Marine Biol. Lab., 1998—. Author: The Retina: An Approachable Part of the Brain, 1987, Neurons and Networks: An Introduction to Neuroscience, 1992, 2d edit., 2001, Creating Mind: How the Brain Works, 1998; contbr. numerous articles on vision to profl. jours. Recipient ann. award N.E. Ophthal. Soc., 1979, award of merit Retina Research Found., 1981, Prentice medal Am. Acad. Optometry, 1991, Von Sallman prize, 1992, The Helen Keller prize for vision rsch., 2000, Gund award Found. Fighting Blindness, 2001. Fellow Am. Acad. Arts and Scis., AAAS; mem. Am. Philos. Soc., Assn. Rsch. in Vision and Ophthalmology (Friedenwald medal 1970), Nat. Acad. Sci., Neurosci. Soc., Soc. Gen. Physiologists. Home: 135 Charles St Boston MA 02114-3264 Office: Harvard U Biology Labs Cambridge MA 02138 E-mail: dowling@mcb.harvard.edu.

DOWLING, MICHAEL PAUL, foundation administrator; b. Norwalk, Conn., Feb. 28, 1953; s. Thomas Edward Dowling and Marion Frances Burke. BS, Yale U., 1975, M in Pub. and Pvt. Mgmt., 1982, M. Forest Sci., 1982. Project mgr. York Rsch. Corp., Stamford, Conn., 1976-78; environ. cons. Envirosphere Co., N.Y.C., 1978-79, energy cons. Newport Beach, Calif., 1980; mgmt. cons. Mgmt. Analysis Ctr., Inc., Cambridge, Mass., 1981, McKinsey & Co., Inc., N.Y.C., 1982-85; sr. v.p., dir. Gen. Atlantic Resources, Inc., Denver, 1985-95; pres. Dowling Found., Denver, 1997—. Chmn., bd. dirs. Colo. Wildlife Fedn., Lakewood, 1998-2000; vice chmn. bd. dirs. Colo. Conservation Trust, Boulder, 2000—; bd. dirs. Colo. Coalition Land Trusts, Golden, 1999-2001; mem. adv. bd. Environ. Def., Boulder, 2000—.

DOWLING, PAUL DENNIS, bilingual special education educator; b. Bryan, Tex., Mar. 10, 1963; s. Dennis William and Dorothy Patricia (Abney) Dowling; m. Lucia Kim, Mar. 17, 2003. BA, U. Tex., 1986, MA, 1988, U. Houston, 1992, EdD, 2000. Cert. tchr., Tex. Behavior intervention expert Houston Schs., 1989-91; learning specialist Goose Creek Schs., Baytown, Tex., 1991-95, bilingual life skills instr., 1995-98; lectr. U. Houston, 1996-98; spl. edn. tchr. Toll Mid. Sch., Glendale, Calif., 1998-99, Beverly Hills H.S., 1999-2000, Providencia Elem. Sch., Burbank, Calif., 2000—02, Stevenson Elem. Sch., Houston, 2002—03, Sepulveda Mid. Sch., 2003—04; 24460. CEO, Coll. Houses Co-ops, Austin, 1986-87; mng. editor TAGS dept. German, U. Tex., Austin, 1983-84. Contbr. articles to newspapers and profl. jours. Pres. Students for Coop. Living, U. Tex., 1985-88; poll watcher Dem. Party, Austin, 1986, 88; bd. rep. Coll. Houses Co-ops, 1986-88; del. Dem. Conv.-Travis County, Austin, 1988. Fellow Phi Delta Kappa; mem. Internat. Reading Assn., Nat. Reading Conf., Nat. Coun. Tchrs. English, World Future Soc., Internat. Soc. Contemporary Legend Rsch., Wissenschaftliche Buchgesellschaft. Avocations: reading, internet, theater, urban legends, foreign languages. E-mail: paulddowling@aol.com.

DOWLING, RODERICK ANTHONY, investment banker; b. N.Y.C., Dec. 29, 1940; s. John Joseph and Anne (Chisholm) D.; m. Lavinia Seibels, May 6, 1977; children: Lavinia Crosby, Roderick A.; children by previous marriage: Anne Chisholm, Katherine Burke. BS, Fairfield U., 1962; JD, Fordham U., 1965. Bar: N.Y. 1965, Ga. 1974. Assoc. Cahill, Gordon & Reindel, N.Y.C., 1965-72; v.p., gen. counsel U.S. Industries N.E. Corp., N.Y.C., 1972-73, Fugua Industries, Inc., Atlanta, 1973-81; chmn. Sun Trust-Robinson Humphrey Inc., Atlanta, 1981—, also bd. dirs. Mem. ABA, Bar Assn. City N.Y., Georgia, Atlanta Bar Assns., S.R., Piedmont Driving Club (Ga.), University Club (N.Y.), Union Club (N.Y.), Capitol City Club, Buckhead Club, Golf Club Ga., Palmetto Club (S.C.), Seabrook Island Club (S.C.). Home: 2525 W Wesley Rd NW Atlanta GA 30327-2033

DOWLING, THOMAS C. pharmacist, educator, pharmacist, researcher; b. Wyandotte, Mich., June 28, 1969; s. Thomas R. and Mary Kay Dowling. PharmD, Ferris State U., 1993; PhD, U. Pitts., 1999. Registered pharmacist Mich., 1993. Lectr. in pharmacokinetics U. Md., Balt., 1997—. Contbr. chapters to books, articles to profl. jours. Recipient Rsch. award, Nat. Kidney Found. - Md., 2000—01. Mem.: Am. Soc. Nephrology. Achievements include development of drug metabolism and kidney function testing in humans pharmacokinetics rsch. Office: Univ Md AHB Rm 540-D 100 N Penn St Baltimore MD 21201 E-mail: taowling@rx.umaryland.edu.

DOWLING, VINCENT JOHN, retired lawyer; b. NYC, Dec. 20, 1927; s. Victor Hurlin and Joan Agnes (Reardon) D.; m. Jane Cooney, Apr. 16, 1958; children: Vincent John Jr., Douglas J., S. Colin, Joseph G. BS, Lehigh U., 1949; JD, U. Conn., 1957. Bar: Conn. 1957, Mass. 1985, Fla. 1986, U.S. Dist. Ct. Conn. 1958, U.S. Ct. Appeals (2d cir.) 1960, U.S. Ct. Claims 1986. Chief mfg. engr. Veeder-Root, Inc., Hartford, Conn., 1949-58; ptnr. Dowling & Dowling, Hartford, Conn., 1958-65, Cooney, Scully & Dowling, Hartford, Conn., 1965—2002; ret., 2001. Lectr. constrn. law. Capt. U.S. Army, 1951-53. Mem. ASME, ABA, Conn. Bar assn. (liaison com. with ctrs., constrn. law com., alt. dispute resolution com., chmn. specialization com.), Am. Arbitration Assn., Nat. Panel Constrn. Arbitrators and Mediators, Nat. Arbitration and Mediation (panel), Fed. Bar Assn., Mass. Bar Assn., Fla. Bar Assn., Internat. Bar Assn., Diocesan Attys. Assn., Hartford Golf Club, Hartford Club, John's Island Club (Vero Beach, Fla.), Quail Valley Club (Vero Beach), Kappa Alpha Soc. Roman Catholic. Address: 111 Stoner Dr West Hartford CT 06107 E-mail: vin@dowling.com.

DOWNEN, ROBERT LYNN, international affairs analyst and political consultant, editor, writer; b. Wichita, Kans., Apr. 18, 1951; s. Lyndall and Ruth Downen; m. Holly Hutchens, Sept. 1, 1980; children: Heather, Lindsey. BA cum laude, Washington U., St. Louis, 1973; MA, George Washington U., Washington, 1975. Legis. asst. to Bob Dole, U.S. Senate, Washington, 1973-79; dir. Pacific stds. Ctr. for Strategic and Internat. Studies/Georgetown U., Washington, 1979-84; dir., spl. projects U.S. State Dept./Asia, Washington, 1984-89; v.p. Neill and Co., Washington, 1989-94; sr. v.p. Jefferson Waterman Internat., Washington, 1994-98; pres. Downen Consulting, 1998—. Author: The Taiwan Pawn, 1979, To Bridge the China Strait, 1984; editor: Multi-System Nations and International Law, 1982, The Emerging Pacific Community, 1984. Mem. adv. group Dole for Pres., Washington, 1996; mem. adv. gorup Reagan for Pres., Washington, 1980; bd. trustees United Bapt. Ch. Named Kans. DeMolay of Yr., Order of DeMolay, 1969, DeMolay Legion of Honor award, 1983; recipient Wolcott Scholar award Internat. High Twelve Clubs, Mo., 1974, Hon. Mem. award Sojourners Lodge AF & AM, Panama Canal Zone, 1978. Mem. Masons, Phi Beta Kappa, Sigma Nu. Republican. Baptist. Avocations: photography, genealogy, study of american history and government, travel.

DOWNER, EUGENE DEBS, JR., editor, publisher; b. Stump Creek, Pa., Dec. 19, 1939; s. Eugene Debs and Vona (Weamer) D. BA, Pa. State U., 1961; MEd, Harvard U., 1989, cert. of advanced study, 1991; MS, Harvard Sch. of Pub. Health, 1994; mediation cert., MIT, 1994. Lic. addictions therapist, cert. alcohol and drug counselor. Asst. advt. dir. Bliss & Laughlin Industries, Oak Brook, Ill., 1964-66; mgr. pub. relations Nat. Can Corp., Chgo., 1966-67; Head Ski Co., Timonium, Md., 1967-68; pres. Osprey Enterprises, Jackson, Wyo., 1968-78; pub., editor Teton Mag., Jackson, 1969—90; owner Teton Bookshop, Jackson, Teton Bookshop Pub. Co., Jackson, 1972—2002; addictions therapist Curran-Seeley Found., Jackson, 2000—02; alcohol and drug counselor Haight Ashbury Free Clinic, San Francisco, 2002—03, Kaiser Permanente Corp., Vallejo, Calif., 2002—. Exhibited in one-man shows Gutman Libr., Harvard U., 1990-91. Mem. Senate Task force on Health, Wyo., 1993; mayoral candidate, Jackson, Wyo., 1994, 96; county commr. candidate, Teton County, Wyo., 1998. Recipient Journalism award AMA, 1974, Journalism award Wyo. State Hist. Soc., 1977, 89. Mem. Harvard Club (N.Y.C.), Harvard Faculty Club. Democrat. Episcopalian. Address: Box 10102 American Canyon CA 94503

DOWNER, ROBERT NELSON, lawyer; b. Newton, Iowa, July 15, 1939; s. Lowell William and Mabel Mary (Hannon) Downer; m. Jane Alice Glafka, May 29, 1971; children: Elise Michele, Andrew Nelson. BA, U. Iowa, 1961, JD, 1963. Bar: Iowa 1963, U.S. Dist. Ct. (so. dist.) Iowa 1963, U.S. Dist. Ct. (no. dist.) Iowa 1964, U.S. Supreme Ct. 1995, U.S. Ct. Appeals (8th cir.) 2001. Assoc. Meardon Law Office, Iowa City, 1963-68; mem. Meardon, Sueppel & Downer PLC and predecessor firms, Iowa City, 1969—. Dir., sec. KZIA, Inc., Cedar Rapids, Iowa, 1975—, Iowa City Tennis & Fitness Ctr., 1987—93; trustee The Oaknoll Found., Iowa City, 1990—98, Herbert Hoover Presdl. Libr. Assn., West Branch, Iowa, 2000—; dir. Christian Retirement Svcs., Inc., Iowa City, 1967—02, Iowa State Bar Found., 1996—2002, Iowa Law Sch. Found., 2000—; bd. regents State of Iowa, 2003—. Mem. Iowa Supreme Ct. Task Force on Domestic Abuse, 1993—94; bd. dirs. Iowa City Area Devel. Group, 1993—2001, chmn., 1996—97, co-chair, 2000—01; dir., sec. Cmty. Found. Johnson County, Iowa, 2000—03; del. Rep. Nat. conv., New Orleans, 1988; mem. Iowa Supreme Ct. comm. Continuing Legal Edn., 1975—83; chair adminstrv. bd. First United Meth. Ch., Iowa City, 1985—87; pres. Greater Iowa City Area C. of C., 1979; bd. trustees Iowa City Pub. Libr., 1971—75, chair, 1973—74. Recipient Excellence in Svc. award, Legal Svcs. Corp. Iowa, 1996. Fellow: Iowa State Bar Found., Am. Bar Found., Am. Coll. Trust and Estate Counsel (state chair 2000—); mem.: ABA, Johnson County Bar Assn. (pres. 1988—89), Iowa State Bar Assn. (chair probate sect. 1990—93, v.p. 1993—94, pres.-elect 1994—95, pres. 1995—96, Merit award 2001), Rotary (pres. 1989—90). Republican. Methodist. Home: 2029 Rochester Ct Iowa City IA 52245-3246 Office: Meardon Sueppel & Downer PLC 122 S Linn St Iowa City IA 52240-1830 E-mail: bobd@meardonlaw.com.

DOWNER, WILLIAM JOHN, JR., retired hospital administrator; b. Springfield, Ill., Sept. 29, 1932; s. William John and Geraldine (Foster) D.; m. Wanda M. Parson, Oct. 3, 1953; children: William E., Lawrence R. BA, Mich. State U., 1954; MHA, U. Mich., 1961. Various mgmt. positions Blodgett Meml. Med. Ctr., Grand Rapids, Mich., 1961-74, pres., CEO, 1974-84; pres., chief exec. officer Columbus Hosp., Great Falls, Mont., 1985-95, sr. cons., 1995-96. Contbr. articles to profl. jours. City commr. City of Gt. Falls, 1996—99; hosp. divsn. chmn. United Way Kent County, Grand Rapids, 1969; mem. cmty. adv. bd. N.W. Mont. for Horizon Air, 1990—97; bd. dirs. No. Rockies Easter Seals/Goodwill, 1995—2000; bd. dirs. Big Sky chpt. ARC, 1986—92, 1996—97; commr. 211th Gen. Assembly Presbyn. Ch. USA, 1999—2000; elder Westminster Presbyn. Ch., Grand Rapids, 1968—85, 1st Presbyn. Ch., Gt. Falls, 1985—2000, Oceanside, Calif., 2001—; mem. com. on ministry Glacier Presbytery, 1996—2000, moderator, 1997. Lt. col. AUS, ret. Fellow Am. Coll. Healthcare Execs. (life, regent for Mich. 1978-84, regent for Mont. 1986-89, Regent's award 1996); mem. Am. Hosp. Assn. (life, mem. governing coun. sect. for met. hosps. 1991-94), Mont. Hosp. Assn. (bd. dirs. 1987-90, chmn. 1989), Mich. Hosp. Assn. (bd. dirs. 1973-82, chmn. 1980-81, Homminga award 1982), Great Falls C. of C. (mem. exec. com. 1988, chmn. 1991-92, mil. affairs exec. com. 1995-99, vice chmn. 1998, chmn. 1999), Rotary, Phi Kappa Phi, Beta Gamma Sigma. Avocations: civil war history, golf, travel. Home: 4001 Arcadia Way Oceanside CA 92056-5139 E-mail: bwdowner@cox.net.

DOWNES, LILLI M. sociologist, social psychologist; b. McKeesport, Pa., Mar. 12; d. Clarence and Margaret Virginia; m. Gary Matesig. BA, U. South Fla., 1985, MA, 1986; PhD, U. Del., 1997. Cert. tchr. Fla. Ful prof. sociology and psychology Hartford C.C., Bel Air, Md., 1989—. Mem. conf. arrangements com. undergrad. edn. com. Ea. Sociol. Soc., 1999. Bd. dirs. Harford Habitat for Humanity, Harford County, Md., 1997—2002. Recipient Tchg. Excellence award, Nat. Inst. for Staff and Orgn. Devel., 1996. Mem.: AAUP, Am. Sociol. Assn. (mem. editl. bd. Teaching Sociology 1998—2002), Pi Gamma Mu, Alpha Kappa Delta, Phi Kappa Phi (life). Office: Harford CC 401 Thomas Run Rd Bel Air MD 21015

DOWNES, NICHOLAS STREET, cartoonist; b. Boston, June 13, 1952; s. Prentice Gilbert and Edna Grace (Faithorn) D. Student, Antioch Coll., 1970-72; BS, Northeastern U., 1976. Freelance mag. cartoonist, Bklyn., 1976—. Del. Nat. Writers Union, 2001—. Author: Big Science, 1992, Whatever Happened to Eureka?, 1994; mag. cartoonist, 1976—. Mem. Cartoonists Assn. (bd. govs. 1987—). Office: PO Box 310107 Brooklyn NY 11231-0107 E-mail: nsdownes@aol.com.

DOWNES, RACKSTRAW, artist; b. Pembury, Kent, Eng., Nov. 8, 1939; came to U.S., 1961; s Henry Alfred and Rosa Kathleen (Rackstraw) D. BA, Cambridge U., 1961; MFA, Yale U., 1964. Asst. prof. U. Pa., Phila., 1967-78; mem.faculty Skowhegan Sch., Maine, 1975; mem. faculty N.Y. Studio Sch., N.Y.C., 1980-82. Editor Fairfield Porter: Art in Its Own Terms, 1979; bd. govs. Skowhegan Sch. Painting and Sculpture, 1981-95. One-man shows Kornblee Gallery, N.Y.C., 1972-82, Hirschl & Adler Modern, N.Y.C., 1982-94, Marlborough Galleries, N.Y.C., London, Madrid, 1996-99, Chinati Found., Marfa, Tex., 1999, Robert Miller Gallery, N.Y.C., 2000—; exhibited in group shows San Antonio Mus., 1981, Pa. Acad., Phila., 1981, Carnegie Internat., Pitts., 1983, Whitney Biennial, N.Y.C., 1981, Mus. Modern Art, N.Y.C., 2000, Snug Harbor Cultural Ctr., S.I., 2001; represented permanent collections, Mus. Modern Art, N.Y.C., Houston Mus. Fine Arts, Whitney Mus. Am. Art, N.Y.C., Hirschorn Mus., Washington, Pa. Acad. Fine Art, Met. Mus. Art, N.Y.C., Phila. Mus. Art, Carnegie Inst., Pitts., Corcoran Gallery Art, Smithsonian Mus., Washington, Ludwig Mus., Cologne; author: In Relation to the Whole, 2000; author Under the Gowanus and Razor-Wire Jour., 2000. Ingram Merrill fellow, 1974; grantee Nat. Endowment for Arts, 1980; recipient Creative Artist's Pub. Svc. award State of N.Y., 1978, Nat. Acad. Arts and Scis. award, 1989; Guggenheim fellow, 1998. Mem. Am. Acad. Arts and Letters.

DOWNEY, ARTHUR HAROLD, JR., lawyer, mediator; b. N.Y.C., Nov. 21, 1938; s. Arthur Harold Sr. and Charlotte (Bailey) D.; m. Gwen Vanden Berg, May 28, 1960; children: Anne Leigh, Neal Arthur, Drew Thomas. BA, Cen. Coll., Pella, Iowa, 1960; LLB, Cornell U., 1963. Bar: Colo. 1963, Wyo. 1991, U.S. Dist. Ct. Colo. 1963, U.S. Dist. Ct. Wyo. 1993, U.S. Ct. Appeals (10th cir.) 1963; diplomate Am. Bd. Forensic Examiners. From assoc. to ptnr. Weller, Friedrich, Ward & Andrew, Denver, 1963-82; ptnr., chief exec. officer Downey Law Firm P.C., Denver, 1982—. Trustee panel Colo. Hosp. Assn., 1988-93; del. Nat. Congress Hosp. Trustees, Am. Hosp. Assn., 1988-93. Contbr. articles to profl. jours. Vice moderator Presbytery of Denver, 1972; past pres. Columbine Village Homeowners Assn., Trails End Homeowners Assn., Upper Village Homeowners Assn., Powderhorn Condominium Homeowners Assn., Breckenridge, Colo.; chmn bd. trustees Bethesda Psychealth Sys., Inc., 1990-93. Fellow Internat. Soc. Barristers (emeritus); mem. ABA, Colo. Bar Assn., Larimer County Bar Assn., Wyo. Bar Assn., Def. Rsch. Inst. (disting. svc. award), Nat. Inst. Trial Advocacy (teaching faculty, team leader 1973—), Colo. Def. Lawyers Assn. (pres. 1977-78), Am. Coll. Legal Medicine (assoc. in law), Nat. Bd. Trial Advocacy (cert.), Am. Arbitration Assn. Republican. Mem. Christian Reformed Ch. In Am. Avocations: photography, woodworking, skiing. Office: Downey Law Firm PC 7688 Promontory Dr Fort Collins CO 80528-9305 E-mail: downeypc@attbi.com.

DOWNEY, ARTHUR THOMAS, III, lawyer; b. N.Y.C., Aug. 17, 1937; s. Arthur T. and Beatrice (Fortune) Downey; m. Mary S. Downey; children: Thomas, Allison, Paulstepchildren: Christopher, Sarah, Matthew. BA, St. Vincent, 1959; LLB, Villanova U., 1962; LLM, Georgetown U., 1963. Bar: D.C. 1964. Atty. U.S. Dept. State, Washington and Berlin, 1964-69; prof. staff The Nat. Security Coun., The White House, Washington, 1969-72; assoc. Morgan. Lewis & Bockius, Washington, 1972-75; dep. asst. sec. U.S. Dept. Commerce, Washington, 1975-77; ptnr. Sutherland, Ashill & Brennan, Washington, 1977-90; shareholder Johnson & Gibbs, 1990—92; v.p. Baker Hughes Inc., Washington, 1992—. Adj. prof. Georgetown U. Law Sch., Washington, 1978—90. Co-author: Freedom From Federal Establishment, 1964. Trustee Am. Univ. Sharjah, 2002—, Fgn. Bondholders Protective Coun., 2002—. Mem.: ABA (vice chmn. sec. internat. law 1984), UN Assn. of USA (bd. govs. 1985—90). Office: Baker Hughes Inc 816 Connecticut Ave NW Fl 2 Washington DC 20006-2706

DOWNEY, BRIAN PATRICK, lawyer; b. Pitts., Sept. 1, 1964; s. Edmond John and Mary Elizabeth (Wallace) D.; m. Linda Alice McKay, Oct. 9, 1993. BA, Dartmouth Coll., 1987; JD, Dickinson Sch. of Law, 1990. Bar: Pa. 1990, U.S. Dist. Ct. (we. dist.) Pa. 1991, U.S. Dist. Ct. (ea. and mid. dists.) Pa. 1994, U.S. Ct. Appeals (3rd cir.) 1994. Assoc. counsel Eckert Seamans Cherin & Mellott, Pitts., 1990-92; asst. counsel Pa. Dept. of Labor, Harrisburg, 1992-94; ptnr. Pepper Hamilton, LLP, Harrisburg, 1994—. Mem. Friends of Tom Foley Com., Harrisburg, 1994; bd. dirs., pres. Open Stage Harrisburg, 2001—. Mem. ABA, Pa. Bar Assn., Dauphin County Bar Assn. Democrat. Roman Catholic. Avocations: creative writing, golf, reading fiction. Office: Pepper Hamilton LLP 200 One Keystone Plz Harrisburg PA 17108 E-mail: downeyb@pepperlaw.com.

DOWNEY, CHRISTINE, state legislator; b. Abilene, Kans., Mar. 26, 1949; children: Amy, Matthew, Erin. Elem. and mid. sch. tchr., 1975-93; mem. Kans. Senate from 31st. dist., Topeka, 1996—. Adj. prof. Bethel Coll., 1990-93; mem. edn. com. Kans. Senate, agriculture com., chldn's issues com., legis. ednl. planning com., ways and means com. Pres., bd. dirs. Newton Cmty. Children's Choir, 1991-92. Mem. Kans. Nat. Edn. Assn. (pres. 1990), Newton Nat. Edn. Assn. (pres. 1989). Home: 10320 N Wheat State Rd Inman KS 67546-8109*

DOWNEY, DEBORAH ANN, systems specialist; b. Xenia, Ohio, July 22, 1958; d. Nathan Vernon and Patricia Jaunita (Ward) D. Assoc. in Applied Sci., Sinclair C.C., 1981, student, 1986-91; BA, Capital U., 1994. Jr. programmer, project mgr. Cole-Layer-Trumble Co., Dayton, Ohio, 1981-82; sr. programmer, analyst, project leader Systems Architects Inc., Dayton, 1982-84, Systems and Applied Sci. Corp. (now Computer Sci. Corp.), Dayton, 1984; analyst Unisys, Dayton, 1984-87; systems programmer Computer Sci. Corp., Fairborn, Ohio, 1987—. Cons. computer software M&S Garage/Body Shop, Beavercreek, Ohio, 1986-87. Mem. NAFE, Am. Motorcyclist Assn., Sinclair C. C. Alumni Assn., Cherokee Nation Okla., Cherokee Nat. Hist. Soc. Democrat. Mem. United Ch. of Christ. Avocations: motorcycles, miniatures, sports, needlework.

DOWNEY, JAMES CECIL, retired music and humanities educator; b. Grand Bay, Ala. s. James Fred and Thelma Hamilton Downey; m. Phyllis Barber, Jan. 25, 1952; children: James Vance, Joy Lyndell, Jennifer Anne, Robert Joel. BA, William Carey Coll., 1963; MMus, U. So. Miss., 1965; PhD, Tulane U., 1968. Prof. music William Carey Coll., Hattiesburg, Miss., 1966-96, prof. humanities, 1989-96, dean Gulfport (Miss.) campus, 1982-85, coord. continuing edn., 1985-86. State officer Am. Musicological Soc., 1966-96. Author: Mingo County Tales, 2003; contbr. articles to profl. jours. Founder, dir. Gulf Coast Cmty. Chorus, Biloxi, Miss., 1982. With U.S. Army, 1954-56. Recipient Jaap Kunst award Soc. for Ethnomusicology, 1964. Democrat. Baptist. Avocation: gentleman farmer. Home: 530 Knight Rd Sumrall MS 39482-3826

DOWNEY, JANET MARION, anthropologist, educator; b. Chgo., May 1, 1946; BA, U. of Minn., 1989; MA, Ariz. State U., 1992. Rsch. asst. Ariz. State U., Tempe, Ariz., 1989—92; residential faculty-anthropology Paradise Valley C.C., Phoenix, 1998—. Cons. Nat. Mus. of Ethiopia, Addis Ababa, Ethiopia, 1998—98, Colo. River Indian Tribes, Parker, Ariz., 1993—93, Quechan Indian Tribe, Yuma, Ariz., 1992—92; rsch. asst. Ariz. State U., Tempe, 1989—92. Fellow Exchange fellow, Paradise Valley C. C., 2002; grantee, Inst. of Human Origins, Ariz. State Univ., 1998, Instrnl. Improvement grant, Mesa C.C., 1998. Mem.: Am. Anthrop. Assn. Office: Paradise Valley Community College 18401 N 32nd St Phoenix AZ 85032 E-mail: j.downey@pvmail.maricopa.edu.

DOWNEY, JOHN ALEXANDER, physician, educator; b. Sept. 16, 1930; BSc in Medicine, U. Man., MD with honors, 1954; PhD, Oxford U., 1962. Diplomate Am. Bd. Phys. Medicine and Rehab. Intern Vancouver Gen. Hosp., Canada, 1953—54; resident phys. medicine and rehab. Columbia Presbyn. Med. Ctr., N.Y.C., 1954—56, resident, 1957—58; asst. resident internal medicine Peter Bent Brigham Hosp., Boston, 1956—57; asst. to med. dir., cons. phys. medicine Blythedale Children's Hosp., Valhalla, NY, 1957—59; rsch. assoc. Columbia U., 1958—59; vis. fellow Presbyn. Hosp., N.Y.C., 1958—59; sr. resident internal medicine Peter Bent Brigham Hosp., 1959—60; vis. worker Med. Rsch. Coun. Group for Body Temperature Control, Oxford, England, 1960—62; assc. prof. rehab. medicine Columbia U. Coll. Physicians ans Surgeons, 1962—64, assoc. prof., 1964—67, prof., 1967—74, Simon Baruch prof., 1974—, chair dept. rehab. medicine, 1974—90, asst. prof. medicine, 1963—64. Asst. attending Presbyn. Hosp., N.Y.C., 1962—64, assoc. attending, 1964—68, attending, 1968—, dir. rehab. medicine svc., 1974—90; vis. prof. dept. human physiology and pharmacology U. Adelaide, Australia, 1969. Author: Stroke: Two to Recover, 1969; co-editor: Physiological Basis of Rehabilitation Medicine, 1971, Physiological Basis of Rehabilitation Medicine, 2d edit., 1994, The Child with Disabling Illness: Principles of Rehabilitation, 1974, The Child with Disabling Illness: Principles of Rehabilitation, 2d edit., 1982, Bereavement of Physical Disability: Recommitment to Life, Health and Function, 1982; mem. editl. bd.: Benneman's Practice of Pediatrics, 1974; contbr. articles to profl. jours.; (films) Rehabilitation: A Patient's Perspective, 1973; I Had a Stroke, 1978; Physiatry: A Physician's Perspective, 1981. Fellow: Royal Coll. Physicians (Can.; mem.: AAAS, APA, AMA, NAS, N.Y. Acad. Medicine, N.Y. Acad. Scis., N.Y. Rheumatism Assn., Am. Rheumatism Assn. Office: Columbia U Dept Rehab Medicine 630 W 168th St New York NY 10032-3795

DOWNEY, JOHN WILHAM, composer, pianist, conductor, educator; b. Chgo., Oct. 5, 1927; s. James Bernard and Augustina (Haas) D.; m. Irusha Czuszakivna; children: Lida, Marc. MusB, DePaul U., 1945; MusM, Chgo. Mus. Coll., 1951; Docteur es Lettres (PhD), U. Paris-Sorbonne, 1957; Prix de Composition (scholar), Paris Conservatory, 1956. Assoc. prof. Chgo. City Coll., 1958-64; prof. music U. Wis., Milw., 1964-86, disting. prof., 1986-98, prof. emeritus, 1999—, 1998—. Lectr. music theory De Paul U., Chgo., 1960-64, Roosevelt U., Chgo., 1961. Author: La Musique Populaire dans l'Oeuvre de Bela Bartok, 1966; composer Eastlake Terrace (piano solo), 1959 (recorded by Master Musician's Collectif, 1998), Chant to Michelangelo, 1959, Edges (piano solo, 1960), Pyramids (piano solo, 1961), Portrait No. 1 (piano solo, 1980), Gasparo Records, Jingalodeon for Orchestra, 1968, recorded with Cala Records, 1991, Harp Concerto, 1968 (recorded by Musician's Collectif 1998, Gasparo Records), Cello Sonata, CRI label, 1968, Symphonic Modules, 1972, Agort, woodwind quintet, recorded with Gasparo label, 1973, Gasparo Records, 1989, Adagio Lyrico: 2 pianos, 1953, What If? (composition for mixed choir, solo timpany and brass octet), 1973, Octet for Winds, 1954, A Dolphin, voice and chamber ensemble, 1974, recorded with Orion Label, 1974, Gasparo Records, 1989, Lydian Suite, 1975, Gasparo Records, Cala Records, 1998, String Quartet II, 1975, Gasparo Records, 1976, Crescendo (for large percussion ensemble), 1977, High Clouds and Soft Rain (for mixed flute choir), 1977, The Edge of Space (Fantasy for Bassoon and Orch.), 1977, CD recorded with Chandos Records, 1989, Silhouette (solo clarinet), 1998, Qu'en Avez-vous Fait? (for voice and piano), 1984, CD recording for Gasparo Records, 1995, Prayer for string trio, 1984, Piano Trio, 1984, Declamations for Large Orch., 1985, recorded with Cala Records, 1991, Discourse for Oboe with String Orch. and Harpsichord, 1986, recorded with Cala Records, 1991, Recombinance for Doublebass and Piano, 1987, Concerto for Doublebass and Orch., 1987,

recorded with Cala Records, 1991, Suite of Psalms for a cappella mixed choir, 1988, Fanfare For Freedom for symphonic winds, 1990, Call for Freedom for symphonic winds, 1991, Yad Vashem-An Impression (piano solo), 1991, Memories (piano solo) 1991, Ode to Freedom, for symphony orchestra, 1992, Symphony No. 1, 1993, Rough Road (guitar and flute), 1994, Angel Talk (for eight cellos), 1995, Rememberance-The Swing Set, Reminder-Hungry Squirrel, Reaffirmation-Red Rose, 1995, Song Suite (high voice and piano), 1995, CD recorded by VAI Recordings, 1997, Ghosts (for 12 violins), 1995, Soliloquy (for solo English Horn, recorded for Cala Records) 1997, For Those Who Suffered (for chamber orch.), 1996, recorded on CD by Master Musicians Collective, 1998, Irish Sonata (for violin and piano) 1998, Mountains and Valleys (solo piano), 2000, incidental music for The Winter's Tale, Bassoon Quintet for bassoon and string quartet, 2001, also electronic and computer music; resident artist, MacDowell Colony, summers 1971, 75-77, 82-83, 92, 94, falls 1978, 85, Millay Colony, summer 1991; rec. artist (album) John Downey Plays John Downey, 1987; 5 orchestral works recorded by the London Symphony Orch.: Jingalodeon, Declamations, Concerto for Double Bass and Orch., Discourse for Oboe, Harpsichord and String Orch., The Edge of Space. Decorated Chevalier de l'Ordre des Arts et des Lettres, France, 1980; scholar Fulbright France, 1952-54, winter, 1979, 80, Fulbright Australia, summer, 1987, French Govt., 1954-55; teaching fellow, 1955-56; German Govt. teaching fellow, 1956-57; Copley Found. grantee, 1956-57, 57-58; recipient awards U. Wis., 1971, 73, 75, 77, 79, 83, 87, 93, 95, Ford Found., 1976, Ctr. for L.Am. Studies of the U. Wis.-Milw. award, 1988, NEA, 1977, 83, 94, Moebius award, 1985, New Music for Young Ensembles award, 1986, Walter Heinrichsen award Am. Acad. and Inst. Arts and Letters, 1990, Meet the Composer awards, 1988, 90, 92, 93; named Music Citizen of Yr. Civic Music Assn. of Milw., 1980, Musician of the Yr. Milw Sentinel, 1993; Wis. Arts Bd. Composition fellow, 1991. Mem. Am. Soc. Univ. Composers, Am. Music Ctr., ASCAP (awards 1974—), Am. Fedn. Musicians, Wis. Contemporary Music Forum (founder, chmn. 1970—), Soc. of Composers, Ctr. 20th Century Studies, De Paul U. Alumni Assn. (Disting. Alumni award 1969), Phi Kappa Phi, Delta Omicron (nat. patron), Mu Phi Alpha (Disting. Musician award 1987, other awards 1974-86), Sigma Alpha Iota (Extraordinary Mus. Achievement award Milw. Alumnae chpt. 1986). Avocations: jogging, bicycling. Office: U Wis Sch Fine Arts Music PO Box 413 Milwaukee WI 53201-0413 E-mail: jwdowney@uwm.edu. *Although styles change and vary with place and time, an artist's sincerity of purpose, depth of feeling, and intellectual finesse are values permeating most works of art regardless of time and fashion.*

DOWNEY, MARGIE LEE COOPER, educator, writer; b. Baltimore, MD, Apr. 4, 1957; d. Jack Crawford and Nancy Lou (Sellers) Cooper; m. Michael Duane Downey, July 7, 1978 (div. Mar. 5, 2003); children: Cynthia Anne, Jennifer Lynn, Justin Jack, Laura Elizabeth, Catherine Amorette. BA, U. Tex. Dallas, 1981. Short-term missionary, 1976—95; office mgr. M. D. Downey, Painting Contractor, Dallas, 1978—83; home sch. educator, 1987—; first lady Global Missions Fellowship, 1987—2002; book distbr. & dist. mgr. Successful Living/David C. Cook Pub., 1987—90; regional spokesman & volunteer Calvert Sch. Home Instruction Dept., Baltimore, Md., 1988—98; Founder & sr. editor Home Sch. Families of Twins, Richardson, Tex., 1998—2003. Science lab asst. Richardson Home School Assn. Teaching Co-op, 1989—94, fine arts coordinator, 1992—96; distbr., dist. mgr. Successful Living, David C. Cook Pub. Editor: Global Missions Fellowship World Update, 1989; author: (course) Missionary SWAT Team Course for Kids, 1993, (5 vol. book) Diamonds, 1998; contbr. Keys to Parenting Multiples, TWINS to QUINTS Incorporated, articles in TWINS Mag.; author & editor (course) Missionary SWAT Team Course for Kids, 1993, Twins and Home School booklet, 1998, Home School Families of Twins survey & report, 2000. Mem. & jr. Am. citizens chmn. Nat. Soc. of DAR, Mary Shirley McGuire Chap., 1996—; Okla. Congl. lobbyist Home Sch. Legal Defense Assn., Oklahoma City, 1986; nat. voting delegate Annual Nat. S. Baptist Convention, Okla., 1984—87; conv. spkr. & vendor, 1982—; mem. & vol. Richardson First Baptist Church, Tex. Recipient Texas Mothers of Multiples' Bette Ade Scholarship, 2003. Mem.: Am. Coun. Law & Justice, Richardson Home Sch. Assn., Am. Ctr. Law and Justice (assoc.), N. Dallas Mothers of Twins, Tex. Mothers of Multiples, Hearth & Home Ministries, Nat. Orgn. of Mothers of Twins Clubs, Am. Coun. Law & Justice (assoc.), N. Tex. Home Educator's Network (assoc.), Tex. Home Sch. Coalition (assoc.), Home Sch. Legal Defense Assn. (assoc.). Christian. Avocations: photography, movies, needlecrafts, reading. Office: Home Sch Families of Twins 1226 Northlake Dr Richardson TX 75080

DOWNEY, MICHAEL S. physician, podiatrist; b. Hartford, Conn., Oct. 29, 1957; s. John Eliot Downey and Jean Hayes Downey Garren; m. Lois F. Downey, May 26, 1984; children: Genevieve, Victoria, Juliana. BS, Mercer U., Macon, Ga., 1979; DPM, Pa. Coll. Podiatric Medicine, Phila., 1983. Diplomate Am. Bd. Podiatric Surgery, Am. Bd. Primary Podiatric Medicine and Orthopedics. Prof., chmn. dept. surgery Temple U. Sch. Podiatric Medicine, Phila., 1988-99; chief divsn. podiatric surgery Presbyn. Med. Ctr., Phila., 1999—. Expert analyst Foot and Ankle Quar., 1990—; mem. faculty The Podiatry Inst., Tucker, Ga., 1986—. Author, co-editor: Comprehensive Textbook of Foot Surgery, 1992; mem. editl. adv. bd.: Jour. Am. Podiatric Med. Assn., 1990—; author: McGlamry's Comprehensive Textbook of Foot & Ankle Surgery, 2001; co-editor: McGlemry's Comprehensive Textbook of Foot & Ankle Surgery, 2001; editor (section): Jour. of Foot & Ankle Surgery; contbr. articles to profl. jours. Named Top Doc, Phila. Mag., 1994, 96, 2002. Fellow Am. Coll. Foot and Ankle Surgeons; mem. Am. Podiatric Med. Assn., Pa. Podiatric Med. Assn., Am. Diabetes Assn. Avocations: golf, chess, medical writing, basketball. Office: Ankle and Foot Med Ctrs 39th and Market Sts Ste 111 Philadelphia PA 19104 E-mail: Dowpod@aol.com.

DOWNEY, RICHARD LAWRENCE, lawyer; b. Washington, Apr. 3, 1948; s. William G. and Laufey A. D.; m. Pamela L. Drewry, July 10, 1971; children: Anna Christine, Laura Michele, Richard Lawrence, Patricia Kathleen. BA, Randolph-Macon Coll., 1970; JD, Hamline U., 1977. Bar: Va. 1978, U.S. Dist. Ct. (ea. dist.) Va. 1978, U.S. Ct. Appeals (4th cir.) 1978, U.S. Supreme Ct. 1983, U.S. Tax Ct. 1990, U.S. Claims Ct. 1990; diplomate Nat. Bd. Trial Advocacy; bd. cert. civil trial adv. Assoc. Downey & Lennhoff, Springfield, Va., 1978-80; pvt. practice Fairfax, Va., 1980-82; sr. ptnr. Duvall, Blackburn, Hale & Downey, Fairfax, Va., 1982-92; prin. Richard L. Downey & Assocs., 1992—. Served to lt. col. USAR. Named Outstanding Young Man of Am. U.S. Jaycees, 1982. Mem. ABA, ATLA, Va. State Bar Assn., Va. Trial Lawyers Assn., Fairfax Bar Assn. (gen. dist. cts. com. 1984-86, cir. ct. com. 1988-89), Nat. Lawyers Assn., Christian Legal Soc., Fairfax County C. of C. (internat. trade com., planning and land use com., legis. com. 1984), Phi Alpha Delta, Rotary. Republican. Address: 4126 Leonard Dr Fairfax VA 22030-5118 Office Fax: 703-273-8800.

DOWNEY, RICHARD RALPH, lawyer, accountant, management consultant; b. Boston, Apr. 22, 1934; s. Paul Joseph and Evelyn Mae (Butler) D.; BS, Northeastern U., 1958; MBA, Harvard U., 1962; JD, Suffolk U., 1979; LLM, Boston U., 1981; children: Richard Ralph (dec.), Janice M., Erin C., Timothy M. Mem. audit staff Price Waterhouse & Co., Boston, 1962-64; assoc. Assos. for Internat. Rsch., Inc., Cambridge, Mass., 1964-68, v.p., 1968—, also dir.; admitted to Mass. bar, 1979, Fed. bar, 1980. Treas., 1580 House Condominium Trust, 1979-80. CPA, Mass., Mem. ABA, Am. Inst. CPAs, Mass. Soc. CPAs, Mass. Bar Assn., Assn. Trial Lawyers Am., Boston Bar Assn., Phi Delta Phi, Algonquin Club, Harvard Club (Boston, N.Y.C.). Home: 25 Washington Ave Cambridge MA 02140-2834 Office: 1100 Massachusetts Ave Cambridge MA 02138-5241

DOWNEY, ROMA, actress; b. Northern Ireland, United Kingdom, May 6, 1963; m. David Anspaugh, 1995 (div. 1998); 1 child, Reilly Marie. BA in Fine Arts, Brighton Art Coll., England, 1983; diploma, London Drama Studio, 1985. Actress CBS Television, L.A. Appeared in Irelands Abbey Theatre, U.S. tour The Playboy of the Western World, 1991; on Broadway in The Circle; Off Broadway in Love's Labour's Lost, Tamara, Arms and the Man; TV appearances include A Woman Named Jackie, Touched by an Angel, 1994-2003, Borrowed Hearts, A Child is Missing; appeared in films including (TV series) A Woman Named Jackie, 1991, Devlin, 1992, A Child is Missing, 1995, Borrowed Hearts, 1997, Monday After the Miracle, 1998, A Test of Love, 1999, A Secret Life, 2000, Second Honeymoon, 2000, Sons of Mistletoe, 2001, Hairy Tale, 2003; exec. prodr. Borrowed Hearts, 1997, Monday After the Miracle, 1998, Second Honeymoon, 2000, Hairy Tale, 2003. Nominee Helen Hayes Best Actress award, 1991, Emmy award, 1997, 98, Golden Globe award, 1997-98; recipient TV Guide award for favorite actress in a drama, 1999. Office: Touched by an Angel care CBS/MTM Studios 4020 Radford Ave North Hollywood CA 91604-2101 Address: Gersh Agy 232 N Canon Dr Beverly Hills CA 90210-5302*

DOWNHAM, THOMAS FLETCHER, dermatologist; b. May 21, 1943; BS, U. Mich., 1966, MD, 1970. Diplomate Am. Bd. Dermatology, Am. Bd. Dermatopathology. Intern Henry Ford Hosp., Detroit, 1970-71; resident Wayne State U. Sch. Medicine, Detroit, 1971-74; dermatologist Henry Ford Hosp., Detroit, 1978—; clin. assoc. prof. Wayne State U. Sch. Medicine, Detroit, 1974—. Contbr. articles to profl. jours. including Jour. Am. Acad. Dermatology, Internat. Jour. Dermatology. Office: Henry Ford Med Ctr 24555 Haig St Taylor MI 48180-3322 Fax: 313-375-2140. E-mail: thomasd@ic.net.

DOWNIE, LEONARD, JR., editor, writer; b. Cleve., May 1, 1942; s. Leonard and Pearl Martha (Evenheimer) D.; m. Barbara Lindsey, July 15, 1960 (div. 1971); children: David Leonard, Scott Leonard; m. Geraldine Rebach, Aug. 15, 1971 (div. 1997); children: Joshua Mark, Sarah Elizabeth; m. Janice Galin, Sept. 12, 1997. BA, Ohio State U., 1964, MA, 1965, LLD (hon.), 1993. Reporter, editor Washington Post, 1964-74, met. editor, 1974-79, London corr., 1979-82, nat. editor, 1982-84, mng. editor, 1984-91; dir. L.A. Times-Washington Post News Svc., 1991—; exec. editor Washington Post, 1991—; dir. Internat. Hearald Tribune, 1985—2002. Author: Justice Denied, 1971, Mortgage on America, 1974, The New Muckrackers, 1976; author: (with Robert G. Kaiser) The News About the News, 2002. Trustee Georgetown Day Sch., 1988-93. Recipient Gavel award ABA, 1967; Alicia Patterson Found. fellow, 1971-72, Goldsmith award for the News About the News, Joan Shorenstein Ctr., Harvard U. John F. Kennedy Sch. of Govt., 2003. Fellow Soc. Profl. Journalists; mem. Am. Soc. Newspaper Editors. Office: Washington Post Co 1150 15th St NW Washington DC 20071-0002

DOWNIE, RICHARD DUNCAN, military officer, government agency administrator; BS, U.S. Mil. Acad., 1976; M In Internat. Rels., U. So. Calif., 1983, D in Internat. Rels., 1995. Fgn. area officer, Latin Am., Colombia, Panama, Mexico and Germany; exch. officer to Colombian Army; comdt. Western Hemisphere Inst. for Security Coop., 2001—. Author: Learning From Conflict: The U.S. Military in Vietnam, El Salvador and the Drug War, 1998; contbr. articles. Decorated Def. Superior Svc.; recipient Orden de Merito Academico, Colombia, Bosnia/Former Yugoslavia NATO medal; fellow, MIT. Office: Western Hemisphere Inst for Security Coop 7011 Morrison Ave Columbus GA 31905-2611

DOWNIE, ROBERT COLLINS, II, lawyer; b. Panama Canal Zone, Feb. 18, 1965; s. Robert Wahl Downie and Margaret Brandon Ausley; m. Robyn Elizabeth McGuire, Sept. 1, 1994. BA in English, Davidson Coll., 1987; JD, Fla. State U., 1989. Bar: Fla. 1990, U.S. Dist. Ct. (mid. and no. dists.) Fla. 1996, U.S. Ct. Appeals (11th cir.) 1996. Assoc. Oertel, Hoffman, Fernandez & Cole, Tallahassee, Fla., 1990-94; shareholder Mathews & Downie, P.A., Tallahassee, 1994-97; assoc. Brown, Ward et al, Orlando, 1997-99; sr. atty. Fla. Dept. Transp., 1999—. Office: Dept Transp 605 Suwannee St # MS58 Tallahassee FL 32399-0458 E-mail: robert.downie@dot.state.fl.us.

DOWNING, BARBARA KAY, school system administrator; b. Lafayette, Ind., Dec. 3, 1951; d. William Julius and Wilma Gladys (Kephart) Wood; m. David Loraine Downing, Nov. 26, 1971; children: Brian Douglas, Andrew David. BS, Ball State U., 1973, MA, 1978, EdS, 1990. Lic. ednl. adminstr., tchr., Ind. Tchr. Anderson (Ind.) Cmty. Sch., 1973-86, dir. student svcs., 1990-94; asst. prin. Madison Hts. H.S., Anderson, 1986-90; prin. Yorktown (Ind.) Mid. Sch., 1994-2000; asst. supt. Jay County Sch. Corp., Portland, Ind., 2000—01, supt., 2001—. Bd. dirs. Jay County Purdue Ext. Svcs., Jay County Step Ahead Coun., 2000-02, Jay County Bd. Health, 2002—. Editor: Anderson Community Schools, 1992 (Merit award Nat. Sch. Publ. and Pub. Rels. Assn. 1992). Bd. dirs. Big Bros./Big Sisters, Anderson, 1990-94, Anderson Area Crime Stoppers, 1990-94, Prosecutors Operation Resolve, Anderson, 1990-94, Jay County Devel. Corp., 2001--, Jay County Purdue Extension, 2000--; active Mayors Commn. Domestic Violence, Anderson, 1992-94. Recipient Met Life/NASSP Ind. Prin. of Yr., 1998; named Ind. Middle Sch. Prin. of Yr., 1997. Mem. ASCD, Ind. Assn. Pub. Sch. Supts., Ind. Prin. Assn. (bd. dirs. acad. competitions 1996-2000), Ind. Mid. Level Educators Assn. (regional chair 1996-98), Portland Area C. of C. (bd. dirs. 2001—), Dunkirk C. of C., Rotary, Phi Delta Kappa (2nd v.p. Ball State U. chpt. 1999, 1st v.p. 2000, pres. 2001-02, pres.-elect Ball State U. chpt. 2002-2003, A. Garland Hardy Leadership Edn. award 2003). United Methodist. Avocations: reading, fishing. Home: 3541 S State Rd Redkey IN 47373 Office: Jay County Sch Corp 404 E Arch St Portland IN 47371 E-mail: bdowning@jayschools.k12.in.us.

DOWNING, DARLENE L. non-for-profit organization executive; b. Cobleskill, N.Y., Jan. 30, 1946; d. Chester W. and Margie G. (Ronk) D.; 1 child, Zachary Boyd Sherry. BA, SUNY, Albany, 1981, postgrad., 1981-82. Program dir., dir. mktg. Rensselaerville (N.Y.) Inst., 1984-88; policy analyst N.Y. Assembly, Albany, N.Y., 1988-90; prin. policy analyst N.Y. Senate, Albany, 1991-97; exec. dir., editor newsletter and mag. Catskill Ctr. for Conservation Devel., inc., Arkville, N.Y., 1997—. Fundraiser Cedar Grove, Thomas Cole's hist. residence, Catskill, 1997-99. Office: Catskill Ctr for Conservation and Devel Rte 28 Arkville NY 12406 Home: 10259 E River St Truckee CA 96161-0336

DOWNING, DAVID CHARLES, retired minister; b. South Gate, Calif., June 24, 1938; s. Kenneth Oliver and Edna Yesobel (Casaday) D.; m. Tommye Catherine Tew, July 11, 1959 (dec. Dec. 11, 1985); children: Sheri Lynn, Teresa Kay, Carla Jeane, Michael David. BA, N.W. Christian Coll., 1961; B in Divinity, Tex. Christian U., 1966, M in Theology, 1973; DMin, San Francisco Theol. Sem., 1987. Ordained to ministry Christian Ch., 1961. Min. Marcola (Oreg.) Ch. of Christ, 1958-59; assoc. min. First Christian Ch., Lebanon, Oreg., 1960-63, min. Ranger, Tex., 1963-65, Knox City, Tex., 1966-68, Fredonia, Kans., 1968-74, Ctrl. Christian Ch., Huntington, Ind., 1974-77; regional min., pres. Christian Ch. Greater Kansas City, Mo., 1978-94; sr. minister Univ. Christian Ch., Disciples of Christ, San Diego, 1994—2001; ret., 2001. Trustee Phillips Grad. Sem., Enid, Okla., 1988-94; bd. dirs. Ch. Fin. Coun., Indpls., Midwest Career Devel. Svc., Chgo.; v.p. bd. dirs. Midwest Christian Counseling Ctr., Kansas City. Author: A Contrast and Comparison of Pastoral Counseling in Rural and Urban Christian Churches, 1972, A Design for Enabling Urban Congregations to Cope with Their Fear of Displacement When Faced with Communities in Transition, 1987. Pres. Kansas City Interfaith Peace Alliance, 1980-82; interim regional min. Pacific S.W. Region Disciples Ch., 2002. Democrat. Mem. Christian Ch. Avocations: swimming, camping, fishing, water skiing, collecting chalices. Home: 4325 Caminito De La Escena San Diego CA 92108-4201 E-mail: davidd624@msn.com.

DOWNING, DIANE VIRGINIA, community health nurse; b. Cin., Dec. 18, 1948; d. Edward Patrick and Virginia Agnes (Heis) Downing. BSN, U. Va., 1971, MSN, 1981; cert. in psychiat. nurse clin. specialist, San Francisco Army Med. Ctr., 1972; postgrad., George Mason JU., 1994—. RN Va. Commd. lt. Nurse Corps U.S. Army, 1967; lt. col. USAR, 1975; chief nurse 343d Combat Support Hosp., Ft. Hamilton, N.Y., 1992-94; sudden infant death syndrome project coord. Ind. State Bd. Health, Indpls., 1981-85, dir. local health stds., 1985-87, dir. maternal and child health div., 1987-90; asst. commr. nursing and quality assurance N.Y.C. Dept. Health, 1990-92; dir. policy rsch. Pub. Health Found., Washington, 1992-93; pub. health program specialist Arlington County Pub. Health Divsn., Dept. Human Svcs., Arlington, Va., 1993—. Tng. officer 531st Med. Co., Balt., 1995—96; nurse staff officer 309th Med. Group, Rockville, Md., 2001—; bd. dirs. Cmty.-Campus Partnerships Health. Vol. Big Sisters-Little Sisters, Indpls., 1982—89; mem. Rappahanock Area ARC Disaster Assistance Team, 2000—. Lt. col. USAR, 1988. Mem.: ANA, APHA (governing coun. representing pub. health nursing sect. 1992—95, chair-elect pub. health nursing sect. 1996, chair 1997, mem. child health task force 1997, mem. at large com. affiliates 1998), Met. Washington Pub. Health Assn. (governing coun. 1996, mem. coun. linkages between acad. and pub. health practice), Nat. Sudden Infant Death Syndrome Found. (chair Greater Indpls. chpt. 1983—85, Outstanding Contbn. award 1986), Ind. Pub. Health Assn. (treas. 1987, v.p. 1988, pres. 1989). Office: Arlington County Pub Health Divsn Dept Human Svcs 1800 N Edison St Arlington VA 22207-1938 E-mail: ddownin1@gmu.edu.

DOWNING, JOAN FORMAN, editor, writer; b. Mpls., Nov. 16, 1934; d. W. Chandler and Marie A. (Forster) Forman; children: Timothy Alan, Julie Marie Downing Giesen, Christopher Alan. BA, U. Wis., 1956. Editl. asst. Sci. Research Assocs., Chgo., 1960-61, asst. editor, 1961-63, Childrens Press, Chgo., 1963-66, assoc. editor, 1966-68, mng. editor, 1968-78, editor-in-chief, 1978-81, sr. editor, 1981-95; propr. Downing Pub. Svcs., Evanston, Ill., 1995—. Dir. Chgo. Book Clinic, 1973-75, publicity chmn., 1973-74 Author: (with Eugene Baker) Workers Long Ago, 1968, Baseball Is Our Game, 1982, Junior CB Picture Dictionary, 1978; project editor: 15 vol. Young People's Story of Our Heritage, 1966 (Graphic Arts Council of Chgo. award), 20 vol. People of Destiny (Chgo. Book Clinic award 1967-68), 20 vol. Enchantment of South and Central America, 1968-70, 36 vol. Open Door Books, 1968, 42 vol. Enchantment of Africa, 1972-78, Hobbies for Everyone: Collecting Toy Trains, 1979 (Graphic Arts award Printing Industries Am.), (multi-vol.) World at War, 1980-87, (52 vol.) America the Beautiful, 1987-91, (52 vol.) From Sea to Shining Sea, 1991-95, (multi-vol.) Rookie Read-About Science, 1994-97, (multi-vol.) Cities of the World, 1995-2001, (multi-vol.) Encyclopedia of First Ladies, 1997-2000. Election judge, Cook County (Ill.), 1974—. Mem. Authors Guild, Authors League Am., Alpha Phi. Democrat. Home and Office: 2414 Brown Ave Evanston IL 60201-2526 E-mail: jd2414@aol.com.

DOWNING, JOHN HENRY, columnist, journalist; b. Toronto, Ont., Can., June 10, 1936; s. John H. and Lena (Hoogstad) D.; m. Mary A. Horvat, July 8, 1961; children: John Henry III, Brett, Mark. B in Applied Arts, Ryerson Polytech., 1958; studies, U. Toronto, 1972-73. Editor White Horse Star, Yukon, 1957; reporter Toronto Telegram, 1958-63, asst. city editor, city editor, asst. mng. editor, 1964-71; polit. columnist Toronto Sun, 1971-84, assoc. editor, 1980-84, editor, 1985-97, columnist, 1997—. Co-author: Mayor of all the People, Member for St. Patrick; contbr. chpts. to books, articles to profl. jours. Bd. dirs. Runnymede Hosp., Toronto; life dir. Toronto Outdoor Art Show; life mem. Metro Conservation Authority, Toronto, 1970—; past pres. Can. Nat. Exhbn.; vice-chmn. Exhbn. Pl. Bd.; bd. dirs. Ontario Safety League; active Royal Winter Fair Assn. Recipient 8 column awards Metro Police Assn., 1975—, Priory award St. John's Ambulance, 1983, Svc. medal City of Toronto Coun., 1991, Centennial medal Gov. Gen. of Can., 1993. Mem. Toronto Press Club (past pres.). Baptist. Avocations: swimming, fishing, reading. Office: The Toronto Sun 333 King St E Toronto ON Canada M5A 3X5 E-mail: jhdii@hotmail.com.

DOWNING, LAWRENCE DEWITT, lawyer; b. McPherson, Kans., Aug. 2, 1936; s. Wayne Curtis and Waneta Corinne (DeWitt) D.; m. Kristi Karen Anderson, June 19, 1960 (div. 1983); children: Kyia, Christopher; m. Ann Marie Lucke, June 2, 1985. BS, Iowa State U., 1958; JD, U. Minn. 1962. Bar: Minn. 1962, U.S. Dist. Ct. Minn. 1962, U.S. Supreme Ct. 1978. Chemist Procter & Gamble, Cin., 1958-59; ptnr. O'Brien, Ehrick, Wolf, Deaner & Downing, Rochester, Minn., 1962-90; pvt. practice Rochester, 1990—. Owner Lawrence Downing & Assocs., Rochester, 1990—. Trustee John Muir Trust, U.K., 1988—, Esalen Inst., 2002—; past mem. Minn. Gov.'s Task Force on Environ. Compact of the States; mem. hon. com. Earth Day, 1990; past mem., chmn. subcom. Minn. Gov.'s Task Force on Energy Policy; past mem. Minn. Gov.'s Power Plan Siting Adv. Com., Olmsted County Environ. Quality Commn. Fellow Am. Acad. Matrimonial Lawyers, 1977—; mem. ABA (family law sect.), Minn. Bar Assn. (bd. dirs. family law sect. 1978-79), 3d Dist. Bar Assn., Olmsted County Bar Assn. (pres. 1985-86), Sierra Club (mem. exec. com. 1984-88, 5th officer 1984-85, sec. 1985-86, v.p. for adminstv. law 1988-92, bd. dirs. 1983-89, pres. 1986-88, pres. Sierra Club Found. 1989-92, mem. numerous nat. coms. and task forces). Achievements include co-inventor Mr. Clean liquid cleaner. Office: Lawrence Downing & Assocs 330 Wells Fargo Ctr 21 1st Ave SW Rochester MN 55902 E-mail: LDowning@Downinglaw.net., LDD@LDowning.com.

DOWNING, M. SCOTT, budget systems analyst; b. Enid, Okla., Aug. 20, 1942; s. Kenneth F. and Maurine (Melvin) D.; m. Ina M. Herrington, June 16, 1963; 1 child, Cynthia Ann. BA, Phillips U., 1963; MA, U. Okla., 1966. Cert. data processor Inst. for Cert. of Computer Profls.; cert. disaster recovery planner Disaster Recovery Inst. Internat.; cert. govt. fin. mgr. Assn. Govt. Accts.; cert. office automation profl.; cert. quality anlyst - Baldridge Stds., Quality Assurance Inst.; cert. quality examiner Baldridge standards Quality Assurance Inst. Instr. Am. history U. Md., Zama, Japan, 1967—69; budget analyst U.S. Bur. of Census, Washington, 1969-70, 1966—67, U.S. Food and Nutrition Svc., Washington, 1970—72; budget systems analyst U.S. Dept. of State, Washington, 1972—74; chief, budget execution Fed. Energy Adminstrn., Washington, 1973—77; sr. budget analyst U.S. Dept. of Energy, Washington, 1977-80; contbg. fin. editor Exec. Publs., Washington, 1972-80; mgmt. analyst Gen. Svcs. Adminstrn., Washington, 1980-81, budget systems analyst, 1981-97; bus. mgr. Sew Classy Assocs., Alexandria, Va., 1996—2002; voiceover Say It Again, Scott, 2000—. Guest instr. Civil Svc. Commn., Washington, 1974, Fed. Regional Couns., 1974-77, Exec. Seminar Ctr., Oak Ridge, Tenn., 1975, Internat. APL Conf., Heidelberg, 1982. Author: (books) The TVA and the Courts, 1966, Dollars and Sense, 1975. Sgt. U.S. Army, 1967-69, PTO. Methodist.

DOWNING, MARGARET MARY, newspaper editor; b. Altoona, Pa., June 3, 1952; d. Irvine William and Iva Ann (Regan) D.; m. Gary Beaver; children: Ian Downing-Beaver, Timothy Downing-Beaver, Abby Downing-Beaver. BA magna cum laude, Tex. Christian U., 1974. Reporting intern Corpus Christi Caller Times, 1973; reporter, bur. chief Beaumont (Tex.) Enterprise & Jour., 1974-76, Dallas Times Herald, 1976-80; reporter, asst. city editor, asst. bus., met. editor, mng. editor Houston Post, 1980—93; mng. editor Jackson (Miss.) Clarion-Ledger, 1993-97; editor-in-chief The Houston Press, 1998—. Jurist Pulitzer Prize Awards, 1992, 93; bd. dirs. News Media Credit Union, 1993, Santa's Helpers, 1992-93; mem. admissions com. Assn. Alternative Newspapers, 2000—. Respite foster parent vol. Harris County Children's Protective Svcs., 1993; chmn. landscape com. Windsor Hills Homeowners Assn.; active Madison Sta. Elem. PTA, 1993—98; coach South Madison County Soccer Orgn., 1997—98; mem. runners club YMCA, 1994, mem. activities adv. bd., 1994, youth soccer and t-ball coach; coach Quail Valley Soccer Assn., 1999—; vol. Houston Taping for the Blind, 2000—02; vestry, mem. children's edn. bd. Grace Episcopal Ch.; bd. dirs. Alvin-Manvel Helping Hands Fund, 2001, Leadership Jackson, 1996—98. Recipient Rick Nelson soccer coaching award, 2001. Mem.: Nat. Youth Sports Assn. (cert. coach), Press Club of Houston (pres. 1984, bd. dirs. 1982—85, 2000—), AP Mng. Editors Assn. (2d v.p. La./Miss. chpt. 1995—96, 1st v.p. 1996—97, pres. 1997—98), Quota Club (bd. dirs. 1996—97). Episcopalian. Home: 3215 Breckenridge Ct Missouri City TX 77459-4907 Office: The Houston Press 1621 Milam St Ste 100 Houston TX 77002-8017 E-mail: margaret.downing@houstonpress.com., downingmargaret@hotmail.com.

DOWNING, ROBERT ALLAN, lawyer; b. Kenosha, Wis., Jan. 6, 1929; s. Leo Vertin and Mayme C. (Kennedy) D.; m. JoAnn C. Cramton, Apr. 14, 1951 (div. Sept. 1977); children: Robert A., Kevin C., Tracey Downing Clark, Gregory E.; m. Joan Govan Reiter, Oct. 29, 1977; 1 child, Charles E. Reiter III. BS, U. Wis., 1950, JD, 1956. Bar: Wis. 1956, Ill. 1956, U.S. Supreme Ct. 1965. Assoc. Sidley & Austin, Chgo., 1956-64, ptnr., 1964-94, counsel, 1994-97, Ruff, Weidenaar & Reidy, Ltd., Chgo., 1997—. Trustee (life), former pres. Episcopal Charities and Cmty. Svcs., Chgo. Diocese. Served to lt. USN, 1950-53, Korea. Fellow Am. Coll. Trial Lawyers; mem. ABA, Soc. Trial Lawyers, Ill. Bar Assn., Chgo. Bar Assn., Wis. Bar Assn., 7th Cir. Bar Assn., Union League Club, Law Club, Legal Club, MidDay Club, Westmoreland Country Club. Republican. Episcopalian. Office: Ruff Weidenaar & Reidy Ltd 222 N Lasalle St Ste 1525 Chicago IL 60601-1003

DOWNING, ROBERT JAMES, artist; b. Hamilton, Ont., Can., Aug. 1, 1935; s. Albert James and Dora Florence (Figgins) D.; m. Miriana Kaludjerovic, Sept. 27, 1980; children by previous marriage: Sara Lynn, Michael John. Police constable City of Hamilton, 1957-60. Lectr. U. Toronto, 1967-68; part-time lectr. Fanshawe Coll. Art and Tech., 1969-71, Ont. Coll. Art and Design, 1971-73, 81-82, Banff Ctr. Sch. Fine Art, 1974, Calif. State U., Long Beach, 1974-78, La Salle, Singapore, 1987-88; vis. lectr. Sheridan Coll., Art's Sake, Ont. Coll. Art and Design, Toronto, 1979-80; art program dir. Appleby Coll., Oakville, 1973; prepared, implemented visual and tactile awareness program for secondary sch. art and design tchrs. Molepolole Coll. Edn., Botswana, 1985-86; artist-in-residence Dynamics Graphics Project, U. Toronto, 1997-99. One-man

shows include Dunkelman Gallery, Toronto, Can., 1963, Galerie Agnes Lefort, Montreal, Can., 1968, Whitechapel Art Gallery, London, 1969, York U. Art Gallery, Toronto, 1970, Gallery House Sol, Georgetown, 1971, Robert McLaughlin Gallery, Oshawa, 1972, U. Alta., Can., 1973, Cultural Resources Ctr., Huntington Beach, Calif., 1978, Coll. Pk., Toronto, 1981, A Room in the Artist's Home, Toronto, 1985, Art Gallery Hamilton, 1992, The Japan Found., Toronto, 1997; group exhbns. include Mil. Hdqrs. Bldg., Ottawa, 1956, John Pace Gallery, Laguna Beach, Calif., 1964, Ont. Arts Coun., 1967, Nat. Gallery Can., 1967, Rothmans Art Gallery, 1968, Montreal Mus. Fine Arts, 1968, Richard DeMarco Gallery, Scotland, 1969, middelheim Pk., Belgium, 1971, Arts Coun. Gt. Brit., 1971, Ont. Soc. Artists, 1972, Winnipeg Art Gallery, 1972, Burnaby Art Gallery, B.C., 1973, Centennial Gallery and Libr., Oakville, Ont., 1973, Long Beach Mus. Art, 1976, Smithsonian Inst., 1978, Pollock Gallery, Toronto, 1978, David Mirvish Gallery, Toronto, 1979, Koffler Ctr., Toronto, 1981, Nat. Gallery Botswana, 1986, Singapore Sci. Ctr., 1988; commns. include Jan Wallace Archtl. Offices, Laguna Beach, Calif., 1964, U. Toronto Med. Scis. Bldg., 1967, Mohawk Coll. Art and Tech., Hamilton, 1968, U. Waterloo Student Svds. Bldg., 1971, Sheraton Conv. Ctr., Toronto, 1972, Valley Bank Nev., Las Vegas, 1975, United Gas Pipe Line Co., Houston, 1976, Jefferson Shopping Mall, Louisville, 1978, Westinghouse Can. Ltd., Toronto, 1981, Esso Singapore Pte. Ltd., 1987, Singapore Sci. Ctr., 1988; completed CD Rom of life's work, 1999; represented in pub. collections. Nat. Gallery Can., Art Gallery Ont., U. Western Ont., Agnes Etherington Art Ctr., Ont. Sci. Ctr., Govt. of Ont., Singapore Nat. Theatre Trust, Can. Confedn. Ctr. Cultural rep. Texaco Can., Inc., 1980-81. Photographer with Royal Can. Navy, 1952-57. Served with Royal Can. Navy, 1952—57. Recipient Ont. Arts Coun. award, 1967, 78, 79, Can. Coun. award, 1967—71, 79, 85. Mem. Can. Artists Rep. (founder 1967), Sculpture Soc. Can., Ont. Soc. Artists (exec. coun. 1979-80), Royal Can. Acad. Arts. Died July 22, 2003.

DOWNS, AMY LOUISE, psychologist; b. Glen Cove, N.Y., Nov. 10, 1956; d. Chester and Hannah Jacqueline (Kaufman) Burger; m. Donald Allen Downs, June 27, 1993. BS, U. Iowa, 1979; MA, U. N.C., 1983, PhD, 1987. Lic. psychologist, N.C. Intern in clin. psychology W.S. Hall Psychiat. Inst., Columbia, S.C., 1984-85; staff psychologist John Umstead Hosp., Butner, N.C., 1987-90; sr. psychologist I in tng. Dorothea Dix Hosp., Raleigh, N.C., 1988; sr. psychologist Crossroads Mental Health, Yadkinville, N.C., 1991, cons., 1991-95. Mem. Am. Psychol. Assn., N.C. Psychol. Assn., Phi Beta Kappa.

DOWNS, ANTHONY, urban economist, real estate consultant; b. Evanston, Ill., Nov. 21, 1930; s. James Chesterfield and Florence Glassbrook (Finn) D.; m. Katherine Watson, Apr. 7, 1956 (dec.May 27, 1998); children: Katherine, Christine, Tony, Paul, Carol; m. Darian Olsen, Nov. 6, 1999. BA, Carleton Coll., 1952, LLD (hon.), 2002; MA, PhD, Stanford U., 1956. With Real Estate Rsch. Corp., Chgo., 1959-77, chmn. bd. dirs., 1973-77; asst. prof. econs. and polit. sci. U. Chgo., 1959-62; econ. cons. Rand Corp., Santa Monica, Calif., 1963-65; sr. fellow Brookings Instn., Washington, 1977—. Bd. dirs. NAACP Legal and Ednl. Def. Fund., Inc., Bedford Property Investors, Gen. Growth Properties, Inc.; mem. Nat. Commn. on Urban Problems, 1967—68, Adv. Commn. on Regulatory Barriers to Affordable Housing, 1990—91; adv. bd. Inst. for Rsch. on Poverty, 1970—78. Author: An Econ. Theory of Democracy, 1957, Inside Bureaucracy, 1967, Urban Problems and Prospects, 1970, 2d edit., 1976, Opening Up the Suburbs, 1973, Fed. Housing Subsidies, 1973, Racism in Am., 1970, Neighborhoods and Urban Devel., 1981, Rental Housing in the 1980s, 1983, The Revolution in Real Estate Fin., 1985, Stuck in Traffic, 1992, New Visions for Met. Am., 1994, A Re-Evaluation of Residential Rent Control, 1996, Polit. Theory and Pub. Choice, 1998, Urban Affairs and Urban Policy, 1998; co-author: Urban Decline and the Future of the Am. Cities, 1982, Costs of Sprawl, 2000, 2003; co-editor: Do Housing Allowances Work, 1981, Energy Costs, Urban Devel. and Housing, 1984. Served with USNR, 1956-59. Mem. Am. Econ. Assn., Am. Soc. Real Estate Counselors, Am. Acad. Arts and Scis., Urban Land Inst., Nat. Acad. Pub. Adminstrn., Anglo Am. Real Property Inst., Phi Beta Kappa, Lambda Alpha. Democrat. Roman Catholic. Home: 8483 Portland Pl Mc Lean VA 22102-1730 Office: 1775 Massachusetts Ave NW Washington DC 20036-2103 E-mail: anthonydowns@csi.com.

DOWNS, BERNARD BOOZER, JR., lawyer; b. Montgomery, Ala., Mar. 15, 1950; s. Bernard B. and Sybil (King) D.; m. Carol Cain, May 27, 1972; children— Boozer Downs, III, Leah C. B.A., U. Ala. 1972, J.D., 1976. Bar: Ala. 1976, U.S. Dist. Ct. (no. dist.) Ala. 1976, U.S. Ct. Appeals (5th and 11th cirs.). Ptnr. Davies, Williams & Wallace, Birmingham, Ala., 1976-84, Harris, Evans & Downs, Birmingham, 1984-90; ptnr. Dominick, Fletcher, Yieldings, Wood & Lloyd. Vestryman, jr. warden All Saints Episcopal Ch., Homewood, Ala., 1981-84. Mem. ABA, Ala. Bar Assn., Birmingham Bar Assn. (exec. com., chmn. pub. relations com. 1983-84, chmn. social welfare com. 1981-83), pres.-elect young lawyers sect. 1984-85), Bench and Bar. Club: Magic City Civitan (bd. dirs. 1982-84, treas. 1981). Home: 2428 Kenvil Cir Birmingham AL 35243-2857 Office: 27447 Highway Five Woodstock AL 35188

DOWNS, CLARK EVANS, lawyer; b. Boston, July 30, 1946; s. Willis A. and Josephine Joyce (Evans) D.; m. Emilie Louise Hartnett, Aug. 17, 1968; children: Elizabeth Morgan, Julia Clark. AB in English Lit., Boston U., 1968, JD cum laude, 1973. Bar: Ill. 1973, D.C. 1981. Assoc. Isham Lincoln & Beale, Washington, 1973-80, ptnr., 1981-87, Jones Day, Washington, 1988—. Trustee, sec. Found. Energy Law Jour., Washington, 1989-93; trustee Mt. Ida Coll., Newton Centre, Mass., 1989-98, chair, 1994-98; trustee Nat. Presbyn. Sch., Washington, 1986-90, Nat. Presbyn. Ch., Washington, 1991-93, Chevy Chase Presbyn. Ch., Washington, 1981-84; bd. visitors Boston U. Sch. Law, 2000-02. Fellow Am. Bar Found.; mem. ABA (ho. of dels. 1995-97), Energy Bar Assn. (chmn. program com. 1985-86, bd. dirs. 1986-89), FERC (Practice Procedure Manual editl. adv. bd. 1996—), D.C. Bar (chmn. lawyers counseling com. 1989), Order St. John (serving brother 2000—). Avocations: cello, folk music, choral music. Office: Jones Day 51 Louisiana Ave NW Washington DC 20001-2113

DOWNS, DONALD ALEXANDER, JR., political scientist, educator; b. Toronto, Ont., Can., Dec. 2, 1948; s. Donald Alexander and Mary Jane (Dutton) D.; m. Susan Yeager, Jan. 30, 1971; children: Jacqueline Marie, Alexander Donald. BS, Cornell U., 1971; MS, U. Ill., 1974; PhD, U. Calif., Berkeley, 1983. Vis. lectr. U. Mich., Ann Arbor, 1981; lectr., then asst. prof. U. Notre Dame, Ind., 1981-85; asst. prof. to full prof. polit. sci. U. Wis., Madison, 1985—, Hawkins prof., 1999—. Bd. dirs. J&D Comms., Charlottesville, Va.; lectr. various univs. and other groups, 1985—; pres. Faculty Com. for Acad. Freedom and Rights, Madison, Wis.; cons. Nat. Endowment Humanities; grant cons. U.S. Dept. Edn., 2002; commentator Wis. Pub. Radio, 1986—, nat. and internat. TV and radio appearances, other radio stas., 1985—. Author: Nazis in Skokie: Freedom Community and the First Amendment, 1985 (Anisfield Wolf award, 1986), The New Politics of Pornography, 1989 (Gladys Kammerer award, 1990), More than Victims: Battered Women Syndrome, Society and the Law, 1996, Cornell '69: Liberalism and the Crisis of the American University, 1999; contbr. Leader, free speech and acad. freedom movement, Madison and nat.; mem. fin. com., strategy com. for congl. candidates Amnesty Internat.; mem. state coord. com. McCain Presdl. Race. Recipient Alumnus Achievement award Wayland Acad., 1992, Disting. Tchg. award U. Wis., 1989. Mem.: So. Poverty Law Ctr., Am. Polit. Sci. Assn. Avocations: coaching basketball, playing basketball, literature, politics, business. Home: 1102 Chapel Hill Rd Madison WI 53711-3102 Office: Univ Wis 110 North St Madison WI 53704-4917

DOWNS, FLOELLA MCINTYRE, civic worker, ferry pilot, instructor and flight examiner; b. Selmer, Tenn., Sept. 19, 1921; d. Edward N. and Ella Pearle (Byrd) McIntyre; m. James Harold Downs, May 27, 1946; children: Linda Downs Ulmer, William Edward, James Patrick. BA, LaVerne U., 1969. Flight instr., comml. pilot FAA, Memphis, 1945-46, pilot flight examiner, 1946; owner, mgr. Basic Tutoring Svc., Ventura, Calif., 1982-86. Civil air patrol pilot, 1956-57 Pres. Naval Officer's Wives, Patuxent River, Md., 1957; active charitable orgns., Md., Italy, Ventura, Calif., 1946—; vol. Children's Home Soc., Ventura and Carpenteria, Calif., 1962-70. Ferry pilot WASP, USAF, 1943-44, WWII, 1st lt. USAFR, 1952-56. Mem. AAUW (area rep. community issues VTA 1980-82), Women's Air Force Svc. Pilots, Toastmistress (pres. Ventura 1982-83). Democrat. Avocations: piano, painting, reading, gardening, theater. Home: 751 Montgomery Pl Ventura CA 93004-2169

DOWNS, HARTLEY H., III, chemist; b. Ridgewood, N.J., Oct. 21, 1949; s. Hartley Harrison and Jennie Mae (Smith) D.; m. Cindy Marie Millen, June 19, 1976; children: Kathryn Marie, Jennifer Anne, Susanna Jayne. BS, Grove City Coll., 1971; MS, Indiana U. of Pa., 1973; PhD, W. Va. U., 1978; postgrad., U. Colo., 1976-77. Postdoctoral rsch. assoc. chemistry dept. U. So. Calif., L.A., 1977-78; staff chemist corp. rsch. labs. Exxon Rsch. and Engring. Co., Linden, N.J., 1978-81, Houston, 1981-83, Annandale, N.J., 1983-86; rsch. scientist, surface chemistry and corrosion sci. group supr. Baker Performance Chems., Houston, 1986-91, rsch. mgr., 1991-92, tech. dir., 1992-97; tech. dir. fluids conditioning tech. Baker Petrolite, Houston, 1997—. Contbr. articles to profl. jours., chpt. to book; patentee in field. Recipient Award for Grad. Rsch., Sigma Xi, 1973, Union Carbide award W.Va. U., 1975, Stan Gillman award U. Colo., 1977, Tech. Merit award Baker-Hughes, 1989, 91, 93. Mem. Am. Chem. Soc., Soc. Petroleum Engrs., Offshore Operators Com. (task force on environ. sci.), NACE Internat. (chmn. task force on oil industry biocides 1996—, symposium chmn. mineral scale deposit control in oilfield ops. 1994, 98, chmn. corrosion/94 and corrosion/98 symposia, vice-chmn. microbiol. control in oil industry ops. corrosion/2000 symposium), Phi Lambda Upsilon. Baptist. Office: Baker Petrolite 12645 W Airport Blvd Sugar Land TX 77478 E-mail: hartley.downs@bakerpetrolite.com.

DOWNS, HUGH MALCOLM, radio and television broadcaster; b. Akron, Ohio, Feb. 14, 1921; s. Milton Howard and Edith (Hick) D.; m. Ruth Shaheen, Feb. 20, 1944; children— Hugh Raymond, Deirdre Lynn. Student, Bluffton (Ohio) Coll., 1938-39, Wayne State U., 1940-41, Columbia, 1955-56. Staff announcer radio sta. WLOK, Lima, Ohio, 1939, program dir., 1939-40; staff announcer radio sta. WWJ, Detroit, 1940-42, NBC, Chgo., 1943-54; co-host 20/20 ABC News, 1978-99; with ABCNews.com. Spl. cons. UN on refugee problems Middle East, 1961-64; cons. Center for Study Democratic Instns.; chmn. bd. Raylin Prodns., Inc., 1960— Free-lance radio and TV broadcaster, 1954—; programs include Home Show, 1954-57, Sid Caesar's Hour, 1956-57, Concentration, 1958-68, Jack Paar show Tonight, 1957-62; host: programs include Today Show, 1962-72, TV Mag. of Air 20/20, 1979-99, ABC; PBS daily series Over Easy; author: Fifty to Forever, 1994, Hugh Downs years Book (with Richard J. Roll), 1982, My Ten Thousand Hours on Television, 1986, Yours Truly, Rings Around Tomorrow, A Shoal of Stars, Potential, Thirty Dirty Lies about Old, Perspectives. Chmn. bd. govs. Nat. Space Soc.; chmn. U.S. com. for UNICEF. Office: Care ABCNews com 77 W 66th St New York NY 10023-6201

DOWNS, JON FRANKLIN, drama educator, director, writer; b. Bartow, Fla., Sept. 15, 1938; s. Clarence Curtis and Frankie (Morgan) D. Student, Ga. State Coll., 1956-58; BFA, U. Ga., 1960, MFA, 1969. Drama dir. Ga. Perimeter Coll. (formerly DeKalb Coll.), Clarkston, 1969-99. Dir., author The Beastly Purple Forest (marionettes) U. Ga., 1968, Dracula: A Horrible Musical, DeKalb Coll., 1971; dir. A Streetcar Named Desire, DeKalb, 1974, Brigadoon, DeKalb, 1981, West Side Story, 1983, Amadeus, 1984, Noises Off, 1986, The Three Musketeers, 1988, A Midsummer Night's Dream, 1990, A Little Night Music, 1991, Hamlet, 1993, over 200 others; actor Wedding in Japan, N.Y.C., 1960, Dark at the Top of the Stairs, N.Y.C. and on tour, 1961, A Life in the Theatre, DeKalb Coll., 1981, numerous others; designer Sweeney Todd, DeKalb Coll., 1970, Romulus, 1971; Grass Harp, 1972, A Funny Thing Happened on the Way to the Forum, 1998, many others; writer, dir. plays Tokalitta, Gold!, The Vigil; on tour of Ga. summers 1973-76; author: The Illusionist, 1979, Rapunzel, 1997; film reviewer So. Flair mag., 1994—, arts editor, 2000—. Grantee arts sect. Ga Dept. Planning and Budget, 1973, 74, State Bicentennial Commn., 1975, Nat. Bicentennial Commn., 1975. Mem. Southeastern Theater Conf. (state rep. 1971-73), Ga. Theater Conf. (exec. bd. 1970-73, 79-82). Office: Ste 110-11 403 W Ponce De Leon Ave Decatur GA 30030-2445

DOWNS, KATHLEEN ANNE, health facility administrator; b. Toledo, Sept. 20, 1951; d. Keith Landis and Cecelia Josephine Babcock; m. Michael Brian Thomas, July 17, 1971 (dec. Oct. 1973); m. David Michael Downs, Aug. 8, 1981. Student, San Diego Mesa Coll., 1968—70; BS, Union Inst., 1989. Cert. med. staff coordinator, provider credentialing specialist, profl. healthcare quality. Sec. Travelodge Internat., Inc., El Cajon, Calif., 1970-73; intermediate stenographer City of El Cajon, 1973-77; adminstrv. asst. MacLellan & Assocs., El Cajon, 1977-78; sr. sec. WESTEC Services, Inc., San Diego, 1978; adminstrv. sec. El Cajon Valley Hosp., 1978-80; asst. med. staff Grossmont Dist. Hosp., La Mesa, Calif., 1980-83, coord. med. staff, 1983-87, mgr., 1987-94; mgr. med. staff Sharp Meml. Hosp., San Diego, 1994; dir. med. staff svcs. Sharp HealthCare, San Diego, 1994-96, sr. specialist med. staff svcs., 1996; dir. med. staff svcs. Alvarado Hosp. Med. Ctr. and San Diego Rehab. Inst., San Diego, 1996-99; mgr. med. staff svcs. Kaiser Permanente Hosp., San Diego, 1999-2001, med. staff svcs. cons., 2001—; dir. med. staff svcs. Paradise Valley Hosp., National City, Calif., 2001—. Tchr. The Vogel Inst., San Diego, 1986; mem. med. staff svcs. adv. com. San Diego C.C. Dist.; adj. faculty Union Inst., 1991-96, Chemeketa C.C., 1991-95; credentials verification orgn. surveyor Nat. Com. Quality Assurance, Washington, 1996—. Mem. Nat. Assn. Med. Staff Svcs. (edn. coun. 1989-93, faculty 1990—, chmn. 1991-93, bd. dirs. 1991-93, editl. bd. Over View 1993-96), Calif. Assn. Med. Staff Svcs. (treas. San Diego chpt. 1984-86, pres. 1986-87, state sec. 1999-2001, pres. 2001-03, pres. 2003—). Avocations: organic gardening, boating, gourmet cooking, yoga, reading, fitness walking.

DOWNS, LESLIE G, music educator, musician; b. Shreveport, La., July 21, 1962; s. Karl and Betty Downs. MusB, Centenary Coll., 1980—84; MusM, Yale U., 1985—87. Music tchr. The Berkeley Carroll Sch., Afterschool Program, Bklyn., 1994—, P.S. 41 Afterschool Program, N.Y.C., 1998—; prin. accompanist N.Y.C. Gay Men's Chorus, 1998—. Musician pianist, solo performer. Deacon Pk. Ave. Christian Ch., N.Y.C., 2000—03. Mem.: Music Teachers Nat. Assn. Mem. Christian Ch. Avocations: reading, cooking, crystal collecting, model trains, travel. Personal E-mail: llesismore@cs.com.

DOWNS, PETER CAMPBELL, small business owner; b. St. Johnsbury, Vt., Jan. 21, 1958; s. John Henry and Virginia Campbell Downs; m. Debra Ann McGrenaghan, May 15, 1964; children: Evan Sinclair, Ava Scott. BA, Amherst Coll., 1982. Pres., owner New Wood Co., Bronx, NY, 1982—. Avocations: collecting classic motorcars and motorcycles, running, hiking, gardening, skiing. Home: 740 W End Ave #66 New York NY 10025 Office: New Wood Co 382 Canal Pl Bronx NY 10451

DOWNS, ROBERT WOODWARD, JR., endocrinologist, researcher; b. Pitts., May 7, 1948; s. Robert W. and Nadine D.; m. Carol Hampton, June 22, 1996; children: Robert, William, Matthew Lindley. BS, Duke U., 1970, MD, 1974. Resident medicine Barnes Hosp., St. Louis, 1974-76; rsch. assoc. NIH, Bethesda, Md., 1976-79, clin. assoc., 1979-83; from asst. prof. to prof. Med. Coll. Va., Va. Commonwealth U., Richmond, 1983—96, prof. divsn. endocrinology, 1996—, dir. clin. curriculum, 1992—97, dir. Ctr. Osteoporosis, 1996—. Mem. Alpha Omega Alpha. Office: Va Commonwealth U Sch Medicine PO Box 980111 Richmond VA 23298-0111

DOWNS, THOMAS EDWARD, IV, lawyer; b. South Amboy, N.J., Sept. 27, 1950; s. Thomas Edward III and Theresa Mary (Jaje) D.; m. Marie Popik, Oct. 6, 1979; children: Thomas Edward V, Lauren Ann. BA, St. Peter's Coll., 1972; JD, Seton Hall U., 1975. Bar: N.J. 1975, U.S. Dist. Ct. N.J. 1975, U.S. Dist. Cts. (so. and ea. dists.) N.Y. 1981. Law clk. to presiding judges Middlesex County, N.J., 1975; assoc. Irving Tabman, Old Bridge, N.J., 1975-76; ptnr. Tabman, Downs & McDonnell, Old Bridge, 1976-77, Tabman & Downs, Old Bridge, 1978-82; pvt. practice Old Bridge, 1982—; South Amboy Mcpl. prosecutor, 1977—; Sayreville Mcpl. prosecutor, 1987—90, 1994—2000; Carteret Mcpl. prosecutor, 2002. Atty. Old Bridge Econ. Devel. Bd., 2002—. Sec. South Amboy Shade Tree com., 1974; co-chmn. South Amboy Blood Bank; pres. South Amboy Young Dem. Orgn.; dep. chmn. Sayreville Dem. Orgn., 1992—; bd. dirs. Middlesex County Social Svcs., 2001-. Mem. Assn. Trial Lawyers Am., N.J. State Trial Lawyers Assn., Middlesex County Bar Assn., N.J. State Bar Assn., Lions (pres. South Amboy chpt. 1984). Roman Catholic. Home: 26 Carter Pl Sayreville PO Box Parlin NJ 08859 Office: PO Box 498 Old Bridge NJ 08857-0498

DOWNS, THOMAS K. lawyer; b. New Albany, Ind., Jan. 10, 1949; BA, Ind. U., 1977, JD magna cum laude, 1980. Bar: Ind. 1980. Ptnr., mcpl. fin. chmn. Ice Miller, Indpls. Mem. editl. bd. Mcpl. Fin. Jour., 1999—; editor Fundamentals of Mcpl. Bond Law: General Law and Professional Responsibility sects., 1994—; exec. editor Ind. Law Jour., 1979-80; contbr. articles to profl. jours. Pres. Ind. Assn. Cities and Towns Found., 1994—; mem. Lt. Gov.'s Jobs Coun. Fellow Am. Coll. Bond Counsel (founding mem., govt. rels. com., co-chmn. bond buyer midwest pub. fin. conf. 1998); mem. Nat. Assn. Bond Lawyers (steering com. 1985-86, 90, 92, 2000, 01, 02, chmn. bond banks workshop 1985-86, tax increment workshop 1989, panelist various workshops, faculty fundamentals mcpl. bond law, opinions and profl. responsibility 1989-90, chair Ann. Washington Conf. 1996, chmn. prof. responsibility com. 2001-03), Ind. Continuing Legal Edn. Forum (chmn. mcpl. law seminars 1984-92, practical impact tax reform act of 1986, panelist mcpl. utility fin. 1988, pub. law 10 1991), Ind. Mcpl. Lawyers Assn., Inc. (bd. dirs. 1983—), Order of Coif, Assn. Ind. Counties (adv. com., gen. counsel), Ind. Assn. Cities and Towns (exec. com., special counsel), Ind. Comn. for the Purchase of Products and Svcs. of Persons with Disabilities (bd. dirs.). Office: Ice Miller Box 82001 1 American Sq Indianapolis IN 46282-0020 E-mail: downs@icemiller.com.

DOWNS, WILLIAM MURRAY, political scientist, educator, researcher; b. Raleigh, NC, Nov. 4, 1966; s. Murray Scott and Virginia Craig Downs; m. Kimberly Harwood, Aug. 5, 1989; children: Rachel Elizabeth, Bradley Craig. BA, NC State U., 1988; MA, Emory U., 1990, PhD, 1994. Vis. prof. and rschr. Odense U., Denmark, 1994—95; vis. prof. of polit. sci. Aarhus Univesity, Denmark, 1995—96, Emory U., Atlanta, 1996—97; prof. of polit. sci. Ga. State U., Atlanta, 1997—. Fulbright fellow Coun. for Internat. Ednl. Exch., Brussels, 1992—93; fellow Belgian-American Ednl. Found., 1992—93; predoctoral fellow Harvard U. Ctr. for European Studies, 1993—94. Author: (research book) Coalition Government Subnational Style: Multiparty Politics in Europe's Regional Parliaments; contbr. articles to profl. jours. Danish Vis. Scientist fellowship program, Danish Rsch. Acad., 1994—95, Hewlett Rsch. Assistantship, African Governance Program Project on Comparative Democratization, Carter Ctr., 1990—91. Mem.: Am. Polit. Sci. Assn., Sigma Iota Rho. Office: Georgia State University Dept of Polit Sci Atlanta GA 30303 Office Fax: 404-651-1434. E-mail: polwmd@panther.gsu.edu.

DOWS, DAVID ALAN, chemistry educator; b. San Francisco, July 25, 1928; s. Samuel Randall and Rita M. (Bowers) D.; m. Wena Hunt Waldner, July 29, 1950; children— Janet Louise, Carol Marie, Joyce Ellen. BS, U. Calif. at Berkeley, 1952, PhD, 1954. Instr. chemistry Cornell U., 1954-56; instr. U. So. Calif., Los Angeles, 1956-57, asst. prof., 1957-59, assoc. prof., 1959-63, prof. chemistry, 1963—, chmn. dept., 1966-72; NATO prof., 1970. Contbr. articles profl. jours. NSF fellow, 1962-63 Mem. Am. Chem. Soc., Am. Phys. Soc., Phi Beta Kappa. Office: U So Calif Dept Chemistry University Park Los Angeles CA 90089-0482 E-mail: dows@usc.edu.

DOWSETT, PETER JOHN, retired obstetrician, gynecologist; b. Portland, Oreg., 1936; BS in Gen. Sci., Lewis and Clark Coll., 1960; MD, U. Oreg., 1965. Diplomate Am. Bd. Ob-Gyn. Intern Valley Med. Ctr., Fresno, Calif., 1965-66; resident in ob-gyn. Emanuel Hosp., Portland, 1967—71, now mem. staff; pvt. practice, Portland, 1971—. Beaverton, Oreg.; ret., 1998. Mem. staff St. Vincent Hosp., Portland, Good Samaritan Hosp., Portland. Mem. AMA, Pacific N.W. Ob-Gyn. Soc., Oreg. Med. Assn., Org. Ob-Gyn Soc.

DOWTY, ALAN KENT, political scientist, educator; b. Greenville, Ohio, Jan. 15, 1940; s. Paul Willard and Ethel Lovella (Harbaugh) D.; m. Nancy Ellen Gordon, Sept. 8, 1961 (div. 1972); children: Merav Aurli, Tamar Eliea, Gidon Yair; m. Gail Gaynell Schupack, Jan. 1, 1973; children: Rachel Miriam, Rafael Jonathan; 1 stepchild, David Freeman. BA, Shimer Coll., 1959; MA, U. Chgo., 1960, PhD, 1963. Lectr. Hebrew U., Jerusalem, 1965-72, sr. lectr., 1972-75; assoc. prof. U. Notre Dame, Ind., 1975-78, prof. polit. sci., 1978—; Kahanoff chair Israeli studies U. Calgary, 2003—. Exec. dir. Leonard Davis Inst., Jerusalem, 1972-74; editl. bd. Middle East Rev., N.Y.C., 1977-90; project dir. Twentieth Century Fund, N.Y.C., 1983-85; reporter experts meeting Internat. Inst. Human Rights, Strasbourg, France, 1989. Author: The Limits of American Isolation, 1971, Middle East Crisis, 1984 (Quincy Wright award 1985), The Arab-Israel Conflict (with others), 1984, Closed Borders, 1987, The Jewish State, 1998; book reviewer Jerusalem Post, 1964-75; contbr. numerous articles to topical publs. Exec. com. Am. Profs. for Peace in Mid. East, 1976-90; witness U.S. Senate Fgn. Rels. Com., Washington, 1976; nat. adv. com. Union of Couns. for Soviet Jews, Washington, 1980-91. Woodrow Wilson fellow, 1959-60; Rothschild fellow Hebrew U., 1963-64; resident fellow Adlai Stevenson Inst., Chgo., 1971-72; Skirball fellow Oxford Ctr. for Hebrew and Jewish Studies, 2000; recipient Charles W. Ramsdell award So. Hist. Assn., 1966; grantee Twentieth Century Fund, N.Y.C., 1983. Mem. Am. Polit. Sci. Assn., Internat. Polit. Sci. Assn., Internat. Studies Assn. (exec. com. 1977-79, Quincy Wright award 1985), Assn. Israel Studies (v.p. 2003—). Jewish. Avocations: travel, jewish studies. Office: U Notre Dame 313 Hesburgh Ctr Notre Dame IN 46556-5677 E-mail: dowty.1@nd.edu.

DOWTY, MARCUS DUAINE, music educator; MusB, Wichita State U., 1972; M Liberal Arts, Baker U., 2003. With Sumner Acad., Kans. City, Kans. Composer: (albums) 22 works published with RBC/Wynn Music, 2 with Fountain Park Music. Mem.: Musician's Union, Kans. Music Edn. Assn., Kans. Am. String Tchrs. Assn.

DOX, IDA, author, medical illustrator; b. Honduras, Central America, July 8, 1927; came to U.S. 1947; d. John and Catherine (Headman) D.; m. B. John Melloni; children: H. Paul, June L., Peter J., Roy G. BFA, Newcomb Coll., New Orleans, 1950; MS, Johns Hopkins U., 1954; PhD, U. Md., 1990. Med. illustrator Georgetown U. Med. Ctr., Washington, 1954-69; med. illustrator select com. on assassinations of J.F. Kennedy and Martin Luther King, Jr. of U.S. Ho. of Reps, Washington, 1978-79; med. illustrator/author Bethesda, Md., 1969—. Author: Melloni's Illustrated Medical Dictionary, 1979 (Best Med. Book award 1979), Diccionario Medico Illustrado de Melloni, 1983, The HarperCollins Illustrated Medical Dictionary, 1993, Melloni's Illustrated Review of Human Anatomy, 1988 (award of excellence 1989), Attorney's Illustrated Medical Dictionary, 1995, Melloni's Student Atlas of Human Anatomy, 1997, Melloni's Illustrated Dictionary of Obstetrics and Gynecology, 1999; contbr. articles to profl. jours. Recipient L.S. Neill prize, Newcomb Coll., 1949, E. Woodward Meml. prize, 1950, Indsl. Graphics Internat. award, 1977. Address: 9308 Renshaw Dr Bethesda MD 20817-2228

DOYAL, LINDA E. clinical pharmacist; b. Villa Rica, Ga., Sept. 10, 1957; d. Wilbur Joe and Charlotte Maize (Moon) D. BS in Pharmacy with honors, U. Ga., 1980; PharmD with honors, Med. U. S.C., 1983. Registered pharmacist, Ga., Tenn. Staff pharmacist Parkway Regional Hosp., Lithia Springs, Ga., 1980-81; faculty Coll. Pharmacy U. Ga., 1983-84; pharmacy dir. HCA Parthenon Pavilion, Nashville, 1987-88, dir. pharmacy, 1988—. Cons. in field. Contbr. articles to profl. jours. Mem.: Tenn. Pharm. Assn. Avocations: needlework, gardening, photography. Office: Centennial Parthenon Pavilion 2401 Parman Pl Nashville TN 37203-1518

DOYEL, CINDY MARIE, information systems specialist; b. Stockton, Calif., Dec. 1, 1964; d. Nathan Cameron Doyel and Charlotte Blanche (Epler) Gezi. Student, Calif. State U., Sacramento, 1982-83; AA, MTI Bus. Coll., Sacramento, 1984. Supr. All Am. Mini Storage, Sacramento, 1988-89; mng. contr. The Royce Cos., Roseville, Calif., 1990-93; contr. Calif. Comml., Sacramento, 1993-95; gen. ptnr., operator Sierra Micro, Fair Oaks, Calif., 1995-98; help desk analyst Shared Med. Sys., Sacramento, Calif., 1998-99; info. tech. specialist Legis. Data Ctr., Sacramento, Calif., 1999—. Mem.: NAFE, NOW. Presbyterian. Avocations: writing, reading, waterpolo, swimming, softball. Office: Legis Data Ctr 1100 J St Ste 200 Sacramento CA 95814-2827

DOYLE, ANTHONY PETER, lawyer; b. Washington, July 13, 1953; s. Francis X. and Anna (Klekotka) D.; m. Maria H. Duda, Aug. 13, 1977; children: Jeffrey Anthony, Joseph Edward, Natalie Maria, Andrew Michael. AA, Berkshire Community Coll., Pittsfield, Mass., 1972-75; BS magna cum laude, Worcester State Coll., 1977; JD, Western New Eng. Coll., 1980. Bar: Mass. 1980; U.S. Dist. Ct. Mass. 1981; U.S. Ct. Appeals (1st cir.) 1981, U.S. Supreme Ct. 1999. Pvt. practice, Pittsfield, 1980-84; ptnr. Doyle & Cormier, Pittsfield, 1985-88, Barry, Doyle & Cormier, Pittsfield, 1989, Barry & Doyle, Pittsfield, 1989—. Pres. Hospice of Cen. Berkshire, Pittsfield, 1988-90; v.p. HospiceCare of the Berkshires, Pittsfield, 1990-92, pres. 1992-2002; bd. dirs. Dalton (Mass.) Youth Ctr., 1986-89, Community Recreation Assn., Dalton, 1989-95; exec.

com. Appalachian Trails Dist. Boy Scouts Am., Dalton, 1989-96; mem. Zoning Bd. Appeals, Dalton, 1995—, chmn., 1997—, Dalton Coun Aging, 1997 . Recipient commendation Western Mass. Pro Bono Referral Svc., 1983-87. Mem. Mass. Bar Assn., Berkshire Bar Assn. (exec. com. 1989-91, v.p. 1997-99res. 1999-2001). Roman Catholic. Avocations: skiing, tennis. Home: 108 Barton Hill Rd Dalton MA 01226-2005 Office: Barry & Doyle 8 Bank Row Ste 2 Pittsfield MA 01201-6224

DOYLE, CONSTANCE TALCOTT JOHNSTON, physician, educator, medical association administrator; b. Mansfield, Ohio, July 8, 1945; d. Frederick Lyman IV and Nancy Jean Bushnell (Johnston) Talcott; children: Ian Frederick Demsky, Zachary Adam Demsky. BS, Ohio U., 1967; MD, Ohio State U., 1971. Diplomate Am. Bd. Emergency Medicine; bd. cert. in emergency crisis response. Intern Riverside Hosp., Columbus, Ohio, 1971-72; resident in internal medicine Hurley Hosp., U. Mich., Flint, 1972-74; emergency physician Oakwood Hosp., Dearborn, Mich., 1974-76, Jackson County (Mich.) Emergency Svcs., 1975-95; cons. Region II EMS, 1978-79, disaster cons., 1983-95; St. Joseph Mercy Hosp., Ann Arbor, 1995—, med. flight physician helicopter life support svcs., 1996-2000; core faculty St. Joseph Merch Hosp./U. Mich. Emergency Residency, Ann Arbor, 1995—; survival flight physician helicopter rescue svc. U. Mich., 1983-91; course dir. advanced cardiac life support and chmn. advanced life support com. W.A. Foote Meml. Hosp., Jackson, 1979-95; dep. dir. emergency svcs. med. ctrl. bd. Washtenaw Livingston County, 2000—; core faculty St. Joseph Mercy Hosp., Ann Arbor, 1996. Clin. instr. emergency svcs., dept. surgery U. Mich., 1981—; faculty combined emergency medicine residency St. Joseph Mercy Hosp.-U. Mich., Ann Arbor, 1995—; asst. med. dir. Region 2 South Biodef. Network, 2002-03, co-med. dir., 2003—; instr. EMT refresher courses, Jackson County, Jackson C.C.; MedFlight physician, 1996-99; Washtenaw County Subcom. on Bioterrorism, 2000—; Washtenaw County Local Emergency Planning Com., 1998—; dep. med. dir. Washtenaw/Livingston County Med. Control Authority, 2000—. Contbg. author: Clinical Approach to Poisoning and Toxicology, 1983, 89, 97, May's Textbook of Emergency Medicine, 1991, Schwartz Principles and Practice of Emergency Medicine, 1992, Reisdorff Pediatric Emergency Medicine, 1993; contbr. articles to profl. jours. Mem. local emergency planning com. Washtenaw County, 1999—, mem. subcom. on bioterrorism, 2000—; asst. med. dir. Region 2S Biodefense Network, 2002, co med. dir., 2003—; mem. Disaster Med. Assistance Team, 2000—. Fellow Am. Coll. Emergency Physicians (pres. Mich. disaster com. 1987-88, bd. dirs. Mich. 1979-88, chmn. Mich. disaster com. 1979-85, mem. nat. disaster med. svcs. com. 1983-85, chmn. 1987-88, cons. disaster mgmt. course Fed. Emergency Mgmt. Agy. 1982, treas. 1984-85, emergency med. svcs. com. 1985, pres. 1986-87, councillor 1986-87, chair steering com. policy sect., 1994—, mem. disaster sect., 1995—, exec. com. disaster sect. 1997—, chair policy sect. disaster 1995—, vice chair sect. careers in emergency medicine 1997—, chair, 2000—), Nat. Assn. Coll. Emergency Physicians (vice chair sect. of disaster med. svcs. 1990-92, nat. disaster subcom. 1989-90, chair subsect. psychol. rehab. svcs., disaster med. svcs. 1992-94, chair policy and legis. 1994-96, task force on hazardous materials 1993—, steering com. sect. disaster medicine 1994—, exec. com. sect. disaster medicine 1995); mem. ACP, Am. Med. Women's Assn., Am. Assn. Women Emergency Physicians, Mich. Assn. Emergency Med. Technicians (bd. dirs. 1979-80), Mich. State Med. Soc., Washtenaw County Med. Soc., Sierra Club. Jewish. Office: 1251 King George Blvd Ann Arbor MI 48108 also: St Joseph Mercy Hosp Dept Emergency Medicine Ann Arbor MI 48109

DOYLE, DAVID PERRIE, lawyer; b. Orange, N.J., May 11, 1960; s. Ralph Thomas and Dorothy (Trevorrow) D.; m. Ana Linda Day, Mar. 7, 1987. BA, Emory U., 1982; JD, Rutgers U., 1985; LLM in Taxation, N.Y.U., 1990. Bar: N.J. 1986, U.S. Dist. Ct. N.J. 1986, U.S. Tax Ct. 1988, U.S. Dist. Ct. (so. dist.) N.Y. 1998. Law clk. to presiding judge Tax Ct. N.J., Trenton, 1985-86; assoc. Pitney, Hardin, Kipp & Szuch, Morristown, N.J., 1986-92, counsel, 1993-94, ptnr., 1995—. Mem. ABA (tax sect., mem. employee benefits com.), N.J. State Bar Assn. (tax sect., past chair employee benefits com.). Office: Pitney Hardin Kipp & Szuch LLP PO Box 1945 Morristown NJ 07962-1945 E-mail: ddoyle@pitneyhardin.com.

DOYLE, DELORES MARIE, retired principal; b. Madison, S.D., July 24, 1939; d. Martin N. and Pearl M. (Anderson) Berkelo; m. Patrick J. Doyle; children: Kathleen, Shawn, Tamara, Timothy. AS, Dakota State Coll., Madison, 1959; BS, Mid. Tenn. State U., 1966, MEd, 1968, EdS, 1975; PhD, Peabody/Vanderbilt U., 1980. Cert. career ladder III tchr. Tchr. 4th grade Meriden-Cleghorn Schs., Meriden, Iowa, 1960-62; tchr. 1st grade Hanover (Ill.) Sch., 1963-66; tchr. 2d grade Hobgood Sch., Murfreesboro, Tenn., 1969-70; tchr. 1st grade Reeves-Rogers Sch., Murfreesboro, 1972-80, tchr. 2d grade, 1981-97, prin., 1997-2000; ret., 2000. Cooperating tchr. Mid. Tenn. State U. Student Tchrs., Murfreesboro, 1972—97, mem. task force edn., 1992—93; summer sch. dir. Murfreesboro City Schs., 1986—98; lead project tutor Reeves-Rogers Sch., Murfreesboro, 1987—90. Active Edn. 2000 Com., Murfreesboro C. of C., 1993; trustee Mid Tenn State U. Found., 1995—2001; bd. dirs. Grace Luth. Ch., Murfreesboro, 1991—93, 2001—03, mem. choir, 1975—. Named Career Ladder III Tchr., Dept. Edn., Nashville, 1984; named to Tenn. Tchrs. Hall of Fame, 2001; recipient Tenn. Tchr. of the Yr. award, Dept. Edn., Nashville, 1992, Murfreesboro City Tchr. of the Yr. award, Murfreesboro City Schs., 1991, Mid-Cumberland Dist. Tchr. of the Yr. award, Dist. Dept. Edn., 1991, Trailblazer award, 1995; Creative Tchg. grantee, State Dept. Edn., 1992, 1993. Mem.: Murfreesboro Edn. Assn. (pres. 1981—82), Tenn. Edn. Assn. (Disting. Classroom Tchr. award 1992, Disting. Adminstr. award 2000), Tenn. State Tchr. of Yr. Orgn. (v.p. 2000—), Nat. State Tchr. of Yr. Orgn., Kappa Delta Pi, Delta Kappa Gamma. Democrat. Avocations: bridge, travel, reading, bicycling. Home: 1710 Sutton Pl Murfreesboro TN 37129-6513 E-mail: pandddoyle@comcast.net.

DOYLE, DENNIS T. lawyer; b. White Plains, N.Y., Apr. 9, 1943; BA, Boston Coll., 1965; JD, Fordham U., 1968. Bar: N.Y. State 1968, U.S. Dist. Ct. (so. and ea. dists.) N.Y. 1978, U.S. Supreme Ct. 1978. Ptnr. O'Connor, McGuiness, Conte, Doyle & Oleson, White Plains, 1969—. Author: You Haven't Got a Prayer. Mem. ABA, Am. Trial Lawyers Assn., N.Y. State, Fedn. Ins. and Corp. Counsel, Trial Lawyers Assn., Appalachian Mountain Club, Adirondeck Mountain Club, Adirondeck Coun. Avocations: bicycling, religious education, hiking, golf. Office: O'Connor McGuiness Conte Doyle & Oleson One Barker Ave Ste 675 White Plains NY 10601-1517 Fax: 914 948-0645. E-mail: ddoyle@omcdoc.com.

DOYLE, DONALD VINCENT, retired state senator, lawyer; b. Sioux City, Iowa, Jan. 13, 1925; s. William E. and Nelsine E. (Sparby) D.; m. Jant E. Holtz, Aug. 9, 1963; 1 child, Dawn Renee. BS, Morningside Coll., Sioux City, 1951; JD, U. S.D., 1953. Bar: S.D. 1953, Iowa 1953. Pvt. practice, Sioux City, 1953—; mem. Iowa Ho. of Reps., 1956-80, Iowa Senate, 1981-93, chmn. judiciary com., 1982-90. Mem. law and justice com. Nat. Conf. State Legis., 1987-89, chmn., 1988-89; chmn. Iowa Boundary Commn., 1991, 92; mem. Commn. Accreditation Law Enforcement Agys., Inc., 1988-95. With USAF, 1943—46. Recipient award Woodbury County Peace Officers, 1974, Restoration Club Sioux City, 1964, Outstanding Elected Ofcl. award Iowa Corrections Assn., 1979. Mem. Iowa Bar Assn., S.D. Bar Assn. (50-Yr. plaque 2003), Woodbury County Bar Assn., CBI Vets. Assn. (past nat. judge adv., Iowa comdr. 1965), Am. Legion, VFW (comdr. post 1997-2001), DAV, 40 and 8 (chef de gare 1999-2001). Office: PO Box 941 Sioux City IA 51102-0941 E-mail: sendvdoyle@aol.com.

DOYLE, EUGENIE FLERI, pediatric cardiologist, educator; b. Bklyn., Oct. 19, 1921; d. Paul Charles and Antoinette (Giovannetti) Fleri; m. Joseph Anthony Doyle, Aug. 19, 1944; children: Christopher, Stephen, Eugenie, Jane Marie, Richard. BS, Marymount Coll., Tarrytown, N.Y., 1943, DSc (hon.), 1993; MD, Johns Hopkins U., 1946; DSc (hon.), Coll. New Rochelle, 1975. Intern in pediatrics Johns Hopkins Hosp., Balt., 1946-47; pediatric resident Bellevue Hosp., N.Y.C., 1947-49; fellow pediatric cardiology NYU Med. Ctr., 1949-53, dir. pediatric cardiology, 1958-93; asst. prof. pediatrics NYU Sch. Medicine, 1953-58, assoc. prof., 1959-70, prof., 1970-92, prof. emerita, 1993—, clin. prof. pediatrics, 1994—. Mem. cardiac adv. com. N.Y. State Health Dept., 1983-92; dir. Vis. Nurse Svc., N.Y.C., 1984—. Editor: Pediatric Cardiology, 1985; contbr. articles to profl. jours. Trustee Marymount Coll., 1983-91, vice chair bd., 1988 91. Mem. Am. Acad. Pediatrics, Am. Pediatric Soc., Am. Coll. Cardiology, Am. Heart Assn., N.Y. Heart Assn. (bd. dirs. 1977-84, pres. 1979-81), Cosmopolitan Club. Roman Catholic. Avocations: gardening, travel, ballet. Home: 32 Washington Sq W New York NY 10011-9156 Office: NYU Med Ctr 550 1st Ave New York NY 10016-6402

DOYLE, FREDERICK JOSEPH, retired government research scientist; b. Oak Park, Ill., Apr. 3, 1920; s. John Frederick and Mary Elizabeth (Meyers) D.; m. Mary Blaskovich, June 18, 1955; children: Frederick J., Margaret, Mary Ellen, George. BCE, Syracuse U., 1951; postgrad., Internat. Tng. Ctr. Aerial Sur, Delft, The Netherlands, 1952; D Eng (hon.), Tech. U., Hannover, Germany, 1976; DSc (hon.), Ohio STate U., 1986, U. Bordeaux, France, 1987; D in Tech., Royal Tech. U., Sweden, 1987. Assoc. prof. geodetic sci. Ohio State U., 1952-60, chmn. dept., 1959-60; chief scientist Raytheon Autometric Co., Alexandria, Va., 1960-69; sci. advisor nat. mapping divsn. U.S. Geol. Survey, Reston, Va., 1969-89, dir. earth resources observation sys. program, 1978-80; ret., 1989. Geodesy cartography adv. com. nat. Acad. Scis., 1967-69; chmn. Apollo orbital Sci. photo team NASA, 1969-73, planetary cartography com., 1974-95; exec. com. divsn. earth sci. NRC, 1973-76. With C.E., AUS, 1943-48, PTO. Recipient Meritorious Svc. award Dept. Interior, 1977, Disting. Svc. medal, 1981, Silver medal City of Paris, 1978; Fulbright fellow Internat. Tng. Ctr. Aerial Survey, 1952, Internat. Tng. Ctr. fellow, 1986. Fellow AAAS; mem. NAE, Internat. Soc. Photogrammetry Remote Sensing (hon., pres. 1980-84, Brock award 1984), Am. Congress Surveying Mapping, Am. Geophys. Union, Am. Soc. Photogrammetry (hon., pres. 1969-70, contbg. author, editor publs., Fairchild Photogrammetric award 1968, Alan Gordon award 1985, Chancellors medal U.Calif. Santa Barbara 2000). Home: 1591 Forest Villa Ln Mc Lean VA 22101-4132

DOYLE, GERARD FRANCIS, lawyer; b. Needham, Mass., Oct. 25, 1942; s. John Patrick and Catherine Mary (Lawler) D.; m. Paula Marie Dervay, may 14, 1983; children: Laura Dervay, Meredith Lawler, Philip John. BS in Indsl. Adminstrn., Yale U., 1966; JD, Georgetown U., 1972. Bar: D.C. 1973, U.S. Dist. Ct. D.C. 1973, U.S. Ct. Fed. Claims 1976, U.S. Ct. Appeals (fed. cir.) 1982, U.S. Supreme Ct. 1982, Va. 2000. Group head for operating submarine reactors and reactor tech Div. Naval Reactors AEC, Washington, 1970-72; atty. Morgan, Lewis & Bockius, Washington, 1972-76; legal counsel Am. Nuclear Energy Coun., Washington, 1975-76; ptnr. Cotten, Day & Doyle, Washington, 1976-87, Doyle & Savit, Doyle, Simmons & Bachman, Doyle & Bachman LLP, Washington, 1987-99, Arlington, Va., 1999—. Legal counsel Assn. Fed. Data Peripheral Suppliers, Washington, 1979; dir. M Internat., Inc.; author and lectr. in field; columnist Federal Computer Week, 1989. Served in USN, 1966-71. Recipient outstanding young man of yr. award, 1976. Mem. ABA (coun. publ. contract law sect. 1989-92), D.C. Bar Assn., Fed. Bar Assn., Am. Arbitration Assn. (panel arbitrators), Nat. Contract Mgmt. Assn., Met. Club (Washington), Yale Club (Washington), Washington Golf & Country Club. Republican. Roman Catholic. Home: 901 Whann Ave Mc Lean VA 22101-1570 Office: Doyle & Bachman LLP 4245 Fairfax Dr Arlington VA 22203-1637 E-mail: gdoyle@doylebachman.com.

DOYLE, GILLIAN, actress; b. Maidenhead, Berkshire, Eng. came to U.S., 1977; d. John Joseph and Joan (Walker) D. BA in Theatre magna cum laude, Am. U., Washington, 1981. Appeared in (off Broadway) Ernest in Love, NYC, 1980; (plays) No Exit, Washington, 1985, Fefu and Her Friends, 1985, The Winters Tale, 1987, A Christmas Carol, 1987, Erpingham Camp, 1989, Turn of the Screw, 1989, Season's Greetings, 1986, Terra Nova, 1987, Mountain, 1990, Old Favorites, 1991, What the Butler Saw, 1993, Fawlty Towers, 1994, Last of the Red Hot Lovers, 1995, The Musical Comedy Murders of 1940, 1996, Move Over Mrs. Markham, 1997, Declarations: Love Letters of the Great Romantics, 1998, Present Laughter, 1999, Two, 1999, U.S.A., 2000, Blithe Spirit, 2002, A Midsummer Night's Dream, 2002, What The Butler Saw, 2003; (musical) The Cradle Will Rock, 2001; (films) Chances Are, 1989, Born Yesterday, 1993, North, 1993, Decade of Love, 1994, Wild Bill, 1994, The Tie That Binds, 1995, Independence Day, 1996, Play Me Again Sam, 1999, Love, 2000; (TV) Ancient Prophecies III, 1995, Friends, 1995, The Martin Short Show, 1995, Days of Our Lives, 1996, Love's Deadly Triangle: The Texas Cadet Murder, 1996, General Hospital, 1997, Port Charles, 1999, The Man Show, 1999, Titus, 2001; (music video) Johnny Sportcoat and the Casuals, 1987; (comml.) United Way, 1988. Mem. SAG, AFTRA, Actors Equity Assn., Phi Kappa Phi. Democrat. Roman Catholic. Avocations: equestrienne, golf, swimming, music, philosophy, scuba diving (cert.). E-mail: gilliandoyle@hotmail.com.

DOYLE, IRENE ELIZABETH, electronic sales executive, nurse; b. West Point, Iowa, Oct. 5, 1920; d. Joseph Deidrich and Mary Adelaide (Groene) Schulte; m. William Joseph Doyle, Feb. 3, 1956. RN, Mercy Hosp., 1941. Courier nurse Santa Fe R.R., Chgo., 1947-50; indsl. nurse Montgomery Ward, Chgo., 1950-54; rep. Hornblower & Weeks, Chgo., 1954-56; v.p. William J. Doyle Co., Chgo., 1956-80, Ormond Beach, Fla., 1980-88. Served with M.C., U.S. Army, 1942-46. Mem. Electronic Reps. Assn. Republican. Roman Catholic. Club: Oceanside Country (Ormond Beach).

DOYLE, JAMES E(DWARD), governor; b. Washington, Nov. 23, 1945; s. James E. and Ruth (Bachhuber) Doyle; m. Jessica Laird, Dec. 21, 1966; children: Augustus, Gabriel. Student, Stanford U., 1963—66; AB in History, U. Wis., 1967; JD cum laude, Harvard U., 1972. Bar: Ariz. 1973, Wis. 1975, U.S. Dist. Ct. N.Mex. 1973, U.S. Dist. Ct. Ariz. 1973, U.S. Dist. Ct. Utah 1973, U.S. Dist. Ct. (we. dist.) Wis. 1975, U.S. Dist. Ct. (ea. dist.) Wis. 1976, U.S. Ct. Appeals (10th cir.) 1974, U.S. Ct. Appeals (7th cir.) 1985, U.S. Supreme Ct. 1989. Vol. Peace Corps, Tunisia, 1967—69; atty. DNA Legal Svcs., Chinle, Ariz., 1972—75; ptnr. Jacobs & Doyle, Madison, Wis., 1975—77; dist. atty. Dane County, Madison, 1977—83; ptnr. Doyle & Ritz, Madison, 1983—90; of counsel Lawton & Cates, Madison, 1990—91; atty. gen. State of Wis., Madison, 1991—2002, gov., 2003—. Mem.: ABA, 7th Cir. Bar Assn. (chmn. criminal law sect. 1988—89), Wis. Bar Assn. (bd. dirs. criminal law sect. 1988). Democrat. Roman Catholic. Office: Office of the Governor 115 E State Capitol Madison WI 53702*

DOYLE, JENNIFER, surgical educator, scholar; b. Milw., Aug. 23, 1952; d. Sylvester Edward and Ethel Anna (Axmann) D. BA, Mt. Mary Coll., 1974; MA, U. Wis., Milw., 1979; postgrad., Brown U., 1979-84, Boston Coll., 2000—. Grad. tchg. asst. U. Wis., 1977-79; fellow Brown U., Providence, 1979-80, grad. teaching asst., 1981-84; adj. instr. Bryant Coll., Smithfield, R.I., 1985; adj. instr. history R.I. Coll., Providence, 1986-90; residency coord. dept. family medicine Brown U., Providence, 1986-87, edn. coord. dept. surgery, 1987-90; assoc. surgery Harvard Med. Sch., Boston, 1990-92, lectr. in surgery, 1992—; asst. dir. surg. edn. Deaconess Hosp., Boston, 1990-96; dir. ednl. devel. and evaluation Beth Israel Deaconess Med. Ctr., Boston, 1996—. Mem. instnl. assessment com. Sch. Medicine Brown U., 2000; inst. scholar Carl. J. Shapiro Inst. for Edn. and Rsch., Boston, 2000—. Dem. committeeman, Wauwatosa, Wis., 1976 78; mem. Big Sisters of R.I., Providence, 1980-88; co-organizer Providence Freeze Coalition, 1982; mem. instnl. assessment com. Brown U. Sch. Medicine, 2000-01. Recipient Charles Edison Meml. fellowship, 1974, Lucetta Bissell Meml. fellowship, 1978, univ. fellowship Brown U., 1979, Wayland Collegium fellowship Brown U., 1988. Mem. Am. Ednl. Rsch. Assn., Assn. Am. Med. Colls., Assn. Surg. Edn., Assn. Program Dirs. in Surgery (assoc.), Assn. of Women Surgeons (assoc.), Assn. for Study of Med. Edn. (U.K.), Generalists in Med. Edn., Am. Evaluation Assn., AAUW, Mass. Consort. on Faculty Devel. Home: 219 Willow St West Roxbury MA 02132-1326 Office: Beth Israel Deaconess Med Ctr Dept Surgery 110 Francis St Ste 3A Boston MA 02215-5501 E-mail: jdoyle@bidmc.harvard.edu., jennifer_doyle@hms.harvard.edu.

DOYLE, JOHN LAWRENCE, artist; b. Chgo., Mar. 14, 1939; s. John W. and Cecelia M. (Tarkowski) D.; children: Lynn, Sean, Morgan. BA, Sch. of Art Inst. Chgo., 1962; MA, No. Ill. U., 1967. Tchr. art Forest View High Sch., Arlington Heights, Ill., 1962-72. Bd. dirs. Toe River Arts Coun., Yancey Libr., Amy Regional Libr. Sys., Yancey History Assn., Yancey Evening Sch. Program, Steering Com., Yancey Mus./Visitor Ctr. Project. One-man shows of prints and/or paintings include: Denver Natural History Mus., Natural Am. Indian Mus., Spokane, Wash., Allen Galleries, Milw., U. N.D., U. S.D., Black Gallery, Taos, N.Mex., Vanderbilt U., Nashville, Tenn., Johns Hopkins U., Balt., Jockey Club Gallery, Miami, Fla., New West Whitney Gallery Western Art, Cody, Wyo., Harvard Med. Library, Lesch Gallery, Mpls., Clev. Clinic, Mayo Clinic, MGM Grand, Las Vegas, Yale U. Hosp., Now and Then Gallery, N.Y.C., Fine Print Unltd., Miami, Grand Gallery, Nev., Galerie Une, Puerto Vallarta, Mex., Welnetz Studio, Wis., Gallery G, Wichita, all 1981; group shows, latest being: U. Miami, Fla., Tex. Tech U., Amarillo and Lubbock, U. Iowa Hosp. and Clinic, Loma Linda U., Calif., Art Resources, Denver, Hayden Hayes Gallery, Colorado Springs, Colo., Southwestern Gallery, Dallas, Nat. Library of Medicine, Bethesda, Md., Cornell Med. Coll., N.Y.C., Columbia U., N.Y.C., U. Kans., Harvard Law Library, Denver Nat. Hist. Mus., William Mitchell Law Sch., Mpls., United Bank of Austin, Tex., others, 1982-85, Inter Art, Nice, France, Loyola U. Sch. Law, New Orleans, Fine Arts Ltd., Miami, U. Dubuque, Iowa, Art Expo Los Angeles, Art Expo N.Y., Degan Bella Gallery, San Antonio, U. Ariz., Tempe, Midwest Mus. Am. Art, Ind., 1986, U. Ill., Chgo., 1987, R. Volid Gallery, Chgo., 1987, Royce Gallery, Denver, 1987, Denver Mus. Nat. History, 1987, No. Ill. U., DeKalb, 1987, Art Expo, N.Y.C., 1987, U. Ill. Chgo., 1988, R. Volip Gallery, Chgo., 1988, Ramses II Denver Mus., N.H., 1988, Royce Gallery, Denver, 1988, Hayden-Hayes Gallery, Colorado Springs, 1988, World Trade Ctr., Mpls.-St. Paul, 1988, Bergren Gallery, Rockford, Ill., 1988, Red Carpet Gallery, Minn., 1988, Yancey County Hist. Mus., N.C., 1988, Minn. World Trade Ctr., St. Paul, 1989, U. Ill., Champaign, 1989, U. Wis., Madison, 1989, Jean Stephen Gallery, Mpls., 1989, New West Cont. Art, Buffalo Bill Hist. Ctr., Cody, Wyo., 1990, White Thunder World Gallery, Milw., 1990, D. Ehrlein Gallery, Milw., 1990, Bank One, Milw., 1990, White Hart Gallery, Steamboat Springs, Colo., 1991, Suzanne Brown Gallery, Scottsdale, Ariz., 1991, Midwest Mus. Am. Art, Elkhart, Ind., 1991, Scripps Meml. Hosp. Schaetzel Ctr., La Jolla, Calif., 1991, Suzanne Brown Gallery, Scottsdale, Ariz., 1992, Walker Art Ctr., Asheville, N.C., 1992; represented in permanent collections: Library of Congress, Washington, Art Inst. Chgo., Indpls., Mus. Art, Carnegie Inst., Pitts., Norton Gallery of Art, West Palm Beach, Fla., Birmingham (Ala.) Mus. Art, Canton (Ohio) Art Inst., Columbus Mus. Fine Art, Columbus, Ohio, Fort Lauderdale (Fla.) Mus. Art, Miss. Art Mus., Whitney Gallery Western Art, Jackson, Nat. Gallery of Art, Washington, U. Mich., Ann Arbor, Savannah (Ga.) Coll. Art and Design, Scripps Meml. Hosp., La Jolla. Bd. dirs. Family Violence Coalition Yancey County Vol. Coop, Toe River Arts Coun., Yancey Libr., Amy Regional Libr., Healty Yancy; pres. Yancey History Assn.; sec., treas. Mus. Visitor Ctr. Project; chair subcom. Land Use Planning Commn.; mem. 21st century cmtys. action com. Yancey County Cultural Resource Commn. Recipient Hon. Mention Internat. Printmakers, 1971; George Brown Travelling fellow, 1962 Address: PO Box 715 Burnsville NC 28714-0715

DOYLE, JOHN ROBERT, lawyer; b. Chgo., May 12, 1950; s. Frank Edward and Dorothy (Bolton) D.; m. Kathleen Julius, June 14, 1974; children: Melissa, Maureen. BA magna cum laude, St. Louis U., 1971; JD summa cum laude, DePaul U., 1976. Bar: Ill. 1976, U.S. Dist. Ct. 1976, U.S. Dist. Ct. (no. dist.) Ill. 1982, Ill. Trial Bar 1982, U.S. Ct. Appeals (7th cir.) 1982. Ptnr. McDermott, Will & Emery, Chgo., 1976—. Mem. ABA, Chgo. Bar Assn. (jud. investigative hearing panel 1986-88), Phi Beta Kappa. Office: McDermott Will & Emery 227 W Monroe St Ste 3100 Chicago IL 60606-5096

DOYLE, JOSEPH ANTHONY, retired lawyer; b. N.Y.C., June 13, 1920; s. Joseph A. and Jane (Donahue) D.; m. Eugenie A. Fleri, Aug. 19, 1944; children: Christopher, Stephen, Eugenie, Jane, Richard. BS, Georgetown U., 1941; LLB, Columbia U., 1947. Bar: N.Y. 1948. Assoc. Shearman & Sterling, N.Y.C., 1947-57, ptnr., 1957-79, 81-97; asst. sec. for manpower, res. affairs and logistics USN, Washington, 1979-81. Bd. dirs. The Fuji Bank and Trust Co. Bd. dirs. USO of Met. N.Y., 1982-90. Lt. USNR, 1941-45. Decorated Navy Cross, D.F.C. with 3 gold stars, Air medal with 7 gold stars; recipient Disting. Pub. Service award Sec. of Navy, 1980. Mem. Met. Club (Washington). Democrat. Roman Catholic. Home: 32 Washington Sq W New York NY 10011-9156

DOYLE, JOSEPH THEOBALD, physician, educator; b. Providence, June 11, 1918; s. Joseph Donald and Gertrude Harriet (Theobald) D.; m. Elizabeth Thompson, Dec. 26, 1944 (dec.); children: Shelagh Thompson, Michael Kedian; m. Joan Gleason Mastrianni, Dec. 30, 1976. AB, Harvard U., 1939, MD, 1943. Successively intern, asst. resident, chief resident in medicine Harvard Med. Service, Boston City Hosp., 1943-44, 47-49; Whitehead fellow in physiology, asst. in medicine and physiology Emory U. Med. Sch., 1950-52; assoc. in medicine Duke U. Med. Sch., 1952; mem. faculty Albany (N.Y.) Med. Coll., 1952—, prof. medicine, 1961—, head div. cardiology, 1961-84, dir. cardiovascular health center, 1952-90, head pvt. diagnostic clinic, 1957-82. Cons. Albany VA Med. Center, 1962-1991. Author papers in field. Served as 1st lt. M.C. AUS, 1944-45. Fellow A.C.P., Am. Coll. Cardiology; mem. AMA, Am. Heart Assn. (chmn. council epidemiology 1969-71), Assn. Univ. Cardiologists, N.Y. Heart Assembly (pres. 1968-69), Med. Soc. County of Albany (pres. 1971-72) Clubs: Ft. Orange, Schuyler Meadows. Presbyterian. Home: 17 Lenox Ave Albany NY 12203-2005 Office: Albany Med Coll Albany NY 12208

DOYLE, JOSEPH THOMAS, preventive health physician; b. Utica, N.Y., 1963; BS, Tufts U., 1984; MD, NYU, 1989; MPH, U. South Fla. Coll., 1993; MBA, Rollins Coll., 1992; MPA, Fla. Atlantic U., 1995, EdS, 1998. Diplomate Am. Bd. Preventive Medicine, Am. Bd. Quality Assurance and Utilization Rev. Physicians. Intern Orlando (Fla.) Regional Med. Ctr., 1989-90; resident HRS/Palm Beach County Pub. Health Unit, West Palm Beach, Fla., 1994-95; pvt. practice Naples, Fla. Mem.: Pub. Health Leadership Inst. Fla., Am. Acad. Profl. Coders, Med. Dirs. Inst./Nat. Assn. Managed Care Physicians, Am. Coll. Physician Execs. Home and Office: PO Box 770208 Naples FL 34107

DOYLE, JUSTIN P. lawyer; b. Rochester, N.Y., Oct. 26, 1948; s. Justin Joseph and Jane Martha (Kreag) Doyle; children: Mary, Joe. BA, Dartmouth Coll., 1970; JD, Cornell U., 1974. Bar: N.Y. 1974. From assoc. to ptnr. Nixon, Hargrave, Devans & Doyle, Rochester, 1974-99; ptnr. Nixon Peabody LLP (formerly Nixon, Hargrave, Devans & Doyle), Rochester, 1999—. Mem.: Monroe County Bar Assn., N.Y. Bar Assn. Home: 252 Overbrook Rd Rochester NY 14618-3648 Office: Nixon Peabody LLP Clinton Sq PO Box 31051 Rochester NY 14603-1051

DOYLE, L. F. BOKER, retired trust company executive; b. N.Y.C., Apr. 23, 1931; Luke Cantwell and Rita (Boker) D.; m. Susanna Stone, Jan. 31, 1959; children: Katharine, Nancy, Victoria, Jessica. BA, Yale U., 1953; postgrad., NYU, 1956-63. 1st v.p., dir., mgr. capital mgmt. dept. Smith Barney & Co., N.Y.C., 1956-74; exec. v.p. Fiduciary Trust Co. Internat., N.Y.C., 1974-83, pres., 1983-94, chmn. exec. com., 1994-96, also dir., 1978-96, cons., 1996. Dir. U.S. LIfe Ins. Co., 1996-97. Trustee Margaret Sanger Rsch. Bur., N.Y.C., 1962-68, N.Y.C. Sch. Vol. Program, 1979-90, New Sch. for Social Rsch., N.Y.C., 1983-91, Taconic Found., N.Y.C., 1989—, Hudson River Found., 1997—; trustee Am. Mus. Natural History, N.Y.C., 1968-2002, hon trustee, 2003—; bd. dirs. Cultural Instns. Retirement Sys., N.Y.C., 1971-96, chmn. bd., 1980-96; trustee Nature Cons., N.Y. State, 1990-2003, chmn., 1993-96; trustee Frick Collection, N.Y.C., 1990, treas., 1992—; trustee Ea. N.Y. chpt. Nature Conservatory, 1998—, chmn., 2003—. 1st lt. USMC, 1953-55. Mem. Century Assn., Anglers Club N.Y. (pres. 1976-77). Avocations: fishing, birding, natural history, conservation, antiques.

DOYLE, MATHIAS FRANCIS, university president, political scientist, educator; b. Malone, N.Y., Nov. 18, 1933; s. Francis J. and Madeline L. (Donnelly) D. BA, Siena Coll., 1955; MA, Cath. U. Am., 1965; PhD, U. Notre Dame, 1968; diploma, Pres.' Assn. of Am. Mgmt. Assn., Inst. Edn. Mgmt., Harvard U. Lectr. St. Francis Coll., Rye Beach, N.H., 1963-65; assoc. prof. polit. sci. Siena Coll., Loudonville, N.Y., 1968-75; pres. St. Bonaventure (N.Y.) U., 1975-90, also trustee., prof. polit. sci., 1992—; Adminstr.'s fellow AID, Washington, 1990-92; dir. human svcs. St. Anthony Shrine, Boston. Trustee Commn. on Ind. Colls. and Univs. Contbr. articles periodicals. Trustee Siena Coll. Arthur Schmidt fellow, 1966-68 Mem. Am., Northeastern polit. sci. assns., Pi Gamma Mu, Delta Epsilon Sigma. Roman Catholic. Home: St Anthony Shrine 100 Arch St Boston MA 02110 Office: Dir of Human Resources Saint Anthony Shrine 100 Arch St Boston MA 02110 E-mail: friarmdoyle@aol.com. *A lifetime spent in education and ministry has taught me how true it is that it is better to give then to receive.*

DOYLE, MICHAEL ANTHONY, lawyer; b. Atlanta, Nov. 4, 1937; s. James Alexander and Wilma (Summersgill) D.; children: John, David, Peter.; m. Bernice H. Winter, Nov. 12, 1977. BA, Yale U., 1959, LLB, 1962. Bar: Ga. 1961, D.C. 1967, U.S. Dist. Ct. D.C. 1967, U.S. Dist. Ct. (no. dist.) Ga. 1962, U.S. Ct. Appeals (5th cir.) 1962, U.S. Ct. Appeals (11th cir.) 1982, U.S. Ct. Appeals (D.C. cir.) 1968, U.S. Supreme Ct. 1972, U.S. Ct. Appeals (4th cir.) 1985. Assoc. Alston, Miller & Gaines, Atlanta, 1962-67; ptnr. Alston & Bird and

predecessor, Atlanta, 1967—. Bd. dirs. Atlanta Legal Aid Soc., 1969-84, pres., 1975-76; bd. dirs. Ga. Legal Services Program; mem. Leadership Atlanta, 1974. Served to lt. USNR, 1964-69. Mem. ABA, State Bar Ga., Atlanta Lawyers Club, Master, Bleckley Inn of Court, Assn. Yale Alumni, Yale Law Sch. Assn. (nat. v.p. 1982-85, mem. exec. com. 1978-85, chmn. planning com. 1988-90, pres. 1991-92, chmn. exec. com. 1992-94). Piedmont Driving Club, Commerce Club, Yale Club Ga. (pres. 1982-84), Yale Club N.Y. Roman Catholic. Office: Alston & Bird 4200 One Atlantic Ctr 1201 W Peachtree St NW Atlanta GA 30309-3424

DOYLE, MICHAEL F. congressman; b. Swissvale, Pa., Aug. 5, 1953; s. Michael Sr. and Rosemarie (Fusco) D.; m. Susan Erlandson; children: Mike Jr., David, Kevin, Alexandra. BS, Pa. State U., 1975. Exec. dir. Turtle Creek (Pa.) Valley Citizens Union, 1977-79; chief of staff State Sen. Frank Pecora, Harrisburg, Pa., 1979-94; co-founder Eastgate Ins. Agy., Pitts., 1983-94; mem. U.S. Ho. of Reps. from 14th Pa. dist., Washington, 1995—; mem. energy and commerce com., founder Congl. Autism Caucus U.S. Ho. of Reps., Washington. Coun. mem. Swissvale (Pa.) Borough Coun., 1977-81. Active Lions Club, Leadership Pitts., Italian Sons & Daughters of Am. Mem. Nat. Dem. Club. Democrat. Roman Catholic. Avocations: golf, italian cooking, piano. Office: US House Reps 401 Cannon HOB Washington DC 20515-3814 Address: 225 Ross St 5th flr Pittsburgh PA 15219 E-mail: doyle@mail.house.gov.*

DOYLE, MICHAEL JAMES, educator, organist; b. Bell, Calif., Aug. 24, 1939; s. Joseph Edward and Irma Louise (Smith) Doyle; m. Mina Katherine Martensen, Feb. 8, 1964; children: Michael James II, Mary Katherine, Matthew John. BA, Whittier Coll., 1961, MEd, 1971. Tchr. El Rancho Unified Sch. Dist., Pico Rivera, Calif., 1961-79, dept. chmn., 1967-74, acting prin., 1979; tchr., asst. prin. Alta Loma (Calif.) Sch. Dist., 1979-86, summer sch. prin., 1985, prin., 1980-93, assoc. faculty Nat. U., Riverside, Calif., 1995-98; adj. prof. Calif. State U., San Bernardino, 1995—, Nat. U., San Bernardino, Calif., 1998—. Organist, dir. various Luth. chs. in So. Calif., 1955-86; organist St. Paul's Luth. Ch., Pomona, Calif., 1986—; mem. Calif. State Program Rev., 1982-83; assoc. mem. Calif. Sch. Leadership Acad., Ontario, 1986-89; v.p. So. Calif. Luth. Music Clinic, 1978-81. Author: Sent Forth by God's Blessing, 1999 (award Concordia Hist. Inst., 2000), Mother of the Valley, 2001 (award Concordia Hist. Inst., 2002), Life and Times of Hans and Lydia Mertensen, 2003. Clk. Zion Luth. Sch. Bd. Edn., Maywood, Calif., 1962-64, chmn., 1966-67; mem. Downey (Calif.) City Water Bd., 1977-78; mem. Luth. High Personnel Commn., La Verne, Calif., 1988-92; asst. archivist Pacific S.W. Dist. Luth. Ch., Mo. Synod, 1999—. Named Outstanding Tchr. of Yr., Burke Jr. High Sch. PTA, Pico Rivera, 1973; recipient hon. svc. award Jasper Sch. PTA, Alta Loma, 1983, continuing svc. award, 1988, Golden Oak Svc. award, 1996, Written Books award Concordia Hist. Inst., St. Louis, 2000, 02; employee recognition award Alta Loma Sch. Dist., 1985. Mem. Assn. Calif. Sch. Adminstrs., Assn. West End Sch. Adminstrs., Calif. Tchrs. Assn., Am. Guild Organists, Downey Hist. Soc., Cucamonga Hist. Soc., Casa de Rancho (Cucamonga, Calif.), Phi Delta Kappa (pres. Mt. Baldy chpt. 1993-97, 2001—, advisor 1997-2000, found. chmn. 1991-93). Democrat. Lutheran. Home and Office: 2085 N Palm Ave Upland CA 91784-1476 E-mail: mdoyle@adelphia.net.

DOYLE, MICHAEL PATRICK, microbiologist, educator, director; b. Madison, Wis., Oct. 3, 1949; s. Donald Vincent and Evelyn (Bauer) Doyle; m. Annette Marie Ripple, Dec. 27, 1971; children: Michael Patrick, Patrick Matthew, Kristen Anne. BS in Bacteriology, U. Wis., 1973, MS in Food Microbiology, 1975, PhD in Food Microbiology, 1977. Sr. project leader Ralston Purina Co., St. Louis, 1977-80; asst. prof. U. Wis., Madison, 1980-84, assoc. prof., 1984-88, prof., 1988-91; prof., dir. U. Ga., Griffin, 1991—, dept. head Athens, 1993-99; chmn. sci. bd. U.S. Food and Drug Admin., 2003—. Regents prof. Bd. Regents Ga. U. Sys., 1997—; mem. food and nutrition bd. Inst. Medicine, NAS, 1991—97, com. to ensure safe food from prodn. to consumption, 1998, chair rev. com. USDA E. coli 0157:H7 in ground beef risk assessment, 2001—02, chair food forum, 2003—; mem. nat. adv. com. on microbiol. criteria for foods USA, Washington, 1988—90, Washington, 1994—2000; trustee Internat. Life Scis. Inst.-n.Am., Washington, 1992—, sci. advisor, 1987—96; mem. Internat. Commn. on Microbiol. Specifications for Foods, 1989—2000; Wis. Disting. prof. bd. regents U. Wis., Madison, 1988—91; James M. Craig Meml. lectr. Oreg. State U., Corvallis, 1990; sci. lectr. Am. Soc. Microbiology Found., 1991—93, 1999—2001; Peter J. Shields lectr. U. Calif., Davis, 1993; G. Malcolm Trout vis. scholar Mich. State U., Lansing, 1994; mem. sci. adv. coun. Refrigeration Rsch. and Edn. Found., 1997—2002; York Disting. lectr. Auburn U., 1999; chmn. com. rev. USDA, 2001—02; chmn. sci. bd. U.S. Food and Drug Adminstrn., 2003—; chmn. food forum Inst. Medicine Nat. Acad. Scis., 2003—. Editor: Food Microbiology: Fundamentals and Frontiers, 1997, Food Microbiology: Fundamentals and Frontiers, 2d edit., 2001, Foodborne Bacterial Pathogens, 1989; contbr. articles to profl. jours. Named one of Top 100 Most Cited Rschrs. Agrl. Scis., Inst. Sci. Info., 2002; recipient award for Profl. Excellence, Am. Agrl. Econs. Assn., 1992, Silver Plow Honor award, USDA, 1998, Ptnrs. in Pub. Health award, Ctrs. Disease Control and Prevention, 2001. Fellow: Am. Acad. Microbiology, Inst. of Food Technologists (Fred W. Tanner lectr. 1986, sci. lectr. 1987—90, exec. com. 2000—03, Samuel Cate Prescott award for rsch. 1987, Nicholas Appert award for preeminence in and contbns. to field of food tech. 1996), Internat. Assn. Food Protection (pres. 1992—93, Norbert F. Sherman article excellence award 1993, NFPA food safety award for outstanding contbn. to food safety rsch. and edn. 1999); mem.: Am. Soc. for Microbiology (chmn. food microbiology divsn. 1987—89, Found. lectr. 1991—93, 1999—2001, P.R. Edwards award for outstanding career achievements 1994), Internat. Assn. Food Protection, Gamma Sigma Delta, Phi Kappa Phi. Roman Catholic. Achievements include patents for for monocional antibody to enterohemorrhagic E. coli; for competitive exclusion bacteria to reduce carriage of enterohemorrhagic E. coli by cattle; development of of methods to control and detect foodborne pathogens. Office: U Ga Ctr Food Safety 1109 Experiment St Griffin GA 30223-1797 E-mail: mdoyle@uga.edu.

DOYLE, MICHAEL W. federal official; b. Honolulu, 1948; Student, USAF Academy; AB, Harvard U, 1970; PhD, Harvard U., 1977. Sanford prof. politics and internat. affairs Woodrow Wilson Sch. Pub. and Internat. Affairs, Princeton U., Princeton, N.J.; dir. Ctr. of Internat. Studies Princeton U.; asst. sec.-gen. spl. adviser to sec. gen. Kofi Annan UN, 2001—. Mem. adv. coms. UN High Commr. for Refugees, Lessons Learned Unit, UN Dept. Peacekeeping Ops. Author Empires, UN Peacekeeping in Cambodia: UNTAC's Civil Mandate, Ways of War and Peace; co-author: Alternatives to Monetary Disorder; co-editor: Escalation and Intervention, Keeping the Peace, Peacemaking and Peacekeeping for the New Century, New Thinking in Internat. Relations Theorys. With Mass. National Air Guard. U Harvard awards include Detur Prize, John Harvard Scholar, Atherton Prize Fellowship; Ford Foundation Rsch. Fellowship, SSRC/MacArthur Found. Fellowship, Membership of the Inst. of Advanced Studies, Ctr. for Advanced Study in the Behavioral Scis. Office: Woodrow Wilson Sch Princeton U Princeton NJ 08544-0001

DOYLE, PATRICK JOHN, otolaryngologist, department chairman; b. Moose Jaw, Sask., Can., Nov. 17, 1926; s. William E. and Bertha L. (Fisher) D.; m. Irene Strilchuk, May 21, 1949; children: Sharon, Patrick, Robert, Barbara, Joseph, Kathleen. BSc, U. Alta., 1947, MD, 1949. Diplomate Am. Bd. Otolaryngology (bd. dirs., v.p. 1986-88, pres. 1988-90). Intern U. B.C. Hosp., 1949-50; resident in medicine and pediatrics, 1950-51; resident in otolaryngology U. Oreg. Hosp., 1958-61; asst. prof., then asso. prof. U. Oreg. Med. Sch., 1965-70; mem. faculty U. B.C. Med. Sch., 1963—, prof. otolaryngology, 1972-91, prof. otolaryngology emeritus, 1992—, head dept., 1972-91, program dir. residency tng. program, 1972-91. Head div. otolaryngology St. Paul's Hosp., mem. numerous nat. med. coms. Author numerous articles in field; mem. editorial bds. profl. jours. Fellow Royal Coll. Surgeons Can., Am. Laryngol., Rhinol. and Otol. Soc. (v.p. western sect. 1988, pres. 1994), Am. Laryngol. Soc., Am. Acad. Otolaryngology-Head and Neck Surgery (v.p. 1984, bd. dirs. 1985-87), Am. Otol. Soc.; mem. Can. Soc. Otolaryngology-Head and Neck Surgery (pres. 1987), Pacific Coast Oto-Ophthal. Soc. (pres. 1977), Soc. Univ. Otolaryngologists, U. Oreg. Otolaryngology Alumni Assn. (pres. 1968-70), Am. Otological Soc., Centurion Club, Tinnitus Rsch. Found. Roman Catholic. Office: # 301-5704 Balsam St Vancouver BC Canada V6M 4B9

DOYLE, PATRICK LEE, retired insurance company executive; s. Lee Patrick and Anne Louise D.; m. Ann Marie Yuhasz, Apr. 26, 1952; children: Robert Christopher, Patrick Brian, David Alan. BA, Ohio State U., 1951. CPCU, Am. Inst. Property Casualty Underwriters CLU Assoc. in Risk Mgmt., Ins. Inst. Am. Life reins. mgr. Nationwide Ins. Cos., Columbus, Ohio, 1965-70, asst. to pres., 1970-79, v.p., adminstrv. asst. to pres., 1980-81, v.p. human resources, 1981-82, v.p. Office Gen. Chmn., 1982-94; instr. Ohio State U., Columbus, 1969-82, Franklin U., Columbus, 1973-82. Mem. exam. com. CPCU, Am. Inst. for Property and Liability Underwriters, Phila., 1969-94; trustee Griffith Found. for Ins. Edn., Columbus, 1975—. .Bd. dirs. Cath. Social Svcs., Columbus, 1981-87, St. Stephen's Cmty. House, 1989-94; trustee Kinder Key, 1973—. Mem. Ins. Inst. Am., Soc. CPCU (ednl. dir. 1965-72, Outstanding Educator award), Soc. CLU, Soc. Ins. Research (dir. 1976-79), Gamma Iota Sigma. Republican. Roman Catholic.

DOYLE, PAUL FRANCIS, lawyer; b. N.Y.C., Sept. 3, 1946; s. Paul Francis and Rita Lilian (Mulcahy) D.; m. Margaret Mary Sullivan, Aug. 23, 1969; children: Karen, Lynn. BA in English, Holy Cross Coll., 1968; JD cum laude, NYU, 1973. Bar: Mass. 1973, N.Y. 1975, U.S. Dist. Ct. (so. and ea. dists.) N.Y. 1975, U.S. Ct. Appeals (2d and 3d cirs.) 1975, U.S. Supreme Ct. 1991, U.S. Dist. Ct. Mass. 1992, U.S. Dist. Ct. (no. dist.) N.Y. 1995. Law clk. Superior Ct. Commonwealth of Mass., Boston, 1973-74; assoc. Kelley, Drye & Warren, N.Y.C., 1974-82, ptnr., 1983—. Instr. Nat. Inst. Trial Advocacy, 1994—95; mem. departmental disciplinary com. Supreme Ct. of N.Y., 1st Jud. Dept., 2003—. Assoc. editor Ann. Survey Am. Law, 1972-73. Mem. Planning Bd., Croton-on-Hudson, N.Y., 1989-92, mem. Comprehensive Plan Com., 1999—; mem. pres.'s coun. Holy Cross Coll. With U.S. Army, 1968-70, Vietnam. Mem. Am. Inns of Ct., Order of Coif. Roman Catholic. Office: Kelley Drye & Warren LLP 101 Park Ave New York NY 10178-0062

DOYLE, ROBERT EUGENE, JR., lawyer; b. St. Simons Island, Ga., Sept. 5, 1948; s. Robert Eugene and Elizabeth Anne (Webb) D.; m. Kristina Maria Kost, Nov. 27, 1971; children: K. Maria, R. Eugene III, Emily Anne. BA, George Washington U., 1970; JD, Stetson U., 1975. Bar: Fla. 1975, U.S. Dist. Ct. (mid. and so. dists.) Fla. 1976, U.S. Ct. Appeals (5th cir.) 1981, U.S. Ct. Appeals (11th cir.) 1985, U.S. Supreme Ct. 1994; cert. Nat. Bd. Trial Advocacy. Ptnr. Asbell, Hains & Doyle, Naples, Fla., 1975-93, Quarles & Brady, Naples, 1993—. Mem. code and rules of evidence com. Fla. Bar, 1988—, chair, 1993-94. Pres. Fillabelly Found., Naples, 1993-95. 1st lt. USMC, 1971-75. Mem. ABA, ATLA, Am. Inns of Ct. (barrister Thomas S. Biggs chpt. 1995), Econ. Devel. Coun. Collier County (chmn. 2001-2002). Democrat. Presbyterian. Avocations: fishing, flying. Office: Quarles & Brady 4501 Tamiami Trl N Ste 300 Naples FL 34103-3023

DOYLE, SHARON THOMAS, school system administrator; b. Maysville, Ky., Apr. 1, 1957; d. Donald Lee and Shirley May (Thomas) T.; m. Allen Darryl Doyle, Nov. 29, 1980. B in Music Edn., Morehead State U., 1979; M in Music Edn., U. Ky., 1980; M in Ednl. Adminstrn., U. S.C., 1995. Cert. elem. and music tchr., Ky. (life), elem. and music tchr., adminstr., supr., S.C. Coord. Danville (Ky.)/Centre String Program Centre Coll. Ky., 1980-84; orch. tchr. Spartanburg (S.C.) Sch. Dist. 7, 1984—2000, acting coord., 1992-93; asst. prin. Cleve. Elem. Sch., 2000—. Staff devel. workshop planning Curriculum Leadership in the Arts, Winthrop Coll., Rock Hill, S.C., 1994; facilitator curriculum leadership in the arts program State Dept., 2001—, mem. task force to rewrite S.C. stds. for performing arts, 2001—; prof. of record Converse Coll., S.C. Arts Leadership for Success Acd., Arts in Basic Edn. Curriculum project; writing team for S.C. Music Curriculum Guide, 2002; facilitator for best practice study groups for Spartanburg Sch. Dist. 7,2001-. Advocate S.C. Alliance for Arts Edn., 1995—. Target 2000 grantee S.C. Dept. Edn., 1995, grantee Spartanburg County Fedn., 1996. Mem. Assn. Supervision and Curriculum Devel., S.C. Arts Edn. Assn., S.C. Arts Alliance, Music Edn. Nat. Conf., S.C. Music Educators Assn. (all-state chmn., v.p., pres.-elect, pres. 1988, mem. exec. bd. 1993-99, treas. 1999—, adminstrv. rep. to state bd.), S.C. Assn. Sch. Adminstrs., Nat. Assn. Elem. Sch. Prins. Avocations: reading, travel. Home: 257 Hollis Dr Spartanburg SC 29307-2463 E-mail: sdoyle@spart7.k12.sc.us.

DOYLE, THOMAS EDWARD, lawyer, educator; b. Washington, Mar. 11, 1963; s. Joseph Thomas Doyle and Elizabeth Brown Preston; m. Ferhan K. Doyle, Oct. 4, 1992; children: Alexis Shannon, Dominic Thomas. BS, U. Md., 1985; JD, George Mason U., 1989. Bar: U.S. Ct. Appeals Md. 1991, U.S. Dist. Ct. Md. 1992, D.C. 1993, U.S. Supreme Ct. 1997, U.S. Dist. Ct. D.C. 1997. Atty., law clk. Van Grack, Axelson & Williamowsky, Rockville, Md., 1989-91; pvt. practice Rockville, 1991-92; ptnr. Siegel & Doyle L.L.C., Rockville, 1992—. Adj. prof. Montgomery Coll., Takoma Park, Md., 1991—; mem. adv. bd. D.C. Consumer Protection Law Ctr., Washington, 1997—; founder, exec. dir. Consumer Law Ctr. Md., Rockville, 1997—. Dir. Joseph T. Doyle Meml. Scholarship, Montgomery Coll., 1992. Recipient Am. Jurisprudence awards for excellence in consumer fin. law and pub. fin. law, 1989. Mem. ATLA, ABA, Md. State Bar Assn., D.C. Bar Assn., Million Dollar Advocates Forum. Office: Siegel & Doyle LLC 101 N Adams St Rockville MD 20850-2217

DOYLE, TOM, sculptor, retired educator; b. Jerry City, Ohio, May 23, 1928; s. John Thomas and Kathleen (Solether) D.; m. Natalie N. Burdette (div. 1957); m. Eva Hesse (dec. 1970); m. Jane Miller. Student, Miami U., Oxford, Ohio, 1948-50; BFA, Ohio State U., 1952, MFA, 1953. Sculptor, N.Y.C., to date. Artist-in-residence La Napoule Art Found., France, 1989. One-man shows include Dwan Gallery, N.Y.C., 1966, 67, 55 Mercer Gallery, N.Y.C., 1972, 74, 76, Picker Art Gallery, Colgate U., Hamilton, N.Y., 1976, Sculpture Now, Inc., N.Y.C., 1978, The Sculpture Ctr., N.Y.C., 1988, Bill Bace Gallery, N.Y.C., 1991, 93-94, Long House Found., East Hampton, N.Y., 1995, Mattatuck Mus., Waterbury, Conn., 1996, Kouros Gallery, N.Y.C., 1999, Nicolaysen Art Mus., Casper, Wyo., 2001, New Arts Gallery, Litchfield, Conn., 2003; exhibited in group shows at Whitney Mus., N.Y.C., 1967, Los Angeles County Mus., 1967, Taft Mus., Cin., 1974, Indpls. Mus. Art, 1974. Recipient commendation GSA, Fairbanks, Alaska, 1980, Jimmy Ernst Lifetime Art Achievement award AAAL, 1994, Ohioana Career award for Lifetime Achievement, 1996; Guggenheim fellow, 1982, Nat. Endowment for the Arts fellow, 1990-91; rsch. grantee CUNY, 1989-90. Mem. Am. Abstract Artists, Nat. Acad. Design. E-mail: tjmdoyle@aol.com.

DOYLE, WENDELL E. retired band director, educator; b. Higbee, Mo., July 8, 1940; s. Travis E. and Hattie Erma (Webb) D.; m. Julia Ann Vail, June 23, 1963; children: Dora Michelle, Michael E., Melissa Kae. BS in Edn., Northeast Mo. State U., 1962; MEd in Music, U. Mo., 1967. Cert. lifetime tchr., Mo. Band dir. Braymer (Mo.) C-4, 1962-68, Brookfield (Mo.) R-3, 1968-72, Platte County (Mo.) R-III, 1972-92; ret., 1992. Exchange tchr. Platte County R-III Schs., Warwickshire, Eng., 1984. Pres. Barry Heights Homes Assn., 1986—; minister of music Park Bapt. Ch., Brookfield, 1968-72, Northgate Bapt. Ch., Kansas City, 1972-85. Mem. Mo. State Tchrs. Assn. (pres. Greater Kans. City dist. 1978), Music Educators Nat. Conf., Mo. Music Educators Assn., Mo. Bandmasters Assn. (sec.), Phi Beta Mu (pres. 1990-91, Outstanding Band Dir. award Lambda chpt., 1993), Mo. Bardmasters Assn. (Hall of Fame 1997). Democrat. Avocations: fishing, reading, golfing, travel. Home: 2330 NW Powderhorn Dr Kansas City MO 64154-1311

DOYLE, WILLIAM B. investment executive; BS in Engring., Princeton U., 1981; MBA, Stanford U., 1985. Investment mgr. McKinsey & Co., Inc., Dallas, 1981-83, Allied Signal Inc., Paris, France, 1985-87, Alex Brown & Sons, Inc., San Francisco, 1987-90, Govett Ltd., San Francisco, 1991-95, Doyle & Boissiere LLC, Burlingame, Calif., 1995—. Bd. dirs. Kojo Worldwide Corp., San Diego, Ocean Pacific Apparel Corp., Irvine, Calif., Naturade, Inc., Irvine. Office: Doyle & Boissiere LLC 330 Primrose Rd Ste 500 Burlingame CA 94010 E-mail: dbllc@dbllc.com.

DOYLE, WILLIAM JAY, II, business consultant; b. Cin., Nov. 7, 1928; s. William Jay and Blanche (Gross) D.; m. Joan Lucas, July 23, 1949; children: David L., William Jay, III, Daniel L. BS, Miami U., Oxford, Ohio, 1949; postgrad., U. Cin., 1950-51, Xavier U., 1953-54, Case Western Res. U., 1959-60. Sales rep. Diebold, Inc., Cin., 1949-52, asst. br. mgr., 1953-57, asst. regional mgr., 1957-62, regional mgr., 1962-74; founder, pres. CEO Ctrl. Bus. Group, Cin., 1974-89, chmn., 1989-95, ret., 1995. Mem. area contractor's coun. Spacesaver Corp., 1985-89; speaker on bus systems, security concepts. Develop new concepts in tng., cash and securities handling, mobile and mechanized storage and filing. Mem. Bus. Systems and Sales Mgmt. Assn. (nat. bd. dirs. 1977-79, 81-85, pres. 1981-83, 84-85), Inst. of Mgmt. Accts., Masons, Shriners. Republican. Home: 1110 Roseate Ct Bradenton FL 34209-7364 E-mail: billjoan49@att.net.

DOYLE, WILLIAM THOMAS, retired newspaper editor; b. Oakland, Calif., May 22, 1925; s. Albert Norman and Catherine (Stein) D.; m. Claire Louise Wogan, Sept. 1, 1946 (dec. Nov. 10, 1984); children: Patrick, Lawrence, Brian, Carrie; m. Mary M. Doren, May 3, 1986. B.Journalism, U. Nev., 1950. Reporter Richmond (Calif.) Independent, 1950-53; reporter Oakland Tribune, 1953-62, asst. state editor, 1962-64, telegraph editor, 1964-67, fin. editor, 1967-79; editor San Francisco Bus. Jour., 1979-81; news dir. Fireman's Fund Ins. Cos., Novato, Calif., 1981-84; mng. editor West County Times, Pinole, Calif., 1984-88. Mem. editorial adv. bd.: Catholic Voice. Pres. Richmond Jr. C. of C., 1957-58; bd. dirs. Cath. Social Svc. Contra Costa County, Calif., 1959-62, Bay Area Coop. Edn. Clearing House, 1977-88, Contra Costa Coll. Found., 1984-88, Richmond Unified Edn. Fund, 1984, Am. Cancer Soc.—West Contra Costa, 1986-96; mem. Richmond Schs. Citizens Adv. Com., 1969; pastoral coun. St. David's Cath. Ch., Richmond, 1994—. With USAAF, 1943-45. Recipient award for best financial sect. daily newspaper Calif., Calif. Newspaper Pubs. Assn., 1968, 70, 72, 74, Knowland award for outstanding performance, 1972, Gen. Excellence award Nat. Newspaper Assn., 1987, Outstanding Editorial Writing award Suburban Newspapers Assn., 1989, 90, 1st Place award for editorial writing Nat. Newspaper Assn., 1992; Hughes fellow Rutgers U., 1969. Mem.: Marine Exch. San Francisco Bay Area, Soc. Am. Bus. Writers, Sons in Retirement, Contra Costa Press Club (pres. 1956, Best News Story award 1965), Contra Costa Club, Elks, Sigma Delta Chi. Home: 2727 Del Monte Ave El Cerrito CA 94530-1507 E-mail: marbildoyle@aol.com.

DOYNO, VICTOR ANTHONY, literature educator; b. Chgo., July 12, 1937; s. Victor A. and Sally B. (Finnegan) D.; m. Ellen Joyce Kuchar, Aug. 22, 1959; children: David, Kenneth, Anna. BA, Miami U. of Ohio, 1959; MA, Harvard U., 1960; PhD, U. Ind., 1966. Instr. Rutgers U., New Brunswick, N.J., 1963-64, Princeton U., 1964-65; prof. SUNY, Buffalo, 1966—. Editor: Mark Twain: American Skeptic, 1985, Random House Huck, 1996, Oxford Huck, 1998; author: Writing Huck Finn, 1992. Recipient Gov.'s award N.Y. Gov. Cuomo, 3 tchg. awards. Office: English Dept SUNY at Buffalo 306 Clemens Buffalo NY 14260-0001 E-mail: doyno@acsu.buffalo.edu.

DOZIER, DAVID CHARLES, JR., marketing public relations and advertising executive; b. Santa Fe, Dec. 4, 1938; s. David Charles Sr. and Zelma (Martin) D.; m. Dianne Flusche, June 1, 1960; children: Deborah, Mary Rebecca, Michael, Constance. BA, U. Dallas, 1960. Editor sports Tex. Catholic, Dallas, 1960-70, gen. sales mgr., 1964-70; dir. classified advt. Dallas Times Herald, 1970-74; pres., chmn. DBG&H Unltd. Inc., Dallas, 1974-88; chmn. Dozier Co., Dallas, 1989—. Innovator, ptnr. Navi Pesanda Indian Blanket Creations, 1992. Author: A Compendium of Endurance, 1989. Mem. Am. Indian, Santa Clara Pueblo Tribe, N.Mex.; cert. athletic trainer Downtown YMCA, 1990-2003. Recipient Disting. Svc. award Pres. U.S. and HUD, 1984. Republican. Roman Catholic. Avocation: completed over 128 marathons. Home: 7102 Wabash Cir Dallas TX 75214-3532 Office: 2021 Farrington St Dallas TX 75207-6607

DOZIER, ELEANOR CAMERON, computer company executive, writer; b. N.Y.C., May 20, 1939; d. Robert Paul and Marion Gill MacNeil; m. Norman Garlan Dozier, June 23, 1989; children: Karen Gonzales, Robert Bennett, Heidi Bennett, Julia, Ian, Jordan. Rep. to British Isles Max Factor, Inc., Hollywood, Calif., 1966—71; co-owner; also songwriter and poet MacNeil Dozier Pub. Co., Pembroke Pines, Fla., 1988—2002; v.p. Computer Dimensions Network Corp., N.Y.C., 1998—. Mktg. dir. Prometheus Devel., San Jose, Calif., 1986—87. Author: (book) O For The Love Of God!, 2003. Recipient commn., Stephen Ministry, Order St. Luke. Episcopalian. Avocations: bicycling, golf, tennis, travel. Address: 250 SW 8th St Dania FL 33004 Office Fax: 954-929-3282. Business E-Mail: call4ecd@bellsouth.net.

DOZIER, ETRULID PRESSLEY, school librarian; b. Anderson, S.C., Sept. 23, 1930; d. Mance and Virgie Mattison Pressley; m. Gibb Dozier (dec. Oct. 1980); children: Shirley Mae, Claudette D. Rouse, Gibb A. III. AB, Benedict Coll., 1954; MSLS, Atlanta U, 1957. Libr. Whittemore H.S.,Conway JR. H.S., Whittemore Park Mid., Conway, SC, 1954—88. Mem. Horry County Trustee Bd., Conway, SC, 2003, HIgher Edn. Comm. Coastal Carolina U, Conway, SC, 2003. Democrat. Bapt. Home: 1915 Racepathe Ave Conway SC 29527

DOZIER, GLENN JOSEPH, diversified financial services company executive; b. Lexington, Ky., Apr. 7, 1950; s. Emmitt and Henrietta Elsie (Geisler) Dozier; m. Paula Jean Cook, June 3, 1974; children: Laura Jean, Diana Leigh. BS in Indsl. Engring. and Ops. Rsch., Va. Poly. Inst., 1972; MBA, U. Va., 1975. Mfg. engr. Tex. Instruments, Dallas, 1972-73; fin. analyst Dravo Corp., Pitts., 1975-76, mgr. corp. fin. analysis, 1976-79, dir. corp. devel., 1980-82, dir. corp. planning and devel., 1982-83; v.p. fin. Dravo Constructors, Inc., Pitts., 1983-87; CFO, treas., asst. sec. AMF Bowling Internat. Inc. and AMF Bowling, Inc., Richmond, Va., 1987-90; v.p., CFO, treas. Owens and Minor, Inc., Richmond, 1990-93, sr. v.p. ops. and systems, CFO, 1991-92, sr. v.p. fin., CFO, 1992-96; CFO Displaytech, Inc., 1997-98; sr. v.p., CFO Hagler Bailly Inc., 1998-99, 1999-2000, This End Up Furniture Co., 2001—; exec. v.p., CFO Upstate Group Inc. Author: (book) Economic Development Finance, 1986, CFO Handbook, 1996, Financial Executives Handbook. Mem. Colonies Civic Assn. Mem.: Colonies Swim and Tennis Club, Tau Beta Pi, Phi Kappa Phi, Alpha Pi Mu, Phi Eta Sigma. Republican. Methodist. Avocations: golf, travel, gardening.

DOZIER, GLORIA ANNE CLIFTON, retired buyer; b. Phila., Jan. 2, 1930; d. James Francis X. and Anna Carolyn (Schrufer) Clifton; m. Joe V. Dozier, Dec. 28, 1954; children: James M., John C., Anne M., Robert E. BS, Drexel U., 1952. Cert. tchr., Tex. Home econs. tchr. Marathon (Tex.) H.S., 1952—55; buyer, salesperson Schreiner Dept. Store, Kerrville, Tex., 1973—85, ret., 1985. Author: Kerr County Texas Death Records 1903-1960, 1988, Kerr County Texas Birth Records 1903-1935 Including 1870-1935, 1998, Kerrville Mt. Sun and Kerrville Advance Obituary and Death Notice Index 1898-1965, 1998, Kerrville Mt. Sun Obituary Index 1966-1985, 1999, All Name Index for History of Bucks County, Pa., 1999, Obituary Index Kerrville, Mt. Sun, 1998-99, 2000, 01, 02 (5 vols.), Kerrville Daily Times, 1986-2002 (17 vols.). Mem. adv. bd. Butt-Holdsworth Meml. Libr., Kerrville, 1999-2000, libr. bd., 2003. Recipient Martha Washington medal SAR, 1999, Cert. Appreciation, 1991, Kerr County Hist. Coun., 1988. Mem. Kerrville Geneaol. Soc. (libr. 1986-91, pres. 1999-2000, 2003—, sec. 1992-93, treas. 2001-02, Cert. Appreciation 1991), Hill Country Preservation Soc. Avocations: genealogy, registered cats.

DOZIER, JAMES LEE, former army officer; b. Arcadia, Fla., Apr. 10, 1931; s. Joseph B. and Leota (Caruthers) D.; m. Judith I. Stimpson, June 30, 1956; children— Cheryl Lyn, Scott Lee BS, U.S. Mil. Acad., 1956; MS in Aerospace Engring., U. Ariz., 1964. Commd. 2d lt. U.S. Army, 1956, advanced through grades to maj. gen., 1984, comdr. 1st Squadron, 1st Cav., 1st Armored Div., 1971-73, staff officer Office of Dep. Chief of Staff for Research, Devel. and Acquisition, 1974-76, also mil. asst. to asst. sec. of army, 1974-76, comdr. 2d Brigade, 2d Armored div. Fort Hood, Tex., 1976-78, chief of staff 2d Armored div., 1978-79, chief of staff III Corps and Ft. Hood, 1979-80, dep. chief of staff logistics and adminstrn. Allied Land Forces So. Europe Verona, Italy, 1980-82, asst. comdt. Armor Sch. Ft. Knox, Ky., 1982-83, dep. comdg. gen. III Corps and Fort Hood Fort Hood, Tex., 1983-85, ret., 1985; pres. Golden Grove Mgmt. Corp., Arcadia, Fla., 1985-87, Suncoast Media Group, Venice, Fla., 1987; gen. mgr. David C. Brown Enterprises, 1988-93; owner JCS Group, Ft. Myers, 1993—. Lectr., condr. seminars on kidnapping experience. Contbg. author: Winter of Fire, 1990; contbr. articles to mil. jours. Decorated Silver Star, Legion of Merit, Bronze Star with V device and 2 oak leaf clusters, Air medals, Purple Heart Avocations: fishing; boating; gardening; woodworking.

DOZIER, NANCY KERNS, retired geriatrics nurse; b. Akron, Ohio, May 31, 1930; d. Guy F. and Alma Jane (Good) Kerns; 1 child, Frederick A. Dietz. AA, Prince George C.C., 1972; student, Catonsville (Md.) Coll., 1976, 78. RN, Ohio, Fla., Md.; cert. in basic and advanced coronary care. Med.-surg., orthopedic staff nurse Childrens Hosp., Balt., 1973-74; nurse med. surg. flr. Bon Secours Hosp., Balt., 1974-76; staff nurse Md. State Maximum Security Penal Inst., Jessup, 1977-78, Bonifay (Fla.) Nursing Home, 1985-86; staff float nurse

predecessor, Atlanta, 1967—. Bd. dirs. Atlanta Legal Aid Soc., 1969-84, pres., 1975-76; bd. dirs. Ga. Legal Services Program; mem. Leadership Atlanta, 1974. Served to lt. USNR, 1964-69. Mem. ABA, State Bar Ga., Atlanta Lawyers Club, Master, Bleckley Inn of Court, Assn. Yale Alumni, Yale Law Sch. Assn. (nat. v.p. 1982-85, mem. exec. com. 1978-85, chmn. planning com. 1988-90, pres. 1991-92, chmn. exec. com. 1992-94). Piedmont Driving Club, Commerce Club, Yale Club Ga. (pres. 1982-84), Yale Club N.Y. Roman Catholic. Office: Alston & Bird 4200 One Atlantic Ctr 1201 W Peachtree St NW Atlanta GA 30309-3424

DOYLE, MICHAEL F. congressman; b. Swissvale, Pa., Aug. 5, 1953; s. Michael Sr. and Rosemarie (Fusco) D.; m. Susan Erlandson; children: Mike Jr., David, Kevin, Alexandra. BS, Pa. State U., 1975. Exec. dir. Turtle Creek (Pa.) Valley Citizens Union, 1977-79; chief of staff State Sen. Frank Pecora, Harrisburg, Pa., 1979-94; co-founder Eastgate Ins. Agy., Pitts., 1983-94; mem. U.S. Ho. of Reps. from 14th Pa. dist., Washington, 1995—; mem. energy and commerce com., founder Congl. Autism Caucus U.S. Ho. of Reps., Washington. Coun. mem. Swissvale (Pa.) Borough Coun., 1977-81. Active Lions Club, Leadership Pitts., Italian Sons & Daughters of Am. Mem. Nat. Dem. Club. Democrat. Roman Catholic. Avocations: golf, italian cooking, piano. Office: US House Reps 401 Cannon HOB Washington DC 20515-3814 Address: 225 Ross St 5th flr Pittsburgh PA 15219 E-mail: doyle@mail.house.gov.*

DOYLE, MICHAEL JAMES, educator, organist; b. Bell, Calif., Aug. 24, 1939; s. Joseph Edward and Irma Louise (Smith) Doyle; m. Mina Katherine Martensen, Feb. 8, 1964; children: Michael James II, Mary Katherine, Matthew John. BA, Whittier Coll., 1961, MEd, 1971. Tchr. El Rancho Unified Sch. Dist., Pico Rivera, Calif., 1961-79, dept. chmn., 1967-74, acting prin., 1979; tchr., asst. prin. Alta Loma (Calif.) Sch. Dist., 1979-86, summer sch. prin., 1985, prin., 1986-95; assoc. faculty Nat. U., Riverside, Calif., 1995-98; adj. prof. Calif. State U., San Bernardino, 1995—, Nat. U., San Bernardino, Calif., 1998—. Organist, dir. various Luth. chs. in So. Calif., 1955-86; organist St. Paul's Luth. Ch., Pomona, Calif., 1986—; mem. Calif. State Program Rev., 1982-83; assoc. mem. Calif. Sch. Leadership Acad., Ontario, 1986-89; v.p. So. Calif. Luth. Music Clinic, 1978-81. Author: Sent Forth by God's Blessing, 1999 (award Concordia Hist. Inst., 2000), Mother of the Valley, 2001 (award Concordia Hist. Inst., 2002), Life and Times of Hans and Lydia Mertensen, 2003. Clk. Zion Luth. Sch. Bd. Edn., Maywood, Calif., 1962-64, chmn., 1966-67; mem. Downey (Calif.) City Water Bd., 1977-78; mem. Luth. High Personnel Commn., La Verne, Calif., 1988-92; asst. archivist Pacific S.W. Dist. Luth. Ch., Mo. Synod, 1999—. Named Outstanding Tchr. of Yr., Burke Jr. High Sch. PTA, Pico Rivera, 1973; recipient hon. svc. award Jasper Sch. PTA, Alta Loma, 1983, continuing svc. award, 1988, Golden Oak Svc. award, 1996, Written Books award Concordia Hist. Inst., St. Louis, 2000, 02; employee recognition award Alta Loma Sch. Dist., 1985. Mem. Assn. Calif. Sch. Adminstrs., Assn. West End Sch. Adminstrs., Calif. Tchrs. Assn., Am. Guild Organists, Downey Hist. Soc., Cucamonga Hist. Soc., Casa de Rancho (Cucamonga, Calif.), Phi Delta Kappa (pres. Mt. Baldy chpt. 1993-97, 2001—, advisor 1997-2000, found. chmn. 1991-93). Democrat. Lutheran. Home and Office: 2085 N Palm Ave Upland CA 91784-1476 E-mail: mdoyle@adelphia.net.

DOYLE, MICHAEL PATRICK, microbiologist, educator, director; b. Madison, Wis., Oct. 3, 1949; s. Donald Vincent and Evelyn (Bauer) Doyle; m. Annette Marie Ripple, Dec. 27, 1971; children: Michael Patrick, Patrick Matthew, Kristen Anne. BS in Bacteriology, U. Wis., 1973, MS in Food Microbiology, 1975, PhD in Food Microbiology, 1977. Sr. project leader Ralston Purina Co., St. Louis, 1977-80; asst. prof. U. Wis., Madison, 1980-84, assoc. prof., 1984-88, prof., 1988-91; prof., dir. U. Ga., Griffin, 1991—, dept. head Athens, 1993-99; chmn. sci. bd. U.S. Food and Drug Admin., 2003—. Regents prof. Bd. Regents Ga. U. Sys., 1997—; mem. food and nutrition bd. Inst. Medicine, NAS, 1991—97, com. to ensure safe food from prodn. to consumption, 1998, chair rev. com. USDA E. coli 0157:H7 in ground beef risk assessment, 2001—02, chair food forum, 2003—; mem. nat. adv. com. on microbiol. criteria for foods USA, Washington, 1988—90, Washington, 1994—2000; trustee Internat. Life Scis. Inst.-n.Am., Washington, 1992—, sci. advisor, 1987—96; mem. Internat. Commn. on Microbiol. Specifications for Foods, 1989—2000; Wis. Disting. prof. bd. regents U. Wis., Madison, 1988—91; James M. Craig Meml. lectr. Oreg. State U., Corvallis, 1990; sci. lectr. Am. Soc. Microbiology Found., 1991—93, 1999—2001; Peter J. Shields lectr. U. Calif., Davis, 1993; G. Malcolm Trout vis. scholar Mich. State U., Lansing, 1994; mem. sci. adv. coun. Refrigeration Rsch. and Edn. Found., 1997—2002; York Disting. lectr. Auburn U., 1999; chmn. com. rev. USDA, 2001—02; chmn. sci. bd. U.S. Food and Drug Adminstrn., 2003—; chmn. food forum Inst. Medicine Nat. Acad. Scis., 2003—. Editor: Food Microbiology; Fundamentals and Frontiers, 1997, Food Microbiology: Fundamentals and Frontiers, 2d edit., 2001, Foodborne Bacterial Pathogens, 1989; contbr. articles to profl. jours. Named one of Top 100 Most Cited Rschrs. Agrl. Scis., Inst. Sci. Info., 2002; recipient award for Profl. Excellence, Am. Agrl. Econs. Assn., 1992, Silver Plow Honor award, USDA, 1998, Ptnrs. in Pub. Health award, Ctrs. Disease Control and Prevention, 2001. Fellow: Am. Acad. Microbiology, Inst. of Food Technologists (Fred W. Tanner lectr. 1986, sci. lectr. 1987—90, exec. com. 2000—03, Samuel Cate Prescott award for rsch. 1987, Nicholas Appert award for preeminence in and contbns. to field of food tech. 1996), Internat. Assn. Food Protection (pres. 1992—93, Norbert F. Sherman article excellence award 1993, NFPA food safety award for outstanding contbn. to food safety rsch. and edn. 1999); mem.: Am. Soc. for Microbiology (chmn. food microbiology divsn. 1987—89, Found. lectr. 1991—93, 1999—2001, P.R. Edwards award for outstanding career achievements 1994), Internat. Assn. Food Protection, Gamma Sigma Delta, Phi Kappa Phi. Roman Catholic. Achievements include patents for for monocional antibody to enterohemorrhagic E. coli; for competitive exclusion bacteria to reduce carriage of enterohemorrhagic E. coli by cattle; development of of methods to control and detect foodborne pathogens. Office: U Ga Ctr Food Safety 1109 Experiment St Griffin GA 30223-1797 E-mail: mdoyle@uga.edu.

DOYLE, MICHAEL W. federal official; b. Honolulu, 1948; Student, USAF Academy; AB, Harvard U, 1970; PhD, Harvard U., 1977. Sanford prof. politics and internat. affairs Woodrow Wilson Sch. Pub. and Internat. Affairs, Princeton U., Princeton, N.J.; dir. Ctr. of Internat. Studies Princeton U.; asst. sec.-gen. spl. adviser to sec. gen. Kofi Annan UN, 2001—. Mem. adv. coms. UN High Commr. for Refugees, Lessons Learned Unit, UN Dept. Peacekeeping Ops. Author Empires, UN Peacekeeping in Cambodia: UNTAC's Civil Mandate, Ways of War and Peace; co-author: Alternatives to Monetary Disorder; co-editor: Escalation and Intervention, Keeping the Peace, Peacemaking and Peacekeeping for the New Century, New Thinking in Internat. Relations Theorys. With Mass. National Air Guard. U Harvard awards include Detur Prize, John Harvard Scholar, Atherton Prize Fellowship; Ford Foundation Rsch. Fellowship, SSRC/MacArthur Found. Fellowship, Membership of the Inst. of Advanced Studies, Ctr. for Advanced Study in the Behavioral Scis. Office: Woodrow Wilson Sch Princeton U Princeton NJ 08544-0001

DOYLE, PATRICK JOHN, otolaryngologist, department chairman; b. Moose Jaw, Sask., Can., Nov. 17, 1926; s. William E. and Bertha L. (Fisher) D.; m. Irene Strilchuk, May 21, 1949; children: Sharon, Patrick, Robert, Barbara, Joseph, Kathleen. BSc, U. Alta., 1947, MD, 1949. Diplomate Am. Bd. Otolaryngology (bd. dirs., v.p. 1986-88, pres. 1988-90). Intern U. B.C. Hosp., 1949-50; resident in medicine and pediatrics, 1950-51; resident in otolaryngology U. Oreg. Hosp., 1958-61; asst. prof., then asso. prof. U. Oreg. Med. Sch., 1965-70; mem. faculty U. B.C. Med. Sch., 1963—, prof. otolaryngology, 1972-91, prof. otolaryngology emeritus, 1992—, head dept., 1972-91, program dir. residency tng. program, 1972-91. Head div. otolaryngology St. Paul's Hosp., mem. numerous nat. med. coms. Author numerous articles in field; mem. editorial bds. profl. jours. Fellow Royal Coll. Surgeons Can., Am. Laryngol., Rhinol. and Otol. Soc. (v.p. western sect. 1988, pres. 1994), Am. Laryngol. Soc., Am. Acad. Otolaryngology-Head and Neck Surgery (v.p. 1984, bd. dirs. 1985-87), Am. Otol. Soc.; mem. Can. Soc. Otolaryngology-Head and Neck Surgery (pres. 1987), Pacific Coast Oto-Ophthal. Soc. (pres. 1977), Soc. Univ. Otolaryngologists, U. Oreg. Otolaryngology Alumni Assn. (pres. 1968-70), Am. Otological Soc., Centurion Club, Tinnitus Rsch. Found. Roman Catholic. Office: # 301-5704 Balsam St Vancouver BC Canada V6M 4B9

DOYLE, PATRICK LEE, retired insurance company executive; s. Lee Patrick and Anne Louise D.; m. Ann Marie Yuhasz, Apr. 26, 1952; children: Robert Christopher, Patrick Brian, David Alan. BA, Ohio State U., 1951. CPCU, Am. Inst. Property Casualty Underwriters CLU Assoc. in Risk Mgmt., Ins. Inst. Am. Life reins. mgr. Nationwide Ins. Cos., Columbus, Ohio, 1965-70, asst. to pres., 1970-79, v.p., adminstrv. asst. to pres., 1980-81, v.p. human resources, 1981-82, v.p. Office Gen. Chmn., 1982-94; instr. Ohio State U., Columbus, 1969-82, Franklin U., Columbus, 1973-82. Mem. exam. com. CPCU, Am. Inst. for Property and Liability Underwriters, Phila., 1969-94; trustee Griffith Found. for Ins. Edn., Columbus, 1975—. .Bd. dirs. Cath. Social Svcs., Columbus, 1981-87, St. Stephen's Cmty. House, 1989-94; trustee Kinder Key, 1973—. Mem. Ins. Inst. Am., Soc. CPCU (ednl. dir. 1965-72, Outstanding Educator award), Soc. CLU, Soc. Ins. Research (dir. 1976-79), Gamma Iota Sigma. Republican. Roman Catholic.

DOYLE, PAUL FRANCIS, lawyer; b. N.Y.C., Sept. 3, 1946; s. Paul Francis and Rita Lilian (Mulcahy) D.; m. Margaret Mary Sullivan, Aug. 23, 1969; children: Karen, Lynn. BA in English, Holy Cross Coll., 1968; JD cum laude, NYU, 1973. Bar: Mass. 1973, N.Y. 1975, U.S. Dist. Ct. (so. and ea. dists.) N.Y. 1975, U.S. Ct. Appeals (2d and 3d cirs.) 1975, U.S. Supreme Ct. 1991, U.S. Dist. Ct. Mass. 1992, U.S. Dist. Ct. (no. dist.) N.Y. 1995. Law clk. Superior Ct. Commonwealth of Mass., Boston, 1973-74; assoc. Kelley, Drye & Warren, N.Y.C., 1974-82, ptnr., 1983—. Instr. Nat. Inst. Trial Advocacy, 1994—95; mem. departmental disciplinary com. Supreme Ct. of N.Y., 1st Jud. Dept., 2003—. Assoc. editor Ann. Survey Am. Law, 1972-73. Mem. Planning Bd., Croton-on-Hudson, N.Y., 1989-92, mem. Comprehensive Plan Com., 1999—; mem. pres.'s coun. Holy Cross Coll. With U.S. Army, 1968-70, Vietnam. Mem. Am. Inns of Ct., Order of Coif. Roman Catholic. Office: Kelley Drye & Warren LLP 101 Park Ave New York NY 10178-0062

DOYLE, ROBERT EUGENE, JR., lawyer; b. St. Simons Island, Ga., Sept. 5, 1948; s. Robert Eugene and Elizabeth Anne (Webb) D.; m. Kristina Maria Kost, Nov. 27, 1971; children: K. Maria, R. Eugene III, Emily Anne. BA, George Washington U., 1970; JD, Stetson U., 1975. Bar: Fla. 1975, U.S. Dist. Ct. (mid. and so. dists.) Fla. 1976, U.S. Ct. Appeals (5th cir.) 1981, U.S. Ct. Appeals (11th cir.) 1985, U.S. Supreme Ct. 1994; cert. Nat. Bd. Trial Advocacy. Ptnr. Asbell, Hains & Doyle, Naples, Fla., 1975-93, Quarles & Brady, Naples, 1993—. Mem. code and rules of evidence com. Fla. Bar, 1988—, chair, 1993-94. Pres. Fillabelly Found., Naples, 1993-95. 1st lt. USMC, 1971-75. Mem. ABA, ATLA, Am. Inns of Ct. (barrister Thomas S. Biggs chpt. 1995), Econ. Devel. Coun. Collier County (chmn. 2001-2002). Democrat. Presbyterian. Avocations: fishing, flying. Office: Quarles & Brady 4501 Tamiami Trl N Ste 300 Naples FL 34103-3023

DOYLE, SHARON THOMAS, school system administrator; b. Maysville, Ky., Apr. 1, 1957; d. Donald Lee and Shirley May (Thomas) T.; m. Allen Darryl Doyle, Nov. 29, 1980. B in Music Edn., Morehead State U., 1979; M in Music Edn., U. Ky., 1980; M in Ednl. Adminstrn., U. S.C., 1995. Cert. elem. and music tchr., Ky. (life), elem. and music tchr., adminstr., supr., S.C. Coord. Danville (Ky.)/Centre String Program Centre Coll. Ky., 1980-84; orch. tchr. Spartanburg (S.C.) Sch. Dist. 7, 1984—2000, acting coord., 1992-93; asst. prin. Cleve. Elem. Sch., 2000—. Staff devel. workshop planning Curriculum Leadership in the Arts, Winthrop Coll., Rock Hill, S.C., 1994; facilitator curriculum leadership in the arts program State Dept., 2001—, mem. task force to rewrite S.C. stds. for performing arts, 2001—; prof. of record Converse Coll., S.C. Arts Leadership for Success Acd., Arts in Basic Edn. Curriculum project; writing team for S.C. Music Curriculum Guide, 2002; facilitator for best practice study groups for Spartanburg Sch. Dist. 7,2001-. Advocate S.C. Alliance for Arts Edn., 1995—. Target 2000 grantee S.C. Dept. Edn., 1995, grantee Spartanburg County Fedn., 1996. Mem. Assn. Supervision and Curriculum Devel., S.C. Arts Edn. Assn., S.C. Arts Alliance, Music Edn. Nat. Conf., S.C. Music Educators Assn. (all-state chmn., v.p., pres.-elect, pres. 1988, mem. exec. bd. 1993-99, treas. 1999—, adminstrv. rep. to state bd.), S.C. Assn. Sch. Adminstrs., Nat. Assn. Elem. Sch. Prins. Avocations: reading, travel. Home: 257 Hollis Dr Spartanburg SC 29307-2463 E-mail: sdoyle@spart7.k12.sc.us.

DOYLE, THOMAS EDWARD, lawyer, educator; b. Washington, Mar. 11, 1963; s. Joseph Thomas Doyle and Elizabeth Brown Preston; m. Ferhan K. Doyle, Oct. 4, 1992; children: Alexis Shannon, Dominic Thomas. BS, U. Md., 1985; JD, George Mason U., 1989. Bar: U.S. Ct. Appeals Md. 1991, U.S. Dist. Ct. Md. 1992, D.C. 1993, U.S. Supreme Ct. 1997, U.S. Dist. Ct. D.C. 1997. Atty., law clk. Van Grack, Axelson & Williamowsky, Rockville, Md., 1989-91; pvt. practice Rockville, 1991-92; ptnr. Siegel & Doyle L.L.C., Rockville, 1992—. Adj. prof. Montgomery Coll., Takoma Park, Md., 1991—; mem. adv. bd. D.C. Consumer Protection Law Ctr., Washington, 1997—; founder, exec. dir. Consumer Law Ctr. Md., Rockville, 1997—. Dir. Joseph T. Doyle Meml. Scholarship, Montgomery Coll., 1992. Recipient Am. Jurisprudence awards for excellence in consumer fin. law and pub. fin. law, 1989. Mem. ATLA, ABA, Md. State Bar Assn., D.C. Bar Assn., Million Dollar Advocates Forum. Office: Siegel & Doyle LLC 101 N Adams St Rockville MD 20850-2217

DOYLE, TOM, sculptor, retired educator; b. Jerry City, Ohio, May 23, 1928; s. John Thomas and Kathleen (Solether) D.; m. Natalie N. Burdette (div. 1957); m. Eva Hesse (dec. 1970); m. Jane Miller. Student, Miami U., Oxford, Ohio, 1948-50; BFA, Ohio State U., 1952, MFA, 1953. Sculptor, N.Y.C., to date. Artist-in-residence La Napoule Art Found., France, 1989. One-man shows include Dwan Gallery, N.Y.C., 1966, 67, 55 Mercer Gallery, N.Y.C., 1972, 74, 76, Picker Art Gallery, Colgate U., Hamilton, N.Y., 1976, Sculpture Now, Inc., N.Y.C., 1978, The Sculpture Ctr., N.Y.C., 1988, Bill Bace Gallery, N.Y.C., 1991, 93-94, Long House Found., East Hampton, N.Y., 1995, Mattatuck Mus., Waterbury, Conn., 1996, Kouros Gallery, N.Y.C., 1999, Nicolaysen Art Mus., Casper, Wyo., 2001, New Arts Gallery, Litchfield, Conn., 2003; exhibited in group shows at Whitney Mus., N.Y.C., 1967, Los Angeles County Mus., 1967, Taft Mus., Cin., 1974, Indpls. Mus. Art, 1974. Recipient commendation GSA, Fairbanks, Alaska, 1980, Jimmy Ernst Lifetime Art Achievement award AAAL, 1994, Ohioana Career award for Lifetime Achievement, 1996; Guggenheim fellow, 1982, Nat. Endowment for the Arts fellow, 1990-91; rsch. grantee CUNY, 1989-90. Mem. Am. Abstract Artists, Nat. Acad. Design. E-mail: tjmdoyle@aol.com.

DOYLE, WENDELL E. retired band director, educator; b. Higbee, Mo., July 8, 1940; s. Travis E. and Hattie Erma (Webb) D.; m. Julia Ann Vail, June 23, 1963; children: Dora Michelle, Michael E., Melissa Kae. BS in Edn., Northeast Mo. State U., 1962; MEd in Music, U. Mo., 1967. Cert. lifetime tchr., Mo. Band dir. Braymer (Mo.) C-4, 1962-68, Brookfield (Mo.) R-3, 1968-72, Platte County (Mo.) R-III, 1972-92; ret., 1992. Exchange tchr. Platte County R-III Schs., Warwickshire, Eng., 1984. Pres. Barry Heights Homes Assn., 1986—; minister of music Park Bapt. Ch., Brookfield, 1968-72, Northgate Bapt. Ch., Kansas City, 1972-85. Mem. Mo. State Tchrs. Assn. (pres. Greater Kans. City dist. 1978), Music Educators Nat. Conf., Mo. Music Educators Assn., Mo. Bandmasters Assn. (sec.), Phi Beta Mu (pres. 1990-91, Outstanding Band Dir. award Lambda chpt., 1993), Mo. Bardmasters Assn. (Hall of Fame 1997). Democrat. Avocations: fishing, reading, golfing, travel. Home: 2330 NW Powderhorn Dr Kansas City MO 64154-1311

DOYLE, WILLIAM B. investment executive; BS in Engring., Princeton U., 1981; MBA, Stanford U., 1985. Investment mgr. McKinsey & Co., Inc., Dallas, 1981-83, Allied Signal Inc., Paris, France, 1985-87, Alex Brown & Sons, Inc., San Francisco, 1987-90, Govett Ltd., San Francisco, 1991-95, Doyle & Boissiere LLC, Burlingame, Calif., 1995—. Bd. dirs. Kojo Worldwide Corp., San Diego, Ocean Pacific Apparel Corp., Irvine, Calif., Naturade, Inc., Irvine. Office: Doyle & Boissiere LLC 330 Primrose Rd Ste 500 Burlingame CA 94010 E-mail: dbllc@dbllc.com.

DOYLE, WILLIAM JAY, II, business consultant; b. Cin., Nov. 7, 1928; s. William Jay and Blanche (Gross) D.; m. Joan Lucas, July 23, 1949; children: David L., William Jay, III, Daniel L. BS, Miami U., Oxford, Ohio, 1949; postgrad., U. Cin., 1950-51, Xavier U., 1953-54, Case Western Res. U., 1959-60. Sales rep. Diebold, Inc., Cin., 1949-52, asst. br. mgr., 1953-57, asst. regional mgr., 1957-62, regional mgr., 1962-74; founder, pres. CEO Ctrl. Bus. Group, Cin., 1974-89, chmn., 1989-95, ret., 1995. Mem. area contractor's coun. Spacesaver Corp., 1985-89; speaker on bus systems, security concepts. Developer new concepts in tng., cash and securities handling, mobile and mechanized storage and filing. Mem. Bus. Systems and Sales Mgmt. Assn. (nat. bd. 1977-79, 81-85, pres. 1981-83, 84-85), Inst. of Mgmt. Accts., Masons, Shri Republican. Home: 1110 Roseate Ct Bradenton FL 34209-7364 E-ma billjoan49@att.net.

DOYLE, WILLIAM THOMAS, retired newspaper editor; b. Oakland, Calif., May 22, 1925; s. Albert Norman and Catherine (Stein) D.; m. Claire Louise Wogan, Sept. 1, 1946 (dec. Nov. 10, 1984); children: Patrick, Lawrence, Brian, Carrie; m. Mary M. Doren, May 3, 1986. BJournalism, U. Nev., 1950. Reporter Richmond (Calif.) Independent, 1950-53; reporter Oakland Tribune, 1953-62, asst. state editor, 1962-64, telegraph editor, 1964-67, fin. editor, 1967-79; editor San Francisco Bus. Jour., 1979-81; news dir. Fireman's Fund Ins. Cos., Novato, Calif., 1981-84; mng. editor West County Times, Pinole, Calif., 1984-88. Mem. editorial adv. bd.: Catholic Voice. Pres. Richmond Jr. C. of C., 1957-58; bd. dirs. Cath. Social Svc. Contra Costa County, Calif., 1959-62, Bay Area Coop. Edn. Clearing House, 1977-88, Contra Costa Coll. Found., 1984-88, Richmond Unified Edn. Fund, 1984, Am. Cancer Soc.—West Contra Costa, 1986-96; mem. Richmond Schs. Citizens Adv. Com., 1969; pastoral coun. St. David's Cath. Ch., Richmond, 1994—. With USAAF, 1943-45. Recipient award for best financial sect. daily newspaper Calif., Calif. Newspaper Pubs. Assn., 1968, 70, 72, 74, Knowland award for outstanding performance, 1972, Gen. Excellence award Nat. Newspaper Assn., 1987, Outstanding Editorial Writing award Suburban Newspapers Assn., 1989, 90, 1st Place award for editorial writing Nat. Newspaper Assn., 1992; Hughes fellow Rutgers U., 1969. Mem.: Marine Exch. San Francisco Bay Area, Soc. Am. Bus. Writers, Sons in Retirement, Contra Costa Press Club (pres. 1956, Best News Story award 1965), Contra Costa Club, Elks, Sigma Delta Chi. Home: 2727 Del Monte Ave El Cerrito CA 94530-1507 E-mail: marbildoyle@aol.com.

DOYNO, VICTOR ANTHONY, literature educator; b. Chgo., July 12, 1937; s. Victor A. and Sally B. (Finnegan) D.; m. Ellen Joyce Kuchar, Aug. 22, 1959; children: David, Kenneth, Anna. BA, Miami U. of Ohio, 1959; MA, Harvard U., 1960; PhD, U. Ind., 1966. Instr. Rutgers U., New Brunswick, N.J., 1963-64, Princeton U., 1964-65; prof. SUNY, Buffalo, 1966—. Editor: Mark Twain: American Skeptic, 1985, Random House Huck, 1996, Oxford Huck, 1998; author: Writing Huck Finn, 1992. Recipient Gov.'s award N.Y. Gov. Cuomo, 3 tchg. awards. Office: English Dept SUNY at Buffalo 306 Clemens Buffalo NY 14260-0001 E-mail: doyno@acsu.buffalo.edu.

DOZIER, DAVID CHARLES, JR., marketing public relations and advertising executive; b. Santa Fe, Dec. 4, 1938; s. David Charles Sr. and Zelma (Martin) D.; m. Dianne Flusche, June 1, 1960; children: Deborah, Mary Rebecca, Michael, Constance. BA, U. Dallas, 1960. Editor sports Tex. Catholic, Dallas, 1960-70, gen. sales mgr., 1964-70; dir. classified advt. Dallas Times Herald, 1970-74; pres., chmn. DBG&H Unltd. Inc., Dallas, 1974-88; chmn. Dozier Co., Dallas, 1989—. Innovator, ptnr. Navi Pesanda Indian Blanket Creations, 1992. Author: A Compendium of Endurance, 1989. Mem. Am. Indian, Santa Clara Pueblo Tribe, N.Mex.; cert. athletic trainer Downtown YMCA, 1990-2003. Recipient Disting. Svc. award Pres. U.S. and HUD, 1984. Republican. Roman Catholic. Avocation: completed over 128 marathons. Home: 7102 Wabash Cir Dallas TX 75214-3532 Office: 2021 Farrington St Dallas TX 75207-6607

DOZIER, ELEANOR CAMERON, computer company executive, writer; b. N.Y.C., May 20, 1939; d. Robert Paul and Marion Gill MacNeil; m. Norman Garlan Dozier, June 23, 1989; children: Karen Gonzales, Robert Bennett, Heidi Bennett, Julia, Ian, Jordan. Rep. to British Isles Max Factor, Inc., Hollywood, Calif., 1966—71; co-owner; also songwriter and poet MacNeil Dozier Pub. Co., Pembroke Pines, Fla., 1988—2002; v.p. Computer Dimensions Network Corp., N.Y.C., 1998—. Mktg. dir. Prometheus Devel., San Jose, Calif., 1986—87. Author: (book) O For The Love Of God!, 2003. Recipient commn., Stephen Ministry, Order St. Luke. Episcopalian. Avocations: bicycling, golf, tennis, travel. Address: 250 SW 8th St Dania FL 33004 Office Fax: 954-929-3282. Business E-Mail: call4ecd@bellsouth.net.

DOZIER, ETRULID PRESSLEY, school librarian; b. Anderson, S.C., Sept. 23, 1930; d. Mance and Virgie Mattison Pressley; m. Gibb Dozier (dec. Oct. 1980); children: Shirley Mae, Claudette D. Rouse, Gibb A. III. AB, Benedict Coll., 1954; MSLS, Atlanta U, 1957. Libr. Whittemore H.S.,Conway JR. H.S., Whittemore Park Mid., Conway, SC, 1954—88. Mem. Horry County Trustee Bd., Conway, SC, 2003, HIgher Edn. Comm. Coastal Carolina U, Conway, SC, 2003. Democrat. Bapt. Home: 1915 Racepathe Ave Conway SC 29527

DOZIER, GLENN JOSEPH, diversified financial services company executive; b. Lexington, Ky., Apr. 7, 1950; s. Emmitt and Henrietta Elsie (Geisler) Dozier; m. Paula Jean Cook, June 3, 1974; children: Laura Jean, Diana Leigh. BS in Indsl. Engring. and Ops. Rsch., Va. Poly. Inst., 1972; MBA, U. Va., 1975. Mfg. engr. Tex. Instruments, Dallas, 1972-73; fin. analyst Dravo Corp., Pitts., 1975-76, mgr. corp. fin. analysis, 1976-79, dir. corp. devel., 1980-82, dir. corp. planning and devel., 1982-83; v.p. fin. Dravo Constructors, Inc., Pitts., 1983-87; CFO, treas., asst. sec. AMF Bowling Internat. Inc. and AMF Bowling, Inc., Richmond, Va., 1987-90; v.p., CFO, treas. Owens and Minor, Inc., Richmond, 1990-93, sr. v.p. ops. and systems, CFO, 1991-92, sr. v.p. fin., CFO, 1992-96; CFO Displaytech, Inc., 1997-98; sr. v.p., CFO Hagler Bailly Inc., 1998-99, 1999-2000, This End Up Furniture Co., 2001—; exec. v.p., CFO Upstate Group Inc. Author: (book) Economic Development Finance, 1986, CFO Handbook, 1996, Financial Executives Handbook. Mem. Colonies Civic Assn. Mem.: Colonies Swim and Tennis Club, Tau Beta Pi, Phi Kappa Phi, Alpha Pi Mu, Phi Eta Sigma. Republican. Methodist. Avocations: golf, travel, gardening.

DOZIER, GLORIA ANNE CLIFTON, retired buyer; b. Phila., Jan. 2, 1930; d. James Francis X. and Anna Carolyn (Schrufer) Clifton; m. Joe V. Dozier, Dec. 28, 1954; children: James M., John C., Anne M., Robert E. BS, Drexel U., 1952. Cert. tchr., Tex. Home econs. tchr. Marathon (Tex.) H.S., 1952—55; buyer, salesperson Schreiner Dept. Store, Kerrville, Tex., 1973—85, ret., 1985. Author: Kerr County Texas Death Records 1903-1960, 1988, Kerr County Texas Birth Records 1903-1935 Including 1870-1935, 1998, Kerrville Mt. Sun and Kerrville Advance Obituary and Death Notice Index 1898-1965, 1998, Kerrville Mt. Sun Obituary Index 1966-1985, 1999, All Name Index for History of Bucks County, Pa., 1999, Obituary Index Kerrville, Mt. Sun, 1998-99, 2000, 01, 02 (5 vols.), Kerrville Daily Times, 1986-2002 (17 vols.). Mem. adv. bd. Butt-Holdsworth Meml. Libr., Kerrville, 1999-2000, libr. bd., 2003. Recipient Martha Washington medal SAR, 1999, Cert. Appreciation, 1991, Kerr County Hist. Coun., 1988. Mem. Kerrville Geneaol. Soc. (libr. 1986-91, pres. 1999-2000, 2003—, sec. 1992-93, treas. 2001-02, Cert. Appreciation 1991), Hill Country Preservation Soc. Avocations: genealogy, registered cats.

DOZIER, JAMES LEE, former army officer; b. Arcadia, Fla., Apr. 10, 1931; s. Joseph B. and Leota (Caruthers) D.; m. Judith I. Stimpson, June 30, 1956; children— Cheryl Lyn, Scott Lee BS, U.S. Mil. Acad., 1956; MS in Aerospace Engring., U. Ariz., 1964. Commd. 2d lt. U.S. Army, 1956, advanced through grades to maj. gen., 1984, comdr. 1st Squadron, 1st Cav., 1st Armored Div., 1971-73, staff officer Office of Dep. Chief of Staff for Research, Devel. and Acquisition, 1974-76, also mil. asst. to asst. sec. of army, 1974-76, comdr. 2d Brigade, 2d Armored div. Fort Hood, Tex., 1976-78, chief of staff 2d Armored div., 1978-79, chief of staff III Corps and Ft. Hood, 1979-80, dep. chief of staff logistics and adminstrn. Allied Land Forces So. Europe Verona, Italy, 1980-82, asst. comdt. Armor Sch. Ft. Knox, Ky., 1982-83, dep. comdg. gen. III Corps and Fort Hood Fort Hood, Tex., 1983-85, ret., 1985; pres. Golden Grove Mgmt. Corp., Arcadia, Fla., 1985-87, Suncoast Media Group, Venice, Fla., 1987; gen. mgr. David C. Brown Enterprises, 1988-93; owner JCS Group, Ft. Myers, 1993—. Lectr., condr. seminars on kidnapping experience. Contbg. author: Winter of Fire, 1990; contbr. articles to mil. jours. Decorated Silver Star, Legion of Merit, Bronze Star with V device and 2 oak leaf clusters, Air medals, Purple Heart Avocations: fishing; boating; gardening; woodworking.

DOZIER, NANCY KERNS, retired geriatrics nurse; b. Akron, Ohio, May 31, 1930; d. Guy F. and Alma Jane (Good) Kerns; 1 child, Frederick A. Dietz. AA, Prince George C.C., 1972; student, Catonsville (Md.) Coll., 1976, 78. RN, Ohio, Fla., Md.; cert. in basic and advanced coronary care. Med.-surg., orthopedic staff nurse Childrens Hosp., Balt., 1973-74; nurse med. surg. flr. Bon Secours Hosp., Balt., 1974-76; staff nurse Md. State Maximum Security Penal Inst., Jessup, 1977-78, Bonifay (Fla.) Nursing Home, 1985-86; staff float nurse

'oy Scouts Am., Dalton, 1989-96; mem. Zoning ... chmn., 1997—, Dalton Coun. Aging, 1997—. ... Western Mass. Pro Bono Referral Svc., 1983-87. ... Assn., Berkshire Bar Assn. (exec. com. 1989-91, v.p. ... 1999-2001). Roman Catholic. Avocations: skiing, tennis. Home: ... Barton Hill Rd Dalton MA 01226-2005 Office: Barry & Doyle 8 Bank Row Ste 2 Pittsfield MA 01201-6224

DOYLE, CONSTANCE TALCOTT JOHNSTON, physician, educator, medical association administrator; b. Mansfield, Ohio, July 8, 1945; d. Frederick Lyman IV and Nancy Jean Bushnell (Johnston) Talcott; children: Ian Frederick Demsky, Zachary Adam Demsky. BS, Ohio U., 1967; MD, Ohio State U., 1971. Diplomate Am. Bd. Emergency Medicine; bd. cert. in emergency crisis response. Intern Riverside Hosp., Columbus, Ohio, 1971-72; resident in internal medicine Hurley Hosp., U. Mich., Flint, 1972-74; emergency physician Oakwood Hosp., Dearborn, Mich., 1974-76, Jackson County (Mich.) Emergency Svcs., 1975-95; cons. Region II EMS, 1978-79, disaster cons., 1983-95; St. Joseph Mercy Hosp., Ann Arbor, 1995—, med. flight physician helicopter life support svcs., 1996-2000; core faculty St. Joseph Merch Hosp./U. Mich. Emergency Residency, Ann Arbor, 1995—; survival flight physician helicopter rescue svc. U. Mich., 1983-91; course dir. advanced cardiac life support and chmn. advanced life support com. W.A. Foote Meml. Hosp., Jackson, 1979-95; dep. dir. emergency svcs. med. ctrl. bd. Washtenaw Livingston County, 2000—; core faculty St. Joseph Mercy Hosp., Ann Arbor, 1996. Clin. instr. emergency svcs., dept. surgery U. Mich., 1981—; faculty combined emergency medicine residency St. Joseph Mercy Hosp.-U. Mich., Ann Arbor, 1995—; asst. med. dir. Region 2 South Biodef. Network, 2002-03, co-med. dir., 2003—; instr. EMT refresher courses, Jackson County, Jackson C.C.; MedFlight physician, 1996-99; Washtenaw County Subcom. on Bioterrorism, 2000—; Washtenaw County Local Emergency Planning Com., 1998—; dep. med. dir. Washtenaw/Livingston County Med. Control Authority, 2000—. Contbg. author: Clinical Approach to Poisoning and Toxicology, 1983, 89, 97, May's Textbook of Emergency Medicine, 1991, Schwartz Principles and Practice of Emergency Medicine, 1992, Reisdorff Pediatric Emergency Medicine, 1993; contbr. articles to profl. jours. Mem. local emergency planning com. Washtenaw County, 1999—, mem. subcom. on bioterrorism, 2000—; asst. med. dir. Region 2S Biodefense Network, 2002, co-med. dir., 2003—; mem. Disaster Med. Assistance Team, 2000—. Fellow Am. Coll. Emergency Physicians (pres. Mich. disaster com. 1987-88, bd. dirs. Mich. 1979-88, chmn. Mich. disaster com. 1979-85, mem. nat. disaster med. svcs. com. 1983-85, chmn. 1987-88, cons. disaster mgmt. course Fed. Emergency Mgmt. Agy. 1982, treas. 1984-85, emergency med. svcs. com. 1985, pres. 1986-87, councillor 1986-87, chair steering com. policy sect., 1994—, mem. disaster sect., 1995—, exec. com. disaster sect. 1997—, chair policy sect. disaster 1995—, vice chair sect. careers in emergency medicine 1997—, chair, 2000—), Nat. Assn. Coll. Emergency Physicians (vice chair sect. of disaster med. svcs. 1990-92, nat. disaster subcom. 1989-90, chair subsect. psychol. rehab. svcs., disaster med. svcs. 1992-94, chair policy and legis. 1994-96, task force on hazardous materials 1993—, steering com. sect. disaster medicine 1994—, exec. com. sect. disaster medicine 1995); mem. ACP, Am. Med. Women's Assn., Am. Assn. Women Emergency Physicians, Mich. Assn. Emergency Med. Technicians (bd. dirs. 1979-80), Mich. State Med. Soc., Washtenaw County Med. Soc., Sierra Club. Jewish. Office: 1251 King George Blvd Ann Arbor MI 48108 also: St Joseph Mercy Hosp Dept Emergency Medicine Ann Arbor MI 48109

DOYLE, DAVID PERRIE, lawyer; b. Orange, N.J., May 11, 1960; s. Ralph Thomas and Dorothy (Trevorrow) D.; m. Ana Linda Day, Mar. 7, 1987. BA, Emory U., 1982; JD, Rutgers U., 1985; LLM in Taxation, N.Y.U., 1990. Bar: N.J. 1986, U.S. Dist. Ct. N.J. 1986, U.S. Tax Ct. 1988, U.S. Dist. Ct. (so. dist.) N.Y. 1998. Law clk. to presiding judge Tax Ct. N.J., Trenton, 1985-86; assoc. Pitney, Hardin, Kipp & Szuch, Morristown, N.J., 1986-92, counsel, 1993-94, ptnr., 1995—. Mem. ABA (tax sect., mem. employee benefits com.), N.J. State Bar Assn. (tax sect., past chair employee benefits com.). Office: Pitney Hardin Kipp & Szuch LLP PO Box 1945 Morristown NJ 07962-1945 E-mail: ddoyle@pitneyhardin.com.

DOYLE, DELORES MARIE, retired principal; b. Madison, S.D., July 24, 1939; d. Martin N. and Pearl M. (Anderson) Berkelo; m. Patrick J. Doyle; children: Kathleen, Shawn, Tamara, Timothy. AS, Dakota State Coll., Madison, 1959; BS, Mid. Tenn. State U., 1966, MEd, 1968, EdS, 1975; PhD, Peabody/Vanderbilt U., 1980. Cert. career ladder III tchr. Tchr. 4th grade Meriden-Cleghorn Schs., Meriden, Iowa, 1960-62; tchr. 1st grade Hanover (Ill.) Sch., 1963-66; tchr. 2d grade Hobgood Sch., Murfreesboro, Tenn., 1969-70; tchr. 1st grade Reeves-Rogers Sch., Murfreesboro, 1972-80, tchr. 2d grade, 1981-97, prin., 1997-2000; ret., 2000. Cooperating tchr. Mid. Tenn. State U. Student Tchrs., Murfreesboro, 1972—97, mem. task force edn., 1992—93; summer sch. dir. Murfreesboro City Schs., 1986—98; lead project tutor Reeves-Rogers Sch., Murfreesboro, 1987—90. Active Edn. 2000 Com., Murfreesboro C. of C., 1993; trustee Mid Tenn State U. Found., 1995—2001; bd. dirs. Grace Luth. Ch., Murfreesboro, 1991—93, 2001—03, mem. choir, 1975—. Named Career Ladder III Tchr., Dept. Edn., Nashville, 1984; named to Tenn. Tchrs. Hall of Fame, 2001; recipient Tenn. Tchr. of the Yr. award, Dept. Edn., Nashville, 1992, Murfreesboro City Tchr. of the Yr. award, Murfreesboro City Schs., 1991, Mid-Cumberland Dist. Tchr. of the Yr. award, Dist. Dept. Edn., 1991, Trailblazer award, 1995; Creative Tchg. grantee, State Dept. Edn., 1992, 1993. Mem.: Murfreesboro Edn. Assn. (pres. 1981—82), Tenn. Edn. Assn. (Disting. Classroom Tchr. award 1992, Disting. Adminstr. award 2000), Tenn. State Tchr. of Yr. Orgn. (v.p. 2000—), Nat. State Tchr. of Yr. Orgn., Kappa Delta Pi, Delta Kappa Gamma. Democrat. Avocations: bridge, travel, reading, bicycling. Home: 1710 Sutton Pl Murfreesboro TN 37129-6513 E-mail: pandddoyle@comcast.net.

DOYLE, DENNIS T. lawyer; b. White Plains, N.Y., Apr. 9, 1943; BA, Boston Coll., 1965; JD, Fordham U., 1968. Bar: N.Y. State 1968, U.S. Dist. Ct. (so. and ea. dists.) N.Y. 1978, U.S. Supreme Ct. 1978. Ptnr. O'Connor, McGuiness, Conte, Doyle & Oleson, White Plains, 1969—. Author: You Haven't Got a Prayer. Mem. ABA, Am. Trial Lawyers Assn., N.Y. State, Fedn. Ins. and Corp. Counsel, Trial Lawyers Assn., Appalachian Mountain Club, Adirondeck Mountain Club, Adirondeck Coun. Avocations: bicycling, religious education, hiking, golf. Office: O'Connor McGuiness Conte Doyle & Oleson One Barker Ave Ste 675 White Plains NY 10601-1517 Fax: 914 948-0645. E-mail: ddoyle@omcdoc.com.

DOYLE, DONALD VINCENT, retired state senator, lawyer; b. Sioux City, Iowa, Jan. 13, 1925; s. William E. and Nelsine E. (Sparby) D.; m. Jant E. Holtz, Aug. 9, 1963; 1 child, Dawn Renee. BS, Morningside Coll., Sioux City, 1951; JD, U. S.D., 1953. Bar: S.D. 1953, Iowa 1953. Pvt. practice, Sioux City, 1953—; mem. Iowa Ho. of Reps., 1956-80, Iowa Senate, 1981-93, chmn. judiciary com., 1982-90. Mem. law and justice com. Nat. Conf. State Legis., 1987-89, chmn., 1988-89; chmn. Iowa Boundary Commn., 1991, 92; mem. Commn. Accreditation Law Enforcement Agys., Inc., 1988-95. With USAF, 1943—46. Recipient award Woodbury County Peace Officers, 1974, Restoration Club Sioux City, 1964, Outstanding Elected Ofcl. award Iowa Corrections Assn., 1979. Mem. Iowa Bar Assn., S.D. Bar Assn. (50-Yr. plaque 2003), Woodbury County Bar Assn., CBI Vets. Assn. (past nat. judge adv., Iowa comdr. 1965), Am. Legion, VFW (comdr. post 1997-2001), DAV, 40 and 8 (chef de gare 1999-2001). Office: PO Box 941 Sioux City IA 51102-0941 E-mail: sendvdoyle@aol.com.

DOYLE, EUGENIE FLERI, pediatric cardiologist, educator; b. Bklyn., Oct. 19, 1921; d. Paul Charles and Antoinette (Giovannetti) Fleri; m. Joseph Anthony Doyle, Aug. 19, 1944; children: Christopher, Stephen, Eugenie, Jane Marie, Richard. BS, Marymount Coll., Tarrytown, N.Y., 1943, DSc (hon.), 1993; MD, Johns Hopkins U., 1946; DSc (hon.), Coll. New Rochelle, 1975. Intern in pediatrics Johns Hopkins Hosp., Balt., 1946-47; pediatric resident Bellevue Hosp., N.Y.C., 1947-49; fellow pediatric cardiology NYU Med. Ctr., 1949-53, dir. pediatric cardiology, 1958-93; asst. prof. pediatrics NYU Sch. Medicine, 1953-58, assoc. prof., 1959-70, prof., 1970-92, prof. emerita, 1993—, clin. prof. pediatrics, 1994—. Mem. cardiac adv. com. N.Y. State Health Dept., 1983-92; dir. Vis. Nurse Svc., N.Y.C., 1984—. Editor: Pediatric Cardiology, 1985; contbr. articles to profl. jours. Trustee Marymount Coll., 1983-91, vice chair bd., 1988-91. Mem. Am. Acad. Pediatrics, Am. Pediatric Soc., Am. Coll. Cardiology, Am. Heart Assn., N.Y. Heart Assn. (bd. dirs. 1977-84, pres. 1979-81), Cosmopolitan Club. Roman Catholic. Avocations: gardening, travel, ballet. Home: 32 Washington Sq W New York NY 10011-9156 Office: NYU Med Ctr 550 1st Ave New York NY 10016-6402

DOYLE, FREDERICK JOSEPH, retired government research scientist; b. Oak Park, Ill., Apr. 3, 1920; s. John Frederick and Mary Elizabeth (Meyers) D.; m. Mary Blaskovich, June 18, 1955; children: Frederick J., Margaret, Mary Ellen, George. BCE, Syracuse U., 1951; postgrad., Internat. Tng. Ctr. Aerial Sur, Delft, The Netherlands, 1952; D Eng (hon.), Tech. U., Hannover, Germany, 1976; DSc (hon.), Ohio STate U., 1986, U. Bordeaux, France, 1987; D in Tech., Royal Tech. U., Sweden, 1987. Assoc. prof. geodetic sci. Ohio State U., 1952-60, chmn. dept., 1959-60; chief scientist Raytheon Autometric Co., Alexandria, Va., 1960-69; sci. advisor nat. mapping divsn. U.S. Geol. Survey, Reston, Va., 1969-89, dir. earth resources observation sys. program, 1978-80; ret., 1989. Geodesy cartography adv. com. nat. Acad. Scis., 1967-69; chmn. Apollo orbital Sci. photo team NASA, 1969-73, planetary cartography com., 1974-95; exec. com. divsn. earth sci. NRC, 1973-76. With C.E., AUS, 1943-48, PTO. Recipient Meritorious Svc. award Dept. Interior, 1977, Disting. Svc. medal, 1981, Silver medal City of Paris, 1978; Fulbright fellow Internat. Tng. Ctr. Aerial Survey, 1952, Internat. Tng. Ctr. fellow, 1986. Fellow AAAS; mem. NAE, Internat. Soc. Photogrammetry Remote Sensing (hon., pres. 1980-84, Brock award 1984), Am. Congress Surveying Mapping, Am. Geophys. Union, Am. Soc. Photogrammetry (hon., pres. 1969-70, contbg. author, editor publs., Fairchild Photogrammetric award 1968, Alan Gordon award 1985, Chancellors medal U.Calif. Santa Barbara 2000). Home: 1591 Forest Villa Ln Mc Lean VA 22101-4132

DOYLE, GERARD FRANCIS, lawyer; b. Needham, Mass., Oct. 25, 1942; s. John Patrick and Catherine Mary (Lawler) D.; m. Paula Marie Dervay, may 14, 1983; children: Laura Dervay, Meredith Lawler, Philip John. BS in Indsl. Adminstrn., Yale U., 1966; JD, Georgetown U., 1972. Bar: D.C. 1973, U.S. Dist. Ct. D.C. 1973, U.S. Ct. Fed. Claims 1976, U.S. Ct. Appeals (fed. cir.) 1982, U.S. Supreme Ct. 1982, Va. 2000. Group head for operating submarine reactors and reactor tech Div. Naval Reactors AEC, Washington, 1970-72; atty. Morgan, Lewis & Bockius, Washington, 1972-76; legal counsel Am. Nuclear Energy Coun., Washington, 1975-76; ptnr. Cotten, Day & Doyle, Washington, 1976-87, Doyle & Savit, Doyle, Simmons & Bachman, Doyle & Bachman LLP, Washington, 1987-99, Arlington, Va., 1999—. Legal counsel Assn. Fed. Data Peripheral Suppliers, Washington, 1979; dir. M Internat., Inc.; author and lectr. in field; columnist Federal Computer Week, 1989. Served in USN, 1966-71. Recipient outstanding young man of yr. award, 1976. Mem. ABA (coun. publ. contract law sect. 1989-92), D.C. Bar Assn., Fed. Bar Assn., Am. Arbitration Assn. (panel arbitrators), Nat. Contract Mgmt. Assn., Met. Club (Washington), Yale Club (Washington), Washington Golf & Country Club. Republican. Roman Catholic. Home: 901 Whann Ave Mc Lean VA 22101-1570 Office: Doyle & Bachman LLP 4245 Fairfax Dr Arlington VA 22203-1637 E-mail: gdoyle@doylebachman.com.

DOYLE, GILLIAN, actress; b. Maidenhead, Berkshire, Eng. came to U.S., 1977; d. John Joseph and Joan (Walker) D. BA in Theatre magna cum laude, Am. U., Washington, 1981. Appeared in (off Broadway) Ernest in Love, NYC, 1980; (plays) No Exit, Washington, 1985, Fefu and Her Friends, 1985, The Winters Tale, 1987, A Christmas Carol, 1987, Erpingham Camp, 1989, Turn of the Screw, 1989, Season's Greetings, 1986, Terra Nova, 1987, Mountain, 1990, Old Favorites, 1991, What the Butler Saw, 1993, Fawlty Towers, 1994, Last of the Red Hot Lovers, 1995, The Musical Comedy Murders of 1940, 1996, Move Over Mrs. Markham, 1997, Declarations: Love Letters of the Great Romantics, 1998, Present Laughter, 1999, Two, 1999, U.S.A., 2000, Blithe Spirit, 2002, A Midsummer Night's Dream, 2002, What The Butler Saw, 2003; (musical) The Cradle Will Rock, 2001; (films) Chances Are, 1989, Born Yesterday, 1993, North, 1993, Decade of Love, 1994, Wild Bill, 1994, The Tie That Binds, 1995, Independence Day, 1996, Play Me Again Sam, 1999, Love, 2000; (TV) Ancient Prophecies III, 1995, Friends, 1995, The Martin Short Show, 1995, Days of Our Lives, 1996, Love's Deadly Triangle: The Texas Cadet Murder, 1996, General Hospital, 1997, Port Charles, 1999, The Man Show, 1999, Titus, 2001; (music video) Johnny Sportcoat and the Casuals, 1987; (comml.) United Way, 1988. Mem. SAG, AFTRA, Actors Equity Assn., Phi Kappa Phi. Democrat. Roman Catholic. Avocations: equestrienne, golf, swimming, music, philosophy, scuba diving (cert.). E-mail: gilliandoyle@hotmail.com.

DOYLE, IRENE ELIZABETH, electronic sales executive, nurse; b. West Point, Iowa, Oct. 5, 1920; d. Joseph Deidrich and Mary Adelaide (Groene) Schulte; m. William Joseph Doyle, Feb. 3, 1956. RN, Mercy Hosp., 1941. Courier nurse Santa Fe R.R., Chgo., 1947-50; indsl. nurse Montgomery Ward, Chgo., 1950-54; rep. Hornblower & Weeks, Chgo., 1954-56; v.p. William J. Doyle Co., Chgo., 1956-80, Ormond Beach, Fla., 1980-88. Served with M.C., U.S. Army, 1942-46. Mem. Electronic Reps. Assn. Republican. Roman Catholic. Club: Oceanside Country (Ormond Beach).

DOYLE, JAMES E(DWARD), governor; b. Washington, Nov. 23, 1945; s. James E. and Ruth (Bachhuber) Doyle; m. Jessica Laird, Dec. 21, 1966; children: Augustus, Gabriel. Student, Stanford U., 1963—66; AB in History, U. Wis., 1967; JD cum laude, Harvard U., 1972. Bar: Ariz. 1973, Wis. 1975, U.S. Dist. Ct. N.Mex. 1973, U.S. Dist. Ct. Ariz. 1973, U.S. Dist. Ct. Utah 1973, U.S. Dist. Ct. (we. dist.) Wis. 1975, U.S. Dist. Ct. (ea. dist.) Wis. 1976, U.S. Ct. Appeals (10th cir.) 1974, U.S. Ct. Appeals (7th cir.) 1985, U.S. Supreme Ct. 1989. Vol. Peace Corps, Tunisia, 1967—69; atty. DNA Legal Svcs., Chinle, Ariz., 1972—75; ptnr. Jacobs & Doyle, Madison, Wis., 1975—77; dist. atty. Dane County, Madison, 1977—83; ptnr. Doyle & Ritz, Madison, 1983—90; of counsel Lawton & Cates, Madison, 1990—91; atty. gen. State of Wis., Madison, 1991—2002, gov., 2003—. Mem.: ABA, 7th Cir. Bar Assn. (chmn. criminal law sect. 1988—89), Wis. Bar Assn. (bd. dirs. criminal law sect. 1988). Democrat. Roman Catholic. Office: Office of the Governor 115 E State Capitol Madison WI 53702*

DOYLE, JENNIFER, surgical educator, scholar; b. Milw., Aug. 23, 1952; d. Sylvester Edward and Ethel Anna (Axmann) D. BA, Mt. Mary Coll., 1974; MA, U. Wis., Milw., 1979; postgrad., Brown U., 1979-84, Boston Coll., 2000—. Grad. tchg. asst. U. Wis., 1977-79; fellow Brown U., Providence, 1979-80, grad. teaching asst., 1981-84; adj. instr. Bryant Coll., Smithfield, R.I., 1985; adj. instr. history R.I. Coll., Providence, 1986-90; residency coord. dept. family medicine Brown U., Providence, 1986-87, edn. coord. dept. surgery, 1987-90; assoc. surgery Harvard Med. Sch., Boston, 1990-92, lectr. in surgery, 1992—; asst. dir. surg. edn. Deaconess Hosp., Boston, 1990-96; dir. ednl. devel. and evaluation Beth Israel Deaconess Med. Ctr., Boston, 1996—. Mem. instnl. assessment com. Sch. Medicine Brown U., 2000; inst. scholar Carl. J. Shapiro Inst. for Edn. and Rsch., Boston, 2000—. Dem. committeeman, Wauwatosa, Wis., 1976-78; mem. Big Sisters of R.I., Providence, 1980-88; co-organizer Providence Freeze Coalition, 1982; mem. instnl. assessment com. Brown U. Sch. Medicine, 2000-01. Recipient Charles Edison Meml. fellowship, 1974, Lucetta Bissell Meml. fellowship, 1978, univ. fellowship Brown U., 1979, Wayland Collegium fellowship Brown U., 1988. Mem. Am. Ednl. Rsch. Assn., Assn. Am. Med. Colls., Assn. Surg. Edn., Assn. Program Dirs. in Surgery (assoc.), Assn. of Women Surgeons (assoc.), Assn. for Study of Med. Edn. (U.K.), Generalists in Med. Edn., Am. Evaluation Assn., AAUW, Mass. Consort. on Faculty Devel. Home: 219 Willow St West Roxbury MA 02132-1326 Office: Beth Israel Deaconess Med Ctr Dept Surgery 110 Francis St Ste 3A Boston MA 02215-5501 E-mail: jdoyle@bidmc.harvard.edu., jennifer_doyle@hms.harvard.edu.

DOYLE, JOHN LAWRENCE, artist; b. Chgo., Mar. 14, 1939; s. John W. and Cecelia M. (Tarkowski) D.; children: Lynn, Sean, Morgan. BA, Sch. of Art Inst. Chgo., 1962; MA, No. Ill. U., 1967. Tchr. art Forest View High Sch., Arlington Heights, Ill., 1962-72. Bd. dirs. Toe River Arts Coun., Yancey Libr., Amy Regional Libr. Sys., Yancey History Assn., Yancey Evening Sch. Program, Steering Com., Yancey Mus./Visitor Ctr. Project. One-man shows of prints and/or paintings include: Denver Natural History Mus., Natural Am. Indian Mus., Spokane, Wash., Allen Galleries, Milw., U. N.D., U. S.D., Black Gallery, Taos, N.Mex., Vanderbilt U., Nashville, Tenn., Johns Hopkins U., Balt., Jockey Club Gallery, Miami, Fla., New West Whitney Gallery Western Art, Cody, Wyo., Harvard Med. Library, Lesch Gallery, Mpls., Clev. Clinic, Mayo Clinic, MGM Grand, Las Vegas, Yale U. Hosp., Now and Then Gallery, N.Y.C., Fine Print Unltd., Miami, Grand Gallery, Nev., Galerie Une, Puerto Vallarta, Mex., Welnetz Studio, Wis., Gallery G, Wichita, all 1981; group shows, latest being: U. Miami, Fla., Tex. Tech U., Amarillo and Lubbock, U. Iowa Hosp. and Clinic, Loma Linda U., Calif., Art Resources, Denver, Hayden Hayes Gallery, Colorado Springs, Colo., Southwestern Gallery, Dallas, Nat. Library of Medicine, Bethesda, Md., Cornell Med. Coll., N.Y.C., Columbia U., N.Y.C., U. Kans., Harvard Law Library, Denver Nat. Hist. Mus., William Mitchell Law Sch., Mpls., United Bank of Austin, Tex., others, 1982-85, Inter Art, Nice, France, Loyola U. Sch. Law, New Orleans, Fine Arts Ltd., Miami, U. Dubuque, Iowa, Art Expo Los Angeles, Art Expo N.Y., Degan Bella Gallery, San Antonio, U. Ariz., Tempe, Midwest Mus. Am. Art, Ind., 1986, U. Ill., Chgo., 1987, R. Volid Gallery, Chgo., 1987, Royce Gallery, Denver, 1987, Denver Mus. Nat. History, 1987, No. Ill. U., DeKalb, 1987, Art Expo, N.Y.C., 1987, U. Ill. Chgo., 1988, R. Volip Gallery, Chgo., 1988, Ramses II Denver Mus., N.H., 1988, Royce Gallery, Denver, 1988, Hayden-Hayes Gallery, Colorado Springs, 1988, World Trade Ctr., Mpls.-St. Paul, 1988, Bergren Gallery, Rockford, Ill., 1988, Red Carpet Gallery, Minn., 1988, Yancey County Hist. Mus., N.C., 1988, Minn. World Trade Ctr., St. Paul, 1989, U. Ill., Champaign, 1989, U. Wis., Madison, 1989, Jean Stephen Gallery, Mpls., 1989, New West Cont. Art, Buffalo Bill Hist. Ctr., Cody, Wyo., 1990, White Thunder World Gallery, Milw., 1990, D. Ehrlein Gallery, Milw., 1990, Bank One, Milw., 1990, White Hart Gallery, Steamboat Springs, Colo., 1991, Suzanne Brown Gallery, Scottsdale, Ariz., 1991, Midwest Mus. Am. Art, Elkhart, Ind., 1991, Scripps Meml. Hosp. Schaetzel Ctr., La Jolla, Calif., 1991, Suzanne Brown Gallery, Scottsdale, Ariz., 1992, Walker Art Ctr., Asheville, N.C., 1992; represented in permanent collections: Library of Congress, Washington, Art Inst. Chgo., Indpls., Mus. Art, Carnegie Inst., Pitts., Norton Gallery of Art, West Palm Beach, Fla., Birmingham (Ala.) Mus. Art, Canton (Ohio) Art Inst., Columbus Mus. Fine Art, Columbus, Ohio, Fort Lauderdale (Fla.) Mus. Art, Miss. Art Mus., Whitney Gallery Western Art, Jackson, Nat. Gallery of Art, Washington, U. Mich., Ann Arbor, Savannah (Ga.) Coll. Art and Design, Scripps Meml. Hosp., La Jolla. Bd. dirs. Family Violence Coalition Yancey County Vol. Coop, Toe River Arts Coun., Yancey Libr., Amy Regional Libr., Healty Yancy; pres. Yancey History Assn.; sec., treas. Mus. Visitor Ctr. Project; chair subcom. Land Use Planning Commn.; mem. 21st century cmtys. action com. Yancey County Cultural Resource Commn. Recipient Hon. Mention Internat. Printmakers, 1971; George Brown Travelling fellow, 1962 Address: PO Box 715 Burnsville NC 28714-0715

DOYLE, JOHN ROBERT, lawyer; b. Chgo., May 12, 1950; s. Frank Edward and Dorothy (Bolton) D.; m. Kathleen Julius, June 14, 1974; children: Melissa, Maureen. BA magna cum laude, St. Louis U., 1971; JD summa cum laude, DePaul U., 1976. Bar: Ill. 1976, U.S. Dist. Ct. 1976, U.S. Dist. Ct. (no. dist.) Ill. 1982, Ill. Trial Bar 1982, U.S. Ct. Appeals (7th cir.) 1982. Ptnr. McDermott, Will & Emery, Chgo., 1976—. Mem. ABA, Chgo. Bar Assn. (jud. investigative hearing panel 1986-88), Phi Beta Kappa. Office: McDermott Will & Emery 227 W Monroe St Ste 3100 Chicago IL 60606-5096

DOYLE, JOSEPH ANTHONY, retired lawyer; b. N.Y.C., June 13, 1920; s. Joseph A. and Jane (Donahue) D.; m. Eugenie A. Fleri, Aug. 19, 1944; children: Christopher, Stephen, Eugenie, Jane, Richard. BS, Georgetown U., 1941; LLB, Columbia U., 1947. Bar: N.Y. 1948. Assoc. Shearman & Sterling, N.Y.C., 1947-57, ptnr., 1957-79, 81-97; asst. sec. for manpower, res. affairs and logistics USN, Washington, 1979-81. Bd. dirs. The Fuji Bank and Trust Co. Bd. dirs. USO of Met. N.Y., 1982-90. Lt. USNR, 1941-45. Decorated Navy Cross, D.F.C. with 3 gold stars, Air medal with 7 gold stars; recipient Disting. Pub. Service award Sec. of Navy, 1980. Mem. Met. Club (Washington). Democrat. Roman Catholic. Home: 32 Washington Sq W New York NY 10011-9156

DOYLE, JOSEPH THEOBALD, physician, educator; b. Providence, June 11, 1918; s. Joseph Donald and Gertrude Harriet (Theobald) D.; m. Elizabeth Thompson, Dec. 26, 1944 (dec.); children: Shelagh Thompson, Michael Kedian; m. Joan Gleason Mastrianni, Dec. 30, 1976. AB, Harvard U., 1939, MD, 1943. Successively intern, asst. resident, chief resident in medicine Harvard Med. Service, Boston City Hosp., 1943-44, 47-49; Whitehead fellow in physiology, asst. in medicine and physiology Emory U. Med. Sch., 1950-52; assoc. in medicine Duke U. Med. Sch., 1952; mem. faculty Albany (N.Y.) Med. Coll., 1952—, prof. medicine, 1961—, head div. cardiology, 1961-84, dir. cardiovascular health center, 1952-90, head pvt. diagnostic clinic, 1957-82. Cons. Albany VA Med. Center, 1962-1991. Author papers in field. Served as 1st lt. M.C. AUS, 1944-45. Fellow A.C.P., Am. Coll. Cardiology; mem. AMA, Am. Heart Assn. (chmn. council epidemiology 1969-71), Assn. Univ. Cardiologists, N.Y. Heart Assembly (pres. 1968-69), Med. Soc. County of Albany (pres. 1971-72) Clubs: Ft. Orange, Schuyler Meadows. Presbyterian. Home: 17 Lenox Ave Albany NY 12203-2005 Office: Albany Med Coll Albany NY 12208

DOYLE, JOSEPH THOMAS, preventive health physician; b. Utica, N.Y., 1963; BS, Tufts U., 1984; MD, NYU, 1989; MPH, U. South Fla. Coll., 1993; MBA, Rollins Coll., 1992; MPA, Fla. Atlantic U., 1995, EdS, 1998. Diplomate Am. Bd. Preventive Medicine, Am. Bd. Quality Assurance and Utilization Rev. Physicians. Intern Orlando (Fla.) Regional Med. Ctr., 1989-90; resident HRS/Palm Beach County Pub. Health Unit, West Palm Beach, Fla., 1994-95; pvt. practice Naples, Fla. Mem.: Pub. Health Leadership Inst. Fla., Am. Acad. Profl. Coders, Med. Dirs. Inst./Nat. Assn. Managed Care Physicians, Am. Coll. Physician Execs. Home and Office: PO Box 770208 Naples FL 34107

DOYLE, JUSTIN P. lawyer; b. Rochester, N.Y., Oct. 26, 1948; s. Justin Joseph and Jane Martha (Kreag) Doyle; children: Mary, Joe. BA, Dartmouth Coll., 1970; JD, Cornell U., 1974. Bar: N.Y. 1974. From assoc. to ptnr. Nixon, Hargrave, Devans & Doyle, Rochester, 1974-99; ptnr. Nixon Peabody LLP (formerly Nixon, Hargrave, Devans & Doyle), Rochester, 1999—. Mem.: Monroe County Bar Assn., N.Y. Bar Assn. Home: 252 Overbrook Rd Rochester NY 14618-3648 Office: Nixon Peabody LLP Clinton Sq PO Box 31051 Rochester NY 14603-1051

DOYLE, L. F. BOKER, retired trust company executive; b. N.Y.C., Apr. 23, 1931; Luke Cantwell and Rita (Boker) D.; m. Susanna Stone, Jan. 31, 1959; children: Katharine, Nancy, Victoria, Jessica. BA, Yale U., 1953; postgrad., NYU, 1956-63. 1st v.p., dir., mgr. capital mgmt. dept. Smith Barney & Co., N.Y.C., 1956-74; exec. v.p. Fiduciary Trust Co. Internat., N.Y.C., 1974-83, pres., 1983-94, chmn. exec. com., 1994-96, also dir., 1978-96, cons., 1996. Dir. U.S. LIfe Ins. Co., 1996-97. Trustee Margaret Sanger Rsch. Bur., N.Y.C., 1962-68, N.Y.C. Sch. Vol. Program, 1979-90, New Sch. for Social Rsch., N.Y.C., 1983-91, Taconic Found., N.Y.C., 1989—, Hudson River Found., 1997—; trustee Am. Mus. Natural History, N.Y.C., 1968-2002, hon trustee, 2003—; bd. dirs. Cultural Instns. Retirement Sys., N.Y.C., 1971-96, chmn. bd., 1980-96; trustee Nature Cons., N.Y. State, 1990-2003, chmn., 1993-96; trustee Frick Collection, N.Y.C., 1990, treas., 1992—; trustee Ea. N.Y. chpt. Nature Conservatory, 1998—, chmn., 2003—. 1st lt. USMC, 1953-55. Mem. Century Assn., Anglers Club N.Y. (pres. 1976-77). Avocations: fishing, birding, natural history, conservation, antiques.

DOYLE, MATHIAS FRANCIS, university president, political scientist, educator; b. Malone, N.Y., Nov. 18, 1933; s. Francis J. and Madeline L. (Donnelly) D. BA, Siena Coll., 1955; MA, Cath. U. Am., 1965; PhD, U. Notre Dame, 1968; diploma, Pres.' Assn. of Am. Mgmt. Assn., Inst. Edn. Mgmt., Harvard U. Lectr. St. Francis Coll., Rye Beach, N.H., 1963-65; assoc. prof. polit. sci. Siena Coll., Loudonville, N.Y., 1968-75; pres. St. Bonaventure (N.Y.) U., 1975-90, also trustee., prof. polit. sci., 1992—; Adminstr.'s fellow AID, Washington, 1990-92; dir. human svcs. St. Anthony Shrine, Boston. Trustee Commn. on Ind. Colls. and Univs. Contbr. articles periodicals. Trustee Siena Coll. Arthur Schmidt fellow, 1966-68 Mem. Am., Northeastern polit. sci. assns., Pi Gamma Mu, Delta Epsilon Sigma. Roman Catholic. Home: St Anthony Shrine 100 Arch St Boston MA 02110 Office: Dir of Human Resources Saint Anthony Shrine 100 Arch St Boston MA 02110 E-mail: friarmdoyle@aol.com. *A lifetime spent in education and ministry has taught me how true it is that it is better to give then to receive.*

DOYLE, MICHAEL ANTHONY, lawyer; b. Atlanta, Nov. 4, 1937; s. James Alexander and Wilma (Summersgill) D.; children: John, David, Peter.; m. Bernice H. Winter, Nov. 12, 1977. BA, Yale U., 1959, LLB, 1962. Bar: Ga. 1961, D.C. 1967, U.S. Dist. Ct. D.C. 1967, U.S. Dist. Ct. (no. dist.) Ga. 1962, U.S. Ct. Appeals (5th cir.) 1962, U.S. Ct. Appeals (11th cir.) 1982, U.S. Ct. Appeals (D.C. cir.) 1968, U.S. Supreme Ct. 1972, U.S. Ct. Appeals (4th cir.) 1985. Assoc. Alston, Miller & Gaines, Atlanta, 1962-67; ptnr. Alston & Bird and

UpJohn Health Care Svcs. U. Md. Hosp. Balt., 1979-81; charge, treatment nurse Monticello (Fla.) Nursing Home, 1983; supr. Estes Nursing Home (Beverly Enterprises), Tallahassee, 1984; with Campbellton-Graceville Hosp., 1984-85, Sun City (Fla.) Med. Ctr. Hosp., 1986; supr. Ponce De Leon Care Ctr., St. Augustine, Fla., 1987-88; charge nurse Graceville (Fla.) Hosp., 1984; charge, patients care plans nurse U. Nursing Care Ctr., Gainesville, Fla., 1988-90.

DOZIER, WILLIAM EVERETT, JR., newspaper editor and publisher; b. Delhi, La., June 12, 1922; s. William Everett and Harriet E. (Miles) D.; m. Eleanor Ruth Roye, Sept. 1, 1944; children: Martha Carolyn Dozier Hunnicutt (dec. July 1995), Sarah Rebecca, Dozeitdi Beratdino. BA in Journalism, La. Tech. U., 1943. Assoc. editor Delhi Dispatch, 1936-39; reporter, state editor New Orleans Times-Picayune, 1946-50; editor Courier-Times-Telegraph, Tyler, Tex., 1952-65; pres., editor, pub. Kerrville (Tex.) Daily Times, 1965-88; pres. Hills o'Texas Publs., Inc., 1982-92; gen. ptnr. Frio-Nueces Publs. Ltd., 1978—99. V.P. Kerrville Music Found. and Performing Arts Soc., 1978-84, also bd. dirs.; bd.d irs. Adm. Nimitz Ctr Found., Fredericksburg, Tex., 1976—; chmn. United Fund campaign, Kerrville, 1967; mem. adv. bd. Salvation Army, 1967—; v.p. Tex. State Arts & Crafts Fair Assn., 1980-90. also bd. dirs., 1972-92; lay leader First United Meth. Ch., Kerrville, 1984-86, past chmn. bd. trustees, chmn. adminstrv. bd.; trustee Schreiner Coll., 1987-96, 97—, v.p., bd. trustees; trustee Sid Peterson Meml. Hosp., 1989-2001; dir. playhouse, 2000-2001—. Served with USN, 1943-46, 50-52, ret. comdr., 1973. Mem. Am. Soc. Newspaper Editors, Am. Newspaper Pubs. Assn., Nat. Newspaper Assn., Tex. AP Mng. Editors Assn. (pres. 1964-65), Tex. Press Assn. (pres. 1979-80), Tex. Daily Newspaper Assn. (dir. 1984-87), Tex. Press Found. (pres. 1982-92), So. Newspaper Pubs. Assn. (chmn. smaller newspaper com. 1983-84, dir. 1984-87), Kerr County C. of C. (pres. 1973-74), W. Tex. C. of C. (regional v.p. 1981-84, pres. 1985-86), Tex. C. of C. (founding dir. 1987-90), Masons (Tyler), Kiwanis (lt. gov. divsn. 5 Tex.-Okla. dist. 1974, pres. Kerrville 1973, Disting. Club Pres. 1973, Disting. Lt. Gov. 1974), Sigma Delta Chi. Home: 2428 Rock Creek Dr Kerrville TX 78028-6504 Office: 815 Jefferson St Ste A Kerrville TX 78028-4581

DRAAYER, SUZANNE RHODES, music educator, writer; b. Hendersonville, N.C., Sept. 23, 1952; d. Ray and Mary Lou Hamilton Rhodes; m. William Ronald Draayer, Mar. 1, 1991. MusB, Furman U., 1973; MS, Vanderbilt U., 1976; MusD, U. of Md., 1987. Asst. prof. So. Utah U., Cedar City, Utah, 1989—93; coll. prof. Winona (Minn.) State U., 1993—. Presenter in field. Musician: Carnegie Hall, 2001; author: A Singer's Guide to the Songs of Joaquín Rodrigo, 1999, 2003; editor: Canciones de España-Songs of Nineteenth-Century Spain, 2003; contbr. articles to profl. jours. Organizer, creator, developer Internat. Rodrigo Festival, Winona, Minn., 1999. Mem.: Nat. Assn. Tchrs. Singing (state pres. 1997—2001, regional gov. 2001—03). Home: 4959 West 6th Winona MN 55987 Office: Winona State University Johnson and Sanborn Streets Winona MN 55987 E-mail: sdraayer@winona.edu.

DRABBLE, MARGARET, writer; b. Sheffield, England, June 5, 1939; d. John Frederick and Kathleen Marie (Bloor) D.; m. Clive Swift, June 27, 1960 (div. 1975); children: Adam, Rebecca, Joseph; m. Michael Holroyd, 1982. BA with honors, Newnham Coll., Cambridge, 1960; DLitt (hon.), U. Sheffield, 1976, U. Manchester, 1987, U. Keele, 1988, U. Bradford, 1988, U. East Anglia, 1994, U. York, 1995. Author: (novels) A Summer Bird-Cage, 1963, The Garrick Year, 1964, The Millstone, 1965 (John Llewelyn Rhys Meml. award 1966), Jerusalem the Golden, 1967 (James Tait Black Meml. book prize 1968), The Waterfall, 1969, The Needle's Eye, 1972 (Yorkshire Post Book of Yr. award 1972), The Realms of Gold, 1975, The Ice Age, 1977, The Middle Ground, 1980 (ALA notable book citation 1981), The Radiant Way, 1987, A Natural Curiosity, 1989, Gates of Ivory, 1991, The Witch of Exmoor, 1996, The Peppered Moth, 2001, Angus Wilson: A Biography, 1995, The Peppered Moth, 2001, The Seven Sisters, 2002; (short stories) Hassan's Tower, 1966, The Reunion, 1968, The Gifts of War, 1970; (non-fiction) Arnold Bennett, A Biography, 1974, For Queen and Country: Britain in the Victorian Age, 1978, A Writer's Britain, 1979; (play) Bird of Paradise, 1969; (screenplays) Laura, 1964, Isadora, 1968, Thank You All Very Much, 1969; (criticism) Wordsworth, 1966; editor: Jane Austen, Lady Susan, The Watsons, and Sanditon, 1975, The Genius of Thomas Hardy, 1976, Oxford Companion to English Literature, 1985, 6th edit., 2000, The Concise Oxford Companion to English Literature, 1987, Angus Wilson a Biography, 1995. Mem.: Am. Acad. Arts and Letters (hon.; fgn. mem., E.M. Forster award 1973). Office: care Peters Fraser & Dunlop Drury House 34-43 Russell St London WC2B 5HA England

DRABIK-NOWAK, RENATA ANNA, internist; b. Radom, Poland, Apr. 28, 1964; d. Tadeusz Stanislaw and Marianna Helena (Smak) Drabik; m. Arthur P. Nowak, Dec. 25, 1993; children: Michelle Katherine, William John. MD, Med. Acad., Warsaw, Poland, 1989. Dipolmate Polish Bd. Internal Medicine, Polish Bd. Ultrasonography, Am. Bd. Internal Medicine. Asst. dept. gastroenterology Med. Ctr. Postgrad. Edn., Warsaw, Poland, 1991-94; resident St. Francis Med. Ctr., Pitts., 1995-98; pvt. practice Wood Med. Clinic, Crossville, Tenn., 1998—. Mem. staff Cumberland Med. Ctr., Crossville. Mem. ACP, Polish Med. Soc., European Soc. Ultrasonography. Roman Catholic. Avocations: tennis, skiing, photography. Office: Wood Med Clinic 194 Cleveland St Crossville TN 38555-4853

DRABISKA, FRANK JOHN, priest, parochial school educator; b. Ellwood, Pa., Oct. 7, 1950; s. Martin and Eugenia (Galat) D. BA in Philosophy, Duquesne U., 1972; MDiv, St. Francis Coll., 1976; MS in Edn., Duquesne U., 1996. Ordained priest Roman Cath. Ch., 1976. Pastor Diocese of Pitts., 1976—, master catechist, 1982—. Roman Catholic. Home and Office: 7446 Mcclure Ave Pittsburgh PA 15218-2339

DRABKIN, MURRAY, lawyer; b. N.Y.C., Aug. 3, 1928; s. Max Drabkin and Minnie Masin; m. Mary Elizabeth Hooper, Nov. 27, 1971. AB, Hamilton Coll., 1950; LLB, Harvard U., 1953. Bar: D.C. 1953, U.S. Ct. Appeals (D.C. cir.) 1954, N.Y. 1966, U.S. Supreme Ct. 1972. Counsel com. on judiciary U.S. Ho. of Reps., Washington, 1957-66; spl. asst. to mayor City of N.Y., 1966-68; pvt. practice N.Y.C. and Washington, 1968-82; ptnr. Cadwalader, Wickersham & Taft, Washington, 1983-92; ret., 1992; of counsel Hopkins & Sutter, Washington, 1992-2000. Dir. Conn. State Revenue Task Force, 1969-71; mem. adv. com. FRS, Washington, 1970-71, D.C. Tax Revision Com., 1976-77. Contbr. articles to profl. jours. Served with USN, 1953-57, to lt. comdr. USNR. Fellow Phi Beta Kappa (bd. dirs. 1996—, pres. 2001—); mem. Nat. Bankruptcy Conf. (chmn. com. on R.R. reorgn. 1984-2000, chmn. com on bankruptcy crimes, 1994-98), D.C. Bar Assn., Harvard Club of Washington (pres. 2000-02, bd. dirs. 1996—), Harvard Club of N.Y.C., Chesapeake Bay Bermuda 40 Assn., Cosmos Club, Nat. Press Club, Delta Sigma Rho.

DRACH, JOHN CHARLES, scientist, educator; b. Cin., Sept. 25, 1939; s. Charles Louis and Edrie B. Drach; m. Elda Jean Flamm, June 20, 1964; children: Laura J., Diane E. BS in Pharmacy, U. Cin., 1961, MS in Pharm. Chemistry, 1963, PhD in Biochemistry, 1966. From assoc. rsch. scientist to rsch. scientist Parke, Davis and Co., Ann Arbor, Mich., 1966-70; asst. prof. U. Mich. Dental Sch., Ann Arbor, 1970-74; assoc. prof. U. Mich., Ann Arbor, 1974-80; assoc. prof. medicinal chemistry U. Mich. Coll. Pharmacy, Ann Arbor, 1978-80; prof. U. Mich., Ann Arbor, 1980—; chmn. dept. oral biology U. Mich. Dental Sch., Ann Arbor, 1985-87, chmn. dept. biologic and materials scis., 1987-95; vis. prof. divsn. virology Burroughs Wellcome Co., Research Triangle Park, N.C., 1994. Cons. Adria Labs., Am. Inst. Chem., Am. Pharm. Assn., AMA, Chartwell, Kimberly-Clark, 1976-83. Author: Clinical Pharmacology, 1986; contbr. numerous articles and revs. to profl. jours.; mem. editorial bd. Elsevier Sci. Pubs., 1984—, Antiviral Chemistry & Chemotherapy, 1996—; patentee antiviral drugs. NSF summer fellow, 1963; NIH grad. fellow, 1964-66; NIH grantee, 1970—. Fellow: AAAS; mem.: Internat. Soc. Antiviral Rsch. (archivist 1992—, chair awards com. 1998—2002, pres. elect 2000—02, pres. 2002—), Am. Soc. Microbiology (mem. editl. bd. 1982—91), Am. Chem. Soc., Am. Assn. Oral Biology, Dental Edn. Assn. (pres. oral biology sect. 1990—91), Am. Assn. Dental Rsch., Sigma Xi, Omicron Kappa Upsilon, Rho Chi. Avocations: jogging, skiing, sailing. Home: 1372 Barrister Rd Ann Arbor MI 48105-2875 Office: U Mich 1011 N University Ave Ann Arbor MI 48109-1078 E-mail: jcdrach@umich.edu.

DRACHMAN, ALLAN WARREN, lawyer, arbitrator; b. Bklyn., Apr. 5, 1937; s. Norman and Marion (Soifer) D.; m. Judy, June 10, 1962; children: Neil, Amy. AB (cum laude), Brandeis U., 1958; LLB, Harvard Law Sch., 1961. Bar: Mass. 1961, U.S. Ct. Appeals (1st cir.) Mass. 1961. Atty. Schneider, Bronstein & Shapiro, Boston, 1961-66; corp. counsel City Boston Law Dept., 1966-70; ptnr. Deutsch, Holtz and Drachman, Boston, 1970-71; atty. sole practice Boston, 1971-73; ptnr., dir. Holtz & Drachman, P.C., 1973-77; dir. Allan W. Drachman, P.C., Boston, 1978-82, Holland, Crowe & Drachman, P.C., Boston, 1982-86, Deutsch Williams et al, Boston, 1986—91, mediator, arbitrator, 2001—03; chmn. Mass. Labor Rels. Commn., Boston, 2003—. Home: 304 Dahlia Dr Wayland MA 01778-2825 Office: 399 Washington St Boston MA 02108-5213

DRACHMAN, DANIEL BRUCE, neurologist, educator; b. N.Y.C., July 18, 1932; s. Julian Moses and Emily (Deitchman) D.; m. Jephta Piatigorsky, Aug. 28, 1960; children: Jonathan Gregor, Evan Bernard, Eric Edouard. AB summa cum laude (N.Y. State scholar), Columbia Coll., 1952; MD (N.Y. State Med. scholar), NYU, 1956. Intern in internal medicine Beth Israel Hosp., Boston, 1956-57, asst. resident in neurology Harvard neurol. unit Boston City Hosp., 1957-58, resident in neurology, 1958-59; resident in neuropathology Harvard neurol. unit and Mallory Inst. Pathology, 1959-60; teaching fellow in neurology Harvard U., 1957-60; clin. assoc. Nat. Inst. Neurol. Diseases and Blindness, NIH, Bethesda, Md., 1960-62, research asso. lab. neuroanat. scis., 1962-63; clin. instr. Georgetown U., 1961-63; asst. prof. neurology Tufts U., 1963-69; assoc. prof. Johns Hopkins U., 1969-73, prof., 1974—, prof. neurosci., 1980—, W.W. Smith Charitable Found. prof. neuroimmunology, 2003—. Attending neurologist Johns Hopkins Hosp.; adv. bd. Multiple Sclerosis Soc., 1981-85; pres. med. adv. bd. Myasthenia Gravis Found.; adv. bd. Familial Dysautonomia Found.; bd. sci. councillors Nat. Inst. Neurol. and Communicative Disorders and Stroke, NIH, 1985-90; med. adv. com. Muscular Dystrophy Assn., 1994-99. Clarinetist.; author publs. on myasthenia gravis, muscular atrophy, muscular dystrophy, clubfoot, devel. disorders, neurology, amyotrophic lateral sclerosis, chamber music; mem. editl. bd. Muscle and Nerve jour., Exptl. Neurology, Autoimmunity. Served with USPHS, 1960-63. Recipient Founders' Day award NYU, 1956, Jacob Javits award, 1986, Berson Disting. Alumnus award NYU Sch. Medicine, 1999; NIH grantee, 1963—, Muscular Dystrophy Assn. grantee, 1969—. Fellow Am. Acad. Neurology, N.Y. Acad. Scis.; mem. AAAS, Internat. Soc. Devel. Biology, Balt. Neurol. Soc., Phi Beta Kappa, Alpha Omega Alpha. Office: Johns Hopkins U Sch Medicine Dept Neurology 600 N Wolfe St Baltimore MD 21287-7519 E-mail: dandrac@aol.com.

DRACHMAN, DAVID ALEXANDER, neurologist; b. NYC, July 18, 1932; s. Julian Moses and Emily Drachman; m. Eleanor Betsy Derby, Nov. 26, 1959; children: Laura Jeanne, Jessica Gail, Douglas Emmet. AB with highest honors, Columbia U., 1952; MD, NYU, 1956. Diplomate: Am. Bd. Psychiatry and Neurology. Intern Duke U. Med. Center, 1956-57; resident in neurology Mass. Gen. Hosp., Boston, 1957-60; clin. assoc. NIH, 1960-63; clin. instr. neurology Georgetown U. Med. Sch., 1961-63; mem. faculty Northwestern U. Med. Sch., 1963-77, dir. neurology clinics, 1963-77, prof. neurology, 1971-77, assoc. chmn. dept., 1972-75; attending physician Passavant Meml. Hosp., Chgo., 1964-72, Northwestern Meml. Hosp., 1972-77; prof. neurology, chmn. emeritus dept. neurology U. Mass.-Meml. Med. Ctr., 1977—. Attending physician U. Mass. Med. Center, St. Vincent Hosp., Worcester; mem. med. adv. bd. Chgo. Multiple Sclerosis Soc., 1971-77, Mass. Multiple Sclerosis Soc., 1979-87, mem. FDA adv. panel on control and peripheral nerve system drugs, 1996—2000; mem. working group on presdl. disability, 1994-96. Mem editl. bd. Neurobiology of Aging, 1979-93, Neurology, Archives of Neurology, 1979-91, Jour. Geriat. Psychiatry and Neurology, Jour. Rehab. and Health; contbr. articles to profl. jours. Fellow Am. Acad. Neurology; mem. AAAS, Am. Neurol. Assn. (hon. mem., pres. 1994-95), Alzheimer's Disease Assn. (chmn. sci. adv. bd. 1986-90, trustee), Am. Neuro-otology Soc., Assn. Univ. Profs. Neurology, Assn. Rsch. Nervous and Mental Diseases, Mass. Assn. Neurology, N.Y. Acad. Scis., Boston Soc. Psychiatry and Neurology (pres. 1980-81), Phi Beta Kappa, Sigma Xi, Alpha Omega Alpha (ea. counselor) Home: 111 Barretts Mill Rd Concord MA 01742-5519 Office: U Mass Med Sch Dept Neurology 55 Lake Ave N Worcester MA 01655-0002

DRACHNIK, CATHERINE MELDYN, recreational therapist, artist, counselor; b. Kansas City, Mo., June 7, 1924; d. Gerald Willis and Edith (Gray) Weston; m. Joseph Brennan Drachnik, Oct. 6, 1946; children: Denise Elaine, Kenneth John. BS, U. Md., 1945; MA, Calif. State U., Sacramento, 1975. Lic. family and child counselor; registered art therapist. Art therapist Vincent Hall Retirement Home, McLean, Va., Fairfax Mental Health Day Treatment Ctr., McLean, Arlington (Va.) Mental Health Day Treatment Ctr., 1971-72, Hope for Retarded, San Jose, Calif., Sequoia Hosp., Redwood City, Calif., 1972-73; supervising tchr. adult edn. Sacramento Soc. Blind, 1975-77; ptnr. Sacramento Divsn. Mediation Svcs., 1981-82; instr. Calif. State U., Sacramento, 1975-82, 92-93, 1999, Coll. Notre Dame, Belmont, Calif., 1975-96; art therapist, mental health counselor Psych West Counseling Ctr. (formerly Eskaton Am. River Mental Health Clinic), Carmichael, Calif., 1975-93; instr. Sacramento City Coll., 1997—. Instr. U. Utah, Salt Lake City, 1988—89; lectr. in field. Author: Interpreting Metaphors in Children's Drawings, 1995; one-woman shows include Vacaville (Calif.) Art Gallery, 1995, Dublier Gallery, Sacramento, 1997, Thistle Dew Gallery, 1998, Jeffery Bldg. Gallery, 2001, Oldham Gallery, 2001, exhibited in group shows at Art of Calif. Mag., 1993, Calif. State Fair, Sacramento, 1995, 1997, 1998, 2000, 2001, Haggin Art Mus., Stockton, Calif., 1994, 1995, 1996, 1997, 1998, 1999, 2000, Haggin Art Mus, 2002, Watercolor West, Brea, Calif., 1998, West Valley Art Mus., Phoenix, 1999, Rocky Mountain Nat. Watercolor, Golden, Colo., 1999, Elliot Fouts Art Gallery, Granite Bay, Calif., 1999—2003, Am. Watercolor Soc., N.Y., 2000, Triton Mus. Art Biennial, Santa Clara, Calif., 2000, 2002, Calif. Watercolor Assn., San Francisco, 1999, 2001. Active charitable orgns. Mem.: Am. Assn. Marriage and Family Therapists, Nat. Art Edn. Assn., No. Calif. Arts, Inc. (master painter), No. Calif. Art Therapy Assn. (hon.; life), Am. Art Therapy Assn. (hon.; life, pres. 1987—89), Omicron Nu, Alpha Psi Omega, Kappa Kappa Gamma Alumnae Assn. (pres. Sacramento Valley chpt. 1991—92). Republican. Avocations: swimming, golf, theater. Home and Office: 4124 American River Dr Sacramento CA 95864-6025 E-mail: cdrach@webtv.net.

DRACKER, ROBERT ALBERT, physician; b. Queens, N.Y., July 28, 1956; s. Albert Donald and Lee (Patruno) D.; m. Maria Elizabeth DiRubbo Dracker; children: Maria Lynn, Robert, Michael. BA in Biology, N.Y.U., 1978; MD, SUNY Health Sci. Ctr., 1982; MS in Health Svcs. Mgmt., New Sch. for Social Rsch., N.Y.C., 1995. Intern dept. pediat. SUNY Health Sci. Ctr., Syracuse, 1982-83, resident dept. pediat., 1983-85, fellow in pediatric hematology and oncology, 1985-87, fellow in blood banking and transfusion medicine, 1987-88, rsch. asst. prof. dept. pathology, 1988-89, dir. transfusion medicine dept. pathology, 1989-93; attending physician ARC, 1994-98; pvt. practice, North Syracuse, N.Y., 1988—; med. dir. and founder Infusacare Med. Svcs., P.C., N. Area Pediat., P.C.; rsch. scientist I Masonic Med. Rsch. Lab., Utica, N.Y., 1989—; med. dir. MetraHealth Ctrl. N.Y., 1995-97; assoc. med. dir. POMCO, Syracuse, 1994-97; med. dir. Viacord Inc., Boston, 1998—. Med. advisor, reviewer Ctrl. N.Y. Blue Cross/Blue Shield, Health Svcs. Adminstrn.; chmn. Ctr. N.Y. Divsn. Review Island Peer Review Orgn., 1988-90; physician reviewer N.Y. State Office of Med. Misconduct; physician reviewer for dispute resolution, Empire State Med. Scientific and Edn. Found.; consulting physician Jowonio Sch., 1983-85, Devillo Sloan Sch. for Handicapped, 1983-85, Walsh Med. Facility, N.Y. State Dept. Corrections, 1991-97; Neonatal Transport Physician, 1983-86; med. dir. MRDS, Syracuse, 1999—. Contbr. numerous abstracts, letters, presentations, articles to profl. jours. Recipient AMA Physicians' Recognition award 1989-92, 92-95, 95-98, 99—, N.Y.U. Alumni award, The Dr. Charipper award, Pediatric Resident Teaching award; grantee Nat. Heart, Lung and Blood Inst, 1984-89, 88-90, Cutter Divsn.of Miles Labs., 1988-89, 90- 91, Pathology Med. Svc. Group SUNY Health Sci. Ctr., 1991-92, Hendricks Fund SUNY Health Sci. Ctr. at Syracuse, 1992. Mem. ARC, AMA, Ctrl. N.Y. AIDS Profl. Group, Vis. Nurse Assn. Ctrl. N.Y., N.Y. State Dept. Health, Ctrl. N.Y. Hosp. Assn., Just For Babies, St. Joseph's Hosp. and Health Ctr., Cmty. Gen. Hosp., Crouse Irving Meml. Hosp., Patients' Choice, Am. Assn. Blood Banks, Am. Acad. Pediatrics, Blood Bank Assn. N.Y. State, Am. Soc. for Apheresis, Med. Soc. N.Y. State, Onondaga County Med. Soc., Onondaga County Pediatric Soc., Internat. Soc. of Hematotherapy and Graft Engring., Am. Soc. for Blood and Marrow Transplantation, Am. Acad. Pediatrics, Phi Beta Kappa, Alpha Omega Alpha. Roman Catholic. Avocations: reading, woodworking, research and development, travel, photography.

DRAEGER, NORMAN ARTHUR, physical chemist, research and development company executive; b. Milwaukee, WI, Aug. 10, 1955; s. Norman A. and Elizabeth A. Draeger; m. Lisa C. Margulski, Sept. 11, 1992. BS, U Wis., Milw., 1977; MS, U Wis., Madison, 1979; PhD in Chemistry, U Wis., Milw., 1987. Rsch. dir. Midwest Rsch. Tech., Inc., Milw., 1988—94; assoc. sci. UW, WCSAR Prog., Madison, Wis., 1994—99; sr. sci. Piezomax Techs., Inc., Madison, Wis., 1999—2000; dir. of tech. Marquette U, Milw., 2000—01; lead materials sci. Platypus Tech., LLC, Madison, Wis., 2001—. Adv. coun. Wis. Small Bus. Devel. Ctr., Madison, Wis., 1990—95; editl. bd. Small Bus. Forum, Madison, Wis., 1992—96. Product devel. (ednl. product) Astroponics, 1998. Recipient Friend of Ext., U of WI, 1992. Mem.: AIAA (sr.), Phi Beta Kappa. Achievements include identified two-dimensional parabolic rate law for reactive surface diffusion; originated "Rose in Space" experiment flown on US Shuttle mission STS-95. Avocations: gardening, home remodeling, collectible automobiles. Home: Mr Norman Draeger PO Box 183 Oregon WI 53575

DRAEGER, SUSANNE YARBROUGH, interior designer; b. Macon, Ga., July 16, 1950; d. Ceasar Augustus and Dorothy Anne (Patrick) Yarbrough; m. Charles Fred Newberry July 29, 1972 (div.); children: Catherine Neil, Charles Fred; m. Eric R. Stanley May, 1988 (div.); m. Lawrence William Draeger Jan. 15, 1996. BSHE in Interior Design, U. Ga., 1972. Cert. ASID, IGD Am. Soc. Interior Designers, Inst. Bus. Designers. Interior designer Et Cetera, Inc., Athens, Ga., 1972-74; with Athens Federal Savings and Loan, Ga., 1974-77; co-owner, sr. designer Athens Interiors, Inc., Athens, Ga., 1974-77; independent interior designer Arlington, Va., 1978-82; interior designer Horizon Trading Co., Inc., Washington, 1983-84; pres., interior designer Nova Internat., Inc., Washington, 1984-94, Nova Europe, Inc., Washington, Paris, France, 1994-96; researcher Interior Design, 1996—. Selected NEA collection Nat. Endowment for the Arts, Am. Consulate Osaka, Japan, 1986. Significant projects with NOVA Europe include: Chevron Oil & Gas, Tengischevroil, Salans, Hertzfeld & Heilbronn, U.S. Agy. for Internat. Devel. in Budapest, Rabat, and Sofia, 1994-96; with NOVA Internat., Inc. U.S. consulate Bldg. Osaka, Japan, Am. consulate staff housing, Hong Kong, SATO for U.S. Mil. in Fed. Repub. West Germany, Mobil Oil, Aldwych House, London, UK, U.S. Dept. State staff housing worldwide, Turner Internat. Industries, N.Y., Peace Vector II Project, Beni Suef, Egypt, US Army Corps of Engrs., Transatlantic Divsn., Am. Internat. Contractors, Ins., Arlington, Va., Peace Vector IV Project, Sakara Egypt, 1984-94; others include Univ. Ga. Law Sch. Offices, Am. Embassies Cairo, Ankara, Islamabad, U.S. Consulate Building Osaka, Japan, Am. Consulate staff housing Hong Kong, Mobil Oil Aldwych House, London, Am. Embassies in Paris, Madrid, Islamabad, Minsk, Sofia and Athens. Vol. Alexandria Hosp., 1985-88. Episcopalian. Avocations: acrobic exercises, swimming, travel, oil painting. Home: 2409 Military Rd Arlington VA 22207-3907

DRAELOS, ZOE DIANA, dermatologist, consultant; b. Milw., Oct. 13, 1958; d. Dimitri Basil and Lorene June (Legan) Kececioglu; m. Michael Draelos, June 14, 1980; children: Mark, Matthew. BSME, U. Ariz., 1979, MD, 1983. Diplomate Am. Bd. Dermatology. Physician in solo dermatology practice, High Point, N.C., 1988—. Cons., owner Dermatology Cons. Svcs., High Point, 1990—. Author: Cosmetics in Dermatology, 1995, Atlas of Cosmetic Dermatology, 2000. Rhodes scholar, Oxford, Eng., 1979. Office: Zoe Diana Draelos MD PA 2444 N Main St High Point NC 27262-7833 E-mail: zdraelos@northstate.net.

DRAGALIN, VLADIMIR, research statistics director; b. Baxani, Soroca, Moldova, Nov. 3, 1958; s. Petru and Nina Dragalin; m. Elena Mazureac, Feb. 7, 1960; children: Veronica, Michaela. MS in Applied Math.(hon.), Moldova State U., Chisinau, 1981; PhD in Probability and Stats., Steklov Math. Inst., Moscow, Russia, 1988. Mgr. GlaxoSmithKline, Collegeville, Pa., 2001—02, dir. rsch. stats., 2002—. Sr. rschr. Inst. of Math., Acad. of Scis., Chisinau, Moldova, 1988—93; rsch. fellow Inst. of Applications in Math. and Informatics, Milan, 1993—94, U. of Wuerzburg, Germany, 1994—96; asst. prof. rsch. Dept. of Biostatistics, U. of Rochester, Rochester, NY, 1997—99; prin. statistician SmithKline Beecham (GlaxoSmithKline), Collegeville, Pa., 1999—2001. CNR Fellowship, Italian Nat. Coun. of Rsch., 1993—94, Fellowship, Alexander von Humboldt Found., 1994—95, Scholarship, NIH, 1996. Mem.: Inst. of Math. Stats., Am. Statis. Assn. Office: GlaxoSmithKline 1250 South Collegeville Rd PO Box 5089 Collegeville PA 19426-0989 Office Fax: 610-917-7994. Personal E-mail: vdragalin@aol.com. E-mail: vladimir.2.dragalin@gsk.com.

DRAGAN, ALEXANDRA, mechanical engineer, consultant, environmental engineer, researcher, engineering educator; d. Ioan and Arety Elena Dragan; 1 child, Miruna Roxanna. BME, MME, U. Bucharest Polytechnica, Romania, 1964; M in Environ. Engring., U. So. Calif., 1993; DEng, U. Constrn., Bucharest, 1998. Registered profl. engr., Calif., N.Y. From engr. to sr. engr. Designing Inst. for Wood Industry, Bucharest, 1963—73; cons. engr. FOREXIM/Technoforest, Bucharest, 1973—76; engr. Jack Stone Engrs., N.Y.C., 1978—81; from sr. engr. to group leader Haines Lundberg Waehler, N.Y.C., 1981—84; from sr. engr. to assoc. Syska and Hennessy, L.A., 1984—86; pvt. practice L.A., Calif., 1984—; chief engr. Donald Dickerson Assoc., L.A., 1986—88; dir. engring. Nat. Air Sys., L.A., 1988; from sr. engr. to supervising mech. engr. III County of L.A. Dept. Pub. Works, Alhambra, Calif., 1988—. Pres. Dragan Engring., L.A., 1984—98; prof. aerospace engring. U. Politehnica of Bucharest, 2000—01, prof. emeritus, 2001—. Author: Thermal Processes and Power Generation in Wood Industry, 1973. Recipient Value Engring. award, County of L.A., 1986, Environ. Sci. and Engring. fellow, AAAS and US EPA, 1992. Mem.: ASHRAE (Cert. of Appreciation 1993—94, Symposium Paper award 2001), Internat. Soc. Indoor Air Quality and Climate, Am. Romanian Acad. for Arts and Scis. (exec. com. 2001). Republican. Avocation: singing. Home: 350 N Palm Dr Apt 402 Beverly Hills CA 90210 Personal E-mail: draganalexandra@yahoo.com.

DRAGAN, FEODOR FEODOROVICH, research scientist; b. Copceac, Moldova, July 14, 1963; s. Feodor G. and Maria I. (Gaidargi) D.; m. Natalia N. Marfina, Nov. 18, 1984; children: Nickolai, Maria. BA (hons.) applied math., Moldova State Univ., Kishinev, Moldova, 1983, MSc (hons.) applied math., 1985; PhD in theoretical computer sci., Inst. Math Belorussian Acad., Minsk, Belarus, 1990. Software engr. Moldavien Acad. Scis., Kishinev, 1982-85; jr. rsch. worker Moldova State Univ. Lab. of Discrete Optimization, Kishinev, 1988-90; asst. prof. Moldova State Univ., Kishinev, 1988-95; sr. rsch. worker Moldova State Univ. Lab. of Discrete Optimization, Kishinev, 1990-96; assoc. prof. Moldova State Univ., Kishinev, 1995-99; rsch. assoc. Univ. Duisburg, Duisburg, Germany, 1994, 95, Univ. Rostock, Rostock, Germany, 1996-99, Univ. Calif., L.A., 1999—. Contbr. articles to profl. jours. Recipient DAAD Rsch. fellowship, 1994, 95, Merit scholarship Moldova State Univ., 1980-85. Avocations: football, traveling, history, bike riding. Office: Univ Calif Computer Sci Dept 3514 Boelter Hl Los Angeles CA 90095-0001 Fax: 310 825 7578. E-mail: dragan@cs.ucla.edu.

DRAGHI, RAYMOND AMADEA, retired postal worker; b. Maple Grove Ohio, Mar. 22, 1927; s. Madea and Emma Maria (Poletti) D.; married, June 14, 1974; children: Michael Joseph, Mary Ann. Degree in bus adminstrn., Bliss Bus. Coll., 1949; degree in acctg., Office Tng. Sch., 1955. Rate clk., then mail clk. U.S. Post Office, Columbus, Ohio, 1957-91; pvt. investigator Columbus, 1958—. Contbr. poems to profl. publs. (Editors Choice awards 1994-96); song writer for Rainbow Records, 1992, Hilltop Records, 1994. With U.S. Army, 1945-46; sgt. USMC, 1950-51. Named to Internat. Poetry Hall of Fame, 1997; recipient Editor's Choice award for outstanding achievement in poetry Poetry.com, Internat. Libr. Poetry, 2002. Republican. Roman Catholic. Avocations: nature trails, wild life, forest and meadow beauty, wild flowers, trees and shrubs. Home: 704 Robinwood Ave Columbus OH 43213-1759

DRAGO, JOSEPH ROSARIO, urologist, educator; b. Jersey City, N.J., Oct. 28, 1947; m. Diane Lavacca; children: Andrea, Daniella, Denise. BS, U. Ill., 1968, MD, 1972. Diplomate Nat. Bd. Med. Examiners, Am. Bd. Urology; cert. Yag Laser, laparoscopic surgery. Intern Pa. State U. Milton S. Hershey Med. Ctr., 1972-73, resident in urology, 1973-77, instr. urology, 1976-77; asst. prof. urology, dir. urology oncology U. Calif., Davis, 1977-79, Milton S. Hershey (Pa.) Med. Ctr., 1979-80, assoc. prof. to prof. of surgery, dir. urologic oncology, 1980-85; assoc. staff Children's Hosp., Columbus, Ohio, 1985—; interim chief of staff elect, prof., dir. urologic oncology Ohio State U. Arthur G. James Cancer Hosp., Columbus, Ohio, 1990-92; with Easton (Pa.) Warren Urology,

Easton, Pa., 1992-95; pvt. practice Washington, N.J., 1995—. Mem. editl. bd. In Vivo Jour.; advisor Internat. Urologic Svcs., Inc., 1987; cons. in field; visiting prof. over 30 univs. and hosps. Author 12 book chpts.; reviewer various profl. jours., 1979—; contbr. articles to profl. jours. Recipient various rsch. grants, 1978-81. Fellow Internat. Coll. Surgeons in Urology; mem. AMA, Am. Coll. Surgeons, Am. Fertility Soc., Am. Inst. Ultrasound in Medicine, Am. Soc. Andrology, Am. Urologic Assn., Assn. Academic Surgery, Assn. Surgical Edn., Hershey Surgical Soc. (sec.-treas. 1983-85), Pa. Med. Soc., Phila. Urologic Soc., others. Home: 4559 Pinehurst Greens Ct Estero FL 33928 Office: 224 Roseberry St Phillipsburg NJ 08865-1632

DRAGON, WILLIAM, JR., footwear and apparel company executive; b. Lynn, Mass., Dec. 1, 1942; s. William and Anne (Stavru) D.; m. Suzanne Gail Behlmer, Feb. 24, 1968; children: Todd Christopher, Heather Anne, Paige Katherine (dec.). BS in Engring. Mgmt., Norwich U., Northfield, Vt., 1964; MS in Mgmt. Scis., Rensselaer Poly. Inst., Troy, N.Y., 1965. With mfg., sales and mktg. staff Gen. Electric Co., Mass. and Ky., 1967-73; dir. product planning and design Samsonite div. Beatrice Corp., Denver, 1973-75, dir. mktg. Samsonite div., 1975-78, v.p. mktg. and sales Buxton div. Springfield, Mass., 1978-81; gen. mgr. Johnston & Murphy Div. Genesco Inc., Nashville, 1981-85, exec. v.p., pres. U.S. Footwear Group, 1985-88, also dir.; v.p. Reebok Internat. Ltd., 1989-92; pres. Avia Group Internat. Inc., Portland, Oreg., 1989-92, Promotion Products Inc., Portland, 1992-94; dir. Deja, Inc., Portland, 1993-94; exec. v.p. DEJA Inc., Portland, 1994-95; pres. Pacific Trail divsn. London Fog Industries, 1995-99; pres., CEO London Fog Industries, 1999—, dir., 1999; chmn., CEO Pacific Trail, 1999—; dir. Lucy, Inc., 2002. Dean's adv. coun. Oreg. State U., 1994-98. Bd. dirs. Nashville Youth Hockey League, 1983-85, Two/Ten Charity Found., 1988-92; vice chmn. Nashville United Way, 1985; mem. men's adv. bd. Cumberland Valley coun. Girl Scouts U.S., 1985-86; mem. adminstrv. bd. Brentwood United Meth. Ch., 1986. 1st lt. U.S. Army, 1965-67, Vietnam. Decorated Bronze Star medal. Recipient Superior Achievement Recognition award Genesco Inc., 1984 Presbyterian. E-mail: bill@pacifictrail.com.

DRAGO-SEVERSON, ELEANOR ELIZABETH E. developmental psychologist, educator, researcher; b. N.Y.C., N.Y., Nov. 25, 1961; d. Rosario Philip and Betty Louise (Brisgal) Drago; m. David Irving Severson, Dec. 30, 1989. BA summa cum laude, L.I.U., 1986; EdM, Harvard U., 1989, EdD, 1990. Cert. biology, chemistry tchr., N.Y. Tchr. math. Palm Beach (Fla.) Acad., 1986-87; h.s. tchr. math., basketball coach Hackley Sch., Tarrytown, N.Y., 1987-88; tchr. biology, dir. human devel. Palm Beach Day Sch., 1990-91, dir. human devel., 1990-91; tchg. fellow Harvard U., Cambridge, Mass., 1993-96, assoc. in edn. Grad. Sch. Edn., 1996—2002, postdoctoral fellow Sch. Edn., 1997-2001, instr., rsch. assoc. Sch. Edn., 1997—2002, lectr. edn. Grad. Sch. Edn., 1998—. Co-dir. J.V. Mara C.Y.O. Sports Camp, Putnam Valley, N.Y., summer 1987. Mem. colloquium com. Harvard U., Cambridge, Mass., 1991-92, chair, 1992, mentor to incoming grad. students, 1992-96. Joseph Klingenstein fellow, 1987, tchg. fellow, 1993-96, doctoral fellow, 1994-96; Spencer sm. grant rsch. award, 2000. Mem. ASCD, APA, AAUW, Am. Ednl. Rsch. Assn., Soc. for Rsch. in Adult Devel., Nat. Staff Devel. Coun., Phi Delta Kappa. Roman Catholic. Home: 39 Kirkland St Apt 403 Cambridge MA 02138-2072

DRAGOUMIS, PAUL, electric utility company executive; b. N.Y.C., Sept. 19, 1934; s. Andrew and Theologie (Pavlou) D.; m. Maria William, Sept. 15, 1957; children— Ann Marie Murtlow, Andrew Paul. BSEE, Poly. Inst. Bklyn., 1956; MS in Nuclear Engring., Internat. Sch. Nuclear Sci. and Engring., Argonne, Ill., 1959; MA in Philosophy, Georgetown U., 1986. Asst. v.p. Am. Electric Power Co., N.Y.C., 1956-70; gen. mgr. corp. exec. staff Allis Chalmers Corp., W. Allis, Wis., 1970-71; v.p. nuclear projects and fossil fuel supply group Potomac Electric Power Co., Washington, 1971-75, v.p. policy, 1976-78, sr. v.p., mem. exec. policy com., 1978-89, exec. v.p., 1989-95; dir. nuclear affairs USFEA, Washington, 1975-76; exec. dir. Pres. Ford's Energy Resources Coun., 1975-76. Mem. mgmt. com. PJM Interconnection, 1980-95; pres. PDA, Inc., 1995-2002. Chmn. emeritus Concert Soc. at Md.; trustee, mem. exec. com. The Washington Opera, 1980—, pres., 1990-94; trustee, mem. exec. com. Greater Washington Rsch. Ctr., 1978-97. Named U.S. Outstanding Young Elec. Engr. Eta Kappa Nu, 1964, Outstanding Young Man of Am. Jaycees, 1966; recipient award for meritorious service USFEA, 1976. Mem. Univ. Club (Washington). Republican. Greek Orthodox. Avocation: sailing. E-mail: dragoum@attglobal.net.

DRAIME, CHARLES DOUGLAS, poet, short story writer, playwright; b. Vincennes, Ind., Feb. 23, 1943; s. Charles Elroy and Lenore Louise Draime; m. Lori Louise Stewart, Dec. 20, 1981 (div. Oct. 10, 1987); children: Aaron Charles, Shawn Stewart; m. Carolyn May Shepherd, Nov. 10, 1995; m. Beth Partlow-Swanson, June 4, 1977 (dec. Oct. 6, 1980). Student, U. Chgo., 1962—63, Fine Arts Acad., Chgo., 1963—64, L.A. City Coll., 1970—71. Laborer Wells Shipping, Vincennes, Ind., 1960; rm. clk. Lake Tower Inn, Chgo., 1962—63; bartender Indpls., 1964; actor, film extra Hollywood, Calif., 1967—70; sales clk. Everybody Book Shop, L.A., 1973—77; proofreader, rschr. Barnes Advtg., Medford, Oreg., 1987—89; asst. tchr. spl. edn. Ashland (Oreg.) Sch. Dist., 1994—. Author: Slaves of the Harvest, 2002; contbr. poems and short stories to various publs. Sgt E-5 U.S. Army, 1964—66. Grantee, PEN Internat., 1988, 1991. E-mail: cddraime@charter.net.

DRAIN, ALBERT STERLING, business management consultant; b. Decatur, Tex., July 5, 1925; s. Albert S. and Bessie (Burk) D.; m. Mauvaline Joyce Beam, Apr. 18, 1946; children: Ronald Dale, Deborah Kay Drain Crawford. Student, Bellville (Ill.) Jr. Coll., Tex. Christian U., Iowa U., Milsaps Coll., Pittsburg (Kans.) Coll. With Armour & Co., 1945-79, regional mgr., 1966-67, mgr. pork div. Chgo., 1967-68, fresh meats div. mgr., 1968-69, corporate v.p., 1968-75, exec. v.p., 1971-73, group v.p. food marketing div., 1973-75; pres. Armour Foods, 1975-79; also dir.; exec. v.p. for Iowa Beef Processors Inc., Dakota City, Nebr., 1979-80; group v.p. Greyhound Corp., Phoenix, 1977—; pres. Sterling Mktg. Inc. (ind. bus. cons. to meat industry), Phoenix, 1980-91; pvt. practice mgmt. cons. meat packing Phoenix, 1991-94; pvt. practice Al Drain Mgmt. Cons., Phoenix, 1994—. Served with USNR, 1943-45. Mem. Am. Soc. Agrl. Cons., Masons, Shriners. Baptist. Home and Office: 24 E San Miguel Ave Phoenix AZ 85012-1337 Fax: 602-266-4797. E-mail: AlDrainl@aol.com.

DRAIN, CECIL B. university dean, nurse anesthetist educator, retired army officer; b. Ft. Worth, Aug. 25, 1943; s. Harry Eugene and F. Colene (McDonald) D.; m. Cynthia M. Pfaff, Aug. 21, 1965; children: Timothy, Stephen, Kathryn. Diploma, St. Joseph Hosp. Sch. Nursing, Ft. Worth, 1967; BSN, U. Ariz., 1976, MS in Med.-Surg. Nursing, NS in Adult Pulmonary Nursing, U. Ariz., 1980; PhD in Ednl. Curriculum and Instrn. in Higher Edn., Tex. A&M U., 1986. RN, Va., Tex.; cert. RN anesthetist. Staff nurse recovery room, head nurse psychiatry St. Joseph Hosp., 1967; commd. 2d lt. U.S. Army, 1968, advanced through grades to col.; chief nurse anesthetist 121st Evacuation Hosp., Seoul, Republic of Korea, 1972—73; staff nurse anesthetist, chief respiratory therapy U.S. Gen. Leonard Wood Army Community Hosp., Ft. Leonard Wood, Mo., 1973-74; staff nurse anesthetist Tucson Med. Ctr., 1974—76, Brooke Army Med. Ctr., Ft. Sam Houston, Tex., 1976—78, spl. project officer, 1986-89; asst. program dir. U.S. Army-SUNY-Buffalo anesthesiology for ANC officers course U.S. Army Acad. Health Sciences, Ft. Sam Houston, 1980-83; program dir. program in anesthesia nursing U.S. Army-Tex. U.S. Army/Tex. Wesleyan U./Acad. of Health Scis., Ft. Sam Houston, 1989-92; dir. program in anesthesia nursing U. Tex. Health Sci. Ctr. Houston/AMEDD Ctr. and Sch., Ft. Sam Houston, 1992-93; prof. clin. nursing U. Tex. Health Sci. Ctr., Houston, 1992-93; prof. Va. Commonwealth U., Med. Coll. Va. Campus, Richmond, 1993—; chmn. dept. nurse anesthesia Med. Coll. Va., Richmond, 1993-96, interim dean Sch. Allied Health Professions, 1996-97, dean Sch. Allied Health Professions, 1997—. Teaching asst. U. Ariz., 1979-80; clin. instr. family medicine U. Okla., 1983; adj. prof. Tex. Wesleyan U., 1989-92; guest lectr. Tex. A&M U., 1986-93; numerous presentations in field; mem. long-term civilian profls. Schooling Selection Bd., Alexandria, Va., 1988; reviewer Clin. Rev. Series in Critical Care Nursing, 1988—. Author: Perianesthesia Nursing: A Critical Care Approach, 4th edit., 2003; mem. editl. bd.: Heart and Lung: Jour. Critical Care, 1977—92, Nurse Anesthesia, 1987—94, Am. Jour. Critical Care, 1992—, Jour. Am. Assn. Nurse Anesthetists, 1980—93, 1992—2000, Jour. Perianesthesia Nursing, 2002—; contbr. articles abstracts and book revs. to profl. jours., chpts. to books. Baseball commr., Ft. Sam Houston, 1980-81; bd. dirs. March of Dimes, San Antonio, 1981-83; umpire USTA, Bryan, Tex., 1985—; trustee Yankton Coll., 2003-. Decorated Legion of Merit, Meritorious Svc. medal with oak leaf cluster. Fellow Am. Acad. Nursing; mem. ANA, AACN (cert. of achievement 1980), Am. Assn. Nurse Anesthetists (jour. faculty 1982-83, bd. dirs. Ednl. and Rsch. Found. 1983-91, cert. of profl. excellence 1976), Am. Soc. Post Anesthesia Nurses (rsch. com. 1986-87), Tex. Assn. Post Anesthesia Nurses (life), 38th Parallel Nurses Soc. (pres. 1971), So. Assn. Allied Health Deans of Acad. Med. Ctrs. (treas. 2002--), Assn. Schs. Allied Health Profls. (treas. 2002--), Ret. Officers Assn. (life), Ret. Army Nurse Corps Assn. (assoc.), Order of Mil. Med. Merit, Downtown Kiwanis, Sigma Theta Tau, Phi Delta Kappa, Sigma Epsilon Chi. Republican. Methodist. Home: 5511 W Bay Rd Midlothian VA 23112-2509 Office: Va Commonwealth U Med Coll Va Campus Sch Allied Health Profs Richmond VA 23298 E-mail: cdrain@hsc.vcu.edu.

DRAKE, ALBERT DEE, writer, educator; b. Portland, Oreg., Mar. 26, 1935; s. Albert Howard and Hildah Leone Drake; married, 1960 (div. 1985); children: Moss, Monica, Barbara Ellen. Student, Portland State Coll., 1956-59; BA in English, U. Oreg., 1962, MFA in English/Writing, 1966. Rsch. asst. Oreg. Rsch. Inst. U. Oreg., Eugene, 1963-64, rsch. asst. dept. English, 1964-65, tchg. asst. dept. English, 1965-66; asst. prof. English Mich. State U., East Lansing, 1966-70, assoc. prof. English, 1970-80, prof. English, 1980-92, prof. English emerita, 1992—. Editor Stone Press, Okemos, Mich., 1968-90; editl. assoc. Writer's Digest Sch., Columbus, Ohio, 1973-75; dir. Clarion Sci. Fiction and Fantasy Writing Workshop, East Lansing, Mich., 1983, 88, 89, 90. Author: The Big 'Little GTO' Book, 1982, Fifties Flashback, 1999, Overtures to Motion, 2003; contbr. over 400 articles to profl. jours. Corp. USNG, 1953-60. Rsch. grantee Mich. State U., 1968, 79, Mich. Coun. for Arts, 1981-82, Nat. Endowment for Arts, 1974-75, 83-84. Home: 9727 SE Reedway St Portland OR 97266-3738 Office: PO Box 66874 Portland OR 97290-6874

DRAKE, ALBERT ESTERN, retired statistics educator, farming administrator; b. Stamping Ground, Ky., June 12, 1927; s. John L and Dullia Zena (Humphrey) D.; m. Katherine Ashby, June 22, 1952; children: Alan Sanford, Paul Steven, Jane, Philip David. Student, Georgetown Coll., 1946-47; BS, U. Ky., 1950, MS, 1951; PhD, U. Ill., 1958; postgrad., N.C. State U., 1959, 63, U. Fla., 1960. Rsch. asst. U. Ill., 1953-55, rsch. assoc., 1955-59; assoc. prof., assoc. biometrician Auburn U., 1959-62, prof., biometrician, 1962-63; dir. computer ctr. W.Va. U., 1963-65, acting coord. stats., 1965-66; prof. stats. U. Ala., 1966-92, coord. quantitative methods, 1966-72, acting head stats and mgmt. sci., 1981, interim assoc. dean undergrad. programs Coll. of Commerce and Bus. Adminstrn., 1988-90, assoc. dean undergrad. programs Coll. of Commerce and Bus. Adminstrn., 1990-92; prof. emeritus, 1992—; part-time mgr. farming enterprise and rock quarry, 1992—. Cons. in field. Contbr. articles to profl. jours., papers to profl. meetings. Bd. dirs. Little League, Auburn, 1961-63; active local council Boy Scouts Am., 1962-63, 66-67. Served with USMC, 1945-46. NSF grantee, 1959, 60, 63; Venture Fund grantee, 1975, 76, 81; inducted to Coll. Commerce & Bus. Adminstrn. U. Ala. Faculty Hall of Fame, 1998. Mem. Biometrics Soc., Am. Statis. Assn. (pres. Ala. chpt. 1972), Decision Scis. Inst. (sec. 1973-74, coun. 1969-72, 75-77, mem. editorial bd. 1969-72), Am. Agrl. Econs. Assn., Phi Kappa Alpha (Disting. Alumni award Omega chpt. 2001). Republican. Home: 5533 E Desert Hills Dr Scottsdale AZ 85254

DRAKE, ALISON BROOKS, physiatrist; b. Galveston, Tex., Mar. 26, 1963; m. David Barrick. BA in Psychology, U. Mich. and U. Tex.; MD, U. Tenn., Memphis, 1990. Fitness program coord. U. Tenn. Sch. Health Scis., Memphis, 1986-88; urgent care physician Group Health Assocs., Cin., 1992-94; staff physician Kennestone Hosp., Marietta, Ga., 1994-96; physiatrist Musculoskeletal Pvt. Practice, Marietta, 1997-98, Pinnacle Orthopaedics, Marietta, 1998—. Mem. AMA, Am. Acad. Phys. Medicine and Rehab., So. Med. Assn., Cobb County Med. Soc. Office: Pinnacle Orthopedics and Sports Med Specialists 652 Church St NW Marietta GA 30060-1139

DRAKE, ANNE KELLY, social worker, educator; b. Peoria, Ill., Nov. 13, 1951; d. Walter Reuel and Ada Frances (Dixon) Wright; m. Daniel L. Drake; children: James, N. Jason, Justin. AA, Lincoln Land C.C., 1975; BA in Child Family Comty. Svc., U. Ill. Sangamon campus, 1978; MEd, U. Ill., 1990. Cert. child protective investigator, child devel. specialist II, Ill.; lic. State of Ill.; cert. child welfare specialist. Case coord. Jacksonville (Ill.) Area Assn. Retarded Citizens, 1975-76; surrogate parent/ednl. advocate Ill. State Bd. Edn., Vermillion County, 1977-79; child care specialist Parents Anonymous, Champaign, Ill., 1990-91, parent facilitator, 1991-93; child devel. specialist Devel. Svcs. Ctr., Champaign, Ill., 1990-94; child protective investigator Ill. Dept. Children and Family Svcs., Charleston, Ill., 1994-2000, licensing quality assurance, day care cons. Savoy, Ill., 2000—, child protective svcs. worker Charleston, Ill., 2001—. Parent group facilitator, sponsor Parents Anonymous, Champaign, Ill., 1990-92; vol. EMT Midleford Vol. Ambulance, Potomac, Ill., 1986-89; surrogate parent/ednl. advocate Ill. State Bd. Edn., Vermillion County, 1986-89; grad. rsch. asst. dept. spl. edn. U. Ill., Champaign, 1987-90; v.p., rep. dept. spl. edn. Coun. Grad. Students in Edn., U. Ill., Champaign, 1987-90. Sec. Middlefork Twp. Vol. Ambulance, Potomac, Ill., 1987—89. Grantee Kappa Delta Pi, U. Ill., Champaign, 1990; Hilton-Perkins scholar, 1993. Mem.: Nat. Assn. Edn. Young Children, Kappa Delta Pi. Republican. Mem. Lds Ch. Home: 1212 Reynolds Dr Charleston IL 61920

DRAKE, BARBARA RUTH, writer; b. N.Y.C., Apr. 7, 1961; d. John Raymond and Ann Lucille D.; m. Jorge Alberto Vera DuBois, Jan. 6, 1996; 1 child, Samuel John Vera. BA with honors, SUNY, Purchase, 1984; postgrad., U. Fla., 2003—. Fellow in fiction Creative Writing Program, U. Fla., 2002—. Author: Destination Guatemala, 1996; author short stories, poetry, essays and cross-genre fiction pub. in N.D. Rev., Iris, The Village Voice; mem. The Volunteers (Celtic rock band), 1991—. Fellow Fontainebleau (France) Ecole des Arts Ams., 1982, Porter fellow Nat. League Am. Pen Women, 2002-2003; grantee Fla. Dept. State Divsn. Cultural Affairs, 1997-98, Artist Access grant Tigertail Prodns./Miami-Dade County Cultural Affairs Coun., 2000.

DRAKE, CHARLES WHITNEY, physicist; b. South Portland, Maine, Mar. 8, 1926; s. Charles Whitney and Katharine Gabrielle (O'Neill) D.; m. Ellen Tan, June 15, 1952; children— Judith Ellen, Robert Charles, Linda Ann. BS, U. Maine, 1950; MA, Conn. Wesleyan U., 1952; PhD, Yale U., 1958. Scientist Westinghouse Atomic Power Div., 1952-53; instr. Yale U., New Haven, 1957-60, asst. prof., 1960-66, rsch. assoc., 1966-69; assoc. prof. Oreg. State U., 1966-74; prof., 1974-93; prof. emeritus, 1993—; chmn. dept. physics, 1976-84. Vis. prof. Oxford U. Clarendon Lab. and St. Peter's Coll., 1972-73, U. Tuebingen (W.Ger.), 1982 Contbr. articles to profl. jours. Served with USNR, 1944-46. Recipient various fellowships and grants. Fellow Am. Phys. Soc.; mem. Am. Assn. Physics Tchrs., Sigma Xi, Tau Beta Pi, Sigma Pi Sigma. Office: Oreg State U Dept Physics Corvallis OR 97331

DRAKE, DIANA ASHLEY, financial planner; b. Poughkeepsie, N.Y., Apr. 28, 1937; d. Albert Jackson and Jane Ashley (Ketchum) D.; m. José Akel Abizaid, Dec. 2, 1956 (div. Nov. 1979); children: Cynthia A. Rush, Allison J. Abizaid, Linda A. Wiener, Carol Lynn Abizaid, Amanda Jo Abizaid, Richard Alan Abizaid; m. Sherrill Cleland, Sept. 3, 1988; stepchildren: Ann Cleland Feldmeier, Douglas S. Cleland, Sarah Cleland Allen, Scott C. Cleland. Student, Cornell U., 1955-56, Am. U. of Beirut, Lebanon, 1956-57; BS in Psychology cum laude, Vassar Coll., 1980; CFP, Inst. Fin. Planners, Denver, 1986. CFP. Divorce mediator Fin. Planning Corp. of Va., McLean, 1983-86; investment advisor Cert. Fin. Svc., McLean, 1986; ptnr. Koelz Drake Advisors, Falls Church, Va., 1987-89; pres. Drake Fin. Svcs., Falls Church, 1986-98; bronze distbr. Nikken health and wellness products, prin. Magnetic Living, 1998—. Sec., mem. Bd. Equalization, Falls Church, 1992-94. Contbr. articles to various mags. Elder Falls Church Presbyn. Ch., 1993-96, chair Christian Edn. Com., 1996, planned giving com. 1997-99, revision com. 1997; co-chmn. 100 yrs. aquatics YMCA, New Orleans, 1986. Recipient Disting. Svc. award for 25 Yrs. svcs. Nat. YMCA, 1986. Mem.: DAR, AAUW, Inst. CFPs, No. Va. Inst. Cert. Fin. Planners (sec. 1994—97, bd. dirs. facilities), Highland Oaks Cir. Assn. (bd. dirs., pres. 2003), Cornell Club of Sarasota, Vassar Club (Sarasota, Fla.), Meadows Chorus (Sarasota), Cornell Club of Washington (mem. investment and audit com. 1990—99), Zonta (dir. Arlington club 1992—99, cmty. svc. coord.), Cornell Club (Sarasota), Delta Gamma. Republican. Avocations: swimming, bridge, writing, photography, travel. Home and Office: 4489 Highland Oaks Cir Sarasota FL 34235 E-mail: dadcleland@aol.com.

DRAKE, DONALD CHARLES, journalist, playwright; b. N.Y.C., Jan. 12, 1935; s. Albert E. and Gloria (Walters) D.; 1 child, Valerie; m. Molly Hindman; 1 step-child, Jennifer. Student, NYU, 1953-56. Copy boy New York Herald Tribune, 1954-55; reporter Patent Trader, Mt. Kisco, N.Y., 1956-57, New Haven Register, 1957-58, Newsday, Garden City, N.Y., 1958-65; med. writer Phila. Inquirer, 1966-93; narrative editor, 1993-2001. Author: Medical School, 1978, (plays) Words, Saintly Mother, Clear and Present Danger, Final Edition, The Last Appointment, Love Knot, The Passage, Aria, Gorked! Recipient Russell L. Cecil Writing award Arthritis Found., 1968, John S. Packard award Pa. Tb. and Health Soc., 1968, Howard W. Blakeslee awards Am. Heart Assn., 1969, 76, 81, Walter J. Donaldson awards Pa. Med. Soc., 1970, 71, Keystone Press awards, 1974-81, 83, 84, 87, 88, 90, 93, 2002, Claude Bernard award Nat. Soc. for Med. Research, 1978, AP Mng. Editors award Pa., 1978, 81, 84, 93, Robert F. Kennedy Journalism award, 1982, Morse award Am. Psychiat. Assn., 1982, Gen. Motors Cancer Rsch. Found. prize, 1990, others. Mem. Nat. Assn. Sci. Writers, Dramatists Guild, Dramatists Ctr. *Journalism would serve a greater good if it sought the truth instead of just the facts, but that's a lot harder to do.*

DRAKE, E. MAYLON, academic administrator; b. Nampa, Idaho, Feb. 8, 1920; s. Austin Henry and Daisy Naomi (Smith) D.; m. Lois Elloise Noble, Oct. 12, 1940; children: E. Christopher, Cameron Lee. BS, U. So. Calif., Los Angeles, 1951, MS, 1954, EdD, 1963. Mgr. Frederick Post Co., San Francisco, 1943-47; asst. supt. Baldwin Park (Calif.) Schs., 1947-51; supt. Duarte (Calif.) Schs., 1951-64, Alhambra (Calif.) City Schs., 1964-70; dep. supt. Los Angeles County Schs., 1970-78; dir. Acad. Ednl. Mgmt., Los Angeles, 1978-80; pres. L.A. Coll. Chiropractic, Whittier, 1980-90, chancellor, 1990-93, chancellor emeritus, 1993—. Adj. prof. U. So. Calif., 1964-90, bd. councilors, 1991—. Author Attaining Accountability in Schools, 1972; contbr. articles to profl. jours. Pres. Industry-Ednl. Council So. Calif., 1978; dir. United Way 1970; dir. Greater Los Angeles Zoo Bd., 1970; dir. Planned Parenthood of Pasadena, Calif., 1996; trustee L.A. Coll. Chiropractic Whittier, Calif., 1996. Recipient Am. Educator's medal Freedom Found.; named Educator of Yr. Los Angeles Chiropratic Soc., 1981. Mem. Coun. on Chiropractic Edn. (pres. 1988-90), Rotary (pres. Duarte 1954-56, bd. dirs. Alhambra 1964-70). Republican. Presbyterian. Avocation: performing arts. Home: Pasadena Highlands 323 1575 E Washington Blvd Pasadena CA 91104 Office: LA Coll Chiropractic PO Box 1166 Whittier CA 90609-1166 E-mail: maylon@webtv.net.

DRAKE, ELISABETH MERTZ, chemical engineer, consultant; b. N.Y.C., Dec. 20, 1936; d. John and Ruth (Johnson) Mertz; m. Alvin William Drake, July 31, 1957 (div. 1984); 1 child, Alan Lee. SB in Chem. Engring., MIT, 1958, ScD in Chem. Engring., 1966. Registered profl. engr., Mass. Staff engr. Arthur D. Little Inc., Cambridge, Mass., 1958-64, sr. staff, 1966-76, mgr. risk analysis, 1977-82, v.p. tech. risk mgmt., 1980-82, 86-89, cons., 1990-94; assoc. dir. new tech. MIT Energy Lab., 1990-2000, dir., 1994-95, cons., 2000—; lectr. U. Calif., Berkeley, 1971; vis. prof. MIT, Cambridge, 1973-74; chmn. chem. engring. dept. Northeastern U., Boston, 1982-86. Corp. mgr. MIT, 1981-86; mem. tech. pipeline safety stds. com. U.S. Dept. Transp., 1980-85; mem. mng. bd. AIChE, 1988-90; vice chair com. on rev. and evaluation on army chem. stockpile disposal program NRC, 1993-98, mem., 2002—. Contbr. articles to profl. jours.; inventor fractionation method and apparatus, 1972. Fellow AIChE (bd. dirs. 1987-90); mem. AAAS, NAE, Am. Chem. Soc., Sigma Xi. Home: 30F Inman St Cambridge MA 02139-2411 E-mail: edrake@alum.mit.edu.

DRAKE, ERVIN MAURICE, composer, author; b. N.Y.C., Apr. 3, 1919; s. Max and Pearl Edith (Cohen) D.; m. Ada Sax, May 28, 1947 (dec. Mar. 1975); children: Linda Shifra, Betsy Jennifer; m. Edith Bein Berman, Nov. 19, 1982. B of Social Sci., CCNY, 1940; studies with Tibor Serly, Jacob Druckman; Mus D (hon.), Five Towns Coll., 1998. Composer popular songs including I Believe, 1998, It Was a Very Good Year, 1999 (recorded by Robbie Williams 2001), Tico Tico, Perdido, Al Di Là, A Room Without Windows, Good Morning Heartache, 1999, Come to the Mardi Gras, The Rickety Rickshaw Man, Across the Wide Missouri, My Friend, Father of Girls, Quando Quando Quando, Sonata, Made for Each Other, Cherry, One God, Now That I Have Everything, Just For Today, There Are No Restricted Signs in Heaven, Marilyn; composer music and lyrics Leslie Uggams CD Painted Mem'ries, 1995, From John Gabriel With Love CD, 1997, One God (recorded by Barbra Streisand), Who Are These Strangers (recorded by Michael Feinstein), 2003; lyricist, co-librettist, composer music Florence of Arabia, 1985; composer music lyrics and co-librettist Songs in Sophisticated Ladies, 1983, 84, Shades of Harlem, 1985, Lady Day, 1987; composer/lyracist Broadway musical What Makes Sammy Run?, 1964-65; composer/lyricist/librettist Her First Roman, 1968; writer, composer and/or prodr. TV programs. Recipient Honor, Friars Club, 2002, Soc. Singers, 2003.

DRAKE, GEORGE ALBERT, college president, historian; b. Springfield, Mo., Feb. 25, 1934; s. George Bryant and Alberta (Stimson) D.; m. Susan Martha Ratcliff, June 25, 1960; children: Christopher George, Cynthia May, Melanie Susan. AB, Grinnell Coll., 1956; Fulbright scholar, U. Paris, 1956-57; AB (Rhodes scholar), Oxford U., 1959, MA, 1963; BD, U. Chgo., 1962, MA, 1963, PhD (Rockefeller fellow), 1965; LLD (hon.), Colo. Coll., 1980, Ripon Coll., 1982; LHD (hon.), Ill. Coll., 1985, Ursinus Coll., 1988, Doane Coll., 1995, Morningside Coll., 1998. Instr. history Grinnell Coll., Iowa, 1960-61, pres., 1979-91, prof., 1979—, trustee, prof., 1991—. Asst. prof., assoc. prof. history Colo. Coll., Colorado Springs, 1964-79, acting dean of Coll., 1967-68, dean, 1969-73 Trustee Grinnell Coll., 1970-79, Penrose Hosp., 1976-79, 80-84, Grinnell Gen. Hosp., 1980-86, mem. Doane Coll. Bd. Trustees, 1995—, Iowa Peace Inst. Bd., 1994—, chair, 1996-99, vol. U.S. Peace Corps, Lesotho, 1991-93; commr. North Ctrl. Assn. Colls. and Schs., 1998-2001; mem. FINE Found. bd., 1998—. NEH fellow, 1974. Mem. Am. Hist. Assn., Am. Ch. History Soc., Nat. Coll. Athletic Assn. (pres. commn. 1984-89), Nat. Merit Scholarship Corp. E-mail: Drake@Grinnell.edu.

DRAKE, HUDSON BILLINGS, aerospace and electronics company executive; b. LA, Mar. 3, 1935; s. Hudson C. and Blossom (Billings) D.; m. Joan M. Johnson, Feb. 9, 1957 (dec. 1997); children: Howard Billings, Paul Marvin; m. Mary H. Vaugier, Nov. 1, 2000. BA in Econs., UCLA, 1957, postgrad., 1990; MBA, Pepperdine U., 1976. Mgr. Autonetics div. Rockwell Inc., Anaheim, Calif., 1958-68; exec. dir. Pres.'s Commn. White House Fellows, Washington, 1969-70; dep. under sec. U.S. Dept. Commerce, Washington, 1970-72; v.p., gen. mgr. Teledyne Ryan Electronics, San Diego, 1972-80, pres., 1980-84; pres., group exec. Teledyne Ryan Aero., San Diego, 1984-88; v.p., group exec. Teledyne Inc., L.A., 1987-88, sr. v.p., group exec., 1988-89, sr. v.p., pres. aerospace and electronics segment, 1989-96; pres. aerospace and electronics segment Allegheny Teledyne Inc., LA, 1996—97; ltd. ptnr. Carlisle Enterprises, La Jolla, Calif., 1997—; dir. Parex Inc., Washington, 1997—. Mem. Def. Procurement Adv. Com. on Trade, Washington, 1988—93; bd. dirs. Compass Aerospace Corp. Contbr. articles to profl. jours. Trustee Children's Hosp., San Diego, 1981-86, chmn. rsch. corp., 1983-86; pres.'s coun. San Diego (Calif.) State U., 1984-90; bd. overseers U. Calif., San Diego, 1985-88; vestry St. James by the Sea, LaJolla, Calif., 1998-2002; bd. dirs. Jonsson Cancer Ctr. Found., UCLA, 1998—. With USNR, 1953-61 Recipient Exec. of Yr. award Nat. Mgmt. Assn., 1995; named Silver Knight of mgmt. Nat. Mgmt. Assn., 1975, Gold Knight of mgmt., 1986; San Diego Bd. Suprs resolution, 1988; White House fellow, 1968. Mem. IEEE, AIAA, Navy League (life), Inst. Navigation, San Diego C. of C. (bd. dirs.), La Jolla Country Club. Republican. Episcopalian. Avocations: golf, fly fishing. Home: 1707 Soledad Ave La Jolla CA 92037 E-mail: hdrake1@san.rr.com.

DRAKE, JAYNE KRIBBS, university administrator, English educator; b. Oil City, Pa., Aug. 3, 1946; d. A. Merle and Edna May Eisenman Kribbs; m. Jeffrey Richard Drake, Dec. 1, 1984; 1 child, Darren Alexander. BA, Clarion (Pa.) U. of Pa., 1968; MA, Pa. State U., 1969, PhD, 1974. Assoc. dean The Grad. Sch. Temple U., Phila., 1984-91, grad. dean Coll. of Liberal, 1991-96, prof. English, 1975—, dir. tchg. improvement ctr., 1996-99, assoc. dean for student svcs., 1997-98, dir. acad. advising, 1998—, vice dean, 1998—. Sec. Golden Cradle Bd. Trustees, Cherry Hill, N.J., 1981—; cons. Phila. Sch. Dist., 1990-94. Author: Critical Essays on John Greenleaf Whittier, 1981, American Literary Periodicals, 1978; editor: MLA International Bibliography, 1969-75. Mem. Beagle Club Civic Assn. (v.p. 1994-2000), Nat. Assn. for Acad. Advising (regional rep. 2000—). Avocations: reading, traveling, boating. Home: 93 Bunning Dr Kirkwood Voorhees NJ 08043 Office: Coll Liberal Arts Deans Office Temple U Philadelphia PA 19122 E-mail: jayne.drake@temple.edu.

DRAKE, JOHN WARREN, aviation consultant; b. Chgo., July 5, 1930; s. Robert Warren and Winifred Elizabeth (Bramhall) D.; m. Miriam Anna Engleman, Dec. 19, 1960 (div. Dec. 1985); 1 child, Robert Warren; m. Mary Pat

O'Kelly, Sept. 24, 2000. BS, Rensselaer Poly. Inst., 1952; MBA, Harvard U., 1954, D.BA, 1972. Research asso. Aero. Research Found., Cambridge, Mass., 1956-57; prin. United Research, Inc., Cambridge, 1957-61; v.p. Systems Analysis and Research Corp., Cambridge, 1961-69; prof. emeritus, air transp. area Sch. Aeros. and Astronautics, Sch. Engring., Purdue U., 1972-92, mem. president's council. Cons. in field; mem. Transp. Research Bd. NRC. Author: The Administration of Transportation Modeling Projects, 1973. Served with U.S. Army, 1954-56. Mem. Air Transp. Rsch. Internat. Forum (coun.), AIAA, Soc. Automotive Engrs. Clubs: University (Washington). Home and Office: 341 Riverview Dr Ann Arbor MI 48104-1847

DRAKE, LAURA, theater director, performer; b. Eureka, Calif., Mar. 1, 1949; d. Stephen Drake and Laura Anne (Filingerie) Morel. BA in Interdisciplinary Creative Arts, San Francisco State U., 1973; MFA in Dramatic Prodn., U. Tex., 1985. Dir., coord. Austin (Tex.) Theatre Artists' Collective, 1984-85; artistic dir. Creatrix Prodns., New Orleans, 1985-89; asst. prof. theatre U. Southwestern La., Lafayette, 1987-91; appt. artist, spare/changes artistic resident Atlantic Ctr. for Arts, 1990; artistic dir. Gabriella Rosetti Prodns., N.Y.C., 1992—. Artist-in-residence Karantena Festival, Dubrovrik, Croatia, 2002; asst. prof. theater Hunter Coll., CUNY, N.Y.C., 2000—. Writer, performer (performance art): Duck/Blind, 1990, Stages: Aphro-Diaspora, 1990 (NEA Inter-Arts award 1990); dir./producer Interdisciplinary Performance Festival, 1988-91 (Lafayette, La.). Morton Brown Rsch. fellow U. Tex., Austin, 1981, 82; recipient Partnership award Acadiana Arts Coun., 1988-91, Inter Arts award Nat. Endowment for the Arts, 1990, New Performance award La. Div. of the Arts, 1990, Ensemble Acting award The Source Theatre, Washington, 2002. Mem. Artists' Alliance (Lafayette, program com. 1989-91, bd. dirs.), Festival Internat. de Louisiane (bd. dirs. 1989-91), Phi Kappa Phi, Alpha Psi Omega. Home: 1691 3d Ave Apt 3A New York NY 10128-2113 E-mail: ldrake@hunter.cuny.edu.

DRAKE, LEE J. public administration executive, writer; b. Leader, Minn., Nov. 5, 1924; s. John Daniel Drake and Elin Amelia Johnson; m. Julia Maurine Hanna, June 19, 1947; children: John Alden, Madeline Anne. BA, Calif. U., Los Angeles, CA, 1952. Prin. analyst LA County, Los Angeles, Calif., 1960—64; asst. county exec. Ventura County, Ventura, Calif., 1964—70; county adminstr. San Joaquin County, Stockton, Calif., 1970—73; owner, mgr. L.J. Drake and Associates, Fresno, Calif., 1974—89, Brookings, SD, 1979—84. Dir. modernization commn. Supervisor's Assn., Sacramento, 1973—74. Author: (novels) Monah, Murder in Muskrat Town, Hiding Gideon Pike. Chmn. Lions Internat., 1965—70, Benevolent and Protective Order Elks, 1983—99. Served with USN, 1943—46, PTO. Recipient Commendation, Bd. Suprs. Assn., 1972, Lee Drake Day, 1973, Liberty Bell award, Bar Assn., 1973. Achievements include design of Personnel Performance Appraisal System; Personnel Classification System. Avocations: lecturing, motivational speaking, woodworking. Home: 750 Valley View Drive #1 Council Bluffs IA 51503 Personal E-mail: landjdrake@qwest.net.

DRAKE, MIRIAM ANNA, librarian, educator, writer; b. Boston, Dec. 20, 1936; d. Max Frederick and Beatrice Celia (Mitnick) Engleman; m. John Warren Drake, Dec. 19, 1960 (div. Dec. 1985); 1 child, Robert Warren. BS, Simmons Coll., Boston, 1958, MLS, 1971; postgrad., Harvard U., 1959-60; LHD (hon.), Ind. U., 1994; DLS (hon.), Simmons Coll., 1997. Assoc. United Rsch., Cambridge, Mass., 1958-61; with mktg. svcs. Kenyon & Eckhardt, Boston, 1963-65; cons. Boston, 1965-72; head rsch. unit libraries Purdue U., West Lafayette, Ind., 1972-76, asst. dir. libraries, prof. library sci., 1976-84; dean, dir. libraries, prof. Ga. Inst. Tech., Atlanta, 1984-2001, prof. emerita, 2001—. Trustee Online Computer Libr. Ctr., Inc., 1978-84, chair, 1980-83; trustee Corp. for Rsch. and Edn. Networking, 1991-94, U.S. Depository Libr. Coun., 1991-94, Simmons Coll., 1999—; trustee, corporator adv. bd. Engring. Info., 1997—. Author: User Fees: A Practical Perspective, 1981, Information Today, 2002; co-author: (with James Matarazzo) Information for Management, 1994; editor: Ency. Libr. Info. Sci., 2nd edit.; mem. editl. bd. Coll. and Rsch. Librs. Jour., 1985-90, Librs. and Microcomputers Jour., 1983-93, Sci. and Tech. Librs., 1989-98, Database, 1989-97; contbr. chpts. to books, articles to profl. jours. Recipient Alumni Achievement award Simmons Coll. Sch. Libr. and Info. Sci., 1985, Kent Meckler Media award U. Pitts., 1994. Fellow: Nat. Fedn. of Abstracting and Indexing Svs. (hon.); mem.: ALA (councilor at large 1985—89, Hugh Atkinson Meml. award 1992), Assn. Info. and Dissemination Ctrs. (pres. 2001—03), Spl. Librs. Assn. (pres.-elect 1992—93, pres. 1993—94, H.W. Wilson award 1983, John Cotton Dana award 2002), Am. Soc. Info. Sci., Am. Mgmt. Assn. Office: Ga Inst Tech Lib Info Ctr Atlanta GA 30332-0900 E-mail: mdrake@library.gatech.edu.

DRAKE, OWEN BURTCH WINTERS, association administrator; b. N.Y.C., May 22, 1941; s. Owen Burtch Winters and Louise Harrison (Gwynn) D.; m. Joan Draper, Dec. 15, 1961 (div. July 1975); children: Burtch Winters, Frederic Malcolm; m. Deborah Edmonson, Jan. 8, 1977; children: Kelley Keresey, Colin Edmonston. Student, U. Va., 1958-61. Sr. v.p., mgmt. supr. Dancer, Fitzgerald & Sample Inc., N.Y.C., 1961-78, pres., gen. mgr. San Francisco, 1981-84; dir. European area Life Savers Inc., London, 1978-80; sr. v.p., group mgmt. supr. Foote, Cone & Belding, N.Y.C., 1981, exec. v.p., gen. mgr., 1985-86; pres. FCB/Leber Katz Ptnrs., N.Y.C., 1986-87; pres. European area Foote, Cone & Belding, London, 1987-89; exec. v.p., chief oper. officer Am. Assn. Advt. Agys., N.Y.C., 1989-94, pres., CEO, 1994—. Bd. dirs. Advt. Coun., 1994—, Nat. Advt. Rev. Coun., 1994—, Advt. Edn. Found., 1994—, AAAA Found. Inc., 1997—. Bd. dir. San Francisco Zool. Soc., 1983-84, Partnership for Drug Free Am., 1994—, Trustee Nat. Childhood Cancer Found., 2003-, served USMCR, 1958-67. Recipient Effie award Am. Advt. Fedn., 1977. Mem.: Racquet and Tennis (N.Y.C.); Rockaway Hunting (Cedarhurst, N.Y.); Lawrence Beach (Atlantic Beach, N.Y.); Coral Beach (Bermuda). Office: Am Assn Advt Agys 405 Lexington Ave New York NY 10174-0002 E-mail: obd@aaaa.org.

DRAKE, PATRICIA EVELYN, psychologist; b. Lewiston, Maine, Feb. 9, 1946; d. Lewis and Anita (Bilodeau) D.; m. Colin Matthew Fuller, May 13, 1973 (div. Aug. 1983); children: R. Matthew, Meaghan Merry. Diploma, St. Mary's Sch. Nursing, 1967; BS, U. Nev., 1985; MA, Calif. Sch. Profl. Psychology, 1987, PhD, 1989. RN. Nurse Maine Med. Ctr., Portland, 1967-73, U. Calif. Sacramento Med. Ctr., 1973-78, Ben Taub Hosp., Houston, 1978-79; psychology intern Shasta County Mental Health Ctr., Redding, Calif., 1988-89, clin. psychologist, 1989-91, tng. dir., chief psychology, 1991—; psychologist pvt. practice, Redding, Calif., 1991—. Mem. AAUW, APA, Calif. Psychol. Assn., Shasta-Cascade Psychol. Assn., Phi Kappa Phi. Democrat. Roman Catholic. Avocations: swimming, cross-country skiing, crafts. Office: Shasta County Mental Health 2640 Breslauer Way Redding CA 96001-4246 E-mail: pdrake@co.shasta.ca.us.

DRAKE, PAUL, detective agency owner; b. N.Y.C., Sept. 6, 1933; s. Austin Drake and Heda Drake; m. Hazel Drake, Oct. 11, 1957. BA in sociology, NYU, 1954. Owner, founder Drake Detective Agy., L.A., 1957—. Chmn. Execs. Against the Internet, N.Y.C., 1995—. Mem. Pvt. Detectives Dirs. Bd. (v.p. 1983—, awards 1989, 93). Avocations: fellowship, reading, travel, working on future book. Office: Drake Agys Inc PO Box 931 New York NY 10116-0931

DRAKE, RICHARD FRANCIS, state legislator; b. Muscatine, Iowa, Sept. 28, 1927; s. Frank and Gladys (Young) R.; m. Shirley Jean Henke; children: Cheryll Dee, Ricky Lee. Student, Iowa State U.; BS, U.S. Naval Acad., 1950. Enlisted man USN, WWII, commd. ensign, 1950; advanced through grades to lt. comdr., 1954; comdg. officer minesweeper USS Crow, 1953—54; ret., 1954; farmer, mgr., 1954—; mem. Iowa Senate from 40th dist., Des Moines, 1968—. Chmn. Young Rep. Orgn. Iowa, 1954-56; adminstrv. asst. Muscatine County Rep. Com., 1956-57, chmn., 1958-66; chmn. 1st Dist. Rep. Com., 1966-72, Nat. Task Force on Rail Line Abandonment and Curtailment; chmn. states and rai problems Midwestern Coun. State Govts., 1978-79. Named One of 10 Outstanding Legislators of Yr., Nat. Rep. Legislators Assn. Mem. VFW, Am. Legion, Farm Bur., Masons, Elks, Order Ea. Star. Lutheran. Office: State Senate State Capitol Des Moines IA 50319-0001

DRAKE, RICHARD PAUL, physicist, educator; b. Washington, Oct. 25, 1954; s. Hugh Hess and Florence Jean (Steele) D.; m. Joyce Elaine Penner, Aug. 30, 1980; children: Katherine Anne, David Alexander. BA in Philosophy and Physics magna cum laude, Vanderbilt U., 1975; PhD in Physics, Johns Hopkins U., 1979. Physicist Lawrence Livermore (Calif.) Lab., 1979-89; assoc. prof. dept. applied sci. U. Calif., Davis, 1989-91, prof., 1991-93; dir. Plasma Physics Rsch. Inst. Lawrence Livermore Nat. Lab., 1990-96; vis. prof. U. Mich., Ann Arbor, 1996-98, prof. space sci., 1998—, dir. Space Physics Rsch. Lab., 1998—2002. Ski instr. Squaw Valley, Calif., 1985-92; referee NSF, Nature, Phys. Rev. Letters, others. Contbr. over 140 articles to profl. jours. Mem. Fellow Am. Phys. Soc. (chmn. topical group on plasma astrophysics 2002); mem. AAAS, Am. Geophys. Union, Am. Astron. Soc., Am. Vacuum Soc., Optical Sci. Am., Phi Beta Kappa. Achievements include rsch. in exptl. astrophysics fundamental experiments and theory on waves, instabilities, and turbulence in plasmas; time-dependent systems. Home: 3204 W Dobson Pl Ann Arbor MI 48105-2580 Office: U Mich Campus 2455 Hayward St Ann Arbor MI 48109-2143 E-mail: rpdrake@umich.edu.

DRAKE, RICHARD REGIS, historian, educator; b. Springfield, Mass., Aug. 23, 1942; s. Floyd Wilbur and Ornella Maria Drake; m. Megen Thompson, Aug. 2, 1979 (div. Apr. 1990); 1 child, Richard Drake Jr.; m. Laure Kay Pengelly, July 14, 2001. BA, St. Michael's Coll., 1963; MA, Brown U., 1965; PhD, UCLA, 1975. Lectr. U. Calif. Irvine, 1976—78, UCLA, 1978—79, Wellesley Coll., Wellesley, Mass., 1979—80, Princeton U., Princeton, NJ, 1980—82; asst. prof., assoc. prof. U. Mont., Missoula, 1982—88, prof., 1988—. Author: Byzantium for Rome: The Politics of Nostalgia in Umbertian Italy, 1980, The Revolutionary Mystique and Terrorism in Contemporary Italy, 1989 (Marraro award, 1989), The Aldo Moro Murder Case, 1995. Fellow, Fulbright, 1972—73, Am. Coun. Learned Socs., 1983, NEH, 1999—2000. Mem.: Am. Hist. Assn., Soc. for Italian Hist. Studies (adv. coun. 1998—2001), Am. Cath. Hist. Assn. Office: Univ Montana Missoula MT 59812

DRAKE, RODMAN LELAND, investment company executive, consultant; b. Terre Haute, Ind., Feb. 2, 1943; s. Leland Rodman and Helen Virginia (Frederick) Drake; m. Lenir Leme-Lambert, July 26, 1975 (div. 1998); children: Stephan Rodman, Philip Lambert; m. Jacqueline B Weld, Dec. 18, 1998. BA, Yale U., 1965; MBA, Harvard U., 1969. Assoc. Cresap, McCormick & Paget, Inc., N.Y.C., 1969-70, Monterrey, Mexico, 1971-72, mng. ptnr. São Paulo, Brazil, 1972-77, v.p., bd. dirs. N.Y.C., 1977-81, mng. dir., CEO, 1981-90; pres. Mandrake Group, Inc., N.Y.C., 1993-97; pres., dir. Continuation Investments Group Inc., N.Y.C., 1997—2002; co-founder Baringo Capital LLC, 2002—. Lead dir. Parsons Brinckerhoff Inc.; bd. dirs. Hotelvision Inc., Excelsior Funds (sponsored by US Trust), Hyperion Total Return Fund, Hyperion 2005 Opportunity Term Trust, Hyperion Strategic Mortgage Income Trust Inc., Clean Fuels Technology, Inc; past bd. Argentina Pvt Equity Fund LP and Garantia LP, Brazil, Alex Brown & Sons, Inc., Mueller Industries; adv. bd. Lebanese Am. U., Lebanon; co-chmn. KMR Power Corp., 1993—96; adv. bd. Silvercrest Asset Mgmt. Mem. drawing com. Whitney Mus. Modern Art; bd. dirs. Animal Med. Ctr. With U.S. Army, 1965—67. Mem.: New Holland Soc., Waccabuc Club (NY), Golf Club Purchase (NY), River Club (NYC). E-mail: rdrake@cipmgmt.com.

DRAKE, STANLEY JOSEPH, association executive; b. New Britain, Conn., Mar. 8, 1916; s. Joseph Nicholas and Alice (Tokarzewska) E.; m. Virginia Allen, Oct. 6, 1940 (dec. Apr. 1993); children: Alice Drake Berg, Janet Drake Gardner, Jane Drake Dover. BS in Bus. Edn., Bryant Coll., Smithfield, R.I., 1937; MS, Temple Bar Coll., Mpls., 1944; PhD, McKinley Roosevelt Inst, Chgo., 1948; D. Pedagogy (hon.), Bryant Coll., 1963; DBA (hon.), Ind. No. U., 1966; Dr.Bus.Adminstrn., Cleary Coll., 1967; LHD, Internat. Fine Arts Coll., 1968; LLD (hon.), Fla. Rsch. Inst., 1970; EdD, Ft. Lauderdale U., 1973. Instr. Mt. Vernon (Ohio) Coll., 1945-48, Broward Coll., Ft. Lauderdale, Fla., 1948-56; pres. Ft. Lauderdale Coll., 1956-76; adj. prof. Tampa (Fla.) Coll., 1977-78, Orlando Coll., 1978-81, Gaston Coll., Dallas, N.C., 1981-94. Author: Thoughts from the Bible, 1991, The Essentials of Esperanto, 1993. Mem. Am. Assn. of Pres. of Ind. Colls. and Univs. (pres. 1967-68, sec. 1969-70), Am. Assn. Specialized Colls. (pres. 1965-67), Internat. Soc. Friendsihp and Good Will (pres. 1982-2002, pres. emeritus 2003—, sec. gen. 1978-82). Republican. Avocations: music, travel. Home and Office: STe 344 Roswell Rd Atlanta GA 30350 E-mail: isfgw@bellsouth.net.

DRAKE, STEPHEN DOUGLAS, clinical psychologist, health facility administrator; b. Iola, Kans., Sept. 8, 1947; s. Harry Francis and Emojean (Price) D.; m. Rebecca Gonzalez, June 1, 1968; 1 child, Michael Paul. BA, U. Tex., 1970; PhD, U. North Tex., 1987. Diplomate Am. Bd. Forensic Examiners; lic. psychologist. Mental health worker Austin (Tex.) State Hosp., 1970-73; claims rep. Social Security Adminstrn., Galveston, Tex., 1974-77, ops. supr. Dallas, 1977-79, staff asst., 1979-80; clin. psychologist Terrell (Tex.) State Hosp., 1987-89, Austin (Tex.) State Hosp., 1989-90; program dir. Austin State Hosp., 1990-92; cons. Tex. Rehab. Commn., 1992-98, chief mental med. cons., 1998—. Contbr. articles to profl. jours. Vice-Chmn. bd. dirs. Galveston (Tex.) Island Mental Health/Mental Retardation Ctr., 1977; v.p. Grad. Assn. Students in Psychology U. North Tex., 1984, grad. rep. exec. com., 1984. Recipient N.A.D.E. 2000/2001 award. Mem. APA, AAAS, Tex. Psychol. Assn., Assn. Advancement Behavior Therapy, Mensa, Phi Kappa Phi. Avocations: Tae Kwon Do, weightlifting, eastern philosophy, foreign languages, travel. Office: Tex Rehab Commn 6102 E Oltorf St Austin TX 78741

DRAKE, SYLVIE (JURRAS DRAKE), theater critic; b. Alexandria, Egypt, Dec. 18, 1930; came to U.S., 1949, naturalized, 1952; d. Robert and Simonette (Barda) Franco; m. Kenneth K. Drake, Apr. 29, 1952 (div. Dec. 1972); children— Jessica, Robert I.; m. Ty Jurras, June 16, 1973. M. Theater Arts, Pasadena Playhouse, 1969. Free-lance TV writer, 1962-68; theater critic Canyon Crier, L.A., 1968-72; theater critic, columnist L.A. Times, 1971-91, theater critic, 1991-93, theatre critc emeritus, 1993—; lit. dir. Denver Ctr. Theatre Co., 1985; pres. L.A. Drama Critics Circle, 1979-81, free lance travel writer, translator, book reviewer. Mem. Pulitzer Prize Drama Jury, 1994; adv. bd. Nat. Arts Journalism Program, 1994-97. Dir. media rels. and publs. Denver Ctr. for the Performing Arts, 1994—; artistic assoc. for spl. projects Denver Ctr. Theatre Co., 1994—. Mem. Am. Theater Critics Assn. Office: Denver Ctr Performing Arts 1245 Champa St Denver CO 80204-2100

DRAKE, VAUGHN PARIS, JR., electrical engineer, retired telephone company executive; b. Winchester, Ky., Nov. 6, 1918; s. Vaughn Paris and Margaret Turney (Willis) D.; m. Lina Louise Wilson, May 5, 1946; 1 child, Samuel Willis. Student, U. Ky., 1936-41. Registered profl. engr., Ky. From asst. engr. to gen. valuation and cost engr. Gen. Tel. Co. Ky., Lexington, 1945-81; ret., 1981. Author: (manual) Conduit Engineering for Telephone Engineers, 1958. Profl. adv. bd. Zoning Commn., Lexington and Fayette County, Ky., 1955-57. Comm. chief, combat engr. group AUS, 1941—45. Decorated Pearl Harbor Commemorative medal. Mem. IEEE (sr., chmn. Lexington sect. 1956-57), NSPE, Ky. Soc. Profl. Engrs. (pres. Bluegrass chpt. 1961-62, chmn. engrs. in industry sect. 1967-68, Outstanding Engr. in Industry award 1979), Ind. Tel. Pioneer Assn. (life), Ky. Hist. Soc., Pearl Harbor Survivors Assn. Home and Office: 633 Portland Dr Lexington KY 40503-2161

DRAKE, W. HOMER, JR., federal judge; b. 1932; AB, Mercer U., 1954, LLB, 1956. Law clk. to Hon. Lewis R. Morgan U.S. Dist. Ct. Ga., 1961-64; ptnr. Swift, Currie, McGhee & Hiers, 1976-79; judge U.S. Bankruptcy Ct., 1964-76, chief judge, 1968-76; bankruptcy judge U.S. Bankruptcy Ct. (no. dist.) Ga., 1979—. Adj. prof. U. Ga. Law Sch., 1971-72, Emory U. Law Sch., Atlanta, 1973-75. Author: Bankruptcy Practice for the General Practitioner, 3d edit., 1995; co-author: Chapter 13 Practice & Procedure, 1983, Chapter 11 Reorganizations, 2d edit., 1998. 1st lt. JAGC, U.S. Army, 1956-59. Recipient David W. Pollard Achievement award Atlanta Bar Assn., 1994; Walter Homer Drake professorship of bankruptcy law established at Walter F. George Sch. Law at Mercer U., 1996, Outstanding Alumnus award Mercer U. Sch. Law, 2003. Fellow: Am. Coll. Bankruptcy; mem.: Nat. Conf. Bankruptcy Judges (pres. 1972—73), Southeastern Bankruptcy Law Inst. (founder, advisor). Address: PO Box 1408 Newnan GA 30264-1408 Office: Lewis R Morgan Fed Bldg US Courthouse 18 Greenville St Newnan GA 30263-2602

DRAKE, WILLIAM FRANK, JR., lawyer; b. St. Louis, Mar. 29, 1932; s. William Frank and Beatrice Drake; m. Martha Minohr Mockbee. BA, Principia Coll., 1954; LLB, Yale U., 1957. Bar: Pa. 1958. Practice, Phila., 1958-68, 84—; mem. firm Montgomery, McCracken, Walker & Rhoads, 1958-68, 87-96, of counsel, 1984-87, 96—; sr. v.p., gen. counsel Alco Std. Corp., 1968-79, 96-98, sr. v.p. adminstrn., 1979-83; chmn., CEO Alco Health Svcs. Corp., 1983-84, vice chmn., 1984-98, also bd. dirs.; vice chmn., gen. counsel Alco Standard Corp. (now Ikon Office Solutions Inc.), 1996-98. Trustee Peoples Light & Theatre Co., Malvern, Pa. With U.S. Army, 1957-58. Mem. ABA, Phila. Bar Assn., Union League (Phila.), Roaring Fork Club (Basalt, Colo.), Wilmington (Del.) Country Club, First Troop, Phila. City Calvary. Office: Montgomery McCracken Walker & Rhoads 123 S Broad St Fl 24 Philadelphia PA 19109-1099

DRAKEMAN, DONALD LEE, biotechnology company executive, lawyer; b. Camden, N.J., Oct. 21, 1953; s. Fred J. and Jean (Faucett) D.; m. Lisa Natale Drakeman, Aug. 23, 1975; children: Cynthia, Amy. AB magna cum laude, Dartmouth Coll., 1975; JD, Columbia U., 1979; MA, Princeton U., 1984, PhD, 1988. Bar: N.J. 1979, U.S. Dist. Ct. N.J. 1979, N.Y. 1980, U.S. Supreme Ct. 1984. Assoc. Milbank, Tweed, Hadley & McCloy, N.Y.C., 1979-82; gen. counsel Essex Chem. Corp., Clifton, N.J., 1982-89, v.p., 1987-89; pres. Essex Med. Products, Clifton, 1988-89; pres., CEO Medarex, Inc., Annandale, N.J., 1987—. Adj. prof. polit. sci. Montclair State Coll., NJ, 1984; rsch. cons. Lilly Found., Inc., 1989—90; lectr. dept. politics Princeton U., 1990—93, 1995—; bd. dirs. Mannkind, Inc., GlycoScis.; chmn. adv. coun. James Madison Program in Am. Ideals and Instn., Princeton U., 2000—; co-chair adv. coun. dept. religion Princeton U.; mem. adv. coun. Index Ventures, Geneva, 2002—03. Author: Church-State Constitutional Issues, 1990; co-editor Church and State in American History, 2d edit., 1986, 3d edit., 2003; contbr. articles to profl. jours. Chmn. Montclair Bd. Adjustment, 1984; trustee, chair Biotech. Coun. N.J., 1996-98; trustee U. Charleston, 1999-2003, Drew U., 2002—; adv. coun. Rutgers Bus. Sch., 2002—; trustee Woodrow Wilson Nat. Fellowship Found., 2003—. Harlan Fiske Stone scholar, Columbia U., 1976-79; inducted N.J. High Tech Hall of Fame, 2000. Mem.: AAAS, ABA, John Maclean Soc., Asssn. Bar City N.Y., Yale Club, Princeton Club, Princeton Alumni Coun. Home: 49 Rolling Hill Rd Skillman NJ 08558-2319 Office: Medarex Inc 707 State Rd Princeton NJ 08540-1437 E-mail: ddrakeman@medarex.com.

DRAKEMAN, LISA N. biotechnology company executive; b. Boston, Oct. 30, 1953; d. Paul and Josephine (Covino) Natale; m. Donald L. Drakeman, Aug. 23, 1975; children: Cynthia Leigh Drakeman, Amy Elizabeth Drakeman. BA, Mt. Holyoke Coll., 1975; MA, Rutgers U., 1983, Princeton U., 1986, PhD, 1988. Chair, v. chair Moncler (N.J.) Redevelopment Agy., 1981-84; vis. scholar Dartmouth Coll., 1988-89; lectr. Princeton U., 1989-92; asst. dir. Alumni Coun. of Princeton U., 1991; dir. adminstrn. Medarex, Inc., Princeton, N.J., 1991-94, v.p. adminstrn., 1994-96, v.p., 1996-98, sr. v.p., head bus. devel., 1998-2000; CEO Genmab A/S, 1999—. Faculty fellow Grad. Coll. Princeton U., 1991-93, mem. adv. coun. dept. religion, 1996—; bd. dirs. Medarex Europe, B.V., GenPharm. Internat., Inc. Biopharm. adv. coun. Tech. Coun. Greater Phila., 1993-96; Gov.'s Biopharm. Task Force N.J. Econ. Master Plan Commn., Trenton, 1994-95; biotech. adv. com. The Franklin Inst., Phila., 1994-96; commr. Prosperity N.J., 1995-2000. Garden State grad. fellow State of N.J., 1981-85; named to N.J. High Tech. Hall of Fame, 2000. Mem. Soc. for Advancement of Women's Health Rsch. (steering com., corp. adv. coun. 1994-97), Biotech. Industry Orgn. (chair nat. capital formation task force 1995-98, Advocate of Yr. award 1995), Biotech. Coun. N.J. (v.p. 1996-2000, Outstanding Industry Woman of Yr. 1996). Home: 49 Rolling Hill Rd Skillman NJ 08558-2319 Office: Genmab A/S Toldbodgade 33 DK Copenhagen Denmark

DRANCE, STEPHEN MICHAEL, ophthalmologist, educator; b. Bielsko, Poland, May 22, 1925; Can. citizen; MB,ChB, U. Edinburgh, Scotland, 1948, MD, 1949; Diploma in Ophthalmology, Royal Coll. Sci., London, 1953; LLD (hon.), Dalhousie U., Halifax, 1995; DSc (hon.), U. Oulu, Finland, 1998, U. B.C., Vancouver, 1998. Intern Western Gen. Hosp., Edinburgh, 1948-49; resident County Hosp., York, Eng., 1952-53, Edinburgh Royal Infirmary, 1953-55, Oxford Eye Hosp., Eng., 1955-57, Oxford U., 1955-57; asst. prof. and assoc. prof. medicine U. Sask., Saskatoon, Can., 1957-63; assoc. prof. ophthalmology U. B.C., Vancouver, Can., 1963-66, prof., 1966-90, dir. ophthalmologic research, 1967-73, head dept. ophthalmology, 1973-90. Cons., lectr. medicine; vis. prof., lectr. numerous univs. Author: (with H. Reed) The Essentials of Perimetry, 2d edit., 1971, (with A. Neufeld) Applied Pharmacology of Glaucoma, 1984, (with D.R. Anderson) Automatic Perimetry in Glaucoma, 1985, (with A. Neufeld, M. van Buskirk) Applied Pharmacology of Glaucoma, 1991; assoc. editor Am. Archives Ophthalmology, 1961-74; mem. editorial bd. Can. Jour. Ophthalmology, 1966; mng. editor Albrecht von Graefe's Archive for Clin. and Exptl. Ophthalmology, 1979-90; editl. bd. Am. Jour. Opthalmology, 1994-99; contbr. articles to profl. jours., chpts. to books Pres. Vancouver Summer Festivals Soc., 1997-2002. With RAF, 1949-51. Decorated officer Order of Can., 1987; recipient numerous awards and grants for excellence in medicine. Fellow Royal Australian Coll. Ophthalmologists U.K. (hon.), Coll. Ophthalmology U.K. (hon.), Royal Soc. Medicine; mem. Can. Assn. Clin. Rsch., Assn. Ophthalmologic Rsch. (U.K.), Assn. for Rsch. in Vision and Ophthalmology, Can. Ophthalmol. Soc. (pres. 1974-75), B.C. Oto-Ophthalmol. Soc., Ophthal. Soc. U.K., Oxford Ophthalmol. Congress, Am. Acad. Ophthalmology (v.p. 1993), Can. Med. Assn., B.C. Med. Assn., Internat. Perimetric Soc. (pres. 1982-88), Glaucoma Soc. Internat. Congrss (pres. 1983-90), Pan-Am. Ophthalmol. Congress, Pan-Am. Glaucoma Soc., Pan-Am. Assn. Ophthalmology, Assn. N.Am. Glaucomatologists, N.Z. Ophthalmol. Soc. (hon.), Academia Ophthalmol. Internat., Internat. Congress Ophthalmology (pres. 1994), Concilium Ophthalmol. Univaersale (visual function com.), Royal Coll. Physicians and Surgeons Can. (sec. 1976-77). E-mail: smd@interchange.ubc.ca.

DRANCHAK, LAWRENCE JOHN, retired mechanical engineer; b. Scranton, Pa., Sept. 1, 1929; s. John J. and Rose (Barron) D.; m. Leota Mae Zimmerman, Aug. 14, 1954 (dec. Aug. 1999); children: Diana Rose, John Lawrence. BSME, Ind. Inst. Tech., 1956, DME (hon.), 1994. Ohio master gardener. Quality control technician Wright Aero. Corp., Woodridge, N.J., 1945; weaver L&M Weaving Corp., Scranton, 1947-50; automotive engr. Ford Motor Co., Dearborn, Mich., 1956-94; ret., 1994. Inventor automobile door magnetic weatherstrip. Cub scout advisor Boy Scouts Am., Taylor, Mich., 1963-68; adult advisor CAP, Dearborn, 1970-79; advisor Jr. Achievement, 1975-76. With U.S. Army, 1950-52, N.G., 1947-50. Mem. Soc. Automotive Engrs., Air Force Assn., Am. Legion, VFW. Republican. Roman Catholic. Avocations: gardening, feline husbandry, radio control model aircraft, computers, old automobile and truck rebuilding. Home: 21810 Road E Continental OH 45831-0165 E-mail: ldrancha@bright.net.

DRANE, A. D. adult education educator; b. Holbrook, W.Va., Apr. 16, 1935; s. Holden and Lela May Drane; m. Betty Sue Shafer, Oct. 25, 1957; 1 child, Anthony Dale. Driver salesmen Superior Dairy Co., West Union, W.Va., 1954—62; driller, tool dresser Spencer Drilling Co., Smithburg, 1962—64; operator, supr. Union Carbide Corp. Long Reach Plant, Bens Run, 1964—93; instr. Washington County Career Ctr., Marietta, Ohio, 1994—. Mem. cmty. adv. panel Cytec Industy, 2003—. Author: Basic Chemical Operator, 2000, Basic Safety Training, 2002. Coun. mem. Belmont City Coun., W.Va., 1967—75; fireman Belmont Vol. Fire Dept., 1967—85, fire chief, 1980—85. Mem.: Ohio Valley Safety Coun. Republican. Methodist. Avocations: fishing, gardening. Home: 301 Emerald St Belmont WV 26134

DRANOVE, DAVID, business educator, consultant, economist; b. N.Y.C., July 25, 1956; s. Alfred and Dorothy Dranove; m. Deborah Salgo, Aug. 21, 1983; children: Daniel, Michael. BA, Cornell U., 1977, MBA, 1979; PhD, Stanford U., 1983. Chmn. Dept. Mgmt. and Strategy Northwestern U., Evanston, Ill., 1996—2000, Walter McNerney disting. prof. of health industry mgmt., 2000—, dir. Ctr. Health Industry Mkt. Econ., 2001—. Bd. dirs. Ped. Faculty Found., Chicago. Author: How Hospitals Survived, 1999, Economics of Strategy, 2003, Economic Evolution of American Health Care, 2001, What's Your Life Worth?, 2003; contbr. articles to profl. jours. Recipient John Thompson prize, Assn. U. Programs in Health Adminstrn., 1993. Mem.: Am. Econ. Assn. Avocations: audiophile, sports enthusiast, fine dining enthusiast. Office: Kellogg Sch of Mgmt 2001 Sheridan Rd Evanston IL 60208 Office Fax: 847-467-1777. Business E-MAIL: d-dranove@kellogg.northwestern.edu.

DRANTZ, VERONICA ELLEN, science educator and consultant; b. Chgo., Sept. 5, 1943; d. Albert William and Veronica Grace (Crowe) D. BS with high honors, U. Ill., Urbana, 1965, MS, 1969; PhD, De Paul U., Chgo., 1987. Biol. sci. forensic analytical chemist Chgo. Police Dept., Chgo., 1970-72, asst. head forensic analytical chemist, 1972-74; instr. Evanston Hosp. Sch. Anesthesia, Chgo., 1975—, East-West Univ., Chgo., 1982-84, dir. biol. and phys. sciences, 1984—, asst. prof., 1987-88, assoc. prof., 1988-91, prof., 1991—, dir. electroneurodiagnostic technology program, 1988—; asst. prof. in MS of nursing

DePaul U., Chgo., 1989—. Spkr. Ill. Assn. Nurse Anesthetists, 1978-80, Ill. Soc. Electroneurodiagnostic Tech., 1986—, Am. Soc. Electroneurodiagnostic Tech., 1994—; sci. cons., spkr. Chgo. Tchrs. Ctr., 1989; instr. Chgo. Heart Assn., 1989—. Co-author: Population Genetics A BSCS Self Instructional Prog., 1969 Recipient Rsch. assistantship NSF, U. Ill., 1965-66, Rsch. Fellowship NSF, U. Ill., 1966-70, Schmidt Acad. fellowship Schmidt Found., DePaul U., 1975-80, Cardiopulmonary Resuscitation award Chgo. Heart Assn., 1990. Mem. Phi Beta Kappa. Avocations: camping, hiking, nature study, photography, computers, gardening. Office: 4942 W School St Chicago IL 60641-4340 E-mail: drdrantz@msn.com.

DRAPALIK, BETTY R. volunteer, artist, educator; b. Cicero, Ill., July 4, 1932; d. Henry William and Jennie Margaret (Robbins) Degen; m. Joseph James Drapalik, Oct. 30, 1951; children: Betty Jennifer Drapalik Coryell, Joseph Henry. Grad., HS, Cicero. Sec., clk. Gt. Lakes (Ill.) Naval Base, until 1982; sect. to asst. dir. Arden Shore Boys' Home, Lake Bluff, Ill., 1984-87; substitute tchr. art Visual Art Ctr., Waukegan, Ill. Exhibited in group shows at Layson Gallery, Waukegan, Ill., 1993, Cmty. Gallery Art, Coll. Lake County, Grayslake, Ill., 1993—94, David Adler Cultural Ctr., Libertyville, Ill., 1994, Women's Works, Old Courthouse Art Ctr., Woodstock, Ill., 1994—95, Anderson Art Ctr., Kenosha, Wis., 1994—2002, one-woman shows include Jack Benny Ctr. Arts, 1995, exhibited in group shows at Cmty. Gallery Art, Coll. Lake County, Grayslake, Ill., 1996—2003, Lake County Mus., Wauconda, Ill., 1996—2003, Hardy Gallery, Ephraim, Wis., 1996—2002 (Purchase award, 1998), North Point Marina, Winthrop Harbor, Ill., 1996—2003 (1st pl. watercolor, 1996, 1999, 2d pl. watercolor, 1997, 1998, Best of Show, 1996, 1997, award of Merit watercolor, 1998, award of Excellence, 1999, 3d pl., 2001, 3d pl. watercolor, 2002), Truman State U., Kirksville, Mo., 1997, Moorehead (Minn.) State U., 1997, David Adler Cultural Ctr., Libertyville, Ill., 1997—2002, Kenosha Art Assn. and Lake County Art League Combined Art Event, 1997 (Best of Show, 1997), Hawthorne Hollow Art Festival, Kenosha, 1997—98, Deer Path Art League Festival, Lake Forest, 1997, N.W. N.Mex Arts Coun., Farmington, 1997, Dellora A. Norris Cultural Arts Ctr., St. Charles, Ill., 1998—2001, Waukegan Visual Arts Ctr., 1998, Kenosha Pub. Mus., 1998 (award of excellence), Spotlight Gallery, Kenosha, 1998—99, Monne's Gallery, 1998, Zion Chamber Orch. Concert and Art Contest, 1998 (Best of Show, 1st pl.), Clausen Art Shop, Wilmette, Ill., 1999, Deer Path Art League Festival, Lake Forest, 1999, Gull Lake Gallery, Richland, Mich., 1999—2002, Nippersink Gallery, Richmond, Ill., 1999—2001, Deer Path Gallery, Lake Forest, 1999—2003, Wauconda Pub. Libr., 1999, one-woman shows include Wauconda Area Pub. Libr., 1999, exhibited in group shows at Green Belt Cultural Ctr., North Chgo., 2000, Women's Works, Old Courthouse Art Ctr., Woodstock, Ill., 2000, Kenosha Art Assn. and Lake County Art League Combined Art Event, 2000 (3d pl., 2000), Kenosha Art Assn. Art Event, 2001—02 (Best of Show, 2001, 3d pl., 2002), City of Zion, Ill., 2001—02, Centennial Days Fine Art Show, 2001, Harring Galleries, Racine, Wis., 2001—03, Guenzel Gallery, Fish Creek, Wis., 2001—02, one-woman shows include Jack Benny Ctr. Arts, 2001, Invitational First Lady Hearts adn Flowers Art Exhbn., Ill., 2001—03, traveling exhbn., America the Beautiful, 2001—03; work published in book Celebrating Door Country's Wild Places, 2001; one-woman shows include Wauconda Area Pub. Libr., 2002, exhibited in group shows at Women's Works, Old Courthouse Art Ctr., Woodstock, Ill., 2002, Wauconda Pub. Libr., 2002, Jack Benny Ctr. Arts, 2003, Colo. Fine Art Ctr., 2003, one-woman shows include GreenBelt Cultural Art Ctr., North Chgo., 2003, Pikes Peak Watercolor Soc. Internat. Watermedia XIII/ Fine Art Ctr., Colo. Springs, 2003, exhibited in group shows at Dellora A. Norris Cultural Arts Ctr., St. Charles, Ill., 2003. Former leader, mem. pub. rels. com. Girl Scouts U.S.; visual arts cons. Green Belt Cultural Ctr. Lake County Forest Preserve Dist.; mem. outreach and evangelism missions bd. First Presbyn. Ch. Waukegan, 2000—02. Recipient Purchase award, Coll. Lake County, Grayslake, 1994, numerous courtesy awards. Mem.: Nat. Mus. Women in the Arts (charter), Bloomin' Artists, N.W. Area Arts Coun., Kenosha Art Assn., Red River Watercolor Soc., Deerpath Art League, Lakes Region Watercolor Guild (past rec. sec., co-program chair, exhibit chair), Lake County Art League (resource person, past pres., various bd. positions, fine arts cons. Green Belt Cultural Ctr. Lake County Forest Preserve), Midwest Watercolor Soc. (life), Internat. Starcraft Camper Club (Ill. chpt. sec./treas. 1975). Evangelical. Avocations: watercolor, photography, camping, gardening, hiking. Home: 2018 W Grove Ave Waukegan IL 60085-1607

DRAPEAU, SUZANNE EVA, art educator, artist; b. Montpelier, Vt., Apr. 8, 1954; d. Norman Emile and Lucille Lorretta (LaBelle) D.; m. Gary William Moylen, Feb. 28, 1976 (div.); 1 child, Benjamin Patrick; m. David Gewanter, Dec. 24, 1988. BA in Visual Studies, Columbia U., 1989; MA in Studio Art, NYU, 1997. Cert. tchr., Conn. Self-employed title abstractor, N.J., 1980-86; title officer Chgo. Title Ins. Co., N.J., 1987; sr. title office mgr. Mountainside, N.J., 1988; art tchr. Master's Sch., West Simsbury, Conn., 1989-93, Hartford (Conn.) Pub. Schs., 1993-95, Avon (Conn.) Pub. Schs., 1996—. Programming coord. Artworks Gallery, Hartford, 1999, pres., 2000—; resident Contemporary Artists Ctr., North Adams, Mass., 1997; workshop leader Avon Continuing Edn., 1999—; presenter in field. One-woman shows at Women's Ctr., U. Hartford, 1993, 80 Washington Sq. East Galleries, N.Y., 1996, Fourwinds Ctr., Farmington, Conn., 1997, Artworks Gallery, Hartford, 1999; exhibited in group shows at Slater Mus., Norwich, Conn., 1992, 98, L'Instituto Universitario d'Architettura di Venezia, Venice, Italy, 1993, 94, Nat. Arts Coun. at Hartford, 1993, Farmington Art Guild, 1994, Casa Italia Zerilli-Marimo, NYU, N.Y.C., 1997, 98, 2000, Artworks Gallery, 1997, 99, 2000, South Windsor (Conn.) Pub. Libr., 1999. Mem. NEA, Nat. Art Edn. Assn., Conn. Art Educators Assn., Conn. Edn. Assn., Internat. Sculpture Ctr., Coll. Art Assn. Home: 6 Tamarack Ln Simsbury CT 06070-2432 Office: Avon Pub Schs 34 Simsbury Rd Avon CT 06001-3714

DRAPER, DANIEL CLAY, retired lawyer; b. Boston, June 7, 1920; s. John W. and Lulu H. (Clay) D.; m. Marcia Humphreys, Nov. 25, 1989. BA, W.Va. U., 1940, MA, 1941; LLB, Harvard U., 1947. Assoc. Kelly, Drye & Warren, N.Y.C., 1947-55; ptnr. Cadwalader, Wickersham & Taft, N.Y.C., 1962-91, ret. Bd. dirs. Union Devel., Montclair, N.J.; adj. prof. history Bloomfield Coll., 1991. Contbr. articles to profl. jours. Mgr. campaign Montclair's Cmty. Com. Candidates, 1964; trustee Montclair Art Mus., 1966-71, Bloomfield Coll., 1974-81, 87-95. With USN, 1942-46. Decorated Bronze Star, European Service Ribbon (3 stars). Mem. N.Y. State Bar Assn. (chmn. banking com. 1981-85), N.Y. County Lawyers Assn. (sec. 1979-81, pres. 1984-87, chmn. banking com. 1968-78, housing and urban affairs and real property coms., chmn. investment com.), St. George Soc., Harvard Club, N.Y.C. Episcopalian. Home: 14 Houston Rd Little Falls NJ 07424-2406

DRAPER, EDGAR, psychiatrist; b. St. Louis, Feb. 5, 1926; s. Neal McLain and Florence Mabel (Meyers) D.; m. Norma Jane Alexander, Mar. 16, 1949; children: Sue Draper Masteller, Anne Draper Klevay, Neal Edgar. AB, Washington U., 1946; BD, Garrett Biblical Inst., 1949; MD, Washington U. Med. Sch., 1953; grad., Inst. for Psychoanalysis, Chgo., 1966. Diplomate Am. Bd. Psychiatry and Neurology. Intern Washington U. Svc. City Hosp., St. Louis, 1953-54; resident in psychiatry U. Cin., 1954-55, 57-59; sr. asst. surgeon USPHS, Ft. Worth, 1955-57; from instr. to assoc. prof. U. Chgo., 1959-68; co-dir. psychiat. outpatient dept., prof. psychiatry U. Mich., Ann Arbor, 1968, dir. psychiat. resident edn., 1968-74, prof. postgrad edn., 1970-75; prof., chmn. dept. psychiatry U. Miss. Med. Ctr., Jackson, 1975-93; prof. psychiatry U. Miss., Jackson, 1993-94; prof. emeritus, 1994—. Cons. in field. Contbr. numerous articles to profl. jours. Bd. dirs. Friends Libr. Named Vis. scholar U. Chgo., 1987, Fellow Soc. for Sci. Study of Religion, 1987, Man of Month Pastoral Psychology, 1970; recipient Physicians Recognition award, 1982-85, Cert. Appreciation Mental Health Assn. Hinds County, 1983, Plaque of Commendation Chgo. Acad. Religion and Mental Health, 1966-67. Fellow Am. Psychiat. Assn. (disting. life fellow), Am. Coll. Psychiatry (life), Am. Soc. Psychoanalytic Physicians, Soc. for Sci. Study of Religion (life), Am. Coll. Psychoanalysts (life, program chmn., bd. regents), So. Psychiat. Assn. (parlimentarian 1980—), Soc. for Study of Psychiatry and Culture; mem. Miss. Psychiat. Assn. (past pres., Disting. Svc. award 2001), Miss. State Med. Soc., Mich. Psychiat. Soc., Washtenaw County Med. Soc., Mich. State Med. Soc., So. Psychiat. Assn., Mich. Psychoanalytic Soc., Mental Health Assn. (bd. dirs. Jackson). E-mail: drapere@iopener.net.

DRAPER, E(RNEST) LINN, JR., electric utility executive; b. Houston, Feb. 6, 1942; s. Ernest Linn and Marcia L. (Saylor) D.; m. Mary Deborah Doyle, June 9, 1962; children: Susan Elizabeth, Robert Linn, Barbara Ann, David Doyle. Student, Williams Coll., 1960-62; BAChemE, Rice U., 1964, BSChemE, 1965; PhD in Nuclear Engring., Cornell U., 1970. Asst. prof. nuclear engring. U. Tex., Austin, 1969-72, assoc. prof., 1972-79; tech. asst. to CEO Gulf States Utilities Co., Beaumont, Tex., 1979, v.p. nuclear tech., 1980-81, sr. v.p. engring, tech. services, 1981-82, sr. v.p. external affairs, 1982-84, sr. v.p. external affairs and prodn., 1984-85, exec. v.p. external affairs and prodn., 1985-86, vice chmn., 1985-87, COO, 1986, pres., CEO, 1986-92, chmn. bd. dirs., 1987-92; pres. AEPCo., Inc.; pres., COO Am. Electric Power Svc. Corp., Columbus, Ohio, 1992-93; chmn., pres., CEO Am. Electric Power Co. and Svc. Corp., Columbus, 1993—. Bd. dirs. Borden Chems. and Plastics. Fellow NSF, 1965-66, AEC, 1967-68. Mem. NAE, Am. Nuclear Soc. (pres. 1984-85), Nuclear Energy Inst. (chmn. 1993-95), Edison Electric Inst. (chmn. 1996-97). Office: Am Electric Power Inc 1 Riverside Plz Columbus OH 43215-2355

DRAPER, GERALD LINDEN, lawyer; b. Oberlin, Ohio, July 14, 1941; s. Earl Linden and Mary Antoinette (Colloto) Draper; m. Barbara Jean Winter, Aug. 26, 1960; children: Melissa Leigh Price, Stephen Edward. BA, Muskingum Coll., 1963; JD, Northwestern U., 1966. Bar: Ohio 1966, US Dist Ct (so dist) Ohio 1966, US Ct Appeals (6th cir) 1975, US Supreme Ct 1980, US Dist Ct (no dist) Ohio 2000. Ptnr. Bricker & Eckler, Columbus, Ohio, 1966-88, Thompson, Hine & Flory, Columbus, 1989-95, Draper, Hollenbaugh, Briscoe, Yashko & Carmany, Columbus, 1996-99, Roetzel & Andress, Columbus, 1999—. Trustee Ohio Bd. Bar Examiners, 1996—99; mem. Ohio Bd. Commn. on Unauthorized Practice of Law, 2002—, Ohio Med. Malpractice Commn., 2003—. Trustee, pres Wesley Glen Retirement Ctr, Columbus, Ohio, 1979—95; trustee Meth Elder Care Servs, Inc, 1995—, Muskingum Coll., New Concord, Ohio, 1988—92, 1993—, vice chair, 1994—; trustee, pres Wesley Ridge Retirement Ctr, 1995—2000, treas, 2001—. Fellow: Am Bd Trial Advs (trustee Ohio chpt. 2001), Am Col Trial Lawyers; mem.: ABA (House Dels 1991—97, 1999—2001), Def Research Inst, Ohio Asn Hosp Attys, Ohio Continuing Legal Educ Inst (trustee 1992—98, chair 1997—98), Nat Conf Bar Found (trustee 1987—90, 1991—94), Columbus Bar Found (pres 1984—86), Columbus Bar Asn (pres 1982—83, Bar Serv Medal 1998), Ohio State Bar Found (trustee 1992—97), Ohio State Bar Asn (pres 1990—91). Avocations: travel, golf, photography. Office: Roetzel & Andress 155 E Broad St Columbus OH 43215-3609 E-mail: gdraper@ralaw.com.

DRAPER, JAMES DAVID, art museum curator; b. Lebanon, Mo., Mar. 6, 1943; s. John Hilton and Hazel (Berg) D. BA, U. Mo., 1965; MA, NYU, 1967, PhD, 1984. Curatorial asst. Met. Mus. Art, N.Y.C., 1969, various positions, 1969-84, dept. curator, 1984—, Henry R. Kravis curator, 1995—. Fellow J. Paul Getty Mus., Malibu, Calif., 1987; exec. dir. The Isaacson-Draper Found., 1999. Author: Bertoldo di Giovanni, Sculptor of the Medici Household, 1992; co-author: (exhbn. catalogs) Augustin Pajou, Royal Sculptor, 1998, La giovinezza di Michelangelo, 1999; editor: (rev. critical edit.) The Italian Bronze Statuettes of the Renaissance (W. von Bode), 1980. Decorated chevalier Order of Arts and Letters (France). Episcopalian. Office: Met Mus Art 1000 5th Ave New York NY 10028-0113 E-mail: james.draper@metmuseum.org.

DRAPER, JAMES WILSON, lawyer; b. Detroit, Dec. 26, 1926; s. Kenneth Draper and Dorothy (Wilson) Barker; m. Alice Patricia Sullivan, May 16, 1953; children: Catherine Draper Clain, Julie Draper Fazekas, James P., Martha Draper Grossman. BA, U. Mich., 1949, JD, 1951. Bar: Mich. 1951, U.S. Dist. Ct. (so. dist.) Mich. 1951, U.S. Ct. Appeals (6th cir.) 1951. Assoc. Dykema, Jones & Wheat and successor firms, Detroit, 1951-61; ptnr. Dykema Gossett, and predecessor firms, Detroit, 1961—. Past chmn. real property law sect. council State Bar Mich. Served with USN, 1944-46 Fellow Am. Coll. Real Estate Lawyers; mem. Mich. State Bar (past chmn. real property law sect., land title stds. com.), Detroit Club, Country Club Detroit (Grosse Point Farms, Mich.). Republican. Presbyterian. Home: 267 Hillcrest Ave Grosse Pointe Farms MI 48236-3622 Office: Dykema Gossett 400 Renaissance Ctr Detroit MI 48243-1603

DRAPER, PENNY KAYE PEKRUL, music educator, piano technician; b. Lansing, Mich., May 14, 1948; d. Edward Emil Pekrul and June Marie Piche-Fahlen; m. William Burle Draper III, June 13, 1970; children: Paige Lindsley, Josselin Bertrand. BA in Choral Edn. cum laude, Mich. State U., 1970, BA in Applied Piano Pedagogy cum laude, 1971, MA in Musicology, 1983, PhD in Musicology, 1997. Cert. tchr., Mich., continuing edn. tchr., Mich. Choral dir. Williamston (Mich.) H.S., 1970-78; dir. Renaissance Singers, East Lansing, Mich., 1979—, Jr. Renaissance Singers, East Lansing, Mich., 1990—; choral dir. East Lansing Schs., 1993-94; pvt. instruction East Lansing, 1993—. Mem. adj. faculty U. Mich., Flint, 1995—96; choral dir. Colonial Choir Plymouth Congl. Ch., 1995—; chair fine arts com. Plymouth Congl. Ch., 1997—2000, chair music sch. com., 1994, mem. organist search com., 2002; choral dir. HOPE Acad., Lansing, Mich., 1996—. Author program notes MSU Symphony Orch., 1980-83, Lansing Symphony Orch., 1981, Elizabethan Musical Feast, 1983-92. Mem. Lansing Matinee Musicale, 1997—, chair performing arts students, 2002—; bd. deacons Plymouth Congl. Ch., 2002—; chair Performing Arts Students, 2002; mem. Lansing Matinee Musicale, 1997—; apptd. humanities profl. Mich. Humanities Coun., 2002—. Piano scholar Mich. State U., 1966-70, Lansing Matinee Musicale, 1965. Mem.: Capital Area Music Tchrs. Assn. (v.p. 1997—99, pres. 1999—2001, Tchr. of Yr. 2003), Mich. Music Tchrs. Assn. (awards chair 2002—, cert., bd. dirs.), Music Tchrs. Nat. Assn. (local chmn. state convention 2003), Pi Kappa Lambda, Sigma Alpha Iota. Home: 513 Woodland Dr East Lansing MI 48823-3273

DRAPER, WILLIAM HENRY, III, import/export company executive; b. White Plains, N.Y., Jan. 1, 1928; s. William Henry and Katherine (Baum) Draper; m. Phyllis Culbertson, June 13, 1953; children: Rebecca, Polly, Timothy. BA, Yale U., 1950, MA (hon.), 1991; MBA, Harvard U., 1954; LLD (hon.), Southeastern U., 1985. With Inland Steel Co., Chgo., 1954-59, Draper, Gaither & Anderson, Palo Alto, Calif., 1959-62; pres. Draper & Johnson Investment Co., Palo Alto, 1962-65; founder, gen. ptnr. Sutter Hill Ventures, Palo Alto, 1965-81; pres., chmn. U.S. Export-Import Bank, Washington, 1981-86; adminstr., CEO, UN Devel. Programme, 1986-93; mng. dir. Draper Richards, San Francisco, 1994—, Draper Internat., San Francisćo, 1994—. Bd. dirs. numerous cos. Nat. co-chmn. fin. com. George Bush for Pres., 1980; bd. dirs., former chmn. Rep. Alliance; chmn. bd. Am. Conservatory Theatre, 1980—81, bd. dirs., 1977—81; chmn. Internat. Inst. Edn. West, 1989—2000; vice chmn. Population Action Internat., 1993—; mem. adv. bd. Stanford Grad. Sch. Bus. Adminstrn., 1980—86; chmn. World Affairs Coun. No. Calif., 2000—02; trustee Yale U., 1991—98, George Bush Libr. Found., 1993—; bd. dirs. Population Crisis Com., 1976—81, Atlantic Coun., 1989—, World Rehab. Fund1988, 1988—92, Ctr. for Econ. Policy Rsch., Stanford U., 1988, Inst. Internat. Studies Stanford U., 1997—99. With U.S. Army, 1946—48, with U.S. Army, 1951—52. Named one of U.S.'s 50 New Corp. Elite, Bus. Week mag., 1985; recipient Alumni Achievement award, Harvard Bus. Sch., 1982, medal of Honor, Ellis Island, 1992. Mem.: Overseas Devel. Coun., Coun. Fgn. Rels., UN Assn. USA (bd. dirs. 2003—), River Club, Chevy Chase Club, Met. Club, Bohemian Club, Pacific Union Club. Home: 91 Tallwood Ct Atherton CA 94027-6431 Office: Draper Richards 50 California St Ste 2925 San Francisco CA 94111-4726 E-mail: bill@draperrichards.com.

DRASKOCZY, PAUL R. psychiatrist; b. Stari Becej, Yugoslavia, Mar. 4, 1926; s. Edward and Maria (Szekely) D.; widowed. MD, Med. U. Szeged, 1951. Diplomate Am. Bd. Psychiatry & Neurology. Asst. prof. pharmacology Med. U. Szeged, Hungary, 1951-56; instr., asst. prof. pharmacology Harvard Med. Sch., Boston, 1958-72; resident in psychiatry Boston City Hosp., 1972-75; staff psychiatrist Solomon Mental Health Ctr., Lowell, Mass., 1975-76, VA Hosp., Bedford, Mass., 1976-97; assoc. prof. psychiatry Boston U., 1977—. Pvt. practice, Weston, Mass., 1975—. Contbr. numerous articles to profl. jours. in pharmacology and psychopharmacology. Mem. Am. Psychiat. Assn., Am. Soc. Pharmacology & Exptl. Therapies. Home: 726 Wellesley St Weston MA 02493-1000

DRASLER, GREGORY JOHN, artist; b. Waukegan, Ill., June 7, 1952; s. John W. and Patricia A. Drasler; m. Nancy B. Davidson, June 15, 1985. BFA, U. Ill., 1980, MFA, 1983. Tchr. Williams Coll., 1994, Princeton U., 1999—. One person shows include Marianne Deson Gallery, Chgo., 1988, R. C. Erpf Gallery, N.Y., 1986, 87, 88, Shea & Beker Gallery, N.Y., 1990, Ctr. for Contemporary Art, Chgo., 1990, Queens Mus., Bulova Ctr., N.Y., 1994, Generous Miracles Gallery, N.Y., 2000, Eyre Moore Gallery, Seattle, Wash., 2000, Fenway Gallery, Chgo., 2000; exhibited in group shows New Mus. Contemporary Art, N.Y.C., 1983, 87, 92, 95, Germans Van Eck Gallery, N.Y., 1984, John Berggruen Gallery, San Francisco, 1985, Jack Tilton Gallery, N.Y.C., 1986, Wellesley (Mass.) Coll. Mus., 1986, Robeson Ctr. Gallery, Rutgers U., Newark, 1987, Ben Shahn Galleries, William Patterson Coll., Wayne, N.J., 1988,, Three Rivers Arts Festival, Carnegie Mus. Art, Pitts., 1989, U. Art Mus., SUNY, Binghamton, N.Y., 1989, Artist Space, N.Y.C., 1990, Flint (Mich.) Inst. Arts, Philharm. Ctr. for Arts, Knoxville Mus. Art, 1991-92, Flint Inst. Arts, 1993; represented in permanent collections Dow Jones Inc., N.Y.C., Krannert Art Mus., Champaign, Ill., Sammuel Lindenbaum, Fisher Bros., U. Ill., Champaign, John W. Heckenger, Barbara Toll, Emily Landau, Henry Luce III Found., Sawyer Miller Group, N.Y.C.; featured in Flint Inst. Arts Cat., Art Press, 1991, Chgo. Tribune, 1990, Art in Am. mag., 1987, 90, N.Y. Times newspaper, 1987, 88, 91, The Independent Press newspaper, 1991, Ben Shahn Gallery cat., 1988, SUNY Binghamton U. Art Mus. cat., Carnegie Mus. Art cat., Artist Space cat., 1990, Mary C. MacLellan fellow, 1980; MacDowell Colony Residence fellow, 1986; art fellow N.Y. Found of Arts, 1991; Nat. Endowment of Arts fellow, 1993; Djerassi Resident Artist Program fellow, 1996.

DRASNER, FRED, newspaper publishing executive; b. Bklyn. m. Cynthia Drasner. JD, NYU. Commd. ensign USN; with J.K. Lasser and Co., N.Y.C.; real estate and tax lawyer Washington; pres., CEO U.S. News and World Report, N.Y.C., 1984—93; co-pub. N.Y. Daily News, N.Y.C., 1993—, CEO, 1993—99, co-chmn., 1998—; chmn., CEO, co-pub. Applied Graphics Techs., 1999—. Recipient Lifetime Achievement award, Guardian Angel, 2002. Office: New York Daily News 450 W 33rd St Fl 3 New York NY 10001-2681

DRAUD, JON E. state representative; b. Nov. 18, 1938; EdD, Univ. of Cincinatti; MA, Xavier Univ.; BA, Ea. Ky. Univ. State Rep. House of Rep., Dist. 63, Ky., 1998—; Supt. Ludlow Pub. Sch., 1978—97. Mem. Crestview Hills City Coun., 1972—77, Kenton County Sch. Bd., 1977—78, Appropriations and Rev.; vice chair Ed.; mem. Licensing and Occupations. Named Outstanding Admin. of the Yr., 1993, Ed. of the Yr., Kenton Co., 1992, named John E. Draud Admin. Ctr., Ludlow Pub. Sch. Admin. Bldg.; recipient Hall of Fame, Ludlow HS, Athletic Dir. Hall of Fame, No. Ky. Mem.: Ky. Assoc. of Sch. Supt. (Bd. of Dir. 1992—97), No. Ky. Bus. Ed. Alliance, 1991-1997, No. Ky. Supt. Assoc. (pres. 1994), No. Ky. Sch. Bd. Assoc. (Sec. 1992—94), Baseball Coach, Holmes HS State champions. Republican. Roman Catholic. Office: Capitol Capitol Annex, Rm 413A Frankfort KY 40601 also: Dist 109 Vernon Dr Crestview Hills KY 41017*

DRAUGHON, SCOTT WILSON, lawyer, social worker, educator; b. Muskogee, Okla., June 17, 1952; s. Arthur Eugene and Helen Carrie (Vanhooser) D. AA, Tulsa Jr. Coll., 1972; BA, Okla. State U., 1974; JD, U. Tulsa, 1977; postgrad., Oxford U., Eng., 1978; MSW, U. Okla, 1992. Bar: Okla. 1979, U.S. Dist. Ct. (no. dist.) Okla. 1980, U.S. Claims Ct., U.S. Tax Ct. 1979, U.S. Ct. Appeals (10th cir.) 1984, U.S. Supreme Ct. 1984; lic. social worker with clin. splty. cert.; lic. tchr. social studies, sch. counselor. Sole law practice, Tulsa, 1979—; stockbroker, 1983-93; pvt. practice fin. planning, 1984—; aftercare dept. coord. Tulsa Boys' Home, 1992-94; pvt. practice social worker, 1994—; legal counsel Tulsa City-County Health Dept., 1996-97; clin. social worker Cushing (Okla.) Regional Hosp., 1996-99; social worker Hospice of Green Country, Inc., 2000—. Founder, exec. dir. The Fin. Hotline, Tulsa, 1984—; adj. faculty Tulsa Jr. Coll., 1986-87; v.p. govtl. and pub. affairs Okla. Credit Union League, Inc., 1988-90, dir. rsch./info. Okla. Credit Union League Affiliates, 1991; founder Internat. Family Providers Alliance, 2000—. Mem. Indian Affairs Commn. City of Tulsa, 1989-91, 20th Anniversary Com. Leadership Tulsa, Inc., 1992—, class IX grad.; mem. exec. bd. Tulsa Assn. Vol. Adminstrs., 1994-95; bd. dirs. Arts and Humanities Coun., Tulsa, 1982-83, Ea. Okla. chpt. March of Dimes, 1989-90, Internat. Coun. Tulsa, 1987-91, Tulsa County Regional Planning Coord. Bd. Svcs. to Children and Youth, 1992-95; mem. exec. com. Corp. Vol. Coun. Greater Tulsa, 1990; chmn. pub. rels. com., exec. com. Tulsa Human Rights Commn., 1987-88; registered lobbyist Okla. Credit Union League Affilliate, 1988-90; grad. Okla. Aging Advocacy Leadership Acad., 2000; vol. docent Tulsa 2000, 1999—; mem. Okla. Human Rights Commn., 1997-2000, vice chmn., 1999. Mem. NASW (past chmn. internat. activities com., Okla. chpt.), Okla. Bar Assn., Masons, Shriners, Phi Delta Phi. Republican. Methodist. Avocations: travel, photography, reading, gardening, cooking. Address: 9071 E 28th St Tulsa OK 74129-6806

DRAY, MARK S. lawyer; b. Alliance, Ohio, Feb. 8, 1943; s. Dwight Leroy and N. Pauline (Clark) Dray; m. Jonadell Pascoe, June 5, 1965; children: Melisa Louise, Justin Clark. BA, Mount Union Coll., Alliance, Ohio, 1965; JD, Coll. William and Mary, 1968, M in Law and Taxation, 1969. Bar: Va. 1968, U.S. Dist. Ct. (ea. dist.) Va. 1970, U.S. Tax Ct. 1971. Tax sr. Price Waterhouse, Washington, 1969-70; assoc. Hunton & Williams, Richmond, Va., 1970-77, ptnr., 1977—. Mem. So. Employee Benefits Conf., 1974—; mem. adv. coun. William and Mary Tax Conf., 1980—88; trustee So. Fed. Tax Inst., 1989—, chair, 1997; spkr. in field. Contbr. articles to profl. jours. Fellow: Va. Law Found., Am. Coll. Employee Benefits Counsel (charter), Am. Coll. Tax Counsel; mem.: ABA (mem. com. employee benefits 1975—, chmn. 1989—90, mem. joint com. employee benefits 1988—91, chmn. 1990—91), Order of Coif, Richmond Bar Assn., Va. Bar Assn., Blue Key, Country Club Va. Episcopalian. Avocation: golf. Office: Hunton & Williams Riverfront Plz East Tower 951 E Byrd St Richmond VA 23219-4074 E-mail: mdray@hunton.com.

DRAY, WILLIAM HERBERT, philosophy educator; b. Montreal, June 23, 1921; s. William John and Florence Edith (Jones) D.; m. Doris Kathleen Best, Sept. 18, 1943; children: Christopher Reid, Jane Elizabeth. BA in History, U. Toronto, 1949; BA in Philosophy, Politics and Econs., Oxford U., 1951, MA, 1955, D.Phil., 1956; LLD (hon.), Trent U., 1987. Lectr. U. Toronto, 1953-55, asst. prof., asso. prof., 1956-63, prof., 1963-68, Trent U., 1968-76, chmn. dept. philosophy, 1968-73; prof. philosophy U. Ottawa, Ont., 1976-85, emeritus, 1986—. Author: Laws and Explanation in History, 1957, Philosophy of History, 1964, 2d edit., 1993, Perspectives on History, 1980, On History and Philosophers of History, 1989, History as Re-enactment, 1995; editor: Philosophical Analysis and History, 1966; co-editor: Substance and Form in History, 1981, Philosophie de l'histiore et la Pratique historienne d'aujourd'hui, 1982, The Principles of History, 1999. Served with RCAF, 1941-46, wing comdr. ret. Am. Council Learned Socs. fellow, 1960-61; Can. Council fellow, 1971-72, 78-79; Killam research fellow, 1980-81; Nat. Humanities Ctr. fellow, 1983-84; recipient Can. Council Molson prize, 1986. Fellow Royal Soc. Can. Home: 818-32 Clarissa Dr Richmond Hill ON Canada L4C 9R7 Office: Dept Philosophy Univ of Ottawa Ottawa ON Canada K1N 6N5

DRAYTON, CAREY M. police administrator; b. New Orleans, Apr. 12, 1961; s. Washignton Howard Drayton. BGS, U. South La., Lafayette, 1985; student, FBI Acad. Asst. dir. pub. safety U. South La., 1986-89; police officer George Washington U., Washington, 1989-90; dir. pub. safety U. Oreg., Eugene, 1990-95; chief of police The Fla. State U., Tallahassee, 1995—. Mem. Internat. Assn. Campus Law Enforcement Adminstrn. (chair comm. com.), Big Bend Basketball Assn. (pres.), Big Bend Football Assn. Office: Fla State U Police Dept 830 W Jefferson St Tallahassee FL 32304-8018 E-mail: cdrayton@admin.fsu.edu.

DRAYTON, JOHN N. publishing executive; b. Adelaide, Australia, Mar. 6, 1944; m. Carol L. Pederson, 1972; 5 children. BA, Brigham Young U., 1969. Missionary Ch. of Jesus Christ of Latter-day Saints, Ctrl. Brit. Mission, 1963-65; mng. editor Brigham Young U. Press, Provo, Utah, 1972-80; asst. dir., editor-in-chief U. Okla. Press, Norman, 1981-97, dir., 1998—. Office: U Okla Press 1005 Asp Ave Norman OK 73019-6051

DRAYTON, JOYCE RENEE, physician; b. Queens, N.Y., May 31, 1964; d. James Arthur and Phyllis Nelson Drayton; m. Michael Anthony Herron, May 5, 1990; children: Daniel Diop Drayton Herron, Brian Kofi Nelson Herron. BS in Zoology, Howard U., 1986, MD, 1988. Diplomate Nat. Bd. Med. Examiners, 1987, in infectious diseases Am. Bd. Internal Medicine, 1994, Am. Bd. Internal Medicine, 2002. Asst. prof. clin. medicine Morehouse Sch. Medicine, Atlanta, 1994—2002; med. dir. Total Life Care, PC, Atlanta, 2002—, Dekalb County Jail, Decatur, Ga. Chmn. infection control com. SW Cmty. Hosp., Atlanta,

1998—2001; sect. head HIV/AIDS Clin. Rsch. Ctr. Morehouse Sch. Medicine, Atlanta, 1998—99; dir. clin. svcs. Nat. Minority AIDS Edn. and Tng. Ctr., Atlanta, 2000—02. Treas., atlanta chpt. The Charmettes, Inc., Atlanta, sec., dekalb county chpt. Nat. Women's Polit. Caucus, Decatur, Ga. Recipient Will Rogers Infectious Disease Fellow award, Will Roger's Found., 1993. Fellow: ACP; mem.: Infectious Disease Soc. Am., Nat. Med. Assn., Alpha Omega Alpha, Phi Beta Kappa, Delta Sigma Theta. Achievements include research in genitourinary tuberculosis and HIV/AIDS; vaccine acceptance among African-Americans; use of Granulocyte Colony Stimulating Factor on outcome of serious infections.

DRAYTON, V. MICHAEL, lawyer, educator; b. Evansville, Ind., Sept. 13, 1953; m. Janet L. Collings, Oct. 10, 1981; children: Christopher Michael, Phillip Arthur George. BA, Valparaiso U., 1976, JD, 1980. Bar: Ind. 1980, Ill. 1980, U.S. Dist. Ct. (so. and no. dists.) Ind. 1980, U.S. Ct. appeals (7th cir.) 1993, U.S. Supreme Ct. 1994; cert. mediator family law, civil litigation. Ptnr. Sallwasser & McCain, La Porte, Ind., 1980—. Adj. prof. law Ind. U., South Bend, 1985—. Mem. ATLA, ABA, Ind. Trial Lawyers Assn., Ind. Bar Assn., Ill. Bar Assn., LaPorte County Assn., La Porte City Bar Assn., Lions. Office: Sallwasser and McCain 820 Jefferson Ave La Porte IN 46350-3410

DRAYTON, WILLIAM, social entrepreneur, lawyer, management consultant; b. N.Y.C., June 15, 1943; s. William A. and Joan (Bergere) D. BA, Harvard, 1965; MA, Oxford (Eng.) U., 1967; JD, Yale, 1970. Bar: N.Y. 1971, D.C. 1976. Cons. McKinsey and Co., Inc., N.Y.C., 1970-77, of counsel, 1981-87; vis. assoc. prof. law Stanford, 1975-76; lectr. John F. Kennedy Sch. of Govt., Harvard U.; also dir. Harvard Regulatory and Mgmt. Group, 1976-77; cons. White House Domestic Coun., 1977; asst. adminstr. for planning and mgmt. EPA, 1977-81; pres. Environ. Safety, Washington, 1981-89, chair, 1989—; pres., founder Ashoka: Innovators for the Pub., Arlington, Va., 1980-2001, chair, CEO, 2001—. Nat. staff mem. Hubert H. Humphrey Presdl. Campaign, Washington, 1968; dir. Corp. for Fiscal Policy, 1971-75; founder, chmn. Yale Legis. Svcs.; mem. adv. coun. Carnegie Commn. Sci., Tech. and Govt., 1990-96. Contbr. articles to profl. jours. Pres. Ams. in India for McGovern, 1972; mem. Carter-Mondale Policy Planning, 1976, Carter-Mondale Govt. Reorgn. Transition Group, 1976-77; dep. dir. for issues Mondale-Ferraro campaign, 1984; mem. energy and environment com. Dem. nat. Com., 1982-86; bd. dirs. Oxfam Am., 1985-89, Appropriate Tech. Internat., 1988-97, chmn. bd. dirs., 1989-97; trustee Black Rock Forest (formerly Harvard Forest), N.Y.; chmn. bd. dirs. Youth Venture, 1994—; founder, chair Get Am. Working!, 1997—; pres. Save EPA, Washington, 1981-83; chair Cmty. Greens, 2000—; founder, dir. Social Entrepreneur Assocs., 1998—. Recipient Ann. award for Entrepreneurial Excellence Yale U. Sch. Mgmt., 1987, Nat. Pub. Svc. award Nat. Acad. Pub. Adminstrn. and Am. Soc. for Pub. Adminstrn., 1995, Pub. Svc. Achievement award Common Cause, 1999, Vanguard Nonprofit Lawyers award ABA, 2002, Edward A. Smith Award for Excellence in Nonprofit Leadership, 2002; Henry fellow, 1965-67, MacArthur Prize fellow, 1984-89. Mem. AAAS (com. on sci. pub. policy 1973-76), Assn. Bar City N.Y., Friends of India Soc. (chmn. 1974-75), Coun. Fgn. Rels., Nat. Acad. Pub. Adminstrn., Am. Acd. Arts and Scis., Asia Soc. (contemporary affairs com. 1987—2000), India Internat. Ctr. (New Delhi), Yale Club N.Y., Harvard Club N.Y., Phi Beta Kappa. Home: 1200 N Nash St Arlington VA 22209-3616 Office: 1700 N Moore St Ste 2000 Arlington VA 22209-1921

DRAZIN, LISA, real estate and corporate investment banker, financial consultant; b. Washington, Nov. 26, 1953; d. Sidney and Bernice Ann (Jeweler) D. AB with honors, Wellesley Coll., 1976; MBA, George Washington U., 1980. Chartered fin. analyst. Securities analyst Geico, Inc., Chevy Chase, Md., 1982; mng. prin. Jefferson Securities Ltd., Bethesda, Md., 1983; chmn., CEO Drazin & Co., Inc., Bethesda, 1983-89, Drazin Properties, Inc., Bethesda, 1985-89, Drazin Securities, Inc., Bethesda, 1985-88, Woodmont Asset Mgmt. Inc., 1989—. Affiliate Montgomery County Bd. Realtors; real estate investment banker Restructuring Fed. Deposit Ins. Corp. Founder Ivy Connection, Washington, 1982; bd. dirs. Friends of Tel Aviv U., actine planning com. Jewish Nat. Fund; active Nat. Truste for Historic Preservation, UJA Fedn. of Greater Washington (young leadership divsn., Ruth Heritage Forum), Am. Friends Hebrew U., Nat. Kidney Found., Shakespeare Theatre Guild. Fellow Wexner Heritage Found., Renaissance Inst., Friends for Life Benefit, Whitman Walker Clinic, Spiritual Ctr. Am., Assn. for Investment Mgmt. and Rsch., Turnaround Mgmt. Assn.; mem. Nat. Assn. Realtors, Comml. Investment Real Estate Coun., Relators Nat. Mktg. Inst., Wash. Soc. Investment Analysts, Inc., Wellesley Club (interns coord., recent grads. rep. 1981-84, Washington), Ben Gurion Club, Beta Gamma Sigma, Tau Zeta Epsilon. Office: Woodmont Asset Mgmt Inc 6403 Kirby Rd Bethesda MD 20817-5523 E-mail: lisadrazin@verizon.net.

DRAZIN, MICHAEL PETER, mathematician, researcher; b. London, June 5, 1929; arrived in U.S.A., 1957; s. Isaac and Leah Drazin; m. Carol Margaret Vaughan, July 20, 1981 (div. Dec. 1994); m. Catherine Annabel Freeman, Oct. 26, 2001. BA with 1st class hons., Cambridge U., 1950, MA, PhD, Cambridge U., 1953. Scientific officer Royal Naval Scientific Svc., Teddington, England, 1953—55; rsch. fellow Trinity Coll., Cambridge, England, 1955—57; vis. lectr. N.W. Univ., Evanston, Ill., 1957—58; sr. scientist Rsch. Inst. Advanced Study, Balt., 1958—62; from assoc. prof. math. to prof. emeritus Purdue U., West Lafayette, Ind., 1962—99, prof. emeritus, 1999—. Hon. rsch. fellow U. Coll., London, 1987—; referee, reviewer NSF. Contbr. articles to profl. jours. Recipient Smith's prize, Cambridge U., 1952. Mem.: Soc. Indsl. & Applied Math., Am. Math. Soc. Achievements include discovery of Drazin inverse, 1958, and of the *-order for systems with involution; extension of Maschke's theorem from groups to semigroups; quasi-inverse; core-quasi-nilpotence. Avocations: photography, music, history of technology, squash. Office: Purdue Univ Math Dept W Lafayette IN 47907 Fax: 765-494-0548.

DRAZNIN, JULES NATHAN, educator; b. Chgo., May 14, 1923; s. Charles G. and Goldie (Malach) D.; m. Shirley Bernstein, Apr. 9, 1950; children: Dean, Jody, Michael. Student, Wright City Coll., Chgo., 1941; BA in Journalism, Calif. State U., Northridge, 1978, MA in Higher Edn., 1984. Various journalism positions City News Bur., Chgo. Am., Chgo., 1941; promotions and publicity Balaban & Katz Theaters, Chgo., 1942-43; asst. dir pub. rels. Combined Jewish Appeal, Chgo., 1944; prin. J.N. Draznin Assocs., Chgo., 1945-50; account supr. Olian & Bronner Advt. Agy., Chgo., 1951-53; dir. advt. Chgo. Defender, Robert S. Abbott Pub. Co., 1953-55; freelance cons. Chgo., 1955-60; v.p. pub. rels. Harshe-Rotman, Chgo., 1956; pub. rels. dir. Abel and Lamensdorf Properties, Chgo., 1960-62; editor-in-chief, assoc. pub. Indsl. News Bender Publs., Calif., 1962-64; labor editor, spl. features writer Valley News and Green Sheet, Calif., 1964; ind. ins. agt. Calif., 1965-74; lectr. pub. rels. UCLA and Calif. State U., L.A.; prof. journalism and pub. rels. L.A. Trade Tech. Coll., 1975-95, chmn. lang. arts dept., 1984-90, prof. emeritus journalism, 2003—. Prof. journalism and pub. rels. L.A. City Coll., L.A. Pierce Coll., L.A. Southwest Coll., East L.A. Coll., L.A. Mission Coll.; guest lectr. Calif. State U., Northridge. Coord. Mass Media AARP/Grass Roots, 1996—, apptd. Calif. legis. adv. team AARP, 1998—, also spokesperson on social security and medicare; mem. L.A. County Commn. on Aging, L.A. County Agy. on Aging. Mem. Assn. for Edn. in Journalism and Mass Comm., Soc. Profl. Journalists. Avocations: classical music, travel. E-mail: julesdraznin@msn.com.

DR. DRE, (ANDRE YOUNG), rapper, record producer; b. L.A. Co-founder Ruthless Records, 1987. Albums include (with N.W.A.) Straight Outta Compton, 1989, 100 Miles and Runnin', 1990 (EP) Efil4zaggin, 1991, (solo) The Chronic, 1993 (Grammy award Best Pop Solo for "Let Me Ride" 1994); prodr. Snoop Doggy Dog's album "Doggy Style", 1993, U Can't Cee Me and California Love singles, 1996; prodr. soundtrack albums Above the Rim, 1994, Murder Was the Case, 1994. Office: care Interscope Records 10900 Wilshire Blvd Fl 12 Los Angeles CA 90024-6501 also: Aftermath Entertainment 10900 Wilshire Blvd Ste 1040 Los Angeles CA 90024-6501

DREBEN, RAYA SPIEGEL, judge; b. Vienna, Dec. 3, 1927; came to U.S., 1928, naturalized, 1936; d. Shalom and Rose (Goldschmiedt) Spiegel; children: Elizabeth, Jonathan. AB magna cum laude, Radcliffe Coll., 1949; LL.B. cum laude, Harvard U., 1954. Bar: Mass. 1957, U.S. Supreme Ct. 1960. Law clk. to Judge Bailey Aldrich, U.S. Dist. Ct. for Mass., 1954-55; Bigelow fellow and instr. U. Chgo. Law Sch., 1955-56; asso. Firm Palmer & Dodge, Boston, 1964-71, partner, 1971-79; assoc. justice Mass. Appeals Ct., Boston, 1979—. Lectr. in copyright Harvard U. Law Sch., 1973-76; mem. adv. com. on copyright registration and deposit Libr. of Congress, 1993. Trustee Radcliffe Coll., 1981-89. Recipient 1st prize Nathan Burkan competition Harvard U. Law Sch., 1954, nat. winner, 1954 Mem. ABA (chmn. com. on authors 1977-79), Am. Law Inst. (adv. on restatement, property-donative transactions), Am. Bar Found., Copyright Soc. U.S.A. (trustee 1973-76, editorial bd. bull. 1974-85), Jud. Inst. Mass. Judiciary (chmn. adv. com. 1988-96). Office: Appeals Ct 1500 Pemberton Sq Boston MA 02108-1701

DREBSKY, DENNIS JAY, lawyer; b. N.Y.C., Sept. 28, 1946; s. Benjamin and Ronnie (Penso) D.; m. Norma Louise Linschitz, Aug. 16, 1970; children: Richard Michael, Joshua William Evan. BBA magna cum laude, CCNY, 1967; JD, Cornell U., 1970. Bar: N.Y. 1971, U.S. Dist. Ct. (so. dist.) N.Y. 1972, U.S. Ct. Appeals (2d cir.) 1971, U.S. Ct. Appeals (5th cir.) 1980, U.S. Ct. Appeals (9th cir.) 1982, U.S. Ct. Appeals (1st cir.) 1981, U.S. Ct. Appeals (10th cir.) 1984, U.S. Ct. Appeals (4th cir.) 1986, U.S. Ct. Appeals (D.C. cir.) 1998. Assoc. Skadden, Arps, Slate, Meagher & Flom, N.Y.C., 1970-77, ptnr., 1978-91, Clifford, Chance, Rogers & Wells, 1991—. Trustee Community Law Offices, N.Y.C., 1980—. Mem. Assn. of Bar of City of N.Y. (mem. com. on corp. reorgn. 1985—). Jewish. Avocations: reading, jogging, theater. Home: 7 Glen Hill Ct Dix Hills NY 11746-4819 Office: Clifford Chance Rogers & Wells 200 Park Ave Fl 8E New York NY 10166-0800 E-mail: dennis.drebsky@cliffordchance.com.

DREBUS, RICHARD WILLIAM, pharmaceutical company executive; b. Oshkosh, Wis., Mar. 30, 1924; s. William and Frieda (Schmidt) D.; m. Hazel Redford, June 7, 1947; children: William R., John R., Kathryn L. Belin. BS, U. Wis., 1947, MS, 1949, PhD, 1952. Tcr. Madison East H.S., 1947-48; Bus. trainee Marathon Paper Corp., Menasha, Wis., 1951-52; tng. mgr. Ansul Corp., Marinette, Wis., 1952-55, asst. to v.p., 1955-58, marketing mgr., 1958-60; dir. personnel devel. Mead Johnson & Co., Evansville, Ind., 1960-65, v.p. corporate planning, 1965-66, internat. pres., 1966-68; v.p. internat. div. Bristol-Myers Co. (merger Mead Johnson & Co. with Bristol-Myers Co.), N.Y.C., 1968-77, sr. v.p., 1977-78, v.p. parent co., 1978-85, sr. v.p. pharm. research and devel. div., 1985-89, ret., 1989. Past bd. dirs. Jr. Achievement S.E. Conn., Meriden Silver Mus.; past bd. dirs. Meriden-Wallngford United Way, chmn. fund raising drive, 1988-89; trustee emeritus Quinnipiac Coll.; bd. visitors emeritus U. Wis. Served with AUS, 1943-45. Decorated Combat Inf. Badge, Purple Heart, Bronze Star. Mem. APA, N.Y. Acad. Scis., U. Wis. Bascom Hill Soc., Oshkosh Country Club, North Shore Country Club, Phi Delta Kappa. Home: 3720 Pau Ko Tuk Ln Oshkosh WI 54902-7332 E-mail: rwdrebus@aol.com.

DREBUSHENKO, DAVID WILLIAM, philosophy educator; b. Clarksville, Tenn., June 28, 1953; s. William Drebushenko and Mary Evelyn Brown. MS, PhD, Ohio State U. Asst. prof. philosophy Ctrl. Mich. U., Mount Pleasant, 1988-91; assoc. prof. philosophy U. So. Ind., Evansville, 1991—. Contbr. articles to profl. jours. Mem. Am. Philosophical Assn., So. Soc. for Philosophy and Psychology. Office: 8600 University Blvd Evansville IN 47712-3534

DRECHNEY, MICHAELENE, secondary education educator; b. Chgo. d. Bill and Pearl (Krupocki) D. BS, Loyola U., Chgo., 1968, MA, 1976. Cert. tchr., Ill., Ohio. Tchr. adult edn. Wright Coll., Chgo., 1983-84; tchr. English, Gordon Tech. High Sch., Chgo., 1977-84; tchr. sci. St. Francis Xavier Sch., Wilmette, Ill., 1973-76; tchr. sci., dir. art St. Monica Sch., Chgo., 1977-93; tchr. Thorp Scholastic Acad., Chgo., 1993—. Grantee Edn. System of People's Republic of China, Woodrow Wilson Found., 1989, Nat. Sci. Tchr.'s Assn., NSF, 1990, NSF, Inst. for Chem. Edn., 1991, Project W.I.Z.E., 1995, Tchrs. as Scholars, 2000, Project Physics, 2002; recipient presdl. award Assn. Sci. Tchrs., Project Lava award 1998. Mem. ASCD, Nat. Sci. Tchrs. Assn. (cert.), Argon Chemistry Tchrs., Nat. Middle Level Sci. Tchrs., Coun. for Elem. Sci. Internat., Nat. Sci. Suprs. Assn., Ill. Sci. Tchrs. Assn. Home: 6514 W Belmont Ave Chicago IL 60634-3995 Office: 6024 W Warwick Ave Chicago IL 60634-2554

DRECHSEL, EDWARD RUSSELL, JR., retired utility company executive; b. Webster, Mass., Dec. 29, 1927; s. Edward R. and Eva A. (Kullas) D.; m. Marcella Marie Japko, Dec. 26, 1950; children: E. Russell, Carl M. BSEE, Worcester Poly. Inst., 1949; MSEE, N.J. Inst. Tech., 1956; grad. pub. utilities exec. program, U. Mich.; intermittent coursework, Rutgers U. Registered profl. engr., N.J.; lic. elec. subcode ofcl., constrn. ofcl. Sales mgr. Jersey Cen. Power and Light Co., Lakewood, N.J., 1959-60, div. engr., 1960-64, dist. supt., 1969-84, supt. div. ops. Old Bridge, N.J., 1984-87, Lakewood, N.J., 1987-91. Ptnr. Cornucopia Enterprises, Wrightstown. Mem. Friends of the Gardens, Monmouth County, Bklyn. Botanic Gardens; bd. dirs. Tom's River (N.J.) C. of C., 1978-84; bd. dirs. N.J. Shade Tree Fedn., New Brunswick, 1982-96, pres., 1991-93; v.p. No. Hanover Twp. Bd. Edn., 1982-83, pres., 1985-86, 86-87, 90-91, 94-95, 97-99; chmn. No. Hanover Shade Tree Commn., 1985-99, Zoning Bd. of Adjustment, No. Hanover, 1985-99; mem. Sayreville Indsl. Commn.; past chmn. Ocean County Traffic Safety Commn., Raritan Valley C. of C.; life mem. Rep. Nat. Com., 1989—; mem. Rep. Presdl. Task Force, 1989—, Rep. Senatorial Com., 1988—, at-large del. party platform planning com. Staff sgt. Signal Corps U.S. Army, 1950-53. Recipient Presdl. Legion of Merit, 1993. Mem. IEEE (sr. mem., life), NSPE, NRA (life), Internat. Soc. Arborists, Internat. Soc. Arbiculture, Am. Forestry Assn., N.J. Soc. Profl. Engrs., N.J. Fedn. Shade Tree Commsn., Air Force Assn. (life), Am. Legion (life), Pa. Horticulture Soc., N.J. Pesticide Assn., Raritan Valley Regional C. of C., Ocean County Employees Legis. Com., Burlington County Employees Legis. Com., Monmouth County Employees Legis. Com. Republican. Roman Catholic. Home: 168 Larrison Rd Wrightstown NJ 08562-2210 E-mail: edrechsel@yahoo.com.

DRECHSEL, ROBERT EDWARD, journalism educator; b. Fergus Falls, Minn., Aug. 7, 1949; BA, U. Minn., 1971, MA, 1976, PhD, 1980. Reporter, city editor Daily Jour., Fergus Falls, 1971-74; instr. dept. journalism S.D. State U., Brookings, 1976-77; asst. prof. dept. tech. journalism Colo. State U., Ft. Collins, 1979-83; from asst. prof. to assoc. prof. Sch. Journalism and Mass Comm. U. Wis., Madison, 1983-91, prof., 1991—, dir., 1991-98; affiliated prof. law U. Wis., Madison, 2000—. Author: News Making in the Trial Courts, 1983; contbr. articles to profl. jours. Mem. Assn. Edn. Journalism and Mass Comm. (Krieghbaum Outstanding Achievement Rsch., Teaching & Pub. Svc. award 1989), Am. Judicature Soc., Wis. Freedom Info. Coun., Internat. Comm. Assn. Office: U Wis Sch Journalism & Mass Comm 821 University Ave Madison WI 53706-1412

DREES, BASTIAAN MEIJER, entomologist; b. Amsterdam, Netherlands, June 28, 1952; s. Jan Meijer and Jacoba Meijer Drees; m. Carol Frost, Oct. 30, 1953; children: Carly Jobes, Erin Lien. BA in Biology, W.Va. U., 1974, MSc in Entomology, 1976; PhD in Entomology, Ohio State U., 1980. Diplomate Am. Bd. Entomology. Ext. entomologist Tex. Agrl. Ext. Svc., Coll. Sta., Tex., 1980—; prof. dept. entomology Tex. A&M U., Coll. Sta., 1993—, coord. Tex. imported fire ant rsch. and mgmt. project dept. entomology, 1997—2002, dir. Tex. imported fire ant rsch. and mgmt. project dept. entomology, 2002—03. Author: (book) A Field Guide to Common Tex. Insects, 1998 (Tex. Reference Source award, Tex. Libr. Assn., 2001); contbr. articles to profl. jour. Recipient Faculty Disting. Achievement award in ext., Assn. Former Students of Tex. A&M U., 1996, Disting. Achievement award in ext., Entomol. Soc. Am., 1997, award for rsch. excellence, Orkin, 2001. Mem.: Southwestern Entomol. Soc. (pres. 2002), Entomol. Soc. Am. (sec. for SW br. 2002). Avocations: photography, music, art. Office: Texas A&M U RM 412 Dept Entomology College Station TX 77843-2475 Office Fax: 979-845-7029. E-mail: b-drees@tamu.edu.

DREES, BETTY, dean, educator; Interim sect. chair in diabetes, endocrinology, and metabolism Truman Med. Ctr. Hosp. Hill, exec. assoc. dean; assoc. prof., docent U. Mo.-Kansas City Sch. Medicine, 1998, interim dean, 2001—. Office: 2411 Holmes Kansas City MO 64108

DREES, STEPHEN DANIEL, marketing professional; b. Livingston, N.J., Mar. 11, 1961; s. Daniel Stevenson and Lois Jean (Litzebauer) D.; m. Sandra Lee Van Dusen, Sept. 28, 1985; children: Madeleine Danielle, Meredith Olivia. BA, Bloomsburg U., 1983; MS, U. Pa., 1989; cert., Nat. Sch. Bank Card Mgmt., 1991; Cert. in Strategic Alliances, U. Pa., 1992; postgrad. cert., Stanford U., 2002. Mktg. mgr. Mfrs. Hanover Corp., Phila., 1986-88; asst. v.p. Mellon Bank Corp., Pitts., 1988-90; v.p. MasterCard Internat., Inc., N.Y.C., 1990-93; prin. Strategic Mktg. Svcs., Inc., Boston, 1993-97; v.p. GE Capital, Cin., 1997-99; pres., CEO Quantum Loyalty Systems, Cin., 1999—. Mem. faculty MasterCard U., 1990-93, chmn. Credit Card Mktg. conf., 1995. Contbr. articles to profl. jours. Mem. World Affairs Coun., Young Pres.'s Orgn., The Penn Club, Zeta Psi. Roman Catholic. Office: 4660 Duke Dr Ste 300 Mason OH 45040-8465 E-mail: stephen@quantumloyalty.com.

DREGER, D. C. academic administrator; b. Bilwaskarma, Zelaya, Nicaragua, Dec. 27, 1950; arrived in U.S., 1962; s. Wilfred Lawrence and Lorraine Amelia Dreger; m. Cathy M. Guillan, Aug. 19, 1972; children: Nate, Seth. BA, Moravian Coll., 1972. Adv. cert. Assn. Fundraising Exec. Exam. Bd., AFCRE. Editor Guy Gannett Pub. Co., Portland, Maine, 1974-85; dir. comm. Stony Brook (N.Y.) Sch., 1985-94; dir. comms. Rabun Gap-Nacoochee Sch., Ga., 1994-96; dir. devel. Covenant Coll., Lookout Mountain, Ga., 1996—. Cons. Rising Fawn, Ga.; mem. advancement com. Chattanooga Christian Sch., 1998—2002. Dir., editl. cons.: book Vision for the 21st Century, 1993. Mem. Chattanooga Planned Giving Coun., sec., 1997—2003. Mem.: Assn. Fundraising Profls. (chair advancment southeastern Tenn. chpt. 1997—2000, mem. award selection com. 2000, mem. curriculum com. 2001, 2003, mem. higher edn. task force 2002, 2003, past pres., chair advancement southeastern Tenn. chpt., chair nat. philanthropy day). Avocations: gardening, etymology, outdoors. Office: Covenant Coll 14049 Scenic Hwy Lookout Mountain GA 30750 Business E-Mail: development@covenant.edu.

DREHER, MELANIE CREAGAN, dean, nursing educator; BSN magna cum laude, L.I. U.; D in Anthropology, Columbia U. Mem. faculty Columbia U., N.Y.C.; dean Sch. Nursing, William Ryan disting. prof. U. Miami; dean Sch. Nursing, prof. U. Mass.; dean Coll. Nursing, prof. U. Iowa; now dean Univ. of Iowa Sch. of Nursing. Mem. editl. bds. various profl. jours. Recipient May A. Brunson award, CASE award. Mem. Sigma Theta Tau (pres. Beta Zeta chpt. 1995). Office: U Iowa Office Dean 101F NB Iowa City IA 52242

DREHER, STANLEY E., JR., state representative; b. Iola, Kans., Apr. 27, 1926; married; 2 children. Soil conservation supr.; mem. Kans. Ho. of Reps., 1997—. Official football and basketball. With USAF. Mem.: Kans. Beef Coun., Kans. Livestock Assn., Kans. Farm Bur., Am. Legion. Republican. Methodist. Office: 110-S State Capitol 300 SW 10th Ave Topeka KS 66612 Address: 1496 2200 St Iola KS 66749*

DREHER, JR. FRANK H. retired optician; b. Philadelphia, Pa., Sept. 21, 1923; s. Frank H. and Mary Catherine Dreher; m. Kathryn Marie Dreher, Aug. 27, 1955; children: Frank H. Dreher, III, George W. Dreher. Modern Bus., Alexander Hamilton Inst., New York, New York, 1962; Optics and Math., Drexel Inst., Philadelphia, Pennsylvania, 1948. Real estate salesperson Craig J. Turnbull Atty., Camden, NJ, 1950—54; opthalmic dispenser Meserall Opticians, Haddonfield, NJ, 1969—77, hearing aid dispenser, 1974—77; opthalmic dispenser Cole Nat. Corp., Willingboro, NJ, 1977—87, Dr. David J. Mellish, O.D., Williamstown, NJ, 1987—98. Creative writing tchr. Salem C.C., Carneys Point, NJ, 1996—97. Contbr. articles to profl. mags. Scout master Boy Scouts of Am., Erial, NJ, 1949—51; sunday sch. supt. Episcopal churches, Clementon and Chews Landing, NJ, 1952—79. T/4 US Armed Forces, 1943—46, New Guinea and Luzon. Mem.: The Internat. Order of St. Luke the Physician Independent. Episcopal Methodist. Avocations: writing, classical music, travel, cooking. Home: 248 Route 40 Lot F5 Newfield NJ 08344

DREIER, DAVID LOUIS, editor, writer; b. Jacksonville, Fla., Mar. 14, 1946; s. Elmer Louis Jr. and Eileen Celeste (Sholin) D.; m. Lynne Virginia Thayer, June 21, 1969; 1 child, Alexandra Louise. BS in Journalism, Northwestern U., 1968. Sci. writer U. Colo. News Svc., Boulder, 1969-70; reporter San Antonio Express & News, 1971-74; editor, writer ADA, Chgo., 1974-79; freelance writer, photographer Chgo., 1979-82; sr. editor annuals World Book Pub., Chgo., 1982-95, mng. editor Year Book, 1995-96, mng. editor Science Year, 1996—2003; mng. editor Science Discovery Ency., 2001—03; freelance writer and editor, 2003—. Contbr. numerous articles to various publs., including Omni, Outside mags. Recipient Mng. Editors award AP, 1973, citation Tex. Ho. of Reps., 1973. Mem. Nat. Assn. Sci. Writers. Avocations: photography, scriptwriting, cartooning. Home and Office: 804 Washington St Evanston IL 60202 E-mail: daviddreier@earthlink.net.

DREIER, DAVID TIMOTHY, congressman; b. Kansas City, Mo., July 5, 1952; s. H. Edward and Joyce (Yeomans) D. BA cum laude, Claremont McKenna Coll., 1975; MA in Am. Govt., Claremont Grad. Sch., 1976. Dir. corp. rels. Claremont McKenna Coll., 1975-78; dir. mktg. and govt. rels. Indsl. Hydro, San Dimas, Calif., 1978-80; mem. U.S. Congress from 26th (formerly 33rd) Calif. dist., 1981—; v.p. Dreier Devel. Co., Kansas City, Mo., 1985—. Vice chmn. rules of the house com., 1995-99, chmn. rules com., 1999—; bd. dirs. Internat. Rep. Inst.; mem. spkrs. steering com. Recipient Golden Bulldog award Watchdogs of the Treasury, 1981-99, Taxpayers Friends award Nat. Taxpayers Union, 1981-99, Clean Air Champion award Sierra Club, 1988. Republican. Office: US Ho Reps 237 Cannon Ho Office Bldg Washington DC 20515-0001*

DREIFKE, GERALD EDMOND, electrical engineering educator; b. St. Louis, June 21, 1918; s. Herman A. and Anna Margaret (Hollenbeck) D.; m. Lorraine Ann Feldhaus, June 9, 1951; children: Mark A., Matthew G., Laura Maria, Anne Marie. *Gerald and Lorraine have eight grandchildren. Mark and his wife Annette have three children: Mark Alexander, Shelby Lyn and Melanie Savannah. Matthew and his wife Patricia have four children Ann Michelle, Catherine Celeste, Joseph Michael and Mary Clare. Xavier L. Bess and Anne Marie Dreifke Bess have one child, Xavier Matthew Bess. Gerald has seven brothers and sisters. In order of birth they are: Herman A. (USAF, Iwo Jima, WWII), Raymond F. (USN Pacific Fleet), Celeste M., Rosalind, Gerald (USN), Dorothea E. Conner, Donald A. (USAF, Purple Heart, POW, Croix de Guerre, Fr. Gov.), Anne Marie Gootee. All eight are first generation Americans of German-born immigrants.* BS, MS, Washington U., 1948, D.Sc. (NSF fellow), 1961. Registered profl. engr., Mo. Layout man Curtiss-Wright Co., St. Louis, 1936-39, design engr., 1939-44; layout man Douglas Aircraft Co., 1939; instr. engring. St. Louis U., 1948-50, asst. prof., 1950-54, asso. prof. elec. engring., dir. grad. program elec. engring., 1954-61, prof. elec. engring., 1961-71; mgr. research and devel. Union Electric Co., 1971-77; cons., 1977—; vis. prof. physics U. Mo.-St. Louis, 1979-94. Cons. Emerson Electric Co., 1951-71, Monsanto Co., 1961-71; mem. tech. staff Bell Telephone Labs. N.J., summer 1963 Editor-in-chief: ISA Transactions, 1966-89; contbr. articles profl. jours. Mem. St. Louis County Bd. Elec. Examiners, Gov.'s Sci. Adv. Com. Mo. Served with USNR, 1944-45. Recipient certificate of merit WPB, 1942; research grants NSF, 1964; research grants NASA, 1965; research grants Monsanto Co., 1965-69; Nancy McNair-Ring Outstanding Faculty award St. Louis U. chpt. Gamma Pi Epsilon, 1965-66 Fellow ISA; mem. Am. Soc. Engring. Edn. (past sec., com. chmn.), IEEE (past chmn. St. Louis sect.), Mo. Soc. Profl. Engrs. (past pres. St. Louis chpt., Engr. of Yr. St. Louis chpt. 1977), St. Louis Elec. Bd. Trade, Sigma Xi, Tau Beta Pi, Eta Kappa Nu, Pi Mu Epsilon, Phi Eta Sigma. Home: 6 Westmoreland Pl Saint Louis MO 63108-1228

DREIMANIS, ALEKSIS, emeritus geology educator; b. Valmiera, Latvia, Aug. 13, 1914; s. Peteris and Marta Eleonora (Leitis) D.; m. Anita Kana, Apr. 18, 1942; children: Mara Dreimanis Love, Aija Dreimanis Downing. Mag. rer. nat., U. Latvia, 1938; D.Sc. (hon.), U. Waterloo, Ont., Can., 1969, U. Western Ont., 1980; D Geography (hon.), U. Latvia, 1991, Habilitation, 1942. Asst. to pvt. docent U. Latvia, 1937-44; mil. geologist Latvian Legion, 1944-45; assoc. prof. geology Baltic U., Hamburg and Pinneberg, Germany, 1946-48; mem. faculty U. Western Ont., London, Can., 1948—, prof. geology, 1964-80, prof. emeritus, 1980—. Pres. Commn. on Genesis and Lithology of Quaternary Deposits, Internat. Union Quaternary Research, 1973-87; cons. in field. Assoc. editor Geosci. Can., 1976-78, Quaternary Sci. Revs., 1981-87, Tech. Rev. (in Latvian), 1978—, Latgeo (in Latvian), 1990-98, Geology Proc. Estonian Acad. Scis., 1991-97, Latvijas Geologijas Vestis, 2000—; contbr. articles to profl. jours. Decorated officer Three Star Order of Latvia; recipient Centennial medal (Can.); Queen Elizabeth II 25th Anniversary medal; Centennial medal Geol. Survey of Finland, U. Helsinki medal; Albrecht Penck medal, teaching award Ont. Confedn. Univ. Faculty Assns., 1978, Centennial medal U. Latvia. Fellow Royal Soc. Can. (Disting.), Geol. Assn. Can. (Logan medal 1978), Geol. Soc. Am. (Disting. Career award Quarternary geology and geomorphology divsn. 1987); mem. Swedish Geol. Soc. (hon. corr. mem.), Can. Quaternary Assn. (W.A. Johnston medal 1989), Am. Quarternary Assn. (pres. 1981-83), Assn. Advancement Baltic Studies, Internat. Union for Quaternary Rsch. (hon.),

Latvian Nat. Fedn. Can. (chmn. coun. 1953-71, hon. mem.), Latvian Acad. Scis. (fgn. hon.), Latvian Cultural Found. (exec. com. 1973-77), London Latvian Soc. (pres. 1948—), Fraternity Lidums (pres. 1935-36, editor newsletter 1969—), Geol. Soc. Finland (hon. corr. mem.), Latvian Am. Assn. Univ. Profs. and Scientists (pres. 1983-85), Geog. Assn. Latvia (hon.), Assn. Latvian Geologists (hon.), Baltic Rsch. Inst. (hon. corr. mem.), Estonian Geol. Soc. (hon.). Home: 287 Neville Dr London ON Canada N6G 1C2 Office: U Western Ont Dept Earth Scis London ON Canada N6A 5B7

DREISBACH, DANIEL LIVINGSTONE, lawyer, educator; b. Yadakunya, Nigeria, July 9, 1959; s. John Ardo and Bettie Short Dreisbach; m. Joyce Cowley, Sept. 5, 1987; children: Mollie Abigail, Moriah Esther. BA, U. S.C., 1981; DPhil, Oxford (Eng.) U., 1985; JD, U. Va., 1988. Jud. clk. U.S. Ct. Appeals (4th cir.), Columbia, S.C., 1988-89; pvt. practice Charlottesville, Va., 1989-91; prof. Am. U., Washington, 1991—. Author: Real Threat and Mere Shadow: Religious Liberty and the First Amendment, 1987, Thomas Jefferson and the Wall of Separation Between Church and State, 2002; editor: Religion and Politics in the Early Republic, 1996; co-editor: Religion and Political Culture in Jefferson's Virginia, 2000. Rhodes scholar, 1981-84; Andrew W. Mellon fellow, 1998-99. Mem. Am. Polit. Sci. Assn., Va. State Bar. Office: Am U Sch Pub Affairs 4400 Massachusetts Ave NW Washington DC 20016-8043 Fax: (202) 885-2907.

DREISBACH, JOHN GUSTAVE, investment banker; b. Paterson, N.J., Apr. 24, 1939; s. Gustave John and Rose Catherine (Koehler) D.; m. Janice Lynn Petitjean; children: John Gustave Jr., Christopher Erik. BA, NYU, 1963. With Dreyfus & Co., 1959-62, Shields & Co., Inc., 1965-68, Model, Roland & Co., Inc., N.Y.C., 1968-72, F. Eberstadt & Co., Inc., N.Y.C., 1972-74; v.p. Bessemer Trust Co., 1974-78; pres. Cmty. Housing Capital, Inc., 1978-80; chmn., pres. John G. Dreisbach, Inc., Santa Fe, 1980—, JDG Housing Corp., 1982—, JGD Mgmt. Corp., 1996—. Gen. ptnr. numerous real estate ltd. partnerships; bd. dirs., pres. The Santa Fe Investment Conf., 1986—; assoc. Sta. KNME-TV. Mem. Santa Fe Cmty. Devel. Commn.; bd. dirs. Friends of Berry Pomeroy Ch With USAFR, 1964. Mem. Internat. Assn. for Fin. Planning, Nat. Assn. Securities Dealers, Inc., NYU Alumni Assn., N.Mex. First, Friends of Vieilles Maisons Francaises Inc., Mensa, Santa Fe C. of C., Augustan Soc., St. Bartholomew's Cmty. Club, Essex Club, Hartford Club, Amigos del Alcalde Club. Republican. Mem. Ch. Of Eng. Avocations: travel, art, arch-design appreciation, classical music, shotokan karate (1st dan). Home: Elm Cottage Hemsford-Littlehempston Totnes Devon TQ9 6NE England Office: 369 Montezuma Ave No 215 Santa Fe NM 87501-2626 Fax: 505-989-7381; Home Fax: (01803) 762-322. E-mail: john@dreisbach.freeserve.co.uk.

DREISBACH, RODNEY LEWIS, structures engineer, researcher; b. Lehighton, Pa., Dec. 6, 1940; s. Lee Llewellyn and Minnie Elsie (Shafnisky) D.; m. Corene Susan Behler, July 14, 1962 (div. Dec. 1980); children: Diana Louise, Chad Lewis; m. Barbara Ann Wilsey, Jan. 2, 1984. BS, Pa. State U., 1962, MS, 1963; PhD, U. Colo., 1969. Registered profl. engr., Colo. Rsch. asst. Pa. State U., State College, 1962-63, instr., 1963-64; tchg. asst. U. Calif., Davis, 1964-66, U. Colo., Boulder, 1966-67, tchg. assoc., 1967-69; structures engr. Boeing Co., Seattle, 1969-93, assoc. tech. fellow, 1993-95, tech. fellow, 1996-98, sr. tech. fellow, 1998—. U. Colo. faculty scholar, 1967, 68. Fellow AIAA (assoc.), Royal Aero. Soc.; mem. Internat. Assn. for Engring. Analysis Cmty., Sigma Xi, Chi Epsilon. Republican. Methodist. Avocations: yard work, walking, woodworking. Home: 24226 135th Ave SE Kent WA 98042-5183 Office: Boeing Co MC 67-HM PO Box 3707 Seattle WA 98124-2207

DRELL, SIDNEY DAVID, physicist, educator; b. Atlantic City, N.J., Sept. 13, 1926; s. Tulla and Rose (White) D.; m. Harriet Stainback, Mar. 22, 1952; children: Daniel White, Persis Sydney, Joanna Harriet. AB, Princeton U., 1946; MA, U. Ill., 1947, PhD, 1949, DSc (hon.), 1981. Rsch. assoc. U. Ill., 1949-50; instr. physics Stanford U., 1950-52, assoc. prof., 1956-60, prof., 1960-63, Lewis M. Terman prof. and fellow, 1979-84; co-dir. Stanford U. Ctr. for Internat. Security and Arms Control, 1983-89; prof. Stanford Linear Accelerator Ctr., 1963-98, dep. dir., 1969-98, exec. head theoretical physics, 1969-86, prof. emeritus, 1998—. Rsch. assoc. MIT, 1952-53, asst. prof., 1953-56, adv. bd. Lincoln Lab., 1985-90; vis. scientist Guggenheim fellow CERN Lab., Switzerland, 1961, U. Rome, 1972; vis. prof., Loeb lectr. Harvard U., 1962, 70; vis. Schrodinger prof. theoretical physics U. Vienna, 1975; vis. fellow All Souls Coll., Oxford, 1979; I.I. Rabi vis. prof. Columbia U., 1984; adj. prof. engring., pub. policy Carnegie Mellon U., 1989-96; cons. Office Sci. and Tech., 1960-73, Office Sci. and Tech. Policy, 1977-82, ACDA, 1969-81; adviser NSC, 1973-81, Office Tech. Assessment U.S. Congress, 1975-90, House Armed Svcs. Com., 1990-93, Senate Select Com. on Intelligence, 1990-93; mem. Jason, 1960—; mem. high energy physics adv. panel Dept. Energy, 1973-86, chmn., 1974-82, energy rsch. adv. bd., 1978-80; mem. Carnegie Commn. on Sci., Tech. and Govt., 1988-93, Pres.'s Fgn. Intelligence Adv. Bd., 1993—; Richtmyer lectr. to Am. Assn. Physics Tchrs., San Francisco, 1978; Danz lectr. U. Wash., 1983; Hans Bethe lectr. Cornell U., 1988; chmn. U.C. pres. coun. on nat. labs., 1992—; chmn. internat. adv. bd. Inst. Global Conflict and Cooperation, U. Calif., 1990-93; mem. bd. dirs. Internat. Sci. Found., 1993-96. Author 8 books; contbr. articles to profl. jours. Trustee Inst. Advanced Study, Princeton, 1974-83; bd. govs. Weizmann Inst. Sci., Rehovoth, Israel, 1970—; bd. dirs. Ann. Revs., Inc., 1976-97; mem. Pres. Sci. Adv. Com., 1966-70. Recipient Ernest Orlando Lawrence Meml. award and medal for rsch. in theoreticl physics AEC, 1972, Alumni award for disting. svc. in engring. U. Ill., 1973, Alumni Achievement award, 1988, Hilliard Roderick prize in sci., arms. control and internat. security AAAS, 1993, Woodrow Wilson award Princeton U., 1994, Ettore Majorana-Erice Sci. for Peace prize, 1994, Gian Carlo Wick medal, 1996, Disting Assoc. award U.S. Dept. Environ., 1997, I. Pomeranchuk prize, 1998, Linus Pauling medal, Stanford U., 1999-2000; MacArthur fellow, 1984-89, Sr. fellow Hoover Inst., 1998—. Fellow Am. Phys. Soc. (pres. 1986, Leo Szilard award for physics in the pub. interest 1980); mem. AAAS, NAS, Am. Acad. Arts and Scis., Am. Philos. Soc., Arms Control Assn. (bd. dirs. 1978-93), Coun. on Fgn. Rels., Aspen Strategy Group (emeritus 1991), Academia Europaea. Home: 570 Alvarado Row Stanford CA 94305-8501 Office: Stanford Linear Accelerator Ctr 2575 Sand Hill Rd Menlo Park CA 94025-7015

DREMSA, THERESA LYNN, military officer, researcher; b. Boscobel, Wis., Apr. 8, 1955; d. Margaret Marie Pettera and Frederick Maximillan Dremsa, Matthew Pettera (Stepfather); children: Maya Esperanza Saudia, Alma Buena Saudia. BSN, U. of Wis., 1977; MSN, U. of Ala., 1989; PhD, U. of Md., 2001. Ccrn, AACN, 1998. Nurse exec. 74th Med. Ops. Critical Care Flight, Wright-Patterson Air Force Base, Ohio, 1996—98; dir., nursing rsch. 59th Clin. Rsch. Squadron, Lackland Air Force Base, Tex., 2001—. Critical care cons. USAF in Europe, Lakenheath Royal Air Force Base, 1993—95. Author: (dissertation) Readiness Estimate and Deployability Index Revised for Air Force Nurses (READI-R-AFN) and READI-R-AFN Short Form : Psychometric Evaluation. Lt. col. USAF, 2001. Decorated Meritorious Svc. medal USAF; grantee Rsch. grant, Tri-Svc. Nursing. Mem.: Sigma Theta Tau Internat. Home: 12242 Netherwood Ln San Antonio TX 78253 Office: 59th Clin Rsch Squadron 1255 Wilford Hall Loop Bldg 4430 Lackland A F B TX 78236 Home Fax: 210-292-6053; Office Fax: 210-292-6053. Personal E-mail: tdremsa@satx.rr.com. E-mail: theresa.dremsa@lackland.af.mil.

DRENGLER, WILLIAM ALLAN JOHN, lawyer; b. Shawano, Wis., Nov. 18, 1949; s. William J. and Vera J. (Simmonds) D.; m. Kathleen A. Hintz, June 18, 1983; children: Ryan, Jeffrey, Brittany. BA, Am. U., 1972; JD, Marquette U., 1976. Bar: Wis. 1976, U.S. Dist. Ct. (ea. and we. dists.) Wis. 1976. Assoc. Herrling, Swain & Drengler, Appleton, Wis., 1976-78; dist. atty. Outagamie County, Appleton, 1979-81; corp. counsel Marathon County, Wausau, Wis., 1981-96, Drengler Law Firm, Wausau, Wis., 1997—. Vice chmn. Wis. Equal Rights Coun., 1978-83, Wis. Coun. on Criminal Justice, Madison, 1983-87. Nat. pres. Future Bus. Leaders Am., 1967-68; mem. nat. Dem. delegation, 1974-76; mem. adminstrv. com. Wis. Dems., Madison, 1977-81, 86-88; chmn. local Selective Svc. Bd., Wausau, 1982-89; mem. adv. bd. Wausau Salvation Army, 1986—; judge adv. officer Wis. Army N.G., 1989-96; bd. dirs. Wausau Youth/Little League Baseball, 1988—, team mgr., 1994-2002. Mem. ABA (chair com. on govt. lawyers sect. state and local govt. 1991-93, bylaws com. govt. and pub. sect. lawyers divsn. 1993-98), KC, Nat. Assn. County Civil Attys. (dir. 1986-88, v.p. 1988-91, pres. 1991-92), Nat. Assn. Counties (bd. dirs. 1991-92, taxation and fin. steering com. 1991-93, deferred compensation adv. com. 1993-95, justice and pub. safety steering com. 1993-94), State Bar Wis. (govt. lawyers divsn., bd. dirs. 1982-86, sec. 1986-87, pres. 1989-91, professionalism com. 1987-91, 92-2000, solo and small firm practice com. 2001--), Kiwanis (lt. gov. 1985-86, club pres. 1989-90, chair past lt. govs. coun. 1990-91), Wausau Elks (parliamentarian 2000-03), Kiwanis Internat. Found. (Hixon Fellowship Award 2001). Roman Catholic. Avocations: baseball, camping, fishing, gardening, tennis. Office: PO Box 5152 609 Scott St Wausau WI 54402-5152

DRENNAN, JERRY M. career officer; BS in Engring. Mgmt., USAF Acad., 1972; MBA, U. Mo., 1976; grad., Squadron Officer Sch., 1976, Armed Forces Staff Coll., 1984, Air War Coll., 1989; program for execs., Carnegie-Mellon U., 1995. Commd. 2d lt. USAF, 1972, advanced through grades to brigadier gen., 1997; missile ops. staff officer Air Staff tng. program Dep. Chief Staff for Ops., Hdqs. USAF, Washington, 1977-78, ground-launched cruise missile plans officer, 1980-82, asst. exec. officer, 1982-84; ops. officer 564th Strategic Missile Squadron, Malmstrom AFB, Mont., 1984-85; comdr. 12th Strategic Missile Squadron, Malmstrom AFB, 1985-86; dep. base comdr. 341st Combat Support Group, Malmstrom AFB, 1986-87; dep. comdr. for ops., vice comdr. 487th Tactical Missile Wing, Comiso Air Sta., Italy, 1989-91; comdr. 842d Combat Support Group, Grand Forks AFB, N.D., 1991-92, 321st Missile Wing, Grand Forks AFB, 1992-93; asst. dir. nuclear ops. Hdqs. Def. Nuclear Agy., Alexandria, Va., 1993-95; dep. dir. plans, dir. logistics Hdqs. Air Force Space command, Peterson AFB, Colo., 1995-96; commandant Air Command and Staff Coll., Maxwell AFB, Ala., 1996-98; comdr. 21st Space Wing, Peterson AFB, 1998—. Decorated Def. Superior Svc. medal, Legion of Merit, Meritorious Svc. medal with 5 oak leaf clusters. Office: 21 SWICC 775 Loring Ave Ste 205 Colorado Springs CO 80914-1290

DRENNAN, MICHAEL ELDON, banker; b. Yakima, Wash., June 24, 1946; s. George Eldon and Jane (Nilsson) D.; m. Alice Marie Seabolt, May 13, 1972; children: Brian, David. BS in Fin., U. Oreg., 1968; grad., Pacific Coast Banking Sch. U. Wash., 1971. Ops. officer First State Bank, Aloha, Oreg., 1972-73, ops., loan officer Portland, Oreg., 1973-74, asst. mgr. Milwaukie, Oreg., 1974-76; asst. v.p. Citizens Bank, Corvallis, Oreg., 1976-80, v.p., 1980-81; pres., chief exec. officer Bank of Corvallis, 1981-87; v.p. dist. mgr. U.S. Bank, Corvallis, Oreg., 1987, sr. v.p. market area mgr. Bend, Oreg., 1988-94, sr. v.p., dist. mgr. Eugene, Oreg., 1994-98; v.p. bus. banking Liberty Fed. Bank, 1998-2000, sr. v.p., 2000—. Bd. dirs. Cascades W. Fin. Svcs. Bd. dirs. United Way Benton County, 1984-88, Cascade Manor Retirement Ctr., 2001—; trustee Good Samaritan Hosp. Found., 1984-88; bd. dirs. Jr. Achievement of Benton County, 1983-85, treas, 1984-85, mem. exec. bd., 1984-85; mem. budget comm. Corvallis Sch. Dist., 1987; bd. dirs. Benton County Family YMCA, 1978-80, sec. 1979, mem. fin. com., 1978-80, mem. pers. com., 1979, active sustaining membership dr.; bd. dirs. Cmty. Club, 1978-83, pres., 1978, treas., 1979-80; active Corvallis Ambs., 1976-88; mem. mgmt. com. Corvallis Conv. and Visitors Bur., 1982-85; fundraising chmn. Com. City Improvement Levy, 1980; mem. exec. com. Pack 17 Boy Scouts Am., 1984-87, treas., 1984-87; mem. adv. bd. Ctrl. Oreg. Econ. Devel. Corp., 1988-90, bd. dirs., exec. bd., treas., 1991-93, v.p., 1993, pres., 1994; bd. dirs. Regional Arts Coun. of Ctrl. Oreg., treas., 1989-92; bd. dirs. Ctrl. Oreg. Air Svc. Task Force, 1989-94, chmn. airline rels. com., 1990; mem. Bend Bus. Assistance Team, 1989-90, United Way Deschutes County, chmn. loaned exec. recruitment, 1992; mem. planning com. St. Charles Med. Ctr. Found., 1993, dir. adminstrn. capital fund drive, 1993; mem. adv. bd. Deschutes County Fair, 1993-94; bd. dirs. Birth to Three, Eugene, 1994-2001, treas., 1995-96, pres.-elect., 1996-97, pres. 1997-98; bd. dirs. Lane Arts Coun., 1995-98, treas. exec. bd., 1996-98; bd. dirs. Conv. and Visitors Assn. Lane County, 1995-, treas. 1998-2000, vice chmn. 2000-2001, chmn. 2001—; bd. dirs. Eugene-Springfield Metro Partnership, 1995-99; chmn. maj. firms campaign cabinet United Way of Lane County, 1996, 97, 2001, 03, team capt. Boy Scout Annual Campaign, 2000; bd. dirs. Oreg. Bach Festival, 1999-2001; fund raising com. Vols. in Medicine, 2003. Lt. USN, 1968-71. Named Jr. First Citizen, Corvallis, 1980. Mem. Bend C. of C. (chmn. mem. dir. task force 1988, chmn. mem. svcs. coun. 1989, chmn. chamber forums com. 1990, Outstanding Leadership award 1989), Corvallis C. of C. (v.p. fin. 1980-83, pres. 1985-86, chmn. bd. dirs. 1986-87, Econ. Devel. award 1978, Chmn. of Bd. award 1979, George award 1980-81, Devel. award 1983), Am. Inst. Banking (cert.), Rotary (bd. dirs. Corvallis club 1981-87, Bend 1988-94, Eugene, 1994—), Risk Mgmt. Assn., Chi Phi, Alpha Kappa Psi, Beta Gamma Sigma. Home: 2574 W 28th Ave Eugene OR 97405-1456 Office: Liberty Bank 355 Goodpasture Island Rd Eugene OR 97401 E-mail: mdrennan@elibertybank.com.

DRENNAN, ROBERT D. archeology educator, researcher; b. Lexington, Ky., Oct. 15, 1947; s. Robert M. and Ruth (Dickerson) D.; m. Jeanne Ferrary, May 3, 1974; 1 child, Margaret. BA in Art and Archeology, Princeton U., 1969; MA in Anthropology, U. Mich., 1970, PhD in Anthropology, 1975. Curator R.S. Peabody Found. Archeology, Andover, Mass., 1974-77; asst. prof. dept. anthropology U. Pitts., 1977-81, assoc. prof. dept. anthropology, 1981-87, prof. dept. anthropology, 1987—, chair dept. anthropology, 1996—99, 2000—03, faculty assoc. Ctr. Latin Am. Studies, 1977—, interim dir. Ctr. Latin Am. Studies, 1992-93, dir. Latin Am. Archeology Publs., 1988—. Assoc. rsch. scientist Mus. Anthropology U. Mich., Ann Arbor, 1976-80; adj. prof. dept. anthropology U. Nacional Colombia, Bogotá, 1988-89; vis. prof. dept. anthropology U. Los Andes, Bogotá, 1983—; rsch. assoc. sect. anthropology Carnegie Mus. Natural History, Pitts., 1978—; organizer, participant in archeol. meetings, confs.; presenter, rschr. in field. Author: Statistics for Archeologists: A Commonsense Approach, 1996, Las Sociedades Prehispanicas del Alto Magdalena, 2000; contbr. numerous articles to profl. jours. Fellow AAAS; mem. Am. Anthropol. Assn. (exec. com. archeology sect., program editor 1986-88), Soc. Am. Archeology (mem. editl. adv. com. Lat. Am. Antiquity 1989-93, mem. editl. bd. 1996—; chair task force Lat. Am. 1993-95; mem. com. on Ams. 1997—, chair 1995-97). Office: U Pittsburgh Dept Anthropology Pittsburgh PA 15260

DRENNEN, WILLIAM MILLER, JR., cultural administrator, film executive, producer, director, mineral resource executive; b. Charleston, W.Va., Nov. 5, 1942; s. William Miller and Margaret (Morton) D.; m. Sarah Polk Wilson, Nov. 27, 1969; children: Zachary Polk, Samuel Boyd. BArch., Yale U., 1964; postgrad., George Washington U., 1977, U. Charleston, 1978, W.Va. Grad. Coll., 1989-92, MA in Humanities, 1993. Freelance writer, film maker, 1967-69; v.p. Communication Corps, Inc., Washington, 1969-79; pres. Briar Mountain Coal and Coke Co., Charleston, 1980-89; founder, pres. Max Media, Inc., Charleston, 1984-89; commr. W.V. Culture and History Div., 1989—97; instr. history W.Va. State Coll., 1997—2001; freelance writer, prodr., cons., 2001—. Mng. gen. ptnr. C&D Enterprises, 1979—; pres. Cox Morton Co., 1980-89; past pres., founder W.Va. Internat. Film Festival, Charleston, 1986-89. Cameraman (film) Evolving Environment, 1972 (Cine Golden Eagle award); editor (film) River of Life, 1975 (U.S. Film Festival award); patentee computerized optical system. Founder, pres. W.Va. Youth Soccer Assn., 1979-84; bd. dirs. Sunrise Mus., Charleston, 1983-86, Renaissance Com., Charleston, 1984-89, Jefferson Co. Hist. Soc., 2002—, Contemporary Am. Theatre Festival, 2002—; mem. Pare Lorentz award panel Internat. Documentary Assn.; trustee U. Charleston, 1985-89; founder W.Va. Assn. Mus., 1990; v.p., sec. W.Va. History Film Project, Inc., 1991-97. Served in USN, 1964-67. Decorated Bronze Star; recipient 2 Cine Eagle awards, cert. Excellence for documentary film work, award Hist. Landmarks Commn. Kanawha County, Tele award, 1997. Mem. Film Arts Guild W.Va. (pres. 1981-87), Orgn. Am. Historians, Am. Hist. Assn., W.V. Hist. Soc., Shepherdstown Rotary, Cress Creek Golf and Country Club. Democrat. Episcopalian. Avocations: tennis, golf, mountain biking, jogging. E-mail: wdrenjr@aol.com., wdrenjr@msn.com.

DRENNON-GALA, DONNEY THOMAS, sociologist, educational consultant, writer; b. Rochester, N.Y., Dec. 20, 1953; s. Donney Lamar and Anna Marie Drennon; m. Katy Rodriguez Gala, May 10, 1980; stepchildren: William G. Bosch, Stephen Bosch, S. Anita Bosch. AAS, Monroe C.C., Rochester, 1974; BS, Rochester Inst. Tech., 1978; MA, U. Ctrl. Okla., 1982; MS in Edn., U. Rochester, 1988, PhD, 1994. Fed. officer Fed. Bur. Prisons, U.S. Dept. Justice, 1983-85, correctional treatment specialist, 1989—; pres. Paragon Homes, Inc., Rochester, N.Y., 1985-88; exec. dir. Fundamental Rsch. and Evaln. in Edn., Inc., Chattanooga, 1999—. Mem. bd. Chattanooga Area Law Enforcement Commn., 1991-2000; assoc. prof. U. N.C., Fayetteville (N.C.) State U., 1995-97; owner, ednl. cons., sociologist practitioner Drennon-Gala & Assocs., Chattanooga, 1995—. Reviewer Free Inquiry in Creative Sociology, 1992—; author: Delinquency and High School Dropouts: Reconsidering Social Correlates, 1995; assoc. editor Free Inquiry in Creative Sociology, 1996—99; contbr. ; contbr.: Sociological Abstracts, 1997, Sociol. Practice, 1999—, Tchg. Sociology, 1999—, Social Commentary, 1999—; contbr. ; Corrections: A Comprehensive View, 2001, Educating All Learners: Refocusing on the Comprehensive Support Model, 2002, Free Inquiry in Creative Sociology, 2002—; contbr. . Bd. dirs. Friends of Moccasin Bend Nat. Park, Chattanooga, 1997—. Sgt. USAF, 1976-80, sgt. USAFR, 1980-82. Master: Masons; mem.: Soc. Profl. Journalists, The Authors Guild, Inc., Acad. Criminal Justice Scis., Am. Correctional Assn. (profl. II), Am. Soc. Criminology, Am. Sociol. Assn., Pi Gamma Mu, Kappa Delta Pi, Alpha Phi Sigma. Avocation: writing. Office: PO Box 302 Chattanooga TN 37343-0302 E-mail: ddgala@doctor.com., ddgala1@comcast.net.

DRENTEA, PATRICIA, educator, researcher; b. Cleve., Sept. 20, 1967; d. Cornell and Dominique Drentea; m. Paul William Tybor, Dec. 28, 1996; 1 child, Hope Elena Drentea-Tybor. BA, U. Wis., 1989; MA, Ohio State U., 1994, PhD, 1999. Rschr. The Lerner Publs. Co., Mpls., 1990—92; rsch. asst. The Ohio State U., Columbus, 1992—99; asst. prof. U. Ala., Birmingham, 1999—. Assoc. scholar Lister Hill Ctr. for Health Policy, Birmingham, 2000—; scientist Ctr. for Aging, Birmingham, 2000—. Contbr. articles to profl. jours. Grantee, U. Ala., Birmingham, 2002—03; Survey Rsch. fellow, The Ohio State U., 1998. Mem.: Sociologists for Women in Soc., Am. Sociol. Soc. Office: Univ Ala Birmingham U 239-I 1530 3rd Ave S Birmingham AL 35294-3350 Office Fax: 205-975-5614. E-mail: pdrentea@uab.edu.

DREPAUL, LORIS OMESH, internist, infectious diseases physician; b. Georgetown, Guyana, Feb. 6, 1960; naturalized U.S. citizen; s. Frank Eric and Iris Ismay Etwaria (Masih-Das) D. BA (honors in philosophy)/BS, Bklyn. Coll., CUNY, 1985; MD, NYU, 1989. Diplomate Am. Bd. Internal Medicine. Intern St. Luke's Hosp.-Columbia U. Coll. Physicians and Surgeons, N.Y.C., 1989-90, resident in internal medicine, 1990-91, Booth Meml. Med. Ctr.-NYU Sch. Medicine, Queens, 1991-92; fellow in infectious diseases Bronx (N.Y.) VA Med. Ctr.-Mt. Sinai Sch. Medicine, 1992-94; attending in infectious diseases Mary Immaculate Hosp, Queens, Cath. Med. Ctr.-Albert Einstein Coll. Medicine, Bronx, 1995-96; mem. faculty, attending in infectious diseases Highland Hosp., Rochester, N.Y., 1997-98; pvt. practice, Rochester, 1997-98. Founder HIV/AIDS Bilingual Primary Care Outreach Program, Bridge Plaza Rehab. Clinic, Queens, N.Y., 1995-96; med. dir. Cmty. Health Network, Inc., Rochester, 1997-98. Mem. AMA, ACP, Med. Soc. State N.Y., Phi Beta Kappa. Avocations: music, bridge, chess, soccer, computers. E-mail: drepaul@pol.net.

DRESBACH, DAVID PHILIP, financial consultant, educator; b. Columbus, Ohio, Feb. 23, 1947; s. Donald Philip and Marilyn Jo (Armstrong) D.; m. Vicki Elaine Smith, Feb. 25, 1966 (div. 1980); children: Chad, Andrew; m. Mary Louise Mathes, Nov. 29, 1980. MA, Ohio U., 1972. Adminstr. Ohio Univ., Athens, 1969-73; regional mgr. State of Ohio, Columbus, 1973-77, adminstr., 1977-79, State of Minn., St. Paul, 1979-82; mgr. Evensen Dodge, Inc., Mpls., 1983-84, v.p., 1985-93, Springsted, Inc., St. Paul, 1993-95, coord. higher edn. group, 1993-95, newsletter editl. bd. mem., 1994; pres. Dresbach & Assocs., Inc., St. Paul, 1995—; sr. v.p. Evensen Dodge Investment Advisors, 2000—03, mgr., 2001—03; sr. mng. cons. Pub. Fin. Mgmt., 2003—. Lectr., adj. prof. Ohio U., Athens, 1969-74, Franklin U., Columbus, 1975, Columbus Tech. Inst., 1976-79, Met. State U., Mpls., 1980, U. Minn., Mpls., 1980-84. Author poetry anthologies, 1970, 90, 91, 93; contbr. articles to profl. jours. Soccer coach, chmn. Grove City Kids Assn., 1977-79; chmn. Dakota County Solid Waste Mgmt. Com., Minn, 1999—. Named Boss of Yr. Am. Businesswomen's Assn., St. Paul, 1980. Mem. Nat. Coun. Higher Edn. Loan Programs, Minn. Soc. Inst. CFPs (bd. dirs.), Am. Assn. Individual Investors, Fin. Planning Assn., Minn. Fin. Planning Assn. (pres. 2000, chair 2001, chair Dakota County Solid Waste Mgmt. adv. com. 2000-), Mpls. Inst. Art, Acad. Am. Poets. Avocations: reading, oil painting, sailing, golf. Office: Dresbach & Assocs Inc 710 Mager Ct Ste 100 Saint Paul MN 55118-4356 E-mail: DPandme@worldnet.att.net.

DRESBACH, MARY LOUISE, state educational administrator; b. St. Paul, Feb. 17, 1950; d. Ernest Joseph and Kathryn Marion (Lauer) Mathes; m. David Philip Dresbach, Nov. 29, 1980. BA, Coll. St. Catherine, 1972; postgrad., U. St. Thomas, 1979-80; MA, Coll. of St. Catherine, 1995. Tchr. St. Paul Pub. Schs., 1974-78; dir. cmty. outreach, human resources and agy. svcs. Minn. Higher Edn. Svcs. Office, St. Paul, 1978—. Speaker Minn. Quality Conf., 1994, chair, 1996. Contbg. author Leading Edge Newsletter. Mem. exec. steering com. Minn. Quality Coll., 1998. Mem.: Assn. for Psychol. Type, Internat. Pers. Mgmt. Assn. (Minn. chpt.), Minn. Coun. Mgrs. (chair 1998), Minn. Ctr. for Women in Govt., Dakota County Quality Initiative, Dakota County Quality Coun., Minn. Quality Initiative, Am. Soc. for Quality, Nat. Assn. Exec. Women, Am. Bus. Womens Assn. (sec. 1979—80), Citizens League-Minn., Met. Mus. Art, Mpls. Inst. Arts, AAUW, Pi Gamma Mu, Phi Beta Kappa.

DRESCHER, DENNIS GEORGE, biochemist, researcher; b. Milw., Wis., Mar. 26, 1942; s. George Gustave and Lillian Frances (Wendlandt) Drescher; m. Marian Jean Partridge, Feb. 1, 1969; children: David Alan, Andrew Jeremy. BS, U. Wis., 1963, MusM, 1964, PhD, 1971; postgrad studies, Harvard U., 1964-66. Rsch. assoc. Ctrl. Inst. for the Deaf, St. Louis, 1971-74; sr. staff fellow NIH, Bethesda, Md., 1974-78; prof. Wayne State U., Detroit, 1978—, dir. molecular rsch. Sch. Medicine, 1978—, chmn. Neurosci. Program. Mem. comm. disorders rev. com. NIH, Bethesda, 1987—90, hearing rsch. study sect., 1996—99, mem. ad hoc rev. coms., 2000—; mem. grant rev. bd. New Zealand Health Rsch. Coun., 1993—. Author: (book) Auditory Biochemistry, 1985; mem. editl. bd.: Hearing Rsch. Jour., 1989—, mem. guest rev. bd.: Jour. Brain Rsch., 1990—. Recipient Senator Jacob K. Javits Neuroscience Investigator Award, NIH, 1986-1990, Claude Pepper Award, Nat. Inst. on Deafness and Other Communication Disorders, NIH, 1990-1994, Intergovernmental Pers. Act Award, NIH, 1990-1991, Wayne State U. Bd. of Governors Faculty Recognition Award, 1987; grantee Rsch. Grant, Identification of Acoustico-Lateralis Transmitters, NIH, 1980-present, Internat. Symposium on Auditory Biochemistry Conf. Grant, 1984-1986. Mem.: Assn. Rsch. in Otolaryngology, Acoustical Soc. Am., Soc. Neurosci., Am. Soc. Neurochemistry, Am. Soc. Biol. Chemists. Achievements include first purification of an inner-ear enzyme; research in inner-ear calcium channels. Avocation: pianist. Home: 461 University Pl Detroit MI 48230-1637 Office: Wayne State U Sch of Medicine 540 E Canfield St Detroit MI 48201-1928

DRESCHER, JACK, psychoanalyst, psychiatrist; b. N.Y.C., Aug. 28, 1951; s. Mayer and Dora (Gajer) D. BA, Bklyn. Coll., 1972; MD, U. Mich., 1980. Diplomate Am. Bd. Psychiatry & Neurology. Internship in psychiatry St. Vincent's Med. Ctr., N.Y.C., 1980-81; residency in psychiatry SUNY Downstate, Bklyn., 1981-83, chief resident in psychiatry, 1983-84, clin. instr. psychiatry, 1984-87, clin. asst. prof. psychiatry, 1987—; dir. affective disorder clinic Downstate Med. Hygiene Assn., Bklyn., 1989-93; pvt. practice N.Y.C., 1985—. Assoc. med. dir. HIV svc. William A. White Psychoanalytic Inst., N.Y.C., 1993-97. Author: Psychoanalytic Therapy and the Gay Man, 1998; editor-in-chief Jour. Gay and Lesbian Psychotherapy; contbr. chpts. to books and articles to profl. jours. Founding mem. Network Profl. Orgns., N.Y.C., 1985. Fellow Am. Acad. Psychoanalysis (trustee 1997-2000), Am. Psychiat. Assn. (disting., past pres. N.Y. br. 2000-01, fellowship award 1995); mem. AMA, Group for Advancement of Psychiatry, William A. White Psychoanalytic Soc. (tng. and supervisory analyst), Am. Coll. Psychiatrists. Avocations: theater, opera, foreign travel, speaking italian. Office: 440 W 24th St Apt 1A New York NY 10011-1350

DRESCHER, JOHN WEBB, lawyer; b. Norfolk, Va., May 13, 1948; s. Otto Charles and Anne Best (Webb) D.; m. Dale McKeithan Moore, June 13, 1970; 1 child, Ryan. BA, Hampden-Sydney Coll., 1970; JD, U. Richmond, 1973. Bar: Va. 1973, U.S. Supreme Ct. 1980, U.S. Ct. Appeals (4th cir.) 1985, U.S. Dist. Ct. (ea. dist.) Va. 1976. Assoc. Brydges, Hammers & Hudgins, Virginia Beach, 1973-74; asst. atty. Office of Commonwealth Atty., Virginia Beach, 1974-75; assoc. Pickett, Spain & Lyle, P.C., Virginia Beach, 1976-78; ptnr. Pickett, Lyle, Siegel, Drescher & Croshaw P.C., Virginia Beach, 1979-87, Breit, Drescher & Imprevento, P.C., Norfolk, 1988—. Trustee Hampden-Sydney Coll., 2003—. Named among best lawyers in Am. Naifeh & Smith, 1995—. Fellow Am. Bd. Trial Advocates; mem. ATLA, Va. Trial Lawyers Assn. (bd. govs. 1990—), Am. Inns Ct., Norfolk-Portsmouth Bar Assn., Hampden-Sydney Alumni Assn. (pres. 1990), U. Richmond Law Sch. Alumni Assn., Virginia Beach Bar Assn. (pres.

1990). Democrat. Episcopalian. Avocations: physical fitness, golf. Home: 925 Holladay Pt Virginia Beach VA 23451-3912 Office: Breit Drescher & Imprevento 1000 Dominion Twr 999 Waterside Dr Ste 1000 Norfolk VA 23510-3304 E-mail: jdrescher@breitdrescher.com.

DRESCHER, JUDITH ALTMAN, library director; b. Greensburg, Pa., July 6, 1946; d. Joseph Grier and Sarah Margaret (Hewitt) Altman; m. Robert A. Drescher, Aug. 10, 1968 (div. 1980); m. David G. Lindstrom, Jan. 10, 1981. AB, Grove City Coll., 1968; MLS, U. Pitts., 1971. Tchr. Hempfield Sch. Dist., Greensburg, 1968-71; children's libr. Cin. Pub. Libr., 1971-72; br. mgr. Cin. Pub. LIbrary, 1972-74; dir. Rolling Meadows (Ill.) Pub. Libr., 1974-79, Champaign (Ill.) Pub. Libr., 1979-85, Memphis/Shelby County Pub. Libr. and Info. Ctr., 1985—. Cons. Providence Assocs., Dallas, 1986-94; Tenn. del. White House Conf. on Librs. and Info. Svcs. Task Force, 1991-92; mem. Tenn. Sec. of State's Commn. on Tech. and Resource Sharing, 1991, 93, steering com. Tenn. Info. and Infrastructure, 1994-97, nat. adv. panel for assessment of role of sch. and pub. librs. U.S. Dept. Edn., 1995-98. Commn. on 21st century Rhodes Coll., Memphis, 1986-88, presdl. adv. com., 1992-2000; active Leadership Memphis, 1987—, selection com., 1992-96; active Memphis Arts Coun., 1989-94; bd. dirs. Literacy Coun., 1986-91, Memphis NCCJ, 1989-93, Memphis Grants Info. Ctr., 1992-97, sec., 1993-95; bd. dirs. Memphis Literacy Found., 1988-92, v.p., 1989-90; bd. dirs. Goals for Memphis, 1988-93, chair edn. com., 1989-91, chair nominating com., 1992, leadership acad., 1999—; bd. dirs. U. Memphis Soc., 1998—; bd. dirs. Cmty. Svcs. Agy., 2002-; exec. adv. bd. Children's Mus., 1988-94, exec. adv. coun. U. Memphis, 1989-99; allocations subcom. United Way, 1989-91, allocations com. Memphis Arts Coun., 100 for the Arts, 1989-91, Libr. Self-study Com. U. Memphis; pres. adv. coun. Lemoyne Coll.; search com. for dean librs. U. Memphis, 1999-2001; adv. com. Memphis Symphony Orch., 2003—. Paul Harris fellow Rotary, Memphis, 2002; recipient Govt. Leader award U. Ill. YWCA, 1981, Communicator of Yr. award Pub. Rels. Soc. Am., 1992, Humanitarian award NCCJ, Memphis, 2003, Charlie Robinson award Pub. Libr. Assn., 2003; named Libr. Coun. Libr. of Yr., 2002-. Mem.: ALA (chmn. intellectual freedom com. 1985—87, mem. coun. 1992—99, mem. nominating com. 2001—02), Assn. Pub. Adminstrs. (midsouth chpt., Adminstr. of Yr. 2002), Pub. Libr. Assn. (v.p., pres. 1994—95), Memphis Libr. Coun., Urban Librs. Coun., Tenn. Libr. Assn., Rotary (bd. dirs. 1992—94, sec. 1993—94, chair membership devel. com. 1994—95), Beta Phi Mu. Home: 1505 Vance Ave Memphis TN 38104-3810 Office: Memphis Shelby County Pub Libr & Info Ctr 3030 Poplar Ave Memphis TN 38111

DRESCHER, SEYMOUR, history educator, writer; b. N.Y.C., Feb. 20, 1934; s. Sidney and Eva Rita (Levine) D.; m. Ruth Lieberman, June 19, 1955; children: Michael, Jonathan, Karen. BA, CCNY, 1955; MS, U. Wis., 1956, PhD, 1960. Instr. history Harvard U., 1960—62; asst. prof. U. Pitts., 1962—65, assoc. prof., 1965—69, prof., 1969—86, Univ. prof., 1986—, chmn., 1980—83; acad. dean. semester-at-sea, 1998, 2002. Vis. disting. prof. CUNY, 1987; Roger T. Anstey Meml. lectr., Canterbury, Eng., 1984; bd. advisors Slavery and Abolition, 1985—; George A. Miller lectr., 1987, Pa. Commonwealth Speakers Program, 1989-91, rsch. fellow Univ. Ctr. Internat. Studies, Pitts., 1992, 00; C-SPAN adv. com., Tocqueville. Author: Tuqueville and England, 1964, Dilemmas of Democracy, 1968, Econocide, 1977, Capitalism and Antislavery, 1986, From Slavery to Freedom, 1999, The Mighty Experiment: Free Labor versus Slavery in British Emancipation, 2002; co-author: The Abolition of Slavery and the Aftermath of Emancipation in Brazil, 1988; editor Jour. Contemporary History, 1991-99; editor: Tocqueville and Beaumont on Social Reform, 1968, Anti-Slavery, Religion and Reform, 1980, Political Symbolism in Modern Europe, 1982, The Meaning of Freedom, 1992, A Historical Guide to World Slavery, 1998, Slavery, 2001, Tocqueville's Memoir on Pauperism, 1997; contbr.: Fifty Years Later: Antislavery, Capitalism and Modernity in the Dutch Orbit, 1995, Is the Holocaust Unique?, 1996, Jews and the Expansion of Europe to the West, 2001; creator film: Confrontation, Paris, 1968, 70. Recipient Pres.'s Rsch. award U. Pitts., 1992; Fulbright scholar, 1957-58; NEH fellow, 1973-74, Guggenheim Found. fellow, 1977-78, Resident fellow Bellagio Ctr. for Scholars, 1980, 90, Woodrow Wilson fellow, 1983-84, sec. European program Wilson Ctr., 1984-85. Mem. Am. Hist. Assn., Hist. Soc., Soc. for French Hist. Studies (v.p. 1978-79), N.Am. Conf. on Brit. Studies, Dutch Royal Inst. Linguistics and Anthropology, Fulbright Assn., Commn. Tocqueville (France). Home: 5550 Pocusset St Pittsburgh PA 15217-1913 Office: U Pitts Dept History Pittsburgh PA 15260

DRESCHHOFF, GISELA AUGUSTE MARIE, physicist, educator; b. Moenchengladbach, Germany, Sept. 13, 1938; came to U.S., 1967, naturalized, 1976; d. Gustav Julius and Hildegard Friederike (Krug) D. PhD, Tech. U. Braunschweig (Ger.), 1972. Staff scientist Fed. Inst. Physics and Tech. Ger., 1965-67; research assoc. Kans. Geol. Survey, Lawrence, 1971-72; vis. asst. prof. physics U. Kans., 1972-74; dep. dir. radiation physics lab. Space Tech. Ctr., 1972-78, assoc. dir., 1979-84, co-dir., 1984-86, dir., 1996—; sr. sci. geology U. Kans., 1991, adj. assoc. prof. physics and astronomy, 1992. Assoc. program mgr. NSF, Washington, 1978-79. Patentee identification markings for gemstones and method of making selective conductive regions in diamond layers. Named to Women's Hall of Fame, U. Kans., 1978; recipient Antarctic Service medal U.S.A., 1979; recipient NASA Group Achievement award, 1983. Fellow Explorers Club; mem. AAAS, Am. Phys. Soc., Am. Geophys. Union, Am. Polar Soc. (pres. 2000-03), Antarctican Soc., Sigma Xi. Home: 2908 W 19th St Lawrence KS 66047-2301 Office: U Kans Dept Physics & Astronomy Lawrence KS 66045-7541 E-mail: giselad@ku.edu.

DRESEN, STEVEN PAUL, music educator; b. Milw., May 11, 1962; s. James Joseph and Judith Sue Dresen; m. Angela Marie Farmer; children: Catherine, Jacob, Nathan, Natasha, Anneka. AA, Ricks Coll., 1985; BA Music Edn., Utah State U., 1990; MMus Choral Conducting, Brigham Young U., 1996. Tchr. South Fremont H.S., St. Anthony, Idaho, 1990—94; tchg. asst. Brigham Young U., Provo, Utah, 1994—96; tchr. Ricks Coll., Rexburg, Idaho, 1996—99; adj. vocal faculty Brigham Young University-Idaho, Rexburg, Idaho, 1999—; tchr. Bonneville H.S., Idaho Falls, 1999—. Co-founder Upper Valley Boy's Choir, Rexburg, IDAHO, 1998—99; co-dir. Upper Valley Civic Chorale, Rexburg, 1997—99. Dir.: (choral conducting graduate students) (Hallady Award, 1995). Fellow: Nat. Assn. of Teachers of Singing; mem.: Idaho Music Educator's Assn. (pres. 1992—94, dist. v.p. 2001—), Am. Choral Dirs. Assn. (life; state jr. coll. chair 1997—99), Gold Key (life), Music Educators Nat. Conf. (dist. v.p. 2001—). Mem. Church Of Jesus Christ Of Latter Day Saints. Avocation: reading, golf, music. Home: 363 East 2nd S Rexburg ID 83440 Office: Bonneville HS 3165 East Iona Rd Idaho Falls ID 83401 Home Fax: n/a; Office Fax: 208 523-7014. Personal E-mail: n/a.

DRESHER, PAUL JOSEPH, composer, music educator, performer; b. L.A., Jan. 8, 1951; s. Melvin J. and Martha (Whitaker) D.; m. Robin Naomi Kirck, Mar. 8, 1986 (dec. 1999); 1 child, Cole Kirck Dresher. MusB, U. Calif., Berkeley, 1977; MA in Composition, U. Calif., La Jolla, 1979. Prof. music Cornish Inst. Arts, Seattle, 1980-83; artistic dir. Paul Dresher Ensemble, Berkeley, 1984—. Cons. Nat. Endowment for the Arts, Calif. Arts Coun., 1982-94, Rockefeller Found. Composer: (opera) Slow Fire, 1987, Power Failure, 1989, (music theater) Pioneer, 1989, (orchestral work) Reaction, 1984; (chamber orch.) Cornucopia, 1990; (dances) Shelf Life, 1987, Age of Unrest, 1991, The Gates, 1993, Outawak, 1997, Kalasam, 2000; (trio) Double Ikat, 1989; (chamber) Din of Iniquity, 1994; (solo piano) Blue Diamonds, 1995, Violin Concerto (chamber), 1996-97, Elapsed Time (for violin and piano), 1998, (music theater) Sound Stage, 2001, (chamber) Cello Concerto Unequal Distemperament, 2001, (dance) In the Name, 2001; works presented by numerous symphonic and other orchs. including N.Y. Philharm. Munich State Opera, London Internat. Festival of Theatre; recordings on New Albion, Lovely, Starkland and New World labels. Bd. dirs. New Langton Arts Orgn., San Francisco, 1984-2002, Am. Music Ctr., 1994-2000. Recipient numerous grants NEA, 1979-2002; Fulbright grantee, 1984; Goddard Lieberson fellow, 1982. Mem. Broadcast Music, Inc., Am. Music Ctr., Opera America, Chamber Music America. Home and Office: 51 Avenida Dr Berkeley CA 94708-2145 E-mail: pauld@dresherensemble.org.

DRESKIN, ERVING ARTHUR, pathologist, educator; b. Jan. 9, 1919; s. Harry and Sarah Molly (Krulvetsky) D.; m. Jeanet Irma Steckler, May 9, 1943; children: Richard Burgas, Stephen Charles, Jeanet Elizabeth, Rena Lynn. BS, Tulane U., 1940, MD, 1943. Diplomate Am. Bd. Pathology, sub-specialty blood banking. Intern Newark Beth Israel Hosp., 1943-44; resident in pathology, instr. pathology U. Ill. Coll. Medicine, Chgo., 1946-49, Am. Cancer Soc. fellow, 1949-50; assoc. pathologist Grant Hosp., Chgo., 1949-50; chief pathologist, dir. labs. and Blood Bank Greenville (S.C.) Hosp. Sys., 1950-85; med. dir. Carolina-Ga. Blood Ctr., 1980—2001. Cons. pathologist to hosps.; clin. prof. pathology Med. U. S.C.; past pres., chmn., exec. com. Pathology Assocs., Greenville, Pa.; bd. dirs. United Way Greenville County, 1973-76; treas. Greater Greenville Community Found., 1980-81, bd. dirs., 1980-83; pres. Temple of Israel, Greenville, 1966-68, Community Found. Greater Greenville, 1990-91, Greenville County Arts Commn., 1993, 95. Lt. M.C., USNR, 1944-46. Recipient SC Order of the Palmetto, 1992. Fellow Am. Soc. Clin. Pathologists, Coll. Am. Pathologists (S.C. regional commr. for lab. accreditation); mem. AMA, Am. Assn. Blood Banks (v.p. 1962, sec. 1963-65, pres. 1965-66), S.C. Soc. Pathologists (pres. 1957-59), S.C. Med. Assn., Alpha Omega Alpha, Rotary (Paul Harris fellow), Poinsett Club. Home: 60 Lake Forest Dr Greenville SC 29609-5038 Office: Carolina-Georga Blood Ctr 515 Grove Rd Greenville SC 29605-4206

DRESSEL, IRENE EMMA RINGWALD, alcoholism and family therapist; b. Enderlin, N.D., Oct. 26, 1926; d. Albert William and Emma Anna Magdelena (Trapp) Ringwald; m. Clarence Irvin Dressel, Jr., Mar. 13, 1946 (div. Nov. 1972), 1 son, Keith Alan. Student pub. schs., Casselton, N.D. Cert. master addiction counselor, N.D.; cert. chem. dependency counselor, Minn. Alcoholism counseling trainee Heartview Found., Mandan, N.D., 1974-75, family therapy intern, 1975-76, family counselor, 1976-77, supr. family mems. program, 1978; designer, supr. family program The Meadows, Wickenburg, Ariz., 1978-79; treatment programs cons., dir. consultation dept. Johnson Inst., Mpls., 1979-81; designer, assoc. dir. chem. dependency unit Presbyn. Hosp., Oklahoma City, 1981-83; designer, supr. adolescent program United Recovery Ctr., Grand Forks, N.D., 1983-85; dir. Irene Dressel Counseling, Grand Forks, 1985-89; designer, program dir. The Dressel Ctr., Fargo, N.D., 1989-90; ret., 1990. FDR/DIR Your Level Best, 1996. Republican. Lutheran. E-mail: irenethebigid@aol.com.

DRESSEL, MARGARET JANE, artist, art educator; b. Brookline, Mass., Aug. 25, 1949; d. Chauncey Lovett Megargle and Esther Laura Field; m. Richard Dressel; children: Bethany, Keith. Student, Moore Coll. Art, 1967-68, Nat. Acad. Art, 1985-86; Assoc. in Occupl. Studies, Pratt Inst., 1985. Owner, artist Peggy Dressel Studio, Oakland, NJ, 1990—; graphic designer Intra Design Inc., Ramsey, NJ, 1990—94; illustrator, asst. Jacqui Morgan Studio, N.Y.C., 1986-90; painting instr. Ramsey Adult Sch., 1996—, Glen Rock (N.J.) Cmty. Sch., 1997—, Art Ctr. No. N.J., New Milford, 1999—2001. Founder Pastel Plus, N.J., pres., 1997—; mem. Blackwell St. Ctr. Arts; chmn. CAA Nat. Juried Exhbns., Ridgewood, N.J., 1993, 94, 95. One-woman shows include St. Peter's Ch., N.Y.C., 1992, Blackwell St. Gallery, Dover, N.J., 1994, Lena DiGangi Gallery, West Paterson, N.J., 1994, Ringwood Manor W. Wing Gallery, N.J. State Pk., 1994, ADP, Inc. Gallery, Roseland, N.J., 1995, Dow Jones & Co., S. Brunswick, N.J., 1994, 96; N.Y. Theol. Sem., N.Y.C., 1998, The Interch. Ctr., N.Y.C., 1998, Kurth Coll. Ridgewood, N.J., 2002; represented in numerous juried exhbns. and pvt. collections; illustrator mags., children's books, brochures, ads, posters; featured artist poster and calendar N.J. Fine Artist Collection, 1998. Recording sec. Oakland Libr. Bd., 1979-80, pres., 1980-82. Recipient Purchase award Degas Pastel Soc., 1992, Merit award Degas Pastel Soc., 1992, Cynthia Goodgal Meml., Ridgewood Art Inst., Nat. Bergen Mus., 1997, others; named Best in Show, Inserria Corp., 1992, Bergen Mus. Music & Art Festival, 2002. Mem. Cmty. Arts Assn. (pres. 1994-96), Southea. Pastel Soc. (signature mem.), Oreg. Pastel Soc. (signature mem.), Am. Artist Profl. League, Degas Pastel Soc. Democrat. Methodist. Avocations: art, music, traveling, gardening. Office: Peggy Dressel Studio 11 Rockaway Ave Oakland NJ 07436-2122 E-mail: pedgartist@aol.com.

DRESSER, MARY T. journalist; b. Chgo., Jan. 24, 1931; d. Bernard Alfred and Florence Harriet (Jorgensen) Rakers; m. David I. Dresser, June 4, 1952 (div. Dec. 1979); children: Michael, Jeanne, Charles, David, Christopher, Mary. Student, Marquette U., 1949—51; BA, Antioch U., 1990. Reporter, city editor Paddock Pub, Arlington Heights, Ill., 1965—69; writer FCC, Washington, 1970—71; info. writer PBS, Washington, 1972—75; news editor Internat. Union Elec. Workers, Washington, 1975—81; editor Internat. Union Bricklayers, Washington, 1984—91. Author: (novels) Stand Fast, 2002, Freedom's Cost, 2003, The Search for Betsy Cory, 2003. Recipient Writing and Editing award, Internat. Labor Commn., 1982, 1989; Study grant, Swedish Inst. Mem.: Nat. Writers Union, Newspaper Guild (sec. 1979—80, Front pg. award 1980, Reporting award 1978—79). Democrat. E-mail: DRESSERINK@aol.com.

DRESSER, NOREEN DEAN O'HARA, civilian army official, artist; b. Cleve., Jan. 2, 1952; d. Forrest James Dresser and Lorraine Anne Culliton. BA, Antioch Coll., 1977; MFA, Claremont Grad. Sch., 1984. Artist-in-residence Watts Towers Art Ctr., L.A., 1978-83; instr. Claremont (Calif.) Grad. Sch., 1983-84; mem. computer graphic planning dept. Western Divsn. Naval Facilities Engring. Command, San Mateo, Calif., 1985-92; realty specialist U.S. Army COE, L.A. and N.Y.C., 1992-98, chief mgmt. and disposal br. real estate divsn. N.Y.C., 1998. Mgr. woman program EEO-Army C.E., N.Y.C., and L.A., 1993-97; artist, spkr. panel of next generation feminist artists White Gallery, UCLA, 1996; v.p. So. Calif. Women's Caucus for Art, 1992-94, v.p. bd. dirs. 2000—. One-woman shows include Women's Bldg., L.A., 1980, W. Gallery, Claremont, Calif., 1984, Hatley Martin Gallery, San Francisco, 1986, 88, 90, Bade Mus., Berkley, Calif., 1987, Inst. Buddhist Studies, Gen. Theol. Union, Berkeley, 1989, Stanford (Calif.) U., 1991, San Francisco State U., 1992, Sch. Theology Claremont, 1993, Congregation Beth Simchat Torah, N.Y., 1995, La Mama's Gallery, N.Y.C., 1997, Gay Meml. Day, N.Y.C., 1999; exhibited in group shows Stella Polaris, L.A., 1983, Miami Valley Arts Coun., Dayton, Ohio, 1986, Calif. Inst. Living Arts, San Francisco, 1991, Spectrum Gallery, San Francisco, 1992, Crete, Greece, 1992, U. Calif., Northridge, 1992, Agnels Gate Cultural Ctr. Gallery, San Pedro, Calif., 1993, Orange County Contemporary Arts Ctr., Calif., 1993, Kohn Turner Gallery, L.A., 1994, Ctr. Arts, Irvine, Calif., 1994, Claremont Grad. Sch., 1994, Calif. State U., L.A., 1995, Holocaust Installation Capital, Washington, 1996, Congregation Beth Cimchat Toray, N.Y.C., 1996, Judson Meml. Ch., N.Y.C., 1997, Richard Anderson Gallery, N.Y.C., 1999, Coll. Art Assn., N.Y., 2000, Air Gallery, N.Y., 2000. Freedom writer Amnesty Internat., Calif., 1992—. Recipient medal Gen King, N.Y.C., 1995. Mem. Coll. Art Assn. (co-chmn. N.Y. exhbn. Gay and Lesbian caucus 2000), Irish Gay and Lesbian Orgn. Jewish. Home: 127 Ludlow St Apt 2C New York NY 10002-3256 Fax: 212-264-0230. E-mail: deand@attglobal.net.

DRESSLER, ALAN MICHAEL, astronomer; b. Cin., Mar. 23, 1948; s. Charles and Gay (Stein) Dressler. BA in Physics, U. Calif., Berkeley, 1970; PhD in Astronomy, U. Calif., Santa Cruz, 1976. Carnegie Instn. of Washington fellow Hale Obs., Pasadena, Calif., 1976-78, Las Campanas fellow, 1978-81; sci. staff Carnegie Obs. (formerly Mt. Wilson and Las Campanas Obs., formerly Hale Obs.), Pasadena, 1981—, acting assoc. dir., 1988-89. Chair origins subcomS NASA, 2000—03. Contbr. to sci. jours. Recipient Pub. Svcs. medal NASA 1999. Fellow Am. Acad. Arts and Scis.; mem. NAS, Am. Astron. Soc. (councilor 1989-91, Pierce prize 1983), Internat. Astron. Union. Office: Carnegie Obs 813 Santa Barbara St Pasadena CA 91101-1232

DRESSLER, DAVID CHARLES, retired aerospace company executive; b. Cleve., June 21, 1928; s. Walter Carl and Beatrice (Albin) D.; m. Dorothea Walker, Dec. 22, 1950; children: David Charles, Bradley, Christopher. BA, Yale U., 1950; grad., Advanced Mgmt. Program, Harvard Bus. Sch., 1973. With Armstrong Cork Co., 1950-51; with Martin Marietta Corp., 1953-92, pres. Master Builders div., 1977-80, pres. Martin Marietta Chem. Co., 1979-81, corp. v.p., 1979-83, sr. corp. v.p., 1983-92; pres. Master Builders Co. Ltd., Toronto, 1977-81, Martin Marietta Aluminum, 1982-85; chmn. bd. Internat. Light Metals, 1985-91; pres. Martin Marietta Materials, Bethesda, Md., 1985-91. Chmn. bd. Martin Marietta Ordnance Sys., 1985—87; chmn. corp. com. Corcoran Mus. Art, 1992; bd. dir. Bowles Fluidics; pres. Dressler Corp., 2001. Served to capt. USMCR, 1951-53. Mem. Congl. Country Club (Washington) (mem. bd. govs. 1990-96), Harvard Bus. Sch. Club (pres. Washington club 1983, chmn. bd. dirs. 1984), Sawgrass Country Club (Ponte Vedra), Phi Beta Kappa. Episcopalian.

DRESSLER, DAVID MICHAEL, psychiatrist; b. Chgo., May 9, 1939; BA, Reed Coll., 1960; MD, U. Chgo., 1964. Diplomate Am. Bd. Psychiatry. Intern San Francisco Gen. Hosp., 1964-65; resident Strong Meml. Hosp., Rochester, N.Y., 1965-68; fellow Yale U., New Haven, 1968-69, asst. prof. psychiatry, 1969-73, chief psychiatry New Britain (Conn.) Gen. Hosp., 1973-92; pvt. practice Woodbury, Conn., 1992—. Office: 51 Sherman Hill Rd Woodbury CT 06798-3648

DRESSLER, MARK CHRISTOPHER, writer; b. Phila., Aug. 1, 1955; s. Bernard Michael and Dolores Marie D. BA, Temple U., 1980. Mideast-related writer, Washington, 1983—87; asst. news editor Castro Valley (Calif.) Forum, 1990-94; newspaper corr. King of Prussia (Pa.) Post, 1995-97; TV govt. corr. UMGA-TV, Montgomery County, Pa., 1997-98; writer Springfield Twp. Enterprise, Montgomery County, 1998—. Mem. Soc. of Profl. Journalists. Avocations: seeing movies, videos, music, conversation. Home. 69 Grove Ave Flourtown PA 19031 E-mail: M1C1D@cs.com.

DRESSLER, OSCAR H. music educator; b. Encarnacion, Itapua, Paraguay, Nov. 17, 1960; s. Reños Dressler and Ilsa Duré; m. Cristina O. Tinao, Apr. 25, 1987; children: Rocio Belen, Mathias Daniel. B in Ch. Music, Internat. Bapt. Theol. Sem., 1986; MusM, Southwestern Bapt. Theol. Sem., 1992, D of Musical Arts in Piano Performance, 1995. Cert. music tchr. Tex., 2001. Asst. prof. music Seminario Internacional Teologico Bautista, Buenos Aires, 1986—90, Ateneo Paraguayo Sch. of Music, Asuncion, Paraguay, 1996—97; tchr. music Steppingstone Christian Acad., Burleson, Tex., 1997—2000; head music dept. Hill Sch., Ft. Worth, 1999—; assoc. pastor music and worship Villa Morra Bapt. Ch., Asuncion, 1996—97. Adj. tchr. piano, artists-in-residence Tex. Wesleyan U./, Ft. Worth, 1998—2000; adj. tchr. piano Southwestern Bapt. Theol. Sem., 2000—02. Author: Teaching Piano to Students with Learning Disabilities. Assoc. min. of music and pianist First Bapt. Ch., Benbrook, Tex., 1997—2002. Recipient Wayne Polly McNeely Piano award, Southwestern Bapt. Theol. Sem., 1992, Academic Achievement award, 1992, 1995; fellow, 1991—95; scholar, U. Music Mozarteum of Salzburg, 1992, Southwestern Bapt. Theol. Sem., 1991, 1992, 1993, 1994, 1995. Mem.: Ft. Worth Music Tchrs. Assn., Tex. Music Tchrs. Assn., Music Tchrs. Nat. Assn., Music Educators Nat. Conf. Achievements include Introduction of piano studies as part of the music curriculum for students with learning disabilities at Hill School of Fort Worth; research in effects and impact on learning skills of piano instruction in students with learning disabilities. Home: 1413 High Ridge Rd Benbrook TX 76126 Office: Hill Sch Ft Worth 4817 Odessa Ave Fort Worth TX 76133 Home Fax: 817-249-2273. Personal E-mail: odressler@msn.com.

DRESSLER, ROBERT A. lawyer; b. Fort Lauderdale, Fla., Aug. 20, 1945; s. R. Philip and Elisabeth Dressler; children: James Philip, Kathryn S. AB cum laude, Dartmouth Coll., 1967; JD cum laude, Harvard U., 1973. Bar: Mass. 1973, Fla. 1974, D.C. 1980, U.S. Dist. Ct. (so. dist.) Fla., U.S. Dist. Ct. Mass., U.S. Ct. Appeals (1st cir.), U.S. Ct. Appeals (5th cir.), U.S. Supreme Ct. Assoc. Goodwin, Proctor & Hoar, Boston, 1973-75; ptnr. Dressler & Dressler, Ft. Lauderdale, 1975-82; mayor City of Ft. Lauderdale, 1982-86; pvt. practice law Ft. Lauderdale, 1982—. Bd. regents State Univ. System, 1987-93; mem. Estate Planning Coun. Broward County; adv. com. Fla. Atlantic U., Broward, 1989—; exec. com. Tchr. Edn. Alliance, 1991-2000. Capt USMC, 1969-72. Named Person of Yr. Fla. Atlantic U., 1993. Mem. Greater Ft. Lauderdale C.of C. (bd. govs. 1982-89), Broward County Bar Assn., Fla. Bar Assn., D.C. Bar Assn., Vietnam Vets. Am., Rotary Internat., Tower Forum (bd. govs. 1983--), Phi Beta Kappa. Presbyterian. Avocations: jogging, scuba diving, hiking. Home: 1215 E Broward BlvdSuite 201 Fort Lauderdale FL 33301 Office: PO Box 2425 Fort Lauderdale FL 33303-2425

DRESSNER, PAUL ROBERT, outside sales and customer service representative; b. Chester, Pa., Feb. 1, 1955; s. Robert Lodge and Mary Louise (Rutt) D.; m. Donna Ellen Smith, June 1, 1980 (div. Feb. 1990); children: Robert Warren, Christopher Ryan. BS in Hotel and Restaurant Mgmt., U. Wis., Stout, 1977. Asst. mgr. Morrisons Cafeteria, Columbia, S.C., 1977-79, Florence, S.C., 1979-80, Wilmington, N.C., 1980-83; night mgr. ARA Svcs., Greensboro, N.C., 1983-84, food svc. dir. Sewanee, Tenn., 1984-86, Americus, Ga., 1986, Frankfort, Ky., 1987, Cleveland, Tenn., 1987-88, Wilmington, N.C., 1988-89; mgr. Dressner's Village Cafe, St. Simons Island, Ga., 1989-90; customer svc. rep., svc. mgr. Island Automotive, St. Simons Island, 1990-95; outside salesman Brooks Auto Parts, Brunswick, Ga., 1995—. Active Coastal Symphony Ga. Named one of Outstanding Young Men of Am., 1985. Avocations: restoring trucks, playing trombone. Home: PO Box 24206 Saint Simons GA 31522-7206

DREW, BERNARD ALGER, writer; b. West Stewartstown, N.H., Jan. 16, 1950; s. Warren Alger and Jennie Roberta (Rose) D.; m. Donna Marie Archambault, July 16, 1977; children: Jessie, Darcie. BA, Northeastern U., 1973. Asst. editor Mart Mag., Pittsfield, Mass., 1973-75; pub. rels. coord. Berkshire Learning Ctr., Pittsfield, 1975-76; freelance writer, 1976-80; reporter, editor Berkshire Courier, Great Barrington, Mass., 1980-96; freelance writer, editor Great Barrington, 1996—. Author: 100 Most Popular Young Adult Authors, 1996, Great Barrington: Great Town * Great History, 1999, A Berkshire Photo Album, 1999, A Century of Headlines, 2000, 100 More Popular Young Adult Authors, 2002; copy editor Lakeville Jour., 1996-. Pres. Great Barrington Hist. Soc., 1982-84; pres. Berkshire County Hist. Soc., Pittsfield, 1986-88; chmn. Great Barrington Hist. Dist. Commn., 1989-98; vol. Housatonic Riverwalk, Great Barrington, 1993—; treas. Upper Housatonic Valley Nat. Heritage Area, Inc. Mem. Soc. Indsl. Archaeology, Great Barrington Land Conservancy, Thoreau Soc. Congregationalist. Avocations: collecting autographs, hiking, photography. Home: 24 Gilmore Ave Great Barrington MA 01230-1438

DREW, CLIFFORD JAMES, university administrator, special education and educational psychology educator; b. Eugene, Oregon, Mar. 9, 1943; s. Albert C. and Violet M. (Caskey) D. BS magna cum laude, Eastern Oreg. Coll., 1965; EdM, U.Ill., 1966; PhD (hon.), U. Oreg., 1968. Asst. prof. edn. Kent State U., Ohio, 1968-69; asst. prof. dir. rsch. and spl. edn. U. Tex., Austin, Tex., 1969-71; assoc. prof. spl. edn. U. Utah, Salt Lake City, 1971-76, prof., 1977—; asst. dean Grad. Sch. Edn., 1974-77, assoc. dean, 1977-79, 89-95, prof. spl. edn., ednl. psychology, 1979—, coord. instrnl. tech., acad. v.p. office, 1995-97, assoc. acad. v.p., 1997—. Cons. HEW, 1969-80; bd. dir. Far West Lab. Ednl. Rsch. and Devel., San Francisco, 1974-80; mem. exec. bd. Salt Lake County Assn. Retarded Children, 1971-72; mem. adv. com. Mental Retardation Counseling Svc., Tex. Dept. Mental Health Mental Retardation, 1969-70. Co-author (with P. Chinn and D. Logan): Mental Retardation: A Life Cycle Approach, 1975; author: Intro. to Designing Rsch. and Evaluation, 1976; co-author (with M. Hardman and H. Bluhm): Mental Retardation: Social and Ednl. Perspectives, 1977; co-author: (with M. Hardman and W. Egan) Human Exceptionality: Soc., Sch. and Family, 1984; author: Designing and Conducting Behavioral Rsch., 1985; co-author (with M. Hardman and D. Logan): Mental Retardation: A Life Cycle Approach to People with Intellectual Disabilities, 1988; co-author: (with B. Wampold) Theory and Application of Stats., 1990; co-author: (with M. Hardman and D. Logan) Mental Retardation: A Life Cycle Approach, 1992; co-author: (with M. Hardman and A. Hart) Designing and Conducting Rsch.: Inquiry in Edn. and Social Sci., 1996; co-author: (with M. Hardman and D. Logan) Mental Retardation: A Life Cycle Approach, 1996; co-author: (with M. Hardman), 2000; co-author: (with M. Hardman and W. Egan) Human Exceptionality: Soc., Sch. and Family, 2002; co-author: (with D. Gelfand) Understanding Child Behavior Disorders, 2003; contbr. NDEA fellow, 1965-66; U.S. Office Edn. fellow, 1966-68. Fellow Am. Assn. Mental Retardation; mem. Am. Psychol. Assn.; Am. Ednl. Rsch. Assn. Office: U Utah Acad V P Office 201 Presidents Cir Rm 205 Salt Lake City UT 84112-9007

DREW, ELIZABETH, television commentator, journalist, author; b. Cin., Nov. 16, 1935; d. William J. and Estelle (Jacobs) Brenner; m. J. Patterson Drew, Apr. 11, 1964 (dec. 1970); m. David Webster, Sept. 26, 1981 (dec. 2003). BA, Wellesley Coll., 1957; LHD, Hood Coll., 1976, Yale U., 1976, Trinity Coll., Washington, 1978, Reed Coll., 1979, Williams Coll., 1981, Georgetown U., 1981, George Washington U., 1994, Trinity Coll., Hartford, 2000. Writer editor Congl. Quar., 1959-64; freelance writer, 1964-67; Washington editor Atlantic Monthly, 1967-73; host TV interview program Thirty Minutes With, 1971-73; commentator TV program Agronsky and Company (now Inside Washington), 1973-92; Washington corr. New Yorker Mag., 1973-92; commentator Monitor Radio, 1992—95. Author: Washington Jour., 1975, Am. Jour., 1977, Senator, 1979, Portrait of an Election, 1981, Politics and Money, 1983, Campaign Jour., 1985, Election Jour., 1989, On the Edge: The Clinton Presidency, 1994, Showdown: The Struggle Between the Gingrich Congress and the Clinton

White House, 1996, Whatever It Takes: The Real Struggle for Political Power in Am., 1997, The Corruption of Am. Politics, 1999, Citizen McCain, 2002; contbr. articles, jours. and periodicals. Recipient award for excellence Soc. Mag. Writers, 1971, Wellesley Alumnae Achievement award, 1973, DuPont award, 1973, Mo. medal, 1979, Sidney Hillman award, 1983, Ambassador of Honor award Books Across the Sea, 1984, Literary Lion award N.Y. Pub. Library, 1985, Edward Weintal prize, 1988. Home and Office: 3000 Woodland Dr NW Washington DC 20008-3543

DREW, ELIZABETH HEINEMAN, publishing executive; b. Evanston, Ill., Aug. 26, 1940; d. Ben Harlow and Marion Elizabeth (Heineman) D. BA, U. Wis., 1961. With Doubleday & Co., Inc., N.Y.C., 1961-84, prodn. asst., 1961-63, personal asst. to editor in chief, 1963-66, adminstrv. asst. to editor in chief, 1966-69, editorial asst. to editor in chief, 1969-71, assoc. editor, 1971-74, editor, 1974-77, sr. editor, 1977-79, exec. editor, editorial dir., 1979-84; v.p., sr. editor William Morrow and Co., N.Y.C., 1984-92; v.p., pub. Lisa Drew Books/Macmillan Pub. Co., N.Y.C., 1993-94; v.p. pub. Lisa Drew Books/Charles Scribner's Sons, N.Y.C., 1994—. Tchr. NYU Sch. Continuing Edn., 1981-82. Bd. dirs. Barbara Bush Found. Family Literacy, 1995—. Mem.: PEN, Assn. Am. Pubs. (internat. freedom to pub. com. 1978—, chmn. 1990—93, freedom to read com. 1988—, chmn. 1994—98), Nat. Press Club, Women's Media Group (treas. 1982—84, pres. 1985—86, bd. dirs. 2000—02), First City Club (Savannah, Ga.), Century Assn. (N.Y.). Democrat. Episcopalian.

DREW, FRASER BRAGG ROBERT, language educator; b. Randolph, Vt., June 23, 1913; s. George Albie and Hazel (Fraser) Drew. AB magna cum laude, U. Vt., 1933; MA, Duke U., 1935; PhD, U. Buffalo, 1952. Instr. Latin Green Mt. Coll., Poultney, Vt., 1936-39; grad. asst. English Syracuse U., 1939-41; instr. English Buffalo State Coll., 1945-47, asst. prof., 1947-52, prof., 1952-73, Disting. Tchg. prof., 1973-83. Author: (book) John Masefield's England, 1973; contbr. articles to profl. jours. Chmn. St. Patrick Scholarship Fund, Buffalo, 1969—79. Recipient Disting. Alumnus award, U. Vt., 1968, Irishman of the Yr award, United Irish Socs. Western N.Y., 1970; grantee, SUNY Rsch. Found., 1960, 1967; St. Patrick scholar, 1967. Mem.: Robinson Jeffers Tor Ho. Found., Hemingway Soc., Boulder Soc., Wilbur Soc., Ira Allen Soc., John Masefield Soc., Housman Soc., Acad. Am. Poets, Green Mountain Cir., Irish Am. Cultural Inst., Am. Com. Irish Studies, Friends Duke U. Chapel, Duke U. Heritage Soc., Friends Bailey/Howe Libr., Friends Hemingway Collection, John F. Kennedy Libr., Iron Dukes, Washington Duke Club, Phi Beta Kappa, Lambda Iota. Home: 47 Nature Cove Ct Williamsville NY 14221

DREW, GEORGE, writer, educator; b. Greenville, Miss., Nov. 3, 1943; s. George Herbert Drew and Willie Sue Logan; m. Lyla Joan Bates, Apr. 25, 1964 (dec. Nov. 7, 1996); 1 child, Christopher; m. Enid Alice Keeler, Apr. 7, 1997; children: Randall, Rena. BA, SUNY, Albany, 1967; MA, Western Wash. U., 1969. Prof. emeritus Hudson Valley C.C., Troy, NY, 1971—2000; exch. prof.Norwich (Eng.) City Coll., 1981—82; exch. prof. Bucks County C.C., Newtown, Pa., 1991. Vis. prof. Tula (Russia) Pedagogical Inst., 1994; poetry readings colls., arts ctrs., bookstores, others. Author: (poetry book) Toads in a Poisoned Tank, 1986, (poetry chapbook) So Many Bones (Poems of Russia), 1997. Mem.: Associated Writers Program, Poets and Writers Inc. Avocations: hiking, running, reading, travel. Home: Box 298 Poestenkill NY 12140-0298

DREW, K. financial advisor, management consultant; b. Freeport, N.Y. d. Harry P. and Kathleen (Isdal) Barton; children: Karen, Donna. BA, U. Ga., 1958; postgrad., U. Ill., 1960-61. Dir. YWCA, Corpus Christi, Tex., 1969-72, Dwoskin Nat. Wallcovering Co., Atlanta, 1974-76; dep. asst. fin. presdl. campaign, 1976-77; dir. fin. Presdl. Inaugural, Washington, 1976; dep. adv. for small bus. SBA, Washington, 1977-80, asst. to adminstr., 1980-82; v.p. Alpha Systems, Inc., Washington and Athens, Greece, 1980-85; human resource cons. MBA Mgmt., Inc., McLean, Va., 1982-84; bus. cons. Drew Cons., McLean, 1984—; cons. assoc. Walling, June & Assocs., Old Town Alexandria, Va., 1986-89; fin. advisor The Family Extended, Washington, 1990—; bus. rep. Nikken, Inc., Washington, 1996, KareMor Internat., Inc., Washington, 1996; cons. The B.O.W.L. Group, Washington, 1996—. Fin. advisor SAKA, Inc., Merrifield, Va., 1991—, Warrenton, Va., 1991-92, DeLeand Assocs., McLean, Va., 1991-92; fin. dir. Disting. Environments, Reston, Va., 1992-94. State rep. poverty program and suicide prevention bds. Corpus Christi Bus. Coun., 1969-71; bd. dirs. YWCA, Washington, 1983-85; head speaker's bur. Fairfax Symphony, 1979-85, mem. exec. devel. com., 1979-86; mem. Mental Health Exec. Bd. dirs., Washington, 1983-88; deacon Nat. Presbyn. Ch., Washington, 1988-90; asst. to exec. dir. T. Monk Found., Jazz Sch., Duke U., 1987-89; event dir. Easter Seal Soc., 1990-91; mem. Youth for Tomorrow devel. com. Joe Gibbs Charities, Washington, 1990-98; presdl. campaign team captain Va. and Ga. Inaugural Com., 1993; Ga. Ball host, Washington, 1993; host Presdl. Inaugural Gala, Washington, 1993; In Kind Svc. to White House Advance Office of Pres., 1993—; cons. advisor Battered Spouses & Their Children, Washington, 1995—; campa pres. team, 1996; pres. inaugural host, Washington, D.C., 1996; fin. mgr. Internat. Fellowship Family Extended, Washington, 1993-98; fin., mkgt. adv., mem. new bowl group Urban Prayer Breakfast, Washington, 1997—; job cons. Homeless Bd. and Symposium, Washington, 1997-98; pres. bd. dirs. WAR Against Broken Hearts, Atlanta, 1998—; hostess Christmas at the White House, Washington, 1999; chmn., newspaper editor Rotonda Pet, McLean, Va., 2000; chmn. Urban Prayer Breakfast for Homeless, Washington, 2000; v.p. Rotonda Assn., McLean, 2002-; pres. Su Casa Mi Casa Nat. Home Mgmt., McLean, Va., 2003. Mem. Nat. League Am. Pen Women (v.p., pres. Washington Capital chpt. 1987-89, nat. bd. dirs. 1987-90, nat. roster chmn. 1989—), Bus. and Profl. Women Washington, Nat. Platform Assn., Alpha Gamma Delta. Office: 8350 Greensboro Dr Ste 1-121 Mc Lean VA 22102-3533

DREW, KATHERINE FISCHER, history educator; b. Houston, Sept. 24, 1923; d. Herbert Herman and Martha (Holloway) Fischer; m. Ronald Farinton Drew, July 27, 1951. BA, Rice Inst., 1944, MA, 1945; PhD, Cornell U., 1950. Asst. history Cornell U., 1948-50; instr. history Rice U., 1946-48, mem. faculty, 1950—, prof. history, 1964—, Harris Masterson, Jr. prof. history, 1983-85, Lynette S. Autrey prof. history, 1985-96, prof. emeritus, 1996—, chmn. dept. history, 1970-80; editor Rice U. (Rice U. Studies), 1967-81, acting dean humanities and social scis., 1973, acting chmn. dept. art and art history, 1996-98. Author: The Burgundian Code, 1949, Studies in Lombard Institutions, 1956, The Lombard Laws, 1973, Law and Society in Early Medieval Europe, 1988, The Laws of the Salian Franks, 1991, also articles; editor: Perspective in Medieval History, 1963, The Barbarian Invasions, 1970; mem. bd. editors Am. Hist. Assn. Guide to Hist. Lit., 1987-94, Am. Hist. Rev. 1982-1985; contbr.: Life and Thought in the Middle Ages, 1967. Guggenheim fellow, 1959; Fulbright scholar, 1965; NEH Sr. fellow, 1974-75 Fellow Mediaeval Acad. Am. (coun. 1974-77, 2d v.p. to pres. 1985-87, del. to Am. Coun. Learned Socs. 1977-81); mem. Am. Hist. Assn. (coun. 1983-86), Am. Soc. Legal History, So. Hist. Assn. (vice chair, chair European sect. 1986-88, exec. com. 1989-91), Phi Beta Kappa. Home: 9333 Memorial Dr # 306 Houston TX 77024-5739 Office: Rice U Dept History MS 42 PO Box 1892 Houston TX 77251-1892 E-mail: kdrew@rice.edu.

DREW, LAWRENCE JAMES, geologist, statistician; b. Dec. 18, 1940; s. James Joseph and Olive Virginia (McAfee) Drew; m. Sheila Moore Collins, Oct. 16, 1965; 1 child, Michael C. BS, U. N.H., 1962; MS, Pa. State U., 1964, PhD, 1966, postdoctoral studies, 1966—67. Statistician Geotech, Inc., Alexandria, Va., 1967—69; geologist Cities Svc. Oil Co., Tulsa, 1969—72, U.S. Geol. Survey, Reston, Va., 1972—82, br. chief, 1982—. Author: Recollections of a Forecaster, 1990, Undiscovered Petroleum and Mineral Resources in Assessment and Controversy, 1997; contbr. Mem.: Am. Statis. Assn., Internat. Assn. Math. Geologists. Presbyterian. Avocation: gardening. Home: 12663 Magna Carta Rd Herndon VA 20171-2710

DREW, PAUL S. entrepreneur; b. Detroit, Mar. 10, 1935; s. Harry and Elizabeth (Schneider) Schlachman; m. Dove Ann Austin, Sept. 9, 1961. BA, Wayne State U., Detroit, 1957. Disc jockey, Port Huron, Mich. and Atlanta, 1955-67; program dir. Sta. WQXI, Atlanta, 1966-67, Sta. CKLW, Detroit, 1967-68; program cons. Storer Broadcasting Co., Phila., 1968-69; program dir. RKO Radio stas. in, Detroit, San Francisco, Washington and L.A., 1970-73; v.p. programming RKO Radio stas., 1973-77; pres. Paul Drew Enterprises, L.A., 1977—; dir. USIA-Radio Marti, 1984-85; pres. USA Japan Co., 1985—, The Mobotron Corp., Hollywood, Calif., 1988—, Fuzzmug Corp., 1991—, 2151 Corp., 1991—. Personal mgr. Pink Lady, outside Japan, 1978; ptnr. Teacup-Teaspoon Music Pub. Co., 1978; chmn. Billboard Internat. Programming Conf., 1976; commr. Calif. Motion Picture Coun., 1979-85. Del. Dem. Nat. Conv., 1976; mem. Dem. Nat. Com., Calif. Dem. Com., Dem. Nat. Fin. Council. Named DeeJay of Year Sixteen Mag., 1965; Program Dir. of Year Bill Gavin Report, 1967; recipient Superior Achievement award RKO Radio, 1973; also numerous gold records for contbs. toward million selling records. Mem. NARAS, Am. Advt. Fedn., Am. Film Inst., Hollywood Radio and TV Soc., L.A. World Affairs Coun., Town Hall Calif., Japan Am. Soc., Variety, Friars, Frat. of Friends, Music Ctr. Home: PO Box 2667 Cumming GA 30028-6508 Office: PO Box 2667 Cumming GA 30028-6508 *Don't make the same mistake once.*

DREW, PHILIP GARFIELD, consultant engineering company executive; b. Dedham, Mass., Jan. 25, 1932; s. Garfield Albee and Katherine Marion (Dowling) D.; m. Anne Spengler, June 10, 1961 (div. 1972); children: Katherine, Philip Garfield; m. Patrice Anne Prall, May 20, 1978 (div. 1998); children: Evlyn Albee, Charles Prescott. BS, Carnegie-Mellon U., 1954; MS, Harvard U., 1959, PhD, 1964. Registered profl. engr., Mass. Staff Arthur D. Little, Inc., Cambridge, Mass., 1964-81; pres. Drew Cons., Inc., Carlisle, Mass., 1981—, Concord (Mass.) Cons. Group, 1996-97, 99—. Contbg. editor: Diagnostic Imaging, 1982—; assoc. sci. editor: Test and Measurement World, 1984-86; contbr. articles to profl. jours. Chmn. bd. overseers Bustins Island Village Corp., Freeport, Maine, 1981-84; pres. Savoyard Light Opera Co., 1988-90, Brown Bag Opera, 1993-2000. Served to 1st lt. AUS, 1954-58. Mem. IEEE, Soc. Photo-Optical Instrumentation Engrs., Soc. Computer Applications in Radiology (chmn. 1996), Harvard Club of Boston. Republican. Home and Office: 101 Bedford Rd Carlisle MA 01741-1817 E-mail: pfrew.ma.ultranet@rcn.com.

DREW, RICHARD ALLEN, retired electrical and instrument engineer; b. Milw., Jan. 10, 1941; s. Frank Emmons and Irene Louise Drew. BSEE, Milw. Sch. Engring., 1970. Registered profl. engr., Wis. Instrument engr. Nekoosa Papers Inc., Port Edwards, Wis., 1970-74, sr. instrument engr., 1974-85, Specialty Systems Inc., Mosinee, Wis., 1985-87, chief elec. and instrument engr. Zimpro Environ. Inc., Rothschild, Wis., 1988-96, ret., 1997. With USAF, 1963—67. Recipient Outstanding Svc. award Pulp and Paper Industry Div., Instrument Soc. Am., 1983, Outstanding Alumnus award Milw. Sch. of Engring., 1985. Mem. Instrument Soc. Am. (sr. mem. chpt. pres. 1974-75), Am. Radio Relay League (life mem.), Milw. Sch. of Engring. Alumni Orgn. (chpt. pres. 1991-95). Achievements include research in pulp and paper industrial control systems and waste treatment control systems. Home: 2610 5th St S Wisconsin Rapids WI 54494-6263

DREW, RUBY LOUISE, speech-language pathologist, consultant; b. Duluth, Minn., Aug. 29, 1944; d. Alfus Bert and Ruth Emerald Dincau; m. Gerald Lester Drew, Dec. 19, 1964; children: Jay Michael, Steven Robert, Joseph Gerald. BS, U. Minn., 1966, MA, 1982; PhD, Northwestern U., 1996. Lic. speech-lang. pathologist, Minn., Ind., Tenn., N.C. Speech-lang. pathologist Proctor Schs., Duluth, 1966-69; speech-lang. cons. North Shore Hosp., Grand Marals, Minn., 1969-74; speech-lang. pathologist Hermantown Schs., Duluth, 1974-83, Nat. Polinsky Rehab. Ctr. Speech Cons., Duluth, 1982-84; clinic dir., asst. prof. Mankato (Minn.) State U., 1984-87; speech-lang. pathologist N.W. Ind. Spl. Edn. Coop., Crown Point, Ind., 1987-91; asst. prof. East Tenn. State U., Johnson City, 1995-99; assoc. prof. Western Carolina U., 1999—. Pvt. practice cons., Superior, Wis., Hobart, Ind., 1982-84, 90-95; cons. Mountain Home (Tenn.) VA Med. Ctr., Asheville VA Med. Ctr. Co-dir. valley writing project Mankato State U., 1987. Mem. Am. Speech and Hearing Assn., Tenn. Assn. Audiologists and Speech-Lang. Pathologists, Acad. Neurol. Comm. Disorders and Scis. Avocations: vocalist, pianist, golf, biking. Home: 2 Glen Cable Rd Asheville NC 28805-9221 Office: Western Carolina U Program Comm Disorders Dept Human Svcs Cullowhee NC 28723 E-mail: drew@wcu.edu.

DREW, SHARON LEE, sociologist; b. L.A., Aug. 11, 1946; d. Hal Bernard and Helen Elizabeth (Hammond) D.; children: Keith, Charmagne. BA, Calif. State U., Long Beach, 1983; postgrad., Calif. State U., Dominguez Hills, 1988—. Clerical support Compton (Calif.) Unified Sch. Dist., 1967-78; case worker L.A. County Dept. Pub. Social Svcs., 1978—. Den mother Boy Scouts Am., Compton, 1971—72; employee vol. Dominguez Sr. H.S., Compton, 1972—73; project coord. Calif. Tomorrow's Parent Edn. Leadership Devel. Project, 1990; mem. L.A. Caregiver's Network, 1993—94; vol. Calif. State U., Dominguez Hills Older Adult Ctr., 1994, AIDS Project, Long Beach, Calif., 2003—; lay min., lay reader St. Luies Episcopal Ch., Long Beach. Recipient cert. Calif. Tomorrow-Parent Edn. Leadership Devel. Project, 1990. Mem. Am. Statis. Assn. (So. Calif. chpt.), Internat. Soc. Exploration of Tchg. and Learning, Calif. Sociol. Assn. (1st gov. at large grad. student 1990-91), Dominguez Hills Gerontology Assn. (chairperson 1990-91), Sociology of Edn. Assn., Nat. Cathedral Assn., Alpha Kappa Delta (Xi chpt. treas. 1992-95). Home: 927 N Chester Ave Compton CA 90221-2105

DREW, THOMAS PAUL, chaplain; b. Harvey, Ill., May 19, 1930; s. Thomas Barnet Dorothy Emma D.; m. LorryJo Drew, May 1, 1954; children: Scott Thomas, Lori-Beth Jackson. BA, Bapt. Christian U., 1981, ThM, 1986; PhB in Philosophy, DePaul U., 1963; ThM, Internat. Bible Inst. and Sem., 1981; D Ministry, U. Biblical Studies, 1989. Underwriter America-Fore, Chgo., 1952-56; ins. broker Prudential, Chgo., 1956-86; chaplain, min., jail evangelist Huntsville (Ala.) Police Dept., 1970—. Counselor Huntsville, 1991—; stress counselor Internat. Critical Incident Stress Found., Huntsville. Author: Here's One Marine, 2000. State chaplain Marine Corps League, Ala., 1999—. Staff sgt. USMC, 1947-52. Independent. Avocations: lapidary, fishing. Home: PO Box 145 Union Grove AL 35175

DREW, WALTER HARLOW, retired paper industry executive; b. Chgo., Feb. 23, 1935; s. Ben Harlow and Marion Elizabeth (Heineman) D.; m. Gracia Ward McKenzie, June 27, 1959; children: Jeffrey, Martha. BS, U. Wis., 1957. With Kimberly-Clark Corp., 1959-88, exec. v.p., 1985-88; pres., CEO Menasha Corp., 1989-92. Bd. dirs. U. Wis. Found.; chmn. bd. visitors U. Wis. Bus. Sch., 1992—93. Mem.: North Shore Golf (Menasha, Wis.) (pres. 1983-85), Amelia Island (Fla.). Republican. Episcopalian.

DREWRY, DON NEAL, fire protection engineer; b. Chgo., Oct. 6, 1949; s. Ruben Neal and Vlasta A. (Waleck) D.; m. Patricia Ann English, Mar. 8, 1975; children: Neal Thomas, Michelle Lynn. BA, Govs. State U., 1978; BS in Engring., U. Hartford, 1984; MS in Fire Protection Engring., Worcester Polytech. Inst., 1986. Mfg. engring./NC programmer Bloomer-Fisk, Chgo., 1974-75; inspector, supr. Hartford Steam Boiler, Chgo., 1975-78; asst. mgr. quality assurance svc. Hartford Steam Boiler Inspection and Ins. Co., 1978-80, project engr., 1980-81, sr. engr., 1982-84, fire protection cons., 1984-87, regional mgmt. property engr., 1987-92, regional manage ins. engr., 1992-94; br. mgr., property program mgr. power generation HSB Profl. Loss Control, Basking Ridge, 1994-97, v.p. industry svcs., 1997-99, v.p. loss control svcs., 1999—. Com. fire protection task force Edison Elec. Inst., Washington, 1995. With USN, 1970-74. Mem. ASME, Soc. Fire Protection Engrs., Nat. Fire Protection Assn. (com. NFPA-850 1985—), Nat. Bd. of Boiler and Pressure Vessel Inspectors. Home: 1401 Sycamore Ave Easton PA 18040-8106 Office: HSB Profl Loss Control 188 Mount Airy Rd Basking Ridge NJ 07920-2021

DREWS, JÜRGEN, pharmaceutical researcher; b. Berlin, Aug. 16, 1933; came to U.S., 1991; s. Walter and Charlotte (Schneider) D.; m. Helga Eberlein, July 24, 1963; children: Ulrike, Karoline, Bettina. MD, Free U. Berlin, 1959; Professorship, U. Heidelberg, Fed. Republic of Germany, 1973. Head chemotherapy Sandoz Rsch. Inst., Vienna, Austria, 1976-79, head of inst., 1979-82; head internat. pharm. rsch. and devel. Sandoz, Ltd., Basel, Switzerland, 1982-85; dir. pharm. rsch. F. Hoffmann-La Roche Ltd., Basel, 1985-86, chmn. rsch. bd., mem. exec. com., 1986-90; pres. internat. rsch. and devel., mem. exec. com. Hoffmann-La Roche Inc., Basel, 1991-97, pres. global rsch., mem. exec com. Nutley, N.J., 1996-97; chmn. Internat. Biomedicine Mgmt. Ptnrs., Basel, 1998—. Prof. medicine U. Heidelberg, 1973—; mem. sci. adv. bd. (jour.) Infection, München, Fed. Republic of Germany, 1973—, Drug News & Perspectives, Barcelona, Spain, 1988—, Klinische Pharmakologie, München, 1989—; bd. dirs. Genentech, Inc., South San Francisco, 1990-97, Protein Design Labs., Mountain View, Calif., MorphoSys GmbH, Munich; bd. dirs., internat. bd. advisors Basel Inst. Immunology, 1986-97; mem. dean's coun. Yale U. Sch. Medicine, 1993—, chmn. sci. panel inter-company collaboration for AIDS drug devel., 1993-96, chmn. bd. participants inter-company collaboration for AIDS drug devel., 1996-97; mem. adv. com. Mass. Gen. Hosp., Boston, 1994-98; chmn. steering com. Sr. Adv. Group Biotech., 1994-96; chmn. bd. mgmt. EuropaBio, 1997-98. Author: Chemotherapie: Grundlagen und Perspektiven, 1979, Immunpharmakologie, Grundlagen und Perspektiven, 1986, Immunopharmacology, Principles and Perspectives, 1990, In Quest of Tomorrow's Medicines, 1999; editor: (with others) Topics in Infectious Diseases, vol. 1, 1975, vol. 2, 1977; also over 250 articles.

DREXEL, BARON JEROME, lawyer; b. Miami Beach, Fla., Sept. 3, 1954; s. Gustave L. and Dorris J. (Haas) D. AA, U. Fla., 1973; BA, U. Calif. Berkeley, 1979; MA in Econs., U. Miami, 1983, JD cum laude, 1985. Bar: Fla. 1985, Calif. 1987, U.S. Ct. Appeals (9th cir.) 1987, U.S. Ct. Appeals (11th cir.) 1989, U.S. dist. Ct. (no. dist.) Calif. 1986, U.S. Dist. Ct. (ctrl. dist.) Calif. 1987, U.S. Dist. Ct. (so. dist.) Calif. 1988. Survey crew mem. U.S. Forest Svc., Hayfork, Calif., 1979; sales rep. real estate Allen Morris Co., Miami, Fla., 1981-82; assoc. Shutts & Bowen, Miami, 1985-88, Lasky, Haas, Cohler & Munter, San Francisco, 1988-89, Aiken, Kramer & Cummings, Oakland, Calif., 1989-92, Bostwick & Tehin, San Francisco, 1992-95; pvt. practice Oakland, 1995—. Recipient J.B. Spence award U. Miami Law Rev. Mem. Order of Coif. Achievements include co-trial couns. for $15.4 million verdict. Office: Ste 1750 1 Kaiser Plz Oakland CA 94612-3688

DREXEL, PETER GEORGE, computer science educator; b. N.Y.C., Sept. 27, 1945; s. George Drexel and Margaret (Vogl) Metzner; m. Kathryn Ahern Drexel, Aug. 12, 1972; children: Josef, Katherine, Peter. AAS in Elec. Tech., Hudson Valley C.C., Troy, N.Y., 1966; BS in Engring., Rochester Inst. Tech., 1969; MS in Engring., Rochester Inst. of Technology, 1980; PhD in Engring., U. N.H., 1993. Mgr. Moose Mt. Lodge, Athol, N.Y., 1970-72; engr. Electronic Automation Systems, Grand Island, N.Y., 1972-74; assoc. engr. IBM Corp., Essex Junction, Vt., 1974-88; prof. Plymouth (N.H.) State Coll., 1988—, chair computer sci., 1998-2001. Reviewer Addison-Wesley, Menlo Park, Calif., 1992—; cons. Drexel Assocs., Plymouth, 1995—; AP Computer Sci. Reader, 1996-2002; summer faculty fellowship program NASA, 1998-99; mem. adv. bd. Computer Info. Sys. N.H. Tech. Inst., Concord, N.H., 2002—. Reviewer McGraw-Hill, 2001—; contbr. articles to profl. jours. Lab. Software grantee Microsoft Corp., 1995-2000; Devel. grant Plymouth State Coll., 1988—, Whiting Found., 1997. Mem. IEEE (sr.), IEEE Computer Soc., ACM, Soc. for Computer Simulation. Roman Catholic. Avocations: amateur radio, photography, cinema. Office: Plymouth State Coll Computer Sci Dept Memorial Hall Plymouth NH 03264 E-mail: peter.drexel@plymouth.edu.

DREXEL, RAY PHILLIPS, lawyer; b. Cleve., Aug. 28, 1949; s. Gordon Arthur and Jean Elizabeth (Phillips) D.; m. Beverly Lynn Beall, June 26, 1971; children: Kate Phillips, Alexander Ray. BS, Ohio State U., 1971; JD, Capital U., 1974. Bar: Ohio 1974, U.S. Dist. Ct. (so. dist.) Ohio 1975, U.S. Supreme Ct. 1978. Staff atty. Buckeye Fed. Savs. & Loan Assn., Columbus, Ohio, 1974-82; ptnr. Hilliard, Ramsey & Drexel, Columbus, 1982-85, Hilliard, Ramsey, Drexel & DePew, Columbus, 1985-86, Hilliard, Drexel & DePew, Columbus, 1986-89, Hilliard & Drexel, 1989-93, Buckley King, Columbus, 1994—2003, Gamble Hartshorn Johnson, LLC, Columbus, 2003—. E2 v.p. Annehurst Village Residents Assn., Westerville, Ohio, 1983-86. Arnold Cohn Meml. scholar, 1970-71. Mem. Columbus Bar Assn., Mid Ohio Lenders Counsel Assn. (pres. 1978-80), Franklin County Trial Lawyers, Nat. Mgmt. Assn. (pres. Buckeye Fed. chpt. 1980-81), Masons. Republican. Methodist. Office: Gamble Hartshorn Johnson LLC 1 E Livingston Ave Columbus OH 43215-5700

DREXLER, FRED, insurance executive; b. Oakland, Calif., Nov. 17, 1915; s. Frederic I. and Jessie (Day) D.; m. Martha Jane Cunningham, Dec. 26, 1936 (dec. June 1987); children: Kenneth, Roger Cunningham, Martha Drexler Lynn. AB, U. Redlands, 1936; JD, Golden Gate U., 1947, LL.D., 1971. Bar: Calif. 1947. Editor Mill Valley (Calif.) Record, 1936-42; employee relations Marinship Corp., 1942-45; office mgr. Bechtel Corp., 1945-46; asst. to pres. Indsl. Indemnity Co., San Francisco, 1946-48, asst. sec., 1948-51, sec., 1951-56, sr. v.p., sec., 1956-67, exec. v.p., sec., 1967-68, pres., 1968-70, chmn. bd., chief exec. officer, 1970-76, chmn. exec. com., 1976-78, dir., 1957-86. Dir. Crum & Forster, 1970-83, Montgomery St. Income Securities, Inc. (dir. 1977, chmn. bd. 1988-91); mem. Calif. Workmen's Compensation Study Commn., 1963-65; founder Calif. Workers Compensation Inst., 1964, pres., 1971-74, honoree testimonial dinner, 1985; pres. Pacific Ins. and Surety Conf., 1967-68 Pres. Marin (Calif.) United Fund, 1956; exec. bd. Marin coun. Boy Scouts Am., 1948-69, adv. bd., 1970—, mem. nat. exec. bd., 1973-87; trustee Marin Country Day Sch., 1960-62, United Bay Area Crusade, 1955-73; trustee Golden Gate U., 1957—, chmn. bd., 1968-70; bd. dirs. San Francisco Bay Area Coun., 1972-76, Buck Inst. for Age Rsch., 1989—; trustee Pacific Presbyn. Med. Ctr., 1974-91; chmn. bd. Inst. Philos. Rsch., 1978-95, trustee, 1973-95; trustee World Affairs Coun. No. Calif., 1973-79, Calif. Pacific Med. Ctr., 1991—. Recipient Silver Beaver, Silver Antelope awards Boy Scouts Am. Mem. Calif. Bar Assn. Clubs: Bankers (San Francisco) (pres. 1976-78), Bohemian (San Francisco), Pacific Union (San Francisco). Baptist. Home: 765 Market Street 23H San Francisco CA 94103 Office: One Post St Ste 2160 San Francisco CA 94104-

DREXLER, JOANNE LEE, art appraiser; b. Washington, Mar. 21, 1944; d. Elias J. and Beatrice Charlotte (Goldberg) D.; m. James R. Cohen, May 31, 1965; children: Terri I., Brett F. Student, Louvre, Paris, 1963-64; BA, Tufts U., 1965; Diamond and Pearl Cert., GIA, N.Y.C., 1974. Tchr. of French Stuyvesant H.S., N.Y.C., 1965-66; decorator, art cons. Joanne Cohen Interiors, Mamaroneck, N.Y., 1967-69; assoc. prof. Hofstra U., L.I., N.Y., 1979-80; pres. Esquire Appraisals, N.Y.C. and Larchmont, N.Y., 1969—. TV appearances include CNN, Sept. 1991; cons., lectr. in field; art judge various contests; art dealer. Organizer, curator N.C. in N.Y. art show Nat. Arts Club, 1993, African Am. art show Nat. Arts Club, 1994; weekly columnist Gannett chain newspapers, 1980-86; contbr. articles to N.Y. Law Jour., Matrimonial Strategist. Mem. Am. Soc. Appraisers (sr.; v.p. Hudson Valley White Plains chpt. 1989, bd. dirs. 1997, pres. White Plains chpt. 1993-94, 97-98), Appraisers' Assn. Am. (cert.), Nat. Arts Club N.Y. (exhbn. com.). Avocations: travel, swimming, horseback riding. Home: 23 Trudy Ln Bedford NY 10506-1337 Office: Esquire Appraisals Inc 630 1st Ave New York NY 10016-3700 E-mail: leedrexler@esquireappraisals.com.

DREXLER, KENNETH, lawyer; b. Aug. 2, 1941; s. Fred and Martha Jane (Cunningham) D. BA, Stanford U., 1963; JD, UCLA, 1969. Bar: Calif. 1970. Assoc. David S. Smith, Beverly Hills, Calif., 1970, McCutchen, Doyle, Brown and Enersen, San Francisco, Calif., 1970-77, Chickering & Gregory, San Francisco, Calif., 1977-80, ptnr., 1980-82, Drexler & Leach, San Rafael, Calif., 1982—. Served with AUS, 1964-66. Mem. Calif. State Bar (resolutions com. conf. of dels. 1979-83, chmn. 1982-83, adminstrn. justice com. 1983-89, chmn. 1987-88, adv. mem. 1990-2000), Marin County Bar Assn. (bd. dirs. 1985-87), Bar Assn. San Francisco (bd. dirs. 1980-81), San Francisco Barristers Club (pres. 1976, dir. 1975-76), Marin Conservation League (bd. dirs. 1985-97, 98—, treas. 2001—). Office: 1330 Lincoln Ave Ste 300 San Rafael CA 94901-2143 E-mail: kdrexler@svn.net.

DREXLER, MARY SANFORD, financial executive; b. Pontiac, Mich., Apr. 19, 1954; d. Arthur H. and Kathryn S. (Sherda) Sanford; m. Brian Day, 1975 (div. 1978); m. York Drexler, 1980. BS, Ea. Mich. U., Ypsilanti, 1976, MA, 1979; postgrad., Walsh Coll., Troy, Mich., 1983. CPA, Mich. Spl. edn. tchr. Oakland Schs., Pontiac, Mich., 1976-83; staff auditor Coopers & Lybrand, Detroit, 1983—84, sr. auditor, 1984—86; asst. contr. Webasto Sunroofs Inc., Rochester Hills, 1986-88; contr. Inalfa Roof Systems, U.S.A., Farmington Hills, Mich., 1988-92; v.p. fin., controller Inalfa Roof Sys., Farmington Hills, Mich., 1992-96, CFO, exec. v.p., 1997—. Bd. dirs. Inalfa Roof Systems, Inc., Inalfa Holding Inc. Bd. dirs. Neighborhood Civic Assn., Troy, 1986—, Coun. for Exceptional Children, Oakland County, 1976-83. Mem. Inst. Mgmt. Accts., Oakland County, Mich. Assn. CPA Mich., Forest Lake Country Club. Avocations: photography, painting, golf, swimming. Office: Inalfa Roof Systems USA 1370 Pacific Dr Auburn Hills MI 48326-1569

DREXLER, MILLARD S. retail executive; b. Bronx, NY, 1944; married. Pres., CEO Ann Taylor Co., New York, NY, 1980—83; exec. v.p. merchandising, pres. Gap Stores div. Gap Inc., San Bruno, Calif., 1983—87; pres. The Gap Inc., San Bruno, 1987—95, pres., CEO San Francisco, 1995—2002; chmn., CEO J. Crew Group, Inc., New York, NY, 2003—. Office: J Crew Group Inc 770 Broadway New York NY 10003*

DREXLER, NORA LEE, retired educator, writer, illustrator; b. Bellefonte, Pa., Nov. 17, 1947; d. Bengt Gerdis and Leanore Francis (Bates) Bjalme; m. Raymond George Drexler, June 27, 1970; 1 child, Michelle Ann. BA of Sci., Villa Maria Coll., 1969; MEd, Gannon U., 1974. Tchr. gifted and talented Millcreek Sch. Dist., Erie, Pa., 1969-99; ret., 1999; pres. Drexler Assocs., Inc., 2003—. Founder, nat. program dir. Coalition Pathways, Inc.; computer tech. facilitator World Confs. and Ednl. workshops; vice chair Pennsylvanians Against Underage Drinking; presenter AMA, Parents Resource Inst. for Drug Edn., 2d Comty. Anti Drug Coalition of Am.; cons. White House Office of Nat. Drug Control Policy, Nat. Youth Anti-Drug Media Campaign, Ctr. for Substance Abuse Prevention, Office of Juvenile Justice and Delinquency Prevention, cons., trainer, Ctr for Substance Abuse Prevention, Nat. Guard Northeast Counter Drug Training Ctr. Recipient 1st Pl. Nat. award for outstanding coalition 1997, Comty. Anti Drug Coalitions of Am., 1997, 1st. Pl. Nat. award Nat. Commn. Against Drunk Driving, 1997, DUI Leadership award, citations Pa. Ho. of Reps. and Pa. Senate, Nat. Exemplary Program award Ctr. for Substance Abuse Prevention, 1999, Disting. Alumni award Gannon U., 2000, Nat. award Nat. Hwy. Traffic Safety Adminstrn., 2001. Mem. NEA, Pa. Edn. Assn. Millcreek Edn. Assn. Democrat. Roman Catholic. Avocations: writing, drawing, pet dog. Home: 5639 Mill St Erie PA 16509-2923 E-mail: ndrexler@erie.net.

DREXLER, RUDY MATTHEW, JR., professional law enforcement dog trainer; b. Elkhart, Ind., Jan. 16, 1941; s. Rudy Matthew Sr. and Elaine Irene (Hardman) D.; m. Patricia Ann Overmyer, Apr. 4, 1981; children: Scott M., Tina S. Thode. Student, Purdue U., 1960-63. V.p. Custom Booth Mfg. Corp., Elkhart, Ind., 1962-80; pres. Orchard Kennels, Elkhart, Ind., 1964-79; pres., treas. Rudy Drexler's Sch. for Dogs, Inc., Elkhart, Ind., 1980—. Lectr. civic orgns.; instr. U. Del. Continuing Edn., Wilmington, 1978. Named to Honorable Order of Ky. Colonels, 1989; named hon. dep. Middlesex County Sheriff's Dept., New Brunswick, N.J., 1984, Daviess County Sheriff's Dept., Owensboro, Ky., 1988, Fairfield County Sheriff's Dept., Lancaster, Ohio, 1982. Mem. Midwest Police K-9 Assn. (founder 1984, tng. dir. 1984-87), Am. Soc. Law Enforcement Trainers (charter mem.), Internat. Narcotics Enforcement Officers Assn. (assoc. mem.), Can. Police K-9 Assn. (assoc. mem.), Nat. Police Res. Officers Assn. (hon. mem.), Moose. Office: Rudy Drexler's Sch for Dogs 50947 County Road 7 Elkhart IN 46514-8853

DREYER, ALEC GILBERT, independent power producer; b. Murphysboro, Ill., Mar. 15, 1958; s. Gilbert Dean and Norma Mae (Cluster) D.; m. Sheri L. Snider, July 26, 1980; children: Hillary Christine, Ahren Grant. BA in Polit. Sci. and Acctg., U. Ill., 1980; MBA with honors, Washington U., 1987. CPA, Ill., Mo. Staff acct. Price Waterhouse, St. Louis, 1980-82, sr. acct., 1982-85, mgr., 1985-88, sr. mgr., 1988-92; contr. Ill. Power Co., Decatur, 1992-94, treas., contr., 1994-95, sr. v.p., 1999-2000; pres. Illinova Generating Co., Decatur, 1995-2000; sr. v.p. Illinova Corp., Decatur, 1999-2000; pres., CEO Generation Dynegy, Inc., 2000—. Asst. treas. Com. To Expand Cervantes Conv. Ctr., St. Louis, 1987-88; mem. Citizens Adv. Coun., Edwardsville, Ill., 1990-91; chmn. pers. svcs. divsn. United Way Macon County, Ill., 1994, bd. dirs., 1995-99, co-chmn. campaign drive, 1995, chmn. campaign drive, 1996, vice chmn. bd. dirs., 1997-98, chmn. bd. dirs., 1999; mem. Cmty. Leaders Coun. United Way Tex. Gulf Coast, 2001—. Mem. AICPA, Ill. Soc. CPAs, Phi Beta Kappa, Beta Gamma Sigma. Republican. Baptist. Avocations: golf, computing, in-line skating, reading. Home: 2631 Tangley St Houston TX 77005-2456 E-mail: alec.dreyer@dynegy.com.

DREYER, JOHN EDWARD, lawyer; b. Feb. 22, 1929; s. Felix Edward and Marie Ann (Bungert) D.; m. Shirley Ann Fenhaus, May 29, 1954 (div.); children: Thomas, Laura, Gregory, Michael; m. Nancy A. Mickelson; stepchildren: Karen Mickelson Ortiz, Kevin W. Mickelson. BS, Loyola U., Chgo., 1951; JD, DePaul U., 1953. Bar: Ill. 1953, U.S. Dist. Ct. (no. dist.) Ill. 1953, U.S. Ct. Appeals (7th cir.) 1953, U.S. Ct. Mil. Appeals 1954. Jr. ptnr. Sears Streit, Tyler & Dreyer, Chgo. and Aurora, Ill., 1961-63; sr. ptnr. Dreyer, Foote & Streit, Assocs., Aurora, 1963-84, Dreyer, Foote, Streit, Furgason & Slocum, PA, 1984-94, of counsel, 1994—. Dir. Valley Nat. Bank Aurora, 1975-86. Bd. editors DePaul Law Rev., 1952-53. Bd. dirs. Family Support Ctr., Aurora, 1975-86. 1st lt. JAGC, U.S. Army, 1953-56. Mem. ABA, Ill. State Bar Assn. (assembly 1972-78), Kane County Bar Assn., Am. Judicature Soc., Ill. Soc. Trial Lawyers, Nat. Assn. R.R. Trial Counsel, Moose, Phi Alpha Delta, Pi Gamma Mu. Home: 3 S 611 Finley Rd Sugar Grove IL 60554 Office: 1999 W Downer Pl Aurora IL 60506

DREYFUS, EDWARD A. psychologist; b. N.Y.C., Mar. 27, 1937; s. Herbert and Estelle Dreyfus; m. Barbara Dreyfus. BBA in Indsl. Psychology, CUNY, 1958, MS in Edn. in Sch. Psychology, 1960; PhD in Clin. Psychology, Kans. U., 1964. Diplomate Am. Bd. Forensic Examiners; diplomate in profl. psychotherapy Internat. Acad. Behavioral Medicine, Counseling and Psychotherapy, Inc.; cert. group psychotherapist AGPA; lic. psychologist, Calif.; lic. marriage, family and child therapist, Calif.; lic. sch. psychologist, N.Y.; registrant Nat. Register Health Svc. Providers in Psychology, Nat. Register Cert. Group Psychotherapists, Nat. Registry Forensic Examiners. Clin. psychology trainee VA Hosp., Kans., 1960-63, clin. psychology intern, 1963-64, clin. psychologist Palo Alto, Calif., 1964-65; pvt. practice clin. psychology, 1965—; founding ptnr. Alternatives: Divorce Mediation, 1995—2003. Clin. psychologist Kans. U. Med. Ctr., Kansas City, Mo., 1961-62, Kans. Reception & Diagnostic Ctr., Topeka, 1962-64; assoc. dir. Student Counseling Ctr., U. Calif., L.A., 1965-73, guest lectr. Sch. Social Welfare, 1968, guest lectr. dept. pscyhology, 1969, instr. Sch. Dentistry, 1971-72;, asst. clin. prof. Ctr. for Legal Psychiatry dept. psychiatry Neuropsychiat. Inst., 1977-80; field assessment officer Peace Corps, 1968-70; cons., instr. Calif. Sch. Profl. Psychology, L.A., 1970-80; field faculty Goddard Coll., Plainsville, Vt., 1971-76, Lindenwood Coll., St. Charles, Mo., 1975-76, Internat. Coll., L.A., 1975-78; presenter in field. Author: Youth: Search for Meaning, 1972, Adolescence: Theory and Experience, 1976, Someone Right For You, 1992, 2003, Keeping Your Sanity, 2000, 2003; contbr. chapters to books, articles to profl. jours. Clin. supr. So. Calif. Counseling Ctr., L.A., 1969-88, bd. dirs., 1975-80; vice chair bd. dirs. New Start, Santa Monica, Calif., 1992-94, chair bd. dirs., 1994; bd. dirs. Kehillath Israel Synagogue, Pacific Palisades, 1994-2000, Jewish Cmty. Rels. Com., Jewish Fedn. L.A., 1996-2000, Jewish Family Svcs., Santa Monica, Calif., 1996. Fellow APA (divsn. psychotherapy and ind. practice, mem. task force on bds. of psychology 1994-2000, mem. task force on psychology and the media 1995-99), Am. Bd. Sexology (diplomate, clin. supr.), Am. Acad. Clin. Sexologists, Internat. Coun. Sex Edn. and Parenthood of the Am. U., L.A. Soc. Clin. Psychologists (co-chair, co-founder Sr. Clinicians Circle 1992—, newsletter editor 1992-97, pres. 1994); mem. Am. Assn. Marriage and Family Therapists, Am. Assn. Sex Educators, Counselors and Therapists (cert. sex therapists, mem. exec. bd. So. Calif. divsn. 1991-92), Calif. State Psychol. Assn. (chair task force on psychol. assts. 1983-85, mem. task force on the bd. of psychology 1993), Calif. Assn. Marriage and Family Therapists, L.A. County Psychol. Assn. (bd. dirs. 1994-96, MCEP steering com., task force on prescription privileges, Disting. Psychologist award 1996), Acad. Family Mediators, Group Psychotherapy Assn. So. Calif. (pres. 2001); mem. Internat. Coaching Fedn. Address: 1421 Santa Monica Blvd Santa Monica CA 90404-1748

DREYFUS, LEE SHERMAN, international speaker; b. Milw., June 20, 1926; s. Woods Orlow and Clare (Bluett) D.; m. Joyce Mae Unke, Apr. 5, 1947; children: Susan Dreyfus Fosdick, Lee S. Jr. BA, U. Wis., 1949, MA, 1952, PhD, 1957; LLD (hon.), Lakeland Coll., Wis., 1978; LHD (hon.), Blackbourne Coll., Ill., 1984; LCD (hon.), Marian Coll., Wis., 1985; LLD (hon.), Hangyang U., Seoul, Korea, 1982. Assoc. prof., gen. mgr. Radio WDET Wayne State U., Detroit, 1952-62; prof., gen. mgr. WHA-TV U. Wis., Madison, 1962-67, chancellor Stevens Point, 1967-79; gov. State of Wis., Madison, 1979-83; pres., COO Sentry Ins. Corp., Stevens Point, 1983-84; pres. L.S.D. Inc., Waukesha, Wis., 1985—; internat. spkr. Washington Spkrs. Bur., Alexandria, Va., 1988—. Interim state supt. pub. instrn., 1993; chief of mission U.S. AID, Vietnam, 1967-74; bd. dirs. Am.-Can. Great Lakes Commn., Washington, 1979-83, Marcus Corp., Assoc. Bank Corp., Nat. Telemedia, Inc.; del. Am. Assn. State Coll. and Univ., China, Taiwan, Poland, 1973-76. Radio child actor regular weekly drama broadcasts Sta. WISN Milw., 1933-44; creator world's 1st intercontinental video classroom, U.S. to France, 1965. Regent U. Wis., Madison, 1990-96; trustee Emerson Coll., Boston, 1988-91; co-chmn. Wis. Sesquicentennial, Madison, 1996-2000; presdl. del. to Benin, Africa, 1991; spl. del. State Dept. Acad. Mission to Cyprus, 1983; chmn. Wis. Cable TV Commn., Madison, 1972; mem. Wis. Land Stewardship Commn., 1998, Wis. Humanities Commn., 1998; spokesman Angelus Ret. Cmtys., 2003. With USNR, 1944-46; comdr.-in-chief Wis. N.G., 1979-83. Recipient Dist. Pub. Svc. medal Dept. Def., 1982, Pres.'s Gold medal U.S. Army, 1984, U. Wis. Sys. Pres.'s medal, 2001; named Man of the Yr., Kappa Sigma, 1980; named to Hall of Fame, DeMolay Internat., 1991, Milw. Washington H.S., 2001. Mem. Nat. Inst. Former Govs. (sec. 1990-94), Am. Legion (life), VFW (life), Masons (33 deg.), Shriner. Republican. Episcopalian. Avocations: charitable fund raising, reading, civic projects, politics. Home: 3159 Madison St Waukesha WI 53188-4409 Fax: 262-544-4933. E-mail: leesr@webtv.net.

DREYFUSS, ERIC MARTIN, allergist; b. Bad Homburg, Germany, July 11, 1930; came to U.S., 1934; s. Walter and Hedwig (Herz) D.; m. Sandra Dale Gasul, June 16, 1957; children: Peter, Lisa. AB, Cornell U., 1953; MD, Chgo. Med. Sch., 1957. Diplomat Am. Bd. Allergy and Immunology. Intern Beth Israel Hosp., N.Y.C., 1957-58; resident in pediats. SUNY, Syracuse, 1958-60; fellow in allergy Rochester, N.Y., 1962-64; allergist Allergy Assocs. Rochester, 1964—. Asst. clin. prof. U. Rochester Sch. Medicine and Dentistry, 1970—. Capt. U.S. Army, 1960-62. Fellow Am. Acad. Allergy and Immunology, Am. Coll. Allergists, Am. Acad. Pediatrics. Office: Allergy Assocs Rochester 300 Goodman St S Rochester NY 14607-3105

DREYFUSS, JOHN ALAN, retired health facility administrator; b. N.Y.C., Dec. 1, 1933; s. Henry and Doris (Marks) D.; m. Katharine Elizabeth Rich, June 28, 1958; children: Karen Elizabeth, James Henry, Kimberly Anne, Katharine Marks. BS in Biology, Boston U., 1959. Tchr. schs. in, Montclair, Pebble Beach and Los Olivos, Calif., 1959-63; reporter, editor San Luis Obispo (Calif.) Telegram Tribune, 1963-64; advt. salesman Ventura County (Calif.) Star-Free Press, 1964-66; gen. assignment writer L.A. Times, 1966-69, 73-75, higher edn. writer, 1969-72, environment writer, 1972-73, architecture and design critic, 1975-84, feature writer View sect., 1984-87, graphics editor View sect., 1987-89, asst. to assoc. editor, 1989-93; v.p., CFO, sec. J. Dreyfuss & Assocs., Santa Monica, Calif., 1993-94; newswriter Sta. KTLA-TV, L.A., 1994-95; pub. info. officer Jonsson Comprehensive Cancer Ctr./UCLA, 1995-96, dir. for comm., 1996-98, dir. for planning and comm., 1998-2000. Ret., 2000. With U.S. Army, 1953-55. E-mail: dreyfuss@ucla.edu.

DREYFUSS, PATRICIA, retired chemist, researcher; b. Reading, Pa., Apr. 28, 1932; d. Edmund T. and Anna J. (Oberc) Gajewski; m. M. Peter Dreyfuss, Jan. 30, 1954; children: David Daniel, Simeon Karl. BS Chemistry, U. Rochester, 1954; PhD, U. Akron, 1964. Postdoctoral fellow U. Liverpool (Eng.), 1963-65; rsch. chemist B.F. Goodrich, Brecksville, Ohio, 1965-71; rsch. assoc. Case Western Res. U., Cleve., 1971-73, sr. rsch. assoc., 1973-74; rsch. assoc. Inst. Polymers Sci., U. Akron, Ohio, 1974-84; sr. rsch. scientist, rsch. prof. Mich. Molecular Inst., Midland, 1984-90; ret. Vis. rsch. fellow U. Bristol, 1972; cons. in field, 1974—; vis. prof. Polish Acad. Scis., Poland, 1974; adj. prof. Cen. Mich. U., Mt. Pleasant, Mich. Tech U., Houghton, 1986-92, Mich. Molecular Inst., Midland, 1990-92. Author: Poly (Tetrahydrofuran), 1982; contbr. numerous articles to profl. jours.; co-author books. Flutist West Suburban Philharm. Orch., Lakewood, Ohio, 1969-75, Midland (Mich.) Cmty. Orch., 1990-97; Explorer advisor Explorer post 2069 Boy Scouts Am., Akron, 1975-81; sec., bd. dirs. Adhesion Soc., 1976-88; treas. LWV, 1959-60; mem. ensemble Blessed Sacrament Ch., Midland; occasional flute soloist. Centennial scholar U. Rochester, 1950-54; Sohio fellow U. Akron, 1960, NSF Coop. Grad. fellow, 1961-63, Internat. fellow AAUW, 1964-65, NIH Spl. fellow, 1972-73; recipient Vol. awrd Odyssey of the Mind, Region V, 1999 2000. Mem. Am. Chem. Soc. (cen. region mtg. chmn. 1984-90, loc. sec. chmn., vice chmn., sec. and bd. dirs. Akron chpt. 1974-84, bd. dirs. Midland chpt. 1985-89, Outstanding Leadership Performance award 1981, Disting. Svc. award Akron chpt. 1985, Outstanding Svc. award Midland sect. 2000), AAUW (bd. dirs. Akron chpt.). Achievements include 4 patents in field. Home: 3980 E Old Pine Trl Midland MI 48642-8891 E-mail: P2Drey@aol.com.

DREYFUSS, RICHARD STEPHAN, actor; b. N.Y.C., Oct. 29, 1947; s. Norman and Gerry Dreyfuss; m. Jeramie Dreyfuss, 1983; children: Emily, Benjamin, Harry. Student, San Fernando Valley State Coll., 1965-67. Motion picture appearances include American Graffiti, 1973, Dillinger, 1973, The Apprenticeship of Duddy Kravitz, 1974, Jaws, 1975, Inserts, 1975, Close Encounters of the Third Kind, 1977, The Goodbye Girl, 1977, The Competition, 1980, Whose Life Is It Anyway?, 1981, Down and Out in Beverly Hills, 1986, Stand By Me, 1986, Tin Men, 1987, Stakeout, 1987, Nuts, 1987, Moon Over Parador, 1988, Let It Ride, 1989, Always, 1989, Postcards from the Edge 1990, What About Bob?, 1991, Once Around, 1991, Rosencrantz and Guildenstern Are Dead, 1991, Lost in Yonkers, 1993, Another Stakeout, 1993, Silent Fall, 1994, Mr. Holland's Opus, 1995 (Acad. award nominee for best actor 1996), The American President, 1995, Mad Dog Time, 1996, James and the Giant Peach, 1996, Night Falls on Manhattan, 1997, Krippendorf's Tribe, 1998, A Fine and Private Place, 1998, The Crew, 2000, The Old Man Who Read Love Stories, 2000, Who Is Cletis Tout?, 2001, Rudolph the Red-Nosed Reindeer and the Island of Misfit Toys (voice), 2001; theatrical appearances include: Julius Caesar, 1978, Othello, 1979, Total Abandon, 1983, Death and the Maiden, 1992; actor, producer: The Big Fix, 1978; actor, TV movies: Two For The Money, 1972, Victory at Entebbe, 1976, The Call of the Wild (voice), 1997, Lansky, 1999, The Day Reagan Was Shot, 2001, producer Quiz Show, 1994, (TV movie) Oliver Twist, 1997; host TV series The Class of the 20th Century, 1991; actor, producer TV series The Education of Max Bickford, 2001-2002. Participant civil rights marches, lobbying for amnesty bills. Served alt. mil. duty Los Angeles County Gen. Hosp., 1969-71. Recipient Golden Globe award, 1978; Academy award as best actor in The Goodbye Girl, 1978 Mem. ACLU, Screen Actors Guild, Equity Assn., AFTRA, Motion Picture Acad. Arts and Scis. Office: William Morris Agy 151 S El Camino Dr Beverly Hills CA 90212-2775*

DREZ, DAVID JACOB, JR., orthopedic surgeon, educator; b. Lake Charles, La., Aug. 21, 1938; s. David Jacob and Hester Adele (Bingham) D.; m. Judith Diane Wolfe, June 5, 1963; children: Susan Drez Joseph, Catherine Ann Self, David Jacob III. BS, Tulane U., 1959, MD, 1963. Diplomate Am. Bd. Surgery, Am. Bd. Orthopaedic Surgery. Intern Charity Hosp., New Orleans, 1963-64, resident in gen. surgery, 1964-68, resident in orthopaedic surgery, 1968-71; resident Scottish Rite Hosp., Atlanta, 1969, USPHS Hosp., New Orleans, 1970; pvt. practice Orthopaedic Assocs., Lake Charles, 1971-82; pvt. practice Orthopaedic and Sports Injury Clinic Knee and Sports Medicine Ctr., Lake Charles, 1982-94; pvt. practice Ctr. for Orthopaedics, Lake Charles, 1994—. Staff Lake Charles Meml. Hosp., 1973—, bd. trustees, 1973, 80-82, sec.-treas., 1977, pres., 1981, chief surgery, 1984, 85; med. staff dept. orthopaedics Children's Hosp., New Orleans, 1988; La. state chmn. Orthopaedic Rsch. and Edn. Found., 1987, 90-92; network of orthopedic surgeons U.S. Gymnastics Fedn., 1988—; physician U.S. Soccer Assn., 1988—; examiner Am. Bd. Orthopaedic Surgery, 1989, 91, 92, bd. dirs.; vis. prof. numerous hosps. and univs.; speaker in field. Author: (with R. D'Ambrosia) Prevention and Treatment of Running Injuries, 1982, Prevention and Treatment of Running Injuries, 2d edit., 1989, (with D.W Jackson) The Anterior Cruciate Deficient Knee-New Concepts in Ligament Repair, 1986, Orthopaedic Sports Medicine: Principles and Practice, 1994 (with Jesse DeLee); author 8 chpts. in books; editor Am. Jour. Sports Medicine, 1988—, Jour. Orthopaedic Techniques, 1993—; co-editor Operative Techniques in Sports Medicine jour., 1993—; mem. editorial bd. Orthopaedics, 1983—, Arthroscopy, 1984-89, Sports Medicine News, 1989—; author 5 video tapes, audio tape; mem. adv. bd. Clin. Update, Sports Medicine, 1983—, Clin. Orthopaedics and Related Rsch., 1987-93; con. rev. bd. Jour. Bone and Joint Surgeons, 1989—; contbr. over 35 articles to profl. jours. Team orthopaedist athletic dept. McNeese State U., Lake Charles, 1974—, pres. 100 Club, 1979; co-dir. Runner's Clinic, La. State U. Sch. Medicine, New Orleans, 1978-81; chief physician NAAU Boxing Championship, Lake Charles, 1979; mem. Gov.'s Coun. on Phys. Fitness and Sports, 1981; bd. dirs. Lake Area Runners, 1989-92. Maj. La. N.G., 1963-71. Named to La. Athletic Trainers Assn. Hall of Fame, 1989, McNeese State U. Hall of Honors, 1990. Mem. Acad. Orthopaedic Soc., Am. Acad. Orthopaedic Surgeons, Am. Acad. Sports Physicians, Am. Coll. Sports Medicine, Am. Coll. Surgeons, Am. Orthopaedic Assn., Am. Orthopaedic Foot Soc., Am. Orthopaedic Foot and Ankle Soc., Am. Orthopaedic Soc. Sports Medicine, Arthroscopy Assn. N.Am., Assn. Bone and Joint Surgeons, Assn. Sports Medicine Fellowship Dirs., Mid. Am. Orthopaedic Assn., Assn. Arthritic Hip and Knee Surgery, Australian-Am. Orthopaedic Soc., Calcasieu Parish Med. Soc., Clin. Orthopaedic Soc., European Soc. Knee Surgery and Arthroscopy, Herodicus Sports Medicine Soc. (past sec., v.p., pres.), Internat. Arthroscopy Assn., Internat. Soc. Knee, La. Orthopaedic Assn. (pres. 1992), La. State Med. Assn., Oscar Creech Surg. Soc., Orthopaedic Rsch. Soc., Soc. Internat. Chirurgie Orthopedique Traumatologie, Soc. Internat. Recherche Orthopedique Tramatologie. Avocations: reading, jogging, traveling, family activities. Office: Ctr for Orthopedics 1717 Oak Park Blvd 3d Fl Lake Charles LA 70601-8990

DREZNER, DANIEL WILLIAM, political scientist, educator; b. Syracuse, N.Y., Aug. 23, 1968; s. Alan David and Esther Barbara Drezner; m. Erika Wynne Golub, May 24, 1997; 1 child, Samuel. BA in Polit. Econ., Williams Coll., 1990; MA in Econ., MA in Polit. Sci., Stanford U., 1995, PhD in Polit. Sci., 1996. Rsch. cons. RAND Corp., Washington, 1994; asst. prof. polit. sci. U. Colo., Boulder, 1996—99; asst. profl. polit. sci. U. Chgo., 1999—; internat. economist U.S. Dept. the Treasury, Washington, 2000—01. Author: The Sanctions Paradox, 1999, Locating the Proper Authorities, 2003. Recipient Internat. Affairs fellow, Coun. on Fgn. Rels., 1999—2001; fellow John M. Olin fellow, Harvard U., 1997. Mem.: Midwestern Polit. Sci. Assn., Coun. Fgn. Rels., Chgo. Coun. on Fgn. Rels., Internat. Studies Assn., Am. Polit. Sci. Assn. Office: Univ Chgo 5828 South University Ave Chicago IL 60637 Office Fax: 773-702-1689.

DRIBIN, LELAND GEORGE, lawyer; b. Washington, Sept. 11, 1944; s. Daniel Macabeus and Tillie (Horowitz) D.; m. Eileen Wilansky, Sept. 28, 1969; 1 child, Julie Marie. B.A., George Washington U., 1965, J.D., 1968, LL.M., 1972. Bar: D.C. 1968, U.S. Ct. Appeals (D.C. cir.) 1969, U.S. Supreme Ct. 1972, Colo. 1973, U.S. Dist. Ct. Colo. 1973, Calif. 1976, U.S. Dist. Ct. (cen. dist.) Calif. 1981, U.S. Ct. Claims 1984, Ill. 1988. Asst. corp. counsel D.C. Govt., Washington, 1970-72; asst. counsel Martin Marietta Corp., Denver, 1972-74, regional counsel, Torrance, Calif., 1975-76; div. counsel Litton Industries, Van Nuys, Calif., 1976-81; assoc. McKenna, Conner & Cuneo, Los Angeles, 1981-83; v.p. legal affairs, aerospace group counsel Morton Thiokol, Chgo., 1983-87, Seyfarth, Shaw, Fairfeather & Geraldson, 1990—. Mem. ABA, Colo. Bar Assn., Los Angeles County Bar Assn., Nat. Contract Mgmt. Assn. Democrat. Home: 325 S Saltair Ave Los Angeles CA 90049-4128 Office: Seyfarth Shaw Fairweather & Geraldson 2029 Century Park E Ste 3300 Los Angeles CA 90067-3019

DRIEBE, MICHAEL D. corporate financial executive; b. Washington, D.C., Sept. 11, 1956; s. William Thomas Driebe, Sr. and Paula Ann Driebe; m. Sylvia Ann Mendoza, Feb. 16, 1985. MS in Leadership and Mgmt., U. of La Verne, Calif., 2002; cert. fundraising mgmt., Ind. U., 2002. Dir. Todd Meml. Chapel, Pomona, Calif., 1992—99; v.p. for devel. LeRoy Haynes Ctr., La Verne, Calif., 1999—. Nat. com. mem. St. Jude Children's Rsch. Hosp., Memphis, 1997—2003; pres. L.A. chpt. ALSAC/St. Jude, 1997—98. Mem.: Pomona Jr. C. of C. (Disting. Svc. award 1995, Jaycee of Yr. 1994), Calif. Jr. C. of C. (sec. 1995—96, Jeren Beeks Meml. award 1994, Outstanding Young Californian 1996), Pomona C. of C. (pres. 1997—98, 1993—94, Pres.'s award 2000), Rotary Club Pomona (pres. 2002—03). Office: LeRoy Haynes Ctr PO Box 400 233 W Baseline Rd La Verne CA 91750-0400

DRIES, KATHLEEN MARIE, social worker; b. Beaver Dam, Wis., Feb. 21, 1946; d. Henry Frank and Eloise Marianne (Rake) D. BS in Sociology, No. Mich. U., 1969. Social worker Dept. Social Svcs., West Bend, Wis., 1969—. Social work cons. Group Home Elderly, Slinger, Wis., 1972-75. Mem. Labor Assn. of Wis., Cath. Knights Ins. Soc. (bd. dirs. 1979-94), Alpha Xi Delta. Roman Catholic. Avocations: tennis, spectator sports, theater, travel. Home: 601 Declark St Beaver Dam WI 53916-1309 Office: Dept Social Svcs 333 E Washington St Ste 3100 West Bend WI 53095-2585

DRIGGS, CHARLES MULFORD, lawyer; b. East Cleveland, Ohio, Jan. 26, 1924; s. Karl Holcomb and Lila Vandeveer (Wilson) D.; children: Ruth, Rachel, Carrie, Karl H., Charles M.; m. Ann Eileen Zargari, Oct. 25, 1991. BS, Yale U., 1947, JD, 1950. Bar: Ohio 1951. Assoc. Squire, Sanders & Dempsey, Cleve., 1950-64, ptnr., 1964-88, of counsel, 1988-91; pvt. practice civil law Cleve., 1991-95; ptnr. Driggs, Lucas, Brubaker & Hogg Co., LPA, Mentor, Ohio, 1995—. Pres. Bratenahl (Ohio) Sch. Bd., 1958-62; mem. adv. coun. Cleve. Ctr. for Theol. Edn., 1978—. Mem. ABA, Ohio Bar Assn., Lake County Bar Assn., Cleve. Bar Assn., Greater Cleve. Growth Assn., Cleve. Law Libr. Assn. (trustee 1977-91), Ct. Nisi Prius (judge 2000), Citizens League Greater Cleve., Geauga County Bar Assn., Phi Delta Phi, Tau Beta Pi, Phi Gamma Delta. Home: 8011 Eagle Rd Kirtland OH 44094 Office: 8522 East Ave Mentor OH 44060 E-mail: charles@driggslaw.com. *Any success I may have achieved I attribute to my continuing attempt to live and conduct my affairs in a manner that my family and friends may later reflect upon with pride.*

DRIGGS, MARGARET, educator; b. Kansas City, Kans., June 30, 1909; d. William Foster and Lillian Edith (Landers) Brazier; m. J.W. Quarrier, Nov. 26, 1933 (div. July 1945); children: John Chilton, Philip Harrington, Camille Elizabeth; m. Howard R. Driggs, Sept. 26, 1948 (dec.). AB, U. Kans., 1930; postgrad., Hofstra Coll., 1960, Grad. Sch. Libr. Sci., Pratt Inst., 1964-65. Adminstrv. asst. to sec., dir. pub. rels. Hofstra Coll., 1956-61, staff adviser Nexus (yrbook.), 1961; mem. faculty Westover Sch., Middlebury, Conn., 1964-65; dir. devel. pub. rels., asst. to dean Cathedral Sch. of St. Mary, Garden City, N.Y., 1965, also yrbook adviser. Nat. dir. pub. rels. Am. Pioneer Trails Assn., 1948; chmn. pub. rels. NYU Faculty Women's Club, 1950-54; nat. 1st v.p. Assn. parents and Friends Kings Point, 1957-58; judge Nat. Svc. Acad. Debate Tournament, 1956; hostess Kings Point Congl. com., 1957; installed Duchess of Richelieu collection St. Mary's Libr., 1973; co-chmn. Guides N.J. Gov.'s Mansion Morven, 1975-82. Contbr. Kansas City Star and Johnson County (Kans.) Herald, 1930-33; editor Am. Trails Series filmstrips; curator Driggs Collection of Americana; represented in Native N. Am. Women Exhbn., Skillman Libr., Lafayette Coll., 1992; editor: New Light on Old Glory, 1950, Pitch Pine Tales, 1951, Nick Wilson, 1951, George, The Handcart Boy, 1952,The Old West Speaks, 1956, When Grandfather was a Boy and Western Cowkid, 1957 (all by Howard R. Driggs); contbg. editor Nat. Assn. Ind. Schs. Archives, Harvard, 1965; editor and photographer Vive Rochambeau, Vive Washington. Chmn. docents N.J. Hist. Soc. at Morven, Princeton, 1982-86; mem. women's coun. Hofstra Coll., 1959-60; mem. U.S. Com. for UN Children's Fund, 1957; mem. Friends of Princeton U. Libr., 1975, Friends of the Winston Churchill Meml. and Libr., Westminster Coll., 1989; mem. Princeton Med. Ctr. Aux.; chmn. Civilian Hostesses 15th Ann. U. S. Army Mus. Conf., Princeton, 1986, Salute to Hall of Fame Ceremony the Voice of Am. Broadcast, Gould Meml. Libr., NYU, 1953; mem. Am. Farm Trust, 1992; mem. Denver Pub. Libr. Friends Found. Recipient Disting. Svc. Citatin Am. Pioneer Trails Assn., 1943, Columbia Scholastic Press Assn. medal, 1970, pin for vol. work in Princeton, 1976, French-Am Alliance medal, cert. and hist. house tile award N.J. Hist. Soc., 1984; Margaret Brazier Driggs Collection of Americana established at U. Kans., 1953, Hofstra Coll., 1961. Mem. Hist. Soc. Gov.'s Mansion Guides, Internat. Platform Assn., Assn. Coll. and Rsch. Librs., Hist. Soc. Princeton, Nat. Trust Hist. Preservation, Smithsonian Assocs., Nat. Parks and Conservatin Assn., Women's Bd. N.J. Hist. Soc., Smithsonian Nat. Mus. of Am. Indian (charter 1999), Met. Mus. Art, Women's Coll. Club Princeton, Woodrow Wilson Internat. Ctr. for Scholars (assoc. 1999), Amiga of Orgn. of Am. States, NYU Faculty Club (hon., life), Libr. of Congress (charter assoc. 1994), Present Day Club (Princeton), Gold Medal Club, Learned Club, Pi Delta Epsilon (grand councilman 1960-61). Home: 2943 W 116th Pl Apt 107 Denver CO 80234-2519

DRINAN, ROBERT FREDERICK, lawyer, former congressman, educator, clergyman; b. Boston, Nov. 15, 1920; s. James Joseph and Ann Mary (Flanagan) D. AB, Boston Coll., 1942, MA, 1947; LL.B., Georgetown U., 1949, LL.M., 1950; Th.D., Gregorian U., Rome, 1954; study, Florence, Italy, 1954-55; LL.D. (hon.), Worcester State Coll., 1970, L.I. U., 1970, R.I. Coll., 1971, St. Joseph's Coll., Phila., 1975, Syracuse U., 1977, Villanova U., 1977, Framingham (Mass.) State Coll., 1978, U. Santa Clara, 1980, Kenyon Coll., 1981, Lowell U., 1981, U. Bridgeport, 1981, Loyola U., Chgo., 1981, Gonzaga U., 1981, Curry Coll., 1982, De Paul U., 1984, U. San Diego, 1984, Mt. St. Mary Coll., 1985, Hebrew Coll., 1987, Notre Dame Coll., Manchester, N.H., 1989, Walsh Coll., Ohio, 1990, Georgetown U., 1991, LLD (hon.), Trinity Coll., 1998, Brandeis U., 2002, CUNY, 2003. Bar: D.C. 1950, Mass. 1956, U.S. Supreme Ct. 1955; ordained priest Roman Cath. Ch., 1953. Asst. dean Boston Coll. Law Sch., 1955-56, dean, 1956-70; vis. prof. U. Tex. Law Sch., 1966-67; mem. 92d-96th

Congresses from 4th Mass. dist.; mem. jud. com., govt. ops. com., house select com. on aging, chmn. subcom. on criminal justice; columnist Nat. Cath. Reporter, 1980; prof., Sch. of Law Georgetown U., Washington, 1980—. Chmn. adv. com. Mass. U.S. Civil Rights, 1962-70; mem. vis. com. Div. Sch., Harvard U., 1975-78; bd. dirs. Bread for the World; founder Nat. Interreligious Task Force on Soviet Jewry.; mem. exec. com. Assn. Am. Law Schs.; vis. lectr. Oxford U., England, 1988. Author: Religion, the Courts and Public Policy, 1963, Democracy, Dissent and Disorder, 1969, Vietnam and Armageddon, 1970, Honor the Promise, America's Commitment to Israel, 1977, Beyond the Nuclear Freeze, 1983. Editor: The Right To Be Educated, 1968, God and Caesar on the Potomac, 1985, Cry of the Oppressed: The History and Hope of the Human Rights Revolution, 1987, Stories from the America Soul, 1990, The Fractured Dream, 1991, The Mobilization of Shame--A World View of Human Richts, 2001; editor in chief Family Law Quar., 1967-70; contbr. editor: nat. Cath. weekly America, 1958-70. Contbr. articles to jours. of opinion. Pres. Ams. for Dem. Action, 1981-84. Fellow Am. Acad. Arts and Scis.; mem. ABA (chmn. sect. individual rights and responsibilities 1990-91, bd. dels. 1993-96, chmn. standing com. professionalism 1996—), NCCJ (nat. trustee), Am. Law Inst., Common Cause (nat. governing bd. 1984-87, 96-99), Mass. Bar Assn. (v.p. 1961), Boston Bar Assn. Office: Georgetown U Law Ctr 600 New Jersey Ave NW Washington DC 20001-2022 Fax: 202-662-9412. E-mail: drinan@law.georgetown.edu.

DRINGENBURG, DUANE CLINTON, health services executive; b. Covington, Ky., Apr. 29, 1948; s. Irvin Clinton and Betty Lee (Lockwood) D. BS in Edn., Ea. Ky. U., 1970, MA in Edn., 1976. Tchr., coach varsity football Dayton (Ky.) Pub. Schs., 1970-75; tchr., grad. asst. Ea. Ky. U., Richmond, 1975-76; tchr., coach varsity football George Rogers Clark H.S., Winchester, Ky., 1976-84; med. sales rep. Wendt Bristol/Foster Med., Columbus, Ohio, 1984-91, Crocker Fels Co., Cin., 1991-92; prin. asst. dept. med. svcs. State of Ky., Frankfort, 1992-93, dep. commr. dept. social svcs., 1993-94, prin. asst. cabinet for human resources, 1994-96, divsn. dir. dept. Medicaid Svcs., 1996—. Mem. Centrist Group, Ky., 1997. Mem. Ky. Coaches Assn. Democrat. Lutheran. Avocations: hunting, fishing, farming. Office: Dept Medicaid Svcs 275 E Main St Frankfort KY 40621-0001

DRINKARD-HAWKSHAWE, DOROTHY LEE, historian, educator, writer; d. Junior Drinkard and Claudia Belle Ashe-Drinkard; m. Richard Ramsey Hawkshawe, Jan. 9, 1963 (dec. July 18, 1989); 1 child, Sharon Belle. BA, Howard U., Washington, D.C., 1960, MA, 1963; PhD, Cath. U. Am., Washington, D.C., 1974. Chair History Dept. East Tenn. State U., Johnson City, 1989—91, prof. of History, dir. of African and African Am. Studies, 1993—. Dir. of teen-age divsn. YWCA, Dayton, Ohio, 1960—61; Chair Dept. History and Politics Bowie (Md.) State U., 1979—82; liaison officer to colls. and univs. Nat. Endowment for the Humanities, Washington, 1983—85; assoc. dean of grad. sch. East Tenn. State U., Johnson City, 1992—95; exec. dir. and CEO Barnhardt & Ashe Pub., Inc., Miami, Fla., 2001—. Author: (book) Illinois Freedom Fighters: A Civil War Saga of the 29th Infantry United States Colored Troops, 1998; editor: The :Legacy of Reconstruction: 1865-1877, 1998. Candidate Howard County Sch. Bd., Columbia, Md., 1986. Named Citizen of the Yr., Theta Zeta chpt. Omega Psi Phi, 1994, Woman of the Year, Pro-to Club, Johnson City. Tenn., 1999; recipient Disting. Program award, Md. Assn. of Higher Edn., 1980. Mem.: AAUW, AAUP, Assn. Am. Publishers, Am. Hist. Assn., Assn. for Study of Afro-Am. Life and History. Liberal. Methodist. Avocations: music, travel, walking. Office: East Tenn State Univ Campus Box 70672 Johnson City TN 37614 Office Fax: 423-439-5373. Personal E-mail: dorodrink@aol.com. E-mail: DoroDrink@aol.com.

DRINKO, JOHN DEAVER, lawyer; b. St. Marys, W.Va., June 17, 1921; s. Emery J. and Hazel (White) D.; m. Elizabeth Gibson, May 14, 1946; children: Elizabeth Lee Sullivan, Diana Lynn Drinko, John Randall, Jay Deaver. AB, Marshall U., 1942; JD, Ohio State U., 1944; postgrad., U. Tex. Sch. Law, 1944; LLD (hon.), Marshall U., 1980, Ohio State U., 1986, John Carroll U., 1987, Capital U., 1988, Cleve. State U., 1990; DHL (hon.), David N. Myers Coll., 1990, U. N.H., 1992, Baldwin-Wallace Coll., 1993, Ursuline Coll., 1994, Notre Dame Coll., 1997, U. Rio Grande, 1999, Marietta Coll., 2001. Bar: Ohio 1945, D.C 1946, U.S. Dist. Ct. (no. dist.) Ohio 1958. Assoc. Baker & Hostetler, Cleve., 1945-55, ptnr., 1955-69, mng. ptnr., from 1969, sr. adviser to mng. com. Chmn. bd. Cleve. Inst. Electronics Inc., Double D Ranch Inc., Ohio; bd. dirs. Cloyes Gear and Products Inc., Orvis Co. Inc., Preformed Line Products Inc. Trustee Elizabeth G. and John D. Drinko Charitable Found., Orvis-Perkins Found., Thomas F. Peterson Found., Mellen Found., The Cloyes-Myers Found., Marshall U. Found.; founder Consortium of Multiple Sclerosis Ctrs., Mellen Conf. on Acute and Critical Care Nursing, Case Western Res. U. Disting. fellow Cleve. Clinc Found., 1991; Ohio State Law Sch. Bldg. named in his honor, 1995, libr. at Marshall U. named in his honor, 1997; inducted into Bus. Hall of Fame, Marshall Univ., 1996. Mem. ABA, Am. Jud. Assn., Bar Assn. Greater Cleve., Greater Cleve. Growth Assn., Ohio State Bar Assn., Jud. Conf. 8th Jud. Dist. (life), Soc. Benchers, Case Western Res. U. Law Sch. Assn., Cleve. Play House, Cleve. Civil War Round-table, Mayfield Country Club, Union Club, The Club at Soc. Ctr., O'Donnell Golf Club, Order of Coif, 33o Scottish Rite Mason, Knight Templar, York Rite, Euclid Blue Lodge No. 599 (Jesters, Shrine, Grotto). Republican. Presbyterian. Home: 4891 Middledale Rd Cleveland OH 44124-2522 also: 1245 Otono Dr Palm Springs CA 92264-8445 Office: Baker & Hostetler LLP 1900 E 9th St Ste 3200 Cleveland OH 44114-3475

DRINNAN, ALAN JOHN, oral pathologist; b. Bristol, Eng., Apr. 6, 1932; came to U.S., 1962, naturalized, 1970; s. Leslie Cyril and Doris May (Porter) D.; m. Marguerite G. Bondolfi, Apr. 4, 1956; children: Michael James, Julia Mary. B.D.S., Bristol U., 1954, M.B.Ch.B., 1962; D.D.S., SUNY, 1964. Tutor oral surgery Bristol U., Eng., 1957-58; asst. prof. SUNY-Buffalo, 1964-68, assoc. prof., 1968-71, prof. dept. oral medicine, chmn., 1971-94, disting. prof., 1994—2000, disting. prof. emeritus, 2000—. Contbr. articles to numerous publs. Served to capt. Royal Army Dental Corps Brit. Army, 1955-57. Fulbright sr. scholar U. Melbourne, Australia, 1981 Mem. ADA, Am. Acad. Oral Pathology (pres.), Internat. Assn. Dental Research, Internat. Assn. Oral Pathologists (pres.). Home: 66 Chestnut Hill Ln Buffalo NY 14221-1702 Office: SUNY Squire Dental Sch Rm 342 Buffalo NY 14214 E-mail: drinnan@buffalo.edu.

DRINNON, JANIS BOLTON, artist, poet, volunteer; b. Pineville, Ky., July 28, 1922; d. Clyde Herman and Violet Ethiele (Hendrickson) Bolton; m. Kenneth Cleveland Drinnon, June 13, 1948; 1 child, Dena Daryl. Student, Lincoln Meml. U., Harrogate, Tenn., 1947-48, Newspaper Inst. Am.; comml. art cert., Art Instrn. Sch., Mpls., 1968. Author: (poems) In HIS Care: A Book of Inspirational Poetry, 1998. Organizer, prodr., dir. religious plays drama dept. Alice Bell Bapt. Ch., Knoxville, Tenn.; mem. New Hopewell Bapt. Ch., Knoxville. Named to Internat. Poetry Hall of Fame, 1996; recipient Editors Choice award, Nat. Libr. Poetry. Mem.: Internat. Soc. Poets (disting. mem.). Republican. Avocations: arts, crafts, oil painting, composing poetry. Home: 7342 Hodges Ferry Rd Knoxville TN 37920-9732 E-mail: kcdrinnon@aol.com.

DRINNON, RICHARD, retired history educator; b. Portland, Oreg., Jan. 4, 1925; s. John Henry and Emma (Tweed) D.; m. Anna Maria Faulise, Oct. 20, 1945; children: Donna Elizabeth, Jon Tweed. BA summa cum laude, Willamette U., 1950; MA, U. Minn., 1951, PhD, 1957. Instr. humanities U. Minn., 1952-53, social sci., 1955-57; instr. Am. history U. Calif., 1957-58, asst. prof., 1958-61; Bruern fellow in Am. studies U. Leeds, 1961-63; faculty research fellow Social Sci. Research Council, 1963-64; asso. prof. history Hobart and William Smith Colls., 1964-66; chmn. dept. history Bucknell U., 1966-74, prof. history, 1974-87, prof. emeritus, 1987—. Vis. prof. U. Paris, 1975 Author: Rebel in Paradise: a Biography of Emma Goldman, 1961, White Savage: The Case of John Dunn Hunter, 1972, Facing West: The Metaphysics of Indian-Hating and Empire-Building, 1980, 90, 97, Keeper of Concentration Camps: Dillon S. Myer and American Racism, 1987; co-editor: Nowhere at Home: Letters from Exile of Emma Goldman and Alexander Berkman, 1974; contbr. articles and revs. to profl. jours. and mags. Served with USNR, 1942-46. NEH sr. fellow, 1980-81 Office: PO Box 1001 Port Orford OR 97465-1001

DRISCOLL, BARBARA HAMPTON, special education educator; b. Natchitoches, La., July 25, 1949; d. Rick Hampton and Frances (Lovell) Davis; children: Kelli Anne, Christopher Mark. BS, Northwestern State U., 1970; MEd in Adminstrn., U. Miss., Oxford, 1977; EdS, Northwestern State U., 1988. Prin. Proprietary Bus. Sch., Shreveport, La., 1979-80; curriculum cons. St. John Berchman's Sch., Shreveport, 1987-88; tchr. severely emotionally disturbed adolescents Caddo Parish Pub. Schs., Shreveport, 1983—2001, 1983-87, juvenile delinquency residential facility tchr., 1987-96, tchr. mild/moderately handicapped, 2001—; pvt. cons. for exceptional children, 1987—. Tchr. Boyce (La.) High Sch., 1970-71, John H, Martyn Vocat.-Tech. High Sch., New Orleans, 1971-73, Northwestern State U., Natchitoches, 1977-78; minister to children Kings Hwy. Christian Ch., 2000—. Mem. bd. deaconesses Kings Hwy. Christian Ch., Shreveport, 1987-91; vol. Hospitality House, Shreveport, 1985-88; active local campaigns, Shreveport, 1980; vol., leader Girl Scouts U.S., Shreveport, 1986-89; asst., vol. Boy Scouts Am., Shreveport, leader, 1986—. Mem. ASCD, Coun. for Exceptional Children, Coun. for Children with Behavioral Disorders. Mem. Christian Ch. (Disciples Of Christ). Avocations: reading, crossword puzzles, church activities. Home: 513 Wayne Shreveport LA 71105-3025 Office: Kings Highway Christian Church 806 Kings Hwy Shreveport LA 71104 E-mail: barbarahampton-driscoll@juno.com.

DRISCOLL, CHARLES FRANCIS, financial services company executive, investment adviser; b. Dubuque, Iowa, July 8, 1943; s. Francis Clarence (dec.)and Grace Ellen (Shanahan) D.; m. Marie Kathleen McGowan, Aug. 19, 1967; children: Sean, Erin. BA in Econs., Loras Coll., 1968. CLU; accredited estate planner. Sr. account mgr. NCR Corp., Davenport, Iowa, 1968-74, St. Louis, 1974-76; fin. planner Mass. Mut. Life Ins. Co., St. Louis, 1976—; pres. Driscoll and Assocs., St. Louis, 1989—. Equity sales coord. MML Investor Svcs., Inc., St. Louis, 1983-88. Chmn. Edgewood Program Alumni Recovery Fund, St. John's Mercy Hosp., St. Louis, 1988-90. Mem. Nat. Assn. Ins. and Fin. Advisors, Soc. Fin. Svc. Profls., Assn. for Advanced Life Underwriters, Estate Planning Coun. St. Lo. Republican. Roman Catholic. Avocations: golf, fishing, nature photography, reading, travel. Home: 2324 Manor Lake Ct Chesterfield MO 63017-7817 Office: 16690 Swingley Ridge Rd Ste 150 Chesterfield MO 63017-0758 E-mail: cdriscoll@finsvcs.com., cdriscoll@mindspring.com.

DRISCOLL, CHARLES FREDERICK, physics educator; b. Tucson, Feb. 28, 1950; s. John Raymond Gozzi and Barbara Jean (Hamilton) Driscoll; m. Suzan C. Bain, Dec. 30, 1972; children: Thomas A., Robert A. BA in Physics summa cum laude, Cornell U., 1969; MS, U. Calif. San Diego, La Jolla, 1972, PhD, 1976. Staff scientist Gen. Atomics, San Diego, 1969; rsch. asst. U. Calif. San Diego, La Jolla, 1971-76, rsch. physicist, sr. lectr., 1976-96, prof. physics, 1996—, assoc. dir. Inst. for Pure and Applied Scis., 1998—. Cons. Sci. Applications, Inc., 1980-81; staff physicist, cons. Molecular Biosystems, Inc., 1981-82. Editor: Non-Neutral Plasma Physics, 1988; contbr. numerous articles to sci. jours. Fellow NSF, 1969-71. Fellow Am. Phys. Soc. (Excellence in Plasma Physics Rsch. award 1991); mem. AAAS, Math. Assn. Am., Phi Beta Kappa. Achievements include development of quantitative analysis of magnetic targeting of microspheres in capillaries, experiments and theory on magnetized electron plasmas, new camera-diagnosed electron plasma apparatus, new laser-diagnosed ion plasma apparatus for in-situ transport measurements; establishment of magnetic containment characteristics of unneutralized plasmas; measurement of collisional transport of heat and particles to thermal equilibrium; observation of new 2D fluid instability and relaxation of 2D turbulence to vortex crystal states. Office: U Calif San Diego Dept Physics 0319 9500 Gilman Dr Dept 0319 La Jolla CA 92093-5004 E-mail: fdriscoll@ucsd.edu.

DRISCOLL, CONSTANCE FITZGERALD, educator, writer; b. Lawrence, Mass., Mar. 29, 1926; d. John James and Mary Anne (Leecock) Fitzgerald; m. Francis George Driscoll, Aug. 21, 1948; children: Frances Mary, Martha Anne, Sara Helene, Maribeth Lee. AB, Radcliffe Coll., 1946; postgrad., Harvard U., U. Hartford, U. Bridgeport, U. Mass. Secondary sch. tchr., North Andover, Mass., 1946-48; book reviewer N.Y.C. and Boston pubs., 1955-64; asst. conf. edn. dir. U. Hartford, 1964-68; lectr. Pace U., N.Y.C., 1973-74; edn. commentary Radio WVOX, New Rochelle, N.Y., 1974-75; asst. ednl. adv. Nat. Girl Scouts, 1972-74; pres., owner, dir. Open Corridor Schs. Cons., Inc., Bronxville, N.Y., 1972-84; pres., dir. Open Corridor Schs., Inc., Oxford, Mass., 1984—2003, Sarasota and Jacksonville, Fla., 2003—, Bradenton, Fla., 2003—. Dir. assoc. grad. edn. program with U. Hartford, Bronxville, N.Y., 1975-82; dir. grad. edn. program Witt U. Bridgeport, Greenwich, Conn., 1975-82; creator in svc. edn. programs pub. schs., Norwalk, Conn., 1983-88; assoc. Worcester State Coll., 1984-85, Fitchburg State Coll., 1986-87; dir. assoc. grad. edn. for tchrs. Anna Maria Coll., Paxton, Mass., 1990-94; assoc. grad. tchr. edn. courses Fitchburg State Coll., 1995-99; English instr. grades 9-12, Bais Chana H.S. for Girls, Worcester, Mass., 2000—; provider long distance learning grad. edn. courses, Antigua and Anguilla, 1997—, U. Bridgeport, Conn., 1995—. assoc. agy. for grad. edn. courses for tchrs., 1995—; profl. devel. points provider Mass. State Dept. Edn., 1995—; tutor, cons. Worcester County Sch. Dists., 1989-95; CEU mgr. for Conn. Dept. Edn. O.C.S., Inc., Conn., 1989—; bi-lingual instr. for Indian and Vietnamese students in grades 5-12, 1988-91; freelance writer newspapers and small jours., 1991—; dir. grad. edn. courses for tchrs. Mass. Coll. Liberal Arts, North Adams, Mass., 1999—; cons. coll./univ. and grad. sch. placement, admissions procedures, 2000—; adviser, cons. Radcliffe Coll. Admissions Coun., 1946-48; summer dir. swim program ARC, North Andover, Mass., 1942-47; cons. Girl Scouts U.S., health guide multicultural program Greater Lawrence, Mass., 1946-48, holiday radio program, Thanksgiving 1774, Antigua and Barbuda; lectr., series for Girl Guides, Antigua, W.I., Nov., 1974. Author curriculum materials; contbr. poetry to Poetry Corner in The Patriot newspaper, 1994—, others. Recipient Educator award Nat. Coun. ARC, Washington, 1985, Edn. award Nipmuc Am. Indian Coun., Webster, Mass., 1985. Office: Open Corridor Schs Inc 3522 53d Ave W Ste 160 Bradenton FL 34210 also: Open Corridor Schs Inc 1015 Atlanta Blvd Ste 273 Atlantic Beach FL 32233

DRISCOLL, DAVID LEE, chiropractor; b. Storm Lake, Iowa, Aug. 3, 1954; s. Glenn Francis and Jeannine Ann (Layer) D.; m. Joan Marie Valle, Sept. 8, 1973; children: Jennifer Marie, Matthew Bryan. D Chiropractic, Logan Coll. Chiropractic, Chesterfield, Mo., 1978. Pvt. practice, Colorado Springs, 1978—. Fellow Internat. Biocranial Acad. (assoc. instr., ednl. dir.), Internat. Acad. Clin. Acupuncture; mem. Am. Chiropractic Assn., Colo. Chiropractic Assn., El Paso County Chiropractic Assn., Internat. Biocranial Acad. (ednl. dir.). Republican. Roman Catholic. Avocations: volleyball, golf, reading. Home: 813 Crown Ridge Dr Colorado Springs CO 80904-1731 Office: Driscoll Chiropractic 1819 W Colorado Ave Colorado Springs CO 80904-3836 E-mail: driscollbct@aol.com.

DRISCOLL, DAWN-MARIE, lawyer; b. Framingham, Mass., Nov. 5, 1946; d. Paul Francis and Wanda Louise (Haznar) D.; m. Norman Marcus. BA, Regis Coll., 1968; JD, Suffolk U., 1973, DHL (hon.), 1989; DCS (hon.), Bentley Coll., 1994; DA (hon.), Regis Coll., 2002. Bar: Mass. 1973. Asst. counsel Mass. Senate, Boston, 1973-78; counsel William Filene's Sons Co., Boston, 1978-80, v.p. corp. affairs, gen. counsel, 1980-88; ptnr. Palmer & Dodge, 1988-90; pres. Driscoll Assocs., 1991—. Exec. fellow Ctr. Bus. Ethics Bentley Coll., 1995—; trustee Scudder Funds, 1987—; dir. 1st Internat. Life Ins. Co., 1990-92, Premier Life Assurance Co. N.Y., 1991-92; mem. bd. govs. Investment Co. Inst., 1995-97, 99—; bd. dirs. CRS Tech.; mem. adv. coun. divsn. employment security State of Mass., 1985-90; bd. dirs., mem. exec. com. Boston Mcpl. Rsch. Bur., 1978-92, chmn., 1988-90; lectr. Law Sch., Suffolk U., 1975, Law Sch., Boston Coll., 1976; bd. dirs. New Eng. Legal Found., Boston, 1980-85, United Way of Mass. Bay, 1989-91; overseer Sta. WGBH-TV, 1988-95, Children's Hosp., 1989-94; mem. adv. bd. Bentley Coll. Ctr. Bus. Ethics, 1991—; mem. adv. bd. Women's Equity Fund Colo., 1992-98; visitor in residence Bunting Inst. Radcliffe Coll., 1990-91. Co-author: Members of The Club: The Coming of Age of Executive Women, 1993, The Ethical Edge: Tales of Organizations That Have Faced Moral Crises, 1996, Ethics Matters: How to Implement Values-Driven Management, 2000. Trustee, mem. exec. com. Regis Coll., Weston, Mass., 1983-90; trustee, bd. dirs. Roxbury Cmty. Coll. Found., 1985-88; mem. Mass. Gov.'s Commn. on Mature Industries, 1983-84; bd. dirs. Downtown Crossing Assn., Boston, 1980-90, chmn., 1980-83; bd. dirs. Better Bus. Bur., 1984, Social Policy Rsch. Group, 1985-89, Mass. Assn. Mental Health, 1985-90. Mass. grad. legis. fellow, Boston, 1969-70. Mem. Nat. Assn. Corp. Dirs., Internat. Women's Forum, Soc. Bus. Ethics, Mass. Women's Forum, Boston Econ. Club. Office: Driscoll Assocs 4909 SW 9th Pl Cape Coral FL 33914-7344

DRISCOLL, EDWARD CARROLL, construction management firm executive; b. Phila., Dec. 25, 1929; s. Leon Francis and Helen (Carroll) D.; m. Nancy Bell, Sept. 22, 1951 (dec.); children: Edward Carroll Jr., David B., Susan H. (dec.); m. Joan Barton, Aug. 14, 2002. AB, U. Pa., 1951. Estimator L.F. Driscoll Co., Phila., 1954-67, sec., 1967-69, pres. Bala Cynwyd, Pa., 1969-75, chief exec. officer, chmn. bd., 1975—. Bd. dirs. Provident Nat. Bank, Phila., Library Co., Phila., Nat. Bldg. Mus., Washington. Trustee Thomas Jefferson U., 1974—, chmn. bd. trustees, 1984-90; trustee Childrens' Heart Hosp., 1976-81; mem. adv. coun. Wills Eye Hosp., 1979—, bd. dirs., 1979-83; bd. dirs. Internat. House, 1978-89; mem. adv. bd., bd. dirs. U. Pa. Ctr. for Study of Aging, 1983—. Served to lt. USN, 1951-54 Mem. Gen. Bldg. Contractors' Assn. (bd. dirs. 1972-85), Chief Exec.'s Orgn., Phila. Pres.' Orgn., Young Pres.' Orgn., Phila. Club, Phila. Cricket Club, Union League Club (Phila.), Sunnybrook Golf Club (Plymouth Meeting, Pa.). Roman Catholic. Office: LF Driscoll Co 9 Presidential Blvd Bala Cynwyd PA 19004-1003

DRISCOLL, GARRETT BATES, retired telecommunications executive; b. Terre Haute, Ind., July 10, 1932; s. James Edgar and Lorraine Emma (Simmons) D.; m. Suzanne Keder O'Reilly, Apr. 30, 1960 (div. Sept. 1984); children: Garrett Edward, Lorraine Elizabeth Driscoll Veltri; m. Ivy Juanita Bryant, Sept. 24, 1985 (div. Aug. 1995); children: Jennifer Louise, Caroline Margaret; m. Janice Patterson Buckalew, Oct. 25, 1996. AA, Broward C.C., Ft. Lauderdale, Fla., 1973; BA, Fla. Atlantic U., Boca Raton, 1979. Tech. supr. TRT Telecom. Corp., Ft. Lauderdale, 1972-80, asst. mgr. N.Y. ops. N.Y.C., 1980-82; asst. v.p. telecom. 1st Am. Bank, Lake Worth, Fla., 1983-86; dir. telecom. R&D John Alden Sys. Co., Miami, Fla., 1986-97; advisor Jan Gar Enterprises, Lake Wales, Fla., 1997—98. Lectr. U. Miami, 1988-97. With USAF, 1951-71. Lutheran. Avocations: reading, woodworking, exercise. E-mail: jangrp@msn.com.

DRISCOLL, GENEVIEVE BOSSON (JEANNE BOSSON DRISCOLL), management and organization development consultant; b. Pitts., Mar. 26, 1937; d. George August and Emma Haling Bleichner; m. John Edwin Bosson, June 17, 1959; 1 child, Matthew Edwin; m. Frederick Driscoll, Oct. 7, 1972; stepchildren: Jennifer Locke, Cynthia Hall, Molly Davis, Julie Ann. BS cum laude, Fla. State U., 1959; postgrad., Nat. Tng. Labs., 1970. Planning asst. Ctr. Planning and Innovation, Dept. Edn. State of N.Y., 1967-71; planning cons. So. Tier Regional Office for Ednl. Planning, Elmira, N.Y., 1971-72; tng. dir. Neusteters, Inc., Denver, 1973-74; orgn. devel. specialist CONNECT, Inc., N.Y.C., 1975-77; cons. Robert H. Schaffer & Assocs., Stamford, Conn., 1977-80; ptnr. Driscoll Cons. Group, Williamstown, Mass., 1980-99; sales tng. mgr. Sheaffer Eaton, Pittsfield, Mass., 1983, mgr. human resources and orgn. devel., 1983-88; dir. human resources Canyon Ranch, Berkshires, 1989-95; dir. The Learning Inst., Bennington, Vt., 1997-99; ret., 1999. Office: 24 Lee Ter Williamstown MA 01267-2039

DRISCOLL, HENRY KEANE, endocrinologist, researcher; b. Boston, Dec. 24, 1953; s. John Joseph and Marie Elizabeth (Keane) D. SB in Life Scis., MIT, 1975, SM, 1976; MD, U. Mass., 1981. Diplomate Am. Bd. Internal Medicine, Bd. on Endocrinology and Metabolism. Asst. prof. medicine Sch. Medicine Marshall U., Huntington, W.Va., 1987-91, assoc. prof. medicine, 1991-96, prof., 1996—. Fellow ACP; mem. Am. Fedn. Med. Rsch., Am. Diabetes Assn. (pres. Heartland region 1999-2001, Clinician of Yr. W.Va. chpt. 1995-96), Endocrine Soc. Achievements include: rsch. in immunology of insulin-dependent diabetes mellitus; hormone secretions from pancreatic islets; actions of retinoids. Office: Marshall U Sch Medicine Dept Medicine Huntington WV 25701-3655

DRISCOLL, JOHN PAUL, civil engineer; b. Asheville, N.C., Mar. 14, 1951; s. John Edward and June (Fenwicke) D. BA in Liberal Arts, Belmont (N.C.) Abbey Coll., 1974; BS in Civil Engring., N.C. State U., 1974; MS in Engring., U. Tex., 1981. Registered profl. engr., N.C., S.C., Fla., Va.; cert. constrn. specifier. Hydraulic engr. U.S. Army Corps Engrs., Savannah, Ga., 1974-76; civil engr. U.S. Forest Svc., Asheville, 1979-80, City of Austin, Tex., 1980-81, Fed. Energy Regulatory Commn., Washington, 1982-84; project engr., mgr. DSA Group, Inc., Tampa, Fla., 1984-88; sr. engr. Law Engring., Inc., Charlotte, NC, 1988-97; sr. tech. cons. Joyce Engring., Inc., Greensboro, NC, 1997—2002; project mgr. City of Charlotte, 2002—. Roman Catholic. Home: 9100 Kings Canyon Dr Charlotte NC 28210-7676 Office: City of Charlotte 600 E Fourth St Charlotte NC 28202-2844

DRISCOLL, KATHLEEN J. writer; b. Boston, May 31, 1946; d. Frederick S. and Catherine T. McNamara D., one child, Catherine. Columnist, journalist The Patriot Ledger, Quincy, MA, 1979-84; editor The Pembroke Mariner, Pembroke, MA, 1984-86; acting pub., columnist South Shore News, Rockland, MA, 1986-94; columnist The Milton Times, Milton, MA, 1995—; feature writer Metro West Daily News, Framington, Mass., 1998—. Author, poetry, Dirty Woman's Rag, 1992, columns, features, NEPA, NFPW, Mass Media Women, etc. Vice pres., Natl. Org. for Women/MA, Mass., 1987-89. Mem., Natl. Writer's Union. Mailing: 451 Beech St Roslindale MA 02131

DRISCOLL, KERRY SUE, language educator; b. Dodge City, Kans., Sept. 20, 1972; d. Phillip Lane Gjerstad and Karen Kay Schubert; m. Ryan Murray Driscoll, July 29, 2000. BA, Coe Coll., 1994; MA, U. Iowa, 1996, MAT, 1998, PhD, 2003. Teaching asst. U. Iowa, Iowa City, 1994—2003; asst. prof. Spanish Augustana Coll., Rock Island, Ill., 2003—. Adj. instr. Coe Coll., Cedar Rapids, Iowa, 1999—2003; cons. Wiley Pubs., 2003. Mem.: Am. Coun. Teaching Fgn. Langs., Modern Lang. Assn., Phi Kappa Phi, Phi Beta Kappa. Avocation: running. Home: 208 Hillcrest Davenport IA 52803

DRISCOLL, MATTHEW J. mayor, restaurant manager, real estate developer; b. 1958; married; 3 children. 2d dist. councilor Syracuse Common Coun., 1987—89, 3d dist. councilor, 1995, pres., 1998—2001; mayor City of Syracuse, 2001—; prin., owner Restaurant. Office: 203 City Hall Syracuse NY 13202-1473*

DRISCOLL, MICHAEL HARDEE, lawyer; b. Houston, Mar. 24, 1946; s. Victor Amadale and Inez Mildred (Hardee) D. B.B.A., U. Houston, 1969, J.D., 1972. Bar: Tex. 1972. Precinct judge Harris County, Tex., 1969-73; justice of peace Harris County, Tex., 1973-78; judge City of Friendswood, Tex., 1978-80; hearing judge Tex. Edn. Agy., 1978-80; ptnr. Burge, Shults & Driscoll, Houston, 1978-80; elected county atty. Harris County, Houston, 1980— . Bd. dirs. Bay Area Drug Abuse Com., 1975-80, Riverside Gen. Hosp., 1977-80; mem. Salvation Army Boys' Club Adv. Council. Mem. State Bar Tex., Houston Bar Assn., Tex. Dist. and County Attys. Assn. (bd. dirs.), Houston C. of C. Democrat. Baptist. Lodges: Rotary, Scottish Rite, Shriners (Houston.). Office: County Atty's Office 1001 Preston St Houston TX 77002-1839

DRISCOLL, RICHARD STARK, retired land evaluation and land use planner; b. Denver, Sept. 16, 1928; s. Myron William and Edith Helene (Stark) D.; m. Joyce Lynn Yarbrough, Jan. 9, 1954; children: Vicki Lynn Driscoll Kiefe, Kelly Sue. BS, Colo. A&M, 1951; MS, Colo. State U., 1957; PhD, Oreg. State U., 1962. Range scientist USDA Forest Svc., Portland, Oreg., 1952-56, rsch. project leader, 1956-62, Washington, 1962-65, Ft. Collins, Colo., 1965-77, R & D program mgr., 1977-83; cons. FMA Internat., Inc., Gardnerville, Nev., 1983-91. Land-use expert UN-FAO, Rome, 1983-89; land use evaluation and planning Fust (Föderung von Umweltstudien), Achenkirch/Tyrol, Austria, 1993. Author, editor: Photo Interpretation for Ranges and Range Management, 1997; contbg. author Remote Sensing-Range Resources: Inventory, Evaluation, Monitoring, 1975; contbr. articles to profl. jours. Dist. chmn. Bend (Oreg.) area Boy Scouts Am., 1961-62, com. chair troop 26, Ft. Collins, Colo., 1969; mem., chair various coms. Westminster Presbyn. Ch. and Timnath Presbyn. Ch., Ft. Collins, 1972—; mem. and moderator com. on ministry Plains and Peaks Presbytery Presbyn. Ch. U.S.A., 1991-99, mem. com. lay pastor group, 1999—. Recipient presdl. citation for meritorious svc. Am. Soc. Photogrammetry and Remote Sensing, 1978, 86. Mem. Am. Inst. Biol. Scis., Soc. Range Mgmt. (Outstanding Achievement award 1983), Nat. Assn. Ret. Fed. Employees (chpt. pres. 1993-95, chair various coms. 1988-2003, pres. Colo. Fedn. 2003—, fed. v.p. for dist. IV 1996-2003), Xi Sigma Pi, Beta Beta Beta, Sigma Xi. Achievements include research on use of remote sensing technology for rangeland inventory and classification, range management planning and management, ecological land classification for land use planning in the U.S., and land evaluation, planning and management in the tropics and central Europe. Home and Office: 2217 Sheffield Dr Fort Collins CO 80526-1640

DRISCOLL, VIRGILYN MAE (SCHAETZEL), retired art educator, artist, consultant; b. Fond du Lac, Wis., May 14, 1932; d. Edward William and Louise (Heider) Schaetzel; m. Patrick A. Driscoll, Aug. 13, 1955; children: Mark P., Craig A., Chris T. BS in Art Edn., Wis. State Coll., 1954; MS in Art, U. Wis., Milw., 1973. Tchr. elem. art Green Bay (Wis.) Pub. Schs., 1954-55, Elm-Brook Pub. Schs., Elm Grove, Brookfield, Wis., 1955-58, supr. elem. art, 1958-66; tchr. secondary art, dept. chair Greendale (Wis.) Pub. Schs., 1967—93; exec. dir. Wis. Alliance Arts Edn., 1993—2000; dir., co-founder Wis. Champions for Arts Edn. Bus. and Cmty. Advs., Inc., 2002—. Arts Edn. Cons., 2000—; art curriculum task force Wis. Dept. Pub. Instrn., 1981—85; mem. task force Wis. Plan Arts Edn., Arts in Sch.s Basic Edn. Grant, 1986—88; mem. State Supts. Commn. Arts Edn., 1988—89; coord. Student Art Exhibit Wis. Assn. Sch. Bd. Joint Conv., 1988—; mem. steering com. arts edn. Wis. Arts Bd., Wis. Alliance Arts Edn., Dept. Pub. Instrn., 1992—; chmn. Wis. Challenging Content Stds. in Arts, 1994—96; coord., facilitator State Supt.'s Blue Ribbon Commn. Arts Edn., 1999—2000; mem. task force Wis. Dept. Pub. Instrn. Integrated Curriculum Guide, 1999—2000; hon. bd. dirs. Wis. Alliance Arts Edn., 2000—. Mem. editl. bd. Spectrum: Jour. Wis. Art Edn., 1986—87, 1988—90; author: (handbook) National Year of Secondary Art, 1990. Named Educator of the Yr., Beloit (Wis.) Coll., 1986, Wis. Rep. Tchr. Inst., 50th Ann. Nat. Gallery Art, Washington, 1991; recipient Excellence in the Arts award, 2000, cert. of Recognition in the Arts and Art Edn., 2000, Disting. Alumnus award, U. Wis., 2001, Distinction award for Dance Edn., 2002. Mem.: NEA, Milw. Area Tchrs. Art (pres. 1982 83), Wis. Painters and Sculptors, Wis. Alliance Art Edn. (pres. 1991—, bd. dirs.), Wis. Art Edn. Assn. (mem. adv. bd. Young Artists Workshop 1982—99, pres. 1985—87, 1987—89, mem. coun., Wis. Art Educator of the Yr. 1989, Career award 2000—), Nat. Art Edn. Assn. (bd. dirs. 1984—89, secondary divsn. dir., mem. exec. com. 1989—91, We. Region Art Educator of Yr. 1990), U. Wis. Milw. Alumni Assn. (1st v.p. 1966—73, pres. 1968—69, pres., emeritus bd. trustee 1996—2000, emeritus trustee 2000—, co-chair Chancellor's Soc. 2000—03, bd. dirs. womens alumni). Avocation: running. Home: 1161 N Lost Woods Rd Oconomowoc WI 53066-8790

DRISKELL, CLAUDE EVANS, college director, educator, dentist; b. Chgo., Jan. 13, 1926; s. James Ernest and Helen Elizabeth (Perry) D., Sr.; m. Naomi Roberts, Sept. 30, 1953; 1 child, Yvette Michele; stepchildren: Isaiah, Ruth, Reginald, Elaine. BS, Roosevelt U., 1950; BS in Dentistry, U. Ill., 1952, DDS, 1954. Practice dentistry, Chgo., 1954—; adj. prof. Chgo. State U., 1971—; dean's aide, adviser black students Coll. Dentistry U. Ill., 1972—. Dental cons., supervising dentist, dental hygienists supportive health services Bd. Edn., Chgo., 1974. Author: The Influence of the Halogen Elements Upon the Hydrocarbon, and their Effect on General Anesthesia, 1962; History of Chicago's Black Dental Professionals, 1850-1983; co-author (with Claude Driskell) Essays on Professor Dr. Earl Renfroe-A Man of Firsts, 2001; author, editor and publisher: Original Forty Club's 75th Anniversary Book (1920-1995); author, editor, archivist, historian Forty Club, 1993-2000; mem. editl. bd. Nat. Dental Assn. Quar. Jour., 1977—; contbr. articles to profl. jours. Vice pres. bd. dirs. Jackson Park Highlands Assn., 1971-73. Served with AUS, 1944-46; ETO. Fellow Internat. Biog. Assn., Royal Soc. Health (Gt. Britain), Acad. Gen. Dentistry; mem. Lincoln Dental Soc. (editor), Chgo. Dental Soc., ADA, Nat. Dental Assn. (editor pres.'s newsletter; dir. pub. relations, publicity; recipient pres.'s spl. achievement award 1969) dental assns., Am. Assn. Dental Editors, Acad. Gen. Dentistry, Soc. Med. Writers, Soc. Advancement Anesthesia in Dentistry, Omega Psi Phi. Home: 6727 S Bennett Ave Chicago IL 60649-1031 Office: 11139 S Halsted St Chicago IL 60628-3910

DRISKELL, LUCILE G. artist; b. NYC, Dec. 20, 1924; d. Charles Albert and Clarice Dorothy (Jung) Gall; m. Richard O. Driskell, Sept. 4, 1946; children: Douglas G., Donald A., David O. AA, Finch Coll., 1945; student, La Jolla Art Ctr., Calif., 1956-63, Fratelli Da Prato Foundry, Pietra Santa, Italy, 1973-78, Art Students League, N.Y.C., 1984-88. Artist, San Diego, Calif., 1950-63, Cin., 1963-67, Aspen, Colo., 1967-72, Greve in Chianti, Italy, 1972-79, Wellsboro, Pa., 1979—, Phila., 1985—. Represented by Environment Gallery, N.Y.C., 1968-84, Rodger Lapelle Gallery, Phila., 1984—, Agora Gallery, N.Y., 1993-2002, Amsterdam Whitney Internat. Fine Arts, N.Y.C., 2002—. Sculptures, 1960—, wall reliefs, 1988—, prints, 1956—. Represented in permanent collections Woodmere Art Mus., Phila. Recipient Purchase award First Union Bank, Wilmington, Del., 1996, Exxon, NYC, 1978, Macy's, Washington, 1989, SAS Inst. Inc., Cary, NC, 2001. Mem. Internat. Sculpture Ctr., Washington Sculpture Group, Art Students League (life). Avocations: hiking, photography, travel. Home: 507 Fischler St Ext Wellsboro PA 16901-8925

DRISKILL, ELITA MARTIN, humanities educator; b. Odessa, Tex., June 9, 1965; d. John Franklin and W.V. Sue Martin; m. Larry Dale Driskill, June 10, 1994. BA English Lang. Arts, Tex. Wesleyan U., Fort Worth, TX, 1988. Teaching Certificate Tex. Educator NW ISD, Justin, Tex., 1988—. Mentor tchr. trainer NW ISD, Justin, Tex., 1998—; 7th grade team leader, faculty coun. mem. NJHS. Contbr. articles on edn. and poetry to profl. jours. Recipient Disting. Tchr. award, N.W. Ednl. Found., 2001. Mem.: Tex. Fedn. of Teachers. Assemblies Of God. Avocations: reading, photography, stained glass, travel.

DRISKILL, JAMES LAWRENCE, minister; b. Rustburg, Va., Aug. 18, 1920; s. Elijah Hudnall and Annie Pharr (Carwile) D.; m. Ethel Lillian Cassel, May 28, 1949; children: Edward Lawrence, Mary Lillian. BA, Pa. State U., 1946; BD, San Francisco Theol. Sem., 1949; ThM, Princeton Sem., 1957; S.T.D., San Francisco Theol. Sem., 1969. Ordained minister in Presbyn. Ch., 1949. Missionary Presbyn. Ch. USA, Japan, 1949-72; stated supply pastor Madison Square Presbyn. Ch., San Antonio, 1973; minister Highland Presbyn. Ch., Maryville, Tenn., 1973-82; supply pastor of Japanese-Am. chs. Presbyn. Ch. USA, Long Beach, Calif., Hollywood, Calif., Altadena, Calif., 1984-99. Vis. prof. religion dept. Trinity U., 1972-73. Author: Adventures in Senior Living, 1997, Christmas Stories from Around the World, 1997, Worldwide Mission Stories for Young People, 1996, Cross-Cultural Marriages and the Church, 1995, Mission Stories from Around the World, 1994, Japan Diary, 1993, Mission Adventures in Many Lands, 1992; contbr. articles to profl. jours. Mem. Sierra Club, Calif., 1988—; trustee Osaka (Japan) Girls Sch., 1952-65, Seikyo Gakuen Christian Sch., Japan, 1953-92. With USN, 1943-46. Mem. Am. Acad. Religion, Presbyn. Writers Guild. Democrat. Presbyterian. Home and Office: 1420 Santo Domingo Ave Duarte CA 91010-2698 *Experience has taught me that, ultimately, the meaning and value of a person's life is determined by the quality of one's personal relationships, especially by the quality of one's relationship to God.*

DRITSCHILO, ANATOLY, radiologist, educator; b. Reigersfeld, Germany, Oct. 10, 1944; s. Peter Prokofovich and Maria (Ivanovna) Dritschilo; m. Joy Ann Dritschilo, Apr. 6, 1968; children: Peter Dale, Andrea Beth, Lisa Ann. BS, U. Pa., 1967; MS, Newark Coll. Engring., 1969; MD, U. Medicine, 1973. Diplomate Am. Bd. Radiology. Fellow Joint Ctr. Radiol. Therapy Harvard Med. Sch., Boston, 1974-77; asst. prof. radiation oncology Tufts New Eng. Med. Ctr., Boston, 1977-79; assoc. prof. radiation medicine Georgetown U., Washington, 1979-85, chmn. dept. radiation medicine, 1980—, prof. radiation medicine, 1985—, dean grad. med. edn., 1994-97, med. dir., 1994-97. Mem. ext. adv. com. U. Wis. Cancer Ctr., Madison, 1992-97; mem. sci. coun. Radiation Rsch., Reston, Va., 2000—; bd. dirs. Neopharm Inc., Bannockburn, Ill. Assoc. editor Radiation Oncology Investigations jour., 1995; patentee in field. Bd. dirs. Nat. Coalition for Cancer Rsch., Washington, 2000—. Fellow Am. Coll. Radiology; mem. NIH (grantee 1987—; mem. radiation study sect. 1990-94, sci. rev. group 1997—), Am. Soc. Clin. Oncologists, Am. Assn. Cancer Rsch., Am. Radium Soc., Radiation Rsch. Soc., Am. Soc. Radiation Oncologists. Russian Orthodox. Avocations: golf, tennis, painting. Office: Georgetown U Hosp 3800 Reservoir Rd NW Washington DC 20007 E-mail: dritschd@georgetown.edu.

DRITSCHILO, WILLIAM, educator; b. Villach, Austria, Nov. 11, 1946; came to the U.S., 1949; s. Peter Prokofiev and Maria Ivanova (Kardash) Schematulsky; m. Jaime Porter Dritschilo, May 16, 1970; children: Gordon Alexander, Christina. BA, BS, U. Pa., 1970; PhD, Cornell U., 1978. Rsch. asst. U. Pa., Phila., 1971-73; rsch. assoc. Washington U., St. Louis, 1977-78; asst. prof. UCLA, 1978-85; sci. tchr. Rutland (Vt.) City Schs., 1985—2002. Adj. prof. Green Mountain Coll., Poultney, Vt., 1996—; cons. in field. Contbr. articles to profl. jours. Mem. AAAS, Sigma Xi.

DRIVER, JENNIFER, communications educator; b. Garland, Tex., Aug. 19, 1974; d. Barry and Virginia Horton; m. Derek Horton, July 4, 1999; children: Baylee Smith-Driver, Brinklee. BA, Tex. A&M Commerce, 1996—98, Med, 2000—02. Standard Prin. Cert. Tex. State Bd. of Educator Certification, 2002, Secondary Language Arts Tchg. Cert. Tex. State Bd. of Educator Certification, 1998. Classroom tchr. Garland Ind. Sch. Dist., Tex., 1998—. Dir. of cheerleading program North Garland H.S., Tex. Home: 1613 Blair Garland TX 75040

DRIVER, JOE L. state legislator, insurance agent; b. Rockwall, Tex., Sept. 29, 1946; s. Marshall Laguin and Alice Elizabeth (Patillo) D.; m. S. DeAnne Browning, Nov. 20, 1993; stepchildren: Eric Browning, Lynsey Browning. BBA, U. North Tex., 1971; grad., Garland Citizen's Police Acad., 1993. With Steak & Ale Restaurants, Dallas, 1971—73; instr. Garland (Tex.) Ind. Sch. Dist., 1972; mgr. Marshall Driver Ins., Garland, 1972-73; owner, agt. Joe Driver Ins.-State Farm, Garland, Tex., 1973 ; mem. Tex. Ho. of Reps., 1993—, mem. energy resources com., 1993—95, 1997—2003, mem. ins. com., 1993-97, mem. pub. safety com., 1995—2003, vice chmn. pub. safety com., 1997-99, chmn. select com. constitutional revision Tex. constitution, 1999—2003, chmn. law enforcement com., 2003—, mem. legis. and adminstrv. procedures com., 2003—. Pres. Christian Singles Unltd., Garland, 1979; bd. dirs. First United Meth. Ch., Garland, 1979-81, Garland Econ. and Devel. Authority, 1986, Garland Crimestoppers, 1985-88, 93—, Am. Heart Assn., 1991-93; bd. dirs. New Beginning Family and Violence Prevention Ctr., 1988-91, v.p., 1990-91; chmn. SITE Found. of Garland, Inc., 1991-92; mem. bd. mgmt. Garland YMCA, 1983-85; fundraising chmn. YWCA, 1992; mem. long-range planning com. City of Garland, 1986-88; mem. devel. coun. Baylor Med. Ctr., Garland, 1991—; mem. Downtown Citizen Rev. Com., 1991-92; active Tex. Conservative Coalition, 1993—, Rep. Caucus Tex. Ho. of Reps., 1993—. Recipient Human Relations award Dale Carnegie Cos., 1978. Mem. Nat. Assn. Life Underwriters (Nat. Quality award 1978-83, 86-92, 2002), Dallas Assn. Life Underwriters, Garland C. of C. (bd. dirs. 1983-87, chmn. 1986, corp. coun. 1988-90), Rowlett C. of C., Sachse C. of C., Tex. Dist. Exch. Clubs (dist. dir. 1984, Outstanding Dist. Dir. award 1985, Pres.'s award 1986), Noon Exch. Club Garland (bd. dirs. 1982-86, 90-91, pres. 1983, 90, Outstanding Svc. award 1986-87), Leadership Garland Alumni Assn. (bd. dirs. 1990-91), U. North Tex. Alumni Assn., Lambda Chi Alpha (pres. 1971). Avocations: golf, weight training. Office: 201 S Glenbrook Dr Garland TX 75040-6227

DRIVER, MARTHA WESTCOTT, English language educator, writer, researcher; b. N.Y.C., Oct. 24; d. Albert Westcott and Martha Louise (Miller) D.; m. Thomas Edward Earl Rhodes, Aug. 4, 2001. BA, Vassar Coll., 1974; MA, U. Pa., 1975, PhD, 1980. Lectr. English Vassar Coll., N.Y.C., 1980-81; from asst. prof. to assoc. prof. Pace U., N.Y.C., 1981-95, prof. English, 1995—, dir. honors program, 1998-2000, disting. prof., 2003—. Cons. N.Y. Pub. Libr., 1984; seminar participant Folger Inst., Folger Shakespeare Libr., 1994. Editor: Jour. of the Early Book Soc., 1998—2003; guest editor: Film & History: The Middle Ages, 1998—99, Literary and Linguistic Computing, 1999; contbr. 35 articles to profl. jours. Mem., lectr. St. John the Divine, N.Y.C., 1995. Recipient Dyson Achievement award, 2003; grantee Rsch. tools grantee, NEH, 1995, travel grantee, Am. Coun. Learned Socs., 1995, NSF, 2001—; Houghton Libr. Harvard U. fellow, 1996—97. Mem. Early Book Soc. (chair 1988), Coll. Art Assn., Medieval Acad. Am., Modern Humanities Rsch. Assn. (U.K.), Medieval Club of N.Y. (conf. coord. 1989-94, pres. 1987-89), Internat. Ctr. Medieval Art, Internat. Arthurian Soc., Medieval Feminist Art History Project, New Chaucer Soc. Episcopalian. Avocations: dancing, museums, theater, concerts. Office: Pace U English Dept 41 Park Row New York NY 10038-1508 E-mail: mdriver@pace.edu.

DRIVER, MICHAELA CLAUDIA, organizational behavior and development educator; b. Berlin, July 2, 1967; arrived in U.S., 1989; d. Michael Hauke and Gabriele-Ines Hoffmann; m. Douglas Lee Driver, Aug. 14, 1989; 1 child, Simon Julien. BA in Mktg., U. Ala., 1993, M. Human Resource Mgmt., 1995, PhD in Orgnl. Behavior, 1997. Prin. cons. PriceWaterhouse LLP, N.Y.C., 1998—; assoc. prof. mgmt. East Tenn. State U., Johnson City, 1998—. Contbr. articles to profl. jours. including Human Rels.; reviewer Mgmt. Learning Jour., Human Rels. Grantee Presdl. grantee, East Tenn. State U., 2002, Instructional grantee, 2002, Instructional Devel. grantee, 1999. Mem.: Bus. Educators Acad., Acad. of Mgmt. Avocations: painting, dressage. Office: East Tenn State Univ Dept Mgmt Box 70625 Johnson City TN 37614

DRIVER, PHYLLIS NELKE, accountant, educator; b. Fort Smith, Ark., Nov. 12, 1941; d. Edward Anton and Anna Sue (Maxey) Nelke; m. Edward Ely Driver III, Aug. 10, 1965. BA, U. Ark., 1963; MBA, U. Tenn., 1973; postgrad., U. Antwerp, 1999. CPA, Tenn. Sys. analyst Genesco Inc., Nashville, 1963-65, Varian Electronics, Palo Alto, Calif., 1966-67; instr. Electronic Computer Programming Inst., Knoxville, Tenn., 1967-69; rsch. asst. Ctr. Bus. and Econ. Rsch. U. Tenn., Knoxville, 1968-72, grad. tchg. asst., 1972-78; asst. prof. acctg. Carson Newman Coll., Jefferson City, Tenn., 1978-85, assoc. prof., 1985—, chair dept. bus. and econ., 1989-92. Evaluator Hiwassee Coll., Athens, Tenn., 1990; tchr. Tenn. Valley Authority, Knoxville, Martin Marietta, Oak Ridge, Tenn., Zheng Zhou U. China, Henan, 1994, Inst. Econ., Baku, Azerbaijan, 1997, Inst. Commerce, Baku, 1997. Mem. task force Shades-Math. and Sci. Mid. Sch. Girls, Knoxville; vol. Habitat for Humanity, Knoxville; v.p. Knoxville Opera Guild, 1998—99, treas., 1999—2000, sec., 2000—01; chmn. budget and fin. com. Presbytery E. Tenn., 2000—; bd. trustees Pellissippi State Tech. Cmty. Coll. Found., 2002—; bd. dir. YWCA, 2000—. Mellon Salzburg Seminar fellow, 1997; named Woman of Yr. in Edn., YWCA Knoxville, 1999. Mem.: AICPA (task force 1989—91, tchr. fin. mgmt. course 1992—93), AAUW (state pres. 1996—98, nat. leadership devel. team 1998—2000, mem. fin. com. Ednl. Found. 1999—2001, nat. mem. svcs. com. 2001—), District Rotary Leadership Acad. (mem. 2003), Inst. Mgmt. Accts. (Knoxville pres. 1995—96, Tenn. Valley coun. pres. 2001—02, nat. mem. svcs. com. 2001—03), Tenn. Soc. CPA (state bd. dir. 1994—97), Am. Acctg. Assn., Rotary (dist. youth exch. 1993—, pres. Jefferson City chpt. 1994—95, chmn. dist. youth exch. com. 2002—03, bd. dir. Bulgarian Child 2002—, Rotarian of Yr. 1995). Avocations: theater, travel, reading, theatre, opera, ballroom dancing. Office: Carson Newman Coll Box 71910 Jefferson City TN 37760 E-mail: pdriver@cn.edu.

DRIVER, ROBERT BAYLOR, JR., opera company administrator; b. Sao Paolo, Brazil, Aug. 26, 1942; came to U.S., 1949, naturalized, 1960; s. Robert Baylor and Mary Louise (Riechman) D.; m. Monica B. Macrae, 1968; 1 child, Katharine. BA, U. Va., 1964; MA, Middlebury (Vt.) Coll., 1971; postgrad., Johns Hopkins U. Asst. stage dir. Die Bayerische Staatsoper, 1966-68; asst. dir. Ky. Opera Assn., 1968-71; assoc. dir. Kansas City Lyric Opera, 1974-75; artistic dir. Opera Theatre, Syracuse, N.Y., 1975-87, Indpls. Opera, 1981-91, Opera Co. Phila., 1991—. Sec. Opera Memphis, Tenn., 1984-91. Mem.: OPERA Am. (bd. dirs.). Office: Opera Co of Philadelphia 1420 Locust St Ste 210 Philadelphia PA 19102-3601 Office Fax: 215-893-7801.

DRIVER, SHARON HUMPHREYS, marketing executive; b. Staten Island, N.Y., Jan. 5, 1949; d. William Edward and Gloria (McCrave) Humphreys; m. William Weston Driver, Jr., June 3, 1972; children: Christopher John, Andrea Nicole. BA, Manhattanville Coll., Purchase, N.Y., 1970; MA, Coll. New Rochelle, N.Y., 1973. Lic. tchr., N.Y. Tchr. Somers (N.Y.) Ctrl. Sch. Dist., 1970-76, Ossining (N.Y.) Village Recreation Dept., 1983-87; media coord., bookkeeper Equation Comm., White Plains, N.Y., 1986-89; media dir. Sims Freeman O'Brien, Elmsford, N.Y., 1989-90; project dir. Rsch. Advantage, Hawthorne, N.Y., 1990-92; asst. v.p. Merson/Greener Assocs., Tarrytown, N.Y., 1992-94; pres. Decision Drivers, Briarcliff, 1994—. Sec. tng. liason, Jr. League, Westchester-on-Hudson, 1982-88; sustainer, trainer-facilitator, Jr. League, Tarrytown, 1988-96; past pres. St. Theresa's Parish Coun., Briarcliff Manor, N.Y.; sec. bd. dirs. Ossining Open Door Health Clinic, 1985-89. Mem. NAFE, Am. Mktg. Assn., Women in Comm. (bd. dirs.), Ad Club of Westchester (bd. dirs.), Qualitative Rsch. Cons. Assn., Sleepy Hollow Toastmasters (charter, sec. exec. com.). Roman Catholic. Avocations: boating, hiking. Home: 197 Macy Rd Briarcliff Manor NY 10510-1017

DRIVER, TOM FAW, theologian, writer, justice/peace advocate, photographer; b. Johnson City, Tenn., May 31, 1925; s. Leslie Rowles and Sarah (Broyles) D.; m. Anne L. Barstow, June 7, 1952; children: Katharine Anne, Paul Barstow, Susannah Ambrose. AB, Duke U., 1950; M.Div., Union Theol. Sem., 1953; PhD, Columbia U., 1957; D.Litt., Denison U., 1970. Ordained to ministry United Meth. Ch., 1951. Dir. youth work Riverside Ch., N.Y.C., 1955-56; faculty Union Theol. Sem., N.Y.C., 1956-93, Paul J. Tillich prof. theology and culture, 1973-93, emeritus, 1993—. Drama critic Christian Century, 1956-62, Sta. WBAI-FM, 1960-61, The Reporter, 1963 64; vis. assoc. prof. English Columbia U., 1964-65; vis. assoc. prof. religion Barnard Coll., 1965-66, Fordham U., 1967; cons. humanities and arts Coll. Old Westbury (N.Y.), 1970; William Evans vis. prof. religion U. Otago, N.Z., 1976; vis. prof. religion Vassar Coll., 1978, Montclair State Coll., 1981; vis. prof. English lit. Doshisha U., Kyoto, Japan, 1983. Author: liberetto for oratorio The Invisible Fire, 1957; The Sense of History in Greek and Shakespearean Drama, 1960, Jean Genet, 1966, Romantic Quest and Modern Query: A History of The Modern Theater, 1970, Patterns of Grace: Human Experience as Word of God, 1977, Christ in a Changing World: Toward an Ethical Christology, 1981, The Magic of Ritual: Our Need for Liberating Rites that Transform Our Lives and Our Communities, 1991, Liberating Rites: Understanding the Transformative Power of Ritual, 1997; editor: (with Robert Pack) Poems of Doubt and Belief, 1964; prodr., photographer (video, with Anne Barstow): Colombia: The Next Vietnam?, 2001 also articles. Bd. dirs. dept. worship and arts Nat. Council Chs., 1958- 63, Found. for Arts, Religion and Culture, 1963-67. Served with AUS, 1943-46. Kent fellow, 1953; Guggenheim fellow, 1962-63 Mem. ACLU, Am. Acad. Religion, New Haven Theol. Group, Soc. Values in Higher Edn., Presbyn. Peace Fellowship, Witness for Peace, Vets. for Peace, Soc. of Arts, Religion & Contemporary Culture, Phi Beta Kappa, Omicron Delta Kappa. Mem. United Methodist Ch. Home: 501 W 123rd St Apt 14G New York NY 10027-5010 E-mail: tfd3@columbia.edu.

DRIVER, WALTER W., JR., lawyer; b. El Paso, Tex., Apr. 10, 1945; s. Walter Williamson and Carolyn Bonds (Mayfield) D.; m. Bettie Townsend Willerson, Dec. 27, 1970; children: Eleanor, Anna, Walter III. AB, Stanford U., 1967; JD, U. Tex., 1970. Bar: Ga. 1970. Ptnr. King & Spalding, LLP, Atlanta, 1976—, chmn. policy com., 1992-94, 98-99, mng. ptnr., chmn., 2000—. Mem. exec. com. Children's Mus. Atlanta, 1990-95; bd. dirs. Ctrl. Atlanta Progress, 1993—; chair Celebration of Life Cancer Soc., 1993. Mem. ABA, State Bar Ga., U.S. Golf Assn. (gen. counsel 1997-99, mem. exec. com. 1999—, treas. 2000-01, v.p. 2001—), Ga. State Golf Assn. (gen. coun., exec. com. 1988-97), Atlanta C. of C. (exec. com., bd. dirs.), Piedmont Driving Club, Peachtree Golf Club (bd. dirs.), Pine Valley Golf Club, Seminole Golf Club. Office: King & Spalding LLP 191 Peachtree St Atlanta GA 30303-1763 E-mail: wdriver@kslaw.com.

DRNEVICH, VINCENT PAUL, civil engineering educator; b. Wilkinsburg, Pa., Aug. 6, 1940; s. Louis B. and Mary (Kutcel) D.; m. Roxanne M. Hosier, Aug. 20, 1966; children: Paul, Julie, Jenny, Marisa. BSCE, U. Notre Dame, 1962, MSCE, 1964; PhD, U. Mich., 1967. Registered profl. engr., Ky., Ind. Asst. prof. civil engring. U. Ky., Lexington, 1967-73, assoc. prof., 1973-78, prof., 1978-91; chmn. civil engring., 1980-84; acting dean engring. U. Ky., Lexington, 1989-90; prof., head Sch. Civil Engring. Purdue U., West Lafayette, Ind., 1991-2000. Dir. joint hwy. rsch. project Purdue U., 1991-95; pres. Soil Dynamics, Instruments, Inc., West Lafayette, 1974—. Inventor in field. Fellow ASCE (chmn. dept. heads coun. exec. com. 1996-2000, vice chmn. com. on edn.-practitioner interface, 1994-98, Norman medal 1973, Huber Rsch. prize 1980), ASTM (exec. com., tech. editor Geotech. Testing Jour. 1985-89, C.A. Hogentogler award 1979, Merit award 1993, Woodland Shockley award 1996); mem. NSPE, Am. Soc. Engring. Edn. (sec./treas. civil engring. divsn. 1995-98, dir. 1999—, vice chair 2002-03, chair 2003—), Transp. Rsch. Bd., Earthquake Engring. Rsch. Inst., Ind. Soc. Profl. Engrs. (pres. A.A. Potter chpt.), Chi Epsilon (Harold T. Larson award 1985, James M. Robbins award 1989). Roman Catholic. Avocations: golf, fishing. Office: Purdue U 550 Stadium Mall Dr West Lafayette IN 47907-2051

DRNJEVIC, JONATHAN MARK, language educator; b. Phoenix, Dec. 20, 1959; s. Mirko and Ruth Drnjevic. PhD, Ariz. State U., 1997. Faculty assoc. English dept. Ariz. State U., Tempe, Ariz., 1998—, libr. specialist. Mem.: MLA. Lutheran. Home: 4032 E St Joseph Way Phoenix AZ 85018-1102 Personal E-mail: jmd@asu.edu.

DROBAC, NIKOLA (NICK DROBAC), educator; b. Rochester, Pa., Feb. 11, 1953; s. Stevan Sr. and Madeline Mildred (Resanovich) D. AS, C.C. of Beaver County, 1975; BS, U. Pitts., 1977; MS, U. So. Calif., 1986. Sr. loss control cons. Fireman's Fund Ins. Cos., Fairfax, Va, 1977-87; risk mgmt. coord. Carnegie-Mellon U., Pitts., 1988-89; ins. mgr. Gen. Nutrition, Inc., Pitts., 1989-90; pers. cons. Tricon Tech., Pitts., 1990-92; lectr. bus. dept. C.C. Beaver County, Monaca, Pa., 1992-93; intermittent intake interviewer unemployment compensation Commonwealth Pa. Dept. Labor and Industry Beaver County Job Ctr., 1992-96; instr. C.C. of Allegheny County, 1994-95; tchr. So. Garrett County H.S., Oakland, Md., 1995—2003; head golf coach So.Garrett County H.S., Oakland, Md., 1995-96; head tennis coach So. Garrett County H.S., Oakland, Md., 1997, asst. mock trial advisor, 2000. Adj. instr. bus./computer applications Garrett C.C., McHenry, Md., 1996, 97. Del. Rep. Presdl. Conv., Washtenaw County, Mich., 1980; vol. basketball coach Carnegie-Mellon U., Pitts., 1988-89; vol. football coach and scout Aliquippa (Pa.) H.S., 1991-92; mem. choir St. Elijah Serbian Orthodox. Ch.; instrument player Kumovi Adult Tamuuritzan Group, Pitts. Mem. Masons (Monaca Ctr.), Am. Serbian Eastern Rite Brothers (3d v.p. 1997-99, 2d v.p. 1999-2001, 1st v.p. 2002—), Shriners. Serbian Orthodox. Avocations: computers, golf, photography, church choir. Home: 1616 Tyler St Aliquippa PA 15001-2036 E-mail: professor@beer.com., professor@teachers.org.

DROBENA, THOMAS JOHN, minister, educator; b. Chgo., Aug. 23, 1934; s. Thomas and Suzanne (Durec) D.; m. Wilma S. Kucharek, Dec. 27, 1980; children: Thomas Samuel, Joshua Michael. BA, Valparaiso U., 1964; ThB, Concordia Theol. Sem., 1961, MDiv, 1974; MA, Hebrew U., Jerusalem, 1968; PhD, Calif. Grad. Sch. Theology, 1975; STM, Luth. Theol. Sem., 1986; DSc (hon.), London U. Ordained to ministry Evang. Luth. Ch. in Am., 1962. English pastor Redeemer Luth. Ch., Jerusalem, 1967-68; prin. St. Mark's Luth. Ch., Bklyn., 1968-69; pastor Ascension Luth. Ch., Binghamton, N.Y., 1969-78, Holy Emmanuel, Mahoney City, Pa., 1981-86, St. John, St. Clair, Pa., 1981-86, Nanticoke, Pa., 1981-86; co-pastor Holy Trinity Luth. Ch., Torrington, Conn., 1986—. Adj. prof. SUNY, Binghamton, 1975-77; chairperson Global Missions, Evang. Luth. Ch. in Am., Chgo., 1985—; v.p., treas. Slavic Heritage Inst., Torrington, 1965—. Co-author: Heritage of the Slavs, 1976; editor The Zion, 1995—, Slovo, 1998—; contbr. articles to profl. jours. Chaplain Civil Air Patrol USAFA, 1964—; bd. dirs. ARC, 1986—; pres. Crimestoppers, 1988—, New Eng. Hist. Soc., 1990 ; co-chair internat. rels. com. ELCA-Slovak Zion Synod, 1995. Grantee U.S. State Dept., Jerusalem, 1967-68, U. Ill. Russian and East European Ctr., Urbana, 1980—. Fellow Istituto Slovacco; mem. Am. Assn. for the Advancement of Slavic Studies, Am. Assn. of Tchrs. of Slavic and East European Langs., Czechoslovak Soc. for the Arts and Scis., New Eng. Luth. Hist. Soc. (pres. 1990—, editor Jour. New Eng. Luth. Hist. Soc. 1995—). Office: Slavic Heritage Inst PO Box 1003 Torrington CT 06790-1003

DROBIS, DAVID R. public relations company executive; Formerly pres., COO Ketchum Pub. Rels., N.Y.C., sr. ptnr. and CEO, 1992—. Office: Ketchum Pub Rels Worldwide 292 Madison Ave New York NY 10017-6307

DROBIZHEV, MIKHAIL ANATOLIEVICH, physicist; b. Moscow, Mar. 8, 1963; s. Anatolii Ivanovich Drobizhev and Nelli Oganesovna Shakhbazyan; m. Irina Pavlovna Kochetkova, May 26, 1990; 1 child, Aleksei Mikhailovich. PhD, Moscow Inst. of Physics and Tech., 1980—86. Rschr. P. N. Lebedev Physics Inst., Moscow, 1986—98; postdoctoral rsch. asst. Mont. State U., 1999—2002, rsch. asst. prof., 2002—. Contbr. articles to profl. jours.; translator: (scientific writings) Optics and Spectroscopy. Recipient to prominent Russian Physicists, Am. Phys. Soc., 1992; grant, Internat. Sci. Found., 1994—95, Los Alamos Nat. Lab., 1995, Internat. Assn. for the Promotion of Cooperation with Scientists from the New Ind. States of the Former Soviet Union, 1995—96. Achievements include research in high-resolution laser spectroscopy of organic molecules and molecular nano-particles; development of time and space domain holography in spectrally-selective media; ultrafast recording of optical information; enlargement of optical memory devices capacity based on nonlinear optical effects; research in nonlinear optical properties of new organic nano-scale materials; ultrafast dynamical processes in complex molecular systems, including aggregates, polymers, and dendrimers. Office: Mont State U Bozeman MT 59717-3840 Office Fax: 406-994-4452. Personal E-mail: drobizhev@physics.montana.edu. E-mail: drobizhev@physics.montana.edu.

DROBNICKI, JOHN ARTHUR, librarian, educator; b. N.Y. AA Liberal Arts, St. John's U., 1983, BA in History, 1986, MA in History, 1988; MLS in Libr. Sci., CUNY, 1992. Cert. pub. libr. N.Y. State Edn. Dept., 1993. Adj. instr. of history St. John's U., Jamaica, NY, 1989—89; libr. Queens Borough Pub. Libr., Jamaica, 1990—95; asst. prof. of libr. svcs. York Coll. CUNY, Jamaica, 1995—2000, assoc. prof. of libr. svcs. York Coll., 2001—03, prof. of libr. svcs. York Coll., 2003—. Exec. bd. York Coll. Chpt. Profl. Staff Congress of CUNY, 2002. Contbr. articles to profl. jours., book reviews to profl. jours. Recipient David Cohen Multicultural award, Queens Coll. Grad. Sch. of Libr. and Info. Studies, 1993. Mem.: Polish Inst. Arts Sci. Am., Polish ALA, Polish Geneal. Soc. of Am., Polish Am. Hist. Assn. Episc. Avocation: genealogy. Office: York College CUNY 94 20 Guy R Brewer Blvd Jamaica NY 11451 Office Fax: 718-262-2997. E-mail: drobnicki@york.cuny.edu.

DROBNY, JIRI GEORGE, chemical engineer; b. Prague, Czech Republic, Feb. 22, 1933; arrived in U.S., 1966; s. Vaclav and Jirina (Landova) D.; m. Elizabeth Anne Douglass, June 15, 1968; children: Mary Martha, Jirina Elizabeth. MSChemE, Tech. U. Prague, 1956; MS in Polymer Sci., U. Akron, 1971, postgrad., 1972; MBA, Shippensburg (Pa.) U., 1977. Group leader Matador Rubber Works, Bratislava, Slovak Republic, 1956-65; rubber chemist Dunlop AG, Hanau, Germany, 1965-66; sr. devel. engr. B.F. Goodrich Internat., Akron, Ohio, 1966-70; mgr. product devel. Carlisle (Pa.) Tire & Rubber Co., 1971-78; asst. rsch. & devel. dir. Beloit Manhattan Inc., Clark Summit, Pa., 1978-82; tech. dir. roofing Plymouth Rubber Co., Canton, Mass., 1982-84; corp. rsch. & devel. mgr. Fulflex Inc., Middletown, R.I., 1984-89; sr. devel. engr. Chemfab Corp., Merrimack, N.H., 1989-95; pres. Drobny Polymer Assocs., Merrimack, 1995—. Adj. faculty dept. plastics engring. U. Mass., Lowell, 1991—. Author: Technology of Fluoropolymers, 2000, Radiation Technology for Polymers, 2002; co-author: Rubber Technology, 1966, SME Handbook of Plastic Part Manufacturing; assoc. editor: FAPU, 2000—; translator: field of polymer tech. Fundraiser Am. Diabetes Assn., 1991—95. Mem. Am. Chem. Soc., Soc. Plastics Engrs., Boston Rubber Group, Assn. Cons. Chemists and Chem. Engrs., Radtech, Soc. for Advancement of Material and Process Engring. Avocations: alpine and nordic skiing, tennis, sailing, languages, music. Home and Office: 11 Quails Way Merrimack NH 03054-2877 E-mail: jgdrobny@attglobal.net.

DROHAN, MARGO ANGELA, pediatric nurse practitioner; b. Yonkers, N.Y., July 21, 1953; d. Edward Anthony and Esther Yvonne (Lockwood) D.; children: Mathew, Jessica, Gavin. BSN magna cum laude, Lehman Coll., 1981, MSN with honors, 1985. RN. Rsch. asst. to corp. nursing chmn. Montefiore Med. Ctr., Bronx, 1983-86; dir. nursing, health svcs. Berkshire Children's Cmty., Great Barrington, Mass., 1989-91; clin. asst. prof. U. Mass., 1992—. Adj. faculty Lehman Coll., Brons, 1982-86, Elizabeth Seaton Coll., Yonkers, N.Y., 1983-84; childhood health cons., 1990—; cons. Boston Children's Hosp., Groton, Mass., 1992; asst. prof. Coll. of Our Lady of the Elms, 1993-97; dir. health and nursing svcs. Kolburne Sch., New Marlborough, Mass., 1998-99. Assoc. editor Alternative Health Practitioner, Jour. Complementary and Natural Care. Bd. dirs., mem. faculty Music for Healing Transition Program, 1996—; coord. Complementary Care Certificate Program Berkshire C.C., Pittsfield, Mass., 1998-2000. Mem. Sigma Theta Tau (pres. 1984-86, v.p. Delta Zeta chpt. 1981-83). Home: HC 65 Box 37 Great Barrington MA 01230-8503

DROKE, EDNA FAYE, elementary school educator, retired; b. Sylvester, Tex., Dec. 4, 1932; d. Ira Selle and Faye Emily (Seckinger) Tucker; m. Louis Albert Droke, June 2, 1951; children: Sherman Ray, Lyndon Allen, Lona Faye Droke Cheairs. BEd, Tarleton State U., Stephenville, Tex., 1983. Cert. ESL and 3d-8th lang. arts tchr., Tex. Tchr. ESL and lang. arts Wingate (Tex.) Ind. Sch. Dist., 1983-86; tchr. 2d grade and ESL Collidge (Tex.) Ind. Sch. Dist., 1986-88; tchr. 4th grade and ESL Peaster (Tex.) Ind. Sch. Dist., 1988-89; tchr. Chpt. I in 1st-6th grades, ESL in K-12th grades Ranger (Tex.) Ind. Sch. Dist., 1989-96, tchr. E.S.L. 3d grade, reading recovery tchr., 1996-98, ret., 1998; substitute tchr. I.S.D., Blanket, Tex.; E.S.L. tchr. 220th CSCD, Comanche, Tex. Tutor Hispanic probationers in English for 220th Dist. Ct., Comanche, Tex., Gustine (Tex.) Ind. Sch. Dist. Reading Improvement, 2000-2003. Mem. ASCD, Kappa Delta Pi, Alpha Chi. Baptist. Avocations: reading, quilting, knitting, playing piano, painting. Home: PO Box 44 Comanche TX 76442-0044

DROLLA, JOHN CASPER DODT, JR., lawyer; b. New Orleans, Sept. 29, 1944; s. John Casper Drolla Sr. and Edna Florence (Bauerfeind) Dempsey. AS, Tarleton State Univ., 1960; BA, Univ. Tex., 1963, JD, 1972. Bar: U.S. Ct. Appeals (fifth cir.) 1976, 82, U.S. Dist. Ct. (we. dist.) Tex. 1974, U.S. Ct. Military Appeals 1988, U.S. Supreme Ct. 1977; bd. cert. legal specialization in comml. and residential real estate law, Tex. Commander 25th Trans Co. and Honor Guard Ft. Sam U.S. Army, Houston, 1965-67; commdr. HHC USAHAC Reaction Forces, Vietnam, 1967-68; briefing clerk Judge Leon Douglas Tex. Ct. Criminal Appeals, Austin, 1972-73, rsch. asst. Judge Leon Douglas, 1973-74; assoc. Philip & Norris, Inc., Austin, 1974-76; rsch. asst. Judge Leon Douglas Tex. Ct. Criminal Appeals, Austin, 1976-77; sr. atty. Law Office of John C.D. Drolla,Jr., Austin, 1977—; commdr. 3d squadron 163d Armored Regiment, 1980-82. Lectr. in field. Contbr. numerous articles to profl. jours. Bd. dirs. Tex. Embassy Mus., 100 Club Ctrl. Tex., 1990—, Track & Field official, Olympic Games, L.A., 1984, U.S. Olympic Com. Adminstrv. staff U.S. Olympic Festival, 1993, Track & Field Official U.S. Olympic Trials 1984, 1992, 2000, USATF Nat. Jr. Olympics, San Jose, Calif., 1995, Houston, 1996, Track & Field Official X Paralympic Games, Atlanta, 1996, coun. mem. Habitat for Humanity, 1993-95; bd. dirs. Tex. Military Forces Mus., Tex., 1996—. Col. USAR 1985. Decorated Silver Star, 1968, Bronze Star, 1968, Def. Meritorious Svc. medal, 1993, Meritorious Svc. medal with two Oak Leaf clusters, 1970, 84, 93, Army Commendation medal with one oak leaf cluster, 1967, 76, Army Achievement medal, 1986, Nat. Def. Svc. medal with one bronze svc. star, 1970, 92, Vietnam Svc. medal with 4 bronze svc. stars, 1970, Armed Forces Res. medal with hour Glass, 1980, 83, Army Res. Components Achievement medal with 3 oak leaf clusters, 1976, 80, 84, Army Svc. ribbon, 1981, Overseas Svc. ribbon, 1981, and others. Fellow Tex. Bar Found., Coll. of the State Bar of Tex.; mem. State Bar Tex., State Bar Tex. (CLE com., real estate, probate and trust sect., family law sect., banking and bus. law sect.), Travis County Bar Assn., Fed. Bar Assn. (treas. 1994-95, prog. com. chair 1994-95, del. nat. conv. 2001, sec. 1995-96, vice pres. 1996-97, pres. elect 1997-98, pres. 1998-99, del. nat. coun. 1999-2003). Avocations: track and field official, stamp collecting, sport cars, outdoor and water related sports. Office: The Town Lake Bldg 512 E Riverside Dr Ste 200 Austin TX 78704-1356 E-mail: lawdroll@texas.net.

DROLLER, MICHAEL JACK, urologist; b. N.Y.C., June 17, 1943; s. Gustav G. and Lotte Judith (Sichel) D.; m. Esther Schweizer, June 27, 1976; children: Miriam Emilie, Daniel Benjamin Jacob. AB summa cum laude, Harvard U., 1964, MD cum laude, 1968; Doctor honoris causa, U. Athens, 2002. Diplomate Am. Bd. Urology. Intern Albert Einstein Coll. of Medicine, 1968-69; jr. asst. resident surgery Peter Bent Brigham Hosp., 1969-70; resident in urology Stanford U. Med. Ctr., 1972-75, chief resident urology, 1975-76; rschr. scientist U. Stockholm, 1976-77; asst. prof. urology Johns Hopkins U. Sch. Medicine, Balt., 1977-80, asst. prof. oncology, 1978-80, assoc. prof. oncology, 1980-84, assoc. prof. urology, 1980-84; attending urologist Johns Hopkins Hosp., Balt., 1977-84; chmn. dept. urology Mt. Sinai Med. Ctr., N.Y.C., 1984—2003; dir. urology Mt. Sinai Hosp., N.Y.C., 1984—2003; prof. oncology Mt. Sinai Med. Ctr., N.Y.C., 1984—. Mem. study sects. nat. cancer Inst., NIH, Bethesda, Md., surg. oncology and clin. trials, and lymphokines and immune response expression; mem. varous hosp. coms.; mem. expert com. WHO Collaborative Project and Consensus Conf., Stockholm, 2000; numerous vis. professorships. Mem. editl. bd. Investigative Urology, 1981-85, 90—, World Jour. Urology, 1982—, Urology, 1985-92, Urol. Rsch., 1989—, Jour. Urology, 1988-94, Urology Survey, 1996—, Progrès en Urologie, 1992—; mng. editor Urologic Oncology, 1995-2000; editor Controversies in Urologic Oncology, 1980, editor-in-chief, 2000—; co-editor-in-chief Urologic Oncology: Seminars and Original Investigations, 2003—; editor: Surgical Management of Urologic Disease: An Anatomic Approach, 1991, Advanced Bladder Cancer, 1992; contbr. articles to profl. jours., including Surg. Forum, Internat. Jour. Urology, Jour. Urology, Contemporary Urology, Brit. Jour. Urology, others. Cons. N.Y. State Dept. Health task force on clin. guidelines and med. tech. assessment, 1995-97; clin. assoc. USPHS, Nat. Inst. Arthritis and Metabolioc Diseases, NIH, 1970-72; mem. vis. com. Mazza Mus., Findlay U., 2000—; mem. devel. com. Harvard U. Libr., 2001—. Recipient various essay awards Am. Urol. Assn. Western Sect., 1975, 76, 78, Rsch. scholar 1976-77, Am. Urological Assn. Grayson Carroll award, hon. mem. German Urological Assn., vis. professorships; Eleanor Roosevelt Cancer Rsch. fellow, Internat. Union Against Cancer, 1976-77. Mem. AAAS, ACS (Schering scholar 1976-77), German Urol. Assn., Am. Assn. Genitourinary Surgeons, Am. Urol. Assn. Mid-Atlantic Sect., Am. Urol. Assn. N.Y. Sect. (exec. com. 1992—, editl. com. chmn. 1993-96, chair med. edn. com. 1994—, program chmn. various meetings and seminars. rep. to Am. Urol. Assn. Rsch. com. 1995-97, treas. 1998-2000, pres. 2001), Urol. Rsch. Soc. (membership chmn. 1984—, pres. 1986), Soc. Urologic Oncology (bylaws chmn. 1990-96, pres.-elect 1996-97, pres. 1997-98), Soc. Basic Urologic Rsch., Soc. Univ. Urologists, Am. Bd. Urology (trustee 1999—), N.Y. State Urol. Soc. (exec. com. 1990—, pres.-elect 1997-2001, pres. 2001-02), N.Y. Acad. Medicine (sec. urology sect. 1991-92, chmn. 1992-93, mem. Edwin Beer Rsch. Com. 1990-96, pres. 1996-97), N.Y. Acad. Scis., Sigma Xi, Phi Beta Kappa, Alpha Omega Alpha. Office: Mt Sinai Medical Ctr One Gustave L Levy Pl 1 Gustave L Levy Pl New York NY 10029-6500

DROLSHAGEN, LEO FRANCIS, III, radiologist, physician; b. Detroit, June 9, 1956; s. Leo Francis Jr. and Janet Marie (Phillppart) D.; m. Barbara Sharon Ritchie, June 29, 1979; children: Leo VI, Colin, Eric, Helena. BA English magna cum laude, U. Detroit, 1977; MD, Wayne State U., 1981; postgrad., Armed Forces Inst. of Pathology, Washington, 1985. Diplomate Am. Bd. Radiology, Nat. Bd. Med. Examiners. Resident in radiology Henry Ford Hosp., Detroit, 1981-85; fellow Vanderbilt U. Hosp. Sch. of Medicine, Nashville, Tenn., 1985-86; radiologist Radiologist P.A., Ft Smith, Ark., 1986—; med. dir., magnectic resonance imaging St. Edward Mercy Med. Ctr., Ft Smith, 1986-90, chief, dept. radiology, 1988-91, vice chief of med. staff elect, 1991-92; v.p. Radiologist P.A., Ft. Smith, 1991-97, pres., 1997—; chief of staff St. Edward Mercy Med. Ctr., 1992—. Clinical asst. prof. of Magnetic Resonance Imaging U. Ark., St. Edward Mercy Med. Ctr. Author: (with others) Magnetic Resonance Imaging of the Normal and Abnormal Female Pelvis, 1986, The Pelvis, 1986, Critical Diagnostic Pathways in Radiology, 1987; contbr. articles to profl. jours. Recipient Tchr. of the Year in Sonography award Vanderbilt U. Med. Ctr., 1985-86, Howard Walsh Meml. award U. Detroit, 1977. Mem. AMA, Am. Roentgen Ray Soc., Radiologic Soc. N.Am., Am. Inst. Ultrasound in Medicine, Am. Coll. Radiology, Soc. Magnetic Resonance Imaging in Medicine, Sebastian County Med. Soc., Mensa, Ft. Smith C. of C., Ducks Unlimited, Bonsai Club. Avocations: volleyball, racquetball, piano, swimming. Home: 8223 Cleburne Ct Fort Smith AR 72903-4362 Office: Radiologist PA PO Box 3887 1501 S Waldron Rd Ste 109 Fort Smith AR 72903-2568 also: St Edward Mercy Med Hosp Dept Radiology Fort Smith AR 72903

DROMS, WILLIAM GEORGE, finance educator, investment advisor; b. Schenectady, Aug. 20, 1944; s. George William and Frances (Maguire) D.; m. JoAnn Gilberti, June 17, 1967; children: Courtney, Justin. AB, Brown U., 1966; MBA, George Washington U., 1971, DBA, 1975. Chartered financial analyst. Prof. Georgetown U., Washington, 1973—, John J. Powers Jr. Chair prof., 1990—, assoc. dean, faculty chair Sch. Bus., 1978-81, 87-89, 92-94, 98-99. Fin. cons., 1975—; pres. Droms Strauss Advisors, Inc., 1994—. Author: Finance and Accounting for Nonfinancial Managers, 1979, 5th edit., 2003, Dow Jones-Irwin No-Load Mutual Funds, 1984, 85, 86; author: (with others) The Dow Jones Irwin Guide to Personal Financial Planning, 1982, 86, Personal Financial Management, 1982, 86, The Life Insurance Investment Advisor, 1988, Investment Fundamentals, 1994; editor: Asset Allocation for Individual Investors, 1987, Managing a Global Investment Program, 1991; contbr. numerous articles to profl. jours. Lt. USN, 1966-70. Mem. Am. Fin. Assn., Eastern Fin. Assn., Assn. for Investment Mgmt. and Rsch., Fin. Mgmt. Assn., D.C. Soc. Investment Analysts, Cosmos Club. Republican. Roman Catholic. Avocations: tennis, golf. Office: Georgetown U Sch Bus Washington DC 20057-0001 E-mail: dromsw@msb.edu.

DRONAMRAJU, KRISHNA RAO, geneticist; b. Pithapuram, India, Jan. 14, 1937; came to U.S., 1963; s. Bapiraju and Rajeswaramma (Vankayalapati) D.; m. Sheila Marion McHarg, Mar. 31, 1962 (div. 1978); 1 child, Raj Gopal. MSc, Agra (India) U., 1957; PhD, Indian Statis. Inst., Calcutta, 1966. Rsch. fellow U. Alberta, Edmonton, Can., 1966-68; asst. prof. U. Saskatchewan, Saskatoon, Can., 1968-69; chief geneticist Lancaster (Pa.) Cleft Palate Clinic, 1969-73; writer, lectr. Balt., 1973-77; pers. cons. City of Balt., 1978-79, job devel. advisor, 1979-81; sr. fellow U. Tex., Houston, 1982-85; pres., dir. Found. for Genetic Rsch., Houston, 1985—. Vis. prof. Hershey (Pa.) Med. Ctr., 1969-73, Osmania U., Indian, 1995; mem. reconbimant DNA adv. com. NIH, Bethesda, Md., 1992—; hon. rsch. fellow U. London, 1994; vis. prof. U. Paris, 1994, Jawaharlal Nehru U., New Delhi, 1994; hon. prof. Albert Schweitzer Internat. U., Geneva; advisor Tex. State Coun. on Biotech., 2002-; mem. adv. bd. to U.S. Sec. Agr., 2002—. Author: Cleft Lip and Palate: Aspects of Reproductive Biology, 1986, The Foundations of Human Genetics, 1989, If I am To Be Remembered, The Life and Work of Julian Huxley with Selected Correspondence, 1993; editor: Haldane and Modern Biology, 1968, Haldane, The Life and Work of J.B.S. Haldane with special reference to India, 1985, The History and Development of Human Genetics: Progress in Different Countries, 1992, Haldane's Daedalus Revisited, 1995, Haldane in India, 1997, Science and Society, 1998, Biological and Social Issues in Biotechnology, 1998, Biological Wealth and Other Essays, 2002, Disease and Evolution, 2002; contbr. articles to profl. jours. Mem. bd. dirs. Sickle Cell Assn., Houston, 1992—. Recipient merit award History of Sci. Soc., 1989, Yellapragada Subbarow award for med. rsch., 1997, Y. Nayudamma award for sci. and tech., India, 1997; Rockefeller U. Archives Grant, 2002. Fellow N.Am. Acad. Arts and Scis.; mem. AAAS, Am. Soc. Human Genetics. Avocations: travel, nature walks. Office: Found for Genetic Rsch PO Box 27701 Houston TX 77227-7701 Fax: (713) 667-5881. E-mail: kdronamraj@aol.com.

DRONEBURG, NANCY MARIE, geriatrics nurse; b. Frederick, Md., Jan. 29, 1953; d. John G. and Marie K. (Stone) D. AA, St. Phillip's Coll., San Antonio, 1979; BSN, U. Tex., San Antonio, 1983. RN, Tex.; cert. geriatrics, med./surg. Bed and staffing coord. Audie L. Murphy VA Hosp., San Antonio, 1983—. With U.S. Army, 1972-79. Home: 513 Mesquite St Converse TX 78109-1313

DRONEY, CHRISTOPHER F. judge; b. June 22, 1954; m. Elizabeth Kelly, Oct. 13, 1979. BA, Coll. Holy Cross, 1976; JD, U. Conn., 1979. Ptnr. Reid & Riege, P.C., Hartford, Conn., 1983-93; U.S. atty. for dist. of Conn. U.S. Dept. Justice, New Haven, 1993-97; judge U.S. Dist. Ct., Conn., 1997—. Notes and comments editor Conn. Law Rev., 1978-79. Mem. U.S. atty. gen. adv. com., 1996-97. Office: 450 Main St Hartford CT 06103-3022

DRONGOWSKI, STEVE, advertising executive; With Fahlgren Inc. (now Icon Marketing), Austin, Tex., 1984—; pres., CEO, 1993-96; CEO, 1996—. Office: Icon Marketing PO Box 6 Austin TX 78767

DROPKIN, CHARLES EDWARD, lawyer; b. NYC, Dec. 17, 1951; s. Harry and Jeanette Dropkin; m. Jeanine Deborah Love, Nov. 5, 1983; children: Melissa Emily, Rebecca Allyson. BA, Williams Coll., 1974; JD, Harvard U., 1977. Bar: N.Y. 1978, U.S. Dist. Ct. (so. and ea. dist.) N.Y. 1978, U.S. Ct. Appeals (2d cir.) 1981, U.S. Supreme Ct. 1981. With Milbank Tweed Hadley & McCloy, N.Y.C., 1977-94; chair banking and fin. instns. dept. Proskauer Rose LLP, N.Y.C., 1994—. Mem. editl. bd. Banking Policy Report, 1994—; contbg. author: Securities Lending and Repurchase Agreements, 1997; contbr. articles to profl. jours. Fellow Am. Coll. Investment Coun.; mem. Assn. of the Bar of the City of N.Y. (uniform state laws com. 2000—), N.Y. State Bar Assn. (exec. com. comml. and fed. litigation sect. 1989-91, creditors rights and banking litigation com. 1995—), B'Nai B'rith. Avocation: golf. Home: 177 Laurel Dr Oradell NJ 07649-2422 Office: Proskauer Rose LLP 1585 Broadway New York NY 10036-8299 E-mail: cdropkin@proskauer.com.

DROSDICK, JOHN GIRARD, oil company executive; b. Hazelton, Pa., Aug. 9, 1943; m. Gloria J. Shenosky, May 10, 1944; children: Scott E., Candice M., Courtney J., Brooke K. BSChemE, Villanova U., 1965; MSChemE, U. Mass., 1968. Crude oil coordinator Exxon USA, Houston, 1973—74, marine planning mgr., 1974—76, corp. analysis mgr., 1978—81, facilities devel. dept. head Baton Rouge, 1976—78, refinery ops mgr., 1981—83; v.p. refining Tosco Corp., Santa Monica, Calif., 1983—85, sr. v.p. refining, 1985—86, exec. v.p., 1986—87, pres., COO, 1987—89, also bd. dirs.; pres., CEO Tosco Refining Co., Santa Monica, Calif., 1989—92, Ultramar, Inc., Long Beach, 1992—96; pres., COO Sunoco, Inc., Phila., 1996—2000, chmn., pres., CEO, 2000—. Mem.: Am. Petroleum Petroleum Refiners Assn. (bd. dirs. 1985—87), Nat. Petroleum Refiners Assn. (bd. dirs. 1985—), Jonathan Wilshire. Roman Catholic. Avocations: running, skiing, tennis, golf. Office: Sunoco Inc 10 Penn Ctr 1801 Market St Philadelphia PA 19103-1699

DROST, MARIANNE, lawyer; b. Waterbury, Conn., Feb. 21, 1950; d. Albin Joseph and Henrietta Jean (Kremski) D. BA, Conn. Coll., 1972; JD, U. Conn., 1975. Bar: Conn. 1975. Assoc. Ritter, Tapper & Totten, Hartford, Conn., 1975-77; sr. atty. GTE Svc. Corp., Stamford, Conn., 1977-84, Chesebrough-Pond's Inc., Greenwich, Conn., 1984-85; corp. sec. GTE Corp., Stamford, Conn., 1985—; v.p., assoc. gen. counsel fin. GTE Svc. Corp., Stamford, Conn., 1991-97, v.p., dep. gen. counsel, 1997-2000; sr. v.p., dep. gen. counsel, corp. sec. Verizon Comm. Inc., NYC, 2000—. Tutor Lit. Vols., Stamford, 1985-90, bd. dirs. Lit. Vols. Am., 1988-94. Mem. ABA, Am. Soc. Corp. Secs. (former pres., bd. dirs. Fairfield-Westchester chpt.).

DROUGHT, JAMES HENRY, healthcare business owner, exercise physiologist; b. Aurora, Ill., Mar. 29, 1957; s. James William and Lorna Beryl (Carlson) D. Student, U.S. Mil. Acad., 1975-77; BS in Phys. Edn., Rutgers U., 1980; MS in Clin. Exercise Physiology, Northeastern U., 1995. Comm. coord. Lake Placid (N.Y.) Olympic Organizing Com., 1980-81; dir. Rainmaker Prodns., Boston, 1982-85; health promotion mgr. City of Boston, 1986-87; owner Personal Trainers Strength & Conditioning Consulting, Boston, 1987—. Cons. City of Boston, 1988-89, State of Mass., Boston, 1988-89, Lotus Devel. Corp., Cambridge, Mass., 1990-91; mem. (C.O.R.P.S.) nat. bd. Reebok Internat., Ltd., Stoughton, Mass., 1992-96; articles cons. SHAPE mag., 1995—, Men's Health mag., 1998—. Exec. editor Conditioning Instr., 1991-93; contbr. articles to profl. jours.; author Ask the Experts Column, Boston Globe, 1990-92. Exec. com. Boston vs. Montreal Fitness Challenge, City of Boston, 1989; James Henry Drought collection donated to Mugar Meml. Libr., Boston U.. Mem. Am. Coll. Sports Medicine, Nat. Strength and Conditioning Assn. (Mass. state dir. 1992-98, nat. bd. dirs. 1998-2001, task analysis com. 1992—, nat. conf. com. 1993-95, chmn. personal trainer com. 1991, exam devel. com., 1994-98, exec. coun., state dirs. com. 1997-98, Challenge Scholarship 1993, State Dir.'s award 1995, Personal Trainer of Yr. award 2000, Nat. Strength and Conditioning Assn. Cert. Commn. award 1993). Avocations: screenwriting, writing, weightlifting, running, tai chi, golf. Home and Office: Kenmore Station PO Box 15601 Boston MA 02215-0011 E-mail: drought@personaltrainers.com.

DROUILHET, PAUL RAYMOND, JR., science laboratory director, electrical engineer; b. San Pedro, Calif., Mar. 11, 1933; s. Paul R. and Elizabeth (Moffatt) D.; m. Betty Bratton; children: Ann, Stephen, Susan. BS, MS in Elec. Engring., MIT, 1955, EE, 1957. Various positions MIT Lincoln Lab., Lexington, 1959-81, div. head, 1981-85, asst. dir., 1985-93; fed. aviation adminstr. Chi Sci. for GPS/CNS, 1994-95, spl. asst. to dir. aviation rsch., 1996; cons. to dir. MIT Lincoln Lab., 1997—. Contbr. articles to profl. jours.; patentee in field. 1st lt. USAF, 1957-59. Fellow IEEE. Avocations: tennis, sailing, travel. Office: MIT Lincoln Lab 244 Wood St Lexington MA 02420-6426 E-mail: drouilhet@ll.mit.edu.

DROULLARD, STEVEN MAURICE, jewelry company executive; b. Pampa, Tex., June 28, 1951; s. Maurice Erskin and Betty (Bonnett) D.; m. Alessia Passalacqua, Dec. 31, 1978. Grad. gemology, Gemological Inst Am., Santa Monica, Calif., 1985; MA in Consciousness Studies, U. of Philos. Rsch., L.A., Calif., 2003. Lic. broadcaster, 1972; lic. securities dealer. Asst. to pres. Standard Coal Co., San Francisco, 1976-78; pres. Adamas Gem Services, Kailua-kona, Hawaii, 1978-82; v.p. Intergem, Inc., Denver, 1982-85, pres., 1985-87, also bd. dirs.; pres., chmn. bd. GMA Inc., 1988—; pres. Steven Maurice Internat. Jewelry, 1993—; broker, mem. exec. rsch. com. Joseph Charles & Assocs., Inc., 1995-99; sr. investment adv. Schneider Securities, Inc., 1999—. Cons. Wells Comms., Denver, 1984—, William Randolph Hearst II, 1997—; strategic planning cons. White & Case, 1997—; mem. bd. advisors Colo. Computing Mag., Boulder, 1985—; chmn. Exec. Jewelry Buyers Club, 1988—. Contbr. articles to mags.; also cons. The Great American Sapphire, 1985; columnist The Adobe Press, 1999—. Named Bus. Assoc. of Yr. Am. Bus. Women Assoc., 1981. Mem. Gemological Inst. Am. Alumni Assn. (charter, pres. Colo. chpt. 1987—), Accredited Gemologists Assn., Am. Gem Trade Assn., Gem Mcht. Assocs. (pres. 1986), Kailua-Kona C. of C. (v.p. 1981), Cherry Creek C. of C. (bd. dir. 1995-97), Y2K preparedness dir., Nipomo, Calif. Avocations: gem faceting, mineral collecting, hiking, skiing. E-mail: SmauriceD@aol.com.

DROWOTA, FRANK F., III, state supreme court chief justice; b. Williamsburg, Ky., July 7, 1938; married; 2 children. BA, Vanderbilt U., 1960, JD, 1965. Bar: Tenn. 1965, U.S. Dist. Ct. Tenn. 1965. Pvt. practice, 1965-70; chancellor Tenn. Chancery Ct. Div. 7, 1970-74; judge Tenn. Ct. Appeals, Middle Tenn. Div., 1974-80; assoc. justice Tenn. Supreme Ct., Nashville, 1980-89, chief justice, 1989-93, assoc. justice, 1993-2001; chief justice, 2001—. Served with USN, 1960-62. Office: Admin Office Cts 511 Union St Ste 600 Nashville TN 37219*

DROZD, LESZEK STANISLAW, composer, performer; b. Warsaw, May 23, 1969; came to U.S., 1994; s. Hanna Eugenia Drozd. Student, Weryho-Radziwillowiczowej, Warsaw, 1991-93; grad., Sch. Music of Fryderyk Chopin. Music composer Sta. WPNA-AM, WSBS-AM, Chgo., 1995-97; music composer, performer STYOPA Productions, Calif., 1998. Soloist, mem. numerous symphonic orchs., bands, choirs. Composer (and performer): (films) (soundtrack) The Innocents, 1999 (Film winner of 3 awards in Nat., Internat. film festivals.); composer: (soundtrack for) (documentary for Time Warner cable) Short Impression About Isolation, 2002. E-mail: ldmusiccomp@aol.com.

DROZD, PHYLLIS ANN, agricultural products supplier; b. Allegan, Mich., July 26, 1932; d. Edward and Wilma (Busfield) Moored; m. Thomas Drozd, June 20, 1953; children: Julie, T. Jon, Jay H. Sec. Cresent Machine Co., Allegan, Mich., 1949-55; farmer Tom & Phyllis Drozd, Allegan, Mich., 1953-85; co-owner Drozd Seed, Inc., Allegan, Mich., 1953—. Pres. Allegan County Sch. Dist., 1978—; treas., 1965-78; sec.-treas. Allegan County Sch. Bds. Assn., 1991-92; pres. Allengan Bus. & Profl. Women, 1986-87, 91-92, 1st sr. v.p., 1984-85; bd. dirs. Mich. Assn. Sch. Bds., 1993—, v.p., 1999-2000, pres.-elect, 2000-01, pres., 2001—; mem. various ednl. coms. Avocations: reading, collecting antiques, walking, travel. Home and Office: 537 32nd St # M40 Allegan MI 49010-9763 E-mail: pdrozd@accn.org.

DROZDA, DONNA JEAN, artist, educator, inventor; b. Cleve., Feb. 15, 1949; d. Joseph Michael and Dorothy Mary (Toth) D. Student, Cleve. Inst. Art, 1971-74. Cert. Internat. Graphoanalysis Soc. Painter, 1980—; gallery owner, 1982-86; lectr., educator, 1982—. Bd. advisors New Orgn. for Visual Arts, Cleve., 1980-82, The Art Studio, Inc., Ctr. for Therapy Through the Arts, 1990—; presenter Creativity Salons; lectr. on the healing power of creativity. Inventor expressive art therapy techniques, including a Personal Energy Guide; exhibited works in numerous group and solo shows; author: 365 Days IMMT, 1993; author, illustrator: Twenty-Two Prayer Poems for Care Givers, 2001. Vol. artist Ctr. for Prevention of Domestic Violence, Cleve., 1990-96, Cleve. Pub. Radio, 1989-92; artist-in-residence Ctr. for Therapy Thru the Arts, 1990-95; vo. Virginia Beach Hospice; mem. staff Contemporary Arts Ctr. Va., Virginia Beach Pub. Schs., Adult Learning Ctr., Assoc. for Rsch. and Enlightenment, Virginia Beach. Recipient various awards for art; grantee NEA, 2003. Avocations: gardening, travel. Office: Wren House Studio PO Box 68324 Virginia Beach VA 23471-8324

DROZDIS, MARIE TRESE, crisis intervention nurse; b. Scranton, Pa., Dec. 8, 1939; d. Stanley and Anna Mary (Rukas) Kwader; m. Anthony Alvin Drozdis, May 16, 1959 (div. Sept. 1986); children: Anthony, Diana, David. BSN magna cum laude, Marywood Coll., 1985. Instr. math. Internat. Correspondence Schs., Scranton, 1957-59; lic. practical nurse Community Med. Ctr., Scranton, 1977-85, RN, 1985-88, Thomas Jefferson U. Hosp., Phila., 1988-2000. Cons. Home Health. Recipient Niemotko medal Marywood Coll. Mem. Internat. Soc. Philos. Enquiry, Mensa Internat., Marywood Coll. Nursing Hon. Soc. (past v.p.), Human Ecology Action League, Kappa Gamma Pi, Delta Epsilon Sigma, Psi Chi. Democrat. Roman Catholic. Home: 3434 Ainslie St Philadelphia PA 19129-1426

DROZDOWSKI, MILADIN PETER LJUBICIC, consulting engineer; b. Zajecar, Yugoslavia, Sept. 28, 1921; came to U.S., 1959; s. Peter Miladin and Martha Jovan (Viktorovic) Ljubicic; m. Dusica Cile Pavic, Sept. 9, 1948. Diploma in engring., U. Belgrade, Yugoslavia, 1951, 52; ancien éleve, Ecole Nationale Superieure de l'Armement, Paris, 1956; MSME, UCLA, 1964, PhD in Mec. Engring., 1971. Design and test engr. Fed. Mogul Bower, El Monte, Calif., 1959-62; chief advanced armament analytical support Hughes Helicopters, Culver City, Calif., 1962-78; engring. supr. Bechtel Power Corp., Norwalk, Calif., 1978-80; engring. adviser Bechtel Espana, Madrid, 1980-87; v.p. Koach Engring., Sun Valley, Calif., 1987; engring. cons. Mission Viejo, Calif., 1987—. Asst. to chmn. continuum mechanics, Belgrade, 1955-56; guest lectr. Sch. Engring. and Applied Sci., UCLA, 1971; prof., Loyola Marymount U., L.A., 1978-80. Contbr. to profl. publs. Avocations: european history, art history, archeology, photography, sculpting. Home and Office: 26426 Lope De Vega Dr Mission Viejo CA 92691-3316

DROZDZIEL, MARION JOHN, aeronautical engineer; b. Dunkirk, N.Y., Dec. 21, 1924; s. Steven and Veronica (Wilk) D.; m. Rita L. Korwek, Aug. 30, 1952; 1 child, Eric A. BS in Aero. Engring., Tri State U., 1947, BSME, 1948; postgrad., Ohio State U., 1948, Niagara U., 1949-51, U. Buffalo, 1951-52. Stress analyst Curtiss Wright Corp., Columbus, Ohio, 1948; project engr. weight analysis Bell Aerospace Textron, Buffalo, 1949-52, stress analyst, 1952-60, asst. supr. stress analysis, 1960-64, chief stress analysis propulsion, 1964-79, chief engr. stress and weights, 1979-84, staff scientist, 1984-85, cons. structures and fractures mechanics, 1985—. Mem. Am. Aerospace Materials Del. to USSR, 1989, Am. Aerospace Industries Del. to People's Republic China, 1991, Am. Aerospace Materials Del. to Czechoslovakia and Commonwealth Ind. States, 1992. Del. Internat. Citizens Ambassador Prog.; active Buffalo Fine Arts Acad., N.Y. Acad. Scis., Disabled Am. Vets.; mem. tech. socs. coun. Niagara Frontier. With U.S. Army, 1944-47. Recipient cert. of achievement NASA-Apollo, 1972, Wisdom award of honor Wisdom Soc. for Advancement of Knowledge, Learning and Rsch. in Edn., 2000; cert. commendation U.K. NATO program, 1982; named to Wisdom Hall of Fame, Wisdom Soc. for Advancement of Knowledge, Learning and Rsch. in Edn., 2000. Mem. AAAS, AIAA (Mem. Chmn.'s award 1988-90, 92-93), Soc. Reliability Engrs. (bd. dirs. 1998-03), U.S. Naval Inst., Am. Space Found., Nat. Conservancy, Nat. Audubon Soc., Sierra Club, Am. Acad. Polit. and Social Sci., Acad. Polit. Sci., Union Concerned Scientists, Air Force Assn., Nat. Space Soc., Soc. Allied Weight Engrs., Planetary Soc., Am. Mgmt. Assn., Bibl. Archeology Soc., Archeol. Inst. Am., Cousteau Soc., Smithsonian Assocs., Buffalo Audubon Soc., Bell Mgmt. Club, Natural History Mus., Internat. Hypersonic Rsch., Disabled Am. Vets, Kosciuszko Found., Polish Arts Club Buffalo, Exch. Club of Tonawandas (sec. 1996-98, bd. dirs. 1999-2000), Nat. Exch. Club (Disting. Sec. award 1996, 97, 98, 99). Republican. Roman Catholic. Achievements include development of criteria and methods of structural analysis extending analyses into the plastic and creep ranges for titanium and columbium rocket nozzle extensions; of criteria and methods of structural analysis for extendable rocket nozzle extensions, including rapid nozzle deployment involving plasticity; of methods of structural analysis for low strength, high ductility steels, aluminums, and teflons as positive expulsion devices for zero gravity application in propellant tanks including bellows, reversing heads, rolling diaphragms devices and collapsing or folding concepts; structural analysis on "X" series of aircraft, on Mercury, Gemini, and Apollo spacecraft reaction control and propulsion systems; structural and weight analysis of programs involving rocket engines, propulsion systems, aircraft, air cushion vehicles, surface-effect ships, laser systems avionics, airborne and ground antennae, Army tanks and fighting vehicles. Home and Office: 152 Linwood Ave Tonawanda NY 14150-4020

DRUCK, KALMAN BRESCHEL, public relations counselor; b. Scranton, Pa., Dec. 6, 1914; s. Jacob L. and Mabelle (Breschel) D.; m. Pearl Spiro, Nov. 26, 1936; children: Ellen Druck Mirtz, Nancy Druck Brassem. BS in Journalism, magna cum laude, Syracuse U., 1936. With Hearst Enterprises, 1936-39, Carl Byoir & Assos., 1939-59; pres., vice chmn. Harshe-Rotman & Druck, Inc., N.Y.C., 1960-81; prin. Kalman B. Druck, Inc., 1981—. Supr. courses pub. rels. Baruch Sch. Bus., CCNY, 1939-55; mem. adv. com. schs. communications Syracuse U., Boston U.; adj. prof. Grad. Sch. Communication, Fairfield (Conn.) U., 1987-88. Pub. Public Relations Career Guide, Impact of High Technology on Public Relations. Bd. dirs. Union Am. Hebrew Congregations, 1956-71, N.Y. Fedn. Jewish Philanthropies, 1957-72, Am. Jewish Com., 1979-87; hon. bd. dirs. Palm Beach Civic Assn.; v.p. Palm Beach Com. for Good Govt.; past chmn. civilian pub. affairs adv. com. U.S. Mil. Acad., West Point, N.Y. Recipient Disting. Alumnus Centennial medal Syracuse U., 1970 Mem. Pub. Rels. Soc. Am. (pres. N.Y. chpt. 1953-55, nat. chmn. 1972, chmn. com. on profl. devel. 1979-80, trustee Found. for Pub. Rels. Rsch. and Edn. 1981-86, Gold Anvil award 1966, named Pub. Rels. Profl. of Yr. 1966). Home: 1208 Devonshire Way Palm Beach Gardens FL 33418-6864 E-mail: kalpearl@aol.com.

DRUCKER, ALAN STEVEN, mechanical engineer; b. Boston, Apr. 22, 1948; s. Eugene Elias and Corrine Ruth (Mintzer) D.; m. Patricia Ellen Sori, Aug. 10, 1974; children: Aaron, Zachary. BS, Cornell U., 1970. Jr. devel. engr. Carrier, Syracuse, N.Y., 1972-78, sr. devel. engr., 1978-82, program mgr., 1982-85, staff engr., 1985-94, sr. staff engr., 1994—. Inventor, patentee in field. Democrat. Jewish. Avocations: diving, scuba, gardening, tennis. Office: Carrier Corp Carrier Pkwy Syracuse NY 13221 E-mail: al.drucker@carrier.utc.com.

DRUCKER, ARNO P. music educator; b. Phila., Dec. 25, 1933; s. Albert Alfred Drucker, Gertrude S. Drucker; m. Ruth L. Landes; children: David, Steven. BMus, U. Rochester, 1954, M in Music, 1955—55; D in Musical Arts, Johns Hopkins U., 1970. Cert. master tchr. Music Tchrs. Nat. Assn. Prof. Essex C. C., Baltimore County, Md., 1967—95. Prin. pianist Balt. Symphony Orchestra, 1972—95; vis. prof. Peabody Conservatory Music, Johns Hopkins U., Balt., 1977—85. Author: American Piano Trios-A Resource Guide, 1999. Sergeant U.S. Army, 1957—59, based in Stuttgart, Germany. Grantee, Fulbright, 1955—56. Mem.: Coll. Music Soc. Avocation: musical stamp collecting. Home: 1 Glencliffe Cir Baltimore MD 21208 Personal E-mail: adrucker@comcast.net.

DRUCKER, BARRY JULES, environmental health specialist; b. St. Louis, Dec. 29, 1940; s. Morris Josef and Geraldine Drucker; m. Sandra Leta Lew, June 10, 1968; 1 child, Melanie. BA, So. Ill. U., 1969; MA, Webster U., 1976; MPH, St. Louis U., 1992. Registered environ. health specialist; cert. profl. environ. health specialist. Chemist St. Louis City Health Dept., 1970-76; sr. research technician Washington U. Sch. Medicine, St. Louis, 1976-77; sanitarian Mo. Dept. Mental Health, St. Louis, 1977-79; sanitarian, supr. Mo. Dept. Health, St. Louis, 1979-82; program mgr. St. Louis County Health Dept., Clayton, Mo., 1982—2001; environ. health supr. St. Charles County Dept. Cmty. Health and Environ., St. Charles, Mo., 2001—. Assoc. dir. Mo. Restaurant Assn., St. Louis, 1982—2001; mem. Mo. Food Adv. Coun., Jefferson City, 1982—, St. Louis County Restaurant Com., 1982—2001; vice chmn. Mo. Bd. Certification for Sanitarians, Jefferson City, 1987—89, Jefferson City, 1990—91, mem., 1986—91, Mo. State Milk Bd., Jefferson City, 1995—2001; mem. adv. bd. Sch. Pub. Health St. Louis U., 1996—; mem. Mo. Food Safety Task Force, Jefferson City, Miss., 1999—. Peer reviewer Jour. of Environ. Health, 1985—; contbr. articles to profl. jours. With USAF, 1960-64. Mem. Mo. Environ. Health Assn. (pres. 1985-86, publ. awards 1986, 87, 88, 93, Sanitarian of Yr. 1987), St. Louis Area Pub. Health Assn. (pres. 1986-87, mem.-at-large 1992—), Mo. Pub. Health Assn. (bd. dirs. 1986-87, pub. award 1988, 93), Nat. Environ. Health Assn. (bd. dirs. 1984-86, Cert. of Merit 1987, Jour. Editor's award 1994). Avocation: vintage advertising. Home: 19250 River Ridge Ln Wildwood MO 63005-3818 Office: St Charles County Dept Cmty Health & Environ 1650 Boone's Lick Rd Saint Charles MO 63301 E-mail: claudius01@msn.com.

DRUCKER, CHRISTINE MARIE, lawyer; b. Sioux City, Iowa, Apr. 16, 1947; d. Sigmund James and Paula Frances (Riedmann) Kulawik; m. John Joseph Drucker, Jr., June 19, 1971; children— Emily, Jeremy. B.A., Webster Coll., 1969; J.D., St. Louis U., 1972. Bar: Mo. 1972, Ill. 1973, Minn. 1977, U.S. Dist. Ct. (no. dist.) Ill. 1972, U.S. Dist. Ct. Minn. 1985. Law clk., Mo. Ct. Appeals, St. Louis, 1972-73; assoc. Walsh, Case & Coale, Chgo., 1973-74; atty. Ill. State's Attys. Assoc., Elgin, Ill., 1974-76; atty., adviser U.S. Dept. Interior, Mpls., 1979-81; sole practice, Mpls., 1983—. Mem. fin. com. Christ the King Parish, Mpls., 1979-81. Mem. ABA, Minn. State Bar Assn., Minn. Women Lawyers, Hennepin County Bar Assn., Minn. Women's Network. Democrat. Roman Catholic. Home: 5121 Bryant Ave S Minneapolis MN 55419-1213 Office: 431 S 7th St Minneapolis MN 55415-1821

DRUCKER, LISA K. editor; b. Bklyn., Mar. 26, 1967; d. Eugene and Dorothy R. Drucker. BA cum laude, Vassar Coll., 1989; MA summa cum laude, New Sch. U., 1992. Dir. adminstrn. Fla. Symphonic Pops, Boca Raton, 1995—96; editl. asst. HCI Books, Deerfield Beach, 1997—98, assoc. editor, 1998—2000, sr. editor, 2000—. Author: Don't Eat the Pomegranates, 2002, The Princess-in-Tng. Manual, 2002, Arise, O Phoenix, 2003. Docent Rockland County Ctr. Holocaust Studies, Spring Valley, NY, 1986—93. Recipient Am. History award, Rockland County Hist. Soc. Avocations: writing, museums, movies, music, crossword puzzles. Office: HCI Books 3201 SW 15th St Deerfield Beach FL 33442

DRUCKER, MARK LEWIS, public administration educator, consultant; b. Sept. 30, 1947; s. Harry and Helen Drucker; children: Michael, Hilary. BA, Columbia U., 1969; MBA, Harvard U., 1971. Asst. prof. urban affairs and policy analysis New Sch. for Social Rsch., N.Y.C., 1971-75; exec. dir. Coun. of Univ. Insts. for Urban Affairs, N.Y.C., 1974-75; vis. asst. prof. urban affairs St. Louis U., 1975-76; Pew fellow in health policy Boston U., 1988-90; assoc. prof pub. adminstrn. and policy analysis So. Ill. U., Edwardsville, 1976—2002, dir. policy analysis grad. program, 1979-88; pvt. practice, 2002—. Cons. East-West Gateway Coordinating Coun., St. Louis, 1998, Springfield (Ill.) Housing Authority, 1995, Urban Inst., Washington, 1995, William M. Mercer, Inc., Chgo., 1991-92. Author: Urban Decisionmaking, 1981; contbr. articles to profl. jours. Pres. Housing Solutions, Inc., St. Louis, 1993-95; chair planning bd. Confluence St. Louis, 1987-88; pres. bd. dirs. Satellite Sch., 1984-85; 1st v.p. Greater St. Louis Health Sys. Agy, 1981-82; mem. Children's Summit, 1998-99; mem. St. Louis 2004 Healthcare Cmty. Action Team, 1996-98. Pew Meml. Trusts fellow, 1988-90; Mortgage Bankers Assn. faculty fellow, 1982-84. Mem. Am. Jewish Congress (v.p. midwest chpt. 1996-99), Mo. Pub. Health Assn. (pres. St. Louis chpt. 1996-97, state bd. dirs. 1996-97). Jewish. Avocations: reviewing mysteries, community affairs, film, theater, baseball. Home: Apt 3N 18 South Kingshighway Saint Louis MO 63108-1330

DRUCKER, MICHAEL STUART, lawyer; b. Brookline, Mass., May 14, 1968; s. C. Gerard and Marjorie (Epstein) Drucker; m. Laura Ann Sugar, June 14, 1997; children: Samuel Evan, Maxwell Rubin. BA, U. Mich., 1990; JD, Suffolk U., 1993. Bar: Ga. 1993, Mass. 1993. V.p., assoc. gen. counsel The Collegiate Licensing Co., Atlanta, 1993—. Avocations: travel, sports, american literature, dining. Office: The Collegiate Lic Co 290 Interstate North Ste 200 Atlanta GA 30339-2205 E-mail: mdrucker@clc.com.

DRUCKER, PETER FERDINAND, writer, consultant, educator; b. Vienna, Nov. 19, 1909; came to U.S., 1937, naturalized, 1943; s. Adolph Bertram and Caroline D.; m. Doris Schmitz, Jan. 16, 1937; children: Kathleen Romola, J. Vincent, Cecily Anne, Joan Agatha. Grad., Gymnasium, Vienna, 1927; LLD, U. Frankfurt, 1931; 25 hon. doctorates. Economist London Banking House, 1933-37; Am. adviser for Brit. banks, Am. corr. Brit. newspapers, 1937-42, cons. maj. bus. corps., 1940—, prof. philosophy, politics Bennington Coll., 1942-49; prof. mgmt. NYU, 1950-72, chmn. mgmt. area, 1957-62; Clarke prof. social sci. Claremont Grad. Sch. (Calif.), 1971—2002; prof. dept. art Pomona Coll., Calif., 1979-85. Author: The End of Economic Man, 1939, new edit. 1995, The Future of Industrial Man, 1941, new edit. 1995, Concept of the Corporation, 1946, new edit., 1993, The New Society, 1950, new edit., 1993, The Practice of Management, 1954, new edit., 1993, America's Next Twenty Years, 1957, The Landmarks of Tomorrow, 1959, new edit., 1996, Managing for Results, 1964, new edit., 1993, The Effective Executive, 1966, new edit., 2002, The Age of Discontinuity, 1969, new edit., 1996, Technology; Management and Society, 1970, Men, Ideas and Politics, 1971, Management: Tasks, Responsibilities, Practices, 1974, new edit., 1993, The Unseen Revolution: How Pension Fund Socialism Came to America, 1976, new edit. (new title: The Pension Fund Revolution, 1996), Adventures of a Bystander, 1979, new. edit., 1998, Managing in Turbulent Times, 1980, new edit., 1993, Toward the Next Economics and Other Essays, 1981, (essays) The Changing World of the Executive, 1982, Innovation and Entrepreneurship, 1985, new edit., 1993, (essays) The Frontiers of Management, 1986, 8th edit., 2000, The New Realities, 1989, new edit., 2003, Managing the Non-Profit Organization, 1990, (essays) Managing for the Future, 1992, 7th edit., 2000, (essays) The Ecological Vision, 1992, new edit., 1997, Post Capitalist Society, 1993, (essays) Managing in a Time of Great Change, 1995, Drucker on Asia: A Dialogue With Isao Nagauchi, 1997, (essays) Drucker on the Profession of Management, 1998, Management Challenges for the 21st Century, 1999, (anthologies) The Essential Drucker on Management, 2001, (essays) Managing in the Next Society, 2002, A Functioning Society, 2003; (fiction) The Last of All Possible Worlds, 1982, The Temptation to Do Good, 1984; co-author: The Song of the Brush: Japanese paintings, 1979; producer: movie series The Effective Executive, 1969, Managing Discontinuity, 1971, The Manager and the Organization, 1977, Managing for Tomorrow, 1981, The Future of Manufacturing, 2000; producer 25 audiocassette series The Non-Profit Drucker, 1988, 5 Online Teaching Devices on Managing Yourself, 2000, 5 Online Teaching Devices on Business Strategies, 2000, 3 Online Teaching Devices on Managing Change, 2003. Recipient gold medal Internat. U. Social Studies, Rome, 1957, Wallace Clark Internat. Mgmt. medal, 1963, Taylor Key Soc. for Advancement Mgmt., 1967, Presdl. citation NYU, 1969, CIOS Internat. Mgmt. gold medal, 1972, Chancellor's medal Internat. Acad. Mgmt., 1987, Evangeline Booth award Salvation Army, 2001, Disting. Leadership medal Nat. Acad. Mgmt., 2001, Presdl. Medal of Freedom, 2002. Fellow AAAS (council), Internat., Am., Irish Acads. Mgmt., Brit. Inst. Mgmt. (hon.), Am. Acad. Arts and Scis.; mem. Soc. for History Tech. (pres. 1965-66), Nat. Acad. Pub. Adminstrn. (hon.).

DRUCKER, STEPHEN, former magazine editor-in-chief; Grad., Vassar Coll.; postgrad., Columbia U. Contbg. editor and exec. editor Travel & Leisure; features dir. HG Mag.; editor The New York Times "Home" sect., 1996—97; creator New York Times "Sunday Styles" sect.; sr. editor Vogue, Self Mag.; editor Martha Stewart Living, N.Y.C., editor-in-chief, 1997—2001; sr. v.p. Martha Stewart Living Omnimedia, N.Y.C.; freelance writer.*

DRUCKMAN, DANIEL, social sciences educator, consultant, researcher; b. N.Y.C., Dec. 14, 1939; s. Irving and Gladys (Marcus) D.; m. Marjorie Kahn, July 22, 1962; children: Kathy Lee Berggren, James N. BA with honors, Mich. State U., 1961; student, Duke U., 1961-62; MS, Northwestern U., 1965, PhD, 1966. Sr. rsch. scientist Inst. Juvenile Rsch., Chgo., 1966-72, program dir., 1972-75; sr. rsch. analyst Mathematica, Inc., Bethesda, Md., 1975-79, math. tech. scientist, 1979-82; sr. scientist, program mgr. Booz-Allen & Hamilton, Bethesda, 1982-85; prin. study dir. Nat. Acad. Scis., Washington, 1985-97; Vernon M. and Minnie I. Lynch prof. conflict resolution George Mason U., Fairfax, Va., 2001, dir. doctoral program, 1997—2002. Vis. faculty IIS Inst. Mgmt., Cochin, India, 1998—; vis. scientist Internat. Inst. Applied Sys. Analysis, Vienna, Austria, 1991-92; cons. Nat. Rsch. Coun., Washington, 1997-2000. Mem. editl. bd. Jour. Conflict Resolution, 1990—, Am. Behavioral Scientist, others; assoc. editor, Negotiation Jour. and Simulation & Games, editor spl. issue Annals of Am. Acad. Polit. and Social Sci., 1995; contbr. over 1250 articles to sci. jours.; author, editor 11 books. Active Nat. Charity Campaigns, Tennis Profls. Tournament Wash. Tennis Patrons, 1990—; coach Montgomery Soccer, Inc., Md., 1979-87. Recipient award U.S. Inst. of Peace, Washington, 1992-93, 96-97, award for enhancing human performance U.S. Army Rsch. Inst., Alexandria, Va., 1986-97, Tchg. Excellence award, George Mason U., 1998. Fellow Soc. Psychol. Study of Social Issues (Otto Klineberg Intercultural and Internat. Rels. award 1995), Soc. Exptl. Social Psychology, Internat. Studies Assn., Internat. Assn. Conflict Mgmt., Sigma Xi. Achievements include research in experimental studies of negotiation and nationalism. Home: 10509 Gainsborough Rd Potomac MD 20854-4045 Office: Inst Conflict Analysis and Resolution George Mason U 4260 Chain Bridge Rd Fairfax VA 22030-4297 Fax: 703-993-1302. E-mail: ddruckma@gmu.edu.

DRUCKREY, INGE HEIDE, graphic designer, educator; b. Berlin, Feb. 6, 1940; came to U.S., 1966; d. Hermann Carl Paul and Annemarie Erna Elisabeth (Eick) D.; m. Edward Rolf Tufte. Diploma in graphic design, Allgemeine Gewerbeschule, Basel, Switzerland, 1965. Designer Studio Halpern, Zurich, 1965-66; design instr. Kansas City (Mo.) Art Inst., 1966-68, Werkkunstschule Krefeld, Germany, 1968-71; asst. prof. Phila. Coll. Art, 1971-73, Yale U., New Haven, Conn., 1973-79, assoc. prof., 1979-82, sr. lectr., 1982-83, vis. prof., 1983-84, sr. design critic, 1984-95. Design cons. Graphics Press, 1982—; part time faculty RISD, Providence, 1987-94; adj. prof. U. of the Arts, Phila., 1995—. Exhibited in group shows at Gewerbe Mus., Basel, 1983, Walker Art Ctr., Mpls., 1985, Moore Coll. Art, R.I. Sch. Design, Va. Commonwealth U., 1986, Mus. Modern Art, N.Y.C., 1988, U. Arts, Phila., 1989, Herb Lubalin Study Ctr., Cooper Union, N.Y., 1989, Walker Art Ctr., Mpls., IBM Gallery Sci. and Art, N.Y., Phoenix Art Mus., Butler's Wharf, London, 1989, Rockefeller Arts Ctr. Gallery, SUNY, Fredonia, 1992; works in numerous publs. and mus. exhbn. catalogs. Grantee Ford Found., 1979-80. Avocations: horseback riding, hiking. Office: U of the Arts Graphic Design Dept 333 S Broad St Philadelphia PA 19107-5839

DRUEHL, LOUIS DIX, biology educator; b. San Francisco, Oct. 9, 1936; naturalized Can. citizen, 1974; s. Louis Dix and Charlotte (Primrose) D.; m. Jo Ann Reeve, Aug. 17, 1967 (div. 1974); m. Rae Kristanne Randolph, Aug. 11, 1983. BSc, Wash. State U., 1958; MSc, U. Wash., 1962; PhD, U. B.C., Vancouver, B.C., 1966. Rsch. advisor Brazil Navy, Cabo Frio, 1975-77; cons. biomass program GE, Catalina, Calif., 1981-83; from asst. prof. to assoc. prof. Simon Fraser U., Burnaby, 1966-88, prof. biology, 1988—2002, prof. emeritus, 2002—, dir. Inst. Aquaculture Rsch., 1988-90; assoc. dir. Bamfield (B.C.) Marine Sta., 1992-96. Rsch. assoc. Inst. Algae Rsch. U. Hokkaido, 1972-73; pres. Can. Kelp Resources Ltd., Bamfield, 1982—. Mem. editorial bd. European Jour. Phycology, 1993-96; contbr. over 50 articles to profl. jours. Recipient Provasoli Best Paper award, Jour. Phycology, 1988. Mem. Western Soc. Naturalists (pres. 1988). Avocation: writing poetry. Home: 4 Port Desire Bamfield BC Canada V0R 1B0 Office: Bamfield Marine Sta Bamfield BC Canada V0R 1B0 E-mail: druehl@sfu.ca.

DRUGAN, CORNELIUS BERNARD, retired school administrator, retired psychologist, musician; b. Youngstown, Ohio, July 23, 1946; s. Francis Edward and Erminia (Costarella) D.; m. Kathleen Anne Cowhard, Aug. 17, 1968; children: Jonelle Kathryn, Noelle Marie. BS, Heidelberg Coll., 1968; AM, John Carroll U., 1970; PhD, Walden U., 1980. Cert. supt.; lic. psychologist. Tchr. Warrensville City Schs., Warrensville Heights, Ohio, 1968-72; intern psychologist Garfield Heights (Ohio) City Schs., 1972-73; psychologist Belmont (Ohio) County Schs., 1973-80; supr. Union Local Schs., Belmont, 1980-83, pupil personnel dir., 1983-87; adminstr. Streetsboro (Ohio) City Schs., 1987—. Tchr. Warrensville Heights Recreation Dept., 1968-72, Southgate Music, Maple Heights, Ohio, 1970-73; instr. Cleve. State U., 1970-72; advisor Belmont County Career Ctr., St. Clairsville, Ohio, 1980-86. Organist St. Peter of the Fields Ch., Rootstown, Ohio, 1989-2000, Western Res. Christian Ch., Hudson, Ohio, 2000—. First place piano competition Portage Music Tchr. Assn., Ravenna, Ohio, 1964. Mem. Am. Guild Organists (exec. bd. Akron, Ohio chpt. 1998-2001, sec. 2002--), Buckeye Assn. Sch. Adminstrs., Jaycees (Jaycee of Month, St. Clairsville, Ohio chpt. 1975), Ohio Ret. Tchrs. Assn., K.C. (coun. 5173). Avocations: part-time profl. musician, guitar and amplifier building/collecting. Home: 3138 Robin Dr Ravenna OH 44266-9548

DRULINER, MARCIA MARIE, education educator; b. Dec. 18, 1946; M in Secondary Edn., U. Nebr., 1974; PhD, Marquette U., 1992. Assoc. prof. edn. Concordia Coll., Bronxville, N.Y., 1993-95; asst. prof. edn. Northwestern Coll., Orange City, Iowa, 1998-2000; instr. Spanish, Gretna (Nebr.) Pub. Schs., 2000—. Home: 20184 Glenmore Dr Apt 76 Gretna NE 68028

DRUM, ALICE, academic administrator, educator; b. Gettysburg, Pa., June 22, 1935; d. David Wentz and Charlotte Rebecca (Kinzey) McDannell; m. D. Richard Guise, June 15, 1957 (div. Aug. 1975); children: Gregory, Brent, Richard, Robert, Clay; m. Ray Kenneth Drum, Mar. 2, 1979; 1 child, Trevor. BA magna cum laude, Wilson Coll., 1957; PhD, Am. U., 1976. Adj. prof. gen. studies Antioch U., Columbia, Md., 1976-78; adj. asst. prof. English Gettysburg (Pa.) Coll., 1977-80; lectr. gen. studies Georgetown U., Washington, 1980-81; lectr. gen. honors U. Md., College Park, 1980-83; asst. prof. English Hood Coll., Frederick, Md., 1981-85, coord. writing program, 1981-83, assoc. dean acad. affairs, 1983-85; dean freshmen Franklin and Marshall Coll., Lancaster, Pa., 1985-88, v.p., 1988-2001, prof., chair womens studies, 2001—. Team mem. Mid. States Accreditation Assn., 1989-2003; cons. in field. Co-author: Funding A College Education, 1996; contbr. chpts. to books, articles and book revs. to profl. jours. Chair Lancaster County DA Commn., Lancaster, 1990-91; mem. Lancaster County Commn. on Youth Violence, Lancaster, 1990-91; bd. trustees Wilson Coll., 1997—, YWCA, Lancaster, Mellon grant, 1979; Davison Foreman fellow, 1975-76. Mem. MLA, N.E. MLA, Deans (pres. 1988-89), Coll. English Assn., Phi Beta Kappa (pres. chpt. 1990-91), Phi Kappa Phi. Democrat. Episcopalian. Avocations: hiking, reading, visiting art museums. Office: Franklin & Marshall Coll Lancaster PA 17604-3003

DRUM, JOAN MARIE MCFARLAND, federal agency administrator, educator; b. Waseca, Minn., Mar. 31, 1932; d. Leo Joseph and Bergetthe (Anderson) McFarland; m. William Merritt Drum, June 13, 1954; children: Melissa, Eric. BA in Journalism, U. Minn., 1962; MEd, Coll. William and Mary, 1975, postgrad., 1984-85. Govt. ofcl. fgn. claims br. Social Security Adminstrn., Balt., 1962-64; freelance writer Polyndrum Publs., Newport News, Va., 1967-73; tchr. Newport News (Va.) Pub. Schs., 1975-79; writer, cons. Drum Enterprises, Williamsburg, Va., 1980-82; developer, trainer communicative skills U.S. Army Transp. Sch., Ft. Eustis, Va., 1982-86; govt. ofcl. test assistance div. U.S. Army Tng. Ctr., Ft. Eustis, 1986, course devel. coord. distributed tng. office, 1992. Adj. faculty English dept. St. Leo Area Coll., Ft. Eustis, 1975-78; del. Communicative Skills Conf., Ft. Leavenworth, Kans., 1983; mem. Army Self-Devel. Test Task Force, 1991-92; task force mem. U.S. Army Tng. FAA; program developer multi-media electronic delivery prototype; tech. tng. facility trainer. Author: Ghosts of Fort Monroe, 1972, Travel for Children in Tidewater, 1974, Galaxy of Ghosts, 1992, Hampton's Haunted Houses, 1998, How to Feed a Ghost, 1998; editor: army newsletter for families, 1968-73, Social Services Resource Reference, 1970; contbr. articles to profl. jours. Chmn. Girl Scouts U.S., Tokyo, 1964-66, Army Cmty. Svc., Ft. Monroe, Va., 1967-68; chmn. publicity Hist. Home Tours, Ft. Monroe, 1971-73; chmn. adv. bd. James City County Social Svcs., 1989-95, chmn. adult svcs., 1989-90; mem. James City County Leadership Devel. Program Bd. Recipient numerous civic awards including North Shore Cmty. Svc. award, Hialeah, Hawaii, 1966, Home Bur. Svc. award, 1975, Svc. award Girl Scouts U.S., Tokyo, 1965, Comdrs. achievement award for civilian svc., 1995, 98. Mem. N Va. Writers Club, Kappa Delta Pi. Home: 9 Bray Wood Rd Williamsburg VA 23185-5504 E-mail: jdrum@hroads.net.

DRUM, SYDNEY MARIA, artist; b. Calgary, Alta., Can., Nov. 20, 1952; d. Ian Mondelet and Dorothy Mary (Weaver) D.; m. Frank DeSalvo, Nov. 7, 1987; 1 child, Christopher. BFA with distinction in art, U. Calgary, 1974; MFA, York U., 1976. Tchr. U. Ill., 1978-83, Govs. State U., 1983-84, Rutgers U., 1984-87. One-woman and 2 person exhibits include Art Gallery Ont., 1978, Condeso/Lawler Gallery, N.Y., 1981, Gallery Pascal, 1983, U. Pitts., 1984, Bau-Xi Gallery, Toronto, 1987, 90, 92, 95, 55 Mercer Gallery, N.Y., 1993, 96, Mus. am Ostwall, Dortmund, Germany, 1994, Hart House-U. Toronto, 1995; represented in pub. collections Can. Coun. Art Bank, U. Toronto, Toronto-Dominion Bank, Petro Can., Mus. Modern Art, N.Y., Phila. Mus. Art, Robert McLaughlin Gallery, Oshawa; commissions include Pope, Ballard, Shepard & Fowle, Chgo., 1983, Zimmerli Mus., Rutgers U., 1990; reviewer art exhibits New Art Examiner, Chgo., 1983-84. Can. Coun. grantee, 1978. Home: 138 W 120th St New York NY 10027-6401

DRUMHELLER, JANET LOUISE, librarian; b. Walton, W. Va., June 23, 1951; d. Nathan Earl and Edna Osial (Dye) Vineyard; m. Fred John Drumheller, Apr. 11, 1971; 1 child, Stephanie Katarina. BS in History, U. Tenn., 1974, MS in Libr. and Info. Scis., 1977. Mgr. Farragut br. Knox County Pub. Librs., Knoxville, Tenn., 1977—81, reference libr., 1983—96, reference svcs. mgr., 1996—. Bd. dirs. Tenn-Share. Bd. dirs. Knoxville-Oak Ridge Regional Network. Mem.: East Tenn. Libr. Assn., Tenn. Libr. Assn. Office: Knox County Libr System 500 W Church Ave Knoxville TN 37902

DRUMHELLER, KIRK, retired engineering company executive; b. Walla Walla, Wash., Jan. 14, 1925; s. William Lewis and Elsie McIver Drumheller; m. Betty Vaara, June 17, 1950; children: Karen, Susan, Ellen, Michael. BS, MIT, 1945; postgrad., Harvard U., 1947—48. Engr. and design mgr., projects mgr. GE, Richland, Wash., 1951—65; R&D mgr. Battelle, Richland, 1965—69, mgr.

Jrsey nuc. project, 1969—70, lab. solar program coord., 1970—84, mgr. industry rels. and industry programs Seattle, 1984—89; pres. Heliostats, Inc., Seattle, 1989—2003; ret., 2003. Prin. investigator Foresight Sci. and Tech., New Bedford, 1998—2001. Contbr. book. Mem., chmn. Wash. State Solar Adv. Group, Olympia, 1979—83. Lt. (j.g.) USN, 1942—46. Recipient Fin. Assistance award, U.S. Dept. Commerce, 1994-1995. Mem.: Am. Solar Energy Soc. Achievements include patents for process of forming an isotopic heat source; child proof latches; heliostat components. Avocations: jogging, skiing, travel, conservation and energy education of the public. Home: 5015 Nicklas Pl NE Seattle WA 98105 E-mail: kirkdrum@alum.mit.edu.

DRUMKE, MICHAEL WILLIAM, lawyer; b. Chgo., Mar. 29, 1966; s. Ronald Alfred and Sandra Drumke; m. Jody L. Pabst, Jan. 2, 1993. BA cum laude, Tufts U., 1988; JD, U. Wis., 1991. Bar: Wis. 1991, Ill. 1992; U.S. Dist. Ct. (we. dist. Wis.) 1991, U.S. Dist. Ct. (no. dist. Ill.) 1992, U.S. Dist. Ct. (ea. dist. Wis.) 1995, U.S. Dist. Ct. (no. and so. dists. Ind.) 1995, U.S. Dist. Ct. (ctrl. dist.) Ill. 1999, Tex. 2001. Intern to chief justice Supreme Ct. of Wis., Madison, 1991; law clk. to presiding judges Dane County Cir. Ct., Madison, Wis., 1991-92; assoc. Taylor, Miller, Sprowl, Hoffnagle & Merletti, Chgo., 92-94, Segal McCambridge Singer & Mahoney, Ltd., Chgo., 1994-2000, Freeborn & Peters, Chgo., 2001—02; ptnr. Schiff Hardin & Waite, Chgo., 2002—. Spkr. in field. Contbr. articles to profl. jours. Fellow Am. Bar Found.; mem. ABA (past chair toxic tort and environ. law com. Tort and Ins. Practice sect., coord. nat. CLE programs), Ill. Bar Assn., State Bar Wis., State Bar Tex. Office: Schiff Hardin & Waite 6600 Sears Tower 233 S Wacker Dr Chicago IL 60606

DRUMMER, DONALD RAYMOND, financial services executive; b. Binghamton, N.Y., Oct. 10, 1941; s. Donald Joseph and Louise Frances (Campbell) D.; m. Rita Kovac, May 22, 1965; children: Shelley Rita, Adam Donn. BS, U. Colo., 1972; MBA, Regis U., 1981. With Lincoln First Bank, Binghamton, 1962-69; asst. comptr. Adams & Horne, Denver, 1969; with Colo. State Bank, Denver, 1969-87, v.p., 1972-81, comptr., 1972-87, sr. v.p., 1981-87; sr. v.p., CFO Wyo. Nat. Bancorp. (formerly Affiliated Bank Corp. of Wyo.), Casper, 1987-91, Wyo. Nat. Bank, Casper, Cheyenne, 1987—91; v.p., contr. Crop Hail Mgmt., Kalispell, Mont., 1991—92; sr. v.p. fin. Am. Nat. Bank, Cheyenne, 1993—95; v.p. Cmty. First Bancorp, Inc., 1994—95, cons., 1995—2001; v.p., CFO Citizens Bank Oviedo, 2001—. Bd. dirs. Wyo. Nat. Bank, Lovell and Kemmerer, 1987-88; corp. sec. Wyo. Nat. Bancorp. (formerly Affiliated Bank Corp. of Wyo.), 1987-91; bd. dirs. Wheatland Ins. Agency, 1989-91; CFO, exec. com. Am. Bankers Assn., 1989-91; adj. faculty Regis U., mem. grad. edn. task force, 1986-87. Editor: Chronicle, 1980-81. Bd. dirs. Girls Club of Casper, 1988. Mem. Inst. Mgmt. Accts. (dir. 1975-79, v.p. 1977-79), Am. Acctg. Assn., Am. Taxation Assn., Denver Sertoma Club (past pres.), City Club (v.p., dir. 1979-83). Office: PO Box 620729 Oviedo FL 32762-0729 E-mail: don@cboviedo.com.

DRUMMOND, CAROL CRAMER, voice educator, singer, artist, writer; b. Indpls., Mar. 5, 1933; adopted d. Burr Ostin and L. Ruth Welch; m. Roscoe Drummond, 1978 (dec. 1983). Student, Butler U., 1951—53; studied voice with Todd Duncan, Frances Yeend, James Benner, Rosa Ponselle, Dr. Peter Herman Adler and John Bullock; studied drama with Adelaide Bishop, Washington, D.C. Original performer Starlite Musicals, Indpls., 1951; singer Am. Light Opera Co., Washington, Seagle Opera Colony, Schroon Lake, N.Y., 1963, 64; soloist St. John's Episcopal Ch., Lafayette Sq., Washington, 5th Ch. of Christ, Scientist, Washington, 1963-78; performer Concerts in Schs. Program, Washington Performing Arts Soc., 1967-99; soloist with Luke AFB band ofcl. opening Boswell Meml. Hosp. Sun City, Ariz., 1970; painter, artist, 1980—; pvt. tchr. voice, 1986—; voice tchr. Ellsworth H.S., Mt. Desert Island H.S., 1986—. Soloist numerous oratorio socs.; appearances with symphony orchs. including Nat. Symphony Orch., Fairfax (Va.) Symphony Orch., Buffalo Philharm. Orch., Concerts in the Pk., Arlington Opera Co., Lake George Opera Co., Glens Falls, NY, The Nat. Cathedral, Washington, Noye's Flood, Lufkin, Tex., 1965, Washington Opera; voiceover radio and TV commls., 1965—84; U.S. Govt. host The Sounding Bd., Sta. WGTS-FM, Washington, 1972—78; dir. ensembles, music/voice cons. Summer Festival of the Arts, S.W. Harbor, Maine, 1992—95, mem. adv. bd., 1986—; dri. Amahl and the Night Visitors, 1992; vocal solo concert The Smithsonian Instn., 1980. Former columnist: Animal Crackers, writer: newspaper and mag. articles and stories; one-woman shows include, Lemon Tree, Bangor, 1995, 1996, Grand Theater, Ellsworth, Maine, 1995, Southwest Harbor (Maine) Pub. Libr., 1997, U. Maine, 1999, Border's, Bangor, 2002; two-woman shows including, Am. Art League, Washington, 1997, two-woman show Cosmos Club, Wash., 1996, Arts Club, 1994, 1995, 1996, artist, owner Dream Come True Notecards, 1997—. Bd. dirs. Washington Sch. Ballet, 1978; life bd. dirs. Internat. Soundex Reunion Registry, Carson City, Nev. Recipient 1st pl. women's divsn. Internat. Printers Ink Contest, 1951. Mem.: Nat. League Am. Pen Women, Beta Sigma Phi, Kappa Kappa Gamma. Republican. Episcopalian. Avocations: cats, knitting, gardening, reading, travel. Home: PO Box 791 79 Clark Point Rd Southwest Harbor ME 04679 Office: 10802 Tradewind Dr Oakton VA 22124-1800 E-mail: ccdrummond@gwi.net.

DRUMMOND, DOROTHY WEITZ, geography education consultant, educator, author; b. San Diego, Dec. 19, 1928; d. Frederick W. and Dora (Weidenhofer) Weitz; m. Robert R. Drummond, Sept. 5, 1953 (dec. June 1982); children: Kathleen, Gael, Martha. AB, Valparaiso U., 1949; MA, Northwestern U., 1951. Cert. tchr., Ind. Social studies tchr. Woodrow Wilson Jr. High Sch., Oxnard, Calif., 1949-50; editorial asst. Am. Geog. Soc., N.Y.C., 1951-53; substitute tchr. Vigo County Sch. Corp., Terre Haute, Ind., 1960-67; social studies tchr. Ind. State U. Lab. Sch., Terre Haute, 1963-64. Geog. edn. cons., author, workshop presenter, Terre Haute, 1953—; adj. asst. prof. geography Saint Mary-of-the-Woods (Ind.) Coll., 1967-99, Ind. State U., Terre Haute, 1990—; dir. project GEO, Ind. State U., 1992-96; cons. McGraw-Hill, Scott-Foresman, Agy. for Instrnl. Tech., Hudson Inst.; grant developer GIS for the Twenty-First Century, Ind. State u., 1996-98. Co-author: The World Today, 3d edit., 1971, World Geography, 1989; author: People on Earth, 3d edit., 1988, Holy Land, Whose Land?, 2002; contbr. numerous articles to profl. jours. Organizer, leader ednl. tours to China, 1986, 1988, 1998, 2001; organizer, leader ednl. tours to Australia, 1993, 1996, 1997, 1999, 2000, 2002; organizer, leader ednl. tours to New Zealand, 2003; bd. dirs. Mental Health Assn. Wabash Valley, Terre Haute, 1984—93, Coun. on Domestic Abuse, Terre Haute, 1987—92, 1997—99, United Ministries Ctr., Terre Haute, 1991—94, 2003—. Fulbright scholar, Burma, 1957-58; grantee Geography Educators Network Ind., 1988-96, Ind. Commn. Higher Edn., 1990, 92, 94, 96, NSF, 1993, 95, 96, 97, U.S. Dept. Edn., 1992-96. Mem. Ind. Coun. Social Studies, Geography Educators Network Ind. (bd. dirs.), Nat. Coun. Geog. Edn. (pres. 1990), Nat. Coun. Social Studies. E-mail: dd2@indstate.edu.

DRUMMOND, GERARD KASPER, lawyer, retired minerals company executive; b. N.Y.C., Oct. 9, 1937; s. John Landells and Margaret Louise (Kasper) D.; m. Donna J. Mason, Sept. 14, 1957 (div. 1976); children: Alexander, Jane, Edmund; m. Sandra Hamilton, Aug. 31, 1985 BS, Cornell U., 1959, LL.B. with distinction, 1963. Bar: Oreg. 1963. Assoc. Davies, Biggs, Strayer, Stoel & Boley, Portland, Oreg., 1963-64; assoc., ptnr. Rives, Bonyhadi, Drummond & Smith, Portland, 1964-77; pres. Nerco, Inc., Portland, from 1977-87, chmn. bd. dirs., CEO, 1987-93; mem. corp. policy group PacifiCorp, 1979-93, exec. v.p., 1987-93, also bd. dirs.; of counsel Stoel Rives, Portland, 1993-98. Pres., chmn. bd. dirs. Tri-County Met. Transit Dist., Portland, 1974-85; Oreg. Investment Coun., 1987-98, 2001— chmn., 1990-98, 2001—; bd. dirs. Oreg. Bus. Coun., 1987—; trustee Reed Coll., 1982-99; bd. dirs. Oreg. Symphony, 1987-93, pres., 1990-92; cmty. bd. dirs. Providence Hosp., 1986-95, chmn., 1993; mem. adv. coun. Cornell U. Law Sch., 1991-95; bd. dirs. Oreg. Shakespeare Festival Assn., 1992-98, Oreg. chpt. Nature Conservancy, 1992-93; trustee Oreg. Symphony Found., 1996—; chmn. bd. dirs. N.W. Bus. Commn. for Arts, 1992-94; trustee Oreg. Shakespeare Festival Found., 1999—, chmn. 2000—. 1st lt. USAR, 1959-67. Mem. Am. Mining Congress (bd. dirs. 1986-92), Arlington Club. Home: 28815 S Needy Rd Canby OR 97013-9570

DRUMMOND, JAMES EVERMAN, defense technology transfer consultant, former army officer; b. Stillwater, Okla., July 13, 1932; s. Garrett Bartlett and Frances Elizabeth (Rigdon) Drummond; m. Helen Wesley Hillman, Dec. 29, 1958 (dec. Aug. 2001); children: James Everman, Sarah Elizabeth. BS, U.S. Mil. Acad., 1955; MS, U. Ariz., 1962; postgrad., Army War Coll., 1975; MA, Central Mich. U., 1982. Commd. 2d lt. U.S. Army, 1955, advanced through grades to maj. gen., served in Europe, Vietnam, Korea, comdr. III Corps Arty., 1979-81, dep. dir. Material Systems Analysis Activity, 1981-82; comdr. TCATA Ft. Hood, Tex., 1983-86; comdr. OTEA Falls Ch., Va., 1986-88; v.p. BDM Corp, Norfolk, Va., 1988-90; pvt. practice cons., 1990-92; v.p. Coe-Truman Tech. Inc., Hampton, Va., 1992-96. Asst. prof. U.S. Mil. Acad., 1962-65 Decorated D.S.M., Legion of Merit with 2 oak leaf clusters, Bronze Star, Air medal, others. Mem. Assn. U.S. Army, Soc. Am. Mil. Engrs., Mil. Order World Wars, Assn. Grads. U.S. Mil. Acad., Internat. Test and Evaluation Assn., Co. of Mil. Historians, Sigma Alpha Epsilon, Masons, Kiwanis. Presbyterian. Home: 173 Loch Cir Hampton VA 23669-5525

DRUMMOND, JOHN C. anesthesiologist, educator; b. Apr. 26, 1949; s. John Cornell and Doris Bradshaw Drummond; m. Hilda Sager Drummond, Nov. 27, 1982; children: Jonathan, Ian, Julie, Bonnie. AB in Biology, Princeton U., 1971; MD, U. Toronto, 1975. Diplomate Am. Bd. Anesthesiology. Med. intern St. Michael's Hosp., Toronto, 1975-76; resident in anesthesiology U. Toronto, 1976-80, clin. instr. dept. anesthesia, 1980; from asst. to full prof., chair dept. anesthesia U. Calif., San Diego, 1981—; staff anesthesiologist VA Med. Ctr., San Diego, 1985—. Contbr. articles to profl. jours., chpts. to books. Diplomate Am. Bd. of Anethesia, Fellow Royal Coll. Physicians of Can.; mem. Am. Soc. Anesthesiologists, Soc. for Neurosurg. Anesthesia and Critical Care, Soc. for Cerebral Blood Flow and Metabolism, Can. Anesthetists' Soc., Calif. Soc. Anesthesiologists, Internat. Anesthesia Rsch. Soc. Office: U Calif San Diego Med Ctr 200 W Arbor Dr Dept 8812 San Diego CA 92103-8812

DRUMMOND, JON, Olympic athlete; b. Phila., Pa., Sept. 9, 1968; m. Celia Drummond, 1997; 1 child. Sprinter U.S.A. Track and Field Team, Atlanta, 1996; co-winner Gold Medal 4X100 meter relay Sydney, 2000; co-winner Silver Medal 4X100 relay U.S. Championships, 1997; U.S. indoor 60m champion, 1993, 2000; placed 1st Penn Relays 4x100m relay, 2003; placed 1st 4x100m relay World Cup, 2002; placed 1st at Adidas Boston indoor games, 2002; ranked #10 in the world (#5 in U.S.) T&FN, 2002; gold medalist 4x100m relay World Outdoors, 2000. Performer: with gospel group Kirk Franklin & The Family (album reached #1 in 1993); singer: backup with Lawrence Johnson, John McEnroe, Alexei Lalas for Bryan Adams, 2000. Office: USA Track and Field Team One RCA Dome Ste 140 Indianapolis IN 46225

DRUMMOND, MALCOLM MCALLISTER, electronics engineer; b. London, Eng., Sept. 22, 1937; came to U.S., 1966, naturalized, 1977; s. George James and Winifred Ethel (Jaye) D.; m. Linda Jerome Banning, May 25, 1968; 1 child, Heather Lynn. BSEE with honors, City U., London. Registered profl. elec. engr. Engr. Brit. Fgn. Office, Cheltenham, Eng., 1964-66; sr. engr. Gen. Dynamics Corp., Rochester, N.Y., 1966-70; tech. rep. Tymshare Inc., Rochester, 1970-72; project engr. Sybron Corp., Taylor Instrument Co., Rochester, 1972-85, Hampshire Instruments Corp., 1985-93, User Friendly Operating Systems, Inc., 1993-2000, Eastman Kodak Co., Rochester, 2000, ENI/MKS, An Emerson Co., Rochester, 2000—. Dir. Care & Svc., Inc., 1982-90, pres. 1986-89. Christian Sci. min. for VA Hosp., 1974-80; chmn., bd. trustees Ch. of Christ Scientst, Rochester, 1993-94, 98-99. Mem. IEEE (life sr. mem., chmn. Rochester sect. 1979-80, past chmn. pension task force 1983-84, Region I PAC coord. 1980-82, Area D chmn. 1982-85, ASIC seminar chmn. 1987-88), Engrs. and Scientists Joint Com. on Pensions (vice chmn. 1983-84), N.Y. State Soc. Profl. Engrs., Engring. Mgmt. Soc. (chmn. 1990—), Computer Soc. (past pres.), Instrument Soc. Am., Rochester Engring. Soc. (emeritus; dir. 1979-83, IEEE rep. 1984—, treas. 1993-2003), Principle Found. Western N.Y. (treas. 1994—), Am. Mgmt. Assns., Inst. Elec. Engrs. (Gt. Brit.), Monroe County Bar Assn. (mem. ethics com. 1994-95). Home: 60 Marberth Dr Henrietta NY 14467-9014 Office: ENI/MKS Instruments 100 Highpower Rd Rochester NY 14623-3498 E-mail: mdrummond@mksinst.com.

DRUMMOND, MARSHALL EDWARD, business educator, university administrator; b. Stanford, Calif., Sept. 14, 1941; s. Kirk Isaac and Fern Venice (McDeritt) D. BS, San Jose State U., 1964, MBA, 1969; EdD, U. San Francisco, 1979. Adj. prof. bus. and edn. U. San Francisco, 1975-81; adj. prof. bus. and info. systems San Francisco State U., 1981-82; prof. MIS, Ea. Wash. U., Cheney, 1985—, exec. dir. info. resources, 1988, assoc. v.p. adminstrv. svcs., chief info. officer, 1988-89, v.p. adminstrv. svcs., 1989-90, exec. v.p., 1990, pres., 1990-98; chancellor L.A. C.C. Dist., 1999—. Cons. Sch. Bus., Harvard Coll., U. Ariz. Contbg. editor Diebold Series; contbr. articles to profl. jours. Democrat. Avocations: running, water sports, equestrian sports., horse breeding and trainging. Office: LA C C Dist 770 Wilshire Blvd Los Angeles CA 90017-3856

DRUMMOND, WILLA HENDRICKS, physiology and medical educator; b. Harrisburg, Pa., Dec. 5, 1945; d. George Edson and Leah Clementine (Connelley) Hendricks; m. Thomas Weston Drummond, June 1966 (div. 1978). BA cum laude, Brown U., 1966; MD, U. Pa., 1970; MS in Med. Informatics, U. Utah, 1999. Resident in pediat. Children's Hosp. Phila., 1970-72, cardiology fellow, 1972-74; instr. pediat. U. Pa., Phila., 1973-74; rsch. fellow perinatology U. Oreg., Portland, 1974-75; staff pediatrician Kaiser-Permanente Clinics, Portland, 1975-76; instr. neonatology, fellow Cardiovasc. Rsch. Inst.-U. Calif., San Francisco, 1976-78; asst. prof. pediat. U. Fla., Gainesville, 1978-82, asst. prof. pediat. and physiology, 1981-82, assoc. prof. pediat. physiology and vet. med. scis., 1982-88, prof., 1988—. Cons. Baxter-Travenol Labs., Deerfield, Ill., 1986-88; co-chair Equine Neonatology Study Group, Gainesville, 1981-91; dir. Neonatology Fellowship Program U. Fla., Gainesville, 1981-85; cons., CIO, ICU DataSys., Inc., Gainsville. Contbr. numerous rsch. papers and abstracts to profl. jours.; poet: Carousel of Progress, 1979. Rsch. grantee (22) including Am. Heart Assn., NIH, Dept. of Def., 1976—; sr. fellow Med. Informatics, 1997-99. Mem. Am. Physiologic Soc., Soc. for Pediat. Rsch., Am. Pediat. Soc., Am. Acad. Pediat., Am. Med. Informatics Assn., Am. Heart Assn., So. Soc. Pediat. Rsch., Internat. Soc. Vet. Perinatology (bd. dirs., pres. 1995-97), Internat. Physicians for Prevention of Nuc. War (collective Nobel Peace Prize 1985), NOW, Sierra Club, other environ., women's and peace orgns. Democrat. Office: U Fla Coll Medicine PO Box 100296 Gainesville FL 32610-0296

DRUMMOND, WINSLOW, lawyer; b. Phila., Jan. 29, 1933; s. Winslow Shaw and Dorothy (Moore) D.; m. Katherine Pace, June 18, 1983; children: Judith L., Kathryn W., Winslow Shaw II. AB, Coll. of Wooster, Ohio, 1954; LLB, Duke U., 1957. Bar: Ark. 1957, U.S. Dist. Ct. Ark. 1957, U.S. Ct. Appeals (8th cir.) 1958, U.S. Supreme Ct. 1992; diplomate Am. Bd. Trial Advs. Mem. firm Wright, Lindsey & Jennings, Little Rock, 1957-82, ptnr., 1962-82, McMath Woods P.A., Little Rock, 1982—. Mem. faculty Coll. Advocacy, Hastings Coll. Law, 1974-89, Nat. Inst. Trial Advocacy, 1979-92; chmn. com. on jury instrns. Ark. Supreme Ct., 1980-89. Co-author: Arkansas Model Jury Instructions-Civil, 1965, 3d edit., 1989. Pres., bd. dirs. Urban League Greater Little Rock; bd. dirs. Little Rock Sch. Dist; trustee U. Ozarks, 1991-99. With U.S. Army, 1957-58. Named Outstanding Lawyer, Pulaski County Bar Assn., 1998, Ark. Bar Assn., 1999. Fellow Am. Coll. Trial Lawyers, Am. Bar Found., Ark. Bar Found., ABOTA Found; mem. ABA, ATLA, Ark. Bar Assn. (past chmn. exec. com., ho. of dels.), Pulaski County Bar Assn., Am. Judicature Soc., Ark. Trial Lawyers Assn. (pres. 1985-86), Am. Inn of Ct. (master of the bench), Order of Coif, Phi Alpha Theta. Democrat. Presbyterian. Home: 1 Tree Tops Ln Little Rock AR 72202-1676 Office: McMath Woods PA 711 W 3rd St Little Rock AR 72201-2201

DRUMMOND BORG, LESLEY MARGARET, clinical geneticist; b. Wellington, New Zealand, Oct. 26, 1948; came to U.S., 1986; d. Grant Allen and Yolanda Drummond; m. Kenneth Irvin Borg; children: Marc, Kyle. MBChB, Otago Med. Sch., New Zealand, 1971, MD, 1983; BSc, Auckland U., New Zealand, 1976. Diplomate Am. Bd. Pediatrics, Am. Bd. Med. Genetics; cert. clin. geneticist. Fellow in clin. genetics U. Auckland Med. Sch., 1974-77, med. geneticist, 1977-79; pediatric resident Hosp. Sick Children, Toronto, Ont., Can., 1980-82; gen. practitioner ARAMCO, Saudi Arabia, 1983-86; sr. fellow med. genetics U. Wash., Seattle, 1986-88; clin. geneticist Genetic Screening and Counseling Svc., Denton, Tex., 1988-95; dir., genetics divsn. Tex. Dept. of Health, Austin, Tex., 1995—. Clin. asst. prof. Tex. A&M U., College Station, 1991-98; cons. staff Odessa (Tex.) Women's Children's Hosp., 1991-96, Cook/Ft. Worth Children's Med. Ctr., 1991-98. Contbr. articles to profl. jours. Fellow Am. Acad. Pediatrics, Am. Coll. Med. Genetics (founder); mem. AMA, Am. Soc. Human Genetics. Avocations: jogging, swimming, hiking. Office: Tex Dept of Health Div Genetic Screening/Case Mgr 1100 W 49th St Austin TX 78756-3160

DRURY, BRADFORD DAVID, surgeon; b. Worcester, Mass., June 24, 1959; MD, U. Mass. Cert. surgery. Resident in surgery Mass. Gen. Hosp., Boston, 1985-90; staff surgeon Landstuhl Army Med. Ctr., Germany, 1990-93; chief gen. surgery Ft. Belvoir, Va., 1993-94; pvt. practice Raleigh, NC, 1994—2003, Morehead City, NC, 2003—. Fellow: ACS. Office: 3714 Guardian Ave Morehead City NC 28557

DRURY, DAVID J. insurance company executive; Chmn. The Prin. Fin. Group, Des Moines. Office: The Principal Financial Grp 711 High St Des Moines IA 50392-0002

DRURY, GERALD IRWIN, periodontist, educator; b. Chgo., July 23, 1944; s. Daniel and Dorothy (Chait) D.; m. Tineke Willy Ten Hagen, Dec. 25, 1970; children: Charles, Justin. BA, U. Ill., 1966; MS, Med. Coll. Van., 1968; BSD, U. Ill., Chgo., 1970, DDS, 1972; cert. in periodontics, La. State U., 1979. Intern N.E. Fla. State Hosp., MacClenny, 1972-73; pvt. practice dentistry Ft. Myers Beach, Fla., 1973-77; resident in anesthesiology VA Hosp., New Orleans, 1978, vis. resident periodontist, 1978-79; instr. Sch. Dentistry La. State U., New Orleans, 1977-79; clin. asst. prof. dept. surg. scis. periodontics sect. Sch. Dentistry U. So. Calif., L.A., 1979, asst. prof., 1979-81, clin. asst. prof. grad. divsn., 1981-85, clin. assoc. prof., 1985-92; mem. provisional med. staff Little Co. of Mary Hosp., Torrance, Calif., 1986; clin. prof. advanced periodontics Sch. Dentistry U. So. Calif., L.A., 1992—, dir. predoctoral periodontal surgery clinic, 1980-81, course dir. current lit. rev. grad. periodontics, 1982—; pvt. practice periodontics Irvine, Calif., 1981, Hermosa Beach, Calif., 1981—85; dir. Am Bd. Periodontology, 2002—. Expert cons. Calif. Bd. Dental Examiners; bd. dirs. Am. Bd. Periodontology. Editor: (Newsletter) Am. Bd. Periodontology. Fellow: Am. Coll. Dentists; mem.: ADA (alt. del.), Internat. Acad. Periodontology (founder), Calif. Dental Assn. (chmn. period peer rev. 1997—, del. 2002), Calif. Soc. Periodontists (regional leader 1991—99, chmn. pub. rels. 1997—, chmn. peer rev. 1997—, sec. 1998, treas. 1999, pres. elect 2000, pres. 2001, Pub. Svc. award 2000), Western Dental Soc. (mem. membership com. 1981—90, mem. peer rev. com. 1992—95, mem. then chmn. ethics com. 1995—), Western Soc. Periodontology (co-chmn. periodontal publs. com. 1977, editor jour. 1999—, bd. dirs. 2002, Platinum citation award for dental editing), Am. Assn. Dental Rsch. (award for excellence in dental rsch.), Am. Acad. Periodontology (mem. local arrangements com., mem. fgn. rels. com., nominating com.). Home: 1100 Pacific Coast Hwy Apt F Hermosa Beach CA 90254 Office: U So Calif Sch Dentistry PO Box 77951 Los Angeles CA 90007-0951

DRURY, KENNETH CLAYTON, biological scientist; b. Madera, Calif., Mar. 27, 1945; s. Carma and Alice (Zollinger) D.; m. Sandra Rosemary hanlon, Apr. 28, 1972; children: Allison Hanlon, Vanessa Laura. BA, Westmont Coll., 1967; PhD, U. Geneva, Switzerland, 1979. Cert. in andrology and embryology high complexity lab. dir. Am. Bd. Bioanalysts. NIH fellow U. Calif., Berkeley, 1979-82; rsch. scientist Codon Corp., South San Francisco, Calif., 1982-84; sr. scientist Microgenics Corp., Concord, Calif., 1984-86; dir. U. Louisville, 1986-92, In Vitro Fertilization and Gamete Physiology Labs. U. Fla., 1992—. Contbr. articles to profl. jours. 1st Lt. U.S. Army, 1969-72, Vietnam. Mem. Am. Fertility Soc., Am. Coll. Reproductive Biology, Am. Soc. Reproductive Medicine. Achievements include first investigator to directly implicate phosphorylation in mechanism of action of maturation promoting factor; one of first investigators to obtain a human live birth after ultra rapid freezing of embryos; successfully performed preimplantation genetic diagnosis to eliminate inherited genetic disease in pregnancy. Office: U Fla Dept Ob-Gyn Divsn Reprod Endocrinology PO Box 100294 Gainesville FL 32610-0294 E-mail: druryk@obgyn.ufl.edu.

DRURY, LEONARD LEROY, retired oil company executive; b. Gillespie, Ill., Nov. 5, 1928; s. Roy August and Regina Loretta (Finnegan) D.; m. Myra Lee Klunk, June 30, 1951; 1 child, Marilyn Jo Drury Chandler. BS in Indsl. Mgmt., St. Louis U., 1950; MBA in Mgmt., U. Houston, 1957. Mgr. systems program info. and computer services Shell Oil Co., N.Y.C., 1966-68, mgr. data processing info. and computer services Menlo Park, Calif., 1968, mgr. acctg. info. and computer services, 1968-69, mgr. MTM bus. systems div. info. and computer services N.Y.C. and Houston, 1969-71, mgr. planning Houston, 1971-73, mgr. planning and tech. info. and computer services, 1973-75, asst. treas. fin., 1975-77, gen. mgr. info. and computer services, 1977-80, liaison Shell Ctr. London, 1980-81, gen. mgr. products fin., 1981-83, v.p. purchasing and adminstrv. services, 1983-86, v.p. info. and computer services, 1986-89, ret., 1989. Mem. United Way, Houston, 1982-89; bd. dirs. South Main Ctr. Assn., Houston, 1986-89. Mem.: Am. Petroleum Inst., Fin. Execs. Inst., Houston Bus. Coun. (pres. 1985—86), West Houston Assn. (bd. dirs. 1984—88), The Houstonian Club, Sigma Iota Epsilon. Roman Catholic. Home: 11711 Flintwood Dr Houston TX 77024-5110

DRURY, MICHAEL, freelance writer; b. 1919; d. Davis A. Drury and Lucile Rood; m. John S. Calderwood, Oct. 2, 1942 (div. 1961). BA, Stanford U., 1939. Staff rschr. Life Mag., N.Y.C., 1941-43; staff editor Harper's Monthly, N.Y.C., 1943-45; asst. fiction editor McCall's Mag., N.Y.C., 1946-47; freelance writer, 1943—. Author 10 books; contbr. numerous articles to mags. including Life, Good Housekeeping, Ladies Home Jour., Glamour, McCalls, many others. Vol. tchr. Vols. in Newport Edn., R.I., 1975-89, Women's Prison of N.Y.C., 1958-60; mem. Com. Against Casino Gambling, Newport, 1980—; vol. tchr. prison for women N.Y.C., 1958-59. Recipient Headline award Theta Sigma Phi, 1958, Outstanding Article Am. Life award Freedoms Found., Valley Forge, Pa., 1973, VIP cert. U. Mo. Mem. Authors Guild (dir. coun. 1955-70), Authors League. Home and Office: 7 Xavier Ter Newport RI 02840 Office: Seth L Schapiro 220 Madison Ave Rm 5G New York NY 10016

DRUSIN, LEWIS MARTIN, physician, educator; b. N.Y.C., Sept. 25, 1939; s. David and Gladys Margaret (Apfel) D. BS, Union Coll., 1960; MD, Cornell U., 1964; MPH, Columbia U., 1974. Med. intern 2nd medicine Bellevue Hosp., N.Y.C., 1964-65; jr. asst. resident in medicine Med. Ctr. Hosp. of Vt., Burlington, 1965-66; sr. asst. resident N.Y. Hosp., N.Y.C., 1968-69; fellow in medicine divsn. allergy and infectious diseases Cornell U. Med. Coll., N.Y.C., 1969-70; asst. prof. pub. health Cornell U., N.Y.C., 1970-77, asst. prof. medicine, 1972-79, assoc. prof. pub. health, 1977-84, assoc. prof. clin. medicine, 1979-98, prof. clin. medicine, 1998—, prof. clin. pub. health, 1984—; dir. dept. epidemiology N.Y. Presbyn. Hosp./Cornell Ctr., N.Y.C., 1970—, assoc. attending physician, 1979-98, attending physician, 1998—. Cons. The Rockefeller Univ. Hosp., N.Y.C., 1981—; regional dir. for N.Am. Internat. Union Against Venereal Diseases and Treponematoses, Leeds, Eng., 1986-95; liaison officer, UN for IUSTI, 1995—. Contbr. book chpts., articles. Task Force Syphilis, N.Y. State Dept. Health, 1990-91. Sr. surgeon USPHS, 1966-68. Fellow ACP, Am. Coll. Preventive Medicine, Infectious Disease Soc. Am., N.Y. Acad. Medicine, Royal Soc. Medicine, Royal Soc. Tropical Medicine and Hygiene, Royal Coll. Physicians; mem. Am. STD Assn. (pres. 1982), Soc. Healthcare Epidemiology Am., Med. Soc. Study of Venereal Diseases (hon. life), Phi Beta Kappa, Sigma Xi, Alpha Omega Alpha. Office: NY Presbyn Hosp Cornell Med Ctr 525 E 68th St New York NY 10021-4885

DRUSS, RICHARD GEORGE, psychiatrist, educator; b. N.Y.C., Aug. 14, 1933; s. Joseph George and Ruth Druss; m. Margery Ellen Kramer, Aug. 28, 1960; children: Benjamin, Elizabeth. AB, Yale Coll., 1955; MD, Columbia U., 1959. Diplomate Am. Bd. Psychiatry and Neurology. Intern Mass. Meml. Hosps., 1959-60; resident Presbyn. Hosp. and N.Y. State Psychiat. Inst., 1960-63; tng. analyst Columbia Psychoanalytic Ctr., N.Y.C., 1975—, assoc. dir., 1981-91; clin. prof. dept. psychiatry Columbia U., N.Y.C., 1983—. Assoc. editor Internat. Jour. Psychoanalytic Psychotherapy, 1974-80, Bull. Assn. Psychoanalytic Medicine, 1974-83, The Psychology of Illness: In Sickness and In Health, 1995, Listening to Patients: Relearning the Art of Healing in Psychotherapy, 2000; contbr. articles and book revs. to profl. jours. Capt. U.S. Army, 1963-65. Recipient George E. Daniels award Assn. Psychoanalytic Medicine, 1990. Fellow Am. Psychiat. Assn., N.Y. Acad. Medicine; mem. AMA, Am. Psychoanalytic Assn. (cert.). Achievements include research in changes in body image following major surgical procedures, healthy and pathologic denial of illness in chronic medical patients. Office: 180 E End Ave New York NY 10128-7763

DRUTCHAS, GEOFFREY GILBERT, minister, historian, writer; b. Detroit, Sept. 18, 1952; s. Gilbert Henry and Elaine Marie Drutchas; m. Eileen Vernor, Apr. 10, 1982; 1 child, Griffin Vernor. BA with high honors, Mich. State U.,

1974; MDiv, Harvard U., 1982; D in Ministry in Christian Ethics, Lancaster Theol. Sem., 1996. Ordained Unitarian-Universalist Assn., 1982, ordained ministerial standing United Ch. of Christ, 1988, basic cert. clin. pastoral edn. Andover-Newton Theol. Sch., 1980, Andover-Newton Theol. Sch., 1982; cert. med. ethics Mich. State U., 1991. Dir. chaplaincy Tufts U., Medford, Mass., 1981—84; ext. min. Harford-York (Pa.) Ministerial Com., 1984—88; sr. pastor St. Paul United Ch. of Christ, Taylor, Mich., 1988—; exec. dir. ChristNet Emergency Shelter, Taylor, 2000—01. Co-convener econs. and clergy conf. Lincoln Filene Ctr. for Citizenship, Tufts U., Medford, 1983; co-convener continental campus ministry conf. Unitarian-Universalist Assn., Boston, 1984; founder, pres., cons. ChristNet Emergency Shelter, Taylor, 1993—; chair Rotating Shelter Roundtable Southeastern Mich., Detroit, 2000—. Author: (book) Is Life Sacred?, 1998 (Reinhold Niebuhr Min. and Scholar award, 1998); contbr. articles to profl. jours. Chair York County United Way Strengthen the Family Task Force, 1987—88, Harford County Food and Nutrition Com., Bel Air, Md., 1986—88; dir. Elisabeth Peabody Settlement Ho., Somerville, Mass. John Haynes Holmes fellow, Cmty. Ch. N.Y., 1981, St. Lawrence fellow, Unitarian Universalist Assn., 1982, Louisville Inst. fellow, Louisville Inst., Louisville Presbyn. Sem., 2001. Mem.: Soc. Christian Ethics (assoc.), Harvard Club Ea. Mich. (v.p. 1997—2001, pres. 2001—03), Phi Beta Kappa. United Church Of Christ. Achievements include discovery of authenticated artist for Michigan State Capitol rotunda; development of founding of county emergency shelter; authored first extensive history of Sanctity of Life concept in Christian ethics. Avocations: art and architectural history research, travel. Home: 24136 Goddard Rd Taylor MI 48180 Office: St Paul United Church of Christ 24158 Goddard Rd Taylor MI 48180 Home Fax: 313-291-3305; Office Fax: 313-291-3305.

DRUTCHAS, GERRICK GILBERT (BARON KHABAROVSKY), investigator; b. Detroit, Sept. 23, 1953; s. Gilbert Henry and Elaine Marie (Rutkowski) D.; 1 child, Gilbert Henry II. BA, Mich. State U., 1975; postgrad., U. Redlands, 1983-85; PhD in Bus. Adminstrn., Yuin U. Dir. Le Baron Investigations, Pasadena, 1992—. Exec. dir. Shared Gifts Found. Exec. dir. Shared Gifts Found. Sgt. USAR, 1981-85. Named Baron, Royal House of Alabona-Ostrogojsk, 1992. Mem. Order of the Swan (chevalier), Order of St. Angilbert (chevalier), K. of P. (past chancellor 1983, 84), Delta Sigma Phi. Unitarian Universalist. Avocations: chess, coin collecting, writing fiction and non-fiction. Home: 601 E California Blvd Pasadena CA 91106-3852 Office: Le Baron Investigations Pasadena CA 91106 E-mail: lebaron@usa.com.

DRUTZ, DAVID JULES, biotechnology executive; b. Knoxville, Tenn, Apr. 20, 1938; s. Abe Morris and Lillian (Billig) D.; m. Lydia Anne Hall, June 28, 1962; children: Gretchen, Adam, Gregory, Jonathan. BA, U. Louisville, 1958, MD, 1962. Cert. Am. Bd. Internal Medicine. Intern Louisville Gen. Hosp., 1962—63; resident Vanderbilt U. Hosp., 1963-65; infectious disease fellow Vanderbilt U. Med. Ctr., 1965-67; chief infectious diseases San Francisco Gen. Hosp., 1969—74; asst. prof. medicine U. Calif., San Francisco, 1969-74; chief infectious diseases U. Tex. Health Sci. Ctr., San Antonio, 1974-86, prof. medicine and microbiology, 1974-86, founder, dir. Ctr. for Cell Regulation, 1984-86; v.p. SmithKline & French Labs., King of Prussia, Pa., 1986-90, Daiichi Pharm. Corp., Ft. Lee, NJ, 1990-94, bd. dir.; pres., CEO, dir. Sennes Drug Innovations, Inc., Houston, 1994-95, Inspire Pharms. Inc., Durham, NC, 1995-99; pres. Pacific Biopharma Assoc., Chapel Hill, NC, 1999—; gen. ptnr. Pacific Rim Ventures Co., Ltd., Tokyo, 1999—. Clin. prof. medicine Seton Hall U. Sch. Grad. Med. Edn., Newark, 1990—, U. Pa. Sch. Medicine, Phila., 1986-90, adj. prof. medicine and microbiology Temple U. Med. Sch., Phila., 1986-90; adj. prof. microbiology Coll. Medicine Baylor U., Houston, 1995—. Editor: Systemic Fungal Infections, 1988-89; contbr. articles and abstracts to profl. jour.; assoc. editor Jour. Infectious Diseases, 1983-88, editorial bd., 1988-91; editorial bd. Am. Rev. Respiratory Diseases, 1979-84, Am. Jour. of the Med. Sci., 1983-91. Chmn. sci. adv. bd. Leonard Wood Memnl., 1984-87. Lt. comdr. USNR, 1967-69, Taiwan, Vietnam. Rsch. grantee NIAID, VA, NSF, 1970-86. Fellow Am. Coll. Physicians, Infectious Diseases Soc. Am. (councillor 1986-88); mem. Am. Soc. for Clin. Investigation, Western Soc. for Clin. Investigation, So. Soc. for Clin. Rsch., Am. Soc. for Microbiology, AMA, Alpha Omega Alpha. Avocations: swimming, skiing, biking. Office: Pacific Biopharma Assocs PO Box 3616 Chapel Hill NC 27515-3616

DRUTZ, JAN EDWIN, pediatrics educator; b. Louisville, Jan. 8, 1942; s. Abe Morris and Lillian (Billig) D.; m. Anne Edwina Sussman, June 7, 1965; children: Jeffrey Benjamin, Lisa Michele, Dana Nicole. BA, U. Louisville, 1964, MD, 1968. Pvt. practice, Houston, 1973-87; intern, then resident Baylor Coll. Medicine, Houston, 1968-71, from clin. asst. prof. to assoc. prof. pediat., 1973—2002, dir. pediat. continuity clinic, 1987—, prof. pediat., 2002—; pres. med. staff Tex. Children's Hosp., 1995, prof. pediats., 2002—. Maj. U.S. Army, 1971-73. Mem. AMA, Harris County Med. Soc., Tex. Pediat. Soc. (adv. com., mem. student preceptorship program 1995-96), Houston Pediat. Soc. (sec. 1984-85, pres. 1988-89), Ambulatory Pediat. Assn. (chmn. continuity clinic spl. interest group 1990-95, edn. com. 1993—). Office: Tex Children Hosp Clin Care Ctr Ste 1540-00 6701 Fannin St Houston TX 77030

DRUYAN, LARA CATHERINE, financial consultant; b. Chgo., July 30, 1967; d. Robert and Mary Ellen Druyan. BA in Econs., U. Chgo., 1989; MBA, Harvard U., 1994. Assoc. Merrill Lynch, N.Y.C., 1994—96; mgr. product Silicon Graphics, Mountain View, Calif., 1996—99; dir. Bus. Devel. eWanted, Santa Clara, Calif., 1999—2000; gen. ptnr. Allegis Capital, Palo Alto, Calif., 2000—. Mem. adv. bd. Big Tribe, San Francisco, 2002—03; bd. dirs. Vernier Networks, Mountain View; bd. observer Z-Force Comm., Santa Clara, 2001—. Mem.: Forum for Women Entrepreneurs. Home: 608 Crescent Ave San Mateo CA 94402 Office: Allegis Capital 100 Hamilton Ste 250 Palo Alto CA 94301

DRUZDZEL, MAREK JOZEF, researcher and educator; b. Radom, Poland, Oct. 7, 1957; s. Edward and Regina (Szymczak) D.; children: Marcin, Stefan, Roman, Julian. MS in Computer Sci. with distinction, Delft U. of Tech., 1985, MSEE with distinction, 1987; PhD, Carnegie Mellon U., 1992. Vis. scientist IBM Thomas J. Watson Rsch. Ctr., Yorktown Heights, N.Y., 1987-88; rsch. asst., adj. prof. Carnegie Mellon U., Pitts., 1988-91, rschr. assoc., 1993; rschr. Rockwell Internat. Sci. Ctr., Palo Alto, 1993; rsch. assoc. Inst. for Decision Systems Rsch., Palo Alto, 1993; assoc. prof. intelligent systems Sch. Info. Scis., U. Pitts., 1993—. Lectr. U. Pitts., Carnegie Mellon U., Imperial Cancer Rsch. Fund, London, U. Utrecht, The Netherlands, Delft U. of Tech., The Netherlands, Free U. of Amsterdam, Rockwell Internat., many others. Contbr. articles to profl. jours. Recipient Career award NSF. Mem. IEEE, Am. Assn. for Artificial Intelligence, Inst. for Ops. Rsch. and Mgmt. Sci., Assn. for Uncertainty in Artificial Intelligence, European Assn. for Decision Making, Sigma Xi. Office: Univ Pitts Dept Info Sci Pittsburgh PA 15260 E-mail: marek@sis.pitt.edu.

DRUZHNIKOV, YURI ILYA, literature educator, writer; b. Moscow, Apr. 17, 1933; m. Valerie Linetsky, June 3, 1983; children: Elena, Ilya. BD, Latvian U., Riga, 1951—53; MD, Moscow Pedagogy U., 1953—55; PhD, HTE Inst., Moscow, 1960. Prof. U. Tex., Austin, 1987—88, U. Calif., Davis, 1988—. Author: Informer 001, 1996, Prisoner of Russia, 1999, Angels on the Head of a Pin, 2003. Named Best Russian Writer of 1998, City of Moscow, 1998; named to the "Author of 10 Best Russian Novels of the XXC" List, U. Warsaw, 1998; recipient Dostoyevsky Prize, Writer's Union of Poland, 2001. Mem.: Internat. Pen Club (v.p. 1993—). Office: German & Russian Dept Univ Calif Davis CA 95616

DRVAR, MARGARET ADAMS, vocational education educator; b. Morgantown, W.Va., Dec. 22, 1953; d. Lester Morris and Daun Collette (Benson) Adams; m. Marvin Lynn Drvar, July 29, 1978; children: Jacob Elias, Jared Nathaniel. BS in Family Resources, W.Va. U., 1977, MS in Family Resources, 1982. Cert. tchr., vocat. family and consumer scis. tchr., W.Va. Substitute tchr. Monongalia County Bd. Edn., Morgantown, 1983-86; tchr. vocat. family and consumer sci. Clay Battelle Jr.-Sr. H.S., Blacksville, W.Va., 1986-89, 91-92, South Mid. Sch., Morgantown, 1992—, treas. faculty senate, 1997—. Instr. culinary arts Monongalia County Tech. Edn. Ctr., Morgantown, 1989-91; youth group adv. Family, Career, Cmty. Leaders Am. (formerly Future Homemakers of Am.), 1986—. V.p. United Meth. Women, Brookhaven, W.Va., 1985-92; sec. bd. trustees Brookhaven United Meth. Ch., 1989-97; bd. dirs., sec. Morgantown AES Fed. Credit Union, 1989—; vol. 4-H leader Brookhaven Bulls 4-H Club, 1992—. Recipient Master Advisor award, Future Homemakers Am. Inc., 1996, Golden Apple Achiever award, Ashland Oil, 1996, Outstanding 4-H Leader Monongalia County award, 1996, Tchr. of Yr. award, W.Va. Family and Consumer Sci. Assn., 2002, Top 10 Tchrs. of the Yr., Am. Assn. of Family and Consumer Scis., 2002, All Star award for yrs. of cmty. svc., W.Va. 4-H, 2003. Mem.: NEA, Monongalia County 4-H Leaders Assn. (pres. 1998—99, 2001—03), W.Va. Vocat. Assn. (historian family and consumer sci. divsn. 1995—96), Assn. for Career and Tech. Edn., Monongalia County Assn. of Family and Consumer Scis., W.Va.Assn. Family and Consumer Scis., Monongalia County Edn. Assn., W.Va. Edn. Assn., Am. Assn. Family and Consumer Scis. (cert.) (Top 10 Tchr. of Yr. 2002), Gamma Phi Beta, Alpha Upsilon Omicron. Avocations: travel, camping. Home: 3307 Darrah Ave Morgantown WV 26508-9187 Office: Monongalia County Schs South Mid Sch 500 E Parkway Dr Morgantown WV 26501-6839 E-mail: mdrvar@access.k12.wv.us.

DRVOTA, MOJMIR, cinema educator, author; b. Prague, Czechoslovakia, Jan. 13, 1923; came to U.S., 1958, naturalized, 1963; s. Jan and Zdenka (Krejcikova) D.; m. Jana Kratochvilova, May 18, 1957; 1 child, Monica. *Daughter Monica Drvota, B.A. 1994 The Ohio State University, J.D. 1998 Capital University Law School, is curretbly employed with the Ohio Department of Education, Office for Exceptional Children. Married in 2000 to Walter James McNamara IV; J.D.; is currently employed with the Ohio Attorney General's Office.* Student, Charles U., 1945-48; PhD, Palacky U., 1953; MS, Columbia U., 1961. Stage dir. state theaters, Czechoslovakia, 1952-56; libr. Bklyn. Pub. Libr., 1958-62; asst. prof. dramatic arts Columbia U., N.Y.C., 1962-69; assoc. prof. cinema NYU, N.Y.C., 1969-72; prof. cinema Ohio State U., Columbus, 1972-92, prof. emeritus, 1992—. Script writer Czechoslovak State Film, Prague, 1948-52; author: Short Stories, 1946, Boarding House for Artists, 1947, Solitaire, 1974, Triptych, 1980, Solitaire, Triptych in Czech, 1993; The Constituents of Film Theory, 1973, in Czech, 1994, How Many ANgels Can Dance on the Tip of a Needle?, in Czech, 2002. Mem. Univ. Film Assn., AAUP, Phi Kappa Phi. Home: 3541 Prestwick Ct Columbus OH 43220-5097 *Everything I stood for was defeated, everything I longed for remained unfulfilled, everything I loved passed beyond reach. In the chasm thus rent I captured a glimpse of what is real and what only is, of what is an act of becoming and what is a mere activity. Henceforth, I made it my task to share in the linking effort of those individuals who communicate in the services of reality: the reality screened by objects into which we are situated.*

DRY, MARSHA G. librarian; b. Monahans, Tex., May 15, 1950; d. Buck N. and Jewel I. (Luxton) Miller; m. William C. Dry, Sept. 19, 1970. BS, Sul Ross State U., 1971; MLS, Tex. Woman's U., 1982. Cert. elem. edn., learning resource specialist, supr. High sch. libr. Alpine (Tex.) Ind. Sch. Dist.; libr. Ector County Ind. Sch. Dist., Odessa, Tex. Mem. PTA (life), ATPE, Tex. Library Assn., Delta Kappa Gamma. Home: 4628 Bonham Ave Odessa TX 79762-4531

DRYANSKY, GERALD Y. writer, editor, film producer, scriptwriter; b. N.Y.C., Jan. 14, 1938; m. Joanne Axelrod; children: André, Larisa. AB, Princeton U., 1959; AM, Harvard U., 1960; MS, Columbia U., 1961. European dir. Fairchild Pubs., Paris, 1965-75; dir. external affairs Bidermann Group, Paris, 1975-77; Paris editor German Vogue, Paris, 1979-81; writer, comm. cons. Paris, 1981-84; editor-at-large European Travel and Life, Paris, 1984-87; European editor Conde Nast Traveler, Paris, 1987—; v.p. Andara Films, Paris, 1995—. Author: (novels) Other People, 1972, The Heirs, 1978, Chant d'Adieu, 2000; co-author (with Joanne Dryansky) Fatima's Good Fortune, 2003; contbr. articles to mags. Bd. dirs. Friends of Florence, Italy, 1998—; chmn. Prince Alumni Schs. Com., Paris, 1983. Mem.: Anglo Am. Press Assn., Harvard Club N.Y.C. Office: Andara Films 96 Ave Kléber 75116 Paris France

DRYCE, H. DAVID, accountant, consultant; b. Bronx, N.Y., Feb. 18, 1930; s. Theodore and Ruth Dryspiel; m. Norma Stein, June 12, 1955; children: Mimi, Arthur, Debra. BA, Yeshiva U., 1952; postgrad., Isaac Elchanan Theol. Sem., N.Y.C., 1955; MBA, CUNY, 1959. CPA, N.Y. 1st lt. U.S. Army, 1955-57, capt., 1957-64; sr. acct. various firms, L.I., NY, 1959-63; prin. H. David Dryce, CPA, Old Bethpage, NY, 1963—98; exec. officer CHB Inc., Buffalo, 1985-96. Instr. SUNY, Farmingdale, 1966-68, cons. Video Art Prodns. Inc., Palm Harbor, Fla., 1986—. Author: Inventory Verification-Extent of Observation and Acceptable Limitations, 1959; contbr. articles to profl. publs. V.p. United Coun. Civil Assns., Oyster Bay, N.Y., 1966-67, Old Bethpage Civic Assn., 1966-67; pres. Metro Region Men's Clubs, N.Y.C., 1970-71; treas. Reggie Lewis Found., 1993-2000. Mem. N.Y. State Soc. CPAs (chmn. mgmt. svcs. com. Nassau County chpt. 1967-69). Home and Office: 4692 Sweetmeadow Cir Sarasota FL 34238-4333 E-mail: nordavid@comcast.net.

DRYDEN, KEN, sports team executive; b. Etobicoke, Ont., Can. m. Lynda Dryden; children: Sarah, Michael. Grad., Cornell U.; JD, McGill U.; LLD (hon.), U. Windsor, U. B.C., York U., Toronto. Goaltender Montreal Canadiens, 1971-79; pres., gen. mgr. Toronto Maple Leafs, 1997—; v.p. Maple Leaf Gardens Ltd., 1997—. Colour commentator Winter Olympic Games ABC-TV, 1980, 84, 88. Author: The Game, Home Game, The Moved and the Shaken: The Story of One Man's Life, In School. Ont. youth commr., 1984—86; initiator Ken Dryden Scholarships. Named to Hockey Hall of Fame, 1983; recipient Conn Smyth Trophy as Most Valuable Player in Playoffs of Stanley Cup, 1971, Calder trophy, 1971—72, Vezina trophy (5). Office: c/o Toronto Maple Leafs 60 Carlton St Toronto ON Canada M5B 1L1

DRYDEN, ROBERT EUGENE, lawyer; b. Chanute, Kans., Aug. 20, 1927; s. Calvin William and Mary Alfreda (Foley) D.; m. Jetta Rae Burger, Dec. 19, 1953; children: Lynn Marie, Thomas Calvin. AA, City Coll., San Francisco, 1947; BS, U. San Francisco, 1951, JD, 1954. Bar: Calif. 1955; diplomate Am. Bd. Trial Advocates (pres. San Francisco chpt. 1997). Assoc. Barfield, Dryden & Ruane (and predecessor firm), San Francisco, 1954-60, jr. ptnr., 1960-65, gen. ptnr., 1965-89; sr. ptnr. Dryden, Margoles, Schimaneck & Wertz, San Francisco, 1989—. Lectr. continuing edn. of the bar, 1971-77; evaluator U.S. Dist. Ct. (no. dist.) Calif. Early Neutral Evaluation Program; master atty. San Francisco Am. Inn of Ct. Mem. bd. counsellors U. San Francisco, 1993—. With USMCR, 1945-46. Fellow Am. Coll. Trial Lawyers, Am. Bar Found., Internat. Acad. Trial Lawyers; mem. ABA, San Francisco Bar Assn., Assn. Def. Counsel (bd. dirs. 1968-71), Def. Rsch. Inst., Internat. Assn. Ins. Counsel, Fedn. Ins. Counsel, U. San Francisco Law Soc. (mem. exec. com. 1970-72), U. San Francisco Alumni Assn. (mem. bd. govs. 1977), Phi Alpha Delta. Home: 1320 Lasuen Dr Millbrae CA 94030-2846 Office: Dryden Margoles Schimaneck & Wertz 101 California St Ste 2050 San Francisco CA 94111-5427

DRYDEN, WOODSON E. lawyer; b. Anadarko, Okla., Dec. 21, 1924; s. Harry Ernest and Ruth Sally (Woodson) D.; divorced; children: Judith, Carol, Kim, Christine, Erich. BBA, Kans. U., 1948; LLB, Tex. U., 1951. Sole practice, Beaumont, Tex., 1951—. With USNR, 1942-46. Mem. Tex. Trial Lawyers Assn. (pres. 1972-73). Democrat. Episcopalian. Home: 6625 Windwood Ln Beaumont TX 77706-4239 Office: 915 Goodhue Bldg Beaumont TX 77706-6229

DRYE, WILLIAM JAMES, JR., business owner; b. Phila., Aug. 27, 1939; s. William James and Louvenia (Spearman) D.; 1 child, William Bradley. Cert. in acctg., U. Pa., 1966, BBA, 1968. Cert. energy reduction specialist. Clk. U. Pa., Phila., 1957-60, acct., 1960-63, asst. to treas., 1966-67, asst. to bus. mgr., 1967-68, acting comptroller, 1974, asst. comptroller, 1968-81, assoc. comptroller, 1981-83; pres. Delaware Valley Energy Conservation, Phila., 1983—. Mem. Springfield Twp. Town Watch, 1987. Served with U.S. Army, 1963-65. Mem. Am. Mgmt. Assn., Nat. Energy Specialist Assn. (performance award 1987). Avocations: sports, travel, cooking. Home and Office: 1211 Meadow Dr Blue Bell PA 19422-3302

DRYER, DOUGLAS POOLE, retired philosophy educator; b. Toronto, Ont., Can., Nov. 27, 1915; s. William Poole and Mabel Elizabeth (McLeod) D.; m. Pegeen Synge, Mar. 22, 1946; children: Dagny, Matthew, Moira; m. Ellice Baird, May 29, 1965; 1 stepdau., Eleanor. AB magna cum laude, Harvard U., 1936, AM, 1939, PhD, 1980. Instr. Union Coll., Schenectady, 1939-41; asst. Harvard Coll., 1943-45; lectr. Tufts Coll., 1944-45; lectr. philosophy U. Toronto, 1945-48, asst. prof., 1948-59, assoc. prof., 1959-63, prof., 1963-81, prof. emeritus, 1981—. Author: Kant's Solution for Verification in Metaphysics, 1966, Introduction to J.S. Mill, Essays on Ethics, Religion and Society, 1969. Fellow Royal Soc. Can.; mem. Am. Philos. Assn., Can. Philos. Assn. Clubs: Alpine of Can, Royal Scottish Country Dancing Soc. Home: 61 Lonsdale Rd Toronto ON Canada M4V 1W4

DRYGA, SERGEY ALEXANDER, biotechnologist; b. Oktyabrskiy, Ryasan Region, Russia, Oct. 16, 1964; s. Alexander Ivanovich and Lidia Aleksandrovna Dryga; m. Olga Anatolievna Duplinskaya, Feb. 9, 1985; children: Dmitriy Sergeyevich, Mariya Sergeyevna. MS, Novosibirsk State U., Russia, 1986; PhD, Inst. Molecular Biology, Novosibirsk, 1994; postgrad., U. N.C., Chapel Hill, 2002—. Scientist Inst. Molecular Biology, Koltsovo, 1990—94; rsch. assoc. Wash. U. Sch. of Medicine, St. Louis, 1994—97; scientist Heska Corp., Ft. Collins, Colo., 1997—98; sr. rsch. scientist Alphavax Human Vaccines, Inc., Research Triangle Park, NC, 1999—. Contbr. articles. Mem.: Am. Soc. Virology. Achievements include patents for recombinant alphavirus-based vectors with reduced inhibition of cellular macromolecular synthesis. Avocations: electronics, amateur robotics, reading. Home: 211 Bonsail Pl Chapel Hill NC 27514 Office: Alphavax Inc PO Box 110307 2 Triangle Dr Research Triangle Park NC 27709-0307 Office Fax: 919-595-0401. Personal E-mail: sergey_dryga@kenan-flagler.unc.edu. E-mail: dryga@alphavax.com.

DRYJSKI, MACIEJ LUKASZ, vascular surgeon, educator; b. Warsaw, Jan. 3, 1951; arrived in Sweden, 1974, came to U.S., 1985; s. Jozef Dryjski and Aniela (Grochowska) Dryjska; m. Hanna Iwona Bielawska, June 4, 1977; children: Dominika, Olivia, Sebastian. MD, Med. Acad., Warsaw, 1974; PhD, Karolinska Inst., Stockholm, 1984. Resident in gen. surgery Karolinska Inst. and Hosp., 1978-83, attending surgeon, instr. surgery, 1983-85; rsch. assoc. in clin. pharm. Duke U., Durham, N.C., 1985-86; asst. prof. medicine and surgery Jefferson U., Phila., 1986-88, resident in gen. surgery, 1988-89; resident in vascular surgery U. South Fla., Tampa, 1989-91; assoc. prof. surgery Karolinska Inst. and Hosp., 1991-94, SUNY, Buffalo, 1994—. Dir. endovascular rsch. Kaleida Health, Buffalo, 1994—; assoc. clinical dir. Surgery Kaleida Health. Editl. bd. Polish Jour. Surgery; contbr. articles to profl. jours., chpts. to boks; jour. referee. Senator SUNY, Buffalo, 1999—. Recipient Swedish Med. Rsch. Coun. award for rsch. in U.S., 1985-87. Fellow ACS, N.Y. Acad. Scis.; mem. Soc. for Vascular Surgery, Eastern Vascular Soc., Western N.Y. Vascular Soc. (pres. 2001-), Buffalo Surg. Soc., Internat. Soc. Cardiovasc. Surgery, Internat. Soc. Thrombosis and Haemostasis, Swedish Med. Soc., Internat. Soc. Applied Cardiovasc. Biology, Internat. Soc. Endovasc. Surgery, Soc. Clin. Vascular Surgery. Roman Catholic. Avocations: tennis, skiing, sailing, golf. Home: 280 Quail Hollow Ln East Amherst NY 14051-1634 Office: SUNY Millard Fillmore Hosp 3 Gates Cir Buffalo NY 14209-1120

DRYMALSKI, RAYMOND HIBNER, lawyer, banker; b. Chgo., June 1, 1936; s. Raymond P. and Alice H. (Hibner) D.; m. Sarah Fickes, Apr. 1, 1967; children: Robert, Paige. BA, Georgetown U., 1958; JD, U. Mich., 1961. Bar: Ill. 1962. Lawyer Chgo. Title & Trust Co., 1963-65; asst. sec., atty. No. Trust Co., Chgo., 1965-68; ptnr. Boodell, Sears, Giambalvo & Crowley, Chgo., 1968-87; mem. Bell Boyd & Lloyd LLC, Chgo., 1987—. Contbr. articles to profl. jours. Bd. dirs. Northwestern Meml. Hosp., Chgo., 1978—, Northwestern Meml. HealthCare, 1987—; vice chmn., sec. Northwestern Meml. Healthcare, 1998—99, chmn., 2000—; bd. dirs. McGaw Med. Ctr. of Northwestern U., 2000—, Lincoln Park Zool. Soc., 1972—, pres., 1980—84; bd. dirs., officer Offield Family Found., 1990—; mem. coun. govs. Northwestern Healthcare Network, 1990—, bd. dirs., 1999. Mem. ABA, Econ. Club Chgo. Roman Catholic. Home: 443 W Eugenie St Chicago IL 60614-5674 Office: Bell Boyd & Lloyd LLC 70 W Madison St Ste 3300 Chicago IL 60602-4244 E-mail: rdrymalski@bellboyd.com.

DRYMAN, AMY, epidemiologist; d. Sylvia and Irving Armin Dryman. BA, Yale U., 1977—81; DSc, Johns Hopkins U., Sch. of Hygiene and Pub. Health, 1982—87. Contbr. articles to profl. jours.

DRYSDALE, JOYCE A, substance abuse counselor; b. Elkhart, Ind., Sept. 21, 1932; d. Chester Arthur Balyeat and Margie Grace Roth; m. Jackson H. Kirkwood, Jun. 13, 1953 (div. 1960); children: Mary Ann Massey, Jeri Ann Tippit, Jenifer Lynn Stone, Jeffrey Alan Kirkwood, Toni Toppel; divorced, 1974. Student, Brevard C.C., 1966-68, Broward C.C., 1970-71, U. Minn., 1974. Addictions counselor USN-Navy Alcohol Safety Action Program, Jacksonville, Fla., 1975-78; aftercare/family coord. Penalta Hosp., Oakland, Calif., 1978-79; addictions counselor Palm Beach Inst., Jupiter and Gulf Breeze, Fla., 1979-83; clin. supr. Renaissance Program Elkhart Gen. Hosp., Elkhart, Ind., 1983-85; program dir. Crossroads Recovery Program, Panama City, Fla., 1985-88, Houston Med. Ctr., Warner Robins, Ga., 1988-92; clin. dir. Recovery Place of Savannah, Ga., 1992-93; coord. outpatient svcs. Charter Lake Hosp., Macon, Ga., 1993-95; coord. special programs Coliseum Psychiatric Hosp., Macon, Ga., 1995-97; addictions counselor, clin. supr. River Edge Recovery Ctr., Macon, Ga., 1997—, facilitator impaired profl. group, 1999—. Clin. supr. Ga. Addiction Counselor Assn., 1993—; mem. adv. bd. Duval County Mental Health, Jacksonville, Fla., 1976-77. Contbr. articles to profl. jours. Lectr. Optomist Club, Warner Robins, Ga., 1992, Kiwanis Internat. Panama City, Fla., 1986, Macon State Univ., 1992. With USAF, 1951-52. Mem. Ga. Addiction Counselor Assn., Nat. Assn. Alcoholism and Drug Abuse Counselors, Employee Assistance Profl. Employee Assistance Assn. Democrat. Roman Catholic. Avocations: travel, reading, arts and crafts, playing organ. Office: River Edge Recovery Ctr 3575 Fulton Mill Rd Macon GA 31206-5117

D'SOUZA, FRANCIS, chemistry educator; b. Sagar, Shimoga, Karnataka, India, Dec. 8, 1960; s. Gabriel and Elizabeth D'Souza; m. Mirabilis Morris, Jan. 10, 1994; children: Preston, Fiona P. PhD, Indian Inst. of Sci., Bangalore, India, 1991. Asst. prof. Wichita (Kans.) State U., Wichita, 1994—99, assoc. prof., 1999—2003, prof., 2003—. Cons. NATO, Brussels, 2001—02. Contbr. articles to profl. jours. Recipient Young Faculty scholarship, Wichita State U., 1998. Mem.: Electrochem. Soc. (vice chmn. Fullerene divsn. 2000—03), Am. Chem. Soc. Office: Wichita State U 1845 Fairmount Wichita KS 67260-0051 Office Fax: 316-978-3431. E-mail: francis.dsouza@wichita.edu.

D'SOUZA, GERARD EUGENE, economist, educator; b. Feb. 20, 1956; s. George I. and Bernadette S. (Coelho) D'S. BS, U. Agrl. Scis., Bangalore, India, 1977; MS, Miss. State U., 1980, PhD, 1983. Rsch. asst. Miss. State U., 1978-84; asst. prof. agrl. econs. W.Va. U., Morgantown, 1984-92, assoc. prof., 1992—99, prof., 1999—. Cons. TVA, Muscle Shoals, Ala., 1983-84; vis. scholar Inst. for Alterative Agr., Greenbelt, Md., 1991. Mem. editorial bd. Agrl. and Resource Econs. Rev.; contbr. articles to profl. jours. Mem. Am. Agrl. Econs. Assn., European Cmty.-Pacific Region Agr. Project Data Working Group, Gamma Sigma Delta. Avocations: computers, sports, reading. Office: WVa U PO Box 6108 Morgantown WV 26506-6108

DU, YIPING P. education educator; b. Hangzhou, Zhejiang, China, May 4, 1960; s. Qianchang Du and Zhiying Han; children: Landon S., Michelle. PhD, U. of Utah, 1994. Cert. Am. Bd. of Med. Physics, 2001. Sys. engr. Shuzhou Optical Instruments Co., Shuzhou, China, 1982—84; post-doctoral fellow U. of Utah, Salt Lake City, 1994—95; scientist GE, Wauksha, Wis., 1995—99; vis. scientist Johns Hopkins Hosp., Balt., 1997—99; asst. prof. U. of Chgo., 2000—02; assoc. prof. U. of Colo. Health Scis. Ctr., Denver, 2002—. Dir. of fmri program U. of Colo. Health Scis. Ctr., Denver, 2002—. Recipient Herbert M. Stauffer award, Assn. of U. Radiologists, 1994, Young Investigator award, Am. Coll. of Cardiology, 2000. Mem.: Am. Assn. of Physicists in Medicine, Orgn. for Human Brain Mapping, Internat. Soc. of Magnetic Resonance in Medicine. Achievements include patents for Nine U.S. patents in magnetic resonance imaging and one Chinese patent in optical microscope. Office: Univ of Color Health Sci Ctr 4200 E 9th Ave Box C-278 Denver CO 80262 E-mail: yiping.du@uchsc.edu.

DUAIME, GINETTE SUZANNE, poet, songwriter; b. Tacoma, Wash., Dec. 9, 1961; d. Richard James and Nancy Lou Duaime; m. Tod Andrew Melotte, Jan. 6, 1984 (div.); children: Danielle Marie Melotte, Cassandra Anne Melotte;1 child, Joseph James Soletski-Duaime. BBH in Internat. Bus. and Langs., St. Norbert Coll., 1983; tchr. cert., U. Wis., Green Bay, 1989. Minister of God Order of the Holy Spirit, 1999. Librn. Camp Pendleton (Calif.) Librs., 1985; instr. U. Wis., Green Bay, 1988—89; substitute tchr. DePere Ashwaubenon Schs., Wis., 1990—95, Green Bay Pub. Schs., 1991—95; instr. Northeast Wis. Tech. Coll., Green Bay, 1998. Mem.: Internat. Soc. Poets, Phi Sigma Iota. Republican. Roman Catholic. Home: 338 S Jackson St Green Bay WI 54301-3908

DUAN, DAYUE, pharmacologist, physiologist; b. Hunan, China, Oct. 9, 1958; came to U.S., 1996; s. Zhao Ping and Xinping (Huang) D.; m. Lingyu Ye, Jan. 6, 1984; children: Marie, Michelle, Alice. MD, Hunan Med. Sch., Changsha, 1982; MSc, Sun-Yat Sen U., Guangzhou, 1987; PhD, McGill U., Montreal, 1996. Intern Hunan Prodince Peoples Hosp., 1982; resident Linwu Co. Traditional Chinese Medicine Hosp., 1983; tchg. asst. Sun Yat-Sen U., Guangzhou, 1984-89, asst. prof., 1989-91; rsch. asst. Montreal Heart Inst., 1991-96; rsch. assoc. U. Nev., Reno, 1996-98, asst. prof., 1998-99, assoc. prof., 1999—. Contbr. articles to profl. jours. including Nature, Jour. Physiology. Grantee NIH, 2000, Am. Heart Assn., 1997-02; fellow Med. Rsch. Coun. (Can.), 1996-98. Mem. Am. Heart Assn. (fellow 2002), AAAS, Internat. Soc. for Heart Rsch. (Pharmacia-Upjohn award 1998), Cardiac Muscle Soc., Biophys. Soc., Am. Physiol. Soc., Phi Beta Delta. Office: U Nev Sch Med Manville Bldg Rm 9 Reno NV 89557 E-mail: dduan@med.unr.edu.

DUAN, DONGSHENG, education educator, researcher; arrived in U.S., 1993; s. Yonglu Duan and Fuhua Zhou; m. Yongping Yue; 1 child, Sean. PhD, U. Pa., Phila., 1997. Asst. rsch. scientist U. Iowa, Iowa City, 1998—2001; asst. prof. U. Mo., Columbia, 2002—02. Contbr. 29 articles to profl. jours. (Am. Soc. of Gene Therapy, 2000). Recipient rsch. grant, NIH, 2003—08; grantee Rsch. grant, Cystic Fibrosis Found., 1998-2000, Rsch. Grant, Muscular Dystrophy Assn., 2001-2003. Mem.: Am. Soc. of Gene Therapy, Am. Soc. of Microbiology. Achievements include patents for Adeno-Associated Virus Vector. Office: M610G Med Sci Buld U Mo One Hos Dr Columbia MO 65212 E-mail: duand@missouri.edu.

DUAN, REN-GUAN, materials scientist; b. Ying Xian, Shan Xi, China, Feb. 15, 1968; arrived in Belgium, 1999, U.S., 2002; s. Le-Rui Duan and Cui-Ying Wang; m. Xia Cao, Apr. 11, 1992; 1 child, Jin-Yi Duan. BS, Tianjin (China) U., 1990; MS, Tsinghua U., Beijing, China, 1996, PhD, 1998. Engr. Liao Yang (China) Electronic Ceramic Factory, 1990-94, dir. Inst., 1991-94; lectr. Tsinghua U., Beijing, 1998-99; postdoctoral fellow Fund for Sci. Rsch., Vlaanderen, Belgium, 1999—2002, U. Calif., Davis, 2002—. Contbr. articles to profl. jours. Jiang Nanxiang scholar Tsinghua U., 1994-95, Liu Xianzhou scholar Tsinghua U., 1995-96, Internat. Engring. Tech. scholar, Colo. Tsinghua U., 1996-97, 12-9 scholar Tsinghua U., 1997-98, Sci. and Tech. scholar Tsinghua U., 1998-99; fellowship Vlaanderen, Belgium, 1999-2000; postdoctoral fellow, Katholieke Univ. Leaven, 2000-01, postdoctoral fellow European Commn., 2001-02, Assn. Univ. of Calif., Davis, 2002—. Achievements include rsch. elec. ceramics, glass-ceramics, PTC film materials, silicon nitride based ceramics, ZrO2/Y2O3 superfine powder, semi-conductor film, nanoceramics, electrically conductive ceramics nanorods, nanowires, and nanotubes, solar cell crystallization of amorphous silicon film deposited on the surface of substrate; US patents in field (electrically conductive nano-silicon ceramics). Office: Dept Chem Engring & Materials Sci U Calif Davis One Shields Ave Davis CA 95616 Home: 1125 H Street #32 Davis CA 95616

DUAN, XIAODONG, engineer; b. Beijing, Jan. 7, 1968; s. Tingyi Duan and Huifen Zhao; m. Wen Wu; 1 child, Xinyu. BS, Tsinghua U., Beijing, China, 1991; MS, Tsinghua U., Beijing,China, 1996; PhD, U. Ctrl. Fla., 2000. Asst. prof. Tsinghua U., 1991—93; rsch. & develop. engr. Beijing Solar Energy Inst., 1996—97; sr. rsch. & develop. engr. Avanex, Corp., Richardson, Tex., 2001—. Tech. referee Optics & Laser Tech., Bournemouth, Dorset, 2001—, Jour. of Physics, 2002—. Contbr. invention, articles and papers; referee: Measurement Sci. and Tech., 2002—. Recipient New Young Scientist award, Inst. Sci. and Tech., Beijing, 1996. Mem.: AAAS, IEEE, Am. Physics Soc. Home: 1515 Rio Grande Drive #1609 Plano TX 75075 Office: Avanex Corp 1801 North Glenville Drive Richardson TX 75081 Home Fax: 469-241-9633; Office Fax: 972-581-3107. Personal E-mail: wuwen99@hotmail.com. Business E-Mail: xiaodong_duan@avanex.com.

DUAN, XIN-RAN, mechanical engineer, educator; b. China; arrived in U.S., 1984; s. Zi-Mei Duan and Xuan-Zhi Yuan; m. Qimin Zhu, 1972; 1 child, Jack. B, Xian Jiao-Tong U., 1968; MS, U. Okla., 1992; PhD, Ind. State U., 2003. Engr. Xian Machine Tool Plant, Xi'an, China, 1968—72, Lanzhou Locomotive Plant, China, 1972—79; asst. prof. Lanzhou Railway U., 1979—84; rsch. asst. Drexel U., Phila., 1984—86; rsch. assoc. Widner U., Chester, Pa., 1986—87; asst. prof. Lanzhou Railway U., 1987—90; instr. U. Okla., Norman, 1990—92; tutor U. Akron, Ohio, 1992—93; prof., dept. chair Ivy Tech State Coll., Columbus, Ind., 1993—. Contbr. Vol. transl. Chinese lang. Columbus Police Dept., 1994—. Mem.: AAUP, ASME, Internat. Engring. Edn. Cmty., Am. Design Drafting Assn., Nat. Assn. Indsl. Techs. Office: Ivy Tech State Coll 4475 Central Ave Columbus IN 47203*

DUAN, YIXIANG, research scientist, chemist; m. Yushu Cheng, Oct. 2, 1984; children: Jiana, Benjamin Cheng. BS, Fudan U., Shanghai, 1981; MS, Chinese Acad. of Scis., Changchun, 1988; PhD, Jilin U., China, 1994. Assoc. prof. Jilin U., Changchun, China, 1991—94; staff mem. Los Alamos Nat. Lab., N.Mex., 1997—. Recipient Award of Sci. and Tech. Progress, Dept. of Health, China, 1987, Jilin Province, China, 1991, Ministry of Edn., China, 1995. Mem.: Soc. for Applied Spectroscopy. Achievements include patents for Microwave plasma monitoring system for real-time elemental analysis, patent number-6, 429, 935; Polyaniline-based optical ammonia detector, patent number: 6, 406, 669; patents pending for Pulsed, atmospheric pressure plasma source for molecular emission spectrometry, S-94, 719; Compact microwave plasma source cavity ring-down spectrometer for ultra-sensitive elemental and isotope analysis; Capillary-discharge based hand-held detector for chemical vapor monitoring, S-99, 942; research in Devel. high-efficiency thermalionization cavity source for mass spectrometry; Plasma source-based field portable monitor for air particulate monitoring. Office: Los Alamos Nat Lab C-Acs Ms K484 Los Alamos NM 87545

DUAN, ZHONG-HUI, education educator, researcher; b. Zhangzhou, Fujian, China, Nov. 30, 1962; arrived in U.S., 1991; d. Tao Duan and GuiLan Xing; m. Ting Shi, Jan. 30, 1988; 1 child, Ivy Shi. MS geo math., Chinese Acad. of Geol. Sci., Beijing, China, 1988; geol. and geophysics, Yale Univ., New Haven, Conn., 1992; MS, PhD, Fla. State Univ., Tallahassee, 1997. Rsch. scientist Anhui Inst. of Geology, Hefei, China, 1982—85, Beijing Computation Inst., Beijing, 1988—91; tchg. asst. Fla. State Univ., Tallahassee, 1992—97; asst. prof. Univ. Mich., Ann Arbor, Mich., 1997—2001, Univ. Akron, Akron, Ohio, 2001—. Referee Jour. of Computational Chemistry, Biophysical Jour. Contbr. scientific papers to profl. jour. Recipient Sci. Achievement award, Min. of Geology and Mineral Resources, China, 1986, 1991; Rackham Faculty Fellowship, Univ. Mich., 1999. Office: Dept Computer Sci Univ Akron Akron OH 44325

DUANY, ANDRES, architectural firm executive; b. N.Y.C., Sept. 7, 1949; Grad., Yale U. Founding ptnr. Arquitectonica, Miami, Fla., 1974—78; founder Duany, Plater Zyberk & Co., 1980—. Tchr. Sch. Arch., U. Miami, 1975—; founding mem. Congress for the New Urbanism. Co-author (with Elizabeth Plater-Zyberk): Suburban Nation. Office: Duany, Plater Zyberk & Co 1023 SW 25 Ave Miami FL 33135

DUARTE, FRANCISCO JAVIER, physicist, researcher; b. Santiago, Chile, Sept. 1, 1954; came to U.S., 1983; s. Luis Enrique and Ruth Virginia (Valenzuela) D. BA with honors, Macquarie U., Sydney, Australia, 1978, PhD in Physics, 1982. Postdoctoral fellow U. NSW, Sydney, 1981-82, Macquarie U., Sydney, 1982-83; asst. prof. physics U. Ala., University, 1983-85; sr. rsch. physicist Eastman Kodak Co., Rochester, NY, 1985—2002, rsch. assoc., 2002—. Analyst U.S. Army (MICOM) Redstone Arsenal, Ala., 1985-97, (AMCOM), 2001-02. Author, co-editor: Dye Laser Principles, 1990; author, editor: High Power Dye Lasers, 1991, Tunable Laser Applications, 1995, Tunable Lasers Handbook, 1995; editor: Selected Papers on Dye Lasers, 1992; topical editor Applied Optics, 1990-96; adv. editor Optics Letters, 1999—, Optics and Photonics News, 2001—; author: Tunable Laser Optics, 2003; contbr. numerous articles to profl. jours. Fellow Australian Inst. Physics, 1987, Optical Soc. Am., 1993, recipient Engineering Excellence Award, Optical Soc. Am., 1995; recipient Commonwealth postgrad. rsch. award Govt. of Australia, 1979. Achievements include rsch. in physics and technology of narrow-linewidth dispersive tunable laser oscillators and interferometric instrumentation; author of generalized multiple-prism dispersion theory; applied Dirac's notation to the description of classical optics; inventions in the fields of optics and lasers. Office: PO Box 26592 Rochester NY 14626 E-mail: fjduarte@opticsjournal.com.

DUARTE, PATRICIA M. real estate and insurance broker; b. Truro, Mass., Feb. 23, 1938; d. Antone Jr. and Marjorie (Beckley) Duarte. Grad. H.S., Provincetown, Mass. Lic. ins. and real estate broker; constrn. supt. Sec. various ins. agys., Amherst, Mass., 1957-60; ins. and real estate agt. Duarte Ins. & Real Estate, Truro, 1960-66, owner, prin. agt., 1966-78; ins. risk mgr. J.L. Marshall & Sons, Inc., Pawtucket, R.I., 1979-92; owner, mgr. Patricia-Duarte Real Estate, Rockport, Maine, 1988-97. Restorer antique homes New Eng., Mass., 1979—. Mem., sec. Truro Planning Bd., 1965-72, chmn., 1974-78; mem. exec. com. Cape Cod Planning and Econ. Devel. Com., 1971-76; mem. Reelect Brawn for Senate Com., Camden, Maine, 1988; mem. Rockport Planning Bd., 1991-94, Rockport Comprehensive Plan Implementation Com., 1991-94; co-chmn. Rockport Capital Improvement Com., 1991-96; bd. dirs. Cape Cod chpt. Am. Heart Assn., 1963-70; mem. Opera House Commn., 1992-94. Mem. Penobscot Bay Bd. Realtors, Profl. Ins. Agts. New Eng. (bd. dirs. 1974-76), Gen. Fedn. Women's Clubs (2d v.p. Camden chpt. 1989), Hist. Preservation Assn. St. Thomas (arts coun. 1998-99, bd. dirs. 1998). Republican. Roman Catholic. Avocations: gourmet cooking, travel, photography, architectural and interior design. Address: PO Box 8 Port Clyde ME 04855 also: Cowpet Bay E Saint Thomas VI 00802

DUAX, WILLIAM LEO, biological researcher; b. Chgo., Apr. 18, 1939; s. William Joseph and Alice B. (Joyce) D.; m. Caroline Townsend Dowell, May 6, 1966; children: Julia, Sarah, William, Stephen. BA, St. Ambrose Coll., 1961; PhD, U. Iowa, 1967. Postdoctoral research fellow Ohio U., Athens, 1967-68; rsch. assoc. Hauptman-Woodward Med. Rsch. Inst. (formerly Med. Found.), Buffalo, 1968-69; head crystallography dept. Med. Found. Buffalo, 1969-70, head molecular biophysics dept., 1970-88, assoc. dir. research, 1983-88, research dir., 1988-93, exec v.p. rsch., 1993-99, v.p., 1998-99, H.A. Hauptman Disting. Scientist, 2000—. Adj. assoc. prof. dept. medicinal chemistry SUNY Buffalo, 1973—, assoc. rsch. prof. dept. biochemistry, 1981—, prof. dept. structural biology, 2001-; dir. distbn. Cambridge Database in U.S., Buffalo, 1983-99; lectr. various internat. confs. Editor: Atlas of Steroid Structure Vol. I, 1975, Vol. II, 1984, Molecular Structure and Biological Activity, 1982, Molecular Structure and Biological Activity of Steriods, 1992, Internat. Union of Crystallography Newsletter, 1993—. Mem. Am. Field Service, Amherst, N.Y. Served with USAR, 1961-67. Fulbright scholar Coun. for Internat. Exchange, 1987; grantee NIH, 1971—; recipient Spl. Merit award Inst. Arthritis and Metabolic Diseases NIH, 1987—, Disting. Alumni award, St. Ambrose Coll., 1983, Clin. Ligand Assay Soc. Disting. Scientist award, 1994. Mem. AAAS, Am. Crystallographic Assn. (v.p. 1985, pres. 1986, exec. officer 1988—, Am. Chem. Soc., Am. Cancer Soc., Biophys. Soc., Endocrine Soc., Peptide Soc., Protein Soc., Internat. Union Crystallography (charter mem., sec. com. on small molecules 1984-90, exec. com. 1999—, pres. 2002-), Am. Inst. Physics (bd. govs. 1987-94, exec. com. 1992), Coun. Sci. Soc. Pres. (govt. and pub. affairs com. 1987), Saturn Club (Buffalo). Democrat. Roman Catholic. Office: Hauptman-Woodward Med Rsch Inst Inc 73 High St Buffalo NY 14203-1196 Fax: 716-852-6086. E-mail: duax@hwi.buffalo.edu.

DUBACK, SALLY WOOD, artist, educator; b. St. Paul, Jan. 19, 1946; d. Thurston and Jane (Washburn) W.; m. Steven Rahr Duback, Aug. 6, 1966 (div. Dec. 1986); children: David, Peter, Andrew. Student, Vassar Coll., 1964; postgrad., U. Wis., Milw., 1969-75; BA, U. Mich., 1968. Tchr. U. Sch. Milw., 1988-93; owner, artist Spectrum 305 Studio, Grafton, Wis., 1983—. Designer, puppetmaster Marquette U. Theatre, Milw., 2000-01; tchr., artist-in-residence Milw. Pub. Schs., 1999-2000; theatrical designer Theatre X, Milw., 1996-98, Bialystock and Bloom, Milw., 1997-98. Author: Hand Papermaking, 1997; artist hand paper sculpture. Founder, The Truck Studio, Artists Working in Edn., Milw., 1999 (bd. dirs., co-pres., 2002-04); bd. dirs., officer Wild Space Dance Co., Milw., 1994-2000, Print Forum Milw. Art Mus., 1993-2002; bd. dirs., past pres. Theatre X, Milw., 1993-2002, bd. dirs. Riveredge Nature Ctr.; mem. North Suburban YMCA. Fellow Vt. Studio Ctr., 2001, 2002, 2004; recipient award Pub. Arts Commn., Wis. Arts Bd., 1996, Gov.'s award for Arts Artists Working in Edn., 2002. Mem. Wis. Acad. Scis., Arts and Letters, Cedarbury Artists Guild. Unitarian Universalist. Avocations: gardening, photography, writing, swimming, music. Office: Spectrum 305 Studio 1350 14th Ave Grafton WI 53024 E-mail: sally@sallyduback.com.

DUBACK, STEVEN RAHR, lawyer; b. Washington, Sept. 4, 1944; s. Paul Hewitt and Natalie (Rahr) D.; children: David, Peter, Andrew. BA, Princeton U., 1966; JD, U. Mich., 1969. Bar: Wis. 1969, U.S. Dist. Ct. (ea. dist.) Wis. 1969, U.S. Ct. Claims 1969, U.S. Tax Ct. 1969. Ptnr. Quarles & Brady LLP, Milw., 1969—. Bd. dirs. Oshkosh (Wis.) B'Gosh, Inc., Commerce Indsl. Chems., Inc. Dir. Ctr. for the Deaf and Hard of Hearing. Mem.: Am. Soc. Corp. Secs., Estate Counselors Forum, Milw. Estate Planning Coun. (dir.), Wis. State and Local Tax Club, Town Club, Milw. Athletic Club, Phi Beta Kappa, Order of Coif. Avocations: golf, tennis. Office: Quarles & Brady LLP 411 E Wisconsin Ave Ste 2550 Milwaukee WI 53202-4497 E-mail: srd@quarles.com.

DUBANIEWICZ, THOMAS H., JR., electrical engineer, bioengineer; BS in Electrical Engring., U. Pitts., 1988, MS in Bioengring., 2000. Registered profl. engr., Pa. Electrical engr. U.S. Bur. Mines, Pitts., 1988-96, NIOSH Pitts. Rsch. Lab., 1996—. Recipient Engring. Literary award U.S. Pub. Health Svc., 2000; named Engr. of Yr. Ctr. Disease Ctrl. and Prevention, Nat. Soc. Profl. Engrs., 2001. Mem. Instrumentation, Systems and Automation Soc. Office: NIOSH Pitts Rsch Lab 626 Cochrans Mill Rd Pittsburgh PA 15236 Office Fax: 412-386-6764. E-mail: tcd5@cdc.gov.

DUBAR, CLAUDE ROGER, sociologist; b. Lille, Nord, France, Dec. 11, 1945; s. Gaston Dubar and Marie-Louise Hubo; s. Elisabeth Marie Charlon, Sept. 9, 1967; (div. 1990); children: Emmanuel, Francois. PhD, Paris-Vincennes, 1970, Paris-Sorbonne, France, 1984, U. Laval, Quebec, 2003. Asst. Faculty of Arts, Lille, 1967-71; prof. Sch. of Letters, Beyrouth, 1971-73; rschr. CNRS, Paris, 1973-77; prof. U. Lille, 1977-90; dept. mgr. CEREQ, Paris, 1990-93; prof. U. Versailles, 1993. Cons. Edn. Ministry, Paris, 1989-93; vice-chmn. U. Lille, 1981-84; director Lab., Lille, 1984-90, Lab. St. Quentin en Yvelines, 1995. Author: La Socialisation, 1991 (Reed award 1995, 2000), La Formation Professionnelle Continue, 1984 (Reedition award 1990, 96, 2000), Sociologie des Professions, 1998, editor: Genèse et dynamique des Groupes professionnels, 1994, Cheminements Professionnels et Mobilité Sociale, 1992, La Crise des identité, 2000 (Reed award 2002). Mem. French Soc. Sociology (pres. 1999). Office: Printemps 47 Blvd Vauban 78047 Guyancourt France E-mail: Claude.Dubar@printemps.uvsq.fr.

DUBAY, THOMAS E. priest, writer; b. Mpls., Dec. 30, 1921; s. Elie Albert Dubay and Leah Caron. MA, Cath. U. Am., Washington, 1952; PhD, Cath. U. Am., 1956. Tchr. Notre Dame Sem., New Orleans, 1952—54, 1956—67, Marist Coll., Washington, 1954—56, Marycrest Coll., Davenport, Iowa, 1967—68, Russel Coll., Burlingame, Calif., 1968—70, Chestnut Hill Coll., Phila., 1970—73; lectr./freeland writer Washington, 1973—. Author: Evidential Power of Beauty, 1999, Fire Within, 1989, Authenticity, 1997. Mem.: Fellowship of Cath. Scholars.

DUBBS, JOHN WILLIAM, III, lawyer, accountant; b. Chgo., July 2, 1951; s. John William, Jr. and Rita Jean (Kucharski) D. B.S. in Fin., U. Ill., 1973; J.D., Northwestern U., 1976; M.B.A. in Fin., U. Chgo., 1981. Bar: Ill. 1976, Fla. 1977, U.S. Dist. Ct. (no. dist.) Ill. 1976; C.P.A., Ill. Tax acct. Arthur Young & Co., Chgo., 1976-80; ptnr. firm Hinshaw, Culbertson, Moelmann, Hoban & Fuller, Chgo., 1980— . Mem. ABA, Ill. Bar Assn., Fla. Bar Assn., Chgo. Bar Assn. Roman Catholic. Office: Hinshaw & Culbertson 222 N La Salle St Ste 300 Chicago IL 60601-1081

DUBÉ, LAWRENCE EDWARD, JR., lawyer; b. Chgo., Sept. 25, 1948; s. Lawrence Edward and Rosemary Nora (Cooney) D.; m. Paula Ann Goodgal, Jan. 10, 1982; 1 child, Charles Bernard. BA in Polit. Sci. cum laude, Knox Coll., 1970; JD with distinction, U. Iowa, 1973. Bar: Ill. 1973, Md. 1982, Pa. 1982, D.C. 1983, U.S. Supreme Ct., 1987. Field atty. NLRB, Chgo., 1973-80, supr. atty., 1980-81; sole practice Balt., 1981-85; assoc. Grove, Jaskiewicz, Gilliam & Cobert, Washington, 1985-87; ptnr. Dubé & Goodgal, P.C., Balt., 1987—. Author: Management on Trial-The Law of Wrongful Discharge, 1987, New Employment Issues: How to Shield your Business from Costly Lawsuits, 1988, Employment References and the Law, 1989; co-author: The Maryland Employer's Guide, 1984. Mem. Nat. Assn. Securities Dealers (arbitrator). Home: 622 W University Pky Baltimore MD 21210-2908 Office: Dubé & Goodgal PC 2400 Boston St Ste 407 Baltimore MD 21224-4787

DUBÉ, RONALD NORMAN, elementary school educator; b. Nashua, N.H., July 13, 1942; s. Norman Francis and Cecile (Soucy) D.; m. Roseanna Dougherty, Oct. 7, 1971; children: John, Ben, Luke. BA, U. N.H., 1964; MS, River Coll., 1976. Cert. tchr., N.H. Zookeeper Benson's Animal Farm, Hudson, N.H., 1963-75; vol. Peace Corps, Niger, Africa, 1964-66; sci. tchr. Salem (N.H.) Sch. Dist., 1967-68, Milford (N.H.) Sch. Dist., 1969-70, Nashua (N.H.) Sch. Dist., 1970-79, North Middlesex Sch. Dist., Townsend, Mass., 1979—, co-chair social studies curriculum, 1996-98. Contbr. articles to profl. publs. Mem. conservation com. Town of Mason, N.H., 1974-76; scoutmaster Boy Scouts Am., 1994—. Mem. Am. Can. Geneol. Soc., Acadian Cultural Soc. Roman Catholic. Avocations: reading, movies, walking, cutting wood.

DUBERMAN, MARTIN, historian, educator; b. N.Y.C., Aug. 6, 1930; s. Joseph M. and Josephine (Bauml) D. BA, Yale U., 1952; MA, Harvard U., 1953, PhD, 1957. Teaching fellow Harvard U., 1955-57; instr. history Yale U., 1957-61; Morse fellow, 1961-62; bicentennial preceptor, asst. prof. Princeton U., 1962-65, asso. prof., 1965-67, prof., 1967-71; Distinguished prof. Lehman Coll., City U. N.Y., 1971—. Founder Ctr. for Lesbian and Gay Studies, Grad. Ctr. CUNY, 1991, dir., 1986-96. Author: Charles Frances Adams, 1807-1886, 1961 (Bancroft prize 1962), In White America (Vernon Rice award 1963-64), James Russell Lowell, 1966 (finalist Nat. Book award 1966), The Uncompleted Past, 1969, Black Mountain: An Exploration in Community, 1972, revised edit., 1993, About Time: Exploring the Gay Past, 1986, rev. edit., 1991, Paul Robeson, 1989, 2d edit., 1996, Cures: A Gay Man's Odyssey, 1991, reissued with new afterword, 2002, Stonewall, 1993, Midlife Queer, 1996, Left Out: The Politics of Exclusion, 1999, reissued, expanded and revised, 2002, Haymarket: a novel, 2003; editor, contbr.; Antislavery Vanguard, 1965, Hidden From History: Reclaiming the Gay and Lesbian Past, 1989, A Queer World, 1997, Queer Representations, 1997; contbr.: (plays) Metaphors in Collision Course, 1968, The Memory Bank, 1970, The Recorder (in the Best Short Plays of 1970), 1971, The Colonial Dudes (in the Best Short Plays of 1972), 1973, Male Armor (Selected Plays 1968-74), 1976, Visions of Kerouac, 1977, Mother Earth: An Epic Drama of Emma Goldman's Life, 1991; mem. bd. Masculinities, Jour. History of Sexuality. Mem. Am. Hist. Assn., Nat. Gay and Lesbian Task Force, ACLU (bd. dirs. N.Y. chpt. 1982-88), Phi Beta Kappa. Address: 475 W 22nd St New York NY 10011-2549

DUBERSTEIN, JOEL LAWRENCE, internist, pulmonologist, educator; b. Bklyn., Jan. 8, 1937; m. Judith Schwartz; children: Laura, Amy. AB, Princeton U., 1957; MD, Columbia U., 1961. Diplomate Am. Bd. Internal Medicine, Am. Bd. Pulmonary Diseases. Intern Mt. Sinai Hosp., N.Y.C., 1961-62, rsch. fellow in medicine, 1962, 65, asst. med. resident, 1963, chief med. resident, 1964, clin. asst., rsch. fellow, 1965-67; asst. chief medicine, chief pulmonary diseases Morrisania Hosp., Montefiore-Morrisania Affiliation, Bronx, N.Y., 1969-71; attending physician dept. medicine Overlook Hosp., Summit, N.J., 1971—, chmn. pulmonary sect., ICU com., med. dir. ICU, 1985-97, divsn. chief pulmonary disease dept. internal medicine; assoc. clin. prof. medicine Columbia U., 1998—. Assoc. vis. physician Morrisania City Hosp., Bronx, 1969-71; mem. staff Morristown Meml. Hosp., 1972—, med. co-dir. respiratory svcs., 1977-82; attending phsician dept. medicine St. Barnabas Med. Ctr., Livingston, N.J., 1971-89, past chmn. pulmonary sect.; mem. staff Newark Beth Israel Med. Ctr., 1971-82; spkr. in field; mem. Essex County Med. Soc. TB Control. Contbr. articles to profl. jours. Maj. U.S. Army, 1967-69. Recipient Recognition award Soc. N.J.'s Physicians. Fellow ACP, Am. Coll. Chest Physicians; mem. AMA (Physician's Recognition award), N.J. Med. Soc., Essex Thoracic Soc., N.J. Acad. Medicine. Office: 315 E Northfield Rd Ste 1D Livingston NJ 07039-4800

DUBES, MICHAEL JOHN, retired insurance company executive; b. Dubuque, Iowa, Oct. 19, 1942; s. Wilmar C. and Cleo (Lenz) D.; m. Glenda Ra. Ackerlund, July 31, 1965; children: Scot (dec.), Heather. BS, Iowa State U., 1966; MS, Am. Coll., Bryn Mawr, Pa., 1981; postgrad., Harvard U., 1987, 90, LIMRA Strategies Inst., 1990. CLU, LLIF; cert. fin. planner; chartered fin. cons. Agt. Northwestern Nat. Life Ins. Co., Des Moines, 1967-68, staff asst., Mpls., 1968-70, tng. mgr., St. Paul, 1970-72, supt. agys., Mpls., 1972-73, asst. mgr., Des Moines, 1973-78, br. mgr., 1978-83, regional mgr., 1983-84, 2d v.p. individual ins. sales, Mpls., 1984-85, v.p. indiv. ins. sales, 1985-87, sr. v.p. individual ins., 1987—; exec. v.p. Northwestern Nat. Life Ins. Sales Co., Mpls., 1984-85, pres., 1985-87; vice chmn., CEO Washington Square Securities, Inc., Mpls., 1984-87; chmn. Washington Sq. Securities, Mpls., 1987—; ret., 2002. Bd. dirs. Mpls., NWNL Found., Washington Sq. Securities Inc., Relia Star Life, Corp. Coun. of the Arts; mem. NWNL cos. Enterprise Coun., mgmt. com.; bd. dirs. No. Life Ins. Co. (a Relia Star co.), Seattle. Amb. Iowa State U.; bd. dirs. Seattle C. of C., 1995—, Seattle Corp. Coun. of the Arts, 1995, Ind. Colls. of Wash., 1995; bd. govs. Iowa State U. With USAR, 1967. Recipient Gene Helton award Des Moines Life Underwriters, 1982. Mem. Nat. Assn. Life Underwriters (bd. dirs. 1983-84), Am. Soc. CLUs, Life Ins. Mktg. and Rsch. Assn. (exec. devel. com. 1985-91, ops. com. 1989—, bd. dirs. 1991-93, chmn. membership com.), Agy. Officer Round Table (meeting chmn. 1994), Gen. Agts. and Mgrs. Assn. (pres. 1983-84), Cert. Fin. Planners, MBA Ins. Mgmt. Adv., U. St. Thomas, Ind. Colls. Wash. (bd. dirs.), Met. Breakfast Club (bd. dirs. 1988-94), Interlachen Country Club (bd. govs.), Desert Mountain Country Club, Rainier Club, Amb. Club (Iowa State U.), Variety Club of Iowa (bd. dirs. 1983-84), Sahalee Country Club, Harvard Bus. Sch. Club Minn., Mpls. Club, Boys and Girls Club Mpls. (bd. dirs., exec. com., devel. com.), Rotary (Paul Harris fellow 1988, bd. dirs.), Seattle C. of C. (bd. dirs.). Home: 5816 Vernon Ln Edina MN 55436-2250 E-mail: dubesmj@aol.com.

DUBEY, VINOD SHANKER, microbiologist, biochemist, researcher; b. Sidharathanagar, Uttar Pradesh, India, July 1, 1970;, 2000; s. Prem Shanker and Subhaymati Dubey; m. Vibha Upadhyay, Feb. 5, 1998; children: Vartika, Shivam. PhD, Lucknow (India) U., 2000. Doctoral rschr. Ctrl. Inst. Medicinal & Aromatic Plants, Lucknow, 1994—2000; post-doctoral rschr. Ohio State U., Columbus, 2000—. Rschr. U. Ctrl. Fla., Orlando, 2003—. Contbr. articles to profl. jours. Jr. and Sr. Rsch. fellow, Coun. Sci. and Indsl. Rsch., India, 1994—99. Achievements include patents in field. Office: Biomolecular Sci Ctr UCF Bldg 20 Rm 132 4000 Central Florida Blvd Orlando FL 32816 Home Fax: 407-823-0956; Office Fax: 407-823-0956. Personal E-mail: vdubey@mail.ucf.edu. E-mail: vdubey@mail.ucf.edu.

DUBIE, BRIAN E. lieutenant governor; b. Burlington, Vt., Mar. 9, 1959; m. Penny Bolio; 4 children. Student, USAF Acad., 1977—80; BS in Mech. Engring., U. Vt., 1982. Aerospace industry project mgr. B.F. Goodrich, Vergennes; capt. Am. Airlines, 1988; lt.gov. State of Vt., 2003—. Emergency preparedness officer Nat. Security Emergency Preparedness Agy.; bd. dirs. Vt. Sys., Inc. Active Essex Junction Sch. Bd., 1995—2000, chair, 1996—2000, sch. dist. moderator, 2000—; active Essex Junction Cmty. Drug Awareness Com., 1993—95; asst. coach Youth Football and Little League. Lt. col. Vt. Air Nat. Guard, col. USAF, 1998. Decorated Meritorious Svc. medal with oak leaf cluster. Office: 115 State St Montpelier VT 05633-5401*

DUBILL, ROBERT A. former newspaper editor; b. Simpson, Pa. BA in Journalism & Mass Comm., St. Benaventure U.; JD, Seton Hall U. Bar: N.J., D.C. Joined AP, 1959, bur. chief N.J. operation, 1959—76; joined Courier Post, 1976; exec. editor The Courier-Post, Cherry Hill, NJ, Gannett News Svc., USA Today, Arlington, Va., 1982—2002. Recipient Pulitzer Prize, 1980.

DUBIN, ARTHUR DETMERS, architect; b. Chgo., Mar. 14, 1923; s. Henry and Anne (Green) D.; m. Lois Amtman, Mar. 10, 1951 (dec. Sept. 1980); children: Peter Arthur, Polly Louise (Mrs. Scott Pollak); m. Phyllis Vollen Burman, Nov. 27, 1981; stepchildren: Garry Arthur, Jill Meredyth, David Yale, Eric Vollen. Student, Lake Forest Coll., 1943-44; B.Arch., U. Mich., 1949. Architect, partner Dubin & Dubin (architects and engrs.), Chgo., 1950-65, Dubin, Dubin & Black (architects and engrs.), 1965-66, Dubin, Dubin, Black & Moutoussamy, 1966-78, Dubin, Dubin & Moutoussamy, 1978-93. V.p., dir. 7337 South Shore Dr. Corp., 1958—81, 7345 South Shore Dr. Corp., 1962—86;

gen. ptnr. 340 Wellington Assocs., 1962—73; mem. adv. bd. Amtrak, 1972—95; v.p. DDBM, Inc., 1975—85; hon. rsch. assoc. Smithsonian Instn., 1975; tech. cons. Paramount Pictures, 1991, TV, 1998—2001; spkr. on confs., U.S. and France. Author: Some Classic Trains, 1964, More Classic Trains, 1974, Pullman Paint and Lettering Notebook, 1997; author: (editor for N.Am.) The Great Trains, 1973; contbr. ; archtl. works include govt. bldgs., rail transit stas. and transp. facilities, mil. installations, banks, indsl. plants, schs. and colls., hosps., housing and urban renewal planning. Chmn. Civic Beautification Com., Highland Park, Ill., 1965—74; mem. Bicentennial Commn., Highland Park, 1974—76, Ill. Commn. on High Speed Rail Transit, 1966—68, Met. Housing and Planning Coun., Chgo., Nat. Coun. Archtl. Registration Bds., 1971—; trustee NORTRAN, Des Plaines, Ill., 1980—91; trustee emeritus George Krambles Transit Scholarship Fund, 1985—, John W. Barriger III Nat. R.R. Libr., St. Louis, 1989—; life mem., friend Art Inst. Chgo. With inf. U.S. Army, 1943—46. Decorated Bronze Star with cluster, Purple Heart; recipient award Gen. Svcs. Adminstrn. for U.S. Custom House, Chgo., 1993. Mem. AIA (emeritus), Am. Pub. Transit Assn., Railway and Locomotive Hist. Soc. (bd. dirs. 1960-93, hon. life dir. 1993), Train Collectors Assn., Steamship Hist. Soc. Am., Cliff Dwellers Club (emeritus, bd. dirs. 1972-75), Builders Club (pres. 1970-71, bd. dirs. 1970-80), Arts Club (Chgo.). Home: 229 Park Ave Highland Park IL 60035 2523

DUBIN, CHARLES LEONARD, lawyer; b. Hamilton, Ont., Can., Apr. 4, 1921; s. Harry and Ethel D.; m. Anne Ruth, Dec. 2, 1951. BA, U. Toronto, Ont., 1941; LL.B., Osgoode Hall Law Sch., 1944. Bar: Ont. 1944, appointed Queen's Counsel 1952. Practiced in, Toronto, 1945-73; judge Ont. Supreme Ct. Appeal, Toronto, 1973—; chief justice Ont. Ct. Appeal, Toronto, 1990-96; counsel Tory Tory Des Lauriers & Binnington Barristers, Toronto, 1996—. Royal Commr. to inquire into air safety in Can., 1979; Head of Inquiry into the practices and procedures of Hosp.for Sick Children, 1983; Royal Commr. to inquire into use of drugs and banned practices in athletics, 1988; apptd. to Bd. of Canadian Centre for Ethics in Sport, 2000; lectr. Osgoode Hall Law Sch., 1945-48 Mem. York Club, Toronto Hunt Club, Toronto Club. Home: 619 Avenue Rd Apt 1702 Toronto ON Canada M4V 2K6 Office: Torys Barristers Toronto Dominion Ctr PO Box 270 #3000 Toronto ON Canada M5K 1N2

DUBIN, DANIEL HERSCHEL ELI, physicist, educator; b. Cochrane, Ont., Can., Sept. 13, 1956; arrived in U.S., 1979; s. Maurice David Dubin, Marion Dubin; m. Adrienne E. Lynch, Aug. 24, 1991; children: Rachel, Alexander. BSc in Theoretical Physics with honors, Queen's U., 1978; PhD in Astrophysics, Princeton U., 1984. Postdoc rschr. U. Calif. San Diego, La Jolla, 1984—87, asst. prof., 1987—94, assoc. prof., 1994—2000, prof., 2000—. Author: Numerical and Analytical Methods for Scientists and Engineers, 2003. Fellow: Am. Phys. Soc. (Excellence in Plasma Physics Rsch. award 2000). Business E-Mail: dhdubin@ucsd.edu.

DUBIN, HENRY C. civilian military employee; b. Paterson, N.J., 1943; BS in Physics, St. Lawrence U., Canton, N.Y.; MA in History and Philosophy of Sci., Ind. U., 1968, PhD in Chem. Physics, 1972. Rsch. physicist U.S. Army Ballistic Rsch. Lab., Aberdeen Proving Ground, Md.; physicist Army Materiel Systems Analysis Activity, 1975—78, ops. rsch. scientist war-gaming br., 1978—81, chief intelligence and electronic warfare br., 1982—83, chief tactical comm. and target acquisition br., 1983—85, tech. study dir., 1985—86, chief artillery analysis br., 1986; tech. dir. Operational Test and Evaluation Command, 1987—98; dir. assessment and evaluation Office of the Asst. Sec. of the Army, 1999—2001, acting dep. asst. sec. for chem. demilitarization, 2001; chief scientist U.S. Army Space and Missile Def. Command, Arlington, Va., 2002—. Participant Tech. Coop. Program Panel on Wound Ballistics, secretariat to the panel on weapon system effectiveness, 1976—79, panel leader 10 nation NATO Anti-artillery Study; U.S. nat. rep. Joint Systems and Analysis Group, 1999—2001, exec. chair, 2001. Recipient Meritorious Presdl. Rank, 1992, 2002. Mem.: Phi Beta Kappa. Office: US Army Space and Missile Defense Command PO Box 15280 Arlington VA 22215-0280

DUBIN, HOWARD VICTOR, dermatologist; b. N.Y.C., Mar. 28, 1938; s. Meyer and Blanche D.; m. Patricia Sue Tucker, June 10, 1962; children—Douglas Scott, Kathryn Sue, David Andrew, Michael Stonier. AB, Columbia U., 1958, MD, 1962. Diplomate: Am. Bd. Dermatology, Am. Bd. Internal Medicine. Intern U. Mich., 1962-63, resident in internal medicine, 1963-64, resident in dermatology, 1968-70, asst. prof., 1970-72, asso. prof., 1972-75, clin. asso. prof., 1975-77, clin. prof., 1977—. Resident in internal medicine Columbia-Presbyn. Med. Center, N.Y.C., 1966-68; practice medicine specializing in dermatology, Ann Arbor, Mich., 1970—2003. Contbr. articles to profl. jours. Trustee Greenhills Sch., Ann Arbor, 1979-87, pres. bd. trustees, 1981-84. Served with U.S. Army, 1964-66. Fellow ACP; mem. Am. Acad. Dermatology, Am. Dermatol. Assn., Soc. Investigative Dermatology, Dermatology Found. (mem. exec. com. 1987-2001, sec.-treas. 1988-91, pres. 1991-98), Mich. Dermatol. Soc. (pres. 1985-87), AMA, Mich. Med. Soc., Washtenaw County Med. Soc., Rotary, Sigma Xi. Office: 2026 Norway Ann Arbor MI 48104

DUBIN, JAMES MICHAEL, lawyer; b. N.Y.C., Aug. 20, 1946; s. Benjamin and Irene (Wasserman) D.; m. Susan Hope Schraub, Mar. 15, 1981; children: Alexander Philip, Elizabeth Joy. BA, U. Pa., 1968; JD, Columbia U., 1974. Bar: N.Y. 1975, D.C. 1984, U.S. Dist. Ct. (so. and ea. dist.s) N.Y. 1975, U.S. Ct. Appeals (2d cir.) 1975. Assoc. Paul, Weiss, Rifkind, Wharton & Garrison, N.Y.C., 1974-82, ptnr., 1982—, chmn. corp. dept., 1995—. Bd. dirs. Conair Corp., Carnival Corp., CTPI Group, Inc., European Capital Ventures, PLC; internat. bd. govs. Tel-Aviv U., 2001—; chmn. bd. govs. Tel-Aviv U. Law Sch., 2001—. Mem. bd. editors Columbia Law Rev., 1973-74. Trustee Solomon Schechter Sch. Westchester, 1991—, vice chmn., 1997—; bd. dirs. Nat. Found. Advancement in Arts, 1991—, vice chmn., 1994—; bd. dirs. Jewish Guild for the Blind, 1989—, chmn., 1995—99, chmn. exec. com., 2000—; bd. dirs. YM-YWHA of Mid-Westchester, Scarsdale, NY, 1983—86. With U.S. Army, 1969—71. Mem.: ABA, Am. Arbitration Assn. (comml. panel arbitrators 1989—), Assn. Bar City N.Y., Snowmass Club, The Dukes Golf Club, Indian Harbor Yacht Club, Sunningdale Country Club (bd. govs. 1989—, pres. 2000—), Queenwood Golf Club, Colony Club, Phi Delta Phi. Office: Paul Weiss Rifkind Wharton & Garrison 1285 Avenue Of The Americas New York NY 10019-6064 E-mail: jdubin@paulweiss.com.

DUBIN, JOSEPH WILLIAM, federal mediator; b. Middletown, Conn., Apr. 7, 1948; s. Emanuel Saul and Hazel (Brenner) D.; m. Brenda Charlotte Ellen Clark, June 27, 1976; children: Brian Joseph Finnegan, Darren Clark Finnegan, Evan Jared. BA, U. Conn., 1970; postgrad., U. Mass., 1970—73. Rsch. asst. U. Conn. Health Ctr., Farmington, 1973-81; organizer Am. Fedn. Tchrs., Hartford, Conn., 1981-82; field rep. Conn. Fedn. Ednl. and Profl. Employees, Rocky Hill, 1982-2000, interest arbitrator, 1990-2000; commr. Fed. Mediation and Conciliation Svc., 2000—. Vice-chmn. Fedn. Nurses and Health Profls. Nat. Steering Com., Washington, 1980-81; v.p. Greater Hartford Labor Coun., AFL-CIO, 1982-84, del., 1980-2000. Contbr. articles to profl. jours. Mem. Boy Scouts Am., 1979—, com. chmn. troop 355, Newington, Conn., 1980-95, mem. advancement com. Nutmeg dist., 1994—. Recipient Dist. award of Merit Long Rivers Coun. Boy Scouts Am., 1992, Spl. Recognition award Univ. Health Profls., 1990, George Meany award AFL-CIO, 1981. Mem. ACLU, Am. Chem. Soc. (student affiliate chmn. 1969-70), Indsl. Rels. Rsch. Assn. (Connecticut Valley chpt. steering com. 1994—, v.p. 2001—), U. Conn. Health Ctr. Profl. Employees Assn. (pres. 1980-81), Staff Union of Conn. (sec.-treas. 1982-87), Nat. Trust Hist. Preservation, Conn. Trust Hist. Preservation, Newington Hist. Soc. and Trust, Inc., Nat. Audubon Soc., Nat. Wildlife Fedn., World Wildlife Fedn., The Wilderness Soc., Friends of Lucy Robbins Welles Libr., Peoples Med. Soc., Conn. Citizens Action Group. Avocations: photography, cooking. Home: 57 Kirkham Pl Newington CT 06111-2408 Office: Fed Mediation Conciliation Svc 333 East River Dr Ste 507 East Hartford CT 06108 Fax: (860) 528-3383. E-mail: jdubin@fmcs.gov.

DUBIN, LEONARD, lawyer; b. Trenton, N.J., July 30, 1934; s. Isadore and Selma (Lotman) D.; m. Marlene B. Bronstein, July 12, 1962; children: Elisa K., David I., Michael B. BS, Temple U., 1956, LLB, 1961. Bar: Pa. 1962. Law clk. Ct. Common Pleas, Phila., 1961-62; assoc. Blank Rome Comisky & McCauley LLP, Phila., 1962-69; ptnr. Blank Rome LLP and predecessor cos., Phila., 1969—. Contbr. articles to profl. jours. Bd. dirs. Juvenile Diabetes Found., 1974-95. 1st lt. U.S. Army, 1956-58. Fellow Am. Bar Found., Pa. Bar Found., Am. Coll. Trial Lawyers, Am. Acad. Matrimonial Lawyers; mem. ABA (ho. of dels. 1988-96), Pa. Bar Assn. (house of dels. 1977—, bd. govs. 1981-84, v.p. 1987-88, pres.-elect 1988-89, pres. 1989-90, chair family law sect. 1991-92), Phila. Bar Assn. (bd. govs. 1975-77). Democrat. Jewish. Office: Blank Rome LLP One Logan Sq Philadelphia PA 19103 E-mail: dubin@blankrome.com.

DUBIN, MARTIN STEVEN, principal; b. Queens, N.Y., July 1, 1950; s. Herman and Fay Dubin; m. Ellen Marlene Kohn, Aug. 18, 1973; children: Rachel Fay, David Isaac. BA, Hofstra U., 1972, MS in Edn. with univ. honors, 1974; D of Edn., Vanderbilt U., 1981. Cert. nursery, kindergarten, grades 1-6, social studies 7-9, spl. classes for emotionally disturbed K-12, Va.; kindergarten, elem. 1-7, spl. edn. for emotional disturbance and learning disabilities, elem. prin., secondary prin. Tchr. emotionally disturbed Mt. Vernon Ctr., Alexandria, Va., 1974-76; head tchr. emotionally disturbed Riverside Elem., Alexandria, 1976-77; resource tchr. emotionally disturbed Franconia Ctr., Alexandria, 1977-81; dept. chmn. learning disabled Robinson Secondary, Fairfax, Va., 1981-83; prin. Armstrong Ctr., Reston, Va., 1988-90, Franconia Ctr., Alexandria, 1990-97, Crestwood Elem., Springfield, Va., 1997-98; adminstrv. prin. Hayfield Secondary, Alexandria, 1998—. Adj. prof. George Mason U., Fairfax, 1988-93; learning disabilities/mild mental retardation specialist Area IV Adminstrv. Office, Fairfax, 1983-88; grant evaluator U.S. Office of Edn., Washington, spring 1991, 93, 95. Pres. Adat Reyim, Springfield, Va., 1997-99; mem. Springfield Coalition, 1997-98. U.S. Office of Edn. rsch. grantee, 1979. Mem. CEC, Nat. Assn. Elem. Sch. Prins., Phi Delta Kappa. Achievements include study in how attitudes of non-disabled students influence the integration and mainstreaming of emotionally disabled students. Office: Hayfield Secondary Sch 7630 Telegraph Rd Alexandria VA 22315-3898 E-mail: 4dubins@prodigy.net., martin.dubin@fcps.edu.

DUBIN, NORMAN HAROLD, endocrinologist; b. Paterson, N.J., Feb. 13, 1942; s. Joseph L. and Madeline J. (Eglowstein) D.; m. Valerie Kresky, July 25, 1964; 1 child, Jessica M. BA, U. Rochester, 1963; PhD, Rutgers U., 1970. Asst. prof. U. Md., Balt., 1971-75; assoc. prof. Johns Hopkins U., Balt., 1975-90; vis. scientist, sr. rsch. assoc. NIH, Bethesda, Md., 1990-91; dir. in vitro fertilization labs. Union Meml. Hosp., Balt., 1991—; sci. dir. MedStar Rsch. Inst., Balt., 2000—. Ad hoc reviewer NIH, NSF, March of Dimes, other granting agys., also for 7 profl. jours. Contbr. over 100 articles to profl. jours. Recipient award Lalor Found., 1971, Excellence in Tchg. award Assn. Profs. Gynecology and Obstetrics, 2000; NSF sr. rsch. fellow, 1990-91. Mem. Am. Soc. Reproductive Medicine, Endocrine Soc., Soc. for Study of Reproduction, Soc. Gynecologic Investigations. Achievements include research in relationship of prostaglandin metabolism to uterine contractions in the mechanism of parturition, statistical interpretation of clinical data. Home: 6210 Biltmore Ave Baltimore MD 21215-3604 Office: Union Meml Hosp 201 E University Pkwy Baltimore MD 21218-2891

DUBIN, STEPHEN VICTOR, lawyer; b. Bklyn., June 17, 1938; s. Herman E. and Rhoda (Fogel) D.; m. Paula L. Dubin, June 28, 1959; children: Jeffrey D., Michelle L. BA, CUNY, 1961; JD, Boston U., 1961. Bar: N.Y. 1961, Ill. 1975, Pa. 1984, U.S. Dist. Ct. (so. and ea. dists.) N.Y. 1966, U.S. Dist. Ct. (no. dist.) Ill. 1975, U.S. Ct. Appeals (2d cir.) 1975, U.S. Supreme Ct. 1970, U.S. Dist. Ct. (ea. dist.) Pa. 1993, U.S. Ct. Appeals (3d cir.) 1993. Assoc. Kronish, Lieb, Weiner & Hellman, N.Y.C., 1965-67; counsel corp. sec Seligman & Latz, N.Y.C., 1967-72; gen. atty. Montgomery Ward & Co., Inc., N.Y.C., 1972-75, regional counsel, asst. sec. Chgo., 1975-78; gen. counsel, exec. v.p., sec. dir. CSS Industries, Inc., Phila., 1978—. Lectr. consumer law Am. Mgmt. Assn., 1974, 79, 81, Practicing Law Inst., 1982, 88. Nassau County Dem. committeeman, 1967-75, mem. county jud. screening com., 1972-75, del. Nat. Dem. Issues Conv., 1974; pres. Phila. chpt. Am. Jewish Com., 1995-97, chmn. 1997-99, nat bd. govs., 1997—, nat. v.p., 2002—. Capt. JAGC AUS, 1961-65. Mem. ABA, N.Y. State Bar Assn., Pa. Bar Assn., Ill. Bar Assn., Chgo. Bar Assn., Phila. Bar Assn., Bar Assn. Nassau County, N.Y. County Lawyers Assn., Am. Soc. Corp. Secs., Masons (master 1982). Office: CSS Industries Inc 1845 Walnut St Philadelphia PA 19103-4708 E-mail: steve.dubin@cssindustries.com.

DUBINA, JOEL FREDRICK, federal judge; b. Elkhart, IN, 1947; BS, U. Ala., 1970; JD, Cumberland Sch. Law, 1973. Pvt. practice law Jones, Murray, Stewart & Yarbrough, 1974—83; law clk. to Hon. Robert E. Varner U.S. Dist. Ct. (mid. dist.) Ala., Montgomery, 1973—74, U.S. magistrate, 1983—86, U.S. Dist. judge, 1986—90; judge U.S. Ct. Appeals (11th cir.), 1990—. Mem.: FBA (pres. Montgomery chpt. 1982—83), Montgomery County Bar Assn. (chmn. Law Day com. 1975, constrn. and bylaws com. 1977—80, grievance com. 1981—83), 11th Cir. Hist. Soc., Ala. State Bar Assn., Supreme Ct. Hist. Soc., Fed. Judges Assn., Nat. Coun. U.S. Magistrate Judges, Cumberland Sch. Law Alumni Assn., Am. Inn of Cts. (pres. Montgomery chpt. 1993—94), Lions, Phi Delta Phi. Office: US Cir Ct Appeals 11th Cir PO Box 867 Montgomery AL 36101-0867 also: US Courthouse Ste C5 1 Church St Montgomery AL 36104

DUBKE, MARIE E. business educator; b. Buffalo, Jan. 30, 1930; d. Harold O. and Eunice F. Dubke; m. Gabriel P. Racz, June 16, 1962 (dec. Nov. 1988). BSBA, SUNY, Buffalo, 1950, MBA, 1955; PhD, Mich. State U., 1961. CPA, Mich., Tenn. Sec., bookkeeper Phillips Wertman & Co., Buffalo, 1950-52; instr. SUNY, Buffalo, 1952-55, Mich. State U., East Lansing, 1955-57; audit staff Deloitte Touche, Detroit, 1957-61; assoc. prof. Ctrl. Mich. U., Mt. Pleasant, 1961-67; prof. U. Memphis, 1967-95; pres., treas. Fall Acctg. Seminars Inc., Memphis, 1990—2002; ret., 2001. Home: 8425 Bussenius Rd Pasadena MD 21122-4607

DUBLIN, STEPHEN LOUIS, secondary school educator, singer, musician; b. L.A., Aug. 17, 1948; s. Thomas Newton and Carole Louise Dublin. BM, Chapman U., 1970; M in Sch. Adminstrn., U. LaVerne, 1988. Vocal music and English tchr. Leland Stanford Jr. H.S., 1973-74; vocal music and gen. music tchr. Walter B. Hill Jr. H.S., 1974-77, 80-88, Woodrow Wilson H.S., 1977-80; govt. and econs. tchr., mem. various sch. coms., mentor tchr., chmn. history dept. Robert A. Millikan H.S., Long Beach, Calif., 1988—. Mem. campaign com. Harriet Williams Bd. Edn., Long Beach, 1988, 90; Calif. tchr. liason Senate Ralph Dells, Long Beach, 1988-92. Scholar Champman U., 1966-70, Bougess White scholar, 1998; named Tchr. of Yr. Millikan H.S., 1993; nominee Tchr. of Yr., League of Calif. High Schs., 1999; named 1 of 5 most popular tchrs., sr. class Millikan H.S., 1999, Most Inspirational Tchr., 1998, tchr. who influenced 2 students most in their lives, 1999, Tchr. of Yr., Long Beach PTA, 1999, Svc. award PTA, 1999; honoree work with homeless children Long Beach USD, raising money Long Beach Red Cross. Mem. Calif. Assn. Econs. (charter), Social Studies Coun., Choral Conductors Guild, So. Calif. Vocal Assn., Constnl. Rights Found. (premier tchr.), Phi Delta Kappa. Avocations: singing, conducting. Home: 4045 E 3d St #112 Long Beach CA 90814

DUBLIN, THOMAS DAVID, retired physician; b. N.Y.C., Jan. 18, 1912; s. Louis I. and Augusta (Salik) D.; m. Christina Macdonald Carlyle, June 3, 1939 (dec. Sept. 1997); children: Sarah Carlyle Dublin Slenczka, Barbara Dublin Van Cleve. AB, Dartmouth Coll., 1932; MD, Harvard U., 1936; M.P.H., Johns Hopkins U., 1940, Dr.P.H., 1941. Diplomate Nat Bd. Med. Examiners, Am. Bd. Preventive Medicine (dir. 1961-71, vice. chmn. for gen. preventive medicine 1965-71). Intern 2d Harvard med. service Boston City Hosp., 1936-38; asst. resident physician Hosp. Rockefeller Inst. for Med. Research, N.Y.C., 1938-39; epidemiologist-in-tng. N.Y. State Dept. Health, 1939-40, asst. dist. health officer, 1940, epidemiologist, 1941-42; instr. preventive medicine Johns Hopkins U. Med. Sch., 1940-41; instr. preventive medicine and public health Albany Med. Coll., 1942; lectr. epidemiology DeLamar Inst. Pub. Health, Coll. Physicians and Surgeons, Columbia U., 1942-45; assoc. prof., 1942-43; prof., exec. officer dept. preventive medicine/cmty. health L.I. Coll. Medicine, Bklyn., 1943-48; epidemiologist Kingston Ave. Hosp., Bklyn., 1943-48; exec. dir. Nat. Health Council, 1948-53; med. cons. Nat. Found. for Infantile Paralysis, 1953-55; med. dir. USPHS, 1955-76, Community Services Programs, Office of Dir., NIH, Bethesda, Md., 1955-60; chief epidemiology and biometry br. Nat. Inst. Arthritis and Metabolic Diseases, Bethesda, 1960-66; research adviser, health service Office Tech. Coop. and Research, AID, 1966-68; dir. Office Health Manpower, HEW, 1968-70; program planning officer Bur. Health Manpower, Health Resources Adminstrn., 1970-72, spl. asst. dep. dir. bur., 1972-76; cons. health manpower supply and edn., 1976-78; cons. div. med. edn. AMA and Coordinating Council on Med. Edn., 1976-78; cons. research and devel. Ednl. Commn. for Fgn. Med. Grads., 1978-86. Mem. expert adv. panel pub. health adminstrn. WHO, 1954-80; mem. Nat. Adv. Com. Epidemiology and Biometry, 1956-60; chm. com. on cert. Am. Bd. Med. Specialists, 1972-77 Contbr. articles on internat. health and health manpower to profl. publs. Fellow Am. Pub. Health Assn. (governing council 1954-60, chmn. research policy com. 1957-60), Am. Coll. Preventive Medicine (regent 1973-76), N.Y. Acad. Medicine; mem. AMA, AAAS, Am. Epidemiol. Soc., Assn. Tchrs. Preventive Medicine (sec. 1944-48), Internat. Epidemiol. Assn., Delta Omega. Home: 2949 Garfield Ter NW Washington DC 20008-3507 E-mail: ThosDDublin@aol.com.

DUBLON, DINA, bank executive; b. Brazil; BA in Econs. and Math., Hebrew U.; MS, Carnegie Mellon U. Exec. v.p. corp. planning Chase Manhattan Corp., N.Y.C., 1996—2000, CFO, exec. v.p.; CFO J.P. Morgan Chase & Co., N.Y.C., 2000—. Bd. dirs. The Hartford Fin. Svc. Group, Inc., govWorks.com, N.Y. Mem. Carnegie Mellon U.'s Grad. Sch. Indsl. Adminstrn.'s Coun. on Finance; mem. adv. bd. St. John U.'s Grad. Sch. Bus. Office: J P Morgan Chase & Co 270 Park Ave New York NY 10260

DUBNER, DANIEL WILLIAM, pediatrician; b. Newark, Apr. 18, 1947; s. Nathan M. and Sara K. (Kuskin) D.; m. Janet Lee, Oct. 5, 1975; children: Sarah, Jeffrey, Emily. BS, Rutgers U., 1969; MD, U. Pa., 1973. Intern, resident Childrens Hosp. Phila., 1973-76; pediatrician Med. Assoc., Chelmsford, Mass., 1978-88, Greater Lowell (Mass.) Pediatrics, 1988—. Author: The Pediatricians' Best Baby Planner for the First Year of Life, 1994. Behavioral Pediatrics fellow U. Wash., Seattle, 1976-77, genetic counseling and birth defect edn. fellow Tufts U., Boston, 1977-78. Fellow Am. Acad. Pediatrics; mem. Mass. Med. Soc. Avocations: running, biking, travel. Office: Greater Lowell Pediatrics 33 Bartlett St Ste 306 Lowell MA 01852-1318 also: 504 Groton Rd Westford MA 01886-1151

DUBOFF, LEONARD DAVID, lawyer; b. Bklyn., Oct. 3, 1941; s. Rubin Robert and Millicent Barbara (Pollach) DuB.; m. Mary Ann Crawford, June 4, 1967; children: Colleen Rose, Robert Courtney, Sabrina Ashley. JD summa cum laude, Bklyn. Law Sch., 1971. Bars: N.Y. 1974, Oreg. 1977, U.S. Dist. Cts. (so. and ea. dists.) N.Y. 1974, U.S. Ct. Appeals (2d cir.) 1974, U.S. Ct. Appeals (9th cir.) 1990, U.S. Customs Ct. 1975, U.S. Supreme Ct. 1977, U.S. Fed. Dist. Ct. 1990. Teaching fellow Stanford (Calif.) U. Law Sch., 1971-72; mem. faculty Lewis & Clark Coll. Northwestern Sch. Law, Portland, Oreg., 1972-94, prof. law, 1977-94; ptnr. DuBoff & Ross, PLLC, Portland, 1994-99, mng. mem. DuBoff, Dorband, Cushing, & King, PLLC, 2000-01, The DuBoff Law Group, LLC, 2001—; instr. Hastings Coll. Law Coll. Civil Advocacy, San Francisco, summers 1978, 79. Founder, past pres. Oreg. Vol. Lawyers for Arts; mem. lawyers' com. ACLU, 1973-78, bd. dirs. Oreg., 1974-76; mem. Mayor's Adv. Com. Security and Privacy, 1974; bd. dirs. Portland Art Mus. Asian Art Council, 1976-77, Internat. Assn. Art Security, N.Y.C., 1976-80; pres. Arts Commn. of Tigard Tualatin and Sherwood, 1990-92; Gov. Oreg. Com. Employment of Handicapped, 1978-81; cons., panelist spl. projects Nat. Endowment for Arts, 1978-79; mem. Mayor's Adv. Com. on Handicapped, 1979-81; mem. Wash. State Atty. Gen's Com. to Reorganize Maryhill Mus.; Oreg. Commn. for Blind, 1987-93; Oreg. Com. for Humanities, 1981-87. Recipient Bklyn. Law Sch. Stuart Hirschman Property, Jerome Prince Evidence, Donald W. Matheson Meml. awards, 1st scholarship prize; Hofstra U. Lighthouse scholar 1965-71; recipient Hauser award, 1967, Howard Brown Pickard award, 1967-69, Oreg. Govs. Arts award, 1990, Dist. award of merit Pioneer Dist., Boy Scouts Am., 1995, Silver Beaver award Boy Scouts Am., 1996, Vigil mem. Order of the Arrow, 1996. Mem. Am. Soc. Internat. Law, Assn. Alumni and Attenders of Hague Acad. Internat. Law, Assn. Am. Law Schs. (standing com. sect. activities 1975, chmn. sect. law and arts 1974-80, 91-93, spl. com. on disabilities 1989-91), ABA, N.Y. State Bar Assn., Oreg. Bar Assn., Delta Kappa Phi, Sigma Pi Sigma, Sigma Alpha. Spl. columnist on craft law, The Crafts Report, 1973-87; editor, contbr. materials to legal and art textbooks; author textbooks and articles for legal and art jours. Office: The DuBoff Law Group LLC 6665 SW Hampton St Ste 200 Portland OR 97223-8357

DUBOIS, ALAN BEEKMAN, art museum curator; b. Forest Glen, N.Y., Dec. 14, 1935; s. Raymond Van Orden and Florence (Beekman) DuB.; m. Joan Edna Burger, Apr. 25, 1959; children: Dean, Ronald, Douglas, Jonathan. BS in Art Edn., SUNY-New Paltz, 1958; MFA in Photography and Related Arts, Ind. U., 1966. Dir. Washington County Mus. Fine Arts, Hagerstown, Md, 1964-66; asst. dir. Mus. Fine Arts, St. Petersburg, Fla., 1966-84, Orlando (Fla.) Mus. Art, 1984-89; curator decorative arts Ark. Arts Ctr., Little Rock, 1989—. Nat. Endowment Arts fellow, 1972, 75 Mem. Nat. Art Edn. Assn., Coll. Art Assn., Am. Assn. Mus. Office: Ark Arts Ctr PO Box 2137 Little Rock AR 72203-2137 E-mail: adubois@arkarts.com.

DUBOIS, MARK BENJAMIN, former utilities executive, educator; b. Peoria, Ill., Sept. 27, 1955; s. Benjamin John and Marjorie Abigail (Black) DuB.; m. Jeri Rene Simmons, May 24, 1975; 1 child, Benjamin Robert. BS with high distinction, U. Ariz., 1977; MA, U. Kans., 1981. Cert. internet bus. strategist, profl. web designer. Rsch. asst. State Biol. Survey Kans., Lawrence, 1978-81; systems programmer Cen. Ill. Light Co., Peoria, 1982-84, operating software supr., 1984-85, gen. supr. data processing ops. sect., 1985-88, gen. supr. applications systems sect., 1988-90, security adminstrn. staff info. systems, 1990-91, gen. supr. data processing ops. sect., 1991-93, staff info. system planning adminstn., 1993-95, sr. market rsch. adminstr., 1995-97; team leader Internet Enhancement Project, 1997-98, sr. bus. cons., 1998-99; sr. cons. Heartland Info. Tech. Svcs., 1999; asst. prof. bus. and info. systems dept. Ill. Ctrl. Coll., East Peoria, 1999—2002, assoc. prof. bus. and info. sys. dept., 2002—. Part-time instr. nat. sci. and computer literacy Midstate Coll., 1987-99, Internet literacy web page design Ill. Ctrl. Coll., 1998-99; rsch. affiliate Ill. Nat. Hist. Survey, Urbana, Ill., 1988—; cons. identifier Ctr. for Insect Identification, Lansing, Mich., 1988-98. Editl. bd. Chpt. of Nature Conservancy, 1997-99; contbr. articles on entomology and personal computer software to profl. jours. Bd. dirs. Spl. People Encounter Christ, Peoria, 1982-83, Midstate Coll., Peoria, Ill., 1998-1999; bd. pres. Sun Found., Washburn, Ill., 1998—; treas. Religious Edn. Activities for Cmty. Handicapped, Lawrence, 1978-81; cons. Jr. Achievement, 1987-88; mem. sch. bd. Father Sweeney Sch. for Academically Gifted, 1989-91; chmn. Utility Info. Systems Exch., 1991-92; amb. Lakeview Mus. Arts Scis., 1991-95, guest curator, 1993-95. Mem. AAAS, Data Processing Mgmt. Assn., Internat. Union for Study Social Insects, Am. Entomol. Soc., Am. Inst. Biol. Scis., Mid-Am. Paleontol. Soc., Cen. States Entomol. Soc., Kans. Acad. Sci., N.Y. Entomol. Soc., Animal Behavior Soc., Cambridge Entomological Club, Soc. Systematic Zoology, World Orgn. of Webmasters (cert. profl. web designer), Internat. Webmasters Assn., Assn. of Internet Profls., Sigma Xi, Phi Kappa Phi, Alpha Zeta, Gamma Sigma Delta. Home: 116 Burton St Washington IL 61571-2509 Office: Ill Central Coll 1 College Dr E Peoria IL 61635-0001

DUBOIS, MICHEL, anesthesiologist; s. Yvon and Renee Dubois; m. Judith Ray Jamison-Dubois, June 25, 1976; children: Marie-Laure, Matthieu. MD, Paris Sch. Medicine, 1968. Diplomate Am. Bd. Anesthesiology, Am. Bd. Pain Medicine, Am. Bd. Pain Mgmt., French Nat. Bd. Anesthesiology, lic. practitioner Gen. Med. Coun., London. Staff anesthesiologist Hospital Henri Mondor, Creteil, France, 1972—74; lectr. in anaesthesia The London Hosp. Med. Sch., 1974—76, sr. lectr. in anaesthesia, 1976—78; instr. anesthesiology Georgetown U. Sch. Medicine, Washington, 1978—80, asst. prof. anesthesiology, 1980—85, assoc. prof. anesthesiology, 1985—92, prof. anesthesiology, 1992—94, NYU Sch. Medicine, 1996—; dir. NYU Pain Program, 1996—. Staff attending NYU Med. Ctr., 1996—; chmn. instl. rev. bd. Georgetown U. Sch. Medicine, 1990—94; dir. clin. investigation unit, dir. pain mgmt. svcs. dept. anesthesia Georgetown U. Hosp., 1988—93; hon. cons. The London Hosp., 1976—77. Editor: Ethics Forum. Mem.: Ea. Pain Assn. (chmn. nomination com. 2002—, pres. 2001—02), France-USA Pain Assn. (pres., founder 1993—95), Am. Acad. Pain Medicine (chmn. ethics com. 1998—2003), Am. Soc. Anesthesiolologists (pain therapy com. 1993—94). Avocations: reading, petanque. Office: NYU Pain Mgmt Ctr 317 E 34th St Ste 902 New York NY 10016

DUBOIS, NANCY Q. elementary school educator; b. St. Petersburg, Fla., June 6, 1960; d. Thomas Malcolm and Barbara Jean (Leitner) Quehl; m. Donald F. Dubois, Nov. 27, 1981; children: Jacquelyn Nicole, Justin Jared. BA, U. South Fla., Tampa, 1983; MEd, U. Fla., 1993; Mid-Mgmt. Cert., Schreiner Coll., 1999. Cert. tchr., Fla., N.Mex., Tex. Tchr. St. Patricks Sch., Fayetteville, N.C., 1984-85, The Most Holy Name Sch., Gulfport, Fla., 1985-88, Kirtland Elem. Sch., Albuquerque, 1988-91; field advisor Coll. Edn., U. Fla., Gainesville, 1991-93; 4th grade tchr. Schulze Elem. Sch., San Antonio, 1993-97; tchr. Bellaire Elem. Sch., San Antonio, 1997-2001; USI peer tchr., 1997-2001. USI

peer tchr., 1997—. Named Tchr. of Yr., Bellaire Elem. Sch., 1998-99; recipient grad. asst. Tchg. award U. Fla., 1993; Trinity U. fellow, 1999-2000. Mem. ASCD, Internat. Reading Assn., Fla. Coun. Tchrs. of Math., Kappa Delta Pi. Republican. Roman Catholic. Avocations: reading, cross-stitch, swimming.

DUBOIS, PAUL MARTIN JOSEPH, non-profit organization executive; b. N.Y.C., Oct. 14, 1945; s. Donald A. and Nancy J. (Grennel) DuB.; children: Kara, Charlene, John, Cynthia, Nate, Joshua, Caleb, Aaron, Rangell, Willie. BA, New Sch. Social Rsch., 1965; PhD, Cornell U., 1975; DHL, Anna Maria Coll., Mass., 1996, Goddard Coll., Vt. Trustee emeritus, hon. pub. Ctr. Living Democracy, Brattleboro, Vt.; exec. dir. Inst. for Cmty. and Race Rels., Rutland, Mass., 1999—2000, Martin Luther King Jr. Meml., Washington, 2000—01; pres., and CEO Am. Slavery Memorial Museum, Washington, 2001—. Author: The Hospice Way of Death, 1977, Modern Administrative Practices, 1980, Handbook of Interracial Dialogue, From Problems to Power, 1997, Personal Repair: Doing the Work that Makes You Effective, 1998, Repairing Your Organization (Making it Match Your Values), 1998, Building the Millennium You Choose, 1999, A Meditation on Our Future (Young People Can't be Problem-Free, but They Can be Problem Solvers), 2000; co-author: The Quickening of America, 1994. Avocation: writing. Home: Marina View Towers SW 1000 Sixth St SW Apt 404 Washington DC 20024

DU BOIS, PAUL ZINKHAN, library consultant, book dealer; b. Ravenna, Ohio, Jan. 5, 1936; s. John Harold and Marie Eggleston (Miller) DuB.; m. Carol Ann Johnson, Aug. 15, 1959; children: Megan, Christopher. *Paul's father, John Harold Du Bois, was a philosophy professor who founded a family business in 1936 which now includes three Ohio University bookstores at Kent State University, Miami University, and University of Cincinnati. His son, Christopher, is a senior executive at American Express in Minneapolis. His daughter, Megan, is mother of Alexander, Campbell, Nathaniel, and Sigourney, and wife to Jonathan Alden, Headmaster of Virginia Beach (Virginia) Friends School.* BA, Hiram Coll., 1959; MA (Crawford scholar), Kent State U., 1960; MA, Western Res. U., 1962, PhD, 1968. Library coordinator Mentor (Ohio) Pub. Sch. System, 1963-64; head librarian N.Y. State Hist. Assn., Cooperstown, 1964-69; asst. dir. Kent State U., 1969-72; dir. library, prof. media communications [illegible] Trenton (N.J.) State Coll., 1972-91; dean libr. svcs. Winthrop U., Rock Hill, S.C., 1991-99; ret.; proprietor PZ Du Bois Antiquarian Books, V.p. DuBois Book Store, Inc., Kent, 1969-85; mem. adv. coun. Princeton U. Libr., 1985-89; cons. N.Y. State Coun. on Arts, Nat. Am. Studies Faculty, NEH, Adirondack Mus., Hist. Gainesville, Bucks County Hist. Soc., Inst. Mus. Svcs., N.J. and Pa. Coms. on Humanities, Mid. States Assn. and others; pres. N.J. Coun. State Coll. and Univ. Librs., 1975-76; mem. N.J. Acad. Libr. Standards Task Force, 1983; mem. adv. bd. N.J. Musto Commn., 1979-80; mem. exec. bd. N.J. Acad. Libr. Network, 1985-91, S.C. Libr. Dirs. Forum, 1993-99, Metrolina Libr. Assn., 1992-94; chair S.C. Coun. Librs., 1993-94. Editor: Librarians' Choice, 1972-81, Paul Leicester Ford, An American Man of Letters, 1977, co-editor Reading and the Art of Librarianship, 1986; contbr. articles and revs. to profl. jours. Pres. Pennsbury Scholarship Found., 1986-88; pres. Episc. Faculty Conf., 1986-2000. Recipient Hugo Alpers award Kent State U., 1960; fellow Seminar for Hist. Adminstrs., Colonial Williamsburg, 1963 Mem. Manuscript Soc., Nat. Assn. Scholars, Nat. Trust Historic Preservation, Beta Phi Mu, Phi Alpha Theta Clubs: Trenton Torch (pres. 1975-76). Home and Office: 29 Morningside Dr Yardley PA 19067-3015 E-mail: cajed608@aol.com.

DUBOIS, PHILIP LEON, university administrator, political science educator; b. Oakland, Calif., Oct. 17, 1950; s. Fernand Edmond and Germaine (Goodrich) D.; m. Lisa Lewis, Aug. 28, 1976; 3 children. AB with highest honors in Polit. Sci., U. Calif., Davis, 1972; MA in Polit. Sci., U. Wis., Madison, 1974, PhD in Polit. Sci., 1978. Asst. prof. polit. sci. U. Calif., Davis, 1976—82, assoc. prof., 1982—87, prof., 1987—91, exec. assoc. dean letters and sci., 1990—91, faculty asst. to vice chancellors, 1982—83; vice chancellor for acad. affairs, provost U. N.C., Charlotte, 1991—97; pres. U. Wyo., 1997—. Cons. (profl. jours., comml. book pubs.); contbr. articles numerous articles, book revs. to law revs. and jours.; author (with Floyd Feeney): Lawmaking by Initiative, 1998; author: From Ballot to Bench: Judicial Elections and the Quest for Accountability, 1980; editor: The Analysis of Judicial Reform, 1982 (Philip L. Dubois), The Politics of Judicial Reform, 1982 (Philip L. Dubois). Fellow, Ford Found., Jud. fellow, U.S. Supreme Ct., 1979—80; scholar, U. Wis. Madison. Mem.: Am. Assn. for Higher Edn., Am. Polit. Sci. Assn. (Edward S. Corwin award 1978), Phi Beta Kappa, Phi Kappa Phi. Democrat. Office: Univ Wyoming Box 3434 University Sta Laramie WY 82071-3434 E-mail: pdubois@uwyo.edu.

DU BOIS, TIM, recording industry executive; b. 1948; MS in Acctg., Okla. State U. Former sr. fin. analyst Fed. Res. Bank, Dallas; pres. Arista/Nashville, 1989—. Hit songs include: Love in the First Degree, When I Call Your Name, She Got the Goldmine (I Got the Shaft). Office: Arista Records 1400 18th Ave S Nashville TN 37212-2809

DU BOIS, WILLIAM, JR., retired public relations professional; b. Hartford City, Ind., Mar. 19, 1933; s. William LeRoy DuBois and Manan Martha Cline; m. Treva Marileen Boise, Apr. 2, 1955; children: Janice Lea and Janelle Lyn (twins), Teresa Ann, Steven Dean. BS in Secondary Edn., Ball State U., 1961, MA in Journalism and Polit. Sci., 1984. Reporter, sportswriter News-Times, Hartford City, 1952-53, 55-56; reporter, sports editor, editor Comml. Rev., Portland, Ind., 1959-60; editor The Graphic, Portland, 1959-60; reporter, copy editor, city editor Muncie (Ind.) Star, 1960-65, mng. editor, 1967-74; info. dir. Ind. C. of C., Indpls., 1965-67; adv. Gov. Otis R. Bowen, exec. asst. to state ch. comm. dir. Ind. Rep. Party, Indpls., 1974-76; exec. asst. to Gov. Bowen State of Ind., Indpls., 1977-80, exec. asst. to Gov. Orr, 1981-83; speechwriter Van P. Smith Ontario Corp., Muncie, 1983-84; exec. dir. State Student Assistance Commn. Ind., 1985-87; pres. Ind. Colls. and Univs. of Ind. Inc., 1987-91; exec. asst. for pub. rels. Ivy Tech. State Coll., Indpls., 1992-98; ret., 1998. Author: Ontario Corporation—A History, 1982, Pyromet, 1983, Descendants and Family of William Cline (1746-1853), Soldier of the American Revolution and American Pioneer, 1990, (with Otis R. Bowen) Doc: Memories From a Life in Public Service, 2000. Mem., bd. dirs., mgmt. com. Ind. Higher Edn. Telecomms. Sys.; mem. exec. com. Midwest Partnership of Ind. Colls.; bd. dirs., publicity chair United Way Delaware County. Named Hon. Jaycee, Muncie Jaycees, 1972; recipient award for advocacy, leadership and sensitivity to problems of the mentally ill Ind. Dept. Mental Health, 1983, award for dedicated svc. to fin. aid profession Ind. Student Fin. Aid Assn., 1987, award for profl. dedication to state student fin. aid programs State Student Assistance Commn. Ind., 1987. Mem. Soc. Profl. Journalists (founding mem. and 1st pres. Ind. East chpt.), Nat. Assn. Ind. Colls. and Univs., State Assn. Execs. Coun., State-Nat. Info. Network (bd. dirs.), Ind. Hist. Soc., Huguenot Hist. Soc., DuBois Family Assn., Ball State U. Alumni Coun., Ball State U. Journalism Alumni Assn. (bd. dirs.), Muncie-Del. County C. of C. (bd. dirs., exec. com.), Indpls. Press Club (bd. dirs.). Avocations: genealogy, indiana history, art. Home: 430 Shady Ln Greenwood IN 46142-8362 E-mail: wdbjr2@msn.com.

DUBOISE, AARON T. music educator; b. Winslow, Ariz., Sept. 1, 1973; s. Terry D. and Diana J. DuBoise; m. Tracy A. Clark, July 23, 1994. BS, Grand Canyon U., 1996, MEd in Ednl. Leadership. Cert. music edn. K-12. Tchr. choral/gen. music St. Johns H.S., St. Johns, Ariz., 1997—. Dir.: Cmty. Handel's, 2001; actor: (opera) Marriage of Figaro, 1992, The Nightingale, 1993, Ariadne auf Naxos, 1993, The Outcasts of Poker's Flat, 1994, The Notorious Jumping Frog, (musical) H.M.S. Pinafore, (opera) The Tempest, 1996. Mem.: Choral Dir.'s Ariz., Ariz.'s Music Educator's Assn. (N.E. regional vocal chair 2001—, N.E. solo and ensemble chmn. 1999—2001). Avocations: hunting, camping, travel, church music ministry, video games, sports. Office: St Johns HS 360 South Redskin Dr Saint Johns AZ 85936 Personal E-mail: aduboise@cybertrails.com. Business E-Mail: aduboise@cybertrails.com.

DU BOISE, KIM REES, artist, photographer, art educator; b. Hattiesburg, Miss., Apr. 7, 1953; d. Samernie and Margaret J. R.; divorced; children: Timothy L., M. Ashley (dec.). BA, U. So. Miss., 1986, M of Art Edn., 1988; postgrad., U. Ala., 1994-95. Art tchr. grades 7-12 Columbia (Miss.) Acad., 1975-76; with prodn./ad design Columbian-Progress/Sunday Mirror (News), Columbia, 1980-81; with advt. design/prodn. Washington Parish ERA-Leader (newspaper), Franklinton, La., 1981; art tchr. grades kindergarten-12 Hattiesburg Prep. Sch., 1984-85; instr. art Pearl River C.C., Poplarville, Miss., 1987-94; artist/photographer Dogwood Studios, 1988-97; artist, photographer PhotoArts Studio, 1997—. Adj. instr. U. So. Miss., 1996-97, 98-2000; festival coord. Very Spl. Arts Festival, SE Dist., Poplarville, Miss., 1989-94; participant regional round-Table on discipline based art edn. Getty Ctr. for Edn. in Arts, Tulsa, 1988. Ann. Bi-State Competition, 1986, Exhibited in group shows at MSC/JCAIA Art Exhbn., 1991, Miss. Cmty. Jr. Coll. Art, 1991—92, Art by Art Tchrs. MAEA, 1992, Art Student League Exhibit, 1995, photography, U. N.Mex., 1995, So. Miss. Art Assn. Annual Juried Competitions, 1996—98, U. So. Miss., 1998, 2000, Hines C.C., Miss., 2000. Chmn. Troop 21 Dixie Com. Boy Scouts Am., Hattiesburg, 1989-93; mem. Miss. Jaycettes/Marion County Jaycettes, Columbia, 1976-84, U.S. Jaycee Women, 1976-84. Named one of Outstanding Young Women of Am., 1981-84, First Lady #83 (Life Mem.) Miss. Jaycettes, 1982, Winner Speak-Up Competition, Miss. Jaycettes, 1981. Mem. New Orleans Mus. of Art (assoc.), So. Miss. Art Assn., Nat. Mus. of Women in the Arts (charter), Nature Conservancy, U. So. Miss. Alumni Assn. (life), Walter Anderson Mus. Art. Episcopalian. Avocations: fishing, reading. E-mail: krd@photoartsstudio.com.

DUBOSE, CHARLES WILSON, lawyer; b. Sumter, S.C., Mar. 2, 1949; s. Frank Elsivan and Fannie Louise (Wilson) DuB.; m. Patricia Holman Rayle, Dec. 5, 1987; children: Charles Wilson Jr., Margaret Louise Rayle, Frank Elsivan IV. AB magna cum laude, Harvard U., 1971; JD, U. Va., 1974. Bar: Ga. 1974, S.C. 1992, U.S. Dist. Ct. (no. dist.) Ga. 1974, U.S. Ct. Appeals (5th cir.) 1976, U.S. Ct. Appeals (4th cir.) 1978, U.S. Supreme Ct. 1979, U.S. Ct. Appeals (11th cir.) 1981, U.S. Dist. Ct. (mid. dist.) Ga. 1982, U.S. Dist. Ct. S.C. 2000. Assoc. Kutak, Rock & Huie and predecessor firms, Atlanta, 1974-79; ptnr. Kutak, Rock & Huie, Atlanta, 1979-84; of counsel Griffin, Cochrane & Marshall, P.C., Atlanta, 1985-86, ptnr., 1986-89, mng. ptnr., 1989-92; ptnr. Schnader, Harrison, Segal & Lewis, Atlanta, 1992—2000, Atlanta mng. ptnr., 1995-2000; ptnr. Winkler, DuBose & Davis LLC, Atlanta and Madison, Ga., 2000—. Mem. Chief Justice's Commn. on Indigent Def., 2000—. Elder Peachtree Presbyn. Ch., Atlanta, Madison (Ga.) Presbyn. Ch.; mem. adv. bd. Atlanta's Table, 1991—, chmn., 1995; exec. vice chmn. Atlanta Billy Graham Crusade. Fellow Found. Ga.; mem. ABA (ho. of dels. 2000—), Am. Law Inst., State Bar Ga. (bd. govs. 1998—, chair ind. def. com. 1997—), Atlanta Bar Assn. (bd. dirs. 1992-97, 2000—, sec. 1993-94, v.p., pres.-elect 1994-95, pres. 1995-96, bd. dirs. litigation sect. 1988-94, chmn. litigation sect. 1992-93), Lawyers Com. for Civil Rights Under Law (Atlanta steering com.), Atlanta Bar Found. (bd. dirs. 1995-96, 2000—), Atlanta Vol. Lawyers Found. (bd. dirs. 1995-96), Inst. Continuing Legal Edn. in Ga. (bd. trustees 1995-96), Am. Arbitration Assn. (comml. arbitration panel, constrn. industry arbitration panel), Lawyers Club of Atlanta, World Trade Ctr. Atlanta. Avocations: photography, piano, architecture, historic preservation. Home: 1050 East Ave Madison GA 30650-1467 Office: 300 Hancock St Madison GA 30650-1380 also: Ste4540 303 Peachtree St NE Atlanta GA 30308-3263 E-mail: wdubose@wddlaw.com.

DUBOSE, ELIZABETH (BETTYE DUBOSE), community health nurse; b. Ozark, Ala., Nov. 11, 1930; d. Samuel D. and Mattie Victoria (Harrell) Preston; m. Charles Raymond Hudson, July 31, 1949; 1 child, Julianne Schenker Adams; m. Frederick William Schenker, Jr., Dec. 15, 1962; m. John Calvin DuBose, July 15, 1978. ADN, Columbus State U., 1973, BSN, 1977. Lab tech. II Ala. Bureau of Labs., Dothan, Ala., 1951-62; student nurse CCU St. Francis Hosp., Columbus, Ga., 1972-73; charge nurse The Med. Ctr., Columbus, 1973-75, infection control nurse, 1975-78; charge nurse The Bradley Ctr., Columbus, Ga., 1974-78; clin. instr. nursing Columbus State U., 1977-78; dir. nursing Oakview Manor Nursing Home, Ozark, Ala., 1979-84; patient care coord. Wiregrass Home Health Agy., 13 Counties in SE Ala., 1984-86; home health coord. Ala. Pub. Health Dept., Abbeville, Ala., 1986-90; home health nurse Dale Co. Health Dept., Ozark, Ala., 1990—2002. Libr. com. mem. The Medical Ctr., Columbus, Ga., 1974-77; chmn. adv bd. Oakview Manor, Ozark, 1980-84. Mem. adv. bd. Henry Co. Health Dept., Abbeville, 1986-88, chmn. adv. bd., 1988-90. Republican. Protestant. Avocations: sewing, knitting, sunday sch. tchr., grandmother. Home: Box 784 Co Rd 122 Ariton AL 36311-9718 Office: Ala State Health Dept Dale Co Ala Home Health Andrews Ave Ozark AL 36360

DUBOSE, FRANCIS MARQUIS, clergyman; b. Elba, Ala., Feb. 27, 1922; s. Hansford Arthur and Mayde Frances (Owen) DuB.; BA cum laude, Baylor U., 1947; MA, U. Houston, 1958; BD, Southwestern Bapt. Sem., 1957, ThD, 1961; postgrad. Oxford (Eng.) U., 1972; m. Dorothy Anne Sessums, Aug. 28, 1940; children: Elizabeth Anne Parnell, Frances Jeannine Huffman, Jonathan Michael, Celia Danielle. Pastor Bapt. chs., Tex., Ark., 1939-61; supt. missions. So. Bapt. Conv., Detroit, 1961-66; prof. missions Golden Gate Bapt. Sem., 1966—, dir. World Mission Ctr., 1979—, sr. prof., 1992; lectr., cons. in 115 cities outside U.S., 1969-82; v.p. Conf. City Mission Supts., So. Bapt. Conv., 1964-66; trustee Mich. Bapt. Inst., 1963-66; mem. San Francisco Inter-Faith Task Force on Homelessness. Mem. Internat. Assn. Mission Study, Am. Soc. Missiology, Assn. Mission Profs. Co-editor: The Mission of the Church in the Racially Changing Community, 1969; author: How Churches Grow in an Urban World, 1978, Classics of Christian Missions, 1979, God Who Sends: A Fresh Quest for Biblical Mission, 1983, Home Cell Groups and House Churches, 1987, Mystic on Main Street, 1994; contbr. to Toward Creative Urban Strategy; Vol. III Ency. of So. Baptists, also articles to profl. jours. E-mail: fddubose@aol.com. Home: 1062 Fulton St 4 San Francisco CA 94117

DUBOSE, GAYLAN RAY, elementary school educator, musician, writer; b. Pearsall, Tex., Oct. 4, 1941; s. Austin Gay and Luning Inez (Hull) DuBose. BA, North Tex. State U., 1964; MA in Classics, U. Minn., 1970. Tchr. Grapevine H.S., Tex., 1964—67, John Jay H.S., San Antonio, 1967—69, 1971—73, Escobar Jr. H.S., San Antonio, 1970, Travis H.S., Austin, Tex., 1973—86, Westwood H.S., Austin, 1986—97, Fulmore Mid. Sch., Austin, 1998—2000, St. Andrew Episcopal Sch., Austin, 2001—03. Author: Farrago Latina, 1997; co-author: Excelability, 2003. Co-chair Tex. State Jr. Classical League, Austin, 1988—99, Dist. Adv. Com., Round Rock, Tex., 1996—97; acad. contest chair Nat. Jr. Classical League, Oxford, Ohio, 1996—2003; organist St. Augustine's Orthodox Cath. Ch. and Procathedral, Pflugerville, Tex., 1998—2003. Named Tchr. of Yr., Travis H.S., 1979, 1983, Westwood H.S., 1996. Mem.: Scottish Rite Bodies. Office: St Andrew's Episcopal Sch 1112 West 31st St Austin TX 78705

DUBOSE, MARY, communication and media professional, educator; b. McRae, Ga., Oct. 7, 1947; d. Alvah M. Goodroe and Talitha Eudora Winkles; m. William W. DuBose, Apr. 21, 1985 (dec. June 1993); children: Cartney C.M., Amber E.; m. J.R. McAliley, Mar. 5, 2001. BFA, U. Ga., Athens, 1969; cert., Ctr. Applied Psychol. Testing, 1987. Asst. assoc. media dir. Tucker Wayne & Co., Atlanta, 1969-70; designer Mead Corp., Atlanta, 1970-72; pres. Maradco Nat. Inc., Atlanta, 1972-89; assoc. dir. creative svcs. Emory U., Atlanta, 1989-91, sr. publ. specialist info. tech., 1992, dir. multimedia divsn., 1993-97, with integrated mktg. comm. divsn., 1997—. Exec. dir. Internet edn. World-Class, 1996. Author: Twelve Days to Jerusalem, 1999, (grant proposal) French in Interaction, 1994; contbr. articles to Info. Tech. Jour. Apptd. by Pres. Carter to comm. coun. The Atlanta Project, 1992; mem. EDUCAUSE, 1992—; key decision maker, mem. adv. bd. Symposium 2000. Mem. NAFE, Am. Inst. Graphics Arts (bd. dirs., v.p., v.p. devel. 1990-95), Assn. Psychol. Type, Univ. and Coll. Designers Assn. (competition com.). Avocations: oil painting, reading, working with children of israel. Office: Emory U 315 Woodruff Libr Atlanta GA 30322-0001

DUBOWITZ, HOWARD, pediatrician; b. Cape Town, South Africa, Jan. 5, 1951; arrived in U.S., 1978; s. Nathan P. and Anita Dubowitz; m. Diana Zuckerman, Apr. 27, 1985; children: Nikki, Andy. MB, BChir, U. Cape Town, 1974; MS, Harvard U., 1983. Family practice Nat. Health Svc., London, 1975—78; pediat. resident North Shore Childrens, Salem, Mass., 1978—79, Boston City Hosp., 1979—81; fellow Boston Childrens, 1981—83, faculty, 1983—85; from asst. to full prof. U. Md. Sch. Medicine, Balt., 1985—. Mem.: Internat. Soc. on Child Abuse and Neglect, Am. Profl. Soc. on Abuse of Children, Am. Pediat. Assn., Am. Acad. Pediat. Avocations: gardening, swimming. Office: U Md Sch Medicine 520 W Lombard St Baltimore MD 21201

DUBREIL, SEBASTIEN, language educator; b. Nantes, France, Nov. 23, 1971; arrived in U.S.A., 1994; s. Gilbert and Marie-Claude Dubreil. BA, Univ. Nantes, Nantes, France, 1993, MBA, 1994; PhD, Emory Univ., Atlanta, Ga., 2002. French, his. tchr. Lycée St.-Martin, Machecoul, France, 1993—94; prof. of French Univ. Notre Dame, Ind., 2002—. Part-time instr. of French Univ. of the So., Sewanee, Tenn., 1994—97. Contbr. articles to profl. jour. Fellow: Nanovic Inst. for European Studies; mem.: Computer Asst. Language Instrn. Consortium, Modern Language Assn., Am. Coun. on the Tchg. of Foriegn Languages. Office: Dept of Romance Languages and Lit 343 O'Shughnessy Hall Notre Dame IN 46556

DUBRIN, ANDREW JOHN, behavioral sciences, management educator, writer; b. NYC, Mar. 3, 1935; s. Albert Edward and Louise Theresa (Walsh) D.; m. Drew, Douglas, Melanie. AB, Hunter Coll., 1956; MS, Purdue U., 1957; PhD, Mich. State U., 1960. Diplomate: Am. Bd. Profl. Psychology; cert. psychologist N.Y. state. Psychologist Data Systems div. IBM, Kingston, N.Y., 1962-63; teaching asst., part-time instr. Purdue U., West Lafayette, Ind., 1956-57; psychol. cons. Clark, Cooper, Field & Wohl, N.Y.C., 1963-64, Rohrer, Hibler & Replogle, N.Y.C., 1964-70, ptnr., 1964-70; assoc. prof. Rochester (N.Y.) Inst. Tech., 1970-72, prof. behavioral sci., 1972—, dept. head mgmt., 1982-84, prof. mgmt., 1984—. Mem. N.Y. State Bd. Psychology, 1979— ; cons. lectr. in field Author: The Practice of Managerial Psychology, 1972, Women in Transition, 1972, The Singles Game, 1973, Fundamentals of Organization Behavior: An Applied Perspective, 1974, Survival in the Sexist Jungle, 1974, The New Husbands and How to Become One, 1976, Casebook of Organizational Behavior, 1979, Human Relations: A Job Oriented Approach, 1978, 5th edit., 1992, Fundamentals of Organizational Behavior: An Applied Perspective, 2d edit., 1978, Winning at Office Politics, 1979, Contemporary Applied Management, 1982, 4th edit., 1994, Essentials of Management, 1986, 6th edit., 2003, The Last Straw, 1987, Human Relations for Career and Personal Success, 3d edit., 1992, 6th edit., 2001, Management and Organization, 1989, 2d edit., 1992, Effective Business Psychology, 1980, 6th edit., 2002, Winning Office Politics: DuBrin's Guide for the '90s, 1990, Bouncing Back: How to Overcome Adversity in the Workplace, 1992, Your Own Worst Enemy: How to Prevent Career Self-Sabotage, 1992, Stand Out! 330 Ways to Gain the Edge with Superiors, Subordinates, Co-workers, and Customers, 1993, Getting It Done: The Transforming Power of Self-Discipline, 1995, The Reengineering Survival Guide, 1995, The Breakthrough Team Player, 1995, Leadership: Research Findings, Practice and Skill, 1995, 98, 2001, 03, Human Relations: Job-Oriented Interpersonal Skills, 2000, 2d edit., 2003, Fundamentals of Organizational Behavior, 1998, 2d edit., 2001, The 10-Min. Guide to Effective Leadership, Personal Magnetism, 1997, Complete Idiot's Guide to Leadership, 1998, 2000, Looking Around Corners, 1999, The Active Manager, 2000. Capt. U.S. Army, 1960-62. Mem. Am. Psychol. Assn., Am. Mgmt. Assn., Acad. of Mgmt. Home: 192 Barclay Square Dr Rochester NY 14618-3140 Office: Rochester Inst Tech 192 Barclay Square Dr Rochester NY 14618 E-mail: ajdbbu@rit.edu., ajdubrin@frontiernet.net.

DUBROFF, HENRY ALLEN, newspaper editor, publisher; b. Neptune, N.J., Nov. 28, 1950; s. Sol and Gilda (Burdman) D.; married, 1980 (div. 1986). AB in History and Lit., Lafayette Coll., 1972; MS in Journalism, Columbia U., 1982. Staff writer Dept. Health and Human Svcs., Washington, 1972-73; tchr. English Holyoke (Mass.) St. Sch., 1974-78; employment & tng. program mgr. Knoxville (Tenn.)-Knox CY Community Action, 1978-81; bus. writer, columnist Springfield (Mass.) Newspapers, 1982-85, The Denver Post, 1985-88, bus. editor, 1988-95; editor Denver Bus. Jour., 1995-99; founder, editor, pub. Pacific Coast Bus. Times, 1999—. Contbg. writer CFO Mag., Boston, 1985-90. Contbr. articles to N.Y. Times, 1982-89. Vol. Russian Resettlement Program Jewish Family & Children's Svcs., Denver, 1989—90; bd. dirs. Ventura County Econ. Devel. Assn., U. Calif. Santa Barbara Econ. Forecast Project, Ptnrs. in Edn., Santa Barbara, Jewish Fedn. Santa Barbara. Recipient N.Y. Fin. Writers Assn. scholarship, 1982, Morton Margolin prize U. Denver, 1988, Bus. Story of Yr. award AP, 1989, Gen. Excellence award Am. City Bus. Jour., 1996, 97, Human Svc. award Am. Jewish Com., 1999. Mem. Soc. Am. Bus. Editors and Writers (past pres., bd. govs., Best in Bus. award 1995, 96, 98, 2000). Avocations: writing, golf, restoring 1975 Porsche. Office: 14 E Carrillo St Ste A Santa Barbara CA 93101 Home (Summer): CO

DUBROFF, RICHARD EDWARD, electrical engineer, educator; b. Chgo., June 14, 1948; s. Warren C. and Suzanne (Stern) DuB.; m. Janet Ellen Rice, Sept. 10, 1978. BS, Rensselaer Polytech. Inst., Troy, N.Y., 1970; MS, U. Ill., 1972, PhD, 1976. Registered profl. engr., Mo. Rsch. assoc. U. Ill., Urbana, 1976-78; rsch. engr. Phillips Petroleum Co., Bartlesville, Okla., 1978-85; prof. ele. and computer engring. U. Mo., Rolla, 1985—. Patentee in field; contbr. articles to profl. jours. Mem. IEEE, Am. Geophys. Union, Eta Kappa Nu (chpt. faculty advisor 1990), Tau Beta Pi, Sigma Xi. Avocations: electronics, music. Office: U Mo Rm 119 Emerson Electric Co Hall Rolla MO 65409

DUBROW, HEATHER, English educator; b. San Antonio, Mar. 5, 1945; d. Hilliard and Helen (Volk) D.; m. Ian Ousby, June 21, 1969 (div. Dec. 1979). BA summa cum laude, Harvard/Radcliffe, 1966; PhD, Harvard U., 1972. Asst. prof. U. Mass., Boston, 1972-73; Leverhulme vis. fellowship U. Kent, Canterbury, Eng., 1973-74; lectr. U. Sussex, Brighton, Eng., 1974-75; from vis. asst. prof. to asst. prof. U. Md., College Park, 1975-80; from assoc. to prof. Carleton Coll., Northfield, Minn., 1980-90; from prof. to John Bascom prof. and Tighe-Evans prof. U. Wis., Madison, 1990—. External rev. team Oberlin Coll., Bryn Mawr Coll. Author: Genre, 1982, Captive Victors, 1987, A Happier Eden, 1990, Echoes of Desire, 1995, Transformation and Repetition, 1997, Shakespeare and Domestic Loss, 1999; contbr. articles to profl. jours. Recipient Capt. Jonathan Fay award, Radcliffe Coll., 1966, Hon. fellow AAUW, 1979—80; sr. fellow Nat. Endowment for the Humanities, 1987—88, Guggenheim Fellow, 2003—. Mem. MLA (mem. editl. bd., exec. coun. 1996-2000), Milton Soc. of Am. (exec. com. 1997-99), Renaissance Soc. Am. (disciplinary rep. 2001-03), Spenser Soc., Phi Beta Kappa. Democrat. Avocations: architecture, art, cooking. Office: U Wis Dept of English 600 N Park St Madison WI 53706-1403

DUBS, PATRICK CHRISTIAN, publisher; b. Paris, Jan. 18, 1947; came to U.S., 1978; s. Robert and Anne Marie D.; m. Anne Kira Znosko-Borovsky, June 17, 2000; children— Vanessa, Olivier. Diplome de droit et scie. economiques, U. Paris, 1967. With Brit. European Airways, Paris, 1969; export dir. Hachette S.A., Paris, 1970-78; pres. Hachette Inc., N.Y.C., 1978—, Regents Pub. Co., Inc., N.Y.C., 1980—; chmn. bd. Arista Corp., Concord, Calif.; mng. dir. Hachette Edition et Diffusion Francophones, 1987-91, 1991—; pres. France-Edition, Paris, 1991-95; mng. dir. Groupe Hatier Internat., Paris, 1995—2001; pres., CEO Hachette Livre-Internat., Paris, 2001—. Bd. advs. M.A. in Pub. program Pace U., 1985 Mem. Am. Assn. Pubs., French-Am. C. of C. (councillor N.Y. chpt.) Clubs: Manursing Island (Rye). Roman Catholic. Office: 21 Rue Jean Bleuzen 92190 Vanves France E-mail: pdubs@hachettelivreinternational.com.

DUBUC, CARROLL EDWARD, lawyer; b. Burlington, Vt., May 6, 1933; s. Jerome Joachim and Rose (Bessette) D.; m. Mary Jane Lowe, Aug. 3, 1963; children; Andrew, Steven, Matthew. BS in Acctg., Cornell U., 1955; LLB, Boston Coll., 1962; postgrad., NYU, 1963-64. Bar: N.Y. 1963, D.C. 1972, Va. 1999; U.S. Dist. Ct. (so. and ea. dists.) N.Y. 1964, U.S. Ct. Appeals (2d cir.) 1965, U.S. Supreme Ct. 1970, D.C. 1972, U.S. Ct. Appeals (D.C. cir.) 1972, U.S. Dist. Ct. D.C. 1973, U.S. Ct. Claims 1975, U.S. Ct. Appeals (4th cir.) 1977, U.S. Ct. Appeals (7th cir.) 1984, U.S. Ct. Appeals (9th cir.) 1985, U.S. Ct. Appeals (5th cir.) 1986, U.S. Ct. Appeals (fed. cir.) 1988, U.S. Ct. Internat. Trade 1988, U.S. Ct. Appeals (6th cir.) 1989, Va. 1999; cert. ct. mediator 1998. Assoc. Haight, Gardner, Poor & Havens, N.Y.C., 1962-70, ptnr., 1970-75; resident ptnr. Finley Kumble Wagner Heine Underberg Manley Myerson & Casey, Washington, 1983-87, Laxalt, Washington, Perito & Dubuc, Washington, 1988-90, Washington, Perito & Dubuc, 1990-91; ptnr. Graham & James, 1991-95, of counsel, 1996-98, Cohen Gettings & Dunham, 1998—. Capt. AC USN, 1954-59. Mem.: ABA (chmn. aviation and space law com. 1985—86, subcom. aviation ins., subcom. internat. practice 1985—87, vice chmn. alternative resolution com., mktg. legal svcs. com. 1991—92, vice chmn. ins. com. 1982—84), ATLA, Internat. Soc. Air Safety Investigators, Internat. Bar Assn. (vice chmn. travel and tourism com. 1998—), Def. Assn. N.Y., Def. Rsch. Inst. (vice chmn. alternative dispute resolution com. 2002—), Fed. Ins. and Corp. Counsel (chmn. alternative dispute resolution sect. 1996—99, aviation transp. 1996—), Internat. Assn. Def. Counsel (past chmn. alternative dispute resolution com.), Maritime Law Assn. U.S., Fed. Bar Coun., Fed. Cir. Bar Assn., Assn. Bar of City of N.Y. (aeroav. com.), Va. Bar Assn., D.C. Bar Assn., N.Y. State Bar Assn. (past chmn. aviation law com.), French-Am. C. of C., Nat. AEro. Assn., Boston Coll. Law Sch. Alumni (pres. Washington chpt. 1992—96), Naval Aviation Command (vice comdr.), Congrl. Country Club, Internat. Aviation Club, Wings Club, Cornell Club, Washington chpt. Aero Club, Sigma Chi.

DUBUC, SERGE, mathematics educator; b. Montreal, Que., Can., Apr. 16, 1939; s. Romuald and Fernande (Desmarchais) D.; m. Pierrette Valois, June 3, 1962; children: Benoit, Martin, Jacinthe. B.Sc. in Math., U. Montreal, 1962, M.Sc. in Math., 1963; PhD in Math, Cornell U., 1966. Asst. prof. math. U. Montreal, 1966-71, assoc. prof., 1973-76, prof., 1976-97, prof. emeritus, 1998—; assoc. prof. U. Sherbrooke, Que., Can., 1971-73. Author: Géométrie Plane, 1971, Problèmes d'Optimisation en Calcul des Probabilités, 1978; editor-in-chief: Annales de Sciences Mathematiques du Quebec, 1975-79, mng. editor, 1979-82; co-editor: Fractal Geometry and Analysis, 1991, Spline Functions and the Theory of Wavelets, 1999. Ford Co. fellow, 1968-69; Can. Arts Council Killam fellow, 1975-76 Mem. Association Mathematique du Que. Roman Catholic. Office: Univ of Montreal Dept Math et Stats Montreal QC Canada H3C 3J7 E-mail: dubucs@dms.umontreal.ca.

DUBUC-SCHINDLER, DEBORAH JO, special education educator; b. Manhattan, Kans., Feb. 7, 1957; d. Philip Louis and Elouise Ann (Vanderbilt) Humbargar; m. Gary Gerard Dubuc, May 31, 1975 (div. July 1976); 1 child, Devin Anthony; m. Joseph Julian Schindler Jr., Mar. 18, 2003. BS Edn. and Psychology magna cum laude, Marymount Coll. Kans., Salina, 1981; MS in Spl. Edn., Kans. State U., 1990. Cert. regular and spl. edn.-learning disabilities tchr. Tchr. 3rd grade Unified Sch. Dist. 475, Geary County Schs., Ft. Riley, Junction City, Kans., 1981-87, self-contained learning disabilities tchr. Junction City, 1987-88, mem. English, reading, math. and sci. task force Ft. Riley, Junction City, 1986-88; learning disabilities itinerant tchr. United Sch. Dist. 305, Salina (Kans.) Pub. Schs., 1989-95, spl. edn. resource tchr. K-12, 1995-97, interrelated spl. edn. instr., 1997—; realtor Broker's Realty, Salina, Kans., 1995—. Univ. supr. on honorarium Kans. State U., 1991; Homebound spl. edn. instr. Unified Sch. Dist. #239, 1992. Co-curriculum guides math., sci., English, reading, 1986-88; contbr. articles to profl. jours. Chair Orgns. Com., Salina, 1979-81, Custer Hill Social Com., Ft. Riley, 1986-87; scout leader Girl Scouts U.S., Salina, 1980-81; asst. leader Cub Scouts, Boy Scouts Am., Manhattan, Kans., 1985-86, comm. officer, 1986-87; mem. choir First Nazarene Ch., Salina, 1989-92; active Salina Area Transition Coun., 1990-97. Mem. Coun. for Exceptional Children (rep. 1988-89, 94-95), Kans. Nat. Ednl. Assn. (alt. del. 1998—), Internat. Reading Assn., Junction City Edn. Assn. (mem. pub. rels. com. 1981, elected mem. profl. devel. com. United Sch. Dist. 305 term 1991-92, 92-93), Assn. Ctrl. Colls. of Kans. (univ. supr. 1991, 93, 94, spl. edn. instr. 1993), Learning Disabilities Assn., Alpha Chi. Avocations: gourmet cooking, travel, vocal music, recreational swimming, writing. Home: 1633 E Beloit Ave Salina KS 67401-8368 Office: Cen Kans Coop in Edn 715 N 9th Salina KS 67401-8038

DUBUQUE, THEODORE JULIEN, JR., retired surgeon; b. St. Louis, 1927; MD, St. Louis U., 1952. Diplomate Am. Bd. Surgery. Intern, resident St. Louis U. Hosps., 1952-58; prof. surgery St. Louis U., 1958-96, emeritus prof. surgery, 1996—. Fellow ACS; mem. AMA, We. Surg. Assn., Alpha Omega Alpha.

DU BUSKE, LAWRENCE M. immunologist, allergist, rheumotologist; b. Jersey City, Oct. 16, 1954; BS, Northwestern U., 1976, MD, 1978; diploma (hon.), Polish Allergy Soc., 2001; diploma in medicine (hon.), Crimean Med. U., 2001; diploma (hon.), Belarussian Inst. Epidemiology and Microbiology, Minsk, Belarus, 2001, Ukrainian Med. U., Russian Fed. Inst. Immunology, Moscow, 2002. Diplomate Am. Bd. Allergy and Immunology, Am. Bd. Internal Medicine, Am. Bd. Rheumatology. Dir. Allergy and Arthritis Family Treatment Ctr., Gardner, Mass., 1984—, dir. Immunology Rsch. Inst. New England, Fitchburg, Mass., 1990—; dir.Immunology Ednl. Inst. New Eng., 1999—. Clin. instr. Harvard Med. Sch., Boston, 1984—; co-dir. allergy fellow tng. program Brigham and Women's Hosp., Boston, 1994—98; adv. bd. Hycor Biomedical, Garden Grove, Calif., 1995—97; hon. prof. Crimean Med. U., 2001, Inst. Immunology, Ministry of Health of Russia, Russia, 2002; cons. Brigham and Women's Hosp., Boston, 1984—, Schering Plough, Kenilworth, NJ, 1994—2002, Hoechst Marion Roussel Pharms., Kansas City, Kans., 1995—97, Hycor Biomedical, Garden Grove, 1995—97, Upjohn Pharms., Mich., 1997, Novartis Pharm., East Hanover, NJ, 2002, Aventis Pasteur Inc., Swiftwater, Pa., 2002, Genentech, San Francisco, 2002. Contbg. editor: Asthma & Allergy Procs., 1994—, Jour. Allergy & Clin. Immunology Supplement, 1996—97, Internat. Allergology Rev., 1997—, Internat. Jour. Immune Rehab., 1998—, Am.Jour. Respiratory Medicine, 2001—; mem. editl. bd. Balkan Allergy Jour., 2002—; contbr. chapters to books, articles. Fellow: ACAAI, ACR, ACP, Am. Acad. Asthma, Allergy and Immunology (chmn. practice and therapeutics com. 1996—2000, chmn. practice stds. coun. 1999—2000). Office: Immunology Rsch Inst New Eng 358 Elm St Gardner MA 01440-3926

DUCANTO, JOSEPH NUNZIO, lawyer, educator; b. Utica, N.Y., Mar. 18, 1927; s. Joseph and Martha (Purchine) D'Acunto; m. Connie Davis (div. May 1990); children: Anthony D. DuCanto, James C. DuCanto; m. Patricia Naegle; children: 1 adopted child, William P. Heiman-DuCanto. BA, Antioch Coll., 1952; JD, U. Chgo., 1955. Bar: Ill. 1955, U.S. Tax Ct. 1960, U.S. Ct. Mil. Appeals 1960, U.S. Supreme Ct. 1960. Rsch. asst. Law and Behavioral Sci. Rsch. Project U. Chgo., 1954-55; assoc. Cotton, Fruchtman & Watt, Chgo., 1955-62; ptnr. Bentley, Campbell, DuCanto & Silvestri, Chgo., 1962-80; prin. Schiller, DuCanto & Fleck, Ltd., Chgo., 1981—; chmn., CEO Securatex, 1982—. Adj. prof. family law Loyola U., Chgo., 1968-2003, vis. prof., 2003; frequent lectr. on family law, taxation, fin. planning and estate planning in connection with divorce. Author: Tax Aspects of Litigation, 1979; contbr. articles, essays on family law and fed. taxation, trusts and estates to profl. publs.; editor, pub. Tax, Fin. and Estate Planning Devels. in Connection with Divorce and Family Law, 1970-85; mem. editl. bd. Fair Share, 1981—, Equitable Distbn. Reporter, 1981—, Matrimonial Lawyer Strategist, 1982—. Served with USMCR, 1944-47, PTO, Guam, Iwo Jima, China. Fellow Am. Acad. Matrimonial Lawyers (nat. pres. 1977-79, chmn.-dir. Inst. Matrimonial Law 1976-85), Am. Coll. Trust and Estate Counsel; mem. Ill. State Bar Assn. (bd. govs. 1983-89, Laureate 2003), Scribes, Cliff Dwellers Club, Union League Club. Republican. Unitarian Universalist. Office: 200 N LaSalle 27th Floor Chicago IL 60601-1089 E-mail: jducanto@sdflaw.com.

DUCAT, SUZANNE BASHA, television producer, communications specialist; b. N.Y.C., Apr. 10, 1953; d. Josef Bert and Ellen Ruth (Wolff) Ducat; m. Stanley M. Cohen, June 26, 1988; 1 child, Hannah Elizabeth. BA, Mount Holyoke Coll., 1975; MA in Comm., U. Pa., 1984. Prodn. asst. Today in Del. WHYY-TV, Wilmington, Del., Phila., 1979-80; rsch. asst. Washington Week in Rev. WETA-TV, Washington, 1981-83, assoc. prodr., 1983-85, prodr., 1986-96, prodr. PBS sp. events coverage, 1987-96, exec.-in-chg. Talking with David Frost, 1990-96, sr. prodr., polit. dir. news and pub. affairs, 1990-96; dir. media rels. The Hawthorn Group, Alexandria, Va., 1996-98; dir. comm. and pub. affairs Coun. for Excellence in Govt., Washington, 1998. Prodr. numerous news spls., documentaries including: Summer of Judgement: The Impeachment Hearings, 1984, On the Air: The United States Senate, 1986, Wartime in Washington, 1985, Dateline Freedom: Civil Rights and the Press, 1988, Caring for Tomorrow's Children, 1989, Headline series, 1989-90, The changing of the Guard, 1993, The Challengers '96: A Washington Week in Review Special, 1995, others. Bd. dirs. Anne Frank House, Washington, 1990—; mem. media adv. com. Inst. for Mental Health, Washington, 1993—, World Child, Inc., Silver Spring, Md., 1996—, Rollingwood Citizens Assn., Chevy Chase, Md., 1996—. Recipient Individual Achievement award (as program rschr.) The Washington Area Emmy awards, 1983 (for Power and the Glory), Silver medal for best analysis, interpretation or commentary Internat. Film and TV Festival of N.Y., 1987, 88, Silver Gavel award (for coverage of Clarence Thomas Confirmation hearings) ABA, 1992, Nat. News and Documentary Emmy awrd NATAS, 1985. Mem. Nat. Press Club. Office: Coun for Excellence in Govt 1301 K St NW Ste 450 West Washington DC 20005 E-mail: sducat@excelgov.org.

DUCATMAN, ALAN MARC, physician; b. Plainfield, N.J., July 19, 1950; s. Fred Paul and Shirley (Buchman) D.; m. Barbara Steinmetz, June 18, 1978; children: Joseph, David, Samuel. BA, Columbia U., N.Y.C., 1972; MSc, CUNY, 1974; MD, Wayne State U., Detroit, 1978. Resident, fellow Mayo Clinic, Rochester, Minn., 1979-82; dir. occupational health Columbia Park Med., Mpls., 1982-83; dir. Environ. Med. Svcs. MIT, 1986-92; prof., dir. Inst. Occupational and Environ. Health W.Va. U., Morgantown, 1992-97, chair dept. cmty. medicine, 1996—. Adj. assoc. prof. Boston U. Sch. Medicine, 1990-92, U. Miss. Sch. Medicine, 1991—; adj. prof. medicine Med. U. S.C., 1994; trustee Am. Bd. Preventive Medicine, 1994—. Contbr. articles to profl. jours. Cmdr. USNR, 1983-86. Fellow ACP, Am. Coll. Occup. and Environ. Medicine (chmn. toxicology com. 1987-92, Adolph G. Kammer Merit Authorship award 1993, Harriet Hardy award 1997). Office: Inst Occupl & Environ Health WVa U/Sch Medicine Morgantown WV 26506-9190

DUCEMAN, MARK EUGENE, planner; b. Shamokin, Pa., Oct. 23, 1960; s. John Albert and Margaret Mary (Deeben) D. AS in Mech. Engring., Pa. State U., 1980, BS in Man-Environment Rels., 1983, BS in Urban Planning, 1983; MBA, James Madison U., 2000. Asst. planner, engr. Northumberland County Planning Dept., Sunbury, Pa., 1983; planner Pa. Dept. Tranps., Harrisburg, 1984-86; real estate svcs. Shamokin Enterprises, Inc., Albany, N.Y., 1987; pres. Jambion Devel., Inc., Toronto, Canada, 1988-89; owner, mgr., exec. Ben & Jerry's Homemade Ice Cream Franchise, Toronto, 1987-89; assoc. planner Lord Fairfax Planning Dist. Commn., Front Royal, Va., 1989-95; planner cmty. devel. dept. Town of Herndon, 1995-97; zoning adminstr./planner Planning and Zoning dept. County of Shenandoah, Va., 1997-2001, erosion and sediment control program adminstr.; transp. planner, dept. cmty. devel. Town of Herndon, Va., 2001—. Mem. Am. Inst. Cert. Planners (cert.), Am. Planning Assn., Potomac Appalachian Trail Club. Democrat. Methodist. Avocations: flying, hiking, swimming, kayaking. Home: 12919 Alton Sq Ste 108 Herndon VA 20170- Office: Town of Herndon Dept Cmty Devel PO Box 427 777 Lynn St Herndon VA 20172 E-mail: mark.duceman@town.herndon.va.us.

DUCH, STEPHEN, bank executive; b. Rochester, N.Y., Aug. 26, 1952; s. Michal and Johanna (Langer) D.; m. Kathleen Ann Haberer, June 21, 1980; children: Sarah, Eric. BS, Cornell U., 1974, MBA, 1975. Fin. analyst Chase Manhattan Bank, N.Y.C., 1975-79, fin. mgr. Europe Inst., 1979-81, v.p., fin. mgr. Internat. Inst., 1981-84, v.p., fin. mgr. Global Electronic Banking, 1984-88, v.p., fin. contr. InfoServ Ops. and Sys., 1988-92, v.p., fin. contr. Retail Banking Tech. Svc. Ctr., 1992-93, v.p., product mgr. Bklyn., 1993-2000; product mgr. J.P.Morgan Chase, 2001—. Avocations: canoeing, nordic skiing, woodworking. Office: Chase Manhattan Bank 55 Water St New York NY 10041 E-mail: stephen.duch@chase.com.

DUCHAMP, DAVID JAMES, retired pharmaceutical company executive, consultant; b. St. Martinville, La., Oct. 15, 1939; s. Clarence Joseph and Marie (Fournet) D.; m. Annette Vivienne Sleigh, May 9, 1964; children: James C., Vivienne A., Joseph E. BS in Math. and Chemistry, U. Southwestern La., Lafayette, 1961; PhD in Phys. Chemistry, Calif. Inst. Tech., 1965. Rsch. asst. Calif. Inst. Tech., Pasadena, 1963-65; rsch. scientist The Upjohn Co., Kalamazoo, Mich., 1965-71, sr. rsch. scientist, 1971-79, disting. scientist, 1979-88, dir. phys. and analytical chemistry, 1988-94, exec. dir. info. tech. R&D, 1994-96. Mem. U.S. Nat. Commn. for Crystallography, NAS, Washington, 1981-83; nat. chmn. Harris User's Exch., 1985-86, 1989-91; cons. D&A Consulting, Kalamazoo, 1996—. Contbr. articles to profl. jours. Active Am. Youth Soccer Orgn. Woodrow Wilson Found. fellow, 1961, NSF fellow, 1961-64; recipient Disting. Svc. award Harris User's Exch., 1987. Mem. Am. Chem. Soc., Am. Crystallographic Assn. (pres. 1990), Assn. Computing Machinery, Analytical Lab. Mgrs. Assn. (pres. 1994). Home: 6209 Litchfield Ln Kalamazoo MI 49009-9159

DUCHEK, MICHAEL GERARD, mechanical engineer; b. St. Louis, May 3, 1966; s. Thomas Jefferson and Mary Alberta Duchek; m. Jennifer Shay Duchek. AA in Math., AA in Engring. Sci., St. Louis Community Coll., 1986; BS in Mech. Engring., Purdue U., 1990; MS in Mech. Engring., U. Mo., Rolla, 1997, MS in Engring. Mgmt., 1999. Registered profl. engr., Mo. Engring. coop. McDonnell Douglas Corp., St. Louis, 1987-90, flight test engr., 1990-91; gen. engr. Def. Mapping Agy. Aerospace Ctr., St. Louis, 1991-93; mech. engr. Def. Mapping Agy. Hydrographic/Topographic Ctr., Washington, 1993-94; resident mech. engr. VA Hosp., Columbia, Mo., 1994-95; grad. teaching asst. U. Mo.-Rolla, 1996-97; sr. engr. The Boeing Co., St. Louis, 1998—. Recipient Congressional award, U.S. Congress, 1988. Mem. ASME (chpt. treas. 1989), Soc. Am. Mil. Engrs., Engrs. Club St. Louis (dir. 2003—), KC, Phi Theta Kappa Internat. Honor Soc. (regional alumni officer 1994-96, alumni chpt. pres. 1996, Stalcup Nat. award 1987, Regional Hall of Honor 1988, regional pres. 1987-88), Soc. of Mfg. Engrs. Roman Catholic. Avocations: softball, soccer, racquetball, martial arts, weight training. Home: 10217 Littie Rd Saint Louis MO 63126-3122 Office: The Boeing Co MC S064-3210 PO Box 516 Saint Louis MO 63166-0516

DUCHIN, PETER OELRICHS, musician; b. N.Y.C., July 28, 1937; s. Edwin Frank and Marjorie (Oelrichs) D.; m. Cheray Zauderer, June 22, 1964 (div. 1982); children: Jason Edwin, Courtnay Oelrichs, Colin Zauderer; m. Brooke Hayward, Dec. 24, 1985. BAU, Yale U., 1958; student polit. scis. and music conservatory, Paris, 1957. Pres. Peter Duchin Orchs., 1963—. Bd. dirs. Chamber Music Soc., Lincoln Ctr., Ballet Theater Found., Citizens Com. for N.Y.C., Inc., N.Y. Found. for the Arts, World Policy Inst., Nat. Jazz Svc. Orgn.; mem. adv. bd. Congl. Arts Caucus Ednl. Program, Planned Parenthood, Musicians Emergency Fund. Mem. Am. Ctr. (bd. dirs.), N.Y. State Coun. on Arts. Clubs: Yale (N.Y.C.); Racquet and Tennis, Century Assn. Office: Peter Duchin Orchs Inc 305 Madison Ave Rm 1526 New York NY 10165-0006

DUCHON, ROSEANN MARIE, business owner, consultant; b. Cleve., Jan. 16, 1950; d. Steve and Mary (Bobak) Gaydos; m. Ronald Joseph Duchon, Oct. 11, 1969 (div. 1994); children: Michelle, Teresa, Megan, Kevin, Jason. Student, Kent (Ohio) State U., 1983-84. Lic. health ins. and annuities agt. Ohio, 2002. Sec. ETC, Inc., Cleve., 1968-69; sec., model Bobbie Brooks, Inc., Cleve., 1969-71; instr. childbirth edn. Childbirth Edn. Assn. Cleve., 1971-83; office mgr. 3690 Corp./Devel. Systems, Beachwood, Ohio, 1984-85, Park Pl. Bus. Services, Hudson, Ohio, 1985-86; owner Hudson Secretarial Services, 1986, Exec. Office Services, Hudson, 1987—, Hudson Telephone Answering Services, Hudson, 1988—; pres. R.M. Duchon, Inc., 1991, Western Reserve Staffing Svcs., 1992—, Cornerstone Mktg., Inc., 2002—. Chmn. Hudson League for Service, 1980-82; active Better Bus. Bur., 1989-90. Recipient Excellence in Competition award Internat. Model and Talent Assn., 1999. Mem. Hudson Bus. and Profl. Women (nominating com. 1985-86, pres. 1986-87, region mem. chmn., Ohio state membership chair 1993-94), Hudson C. of C., Nat. Assn. Secretarial Svcs., Nat. Fedn. Indep. Bus., Women's Network. Roman Catholic. Office: Exec Office Svcs PO Box 541 Hudson OH 44236-0541

DUCHOSSOIS, CRAIG, manufacturing executive, heavy; BBA, MBA, So. Meth. U.; BA, MBA, So. Meth. U., Dallas. CEO, pres. Duchossois Industries, Elmhurst, Ill. Vice chmn. bd. trustees Ill. Inst. Tech.; chmn. bd. dirs. Thrall Car Mfg. Co. Office: Duchossois Industries 845 N Larch Ave Elmhurst IL 60126*

DUCHOSSOIS, RICHARD LOUIS, manufacturing executive, racetrack executive; b. Chgo., Oct. 7, 1921; s. Alphonse Christopher and Erna (Hessler) D.; children: Craig J., Dayle, R. Bruce, Kimberly. Student, Washington and Lee U. Chmn. bd. dirs. Duchossois Industries, Inc., Elmhurst, Ill., chmn.; chmn., dir. Chamberlain Tech. Cos.; chmn. Arlington Park Racecourse, Ltd., Arlington Heights, Ill. Bd. dirs. Chamberlain Consumer Products, Hill 'n Dale Farm. Served with U.S. Army, 1942-46, ETO. Decorated Purple Heart, Bronze Star. Mem. Chief Execs. Orgn., Economic Club, Execs. Club (bd. dirs.), Jockey Club N.Y.C. Republican. Methodist. Office: Duchossois Industries Inc 845 N Larch Ave Elmhurst IL 60126-1196 E-mail: duchossois@arlingtonpark.com.

DUCHOWNY, MICHAEL S. physician, educator; b. N.Y.C., Nov. 17, 1945; s. Boris M. and Helen J. Duchowny; children: Alexandria, Catherine, Margot. AB, Cornell U., 1966; MD, Albert Einstein Coll. Medicine, 1970. Cert. Am. Bd. Pediat., Am. Bd. Neurology (spl. competency in child neurology), Am. Bd. Clin. Neurophysiology. Intern in pediat. U. Chgo., 1970—71; resident in pediat. Montefiore Hosp., N.Y.C., 1971—72; rsch. assoc. NIH, 1972—74; resident in neurology Harvard U., Boston, 1974—77, asst. prof., 1979—80; dir. epilepsy program Miami Childrens Hosp., 1987—; clin. prof. neurology & pediat. U. Miami, Fla., 1992—. Academic chair pediatric epilepsy Miami Children's Hosp., 1999. Editor (assoc. editor): Jour. Child Neurology; mem. editl. bd.: Epileptic Disorders Pediatric Neurology, Epilepsy Currents; editor: (book) Intractable Focal Epilepsy, 2000; contbr. articles to profl. jours. Fellow: Am. Acad. Neurologists, Am. Acad. Physicians. Avocations: banjo, racquetball, fly fishing, photography, hiking. Office: Miami Childrens Hosp 3200 SW 60th Ct Miami FL 33155 Business E-Mail: michael.duchowny@mch.com.

DUCK, PATRICIA MARY, librarian; b. Bklyn., Jan. 22, 1951; d. Warren James and Virginia Susan (Noonan) Johnson; m. John Jacob Duck, Feb. 2, 1973; children: Michael, Jennifer, Matthew. BA, George Washington U., 1974; MLS, U. Pitts., 1980, PhD in Libr. Sci., 1992. Libr., serials cataloger U. Pitts., 1980-84, libr., coord., 1984-85, libr., project supr., 1985-86; dir. libr. U. Pitts. Greensburg, 1986—. Facilitator region 10 Gov.'s Conf. Libr. and Info. Svcs., Pitts., 1990. Contbr. articles to profl. jours. Leader troop 47 Girl Scouts U.S., 1990-91; trustee Penn Area Libr., Level Green, Pa., 1989-91. Mem. ALA, Beta Phi Mu. E-mail: pmd1@pitt.edu Avocations: art. Office: U Pitts Greensburg Campus 1150 Mount Pleasant Rd Greensburg PA 15601-5860

DUCK, VAUGHN MICHAEL, software company executive; b. Rockford, Ill., Sept. 13, 1943; s. Vaughn Victor and Virginia Stella (Cielisz) D.; m. Sandra Jean Carlstrom, Jan. 27, 1968; children: Kirsten Lee, Kendra Edith. Assocs., Inst. Automation, Chgo., 1963. Dir. MIS G.C. Electronics, Rockford, 1964-67; gen. mgr., v.p. Computer Svcs. Ctr., Rockford, 1968-79; pres. Integrated Micro Systems, Rockford, 1980-82, Govtl. Data Systems, Rockford, 1983-85; exec. v.p. Bus. Records Corp., Dallas, 1986-87; pres. Interactive Software Products, Rockford, 1988—; v.p. Tyler Techs., Inc., Dallas, 2000—. Developer: (software) Election Mgmt. System, 1984, Retail Operations System Exec., Rose, 1988, Unix Retail POS System, UX/POS, 1991; Inventor election ballot processor, PEPS, 1980. Republican. Avocations: golf, reading, travel. Office: Interactive Software Products 2704 Broadway Rockford IL 61108-5800

DUCKER, BRUCE, novelist, lawyer; b. N.Y.C., Aug. 10, 1938; s. Allen and Lillian Ducker; m. Jaren Jones, Sept. 1, 1962; children: Foster, Penelope, John. AB, Dartmouth Coll., 1960; MA, Columbia U., 1963, LLB, 1964. Bar: Colo. 1964, U.S. Dist. Ct. Colo. 1964, U.S. Ct. Appeals (10th cir.) 1964. Gen. counsel Great Western United Corp., Denver, 1972-73; pres., chmn. bd. dirs. Great Western Cities Inc., Denver, 1974-75; pres. Ducker, Montgomery Lewis & Aronstein P.C., Denver, 1979-97. Author: (novels) Rule by Proxy, 1976, Failure at the Mission Trust, 1986, Bankroll, 1989, Marital Assets, 1993, Lead Us Not Into Penn Station, 1994, Bloodlines, 2000, Mooney in Flight, 2003; contbr. articles, poetry and short stories to lit. jours. Former trustee Legal Aid Found. of Colo., Denver Symphony Assn., Kent Denver Country Day Sch. Mem. ABA, PEN/America, Authors' Guild, Poetry Soc. Am., Denver Club, Cactus Club. Office: Ducker Montgomery et al 1560 Broadway Ste 1400 Denver CO 80202-5151

DUCKETT, BERNADINE JOHNAL, retired elementary principal; b. Flint, Mich., Aug. 7, 1939; d. John and Bernice (Robinson) Edwards: m. Ellis Duckett Jr., Apr. 15, 1963; children: Bruce Devlon, Janeen Jae; 1 stepchild, Ellis III; m. Charles Teaberry (div. June 1960). BS in Edn., Ctrl. Mich. U., 1962; MA in Ednl. Adminstrn., U. Mich., 1966; Reading Specialist, Mich. State U., 1970; postgrad., Flint (Mich.) C.C., 1989-92. Cert. elem. tchr., Mich. Classroom tchr. Dort Elem. Sch., Flint, 1959-65; reading tchr. Dort & Dewey Elem. Sch., Flint, 1965-67; instrnl. specialist Doyle and Dewey Elem. Sch., Flint, 1967-71; asst. prin. Dewey, Merrill & Cook Elem. Sch., Flint, 1971-74; prin. Garfield & Elem. M.L. King, Flint, 1974-96; ret., 1996. Presenter, mem. Internat. Ednl. Symposium, Rome, 1988-92, Flint Schs. Employee of Month Program, 1985-92. Author: Dict on the Lighter Side, 1988, My Grandparents Said Go 4 It, 1989; author joint books: Bicentennial Sch. Cookbook, 1976, Tapestry, 1988, URA Winner, 1994; presenter Tribute to Georgia Hyche, 2003; contbr. articles to mags. and newspapers. Mem. Faith Tabernacle Choir, 2003; fundraiser walk-a-thons United Negro Coll. Fund, Children's Miracle, Flint, 1991, Crim Race for Spl. Children, Flint, 1989—2003, Riverbend Striders, Flint, 1993—; mem., presenter Consortium to Prevent Child Abuse, 1990; vol. St. Joseph Hosp. Aux., Flint, 1990—98; walker March of Dimes, 2002; walker, medalist marathon Arthritis Found., 2000. Named to Greater Flint Afro-Am. Sports Hall of Fame, 1992—2003; recipient Outstanding Educator plaque, NAACP, Flint Intern Plaque, 1986, Flint OBE Pioneer Plaque, 1993, Ednl. Contbns. as Family award, 1993, Walker medal, Leukeima Soc., 1996, Walker-Prevention of Breast Cancer medal, 2000—01, medal, Nat. Arthritis Hawaii Marathon Walker, 2001; grantee, Flint Cmty. Schs., 1990—93. Mem. Nat. Assn. Elem. Sch. Prins. (dir. founds. 1992-96, cons., student discipline Focus Group on Ethnic Minorities 1981, 92, 94, Outstanding Svc. Plaque 1993), Nat. Assn. Media Women (sec. Flint chpt. 1989-92, Media Woman of Yr. 1990), Mich. Assn. Elem. and Mid. Sch. Prins. (chairperson awards, mem. conf. planning and summer camp com., treas., membership chair, del., presenter 1977-92, certs. 1985, 87, 91, plaque 1990), Nat. Alliance Black Sch. Educators (presenter 1993), Internat. Platform Assn., Flint Assn. Elem. Prins. (sec., election chair, social chair 1980-96), Global Network of Schs., U. Mich. Alumni Assn., Nat. Leukemia Soc. (Alaskan marathon walker, medalist 1996), Quota Club Internat. (mem. com. aiding hard of hearing, 1994-2003). Avocations: marathon walking, writing poetry, reading, flower gardening, singing. Home: 3720 Circle Dr Flint MI 48507-1879

DUCKETT, JOAN, law librarian; b. Bklyn., Oct. 21, 1934; d. Stephen and Mary (Wehrum) Kearney; m. Richard Duckett, Aug. 25, 1956; children: Richard, David, Daniel, Deirdre. BA, Kean Coll., 1974; MLS, Rutgers U., 1977; JD, Suffolk U., 1983; postgrad., Oxford (Eng.) U., 1986. Bar: Mass. 1983, U.S. Ct. Appeals (fed. cir.) 1984. Media specialist Oak Knoll Sch., Summit, N.J., 1976-80; law clk. Dist. Atty. Suffolk County, Boston, 1982; vol. atty. Cambridgeport Problem Ctr., Cambridge, Mass., 1984-85; reference libr. Harvard Law Sch. Libr., Cambridge, 1982-84, coord. The New Eng. Law Libr. Consortium, 1984-87, head reference svcs., 1987—, profl. devel. com., chmn. Bryant fellowship award panel, 1987—. Contbr. articles to profl. jours. Protocol hostess L.A. Olympic Com., 1984. Fellow Mass. Bar Found.; mem. Mass. Bar Assn., Boston Bar Assn., Am. Assn. Law Librs., Law Librs. New Eng., Assn. Boston Law Librs., Alpha Sigma Lambda, Beta Phi Mu. Office: Harvard Law Sch Libr Langdell Hall Cambridge MA 02138

DUCKETT, LILA WHEELER, retired language educator, writer; b. N.Y.C., Jan. 6, 1935; d. DePriest Edward Wheeler and Lila Sylvia Hollowell; m. Philip Chandler Duckett, June 13, 1959; children: John Chandler, Dawn Christine, Anais Court. BS in Edn., CCNY, 1958. Tchr. N.Y. Pub. Schs., N.Y.C., 1958—65; reading tchr. Beersley Reading Academy, Flushing, NY, 1965—86; ESL tchr. Japanese Sch. of N.Y., Flushing, 1986—90, Greenwich (Conn.) Japanese Sch., 1990—96. Lectr. in field; coord. Freedom Schs., Jamaica, NY. Panelist Queens Coun.on the Arts, 1993, 1994; pres. Fresh Meadows Poets, Flushing, 1995—97, chmn. judging com., 1992—94; judge First Poet Laureate of Queens, 1995. Mem.: Svcs. to Parents of Exceptional Asian Children. Avocations: writing, poetry, jewelry design. Home: 196 05 B 65th Crescent Fresh Meadows NY 11365 E-mail: piezoengine@juno.com

DUCKETT, WARREN BIRD, JR., state's attorney; b. Annapolis, Md., Aug. 28, 1939; s. Warren B. Sr. and Mary Knight (Linthicum) D.; m. Judith Livingstone, Mar. 25, 1961; children— Pamela, Stephanie, Warren. A.B., U. Md., 1962, J.D., 1966. Bar: Md. 1967, U.S. Ct. Appeals (4th cir.) 1967, U.S. Supreme Ct. 1972. Asst. state's atty. Anne Arundel County, Annapolis, Md., 1967-69, state's atty., 1973— ; ptnr. Turk, Manis & Duckett, Annapolis, 1968-75; prof. law and evidence Anne Arundel Community Coll.; mem. Anne Arundel County Council, Annapolis, 1970-73. Del. Democratic Nat. Conv., 1972; pres. Anne Arundel County YMCA, 1985-87. Named Outstanding Young Annapolitan, Jaycees, Annapolis, 1970; Prosecutor of Yr., Washington Bd. Trade, 1978; recipient Human Relations award Frontiers Internat., Annapolis, 1981, Exceptional Service award HHS, 1986. Mem. Nat. Dist. Attys. Assn. (dir. 1975-77, 82-86), Md. State's Attys. Assn. (dir. 1973—, pres. 1975-77, 82-86), Md. Bar Assn., Anne Arundel County Bar Assn. Episcopalian. Club: Touchdown (sec. 1985—) (Annapolis). Lodges: Lions (sec. Annapolis 1968-70), Rotary. Home: 208 Wardour Dr Annapolis MD 21401-1249 Office: State Attys Office Anne Arundel County 101 South St Annapolis MD 21401-2635

DUCKSTAD, JON ROBERT, lawyer, educator; b. Beaver Creek, Minn., June 4, 1934; s. Norman Brown and Mary Josephine (Holbert) D.; children: Julie, Patricia, Marjorie Duckstad Coluccio. BA, Luther Coll., 1956; LLB, JD, William Mitchell Coll. Law, 1962. Bar: Minn. 1962, U.S. Dist. Ct. Minn. 1967, U.S. Ct. Appeals (8th cir.) 1968. Asst. St. Paul City Atty., 1963-70; asst. pub. defender Ramsey County, St. Paul, 1973—; pvt. practice St. Paul, 1962—; adj. prof. William Mitchell Coll. Law, St. Paul, 1983—. Mem., atty. civil commitment def. panel Probate Ct., Ramsey County, Minn., 1971—; mental illness and dangerous def. atty. jud. appeal panel Minn. Supreme Ct., 1973—. Mem. St. Paul Charter Commn., 2000—, vice chair, 2002—; mem. St. Paul Zoning Bd. Appeals, 2000—, sec., 2002—; co-chair safe and drug-free schs. St. Paul Pub.

Schs., 2000—. With M.C., U.S. Army, 1956-58, Germany. Mem. ABA (del. 1995-99), Ramsey County Bar assn. (pres. 1995-96), Minn. State Bar Assn. (pres. 2002-03). Avocations: hunting, fishing. Office: 2334 University Ave W #190 Saint Paul MN 55114

DUCKWILER, GARY ROSS, physician; MD, UCLA, 1983. Lic. Calif. Med. Bd., 1983. Prof. UCLA Med. Sch., 1984—. Mem.: Am. Soc. Interventional and Therapeutic Neuroradiology (v.p. 2002—03). Office: UCLA Med Ctr 10833 Le Conte Ave Los Angeles CA 90095

DUCKWORTH, GUY, musician, pianist, educator; b. L.A., Dec. 19, 1923; s. Glenn M. and Laura (Lysle) D.; m. Ballerina Maria Farra, May 23, 1948. BA, UCLA, 1951; MusM, Columbia U., 1953, PhD, 1969. Piano soloist Metro Goldwyn Mayer Studios, 1936-41, Warner Bros. Studios, 1936-41, Sta. KFI, L.A., 1938, Sta. KNX, L.A., 1939, Sta. KHJ, L.A., 1940; artist Columbia Artists, 1942-49; asst. prof. music. U. Minn., Mpls., 1955-60, assoc. prof., 1960-62; prof. piano, fellow Northwestern U., Evanston, Ill., 1962-70, chmn. dept. preparatory piano, 1962-70; prof. music U. Colo., Boulder, 1970-88, prof. emeritus, 1988, originator, coordinator masters and doctoral programs in mus. arts. Piano concert tours in U.S., Can., Mexico, 1947-49; condr. various music festivals, U.S., 1956—; dir. Walker Art Children's Concerts, Mpls., 1957-62; nat. piano chmn. Music Educators Nat. Conf., 1965-71; vis. lectr., scholar 96 univs., colls. and conservatories, U.S. and Can., 1964—; cons. to Ill. State Dept. Program Devel. for Gifted Children, 1968-69; vis. prof. U. Colo., 1988-90. Creator, performer: TV series "A New Dimension in Piano Instruction", 1959 (Nat. award for outstanding ednl. TV series from Nat. Ednl. TV); author: Keyboard Explorer, 1963, Keyboard Discoverer, 1963, Keyboard Builder, 1964, Keyboard Musician, 1964, Keyboard Performer, 1966, Keyboard Musicianship, 1970, Guy Duckworth Piano Library, 1974, Guy Duckworth Musicianship Series, 1975, Keyboard Musician: The Symmetrical Keyboard, 2 vols., 1987-88, Keyboard Musician: The Symmetrical Keyboard, 1988, rev. edit., 1990; contbr. to over 6 books, 23 articles on pedagogy of music to various jours.; prodr., performer video tapes on piano tchg.; prodr., writer (film) The Person First: A Different Kind of Teaching, 1984 Nominator Irving S. Gilmore Internat. Keyboard Festival, Gilmore Artist and Young Artist Awards. With U.S. Army, 1943-46. Recipient All-Univ. Teaching award for excellence, U. Colo., 1981, Pedagogy Honors award Nat. Conf. Piano Pedagogy, Chgo., 1994; named Pioneer Pedagogue Nat. Corp. Piano Pedagogy, Princeton U. Retrospective, 1992. Mem. Music Tchrs. Nat. Assn., Colo. State Music Tchrs. Assn., Coll. Music Soc., Music Educators Nat. Conf., Music Teachers Assn. Calif., Phi Mu Alpha, Pi Kappa Lambda. Office: U Colo Coll of Music Boulder CO 80302

DUCKWORTH, JERRELL JAMES, electrical engineer; b. Ft. Payne, Ala., July 22, 1940; s. James K. and Maggie Lee (Hartline) D.; m. Yvonne Cheryl Jones, Nov. 2, 1974; one child, Shelby Elizabeth. AAS in Elec. Engring., DeVry Inst. Tech., 1963. Gen. engr. McDonnell Aircraft Corp., St. Louis, 1963-66; sr. assoc. engr. IBM Corp. Space Systems Ctr., Huntsville, Ala., 1966-72; chief engr. Electric Systems Inc., Chattanooga, 1972-80; dir. elec. engring. Chattanooga Corp., 1980-91; dir. engring. Chattanooga Group Inc., 1991-95; v.p. of engring. GoPro, Inc., Hendersonville, Tenn., 1995-2000; program mgr. ISC, Inc., Hendersonville, 2000—01; cons., 2001—. Served with U.S. Army, 1958-61. Recipient Apollo 8 medallion NASA, 1968, Apollo 11 medallion, 1969, Apollo Achievement award, 1970. Mem. IEEE, Engring. in Medicine and Biology Soc., Assn. for the Advancement of Med. Instrumentation, Instrument Soc. Am., U.S. Space Found. Mem. Ch. of God. Achievements include development of the Recent History Storage Unit used to locate both hardware and software faults, AC and DC drive systems and a therapeutic ultrasound generator with a multiple-frequency transducer. Home and Office: 7916 Shallowmeade Ln Chattanooga TN 37421-1930

DUCKWORTH, MARVIN E. lawyer, educator; b. Aug. 16, 1942; s. Marvin E. and Maryann Duckworth; children: Matthew, Brian, Jennifer, Jeffrey. BS in Indsl. Engring., Iowa State U., 1964; JD, Drake U., 1968. Bar: Iowa 1968, U.S. Dist. Ct. (no. and so. dists.) Iowa 1969. Assoc. Davis, Huebner, Johnson & Burt, Des Moines, 1968-70; asst. prof. Drake U., 1970-71, lectr. law, 1971-85, assoc. dean clin. programs, 1986-87, adj. prof., 1987—; shareholder Hopkins & Huebner, P.C., Des Moines, 1971—. Spkr. in field. Pres. Drake Law Bd. Counselors, 1991-92, Drake Law Endowment Trust, 1995-96. Named Alumnus of Yr. Drake Law Sch., 1997. Fellow Iowa Bar Found.; mem. ABA (chmn. workers compensation and employers liability law 1986-87, vice hmn. toxic and hazardous substances and environ. law com. 1989-93), Iowa Bar Assn. (pres. young lawyers sect. 1977-78, Merit award 1982, chair workers compensation sect. 1992-93), Def. Rsch. Inst., Fedn. Ins. and Corp. Counsel (workers compensation com.), Iowa Assn. Workers Compensation Lawyers (pres. 1988-89), Iowa Acad. Trial Lawyers, Order of Coif. Office: 2700 Grand Ave Ste 111 Des Moines IA 50312-5215

DUCKWORTH, PAULA OLIVER, secondary school educator, freelance artist, writer, photographer; b. Dallas, Aug. 5, 1940; d. Allen Oliver and Minnie Lila (Paul) D. BA, U. Tex., 1963; MA, So. Meth. U., 1968; postgrad., U. London, 1972, R.I. Sch. Design, 1983, U. North Tex., 1985—87. Tchr. English San Antonio Ind. Sch. Dist., 1963-65; tchr. art and English Highland Pk. Ind. Sch. Dist., Dallas, 1965—2001; tchr. art Yarneh Acad., Dallas, 2001—. Tchr. Perkins Sch. of Theology, So. Meth. U., 1995-97. Illustrator: A Cotton Feast, 1982; paintings exhibited in several shows and pvt. collections. Patron, Kimball Art Mus., Dallas Mus. Art, Meadows Mus. at So. Meth. U.; elder Highland Pk. Presbyn Ch. Mem. Nat. Art Edn. Assn., So. Meth. U. Alumni Assn., Highland Pk. Alumni Assn., Kappa Alpha Theta, Delta Kappa Gamma (Sim Green scholar 1973). Democrat. Presbyterian.

DUCKWORTH, TARA ANN, insurance company executive; b. Seattle, June 7, 1956; d. Leonard Douglas and Audrey Lee (Limbeck) Hill; m. Mark L. Duckworth, May 16, 1981; children: Harrison Lee III, Andrew James, Kathryn Anne. AAS, Highline C.C., Seattle, 1976. From acctg. clk. to info. sys. supr. SAFECO Ins. Co., Seattle, 1977-90, rate sys. mgr., 1990-94; sys. mgr. SAFECO Mut. Funds, SAFECO Credit, PNMR, Seattle, 1994-97, mktg. comm. and incentives, quality assurance mgr., 1997-98, dir. comml. lines sys., 1998—2001, dir. quality assurance, 2001—03, dir. personal policy sys., 2003—. Mem. tech adv. com. for the computer info. svcs. program North Seattle Community Coll., 1984-96, chairperson tech. adv. com., 1988-90. Mem. Star Lake Improvement Club, 1988-94; mem. fellowship com. St. Lukes Luth. Ch., 1986—; mem. Boy Scouts Am., 1996-2003. Mem. NAFE, Nat. Assn. for Ins. Women, Soc. for State Filers, Nat. PTA. Office: SAFECO Ins Co Safeco Plz Seattle WA 98185-0001

DUCKWORTH, WALTER DONALD, museum executive, entomologist; b. Athens, Tenn., July 19, 1935; s. James Clifford and Vesta Katherine (Walker) D.; m. Sandra Lee Smith, June 17, 1955; children: Clifford Monroe, Laura Lee, Brent Cullen. Student, U. Tenn., 1953-55; BS, Middle Tenn. State U., 1955-57; MS, N.C. State U., 1957-60, PhD, 1962. Entomology intern Nat. Mus. Nat. History, Washington, 1960-62, asst. curator, 1962-64, assoc. curator, 1964-75, entomology curator, 1975-78, spl.asst. to dir., 1975-78; spl. asst. to asst. sec. Smithsonian Inst., Washington, 1978-84; dir. Bishop Mus., Honolulu, 1984-86, pres., dir., 1986—2001; pres., CEO Hawaii Maritime Ctr. subs. Bishop Mus.; sr. counsel The Nat. Group LLP, Washington, 2001—. Trustee Sci. Mus. Va., Richmond, 1982-86, bd. dirs., 1982-84, Hawaii Maritime Mus., Honolulu, 1984-95; mem. Sci. Manpower Commn., Washington, 1982-84. Co-editor: Amazonian Ecosystems, 1973; Am. editor: Dictionary of Butterflies and Moths, 1976; author, co-author numerous monographs and jour. articles in systematic biology. Pres. Social Ctr. for Psychosocial Rehab., Fairfax, Va., 1975. N.C. State U. research fellow, 1957-62, fell of the Pacific, Hawaii Pacific U., 1999; recipient numerous grants NSF, Am. Philos. Soc., Smithsonian Research Found. Assn., Exceptional Service awards Smithsonian Inst., 1973, 77, 80, 82, 84, Disting. Alumnus award Middle Tenn. State U., 1984. Mem. Am. Inst. Biol. Scis (pres. 1985-86, sec.-treas. 1978-84), Entomol. Soc. Am. (pres. 1982-83, governing bd. 1976-85, Disting. Svc. award 1981), Assn. Tropical Biology (exec. dir. 1971-84, sec.-treas. 1976-81), Hawaii Acad. Sci. (coun. 1985—), Arts Coun. Hawaii (legis. com. 1986-87), Assn. Sci. Mus. Dirs., Social Sci. Assn., Assn. Systematic Collections (v.p. 1988-89, pres. 1990-91, Disting. Svc. award 1992), Pacific Sci. Assn. (pres. 1987-91, pres. Pacific Sci. Congress, Honolulu 1991). Lodges: Rotary, Masons, Order Eastern Star. Democrat. Presbyterian. Office: Ste 1100 818 Connecticut Ave NW Washington DC 20009

DUCKWORTH, WINSTON HOWARD, retired ceramic engineer; b. Greenfield, Ohio, Oct. 15, 1918; s. Benton Raymond and Carrie Lois (Schrock) D.; m. Clara Elizabeth Ayres, Dec. 15, 1941 (dec. July 1999); children— Winston (dec.), Christopher. BChemE, Ohio State U., 1940, MS, 1941. Registered profl. engr., Ohio. With Battelle Meml. Inst., Columbus, Ohio, 1946-94, research engr., 1946-48, asst. chief ceramic research, 1948-52, chief ceramic research, 1952-66, fellow, 1966—; dir. Battelle Meml. Inst. (Def. Ceramic Info. Center), 1967-71, mem. research council, 1979-85. Mem. Engrs. Joint Council, 1968-78, trustee, 1975-77 Author: Engineering Properties of Ceramics; also numerous articles. With AUS, 1941-46; lt. col. USAF; Ret. Fellow Am. Ceramic Soc. (Cramer award 1974, trustee 1968-74, v.p. 1976, disting. life mem. 1985); mem. Nat. Inst. Ceramic Engrs. (pres. 1964, trustee 1963-74, permanent sec. 1978-91, Greaves-Walker award 1987), Can. Ceramic Soc., AAAS, Ohio Acad. Sci., Keramos, Sigma Xi. Home: 63 Brevoort Rd Columbus OH 43214-3823

DUCLOW, DONALD FRANCIS, philosophy educator, researcher; b. Chgo., Jan. 11, 1946; s. Francis Harold Duclow and Josephine Theresa (Schutzenhofer) Duclow-Baudler; m. Geraldine Anne Hodzima, July 11, 1970. BA, DePaul U., 1968, MA, 1969, Bryn Mawr Coll., 1972, PhD, 1974. Asst. prof. philosophy Gwynedd-Mercy Coll., Gwynedd Valley, Pa., 1974-79, assoc. prof. philosophy, 1979-89, prof. philosophy, 1989—. Vis. prof. Fordham U., Bronx, N.Y., 1978. Mem. editl. bd.: Listening, 1981—89; contbr. articles to profl. jours. Mellon fellow in the Humanities, U. Pa., Phila., 1980-81, sr. fellow Inst. Advanced Study Religion, Divinity Sch., U. Chgo., 1998; grantee NEH, 1987, 93. Mem. AAUP (pres. Gwynedd-Mercy chpt. 1996-97, exec. com. Pa. divsn. 2000-2003), Am. Acad. Religion, Am. Philos. Assn., Medieval Acad. Am., Am. Cusanus Soc. (sec. 1985—), German Cusanus Soc. (adv. bd. 1993—), Amnesty Internat., Common Cause. Episcopalian. Office: Gwynedd-Mercy Coll PO Box 901 Gwynedd Valley PA 19437-0901 E-mail: duclow.d@gmc.edu.

DUCLOW, GERALDINE, historian, theatre and film librarian; b. Chgo., Sept. 20, 1946; d. Steve and Irene (Halat) Hodzima; m. Donald F. Duclow, July 11, 1970. BA in English magna cum laude, DePaul U., 1968; MLS, Rosary Coll. (now Dominican U.), 1969. Reference libr. Chgo. Pub. Libr., 1969-70, Free Libr. Phila., 1970-71, head theatre collection, 1972—. Coord. conf. Preservation Mgmt. for Performing Arts Collections, 1982; cons. Lubin Film Co. exhibit at Nat. Mus. Am.-Jewish History, 1984; cons. and speaker in field. Contbr. articles to profl. jours. Mem. Am. Soc. for Theatre Rsch., Spl. Libr. Assn., Theatre Libr. Assn. (mem. exec. bd. 1980-95, pres. 1995—), Theatre Assn. Pa. Avocation: art. Office: Free Libr Phila 1901 Vine St Philadelphia PA 19103-1189

DUCOSTE, JOEL J. research scientist, educator; b. Port au Prince, Haiti, Aug. 14, 1966; PhD, U. Ill., 1996. Contbr. articles to profl. jours.

DUCOTE, CHARLOTTE ANNE, allied health services administrator; b. Baton Rouge, Oct. 21, 1951; d. Gaston Camille and Edna Lora (Bossier) D. BA in Speech and Hearing Therapy, La. State U., 1972, PhD in Speech-Lang. Pathology, 1983; MA in Speech and Hearing Scis., Vanderbilt U., 1973. Cert. clin. competence in speech-lang. pathology; lic. speech-lang. pathology, La. Speech-lang. clinician Met. Schs. of Nashville and Davidson County, 1973-74; speech and hearing cons., acad. instr. dept. spl. edn. U. New Orleans, 1974-78; speech-lang. pathologist, coord. speech and hearing svc. dept. pediatrics and adult units Earl K. Long Meml. Hosp., Baton Rouge, 1978-81; head sect. speech-lang. pathology La. Rehab. Inst. of Charity Hosp., New Orleans, 1982-87; asst. prof. medicine rehab. medicine sect./dept. medicine La. State U. Sch. Medicine, 1986-87; assoc. program dir. New Medico Rehab. Ctr. La., Folsom, 1987, program dir., 1987-88; program dir. post-acute brain injury program Touro Rehab. Ctr., New Orleans, 1989-94; dir. divsn. communicative disorders Ochsner Clinic Found., New Orleans, 1994—. Speech-lang. pathology cons. dept. pediat. Ochsner Med. Ctr., 1978; instr. speech dept. La. State U., Baton Rouge, 1979, clin. supr. articulation disorders and cleft palate clinics, 1979, 81-82; speech-lang. pathologist Upjohn Home Health Care Svc. and Americare Home Health Svc., Baton Rouge, 1981-82; speech-lang. pathology cons. Greenwell Springs Hosp., Baton Rouge, 1981-82; mem. utilization review com. St. Tammany Parish Home Health Svcs., Covington, La., 1980, Am. Healthcare Svc., Baton Rouge, 1981-82; clin. supr. off-site clin. tng. program La. State U. Med. Ctr., 1983-86; program com. chair Gov.'s task force La. Conf. for Disabled Persons, 1986; mem. Hosp./Sch. Linkage Com., 1991-95; mem. program com. Internat. Brain Injury Symposium, 1991; adj. instr. comm. disorders La. State U. Med. Ctr., 1992-95. Contbr. articles and revs. to profl. publs. Mem. Coalition for Citizens with Disabilities, 1983-95; vol. speech pathologist Op. Smile, 1996—; chair Op. Smile Speech Pathology Coun., 1998—; co-founder Op. Smile Speech Therapy, Vietnam, 1998—. Phi Mu-Mary King Shepardson fellow, 1978; recipient Disting. Alumnus award, Vanderbilt U. Med. Ctr., Divsn. Hearing and Speech Scis., 2002. Mem. Am. Speech-Lang.-Hearing Assn. (clin. reviewer 1977-85, assoc. editor 1986-90, spl. interest groups speech scis. and orofacial disorders, neurol. scis. and disorders, swallowing and swallowing disorders, lang. and multicultural populations), Am. Speech and Hearing Found. (Louis DiCarlo award for recent clin. achievement 2001, State award for recent clin. achievement 2001), Brain Injury Assn., La. Speech and Hearing Assn. (rehab. and med. agys. com. 1984-2000, chair 1996-98, Spl. Recognition award 2000, La. DiCarlo Clin. Achievement award 2001), La. Head Injury Found. (co-founder 1983, coord., pres. 1983-86, bd. dirs. 1986-95, sec., bd. dirs. 1987-90, program co-chair ann. conf. 1990, 91, 92, pres. 1993-94, Profl. of Yr. 1991), New Orleans Neuropathology Interest Group. Avocations: traveling, reading, music, family, friends. Office: Ochsner Clinic Found 6-South 1514 Jefferson Hwy New Orleans LA 70121-2483 E-mail: caducote@yahoo.com., caducote@aol.com., cducote@ochsner.org.

DUCRAN, CLAUDETTE DELORIS, retired financial analyst; b. Trinityville, St. Thomas, Jamaica, July 23, 1941; came to U.S., 1962; d. Wellesley Provan and Hilda Maude (Beckford) DuC. Student, Corcoran Sch. Art, Washington, 1967; cert. of diploma, USDA Grad. Sch., Washington, 1972; student, Harvard U., 1976; BBA, George Washington U., 1982; postgrad., Columbia U., 1987. Adminstrv. asst. World Bank, Washington, 1964-75, fin. asst., 1975-85, ops. asst., 1985-88, disbursement asst., 1988-94, disbursement analyst, 1994-96; ret., 1996. Mem. adv. com. Very Spl. Arts Kennedy Ctr., Washington, 1990-93, Hands Across Hemisphere Craft Ctr., Washington, 1991; founder, pres. Let's Learn by Reading, Jamaica, 1990-2000. Author: Exhibitors Guidelines, 1989, 2d edit., 1990. Bd. dirs. Craft Ctr., Washington, 1991-99; panelist Career Week George Washington U., Washington, 1991, Women's Ctr., McLean, Va., 1991; founder, pres. The Claudette D. Ducran Found., Inc., Kingston, Jamaica, W.I., 1995-2001, Eureka Alliance, Inc., Washington, 1995—. Recipient 1st prize Writer's League, Washington, 1967, Internat. Order of Merit, 1994; named Internat. Woman of Yr., 1993-94. Mem.: World Bank 1818 Soc., World Bank Art Soc. (v.p. 1986—88, pres. 1988—93), Soc. for Internat. Devel., World Affairs Coun., Jamaica C. of C. (hon. Washington rep. 1997—). Avocations: performing and visual arts, children, travel, working with handicapped, international development. Home: The Brighton 2123 California St NW Apt B1 Washington DC 20008-1804

DUCREST, WILLIS FRANCIS, retired music educator; b. St. Martinville, La., Dec. 13, 1910; s. Frank Martin D. and Anna Loretta Moutom; m. Grace Simons, Dec. 23, 1948; children: Stephen, Frank David, Ted Albert. BM, La. State U., 1932, MM, 1933; postgrad., Ind. U., Bloomington, 1950. Instr. voice (chorus) La. State U., Baton Rouge, 1934—37; asst. prof. voice (choir) Okla. Coll. for Women, Chickasha, 1940—43; assoc. prof. voice (choir) U. Southwestern La., Lafayette, La., 1943—45, prof., dir. music, head dept., 1945—77, prof. emeritus, 1977. Arranger: choral music 18 arrangement fro G. Schirmer 1963—69. Mem. Lafayette Auditorium Commn., Cajun Dome Bldg., Bldg. Com. Sgt. USN, 1944—45. Named to La. Music Edn. Hall of Fame, 1984—85; recipient honor, Endowed Music Scholarship, 1999, Ducrest Young Artist Internat. Competition established in his honor, Acadiana Symphony Assn., 1999, award for outstanding contribution music in band field, Phi Beta Mu. Mem.: La. Music Tchrs. Assn. (hon. Citation 1977), Nat. Arts Assn. (hon.), Music Tchrs. Nat. Assn. (life; nat. treas. 1979—87, pres. 1965—67, 1967—69), La. Music Tchrs. Assn. (life), Nat. Arts Assn. (life), Phi Kappa Phi, Phi Mu Alpha Sinfonia (hon.), Phi Mu Alpa Sinfonia (life), Sigma Alpha Iota (hon.), Democrat. Roman Catholic. Avocations: genealogy, philately. Home: 103 Tackaberry Rd Lafayette LA 70503

DUDA, JOHN LARRY, chemical engineering educator; b. Donora, Pa., May 11, 1936; s. John Jr. and Nellie (Tihanski) D.; m. Margaret K. Barbalich, Jan. 27, 1962; children: John Eric, David Andrew, Paul Laurence, Laura Margaret. BSChE, Case Inst. Tech., Cleve., 1958; MSChE, U. Del., 1961, PhD in Chem. Engring., 1963. Chem. engr. Dow Chem. Co., Midland, Mich., 1963-64, rsch. engr., 1964-69, sr. rsch. engr., 1969-71; assoc. prof. chem. engring. Pa. State U., University Park, 1971-75, prof., 1975—, head dept., 1983-2000. Contbr. articles to profl. jours. Fellow AIChE (co-recipient William H. Walker award 1981, Charles Stine award 1989, dir. materials divsn. 1990—, mem. coun. 1996—, dir. nat. 1996—); mem. Am. Chem. Soc. (E.V. Murphree award, 2000), Am. Soc. Engring. Edn. (Lectureship award 1989, Nat. Acad. Engring. W.K. Lewis award 1994), Soc. Petroleum Engrs., Soc. Plastic Engrs., Soc. Tribology and Lubrication Engrs. Home: 602 Holmes St State College PA 16803-3619 Office: Pa State U Dept Chem Engring 160 Fenske Lab University Park PA 16802-4400 E-mail: jld@psu.edu.

DUDA, RICHARD FRANK, architect, engineering executive; b. New York, Sept. 23, 1923; s. Frank and Emma Louise Duda; m. Wynema Jane Bond, May 3, 1945; children: Wynema Jane, Richard Frank, Lesley June, Desiree Joan. Cert. in Meteorology, NYU, 1944; BS in Chem. Engring., Rensselaer Poly. Inst., 1948. Registered profl. engr., NY. Project engr. Kellex-Vitro Engring. Co., NYC, 1948-54; project mgr. Vitro Engring. Co., NYC, 1954-62, chief process engr., mgr. chem. programs, 1962-67; project mgr. Parsons-Jurden, NYC, 1967-68; project dir. Nuc. Materials and Equipment Co., Apollo, Pa., 1968-70; mgr. facilities design and constrn. nuc. fuel divsn. Westinghouse Power Sys., Monroeville, Pa., 1970-73, engring. mgr. Recycle Fuels Group, nuc. fuel divsn., 1973—79, mgr. fuel cycle planning Advanced Energy Sys. divsn., 1980-84; cons. Fuel Cycle Svc. Inc., Greensburg, Pa., 1984-85; project mgr. Ralph M. Parsons Co., Pasadena, Calif., 1985-90, v.p., 1990-94; cons. Westinghouse-Savannah River, Aiken, SC, 1994-99, SC&A Inc., McLean, Va., 1994-99. Liaison chmn. industry interface State Dept. and Arms Control Agy., 1983-84; nuclear industry expert US Internat. Nuclear Fuel Cycle Evaln. Asst. scoutmaster Boy Scouts Am., Paramus, NJ, 1960-62, cubmaster, 1960. 1st lt. USAF, 1943-46. Mem. ASTM, Am. Nuc. Soc. (mem. com. 1981-82, mem. std. N287 cirteria for design of mixed oxide fuel plants com. 1982-83, mem. com. fuel cycle and waste mgmt. divsn. 1982-84, tech. reviewer Nuc. Tech. 1983-85), ASTM (chmn. std. E909-83 1983), Inst. Nuc. Materials Mgmt. (mem. exec. com. 1983-84, chmn. sub-com. govt. liason 1984) Republican. Presbyterian. Achievements include project engineering for 1st Pu reprocessing plant, for first nerve gas plant, for many first-of-a-kind plants. Avocations: gardening, reading. Home: 4421 Calm Water Ct Orlando FL 32817

DUDASH, KAREN SHREFFLER, community health nurse; b. Melrose Park, Ill., Mar. 15, 1947; d. Keith Donald and E. Ruth (Kraemer) Shreffler; m. Joseph F. Dudash, Feb. 23, 1985; 1 child, Ryan Matthew. BS in Nursing, Northeast Mo. U., 1970. Staff nurse gastro-intensive ICU Hines (Ill.) VA Hosp., 1970; staff/charge nurse Story County Hosp., Nevada, Iowa, 1972-73; sch. nurse Lenox (Iowa) Community Sch. System, 1971-72; staff/charge nurse med.-surg. Mercy Hosp., Cedar Rapids, Iowa, 1973-85; Staff/charge nurse oncology med.-surg. Franklin Square Hosp., Balt., 1985-86; home health nurse Balt. County Health Dept., Balt., 1987—, Johns Hopkins Home Health, 1993—. Mem. Assn. for Home Care, Inc. (rep.), Northeast Mo. U. Alumni Assn.

DUDASH, LINDA CHRISTINE, insurance executive; b. Pitts. d. Andrew Daniel and Lillian (Reynolds) D. BA in English, Point Park Coll., 1969. Tech. writer Am. Insts. for Rsch., Pitts., 1968-69; claim svc. rep. Reliance Ins. Co., Pitts., 1969-70, claim rep., 1970-71, claim mgr. Jacksonville, Fla., 1971-73, Harrisburg, Pa., 1973-80, Chgo., 1980-86; maj. case unit mgr. Zurich Ins. Co., Schaumburg, Ill., 1986-88, asst. v.p., mgr. liability claims, 1988-91, asst. v.p., mgr. claims continuous improvement, 1991-92; v.p. dir. field ops. Zurich-Am. Ins., Schaumburg, Ill., 1992-95; sr. v.p. claims Casualty Ins. Co., divsn. Fremont Compensation Ins. Co., Chgo., 1995—2000; sr. v.p., chief claims officer Fremont Compensation Ins. Group, Glendale, Calif., 2000—. Office: Fremont Compensation Ins Group 500 N Brand Blvd Glendale CA 91203-3392 E-mail: ldudash@fremontcomp.com.

DUDDECK, HEINZ WERNER, civil engineering educator; b. Sensburg, Germany, May 14, 1928; m. Marianne Lindhofer, 1956; children: Beat, Fabian. Diploma in civil engring., Tech. U. Hannover/U. Bristol, Eng., 1955, Habilitation, 1963; DEng, Tech. U. Hannover, Germany, 1959; DEng (hon.), U. Karlsruhe, Germany, 1988. Teaching asst. Tech. U. Hannover, 1956-59; rsch. assoc. Stanford (Calif.) U., 1959-61; cons. engr. Emch and Berger, Bern, Switzerland, 1961-63; engring. specialist Beton and Monierbau AG, Düsseldorf, Germany, 1963-65; prof. structural analysis Tech. U. Braunschweig, Germany, 1966-96. Cons. civil engr., Braunschweig, 1980—; chmn. Reform Edn. in Civil Engring., 1979-90; mem. senate Deutsche Forschungsgemeinschaft, 1978-84. Contbr. over 200 articles on analysis, edn. and tunnelling to profl. jours., chpts. to books. Mem. Internat. Assn. Rock Mechanics, Austrian Soc. Geomechanics, Internat. Assn. Bridges and Structural Engring., Internat. Assn. Tunnelling Design (chmn. working group 1978-95), Braunschweig Sci. Assn., Berlin-Brandenburg Acad., Acad. Europaea. Home: Greifswaldstr 38 38124 Braunschweig Germany Office: Tech U Braunschweig Beethovenstr 51 D-38106 Braunschweig Germany

DUDDEN, ARTHUR POWER, historian, educator; b. Cleve., Oct. 26, 1921; s. Arthur Clifford and Kathleen (Bray) D.; m. Adrianne Churchill Onderdonk, June 5, 1965; 1 child, Alexis Dudden; children by previous marriage: Kathleen Dudden Rowlands, Candace L. Dudden (Schweitzer). AB, Wayne State U., 1942; A.M., U. Mich., 1947, PhD, 1950. Faculty Bryn Mawr Coll., 1950—, prof. history, 1965-92, Fairbank prof. humanities, 1989-92, Katharine E. McBride prof. history, 1992-95, 98-99, prof. emeritus history and Fairbank prof. emeritus humanities, 1992—. Instr. CCNY, summer 1950; vis. asst. prof. Am. civilization U. Pa., 1953-54, ednl. coord. spl. program Am. civilization, 1956, mem. faculty Inst. Humanistic Studies for Execs., 1953-59, vis. assoc. prof. history, summers, 1958, 62-65, vis. prof. history, 1965-68; vis. assoc. prof. Princeton (N.J.) U., 1958-59, Haverford Coll., 1962-63; vis. prof. Trinity Coll., summer 1965; cons. Peace Corps, 1962-66; mem. Bicentennial Com. on Internat. Confs. of Americanists, 1973-76; founding pres. Fulbright Assn. of Alumni, 1976—, exec. dir., 1980-84; cons. Nat. Archives, 1993-95; adj. prof. history Lehigh U., 1993-95. Author: Teachers Manual to the American Republic, vols. I and II, 1959, 60, 70, Understanding the American Republic, vols. I and II, 1961, 70, Objective Tests, The American Republic, 1962, The Assault of Laughter, 1962, The United States of America: A Syllabus of American Studies, 2 vols, 1963, The Instructor's Guide to the United States, 3d edit, 1972, The Student's Guide to the United States, 2d edit, 1967, Joseph Fels and the Single Tax Movement, 1971, Pardon Us, Mr. President!, 1975, The Fulbright Experience, 1946-1986, 1987, American Humor, 1987, The American Pacific, 1992, paperback edit., 1993; editor: Woodrow Wilson and the World of Today, 1957, The Logbook of the Captain's Clerk, 1995; compiler: International Directory of Specialists in American Studies, 1975; contbr. Ency. Am. Social History, 1993, Ency. U.S. Fgn. Rels., 1997. Served with USNR, 1942-45. Sr. Fulbright scholar Denmark, 1959-60 and West Europe, 1992. Mem. Fellows Am. Studies (sec.-treas. 1957-59, pres. 1960-61), Am. Studies Assn. (treas. 1968, 72, exec. sec. 1969-72, Bode-Pearson prize 1991), Am. Hist. Assn., Orgn. Am. Historians (local arrangements chmn. Phila. 1969), Harriton Assn. (bd. dirs. 1962—), Hist. Soc. of Pa. (trustee 1993-99). Home: 829 Old Gulph Rd Bryn Mawr PA 19010-2910 E-mail: adudden@brynmawr.edu.

DUDEK, HENRY THOMAS, management consultant; b. Queens, N.Y., Dec. 29, 1929; s. Wojciech and Magdalena (Swiader) D.; m. Olga Waranitsky, June 14, 1953; children: Kathryn, Nancy, Linda, Andrew, Henryk. BBA, CCNY, 1955. Acctg. mgr. A.D.T. Co., N.Y.C., 1948-54; asst. controller Dancer Fitzgerald Sample, Inc., N.Y.C., 1955-60; chief fin. officer Wunderman Ricotta & Kline, Inc., N.Y.C., 1961-69, Van Brunt & Co., N.Y.C., 1970; controller, stockholder Compton Advt., Inc., N.Y.C., 1971; pres., chief exec. officer Henry T. Dudek & Assocs., Inc., Floral Park, N.Y., 1972—. Frequent speaker on finance and advt. Mem. Advt. Agy. Fin. Mgmt. Assn. (bd. dirs.). Roman Catholic. Home: 90 Beech St Floral Park NY 11001-3103 Office: PO Box 478 Floral Park NY 11002-0478

DUDEK, RICHARD ALBERT, engineering educator; b. Clarkson, Nebr., Sept. 3, 1926; s. Emil E. and Jennie (Indra) D.; m. Helen M. Staver, Dec. 19, 1954; children: Richard Emil, Rustin Max. BS in Mech. Engring., U. Nebr.,

1950; MS in Indsl. Engring., U. Iowa, 1951, PhD, 1956. Plant indsl. engr. Fairmont Foods Co., Sioux City, Iowa, 1951-52, div. indsl. engr. Omaha, 1952-53; research asst. U. Iowa, 1953-54; asst. prof. mech. engring. U. Nebr., 1954-56; research assoc. Sch. of Health Professions, also asso. prof. indsl. engring. U. Pitts., 1956-58; prof., head dept. indsl. engring. Tex. Tech U., Lubbock, 1958-86; dir. Ctr. of Biotech. and Human Performance, 1969-74, P.W. Horn prof., 1970-92, P.W. Horn prof. emeritus, 1992—. Tech. cons. industry, instns., religious orgns., hosps., 1951—; instr. TV courses; dir. Found. Internat. Rsch. and Devel., Lubbock, 1960-65, MASET, Inc., Lubbock, 1974-85, Jay Bee Mfg. Inc., Tyler, Tex., 1984-86, Cellular Tech., Inc., Lubbock, 1984-88, Rowden Gas Inc., Lubbock, 1986-92, Sone Energy, Inc., Dallas, 1988-94. Mem. editl. bd. Engring. Costs and Prodn. Econs., 1980-94; contbr. articles to profl. jours. Bd. dirs. South Plains chpt. Muscular Dystrophy Assn. Am., 1966-76, campaign chmn., 1968. Recipient Faculty Recognition award, 1978, Disting. Scientist award Achievement Rewards for Coll. Scientists, 1984, award of Excellence Halliburton Edn. Found., 1987; named South Plains Engr. of Yr. Tex. Soc. Profl. Engrs., 1986. Fellow Am. Inst. Indsl. Engrs. (pres. Great Plains chpt. 1960-61, chmn. nat. student chpt. 1961-63, ECPD guidance rep. 1965-68, research com. 1967-69, regional v.p. 1969-71, Appreciation award 1970, spl. service award 1971); mem. Council Indsl. Engring. Acad. Dept. Heads (asst. sec. 1980, sec. 1981-82, vice chmn. 1982-83, chmn. 1983-84), Am. Soc. Engring. Edn. (editor indsl. engring. div. 1965-66, sec. indsl. engring. div. 1966-67, vice chmn. 1967-68, chmn. 1968-69, chmn. planning com. of council of tech. divs. 1970-71, sec. council 1972-73), Inst. Mgmt. Sci., ASME, Human Factors Soc., Tech. Assessment Soc., Sigma Xi (pres. Tex. Tech. chpt. 1971-72), Tex. Tech. Acad. Indsl. Engrs., Phi Kappa Phi (chpt. pres. 1967), Pi Mu Epsilon, Pi Tau Sigma, Alpha Pi Mu, Tau Beta Pi, Phi Beta Delta. Home: 3707 46th St Lubbock TX 79413-3446 E-mail: kgric@ttacs.ttu.edu.

DUDEN, PAUL RUSSELL, lawyer, managing partner; b. Portland, Oreg., Sept. 1, 1940; s. Harold Pennoyer Duden and Helen Pearson Campbell; m. Martha Anderson, Nov. 9, 1985 (dec.); children: Emily, Andrew, Lessie, Gurney; m. Francesca Frost, June 29, 2003. BS, U. Oreg., 1963, LLB, 1966. Bar: Oreg. 1966, U.S. Dist. Ct. Oreg. 1966, U.S. Ct. Appeals (5th cir.) 1966, U.S. Supreme Ct. 1977. Assoc. Tooze, Kerr, Tooze & Peterson, Portland, 1966-70, ptnr., 1970-72; mng. ptnr. Tooze, Duden, Creamer, Frank & Hutchinson, Portland, 1972—2002; ptnr. Duden Neiman LLP, Portland, 2003—. Bd/. dirs. Riverdale Sch. Dist., Portland, 1972-80; commr. Palatine Hill Water Act, Portland, 1982—; bd. dirs. Easter Seal Soc. Oreg., 1967—. Fellow Am. Coll. Trial Lawyers; m. Am. Bd. Trial Advocates, Internat. Assn. Def. Counsel, Def. Rsch. Inst. Home: 250 SW Carey Ln Portland OR 97219-7973 Office: Duden Neiman LLP 333 SW Taylor St Portland OR 97204-2413 E-mail: pduden@duden-neiman.com.

DUDENHOEFFER, FRANCES TOMLIN, physical education educator; b. San Antonio, Aug. 8, 1943; d. Arthur Reader and Annie Beatrice (Everett) Tomlin; m. Arthur Wood Dudenhoeffer, July 17, 1976. BS in Edn., S.W. Tex. State U., San Marcos, 1965; MS in Phys. Edn., U. N.C., Greensboro, 1967; PhD, U. Tex., 1977. Cert. recreational sports specialist; cert. tchr., Tex.; mem. cast My Three Angels prodn. Eastside Ch. of Christ, 2002. Grad. asst. U. N.C., Greensboro, 1965-66; instr. U. Okla., Norman, 1966-70, asst. prof., 1970-72; recreational sports specialist U. Tex., Austin, 1971-72, grad. asst., 1973-74; lectr., women's intramural dir. U. North Tex., Denton, 1974-76; intramural dir. N.Mex. State U., Las Cruces, 1976-97; field staff Kappa Delta Pi Internat., 1998-2000. Mem. intramural task force Las Cruces Pub. Schs., 1987-89; content rev. panel N.Mex. Dept. Edn., Santa Fe, 1984; expert witness Lea County Atty., Lovington, N.Mex., 1988. Author: (manual) Intramural Staff Handbook, 1992; editl. com.: Navigating the Tides of Change, 1994; editor/author: (pamphlet) Guidelines for Intramural Programs, 1992; contbr. articles to profl. jours. Bd. dirs. Los Amigos de Krwg, Las Cruces, 1994-97. Recipient Excellence in Programming Nat. Intramural Sports Coun., Reston, Va., 1989, Disting. Alumnus in Phys. Edn. award S.W. State U., San Marcos, Tex., 1990, Disting. Svc. award Nat. Assn. Sports and Phys. Edn., Reston, Va., 1993, Ft. Bliss Fed. Credit Union Svc. award for N.Mex. State U. Profl. Staff, 1996. Mem. AAHPERD (pres. S.W. dist. 1992-93, Honor award 1994, reviewer Jour. of PERD 1997—), Nat. Intramural Recreational Sports Assn. (state dir. 1994-96, editl. bd. NIRSA Jour. 1996-99), N.Mex. Assn. Health, Phys. Edn., Recreation and Dance (pres. 1988-89, Honor award 1989), Kappa Delta Pi (chpt. counselor 1987-97), Phi Delta Kappa, Alpha Xi Delta Alumnae Assn. (publicity chair Pike's Peak chpt. 1999-2003, pres. 2003—). Avocations: stamp collecting and exhibiting, racquetball, golf, badminton. Home: 4980 Molly Pond Ct Colorado Springs CO 80917-1045 E-mail: f.dudenhoeffer@att.net.

DUDERSTADT, JAMES JOHNSON, academic administrator, engineering educator; b. Ft. Madison, Iowa, Dec. 5, 1942; s. Mack Henry and Katharine Sydney (Johnson) D.; m. Anne Marie, June 24, 1964; children: Susan Kay, Katharine Anne. B in Engring. with highest honors, Yale U., 1964; MS in Engring. Sci, Calif. Inst. Tech., 1965, PhD in Engring. Sci. and Physics, 1967. Asst. prof. nuclear engring. U. Mich., 1969—72, assoc. prof., 1972—76, prof., 1976—81; dean U. Mich. (Coll. Engring.), 1981—86; provost, v.p. acad. affairs U. Mich., 1986—88, pres. univ., 1988—96, pres. emeritus, prof. sci. engring., 1996—. Dir. Millennium Project, 1996—. AEC fellow, 1964-68; recipient E. O. Lawrence award U.S. Dept. Energy, 1986, Nat. medal of Tech., 1991; named Nat. Engr. of Yr., NSPE, 1991. Fellow Am. Nuclear Soc. (Mark Mills award 1968, Arthur Holly Compton award 1985); mem. NAE (coun.), Am. Phys. Soc., Nat. Sci. Bd. (chair 1991-94), Am. Acad. Arts & Scis., Sigma Xi, Tau Beta Pi, Phi Beta Kappa. Office: Millennium Project 2001 Media Union Ann Arbor MI 48109*

DUDGEON, THOMAS CARL, judge; b. Oak Park, Ill., Oct. 3, 1952; s. Harold Arthur and Elizabeth Ann (Bode) D.; m. Britt Lin Gilbertz, Sept. 12, 1981; children: Elizabeth Lin, Grant Arthur. Student, Am. U., 1972; BA summa cum laude, Augustana Coll., 1974; JD, Drake U., 1977. Bar: Ill. 1977, U.S. Dist. Ct. (no. dist.) Ill. 1977, U.S. Ct. Appeals (7th cir.) 1988. Assoc. O'Reilly & Cunningham, Wheaton, Ill., 1977-85; ptnr. O'Reilly, Cunningham, Duncan & Huck, Wheaton, 1985-87, Richter, Jaros & Dudgeon, Oak Brook, Ill., 1987-92; assoc. judge 18th Jud. Cir. Ct., DuPage County, Ill., 1992—. Mem. Ill. Bar Assn., DuPage County Bar Assn., Phi Beta Kappa, Omicron Delta Kappa. Lutheran. Avocations: bicycling, reading, backpacking, photography. Office: 505 N County Farm Rd Wheaton IL 60187-5112

DUDICK, MICHAEL JOSEPH, retired bishop; b. St. Clair, Pa., Feb. 24, 1917; s. John and Mary (Jurick) D.. BA, Ill. Benedictine Coll., Lisle, 1943; postgrad., St. Procopius Sem., Lisle, 1943—45; HHD (hon.), Kings Coll., 1987; DD (hon.), Scranton U., 1989. Ordained priest Roman Cath. Ch., 1945. Vice chancellor Exarchate of Pitts., 1946—55; chancellor Diocese of Passaic, NJ, 1963—68, bishop, 1968—96; ret., 1996. Mem. N.J. Coalition of Religious Leaders; cons. ecumenical and interreligious com. Nat. Conf. Cath. Bishops, 1986—96. Bd. regents Seton Hall U. Seton Hall U., 1968—96. Roman Catholic.*

DUDICS-DEAN, SUSAN ELAINE, interior designer; b. Perth Amboy, N.J., Oct. 22, 1950; d. Theodore W. and Joyce M. (Ryals) D.; m. Rick Dean, Apr. 30, 1989; 1 child, Merissa Joyce. BS in Sociology, W.Va. U., 1972; postgrad., Rutgers U., 1975-78, U. Calif., Irvine, 1979-81, Can. Coll., 1981-89. Programmer Prudential Life, Newark, 1972-73; sr. sys. analyst Johnson & Johnson, New Brunswick, N.J., 1978-78, Sperry Univac, Irvine, 1978-80; sr. sys. analyst, project leader Robert A. McNeil, San Mateo, Calif., 1981-83; dist. design dir. TransDesigns, Woodstock, Ga., 1982-93; prin. Celestial Designs, 1980—; cons. So. Living at Home, 2001—. Lectr., spkr. in the field of interior design, sales and Feng Shui, 1986—; dir. So. Living at Home. Writer Drapery and Window Coverings, Design Lines, Window Fashions Mag., Designer Lines; guest on TV shows House Doctor, Marketplace Sta. KGO-TV; contbr. articles to profl. jours. High sch. mentor Directions, San Francisco, 1985-95. Recipient awards TransDesigns, Woodstock, 1984-87, 89-91, MoonRise Galleries, 1994-99. Mem. Women Entrepreneurs (membership com., treas. 1983-87), Romance Writers Am., Washington Romance Writers, Ctrl. N.J. Alumni Assn. Delta Gamma (assoc. sec., founder, pres.), Am. Soc. Interior Designers (allied mem. 1989-92), Profl. Bus. Women's Assn., Delta Gamma. Avocations: sewing, scuba diving, ballet, handcrafts.

DUDLEY, BROOKE FITZHUGH, educational consultant; b. East Orange, NJ, Oct. 22, 1942; s. Benjamin William and Jean (Peeples) D.; m. Elizabeth Slater; 1 child, Catherine Sanford. AB in Econs., Colgate U., 1966. Sales mgr. De La Rue Instruments, Phila., 1968-71; comml. banker Bankers Trust Co., N.Y.C., 1966-68, Provident Nat. Bank, Phila., 1972-74; dir. admissions/fin. aid St. Stephen's Episc. Sch., Austin, Tex., 1974-78; exec. dir. U. Tex. Law Sch. Found., Austin, 1978-85; ednl. cons., 1982—; founding ptnr. The Edn. Group Southwest, Inc., 1989-92; exec. dir. San Antonio Art Inst., 1992-93; founding ptnr. Peninsula Group, 1999—. Chmn. bd. trustees Austin Evaluation Ctr.; trustee Austin Repertory Theater; chmn. bd. dirs. All Saints Episc. Day Sch., Austin; Bishop's com. St. Michael's and All Angels Episcopal Ch., Blanco, Tex.; bd. dirs. Symphony Sq., Austin Child Guidance and Evaluation Ctr.; adv. trustee Winston Sch., San Antonio; Rep. campaign mgr., NYC, 1966-68; trustee Rio Blanco Montessori Sch.; founding chmn. bd. trustees Ind. Ednl. Cons. Found. With U.S. Army, 1962-64. Mem. Ind. Ednl. Cons. Assn. (past chmn. bd. trustees, found. chmn. bd. trustees), Hill Sch. Alumni Assn. (exec. com. 1968-71), Edna Gladney Austin Aux. (past pres.). Episcopalian. Office: PO Box 867 Blanco TX 78606 E-mail: dudley@moment.net.

DUDLEY, CRAIG JAMES, retired executive recruiter; b. Pendleton, Oreg., July 19, 1930; s. Craig James and Elizabeth (Thieman) Dudley; m. Alta Mae McKelvey, June 21, 1952 (div. Nov. 1974); children: Erin Maureen, Craig James; m. Grace Vota, May 30, 1975. BS, U. Oreg., 1955; B in Fgn. Trade, Am. Inst. Fgn. Trade, 1958. Counselor Marion County Juvenile Dept., Salem, Oreg., 1955-57; v.p., gen. mgr. ESB Inc., Phila., Monterrey, Mex., 1958-69; v.p. Boydon Latin Am., Mexico City, 1970-75; pres., ptnr. Conrey-Paul Ray, Mexico City, 1975—2002; ret., 2002. Bd. dirs. Ray & Berndtson Internat. Chmn. United Way, Mexico City, 1987, 1988. With U.S. Army, 1952—54. Named one of Am.'s Top 150 Exec. Recruiters, Career Makers, 1994—. Mem.: Am. C. of C. Mex. (bd. dirs. 1983—85, 1987), Am. Soc. Mex. (pres. 1989, 1990), Club Indsl.-Mex. Republican. Avocations: hiking, golf, fishing.

DUDLEY, DON, broadcast journalist, communications consultant; b. Beaufort, N.C., Oct. 18, 1961; s. Donnie L. and Sara Parkin (Brooks) D. BS in Broadcast Journalism, Boston U., 1984. Reporter, bur. chief Sta. WCSH-TV, Portland, Maine, 1984-85, Stas. WBTW-TV/WSPA-TV, Columbia, S.C., 1985-93; anchor, reporter Sta. WSPA-TV, Spartanburg, S.C., 1993-94; prodr., reporter News Channel 8, Washington, 1994-96; sr. prodr. programming NET Polit. News Talk Network, Washington, 1996-97; news dir., corr. Network USA Aviation News, Washington, 199-99; pres. Don Dudley Group, LLC, 1999—2000; exec. prodr. News 12 Networks, News 12 Westchester, N.Y.C., 2002—. Adj. prof. journalism Coll. Journalism, U. Md., 1998-99. Author: The Dynamic Action Diet: Discover Your Diet Personality, 1994. Bd. dirs. Dynamic Concepts, Inc., Spartanburg, 1993-95, The Agy. for Internat. Understanding, Spartanburg, 1993-95, Piedmont chpt. ARC, Spartanburg, 1993, co-chmn. cmty. rels. bd., 1992-93; hon. chmn. Mobil Meals Found., Greenville-Spartanburg, 1993; master of ceremonies Miss S.C. Pageant, Greenville, 1993-94. Recipient Vol. award ARC, Spartanburg, 1993, Spot News Coverage 1st pl. award Maine Assn. Broadcasters, Portland, 1985, Pub. Svc. award Carolina Power Squadron, Greenville, 1993. Mem. NATAS, Soc. Profl. Journalists (bd. dirs. D.C. Pro chpt. 1997-98, v.p. 1999, pres. 1999-00, immediate past pres., Dateline Awards Banquet chair), Nat. Press Club, Radio-TV News Dirs. Assn., Washington Corrs. Assn., Nat. Press Club. Episcopalian. Home: 1155 Warburton Ave Ste 4G Yonkers NY 10701 Office: 6 Executive Plz Yonkers NY 10701 E-mail: dldudley@news12.com.

DUDLEY, DORIS S. music educator, small business owner; b. Honolulu, July 11, 1931; d. Matsutaro and Yoshiko Kamioka; m. Michael Kioni Dudley, Aug. 11, 1981; children from previous marriage: Luis Kazuo San Miguel, Daniel Kenji San Miguel. At, Oberlin Conservatory of Music, Ohio, 1949—52, Geneva Conservatory of Music, Switzerland, 1951; MusB in edn., U. Colo., Boulder, 1962. Cert. profl. in music edn. Hawaii, 1965. Sch. music specialist Dept. of Edn., Honolulu, 1967—80, dist. resource music tchr., 1981—83, sch. music specialist, 1983—87; instr. keyboard and piano Leeward CC, Pearl City, Hawaii, 1988—92, Spl. Sr. Program, Pearl City, Hawaii, 1988—92, self-employed, Kapolei, 2000—; piano tchr. Barberis Pt. Elem. Sch., Kapolei, 2003—; piano instr. Kapoli Comty. Sch. Adults, 2000—. Adjudicator Leeward dist. Spring Festival Dept, of Edn., Honolulu, 1981—87; adjudicator Sterling award Brigham Young U., Laie, 1983—84; condr. Pianomania at Concert Hall, Honolulu, 2002. Dist. 20 chmn. Rep. Party of Hawaii, 1997—99; bd. sec. Palehua Vista Assn., Kapolei, 2000—02. Recipient Tchr. of the Yr., Mai'ili Elem. Sch., 1979. Mem.: Hawaii Music Tchrs. Assn. Avocations: musical activities, fitness, plants, church choir and accompanist. Home: 92-1365 Hauone St Kapolei HI 96707

DUDLEY, DURAND STOWELL, librarian; b. Cleve., Feb. 28, 1926; s. George Stowell and Corinne Elizabeth (Durand) D.; m. Dorothy Woolworth, July 3, 1954; children: Jane Elizabeth, Deborah Anne. BA, Oberlin Coll., 1948; MLS, Case Western Res. U., 1950. Librarian, Marietta (O.) Coll. Library, 1953-55, Akron (O.) Pub. Library, 1955-60; librarian Marathon Oil Co., Findlay, O., 1960-74, sr. law librarian, 1974-86; supr. tech. services dept. Findlay-Hancock County Pub. Library, Findlay, 1986-88. Mem. Spl. Libraries Assn. Presbyterian (deacon). Home: 807 Red Maple Ct Bluffton OH 45817-8551

DUDLEY, ELIZABETH HYMER, retired security executive, community volunteer; b. Hibbing, Minn., Mar. 12, 1937; d. Howard Golden and Esther Juliette (Wanner) Hymer; m. Richard Walter Dudley, 1962. BA, Brown U., 1959; postgrad., U. Calif., Berkeley. With AT&T Bell Labs., MurrayHill, N.J., 1959-89, systems programmer, personal info., 1965-67, systems analyst, personnel info., 1967-71, sr. systems analyst, mgmt. info. and adminstrv. systems, 1971-77, applications systems coord. mgmt. info./adminstrv. systems, 1977-78, group supr. affirmative action compliance and reports, 1978-81, group supr. service ops. system support group, 1982-84, mgr. security, 1984-85, mgr. govt. security, 1986-89, ret., 1989. Bd. dirs. Boca Ballet Theatre Co., 1994—, 1st v.p., 1998—; treas. Fla. Atlantic U. Vol. League, 1993-94; chmn. boutique Boca Ballet Guild, 1994, pres. 1994-97, v.p. membership, 1997-98, treas. 2000-02; treas. Boca Raton Hist. Soc. Gala, 2003. Recipient Boca Ballet Vol. of Yr. award, 2001. Mem. Humanitarian Soc., Nat. Soc. Arts and Lettters (2d v.p. 1998-99, v.p. 1999-2000, chair South Fla. ballet competition), Brown Nat. Alumni Sch. Coms., Nat. Security Indsl. Assn., Women's Rights Assn. (treas. 1977, v.p. 1978), Am. Soc. Indsl. Security, Nat. Classification Mgmt. Soc., Brown Network, Royal Palm Improvement Assn. (bd. govs., chair environ. inspection 1993-94, v.p., 1994, pres. 1994-96, chmn. security 1994), Friends of Boca Pops (governing coun.), Pembroke Coll. of N.J. Club (publicity chmn. 1965-69, v.p. 1969-70), U. Club Fla. Atlantic U. (corr. sec. 1999-2000), Lucia Chase Soc. (Am. Ballet Theatre).

DUDLEY, GARY EDWARD, clinical psychologist; b. Columbus, Ohio, July 19, 1947; s. Ray Leonard and Mary Virginia (Russi) D.; m. Linda Jean Patterson, June 21, 1969; children: Michelle Denise, Karen Elizabeth. BS, Ohio State U., 1969; MS, U. Miami, 1972, PhD, 1975. Lic. psychologist, Ga., Fla. Tchr. Columbus pub. schs., 1969-70; intern in clin. psychology Mt. Zion Hosp. and Med. Ctr., San Francisco, 1972-73; clin. psychologist Met. Dade County Jail, Miami, Fla., 1974-76, Southeast Inst. Criminal Justice, Miami, 1974-76, Ga. So. U., Statesboro, 1976-80; pvt. practice clin. psychology Marietta, Ga., 1980—. Cons. Child Devel. Ctr., Ga. Psycho-Ednl. Network, Atlanta; exec. v.p. The Psychol. Advantage, Inc.; dir. svcs. Atlanta Area Psychological Assocs., P.C.; pres. Accurate Assessment Svcs. Atlanta. Contbr. articles to profl. jours. NIMH fellow, 1971, 73, VA fellow, 1971. Mem. Am. Psychol. Assn., Nat. Acad. Neuropsychologists, Am. Bd. Med. Psychotherapists, Southeastern Psychol. Assn., Ga. Psychol. Assn., Nat. Honor Soc. Psychology, Sigma Xi. Office: Doctors Bldg/Windy Hill 2520 Windy Hill Rd Ste 203 Marietta GA 30067-8650 E-mail: gdudleys@mindspring.com.

DUDLEY, GEORGE AUSTIN, architect, planning consultant, educator; b. Pitts., Dec. 24, 1914; s. Samuel William and Mabel Eva (Allen) D.; children: George Bergin, Sally Jean, John Phillips, Samuel William III. BA, Yale U., 1936, B.F.A. in Arch, 1938, M.F.A. in City Planning, 1940. With Office Coordinator of Inter-Am. Affairs, 1941-45; dir. research Conn. Post War Planning Bd., 1944-45; with archtl. firm Harrison & Abramovitz, N.Y.C., 1945-48, 59-60; sec. internat. bd. design UN Hdqrs., 1945-46; pres. IBEC Housing Corp., 1948-59; cons. Internat. Devel. Adv. Bd., 1951; dir. N.Y. State Office Regional Devel.; also sec. Planning Coordination Bd., 1960-62; trustee N.Y. State U. Constrn. Fund; planning coordinator N.Y. State South Mall, 1962-65; dean Sch. Architecture, Rensselaer Poly. Inst., 1962-65; founding dean Sch. Architecture and Urban Planning, U. Calif. at Los Angeles, 1965-68; chmn. N.Y. State Pure Waters Authority, 1967-70; pres. N.Y. State Environ. Facilities Corp., 1970-72; chmn., chief exec. officer N.Y. State Council on Architecture, 1967-75; sr. cons. and phys. planning officer Kuwait Inst. Sci. Research, 1977-80; cons. master planning Saudi Arabian Nat. Center Sci. and Tech., Riyadh, 1980-84, Amanat Al-Asima, Baghdad, Iraq, 1980-85; advisor master planning King Abdulaziz U., Jeddah, Saudi Arabia, 1986-88. Lectr. USIS/ICA, Brazil, Venezuela, Trinidad, Honduras, Mexico, India, Singapore, Malaysia, Indonesia, S. Korea, Hong Kong, Japan; mem. U.S. del. UN Conf. Human Settlement, Vancouver, 1976 Author: A Workshop for Peace/Designing the United Nations Headquarters, Architectural History Foundation, 1994, Dudley's Drawings, A Retrospective View, 2001; co-author: he Case for Regional Planning, 1947; contbg. editor: Architecture Plus. Trustee Inst. Architecture and Urban Studies, 1968-78; bd. dirs. AIA Found.; mem. overseers vis. com. Harvard Grad. Sch. Design, 1974-79; chmn. Yale Council Com. for Architecture and Art, 1970-75. Fellow AIA; mem. Nat. Acad. Design (assoc.). Home: Hickory Hill Rensselaerville NY 12147 also: 1 W 67th St New York NY 10023-6200 E-mail: gadudley@aol.com.

DUDLEY, GEORGE ELLSWORTH, lawyer; b. Earlington, Ky., July 14, 1922; s. Ralph Emerson and Camille (Lackey) D.; m. Barbara J. Muir, June 28, 1950 (dec. Feb. 1995); children: Bruce K., Camille Dudley McNutt, Nancy S., Elizabeth Dudley Stephens. BS in Commerce, U. Ky., 1947; JD, U. Mich., 1950. Bar: Ky. 1950, D.C. 1951, U.S. Dist. Ct. (we. dist.) Ky. 1962, U.S. Ct. Appeals (6th cir.) 1987. Assoc. Gordon, Gordon & Moore, Madisonville, Ky., 1950-51; pvt. practice law Louisville, 1952-59; ptnr. Brown, Ardery, Todd & Dudley, Louisville, 1959-72, Brown, Todd & Heyburn, Louisville, 1972-92, of counsel, 1992—, mem. mgmt. com., 1972-90, chmn., 1989-90. Pres. Ky. Easter Seal Soc., Louisville, 1971-72; treas. Ky. Dem. Party, Frankfort, 1971-74; bd. dirs. Alliant Adult Health Svcs., Louisville, 1976—; 1st v.p. Nat. Easter Seal Soc., Chgo., 1981. Capt. inf. U.S. Army, 1943-46, ETO; capt. JAGC, U.S. Army, 1951-52. Mem. ABA, Ky. Bar Assn., Louisville Bar Assn., U.S. 6th Cir. Jud. Conf. (life), Harmony Landing Country Club (pres. 1978-79), Tavern Club, Barristers Soc., Omicron Delta Kappa. Presbyterian. Avocations: golf, tennis, travel, sports spectator. Home: 1905 Crossgate Ln Louisville KY 40222-6405 Office: Frost Brown Todd 3200 Aegon Center Louisville KY 40202

DUDLEY, KATHRYN MARIE, anthropology and American studies educator; b. Dec. 9, 1958; BA in Psychology, U. Wis., Milw., 1984; MA in Anthropology, Columbia U., 1987, PhD in Anthropology, 1991. Adj. asst. prof. anthropology Columbia U., N.Y.C., 1991—93; from asst. prof. to assoc. prof. anthropology Yale U., New Haven, 1993—2002, prof. anthropology and Am. studies, 2002—. Author: The End of the Line: Lost Jobs, New Lives in Post-Industrial America, 1994, Debt and Dispossession: Farm Loss in America's Heartland, 2000. Recipient Harry Chapin Media award, 1995, Margaret Mead award, 2000. Mem. Phi Beta Kappa. Office: Yale U Dept Anthropology PO Box 208277 New Haven CT 06520-8277

DUDLEY, KENNETH EUGENE, manufacturing company executive; b. Bellville, Ohio, Nov. 26, 1937; s. Kenneth Olin and Ethel Elizabeth (Poorman) D.; m. Judith Ann Brown, Apr. 15, 1972; children: Camaron J. McCluggage, Kenneth Alan. Inventory control mgr. Gorman-Rupp Industries, Bellville, 1958-67, prodn. mgr., 1967-69, mgr. data processing, 1969-74, cost mgr., 1974-78, contr., 1978-82; treas., chief fin. officer Gorman-Rupp Co., Mansfield, Ohio, 1982—. With USAF, 1962-63. Republican. Lutheran. Home: 1855 Chapelwood Blvd Mansfield OH 44907-2205

DUDLEY, PERRY, JR., retired electronics executive; b. New Haven, June 5, 1928; s. Perry and Ella (Leach) D.; m. June Ungar, Feb. 13, 1993; children: Bruce Lawrence, Virginia Barbara (from previous marriage). BSEE, Purdue U., 1952; MBA, Santa Clara U., 1966. Sales engr. Reliance Elec. Co., Cleve. and L.A., 1952-60, GTE Sylvania, Burlingame, Calif., 1960-65; sr. applications engr. Varian Assocs., Palo Alto, Calif., 1965-68; product mgr. Ampex Corp., Redwood City, Calif., 1968-70; program mgr. Genesys Sys., Inc., 1972-73; indsl. real estate broker, salesman, 1974-80; program mgr. Dalmo Victor Ops., Bell Aerospace Divsn., Textron, 1980-85; mktg. and program mgr. Loral Data Sys., San Diego, 1986-88; mgmt. cons. San Diego, 1989-94; real estate agent Prudential Atlanta Realty, 1995-96; program mgr. EMS Scis., Norcross, Ga., 1996-97; plan owner GTE Wireless, 1997-2000; financial svcs. rep. South Trust Bank, 2000—02, ret., 2002. Instr. mktg. and mgmt. San Francisco State U., 1982, West Coast U., 1990-94. Pres. Young Rep. Club, Pasadena, Calif., 1959; precinct capt. Menlo Park (Calif.) Rep. Com., 1961-72; elder Presbyn. Ch. With USN, 1946-48. Mem. Nat. Assn. of Mgmt., Assn. of Old Crows, North Fulton County Rep. Club, Purdue Alumni Club (pres. 1959), Mensa, Phi Gamma Delta. Avocations: sailing, cruising. Home: 12130 Winding Woods Way Bradenton FL 34202-2872

DUDLEY, RICHARD GEORGE, fisheries and natural resources consultant; b. New Rochelle, N.Y., Mar. 25, 1945; s. John Chapman and Flora Helen (Ehrsam) Dudley; m. Carol Jean Pierce-Colfer, Feb. 2, 1985; m. Christina Cranston Gillis, July 6, 1968 (div. 1982); children: Brian, Amy. BS, Cornell U., 1967, MS, 1969; PhD, U. Idaho, 1972. Cert. fishery scientist Am. Fisheries Soc. Asst. prof. U. Ga., Athens, 1972—80, Oreg. State U., Corvallis, 1980—82, Semarang, Indonesia, 1982—85, assoc. prof. Muscat, Oman, 1986—90; pvt. practice internat. cons., 1990—. Small scale fisheries cons. USAID/Oreg. State U., Semarang, 1982—85, team leader fishery rsch., Muscat, 1986—90; team leader conservation ODA/Wetlands Internat., Sintang, Indonesia, 1992—93; team leader marine sci. edn. ADB/Eduplus, Jakarta, Indonesia, 1994—95. Contbr. articles to profl. jours. Fellow: Am. Inst. Fishery Rsch. Biologists. Avocations: sailing, gardening, fishing, photography.

DUDLEY, RICHARD MANSFIELD, mathematician, educator; b. East Cleveland, Ohio, July 28, 1938; s. Winston Mansfield and Charlotte Mae (Wheaton) D.; m. Elizabeth Allen Martin, June 3, 1978. AB, Harvard U., 1959; PhD, Princeton U., 1962. Asst. prof. math. U. Calif., Berkeley, 1963-66; asso. prof. MIT, 1967-72, prof., 1972—. Author: Real Analysis and Probability, 1989, 2d edit., 2002, Uniform Central Limit Theorems, 1999; editor: White Mountain Guide, 1979, Annals of Probability, 1979—81. Alfred P. Sloan Found. fellow, 1966-68, Guggenheim Found. fellow, 1991. Fellow AAAS, Am. Stats. Assn., Inst. Math. Stats.; mem. APHA, Am. Math. Soc., Bernoulli Soc., Internat. Stats. Inst. Democrat. Home: 92 Lewis St Newton MA 02458-1840 Office: MIT 77 Massachusetts Ave Rm 2-245 Cambridge MA 02139-4307

DUDLEY, RICK, professional hockey coach; b. Jan. 31, 1949; Player Am. Hockey League, Internat. Hockey League, World Hockey Assn., Cleve., Cin., 1969-79, Buffalo Sabres, NHL, 1979-80, head coach, 1989-96; player Winnipeg (Man., Can.) Jets, NHL, 1981; coach Atlantic Coast Hockey League, Internat. Hockey League, Am. Hockey League, 1982-89; v.p., gen mgr Ottawa Senators, 1996-99; gen. mgr., v.p. Tampa Bay Lightning, 1999—. Office: Tampa Bay Lightning 401 Channel Dr Tampa FL 33606

DUDLEY, WILLIAM SHELDON, historian; b. Bklyn., July 14, 1936; s. William Henry and Dorothy (Lawson) D.; m. Julia Bartel, Aug. 21, 1965 (dec.); children: Jennifer Bee, Mary Megan; m. Donna Tully, Feb. 20, 2001 BA, Williams Coll., 1958; MA, Columbia U., 1966, PhD, 1972. History tchr. Poly. Prep. County Day Sch., Bklyn., 1963-66; asst. prof. History So. Meth. U., Dallas, 1970-77; supervisory historian Naval Hist. Ctr., Washington, 1977-82, head early history br., 1982-90, sr. historian, 1990-95, dir., sr. exec. svc., 1995—. Editor: Naval War of 1812, vol. 1, 1985, vol. 2, 1992, vol. 3, 2002. Pres. Bach Meistersingers, Annapolis, 1985-87; mem. Md. Adv. Com. for Archaeology. Lt. USNR, 1959-63. Recipient Samuel Eliot Morison award USS Constitution Mus., 1993, Nat. Trust for Historic Preservation, Nat. Pres. awards U.S.S. Constn., 1997, H.L. Hunley Recovery, 2002. Mem. Am. Revolution Roundtable (pres. 1987), Soc. History in the Fed. Govt. (pres. 1989-90, Thomas Jefferson prize 1993), Md. Hist. Soc. (maritime com. 1994—), N.Am. Soc. Oceanic History (pres. 1999—), Mass. Hist. Soc. (corr. mem.). Avocations: sailing, gardening, choral music. Home: 4420 Cobalt Dr Harwood MD 20776 Office: Naval Hist Ctr 805 Kidder Breese St SE Washington DC 20374-0001

DUDMAN, RICHARD BEEBE, journalist; b. Centerville, Iowa, May 3, 1918; s. Virgil Ernest and Wilma (Beebe) D.; m. Helen Sloane, Mar. 14, 1946; children: Iris Janet Sloane, Martha Tod. BA, Stanford U., 1940; LLD (hon.), U. Mo., St. Louis, 1979. Reporter, photographer Oroville (Calif.) Mercury-Register, 1937; reporter Denver Post, 1945-49, St. Louis Post-Dispatch, 1949-53, Washington corr., 1954-68, bur. chief, 1969-81; chmn. bd., treas. Dudman Communications Corp., Ellsworth, Maine, 1981-92, chmn. emeritus, 1992-99. Mem. adv. com. Nieman Found. for Journalism, 1977-81; trustee South-North News Svc., 1985-95, pres., 1987-90, mng. editor, 1987-95; cons. to Washington Bur., St. Louis Post Dispatch, 1997; editl. writer Bangor (Maine) Daily News, 2000--. Author: Men of the Far Right, 1962, 40 Days with the Enemy, 1971, also articles. Trustee Washington Journalism Ctr., 1974-92, Inst. Current World Affairs, 1983-89, 95-98; bd. dirs. Downeast Family YMCA, Ellsworth, 1987-91; pub. mem. Maine Lobster Promotion Coun., 1991-2000. With USNR, 1942-45. Recipient award Asia Overseas Press Club, 1972, Edward Weintal award, 1979, Mo. medal U. Mo., 1981, Gold Polk Career award, 1993; Nieman fellow Harvard U., 1953-54, Knight Internat. Press fellow, South Africa, 1994, 96. Mem. Nat. Assn. Broadcasters (First Amendment com. 1985-89). Clubs: Gridiron (Washington). Lodges: Rotary. Avocations: sailing, boat building.

DUDNIKOV, VADIM G. physicist, researcher; b. Gunda, Buryat, Russia, Sept. 15, 1943; came to U.S., 1995; s. Georgy V. and Klavdiya P. (Bambakova) D.; m. Galinai Sapozhnikova; children: Andrei, Irina. M degree, Novosibirsk State U., 1965; PhD, Inst. Nuclear Physics, Novosibirsk, 1967. Sr. scientist Inst. Physics, Novosibirsk, 1967-78, head lab., 1978-92; prof. Novosibirsk State U., 1986-89, head gen. physics, 1989-92, prof., 1993-95; vis. scientist Oak Ridge (Tenn.) Nat. Lab., 1993, Brookhaven Nat. Lab., Upton, N.Y., 1992-93, U. Md., College Park, 1995; chief scientist Superior Design, Inc., Peabody, Mass., 1995-98; pres. Sci. Tech. Cons., Beverly, Mass., 1998; scientist Fermi Nat. Accelerator Lab., Batavia, Ill., 1999—. Inventor charge exch. injection, method negative ion prodn., and surface-plasma sources. Mem. Am. Phys. Soc. Avocation: history. Home and Office: 202 Townehouse Dr Coram NY 11727 E-mail: dvg43@yahoo.com.

DUDRICK, STANLEY JOHN, surgeon, scientist, educator; b. Nanticoke, Pa., Apr. 9, 1935; s. Stanley Francis and Stephania Mary (Jachimczak) D.; m. Theresa M. Keen, June 14, 1958; children: Susan Marie, Paul Stanley, Carolyn Mary, Stanley Jonathan, Holly Anne, Anne Theresa. BS cum laude, Franklin and Marshall Coll., 1957; MD, U. Pa., 1961; MA (hon.), Yale U., 1999. Diplomate Am. Bd. Surgery. Intern Hosp. of U. Pa., Phila., 1961-62, resident in gen. surgery, 1962-67; acad. practice specializing in surgery Phila., 1967-72, 88-90, Houston, 1972-88, 90-94, Waterbury, New Haven, 1994—, Bridgeport, 2000—; chief surg. svcs. Hermann Hosp., Houston, 1972-80, surgeon in chief, dir. Ctr. Cardiovascular Disease, dir. nutritional support svcs., dir. Nutritional Sci. Ctr., 1990-94; prof. surgery U. Tex. Med. Sch., Houston, 1972-82, clin. prof. surgery, 1982-95, chmn. dept. surgery, 1972-80. Cons. in surgery M.D. Anderson Hosp. and Tumor Inst., 1973-88, clin. prof. surgery, cons. to pres., 1982-88; sr. cons. surgery and medicine Tex. Inst. for Rehab. and Rsch., 1974-88; mem. Anatomical Bd., State of Tex., 1973-78; examiner Am. Bd. Surgery, 1974-78, bd. dirs., 1978-84, sr. mem. 1984-2000, also mem. and chmn. various coms.; chmn. sci. adv. com. Tex. Med. Ctr. Libr., 1974; mem. food and nutrition bd. NRC-Nat. Acad. Scis., 1973-75; mem. sci. adv. com. Nat. Found. for Ileitis and Colitis; mem. surgery, anesthesia and trauma study sect. NIH, 1982-86; chmn. dept. surgery Pa. Hosp., Phila., 1988-90, surgeon in chief, 1988-91, hon. surgery staff, 1991—; clin. prof. surgery U. Pa., 1988-93; assoc. chmn. dept. surgery, 1994-2000, 02--, dir. surgery program, 1994-2000, 02--, dir. Med. Edn., 1995-2000, 02--, St. Mary's Hosp., Waterbury, Conn.; clin. prof. surgery, Yale U., New Haven, Conn., 1995-99, prof. surgery, 1999—; chmn. dept. surgery, dir. surg. edn. Bridgeport Hosp.-Yale U. New Haven Health Sys., 2000-02; adj. prof. surgery Quinippiac U., 1996—. Editor: Manual of Surgical Nutrition, 1975, Manual of Preoperative and Postoperative Care, 1983, Current Strategies in Surgical Nutrition, 1991, Practical Handbook of Nutrition in Clinical Practice, 1994, Surgical Nutrition: Strategies in Critically Ill Patients, 1995; assoc. editor Nutrition in Medicine, 1975—; editorial bd. Annals of Surgery, 1975—, Infusion, 1978—, Nutrition and Cancer, 1980—, Nutrition Support Services, 1980-86, Jour. Clin. Surgery, 1980-83, Nutrition Research, 1981—, Intermed. Communications Nursing Services, 1981—, Postgraduate General Surgery, 1992—; others; contbr. chpts. to books, articles to profl. jours.; inventor of new technique of intravenous feeding and anti-cholesterol therapy. Bd. dirs. Found. for Children, Houston, Harris County unit Am. Cancer Soc., Phila. chpt., 1988-90; trustee Franklin and Marshall Coll., 1985—, mem. student life, art collection, and trusteeship coms., 1986-2002, mem. overseers bd., 1986-2002, exec. com. 1986-2002, alumni programs and devel. com., 1991—, pres. regional adv. coun., 1992—, vice chmn. 1994-2002, John Marshall Soc., 1993—; founder Benjamin Rush Soc., 1987, hon. chmn., 1999—, campaign nat. chmn., 1995-2002, campaign exec. com. chmn., 1995—, mem. bldgs. and grounds com., 2002--. Decorated knight Order St. John of Jerusalem Knights Hopitalier; recipient VA citation for significant contbn. to med. care, 1970; Mead Johnson award for rsch. in hosp. pharmacy, 1972; Seale Harris medal So. Med. Assn., 1973; AMA-Brookdale award in medicine, 1975; Great Texan award Nat. Found. Ileitis and Colitis, 1975; Modern Medicine award, 1977; Disting. Alumnus citation Franklin and Marshall Coll., 1980; WHO, Houston, 1980; Stinchfield award Am. Acad. Orthopedic Surgery, 1981; Bernstein award Med. Soc. State of N.Y., 1986, Alumni Svc. award U. Pa. Med. Sch., 1996, Excellence in Surgical Tchg. Awd., St. Mary's Hosp., 1999, Roswell Park award Buffalo Surgery Soc., 2000, numerous others. Fellow ACS (vice chmn. pre and post operative com. 1975, gov. 1979-85, com. on med. motion pictures 1981-90, SESAP com. 1990-94, co-chmn. multiple choice com. 1993-94, mem. Conn. chpt.), Philippine Coll. Surgeons (hon.), Coll. Medicine and Surgery of Costa Rica (hon.), Am. Coll. Nutrition (Grace A. Goldsmith award 1982), Phi Beta Kappa; mem. AMA (council on food and nutrition 1971-76, exec. com. 1975-76, council on sci. affairs 1976-81, Goldberger award in clin. nutrition 1970), AAAS, AAUP, Am. Surg. Assn. (Flance-Karl award 1997), Am. Acad. Pediatrics (hon., Ladd medal 1988), Am. Pediatric Surg. Assn. (hon.), Am. Soc. Nutritional Support Services (bd. dirs. 1982-87, pres. 1984, Outstanding Humanitarian award 1984) Soc. Univ. Surgeons (exec. council 1974-78), Assn. for Acad. Surgery (founders group), Internat. Soc. Surg., Internat. Fedn. Surg. Colls., Internat. Soc. Parenteral Nutrition (exec. council 1975-81, pres. 1978-81), Internat. Fedn. Surgery Soc., So. Med. Assn. (chmn. surgery sect. 1984-85), Houston Gastroent. Soc., Houston Surg. Soc., Tex. Surg. Soc., Tex. Med. Assn. (com. nutrition and food resources), Tex. Med. Found., Harris County Med. Soc., New Haven (Conn.) County Med. Soc., Conn. Soc. Am. Bd. Surgeons, New England Surg. Soc., Am. Radium Soc., Am. Soc. Clin. Oncology, Am. Soc. Parenteral and Enteral Nutrition (pres. 1977, bd. advs. 1978—, chmn. bd. advisers 1978, Vars award 1982, Rhoads lectr. 1985, Dudrick Rsch. Scholar award named in his honor), Penn. Nutritionists Soc. (pres. 1985), Am. Gastroent. Assn., Soc. Surg. Oncology, James Ewing Soc., Ravdin-Rhoads Surg. Assn., Excelsior Surg. Soc. (Edward D. Churchill lectr. 1981), Soc. Laparoendoscopic Surgery, Soc. Surg. Chairmen, So. Surg. Assn., Southwestern Surg. Congress, Southeastern Surg. Congress, Surg. Biology Club II, Surg. Infection Soc. (chmn. membership com. 1987-90), Western Surg. Soc., Halsted Soc., Allen O. Whipple Surg. Soc., Am. Inst. Nutrition, Soc. Clin. Surgery, Am. Soc. Clin. Investigation, Soc. for Surgery of Alimentary Tract, Am. Trauma Soc. (founders group), Am. Assn. for Surgery of Trauma, Soc. Clin. Surgery, Am. Soc. Clin. Nutrition, Fedn. Am. Soc. Exp. Biology, Am. Burn Assn., Assn. Program Dirs. Surgery (bd. dirs. 1998—), John Marshall Soc., Coll. Physicians Phila., Phila. Acad. Surgeons, George Hermann Soc., Union League Phila., Med. Club Phila., Franklin Club Phila., Houston Doctors Club (gov. 1973-76), Nat. Alumni Coun. U. Pa. Med. Sch. (chmn. 1994-2001), Conn. United for Rsch. Excellence (bd. dirs. 1995-2001), Waterbury Symphony Orch. (bd. dirs. 1999—, chmn. endowment com. 2002—), Cosmos Club, Athenaeum, The Penn Club (charter), Phi Beta Kappa Assocs., Sigma Xi, Alpha Omega Alpha. (sec.-treas. Houston chpt. 1982-83), Home: 40 Beecher St Naugatuck CT 06770-2721 Office: St Mary's Hosp 56 Franklin St Waterbury CT 06706- E-mail: sdudrick@stmh.org.

DUDROW, PETER WARREN, human resources executive, consultant; b. Bath, Maine, Oct. 13, 1935; s. Daniel Edward and Barbara Joan (Lemen) D.; m. Jewell Gloria Glover, Mar. 31, 1955 (div. Apr. 1975); children: Rebecca, Michelle, Laura, Leah, William; m. Nancy Carol Chirdon, Apr. 1, 1978 (div. May 1988). BSBA in Pers. Mgmt., La. State U., 1960; MBA, Wayne State U., 1964. Pers. mgmt. Chrysler Corp., Highland Park, Mich., 1960-66; sr. cons. A. T. Kearny & Co., Inc., Chgo., 1966-72; dir. compensation and benefits Northwest Industries, Chgo., 1972-75; cons. Dept. Def., Washington, 1975-78; mgr. exec. compensation and pers. practices Peat, Marwick, Mitchell & Co., N.Y.C., 1978-81; v.p. Mgmt. Consulting Divsn. Alexander and Alexander, Greenwich, Conn., 1981-83; prin. Human Resource Assocs. Am., Denville, N.J., 1983—. Contbr. articles to profl. jours. Mem. Dist. 57 Pub. Sch. Bd., Mount Prospect, Ill., 1970-73; bd. dirs., chmn. pers. com. Somerset Coun. Alcoholism and Drug Abuse, Somerville, N.J., 1992-95; bd. dirs., steering com. YMCA, local ch. Career Forum, Bernardsville, N.J., 1991-95; past chmn. bd. dirs. Encompass, the Music Theater, 1979-81. Col. U.S. Army, ret., 1955-95. Mem. Free Masons, Sojourners. Republican. Presbyterian. Avocations: golf, squash, bridge, nature hiking. Home: 68 Franklin Rd Denville NJ 07834-1557 E-mail: petedudrow@aol.com.

DUDUIT, MICHAEL, editor, university administrator; b. Sandwich, Ill., Aug. 18, 1954; s. James Loren and Sarah Lee (Baker) D.; m. Laura Ann Niemann, Aug. 10, 1959; 1 child, James Robert. BA in Speech, Stetson U., 1975; MDiv, So. Bapt. Sem., Louisville, 1979; PhD in Humanities, Fla. State U., 1983. Ordained to ministry Bapt. Ch., 1977. News dir. So. Bapt. Sem., Louisville, 1975-77; dir. pub. affairs Palm Beach Atlantic Coll., West Palm Beach, Fla., 1977-80; asst. to pres. Cuneo Advt., Tallahassee, 1980-81; assoc. pastor Immanuel Bapt. Ch., Tallahassee, 1981-84; dir. comms .So. Bapt. Sem., 1984-87; dir. devel. Samford U., Birmingham, Ala., 1987-93; exec. v.p. Union U., Jackson, Tenn., 1996—2001; pres., CEO Preaching Resources, Inc., Brentwood, Tenn., 2002—; editor Preaching Mag., Jackson, 1985—. Author: Joy in Ministry, 1991; editor: Handbook of Contemporary Preaching, 1993, Abingdon Preaching Annual, 1995, 96, 97, 98, 99, Communicate with Power, 1996. Mem. Bapt. Communicators Assn. (pres. 1994-95), Acad. of Homiletics, Religious Speech Comm. Assn., Evang. Homiletics Soc., Rotary. Office: Preaching Resources Inc 1600 Westgate Cir Ste 275 Franklin TN 37067 E-mail: mduduit@ix.netcom.com.

DUDUKOVIC, MILORAD P. chemical engineering educator, consultant; b. Beograd, Yugoslavia, Mar. 25, 1944; arrived in U.S., 1968; s. Predrag R. and Melita Maria Dudukovic; m. Judith Ann Reiff, Dec. 27, 1969; children: Aleksandra Anne, Nicole Maria. BS in Engring., U. Beograd, 1967; MS, Ill. Inst. Tech., 1970, PhD, 1972. Rsch. engr. Process Design Inst., Beograd, 1967-68; instr. Ill. Inst. Tech., Chgo., 1970-72; asst. prof. Ohio U., Athens, 1972-74; assoc. prof. Washington U., St. Louis, 1974-80, prof., dir., 1980—, Laura and William Jens prof. environ. engring., 1993—, chmn. dept. chem. engring., 1998—. Cons. in field. Assoc. editor: Indsl. and Engineering Chemistry Research, 1991—; contbr. articles to profl. jours. Recipient Burlington No. Found. Tchg. award, 1986, Nat. Catalyst award Chem. Mfrs. Assn., 1988, St. Louis award ACS, 1995, Malcolm E. Pruitt award Coun. Chem. Rsch., 1999; 2 NASA certs. of recognition and citations; Fulbright scholar Inst. for Higher Edn., 1968. Fellow AIChE (R.H. Wilhelm award 1994), St. Louis Acad. Scis.; mem. AAAS, Am. Chem. Soc., Am. Assn. Engring. Edn., Yugoslav Acad. Engring. (fgn. mem.), Sigma Xi, Century Club (St. Louis). Achievements include pioneering work on trickle bed reactors, bubble columns; research in Czochralski crystal growth, novel experimental techniques for multiphase reactors; environmentally benign processing. Office: Washington U Dept Chem Engring Campus Box 1198 One Brookings Dr Saint Louis MO 63130-4899 E-mail: dudu@poly1.che.wustl.edu.

DUDYCHA, ANNE ELIZABETH, retired special education educator; b. Rockford, Ill., Aug. 15, 1934; d. O. Garfield and Agnes Marie (Anderson) Beckstrand; m. W. Johnson, 1956 (div. Nov. 1978); children: Carole, Deanna, Sheila; m. Lee Dudycha, Feb. 1993. BA, Carthage Coll., 1956; MEd, U. Minn., 1982. Cert. tchr., emotional/behavioral disorders, dir. spl. edn., learning disabilities. Tchr., English Edn. Han. Jr. H.S., Lancaster, Pa., 1956-57; home bound. Hopkins and St. Louis Park (Minn.) Sch. Dists., 1971; tchr., spl. edn., adolescent therapy program Golden Valley (Minn.) Health Ctr., 1972-77, tchr., spl. edn., 1977-80, 82-85; tchr., spl. edn., emotional and behavioral disorders Robbinsdale (Minn.) Jr. H.S., 1977-79, Sandburg Mid. Sch., Golden Valley, 1979-93, spl. edn. adminstrv. liaison, 1990-92, behavior specialist, cons., 1992-93, dist. spl. edn. coord., 1993-96; ret., 1996. Lectr. Carthage Coll., Kenosha, Wis., 1996-2002; program com. mem. Devel. Severely Emotionally Disordered, Robbinsdale, 1985-86, 90-96; com. mem. Program and Curriculum for Implementation of Mid. Sch., Robbinsdale, 1986-87. Mem. design com. Holy Nativity Luth. Ch., New Hope, Minn., 1987-90, co-chmn. fund drive, 1987, mem. coun., 1988-93, pers. com., 1985-96, mem. choir, 1970-96. Mem. Minn. Educators Emotionally Disordered (profl. growth chmn. 1982-83), Minn. Coun. Children-Behavioral Disorders (pres. 1987-88, advocacy com. 1989-96), Minn. Assn. Mid. Level Edn. (bd. dirs. 1991-94), Phi Kappa Phi. Avocations: concerts, plays, reading, walking, hand work.

DUDZIAK, DONALD JOHN, nuclear engineer, educator; b. Alden, N.Y., Jan. 6, 1935; s. Joseph and Josephine Mary (Ratajczak) D.; m. Judith Ann Staib, Aug. 22, 1959; children: Alan Joseph, Matthew John, Karin Marie. BS in Marine Engring., U.S. Mcht. Marine Acad., 1956; MS in Radiation Biology/Radiol. Physics, U. Rochester, 1957; PhD in Applied Math., U. Pitts., 1963. Registered profl. engr., Calif. Commd. ensign USN, 1956, advanced through grades to capt.; sr. engr. Bettis Atomic Power Lab., Pitts., 1957-65; staff mem. U. Calif.-Los Alamos (N.Mex.) Nat. Lab., 1965-68, 69-74, assoc. and alt. group leader, 1974-78, group leader, 1978-82, dep. group leader, sect. leader, 1982-88, lab. fellow, 1988—; ret. USN, 1995; prof., head dept. nuclear engring. N.C. State U., Raleigh, 1990—2001; pres. Pinorealosa Corp, 1989-90. Vis. prof. U. Va., Charlottesville, 1968-69; adj. prof. U. N.Mex., 1966, Kans. State U., 1989-90; guest scientist Swiss Fed. Inst. Reactor Rsch., Wuerenlingen, 1981-82; mem. lab. microfusion facility steering com. U.S. Dept. Energy, 1986-90, inertial confinement fusion adv. com., 1992-96; vice-chair accelerator prodn. of tritium rev. panel Los Alamos Nat. Lab., 1995-98; chmn. fusion tech. working group Neutronics, Brookhaven, N.Y., 1975; mem. Nat. Nuc. Accrediting Bd., Nat. Acad. Nuc. Tng., 1998—; cons. nuclear power schs. USN, 1962-65; cons. Oak Ridge Nat. Lab., 1993-96, TSI Rsch. Co., 1992—, U.S. Nuclear Regulatory Commn., 1997, Am. Coun. on Edn., 1995—, Duke U., 1997-98. Editor: Reactor Principles, 1964, Radiation Shielding, 1964, Progress in Nuclear Energy, 1992—; contbr. editor Fusion Tech., 1987—; contbr. articles to profl. jours. Vice-chmn. Los Alamos County Planning and Zoning Commn., 1969-74. Fellow Am. Nuclear Soc. (divsn. chair 1972-73, 77-78, 92-93, gen. chair fusion energy divsn. nat. meeting 1994); mem. Am. Soc. Engring. Edn., U.S. Naval Inst., Los Alamos Sunrise Kiwanis (treas. 1987-89), Sigma Xi, Phi Kappa Phi. Office: Los Alamos Nat Lab Tech Assessment Group D-2 MS F609 Los Alamos NM 87545

DUDZIAK, MARY LOUISE, law educator, lecturer; b. Oakland, Calif., June 15, 1956; d. Walter F. Dudziak and Barbara Ann Campbell; 1 child, Alicia. AB in Sociology with highest honors, U. Calif., Berkeley, 1978; JD, Yale Law Sch., 1984; MA, MPhil in Am. Studies, Yale U., 1986, PhD in Am. Studies, 1992. Adminstrv. asst. to dep. dir. Ctr. Ind. Living, Berkeley, 1978-80; law clk., nat. legal staff ACLU, N.Y.C., 1983; law clk. Judge Sam J. Ervin, III Fourth Cir. Ct. Appeals, Morganton, N.C., 1984-85; assoc. prof. coll. law U. Iowa, Iowa City, 1986-90, prof. coll. law, 1990-98. Vis. prof. U. So. Calif., 1997-98, prof. U. So. Calif., 1998-2002, Judge Edward J. and Ruey L. Guirado prof. law and history, 2002-; mem. faculty senate task force on faculty devel. U. Iowa, 1989-90, mem. faculty welfare com., 1990-92, mem. faculty senate task force on faculty spouses and ptnrs., 1991-92, mem. presdl. lecture com., 1992-95; v.p. rsch. adv. com. in social scis., 1992-94; fellow law and pub. affairs program Princeton U., 2002; presenter in field. Author: Cold War Civil Rights: Race and the Image of American Democracy, 2000; editor, co-author: September 11 in History: A Watershed Moment?, 2003; mem. bd. mng. editors Am. Quar., 2003—; contbr. articles to profl. jours. Bd. dirs. Iowa Civil Liberties Union, 1987-88; chairperson office svcs. for persons with disabilities program rev. com., U. Iowa, 1987-88, law sch. ombudsperson, 1991. Charlotte W. Newcombe Doctoral Dissertation fellow Woodrow Wilson Fellowship Found., 1985-86; Old Gold fellow U. Iowa, 1987, 88, 89, Moody Grant Lyndon Baines Johnson Fdn., 1998, Theodore C. Sorenson Fell., JFK Libr. Fdn., 1997, Orgn. Am. Historians-Japanese Assn. for Am. Studies fellow 2000; travel grantee Eisenhower World Affairs Inst., 1993; recipient Scholars Devel. award Harry S. Truman Libr. Inst., 1990. Mem. Am. Soc. Legal History (mem. com. on documentary preservation 1988-2000, mem. program com. for 1988 conf., mem. exec. com., bd. dirs. 1990-92, 95-97, chairperson program com. 1993, mem. nominating com. 1999-2001, chair nominating com. 2001), Am. Hist. Assn. (Littleton-Griswold rsch. grantee 1987), Am. Studies Assn. (mem. nominating com. 1999-2002, chair nominating com. 2002), Assn. Am. Law Schs. (sec.-treas. legal history sect. 1987, vice chair 1988, chair 1989), Law and Soc. Assn. (mem. Hurst prize com. 1992), Orgn. Am. Historians, Soc. Am. Law Tchrs., Soc. for Historians Am. Fgn. Rels. Democrat. Office: U So Calif Law Sch Los Angeles CA 90089-0001 E-mail: mdudziak@law.usc.edu.

DUE, JEAN MARGARET, agricultural economist, educator; b. Peterborough, Ont., Can., Sept. 19, 1921; d. Allan B. and Katherine Jean (Calder) Mann; m. John F. Due, Aug. 18, 1950; children: Allan Malcolm, Kevin John Burritt. B.Com., U. Toronto, 1946; MS, U. Ill., 1950, PhD, 1953. Economist Dept. Agr., Ottawa, Ont., 1946-49; research asso. in home econs. U. Ill., 1959-61, vis. prof., 1965-70, prof. dept. agr. econs., 1970-90. Contbr. articles to profl. jours. Mem. African Studies Assn., Am. Econ. Assn., Am. Agrl. Econs. Assn., Internat. Assn. Agrl. Econs., Assn. Women Internat. Devel. Home: 1208 Clark Lindsey Village 101 W Windsor Rd Urbana IL 61802-6663 Office: Univ Illinois 305MH 1301 W Gregory Dr # 305mh Urbana IL 61801-9015 E-mail: jdue@uiuc.edu.

DUE, JOHN FITZGERALD, economist, educator emeritus; b. Hayward, Cal., July 11, 1915; s. Jackson Angelo and Emmarene (Hurd) D.; m. Margaret Jean Mann, Aug. 18, 1950; children: Nancy, Allan, Kevin. AB, U. Calif.-Berkeley, 1935, PhD, 1939; A.M., George Washington U., 1936. Instr. U. Utah, 1939-42, asst. prof., 1945-48; economist Treasury Dept., 1942; faculty U. Ill., 1948-86, prof. econs., 1951-86, prof. emeritus, 1986—, chmn. dept. econs., 1963-67, 71-72; acting dean Coll. Commerce U. Ill., 1976, 85-86. Author: Taxation and Economic Development in Tropical Africa, 1963, Indirect Taxation in Developing Economies, 2d edit., 1988; co-author: Sales Taxation: State and Local Structure and Operation, 1983, rev., 1994, The Electric Interurban Railway in America, 1960, Rails to The Ochoco Country-The City of Prineville Railway, 1968, Government Finance, 7th edit, 1981, Rails to the Mid Columbia Wheatlands, 1979, Roads and Rails South from the Columbia, 1991. Served with USMCR, 1942-45. Mem. Am. Econ. Assn., Nat. Tax Assn., Phi Beta Kappa. Home: 101 W Windsor Rd Apt 1208 Urbana IL 61802-6663 Office: Univ Ill Wohlers Hall 1206 S 6th St Champaign IL 61820-6978 E-mail: jdue@uiuc.edu.

DUECKER, ROBERT SHELDON, retired bishop; b. Medina County, Ohio, Sept. 4, 1926; s. Howard LaVerne and Sarah Faye (Simpson) D.; m. Marjorie Louise Clouse, June 13, 1948; children: Philip Lee, Christine Cay Duecker Isle. B in Religion, AB, Indiana Wesleyan U., 1948; BD, MS, Christian Theol. Sem., Indpls., 1952, DD (hon.), 1969; D in Pub. Svc. (hon.), Kendall Coll., 1996. Ordained to ministry United Meth. Ch., 1952. Pastor Dyer (Ind.) United Meth. Ch., 1952-54; sr. pastor Gethsemane United Meth. Ch., Muncie, Ind., 1954-62, Grace United Meth. Ch., Hartford City, Ind., 1962-65, 1st United Meth. Ch., Warsaw, Ind., 1965-70, Simpson United Meth. Ch., Ft. Wayne, Ind., 1970-72; dir. No. Ind. Conf. Coun. Ministries United Meth. Ch., Marion, 1973-77, dist. supt. No. Ind. Conf. Ft. Wayne, 1977-82; sr. pastor High St. United Meth. Ch., Muncie, 1982-88; bishop Chgo. area United Meth. Ch., 1988-96; ret., 1996; instr. Christian Theol. Sem., Indpls., 1998. Trustee United Theol. Sem., Dayton, Ohio, 1985-88, Kendall Coll., Evanston, Ill., 1988-96, North Ctrl. Coll., Naperville, Ill., 1988-96, Garrett Theol. Sem., Evanston, 1988-96; mem. gen. bd. publ. United Meth. Ch., 1988-92, gen. bd. higher edn. and ministry, 1992-96, univ. senate, 1992-96; mem. adv. coun. Ams. United for Separation of Ch. and State; instr. Christian Theol. Sem., Indpls., 1998. Author: Tensions in the Connection, 1982; also monographs. Mem. Kosciusko County Health Planning Coun., Warsaw, Ind., 1968—70; former pres. Delaware County Mental Health Assn., Muncie; bd. dirs. Goodwill Industries, Ft. Wayne, Ind., 1977—88, Parkview Hosp. Found., 1997—. Named Sagamore of the Wabash Gov. of Ind., 1988. Mem. Coun. of Religious Leaders of Met. Chgo. (pres. 1996—), Coun. Bishops United Meth. Ch., North Ctrl. Jurisdiction Coll. Bishops, Kiwanis, Rotary, Theta Phi. Methodist. Avocations: stamp collecting, golf. E-mail: rsduecker@aol.com.

DUEL, WARD CALVIN, retired health care consultant; b. Fond du Lac, Wis., Mar. 13, 1924; s. Myrton M. and Matie Rose (Tidyman) D.; m. Madelyn Mae Kressin, Oct. 1, 1950; children: Ward Rick, Christine Selma, Roxanne Matie, Beth Dawn. BS, U. Wis., 1950; postgrad., Marquette U., 1955-57; MPH, U. Calif., Berkeley, 1959. Registered environ. health specialist, Calif., Nat. Environ. Health Assn. Sanitarian City of Kenosha (Wis.), 1951-59; br. office mgr. Lake County Health Dept., Waukegan, Ill., 1959-65; dir. health Skokie (Ill.) Dept. Health, 1965-68, McHenry County Health Dept., Woodstock, Ill., 1968-70; asst. dir. pub. and environ. health AMA, Chgo., 1971-81; chief environ. health City of Chgo., 1981-82; dir. Mid-Ohio Valley Dept. Health, Parkersburg, W.Va., 1982-83; dir. environ. health, pub. and mental health Choctaw Indians, Philadelphia, Miss., 1984-85; cons. on environ. health to prisons, juv. detention ctrs. and mental hosps. in 44 states and D.C., 1985—2002; ret., 2002. Active Nat. Com. on Correctional Health Care; capt. U.S. Pub. Health Svc. Commn. Corps Res., 1958—; cons. in field; lectr. in field. Co-editor: Clinical Implications of Air Pollution Research; author monographs: Physicians Guide to Solid Waste, 1975, Physicians Guide to Air Pollution, 1973-80, Flood Area Health Guide, 1961; contbr. articles to profl. jours. Served in U.S. Army, 1945-46. Decorated 3 Battle Stars and Bronze Star for heroism; recipient Theta award Defenders, 1969, Samuel J. Crumbine award Single Svc. Inst., 1963, Walter S. Mangold award Nat. Environ. Health Assn., 1978, Outstanding Citizen award Ill. Dept. Edn., 1984, Jour. Environ. Health Editors award, 1979. Fellow Am. Pub. Health Assn. (task force correctional standards); mem. Nat. Environ. Health Assn. (pres. 1967-68), Wis. Environ. Health Assn. (pres. 1957-58), Ill. Environ. Health Assn. (pres. 1964-65), Am. Correctional Assn., Am. Jail Assn. (nat. stds. com. 1993—). Lutheran. Home and Office: 4907 N West St Mchenry IL 60050-7968 Fax: 847-497-3971.

DUELFER, CHARLES A. diplomat; b. Stamford, Conn., Sept. 18, 1952; s. Charles A. and Grace H. Duelfer; m. Michele McAuliff. BA, U. Conn., 1974; MS, MIT, 1977. Nat. security analyst Office of Mgmt. and Budget, Washington, 1977—82; polit.-mil. affairs officer U.S. State Dept., Washington, 1982—85; dir. Office of Internat. Security Policy U.S. Dept. State, Washington, 1985—90, dep. to asst. sec. of state, 1990—93; dep. chmn. UN spl. commn. on Iraq UN, N.Y.C., 1993—2000. Polit.-mil. expert various TV and radio programs, 2000—; vis. scholar Ctr. for Strategic and Internat. Studies, Washington, 2000—. Contbr. Mem.: Coun. Fgn. Rels. Avocations: skydiving, ice hockey, painting. Office: Ctr for Strategic and Internat Studies 1800 K St NW Washington DC 20006 Office Fax: 202-466-4740. Business E-Mail: cduelfer@csis.org.

DUELL, DANIEL PAUL, artistic director, choreographer, lecturer; b. Rochester, N.Y., Aug. 17, 1952; s. Seth Joseph and Ellen Catharine (Newton) D. Diploma, Profl. Children's Sch., N.Y.C., 1970; scholarship student, Sch. Am. Ballet, 1969-72. Mem., N.Y.C. Ballet, 1972-87, soloist, 1977-79, prin. dancer, 1979-87; choreographer in repertoire of Ballet Hispanico, N.Y., Dayton Ballet, Ballet Chgo.; mem. edn. dept., N.Y.C. Ballet; now artistic dir., choreographer Sch. Ballet Chgo. Mem. Sch. Am. Ballet Assn., Dance/USA, Chgo. Dance Coalition. Office: Ballet Chgo 218 S Wabash Ave Ste 300 Chicago IL 60604

DUEMLING, ROBERT WERNER, diplomat, museum director; b. Ann Arbor, Mich., Feb. 8, 1929; s. Werner William and Anne (Lindemulder) D.; m. Louisa duPont Copeland, May 15, 1982. BA, Yale U., 1950, MA, 1953; student, Cambridge U., Eng., 1950-51. Joined fgn. service Dept. State, Washington, 1957, with, 1957-60, 66-70, Am. embassy, Rome, 1960-63, Kuala Lumpur, 1963-65, Tokyo, 1970-74; U.S. consul Kuching, Malaysia, 1965-66; exec. asst. to dep. sec. state Dept. State, Washington, 1974-76; dep. chief of mission with rank of minister Am. embassy, Ottawa, Ont., Can., 1976-80; chief Fgn. Contingents, Multinat. Force and Observers, Sinai, 1981-82; U.S. ambassador to Suriname, to Paramaribo, 1982-84; dir. Nicaraguan Humanitarian Assistance Office, Dept. State, 1985-87; pres., dir. Nat. Bldg. Mus., Washington, 1987-94. Sr. fellow Washington Coll., 1983—, adj. prof., 2000—. Trustee Cafritz Found., Washington Nat. Monument Assn., Nat. Gallery of Art, Soc. Archtl. Historians. Served in U.S. Navy, 1953-57. Henry fellow, 1950-51; decorated Order of the Palm (Suriname). Fellow Royal Soc. for Arts (U.K.); mem. Washington Inst. Fgn. Affairs, Met. Club, Century Assn., Alibi Club. Home: 2950 University Te[illegible] NW Washington DC 20016-3461

DUENAS, LAURENT FLORES, health and nursing consultant; b. Yigo Guam, Jan. 9, 1947; d. Joaquin Garcia and Maria Acosta (Calvo) Flores; m Jimmy J. Duenas, Jan. 9, 1971; children: James Richard, Sherry Marie, Kenneth Ray. ADN, U. Guam, 1968; BSN, Mont. State U., 1969; MPH, U. Hawaii a

Manoa, 1984. RN, Guam, Mont.; CNA, NLN; cert. SMDP trainer, Internat. Pub. Health. Staff nurse nursing sect. Dept. Pub. Health and Social Svcs., Guam, 1969-70, nurse supr. I, 1970-71, nurse supr II, 1972-78, asst. adminstr. Bur. Community Health and Nursing Svcs., 1978-89, detailed adminstr., 1986-88, adminstr., 1989-95, ret., 1995. Health and nursing cons. Guam Legislature and U. Guam, 1996—; bd. dirs., chair Pacific Basin Maternal Child Health Resource Ctr., Mangilao, Guam, 1984-96, Pacific Basin MCH coord., Honolulu, 1984-95; mem. State and Territorial Dirs. Nursing, 1987-98; mem. Interagy. Leadership Consortium for Individual's with Spl. Needs, 1990—; mem. Maternal Child Health Task Force, 1996—, Gov.'s Vision 2000 Health Task Force, 1996-2000; chair Nurse Leaders Com., 1995-98, mem., 1998—; preceptor nursing students U.Guam, 1995—; presenter in field. Author: Caring for Young Children, modified version, 1998. Recipient Centennial award Nat. League of Nursing, 1994, Gov.'s Chief Gadao Disting. award, 1995. Mem. ANA, APHA, Y'netnon Famaloan-Dem. Women Leaders, Am. Pacific Nursing Leaders (coun. pres. 2001-, treas., 1986-92, vice mem. 1986—), Commn. on Licensure, Guam Bd. Nurses Examiners (bd. dirs., chair 1981-90), Guam Nurses Assn. (bd. dirs. 1992-94, Leadership award 1988, Nursing Excellence award 1990, Guam Nurse of Yr. 1993, Pub. Health Unit award 1994, Guam Legis. Resolution 1995, 98), Orgn. Health and Med. Prof. Women (treas. 2003—). Democrat. Roman Catholic. Avocations: crocheting, collecting recipes, baking, campaigning strategies, visiting sick. Home: 3 NC Yigo GU 96929 Office: 107-3 N Cupa Perez Acres Yigo GU 96929-0142 also: Univ of Guam Micronesian Health & Aging Studies UOG Station Mangilao GU 96923

DUENSING, DOROTHY JEAN, music educator, vocalist; d. George Prescott Duensing I and Patricia Ann (dec.) Gasthoff-Duensing, Catherine Dew-Duensing (Stepmother); m. Michael William Miller, Nov. 9, 1997; m. Thomas Andrew Cormie, Oct. 10, 1987 (div. Oct. 3, 1996); children: Morgan Elizabeth Miller, Mason Andrew Cormie. MusB, Ind. U., 1984; MusM, U. of Mich., 1990. Orff Schulwerk Music-Level I Madonna U., Livonia, Mich., 2001, Orff Schulwerk Music-Level II Madonna U., Livonia, Mich., 2002. Adj. prof. voice Wayne State U. Dept. of Music, Detroit, 1999—; educator, primary music dir. Acad. of the Sacred Heart, Bloomfield Hills, Mich., 2000—. Soprano soloist, sect. leader Christ Episcopal Ch., Dearborn, Mich., 1986—94; part-time voice faculty Ctr. for Creative Studies' Inst. of Music and Dance, Detroit, 1990—2000; alto soloist, sect. leader Temple Israel, West Bloomfield, Mich., 1991—97; artist-in-residence Toledo Opera Co., 1991—99; performing artist Omni Arts in Edn., Southfield, Mich., 1992—; full-time vocal music substitute U. Liggett Mid. and Upper Schools, Grosse Pointe Farms, Mich., 1996; part-time voice, piano faculty Ward Church's Christian Sch. of Fine and Performing Arts, Northville Twp., Mich., 1998—2002; adj. prof. voice William Tyndale Coll., Farmington Hills, Mich., 2001—02; alto soloist, sect. leader Met. United Meth. Ch., Detroit, 2001—02; soprano soloist, sect. leader First Presbyn. Ch., Royal Oak, Mich., 2002—. Choral music dir. Music Study Club, Detroit, 1995—96, Bel Canto Choral Group, Southfield, Mich., 1998—2001; deacon Faith Cmty. Presbyn. Ch., Novi, Mich., 1998—2000; teen choir dir. Faith Cmty. Presbyn., Novi, Mich., 1999—2000. Recipient Hazel Mueller Meml. award, Interlochen Ctr. for the Performing Arts, 1979, 1980, First Pl. Vocalist in the State of Mich., Mich. Schs. Vocal Music Assn., 1980, Dist. Finalist, Met. Opera Assn. (Midwest Dist.), 1991, Second Pl. Winner, Harold Haugh Light Opera Vocal Competition, Ann Arbor, MI, 2001; scholar Interlochen Alumnae Scholarship for Half Tuition at Nat. Music Camp, Interlochen Ctr. for the Performing Arts, 1979, Scholarship, Iota Epsilon Patroness Chpt., Bloomington, IN, 1983, Patricia Brinton-Becirovic Meml. Scholarship, Am. Inst. of Musical Studies, Austria, 1989. Mem.: Livonia Area Piano Tchrs. Forum, Mich. Music Tchrs. Assn., Music Tchrs. Nat. Assn., Detroit Orff Schulwerk Assn., Nat. Orff Schulwerk Assn., Nat. Assn. of Tchrs. of Singing, Nat. Fedn. of Music Clubs' Tuesday Musicale of Detroit, PEO Sisterhood, Chpt. FE, Novi, MI (life; chaplain 2001—02), Sigma Alpha Iota (life; iota epsilon chpt. pres. 1982—83, Sword of Honor 1983). Office: Wayne State U Dept of Music 1321 Old Main Bldg Studio #2315 Detroit MI 48202 Office Fax: 313-577-5420. Personal E-mail: divaduensing@aol.com.

DUER, ELLEN ANN DAGON, anesthesiologist, general practitioner; b. Balt., Feb. 3, 1936; d. Emmett Paul and Annie (Sollers) Dagon; m. Lyle Jordan Millan IV, Dec. 21, 1963; children: Lyle Jordan V, Elizabeth Lyle, Ann Sheridan Worthington.; m. T. Marshall Duer, Jr., Aug. 23, 1985. AB, George Washington U., 1959; MD, U. Md., 1964; postgrad., Johns Hopkins U., 1965-68. Intern Union Meml. Hosp., Balt., 1964-65; resident anesthesiology Johns Hopkins Hosp., Balt., 1965-68, fellow in surgery, 1965-68; practice medicine specializing in anesthesiology Balt., 1968—; faculty Church Home and Hosp., Balt., 1969—; attending staff Union Meml. Hosp., Church Home and Hosp., Frankling Sq. Hosp., Children's Hosp., James Lawrence Kernan Hosp., Balt., 1982-94; co-chief anesthesiology James Kernan Hosp., 1983-94, med. dir. out-patient surgery dept., 1987-94. Mem. med. exec. com. Kernan Hosp., 1988-94; affiliate cons. emergency room Church Home and Hosp., Balt., 1969—, mem. med. audit and utilizaions com., 1970-72, mem. emergency and ambulatory care com., 1973-74, chief emergency dept., 1973-74; cons. anesthesiologist Md. State Penitentiary, 1971; fellow in critical care medicine Md. Inst. Emergency Medicine, 1975-76; mem. infection control com. U. Md. Hosp., 1975—; instr. anesthesiology U. Md. Sch. Medicine, 1975—; staff anesthesiologist Mercy Hosp., 1978—, audit com., 1979-80, 82; asst. prof. anesthegiology U. Md. Med. Sch., 1989-94; mem. med. exec. com. Kernan Hosp., 1990-94, v.p. 1990, chief of staff, 1992—; mem. Tappahannock Family Practice, 1994-96, Rappahannock Gen. Hosp. Family Practice, 1996—; active staff Rappahannock Gen. Hosp., 1996—, ethics com., 1997—; med. examiner No. Neck of Va., 1996—; mem. Commonwealth of Va. Med. Bd. Mem. AMA, Am. Coll. Emergency Physicians, Am. Acad. Gen. Practitioners, Met. Emergency Dept. Heads Am., Md. Soc. Anesthesiologists, Balt. County Med. Soc., Mid. Peninsula Med. Soc., No. Neck Med. Soc., Med. Soc. Va., Med. and Choir Faculty Med., Chiurgical Soc., Internat. Congress Anaesthesiologists, Internat. Anesthesia Rsch. Soc., Am. L'Hirondelle Club, Annapolis Yacht Club, Chesapeake Bay Yacht Racing Assn, Rappahannock River Yacht Club. Anglican. Address: 347 Coppedge Farm Rd White Stone VA 22578-2021

DUERBECK, HEIDI BARBARA, lawyer; b. Duisburg, Fed. Republic of Germany, July 19, 1947; came to U.S., 1956; d. Kurt and Irmgard (Gottsche) D.; m. Jenik R. Radon, June 10, 1971; 1 child, Kaara. BA cum laude, UCLA, 1968, MA, 1969, student Gottingen U., Fed. Republic Germany, 1967-68; JD, Stanford U., 1972. Bar: Calif. 1973, N.Y. 1975, U.S. Dist. Ct. (so. dist.) N.Y. 1975. Atty. Sullivan & Cromwell, N.Y.C., 1972-77; ptnr. Walter, Conston, Alexander & Green, P.C., N.Y.C., 1980—. contbr. articles to German legal bus. jours.; Bd. dirs. Hugh O'Brien Youth Found., N.Y.C., 1984—; mem. N.Y. State Trade Mission, Europe, 1982, N.Y.C. Trade Mission, Europe, 1983; mem. Am. Council on Germany, N.Y.C., German Forum, N.Y.C. Soroptimist fellow, 1970. Mem. German-Am. Law Assn. (bd. dirs. 1982-86, pres. 1982—), ABA, Assn. of Bar of City of N.Y. Lutheran. Home: 269 W 71st St New York NY 10023-3701 Office: Walter Conston Alexander & Green PC 90 Park Ave Fl 14 New York NY 10016-1301

DUERINCK, LOUIS T. retired railroad executive, attorney; b. Chgo., Aug. 1, 1929; s. Aloys L. and Thais E. (De Backer) D.; m. Patricia A. Bird, June 27, 1953; children: Louis M., Kathleen M. Lutgen, Kevin F., Mark V., Lynn P. Dressel, Brian T., Paul S. Student, U. Notre Dame, 1947-48; JD, DePaul U., Chgo., 1952. Bar: Ill. 1952. Commerce atty. N.Y. Cen. R.R., Chgo., 1955-65; gen. atty. Nat. Ry. Labor Conf., Chgo., 1967-68; with C&NW Ry. Co., Chgo., 1965-67, 68-89; sr. v.p. law and real estate C&NW Transp. Co., 1979-83, sr. v.p. traffic, 1983-88, sr. v.p., 1988-89, also bd. dirs. Served with AUS, 1952-55. Mem. ABA, Assn. Transportation Law, Logistics and Policy, Ill. Bar Assn., Glen Oak Country Club, Wyndemere Country Club (Naples). Roman Catholic. Home and Office: 718 Midwest Club Pky Oak Brook IL 60523-2531

DUERKSEN, GEORGE LOUIS, music educator, music therapist; b. St. Joseph, Mo., Oct. 29, 1934; s. George Herbert and Louise May (Dalke) D.; m. Patricia Gay Beers, June 3, 1961; children— Mark Jeffrey, Joseph Scott, Cynthia Elizabeth Student, Tabor Coll, 1951-52; BMusEdn, U. Kans., 1955, MMusEdn, 1956, PhD, 1967. Cert. music educator Kans., Mo., registered music therapist Nat. Assn. Music Therapy, bd. cert. music therapist Bd. for Music Therapists, 1988. Tchr. music Tonganoxie High Sch., Kans., 1955-56, Stafford Jr. and Sr. High Sch., Kans., 1959-60, Labette County High Sch., Altamont, Kans., 1960-62, Shawnee Mission (Kans.) North High Sch., 1962-63; asst. prof., dir. psychology of music lab. Mich. State U., East Lansing, 1965-69; prof., chmn. dept. art and music edn. and music therapy U. Kans., Lawrence, 1969-93, dir. Singing Jayhawks, 1979-83, prof., dir. music edn. and music therapy divsn., 1993—, prof., interim chair dept. music and dance, 2000-01, dir. Ctr. for Rsch. on Music Behavior, 2001—; assoc. dir. Kans. North Ctrl. Assn. Colls. and Schs., 1992-2000. Cons., vis. prof. U. Hawaii, Honolulu, summer 1978; cons., vis. prof. U. Melbourne, Australia, summer 1981; cons., lectr. N.Z. Soc. for Music Therapy, Wellington, 1983, Ctr. for Contemporary Music Rsch., Athens, 1991, U. Thessaloniki, Greece, 1993, Korean Assn. for Music Therapy, 1994, 97, Sook Myung U., Seoul, 1997; cons. functional music applications, 1967—, Deakin U., Geelong, Victoria, Australia, 1990. Author: (monograph) Teaching Instrumental Music, 1973; Music for Exceptional Children, 1981; contbr. articles to profl. jours. Fulbright scholar Inst. for Internat. Edn., Australia, 1956-57; U.Kans. fellow, Lawrence, 1963-64; U.S. Office Edn. grantee, 1966-67, 73-75, 78-81 Mem. AAAS, Music Educators Nat. Conf., Am. Music Therapy Assn.(award of merit, 2000), Music Edn. Rsch. Coun. (chmn. 1980-82), Brit. Soc. for Music Therapy, Coun. for Rsch. in Music Edn., Pi Kappa Lambda, Phi Mu Alpha, Phi Delta Kappa. Avocations: photography, boating, travel. Office: U Kans Music Edn and Music Therapy Div 448 Murphy Hall 1530 Naismith Dr Lawrence KS 66045-3102 E-mail: gduerksen@ku.edu.

DUERR, DAVID, civil engineer; b. Newark, July 4, 1953; s. Warren August and Dorothy (Lanzillo) D.; m. Roberta Kay Apolant, Oct. 12, 1991. B of Engring., Pratt Inst., 1975; MS, U. Houston, 1985. Registered profl. engr. Project engr. Hoffman Internat., Pt Newark, N.J., 1974-76; chief engr. Williams Crane & Rigging, Richmond, Va., 1976-79; sr. structural engr. Hudson Engring Corp., Houston, 1980-86; pres. 2DM Assocs., Inc., Houston, 1986—. Frequent lectr. constrn. industry seminars. Contbr. tech. papers to profl. jours. Mem.: ASME (mem. BTH stds. com. on below-the-hook lifting devices), ASCE, Specialized Carriers and Rigging Assn., Soc. Naval Archs. and Marine Engrs., Soc. Automotive Engrs., Am. Coun. Engring. Cos. Achievements include research in the design of pinned connections and development of standards for the design of telescopic hydraulic gantries. Home: 8439 Hunters Creek Dr Houston TX 77024-3204 Office: 2DM Assocs Inc 9235 Katy Freeway Ste 350 Houston TX 77024-1526

DUERR, DIANNE MARIE, educator, sports medicine consultant; b. Buffalo, July 14, 1945; d. Robert John and Aileen Louise D. BS in Health and Phys. Edn., SUNY, Brockport, 1967; cert., SUNY, Oswego, 1982; postgrad., Canisius Coll., 1970-71. Cert. tchr., N.Y. Tchr. North Syracuse (N.Y.) Sch. Dist., 1967—; tchr. dept. orthopedic surgery SUNY Upstate Med. U., Syracuse, 1982—2003; creator Inst. for Human Performance SUNY Health Sci. Ctr., Syracuse, 1988. Coord. scholastic sports injury reporting system project SUNY, 1985-98; mem. com. on scholastic sports-related injuries NIH Inst. Arthritis, Musculoskeletal and Skin Diseases, 1993-96. Author: SSIRS Pilot Study Report, 1987, SSIRS Fall Study Report, 1988, SHASIRS Report, 1991; creator Scholastic Sports Injury Reporting System, 1985, Scholastic Head and Spine Injury Reporting System, 1989. Co-chmn. sports medicine USA Amateur Athletic Union, Nat. Jr. Olympic Games, Syracuse, NY, 1987; vol. sports medicine N.Y. State Sr. Games, 1990—95, sports medicine coord., 1990—95, U.S. Roller Skating Nat. Championships, 1995, N.Y. State Womens Lacrosse Championships, 1995, U.S. Nat. Precision Ice Skating Championships, 1997, Youth Basketball of Am., Northeast Regional Tournament, 1999; co-chmn. healthcare, security Empire State Games, Syracuse, 2002; mem. com. sports injury surveillance Ctrs. for Disease Control, 1995; cons. N.Y. Sci., Tech. and Soc. Edn. Project, 1995. Mem. AAUW, N.Y. State AAHPERD (pres. exercise sci. and sports medicine sect., 1994-98), Am. Coll. Sports Medicine, United Univ. Profs., Women's Sports Fedn., Am. Fedn. Tchrs., N.Y. United Tchrs., North Syracuse Tchrs. Assn., Phi Kappa Phi. Avocations: swimming, cycling, ice skating, reading, photography. Office: 418 Buffington Rd Syracuse NY 13224-2208 E-mail: dmduerr@twcny.rr.com.

DUERR, HERMAN GEORGE, retired publishing executive; b. Nagold, Germany, June 24, 1931; came to U.S., 1949, naturalized, 1975; s. Adolf Gustav and Wilhelmine Dorothea (Walz) Durr; m. Shirley Yvonne Jones, June 29, 1957; children: Suzanne, Steffan, Krista. B.F.A., Wayne State U., 1958. Publs. designer Ceco Comm. Inc., Warren, Mich., 1958-60; art dir. Am. Youth mag., 1960-67, Friends mag., 1967-86, exec. editor, 1978-87; v.p. Ceco Comm., Inc., 1981-91; dir. mktg. prodn. Ceco Pub. Co., 1987-91; publ. cons. Harrison, Mich., 1991—. Adj. faculty Mid Mich. C.C., 1991—. Served with U.S. Army, 1952-55.

DUERR, JOHANNES KLAUS, research scientist; b. Friedrichshafen, Baden-Wuerttemberg, Germany, Aug. 6, 1970; s. Walter Herbert and Gisela D. M in Aerospace Engring., U. Stuttgart (Germany), 1996. Rsch. engr. Daimler-Benz Aerospace,Dornier Daimler-Benz R&T, Friedrichshafen, 1997-99; project mgr. R&T T. Dornier GMBH, Friedrichshafen, 1999—. Mem. program com. Adaptronic Congress, Berlin, 2001—03. Contbr. 17 articles to profl. jours. Lt. mountain rocket artillery, 1989-91. Named Best of Tng. Course German Fed. Armed Forces Artillery Sch., 1990, 91; recipient of the Sci. award of Donor's Assn. for the Promoting of Scis. and Humanities in Germany, 2000. Mem. SPIE (mem. program com. Indsl. and Comml. Applications of Smart Structures Techs.). Avocations: soccer, paragliding, skiing, motorcycling. Office: Daimler-Chrysler R&T An der Bundesstr 31 Friedrichshafen 88039 Germany Fax: 49-7545-814254. E-mail: johannes.duerr@daimlerchrysler.com.

DUERSTOCK, BRADLEY S. neurobiologist, researcher; b. Indpls., Dec. 1, 1970; s. Marvin A. Duerstock and Sabra D. Carmack. BS in Engring., Purdue U., Ind., 1994, PhD, 1999. NIH post-doctoral rsch. assoc. Ctr. for Paralysis Rsch., West Lafayette, Ind., 2000—03. Grantee Program for Persons with Disabilities, NSF, 2002—. Mem.: Neurotrauma Soc. Office: Purdue U 408 South University St West Lafayette IN 47907-2065 E-mail: bsd@purdue.edu.

DUESENBERG, RICHARD WILLIAM, lawyer; b. St. Louis, Dec. 10, 1930; s. (John August) Hugo and Edna Marie (Warmann) D.; m. Phyllis Evelyn Buehner, Aug. 7, 1955; children: Karen, Daryl, Mark, David. BA, Valparaiso U., 1951, JD, 1953, LLD, 2001; LLM, Yale U., 1956. Bar: Mo. 1953. Prof. law NYU, N.Y.C., 1956-62, dir. law ctr. publs., 1960-62; sr. atty. Monsanto Co., St. Louis, 1963-70, asst. gen. counsel, asst. sec., 1975-77, sr. v.p., sec., gen. counsel, 1977-96. Dir. law Monsanto Textiles Co., St. Louis, 1971-75; corp. sec. Fisher Controls Co., Marshalltown, Iowa, 1969-71, Olympia Industries, Spartanburg, S.C., 1974-75; vis. prof. law U. Mo., 1970-71; faculty Banking Sch. South, La. State U., 1967-83; vis. scholar Cambridge U., England, 1996; vis. prof. law St. Louis U., 1997-98. Author: (with Lawrence P. King) Sales and Bulk Transfers Under the Uniform Commercial Code, 2 vols, 1966, rev., 1984, New York Law of Contracts, 3 vols, 1964, Missouri Forms and Practice Under the Uniform Commercial Code, 2 vols, 1966; editor: Ann. Survey of Am. Law, NYU, 1961-62; mem. bd. contbg. editors and advisors: Corp. Law Rev, 1977-86; contbr. articles to law revs., jours. Mem. lawyers adv. coun. NAM, Washington, 1980, Adminstrv. Conf. U.S., 1980-86, legal adv. com. N.Y. Stock Exch., 1983-87, corp. law dept. adv. coun. Practising Law Inst., 1982; bd. dirs. Bach Soc., St. Louis, 1985-86, pres., 1973-77; bd. dirs. Valparaiso U., 1977—, chmn. bd. visitors law sch., 1966—, Luth. Charities Assn., 1984-87, vice chmn., 1986-87; bd. dirs. Luth. Med. Ctr., St. Louis, 1973-82, vice chmn., 1975-80; bd. dirs. Nat. Jud. Coll., 1984-90, St. Louis Symphony, 1988-2002, Opera Theatre St. Louis, 1988—, Luth. Brotherhood, Mpls., 1992-2000, Liberty Fund, Inc., Indpls., 1997—. Served with U.S. Army, 1953-55. Decorated officer's cross Order of Merit (Germany); named Disting. Alumnus, Valparaiso U., 1976. Fellow Am. Bar Found.; mem. ABA (chmn. com. uniform comml. code 1976-79, coun. sect. corp., banking and bus. law 1979-83, sec. 1983-84, chmn. 1986-87), Mo. Bar Assn., Am. Law Inst., Mont Pelerin Soc., Nat. Jud. Coll. (bd. dirs. 1984-90), Order of Coif, Bach Soc., Am. Soc. Corp. Sec. (bd. chmn. 1987-88), Assn. Gen. Coun., Am. Arbitration Assn., St. Louis Club. Home: 1 Indian Creek Ln Saint Louis MO 63131-3333

DUESENBERG, ROBERT H. retired lawyer; b. St. Louis, Dec. 10, 1930; s. Hugo John August and Edna Marie (Warmann) D.; m. Lorraine Freda Hall, July 23, 1938; children: Lynda Renee, Kirsten Lynn, John Robert. BA, Valparaiso (Ind.) U., 1951, LLB, 1953; LLM, Harvard U., 1956. Bar: Mo. 1953, U.S. Supreme Ct. 1981, Va. 1993. Pvt. practice, St. Louis, 1956-58; atty. Wabash R.R. Co., St. Louis, 1958-65, Norfolk & Western Ry. Co., St. Louis, 1962-65; atty., assoc. gen. counsel Pet Inc., St. Louis, 1965-77, v.p., assoc. gen. counsel, 1977-80, v.p., gen. counsel, 1980-83, Gen. Dynamics Corp., Falls Church, Va., 1984-91, sr. v.p. and gen. counsel, 1991-93; ret., 1993. Bd. dirs. Valparaiso (Ind.) U.; adv. bd. ELawForum, Inc., Washington. Contbr. numerous articles to profl. jours. Sec., treas., legal advisor Am. Kantorei, St. Louis, 1970-75; mem. Coun. on World Affairs, St. Louis, 1975—, Mo. Coordinating Bd. for Higher Edn., Jefferson City, 1976-83, chmn., 1978-81; mem. pres.'s coun. Valparaiso (Ind.) U., 1979—, bd. dirs., 1995—; bd. dirs. Higher Edn. Loan Authority, 1982-84; mem. adv. bd. Northwestern U. Corp. Counsel Ctr., 1988—, chmn. adv. bd., 1992; bd. dirs. Opera Theatre of St. Louis, 1988—; bd. dirs. Luther Inst., Washington, 1999—, chair, 2000-03; mem. adv. bd. ELawForum, Washington. Cpl. U.S. Army, 195355. Recipient Disting. Alumnus award Valparaiso U., 1982. Mem. ABA, Va. Bar Assn., Mo. Bar Assn., St. Louis Bar Assn. (chmn. antitrust com. 1971-73, v.p. bus. law sect. 1972-73, chmn. 1973-74), Am. Law Inst., Gen. Counsels Assn., Machine and Allied Products Inst. (legal counsel 1986—), Am. Corp. Counsel Assn., S.W. Legal Found. (adv. bd.), Aerospace Industry Assn. (legal com. 1981-88), Bach Soc. of St. Louis (bd. dirs.). Republican. Lutheran. Home: 10171 Castlewood Ln Oakton VA 22124-3027

DUETSCH, JOHN EDWIN, lawyer; b. Newark, Sept. 25, 1915; s. John J. and Barbara A. (Nickl) D.; m. Gertrude A. Stewart, Aug. 31, 1940; children: John E., Karen A. Duetsch Gammond, Thomas F. LLB, Fordham U., 1941. Bar: N.Y. 1941. Clk. Ira Haupt & Co., N.Y.C., 1933-34; with Morris & McVeigh, N.Y.C., 1934—, ptnr., 1961-85, of counsel, 1985-90. Mem. planning bd. Township of Livingston, N.J., 1955-56, mayor, councilman, 1957-64; bd. dirs. Jacaranda Homeowners Assn. With U.S. Army, 1945. Mem. ABA, N.Y. Bar Assn., Am. Arbitration Assn. (panel), Guild Cath. Lawyers, N.J. State Srs. Golf Assn. (assoc., v.p., bd. dirs.), Am. Legion, Spring Brook Country Club (hon. life, pres. 1970-77) (Morristown, N.J.), Country Club of Jacaranda West (Venice, Fla.), KC (hon., life). Home: 900 N Doral Ln Venice FL 34293-3805 Office: Morris & McVeigh 767 3rd Ave New York NY 10017-2023

DUFF, DORIS EILEEN (DORIS SHULL), critical care nurse; d. Harley Ray and Eloise (Whitmer) Shull; m. William DeLaney Duff; 2 children. BS in Gen. Sci., Radford (Va.) U., 1983; diploma in nursing, Roanoke (Va.) Meml. Hosps., 1985. RN III, Va.; cert. emergency nurse. Med.-surg. nurse Roanoke Meml. Hosp., 1985-87, nurse emergency-trauma dept., 1987—, dir. quality mgmt. emergency dept. Mem. Emergency Nurses Cancel Alchohol Related Emergencies (ENCARE). Mem. Emergency Nurses Assn., Roanoke Meml. Hosps. Sch. Nursing Alumni Assn. (mem. hosp. ethics com.), Nursing Honor Soc. Roanoke Valley. Office: Roanoke Meml Hosp Belleview at Jefferson Sts Roanoke VA 24033

DUFF, ERNEST ARTHUR, political scientist, educator; b. Charlottesville, Va., Dec. 27, 1929; s. Ernest Ragland and Emma Ruth (Bennett) D.; m. Barbara Ellen Jones, Aug. 30, 1955; children: Ernest A. Jr., Melanie Duff Badesch, Cameron John, Valerie Duff-Strautmann. BA, U. Va., 1952, MA, 1957, PhD, 1964. Fgn. svc. officer Dept. of State, Havana, Cuba, 1957-60, Washington, 1960-62, Bogota, Colombia, 1962-63; prof. Randolph-Macon Woman's Coll., Lynchburg, Va., 1964-97, Charles Dana prof., 1986, prof. emeritus, 1997—. Spl. field rep. Rockefeller Found., Cali, Colombia, 1966-67; vis. Fulbright prof. U. of Mexico, Mexico City, 1979-80. Author: Agrarian Reform in Colombia, 1968, Violence and Repression in Latin America, 1974, Leader and Party in Latin America, 1984; reviewer Choice mag. Am. Libr. Assn. Polit. analyst WSET-TV, Lynchburg, Va., 1987—. Lt. USN, 1952-55, Korea. NROTC scholar USN and U. Va., 1948-52; Helen Wessell fellow, U. Va., 1963-64, NEH summer fellow, Brown U., Providence, 1990. Mem. Latin Am. Studies Assn., So. Polit. Sci. Assn., Southeastern Coun. Latin Am. Studies, Va. Polit. Sci. Assn. Baptist. Avocations: tennis, gardening. Home: 1633 Dogwood Ln Lynchburg VA 24503-1923 E-mail: ebdu@earthlink.net.

DUFF, JAMES GEORGE, retired financial services executive; b. Pittsburg, Kans., Jan. 27, 1938; s. James George and Camilla Matilda (Vinardi) D.; m. Linda Louise Beeman, June 24, 1961 (div.); children: Michele, Mark, Melissa; m. Beverly L. Pool, Nov. 16, 1984. BS with distinction, U. Kans., 1960, MBA, 1961. With Ford Motor Co., Dearborn, Mich., 1962-97, various positions fin. staff, 1962-71; dir. product, profit, price, warranty Ford of Europe, 1972-74; controller Ford Div., 1974-76, controller car ops., 1976, controller car product devel., 1976-80; exec. v.p. Ford Motor Credit Co., 1980-88, bd. dirs.; pres., COO U.S. Leasing Internat. Inc., San Francisco, 1988-89; pres., CEO U.S. Leasing Internat. Inc. (now USL Capital), San Francisco, 1990-91; chmn., CEO USL Capital, San Francisco, 1991-97, also bd. dirs. Bd. dirs. Boulder Total Return Fund, 1997-99; mem. Conf. Bd., 1990-97. Mem. adv. bd. U. Kans. Sch. Bus., 1980-98; bd. dirs. Bay Area Coun., 1990-97; trustee San Francisco Mus. Modern Art, 1990-97; chmn. bus. devel. unit Detroit United Fund, 1980-85, chmn. edn. and local govt. unit Detroit United Fund, 1986-88. Sunray Mid-Continent scholar, Bankers scholar, to 1960. Mem. San Francisco C. of C. (bd. dirs. 1990-91). Home: 7544 S Dunns Farm Rd Maple City MI 49664-8718 also: 1 The Courtyard 65 Old Church St London SW3 5BS England E-mail: onmyduff@msn.com.

DUFF, JAMES HENRY, museum director, environmental administrator; b. Pitts., Oct. 11, 1943; s. James Sylvester and Virginia (Henry) D.; m. Sally Kathryn Tredwell, Sept. 14, 1963; children: Abigail Margaret, Jessica Lauren. BA, Washington and Jefferson Coll., 1965; MA, U. Mass., 1970. Teaching asst. U. Mass., Amherst, 1965-66; dir. Mus. of Hudson Highlands, Cornwall-on-Hudson, N.Y., 1966-73, Brandywine River Mus., Chadds Ford, Pa., 1973—; exec. dir. Brandywine Conservancy, Chadds Ford, 1976—. Cons. N.Y. State Coun. on Arts, 1970-72; panel mem. Pa. Coun. on Arts, 1976-79, 83-85; mem. adv. coun. Nat. Mus. Act, 1982-85; mem. Nat. Mus. Svcs. Bd., 1986-95. Author: The Western World of N. C. Wyeth, 1980, Landscapes, Still Lifes and Portraits by N. C. Wyeth, 1982, An American Vision, 1987; contbr. articles on mus. programs to profl. jours. Trustee Wyeth Endowment for Am. Art, 1986-95, Am. Arts Alliance, 1995-96, Greater Phila. Cultural Alliance (trustee 2001—). With U.S. Army, 1967-69. Mem. Mid-Atlantic Assn. Mus. (pres. 1983-85, The Katherine Coffey award 1992), Assn. Art Mus. Dirs. (trustee 1993-98, 2001—, v.p. 1995-96, pres. 1996-97), Am. Assn. Mus. (trustee 1983-88). Home: PO Box 297 Chadds Ford PA 19317-0297 Office: Brandywine River Mus Brandywine Conservancy PO Box 141 Chadds Ford PA 19317-0141 E-mail: bmuse1@brandywine.org.

DUFF, JOHN BERNARD, college president, former city official; b. Orange, N.J., July 1, 1931; s. John Bernard and Mary Evelyn (Cunningham) D.; m. Helen Mezzanotti, Oct. 8, 1955 (div.); children: Michael, Maureen, Patricia, John, Robert, Emily Anne; m. Estelle M. Shanley, July, 1991. BS, Fordham U., 1953; MA, Seton Hall U., 1958; PhD, Columbia U., 1964; DHL (hon.), Seton Hall U., 1976, Northeastern U., 1982, Emerson Coll., 1983, Lincoln Coll., 1993. Sales rep. Remington-Rand Corp., 1955-57, dist. mgr., 1957-60; mem. faculty Seton Hall U., 1960-70, prof. history, 1968-70, acad. v.p., 1970-71, exec. v.p., acad. v.p., 1971-72, provost, acad. v.p., 1972-76; pres. U. Lowell, Mass., 1976-81; chancellor of higher edn. State of Mass., 1981-86; commr. Chgo. Pub. Libr. System, 1986-92; pres. Columbia Coll., Chgo., 1992-2000, ret., 2000—. Mem. Gov.'s Commn. to Study Capital Punishment, 1972-73; chmn. bd. dirs. Mass. Corp. Edni. Telecommunications, 1983— ; dir. Mass. Tech. Park Corp. Author: The Irish in the United States, 1971, also articles.; Editor: (with others) The Structure of American History, 1970, (with P.M. Mitchell) The Nat Turner Rebellion: The Historical Event and the Modern Controversy, 1971, (with L. Greene) Slavery: Its Origin and Legacy, 1975. Dem. candidate to U.S. Congress, 1968; mem. State Bd. Edn., 1981-86; chmn. Livingston Town Dem. Com., 1972-76; bd. dirs. Merrimack Regional Theatre, 1981-84, Mass. Higher Edn. Assistance Corp., 1981-86, Chgo. Metro History Fair ; trustee Essex County Coll., 1966-70, Mass. Community Coll. System., St. John's Prep. Sch., Danvers, Mass.; chmn. Lowell Hist. Preservation Commn., 1979-86; mem. adv. bd. Wang Inst., 1979-81; mem. bd. visitors Emerson Coll., 1986-90; pres. Nat. Coun. of Heads of Public Higher Edn. Systems; mem. nat. adv. com. on accreditation and indsl. eligibility U.S. Dept. Edn., 1981-82; mem. Ill. Lit. Coun., 1986-92, adv. com. Ill. State Libr., 1986-92; chmn. Fedn. Ind. Ill. Colls. and Univs., 1996-98. With U.S. Army, 1953-55. Mem. Univ. Club, Tavern Club.

DUFF, JOHN EWING, sculptor; b. Lafayette, Ind., Dec. 2, 1943; s. John Ewing and Ruth (Miller) D. B.F.A., San Francisco Art Inst., 1967. One man shows include: Margo Leavin Gallery, L.A., 1981, Blum-Helman Gallery, N.Y.C., 1985-90, L.A., 1987, 91, San Jose (Calif.) Mus. Art, 1991, Gallery 57, Madrid, 1992, Salama Caro Gallery, London, 1992, David McKee Gallery, 1995, JohnsonCounty C.C. Gallery Art, 1995, Knodler Gallery, N.Y.C., 1997, Hill Gallery, Birmingham, Mich., 1999, Brantley Gallery, Scottsdale, Ariz.,

1999, Ingred Rabb Gallery, Berlin, 1999, Knodler Gallery, N.Y.C., 2001 (early work), Manfred Baumgartner Gallery, N.Y.C. 2001 (recent work); two-person show at Hill Gallery, Birmingham, Mich., 1996; group exhbns. include Whitney Mus., N.Y.C., 1969, 81, David Whitney Gallery, N.Y.C., 1970, 71, Irving Blum Gallery, L.A., 1972, John Bernard Meyers Gallery, N.Y.C., 1972, 73, Willard Gallery, N.Y.C., 1975-78, Whitney Mus. Equitable Ctr., 1987, The Edward R. Broida Collection, Orlando Mus. of Art, 1998, Anderson Gallery, Va. Commonwealth U., 2000, Am. Acad. Invitational Exhbn. of Painting and Sculpture, 2002; represented in public collections Kaiser Wilhelm Mus., Krefeld, Fed. Republic Germany, Mus. Modern Art, N.Y.C., Walker Art Ctr., Mpls., Met. Mus. Art, N.Y.c., Solomon R. Guggenheim Mus., N.Y.C., L.A. Mus. Contemporary Art, Mus. Contemporary Art, Chgo. Recipient Theodoren award Guggenheim Mus., 1977, award Am. Acad. and Inst. Arts and Letters, 1981, John Simon Guggenheim fellowship, 1979-80, Brandeis U. Creative Arts award Citation in Sculpture, 1987. Home and Office: 7 Doyers St New York NY 10013-5112

DUFF, JOHN MICHAEL, neurosurgeon; b. Dublin, June 12, 1963; s. Donal Michael and Gina Ann Duff; m. Annamaria Luisa Cafolla; children: Mark, John Kevin, Lara. MD, Royal Coll.Surgeons Ireland, Dublin, 1988. Diplomate Am. Bd. Neurol. Surgery, 1997, cert. European Assn Neurosurg. Socs., 1999. Resident in surgery The Johns Hopkins Hosp.ital, Balt., 1990—92; resident neurosurgery Mayo Grad. Sch. of Medicine, Rochester, Minn., 1992—97; fellow pediatric neurosurgery The New Childrens Hosp, Sydney, Australia, 1995; fellow cranial base surgery George Washington Univ.Hosp., Washington, 1997—98; chef de clinique adjoint Univ. Hosps. Geneva and Lausanne, Geneva, 1998—2000; asst. prof. neurosurgery Tufts U. Sch. of Medicine, Boston, 2000—03. Mem.: Am. Assn. Neurol. Surgeons. Office: St Elizabeth's Med Ctr Med Office Bldg 402 Boston MA 02135 Office Fax: 617-782-2439. E-mail: John_Duff@cchcs.org.

DUFF, MICHAEL JAMES, physicist; b. Manchester, Jan. 28, 1949; s. Edward and Elizabeth (Kaylor) D.; m. Lesley Yearling, 1984; children: Jessica, Matthew. BS, Queen Mary Coll., U. London, 1969; PhD, Imperial Coll., U. London, 1972. Postdoctoral fellow in theoretical physics Internat. Ctr. Theoretical Physics, Trieste, Italy, Oxford (Eng.) U., U. London, Brandeis U., Waltham, Mass., 1972-79; faculty mem. Imperial Coll., 1979-88; sr. physicist CERN, Geneva, 1984-87; prof. physics Tex. A&M U., College Station, 1988-92, Disting. prof. physics, 1992-99; Oskar Klein prof. physics U. Mich., Ann Arbor, 1999—; dir. Mich. Ctr. for Theoretical Physics, 2000—. Contbr. articles to profl. jours. Fellow Am. Phys. Soc. Avocations: water colors, golfing. Home: 846 Arboretum Dr Saline MI 48176-1354 Office: U Mich Dept Physics 3425 Randall Lab Ann Arbor MI 48109-1120

DUFF, WILLIAM BRANDON, lawyer; b. Flushing, N.Y., June 1, 1949; s. Daniel Vincent and Priscilla (Booth) D.; m. Terri Ann Sherman, June 16, 1985; children: Elizabeth, Madeleine. AB, Coll. of Holy Cross, 1971; JD, Georgetown U., 1975. Bar: D.C. 1975, U.S. Dist. Ct. (D.C.) 1975, U.S. Ct. Appeals (D.C. cir.) 1975, N.Y. 1983. Assoc. McChesney & Pyne, Washington, 1975-78, Carter, Ledyard & Milburn, N.Y.C., 1980-84; pvt. practice, N.Y.C., 1984-86; ptnr., dept. head DeForest & Duer, N.Y.C., 1986-96, Baer, Marks & Upham, N.Y.C., 1996-2000; ptnr. Jenkens & Gilchrist Parker Chapin LLP, N.Y.C., 2000—02, KMZ Rosenman, N.Y.C., 2002—. Instr. fed. employee benefit plans law Georgetown U. Sch. Continuing Edn., Washington, 1977, 78. Mem. legislature City of Greenwich, Conn., 1994-98. Office: KMZ Rosenman 575 Madison Ave New York NY 10022 E-mail: william.duff@kmzr.com.

DUFF, WILLIAM GRIERSON, electrical engineer, educator; b. Alexandria, Va., Dec. 16, 1936; s. Johnnie Douglas and Annetta Osceola (Rind) D.; m. Sandra K. Via, June 25, 1983; children: Warren David, Valerie Lynn, Dawn Elizabeth, Deborah Arleen, Kelly Juanita. BEE, George Washington U., 1959, postgrad., 1959-72; MS, Syracuse U., 1969; DSc in Elec. Engring., Clayton U., 1977. Chief tech. officer SENTEL, Alexandria, Va., 1959—. Asst. prof. Capitol Inst. Tech., Greenbelt, Md., 1972—; instr. Interference Control Technologies, Don White Cons., Inc., Gainesville, Va. Author: EMI Handbook, vol. 5, EMI Prediction and Analysis Techniques, 1972, Mobile Communications, 1976, Fundamentals of EMC, 1988, EMC in Telecommunications, 1988; contbr. articles to profl. jours. Counselor Meth. Sr. High Youth Group, 1965-73. Recipient Good Citizenship award DAR, 1955, Math. award George Washington H.S., Alexandria, 1955. Fellow IEEE (pres. EMC Soc., assoc. editor group newsletter 1970—); mem. AIEE (Best Paper award 1961), George Washington U. Engring. Alumni Assn. (pres. 1963-64, Engring. Alumni Svc. award 1980), Springfield Golf and Country Club, Occoquan Water Ski Club (pres. 1976), Sigma Tau, Theta Tau. Home: 7601 S Valley Dr Fairfax VA 22039-2965 Office: Sentel 7601 S Valley Dr Fairfax Station VA 22039 E-mail: wduff@sentel.com.

DUFF, WILLIAM LEROY, JR., university dean emeritus, business educator; b. Oakland, Calif., Sept. 14, 1938; s. William Leroy and Edna Francis (Gunderson) D.; m. Arline M. Wight, Sept. 1, 1962; children— Susan M., William Leroy III. BA, Calif. State U.-, San Francisco, 1963, postgrad., 1963-64; MSSc., Nat. Econs. Inst., U. Stockholm, 1965; PhD, UCLA, 1969. Research assoc. C.F. Kettering Found., 1967-69; asst. JOBS program Nat. Alliance Businessmen, 1969-70; prof. U. No. Colo., Greeley, 1970—, dir. Sch Bus., Bur Bus. and Pub. Research, 1972-75, dean Coll. Bus. Adminstrn., 1984—, interim v.p. acad. affairs, 1987, chmn. faculty senate, 1981-82. On leave as UN adviser to Govt. of Swaziland, 1975-77; cons. in field. Contbr. articles to profl. jours. Mem. Greeley Planning Commn., 1972-75, chmn., 1974-75; trustee U. No. Colo., 1983; mem. Greeley Water and Sewer Bd., 1994-98, Greeley City Coun., 2000; bd. dirs. Centennial Svcs., 2003, United Way of Weld County, 2003, exec. bd. and investment com., UNC Found., 2003. With U.S. Army, 1958-60. Mem. Greeley Rotary Club (bd. dirs.), Greeley Area C. of C. (bd. dirs.). Home: 1614 Lakeside Dr Greeley CO 80631-5343 Office: U No Colo Coll Bus Adminstrn Kepner Greeley CO 80639-0001

DUFFETT, BENTON SAMUEL, JR., lawyer; b. Kansas City, Mo., Dec. 22, 1936; s. Benton S. Sr. and Carabel (Marvin) D.; m. Virginia M. Keys, June 23, 1962 (dec. Mar. 1998); children: Benton S., III, Robert J., David J.; m. Deborah B. Tighe, July 10, 1999. BS in Chem., U. Kans., 1959; JD in Law, U. Mich., 1962. Bar: D.C. 1963, Va. 1978. From assoc. to partner Burns, Doane, Swecker & Mathis LLP, Alexandria, Va., 1963—. Mem. ABA, Am. Intellectual Property Law Assn., Nat. Assn. Plant Patent Owners, Am. Chem. Soc., Am. Soc. Hort. Sci., Am. Hort. Soc., Royal Hort. Soc., Can. Ornamental Plant Found., Internat. Community of Breeders of Asexually Reproduced Ornamental and Fruit-Tree Varieties. Office: Burns Doane Swecker Mathis LLP 1737 King St Ste 500 Alexandria VA 22314-2727

DUFFETT, MICHAEL FRANK, humanities educator, poet; b. London, Feb. 23, 1943; arrived in U.S., 1980; s. Jack Anthony and Doris Ann Lilian Duffett; m. Debra Faye Jones, July 31, 1982; children: Kimberley, Heather, Matthew, Jack, Chaela, Peter. BA with honors, Cambridge U., Eng., 1964, MA, 1968; LittD (hon.), Gakushuin U., Japan, 1977. Tchr. English, British Coun., Saudi Arabia, 1964—66, 1968—70, Kanda Fgn. Lang. Inst., Tokyo, 1970—73; assoc. prof. English, Kawamura Gakuen U., Tokyo, 1973—80; asst. prof. Chaminade U., Honolulu, 1980—83; contract artist Calif. Dept. Corrections, Jamestown, 1988—93; prof. humanities Humphreys Coll., Stockton, Calif., 1996—. Writer-in-residence Calif. Youth Authority, Stockton, 1990—93. Author: Evolution-A Japanese Journal, 1977, The Variety of English Expression, 1978, Forever Avenue, 1986; editor: River News Herald, 1995—96; columnist: Union Dem., 1999—2000. Min. Ch. of Christ, Rio Vista, Calif., 1986—91; sub-deacon St. Matthew's Epis. Ch., San Andreas, Calif., 2001—. Recipient award for poetry, Tokyo English Lit. Soc., 1975. Mem.: Poetry Soc. Am., Cambridge Soc. Anglican. Avocation: reading. Home: 3201 Laurie Ct Valley Springs CA 95252 Office: Humphreys Coll 6650 Inglewood Ave Stockton CA 95207 Office Fax: 209-478-8721. Business E-Mail: mduffett@humphreys.edu.

DUFFEY, GEORGE HENRY, physics educator; b. Manchester, Iowa, Dec. 24, 1920; s. Henry Alfred and Marion Ella (Barr) D.; m. Helen Susie Hooper, Sept. 17, 1945; children: Ann Elizabeth, James Roy, Mary Kay. BA, Cornell Coll., 1942; PhD, Princeton (N.J.) U., 1945. Asst. prof. chemistry S.D. State Coll., Brookings, 1945-49, assoc. prof. chemistry, 1949-55, prof. chemistry, 1955-58; prof. chemistry physics U. Miss., Oxford, Miss., 1958-59; prof. physics S.D. State U., Brookings, 1959—; vis. prof. physics U. Western Australia, Perth, 1977. Author: Physical Chemistry, 1962, Theoretical Physics, 1980, A Development of Quantum Mechanics, 1984, Quantum States and Processes, 1992, Applied Group Theory, 1992, Modern Physical Chemistry, 2000; editor: Poems from the 1830s by a Poor Son of Ireland, 1977; contbr. articles to profl. jours. including Jour. Chem. Physics, Phys. Rev., Jour. Phys. Chemistry, Founds. of Physics and Jour. Chem. Edn. Recipient Excellence in Teaching award Western Elec. Fund, 1971-72. Mem. AAAS, Am. Phys. Soc., Am. Chem. Soc., Societa Italiana di Fisica, Philosophy of Sci. Assn. Baptist. Home: 628 11th Ave Brookings SD 57006-1526 Office: SD State U Dept Physics Brookings SD 57007-0001

DUFFEY, JOSEPH DANIEL, academic administrator; b. Huntington, W.Va., July 1, 1932; s. Joseph I. and Ruth (Wilson) Duffey; m. Anne Wexler, 1974; children: Michael, David, Danny Wexler, David Wexler. BA, Marshall U., 1954; STM, Yale U., 1963; BD, Andover Newton Theol. Sch., 1958; PhD, Hartford Sem. Found., 1969; LHD, CUNY, 1978, U. Cin., 1978, U. Mass., 1991; LittD, Dickinson Coll., Pa., 1978, Centre Coll., Ky., 1977, Gonzaga U., Wash., 1980, Monmouth Coll., 1980, CCNY; LLD, Amherst Coll., Bethany Coll., Austin Coll., Ritsuimaneu U., Kyoto, Japan, 1993; LittD, Alderson-Broadus Coll., Adelphi U., Central Fla. Asst. prof. Hartford (Conn.) Sem., 1960—63; assoc. prof., dir. Ctr. Urban Studies, 1965—70; fellow Harvard U. Kennedy Sch. Govt., 1971; adj. prof. and fellow Calhoun Coll., Yale U., 1971—73; exec. officer AAUP, 1974—77; asst. sec. for edn. and cultural affairs Dept. State, 1977; chmn. NEH, 1978—81; chancellor U. Mass., Amherst, 1982—, pres., 1990—91, Am. U., Washington, 1991—93; dir. U.S. Info. Agy., Washington, 1993—98; sr. exec., chmn. internat. univ. project Sylvan Learning Sys., Washington, 1999—. Mem. U.S. dept. 20th and 21st gen. confs. UNESCO, 1978, 80; mem. exec. com. Nat. Coun. Competitiveness Govt. and Industry Univ. Panel Nat. Acad. Scis.; bd. dirs. Bay Bank, Springfield, Mass. Contbr. articles to profl. jours. Bd. dirs. Woodrow Wilson Internat. Ctr. Scholars, East-West Ctr., Western Mass. Area Devel. Corp., Jewish Theol. Sem. Libr., Springfield Symphony. Decorated Order of Leopold IV Belgium; recipient Tree of Life award, Nat. Jewish Fund, 1987; scholar, Rockefeller Found., 1966—68. Mem.: Century Assn., Coun. Fgn. Rels., Cosmos Club. Office: Sylvan Learning Sys 2801 New Mexico Ave NW Apt 311 Washington DC 20007-3913 E-mail: jdoffey@earthlink.net.

DUFFEY, LEE, communications company executive; BA, U. Ga. Pres. Duffey Comms., Inc., 1984—. Officer, mem. exec. com. Buckhead Coalition, Atlanta, 1985. Address: Duffey Communications Nc 3379 Peachtree Rd NE Atlanta GA 30326-1020

DUFFEY, WILLIAM SIMON, JR., lawyer; b. Phila., May 9, 1952; s. William Simon and Elinor (Daniluk) D.; m. Betsy Byars, Dec. 17, 1977; children: Charles, Scott. BA in English, honors, Drake U., 1973; JD cum laude, U. S.C., 1977. Bar: S.C. 1977, Ga. 1982, U.S. Dist. Ct. (no., mid. and so. dists.) Ga. 1982, U.S. Ct. Appeals (llth cir.) 1983, U.S. Supreme Ct., 1992. Atty. Nexson, Pruet, Jacobs & Pollard, Columbia, S.C., 1977-78, King & Spalding, Atlanta, 1982-94, ptnr., 1995—2001; dep. ind. counsel Office of the Ind. Counsel, Little Rock, 1994-95; U.S. Atty. No. Dist. Ga., Atlanta, 2002—. Adj. prof. U. S.C. Law Sch., 2000—01. Articles editor S.C. Lawyer, 1990-94. Pres. Pine Hills Civic Assn., Atlanta, 1984-88; trustee Drake U.; Ga. Rep. Found., Leadership Atlanta; bd. dirs. Ga. Wilderness Inst., 1992-2001; mem. Peachtree Rd. Race Com., 1993—, chmn. Ga. Good Govt. Com., 1995-2001; chmn. bd. advisors Coverdell Leadership Inst., 1995-2002; bd. mem. North Ga. Walk to Emmaus, 1999-2001; bd. advisors Camp Hope, 2000-01; founder New Century Forum. Mem. Altanta Bar Assn. (chmn. alt. dispute resolution com. 1984-88), Lawyers Club, Atlanta Track Club (gen. counsel 1993—). Republican. Avocations: running, cooking, woodturning. Home: 4825 Franklin Pond NE Atlanta GA 30342-2765 Office: Office US Atty US Courthouse Ste 600 75 Spring St Atlanta GA 30303

DUFFIE, JOHN ATWATER, chemical engineer, educator; b. White Plains, N.Y., Mar. 31, 1925; s. Archibald Duncan and Lulie Adele (Atwater) Duffie; m. Patricia Ellerton, Nov. 22, 1947; children: Neil A., Judith A. Duffie Schwarzmeier, Susan L. Duffie Buse. B.Ch.E., Rensselaer Poly. Inst., 1945, M.Ch.E., 1948; PhD, U. Wis., 1951. Registered profl. engr., Wis. Instr. chem. engring. Rensselaer Poly. Inst., 1946-49; research asst. U. Wis., 1949-51; research engr. DuPont Co., 1951; sci. liaison officer Office Naval Research, 1952-53; mem. faculty dept. chem. engring. U. Wis.-Madison, 1954—, prof., 1957-88, prof. emeritus, 1988—, dir. solar energy lab., 1956-88. Author (with W.A. Beckman, S.A. Klein): Solar Heating Design, 1977; author: (with W.A. Beckman) Solar Energy Thermal Processes, 1974; author: Solar Engineering of Thermal Processes, 1980, 1991. With USN, 1943—46, with USN, 1952—53. Fellow Hon. Sr. Research, U. Birmingham, 1984; scholar Fulbright, U. Queensland, Australia, 1964, Sr. Fulbright-Hays, Commonwealth Sci. and Indsl. Research Orgn., Australia, 1977. Fellow: Am. Inst. Chem. Engrs.; mem.: Internat. Solar Engergy Soc. (past pres., editor Solar Energy Jour. 1985—93, Charles G. Abbott award Am. sect. 1976, Farrington Daniels award 1987). Office: Univ Wis 1500 Engineering Dr Madison WI 53706-1609

DUFFIÉ, MARY KATHARINE, anthropologist, researcher, educator; b. Phila., June 23, 1963; d. Claire Alfred Pelton III and Nikki Joan (Newcomb) D. BA, U. Ariz., 1985, MA, 1989; PhD, Wash. State U., Pullman, 1994. Asst. prof. Mont. State U., Bozeman, 1995-97; asst. prof. anthropology UCLA, 1997—. Prin. investigator UCLA/Calif. Dept. Health Svcs., 1997-98, CDC, Atlanta, 1996-97, Ariz. Humanities Coun., Tucson, 1989-90. Author: Heeni: A Tainui Elder Remembers, 1997, Through the Eye of the Needle: A Maori Elder Remembers, 2001. Chair So. Calif., Am. Indian Health Working Group, L.A., 1997—; vol. Together, Inc., Glassboro, N.J., 1976-81, Hospice, Tucson, 1987-89. Recipient W.H.R. Rivers award Soc. for Med. Anthropology, 1993; book recognized among top 20 titles for 1997 Listener Women's Book Festival, Auckland, New Zealand, 1997; nominated Victor Turner award Am. Anthropology Assn., 2001. Democrat. Presbyterian. Avocations: reading, writing, horseback riding, hiking. Home: 8050 Lupine Ln Bozeman MT 59718

DUFFIE, VIRGIL WHATLEY, JR., retired state agency administrator; b. Greenwood, S.C., Sept. 10, 1935; s. Virgil Whatley and Lorena (Ouzts) D.; m. Mary Hartzog, Oct. 6, 1962 (dec. Sept. 2001); children: Rebecca Louise, Mary Page, Virgil W. III. BA, U. S.C., 1957, JD, 1959. Bar: S.C. 1959. Trust officer Bankers Trust S.C., Columbia, 1959-67, sr. trust officer, 1967-70, sr. v.p., 1970-73, exec. v.p., 1973-84, 1st exec. v.p., 1984-86; sr.v.p., trust officer NCNB S.C., Columbia, 1986; sr. v.p. Interstate Securities Corp., Columbia, 1987-88; dir. spl. gifts U. S.C., Columbia, 1988-89; apptd. commr. S.C. Dept. Labor, Columbia, 1989-94, appt. dir. labor, licencing and regulations, 1994-95, dept. dir. labor, licensing and regulations, 1995—99. Bd. dirs. Index-Pub. Co., Greenwood, Stier Supply Co., Columbia, George W. Park Seed Co., Greenwood. Bd. dirs. Palmetto Boys State, Charleston, S.C., 1954-74; chmn. bd. Carolina Children's Home, Columbia, 1976; sec. bd. dirs. Richland Meml. Hosp., Columbia, 1970-73. Mem. ABA, S.C. Bar Assn., S.C. Bankers Assn. Home: 34 Quinine Hl Columbia SC 29204-3414

DUFFNER, LEE R. ophthalmologist; b. June 3, 1936; m. Alvina Bross, Aug. 31, 1957; children: Fay, Rachel, Tamar. BS Engring., Purdue U., 1957; MS Physiology, Marquette U., 1961; MD, Med. Coll. Wis., 1962. Diplomate Am. Bd. Ophthalmology. Intern Stanford U., 1962—63; resident U. Miami, Fla., 1966—69; practice medicine specializing in ophthalmology Hollywood, Fla., 1969—; clin. prof. ophthalmology U. Miami Sch. Medicine, 1969—; dir. Am. Bd. Ophthalmology, 1995—2002. Pres. town coun. Town of Golden Beach, Fla., 1983—95. Capt. USAF, 1963—66. Fellow: ACS, Am. Acad. Ophthalmology; mem.: Miami Ophthal. Soc. (pres. 1983—84). Avocation: racewalking. Home: 185 Ocean Blvd Golden Beach FL 33160-2208 Office: 2740 Hollywood Blvd Hollywood FL 33020-4826

DUFFY, BRIAN, editor; Investigative editor The Wall St. Jour., 1996—98; nat. editor US News & World Report, Washington, 1996—2001, exec. editor, 1998—2000, editor, 2001—. Office: US News & World Report 1025 Vermont Ave NW Washington DC 20005

DUFFY, CHERYL HOFSTETTER, language educator; b. Hill City, Kans., June 23, 1959; d. Paul Louis and Deloris Luhman Hofstetter; m. Robert Edward Duffy, June 5, 1999; m. John Oliver Towns, Aug. 17, 1978 (dec. June 18, 1995); 1 child, Anna Marie Towns. At, Colby CC, Kans., 1977—78; BSE in English, Emporia State U., Kans., 1981; MA in English, Fort Hays, Kans., 1984; PhD in English, U. Kans., Lawrence, 1996. Writing ctr. tutor Emporia State U., 1978—80; English instr. Colby CC, 1981—86; disabled student svcs. coord. Ft. Hays State U., 1986—88, English instr., 1988—89; curriculum writing specialist Kans. State Dept. Edn., Topeka, 1989—90; gta U. Kans., 1991—92; assoc. prof. English Ft. Hays State U., 1992—. Svc.-learning faculty cons. comty. svc. program Kans. State U., 2002—. Contbr. articles to profl. jours. Mem.: Nat. Coun. of Tchrs. of English. Office: Fort Hays State U English Dept 600 Park St Hays KS 67601 Office Fax: 785-628-4087.

DUFFY, EARL GAVIN, hotel executive; b. Boston, Oct. 11, 1926; s. William Emmett and Mary Irene (Costello) D.; m. Bernice Rose MacMaster, Feb. 14, 1948; children— Earl Gavin, Joan Irene, Mark Charles, Neil William, Lynn Anne. Student public schs., Boston. In various hotel positions, Boston, 1941-52; sales mgr. Somerset Hotel, Boston, 1952-56; eastern sales mgr. Hotel Corp. Am., Boston, 1956-59, asst. nat. sales mgr., 1959-61, nat. sales mgr., 1961-64; v.p., gen. mgr. Hotel America, Houston, 1964-67, Hartford, Conn., 1967-69, Royal Sonesta Hotel, New Orleans, 1969-71, Soneta Beach Hotel, Key Biscayne, Fla., 1971-76, Boston Park Plaza Hotel, 1977-80; pres. Earl G. Duffy & Assos., 1981—. Guest lectr. Cornell U., 1961, U. Houston, 1965, Wash. State U., 1966, Fla. Internat. U., 1971-76; pres. Greater Hartford Conv. and Visitor's Bur., 1969 Chmn. div. bus. and industry Harris County (Tex.) March of Dimes, 1964-67; pres. New Orleans Jazz Festival, 1970-71. Served with USN, 1943-46. Recipient Golden Host award Wash. State U., 1964 Mem. Skal Club, Am. Hotel and Motel Assn., Hotel Sales Mgmt. Assn. Internat., Greater Boston Hotel and Motor Inn Assn., Mass. Hotel and Motel Assn., New Eng. Innkeepers Assn., Boston Exec. Club. Clubs: Rotary. Roman Catholic. Home and Office: 345 W Enid Dr Key Biscayne FL 33149-2005 *There is no question in my mind that anyone who wants to "make it" in America can do so.*

DUFFY, EDMUND CHARLES, lawyer; b. N.Y.C., Jan. 16, 1942; s. Thomas and Helen (Fisher) D.; m. Terry L. Davis, Oct. 21, 1973; children: Elisabeth, Margot. AB in Eng., Boston Coll., 1963; LLB, Columbia U., 1966. Bar: N.Y. 1967. Assoc. Cravath, Swaine & Moore, N.Y.C., 1968-77; from assoc. to ptnr. Skadden, Arps, Slate, Meagher & Flom, N.Y.C., 1977—. Served to capt. U.S. Army, 1966-68, Vietnam. Mem. ABA, N.Y. State Bar Assn. Office: Skadden Arps Slate Meagher & Flom LLP 4 Times Sq New York NY 10036-6595

DUFFY, JAMES HENRY, writer, former lawyer; b. Lowville, N.Y., Feb. 3, 1934; s. William Christopher and Phyllis Catherine (Rofinot) D.; m. Martha McDowell, May 25, 1968 (dec. 1997). AB, Princeton U., 1956; LLB, Harvard U., 1959. Bar: N.Y. 1960. Assoc. Cravath, Swaine & Moore, N.Y.C., 1959-67, ptnr., 1968-88. Bd. dirs. Albanian-Am. Enterprise Fund, Am. Bank of Albania. Author: Domestic Affairs: American Programs and Priorities, 1979, Dog Bites Man: City Shocked, 2001, (under pseudonym Haughton Murphy) Murder for Lunch, 1986, Murder Takes a Partner, 1987, Murders and Acquisitions, 1988, Murder Keeps a Secret, 1989, Murder Times Two, 1990, Murder Saves Face, 1991, A Very Venetian Murder, 1992. Mem. Mayor's Commn. Cultural Affairs, 1981-91; bd. dirs. Nat. Corp. Fund for Dance, Inc., 1981-88, Sch. Am. Ballet, Commonweal Mag., Alliance for the Arts, N.Y.C., Inst. for Advanced Cath. Studies; bd. trustees N.Y.Pub. Libr. Mem. Assn. of Bar of City of N.Y., Coun. Fgn. Rels., Mystery Writers Am. (bd. dirs. 1986-92, treas. 1992), Authors Guild (mem. coun. 1993—), Crime Writers Assn. (U.K.), Century Assn. Democrat. Roman Catholic. Address: 116 E 68th St New York NY 10021-5955 E-mail: jduffy@attglobal.net.

DUFFY, JAMES EARL, JR., lawyer; b. St. Paul, June 4, 1942; s. James Earl and Mary Elizabeth (Westbrook) D.; m. Jeanne Marie Ghiardi, June 7, 1969; children— Jennifer, Jessica. B.A., Coll. St. Thomas, 1965; J.D., Marquette U., 1968. Bar: Wis. 1968, Hawaii 1969. Assoc. Cobb & Gould, Honolulu, 1968-71, Chuck & Fujiyama, Honolulu, 1972-74; ptnr. Fujiyama, Duffy & Fujiyama, Honolulu, 1975— ; mem. Am. Bd. Trial Advocates. ; mem. med. ethical resources com. Kapiolani Children's Med. Ctr., 1984— . Mem. Hawaii Bar Found. (bd. dirs. 1984—), Hawaii Bar Assn. (pres. 1982), Hawaii Trial Lawyers Assn. (pres. 1981), Hawaii Supreme Ct. Jud. Coun., Trial Lawyers Assn. Am. (bd. govs. 1982-85), Hawaii Acad. Plaintiff's Attys. (pres. 1986-93), Am. Inns of Court IV. Roman Catholic. Home: 1567 Ulueo St Kailua HI 96734-4408 Office: Fujiyama Duffy & Fujiyama 1001 Bishop St Honolulu HI 96813-3429

DUFFY, JAN, law educator, lawyer; b. Wichita, Kans., Apr. 27, 1950; d. Dwight C. and Helen J. Hornberger; AB, Stanford U., 1972; JD, Case Western Res. U., 1976. Bar: Ohio 1976, Calif. 1978. Assoc. Jones Day Reavis & Pogue, Cleve., 1976-77, Orrick, Herrington & Sutcliffe, San Francisco, 1978-80; prof. Calif. Poly. State U., San Luis Obispo, 1980-98; of counsel Sinsheimer, Schiebelhut & Baggett, San Luis Obispo, 1983-91; prin. Mgmt. Practices Group, Inc., 1998—. Contbr. articles to legal jours. Chair Calif. Minimum Wage Bd., 1984. Mem. ABA (co-chair workplace privacy subcom. 1981-94, co-chair employee rights and responsibilities com. 1994-97, co-chair technology com. 2000-03), Calif. Women Lawyers, XBHR (founding mem.). Democrat. Office: Ste 207 355 Bryant St San Francisco CA 94107-4141 E-mail: janduffy@managementpractices.com.

DUFFY, JOHN CHARLES, psychiatric consultant; b. Cleve., June 19, 1934; s. John Joseph and Hannah (McIllwee) D.; m. Francoise C. Antonini; children: Charles, Robert, John. Grad., Boston Coll., 1956; MD, N.Y. Med. Coll., 1960. Intern Henry Ford Hosp., Detroit, 1960-61; resident Mayo Clinic, Rochester, Minn., 1963-67; exec. dir. Tucson Child Guidance Ctr., 1971-74; commd. med. officer USPHS, 1974; prof., assoc. chmn. Uniformed Svcs. U. Sch. Medicine, Bethesda, Md., 1974-81; assoc. commr. health affairs FDA, cons. Surgeon Gen., Rockville, Md., 1981-88; asst. surgeon gen. USPHS, 1983-92, chief physician officer, 1983-88; dir. C. Everett Koop Inst. Dartmouth Coll., Hanover, N.H., 1992-94; prof. psychiatry Uniformed Svcs. U. Sch. Medicine, Bethesda, 1981-94, clin. prof., 1994—, joint commr. on accreditation of healthcare orgns. Surveyor Joint Commn. on Accreditation of Healthcare Orgns., 1998—; founder Integrative Healthcare Solutions. Author: Psychiatric Morbidity of Physicians, 1964, Psychiatric Issues in the Lives of Physicians, 1966, Child Psychiatry, 1972, 86, Psychiatric Reviews, 1976; founding editor-in-chief Child Psychiatry and Human Devel., 1970-83; editor: Ship's Medical Chest, 1984; editor-in-chief Mil. Medicine; mem. editl. bd. MD mag., 1976—. Recipient OutstandingSvc. medal Bd. Regents Uniformed Svcs. U., 1981, Surgeon Gen.'s medallion. Fellow Am. Psychiat. Assn. (life), Aerospace Med. Assn. (assoc.; Longacre medal); mem. Assn. Mil. Surgeons U.S., Sigma Xi. Roman Catholic. Home: 2402 Golf Vista Blvd Viera FL 32955

DUFFY, JOHN JOSEPH, retired academic administrator, history educator; b. Charleston, S.C., Apr. 25, 1931; s. John Joseph and Mary (McMahon) D.; m. Marcia Fletcher Tinkham, Aug. 15, 1959; children: Katharine, John Joseph, Eleanor. BA in History, Coll. Charleston, 1952; MA in History, U. S.C., 1955, PhD in History, 1963. Dir. U. S.C., Beaufort, 1959-66, assoc. prof. history Columbia, 1964-98, acad. coord. Coll. Gen. Studies, 1966-67, asst. provost regional campuses, 1967-68, assoc. provost regional campuses, 1968-72, assoc. v.p. regional campuses, 1972-77, system v.p. univ. campuses and continuing edn., 1977-88, chancellor univ. campuses and continuing edn., 1988-91; vice provost for regional campuses and continuing edn., 1991-92; vice provost, exec. dean regional campuses/continuing edn. U. S.C., Columbia, 1992-98; ret., 1998. Author: (radio script) Secession Convention of 1860, 1960; (pamphlet) A Short History of Beaufort County, 1975, also articles. Dist. chmn. Midlands coun. Boy Scouts Am., 1969-71; sustaining mem. S.C. Dem. Party. Recipient Disting. Svc. award Garnet and Black of U. S.C., 1969, Outstanding Edn. Profl. award S.C. Assn. Higher Continuing Edn., 1983, Disting. Svc. award Ednl. Found. U. S.C., 1989; named Young Man of Yr. Jaycees, Beaufort County, S.C., 1964 Mem. So. History Assn., S.C. History Assn., Nat. Univ. Continuing Edn. Assn. (chair region III 1980-82), Nat. Assn. State Univs. and Land Grant Colls., Rotary, Phi Beta Kappa Roman Catholic. Avocations: reading, music.

DUFFY, JOHN LEWIS, retired Latin, English and reading educator; b. Whittemore, Iowa, Oct. 6, 1934; s. Lewis A. and Dorothy (Bestenlehner) D.; m. Anne O'Brien, July 19, 1958; children: Jane, Paul, Sarah, Steven. BA, Loras Coll., Dubuque, Iowa, 1956; MS Ed, Creighton U., 1961; student, U. Minn., summer 1967. Jr. and sr. H.S. tchr., coach Presentation Acad., Whittemore, Iowa, 1957-58; H.S. tchr. Clear Lake (Iowa) Cmty. Schs., 1958-61; teaching asst. U. Iowa, Iowa City, 1961-62; tchr. Latin Larkin H.S., Elgin, Ill., 1962-96,

students' coun. advisor, 1965-71, chmn. English and fgn. langs., 1969-77, chmn. English and reading divsn., 1977-96. Tchr. prep. courses for ACT, PSAT and SAT Elgin YWCA and Larkin H.S., Elgin, 1977-96. Summer chef's asst. The Frugal Gourmet, WTTW-TV, Chgo., 1983. Bd. trustees Elgin C.C., 1975—, chmn., 1980-81, 85-87, 97-2001, vice-chmn., 1981-84, 94-95; bd. dirs. Elgin Area Cath. Social Svcs., 1981-90, pres., 1986-88; mem. St. Laurence Parish Bd., 1974-79, Edn. Commn., 1972-79, chmn. Edn. Commn., 1974-79; state advisor Iowa Jr. Classical League, 1960-61. Named Kane County Disting. Educator of Yr., 1982, Outstanding Young Men in Am., 1970; recipient Outstanding Young Educator award Elgin Jaycees, 1969. Mem.: Am. Assn. Cmty. and Jr. Colls., Ill. Coun. Tchrs. English, Nat. Coun. Tchrs. English, Ill. Classical League, Am. Classical League, Elgin Assn. Sch. Adminstrs., Elgin Tchrs. Assn. (welfare chmn. and chief negotiator 1963—65, pres. 1966—67), Ill. Edn. Assn. (legis., chmn. northeastern divsn. 1968—71, chmn. ad hoc com. on tchr. tenure 1972—73), Ill. C.C. Trustees Assn. (exec. com. 1981—84, chmn. west suburban region 1981—84, chmn. fed. rels. com. 1982—87, bd. rep. 1986—95, 1997—, exec. com. 1998—2000, chmn. west suburban region 1998—2000, exec. com. 2002—04, chmn. west suburban region 2002—04, Trustee of Yr. award 2002), Am. Assn. C.C. (bd. dirs. 1990—93), Assn. C.C. Trustees (chmn. ctrl. region nominating com. 1981—82, sgt.-at-arms ann. conv. 1982, mem. com. on internat. rels. 1983—84, bd. dirs. 1983—89, chmn. future directions com. 1984—86, fed. rels. commn. 1985—93, chmn. ctrl. region 1987—88, vice-chmn. fed. rels. commn. 1987—88, chmn. fed. rels. commn. 1988—89, chmn. ctrl. region nominating com. 1992—93, Ctrl. Region Trustee of Yr. award 1991, 2002). Home: 192 Kathleen Dr Elgin IL 60123-5914 also: 4840 Heron Run Cir Leesburg FL 34748-7819 Fax: (847) 429-0408.

DUFFY, LAWRENCE KEVIN, biochemist, educator; b. Bklyn., Feb. 1, 1948; s. Michael and Anne (Browne) D.; m. Geraldine Antoinette Sheridan, Nov. 10, 1972; children: Anne Marie, Kevin Michael, Ryan Sheridan. BS, Fordham U., 1969; MS, U. Alaska, 1972, PhD, 1977. Tchg. asst. dept. chemistry U. Alaska, 1969-71, rsch. asst. Inst. Arctic Biology, 1974-77; postdoctoral fellow Boston U., 1977-78, Roche Inst. Molecular Biology, 1978-80; rsch. asst. prof. U. Tex. Med. Br., Galveston, 1980-82; asst. prof. neurology (biol. chemistry) Med. Sch. Harvard U., Boston, Mass., 1982-87, adv. biochemistry instr. Med. Sch., 1983-87; instr. gen. and organic chemistry Roxbury C.C., Boston, 1984-87; prof. chemistry and biochemistry U. Alaska, Fairbanks, 1992—, head dept. chemistry and biochemistry, 1994-99; assoc. dean for grad. studies and outreach Coll. Sci. Engring. and Math., U. Alaska, Fairbanks, 2000—. Coord. program biochemistry and molecular biology for summer undergrad. rsch., 1987-96; pres. U. Alaska Fairbanks Faculty Senate, 2000-01. Mem. editl. bd. Sci. of Total Environment. Pres., bd. dirs. Alzheimer Disease Assn. of Alaska, 1994-95; mem. instnl. rev. bd. Fairbanks Meml. Hosp., 1990; sci. adv. bd. Am. Fedn. Aging Rsch, 1991-95. Lt. USNR, 1971-73. NSF trainee, 1971, J.W. McLaughlin fellow, 1981; W.F. Milton scholar, 1983; recipient Alzheimers Disease and Related Disorders Assoc. Faculty Scholar award, 1987; Carol Fiest Outstanding Advisor award, 1994, 97, Nat. Inst. Deafness & Commn. Disorders, NIH Cert. of Merit for mentoring, 1996, North Star Bough Sch. Dist. Svc. award, 1998, Alumni Achievement award for profl. activity U. Alaska-Fairbanks, 1999, Usibelli award for rsch., 2002. Fellow: Am. Inst. Chemists (mem. editl. bd. Sci. of Total Environment 1999, assoc. editor Jour. Alzheimer's Disease 2000, bd. dirs. 2002—, cert. profl. chemist, sec. bd. dirs. 2003); mem.: AAAS (arctic divsn. exec. dir.), Soc. Environ. Toxicologists and Chemists, Am. Soc. Circumpolar Health (bd. dirs. 1999—2001, 2003), Internat. Soc. Toxinologists, Am. Chem. Soc. (Analytical Chemistry award 1969), N.Y. Acad. Scis., Am. Soc. Biol. Chemists, Am. Soc. Neurochemists, Sigma Xi (assoc. regional dir. 2000—02, pres. 1991 Alaska club, nominating com.), Phi Lambda Upsilon. Roman Catholic. Office: U Alaska Fairbanks Dept Chemistry and Biochemistry Box 756160 Fairbanks AK 99775

DUFFY, MARTIN EDWARD, management consultant, economist; b. Fall River, Mass., May 24, 1940; s. Arthur Louis and Edna Marie (Cunneen) D.; m. Irene Patricia Daley, Aug. 24, 1968 (div. Jan. 1980); 1 child, Kathryn; m. Priscilla Claire Stieff, May 14, 1988; 1 child, Brianna. BS in History, BSEE, Tufts U., 1963; MBA, U. Pa., 1967. Asst. dean U. Pa., 1967-71; asst. dir. Fels Ctr., U. Pa., 1971-73; v.p. Data Resources, Lexington, Mass., 1975-84; v.p., gen. mgr. MRCA Info. Svcs., Cambridge, 1984-86; pres. The Perseus Group/RCG, Boston, 1986—; co-founder AllSeasons Investments, 1999—. Planning com. White Ho. Conf. on Aging, Washington, 1981; cons. La in 2001, Baton Rouge, 1982; lectr. in field; adj. prof. mgmt. Emmanuel Coll., Suffolk U.; conf. leader Presdl. Summit for Am.'s Future, 1997. Author: The Elderly in Future Economy, 1981. Lt. USN, 1963-65. Mem. Am. Econs. Assn., Nat. Assn. Forensic Economists, Cambridge Sports Union, Tufts U. Alumni Assn. (pres. 1985, exec. com. 1982-87, mem. coun. 1978—), Nat. Bus. Travelers Assn. (bd. dirs. ednl. com. 1988-93). Roman Catholic. Avocations: running marathons, mountain climbing, biking. *A career is an unfolding process, like the gradual opening of an exotic design, demanding only our presence, attention and determination to do well.*

DUFFY, MARTIN PATRICK, lawyer; b. Louisville, Feb. 2, 1942; s. Martin Joseph and Elsie (Shrader) D.; m. Virginia Schoo, Mar. 20, 1970; children: Timothy Brian, Kathleen Kelly. AB in English, U. Notre Dame, 1964; JD, U. Louisville, 1975. Bar: Ky. 1975, U.S. Tax Ct. 1980. Ptnr. Olson, Baker, Henriksen & Duffy, Louisville, 1978-79, Wyatt, Tarrant & Combs, Louisville, 1979-. Bd. dirs. Bellarmine Coll. Overseers, Louisville, 1974-80; trustee St. Mary & Elizabeth Hosp., Louisville, 1980-86, chmn. bd. 1982-85. With U.S. Army, 1964-65, 68-69. Mem. ABA, Ky. Bar Assn., Louisville Bar Assn. Democrat. Roman Catholic. Avocations: running, golf. Office: Wyatt Tarrant & Combs 2700 Citizens Plz Louisville KY 40202 Fax: 502-589-0309. E-mail: pduffy@wyattfirm.com.

DUFFY, MARY KATHLEEN, neonatal nurse; b. Oak Park, Ill., Aug. 10, 1949; d. William F. and Mary F. (Lang) D. ADN, Triton Coll., River Grove, Ill., 1976; BSN with honors, Ill. Benedictine Coll., Lisle, 1986. Staff nurse gen. med./surg. unit MacNeal Hosp., Berwyn, Ill., 1976-80, staff nurse, level II nursery, 1980-86; staff nurse, neonatal intermediate intensive care nursery DeKalb Gen. Hosp., Decatur, Ga., 1986-87; staff nurse level II nursery MacNeal Hosp., Berwyn, 1987-88; staff nurse level III neonatal intensive care unit Good Samaritan Hosp., Downers Grove, Ill., 1988—. Mem. Nat. Assn. Neonatal Nurses, Sigma Theta Tau. E-mail: mkd50@earthlink.net.

DUFFY, MICHAEL F. commissioner; BA, Catholic U. Am., 1971; JD, George Washington U., Nat. Law Ctr., 1976. Bar: Am., DC. Atty. Fed. Mine Safety Health Rev. Commn., 1977—79; sr. counsel Am. Mining Congress, 1979—87; counsel to chmn. Fed. Mine Safety Health Rev. Commn., 1987—93; dep. gen. counsel Nat. Mining Assn., 1993—2002; commr. Fed. Mine Safety Health Rev. Commn., 2002—. Author: Resolution of MSHA Disputes The Need for Change and Suggestions for a More Productive Approach, 1993, Safety and Health Beyond the Gates The Overlap of EPA and MSHA Standards on Explosives: A Case Study, 1994, Prometheus Re-Bound: How Adoption of the Kyoto Protocol on Climate Change Would Devastate the Western U.S. Coal Industry, 1999. Office: Fed Mine Safety Health Rev Commn 601 New Jersey Ave Washington DC 20001*

DUFFY, PATRICK SEAN, events producer, real estate consultant; b. Long Beach, Calif., Sept. 16, 1964; s. Thomas Peter Duffy and Maureen Lucille (McNerney) Habel. BA in Econs., U. Calif., San Diego, 1986. Asst. to v.p. and gen. mgr. Kaiser Devel. Co., Carlsbad, Calif., 1986; treasury adminstrn. specialist Imperial Corp. Am., San Diego, 1986—93; v.p. Market Profiles San Diego, 1987-93; owner, mgr. Cmty. Info. Systems, San Diego, 1992-94; corp. mktg. rsch. mgr. INCO Homes Corp., Upland, Calif., 1993-94; pub. The New Home Report, 1994-96; project mgr. digital studios divsn. Sony Pictures Entertainment, 1996-98; prodn. mgr. LMNO Prodns., 1999—2000; v.p. Market Pointe Realty Advisors, 2000—; pub. Residential Tech Trends; v.p. Bergman Orgn., L.A., 2002—. Contbr. articles to profl. publs. Bd. dirs., treas. San Diego Uptown Cmty. Planning Com., 1991—93; bd. dirs. ReVisions Resources, 1991—94; mem. host com. AIDS Found. San Diego, 1993; grad. L.E.A.D. San Diego, 1994; ann. sitcom event chair AMFAR, 1999—2001; founder BIAISC Tech. Task Force; mem. nat. steering com. Gore 2000. Mem. Constrn. Industry Fedn. San Diego (alt. mem. polit. policies com. 1993, mem., co-chmn. fund raising subcom. 1993), Bldg. Industry Assn. San Diego (mem., column editor real estate fin. com. 1990-91, planning retreat com. 1992, co-chmn. SAM awards com. 1993), Toastmasters (v.p. pub. rels. 1992, chmn. exec. com. 1997—). Avocations: piano, writing, volunteer activities, fundraising events, politics. Address: 3924 E 8th St Long Beach CA 90804-5317 E-mail: sarckar@aol.com.

DUFFY, ROBERT ALOYSIUS, aeronautical engineer; b. Buck Run, Pa., Sept. 9, 1921; s. Joseph Albert and Jane Veronica (Archer) D.; m. Elizabeth Reed Orr, Aug. 19, 1945 (dec.); children: Michael Gordon, Barclay Robert (dec.), Marian Orr (dec.), Judith Elizabeth Parsons, Patricia Archer; m. Jenifer Williams Pickett, Nov. 28, 1992. BS in Aero. Engring., Ga. Inst. Tech., 1951. Commd. 2d lt. U.S. Army, 1942; commd. U.S. Air Force, advanced through grades to brig. gen., 1967; vice comdr. USAF Space and Missile Systems Orgn., L.A., 1970-71; ret., 1971; v.p., dir. Draper Lab. div. MIT, Cambridge, Mass., 1971-73; pres., chief exec. officer Charles Stark Draper Lab., Inc., 1973-87, dir., 1973-91, dir. emeritus, 1991—. Contbr. articles to profl. jours. Decorated Disting. Svc. medal, Legion of Merit; recipient Thomas D. White award Nat. Geog. Soc., 1970; named to Ga. Tech. Engring. Hall of Fame, 1994. Fellow AIAA; mem. NAE, Internat. Acad. Astronautics, Inst. Navigation (Thurlow award 1964, pres. 1976-77), Air Force Assn., Tau Beta Pi. Home: 1001 Arbor Lake Dr #1108 Naples FL 34110 Office: Charles Stark Draper Lab 555 Technology Sq Cambridge MA 02139-3539 E-mail: fortressd@aol.com.

DUFFY, RUTH ANNE, pharmacologist; b. Jersey City, N.J., June 6, 1960; d. William John Harney and Joan B. Brennan; m. Mark Thomas Duffy, Oct. 22, 1988; children: Megan Elizabeth, Christopher William. BA magna cum laude, Chatham Coll., 1982; MA, CUNY, 1988, PhD, 1996. Assoc. scientist Schering-Plough Rsch., Bloomfield, NJ, 1989—92; from rsch. scientist to sr. scientist Schering Plough Rsch. Inst., Kenilworth, NJ, 1992—2000, sr. scientist, 2000—03, assoc. prin. scientist, 2003—. Contbr. articles to profl. jours. Recipient Foltin award, Chatham Coll., 1982. Mem.: Am. Soc. of Pharmacology and Exptl. Therapeutics, N.Y. Acad. of Scis., Soc. for Neuroscience. Avocations: reading, travel, painting. Office: Schering-Plough Research Institute 2015 Galloping Hill Road Kenilworth NJ 07033 Office Fax: 908-740-2383. E-mail: ruth.duffy@spcorp.com.

DUFFY, TERRENCE A. brokerage house executive; married. BS in bus. adminstrn., U. Wis. - Whitewater, 1980. Pres. TDA Trading, Inc., 1981—; vice chmn. Chgo. Merc. Exch. Holdings Inc., 2001—02, chmn. bd., 2002—; vice chmn. Chgo. Merc. Exch. Inc., 1995—2002, chmn. bd., 2002—. Mem. Chgo. Merc. Exch., 1981—, bd. dirs., 1995—, chmn. bd., 2002—. Office: Chgo Merc Exch 30 S Wacker Dr Chicago IL 60606*

DUFFY, THOMAS PATRICK, retired poet; b. Chgo., Ill., Aug. 3, 1950; s. Thomas Patrick and Agnes Mary Duffy; m. Sharen Eileen Kilty, May 18, 1972 (div. Aug. 17, 1984); children: Carrie Anne, Jamie Marie; m. Cheryl Beatrice Frearson, Aug. 8, 1989. AA Liberal Arts, Glendale C.C., Ariz., 1986; BS Ops. Prodn. Mgmt., Ariz. State U., Tempe, 1992. Journeyman Electrician AT&T/ Ill., 1972. Electrician Western Electric, Chgo., 1968—73, Western Electric / AT&T, Phoenix, 1973—84; electronic technician AT&T, Phoenix, 1984—94; mgr. Lucent Technologies, Orlando, Fla., 1995—2000; process analyst AT&T, Orlando, Fla., 1994—95; poet Pho-R-Try, Orange City, Fla., 2000—. V.p. trades Comm. Workers of Am., Phoenix, 1984—92. Author: (poetry) Years Worth of yFFUD Volume I, Years Worth of yFFUD Volume II; author: (artist) poetry/photography. Precinct capt. Dem. Party, Glendale, Ariz., 1981—82, 1981—82. Avocations: car collector, house restoration, saxophone, in band. Home: PO Box 1089 Zellwood FL 32798

DUFFY, W. LESLIE, lawyer; b. NYC, Dec. 31, 1939; s. William L. and Edna (Torseillo) D.; 1 child, Alexander Durand. BA, U. Notre Dame, 1961; LLB, Columbia U., 1964; LLM, NYU, 1967. Assoc. Cahill, Gordon & Reindel, N.Y.C., 1965-73, ptnr., 1973—. Bd. dirs. various pub. cos. Contbr. articles to profl. jours. Served to lt. USNR. Mem. ABA, N.Y. State Bar Assn. Office: Cahill Gordon & Reindel LLC 80 Pine St Fl 17 New York NY 10005-1790

DUFFY, WILLIAM EDWARD, JR., retired education educator; b. Fostoria, Ohio, Aug. 30, 1931; s. William Edward and Margaret Louise (Drew) D.; m. Sally King Wolfe, Nov. 21, 1958 (div. 1978). BS, Wayne State U., 1958, MEd, 1960; PhD, Northwestern U., 1967. Tchr. social studies Detroit Pub. Schs., 1957-61; instr. Northwestern U., Evanston, Ill., 1961-65; asst. prof. gen. edn. U. Iowa, Iowa City, 1965-70, assoc. prof., 1970-94, coord. Soc. Found. Edn. program, 1978-93, chmn. divsn. founds., postsecondary edn., 1981-88; ret., 1994. Lectr. in field. Mem. editl. bd. Ednl. Philosophy Theory, 1969-71; contbr. book revs. and articles to profl. jours. With USAF, 1951-54. Fellow John Dewey Soc., Philosophy Edn. Soc.; mem. Am. Ednl. Rsch. Assn. Home: 376 Samoa Pl Iowa City IA 52246-3632

DUFFY-KING, JAN (JOHN MITCHELL MAVER WALLACE), journalist, information architect, public speaker; b. Edinburgh, Scotland, July 21, 1965; came to U.S., 1991; s. John and Annie Elizabeth (Devine) Wallace; 1 child, Shelley (dec.); m. Laurie Meredith Haughton. BA with honors, U. Oxford, Eng., 1987. Journalist Mirror Group Newspapers, London, 1987-90, editor Amsterdam, 1990-91; author JWE Internat., N.Y.C., 1991-93; info. architect eurotrash-.com., N.Y.C., also Cologne and Edinburgh, 1993—. Bd. dirs. Johnboy Records, London, eurotrash.com Inc., N.Y.C., eurotrash.com Ltd., Eng., perfectit.com Ltd., N.Y., Edinburgh, perfectit.com GmbH, Cologne, JWE Internat., Edinburgh, Brian Roache Archtl.Svcs.; chmn. Consili Ltd., Edinburgh; e-bus. advisor Scottish Parliament. Author: Zuid-Amerikaanse Reis Gids, 1993, Knowledge Management for E-Business Performance, 2001, e-Initiatives for Europe 2005, 2003, Information Architecture, Its Place in the Business Plan, 2002, (with Laurie Haughton) Search Engine Optimization, 2001. Lt. Dutch Army, 1983-87. Named Journalist of Yr., Nat. Union of Journalists, 1990. Avocations: flying helicopters, free-fall parachuting, travel. Office: 20 River Rd New York NY 10044-1100 also: 107 Magdalene Gardens Edinburgh EH15 3DS Scotland E-mail: jan@eurotrash.com.

DUFNER, EDWARD JOSEPH, editor; b. Reading, Pa., May 26, 1960; s. Edward J. Sr. and Marcia (Keiser) D.; m. Connie Elizabeth Pryzant, July 29, 1984; children: Elena Miriam, Adam Joseph. BS in Journalism, Northwestern U., 1982. Reporter, asst. regional editor Abilene (Tex.) Reporter-News, 1982-83; news editor Arlington (Tex.) Daily News, 1983, editor, 1984; copy editor The Dallas Morning News, 1984-86, asst. nat. editor, 1986-89, nat. editor, 1990-91, 93-95, polit. editor, 1992, 96, bus. reporter, 1997-99, bus. editor, 1999—. Trustee Temple Emanu-El, Dallas, 1996-2000. Mem. Soc. Am. Bus. Editors and Writers. Jewish. Avocations: running, swimming, piano, history. Office: The Dallas Morning News Comms Ctr PO Box 655237 Dallas TX 75265-5237

DUFOUR, JEAN-MARIE, economics researcher, educator; b. Montreal, Que., Can., Dec. 27, 1949; s. Jean-Marie Dessureault and Bella Dufour. BA, U. Montreal, 1969; BSc in Math., McGill U., Montreal, 1971; MSc in Stats., U. Montreal, 1973; MA in Econs., Concordia U., 1974, U. Chgo., 1978, PhD in Econs., 1979. Lectr. stats. U. Que., Trois-Rivières, 1972-73; prof. math. Coll. Édouard-Montpetit, Montreal, 1973-75; rsch. assoc. Inst. Applied Econ. Rsch. Concordia U., 1978-79; lectr. econs. U. Montreal, 1978-79, mem. rsch. staff ctr., 1979—85, sr. mem. rsch. staff, dir. rsch. program in econometrics and macroecons. ctr. de recherche et développement en économique, 1985-90, asst. prof., 1979-83, assoc. prof., 1983-88, prof., 1988—, dir. ctr. recherche et développment en économique, 1988—95, 1997—98, chmn. dept. econs., 1995—97, Can. rsch. chair in econometrics, 2001—; fellow CIRANO, 1998—. Vis. scholar MIT, 1980, Queen's U., 1986, CEPREMAP, Paris, 1986, U. Libre de Bruxelles, 1988, 89, 90, 91, 93, Ecole Nat. des Stats. et l'Adminstrn. Economique, Paris, 1990, 91, 93, 95, 2000, 2001, U. Scis. Sociales de Toulouse, France, 1992, 94, 2002, Humboldt U. Berlin, 1994, Deutsche Bundesbank, Frankfurt, 2001-02; cons. Econ. Coun. Can., 1981, Office de Planification et Devel. economique du Que., 1982, Royal Commn. Econ. Union and Devel. prospects for Can., 1983-84; invited prof. U. de Toulouse I, 1983, 94, 2002, U. Pa., 1992, U. Lausanne, 1995; rsch. fellow Ctr. Ops. Rsch. and Econometrics U. Cath. de Louvain, 1985-86; bd. dirs. Soc. Can. de Sci. Economique, 1984-87; Benjamin Meaker chair, U. Bristol, 1993, 99; vis. prof. Stanford U., 1999, Tilburg U., 2000, Technische U. Dresden, 2000. Assoc. editor Econometrica, 1996—2002, Jour. Econometrics, 1994—, Empirical Econs., 1994—, Econometric Theory, 1991-93, Econometric Reviews, 1991-96, 98—, Annales d'Économie et de Statistique, 1990—, Cahiers de Centre d'Études de Recherche Opérationnelle, 1989—, Can. Jour. Econs., 1984-88; guest editor Jour. Econometrics, 1992-93, Empirical Econs., 1993—; contbr. 75 articles to profl. jours. Recipient Excellence in Rsch. award Soc. Can. de Sci. Économique, 1988, 2000, Leave fellowship Social Scis. and Humanities Rsch. Coun. Can., 1985-86, Doctoral fellowship Can. Coun., 1975-78, Doctoral fellowship Govt. Que., 1975-78, Scholarship, U. Montreal, 1971-72; rsch. grantee Ministry Edn. Que., 1979-80, 80-81, 81-82, Social Scis. and Humanities Rsch. Coun. Can., 1980-81, 83, 83-85, 87-89, 89-91, 91-94, 94-97, 97—, U. Montreal 1979-80, Econ. Coun. Can., 1981, Govt. Que., 1982-83, 83-84, 84-85, 85-86, 86-87, 87-90, 90-93, 96-96, 96—, Royal Commn. on Econ. Union and Devel. Prospects per Can., 1983-84, Natural Scis. and Engring. Rsch. Coun. Can., 1983-86, 87-90, 89-91, 91-94, 94-97, 97—, Govt. Que. and Communauté française de Belgique, 1989-90, Govt. Que. and Govt. France, 1990-92, Can. Internat. Devel. Agy., 1991-93; Killam fellow Can. Coun. for Arts, 1998-2000. Fellow: Econometric Soc., Royal Soc. Can.of Econometrics; mem.: Can. Econ. Assn. (v.p. 2000—01, Rsch. Chair in Econs. 2001—03, pres. 2001—03), Société canadienne de sci. économique (bd. dirs. 1984—87, pres. 1998—2001), Inst. Mathematical Stats., Econometric Soc., Internat. Statis. Inst., Can. Econometric Study Group Bd. (dir. 2002—, dir. 2002—), Statis. Soc. Can. (rsch. com. 1988—), Can. Econs. Assn. (spl. prize outstanding rsch. 1994), Am. Statis. Assn., Am. Econ. Assn. Home: 1060 Ave Bernard Apt 5 Outremont QC Canada H2V 1V2 Office: U Montreal C R D E Case Postale 6128 Succursale Centre-Vill Montreal QC Canada H3C 3J7 E-mail: Jean.Marie.Dufour@umontreal.ca.

DUFRESNE, ARMAND FREDERICK, management and engineering consultant; b. Manila, Aug. 10, 1917; s. Ernest Faustine and Maude (McClellan) DuF.; m. Theo Rutledge Schaefer, Aug. 24, 1940 (dec. Oct. 1986); children: Lorna DuFresne Turnier, Peter; m. Lois Burrell Klosterman, Feb. 21, 1987. BS, Calif. Inst. Tech., 1938. Dir. quality control, chief product engr. Consol. Electrodynamics Corp., Pasadena, Calif., 1945-61; pres., dir. DUPACO, Inc., Arcadia, Calif., 1961-68; v.p., dir. ORMCO Corp., Glendora, Calif., 1966-68; mgmt., engring. cons. Duarte and Cambria, Calif., 1968—. Dir., v.p., sec. Tavis Corp., Mariposa, Calif., 1968-79; dir. Denram Corp., Monrovia, Calif., 1968-70, interim pres., 1970; dir., chmn. bd. RCV Corp., El Monte, Calif., 1968-70; owner DUFCO, Cambria, 1971-82; pres. DUFCO Electronics, Inc., Cambria, Calif., 1982-86, chmn. bd. 1982-92; pres. Freedom Designs, Inc., Simi Valley, Calif., 1982-86, chmn. bd. dirs., 1982-97; owner DuFresne Consulting, 1992—; chmn. bd., pres. DUMEDCO,Inc., 1993-95. Patentee in field. Bd. dirs. Arcadia Bus. Assn., 1965-69; bd. dirs. Cambria Community Services Dist., 1976, pres., 1977-80; mem., chmn. San Luis Obispo County Airport Land Use Commn., 1972-75. Served to capt. Signal Corps, AUS, 1942-45. Decorated Bronze Star. Mem. Instrument Soc. Am. (life), Arcadia (dir. 1965-69), Cambria (dir 1974-75), C. of C., Tau Beta Pi. Home: 61 Broad St Apt 211 San Luis Obispo CA 93405-1772

DUGAN, CINDY, music educator, organist; b. Grenada, Miss., Aug. 6, 1953; d. Clovis Jr. and Geraldine McGregor) Harden; m. Lawrence Clayton Dugan Jr.; children: Dawn Dugan Looney, Clayton Hunter. B Music Edn. cum laude, U. Miss., 1975, M Music Edn., 1993. Pvt. tchr. piano, Grenada, 1975—; tchr. music Kirk Acad., Grenada, 1975—; organist 1st Bapt. Ch., Grenada, 1978—; prof. music Holmes C.C., Grenada, 1993—. Former mem., bd. dirs. Fine Arts Coun., Grenada 1985-90. Mem. Nat. Music Tchrs. Assn. (nat. cert. tchr.), Nat. Piano Guild (piano adjudicator 1992—), Miss. Music Tchrs. Assn. (piano adjudictor 1993—), Former 20th Century Club (membership officer 1999), Phi Kappa Phi. Baptist. Avocations: reading, walking. Home: 311 Snider St Grenada MS 38901-4224

DUGAN, FORTUNE ANTHONY, cardiologist, consultant; b. Dallas, Aug. 31, 1944; s. Albert Francis and Ruth (Welsch) D.; m. Sandra Mary Duracher, 1968; children: Fortune Anthony, Bridget Ann. BS cum laude, La. State U., New Orleans, 1966, MD, 1968. Diplomate in internal medicine and cardiovascular disease Am. Bd. Internal Medicine; bd. cert. in interventional cardiology. Straight med. intern La. State U. divsn. Charity Hosp. of La., New Orleans, 1968-69, resident in medicine, 1969-71; fellow in cardioloy Duke U. Med. Ctr., Durham, N.C., 1973-75; chief cardiovascular lab. Vets. Hosp., Durham, 1975-76; assoc. in medicine, dept. int. medicine Duke U. Med. Ctr., Durham, 1975-76; mem. staff dept. cardiology East Jefferson Gen. Hosp., Metairie, La., 1979—; clin. assoc. prof. dept. medicine Tulane U. Sch. medicine. New Orleans, 1979—, med. dir. cardiology, 1998—, med. dir. cardiac catheterization lab., 1998—. Vis. staff Chairty Hosp., New Orleans, 1979—. Contbr. articles to profl. jours. Named as top cardiologist New Orleans Mag., 1994; recipient Bel award, 1968, others. Fellow ACP, Am. Coll. Chest Physicians, Am. Coll. Cardiology (v.p. La. chpt. 1991, pres. 1993-96, gov. 1993-96), Soc. for Cardiovasc. Angiography and Interventions, Internat. Soc. Cardiovasc. Interventionists; mem. AMA, Am. Heart Assn. (fellow coun. on clin. cardiology, Silver Torch award 1994), New Orleans Acad. Internal Medicine (pres. 1989-90), Am. Coll. Sports Medicine, Am. Soc. Internal Medicine, Alpha Omega Alpha, Omicron Delta Kappa, Phi Kappa Phi. Avocation: exercise. Home: 3009 Palm Vista Dr Kenner LA 70065-1560 Office: East Jefferson Gen Hosp 4200 Houma Blvd Metairie LA 70006-2996 E-mail: fdoc@msn.com.

DUGAN, GORDON F. investment banker; b. Bogota, Colombia, June 7, 1966; s. Gordon Joseph and Gloria (Vidotto) D. BS, U. Pa., 1988. Asst. to chmn. W.P. Carey & Co., Inc., N.Y.C., 1988-89, 1st v.p., 1989—94, sr. v.p., 1994—95, 1997—99, pres., 1999—2002, co-CEO, 2002—. Mem. St. Elmo Club of Phila. (undergrad. pres. 1987-88), Racquet & Tennis Club (N.Y.C.), Deepdale Golf Club (Manhasset, N.Y.), The Mashomack Preserve Club (Millbrook, N.Y.). Office: WP Carey & Co Inc 50 Rockefeller Plz New York NY 10020-1605

DUGAN, JOHN LESLIE, JR., foundation executive; b. Phila., Nov. 6, 1921; s. John Leslie and Ellen May (Reid) D.; m. Barbara McClelland Day, Dec. 21, 1946; children: Barbara Nicholas, Geoffrey McClelland, Sara Ellen. BS, Swarthmore Coll., 1943; postgrad., Harvard U., 1947-48; MBA, U. Pa., 1950. Instr. Swarthmore Coll., 1946-47, U. Pa., 1948-50; cons. Booz, Allen and Hamilton, 1951-55; asst. to pres. Grace Nat. Bank, N.Y.C., 1955-58; treas. Underwood Corp., N.Y.C., 1958-60; v.p. fin. Chicopee div. Johnson & Johnson, New Brunswick, N.J., 1960-75; dir., adminstr. Robert Wood Johnson Found., Princeton, N.J., 1975 77; exec. v.p. Am. Diabetes Assn., Inc., N.Y.C., 1977-80; exec. dir. Fin. Analysts Fedn., N.Y.C., 1981-84; pres. The Greenwall Found., N.Y.C., 1981-90; founder, pres. Buck Hill Conservation Found., 1992-97, trustee, 1992-99. Adj. prof. mgmt. St. Peter's Coll., 1975-81 Committeeman Millburn Twp., N.J., 1975-79, commr. fin. and welfare, 1976-79; vestryman, warden, lay reader Christ Ch. in Short Hills, N.J. Served to lt. comdr. USNR, 1943-46. Mem. Tau Beta Pi. Clubs: Baltusrol Golf, Short Hills, Ozone, Buck Hill Golf. Republican. Home: PO Box 851 New Vernon NJ 07976-0851

DUGAN, LEROY, chemist, educator; b. Petersburg, Ind., Aug. 18, 1915; s. LeRoy and Edith Louise Dugan; m. Dorothy Elizabeth Dooley; children: Ronald L., Terry S., Maureen K. Angelo. BS Chem., Ind. Univ., Bloomington, IN, 1937; PhD Org. Chem., Univ. Wash., Seattle, WA, 1942. Organic chemist, chief divsn. organic chemistry Am. Meat Inst. Found., Chicago, Ill., 1946—61; assoc. prof. food sci. Mich. State Univ., East Lansing, 1961—64, prof., 1964—81, asst. dean, grad. sch., 1970—81, prof., asst. dean emeritus, 1981—. Pres. north ctrl. sect. Am. Oil Chemists Soc., Chicago, Ill., 1960. Maj. Chem. Corps. AUS, 1942—46, ret. col. Chem. Corps. AUS, 1970. Achievements include Author/Co-Author, Book Chapters/Journal Articles, 1946-1985; patents for 2 Patents: Antioxidants For Fats And Oils. Avocations: gardening, reading, fishing, hunting. Home: 1889 Ridgewood Dr East Lansing MI 48823-2939 Office: Michigan State Univ East Lansing MI 48824

DUGAN, MICHAEL JOSEPH, former career officer, health agency executive; b. Albany, N.Y., Feb. 22, 1937; s. D. Joseph and Dorothy M. (Krebs) D.; m. Grace A. Robinson, Aug. 9, 1958; children: Colleen, Erin, Mike, Sean, Kathleen, Kevin. BS, U.S. Mil. Acad., 1958; MBA, U.Colo., 1972. Commd. officer USAF, 1958, advanced through grades to gen.; comdr.-in-chief U.S. Air Forces Europe, 1989-90; comdr. Allied Air Forces Cen. Europe, 1989-90; chief of staff USAF, 1990, ret., 1991; lectr. in strategic studies Johns Hopkins U., Washington, 1991-92; pres., CEO Nat. Multiple Sclerosis Soc., N.Y.C., 1992—. Decorated D.S.M., Silver Star, Legion of Merit, D.F.C., Purple Heart; Knight's Cross (Germany). Home: 36 James Ct Dillon CO 80435 Office: NMSS 700 S Broadway Ste 810 Denver CO 80203-3442 E-mail: mike.dugan@nmss.org.

DUGAN, PATRICK RAYMOND, microbiologist, university dean; b. Syracuse, N.Y., Dec. 14, 1931; s. Francis Patrick and Joan Irma (Clause) D.; m. Patricia Ann Murray, Sept. 22, 1956; children: Susan Eileen, Craig Patrick, Wendy Shawn, Carolyn Paige. BS, Syracuse U., 1956, MS, 1959, PhD, 1964. Asso. research scientist Syracuse U. Research Corp., 1956-63; mem. faculty Ohio State U., Columbus, 1964—, asso. prof., 1968-70, prof., chmn. dept. microbiology, 1970-73; acting dean Ohio State U. (Coll. Biol. Scis.), 1978-79, dean, 1979-85; prin. scientist EG&G Idaho Nat. Engring. and Environ. Lab., Idaho Falls, 1987-91, sci. and engring. fellow, 1991-94, dir. Ctr. for Bioprocessing Tech., 1987-94; ret., cons., 1994—. Author: Biochemical Ecology of Water Pollution, 1972. Trustee Columbus Zool. Assn. and Zoo, 1982—87. Fellow Am. Acad. Microbiology; mem. AAAS, Am. Soc. Microbiology (Ohio pres. 1968-70), Soc. Indsl. Microbiology, Am. Chem. Soc. E-mail: pduganzz@aol.com.

DUGAN, ROBERT PERRY, JR., retired minister, religious organization administrator; b. Morristown, N.J., Jan. 19, 1932; s. Robert P. and Marion Frances (Sahrbeck) D.; m. Marilyn I. Wertz, Aug. 8, 1953; children: Robert Perry III, Cheryl. AB, Wheaton Coll., 1953; MDiv, Fuller Theol. Sem., 1956; DD, Denver Conservative Bapt. Sem., 1985; LHD, Geneva Coll., 1985; LLD, Roberts Wesleyan Coll., 1990. Ordained to ministry Conservative Bapt. Assn. Am. 1957. Postgrad. teaching fellow in Hebrew Fuller Theol. Sem., 1954-57; minister of youth ch. Bloomfield, N.J., 1957-58; pastor Rochester, N.H., 1959-63, Elmhurst, Ill., 1963-69, Trinity Baptist Ch., Wheat Ridge, Colo., 1970-75; chaplain Senate of State of Colo., 1974-75; pres. Conservative Baptist Assn. Am., 1973-76; v.p. Rockmont Coll., Lakewood, Colo., 1976-78; dir. Office of Pub. Affairs, Nat. Assn. Evangelicals, Washington, 1978-96; v.p. governmental affairs Nat. Assn. Evangelicals, Washington, 1996-98; ret., 1999. Bd. dirs. Denver Sem., chmn., 1998-2001; Staley disting. Christian scholar lectr., 1973, 82, 84, 86, 88, 94; participant Internat. Congress on World Evangelism, Lausanne, Switzerland, 1974. Author: Winning the New Civil War: Recapturing America's Values, 1991, Stand and Be Counted: A Washington Insider Tells How to Preserve America's Liberties for You and Your Children, 1995; editor monthly newsletter NAE Washington Insight, 1979-97. Candidate for U.S. Congress, 1976; mem. ethics adv. bd. USIA, 1982-84; bd. dirs. Justice Fellowship, 1983-91, Transformation Internat., 1987-91; bd. trustees Williamsburg Charter Found., 1988-89. Home: 37784 Pineknoll Ave Palm Desert CA 92211-2128 E-mail: RPDuganJr@juno.com.

DUGAN, SEAN FRANCIS XAVIER, lawyer; b. Bklyn., June 21, 1951; s. Thomas Joseph and Maureen (Brett) D.; m. Martha S. Dones, 1981; children: Vanessa, Shivaun, Brandon, Ann Veronica. BA, SUNY, Oneonta, 1973; JD, Bklyn. Law Sch., 1977; LLM in Environ. Law, Pace U., 1991. Bar: N.Y. 1978, U.S. Dist. Ct. (so. and ea. dists.) N.Y. 1979, U.S. Ct. Appeals (2d cir.) 1993, U.S. Supreme Ct. 1988. Assoc. Martin, Clearwater & Bell, N.Y.C., 1978-84, ptnr., 1985—. Co-author: (chpt.) Automated Cervical Cancer Screening, 1994, Legal Manual for New York Physicians, 2003; author: (chpt.) Legal Manual for New York Physicians, 2003; contbr. articles to profl. jours. Mem. Environ. Council Village Sleepy Hollow, N.Y., 1987; pro bono mediator U.S. Dist. Ct. (so. dist.), N.Y. Mem. ABA (com. toxic and hazardous substances and environ. law), N.Y. State Bar Assn. (mpcl. law sect., solid and hazardous waste mgmt. com., com. product liability ins., com. profl. discipline), Assn. of Bar of City of N.Y., Nat. Inst. Trial Advocacy, Westchester County Bar Assn. (mpcl. law com.), NY State Med. Def. Bar Assn., Defense Rsch. Inst., Soc. Friendly Sons of St. Patrick. Home: 9 Birch Close Sleepy Hollow NY 10591-1001 Office: Martin Clearwater & Bell 220 E 42nd St New York NY 10017-5806 E-mail: DuganS@MCBlaw.com.

DUGAS, LOUIS, JR., lawyer; b. Beaumont, Tex., Dec. 12, 1928; s. Louis and Loney (Duron) D.; m. Frances Elizabeth Tuley, Feb. 3, 1956; children: Mary Hester Dugas Koch, Kerry Beth Dugas Davidson, Louis Claiborne, Evin Garner, Reagan Taylor. AA, Lamar Jr. Coll., 1950; BBA in Banking and Fin., U. Tex., 1956, LLB, 1960. Bar: Tex. 1960, U.S. Ct. Appeals (5th cir.) 1972, U.S. Ct. Appeals (11th cir.) 1984, U.S. Supreme Ct. 1967. Pvt. practice, 1960—. Mem. Tex. Ho. of Reps., 1954-60; justice of the peace, Orange County, Tex., 1963; spl. counsel D.C. com. U.S. Ho. of Reps., 1967; dist. and county atty., Orange County, 1968-72; former tchr. Tex. history and govt., Lamar U. Former columnist The Opportunity Valley News; columnist Orange County Record, 1993—. Regent Nat. Criminal Def. Coll., Mercer Law Sch., Macon, Ga.; explorer leader Boy Scouts Am., 1963; comdr. Am. Legion Post, 1967; mem. Bd. Adjustments, City of Orange, 1967; founder "Les Acadiens du Texas"; pres. Orange County Hist. Soc., 1974-76; active Orange Art League; bd. dirs. Orange Cmty. Players, 1977-82; tchr. Cajun French Orange City Parks and Recreation Dept., 1980-81; nominee Rep. Party for 2d Congl. Dist., Tex., 1984; pres. Lamar U. Friends of Arts, 1985-86; mem. adminstrv. bd. 1st United Meth. Ch., Orange, 1983, 84, 85, also trustee; pres. S.E. Tex. Vets. Coalition, 1999—. Sgt. USMC, 1950-52, Korea. Mem. Tex. Bar Assn. (sec. criminal law sect. 1969, 72), Orange County Bar Assn. (pres. 1979), Nat. Assn. Criminal Def. Lawyers (bd. dirs. 1982-88), Tex. Criminal Def. Lawyers Assn. (bd. dirs. 1976-88, pres. 1985-86, contbr. to pub. The Voice), Tex. Criminal Def. Lawyers Inst. (pres. 1986), Tex. Assn. Bd. Cert. Specialists in Criminal Law (pres. 1983), Tex. Criminal Def. Lawyers (sec.-treas. 1981), VFW, Gulf Coast Leathernecks (founder 1995), Optimists Club, Phi Alpha Delta Avocations: historical research, bird watching, photography, conchology, writing. Home: 1802 16th St Orange TX 77630-3309 Office: 1804 16th St Orange TX 77630-3309 E-mail: lugas@pnx.com.

DUGGAN, CAROL COOK, research director; b. Dillon, SC, May 25, 1946; d. Pierce Embree and Lillian Watkins (Eller) Cook; m. Kevin Duggan, Dec. 29, 1973. BA, Columbia Coll., 1968; MS, U. Ky., 1970. Reference asst. Richland County Pub. Libr., Columbia, S.C., 1968-69, asst. to dir., 1970, chief adult svcs., 1971-82; dir. Maris Rsch., Columbia, 1982—. Lectr. Greater Columbia (S.C.) Literacy Coun., 1973—75. Author: A History of the City of Forest Acres, S.C., 1998. Treas. Friends of S.C. Libr., 1995—; zoning bd. appeals City of Forest Acres, 1999—; worship com. Washington St. United Meth. Ch., Columbia, SC, 1985—86, 1999—, staff-parish rels. com., 1985—91, trustee, 1995—98, chair, 1993, mem. adminstr. bd., 1983—86, mem. adminstr. br., 1988—91, mem. adminstr. bd., 1993; exec. bd. United Meth. Women, 1983—2001, treas. unit 7, 1989—91, pres. unit 5, 1992—97, treas., 1998—; chmn. Washington St. United Meth. Ch., Columbia, SC, 1993—, adminstrv. bd., 1988—91, 1993. Recipient Sternheimer award, Columbia Coll., 1968. Mem.: PEO (pres. 1983—85, chmn. amendments and recommendations com. 1983—85, historian 1986—87, treas. state conv. 1987—88, historian 1990—92, v.p. 1998—99, del. internat. conv. 1999, historian 2002—), DAR, ALA (chmn. state membership com. 1979—83, councilor 1980—82), S.C. Pub. Libr. Assn. (pres. 1980—81), S.C. Libr. Assn. (sec. 1976, exec. bd. 1976, 1978—82), Columbia Coll. Alumnae Assn. (alumnae coun. spl. events com. 1996—, Columbia Coll. Commn. 150 2003), Beta Phi Mu. Methodist. Home: 2101 Woodmere Dr Columbia SC 29204-4341

DUGGAN, DENNIS MICHAEL, newspaper editor; b. Detroit, Oct. 12, 1927; s. Michael and Anne (Judge) D.; divorced; 1 child, Nancy Ellen. AB, Wayne U., Detroit, 1952. Wall St. columnist N.Y. Herald Tribune, 1960-61; asst. real estate editor N.Y. Times, 1961-62; fin. writer N.Y. Daily News, 1967; sr. editor, N.Y. bur. chief Newsday, 1973-83; columnist, 1983—. Recipient Meyer Berger award Columbia U. Grad. Sch. Journalism, 1987; co-recipient Pulitzer prize N.Y. Newsday, 1991. Mem. Inner Circle, Soc. Silurians (pres., Peter Kihss award), Dutch Treat Club. Home: 235 W 11th St New York NY 10014-2277 Office: 780 3rd Ave New York NY 10017-2024 E-mail: dinkydiz@aol.com.

DUGGAN, EDWARD MARTIN, secondary science education educator; b. Tacoma, Sept. 23, 1953; s. John and Catherine Patricia (Fitzgerald) D.; children: Rory Emmett, Orlaith Catherine Mary. BS in Psychology, BA in Zoology, U. Wash., 1979, BS in Botany, 1980, MEd in Sci. Edn., 1982. Cert. tchr., Wash., police commr., Wash., EMT. Sci. tchr. Federal Way (Wash.) Pub. Schs., 1982—, traffic safety instr., 1982—, track coach, 1996; gymnastics coach Tacoma Pub. Schs., 1982-84, track coach, 1982-88, cross country coach, 1983-88; police officer, 1996—2001; traffic safety instr., 1998—. Mem. NSTA, Audubon Soc., Nat. Wildlife Fedn. Roman Catholic. Avocations: skiing, sailing, scuba diving, science, biking. Home: 2729 SW 349th Pl Federal Way WA 98023-3090

DUGGAN, JAMES E., JR., state supreme court justice; b. 1942; Prof. Franklin Pierce Law Ctr., 1977—2001, interim dean, 1992—93; chief appellate defender State of NH, 1981—2001; assoc. justice NH Supreme Ct., 2001—. Office: Supreme Ct Bldg One Noble Dr Concord NH 03301-6160*

DUGGAN, JOHN DAVID, JR., computer technician; b. Battleboro, Vt., Nov. 21, 1972; s. John David and Martha Jane Duggan; m. Sara Ruth Wodell, Sept. 18, 1999; children: John David III, Charles Barry. BS in Biology, Salve Regina U., 1995. Validation specialist Glaxo Welcome, West Greenwich, RI, 1996—98; sr. celidanon engr. VelSource, Inc., Downingtown, Pa., 1998—2000; assoc. mgr. computer validanon Amgen, Inc., West Greenwich, 2000—. Mem.: Inst. Validanon Tech., Parenal Drug Assn. Democrat. Unitarian. Office: Amgen Corp 40 Tech Way West Greenwich RI 02817 Fax: 401-392-3740. E-mail: dugganj@amgen.com.

DUGGAN, JOSEPH PATRICK, federal agency administrator; b. St. Louis, July 5, 1955; s. Martin Lawler and Mary Margaret (Mae) D.; m. Juanita Sheryl Donaghey, Oct. 29, 1983 (div. July 1996); children: James Joseph Lawler, Edward Scott Wilson. BA in Classics magna cum laude, U. Dallas, 1976. Editl. writer The Greensboro (N.C.) Record, 1977-79; asst. editor editl. page Richmond (Va.) Times-Dispatch, 1979-81; spl. asst. to ambassadors Jeane Kirkpatrick & Edward Rowny U.S. Dept. of State, Washington, 1981-85, 86-91; speechwriter to Pres. The White House, Washington, 1991-92; budget & econ. policy advisor Office of U.S. Rep. Christopher Cox, Washington, 1993-94; comm. & policy dir. U.S. Senate Commerce Com., Washington, 1994-95; v.p., dir. media rels. Powell Tate, Washington, 1995-98; sr. v.p. The DCS Group, Washington, 1998—2002; sr. polit. advisor U.S. AID, Washington, 2002—. Mem. bd. visitors Georgetown U. Inst. Polit. Journalism, Washington, 1985, Inst. Comparative Politics and Econs., 1983-84. Founder, chmn. Washington Cath. Forum, 1985; comm. advisor Rep. Nat. Conv., San Diego, 1996. Mem. U.S. Senat Press Secs. Assn., European Inst., Cosmos Club. Roman Catholic. Home: 3632 Jenifer St NW Washington DC 20015-1752 Office: US AID Ronald Reagan Bldg Washington DC 20523

DUGGAN, KEVIN, information technology professional; b. St. Louis, Feb. 29, 1944; s. Leo Patrick and Jean Claire (McHenry) D.; m. Lillian Carol Cook, Dec. 29, 1973. BA, U. S.C., 1977; MA, Webster U., 1988. With S.C. Nat. Bank, Columbia, 1970-79; mgr. tech. support, 1978-79; dir. info. sci. tech. Midlands Tech. Coll., Columbia, 1979-97; faculty mem. Info. Sys. Tech., 1998—. Cons. electronic data processing. Mem. Richland County Friends of Libr., Literacy Coun. S.C.; chmn. fin. com. Washington St. Meth. Ch., 1987-90, chmn. stewardship com., 1982-86, mem. evangelism and membership coms., 1982-86, mem. coun. on ministries, 1982-96, mem. exec. com., 1987-90, mem. adminstrv. bd., 1982-96, 99—, lay leader, 1992-96, mem. Missions, 1997-99. Served with USMC, 1963-67. Decorated Bronze Star (3). Mem. Assn. Sys. Mgr., IBM Users Group, Data Processing Mgmt. Assn., Palmetto Fencing Soc., Amateur Fencing League Am., Rotary. Methodist. Office: PO Box 2408 Columbia SC 29202-2408

DUGGAN, PATRICK JAMES, federal judge; b. 1933; BS in Econs., Xavier U., 1955; LLB, U. Detroit, 1958. Pvt. practice Brashear, Duggan & Tangora, 1959-76; judge Wayne County Cir. Ct., 1977-86, U.S. Dist. Ct. (ea. dist.) Mich., Detroit, 1987—. Adj. prof. Madonna U., Livonia, Mich., 1975-93. Chmn. Livonia Family YMCA, 1970-71; bd. trustees Madonna U., 1970-79; pres. Livonia Bar Assn., 1975-76. Mem. Mich. Jaycees (pres. 1967-68), Am. Inn of Ct. U. Detroit Law Sch. (pres.) Office: US Dist Ct 867 Theodore Levin Cthouse 231 W Lafayette Blvd Detroit MI 48226-2700

DUGGAN, THOMAS PATRICK, management consultant; b. Hartford, Conn., Mar. 17, 1946; s. Edward O. and Mildred B. (Balf) Duggan; m. Marcia McCormack, Aug. 31, 1968 (div. 1978); children: Mary Christina, T. Patrick; m. Ann Hailey, Sept. 21, 1985; 1 child, Christopher T. AB, Providence Coll., 1968; postgrad. studies in Mgmt., We. N. Eng. Coll., 1969-71. Mgr. Travelers Mgmt. Svcs., Hartford, Conn., 1968-75; mgr. mgmt. cons. svcs. Coopers & Lybrand, N.Y.C., 1975-79; prin., dir. ins. mgmt., cons. svcs. Hay Assocs., N.Y.C., 1979-84; exec. v.p., nat. dir. bus. strategy cons. group Alexander & Alexander Mgmt. Cons. Svcs., N.Y.C., 1984; pres. Duggan Cons. Assocs., New Albany, Ohio, 1984—. 1st lt. USAR, 1968-75. Mem. Human Resource Planning Soc., Am. Mgmt. Assn., Ins. Acctg. and Statis. Assn. (session chmn. 1975-79), New Albany Country Club. Home: 7531 Ehret Round New Albany OH 43054-8926

DUGGER, RICHARD CHARLES, music educator; b. Tulsa, Okla., June 11, 1950; s. James Marvin and Ninah Joy Dugger. MusB, Okla. State U., 1972, B in Music Edn., 1977; M in Horn Performance, Ind. U., 1974; PhD, U. North Tex., 1992. Dir. of bands Ctrl. Jr. H.S., Sand Springs, Okla., 1977—81; dir. of bands, supr. instrumental music Okmulgee (Okla.) H.S., 1984—88; asst. prof. music edn. U. of the Pacific, Stockton, Calif., 1990; assoc. prof. music U. New Orleans, 1992—2001; assoc. prof. of music U. Louisville, 2001—. Asst. prin. horn Tulsa Philharm. Orch., 1978—81; French horn Audubon Wind Quintet, New Orleans, 1996—2001; condr. and musical dir. New Orleans Concert Band, 1998—2001; 2d horn Jefferson Parish Arts Soc. Symphony, New Orleans, 1999—2001. Contbr., articles to profl. jours. Mem.: Coll. Band Dirs. Nat. Assn., Am. Sch. Band Dirs. Assn., Music Educators Nat. Conf., Phi Mu Alpha Sinfonia, Kappa Kappa Psi (life). Home: 3122 W Horton Ave Louisville KY 40220 Office: U Louisville Sch of Music Louisville KY 40292 Office Fax: 502-852-0520. E-mail: rdugger@louisville.edu.

DUGGER, TOMMY RAY, academic administrator; b. Carlinville, Ill., Dec. 6, 1948; s. Junior Ray and Luella Jane Dugger; m. Kathy Lee Dugger, Apr. 4, 1970; children: Jason Thomas, Justin Matthew. AA, Hannibal-LaGrange Coll., 1976; BS in Ch. Recreation, S.W. Bapt. U., 1978; MA in Bus. Mgmt., Webster U., 1991. Gen. mgr. WeatherFORD Motors, Carlinville, Ill., 1970-72; nursing home adminstr. Weatherford Nursing Home, Carlinville, Ill., 1972-74; youth min. Immanual Bapt. Ch., Hannibal, Mo., 1976; recreation facility dir. First Bapt. Ch., Bolivar, Mo., 1976-77; recreation intern Trinity Bapt. Ch., Lake Charles, La., 1977; min. activities Concord Bapt. Ch., Jefferson City, Mo., 1978-79; assoc. dir. admissions Hannibal-La Grange Coll., 1979-84, dean student affairs, 1984-95, v.p. for bus. and student affairs, 1995—. Deacon Calvary Bapt. Ch.; mem. Leadership Hannibal. With U.S. Army, 1968—70, Vietnam. Mem. Bapt. Assn. Student Affairs (pres.-elect 1997, pres. 1998, sec.-treas. 2001-2003). Avocations: classic cars, boating. Office: Hannibal-LaGrange Coll 2800 Palmyra Rd Hannibal MO 63401-1999

DUGGER, WILLIAM MAYFIELD, economics educator; b. Garden City, Kans., Nov. 7, 1947; s. Charles B. and Mary Genevieve (Cline) D.; m. Pauline June Laddusaw, Mar. 24, 1967. BS, U. Tulsa, 1970; PhD, U. Tex., Austin, 1974. Asst. prof. econs. North Tex. State U., Denton, 1974-79, assoc. prof., 1980-81, DePaul U., Chgo., 1981-84, prof., 1985-93; prof. Econs. U. Tulsa (Okla.), 1993—. Cochran-Hersh meml. lectr. U. North Tex., Denton, 1988. Author: Alternative to Retrenchment, 1984, Corporate Hegemony, 1989, Underground Economics, 1991; co-author: (with Howard Sherman) Reclaiming Evolution, 2000; editor: Radical Institutionalism, 1989, Inequality, 1996; co-editor: (with William Waller) The Stratified State, 1992, co-editor: (with Howard Sherman) Evolutionary Theory in the Social Sciences, 4 vols., 2002. Recipient Thomas Divine award in social econs., 2002. Mem. AAUP (pres. DePaul U. chpt. 1991—93), Assn. Social Econs. (pres. 1984-85, exec. coun. 1980-82), Assn. Evolutionary Econ. (pres. 1997, bd. dirs. 1990—), Assn. Instl. Thought (pres. 1987-88), Union Radical Polit. Econs., Western Social Sci. Assn. Avocations: bass fishing, hiking, traveling. Office: Dept Economics U Tulsa Tulsa OK 74104-3189

DUGGINS, DAVID DRYDEN, lawyer; b. Wichita, Kans., June 9, 1937; s. Frank Hall and Camille (Wilson) Duggins; m. Elizabeth Lauderman, Nov. 4, 1967; children: David Dryden II, William Scott. BA, Tulane U., 1960, LLB, 1962. Bar: La. 1962. Landman Chevron Oil Co., 1962; ptnr. Newman, Duggins, Drolla & Gamble, 1967-74; pvt. practice New Orleans, 1974—. V.p. adv. bd. Salvation Army New Orleans, pres., 1994—95; mem. La. Civil Svc. League, Jefferson Parish Charter Adv. Bd., Velocity Found., La. Coun. Music and Peforming Arts, La. State Civil Svc. Commn., Preservation Resource Ctr.; founder, past pres. Jeuness D'Orleans; mem. adv. bd. St. Martins Episcopal Sch.; past chmn. bd. dirs. St. George's Episcopal Sch.; mem. alumni bd. Metairie Park Country Day Sch.; mem. arson com. New Orleans Fire Dept. Named Vol. of the Yr., Salvation Army, 1992; recipient Monte M. Leman award, La. Civil Svc. League. Mem.: Rotary (pres. New Orleans chpt. 1995—96). Republican. Methodist. Avocations: hunting, fishing, gourmet cooking, renovations, antiques. Home: 32 Orpheum Ave Metairie LA 70005-4524 Office: 1011 Julia St New Orleans LA 70113-1904 E-mail: dduggins@bellsouth.net.

DUGGIRALA, RAVINDRANATH, geneticist, researcher; b. Ongole, India, Jan. 18, 1956; s. Moses Tirupathi and Suvarnamma Duggirala; m. Juliet Amuche Ezeilo, Nov. 18, 1959; children: Moses Amala Neville, Edwin Emeka Gautham. PhD, U. Kans., 1995. Asst. prof., rschr. dept. medicine U. of Tex. Health Sci. Ctr. at San Antonio, Tex., 1997—2002; assoc. scientist dept. genetics S.W. Found. for Biomed. Rsch., San Antonio, 2002—. Contbr. articles. Recipient One of five finalists for Young Investigator award, North Am. Assn. for the Study of Obesity, 1995; fellow U. Grants Commn. (UGC) Rsch. Fellowship, UGC, India/Dept. of Anthropolgy, 1982—85, Ludwig G. Broman Fellowship in Mus. Studies, 1987; grantee Two R01s, NIH, 1 R01: 1998-2003 and 2 R01: 2001-2006. Mem.: Am. Assn. of Anthrop. Genetics, Am. Diabetes Assn. Achievements include research in genetic epidemiology of complex diseases or phenotypes such as type 2 diabetes, obesity, gallbladder disease, coronary heart disease, diabetic nephropathy, and aging; identification of susceptibility genes for type 2 diabetes, obesity, diabetic nephropathy, gallbladder disease, coronary heart disease, and related phenotypes. Avocations: reading, world politics and politics of social stratification, NCAA basketball (Kans. Jayhawks), family. Office: SW Found for Biomedl Rsch P O Box 760549 San Antonio TX 78245-0549

DUGHI, LOUIS JOHN, JR., lawyer; b. Westfield, N.J., June 22, 1946; s. Louis John and Maybelle Helen (Albano) D.; m. Virginia Kiss, Aug. 9, 1974; stepchildren: Christopher Polek, David Polek; 1 child, Christina Blair. BA, Cornell U., 1969, JD, 1972. Bar: N.J. 1972, U.S. Dist. Ct. N.J. 1972. Assoc. Shanley & Fisher, Newark, 1972-79; ptnr. Dughi & Hewit, Cranford, Mt. Laurel, N.J., 1979—. Lectr. Inst. Continuing Legal Edn., Newark, 1973—. Trustee, Blair Acad., Blairstown, N.J., 1975-85, Kent Place Sch., Summit, N.J., 1986—. Mem. ABA, N.J. State Bar Assn., Fed. Bar Assn., Am. Bd. Trial Advocates, Def. Rsch. Inst., Echo Lake Country Club (Westfield), Bayhead Yacht Club, Beacon Hill Club (Summit). Episcopalian. Home: 921 Kimball Ave Westfield NJ 07090-1938

DUGLE, VIVIAN RACHELLE, education educator; b. Richmond, Ind., June 25, 1973; d. E. B. and Adna Clemons; m. Donald Ricky Dugle, Sept. 5, 1973. MA, Ball State U., 2000. Tchr. Fayette County Sch. Corp., Connersville, Ind., 1996—2000; asst. prof. edn. Cedarville (Ohio) U., Cedarville, 2000—. Scholar, U. Cin., 2001, 2002, 2003. Mem.: Phi Delta Kappan, Coun. Exceptional Children. Home: 72 Shawnee Ct Franklin OH 45005 Office: Cedarville University 251 N Main Cedarville OH 45314 Office Fax: 937-766-7769. Personal E-mail: duglev@earthlink.net. E-mail: duglev@cedarville.edu.

DUGOFF, HOWARD JAY, business consultant; b. Yonkers, N.Y., Nov. 23, 1936; s. Benjamin and Bessie (Ettinger) D.; divorced; children: Lorraine, Richard, Julie. M.E., Stevens Inst. Tech., 1958, MS in Physics, 1960. Research engr. Davidson Lab.-Stevens Inst. Tech., Hoboken, N.J., 1959-67, Hwy. Safety Research Inst.-U. Mich., Ann Arbor, 1967-71; chief research-analysis br. U.S. Army Tank Automotive Command, Warren, Mich., 1971-74; assoc. adminstr. Nat. Hwy. Traffic Safety Adminstrn.-U.S. Dept. Transp., Washington, 1974-77, dep. adminstr., 1977-79, research and spl. adminstr., 1979-84, Sci. and tech. advisor to sec. transp., 1984-85; sr. v.p. ICF, Inc., Washington, 1985—. Adv. com. for injury prevention and control of Ctrs. for Disease Control, HHS; mem. U.S. Radiation Policy Coun., 1979-80; mem. exec. policy bd. Alaska Natural Gas Transp. System, 1979-80; U.S. rep. European coun. of Ministers of Transport, Paris, 1979 Curtiss-Wright Corp. fellow, 1959; recipient U.S. Army Research & Devel. award, 1973; named Meritorious Fed. Exec. Pres. of U.S., 1980 Mem. Soc. Automotive Engrs. (dir. 1977) Home: 3225 Grace St NW Washington DC 20007-3641 Office: ICF Inc 1850 K St NW Washington DC 20006-2213 *I find a request to write on the subject "Thoughts on my life" thoroughly intimidating. After some consideration, and in all due immodesty, I've decided to try to record a "thought" about my approach to my work. The essence of that approach is a real commitment to the interests of the organization for which I work. I come by that commitment, which I've felt in every job I've ever had, not through intellectual or moral conviction, but by instinct. And the instinct serves me well. I've enjoyed personal gratification and success as by-products of my efforts thus motivated, to a degree far greater than I believe I could achieve by directly pursuing personal goals.*

DUGONI, ARTHUR A. orthodontics educator, university dean; b. San Francisco, June 29, 1925; s. Arthur B. and Lina Marie (Bianco) D.; m. Katherine Agnes Groo, Feb. 5, 1949; children: Steven, Michael, Russell, Mary Diane, Arthur, James. DDS, Coll. Physicians and Surgeons, San Francisco, 1948; MSD, U. Wash., 1963; BS, Gonzaga U., 1986; DHL honoris causa, U. Detroit, 1997. Diplomate Am. Bd. Orthodontics (bd. dirs., pres. 1979-86). Clin instr. operative dentistry Coll. Physicians and Surgeons, San Francisco, 1951-55, asst. clin. prof. operative dentistry, 1955-60, asst. clin. prof. orthodontics 1963-64, chair dept. orthodontics, 1963-67; assoc. prof. orthodontics U. Pacific San Francisco, 1966-77, prof., 1977—, dean sch. dentistry, 1978—. Chair coun deans Am. Assn. Dental Schs., Washington, 1985; active Pew Commn. for the Health Professions, 1993-96. Recipient award San Mateo County Dental Soc. 1971, Disting. Svc. award Pacific Coast Soc. Orthodontists, 1976, Disting Practitioner award Nat. Acads. Practice Press Club, 1987, Hinman medallion 1989, medallion of distinction U. Pacific, 1989, Orthodontic Edn. and Rsch Found. disting. merit award, 1993, Albert H. Ketcham award Am. Bd Orthodontics, 1994, Chmn.'s award Am. Dental Trade Assn., 1994, Dr. Irving E. Gruber award, 1997, List of Honor of FDI World Dental Fedn., 1998, award of merit Pacific Coast Soc. Orthodontists, 2001, Disting. Svc. award Calif Assn. Orthodontist, 2002; named Person of Yr., South San Francisco, 1960 Alumnus of Yr., U. Pacific Sch. Dentistry, 1983, U. Wash., 1984, U. San Francisco, 1988, Gonzaga U., 1992, Gold medal Pierre Fauchard Acad., 1996 Callahan Internat. award Ohio Dental Assn., 1999, Disting. Svc. award Calif Assn. Orthodontists, 2002. Fellow Am. Coll. Dentists (William John Gies award 2001, Willard C. Fleming Meritorious Svc. award, No. Calif. sect., 2003) Internat. Coll. Dentists (award of Excellence in Dentistry, 13th dist. 2002) Pierre Fauchard Acad., Acad. Dentistry Internat., Acad. Gen. Dentistry (hon fellow 1992); mem. ADA (trustee 1984-87, treas. 1987-88, pres. 1988-89 Pres.'s citation 1994, 99, Disting. Svc. award 1995), Fedn. Dentaire Internat (councilor 1989-92, treas. 1992-98, List of Honour 1999), Am. Assn. Dental Schs. (pres. 1995, Disting. Svc. award 2000), Calif. Dental Assn. (pres 1982-83), Concordia-Argonaut Club, Peninsula Golf and Country Club, Phi Kappa Phi, Omicron Kappa Upsilon, Tau Kappa Omega, Xi Psi Phi. Republican. Roman Catholic. Avocation: golf. Office: U Pacific 2155 Webster St San Francisco CA 94115-2333 E-mail: adugoni@sf.uop.edu.

DUGUA, PIERRE-YVES, journalist; b. Bône, Algeria, Nov. 10, 1960; came t U.S., 1982; s. Georges Jean and Denise Henriette (Harger) D.; m. Lisa An Utley, Jan. 11, 1986; children: Georges, Celia, Elise. Diploma, Inst. d'Etude Politiques, Paris, 1981; MA, Johns Hopkins U., 1984. Dep. rep. Banqu Paribas, Washington, 1984-89; U.S. corres. La Cote DesFossés-L'Agefi, Washington, 1990-96; U.S. bus. corres. Le Figaro, Washington, 1995—, Radi France, Washington, 1991—. Fundraiser Medicine for Autism Today, Washington, 1998—. Mem. Sc.-Po Alumni of Washington (pres., co-founder 1997-99 Home: 4208 Dresden St Kensington MD 20895-3816

DUGUID, IAIN MOIR, education educator; b. Coulsdon, United Kingdom Oct. 15, 1960; s. James Moir and Eileen Middleton Petrie Duguid; m. Barbar Ruth Befus, Sept. 1, 1984; children: James Cameron, Samuel Peter, Hanna Patricia, Robert Moir, Sarah Rose. BSc, U. of Edinburgh, 1978—81; MDi Westminster Theol. Sem., 1985—89; PhD, U. of Cambridge, 1989—92. Asso prof. of old testament Westminster Sem. in Calif., Escondido, 1996—; past Grace Presbyn. Ch. Fallbrook, Calif., 2000—03. Author: (biblical study) Th Gospel According to Abraham, Hero of Heroes, The Gospel In the Lives Isaac and Jacob. Mem.: Evang. Theol. Soc., Soc. for Bibl. Lit. Home: 292 Lakemont Dr Fallbrook CA 92028 Office: Westminster Seminary in Californi 1725 Bear Valley Pkwy Escondido CA 92028 Home Fax: 760-480-0252; Offic Fax: 760-480-0252. Personal E-mail: iduguid@wtscal.edu. E-mai iduguid@wtscal.edu.

DUGUNDJI, JOHN, aeronautical engineer; b. N.Y.C., Oct. 25, 1925; s. Basile and Rosa (Finale) D.; m. Wraye Polkey, July 25, 1965; children: Elenna Rose, Elisa Anthe. BAE, N.Y. U., 1944; MS in Aero. Engring, M.I.T., 1948, Sc.D. in Aero. Engring, 1951. Research engr. Grumman Aircraft Co., Bethpage, N.Y., 1948-49; dynamics engr. Republic Aviation Corp., Farmingdale, N.Y., 1951-56; research asso. M.I.T., 1956-57, asst. prof. aero. engring., 1957-62, asso. prof., 1962-70, prof., 1970-93, sr. lectr., 1993-2001. Served with USN, 1944-46. Mem. AIAA, Sigma Xi, Tau Beta Pi. Greek Orthodox. Home: 39 Albert Ave Belmont MA 02478-4203 Office: MIT Dept Aeros & Astronautics Cambridge MA 02139

DUHAIME, NINA LEE, research and development company executive; b. Westbrook, Tex., Feb. 13, 1926; d. Walter Frank Hupaylo and Mary Agnes (Shockley) Hupaylo-Hampton; 2 children. Lic. real estate. Social svc. enterainer USO, Colo., Calif.; retail bus., gen. mdse. Montgomery Ward, Broomes Furniture, Santa Fe, 1952—59; self employed, journalism land acquistion & devel., writing, Santa Fe, 1951—; exec. v.p. Atom, Inc., Santa Fe, 1968—81; owner, real estate agy. Sun Mountain. Agy., Santa Fe, 1964—84; owner, rancher, farmer Bar V Ranch, N.Mex., 1946—69; sale rsch., tech. writer and journalist R.W. Bryant Co., Austin, Tex., 1966 78. Contbr. columns in newspapers, articles to profl. jour. Presdl. task force advisor U.S. Gov., Washington, 1980—. Mem.: N.Y. Acad. of Sci. Achievements include U.S. presdl. fitness award, 1973 swimming; introducing the drying and mktg. of tropical fruits 1979. Avocations: cooking, gardening, singing, acting, physical fitness. Home and Office: 645 Camino Lejo Santa Fe NM 87505-7517

DUHAIME, RICKY EDWARD, music educator, woodwind specialist; b. Rochester, N.H., Jan. 3, 1953; s. Edward Francis and Ruth Frances (Lyons) D. BA, BS, U. N.H., 1976; MusM, U. Ill., 1978; D Musical Arts, U. North Tex., 1986. Lectr. U. N.H., Durham, 1976; grad. asst. U. Ill., Urbana, 1976-78; instr. music Austin Coll., Sherman, Tex., 1978-80, prof., 1980—, dir., performer instrumental ensembles, 1978—, chmn. dept. music, 1992-2000, Mildred S. Mosher prof. of music, 1993—. Vis. prof. Haydn Konservatorium, Austria, 1996, guest performing artist, 1998; prin. clarinet mid-Am. Tour Am. Wind Symphony Orch., 1973, Latin Am. Tour U. Ill.-U.S. Dept. State, 1977, Sherman Symphony Orch., 1978— Am. Chamber Winds, 1991, Austrian Classical Music Seminar Festival, Vienna, 1992—; guest soloist Walden String Quartet, 1977, Galliard String Quartet, 1986, New Millennium Quartet, 1996, Trio Eisenstadt, 2003; concerto soloist Sherman Symphony Orch., 1978, 85, 91, 93, 99, U. N.H. Wind Symphony, 1988; founding dir., performer Grand Avenue Trio, 1989—; faculty Eisenstädter Sommerakademic, Austria, 2000—. Editor modern edits. 18th century woodwind concerti; contbr. articles and revs. to profl. jours. Mem. Nat. Assn. Coll. Wind and Percussion Instrs., Internat. Clarinet Soc., Phi Kappa Phi, Pi Kappa Lambda. Office: Austin Coll 900 N Grand Ave Sherman TX 75090-4440 E-mail: rduhaime@austinc.edu.

DUHE, JOHN MALCOLM, JR., judge; b. Iberia Parish, La., Apr. 7, 1933; s. J. Malcolm and Rita (Arnandez) D.; children: Kim Duhe Holleman, Jeanne Duhe Sinitier, Edward M., M. Bofill. Student Washington and Lee U., 1951-53, BBA, Tulane U., 1955, LLB, 1957. Atty. Helm, Simon, Caffery & Duhe, New Iberia, La., 1957-78; dist. judge State of La., New Iberia, 1979-84, judge U.S. Dist. Ct. (we. dist.) La., Lafayette, 1984-88; cir. judge, U.S. Ct. Appeals (5th cir.), Lafayette, 1988-99, sr. judge, 1999—. Assoc. editor Tulane Law Rev., 1956, editor-in-chief, 1967. Mem. Order Coif, Omicron delta Kappa, Kappa Delta Phi. Office: US Ct Appeals 800 Lafayette St Ste 5200 Lafayette LA 70501-6865*

DUHL, LEONARD, psychiatrist, educator; b. N.Y.C., May 24, 1926; s. Louis and Rose (Josefsberg) D.; m. Lisa Shippee; children: Pamela, Nina, David, Susan, Aurora. BA, Columbia U., 1945; MD, Albany Med. Coll., 1948, postgrad., 1956-64. Diplomate Am. Bd. Psychiatry and Neurology (examiner 1977, 85). With USPHS, 1951-53, 54-72, med. dir., 1954-72; fellow Menninger Sch. Psychiatry Menninger Sch. Psychiatry, Winter VA Hosp., Topeka, 1949-51, resident psychiatry, 1953-54; asst. health officer Contra Costa County (Calif.) Health Dept., 1951-53; with USPHS, 1949-51, 53-54; psychiatrist profl. svcs. br., chief office planning NIMH, 1954-66; spl. asst. to sec. HUD, 1966-68; cons. Peace Corps, 1961-68; assoc. psychiatry George Washington Med. Sch., 1961-63, asst. clin. prof., 1963-68, assoc. prof., 1966-68; prof. public health Sch. Pub. Health U. Calif., Berkeley, 1968—93; prof. city planning Coll. Environ. Design U. Calif., Berkeley, 1968-92; dir. dual degree program in health and med. scis. U. Calif., Berkeley, 1971-77, clin. prof. psychiatry San Francisco, 1969—; pvt. practice psychiatry Berkeley; sr. assoc. Youth Policy Inst., Washington. Mem. sci. adv. coun. Calif. Legis., 1970-73, sr. cons. Assembly Office of Rsch., 1981-85; cons. Health Cities Program, Environ. Health, WHO, UNICEF, ICDC, Florence, Global Forum of Parliamentarians and Spititual Leaders, 1989—, Ctr. for Fgn. Journalists, 1987-90, Am. Hosp. Assn. Health Rsch. and Edn. Trust, 1995—. Author: Approaches to Research in Mental Retardation, 1959, The Urban Condition, 1963, (with R.L. Leopold) Mental Health and Urban Social Policy, 1969, Health Planning and Social Change, 1986, Social Entrepreneurship of Change, 1990, 1995, Health and the City, 1993; bd. editors Jour. Community Psychology, 1974, Jour. Cmty. Mental Health, 1974—, Jour. Mental Health Consultation and Edn., 1978—, Jour. Prevention, 1978—, Nat. Civic Rev., 1991—; contbr. articles to tech. lit. Trustee Robert F. Kennedy Found., 1971-83; bd. dirs. Citizens Policy Ctr., San Francisco, 1975-85, New World Alliance, 1980-84, Calif. Inst. for Integral Studies, 1991-95, Ptnrs. for Dem. Change, 1990—; chair First Internat. Healthy Cities Conf., San Francisco, 1993; exec. trustee Nat. Inst. for Citizen Participation and Negotiation, 1988-90; trustee Menninger Found., Topeka, 1994—, bd. dirs., 1995—; bd. dirs. Louis August Jonas Found. (Camp Rising Sun), 1990—, Ctr. for Transcultural Studies, 1996—; exec. dir. Internat. Healthy Cities Found., 1993—. Recipient World Health Day award, WHO, 1996, Health Cities award for Coalition of Healthier Cities and Cmtys., 1999, A. Horwitz award, 2002. Fellow Am. Psychiat. Assn. (life), Am. Coll. Psychiatry (life), No. Calif. Psychiat. Soc. (life), Group for Advancement in Psychiatry (chmn. com. preventive psychiatry 1962-66), APHA. Home: 639 Cragmont Ave Berkeley CA 94708-1329 Office: U Calif Sch Pub Health 410 Warren Hl Berkeley CA 94720-0001 E-mail: len-duhl@socrates.berkeley.edu.

DUHL, OLGA ANNA, literature educator, researcher; arrived in U.S., 1984; d. Emeric and Olga Kiss; m. Joseph Samuel Duhl, Oct. 17, 1981; 1 child, Esther Annamaria. MA, U. Cluj-Napoca, Romania, 1979; PhD, Rutgers U., 1992. Instr. Barnard Coll., N.Y.C., 1991; French lit. cons. Jane Voorhees Zimmerli Art Mus., New Brunswick, NJ, 1991; head tchg. asst. Rutgers U., New Brunswick, NJ, 1991; vis. prof. Eotvos Lorand U., Budapest, Hungary, 1998; adj. asst. prof. Columbia U., N.Y.C., 1999; instr. Lafayette Coll., Easton, Pa., 1992—93, asst. prof., 1993—2000, assoc. prof., 2000—03. Lit. cons. Jane Voorhees Zimmerli Art Mus., New Brunswick, NJ, 1991; mem. U. Burgundy Rsch. Ctr., 1998—. Author: Folie et Rhétorique-Dans la Sottie, 1994; editor: Le Théâtre Français Des Années, 2002; editl. bd. (other) Revue d'Etudes Françaises, 1998—; contbr. articles to profl. jours. Grantee, The Renaissance Soc. Am., 2003. Mem.: MLA. Avocations: music, theater.

DUHME, CAROL MCCARTHY, civic worker; b. St. Louis, Apr. 13, 1917; d. Eugene Ross and Louise (Roblee) McCarthy; m. Sheldon Ware, June 12, 1941 (dec. 1944); 1 child, David; m. H. Richard Duhme, Jr., Apr. 9, 1947; children: Benton (dec.), Ann, Warren (dec.). AB, Vassar Coll., 1939; DHL (hon.), Eden Theol. Sem., 2002. Tchr. elem. sch., 1939-41, 42-44; moderator St. Louis Assn. Congl. Chs., 1959—62; trustee 1st Congl. Ch., 1964—66; mem. ch. coun. St. Louis Assn. Congl. Ch., 1974-75, 84-85, 87-89, bd. deaconesses, 1978-81, bd. deacons, chmn. bd. Christian Edn., 1987-88. Former bd. dirs. Community Music Schs., St. Louis, Community Sch., Ch. Women United, John Burroughs Sch., St. Louis Bicentennial Women's Com., St. Louis Jr. League; pres. St. Louis Vassar Club; pres., bd. dirs. YWCA, St. Louis, 1973-76, chmn. ann. fund, 1989-90; bd. dirs. North Side Team Ministry, 1968-84, Chautauqua (N.Y.) Instn., 1971-79, mem. adv. coun. to bd., 1987—. Mem. adv. coun. Mo. Bapt. Hosp., 1973—89; mem. exec. com. bd. dirs. Eden Theol. Sem., 1981—95, presdl. search com., 1986—87, 1992—93, v.p., bd. dirs., 1991, chmn. 150th ann. com., 1996—2000; sec. bd. dirs. UN Assn., St. Louis, 1976—84, coun. advisors, 1993—, nat. coun., 1995—; mem. nat. coun. UN-USA, 1995—2001; pres. bd. dirs. Family and Children's Svc. Greater St. Louis, 1977—79; mem. chancellor's long range planning com. Wash. U., 1980—81, mem. Nat. Coun., Sch. Social Work, 1987—; chmn. Benton Roblee Duhme Scholar Fund; trustee Joseph H. and Florence A. Roblee Found., St. Louis, 1984—, pres., 1984—90; bd. dirs.; chmn. Chautauqua Bell Tower Scholar Fund, 1961—; bd. dirs. Nat. Inland Waterways Libr., St. Louis Merc Libr.; mem. corp. assembly Blue Cross Hosp. Svc. Mo., 1978—86; pres. Joseph H. and Florance A. Roblee Found., 2002. Recipient Mary Alice Messerley award for volunteerism Health and Welfare Coun. St. Louis, 1971, Vol. of Yr. award, YWCA, 1976, Woman of Achievement award St. Louis Globe Democrat, 1980, Outstanding Lay Women nomination Mo. United Ch. of Christ, 1991, Outstanding Alumna award John Burroughs Sch., 1992, Humanitarian award Planned Parenthood St. Louis, 2000. Home: 8 Edgewood Rd Saint Louis MO 63124-1817

DUHME, H(ERMAN) RICHARD, JR., sculptor, educator; b. St. Louis, May 31, 1914; s. Herman Richard and Ruth Frances (Leggat) Duhme; m. Carol Louise McCarthy, Apr. 9, 1947; children: David W., Benton Roblee(dec.), Ann Duhme Nelson, Warren L.(dec.). Student, Pa. Acad. Fine Arts, 1932-38, U. Pa., 1934, Am. Sch. Classical Studies, Athens, Greece, 1951; B.F.A., Washington U., St. Louis, 1953. Prof. sculpture Washington U., St. Louis, 1947-82, prof. emeritus, 1982—; head sculpture dept. Chautauqua Instn. Summer Sch., 1953-85, Syracuse U. Chautauqua Center, 1953-69. Numerous sculpture commns. including St. Martin and the Beggar, Episcopal Cathedral, Erie, Pa., Lion Cub Fountain, Mycenae, Greece, Bears, Washington U., St. Louis, fountain Boy with Recorder, Chautauquq, NY, Pettus Meml. Fountain in Mo. Bot. Garden, St. Louis, Busts, John Horan, Merck Chem. Co., Rahway, N.J., George Kassabaum, St. Louis, Dr. Koici Iwadare, Tokyo, Dr. William H. Danforth, St. Louis, others. Served with USAAF, 1942-46. Decorated Bronze Stars; designed medals Shepherd's award Nat. Coun. Chs., Mo. Sesquicentennial, Chatutauqua Centennial, Dr. Evarts A Graham medal, Christi Vivit medal Concordia Sem., others. Fellow Nat. Sculpture Soc.; mem. Allied Artists Am., Lauderdale Yacht Club, Town Club (Jamestown, N.Y.), St. Louis Country Club, Univ. Club St. Louis. Home: 8 Edgewood Rd Saint Louis MO 63124-1817 Office: Sculpture Dept Washington U Saint Louis MO 63130 *I feel that an artist's life and work is of no importance unless it touches those around him and gives pleasure, help, or increased knowledge and enrichment in so doing. I have tried to remember this in creating my sculpture and in my contacts with my students.*

DUHNKE, ROBERT EMMET, JR., retired aerospace engineer; b. Manitowoc, Wis., Jan. 28, 1935; s. Robert Emmet and Vivian Dorothy (Abel) D.; m. Patricia R. Ebben, 1956 (div. 1972); children: Kim Marie, Lori Ann, Dawn Diane, Robert III, Mary Lynn; m. Judy Anne Lind, Feb. 14, 1978. BS in Aero. Engring., Purdue U., 1957. Assoc. engr. Convair/Aerodyns. Group, Pomona, Calif., 1957-58; assoc. engr., instr. Boeing Co., Seattle, 1964-66, instr. maintenance tng., 1972-83, navigation sys. analyst, 1983-90, sr. specialist engr., instr. comml. maintenance tng. ctr., 1990-95; flight navigator Flying Tigers, San Francisco, 1966-68; salesman various real estate and ins. cos., Seattle, 1968-72; shuttler Hertz, Seattle, 1996-97; reservation sales agt. Alaska Airlines, Phoenix, 1997—; contract aerospace engr. Superior Design Co., Inc., Kirkland, Wash., 1996—. Author poems in English, German, French and Spanish. Sponsor World Vision, Pasadena, Calif.; mem. Citizens Against Govt. Waste. Capt. USAF, 1958-64. Recipient Hon. Freedom Fighter award Afghan Mercy Fund, 1987. Mem. Internat. Soc. Photography (disting.), Inst. Navigation, Air Force Assn. Avocations: photography, fishing, biking, kayaking. Home: Apt 19-206 30 W Carter Dr Tempe AZ 85282-7712

DUHON, DAVID LESTER, business educator, management consultant; b. Crowley, La., Oct. 21, 1948; s. J. Lester and Winona Faye Duhon; m. Roxanne Istre, Jan. 25, 1970; children: Jonathan, Leah, Sarah. BS in Bus., U. Southwestern La., 1970; MBA, La. State U., 1975, PhD in Mgmt., 1981. Instr. mgmt. La. State U., Baton Rouge, 1978-80; from asst. prof. to assoc. prof. U. Southwestern La., Lafayette, 1980-88, petroleum land mgmt. coord., 1981-88; from asst. prof. to assoc. prof. U. So. Miss., Hattiesburg, 1988—, dir. external rels. Coll. Bus., 1995-99. Ptnr. People Solutions LLC, Hattiesburg, Miss.; cons. Jaws Offshore, Lafayette, 1984-88, Continuing Edn. U. So. Miss., Hattiesburg, 1988—, Miss. Personnel Bd., Jackson, 1990—, Pine Belt Mental Health, Hattiesburg, 1992—; interim chair divsn. bus. U. S. Miss.-Gulf Coast, Long Beach, 1996-97; vis. lectr. Ecole Superieure de Commerce, Fontainbleu, France, 1997, 98; instr. Brit. studies program, London, 2001—. Contbr. articles to profl. jours. Chair fin. com. Ch. of the Nazarene, Hattiesburg, 1992-99, chair lay retreat com., Jackson, 1994-96; pres. faculty senate, U. So. Miss., Hattiesburg, 1997-98, co-chair United Way campaign, 1998-99. Summer Instrn. grantee U. So. Miss., 1992, 95. Fellow E./W. Centre-Honolulu; mem. Area Devel. Partnership, Acad. Mgmt., Allied Acads., So. Mgmt. Assn. Republican. Avocations: reading, traveling, hunting, fishing. Home: 2264 Old Highway 24 Hattiesburg MS 39402-7751 E-mail: duhon@cba.usm.edu.

DUHOV, BENJAMIN, consulting group executive; b. St. Louis, Feb. 3, 1928; s. Sidney M. and Sara (Niachin) D.; m. Oro Lucy Garzon; 1 child, Tamara. BSEE, Washington Univ., St. Louis, 1948. Design engr. McDonnell Aircraft, St. Louis, 1948-49; with sales Broadwell & Co., St. Louis, 1950-51; electronics officer patrol squadron USN Air Corps., 1951—55; applications engr. Westinghouse Lamp, St. Louis, 1955-58; mktg. mgr. Aero Gen., Azusa, Calif., 1958-71; dir. mktg. CBS Labs., Stamford, Conn., 1972-75; v.p. Thomson-CSF, Inc., Alexandria, Va., 1975-93; pres. Stamford Consulting Group, 1993—. Mem. United Jewish Fedn., Stamford. Lt. (j.g.) USN, 1951-54. Avocations: skiing, geopolitics. Home and Office: 30 Winesap Rd Stamford CT 06903-1814 Fax: (203) 322-9279.

DUIGAN, JOHN, film director; b. Hartley Wintney, Hampshire, Eng., June 19, 1949; MA in Philosophy, U. Melbourne, Australia, 1973. Faculty U. Melbourne, Latrobe U. Dir., writer exptl. short: The Firm Man, 1974; novels include: Badge, Players, Room to Move; dir., writer (films) The Trespassers, 1976, Mouth to Mouth, 1978, Winter of our Dreams, 1981 (Australian Writers Guild award), Far East, 1983, One Night Stand, 1984, Room to Move, 1985, The Year My Voice Broke (Australian Acad. Awards for best dir. and best screenplay, Australian Writers Guild best screenplay), Flirting, 1990, Sirens (also actor), 1994; dir.: (films) Dimboola, 1979, Romero, 1989, Wide Sargasso Sea, 1992, The Journey of August King, The Leading Man, 1996, Lawn Dogs, 1997, Molly, 1999, Paranoid, 1999, The Parole Officer, 2001; co-dir. TV mini-series Vietnam, (film) Fragments of War: The Story of Damien Parer, co-writer: Australian Penguin TV Awd., best dir., Byron Kennedy Awd. for contribution to Australian Cinema.

DUIKER, SJOERD WILLEM, soil scientist, educator; b. Jutryp, Fryslan, Netherlands, Aug. 11, 1966; s. Willem and Suzanna Duiker; m. Maria Alvarez, Sept. 17, 1994; children: Suzanna Esther, Lina Ruth, Maria Rebecca, Willem Antonio. MSc, Landbouwuniversiteit, Wageningen, Netherlands, 1990; PhD, Ohio State U., 2000. Rsch. asst. Internat. Ctr. for Rsch. in Semi Arid Tropics, Niamey, Niger, 1987, Tropenbos Found., Ede, Netherlands, 1991—92; conf. asst. Wageningen Agrl. U., 1993—94; rsch. asst. Internat. Ctr. for Nat. Agrl. Rsch., The Hague, Netherlands, 1994—96; asst. prof. Pa. State U., University Park, 2000—. Contbr. articles to profl. jours. Mem.: Soil and Water Conservation Soc., Am. Soc. Agronomy, Soil Sci. Soc. Am. Office: Dept Crop & Soil Scis Pa State U 116 ASI Bldg University Park PA 16802 Office Fax: 814-863-7043. E-mail: swd10@psu.edu.

DUJACK, STEPHEN RAYMOND, editor; b. N.Y.C., Apr. 7, 1953; s. Raymond Leon and Inge (Wassermann) D. BA, Princeton U., 1976. Assoc. editor Princeton (N.J.) Alumni Weekly, 1976-80; graphic artist Forte, Inc., Alexandria, Va., 1980-81; editor Fgn. Svc. Jour., dir. comms. Am. Fgn. Svc. Assn., Washington, 1981-88; dir. comms. Worldwatch Inst., Washington, 1988-90. Lectr. George Washington U., 1983 88. Editor: The Environ.. Forum, 1990—; contbr. articles on pub. policy to The Washington Post, The L.A. Times, The New Republic, The Christian Sci. Monitor, Gannett Syndicate, L.A. Times Syndicate. Recipient Allen Furniss award Daily Princetonian, Princeton, 1976; Best Feature Article, Soc. Nat. Assn. Publs., 1983, Best Spl Issue, 1983, Most Improved Mag., 1992, Best Ann. Report, 1994, 96, 98, 99, 1st pl. Master's Divsn., TriAtlantic Biathlon Series, 1994, 3d pl. 45-49 divsn., 1998, 1st pl., 2000. Office: Environ Law Inst 1616 P St NW Ste 200 Washington DC 20036-1423 E-mail: dujack@eli.org. *Honor is the central principle of a moral life.*

DUJARDIN, RICHARD CHARLES, journalist; b. Queens, N.Y., Dec. 20, 1944; s. Julien Camille and Veronica (Venesoen) D.; m. Rosemarie Catherine Levesque, Jan. 20, 1947; children: Julianne, Peter, Philip, Joelle, Jean-Paul, Jeffrey. BA in Comm. Arts, Fordham U., 1966. Reporter Providence Jour.-Bulletin, 1966-68, 71-75, bureau mgr., 1975-77, religion writer, 1977—. V.p. Action for Franco-Ams. in N.E., 1991-93, dir., 1986-94; dist. pres. Union St. Jean Baptiste, 1990-94. Lt. (j.g.) USN, 1968-71. Recipient Wilbur award Religious Pub. Rels. Coun., 1986, 91, 95. Mem. Religion Newswriters Assn. (treas. 1989-90, v.p. 1990-94, pres. 1994-96, Supple Meml. award 1986, Templeton Reporter of Yr. award 1991). Roman Catholic. Home: 129 Hillside Ave Providence RI 02906-2900 Office: Providence Jour Bull 75 Fountain St Providence RI 02902-0050 E-mail: rdujardi@projo.com., rcdujardin@cox.net.

DUKE, ANTHONY DREXEL, sociologist, educator, philanthropist; b. N.Y.C., July 28, 1918; s. Angier Buchanan and Cordelia (Biddle) D.; children by previous marriage: Anthony D. Jr., Nicholas R., Cordelia Duke Jung, Josephine Duke Brown, December Duke McSherry, John O., Douglas D.; m. Maria Luly de Lourdes Alcebo, Sept. 27, 1975; children: Lulita C., Washington A., James B. Student, Princeton U., 1941; DHL (hon.), Adelphi Coll., 1957, L.I. U., 1988, Drexel U., 1991. With Import Export Co., 1946-50; prin. A.D. Duke Realty, Inc., 1955-65. Chmn. bd. dirs., pres., founder Boys Harbor Inc., 1937—. Trustee Big Brother Movement, 1951-63; past trustee Henry St. Settlement, N.Y.C.; del. Internat. Conf. Pvt. Sector Initiatives, 1986; hon. commr. Manhattan Borough Projects, 1954-57, Civic Affairs and Pub. Events, N.Y.C.; mem. N.Y.C. Youth Bd., 1955-58; rep. Internat. Rescue Com., Vietnam War, Meriel refugee crisis Cuba, 1983; active Save the Children, Pomfret Sch., Duke U., U.S. Naval Acad. Lt. comdr. USNR, 1941-46, PTO, ATO, ETO. Decorated Bronze Star. Recipient Town and Country Most Generous Am. award 1988, Save the Children award, 1977; Presdl. citation for pvt. sector commendation, 1986, Citation for Promotion of Human Welfare Commonwealth of Mass., 1987. Mem. Bodman and Achelis Found., Nat. Com. on Am. Fgn. Policy, Maidstone Club (former gov.), Piping Rock (former gov.), River Club, Racquet and Tennis Club, Beaver Dam Club. Home: PO Box 177 East Hampton NY 11937-0177 Office: Boys Harbor Inc PO Box 3000 New York NY 10029-0300

DUKE, CHARLES BRYAN, electronics executive, physicist, educator; b. Richmond, Va., Mar. 13, 1938; s. Charles Joseph Jr. and Virginia (Welton) Duke; m. Ann Evans, July 1, 1961; children: Amy Dickerson, Emily Elizabeth. BS in Math., Duke U., 1959; PhD in Physics, Princeton U., 1963. Staff cor. rsch. GE, Schenectady, N.Y., 1963-69, cons., 1969-72; prof. physics U. Ill., Urbana, 1969-72; mgr., sr. fellow Xerox Corp., Webster, NY, 1972-88, sr. rsch. fellow, 1989-96, v.p., sr. rsch. fellow, 1996—; dep. dir., chief scientist Battelle Pacific Northwest Div., Richland, Wash., 1988-89. Bd. govs. Am. Inst. Physics, N.Y.C., 1976—82, N.Y.C., 1984—87; adj. prof. physics U. Rochester, NY, 1972—88; affiliate prof. physics U. Wash., Seattle, 1988—89; gen. chmn. Phys. Electronics Conf., 1997—2000. Author: (book) Tunneling in Solids, 1969, Surface Science: The First Thirty Years, 1994, Color Systems Integration, 1998, Frontiers in Surface and Interface Science, 2002; editor-in-chief: Jour. Materials Rsch., 1985—86, Surface Sci., 1992—2001; contbr. articles to profl. jours. Named one of 1000 Most Cited Scientists, Inst. Sci. Info., 1981. Fellow: IEEE, Am. Phys. Soc. (councillor 1995—98, exec. bd. 1997—98), Am. Vacuum Soc. (hon.; bd. dirs. 1973—76, pres. 1979, trustee 2003—, pres. 2003—, M. W. Welch award in vacuum sci. and tech. 1977); mem.: NAS, NAE, Materials Rsch. Soc. (councillor 1988—90, treas. 1991—92, councillor 1995—97). Office: Xerox Wilson Ctr for R & T 800 Phillips Rd # 114-38D Webster NY 14580-9720 E-mail: cduke@crt.xerox.com.

DUKE, CHARLES RICHARD, academic dean; b. West Stewartstown, N.H., July 6, 1940; s. George Tunicliffe and Evelyn Agnes (Murray) D.; m. Leona Ruth Hubbard, June 1, 1963. BE, Plymouth (N.H.) State Coll., 1962; MA, Middlebury (Vt.) Coll., 1968; PhD, Duke U., 1972. Tchr. English, head dept. Sunapee (N.H.) High Sch., 1962-68; prof. English Plymouth State Coll., 1968-78, Murray (Ky.) State U., 1978-84; prof., head dept. secondary edn. Utah State U., Logan, 1984-89; dean Coll. Edn. and Human Svcs. Clarion (Pa.) U., 1989-94; dean Coll. Edn. Appalachian State U., Boone, N.C., 1995—. Dir. West Ky. Writing Project, 1980-84; co-dir. Utah Writing Project, 1984-89, Clarion U. Student Literacy Corps, 1990-94. Author: Creative Dramatics and English Teaching, 1974, Writing Through Sequence, 1983, Strategies for teaching, 1987; contbr. articles to profl. jours; editor: Exercise Exchange, 1979—2001, Poets Perspectives, 1992, American Overseas Education, 2000, Assessing Writing Across the Curriculum, 2001. Am. Studies fellow Coe Found., 1964; recipient Alumni Outstanding Svc. award Plymouth State Coll., 1977. Mem. ASCD, Internat. Reading Assn., Nat. Coun. Tchrs. English, Am. Assn. Colls. Tchr. Edn., Assn. Tchr. Educators, Phi Delta Kappa. Office: Appalachian State U 222 Duncan Hall PO Box 32038 Boone NC 28608-2038

DUKE, DONALD NORMAN, publishing executive; b. L.A., Apr. 1, 1929; s. Roger V. and Mabel (Weineger) D. BA in Ednl. Psychology, Colo. Coll., 1951. Comml. photographer, Colorado Springs, Colo., 1951-53; pub. rels. Gen. Petroleum, L.A., 1954-55; agt. Gen. S.S. Corp., Ltd., 1956-57; asst. mgr. retail advt., sales promotion Mobil Oil Co., 1958-63; pub. Golden West Books, Alhambra, Calif., 1964—. Dir. Pacific R.R. Publs., Inc., Athletic Press; pub. relations cons. Santa Fe Ry., 1960-70. Author: The Pacific Electric: A History of Southern California Railroading, 1958, Southern Pacific Steam Locomotives, 1962, Santa Fe...Steel Rails to California, 1963, Night Train, 1961, American Narrow Gauge, 1978, RDC: the Budd Rail Diesel Car, 1989, The Brown Derby, 1990, Camp Cajon, 1991, Fred Harvey: Civilizer of the American West, 1994, editor: Water Trails West, 1977, Branding Iron, 1988-91, Santa Fe...The Railroad Gateway to the American West, Vol. 1, 1995, Vol. 2, 1997, Incline Railways of Los Angeles and Southern California, 1998, Electric Railroads of San Francisco Bay, Vols. 1 and 2, 1999, Pacific Electric Railway (The No. Divsn), vol. 1, 2001, Pacific Electric Railway (The Ea. Divsn.), vol. 2. Recipient Spur award for Trails of the Iron Horse Western Writers Am., 1975 Mem. Ry. and Locomotive Hist. Soc. (dir. 1944-98), Western History Assn., Newcomen Soc., Lexington Group of Transp. History, Western Writers Am., P.E.N. Internat. (v.p. 1975-77), Authors Guild Am., Book Pubs. Assn. So. Calif. (dir. 1968-77), Cal. Writers Guild (dir. 1976-77), Calif. Book Pubs. Assn. (dir. 1976-77), Westerners Internat. (hon., editor Branding Iron 1971-80, 88-91), Hist. Soc. So. Calif. (dir. 1972-75), Henry E./Arabella Huntington Soc., Kappa Sigma (lit. editor Caduceus 1968-80). Home: PO Box 80250 San Marino CA 91118-8250 Office: Golden West Books 525 N Electric Ave Alhambra CA 91801-2032 E-mail: Trainbook@Earthlink.net., www.goldenwestbooks.com.

DUKE, ELIZABETH M. health facility administrator; B Polit. Sci., M Polit. Sci., Rutgers U.; M African Studies, Northwestern U.; PhD, George Washington U. Dir. gov. affairs inst. office exec. and mgmt. devel. Health Resources and Svcs. Adminstrn., HHS, 1978—84; dep. asst. dir., dir. policy and sys. office tng. and devel. U.S. Office Pers. Mgmt., 1984—86; dep. asst. sec. adminstrn. Adminstrn. Children and Families U.S. Dept. Health and Human Svcs., CFO, mgmt. control officer, chief grants officer, chief info. officer Adminstrn. Children and Families, head grants policy, fin. mgmt. internal and state sys., human resources, other adminstrv. duties Adminstrn. Children and Families; acting adminstr. Health Resources and Svcs. Adminstrn., HHS, 2001—; adminstr. Health Resources and Svs. Adminstrn., HHS, 2002—. Rsch. writer Congressional Quarterly. Office: Health Resources and Svs Adminstrn US Dept Health & Human Svcs Parklawn Bld 5600 Fishers Ln Rockville MD 20857

DUKE, ELLEN KAY, planned giving administrator; b. Indpls., June 7, 1952; d. Richard Thomas and Ruby Mae (Wright) D. Student, Chapman Coll., Orange, Calif., 1972; BS in Pub. Affairs, Ind. U., Bloomington, 1975; postgrad., Portland State U., 1980—81; MPA, Calif. State U., 1998. Cert. playground safety specialist/inspector; cert. Dale Carnegie Pub. Speaking instr., 1987-93. Newsreporter Salem Statesman, Corvallis, Oreg., 1976-78; com. adminstr. Oreg. State Legislature, Salem, 1979-80; pub. involvement coord. Met. Regional Svc. Dist., Portland, 1981-82; account mgr. Thunder & Visions, Portland, 1982-83; project asst. Amdahl Corp., Sunnyvale, CAlif., 1983-84; spl. project coord. Computerland Corp., Hayward, Calif., 1984-89; prodr., lead facilitator Sage, Inc., Walnut Creek, Calif., 1982—; loan broker Capital Trust Mortgage, Campbell, Calif., 1994—. Co-author (ednl. film) Communication Skills, 1975. Pub. rels. dir. local YMCA; chairperson Corvallis Budget Commn., Oreg., 1978; commr. Hayward Libr., 1985—, Alameda County Consumer Affairs, Oakland, 1985; rep. Nat. Dem. Conv., N.Y.C., 1982. Named Able Toastmaster, Toastmasters Internat., 1981; grad. Leadership Oakland, 1991. Mem. NAFE,

ASTD, Pub. Rels. Soc. Am., Nat. Planned Giving Coun., Nat. Soc. for Fund Raising Execs. (planned giving coun.), Kansas City Coun. on Philanthropy, Sierra Club (San Francisco). Office: Assn Unity Churches 401 SW Oldham Pkwy Lees Summit MO 64081-2747

DUKE, GARY JAMES, electronics executive; b. Norman, Ark., Aug. 3, 1947; s. Arley Matthew and Evelyn Ethia (Cogburn) D.; m. Evonne Pearson, Oct. 7, 1966; children: Arlon Matthew, Anton Lee, Angela Michelle. Student, U. Ark., Little Rock, 1969-70. With Diebold Inc., 1970—, dist. mgr., 1974-75, Charleston, W.Va., 1975-76, area tech. specialist Little Rock, 1976, tech. mgr. south cen. area Memphis, 1977-87, tech. mgr. southwestern area Dallas, 1988, tech. mgr. so. div. Atlanta, 1988-90, customer svc. mgr. Memphis, 1990—2000; owner Networking Teams, Collierville, Tenn., 2000—. Mem. gen. adv. coun. State Tech. Inst. at Memphis, 1984-86; mem. Tenn. Gov.'s Task Force, 1984; v.p.-employer Tenn. Coll. Placement Assn., 1985. Contbr. articles to various publs. Brotherhood dir. 1st Bapt. Ch., Collierville, Tenn., 1985-88, Shelby Bapt. Assn., Memphis, 1987-88; v.p. Bapt. Men, Tenn. Bapt. Brotherood, 1987-88. Sgt. USMC, 1965-69. Recipient honor award Armed Forces Communications and Electronics Assn., 1966, Exceptional Svc. award State Tech. Inst. at Memphis, 1985. Avocations: computers, geneaology, photography. Home: 1213 Greenview Rd Collierville TN 38017-1161 Office: 622 W Poplar # 316 Collierville TN 38017

DUKE, GEORGE F. lawyer; b. N.Y.C., Aug. 21, 1935; s. David S. and Marlene D.; m. Eugenie Arnold (div. 1985); children: Jonas, Nina; m. Shirley Kison, Sept. 4, 1988. BA magna cum laude, Tufts U., 1956; JD, Harvard U., 1959. Law clk. Calif. Ct. of Appeal, 1960-61; assoc. Leonard, Dole & Formichelli, San Francisco, 1961-66; directing atty. Calif. Rural Legal Assistance, Santa Rosa, 1966-67; dir. Calif. Indian Legal Svcs., Berkeley, 1968-71; cons. Carnegie Endowment for Internat. Peace, Geneva, Switzerland, 1972; pvt. practice law San Francisco, 1973—. Lectr. Boalt Hall Law Sch., Berkeley, 1975-78, U. Calif., Davis, 1980. Ford Found. grantee, 1971-72. Mem. Calif. Bar Assn., Bar Assn. of San Francisco, Phi Beta Kappa. Avocations: music, hiking. Office: 31 Maywood Way San Rafael CA 94901-1100 Office Fax: 415-456-6078. Business E-Mail: dukelaw@svn.net.

DUKE, GEORGE WESLEY, financial executive; b. Nashville, Dec. 27, 1953; s. Harold Wesley and Justine Hope (Perry) D.; m. Lucy Neale; children: Elizabeth, Margaret, Hope. BBA, Coll. William and Mary, 1976; M Taxation, Va. Commonwealth U., 1981; MBA, Darden Sch., 1983; MEd, Vanderbilt U., 1989; M of Liberal Arts, Johns Hopkins U., 1992. CPA, Va. Acct. KPMG Peat Marwick, Richmond, Va., 1976-81; v.p. Jacques-Miller, Nashville, 1983-86; sr. v.p. Alex Brown Kleinwort Benson, Balt., 1986-94; prin. LaSalle Ptnrs. (formerly Alex Brown Kleinwort Benson), Balt., 1994-99; mng. dir. LaSalle Investment Mgmt. (formerly LaSalle Ptnrs.), Balt., 1999—. Mem. AICPA, Pension Real Estate Assn., Ctr. Club, Darden Sch. Alumni Assn. (past pres. alumni bd.). Office: LaSalle Investment Mgmt 100 E Pratt St Baltimore MD 21202-1009 E-mail: George.Duke@LaSalle.com.

DUKE, JAMES T, art educator, consumer products company executive; b. Chicago, Ill., Feb. 21, 1937; s. James E. and Anna M. Duke. Owner, operator Duke Sign, Chicago, Ill., 2002—02; sign co. exec. U.S.A. Sign, Fort Lauderdale, Fla., 2002—; pub. sch. educator Broward County, Fort Lauderdale, Fla., 2002—. Specialist 4 class US Army. Avocations: martial arts, fine art, commercial art, gourmet cooking. Home: 609 NE 14th Place Fort Lauderdale FL 33304 Office: Duke Sign 609 NE 14th Place Fort Lauderdale FL 33304 Home Fax: 954-462-8632; Office Fax: 954-462-8632.

DUKE, ROBERT DOMINICK, lawyer; b. Goshen, N.Y., Oct. 14, 1928; s. Robert DeWitt and Elma Christina (Dominick) D.; m. Jeannette Parham, Apr. 24, 1954; children: Katherine Campbell, Robert Dominick, Peter Benjamin DeWitt, Lois Christina. BA, Va. Mil. Inst., 1947; LL.B., Yale U., 1950; MBA, U. Pa., 1952. Bar: N.Y. 1950, Conn. 1989. With Cravath, Swaine & Moore, N.Y.C., 1951-52, 54-64, Freeport-McMoRan Inc. and predecessors, N.Y.C., 1964-84, gen. counsel, 1970-84, sr. v.p., 1973-84; sr. v.p., gen. counsel The Pittston Co., Stamford, Conn., 1984-93, sr. counsel, 1993—2002, also bd. dirs., 1991-93. Served as 1st lt. JAGC, U.S. Army, 1952-54. Mem.: ABA, Assn. Bar City NY, Silver Spring Golf Club, Silvermine Golf Club, Yale Club (N.Y.C.). Presbyterian. Home: 67 Ridgefield Rd Wilton CT 06897-3006

DUKE, ROBIN CHANDLER TIPPETT, retired public relations executive; b. Balt., Oct. 13, 1923; d. Richard Edgar and Esther (Chandler) Tippett; m. Angier Biddle Duke, May 1962; children: Jeffrey R. Lynn, Letitia Lynn, Angier Biddle Jr. Fashion editor N.Y. Jour. Am., N.Y.C., 1944-46; freelance writer N.Y.C., 1946-50; rep. Orvis Bros., N.Y.C., 1953-58; mem. pub. rels. staff Pepsi Cola Co., Internat., N.Y.C., 1958-62; amb. to UNESCO, Belgrade, 1980; amb. U.S. to Norway, 2000—01. Bd. dirs. Am. Home Products, N.Y.C., Internat. Flavors & Fragrances, N.Y.C., East River Bank, New Rochelle, NY; bd. dirs. emeritus Inst. Internat. Edn.; dir. Rockwell Corp., 1977—95. Co-chmn. Population Action Internat., N.Y.C., 1975-96; Met. Club Washington; bd. dirs. David Packard Found., U.S. Japan Found. Recipient Albert and Mary Lasker Social Svc. award, 1991, Margaret Sanger Woman of Yr. Valor award, 1995. Mem. Coun. on Fgn. Rels., Acad. Arts & Scis., World Affairs Coun. L.I. (co-chmn.), Colony Club, River Club. Democrat. Avocations: skiing, swimming. Home: 435 E 52nd St New York NY 10022-6445

DUKE, STEPHEN OSCAR, physiologist, researcher, educator; b. Battle Creek, Mich., Oct. 9, 1944; s. Oscar and Azalee Rosa (Tallant) D.; m. Barbara Alice Rowe, June 2, 1967 (div. Dec. 1993); children: Gregory Ivan, Robin Anne. BS, Henderson State U., 1966; MS, U. Ark., 1969; PhD, Duke U., 1975. Plant physiologist So. Weed Sci. Lab., USDA, Stoneville, Miss., 1975-84, rsch. leader, 1984-87, lab. dir., 1987-96, rsch. leader Oxford, Miss., 1996—. Adj. prof. U. Miss., Oxford, 1996—. Co-author: Physiology of Herbicide Action, 1993; editor: Weed Physiology, 2 vols., 1985, Pest Control with Enhanced Environmental Safety, 1993, Porphyric Pesticides, 1994, Herbicide Resistant Crops, 1995; contbr. articles to profl. jours. Head referee Greenville Youth Soccer Assn. (Miss.), 1982-96; soccer coach Washington Sch., Greenville, 1986-88. Served to 1st lt. U.S. Army, 1968-70, Vietnam. Decorated Bronze Star; recipient Edminster award USDA, 1986, Disting. Alumnus award Henderson State U., 1989, CIBA-GEIGY/Weed Sci. Soc. Am. award CIBA-GEIGY Corp., 1990, Outstanding Sr. Scientist award USDA, Agr. Rsch. Svc., 2001, Extraordinary Prof. award U. Pretoria RSA, 2002-, Molisch award Internat. Allelopathy Soc.; elected Henderson State U. Acad., 2001. Fellow AAAS, Weed Sci. Soc. Am. (assoc. editor 1978-83, pres. 1996, Outstanding Young Scientist award 1984, Outstanding Article award 1984, Rsch. award 1990); mem. Am. Soc. Plant Physiology (chmn. so. sect. 1985-86), Coun. for Agrl. Sci. and Tech. (bd. dirs. 1993-94), Am. Chem. Soc., So. Weed Soc. (pres. 1995, disting. svc. award 1998), Internat. Weed Sci. Soc. (pres. 2000—). Avocations: gardening, writing. Home: 9 Private Rd 3078 Oxford MS 38655 E-mail: sduke@olemiss.edu.

DUKE, STEVEN BARRY, law educator; b. Mesa, Ariz., July 31, 1934; s. Alton and Elaine (Altman) D.; m. Janet Truax, 1956 (div. 1971); children: Glenn, Warren, Alison, Sally; m. Margaret Munson, 1984 (div. 1999); children: Jennifer, Lauren. BS, Ariz. State U., 1956; JD, U. Ariz., 1959; LL.M., Yale U., 1961. Bar: Ariz. 1959. Law clk. to Supreme Ct. Justice Douglas, 1959; grad. fellow Yale Law Sch., 1960, mem. faculty, 1961—, prof. law, 1966—, Law of Sci. and Tech. prof., 1982—99. Vis. prof. U. Calif.-Berkeley, 1965, Hastings Coll. Law, 1981, Ariz. State U., 1986; Bd. dirs. New Haven Legal Assistance Assn., 1968-70; cons. Commn. to Revise Fed. Criminal Code; mem. Conn. Commn. on Medicolegal Investigations, 1976—; bd. visitors Fordham U. Law Sch., 1986-1999. Author: (with A. Gross) America's Longest War: Rethinking Our Tragic Crusade Against Drugs, 1993; editor-in-chief Ariz. Law Rev.; contbr. articles to profl. jours. Mem. Woodbridge (Conn.) Bd. Edn., 1970-72; mem. Woodbridge Democratic Town Com., 1967-72. Mem. Nat. Assn. Criminal Def. Lawyers, Am. Trial Lawyers Assn., ACLU, Phi Kappa Phi, Alpha Tau Omega. Home: 250 Grandview Ave Hamden CT 06514-3028 Office: Yale Law Sch PO Box 208215 New Haven CT 06520-8215 E-mail: steven.duke@yale.edu.

DUKE, WILLIAM EDWARD, public affairs executive; b. Bklyn., July 18, 1932; m. Leilani Kamp Lattin. BS, Fordham U., 1954. City editor Middletown (N.Y.) Record, 1956—60; asst. state editor Washington Star, 1961—63; exec. asst. U.S. Sen. Jacob K. Javits, Washington, 1963—69; dir. pub. affairs Corp. Pub. Broadcasting, Washington, 1969—72; dir. fed. govt. rels. Atlantic Richfield Co., Washington, 1973—78, mgr. pub. affairs L.A., 1978—91; mgr. external affairs We. States Petroleum Assn., 1993—95; pres. W.E. Duke and Co., 1996—. Lectr. U. So. Calif. Grad. Sch. Journalism, 1988—; cons. in field. Fellow: Pub. Rels. Soc. Am., Capitol Hill Club, Nat. Press Club.

DUKE DE LEONEDES OF SPAIN SICILY GREECE, HIS ROYAL HIGHNESS See SANCHEZ, LEONEDES MONARRIZE WORTHINGTON

DUKE OF NEMI, GRANDEE OF SPAIN, See THEODOLI-BRASCHI, GIOVANNI

DUKER, NAHUM JOHANAN, pathologist, educator; b. NYC, Oct. 27, 1942; s. Abraham and Lillian (Sandrow) D.; m. Naomi Maisel, June 13, 1972 (div.); children: Eli Avishai, Joshua Jair, Jonathan Jacob, Ezra Aryeh; m. Vita Khayyat, Apr. 12, 1992. BS, U. Ill., 1962; MD, U. Ill., Chgo., 1966. Diplomate pathologic anatomy and clin. pathology Am. Bd. Pathology. Intern Bellevue Hosp., N.Y.C., 1966-67; resident NYU Med. Sch., N.Y.C., 1970-76, instr., 1976-77; asst. prof. Temple U. Med. Sch., Phila., 1977-82, assoc. prof., 1982-87, prof., pathology, 1987—. Contbr. articles to profl. jours. Capt. U.S. Army, 1967-69. Recipient Career Devel. award, Nat. Cancer Inst., 1983. Republican. Jewish. Avocation: music. Office: Temple U Med Sch 3400 N Broad St Philadelphia PA 19140-5104

DUKES, DEBORAH FEAGANS, counselor, administrator; b. Ashland, Ky., June 13, 1952; d. Robert Geary and Louise (McCalvin) Feagans; m. J.W. Buckner, May 22, 1982 (div. Dec. 1989); 1 child, Zachary Robert; m. Jeffery Miram Dukes, May 24, 1996. AA in English, U. S.C., 1972, BA in Psychology, 1974; MA in Profl. Counseling, Liberty U., 1995. Lic. profl. counselor. Clin. counselor State of S.C. Dept. Mental Health, Columbia, 1976-84; alcohol and drug safety action program coord. Rubicon Counseling Ctr., Hartsville, S.C., 1984-87, adolescent counselor, 1986-87; clin. counselor Aiken (S.C.) Ctr. for Alcohol and Drug Abuse, 1987-95; clin. coord. Mentor Inc., Aiken, 1995-96; dir. Shiflet Ctr. John de la Howe Sch., McCormick, S.C., 1996-2000; counselor, dir. child, adolescent, family divsn. Aiken Barnwell Mental Health Ctr., 2000—. Mem. adv. bd. Darlington County Youth Home, 1984-87; mem. Darlington County Treatment Adv. Team, 1986-87; mem. dist. core team Aiken County Student Assistance Program, 1990-96; mem. McCormick Cmty. Coordinating Coun., 1996-2000; chair parent adv. coun. John de la Howe Sch., 1996-2000. Mem. Aiken County Child Task Force, 2001—. Grantee U.S. Dept. Forestry, 1998. Mem.: Nat. Assn. Alcohol and Drug Abuse Counselors, SC Assn. Alcohol and Drug Abuse Counselors. Avocations: reading, swimming, refinishing furniture, quilting. E-mail: jaddukes@atlantic.net.

DUKES, KATHARINE LEE, lawyer; b. Washington, July 31, 1968; d. Mack Gerald and Elizabeth (McClellan) Fleming; m. Glenn Edward Dukes, Sept. 4, 1993. BA in History, Rice U., 1990; JD, U. Tex., 1993. Bar: Tex. 1993, U.S. Dist. Ct. (ea. dist.) Tex. 1994, U.S. Ct. Appeals (5th cir.) 1994, U.S. Dist. Ct. (we. dist.) Tex. 1995, U.S. Supreme Ct. 1998. Jud. law clk. U.S. Dist. Ct. (ea. dist.) Tex., Marshall, Tex., 1993-94, U.S. Ct. Appeals (5th cir.), Tyler, Tex., 1994-95, Austin, 1995-96; assoc. Cantilo Maisel & Hubbard LLP, Austin, 1996-98; staff atty. 3d Ct. Appeals, Austin, 1998-99; jud. law clk. U.S. Magistrate Ct. (we. dist.) Tex., Austin, 1999—2003; assoc. Clark, Thomas & Winters, P.C., Austin, 2003—. Mem. Travis County Bar Assn., Austin Young Lawyers Assn. Democrat. Presbyterian. Avocations: musical theater, vocal ensemble. Office: Clark Thomas & Winters PC 300 W 6th St 15th Fl Austin TX 78701 E-mail: kld@ctw.com.

DUKES, MICHAEL, consumer products company executive; b. Augusta, Ga., Oct. 5, 1960; s. George Alonzo Dukes, Sr. and Essie Minick Dukes; m. Jacquelyn Denise Shields, Apr. 25, 1992 (dec. Oct. 1993); m. Gabriele Constanze Beurer, Nov. 19, 1995; children: Christopher Floyd, Ellen Anatolia, Michael Juergen. BS, Ga. So. U., 1991, So. Ill. U., 1995; MBA, Nova Southeastern U., 1999. Electronics mgr. Westinghouse, Aiken, SC, 1985—98, rep. dept. fin. and budget, 1998—2000, facilities program mgr., 2000—. Co-chmn. campaign United Way, Aiken, 2002, chmn., 2003. Avocations: golf, basketball, travel, scuba diving. Home: 2314 Laurel Ln Augusta GA 30904

DUKES, PATRICK RYAN, secondary school educator; b. Athens, Ga., Aug. 4, 1971; s. Wayne Richard and Marsha Kay Dukes; m. Nora Elizabeth Hoyt, Dec. 30, 1994; children: Brendan Ward, Katherine Grace, Cecilia Elizabeth. B in Music Edn., Augusta (Ga.) Coll., 1994; MS, Troy State U., Augusta, 2001. Cert. tchr. Ga., master's level tchr. Ga. Elem. gen. music tchr. Sue Reynolds Elem. Sch., Augusta, 1994—95; band dir. Langford Mid. Sch., Augusta, 1995—98, asst. baseball coach, 1996—98; band dir. Westside H.S., Augusta, 1998—2001, Washington-Wilkes Comprehensive H.S., Washington, Ga., 2001—, asst. baseball coach, 2001—. Co-developer mid. sch. band curriculum Richmond County Bd. of Edn., Augusta, 1996. Mem.: ASCD, PAGE, Music Educators Nat. Conf., Ga. Music Educators Assn. (Dist. 10 instrumental chmn. 2000—02). Republican. Roman Catholic. Avocations: baseball, basketball. Office: Washington-Wilkes Comprehensive HS 304 Gordon St Washington GA 30673 Office Fax: 706-678-2628. Personal E-mail: dukesrn4@nu-z.net. E-mail: dukesr@wilkes.k12.ga.us.

DUKES, REBECCA WEATHERS (BECKY DUKES), musician, singer, songwriter; b. Durham, N.C., Nov. 21, 1934; d. Elmer Dewey Weathers and Martha Rebecca (Kimbrough) Weathers-Hall; m. Charles Aubrey Dukes Jr., Dec. 20, 1955; children: Aurelia Ann, Charles Weathers, David Lloyd. BA, Duke U., 1956; AA (hon.), Md. Coll. Art and Design, 2002. Lic. elem. sch. tchr. Tchr. Durham City Schs., 1956-57; sec. USMC, Arlington, Va., 1957-58; tchr. Arlington County Schs., 1958-59; office mgr. Dukes and Kooken, Landover, Md., 1976; musical performer Washington and various locations, Va., Md., 1982—. Prin. R.W. Dukes Music Inc. Vocal student Todd Duncan; pianist, vocalist Back Alley Restaurant Lounge, 1982, various hotels, lounges, 1982—; original program, A Life Cycle in Song, presented throughout mid-Atlantic states and Washington; full operatic solo recital, 1983; featured performer benefit for Nat. Symphony Orch., Prince George's Philharmonic; performer Capital Ctr., Cole Field House, George Washington U., Smith Ctr.; operatic solo concert with pianist Glenn Sales, 1985; benefit appearance U. Md. Concert Series, 1986-87; composer over 100 original songs including Between the Lovin' and the Leavin', Covers of My Mind, Gentle Thoughts (lead song Nat. Capitol Area Composers Series), Headin' Home Again, I Would Like to Be Reborn, Miss You, Tears, You Played a Part in My Life, Christmas Memories, Mood Rhapsody, Let Freedom Ring; songwriter, vocalist (album releases-12 songs) Alive, 1992, Rainbow, 1994, Borrow The Sun, 1995, Almost Country, 1999, Rhapsody of Moods, 2000; author: (poems) Pottery, Canyons and Connections, Let the Trees of the Forest Rustle with Praise; contbr. poems to A Question of Balance, 1992, Treasured Poems of America, 1993, Distinguished Poets of 1994. Pres. Nat. Capitol Law League, Washington, 1976-77; pres. women's group, deacon, elder Riverdale Presbyn. Ch., Hyattsville, Md., 1968-94, elder, 1994; chmn. event honoring wives of Supreme Ct. justices, 1981; exec. com. women's com. Nat. Symphony, 1999-2003, bd. dirs.; chmn. awards event Marian Anderson Internat. Vocal Arts Competition, 1991, 95; bd. dirs. Md. Coll. Art and Design; mem. leadership coun. Clarice Smith Performing Arts Ctr. U. Md., 2002-. Recipient Friend of Yr. award Md. Summer Inst. for Creative and Performing Arts, U. Md., 1986, award for Vol. Svcs., Duke U., 1992, Hon. Mention award For the Children of the World Billboard mag., 1996, Billboard Hon. Mention for It's Own Time, 1999; named Hon. trustee Prince George's (Md.) Arts Coun., 1984-96, one of Women of Outstanding Achievement, Prince George's County, 1994. Mem. ASCAP (Popular Music award 1994-2001), Nat. Acad. Recording Arts and Scis., Nashville Songwriters Assn. Internat., Songwriters Assn. Washington, William Preston Few Assn. of Duke U. (pres. couns., exec. bd. of ann. fund), Internat. Platform Assn., Pres.'s Club of U. Md., Univ. Club, Founders Club of Duke U. Republican. Home and Office: 7111 Pony Trail Ln Hyattsville MD 20782-1031 Fax: 301-927-4073.

DUKES, VANESSA JOHNSON, dietitian; b. Charleston, S.C., Aug. 4, 1955; d. Rubin and Christena (Weston) Johnson; m. Warren L. Dukes, May 21, 1983. BS, S.C. State U., 1977, MEd, 1979. Registered and lic. dietitian. Grad. asst. in home econs. S.C. State Coll., Orangeburg, 1977-79; nutritionist Services Council Day Care Ctr., Aiken, S.C., 1980-83; food service supr. III S.C. Dept. Correction, Ridgeville, 1987—; tchr. emotionally handicapped Charleston County Sch. Dist., 1987-97; diet technician, dietitian Sodexho Mariott, Des Moines, 1997—; food svc. supr., diet tech., Mariott, Des Moines, 1997—. Dietary asst. S.C. Dept. Health and Environ. Control, Columbia, 1978; substitute tchr. Charleston County Sch. Dist., 1985—; nutritionist Franklin C. Fetter Health Clinic, Charleston, 1988—; companion, homemaker Med. Pers. Pool, Des Moines; asst. food svc. mgr. Fountain West Health Care Ctr., Des Moines, 1995—. Vol. Meals on Wheels, Aiken, 1976, Mercy House Diabetic Clinic, 1999—; vol. Project NOW Broadlawns Med. Ctr., 2001; alt. del. S.C. Dem. conv., 1980; voter registrar Aiken, SC, 1980—82. Recipient John H. Cromer Meml. scholarship S.C. Dietetic Assn., 1977. Mem. Am. Dietetic Assn., Ctrl. Iowa Dietetic Assn., Iowa Dietetic Assn., Kappa Omicron Phi. Avocations: reading, creative cooking, gardening, crafts. Home: 4046 Plainview Dr Des Moines IA 50311

DUKE-WHITAKER, LOIS, government and public relations educator, consultant, educator, researcher; b. Bessemer City, N.C., Feb. 13, 1935; d. Fred R. and Pearl (Kiser) Lovelace; married; children: Bruce F., Mary Louanne. BA, U. S.C., 1976, MA, 1979, PhD, 1986. Prof. Am. Govt. and polit. theory U. S.C., Auburn U., Mont., Ala., 1987—89; asst. prof. U. Ala., Tuscaloosa, 1989—90; assoc. prof. Clemson U., 1990—94, prof., 1994—96; prof., chmn. Ga. So. U., Statesboro, 1996—99, prof., 1999—; cons. pub. rels. Pub. Rels./Mktg. Assocs., Charlotte, NC, 1982—85; chief, pub. info. and cmty. rels. officer Pub. Affairs Office, Fort Jackson, SC, 1973—82. Author: Women in Politics: Outsiders or Insiders; co-editor (book with James Burns, William Crotty, Lawrence Longley) The Democrats Must Lead: The Case for a Progressive Democratic Party; contbr. other pieces on women and politics and on U.S. nat. govt. Organist, choir dir. United Meth. Ch.; officer PTO; leader Indian Waters Coun. Boy Scouts Am., Congaree area Girl Scouts Am. Recipient Merit award distinctive contbns. to acad. profession, AAUP Clemson chpt., 1992. Mem.: Beta Sigma Phi, Pi Sigma Alpha, Sigma Delta Chi, Am. Women in Radio and TV (pres. Palmetto chpt.), Pub. Rels. Soc. Am. (pres.), Columbia Media, Columbia Advt., Gamma Tau Alpha. Achievements include research in mass media and politics and state and local govts. Home: 6106 Crabtree Rd Columbia SC 29206 Office: Dept Polit Sci Ga So U PO Box 8101 Statesboro GA 30460

DUKMEJIAN, MICHAEL, publishing executive; Advt. mgr., mgr. bus. devel. Time Mag., 1980—93; dir. sales devel. Sports Illustrated, 1993—98; pub. Mut. Funds Mag., 1999—2002, Money Mag., N.Y.C., 2002—. Office: Money Mag 1271 Ave of the Ams New York NY 10020-1300

DULA, ARTHUR MCKEE, III, lawyer; b. Arlington, Va., Feb. 6, 1947; s. Arthur McKee D.; m. Tamea A. Smith, Dec. 27, 1971. BS, Eastern N.Mex. U., 1970; JD, Tulane U., 1975. Bar: Tex. 1975. Assoc. Butler & Binion, Houston, 1975—79; mem. Law Office of Art Dula, Houston, 1979—. Faculty law U. Houston, 1977-2003, South Tex. Coll. Law, 1985-97; vis. disting. prof. law U. Akron, 1992-93, Academic Law U., Moscow, Russia, 1992—; trustee Heinlein Prize Trust, 1991—. Mem. editl. bd. U. Houston Law Rev., 1978-84; contbr. articles to profl. jours. Trustee Robert A. & Virginia Heinlem Prize Trust, 1991—. Fellow AIAA (assoc.), Brit. Interplanetary Soc.; mem. ABA (sci. and tech. sect. chmn. 1982-83, award 1982), Internat. Inst. Space Law (Paris). Home: 3102 Beauchamp St Houston TX 77009-7206 Office: 3106 Beauchamp St Houston TX 77009-7206 E-mail: art@dula.com.

DULANEY, RICHARD ALVIN, lawyer; b. Charlottesville, Va., Oct. 18, 1948; s. Alvin Tandy and Susie Lucille (Sims) D. BA, Yale U., 1971; JD, Coll. William and Mary, 1977. Bar: Va. 1977, U.S. Dist. Ct. (ea. dist.) Va. 1978. V.p. Christian Ctr., Charlottesville, Va., 1972-73; rsch. asst. Marshall-Wythe Sch. Law, Williamsburg, Va., 1975; assoc. Niles & Chapman, Remington, Va., 1977-79; gen. ptnr. Niles, Dulaney & Parker, Culpeper, Va., 1980-92; of counsel Chandler, Franklin, and O'Bryan, Culpeper, Va., 1988—; ptnr. Niles Dulaney Parker and Lauer LLP, Culpeper, 1992-98, Dulaney, Parker, Lauer & Thomas LLP, Culpeper, 1999-2001, Dulaney, Lauer & Thomas LLP, Culpeper, 2001—. Bd. dirs. Rappahanock Legal Svcs., Fredericksburg, Va., 1981-83. Bd. dirs. Christian Ctr., Syria, Va., 1974-89, U. Sci. and Philosophy Swannanoa, Waynesboro, Va., 1985-2002, The Quest Inst., Charlottesville, Va., 1986-87; mem. Bd. Zoning Appeals, Culpeper County, Culpeper, Va., 1983-90. Mem. Piedmont Bar Assn., Va. Bar Assn., Va. Trial Lawyers, Assn., Am. Trial Lawyers Assn., Culpeper Bar Assn. (pres. 1985-86), New Haven chpt. Pierson Fellowship Club, Omicron Delta Kappa. Home: PO Box 511 Culpeper VA 22701-0511 Office: Dulaney Lauer & Thomas LLP PO Box 190 Culpeper VA 22701-0190 E-mail: dulaneylaw@aol.com.

DULANY, DONELSON EDWIN, JR., psychology educator; b. Shreveport, La., Dec. 9, 1928; s. Donelson Edwin and LaVera (Jackson) D.; m. Elizabeth Carolyn Gjelsness, Mar. 19, 1955; 1 child, Christopher Daniel. AB, U. Tenn., 1948; PhD, U. Mich., 1955. Rockefeller rsch. fellow in philosophy U. Mich., Ann Arbor, 1951-52, instr. psychology, 1952—54; rsch. fellow Harvard U., Cambridge, Mass., 1958; asst. prof. psychology U. Ill., Urbana-Champaign, 1956-59, assoc. prof., 1959-64, prof. psychology, 1964-98, prof. emeritus, 1998—. Inst. affiliate Beckman Inst., U. Ill., 1990—. Co-author: A Method for Teaching English to Spanish Speaking Military Personnel, 1956; editor: Contributions to Modern Psychology, 1963; editor Am. Jour. Psychology, 1988—; contbr. articles to profl. publs. With U.S. Army, 1954—56. Grantee NSF, NIH. Fellow APA (chmn. com. on equal opportunity and condtions of employment 1970), Am. Psychol. Soc. Avocations: reading, photography, travel, music. Office: U Ill Dept Psychology 603 E Daniel St Champaign IL 61820-6232

DULANY, ELIZABETH GJELSNESS, university press administrator; b. Charleston, S.C., Mar. 11, 1931; d. Rudolph Hjalmar and Ruth Elizabeth (Weaver) Gjelsness; m. Donelson Edwin Dulany, Mar. 19, 1955; 1 son, Christopher Daniel. BA, Bryn Mawr Coll., 1952. Editor, R.R. Bowker Co., 1948-52; med. editor U. Mich. Hosp., Ann Arbor, 1953-54; editorial asst. E.P. Dutton & Co., N.Y.C., 1954-55, U. Ill. Press, Champaign, 1956-59, asst. editor, 1959-67, assoc. editor, 1967-72, mng. editor, 1972-90, asst. dir., 1983-90, assoc. dir., 1990—98, editor, 1998—. Democrat. Episcopalian. Home: 73 Greencroft Dr Champaign IL 61821-5112 Office: U Ill Press 1325 S Oak St Champaign IL 61820-6903 E-mail: edulany@uillinois.edu.

DULANY, WILLIAM BEVARD, lawyer; b. Sykesville, Md., Sept. 4, 1927; s. William Washington and Helen Marie (Bevard) D.; m. Anna Winifred Spencer, Aug. 16, 1952; children: William Bryant, Thomas Patrick, Anne French. AB, McDaniel Coll., 1950, LLD (hon.), 1989; postgrad., U. Mich., 1950—51; JD, U. Md., 1953. Bar: Md. 1953, U.S. Dist. Ct. Md. 1954, U.S. Tax Ct. 1979, U.S. Supreme Ct. 1990. Assoc. Baldwin, Jarman & Norris, Balt., 1953-59; sr. ptnr. Dulany, Leahy, Curtis & Williams, LLP, Westminster, Md., 1959—. Mem. character com. Md. Ct. Appeals, Annapolis, 1974—93; chmn. bd. dirs. Mut. Fire Ins. Carroll County. Mem. Md. Ho. of Dels., Annapolis, 1962-66, Md. Constl. Conv., Annapolis, 1967-68, Md. Regional Planning Coun., 1964-66; chmn. Md. Fair Campaign Practices Commn., 1975-78; chmn. adv. com. Carroll County C.C., 1976; trustee McDaniel Coll., Westminster, Md., 1976—; bd. dirs. nat. office Am. Heart Assn., Dallas, 1982-89, chmn., 1987-88; bd. dirs. Episcopal Ministries to Aging, Inc., Fairhaven, 1982—, chmn., 1986—; former commr. Md. Human Rels. Commn.; vice chmn. Md. Spl. Com. on Gen. Equality, 1989-91; mem. commn. on Racial and Ethnicity Fairness in Judicial Process, 2002—; trustee Md. Hist. Soc., 1991-2001; past pres. Hist. Soc. Carroll County; former mem. Vestry Ascension Episc. Ch. Named one of Outstanding Young Men of Am., Westminster chpt. Jaycees, 1961, Alumnus of Yr. McDaniel Coll., 1986; recipient Outstanding Citizen award Westminster chpt. Rotary, 1985, Trustee of Yr. award Am. Assn. Homes and Svcs. for the Aging, 2002. Fellow Md. Bar Found. (pres. 1986-88, bd. dirs.); mem. ABA, Md. Bar Assn. (v.p. 1970-71), Carroll County Bar Assn. (pres. 1966-67), Am. Judicature Soc., Am. Bar Found., Bachelor's Cotillon Club (Balt.), Phi Alpha Delta. Avocations: travel, volunteer work in non-profit organizations. Home: 1167 Old Taneytown Rd Westminster MD 21158-3605 Office: Dulany Leahy Curtis & Williams LLP 127 E Main St Westminster MD 21157-5012 E-mail: dulany@dulany.com.

DULAUX, RUSSELL FREDERICK, lawyer; b. West New York, N.J., Dec. 30, 1918; s. Frederick and Theresa A. (Noble) L.; m. Ann deFriedberg, Aug. 22, 1962 (dec.); m. Eva DeLuca, Dec. 24, 1985. Student, Drake's Bus. Sch., 1937; Pace Inst., 1938-40, Fordham U., 1946-48; LLB summa cum laude, N.Y. Law

Sch., 1950; postgrad., Pace Coll., 1951, Columbia U., 1955; DBA (hon.), Adam Smith U. Am., 2001. Bar: N.Y. 1951, U.S. Dist. (so. dist.) N.Y. 1951, U.S. Ct. Appeals (2d cir.) 1951, U.S. Ct. Claims 1952, U.S. Tax Ct. 1952, U.S. Dist. Ct. (ea. dist.) N.Y. 1953, U.S. Ct. Customs and Patent Appeals 1963, U.S. Ct. Mil. Appeals 1963, U.S. Supreme Ct. 1963. Mem. staff N.Y. State Dept. Law, Richmond County Investigations, 1951-54, N.Y. State Exec. Dept. Office of Commr. of Investigations, 1954-57; comptroller-counsel Odyssey Productions, Inc., 1957-59; ptnr. Ryan, Murray & Laux, N.Y.C., 1951-61, Ryan & Laux, N.Y.C., 1961; pvt. practice N.Y.C., 1961—; prof. of bus. law and legal studies Adam Smith Univ., 2001. Served with AUS, 1940-46; capt. JAG, vet. corps. of arty. State of N.Y., 1975-92, maj., 1992—; spl. agt. counter intelligence corps and security intelligence corps; col. U.S. Army. Recipient Eloy Alfaro Grand Cross Republic of Panama, Cert. of World Leadership for Leadership and Achievement, 1987, Cert. of Merit for Disting Achievement, 1984, Cert. for Internt. Contemporary Achievement for Outstanding Contbr. to Soc., 1984, Disting. Leadership award for Contbns. to the Legal Profession, Award of Merit for Outstanding Profl. and Pub. Svc., Guglielono Marconi Bronze award, 1987, 1st Century award for achievements in bus. adminstrn. and law, 2001; inducted Hall of Fame for Contbn. to Legal Profession, recipient, Am. Medal of Honor, ABA, 2002., Outstanding People of 21st Century award, England Internat. Bar Assn., 2002. Mem. NATAS, Bronx County Bar Assn. (Townsend Wandell Gold medal), Met. Opera Guild, Internat. Platform Assn., VFW (adjutant Floyd Gibbons Post 500, Cert. of Recognition and Appreciation Polit. Action Com. 1990, Cert. of Svc. on Pres. Rehab. Com. Vets. sect.), Order of Lafayette, Am. Def. Preparedness Assn., Sons Union Vets. Civil War, Soc. Am. Wars, Nat. Sojourners, Heroes of '76, Navy League, St. Andrews Soc. N.Y., St. George Soc. N.Y., Soc. Friendly Sons St. Patrick, English Speaking Union, Asia Soc., China Inst. Am., Army and Navy Union USA, Am. Legion (past post comdr. admen's post 209), Mid Manhattan C. of C., Res. Officers Assn. U.S. (col.), Humanity Against Hatred, Delta Theta Phi, Lambs Club, Knights Hospitaller of St. John of Jerusalem, Grand St. Boys' Club, Soldiers' Club, Sailors' and Airmen's Club, Order Ea. Star, Masons (past comdr. N.Y. Masonic War Vets), Shriners, Knights of Malta, Knights of St. George, Sovereign Mil. Order of Temple of Jerusalem. Office: FDR Station PO Box 477 New York NY 10150-0477

DULBECCO, RENATO, biologist, educator; b. Catanzaro, Italy, Feb. 22, 1914; arrived in U.S., 1947, naturalized, 1953; s. Leonardo and Maria (Virdia) D.; m. Gulseppina Salvo, June 1, 1940 (div. 1963); children: Peter Leonard (dec.), Maria Vittoria; m. Maureen Rutherford Muir; 1 child, Fiona Linsey. MD, U. Torino, Italy, 1936; D.Sc. (hon.), Yale U., 1968, Vrije Universiteit, Brussels, 1978; LL.D., U. Glasgow, Scotland, 1970. Asst. U. Torino, 1940-47; research asso. Ind. U., 1947-49; sr. research fellow Calif. Inst. Tech., 1949-52, asso. prof., then prof. biology, 1952-63; sr. fellow Salk Inst. Biol. Studies, San Diego, 1963-71; asst. dir. research Imperial Cancer Research Fund, London, 1971-74, dep. dir. research, 1974-77; disting. research prof. Salk Inst., La Jolla, Calif., 1977—, pres., 1989-92, pres. emeritus, 1993—; prof. pathology and medicine U. Calif. at San Diego Med. Sch., La Jolla, 1977-81, mem. Cancer Ctr.; with Nat. Rsch. Coun. Milan. Vis. prof. Royal Soc. G.B., 1963—64; Leeuwenhoek lectr., 1974; Clowes Meml. lectr., Atlantic City, 61; Harvey lectr. Harvey Soc., 1967; Dunham lectr. Harvard U., 1972; 11th Marjory Stephenson Meml. lectr., London, 73; Harden lectr., Wye, England, 73; Am. Soc. for Microbiology lectr., L.A., 79; mem. Calif. Cancr Adv. Coun., 1963—67; mem. vis. com. Case Western Res. Sch. Medicine; adv. bd. Roche Inst., 1968—71, Inst. Immunology, Basel, Switzerland; esperto Italian Nat. Rsch. Coun.; trustee Am.-Italian Fedn. for Cancer Rsch.; bd. dirs. Scientific Counselors Dept. Etiology NCI; cons. Nat. Rsch. Coun. ESPERTO, 1994—. Trustee La Jolla Country Day Sch., Am.-Italian Fedn. for Cancer Rsch.; bd. mem. sci. counselors dept. etiology Nat. Cancer Inst. Decorated grand ufficiale Italian Republic; co-recipient (with David Baltimore and Howard Martin Temin) Nobel prize in medicine, 1975; named Man of Yr., London, 1975, Italian Am. of Yr., San Diego County, 1978, hon. citizen, City of Imperia (Italy), 1983, City of Arezzo, City of Sommariva Perno, City of Catanzaro, City of Torino, hon. founder, Hebrew U., 1981; recipient John Scott award City Phila., 1958, Kimball award Conf. Pub. Health Lab. Dirs., 1959, Albert and Mary Lasker Basic Med. Rsch. award, 1964, Howard Taylor Ricketts award, 1965, Paul Ehrlich-Ludwig Darmstaedter prize, 1967, Horwitz prize, Columbia U., 1973, Targa d'oro Villa San Giovanni, 1978, Mandel Gold medal, Czechoslovak Acad. Scis., 1982, Via de Condotti prize, 1990, Cavaliere di Gran Croce Italian Rep., 1991, Natale Di Roma prize, 1993, Columbus prize, 1993, Spl. Oscar of Italian TV, 1999; fellow Guggenheim and Fulbright fellow, 1957—58. Mem.: NAS, Am. Acad. Arts and Scis., Fedn. Am. Scientists, Royal Soc. (fgn.), Academia Nazionale del Lincel (fgn.), Am. Philos. Assn., Internat. Physicians for Prevention Nuclear War, Am. Assn. Cancer Rsch., Comitato di Collaborazione Culturale (hon.), Academia Ligure di Scienze e Lettre (hon.), Alpha Omega Alpha. Home: 7525 Hillside Dr La Jolla CA 92037-3941 Office: Salk Inst PO Box 85800 San Diego CA 92186-5800

DULCHINOS, PETER, lawyer; b. Chicopee Falls, Mass., Feb. 2, 1935; s. George and Angeline D.; children: Matthew George, Paul Constantine, Gregory Peter. BSEE, MIT, 1956, MSEE, 1957; MS in Engring. Mgmt., Northeastern U., 1965; JD, Suffolk U., 1984. Bar: Mass. 1984, U.S. Dist. Ct. (Mass.) 1984, U.S. Ct. Appeals (1st cir.) 1985, U.S. Supreme Ct. 1988, U.S. Patent and Trademark Office 1989, U.S. Claims Ct. 1989. With Sylvania Co., Waltham, Mass., 1957-61, Needham, Mass., 1963-66, Tech Ops, Burlington, Mass., 1961, RCA, Burlington, 1962-63, Raytheon Co., Lexington, Mass., 1966—. Computer ops. mgr. tactical software devel. facility Patriot Ground Computer System, 1977-86, intellectual property mgr., 1986—; lectr. Fitchburg State Coll., 1985-90; corporator Ctrl. Savs. Bank, Lowell, Mass., 1980-92; sec.-treas. U. Lowell Bldg. Authority, 1974-85; mem. statewide adv. coun. Dept. Mental Health, 1996—. Mem. statewide adv. coun. Dept. Mental Retardation, 1993-96; mem. human studies subcom. Bedford VA Hosp., 1987-90; pres. Chelmsford Rep. Club, 1964-70; chmn. Chelmsford Rep. Town Com., 1972-76, 80—, chmn., 2000—; assoc. town counsel Tyngsborough, Mass., 1985-87; mem., chmn. Chelmsford Bd. Health, 1972-87, 93—; mem. Nashoba Tech. High Sch. Com., 1970-71; trustee, chmn. Medfield State Hosp., 1993-2003, Westborough State Hosp., 2003—; v.p. Greater Lowell Comprehensive Cmty. Support Systems Bd. Dept. Mental Health, 1994-99; mem. State Mental Health Planning Coun., 1999—. 2d lt. U.S. Army, 1957-58. Mem. Mass. Bar Assn., Boston Patent Law Assn., Raytheon Employees Profl. Assn. (treas. 1998, pres. 1999). Republican. Greek Orthodox. Home: 17 Spaulding Rd Chelmsford MA 01824-1021 Office: Raytheon Co 141 Spring St Lexington MA 02421-7899 E-mail: peter_dulchinos@raytheon.com.

DULEY, CHARLOTTE DUDLEY, vocational counselor; b. Lincoln, Nebr., Oct. 2, 1920; d. Millard Eugene and Inez Kathryn (Miller) Dudley; m. Phillip D. Duley, Mar. 28, 1942 (dec. Sept. 1984); children: Michael Dudley (dec.), Patricia Kaye; m. P. Fredrik Nordgaard, Sept. 1, 1990. Student, U. Nebr., 1938-41; BS, Lewis and Clark State Coll., 1973; MA in Guidance Counseling, U. Idaho, 1977. Tchr. Nebr. schs., 1951-56; with Dept. Employment, Lewiston, Idaho, 1958-81, local office counselor handling fed. tng. programs, 1958-81; ind. job. cons., counselor; part-time counselor, tester, 1981—. Avon sales rep. 1988— Pres., bd. dirs. Civic Arts, Inc., 1972-81; mem. women's svc. league Wash. Idaho Symphony Orch., 1972-96; bd. dirs. YWCA, 1980-88, treas., 1981-88; vol. tchr. YWCA programs, 1975—; mem. adv. bd. Salvation Army, 1980-94; dir. artist series Lewis and Clark State Coll., 1984-90; vol. INWBC blood dr., 1985—. Recipient Altrusa Woman of Achievement award, 1984. Mem. Am. Pers. Guidance Assn., Idaho Pers. Guidance Assn., Idaho State Employees Assn., Internat. Assn. Employees in Employment Security, Am. Assn. Counseling and Devel., Idaho State Employment Counselors Assn. (pres. 1979-80), Stateline Guidance and Counseling Assn. (sec.-treas. 1964, 76-77), Lewiston Cmty. Concert Assn. (bd. dirs. 1980-96, pres. 1980-94), Greater Lewiston C. of C. (chmn. conv. and tourism com. 1984-95), Altrusa (bd. dirs.), Ladies of Elks (pres. 1986-87, exec. bd. dirs. 1985-88, 1st v.p. 1993-95, ladies of Elks pres. 1987-89, 95-96, bd. dirs. 1996-98, 2001-02, chmn. or registrar-judge 1988—). Baptist. Home: 1819 Ridgeway Dr Lewiston ID 83501-3890 E-mail: cduley@lewiston.com.

DULIN, MAURINE STUART, volunteer; b. Lonerock, Iowa, Feb. 16, 1919; d. Frank Meagher and Fern Adrienne (Wetzel) Stuart; m. William Carter Dulin, Oct. 5, 1940; children: Jacquelyn Dulin Wilson, Patricia F., Stuart M. AB in Polit. Sci./Econs., The Coll. of William and Mary, 1939. Coll. cons. Woodward and Lothrop, Washington, 1939-40; adminstr. asst. Sightler and Cox, Washington, 1942-43; acctg. dept. asst. The Am. U., Washington, 1964-69; corp. sec. Bittinger and Dulin, Arlington, Va., 1949-73; ptnr. 41 Limited Partnership, Bethesda, Md., 1979—, Montrose-270 Ltd. Partnership, Bethesda, 1979—. Mem. Rock Creek Womens Rep. Club, Bethesda, 1951-57; sgt.-at-arms Montgomery County Fed. of Rep. Women, Bethesda, 1952-53, State Fedn. of Womens Rep. Club, 1953-54; charter mem., com. chmn. Nat. Mus. of Women in the Arts; mem. Women's Bd.Cathedral Choral Soc. 1975—, com. chmn., 1988-90; mem. Women's Bd. George Washington U. Hosp., 1970—, Save Our Seminary at Forest Glen, Md., 1989—. Mem. The Town Club (pres. 1958-59), Pi Beta Phi (nat. com. chmn. 1971-75, province officer 1967-71). Episcopalian. Home: 9707 Old Georgetown Rd Apt 1416 Bethesda MD 20814

DULING, EDWARD BURGER, music education educator; b. Coshocton, Ohio, Dec. 6, 1954; s. Edwin Tracy and Mary Helen (Burger) D. MusB, Capital U., 1977; MA, Ohio State U., 1987, PhD, 1992. Cert. elem. tchr., music tchr., supr., Ohio. Tchr. music, English Cedar Cliff Local Schs., Cedarville, Ohio, 1984-89; grad. teaching assoc. Ohio State U., Columbus, Ohio, 1989-91, lectr. music edn. Newark, Ohio, 1991-93; asst. prof. Morehead (Ky.) State U., 1993-94; co-dir. Southeast Inst. Edn. in Music, Chattanooga, 1994-95; tchr. gen. music Chattanooga (Tenn.) City Schs., 1995-96; asst. prof. Bowling Green (Ohio) U., 1996—2002, U. Toledo, 2002—. Facilitator Southeast Inst. for Edn. in Music, Chattanooga, 1996, discipline-based expert, New Orleans, 1997-02; presenter in field; church organist 24 yrs., tubist, trombonist. Contbr. article and book revs. to profl. jours. Recipient Outstanding Faculty Svc. award ProMusica of Coll. of Musical Arts, Bowling Green State U., 1996-97, Disting. Faculty award Phi Mu Alpha Sinfonia, 1997-98, Dean's award, 1999. Mem. Ohio Music Edn. Assn. (editor jour. Triad 2001-03), Internat. Tuba and Euphonium Assn., Internat. Trombone Assn., Music Educators Nat. Conf., Phi Mu Alpha (chpt. advisor 1996-2001). Methodist. Avocations: art pottery, gardening, collecting sheetmusic and memorabilia. Office: U Toledo Ctr for Performing Arts Toledo OH 43606-3390 E-mail: ebd2140@aol.com.

DULIT, EVERETT PAUL, psychiatrist, educator; b. Bklyn., May 2, 1929; s. Benjamin and Florence Dulit; m. Elinor Greenspun, Sept. 12, 1954; children: Rebecca, Kathryn, Alan. BS, MIT, 1950, PhD in Physics, 1957; MD, U. Minn., 1958; grad., N.Y. Psychoanalytic Inst., 1968. Intern Kaiser Found. Hosp., San Francisco, 1958—59; resident in psychiatry Bronx Mcpl. Hosp. Ctr., 1959—61, chief resident dept. psychiatry, 1961—62; rsch. fellow Albert Einstein Coll. Medicine, 1962—65, instr. in psychiatry, 1965—68, asst. clin. prof. psychiatry, 1968—74, assoc. clin. prof. psychiatry, 1974—76, 1980—2000, dir. overall divsn. child and adolescent psychiatry, 1984—87, assoc. clin. profl. pediat., 1988—2000, assoc. clin. prof. emeritus, 2000—; assoc. clin. prof. psychiatry Cornell Med. Coll., 1976—80; psychiat. cons. divsn. adolescent medicine Montefiore Med. Ctr., 1980—2000, acting dir. child and adolescent psychiatry, 1983—84, dir., 1984—87, psychiat. cons. child protective svcs., 1991—95, psychiat. cons. dept. pediat., 1994—2000; psychiat. cons. Westchester Family Svc., White Plains, NY, 1997—. Dir. sch. consultation svc. Bronx H.S. Sci., 1963—76; overall dir. h.s. consultation project Albert Einstein Coll. Medicine and N.Y.C. Bd. Edn., 1965—76; fellow in child psychiatry Albert Einstein Coll. Medicine, 1966—70, dir. ann. Ed Hornick Meml. lecture, 1985—, dir. child psychiatry Ground Rounds series, 1987—2000; dir. divsn. adolescent psychiatry Albert Einstein Coll. Medicine-Bronx. Mcpl. Hosp. Ctr., 1969—76, acting dir., 1971—72, 1974—75, assoc. dir., 1971—75; dir. adolescent psychiatry Westchester divsn. N.Y. Hosp. Cornell Med. Sch., 1976—80, coord., moderator Grand Rounds vis. lecture series, 1977—80; vis. prof. numerous hosps. and univs., spkr. numerous confs.; lectr. in field, 1967—89. Author: (chpt.) Personality Development and Deviation, 1975, Clinical Update in Adolescent Psychiatry, 1983; contbr. articles and book revs. to profl. jours. Named Shell fellow in Physics, MIT Grad. Sch., 1951—52, Sol Ginsberg fellow, Group for Advancement Psychiatry, 1961—62; recipient Rsch. Career Devel. award, NIMH, 1962—67. Fellow: APA (task force preparing DSM3 1976—80, com. on childhood and adolescence 1976—80, com. on DSM3 ASAP 1976—80); mem.: Am. Bd. Adolescent Psychiatry (founding mem.), Am. Soc. Adolescent Psychiatry, Sigma Xi. Avocations: jazz, clarinet, saxophone, skiing. Home and Office: 16 Sage Terr Scarsdale NY 10583

DULL, CLIFFORD JOHN, religious groups analyst; b. Richland Ctr., Wis., Jan. 11, 1946; s. Clifford LaVerne and Olive Clare (McKittrick) D.; m Helen Marie Kirkpatrick, June 12, 1970. BA in History, Milligan Coll., 1968; MA in Classics, U. Wis., 1970, PhD in History, 1975; Cert. in Book Pub., NYU, 1980. Vis. asst. prof. U. Colo., Boulder, 1975-76; faculty mem. Roanoke Bible Coll., Elizabeth City, N.C., 1976-77; lectr. Carthage Coll., Kenosha, Wis., 1977-78; editorial cons. Standard Pub., Cin., 1978-79; lectr. U. Wis.-Washington County, West Bend, 1980; computer specialist Def. Logistics Agy., Columbus, Ohio, 1980—. Contbr. articles and book revs. to profl. jours. and articles to books. Elder Upper Arlington Christian Ch., Columbus, 1983—. Mem. Assn. Ancient Historians, Am. Inst. Archaeology, Disciples of Christ Hist. Soc., Am. Soc. Ch. History, State Hist. Soc. Wis. Avocations: playing organ and piano, wallyball, collecting videos of b-movies, attending operas, visiting turreted victorian homes. Home: 225 Tibet Rd Columbus OH 43202-1439 E-mail: cjdullrm@cs.com.

DULL, PAMELA, physician, educator; BA, Hiram Coll., 1981; MD, Ohio State U., 1984. Lic. American Board of Family Practice Am. Bd. Family Practice. Asst. clin. prof. Ohio State U. Family Practice, Columbus, 1995—. Mem.: Am. Acad. Family Physicians, Ohio Assn. Family Physicians. Office: Ohio State U Family Practice 2231 N High St Columbus OH 43201 Office Fax: 614-293-2720. E-mail: dull-1@medctr.osu.edu.

DULL, WILLIAM MARTIN, retired engineering executive; b. Buchanan, Mich., June 24, 1924; s. Curtis Frank and Daisy Julia (Sharp) D.; m. Margaret Ann McMillan, Apr. 10, 1976; children: Richard William, Beverly Ann, William McMillan. BSME, U. Mich., 1945. Registered profl. engr., Mich. Dir. tech. staff Detroit Edison, 1951-66, asst. gen. supt. cen. plants, 1966-70, gen. supt. underground lines, 1970-71, mgr. employee relations, 1971-74, mgr. orgn. planning and devel., 1974-89; pres. Charleston Engring. Cons., 1990-92; ret., 1992. Chmn. Charleston Engrs. Joint Coun., 1991—, chmn. 1993-94. Bd. dirs. World Med. Relief, Detroit, 1971-90, chmn., 1988-90; bd. dirs. Jr. Achivement, Southeastern Mich., 1971-90; trustee Detroit Sci. Ctr., Inc., 1979-85. Served to lt. (s.g.) USN, 1942-51, PTO. Recipient Gold Leadership award Jr. Achievement, 1985. Fellow Engring. Soc. Detroit (pres. 1970-71, Disting. Svc. 1980, life); mem. ASHRAE (pres. 1964-65, Outstanding Engr. award 1965, life), ASME (life), IEEE (chmn. nat. conf. 1971), NSPE (life), Architects, Engrs., Surveyors Registration Coun. (chmn. 1968-69), Mich. Soc. Profl. Engrs. (bd. dirs. 1973-75, Disting. Engr. 1980), S.C. Soc. Profl. Engrs. (bd. dirs. 1994-95), Charleston Engrs. Joint Coun. (chmn. 1993-94), U. Mich. Alumni Assn. (v.p., bd. dirs. 1964-71, Disting. Svc. award 1970), Charleston Navy League (v.p., bd. dirs. 1993—), Detroit Yacht Club. Republican. Methodist. E-mail: mwmdull@aol.com.

DULLES, AVERY, cardinal, theologian; b. Auburn, NY, Aug. 24, 1918; s. John Foster and Janet Pomeroy (Avery) D. AB, Harvard U., 1940, postgrad. in law, 1940-41; PhL, Woodstock Coll., 1951, STL, 1957; STD, Pontifical Gregorian U., Rome, 1960; LLD, St. Joseph's Coll., Phila., 1969; LHD, Georgetown U., 1977; ThD, U. Detroit, 1978; LLD, Iona Coll., New Rochelle, N.Y., 1980; DD, St. Anselm Coll., Manchester, N.H., 1981; LHD, Creighton U., 1983; DD, Jesuit Sch. Theology, Berkeley, Calif., 1984, Protestant Episcopal Theol. Sem., Alexandria, Va., 1986; LHD, Seton Hall U., 1989, Stonehill Coll., 1990, Loyola U., Chgo., 1990; STD (hon.), Providence Coll., 1991; DD, Carthage Coll., Kenosha, Wis., 1991; ThD, U. Dayton, 1992; LHD, Christ the King Seminary, East Aurora, N.Y., 1994; DD, Nashotah House, Nashotah, Wis., 1996; LittD, Fordham U., 1996; post grad, John Carroll U., Cleveland, Ohio, 1997; LLD, U. Mass., Boston, 1998, U. Notre Dame, 2001; LHD, St. Francis Coll., Bklyn., 1999; ThD, Theol. Faculty Paderborn, Germany, 2000; LHD (hon.), LeMoyne Coll., Syracuse, NY, 2001, Univ. St Thomas, Miami, 2001, Seminary St. Charles Barromeo, Overbrook, Pa., 2002, Univ. St. Thomas,St. Paul, Minn., 2002; ThD (hon.), Univ. Scanton, Pa., 2002; post grad., Franciscan Univ., Steubenville, Ohio, 2002; post grad, St. Joseph's Coll., Renssalear, Ind., 2003, Christendom Coll. Front royal, Va., 2003, Coll. of the Holy Cross, Worcester, Mass., 2003, Sena Coll., Londonville, NY, 2003. Joined S.J., Roman Cath. Ch., 1946, ordained priest, 1956, elevated to cardinal, 2001. Instr. philosophy Fordham U., 1951-53, vis. lectr., 1970, Laurence J. McGinley prof. religion and society, 1988—; mem. faculty Woodstock Coll., NYC, 1960-74, prof. theology, 1969-74, Cath. U. Am., Washington, 1974-88; Gasson prof. theology Boston Coll., Boston, 1981-82; prof. emeritus Cath. U. Am., Washington, 1988— Vis. lectr. Weston Coll., 1971, Union Theol. Sem., 1971-74, Princeton Theol. Sem., 1972, Pontifical Gregorian U., 1973, 90, 93, Episcopal Theol. Sem., 1975, Luth. Sem. Pa., 1978; Martin C. D'Arcy lectr. Campion Hall, Oxford (Eng.) U., 1983; vis. John A. O'Brien prof. theology Notre Dame U., 1985; vis. prof. theology Cath. U. of Leuven, 1992; vis. prof. religious studies Yale U., New Haven, 1996; fellow Woodrow Wilson Internat. Ctr. for Scholars, 1977; mem. Commn. on Christian Unity, Archdiocese of Balt., 1962-70, Cath. Bishops' Adv. Coun., 1969-75; consultor to Papal Secretariat for Dialogue with Non-Believers, 1966-73, mem. USA Luth.-Cath. Dialogue, 1972-92; cons. to Com. on Doctrine, Nat. Conf. Cath. Bishops, 1991—; mem. Internat. Theol. Com., 1992-97; mem. Luth.-Roman Cath. Coord. Com., 1994-96. Author: Princeps Concordiae, 1941, A Testimonial to Grace, 1946, (with others) Introductory Metaphysics, 1955, Apologetics and the Biblical Christ, 1963, The Dimensions of the Church, 1967, Revelation and the Quest for Unity, 1968, Revelation Theology: A History, 1969, (with others) Spirit, Faith and Church, 1970, The Survival of Dogma, 1971 (Christopher award 1972), A History of Apologetics, 1971, Models of the Church, 1974, 2d rev. edit., 1987, Church Membership as a Catholic and Ecumenical Problem, 1974, The Resilient Church, 1977, A Church to Believe In, 1982, Models of Revelation, 1983, 2d rev. edit., 1992, (with Patrick Granfield) The Church: A Bibliography, 1985, The Reshaping of Catholicism, 1988, The Craft of Theology, 1992, expanded edit., 1995 (Best Book in Theology Cath. Press Assn. 1993), The Assurance of Things Hoped For, 1994, A Testimonial to Grace and Reflections on a Theological Journey, 1996, The Priestly Office, 1997, (with Patrick Granfield) The Theology of the Church: A Bibliography, 1999, The Splendor of Faith: The Theological Vision of Pope John Paul II, 1999, The New World of Faith, 2000, Newman, 2002; assoc. editor for ecumenism Concilium, 1963-70, adv. editl. bd., 1970-92; adv. editl. bd. Midstream: An Ecumenical Jour., 1974—; mem. editl. bd. Logos: A Jour. of Cath. Thought and Culture, 1997—; contbr. column to Theology for Today, America, 1967-68; contbg. editor New Oxford Rev., 1990—; cons. Theology Digest, 1985—; mem. adv. coun. Pro Ecclesia, 1991—; contbr. articles to theol. publ. Bd. dirs. Georgetown U., 1966-68, Woodstock Theol. Ctr., 1974-79; trustee Fordham U., 1969-72, St. Mary's Sem. and Univ., Balt., 1992-98; acad. coun. Irish Sch. Ecumenics, 1971-78. Served to lt. USNR, 1942-46. Decorated Croix de Guerre with silver star (France); scholar-in-residence St. Joseph's Sem., Dunwoodie, NY, 1996; recipient Cardinal Spellman award for disting. achievement in theology, 1970, Religious Edn. Forum award Nat. Cath. Edn. Assn., 1988, Campion award Cath. Book Club, NY, 1989, F. Sadlier Dinger award, 1994, Choate Alumni Seal prize Choate Rosemary Hall, 1995, Christus Magister medal U. Portland, 2001, James Cardinal Gibbons medal Cath. U. Am., Washington, 2001, Gold Medal award Nat. Inst. Social Sci., N.Y.C., 2001, John Henry Newman award Cardinal Newman Soc., 2001, John Carroll Soc. Medal, Washington, 2002, John Paul II award Inst. for Social Sci., Arlington, Va., 2002, Jerome award Cath. Libr. Assoc., 2002. Mem. Cath. Theol. Soc. Am. (bd. dir. 1970-72, 74-77, v.p. 1974-75, pres. 1975-76), Am. Theol. Soc. (v.p. 1977-78, pres. 1978-79), Cath. Commn. on Intellectual and Cultural Affairs (exec. com. 1991-94), Phi Beta Kappa. Roman Catholic. Office: Fordham U Faber 255 Bronx NY 10458

DULLES, FREDERICK HENDRIK, lawyer; b. NYC, Mar. 12, 1942; s. William Winslow and Joanna (deLeu) D.; m. Martine Pred'homme, Aug. 26, 1977; 1 child, Emilie Pred'homme. AB cum laude, Harvard U., 1964; JD, MBA, Columbia U., 1968. Bar: D.C. 1971, N.Y. 1972. Assoc. Shearman & Sterling, N.Y.C. and Paris, 1971-80; counsel Philip Morris Inc., N.Y.C., 1980, asst. gen. counsel, 1981-83; dir. regional counsel EFTA-Eastern Europe-Middle East-Africa region, Lausanne, Switzerland, 1983-92; counsel Pirenne Python Schifferli Peter & Ptnrs., Geneva, 1993-94; ptnr. McDermott, Will & Emery, Chgo., 1994-96; of counsel Jackson & Nash, LLP, N.Y.C., 2000; ptnr. McFadden, Pilkington & Ward, LLP, London, N.Y.C., 1997—. Trustee Mass. Fin. Svcs.-Sun Life Compass mut. funds, 2001--; internat. exec. Assn. Internat. des Etudiants en Sciences Economiques et Commerciales, 1961-66, U.S. gen. counsel, 1977-80. Trustee Am. U. of Paris, 2001--. Lt. Security Group Command, USNR, 1968-71. Decorated Navy Achievement medal. Mem. Am. Bar Assn., Assn. Bar City N.Y., Swiss Arbitration Assn., Am. Mgmt. Assn., Internat. Bar Assn., Harvard Club (N.Y.C., Boston). Republican. E-mail: dulles@post.harvard.edu.

DULLES, JOHN WATSON FOSTER, history educator; b. Auburn, N.Y., May 20, 1913; s. John Foster and Janet Pomeroy (Avery) D.; m. Eleanor Foster Ritter, June 15, 1940; children: Edith, John, Ellen, Avery. AB, Princeton U., 1935; MBA, Harvard U., 1937; BS in Metall. Engring., U. Ariz., 1943, Metall. Engr., 1951. Clk. The Bank of N.Y., N.Y.C., 1937-38; miner Callahan Zinc-Lead Co., Patagonia, Ariz., 1938-41; head ore dept., smelter operator Cia Minera de Peñoles, S.A., Monterrey, Mex., 1943-49, head comml. divsn., 1949-51, asst. gen. mgr., 1951-59, exec. v.p., 1959; v.p. Cia Mineração Novalimense, Belo Horizonte, Brazil, 1959-62; prof. history U. Ariz., Tucson, 1966-91; univ. prof. L.Am. studies U. Tex., Austin, 1962—. Advisor to U.S. delegation to OAS Conf., Vina Del Mar, Chile, 1967; cons. U.S. Dept. State, Bur. Intelligence and Rsch., 1968-72. Author: Yesterday in Mexico, 1961, Vargas of Brazil, 1967, Unrest in Brazil, 1970, Anarchists and Communists in Brazil, 1973, Castello Branco: The Making of a Brazilian President, 1978, President Castello Branco, 1980, Brazilian Communism, 1935-1945, 1983, The São Paulo Law School, 1986, Carlos Lacerda: Brazilian crusader, Vol. 1, 1991, Vol. 2, 1996 (Brazilian Union Writers and Carioca Acad. Leters prize 2000), Sobral Pinto: The Conscience of Brazil, 2002. Pres. exec. bd. Union Ch. Monterrey, Mexico, 1948—49, elder, 1957—59. Recipient Achievement medal U. Ariz., 1960, Ptnrs. of the Alliance Medal, Brazilian Govt., 1966. Fellow Calif. Inst. Internat. Studies; mem. The Am. Soc. of the Most Venerable Order of the Hosp. of St. John of Jerusalem (knight), Am. Hist. Assn., Tex. Inst. of Letters, Theta Tau (Alumni Hall of Fame), Inst. History and Geography Brasil. Avocation: tennis. Office: U Texas PO Box 7934 Austin TX 78713-7934 E-mail: dulles@mail.utexas.edu.

DUMA, RICHARD JOSEPH, microbiologist, physician, pathologist, researcher, educator; b. Bethlehem, Pa., Apr. 2, 1933; s. Joseph Anthony and Helen Veronica (Bartek) D.; m. Mary Alyce Fridley, Apr. 18, 1957; 1 child, Scott. BA, Va. Poly. Inst., 1955; MD, U. Va., 1959; PhD, Va. Commonwealth U.-Med. Coll. Va., 1978. Diplomate Am. Bd. Internal Medicine; lic. physician, Fla., Va.; lic. pvt. pilot. Intern, then resident in medicine U. Ala. Med. Center, Birmingham, 1959-60, 62-65; research fellow Harvard U. Med. Sch.-Mass. Gen. Hosp., 1965-67; mem. faculty Med. Coll. Va., Richmond, 1967-91, chmn. div. infectious diseases, 1974-92, prof. medicine and pathology, 1975-92, prof. microbiology, 1977-92. Mem. U. S. Pharmacopeia Adv. Panel on Hosp. Practices, 1971-82, chmn. subcom. rsch., 1976-82, clin. prof. medicine and infectious diseases Med. Coll. Richmond, 1992—; exec. dir. Nat. Found. for Infectious Diseases, 1991-94, v.p. bd. dirs., 1973-75, pres., 1975-91, trustee, 1994—; chmn. Nat. Coalition for Adult Immunization, 1988-94; didr. infectious diseases Halifax Med. Ctr., Daytona Beach, Fla., 1995—. Mem. bd. visitors Embry-Riddle Aero. U., 1999—. Served with M.C., USNR, 1960-62. Fellow ACP, Infectious Disease Soc. Am., Royal Soc. Tropical Medicine and Hygiene, Am. Soc. Tropical Medicine and Hygiene, Am. Soc. Rickettsiology, Fla. Infectious Disease Soc. (pres. 1997-99); mem. AAAS, Am. Fedn. Clin. Rsch., Am. Soc. Microbiology, Va. Soc. Microbiology, Am. Soc. Internal Medicine, Va. Soc. Internal Medicine, Richmond Soc. Internal Medicine, So. Soc. Clin. Investigation, Am. Thoracic Soc., Royal Soc. Medicine, Med. Soc. Va., Richmond Acad. Medicine, Acad. of Medicine, Volusia, Med. Assn. Fla., Volusia Med. Soc., Sigma Xi, Tau Beta Pi. Home: 1 Capri Ct Palm Coast FL 32137- Office: Halifax Medical Ctr 303 N Clyde Morris Blvd Daytona Beach FL 32114-2700

DUMAINE, ROBERT, research scientist, educator; b. Acton Vale, Quebec, Canada, Mar. 23, 1958; s. Jean-Claude Dumaine and Denise Tellier; m. Sylvie Bergeron, June 17, 1993; children: Hugo, Sarah Marie. PhD, U. Sherbrooke, Can., 1986—93. Head molecular biology dept. Masonic Med. Rsch. Lab., Utica, NY, 1996—. Recipient Best Sci. Work, French Can. Assn. for Advancement of Sci., 1992, Gordon K. Moe Young Investigator, NY state EP Soc./Am. Heart Assn., 1999; fellow, Heart and Stroke Found. Can., 1993—95, Fonds de la Recherche en Santé du Québec, 1995—96. Mem.: Am. Heart Assn. (rsch. coun. mem. 1999—2003), Biophysical Soc. Achievements include discovery of an electrophysiological characterization of cardiac gene defects causing Long QT and Brugada syndromes. Office: Masonic Medical Rsch Lab 2150 Bleecker Utica NY 13501 Office Fax: 315-735-5648. E-mail: rdumaine@mmrl.edu.

DUMAIS, ARLENE, psychiatric mental health and critical care nurse; b. Norwich, Conn., Nov. 27, 1939; d. Warren Frank and Harriett Pearce; m. Joseph D. Dumais, Aug. 24, 1970; children: Arlene Goodwin Starke, Wayne Goodwin. Diploma, Lynn Hosp. Sch. Nursing, Mass., 1961; BSN, U. Hartford, 1986; MSN, St. Joseph Coll., Hartford, Conn., 1989. RN, Conn.; cert. hypnotherapy practitioner, advanced practice RN; cert. in case mgmt. Nurse ICU, CCU, emergency rm. Lawrence & Meml. Hosp., New London, Conn., 1967-89; psychiat. nurse clinician Natchaug Hosp., Mansfield Center, Conn., 1989-92; dir. behavioral health dept. Mashantucket Pequot Health Dept. (Indian Reservation), Ledyard, Conn., 1995; managed disability nurse Benefit Mgmt. Svcs./The Hartford, Simsbury, Conn., 1995—. Mem. ANA, Conn. Nurses Assn., Sigma Theta Tau. Home: 14 Cove Rd Preston CT 06365-8301 Office: The Hartford 200 Hopmeadow St Simsbury CT 06089-9793

DUMAS, H. SCOTT, mathematician; BA, Rice U., 1979; MA, U. of Colo., 1981; PhD, U. N.Mex, 1988. Engr. II Jet Propulsion Lab., Pasadena, Calif., 1982; rsch. asst. Naval Rsch. Lab., Washington, 1984—85; asst. prof. of math. and physics SUNY, Albany, 1988—89; postdoctoral mem. Inst. for Math. and its Applications, Mpls., 1989—90; asst. prof. of math. U. of Cin., Cincinnati, Ohio, 1990—94, assoc. prof. of math., 1994—2000, prof. of math., 2000—. Fulbright scholar Ecole Normale Superieure, Paris, 1986—87; vis. assoc. prof. math. U. Picardy, Amiens, France, 1991—92; vis. prof. math. Ecole Normale Superieure, Cachan, France, 1994; vis. astronomer Bur. Longitudes, Paris, 1996; vis. prof. math. U. Cergy-Pontoise, France. Translator: (mathematics text) Multiphase Averaging for Classical Systems, by P. Lochak and C. Meunier; editor: Hamiltonian Dynamical Systems: History, Theory, and Applications (H.S. Dumas, K.R. Meyer, and D.S. Schmidt, Eds.). Grantee, NSF, 1992—94, 1995—98. Office: U Cin Dept Math Scis Cincinnati OH 45221-0025

DUMAS, MICHAEL GODFREY JOSEPH, artist; b. Whitney, Ontario, Canada, Sept. 20, 1950; s. Alphyr Adrian and Caroline Anna (Cenzura) D.; m. Ellen Kocsis, July 19, 1975; 1 child, Shae Shannon-Mae. Student, Art Instrn. Sch., Mpls., 1968, Humber Coll., 1970, postgrad., 1971, Cornell U., 1984. Apprentice to his. painter Lewis Parker Lazare & Parker Studios, 1971-72. Adv. bd. mem. Art Impressions mag., 1993-97. Major exhibits include Nat. Mus. Nat. Sci., Ottawa, Ont., 1977, Theodore Roosevelt Inaugural Nat. Hist. Site, Buffalo, NY, 1977, McMichael Can. Coll., Kleinburg, Ont., 1981, Royal Botanical Gardens, Hamilton, 1985, R.O.M., 1987-88, Yamanaakako-Takamura Mus. Art, 1991-2001, Mitsukoshi Galleries, Tokyo, 1994-2002, Algonquin Gallery, Algonquin Pk., Ont., 1995-2002, Suntory Mus. Art, Osaka, 1995, Suntory Mus. Art, Tokyo, 1996, Matsuya Gallery, Tokyo, 1997, Sogo Gallery, Osaka, 1997, Yumehodaka Mus., Nagano, 1997, Spanierman Gallery, NY, 1998, Mitsukoshi Gallery, Sendai, 1999-2003, Arai Gallery, Tokyo, 2003, Cedar Ridge Creative Ctr., Scarborough, 1999; represented in permanent collections including Internat. Mus. Art Inspired By Nature, Gloucester, Eng., Yamanakako-Takamura Mus. Art, Japan, Imaoka Collection, Japan, Ont. Provincial Collection, Queen's Park, Ont.; major conservation events include The Spirit of the Wild fundraiser and exhibit, 1982, Kenya Wild Elephant fundraiser, Toronto, 1987, 91, Bird Preservation fundraiser, Osaka, Japan, 1990, Save the Rhino Trust, Namibia, 1998; commd. to design four coins for Royal Can. Mint, 1994, commd. to design Can. commemorative postage stamps; author: Nature in Art, 1991; columnist Angler & Hunter, 1976-83; contbr. articles to mag. Recipient Waterfowl Art award Ducks Unltd., 1983-84, Carling-O'Keefe Profl. Conservation award, 1986, Wildlife Conservation award Ont. Min. Natural Resources, 1987, Bronze Teal Conservation award Ducks Unltd., 1989; named Artist of the Yr., Can. Collector's Clubs, 1987, first winner by competion Wildlife Habitat Can., 1990, Internat. Flyway Artist, Ducks Unltd., Inc., 1992, Artist of the Yr., Ont. Fedn. Anglers and Hunters, 1993-2004, Outdoor Card Program award Ont. Ministry of Natural Resources, 1998, Twentieth Century Achievement award Am. Biog. Inst., 2000. Fellow Internat. Biog. Assn. (Eng., life); mem. Soc. Animal Artists, Soc. Wildlife Art of the Nations (charter). Avocations: travel, photography, camping. Address: PO Box 8314 RR 1 Peterborough ON Canada K9J 6X2 E-mail: natures.studio.inc@sympatico.ca.

DUMAS, RHETAUGH ETHELDRA GRAVES, university official; b. Natchez, Miss., Nov. 26, 1928; d. Rhetaugh Graves and Josephine (Clemmons) Graves Bell; m. A.W. Dumas, Jr., Dec. 25, 1950; 1 child, Adrienne. BS in Nursing, Dillard U., 1951; MS in Psychiat. Nursing, Yale U., 1961; PhD in Social Psychology, Union Grad. Sch., Union for Experimenting Colls. and Univs., Cinn., 1975; also various other courses; D Pub. Svc. (hon.), Simmons Coll., 1976, U. Cin., 1981; LHD (hon.), Yale U., 1989; LLD (hon.), Dillard U., 1990; LHD (hon.), U. San Diego, 1993, Georgetown U., 1996; DPub. Svc., Fla. Internat. U., Miami, 1996; DSc (hon.), Ind. U., Gary, 1996; JD (hon.), Bethune-Cookman Coll., 1997; LHD (hon.), U. Mass, 1997. Instr. Dillard U., 1957-59, 61; research asst., instr. Sch. Nursing Yale U., 1962-65, from asst. prof. nursing to assoc. prof., 1965-72, chmn. dept. psychiat. nursing, 1972; dir. nursing Conn. Mental Health Ctr., Yale-New Haven Med. Ctr., 1966-72; chief psychiat. nursing edn. br. Div. Manpower and Tng. Programs, NIMH, Rockville, Md., 1972-76; dep. dir. Div. Manpower and Tng. Programs NIMH, 1976-79, dep. dir. alcohol, drug abuse and mental health adminstrn., 1979-81; dean, prof. U. Mich. Sch. Nursing, 1981-94; vice provost health affairs U. Mich., 1994-97, Lucille Cole prof. sch. nursing, 1994—, vice provost emerita, 1997—, dean emerita, 1997—. Dir. Group Rels. Confs. in Tavistock Model; cons., speaker, panelist in field; fellow Helen Hadley Hall, Yale U., 1972, Branford Coll., 1972; dir. Community Health Care Ctr. Plan, New Haven, 1969-72; mem. U.S. Assessment Team, cons. to Fed. Ministry Health, Nigeria, 1982; mem. adv. com. Health Policy Agenda for the Am. People, AMA, 1983-86; cons. NIH Task Force on Nursing Rsch., 1984; mem. Nat. Commn. on Unemployment and Mental Health, Nat. Mental Health Assn., 1984-85; mem. com. to plan maj. study of nat. long-term care policy Inst. Medicine, 1985; mem. adv. com. to dir. NIH, 1986-87; mem. Sec.'s Nat. Commn. on Future Structure of VA Health Care System, 1990-91; mem. coun. on grad. med. edn. Nat. Adv. Coun. on Nurse Edn. and Practice Workgroup on Primary Care Workforce Projection, Divsn. Nursing, 1994; mem. com. to rev. breast cancer rsch. program U.S. Army Med. Rsch. and Material Command, Inst. of Medicine, 1996-97; mem. Pres.'s Nat. Bioethics Adv. Commn., 1996—. Author profl. monographs; contbr. over 40 articles to profl. publs.; mem. editorial bd. Community Mental Health Rev., 1977-79, Jour. Personality and Social Systems, 1978-81, Advances in Psychiat. Mental Health Nursing, 1981. Bd. dirs. Afro Am. Ctr., Yale U., 1968-72; mem. New Haven Bd. Edn., 1968-71, New Haven City Demonstrations Agy., 1968-70, Human Rels. Coun. New Haven, 1961-63, Nat. Neural Circuitry Database Com., Inst. Medicine, Nat. Acad. Scis., mem. bd. scientific advisors, 1985—; mem. commn. on future structure of vets. health care U.S. Dept. Vets. Affairs, 1990; mem. Pres. Clinton's Nat. Bioethics Adv. Commn., 1996-01. Named Disting. Alumna, Dillard U., 1966; recipient various awards, including cert. Honor NAACP, 1970, Disting. Alumnae award Yale U. Sch. Nursing, 1976, award for outstanding achievement and service in field mental health D.C. chpt. Assn. Black Psychologists, 1980, Pres. 21st Century award The Nat. Women's Hall of Fame, 1994, Lifetime Achievement award, nat. Black Nurses Assn., 2000—. Fellow A.K. Rice Inst., Am. Coll. Mental Health Adminstrs. (founding), Am. Acad. Nursing (charter, pres. 1987-89); mem. Inst. Medicine NAS, Am. Nurses Assn., Nat. Black Nurses Assn., Am. Assn. Colls. Nursing (govtl. affairs com. 1990-93), Am. Pub. Health Assn., Nat. League Nursing (pres. 1997-99), Nat. Bioethics Adv. Commn., Sigma Theta Tau Internat. (mentor award 1989), Delta Sigma Theta. Office: U Mich 400 N Ingalls St Rm 4320 Ann Arbor MI 48109-2003

DUMAS, SANDRA LEE, medical technologist, microbiologist; b. Amsterdam, N.Y., Nov. 15, 1949; d. Richard Carl and Eunice Yetive Teschka; children: Stacey Ann Warner, Joseph William; m. C. Clifford Jr. A in Clin. Lab. Sci., Empire State Coll., Saratoga Springs, N.Y., 1987, BS in Biology, 1991. Cert. clin. lab. scientist Nat. Cert. Agy. for Med. Lab. Pers. Med. tech. Johnstown (N.Y.) Hosp., 1968-70, Nathan Littauer Hosp., Gloversville, N.Y., 1967-68; med. tech. in microbiology Nathan Littaver Hosp., Gloversville, N.Y., 1975—. Avocations: oil painting, golfing, boating, photography.

DUMBLETON, DUANE DEAN, college president, educator; b. Shiocton, Wis., May 30, 1939; s. Reginald William and Marguerite Eva (Testin) D.; m. Nancy M. Cavins; children: Laura Layli, Mary Bahiyyih, Rama Ali Sequoyah, Nuriyyih Alexandra, Benjamin Idal. BS, U. Wis., 1962; MA, Syracuse (N.Y.) U., 1969; EdD, U. Ga., 1973. Tchr. geography Hillsborough County Pub. Schs., Tampa, Fla., 1962-63; tchr. English, Geneva (N.Y.) Pub. Schs., 1964-65; tchr. world culture Onondoga County Pub. Schs., Syracuse, 1965-70; tchr. English, Clarke County Pub. Schs., Athens, Ga., 1970-71; mem. faculty Fla. C.C., Jacksonville, 1973—, div. chmn. humanities dept., prof. Asian humanities, edn., 1978-83; campus pres. Fla. Community Coll., Jacksonville, 1988—. Author: Education for American Indians, 1973; contbr. articles to profl. jours. Mem. Jacksonville Cmty. Coun., Inc., 1986—; mem. com. Pine Castle, Inc., 1994—99, Sister Cities Assn., Jacksonville, 1989—92, Urban Core Citizens Planning Adv. Com.; mem. com., bd. pres. Interfaith Coun., Jacksonville, 1989—; mem. com. Spiritual Assembly of Bahais of Jacksonville, 1974—2000; mem., chair Spiritual Assembly of the Bahais of Clay County, 2001—. Recipient Svc. award Jacksonville Jaycees, 1978, Clay County Bahai Community, 2000—. Mem. Cmty. Colls. for Internat. Devel. (bd. dirs., sec. 1988-92), Assn. Bahai's Studies, Fla. Assn. Community Colls., Leadership Jacksonville Alumni Assn., Urban League (bd. dirs.), Learn to Read (bd. dirs. 2000-). Avocations: writing poetry and essays, public speaking. Home: 526 Los Palmas Dr Orange Park FL 32003-8207 Office: Fla CC 3939 Roosevelt Blvd Jacksonville FL 32205-8945 Fax: 908-673-1179. E-mail: ddumbltn@fccj.edu.

DUMBRAVA, ADRIAN, chemical engineer, process engineer; b. Gagesti, Vrancea, Romania, June 14, 1952; s. Victor and Florica (Purice) D.; m. Luminita Spirescu, Apr. 30, 1977; children: Diana Cristina, Dan Octavian. MSc in petroleum tech. and petrochem., Petroleum & Gas Inst., Ploiesti, Romania, 1976, PhD in Chem. Engring., 1992; Diploma Advanced Process Analysis, Tokyo Inst. Tech., 1986; Cert. in Energy Mgmt., Twente U., The Netherlands, 1993. Process engr. Brazi Petrochem. Works, Ploiesti, 1976-79, ICITPR/IPIP Oil Engring. Co., Ploiesti, 1979-90; sr. rsch., head of dept. Rsch. Inst. for Oil Refining & Petrochemistry, Ploiesti, 1990-99; asst. prof. Petroleum and Gas Inst., Ploiesti, 1979-83; sr. process engr. Optima Engrs. and Constructors, Calgary, Alta., Can., 2000—. Expert in tech. coop. program UN for Indsl. Devel. Orgn., Vienna, 1991-2000. Editl. bd. Romanian Petroleum Jour. Cimpina, 1993-00; co-author: The Ency. of chemistry, Vol. IV, 1987; contbr. articles to profl. jours.; patentee in field. Mem. Can. Soc. Chem. Engrs., Instn. of Chem. Engrs. U.K., Romanian Catalysis Soc., Romanian Chem. Engrs., Can. Prairie Group Chartered Engrs. Orthodox Ch. Avocations: chess, puzzles, classical music, history, mountain excursions. Home: 71 Kingsland Villas SW Calgary AB Canada T2V 5J9 E-mail: dumbrava.andy@optimaepc.com., dumbrava@telus.net.

DUMERER, LORRAINE JOANNE LORI, social studies educator, clinician, consultant; b. Providence, July 10, 1946; d. John and Edith (Flippin) Florio; m. James Edward Dumerer, Nov. 23, 1966; children: James, Marc, Jennifer, Matthew, Paul. Student, Seton Hill Coll., 1964-66, St. Louis U., 1966; AB, U. Ill., 1969, MAT, 1972; postgrad., Tex. Women's U., 1987-88, U. Tex., Dallas, 1993, So. Meth. U., 1999-2001. Cert. social studies tchr. talented and gifted Tex., coll. bd. endorsed Advanced Placement cons. Tchr. Dayton (Ohio) Pub. Schs., 1970—71, St. Benedicts Sch., San Antonio, 1979—80, Incarnate World H.S., San Antonio, 1980—81, Diocese of Dallas, 1981—88, Dallas Ind. Sch. Dist., 1988—97; tchr., chmn. social studies dept., dean of faculty Long Trail Sch., Dorset, Vt., 1997—98; tchr. govt. and politics, macro and microecons., law studies Carrollton-Farmer's Branch Ind. Sch. Dist., 1998—. Coach Fed Challenge econs. competition, 1998-2001, North Dallas H.S. CIS-site based team, 1996-97; mem. R.L. Turner H.S. CIC-site based team, 1999—; mem. train the writers program US Dept Edn. Nat. Coun. for Econ. Edn., Romania, 2003; coach model UN teams, 2000—; clinician Acad. Clin. Svc., Dallas, 1985—; coord. nat. history day Diocese of Dallas, 1985-87; coord. Jane Goodall CHIMP project, 1991; chmn. dept. social studies, student coun. advisor North Dallas H.S., 1993-97; ednl. cons., presenter Specialty Limited English Proficient Integration, 1990—, Tex. Coun. Social Studies, Advanced Placement Reading Strategies, Cross-grade Level Curriculum Integration; Creating an Inclusive AP and Pre-AP Program, Integrating State Mandates in Pre-AP and AP Programs, Nat. Coun. for the Social Studies, AP Econ. Strategies, AP Govt., others; participant NEH Inst., 1995, Woodrow Wilson Inst., U. Tex., Dallas, 1993-1995, Congress in the Classroom Dirkson Ctr., Ill., 2003, Econs. for Leaders Found. for Tchg. Econs., So. Meth. U., 2000; reader Coll. Bd. Am. Govt., 2001-03; nat. endorsed Coll. Bd. cons.; selected for Tng. of Writers Project, Nat. Coun. Econ. Edn., U.S. Depts. of State and Edn., Bucharest, Romania, 2003; presenter in field Author: (essays) Economic Forces in American History, Foundation for Teaching Economics, 2001, numerous poems; contbr. chapters to books. Referee coord. N.E. Youth Soccer Assn., 1979-80, coach, 1979-80; coach, referee Mesquite Soccer Assn., 1981-86, referee liaison, 1981-82, sec., 1982-83, commr. of coaches, 1982-83. Mellon grantee, 1994; named Tchr. of Yr. Dallas Coun. for Social Studies, 1996, Outstanding HS Social Studies Tchr. of Yr., Tex. Coun. for Social Studies, 2002; named one of 50 Elite Tchrs., Tex. Coun. Econ. Edn., 2001. Mem. Nat. Coun. Social Studies, Tex. Coun. for Social Studies (sec. Peter's Colony Coun. for social studies 1998-99, v.p. 2000, pres. 2001-03), North Tex. Women's Soccer Assn. (capt. 1989-95), Ctr. for Applied Linguistics (cons. World Culture Project 1996), Nat. Coun. Econ. Edn. Avocations: writing, soccer, travel. Home: 3535 Misty Meadow Dr Dallas TX 75287-6027 E-mail: dumererl@cfbisd.edu, dumererl@earthlink.net.

DUMITRESCU, DOMNITA, Spanish language educator, researcher; b. Bucharest, Romania; came to U.S., 1984; d. Ion and Angela (Barzotescu) D. Diploma, U. Bucharest, 1966; MA, U. So. Calif., 1987, PhD, 1990. Asst. prof. U. Bucharest, 1966-74, assoc. prof., 1974-84; asst. prof. Spanish Calif. State U., L.A., 1987-90, assoc. prof., 1990-94, prof., 1995—. Author: Gramatica Limbii Spaniole, 1976, Indreptar Pentru Traducerea Din Limba Romana in Limba Spaniola, 1980; translator from Spanish lit. to Romanian; assoc. editor: Hispania, 1996—; contbr. articles to profl. jours. Fulbright scholar, 1993—. Mem. MLA, Linguistic Soc. Am., Internat. Assn. Hispanists, Linguistic Assn. S.W., Am. Assn. Tchrs. Spanish and Portuguese (past pres. So. Calif. chpt., Tchr. of Yr. award 2000), Sigma Delta Pi (v.p. West 1996—). Office: Calif State U 5151 State University Dr Los Angeles CA 90032-4226 E-mail: ddumitr@calstatela.edu.

DUMKE, MELVIN PHILIP, dentist; b. Sleepy Eye, Minn., Jan. 23, 1920; s. Herman Gustav and Else Ida (Battig) D.; m. Phyllis Lorraine Steuck, June 25, 1950; children: Pamela, Bruce, Shari. DDS, U. Minn., 1943. Practice dentistry, Sleepy Eye, 1946-50, Morgan, Minn., 1950-66, Mankato, Minn., 1966—. Lectr. dental assts. Mankato State Coll., 1967-69. Mem. Town Coun., Morgan, 1960-65; bd. control Martin Luther Acad., New Ulm, Minn., 1965-79; bd. dirs. The Luth. Home, Belle Plaine, Minn., 1981-96, Orgn. Wis. Luth. Svcs.; pres. Luth. Congregation, 1970, 86-87. Served to capt., Dental Corps, AUS, 1943-46. Fellow Royal Soc. Health, Internat. Coll. Dentists, Am. Coll. Dentists, Pierre Fouchard Acad.; mem. ADA (ho. of dels. 1977-87), Minn. Dental Assn. (chmn. peer rev. com. 1973-79, mem. ho. of del. 1978-89, prse. 1983-84, guest of honor 1993), So. Dist. Dental Soc. (exec. coun., trustee 1988-89, guest of honor 1986), South Cen. Dental Study Club (pres. 1970), Fedn. Dentaire Internationale, U. Minn. Alumni Assn., VFW (Disting. Svc. award 1966, comdr. 1965), Am. Legion, Lions (pres. 1965, 74, zone chmn. 1975, Melvin Jones fellow 1999), Mankato Golf Club, St. Paul U. Club, U. Minn. Sch. Dentistry Century Club, Psi Omega. Home: 364 Carol Ct Mankato MN 56003-3300 Office: 430 S Broad St Mankato MN 56001-3703 Personal E-mail: dumkes@i.c.mankato.mn.us.

DUMM, ROBERT WAYNE, musician, educator, writer; b. East McKeesport, Pa., May 21, 1928; s. Claude Alvin and Garnet Sarah (Weaver) D.; m. Mary Elizabeth Covert, Dec. 24, 1952 (div. June, 1981); children: Dexter Hearn, Claudia Ann. MusB with honors, U. Mich., Ann Arbor, 1949, MusM in Piano and Theory, 1952, postgrad., 1953-57. Tchr. piano, Ann Arbor, Mich.; dean Boston Conservatory, 1958-68; editor Boston Music Co., 1958-68; critic Christian Sci. Monitor; prof. piano, head piano pedagogy Cath. U., Washington, 1968-79. Tchr. music courses Ann Arbor Adult Edn. Program, 1950-57; condr. combined piano ensembles Nat. Music Camp, Interlochen, Mich., 1956-57; founder libr. concerts Twinbrook Lib., Rockville, Md., 1979-81; tchr. courses Elderhostel, Shenandoah U., Winchester, Va., 1995-98; judge numerous competitions; founder, dir. numerous music workshops; conducted 500 taped interviews with pianists for Internat. Piano Archive, U. Md. Author: Adult Piano Course, 1981, Instead of Scales, 2001, Pumping Ivory, 1989; contbg. editor Clavier mag., 2000—, (also cover photo feature); author technique column Piano Today, 1979—; contbr. articles to profl. jours. Mem. Am. Liszt Soc. (founding mem.), Phi Beta Kappa, Phi Sigma Phi, Phi Mu Alpha, Music Tchrs. Nat. Assn. (lifetime cert.) Democrat. Presbyterian. Avocations: gardening, walking, wide reading. Home: 333 Sheridan Ave Winchester VA 22601 E-mail: pianoman@visuallink.com.

DUMMER, WILLIAM L, lawyer, writer; b. Los Angeles, California, Aug. 3, 1947; s. Jerome Martin Dummer and Mary Caroline Seeger; m. Sheila Marie Thompson, Aug. 23, 1969 (div. Apr. 24, 1980); children: Wendy, David. BA, U. of San Francisco, 1965—72; JD, Golden Gate U., 1975—78. Atty. self-employed, San Mateo, Calif., 1978—80, Coopers & Lybrand, San Francisco, 1980—84, Trust Cons., Inc., San Mateo, 1984—90, Independence Funding Group, South San Francisco, 1990—99, Sutro and Co., San Francisco, 1999—2002, Metaranto Svc., San Mateo, 2002—. Bd. of dirs. Independence Funding Group, South San Francisco, 1990—99. Author: (book) Carolina Kane, 2003. Mem.: PSCA. Democrat. Catholic. Office: WLD Consulting 1830 S Norfolk #115 San Mateo CA 94403

DUMMETT, CLIFTON ORRIN, dentist, educator; b. Georgetown, British Guiana, May 20, 1919; s. Alexander Adolphus and Eglantine Annabella (Johnson) Dummett; m. Lois Maxine Doyle, Mar. 6, 1943; 1 child, Clifton Orrin Jr. BS in Psychology, Roosevelt U., Chgo., 1941; DDS, Northwestern U., 1941, MScD, 1942, DSc (hon.), 1976; MPH, U. Mich., 1947; ScD (hon.), U. Pa., 1978. Diplomate Am. Bd. Periodontology, Am. Bd. Oral Medicine. Dean, prof. periodontology Meharry Med. Coll., Nashville, 1945-49; chief dental service VA Hosp., Tuskegee, Ala., 1949-65, assoc. chief staff for rsch. and edn., 1958-65, chief dental service Chgo., 1965-66; dental dir., dir. ctr. Watts Health Ctr., L.A., 1966-69; assoc. dean, chmn. dept. cmty. dentistry U. So. Calif. Sch. Dentistry, L.A., 1969-75, prof., 1969-89, prof. emeritus, 1989-96, disting. emeritus prof., 1997—. Adj. prof. Northwestern U. Dental Sch., 1989; vis. prof., cons. Sch. Vet. Medicine Tuskegee Inst., 1962—65; vis. prof. Meharry Med. Coll., 1989—; trustee Am. Fund Dental Health, Chgo., 1968—78; chem. devel. component rev. panel Calif. Regional Med. Programs, L.A., 1975—77; mem. Pres.'s Com. on Nat. Health Ins., 1977; sr. reviewer U.S. Surgeon Gen. Report on Oral Health, 2000. Author: Community Dentistry, 1974, Afro-Americans in Dentistry: Sequence and Consequence of Events, 1977, Charles Edwin Bentley, 1982, Dental Education at Meharry Medical College: Origin and Odyssey, 1992, Culture and Education in Dentistry at Northwestern University, 1993, NDA.II The Story of America's Second National Dental Associan, 2000, (editl.) Nor Yet the Last, 1962 (W.J. Gies award, 1963), The Hillenbrand Era, 1986; editor: Nat. Dental Assn., 1953—75; contbr. . Chmn. adv. bd. Econ. and Youth Opportunity Agy. Project Head Start, Tuskegee, Ala., 1961—65; mem. spl. health adv. com. Calif. Bd. Edn., L.A., 1972—74; mem. L.A. regional hearing planning coun. Pres.'s Com. on Health Edn., L.A., 1973—74. Lt. col. USAF, 1955—58. Named to, U. So. Calif. Dental Hall of Fame, 1997; recipient Alumni Merit award, Northwestern U., 1971, Fones Gold medal, Conn. Dental Assn., 1976, Pierre Fauchard Gold medal, Pierre Fauchard Acad., 1980, John R. Callahan award, Ohio Dental Assn., 2003. Fellow: AAAS (chmn. dental sect. 1975—76, 1987—88), APHA (v.p. for U.S. 1995—96, John W. Knutson Disting. Svc. award 1992), Am. Acad. History of Dentistry (pres. 1982—83, Hayden and Harris award 1987), Internat. Coll. Dentists; mem.: ADA (hon.), Am. Dental Edn. Assn. (Presdl. citation 2003), Inst. Medicine of NAS (sr. mem.), Nat. Acads. Practice (Disting. Practitioner 1987), Am. Assn. Dental Editors (editor 1963—72, pres. 1974—75, Disting. Svc. medal 1976), Assn. Mil. Surgeons (life), Internat. Assn. Dental Rsch. (pres. 1969—70), Am. Coll. Dentists (Wm. J. Gies award 1992), Sigma Xi, Omicron Kappa Upsilon (pres., founder Nashville chpt. 1947—49), Delta Omega, Alpha Phi Alpha, Sigma Pi Phi. Democrat. Episcopalian. Avocations: music, politics, track. Home: 5344 Highlight Pl Los Angeles CA 90016-5119 Office: U So Calif Sch Dentistry PO Box 77006 Los Angeles CA 90007-0006

DUMONT, ALLAN ELIOT, retired physician, educator; b. N.Y.C., Oct. 8, 1924; m. Joan Auerbach, Oct. 1, 1949; children: Mark E., James A., David H. BA, Hobart Coll., 1945; MD, NYU, 1948. Diplomate Am. Bd. Surgery. Intern Bellevue Hosp., N.Y.C., 1948-49, resident, 1949-51, 53-54, chief resident, 1954-55; instr. surgery NYU, 1955-59, asst. attending surgeon Univ. Hosp., asst. vis. surgeon 3d and 4th surg. divs. Bellevue, 1955-60, asst. prof. surgery, 1959-62, assoc. vis. surgeon 3d and 4th surg. div. Bellvue, 1961-65; attending surgeon Manhattan VA Hosp., N.Y.C., 1958-67, cons. surgeon, 1967-90; assoc. attending surgeon Univ. Hosp. NYU, 1961-68, attending surgeon, 1968-90, assoc. prof. surgery, 1962-68, prof. surgery, 1968-73, Jules Leonard Whitehill prof. surgery, 1973-90, prof. emeritus, 1990—; clin. prof. surgery U. Conn. Sch. Medicine, 1991. Career scientist N.Y.C. Health Research Council, 1959-62; univ. senate NYU, 1966-69; vis. surgeon Bellevue Hosp., 1965-90, assoc. dir. surg. service, 1975-90; cons. surgeon St. Francis Hosp., Hartford, 1990—. Editor: Lymphology. 1974-84. Served to lt (j.g.) USN, 1951-53. Recipient Research Career Devel. award USPHS, 1961-71, Purkinje medal, Czechoslovakia, 1977. Mem. Am. Coll. Surgeons, New Eng. Surg. Soc., Harvey Soc., N.Y. Surg. Soc. (pres. 1987-88), Am. Physiol. Soc., Soc. Univ. Surgeons, Soc. for Surgery Alimentary Tract, Internat. Soc. Lymphology (pres. 1979-83), Am. Surg. Assn.

DU MONT, ALLEN ANDRÉ, psychotherapist, educator; b. N.Y.C., Nov. 17, 1942; s. Phillip J. DuMont and Gabrielle Dumas; m. Marilyn Sciacca, May 28, 1983; 1 child, James. BA, CUNY, Queens, 1965; MSW, Adelphi U., 1974; PhD, NYU, 1984. Cert. social worker, clin. social worker; bd. cert. diplomate Am. Bd. Examiners in Clin. Social Work; cert. psychoanalytic psychotherapy L.I. Inst. Mental Health; primary cert. Inst. Rational Emotive Therapy; cert. object rels. couples therapy Met. Ctr. for Objective Relative Therapy. Clin. field instr. office staff devel. N.Y.C. Human Resources Adminstrn., 1985-89, psychotherapy supr., 1986—; dir. Child and Family Therapy Ctr of Bayside, 1983—; sch. social worker N.Y.C. Bd. Edn., 1989—98. Child and family therapist L.I. Consultation Ctr., Rego Park, N.Y., 1985-90, St. Anthony's Guidance Clin., Mineola, N.Y., 1977-82; dir. spl. asst. for tng. office field svcs. Child Welfare Adminstrn., N.Y.C., 1980-84. Recipient Cath. Charities Svc. award, 1982; fellow L.I. Inst. Mental Health, 1979; grad. assistantship Adelphi U., 1973. Fellow Am. Orthopsychiat. Assn.; mem. NASW, N.Y. Soc. Clin. Social Work Psychotherapists (diplomate, 1st v.p., state treas., mem.-at-large Queen's chpt. pres.), NY Soc. Clin. Social Work (pres. 1998-2001, diplomate), Clin. Social Work Fedn. (fin. chmn. 2000-02, pres.-elect 2002—). Home and Office: 39-06 219th St Bayside NY 11361-2344

DUMONT, JAMES KELTON, JR., actor, theater producer; b. Chgo., Aug. 12, 1965; s. James Kelton and Judith Katherine (Johnson) DuMont; m. Wendel Faith Hall, Dec. 14, 1968; 1 child, Sinclair Marie. Student, Boston U., 1983-85. Field recruiter Nat. Rsch. Group, Hollywood, Calif., 1993-2000; pres., CEO DuMont Entertainment Group, Hollywood, 1994—; v.p. sales and mktg. PACE Am., Hollywood, 2000—. Mem. Ensemble Studio Theatre, N.Y.C., 1989—; co-artistic dir. L.A. Project, 1996. Actor: (Broadway plays) Six Degrees of Separation, 1990—93, (off-Broadway play) Tony & Tina's Wedding, 1989—90; (films) Speed, 1993, Combination Platter, 1993, Bombshell, 1996, The Peacemaker, 1996, Primary Colors, 1996, Erasable You, 1997, In Quiet Night, 1997 Bellyfruit, 1998, Love & Basketball, 1999, Catch Me if You Can, 2002 S.W.A.T., 2003, Seabiscuit, 2003, Captured; (TV series) NYPD Blue, 1995 Lois & Clark, 1996, Chgo. Sons, 1996, Tracy Takes on, 1995, Fallen Angels 1995, The Client, 1995, Sweet Justice, 1995, Can't Hurry Love, 1995, Arliss 1998, Then Came You, 1999, The West Wing, 2000, Becker, 2000, Titus, 2001 That's Life, 2001, That Was Then, 2002; (TV films) Pentagon Wars, 1998 Winchell, 1999, Gotta Kick It Up, 2001; prodr., actor : (films) The Confession 1996. Democrat. Buddhist. Avocation: writing prose and short stories, plays and screenplays. Office: Ensemble Studio Theatre 137 N Larchmont Blvd # 134 Los Angeles CA 90004-3704 E-mail: dumontentgrp@earthlink.net. jdumont@paceamerica.org.

DU MONT, NICOLAS, psychiatrist, educator; b. San Juan, P.R., Dec. 22 1954; s. Joseph Henri and Isabel (Solano) Du M. Postgrad. adult psychiatry Columbia U., 1990; MD, U. P.R., 1986; postgrad. child, adolescent psychiatry Columbia U., 1992, postgrad. pub. cmty. psychiatry, 1993. Assoc. prof Polytech. U., San Juan, 1984-88, InterAm. U., San Juan, P.R., 1986-87; med dir. Holistic Med. Ctr., N.Y.C., 1993-94; asst. prof. Albert Einstein Coll. of Medicine, N.Y.C., 1991-96, Mt. Sinai Sch. of Medicine, N.Y.C., 1993-96 Columbia Physicians and Surgeons Coll. Medicine, N.Y.C., 1997—; asst attending physician Elmhurst Med. Ctr., N.Y.C., 1993-94; asst. physician Mt Sinai Med. Ctr., N.Y.C., 1993-96; v.p., CEO Engring. Med. Support, Inc. N.Y.C., 1992—; asst. prof. Columbia Physicians and Surgeons Coll. Medicine N.Y.C., 1997—. Attending physician Westchester Jewish Med. Svcs., Hartsdale N.Y., 1990-95, Montefiore Med. Ctr., N.Y.C., 1991-96, Albert Einstein Coll Medicine, 1991-96, Puerto Rican Family Inst., 1994—; asst. attending physician and med. dir. Tavares Hispanic Mental Health Clin. at Columbia Presbyn

Med. Ctr., 1997—. Assoc. editor: Jour. Pagan Studies (N.Y. edit.), 1990—. Vis. fellow N.Y. State Psychiat. Inst., 1992-93. Mem. Assn. Hispanic Mental Health Profls. (exec. bd. dirs. 1999—, treas.). Office: Engring Med Support Inc 200 W 70th St Ste 8F New York NY 10023-4326 E-mail: info@dumont.org.

DUMONTIER, CLARISSA WILLIAMS, lawyer; b. Jefferson City, Mo., Apr. 13, 1957; d. James Albert and Ann Marguerite (Dyer) Williams; m. Bruce John DuMontier, July 19, 1980; children: Benjamin John, Clark William. BS in Edn., U. Mo., 1977, JD, 1982. Bar: U.S. Dist. Ct. (we. dist.) Mo. 1982. Assoc. atty. Harlan, Harlan, and Still, Boonville, Columbia, Mo., 1982-84; asst. pros. atty. Cooper County, Mo., 1986-2000, Howard County, Fayette, Mo., 1994-2000, Randolph County, Moberly, Mo., 1994-2000, Chariton County, Keytesville, Mo., 1994-2000. Mem. Child Support Adv. Com. Child Support Enforcement divsn., Jefferson City, 1991-94, Child Support Guidelines Com. Mo. Supreme Ct., Jefferson City, 1993, Pros. Atty's. Adv. Com. Child Support Enforcement divsn., Jefferson City, 1998-2000, Change Ctl. bd. Child Support Enforcement, Jefferson City, 1999-2000. Chmn. Mo. River Festival Arts, Boonville, 1993-94; pres. SS. Peter and Paul Home and Sch., Boonville, 1997-98. Recipient Cert. of Appreciation Mo. Child Support Enforcement Assn., 1997. Mem. Mo. Bar Assn., Wis. Bar Assn., Cooper County Assn. (treas. 1992, 98, v.p. 1998-2000, pres. 2000-01). Republican. Roman Catholic. Avocations: piano, watercolor painting, writing, being a church organist.

DUMVILLE, JOHN P. historic site director; b. Hanover, N.H., Feb. 17, 1950; BA, U. Vt., 1972, MA, 1976. Tchr. Turnbridge (Vt.) Sch. Sys., 1974-75; arch. historian State of Vt., 1976-79; dir. Vt. State Historic Sites, Montpelier, 1979—. Trustee Vt. Hist. Soc., 1976-82, 86-92, Royalton Meml. Libr., 1969-97; selectboard Town of Royalton, Vt., 1994—. Office: Historic Preservation Nat Life Bldg Drawer 20 Montpelier VT 05620-0001 E-mail: John.Dumville@state.vt.us.

DUNAEVSKY, VALERY, mechanical engineer, researcher; b. USSR, Dec. 25, 1942; came to U.S., 1979, naturalized, 1985; s. Victor and Alla (Shmulian) D.; m. Ada Shalyt; 1 child, Victoria. MSME, Riga (Latvia) Tech. U., 1965, PhD in Tribology, 1975. Sr. technol./test engr. Diesel Engine Plant, Riga, 1969-76; sr. designer Diesel Locomotive Plant, Riga, 1977-79; sr. staff engr. Westinghouse Air Brake Co., Wilmerding, Pa., 1980-87; tribology group leader Copeland Corp., Sidney, Ohio, 1988-92; sr. staff engr., group leader compressor engring. Bendix Comml. Vehicle Sys., Elyria, Ohio, 1993—. Editor translation: Handbook of Friction Units of Machines, 1987, Accuracy of Metal-Cutting Tools, 1988; co-author: CRC/STLE Tribology Data Handbook, 1997; contbr. articles to Jour. Tribology, Tribology Trans, SAE Papers. Mem. ASME, Soc. Tribologists and Lubrication Engrs. Achievements include pioneering development of three-dimensional theory of conformability of the piston rings. Office: Bendix Comml Vehicle Sys 901 Cleveland St Elyria OH 44035-4153 E-mail: val.dunaevsky@bendix.com.

DUNAGAN, WALTER BENTON, lawyer, educator; b. Midland, Tex., Dec. 11, 1937; s. Clinton McCormick and Allie Mae (Stout) D.; m. Tera Childress, Feb. 1, 1969; children: Elysha, Sandi. BA, U. Tex., 1963, JD, 1965, postgrad., 1965-68. Bar: Tex. 1965, Fla. 1970, U.S. Dist. Ct. (mid. dist.) Fla. 1971, U.S. Ct. Appeals (11th cir.) 1982. Corp. atty. Gulf Oil, New Orleans, 1968-69, Getty Oil Co., L.A., 1969—, Westinghouse/Econocar, Internat., Daytona Beach, Fla., 1969-72; assoc. Becks & Becks, Daytona Beach, 1973-75; prin. Walter B. Dunagan, Daytona Beach, 1975—. Cons. Bermuda Villas Motel, Daytona Beach, Buccaneer Motel, Daytona Beach, Pelican Cove West Homeowners Assn., Edgewater, Fla. Organizer Interfaith Coffee House, New Orleans; tchr., song leader various chs.; chief Indian guide/princess program YMCA, Daytona Beach; bd. dirs. Legal Aid, Daytona Beach. Lance cpl. USMC. Mem. Volusia County Bar Assn., Lawyers Title Guaranty Fund, Phi Delta Phi. Avocations: reading, languages. Home and Office: 714 Egret Ct Edgewater FL 32141-4120 Fax: 386-409-3710. E-mail: wbdunfla@msn.com.

DUNAIEF, LEAH S. newspaper editor, publisher, writer; b. N.Y.C., Aug. 21, 1940; d. Rudolph and Mollie Salmansohn; m. Ivan F. Dunaief, Feb. 24, 1963; children: Joshua, Daniel, David. BA, Barnard Coll., 1962; MBA, Columbia U., 1982. Writer, rschr. Time Inc., N.Y.C., 1963-67; exec. founder, editor, pub. Village Times, Setauket, 1976—, now pres., chmn. bd.; founder, editor, pub. North Shore Homes, 1978—, Village Beacon, Rocky Point, N.Y., 1986—, St. James N.Y. Times, 1988—, Port Times, Port Jefferson, N.Y., 1989—, Times of Smithtown, N.Y., 1993—, Times of Nesconset, 1993, Port Jefferson Record, 1994—, North Shore Record, 1994—, Prime Times, "For Those Who Weren't Born Yesterday", 1995, Parent Connection, 1998. Bd. dirs. N.Y. Press Svc. Contbr. N.Y. Times, Time-Life Sci. Libr.; contbr., pub. Women's Bar News of State of N.Y. Active Spkr. Stanley Fink's Small Bus. Commn. for L.I., Congressman Mrazek's Women's Issues Com.; assoc. trustee Dowling Coll., Oakdale, N.Y.; edn. com. Mus. at Stony Brook; bd. dirs. Stony Brook Found. Realty, SUNY; adv. bd. W. Averill Harriman Coll. Policy Analysis and Pub. Mgmt. SUNY at Stony Brook; chmn. adv. com. Barnard Mag. Barnard Coll., Columbia U.; v.p. Three Village C. of C.; dir. Coun. Dedicated Mchts., Miller Pl. Recipient media awards for state and nat. press assns. including more than 300 awards for Journalistic Excellence N.Y. Press Assn., 1976, Proclamation of N.Y. State Senate, 2000; named Woman of Yr. in Comms., Town of Brookhaven, 1987, Honoree of Yr., Greater Port Jefferson Arts Coun., 1997, Miller Place-Mt. Sinai Hist. Soc., 2000, Proclamation of County of Suffolk, 2000, Mem. of Yr., Three Village C. of C., 2001, 1st in N.Y. State for Advt. Excellence award N.Y. Press Assn., 2001, cert. of congratulations Brookhaven Town Bd., 2001, Legis. Resolution, N.Y. State Senate, 2001, citation N.Y. State Assembly, 2001, Resolution, County of Suffolk Legislature, 2001, Cmty. Svc. award, Three Village CYS Boys and Girls, 2002. Mem. N.Y. Press Assn. (pres. 1984-85, 3rd pl. Best Column award 1994, 2nd pl. Best Column award 1995, ex-officio mem. bd. dirs.), Nat. Newspaper Assn. (state chmn. 1982—, 1st pl. award for investigative reporting 1985), L.I. Press Club (1st pl. award for best weekly column 1987). Office: Village Times Box 707 185 Route 25A Setauket NY 11733-2946

DUNAIF, ANDREA ELIZABETH, endocrinologist; b. N.Y.C., Feb. 26, 1952; d. Samuel Lewis and Nancy Marie (Peters) D. BA, Sarah Lawrence Coll., 1973; MD, Columbia U., 1977. Diplomate Am. Bd. Internal Medicine, Am. Bd. Endocrinology, Diabetes and Metabolism. Intern, resident in medicine Presbyn. Hosp., N.Y.C., 1977-80; clin. and rsch. fellow in endocrinology Mass. Gen. Hosp., Boston, 1980-81, clin. and rsch. fellow in medicine and gynecology, 1981-82; instr. in ob-gyn., reproductive sci. and medicine Mt. Sinai Sch. Medicine, N.Y.C., 1982-88, asst. prof. medicine, ob gyn., reproductive sci., 1985-88, assoc. program dir. clin. rsch. ctr., assoc. prof. medicine, 1988-91, assoc. prof. ob-gyn. and reproductive scis., 1989-91; prof. medicine and cellular and molecular physiology Pa. State Coll., Hershey, 1991-96, program dir. gen. clin. rsch. ctr., 1995-96, dean's lectr., 1995; assoc. dir. Nat. Ctr. for Infertility Rsch. Brigham and Women's Hosp., Boston, 1996—, dir. and chief medicine and ob-gyn divsn. women's health, 1997-2001, sr. physician, 1997—; dir. Nat. Ctr. Excellence in Women's Health Harvard Med. Sch., 1998-2001; chief divsn. of endocrinology metabolism/molecular medicine, Charles F. Kettering prof. medicine Northwestern U. Med. Sch., Chgo., 2001—. Asst. attending physician Mt. Sinai Hosp., N.Y.C., 1982-88, assoc. attending physician, 1988-91; attending physician medicine Hershey (Pa.) Med. Ctr., 1992-96; sr. dir. Diabetes, Med. and Sci. Affairs, Parke-Davis, Morris Plains, N.J., 1996-97. Editor (with others, book) The Polycystic Ovary Syndrome, 1992; assoc. editor Jour. Clin. Endocrinology and Metabolism, 1993-2000; contbr. numerous articles to profl. jours, also abstracts and revs.; mem. editl. bd. Molecular and Cellular Endocrinology. Named Kelly West lectr., U. Okla., Okla. City, 1995; recipient Sinsheimer Scholar award, 1986—89, Pennsylvanians of Vision award, Tri-County chpt. Am. Diabetes Assn., Pa. affil., 1995, Citation for alumnae achievement, Sarah Lawrence Coll., 1996, Woman of Achievement award, Big Sister Assn. Greater Boston, 1999; fellow Charles H. Revson fellow, 1983—85; grantee NIH, 1985—2002, others. Mem.: Assn. Am. Physicians, Am. Soc. Clin. Investigation, Am. Fedn. Med. Rsch. (future directions com. 1997), Endocrine Soc. (mem. clin. initiatives com. 1992—94, steering com. recent progress in hormone meeting 1995—97, mem. coun. 1998—2001), Am. Diabetes Assn. (chair 1992—93, liason com. with endocrine soc.), Women in Endocrinology (chair program com. 1990—94). Avocation: opera. Office: Northwestern U Med Sch Tarry 15-709 303 E Chicago Ave Chicago IL 60611-3008 Fax: 312-908-3870. E-mail: a-dunaif@northwestern.edu.

DUNATHAN, HARMON CRAIG, college dean; b. Celina, Ohio, July 25, 1932; s. Harry V. and Mildred B. (Greek) D.; m. Katy Mary Dragati, Mar. 15, 1956 (div. July 1990); children: Christine, Susan, Amy, Andrea; m. Mary Frances Pitts, Sept 29, 1990. BA, Ohio Wesleyan U., 1954; MS, Yale U., 1956, PhD, 1958. Mem. faculty Haverford (Pa.) Coll., 1957-75, assoc. prof. chemistry, 1964-70, prof., 1970-75; provost, dean faculty Hobart and William Smith Colls., Geneva, N.Y., 1975-84, acting pres., 1978-79; dean faculty Hampshire Coll., 1984-87; dean acad. affairs Rhodes Coll., Memphis, 1987-93; prof. chemistry, dir. rsch. and sponsored programs LeMoyne-Owen Coll., Memphis, 1993-95, prof. chemistry, interim v.p. instl. advancement, 1996-97, 00-01, prof. chemistry, dir. internat. rsch., 1997—. Home: 2014 Hallwood Dr Memphis TN 38107-4703

DUNAU, ANASTASIA THANNHAUSER, retired administrative law judge; b. Munich, Bavaria, Germany, July 16, 1919; came to U.S., 1935; d. Siegfried Joseph and Franziska (Reiner) Thannhauser; m. Bernard Dunau, July 10, 1950 (dec. Mar. 1975); children: Mark, Frank, Miriam, Andrew. BA, Smith Coll., 1941; LLB, Yale U., 1943. Bar: N.Y. 1945, D.C. 1958, U.S. Supreme Ct. 1958. Assoc. Hughes, Hubbard & Ewing, N.Y.C., 1943-47; atty. advisor NLRB, Washington, 1947-52; pvt. practice Washington, 1952-63; atty. U.S. Dept. Labor, Washington, 1963-79, adminstrv. law judge, 1979-85, ret., 1985. Mediator U.S. Dist. Ct., Washington, 1992—; vol. atty. LCE-AARP, Washingtno, 1993—. Mem. Nat. Assn. Women Judges (life, chair resolutions com. 1985, 86). Democrat.

DUNAVANT, WILLIAM BUCHANAN, JR., textiles executive; b. Memphis, Dec. 19, 1936; s. William Buchanan Sr. and Dorothy D. (Knight); m. Lillian Dobson (div. May 1975); children: Elizabeth Corneil Dunavant Adams, Dorothy Dobson Dunavant Fisher, William Buchanan III, John Dobson; m. Ann Querbes (div. Apr. 1989); children: Forest Buchanan, Buchanan Dobson, Woodson Querbes. Student, Vanderbilt U.; BBA, Memphis State U.; HHD (hon.), Rhodes Coll. Jr. ptnr. T.J. White & Co. (now W.B. Dunavant & Co.), Memphis, 1952-56, ptnr., 1956-60; chmn. bd. dirs., chief exec. officer Dunavant Enterprises, Memphis, 1957—. Bd. dirs. Nat. Bank of Commerce, Promus, Ptnrs., Inc., Browning Ferris Industries, Inc.; mem. Nat. Adv. Com. on Cotton Mktg. King of Memphis Cotton Carnival, 1973. Recipient Chickasaw Coun. Scout Ctr. named in his honor, Boy Scouts Am., 1983, Outstanding Community Salesman of the Yr. award, Sales and Mktg. Execs. of Memphis, 1980, Spirit of Life award, NCCJ, 1984, Outstanding Citizen of the Yr. award, Civitan Club, 1984, Master of Free Enterprise award, Jr. Achievement, 1984, Humanitarian of the Yr. award, Rhodes Coll., 1984, Disting. Alumnus award, McCallie Sch., 1986, Alumnus of the Yr. award, Memphis State U., 1989. Mem.: Am. Cotton Exporters Assn. (bd. dirs.), Southern Cotton Assn. (past pres. and bd. dirs.), Memphis Cotton Exch. (past bd. dirs.), New Orleans Commodity Exch. (past bd. dirs.), Am. Cotton Shippers Assn. (past pres. and bd. dirs.), Nat. Cotton Coun. (chmn. bd. dirs., past pres. and bd. dirs.), Cotton Coun. Internat. (past bd. dirs.)), N.Y. Cotton Exch. (bd. mgrs.). Presbyterian. Avocations: tennis, hunting, golf. Office: Dunavant Enterprises Inc PO Box 443 Memphis TN 38101-0443*

DUNAWAY, CAROLYN BENNETT, retired sociology educator; b. Atlanta, Mar. 3, 1943; d. Clarence Rhodes and Gay (McKenzie) Bennett; m. William Preston Dunaway, Aug. 26, 1967; 1 child, Robert Bennett Dunaway. BA English, Auburn U., 1966; MA English, U. Ala., Tuscaloosa, 1967; EdD, Auburn U., 1983. Instr. sociology Jefferson State C.C., Birmingham, Ala., 1967-69; prof. Auburn U., Montgomery, Ala., 1970-71; prof. sociology and gerontology dept. Jacksonville (Ala.) State U., 1971-95, prof. emeritus, 1999—. Student counselor Jacksonville State U., Ala., 1971—. Contbd. articles to profl. jours. Cons., trainer Calhoun County Hospice Anniston, Ala., 1983—; presenter Calhoun County Gerontology, Anniston, 1985—; officer Jacksonville Book Club, Ala., 1984; elder, tchr. First Presbyn. Ch., Jacksonville, 1993. Recipient 100 Most Outstanding Women Alumna award Auburn U., 1991, U. Rsch. award Jacksonville State U., 1989. Mem. Ala.-Miss. Sociol. Assn. (v.p. 1975-76, Sociology Club, Inter-Se Study Club, Ala. Fedn. Womens Club (dist. sect.), Phi Kappa Phi, Kappa Delta Pi, Delta Delta Delta, Phi Delta Kappa. Democrat. Presbyn. Avocations: flower arranging, gardening, reading. Home: 902 11th St NE Jacksonville AL 36265-1230

DUNAWAY, FRANK ROSSER, III, emergency physician; b. Albuquerque, Sept. 2, 1953; s. Frank Rosser and Constance (Durham) D.; m. Marcia Lee Moore, May 24, 1975 (div. 1990); children: Melissa Sommer, Amanda Durham, Vanessa Lee; m. Amy Jane Rutledge, Apr. 7, 1990; children: Kiera Elizabeth Eirwyn, Reagan Kailean Maira. BS, Duke U., 1975; MD, U. Ill., 1988. Diplomate Am. Bd. Emergency Medicine, Nat. Bd. Med. Examiners. Resident inspector nuclear engr. U.S. Nuclear Regulatory Commn., Glen Ellyn, Ill., 1982-84; resident emergency physician St. Francis Med. Ctr., Peoria, Ill., 1988-91; attending emergency physician Qualified Emergency Specialists Inc., Cin., 1991-93; med. dir. emergency svcs., chmn. dept. emergency medicine Proctor Hosp, Peoria, 1993—; attending emergency physician Proctor Hosp., Peoria, 1993—, assoc. chmn. interventional dept., 1997—99; v.p. Proctor Emergency Physicians, P.C., Peoria, 1995-97, pres., 1997—; consulting physician Hyperbaric Medicine, Peoria, 1996—2000; med.-legal cons. in emergency medicine, 1998—. Mem. faculty Ill. Coll. Emergency Physicians Oral Bd. Rev. Course, 1995—, AHA, 1985—; chmn. dept. emergency medicine Proctor Hosp., 1993—; assoc. project med. dir. Peoria Area Emergency Med. Svcs., 1994—. Contbr. articles to profl. jours. Lt. USN, 1975—82, capt. USNR, 1982—2002. Fellow: Am. Coll. Emergency Physicians; mem.: SAR, Shriners, Masons. Republican. Episcopalian. Avocations: snow skiing, sailing, scuba, backcountry canoeing.

DUNAWAY, MARGARET ANN (MAGGIE DUNAWAY), retired state agency consultant; b. Fresno, Calif., Feb. 10, 1943; d. Joseph John and Anna Frances (Dice) Cumero; children from previous marriage: Christian Anthony Freitag, Erika Lynn Bullard; m. Michael Earl Babcoke, Oct. 6, 1990; 1 stepchild, Jason Ethan Babcoke. Student, U. Calif., Davis, 1960-62, U. Calif., Berkeley, 1962-63. Supr. Gov's Office, Sacramento, 1969-72; office mgr. State Health and Welfare Agy., Sacramento, 1972-73; analyst regulations devel. Calif. State Depts. Health and Social Svcs., Sacramento, 1974-84, cons. adult and children's svcs., 1984-90, rep. adult svcs., 1984-90, with food drive com., 1987-88, rep. ind. living program com., 1989-90; community program specialist Calif. State Dept. Devel. Svcs., Sacramento, 1990-2000; ret., 2000. Project coord. SDSS L.A. County Children's Svcs. Caseload, 1989-90; primary cons. SDDS Study Family Home Agy. Program, 1998-2000. Active Southpark Homeowner's Assn., Sacramento, 1974-78; presenter Adult Svcs. Ann. Asilomar Conf., 1987; coord., presenter Adult Family Home Confs., L.A., 1999, 2000; owner Maggie's Memories Collectibles, 1975-. Recipient Superior Accomplishment award, SDSS, 1999. Fax: (530) 644-6938. E-mail: maggiesmemories@webbox.com.

DUNAWAY, WILLIAM PRESTON, retired educator; b. Lineville, Ala., June 30, 1936; s. Robert Johnson and Zylpha Mae (Preston) D.; m. Carolyn Bennett, Mar. 3, 1943; 1 child, Robert Bennett. BS, Jacksonville (Ala.) State U., 1959; MEd, Auburn (Ala.) U., 1966; AA, U. Ala., 1972; EdD, U. Miss., 1974. Tchr. math. Clay County High Sch., Ashland, Ala., 1960-61, Benjamin Russell High Sch., Alexander City, Ala., 1961-65; asst. supt. Alexander City Bd. Edn., 1965-67; asst. prin. Erwin High Sch., Birmingham, Ala., 1967-70; headmaster St. James Sch., Montgomery, Ala., 1970-71; prin. Anniston (Ala.) High Sch., 1971-73; prof. Sch. Adminstrn. Jacksonville (Ala.) State U., 1974-91, prof. emeritus, 1993—. Cons. in field; computer edn. dir. Jacksonville State U., 1983-91. Contbr. articles to profl. jours. Boy scout and cub scout master, bd. dirs. coun. Boy Scouts Am., Anniston, contbr. Handicapped Scouting Manual 1980; officer, tchr., First Presbyn. Ch., Jacksonville, 1975—; mem. Jacksonville Housing Authority Commn., 1992—, vice chair, 1993—; founding mem. Nat. Campaign for Tolerance, Wall of Tolerance. Capt. U.S. Army Res. and N.G., 1954-68. Recipient Jacksonville State U. Research award, 1988, Citizen of Yr. award, 1984; grantee Ala. Commn. on Higher Edn., 1986. Mem. Nat. Assn. Secondary Sch. Prins., Am. Assn. Sch. Adminstrs., Coun. for Computer Edn., Assn. Pub. Housing and Devel., Kiwanis, Sierra Club, Kappa Delta Pi, Phi Delta Kappa. Democrat. Avocations: computer enthusiast, landscape gardening, environmental issues, church and civic activities. Home and Office: 902 11th St NE Jacksonville AL 36265-1230

DUNBAR, BRUCE STEPHEN, photographer, gallery administrator; b. Stratford, Conn., Aug. 12, 1967; BA, Boston U., 1989; MA, NYU, 2002. Gallery mgr. Silvermine Guild Arts Ctr., New Canaan, Conn., 1995-2000; photography instr. Silvermine Sch. Art, 1998—; gallery asst. Grey Art Gallery, N.Y.C., 2000—02. Freelance photographer, Stratford, Conn., 1996—. Contbr. photographs to Greenwich Mag., Metroline.

DUNBAR, DAVID WESLEY, bank executive; b. New Haven, June 23, 1952; s. Carl Owen and Ann Harris (Peck) D; m. Cynthia Susan Minnick, Mar. 8, 1980. BS in Fin., Acctg., Fla. State U., 1974; Cert. Commt. Lender in Comml. Lending and Fin., U. Okla., 1977; cert. in banking and fin., La. State U., 1982. Legis. analyst Fla. State Ho. of Reps., Tallahassee, 1973-74; mgmt. trainee S.E. Banking Corp., Miami, 1975; asst. v.p. S.E. Bank of St. Petersburg (Fla.), 1976; v.p. S.E. Bank of Pinellas, Largo, Fla., 1977-80; v.p. regional S.E. Banking Corp., Tampa, Fla., 1980-81, pres., CEO Republic Bank, Clearwater, Fla., 1981-88, 91-93; pres. Dunbar Corp., Palm Harbor, Fla., 1989-91; exec. v.p., bd. dirs. Peoples State Bank, New Port Richey, Fla., 1993-95; chmn., CEO, founder Peoples Bank, Palm Harbor, Fla., 1995—; chmn., CEO Peoples Ins. LLC, 2000—, So. Mortgage Corp., 2001—. Bd. dirs. CNL Retirement Properties, Inc., trustee, 2000—, Bay Care Health Sys. Treas. Morton Plant-Mease Hosp. Found., Clearwater, 1986-88, 94-96; mem. Donald Roebling Soc., dress circle Performing Arts Ctr. Theater; bd. dirs. Retarded Citizens Found., Clearwater, 1982-90, 98-99, Pinellas County Edn. Found., Largo, 1986-92, Pinellas County Arts Coun., 1985-86; gov.'s appointee as commr. to Taxation and Budget Reform Commn. State of Fla., 1990-2000; chmn., trustee Morton Plant-Mease Hosp., 1997—, Morton Plant Mease Health Care, 1997—, North Bay Hosp., 1998-2002, New Port Richey, Fla.; gov. apptd. commr. Fla. Elections Commn., 1998-2001; chmn. Fla. Bankpac Bankers Assn., Tallahassee, 1985-87. Named one of Outstanding Young Men of Am., U.S. Jaycees, 1980, Fla. Advance Team Mem., U.S. White House, 1980. Mem. Fla. State U. Found. (Pres.'s Club), Weston Innisbrook Resort, Cypress Run Country Club. Avocations: golfing, sport fishing. Office: Peoples Bank 32845 US Highway 19 N Palm Harbor FL 34684-3140 E-mail: dunbar@peoplesflorida.com.

DUNBAR, GARY LEO, psychology educator; b. Cadillac, Mich., Feb. 5, 1949; s. Leo Arthur and Betty Jean (Norden) D.; m. Deborah Sue Prevost, Dec. 25, 1976; children: Darbi Sue, Gary Leo Jr. BA, Eckerd Coll., 1971, BS, 1975; MA, MS, Ctrl. Mich. U., 1976, 77; PhD, Clark U., 1988. Grad. asst. Ctrl. Mich. U., Mt. Pleasant, 1975-77, instr. psychology, 1977-83, 87-88, asst. prof., 1988-91, assoc. prof., 1991-95, prof., 1995—; Clark U. scholar Clark U., Worcester, Mass., 1983-85, rsch. fellow, 1985-87. Author: Psychology and Human Behavior, 1978, book chpts.; contbr. articles to profl. jours. Named Mich. Prof. of Yr., 1997. Mem. Am. Psychol. Soc., Soc. Neurosci. (past pres. faculty undergrad. neurosci., pres. Mich. chpt.). Achievements include rsch. in pharmacological treatment of behavioral deficits caused by damage to the brain or neurodegenerative diseases. Home: 3314 Saratoga Springs Dr Mount Pleasant MI 48858-9696 Office: Ctrl Mich U Psychology Dept Mount Pleasant MI 48859-0001 E-mail: gary.dunbar@emich.edu.

DUNBAR, HOLLY JEAN, communications and public relations executive; b. Plainfield, N.J., May 15, 1960; d. Robert Kenneth and Marian (DuBets) D. BA, Rutgers U., 1982. Graphic designer Chubb & Son, Inc., Warren, N.J., 1983-86; freelance writer, 1984—; pub. rels. rep., archivist AT&T Bell Labs., Warren, 1987; self-employed graphic designer North Plainfield, N.J., 1987-88; direct response mktg. coord. U.S. and Can. Beneficial Mgmt. Corp. of Am., Peapack, NJ, 1988-94; internal comms. mgr. Beneficial Mgmt. Corp., Peapack, NJ, 1994—98; dir. comms. and mktg. Somerset County United Way, Somerville, NJ, 1998—. Photographer: (survey) Tark Farm Site Monmouth Battlefield, 1982, Ellis Island Restoration, 1988-92; designer: Official Logo and Slogan of Somerset County, N.J., 1985 (Winning entry). Recipient Photography awards Cook Coll., New Brunswick, N.J., 1981, Chubb & Son, Inc., Warren, 1984, N.J. Agrl. Fair, 1994; Outstanding Svc. to 4-H award Somerset County 4-H, Somerville, 1996, Outstanding Alumna, Somerset Co. 4-H, 1999; cited for Distinctive Contbr. N.J. Culture and History Am. Studies Dept., Douglass Coll., New Brunswick, 1982, numerous others; recognized for vol. efforts and participation Somerset County Bd. Chosen Freeholders, Somerville, N.J., 1996. Mem. DAR (nat. vice chmn. pub. rels.-print media 2001--,dep. rep. Nat. Soc to Vet. Affairs Vol. Svc., 1983-92, state chmn. Am. Heritage-Art N.J. Soc. 1989-92, state chmn. N.J. Jr. Mem. Centennial Project N.J. Soc. 1991-92, nat. and N.J. state page 1983-2000, regent Elizabeth Snyder chpt. 1992-95, registrar, 1991-92, Continental Congress Thatcher award 1992, state chmn. DAR Mag. Advt. N.J. Soc. 1992-95, Ad Excellence award, 1993, 94, state corr. sec. N.J. soc. 1995-98, state chmn. Conservation N.J. Soc., 1998—, Outstanding Jr. Mem. N.J. Soc. 1996), N.J. Audubon Soc., Internat. Assn. Bus. Communicators, Douglass Coll. Alumnae Assn., Somerset County 4-H Assn. (4-H fair publicity com.), Am. Birding Assn., Clan Dunbar. Avocations: N.J. history and genealogical rsch., liturgical art, birding, travel, gardening. Home: 725 Ayres Ave North Plainfield NJ 07063-1607 Office: Somerset County United Way 205 W Main St Somerville NJ 08876

DUNBAR, JEFFREY BARTLETT, social services administrator; s. Richard Lewis Dunbar and Nancy Barrows; m. Mary Jane Greenawalt, Nov. 21, 1973; children: Kiersten Lynn, Jeffrey Bartlett Dunbar, Jr, Jesse Barrows. PhD, U. Md., 1974. Cert. Teaching & Supervision State of Md., 1965. Tchr. Montgomery County Pub. Schs., Rockville, Md., 1966—70; grad. instr. U. Md., College Park, 1970—74; team leader, tchr. Montgomery County Pub. Schools, 1974—78; chair, dept. of edn. Allegheny Coll., Meadville, Pa., 1978—98; assoc. prof. of edn. Calif. U. of Pa, California, Pa., 1999—2001; chair, dept. of tchg., social svcs. Bethany Coll., Bethany, W.Va., 2001—. Chair, instl. program rev. Allegheny Coll., Meadville, Pa., 1987—89; coord. Bethany Coll., Bethany, W.Va., 2001—. Stewardship cons. Nat. Episcopal Ch., NYC, 1995—97. Grantee WV:IMPACT - Coll./Schs. Performance Assessment, W.Va. Dept. of Edn., 2001. Mem.: Phi Delta Kappa. D-Liberal. Episcopal. Achievements include research in Coalition of Essential Schools. Avocations: sailing, hiking, tennis. Office: Bethany Coll WV Steinman Hall 201 Bethany WV 26032-0417 Office Fax: 304-829-7192. E-mail: jdunbar@bethanywv.edu.

DUNBAR, LESLIE WALLACE, writer, consultant; b. Lewisburg, W.Va., Jan. 27, 1921; s. Marion Leslie and Minnie (Crickenberger) Le; m. Peggy Rawls, July 5, 1942; 1 foster child, Nha Van children: Linda Dunbar Knox, Anthony Paul. MA, Cornell U., 1946, PhD, 1948. Asst. prof. polit. sci. Emory U., Atlanta, 1948-51; chief community affairs Savannah River plant AEC, Aiken, S.C., 1951-54; asst. prof. polit. sci. Mt. Holyoke Coll., 1955-58; dir. research So. Regional Council, Atlanta, 1958-61, exec. dir., 1961-65; exec. dir., sec. Field Found., N.Y.C., 1965-80; vis. prof. polit. sci. U. Ariz., 1981. Cons. Fund for Peace, Nat. Urban League, 1981-84; sr. project assoc. social welfare policy, 1985-87, Ford Found.; guardian ad litem State of N.C., 1993 2001. Author: A Republic of Equals, 1966, The Common Interest, 1988, Reclaiming Liberalism, 1990, The Shame of Southern Politics, 2002; co-author, editor: Minority Report, 1984; book rev. editor So. Changes, 1989-93. Deacon Watts St. Bapt. Ch., Durham, 1998—2001; bd. dirs. Nation Inst., 1980—86, pres., 1980—84; bd. dirs. Village of Pelham Libr. Bd., 1980—84, pres., 1982—84; bd. dirs. Children's Found., 1980—86, pres., 1982—84, Franklin and Eleanor Roosevelt Inst., 1987—2001, v.p., 1987—92; bd. dirs. Eleanor Roosevelt Inst., 1976—87, Field Found., 1978—80, Minority Rights Group, N.Y.C, 1980—85, Ctr. Nat. Security Studies, 1980—87, Amnesty Internat./U.S.A., 1984—86, Winston Found. for World Peace, 1985—89, Voter Edn. Project, 1987—90, N.C. Coun. Chs., 1991—93, Southeastern Efforts Developing Sustainable Staples, Inc., 1998—2001, Ruth Mott Fund, 1988—99, chair, 1992—94; bd. dirs., mem. selection com. Windcall REsident Program, 1990—94. Guggenheim fellow, 1954-55; United Negro Coll. Fund scholar-at-large, 1984-85. Fellow So. Regional Coun. (life). Home: 3050 Military Rd NW Washington DC 20015 E-mail: ldunbar@aol.com.

DUNBAR, MARY ASMUNDSON, communications executive, investor and public relations consultant; b. Sacramento, Calif., Feb. 6, 1942; d. Vigfus Samundur and Aline Mary (McGrath) Asmundson; m. Robert Copeland Dunbar, June 21, 1969; children: Geoffrey Townsend, William Asmundson. BA in English Lit., Smith Coll., 1964; MA in Communications, Stanford, 1967; MBA in Fin., Case Western Res. U., 1985. Cert. pub. rels. profl. Tchr. Peace Corps, Cameroun, Africa, 1964-66; writer, editor Ednl. Devel. Corp., Palo Alto, Calif., 1967-68, Addison-Wesley, Menlo Park, Calif., 1969-70; free lance writer, editor various, Cleve., 1970-85; account exec. Edward Howard & Co.,

Cleve., 1985-87, Dix & Eaton, Inc., Cleve., 1987-89, sr. account exec., 1990-92, v.p., 1992-96, sr. v.p., 1997—. Author publs. in field. Trustee Cleve. Coun. World Affairs, 1994—99. Smith Coll. scholar, Northampton, Mass., 1960-64; fellowship Stanford Univ., Palo Alto, Calif., 1967; recipient Internat. Assn. Bus. Comm. award, 1987, Women in Comm. award, 1987, Arthur Page award, 1990. Mem. Smith Coll. Club Cleve., Pub. Rels. Soc. Am. (Silver Anvil award 1997), Nat. Investor Rels. Inst. (past pres. Cleve.-No. Ohio chpt., elected to nat. bd. dirs. 2002), Cleve. Soc. Security Analysts. Republican. Episcopalian. Avocations: jogging, music. Home: 2880 Fairfax Rd Cleveland OH 44118-4014 Office: Dix & Eaton Inc 1301 E 9th St Ste 1300 Cleveland OH 44114-1820 E-mail: mdunbar@dix-eaton.com.

DUNBAR, MAURICE VICTOR, English language educator; b. Banner, Okla., May 24, 1928; s. Moyer Haywood and Louise Edna (Curry) D.; m. Carol Ann Cline, July 28, 1948 (div. 1963); children: Kurt, Karl, Karla, Karen, Kristen. AA, Compton Jr. Coll., 1948; BA, U. Calif., Berkeley, 1952; MA, Calif. State U., Sacramento, 1965. Elem. tchr. Lone Tree Sch., Beale AFB, Calif., 1962-64; tchr. Anna McKenney Jr. H.S., Marysville, Calif., 1964-66, Yuba City (Calif.) H.S., 1966-67; instr. Foothill Coll. Jr. Coll., Los Altos Hills, Calif., 1967-82; prof. English, De Anza Coll., Cupertino, Calif., 1982-98; ret., 1998. Author: Fundamentals of Book Collecting, 1976, Books and Collectors, 1980, Collecting Steinbeck, 1983, Hooked on Books, 1997; contbr. articles to profl. jours. With U.S. Army, 1948-58, PTO. Mem. Masons, Shriners (orator, libr. 1982—), B'nai B'rith. Avocations: book collecting, reading, travel, visiting university campuses. E-mail: mvdkcch@attbi.com.

DUNBAR, SHIRLEY EUGENIA-DORIS, small business owner, author, lecturer; b. Haverhill, Mass., Apr. 26, 1930; d. Clement and Doris (Riel) Allard; m. Everett Allan Dunbar, Feb. 18, 1967; children: Linda, Andrew, Susan. BA magna cum laude, U. Mass., 1974; MA, U. N.H., 1975; EdD, Nova U., 1979. Grad. gemologist. From instr. to prof. comm. Bunker Hill C.C., Boston, 1975-89, prof. emeritus, 1989—, owner Treasure Coast Gem Lab. Dir. tchg. tng. program, Taipei, Taiwan, 1983-84; dir. Learn to Read, Port St. Lucie County, 1989-91; owner Dunbar Enterprises, St. Lucie, Fla., 1988-96, Treasure Coast Gem. Lab., Port St. Lucie, 1996—; cons. in field. Author: Heisey Glass: The Early Years, 1896-1924, 2000. Judge Young Floridian awards, St. Lucie County, 1998—. Recipient Pub. Svc. award Ministry of Edn., Taiwan, 1982-83, citation for oustanding performance Gov. Michael Dukakis, 1985, Nat. Competition non-fiction award, 2001, First Place award Mid-Adminstrn. Congress, Non-Fiction Pub. Adult Book First Place award Fla. State, 2001; CAEL fellow in comm., U. Ohio, 1984, Best in Show award Rock and Gem Club, Fort Pierce, Fla., 2003. Mem.: AAUW (founding br. pres.), Nat. Assn. Jewelry (cert. appraiser), Nat. League Am. Pen Women, Fla. Women's Consortium. Avocations: silversmithing, goldsmithing. Home: RR 2 Box 524 Bridgton ME 04009-9530 E-mail: shirley400@aol.com.

DUNCALF, DERYCK, retired anesthesiologist; b. York, Eng., Nov. 14, 1926; arrived in U.S., 1956; s. Hubert Claude and Anne Elizabeth D.; m. Mira Novakovic, July 23, 1978; children: Richard Michael, Tamara, Sharon. MB, ChB, U. Leeds, 1950. Diplomate Am. Bd. Anesthesiology. Resident in anesthesia St. James Hosp. and Gen. Infirmary, Leeds, 1950-54, Cardiff Royal Infirmary, Wales, 1954-56; fellow faculty anaesthetists Royal Coll. Physicians and Surgeons, 1954; fellow in anesthesiology Mercy Hosp., Pitts., 1956-57, Montreal Children's Hosp., Que., Can., 1958-59; staff anesthesiologist Kings County Hosp., Bklyn., 1959-62, Montefiore Med. Ctr., Bronx, 1962-97, chmn. dept. anesthesiology, 1975-85; prof. anesthesiology Albert Einstein Coll. Medicine, Bronx, 1971-97, vice-chmn. dept. anesthesiology, 1985-94, emeritus prof., 1997—. Cons. Wyckoff Heights Hosp., Bklyn., 1966-85. Author: (with D.H. Rhodes) Anesthesia in Clinic Ophthalmolgy, 1963; contbr. articles to profl.jours. Fellow Am. Coll. Anesthesiologists; mem. Am. Soc. Anesthesiologists, N.Y. State Soc. Anesthesiologists, Pan Am. Med. Assn. (diplomate and hon. life mem. sect. anesthesiology), Assn. Univ. Anesthetists, Ecuatoriano de Anesthesiologia (hon.). Home: 33 Ferncliff Rd Cos Cob CT 06807-1206 E-mail: deryckduncalf@cs.com.

DUNCAN, A. BAKER, investment banker; b. Waco, Tex., Dec. 29, 1927; s. A. Baker and Frances (Higginbotham) Duncan; m. Sally P Witt, Jan. 31, 1953; children: Addison Baker III, Richard Witt, Andrew Prescott. Grad., Woodberry Forest (Va.) Sch., 1945; BA, Yale U., 1949; MA, U. Tex., 1952. Master Hill Sch., Pottstown, Pa., 1949-51; ptnr. Rotan Mosle & Co. (investment bankers), Houston, 1953—61; headmaster Woodberry Forest Sch., 1962-70; sr. v.p., dir. Rotan Mosle Inc., 1970-78; chmn. Duncan-Smith Co., 1978—. Bd dirs SW Research Inst; gov emeritus Tex Mil Inst; chmn. devel. com. Episcopal Diocese W. Tex. Mem.: Chi Psi. Democrat. Episcopalian. Home: 610 Garraty Rd San Antonio TX 78209-6149 Office: 711 Navarro Ste 740 San Antonio TX 78205-1786 E-mail: duncansm@swbell.net.

DUNCAN, AARON W. media specialist, minister; b. St. Louis, Oct. 5, 1976; s. Darrell W. and Joyce E. Duncan; m. Holly R. McClintock, Apr. 19, 1997; 1 child, Courtney R. Internet analyst Hasco Internat.; mgr. e-commerce Trans World Airlines, St. Louis; pres. Three Point Media, Wentzville, Mo., 2000—. Asst. pastor New Life Ctr., Warrenton, Mo.; exec. bd. dirs. Gateway Golfer, Inc. Recipient Lachance, Creative Design award, Advanced Web Design award, Golden Web award, IAWMD, 2000, 2003, Advanced Web Design award, Landmarks Tech., 2002. Republican. United Pentecostal. Avocations: golf, travel. Office: Three Point Media 73 Casey Ct Wentzville MO 63385 E-mail: awduncan@threepointmedia.com.

DUNCAN, ALLYSON K. judge; b. Durham, NC, Sept. 5, 1951; BA, Hampton U., 1972; JD, Duke U., 1975. Bar: N.C. 1975, D.C. 1977. Assoc. editor Lawyers Coop. Publ. Co., 1976—77; law clk. to Hon. Julia Cooper Mack DC Ct. Appeals, 1977—78; appellate atty., asst. to dep. gen. counsel, asst. to chmn. EEOC, 1978—86; assoc. prof. NC Ctrl. U. Sch. Law, 1986—90; assoc. judge NC Ct. Appeals, 1990; commr. NC Utilities Commn., 1991—98; ptnr. Kilpatrick Stockton LLP, Raleigh, NC, 1998—2003; judge US Cir. Ct. Appeals 4th Cir., 2003—. Mem.: Wake County Bar Assn. (pres. 2002—03), N.C. Bar Assn. (pres.-elect 2002). Office: Kilpatrick Stockton LLP Ste 400 3737 Glenwood Ave Raleigh NC 27612

DUNCAN, CHARLES TIGNOR, lawyer; b. Washington, Oct. 31, 1924; s. Robert Todd and Nancy Gladys (Jackson) D.; m. Dorothy Adelena Thrasher, July 31, 1947 (dec. Dec. 1972); 1 child, Charles Todd; m. Pamela Jo Thurber, Aug. 10, 1996. BA, Dartmouth Coll., 1947, LLD (hon.), 1986; JD, Harvard U., 1950. Bar: N.Y. 1951, D.C. 1953, U.S. Supreme Ct. 1954, Md. 1955. Assoc. Rosenman, Goldmark, Colin & Kaye, N.Y.C., 1950-53; partner Reeves, Robinson & Duncan, Washington, 1953-60; prin. asst. U.S. atty. Washington, 1961-65; gen. counsel U.S. Equal Employment Opportunity Commn., Washington, 1965-66; corp. counsel D.C., D.C., 1966-70; acting dir. pub. safety, 1969; partner Epstein, Friedman, Duncan & Medalie, Washington, 1970-74; dean, prof. law Sch. Law Howard U., 1974-78; ptnr. Peabody, Lambert & Meyers, Washington, 1978-84, Reid & Priest, Washington, 1984-90, sr. counsel, 1990-94; mem. Iran-U.S. Claims Tribunal, The Hague, 1994—2000. Trustee Northfield Mt. Hermon Sch., 1980—90, chmn., 1987—90; sr. dir. NAACP Legal Def. and Edn. Fund. With USNR, 1944—46. Recipient Distinguished Service award D.C. Bar, 1974 Fellow Am. Bar Found. (life); mem. ABA, Nat. Bar Assn., D.C. Bar Unified (Pub. Service award 1974, pres. 1973-74), Phi Beta Kappa, Alpha Phi Alpha, Sigma Pi Phi, Delta Theta Phi. Lodges: Masons (32 deg.). Democrat. Achievements include being an active participant in preparation and presentation of sch. desegregation cases before U.S. Supreme Ct., 1953-55. Home: 1362 Myrtle Ave Annapolis MD 21403-4952

DUNCAN, CHARLES WILLIAM, JR., investor, former government official; b. Houston, Sept. 9, 1926; s. Charles William and Mary Lillian (House) D.; m. Thetis Anne Smith, June 10, 1957; children: Charles William III, Mary Anne. BSChemE, Rice U., 1947; postgrad. mgmt., U. Tex., 1948-49. Roustabout, chem. engr. Humble Oil & Refining Co., 1947; with Duncan Foods Co., Houston, 1948-64, adminstrv. v.p., 1957-58, pres., chmn. adv. bd., 1958-64; pres. Coca-Cola Co. Food Div., Houston, 1964-67; chmn. Coca-Cola Europe, 1967-70; exec. v.p. Coca-Cola Co., Atlanta, 1970-71, pres., 1971-74; chmn. bd., dir. Rotan Mosle Fin. Corp., Houston, 1974-77; dep. sec. Dept. Def., Washington, 1977-79; sec. Dept. Energy, Washington, 1979-81. Bd. dirs. Newfield Exploration Co. Trustee emeritus, immediate past chmn. Rice U.; bd. dirs. Welch Found., The Meth. Hosp.; treas. The Meth. Hosp. With USAAF, 1944-46. Mem. Coun. Fgn. Rels., Houston Country Club, River Oaks Country Club, Allegro Club, Sigma Alpha Epsilon, Sigma Iota Epsilon. Methodist. Home: 9 Briarwood Ct Houston TX 77019-5801 Office: 600 Travis St Ste 6100 Houston TX 77002-3007

DUNCAN, CHERYL L. critical care and cardiac catherization nurse; b. Fayette County, Ky., Apr. 26, 1960; d. Thomas Jr. and Nadine (Johnson) Dabney; m. Anthony W. Duncan, Aug. 30, 1986; children: Anthony Thomas, Ashley Jadine. BSN, Ea. Ky. U., Richmond, 1983. RN, Ky., Tex.; cert. BCLS, ACLS, CPR instr. Nurse level I critical care unit Meth. Hosp., Houston, 1984-85, 86-87, asst. head nurse 3-11 shift coronary care unity, 1987-89, staff nurse level II cardiac catherization lab., 1989—; clin. level I nurse St. Joseph Hosp., Lexington, Ky., 1983-84, 85-86, patient care coord., cardiac catheterization lab., 2000—. Mem. ANA, AACN, Am. Heart Assn., N.Am. Soc. Pacing and Electrophysiology, Networks for Health Awareness, Soc. Critical Care Medicine, Sigma Theta Tau. Home: 7919 Candle Ln Houston TX 77071-2010

DUNCAN, CONSTANCE CATHARINE, psychologist, educator, researcher; b. Watertown, Wis, Nov. 2, 1948; d. Howard Burton and Mary Elizabeth (Fagan) Duncan; m. R.E. Johnson, Jr., 1974 (div. 1984); m. Allan Franklin Mirsky, July 4, 1986. BA, Northwestern U., 1970; AM, U. Ill., 1973, PhD, 1978. Sr. rsch. analyst Adolf Meyer Mental Health Ctr., Decatur, Ill., 1971-73; asst. in rsch. and tchg. dept. psychology U. Ill., Champaign, 1974-78; NIMH postdoctoral fellow in neurosis. Stanford U. Sch. Medicine, Palo Alto, Calif., 1978-81; rsch. psychologist VA Med. Ctr., Palo Alto, 1978-81; sr. staff fellow Lab. Psychology and Psychopathology, NIMH, 1981-88; chief unit on psychophysiology NIMH, Bethesda, Md., 1982-89, rsch. psychologist, 1988-89, rsch. specialist, 1989-93; pvt. practice Bethesda, Md., 1981—. Adj. assoc. prof. Johns Hopkins Sch. Hygiene and Pub. Health, Balt., 1987—; guest rschr. Lab. Psychology and Psychopathology NIMH, 1993—97, Sect. on Clin. and Exptl. Neuropsychology NIMH, 1997—; rsch. assoc. prof. Uniformed Svc. Univ. Health Sci., 1993—. Assoc. editor Psychophysiology, 1987-91; mem. editl. bd. Internat. Jour. Psychophysiology, 2002—; cons. editor numerous sci. jour.; contbr. articles to profl. jour., chpt. to books. Found. assoc. Nat. Women's Econ. Alliance; mem. NIMH/NINCDS Assembly of Sci. Coun., 1982-84. Recipient Nat. Rsch. Svc. award, NIMH, 1978-81, Golden Anniversary Scholarship award, AAUW, 1974; NIMH fellow, 1970-74. Fellow: APA (awards com. 2001—), Internat. Orgn. Psychophysiology, Am. Psychol. Soc.; mem.: EEG and Clin. Neurosci. Soc., Am. Psychopathol. Assn., Internat.Neuropsychol. Soc., Soc. for Neurosci., Soc. for Rsch. in Psychopathology (bd. dirs. 1986—88, membership com. 1987—88), Soc. for Psychophysiol. Rsch. (program com. 1979, 1980, nominating com. 1981, chmn. early career award com. 1981—84, program com. 1982, bd. dirs. 1982—85, nominating com. 1983, chmn. conv. com. 1983—87, program com. 1986, chmn. program com. 1987, program com. 1988, nominating com. 1989, Blue Ribbon Panel on state of soc. in Yr. 2000 1990—93, chmn. enhancement com. 1992—93, chmn. early career award com. 1994—96, conv. com., sec.-treas. 1996—99, com. governance and ops. 2000—01, program com. 2001, sr. awards com. 2001—, chair sr. award com. 2002—, pres. 2002—, Early Career Contbn. award 1980), Phi Beta Kappa, Pi Mu Epsilon, Alpha Lambda Delta, Phi Kappa Phi, Sigma Xi, Shi-Ai, Mortar Bd. Achievements include electrophysiological and neuropsychological research on normal and disordered attn. and cognition. Office: Uniformed Svc U Health Sci Clin Psychophysiology and Psychopharm Lab 4301 Jones Bridge Rd Bethesda MD 20814-4799

DUNCAN, DALE A. publishing executive; b. Detroit; BA in Journalism, Ctrl. Mich. U., 1976; postgrad., Am. Press Inst., 1980, Am. Press Inst., 1983, Am. Press Inst., 1986, Northwestern U., 1996. Reporter Belleville (Ill.) News-Dem. and Oakland Press, Pontiac, Mich., 1976—80; exec. editor, city editor Times Leader, Wilkes-Barre, Pa., 1980—86, pres., pub., 1986—94, Oakland Press, Pontiac, 1995—97; v.p. ABC Pub. Group, 1995—97; pres., gen. mgr. Indpls. Newspapers, Inc., 1998—99, pres., pub., 1999—2001; bd. advisors, bd. dir. iCopyright.com. Bd. chmn. Salvation Army; dir. F. M. Kirby Ctr. for Performing Arts; adv. bd. Clinton Valley coun. Boy Scouts Am.; co-chair minority journalism fundraising com. Ctrl. Mich. U.; mem. ch. and soc. task force St. Paul's United Meth. Ch.; bd. dirs. United Way Oakland County. Recipient 3 nat. journalism awards, Scripps-Howard, 4 Pa. state awards for editl. writing, Disting. Citizen award, Penn Mountains coun. Boy Scouts Am., 1995. Mem.: Pa. Newspaper Pub.'s Assn. (bd. dirs., chmn. diversity com.), C. of C. Office: Ste 525 100 S King St Seattle WA 98104 Fax: 317-633-9331.

DUNCAN, DAN L. gas company executive; Chmn. Enterprise Products Ptnrs., L.P., Houston. Office: Enterprise Products Ptnrs LP 2727 N Loop W Ste 700 Houston TX 77008-1037

DUNCAN, DAVID FRANK, community health specialist, educator; b. Kansas City, Mo., June 26, 1947; s. Chester Frank and Maxine (Irwin) D.; B.A., U. Mo., Kansas City, 1970; postgrad. Sam Houston State U., 1971; Dr.P.H., U. Tex., 1976; diploma, Brown U., 1996. 1 foster son, Kevin Rheinboldt. Research asst. U. Kans. Bur. Child Research, 1967-68; supr. Johnson County Juvenile Hall, Olathe, Kans., 1968-70; asst. to warden Draper Correctional Center, Elmore, Ala., summer 1970; supr. Harris County Juvenile Hall, Houston, 1970-71; project dir. Who Cares, Inc. Drug Abuse Treatment Center, Houston, 1971-73; exec. dir. Reality Island Halfway House, Houston, 1974-75; research assoc. Tex. Gov.'s Office, Austin, summer 1975; research assoc. Inst. Clin. Toxicology, clin. toxicologist Ben Taub Gen. Hosp., Houston, 1975-76; asst. prof. health sci. SUNY, Brockport, 1976-78, assoc. prof., 1978, acting chmn. dept. health sci., summer 1978; vis. prof. health environ. research U. Cologne, Fed. Republic Germany, 1986; prof. health edn., coord. cmty. health program So. Ill. U., Carbondale, 1978-92; chmn. So. Ill. Health Edn. Task Force, 1979-92; rsch. fellow Brown U., Providence, 1992-96, assoc. prof. med. sci., 1997—; sr. pub. health epidemiologist R.I. Dept. Health, 1996—; bd. dirs. Ill. Pub. Health Continuing Edn. Council; cons. to numerous health, edn. instns. Mem. Am. Public Health Assn. (past chmn. sect. mental health), Ill. Public Health Assn. (exec. council), Am. Coll. Epidemiology, Soc. Epidemiologic Research, AAAS, Ill. Acad. Sci., N.Y. Acad. Sci. Democrat. Methodist. Author: Drugs and the Whole Person, 1982, Health Education: A Transatlantic Perspective, 1987, Epidemiology-Basis for Disease Prevention and Health Promotion, 1988; contbr. articles to profl. jours.; editorial bd. Health Values, 1980—, also assoc. editor, Jour. Drug Edn., 1981—, Internat. Jour. Mental Health, 1982-83. Office: Brown U Ctr Alcohol & Addiction Studies Box G-BH Providence RI 02912 E-mail: david.duncan@accessky.net.

DUNCAN, DEBBIE, writer; b. Pasadena, Apr. 28, 1953; d. Donal Baker and Lavon (Johnson) Duncan; m. William E. Stone, June 19, 1981; children: Jennifer Duncan Stone, Allison Duncan Stone, Molly Duncan Stone. AB, Stanford U., 1976. Adminstr. Stanford U., Calif., 1977—89. Author: (book) When Molly Was in the Hospital, 1994 (Benjamin Franklin award, 1995), Joy of Reading; contbr. essays. Avocations: singing, sports, baseball. Home and Office: 1061 Cathcart Way Stanford CA 94305

DUNCAN, DEBORAH L. finance company executive; BA in Econs., Smith Coll.; MS in Acctg., NYU. With Chase Manhattan, N.Y.C., 1979—2000; numerous positions including corp. treas., co-head global markets, We. Hemisphere treas., treas. Chase Tokyo, others; sr. v.p. Chase Manhattan, N.Y.C., 1991-94; exec. v.p. markets, We. Hemisphere treas., treas. Chase Tokyo, others, 1994—; CEO, mng. dir. Freemont Investment Advisors, 2001—03, chmn., 2003—. Bd. dirs. Investment Co. Inst. Bd. dirs. United Way of Tri-State, YMCA of Greater N.Y., Ronald McDonald House. Office: Freemont Investment Advisors 333 Market St Ste 2600 San Francisco CA 94105-2127*

DUNCAN, DONALD WILLIAM, lawyer; b. Baldwin, Md., May 18, 1932; s. William Rush and Mary Alice (MacBlane) D.; children: David (dec.), Lisa; m. Auria Adorno Duncan; 1 child, Roberto Millan. AA, U. Balt., 1956, JD, 1960. Bar: Md. 1960, Fla. 1992; County Ct. mediator. Asso. Haynie & McFerrin, C.P.A., Balt., 1956-61; controller H.C. Weiskettel Co., Balt., 1961-62; v.p., counsel, sec., Balt. Aircoil Co., Inc., 1962-87; pvt. practice Palm Coast, Fla., 1987—. Mem. Md. Bar Assn., Fla. Bar. Republican. Presbyterian. Office: Donald W Duncan PA PO Box 352411 Palm Coast FL 32135-2411 E-mail: dwduncan@pcfl.net.

DUNCAN, DORIS GOTTSCHALK, information systems educator; b. Seattle, Nov. 19, 1944; d. Raymond Robert and Marian (Onstad) D.; m. Robert George Gottschalk, Sept. 12, 1971 (div. Dec. 1983). BA, U. Wash., Seattle, 1967, MBA, 1968; PhD, Golden Gate U., 1978. Cert. data processor, systems profl., computer profl., data educator. Comm. cons. Pacific N.W. Bell Tel. Co., Seattle, 1968-71; mktg. supr. AT&T, San Francisco, 1971-73; sr. cons., project leader Quantum Sci. Corp., Palo Alto, Calif., 1973-75; dir. co. analysis program Input Inc., Palo Alto, 1975-76; lectr. acctg. and info. systems Calif. State U., Hayward, 1976-78, assoc. prof., 1978-85, prof., 1985—, coord. computer info. sys., 1994-97; dir. info. sci. dept. Golden Gate U., San Francisco, 1982-83, mem. info. systems adv. bd., 1983-85, co-advisor grad. program Computer Inf. Sys., e-bus. programs, 1999—. Cons. pvt. cos., 1975—; vis. prof. U. Wash., Seattle, 1997-98; internat. spkr. profl. groups and confs. Author: Computers and Remote Computing Services, 1983; contbr. articles to profl. jours.; mem. editl. rev. bd. Jour. Info. Systems Edn., 1992-97, Jour. Informatics Edn. Rsch., 2000—. Loaned exec. United Good Neighbors, Seattle, 1969; nat. com. woman bd. dirs. Young Reps., Wash., 1970-71; advisor Jr. Achievement, San Francisco, 1971-72; mem. nat. bd. Inst. for Certification of Computer Profls. Edn. Found., 1990-93; bd. dirs. Computer Repair Svcs., 1992-94, mem. adv. bd. Ximnet Corp., 2000-02. Recipient Disting. Rsch. award Allied Acads., 1999; named Computer Educator of Yr., Internat. Assn. Computer Info. Systems, 1997. Mem. Data Processing Mgmt. Assn. (Meritorious Svc. award, Bronze award 1984, Silver award 1986, Gold award 1988, Emerald award 1992, Diamond award 1994, Double Diamond award 1999, Triple Diamond award 2001, Nat. grantee, 1984, dir. edn. chmn. San Francisco chpt. 1984-85, sec. and v.p. 1985, pres. 1986, assn. dir. 1987, by-laws chmn. 1987, chair awards com. 1992-95, nat. bd. dirs. spl. interest group in edn. 1985-87), Am. Inst. Decision Scis., Western Assn. Schs. and Colls. (accreditation evaluation team 1984-85), Assn. Computing Machinery, Jr. Club of Seattle (Beautiful Home award Foster City 1994, 95, winner Tournament of Christmas Lights 1996), Bus. Honor Soc., Beta Gamma Sigma. Achievements include subspecialties: Information systems (information science). Current work: curriculum development, professional certification, industry standards, computer literacy and user education, system analysis and design, design of databases and data banks, electronic commerce. Office: Calif State U Sch Bus & Econs Hayward CA 94542

DUNCAN, ED EUGENE, lawyer; b. Gary, Ind., Dec. 10, 1948; s. Attwood and Freddie Leon (Ballard) D.; m. Patricia Louise Revado, Sept. 8, 1973 (div.); children: Kristin, Anika, Gregory. BA, Oberlin Coll., 1970; JD, Northwestern U., 1974. Bar: Ohio 1974, U.S. Dist. Ct. (no. dist.) Ohio 1977, U.S. Supreme Ct. 1977. Assoc. Arter & Hadden, Cleve., 1974-82, ptnr., 1982—. Bd. mem. Glenville br. YMCA, Cleve., 1979—, Ohio Bd. of Bldg. Standards, Columbus, 1986-89; trustee Legal Aid Soc., Cleve., 1990-91. Mem.: Cleve. Bar Assn., Ohio Bar Assn. Avocations: writing, reading. Home: 935 Roland Rd Cleveland OH 44124-1033 Office: Arter & Hadden 925 Euclid Ave Ste 1100 Cleveland OH 44115-1475 E-mail: ed.duncan1@arterhadden.com.

DUNCAN, ELIZABETH CHARLOTTE, retired marriage and family therapist, educational therapist, educator; b. L.A., Mar. 10, 1919; d. Frederick John de St. Vrain and Nellie Mae (Goucher) Schwankovsky; m. William McConnell Duncan, Oct. 12, 1941 (div. 1949); 1 child, Susan Elizabeth Duncan St. Vrain. BA, Calif. State U., Long Beach, 1953; MA, UCLA, 1962; PhD, Internat. Coll., 1984. Cert. marriage and family therapist; cert. clin. psychopathologist, Wash. Dir. gifted program Palos Verdes (Calif.) Sch. Dist., 1958-64; TV tchr., participant ednl. films Los Angeles County, 1961-64; dir. U. So. Calif. Presch., L.A., 1965-69, Abraham Maslow rsch. assoc., 1962-69; pvt. practice family counseling Malibu, Calif., 1979—2003, Ventura, 1979—2003, Eastsound, 1979—2003, Seattle, 1979—2003; pvt. practice psychotherapy West Seattle, 1994—2003; ret., 2003. Psychotherapist Children's Program North Sound Regional Support Network, 1992; resident psychologist for film series Something Personal, 1987—; mem. Rsch. Inst. of Scripps Clic, La Jolla, Calif.; charter mem. Inst. Behavioral Medicine, Santa Barbara, Calif.; pub. spkr., lectr. comm.; cons. in field. TV performer in documentary The Other Side, 1985; creator: Persephone's Child, 1988. Active Chrysalis Ctr., L.A., 1984-86; mem. Ventura County Mental Health Adv. Bd., 1985-86, United Way, L.A., 1985-92; mem. Menninger Found. San Juan County, Wash., 1992; mem. adv. bd. North Sound Regional Support Network, 1992, Amb.'s People to People, San Juan County Network, 1998-00. Recipient Emmy award for best documentary Am. Acad. TV Arts and Scis., 1976; named Child Adv. of Yr., Calif. Mental Health Adv. Bd., 1987. Mem. AACD (Disting. Svc. award 1990), Transpersonal Psychol. Assn., Calif. State Orgn. Gifted Edn. (sec. 1962-64), Internat. Platform Assn., Am. Assn. for Marriage and Family Therapy (supr. licenses). Democrat. Avocations: swimming, plays, concerts, boating, political issues, especially women and child abuse. Home: 4455 Providence Point Pl SE Issaquah WA 98029 E-mail: drduncan@foxinternet.com.

DUNCAN, FRANCIS, historian, retired government official; b. Oak Park, Ill., July 12, 1922; s. Fred B. and Olive (Whitney) Duncan; m. Frances M. Mergus, Aug. 16, 1947 (dec. June 2002); children: Evan, April. BA, Ohio Wesleyan U., 1944; MA, U. Chgo., 1947, PhD, 1954. Instr. history Wayne State U., Detroit, 1947-50; civilian employee Office of Intelligence, USAF, Washington, 1950-57; analyst Office of Controller, AEC, Washington, 1957-62, asst. historian, 1962-74; asso. historian div. naval reactors ERDA, 1974-77; historian div. naval reactors Dept. Energy, 1977-86, cons. hist. divsn., 1986-96. Author: Rickover and the Nuclear Navy, the Discipline of Technology, 1990, Rickover: The Struggle for Excellence, 2001; author: (with Richard G. Hewlett) Atomic Shield, 1969, Nuclear Navy 1946-1962, 1974; contbr. articles on naval history to profl. jours. Served with USNR, 1943-46. Recipient David D. Lloyd Prize in History 1970, Theodore and Franklin D. Roosevelt Naval History Prize, 1991. Mem. AAAS, U.S. Naval Inst., Naval Hist. Found., Nat. Coun. on Pub. History. Home: 9209 Ewing Dr Bethesda MD 20817-3313 E-mail: ffrncdunc9@aol.com.

DUNCAN, GEORGE, marketing consultant; b. N.Y.C., Apr. 16, 1935; s. George Edward and Beatrice Duncan; m. Sally Anne Pickhardt, Jan. 26, 1980; 1 child, Laura. B Social Sci., Fordham U., 1957. Ind. cons. Duncan Direct Assocs., Peterborough, N.H., 1976—; co-founder, pres. Vt.-N.H. Direct Mktg. Group, Concord, N.H., 1987—. Author: Streetwise Direct Marketing, 2001. Pres. Rotary Club, Peterborough, 1994-95. Capt. U.S. Army, 1957-63. Recipient John Caples award Direct Mktg. Writers Guild, 1978, 83, John Howie Wight Cup, Mail Advt. Svc. Assn., 1983, Echo Leader award Direct Mktg. Assn., 1986, first place New Eng. Direct Mktg. Assn., 1990, Wood Badge, Boy Scouts Am., 1990. Democrat. Home: 16 Elm St Peterborough NH 03458 Office: Duncan Direct Assocs 16 Elm St Peterborough NH 03458 Office Fax: 603-924-8511. E-mail: gduncan@pobox.com.

DUNCAN, GEORGE THOMAS, statistician, educator; b. Chgo., Ill., Aug. 7, 1942; s. Thomas Presley Duncan and Alice Anna Michaelson; m. Sheryl F. Kelsey, Jan. 4, 1985; m. Mary Allison, Dec. 21, 1968 (div. 1984); children: Christina Kim, Gregory. BS, U. of Chgo., 1963, MS, 1964; PhD, U. of Minn., 1970. Sr. statistician Texaco Rsch., Beacon, 1964—65; asst. prof. of math. U. of Calif., Davis, Calif., 1970—74; prof. of stats. Carnegie Mellon U., Pitts., 1974—. Vis. faculty Los Alamos Nat. Lab., Los Alamos, N.Mex., 1999—. Author: Private Lives and Public Policies, 1993. Vol. Peace Corp., Marawi City, Philippines, 1965—67; bd. dir. Ctrl. Blood Bank, Pitts., 1984—2002. Fellow: AAAS, Am. Statis. Assn. (Disting. Paper award Jour. of Am. Statis. Assn. 1985, Statis. of Yr. award Pitts. chpt. 1996); mem.: Internat. Statis. Inst. Avocation: art. Office: Carnegie Mellon University 5000 Forbes Avenue Pittsburgh PA 15213 Office Fax: 412-268-5338. Business E-Mail: gd17@andrew.cmu.edu.

DUNCAN, GWENDOLYN MCCURRY, elementary education educator; b. Walhalla, S.C., Feb. 24, 1943; d. Benjamin Harrison and Lucy Rosa (Quarles) McCurry; m. Harold Edward Duncan, July 29, 1962; children: Gregory Scott, Michael Lane. BA in Elem. Edn., Clemson (S.C.) U., 1984, MA in Elem. Edn., 1999. Cert. tchr. S.C., Nat. Bd. Tchr. Cert., 2002. Tchr. Westminster (S.C.) Elem. Sch., 1984-97, Orchard Park Elem. Sch., Westminster, 1997—. Sunday sch. tchr. Mountain View Bapt. Ch., Walhalla, 1968—; mem. Westminster Elem. PTA, 1984-97, Orchard Park Elem. PTA, 1997—. Mem. NEA, Oconee County Edn. Assn., S.C. Edn. Assn., S.C. Tchrs. of Math., Nat. Coun. of Tchrs. of Math., Kappa Delta Pi. Baptist. Avocations: reading, camping, traveling, growing roses. Home: 389 Fowler Rd West Union SC 29696-3122 Office: Orchard Park Elem Sch 600 Toccoa Hwy Westminster SC 29693-1638

DUNCAN, JEFFREY BURT, computer systems engineer; b. Plainfield, N.J., Nov. 20, 1941; s. George W.B. and Alice R. (Gerhold) D.; m. Patricia J. Jackson, Aug. 7, 1965; 1 child, Kim D. AS, Newark Coll. Engring., 1961; BS, Rensselaer Poly. Inst., 1965; MS, Union Coll., Schenectady, 1971. Registered profl. engr., N.Y. Engr. Empire Rsch. Corp., Cohoes, N.Y., 1965-66; engr., ptnr. Heatco, Inc., Stillwater, N.Y., 1966-67; devel. engr. W.T. La Rose & Assocs., Inc., Cohoes, 1967-69; project engr. Systomation, Inc., Elnora, N.Y., 1969-73; engr., mgr. quality control Xciton Corp., Latham, N.Y., 1973-75; project engr. engineered systems div. Albany Internat. Corp., Glens Falls, N.Y., 1975-81, sr. project engr. Albany, N.Y., 1981—. Cons. Ultramics, Inc., Albany, 1973-86, TechMark, Inc., Newport, R.I., 1983-85; tech. editor Litton Ednl. Pub. Co., Albany, 1974-77. Patentee paper equipment, computerized weave loom, also others. Com. mem. Concerned Argyle (N.Y.) Citizens, 1987-89. Mem. IEEE (sr.), Instrument Soc. Am. (sr.), Eta Kappa Nu, Tau Beta Pi, Phi Eta Sigma. Avocations: hiking, camping, canoeing, skiing, ballroom dancing. Home: 927 Rte 197 Argyle NY 12809-9703 Office: Albany Internat Corp PO Box 1907 Albany NY 12201-1907

DUNCAN, JENNINGS LIGON, III, minister; b. Greenville, S.C., Nov. 29, 1960; s. Jennings Ligon and Shirley Anne (Ledford) D.; m. Marjorie Anne Harley, Jan. 25, 1992; children: Sarah Kennedy, Jennings. BA, Furman U., 1983; MDiv, Covenant Theol. Sem., St. Louis, 1986, MA, 1987; PhD, U. Edinburgh, 1995. Ordained Presbyn. minister, 1990. Asst. pastor Trinity Presbyn. Ch., Jackson, Miss., 1990-95; prof. theology Reformed Theol. Sem., Jackson, 1990-96; sr. minister First Presbyn. Ch., Jackson, 1996—. Interim pastor 1st Presbyn. Ch., Yazoo City, Miss., 1993; founder, editl. dir. Reformed Acad. Press, Greenville, S.C., 1993—; adj. prof. Reformed Theol. Sem., 1996—; mem. reference Christian Witness to Israel. Author: Common Sense and American Presbyterianism, 1987, The Covenant Idea in Ante-Nicene Theology, 1995, Moses' Law for Modern Government, 1996; co-author: The Westminster Assembly: A Guide to Basic Bibliography, 1993, A Short History of the Westminster Asembly, 1993, The Genesis Debate: Three Views of the Days of Creation, 2000; contbg. author: The Practice of Confessional Subscription, 1995; editor: Introduction to Theological Studies, 1991, The Humiliated and Exalted Lord, 1994, Method for Prayer, 1994, The Federal Theology, 1994, The Broken Home: Lessons in Sorrow, 1994, Everyday Work of the Westminster Assembly, 1994, The Character of a True Theologian, 1995, A Place for Truth, 1998, Reformed Worship, 1998, A Scientific Man and the Bible, 2000, Preaching: The Man, the Message, and the Method, 2003, Give Praise to God: Sola Scriptura et Soli Deo Gloria, 2003; co-author, editor: The Westminster Confession into the 21st Century 2003; contbr. articles to profl. publs.; founder, editl. dir. Reformed Acad. Press. Bd. dirs., exec. com. Belhaven Coll., Jackson, 1998—; adv. bd. Values Investing Forum, Jackson, 1997—. Reformation Societies Internat. Inc., Indpls., Kindness Found., Hattiesburg, Miss., 1997—; sec. bd., exec. com. Ctr. Ch. Reform, Washington, bd. dirs.; sec. bd., mem. exec. com. The Highland Theol. Coll. U. Highlands and Islands, Dingwall, Scotland; pres., bd. dirs. Coun. Biblical Manhood and Womanhood, Alliance for Confessing Evangelicals, Institutional Rev. Bd. Miss. Bapt. Med. Ctr., Jackson, Word Ministries, Sardinia, S.C.; bd. dirs. Christian Witness to a Pagan Planet. Fellow Ctr. Advancement Paleo-Orthodoxy, Carl F.H. Henry Inst. for Evang. Engagement; mem. Scottish Evang. Theology Soc., Rutherford House Fellowship, N.Am. Patristic Soc., Evang. Theol. Soc., S.C. Hist. Soc. Presbyterian. Avocations: reading, music, chess, basketball, tennis. Office: 1st Presbyn Ch 1390 N State St Jackson MS 39202-2005 E-mail: lduncan@fpcjackson.org.

DUNCAN, JOHN J., JR., congressman; b. Lebanon, Tenn., July 21, 1947; m. Lynn Hawkins; children: Tara, Whitney, John J. III, Zane. BS in Journalism, U. Tenn., 1969; JD, George Washington U., 1973. Bar: Tenn. 1973. Pvt. practice, Knoxville, Tenn., 1973-81; state trial judge, 1981-88; mem. U.S. Congress from 2nd Tenn. dist., Washington, 1989—; mem. transp. and infrastructure com., resources com., govt. reform com. Bd. dirs. or past bd. dirs. ARC, YWCA, Sunshine Ctr. for Mentally Retarded, Beck Black Heritage Ctr., Knoxville Union Rescue Mission, St. Citizens Home Aid Svc., Knoxville Girls Club, others; active elder Eastminster Presbyn. Ch. Capt. U.S. N.G. and Res. Named One of Top 5 Most Fiscally Conservative Mems. of House and Senate, Nat. Taxpayers Union; recipient Super Hero award Citizens Against Govt. Waste, Golden Bulldog award Watchdogs of Treasury, Inc., Hartranft award Airline Operators and Pilots Assn., 1998; honored by Ams. for Tax Reform, Nat. Fefn. Ind. Bus., Concord Coalition, U.S. C. of C., Citizens for Sound Economy. Mem. Am. Legion, Elks, Sertoma Club, 40&8, Masons, Shriners. Republican. Office: US Ho of Reps 2267 Rayburn House Office Bldg Washington DC 20515-4202*

DUNCAN, JOHN M. federal agency administrator; m. Marcia Duncan; 1 child. Degree in indsl. adminstrn., U. Ill.; MS. Served with Am. Peace Corps; with CNA Fin., Continent Casualty Co.; profl. staff mem. Subcom. on Intergovtl. Rels. and Human Resources House Com. on Govtl. Opers., staff idr., 1978—84; maj. staff dir. U.S. Senate Com. on Govtl. Affairs, Washington, 1984—85, chief of staff, legis. dir. for U.S. Sen. William Roth, 1985—2001; treas. asst. sec. legis. affairs U.S. Dept. Treas., Washington, 2001—. Office: US Dept Treasury Legis Affairs 1500 Pennsylvania Ave NW Washington DC 20220

DUNCAN, JOHN PATRICK CAVANAUGH, lawyer; b. Kalamazoo, Mich., Jan. 25, 1949; s. James H. and Colleen Patricia (Cloney) D.; children: Sarah Ellen, James Patrick Cloney. BA cum laude, Yale U., 1971; JD, U. Chgo., 1974. Bar: Ill. 1974, U.S. Dist. Ct. (no. dist.) Ill. 1974, U.S. Ct. Appeals (7th cir.) 1975, U.S. Supreme Ct. 1979. Assoc. firm Holleb & Coff, Chgo., 1974-79; mem., 1979-87; ptnr. Jones, Day, Reavis & Pogue, Chgo., 1987-99; leader banking and investment practice area, 1996-99; prin. Duncan Assocs., LLC, 2000—. Adj. prof. IIT Chgo.-Kent Coll. Law Fin. Svcs. LLM Program, 1988—; mem. Fulbright Vis. Scholar Adv. Bd., 1995—98; mem. Chgo. com. Chgo. Coun. on Fgn. Rels., 1998—2000; author fed. and state trust co. laws. Contbr. articles to profl. jours. Fellow NSF, 1970. Fellow: Ill. Bar Found.; mem.: ABA (chmn. securities activities banks subcom. 1995—98, privacy task force 1998—2001, banking com.), Ill. Bankers Assn. (legal affairs com. 1986—87), Chgo. Bar Assn. (chmn. fin. insts. com. 1985—86), Yale Club (Chgo., N.Y.). Home: 3814 N Paulina St Chicago IL 60613-2716 Office: Duncan Assocs LLC 180 N LaSalle Ste 2410 Chicago IL 60601-2704 E-mail: jpcd@jpcdlaw.com.

DUNCAN, LELAND RAY, retired mission administrator; b. Bee Branch, Ark., Nov. 9, 1929; s. Enoch R. and Julia C. (Lane) D.; m. M. Ruth Tindall, May 28, 1952; children: Wallace L., Gregory A. BA, Oakland City U., 1962; postgrad., So. Theol. Sem., 1966-67; DD, Oakland City U., 1974. Owner, oper. Twin City Radio & TV, North Little Rock, Ark., 1956-59; pastor Gen. Bapt. Chs., Ind., Ark., Ky. & Mo., 1959-71; exec. dir. Gen. Bapt. Home Missions, Poplar Bluff, Mo., 1972-97, pres., until 1997; ret., 1997. Chmn. com. to revise Gen. Bapt. Statements of Faith, 1968-71; founder Gen. Bapt. Investment Fund, Popular Bluff, 1974, pres., 1974—; chmn. nominating com. N.Am. Bapt. Fellowship, Washington, 1978, chmn. cons. on ch. planting, 1979; mem. Connect Mo., Jefferson City, 1994. Mem. Poplar BLuff PTA, 1969-73; pres. Poplar BLuff Min.'s Assn., 1971. With 7th infantry divns. U.S. Army, 1951-52, Korea. Mem. VFW, Am. Legion, Am. Woodcarvers Assn. Avocations: wood carving, gardening, walking, reading. Home: 3643 Mclane Dr Poplar Bluff MO 63901-8752

DUNCAN, LINDSAY VERE, actress; b. Edinburgh, Scotland, Nov. 7, 1950; m. Hilton McRae; 1 child, Callum. Attended, Ctrl. Sch. Speech and Drama, London. Actor: (films) Loose Connections, 1983, Prick Up Your Ears, 1987, Manifesto, 1988, Body Parts, 1991, The Reflecting Skin, 1991, A Midsummer Night's Dream, 1996, City Hall, 1996, An Ideal Husband, 1999, Mansfield Park, 1999, Star Wars: Episode 1 - The Phantom Menace, 1999; (TV series) Just William, 1977—78, Ace of Spies, 1983, Dead Head, 1986, Traffik, 1989 (FIPA Golden award, Cannes Internat. Film Festival, 1990), Jake's Progress, 1995, Get Real, 1998; (TV miniseries) A Year in Provence, 1993, The History of Tom Jones, 1997, Oliver Twist, 1999; (Broadway plays) Les Liaisons Dangereuses (award, 1987, Tony award nomination, 1987, Theatre World award, 1987), Top Girls (Obie award, 1982), A Midsummer Night's Dream, Ashes to Ashes (Drama Desk nomination), Celebration, The Room, Private Lives (winner Tony award for Best Performance by a Leading Actress in a Play, 2002, Drama Desk Best Actress award, 2002); (films) Under the Tuscan Sun, 2003; (TV miniseries) Shooting the Past, Perfect Strangers. Office: ICM Oxford House 76 Oxford St London W1D 1B5 England

DUNCAN, LIONEL SEBASTIAN, artist, educator; b. Cristobal, Canal Zone, Panama, Oct. 24, 1929; s. Lionel Joseph and Ruby Veronica Duncan; children: Valerie Babb, Joseph, Damaris, Zena. Lic. Physics, U. Argentina, 1965; MFA Painting, Towson State U., 1998; PhD Edn., U. So. Calif., 1971. Cert. Sch. Adminstr., L.A, 1973. Prof. edn. Morgan State U., Balt., 1971—, dir. distance edn., 1995—2001. Cons. US Agencies of Ed. Devel., Washington. Exhbn., Howard County of the Arts Exhibiton, 1997 (Honarary Mention, 1997). Bd. dirs. Internat. Associaton Knowledge Engrs., Washington. Grantee UN Fellowship to Argentina, Unesco, 1963—65. Mem.: Fulbright Alumni Assn. (life Fulbright Fellow 1976, 1985, 1998). Green Party. Roman Catholic. Avocation: travel. Home: 1444E Baltimore St Ste 2A Baltimore MD 21231 Office: Morgan State U 1700 E Cold Spring Ln Baltimore MD 21251 Home Fax: 410 319 3698; Office Fax: 410 319 3698. Personal E-mail: lionelsduncan@aol.com. Business E-Mail: lduncan@moac.morgan.edu.

DUNCAN, MARGARET CAROLINE, physician; b. Salt Lake City, June 9, 1930; d. Donald and Margaret Aileen (Eberts) D.; m. N. Paul Arceneaux, Dec. 26, 1958; children: David Paul, Eleanor Anne, Stephen Louis, Andre. BA, U. Tex., 1952, MD, 1955. Intern Kings County Hosp., Seattle, 1955-56; resident in pediatrics John Sealy Hosp., Galveston, Tex., 1956-58; resident in neurology Charity Hosp., New Orleans, 1958-60; fellow child neurology Johns Hopkins Hosp., 1960-61; mem. faculty La. State U. Med. Center, New Orleans, 1961—, prof. neurology and pediatrics, 1973-2000, prof. neurology emeritus, 2000—. Chmn. La. Com. Epilespy and Cerebral Palsy, 1976-79. Fellow Am. Acad. Neurology, Am. Acad. Pediatrics; mem. Child Neurology Soc., Profs. Child Neurology, Alpha Omega Alpha. Episcopalian. Office: 1542 Tulane Ave New Orleans LA 70112-2825

DUNCAN, MARK, air transportation executive; BME, Royal Mil. Coll., 1968; Diploma of Pub. Adminstrn., Dalhousie U., 1975; MA in Pub. Adminstrn., Carleton U., 1981. Comml. pilot, 1974; registered profl. engr., Ont. Supt. airport sys. Transport Can., Ottawa, Ont., 1975-78, dep. airport gen. mgr., mgr. ops. Lester B.Pearson Airport Toronto, 1978-87, regional dir. gen. Airports Group Vancouver, 1987-96, regional dir. gen. Pacific Region, 1996—2002; v.p. ops. Can. Air Transp. Security Authority, Ottawa, 2002—03, v.p. and COO, 2003—. Recipient Achievement award Internat. N.W. Aviation Coun., 1995. Mem.: Union Club Brit. Columbia. Home: 374 Cooper St Apt 701 Ottawa ON Canada K2P 2P4 Office: Can Air Transp Security Authority 99 Bank St 13 Fl Ottawa ON Canada K1P 6B9

DUNCAN, MAURICE GREER, accountant, consultant; b. Marshall, Mo., July 16, 1928; s. Carl I. and Marguerite (Greer) D.; m. Sara Bangert, Aug. 29, 1959; children: Nancy L., Guerry M., Barbara D. Balke. BSBA, U. Okla., 1950. CPA, Okla. Staff acct. Amoco Corp., Houston, 1951-52, B.W. Vetter & Co., CPAs, Tulsa, 1953-58, ptnr., 1959-73, Hurdman & Cranston, CPAs, Tulsa, 1974-79; mng. ptnr. Main Hurdman, CPAs, Tulsa, 1979-87; ptnr. KPMG Peat Marwick, CPAs, Tulsa, 1987-88; cons. Maurice G. Duncan, CPA, Tulsa, 1988—. Mem. Tulsa Estate Planning Forum, 1978-88, pres. 1981. With USNR, 1950-59. Mem. AICPAs, Okla. Soc. CPAs, Tulsa Execs. Assn. (pres. 1985), Kiwanis, Tulsa Men's Club (treas.) RSVP (adv. bd.). Republican. Methodist. Home: 4325 E 87th St Tulsa OK 74137-2726 Office: Corporate Place # 600 5800 E Skelly Dr Tulsa OK 74135

DUNCAN, MICHAEL CLARKE, actor; Actor, 1987—. Actor: (TV series) The Bold and the Beautiful, 1992—94, Skwids, 1996; (films) Friday, 1995, Back in Business, 1997, Caught Up, 1998, The Players Club, 1998, Bulworth, 1998, Armageddon, 1998, A Night at the Roxbury, 1998, Breakfast of Champions, 1999, The Green Mile, 1999, The Underground Comedy Movie, 1999, The Whole Nine Yards, 2000, Wrestlemania 2000, 2000, Soldier of Fortune, 2000, See Spot Run, 2001, The Immigrant Garden, 2001, Cats & Dogs, 2001, Planet of the Apes, 2001, They Call Me Sirr, 2001, Hollywood Digital Diaries, 2001, The Scorpion King, 2002, George and the Dragon, 2002, numerous TV guest appearances. Office: c/o Dolores Robinson Entertainment 112 S Almont Dr Los Angeles CA 90048

DUNCAN, POPE ALEXANDER, college administrator; b. Glasgow, Ky., Sept. 8, 1920; s. Pope Alexander and Mabel (Roberts) D.; m. Margaret Flexer, June 30, 1943; children— Mary Margaret Jones, Annie Laurie Kelly, Katherine Maxwell Aimone. BS, U. Ga., 1940, MS, 1941; Th.M., So. Bapt. Theol. Sem., 1944, PhD, 1947; postgrad., U. Zurich, 1960-61; LLD (hon.), Rollins Coll., 1987; LittD (hon.), Limestone Coll., 1987; LLD (hon.), Stetson U., 1987; EdD (hon.), Alderson-Broaddus Coll., 1994; LLD (hon.), William Jewell Coll., 1999. Instr. physics U. Ga., 1940-41; fellow So. Bapt. Theol. Sem., 1944-45; dir. religious activities Mercer U., 1945-46, Roberts prof. ch. history, 1948-49; prof. religion Stetson U., 1946-48, 49-53; prof. ch. history Southeastern Bapt. Theol. Sem., 1953-63; dean Brunswick Coll., 1964; pres. South Ga. Coll., Douglas, 1964-68; v.p. Ga. So. U., Statesboro, 1968-71, pres., 1971-77, Stetson U., DeLand, Fla., 1977-87, chancellor, 1987—2002, chancellor emeritus, 2002—. Author: Our Baptist Story, 1958, The Pilgrimage of Christianity, 1965, Hanserd Knollys, 1965, Memoirs, 2002 Pres. Wake Forest Civic Club, 1959-60, Ga. Assn. Colls., 1968-69; pres. Coastal Empire council Boy Scouts Am., 1973-74; chmn. council of presidents So. Consortium for Internat. Edn., Inc., 1974-75; mem. commn. on colls. So. Assn. Colls. and Schs., 1978-82; bd. dirs. Fla. Endowment for Humanities, 1978; chmn. pres.'s council Ind. Colls. and Univs. Fla., 1982-84 ; chmn. Fla. Ind. Colls. Fund, 1980-81; mem. exec. com. So. Univ. Conf., 1981-85. Mem. Am. Hist. Assn., Am. Soc. Ch. History, Douglas Coffee County C. of C. (dir. 1966-68), DeLand (Fla.) C. of C. (dir. 1978-81), Nat. Assn. Ind. Colls. and Univs. (dir. 1979-83), Fla. Assn. Colls. and Univs. (bd. dirs. 1978-85, v.p. 1981-82, pres. 1982-83, Disting. Service award 1987), Nat. Collegiate Athletic Assn. (pres.'s commn. 1985-87), Assn. So. Bapt. Colls. and Schs. (pres. 1980-81), Assn. Ch. Related Colls. and Univs. of the South (pres. 1984-85), Phi Beta Kappa, Omicron Delta Kappa, Phi Kappa Phi, Phi Delta Kappa, Kappa Delta Pi, Pi Mu Epsilon, Phi Eta Sigma, Sigma Phi Sigma. Lodges: Rotary (dir. 1965-66, 70-72, pres. 1967-68). Democrat. Baptist.

DUNCAN, RICHARD ALAN, lawyer; b. Mpls., July 8, 1963; BA in Econs. summa cum laude, Yale U., 1985, JD, 1988. Bar: Minn. 1988, U.S. Ct. Appeals (8th cir.) 1988, U.S. Ct. Appeals (9th cir.) 1990, U.S. Ct. Appeals (10th cir.) 1998, U.S. Ct. Appeals (fed. cir.) 2000,, U.S. Ct. Appeals (11th cir.) 2001, U.S. Supreme Ct. 1991. Assoc. Faegre & Benson, LLP, Mpls., 1988-95, ptnr., 1996—. Adj. prof. law U. Minn. Law Sch., 1998—. Mem. exec. com. North Star chpt. Sierra Club, 1988-91, 95-98, 2001-03. Mem. Phi Beta Kappa. Office: Faegre & Benson LLP 90 S 7th St Ste 2200 Minneapolis MN 55402-3901 E-mail: rduncan@faegre.com.

DUNCAN, RICHARD LEO, communications educator; b. Plymouth, Ill., Dec. 7, 1936; s. Gilbert Leo and Vera Viola (Payne) D.; m. Mary Rose Hackett, Dec. 16, 1962 (div. Nov. 1981); m. Eva Elena Hargis, Mar. 26, 1994 (div. Mar. 2000); 1 child, Sean Mackenzie. BA in Chemistry, Knox Coll., 1958; MDiv, Pacific Sch. Religion, 1969; postgrad., San Diego C.C., 1977-81; DMin, United Theol. Sem., 2001. Ordained United Ch. of Christ, 1970. Min. youth and edn. Kensington Cmty. Ch., San Diego, 1969-74; campus min. Calif. State U., Long Beach, 1975-77; exec. dir. Religious Media Ministry-United Ch. of Christ, San Diego, 1977-88; pastor media ministry Shiloh Ch.-United Ch. of Christ, Dayton, Ohio, 1988-94; faculty, dir. Comm. Ctr. United Theol. Sem., Dayton, 1994—. Danforth assoc. San Diego State U., 1972-78; prodr. KGTV (ABC), San Diego, 1977-88; host, prodr. KFMB-TV (CBS), San Diego, 1978-88; v.p., bd. dirs. ECUMEDIA-Coun. of Chs., L.A., 1980-88, interim exec., 1982; bd. dirs. NATAS, San Diego, 1987-88. Mem. editl. com.: You Own More Than Your TV Set, 1983. Mem. adv. bd. Congressman Jim Bates, San Diego and Washington, 1984, Calif. Assemblywoman Lucy Killea, San Diego and Sacramento, 1984. Capt. U.S. Army, 1960-68. Recipient Gabrial Cert. of Merit, U.S. Cath. Conf./UNDA, 1978, Emmy awards NATAS, San Diego, 1980, 84, Award of Merit, Religious Pub. Rels. Coun., 1983, Merit award Internat. TV Assn., San Diego, 1985. Mem. Nat. Assn. for Better Broadcasting (bd. dirs. 1981-2001), Internat. TV Assn., N.Am./World Assn. Christian Communicators (mem. nat. steering com. 1995-97), Telecom. Consumer Coalition, United Ch. of Christ Conf.-Ohio/SONKA Assn. Democrat. Avocations: snow skiing, whitewater rafting, skydiving, camping, glass blowing, stained glass art. Office: United Theol Sem 1810 Harvard Blvd Dayton OH 45406-4539

DUNCAN, RICHARD RAY, history educator; b. Cin., Aug. 30, 1931; s. Ray Howard and Emma (Swing) D. BA, Ohio U., 1954, MA, 1955; PhD, Ohio State U., 1963. Instr. Kent State U., 1961-64; asst. prof. U. Richmond, Va., 1964-67; prof. Georgetown U., Washington, 1967-2000, prof. emeritus, 2000—. Vis. assoc. prof. Ohio State U., Columbus, summer 1971; chmn. bd. dirs. Duncan Bros. Tire Co., Winchester, Va. Author: Lee's Endangered Left, 1998; editor: Alexander Neil and the Last Valley Campaign, 1996, Maryland Historical Magazine, 1967-74; compiler: Theses and Dissertations on Virginia History, 1986; contbr. articles to profl. jours. Episcopalian. Home: 6101 Edsall Rd Apt 1802 Alexandria VA 22304-6009 Office: Georgetown U History Dept Washington DC 20057-0001

DUNCAN, ROBERT BANNERMAN, strategy and organizations educator; b. Milw., July 4, 1942; s. Robert Lynn and Irene (Hoenig) D.; m. Susan Jean Phillips, June 12, 1965; children: Stephanie Olcott, Christopher Robert. BA, Ind. U., 1964, MA, 1966; PhD, Yale U., 1971. Asst. prof. Northwestern U. Kellogg Grad. Sch. Mgmt., Evanston, Ill., 1970-73, assoc. prof. orgn. behavior, 1973-76, prof., 1976, Earl Dean Howard prof. orgn. behavior, 1980-83, J.L. Kellogg disting. prof. strategy and orgns., 1983-86, 92—, J. Allen disting. prof. strategy and orgns., 1986-89; Richard L. Thomas prof. leadership orgnl. change Northwestern U., Evanston, 1996—2002; assoc. dean acad. affairs Northwestern U. Kellogg Grad. Sch. Mgmt., Evanston, Ill., 1975-76, 80-82, 84-86; provost, chief acad. affairs Northwestern U., Evanston, 1987-92; Eli and Edythe L. Broad dean Eli Broad Coll. Bus. Mich. State U., East Lansing, 2002—. Co-author: Innovations and Organizations, 1973, Strategies for Planned Change, 1977; also numerous articles in profl. jours. Fellow Acad. Mgmt. (chair nat. program 1980-81, pres. 1983-84). Avocation: sailing.

DUNCAN, ROBERT CLIFTON, retired government official; b. Jonesville, Va., Nov. 21, 1923; s. Robley Evans and Selva (Cooney) D.; m. Rosemary Fleming, Mar. 19, 1949; children: Melissa, Babette Duncan Wilson, Robert, Scott. BS, U.S. Naval Acad., 1945, U.S. Naval Postgrad. Sch., 1953; S.M., MIT, 1954, Sc.D., 1960. Commd. ensign USN, 1945, advanced through grades to comdr., naval aviator fighters and heavy attack aircraft; chief space programs br., chief naval ops. Washington, 1960-61; staff asst., dir. def. research and engring., 1961 64; ret., 1965; chief guidance and control div. Manned Spacecraft Ctr., NASA, Houston, 1964-67; asst. dir. Electronics Research Ctr., NASA, Cambridge, Mass., 1967-68; v.p. Polaroid Corp., Cambridge, 1968-85; dir. Def. Advanced Research Projects Agy., Washington, 1985-88; asst. sec. def. for research and tech. U.S. Dept. Def., Arlington, Va., 1986-87; dir. def. research and engring. The Pentagon, Washington, 1987-89, dir. operational test and evaluation, 1989-93; v.p. Hicks & Assocs. Inc., McLean, Va., 1993—. Dir. Charles Stark Draper Lab., Cambridge, 1974-85 Author: Dynamics of Atmospheric Entry, 1962; contbr. articles to profl. jours. Dist. chmn. Norumbega council Boy Scouts Am., Weston, Mass., 1969-72, exec. bd., Waban, Mass., 1969-85; mem. indsl. and profl. adv. council Pa. State U., 1973-78; deacon Trinitarian Congregation Ch., Wayland, Mass., 1981-85; trustee Forsyth Dental Ctr., Boston, 1967-85; pres. Polaroid Found., Cambridge, 1978-82 Decorated Legion of Merit; recipient Hayes award Inst. Navigation, Exceptional Svc. medal NASA, 1968, Silver Beaver and Disting. Eagle Scout award Boy Scouts Am., 1984, Disting. Pub. Svc. medal Dept. Def., 1987, 89, 93. Mem. Nat. Acad. Engring. Republican. Avocations: backpacking, hiking, camping. Home: 5109 Yuma St NW Washington DC 20016-4336 Office: Hicks & Assocs Inc 1710 Goodridge Dr Ste 1300 Mc Lean VA 22102-3700

DUNCAN, ROBERT MICHAEL, banker, lawyer, Republican national committeeman; b. Oneida, Tenn., Apr. 14, 1951; s. Robert C. and Barbara (Taylor) D.; m. Joanne Kirk, June 3, 1972; children: Robert Michael. BA, Cumberland Coll., 1971; JD, U. Ky., 1974; postgrad., U. Wis., 1977-80; LLD (hon.), Cumberland Coll., 1990; owner pres. mgmt. program, Harvard U., 1990; D Pub. Svc. (hon.), Coll. of Ozarks, 1992. Cert. lener-bus. banking, 1994. V.p. Inez (Ky.) Deposit Bank, 1974—77, exec. v.p., 1977—81, chmn., 1981—, Cmty. Holding Co., Inez, 1983—; with First Nat. Bank (now Inez Deposit Bank FSB), Louisa, Ky., 1984—. Dir. Cin. Br. of Cleve. Fed. Res. Bank, 1987-90; chmn. Morehead State U., 1985-86; trustee, chmn. Alice Lloyd Coll., Pippa Passes, Ky., 1978—, acting pres., 1993-94; mem. class XX Pres.'s Commn. on Exec. Exch. assigned to White House Office Pub. Liaison as asst. dir.; dir. Christian Appalachian Project, 1995—; mem. Pres.'s Commn. on White House Fellows, 2001—; polit. commentator WYMT-TV, 1999--. Del. Rep. Nat. Conv., 1972, 76, 92, 96, 2000, chair contest com. 2000 conv.; nat. committeeman for Ky., 1992—, Rep. Nat. Com., vice chmn. so. region, 1992-2001, treas., 2001-02, gen. cousnel, 2002--, exec. com., 1996; chmn. Ky. Rep. Com., 1995; trustee Highlands Regional Med. Ctr., 1977—, sec., 1994; active Govt. Rels. Coun., White House Conf. on Small Bus., 1995; chmn. Govs. Scholars, 1995—, bd. dirs. 1996—; chmn. East Ky. Corp., 1996, vice chmn. Ctr. Econ. Devel.; chmn. Bunning for U.S. Senate campaign, 1998; midwest regional chmn. Bush Presdl. campaign, 1999. Named Cumberland Coll. Outstanding Alumnus, 1976, Outstanding Young Man, Ky. Jaycees, 1982; U. Ky. fellow, 1978, White House fellow finalist, 1989; recipient Cmty. Leadership award McConnell Scholars U. Louisville, Cmty. Leadership award, 1999; named to U. Ky. Coll. of Law Hall of Fame, 2002. Mem. Am. Bankers Assn., Ky. Bankers Assn. (pres. 1985-86, dir.), Ky. Bar Assn., Ky. C. of C. (dir.), Kiwanis (lt. gov. 1983-84). Baptist. Home: PO Box 331 Inez KY 41224-0331 Office: PO Box 365 Inez KY 41224-0365 E-mail: mduncan@inezdepositbank.com.

DUNCAN, RONNY RUSH, agriculturist, turf researcher, consultant; b. Hereford, Tex., May 21, 1946; s. George Wesley and Nancy Marie (Olson) D.; m. Nancy Elizabeth Douglass, June 10, 1971; children: Cady Meyer, Drew Wesley, Carey Elizabeth. BS, Tex. Tech. U., 1969; MS, Tex. A&M U., 1974, PhD, 1977. Grad. rsch. asst. Tex. A&M U., College Station, 1969, 73-77; asst. prof. U. Ga., Griffin, 1977-82, assoc. prof., 1982-88, prof., 1988—2003. Cons. environ. stress problems on recreational/landscape turf; specialist in salt-affected soils, effluent or ocean water irrigation, paspalum turfgrass. Co-author: Salt Affected Environments—Assessment and Management, 1998, Seashore Paspalum-The Environmental Turfgrass, 2000; editor: Crops As Enhancers of Nutrient Use, 1990; editor Sorghum Newsletter, 1990-95. Sgt. USAF, 1969-73. Mem. Am. Soc. Agronomy, Crop Sci. Soc. Am., Internat. Turfgrass Soc., Coun. for Agr., Sci. and Tech., Sports Turf Mgrs. Assn., Golf Course Supts. Assn. Am., Turfgrass Prodrs. Internat., Gamma Sigma Delta, Sigma Xi. Democrat. Baptist. Achievements include development of environmentally friendly turfgrasses with low fertilizer and pesticide requirements, which grow with recycled or ocean water; specialist in breeding and stress physiology of grasses including turfgrasses, salinity problems and water issues. Office: U Ga 1109 Experiment St Griffin GA 30223-1797 E-mail: duncanturf@hotmail.com.

DUNCAN, ROYAL ROBERT, publisher; b. Bloomington, Ill., May 6, 1952; s. Robert E. and Audrey L. Gresham (Mossberger) D. AA, Rock Valley Coll., Rockford, Ill., 1972; BS, Bradley U., 1974. Sales mgr. Sports Svcs., Peoria, Ill., 1975-77, 4-B Advt., East Peoria, Ill., 1977-78; pres. Royal Pub., Peoria, 1978—. Home: 428 W Collingwood Cir Peoria IL 61614-2069 Office: 7620 Harker Dr Peoria IL 61615-1849

DUNCAN, SAM K. retail executive; With Albertson's Inc., 1969—92, Fred Meyer, Inc., 1992—2001; dir. ShopKo Stores Inc., 2002—. Office: 700 Pilgrim Way Green Bay WI 54304*

DUNCAN, SARAH BAKER, judge; b. Waco, Tex., May 23, 1955; d. Malcolm Perry and Mary Ruth (Norris) D. BA with honors, U. Tex., 1977, JD with honors, 1984. Bar: Tex. 1984; cert. in civil appellate law Tex. Bd. Legal Specialization. Assoc. Fulbright & Jaworski, Austin and Houston, 1984-88, Minton, Burton, Foster & Collins, Austin, 1988-89; assoc., participating assoc. Soules & Wallace, P.C., San Antonio, 1989-90; pvt. practice San Antonio, 1990-91; of counsel Fulbright & Jaworski, LLP, San Antonio, 1991-93, Denton McKannie & Navarro, San Antonio, 1994; justice Fourth Ct. Appeals, San Antonio, 1995—. Mem. Supreme Ct. Adv. Com. on the Rules of Civil Procedure, Austin, 1993-2002; tri-chair Gender Bias Task Force, San Antonio, 1995—; mem. Task Force on Funding Jud. Efficiency Commn., Austin, 1995-96; coun. mem. Appellate Practice Sect., State Bar Tex., 1996-98. Contbg. author: Texas Appellate Practice Manual, 1993; mem. Tex. Law Rev./U. Tex. Sch. Law, Austin, 1982-84. Fellow Am. Bar Found., Tex. Bar Found., San Antonio Bar Found.; mem. State Bar Tex. (appellate sect., jud. sect.), San

Antonio Bar Assn. (appellate sect.), Bar Assn. Fifth Fed. Cir., Bar U.S. Supreme Ct. Avocations: gardening, reading, computers, cross-country skiing. Office: Fourth Ct Appeals 300 Dolorosa Ste 3200 San Antonio TX 78205-3037

DUNCAN, TIM, professional basketball player; b. Apr. 25, 1976; Center San Antonio Spurs, 1997—. Recipient Naismith award, 1996, Wooden award, NCAA, 1996. Office: 100 Montana St San Antonio TX 78203-1033

DUNCANSON, DONALD GEORGE, retired encyclopedia editor; b. L.A., Feb. 26, 1928; s. George H. and Addie (Biddison) D. BA, U. So. Calif., L.A., 1953; MA, Harvard U., 1954; postgrad., U. Chgo., 1954-56. Lexicographer Funk & Wagnalls Inc., N.Y.C., 1956-57; assoc. editor Scott, Foresman & Co., Chgo., 1958-64, Sci. Rsch. Assocs., Inc., Chgo., 1964-67; editor Ency. Britannica, Inc., Chgo., 1967-73, 77-93. With USN, 1946-49. Democrat. Avocations: reading, travel. Home: 3605 Sarah St Franklin Park IL 60131-1632 E-mail: dj2849@comcast.net.

DUNCOMBE, PATRICIA WARBURTON, retired social worker; b. London, Jan. 30, 1925; came to U.S., 1940. d. P.G. Eliot and Mary Louise (Thompson) Warburton; m. David S. Duncombe, July 11, 1947 (dec. Apr. 1976); children: Elizabeth, Mari, Edward, David, Peter. BA, Barnard Coll., 1944; MS in Social Work, Columbia U., 1947. Cert. social worker. Social worker YWCA, Chgo., Evanston, Ill., 1947-50, B.I.A., Elko, Nev., 1966-67, Nev. State Welfare Div., Elko, Nev., 1967-69; dir. St. Michael's Youth Residence, Ethete, Wyo., 1970-76; asst. prof. U. Wyo., Laramie, 1976-83; program dir. St. Jude's Ranch, Boulder City, Nev., 1983-85; med. social worker home health agys., Las Vegas, Nev., 1985-95; retired. Mem. Wyo. Commn. for Women, 1971-83, chmn., 1975-77; bd. dirs. SE Wyo. Mental Health, 1980-83; founder Lend-A-Hand Program, Boulder City, 1989 (awarded 700th Point of Light, 1992). Recipient Gov.'s award, 2000. Mem. NASW (chpt. pres. 1979, 81, commn. on women 1977-79, exec. dir. Nev. chpt. 1985-90, Social Work of Yr. award Wyo. chpt. 1980, Nev. chpt. 1989, lifetime achievement award 1992), AAUW (nat. bd. dirs. 1983-85), Mesquite Club (Las Vegas, pres. 1998-99), Phi Theta Kappa. Democrat. Episcopalian. Avocations: gardening, travel, reading, art.

DUNCOMBE, RAYNOR LOCKWOOD, astronomer; b. Bronxville, N.Y., Mar. 3, 1917; s. Frederic Howe and Mabel Louise (Taylor) D.; m. Julena Theodora Steinheider, Jan. 29, 1948; 1 son, Raynor B. BA, Wesleyan U., Middletown, Conn., 1940; MA, State U. Iowa, 1941; PhD, Yale U., 1956. Astronomer U.S. Naval Obs., Washington, 1942-62; dir. Nautical Almanac Office, 1963-75; prof. aerospace sci. U. Tex., Austin, 1976—. Research assoc. Yale U. Obs., 1948-49; lectr. dynamical astronomy U. Md., 1963, Yale Summer Inst., 1959-70, Office Naval Research Summer Inst. in Orbital Mechanics, 1971, NATO Advanced Study Inst., 1972; cons. orbital mechanics Projects Vanguard, Mercury, Gemini, Apollo, USN Space Surveillance System; mem. NASA space scis. steering com., NASA research adv. panel in applied math., 1967; adviser Internat. Com. on Weights and Measures, Internat. Radio Consultative Com., Internat. Telecommunications Union; mem. NAS-NRC astronomy survey com., 1970-72, Hubble Space Telescope Astrometry Team, 1976—. Author: Motion of Venus, 1958, Coordinates of Ceres, Pallas, Juno and Vesta, 1969; editor: (with V.G. Szebehely) Methods in Celestial Mechanics, 1966, Dynamics of the Solar System, 1979; (with D. Dvorak and P.J. Message) The Stability of Planetary Systems, 1984; assoc. editor: Fundamentals of Cosmic Physics, 1971; exec. editor: Celestial Mechanics, 1977-85; contbr. articles to profl. jours. Fellow Royal Astron. Soc., AAAS (sect. chmn.); assoc. fellow AIAA; mem. Internat. Astron. Union (pres. com. on ephemerides), Minor Planet 3368 named Duncombe, 1988), Am. Astron. Soc. (chmn. div. dynamical astronomy 1970), Inst. Navigation (councillor 1960-64, v.p. 1964-66, pres. 1966-67, Superior Achievement award 1967, Hays award 1975), ASME (sponsor applied mechanics div. 1968-70), Internat. Assn. Insts. Nav. (v.p.), Assn. Computing Machinery, Sigma Xi. Home: 1804 Vance Cir Austin TX 78701-1035 Office: U Tex Dept Aerospace Engring Austin TX 78712

DUNDAS, PHILIP BLAIR, JR., lawyer; b. Middletown, Conn., Apr. 29, 1948; s. Philip Blair and Madolyn Margaret Dundas; m. Elizabeth Anne Adorno, Aug. 9, 1969; children: Philip Blair III, Chapman P. BA, Wesleyan U., Conn., 1970; JD, Washington and Lee U., 1973. Bar: N.Y. 1974. Assoc. Shearman & Sterling, N.Y.C., 1973-81, ptnr., 1981—, ptnr. in charge of Abu Dhabi, United Arab Emirates Office, 1981—. Mem. ABA, Internat. Bar Assn., N.Y. State Bar Assn., Assn. Bar City N.Y., Union Internationale des Avocats, Clinton Country Club. Home: 599 Lexington Ave New York NY 10022-6030

DUNDES, ALAN, writer, folklorist, educator; b. NYC, Sept. 8, 1934; s. Maurice and Helen (Rothschild) D.; m. Carolyn M. Browne, Sept. 8, 1958; children: Alison, Lauren, David. BA, Yale U., 1955, MAT., 1958; PhD, Ind. U., 1962. Instr. English U. Kans., 1962-63; asst. prof. anthropology U. Calif., Berkeley, 1963-65, assoc. prof., 1965-68, prof. anthropology and folklore, 1968—. Author: The Morphology of North American Indian Folktales, 1964, Analytic Essays in Folklore, 1975, Essays in Folkloristics, 1978, Interpreting Folklore, 1980, Life is Like a Chicken Coop Ladder: A Portrait of German Culture Through Folklore, 1984, Cracking Jokes: Studies of Sick Humor Cycles and Stereotypes, 1987, Parsing Through Customs: Essays by a Freudian Folklorist, 1987, Folklore Matters, 1989 From Game to War and Other Psychoanalytic Essays on Folklore, 1997, Two Tales of Crow and Sparrow: A Freudian Folkloristic Essay on Caste and Untouchability, 1997, Holy Writ as Oral Lit: The Bible as Folklore, 1999, The Shabbat Elevator and Other Sabbath Subterfuges: An Unorthodox Essay on Circumventing Custom and Jewish Character, 2002, Bloody Mary in the Mirror: Essays in Psychoanalytic Folkloristics, 2002, Fables of the Ancients? Folklore in the Qur'an, 2003; co-author: La Terra in Piazza: An Interpretation of the Palio of Siena, 1975, Urban Folklore from the Paperwork Empire, 1975, The Art of Mixing Metaphors: A Folkloristic Interpretation of the Netherlands Proverbs of Pieter Bruegel the Elder, 1981, First Prize: Fifteen Years! An Annotated Collection of Romanian Political Jokes, 1985, When You're Up to Your Ass in Alligators: More Urban Folklore from the Paperwork Empire, 1987, Never Try to Teach a Pig to Sing: Still More Urban Folklore from the Paperwork Empire, 1991, Sometimes The Dragon Wins: Yet More Urban Folklore from the Paperwork Empire, 1996, Why Don't Sheep Shrink When It Rains: A Further Collection of Photocopier Folklore, 2000; editor: The Study of Folklore, 1965, Every Man His Way: Readings in Cultural Anthropology, 1968, Mother Wit from the Laughing Barrel: Readings in the Interpretation of Afro-American Folklore, 1972, Varia Folklorica, 1978, The Evil Eye: A Folklore Casebook, 1981, Cinderella: A Folklore Casebook, 1982, Sacred Narrative: Readings in the Theory of Myth, 1984, The Flood Myth, 1988, Little Red Riding Hood: A Casebook, 1989, The Blood Libel Legend: A Casebook in Anti-Semitic Folklore, 1991, The Cockfight: A Casebook, 1994, The Walled-Up Wife: A Casebook, 1996, The Vampire: A Casebook, 1998, International Folkloristics: Classic Contributions by the Founders of Folklore, 1999; co-editor: The Wisdom of Many: Essays on the Proverb, 1981, Oedipus: A Folklore Casebook, 1983, The Wandering Jew: Essays in The Interpretation of a Christian Legend, 1986, Folk Law: Essays in the Theory and Practice of Lex Non Scripta, 1994; compiler: Folklore Theses and Dissertations in the United States, 1976; contbr. articles to Ency. Britannica, Worldbook Ency., The Book of Knowledge, profl. jours. With USNR, 1955-57. Recipient Chgo. Folklore 2d prize 1962, 1st prize 1976, Pitrè Prize, Sigillo d'oro, 1993; Guggenheim fellow, 1966-67, NEH sr. fellow, 1972-74. Mem. AAAS, Am. Folklore Soc. (pres. 1980), Fellows of the Am. Folklore Soc. (pres.) Calif. Folklore Soc., Internat. Soc. Folk Narrative Rsch. Home: 1590 La Vereda Rd Berkeley CA 94708-2036 Office: U Calif Dept Anthropology 201 Kroeber Hall Berkeley CA 94720-3711 *As a psychoanalytic folklorist, my professional goals are to make sense of nonsense, find a rationale for the irrational, and seek to make the unconscious conscious.*

DUNDES, LAUREN, education educator; b. Miami, Fla., May 16, 1962; d. Carolyn and Alan Dundes; m. Michael Streiff; children: Zachary Streiff, Madeline Streiff. BA, Stanford U., 1984; MHS, Johns Hopkins Bloomberg Sch. of Pub. Health, 1986, DSc, 1989. Post-doctoral assoc. Ctr. for Studies in Criminology and Law, U. of Fla., 1989—91; asst. prof. of sociology Goucher Coll., Towson, Md., 1992—96; assoc. prof. of sociology McDaniel Coll., Westminster, Md., 1996—. Coord. of mid. sch. girls mentoring program Fields of Wings of McDaniel Coll., Westminster, Md., 1998—. Author: (book) The Manner Born: Birth Rites in Cross-Cultural Perspective; contbr. articles to profl. jours.; also reference books. Fellow Summer Rsch. fellowship, Nat. Inst. of Justice, 1990; grant; Racial and Ethnic Bias in the Criminal Justice Sys., Racial and Ethnic Bias Study Commn., established by the Fla. Supreme Ct., 1990, 1991, grant; Summer program for youths at-risk in East Balt., State of Md., Dept. of Juvenile Justice, 1996, Johns Hopkins Hosp. Corp. and Cmty. Rels., Goldsmith Family Found., The Chesapeake Bay Trust, The Md. Food Com., 1997, grant; Fields of Wings mentoring program, Carroll County Pub. Schools, 1999—2003. Office: Dept of Sociology McDaniel College 2 College Hill Westminster MD 21157-4390 E-mail: ldundes@mcdaniel.edu.

DUNDON, MARGO ELAINE, museum director; b. Cleve., July 3, 1950; d. Elmer Edward and Ruth Ann (Dreger) Buckeye. BS in Communications,cum laude, Ohio U., 1972; postgrad. in Mus. Studies, U. Okla, 1987. Mem. gen. staff Grout Mus. History and Sci., Waterloo, Iowa, 1974-75, coordinator edn., 1976-78, co-dir., 1979-87, dir., 1988-90; exec. dir. Mus. Sci. and History, Jacksonville, Fla., 1990-99, pres., 1999—. Apptd. grievance com. Fla. Bar 4th Jud. Cir., 2002—. Chairperson Waterloo Hist. Preservation Commn., 1987—88; cultural com. Visitors and Conv. Bur., Waterloo, 1988—90, My Waterloo Days, 1982, 1983; mem. Jacksonville Women's Network, Non-Profit Execs. Round Table, 1990—95; bd. dirs. Resource Plus, Waterloo-Cedar Falls, Iowa, 1986—88, CJI, Girls Inc. of Jacksonville, 1994—95, Ritz Theater & LaVilla Mus., 1998—2000, Jacksonville and the Beaches Conv. and Vis. Bur., 2001—. Am. Law Inst.-ABA scholar, 1979, 86; recipient Mayor's Vol. Performance award, Waterloo, 1983, Vol. award Gov. of Iowa, 1990. Mem.: Iowa Mus. Assn. (pres. 1984—86), Fla. Attractions Assn. (bd. dirs. 1997—98), Fla. Assn. Mus. (pres. 1995—96), Southeast Mus. Conf., Midwest Mus. Conf. (pres. 1988—90), Am. Assn. Mus. (site surveyor mus. assessment program 1982—, site examiner mus. accreditation commn. 1987—, regional councilor 1988—90, Peer Reviewer award 2000), Jacksonville C. of C., Quota Club (pres. 1982), Rotary. Avocations: snorkeling, scuba diving, travelling, gardening. Office: Mus Sci & History 1025 Museum Cir Jacksonville FL 32207-9053 *Share your life with a cat. When life is cold and hard edged, a cat is warm and soft. Cats do not fawn over our successes or judge us lacking for our failures. Cats remind us of the importance of life's simple gifts: a good meal, a warm nap, a relaxing bath, and an interesting bird at the window. For balance, there is nothing like living with a cat.*

DUNDZILA, RUDRA VILIUS, language educator, minister; b. Chgo., Oct. 22, 1962; s. Antanas Vytautas Dundzila and Dalia Joana Povilaitis. BA, U. Ill., Chgo., 1982, MA, 1985; PhD, U. Wis., Madison, 1991; MPS, Loyola U., Chgo., 2002. Ordained seniunas elder Lithuanian Ethnic Ch., 1991. Postdoctoral rsch. Vilnius (Lithuania) U., 1991; vis. docent Vytautas Magnus U., Kaunas, Lithuania, 1991—92; mgr. Images of the World, Chgo., 1993—95; DDP specialist Kemper, Long Grove, Ill., 1995—97; cons. Andersen Consulting, Northbrook, Ill., 1997—99; asst. prof. occupl. devel. Truman Coll., Chgo., 1999—; trainer Comp USA, Skokie, Ill., 1992—93; instr. Beloit Coll., Wis., 1989—91; tchg. asst. Univ. Wis., 1990—91; instr. Madison Area Tech Coll., 1990—91, Berlitz Language Ctr., Chgo., 1984—85; tchr. Chgo. Lithuanian High Sch., 1981—82. Pres. Lithuanian Ethnic Ch. Romuva of U.S., Chgo., 1992—2002; chaplain AIDS Pastoral Care Network, Chgo., 1999—. Author: books; contbr. articles to profl. jours. Fellow: Assn. Advancement of Baltic Studies (sec.-treas. 1994—97). Office: Truman College 1145 W Wilson Ave Chicago IL 60660 Office Fax: 773-907-4464. E-mail: rdundzila@ccc.edu.

DUNE, STEVE CHARLES, retired lawyer; b. Vithkuqi, Korca, Albania, June 15, 1931; s. Costa Pappas and Evanthia (Vangel) D.; m. Irene Duff Boudreau, Sept. 4, 1955; children: Michelle Dune Gesky, Christopher Michael. AB, Clark U., 1953; JD, NYU, 1956. Bar: N.Y. 1957. Law clk. U.S. Ct. Appeals 1st Cir., 1956-57; from assoc. to ptnr. Cadwalader, Wickersham & Taft, N.Y.C., 1957-95; counsel Albanian-Am. Enterpise Fund, 1995-96. Trustee Clark U., Worcester, Mass., 1974-86, 93-97, hon. trustee, 1997-2001, vice-chmn. bd. dirs., 1980-84, chmn. bd. dirs., 1984-86, chmn. presdl. search com., 1983-84, mem. pres.'s coun., 1987-90; dir. Albanian Children Fund, 1998-2002, chmn. Albanian-Am. C. of C., 1995-96. Recipient Disting. Svc. award, Clark U. Alumni Assn., 2003; Root-Tilden scholar, 1953—56. Mem.: ABA (divsn. sr. lawyers), Assn. Bar City NY, NY State Bar Assn. (com. on Ea. European affairs 1992—95, admiralty com. 1976—79, 1987—90), India House, Phi Beta Kappa. Home and Office: PO Box 456 98 Barrett Hill Rd Brooklyn CT 06234-1500 E-mail: scdune@snet.net. *Commitment, determination and perseverance are a person's best allies in solving any problem, meeting any challenge and realizing upon any opportunity of life.*

DUNEA, GEORGE, nephrologist, educator; b. Craiova, Rumania, June 1, 1933; came to U.S., 1964; s. Charles L. and Gerda (Low) D.; 1 dau., Melanie. MD, U. Sydney, Australia, 1957. Diplomate Am. Bd. Internal Medicine, Am. Bd. Nephrology. Intern Royal North Shore Hosp., Sydney, 1958-59; resident in internal medicine Australia and Eng., 1959-63; fellow in nephrology Cleve. Clinic, Presbyn.-St. Luke's Hosp., Chgo., 1964-66; practice internal medicine specializing in nephrology Chgo., 1972—; attending physician Cook County Hosp., Chgo., 1966—, dir. dept. nephrology-hypertension, 1969—; prof. medicine U. Ill., Chgo., 1986—; exec. dir. Hektuen Inst. of Med. Rsch., 1991—. Vis. prof. medicine Rush Med. Sch., Chgo., 1976—. Contbr. chpts. to books, articles to profl. pubs. Fellow A.C.P., Royal Coll. Physicians (London, Edinburgh); mem. AMA, Am. Soc. Nephrology, Brit. Med. Assn., Soc. Med. History. Home: 222 E Chestnut St Chicago IL 60611-2360 Office: 1835 W Harrison St Chicago IL 60612-3701 E-mail: geodunea@aol.com.

DUNFEE, THOMAS WYLIE, law educator; b. Huntington, W.Va., Nov. 15, 1941; s. Wylie Ray and Chloe Edith (Wylie) D.; m. Dorothy Jane Taylor, Aug. 26, 1967; children: John Wylie, Jennifer Sue, Shannon Elizabeth. AB, Marshall U., 1963; JD, NYU, 1966, LLM, 1969. Instr. N.Y. Inst. Tech., 1965-68; asst. prof. Ill. State U., Normal, 1968-70, Ohio State U., Columbus, 1970-72, assoc. prof., 1972-74; assoc. prof. legal studies Wharton Sch., U. Pa., Phila., 1974-79, prof., 1979—, Kolodny prof. social responsiblity, 1982—, chmn. dept. legal studies, 1980-84, 87-91, dir. Wharton ethics program, 1995-96, dir. Zicklin Ctr. for Bus. Ethics Rsch., 1997-2000, vice dean, 2000—03. Vis. prof. U. Fla., 1989, U. Newcastle, Australia, 1981, 85, Georgetown U., 1994, U. Mich., 2000; cons. United Way of Am., McGraw-Hill, Ind. Stds. Bd., Citibank, GM, Honda, GlaxoSmithKline, AT&T. Author: Business and Its Legal Environment, 1992, Modern Business Law, 1996; co-editor: Business Ethics: Japan and the Global Economy, 1993; co-author: (with Thomas Donaldson) Ethics in Business and Economics, 2 vols., 1997, Ties That Bind: A Social Contracts Approach to Business Ethics, 1999; editor-in-chief Am. Bus. Law Jour., 1976-79; contbr. articles to profl. jours. Grantee Exxon Found., 1985-86, Kemper Found., 1993. Mem. Acad. Legal Studies in Bus. (pres. 1989-90, Disting. Sr. Faculty award for Excellence 1991), Soc. Bus. Ethics (pres. 1995-96). E-mail: dunfeet@wharton.upenn.edu.

DUNGAN, GLORIA KRONBECK, critical care nurse; b. Little Falls, Minn., July 4, 1938; d. Hans Emil and Marie (Hahn) Kronbeck; divorced; 1 child, Kirk. Diploma, Abbott Hosp. Sch. Nursing, Mpls., 1958; BS in Nursing, U. Alaska, 1978. CCRN. Nurse at hosps., Mpls., Anchorage, 1958-63; staff nurse, charge nurse Narrabri (Australia) Hosp., 1963-64; night supr., staff nurse, charge nurse Providence Hosp., Anchorage, 1964-65; night supr., staff nurse Anchorage Community Hosp., 1966-67, Greater Juneau Borough Hosp., Juneau, Alaska, 1968-69; asst. head nurse nights intensive care unit Providence Hosp., Anchorage, 1970-77; staff nurse Alaska Nurses Registry, Anchorage, 1977-78; from nurse mgr. to staff nurse intensive care unit Providence Hosp., Anchorage, 1978-83; staff nurse intensive care unit King Fahd Mil. Hosp., Jeddah, Saudi Arabia, 1983-84; staff nurse intensive care Providence Hosp., Anchorage, 1984-90; staff nurse critical care Am. Critical Care Svcs., Anchorage, 1990-92, Humana Hosp. Alaska, Anchorage, 1992, Alaska Native Med. Ctr., 1992-2000, ret., 2000. Mem. Sigma Theta Tau.

DUNGAN, JOHN RUSSELL, JR., (TITULAR VISCOUNT, DUNGAN OF CLARE, HEREDITARY PRINCE OF ERMOY AND ARRA), anesthesiologist, health facility administrator; b. Boston, Dec. 12, 1953; s. John Russell and Nancy Pauline (Beaton) Dungan; m. Nancy Elizabeth Perkins, July 12, 1986 (div. 1997); children: Elizabeth Adelaide, Thayer Warren, Eleanor Grace Appleton. AB magna cum laude, Harvard U., 1977, EdM, 1978; DDS, Baylor U., 1984; MD cum laude, Creighton U., 1989. Diplomate Nat. Bd. Anesthesiology (dir. 1989-92, 97-, v.p. 1997-), Am. Acad. Pain Mgmt. Instr. anesthesiology Boston U. Sch. Medicine, 1986-89; attending staff anesthesiologist, residency instr. Boston City Hosp., 1986-89; anesthesiologist, chief Tobey Hosp., Wareham, Mass., 1989-91; chief anesthesia Mary Lanning Hosp., Hastings, Nebr., 1991—, chief surgery, 1995, 2001; pres. Hastin[gs Anesthesi]ology Assocs., 1992—. Chmn. pharmacy and therapeutics, 1993[—]. Author: (book) The Kings of the Picts and Dál Riads, 1976, The B[...] Angus MacDonald, 1977; contbr. articles to profl. jours. Rsc[h. ...] Restoration of Celbridge Chapel and Cemetery, Kildarie, Ireland, [...] to, Honorable Order Ky. Cols.; head and comdr., Mil. Order Knigh[ts ...] John Eliot scholar, 1967, Nat, Merit scholar, 1971, Harvard [...] 1975—77, John Harvard scholar, 1976. Mem.: Soc. Interv[entional Pain] Physicians (pres. 2003—), Adams County Med. Soc. (pres. 200[...]) Anesthesiologists, Am. Soc. Anesthesiologists, Cum Laude Soc., United Empire Loyalists Assn. (Can.), New Eng. Hist. Geneal. S[oc. ...] History Roundtable, English-Speaking Union U.S. (Internat. fello[w ...]) N.Y. Biog. and Geneal. Soc., Harvard Club Nebr., Clan Dungan [...] pres. 1998—), Wild Geese, Old Tonbridgian Soc., Hasty Puddin[g ...] Phi Beta Kappa. Republican. Episcopalian. Avocations: medieval [...] british history research, family history. Home: Heartwell Park 92[34] Hastings NE 68901-4021 Office: Hastings Anesthesiology Ste 101 [...] Hastings NE 68901-7551

DUNGAN, WILLIAM JOSEPH, JR., insurance broker, economi[c ...]; b. New London, Conn., Mar. 19, 1956; s. William Joseph and Alph[...] D.; m. Janet Dudek, May 28, 1983. BS in Biology, Old Dominion [U. ...] postgrad. in Econs., 1978-80; postgrad., U. Pa., 1984-85, Coll. for Fin. [Planning ...] 1983-84; MS in Fin. Svcs., Am. Coll., 1988, MS in Mgmt., 199[...] chartered fin. cons., cert. fund. specialist. Rep. Prudential Ins. Co., Nor[folk ...] 1979-80; assoc. Russ Gills and Assocs., Virginia Beach, Va., 1980-8[...] Tidewater C.C., Virginia Beach, Va., 1979-86; v.p. life and employee [...] Henderson & Phillips Inc., Norfolk, Va., 1988—; founding prin. Fi[n. ...] Resources, 1987—. Instr. employee benefits and econs. Inst. Mgmt. [...] Dominion U., 1988—, chmn. cert. employee benefit specialists adv. bd.; [...] employee benefits U. Va., 2000—; instr. CEBS program U. Va., 2000—; [...] dirs. Epilepsy Assn. Va.; trustee Old Dominion U. Ednl. Found., 1991-9[...] Epilepsy Assn. Va.; treas. Hampton Roads Youth Hockey Assn., 1999-94 [...] Internat. Assn. Fin. Planning (pres. Hampton Rds. chpt.), Nat. Assn. [...] Underwriters, Assn. for Advanced Life Underwriting, Inst. Cert. Fin. Plann[ers ...] Inst. Cert. Employee Benefits Specialists, Am. Soc. CLUs, Norfolk Assn. L[ife] Underwriters (bd. dirs.), Monarch Bus. Soc., Old Dominion Univ.'s Ins. a[nd] Fin. Svcs. Ctr., Epilepsy Assn. Va. (bd. dirs.), Million Dollar Round Tab[le]. Republican. Avocations: tennis, travel, reading. Home: 4201 Mercedes [...] Virginia Beach VA 23455-5649 Office: Henderson & Phillips Inc 235 E Plum [...] St Norfolk VA 23510-1755

DUNGY, KATHRYN R. humanities educator; b. Stanford, Calif., Sept. 21, 1969; d. Claibourne I. and Madgetta Thornton Dungy; life ptnr. Timothy Voigt. BA magna cum laude, Spelman Coll., Atlanta, 1991; MA, Duke U., Durham, N.C., 1993, PhD, 2000. Vis. lectr. U. of Vt., Burlington, 1999—2000, asst. prof. Latin Am. and Caribbean history, 2000—. Author: (jour.) The So. Friend: Jour. of the N.C. Friends Hist. Soc., (dissertation) A Fusion of the Races: Free People of Color and the Growth of Puerto Rican Soc., 1795-1848; contbr. book; biographical compiler (book) To Conserve a Legacy: American Art from Historically Black Colleges and Universities. Fellow Minority Fellowship, Dana Found., 1989—91, Ford Found. Predoctoral Fellowship for Minorities, Ford Found., 1991—94, Latin Am. Studies Fellowship, Duke U., 1994—96; grantee Tinker Found. Summer Rsch. Grant, 1993, George Washington Henderson Fellowship, U. of Vt., 1998—99, Travel Grant, Women's Studies Program, U. of Vt., 2001; scholar Internat. Student Identity Card Scholarship, CIEE, 1989—90, Fgn. Study Scholarship, Spelman Coll./Charles A. Merrill Found., 1989—90. Mem.: Pres's. Coun. on Racial Equality (co-chair 2000—02, Outsanding Faculty Diversity award 2002), Am. Hist. Assn., Caribbean Studies Assn., Assn. of Caribbean Historians, Mortar Bd. Sr. Honor Soc., Sigma Delta Epsilon Spanish Honor Soc. (v.p., spelman coll. chpt. 1990—91), Phi Alpha Theta History Honor Soc. (life; pres., spleman coll. chpt. 1990—91), Delta Sigma Theta Sorority, Inc. Avocations: photography, travel. Office: U of Vt 133 So Prospect Wheeler House Burlington VT 05403 Office Fax: 802-656-8794. Personal E-mail: kathryn.dungy@uvm.edu.

DUNGY, TONY, professional football coach; b. Jackson, Mich., Oct. 6, 1955; Def. asst. Pitts. Steelers, 1981-83, def. back coach, 1982-83, def. coord., 1984-88; def. backs coach Kansas City Chiefs, 1989-91; def. coord. Minn. Vikings, 1992-95; head coach Tampa Bay (Fla.) Buccaneers, 1996—2001, Indpls. Colts, 2002—. Mem. Super Bowl Championship Team, 1978. Office: Indianapolis Colts 7001 West 56th Street Indianapolis IN 46254

DUNHAM, ARCHIE WALLACE, petroleum and chemical products company executive; b. 1938; BS, MBA, U. Okla. Assoc. engr. Conoco Inc., 1966—73, mgr. gas prodn., 1978—81, v.p. logistics and downstream planning, 1981—83, v.p. transp. natural gas, gas products, 1983—85, exec. v.p. div., 1985; exec. v.p. Douglas Oil Co., 1976—79, pres., 1979; group v.p. chems. and pigments E.I. du Pont de Nemours & Co., Wilmington, Del., 1987—96; v.p. Exploration Products, Houston, 1992—96; pres., CEO Conoco Inc., Houston, 1996—, chmn., 1999—. Bd. dirs. LA Pacific Corp., Phelps Dodge Corp., Union Pacific Corp., API, Energy Inst. of Ams. Bd. dirs. Smithsonian Inst.; trustee George Bush Presdl. Libr. Found. Recipient Horatio Alger award, 2001, inducted in Okla. Hall of Fame, 1998. Office: ConocoPhillips 600 N Dairy Ashford Houston TX 77079-1175

DUNHAM, BENJAMIN STARR, editor, art association administrator; b. N.Y.C., Sept. 19, 1944; s. George Roscoe and Portia Elizabeth (Play[...]) Dunham; m. Wendy H. Rolfe, Apr. 12, 1986; 1 child, Samuel Edward Rolf[e ...] Mimi Cox, Sept. 9, 1978 (div.). BA, Harvard U., 1966; postgrad., Bosto[n ...] 1970, Cath. U., 1971-73. Asst. editor Music Educators Jour., Washi[ngton], 1967-70; editor Symphony News, Vienna, 1971-78; dir. spl. projects Ch[amber] Music Soc. Lincoln Ctr., N.Y.C., 1982; exec. dir. Chamber Music Am., [...] 1978-82, Am. Symphony Orch., N.Y.C., 1982-84; exec. v.p. Nat. Music [...] N.Y.C., 1984-90; editor Am. Recorder, 1990—2002, Early Music A[m. ...] 2002—. Cons. to TV, fundraising and mktg. in chamber music, pubs. [...] pvt. tchr. recorder, 1971—78; mem. music faculty Trinity Coll., W[...] 1973—75; pvt. tchr. recorder MusciCo-op, Wareham, Mass., 1986 [...] berry Concerts, 1993—; cons. on period instrument orch. program [...] Mellon Found., 1989—91; lectr. in field. Contbr. articles to profl. [...] recorder performer: Handel Festival Orch., 1977—78. Mem. Warek[...] Humanities Coun., 1986—90, 1992—94; Hist. Dist. Commn. [...] 1986—97; bd. dirs. Marion Art Ctr., 1996—99; Sippican Elem. [...] 1998—2001. Named Arts Adminstr. of the Yr., Arts Mgmt. Mag., [...] Mem.: Am. Recorder Soc. (bd. dirs. 1984—89), Nat. Guild C[...] (trustee 1982—87), Early Music Am. (bd. dirs. 1988 [...] 2000—02, treas. 1993—95).

DUNHAM, BYRON S. writer; b. Toledo, Apr. 1, 1940; s. Be[...] Priser Dunham. Student, Kenyon Coll., 1958—61; PhB in Hi[...] ern U., 1973. Reporter, photographer U.S. Army, Ft. Bennin[g ...] staff writer The Toledo Blade, 1965—68; asst. editor Rotari[an ...] Ill., 1968—72, mng. editor, 1972—78; convention stage m[...] Evanston, 1973—78; publicity dir. Savannah (Ga.) Sy[...] Author: (short stories) Genre Mag., 2000 (Nat. Mag. a[...] Western Publs. Assn., 2001), (novellas) Tales of Teddy, [...] coun. U. Ill. Found. Mem.: Nat. Trust for Hist. Pres[...] Episcopalian. Avocations: patron and collector of modern [...] RR enthusiast. Home: 15 Monastery Rd W Savannah [...]

DUNHAM, CHRISTOPHER SCOTT, librarian; b. [...] Curtis Lee and Susan Ingrid (Meyer) D.; m. Colleen Ma[...] (div. Apr. 2002). BA, Rutgers U., 1986, MLS, 1994. [...] Am., Denville, N.J., 1987-91; trips dir. Citta Scout R[...] Barnegat, N.J., 1991, aquatics dir., asst. camp dir., 199[...] New Brunswick, NJ, 1992-94, reference libr., 1993-[...] Newton, N.J., 1993-97, Montclair State U., Upper M[...] electronic resources libr. Passaic County C.C., Paters[on ...] ence and interlibr. svcs. libr. Fairfield (Conn.) U., 199[...] U. Sch. Comm. Info. and Libr. Studies Alumni Assn. [...]

Women Lawyers of Franklin County (trustee, treas. 1990-93, 91-92), Am. Health Lawyers Assn., Soc. of Ohio Hosp. Attys., Order of the Coif. Roman Catholic. Avocations: cooking, hiking, camping, reading. Office: Schottenstein Zox & Dunn 41 S High St Ste 2600 Columbus OH 43215-6109 E-mail: cdunlay@szd.com.

DUNLEAVY, MICHAEL JOSEPH, professional basketball coach; b. Brooklyn, NY, Mar. 21, 1954; m. Emily Dunleavy; children: Michael, William Baker, James. Ed., Univ. S.C. Player Phila. 76ers, NBA, 1976-77; former player-coach Carolina Lightning, All-Am. Basketball Alliance; player Houston Rockets, NBA, 1978-83, San Antonio Spurs, NBA, 1982, Milw. Bucks, 1984, asst. coach, to 1990; head coach L.A. Lakers, 1990-92, Milw. Bucks, 1992-93, gen. mgr., v.p. basketball ops., 1993-96; head coach Portland (Oreg.) Trailblazers, 1997—. Office: Portland Trailblazers One Center Ct Ste 200 Portland OR 97227

DUNLOP, DAVID JOHN, geophysics educator, researcher; b. Toronto, Ont., Can., Jan. 30, 1941; s. Harry John Ewart and Mary Scott Dunlop; children: Lisa Karen, Jennifer Michelle; m. Özden Özdemir, June 2, 1987. BASc, U. Toronto, 1963, MA, 1964, PhD, 1968. Postdoctoral studies U. Tokyo, 1968-69; rsch. fellow Université de Paris VI, 1969-70; asst. prof. U. Toronto, 1970-73, assoc. prof., 1973-78, prof., 1978—. Vis. scientist NASA Johnson Space Ctr., Houston, 1972; sr. vis. scientist CSIRO, Sydney, Australia, 1992; assoc. prof. U. Montpellier, France, 1997. Editor: Origin of Thermomagnetism, 1977; assoc. editor Can. Jour. Earth Scis., 1983-94; co-author: Rock Magnetism Fundamentals and Frontiers, 1997, 2d edit., 2001. Killam Found. fellow, Can. Coun., 1983-85, USSR Acad. Scis. fellow, 1988, Sr. Rsch. fellow Tokyo Inst. Tech., 1988-89, DAAD rsch. fellow Munich, 1990; sr. rsch. fellow Kyoto (Japan) U., 1997; recipient Louis Néel medal European Geophys. Soc., 1999. Fellow Royal Soc. Can., Am. Geophys. Union (sect. pres. 1992-94), Geol. Assn. Can. (councillor 1985-87); mem. Can. Geophys. Union (pres. 1985-87; Tuzo Wilson medal 1999). Avocations: canoeing, hiking, lepidoptera, photography, restoring old houses. Office: U Toronto Dept Physics Toronto ON Canada M5S 1A7

DUNLOP, DAVID WALLACE, economist, educator; b. Placerville, Calif., July 6, 1942; s. William Wallace and Sarah Nevada (Ross) D. BS, U. Calif., Berkeley, 1965; MA, Mich. State U., 1969, PhD, 1973. Lectr. dept. agrl. econs. Mich. State U., East Lansing, 1971-72; asst. prof. econs. dept. Vanderbilt U., Nashville, 1972-79; asst. prof. dept. cmty. medicine Meharry Med. Coll., Nashville, 1972-79; economist, health economist U.S. Agy. for Internat. Devel., Washington, 1979-82; vis. prof. dept. community medicine Dartmouth Med. Sch., Hanover, N.H., 1979-82; vis. prof. dept. fin. and econs. and program in health mgmt. Boston U., 1983-86, assoc. rsch. fellow, 1984-92; sr. economist ABT Assocs., Inc., Cambridge, Mass., 1986-88; health economist Econ. Devel. Inst World Bank, Washington, 1988-91, cons. and health economist East Asia region, 1992—95, task mgr. for health programs in Ethiopia and Eritrea, Africa region, 1995—97. Mem. exec. com., bd. govs. Nat. Coun. Internat. Health, Washington, 1984-90; convenor Faculty Forum on Internat. Health, Assn. Univ. Programs in Health Adminstrn., Washington, 1984-88; adj. prof. Sch. of Pub. Health U. North Carolina, 1979-93; adj. prof. dept. community and family medicine Dartmouth Med. Sch., 1982—; health svcs. specialist White River Junction VA Med. Ctr., 2001—; cons. health economist to UK., Japan govts., Asian Devel. Bank, 1999—. Co-editor: Health: What is it Worth?, 1979, An International Assessment of Health Care Financing: Lessons for Developing Countries, 1995; editor Jour. Social Sci. and Medicine, 1977-82. Grantee Midwestern U. Consortium for Internat. Activities, 1970, U.S. Nat. Ctr. for Health Svcs. Rsch., 1975. Mem. Am Econs. Assn., Am. Pub. Health Assn. Avocations: running, hiking, travel. Office: Dartmouth Med Sch Dept Cmty & Family Medicine Strassenburgh Hall Hanover NH 03755

DUNLOP, DOROTHY D. statistician; BS, Wheaton Coll., 1972; MHS, Johns Hopkins U., 1974; PhD, Northwestern U., 1990. Statistician Northwestern U., Evanston, Ill., 1991—. Author: (book) Statistics and Data Analysis, 2000. Mem.: Am. Statis. Assn. (pres. Northeastern Ill. chpt. 2000—00, Chpt. Svc. award 2002).

DUNLOP, EDWARD ARTHUR, computer company executive; b. Wilmington, Del., 1951; s. Edward C. and Eleanor (Smith) D.; m. Gladys Englehart, July 21, 1984; 1 child, Elizabeth. BS, U. Del., 1978, postgrad., 1978-79. Rsch. asst., U. Del., Newark, 1972-78; pres. Technology Logistics, Newark, 1978-85, West Chester, Pa., 1989—; asst. to v.p. Continental Ins. Co., Neptune, N.J., 1985-88; sr. project mgr., asst. to vice chmn. Roy F. Weston Inc., West Chester, 1988-89. Voting mem. Nat. Standards com. on Local and Metro. Area Networks, 1994—; advisor Nat. Computer Security Ctr., U.S. Govt., Nat. Security Agy., Nat. Inst. Stds. and Tech., 1985—. Mem. Coun. on Environ Control State of Del., 1975-81. Univ. fellow bus. and govt. ethics U. Del., 1983-85. Mem. IEEE, IEEE Computer Soc., Assn. for Computing Machinery, Ea. Tech. Coun. Office: Technology Logistics 1265 Estate Dr West Chester PA 19380-1258 E-mail: ed@computer.org.

DUNLOP, FRED HURSTON, lawyer; b. Clarksville, Tenn., May 3, 1946; s. William Barrett and Nelle Major (Hurston) D.; m. Jacqueline Rae Thompson, Aug. 17, 1968; children: Holt McKinney, Lindsay Barrett. BA, Vanderbilt U., 1968, JD, 1971. Bar: Tenn. 1971, Tex. 1972; comml. mediator, arbitration cert. Internat. Ctrs. Arbitration. Assoc. Baker Botts LLP, Houston, 1972—78, ptnr., 1979—. 1st lt. U.S. Army, 1971-72. Fellow Tex. Bar Found.; mem. ABA, Am. Coll. Real Estate Lawyers, State Bar Tex., Houston Bar Assn., Houston Real Estate Lawyers Coun., Coll. of State Bar of Tex. Avocations: golf, hunting, skiing. Home: 5609 Tupper Lake Dr Houston TX 77056-1628 Office: Baker Botts LLP 1 Shell Pla 910 Louisiana St Ste 3100 Houston TX 77002-4916 E-mail: fred.dunlop@bakerbotts.com.

DUNLOP, JOHN BARRETT, foreign language educator, research institution scholar; b. Boston, Sept. 10, 1942; s. John Thomas and Dorothy Emily (Webb) D.; m. Olga Verhovskoy, Sept. 12, 1965; children: Maria, John, Olga, Catherine. BA, Harvard Coll., 1964; MA, Yale U., 1965, PhD, 1973. Prof. Russian Oberlin Coll., Ohio, 1970-83, chmn. dept. German and Russian, 1976-82; sr. fellow Hoover Instn., Stanford U., Calif., 1983—, assoc. dir., 1983-87; editor Chechnya Weekly (Jamestown Found.), Wahington, 2000—02. Mem. Soviet Union in the Eighties Project, CSIS, Georgetown U., 1982-83; mem. Eastern Great Lakes regional selection com. Mellon Fellowships in Humanities, 1982-83, applicant evaluations com. Woodrow Wilson Internat. Ctr. for Scholars, 1989-93; exec. coun. Midwest Slavic Conf., 1977-79; mem. editl. bd. Russian Archives Preservation Project, 1992—; mem. rsch. coun. Internat. Forum Democratic Studies Nat. Endowment for Democracy, 1994—; mem. exec. com. Assn. Study of Nationalities, 1994-97, mem. adv. com., 1997—; mem. steering com. Ctr. Russian and East European Studies Stanford U., 1995-97, 2000—; mem. overseers' com. Vis. to Kathryn W. and Shelby Cullom Davis Ctr. for Russian Studies, Harvard U., 1997-2003; disting. vis. U. Alta., 1995. Author: Staretz Amvrosy, 1972, 2d edit. 1975; The New Russian Revolutionaries, 1976; The Faces of Contemporary Russian Nationalism, 1983, The New Russian Nationalism, 1985, The Rise of Russia and the Fall of the Soviet Empire, 1993, 2d edit. 1995, Russia Confronts Chechnya, 1998; co-editor: Aleksandr Solzhenitsyn, 1973, 2d edit. 1975, Solzhenitsyn in Exile, 1985; editor Chechnya Weekly, 2000-02. Recipient Edward Chandler Cumming prize Harvard Coll., 1964; Woodrow Wilson fellow, 1965, Younger Humanist fellow, 1974-75, Hoover Instn. nat. fellow, 1978-79, Olin vis. sr. Fellow Radio Liberty, Munich, 1991-92; rsch. scholar Kennan Inst., 1987. Mem. Am. Assn. for Advancement of Slavic Studies, Western Slavic Assn. Eastern Orthodox. Office: Stanford U Hoover Instn Stanford CA 94305

DUNLOP, JOHN THOMAS, economics educator, former secretary of labor; b. Placerville, Calif., July 5, 1914; s. John W. and Antonia (Forni) D.; m. Dorothy Webb, July 6, 1937; children: John Barrett, Beverly Claire, Thomas Frederick. AB, U. Calif., 1935, PhD, 1939; LLD, U. Chgo., 1968, U. Pa., 1976, Harvard U., 1987. Acting instr. Stanford U., 1936-37; instr. Harvard U., 1938-45, assoc. prof. econs., 1945-50, prof. econs., 1950-85, Lamont U. prof., 1970-85, dean faculty arts and scis., 1970-73; Served as vice chmn. Boston Regional War Labor Bd., 1944-45; chmn. Nat. Joint Bd. for Settlement of Jurisdictional Disputes in bldg. and constrn. industry, 1948-57. Cons. Office Econ. Stabilization, 1945-47, NLRB, 1948-52, Atomic Energy Labor Panel, 1948-53; mem. bd. inquiry Bituminous Coal Industry, 1950; pub. mem. ESB, 1950-52; mem. Emergency Bds. 109, 130, 167; mem. Presdl. R.R. Commn., 1960-62, Missile Sites Labor Commn., 1961-67, Pres.'s EEOC, 1964-65; impartial chmn. Constrn. Industry Joint Conf., 1959-68; dir. Cost of Living Coun., 1973-74; sec. labor, 1975-76; chmn. Mass. joint com. Mcpl. Police and Fire, 1977—; chmn. Pay Adv. Com., 1979-80, Social Security Coun., 1989-91; chmn. Future Worker/Mgmt. Rels. Com., 1993-95, Mass. Blue Ribbon Commn. on Older Workers, 1997-2000, Att. Gen. internat. adv. com., 1997-2000. Author: Wage Determination under Trade Unions, 1944, Collective Bargaining: Principles and Cases, 1949, 2d edit., 1953, Industrial Relations Systems, 1958, 2d edit., 1993, (with D.C. Bok) Labor and the American Community, 1970, The Lessons of Wage and Price Controls, 1977, Business and Public Policy, 1980, Dispute Resolution: Negotiation and Consensus Building, 1984, The Management of Labor Unions, 1990, (with A.M. Zack) Mediation and Arbitration of Employment Disputes, 1997, (with others) A Stitch in Time, 1999; editor Wertheim Series in Industrial Relations, 1945—. Named to Nat. Housing Hall of Fame; recipient Murray, Meany, Green award AFL-CIO, 1987, gold medal award Nat. Policy Assn., 2000. Mem. Am. Acad. Arts and Scis., Am. Philos. Soc., Inst. Medicine (life), Nat. Acad. Arbitrators, Nat. Acad. Human Resources. Home: 509 Pleasant St Belmont MA 02478-3238 Office: Harvard U 208 Littauer Ctr Cambridge MA 02138

DUNLOP, MARIANNE, retired English as second language educator; b. Niobrara, Nebr, Mar. 14, 1933; d. Harvey Wesley LaBranche and Karen Sanna Arneson; m. Richard Campbell Dunlop, Apr. 26, 1959; 1 child, Christopher Campbell. BA, Vt. Coll., 1985, MA, 1989. Bd. dir./bd. mem. The Sargent House Mus., Gloucester, Mass., 1992-96; ESL educator Penasquitos Laubach Literacy Ctr., San Diego, 1999—2002; ret., 2002. Author: (book) Judith Sargent Murray: Champion of Social Justice, 1993; editor: (book) Judith Sargent Murray: Her First 100 Letters, 1995; writer, contbr.: (book) Standing Before Us: Unitarian Universalist Women and Social Reform 1776-1936, 1999; spkr., contbr. (documentary) Judith Sargent Murray: 18th Century Feminist. Officer, bd. dirs. Sargent House Mus., Gloucester, Mass., 1992—96, mem. adv. bd., 1996—; ESL educator Penasquitos Laubach Literacy Ctr., San Diego, 1999—2002; mem. Sargent House Mus. Mem. Virginia Woolf's Outsider Soc., Unitarian Universalist Women's Heritage Soc. Unitarian Universalist. Avocation: honoring otherness. Home: 11032 Ipai Ct San Diego CA 92127-1382

DUNMEYER, SARAH LOUISE FISHER, retired health care consultant; b. Ft. Wayne, Ind., Apr. 13, 1935; d. Frederick Law and Jeanette Blose (Stults) Fisher; m. Herbert W. Dunmeyer, Sept. 9, 1967; children: Jodi, Lisa. BS, U. Mich., 1957; MS, Temple U., 1966; EdD, U. San Francisco, 1983. Lic. clin. lab. technologist, Calif. Instr. med. tech. U. Vt., Burlington, 1966-67, Northeastern U., Boston, 1967-68, instr. lab. asst. program, 1968-70; educator, coord. sch. med. tech. Children's Hosp., San Francisco, 1970-73; dir. course devel. for continuing edn. program Pacific Presbyn. Med. Ctr., San Francisco, 1974-82, project mgr., cons. Peabody Mktg. Decisions, San Francisco, 1983-87; sr. rsch. assoc. Inst. for Health and Aging, U. Calif., San Francisco, 1986-89; rsch. analyst student acad. svcs. U. Calif., San Francisco, 1991-94; external cons. Health Care Consulting Svcs., San Francisco, 1986-97; clin. lab. scientist Kaiser Hosp., San Francisco, 1989—2002, ret. Seminar presenter Am. Assn. Blood Banks, San Francisco, 1976, Am. Soc. Clin. Pathologists, Miami Beach, Fla., 1977, Ann. Meeting of Am. Soc. Med. Technology, Atlanta, 1977; site surveyor Nat. Accrediting Agy. for Clin. Lab. Scis., Chgo., 1974-80. Contbr. articles to profl. jours.

DUNMIRE, WILLIAM WERDEN, writer, photographer, naturalist; b. Alameda, Calif., Feb. 24, 1930; s. Samuel P. Dunmire and Margaret L. (Dickinson) D.; m. Marjorie S. Schoder, June 14, 1954 (div. 1972); children: Glenn E., Peter P.; m. Evangeline L. Blinn, Oct. 17, 1972. BA, U. Calif., 1954, MA, 1957. Chief park naturalist Nat. Park Svc., Badlands Nat. Monument, S.D., 1961-63, Isle Royale Nat. Park, Mich., 1963-66, Yellowstone Nat. Park, Wyo., 1968-72; chief interpretation Nat. Park Svc., Washington, 1973-77; supt. Coulee Dam NRA, Washington, 1977-81, Carlsbad Caverns/Guadalupe Mountains Nat. Parks, N.Mex., 1981-85; N.Mex. pub. lands coord. The Nature Conservancy, Santa Fe, 1985-92; curatorial assoc. Mus. Southwestern Biology, U. N.Mex., 1992—; adj. naturalist N.M. Museum of Natural History & Sci., 1997—; assoc. in biology U. N.Mex., 1998—. Co-author: Wild Plants of the Pueblo Province, 1995, Wild Plants and Native Peoples of the Four Corners, 1997; author more than 60 tech. and popular booklets and articles. Bd. dirs. United Way, Carlsbad, 1981-84, div. chmn., 1983-84. Served to cpl. U.S. Army, 1954-56. Recipient Meritorious Svc. award U.S. Dept. Interior, 1973. Home: 12 Camino A Las Estrellas Placitas NM 87043-8804 E-mail: bdunmire@unm.edu.

DUNN, ADOLPHUS WILLIAM, orthopedic surgeon; b. Eden, N.C., Nov. 23, 1922; s. Adolphus William and Sally Grey (Ivie) D.; m. Doris Margery Nash, June 23, 1945 (div. 1975); children: John B.R., Adolphus W. III; m. Clara Delores Kelly, Sept. 3, 1977 (deceased March 10, 2000). BS, Wake Forest Coll., 1942; MD, Duke U., 1945. Diplomate Am. Bd. Orthopaedic Surgery. Commd. ensign USN, 1943, advanced through grades to capt., 1959, ret., 1965; intern Yale U. Hosp., New Haven, Conn., 1945; resident U.S. Navy Hosp., San Diego, 1948, Bethesda, Md., 1952-53, Children's Hosp., Boston, 1954; chmn. dept. orthopaedic surgery Ochsner Med. Instns., New Orleans, 1965-88; clin. prof. dept. orthopaedics sch. medicine Tulane U., New Orleans, 1965-88; ret., 1988. Contbr. numerous articles to profl. jours. Fellow Am. Acad. Orthopaedic Surgeons (emeritus); mem. Am. Orthopaedic Assn. (emeritus), Phi Beta Kappa. Republican. Avocations: travel, swimming, bicycling, reading. Home: One Kingfisher Cove Saint Helena Island SC 29920

DUNN, ARNOLD SAMUEL, biochemistry educator; b. Rochester, N.Y., Jan. 31, 1929; s. Alexander and Dora (Cohen) D.; m. Doris Ruth Frankel, Sept. 14, 1952; children: Jonathan Alexander, David Hillel. BS, George Washington U., 1950; PhD, U. Pa., 1955; LHD (hon.), Hebrew Union Coll., 1995. Research assoc. Michael Reese Hosp. Research Inst., Chgo., 1955-56; asst. prof. NYU Sch. Medicine, N.Y.C., 1956-62; vis. prof. Weizmann Inst. Sci., Rehovot, Israel, 1972-73, 83-84, Hebrew U., Jerusalem, 1972-73; prof. molecular biology U. So. Calif., Los Angeles, 1962—, dir. molecular biology L.A., 1982-90, assoc. dean, 1990-92; vis. fellow history sci. Princeton U., 1993. Contbr. articles to profl. jours.; mem. editorial bd.: Am. Jour. Physiology, 1979—, Analytical Biochemistry, 1980— . Recipient award for Teaching Excellence U. So. Calif., 1969; recipient award for Research Excellence U. So. Calif., 1972, Raubenheimer award U. So. Calif., 1981; UPSHS fellow, 1972, 83; Meyerhoff fellow Weizmann Inst. Sci., 1983 MEm. Am. Physiol. Soc., Am. Soc. Biol. Chemists, Endocrine Soc., Phi Beta Kappa, Sigma Xi, Phi Kappa Phi, Golden Key. Office: U So Calif University Park Los Angeles CA 90089-0001

DUNN, BERNARD DANIEL, former naval officer, consultant; b. Providence, Feb. 10, 1934; s. Alexander Gerard and Mary Alice (Fitzpatrick) D.; m. Hilda Hughes Tunney, Jan. 4, 1958; children: Bernard Daniel Jr., Brian Lindsay, Mary Catherine, J. Alexander. BS in Econs., Villanova U., 1956; MBA in Transp., Mich. State U., 1971. Commd. ensign USN, 1956, advanced through grades to capt.; asst. supply and disbursing officer USS Rushmore, Little Creek, Va., 1957-58; asst. material divsn. officer, stock control divsn. officer Sub Base New London, Groton, Conn., 1958-61; material and fiscal divsn. supt. Ship Repair Facility, Guam, 1961-63; nuclear weapons material divsn. officer Naval Supply Ctr., Oakland, Calif., 1963-64; supply ops. officer Nuc. Weapons Supply Annex, Oakland, Calif., 1964-65; commn. supply officer USS Fox, 1965-68; project officer Naval Supply Sys. Command, Washington, 1968-70; asst. for sea transp. Office Chief Naval Ops., Washington, 1971-73; sr. mem. Mobile Tng. Team to Colombian Navy, Bogota, Colombia, 1973; dir. warehousing, chief transp. office Def. Depot, Tracy, Calif., 1973-76; dep. project mgr., Navy rep. Joint Container Steering Group Office of Sec. of Def., Washington, 1976-77; dir. transp. field ops. divsn. Naval Supply Sys. Command, Washington, 1977-78; head transp. mgmt. and policy br. Office Chief Naval Ops., Washington, 1978-83; comptr./dir. supply Naval Edn. and Tng. Command, Newport, R.I., 1983-85; A-76 program officer Mil. Sealift Command, Washington, 1985; acting dir./chief staff commn. on Merchant Marine and Def., Alexandria, Va., 1985-88; bd. dirs., corp. sec. Greenwich Ctr., Inc., East Greenwich, RI, 1988—2002. Cons., Alexandria, Va., 1988-91; chief program analyst Resource Cons., Inc., Vienna, Va., 1991-94, sr. supply specialist, 97-98. Life mem. East Greenwich (R.I.) Fire Dept., 1953—. Decorated Def. Meritorious Svc. medal, Meritorious Svc. medal, Joint Svc. Commendation medal with oak leaf cluster, Navy Meritorious Unit commendation, Air Force Outstanding Unit award, Humanitarian medal, Nat. Def. Svc. medal, Vietnam Svc. medal with one bronze star, Rep. of Vietnam Campaign medal. Mem. U.S. Naval Inst., Nat. Def. Transp. Assn. (pres. San Joaquin chpt. 1974-75), USCG Acad. Found., East Greenwich Vets. firemen Assn., Mil. Officers Assn., Washington Area Supply Corps Assn., Naval Submarine League, USS Rushmore Assn. (founder and charter mem., assoc. treas.1995-2001). Roman Catholic. Avocations: stamp collecting, ice hockey, running, volunteer fireman, golf. Home: 5817 Shalott Ct Alexandria VA 22310-1427 E-mail: bddunn@erols.com.

DUNN, BONNIE BRILL, chemist; b. Bethesda, Md., Mar. 10, 1953; m. William H Dunn, July 13, 1974 (div.); children: Daniel Brill, Vanessa Thompson; m. Ronald G Manning, Aug. 2, 1996. AA, Montgomery Coll., 1972; BS in Food Sci., U. Md., 1974, MS in Food Chemistry and Stats., 1978, PhD in Food Chemistry, 1982. Rsch. asst. U. Md., College Park, 1976-79, tchg. asst., 1977-80; rschr. divsn. chemistry and physics U.S. FDA, Washington, 1979; statistian USDA, Beltsville, Md., 1980, rschr., 1980-82; radiochemist Positron Emission Tomography; head quality assurance NIH, Bethesda, 1984-93; rev. chemist FDA, Rockville, Md., 1993-95, expert scientist, 1996, dep. dir. divsn. new drug chemistry, 1996—2003; scientfic review adminstr. NIH, Bethesda, Md., 2003—. Mem adv bd on intramural woman scientists NIH, rev. ad admin., Md., 2003—. Contbr. articles to profl jours. Secy, vpres PTA, 1988—94; mem PTA Forest Knolls Elem, Montgomery County, Md., 1988—94; mem exec bd dirs PTA Eastern Mid Sch, Montgomery County, Md., 1992—94; leader Girl Scouts US, 1988—91; bd dirs Olney Children Ballet Theater, 1996—99. Recipient Performance Award, NIH, 1987—92, USPHS, 1993—96; fellow Nat Leadership, 1997—98. Mem.: Soc Nuclear Med, Am Chemistry Soc. Home: 9901 Indian Ln Silver Spring MD 20901-2521 Office: NIH 6707 Democracy Blvd Bethesda MD 20892-0001 Business E-Mail: dunnbo@mail.nih.gov.

DUNN, BOYD, mayor, lawyer; m. Nancy Dunn; children: Andrew, Kevin. BA, JD, Ariz. State U. Bar: Ariz. 1979. Mem. Chandler City Coun., 1994—2002; pvt. practice; mayor City of Chandler, Ariz., 2002—. Mem. East Valley Behavioral Health Assn., Maricopa Assn. Govts. Regional Devel. Policy Com., Airport Commn.; mem., past chmn. Planning & Zoning Commn.; liaison City of Chandler's Fin., Pub. Safety & Cmty. Svcs. Coms. Treas., bd. dirs. Phoenix Coun. Navy League; bd. dirs. Downtown Chandler Cmty. Partnership, Greater Phoenix Econ. Coun. Mem.: Christian Legal Soc., Ariz. State U. Alumni Assn. Office: 55 N Arizona Pl Ste 301 Chandler AZ 85225 E-mail: boyd.dunn@ci.chandler.az.us.*

DUNN, BRUCE SIDNEY, materials science educator; b. Chgo., Apr. 22, 1948; s. George Bernard and Goldye Rosalyn (Opper) D.; m. Wendy Joan Rader, June 7, 1970; 1 child, Julianne. BS in Ceramic Engring., Rutgers U., 1970; MS in Materials Sci., UCLA, 1972, PhD in Materials Sci., 1974. Staff scientist GE, Schenectady, N.Y., 1976-80; assoc. prof. materials sci. UCLA, 1981-85, prof., 1985—, Nippon Sheet Glass chair materials sci., 2003. Cons. to numerous corps.; invited prof. U. Paris, 1986, 91, 92, 93, 98, U. Bordeaux, 2000 Contbr. articles to profl. jours. Fulbright fellow, 1985-86. Fellow Am. Ceramic Soc.; mem. Electrochem. Soc., Materials Rsch. Soc. Achievements include patents in field. Office: UCLA Dept Materials Scis & Engring 6532 Boelter Hl Los Angeles CA 90095-0001

DUNN, CAROLA, writer; b. London, Eng., Apr. 1946; d. Margaret and Max Brauer; 1 child, Joseph. BA, U. Manchester, Eng., 1967. Author: (novels) Toblethorpe Manor, 1981, Lavender Lady, 1983, (novel) Angel, 1984, The Miser's Sister, 1984, Lord Iverbrook's Heir, 1986, The Man in the Green Coat (aka Gabrielle's Gamble), 1987, Smugglers' Summer, 1987, Miss Hartwell's Dilemma, 1988, Black Sheep's Daughter, 1989, A Poor Relation, 1990, Lady in the Briars, 1990, A Susceptible Gentleman, 1990, Two Corinthians, 1990, A Lord for Miss Larkin, 1991, Byron's Child, 1991, Polly and the Prince, 1991, The Fortune Hunters, 1991, The Frog Earl, 1992 (Reviewer's Choice Best Regency Comedy Award of Excellence, 1992), The Road to Gretna, 1992, Miss Jacobson's Journey, 1992, My Lord Winter, 1992, Thea's Marquis, 1993, Ginnie-Come-Lately, 1993, His Lordship's Reward, 1994, The Captain's Inheritance, 1994, Death at Wentwater Court, 1994, The Lady and the Rake, 1995, The Winter Garden Mystery, 1995, The Tudor Secret, 1995, Requiem for a Mezzo, 1996, Damsel in Distress, 1997, The Babe and the Baron, 1997, Mayhem and Miranda, 1997, Murder on the Flying Scotsman, 1997, Dead in the Water, 1998, The Improper Governess, 1998, Crossed Quills, 1998, Styx and Stones, 1999, Rattle His Bones, 2000, To Davy Jones Below, 2001, The Case of the Murdered Muckraker, 2002, Mistletoe and Murder, 2002 (IMBA bestseller), (novels) Die Laughing, 2003, numerous others. Reader SMART, Eugene, 1998—2003. Mem.: Sisters in Crime. Avocations: gardening, reading, walking, travel, dogs. Personal E-mail: carola@sinc-ic.org.

DUNN, CHARLES DEWITT, academic administrator; b. Magnolia, Ark., Dec. 2, 1945; s. Charles Edward and Nora Lucille (Bailey) D.; m. Donna Jane Parsons, Apr. 9, 1966; children: Aimee, James, Joseph, Mary Elizabeth. BA, So. Ark. U., 1967; MA, North Tex. State U., 1970; PhD, So. Ill. U., 1973; cert. inst. ednl. mgmt., Harvard U., 1991. Instr. polit. sci. U. Ark., Monticello, 1969-72, asst. prof., 1972-75; assoc. prof. U. Ctrl. Ark., Conway, 1975-80, prof., 1980—, chmn. dept. polit. sci., 1976-82, dir. govt. rels., 1982-86; pres. Henderson State U., Arkadelphia, Ark., 1986—. Chmn. Commn. for Ark.'s Future, 1989-93; chmn. Ark. Higher Edn. Coun., 1992-96; chmn. fin. com. Ark. Cmty. Found. Bd. Dirs., v.p., 2000-02, pres., 2002-03; active Blue Ribbon Commn. on Pub. Edn., 2001-02. Mem. Am. Assn. State Coll. and Univs., NCAA (pres.'s commn. 1996-97, pres.' coun. 1997-2001, pres. Gulf South conf. 1998-2000), Ark. Polit. Sci. Assn. (pres. 1976-77), Conway C. of C. (bd. dirs. 1984-85, v.p. 1985-86), Arkadelphia C. of C. (bd. dirs. 1987-91), Rotary. Methodist. Office: Henderson State U PO Box 7532 1100 Henderson St Arkadelphia AR 71999-0001 E-mail: cddunn@hsu.edu.

DUNN, CHRISTOPHER JOSEPH, telecommunications industry executive; b. Oak Park, Ill., June 20, 1952; s. Paul Joseph and Kathryn Dooley Dunn; m. Elizabeth Catherine Hanley; children: Christopher Patrick children: John Fitzgerald. BA, U. Ill., Chgo., 1974; MA, U. Chgo., 1976; JD, DePaul U., 1982. Bar: Ill. 1982, U.S. Dist. Ct. (no. dist.) Ill. 1982. Cen. states regional dir. external affairs AT&T Wireless, Chgo., 1995—2003; exec. asst. to adminstr./White House liaison NASA, Washington, 1993—95; search mgr. Office of Presdl. Pers. The White House, Washington, 1993—93; spl. asst. to adminstr./White House liaison U.S. Gen. Svcs. Adminstrn., Washington, 1993—93; dir. state regulatory affairs City of Chgo., 1991—93; gen. counsel U.S. Sen. Paul Simon U.S. Senate, Washington, 1989—91; counsel subcom. on Constn., minority counsel subcom. on juvenile justice U.S. Senate Com. on the Judiciary, Washington, 1985—89; atty. Law Offices Gerhard E. W. Kelter, Jr., Chgo., 1982—85; environmentalist U.S. Dept. Commerce - Econ. Devel. Adminstrn., Chgo., 1977—80. Commr., vice chair Bd. Police and Fire Commrs. - Village of Wilmette, Ill., 1999—; chmn. Govt. Assistance Program at DePaul U., Chgo., 1999—; alt. del. to Dem. Nat. Conv. Ill.'s 10th Congl. Dist., L.A., 2000—00, mem. standing com. on rules Dem. Nat. Conv., Chgo., 1996—96. Roman Catholic. Avocations: travel, reading. Home: 1616 Highland Ave Wilmette IL 60091 Office: AT&T Wireless Ste 4 227 W Monroe Chicago IL 60606

DUNN, CRAIG ANDREW, entertainer, conductor, composer, writer, educator; b. Point Pleasant, N.J., Nov. 11, 1947; s. Andrew Robert and Ruth Agnes (Schott) D.; m. Crystal Lynn Kesler, May 26, 1970. MusB, U. Cin., 1972; MusM, Ohio U., 1973; EdD, Nova Southeastern U., 1996. Cert. tchr., Fla. Dir. bands Greenville (S.C.) Sr. H.S., 1973-74, Bayonne (N.J.) H.S., 1974-75; studio instr. Buddy Rogers Music Studios, Inc., Cin., 1975-78; music specialist, music dir. Diocese of St. Petersburg, Fla., 1979-88; music specialist Sch. Dist. of Hillsborough County, Tampa, Fla., 1988—; performing artist, entertainer, 1972—; mem. faculty music St. Petersburg Coll., Fla., 2001—. Mem. adv. bd. Am. Youth Symphony Band and Chorus, Pitts., 1980-85, artistic advisor, coach, 1980, 83, 85; dir. sch. dance and choral ensembles Fla. State Fair, 1992—. Composer: The Devil's Jester, 1971, Come to Me, 1971, Fishers of Men, 1976, The One-Hundred Fiftieth Psalm, 1976, A Mass for the Feast of the Triumph of the Cross, 1981; contbr. articles to profl. jours. Mem. Music Educators Nat. Conf., Fla. Music Educators Assn., Nat. Acad. Songwriters (pub. composer, author). Avocations: orchestrating, writing, reading. Home: 11800 4th St E Isle of Capri Treasure Island FL 33706

DUNN, DANA-LORI, counselor; b. Covina, Calif., Aug. 6, 1957; d. Lowell Roland Butterfield and Dorothy Jane Whay Butterfield; m. Mark Philip Dunn, Nov. 3, 1979; children: Ian Roland, Brittany Jane. Cert. Program land devel. cmty. planning, U. Calif., Irvine, 1991; PhD in Metaphysics, U. Metaphysics,

Studio City, Calif., 1996. Ordained Metaphys. min. Internat. Metaphys. Ministry, 1995; bd. cert. pastoral counselor; cert. hypnotherapist Am. Bd. Hypnotherapy. Sec. Garrett Airesearch, Torrance, Calif., 1975-78; adminstrv. asst. Panel-Air Corp., Costa Mesa, Calif., 1979-81; exec. sec. Rockwell Internat., Newport Beach, Calif., 1984-86; adminstrv. asst. Las Flores Group, Inc., Dana Point, Calif., 1990-92, Cymbolic Scis. Internat., Aliso Viejo, Calif., 1992-93; acctg. asst. Quigley Ins. Svcs., Mission Viejo, Calif., 1993-95; pvt. practice Aliso Viejo, 1995—. Author: A Leap of Faith: Back to the Garden, 1998, The Power and the Glory of the RAYS, 1998. Active Nat. Campaign for Tolerance. Recipient Bus. award Bank of Am., 1975, Meritorious Achievement award IBC, 2000. Mem. Lucis Trust, United Lodge of Theosophists, Planetary Soc. Republican. Avocations: pianist, composer, hiking, skiing. Home: 23572 El Rio Aliso Viejo CA 92656-1110

DUNN, DAVID B. ambassador; b. Great Falls, Mont. s. Elmer and Marjory Dunn; m. Maria-Elena Dubourt; two children: Tom, Brian. AB, Occidental Coll.; MA, Am. U.; MS, Nat. War Coll. Entered U.S. Fgn. Svc., 1979, dir. for East African Affairs, U.S. State Dept. African Bur., U.S. ambassador to Republic of Zambia, 1999—2002; U.S. Counsel Gen. Johannesburg, 2002—. Office: US Consulate Gen 1 River St Johannesburg South Africa E-mail: DunnDB@state.gov.

DUNN, DAVID CAMERON, entrepreneur, business executive; b. Juneau, Alaska, Dec. 8, 1941; s. Robert Charles and Kay (Watson) D.; m. Karen Ann Leonard, Jan. 17, 1970 (div. 1990); m. Shari Carter, Mar. 10, 2001; children: David Cameron Jr., Paige. BA, Stanford U., 1963; MBA, U. Pa., 1968. Account exec. J. Walter Thompson, N.Y.C., 1968-70; product mgr. Gen. Foods, White Plains, N.Y., 1970-73; dir. mktg. Heublein, San Francisco, 1973-77; exec. v.p. Perelli-Minetti Winery, San Francisco, 1977-79; sr. v.p., bd. dirs. Valchris Farms, Modesto, Calif., 1980-84, DFS Advt., San Francisco, 1984-87; pres. Thomas-Rahm Advt., Oakland, Calif., 1987-89, e-agency, Inc., Oakland, 1990—. Co-founder Re-Con Sys. (OTC) 1968; bd. dirs. PC Guardian, San Rafael, Calif., Leftgrear.com, West Hollywood, Calif. Trustee Oakland Symphony, 1989-90, Orinda (Calif.) Edn. Found., 1986-87; vice chair Oakland Conv. and Visitors Bur., 2003. 1st lt. U.S. Army, 1964-66, Germany. Mem. Oakland C. of C. (Small Bus. of Yr. 1991, Entrepreneur of Yr. 2002). Republican. Roman Catholic. Avocations: coin collecting, rare books. Office: e-agency Inc 299 3rd St Ste 101 Oakland CA 94607-4350

DUNN, DAVID E. university dean; b. Dallas, Oct. 13, 1935; s. Nelson E. and Lemoine (Kellett) Dunn Neal; m. Gretchen Yost, Jan. 24, 1958 (dec. 1987); children: Dusty, Peter; m. Sarah Sue Holmes, Dec. 25, 1990. BS in Geology, So. Meth. U., 1957, MS, 1959; PhD, U. Tex., 1964. Cert. profl. geologist. Instr. geology U. Tex., Austin, 1960-61; asst. prof. geology Tex. Tech. Inst., Lubbock, 1962-63, U. N.C., Chapel Hill, 1963-66, assoc. prof., 1967-73, prof., 1973-79; dean coll. sci. U. New Orleans, 1979-84; dean Sch. Natural Sci. and Math. U. Tex.-Dallas, 1984-97, prof., dean emeritus, 1998—. Cons. various legal firms, N.C., 1967-79, Pennzoil, Houston, 1980-87, Amoco, Houston, 1982-89. Oryx. 1991-92; chmn. La. Univs. Marine Consortium, Baton Rouge, 1981-83; chmn. bd. dirs. Drilling, Observation and Sampling of Earth's Continental Crust Inc. 1991-93; chmn. steering com. VIIth Internat. Symposium on Continental Sci. Drilling, 1994. Co-author: A Characterization of Faults in the Appalachian Foldbelt, 1980; contbr. chpt. to book, articles to sci. jours. Fund-raiser numerous candidates, Chapel Hill, 1969-75. Fellow Geol. Soc. Am. (chmn. structure and tectonics div. 1983, councilor 1985-87, 92-2001, treas. 1992-2001, Disting. Svc. award 2002); mem. AAAS, Am. Geophys. Union, Am. Inst. Profl. Geologists, Geol. Soc. Am. Found. (trustee 2001—), Carolina Geol. Soc. (chmn. 1968-69). Home: 6 Crown Pl Richardson TX 75080-1603 Office: Univ of Tex at Dallas Dept Geoscis PO Box 688 Richardson TX 75083-0688 E-mail: ddunn@utdallas.edu.

DUNN, DAVID JOHN, human resources executive; b. New Hartford, NY, May 24, 1943; s. Leslie Sherwood and Mary Frances (Spreaker) D. BS, Rensselaer Polytech. Inst., 1965; MBA, U. Mo., 1976. Dir. bus. placement U. Mo., Columbia, 1973-76; pres. Am. Med. Mgmt., Inc., Columbia, Mo., 1979-81; v.p. mgmt. services Med. Corp. Am., Kansas City, Mo., 1981-82; dir. corp. devel. Forum Group, Inc., Indpls., 1982-84; v.p. fin. DRG, Inc., Kansas City, 1984-86; v.p. devel. Inst. Tech. Devel. Living Systems div., Oxford, Miss., 1986-87; pres., gen. mgr. Mgmt. Recruiters of Columbia, 1988-94; v.p. Drake Beam Morin Inc., Memphis, 1994-95; mng. dir., sr. v.p. Russell, Montgomery & Assocs., Memphis, 1995-98; mng. dir. Worldwide Selection, LLC, Columbia, Mo., 1998—. Ward committeeman Boone County Rep. Cen. Com., 1985-86. Served to capt. USAF, 1967-73. Recipient NASA Achievement award Apollo Mission Control, 1969; Regents scholar, 1961-65; faculty fellow U. Mo., 1973. Mem. Soc. for Human Resources Mgmt., Rotary. Roman Catholic. Avocations: sailing, aviation. Home and Office: Worldwide Selection PO Box 38562 Colorado Springs CO 80937 E-mail: david@wwselect.com.

DUNN, DAVID JOSEPH, financial executive; b. Bklyn., July 30, 1930; s. David Joseph and Rose Marie (McLaughlon) D.; m. Marilyn Percaccia, June 1955 (div.); children: Susan, Steven, Linda; m. Marilyn Bell, Apr. 1994. BS, U.S. Naval Acad., 1955; MBA, Harvard U., 1961. Investment banker G.H. Walker & Co., N.Y.C., 1961-62; ptnr. J.H. Whitney & Co., N.Y.C., 1962-70; mng. ptnr. Idanta Ptnrs., San Diego, 1971—. Chmn. bd. Iomega Corp., San Diego, Calif., Munchkin, Inc., Van Nuys, Calif.; bd. dirs. Torrex, Livermore, Calif. With USMC, 1950-51, 55-59. Mem. Univ. Club (N.Y.C.), San Diego Yacht Club, LaJolla Country Club, Vintage Club, DelMar Country Club, Glenwild Country Club. Office: Idanta Ptnrs Ste 925 9255 Towne Centre Dr San Diego CA 92121-3066

DUNN, DELMER DELANO, political science educator; b. Sentinel, Okla., Oct. 31, 1941; s. Robert Patrick and Mildred Marion D.; m. Ann Gregg Swinford, May 15, 1971; children— John Swinford, Kielly McKee BA, Okla. State U., 1963; MS, U. Wis., 1964, PhD, 1967. Asst. prof. polit. sci. U. Ga., Athens, 1967-71, assoc. prof., 1971-77, prof., 1977-82, Regents prof., 1982—, dir. Inst. Govt., 1973-82, acting head dept. polit. sci., 1987-88, assoc. v.p. acad. affairs, 1988-91, dir. Inst. Higher Edn., 2001—02; rsch. assoc. The Brookings Instn., Washington, 1969-70. Vis. fellow dept. polit. sci. faculty of arts The Australian Nat. U., Canberra, 1992; v.p. Instruction, 2002-. Author: Public Officials and the Press, 1969, Financing Presidential Campaigns, 1972, Politics and Adminstration at the Top: Lessons from Down Under, 1997 (Charles Levine Book award for best book in pub. policy and adminstrn. 1998); mem. editl. bd. Social Sci. quar., 1988-94; contrbr. articles to profl. jours. Trustee Leadership Ga., 1976-82; pres. Clarke/Oconee unit Am. Cancer Soc., 1981-82, chmn., 1982-83 Mem. AAAS, Am. Polit. Sci. Assn. (Congl. fellow, 1968-69), Nat. Assn. Schs. of Pub. Affairs and Adminstrn. (pres. 1987-88), Am. Soc. Pub. Adminstrn., Pi Alpha Alpha (nat. pres. 1983-85). Presbyterian. Office: Univ Ga Sch Pub and Internat Affairs Athens GA 30602

DUNN, DENNIS STEVEN, artist, illustrator; b. San Diego, Apr. 30, 1951; s. Dean Stanley and Phyllis Marie (Pratt) D.; m. Donna Rae Krogh, Dec. 29, 1973; 1 child, Claire Estelle. BA with distinction, San Diego State U., 1973. Master printer, intaglio Orr's Gallery, San Diego, 1973-74, instr. intaglio, 1974; graphic artist NARF/North Island Naval Air Sta., Coronado, Calif., 1974-76; illustrator NETSCPAC/Naval Tng. Ctr., San Diego, 1976-81, Fleet Combat Tng. Ctr., Point Loma, Calif., 1981-82, FASO Det/Miramar Naval Air Sta., San Diego, 1982-86, DTRA/Kirtland AFB, Albuquerque, 1986—. Life drawing instr. U. N.Mex., Albuquerque, 1986-87. Group exhibits include Traveling Exhbn. to Turkey and Greece, 1975, San Diego Print Club, 1984, Spectrum Gallery, San Diego, 1986, Stables Art Gallery, Taos, N.Mex., 1986, The Wedge Gallery, Rochester, N.Y., 1988, Print Club of Albany, N.Y., 1989, Clary Minor Gallery, Buffalo, 1990, U. Anchorage, 1990, Bradley U., Peoria, Ill., 1991, Artlink Gallery, Ft. Wayne, Ind., 1991, Garret Gallery, St. Louis, 1993; works included in various mags. Recipient Letter of Commendation USN, 1985. Mem. Albuquerque United Artists (bd. dirs. 1987-88), SIGGRAPH. Avocations: composing and editing music, playing and performing renaissance music. Home: 6209 Arvilla Ave NE Albuquerque NM 87110-2651

DUNN, DONALD JACK, law librarian, law educator, dean, lawyer; b. Tyler, Tex., Nov. 9, 1945; s. Loren Jack and Clara Inez (Milam) Dunn; m. Cheryl Jean Sims, Nov. 24, 1967; 1 child, Kevin. BA., U. Tex.-Austin, 1969, MLS, 1972; JD, Western New Eng. Coll., 1983. Asst. to law libr. U. Tex., 1969-72, supervising libr. Criminal Justice Reference Libr., 1972-73; law libr., prof. law Western New Eng. Coll., Springfield, Mass., 1973-96, interim dean, 1996-98, dean, 1998—2001, assoc. dean for libr. and info. resources, prof. law, 2002—03; dean, prof. law U. La Verne Coll. Law, Ontario, Calif., 2003—. Editor (with Flynn): Immigration and Nationality Law Rev., vols. 3-7, 1979—84; editor: (with Mersky) Fundamentals of Legal Research, 8th edit., 2002. Bd. dirs. Pioneer Valley chpt. ARC; pres. Scribes, 2001—. Fellow: Am. Bar Found.; mem.: ABA (chair law librs. com. 1988—92), ALA, Am. Law Inst., Law Librs. New Eng. (pres. 1982—83), Spl. Libr. Assn., Am. Assn. Law Librs. (chair acad. law librs. spl. interest sect. 1989—90), Scribes (pres. 2001—03). Democrat. Episcopalian. Office: U La Verne Coll Law 320 East D St Ontario CA 91764 E-mail: dunnd@ulv.edu.

DUNN, DORIS, retired critical care nurse, artist, rancher; b. Enid, Okla., June 13, 1935; d. Glen Olen Powell and Emma Jean Dunn; m. Lynn E. Dunn, Sept. 13, 1989 (dec. Sept. 17, 1993); m. George Leroy Doerfler, Sept. 7, 1961 (div. Apr. 1971); children: James G., Deborah, Mitchell, Christopher, Vicki. At, Enid Bus. Coll., 1959; at in nursing, Barton County CC, Great Bend, Kans., 1979. RN. Charge nurse CCU, Great Bend, Kans.; head nurse GYN Wesley Med. Ctr., Wichita, Kans., 1973—90. charge CCRN, 1973—90; CCRN St. Francis Med. Ctr., Wichita, 1975—87; horse breeder, 1987—. Lectr. Life Ins. Joint Member, Wichita, 1994—95; instr. Steve Colgate's Offshore Sailing Sch., Tortola, British Virgin Islands, 1989. Author: Painting Your First Portrait - For the Beginner, 2001. Vol. RN to Guatemala; career counselor U.S. Coast Guard Acad. Mem.: Coast Guard Aux. Divsn. 31 (vessel examiner, staff officer, coxswain-career, vice capt. 1989, Outstanding Individual 1996, Outstanding Divsn. staff officer 1995—96). Democrat. Avocations: painting, horseback riding, sailing. Home: 4135 E Blaney Rd Peyton CO 80831

DUNN, DORIS MARJORY, retired educator, volunteer; b. Chgo., Jan. 7, 1921; d. William Christian and Mary Esther (Hoffman) Rose; m. Jack Harold Wheeler Dunn, Sept. 19, 1945 (dec. June 1978); children: Randall L., Jon G., Bonham. BS in Edn., Ind. U., 1942; postgrad., Northwestern U., 1943-44; MS, Valparaiso U., 1973. Life lic. in teaching, Ind. Tchr. Crown Point (Ind.) High Sch., 1963-74, Lowell (Ind.) High Sch., 1942-45; sch. tchr., jr. coll. tchr., 1976-78. Asst. to engring.libr. U. Tex., Austin, 1947-49. Pres. LWV, Crown Point, 1974; pres.-elect Good Samaritan Hosp. Aux., v.p., 1988-89, pres., 1989-90; buyer Good Samaritan Gift Shop, 1989—; chmn. ways and means Assistance League, 1988-89, regional coun. rep., 1990-91, mem. resource devel. nat. bd., 1991-98; pres. Luckiamute Water Bd., 1988—; mem. Republican Senatorial Inner Circle, State of Oreg., 1997-98. Mem. P.E.O. (pres. 1989-90), Corvallis Country Club. Ladies Orgn. (pres. 1989-90), Kappa Kappa Kappa (pres. 1975), Delta Kappa Gamma. Methodist. Avocations: wood carving, golf, flying, stained glass creation, travel. Home: 12260 Rolling Hills Rd Monmouth OR 97361-9758

DUNN, DWAYNE EARLE, music educator; b. Joplin, Mo., Mar. 7, 1962; s. Lloyd Wayne and Dorothy Sue Dunn, Kay (Francis) Dunn (Stepmother); m. Cynthia Melissa Colwell, Mar. 11, 1996; m. Donna Lee Wilson, May 21, 1983 (div. Mar. 18, 1992); children: Bryce Colwell Cahoon, Danielle Sue. PhD of Music Edn., La. State U., 1995; MusM in Performance, SW Tex. State U., 1992; MusB in Edn. summa cum laude, Tex. Christian U., 1984. Dir. choral activities Olathe East H.S., Olathe, Kans., 2001—; dir. music grades 5-12 Barstow Sch., Kansas City, Mo., 2000—01; asst. prof. music edn. U. Ariz., Tucson, 1995—2000; asst. dir. choral activities Harlingen Consol. Ind. Sch. Dist., Harlingen, Tex., Saint Helena, 1988—91. Musical dir., accompanist Barn Players, Shawnee-Mission, Kans., 2001—. Dir.(founder): (performing ensemble) University of Arizona High School Outreach Choir (Dean's Fund for Excellence Grant, 1996); contbr. Sr. city counselor Tex. Am. Legion Boys State, Austin, Tex., 1989—2000; elder Pusch Ridge Christian Ch., Tucson, Ariz., 1997—2000. Recipient Outstanding Grad. Student - Sch. of Fine Arts and Comm., SW Tex. State U., 1993; Alumni Fellowship for Doctoral Study, La. State U., 1992—95. Mem.: Am. Choral Directors Assn., Music Educators Nat. Conf. (ariz. state chairperson: nat. menc collegiate adv. coun. 1995—2000, Chairperson Ariz. chpt., Collegiate adv. coun. 1995—2000), Ariz. Collegiate Music Educators (pres. 1999—2000, pres. 1999—2000), Ariz. Music Educators Assn. (music tchr. edn. chair 1997—99, George C. Wilson Leadership, Svc. award 2000, chair Music Tchr. Edn. 1997—99), Kans. Music Educators Assn., Pi Kappa Lambda, Phi Mu Alpha (chpt. pres. 1982—83, Louden Meml. Scholarship 1983, chpt. pres. 1982—83). Avocations: piano, reading, golf. Office: Olathe East High School 14545 W 127th St Olathe KS 66062 E-mail: ddunnoe@mail.olathe.k12.ks.us.

DUNN, EDWARD K., JR., banker; b. Balt., May 20, 1935; s. Edward K. and Anne (Butler) D.; m. Janet Evans, June 14, 1958; children: J. Holliday, Edward K., Peter C. AB, Princeton U., 1958; MBA, Harvard U., 1960. Chartered fin. analyst. Securities analyst Robert Garrett & Sons, Balt., 1960-64, various positions, 1964-73, pres., 1973-74; gen. ptnr. Alex Brown & Sons, Balt., 1974-88; mng. dir. Alex Brown & Sons Inc., 1985-88; chmn. exec. com., bd. dir. Mercantile-Safe Deposit & Trust Co., Mercantile Bankshares, 1988-90; pres., bd. dir. Mercantile Bankshares; vice chmn., bd. dir. Mercantile-Safe Deposit & Trust Co., 1991-95, pres., COO, 1995-97; pres. Mercantile Bankshares, 1995-97; chmn. bd. dirs. Mercantile Mktg. Corp., 1997-2000. Mem. corp. adv. bd. Nat. Assn. Security Dealers. Chmn. bd. Johns Hopkins Medicine, Johns Hopkins Hosp., Johns Hopkins Health Sys.; vice chmn. bd. Johns Hopkins U.; pres. Robert Garrett Fund for Surg. Treatment of Children; treas. Evergreen House Found.; bd. dirs. Thomas Wilson Sanitarium, Anna Emory Warfield Fund, Marion Burk Knott Scholarship Fund; mem. bd. fin. adminstrn. Archdiocese of Balt.; dir. Aegon USA, AIM Funds, Balt. Equitable Soc., Ward Machinery; trustee Inst. Christian and Jewish Studies, Johns Hopkins Hosp. Endowment Fund, Green Mt. Cemetery, Balt. Cmty. Found., Ralph C. Heller Found., Gottschalk Found. Democrat. Roman Catholic. Home: Vesper Hill 7315 Bellona Ave Baltimore MD 21212-1009 Office: Mercantile Mortgage Corp PO Box 1477 Baltimore MD 21203-1477

DUNN, EDWIN RYDELL, lawyer; b. Boston, July 24, 1942; s. Richard Joseph and Clara Hudson (Rydell) Dunn; m. Kathleen Lynch, July 23, 1966; children: Jeanne, Kathleen, Anne, Daniel. BA U. Notre Dame, 1964; JD cum laude, Northwestern U., Chgo., 1967. Bar: Ill. 1967. Assoc. Baker & McKenzie, Chgo., 1967—73, ptnr., 1973—. Mem. law bd. Northwestern U. Law Sch., 1996—; bd. dirs. Nr. West Side Cmty. Devel. Corp., 1991—. Mem. bd. advisors Cath. Charities, Chgo., 1999—. Mem.: ABA, Ill. Bar Assn., Chgo. Bar Assn. Office: Baker & McKenzie 1 Prudential Pla 130 E Randolph St Ste 3700 Chicago IL 60601-6342

DUNN, ERIN C. psychologist, researcher; b. Rochester, N.Y., Mar. 27, 1974; d. Suzanne B. Dunn, Stephen T. Dunn. BA summa cum laude, Emory U., 1996; MS, U. Ill., 1998, U. Wash., 2000, postgrad., 2002—. Rsch. asst. Emory U., Atlanta, 1994—96, U. Ill., Urbana, 1996—98, U. Wash., Seattle, 1998—. Therapist U. Wash., 1998—. Contbr. articles. Scholar, Stanley Found., 2001. Mem.: Soc. Behavioral Medicine, Assn. Advancement of Behavior Therapy, Am. Psychol. Assn., Psi Chi (life), Phi Beta Kappa (life). Avocations: travel, interior decorating, reading, exercise. Office: Univ Wash Box 351525 Seattle WA 98195-1525

DUNN, FLOYD, biophysics and biomedical engeering educator; b. Kansas City, Mo., Apr. 14, 1924; s. Louis and Ida (Leibtag) Dunn; m. Elsa Tanya Levine, June 11, 1950; children: Andrea Susan, Louis Brook. Student, Kansas City Jr. Coll., 1941-42, Tex. A&M U., 1943; BS, U. Ill., Urbana, 1949, MS, 1951, PhD, 1956. Rsch. assoc. elec. engring. U. Ill., Urbana, 1954-57, rsch. asst. prof. elec. engring., 1957-61, assoc. prof. elec. engring. and biophysics, 1961-65, prof., 1965—, prof. elec. engring., biophysics and bioengring., 1972-95, faculty mem. Beckman Inst. Advanced Sci. and Tech., prof. emeritus, 1995—, dir. bioacoustics rsch. lab., 1976-95, chmn. bioengring. faculty, 1978-82. Vis. prof. U. Coll., Cardiff, Wales, 1968—69, Inst. Chest Diseases and Cancer, Tohoku U., Sendai, Japan, 1982, Sendai, 1989—90, U. Nanjing, China, 1983; mem. bioengirng., radiation and diagnostic radiology study sects. NIH, 1970—81; steering com. workshop interaction ultrasound and biol. tissues NSF, 1971—72; vis. sr. scientist Inst. Cancer Rsch., Sutton, Surrey, England, 1975—76, Sutton, 1982—83, Sutton, 1990; chmn. working group health aspects exposure to ultrasound radiation WHO, London, 1976; mem. tech.-elec. products radiation stds. com. FDA, 1974—76; adj. prof. radiation oncology U. Ariz., Tucson, 1996—; mem. Nat. Coun. Radiation Protection and Measurement, 1980—. Mem. editl. bd. Jour. Acoustical Soc. Am., 1968—, Ultrasound Medicine and Biology, 1981—, Ultrasonics, 1981—, Handbook of Acoustics, 1981—, Encyclopedia of Applied Physics, 1981—, Am. Inst. Physics Series Modern Acoustics and Signal Processing, 1990—97; contbr. articles to profl. jours. Trustee Hensley Twp., Ill., 1980—81. With AUS, 1943—46. Recipient Spl. Merit medal, Acoustical Soc. Japan, 1988, History Med. Ultrasound Pioneer award, AIUM/WFUMB, 1988; fellow, Japan Soc. Promotion Sci., 1982, 1996, Fogarty Internat., 1990; Spl. Rsch. fellow, NIH, 1968—69, Eleanor Roosevelt-Internat. Cancer fellow, Am. Cancer Soc., 1975—76, 1982—83, Fulbright fellow, 1982—83. Fellow: AAAS, IEEE (life Engring. Medicine and Biology Soc. Career Achievement award 1995, Edison medal 1996), Inst. Acoustics (U.K.), Am. Inst. Ultrasound in Medicine (William J. Fry meml. award 1984, Joseph H. Holmes Basic Sci. Pioneer award 1990), Acoustical Soc. Am. (Silver medal 1989, Gold medal 1998), Am. Inst. Med. Biol. Engring. (assoc. editor Jour. 1968-, exec. coun. 1977-80, v.p. 1980-81, pres. 1985-86, chmn. pub. policy com. 1994-), Internat. Acad. Med. Biol. Engring.; mem.: NAE, NAS, Biophys. Soc., Rochester Soc. Biomed. Ultrasound (hon.), Japan Soc. Ultrasound in Medicine (hon.), Am. Inst. Physics (mem. editl. bd. series in modern acoustics and signal processing 1990—97, publs. policy com. 1992—2000), Phi Sigma Phi, Phi Sigma, Pi Mu Epsilon, Tau Beta Pi, Eta Kappa Nu, Sigma Tau, Sigma Xi. Home: 2631 E Avenida de Maria Tucson AZ 85718-3081 *Excellent, dedicated and understanding teachers, bright and energetic students, and a single-mindedness to see a problem to solution are the ingredients for a modest success.*

DUNN, FLOYD EMRYL, psychiatrist, neurologist, consultant; b. Wilkes-Barre, Pa., Apr. 25, 1910; s. Adrian Anson and Frances Amanda (Culver) D.; m. Wilda Kathryn Lauer, Aug. 14, 1943 (dec. July 1991); children: Kathryn Alice (dec.), Deborah Lee; m. Nova Judy Halopoff, Mar. 22, 2003. Student, Temple U., 1929-32; DO, Phila. Coll. Osteo. Medicine, 1936. Diplomate Am. Osteo. Bd. Neurology and Psychiatry. Resident in neurology, psychiatry Still-Hildreth Hosp., 1941-45, staff psychiatrist, 1945-49; chmn. divsn. neurology, psychiatry Kirksville Coll. Osteo. Medicine, 1945-48, Kansas City Coll. Osteo. Medicine, U. Health Scis., Mo., 1949-68; mem. staff VA Hosp., Knoxville, Iowa, 1968-76, chief psychiatry svc., 1970-76; clin. prof. neurology, psychiatry Coll. Osteo. Medicine, Des Moines, 1970-74. Mem. Nat. Bd. Examiners for Osteo. Physicians and Surgeons, 1965-74, Excellence award, 1974; cons. neurology, psychiatry, Chgo., 1974-90, cons., examiner sect. of disability determinations Mo. Dept. Elem. and Secondary Edn., Jefferson City, 1985-96. Author: (monograph) History of the American College of Neuropsychiatrists, 1984; contbr. articles to profl. jours. Mem. Iowa Adv. Coun. on Mental Health Ctrs., Des Moines, 1972-78, Cen. Regional Adv. Coun. for Comprehensive Psychiat. Svcs., Columbia, Mo., 1978-86. Fellow Am. Coll. Neuropsychiatrists (life, sec.-treas. 1948-52, pres. 1954-55, 63-64, Disting. Svc. award 1967, Disting. Fellow award 1984, 1st Fellows' Lecture Honoree 1989), Am. Assn. on Mental Deficiency; mem. AMA (life), Am. Osteo. Assn. (life, editl. cons. publs. 1958-95, del. 1960-69, pres.'s adv. coun. 1973), Am. Coll. Neuropsychiatrists (life), Am. Osteopathic Assn. (life, cons. examiner of neurology and psychiatry residency tng. programs 1988-91), Mo. Assn. Osteo. Physicians and Surgeons (hon. life, del. 1958-69, v.p. 1969-70, Appreciation plaque 2000), Lions (pres. Gravois Mills, Mo. chpt. 1984-85, sec. 1985-88, del. to internat. conv. 1985, 86, 87), Masons (32d degree), Abou Ben Adhem Temple, Elks (life), Alpha Phi Omega, Phi Sigma Gamma (pres. grand coun. 1952-53, coun. sec.-treas. 1953-59, editor Speculum 1959-65, 95—, Meritorious Svc. award 1965, 87-91, exec. sec.-treas. grand coun. 1980-95). Republican. Methodist. Avocations: photography, travel, journalism. Home: 30171 Millcreek Loop Gravois Mills MO 65037-4118

DUNN, FRANK A. communications executive; B Commerce, McGill U. Cert. mgmt. acct. With Nortel Networks, Brampton, Canada, 1976—, sr. v.p. fin. and planning, v.p. ops., fin. and planning, v.p. fin. Nortel N.Am., v.p., corp. contr., v.p. wireless product group, CFO, 1999, CEO. Office: Nortel Networks Ltd 8200 Dixie Rd Ste 100 Grampton ON Canada L6T 5P6

DUNN, GEORGE J. lawyer, oil company executive; b. Cleve., Apr. 29, 1935; married. BS, Yale U., 1957; JD, Harvard U., 1960. With McAfee, Hanning, Newcomer & Hazlett, 1960—67, Squire, Sanders & Dempsey, 1967; legal dept. Std. Oil (Ohio Corp.), Cleve., 1968—74, v.p., gen counsel, 1974—90; sr. v.p., gen counsel BP Am., Inc. (formerly Std. Oil Co.), Cleve., 1990—. Office: BP America Inc 200 Public Sq Cleveland OH 44114-2375

DUNN, GLENNIS MAE, retired writer, lyricist; b. Montevideo, Minn., Sept 11, 1938; d. James Arnold and Mabel Helmina (Anderson) Haugerud; m. Edward Henry Roske, Mar. 19, 1956 (div. Mar. 1975); children: Daniel Edward Roske, Deborah Kay Roske Hawthorne, Judith Ann Roske Rinker, Kristine Jean Roske McMackin, James William Roske, William Benjamin Roske; m. George Maurice Dunn, Sept. 1, 1984 (dec. Dec. 1992). Grad., Montevideo High Sch. Cert. pvt.-instrument pilot, basic ground flight instr. Comml.-instrument ground instr. Sawyer Aviation, Phoenix, 1976—78; pvt.-instrument pilot West Air Flight Club, Phoenix, 1976—; sales telemarketer Lone Star Performing Arts, 1994—, group sales rep., 1996; entrepreneur, 1996; travel cons., 1997 customer svc. rep. Carnival Cruises Holland Am. Cruises, Galveston 2001—02. Security pub. adminstrn. officer Star of Tex., Galveston, 1994; flight program specialist Embery Riddle Aero. U., Daytona Beach, Fla., 1980-83; ind. contractor, tour condr. Am. Hawaii Cruises, 1998—. Author: You Never Need to Worry-If You Forget to Grow Up, 1985, Someday Darling, Under My Wings We'll Fly, 1993; author, lyricist (song) A Vet's Song, 1992, My Red, White and Blue, 1993, Little Crystal Town, 1993, Riverwalk Christmas, 1993, Santa Keeps an Eye on Me, 1993, One for the Duck, One for Mother, 1993, Texas Auction at the Wheel, 1993, Love your Irish Blue Eyes, 1994 Named to Tex. Hall of Fame, 1996. Mem. Nat. FAA Pilot Assn. (radio operator), Internat. Platform Assn., Am. Legion Aux., Fraternal Order Eagles Aux. Republican. Avocations swimming, writing, golf, jogging, singing. Home and Office: PO Box 1643 12 Seadrift Dr Crystal Beach TX 77650

DUNN, GLORIA JEAN, artist; b. Detroit, Apr. 21, 1927; d. Donald Stanton and Etta Florence (Barber) Hopkins; m. Eugene Oliver Dunn, Dec. 28, 1944; children: Michael Eugene, Patricia Ann. Student, Wayne County C.C., Taylor, Mich., 1987-90. Instr. arts and crafts YWCA, Wyandotte, Mich., 1963-86; instr. painting and calligraphy, adult edn. Lincoln Park (Mich.) Sch. Sys., 1982-90; owner, mgr. Pen, Brush and Anvil Studio, Southgate, Mich., 1975-95, Gloria Hopkins Dunn Studio of Fine Art, Wyandotte, 1995—; represented by Home Gallery, Taylor, Mich., Swann Gallery, Lincoln Park, Mich., Fuenteo Gallery, Wyandotti. Mem. adv. bd. Wyandotte St. Art Fair, 1962—, organizer, co-chair 1962-81. One-woman shows include Taylor (Mich.) Cmty. Libr., Southgate (Mich.) City Hall, Swann Gallery, Detroit, Taylor (Mich.) City Hall, Trenton (Mich.) City Hall. Mem. Southgate Cultural Commn., 1974-82, 91-99. Recipient Cmty. Svc. award City of Southgate, 1978, Hon. Tribute, City of Wyandotte 1982, 20 Yrs. Dedication to Art award City of Wyandotte, 1991, Salute to Excellence award Downriver Coun. for the Arts, 2003. Mem. Acanthus Art Soc. Wyandotte (pres. 1994—), Downriver Arts and Crafts Guild (exhibit chair 1995, 96, 97, 98, 99, 2000, jury chair 2000-01), Art Ambience (historian 1993—, bd. dirs., v.p. 1999—, pres. 2001-02, Downriver Coun. Arts Salute to Excellence award, 2003), Nat. Assn. Fine Arts. Avocations: swimming, photography, gardening, riding. Office: 2930 Biddle St Wyandotte MI 48192-521

DUNN, HELEN ELIZABETH, retired secondary school educator; b. Peoria, Ill., July 14, 1930; d. Albert Edward and Corinne Ada (Rudel) Joos; m. Harry Christie Dunn, Feb. 4, 1951; children: Pamela Elizabeth Dunn Baumann, Patricia Louise Dunn Marshall. BS in Edn., Bradley U., 1951, MA in Guidance/Counseling, 1969. Tchr. Pub. Schs. of Hawaii, Lanai City, 1951-54, Ulupalakua, 1954-56, Pub. Schs. of Peoria, 1956-69; English LaSalle (Ill.)-Peru H.S., 1970-71; counselor, tchr. Peru (Ill.) Pub. Schs., 1971-89; ret., 1989. Contbr. poems to books: The Best Poems of the '90s, 1992, Distinguished Poets of America, 1993, Best Poems of 1995, 1995. Presenter programs on Hawaii, Peoria. Mem.: PEO, LWV (bd. dirs. 1973—89, treas. 1982—89), NEA (del. 1951—56, rep. 1957—69), Ret. Tchrs. Assn. (legis. com. 1991—98), Peoria Area Ret. Tchrs. Assn. (sec. 2001—02), Peoria Women's Club (corr. sec. 2000—03), Phi Lambda Theta, Sigma Kappa (alumni chpt., pres. 1962, 1991), Delta Kappa Gamma (pres. 1968—70, 1978—80, 1992—94). Methodist. Avocations: writing poetry, tennis, dancing, reading, singing.

DUNN, HERBERT IRVIN, lawyer; b. Balt., July 19, 1946; s. Albert M. and Hilda F. (Winakur) D.; m. Marsha Edith Greenfield, Apr. 1, 1979; children: Marla Phyllis, Jonathan Howard. BS with high honors, U. Md., 1969, JD, 1971. Bar: Md. 1971, D.C. 1971, U.S. Ct. Claims 1972, U.S. Tax Ct. 1972, U.S. Dist. Ct. D.C. 1971, U.S. Ct. Appeals (D.C. cir.) 1971, U.S. Supreme Ct. 1975. Atty.-adviser Office of Gen. Counsel U.S. Gen. Acctg. Office, Washington, 1971-83, sr. atty., 1983—. Served with USAR, 1968-74. Fellow: Found. of the FBA (charter) (advisor 1999—, bd. dirs. 2002—, sec. 2002—); mem.: Northwest Br. Citizens Assn. (sec. 1988 95, 1st v.p. 1995—99), Md. Bar Assn., FBA (Capitol Hill chpt. exec. coun. 1975—83, treas. younger lawyers divsn. 1977—79, nat. coun. 1978—79, v.p. 1990—91, nat. coun. 1991—, pres. 1992—93, v.p. D.C. cir. 1994—, nat. exec. com. 1999—2000, v.p. for the cirs. chmn. 1999—2000, bd. dirs. 2002—, sec. 2002—), Omicron Delta Epsilon. Office: 441 G St NW Washington DC 20548-0001

DUNN, HORTON, JR., organic chemist; b. Coleman, Tex., Sept. 3, 1929; s. Horton and Lora Dean (Bryant) D. BA summa cum laude, Hardin-Simmons U., 1951; MS, Case Western Res. U., 1975, PhD, 1979. Instr. chemistry Hardin-Simmons U., 1951; ONR fellow Ohio State U., Columbus, 1951-52; teaching fellow in chemistry Purdue U., Lafayette, Ind., 1952-53; rsch. chemist Lubrizol Corp., Cleve., 1953-70, dir. tech. info. ctr., 1970-79, supr. rsch. divsn., 1980-98, cons. in chemistry, 1998—. Chmn. bd., bus. mgr. Isotopics, Cleve., 1964-67, editor, 1961-63, supr. rsch. divsn., 1989-97, cons. in chemistry, 1998—. Contbr. articles to profl. jours.; patentee in field. Treas. Cleve. Cir. Decorative Arts Trust, 1990-91, 93—, v.p., 1992-93; bd. mgrs. One Bratenahl Place, 2001—; mem. TRIDECA Soc. of Cleve. Mus. Art; active Cleve. Art Assn., Rock and Roll Hall of Fame, Mus. Founders Club; mem., vol. Great Lakes Sci. Ctr., Cleve. Mus. Natural History; mem. Cleve. Bot. Garden, Condr.'s Cir. of Cleve. Orch., English Speaking Union (Cleve. br.), mem. Trideca Soc. of Cleve. Mus. of Art. Fellow Am. Inst. Chemists; mem. AAAS, SAR (life), Am. Chem. Soc. (treas. Cleve. chpt. 1968-70, chmn. 1987, bd. dirs. 1990—), Am. Soc. for Info. Sci. (chpt. pres. 1973-74), Royal Soc. Chemistry (life), Soc. Tribologists and Lubrication Engrs., Nat. Coun. Met. Opera, Royal Oak Soc. (life), Cleve. Tech. Soc. Coun. (treas. 1987), Cleve. Art Assn., Univ. Club, Cleve. Club, Cleve. Play House Club, Rock and Roll Hall of Fame Mus. Founders Club (charter), English Speaking Union, Trideca Soc. of Cleve. Mus. Art, Cleve. Skating Club. Home and Office: 1 Bratenahl Pl Apt 103 Bratenahl OH 44108-1152 Office: Lubrizol Corp 29400 Lakeland Blvd Wickliffe OH 44092-2298 Fax: 216-541-6431.

DUNN, JACKSON THOMAS, JR., lawyer, legal educator; b. Charlotte, NC, Nov. 30, 1943; s. Jackson Thomas and Dorothy Holland (Schweiger) D.; m. Mary Louise Miller, Apr. 23, 1944; children: Jackson Thomas, Michael Lansing, Mary Katharine Holland. AB, Belmont Abbey Coll., 1965; JD, U. N.C., 1968. Bar: N.C. 1968, U.S. Dist. Ct. (mid. dist.) N.C. 1977, U.S. Dist. Ct. (we. dist.) N.C. 1974, U.S. Supreme Ct. 1982. Asst. prof. East Carolina U., Greenville, N.C., 1968-69, U. Ga., Athens, 1969-75; ptnr. Edwards & Dunn, Charlotte, N.C., 1975; counsel The Ervin Co., Charlotte, N.C., 1976; v.p., sr. counsel Northwestern Fin. Corp./Northwestern Bank, North Wilkesboro, N.C., 1976-85; sr. v.p., dep. gen. counsel 1st Union Corp./1st Union Nat. Bank, Charlotte, 1985-2000; ptnr. Moore & Van Allen PLLC, Charlotte, 2000—. Instr. NC Bankers Assn. Seminars. Contbr. articles to profl. jours. Bd. govs. U. N.C. Law Sch. Alumni Assn.; mem. bd. advisors U. N.C. Law Sch. Banking Inst. Mem.: ABA, N.C. Bankers Assn., Am. Law Inst., N.C. Carolina Bar Assn., N.C. Bar Assn. (chmn. fin. Instns. com., chmn. bank counsel com., bus. law coun.). Democrat. Office: Moore & Van Allen PLLC 100 N Tryon St Ste 4700 Charlotte NC 28202 E-mail: tomdunn@mvalaw.com.

DUNN, JAMES EDWARD, JR., corporate consultant, lawyer; b. Pitts., May 31, 1947; s. James Edward and Anne Elizabeth (O'Connor) D.; m. Sally Skeehan, June 6, 1970; children: Meghan, Mark. BS, St. Joseph's Coll., 1969; JD, Duquesne U., 1972. Bar: Pa. 1972, Ohio 1973, Fla. 1981, Ga. 1999. Assoc. atty. IRS, Cleve., 1972-76; asst. gen. atty. Chessie System, Cleve., 1976-79; asst. to treas. Harris Corp., Melbourne, Fla., 1979-83; treas. Harris Graphics, Melbourne, Fla., 1983-86; prin. Ernst & Whinney, Atlanta, 1986—. Mem. Estate Planning Council Brevard County; bd. dirs. Space Coast Sci. Ctr., Melbourne, 1986; vice chmn. devel. council Holmes Regional Med. Ctr., Melbourne, 1986. Mem. ABA, So. Pension Conf. Home: 8360 Greensboro Dr Apt 603 Mc Lean VA 22102 Office: Ernst & Whinney 225 Peachtree Ctr South Tower 8484 Westpark Dr Mc Lean VA 22102

DUNN, JAMES MILTON, religious organization administrator; b. Ft. Worth, Tex., June 17, 1932; s. William Thomas and Edith (Campbell) Dunn; m. Marilyn McNeely, Dec. 19, 1958. BA, Tex. Wesleyan Coll., 1953; BD, Southwestern Bapt. Theol. Sem., 1957, ThD, 1966, PhD, 1978; LLD, Alderson-Broaddus Coll., William Jewell Coll.; DHL, Linfield Coll.; DD, Crl. Bapt. Theol. Sem., Furman U. Ordained to ministry So. Bapt. Conv. and Am. Bapt. Ch. in U.S.A., 1955. Assoc. pastor First Bapt. Ch., Weatherford, Tex., 1955-57; pastor Emmanuel Bapt. Ch., Weatherford, 1957-61; religion instr., campus minister W. Tex. State U., Canyon, 1961-66; dir. christian life commn. Bapt. Gen. Conv. Tex., Dallas, 1967-80; exec. dir. Bapt. Joint Com. on Pub. Affairs, Washington, 1981-99, pres., 1999—. Sec. bd. Ams. United for Separation Ch. & State, Silver Spring, Md., 1978-88; bd. dirs. Bread for the World, Washington, pres., 1987; chmn. ethics commn. Bapt. World Alliance, McLean, Va., 1975-80; bd. dirs. Ch.'s Ctr. for Theology and Pub. Policy, Washington, 1993—; vis. prof. Wake Forest Div. Sch., 1999—. Editor, co-author: Politics a Guidebook for Christians, 1970, Endangered Species, 1976; co-author: An Approach to Christian Ethics, 1979, Teacher Renewal, 1987; author: (with others) Equal Separation, 1990, The Fundamentalist Phenomenon, 1990, Defining Baptist Convictions, 1996, Proclaiming the Baptist Vision, Religious Liberty, 1997, Why I Am a Baptist, 1999, Baptists in the Balance, 1997, Soul Freedom: Baptist Battle Cry, 2000. Sec. Anti-Crime Coun. Tex., Dallas, 1968-80; founding mem. Dallas Dem. Forum, 1976-80; mem. Fair Campaign Practices Com., Dallas, 1972-76, Gov.'s Juvenile Coun., State of Tex., Austin, 1976-77. Recipient Disting. Svc. award Christian Life Commn. of So. Bapt. Conv., 1979, Moore-Bowman Award of Excellence, Tex. Coun. on Family Relations, 1979, Disting. Svc. award Chs. Ctr. for Theology and Pub. Policy, 1993, T.B. Maston Christian Ethics award, 1995, Abner V. McCall Religious Liberty award Baylor U., 1998, Disting. Svc. award Christian Life Commn. Bapt. Gen. Conv. Tex., 1998, Madison-Jefferson award Americans United, 1999, Disting. Svc. medal Colgate Rochester Divinity Sch., 2000. Mem. Soc. for the Sci. Study of Religion. Baptist. Avocation: music. Office: Baptist Joint Com 200 Maryland Ave NE Ste 302 Washington DC 20002-5797 E-mail: dunnj@wfu.edu. *All freedom is rooted in our being made in the image of God and is one aspect of the two-sided coin of freedom and responsibility. The two go together inextricably.*

DUNN, JEFFREY EDWARD, neurologist; b. Shaker Heights, Ohio, Nov. 27, 1960; s. John Kenneth and Mary Margaret (O'Neill) D.; m. Sandra Lee Judy, Feb. 3, 1990; children: Caitlin Irene, Bronwyn Leigh, Colin John Donald. BA in French Lit., Haverford (Pa.) Coll., 1983; MD, Temple U., 1989. Diplomate Am. Bd. Psychiatry and Neurology. Molecular immunologist Fox Chase Cancer Ctr., Phila., 1984-85; intern Ea. Va. Grad. Sch., Norfolk, 1989-90; resident in neurology U. Wash., Seattle, 1990 93; attending physician Neurol. Assocs. of Wash., Bellevue, 1993—; clin. asst. prof. neurology U. Wash., Seattle, 1993—; founder, med. dir. Overlake Multiple Sclerosis Ctr., Bellevue, Wash., 1996—. Guest physician TV: MS Update, Denver, 1994, ALS Update, Seattle, 1995, MS Ctr. Vision, Seattle, 2001. Recipient Cert. of Excellence in MS Rx, Prodigy Online Com., 1995; named to Outstanding Young Men of Am., 1996. Fellow Royal Soc. Medicine; mem. Am. Acad. Neurology, Am. Neurol. Assn., World Congress Neurology, North Pacific Soc. of Psychiatry and Neurology, Pacific N.W. Alliance of MS Ctrs. Avocations: golf, skiing, camping, outdoor recreation. Office: Neurol Assocs of Wash 13107 121st Way NE Kirkland WA 98034-3051

DUNN, JENNIFER BLACKBURN, congresswoman; b. Seattle, Wash., July 29, 1941; d. John Charles and Helen (Gorton) Blackburn; div.; children: Bryant, Reagan. Student, U. Wash., 1960-62; BA in English Lit., Stanford U., 1963. Sys. engr. IBM, 1964-69; with King County Dept. of Assessments, 1979-80; former chmn. Rep. Party State of Wash., 1981-92; mem. U.S. Congress from 8th Wash. dist., Washington, 1993—. Bd. dirs. Nat. Endowment Democracy; mem. ways and means com., homeland sec. com., econ. com.; mem. adv. bd. Internat. Rep. Inst.; participant Preparatory Commn. World Conf. Status of Women, Nairobi, 1985, World Econ. Forum, Davos, Switzerland, 2000. Del. Rep. Nat. Conv., 1980, 84, 88; presdl. apptd. adv. coun. Historic Preservation, adv. coun. volunteerism SBA; apptd. presdl. commn. on debates; N.W. Regional Dir. Met. Operal Regional Auditions; mem. Jr. League of Seattle Named one of 25 Smartest Women in Am., Mirabella mag., one of 10 Most Powerful Women in Wash., Washington Law and Politics mag. Mem. Internat. Women's Forum (Wash. chpt.), Gamma Phi Beta. Republican. Office: US Ho Reps 1501 Longworth Ho Office Bldg Washington DC 20515-4708*

DUNN, JOE, state representative; b. Bayonne, NJ, Feb. 1, 1968; m. Karen Dunn; children: Joe, Jack. BS, Northern Ill. Univ., 1990; MBA, DePaul Univ., 1998. State Rep. House of Representatives, District 96, 2002; v.p. Dyson Dyson & Dunn Inc., 1995—; pres., found. Gen. Aviators, 1992—2002. Trustee, elected mem. Twp. Bd., 2000—; mem. Comm. At-Large, Rep. Party, Twp. Fin. and Plan Comm.; Appropriations- Gen. svc.; Fin. Inst.; mem. Ins., Gaming. Republican. Catholic. Office: Capitol 213-N Stratton Office Bldg Springfield IL 62706 also: District 552 S Wash 119 Naperville IL 60540*

DUNN, JOHN BENJAMIN, lawyer; b. Washington, July 12, 1948; s. Read P. and Barbara (Butts) D.; m. Virginia Ann Hughes, July 3, 1983; children: Lily Conti, Noah Benjamin. BA, Ohio Wesleyan U., 1970; JD, George Washington U., 1973. Bar: D.C. 1973, Md. 1974. Assoc. Schultz & Overby, Washington, 1973-76, Law Offices of Daniel E. Schultz, Washington, 1976 80; prin. Schultz & Dunn Chartered to Schultz Dunn & Murray Chartered, Washington, 1980-85; sole practice Takoma Park, Md., 1985—. Office: 7030 Carroll Ave Ste 2 Takoma Park MD 20912-4448 E-mail: jbdunn@erols.com.

DUNN, JOHN FRANCIS, lawyer, state representative; b. Logansport, Ind., Dec. 24, 1936; s. John Francis and Bertha (Newman) D.; m. Barbara Burke, Feb. 10, 1962; children: John F. III, Robert E., William M., Nancy L. BS in Chem. Engring., U. Notre Dame, 1958, JD, 1961. Bar: Ill. 1961, Ind. 1961, U.S. Dist. Ct. (so. dist.) Ill. 1961, U.S. Ct. Appeals (4th cir.) 1962. Atty. Standard Oil Ind. (now Amoco), Chgo., 1961-64; assoc. Morey and Dunn, Attys., Decatur, Ill., 1964-74; ptnr. Dunn and Fichter, Attys., Decatur, Ill., 1975-85; pvt. practice Decatur, Ill., 1986—. State rep. Ill. Gen. Assembly, Springfield, 1974-94, asst. majority leader; city councilman City of Decatur, 1971-74. Democrat. Roman Catholic. Avocations: bicycling, jogging. Office: 301 Millikin Ct Decatur IL 62523-1399

DUNN, JOHN RAYMOND, JR., stockbroker; b. Pittsfield, Mass., Aug. 24, 1937; s. John Raymond and Margaret Mary (Coyne) D.; 1 child, John Raymond III. AB, Boston Coll., 1960. Ins. agt. John Hancock Ins. Co., Boston, 1964-67; dist. mgr. Nat. Life Ins. Co., Montpelier, Vt., 1967-74; gen. agt. United Life & Accident Ins. Co., Concord, N.H., 1974—; stockbroker, regional mgr. Cornerstone Fin. Svcs., Inc., Boston, 1974-80; stockbroker, br. mgr. Weinrich, Zitzman, Whitehead Fin. Svcs., Inc., St. Louis, 1980—; pres. Dunn Assocs., Amherst, Mass., 1965—; br. mgr. Jefferson Pilot Securities Corp., 1998—. Field adv. mem. Pres. Adv. Coun. CFS-Div. Weinrich, Zitzman, Whitehead, Inc., 1982—; named to gen. agts. adv. com. Chubb Life Am./Chubb Securities Corp., 1988-89; dist. mgr. Chubb Securities Leaders' Club; lectr. in field. Author seminar: Let's Make Money; freelance writer Investment Dealer Digest, 1980; film prodr. Ernest Hemingway documentary. Dir. Parents and Tchrs. for Social Responsibility, Moretown, Vt., 1982-85. Mem. White Mountain Club (Club award 1984-92), Summit Club, Life U.S.A. Club, Chmns. Club., Pres. Club. Roman Catholic. Fax: 413-253-9356.

DUNN, JON MICHAEL, informatics educator, dean; b. Ft. Wayne, Ind., June 19, 1941; s. Jon Hardin and Philomena Elizabeth (Lauer) D.; m. Sarah Jane Hutchison, Aug. 8, 1964; children— Jon William, Jennifer Anne AB, Oberlin Coll., 1963; PhD, U. Pitts., 1966. Asst. prof. philosophy Wayne State U., Detroit, 1966-69; vis. asst. prof. philosophy Yale U., New Haven, 1968-69; assoc. prof. philosophy Ind. U., Bloomington, 1969-76, prof., 1976—, Oscar Ewing prof. philosophy, 1989—, chmn. dept. philosophy, 1980-84, 94-97, adj. prof. computer sci., 1987-89, prof., 1989—, assoc. dean Coll. Arts and Scis., 1988-91, exec. assoc. dean, 1991-93, dir., dean Sch. Informatics, 1999—2000, prof. informatics, 2002—. Vis. fellow Inst. Advanced Studies, Australian Nat. U., Canberra, 1975-76; sr. visitor Math. Inst., U. Oxford, Eng., 1978; faculties vis. scholar U. Melbourne, Australia, 1983; fellow Ind. U. Inst. for Advanced Study, 1984; sr. visitor Ctr. for Philosophy of Sci., U. Pitts., Nov. 1984; adj. prof. U. Mass., Amherst, spring 1985. Author: (with G. Hardegree) Algebraic Methods in Philosophical Logic, 2001; contbg. author: Entailment, Vol. I, 1975, co-author Vol. II, 1992; editor: (with A. Gupta) Truth of Consequences: Essays in Honor of Nuel Belnap, 1990, (with G. Epstein) Modern Uses of Multiple-Valued Logic, 1975, (with G. Hardegree) Algebraic Methods in Philosophical Logic, 2001; editor Jour. Symbolic Logic, 1982-87; chief editor Jour. Philos. Logic, 1987-95; mem. editl. bds. Jour. Philos. Logic, 1979-87, Nous, 1968—, Studia Logica, 1978—, Jour. Non-Classical Logic, 1985-91. Am. Council Learned Socs. fellow, 1984-85; NSF prin. investigator, 1969-74; Fulbright-Hays research sr. scholar, 1974 Mem. Assn. Symbolic Logic (exec. com. 1978-81, council 1982—), Soc. Exact Philosophy (treas. 1982-84, v.p. 1986-88, pres. 1988-90), Am. Philos. Assn. (com. research and publs. 1985-88). Office: Ind U Sch Informatics 901 E 10th St Bloomington IN 47408

DUNN, JOSEPH, state legislator; b. 1958; m. Diane Dunn; 2 children. BA, Coll. St. Thomas, 1980; JD, U. Minn., 1983. Atty. in pvt. practice; mem. Calif. State Senate, 1998—, mem. edn., budget, govtl. orgn. and vets. affairs coms., vice chmn. transp. com. Named Outstanding State Senator, Calif. chpt. VFW. Democrat. Avocations: racquetball, long distance bicycling. Office: Calif State Senate State Capitol Rm 2068 Sacramento CA 95814 also: 12397 Lewis St Ste 203 Garden Grove CA 92840-4679*

DUNN, KEITH A. government agency administrator; b. Cape Girardeau, Mo., Feb. 13, 1948; s. Lyman Hamby Dunn, Louise Pender Dunn; m. Terry Kelly Dunn, Sept. 6, 1975; children: Chris Vile, Drew. MA, U. Mo., 1969, PhD History, 1973. Sr. policy analyst, polit. scientist Strategic Studies Inst., U.S. Army War College, Carlisle Barracks, Va., 1977—85; sr. fellow Inst. Nat. Strategic Studies, Nat. Def. U., Washington, 1985—90; dir. def. plans divsn. U.S. Mission to NATO, 1990—95, dep. def. advisor, 1995—96; prin. dir. Inter-Am. Affairs Office of the Sec. Def., Washington, 1997—98; sec. def. rep., spl. asst. to exec. dir. U.S. Commn. Nat. Security/21st Century, Arlington, Va., 1998—2001, staff mem. Bush-Cheney Transition Nat. Security Coun., Washington, 2001, office of sec. def. enduring freedom coalition coord., 2001—. Author: (book) In Defense of NATO: The Alliance's Enduring Value, 1990, The Strategic Implications of the Continental-Maritime Strategy Debate, 1984; editor: NATO's Fifth Decade, 1990, Military Strategy and Conflict Termination: Persuasion, Coercion and War, 1987, Alternative Military Strategies for the Future, 1985, Military Strategy in Transition--Defense and Deterrence in the 1990s, 1984; contbr. articles to profl. jours. Capt. U.S. Army, 1973—77. Presbyterian. Avocation: golf. Home: 153 John Browning Willliamsburg VA 23185 Office: Office of Sec of Def 2000 Defense Pentagon Washington DC 20315 Business E-Mail: kdunn@mail.policy.osd.mil.

DUNN, KENNETH RALPH, insurance company executive; b. Paterson, N.J., Apr. 9, 1958; s. Ralph and Florence Louise (May) D.; m. Martha Jean Davis, Sept. 6, 1980; children: Laura Jean, Jonathan Ralph, David Allan. BS, Messiah Coll., 1980. Cert. in gen. ins.; lic. resident property and liability ins. agt., N.C.; lic. surety ins. agt., N.C.; lic. surety ins. agt., N.C., Hawaii. From external auditor to br. bond mgr. Selective Ins. Co. Am., Branchville, N.J., 1980-95; corp. bond mgr. Aegis Security Ins. Co., Harrisburg, Pa., 1995-99; pres. S.E. Contract Bond Svcs. of Carolinas, Inc., Pineville, N.C., 1999-2001; regional surety bond mktg. rep. Ohio Casualty Ins. Group, 2001—. Author: Messiah College Baseball Encyclopedia, 1991. Treas., deacon, softball coach, youth leader Newton (N.J.) 1st Bapt. Ch., 1980-84; ordained deacon, chmn. pastoral search com., recreation dir., chm. tng. dir., softball coach Calvary Bapt. Ch., Belair, Md., 1984-90; chmn. personnel com., ordained deacon, body life coord., softball coach, recreation dir., Covenant Bapt. Ch., Charlotte, N.C., 1990-95; sec., pres. Sussex County Softball League, Newton, 1982-84; adv. bd. Messiah Coll. Falcon Club, 1994; active Rep. Nat. Com., 1994—; sec. Constitution Party, N.C., 2003. Mem. Mid-Atlantic Surety Assn. (by-law com. 1987, sec. 1988, treas. 1989), Messiah Coll. Baseball Assn. (founder, pres./sec. 1989, sec. 1990, newsletter editor 1989-94, pres. 1994), Carolinas Surety Underwriters Assn. (treas. 1992, sec. 1993, v.p. 1994, pres. 1995), Geneal. Rsch. Soc. Northeastern Pa. Baptist. Avocations: coin collecting, baseball card collecting, athletics, ch. choir mem. Home: 14316 Blue Granite Rd Pineville NC 28134-8312 Office: Ohio Casualty Ins Group PO Box 489 Pineville NC 28134-0489 E-mail: KenMarDunn@aol.com.

DUNN, LARRY K. lawyer; b. Oaha, Hawaii, Apr. 3, 1948; s. Norman Dunn and Anne Martin; m. Kathleen Lillo, March 23, 1968; children: Jennifer, Karena, Jeffrey, Lindsay. AA, Western Nev. Cmty. Coll., 1977; BA, U. Nev., 1980; JD, McGeorge Sch. Law, 1984. Bar: Nev. 1984. Law clerk County Pub. Defenders Office, Sacramento, Calif., 1982-84; deputy dist. attorney Washoe County Dist. Attorney, Reno, Nev., 1984-86; criminal defense attorney Larry K. Dunn Chartered, Reno, Nev., 1986—. Lectr. High Sierra Police Acad., Reno, 1994—. With U.S. Army, 1967-72. Mem. Am. Legion. Republican. Episcopalian. Avocations: golf, ocean fishing, guitar. Office: Larry K Dunn Chartered 1385 Haskell St Reno NV 89509-2843 E-mail: lkdesq@aol.com.

DUNN, LEO JAMES, obstetrician, educator, gynecologist, educator; b. Trenton, N.J., May 23, 1931; s. Augustine Leo and Molly (McDaid) Dunn; m. Betty Beatrice Buchanan, Aug. 28, 1954; children: Laurie, Cary. AB, Hofstra U., 1952; MD, Columbia U., 1956. Diplomate Am. Bd. Ob-Gyn., Am. Bd. Gyn. Oncology. Intern Cin. Gen. Hosp., 1956—57; resident Sloane Hosp for Women, Columbia-Presbyn. Med. Ctr., 1957—62; asst. prof. ob-gyn U. Iowa Coll. Medicine, Iowa City, 1962—65, assoc. prof. ob-gyn, 1965—67; prof., former chmn. dept. Med. Coll. Va., Richmond, 1967—, interim dean, chmn. of dept. Ob-Gyn., 1983—85, prof. emeritus; pres. Am. Bd. Med. Specialties, 1998—2000. Bd. dirs. Am. Bd. Ob-Gyn, 1975—, pres., 1982—; mem. Nat. Bd. Med. Examiners, 1979—83. Recipient Silver medal as disting. alumnus, Columbia U. Coll. Physicians and Surgeons, 1967; scholar Markle, 1963. Fellow: ACOG (dist. v.p. 1976—78); mem.: Va. Ob-Gyn. Soc. (pres. 1981—82), Am. Assn. Ob-Gyn. (coun. 1975—79, pres. found. 1980—82, trustee 1975—82), Soc. Gynecol. Oncology (chmn. program com., v.p.), Phi Beta Kappa. Office: Med Coll Va MCV Station PO Box 980034 Richmond VA 23298-0034

DUNN, LIN, professional basketball coach; b. Nashville, May 10, 1947; BS in Health and Phys. Edn., U. Tenn., Martin, 1969; MS in Phys. Edn., U. Tenn., 1970. Women's basketball coach Austin Peay State, 1970-76, U. Miss., Oxford, 1977-78, U. Miami, 1979-87, Perdue U., W. Lafayette, Ind., 1987-96; head coach Portland Power, Oreg., 1996-98; draft consultant & assist. coach Houston Comets, 1998-99; head coach & gen. mgr. Seattle Storm, 1999—. Asst. coach silver-medal winning Select Team, 1986, gold-medal winning Pam Am. Games, 1987, Select Team, 1989, gold-medal winning Goodwill Games, gold-medal winning World Championship teams, 1990, Olympic bronze-medal winning team, Barcelona, Spain, 1992; head coach bronze-medal winning R. Williams Jones Cup team, Taipei, Taiwan, 1995; mem. Player Selection Com. that overseas the selection of players for all U.S.A. basketball teams. Achievements include being the first Big Ten coach to serve on an Olympic staff. Office: Seattle Storm 351 Elliott Ave W Seattle WA 98119-4101 E-mail: info@portlandpower.com.

DUNN, LYNDA M. music educator; b. Toledo, Ohio, Jan. 15, 1941; d. Claire C. and Adelaide M. (Stright) D.; m. Paul Wyatt, June 17, 1963 (div. June 1983); children: Paige M., Pamela L.; m. William F. Dais, Aug. 22, 1987. BS in Music Edn., Coll. Conservatory of Music, Cin., 1963, MusM in Piano Performance, 1989; PhD, Ohio State U., 1992. Tchr. Toledo (Ohio) Pub. Schs., 1963 65, 83-87; tchr. music and spl. edn. Genoa (Ohio) Area Local Schs., 1966-83; grad. tchg. asst. Ohio State U., Columbus, 1990-92; instr. music No. Ill. U., DeKalb, 1992-94; assoc. prof. music Carson-Newman Coll., Jefferson City, Tenn., 1994—. Adjudicator East Tenn. Vocal Edn., Knoxville, 1996. Piano soloist. Mem. Ohio Music Educators Assn. (clinician), Tenn. Music Edn. Assn. (clinician), Music Educators Nat. Conf., Music Tchrs. Nat. Assn. (adjudicator), East Tenn. Vocal Assn., Orgn. Am. Kodaly Educators, Phi Kappa Phi, Pi Kappa Lambda, Phi Delta Kappa. Methodist. Avocations: swimming, power walking, nordic trac. Home: 910 Buckeye St Genoa OH 43430-1523 Office: Carson-Newman Coll Box 71967 Jefferson City TN 37760

DUNN, MARIJA GAVRILOVA, psychologist, educator; b. Skopje, Macedonia, Oct. 19, 1949; d. Eftim Serafim Gavrilovski and Jordanka Stefan Gavrilova; m. William Newlin Dunn, Dec. 24, 1971 (div. Sept. 10, 1999); children: Alexander Eftim, Elizabeth Danica. BA, U Cyril & Methodius, Skopje, Macedonia, 1969—73; MA, U of Pitts., Pitts., PA, 1987—90, PhD, 1990—96. Rsch. asst. prof. of pharm. sci. and devel. psychology U of Pitts., Pitts., 2000—; sci. dir. Rsch. Coordinating Ctr. For Substance Abuse Prevention, Pitts.; instr. U Of Pitts. Sch. Of Edn., Pitts., 1996—2000, U Of Pitts. Dept. Of Slavic Languages And Literatures, Pitts., 1984—86. Adv. bd. mem. Grad. Sch. of Pub. and Internat. Affairs, U of Pitts., Pitts., 2001—; cons. Bikirkoy Psychiat. Hosp., Isambul, Turkey, 1989. Author: (scientific research article) Clin. Psychology Rev., Jour. of Child and Adolescent Substance Abuse, Psychology of Addictive Behaviors, (scentific research article) Prevention Sci., (scinetific research article) Jour. of Child Psychology and Psychiatry, (book chapter) Preventing Substance Abuse: Ages 3-14; translator: (book) Workers Self-mgmt. and Orgnl. Power in Yugoslavia. Recipient comprehensive exam for the PhD degree completed with distinction, U Of Pitts., 1994, PhD grad. work completed with a QPA of 4.00+, U of Pitts., 1994; fellow Tchg. Fellow In Devel./ednl. Psychology, U Of Pitts., 1992-1993. Mem.: Fed. Child Neglect Rsch. Consortium, Soc. for Prevention Rsch., APA. Avocations: writing, attending symphony concerts, walking, cycling.

DUNN, MARVIN IRVIN, physician; b. Topeka, Dec. 21, 1927; s. Louis and Ida (Leibtag) D.; m. Maureen Cohen, Mar. 10, 1956 (dec. Nov. 1988); children: Jonathan Louis, Marilyn Paulette. BA, U. Kans., 1950, MD, 1954. Intern USPHS, San Francisco, 1954-55; resident U. Kans., 1955-58, fellow, 1958-59, instr. medicine, 1958-60, assoc. in medicine, 1960-62, asst. prof. medicine, 1962-65, assoc. prof., 1965-70, prof., 1970-2000, prof. emeritus, 2001—, Franklin E. Murphy Disting. prof., 1978-2000, dir. Cardiovascular Lab., head sect. Cardiovascular Disease Med. Center, 1963-92, dean Sch. of Medicine, 1979-84. Cons. USAF, 1971-95; spl. cons. to fed. air surgeon of FAA, 1990—. Author: Home Study Course: Difficult EKG Diagnosis, 1969, Translator Deductive and Polyparametric Electrocardiography, 1970; (with others) Clinical Vectorcardiography and Electrocardiography, 2d edit., 1977, Clinical Electrocardiography, 8th edit., 1989; editor in chief Cardiovascular Perspectives, 1985-89; mem. editl. bd. Am. Jour. Cardiology, 1970-75, Catheterization and Cardiovascular Diagnosis, 1980-87, AMA Archives Internal Medicine, 1984-94, Jour. Am. Coll. Cardiology, 1983-89, Biomedicine and Pharmacotherapy, 1985-90, Am. Jour. Noninvasive Cardiology, 1985-89, Chest, 1984-89, 94-98, Practical Cardiology, 1980-88, Heart and Lung, 1986-88, Bd.-Advanced in Therapy, 1992, Slovak Jour. Noninvasive Cardiology, 1993, Griffith Resource Libr., 1980-90, Am. Heart Jour., Jour. Acoustical Soc. Bd. dirs. Hebrew Acad. Jewish Geriatric and Convalescent Center, Beth Shalom Synagogue. Served with AUS, 1946 47. Recipient Alumnus of Yr. award U. Kansas Sch. Medicine, 1987, silver medal U. Socrates, Thessaloniki, Greece, 1992. Master Am. Coll. Chest Physicians (mem. bd. regents, pres. 1988-89, gov. State of Kans.); fellow ACP (Laureate award 1990), Am. Coll. Cardiology (trustee), Am. Heart Assn., Royal Acad. Medicine (Ireland), Royal Coll. Physicians (Valencia, Spain); mem. Am. Physicians Fellowship (dir.), Univ. Cardiologists, Alpha Omega Alpha, Phi Chi (cited Best Doctors in Am., 1998). Home: 3205 Tomahawk Rd Shawnee Mission KS 66208-1861 Office: U Kans Hosp 3901 Rainbow Blvd Kansas City KS 66160-0001 *My small modicum of success was achieved by hard work, dedication to a single goal, and an application of total energy in achieving this goal. Open-mindedness, imaginativeness, and fair play have helped to make the road easier.*

DUNN, MICHAEL J. dean; m. Patricia O'Reilly; 5 children. MD, Med. Coll. of Wisconsin, 1962. Intern Johns Hopkins Hosp, Baltimore, 1962—63, resident, 1963—65; asst. prof. & co-dir., nephrology unit U. Vermont Coll. Medicine, 1969—77; various pos. Case Western Reserve, 1977—95; dean, prof. of med. and exec v.p. Med. Coll. Wis., Milw., 1995—. Grantee Fogarty Senior International Fellow. Mem.: Am. Soc. Nephrology (pres. 1989—90). Office: Med Coll Wis Office of the Dean 8701 W Watertown Plank Rd Milwaukee WI 53226-3548*

DUNN, MICHAEL M. military officer; BS in Astrodynamics, USAF Acad., 1972; grad., Squadron Officer Sch., 1976; MS in Sys. Mgmt., U. So. Calif., 1981; grad., Air Command and Staff Coll., 1983; nat. security mgmt. course,

1984; grad., Air War Coll., 1986. Commd. 2d lt. USAF, 1972, advanced through grades to maj. gen., 1996; action officer Air Staff tng. program, sec. Air Force legis. liaison, Washington, 1978-79; instr. pilot, chief of tactics, R&D Interceptor Weapons Sch., Tyndall AFB, Fla., 1979-82; F-15 pilot, chief plans, programs, spl. projects 18th Tactical Fighter Wing, Kadena Air Base, Japan, 1983-85; F-15 pilot, dir. fighter ops. Hdqs. 5th Air Force, Yokota Air Base, Japan, 1983-85; div. chief Pacific East divsn., dir. plans, dep. chief staff Hdqs. USAF, Washington, 1989-90, dep. asst. dir. Joint Nat. Security Coun. Matters, 1991, exec. asst. to dep. chief of staff, plans and ops., 1991-92; comdr. 1st Ops. Group 1st Fighter Wing, Langley AFB, Va., 1992-93; divsn. chief strategy, resources, legis. affairs divsn. Hdqs. U.S. European Command, Stuttgart, Germany, 1993-94; exec. officer to dep. comdr. in chief U.S. European Command, Stuttgart, Germany, 1994-95; sr. mil. fellow Coun. on Fgn. Rels., N.Y.C., 1995-96; sr. mil. asst. to dep. sec. of def. The Pentagon, Washington, 1996-97; dir. plans and programs Hdqs. Pacific Air Forces, Hickam AFB, Hawaii, 1997-99; dep. chief staff UN Command and Forces Korea Youngsan Army Garrison, South Korea, 1999—. Decorated Def. Disting. Svc. medal, Def. Superior Svc. medal, Meritorious Svc. medal with 3 oak leaf clusters. Office: DCS/UNC-USFK Yongsan Army Garrison Apo AP 96205-0010

DUNN, M(ORRIS) DOUGLAS, lawyer; b. Ionia, Mich., Nov. 1, 1944; s. Morris Frederick and Lola Adella (Gee) D.; m. Jill Lynn Fasbender, July 22, 1967; children: Brooks, Gillian, Joshua. BSME, U. Mich., 1967; JD, Vanderbilt U., 1970. Bar: U.S. Dist. Ct. (so. dist.) N.Y. 1972, U.S. Ct. Appeals (2d cir.) 1973, U.S. Supreme Ct. 1978. Assoc. Winthrop Stimson, Putnam & Roberts, N.Y.C., 1970-78, ptnr., 1978-84; sr. v.p., mng. dir. Shearson Lehman Bros., Inc., N.Y.C., 1984-85; ptnr. Milbank, Tweed, Hadley & McCloy, N.Y.C, 1985—. Contbr. articles to profl. jours. Fellow: Am. Bar Found.; mem.: ABA (fed. regulation of securities com. bus. law sect. 1981—, chair pub. utility, comms. and transp. law sect. 1997—98, bd.govs. 1998—2001), Internat. Bar Assn. (com. chmn. 1990—94), Assn. Bar City NY, Grey Oaks Country Club, Loch Lomond Golf Club, Canoe Brook Country Club, Down Town Assn. Office: Milbank Tweed Hadley & McCloy LLP 1 Chase Manhattan Plz Fl 47 New York NY 10005-1413

DUNN, NEIL F. retired computer science educator; b. Danvers, Mass., Aug. 11, 1934; s. Cornelius F. and Helena D. (Cashman) D.; m. Marian F. Bolger, Feb. 16, 1974. BS in Physics, Boston Coll., 1956, MS in Physics, 1958; MEd, Salem State Coll., 1965, Cert. secondary edn. tchr., Mass. Physics tchr. Burlington (Mass.) H.S., 1961-67; computer programmer Salem (Mass.) State Coll., 1970-75; sr. computer programmer/analyst Boston U., 1976-82; prof. computer sci. Mass. Bay C.C., Wellesley Hills, Mass., 1982-2000; ret., 2000. Mem. Sigma Pi Sigma (life). Avocations: amateur "ham" radio, classical music, reading, travel.

DUNN, NORMAN SAMUEL, plastics and textiles company executive; b. Woonsocket, R.I., Sept. 17, 1921; s. Israel M. and Ida (Mayerson) D.; m. Mildred M. Michaels, Aug. 31, 1975; 1 son, by previous marriage, Jeffrey Mark. Ph.B. cum laude, Providence Coll., 1942. Purchasing agt. Uniroyal Inc., Conn., 1942-48; pres. Emerson Textile Co., Chelsea, Mass., 1948-64; exec. v.p., treas. Chelsea Industries Inc., 1948-84, officer, bd. dirs., 1948—; chmn. bd. Am. Shacks Inc., 1982—. Dir. NFA Corp. Trustee Combined Jewish Philanthropies; overseer Beth Israel/Deaconess Hosp., Boston; past chmn. 330 Beacon St. Condominium Trust; hon. trustee The Rehab. Ctr. for the Aged, Boston. Mem. Two Ten Nat. Found. Clubs: Belmont Country (Mass.); Rockrimmon Country (Stamford, Conn.). Home: 330 Beacon St Boston MA 02116-1153 also: Bayberry Way Pound Ridge NY 10576 Office: PO Box 505807 181 Spencer Ave Chelsea MA 02150-3006

DUNN, PATRICIA C. retired social work educator; b. Gastonia, N.C., Jan. 27, 1938; d. Thomas S. and Hazel (Twitty) Crawford; m. Ernest F. Dunn, Sept. 8, 1962; children: Celeste, Amina. BA, Va. Union U., 1960; MSW, Mich. State U., 1967; EdD, Rutgers U., 1985. Social worker Ingham County (Mich.) Dept. Social Svc., Lansing, 1963-65; clin. social worker Family Svc. Agy., Lansing, 1967-69; dir. acad. found. Livingston Coll., New Brunswick, N.J., 1969-71; asst., then assoc. prof., dir. continuing edn. program Sch. Social Work, Rutgers U., New Brunswick, 1972—2000, assoc. dean, 1993-94; ret., 2000. Cons. Pub. Health Sch. N.J., U. Medicine and Dentistry N.J., 1998-2000. Chmn. cmty. task force for sch. reform, Plainfield (N.J.) Bd. Edn., 1995-99. Named NJ Social Worker of Yr., 2000. Mem. NASW (sect. alcohol, tobacco and other drugs, chmn. Acad. Cert. Social Workers exam. rev. bd. 1997-99, chmn. task force for Alcohol, Tobacco and Other Drugs cert., mem. splty. edn. task force). Democrat. Congregationalist. Avocations: reading, bead making, photography, travel.

DUNN, PETER COLT, not-for-profit developer; b. Balt., July 17, 1965; s. Edward Klein Dunn Jr. and Janet Evans Dunn. BA, Tufts U., 1989. Owner/mgr. Homewood Landscaping Inc., Monkton, Md., 1993—98; devel. dir. Cmty. Action Marin, San Rafael, Calif., 2000—. Prodr.: (documentaries) A Vision of Us. Vol. Grace Cathedral, San Francisco, 1998—2003. Mem.: Marin Devel. Dirs. Democrat. Episcopalian. Avocations: kayaking, hiking, gardening. Personal E-mail: pdunn@camarin.org.

DUNN, RANDALL L. federal judge; Apptd. bankruptcy judge U.S. Dist. Oreg., 1998. Office: 1001 SW 5th Ave Ste 700 Portland OR 97204-1141

DUNN, RICHARD JOSEPH, retired investment counselor; b. Chgo., Apr. 5, 1924; s. Richard Joseph and Margaret Mary (Jennett) Dunn; m. Marygrace Calhoun, Oct. 13, 1951 (dec. May 2000); children: Richard Robert(dec.), Marianne, Anthony, Gregory, Noelle. AB, Yale U., 1948; LLB, Harvard U., 1951; MBA, Stanford U., 1956. Bar: Tex. 1952. Mem. Carrington, Gowan, Johnson & Walker, Dallas, 1951-54; investment counselor Scudder, Stevens & Clark, San Francisco, 1956-84, gen. ptnr., 1974-84, ret. With AUS, 1943—46. Decorated Combat Infantry Badge, Bronze Star, Purple Heart, knight Sovereign Mil. Hospitalier Order St. John of Jerusalem of Rhodes and of Malta, Western Assn., 1978, chancellor, 1987-93, pres. 1993-99, sovereign coun., 1999, knight of obedience, 1990, Grand Cross The Sacred Mil. Constantinian Order of St. George, 1995, Grand Cross of Merit, 1999, Grand Cross of Grace and Devotion in Obedience, 2000, with sash, 2003, knight of St. Gregory, 2000; recipient Assumpta award Archdiocese of San Francisco, 1996. Roman Catholic. Home: 530 Junipero Serra Blvd San Francisco CA 94127-2727

DUNN, ROBERT ELBERT, education consultant, principal; b. Newark, May 26, 1928; s. George Elbert and Ruth Marie (Barker) D.; m. Gladys Annette Bovino, June 28, 1958. BA, Bates Coll., 1950; MA, U. Conn., 1951, PhD, 1955; spl. cert., U. Birmingham, Eng., 1952; D (hon.), Bates Coll., 1999. Tchr. of sociology Hall H.S., West Hartford, Conn., 1952-54, guidance counselor, 1953-55, asst. prin., 1955-57, vice prin., 1957-62, prin., 1962-90; dept. head West Hartford Schs., 1953-54; dep. headmaster, ednl. cons. Seoul (Korea) Internat. Schs., 1990-95. YM-YWCA Bd. YMCA, West Hartford, 1965-85; chmn. sch. and cmty. orgns., 1965-85. Rotary Found. fellow, 1951-52, Whitehead fellowship Harvard U., 1970-71, Paul Harris fellow Rotary Internat., 1993; recipient Noah Webster award C. of C., 1989, Prin. of Yr. State of Conn., 1989-90. Mem. West Hartford Rotary Club (hon.). Congregationalist. Avocation: travel. Home: 37 Ranger Ln West Hartford CT 06117-3040 E-mail: thedunns37@cs.com.

DUNN, ROBERT GIDDINGS, writer, educator; b. Santa Monica, Calif., Nov. 16, 1950; s. Gerald Rohrer and Mary Benjamin Dunn; m. Patricia Woodbridge. AB, U. Calif., Berkeley, 1973. Pub. Coral Press, N.Y.C., 2001—; writing prof. The New Sch., N.Y.C., 1986—. Copyreader Sports Illustrated, N.Y.C., 1984—; writing prof. Dickinson Coll., Carlisle, Pa., 1982—83; editl. asst. New Yorker Mag., N.Y.C. Author: The Sting Rays, 2000, Pink Cadillac, 2001, Cutting Time, 2003; musician: (compact disc) Thin Wild Mercury, 2002. Recipient O. Henry Prize Short Story, Doubleday, 1980. Personal E-mail: rgdunn@aol.com.

DUNN, ROBERT LAWRENCE, lawyer; b. Westerly, R.I., Jan. 2, 1938; m. Sammie Louise Sanford (dec. Sept. 1999); children: Christopher Jon, Geoffrey Robert; m. Linda Elizabeth Barry, 2003. BA, Cornell U., 1958; JD magna cum laude, Harvard U., 1962. Bar: N.Y. 1962, Calif. 1966, U.S. Dist. Ct. (no. dist.) Calif. 1966, U.S. Ct. Appeals (9th cir.) 1966, U.S. Dist. Ct. (ea. dist.) Calif. 1970, U.S. Supreme Ct. 1984, U.S. Dist. Ct. (cen. dist.) Calif. 1987. Law clk. to cir. judge U.S. Cir. Ct., Hartford, Conn., 1962-63; assoc. Paul, Weiss, Rifkind, Wharton & Garrison, N.Y.C., 1963-65, Bancroft, Avery & McAlister, San Francisco, 1965-71; ptnr. Bancroft & McAlister, San Francisco, 1971-93, Cooper, White & Cooper, San Francisco, 1993-99; corp. counsel Real Restaurants, Sausalito, Calif., 1999—. Author: Recovery of Damages for Lost Profits, 1978, rev. edit., 1998, Recovery of Damages for Fraud, rev. edit., 1995, Expert Witnesses: Law and Practice, 1996, rev. edit., 2003, Effectove Use of Expert Witnesses in Commerical Litigation,2003; contbr. articles to profl. jours. Mem. planning commn. Town of Corte Madera, Calif. 1974-78, mem. town coun., 1978-84, mayor, 1979, 82; bd. dirs. Merola Opera Program, 1995—, Philharmonia Baroque Orch., San Francisco, 1991-94. 1st lt. U.S. Army, 1958-59. Avocations: travel, scuba diving, opera, literature.

DUNN, ROBERT S. writer, artist; b. Bklyn., Feb. 16, 1959; s. David and Marcia Dunn. BFA Media Arts, Sch. of Visual Arts, N.Y.C., 1980; MA English, CUNY, Queens Coll., Flushing, N.Y., 1993. Author: Zen Yentas in Bondage, 1997, Guilty as Charged, 1999, Playing in Traffic, 2000, Sunspot Boulevard, 2000, Horse Latitudes, 2003.

DUNN, RONALD HOLLAND, civil engineer, management executive, consultant; b. Balt., Sept. 15, 1937; s. Delmas Joseph and Edna Grace (Holland) D.; m. Verona Lucille Lambert, Aug. 17, 1958; children: Ronald H., Jr. (dec.), David R., Brian W. BS in Engring., Johns Hopkins U., 1969. Registered profl. engr., Va., D.C.; diplomate forensic engring. Field engr. Balt. & Ohio R.R., Balt., 1958-66; chief engr. yards, shops, trackwork DeLeuw, Cather & Co., Washington, 1966-73; mgr. engring. support Parsons-Brinckerhoff-Tudor-Bechtel, Atlanta, 1973-76; dir. railroad engring. Morrison-Knudsen Co., Inc., Boise, Idaho, 1976-78; v.p. Parsons-Brinckerhoff-Centec, Inc., McLean, Va., 1978-83; v.p., area mgr., tech. dir. railway engring., profl. assoc. Parsons Brinckerhoff Quade & Douglas, Inc., McLean and Pitts., 1983-84; dir. transp. engring. R.L. Banks & Assocs., Inc., Washington, 1984; pres. R.H. Dunn & Assocs., Inc., Fairfax, Va., 1984-91, Williamsburg, Va., 1991—. Insp., rail transit facilities, Europe, 1980, 82, 84, 99, China and Hong Kong, 1985; involved in engring. of 18 railroads and 17 rail transit systems throughout N.Am., in over 45 states, Washington D.C. and 6 provinces; guest Japan Railway Civil Engring. Assn., 1972, French Nat. Railroads and Paris Transport Authority, 1988; mem. adv. com. track engrs. U.S. Dept. Transp., 1968-71. Chmn. Cub Scout Pack, Boy Scouts Am., 1972-73, committeeman, 1973-75, troop committeeman, 1979-85. Fellow ASCE, Inst. Transp. Engrs., Nat. Acad. Forensic Engrs., mem. NSPE, NAS (mem. select panel), Arbitration Assn., Am. Mgmt. Assn., Am. Rlwy. Engring. Assn. (life), Am. Pub. Transit Assn., Soc. Am. Mil. Engrs., Roadmasters and Maintenance of Way Assn. Am., Am. Rlwy. Bridge and Bldg. Assn., Constrn. Specifications Inst., Transp. Rsch. Bd., Nat. Assn. R.R. Safety Cons. and Investigators, Can. Soc. Civil Engring., Va. Soc. Profl. Engrs., Can. Urban Transit Assn., Rlwy. Tie Assn., Inst. Rapid Transit, Phi Kappa Sigma. Methodist. Office: PO Box 3106 Williamsburg VA 23187-3106 E-mail: rhdunninc@widomaker.com.

DUNN, ROY J. landscape architect; b. Camden, N.J., July 23, 1946; s. John S. and Almira G. (Dott) D. BS, Rutgers U., 1968. Registered landscape arch., N.J., Pa. Landscape architect Edward R. Bachtle, ASLA, Wilmington, Del., 1968-70, Land Design, Inc., Cherry Hill, N.J., 1970-76, Robert Kraeger, Inc., Horsham, Pa., 1976-77, Taylor, Wiseman & Taylor, Mt. Laurel, N.J., 1977-85; prin. Roy Dunn & Assocs., Inc., Medford, N.J., 1985—. Chmn., mem. Unified Nat. Exam. Com., Syracuse, N.Y., 1978-81, N.J. Bd. Landscape Archs., Newark, 1984-93. Trustee Rutgers U., 1989-95, chair bldgs. and grounds com., 1994-95; bd. dirs. Landscape Arch. Found., Washington, 1991-92. Named Outstanding Alumni of Yr., Cook Coll. Landscape Architecture Dept., 1990; recipient Dean's Svc. award, Cook Coll., 1996, Meritorious Svc. award Rutgers U, 1997. Fellow Am. Soc. Landscape Archs. (trustee 1978-85, nominating com. 1988-89, chair ann. meeting program 1991, Pres. medal 1992, N.J. Chpt. Svc. award 1986). Cook Coll. Agr. and Environ. Scis. Alumni Assn. (bd. dirs. 1984—, pres. 1988-89). Office: Roy Dunn & Assocs 200 Woodland Ave Medford NJ 08055-3460

DUNN, SHANNON, Olympic athlete; b. Steamboat Springs, Colo., Nov. 26, 1972; Mem. U.S. Olympic Snowboarding Team. Named 4th pl., World Championships, 1997, 1st pl., World Cup, 1996, 5th pl., 1995, 4 time winner, U.S. Snowboard Grand Prix; recipient Bronze medal Snowboarding Halfpipe, Nagano Olympics, 1998. Achievements include one of the dominant halfpipe competitors in the world; key athlete in the progression of women's snowboarding. Office: c/o US Ski and Snowboarding Assn PO Box 100 Park City UT 84060-0100

DUNN, TERRENCE P. manufacturing executive; b. Oct. 14, 1949; BA, Rockhurst Coll.; MBA, U. Miss. With Dunn Industries (formerly J.E. Dunn Construction Co.), 1974—; pres., CEO Dunn Industries, Kansas City, Mo. Office: Dunn Industries 929 Holmes St Kansas City MO 64106-2639*

DUNN, VIRGINIA, artist, community volunteer; b. Long Island, N.Y., Dec. 11, 1951; d. James Joseph and Margaret Virginia Dunn. Student, Lynn U., 1970—71, SUNY, Purchase, 1972-75, Propersie Sch. of Art, 1975-76, Lynn U., Boca Raton, Fla. Nurse's aide St. Joseph's Hosp., Stamford, Conn., 1967-70; with advt. dept. Cuisinart, Greenwich, Conn., 1977-89. One-woman shows include Greenwich Hosp., 2002, Garden Cafe, Greenwich, 2002, Nathaniel Witheral, exhibitions include Hurlbutt Gallery, Greenwich (Conn.) Libr., various yrs., Gertrude White Gallery, Greenwich, 1998—2002, Greenwich Garden Ctr., Cos Cob, Conn., 1989—2002 (honorable mention, 2002, 2d place, 2 honorable mentions), Ferguson Libr., Stamford, Conn., 1993—2002, Hammond Mus. & Japanese Stroll Garden, North Salem, N.Y., 1993—2001, Whitby Sch., Greenwich, 1994, Rush-Holley House, Cos Cob, 1994, Wilton (Conn.) Libr., 1995—96, E.C. Potter Gallery, Greenwich, 1996—2002, The Coffee Shoppe, Greenwich Hosp., 1997, Stamford Art Assn., 1999 (3d Pl. award), Greenwichart, Stamford, 1999, Art Soc. Old Greenwich Sidewalk Shows, 1999—2002, Stamford Art Assn., 2001, Westfield Ct., 2001, Greenwich Libr., Flinn Gallery, 2001, 2002, Landson Park, Katona, N.Y., 2001, Flynn Gallery, Greenwich Libr., 2001—02, Landson Park, Katona, N.Y., 2002, St. Raphael's Hosp., New Haven, 2002, Hammond Mus., 2002, Circe d'Art Gallery, Rowayton Art Ctr. Recipient Honorable Mention award Greenwich Art Soc., 1999, other awards for art. Mem. Oriental Brush Artist Guild (mailing com. 1993-2002), Eastern Arts Connection, The Greenwich Art Soc. (mailing com. 1988-89, Second Place award 2000), The Art Soc. of Old Greenwich (hostess 1988-89, 2d place award 2002, numerous honorable mentions), Conn. Graphic Art Ctr., Greenwich Arts Coun., The Stamford Art Assn., The Hammond Mus., Women in the Arts, Rowayton Art Assn. Avocations: art, music, travel, cats, American Indian flute. Home: 19 Miltiades Ave Riverside CT 06878-2007

DUNN, WALTER SCOTT, JR., writer, former museum director, consultant; b. Detroit, Apr. 5, 1928; s. Walter Scott and Minnie (Van Lahr) D.; m. Jean Wendeberg, July 11, 1959. BA, U. Durham, Eng., 1951; MA, Wayne State U., 1953; PhD, U. Wis., 1971. Curator indsl. history Detroit Hist. Mus., 1952-56; chief curator State Hist. Soc. Wis., Madison, 1956-63; mus. cons., 1962—; dir. Buffalo and Erie County Hist. Soc., 1963-78, Des Moines Ctr. Sci. and Industry, 1978-84, Nat. Mus. Transport, St. Louis, 1984-86, Dog Mus., St. Louis, 1987-89. Author: Western Commerce, 1760-1774, 1971, Second Front Now, 1943, 80, Hitler's Nemesis: The Red Army, 1994, The Soviet Economy and the Red Army 1930-1945, 1995, Kursk: Hitler's Gamble, 1943, 1997, Frontier Profit and Loss, 1760-1764, 1998, Views of America: Walworth County, 1998, Soviet Blitzkrieg, 2000, The New Imperial Economy, 2000, Opening New Markets, 2002, Heroes or Traitors, 2003; host several Pub. TV series on mil. history, Madison, Wis. and Buffalo, 1959-78. Served with AUS, 1946-47. Mem. Walworth County Hist. Soc. (pres. 1996). Home: N6539 Peck Station Rd Elkhorn WI 53121-3246 *Human progress can be achieved only through constant questioning of the past and innovative action to solve the problems of the future.*

DUNN, WARREN HOWARD, retired lawyer, brewery executive; b. Omaha, Sept. 25, 1934; s. John Ralph and Frances (Liddell) D.; m. Nancy Ann Nolan, July 2, 1955; children— Kathleen, Erin, Theresa, Maureen. BS in Bus. Adminstrn, Creighton U., Omaha, 1956, JD, 1958. Bar: Nebr. 1958, Wis. 1967. Claims adjuster U.S. Fidelity & Guarantee Co., Omaha, 1958-59; spl. agt. FBI, 1959-66; with Miller Brewing Co., Milw., 1966-94, v.p., gen. counsel, 1973-84, sr. v.p. adminstrn., 1984-90, exec. v.p., 1990-91, pres., CEO, 1991-92, chmn., CEO, 1992-93; ret., 1994. Mem.: Nebr. Bar Assn., Wis. Bar Assn.

DUNN, WARRICK, football player; b. Baton Rouge, La., Jan. 5, 1975; Running back Atlanta Falcons, 2002—, Tampa Bay Buccaneers, 1997—2001. Office: Atlanta Falcons 4400 Falcon Pky Flowery Branch GA 30542

DUNN, WILLIAM A., JR., cell biologist, educator; b. Pitts., Jan. 2, 1953; s. William and Mary Dunn; m. Constance Rae Uphold, Aug. 25, 1979; children: Lindsay Rae, Nicholas William. BA, Thiel Coll., 1974; PhD, Pa. State U., 1979. Post-doctoral fellow Albert Einstein Coll. Medicine, Bronx, NY, 1979—81, Johns Hopkins Med. Sch., Balt., 1981—83, rsch. assoc., 1984—86; asst. prof. U. Fla. Coll. Medicine, Gainesville, 1987—93, assoc. prof. cell biology, med. histology, 1993—. Contbr. chapters to books, articles to profl. jours. Grantee, NIH, 1984—98, 2002—, NSF, 1999—2002. Mem.: AAAS, Am. Soc. for Biochemistry and Molecular Biology, Am. Soc. Cell Biology. Republican. Methodist. Achievements include research in Molecular Biology of Cellular Autophagy. Office: Univ Florida PO Box 100235 JHMHC Gainesville FL 32610-0235 Office Fax: 352-392-3305. E-mail: dunn@ufl.edu.

DUNN, WILLIAM BRADLEY, lawyer; b. Newark, Dec. 2, 1939; s. Ernest William and Ruth Harriet (Bradley) D.; m. Judy Ann Shepherd, Aug. 2, 1988; children: John, Peter, Brian, Kelly. AB, Muskingum Coll., 1961; JD, U. Mich., 1964. Bar: Mich. 1964. Mem. Clark Hill PLC (formerly Clark, Klein & Beaumont), Detroit, 1964—. Mem. subcom. on profl. ethics State Bar of Mich., 2002—; lectr. in field. Contbr. articles to legal jours. Mem.: ABA (chair sect. real property, probate and trust law 1989—90, mem. ho. of dels. 1990—98, mem. standing com. on professionalism 1993—96, mem. standing com. on ethics and profl. responsibility 1998—2001, spl. adv. standing com. on ethics and profl. responsibility 1998—2001, 2003—), Internat. Assn. Attys. and Exec. Corp. Real Estate, Am. Coll. Real Estate Lawyers (pres. 1983—84). Episcopalian. Home: 6398 Catalpa Ct Troy MI 48098-2231 Office: Clark Hill PLC 500 Woodward Ave Ste 3500 Detroit MI 48226-3435 E-mail: wdunn@clarkhill.com.

DUNN, WILLIAM BRUNA, III, journalist; b. Streator, Ill., Jan. 26, 1947; s. William Bruna and Mary Elizabeth (Allgaier) D.; m. Sandra Lee Ann Klein, Aug. 23, 1969; 1 child, William IV. BS in Journalism, U. Fla., 1969. Reporter Orlando (Fla.) Sentinel, 1967-69, mng. editor, 1970-80, dep. mng. editor, 1979-81, mng. editor, 1981-91, assoc. mng. editor, photos, graphics and design, 1991-2001; design editor Orlando (Fla.) Sentinel, 2001—02. Author: Kidding Around, 1973; editor: SHAQ! That Magical Rookie Season, 1993; editor: Martin Andersen: Editor, Publisher, Galley Boy, 1996. Recipient Silver Gavel award ABA, 1974; Gold and Silver medals Soc. News Design, 1984. Mem. Nat. Press Photographers Assn., Soc. Profl. Journalists (past pres. Cen. Fla. chpt.), Soc. of News Design. Roman Catholic. Home: 4 E Vanderbilt St Orlando FL 32804-5925

DUNN, WILLIAM JACKSON, dental educator, researcher; b. Ozark, Ala., Oct. 13, 1959; s. Leo Miner and Sue Dunn; m. Betsy Diane Eberly, Apr. 18, 1987; children: Thomas Destin, William Jackson, Darien James. BA, Tex. Tech U., 1981; DDS, U. Tex., Houston, 1986. Diplomate Fed. Services Bd. Dentistry, Am. Bd. of Dentistry. Comdr. 320 Aeromedical Dental Squadron, Seeb Air Base; dir. of rsch. 59 Dental Squadron, Lackland AFB, Tex., 2000—; chair med. bioethics Wilford Hall Med. Ctr., Lackland AFB, Tex., 2001—. Cons. to surgeon gen. USAF, Washington, 2000—; alt. chair Instl. Rev. Bd., Wilford Hall Medical Center, Tex., 2000—; del. ADA, Chgo., 1998—; dep. regent Internat. Coll. of Dentists, San Antonio, 2002—. Author: (scientific research) Journal of the American Dental Association, American Journal of Dentistry, Journal of Prosthodontics, American Journal of Orthodontics. Lt. col. USAF, 1987—2002. Decorated Meritorious Svc. medal USAF; recipient Fellow award, Internat. Coll. of Dentists, 2001, Peirre Fauchard Honor Acad., 1998. Fellow: Am. Coll. of Dentists; mem.: ADA (del. Chgo. 1998—2002), Lion's Club Internat. (life; del. 1998—2002, Life award 2002). Conservative. Presbyterian. Achievements include research in Polymer Chemistry/Dental; Orthodontic Bonding; Light-Emitting Diodes. Avocations: golf, tennis, running. Home: 9406 Tranquil Park Dr San Antonio TX 78254 Office: 59 DS/MRDGB 1615 Truemper St Lackland A F B TX 78236-5551 Home Fax: 210-292-2740. Personal E-mail: wjdarkhorse@aol.com. E-mail: william.dunn@lackland.af.mil.

DUNNE, WILLIAM WYLY, corporate lawyer; b. N.Y.C., Mar. 7, 1925; s. Beverly Charles and Helen Ward (Fay) D.; m. Rosemarie Boehme, Sept. 4, 1947; 1 child, Fred Wyly. BA cum laude, Harvard U., 1947, JD cum laude, 1950. Bar: D.C. 1950, U.S. Cir. Ct. D.C. 1958, N.Y. 1982. Atty.-advisor USAF, Wiesbaden, 1951-58; mng. dir. Collins Radio GmbH, Frankfurt, Fed. Republic of Germany, 1958-61; dir. contracts Litton Industries GmbH, Hamburg and Bonn, Fed. Republic of Germany, 1962-64; mgr. Paris office LTV, Inc., 1964-68, dir. European affairs, 1969-70; gen. counsel Mobil Oil Francaise, Paris, 1970-81; sr. counsel Mobil Oil Corp., N.Y.C., 1981-86. Exec. v.p. Assn. of Ams. Resident Overseas, Paris, 1980-81; co-chmn, corp. counsel subcom. Am. C. of C., Paris, 1981. Served to 1st lt. U.S. Army, 1944-47. Recipient Saltonstall prize Law Sch., Harvard U., Cambridge, Mass., 1947, Sheldon prize Harvard U., Cambridge, 1948. Mem. ABA, N.Y. Bar Assn., D.C. Bar Assn., Farmington Country Club (Charlottesville, Va.). Republican. Avocations: golf, dancing, classical music. Home: 116 Shasta Ct Charlottesville VA 22903-4216 E-mail: wwd5t@earthlink.net.

DUNNE, DANA PHILIP C. management consultant; b. NYC, July 30, 1963; s. Philip M. and Diane (Cantine) D. BA, Wesleyan U., 1985; MBA, Wharton Sch., 1990; MA in Internat. Studies, U. Pa., 1990. Asst. treas. Chase Manhattan Bank, N.Y.C., 1985-87; sr. engagement mgr. McKinsey & Co., Inc., 1990-98; v.p. strategy of comm. group US West Media, Inc., Denver, 1998—2002; pres. Belgacom Telecomm., 2002—. Author: Financial Instability: An Empirical Analysis; editor-in-chief Wesleyan Economic Review. Mem. Meals for Homeless St. James' Ch., 1985—; mentor Underprivileged Youths in South Bronx, 1986. Named Disting. Internat. Young Leader Cambridge U. Am. Biog. Inst., Eng., 1987. Episcopalian. Avocations: art history, skiing, squash, crew. Home: 750 Park Ave New York NY 10021-4252

DUNNE, DIANE C. marketing executive; b. Milw. d. Francis and Ruth Borman Cantine; 1 child, Dana Philip. BS, Marquette U.; MBA, NYU, 1985. Mgr. advt. NBC, N.Y.C., 1975-77; dir. mktg. CBS, N.Y.C., 1977-80; dir. funding Bloomingdale's, N.Y.C., 1980—; real estate cons. The Corcoran Group. Dir. 750 Park Ave. Corp., N.Y.C., 1999—; dir. Women's Econ. Round Table, 1988—; v.p. events, bd. dirs. The Oxford U. Alumni Assn. N.Y., 1993—. Author: Guidelines to Advertising All News Radio, 1976, Guidelines for Catalogue Copywriters, 1985; asst. editor Am. Cancer Soc., Gourmet Guide for Busy People by Famous People, 1985, The International Directory of Distinguished Leadership; columnist The N.Y. Sun; contbr. articles to profl. jours. Mem. Am. Cancer Soc., N.Y.C., 1980—; chair Feed the Homeless com. St. James Ch., N.Y.C., 1984-87; mem. pastoral and cmty. ministry com. St. James Altar Guild. Mem. Fashion Group (co-chair regional com.), Women's Econ. Roundtable (bd. dirs. 1988), NYU Exec. MBA Assn. Episcopalian. Avocations: opera, jogging, skiing, rollerblading. Home: 750 Park Ave New York NY 10021-4252 Office: Bloomingdales 770 Lexington Ave New York NY 10021-8165

DUNNE, DONALD REDMOND, military officer; b. Toms River, N.J., July 16, 1959; s. Donald James and Jane Irene Dunne; m. Mi Suk Kim, Mar. 17, 1987; children: Morgan, Jacqulaine, Brittany, Megan. BA in Polit. Sci., SUNY, Geneseo, 1981; MA in Nat. Security Studies, Calif. State U., San Bernardino, 2003. Commd. 2d lt. U.S. Army, advanced through grades to maj., 1997; nuclear weapons platoon leader 27th U.S. Army Field Arty. Detachment, Turkey, 1987—88, 6-37 Field Arty. Bn., Uijongbu, Republic of Korea, 1988—89; all source intelligence officer 4-21 Infantry Bn., Ft. Ord, Calif., 1990—91; intelligence tng. officer 7th Infantry Divsn. (Light), 1991—92; signals intelligence officer 122d Signal Bn., Tongduchon, Republic of Korea, 1992—93; asst. intelligence ops. officer 102d Mil. Intelligence Bn., 1993—94; all source intelligence co. comdr., 1994—95; intelligence adminstrn. exec officer 372d Mil. Intelligence Bn., Oakland, Calif., 1995—96; fin. planner Am Express, San Rafael, 1996—97; asst. chief counterterrorism analyst 7th Army Chief of Staff Intelligence, Heidelberg, Germany, 1997; lang. bn. ops. officer 372d Mil. Intelligence Bn., Bell, Calif., 1997—99; detailed insp. gen. 63d Regional Support Command, Los Alamitos, 1999—. Recipient Knowlton award Mil. Intelligence Corps Assn., 1997. Mem. Turkish-Am. Soc. Roman Catholic

Home: 13363 Rusty Fig Cir Cerritos CA 90703-1311 Office: 63 Regional Support Command 4235 Yorktown Ave Los Alamitos CA 90720 Office Fax: 562 795 2269. E-mail: donald.dunne@usarc-emh2.army.mil.

DUNNE, GERARD FRANCIS, lawyer; b. Huntington, N.Y., Aug. 23, 1947; s. Frank and Adele A. (Malerba) D.; m. Judith Ellen Gordon, Dec. 5, 1976; 1 child, Heather Chelsey. B in Engring., Manhattan Coll., 1969; JD, U. Balt., 1974. Bar: D.C. 1974, N.Y. 1974, U.S. Patent Office, U.S. Dist. Ct. (ea. and so. dists.) N.Y. 1976, U.S. Ct. Appeals (fed. cir.) 1982, U.S. Ct. Appeals (2d, 3d, 8th, 9th and Fed. cirs.), U.S. Supreme Ct. 1987. Examiner patents U.S. Patent Office, Washington, 1969-74; assoc. Law Offices of Albert C. Johnston P.C., N.Y.C., 1974-76, Wyatt, Gerber, Burke & Badie, N.Y.C., 1976-82, ptnr., 1982-94; sole practice law N.Y.C., 1995—. Mem. ABA, Assn. of Bar of City of N.Y., Fed. Bar Council, Am. Intellectual Property Law Assn. Home: 89-04 63rd Ave Rego Park NY 11374-2815 Office: 156 5th Ave Ste 1223 New York NY 10010-7002 E-mail: gfdunne@rcn.com.

DUNNE, JAMES ROBERT, academic administrator, management consultant, business educator; b. Cleve., July 8, 1929; s. Carroll Joseph and Wilma Agnes (Sutmore) D.; m. Nancy Anne McSween, Oct. 28, 1952; children: James Jr., Stephen. BA, Albion Coll., 1951; MA, SUNY, Albany, 1964, PhD, 1972; postgrad., Nova Southeastern U., Webster U., Nat. Def. U. Sect. mgr. news bur. GE, Schenectady, N.Y., 1955-63; asst. to chancelor SUNY, Albany, 1963-68; dir. pub. affairs N.Y. State Office Gen. Svcs., Albany, 1968-73; v.p. mktg. N.Y. State Higher Edn. Assistance Corp., Albany, 1973-76, exec. on loan N.Y. State U.S. Office Edn., 1976-78; pres. J.R. Dunne, Inc., Orlando, Fla., 1978-94; program mgr. Eagle Tech., Inc., Orlando, 1983-85; asst. prof. mgmt., acad. program chmn. Fla. Inst. Tech., Orlando, 1985-89; sr. mgmt. analyst Star Mountain, Inc., 1989-90; regional dir. Webster U., Orlando, Fla., 1990-98, spl. asst. devel. to exec. v.p., 1998-2000; dir. Sarasota Met. Campus and Bradenton Classrm. Ctr., 1999-2000; assoc. emeritus Webster U., 2000—. Adj. prof. Schenectady C.C., 1968-76, SUNY, Brockport, 1970-72; adj. instr. Valencia C.C., Orlando, 1980-94, Fla. So. Coll., Orlando, 1980-81, Brevard C.C., Titusville, Fla., 1979-80, Columbia Coll., Orlando, 1980-94; mem. nat. faculty Nova U., Ft. Lauderdale, Fla., 1980-91; acad. assoc. Atlantic Coun., 1982-96; advisor doctoral dissertation Nova U., 1988-2001; cons. Am. Schs. Corp., 1998-2000; bd. dirs., tutor K-5 grades Anna Maria Island Cmty. Ctr., 2001-03, tutor, 2003—. Pres. Westbay Point and Moorings Condo Assn., 2003—; mem. steering com. Manatee Visioning Program, 2002—03; dirs. Manatee-Sarasota chpt., United Nations Assn., 2003—; mem. Parks and Beautification Com., City of Holmes Beach; lector, eucharist min. St. Bernard's Roman Cath. Ch., Holmes Beach, Fla.; bd. dirs. South Fla. Mus., 2002—. With USN, 1952—55, capt. USNR, 1955—89. Paul Harris fellow, 1989. Mem.: VFW, Mil. Officers of Am., Rotary (chmn. dist. youth exch. 1981—91, mem. Paul Harris Sch. com. 1988—89, pres. Anna Maria Island chpt. 2001—03, Dist. 6960 Paul Harris Ambassadorial Scholarship com. 2001—, Area 8 dep. dist. gov. 2003—, Rotarian of Yr. Altamonte Springs chpt. 1981, 1983, 1985). Republican. Roman Catholic. Avocations: golf, travel. Home: 6400 Flotilla Dr Apt 31 Holmes Beach FL 34217-1425

DUNNE, JOHN GREGORY, writer; b. Hartford, Conn., May 25, 1932; s. Richard Edwin and Dorothy (Burns) D.; m. Joan Didion, Jan. 30, 1964; 1 child, Quintana Roo. AB, Princeton U., 1954. Writer, editor Time mag., N.Y.C. Columnist: New West, Saturday Evening Post, 1967-69, Esquire, 1976-77, 1986-87; author: books, including: Delano: The Story of the California Grape Strike, 1967, The Studio, 1969, Vegas: A Memoir of a Dark Season, 1974, True Confessions, 1977, Quintana and Friends, 1978, Dutch Shea, Jr., 1982, The Red White and Blue, 1987, Harp, 1989, Crooning, 1990, Playland, 1994, Monster: Living Off the Big Screen, 1997; (with Joan Didion) screenplay Panic in Needle Park, 1971, Play It As It Lays, 1973, A Star is Born, 1976, True Confessions, 1981, Hills Like White Elephants, 1991, Broken Trust, 1995, Up Close & Personal, 1996; contbr. articles to mags., including New Yorker, New York Rev. Served with U.S. Army, 1954-56. Office: Janklow & Nesbit Assocs 445 Park Ave New York NY 10022-2606*

DUNNE, KEVIN JOSEPH, lawyer; b. Pitts., Sept. 22, 1941; s. Matthew S. and Marjorie (Whelan) D.; m. Heather Wright Dunne, Sept. 27, 1963; children: Erin, Kevin Jr., Patrick, Sean. BA, U. Conn., 1963; JD, Georgetown U., 1966. Bar: Calif. 1967, U.S. Dist. Ct. (no. dist.) Calif., 1967, U.S. Dist. Ct. (ea. dist.) Calif. 1969, U.S. Dist. Ct. (ctrl. dist.) Calif. 1971, U.S. Ct. Appeals (9th cir.) 1971. Assoc. Sedgwick, Detert, Moran & Arnold, San Francisco, 1968-75, ptnr., 1975—, chmn., 2001—. Adj. prof. U. San Francisco Sch. Law, 1980-86; bd. editorial advisors Bender's Drug Product Liability Reporter, 1988-92. Author: Dunne on Depositions, 1995; contbr. articles to profl. jours. Capt. U.S. Army, 1966-68, Vietnam. Recipient Bronze Star, Army Commendation medal; recipient Exceptional Performance award Def. Rsch. Inst., 1988. Fellow: Am. Coll. Trial Lawyers, Internat. Acad. Trial Lawyers; mem.: Lawyers for Civil Justice (pres. 1998—2000), Am. Bd. Trial Advocates, Internat. Assn. Def. Counsel (pres. 1994—95), No Calif. Assn. Def. Counsel (pres. 1987—88). Roman Catholic. Avocation: golf. Office: Sedgwick Detert Moran & Arnold 1 Embarcadero Ctr Ste 1600 San Francisco CA 94111-3716

DUNNE, NANCY ANNE, retired social services administrator; b. Ionia, Mich., Aug. 5, 1929; d. Warner Kingsley and Hazel Fern (Alliason) McSween; m. James Robert, Oct. 28, 1952; children: James Robert Jr., Stephen Michael. BA, Albion (Mich.) Coll., 1951. Tchr. Oakdale Elem., Grand Rapids, Mich., 1951-53, Lakeside Sch., East Grand Rapids, Mich., 1953; clk. Office of Naval Rsch., Washington, 1954-55; dir. pub. rels. Diocesan Office Health and Social Svcs., Albany, N.Y., 1971-74; dir. vol. action dept. Coun. of Human Resources, Schenectady, N.Y., 1974-76; pers. asst. Am. Soc. Assn. Execs., Washington, 1977-78; adminstrv. asst. N.Y. Soc. Cons. Engrs., N.Y.C., 1978-79, Assessment Designs, Inc., Orlando, Fla., 1980-82, Catholic Social Svcs., Orlando, Fla., 1982-84, ret., 1984. Only female mem. N.Y. State Comm. Cultural Resources, Albany, 1970-73; bd. dirs. Coalition for the Homeless, Orlando, 1983-87; tutor, mentor After Sch. Program, Anna Maria Island, Fla.; vol. Blake Meml. Hosp., Bradenton, Fla., 1999-2003, Imagine Manatee Task Force, Bradenton, 2003; mem. Anna Maria Island Cmty. Ctr., 2000-01; bd. dirs. Anna Maria Island Symphony Orch., 2003—; 1st v.p. Performing arts Downtown Manatee County, Inc., 2003-03; devel. dir., bd. dirs. Anna Maria Island Orch. and Chorus, 2003-04. Mem. AAUW (pres. Manatee County br. 2001-03), Jr. League of Schenectady (Vol. of Yr. award 1965-66), Schenectady Symphony Orch. (pres. 1969-70), Ladies of Charity (pres. Albany chpt. 1970-72, pres. Orlando chpt. 1984-86, nat. pres. 1990-94, nat. bd. dirs. 2001-02, v.p. internat. 1990-94, bd. dirs. 1994-2000). Roman Catholic. Avocations: reading, traveling, golfing, bridge, entertaining friends. Home: 6400 Flotilla Dr Apt 31 Holmes Beach FL 34217-1425

DUNNE, THOMAS, geology educator; b. Prestbury, U.K., Apr. 21, 1943; arrived in U.S., 1964; s. Thomas and Monica Mary (Whitter) D. BA with honors, Cambridge (Eng.) U., 1964; PhD, Johns Hopkins U., 1969. Rsch. assoc. USDA-Agrl. Rsch. Svc., Danville, Vt., 1966—68; rsch. hydrologist U.S. Geol. Survey, Washington, 1969; asst. prof. McGill U., Montreal, Canada, 1969—73; from asst. prof. to prof. U. Wash., Seattle, 1973—95, chmn. dept., 1984—89; prof. sch. environ. scis. & mgmt. U. Calif., Santa Barbara, 1995—. Vis. prof. U. Nairobi, Kenya, 1969-71; cons. in field, 1970—. Author (with L.B. Leopold) Water in Environmental Planning; (with L.M. Reid) Rapid Evaluation of Sediment Budgets, 1996. Fulbright scholar 1984; grantee NSF, NASA, Rockefeller Found., 1969—; named to NAS, 1988, Guggenheim fellow, 1989-90. Fellow AAAS, Am. Acad. Arts and Scis., Am. Geophys. Union (Robert E. Horton award 1987, Langbein lectr. 2003), Calif. Acad. Scis.; mem. NAS (G.K. Warren prize in Fluviatile Geology 1998), Geol. Soc. Am., Sigma Xi. Office: U Calif Donald Bren Sch Environ Scis & Mgmt 4670 Physical Sciences N Santa Barbara CA 93106

DUNNELL, ROBERT CHESTER, archaeologist, educator; b. Wheeling, W.Va., Dec. 4, 1942; s. Arthur and Kathryn (McCarter) D.; m. Mary Jewett Davidson, June 4, 1966. BA, U. Ky., 1964; PhD (Woodrow Wilson fellow/Univ. fellow), Yale U., 1967. Asst. prof. anthropology U. Wash., Seattle, 1967-71, assoc. prof., 1971-74, prof., 1974—98, prof. emeritus, 1998—, chmn. dept. anthropology, 1973-85; prin. investigator Nat. Park Svc. contracts, U.S. Army Corps Engrs. contracts; adj. curator N.Am. archaeology Burke Meml. Wash. State Mus., 1971-97; mem. sci. com. Wash. Archeol. Rsch. Ctr., 1975-79; adj. prof. Quaternary Rsch. Ctr., 1976—. Mem. coun. from Anthropology to Quaternary Rsch. Ctr. Adn. Coun., 1976-79; curatorial affiliate in anthropology Peabody Mus. Naturay History, Yale U., 1985—; mem. nat. adv. coun. Desert Rsch. Inst., 1987-89; adj. prof. U. Tenn., 1997—, Miss. State U., 1997—. Mem. editl. bd.: Advances in Archaeological Theory and Method, 1977-87, Studies in Archaeol. Method and Theory, 1987 2002, Jour. Field Archaeology, 1985-2002. Fellow AAAS (rep. to sect. H exec. bd. 1988-90); mem. Soc. for Am. Archaeology, Assn. Field Archaeology (pres. 1985-88), Sigma Xi. Office: 21 Pruett Rd Natchez MS 39120-9427

DUNNER, DAVID LOUIS, medical educator; b. Bklyn., May 27, 1940; s. Edward and Reichel (Connor) D.; m. Peggy Jane Zolbert, Dec. 27, 1964; children: Laura Louise, Jonathan Michael. AA, George Washington U., 1960; MD, Washington U., St. Louis, 1965. Diplomate Am. Bd. Psychiatry and Neurology. Intern Phila. Gen. Hosp., 1965-66; resident in psychiatry Barnes Renard Hosp. of Washington U., St. Louis, 1966-69; research psychiatrist N.Y. State Psychiat. Inst., N.Y.C., 1971-79; from asst. prof. to assoc. prof. clin. psychiatry Columbia U., N.Y.C., 1972-79; chief psychiatry Harborview Med. Ctr., Seattle, 1979-89, dir. outpatient psychiatry, 1989-97; prof. psychiatry and behavioral scis. U. Wash., Seattle, 1979—, vice chmn. clin. svcs., 1989-97; dir. Ctr. for Anxiety & Depression, 1997—. Cons. Found. for Depression and Manic Depression, N.Y.C., 1974—. Editor-in-chief Comprehensive Psychiatry, 1997—; contbr. articles to profl. jours. Served to lt. comdr. USPHS, 1969-71. Fellow Am. Psychiat. Assn., Am. Psychopathol. Assn. (pres. 1986), Am. Coll. Neuropsychopharmacology, West Coast Coll. Biol. Psychiatry (charter, pres. 1987); mem. Psychiat. Research Soc. (pres. 1984). Office: Ctr for Anxiety & Depression 4225 Roosevelt Way NE Ste 306C Seattle WA 98105-6099 E-mail: ddunner@u.washington.edu., dldunner@attbi.com.

DUNNER, DONALD ROBERT, lawyer; b. Bklyn., 1931; s. Edward Dunner and Mollie Friedman; m. Jenny Sue Dailey, 1957; children: Jennifer D. Weaver, Lisa A. BSChemE, Purdue U., 1953; JD, Georgetown U., 1958. Bar: D.C. 1958, U.S. Supreme Ct. 1963, U.S. Ct. Appeals (fed. cir.) 1982. Patent examiner U.S. Patent & Trademark Office, Washington, 1955-56; law clk. U.S. Ct. Customs and Patent Appeals, Washington, 1956-58; assoc. Strauch, Nolan & Neale, Washington, 1958-60; assoc., ptnr. Diggins & Le Blanc, Washington, 1960-62; ptnr. Lane, Aitken, Dunner & Ziems, Washington, 1962-78; of counsel Finnegan, Henderson, Farabow & Garrett, Washington, 1978-79; ptnr. Finnegan, Henderson, Farabow, Garrett & Dunner, Washington, 1979—. Mem. Pres. Adv. Com. on Indsl. Innovation, 1978-79; professorial lectr. in law George Washington Law Ctr., 1969-82; adj. prof. Washington Coll. of Law, Am. U., 1992-99. Co-author: Patent Law Perspectives, 1970-89, Court Review of Patent Office Decisions: CCPA, 1973, Court of Appeals for the Federal Circuit: Practice and Procedure, 1985. Chmn. Fed. Cir. Adv. Com., 1982-92; mem. adv. commn. on Patent Law Reform, 1991-92. With U.S. Army, 1953-55. Recipient Best Article of Yr. award Patent Office Soc., 1980, award Patent Resources Group, 1980. Fellow Am. Coll. Trial Lawyers; mem. ABA (chair intellectual property law sect. 1995-96, ho. of dels. 2002—), Am. Intellectual Property Law Assn. (pres. 1979-80), D.C. Bar Assn. (chmn. patent, trademark and copyright law sect. 1964-65), D.C. Bar (chair patent, trademark and copyright law sect. 1976-77), Fed. Cir. Bar Assn. (bd. dirs. 1999-2002), Am. Inn of Ct. (pres. Giles S. Rich Inn 1994-95), Cosmos Club. Avocations: tennis, skiing, sailing. Office: Finnegan Henderson Farabow 1300 I St NW Washington DC 20005-3315 E-mail: dunnerd@finnegan.com.

DUNNETT, DENNIS GEORGE, retired state official; b. Auburn, Calif., Aug. 5, 1939; s. George DeHaven and Elizabeth Grace (Sullivan) D. AA in Elec. Engring., Sierra Coll., 1959; AB in Econs., Sacramento State Coll., 1966. Engring. technician State of Calif., Marysville, 1961-62, data processing technician Sacramento, 1962-67, EDP programmer and analyst, 1967-74, staff services mgr. and contract adminstr., 1974-76, hardware acquisition mgr., 1976-86, support services br. mgr., information security officer, 1986-90, chief Office Security and Operational Recovery, 1990-92, spl. projects mgr., 1992-93, customer support ctr. mgr., 1994, procurement mgr., 1994-97, chief bur. adminstrn., 1997-2000, ret., 2000—. Patron San Francisco Opera, TV Sta. KVIE. Mem. AARP, IEEE, ACLU, IEEE Computer Soc., Fine Arts Mus. of San Francisco, Crocker Art Mus., Calif. State U.-Sacramento Alumni Assn. (life). Home: 729 Blackmer Cir Sacramento CA 95825-4704 E-mail: dpdennis39@comcast.net.

DUNNIGAN, BRIAN LEIGH, military historian, curator; b. Detroit, July 11, 1949; s. James Patrick and Dorothy Jane (McKay) D.; m. Carol Lynn Fredriksen, Sept. 21, 1974 (div. Oct. 1988); m. Candice Maria Cain, Apr. 22, 1989; children: James Cain, Claire Beausom. BA in History, U. Mich., 1971, MA in History, 1973; MA in History and Museum Studies, Cooperstown Grad. Programs, 1979. Curator Mackinac Island (Mich.) State Park Commn., 1971-74; mng. dir. Historic Fort Wayne, Ind., 1974-79; exec. dir. Old Fort Niagara Assn., Youngstown, N.Y., 1979-96; curator of maps William L. Clements Libr. U. Mich., Ann Arbor, 1996—. Author: History and Guide to Old Fort Niagara, 1985, Siege-1759, 1986, rev. edit., 1996, Glorious Old Relic, 1987, Forts Within A Fort, 1989, Old Fort Niagara in Four Centuries, 1991; editor: Pouchot's Memoirs on the Late War in North America, 1994, Niagara, 1796, 1996, Frontier Metropolis, 2001. Fellow Co. Mil. Historians. Home: 4531 Maute Rd Grass Lake MI 49240 Office: William L Clements Libr 909 S University Ave Ann Arbor MI 48109-1190

DUNNIGAN, EARL JOSEPH, nephrologist; b. Detroit, Feb. 27, 1958; s. Ralph Joseph and Bernadette Marie D.; children: Matthew Ryan. BS, U. N.D., 1979, MD, 1983. Diplomate Am. Bd. Internal Medicine, Am. Bd. Nephrology. Med. dir. St. Alexius Renal Svcs., Bismarck, N.D., 1989—, St. Alexius Med. Ctr., Bismarck, 1989—. Clin. prof. medicine U. N.D. Sch. Medicine. Fellow ACP. Avocations: hunting, fishing, woodworking. Office: Nephrology Clinic St Alexius Med Ctr 900 E Broadway Ave Bismarck ND 58501-4520

DUNNIGAN, MARY ANN, former educational administrator; b. St. Maries, Idaho, Sept. 7, 1915; d. William Henry and Mary Ellen (Kelly) D. BA, Holy Names Coll., Spokane, Wash., 1942; MA, Gonzaga U., Spokane, 1957; postgrad., U. Idaho, UCLA. Tchr. rural schs. Bonner County, 1936-41; tchr. elem. schs., 1941, 45-59; tchr. high sch., 1942, 45; coord. elem. edn., 1959—81; rsch., devl. program special edn. program, 1975—81; rsch., devl. kindergarten program, 1978—81; prin. kindergarten Sch. Dist. 271, Coeur d'Alene, Idaho, 1978-81; instr. extension classes U. Idaho. Curriculum chmn. Idaho Gov.'s Conf. on Edn.; mem. adv. coun. Head Startl bd. dirs. Coeur d'Alene Tchrs. Credit Union, 1958-87, pres., treas., 1976-89. Mem. adv. coun. Coun. for Aging; mem. North Idaho Mus., Cmty. Coun., Cmty. Concerts, Cmty. Theater, North Idaho Booster Club, Mayor's Com. on Handicapped; mem. task force and diocesan bd. Cath. Edn. Idaho, 1969-74; mem. Coeur d'Alene U.S. Constn. Bicentennial Com., 1986-91; hist. chmn. Coeur d'Alene Centennial, 1986-89, chmn. hist. com., 1988; mem. staff centennial com. for Kootenai County, 1990; parliamentarian Idaho Coun. Cath. Women State Conv., 1993, Idaho Cath. Daus. of Am. State Conv., 1994; mem. steering com. New Holy Family Cath. Sch. in Kootenai County, 1994; parliamentarian Idaho Coun. Cath. Women, 1992. Named Citizen of Yr., North Idaho Coll., 1974, Idaho Cath. Dau. of Yr., 1968, Educator of Yr., Kootenai County Women's Forum, 1998, Woman of Distinction in Edn. award Kootenai County Women's Forum, Inc., North Idaho Coll., Lewis and Clark State Coll., and U. Idaho, 1998; named to Idaho Ret. Tchrs. Hall of Fame, 1987; recipient hon. alumnus award North Idaho Coll., 1987, Nat. Cmty. Svc. award AARP/NRTA, 1988. Mem. NEA, Idaho Edn. Assn., Idaho Nat. Tchrs. Assn. (state chmn. pre-retirement 1985-92), Kootenai County Ret. Tchrs. Assn. (pres. 1983-87),Toastmasters Intenat. Kootenai County (pres. 1960-1962), Cath. Daugs. Am. (state regent 1956-62, 50 Yr. Pin 1997), China Painters Club, Rambling Rovers, Delta Kappa Gamma (charter, pres. Zeta chpt. 1947-92, Silver Bell award for 50 yrs. svc. 1997). Home: 720 N 9th St Coeur D Alene ID 83814-4259

DUNNIGAN, T. KEVIN, electrical and electronics manufacturing company executive; b. Montreal, Que., Can., Jan. 31, 1938; s. John George and Olive Mary (Brophy) D.; m. Beverley Alice Laramee, Apr. 11, 1960 (div. June 1980); children: David, Kathleen; m. Leah Anne Merlo. BA in Commerce, Loyola U., 1971. With Can. Elec. Distbg. Co., prior to 1962; salesman No. Telecom, Montreal, 1956-60; purchasing agt. Black-MacDonald, Montreal, 1960-62; salesman Thomas & Betts Corp., Iberville, Que., 1962-67, v.p. sales, 1967-70, pres., 1970-73, div. pres. Bridgewater, N.J., 1974-78, corp. exec. v.p. electronics, 1978-80, pres., 1980—, chief oper. officer, 1980-85, chief exec. officer, 1985-97, chmn. bd. Memphis, 1992—. Bd. dirs. C.R. Bard Inc., Decre & Co., Imagistics Inc., Pro-Mach, Inc. Office: Thomas & Betts Corp 8155 T&B Blvd Memphis TN 38125

DUNNING, KENNETH LAVERNE, research physicist; b. Yale, Iowa, Sept. 24, 1914; s. Howard Grant and Gertrude Estelle (Dygert) D.; m. Ruth Ellen Pyle, Sept. 2, 1941; children: David M., Jane B., John K., Marion Leigh. BEE, U. Minn., 1938; MS in Physics, U. Md., 1950; PhD in Physics, Cath. U. Am., 1968. Engr. Western Union, N.Y.C., 1938-41; physicist U.S. Naval Research Lab., Washington, 1945-80; cons. Port Ludlow, Wash., 1981—2001. Contbr. articles to profl. jours. Pres. Highland Greens Condominium Assn., Port Ludlow, 1983-84, v.p. 1984-85. Served to maj. U.S. Army, 1941-45. Recipient Research Pub. award Naval Research Lab., 1971. Mem. IEEE, Am. Phys. Soc., Sigma Xi, Tau Beta Pi, Eta Kappa Nu. Home and Office: 157 Holly Hills Dr Williamsburg VA 23185-3386

DUNN KELLY, RUTH EMMA, management consultant; b. Tuskegee, Ala., Apr. 26, 1945; d. Moses and Annie Virgia Dunn; m. Bernard Kelly, June 2, 2001. BS, Wayne State U., 1985; MS, Ctrl. Mich. U., 1989. Analyst Gen. Motors, Detroit, 1969—99; test adminstr. Aon Cons., Finley, Ohio, 1998—; counselor Macomb County Crisis Ctr., Warren, Mich., 1994—95.

DUNPHY, EDWARD JAMES, crop science extension specialist; b. Frederick, Md., Nov. 14, 1940; s. Edward John and Marie W. (Barlow) D.; m. Judith Kay Mitchell, Aug. 18, 1962; children: Kevin James, Brian Patrick, Cory Edward. MS, U. Ill., 1964; PhD, Iowa State U., 1972. Rsch. asst. U. Ill., Urbana, 1962-64; agronomist Dunphy's Feed & Fertilizer, Sullivan, Ill., 1964-66; rsch. asst. Iowa State U., Ames, 1969-72, crop prodn. specialist Des Moines, 1972-75; extension specialist soybeans N.C. State U., Raleigh, 1975—, prof. crop sci., 1986—. Instr. soybean prodn. N.C., 1975—; mem. N.C. Land Use Value Adv. Bd., Raleigh, 1987—. Author 4 computer programs; contbr. numerous articles to profl. jours. Cubmaster Boy Scouts Am., Raleigh, 1976-81, troop com. chair, 1979-98; officer Athens Dr. Band Boosters, Raleigh, 1983-90. Sgt. U.S. Army, 1966-69. Recipient Meritorious Svc. award N.C. Soybean Producers. Mem. Am. Soc. Agronomy (com. chair, fellow, Agronomic Extension Edn. award), Crop and Soil Sci. Socs. Am., Am. Soybean Assn. (mem. S.Am. soybean mission), Coun. for Agrl. Sci. and Tech., Alpha Zeta, Epsilon Sigma Phi, Gamma Sigma Delta, Phi Eta Sigma, Phi Kappa Phi, Sigma Xi. Achievements include research on soybean varieties, production, management and econ. Home: 3708 Swift Dr Raleigh NC 27606-2572 Office: NC State U Box 7620 Raleigh NC 27695-7620 E-mail: jim_dunphy@ncsu.edu.

DUNPHY, MAUREEN MILBIER, educator; b. Springfield, Mass., Feb. 25, 1949; d. Donald J. and Mary C. Milbier; m. Terrence Michael Dunphy. BS in Edn., Westfield State Coll., 1971, MEd, 1975, Cert. Advanced Grad. Study, 1988; cert. paralegal, 1996. Tchr. Thornton Burgess Intermediate Sch., Hampden, Mass., 1971-75; reading specialist, reading dept. head West Springfield Jr. H.S., 1975—2002; reading supr. K-12 Westfield (Mass.) Pub. Schs., 2002—. Acting asst. prin. W. Springfield Jr. HS, 1989; cons. Nat. Evaluations Systems, Amherst, Mass. Mem. editl. bd.: MRA Primer, 1999—. Mem. Long Range Bldg. Needs Com., Westfield, 1986-87, 2000-02. Mem. Pioneer Valley Reading Coun. (pres. 1977-79), Mass. Reading Assn. (dir. 1977-81), West Springfield Edn. Assn. (negotiations sec.), Mass. Tchrs. Assn., Hampden County Tchrs. Assn. Home: 282 Steiger Dr Westfield MA 01085-4934 Office: North Mid Sch 350 Southampton Rd Westfield MA 01085

DUNSIRE, P(ETER) KENNETH, insurance company executive; b. Spearhill, Man., Can., Mar. 1, 1932; came to U.S., 1969; s. Robert Anderson and Margaret (Kinnear) D.; m. Lily Martha Bell (div. Nov. 1971); children: Robert K., Barbara L. Dunsire Belanger; m. Stephanie Alice Mooradian. Student, U. B.C., Can., 1949-50, U. Alta., 1955-56. V.p. Avco Fin. Services, Newport Beach, Calif., 1961-71; exec. v.p. Carte Blanche, Los Angeles, 1971-74, pres., 1974-78; chmn. Am. Benefit Plan Adminstrn., Los Angeles, 1978-80; exec. v.p. Paul Revere Life Ins. Co., Worcester, Mass., 1980-84, Lincoln Nat. Life Ins. Co., Ft. Wayne, Ind., 1984-86, also bd. dirs.; exec. v.p. Lincoln Nat. Corp., Ft. Wayne, Ind., 1986-95, ret., 1995. Bd. dirs. Ft. Wayne Med. Soc. Found., Ft. Wayne C. of C. Found., Nat. Auto & Truck Mus.; chmn. Cannon Lincoln Plc., London, 1984-90, chmn. bd., 1992-95. Chmn. bd. Sta. WFWA-TV, Ft. Wayne, 1985-91, Auburn Cord Duesenberg Mus., Ind., 1986-2001, Ft. Wayne Civic Theater, 1985-86. Mem. Ft. Wayne C. of C. (vice-chmn. 1989-91, chmn. 1991-92). Republican. Avocation: automobile collecting. Home: 8140 Auburn Rd Fort Wayne IN 46825-3016 E-mail: pkdunsire@aol.com.

DUNSKER, STEWART B. physician, neurosurgeon; b. Cin. s. Shiel and Tillie Dunsker; m. Ellen Lothian Treiman, July 2, 1966. BA, Harvard U., 1956; MD, U. Cin., 1960. Diplomate Am. Bd. Neurol. Surgery (pres.). Intern U. Ill., Chgo., 1960-61; resident in internal medicine U. Cin., 1961-62, resident in gen. surgery, 1964-65; resident in neurol. surgery Washington U., St. Louis, 1965-69; prof. clin. neurosurgery U. Cin.; treas. Mayfield Clinic, Cin. Capt. U.S. Army, 1962-64. Fellow: ACS; mem.: Am. Bd. Neurol. Surgeons (vice chair), Am. Acad. Neurol. Surgeons (v.p.), Am. Assn. Neurol. Surgeons (pres., Harvey Cushing medal 2003), Ohio State Neurosurg. Soc. (pres.), Soc. Univ. Neurosurgeons (pres.), Ohio State Med. Assn. (pres., named Ohio Neurosurgeon of the Bear 1992, Evans award 1998). Office: Mayfield Clinic 2123 Auburn Ave # 441 Cincinnati OH 45219-2906

DUNSKY, MENAHEM, retired advertising agency executive, communications consultant, painter; b. Montreal, Que., Can., July 5, 1930; s. Shimson D. and Esther Dunsky; children: Ron Abraham, Ilan Isaac, Dan David Gil. Teaching diploma, Jewish Tchrs. Sem., Montreal, 1948; BA, Concordia U., Montreal, 1952; MA, NYU, 1954; hons. diploma, Parsons Sch. Design, 1956. Tchr. Jewish People's Schs., Montreal, 1948-52; asst. art dir. L.W. Frohlich Advt., N.Y.C., 1956-58; creative dir. Gordon, Lewinson Advt., Tel Aviv, 1958-59; lectr. art history Saidye Bronfman Cultural Centre, Montreal, 1960-63; founder, pres. Dunsky Advt. Ltd., Westmount, Que., Can., 1960-87. Cons. Govt. of Man., Winnipeg, 1970-77, Govt. of Sask., Regina, 1971-82, Govt. of B.C., Victoria, 1972-75; panelist pub. symposium Politics and the Media, 1980 Published Jewish Iconography, 1961; paintings exhibited at Jewish Pub. Libr., Montreal, 1964; retrospective Le Waldorf, Montreal, 2002. Chmn. bd. Saidye Bronfman Cultural Centre, 1969-70; officer Jewish People's Sch. System, Montreal, 1982-85; chmn. edn. com. Bialik High Sch., Montreal, 1981-85, chmn. personnel com., 1983-85; exec. mem. YM/YWHA, Montreal, 1969-71; chmn. nat. edn. com. Can. Zionist Fedn., 1984-88; mem. nat. exec. com., 1985-88; bd. dirs. Jewish Edn. Coun., 1986-88; chmn. pub. rels. com. Can. Ben Gurion Centennial Celebration, 1986-87. Mem. Trans Can. Advt. Agy. Network-Toronto (founding mem.), Trans. Can. Advt. Agy. Network-Toronto (bd. dir. 1962-87), Trans Can. Advt. Agy. Network-Toronto (pres. 1965), Inst. Can. Advt.-Toronto (dir. 1972-75), Inst. Can. Advt. (chmn. profl. com. 1974-75), Advt. Agy. Coun. Que. (founding mem., exec. com. 1969-75) Jewish. E-mail: menahemdunsy@aol.com. *The extent to which one manages to meld the pursuit of one's career interests with considerations of a broader social and cultural nature has always served me as a principal concern. As well, I have kept career considerations from diminishing the time and quality of attention which family and self deserve and require.*

DUNST, ISABEL PAULA, lawyer; b. N.Y.C., Feb. 21, 1947; d. Philip R. and Mae F. Dunst. BS, U. Wis., 1967; JD, NYU, 1971; MPH, Harvard U., 1979. Bar: N.Y. 1971, D.C. 1973. Staff atty. Office Gen. Counsel HEW, Washington, 1971-75, sr. aggy., 1975-79, assoc. gen. counsel, 1979—. Dep. gen. counsel, 1987-90; ptnr. Hogan & Hartson, Washington, 1990—. Bd. dirs. Women's Legal Def. Fund, 1973—75, pres., 1973-74. Mem. ABA, Am. Health Lawyers Assn. E-mail: ipdunst@hhlaw.com.

DUNST, KIRSTEN, actress; b. Point Pleasant, N.J., Apr. 30, 1982; d. Klaus and Inez Dunst. Appeared in films Bonfire of the Vanities, 1990, High Strung, 1991, Greedy, 1994, Interview with the Vampire, 1994, Little Women, 1994, Jumanji, 1995, Wag the Dog, 1997, (voice) Anastasia, 1997, Drop Dead Gorgeous, 1999, Dick, 1999, The Virgin Suicides, 1999, Bring It On, 2000, crazy/beautiful, 2001, The Cat's Meow, 2001, Spider-Man, 2002; appeared on TV in Storytime, 1994, Darkness before Dawn, 1993, Saturday Night Live, others. Recipient Golden Globe Award nomination for best supporting actress,

1995, Boston Soc. of Film Critics Award for best supporting actress, 1994, Chicago Film Critics Assn. Award for most promising actress, 1994. Office: c/o Iris Burton Agy 8916 Ashcrof Ave Los Angeles CA 90069-1327*

DUNST, LAURENCE DAVID, advertising executive; b. N.Y.C., Feb. 21, 1941; s. Philip R. and Mae (Fruchthendler) D.; m. Diane Gordon, Dec. 22, 1962; children: Lee Gordon, Melissa Susan. BA, Syracuse U., 1961. Advt. copywriter R.H. Macy & Co., 1961-63; with Daniel & Charles, N.Y.C., from 1963; pres. Laurence, Charles, Free & Lawson, Inc., N.Y.C., 1969-86, chmn., 1986-91, pres., CEO, 1991-95; chmn, CEO Gotham Inc., N.Y.C., 1995—. Mem. Young Pres.'s Orgn., The Met. Club. Home: 900 Fifth Ave New York NY 10021- Office: Gotham Inc 100 5th Ave Fl 16 New York NY 10011-6996

DUNSTAN, LARRY KENNETH, insurance company executive; b. Payson, Utah, May 26, 1948; s. Kenneth Leroy Dunstan and Verna Matilda (Carter) Taylor; m. Betty K. Limb, Sept. 23, 1966 (div. June 1975); children: Tamara, Thane; m. Jacqueline Lee Darron, Oct. 7, 1975; children: Tessa, Matthew, Bennett, Spencer, Adam. CLU, CPCU, chartered fin. cons., registered health underwriter, life underwriter tng. council fellow. Mgr. Diamond Bar Inn Ranch, Jackson, Mont., 1972-73; agt. Prudential Ins. Co., Missoula, Mont., 1973-77, devel. mgr. Billings, Mont., 1977-78, div. mgr. Gt. Falls, Mont., 1978-83; pres. Multi-Tech Ins. Services, Inc., West Linn, Oreg., 1983—; agy. mgr. Beneficial Life Ins. Co., Portland, Oreg., 1983-88. Mem. planning commn. City of West Linn, Oreg., 1985-87; mem. bishopric Ch. Jesus Christ of Latter Day Sts., West Linn, 1984-86, exec. sec. Lake Oswego Oreg. Stake, 1987-89; scouting coord. Boy Scouts Am., West Linn, 1984-86, scoutmaster various troops; pres. West Linn Youth Basketball Assn., 1991-97, West Linn/Wilsonville Youth Track Club, 1993-96. Named Eagle Scout Boy Scouts Am., 1965, recipient Heroism award 1965. Fellow Life Underwriter Tng. Coun. (bd. dirs. local chpt. 1980-81); mem. Gen. Agts. and Mgrs. Assn. (bd. dirs. local chpt. 1981-82), Am. Soc. CLU (pres. local chpt. 1982-83). Republican. Avocations: sports, stamp collecting, hunting, gardening, photography. Home: 19443 Wilderness Dr West Linn OR 97068-2005 Office: Multi-Tech Ins Svcs 19125 Willamette Dr West Linn OR 97068-2019

DUNTON, GARY C. insurance company executive; In sr. positions Aetna Life & Casualty Co., 1980s; pres. Family and Bus. Ins. Group, USF&G Ins., 1997—; with MBIA, 1997—; pres., COO MBIA Inc., 1999—, also bd. dirs. Office: MBIA Ins Inc 113 King St Armonk NY 10504-1610

DUNTON, JAMES RAYNOR, publisher; b. Wilmington, Del., June 17, 1955; s. Guthrie Raynor III and Jane (Hill) D. BA, U. Va., 1977; MBA, Boston U., 1981. Editor Quorum Books, Westport, Conn., 1984-87; sr. editor Praeger Pubs., N.Y.C., 1987-91, editor-in-chief, 1991-94; pub. acad. and trade Greenwood Pub. Group, Westport, 1994-96; dir. publs. Ctr. for Strategic and Internat. Studies, Washington, 1996—; consulting editor Praeger Pubs., Washington, 1996—, Brassey's, Inc., Washington, 2003—. Mem.: Washington Book Pubs., Soc. for Scholarly Pub., Va. Club of N.Y. Home: 1520 16th St NW Apt 704 Washington DC 20036-1448 Office: Ctr for Strategic and Internat Studies 1800 K St NW Washington DC 20006-2202

DUNWICH, GERINA, writer, magazine editor, astrologer; b. Chgo., Dec. 27, 1959; d. W.E. Novotny (dec.) and Teri Enies (LoMastro) D. Ordained min. Univ. Life Ch., 1998. Freelance writer, 1975—; editor, pub. Golden Isis mag., 1980—. Guest spkr. Craftwise Pagan Gathering, Waterbury, Conn., 1996, The Real Witches' Ball, Columbus, Ohio, 1997, Pagan Day Festival, Westwood, Calif., 2000, West Hollywood, Calif., 2001, 02; spokesperson Wiccan/Neo-Pagan Cmty. Author: Candlelight Spells, 1988, The Magick of Candleburning, 1989, Circle of Shadows, 1990, The Concise Lexicon of the Occult, 1990, Wicca Craft, 1991, Secrets of Love Magick, 1992, The Wicca Spellbook, 1994, The Wicca Book of Days, 1995, The Wicca Garden, 1996, The Wicca Source Book, 1996, Wicca Love Spells, 1996, Wicca Candle Magick, 1996, Everyday Wicca, 1997, A Wiccan's Guide to Prophecy and Divination, 1997, Wicca A to Z, 1997, Magick Potions, 1998, The Wicca Source Book, rev. 2d edit., 1998, Your Magickal Cat: Feline Magick, Lore and Worship, 2000, The Pagan Book of Halloween, 2000, Exploring Spellcraft, 2001, The Cauldron of Dreams, 2002, A Witch's Guide to Ghosts and the Supernatural, 2002, Dunwich's Guide to Gemstone Sorcery, 2003; editor, pub. Aquarius Anthology, 1986, The Liberated Voice, 1987, Coven, 1987, Evil Genius Poetry Jour., 1987-88; appeared on numerous radio talk shows across U.S. and Can.; contbr. articles to profl. jours.; contbr.: Circles, Groves and Sanctuaries, 1992, Llewellyn's Witches' Calendar, 1999, 2000, 2001, Witches' Datebook, 1999, 2000, 2001, Llewellyn's Magical Almanac, 1999, 2000, 2001, Llewellyn's Spell-A-Day Calendar, Llewellyn's Herbal Almanac, The Cat Book of Lists, 2001, A Witch Like Me, 2002, Haunted Northern New York, 2002, The Action Hero's Handbook, 2002. High Priestess and founder Circle of the Old Ways (formerly Coven Mandragora); founder North Country Wicca, 1996; founder Wheel of Wisdom Sch.; bd. advisors Am. Biog. Inst. Mem. Pagan Poets Soc. (founder), Circle, The Fellowship of Isis, The Authors Guild, The Authors League Am. Office: Golden Isis Press PO Box 4263 Chatsworth CA 91313-4263 E-mail: witchywoman13@paganpoet.com.

DUNWODY, EUGENE COX, architect; b. Macon, Ga., July 19, 1933; s. William Elliott and Mary Bennet (Cox) D.; m. Susan Howe Foxworth, June 15, 1957; children: Susan, Eugene Jr., George, Mary Bennet. BS, Ga. Tech., 1955, BArch, 1956. Registered architect, Ga., Fla. V.p., treas. W. Elliott Dunwody Jr., Macon, 1959-69; pres. Dunwody and Co., Macon, 1969-81, Dunwody, Beeland and Henderson Architects Inc., Macon, 1981-97, Dunwody, Beeland, Azar, Walsh, and Matthews, Architects Inc., Macon, 1997-2000, Dunwody/Beeland, Archs., 2000—. Pres. Rotary, Macon, 1974, City Coun., Macon, 1975-87, C. of C., Macon, 1977; dir. Ga. Mcpl. Assn., Atlanta, 1982-83, Nat. League Cities, Washington, 1985-87; chmn. Macon-Bibb County Indsl. Authority, 1992-93, 99, 2000, Macon Econ. Devel. Commn., 1992-93, 99, 2000; pres. Macon Symphony Orch., 2000-2002; deacon Presbyn. Ch. Named Community leader of Yr. Robins Air Logistics Ctr., Warner Robins, Ga., 1987; recipient Motie Wiggins award for Outstanding elected ofcl. Ga. Mcpl. Assn., Atlanta, 1987, Ga. Tech.'s Dean Griffin Cmty. Svc. award, 2000, Macon Arts Alliance Cultural award, 2002. Fellow AIA; mem. Middle Ga. chpt. AIA (pres. 1993), Ga. Assn. AIA (dir. 1992-93). Democrat. Presbyterian. Avocations: golf, piano, choir. Office: Dunwody Beeland 484 Mulberry St Ste 220 Macon GA 31201-7922

DUNWOODY, KENNETH REED, magazine and book editor; b. Washington, Iowa, Oct. 1, 1953; s. Kenneth W. and Marilyn Jane (Green) D.; m. Patricia P. Seale, July 7, 1990 BS in Journalism with honors, U. Ill., 1976. Sports announcer Sta. WPGU, Champaign, Ill., 1972-75; sports editor Free Press Newspaper Group, Carpentersville, Ill., 1976-79, Daily Crystal Lake Herald, Ill., 1979-82; mag. editor Fur-Fish-Game mag. A.R. Harding Pub. Co., Columbus, Ohio, 1982-86, art dir., 1982-86; mag. editor Game & Fish Pub., Marietta, Ga., 1986-88, editorial dir., 1989—. Contbr. articles to mags. Recipient Journalist of Yr. award Free Press Newspapers, 1977, 79, Sports Photography award Ill. Press Assn., 1978, Best Sports Writing award UPI, Ill. Press Assn., 1979, 80, Best Sports Column award UPI, 1979, 80, 81 Mem. Outdoor Writers Assn. Am. Avocations: photography, writing, fishing, baseball. Home: 2381 N Forest Dr Marietta GA 30062-6553 Office: Game & Fish Pub 2250 New Market Pkwy SE Ste 110 Marietta GA 30067-9394 E-mail: kdunwoody@cowles.com., pdunwood@mindspring.com.

DUNWOODY, SHARON LEE, journalism and communications educator; b. Hamilton, Ohio, Jan. 24, 1947; d. Walter Charles and Fanchon (Kapp) D. MA, Temple U., 1975; PhD, Ind. U., 1978. Asst. prof. journalism Ohio State U., Columbus, 1977-81; from asst. prof. to prof. Sch. Journalism and Mass Comm. U. Wis., Madison, 1981—, dir. Sch. Journalism and Mass Comm., 1998—2003, assoc. dean Grad. Sch., 2003—. Instr. Inst. Environ. Studies U. Wis., Madison, 1985—, head acad. programs, 1995-98. Co-editor: Scientists and Journalists, 1986, Communicating Uncertainty, 1999. Mem. AAAS (chair sect. on gen. interest in sci. and Eng. 1992-93), Soc. for Social Study of Sci., Midwest Assn. for Pub. Opinion Rsch. (pres. 1989-90). Home: 1306 Seminole Hwy Madison WI 53711-3728 Office: Univ Wis Sch Journalism & Mass Comm 821 University Ave Madison WI 53706-1412

DUNWORTH, JOHN, retired college president; b. L.A., Jan. 6, 1924; s. Charles William and Alice (Morris) D.; m. Lavona Anita Walden, July 7, 1956. BA, U. Calif.-Berkeley, 1949, MA, 1953; EdD, U. So. Calif., 1959. Cons. spl. edn. San Diego County pub. schs., 1949-51; speech therapist Walnut Creek (Calif.) Sch. Dist., 1952-54; tchr., vice prin., then prin. Torrance (Calif.) Unified Sch. Dist., 1954-59; asst. supt. Lawndale (Calif.) Sch. Dist., 1959-62; supt. schs. Beaumont (Calif.) Unified Sch. Dist., 1962-64; supt. dependents schs. Dept. Def., Pacific and Far East, 1964-66; dean Tchrs. Coll., Ball State U., Muncie, Ind., 1966-73; pres. George Peabody Coll. for Tchrs., Nashville, 1974-79; dean Coll. Edn., U. West Fla., Pensacola, 1979-82; supt. Santa Ana (Calif.) Unified Sch. Dist., 1982-85; Jones disting. univ. prof. Emporia (Kans.) State U., 1987-89; interim dean Sch. Edn., Calif. State U., San Bernardino, 1990-91; prin. Munson (Fla.) Elem. Sch., 1997-98. Lectr. U. Redlands, 1963, U. Hawaii, 1965, U. So. Calif., 1968; del. World Conf. on Edn., Switzerland, 1975; commr. Ind. Sch. Fund Commn., 1969-73 Author (with E. Stoops): Classroom Discipline, 1958; author: (with T. Drysdale) Millions of People, 1965; author: Kindergarten Overseas, 1967; author: (with L. Dunworth and E. Stoops) (bimonthly periodical) Discipline, 1962—93; author: The Dollar-A-Year Principal, 2000. Bd. dirs. Nashville Symphony, 1975-79, Pensacola Symphony, 1992-97, Tenn. Coun. Econ. Edn., 1976-79, Aerospace Edn. Found., 1981-83; pres. Beaumont C. of C., 1963-64. With U.S. Maritime Svc., 1943-46. Recipient svc. award L.A. Community Chest, 1961, Am. Educator medal Freedoms Found., Valley Forge, 1960, Outstanding Pub. Svc. medal U.S. Sec. Def., 1976, Outstanding Ret. Sch. Adminstr. award Phi Delta Kappa N.W. Fla., 1998, Outstanding Older Worker for Santa Rosa County award N.W. Fla. Agy. on Aging, 1999; honored by Fla. Ho. Reps., 1999. Mem. Ind. Assn. Colls. for Tchr. Edn. (pres. 1970-71), Am. Assn. Sch. Adminstrs., Council Ednl. Facility Planners (dir. 1969-72), So. Assn. Colls. and Schs. (commn. on colls.), Am. Assn. Colls. for Tchr. Edn. (pres. 1975-76) Episcopalian.

DUNYE, CHERYL, artist, film maker; b. Phila. BA, Temple U.; MFA, Rutgers U. Part-time instr. dept. media studies Pitzer Coll., Calif. Film maker (short film films) Greetings from Africa, 1994, (video films) The Potluck and the Passion, creator (films) The Watermelon Woman, contbr. articles to profl. jours. Recipient Major Artists award, MARMAF Pa., 1993; fellow, Rutgers U., 1990, 1991, Art Matters, Inc., 1992, grantee, Astrea Found., 1992 Frameline, 1992, NEA, 1995. Office: c/o Media Studies Pitzer Coll Scott Hall Basement 1050 N Mills Ave Claremont CA 91711-3908

DUONG, CONG NGHIEP, aeronautical engineer; s. Quy H. Duong and Loan T. Do; m. Thanh T. Mac, July 12, 1997; children: Clara Ai-Dan, Nathan Vi-Khang. PhD, Calif. Inst. of Tech., 1994. Engr. Boeing Co. (MDC Heritage), Huntington Beach, Calif., 1986—. Fellow, Calif. Inst. of Tech., 1989. Mem.: AIAA. Democrat. Buddist. Achievements include research in aircraft bonded repair technology and damage assessment of aging aircraft. Office: Boeing Company 5301 Bolsa Ave Huntington Beach CA 92647-2099 Office Fax: 714-896-6509. E-mail: cong.n.duong@boeing.com.

DUPEY, MICHELE MARY, communications specialist; b. Bronx, NY, Feb. 26, 1953; d. William B. and Sandra Nancy (Raia) D.; m. Daniel Michael Gieser, July 14, 1980 (div. May 1991). BA, Montclair State Coll., 1975; cert. in copywriting, NYU, 1988. Sec. DDB Needham Worldwide Inc. Advt. (formerly Doyle Dane Bernbach Advt. Co.), N.Y.C., 1985—88; asst. pub. info. officer Hudson County (N.J.) Bd. Chosen Freeholders, 1988-2000; media specialist Englewood Hosp. and Med. Ctr., 2000—01; freelance copywriter Jersey City, 1988—. Creator ann. Hudson County Women's History Month Program; in-house planning chair 150th Anniversary Celebration of Hudson County; participant Comm. Gay Games IV, N.Y.C., 1991—94; mem. planning com., pub. rels. Hudson County Am. Heritage Festival, 1994—95; program prodr. pub. rels. 1996 Olympic Torch Relay Hudson County, 1996; developer Hudson County ADv. Commn. on Women; developer seminars, prodr. video What is a Freeholder?; spkr. in field. Contbr. articles to profl. publs. Recipient Gov.'s award, Hudson County Am. Heritage Festival, 1995; fellow Leadership N.J., 1995. Democrat. Roman Catholic. Home and Office: Copy on Target 206 Washington St Apt 3A Jersey City NJ 07302-4566 E-mail: wittywoman@aol.com.

DUPIES, DONALD ALBERT, retired civil engineer; b. Waukegan, Ill., Apr. 17, 1934; s. Renie Bernard and Catherine Marie (Dowe) D.; m. Margaret T. McKibbin, Sept. 29, 1962; children: Mark, Patrick, Peggy, Colleen. BCE, Marquette U., 1957. With Howard, Needles, Tammen & Bergendoff, Milw., 1959—, office engr., 1969-71, engr. in charge, 1971-74, assoc., 1974-79, cons. engr., ptnr., 1980-95. Pres. Great Lakes divsn. HNTB Corp., ret., 1995. Bd. dirs. Centurions of St. Joseph Hosp., Milw., 1971-76; cubmaster Milw. County coun. Boy Scouts Am., 1973-75; mem. Bd. Appeals, Town of Delafield, Wis., 1996-2002. Served with C.E. U.S. Army, 1957-59. Mem. ASCE (nat. dir. 1982-85), Internat. Inst. of Transportation Engrs., Marquette Club of Milwaukee, Marquette U. Engring. Alumni Assn. (dir. Milw. 1976-83pres. 1981-82), Tau Beta Pi, Chi Epsilon. Roman Catholic. Home: 1480 Fairways Cir Oconomowoc WI 53066

DUPLANTIER, ADRIAN GUY, federal judge; b. New Orleans, Mar. 5, 1929; s. F. Robert and Amelie (Rivet) D.; m. Sally Thomas, July 15, 1951; children: Adrian G., David L., Thomas, Jeanne M., Louise M., John C. JD cum laude, Loyola U., New Orleans, 1949; LLD, Loyola U., 1993; LLM, U. Va., 1988. Bar: La. 1950, U.S. Supreme Ct. 1954. Pvt. practice law, New Orleans, 1950-74; judge Civil Dist. Ct. Parish of Orleans, 1974-78, U.S. Dist. Ct., New Orleans, 1978-94, sr. judge, 1994—. Part-time prof. code of civil procedure Loyola U., 1951—, lectr. dental jurisprudence, 1960-67, lectr. English dept., 1948-50, chmn. law sch. vis. com., 1995-97, adj. prof. law, 1952—; prof. summer sch. abroad Tulane Law Sch., Rhodes, Greece, 1992, Cambridge, England, 1993, Loyola Law Sch., Vienna, Austria, 1996; mem. La. State Senate, 1960-74; 1st asst. dist. atty. New Orleans, 1954-56; mem. Jud. Conf. of U.S. Bankruptcy Rules Adv. Com., 1994-96, chmn. 1997—; elected La. State Senate, 1960-74; 5th cir. dist. judge rep. Jud. Conf. U.S., 1993-94, com. bicentennial of constn., 1986-91; chmn. Bill of Rights Bicentennial Conf. Fed. Judges, 1991. Editorial bd.: Loyola Law Rev, 1947-48; editor-in-chief, 1948-49. Del. Democratic Nat. Conv., 1964; pres. Associated Cath. Charities New Orleans, Social Welfare Planning Council Greater New Orleans; mem. adv. bd. St. Mary's Dominican Coll., 1970-71, Ursuline Acad., 1968-73, Mt. Carmel Acad., 1965-69; chmn. pres.'s adv. coun. Jesuit H.S., 1980-81, mem., 1976—; chmn. bd. dirs. Boys Hope, 1980—, nat. bd. dirs., 1982-92, coun., 1992—; active Assn. Retarded Children. Recipient Meritorious award New Orleans Assn. Retarded Children, 1965, Gov.'s Cert. of Merit, 1970, Outstanding Alumnus award Loyola U., 1985, Vol. Activist award Outstanding Vol. Svc., 1986. Mem. ABA (award 1960), La. Bar Assn., New Orleans Bar Assn., Loyola Law Sch. Vis. Com. (chmn. 1993-96), Jud. Conf. of U.S., Loyola Law Sch. Alumni Assn. (St. Ives award 1998), U.S. Adv. Com. (jud. conf. on bankruptcy rules 1993—, chmn. 1996—), Order of Coif, Alpha Sigma Nu. Office: US Dist Ct C-205 US Courthouse 500 Camp St New Orleans LA 70130-3313

DUPLESSIS, AUDREY JOSEPH, school system administrator; b. New Orleans, June 23, 1920; d. Louis Joseph and Sidonie Josephine (DeLaRose) Boyer; m. Norwood Jerome Duplessis, Sr., June 27, 1984. B in Vocat. Edn., So. U., Baton Rouge, 1942; BA, Calif. State U., 1959, MA, 1966. Tchr., dir. Tri State Coll., New Orleans, 1948-50; from elem. tchr. to dir. Magnet Sch. L.A. Unified Schs., 1954—2002, dir. Magnet Sch., 2002—. Playground L.A. Unified Schs., 1956-59, reading resource tchr., 1965-70, curriculum coord., 1972-78, dir. L.A. Unified Magnet Sch., 1978-02; reading tchr. Calif. Lutheran Coll., Thousand Oaks, 1968-70. Mem. United Tchrs. PAC, L.A., 1980-88. Recipient svc. award Congress of Parents, L.A., 1988, spl. recognition U.S. Congress, 1988. Mem. Internat. Assn. Childhood Edn. (state pres. 1987-89, appreciation award 1989), St. Brigid Edn. Com., Delta Sigma Theta. Democrat. Roman Catholic. Avocations: reading, sewing, traveling, opera, listening to music.

DU PLESSIS, ERIC HOLLINGSWORTH, literature educator, language educator; b. Albertville, France, Sept. 19, 1950; s. Jean-Pierre Leopold and Simone Jeanne Babu; children: Harrison Asher, Miriam Isabelle, Carey Jennifer Benton, David Lindsey Bendiksen, Kenneth Jean-Pierre Bendiksen. Attended Univ. Paris, France; BA, Va. Commonwealth U., 1973; MA, Univ. of Richmond, 1975; Ph.D., Univ. of Va., Charlottesville, 1979. Asst. prof. Tex. A&M U., 1979—87; prof. Radford U., Va., 1987—. Translator: Balzac's The Last Fay, The Nightcharmer and other Tales of Claude Seignolle; author: Nietzsche in France, 1892-1915; contbr. European Studies Jour., Poe Studies, World Education Encyclopedia, World Press Encyclopedia, Revue De Litterature Comparee. Independent. Roman Catholic. Avocations: aikijitsu, flying, photography, hiking. Home: 523 Maple St Dublin VA 24084 Office: Radford U Box 6937 Radford VA 24142-6937 E-mail: ehduples@radford.edu.

DUPLESSY, JEAN CLAUDE, research scientist; b. Paris, Oct. 3, 1942; s. Andre and Lucette (Fauvet) D.; m. Sylwia Kowalska, Sept. 21, 1968; children: Jacques-Eric, Catherine. Agrégation Physics, Ecole Normale Sup., Paris, 1967; D. Geology, U. Paris, 1967, D. Scis./Physics, 1972. Rsch. intern Ctr. Natl. de la Recherche Scientifique, Gif Sur Yvette, France, 1967-68, rsch. attaché, 1968-73, rsch. asst., 1973-76, rsch. master, 1976-84, dir. rsch., 1984-91, dir. rsch.-exceptional class, 1991—. Dir. Ctr. des Faibles Radioactivites, Gif Sur Yvette, 1985-96. Co-Author: Gros Temps Sur la Planete, 1990; co-editor: (2 book series) Nato, 1989-94. Recipient prix Aime Berthe, French Acad. Sci., 1987, Milankovitch medal European Geophys. Soc., 1995. Mem. Acad. Europaea. Office: Lab des Scis Climat et L'environnement Parc Du CNRS 91198 Gif-sur-Yvette France

DUPONT, COLYER LEE, television and film producer, video and film distributing company executive; b. Golden, Colo., Oct. 23, 1957; s. Alfred Lee and Frances Dudley (Smith) D. BA, More U., 1980. Advt. mgr. Magical Blend mag., San Francisco, 1981-83; owner, mgr. Newave Co., San Francisco, 1983; mktg. dir. Venture Rsch., Inc., San Francisco, 1983-84; assoc. producer Left Coast Prodns., San Francisco, 1984-86; owner, mgr. Cinemagic Prodns., San Francisco, 1986—. Writer, producer, dir. TV spl. Computer Magic, 1987; videoworks exhibited Mus. Modern Art, N.Y.C., Nat. Mus. Natural History, Smithsonian Inst., Washington, N.Y. Hall of Sci., Corona, Fine Arts Mus. L.I., Hempstead, N.Y.; inventor belt-attached carrier. Recipient Chris award 34th Columbus (Ohio) Internat. Film and Video Festival, 1986, Silver medal Internat. Film and TV Festival N.Y., 1986, Joey award of merit Profl. Media Network, 1986, Golden Eagle award Coun. for Internat. Non-theatrical Events, 1987, Gold Electra award Birmingham (Ala.) Internat. Edn. Film Fetival, 1987, Silver plaque Chgo. Internat. Film Festival, 1987. Mem. Bay Area Video Coalition, Ind. Filmmakers No. Calif. (founder), Film Arts Found., Visual Communicators Calif., San Francisco Advt. Club (Excellence award 1987). Avocations: art, scuba diving, travel. Office: Cinemagic Prodns 537 Jones St Ste 898 San Francisco CA 94102-2007

DUPONT, HERBERT LANCASHIRE, medical educator, researcher; b. Toledo, Nov. 12, 1938; s. Robert L. and Martha (Lancashire) DuP.; m. Margaret Wright, June 9, 1963; children: Denise Lorraine, Andrew Wright BA, Ohio Wesleyan U., 1961; MD, Emory U., 1965. Diplomate Am. Bd. Internal Medicine. Resident U. Minn. Med. Ctr., Mpls., 1965-67; officer epidemic intelligence service CDC Atlanta, infectious disease fellow U. Md. Sch. Medicine, Balt., 1967-69; faculty, prof., dir. Ctr. for Infectious Diseases U. Tex., Houston, 1973-94, prof. Sch. Pub. Health, 1975—, prof. medicine M.D. Anderson Cancer Ctr., 1988—, Mary W. Kelsey prof. med. sci., 1988—, interim chmn. dept. internal medicine, 1987-89; chief internal medicine svc. and Baylor Coll. Medicine, H. Irving Schweppe chair in internal medicine St. Luke's Episcopal Hosp., Houston, 1995—; clin. prof. dept. medicine Baylor Coll. Medicine, Houston, 1995—; dir., ctr. for infectious diseases, prof. epidemology U. Tex. Sch. Pub. Health, 2002—; faculty, prof., dir. Ctr. for Infectious Diseases U. Tex., 2002—. Clin. prof. dept. medicine and adj. prof. dept. microbiology and immunology Baylor Coll. Medicine, Houston, 1995—; vaccines and related biologic products adv. com. U.S. FDA, 1989—93; sci. adv. com. Inst. Medicine, NAS, 1989—94; bd. sci. counselors Nat. Ctr. for Infectious Diseases, CDC, 1992—96; mem. standing sci. adv. com. Thrasher Rsch. Fund, 1993—96; bd. mem. Kelsey Rsch. Found. Author various med. books; editor (assoc.): Am. Jour. Epidemiology, 1978—81; assoc. editor: Jour. Infectious Diseases, 1983—88; mem. editl. bd. Clin. Infectious Diseases, 1990—95, Infectious Diseases in Clin. Practice, 1992—, internat. advisor Jour. of Infection, 1997—, editl. bd., 2002—; contbr. articles. Lt. comdr. USAF, 1967—69. Rsch. grant NIH, 1975-97. Fellow ACP-Am. Soc. Internal Medicine (regional gov. elect 2002-03, 03-07); mem. Am. Soc. Clin. Investigation, Infectious Diseases Soc. Am. (counselor 1978-81, sec. 1982-87, pres. 1989-90), Nat. Found. Infectious Diseases (bd. dirs. 1981—2002, v.p. 1994-97, pres. 1997-99), Am. Clin. and Climatol. Assn. (recorder, coun. mem. 2000—), Am. Epidemiology Soc., Assn. Am. Physicians, U.S. Mex. Found. Sci. and Tech. (com. chair health 1994-99), Tex. Acad. Internal Medicine (bd. dirs.), Internat. Soc. Travel Medicine (pres. 1991-93), Am. Coll. Phys. (bd. dirs. 2001-), Alpha Omega Alpha. Republican. Methodist. Home: 1111 Hermann Dr Apt 19F Houston TX 77004-6931 Office: St Luke's Episcopal Hosp # MC 1-164 6720 Bertner St Houston TX 77030-2697 E-mail: hdupont@sleh.com.

DUPONT, NICOLE, artist; b. Wilmington, Del., July 24, 1957; d. Henry E.I. duPont and Deborah (Eldredge) duPont Hogan. Artist, CEO Visionary Art Studios, Novato, Calif., 1989-93, Creative Light Prodns., Kapa'a, Hawaii, 1993—. Artist; creator Hawaiian Legend Leis; leis collected in museums including Bishop Mus., Honolulu. Adminstrv. for cmty. classes in Hawaiian culture, Kapa'a, 1994-95. Winner 1st Place award Mokihana Festival Lei Contest, 1997, 98. Mem. Kaua'i Soc. Artists, Garden Island Arts Coun., Kaua'i C. of C. Office: Creative Light Prodns 1191 Kuhio Hwy 116 Kapaa HI 96746 E-mail: hnd@aloha.net.

DUPONT, RALPH PAUL, lawyer, educator; b. Fall River, Mass., May 21, 1929; s. Michael William and Gertrude (Murphy) Dupont; children: Ellen O'Neill, Antonia Chafee, William Albert, Christen Paul. AB in Am. Civilization cum laude with highest honors, Brown U., 1951; JD cum laude, Harvard U., 1956. Bar: Conn. 1956, U.S. Supreme Ct. 1967, diplomate: Nat. Bd. Trial Advocacy, cert.: Conn. (civil trial specialist). Assoc. Davies, Hardy & Schenck, N.Y.C., 1956-57; ptnr. Copp & Dupont, New London, Conn., 1957-60; mem. Suisman, Shapiro & Wool, New London, 1961-63; ptnr. Dupont & Dupont (and successor firms), New London, 1963-91; of counsel Durant, Nichols, Houston, Mitchell & Sheahan, Bridgeport, Conn., 1992-97; ptnr. Dupont and Radlauer LLP, New London, Stamford, 1997—. Instr. Am. history and bus. law Mitchell Coll., New London, 1955, New London, 1957—58, trustee, 1991—94; vis. prof. Northeastern U. Sch. Law, 1977—78; lectr.-on-law U. Conn. Sch. Law, 1980—86; mem. adv. coun. Conn. Legal Svcs., 1980—82; trustee Anne S. K. Brown Mil. Collection Brown U., 1988—94, presiding trustee, 1990—92; vis. prof. law Bridgeport Law Sch. Quinnipiac Coll., 1991—92, mem. exec. bd., adj. prof. Sch. Law, Hamden, Conn., 1994—96; vis. prof. We. New Eng. Coll. Law, 1992—94; instr. bus. law U. New Haven, 1998. Author: (book) Litigation in 1 Attorney's Desk Library, 1994, Dupont on Connecticut Civil Practice, 2003. Mem. New London Bd. Edn., 1959—61; Dem. candidate Conn. Senate, 1960; trustee U.S. Atlantic Tuna Tournament, 1984—85, pres., 1988—90, chmn., 1991—92. Lt. (j.g.) USNR, 1951—53. Named Outstanding Young Man of the Yr., Conn. Jr. C. of C., 1960; recipient Disting. Svc. award, Greater New London Jr. C. of C., 1960. Fellow: Am. Coll. Trust and Estate Coun.; mem.: ABA, Internat. Acad. Estate and Trust Law, Conn. Bar Found. (bd. dirs. 1975—79), Conn. Bar Assn., Harvard U. Law Sch. Assn., Harvard Club, Kappa Sigma, Delta Sigma Rho. Roman Catholic. Home: PO Box 710 New London CT 06320-0710 Office: Dupont and Radlauer LLP PO Box 710 165 State St New London CT 06320-6397 E-mail: radlaw2001@aol.com.

DUPONT, ROBERT LOUIS, psychiatrist, physician; b. Toledo, Mar. 25, 1936; s. Robert Louis and Martha Ireton (Lancashire) DuP.; m. Helen Gayden Spink, July 14, 1962; children: Elizabeth, Caroline. BA, Emory U., 1958; MD, Harvard U., 1963. Diplomate Am. Bd. Psychiatry and Neurology. Intern Western Res. U., 1963-64; resident in psychiatry Harvard Med. Sch., 1964-66; clin. assoc. NIH, 1966-68; research psychiatrist, acting assoc. dir. for community services D.C. Dept. Corrections, Washington, 1968-70; practice medicine specializing in psychiatry, 1968—. Adminstr. Narcotics Treatment Adminstrn., D.C. Dept. Human Resources, 1970-73; acting adminstr. Alcohol, Drug Abuse and Mental Health Adminstrn., HEW, Rockville, Md., 1974; dir. Nat. Inst. on Drug Abuse, HEW, Rockville, 1973-78, Spl. Action Office for Drug Abuse Prevention, Exec. Office Pres., Washington, 1973-75; pres. Inst. for Behavior and Health Inc., 1978—, Am. Council for Drug Edn., 1980-85; U.S. del. UN Commn. on Narcotic Drugs, 1973-78; mem. Coordinating Council on Juvenile Justice and Delinquency Prevention, Dept. Justice, 1974-78; assoc. clin. prof. psychiatry and behavioral scis. George Washington Med. Sch., 1972-80; clin. prof. psychiatry Georgetown U. Med. Sch., 1980—; vis. assoc. clin. prof. psychiatry Harvard U. Med. Sch., 1978-84; chmn. Ctr. Behavioral Medicine,

1978-89; v.p. Bensinger, DuPont Assocs., Inc, 1982—. Contbr. articles in fields of drug abuse, criminology and mental health to profl. jours.; appeared on Good Morning America, ABC-TV, 1978 80. Bd. dirs. Washington Soc. for Performing Arts, 1972 76; mem. adv. com. Washington Jr. League, 1972-76. Served to surgeon (maj.) USPHS, 1966-68. Fellow Am. Psychiat. Assn.; mem. Washington Psychiat. Soc., World Psychiat. Assn., Pan Am. Med. Assn., Anxiety Disorders Assn. Am. (pres. 1982-85), Am. Soc. Addiction Medicine (diplomate). Home: 8708 Susanna Ln Chevy Chase MD 20815-4714 Office: 6191 Executive Blvd Rockville MD 20852-3901 *As a practicing physician dealing with addiction and anxiety disorders, I have seen first-hand the intense suffering experienced by those afflicted and by those who love them. As a public health practitioner, I have seen the immense cost of these disorders. The miracle of recovery has been the inspiration of my career.*

DUPONT, TODD F. mathematics and computer science educator; b. Houston, Aug. 29, 1942; s. T.F. and Nan G. D.; m. Judy Smith, Aug. 20, 1964; children: Michelle, Todd K. BA, Rice U., 1963, PhD, 1968. Research mathematician Esso Prodn. Research, Houston, 1968; instr. U. Chgo., 1968-69, asst. prof., 1969-72, assoc. prof., 1972-75, prof. math., 1975—, prof. computer sci., 1985—, chmn. computer sci., 1994-97. Prin., officer, past bd. dirs. DREM (formerly Dupont-Rachford Engring. Math. Co.), Houston, 1969-92; prin. tech. adv. Stoner Assocs., Inc., 1992—. Assoc. editor Math. of Computation, 1977—84, SIAM Jour., 1976—86. Home: 1335 E Park Pl Chicago IL 60637-1767 Office: Univ Chgo Dept Computer Sci 1100 E 58th St Chicago IL 60637-1588

DUPONT, WILLIAM DUDLEY, biostatistician, educator; b. Montreal, Que., Can., Nov. 6, 1946; came to U.S., 1971; s. Charles Thomas and Jean (White) Dupont; m. Susan Miller McChesney, July 20, 1974; children: Charles Thomas, Peter William. BSc, McGill U., 1969, MSc, 1971; PhD, Johns Hopkins U., 1976. Lectr. U. Md., Balt., 1976-77; asst. prof. biostats. Vanderbilt U. Sch. Medicine, Nashville, 1977-85, assoc. prof., 1986-92, prof., 1992—, dir. divsn. biostats., 1989—. Nat. Cancer Inst. grantee, 1980—. Mem. AAAS, Am. Statis. Assn., Biometric Soc., Soc. Clin. Trials, Soc. Epidemiol. Rsch. Office: Vanderbilt U Med Sch Dept of Preventive Medicine A-1124 Med Ctr N Nashville TN 37232-0001 E-mail: william.dupont@vanderbilt.edu.

DUPPS, JOHN AVERY, JR., process machinery company executive; b. Middletown, Ohio, Sept. 1, 1942; s. John Avery and Mary (Norris) D.; m. Patricia Murphy, Oct. 5, 1968; children: Emily Kathleen, Julia Marie, Mary Katherine. BSChemE, U. Notre Dame, 1964. V.p. The Dupps Co., Germantown, Ohio, 1966-82, pres., 1982—. Bd. dirs. First Nat. Bank, Germantown. Chmn. Mid Miami Healthcare Found., Middletown, 1994-99, chmn. C-J H.S. Devel. Adv. Coun., Dayton, Ohio, 1998-03. Mem. Am. Oil Chemists Soc., Meat Industry Suppliers Assn. (pres. 1988-89), Process Equipment Mfrs. Assn. (pres. 1999-2000). E-mail: info@dupps.com.

DUPPSTADT, ANDREW EARL, historic site staff member; b. Camp Lejeune, N.C., Mar. 21, 1973; s. Claude Earl and Gwendolyn Gail Duppstadt. BA in History, U. N.C. Wilmington, 1996, MA in History, 1999. Exec. dir. Carteret County Hist. Soc., Morehead City, NC, 1999—2000; asst. site mgr. CSS Neuse State Hist. Site, Kinston, NC, 2001—. Character interpreter Tryon Palace Hist. Site and Gardens, New Bern, NC, 2000. Mem.: So. Hist. Assn., Orgn. Am. Historians, Phi Alpha Theta. Libertarian. Presbyterian. Avocations: tennis, basketball, music, disc golf, Civil War reenacting. Office: CSS Neuse State Hist Site 2612 W Vernon Ave Kinston NC 28504

DUPRÉ, LOUIS, retired philosopher, educator; b. Veerle, Belgium; came to U.S., 1958, naturalized, 1966; s. Clement and Francisca (Verlinden) D. PhD, U. Louvain, Belgium; PhD (hon.), Loyola Coll., 1989, Sacred Heart U., 1992, Georgetown U., 1996, Siena Coll., 1997, Regis Coll., U. Toronto, 1998, St. Michael's Coll., 2002. From asst. prof. to prof. philosophy Georgetown U., Washington, 1959-73; T. Lawrason Riggs prof. philosophy of religion Yale U., New Haven, 1973-98. Author: Kierkegaard as Theologian (also in Dutch), 1963, The Philosophical Foundations of Marxism, 1966, Dutch edit., 1970, Korean edit., 1982, The Other Dimension, 1972, French edit., 1977, Chinese edit., 1986, Polish edit., 1990, Dutch edit., 1991, Korean edit., 1995, Spanish edit., 1999, Transcendent Selfhood, 1976, Dutch edit., 1981, A Dubious Heritage, 1979, The Deeper Life, 1981, Polish edit., 1994, German edit., 2002, Marx's Social Critique of Culture, 1983, The Common Life, 1984, Polish edit., 1994, Passage to Modernity, 1993, Metaphysics and Culture, 1994, Religious Mystery and Rational Reflection, 1997, Symbols of the Sacred, 2000; editor: Faith and Reflection, 1968; co-editor: Light from Light, 1987, 2d edit., 2001; contbr. articles to profl. jours. Recipient Phi Beta Kappa medal as Tchr. of Yr. at Yale U., 1996, Aquinas medal, Am. Cath. Philos. Assn., 1997. Mem. Am. Cath. Philos. Assn. (pres. 1971), Hegel Soc. Am. (pres. 1972-73), Am. Acad. Arts and Scis., Belgian Acad. Letters, Arts, & Scis. Roman Catholic. Home: 67 N Racebrook Rd Woodbridge CT 06525-1407 Office: 451 College St New Haven CT 06520 E-mail: louis.dupre@yale.edu.

DUPREE, SANDRA KAY, librarian; b. Warren, Ark., July 17, 1956; d. Erie Ingram; 1 child, David Dupree Russell. BA, U. Ark., 1978; MLS, Atlanta U., 1979. Intern Pub. Libr. of Columbus (Ohio) and County of Franklin, 1979-80; dir. libr. County of Bradley, Warren, 1980-81; specialist Southeast Ark. Regional Libr., Monticello, 1982-83; instr. U. Ark., Pine Bluff, 1982, asst. libr. Monticello, 1984—2001; dir. U. Ark. Monticello Libr., 2001—. Bd. dirs. Delta Counseling, Monticello, 1981, Ark. Endowment for Humanities, Little Rock, 1986-89; vol. pub. rels. com. Bradley County Civic League, Warren, 1980-82. Mem. AAUW, Am. Libr. Assn., Ark. Libr. Assn., Ark. Audiovisual Assn., Monticello Book Club, (hon.) Phi Kappa Delta, Beta Phi Mu. Democrat. Methodist. Avocations: backgammon, cross-stitch, latch hook. Home: PO Box 312 Monticello AR 71657-0312 Office: U Ark PO Box 3599 Monticello AR 71656-3599

DUPREE, STANLEY M. lawyer; b. Thomaston, Ga., Sept. 7, 1946; BA, Stanford U., 1971; JD, U. Calif., 1974. Bar: CAlif. 1974. Instr. U. Calif., 1976-82; law clerk, acting ct. commr. San Francisco Superior Ct., 1974-76; ptnr. Schultz & Dupree, San Francisco, Dupree & Colvin. Mem. ABA, State Bar Calif., Bar Assn. San Francisco. Office: Dupree & Colvin Ste 200 777 E Tahquitz Canyon Way Palm Springs CA 92262-6797

DUPREE, THOMAS ANDREW, forester, state official; b. Cambridge, Mass., Jan. 18, 1950; s. Glenn Stewart and Elvira (Pacifici) D.; m. Sandra Ann Becker, Aug. 31, 1975; 1 child, Steven. BS in Forestry, U. Mass., 1972. Svc. forester R.I. Div. Forest Environ., Hope Valley, 1974-76, sr. forester, 1976-78, prin. forester, 1978-86, chief Scituate, 1986—. Chmn. R.I. Tree Farm Com., 1976-78; chmn. Arcadia Mgmt. Coun., 1981-86. Bd. mem. USS Mass. Meml. Com., Fall River, 1987-2000; commr. Northea. Forest Fire Protection Commn., 1986—, vice chmn., 1988-89, chmn., 1990-92; pres. So. New England Forest Consortium, Inc., 1990—; mem. forest productivity working group N.E. Govs.' and Ea. Can. Premiers, 1986-91; bd. dirs. R.I. Tree Coun., Inc., 1993—, R.I. Resource Conservation and Devel. Area, Inc., 1996—; coach Coventry Basketball Assn., 1994-2000, sec., 1997-98. Mem.: R.I. Landscape Archs. Bd. Examiners, R.I. Fire Chiefs Assn., N.E. Area Assn. State Foresters (sec.-treas. 1990, v.p. 1991, pres. 1992, chmn. R.I. rural lands coalition 1997—), New Eng. Soc. Am. Foresters (exec. com. 1982—90), Nat. Assn. State Foresters (v.p. found. 1988—2000, exec. com. 1992—93, chmn. forest health com. 1992—96, bd. dirs. found. 1995—, chmn. stats com. 1998—2000, pres. found. 2000—01, chmn. working lands conservation com. 2000—, pres. found 2003—), Am. Forestry Assn. (mem. Yankee divsn.), Soc. Am. Foresters (sec.-treas. 1986, vice chmn. 1987). Avocations: golf, hiking, hunting, fishing, coaching basketball. Home: 20 Gentry Farm Rd Coventry RI 02816-6952 Office: RI Div Forest Environ 1037 Hartford Pike North Scituate RI 02857-1030

DUPRIEST, DOUGLAS MILLHOLLEN, lawyer; b. Ft. Riley, Kans., Dec. 28, 1951; s. Robert White and Barbara Nadine (Millhollen) DuP. AB in Philosophy with high honors, Oberlin Coll., 1974; JD, U. Oreg., 1977. Bar: Oreg. 1977, U.S. Dist. Ct. Oreg. 1977, U.S. Ct. Appeals (9th cir.) 1977. Assoc. Coons & Anderson and predecessors, Eugene, Oreg., 1977—81, Hutchinson, Harrell et al, 1981; ptnr. Hutchinson, Cox, Coons, DuPriest, Orr, and Sherlock and predecessors, 1982—. Adj. prof. sch. law U. Oreg., 1986; mem. task forces Wetlands Mgmt., 1988-89, 92-93. Author: (with others) Land Use, 1982, 2000, Administrative Law, 1985; contbg. editor Real Estate & Land Use Digest, 1983-86; articles editor, mng. bd. mem. U. Oreg. Law Rev., 1976-77. Bd. dirs. Home Health Agy., Eugene, 1977-79, pres., 1978-79; bd. dirs. Oreg. Environ. Coun., Portland, 1979-84, pres., 1980-81, McKenzie River Trust, 1998—; chair voters pamphlet com. Eugene City Club, 1993. Recipient Disting. Svc. award Oreg. Environ. Coun., 1988. Mem. Oreg. Bar Assn. (exec. com. real estate and land use sect. 1978-81). Home: 225 Dartmoor Dr Eugene OR 97401-6620 Office: Hutchinson Cox Coons DuPriest Orr & Sherlock 777 High St Ste 200 Eugene OR 97401-2750

DUPUIS, KATERI THERESA, retired elementary education educator; b. Menominee, Mich., Dec. 1, 1941; d. Edmund Bruno and Emelie Josephine (Archambault) D. BA, Cardinal Stritch Coll., 1964; MS, Lesley Coll., 1989. Cert. elem. tchr. 4-8, Wis. Tchr. grade 5 St. Michael's Indian Sch., St. Michael, N.D., 1964-65; tchr. grades 4, 6 and 8 Cudahy (Wis.) Pub. Schs., 1965-99; ret., 1999. Mem. French Can./Acadian Genealogists of Wis. (treas. 1992-93, pres. 2001—), Cudahy Edn. Assn. (pres., v.p., sec., negotiator, com. chair 1967-82). Avocations: genealogy, photography, computers, tiffany glass work. Home: 10506 W Concordia Ave Wauwatosa WI 53222-3355

DUPUIS, ROBERT SIMEON, sales executive; b. Palmer, Mass., Aug. 31, 1941; s. Bertrand Leonard and Hanora Theresa (Crean) D.; m. Dianne Cecile Gibouleau, Aug. 20, 1960; children: Kathleen, Corinne, Lynn, Robert. Student, Springfield Tech. C.C. Laborer Springfield (Mass.) Foundry, 1959-60; warehouse forklift operator Ludlow (Mass.) Industries, 1960-62; machinists, mechanic Tambrands, Inc., Palmer, Mass., 1962-64; apprentice toolmaker Pratt & Whitney Aircraft, East Hartford, Conn., 1964-66; toolmaker Target Tool Co., Three Rivers, Mass., 1966-68; tool and die maker Brookfield Machine Corp., West Brookfield, Mass., 1968-75, Prodn. Tool & Die, Springfield, 1975-77; tool and die engr. Vogform Tool & Die, West Springfield, 1977-85; regional mgr. Dayton (Ohio) Progress Corp., 1985—. Cons., speaker Worcester (Mass.) Poly. Inst., 1991—. Chmn., vice chair Palmer (Mass.) Sch. Com., 1977—; sec. Three River Prudential Fire Dept. Com., 1978-80; chmn., subcom. Palmer Fin. Com., 1971-77; mem. Palmer Libr. Com., 1988-90. Mem. SME (sr., speaker), Precision Metal Forming Assn. (tech. cons., speaker 1985—), Three Rivers C. of C. Roman Catholic. Avocations: deep sea fishing, scuba diving, hiking, biking, golf, boating. Home and Office: Dayton Progress Corp 322 Flynt St Palmer MA 01069-1657 Fax: 413-283-5521. E-mail: bdupuis@daytonprogress.com.

DUPUIS, VICTOR LIONEL, retired curriculum and instruction educator; b. Chgo., Oct. 30, 1934; s. Edward G. and LaVerne Ann (Brown) D.; m. Mary Jean Miles, Aug. 11, 1956; children: Mary Catherine, Victor Edward, Elizabeth Ann. BS, Northwestern U., 1956; MA, Am. U., 1961; PhD, Purdue U., 1965. Tchr. jr. high sch., Arlington, Va., 1956-61; tchr. Klondike Sch. Dist., West Lafayette, Ind., 1961-63, curriculum dir., 1962-63; grad. instr. Purdue U., West Lafayette, 1963—65; asst. prof. Pa. State U., University Park, 1967—70, assoc. prof. curriculum, 1970—74, prof., chmn. curriculum and supervision, 1974—91, prof. edn. curriculum and instrn., 1989-91, Waterbury prof. secondary edn., 1990-92, chmn. curriculum and suprvision, 1991, prof. emeritus curriculum and instrn., 1992—; CEO, Dupuis Assocs. Cons. to various pvt. and public schs., state depts. edn. Native Am. programs. Author (with others): (education text) Introduction to the Foundations of American Education, 1966; author: (education texts) Introductory Readings in the Foundation of American Education, 1966, Resource Booklet and Overhead Transparency Masters for Foundation of American Education, 1966, (education textbook) An Introduction to the Foundations of American Education, 1969, (Education text), 2002, (education texts) Foundation of American Education: Readings, 1969, 1985, Issues in Education, 1991, Resource Booklet: Foundations of American Education, 2002. Chmn. Patton Twp. (Pa.) Park Bd., 1969-70, Patton Twp. Planning Commn., 1971-73; Democratic precinct committeeman Patton Twp., 1971-76, chmn., twp. supr., 1973-92. Served to 2d lt. inf. U.S. Army, 1957-59. Mem. ASCD, Am. Ednl. Rsch. Assn., Nat. Staff Devel. Coun., Pa. Assn. for Supervision and Curriculum Devel., Phi Delta Kappa. Home: 3203 Buffalo Run Rd Bellefonte PA 16823-9027

DUQUES, RIC, information services executive; Chmn., CEO First Data Corp., Atlanta. Office: First Data Corp Ste 1400 5660 New Northside Dr NW Atlanta GA 30328-5825

DUQUET, SUZANNE FRANCES, special education educator; b. Detroit, July 15, 1954; d. Nicholas John and Frances Catherine (Muscat) Calleja; m. Michael Patrick Duquet, Aug. 26, 1978; children: Michael II, James, Michelle, Christopher. AA, Siena Heights Coll., 1974, BA, 1976; continuing edn. & spl edn. endorsement, Ea. Mich. U., 1980; MAT with LD Specialty, Madonna U., 1996. Sec. to dean of students Siena Heights Coll., Adrian, Mich., 1973-76; tchr. Boysville of Mich., Clinton, 1976-81, asst. prin., 1981-85; tchr. spl. edn., tchr. cons. Pinckney (Mich.) Cmty. Schs., 1985—. Cons. Livingston Pediat. Ctr., Brighton, Mich., 1990-00; mem. adv. com. dept. student tchrs. Siena Heights Coll. Edn., Adrian, 1983-93. Author: (curriculum) Human Sexuality Program, 1983, K-12 Special Education Curriculum, 1991, Transition of Learning Disabled Students from High School to Adult Life: A Survey of Former Students, 1996. Eucharistic min., lector Holy Spirit Cath. Ch., Hamburg, Mich., 1986—, mem. parish leadership coun., 2002-03, mem. ednl. commn., 2003—; mem. MADD, Brighton, 1990—; faculty advisor Students Against Driving Drunk, Pinckney H.S., 1987—; sponsor internat. student travel Pinckney Cmty. Schs., 1998—. Scholar Daus. of Korean Conflict, 1972, Walsh scholar Siena Heights Coll., 1973; tuition grantee State of Mich., 1972-76; named SADD-Mich. advisor of Yr., 1999-2000. Mem.: Coun. for Exceptional Children, Mich. Edn. Assn. Avocations: reading, boating, ceramics, theater, traveling. Home: 9456 Lakecrest Dr Whitmore Lake MI 48189-9388 Office: Pinckney Cmty Schs 10255 Dexter Pinckney Rd Pinckney MI 48169-8918 E-mail: duquet@pcs.k12.mi.us.

DUQUETTE, DAVID JOSEPH, materials science and engineering educator; b. Springfield, Mass., Nov. 4, 1939; s. Joseph Albert and Jeannette Marie (Bernier) D.; m. JoAnn Nazarko, July 31, 1982; children: David Joseph Jr., Peter James. BS, USCG Acad., 1961; PhD, MIT, 1968. Commd. officer USCG, 1961, advanced through grades to lt., 1965; rsch. asst. MIT, Cambridge, Mass., 1965-68; sr. rsch. assoc. Adv. Materials R&D Lab. Pratt & Whitney, Middletown, Conn., 1968-70; faculty mem. Rensselaer Poly. Inst., Troy, N.Y., 1970—, assoc. dir. Ctr. for Advanced Interconnects Sci. and Tech., 1999—, dept. head., 2000—. Vis. prof. Imperial Coll. of Sci. and Tech., U. London, 1973; vis. sr. scientist Max Planck Institut fur Eisenforschung, Dusseldorf, 1983-84; mem. 5 panels on material performance NAS/NAE, Washington, 1980—, NASA Space Processing Rev. Com., Huntsville, Ala., 1978-83; mem. U.S. Nuc. Waste Tech. Rev. Bd., 2002—. Contbr. 190 articles to tech. jours. Mem. North Colonie Bd. of Edn., 1974-79, Albany County Airport Adv. Com., 1976-79. Recipient Excellence award ALCOA Found., 1978, 79, Humboldt prize Alexander von Humboldt Found., 1983, Willis Rodney Whitney award Nat. Assn. of Corr. Eng., Tex., 1990, Centennial scholar Case Inst. of Tech., Cleve., 1980, fellow ASM Internat., Metals Park, Ohio, 1986. Fellow Nat. Assn. Corrosion Engrs. Internat.; mem. Alpha Sigma Mu (hon.) Avocations: skiing, sailing. Office: Rensselaer Poly Inst Materials Sci and Engring Dept Troy NY 12180 E-mail: duqued@rpi.edu.

DUQUETTE, DAVID JOSEPH, JR., lawyer, investor; b. Boston, May 12, 1964; s. David Joseph and Joan (Culverhouse) D.; m. Patricia Mae Doykos; 1 child, John Culver. AB, Princeton U., 1986; JD, U. Va., 1991. Bar: N.Y. 1992, Mass. 1992, N.J. 2002. Assoc. Rogers & Wells, N.Y.C., 1991-96; ptnr. Duquette & Tipton LLP, N.Y.C., 1996—2001, Saul Ewing LLP, Princeton, NJ, 2002—. Dir. Am. Canyon Ptnrs. LLC, San Francisco; advisor Lux Capital LLC, N.Y.C. Mem.: Racquet & Tennis Club N.Y.C. Office: 214 Carnegie Ctr Princeton NJ 08540

DUQUETTE, JEAN-PIERRE, French language and literature educator; b. Valleyfield, Que., Can., June 27, 1939; s. J.-Armand and Marguerite (Besner) D. BA, Université de Montréal, Can., 1960, L ès L, 1963; Doctorat 3e cycle, Paris X, France, 1969. Asst. prof. French McGill U., Montréal, 1969-73, assoc. prof. French, 1973-83, prof. French, 1983—. Author: Flaubert, 1972, Germaine Guèvremont, 1973, Fernand Leduc, 1980, Colette, 1984, L'Espace du regard, 1994. Decorated chevalier Order Nat. de Quebec. Mem. Acad. of Letters of Que., Internat. PEN Que., McGill U. Faculty Club. Office: McGill U Dept of French Lang 3460 McTavish St Montreal QC Canada H3A 1X9 E-mail: jean.duquette@mcgill.ca.

DUR, PHILIP ALPHONSE, defense aerospace executive, retired naval officer; b. Bethesda, Md., June 22, 1944; s. Philip Francis and Elena (Delgado) D.; m. Kathleen Mary Donovan, June 6, 1966; children: Courtney Morris, Philip Ralston. BA, U. Notre Dame, 1965, AM, 1966; MPA, Harvard U., 1973, PhD, 1976. Commd. ensign USN, 1965, advanced through grades to rear adm., 1991, strategic planner Office of the Chief Naval Ops., 1977-79, mil. asst. Office of Sec. Def., 1979-80, dir. polit. mil. affairs Nat. Sec. Coun., 1982-84, exec. asst. Chief Naval Ops. plans, policy, ops., 1984-86, exec. asst. sec. of navy, 1988-89, commanding officer USS Comte De Grasse Norfolk, Va., 1980-82, commanding officer USS Yorktown, 1986-88, 91-93; U.S. def. attache Am. embassy Paris, 1989—91; comdr. Cruiser Destroyer Group Eight, 1991-93; dir. strategy and policy Office of the Chief Naval Ops., Washington, 1993—94, dep. asst. CNO plans, policy and ops., 1994—95; retired USN, 1995; v.p. Tenneco Inc., Houston, 1995-96; exec. v.p. Walker-Gillet Europe, Edenkoben, Germany, 1996-97; v.p. worldwide bus. devel. & strategy Tenneco, Inc., Lake Forest, IL, 1997-2000; v.p. program ops. Northrop Grumman, Balt., 2000—01; pres. Northrop Grumman Ship Sys., 2001—. Scoutmaster Boy Scouts Am., Gaeta, Italy, 1967. Decorated Def. Disting. Svc. medal, Navy Disting. Svc. medal, Def. Superior Svc. medal, Legion of Merit; comdr. Ordre Nat. du Merite (France). Mem. U.S. Naval Inst. Found., Coun. on Fgn. Rels., Cercle de l'Union Interalliee, Surface Navy Assn., Marine Acad. (France), Nat. Eagle Scouts Assn., Notre Dame Alumni Club, Army-Navy Club, Harvard Club. Avocations: history, golf, foreign languages. Office: Northrop Grumman Ship Sys PO Box 149 Pascagoula MS 39568

DUR, PHILIP FRANCIS, political scientist, educator, retired foreign service officer; b. St. Louis, June 30, 1914; s. Alphonse and Sarah (Ralston) D.; m. Elena Delgado, June 30, 1942; children: Elena (Mrs. Philip A. Morris), Philip, Stansbury, Carmen (Mrs. Norman B. Conley, Jr.), Jacqueline (Mrs. James Chase Sheppard), John. AB, Harvard U., 1935, PhD, 1941; postgrad., Fgn. Service Inst., 1961. Consul, pub. affairs officer, Lyon, France, 1948-51; chief Office Pub. Affairs, Office U.S. High Commr. for Germany, Bonn, 1951-52; consul, exec. officer Am. Consulate Gen., Bremen, Germany, 1952—53; comml. controls officer Mil. Security Bd., Coblenz, Germany, 1953-54; consul Colon, Panama, 1954-55, Yokohama, Japan, 1954—58; pub. affairs adviser Dept. State, 1958-61; consul Nagoya, Japan, 1961 -65, Jefferson Caffery prof. polit. sci. U. Southwestern La., Lafayette, 1965-84, prof. emeritus, 1984—, faculty senate, 1969-84. Adviser Council for Devel. of French in La., 1968— ; mem. U. Southwestern La. Found., 1969-71; pres. France-Amerique de la Louisiane Acadienne, 1970-72; resident dir. La. Consortium Colls. and Univs., Montpellier, France, 1976-77; organizer, exchange prof. La. Ctr. for Studies, U. Paul Valéry, Montpellier. Served to lt. comdr. USNR, 1942-46. Decorated Acad. Palms (France); recipient Nat. Medal of Honor, DAR, 1983, 1st prize French poetry Deep South Writers Conf., 1995. Mem. Am. Fgn. Service Assn., La. Historical Assn., Phi Beta Kappa. Home: 517 Woodvale Ave Lafayette LA 70503-3435 E-mail: pfd2009@louisiana.edu.

DURACZYNSKI, DONNA MOORE, retired accountant; b. Homer, La. d. William Franklin and Maybelle (Adams) Moore; m. Edward Julian Duraczynski, Jan. 11, 1957; children: Deborah Bulliard, Donna Reyenga, Edward J. Jr. AA, Merced Coll., 1966; BA, La. State U., 1984. Cert. sec. Profl. Secs. Internat. Inst. Loan officer Fin. & Thrift Co., Merced, Calif., 1964-66; bookkeeper Homer Nat. Bank, Homer, La., 1966-67; ednl. adminstr. Raytheon, Bedford, Mass., 1967-75; gas acct. Crystal Oil Co., Shreveport, La., 1976-95; v.p. AAA Mortgage, Shreveport, La., 1997-99. Mem. state civl. com. Dem. Party, Baton Rouge, 1984-2000; founding pres. Ark La Tex Paint Horse Club, 1984, treas. 1985-86, active 1984-88; active Girl Scouts U.S., 1967-75; hospitality chmn. Town of Concord, Mass. Bicentennial Celebration, 1975. Mem. Shreveport C. of C., Southside Riding Club (hon. mem., pres. 1985-95, treas. 1977-85). Roman Catholic. Avocations: sewing, horses, roses. Home: 6103 Colquitt Rd Keithville LA 71047-8963

DURAKOVIC, ASAF, nuclear medicine physician, consultant; b. Stolac, Herceg, Croatia, May 16, 1940; arrived in U.S., 1970; s. Bekir Durakovic and Remza Fest; m. Tania Rebecca Durakovic, Aug. 10, 1997; 1 child, Adiya. DVM, MSc, U. Zagreb, Croatia, 1965, PhD, 1969; MD, McMaster U., Can., 1975. Diplomate Am. Bd. Nuc. Medicine. Intern Toronto (Can.) Gen. Hosp., 1975—76; resident and fellow in internal medicine Georgetown U. Hosp., Washington, 1976—77; resident in radiology and nuc. medicine Strong Meml. Hosp. Rochester (N.Y.) U., 1977—79; fellow in nuc. cardiology VA Hosp., State U., Buffalo, 1979—80; assoc. chief divsn. nuc. medicine Walter Reed Hosp., Washington, 1980—83; chief exptl. nuc. medicine Armed Forces Radiobiology Rsch. Inst. Def. Nuc. Agy., Bethesda, Md., 1984—87; chief radiol. sci., divsn. med. and health sci. Oak Ridge (Tenn.) Associated U., 1987—89; dir. World Life Inst., Waterport, NY, 1987—2002; chief nuc. medicine VA Regional Med. Ctr., Wilmington, Del., 1989—98; chief nuc. medicine, cons. King Faisal Hosp., Riyadh, Saudi Arabia, 1999—2001; dir. Uranium Med. Rsch. Ctr., Toronto and Washington, 1999—. Advisor Children Chernobyl, Jerusalem, 1987; prof. U. Zagreb, Croatia, 1994—. Author: (book) Saramatian Trials, 1993, Sand Dunes, 1994, Mountain Kaf, 1995, Great Waters, 1996. Dir. Project Life, Toronto, 1994—. Col. U.S. Army, 1980—91. Fellow: ACP; mem.: AMA, Nuc. Medicine Soc., Am. Coll. Radiology, B. B. French Blue Lodge, Scottish Rite. Avocations: poetry, classical music, horses, humanities. Home: 10200 Forest Grove Silver Spring MD 20902 Office: Uranium Med Ctr 3430 Connecticut Ave Washington DC 20008 Business E-Mail: asaf@umrc.net.

DURAN, ANGELICA ALICIA, literature educator; b. L.A., July 18, 1966; d. Alicia Hernandez; m. Sean Thomas O'Connor; children: Jacqueline Alicia Cassutt, Paul Leon Cassutt. BA, U. Calif., Berkeley, 1987, MA, 1988; PhD, Stanford U., 2000. Instr. dept. English Stanford U., Palo Alto, Calif., 1996—2000; asst. prof. dept. English Purdue U., West Lafayette, Ind., 2000—03. Troop leader Girl Scouts Am., West Lafayette; dir. Purdue Latino and Faculty Assn., West Lafayette, 2002—03; coord. Stanford Ptnrs. for Acad. Excellence, Palo Alto; faculty advisor Purdue chpt. Delta Phi Mu Sorority, West Lafayette, 2002—03; faculty advisor Purdue's Fathers And Mothers, West Lafayette, 2000—03. Named Outstanding Leader, Girl Scouts of Sycamore County, 2002; named to Cmty. Honor Roll, City of West Lafayette, 2001; recipient Mary Patterson award, Girl Scouts of Sycamore County, 2003, Salute to Women award, YWCA, 2003; fellow, Mellon Found., 1994—98; scholar, Nat. Hispanic Assn., 1984—85; Mellon Dissertation fellow, Mellon Found., 1998—99. Mem.: MLA (assoc.), Milton Soc. Am. (assoc.). Roman Catholic. Office: English Dept Purdue U 500 Oval Dr West Lafayette IN 47907

DURAN, JAIME, language educator; b. Oviedo, Asturias, Spain, Mar. 4, 1967; s. Jaime Durán and Luisa Fernanda Díaz; m. María Leticia Meana, Dec. 29, 2000. Licenciado, Universidad de Oviedo, Spain, 1989—95; MA, Villanova U., 1995—97, PhD, Temple U., 1997—2000. Asst. prof. Villanova U., 2000—03. Recipient Bridgebuilder Award, Villanova U., 2003. Mem.: Modern Languages Assn. Home: 1014 Spruce St 5-4 Philadelphia PA 19107 Office: Villanova U 800 Lancaster Ave Villanova PA 19085 E-mail: jduran@villanova.edu.

DURAN, KARIN JEANINE, librarian; b. Burbank, Calif., Aug. 31, 1948; d. Jose Antonio and Sophia (Cortez) D.; m. Richard Mark Nupoll, Sept. 5, 1971. AA, L.A. Pierce Coll., Woodland Hills, Calif., 1968; BA, Calif. State U., 1970; MLS, U. So. Calif., 1972, PhD, 1986. Libr. Calif. State U., Northridge, 1972—. Lectr. Calif. State U., Northridge, 1977—. Mem. Comision Femenil San Fernando Valley, Calif., 1987—. Named Woman of Year Calif. Women Higher Edn., Northridge, 1989, Bicentennial Woman, L.A. Human Rels. Com., 1976. Mem. ALA, Nat. Assn. Chicano Studies, Calif. Libr. Assn., Calif. Acad. Rsch. Librs., REFORMA. Avocations: travel, theatre, reading. Office: Calif State U Northridge Libr 18111 Nordhoff St Northridge CA 91330-8327

DURAN, MATIAS MARTIN, adult education educator; b. Valladolid, Yucatan, Mexico, Feb. 24, 1922; s. Marcelo Duran, Aureliana Martin; m. Faasoa Togiaso Duran, Nov. 15, 1980; children: Mary F., Martin T., Marcelo, Matthias. Aa, Riverside City Coll., Calif., 1970; BA, U. Calif., Riverside, 1974; MA, U. Dominguez Hills, Long Beach, Calif., 1988. Psychiat. technician Met.

State Hosp., Norwalk, Calif., 1965; correctional officer Calif. Rehab. Ctr., Norco, 1966—72; probation officer Riverside County Probation, Blythe, Calif., 1975—77; ESL tchr./bilingual crosscultural instr. Compton Unified Sch. Dist., Calif., 1977—93. Mem.: K.C. (warden of coun. 1999—). Home: 140 W Barclay St Long Beach CA 90805-2108

DURAN, MICHAEL CARL, bank executive; b. Colorado Springs, Colo., Aug. 27, 1953; s. Lawrence Herman and Jacqueline Carol (Ward) D. BS magna cum laude, Ariz. State U., 1980. With Valley Nat. Bank (name now Bank One, Ariz., N.A.), Phoenix, 1976—; corp. credit trainee Bank One Ariz. (formerly Valley Nat. Bank Ariz.), Phoenix, 1984-85; comml. loan officer Valley Nat. Bank Ariz. (name now Bank One Ariz.), Phoenix, 1985-86; br. mgr., asst. v.p. Valley Nat. Bank Ariz. (name now Bankone, Ariz.), Phoenix, 1986-90, comml. banking officer, asst. v.p., 1990-93, credit mgr., v.p., 1993-99, relationship mgr., v.p., 1999—. Cons. various schs. and orgns., 1986—; incorporator Avondale Neighborhood Housing Svcs., 1988. Mem. Cen. Bus. Dist. Revitalization Com., Avondale, Ariz., 1987-88, Ad-Hoc Econ. Devel. Com., 1988; coord. Avondale Litter Lifters, 1987-88; vol. United Way, Phoenix, 1984; bd. dirs. Jr. Achievement, Yuma, Ariz., 1989-91, vol., Phoenix, 1993—; yokefellow 1st So. Bapt. Ch. of Yuma, 1990-91; treas. Desert View Bapt. Ch., Gilbert, Ariz., 1998—. Recipient Outstanding Community Svc. award City of Avondale, 1988. Mem. Robert Morris Assocs., Ariz. State U. Alumni Assn. (life), Toastmasters, Kiwanis (local bd. dirs. 1986-88), Beta Gamma Sigma, Phi Kappa Phi, Phi Theta Kappa, Sigma Iota Epsilon. Democrat. Baptist. Avocations: art, photography, hiking, jogging. Home: 925 N Quartz St Gilbert AZ 85234-3661

DURAND, CHARLES ERIC, psychologist, educator; b. Ponchatoula-Hammond, La., Nov. 21, 1964; s. Charles Lucius and Marilyn Glynn (Williams) Durand. ADJ, ThD, PhD, So. Christian Coll., Ponchatoula, 1986. Lic. tchr. La. Track equip. mgr. Southeastern La. U., Hammond, 1982; rschr., instr. So. Christian U., Ponchatoula, 1982—86; rschr., prof., adminstr. UNIGLOE U. Sys., Hammond, 1986—. Rschr., clinician The Love Insts., Hammond, 1986—; founder The $75 Educate Am. Program. Author: Dr. Durand's Absolute Bibles, 1985, Absolute Psych, 1986, Absolute Love, 1984—86. Pres., cand. Anti-Dictatorial Party, 1992, 1996, 2000, civil prosecutor, 1990, co-founder, 1989—. With USN, 1982—83. Named Ct. Proven Lover, The Beauties Hall of Fame, 1986; grantee rsch. grante, Andrew Carnegie Sch. Bus., 1984. Mem.: Internat. Assn. Hypnoanalysts (diplomate). Avocation: martial arts. Home: 509 Brickyard Rd Hammond LA 70401 Office: UNIGLOE University System LTF #LA76 11265 Redbird Ln Hammond LA 70401

DURANT, GRAHAM JOHN, medicinal chemist, drug researcher; b. Newport, Gwent, U.K., Mar. 14, 1934; s. Edgar Counsell and Florence (Pocock) D.; m. Rosemary Margaret Towle, Apr. 14, 1962; children: Julian Clive, Adrian Charles. BSc in Chemistry with honors, U. Birmingham, U.K., 1955, PhD, 1958; postdoctoral study, State U. Iowa, Iowa City, 1958-59. Sr. rsch. officer Smith Kline & French Rsch., Welwyn Garden City, Hertfordshire, U.K., 1960-75, head dept. medicinal chemistry, 1975-85, head rsch. adminstrn., 1985-86; Disting. prof. medicinal chemistry Coll. Pharmacy, U. Toledo, Ohio, 1987-92, dir. Ctr. for Drug Design and Devel., 1987-92; sr. dir. chemistry Cambridge (Mass.) Neurosci., Inc., 1992-98; pharm. cons., 1998—. Contbr. articles to profl. jours.; co-holder over 100 patents. Trustee Inventure Place, Akron, Ohio, 1990-98. Inducted into Nat. Inventors Hall of Fame, 1990. Fellow Royal Soc. Chemistry (Medicinal Chemistry award 1983, mem. fine chems. group com. 1985-87). Avocations: genealogy, travel. Home and Office: GJD Consulting 5 Wingfield Thurlestone Kingsbridge TQ7 3TE England E-mail: gradurant@aol.com.

DURANT, JOHN RIDGEWAY, retired physician, consultant; b. Ann Arbor, Mich., July 29, 1930; s. Thomas Morton and Jean Margaret (deVries) D.; m. Mary Sue Avery Dillon, Jan. 13, 1990; children by previous marriage: Christine Joy, Thomas Arthur (dec.), Michele Grace, Jennifer Margaret. BA, Swarthmore (Pa.) Coll., 1952; MD, Temple U., Phila., 1956; hon. degree, U. Ala., 1993. Diplomate: Am. Bd. Internal Medicine. Intern, then jr. asst. resident in medicine Hartford (Conn.) Hosp., 1956-58; resident in medicine Temple U. Med. Center, 1960-62; spl. fellow med. neoplasia Meml. Hosp. for Cancer and Allied Diseases, N.Y.C., 1962-63; Am. Cancer Soc. advanced clin. fellow Temple U. Health Scis. Center, 1964-67, instr., then asst. prof. medicine, 1963-67; clin. assoc. chemotherapy Moss Rehab. Hosp., Phila., 1964-67; research assoc. Fels Research Inst., Phila., 1965-67; mem. faculty U. Ala. Med. Center, Birmingham, 1968-82, prof. medicine, dir. comprehensive cancer center, 1970-82, prof. radiation oncology, 1978-82, chmn. Southeastern coop. cancer study group at univ., 1975-82, Disting. faculty lectr., 1980; pres. Fox Chase Cancer Ctr., Phila., 1982-88; sr. v.p. health affairs and dir. med. ctr. U. Ala., Birmingham, 1988-95; exec. v.p. Am. Soc. Clin. Oncology, Alexandria, Va., 1995-2000; cons. med. dir. Walther Cancer Inst., Indpls., 2000—; cons. Baptist Health Sys., Birmingham, Ala., 2000—. Chmn. coop. group exec. com. Nat. Cancer Inst., NIH, 1977-82, chmn. coop. group chairmen, 1979-82; cons. VA Hosp., Tuskegee, Ala., 1970-82; exec. com. Birmingham chpt. ARC, 1972-77; mem. Nat. Cancer Adv. Bd., 1986-92. Mem. editorial bd. Cancer Clin. Trials, 1979-82, assoc. editor, 1982—; editorial bd. Med. and Pediatric Oncology News, 1975-90; assoc. editor Cancer, 1984-92; contbr. numerous articles to med. jours. Mem. adv. coun. for sci. Notre Dame U., 2002—. Served as officer M.C. USNR, 1958-60. Recipient Oncologist of Yr. award So. Oncology Assn., 1999; named Temple U. Med. Sch. Alumnus Yr., 1982, Cancer Fighter of Yr., Cancer Fighter Awards Trust, 2000. Fellow ACP, Coll. Physicians Phila.; mem. Am. Cancer Soc. (vice chmn. advanced clin. fellowship com. 1974-76, 85-87, mem. instl. rsch. grant com. 1979-82, pres. Ala. divsn. 1973-75, 77-79, mem. blue ribbon com. to rev. nat. rsch. program 1994-95), Am. Assn. Cancer Rsch., Am. Radium Soc. (pres. 1984), Am. Bd. Int. Med. Oncology (subcom. 1979-85, chmn. 1983-85), Assn. Am. Cancer Insts. (dir. 1978—, pres. 1982-83), Assn. Cmty. Cancer Ctrs. (dir. 1979-81), Am. Soc. Clin. Oncology (chmn. pub. rels. com. 1976-79, bd. dirs. 1979-82, 84-87, pres. 1985-86, Spl. Recognition award 1999), others. Methodist. E-mail: msdurant@aol.com.

DURANT, MARC, lawyer; b. N.Y.C., Jan. 17, 1947; s. Sidney Irwin and Estelle (Haas) D.; m. Karen Rose Baker, June 9, 1968 (div. 1975); children: Lauren, Elyssa; m. Rita Mary Tatar, Dec. 31, 1979; children: David, Alexander. BS, Cornell U., 1968; JD, Harvard U., 1968-71. Bar: Pa. 1972, U.S. Dist. Ct. (ea. dist.) Pa. 1972, U.S. Supreme Ct. 1980, U.S. Ct. Appeals (3d cir.) 1981, N.Y. 1991. Law clk. U.S. Dist. Ct., Wilmington, Del., 1971-72; assoc. Schnader, Harrison, Segal & Lewis, Phila., 1972-75; asst. U.S. Atty. U.S. Dept. Justice, Phila., 1975-77; dep. chief criminal divsn.v. U.S. Atty.'s Office, Phila., 1977-81; ptnr. Durant and Durant, Phila., 1981—. Mem.: ABA, Phila. Bar Assn., Pa. Bar Assn., Nat. Assn. Criminal Def. Lawyers, Fed. Bar Assn. Office: Durant & Durant 325 Chestnut St Philadelphia PA 19106-2614 E-mail: mdurant@durantlaw.com.

DURANT, PENNY LYNNE RAIFE, writer, speaker, educator; b. Albuquerque, May 22, 1951; d. John Carl and Patricia Fay (Bremermann) Raife; m. Omar Duane Durant, Jan. 2, 1971; children: Geoffrey Alan (dec.), Adam Omar. Student, Lawrence U., Appleton, Wis., 1969-70; BS, U. N.Mex., 1973, MA, 1980. Mem. adv. bd. Soc. Children's Book Writers and Illustrators/N.Mex., Albuquerque, 1996-2000. Author: Make a Splash!, 1991, Prizewinning Science Fair Projects, 1991, When Heroes Die, 1993 (Lambda Lit. award 1993, 1st prize juvenile novel Nat. League Am. Pen Women 1993, award of excellence N.Mex. Press Women 1993), Bubblemania!, 1995, Exploring the World of Plants, 1995, Exploring the World of Animals, 1995, More Prizewinning Science Fair Projects, 1998; works put to music, performed include We Are One, Aki's Story, Mayhem and Malarkey; conbr. articles to Parents Mag., Durango Mag., Working Parents, The Luth, Southwest Sage. Sec. bd. dirs. Albuquerque Children's Theatre, 1995-98. Mem. Nat. League Am. Pen Women (v.p. Albuquerque br. 1990, sec. 1996, state letters chair 1996), S.W. Writers, Soc. Children's Book Writers and Illustrators (mem. adv. bd. N.Mex. chpt. 1997-2000). Democrat. Lutheran. Home: 305 Quincy St NE Albuquerque NM 87108-1344 E-mail: pennydurant22@msn.com.

DURAY, JOHN ROBERT, physicist; b. East Chicago, Ind., Jan. 28, 1940; s. John S. and Margaret A. D.; m. Elizabeth A. Meyer, Nov. 19, 1966; children: Sam, Vince, Mike. BS, Benedictine U., 1962; PhD, U. Notre Dame, 1968. Postdoctoral fellow Ohio State Univ., Columbus, 1968-70; instr. Princeton (N.J.) Univ., 1970-75; asst. prof. Ind. Univ. N.W., Gary, 1975; mgr. subsurface sys. Bendix Field Engring., Grand Junction, Colo., 1975—81; sr. mgr. tech. programs Rust Geotech, Grand Junction, 1981—96; prin. scientist Sensible Environ. Solutions, Grand Junction, 1996—; sr. program mgr. Rust Geotech, 1986—96. Chmn. bd. dirs. Holy Family Edn. Found. Mem. Am. Phys. Soc., Sigma Xi. Office: 2137 Banff Ct Grand Junction CO 81503-1032 E-mail: jrduray3@attbi.com.

DURBETAKI, N. JOHN, software company executive; b. Rochester, N.Y., Oct. 7, 1955; s. Pandeli and Elisabeth (Megerle) D.; m. Jeanne Feng, June 16, 1984; children: Lee Daniel, Mark John. BEE, Ga. Inst. Tech., 1977. Product engr. Nat. Semiconductor, Santa Clara, Calif., 1977-78, Intel, Aloha, Oreg., 1978-80, test engr., 1980-83, cons. Hillsboro, Oreg., 1983-84; chmn. bd., pres. OrCAD Systems Corp., Hillsboro, 1984-86, chmn. bd., chief exec. officer, 1986-89; chief exec. officer OrCAD L.P. and predecessors, 1989-91; bd. dirs., v.p. R&D OrCAD, Inc., 1991-93; founder The Gaston (Oreg.) Works, 1993-99. Founder Bison Ventures, Lake Oswego, Oreg., 1996-2000, Tantonka Woods, 1998—, Bison CAD, 2001—; dir. embedded sys. iMove, Inc., 2002—. Cubmaster pack 729 Boy Scouts Am., 1996-2000, com. mem. troop 855, 1995-96, asst. scoutmaster, 1996-97, scoutmaster, 1997—, 1st asst., scoutmaster Cascada Pacific coun. Jamboree, 1999-2001, staff Tuality Dist. Camporee, 1999—, roundtable, 1999—, Woodbadge, Buffalo Patrol, 1999. Mem. Nat. Bison Assn., Northwest Bison Assn., Internat. Hurling Soc., Delta Tau Delta. Republican. Lutheran.

DURBIN, CHARLES G., JR., anesthesiologist, intensivist, educator; b. Phila., Jan. 7, 1948; s. Charles G. and Eleanor M. Durbin; m. Bertha M. Durbin, June 7, 1969; children: Brandy, Jennifer, Michael. BA, Johns Hopkins U., 1970, MD, 1973. MD, Va. Prof. U. Va., Charlottesville, 1983—, med. dir. respiratory care. Mem. Am. Assn. Respiratory Care (hon.). Avocation: cross country and mountain biking. Home: 4522 Catterton Rd Free Union VA 22940 Office: U Va Dept Anesthesiology Box 800710 Charlottesville VA 22908 E-mail: CGD8V@Virginia.edu.

DURBIN, RICHARD JOSEPH, senator; b. East St. Louis, Ill., Nov. 21, 1944; s. William and Ann D.; m. Loretta Schaefer, June 24, 1967; children: Christine, Paul, Jennifer. BS in Econs., Georgetown U., 1966, JD, 1969. Bar: Ill. 1969. Chief legal counsel Lt. Gov. Paul Simon of Ill., 1969; mem. staff minority leader Ill. Senate, 1972-77, parliamentarian, 1969-77; practice law, 1969—; assoc. prof. med. humanities So. Ill. U., 1978—; mem. 98th-104th Congresses from 20th Dist. Ill., 1983-97; U.S. senator from Ill., 1997—; mem. judiciary com., govtl. affairs com., budget com. Mem. appropriations com., subcoms. on agriculture, rural devel. and related agys., def., legis. br., and D.C. (ranking mem.), 1999—; mem. budget com.; mem. govt. affairs com. subcom. on oversignt of govt. mgmt., restructuring and the D.C., 1999—, and permanent subcom. on investigations, 1997—; mem. select com. on ethics, 1999—; asst. Dem. fl. leader. Campaign worker Sen. Paul Douglas of Ill., 1966; staff Office Ill. Dept. Bus. and Econ. Devel., Washington; candidate for Ill. Lt. Gov., 1978; staff alt. Pres.'s State Planning Council, 1980; advisor Am. Council Young Polit. Leaders, 1981; mem. YMCA Ann. Membership Roundup, YMCA Bldg. Drive, Pony World Series; bd. dirs. Cath. Charities, United Way of Springfield, Old Capitol Art Fair, Springfield Youth Soccer; mem. Sch. Dist. 1986 Referendum Com., Springfield NAACP. Democrat. Roman Catholic. Office: US Senate 332 Dirksen Sen Office Bldg Washington DC 20510-0001*

DURBIN, RICHARD LOUIS, SR., healthcare administration consultant; b. Millersport, Ohio, Aug. 28, 1928; s. Clark Babe and Mabel (Bushee) Durbin; m. Carolyn Bohrer, Mar. 18, 1955; children: Richard Louis, Margot Jane, Melissa Bushee. BA, Ohio State U., 1949; MBA, U. Chgo., 1956; MPA, U. Ariz., 1969; postgrad., Pace Coll., 1973; MPH, U. Tex. Sch. Pub. Health, 1992, postgrad, 1999—. Cert. govt. fin. mgr., Assn. Govt. Accts.; profl. sanitarian. Research chemist Battelle Meml. Inst., Columbus, Ohio, 1949—50; sales rep. Am. Cyanamid Co., N.Y.C., 1953—54; adminstrv. asst. Lancaster (Ohio)-Fairfield Hosp., 1954; with Bus. Devel. Outreach Helath, Austin, 1995—; asst. adminstr. City of Memphis Hosps., 1956—58, assoc. adminstr., 1958—60; dir. outpatient and profl. services Presbyn.-St. Luke's Hosp., Chgo., 1960—61; assoc. dir. grad. program in hosp. adminstrn., faculty U. Chgo. Grad. Sch. Bus., 1961—62; exec. sec. Am. Assn. Univ. Programs in Hosp. Adminstrn., 1960—62; assoc. prof. bus. adminstrn. Temple U., 1967—69, prof. mgmt., 1969—70; exec. dir. Lubbock (Tex.) County Dist. Hosp., 1970—71; v.p. Coll. Medicine and Dentistry N.J., 1971—75; also v.p. Acad. Health Center; asst. prof. N.J. Med. Sch., 1973—75; pres., CEO Harris County Hosp. Dist., Houston, 1975—89; asst. regional dir. region #6 Tex. State Dept. Health, 1989—92; adminstr. Tex. Alcoholic Beverage Commn., Austin, 1992—93; pres., CEO Durbin Internat., San Marcos, Tex., 1993—; health dir. Cameron County Health Dept., San Benito, Tex., 1995—; CEO/dir. Maverick County Hosp. Dist., Eagle Pass, Tex.; dir. Maverick County Health Dist., Eagle Pass; pres. Health Edn. Found. for Deserving Students, Eagle Pass; CEO, Montgomery County Hosp. Dist.; pres. Vineyard Inc., Houston, 2003—. Founder, dir. grad. program in health care adminstrn., 1967—70; exec. dir., 1966—70; cons. in field; pres. D&H Enterprises, Durbin Internat.; project dirl., chief planner, exec. dir. Newark Comprehensive Health Plan, 1974; cons. divsn. hosp. and med. facilities HEW, 1967—; design adv. group, nat. rev. com., cons. exptl. health systems, 1971—73; cons. Nat. Commn. on Productivity, U.S. Bur. Prisons, 1968—; mem. Hosp. Devel., Inc. N.J. Gov.'s Correctional Health Svc. Investigations Com.; mem. adv. bd. Comprenetics, Inc., 1967—; steering com. Tucson Hosp. and Health Planning Commn., 1962—, Assoc. Hosp. Svcs. Ariz., 1963—64; treas. Ariz. League Nursing, 1963—64; adj. assoc. prof. Tex. Woman's U.; mem. coordinating coun. Tex. Health and Human Svcs., 1986—; appraisal rev. bd. Travis Ctrl. Appraisal Dist., 1994—; dir. bus. devel. Outreach Health Svcs., 1995—; adj. assoc. prof. U. Tex. Sch. Pub. Health, 1996—2003; med. adv. com. Tex. Workman's Compensation Commn. Author: A Statistical Methodology of Evaluating a Medical Staff, 1961, New Ideas and Concepts in Outpatient Management, 1963; author: (with others) Ivory Tower to Workshop, 1964; author: Ambulatory Care Development, 1966; author: (with W.H. Springall) Organization and Administration of Health Care, 1974; author: (with Springall, P. High) Manual for Hospital Program and Performance Budgeting at the Operating Level, 1968; author: (with G. Connor) Design of a City-Wide HMO, 1974; author: Border Issues, 2000; cons. editor Hosp. Topics, editor The Forum, What's Going On: Hospital Topics, mem. editl. bd. Physician Weekly; contbr. articles to profl. jours. Mem. Phila. Crime Commn., 1967—, Tex. Indigent Care Task Force; chmn. Harris County Jail com., 1987—88, Health Svcs. com. AIDS panel; ch. deacon; bd. dirs. Ariz. Blue Cross, Mexic-Arte Mus., 1994—. Lt. USNR, 1945—46, lt. USNR, 1950—53. Recipient Editl. award, Hosp. Mgmt. mag., 1961, 1963, 1965, cert. of merit, Gov. Ariz., 1967, 1968, Silver medal (DeBakey) award, Baylor Coll. of Medicine, 1986. Fellow: Am. Coll. Hosp. Adminstrs. (cert.); mem.: AAUP, Tex. Pub. Health Assn., Am. Coll. Managed Care Adminstrs., Am. Coll. Healthcare Assn. (chmn. book award com. 1983, membership com. 1986), Am. Mgmt. Assn. (Excellence award 1968), Internat. Hosp. Fedn., Am. Inst. Mgmt., Am. Soc. Pub. Adminstrn., Am. Criminology Soc., So. Ariz. Hosp. Coun. (pres. 1963), Tex. Hosp. Assn. (bd. dirs., mem. exec. com. 1987—88), Pa. Hosp. Assn., Am. Hosp. Assn. (coun. pub. hosps.), Nat. Assn. Clinic Mgrs., Am. Chem. Soc., Nat. Assn. Pub. Hosps. (dir., founder), Blanton Art Mus., Texans Standing Tall, U. Tex. Recreational Sports (life), Tucson Press Club (life), U. Tex. Faculty Ctr., Quadrangle Club (U. Chgo.), Midway Club (Chgo.), Buckeye Lake Yacht Club, Columbian Yacht Club (Chgo.), Pa. Soc. Club, Army-Navy Capitol Hill Club (Washington), Houston Yacht Club, Headliners Club (Austin, Tex.), Hillcrest Country Club, Rotary, Houston C. of C. (health com.), Sigma Xi, Sigma Alpha Epsilon. Presbyterian. Home: 505 W 7th St Apt 319 Austin TX 78701-2836 Office: 9415 Burnet Rd Ste 300 Austin TX 78758-5266

DURBIN, RICHARD LOUIS, JR., lawyer; b. Gary, Ind., Dec. 23, 1955; s. Richard Louis and Carolyn Martha (Bohrer) D.; m. Diana Cabaza Durbin, June 2, 1979; children: Louis Eloy, Laura Elena. Student, Rutgers U., 1973-75; BA, U. Chgo., 1977; JD, U. Tex., 1980. Bar: Tex. 1980. Law clk. to presiding judge U.S. Dist. Ct. (we. dist.) Tex., San Antonio, 1980-82; assoc. Susman, Godfrey & McGowan, Houston, 1982-83; asst. U.S. atty. U.S. Atty.'s Office (we. dist.) Tex., San Antonio, 1983—, chief criminal sect., 1988-90, 98—, chief narcotics sect., 1990-92, 97-98, chief appellate sect., 1992-98; adj. prof. law St. Mary's U. Sch. of Law, 1995—. Instr. U.S. Atty. Gen. Adv. Inst., Washington, 1987—; Dept. of Justice Nat. Advocacy Ctr., 1998—; speaker San Antonio Bar Assn. Criminal Law Inst. 1999— Editor Tex. U. Law Rev., 1979-80. Interviewer U. Chgo. Alumni Schs. Com., San Antonio, 1984—. Recipient Dir.'s award Tex. Dept. Pub. Safety, Austin, 1985. Mem. Tex. State Bar, Coll. State Bar Tex., Order of Coif, Phi Beta Kappa. Office: US Attys Office 601 NW Loop 410 Ste 600 San Antonio TX 78216-5512 E-mail: richard.durbin@usdoj.gov.

DURBIN, TIMOTHY TERRELL, music educator; b. Lexington, Ky., June 14, 1957; s. Ferrell James Durbin and Vera Louise (Baldridge) Brock; m. Sandra Elizabeth Stone, June 13, 1981; children: Josef Amadeus, Heather Elizabeth, April. MusB in Violin Performance, U. Ala., 1979; MusM in Violin Performance, U. Ill., 1982. Tchg. asst. U. Ill., Champaign, 1979-82; asst. concertmaster Lexington Philharm. Orch., 1982-86; violin instr. Lexington Talent Edn. Assn., 1982-87; pvt. instr. violin Lexington, 1982—; violin instr. Morehead (Ky.) State U., 1984-90; .; clinician Suzuki Assn. Ams., Inc., Muscatine, Iowa, 1984—2002; dir. string studies Azusa (Calif.) Pacific U., 2002—. Dir. Morehead State U. Orch., 1987-89, 1999-2002, Lexington Cmty. Orch., 1984-87; adj. instr. Transylvania U., Lexington, Ky., 1985-87, 99—, Composer overture for violin and string orch., 1991, Fanfare for 4 violins, 1991, brass quinted percussion piece, 1976, Suite for Strings, 2001. Mem.: Suzuki Assn. Ams., Inc. Democrat. Episcopalian. Avocations: Karate, aviation, computers, science fiction. Home: 627 South Santa Fe Apt D Glendora CA 91740 Office: Azusa Pacific Univ 901 E Alosta Ave Azusa CA 91702 E-mail: Hdurbin@aol.com.

DURCA, ERIC MARCEL, physician for addictions; b. Paris, Oct. 12, 1957; s. Ludovic and Nicole Aimée (Coullet) D.; m. Bettina Doris Begyn, Apr. 8, 1986. MD, U. Paris XIII, 1987; cert. de toxicomanies, U. Montréal, Que. Resident various hosps., Paris, 1984-87, sr. physician for alcoholic diseases, 1987-90; sr. physician, head Westfälische Klinik für Psychiatrie, Germany, 1990-92; sr. physician, med. supt. gerontology Med. Ctr. Belligneux, Hauteville, France, 1993-94; sr. physician for alcoholic diseases Centre Hospitalier, Lorrain, Martinique, 1994-96; with C.M.P., Orval, France, 1996-2000; sr. physician for addictions Hôpital Dept. de Felleries-Liessies, Solre-Le-Chateau, France; sr. physician for addiction and psychiatry Hopital de Hull, Canada, 2001; sr. physician for psychiatry Hopital Montpon, France, 2002—. Instr. nursing sch., Germany, 1991-92, France, 1993-94. Mem. N.Y. Acad. Scis., ASAM, Soc. Francaise Alcoologie. Roman Catholic. Avocations: hiking, skiing. Office: Hopital de Montpon 24700 Montpon France Office Fax: 33 533 801483.

DURCAN, DEBORAH ANN, finance company executive; b. Des Moines, Iowa, Nov. 22, 1952; d. Jerry Ralph and Anne Lucille Durcan; m. Eli Howard Schmukler, Aug. 28, 1988; children: Eric Leaf, Glenn Schmukler, Ryan Schmukler. BBA, Univ. Wis.-Madison, Madison, Wis., 1974. CPA, CGFM. Auditor State Dept of Revenure, Madison, Wis., 1975—76; staff acct. Univ. Wis. in Sys., Madison, Wis., 1976—84, asst. dir. fin. reporting, 1984—85, assoc. contr., 1985—87, contr., 1987—92, assoc. v.p. for fin. admin., 1992—99, v.p. for fin., 1999—. Sec., bd. mem. Ctrl. Assn, of Coll. Univ. Bus. Officers, Chgo., 1996—2002; bd. mem. Coll. Savings Bd., Madison, Wis., 2000—03. Mem.: Soc. of Coll. & Univ. Planning, Nat. Assn. of Coll. & Univ. Bus. Offices, Ctrl. Assn. of Coll. & Univ. Bus. Offices. Avocations: sailing, skiing, travel. Office: Univ Wis Sys 1200 Linden Dr/ 1752 Van Hse Hall Madison WI 53706

DURCHSLAG, STEPHEN P. lawyer; b. Chgo., May 20, 1940; s. Milton Lewis and Elizabeth (Potovsky) D.; m. Ruth Florence Mayer, Nov. 21, 1976; children: Rachel Beth, Danielle Leah. BS, U. Wis., 1963; LLB, Harvard U., 1966. Bar: Ill. 1966. Assoc. Sidley & Austin, Chgo., 1966-72, ptnr., 1972-89, Winston & Strawn, Chgo., 1989—. Contbr. articles to profl. jours. Trustee Nathan Cummings Found., 1996—, Anshe Emet, Chgo., 1983—, pres., 2000—02. Mem. ABA (AAF legal com.), Promotion Mktg. Assn. (bd. dirs.), Am. Standard Club, East Bank Club. Jewish. Avocations: skiing, running, tennis, rare books. Office: Winston & Strawn 35 W Wacker Dr Ste 3600 Chicago IL 60601-1695 E-mail: sdurchsl@winston.com.

DURDAHL, CAROL LAVAUN, psychiatric nurse; b. Crookston, Minn., Jan. 18, 1933; d. Elmer Oliver and Ovidia (Olson) Durdahl; m. Hans A. Dahl, May 22, 1956 (div. 1983); children: Hana Sorensen-O'Neill, Carla Pederson. RN, St. Lukes Hosp., Duluth, Minn., 1953; BA in Human Svcs., Met. State U., St. Paul, 1982. Staff nurse various hosps., Minn., 1953-59; human svcs. tech. Willmar (Minn.) State Hosp., 1970-74, supplemental tchr., 1974-83; staff nurse Rice Meml. Hosp., Willmar, 1983-86; utilization rev. various nursing homes, Willmar, 1985-86; tchr. Willmar Area Vocat. Tech. Inst., 1986; dir. nurses Glenmore Recovery Ctr., Crookston, Minn., 1986-88; shift supr. Golden Valley (Minn.) Health Ctr., 1988-92; with crisis dept. Hennepin County Med. Ctr., 1988—; managed care of psychiat. and substance abuse MCC Managed Behavioral Care, Mpls., 1992. Contbr. articles to profl. jours. Mem. AAUW, Bus. and Profl. Women, League Women Voters (pres. and state bd.), Federated Women, Does. Republican. Lutheran. Avocations: reading, walking, crafts. Home: 3720 Independence Ave S Apt 41 Minneapolis MN 55426-3767 Office: Hennepin County Med Ctr 701 Park Ave Minneapolis MN 55415-1623 E-mail: cdurdahl@aol.com.

DURDANOVIC, IGOR, researcher; b. Zagreb, Croatia, Mar. 14, 1966; s. Zarko and Marija Durdanovic; m. Vedrana Krstic, May 29, 2000; 1 child, Dora Durdanovic Krstic. BS, U. Zagreb, Croatia, 1990. Rsch. asst. U. Paderborn, Germany, 1994—96; associated rsch. staff mem. NEC Labs. USA, Inc., Princeton, NJ, 1996—. Mem.: European Assn. for Computer Sci. Logic, N.Y. Acad. of Sci. Office: NEC Labs USA Inc 4 Independence Way Princeton NJ 08540 Office Fax: 1-609-951-2488. E-mail: igord@nec-labs.com.

DURDEN, ROME L. aircraft manufacturing company executive; b. L.A., Apr. 5, 1935; s. Rome and Hortense (Anderson) D.; m. Priscilla Louise Bibby, Oct. 27, 1962; children: Suzette, Steven. B of Laws, La Salle Extension U., 1971; DD (hon.), Universal Life, Modesto, Calif., 1980. Tech. writer Hughes Aircraft Co., Culver City, Calif., 1962-72, sr. tech. editor, 1972-79, sr. mgmt. systems specialist, 1979-89. Author: (Manuals) Guide for Drafting Procedure, 1981, Simplified Drawing Substitutions, 1984. Treas. Marysville United Meth. Ch., 1997-99; mem. Lake Stevens Governance Coun., 1999, 2000. Recipient Presentation gavel Ramona Park Adv. Coun., Long Beach, Calif., 1971. Mem. Harmony Woods Homeowners Assn. (bd. dirs., treas. 1996-99, v.p. 2000-02). Home: PO Box 1322 Lake Stevens WA 98258-1322

DURDEN, WILLIAM G. academic administrator; Grad., Dickinson Coll., 1971; MA in German Lit. and Lang., PhD in German Lit. and Lang., Johns Hopkins U.; postgrad., U. Freiburg, Germany, U. Münster, U. Basle, Switzerland. Exec. dir. Inst. for the Acad. Advancement of Youth; faculty mem. German dept. Johns Hopkins U.; pres. Sylvan Acad., Sylvan Learning Sys. Inc., Dickinson Coll., Carlisle, Pa., 1999—. Sr. edn. cons. U.S. Dept. State, chair adv. com. exceptional children and youths. Actor: (books); contbr. articles to prof. jours. Recipient Klingenstein award, Tchrs. Coll., Columbua U.; fellow Klingenstein fellow, Wis. Policy Rsch. Inst.; grantee, Am. Coun. Learned Socs., Volkswagen Found., German Soc. Md.; scholar, Fulbright. Office: Dickinson Coll PO Box 1773 Carlisle PA 17013-2896 Fax: 717-245-1457.

DURE, ROBERT SAMUEL, music educator; b. La Porte, Ind., June 12, 1976; s. Robert George and Rose Marie Dure; m. Lisa Marie Cassell, May 15, 1999. BS, Ball State U., 1999. Cert. K-12 music tchr. Ind. Dir. of bands Tri-County Mid./Sr. H.S., Wolcott, Ind., 1999—. Freelance french hornist, Ind., 1995—. Mem.: Internat. Horn Soc., Music Educators Nat. Conf., Ind. Music Educators Assn. (local arrangements chmn. 1999), Phi Mu Alpha Sinfonia (treas. 1997—99). Home: 340 Blakely Dr Lafayette IN 47905 Personal E-mail: rdure340@insightbb.com.

DUREK, DOROTHY MARY, retired English language educator; b. Pitts., Jan. 23, 1926; d. Joseph Adam and Helen Barbara (Ondich) D. BS in Edn., Youngstown State U., 1962; MS in Edn., Westminster Coll., 1969. Cert. English tchr., Ohio, comprehensive English cert., Pa. Tchr. English Brookfield (Ohio) Schs., 1962-64, Sharon (Pa.) City Schs., 1964-88. Mem., pres. Coll. Club Sharon, 1993-94. Charter mem., bd. dirs. LWV Mercer County, Pa., 1993—97; docent Butler Inst. Am. Art, Youngstown, 1988—; mem. Shenango Valley Women's Interfaith Coun., Jewish-Christian Dialogue Group, Sharon; charter mem. Mus. Women's Art, Washington, Nat. Mus. of the Am. Indian, Washington; mem., bd. dirs. Christian Assocs. Shenango Valley. Mem.: AAUW, NEA,

Read and Discuss Group, Sharon Lifelong Learning Coun. (bd. dirs. 1995), Cath. Collegiate Assn., Sharon Tchrs. Assn., Pa. State Educators Assn., Prospect Heights Lit. Club. Roman Catholic. Home: 260 S Buhl Farm Dr Apt 236 Hermitage PA 16148-2528

DUREK, THOMAS ANDREW, computer company executive; b. Sharpsville, Pa., July 1, 1929; s. Joseph Adam and Helen Barbara (Ondish) D.; m. Phyllis H. Norris, Aug. 1, 1987. BA, Pa. State U., University Park, 1953; MA, Baylor U., 1957; MS, Stanford U., 1959. Mgmt. scientist USAF, Pentagon, Washington, 1959-65; project engr. North Am. Rockwell Corp., Washington, 1965-68; systems engr. TRW, Inc., Washington, 1968-81, facility mgr. Patuxant, Md., 1981-82, project mgr. Washington, 1982-86; project mgr., prin. mem. tech. staff Software Productivity Consortium, Herndon, Va., 1986-89; sr. tech. staff, software technologist Systems Integration Group TRW, Inc., Fairfax, Va., 1989-92; founder, prin. TAD Assocs., Bethesda, Md., 1992—. Personal investment software developer; professorial lectr. George Washington U., 1960-66, George Mason U., 1991; chair software reusability conf. Nat. Inst. for Software Quality and Productivity, 1989-91, mem. adv. bd., 1991-96, chair info. systems engrng. for downsizing conf., 1993; speaker in field of software reuse and productivity. Contbr. articles to profl. jours. Mem. parish coun. Church of St. Stephen Martyr, Washington, 1970-78, pres. 1975-78, liturgical min., 1973-87, mem. pastoral coun. Shrine Most Blessed Sacrament, Washington, mem. continuing edn. com., 1993-96; established religious edn. audio-cassette libr., 1995-2001; leader Action in Montgomery, 2000—. With USAF, 1953-65; to col. USAFR, ret., 1984. Decorated Meritorious Svc. medal, 1984. Roman Catholic. Home and Office: 7915 Quarry Ridge Way Bethesda MD 20817-6956 E-mail: tadurek@aol.com.

DURELL, JACK, psychiatrist; b. N.Y.C., July 5, 1928; s. Sam and Helen (Schwartzman) D.; m. Viviane M. diGioja, May 19, 1955. BA summa cum laude, Harvard U., 1949; MD cum laude, Yale U., 1953. Rsch. biochemist NIMH, Bethesda, Md., 1954-57, chief, sect. of psychiatry, 1963-67; v.p. med. affairs, clin. dir. The Psychiat. Inst., Washington, 1967-72, pres., med. dir., 1972-78; assoc. dir. sci. Nat. Inst. Drug Abuse, Rockville, Md., 1979-86; med. dir. clin. affairs div. Ea. Va. Med. Authority, Norfolk, 1986-87; chmn. dept. psychiatry Mercy Cath. Med. Ctr., Phila., 1987-92; prof. psychiatry U. Pa., Phila., 1987—. Exec. dir. Treatment Rsch. Inst., 1992—; pres. Delta Metrics, 1994—; pres. The Psychiat. Inst. Found., Washington, 1973-78; trustee Phila. Mental Health Care Connection, 1987-89. Editor: The Changing Clinical Picture of Schizophrenia, 1977; asst. editor-in-chief Jour. Psychiat. Rsch., 1966-82, mem. editorial bd., 1982—; contbr. to numerous med. publs. With USPHS, 1953-86. Fellow Am. Psychiat. Assn.; mem. Am. Acad. Psychiatrists in Alcoholism and Addictions (sec.-treas. 1985-93), Am. Psychopathological Assn., Am. Coll. Neuropsychopharmacology. E-mail: jdurell@deltametrics.com.

DURFEE, MICHAEL JOHN, child psychiatrist; b. Worcester, Mass., May 4, 1942; s. Marion Birch and Juanita Jean (Livingston) D.; children: Mark, Kirsten, Joshua; m. Deanne Mistretta Tilton, Aug. 18, 1985. BA, Colo. Coll., 1964; MD, U. So. Calif., 1968, cert. in child psychiatry, 1975. Diplomate Am. Bd. Psychiatry and Neurology. Psychiatrist MacLaren Children's Ctr., L.A., 1975-79; child abuse prevention coord. L.A. County Dept. Mental Health, 1979-81; child abuse prevention dir. L.A. County Dept. Health Svcs., 1981—; asst. clin. prof. dept. pediatrics and child psychiatry U. So. Calif. Sch. Medicine, L.A., 1979—. Cons. founder Nat. Ctr. on Child Fatality Rev., L.A., 1996—; nat. and internat. cons. in field, 1978—. Co-author: Sex Abuse of the Young Child, 1986; contbr. articles on child abuse/neglect to profl. publs. Bd. dirs. Calif. Consortium to Prevent Child Abuse, 1980—. Capt. MC, U.S. Army, 1969-72. Mem. APHA, Am. Acad. Forensic Scis. Avocation: swimming. Office: LA County Dept Health Svcs Child Abuse Prev Prgm 8thFl 600 S Commonwealth Ave Los Angeles CA 90005-4001

DURFIELD, TIMOTHY RICHARD, legal assistant; b. Van Nuys, Calif., Feb. 23, 1972; s. Richard and Renee Alberta Durfield. BS in Mktg., Azusa Pacific U., 1994, MBA, 2002; JD, Western State U., 1998. Mgr. Nordstom, Montclair, Calif., 1993—94; law clk. U.S. Fed. Bankruptcy Ct., San Bernardino, Calif., 1997, Fair Housing Dept., Santa Ana, Calif., 1997—98, Law Office Keith C. Holmes, Diamond Bar, Calif., 1997—98; sr. law clk. Orange County Dist. Atty., Santa Ana, 1998—; prof. bus. law Mt. San Antonio Coll., Walnut, Calif., 2003—. Cert. mediator Fair Housing Coun., Orange County, Calif., 1997—98. Republican.

DURGIN, FRANK HERMAN, II, aeronautical engineer; b. Exeter, N.H., Aug. 24, 1926; s. John Frank and Eudora Bissette (Gallant) D.; m. Marianne Hamilton, June 15, 1953; children: John, Jane, Laura, Sally, Frank. SB, MIT, 1948, SM, 1954, aero. engr., 1957. Rsch. engr. Naval Supersonic Lab. MIT, Cambridge, Mass., 1948-61, sr. scientist Aeroelastic Lab., 1961-69, assoc. dir. Wright Bros. Wind Tunnel, 1969-91; pvt. cons., Belmont, Mass., 1991—. Contbr. articles to profl. publs. Mem. Town Meeting, 1963-96; mem. Ran Sch. Com., Belmont, 1966; active Waverly Congl. Ch., 1960-95. With U.S. Army, 1946-47. Mem. AIAA, NSPE, ASCE (chmn. manual of practice for wind tunnel testing of bldg. and structures 1981-86, chmn. manual update 1991-98). Achievements include research in solving major engineering problems at John Hancock Bldg., Boston, Sears Tower, Chgo., Coll. Life Ins. Co. Hdqrs., Indpls., pedestrian wind assessments for many buildings in Boston. Home and Office: 19 Payson Rd Belmont MA 02478-2720 E-mail: fhdurgin@aol.com.

DURGOM-POWERS, JANE ELLYN, lawyer; b. Denver, Sept. 1, 1948; d. John Albert and Rosemarie (Scordino) Durgom. BSIM in Econs., Purdue U., 1971; JD, Georgetown U., 1974. Bar: N.Y. 1975, U.S. Dist. Ct. (so. dist.) N.Y. 1975, U.S. Ct. Appeals (2d cir.) 1975, U.S. Supreme Ct. 1978, Ill. 1981, D.C. 1987, U.S. Dist. Ct. (no. dist.) Ill. 1989, Wyo. 1994. Asst. dist. atty., N.Y.C., 1974-76; spl. asst. narcotics prosecutor Office of Spl. Prosecution, N.Y.C., 1976-78; atty. GM Corp., N.Y.C., 1978-81; gen. counsel Genway Corp., Chgo., 1981-83, Nissan Motor Acceptance Corp., Carson, Calif., 1983-87; cons. Nissan Motor Corp., Ltd., Carson, 1987-88; ptnr. Williams and McCarthy law firm, Rockford, Ill., 1988-97; pres., gen. counsel Antel Internat., Inc., 1997-98; pres., CEO Warren Industries LLC, 1998—2001. Bd. dirs. Internat. Sch. Rock Valley Coll., Rockford. Co-author: (books) Federal Regulation of Consumer Credit, 1981, Jury Instructions for Civil-Criminal RICO Cases. Gen. counsel Nat. League Families POW/MIA in S.E. Asia, Washington, Raoul Wallenberg Humanitarian Inst. Chosen by Rockford mag. as one of city's most interesting people, 1989; recipient cert. Spl. U.S. Congressional Recognition for Outstanding & Invaluable Cmty. Svc., 1995, Nat. Humanitarian Svc. award to Am. MIA's and POW's of the SE Asia War Nat. League of Families, 1995. Mem. ABA (vice chair human rights com. 2000—, chair humanitarian subcom. 2000—), N.Y. Bar Assn., Washington D.C. Bar Assn., Ill. Bar Assn., Rockford C. of C. (bd. dirs.). Avocations: collecting art, antiques. E-mail: jed-p@worldnet.att.net.

DURHAM, BETTY BETHEA, therapist; b. S.C., Jan. 27, 1933; d. Liston Fenton and Rosalie (Bracey) Bethea; m. John Lewis Cottrell, June 8, 1952 (div. June 1972); children: John Lewis Jr., Gregory Bethea; m. John I. Durham, Apr. 29, 1988. BS, U.N.C. at Pembroke, 1974; MSW, U. Ga., 1981. Psycho-social specialist Dublinaire Nursing Care, Dublin, Ga., 1979-80; med. social worker C. Vinson V.A. Med. Ctr., Dublin, 1982-86; therapist Raleigh (N.C.) employee's assistance program Raleigh Cmty. Hosp., 1987-88; pastoral counselor Greenwich (Conn.) Bapt. Ch., 1988-94; therapist Big Island, Va., 1995—. Marriage and family counselor Bapt. Ch., Greenwich, 1988-94; supr. grad. studies U. Ga., Fla. State U., Dublin, 1982-86. Editor Hospital Social Svc. manuals, 1982-86. Mem. Laurens County Ga. Mental Health Bd., 1975-76, Ga. Grand Jury and Gov. Com. on Drug Abuse, 1977; survey and coord. of nursing home svcs., 52 counties in Ga., 1982-86. Recipient Citation for Developing Nursing Home Fund Drive Nat. Heart Assn., 1979, Hands and Heart award VA, 1984. Mem. AAUW, Nat. Mus. of Women in the Arts (tour leader Europe and Mid. East 1988—), Nat. Women's History Mus. (charter). Mem. United Meth. Ch. Avocations: needlepoint, painting, horticulture, reading the classics. Home: 1509 Tolley Meadow Rd Big Island VA 24526-2977 E-mail: johnandbettyd@aol.com.

DURHAM, BETTY LOUISE, poet; b. Hamilton, Ohio, Sept. 11, 1944; d. Gertrude Durham, Ralph Durham. Author: (poetry) Place in the Sun, 1992, Passages-An Anthology of Contemporary Lit., 1992, Reflections-The Poetry Ctr., 1992, The Best Poems of the 90's, 1992, Great Poems of Our Time, 1993, Treasured Poems of Am., 1993. Sgt. USMC, 1967—70. Recipient Songwriter award, I.M.X Recording Co., 1995; scholar Golden Poet scholar, World Of Poetry, 1990—93. Avocations: reading, gardening, writing poetry. Home: 355 E School St #B Covina CA 91723 Personal E-mail: bettyd24@juno.com.

DURHAM, BRADLEY PAUL, financial publisher; b. Dec. 29, 1962; BA, U. Okla., 1985; MS, Boston U., 1987; JD, Suffolk U., 1991. Mng. editor The World Paper, Boston, 1987-89; editor, cons. Kommersant, Moscow, 1990-91; fin. corr. Hearst Corp., Washington, 1992-94; co-founder, pres. Global Investor Pub., Inc., Cambridge, Mass., 1995—; founder, EmergingPortfolio.com Fund Rsch., Cambridge, Mass., 1999—. Office: 50 Follen St Ste 14 Cambridge MA 02138-3501 E-mail: durham@epfr.com.

DURHAM, CAROL ELISE, musician, educator; b. Jackson, Miss., Apr. 10, 1945; d. William Ernest and Elise (Green) Strange; m. James David Durham, Sept. 7, 1968; children: Rachel Elise, David William, Carol Elizabeth. MusB, Miss. Coll., 1966; MusM, U. Tenn., 1968. Organist Grace Luth. Ch., Oak Ridge, Tenn., 1967-69, 1st Bapt. Ch., Auburn, Ala., 1970; adj. music instr. Miss. Coll., Clinton, 1970-72, coach, accompanist, 1990—; organist Raymond (Miss.) United Meth. Ch., 1971-75, Morrison Heights Bapt. Ch., Clinton, 1976—, kindergarten music tchr., 1978-80; piano tchr. Clinton, 1984—; adj. instr. music Hinds C.C., Clinton, 1990. Leader Bapt. Keyboard Festival, Bapt. Music Conv., Jackson, 1994, 97; piano, adjudicator Bapt. Keyboard Festivals, Miss., 1970—. Miss. Music Tchrs. Assn. Auditions, Jackson, Meridian and Vicksburg, Music Forum Bach Festival, Jackson, Miss. Federated Jr. Festivals, Clinton and Canton. Dir. 2d grade choir Morrison Heights Bapt. Ch., Clinton, 1984—, trainer Evangelism Explosion, 1994-97. Mem. Am. Guild Organists (sub-dean publicity Jackson chpt.), Music Tchrs. Nat. Assn., Miss. Music Tchrs. Assn. (area chmn. pre-coll. auditions), Music Forum of Jackson (chmn. sonata festival, Bach festival), MacDowell Music Club (3d v.p.), Alpha Lambda Delta, Alpha Chi, Delta Omicron. Home: 304 Camp Garaywa Rd Clinton MS 39056-5406 Office: Morrison Heights Bapt Ch 201 Morrison Dr Clinton MS 39056-5299 E-mail: csdurham@aol.com.

DURHAM, CAROLYN RICHARDSON, foreign language and literature educator; b. Bklyn., Jan. 13, 1947; d. Herbert Nathaniel and Fannie Elaine (Franklin) Richardson; m. Edward Cassell Durham; children: Diana Kristine, Dara Marie. BA, Drew U., Madison, N.J., 1968; MA, Rutgers U., 1972, PhD, 1987. Rsch. analyst Equitable Life Assurance Soc., N.Y.C., 1968-69; instr. Hampton (Va.) U., 1977-76, asst. prof. fgn. lang. and lit., 1976-91, coordinator modern fgn. lang., 1981-91; assoc. prof. Tex. Christian U., Ft. Worth, 1991—2002; chairperson dept. Fgn. Langs. N.C. Agrl. & Tech. State U., Greensboro, 2003—. Cons. Archdiocese of N.Y. Schs., N.Y.C., 1982, U.S. Dept. Edn., 1992, 95, NEH, 1992. Author, co-editor, translator: Finally Us: Contemporary Black Brazilian Women Writers, 1995; contbg. author: Africana: St. James Guide to Black Artists, 1997, Microsoft Encarta Africana, 1998, The Encyclopedia of the African and the African-American Experience, 1999Microsoft Encarta Africana, 2001; contbr. articles to profl. jours. Bd. dirs. Adv. Bd. on Black Adoptions, Va., 1983-85; interpreter ARC, Yorktown, Va., 1981—; del. nominating conv. Dem. Party, 1984, 86. Ford Found. fellow, 1990; Fulbright-Hays awardee, 1989; recipient Seminar award NEH, 1989, Russell fellow, 1972, NEH Inst. award, 2001; Cert. of Recognition, State of Va., 1984, TCU Rsch. award 1991, 94, 96-98, 2000, Edn. in a Global Soc. award TCU, 1993, 97, Rsch. award, 2001, Edn. in a Global Soc. award, 2001. Mem. MLA, Brazilian Studies Assn., Afro-Latin Am. Rsch. Assn., Am. Coun. on Tchg. and Fgn. Lang., Am. Assn. Tchrs. Spanish and Portuguese, Coll. Lang. Assn., South Ctrl. MLA, Assn. Acad. Programs in Latin Am. and the Caribbean, Feministas Unidas, Assn. of Caribbean Women Writers and scholars, Phi Sigma Iota, Sigma Delta Pi. Democrat. AME Zion Ch. Office: NC U A&T State U Dept Fgn Langs Greensboro NC 27411

DURHAM, CHARLES WILLIAM, civil engineer, director; b. Chgo., Sept. 28, 1917; s. John Barnett and Monica (O'Dea) Durham; m. Margre Ann Henningson, Oct. 12, 1940; children: Steven, Mary Helen, Lynn Barnett, Debra Ann. BS in Gen. Engring., Iowa State U., 1939, BSCE, 1940. Registered profl. engr., 30 states and D.C., Diplomate, Am. Acad. Environ. Engrs. Civil engr. Henningson Engrng. Co., Omaha, 1939—46, ptnr., 1946—50; pres., CEO Henningson, Durham & Richardson, Omaha, 1950—76, chmn. bd., CEO, 1976—. Chmn. bd. Gt. Plains Natural Gas Co.; dir. Omaha Nat. Bank, ONB Realbanc, Minn. Enterprises Inc. Bd. dirs. Iowa State U. Found.; mem. engring. adv. coun. U. Nebr.; mem. adv. com. SAC. Fellow: ASCE, Cons. Engrs. Coun.; mem.: NSPE, Chief Execs. Forum (past pres.), Water Pollution Control Fedn., Nebr. Soc. Profl. Engrs. (past pres., nat. dir.), Soc. Am. Mil. Engrs., Am. Pub. Works Assn., Knights of Ak-Sar-Ben (gov.), U.S. C. of C. (dir.), Beavers, Omaha C. of C. (past pres., past dir.), Jesters, Shriners, Masons. Office: Durham Resources Inc 8401 W Dodge Rd Ste 100 Omaha NE 68114-3438

DURHAM, CHRISTINE MEADERS, state supreme court chief justice; b. L.A., Aug. 3, 1945; d. William Anderson and Louise (Christensen) Meaders; m. George Homer Durham II, Dec. 29, 1966; children: Jennifer, Meghan, Troy, Melinda, Isaac. AB, Wellesley Coll., 1967; JD, Duke U., 1971. Bar: N.C. 1971, Utah 1974. Sole practice law, Durham, N.C., 1971-73; instr. legal medicine Duke U., Durham, 1971-73; adj. prof. law Brigham Young U., Provo, Utah, 1973-78; ptnr. Johnson, Durham & Moxley, Salt Lake City, 1974-78; judge Utah Dist. Ct., 1978-82; assoc. justice Utah Supreme Ct., 1982—2002, chief justice, 2002—. Pres. Women Judges Fund for Justice, 1987-88. Fellow Am. Bar Found.; mem. ABA (edn. com. appellate judges' conf.), Nat. Assn. Women Judges (pres. 1986-87), Utah Bar Assn., Am. Law Inst. (coun. mem.), Nat. Ctr. State Courts (bd. dirs.), Am. Inns of Ct. Found. (trustee). Office: Utah Supreme Ct PO Box 140210 Salt Lake City UT 84114-0210*

DURHAM, DONA ANITA, special education educator; b. Midland, Tex., Apr. 17, 1948; d. Charles Albert and June Maxine Durham; m. W. Thomas Fairbourn, Nov. 18, 1989; 1 stepchild, Paul Lagoe. BA, U. Tex., 1966, MA, 1972, PhD, 1984. Cert. tchr. Tex., Va., Maine. Asst. prof. U. Ky., Lexington, 1984—85, George Washington U., Washington, 1986—92; rsch. coord. Acad. of Ednl. Devel., Washington, 1985—86; resource tchr. Arlington (Va.) Pub. Schs., 1991—92, Cape Elizabeth (Maine) Schs., 1992—93; learning strategist Portland (Maine) Pub. Schs., 1993—2003, SST coord., 2003—. Adj. prof. Lesley U., Cambridge, Mass., 2001—; profl. devel. specialist for ednl. instns. Portland Pub. Schs., 2001—. Mem. Conservation Commn., 1997; chmn. Scarborough (Maine) Conservation Commn., 1997—99; mem. Open Space Com., 2000. Grantee, Portland Pub. Schs., 2000—01; ESL/spl. edn. grantee, Maine Support Network, 1999—2001. Mem.: NEA, New England Bilingual Spl. Edn. Support Network, Educators for Social Responsibility. Democrat. Avocations: travel, yoga, reading, gardening, kayaking. Home: 10 Wynmoor Dr Scarborough ME 04074 E-mail: DDurham207@aol.com.

DURHAM, DREW TAYLOR, lawyer; b. Big Spring, Tex., July 3, 1949; s. Worth Barton and Mary Jo (Nance) D.; m. Patricia Enright, May 29, 1976; children— Alexis, Benjamin. B.A., U. Tex., 1971; J.D., St. Mary's U., San Antonio, 1975. Bar: Tex. 1976. Briefing atty. Fed. Dist. Judge, Lubbock, Tex., 1976-77; asst. county atty. Sterling County (Tex.), 1977-78, county atty., 1978— ; owner Durham & Durham, Sterling City, 1977— . Mem. ABA, Tex. Bar Assn., Phi Alpha Delta. Democrat. Methodist. Home: PO Box 900 Sterling City TX 76951-0900 Office: Durham & Durham PO Box 7 Sterling City TX 76951-0007

DURHAM, FLOYD WESLEY, JR., economist, educator; b. Yuma, Ariz., Feb. 9, 1930; s. Floyd Wesley and Inez (Irvin) D.; BA, North Tex. State U., 1951, MA, 1952; PhD, U. Okla., 1963; m. Patricia Keehan, May 24, 1973; children— Mark Kipling, Ronald Chappell. Claimsman, Liberty Mutual Ins. Co., Boston and Ft. Worth, 1955-58; mem. faculty dept. econs. Tex. Christian U., Ft. Worth, 1960—, prof., 1971— ; cons., 1964— . Pres., Suicide Prevention Tarrant County, 1968-69. Bd. dirs. Ft. Worth Literacy Council, 1963-70, Cen. Tax Authority, Parker County, Tex. Served with AUS, 1953-55. Danforth Found. grantee, 1969-70. Mem. AAUP, Am. So. Econ. Assns., Southwestern and Western Social Sci. Assns., Western Writers Am., Beta Gamma Sigma, Omicron Delta Epsilon, Lambda Chi Alpha. Author: A Pilot Methodological Study to Determine Dibilitating Conditions, 1967; The Trinity River Paradox; Flood and Famine, 1976. Contbr. articles to profl. jours. Home: 6025 Wrigley Way Fort Worth TX 76133-3535 E-mail: durham8@charter.net.

DURHAM, HARRY BLAINE, III, lawyer; b. Denver, Sept. 16, 1946; s. Harry Blaine and Mary Frances (Oliver) Durham; m. Lynda L. Durham, Aug. 4, 1973; children: Christopher B., Laurel A. BA cum laude, Colo. Coll., 1969; JD, U. Colo., 1973. Bar: Wyo. 1973, U.S. Tax Ct. 1974, U.S. Ct. Appeals (10th cir.) 1976. Assoc. Brown, Drew, Apostolos, Massey & Sulllivan, Casper, Wyo., 1973-77; ptnr. Brown & Drew, Casper, 1977-98, Brown, Drew & Massey, LLP, Casper, 1998—. Articles editor: U. Colo. Law Rev., 1972—73. Bd. dirs. Natrona County United Way, 1974—76, pres., 1975—76; mem. City of Casper Pks. and Recreation Commn., 1985—94, vice chmn., 1987—94; Rep. precinct committeeman, 1999—2002; bd. dirs. Casper Symphony Assn., 1974—88, vice chmn., 1979—82, pres., 1983—87. Named Permanent Class Pres., Class of 1969, Colo. Coll., Mem. Nat. Alumni Coun.; recipient State Heroes award, Sporting Goods Mfg. Assn., 1997. Mem.: ABA, Nat. Assn. R.R. Trial Counsel, Natrona County Bar Assn., Wyo. Bar Assn., Wyo. Amateur Hockey Assn. (bd. dirs., sec. 1974—85, pres. 1985—88), Casper Amateur Hockey Club (bd. dirs. 1970—77, sec. 1974—77), Phi Beta Kappa. Home: 3101 Hawthorne Ave Casper WY 82604-4975 Office: 159 N Wolcott St Ste 200 Casper WY 82601-7009

DURHAM, HARVEY RALPH, academic administrator; BS, Wake Forest U., 1959; MA, U. Ga., 1962, PhD in Math., 1965. Asst. prof. math. Appalachian State U., Boone, N.C., 1965-67, assoc. prof., chair dept. math., 1967-71, prof. math., 1971-74, assoc. dean faculty, 1971-74, assoc. vice chancellor for acad. affairs, 1974-79, acting vice chancellor for acad. affairs, 1979-80, vice chancellor for acad. affairs, 1980-89, provost, exec. vice chancellor, 1989—. Office: Appalachian State U Office Acad Affairs Boone NC 28608-0001 E-mail: durhamhr@appstate.edu.

DURHAM, JAMES MICHAEL, SR., marketing executive, retired army officer; b. Shreveport, La., May 27, 1937; s. Judson Burney and Edith Eloise (Whittington) D.; m. Constance Manuela Alvarez, June 4, 1960; children: Jennifer Paige Esperanza Kessler, James Michael Jr., Christopher Jon, David Bradley, Matthew Craig. BS in Math., Centenary Coll. of La., 1959; MSME, N.Mex. State U., 1963; MS in Sys. Mgmt., U. So. Calif., 1981; MBA, Mich. State U., 1988. Commd. 2d lt. U.S. Army, 1959, advanced through grades to col., 1979, mgmt. analyst Army Office Chief of Staff, 1972-74; command and staff positions 3d Infantry Div. U.S. Army, Wurzburg, Germany, 1974-77; student U.S. Army War Coll., Carlisle Barracks, Pa., 1977-78; product mgr. U.S. Army Tank-Automotive Materiel Readiness Command, Warren, Mich., 1978-80; commander Mainz Army Depot, Mainz, Germany, 1980-83; exec. officer to deputy commanding gen. U.S. Army Devel. and Readiness Command, Alexandria, Va., 1983; program mgr., tactical vehicles U.S. Army Tank-Automotive Command, Warren, Mich., 1984-86; ret. U.S. Army Tank Automotive Command, Warren, Mich., 1986; dir. tank automotive programs Cypress Internat., Troy, Mich., 1986-89; v.p. govt. business Cummins Engine Co., Inc., Columbus, Ind., 1989-92, v.p. govt. products, 1992-95, ret., 1995; pres. Cummins Mil. Sys. Co., Inc., Columbus, 1992-93, JD Interests Inc., Farnham, Va., 1995—; v.p. mktg. and bus. devel. Lear Siegler Svcs., Inc., Annapolis, Md., 2002. Guest lectr. Wayne State U. Chmn. Bartholomew County Solid Waste Mgmt. Dist. Citizens Adv. Com., 1991-95, Bartholomew County Solid Waste Mgmt. Authority, 1993-95, Bartholomew County Landfill Site Selection Com., 1993; co-chmn. Project Water, Columbus, 1990-95; chmn. bd. dirs. Am. Youth Activities Assn., Mainz, Germany, 1980-83, pres. Am. Youth Activities Assn., Kitzingen, Germany, 1975-77; bd. dirs. Indpls. Mus. Art-Columbus Gallery, 1995; chmn. devel. com. Richmond County (Va.) Habitat for Humanity, 1996-2002, bd. dirs., 1997-2002, v.p., 1998, pres., 1999-2001; trustee No. Neck chpt. Assn. for the Preservation of Va. Antiquities, 1999, vice dir., 2000-01, dir., 2001-2002. Decorated Legion of Merit with oak leaf cluster, Bronze Star, Vietnam campaign medal with 60 device, Vietnamese Cross of Gallantry with palm. Mem.: ASME, Hist. Soc. No. Neck of Va. (bd. dirs. 1998—2002), U.S. Army Ordnance Corps Assn., Ret. Officers Assn. (sec. Potomac chpt. 1997—98, dir. 1999—2001), Soc. Automotive Engrs., Soc. Mfg. Engrs., Assn. U.S. Army, Nat. Def. Indsl. Assn. (exec. bd. tank and automotive sys. divsn. 1991—, steering com. combat vehicle sys. divsn. 1988—, chmn. 1991—95, steering com. tactical vehicle sys. sect. 1986—95, Silver medal 2000). Republican. Avocation: reading. Home: 2494 Simonson Rd Farnham VA 22460-2212 E-mail: JMD527@aol.com.

DURHAM, JAMES W. lawyer; b. Nov. 18, 1937; m. Kathleen B. Wollman; children: Linda, Cynthia, Andrea. BSBA, Pa. State U., 1959; MBA in Bus. Adminstrn., U. Portland, 1962; JD, Pa. State U., 1965. Bar: Oreg. 1965, U.S. Dist. Ct. Oreg., U.S. Ct. Appeals (9th cir.), U.S. Supreme Ct. Assoc. Davies, Biggs, Strayer, Stoel & Boley, Portland, Oreg., 1965—68; ptnr. Durham, Smith, Todd & Ball, Portland, 1968—70; atty. Oreg. Dept. Justice, Salem, Oreg., 1970—78; sr. v.p., gen. counsel, sec. Portland Gen. Electric Co., 1978—87; sr. v.p., gen. counsel Phila. Electric Co. (now Exelon Corp.), Phila., 1988—2001, mediator, arbitrator, 2001—. Chmn. bd. dir. Oreg. Pub. Broadcasting Found., 1984—88; chmn. Oreg. Pub. Defender Com., 1984—85. Chmn., bd. dir. Columbia-Willamette YMCA; bd. dir., trustee Franklin Inst., 1991—2001; bd. dir. Del. Valley Citizens Crime Commn., vice chmn., 2000—02, chmn., 2002—; mem. legal adv. com. Rep. Com. Oreg., 1984—86. Mem.: ABA, Phila. Bar Found. (trustee 1991—94), Del. Valley Corp. Counsel Assn. (bd. dir. 1989—, pres. 1998), Phila. Bar Assn., Pa. Electric Assn. (chmn. 1993—94), Pa. Bar Assn., Oreg. Law Found. (bd. dir. 1986—88, pres. 1988), Oreg. State Bar (bd. govs. 1983—86, pres. 1985—86), Rotary, Tau Kappa Epsilon (fraternity alumnus of yr. 1987). Office: 2620 N Providence Rd Media PA 19063

DURHAM, JEANETTE RANDALL, artist, educator; b. Plainfield, N.J., June 17, 1945; d. F. Gilbert and Alice (Petricek) Randall; m. Ormonde G. Durham III, June 26, 1971; 1 child, O. Ethan. BA in Fine Arts, Montclair State U., 1967; postgrad., Art Students League, 1970, 71, 72, Westchester Art Workshop, 1980-81; MS in Edn., SUNY, Oneonta, 1991. Cert. art tchr. N.Y., N.J., reading tchr. N.Y. Art instr. Mohawk Valley Ctr. Arts, Little Falls, N.Y., 1983, Owen D. Young Cen. Sch., Van Hornesville, N.Y., 1987-92; adj. humanities instr. Herkimer County C.C., 1998—. Mem. decentralization grants panel Ctrl. NY Cmty. Arts Coun., Utica, 1999—2001, mem. exhbn. coms., 2001—; mem. exhbn. com. Mohawk Valley Ctr. for the Arts, 1995—. One person shows include Gallery 57, Cambridge (Mass.) Arts Coun., 1984, Gannett Gallery, SUNY Tech., Utica, N.Y., 1988, South Shore Arts, Little Falls, N.Y., 1991, Pleiades Gallery, N.Y.C., 1993, Mohawk Valley Ctr. for Arts, Little Falls, 1994, Rensselaer Poly. Inst., Troy, 1997, Herkimer County C.C., 1997, Arts Ctr. Old Forge, N.Y., 1998; two-person show at Cazenovia (N.Y.) Coll., 2001; exhibited in group shows at Art of N.E. U.S.A., Silvermine, New Canaan, Conn., 1986, 98 (award), WMHT Exhbn. N.Y. State Mus., Albany, 1988, 56th Ann. Nat. Exhbn. The Cooperstown Art Assn., 1991, 94, 97, 99, 56th Midyear Ann. Butler Inst. Am. Art, 1992, Albany Inst. History and Art, 1993, 96 (award), Arts Coun. Ctrl. N.Y., Utica, 1994, 2001, Pleiades Gallery, N.Y.C., 1991—, Schweinfurth Art Ctr., 1998, Albany Ctr. Galleries, 1999, Gallery 210, Syracuse, 1999, South Shore Art Gallery, Little Falls, N.Y., 1987-2001. SOS grantee N.Y. Found. for Arts, 1997. Mem. Nat. Assn. Women Artists (William Meyerowitz Mcml. award 1991, Florence Andreson award 1998), N.Y. Artist Equity, Coll. Art Assn. Home: 111 Hoke Rd Jordanville NY 13361-2017 E-mail: durhamjr@hccc.suny.edu., jrdurham@ntcnet.com.

DURHAM, JO ANN FANNING, artist; b. Sulphur Springs, Tex., May 31, 1935; d. William Jeffress and Merle Jo (Barrett) Fanning; m. William E. Durham (dec.); children: William, John Lee (dec.). BS, Tex. A&M U., 1956; postgrad., U. Tex., Austin, 1953-55, Tex. Woman's U., Denton, Tex., 1953-55; docteur honoris causa in arts, 1994. Exhibited in group shows at Galerie Jean Lammelin, Paris, 1991, Salon D'Automne Grand Palais, Paris, 1992, 93, Vanderbilt Museum, Long Island VIU, N.Y., 1995, Lever House, VIU, N.Y., 1995, Pen and Brush Club, 1995,96, VIU, N.Y., 1996, Templeton, Fort Worth Artists and Co., Fort Worth, 1996, Sumner Art Museum, Washington, 1996, Belgium Grand Prix, De Paadestallen Van Het Park Van Enghien, Belgium, 1996, Soc. Internat. Des Beaux Arts, Paris, 1996,97, Southwestern Watercolor Soc., D-Art, Dallas, 1996, 97, Anthology Art Gallery, Lebanon, 1997, Longboat Key Art Ctr., North Tex. Health Sci. Ctr., 1997, Atrium Gallery, Fort Worth, 1998, Laura Knott Gallery, Bradford Coll., Mass., 1998, Lee Scarfone Gallery, U. Tampa, Fla., 1998, Fort Mason, San Francisco, 1998, Yale Med. Sch. Libr., 2000, La Chapelle des Penitents, Gordes, France, 2000, Columbia U., 2000, Huntsville (Ala.) Mus. Art, 2001, Salmagundi Club, 2002, 03, ISEA, Chgo. and Aberdare, Wales; The Artist's Magazine, Dec. 2001, Nautilus Fellowship, ISEA, Oct. 2001, Encaustic Works Biennial, 2001, ISEA Dennos Museum,

Traverse City, 2001, Minetrista Cultural Ctr, Muncie, 2002, Salmagundi Club, N.Y.C., 2002, 03, ISEA-WALES, Aberdare, 2003—, Splash 8, 2003. Recipient Gold medal Belgium Grand Prix, 1993. Mem. Soc. Watercolor Artists (signature), Internat. Soc. Exptl. Artists (signature; pres. 1999), Soc. Layerists in Multimedia (signature), Allied Artists, Tex. Fine Arts Assn. (past pres., regional dir., exec. bd.), D Art, Dallas Women's Caucus for the Arts, Dallas Artists Rsch. and Exhbn., Southwestern Watercolor Soc. (signature), Tex. Visual Artists Assn., Fort Worth Woman's Club Art Dept., Templeton Art Ctr., Nat. League of Am. Pen Women, Contemporary Art Ctr., Christians in the Visual Arts, Nat. Coll. Soc., Salmagundi Club. Home: 4300 Plantation Dr Fort Worth TX 76116-7607 Fax: 817-737-6520.

DURHAM, JOHN I. retired religious studies educator; b. Bucyrus, Ohio, May 29, 1933; s. John Isaac and Lula Frances (Jackson) D.; m. Betty Ann Bethea, Apr. 29, 1988; children: Gwynne, Jeremy. BA magna cum laude, Wake Forest U., 1955; BD, Southeastern Sem., Wake Forest, 1959, THM, 1961; DPhil, U. Oxford, Eng., 1963. Pastor Sharon & Dobson's Chs., Chinquapin, N.C., 1955-61; acting instr., Latin Meredith Coll., Raleigh, N.C., 1955-56; prof. Hebrew and Old Testament Studies Southeastern Sem., Wake Forest, N.C., 1963-88; pastor Greenwich (Conn.) Bapt. Ch., 1988-94. Mem. Gov.'s Com. on Art and Religion, N.C., Raleigh, 1977-81; lectr. in Bibl. studies Regent's Park Coll., Oxford, 1981; Albritton lectr. Wake Forest U., Winston-Salem, N.C., 1987; lectr. art and architecture Europe and Biblical History in the Middle East tours. Cons. editor: Broadman Bible Commentary, Nashville, 1967-72; author: Psalms Commentary, 1970, Commentary on Exodus, 1987, Understanding the Basic Themes of Exodus, 1991; contbg. author Oxford Companion to the Bible, 1993, Mercer Commentary on the Bible, 1995; co-editor Proclamation and Presence, 1970; editor Worship Beyond the Usual, 1993. Grantee Am. Assn. of Theol. Schs., 1969-70; Sabbatical scholar Fgn. Mission Bd., Rüschlikon, Switzerland, 1976-77, others. Mem.: Phi Beta Kappa. Avocations: classical music, gardening, Rembrandt, Bible study. Home: 1509 Tolley Meadow Rd Big Island VA 24526-2977 E-mail: johnandbettyd@aol.com.

DURHAM, J(OSEPH) PORTER, JR., lawyer, educator; b. Nashville, May 11, 1961; AB in Polit. Sci. and History cum laude, Duke U., 1982, JD, 1985. Bar: Tenn. 1985, Md. 1988. Ptnr. Miller & Martin, Chattanooga, 1990-96, Baker, Donelson, Bearman & Caldwell, Chattanooga, 1997—2003, chmn. corp. dept., 1998—2003. Adj. prof. dept. acctg. and fin. U. Tenn., Chattanooga, 1992-98; participant Russian tax code adv. group, 1999; assoc. dir. edn. divsn. and gen. coun. Duke Endowment, 2003—. Editor Duke Law Mag., 1984-85; contbr. articles to profl. jours. Mem. Balt. Citizens Planning and Housing Assn., 1988-90; career edn. spkr. Explorer Scout program Boy Scouts Am., 1985, 88, 90-92; mem., v.p. bd. dirs., chmn. fin. com. Waxter Ctr. Found., 1989-91; mem., sec. bd. dirs. Assn. for Visual Artists, 1993-96; trustee Good Shepherd Sch., 1992-93; chmn. spl. mgmt. com. Nashville Rehab. Hosp., 1995; trail maintenance vol. U.S. Pk. Svc., 1993-95; mem. adv. com. Chattanooga State Tech. C.C.; bd. dirs. Sr. Neighbors, Inc., 2001-03. Recipient Outstanding Svc. award Waxter Ctr. Found., 1991. Mem. ABA, Tenn. Bar Assn., Md. Bar Assn., Duke U. Law Sch. Alumni Assn. (bd. dirs. 1994-97), Duke U. Gen. Alumni Assn. (bd. dirs. 1986-92, exec. com. 1989-92). Office: The Duke Endowment 100 N Tryon St Ste 3500 Charlotte NC 28202-4012

DURHAM, LYNDA LAURENE, language educator; b. Boulder, Colo., Oct. 6, 1949; d. Roger William and Alice Lorraine Cozens; m. Harry B. Durham III, Aug. 4, 1973; children: Christopher B., Laurel A. BA in Latin am. studies, U. Colo., 1971; MA in Spanish, U. North Colo., 1986. Spanish instr. Cherry Creek HS, Denver, 1971—73; Spanish prof. Casper Coll., Casper, Wyo., 1984—. Chair Wyo. Chpt. Am. Assn. Teachers of Spanish and Portuguese, Casper, Wyo., 1995, Fulbright Tchr. Exch., Casper, 1986—2001, Casper Coll. Humanities Festival, 1992; pres. Chpt. AC PEO, 1983—84; dir. Wyo. Symphony Orch., 1998—2001; Rep. precinct com. woman Casper, 2000—02; ctrl. com. Natrona County Rep. Party, Casper, 1997—2001. Mem.: First United Meth. Ch., Casper Coll. Theater, Alpha Chi Omega (province alumni chair 1989—2002). Republican. Methodist. Avocations: music, cooking, horseback riding. Home: 3101 Hawthorne Casper WY 82604 Office: Casper Coll 125 Coll Dr Casper WY 82601

DURHAM, ORMONDE GEORGE, III, manufacturing executive; b. Glen Ridge, N.J., Oct. 22, 1946; s. Ormonde and Dolores (Cannon) D.; m. Jeanette Louise Randall, June 26, 1971; 1 child, Ormonde Ethan. BS in Engring., Stevens Inst. Tech., 1971; postgrad., Vassar Coll., 1972-73. Engr. IBM, 1971-77, mktg., 1978-84; v.p. High Tech. Solutions, N.Y., 1985; pres., CEO Opto Generic Devices, Van Hornesville, N.Y., 1986—. Author, spkr. I.E.C.O.N., San Jose, 1999. Patentee in field; contbr. articles to profl. jours. Recipient N.Y. State Tech. award, 1994, Nat. Innovation award Data Automation/DSN Monitor, 1995; rsch. grantee N.Y. State Rsch. Devel. Authority, 1994, U.S. DOE, 2001. Mem. Audi Quattro Club. Home: 111 Hoke Rd Jordanville NY 13361-2017 Office: Opto Generic Devices PO Box OGD Pumpkin Hook Rd Van Hornesville NY 13475

DURHAM, ROBERT DONALD, JR., state supreme court justice; b. Lynwood, Calif., May 10, 1947; s. Robert Donald Durham and Rosemary Constance (Brennan) McKelvey; m. Linda Jo Rollins, Aug. 29, 1970; children: Melissa Brennan, Amy Elizabeth. BA, Whittier Coll., 1969; JD, U. Santa Clara, 1972; LLM in the Judicial Process, U. Va., 1998. Bar: Oreg. 1972, Calif. 1973, U.S. Dist. Ct. Oreg. 1974, U.S. Ct. Appeals (9th cir.) 1980, U.S. Supreme Ct. 1987. Law clk. Oreg. Supreme Ct., Salem, 1972-74; ptnr. Bennett & Durham, Portland, Oreg., 1974-91; assoc. judge Oreg. Ct. Appeals, Salem, 1991-94; state supreme ct. assoc. justice Oreg. Supreme Ct., Salem, 1994—. Adv. com. Joint Interim Judiciary Com., 1984-86; chmn. Oreg. Commn. on Adminstrv. Hearings, 1988-89; faculty Nat. Jud. Coll., Reno, Nev., 1992; mem. Case Disposition Benchmarks Com., 1992-93, Coun. on Ct. Procedures, 1992-93, 95—; mem. Oreg. Rules of Appellate Procedure Com., 1998-2002; bd. dirs. Oreg. Law Inst.; chmn. commn. on jud. rule 4 Oreg. Supreme Ct., 1995-97, 2002— Mem. ACLU Lawyer's Com., Eugene and Portland, Oreg., 1978-91. Recipient award for civil rights litigation ACLU of Oreg., 1988, Ed Elliott Human Rights award Oreg. Edn. Assn., Portland, 1990. Mem. Am. Acad. Appellate Lawyers (ninth cir. screening com. 1991—, rules com. 1994, co-chair appellate cts. liaison com. 1994), Oreg. Appellate Judges Assn. (pres. 1996-97), Oreg. State Bar (chair labor law sect. 1983-84, adminstrv. law com. govt. law sect. 1986), Willamette Valley Inns of Ct. (master of bench, team leader 1994—). Office: Oreg Supreme Ct 1163 State St Salem OR 97310-1331

DURHAM, SIDNEY DOWN, lawyer; b. Detroit, Dec. 27, 1943; s. Robert Harris and Mary Louise (Edwards) D.; m. Julia Crane; 1 child, Emily Bartlett Crane Durham. BA, U. Mich., 1966; JD, Wayne State U., 1969. Bar: Mich. 1969, U.S. Dist. Ct. (we. dist.) Mich. 1969. Ptnr. Butler, Durham & Toweson PLLC, Kalamazoo, Mich., 1989—. Fellow Internat. Acad. Matrimonial Lawyers, Am. Acad. Matrimonial Lawyers, Mich. State Bar Found.; mem. ABA (family law sect.), State Bar Mich. (family law, real property and probate law sects.), Fedn. of Fly Fishermen, Ducks Unltd. (chmn. S.W. Mich. chpt., sponsor), Safari Club Internat. Episcopalian. Avocations: horseback riding, duck hunting, trout fishing, big game hunting. Home: 6820 N 37th St Richland MI 49083-9687 Office: Butler Durham & Toweson PLLC 202 N Riverview Dr Kalamazoo MI 49004-1310 E-mail: sid@lawlords.net.

DURHAM, SUSAN K. research scientist; b. Stafford, Kans., May 18, 1957; d. Rolla Evern and Betty Florence Durham. BS, Kans. State U., 1979, MS, 1981; PhD, Iowa State U., 1991. Postdoctoral fellow Mayo Clinic, Rochester, Minn., 1991-94, Baylor Coll. Medicine, Houston, 1994-98, rsch. assoc., 1998—; tech. svcs. coord. Diagnostic Systems Lab. Inc., Webster, Tex., 1999—. Mem. Endocrine Soc., Women in Endocrinology (travel award 1993), Am. Soc. Animal Sci. Avocations: reading, antiques, animals. Office: Baylor Coll Medicine 6621 Fannin St Houston TX 77030

DURHAM, THENA MONTS, microbiologist, researcher, management executive; b. Bradenton, Fla., July 10, 1945; d. Turner and Silverrene (Taylor) M.; m. Millard Durham, Aug. 30, 1969; children: Bryce Vincent-Barnard, Brittanie Yvonne. BS, Fisk U., 1966; MS, Purdue U., 1968. Rsch. microbiologist Ctrs. for Disease Control, Atlanta, 1968-86, assoc. dir. for programs Nat. Ctr. for Prevention Svcs., 1988-95; program analyst Office Dir., Ctr. for Health Promotion and Edn., 1986-88; dir. exec. secretariat Ctrs. for Dis. Control and Prevention, Atlanta, 1995—2001; dep. dir. for policy Nat. Ctr. for HIV, STD, and TB Prevention for CDC, Atlanta, 2001—. Cons. FDA. Author numerous tech. papers; contrb. articles to profl. jours. Mem. NAACP, Neighborhood Planning Unit. Recipient Sec.'s award for Disting. Svc., Dept. HHS, 2001. Mem. AAAS, Sci. Rsch. Soc., Am. Soc. Microbiologists, CFC Assn. Exec. Women (founder, co-chmn.), Women in Sci. and Engring., Sigma Xi. Democrat. E-mail: tmd1@cdc.gov.

DURHAM, THOMAS L. music educator, director; b. Salt Lake City, Utah, Aug. 26, 1950; s. Lowell Marsden and Betty Dee (Divers) Durham; m. Rebecca Christensen Durham, Dec. 14, 1973; children: Carter Paul, Laura Lee, Lisa Marie. MusB, U. of Utah, 1974, MusM, 1975; PhD, U. of Iowa, 1978. Prof. Brigham Young U., 1978—, assoc. dir, sch. of music, 1996—, exec. dir., Barlow Endowment for music composition, 1998—. Pres. Deseret Music Publishers, Sandy, Utah, 1992—; question leader Advanced Placement, Trenton, NJ, 1996—. Composer: (choral works) Desert Music Publishers, 1980—; author: (ear tng. text) Beginning Tonal Dictation, 1994. Mem. Mormon Tabernacle Choir, Salt Lake City, 1980—2002. Mem.: Am. Soc. of Composers, Authors, Publishers (ASCAP std. award 1989—2003). Avocations: cooking, gardening, golf, travel. Home: 11640 Littler Rd Sandy UT 84092 Office: Brigham Young U E-553 HFAC Provo UT 84602

DURHAM, WILLIAM ANDREW, lawyer; b. Paris, Tex., Mar. 21, 1956; s. James David and Ruby (Bartlett) D.; m. Susan Margaret Gallagher, Sept. 30, 1982; children: Andrew Gallagher, Margaret Rudyard. BA cum laude, Tex. A&M U., 1978; JD cum laude, U. Houston, 1981. Bar: Tex. 1981, U.S. Dist. Ct. (so. and ea. dists.) Tex. 1981, U.S. Ct. Appeals (5th cir.) 1982, U.S. Dist. Ct. (no. dist.) Tex. 1983, U.S. Supreme Ct. 1990. Assoc. Eastham, Watson, Dale & Forney, Houston, 1981-84, ptnr., 1984-98, mng. ptnr., 1998—. Bd. dirs. Casa Juan Diego, Houston, 1986—. Mem. State Bar Tex., Houston Bar Assn., Maritime Law Assn. Republican. Episcopalian. Office: Eastham Watson Dale & Forney Niels Esperson Bldg 20th 808 Travis St Houston TX 77002-5706 E-mail: wdurham@aol.com.

DURIG, JAMES ROBERT, chemistry educator; b. Washington, Pa., Apr. 30, 1935; s. and Roberta Wilda Mounts; m. Kathryn Marlene Sprowls, Sept. 1, 1955; children: Douglas Tybor, Bryan Robert, Stacey Ann. BA, Washington and Jefferson Coll., 1958, D.Sc. (hon.), 1979, PhD, M.I.T., 1962. Asst. prof. chemistry U. S.C., Columbia, 1962-65, asso. prof., 1965-68, prof., 1968-93, Ednl. Found. prof. chemistry, 1970-73, dean Coll. Sci. and Math., 1973-93; dean Coll. Arts & Scis. U. Mo., Kans. City, 1993—2000, prof. chemistry & geosci., 1993—. Editor: Vibrational Spectra and Structure, 24 vols., 1972—, Jour. Raman Spectroscopy, 1979-94; mem. editl. bd. Jour. Molecular Structure, 1972—; contbr. articles to profl. jours. Served with Chem. Corps U.S. Army, 1963-64. Recipient Russell award U.S.C., 1968; Alexander von Humboldt Sr. Scientist award W. Ger., 1976; award Spectroscopy Soc. of Pitts., 1981; U. S.C. Ednl. Found. award, 1984 Mem. Am. Chem. Soc. (So. Chemist award Memphis sect. 1976, Charles A. Stone award S.E. Piedmont sect. 1975), Am. Phys. Soc., Soc. for Applied Spectroscopy (Pitts. sect. award 1981), Coblentz Soc. (mem. governing bd. 1972-76, pres. 1974-76, award for outstanding research in molecular spectroscopy 1970), Internat. Union Pure and Applied Chemistry (chmn. sub-commn. on infrared and Raman spectroscopy 1975-95, mem. commn. molecular spectra and structure 1978-89, sec. 1981-83, chmn. 1983-89, editor Spectrochimica Acta 1999—), Blue Key Soc., Phi Beta Kappa (pres. Alpha chpt. S.C. 1970), Sigma Xi, Phi Lambda Upsilon. Presbyterian. Home: 1213 W 64th Ter Kansas City MO 64113-1516 Office: Univ Mo 410 RHFH Kansas City MO 64110 *Everything has a lighthearted side which is sometimes difficult to recognize. Never lose your sense of humor.*

DURINGER, DAVID ROBERT, lawyer; b. Coronado, Calif., June 28, 1964; m. Lena Nicolaevna Duringer; 1 child, Ayn. BA in Econs., U. Calif., San Diego, 1986, JD, 1989. Bar: Calif. 1989, Wash. 1997; lic. real estate broker, Calif. Sole practice, Orange County, Calif., 1989-95; owner, broker Adv. Realty Mgmt., Vancouver, Wash., 1995-97; gen. counsel Genisys Fin. Corp., San Diego, 1997—2001; atty., pres. Law News.TV, P.C., Carlsbad, Calif., 1999—. Mem. Calif. Bar Assn. (estate planning, trust and probate section), San Diego County Bar Assn., Bar Assn. No. San Diego County, Federalist Soc., Nat. Eagle Scout Assn., Calif. Rifle and Pistol Assn. Republican. Office: LawNews TV PC PO Box 130836 Carlsbad CA 92013-0836 E-mail: info@lawnews.tv.

DURIO, WILLIAM HENRY, lawyer; b. Crowley, La., May 15, 1947; s. Lennard Edwin and Helen Hazel (Miller) D.; m. Rita Jane Putch, June 6, 1971; children: Matthew, Caroline. BS, U. La., Lafayette, 1970; JD, La. State U., 1975. Pvt. practice, Lafayette, La., 1976-78, 83-89; ptnr. Hughes Durio & Grant, Lafayette, 1978-83; gen. counsel Global Industries Ltd., Maurice, La., 1990-91; pvt. practice. Lafayette, 1991—. Adj. prof. mineral law U. La., Lafayette, 1983-84. With U.S. Army, 1970-72. Mem. La. Bar Assn., Lafayette Town House Club, Order of Troubadours. Avocations: running, fishing, scuba diving, hunting, traveling. Home: 608 Claymore Dr Lafayette LA 70503-4020

DURKEE, JACKSON LELAND, civil engineer; b. Tatanagar, India, Sept. 20, 1922; s. E. Leland and Bernice J. (Jackson) D.; m. Marian H. Carty, Feb. 20, 1943; children: Janice D. Parry, Judith D. Burton, Christine D. Simpson. BSCE, Worcester Poly. Inst., 1943, CE, 1951; MCE, Cornell U., 1947. Registered profl. engr., Calif., Conn., N.Y., Pa.; chartered engr., U.K. Designer Douglas Aircraft Co., 1943-44; various engring. positions Fabricated Steel Constrn. div. Bethlehem Steel Corp., 1947-65, chief bridge engr., 1965-76; vis. prof. structural engring. Cornell U., 1976; ptnr. Modjeski and Masters, cons. engrs., Harrisburg, Pa., 1977-78; cons. structural engr. Bethlehem, Pa., 1978—. Mem. numerous tech. and profl. coms. Contbr. articles on bridge structural analysis, rsch., design, constrn., contracting, innovation and history to profl. jours., and chpts. on steel bridge constrn. to structural engring. handbooks; originator, dir. devel. of shop-fabricated parallel-wire-strand method for constrn. of suspension bridge cables, and pipe-assembly anchorage method and plastic-type weather protection sys. for such cables; patentee suspension bridge cable constrn., anchorage and weather protection techniques. Served to lt. USNR, 1944-46, PTO. Recipient constrn. industry citation Engring. News-Record, 1968, Robert H. Goddard award Worcester Poly. Inst., 1998, John A. Roebling medal Engrs. Soc. Western Pa., 2002. Fellow ASCE (Ernest E. Howard award 1982, hon. mem. 1996), Instn. Civil Engrs. (U.K.), Instn. Structural Engrs. (U.K.); mem. Nat. Soc. Profl. Engrs., Am. Ry. Engring. and Maintenance-of-Way Assn., Am. Welding Soc., Structural Stability Rsch. Coun., Internat. Assn. for Bridge and Structural Engring., Nat. Acad. Engring. (cited for origination and devel. of innovations in fabrication and erection engring. of longspan bridges), Tau Beta Pi, Sigma Xi. Republican. Mem. Moravian Ch. Clubs: Silver Creek Country (Hellertown, Pa.); Cosmos (Washington); St. Andrews Golf, New Golf (St. Andrews, Scotland). Home and Office: 217 Pine Top Trl Bethlehem PA 18017-1729

DURKEE, JOE W(ORTHINGTON), JR., nuclear engineer; b. Albuquerque, Mar. 10, 1956; s. Joe W. Sr. and Hallie Mae Durkee. BS, Tex. A&M U., 1978, ME, 1981, PhD, 1983. Staff mem. Los Alamos (N.Mex.) Nat. Lab., 1983-95; asst. prof. radiology U. Tex. Southwestern Med. Sch., Dallas, 1995—2002, Los Alamos Nat. Lab., N.Mex., 2002—. Rsch. proposal reviewer LANL, 1986-87, Dept. Energy/ER Nuc. Engr. Proposal Rev. Panel, 1988-94. Invited rsch. paper reviewer Jour. Nuclear Tech., 1987, Jour. Biomech. Engr., 1991; contbr. articles to Jour. Physics in Medicine and Biology, Progress in Nuclear Energy, Annuals Nuclear Energy, Jour. Nuclear Tech. Mem. Am. Nuclear Soc. (admissions com. 1986-99, chair 1990-99), Tex. A&M Former Student Assn., Nat. Space Soc., N.Y. Acad. Sci. Achievements include development of Sn and Monte Carlo reactor physics design calculations for a number of thermal and fast nuclear reactor designs, of mathematical models depicting heat transport in the human body; notation of bifurcating behavior of multiregion bioheat and neutron diffusion equations and development of techniques to solve and computationally evaluate these expressions; research in space-time neutron diffusion and fission-product convective diffusion, reactor physics calculations for LANL Omega West Reactor reconfiguration to product radioisotopes for medical applications; design of medical imaging devices, biochemical reactive diffusion modeling, computational fluid dynamics modeling. Office: Group D-5 MS K575 Los Alamos Nat Lab Los Alamos NM 87545

DURKEE, WILLIAM ROBERT, retired physician; b. Kansas City, Mo., Apr. 12, 1923; s. Dwight and Bessie Deane (Williams) D.; m. Billie Maxine Schreiner, Sept. 19, 1946; m. Jeanne Elizabeth Wells, June 7, 1975; children— Bruce William, Ellen Jeanne AA, Kansas City Jr. Coll., 1941; student, U. Chgo., 1941-42; MD, U. Kans., 1945. Diplomate Am. Bd. Internal Medicine. Intern U. Kans. Med. Ctr., Kansas City, 1945-46, resident, 1948-51; practice medicine specializing in internal medicine Manhattan, Kans., 1951-91; ptnr. Ball Meml. Clinic, 1951-76, Drs. Durkee and Boese, 1976-91; med. dir. Kans. Farm Bur. Life Ins. Co., Manhattan, 1963-91; ret., 1991. Mem. staff Mercy Health Ctr.; trustee Meml. Hosp., Manhattan, Kans., 1994-03, chmn. 2001-03. Bd. dirs. Friends of McCain, 1988-95, Sunset Zoo Wildlife Conservation Trust, Manhattan, 1995-2002, pres., 1998; mem. adv. bd. Friends of Libr., Kans. State U., 1993-2002. Capt. U.S. Army, 1943-48. Fellow ACP, Am. Coll. Cardiology (assoc.); mem. AMA, Riley County Med. Soc., Kans. Med. Soc., Am. Soc. Internal Medicine, Manhattan C. of C., Pres.'s Club Kans. State U., Manhattan Country Club, Rotary. Republican. Methodist. Home: 440 Oakdale Dr Manhattan KS 66502-3736

DURKIN, DENNIS JOHN, librarian; b. El Paso, Tex., Oct. 11, 1954; s. Edward Patrick and Adele Gould Durkin; m. Megan Monaghan, May 22, 1982; children: Brendan John, Daniel George. BA in English, Met. State Coll., 1984; MLS, Emporia State U., 1992. Reference libr. Denver Pub. Libr., 1987—. Author: Don't Be Angry At The Sun, 2001. Home: 4725 E Highline Place Denver CO 80222 Office: Denver Public Library 305 Milwaukee Denver CO 80206 Personal E-mail: buckyd55@aol.com.

DURKIN, DIANE L. nurse; b. Youngstown, Ohio, Feb. 1, 1952; d. Harold Henry and Helen Michelle Durkin. Diploma, St. Elizabeth Sch. Nursing, Youngstown, 1973. RN; cert. in neonatal intensive care nursing. Staff nurse St. Christopher Children's Hosp., Phila., 1979-80, Jackson Meml. Hosp., Miami, Fla., 1973-79, 80-81, assoc. head nurse newborn intensive care, 1981—, neonatal transport nurse, 1975-79, 80—. Contbr. articles to profl. jours. Mem. comty. adv. com. WPBT Pub. Broadcast, Miami, Fla., 1999. Mem.: Fla. Assn. Flight Nurses, S.E. Fla. Assn. Neonatal Nurses (mem. steering com. 1993—94, treas. 1994—96, v.p. 1996—98, pres. 1999, co-founder), Nat. Assn. Neonatal Nurses (NANN pages editor 2000, Central Lines editor 2002—03, chair comms. com.). Republican. Roman Catholic. Avocations: reading, walking. Office: U Miami/Jackson Meml Hosp 1511 NW 12th Ave Miami FL 33136 E-mail: plemented@aol.com.

DURKIN, DOROTHY ANGELA, university official; b. Glen Cove, NY, June 23, 1945; d. Frank Vincent and Rose Marie Durkin; 1 child, David Francis. BA SUNY, Stony Brook, 1968; MA, NYU, 1974. Adminstrv. asst. SUNY, Stony Brook, 1965-67; prodn. editor Holt, Rhinehart & Winston, Inc., Stony Brook, 1967-69; editor Hill & Wang Pub., Inc., NYC, 1969-70; asst. dir. pub. info. NYU Sch. Continuing Edn., 1970-72; assoc. dean pub. affairs and student svc. Sch. Continuing and Profl. Studies NYU Sch. Continuing Edn. and Profl. Studies, 1983—. Cons. NYC Ctr. for Lifelong Learning, 1974; producer TV series Continuum, Sta. WNYC, 1974. Editor: NSF student mag., 1961. Recipient Merit award Andy Advt., 1972, Art Dirs. Club, 1980, Soc. Illustrators, 1980, Big Apple award NY Radio Broadcasters Assn., 1985, Admissions Mktg. Report awards, 1987-88, 98-2001, Catalog Age awards, 1988, 93. Mem. Univ. Continuing Edn. Assn. (chair info. svc. 1980-81, nat. award chair, chair mktg. adv. com. 1989-98, group leader Learn From Success series 1989-90, bd. dir. 1991-93, membership com. 1994-95, mktg. conf. planning com. 1993-00, presenter, Bronze, Silver and Gold awards 1978, 81-2001, Internat. Leadership in Continuing Edn. award 1999), Am. Coll. Pub. Rels. Assn. (nat. award 1973), Coun. for Advancement and Support of Edn. (awards 1982-83, 85-87, 89-90, 92-94), Women in Comms. (job chair), Pub. Rels. Soc. Am. (Am. demographics adv. bd. 1989-90), Direct Mktg. Assn. (Echo Leadership award 1987, 88), Internat. Direct Mktg. Assn., SUNY Alumni Assn. (bd. dir.), The College Bd. (speaker, cons.), Learning Resources Network. Office: NYU Sch Continuing Edn 7 E 12th St Fl 11 New York NY 10003-4475 E-mail: dorothy.durkin@nyu.edu.

DURKOP, GEORGIA F. interior designer; b. Alexandria, La., Aug. 03; d. John D. and Nanny Landis (Barton) Freeman; m. Clarence Franklin Fielden, July 16, 1942 (wid. Dec. 1980); children: Clarence Franklin III, Landis Fielden Vance; m. Henry George Durkop, Aug. 3, 1994. BS, Vanderbilt U., 1941; postgrad., N.Y. Sch. Interior Design. Cert. designer ASID. Dept. head Camp Bon Air, Sparta, Tenn., 1939-42; art tchr. pub. schs., Jackson, Miss., 1940-41; assoc. designer J. Marshall Morin Interiors, Colorado Springs, Colo., 1953-56; owner, designer Georgia Fielden Interiors, Denver, 1956—. Pub. dir. Am. Inst. Interior Design, Rocky Mountain, 1957-58, sec., 1959-60; mem. nat. com. pub. rels., ASID, N.Y., 1959-61. Exhbn. Colo. Springs Fine Art Mus., 1958; contbr. decorating and home fashion mags. Mem. ASID, DAR, PEO, Colonial Dames of Am., Soroptimist, Rotary Assocs. (local v.p. 1959-60). Presbyterian. Avocations: organ, genealogy. Home: PO Box 441083 Aurora CO 80044-1083

DURLAND, JACK RAYMOND, retired lawyer; b. Taylor, Tex., Sept. 21, 1916; s. Den D. and Percy (Langrill) D.; m. June Kathryn Cain, Feb. 5, 1937; children: Jack Raymond, Diane Elizabeth. LLB, U. Okla., 1941. Bar: Okla. 1941. Spl. agt. FBI, 1942-46; sole law practice Oklahoma City, 1946-50; asst. to pres. Cain's Coffee Co., Oklahoma City, 1950-52, pres., 1952-82, Gallery at Nichols Hills Inc., Oklahoma City, 1982-87. Chmn. bd. Nat. Coffee Assn., 1961-62 Bd. dirs. Met. YMCA, Oklahoma City. Mem. ABA, Okla. Bar Assn., World Pres. Orgn. Home: 1620 Queenstown Rd Oklahoma City OK 73116-5523

DURLESSER, JAMES ARTHUR, clergyman, writer, lecturer; b. New Castle, Pa., Sept. 15, 1953; s. Arthur P. and Louise E. Durlesser; m. Joy Devine, Nov. 22, 1977. BA in Religion, Westminster Coll., New Wilmington, Pa., 1975; MDiv, Pitts. Theol. Sem., 1978, ThM, 1980; PhD in Religious Studies, U. Pitts., 1988. Ordained to ministry United Meth. Ch., 1979. Pastor United Meth. Ch., Scottdale, Pa., 1978-81, Butler, Pa., 1981-84, Scenery Hill, Pa., 1984-88, Uniontown, Pa., 1988-92, Indiana, Pa., 1992-95, New Wilmington, 1995-2001, Meadville, Pa., 2001—. Instr. Lay Leadership Schs., Western Pa. Conf. United Meth. Ch., 1989—92, 2002, 03; tchr. Bible Coop. Sch. Christian Mission, 1995; instr. study course Meth. Theol. Sch. in Ohio, Del., 1995—97, 1998—2000; adj. prof. Pitts. Theol. Sem., 1999—. Co-author: Adult Bible Studies Teacher, 1992, 1994, 1999, 2000, 2001, Approaching the New Millennium, 1995, 1 Samuel and 2 Samuel, 1995, Daily Bible Study, 2003; contbr. articles to religious jours. Dean's grantee U. Pitts., 1987, 88. Mem. Am. Schs. Oriental Rsch., Soc. Bibl. Lit., Mu Delta Epsilon. Avocations: piano, swimming, snowshoeing. Home: 516 Chestnut St Meadville PA 16335

DURNBAUGH, DONALD FLOYD, church history educator, researcher; b. Detroit, Nov. 16, 1927; s. Floyd Devon and Ruth Elsie (Tombaugh) D.; m. Hedwig Therese Raschka, July 10, 1952; children: Paul D., Christopher S., Renate E. BA, Manchester Coll., Ind., 1949, LHD (hon.), 1980; MA, U. Mich., 1953; PhD, U. Pa., 1960; LHD (hon.), Juniata Coll., Pa., 2003. Dir. program Brethren Svc. Commn., Austria, 1953-56; asst. prof. history Juniata Coll., Huntingdon, Pa., 1958-62, J. Omar Good disting. prof. evang. Christianity, 1988-89, archivist, 1992—; assoc. prof. ch. history Bethany Theol. Sem., Oak Brook, Ill., 1962-69, prof. ch. history, 1970-88; Carl W. Zeigler prof. religion and history Elizabethtown (Pa.) Coll., 1989-93; dir. in Europe Brethren Colls. Abroad, France, Germany, 1964-65. Cons. Brethren Hist. Com., Elgin, Ill., 1982—; moderator Ch. of the Brethren, 1985-86 Author: European Origins of the Brethren, 1958, 4th edit., 1986, The Brethren in Colonial America, 1967, 3rd edit., 1996, Guide to Research in Brethren History, 1968, The Believers' Church: The History and Character of Radical Protestantism, 1968, 2nd edit., 1985, Every Need Supplied: Mutual Aid and Christian Community in the Free Churches, 1525-1675, 1974, Pragmatic Prophet: The Life of M.R. Zigler, 1989, Brethren Beginnings: The Origin of the Church of the Brethren in Early Eighteenth-Century Europe, 1992, Fruit of the Vine: A History of the Brethren, 1708-1995, 1997; editor: Die Kirche der Brueder: Vergangenheit und Gegenwart, 1971, The Church of the Brethren: Past and Present, 1971, To Serve the Present Age: The Brethren Service Story, 1975, On Earth Peace: Discussion on War/Peace Issues Between Friends, Mennonites, Brethren and European Churches, 1935-1975, 1978, Church of the Brethren: Yesterday and Today, 1986; editor-in-chief The Brethren Ency., Inc., 1978-84; contbr. articles, book revs. to scholarly jours., periodicals. Alternative svc. as conscientious objector, 1953-56. U. Pa. Scholar, 1956-57, fellow, 1957-58; NEH sr. fellow, 1976-77; fellow Assn. Theol. Schs., 1986-87; recipient Alumni award Manchester Coll., 1978. Fellow Young Ctr. for Study of Anabaptist and Pietist Groups; assoc. Inst. of Mennonite Studies; mem. Am. Soc. Ch. History, Brethren Jour. Assn., Soc.

German Am. Studies, Communal Studies Assn., Pa. German Soc. Mem. Ch. Of The Brethren. Home: PO Box 484 James Creek PA 16657-0484 Office: Juniata Coll PO Box 948 Huntingdon PA 16652-0948 E-mail: durnbaughd@juniata.edu.

DURNEY, MICHAEL CAVALIER, lawyer; b. Piedmont, Calif., May 20, 1943; s. James Joseph and Camille (Cavalier) D.; m. Ann E. Belanger, Nov. 27, 1971 (dec. Oct. 2001); 1 child, Christine Cavalier; m. Carla Voetsch, June 6, 2002; 1 child, James McIvor. BA, U. Calif., Berkeley, 1965; JD, U. Calif.-Hastings Coll. of Law, 1968. Bar: Calif. 1969, D.C. 1972, U.S. Supreme Ct. 1972. Trial atty. Tax div. Dept. Justice, Washington, 1968-72, dep. asst. atty. gen. Tax div., acting asst. atty. gen., 1986-88; assoc. Hamel and Park, Washington, 1972-78, ptnr., 1978-86, Myerson, Kuhn & Sterrett, Washington, 1988-89, Law Offices of Michael C. Durney, Washington, 1990—. Chmn. bd. trustees St. Patrick's Episcopal Day Sch., Washington, 1989-92. Mem. ABA (tax and litigation sects.), Fed. Bar Assn. (chmn. tax sect. 1982-84), Calif. Bar Assn., D.C. Bar Assn. Clubs: Metropolitan (Washington), Burning Tree. Republican. Episcopalian. Avocation: golf. Home: 6732 Selkirk Dr Bethesda MD 20817-4955 Office: 1072 Thomas Jefferson St NW Washington DC 20007-3832 E-mail: mcd@mdurney.com.

DURNIL, GORDON KAY, lawyer, diplomat, arbitrator, political party official; b. Indpls., Feb. 20, 1936; s. J. Ray and E. Merle Durnil; m. Lynda L. Powell, Mar. 1, 1963; children: Guy S., Cynthia L. BS, Ind. U., 1960, JD, 1965. Bar: Ind. 1965. Sales rep. Franklin Life Ins. Co., 1956; v.p. Ind. Ornamental Iron Works, Inc., 1960-65; sales rep. Moore Bus. Forms, Inc., 1960; pvt. practice, Indpls., 1965—. Dep. atty. gen. State of Ind., 2001—; dep. prosecutor Marion County, Ind., 1965—66; legal counsel Ind. Fedn. Young Reps., 1965—68; spl. asst. Office Bus. Svc. U.S. Dept. Commerce, 1971; profl. arbitrator, mediator, Indpls., 1993—; chmn. Internat. Joint Commn. U.S. and Can., 1989—; head del. UN Conf. on Environ. and Devel., Rio de Janeiro, 1992, v.p. Author: The Making of a Conservative Environmentalist, 1995, Is America Beyond Reform?, 1997, Soft Money, 1998, Throwing Chairs and Raising Hell, 1999; editor: Marion County Rep. Reporter, 1966—71. Justice of peace Washington Twp., Ind., 1967—70; bd. dirs. Our House Inc. (Ind. Ronald McDonald House); mem. exec. coun. Rep. Nat. Com., 1985—89; active Rep. Party, 1960—; mem. publicity com. Marion County Rep. Com., 1966—67; mem. campaign coordinating com. Ind. Rep. Com., 1968—80, mem. congl. coordinating com., 1972—74, campaign dir., 1978, state chmn., 1981—89; campaign mgr. for numerous candidates; chmn. Midwestern Rep. State Chairmen Assn., 1988—89; chmn. Ind. del., del. Rep. Nat. Conv., 1984, 1988; chmn. Marion County Election Bd., 1978—81. With U.S. Army, Korea. Mem.: Ind. Bar Assn., Soc. Profls. in Dispute Resolution, Am. Assn. Polit. cons., Emmerich Manual H.S. Alumni Assn. (pres. 1968, named Alumnus of Yr. 2000). Office: Internat Joint Commn 1250 23d St NW Ste 100 Washington DC 20037-1100 E-mail: gdurnil@aol.com.

DURNIN, RICHARD GERRY, education educator; b. Haverhill, Mass., Mar. 9, 1920; s. William Edward and Ethel (Millett) Durnin. BS, Columbia U., 1947; MEd, Harvard U., 1950; postgrad. summers, U. Nottingham, 1950, U. Oxford, 1956; EdD, U. Pa., 1968. Tchr. pub. schs. N.J., Mass., 1946-49; instr. State Coll. at Fitchburg (Mass.), 1949-51; dir. Antioch Sch., Yellow Springs, Ohio, 1951-52; asst. prof. SUNY, Buffalo, 1952-58; vis. lectr. edn. Tufts U., spring 1957; dir. Smith Coll. Day Sch., 1958-59; asst. prof. edn. Rutgers U., 1959-65; prof. social and hist. founds. of edn. CCNY, 1965-90, prof. emeritus, 1990—. Instr. U. Nev., U. N.H., Coll. William and Mary, Johns Hopkins U., 1951—68. Author: (book) American Education: A Guide to Information Sources, 1982; contbr. articles to profl. jours. Mem. nat. coun. Travelers Aid Internat. Social Svc., 1972—77; mem. coun. Middlesex County (N.J.) Cultural and Heritage Commn., 1976—95; mem. adv. commn. Mercer County (N.J.) C.C., 1980—87; Rep. committeeman Middlesex County, 1992—; bd. dirs. Internat. Social Svc.-WAIF; trustee Proprietary Ho. Assn., NJ, 1977—97; mem. adv. con. Old Barracks, Trenton, NJ, 1982—88, trustee, 1992—98. 1st lt. USAF, 1942—46. Mem.: SAR, Soc. Colonial Wars, Jamestowne Soc., Soc. War of 1812, N.J. Hist. Soc., Nat. R.R. Hist. Soc., New Brunswick Hist. Soc. (pres. 1969—71), History Edn. Soc., Mil. Order Fgn. Wars, Essex Inst., English-Speaking Union (pres. New Brunswick br. 1991—93), Joyce Kilmer Centennial Commn. (v.p. 1986—), St. George Soc. N.Y., Soc. Mayflower Descs., Colonial Order Acorn, Phi Delta Kappa, Kappa Delta Pi. Episcopalian. Home: 50 Chester Cir New Brunswick NJ 08901-1526

DURNYA, LOUIS RICHARD, lawyer; b. Plainfield, N.J., July 24, 1950; s. Louis and Mary Ann (Pellegrino) D.; m. Elizabeth Trabue Shelton, July 16, 1977; children: Cameron, Sarah. BBA, Seton Hall U., 1972, student Brookings Instn., 1998; JD, U. Richmond, 1975; postgrad. Command and Gen. Staff Coll., 1990. Bar: N.J. 1975, U.S. Dist. Ct. N.J. 1975, U.S. Ct. Mil. Appeals 1976, U.S. Supreme Ct. 1979, U.S. Ct. Claims 1981, Ct. Appeals (Fed. cir.) 84. Assoc. Orlando & McGimpsey, Esquires, New Brunswick, N.J., 1975-76; atty. Office of Chief Counsel Kennedy Space Ctr., Fla., 1979-82; assoc. chief counsel Marshall Space Flight Ctr., Ala., 1982-96, asst. chief counsel, 1996—. Col. JAGC, USAR, 1994—, staff judge advocate, 2002—. Recipient Superior Achievement award NASA, 1982, Merit award, 1989, Exceptional svc. medal, 1996, Silver Snoopy award U.S. Astronaut Corps., 1988; named an Outstanding Young Man of Am., Jaycees, 1977. Mem. Fed. Bar Assn. (past pres. North Ala. chpt.), Ky. Col. Assn., Delta Theta Phi (scholarship key 1973-74). Home: 1005 Appalachee Dr SE Huntsville AL 35801-2202 Office: Office of Chief Counsel Marshall Space Flight Ctr Huntsville AL 35812

DUROCHER, FRANCES A. physician, educator; b. Woonsocket, R.I., Mar. 11, 1943; d. Armand D. and Teresa (Leverone) DuRocher. BA with honors, Trinity coll., 1964; MS, Brown U., 1966; postgrad., Woman's Med. Coll., 1970. Med. resident Phila. VA Hosp. and Med. Coll. Pa., 1971-73; assoc. in internal med. Guthrie Clinic Ltd., Sayre, Pa., 1973-79, Annandale (Va.) Group Health Assocs., 1979-87; assoc. chair internal med. Annandale Group Health Assoc., 1986-87; pvt. practice Fairfax, Va., 1987—. Clin. asst. prof. med. and health svcs. George Washington U. Med. Sch., Washington, 1994—. Bd. dirs. Fairways of Penderbrook Homeowners Assn., 1993—, sec., 1995-96, pres., 1996—. Mem. AMA, ACP-Am. Soc. Internal Medicine, Am. Med. Women's Assn. (exec. bd. br. I, 1985-91, pres. 1987-88), Med. Soc. Va., Fairfax County Med. Soc. Avocations: reading, traveling. Office: 9926 Main St Fairfax VA 22031-3901

DU ROCHER, JAMES HOWARD, lawyer; b. Racine, Wis., Aug. 4, 1945; s. Howard James and Frances Ann (Rasmussen) Du R.; m. Rosalyn Ann, Sept. 2, 1972; children: Jessica Lynn, James Howard, Emily Rosalyn. Student, U.S. Mil. Acad., 1963-65, Ripon Coll., 1965-66; JD, U. Wis., 1969. Bar: Wis. Assoc. Stewart, Peyton, Crawford & Josten, Racine, 1969-78; pres. Du Rocher, Murphy, Murphy & Schroeder, S.C., Racine, 1978-96, Du Rocher Law Offices, S.C., 1996—. Bd. dirs., Careers Industries, Inc., pres., 1988-89. Bd. dirs. Racine Area United Way, 1973-79, v.p., 1977-79; chmn. Park Trails Dist. Boy Scouts Am., 1979-82; bd. dirs. Careers for Retarded Adults, Inc., 1982, pres., 1983, 90; bd. dirs. A-Center of Racine, Inc., 1978-85, pres., 1985; bd. dirs. Careers Industries Support Found., Inc., 1993-2000; deacon Atonement Luth. Ch., Racine, 1978-81; mem. adv. bd. Children's Svc. Soc. Wis.; treas. Faith Cmty. Ch., Racine, 2002—. Capt. JAGC, U.S. Army, 1969-73. Decorated Bronze Star. Mem. State Bar Wis., Mason, Rotary (pres. Racine-West club 1998-99). Home: 5531 Whirlaway Ln Racine WI 53402-1865 Office: 827 Main St Racine WI 53403 E-mail: durlaw@execpc.com.

DUROSE, STANLEY CHARLES, JR., insurance executive; b. Joliet, MT, Oct. 26, 1923; s. Stanley Charles and Wilhelmena Amelia (Zwicky) DuR.; m. Lorraine Homan, May 27, 1977. BS, U. Wis., 1948. Various positions Wis. Dept. Ins., Madison, 1948-65; dep. commr. ins. State of Wis., Madison, 1965-69, commr. ins., 1969-75; v.p. govt. rels. Cuna Mut. Ins., Madison, 1976-80; sr. v.p. adminstrn. Cumis Ins. Soc., 1980-86, sr. v.p. reinsurance, 1986-88; dep. commr. of ins. State of Wis., 1989-91; ret., 1991. Contbr. articles to profl. pubs. With USAF, 1943-45, 51-52. Mem. Casualty Actuarial Soc., Am. Acad. Actuaries. Home: 201 Durose Ter Madison WI 53705-3322

DURR, KENNETH D. historian; b. Salem, Ohio, Oct. 23, 1960; s. Donald Joseph Durr and Marilyn Anne Jones; m. L. Jean Patterson, Sept. 10, 1988; 1 child, Olivia Anne. BA in Am. Studies, Kent State U., 1983; MA in History, Am. U., 1992, PhD in History, 1998. Historian History Assoc., Inc., Rockville, Md., 1991—95; cons. PHR Environ. Assoc., Silver Spring, Md., 1996; sr. historian History Assoc., Inc., Rockville, 1997—; adj. prof. Am. U., Wash., DC, 1998—99; dir., history div. History Assoc., Inc., Rockville, 2000 . Author: (article) Labor History, 1996, (books) Behind the Backlash, 2003; co-author: The Roadway Story, 1996, Never Stand Still, 1999. Avocations: hiking, music. Office: History Assoc Inc 300 N Stonestreet Ave Rockville MD 20850-1655

DURR, LESLIE MARTINA, nurse, psychotherapist; b. Jamaica, N.Y., May 23, 1945; d. Leonard John Durr and Ida Martina Wissel; m. Floyd Hurt, Aug. 8, 1970 (div. 1990); children: Eric Marshall Hurt, Morgan Leslie Hurt. BSN, Syracuse U., 1967; MSN, Hunter Coll., 1973; PhD, Va. Commonwealth U., 1998. Cert. clin. nurse specialist, Am. Nurses' Credentialing Ctr. Clin. nurse specialist DeJarnette Ctr., Staunton, Va., 1992-96; mgr., clin. nurse specialist Martha Jefferson Home Care, Charlottesville, Va., 1996-98; adminstr. Lafayette Acad. & Treatment Ctr., Charlottesville, Va., 1998-99; pvt. practice psychotherapist Charlottesville, Va., 1988—. Nurse mgr., We. State Hosp., Staunton, Va., 2000—; pvt. practice med.-legal nurse cons., Charlottesville, 1997—. Contbr. articles and revs. to profl. jours. Mem. bd. Monticello Area Cmty. Action Agy., Charlottesville, 1997-2000; vol. debriefer Thomas Jefferson Emergency Svcs. Coun., Charlottesville, 1985-93; vol. nat. depression screening, Charter Hosp., Charlottesville, 1997. Mem. Charlottesville-Albemarle Mental Health Assn. (bd. mem. 1987-90). Episcopalian. Home: 3074 Doctors Xing Charlottesville VA 22911-5733 Office: 918 9 1/2 St NE Charlottesville VA 22902-5311

DURR, ROBERT JOSEPH, construction firm executive, mechanical engineer; b. N.Y.C., June 25, 1932; s. Otto and Veronica U. (Quinlan) D.; m. Julia Loretta, Apr. 16, 1955; children— Kathryn A., Robert J. Jr., Kenneth A., Jennifer L. BBA, Iona Coll., 1954; Cert. in Mech. Engring., NYU, 1957. Mem. staff Courter & Co., Inc., N.Y.C., 1955-60, mgr., 1960-71, v.p., 1971-81, pres. Secaucus, NJ, 1981-85, Durr Mech. Constrn., Inc., N.Y.C., 1986-98, chmn., 1998—. Chmn. Nat. Joint Steamfitter Apprenticeship Com., Washington, 1980-84; trustees Nat. Cert. Pipe Welding Bur., Washington, 1983—. Recipient Recognition award Nat. Cert. Pipe Welding Bur., 1980 Mem. Subcontractors Trade Assn., Mech. Contractors Assn. Am. (bd. dirs. 1989—, mem. exec. bd. 1993, pres. 1996), Mech. Contractors Assn. N.Y. (bd. dirs., pres. 1976-82, Appreciation award 1982), N.Y. Bldg. Congress (bd. govs. 1978-84), Bldg. Trade Employers Assn. N.Y. (Greater N.y. welding chpt. 1975-88, chmn. 1979-88), Upper Montclair (N.J.) Country Club. Roman Catholic. Avocations: golf, swimming, sailing.

DURRANI, SAJJAD HAIDAR, retired space communications engineer; b. Pakistan, Aug. 27, 1928; came to U.S., 1959, naturalized, 1966; s. Inayat Ullah and Hameedah Khanum D.; m. Brita Katarina Yasmin Portin, May 21, 1959; children: Zarina, Amina, Arif. BA, Govt. Coll., Lahore, Pakistan, 1946; BSc in Elec. Engring. with honors, Engring. Coll. Lahore, 1949; MScTech, Coll. Tech., Manchester, Eng., 1953; ScD, U. N.Mex., 1962. Lectr., asst. prof. Engring. Coll., Lahore, 1949-59; instr., research assoc. U. N.Mex., Albuquerque, 1959-62; sr. engr. Gen. Electric Co., Lynchburg, Va., 1962-64; prof., chmn. dept. elec. engring. Engring. U. Lahore, 1964-65; assoc. prof. Kans. State U., Manhattan, 1965-66; sr. engr. RCA Space Center, Hightstown, N.J., 1966-68; staff scientist, br. mgr. COMSAT Labs., Clarksburg, Md., 1968-73; sr. scientist Ops. Research, Inc., Silver Spring, Md., 1973-74; sr. engr. NASA-Goddard Space Flight Center, Greenbelt, Md., 1974-79; mgr. for system planning, tracking and data relay satellite system NASA-GSFC, 1981-84; mgr. research and planning NASA Communications Div., 1984-88; chief communications scientist NASA Hdqrs., Washington, 1979-81, program mgr., Advanced Systems Office, 1988-92; consulting engr. Computer Scis. Corp., Beltsville and Seabrook, Md., 1992-98; ret., 1998. Vis. prof. U. Md., 1972, adj. prof. Univ. Coll., 1997—. ; adj. prof. George Washington U., 1980-82, 86, 87, rsch. prof., 1993-97; mem. Engring. Manpower Commn., Am. Assn. Engring. Socs., 1981; cons. Space Applications and Rsch. Ctr., Space and Upper Atmosphere Rsch. Commn., Pakistan, UN Devel. Program, 1999; exec. fellow and advisor to FCC, 2000-2001. Mem. editorial bd.: COMSAT Tech. Rev., 1972, IEEE Spectrum, 1975-78, IEEE Procs., 1988-92. Pres. Muslim Cmty. Ctr., Silver Spring, Md., 1976-82, trustee, 1989-94, 95-2000, chmn., 1998-2000. Recipient spl. achievement award NASA, 1977, 78, 90, Amb. award Computer Scis. Corp., 1996. Fellow: IEEE (bd. govs. aerospace and electronic sys. soc. 1977—93, pres. 1982—83, dir. Divsn. IX 1984, 1985, publs. bd. 1986, 1987, 1991, bd. dirs. nat. telesys. conf. 1991—94, publs. bd. 1992, bd. govs. aerospace and electronic sys. soc. 1997—2003, Citation of Honor U.S. Activties Bd. 1980, Outstanding Mem. Region 2 1982, Meritorious Achievement in Continuing Edn. award 1994, Millennium medal 2000, Profl. Activities award 2001, Centennial medal 1984), AIAA (assoc.). E-mail: s.durrani@ieee.org.

DURRANT, GEOFFREY HUGH, retired English language educator; b. Pilsley, Eng., July 27, 1913; s. John and Charlotte (Atkinson) D.; m. Barbara Joan Altson, June 2, 1942; children: John Guy, Catherine Jane. BA, Cambridge (Eng.) U., 1932-35; diploma in edn., London U., 1935-36; student, Tuebingen (W. Ger.) U., 1937-39. Prof., English U. Natal, South Africa, 1945-60, head dept. English; prof. U. Man., Winnipeg, Can., 1961-66; now prof. emeritus U. B.C., Vancouver, Can., master tchr., 1973. Author: William Wordsworth, 1969, Wordsworth and the Great System, 1970. Served with South African Armed Forces, 1940-44. Carnegie fellow, 1960; Killam sr. fellow, 1976 Fellow Royal Soc. Can.; mem. Assn. Can. Univ. Tchrs. English. Anglican. Home: 3994 W 34th Ave Vancouver BC Canada V6N 2L5

DURRANT, MATTHEW B. state supreme court justice; JD, Harvard U., 1984. Adj. prof. Brigham Young U., Salt Lake City; law clerk U.S. Supreme Ct. Appeals (10th cir.), Salt Lake City; shareholder Parr, Waddoups, Brown & Gee, Salt Lake City; judge Third Dist. Ct., Salt Lake City, 1997-2000; justice Utah Supreme Ct., 2000—. Office: Utah Supreme Ct PO Box 140210 Salt Lake City UT 84114-0210*

DURRETT, JAMES FRAZER, JR., retired lawyer; b. Atlanta, Mar. 23, 1931; s. James Frazer and Cora Frazer (Morton) D.; m. Lucretia McPherson, June 9, 1956; children: James Frazer III, William McPherson, Lucretia Heston Miller, Thomas Ratcliffe. AB, Emory U., 1952; postgrad., Princeton U., 1952-53; LLB cum laude, Harvard U., 1956. Bar: Ga. 1955. Ptnr. Alston & Bird (and predecessor firm), Atlanta, 1956-97, retired, 1997. Adj. prof. Emory U. Law Sch., 1961-77. Trustee emeritus Student Aid Found., The Howard Sch. Mem. Am. Law Inst. (life, adv. estate and gift tax project, restatement, second property, Fed. Income Tax project), Capital City Club, Harvard Club (Atlanta). Presbyterian. Home: 3483 Ridgewood Rd NW Atlanta GA 30327-2417 Office: Alston & Bird 1 Atlantic Ctr Atlanta GA 30309-3400

D'URSO, JOSEPH PAUL, interior designer; b. Newark, Apr. 8, 1943; s. Dominick and Rose (Maffiore) D'U. BFA, Pratt Inst., 1965. Pres., sole designer D'Urso Design Inc., 1967—. Major projects include 4 showrooms Calvin Klein, Esprit store, Washington, Esprit store and showroom, Los Angeles, furniture collection Knoll Internat. and Donghia, 2000. Fellow Royal Coll. Art, London, 1967, Manchester (Eng.) Poly., 1969; named to Interior Design Hall of Fame Interior Design mag., 1986; recipient Prix Di Rome, Am. Acad. Rome, 1987; named among Top Ten Designers in Am., House Beautiful, 1999. Avocations: collecting books, antiques, travel. Home and Office: PO Box 1154 Water Mill NY 11976-1154

DURSO, SAMUEL CHRISTOPHER, physician, educator, academic administrator; b. Galveston, Tex., Feb. 1, 1954; s. Joseph and Kathleen Durso; m. Lorna Sribnick, May 21, 1981; children: Emily, Michele. Student, U. Tex., Austin, 1972-75; MD cum laude, Baylor Coll., 1978. Clin. asst. prof. family practice U. Tex. Med. Br., Galveston, 1981-83; pvt. practice Columbia, S.C., 1983-95; instr. Johns Hopkins U., Balt., 1995-97, asst. prof. medicine, 1997—2003, assoc. prof. medicine, 2003—; med. dir. geriatrics John Hopkins Geriatrics Oak Crest Village, Balt., 1995-98, John Hopkins Geriatrics Putty Hill, Balt., 1999-00; med. dir. primary and speciality care Johns Hopkins, White Marsh, 2000—, dep. dir. edn., co-dir. geriatric fellow tng. Author: Teaching Ambulatory Medicine: Moving Medical Education into the Office, 2002. Med. dir. Columbia Free Med. Clini, 1987-95. Mem.: Columbia Med. Soc., Am. Geriatric Soc. (chmn. clin. practice com. 2001—, Clinician of Year award 1999, Cmty. Faculty Tchg. award 2001), Alpha Omega Alpha. Jewish. Avocations: writing, bicycling. Office: Divsn Geriatric Medicine & Gerontology John R Burton Pavillion 5505 Johns Hopkins Bayview Cir Baltimore MD 21224 E-mail: sdurso@jhmi.edu.

DURST, CAROL GOLDSMITH, educator; b. Bklyn., Mar. 1, 1952; d. Hyman and Florence (Weisblatt) Goldsmith; m. Marvin Ira Durst, June 18, 1972 (div. Sept. 1977); m. Leslie Mark Wertheim, Apr. 1, 1984; 1 child, William David. BA, Hamilton Kirkland Coll., 1973; MA, Columbia U., 1974; postgrad., Union Inst., 2000—. Career counselor Hofstra U., Hempstead, N.Y., 1974-75, Ocean County C.C., Toms River, N.J., 1975-76; rsch. assoc. Catalyst, N.Y.C., 1975-77; coord. displaced homemakers program N.Y. State Dept. Labor, N.Y.C., 1977-79; dir. N.Y. restaurant sch. New Sch. Social Rsch., N.Y.C., 1979-83; owner New Am. Catering Corp., N.Y.C., 1983-98; tchr., career counselor Peter Kump's N.Y. Cooking Sch., N.Y.C., 1988-98. Adj. prof. food studies dept. NYU, 1997—, Westchester C.C., 2001—, Kingsborough C.C., 2003. Author: I Knew You Were Coming So I Baked a Cake, 1997. Mem. AAUW, N.Y. Women's Culinary Alliance (new mem. chair 1995-96), Women Chefs and Restaurateurs (co-chair mentoring program 2003-2004), Nat. Mus. Women in the Arts, Am. Mus. Natural History, Met. Mus. Art. Avocations: fine arts, piano, opera, ice skating. Home and Office: PO Box 270 Millwood NY 10546-0270

DURST, ROBERT JOSEPH, II, lawyer; b. Pitts., Jan. 23, 1943; s. Robert J. and Catherine (Thomas) D.; m. Sandra A. Cattani; children: Thomas Sandberg, Eric Francis. BA, Gettysburg Coll., 1964; JD, Villanova U., 1967. Bar: Pa. 1967, N.J. 1968, U.S. Dist. Ct. (we. dist.) Pa. 1967, U.S. Dist. Ct. (N.J.) 1968, U.S. Supreme Ct. 1973. Corp. staff atty. Alcoa, Pitts., 1967; assoc. Herr & Fisher, Flemington, N.J., 1967-76; ptnr. Bernhard, Durst & Dilts, Flemington, 1976-89, Stark & Stark, Princeton, N.J., 1989—. Board cert. matrimonial atty. N.J. Supreme Ct., 1982— ; lectr., author on divorce and family law. With USMC, 1960—64. Fellow Am. Acad. Matrimonial Lawyers (pres. N.J. chpt. 1998-99); mem. ABA, Am. Trial Lawyers Assn., N.J. Bar Assn. (mem. exec. com. family law sect., Saul Tiscuier award Lifetime Contbn. Family Law 2003), Hunterdon County Bar Assn., Mercer County Bar Assns., Am. Coll. Family Trial Lawyers (diplomate). Home: 28 Marvin Ct Lawrenceville NJ 08648-2112 Office: Stark & Stark PO Box 5315 Princeton NJ 08543-5315

DURYEE, HAROLD TAYLOR, insurance consultant; b. Willoughby, Ohio, Feb. 11, 1930; s. Gerald Fancher and Margaret Grace (Taylor) D.; m. Phyllis Annette Painter, June 18, 1966. AB, Kenyon Coll., 1951. Field rep. Mahoning Valley Coun., Boy Scouts Am., Youngstown, Ohio, 1951-56; mgr. claims svcs. Nationwide Ins. Cos., Canton, 1956-65; legis. and field dir. Ohio Rep. Party, Columbus, 1965-70, exec. dir., 1970-77, cons., 1980-81; dep. adminstr. Ohio Bur. Workers' Compensation, Columbus, 1977-84; exec. dep. adminstr. Fed. Ins. Adminstrn., Washington, 1984-86; adminstr. fed. ins. Fed. Emergency Mgmt. Agy., Washington, 1986-90; dir. Ohio Dept. Ins., 1991-99; sr. advisor Internat. Ins. Found., 1999—. Trustee, exec. com. Griffith Found. for Ins. Edn.; mem. Ohio Elections Commn., 1980-84. Vice chmn. North Canton City Planning Commn., 1958-67; precinct committeeman Stark County Cen. Com., 1958-72; organizer North Canton Rep. Com., 1958, chmn., 1960-72; sec. North Canton Area Devel. Com., 1959-64; chmn. North Canton City Charter Commn., 1960; campaign mgr. U.S. Rep. Frank T. Bow, 1962, Oliver P. Bolton for U.S. Congress, 1964, Clarence J. Brown, Jr. for U.S. Congress, 1965; state chmn. Ohio League Young Rep. Clubs, 1962-63; nat. vice chmn. Young Rep. Nat. Fedn., 1963-65; former chmn. bd. trustees Nat. Assn. Ins. Commrs. Edn. and Rsch. Found.; former trustee ASFPM Edn. and Rsch. Found. Recipient Disting. Svc. award Jaycees, 1961, Civic Affairs award Rotary, 1964, Meritorious Svc. award Fed. Emergency Mgmt. Agy., 1989, Disting. Civilian Svc. medal, Fed. Emergency Mgmt. Agy., 1990. Mem. Acad. Polit. Sci. Episcopalian. Avocation: genealogy. Home: 925 City Park Ave Columbus OH 43206-2511 E-mail: hduryee@columbus.rr.com.

DUSANENKO, THEODORE ROBERT, retired educator, county official; b. Bronx, N.Y., Jan. 28, 1942; 010s. Teddy B. and Harriet T. Dusanenko; m. Dolores A. James, Aug. 31, 1986; children: Debra Garvey, Roger L. James. BS, SUNY, Albany, 1964, MS, 1967. Cert. secondary math. tchr., N.Y. Tchr. math. Clarkstown North H.S., New City, N.Y., 1964-80, 82-83, 85-96, wrestling coach, 1964-73; ret., 1996; legislator Rockland County, New City, 1970—85, 1989—; real estate salesman ERA Kennedy & Kennedy Real Estate, Piermont, NY, 1986—. Mem. New City Vol. Ambulance Corps, 1964-76, Rockland County Rep. Com., 1964—, O'Grady Brown Scholarship Com., 1981—; supr. Town of Clarkstown, New City, 1980-85, councilman, 1992-95; mem. Hudson River Valley Econ. Devel. Commn.; mem. region III N.Y. State Fish and Wildlife Bd.; initiator Clarkstown Youth Ct., 1981—. Mem. Elks. Roman Catholic. Avocations: gardening, grandparenting. Home: 462 Storms Rd Valley Cottage NY 10989-1213 Office: ERA Kennedy & Kennedy Real Estate 540 Piermont Ave Piermont NY 10968-1035

DUSANIC, DONALD GABRIEL, parasitology educator, microbiologist; b. Chgo., Dec. 15, 1934; s. Gabriel John and Harriet (Rojewski) D.; m. Roberta Leona Drost (dec. Feb. 1970); children: Donald, Robert; m. Jane Mitchell Haw, June 11, 1971; children: Belinda Conrad, Karla Conrad, Allan Conrad. BS, U. Chgo., 1957, MS, 1959, PhD, 1963. Instr. U. Chgo., 1963-64; asst. prof. U. Kans., Lawrence, 1964-68, assoc. prof., 1968-71, prof., 1971-72; prof. parasitology Ind. State U., Terre Haute, 1972-95, dir. Interdisciplinary Ctr. for Cell Products and Techs., 1987-95; prof. emeritus, 1995—. Vis. prof. U. Philippines Sch. Medicine, Manila, 1964, Nat. Taiwan U. Sch. Medicine, Taipei, 1971, Nat. Sun Yat-sen U., Kaohsiung, Taiwan, 1991; adj. prof. Ind. U. Sch. Medicine, Terre Haute, 1982-95. Contbr. numerous articles on biochemistry and immunology of schistosomes, nematodes, amebae, and trypanosomes to sci. jours., chpts. to books. Recipient rsch. and creativity award Ind. State, 1982, Coll. Arts and Scis. Disting. Prof. award, 1990; rsch. grantee NIH, NSF, Office Naval Rsch. Mem. Am. Soc. Parasitologists, Am. Soc. Tropical Medicine and Hygiene, Am. Soc. Protozoologists, Am. Assn. Immunologists, N.Y. Acad. Scis., Sigma Xi. Home: 5726 E Cougar Dr Terre Haute IN 47802-8533 E-mail: dusanic@mama.indiastate.edu.

DUSANSKY, RICHARD, economist, educator; b. Bklyn., Dec. 23, 1942; s. Abraham and Mary (Strawitz) D.; m. Abigail November, July 3, 1965; children: Eric, Deborah. BA cum laude, Bklyn. Coll., 1964; PhD in Econs., Brown U., 1969. Asst. prof. econs. SUNY, Stony Brook, 1968-72, assoc. prof, 1972-74, prof., 1974-84, dir. Econ. Rsch. Bur., 1977-82; prof., head dept. econs. U. Ga., 1984-89; Powell Centennial prof. dept. econs. U. Tex., Austin, 1989-91, Richard Gonzalez Regents Chair prof. econs., 1991—, chmn., 1989-97,98-2000, dir. Ctr. for Applied Rsch. in Econs., 1999—. Vis. scholar dept. econs U. Calif., Berkeley, 1973, 78, 96; vis. prof. dept. econs. U. Wis., Madison, 1974-75. Contbr. articles on econs. to profl. jours. Ford Found. fellow, 1967-68. Mem. Am. Econs. Assn., Econometric Soc. Office: U Tex Dept Econ Austin TX 78712 E-mail: dusansky@econ.utexas.edu.

DUSCHA, JULIUS CARL, journalist; b. St. Paul, Nov. 4, 1924; s. Julius William and Anna (Perlowski) D.; m. Priscilla Ann McBride, Aug. 17, 1946 (dec. Sept. 1992); children: Fred C., Steve D., Suzanne, Sally Jean; m. Suzanne Van Den Heurk, June 21, 1997. Student, U. Minn., 1943-47; AB, Am. U., 1951; postgrad., Harvard Coll., 1955-56. Reporter St. Paul Pioneer Press, 1943-47, Congl. Quar., 1947—48; publicist Dem. Nat. Com., 1948, 52; writer Labor's League for Polit. Edn., AFL, 1949-52, Internat. Assn. Machinist, 1952-53; editorial writer Lindsay-Schaub Newspapers, Ill., 1954-58; nat. affairs reporter Washington Post, 1958-66; assoc. dir. profl. journalism fellowships program Stanford (Calif.) U., 1966-68; dir. Washington Journalism Ctr., 1968-90; columnist, freelance journalist, West Coast corr. Presstime mag., San Francisco, 1990-99; sr. corr. News Inc., San Francisco, 1998—. Author: Taxpayer's Hayride: The Farm Problem from the New Deal to the Billie Sol Estes Case, 1964, Arms, Money and Politics, 1965, The Campus Press, 1973; editor: Defense Conversion Advisory; contbr. articles to mags., including Washingtonian, N.Y. Times Mag., Changing Times, Harper's, Reporter, Progressive, New Leader. Recipient award for distinguished Washington corr. Sigma Delta Chi, 1961 Mem. Cosmos Club (Washington), Kappa Sigma. Home: 2200 Pacific Ave Apt 7D San Francisco CA 94115-1412 E-mail: juliusduscha@aol.com.

DUSEL-BACON, CYNTHIA, geologist, researcher; b. San Jose, Calif., Aug. 16, 1946; d. William John and Pauline Stevens Dusel; m. Charles R. Bacon, Mar. 5, 1977; 1 child, Ian C. Bacon. BA in Spanish, U. Calif., Santa Barbara, 1968; BA in Geology, San Jose State U., 1975. Cert. secondary edn., Spanish tchr. Calif. Spanish tchr. Healdsburg (Calif.) H.S. Dist., 1970—72; phys. sci. technician U.S. Geol. Survey, Menlo Park, Calif., 1975—80, rsch. geologist, 1980—. Author: (geologic map) Metamorphic Facies Map of Alaska, 1994, (chpts.) Metamorphic History of Alaska. Chair Environ. Beautification Commn., Menlo Park, 1981—86. Recipient Outstanding Disabled Employee award, U.S. Govt., 1981, Disting. Alumni award, Sonoma State U., 1999. Fellow: Geol. Assn. Can.; mem.: Soc. Econ. Geologists, Geol. Soc. Am. (assoc. editor Geol. Soc. Am. Bull. 1993—99). Avocation: chromatic harmonica. Office: US Geol Survey 345 Middlefield Rd Menlo Park CA 94025

DUSENBERY, WALTER CONDIT, sculptor; b. Alameda, Calif., Sept. 21, 1939; s. Walter A. and Allegra V. (McIlrath) D.; m. Irene McManus, Jan. 25, 1986. Student, San Francisco Art Inst., 1961; M.F.A., Calif. Coll. Arts and Crafts, Oakland, 1969. Instr. U. Calif. Extension-San Francisco, 1967-69; vis. sculptor Grad. Sch. Design-Harvard U., Cambridge, Mass., 1979—; dir. Stone divsn. Johnson Atelier, 1996—. Exhibitor one-man shows, Laumeir Internat. Sculpture Park, St. Louis, 1983, Va. Commonwealth U., Richmond, 1983, Harvard U. Grad. Sch. Design, 1982, Nassau County Mus. Fine Art, Roslyn, N.Y., 1981, Hamilton Gallery Contemporary Art, N.Y.C., 1978, 80, Fendrick Gallery, Washington, 1986, 88; represented in permanent collections, Carnegie Inst., Pitts., Columbus (Ohio) Mus. Art, Commune of Glostrup, Denmark, Solomon R. Guggenheim Mus., N.Y.C., Huntington (W. Va.) Galleries, Met. Mus. Art, N.Y.C., San Francisco Mus. Modern Art, U. N.Mex. Mus., Albuquerque, Jerusalem Found, Israel, City of Portland Oreg., U. No. Iowa, Cedar Falls, Rainier Bank, Seattle; author: The Story of the Bed, 1970. Recipient Meml. prize Augustus St. Gaudens Found.; fellow Creative Artists Program Svc., N.Y.C., 1980, Nat. Endowment for Arts, 1980. Home: 109 Cemetery Rd Fly Creek NY 13337-2101 E-mail: sculptor@stonedivision.com.

DUSENBURY, RUTH COLE, business owner; b. Balt., June 19, 1929; Social worker Balt. City Welfare Dept., 1950-51; civil rights desk clk. FBI, 1951; asst. buyer, br. store sect. mgr., rsch. supr. Hutzler Bros. Dept. Store, Balt., 1951-58, pub. rels. rep., 1969-72; real estate rep. Robert Knatz Agy., 1969-70; sec., treas., officer mgr., co-owner Speer Cushion Co., Holyoke, Colo., 1974—. Active Rep. Party, 1968—, Bus. and Profl. Women's Orgn., 1976-87, Colo. Workforce Devel. Coun., 1999-2001; bd. dir. Holyoke Cmty. Arts Coun., 1976-2002; charter mem. bd. Colo. Arts Consortium, chmn., hon. bd. dir.; pres. Colo. Arts Coalition; del. White House Conf. on Small Bus., Washington, 1995; apptd. Congressman Bob Schafer's Bus. Adv. Com., 1998.

DUSHKINA, NATALIA MITKOVA, physicist, researcher; b. Sliven, Bulgaria, June 1, 1960; arrived in Japan, 1995; d. Mitko Nikiforov and Gunka Nikolova (Deneva) Kartcheva; m. Ceco Danov Dushkin; children: Danail Cecov, Magdalena Cecova. MS, U. Sofia, Bulgaria, 1984; PhD, Bulgarian Acad. Scis., Sofia, 1993. Tchr. High Tech. Sch. Optics and Fin Mechanics, Sofia, 1984-88; rschr. Ctrl. Lab. Optical Storage and Processing Info., Sofia, 1992-95; Monbusho fellow U. Tokyo, 1995-97; Agy. Indsl. Sci. and Tech. fellow Mech. Engring. Lab.-Ministry Internat. Trade and Industry, Tsukuba, Japan, 1997-98; rschr. Tsukuba, 1998-99; vis. prof. Tokyo U. Agriculture and Tech., 1999-2000; vis. rschr. Ctr. for Materials Sci. Bowling Green (Ohio) State U., 2000—01; mgr. laser applications lab. GCE Techs., Dayton, Ohio, 2001—. Cons. Ministry of Edn., Sofia, 1985-91, mem. program com., 1985-88. Author: Lasers and Lasers Technologies, 1992; contbr. articles to profl. jours.; patentee in field. Mem. Optical Soc. Australia, Union Scientists in Bulgaria, Internat. Soc. Optical Engring. Avocations: swimming, hiking, linguistics, science management. Home: VL Ochkov Str 3 Ap 49 8800 Sliven Bulgaria Office: GCE Techs 1425 N Keowee St Dayton OH 45404 E-mail: ndushkina@hotmail.com.

DUSKA, BRENDA SHAY, accountant, academic financial administrator; b. Staten Island, N.Y., Apr. 15, 1965; d. James George and Catherine Maureen (Lee) Shay; m. Ronald F. Duska, Dec. 29, 1990; 1 child, Elizabeth Catherine. BS in acctg., Rosemont Coll., 1987; M in taxation, Villanova U., 1996. CPA, Pa. Acct., supr. Han & Assocs., Bethesda, Md., 1992-95; pvt. practice Villanova, Pa., 1995—, Del Pizzo & Assocs., Ardmore, Pa., 1997—2001; v.p. fin. and adminstrn. Rosemont (Pa.) Coll., 2001—. Co-author: Accounting Ethics (with Ronald F. Duska), 2002, Accounting Ethics, 2002. Mem. AICPA, Pa. Inst. CPA's. Roman Catholic. Home: 518 Conestoga Rd Villanova PA 19085-1131 Office: Rosemont Coll 1400 Montgomery Ave Bryn Mawr PA 19010 Fax: 610-527-0341. E-mail: bduska@rosemont.edu.

DUSOLD, LAURENCE RICHARD, chemist, computer specialist; b. Chgo., Nov. 15, 1944; s. Henry E. and Colette M. Dusold; m. Karen A. Marsh, Aug. 29, 1970; children: Amy, Lauren, Patricia, Amanda. BS in Chemistry, Purdue U., 1966; MS, U. N.C., 1969; postgrad., Wayne State U., 1969-71. Rsch. chemist, residue analysis and methods investigation br. Bur. Foods FDA, Washington, 1971-75, chemist, computer specialist, div. chemistry and physics, 1975-81, sr. chemist, computer specialist, div. of chemistry and physics, 1981-86, chief telecomms. and sci. computer support, 1986—. Faculty, evening divsn. U. Md., 1973-2000; fed. engring. planning group Dept. HHS, 1990-95. Mem. editl. bd. Sci. Computing and Automation, 1990-2003; contbr. articles to profl. jours., chpts. to books. Mem. AAUP, Am. Chem. Soc., Internet Soc., IEEE, IEEE Computer Soc., Assn. Computing Machinery (chmn. SIGAPL, D.C. chpt. 1978-91, vice chmn. Potomac chpt. 1993-96), Greater Washington Fed. Agy. APL Users Group (co-chmn. 1977-87), Alpha Chi Sigma, Phi Lambda Upsilon. Republican. Roman Catholic. Office: FDA 5100 Paint Branch Pky College Park MD 20740-3835 E-mail: Laurence.Dusold@cfsan.fda.gov.

DUSSART, FRANCOISE, anthropologist, educator; b. Paris, May 14, 1959; came to U.S., 1988; d. Jean Gilbert Dussart and Yvonne Constance Guet; m. Allen Jay Kurzweil, Feb. 22, 1991; 1 child, Maximilian Kurzweil. BA in Sociology, Sorbonne, Paris, 1980, MA in Anthropology, 1981; PhD in Anthropology, Australian Nat. U., Canberra, 1989. Asst. prof. anthropology Rutgers U., Newark, N.J., 1989-91, NYU, N.Y.C., 1990-91, U. Conn., Storrs, 1991-97, assoc. prof. anthropology, women studies, 1997—. Curatorial cons., Mus. Popular Art, Haut Languedoc, France, 1979-80, Asia Soc., N.Y.C., 1987-88; co-curator South Australian Mus., Adelaide, 1988, Musée des Arts Africains et Oceaniens, Paris, 1993. Author: La Peinture des Aborigènes d'Australie, 1993, The Politics of Ritual in an Aboriginal Settlement, 2000. Rsch. grantee Wenner Gren, N.Y., 1991; NEH fellow, 1995-96. Mem. Am. Anthropol. Assn., Australian Inst. Aboriginal Studies (rsch. grantee 1984, 87, 91), European Soc. Oceanists, French Soc. Oceanists, Women's Studies Program (Storrs). Avocations: nature walks, horseback riding, reading. Home: 20 Benefit St Providence RI 02904 Office: U Conn Dept Anthropology Beach Hall U-2176 Storrs Mansfield CT 06269-2176 E-mail: dussart@uconnvm.uconn.edu.

DUSSAULT, JEAN H. endocrinologist, medical educator; b. Que., Apr. 6, 1941; BA, U. Montreal, 1960; MD, Laval U., 1965; MSc, U. Toronto, 1969. Intern Hosp. Enfant-Jesus, 1964-65, chief resident, 1965-67; Med. Rsch. Coun. Can. sr. rschr. in endocrinology U. Toronto/Wellesley Hosp., 1967-69, UCLA Sch. Medicine/Harbor Gen. Hosp., 1969-71; from asst. prof. to assoc. prof. Laval U. Sch. Medicine, Quebec City, 1971-81, prof. medicine, from 1981; dir. rsch. unit ontogenesis and molecular genetics Ctrl. Hosp./Laval U., 1986-96. Recipient Ross award Am. Acad. Pediatrics, 1976, Manning award Can. Assn. Endocrinology and Metabolism/Can. Diabetes Assn., 1987, 88, Spl. Rhône-Poulenc Sante Pediat. award, 1987, Wallae Robert Guthrie prize ISNS, 1999; named to Ordre du Can., 1988, Ordre Nat. du Que., 2000. Fellow Royal Coll. Physicians (Can.); mem. Am. Thyroid Assn. (Van Meter-Armour award 1980), Can. Med. Assn., Am. Fedn. Clin. Rsch., Endocrine Soc., Can. Soc. Clin. Rsch., Can. Soc. Endocrinology and Metabolism, Soc. Pediatric Rsch., N.Y. Acad. Sci. Died Mar. 2002.

DUSSEAU, RALPH ALAN, civil and environmental engineering educator; b. Flint, Mich., Jan. 19, 1955; s. Richard Joseph and Bertha Ann (Dreuth) D.; m. Ann Marie Hallenbeck, Sept. 17, 1977; children: Robert Anthony, Edward Maurice. BS, Mich. State U., 1978, MS, 1981, PhD, 1985. Registered profl. engr., Mich. Truck mileage tax bookkeeper Bels Produce Co., Inc., Montrose, Mich., 1972-75; design aide Johnson & Anderson Inc., Pontiac, Mich., 1976-77; undergrad. teaching asst. Mich. State U., East Lansing, 1977, grad. teaching asst., 1979-83, grad. rsch. asst., 1980-85; staff estimator Bechtel Power Corp., Ann Arbor, Mich., 1978; asst. prof. Wayne State U., Detroit, 1985-91, assoc. prof. civil and environ. engring., 1991-95; prof. and chair civil and environ. engring. Rowan Univ. of N.J., Glassboro, N.J., 1995—. Cons. Ghafari and Assocs., Livonia, Mich., 1988. Contbr. articles to profl. jours. Mem. ASCE, NSPE, Earthquake Engring. Rsch. Inst., Am. Soc. Engring. Edn. Achievements include research on earthquake engineering and computers and structures. Office: Rowan Univ of New Jersey Coll Engring 201 Mullica Hill Rd Glassboro NJ 08028-1700

DUST, MARGARET CECILE, psychology educator; b. East Chicago, Ind., Aug. 1, 1947; d. Isidor Gerhardt and Nettie Zelenda (Klingspor) D. BA in Polit. Sci., Loyola U., Chgo., 1969; postgrad., John Marshall Law Sch., 1970-71; BA in Psychology, Purdue U. Calumet, 1977; MS in Indsl. Psychology, Ill. Inst. Tech., 1985; PhD in Ednl. Psychology and Stats., Andrews U., 1995. Lic. secondary sch. tchr., Ind. Field worker ARC, Vietnam, 1969-70; coord. of advising Purdue U. Calumet, Hammond, Ind., 1978-82, instr. psychology, 1978-88, asst. prof. psychology, 1988-90; assoc. prof. psychology Chgo. State U., 1990—. Assessment cons. Calumet Coll., Whiting, Ind., 1999-2000; mem. Ill. State Steering Panel; co-chair Behavioral Sci. Panel, State of Ill.; faculty senator, Chgo. State U., coord., dept. team, undergrad. com. psychology, grad. com. psychology; presenter in field Contbr. articles to profl. jours. Grantee for data analyis NSF, San Francisco, 1994; grantee for rsch. tng. and minority students Corp. for Tng. Minority Students, Chgo., 1998, 99. Mem. APA, Soc. for Computers in Tech., Ind. Coun. for the Humanities, Vietnam Vets. Am. (post traumatic stress disorder chair chpt. 285). Avocations: photography, gardening, world traveling. Home: 215 Greiving St Dyer IN 46311-1810 Office: Chgo State Univ 9501 S King Dr Chicago IL 60628-1501 E-mail: m-dust@csu.edu.

DUSZYNSKI-WALDBILLIG, CYNTHIA, piano teacher, performer, adjudicator; b. Milw., Jan. 5, 1958; d. James and Dianne Duszynski; m. Terence Joseph Waldbillig, July 27, 1985; children: Abbey Lynn, Benjamin Jacob. BS, Carroll Coll., 1990. Pvt. tchr. piano C. Duszynski Studio Music, New Berlin, Wis., 1972—. Vocalist Eisenhower Choral Group, New Berlin, 1972-76, Waukesha Choral Union, 1976-77, various solo functions, Milw., 1974—; pianist Bob Hope Talent Search, St. Louis, 1977; pianist, vocalist, dancer Friendship of Ambs., Italy, Austria, Romania, Hungary, 1976; pianist, organist various hotels and chs., Milw., 1972—; adjudicator various music orgns., Milw., 1985—; lectr. various music functions, Chgo., 1990, Milw., 1990—; creator music programs Shared Leadership Program, 1999. Composer: (film music) Go Walk the Hallowed Ground Someday, 1990. Active Youth on Parade, New Berlin Jaycees, 1974; founder, chair LOVE P.A.T.S. Mem.: Milw. Music Tchrs. Assn. (adjudicator 1995), Wis. Music Tchrs. Nat. Assn. (v.p. 1992—96, judge coord. 1999—2000, v.p. 1999—2001, pres. 2000, Most Outstanding Piano Tchr. award 2000—01, 2002—03, Oustanding Tchr. award 2001—02), Nat. Guild Piano Tchrs. (adjudicator 1994—), Assn. Piano Tchrs. (judge coord. 1999—2000), Nat. Fedn. Music Clubs (adjudicator 1984—), Music Tchrs. Nat. Assn. (lectr. 1990—, state and nationally cert.). Avocations: stained glass, gardening, reading, interior decoration. Home and Office: 5900 S Aberdeen Dr New Berlin WI 53146-5210

DUTCHER, BRANDON TYLER, think tank research director, columnist; b. Tulsa, Okla., Aug. 16, 1966; s. Harris A. Jr. and Dona (Beesley) D.; m. Susan Elizabeth Woodard, Dec. 27, 1991; children: Lincoln, Elizabeth, Mary Margaret, Jack Henry. BA in Polit. Sci., U. Okla., 1988; MA in Pub. Policy, Regent U., 1991, MA in Journalism, 1992. Editor, pub. Bartlesville (Okla.) Times, 1992-94; rch. dir. Okla. Coun. Pub. Affairs, Oklahoma City, 1995—. Founding mem. opinion bd. contbrs. Daily Oklahoman, Oklahoma City, 1999-01. Contbr. numerous articles to newspapers; editor: Oklahoma Policy Blueprint, 2002; host weekly radio feature on IO stas. Recipient Excellence in Ednl. Journalism award, 2001, Amy Found. award of Outstanding Merit, 2001. Mem. Soc. Profl. Journalists (award 1994, 97, 99-02) Mem. Reformed Ch. in Am. Avocations: reading, home schooling. Home: 1512 Wild Plum Ct Edmond OK 73003 Office: Okla Coun Pub Affairs 100 W Wilshire Blvd Ste C-3 Oklahoma City OK 73116 E-mail: brandondutcher@yahoo.com.

DUTCHER, JANICE JEAN PHILLIPS, oncologist; b. Bend, Oreg., Nov. 10, 1950; d. Charles Glen and MayBelle (Fluit) Phillips; m. John Dutcher, Sept. 8, 1971 (div. 1980). BA with honors, U. Utah, 1971; MD, U. Calif., Davis, 1975. Diplomate Am. Bd. Internal Medicine, Am. Bd. Med. Oncology. Intern Rush-Presbyn. St. Luke's Hosp., Chgo., 1975-76, resident, 1976-78; clin. assoc. Balt. Cancer Rsch., Nat. Cancer Inst., 1978-81, sr. investigator, 1981-82; asst. prof. U. Md., Balt., 1982, Albert Einstein Coll. Medicine, N.Y.C., 1983-86, assoc. prof., 1986-92, prof., 1992-98, course co-dir. Advances in Cancer Treatment Rsch. Manhattan, 1984-96; prof. medicine N.Y. Med. Coll., 1998—; assoc. dir. for clin. affairs Comprehensive Cancer Ctr., Our Lady of Mercy Med. Ctr., 1998—. Chmn. biol. response mod. com. Ea. Coop. Oncology Group, Madison, Wis., 1989-95, mem. exec. com., 1995-97, chair renal subcom., 1998—; mem. data safety com. Nat. Heart Lung Blood Inst., Bethesda, Md., 1990-95; mem. biologic response modifier study sect. Nat. Cancer Inst., Bethesda, 1988, 90, 94, 96; mem. NIH Consensus Panel on Early Melanoma, 1992; mem. FDA Oncology Drug Adv. Bd., 1995-99, chair FDA-ODAC, 1996-99, NCI subcom. D for program project rev., 1995-98, mem. subsplty. med. oncology bd. Am. Bd. Internal Medicine, 1997-2003; mem. NCI subcom. A for Cancer Ctrs., 1998-2002. Editor: Handbook of Hematology/Oncology Emergencies, 1987, Modern Transfusion Therapy, 1990; sect. editor: Neoplastic Diseases of the Blood, 3d edit., 1996, 4th edit., 2003; mem. editl. bd. Jour. Immunotherapy, Med. Oncology, Jour. Clin. Oncology, Jour. Clin. Pharm., Ann. Intern. Med.; sect. editor Current Treatment Options in Oncology Chronic Leukemia, 2000—, Chronic Leukemia; contbr. articles to Blood, Leukemia, Jour. Clin. Oncology, Jour. Immunotherapy, Clin. Cancer Rsch., Soc. Am. Cancer Jour. Recipient Beecham award in Hematology So. Blood Club, 1983, Henry C. Moses Clin. Rsch. award Montefiore Med. Ctr., 1989, Outstanding Alumnus award U. Calif., Davis, 1989; named Outstanding Young Investigator Ea. Coop. Oncology Group, 1993; recipient numerous grants. NIM Progress Review Group on Kidney Cancer, 2001 Achievements include findings related to management of alloimmunization to platelet transfusions, intensive maintenance of patients with acute leukemia, studies of new biologic response modifiers as antitumor drugs, management of renal cell cancer and breast cancer, study and treatment with biologic antitumor agents. Address: Our Lady of Mercy Medical Cen Comprehensive Cancer Cen 600 E 233rd St Bronx NY 10466-2604

DUTKO, MICHAEL EDWARD, lawyer; b. Memphis, Jan. 18, 1954; s. Edward James and Norma Dean (Sparks) D.; m. Bettie Ballowe, Mar. 14, 1981; children: Michael, Christina, Ashley. BA, Biscayne Coll., 1978; JD, Nova U., 1984. Police officer, detective Ft. Lauderdale (Fla.) Police Dept., 1976-81; pros., asst. state atty. Broward State Atty.'s Office, Ft. Lauderdale, 1984-86; assoc. Kay & Bogenschutz, P.A., Ft. Lauderdale, 1986-90; ptnr. Kay, Bogenschutz & Dutko, Ft. Lauderdale, 1990-92, Bogenschutz & Dutko, P.A., Ft. Lauderdale, 1992—. Mem. Broward Assn. Criminal Def. Lawyers, Fla. Assn. Criminal Def. Lawyers, Nat. Assn. Criminal Def. Lawyers, St. Thomas More Soc. South Fla. (bd. govs.), Canon Law Soc. Am. (assoc.). Democrat. Roman Catholic. Avocations: golf, boxing, motorcycles. Office: Bogenschutz & Dutko PA 600 S Andrews Ave Ste 500 Fort Lauderdale FL 33301-2851

DUTOIT, CHARLES, conductor; b. Lausanne, Switzerland, Oct. 7, 1936; Studied at, Conservatory of Lausanne, Acad. Music, Geneva, Academia Musicale Chigiana, Siena, Conservatory Benedetto Marcello, Venice, Italy; attended session in conducting, Berkshire Music Ctr., Tanglewood, Mass.; MusD (hon.), McGill U., Montreal U., Laval U. Prin. condr. NHK Symphony Orch., N.Y.C., 1996, Montreal Symphony Orch. Formerly violinist with Lausanne Chamber Orch., debut as condr. with Bern (Switzerland) Symphony Orch., 1963, condr. and asst. music dir., later music dir., 1964, condr. and artistic dir. Radio-Zurich Orch., Switzerland, 1967, also guest condr. Vienna Opera, music dir. Nat. Symphony Orch. of Mex., Orch. Nat. de France, 1991—, apptd. chief condr. Goteborg Orch., Sweden, 1975, music dir., condr. Montreal Symphony Orch., 1977—2002, prin. guest condr. Minn. Orch., 1982—85, prin. condr., artistic dir. Phila. Orch., 1990—91, artistic dir., prin. condr. summer festivals Phila. Orch. at Mann Ctr. for Performing Arts, Saratoga Performing Arts Ctr., prin. condr. NHK Symphony Orch., Tokyo, 1996, guest condr. all maj. orchs., S.Am., Europe, Japan, Australia, U.S., Can. and Israel, rec. Deutsche Gramophon, Erato, CBS, Decca/London, Phillips, EMI, with Bavarian Radio Symphony, Boston Symphony Orch., Montreal Symphony Orch., L.A. Philharm., many London orchs., others. Recipient Can. Music Coun. medal, 1988. Office: KM Artits LTD 40 W 57th St New York NY 10019-4001 also: NHK Symphony Orchestra 2-16-49 Takanawa, Minato-ku Tokyo 108-0074 Japan*

DU TOIT, CORNELIS FREDERIK, electronic engineer; b. Vereeniging, South Africa, May 3, 1962; arrived in New Zealand, 1993; s. Frederik Johannes and Maria Jacoba Elizabeth (Lategan) Du T.; m. Elizabeth Barnard, Dec. 16, 1984; 1 child, Charl Nicolaas. B of Engring. cum laude, U. Stellenbosch, South Africa, 1984, M of Engring. cum laude, 1986; PhD in Engring., U. Stellenbosch (South Africa), 1992. Rsch. asst. U. Stellenbosch, Stellenbosch, 1988-92; antenna engr. Plessey Tellumat, Cape Town, South Africa, 1993; antenna rsch. engr. Deltec Telesystems, Wellington, 1994-99; sr. antenna engr. Paratek Microwave, Inc., Columbia, Md., 1999—. Patentee in field; contbr. articles to profl. jours. Harry Crossley Fund scholar, 1985-87. Mem. IEEE. Avocations: music, piano, amateur astronomy, tramping. Home: 9941 Frederick Rd Ellicott City MD 21042-3647 Office: Paratek Microwave Inc 6935 Oakland Mills Rd Ste N Columbia MD 21045-4719 E-mail: cdutoit@paratek.com.

DUTRA, JOHN A. state legislator; b. Oakland, Calif., Oct. 15, 1935; m. Bernadine Dutra; children: John J., Cynthia Dutra-Brice, Dominic, Diana. AA, Diablo Valley Jr. Coll., 1961; BS in Bus. and Indsl. Mgmt., San Jose State U., 1964, MBA, 1967. 2nd class hosp. corpsman USN, 1952—56; cert. fluorescent penetrant and magnetic particle inspector Magnaflux Corp., 1956—58; prin. rsch. apparatus technician U. Calif.-Lawrence Radiation Lab., 1961—64; technologist San Francisco Naval Shipyard, 1964—66, engring. technician, 1966—67; nondestructive tester Union Carbide Corp., 1967—68; indsl. educator hazards control dept. U. Calif., 1968—75; CEO Dutra Realty Enterprises, Inc., 1972—; chmn. bd.; instr. Ohlone Jr. Coll., 1975—79; mem. state ctrl. com. Dem. Party; planning commr. City of Fremont, Calif., 1981—84, vice mayor, 1987—88, 1989—90, 1992, 1993—94, 1995—96, councilmember, 1986—96; mem., dist. 20 Calif. State Assembly, 1998—. Mem. Jud. Coun. on Ct. Technology, 1998—, Electronic Beneifts Transfer Caucus, 1998—, Earthquake Safety and Preparedness Caucus, 1998—, Constrn. Fraud Caucus, 1998—, Aerospace Industry Caucus, 1998—, Budge Com., Housing and Cmty. Devel. Com., Human Svcs. Com., Ins. Com., Jud. Com.; chair Transp. Com. Mem. Fremont Parks Facilities Corp., Govt. Issue Forum; mem. bldg. com. St. Joseph's Ch. Served 2nd class hosp. corpsman USN, 1952—56. Mem.: Calif. Assn. Realtors, So. Alameda County Assn. Realtors. Democrat. Roman Catholic. Mailing: PO Box 942849 Rm 3091 Sacramento CA 94249 Office: 39510 Paseo Padre Pkwy Ste 80 Fremont CA 94538*

DUTRO, JOHN THOMAS, JR., geologist, paleontologist; b. Columbus, Ohio, May 20, 1923; s. John Thomas and Dorothy Durstine (Smith) D.; m. Nancy Ann Pence, Jan. 2, 1948; children: Sarah Dutro Cormier, Christopher, Susan Dutro Hultman. BA, Oberlin Coll., 1948; MS, Yale U., 1950, PhD, 1953; DSc, Denison U., 1993. Geologist, U.S. Geol. Survey, 1948-94, chief paleontology and stratigraphy br., 1962-68, mem. geologic names com., 1962-83; ret., 1994; emeritus vol. U.S. Geol. Survey, 1994—; rsch. assoc. Smithsonian Instn., 1962—. Vis. lectr. Am. U., 1957-59, George Washington U., 1962-63; mem. geology panel Bd. Civil Svc. Examiners, 1958-65; dir., field trip chmn. 9th Internat. Carboniferous Congress, 1979. Active area PTA, 1959-69, Boy Scouts Am., 1963-66, Fairlington Players, 1965-75. With Army Air Corps, 1943-46. Recipient Meritorious Svc. award U.S. Dept. Interior, 1983, Disting. Svc. award, 1996; Sterling fellow, 1949. Fellow AAAS (sec. sect. E 1981-85, Pacific divsn. pres. 1996-97), Arctic Inst. N.Am., Geol. Soc. London, Geol. Soc. Am. (assoc. editor 1974-82); mem. Am. Geol. Inst. (vis. geoscientist 1961-67, bd. dirs., sec.-treas. 1965-71), Palaeontol. Soc. (tech. editor 1991), Palaeontol. Assn., Palaeontol. Rsch. Inst. (trustee 1986—, v.p. 1990-91, pres. 1992-94), Internat. Paleontol. Assn., Palaeontol. Soc. Washington (pres. 1955-56), Geol. Soc. Washington (sec. 1959-60, pres. 1978), Assn. Earth Sci. Editors (pres. 1989-90), Am. Polar Soc., Alaska Geol. Soc., Sigma Xi, Pick and Hammer Club, Cosmos Club, Yale Club (Washington). Democrat. Achievements include research in brachiopoda, Paleozoic biostratigraphy and biogeography of Arctic regions and western hemisphere, biostratigraphy of east Asia, and history of paleontology. Home: 5173 Fulton St NW Washington DC 20016-3448 Office: US Nat Mus Natural History Washington DC 20560-0137 Fax: 202 343 8620. E-mail: dutro.tom@nmnh.si.edu.

DUTSON, THAYNE R. university dean; b. Idaho Falls, Oct. 3, 1942; s. Rollo and Thelma (Fugal) D.; m. Joyce Cook, Dec. 19, 1962 (div. 1980); 1 child, Bradley; m. Margaret McCallum, June 23, 1989; children: Taylor, Alexandra. BS, Utah State U., 1966; MS, Mich. State U., 1969, PhD, 1971. Postdoctoral fellow U. Nottingham, Sutton Bonnington, Eng., 1971-72; prof. Tex. A&M U., College Station, 1972-83; dept. head Mich. State U., East Lansing, Mich., 1983-87; dir. agrl. exptl. sta. Oreg. State U., Corvallis, 1987-93, dean, dir. Coll. Agrl. Sci., 1993—. Editor: Advances in Meat Research (11 vols.) 1985-97; contbr. articles to profl. jours. Scoutmaster Boy Scouts Am., Mich., 1966-71. Fellow Inst. Food Technologists; mem. Am. Meat Sci. Assn. (bd. dirs. 1979-81, Disting. Rsch. award 1985), Am. Soc. Animal Sci. (Meat Rsch. award 1981), Coun. for Agr. Sci. and Tech. (pres. 1988), Phi Kappa Phi, Sigma Xi. Avocations: fly-fishing, running, exercise, golf.

DUTT, KAMLA, medical educator; b. Lahore, Punjab, India; came to U.S., 1969; d. Gulzari Lal and Raj Bansi Dutt. BS with honors, Panjab U., Chandigarh, India, 1961, MS in Zoology with honors, 1962, PhD, 1970. Rsch. assoc. Harvard Med. Sch. Sidney Farber Cancer Ctr., Boston, 1972-76; rsch. assoc. Eye Inst. Retinal Fedn., Boston, 1977-80; sr. rsch. assoc. Yale Med. Ctr., New Haven, 1980-81, Emory U., Atlanta, 1981-82; asst. prof. Morehouse Sch. Medicine, Atlanta, 1983-89, assoc. prof., 1989—2001, prof., 2001—. Sci. adv. bd. Fernbank Sci. Ctr., Atlanta. Contbr. numerous articles to sci. jours.; author short stories (in Hindi); prodr., actor 3 maj. plays, Atlanta; actor 11 maj. plays, India. Bd. dirs. VSEI (vol. fundraising orgn. for edn. in India), 1973-78; v.p. Indian Am. Cultural Assn., 1985; podium spkr., participant King Week, 1990, 91, 93; spkr. Gandhi Day Celebration, 1984, 85; key participant Intercultural Conf., 1990; main participant joint document Women's Perspective; active human rights issues; stake holder Vision 20/20 Collaborative State of Ga., diversity and edn. coms., 1995. Hindu. Achievements include establishment of human ocular cell lines by gene trasfaction, used as model for study of eye diseases and tissue engineering. Office: Morehouse Sch Medicine 720 Westview Dr SW Atlanta GA 30310-1458

DUTTA, HIRAN MOYEE, biologist, educator; b. Patna, Bihar, India; came to the U.S., 1966; s. Trailokha N. and Sarujobala (Dutta) D.; m. Ashok K. Dutt, Jan. 19, 1958; children: Rinku Dutt, Jhumku D. Kohtz. PhD, Leiden U., 1968. Asst. prof., chmn. dept. sci. N.H. Coll., Manchester, 1966-68; asst. prof., chmn. dept. biology Walsh Coll., North Canton, Ohio, 1968-70; vis. asst. prof. Kent (Ohio) State U., 1970-75, asst. prof., 1975-80, assoc. prof., 1981-89, prof., 1990—. Dir. exchange student program Kent State U. and Leiden U. (The Netherlands), 1978—; vis. prof. Inst. Zoology Jagellonian U., Krakow, Poland, 1987, Polish Acad. Scis. Inst. Zoology, 1989, Paradenia U., Sri Lanka, 1991; invited spkr. ann. conf. India Sci. Congress Assn., 1994, 2001, India Inst. Sci., 1995, Internat. Symposium on Water/Air Transitions in Biology, 1996. Author: Functional Morphology of the Head of Anabas Testudineus, 1968; editor: Fish Morphology Horizon of New Research, 1996, Vertebrate Functional Morphology: Horizon of Research in the 21st Century, 2001; contbr. chpts. to books, articles to profl. jours. Faculty advisor Kent State Indian Assn., 1976-82, Kent State U. Bangladesh Student Assn., 1983-89. Fulbright lecturing/rsch. fellow, 1991; Smithsonian Instn. grantee, 1990-93. Mem. AAAS, Indian Assn. Freshwater Biology (mem. editorial bd.), Ichyologists and Herpetologists, Ohio Acad. Sci., Soc. Environ. Toxicology & Chemistry, Soc. for Integrative and Comparative Biology, Indian Assn. Greater Ak ron (v.p. 1979, pres. 1980), Cleve. Bengali Cultural Soc. (bd. trustees 1998—). Avocations: music, travel. Office: Kent State U Dept Biology 256 Cunningham Hl Kent OH 44242-0001 Fax: 330-672-3713. E-mail: hdulta@kent.edu.

DUTTA, INDRANATH, metallurgical engineer, educator; b. Calcutta, India, Oct. 31, 1960; s. Nirmalya Nath and Pratima D.; m. Geeta Ahuja, Dec. 12, 1989; children: Shouvik, Koushik. B in Tech., Indian Inst. Tech., Kharagpur, 1983; MS, Case Western Res. U., 1985; PhD, U. Tex., 1988. Prof. Naval Postgrad. Sch., Monterey, Calif., 1988—; cons. Motorola Inc., Tempe, Ariz., 2000-01. Vis. faculty Intel Corp., Chandler, Ariz., 2001—; vis. fellow U. Oxford, Eng., 1996; fellow Air Force Rsch. Lab., Dayton, Ohio, 1995; coun. mem., membership devel. rep. electronic, magnetic and photonic materials divsn. TMS-AIME,

2002-; tech. adv. bd. Trans-Tech Pubs., Switzerland, 1996—; proposal reviewer, panelist NSF, Arlington, Va., 1996—; postdoctoral advisor Naval Postgrad. Sch., NRC, Monterey; presenter in field. Tech. advisor Jour. Metals, Metall. Soc., Warrensdale, Pa., 2001—; tech. rev. panel Acta Materialia, Jour. Am. Ceramics Soc., Materials Rsch. Soc., ASME, Jour. Electronic Materials, Metall. and Materials Transactions, Materials Sci. and Engring., 1995—; contbr. over 30 articles to profl. jours. Vol. tchr. Deseret Montessori Sch., Monterey, Calif., 1996-98; judge Monterey County Sci. Fair, 1995-97; vol. Monterey Bay Aquarium, 1995-97; host Discovery Day Monterey Peninsula Unified Sch. Dist. Recipient Carl E. and Jessie W. Menneken Excellence award Naval Postgrad. Sch. Found., 1998. Mem.: Assn. Sci.-Tech. Ctrs. Inc., Minerals, Metals and Materials Soc. (mem. exec. coun. electronic, magnetic and photonic materials divsn.), Am. Soc. Materials, Materials Rsch. Soc., Metall. Soc. of AIME (Young Leader award 1996), Amnesty Internat., Beta Alpha Phi, Phi Kappa Phi, Tau Beta Pi. Hindu. Achievements include patents for constant-depth scratch test for quantification of interfacial shear strength of film-substrate systems, surface modification of CVD diamond substrates for producing adherent thick and thin film metallizations for electronics packaging. Office: Naval Postgrad Sch 700 Dyer Rd Monterey CA 93943

DUTTA, MANORANJAN, economics educator; b. India, Oct. 1, 1925;, naturalized, U.S., 1972; m. Kanak Dutta; 1 child, Kavery Dutta Kaul. PhD, U. Pa., 1962. Asst. prof. econs. Rutgers U., New Brunswick, N.J., 1962-64, assoc. prof. econs., 1964-76, prof. econs., 1976—. Hon. rsch. prof. Shanghai Acad. Social Scis., 1988; vis. scholar Japan Ministry Fin., De Nederlandsche Bank, Der Deutsche Bundesbank, Banque de France, 2000; lectr., asst. prof. various colls. W. Bengal Edn. Svc. affiliated to U. Calcutta, 1951—58; cons. Mathematica, Princeton, NJ, 1969—70; adj. prof. Pace U., NY, 1975; dir., pres. bd. trustees Am. Com. Asian Econ. Studies; dir. Coun. State Econ. Studies; chmn. Nat. Adv. Coun. S. Asian Affairs; spkr., presenter and vis. lectr.in field at various univs. in Europe, N.Am., Asia, Australia. Editor: Jour. of Asian Economics, 1990—; contbr. articles to profl. jours. and books; author, co-author, editor, co-editor: Econometric Methods, 1976, Economic Regionalization in the Asia-Pacific, 1999; editor: (jour.) Rsch. Asian Econ. Studies, 1985—2002. 1980 census adv. com. for Asia-Pacific Ams. Recipient cert. of Appreciation, Bur. Census U.S. Dept. Commerce, 1982, Honor award, Assn. Asian Indians in Am., 1986, Honored Am. award, Congl. resolution signed by Pres. Reagan, 1986; fellow Fulbright-Smith-Mundt, 1958, 1959, Faculty Rsch., Rutgers U., 1967, 1987, Nat. Sci. Found., 1973, 1976; grantee, U.S. Dept. Labor, 1978, Rutgers U. Rsch. Coun., 1979, N.J. State Dept. Industry and Labor, 1979, Ford Found., 1980, 1981, Port Authority N.Y. and N.J., 1981, 1985, AT&T, 1981, John D. and Catherine T. MacArthur Found., 1988, USAID, 1994, U.N. Devel. Program, 1996, Asia Devel. Bank, 1998. Mem.: AAUP, AAAS, Fulbright Sr. Specialists' Program, Calif. Inst. Internat. Studies, N.Y. Acad. Scis., Econometric Soc., Ea. Econ. Assn., Am. Com. Asian Econ. Studies, Assn. Indian Econ. Studies, Asia Soc. N.Y., Am. Assn. Asian Studies, Am. Statis. Assn., Am. Econ. Assn. Office: Rutgers U Faculty Arts and Scis 75 Hamilton St New Brunswick NJ 08901-1248 Fax: 732-932-1558. E-mail: mdutta@rci.rutgers.edu.

DUTTA, NRIPENDU, stress analyst, consultant; b. Calcutta, India, Mar. 15, 1950; came to U.S., 1990; s. Narendra Nath and Parul Dutta; m. Keya Dutta, Jan. 16, 1978; children: Soumak, Shayok. BSc in Mech. Engring., Banaras Hindu U., Varanasi, India, 1973; MSME, Tex. Tech. U., 1995, PhD, 1997. Registered profl. engr., Tex. Instr. Tex. Tech. U., Lubbock, 1994-97; dep. chief engr. Devel. Cons., Calcutta, India, 1974-90; sr. mech. engr. The Kuljian Corp., Phila., 1990-93; assoc. Stress Engring., Houston, 1998—. Contbr. articles to profl. jours. Recipient rsch. awards Tex. Tech. U., 1996, 97. Mem. ASME, Soc. for Exptl. Mechanics, Soc. for Design and Process Sci., Operational Rsch. Soc., Brit. Soc. for Strain Measurement. Office: Stress Engring Svcs 13800 Westfair East Dr Houston TX 77041-1101 Home: 21211 Branford Hills Ln Katy TX 77450-6119

DUTTERER, DENNIS ALTON, lawyer; b. Hanover, Pa., July 12, 1944; s. Alton J. and Garma S. (Barnhart) D.; m. Judith Barnett, Nov. 11, 1972; children: Andrew, Emily. BS, U. Md., 1967; JD, Am. U., 1970; LLM, George Washington U., 1971. Bar: D.C. 1970, N.Y. 1984, U.S. Ct. Claims 1974, U.S. Ct. Appeals (D.C. cir.) 1974, U.S. Ct. Appeals (7th cir.) 1982, U.S. Ct. Appeals (9th cir.) 1981, U.S. Ct. Appeals (10th cir.) 1979, U.S. Supreme Ct. 1973. Trial atty. lands and natural resources divsn. Dept. Justice, Washington, 1972-77, asst. U.S. atty., 1977-81; dep. chief civil divsn. U.S. Attys. Office, 1979-81; gen. counsel Commodity Futures Trading Commn., 1981-83; ptnr. Wiley & Rein, 1983-85; v.p., gen. counsel Bd. Trade Clearing Corp., Chgo., 1985-87; from sr. v.p., gen. counsel to exec. v.p., gen. counsel Bd. of Trade Clearing Corp., 1987-98, pres., CEO, 1998—. Interim pres., CEO Chgo. Bd. Trade, 2000-2001. Mem. ABA, D.C. Bar Assn., N.Y. Bar Assn., Ill. Bar Assn., Chgo. Bar Assn. Home: 21 Woodley Rd Winnetka IL 60093-3738 Office: 141 W Jackson Blvd Chicago IL 60604-2992 E-mail: dennis.dutterer@botcc.com.

DUTTON, CAROL TYMINSKI, accounting and business educator; b. Port Chester, N.Y., June 29, 1946; d. Joseph Andrew and Rosalie Cecelia (Kolakowski) Tyminski; m. Edmund Lee Dutton, July 15, 1967; 1 child, Vandy Elizabeth. AA, Washington State C.C., 1978; BA, Marietta Coll., 1985; MBA, W.Va. U., 1990; postgrad. studies, Nova Southeast U. CPA, Ohio, Fla. Purchasing clk. Forma Sci., Marietta, Ohio, 1966-68; bookkeeper various temp. svcs., Marietta, 1978-80; office mgr. E-tek, Marietta, 1981-82, pvt. practice med. office, Marietta, 1983-84; bus. office/bookstore mgr. Wash. State C.C., Marietta, 1982-83; substitute tchr. Marietta City Schs., 1985-86; field exec. Heart of Ohio coun. Girl Scouts U.S., Zanesville, 1986; office mgr. pvt. practice acctg. and tax svc. Marietta, 1986-89; assoc. prof. acctg. and bus. mgmt. Wash. State C.C., Marietta, 1986-97, prof. acctg. & bus., South Fla. C.C., Avon Park, 1997—. Chmn. dept. bus. techs. South Fla. C.C. Mem.: AICPA, Fla. Inst. CPAs, Inst. Mgmt. Accts. (exec. v.p. 1990—92, pres. 1992—), Am. Acctg. Assn. Avocations: computers, mystery novels, travel, scuba diving. Office: South Fla CC 600 W College Dr Avon Park FL 33825-9356

DUTTON, CLARENCE BENJAMIN, retired lawyer; b. Pitts., May 31, 1917; s. Clarence Benjamin and Lillian (King) D.; m. Marian Jane Stevens, June 21, 1941; children: Victoria Lynn Dutton Sheehan, Barbara King Dutton Morgan. BS with distinction, Ind. U., 1938, JD with high distinction, 1940, LLD, 1970. Bar: Ind. 1940. Instr. bus. law Ind. U. Sch. Bus., 1940-41; atty. E.I. duPont de Nemours & Co., Inc., Wilmington, Del., 1941-43; asst. prof. law Ind. U. Sch. Law, 1946-47; pvt. practice Indpls., 1947—2000; ret. Bd. dirs. Sarkes Tarzian, Inc.; mem. Ind. Jud. Study Commn., 1965-74; regional adv. group Ind. U. Sch. Medicine, 1966-75; mem., sec. Ind. Civil Code Study Commn., 1967-73; mem. Ind. Commn. on Uniform State Laws, 1970—, chmn., 1980-91, life mem., Nat. Conf. Commrs., 1991. Author: (bus. law sect.) Chemical Business Handbook, 1954; contbr. articles to profl. jours. Bd. dirs. Found. Ind. U. Sch. Bus., Found. Econ. and Bus. Studies; mem. bd. visitors Ind. U. Sch. Law, 1971—, chmn., 1974-75; bd. dirs. Soc. for Advanced Study, Ind. U., 1984—, pres., 1985-87; mem. Acad. Alumni Fellows, Ind. U. Sch. Law, 1988. Comdr. USNR, 1943-45. Recipient Ind. Bar Found. 50-Yr. award, 1992, Ind. U. Disting. Alumni Svc. award, 1995. Mem. ABA (ho. of dels. 1960-62, state del. 1967-72, bd. govs. 1971-74, chmn. gen. practice sect. 1971-72), Ind. State Bar Assn. (bd. mgrs. 1957-63, pres. 1961-62), Indpls. Bar Assn. (v.p. 1957), Lawyers Club (pres. 1959-60), Indpls. Country Club (pres. 1955), Columbia Club, Woodstock Club, Wilderness Country Club (Naples, Fla., dir. 1991-94). Republican. Presbyterian. Home: 1402 W 52d St Indianapolis IN 46228-2317

DUTTON, DIANA CHERYL, lawyer; b. Sherman, Tex., June 27, 1944; d. Roy G. and Monett D.; m. Anthony R. Grindl, July 8, 1974. BS, Georgetown U., 1967; JD, U. Tex., 1971. Bar: Tex. 1971. Regional counsel U.S. EPA, Dallas, 1975-79, dir. enforcement div., 1979-81; ptnr., head firm-wide environ. practice, mem. Dallas practice com. Akin, Gump, Strauss, Hauer & Feld, L.L.P., Dallas, 1981—. Bd. dirs. Dallas Nature Ctr., 2001-02; chair Greater Dallas Chamber Environ. Com., 2001. Named One of Best Lawyers in Dallas D Mag., 2001, Best Lawyers in Am., 2003, Ams. Leading Bus. Lawyers Chambers USA, 2003-. Mem. ABA, Tex. Bar Assn. (chmn. environ. and natural resources law sect. 1985-86), Dallas Bar Assn. (chmn. environ. law sect. 1984), Dallas Bar Found.. Episcopalian. Office: Akin Gump Strauss Hauer & Feld LLP 1700 Pacific Ave Ste 4100 Dallas TX 75201-4675 E-mail: ddutton@akingump.com.

DUTTON, DOMINIC EDWARD, lawyer; b. New Orleans, Aug. 21, 1944; s. Lee M. and Fara C. Dutton. BS, Lamar Coll. Tech., 1968; JD, U. Houston, 1973. Bar: Tex. 1973, N.Mex., U.S. Dist. Ct. (we. dist.) Tex., U.S. Dist. Ct. N.Mex., U.S. Tax Ct., U. S. Ct. Appeals (10th cir.). Assoc. Bivins, Wienbrenner P.A., Las Cruces, N.Mex., 1973—76; ptnr. Dutton, Wincheste, Las Cruces, N.Mex., 1976—81, Underwood & Dutton Ltd., Ruidoso, N.Mex., 1982—85, Underwood, Dutton & Griffin, Ltd., Ruidoso, N.Mex., 1985—91, Dutton, Griffin & Hakanson, Ltd., Ruidoso, N.Mex., 1991—94, Dutton & Hakanson, Ltd., Ruidoso, N.Mex., 1994—96, The Dutton Firm, Ltd., Ruidoso, N.Mex., 1997—. Village atty., Ruidoso Downs, N.Mex., 1982—86, Carrizozo, N.Mex., 1983—85, Capitan, N.Mex., 1987—2002; bd. mem. N.Mex. Gaming Control Bd., 2003—. Del. Dem. State Conv., 1980, 1984; bd. dirs. Open Door Ctr., Inc., Las Cruces, 1976—80. Mem.: N.Mex. State Bar Assn. (chmn. ethics com. 1976—77), Lincoln County Bar Assn. (sec.-treas. 1983—84, pres. 1985—87), Dona Ana County Bar Assn., Tex. State Bar Assn., Alto Lakes Country Club (Alto, N.Mex.), Cree Meadows Country Club (Ruidoso), Lions (past bd. dirs. Las Cruces club). Home: 200 Racquet Ct Ruidoso NM 88345-1668 Office: The Dutton Firm Ltd 1096 Mechem Dr Ste 229 Ruidoso NM 88345-7068

DUTTON, FRANK ELROY, data processing executive, writer; b. Warren, Ohio, Nov. 16, 1946; s. Robert Wade and Ann Victoria (Sessions) D.; m. Nancy June Gephart, Nov. 6, 1965 (div. 1981); children: Cynthia, Frank, Robert; m. Margaret Elizabeth Sessions, Dec. 16, 1981 (div. Dec. 1987); m. Paula Kay Gately, Feb. 14, 1992 (div. Sept. 1994). With sales dept. Zylco Cutlery Rena Ware Distrs., Warren, 1964-68; advt. salesman Directory Dept. Ohio Bell Telephone Co., Cuyahoga Falls, 1968-69; pvt. practice residential constrn. Warren and Hammond (La.), 1970-74; technician J. Ray McDermott & Co., New Orleans, 1974-83, McDermott Internat., Antwerp, Belgium, 1975, McDermott SE Asia, Singapore, 1981-83; owner Computer Time, Inc., Hammond, 1983-85; mgr. tech. services Industry Programs, Inc., Houston, 1985-86; owner Affordable Automation, Houston, 1987-89; program. analyst The Phillips Group, Stafford, Tex., 1989-92; owner software and hardware integrator IHMS Software Support, Many, La., 1992—; owner computer software, internet web site design hosting Fred Software, Many, 1998—. Cons. in computer communications Southmark Industries, Houston, 1986-87, Crown Broadcasting, Hammond, La., 1987-89, Bee-Line Delivery Svc., Houston, 1986-89. Author, designer various computer games, utility software programs, computer software for radio stas., computer software for retail furniture stores, Turbo Pascal Toolbox, 1988 (award of disting. tech. communication 1989, award of excellence Internat. Soc. Tech. Communication 1989). French transl., 1988, Portuguese trans., 1990, French trans., 1990; contbr. articles to profl. jours. Served with USAR, 1966—72. Recipient semi-finalist award, Global Info. Infrastructure, 1999. Mem.: Am. Mensa Soc. Avocations: astrology, photography. Home and Office: 80 Anna St Many LA 71449

DUTTON, FREDERICK GARY, lawyer; b. Julesburg, Colo., June 16, 1923; s. F. G. and Lucy Elizabeth (Parker) D.; m. June Klingborg (div.); m. Nancy Hogan; children: Christopher, Lisa, Eve, Stacy, Christina. BA with honors, U. Calif. at Berkeley, 1946; LL.B. (bd. editors Law Rev.), Stanford, 1949. Bar: Calif. 1949, D.C. 1975. With firm Kirkbride, Wilson, Harzfeld & Wallace, San Mateo, Calif., 1949-50; 1st asst. counsel So. Counties Gas Co. Calif., 1952-56; chief asst. atty. gen. Calif., 1957-58; exec. Sec. to gov. Calif., 1959-60; spl. asst. to Pres. Kennedy, 1961; asst. sec. of state for congl. relations, 1962-64; with firm Clifford & Miller, 1966-67; pvt. practice, Washington, 1967—2003; firm Dutton & Dutton, 1979—. Exec. dir. Robert F. Kennedy Meml. Found., 1968-70; editor Los Angeles Bar mag., 1955; spl. counsel judiciary com. Calif. Senate, 1956-57; So. Calif. chmn. Stevenson presdl. campaign, 1956; Calif. campaign chmn. Brown for Gov., 1958; dep. nat. chmn. Citizens for Kennedy and Johnson campaign, 1960; exec. dir. platform com. Democratic Nat. Conv., 1964; dir. research and planning nat. Dem. presdl. campaign, 1964, in charge Senator Robert F. Kennedy's travel campaign in primaries, 1968, mem. Dem. delegation selection (reform) com., 1969-72; aide to Senator George McGovern, 1972; organizing dir. John F. Kennedy Meml. Library Oral History Project, 1964-65. Contbr. articles to legal jours., mags.; author: Changing Sources of Power: American Politics in the 1970's, 1971, Election Guide for 1972, 1972. Bd. dirs. American Center for Community Devel. and Citizens Adv. Com., 1969-70; Am. U. Cairo, 1983-87; bd. regents U. Calif., 1962-76. Served with inf. AUS, World War II; prisoner of war Germany; served with Judge Adv. Gen. Corps, Korean Emergency, Japan. Decorated Bronze Star, Purple Heart, Combat Inf. Badge. Mem. State Bar Calif., D.C. Bar Assn., Delta Tau Delta. Office: Dutton & Dutton 5017 Tilden St NW Washington DC 20016-2333

DUTTON, JOHN ALTNOW, meteorologist, educator; b. Detroit, Sept. 11, 1936; s. Carl Evans and Velma (Altnow) D.; m. Frances Elizabeth Andrews, Jan. 13, 1962; children— Christopher Evan, John Andrews, Jan Frederik. BS, U. Wis., 1958; MS, 1959, PhD, 1962. Mem. faculty Pa. State U., University Park, 1965—2002, assoc. prof. meteorology, 1968-71, prof., 1971—2002, head dept. meteorology, 1981-86, dean Coll. Earth and Mineral Scis., 1986—2002. Expert aero. system div. USAF, 1965-71; vis. scientist Riso Rsch. Establishment, Roskilde, Denmark, 1971-72, summer 1975, 78-79; vis. prof. Tech. U., Denmark, 1978-79; v.p. UCAR Found., 1986-87, pres., 1987-95, chmn. bd. dirs., 1995-2001. Author: The Ceaseless Wind: An Introduction to the Theory of Atmospheric Motion, 1976, 2d edit., 1986 (reprinted as Dynamics of Atmospheric Motion, 1995), (with H.A. Panofsky) Atmospheric Turbulence: Models and Methods for Engineering Applications, 1984; assoc. editor: Meteorol. Monographs, 1973-79, editor, 1979-84; contbr. articles to profl. jours. Trustee Univ. Corp. for Atmospheric Rsch., 1974-81, sec., 1977, treas., 1978-79, vice-chmn., 1980-84, chmn. unidata steering com., 1982-86, chmn. unidata policy com., 1986-88; chmn. long-range planning com. NSF-Univ. Corp. for Atmospheric Rsch., 1986-87; mem. bd. atmospheric scis. and climate NRC, 1982-83, 88-97, chmn. bd., 1989-97, mem. internat. space yr. planning com., 1986-89, panel of experts on earth sci. and tech. Internat. Space Yr. in 1992, 1989-92, space sci. bd. com. on earth scis., 1987-89, mem. space studies bd., 1989-93, chmn. task group priorities space rsch. of space studies bd., 1989-94, mem. nat. weather svc. modernization com., 1989-95; mem. Nat. Aviation Weather Svcs. Com., 1994-95; mem. com. long-term retention sci. and tech. records of fed. govt., 1993-95; ex-officio mem. Com. on Global Change Rsch., 1995-97, chmn. com. on aeronautics rsch. and tech. for environ. compatibility, 2000-02; mem. space and earth scis. adv. com. NASA, 1982-86, earth system sci. com., 1983-87, ctr. sci. assessment team, 1986-88. 1st lt. USAF, 1962-65. Fellow AAAS (sect. atmospheric and hydrospheric scis.), Am. Meteorol. Soc. (councillor 1986-88, chmn. publs. commn. 1984-85); mem. Math. Assn. Am., Soc. Indsl. and Applied Math., Sigma Xi, Phi Kappa Phi, Theta Delta Chi. Home: 240 Mount Pleasant Dr Boalsburg PA 16827-1810 Office: 508 Walker Bldg University Park PA 16802-2710

DUTTON, MARK ANTHONY, lawyer; b. Moulton, Ala., Jan. 24, 1964; s. William B. and Judith C. (Barrett) D. BA, Huntingdon Coll., Montgomery, Ala., 1987; JD, Samford U., 1990. Bar: Ala. 1991, U.S. Dist. Ct. (no. dist.) Ala. 1991, U.S. Ct. Appeals (11th cir.) 1991. Pvt. practice, Moulton, Ala., 1991—. Exec. committeeman Dem. Party, Lawrence County, Ala., 1993-, former pres. of Lawrence Continental, Al. Bar Assn.. Mem. Ala. Bar Assn., Ala. Trial Lawyers Assn., Masons, The Players Club (N.Y.C.). Democrat. Baptist. Avocations: racquetball, politics, reading. Home: 14220 Market St Moulton AL 35650-1442 Office: 714 East St Moulton AL 35650-1668

DUTTON, PAULINE MAE, fine arts and reference librarian; b. Detroit; d. Thoralf Andreas and Esther Ruth (Clyde) Tandberg; m. Richard Hawkins Dutton, June 21, 1969; 1 child, Nancy Katherine. BA in Art, Calif. State U., 1967; MLS, U. So. Calif., 1971. Elem. tchr., Anaheim, Calif., 1967-68, Corona, Calif., 1968-69; fine arts libr. Pasadena (Calif.) Pub. Libr., 1971-80; art cons., rschr., 1981-87; mgr. adult svcs. and ref. dept. Altadena Libr. Dist., adult svcs. coord., 1985—. Ref. chair Met. Coop. Libr. Sys., 1998-99. Mem. Am. Film Inst., Am. Entrepreneurs Assn., NAFE, Calif. Libr. Assn., Calif. Soc. Librs., Art Librs. N.Am., Pasadena Librs. Assn. (sec. 1978, treas. 1979-80), Telling Tales Theatre, Gilbert and Sullivan Soc., Toastmistress, Alpha Sigma Phi. Office: Altadena Libr Dist 600 E Mariposa St Altadena CA 91001-2211

DUTTON, P(ETER) LESLIE, biochemist, educator; b. Ashton-Under-Lyne, Lancashire, U.K., Mar. 12, 1941; came to U.S., 1968; s. Arthur Bramwell and Mary (Drake) D.; mn. Julia R. Dwyer, July 19, 1965; children: Michael, Sara, Simon. BSc in Chemistry with honors, U. Wales, 1963, PhD in Biochemistry, 1967. Postdoctoral fellow with W. Charles Evans U. Wales, U.K., 1967; postdoctoral fellow Johnson Rsch. Found., U. Pa., Phila., 1968, asst. prof., 1971-75; assoc. prof. dept. biochemistry and biophysics U. Pa., Phila., 1976-80, prof. dept. biochemistry and biophysics, 1981—. acting chmn. dept., 1993-94, chmn. dept., 1994—, dir. Johnson Rsch. Found., 1991—. Inst. on Aging fellow. Vis. prof. Imperial Coll., London, 1994, Univ. Coll., London, 1995. Author: Frontiers of Biological Energetics: From Electrons to Tissues, 1978, Protein Structure: Molecular and Electronic Reactivity, 1987; patentee in field; mem. editorial bd. Archives of Biochemistry, 1976-79; editor FEBS Letters, 1981-89; mng. editor Bioenergetics Revs. Sect. Biochimica et Biophysica Acta, 1981-96, Biochimica et Biophysica Acta, 1989-96. Mem. NIH adv. com. Molecular and Cellular Biophysics Study Sect., 1986-90; reserve mem. NIH Adv. Coms., 1990-94. Fellow Royal Soc. London. Office: Johnson Rsch Found 1005 Stellar Chance Labs 422 Curie Blvd Philadelphia PA 19104-6059

DUTTON, ROBERT D. state official; b. Lincoln, Nebr., Oct. 13, 1950; m. Andrea Dutton; 1 child, Kara. AA, L.A. Valley Coll., 1972. Pres., CEO property mgmt. co., 1972—; pres., CEO Dutton & Assocs., Inc., 1992—; mem. Calif. Rep. Party, 1990—; state assembly mem. Dist. 63 Calif. State Assembly, 2002—. Mem. health com.; mem. ins. com.; vice chair VA com.; commr. Rancho Cucamonga Pks. and Recreation Commn.; chair Rancho Cucamonga Cmty. Found.; commr. Rancho Cucamonga Pub. Safety Commn., San Bernardino County Econ. and Cmty. Devel., Inland Empire of Calif., 1998—; mem. Calif. Rep. Party, 1990—. Mem. San Bernardino County Sheriff's Coun., 1990—; chair West End and Rancho Cucamonga Family YMCA. Sgt. USAR, 1969—74. Mem.: Rancho Cucamonga C. of C. (past pres. 1982—), Calif. State Chamber Small Bus. Com., Rep. Nat. Com. (life). Republican. Roman Catholic. Mailing: Rm 3149 PO Box 942849 Sacramento CA 94249 Office: Ste 210 8577 Haven Ave Rancho Cucamonga CA 91730

DUTWIN, PHYLLIS, writer, scholarly; b. Newark, N.J. d. Bernard I. and Miriam Samuels; m. Marcel Dutwin, Jan. 24, 1960; children: Pamela, David. BS in edn., U. Wis., 1957; reading specialist, Kean Coll., 1968; MA, U. R.I., 1995. cert. reading specialist. Tchr. english/jr. high., h.s. S. Orange Maplewood Sch. Sys., 1960-65; v.p. Reading/Ednl. Svcs., Irvington, N.J., 1968-85; ednl. cons. Jewish Family Svc., Providence, R.I., 1980-85; pres. Dutwin Assocs., N. Kingstown, R.I., 1993—. Bd. dirs. R.I. Adult Literacy Coun., Providence, 1983—. Author: (books) Grammar In Plain English, 4th edit., 1997, GED The Science Test, 1985, English The Easy Way, 3rd edit., 1996, Writing the Easy Way, 3rd edit., 1999, Read to Work: Health Occupations, 1997, Read to Work: Business Occupations, 1997, The ABCs of Evaluation: Timeless Techniques for Program and Project Managers, 1999, TABE Test of Adult Basic Education: The First Step to Lifelong Success, 2003. Mem. Am. Soc. Tng. & Devel., Am. Assn. Adult & Continuing Edn., R.I. Adult Literacy Coun. Avocations: reading, music, travel. Office: Dutwin Assocs 97 Oceanwoods Dr North Kingstown RI 02852-7100 E-mail: pdutwin@cox.net.

DUUS, GORDON COCHRAN, lawyer; b. Ridley Park, Pa., Oct. 17, 1954; s. Frank Martin and Shirley (Cochran) D.; m. Mary Ellen Moses, Nov. 9, 1985; children: Alexander, Hannah, Julianne. BA in Aquatic Biology magna cum laude, U. Pa., 1977; JD with honors, George Washington U., 1981. Bar: D.C. 1981, N.J. 1982, Calif. 1987, U.S. Dist. Ct. N.J. 1982, U.S. Supreme Ct. 1989. Assoc. Previti, Todd, Gemmel, Fitzgerald & Nugent, Linwood, N.J., 1982-87; ptnr., chmn. environ. law dept. Margolis, Chase, Kosicki, Aboyoun & Hartman, Verona, N.J., 1987-90, Cole, Schotz, Meisel, Forman & Leonard, Hackensack, N.J., 1990—. Mem. faculty Cook Coll. of Rutgers U., New Brunswick, N.J., 1991-2002, Nat. Bus. Insts., Saddlebrook, N.J., 1992, Govt. Inst., Atlantic City, 1995; spkr. in field. Contbr. articles to profl. jours. Mem. ABA, N.J. Bar Assn., Bergen County Bar Assn. Office: Cole Schotz Meisel Forman & Leonard 25 Main St Hackensack NJ 07601-7015 E-mail: gduus@coleschotz.com.

DUUS, PETER, history educator; b. Wilmington, Del., Dec. 27, 1933; s. Hans Christian and Mary Anita (Pennypacker) D.; m. Masayo Umezawa, Nov. 25, 1964; 1 child, Erik. AB magna cum laude, Harvard U., 1955, PhD, 1965; MA, U. Mich., 1959. Asst. prof. history Washington U., St. Louis, 1964-66, Harvard U., Cambridge, Mass., 1966-70; assoc. prof. history Claremont (Calif.) Grad. Sch., 1970-73, Stanford (Calif.) U., 1973-78, prof., 1978—. Author: Party Rivalry and Political Change in Taishō Japan, 1968, Feudalism in Japan, 1969, The Rise of Modern Japan, 1976, The Cambridge History of Japan, Vol. 6: The Twentieth Century, 1989, The Japanese Informal Empire in China, 1989, The Abacus and the Sword: The Japanese Penetration of Korea, 1995, The Japanese Discovery of America, 1996, Modern Japan, 1997. Exec. sec. Inter-Univ. for Japanese Lang. Studies, Tokyo, 1974-90; bd. dirs. Com. for Internat. Exchange of Scholars, Washington, 1987-91. Served with U.S. Army, 1955-57. NEH sr. fellow, 1972-73, Japan Found. postdoctoral fellow, 1976-77, Fulbright rsch. fellow, 1981-82, 94-95, Japan Found. rsch. fellow, 1986-87. Fellow AAAS, mem. Assn. for Asian Studies (bd. dirs. 1972-75, nominating com. 1983, v.p. 1999-2000, pres. 2000—), Am. Hist. Assn. (bd. editors 1984-87). Home: 818 Esplanada Way Palo Alto CA 94305-1015 Office: Stanford U History Dept Stanford CA 94305 E-mail: pduus@leland.stanford.edu.

DUVAL, ALBERT FRANK, paper company executive; b. Holyoke, Mass., Oct. 31, 1920; s. Albert Frank and Lena (Potvin) D.; m. Mary Tague, Apr. 12, 1947; children: Denise, Richard, Nanette, Robert, Carolyn, Michele, Kathleen. BA, Amherst Coll., 1943. Mgr. Calif. div. U.S. Envelope Co., 1946-52, sales mgr., 1952-55, v.p. sales, 1955-60, pres., 1960; v.p. Hammermill Paper Co., Erie, Pa., 1960-69, sr. v.p., 1969, pres., 1970—, chief exec. officer, 1971-85, chmn., 1983-85. Trustee Mercyhurst Coll.; trustee St. Vincent's Hosp., chmn., 1976. Served with USAAF, 1944-46, ETO. Mem. Envelope Mfrs. Assn. (pres. 1963-65), Am. Paper Inst. (chmn. 1976) Clubs: Kahkwa (Erie) (pres. 1969—). Home: 3220 Georgian Ct Erie PA 16506-1116

DUVAL, DANIEL WEBSTER, manufacturing company executive; b. Cin., May 27, 1936; s. Harry A. and Wilda (Webster) V.; m. Sue Ann Howard, July 20, 1962; children: Laurie Ann, Paula Lee, Christopher Webster. BA, U. Cin., 1960. V.p. staff elec. products div. Midland-Ross, Cleve., 1976-78, group v.p., 1979-81, exec. v.p., 1981-83, pres., chief operating officer, 1983-86; pres., chief exec. officer Robbins & Myers Inc., Dayton, Ohio, 1986-98, also bd. dirs., ret. vice chmn., bd. dirs., 1999. Bd. dirs. Arrow Electronics, Gosiger, Inc., Dayton, The Manitowac Co., Wis.; chmn. Arrow Electronics, Inc., N.Y.C., 2002—. Patentee container coupling mechanism. Bd. trustees Wright State U., 1991-2000, Wright State U. Found.; pres. Civitan Found., Ariz., 1973-74, Dayton Ballet Assn., 1990-93; participant Leadership Cleve.; bd. dirs. U.S. Air and Trade Show. Mem. Dayton Racquet Club. Republican. Roman Catholic. Home: 829 Timberlake Ct Kettering OH 45429 Office: 1480 Kettering Tower Dayton OH 45423-1001

DUVAL, DAVID ROBERT, professional golfer; b. Jacksonville, Fla., Nov. 9, 1971; Student, Ga. Tech. Profl. golfer PGA, 1993—. Mem. Walker Cup team, 1991, Presidents Cup team, 1996, 98, Ryder Cup team, 1999. Winner Nike Wichita Open, 1993, Nike Tour Championship, 1993, Michelob Championship at Kingsmill, 1997, Walt Disney World/Oldsmobile Classic, 1997, The Tour Championship, 1997, Tucson Chrysler Classic, 1998, Shell Houston Open, 1998, NEC World Series of Golf, 1998, Michelob Championship at Kingsmill, 1998, Mercedes Championship, 1999, Bob Hope Chrysler Classic, 1999, The Players Championship, 1999, Bell South Classic, 1999, Ryder Cup, 1999; recipient Dave Williams award, 1993, Jasper award, Jacksonville, 1996; named Collegiate Player of Yr., 1993. Avocations: reading, fly fishing, surfing, skiing, baseball. Office: PGA of Am Box 109601 100 Ave of Champions Palm Beach Gardens FL 33410

DUVAL, STANWOOD RICHARDSON, JR., judge; b. New Orleans, Feb. 8, 1942; m. Deborah Barnes, Jan. 20, 1979. BA, La. State U., 1964, JD, 1966. Assoc. Duval, Arceneaux & Lewis, 1966-94; ptnr. Duval, Funderburk, Sundberry & Lovell, L.L.P., 1966-94; asst. city atty. Terrebonne Parish Consol. Govt., 1970-72, parish atty., 1988-92; dist. judge U.S. Dist. Ct. (ea. dist.), New Orleans, 1994—. Mem. Indigent Def. Bd., 1976-82; elected La. Constnl. Conv., 1973, mem. exec. br. com., com. to write rules of procedure. Mem. Terrebone Parish. Mem. ABA (adv. com. appellate rules 1997-2003), La. Law Inst. (coun. 1996-2001), La. State Bar Assn., Terrebonne Parish Bar Assn., Tulane Inns of Ct. Avocations: traveling, scuba diving, fishing, performing arts. Office: US Dist Ct Ea Dist 500 Camp St Rm C-368 New Orleans LA 70130-3313

DUVAL-CARRIÉ, EDOUARD, artist; b. Haiti, 1954; Student, Ecole Nat. Superieure des Beaux Arts, Paris, 1988—89; BA, U. Loyola Montreal, 1978; student, McGill U., U. Montreal. Resident Arts Internat., Found. Claude Monet, Giverny, France, 1998. One-man shows include Art Ctr., Port-au-Prince, Haiti, 1980, Franz Bader Gallery, Washington, 1982, Paul Waggoner Gallery, Chgo., 1983, Anderson Gallery, Va. Commonwealth U., Richmond, 1986, Brent Gallery, Houston, 1987, Nicole Gallery, Chgo., 1987, Malraux Gallery, L.A., 1991, Armand Gallery, Paris, 1991, Mus. de Arte Contemporaneo de Monterrey, Mex., 1992, Porter Randall Gallery, San Diego, 1994, Lakaye Gallery, L.A., 1994, 1998, Galeria Fernando Quintana, Bogota, Colombia, 1994, Gutierez Fine Arts, Miami Beach, Fla., 1994, Mus. du Coll. St. Pierre, Port-au-Prince, 1996, Polk Mus. Art, Lakeland, Fla., 1997, Quintana Gallery, Miami, 1997, David Beitzel Gallery, Project Room, N.Y.C., 1997, exhibited in group shows at Southeastern Ctr. Contemporary Art, Winston-Salem, 1997, Palacio del Segundo Cabo, Havana, Cuba, 1997, Mus. African Am. Art, Tampa, Fla., 1998, Internat. Arts Club, Chgo., 1973, Ramscale Gallery, N.Y.C., 1998, Taller Boricua Gallery, Julia de Burgos Cultural Ctr., 1998, Miami-Dade Cultural Ctr., 1999, Miami Art Mus., 2000, New Work Gallery, 2000, Bernice Steinbaum Gallery, Miami, 2002, numerous others, Represented in permanent collections; illustrator Imagen mag., 1995; illustrator Cantos to Blood and Honey, 1997, numerous others; contbr. South Fla. Cultural Consortium Visual Art fellow, 1995, So. Arts Fedn. Visual Art fellow, 1996.

DUVALL, BERNICE BETTUM, artist, exhibit coordinator, jewelry designer; b. Washington, Mar. 17, 1948; d. William A. and Bergny (Farovig) Bettum; m. Donald Dunn Duvall, Oct. 5, 1968; children: Gregory Thomas, Peter Brian. Grad. high sch., Washington, 1966; art edn. pvt. study, 1970-74. Artist watercolor, acrylic, needlework design, Chevy Chase, Md., 1972—; exhibit coord. Discovery Channel, Learning Channel, Discovery Comms., Inc., Bethesda, Md., 1993—, N.Y.C., Miami, L.A., 2000—, Your Choice TV, Bethesda, Md., 1995-97, Discovery Com., Inc., Chgo., 2001—, Charlotte, NC, 2003—. Pub. rels. and publicity Town Ctr. Gallery, Rockville, Md., 1986-89; banner designer St. Paul's Luth. Ch., Washington, 1985—; sch. art project coord. Am. Speech-Lang.-Hearing Assn., Rockville, Md., 1998-99; spkr. in field. Exhbns. include Capricorn Gallery, Bethesda, 1982, Westmoreland Mus. Art, Greensburg, Pa., 1982, 87, Hull Gallery, Washington 1983, 85, Butler Inst. Am. Art, Youngstown, Ohio, 1983, DeLand (Fla.) Mus., 1984, Springfield (Mo.) Art Mus., 1988, 95, 98, Newberry Gallery, Pa., 1989, Broadway Gallery, Va., 1989, Watergate Gallery, Washington, 1990, Fine Art Mus. of South, Mobile, Ala., 1990, Images Internat. Gallery, Bethesda, 1991-93, So. Watercolor Soc., 1993, 99, Charles Sumner Sch. Mus., Washington, 1994, Sugar & Frichtl Gallery, Kensington, Md., 1994, Univ. Club, Washington, 1995, NIH, Bethesda, 1995, Margaret Smith Gallery, Ellicott City, Md., 1995, Office Gov. State of Md., Balt., 1996, Md. State House, Annapolis, 1996, Fine Arts Invitational, Oxford, Md., 1996-97, 99-02, Hughes Network Sys., Germantown, Md., 1996, Arlington County Sch. Bd., Arlington, Va., 1997, Delaplaine Visual Art Ctr., Frederick, Md., 1998, Mt. St. Mary's Coll., Emmittsburg, Md., 1998, Howard County Pub. Sch. Adminstrn. Gallery, Ellicott City, Md., 1999; one-woman shows include Wash. County Mus. Art, Hagerstown, Md., 1999; exhibited in group shows at Internat. Artists in Watercolor, London, 1981, Glenview Mansion Civic Ctr. Art Gallery, Rockville, Md., 2000, Dorchester Art Ctr, 2001, Sandy Spring (Md.) Mus., 2003; prin. works represented in pub. and pvt. collections including Montgomery County Contemporary Art Acquisitions, New Eng. Life Ins. Co., Pelavin Assocs., Inc., Capricorn Gallery, Univ. Club Washington; contbr. articles to Am. Artist, Watercolor, The Artist mag. Vol. artist Nat. Zoo, Washington, 1985-91; art judge Art in Schs., Parks, Pub. Places, Montgomery County, Md., 1988-90. Recipient Award of High Commendation Internat. Artists in Water Colors, 1981, Arthur Alexander award So. Water Color Soc., 1981, Award of Merit Md. Fedn. Art, 1980, Liquitex award Adirondacks Am. Watercolorists, 1989, Bendann Gallery award Balt. Water Color Soc., 1990, Washington Water Color Assn. award, 1993, Patron's award Watercolor U.S.A., 1995, First Place award Fed. Reserve, 1995. Mem. Pa. Watercolor Soc., Art League (bd. dirs. 1982-86), Washington Water Color Assn. (bd. dirs. 1986-87, award 1993), Town Ctr. Gallery (bd. dirs. 1986-89), Potomac Valley Watercolorists (bd. dirs. 1993—), Artists Equity, Arts Coun. Montgomery County, So. Watercolor Soc. (co-chmn. ann. juried exhibit 1993), Balt. Watercolor Soc., Strathmore Arts Found., Women's Club Chevy Chase. Lutheran. Avocations: gardening, horseback riding, needlework. Home: 3414 Taylor St Chevy Chase MD 20815-4024 Fax: 301-657-2291. E-mail: bbduvall.art@starpower.net.

DUVALL, CHARLES PATTON, retired internist, oncologist; b. Evanston, Ill., June 16, 1936; s. Charles Fleming and Edith (Osgood) D.; m. Nancy Ash, June 21, 1958; children: Lawrence Charles, Stephen Rogers, Douglas Patton, Lauren Duvall Meacham. AB, Cornell U., 1958; MD, U. Rochester, N.Y., 1962. Diplomate Am. Bd. Internal Medicine, Am. Bd. Med. Oncology. Intern Yale New Haven Med. Ctr., 1962-63; resident in internal medicine U. Rochester, 1963-64; clin. assoc. Nat. Cancer Inst., NIH, Bethesda, Md., 1964-66; resident in medicine Georgetown U. Hosp., Washington, 1966-67, USPHS spl. fellow in hematology, 1967-68; physician Foxhall Internists, Washington, 1968-2000; ret., 2000. Clin. prof. medicine Georgetown U. Hosp., Washington, 1968-2000; vice chmn. dept. medicine Sibley Hosp., Washington, 1987-90, chmn., 1990-91; mem. emeritus staff Washington Hosp. Ctr., 1988—. Contbr. articles to profl. jours. Elder Bradley Hills Presbyn. Ch., Bethesda, 1974-77; Stephen min., deacon 1st Presbyn. Ch., Hilton Head Island, SC, 2003—, v.p. men of the ch.; chmn. bd. Blue Cross Blue Shield Nat. Capital area, Washington, 1986-94, Group Hospitalization Med. Svcs., Inc., Washington, 1986-94; vice chmn., bd. trustees Vols. in Medicine Inst., Hilton Head, S.C., 1998-2002. Lt. comdr. USPHS, 1964-66. Recipient 5 Yr. Svc. award Am. Cancer Soc., 1978. Fellow ACP (Outpatient Tchg. award 1998, Laureate award 2000); mem. Am. Soc. Internal Medicine (DC chpt. pres. 1977, pres. rsch. found. 1987-88, pres.-elect 1988-89, pres. 1989-90, speaker ho. of dels. 1991-95, chmn. federated coun. internal medicine 1989-90, Spl. Recognition award 1979), AMA (del. 1988-93, coun. on legislation 1991-2000, coun. on legislation chmn. 1996-97), Spltys. and Svcs. Soc. (pres. 1990-91, sect. coun. IM), Sect. Coun. Internal Medicine (chmn. 1987-88), Osler Soc. D.C. (pres. 1978-79), Clin. Pathologic Soc. (pres. 1995-96), Congl. Country Club, Country Club of Hilton Head (S.C.), Bear Creek Club (S.C., v.p.), Alpha Omega Alpha, Sigma Chi. Republican. Presbyterian. Avocations: golf, skiing, photography, painting. Home: 316 Seabrook Dr Hilton Head Island SC 29926-1979

DUVALL, GENE ROBERT, radiologist; b. Hutchinson, Kans., 1922; MD, Stanford Univ., 1950. Intern San Francisco Hosp., 1949-50; resident radiology Stanford Univ. Hosp., 1950-51, San Francisco Hosp., 1952; fellow radiology Stanford Univ. Hosp., 1953.

DUVALL, HENRY FRANKLIN, JR., public relations executive; b. Washington, Jan. 3, 1949; s. Henry Franklin and Ruth (Catlett) D.; m. Deborah Hawkins, Aug. 12, 1975; 1 child, Cherie Reneé. BS, U. Md., 1975. Copy editor Albuquerque Jour., 1975-76; staff writer U. Md., College Park, 1976-77; writer Potomac Electric Power Co., Washington, 1978; editor Howard U., Washington, 1978-81, media coord., 1981-89, info. officer, 1989-91; media rels. assoc. ARC, Washington, 1991-92; dir. communications Coun. Great City Schs., Washington, 1992—. With USN, 1968-70, Vietnam. Scholar Am. Newspaper Pubs. Assn., 1974. Mem. Capital Press Club (bd. dirs. 1978-92), Nat. Assn. Black Journalists, Nat. Press Club, Edn. Writers Assn., Nat. Sch. Pub. Rels. Assn., Am. Soc. Assn. Execs. Office: Coun Great City Schs 1301 Pennsylvania Ave NW Washington DC 20004-1701 E-mail: hduvall@cgcs.org.

DUVALL, HOLLIE JEAN, music educator; b. Greensburg, Pa., Dec. 8, 1953; d. William Gilbert Smail and Betty Jane Rygiel; m. Charles Timothy Duvall, Feb. 18, 1977; children: Charles Timothy, Renee Jean. B in Music Edn., Seton Hill Coll., 1995; MA, Ind. U. of Pa., 1997. Pa. instrnl. cert. in music edn. Music dir. Ch. of God (Holiness), Greensburg, Pa., 1970—; wedding and fashion show cons. Greensburg, 1982-98; interior designer, 1982—; freelance pianist, 1985—; instr. piano and voice Pvt. Studio, Greensburg, 1985—; prof. music Westmoreland County C.C., Youngwood, Pa., 1996—, music coord., 1998—; prof. music C.C. of Allegheny County, West Mifflin, Pa., 1999—, Pa. State U., Fayette, Pa., 2002—. Judge-fine arts Keystone Christian Edn. Assn., Pa., 1989—, Ea. Nazarene Regional Div., Greensburg, Pa., 1990, Am. Fedn. Women's Clubs, Greensburg, 1995-97. Reviewer in field. Sunday sch. tchr. Ch. of God (Holiness), Greensburg, 1975—. Recipient scholarship award AAUW, 1993, scholarship award PEO Sisterhood, 1994. Mem. Profl. Music Educator's Assn., Alpha Sigma Lambda (Scholarship award 1992). Republican. Avocations: reading, floral arranging, decorating. Office: Westmoreland County CC 400 Armbrust Rd Youngwood PA 15697-1801 E-mail: duvallh@astro.westmoreland.cc.pa.us., hollie_duvall@yahoo.com.

DUVALL, LORRAINE, recreation center owner; b. Hamilton, Ohio, Jan. 31, 1925; d. Saul and Martha Jane (Huff) Baker; m. Ray DuVall, June 12, 1951; children: Sharon DuVall Keese, Deborah D. Velchoff, Steve, Annette. BA, U. Cin., 1951; MA, Tex. A&I U., 1963; postgrad., Miami U., Oxford, Ohio, 1958, U. Toledo, 1959, U. Tex.-Austin, 1968. Elem. tchr., Larkmoor, Lorain, Ohio, 1956-60; tchr. math Incarnate Word High Sch., Corpus Christi, 1964-70; owner, instr. Aerobic Fitness, Corpus Christi, 1973-93; owner, coach Corpus Christi Marlin Swim Team, 1972—. Mgr. Corpus Christi Country Club Pool, 1973-88; pres., mgr. Club Estates Pool Chems., Corpus Christi, 1980-89, Club Estates Recreation, Corpus Christi, 1977—. Vol. psychiat. ward Meml. Hosp., Corpus Christi, 1966-70, U.S. Swimming Club Devel., 1993-97; harpist First Bapt. Ch. Orch., 1995—; adminstrv. gen. chair South Tex. Swimming, 1996-99; liaison to U.S. Swimming Club Devel. Com, 1995; bd. dirs. vol. YWCA, Corpus Christi, 1970-77; water safety trainer ARC, Corpus Christi, 1975-82; CPR instr. Am. Heart Assn., Corpus Christi, 1980-84; vol. children's choir dir. St. John Methodist Ch., Corpus Christi, 1966-78, Asbury United Meth. Ch., 1980-93; vol. harpist 1st Bapt. Ch., 1995—. NSF grantee U. Tex.-Austin, 1968. Mem. Am. Swim Coaches Assn., Am. Harp Soc. Avocations: music, swimming, tennis, skiing, backpacking. Home: 6709 Pintail Dr Corpus Christi TX 78413-2337 Office: 4902 Snowgoose Dr Corpus Christi TX 78413-2328 E-mail: l-r-duvall@prodigy.net.

DUVALL, MARJORIE L. English and foreign language educator; b. Lehighton, Pa., Dec. 2, 1958; d. Charles Jacque and Carole Faye (Eckhart) Lusch; m. Glenn Edward Duvall, July 26, 1954. BA in German, Lafayette Coll., 1980; MA in German, U. Fla., 1998; postgrad., East Stroudsburg U., 1982, Ga. So. U., Middlebury Coll., 1988, Augusta State U., U. Pa., 1994, U. S.C., 1993; degree, Goethe-Inst., Germany, 2003; student, Accord Lang. Sch., Paris, France, 2003. German and French tchr. Evans (Ga.) Mid. Sch., 1987-89, Harlem (Ga.) Mid. Sch., 1989-92; ESOL tchr. Lakeside Mid. and H.S.'s, Evans, Ga., 1992-97; ESL tchr. Davidson & Murphy H.S.'s, Mobile, Ala., 1997-99; German tchr. Brookwood H.S., Snellville, Ga., 1999-00; tchr. ESOL and lang. arts for gifted Freedom Middle Sch., Stone Mountain, Ga., 2000—03; tchr. English, Dunwoody (Ga.) H.S., 2003—. Contbr. articles to profl. jours. Recipient scholarship Profl. Assn. Ga. Educators, 1994. Mem.: TESOL, Fgn. Lang. Assn. Ga., Ga. Assn. Gifted Children, Nat. Coun. Tchrs. English, Am. Assn. Tchrs. of French, Am. Assn. Tchrs. of German, Friends of Goethe, DeKalb County Supporters of the Gifted, Mensa. Lutheran. Avocations: choral music, piano, swimming, baton twirling, dance. Home: 4452 Beacon Hill Dr SW Lilburn GA 30047 Office: Dunwoody HS 5035 Vermack Rd Dunwoody GA 30338 E-mail: pardette80@aol.com.

DUVALL, PATRICIA ARLENE, secondary education educator; b. Pitts., June 27, 1950; d. William Richard and Willene Alberta (Goode) Addison; 1 child, Tiyonda Aikee. BA in Math., Carnegie-Mellon U., 1972; MEd, U. Pitts., 1981. Long distance telephone operator AT&T, Pitts., 1968-71; switchboard operator Union Nat. Bank, Pitts., 1972; tchr. math. Allegheny Intermmediate Unit, Pitts., 1978-79; math. skills program Chatham Coll., Pitts., 1983—; tchr. math. Pitts. Bd. Pub. Edn., 1972—. Math instr. Kids and Teens coll. program Community Coll. Allegheny County, summer 1986, 87; tennis coach Allegheny High Sch., Pitts., 1979-81. Mem. U.S. Tennis Assn., Am. Alliance Health Phys. Edn., Recreation and Dance, Women's Tennis Assn., Nat. Coun. Tchrs. Math. Jehovah'S Witness. Avocations: stamp collecting, tennis, reading, collecting comic books, home computers. E-mail: parelene@netscape.net.

DUVALL, ROBERT, actor; b. San Diego, Calif., Jan. 5, 1931; s. William Howard Duvall; m. Gail Youngs, m. Sharon Brophy, May 1, 1991. Grad., Principia Coll., Ill.; student, Neighborhood Playhouse, N.Y. Film appearances include To Kill a Mockingbird, 1963, Captain Newman, M.D., 1964, The Chase, 1965, Countdown, 1968, The Detective, 1968, Bullitt, 1968, True Grit, 1969, The Rain People, 1969, M*A*S*H, 1970, The Revolutionary, 1970, THX-1138, 1971, Lawman, 1971, The Godfather, 1972 (N.Y. Film Critics award for best supporting actor 1972, Acad. award nominee for best supporting actor), Tomorrow, 1972, The Great Northfield, Minnesota Raid, 1972, Joe Kidd, 1972, Lady Ice, 1973, Badge 373, 1973, The Outfit, 1974, The Conversation, 1974, The Godfather Part II, 1974, Breakout, 1975, The Killer Elite, 1975, Network, 1976, The Seven Per Cent Solution, 1976, The Eagle Has Landed, 1977, The Greatest, 1977, The Betsy, 1978, Apocalypse Now, 1979 (Acad. award nominee for best supporting actor), The Great Santini, 1980 (Acad. award nominee for best actor 1981), True Confessions, 1981, The Pursuit of D.B. Cooper, 1981, Tender Mercies, 1983 (Acad. award for best actor 1984), The Stone Boy, 1984, The Natural, 1984, The Lightship, 1986, Let's Get Harry, 1986, Belizaire the Cajun, 1986, Colors, 1988, Convicts, Roots in a Parched Ground, The Handmaid's Tale, 1990, A Show of Force, 1990, Days of Thunder, 1990, Rambling Rose, 1991, Newsies, 1992, Falling Down, 1993, Geronimo, 1993, Wrestling Ernest Hemingway, 1993, The Paper, 1994, The Stars Fell on Henrietta, 1995, The Scarlet Letter, 1995, Sling Blade, 1996, Phenomenon, 1996, A Family Thing, 1996, Gingerbread Man, 1997, The Apostle, 1997 (also prodr., dir., writer) (nominated Oscar for best actor), Deep Impact, 1998, A Civil Action, 1999, Gone in Sixty Seconds, 2000, A Shot at Glory, 2000 (also prodr.), The Sixth Day, 2000, John Q, 2002, Assassination Tango, 2002 (also prodr., dir., writer), Gods and Generals, 2003, Open Range, 2003, Secondhand Lions, 2003; TV movies include Fame is the Name of the Game, 1966, The Terry Fox Story, 1983, Stalin, HBO, 1992 (Emmy nomination, Lead actor -Miniseries, 1993); plays including A View From the Bridge, 1965 (Obie award), Wait Until Dark, 1966, American Buffalo, 1977; TV miniseries include Ike, 1979, Lonesome Dove, 1989; dir.: film We're Not the Jet Set; actor, dir. film: Angelo My Love, 1983; rec. artist: Triad Records. Recipient Golden Globe award, Brit. Acad. award, Nat. Assn. Theatre Owners award. Office: William Morris Agy 151 El Camino Dr Beverly Hills CA 90212-2775*

DUVA-MIKHAIL, DONNA MARIE, financial executive; b. Paterson, N.J., June 28, 1956; d. Alfred Dominick and Frances P. (D'Andrea) D. AAS, Bergen Community Coll., 1976; BS in Acctg., Ramapo Coll., 1985. Bookkeeper Passaic County Treas. Office, Paterson, 1973-77; acctg. tutor Bergen Community Coll., Paramus, N.J., 1974-76; full charge bookkeeper Weisz Supermarket, Inc., Clifton, N.J., 1977-79; acct. Beecham, Inc., Clifton, 1980-85; CFO, contr. Al Duva Enterprises, Inc., Paterson, 1976—, Power Battery Corp., Paterson, 1986-96, Atlantic Battery Corp., 1986-96, Power Auto & Truck Parts of Fla., 1986-96, Power Battery & Truck Parts of Vt., 1986-96; pvt. practice, 1997—. Author newspaper editorials Paterson Evening News, 1976. Mem. N.J. Soc. Notary Pubs., Ramapo Coll. Alumni Assn., Bergen Community Coll. Alumni Assn., Nat. Assn. Female Execs. Democrat. Roman Catholic. Avocations: games of chance, bowling, tennis, travel. Home and Office: 8284 Orange Vale Ave Las Vegas NV 89131

DUVERNOY, WOLF F.C. cardiologist; b. Stuttgart, Germany, Apr. 16, 1935; came to U.S., 1960; s. Friedrich Ludwig and Hedwig Luise (Elben) D.; m. Eva Sibylle Hummel, Feb. 27, 1960; children: Christian L., Claire S. Abitur, Wilhelms Gymnasium, Stuttgart, 1954; MD, U. Tubingen, Germany, 1959. Diplomate Am. Bd. Internal Medicine, Am. Bd. Cardiovascular Disease. Intern Flower Hosp., Toledo, 1960-61; resident in internal medicine Henry Ford Hosp., Detroit, 1962-65, resident in cardiology, 1965-66, staff cardiologist, 1969-75, dir. EKG Lab., 1973-75; chief sect. cardiology Providence Hosp., Southfield, Mich., 1984-2000, pres. med. staff, 1985-86; ptnr. pvt. practice Southfield. Clin. prof. internal medicine Wayne State U., Detroit, 1994-2000; clin. prof. medicine divsn. cardiology U. Mich., Ann Arbor, 2001. Contbr. articles to profl. publs. Mem. tech. adv. panel Greater Detroit Area Health Coun., 1993-99; mem. profl. edn. com. Mich. Heart Assn., Detroit; pres. Detroit Heart Club, 1984. Maj. U.S. Army, 1966-69. Fellow ACP, Am. Coll. Cardiology (gov. Mich. 1993-96, pres. Mich. chpt. 1993-96), Am. Coll. Chest Physicians, Am. Heart Assn. (Forest Dewey Dodrill award for excellence 1999). Address: 1527 Newport Creek Dr Ann Arbor MI 48103 E-mail: duvernoy@comcast.net.

DUVICK, DONALD NELSON, plant breeder; b. Sandwich, Ill., Dec. 18, 1924; s. Nelson Daniel and Florence Henrietta (Appel) D.; m. Selma Elizabeth Nelson, Sept. 10, 1950; children: Daniel, Jonathan, Randa. BS, U. Ill., 1948; PhD, Washington U., St. Louis, 1951. With Pioneer Hi-Bred Internat., Inc., Johnston, Iowa, 1951-90, corn breeding coordinator Ea. and So. div., 1965-71, dir. corn breeding dept., 1971-75, dir. plant breeding div., 1975-85, v.p. research, 1985-86, sr. v.p. research, 1986-90, co. dir., 1982-90; affiliate prof. Iowa State U., 1990—. Chmn. nat. plant genetic resources bd. USDA, 1990-91, vice-chmn. nat. genetic resources adv. com., 1992-93; trustee Internat. Ctr. for Maize and Wheat Improvement, 1988-94, trustee Internat. Rice Rsch. Inst., 1996-98; lectr. in field. Assoc. editor: Plant Physiology Jour., 1977-78; contbr. articles to profl. jours. on genetics and plant breeding, devel. anatomy and cytology, cytoplasmic inheritance, quantititive genetics and biodiversity. Pres. Johnston Consol. Sch. Bd., 1965-67. Served with AUS, 1943-46. Pioneer Hi-Bred fellow U. London, 1968; Disting. fellow Iowa Acad. Sci. Fellow AAAS, Crop Sci. Soc. Am. (pres. 1986), Am. Soc. Agronomy (pres. 1992), Iowa Acad. Sci.; mem. NAS, Coun. Agrl. Sci. and Tech. (bd. dirs. 1987-90), The Nature Conservancy (chair bd. trustees Iowa chpt. 1994). Democrat. Mem. United Ch. Christ. Achievements include identification of intra cellular site of zein storage in maize endosperm; research in maize cytoplasmic male sterility, in plant breeding's effects on crop plant genetic diversity, in changes in productivity of hybrid maize since 1930. Office: 6837 NW Beaver Dr Johnston IA 50131-1446 E-mail: dnd307@aol.com. *Love science and humanity with equal fervor. Pursue knowledge for its own sake but also seek to apply it to useful ends.*

DUVIN, ROBERT PHILLIP, lawyer; b. Evansville, Ind., May 18, 1937; s. Louis and Henrietta (Hamburg) D.; m. Darlene Chmiel, Aug. 23, 1961; children: Scott A., Marc A., Louis A. BA with honors, Ind. U., 1958, JD with highest honors, 1961; LLM with highest honors, Columbia U., 1963. Bar: Ohio 1964. Since practiced in, Cleve.; pres. Duvin, Cahn & Hutton, 1972—. Lectr. law schs.; labor adviser corps., cities and hosps. Contbr. to books and legal jours.; bd. editors: Ind. Law Jour., 1961, Columbia Law Rev., 1963. Served with AUS, 1961-62. Mem. ABA, FBA, Ohio Bar Assn., Cleve. Bar Assn., Cleve. Racquet Club, Beechmont Country Club, Soc. Club, Canterbury Golf Club, Sanctuary Golf Club. Jewish. Home: 2775 S Park Blvd Cleveland OH 44120-1669 Office: Duvin Cahn & Hutton Erieview Tower 1301 E 9th St Ste 2000 Cleveland OH 44114-1886 E-mail: rduvin@duvin.com.

DUVIVIER, JEAN FERNAND, management consultant, consultant; b. Niteroi, Brazil, Dec. 17, 1926; came to U.S., 1954; s. Herman Felix and Eugenie A. (Dits) D.; m. Barbara Johanne Doucet, June 9, 1956; children: Christine, Michele, John, Elizabeth, Marc. BSc, Boston U., 1955; SM, MIT, 1958, Engr. in Aeronautics & Astronautics degree, 1966. Project leader MIT Aeroelastic Lab., Cambridge, 1955-61; sr. staff Ctr. Naval Analyses, Cambridge, 1961-66; cons. Rsch. Analysis Corp., McLean, Va., 1966; sr. engr. Electric Boat divsn. Gen. Dynamics, Quincy, Mass., 1966-68; mgr. rsch. and devel., dir. mktg. for Latin Am. Boeing Vertol Co., Phila., 1968-82; v.p. internat. mktg. Fairchild Republic, Farmingdale, N.Y., 1982-85; v.p. aerospace systems Lear Siegler Internat., Stamford, Conn., 1985-88; dir. systems mktg. Smiths Industries, Stamford, 1988-90; gen. mgr. Duvivier Assocs., Georgetown, Conn., 1990—; v.p. HELTEC Inc., Ridgefield, Conn., 1992—. With Brazilian Air Force, 1944-45. Mem. AIAA (assoc. fellow, chmn. Conn. sect. 1991-92), U.S. Naval Inst. Republican. Roman Catholic. Home: 12 Granville Way Exton PA 19341 Office: 12 Granville Way Exton PA 19341

DUVIVIER, JEAN-PAUL, investment banker, educator; b. N.Y.C., Feb. 6, 1971; s. Roger Duvivier and Edna Lucrecia Duvivier Salguero. BA, Conn. Coll., 1993; MA, Johns Hopkins U., 1996. Registered securities rep. Ops. asst. WestHem Internat., Inc., N.Y.C., 1994; intern U.S. Govt., Washington, 1995; mktg. asst. Coutts Internat., Miami, Fla., 1997—99; regional mgr. Swiss Investment Group, Miami, 2000—. Vol. Am. Field Svc., 1998—. Fellow, US-Indonesia Soc., 1996. Roman Catholic. Avocations: philately, soccer, linguistics, squash, travel. Office: Swiss Investment Group 999 Brickell Ave Ste 700 Miami FL 33131

DUVIVIER, KATHARINE KEYES, lawyer, educator; b. Alton, Ill., Jan. 1, 1953; d. Edward Keyes and Marjorie (Attebery) DuVivier; m. James Wesley Perl, Mar. 30, 1985 (div. Aug. 1997); children: Alice Katharine, Emmett Edward Perl. BA in Geology and English cum laude, Williams Coll., 1975; JD, U. Denver, 1982. Bar: Colo. 1982, U.S. Dist. Ct. Colo. 1982, U.S. Ct. Appeals (10th cir.) 1982. Intern-curator Hudson River Mus., Yonkers, N.Y., 1975; geologist French Am. Metals Corp., Lakewood, Colo., 1976-79; assoc. Sherman & Howard, Denver, 1982-84, Arnold & Porter, Denver, 1984-87; atty. Office of City Atty., Denver, 1987-90; sr. instr. sch. law Univ. Colo., 1990-00; reporter of decisions Colo. Ct. of Appeals, Denver, 2000; asst. prof., dir. Lawyering Process Program U. Denver Coll. Law, 2000—. Chair Appellate Practice Subcom., 1998—2000, vice-chmn., 1996—98, 2000—. Contbr. articles to profl. jours. Mem. Denver Botanic Gardens, 1981—88; vol. Outdoor Colo., Denver, 1985—87, 1998—. Mem.: ABA (vice chmn. subcom. 1985—91), Boulder Women's Bar Assn. (pres. 1991—93), Colo. Bar Assn., Alliance Profl. Women (bd. dirs. 1985—90, pres. 1988—89), Work and Family Consortium (bd. dirs. 1988—90), St. Ives, William Coll. Alumni Assn. (co-pres. Colo. chpt. 1984—86), Phi Beta Kappa. Avocation: Avocations: geology, skiing, dancing, swimming. Home: 4761 McKinley Dr Boulder CO 80303-1142 E-mail: kkduvivier@law.du.edu.

DUVO, MECHELLE LOUISE, oil company executive, consultant; b. East Stroudsburg, Pa., Apr. 25, 1962; d. Nicholas and Arlene Birdie (Mack) D. AS, Lehigh County Community Coll., 1982. Rehab. counselor Phoenix Project, Bakersfield, Calif., 1982-84; nat. sales mgr. Olympia Advt., L.A., 1984-85; oil exploration cons. Cimmaron Mgmt., Nashville, 1985-86; exec. sec. Pueblo Resources Corp., Bowling Green, Ky., 1986-87; nat. oil cons. El Toro, Inc., Bowling Green, 1986-87; founder, pres. and CEO Majestic Mgmt. Corp., Glasgow, Ky., 1987—; nat. oil cons. Impact Oil, Inc., Glasgow, 1987—. Lease procurator El Toro, Inc., 1986-87; spkr. Nat. Investment Seminars, 1994—. Editor, pub.: (newsletter) The Majestic Field Copy, 1994—. Fundraiser Am. Cancer Soc., LA, 1984-85; vol. Humane Soc., Nashville, 1985-86, Humane Soc., Bowling Green, 1986-87, Boy Scouts Am., 2001-02; counselor Salvation Army, Bakersfield, 1982-84; vol. mgr. Food Pantry Outreach Program, 1999-2001, Relay for Life, 2001—. Mem. NAFE (exec. program), Internat. Platform Assn., Ky. Oil & Gas Assn. Avocations: house plants, gardening, music, gourmet cooking. Home and Office: Majestic Mgmt Corp 1202 S Green St Glasgow KY 42141-2014 E-mail: majestic-mgmt-corp@glasgow-ky.com.

DUXBURY, THOMAS CARL, planetary scientist; b. Fort Wayne, Ind., Dec. 8, 1941; s. John Lawrence and Justine Agnus (Jaron) D.; m. Natalia Duxbury, Nov. 8, 1990; children: Brett Harding, Katerina. BSEE, Purdue U., 1965, MSEE, 1966. Planetary scientist Jet Propulsion Lab., Pasadena, Calif., 1966—. Co-author: Television Investigations of Phobos, 1994. Recipient Sci. Achievement medal NASA, Washington, 1972, Space Mission Svc. medal Russian Lavochkin Assn., The Hague, The Netherlands, 1991, Burka award Inst. of Navigation, 1973, Achievement awards NASA, 1980, 82. Mem. Am. Geophysical Union, 1978—, Am. Astronomical Soc., 1980—, Russian Assn. for Space Sci. & Tech., 1993—. Achievements include prodn. of first map of another planet's moon, 1972; discovery of the Groove Network on Phobos (Mars moon), 1978; co-discovery of the Rings of Jupiter, 1979, of the Jupiter Lightning, 1979; selection by NASA/Soviet Union to participate in the Soviet PHOBOS Mission to Mars, 1988-89. Dept. Def. (DOD) Clementing Sci. Team for Lunar Exploration, 1992-94, Russian Mars 1994-96 Mission Sci. Team, 1992-97, project dir. NASA STARDUST Mission, 1996—, participating scientist Mars Global Surveyor Mission, 1996—, USAF/NASA Sci. Definition Team Deputy Leader, 1997-98, interdisciplinary scientist on European Space Agy. Mars Express Mission, 1999—. Office: Jet Propulsion Lab 4800 Oak Grove Dr # 264-379 Pasadena CA 91109-8099 E-mail: tduxbury@jpl.nasa.gov.

DUYCK, KATHLEEN MARIE, poet, musician, retired social worker; b. Portland, Oreg., July 21, 1933; d. Anthony Joseph Dwyer and Edna Elisabeth Hayes; m. Robert Duyck, Feb. 3, 1962; children: Mary Kay Boeyen, Robert Patrick, Anthony Joseph. BS, Oreg. State U., 1954; MSW, U. Wash., 1956. Cert. NASW, Oreg. Adoption worker Cath. Svcs., Portland, 1956-61, Cath. Welfare, San Antonio, 1962; musician Tucson Symphony, 1963-65; prin. cellist Phoenix (Ariz.) Coll. Orch., 1968-78, Scottsdale (Ariz.) Symphony, 1974-80; poet, 1993—. Author: (poetry cassettes) Visions, 1993 (Contemporary Series Poet 1993), Visions II, 1996 (Contemporary Series Poet 1996); author numerous poems. Rep. worker Maricopa County Reps., Phoenix, 1974; mem. Scottsdale Cultural Coun.; NASW bd. Cath. Charities Rep., Portland, 1959-61. Recipient

Golden Poet award World of Poetry, 1991, 92, Editor's Choice awards Nat. Libr. Poetry, 1993-2003, Sec. gift Phoenix Exec. Bd., 1976. Recognition award Archbishop Howard, 1961, 5-Yr. Kathleen Duyck award Cello Congress V, 1996, Internat. Poet of Merit award Internat. Soc. Poets, 2003. Mem. Internat. Poetry Hall Fame, Ariz. Cello Soc., Nat. Libr. Poetry, Internat. Soc. Poets, Phoenix Symphony Guild (exec. bd. 1970-80). Republican. Roman Catholic. Avocations: piano, photography, poetry, artistic collections, concerts. Home: 4545 E Palomino Rd Phoenix AZ 85018-1719

DUZEY, ROBERT LINDSEY, lawyer; b. Long Beach, Calif., Nov. 15, 1960; s. Donald Bohdan and Noreen (Rosen) D.; m. Susan Misook Yoon, Mar. 14, 1987; children: Dylan Grey, Zenon Drake. BA, U. Calif., Irvine, 1984; JD, Western State U., Fullerton, Calif., 1994. Bar: Calif. 1994., U.S. Dist. Ct. (so., ctrl., ea. and no. dists.) Calif., U.S. Ct. Appeals (9th cir.), U.S. Supreme Ct. Claims rep., mgr. Farmers Ins. Group, Santa Ana, Calif., 1985-89; risk mgr. Dollar Rent A Car, Irvine, 1989-93; law clk. Callahan, McCune & Willis, Tustin, Calif., 1994-96; atty. Madigan, Evans & Boyer, Costa Mesa, Calif., 1996-98, Law Offices of Robert Lindsey Duzey, Downey, Calif., 1998—. Recipient Am. Jurisprudence award. Mem. ATLA, ABA, Orange County Bar Assn., Fed. Bar Assn., Orange County Barristers, L.A. County Bar Assn., Delta Theta Phi. Avocations: bicycling, badminton, home decorating. Office: Law Offices Robert Lindsey Duzey 9900 Lakewood Blvd Ste 250 Downey CA 90240-4038 Fax: (562) 862-7721. E-mail: RDuzey@earthlink.net.

DVORA, SUSAN (SUSAN BERNSTEIN), non-profit organization professional; b. Chgo., May 17, 1938; d. Herman and Frances Dobkin Powell; m. Phillip Bernstein, Sept. 4, 1957 (div. July 1995); children: Kenneth, Robert, Michael. BA in Human Svcs., Northeastern Ill. U., 1978, postgrad., 1978-80. Real estate salesperson Martin-Marbry, Skokie, Ill., 1971—; exec. dir. Land of Lakes region B'nai Brith Women Internat., Chgo., 1978-83; founder, pres. Nat. Forum Women, Woodstock, Ill., 1980-83; dir. resource devel. Travelers & Immigrants Aid, Chgo., 1983-86; dir. Ctr. Ch.-State Studies, DePaul U. Sch. of Law, Chgo., 1986-90; cons. to non-profit orgns., Chgo., Md., Israel, and South Africa, 1986—. Owner, mgr. Siza Gallery, Evanston, Ill., 1989—92. Dir., prodr. (documentary) Legacy of Charlotte Perkins Gilman, 1996. Dir. alumni rels. Agrl. Edn. Found., Templeton, Calif., 1995-97; active Ill. Women's Agenda, Chgo., 1978-82; mem. Gov.'s Commn. on Status of Women, Ill., 1981; asst. to sculptor Andries Botha human rights work, South Africa, 1986—; sec., treas. Create Africa South. Named Citizen of Yr., Lerner-Life Newspapers, Skokie, 1979-80. Democrat. Jewish. Avocations: swimming, reading, travel. Address: PO Box 2311 Avila Beach CA 93424 E-mail: susandvora@aol.com.

DVORAK, ALLEN DALE, radiologist; b. Dodge, Nebr., Mar. 13, 1943; s. Rudolph Charles and Mildred B. (Misek) D.; m. Carol Ann Cockson, July 22, 1967; children: Kristin Ann, Andrea Marie, Ryan Allen. Grad., Creighton Coll. Arts and Scis., Omaha, Nebr., 1961-64; MD, Creighton Sch. Medicine, Omaha, Nebr., 1969. Intern Creighton Meml. St. Joseph Hosp., Omaha, 1969-70; resident Ind. U. Med. Ctr., Indpls., 1970-73, chief resident, 1972—73; asst. prof. radiology Creighton U. Sch. Medicine, Omaha, 1973-83; diagnostic radiologist Nebr.-Iowa Radiology Cons., Papillion, Nebr., 1983—, mng. ptnr., 1987—. Staff radiologist Alegent Midlands Cmty. Hosp., Papillion, 1983—, med. staff exec. bd., 1996—, pres. med. staff, 2000-02, med. staff exec. bd. Nebr. Bd. Health, 1995-2000; bd. dirs. Blue Cross Blue Shield Nebr., 2000—, bd. dirs. PRIME Therapeutics, Inc., 2002—. Author: (chpt.) Ultrasound, 1981; contbr. articles to profl. jours. Chmn. Midlands Area Health Adv. cuon., State of Nebr., 1982-86; trustee Duchesne Acad., 1988-91, Boys Town Nat. Coun. Friends, 1989—; bd. dirs. Safety and health Coun. of Greater Omaha, 1990-91; mem. Gov.'s Blue Ribbon Coalition to Study Health Care in Nebr., 1991-98; mem. Creighton Med. Sch. Alumni Adv. Bd., 1993—, pres., 1998-2000. Fellow Am. Coll. Radiology; mem. AMA (alt. del. 1992-98, del. 1999-2000), Nebr. Radiol. Soc. (pres. 1980-81), Omaha Midwest Clin. Soc. (pres. 1982), Nebr. Assn. Nuclear Physicians (pres. 1976-78, del. 1984—), Met. Omaha Med. Soc. (exec. com. 1980-2000, pres. 1990), Nebr. Med. Assn. (del. 1986—, pres. 1997-98), Regency Lake and Tennis Club (bd. dirs. 1981-85, chmn. bd. 1983-85), Happy Hollow Country Club. Avocations: tennis, boating. Home: 9733 Brentwood Rd Omaha NE 68114-4970 Office: Nebr-Iowa Radiology Cons Mng Ptnr 401 E Gold Coast Rd Ste 102 Papillion NE 68046-4194

DVORAK, JOSEF CERMIN, endocrinologist; b. Prague, Czechoslovakia, July 20, 1945; came to U.S., 1969; s. Josef and Milena (Frankova) Dvorak; m. Vera Cermin, Sept. 26, 1970; children: Marek, Andrea. MD, Charles U., 1969. Bd. cert. in internal medicine, endocrinology, and geriatric medicine. Intern Med. Coll. Va., 1970-71; resident U. Okla., 1971-74; rsch. fellow U. Pa., 1974-76; clin. asst. prof. medicine Georgetown U., 1977—. Cons. in endocrinology and metabolism, Arlington, Va. Office: 1635 N George Mason Dr Ste 350 Arlington VA 22205-3616

DVORAK, ROGER GRAN, health facility executive; b. St. Paul, Aug. 30, 1934; s. William Anthony and Evelyn Carolyn (Gran) D.; m. Gail Ann Peterson, Dec. 30, 1960; children: Karen, Mark. BBA, U. Minn., 1955, MHA, 1957. Asst. adminstr. Glenwood Hills Hosp., Mpls., 1958-61; asst. hosp. adminstrv. svcs. dir. Phila. Gen. Hosp., 1961-65; asst. dir. Presbyn. U. Pa. Med. Ctr., Phila., 1965-67, assoc. dir., 1967-72; adminstr. Symmes Hosp., Arlington, Mass., 1972-78; exec. dir. Lawrence Hosp., Bronxville, N.Y., 1978-86, pres., 1986-2000; ret., 2000. Mem. session Hitchcock Presbyn. Ch., Scarsdale, NY; chmn. adv. bd. The Counseling Ctr. of So. Westchester, 2000—02. Fellow Am. Coll. Healthcare Execs. Presbyterian. Avocations: painting, running, music. Home: 11 Rolling Ridge Rd White Plains NY 10605-4526

DVORETZKY, ISRAEL, dermatologist; b. Jerusalem, June 4, 1944; came to U.S., 1976; s. Itzak and Zippora (Levit) D.; m. Ayala Chenstochovsky, Oct. 11, 1970; 1 child, Shay. MD, Tel Aviv U., 1971. Intern Meir Kfar-Saba Hosp., Tel-Aviv, Israel, 1971-72; resident in dermatology Chaim Sheba Med. Ctr., Tel-Aviv, 1973-76; 2d resident in dermatology Yale New Haven Hosp., 1976-78; vis. assoc. At. Cancer Inst. NIH, Bethesda, Md., 1978-82; asst. clin. prof. dermatology Yale U. Sch. Medicine, New Haven, 1982-88, assoc. clin. prof., 1988-97, clin. prof. dermatology, 1997—. Pvt. practice Ansonia, Conn., 1982—. Author: Chemistry and Biology of Interferon, 1982; contbr. articles to profl. jours.; patentee in wart therapy. Fellow Am. Acad. Dermatology, Soc. Dermatol. Surgery, Soc. Pediat. Dermatology, Soc. Internat. Dermatology, Soc. Investigative Dermatology; mem. New Eng. Dermatol. Soc., Am. Contact Dermatitis Soc., Dermatology Found. Avocations: classical music, jazz, international music, reading, writing. Office: 22 Westfield Ave Ansonia CT 06401-1158

DWAN, DENNIS EDWIN, broadcast executive, photographer; b. St. Joseph, Mich., Oct. 6, 1958; s. Edwin O. and Elizabeth L. (Miller) D.; m. Tami L. Nixon, Oct. 13, 1984; children: Megan, Kaitlyn. BA, Mich. State U., 1981. Photographer Sta. WJIM-TV, Lansing, Mich., 1981-83, Sta. KAYU, Spokane, Wash., 1984-86, Sta. KREM-TV, Spokane, 1984-87; ops. mgr. Sta. KOMO TV, Seattle, 1987—. Mem. Nat. Press Photographers Assn. E-mail: DennisD@Komotv.com.

DWEIK, RAED A. physician, researcher, educator; b. Hebron, Jordan, Aug. 20, 1964; came to U.S., 1990; s. Abdul-Rahim a. and Fikrat (Salhi) D.; m. Erin Makley, Sept. 23, 1995; children: Zayn, Sana, Qyce. MB BS, U. Jordan, 1988. Diplomate Am. Bd. Internal Medicine, Am. Bd. Pulmonary Disease, Am. Bd. Critical Care Medicine. Resident Wright State U., Dayton, Ohio, 1990-93; fellow Cleve. Clinic Found., 1993-96; staff physician Cleve. Clinic, 1996—. Contbr. aticles to profl. jours. Fellow ACP, Am. Coll. Chest Physicians, Royal Coll. Physicians and Surgeons; mem. AMA, AAAS, Am. Thoracic Soc., Soc. Critical Care Medicine. mem. Am. Physiol. Soc., Am. Fed. for Med. Rsch.. Achievements include investigating regulation of nitric oxide production in the lungs by oxygen and the role of nitric oxide in lung physiology and pathology. Office: Cleve Clinic Found A-90 9500 Euclid Ave Cleveland OH 44195-0001

DWEK, CYRIL S. bank executive; b. Kobe, Japan, Nov. 9, 1936; s. Nessim S. and Alice (Stambouli) Dwek; children: Nevil, Alicia. BS, U. Pa., 1958. With Trade Devel. Bank, Geneva, 1962-65; with Republic Nat. Bank of N.Y., 1966-99, dir., 1967—, exec. v.p., 1973—, vice chmn., 1983-99; dir. Republic N.Y. Corp., 1974—, vice chmn., 1983-99; chmn. HSBC Republic Adv. Bd., N.Y.C., 2000—, Bd. dirs. HSBC Republic, Mexico, France, dir., vice chmn., Monaco. Mem.: Racing Club de France (Paris). Office: HSBC USA 2nd Flr 452 5th Ave New York NY 10018-2706

DWIGGINS, CLAUDIUS WILLIAM, JR., chemist; b. Amity, Ark., May 11, 1933; s. Claudius William and Lillian (Scott) D. BS, U. Ark., 1954, MS, 1956, PhD, 1958. With U.S. Dept. of Energy Bartlesville Tech. Ctr., Okla., 1958-83, chemist, 1958-60, project leader surface physics project, 1960-65, project leader petroleum composition rsch. project, 1965-80, supervisory rsch. chemist, thermodynamics divsn., 1980-83; sr. chemist Nat. Inst. Petroleum and Energy Rsch., 1983-84, cons., 1984—. Contbr. articles to profl. jours. Am. Oil Co. fellow, Coulter-Jones scholar. Mem. Am. Chem. Soc., N.Y. Acad. Scis., AAAS, Am. Crystallographic Assn., Am. Inst. Physics, Sigma Xi (sec. 1966-67), Alpha Chi Sigma, Delta Sigma Phi (treas. 1952). Home: 1211 S Keeler Ave Bartlesville OK 74003-4756

DWIGHT, DONALD RATHBUN, newspaper publisher, corporate communications executive; b. Holyoke, Mass., Mar. 26, 1931; s. William and Dorothy Elizabeth (Rathbun) D.; m. Susan Newton Russell, Aug. 9, 1952 (div. Aug. 1982); children: Dorothy Campbell, Laura Newton, Eleanor Addison, Arthur Ryan, Stuart Russell.; m. Nancy John Sinnott, Dec. 18, 1982; children: Christopher Sinnott, Helen Rathbun. AB, Princeton U., 1953; DSc (hon.), U. Mass., Lowell, 1974. Reporter, asst. to pub. Holyoke (Mass.) Transcript-Telegram, 1955-63, assoc. pub., 1966-69; assoc. commr. Mass. Dept. Pub. Works, Boston, 1963-66; commr. adminstrn. Commonwealth Mass., Boston, 1969-70, lt. gov., 1971-75; assoc. pub., v.p. Mpls. Star and Tribune, 1975-76, pub., sr. v.p., 1976-81; pres., pub. Star & Tribune Newspapers, Mpls., 1981-82; exec. v.p., dir. Cowles Media Co., 1981-82; chmn. Newspapers of New Eng., Inc., 1982-98, chmn. emeritus, 1999—; assoc. The Prospect Group, N.Y.C., 1983-88; chmn., mng. ptnr. Clark, Dwight & Assocs., Inc., 1988-90; pres. Dwight Ptnrs., Inc., Lyme, N.H., 1988—. V.p. Wood River Capital Corp., 1984—88; exec. v.p. Entretech Inc., 1988—90; trustee Eaton Vance Mut. Funds, Boston, 1986—2003, The Royce Funds, NYC, 1998—. Mem. Town Meeting, South Hadley, Mass., 1957-69; bd. dirs. Mpls. Soc. Fine Arts, 1976-82; trustee Twin Cities Pub. TV, 1976-82; chmn. bd. Guthrie Theater Found., 1978-81; v.p., dir. Nat. Corp. Theatre Fund, 1985-88; dir. Joint Action in Cmty. Svc., Washington, 1989-92, Lyme (N.H.) Found., Inc., 1994-98; trustee Trust Funds, Lyme, N.H., 1997-2000; mem. vestry St. Thomas Episcopal Ch., Hanover, N.H., 1998-2001. 1st lt. USMCR, 1953-55. Mem. Newspaper Assn. of Am., Princeton Club, Knickerbocker Club N.Y.C., Round Hill Club Greenwich, Hillsboro Club Fla. Republican. Episcopalian. Home and Office: 16 Clover Mill Ln Lyme NH 03768-3301 E-mail: dwight.partners@valley.net.

DWIGHT, HARVEY ALPHEUS, retired small business owner; b. Albany, N.Y., Apr. 21, 1928; s. Harvey Alpheus and Tessa Blanche (Gellert) D.; m. Helen Jean Fowler, Apr. 20, 1951 (dec. Sept. 1992); children: Diana, Lesley, Jessie, Harvey. Grad. H.S., Albany, N.Y., 1947; grad. in Mech. Engring., Rochester Inst. Tech., 1951. Lic. master plumber, N.Y. Owner Dwight Heating Supply Co., Rensselaer, N.Y., 1943-93; pvt. practice mech. cons., 1993—. With Army N.G., 1949-58. Mem. Albany Lic. Plumbers (v.p. 1985-86), Shriners. Avocations: hunting, fishing, flying, gardening.

DWIGHT, REGINALD KENNETH See JOHN, ELTON

DWINELL, ANN JONES, retired special education educator; b. Lowell, Mass., Oct. 28, 1934; d. George Hubert and Bridget Jones; m. Roland A. Dwinell, Dec. 23, 1956; children: Theresa, Joseph, Richard, John. BA, Framingham State Coll., 1972; MEd, Lesley Coll., 1974; PhD, Boston Coll., 1991. Cert. Eng. tchr., moderate spl. needs instr., Mass., adminstr., supt., spl. edn. adminstr., R.I. Spl. edn. tchr., adminstr. Marlborough (Mass.) Pub. Sch., 1972-78; core chairperson Malden (Mass.) Pub. Schs., 1978-80, spl. edn. specialist, 1980—2001. Contbr. articles to profl. jours. Mem. NEA, Mass. Tchrs. Assn. (rep. 1983-85, liaison 1987—), Phi Delta Kappa. Roman Catholic. Avocations: dancing, music, boating, reading.

DWON, LARRY, retired electrical engineer, educator, consultant; b. N.Y.C., May 2, 1913; s. Lucas and Mary (Woytowich) Dzwonczyk; m. Mary Jean Skala, Feb. 14, 1941; children: Lawrence A. Dwon, Roger R. Dzwonczyk. D in Electrical Engring., Cornell U., 1935; MBA, NYU, 1954. Registered profl. engr., N.Y., N.C. Engr. Diehl Mfg. Co., Elizabethport, N.J., 1935-37, Holophane Lighting, Inc., Newark, Ohio, 1937-38; mem. tech. staff Office Sci. and Rsch. Devel. Harvard Radio Rsch. Lab., Bell Telephone Labs., N.Y.C., 1942-45; engr. Am. Electric Power Svc. Corp., N.Y.C., 1938-45, sr. engr., 1945-52, operating sponsor (reporting to operating exec. v.p.), 1952-55, adminstrv. asst. to exec. v.p. ops., 1955-57, mgr. engring. manpower, 1957-78. Cons., cons. instr. N.C. State U., Raleigh, 1978—, N.C. State U. Coll. Engring., 1979—; self-employed cons., Apex, N.C., 1978—. Author: History of Eta Kappa Nu, 1976; contbr. over 200 tech. and profl. papers to many profl. jours. Recipient Plummer lecture medal, Am. Welding Soc., 1975, Disting. Svc. award, Power Engring. Edn. Com., 1977, Spl. Citation, Edison Elec. Inst., 1977, Disting. Svc. award, 1976, Cert. of Distinction, Assn. of Coll. Honor Socs., 2001, IEEE-USA Bd. recognition for SPAC founder and yrs. of leadership, 2002. Fellow IEEE (chmn. various coms. from 1969, U.S. Activities Bd. award 1982, Centennial medal 1984, Lit. Contbns. award 1988); mem. Am. Assn. Concerned Engrs. (bd. dirs.), Cornell Engring. Soc., Eta Kappa Nu (v.p. 1958, pres. 1959, emminent mem. 1984, Disting. Svc. award 1976). Avocations: classical music, writing, speaking. Home and Office: PO Box 216 West Kill NY 12492-0216 E-mail: LarryDwon@aol.com.

DWORETZKY, JOSEPH ANTHONY, lawyer, city official; b. N.Y.C., Sept. 17, 1951; s. Lawrence H. and Grace W. (Jackson) D.; m. Amy L. Banse; children: Lydia Light, Adam Eliot, Alex John, Anna Grace. BA with distinction, Purdue U., 1972; JD summa cum laude, Villanova U., 1977. Bar: Pa. 1977, D.C. 1978. Law clk. to judge U.S. Ct. Appeals 2d Cir., N.Y.C., 1977-78; assoc. Drinker Biddle & Reath, Phila., 1978-84, ptnr., 1984-93, mng. ptnr., 1992-93; chmn. corp. group law dept. City of Phila., 1993, city solicitor, 1994-96; shareholder Hangley Aronchick Segal & Pudlin, 1997—, exec. com., 1998—. Adj. prof. Rutgers U. Sch. Law, Camden, 1986-93. V.p., bd. dirs. Phila. Vol. Lawyers for Arts, 1981-84, Phila. Bd. Pensions, 1994-96, Phila. Indsl. Devel. Corp., 1994-96, Phila. Theatre Co., 1998-2000, William Penn Found., 2001—, Moore Coll. Art and Design, 2003—; sec.-treas., bd. dirs. Consumer Bankruptcy Assistance Project, 1992—, Acad. for Law, Pub. Adminstrn. and Criminal Justice, 1995-98; chair East Dist. Pa. Bankruptcy Conf., 2001. Fellow Am. Coll. Bankruptcy (regent); mem. ABA, Pa. Bar Assn., Phila. Bar Assn., Order of Coif, Phi Beta Kappa. Home: 7801 Huron St Philadelphia PA 19118-4218 E-mail: jad@hangley.com.

DWORETZKY, MURRAY, physician, educator; b. N.Y.C., Aug. 18, 1917; s. Samuel and Frieda (Newhoff) D.; m. Barbara Ratner, June 11, 1943; children: Thomas Alan, Joan Mara. BA, U. Pa., 1938; MD, SUNY, Coll. Medicine, N.Y.C., 1942; MS in Medicine, U. Minn., 1950. Diplomate: Am. Bd. Internal Medicine (examiner allergy subbd. 1967-71), Am. Bd. Allergy and Immunology (founding mem., dir. 1971-74), Pan Am. Med. Assn. Intern City Hosp., N.Y.C., 1942-43, asst. resident pathology, 1943, fellow in pathology, 1946-47; resident pathology U. Chgo., 1947-48; fellow in medicine Mayo Found., Rochester, Minn., 1948-50; practice medicine, specializing in internal medicine, allergy and clin. immunology N.Y.C., 1951—; asst. physician N.Y. Hosp., 1951, physician, 1951-56, asst. attending physician, 1956-61, assoc. attending, 1961-66, attending physician, 1966—, physician-in-charge Allergy Clinic, 1961-88; asst. in medicine Cornell U. Med. Coll., 1951-52, instr. medicine, 1952-56, clin. asst. prof., 1956-61, clin. asst. prof. pub. health, 1957-62, clin. assoc. prof. medicine, 1961-66, dir. tng. program div. allergy and immunology, 1961-88, clin. prof. medicine, 1966—; attending physician Manhattan Eye, Ear and Throat Hosp., 1953-62. Med. dir.-at-large Asthma-Allergy Found. Am., 1963-64, bd. dirs., 1964-78, mem. exec. com., 1964-77; founding mem. bd. dirs. Am. Bd. Allergy and Immunology, 1971-74; examiner sub-bd. allergy Am. Bd. Internal Medicine, 1967-71. Co-editor Allergy Archives, Jour. Allergy and Clin. Immunology, 2001—; contbr. articles to profl. jours. Served to capt., M.C. AUS, 1943-46. Recipient Frank L. Babbott M.D. Meml. award Alumni Assn. Coll. Med. SUNY, 1992. Fellow: ACP, N.Y. Acad. Medicine, Am. Acad. Allergy and Immunology (past pres. 1968, Disting. Svc. award 1989, Spl. Achievement award 2002); mem.: AMA (chmn. allergy sect. coun. 1974—77, residency rev. com. for allergy and immunology 1980—85), Am. Assn. Immunologists, Am. Fedn. Clin. Rsch., Harvey Soc., Soc. Exptl. Biology and Medicine, N.Y. Allergy Soc. (past pres., exec. com. 1958—94, tchg. day dedicated in his honor 1995), N.Y. County Med. Soc., Sigma Xi. Home: 21 E 87th St New York NY 10128-0506 Office: 115 E 61st St New York NY 10021-8183

DWORIN, MICKI (MAXINE DWORIN), automobile dealership executive; widowed; children: Judy, Diane. V.p. Dworin Chevrolet, Inc., East Harford, Conn., 1955-83, Dworin Auto Leasing. Pres. Eastern Auto Ins., Conn. Chevrolet Dealers Assn., Tarrytown Zone Dealer Coun., Atlantic Coast Region Dealer Coun., Boulevard, Inc. Sec. BBB, Hartford, Conn.; vol. coord. Vol. Broward, 1998-99, Children's Diagnostic and Treatment Ctr., 1996-98, Am. Cancer Soc., 1994-96, Kids in Distress, 1991-95; hon. trustee Hartford Coll. for Women; sec., bd. govs. Point of Am. Condominium; coord. Trinity Coll.; bd. dirs. Combined Health Appeals; chmn. King David Soc., 1995-96. Mem. Advt. Assn. Grtr. Hartford. Fax: 954-522-6770. E-mail: volbrow@safari.net.

DWORKIN, ANTHONY GARY, sociologist, educator; b. L.A., Nov. 22, 1942; s. Harry Arnold and Dorothy (Dropkin) D.; m. Rosalind Jean Barbagallo, Mar. 21, 1966; 1 child, Jason Peter. A.B., Occidental Coll., 1964; M.A., Northwestern U., 1966, Ph.D., 1970. From instr. to asst. prof. U. Mo., Columbia, 1968-73; prof. U. Houston, 1973—; chmn. dept. sociology, 1988-94, dir. Sociology Edn. Rsch. Group, 1997—; vis. fellow, The Australian Nat. U., 2001. Co-editor: The Blending of Races, 1972; author: When Teachers Give Up, 1985; Teacher Burnout in the Public Schools, 1986; co-author: The Minority Report, 1976, 82, 99; The Female Revolt, 1986, Giving Up in School, 1991. Recipient Bobbs-Merrill award, 1966; Woodrow Wilson fellow, 1964, 67; grantee NSF, NIMH, Hogg Found., Nat. Inst. Edn. Mem. Am. Sociol. Assn. (mem. coun. sociology of edn. sect.), S.W. Social Sci. Assn., S.W. Sociol. Assn. (v.p., pres. elect 1987-90), Midwest Sociol. Soc. (assoc. editor 1969-73), Soc. Study Social Problems, Soc. Psychol. Study Social Issues, Phi Beta Kappa. Avocations: astronomy; golf; computers. E-mail: gdworkin@mail.uh.edu. Office: U Houston Dept Sociology 450 Phillip G Hoffman Hall Houston TX 77204-3012

DWORKIN, GARY STEVEN, insurance company executive; b. N.Y.C., July 7, 1947; s. Irving Milton and Grace Wilhelmina (Korn) D.; student Hofstra U., 1965-68, NYU, 1969-71; m. Linda Lee Fuchs, Aug. 28, 1970; children: Robert Benjamin, Alexandra Tenille. Sales mgr. Chatham Blankets, N.Y.C., 1968-70; ins. agt. Travelers Ins. Co., Hartford, Conn., 1970-74; broker Dworkin Assos., Rochester, N.H., 1974-76; pres. Dworkin Assos., Inc. (DAI), Rochester, 1976—. Registered health underwriter; chartered life underwriter. Mem. Nat. Assn. Ins. Fin. Advisors, LIFE, Inc., Lifemark Ptnrs. Inc., Home Office Life Underwriters Assn., Southeastern N.H. NAIFA, New Eng. Forum, Nat. Assn. Health Underwriters, Am. Risk and Ins. Assn., Risk Appraisal Forum, Nat. Assn. Ind. Life Brokerage Agys. (charter), Soc. Fin. Svcs. Profls. Republican. Office: PO Box 2000 Rochester NH 03866-2000 E-mail: gsd@dworkin.com.

DWORKIN, HOWARD JERRY, nuclear medicine physician, educator; b. Bklyn., Oct. 29, 1932; s. Joseph Henry and Mollie M. (Hodas) Dworkin; m. Gina Gora; children: Rhonda Fran, Steven Irving, Paul J., Edward Joshua, Joseph Jacob. BSChemE, Worcester Poly. Inst., 1955; MD, Albany Med. Coll., 1959; MS in Radiation Biology, U. Mich., 1965. Diplomate Am. Bd. Internal Medicine, Am. Bd. Nuclear Medicine. Intern Albany Hosp., NY, 1959-60; resident Rochester (N.Y.) Gen. Hosp., 1960-62, U. Mich. Hosps., 1962-65, asst. coord. nuclear medicine unit, 1963-66, instr., 1965-66; asst. prof. medicine U. Toronto, Canada, 1966, assoc. prof., 1967; head dept. nuclear medicine Princess Margaret Hosp., Toronto, 1967; head nuclear medicine sect., radiology Nat. Naval Med. Ctr., Bethesda, Md., 1967-69; dir. sch. nuclear medicine tech. William Beaumont Hosp., Royal Oak, Mich., 1969—, chief dept. nuclear medicine, 1969—2002, dir. nuclear medicine resident tng. program, 1970—, chmn. CME com., 1993—. Clin. asst. prof. dept. medicine Wayne State U. Med. Sch., Detroit, 1970—; clin. assoc. prof. dept. radiology Mich. State U., East Lansing, 1976—; clin. prof. med. physics Ctr. Health Scis. Oakland U., Rochester, Mich., 1977—. Author (with N. Aspin and R. G. Baker): (book) Use of Isotopes in the Physics of Radiology, 1969, Part Two, Clinical Procedures in Radioisotope Laboratory Procedures, 1969; contbr. articles and chpts. to med. jours. and texts. With USN, 1967—69. Mem.: AMA, Mich. State Med. Soc. (chmn. continuing med. edn. com. 1999—), Am. Coll. Nuc. Physicians (sec. 1974—75, pres. 1978—79), Endocrine Soc., Am. Thyroid Assn., Soc. Nuc. Medicine (trustee 1973—81, v.p. 1982, pres. 1986—87), Am. Bd. Nuc. Medicine (treas. 1982—84), Accrediation Coun. Continuing Med. Edn. (chmn. 1998). Achievements include patents for in radioactive labeled protein material process and apparatus. Office: William Beaumont Hosp Dept Nuclear Medicine Royal Oak MI 48073 E-mail: hdworkin@beaumont.edu.

DWORKIN, MARTIN, microbiologist, educator; b. N.Y.C., Dec. 3, 1927; s. Hyman Bernard and Pauline (Herstein) D.; m. Nomi Rees Buda, Feb. 2, 1957; children: Jessica Sarah, Hanna Beth. BA, Ind. U., 1951; PhD (NSF predoctoral fellow), U. Tex., Austin, 1955. NIH research fellow U. Calif., Berkeley, 1955-57, vis. prof., summers 1958-60; asst. prof. microbiology Ind. U. Med. Sch., 1957-61, assoc. prof., 1961-62, U. Minn., 1962-69, dir. MD/PhD tng. program, 1990-97, prof., 1969—. Vis. prof. U. Wash., summer 1965, Stanford U., 1978-79; vis. scholar Oxford (Eng.) U., 1970-71; Found. for Microbiology lectr., 1973-74, 76-77, 81-82; Sackler scholar Tel Aviv U., 1992. Author: Developmental Biology of the Bacteria, 1985, Microbial Cell-Cell Interactions, 1991; contbr. numerous articles, revs. to profl. publs.; mem. editorial bd. Jour. Bacteriology, 1967-74, 86-88, Ann. Revs. Microbiology, 1975-79, The Prokaryotes, 2d edit., editor-in-chief 3d edit. Alt. del. Democratic Nat. Conv., 1968; mem. Minn. Dem. Farm Labor Central Com., 1969-70. Served with U.S. Army, 1946-48. Recipient Career Devel. award NIH, 1963-68, 68-73; John Simon Guggenheim fellow, 1978-79 Fellow Am. Acad. Arts and Scis. (chmn. Midwest ctr., v.p., 2002); mem. Am. Soc. Microbiology (vice chmn. div. gen. microbiology 1977-78, chmn. 1978-79, div. councillor 1980-82), Soc. Gen. Microbiology (Eng.). Home: 2123 Hoyt Ave W Saint Paul MN 55108-1314 Office: U Minn Dept Microbiology Minneapolis MN 55455

DWORKIN, MICHAEL LEONARD, lawyer; b. Bridgeport, Conn., Oct. 10, 1947; s. Samuel and Frances (Stein) D.; m. Christina Lyn Hildreth, Sept. 25, 1977; children: Jennifer Hildreth, Amanda Hildreth. BA in Govt. with honors, Clark U., 1969; JD with honors, George Washington U., 1973. Bar: D.C. 1973, Calif. 1975, U.S. Supreme Ct. 1978, U.S. Ct. Appeals (9th cir.) 1982, U.S. Claims Ct. 1983. Atty. FAA, Washington, L.A., 1973-77, United Airlines, San Francisco, 1977-81; pvt. practice San Francisco, 1981-95, San Mateo, Calif., 1995—. Instr. Embry Riddle Aeronautical U., San Francisco, 1980 81; dir. Poplar Ctr., San Mateo, Calif., 1979-86. Benefactor Hiller No. Calif. Aviation Mus. Jonas Clark scholar Clark U., 1966-69. Mem. ABA, Lawyer Pilots Bar Assn., Nat. Transp. Safety Bd. Bar Assn. (regional v.p. 1986-87, 90-99, chmn. rules com. 1985-99, pres. 2000-02), Aircraft Owners and Pilots Assn., Conn. Aviation Hist. Assn., Benefactor-Hiller Aviation Mus., San Mateo County Bar Assn., Bar Assn. San Francisco, Internat. Soc. Air Safety Investigators (bd. dirs. San Francisco regional chpt. 1988-89), State Bar Calif., D.C. Bar Assn., Regional Airline Assn., Commonwealth Club of Calif., New England Air Mus., Aero Club of No. Calif. Jewish. Office: 465 California St Ste 210 San Francisco CA 94104 E-mail: law@avialex.com.

DWORKIN, PAUL HOWARD, pediatrician; b. Paterson, N.J., Oct. 22, 1947; s. Bernard and Ruth (Steinhauer) D.; m. Sheila Ann Maher, Oct. 7, 1979; children: Molly Maher, Eamon Timothy. AB, Rutgers U., 1969; MD, Johns Hopkins U., 1973. Diplomate Am. Bd. Pediatrics. Pediatric registrar Paddington Green Children's Hosp./St. Mary's Med. Sch., London, 1976; resident in pediatrics Children's Hosp., Boston, 1973-75, fellow in ambulatory pediatrics, 1976-78; asst. prof. pediatrics W.Va. U. Sch. Medicine, Morgantown, 1978-81; prof./asso. chair pediats., head div. gen. peds., asst. dean U. Conn. Sch. Medicine, Farmington, 1981-98, prof./chair pediats., 1998—. Dir., chair pediats. St. Francis Hosp. and Med. Ctr., Hartford, Conn., 1992—; physician-in-chief Conn. Children's Med. Ctr., Hartford, 1998—. Author: Learning and Behavior Problems of Schoolchildren, 1985; editor: Pediatrics: National Medical Series for Independent Study, 1987, 4th edit., 2000; editor Jour. Devel. & Behavioral Pediats., 1996-2002; editl. bd. Pediats., 1991-98, Ambulatory Child Health, Current Pediatrics, 1991—. Vol. Salvation Army Shelter Pediat. Clinic,

Hartford, 1991—. Fellow Am. Acad. Pediats. (chair com. on scientific mtgs. 1994-98); mem. Ambulatory Pediat. Assn., Soc. Devel. and Behavioral Pediats. Office: Conn Children's Med Ctr 282 Washington St Hartford CT 06106-3322

DWORKIN, SAMUEL FRANKLIN, dentist, psychologist; b. Freedom, Ohio, Sept. 26, 1933; s. Louis and Minnie (Katz) D.; m. Mona Mae Moskowitz, Dec. 23, 1956; children: Adam, Ted. BS, CCNY, 1954; D.D.S., NYU, 1958, PhD, 1969. Practice dentistry, N.Y.C., 1959—74; Nat. Inst. Dental Research spl. fellow, 1965-69; asst. prof. dept. preventive dentistry and community health NYU Coll. Dentistry, 1969-70; assoc. prof. div. preventive dentistry, dir. office of edn. and behavioral research Columbia U. Sch. Dental and Oral Surgery, 1970-74; prof. oral surgery, assoc. dean acad. affairs U. Wash. Sch. Dentistry, Seattle, 1974-77; prof. psychiatry and behavioral sci. U. Wash. Sch. Medicine, 1977—; prof. oral medicine, 1977—; dir. psychophysiologic liaison clinic dept. psychiatry and behavioral sci. U. Wash. Sch. Medicine, 1978-89, Washington dental svc. disting. prof. dentistry, 1999—. Clin. dir. Regional Clin. Dental Rsch. Ctr., U. Wash., 1992-99; cons. NIH, mem. behavioral medicine study sect., 1985-90, mem. rsch. adv. coun. 1999—; cons. ADA, Am. Dental Hygiene Assn. Cons. editor Jour. Dental Edn., 1976—, Jour. Dental Rsch., 1976—, Pain, 1984—, Clin. Jour. Pain, 1989—, Psychosomatic Medicine, 1989—; guest editor Jour. Preventive Dentistry, 1977, Jour. ADA, Pain; contbr. articles to profl. jours. Co-founder, pres. League of Parents of Hearing Impaired Infants, N.Y.C., 1966-70; v.p. N.Y. State Parents of Hearing Impaired Children, 1970-74; adv. coun. Lexington Sch. of Deaf, N.Y.C., 1970-74; bd. dirs. Seattle Pro-Musica, 1977, v.p., 1978-81, treas., 1991-98, pres. 1995-98, pres. emeritus, 1999. Grantee, NIH, 1979—. Fellow Internat. Assn. for Study of Pain, Am. Pain Soc.; mem. ADA (coun. dental health edn., coun. nat. bd. exams. 1974-79), AAAS, APA, Am. Assn. Dental Schs., Behavioral Scientists in Dental Rsch. (pres. 1975, 90), Internat. Assn. for Dental Rsch. (Disting. Scientist award behavior and health svcs. rsch., Dental Rsch. Giddon award), Internat. Soc. Clin. and Exptl. Hypnosis, Behavioral Scis. Group (Disting. Rschr. award), Behavioral and Health Svcs. Rsch. Group (pres. 1990-91). Office: U Wash Dept Psychiatry Seattle WA 98195-0001 E-mail: dworkin@u.washington.edu.

DWORNIK, FRANCES PIERSON, lawyer; b. Newport News, Va., Nov. 5, 1956; d. John Clayton and Frances Ann Pierson; m. David Dwornik, Mar. 9, 1991. BA with distinction, U. Va., 1979; JD, Coll. William and Mary, 1985. Bar: Va. 1985, U.S. Dist. Ct. (ea. dist.) Va. 1986. Assoc. Odin, Feldman and Pittleman, P.C., Fairfax, Va., 1985-89, ptnr., 1989—. Symposium editor, exec. bd.: William and Mary Law Review, 1985. Mem. ABA (regional III trial competition organizing com. 1988, 90), Va. Bar Assn. (labor and employment sect.), No. Va. Young Lawyers Assn. (v.p. 1986-87, pres. 1987-88), Am. Soc. for Human Resource Mgmt., Am. Soc. Assn. Execs. Office: Odin Feldman and Pittleman 9302 Lee Hwy Ste 1100 Fairfax VA 22031-1215

DWORNIK, JULIAN JONATHAN, anatomist, researcher; b. Colonsay, Saskatchewan, Can., Mar. 11, 1938; s. Marie Jay and Peter Klamut(Stepfather); m. Diane Joan St. Goddard Dwornik; 1 child, Pamela M.J. BA in Zoology, Andrew's U.; MSc, U. Man., 1964, PhD, 1969. From instr. to asst. prof. U. Louisville, 1967—70; prof. Coll. of Med. U. So. Fla., Tampa, Fla., 1970—, assoc. dean admissions Coll. of Med., 1972—88. Mem.: Am. Assn. Clin. Anatomists. Protestant. Avocations: radio controlled boating, swimming, piano. Office: Univ So Fla Coll Med Dept Anat MDC Box 6 12901 Bruce B Downs Blvd Tampa FL 33612-4799

DWORSKI, SYLVIA, modern languages educator; b. New Haven, Conn., Apr. 10, 1915; d. Louis and Ida (Miller) D. BA with highest honors, Conn. Coll. for Women, 1935; MA with distinction, Yale U., 1937, PhD, 1941; cert., U. Paris, 1939. Instr. Spanish New Haven State Tchrs. Evening Coll., 1941-44; tchr. French, Spanish and English East Haven (Conn.) H.S., 1942-44; instr. Romance langs. Sweet Briar (Va.) Coll., 1944-46, St. Helena Ext. Coll. William and Mary, Norfolk, Va., 1946-48; asst. prof. French Wilkes Coll., Wilkes-Barre, Pa., 1948-54, assoc. prof. modern langs., 1954-63, St. Mary's Coll., Notre Dame, Ind., 1963-64, co-chmn. dept. modern langs., 1963-65, prof. modern langs., 1964-80, chmn. dept. French, 1965-67, prof. emeritus modern langs., 1980—. Vis. faculty mem. grad. sch. langs. U. Notre Dame, summers 1967, 68. Grantee Spanish Lang. Inst. U. Mex., summer 1944; vis. fellow Romance langs. Yale U., New Haven, 1941-42, French Traveling fellow Yale U., 1938-39; Winthrop scholar Conn. Coll., 1934; Sylvia Dworski Endowed Scholarship Fund established in honor, Wilkes U., Wilkes-Barre, Pa., 2001. Mem. AAUP (St. Mary's Coll. chpt. founding mem. 1965, sec.-treas. 1965-66, 78-79, exec. bd. 1966-67, 79-80), Am. Assn. Tchrs. French (hon. life mem.), Gray Panthers (exec. bd. Montgomery County chpt. 1988-96), Phi Beta Kappa. Jewish. Avocations: reading, music, opera, theatre, movies. Home: 70 Byron Pl New Haven CT 06515-2406

DWORSKY, CLARA WEINER, lawyer, former merchandise brokerage executive; b. N.Y.C., Apr. 28, 1918; d. Charles and Rebecca (Becker) Weiner; m. Bernard Ezra Dworsky, Jan. 2, 1944; 1 child, Barbara G. Goodman. BS, St. John's U., N.Y.C., 1937, LLB, 1939, JD, 1968. Bar: N.Y. 1939, U.S. Dist. Ct. (ea. dist.) N.Y. 1942, U.S. Dist. Ct. (so. dist.) Tex. 1993, U.S. Ct. Appeals (9th cir.) 1994, U.S. Ct. Appeals (5th cir.) 1995. Pvt. practice, N.Y.C., 1939-51; assoc. Bessie Farberman, N.Y.C., 1942; clk., sec. U.S. Armed Forces, Camp Carson, Colo., Camp Claiborne, La., 1944-45; abstractor, dir. Realty Title, Rockville, Md., 1954-55; v.p. Kelley & Dworsky Inc., Houston, 1960—. Appeals agt. Gasoline Rationing Apls. Bd., N.Y.C., 1942; bd. dirs. Southlan Sales Assocs., Houston. Vol. ARC, N.Y.C.; vice chmn. War Bond pledge drive, Bklyn.; vol. Houston Legal Found., 1972-73; pres. Women's Aux. Washington Hebrew Acad., 1958-60, v.p. bd. trustees, 1959-60; co-founder, v.p. S. Tex. Hebrew Acad. (now Hebrew Acad.), Houston, 1970-75, hon. pres. women's divsn., 1973. Recipient Cert. award Treas. of U.S., 1943; Commendation Office of Chief Magistrate of City N.Y., 1948; Pietas medal St. Johns U., 1985. Mem.: ABA (chmn. social security com., sr. lawyers divsn. 1989—93, mem. sr. lawyers divsn. coun. 1989—95, chairsubcom. 1993—95, chmn. social security com., sr. lawyers divsn. 1995—, mem. editl. bd. sr. lawyers divsn. pub. Experience), Nat. Assn. Women Lawyers (chmn. organizer Juvenile Delinquency Clinic N.Y. 1948—51), Houston Bar Assn. (sec. social security sect. 1995—96), Fed. Bar Assn. (vice chair programs, sr. lawyers divsn. 1994—96, dep. chair 1996—97, chmn. 1997—98, chair sr. lawyers com. south Tex. chpt. bd. 1998—, chmn. soc. sec. com., sen. lawyers divsn., co-editor sr. citizens handbook 2002), N.Y. State Bar Assn., St. Johns U. Alumni Assn. (coord. Houston chpt. 1983—, pres. 1986), Amit Women Club, Delphians Past Pres.'s Club, Hadassah. Jewish. Home: 9726 Cliffwood Dr Houston TX 77096-4406

DWORSKY, DANIEL LEONARD, architect, educator; b. Mpls., Oct. 4, 1927; s. Lewis and Ida (Fineberg) D.; m. Sylvia Ann Taylor, Aug. 10, 1957; children: Douglas, Laurie, Nancy. B.Arch., U. Mich., 1950. Practice architecture as Dworsky Assocs., L.A., 1953-2000, Cannon Dworsky, L.A., 2000—; design critic, lectr. arch. U. So. Calif., U. Mich., UCLA, 1983-84. Chmn. archtl. rev. panel Fed. Res. Bank. Recipient Design citation Progressive Arch. mag. 1967, Gov. Calif. award 1966, 3 Los Angeles Grand Prix awards So. Calif. AIA and City of Los Angeles 1967; prin. works include Angelus Plaza Elderly Housing, Los Angeles, 1981, Ontario (Calif.) City Hall, 1980, CBS Exec. Office Bldg, North Hollywood, Calif., 1970, U. Calif. at Los Angeles Stadium, 1969, Fed. Res. Bank Bldg., Los Angeles, 1987, U. Mich. Crisler Arena at Ann Arbor, 1966, Dominguez Hills State U. Theatre, 1977, Ventura County Govt. Center, 1979, Northrop Electronics Hdqrs., Los Angeles, 1983, Hewlett-Packard Region Office, North Hollywood, 1984, Los Angeles County Mcpl. Cts. Bldg., 1985, Tom Bradley Internat. Terminal L.A. Airport, 1984, City Tower, City Orange Calif., 1988, Fed. Office Bldg., Long Beach, Calif., 1992, Las Vegas Fed. Cts. Bldg., 2000. Fellow AIA (more than 100 awards including 24 awards Calif. chpts., Nat. Honor award 1974, 68-69, Firm award Calif. chpt. 1985, L.A. Gold Medal award 1994). Home: 9225 Nightingale Dr Los Angeles CA 90069-1117 Office: Cannon Design 1901 Ave of States Ste 175 Los Angeles CA 90067 E-mail: dan@cannondesign.com.

DWYER, CORNELIUS J., JR., lawyer; b. New Rochelle, N.Y., Sept. 3, 1943; s. Cornelius John and Mary Cecelia (McDonough) D.; m. June Forsythe Sonnekalb, Sept. 14, 1968; children: Cornelius William, Colin Micheal. BA, Yale U., 1965; LLB, Harvard U., 1968. Bar: N.Y. 1968, U.S. Dist. Ct. N.Y. 1969. Assoc. Shearman & Sterling, N.Y.C., 1968-76, ptnr., 1976—. Democrat. Roman Catholic. Office: Shearman & Sterling 599 Lexington Ave Fl C2 New York NY 10022-6069 E-mail: cdwyer@sharman.com.

DWYER, DARRELL JAMES, finance company executive; b. Vermillion, S.D., Nov. 27, 1946; s. Michael Leroy and Faye Awilda (Hansen) Dwyer; m. Helen K. Howard, 1989; 1 child, Sean Patrick. BS, Minn. State U., 1977; MBA, U. Calif., Berkeley, 1978. CPA, cert. mgmt. acct., internal auditor; data processor. Acct. Touche Ross & Co., Salem, Oreg., 1978-79; cons. Arthur, Persons Co., Salem, 1980-82; v.p. fin. Evergreen Internat. Airlines Inc, McMinnville, Oreg., 1982-87; CFO Erickson Group Ltd., Medford, Oreg., 1987-89; sr. v.p., corp. sec. Evergreen Internat. Aviation, Inc., McMinnville, 1989-90; pres., CEO Dwyer Co., Rocklin, Calif., 1990—. Recipient award of merit, Evergreen Internat. Aviation, McMinnville, 1984; Calif. State scholar. Mem.: Inst. Cert. Mgmt. Accts., Calif. Soc. CPA. Republican. Episcopalian. Avocations: skiing, tennis, travel. Office: Dwyer Co 3111 Sunset Blvd Rocklin CA 95677 E-mail: djdwyer@pacbell.net.

DWYER, DENNIS D. information technology executive; b. Oak Park, Ill., July 19, 1943; s. John J. and Jessie M. Dwyer; m. Carolyn R. Schultz, Apr. 29, 1967; children: David, Julianne. Various positions Harris Bank, Chgo., 1967-83, mgr. info. tech. planning, 1983-86, v.p. tech. facilitation, 1986—. Resolutions chmn. Cooperating Users of Burroughs Equipment, Detroit, 1978-82; cons. Unisys mainframe computers. Pres. Hunting Ridge Homeowners Assn., 1983-85; mem. Palatine Plan Commn., 1984—, chmn., 1989—. Recipient Tom Grier award for Excellence Unisys Users Group, 1988. Home: 1032 Raven Ln Palatine IL 60067-6649 Office: Harris Bank PO Box 755 Chicago IL 60690-0755 E-mail: dennis.dwyer@harrisbank.com., dennis-carolyn@ravenlane.com.

DWYER, DENNIS MICHAEL, microbiologist; b. Passaic, N.J., Feb. 26, 1945; s. Alexander James and Julie (Sinkovitz) D.; m. Nancy Kinerson, Dec. 28, 1969; children: Jeffrey Scott, Matthew James. BA in Biology, Montclair State Coll., 1967; MS in Zoology, U. Mass., 1970, PhD in Zoology, 1971. Postdoctoral fellow Rockefeller U., N.Y.C., 1971-73, asst. prof., 1973-76, assoc. prof., 1976-81; rsch. microbiologist lab. parasitic diseases Nat. Inst. Allergy and Infectious Diseases, NIH, Bethesda, Md., 1976-80, supr. microbiology, 1980-94, head cell Biology sect. Lab. of Parastitic Disease, 1994—. Adj. assoc. prof. U. Mass., Amherst, 1978— ; cons. WHO, Geneva, 1982— ; sci. reviewer jours., books, grants, 1980— . Editl. bd. Jour. Protozoology, 1978-83, Infection and Immunity, 1981-88, Exptl. Parasitology, 1984—, Jour. Eukaryotic Microbiology, 1993—, Tropical Medicine Abstracts, 1990—; contbr. numerous articles, chpts. to profl. publs., 1970—. Active PTA, Rockville, Md., 1980-98; leader Cub Scouts, Rockville, 1984-91, Boy Scouts Am., 1987—. Recipient Alumni Citation award Montclair State Coll., 1983, Dir.'s award NIH, 1987. Mem. AAAS, Protozoologists, Am. Soc. Parasitologists, (Henry Baldwin Ward medal 1980), Am. Soc. Cell Biologists, Am. Soc. Tropical Medicine and Hygiene, N.Y. Acad. Scis., Phi Kappa Phi. Democrat. Methodist. Avocations: down hill skiing, camping, fishing, hiking, jogging. Home: 13416 Bartlett St Rockville MD 20853-2938 Office: Nat Inst Allergy and Infectious Diseases Lab Parasitic Diseases Bldg 4 Rm 126nih Bethesda MD 20892-0001

DWYER, DIANE MARIE, lawyer, judge; b. Amityville, N.Y., Nov. 5, 1958; d. Joseph R. and Geraldine (Burchell) D. BA, Molloy Coll., 1980; JD, St. John's U., 1983. Bar: N.Y. 1983, U.S. Supreme Ct. 1991. Assoc. Deutsch & Schneider, Bklyn., 1983—84; pvt. law practice Wantagh, NY, 1984—91; dist. ct. judge, 1999; hearing examiner Nassau County Family Ct., 2000—. Dep. county atty. Nassau County, 1984—91; advisor cmty. legal instrn. program St. John's U., Jamaica, NY, 1984. Mem. ABA, N.Y. State Bar Assn., Nassau County Bar Assn. (com. mem. 1987—), Nassau County Women's Bar Assn. (bd. dirs. 1993—, pres. 2000-01), Molloy Coll. Alumni Assn. (v.p. 1986-89, pres. 1989-92, admissions recruiter 1988-94). Office: 1200 Old Country Rd Westbury NY 11590-5630

DWYER, DORIS DAWN, adult education educator; b. Cin., Feb. 19, 1948; d. James Daniel and Marjorie Elaine (Fisher) D. ABin Social Sci., Ea. Ky. U., 1970, MA in History, 1971; PhD, Miami U., Oxford, Ohio, 1979. Instr. social sci. Ea. Ky. U., Richmond, 1971-74; doctoral fellow Miami U., Oxford, 1974-78; asst. prof. social sci. Coll. Ganado (Ariz.), 1979-80; prof. history Western Nev. C.C., Fallon, 1980—. Bd. dirs. Nev. Humanities Com., Reno, 1983-89, mem. chautauqua performance, Nev. and Calif., 1994—. Author: A Century of City-Building, 1983; editl. adv. bd. U. Nev. Press, 1997-2000. Mem. Western History Assn., Nev. Hist. Soc., Nev. Women's History Project; mem. women's archives bd. Reno Libr., U. Nev., 1995—; vice-chmn. bd. dirs. Nev. State Mus. and History, Carson City, 1994-99; bd. dirs. Nev. Hist. Preservation, Carson City, 1990-94; chmn. bd. trustees Churchill County Libr., Fallon, Nev., 1989-96. Recipient Gov.'s Humanities award, 2000; named Cmty. Woman of the Yr. Fallon Bus. and Profl. Women, 1992. Democrat. Roman Catholic. Avocations: travel, walking. Office: Western Nev C C 160 Campus Way Fallon NV 89406-2661 E-mail: ddwyer@wncc.edu.

DWYER, GERALD PAUL, JR., economist, bank executive; b. Pittsfield, Mass., July 9, 1947; s. Gerald Paul and Mary Frances (Weir) Dwyer; m. Katherine Marie Lepiane, Jan. 15, 1966; children: Tamara K., Gerald P. III, Angela M., Michael J. L., Terence F. BBA, U. Wash., 1969; MA in Econs., U. Tenn., 1973; PhD in Econs., U. Chgo., 1979. Economist Fed. Res. Bank, St. Louis, 1972-74, Chgo., 1976-77, asst. v.p. Atlanta, 1997-98, v.p., 1998—; asst. prof. Tex. A&M U., College Station, 1977-81, Emory U., Atlanta, 1981-84, sr. rsch. assoc. Law and Econ. Ctr., 1982-84; assoc. prof. U. Houston, 1984-89; prof. Clemson (S.C.) U., 1989-99, acting head dept. econ., 1992-93. Cons. Arthur Bros., Corpus Christi, Tex., 1980—81, FTC, Washington, 1983—84, Amerigas, Houston, 1985, We. Container Corp., 1987, Metrica, Inc., Bryan, Tex., 1989—93; vis. scholar Fed. Res. Bank, Atlanta, 1982—84, St. Louis, 1987—89, Atlanta, 1994—97, Mpls., 1995; vis. fin. economist Commodity Futures Trading Commn., Washington, 1990; vis. faculty Ga. State U., 1997, U. Ga., 1999—2000, 2003—, Univ. Rome, 2000—. Contbr. articles to profl. jours. Fellow, Earhart Found., 1975—77; Weaver fellow, Intercollegiate Studies Inst., 1974—75, Rsch. grantee, Earhart Found., NSF. Mem.: Econometric Soc., Am. Stats. Assn., Am. Fin. Assn., Am. Econ. Assn., Phi Kappa Phi, Beta Gamma Sigma. Avocation: sailing.

DWYER, JIM, reporter, columnist; b. N.Y.C., Mar. 4, 1957; s. Philip and Mary (Molloy) Dwyer; m. Catherine Muir; 2 children. BS, Fordham Coll., 1979; MS, Columbia U., 1980. Reporter Hudson Dispatch, Union City, NJ, 1980—82, Elizabeth (N.J.) Jour., 1982, Bergen Record, Hackensack, NJ, 1983—84; reporter, columnist N.Y. Newsday, N.Y.C., 1984—95; columnist N.Y. Daily News, 1995—. Author (with others): (songs) (book) Journalism Collection of Best Newspaper Writing, 1991, Two Seconds Under the World, 1994, Actual Innocence, 2000. Recipient Outstanding Column award, Nat. Headliners Soc., 1987, 1988, Meyer Berger prize, Columbia U., 1988, Writing award for commentary, Am. Soc. Newspaper Editors, 1991, Pulitzer Prize for commentary, 1995. Mem.: Graphic Comms. Internat. Union. Roman Catholic. Office: Daily News 450 W 33rd St Fl 3 New York NY 10001-2681

DWYER, JOHN CHARLES, lawyer; b. San Francisco, Mar. 26, 1962; s. Richard Thomas and Dorothy (Blake) D. BS, U. Calif., Berkeley, 1984; JD, Harvard U., 1988. Bar: Calif. 1988, U.S. Dist. Ct. (no. dist.) Calif. 1988, U.S. Ct. Appeals (9th cir.) 1988, U.S. Supreme Ct. 1996. Assoc. Jackson, Tufts, Cole & Black, San Francisco, 1989-93; dep. assoc. atty. gen. U.S. Dept. Justice, Washington, 1993-96, acting assoc. atty. gen., 1997; ptnr. Cooley Godward LLP, Palo Alto, Calif., 1998—. Democrat. Roman Catholic. Office: Cooley Godward LLP 3000 El Camino Real Palo Alto CA 94306

DWYER, JOHN JAMES, mechanical engineer; b. Jersey City, Mar. 1, 1928; s. John J. and Margaret (Casey) D.; m. Joan Catherine Hyde, June 26, 1954 (div. Jan. 1984); children: William J., Kathleen M., Barbara A.; m. JoAnna Mary Kuta, Feb. 4, 1989 (dec. July 5, 1994). BS, N.J. Inst. Tech., 1957; MBA, Lehigh U., 1972. Registered profl. engr., Pa., Tex. Machinery engr. Air Products and Chems., Inc., Allentown, Pa., 1957-63, mgr. machinery engring., 1963-83; cons. Houston, 1983-97. Sgt. U.S. Army, 1950-52, Korea. Mem. ASME (mem. performance test code for centrifugal compressors com. 1975-98), NSPE, Tex. Soc. Profl. Engrs. Roman Catholic. Home: 5745 Springhaven Ln Macungie PA 18062 E-mail: johndwyer@juno.com.

DWYER, JOHN M. mathematician, statistician, computer scientist; b. Ann Arbor, Mich., June 8, 1937; s. Paul Sumner and Florence Baylis (Brown) D.; children: Anne Louise, Laura Beth. BA, U. Mich., 1959, MS, 1965; PhD, Tex A&M U., 1971. Asst. prof. stats. U. Wyo., Laramie, 1962-66; asst. prof. math. U. Detroit, 1969-73, assoc. prof. math., 1974—, chair, 1974-77, interim chair, 1989-91. Vis. assoc. prof. dept. mgmt. and mktg. Northern Mich. U., Marquette, 1983-84; dir. rsch. Detroit Inst. Abuse Rsch. and Tng., 1973-74; cons. Detroit Tax Assessor's Office, 1971; expert witness Focus: HOPE, Detroit, 1981-86; panelist "Ask the Professor" radio show U. Detroit, 1977-83. Mem.: AAAS, Computer Profls. for Social Responsibility (co-founder Mich. chpt. 1997, chair 1998—2001, bd. dirs. 2001—, treas. 2002), Assn. Computing Machinery, Union of Concerned Scientists, Math. Assn. Am. Office: U Detroit Mercy Dept Math and Computer Sci P O Box 19900 Detroit MI 48219-0900 E-mail: dwyerjm@udmercy.edu.

DWYER, JOHN THOMAS, JR., educator, researcher; b. Memphis, June 4, 1953; s. John Thomas and Leona (DeMere) D.; children: John T. III, Caryn Desiree. AA, Shelby State C.C., 1975; diploma, Memphis Police Acad., 1975; BA, U. Memphis, 1983. Officer Memphis Police Dept., 1975-94, sr. rschr., 1986-91, divsn. coord., 1992-94; substitute tchr. Fayette County (Tenn.) Schs., 1996—. Cons. S.Y. Wilson & Co., Arlington, Tenn., 1994-97; rschr. initiator crisis intervention unit. Organizer 1st gun buyback program, 1993. Recipient Lifesaving medal City of Memphis, 1983, Medal of Merit, City of Memphis, 1988, Patriotism medal Nat. Assn. Chiefs of Police, 1993. Mem. Gen. Soc. Colonial Wars, Children of the Confederacy, Memphis Police Assn. Democrat. Roman Catholic. Home: 3605 Ivy Rd Eads TN 38028-3223

DWYER, MARY JO, medical librarian; b. Chgo., Mar. 19, 1941; d. William Michael and Helen Lucille (Ramsden) D.; m. James Thomas Miller, Aug. 19, 1977. BA, St Xavier Coll., 1963; MALS, Rosary Coll., 1976. Papal vol. Latin Am. Colegio Monte María, Guatemala City, 1964-68; rsch. assoc. AMA, Chgo., 1968-76, reference libr., 1976-82, assoc. dir. reference, 1982-84; circuit libr. Victoria (Tex.) Coll., U. Houston, 1985-89, U. Tex. Health Sci. Ctr., San Antonio, 1989—, sr. circuit libr., 1995—. Bd. dirs. Nat. Network Librs. of Medicine/South Ctrl. Region, Houston, 1991-92. Presenter, producer (video) Library Video Magazine, 1989. Recipient DeBakey Libr. Svcs. Outreach award Friends, Nat. Libr. of Medicine, Washington, 1993. Mem. Am. Libr. Assn., Med. Libr. Assn. (hosp. librs. sect. govt. rels. com., s. ctrl. chpt. govt. rels. com.), Democrat. Roman Catholic. Office: U Tex Health Sci Ctr 7703 Floyd Curl Dr San Antonio TX 78284-6200

DWYRE, WILLIAM PATRICK, journalist, public speaker; b. Sheboygan, Wis., Apr. 7, 1944; s. George Leo and Mary Veronica (O'Brien) D.; m. Jill Ethlyn Jarvis, July 30, 1966; children— Amy, Patrick BA, U. Notre Dame, Ind. Sports copy editor Des Moines Register, 1966-68; sports writer, asst. sports editor, sports editor Milw. Jour., 1968-81; asst. sports editor, sports editor Los Angeles Times, 1981—. Columnist Referee Mag., 1977-02; voting mem., bd. dirs. Amateur Athletic Found. Nat. Sports Hall of Fame, 1981—. Bd. dirs. Honda-Brockerick Cup Women's Collegiate Athlete of Yr.; bd. dirs. Casa Colina Hosp. Rehab., Pomona. Named Sportswriter of Yr., Wis. Nat. Sportscasters and Sportswriters Assn., 1980; Nat. Editor of Yr., Nat. Press Found., 1985; recipient award for Sustained Excellence by Individual, L.A. Times, 1985, Red Smith award AP sports Editors, 1996. Mem. Nat. Sportscasters and Sportswriters Assn. (bd. dirs., Powerade Sport Story of Yr. award 1999), Assoc. Press Sports Editors (pres. 1989), Nat. Baseball, Pro Basketball and Football Writers Assn. Clubs: Milw. Pen and Mike. Avocation: tennis. Office: Los Angeles Times Times Mirror Sq Los Angeles CA 90012 E-mail: bill.dwyre@latimes.com.

DY, DEANA LIM, allergist; b. Manila, Philippines, 1947; MD, U. Santo Tomas, 1972. Diplomate Am. Bd. Allergy and Immunology. Intern U. Santo Tomas Hosp., Manila, Philippines, 1972-73; resident in pediats. Children's Hosp. Mich., Detroit, 1974-76; fellow in pediat. hematology/oncology William Beaumont Hosp., Royal Oak, Mich., 1976-78; fellow in allergy & immunology Grant Hosp., Chgo., 1980-82; staff Columbia Grant Hosp., Chgo., 1982—. Mem. staff Centegra Meml. Med. Ctr., Woodstock, Ill., 1986—, No. Ill. Med. Ctr., McHenry, Ill., 1986—. Mem. AMA, Am. Acad. Allergy, Asthma & Immunology, ISACI, Ill. State Med. Soc., Chgo. Med. Soc. Office: Allerclinic Ltd 25 S Virginia St Ste 203 Crystal Lake IL 60014-5800

DYAKONOV, ALEXANDER J. physical chemist, researcher; b. Ivanovo, Russia, June 30, 1953; came to U.S., 1993; s. July B. Dyakonov and Tatyana E. Envold; m. Tatyana A. Mikirov, Apr. 29, 1975; 1 child, Artem A. MS with honor, Moscow Inst. Petrochem. and Gas Industry/Russian Acad. Scis., 1975, PhD, 1980. Jr. rsch. fellow Inst. Petrochem. Synthesis, Russian Acad. Scis., Moscow, 1980-83, rsch. fellow, 1983-85, sr. rsch. fellow, 1985-93, dep. head lab., 1987-93; rsch. fellow Wichita (Kans.) State U., 1993-96; rsch. chemist A. W. Spears Rsch. Ctr. Lorillard Tobacco Co., Greensboro, N.C., 1996-99, sr. rsch. chemist, 1999—. Editor publs. Russian Acad. Scis., 1970-93; presenter in field. Contbr. numerous articles to profl. jours.; 20 patents in field. NSF-Exptl. Program to Stimulate Competitive Rsch. grantee, 1993-96. Mem. AIChE, Am. Chem. Soc., N.Am. Catalysis Soc., Soc. Free Radical Biology and Medicine. Avocations: bicycling, marathon running. Office: AW Spears Rsch Ctr Lorillard Tobacco Co 420 N English St Greensboro NC 27405-7310 Home: 702 Ivy Meadow Ln Durham NC 27707-6183

DYAL, EDITH COLVIN, retired music educator; b. El Dorado, Ark., Mar. 9, 1928; d. Otis Herbert and Irene (Hammons) Colvin; m. William M. Dyal, May 13, 1950; children: Kathy Dyal Schwab, Deborah Dyal DeMeo, Lisa Dyal Reese. BA, Baylor U., 1949; MA, Columbia U., 1984, MEd, 1985, EdD, 1991. Pvt. piano studio mgr. and tchr. Edith Dyal Studio, Alexandria, Va., 1971-81, Kiawah Island/Charleston, S.C., 1986-94; pvt. piano instr. Panama City, Panamá, 1995-97; ret., 1997. Adj. assoc. prof. music Sch. of the Arts, U. Charleston, 1986-94; cons. Internat. Piano Tchg. Found., N.Y.C., 1986-92. Mem. Music Tchrs. Nat. Assn. (local pres. 1988-90), Nat. Fedn. Music Clubs (local pres. 1991-93). Democrat. Baptist.

DYAL, LUCIUS MAHLON, JR., lawyer; b. Gadsden, Ala., Mar. 30, 1937; s. Lucius M. and Juliet (McCall) D.; m. Kay Rankin, Jan. 27, 1968; children: Juliet, Caroline, Lucius M. III. BSCE, Auburn U., 1959; JD, U. Fla., 1966. Bar: Fla. 1966, U.S. Dist. Ct. (mid. dist.) Fla. 1966, U.S. Ct. Claims 1995, Internat. Ct. Trade 1995; cert. internat. and civil law, Fla.; bd. cert. in internat. law. Commd. 2d. lt. U.S. Army, 1959, advanced through grades to capt., 1965, resigned, 1967; atty. Shackleford, Farrior, Stallings & Evans, PA, Tampa, Fla., 1966—, pres., 1989-93, 99-2000, mng. ptnr., 2000—02. Chmn. bd. U. South Fla. Coll. Engring., 1998—. Mem. ABA, Am. Bar Found., Bar of Lima Peru, Bar of Rep. Honduras, Soc. Internat. Bus. Fellows (pres., chmn. 1995-97), Mus. Sci. Industry Found. (pres., chmn. 1994-96), Tampa C. of C. Office: NCE Corp 1900 5th St NW Winter Haven FL 33881

DYAL, PALMER, retired physicist; b. Odon, Ind., Oct. 27, 1933; s. Roland Lewis and Stella Sims Dyal; m. Gladys Irene Wiley, Aug. 14, 1955; children: Debra, Gordon. BA, Coe Coll., 1955, DSc (hon.), 1978; PhD, U. Ill., 1959. Project mgr. USAF Spl. Weapons Ctr., Albuquerque, 1959—61, rsch. physicist, 1961—66; rsch. scientist NASA/Ames Rsch. Ctr., Moffett Field, Calif., 1966—73, astrophysical experiments br. chief, 1974—82, asst. dir. projects, 1982—91, dep. dir. space rsch., 1991—96; sr. scientist Orbital Scis. Corp., Mountain View, Calif., 1996—2001; cons. Mission Rsch. Corp., Santa Barbara, Calif., 2001—02; ret., 2002. Cons. Los Altos Hills, Calif., 2001—02. Mgr. Little League Baseball, Los Altos Hills, 1972—73; leader Sierra Club Peak Climbing Sect., San Francisco, 1993—2002. Capt. USAF, 1959—61. Fellow Hugh L. Dryden Meml., NASA, 1973, Dryden, U. Calif., Berkeley, 1973—74. Mem.: Am. Astron. Soc., Am. Phys. Soc., Am. Geophys. Union (sec. planetology sect. 1975—77), Explorers Club, Sigma Xi, Phi Kappa Phi. Avocations: mountain climbing, kayaking. Home: 26405 Ascension Dr Los Altos Hills CA 94022 Personal E-mail: pdyal@pacbell.net.

DYAL, WILLIAM M., JR., retired federal agency administrator; b. Austin, Tex., May 13, 1928; s. William M. and Midlred Eleanor (Taylor) D.; m. Edith Colvin, May 6, 1950; children: Kathy Lynn Dyal Schwab, Deborah Irene Dyal DeMeo, Maria Lisa Dyal Reese. AB, Baylor U., 1949; ThM, So. Theol. Sem., 1953. With Fgn. Mission Bd., Costa Rica, Guatemala and Argentina; dir. orgn. Christian Life Commn., 1962-66; dir. Peace Corps, Colombia, 1966-69, regional dir., 1969-71; pres. Inter-Am. Found., Rosslyn, Va., 1971-80; advisor to pres. Ford Found., N.Y.C., 1980-81; pres. Am. Field Service

Internat./Intercultural Programs, N.Y.C., 1981-86, St. John's Coll., Annapolis, Md., 1986-90, ret., 1990; dir. Peace Corps, Panama, 1995-97; ret., 1997. Author: It's Worth Your Life, 1967, Un Desafío al Discipulado, 1970, also articles. Recipient Santander Gold medal Colombia, 1968. Home: 611 Fauquier St Fredericksburg VA 22401-3745

DY-ANG, ANITA C. pediatrician; b. Cavite, The Philippines, Feb. 21, 1943; came to U.S., 1970; m. Raymundo Ang., May 1, 1977; children: Aileen Ang, Audrey Ang. MD, U. East Ramon Magsaysay, Quezon City, Philippines, 1967. Diplomate Am. Bd. Pediatrics. Pediat. resident Tulane U. Charity Hosp. New Orleans, 1973; pvt. practice Warsaw, N.Y. Mem. attending staff Wyoming County Cmty. Hosp. Mem. Wyoming County Med. Soc. Office: 78 N Main St Warsaw NY 14569-1329

DYBCZAK, ZBIGNIEW WLADYSLAW, dean, educator, mechanical engineer; b. Zaleszczyki, Poland, June 27, 1924; s. Franciszek and Sylwia (Rozborska) Dybczak; m. Karolina Czarnota Dybczak, Apr. 27, 1957; children: Maria Karolina, Mark Zbigniew. BSc in engring., U. London, Eng., 1950; PhD, U. Toronto, Can., 1959. Registered profl. engr., Ala., Ont. Design engr., Lincoln, England, 1949—51; rsch. asst. U. Toronto, 1952—54, instr., 1952—54, lectr., 1954—59; assoc. mech. engr. Argonne Nat. Lab., 1960, resident rsch. assoc., summers, 1961—65; prof., dept. head, dean of engring. Tuskegee Inst., 1960—81; prof. mech. engring. Tuskegee Inst., 1981—85, U. Fla., 1981—85. Stress analyst, cons. govt., founds., industry. Contbr. articles to profl. jours.; book reviewer. Dir. mixed voice choir, Toronto, 1953—59; chmn. Ho. of Providence Fund, Toronto, 1958—59; bd. dirs. Montgomery Bd. Edn., pres.; chmn. bd. Southeastern Consortium for Minorities in Engring. 2nd lt. Polish RAF, 1941—46, ETO. Mem.: ASME, Am. Nuc. Soc., Am. Soc. Engring. Edn., War Vets. Assn. (Polish pres. 1949—51), Tau Beta Pi, Eta Kappa Nu, Pi Tau Sigma, Sigma Xi. Independent. Roman Catholic. Avocations: history, music, tennis, golf, chess. Home: 129 Arrowhead Dr Montgomery AL 36117 Home Fax: 334-277-0622. E-mail: dybczakz@knolocy.net.

DYBECK, ALFRED CHARLES, labor arbitrator; b. Camden, Del., Nov. 16, 1928; s. George L. and Freda (Alexander) D.; m. Leah Anne Pestell, June 28, 1952; 1 son, Alfred Arthur. Student, Emmanuel Missionary Coll., 1946-49; BA, George Washington U., 1955, JD, 1958. Bar: Va. 1958. Field atty. NLRB, Pitts., 1958-63, supervising atty., 1963-65, asst. regional atty. Milw., 1965; assoc. chmn. bd. arbitration United Steelworkers Am., U.S. Steel Corp., Pitts., 1965-78, chmn. bd. arbitration, 1979-96. Exec. sec. Nat. Acad. Arbitrators, 1971-77, pres., 1989-90. With AUS, 1951-53. Mem. Order Coif. Home: 11 Dover Ct Carnegie PA 15106-1588 Office: 2101 Greentree Rd Pittsburgh PA 15220-1400

DYBEK, STUART, English educator, writer; b. Chgo., Apr. 10, 1942; s. Stanley and Adeline (Sala) S.; m. Caren Bassett, Feb. 7, 1967; children: Anne, Nicholas. BS, Loyola U., Chgo., 1964, MA, 1967; MFA, U. Iowa, 1973. Tchr. U.S. V.I. Sch., St. Thomas, 1968-70, U. Iowa, Iowa City, 1970-73; prof. English Western Mich. U., Kalamazoo, 1973—. Vis. prof. creative writing Princeton (N.J.) U., 1991, U. Calif., Irvine, 1995, U. Iowa, 1998, Northwestern U., 2001. Author: (poetry) Brass Knuckles, 1979; (fiction) Childhood and Other Neighborhoods, 1980, The Coast of Chicago, 1990, I Sailed With Magellan, 2003. Guggenheim fellow, 1982; recipient Whiting Writers award, 1985, O. Henry first prize, 1985, Acad. award in fiction Am. Acad. Arts and Letters, 1994, PEN/Malamud award, 1995, Lannan Lit. prize, 1998. Mem. PEN. Home: 320 Monroe St Kalamazoo MI 49006-4436 Office: Western Michigan U Dept English Kalamazoo MI 49008 also: care Amanda Urban Intl Creative Mgt 40 W 57th St New York NY 10019-4001 E-mail: sdybek@earthlink.net.

DYBELL, ELIZABETH ANNE SLEDDEN, clinical psychologist; b. Buffalo, Sept. 25, 1958; d. Richard Edward and Angela Brigid (Scimone) Sledden; m. David Joseph Dybell, Nov. 30, 1985. BA in Psychology summa cum laude, U. St. Thomas, Houston, 1980; PhD in Psychology, Tex. Tech. U., 1986. Lic. clin. psychologist, Tex. Rsch. asst. health sci. ctr. Tex. Tech. U., Lubbock, 1983-84, psychol. cons. health sci. ctr. neurology dept., 1982-84; psychology intern U. N.Mex. Med. Sch., Albuquerque, 1984-85; psychotherapist Katz & Assocs. P.C., Houston, 1985-88, Meyer Ctr. for Devel. Pediatrics Tex. Children's Hosp., Houston, 1988-92; pvt. practice Houston, 1990—. Author: (monograph) When Will Life Be Normal?, 1989, Myths of the Super Parent, 2003; contbr. articles to numerous publs. Choir mem. St. Thomas More Ch., Houston, 1974-87. Mem. APA, Md. Psychol. Assn., Assn. for the Care of Childrens Health, Nat. Ctr. Clin. Infant Programs, Soc. Pediatric Psychology, Southwestern Psychol. Assn., Tex. Psychol. Assn., Houston Psychol. Assn., Am. Psychol. Soc. (charter). Roman Catholic. Avocations: water gardening, horticulture, nature studies, ornamental koi raising, ecology. Home and Office: PO Box 609 Jefferson MD 21755-0609

DYBMAN, NICK NISON (NICK CHINA), poet; b. Tientsin, China, Dec. 23, 1945; Came to U.S., 1950; s. Gregory and Alla D. BA, Queens Coll., 1972. Pres. Aleza Records, Forest Hills, N.Y., 1989. Composer over 300 songs and poems including Ms. Hooker is Running Free, Sweet Recovery, There she Goes Again, Blessed Be the Refugee. Avocation: drawing. Home: 66-36 Yellowstone Blvd Forest Hills NY 11375-2514 E-mail: Elkin@cs.com.

DYCHE, DAVID BENNETT, JR., retired management consultant; b. Port Chester, N.Y., July 23, 1932; s. David B. and Julia H. D.; m. Mary J. Moorman, Apr. 28, 1956; children— David B. III, Williard H. AB, Dartmouth Coll., 1954; MBA, U. Pa., 1958. Chartered fin. analyst. With J.P. Morgan & Co., and Morgan Guaranty Trust Co., N.Y.C., 1958-81; dir. fin. industries Arthur D. Little, Inc., 1981-98. Chmn., commr. Boca Grande Fire Control Dist. With U.S. Army, 1954-56. Mem. Assn. Investment Mgmt. Rsch., N.Y. Soc. Security Analysts. Home: Box 502 Boca Grande FL 33921-0502

DYCHES, TINA TAYLOR, special education educator, consultant; b. Las Vegas, Nev., July 17, 1962; d. Richard Blackburn and Charlene Flora (Belknap) Taylor; m. David Terry Dyches, Sept. 18, 1987; 1 child, Logan Taylor. BS, Brigham Young U., 1986; MS, Utah State U., 1990; EdD, Ill. State U., 1995. Cert. spl. edn., elem. edn., gen. adminstrv., Utah. Tchr. spl. edn. Salt Lake City Sch. Dist., 1986-91, Unit 5 Sch. Dist., Normal, Ill., 1991-94; clin. instr. Ill. State U., Normal, 1994-95; from clin. instr. dept. spl. edn. to assoc. prof. Brigham Young U., Provo, Utah, 1995—2002, assoc. prof., 2002—. Autism cons., Utah, 1995—; external evaluator Utah Gov.'s Coun., Salt Lake City, 1998—2000. Co-author: Guide To Writing Quality Individualized Education Programs, 1999, (CD ROM) What's Best for Matthew?, 1999; contbr. chapters to books, articles to profl. jours. Mem.: Tchr. Edn. Divsn., Utah Subdivsn. Devel. Disabilities (pres. 1997—98), Divsn. Devel. Disabilities (chmn. literary Dolly Gray award com. 1999—, mem. FarWest regional bd. 2001—, John W. Kidd subdivsn. award 1998), Autism Soc. Utah (exec. bd. 1996—99), Coun. for Exceptional Children (publicity chmn. Utah Fedn. 1998—), Autism Soc. Am. Mem. Lds Ch. Avocations: reading, playing with and teaching children, snowboarding, working on computer, genealogy. Office: Brigham Young U 340-F MCKB Provo UT 84602

DYCK, ANDREW ROY, philologist, educator; b. Chgo., May 24, 1947; s. Roy H. and Elizabeth (Beck) D.; m. Janis Mieko Fukuhara, Aug. 20, 1978. BA, U. Wisc., 1969; PhD, U. Chgo., 1975. Sessional lectr. U. Alta., Edmonton, Can., 1975-76; asst. prof. U. Minn., Mpls., 1977-78; vis. asst. prof. Classics UCLA, 1976-77, asst. prof., 1978-82, assoc. prof., 1982-87, prof., 1987—, chmn. dept. classics, 1988-91. Mem. Inst. for Advanced Study, Princeton, 1991-92; vis. fellow All Souls Coll., Oxford, 1998, Clare Hall, Cambridge, 1999. Author: A Commentary on Cicero, De Officiis, 1996; editor: Epimerismi Homerici, 2 vols., 1983, 95, Essays on Euripides and George of Pisidia and on Heliodorus and Achilles Tatius (Michael Psellus), 1986, Cicero, De Natura Deorum I, 2003; co-editor: Studies in Classics: Outstanding Dissertations, 2002-. Alexander von Humboldt-Stiftung fellow, Bonn, Fed. Republic of Germany, 1980-89; NEH fellow, 1991-92. Mem. Am. Philol. Assn., Calif. Classical Assn., U.S. Nat. Com. on Byzantine Studies. Office: UCLA Classics Dept 405 Hilgard Ave Los Angeles CA 90095-9000 E-mail: dyck@humnet.ucla.edu.

DYCK, ARTHUR JAMES, ethicist, educator; b. Saskatoon, Sask., Can., Apr. 27, 1932; s. Jacob Peter and Mary (Zacharias) D.; m. Sylvia Willms, Sept. 2, 1952; children— Sandra Lynn and Cynthia Ann (twins). BA, Tabor Coll., 1953; MA, U. Kans., 1958, MA, 1959; PhD, Harvard, 1966. Research asst. psychology U. Kans., 1957-60; spl. lectr. philosophy U. Sask., 1964-65; asst. prof. social ethics Harvard Div. Sch., 1965-69; Mary B. Saltonstall prof. population ethics Harvard Sch. Pub. Health, 1969—, Co-dir. Kennedy Interfaculty Program in Med. Ethics, 1971—, mem. Ctr. for Population Studies and Div. Sch. Faculty, 1965—. Author: On Human Care: An Introduction to Ethics, 1977, Rethinking Rights and Responsibilities: The Moral Bonds of Community, 1994, When Killing is Wrong: Physician Assisted Suicide and the Courts, 2001, Life's Worth: The Case Against Assisted Suicide, 2002; editor (with S.J. Reiser, W.J. Curran): Ethics in Medicine, 1977; assoc. editor: Jour. Religious Ethics, mem. editl. bd.: Linacre Quar.; contbr. articles to profl. jours. Mem. Am. Soc. Christian Ethics, The Hastings Ctr., Soc. European Culture, Am. Pub. Health Assn., N.Am. Soc. for Social Philosophy, Phi Beta Kappa. Congregationalist. Home: RR 1 Box 236A Alton NH 03809-9738 Office: 45 Francis Ave Cambridge MA 02138-1911 E-mail: adyck@hds.harvard.edu. *I do not measure success apart from what moral principles require of me. To do my chosen scholarly work honestly, fairly, enthusiastically, and in ways that contribute, however modestly, to learning, knowledge and social justice is success. The most important measures of success are the increase of love for others and for the divine power that makes the moral life possible on earth. This is true in my family as well as in my vocation.*

DYCK, GEORGE, psychiatry educator; b. Hague, Sask., Can., July 25, 1937; came to U.S., 1965; s. John and Mary (Janzen) D.; m. Edna Margaret Krueger, June 27, 1959; children: Brian Edward, Janine Louise, Stanley George, Jonathan Jay. Student, U. Sask., 1955-56; B of Christian Edn., Can. Mennonite Bible Coll., 1959; MD, U. Man., 1964; postgrad., Menninger Sch. Psychiatry, 1965-68. Diplomte in psychiatry and geriatric psychiatry Am. Bd. Psychiatry and Neurology; cert. psychiatrist Royal Coll. Physicians and Surgeons, Can. Fellow cmty. psychiatry Prairie View Mental Health Center, Newton, Kans., 1968-70; clin. dir. tri-county svcs. Prairie View Mental Health Ctr., 1970-73; prof. dept. of psychiatry U. Kans.-Wichita, Wichita, 1973—2002, chmn. dept. of psychiatry, 1973-80, 98-99; dir. geriatric psychiatry U. Kans., 1993-2001, prof. emeritus, 2002—; med. dir. Prairie View, Inc., 1980-89. Cons. Shenyang Psychiat. Hosp., People's Republic of China, 1990, Palestinian Mental Health Program, West Bank, 1990; mem. Kans. Hosp. Closure Commn., 1995; bd. dirs. Kidron Bethel Retirement Svcs., Newton, Kans., 1994-2002, chmn., 2001-02. Bd. dirs. Mennonite Mut. Aid, Goshen, Ind., 1973-85, Chmn., 1982-85; bd. dirs. Mid-Kans. Cmty. Action Program, 1970-73, Wichita Council Drug Abuse, 1974-76, Kauffman Mus. North Newton, 1995-98. Fellow Am. Psychiat. Assn. (pres. Kans. chpt. 1982-84, dep. rep. 1984-86, rep. 1986—, cert. in adminstrv. psychiatry 1984); mem. AMA, Kans. Med. Soc., Kans.-Paraguay Ptnrs. (treas. 1986-89). Mennonite. Home: 1505 Hillcrest Rd Newton KS 67114-1340 E-mail: gdyck@cox.net.

DYCK, MARTIN, literary theorist, German literature theorist, mathematics historian; b. Grünfeld, Ukraine, Jan. 16, 1927; came to U.S., 1956; s. Martin and Helene (Peters) Sommer D.; m. Marie Wiens, June 12, 1949 (div. 1983); children: Vernon, Victor, Martin Christopher Columbus and Ingrid Rose Marie (twins). BA German and Pure Math. (double hons.), U. Manitoba, Can., 1953, MA in German and Math., 1954; PhD in German Lit., U. Cin., 1956. Grad. asst. math. U. Manitoba, 1952-53, sessional lectr. in Germn, 1953-54; Taft Meml. fellow U. Cin., 1954-56; asst. prof. German and Russian MIT, Cambridge, 1956-58, prof. German and humanities, 1965-87, prof. emeritus, 1987—; from asst. to prof. German U. Mich., Ann Arbor, 1958-65. Author: Goethe und die Mathematik, 1954, Novalis and Mathematics, 1960, 70, Die Gedichte Schillers, 1967; mem. editorial bd. Historia Mathematica, 1972-76; contbr. articles to profl. jours. and book chpts. Fellow Guggenheim, 1961-62, Am. Coun. Learned Socs., 1961-62; grantee Am. Philos. Soc., 1969. Mem. MLA (del. assembly 1979-81), Modern Humanities Rsch. Assn., Assn. Lit. Scholars and Critics, History of Sci. Soc., Lessing Soc., Am. Soc. for Eighteenth Century Studies, Am. Assn. Tchrs. German, German Studies, Assn., N.E. MLA. Avocations: mountain climbing, walking, reading. Home: PO Box 1179 Lincoln NH 03251-1179 Office: MIT 77 Massachusetts Ave Rm E38-277 Cambridge MA 02139-4307 *I have striven to test and taste the poetry, comedy, and mathematics of man against matter and nothingness.*

DYCK, PETER JAMES, neurologist, researcher, educator; b. So. Caucasis, Russia, Oct. 20, 1927; came to U.S., 1959; s. Jacob and Katherine (Janzen) D.; m. Janet Isabelle Dyck, Sept. 11, 1954; children: Ernest C., Fred H., P. James B., Kathy E. BA, U. Sask., SAskatoon, Can., 1951; MD, U. Toronto, Ont., Can., 1955; D hon. c25606633, U. Aix-Marseilles, France, 1992. Lic. Med. Coun. Can., Minn.; diplomate Am. Bd. Psychiatry and Neurology. Rotating intern U. Hosp., Saskatoon, Saskatch., Can., 1955-56, asst. resident internal medicine, 1956-57, registrar O.P.D. internal medicine, 1957-58, fellow in neurology, 1958-59, Mayo Found., Rochester, Minn., 1959-61; cons. in neurology Mayo Clinic, Rochester, 1961—; instr. neurology Mayo Grad. Sch. Medicine U. Minn., Rochester, 1963-67, asst. prof., 1967-69, assoc. prof., 1969-73; prof. Mayo Med. Sch., Rochester, 1973—. Mem. editl. bds, Minn. Medicine, 1963-66, Neurology, 1975-80, Muscle and Nerve, 1977-81, Neurochem. Pathology, 1983—, Peripheral Nerve Repair and Regeneration, 1986-87, Jour. Cranomadibular Disorders: Facial and Oral Pain, 1986-88, Jour. Neuropathology and Exptl. Neurology, 1987-92, European Neurology, 1988—, Diabetes, 1990—, Jour. Neurosci., 1990—, Can. Jour. Neurol. Scis., 1993—; cons. to Shell Internat. Neuropathol. Assessment of Toxicity from Pyerthroids; mem. adv. com. on fellowships, Multiple Sclerosis Soc., NIH Rev. Com. Study sect. 1978-81, ctrl. and preripheral nervous system work group Nat. Diabetes Adv. Bd., 1979-80, Med. Sci. Rev. Com., Diabetes Rsch. Found., 1989—; chairperson AAN com. on Neuromuscular Pathology, 1995— and many other nat. and internat. med. groups; participant in numerous national and internat. symposiums and seminars, vis. lectr. at about 100 internat. univs. and medical assns. including Max Planck Inst. Frankfurt, Germany, U. Tokyo, Japan, Johns Hopkins U., Balt., U. Chgo., NYU Med. Ctr.Univd. of Rome, Genoa and Milan, U. Mich., Mass. Gen. Hosp., Boston. Editor: (with others) Peripheral Neuropathy, 1975, 3d rev. edit., 1993, Diabetic Neuropathy, 1987, 1999, Neurologic Clinics, 1992; contbr. over 300 articles and 75 revs. to profl. jours. Named Roy E. and Merle Meyer Prof. Neuroscience, Mayo Med. Sch., 1988—, fgn. corr. Acad. Royale de Medecine de Belgique, 1981—, Paddison Lectr., La. State U., New Orleans, 1987, Alan Bailey Meml. Lectr., Baker Lectr. Hennepin County Med. Ctr., Mpls., 1985; hon. mem. Am Neurol. Assn., 1996, Can. Soc. Clin. Neurophysiologists, 1997; recipient NIH Jacob Javits Investigator award, 1997 and other honors. Fellow ACP, Am. Acad. Neurology (mem. various coms., chmn. com. on neuromuscular pathology 1995—, Wartenberg lectr. 1988); mem. Minn. State Med. Assn., Am. Assn. Neuropathologists, Am. Assn. Electromyography and Electrodiagnosis (Lambert lectr. 1986), Am. Soc. for Cell Biology, Am. Neurol. Assn. (numerous coms. and offices including pres. 1992-93), Zumbro Valley Med. Assn., Peripheral Nerve Study Group (founding mem. mem. ad hoc com. 1975-93, chmn. 1976), Peripheral Neuropathy Assn. (founding mem., pres. 1984-94 organizer meetings, symposia, congresses, 1984-92), Peripheral Nerve Soc. (bd. dirs. 1995—), Lyra Inc. (St. Paul, bd. dirs., com. mem.), Sigma Xi. Office: 200 1st St SW Rochester MN 55905-0001 E-mail: dyck.peter@mayo.edu.

DYCK, WALTER PETER, gastroenterologist, educator, university official; b. Winkler, Man., Can., 1935; MD, U. Kans., 1961. Diplomate Am. Bd. Internal Medicine, Am. Bd. Gastroenterology. Intern Henry Ford Hosp., Detroit, 1961-62, resident in internal medicine, 1962-63, 65-66; rsch. fellow gastroenterology U. Zurich, Switzerland, 1963-64; fellow enzymology rsch. U. Toronto, Ont., Can., 1964-65; fellow gastroenterology Mt. Sinai Sch. Medicine, N.Y.C., 1966-68; mem. sr. staff Scott and White Clinic, Temple, Tex., 1968—, chmn. dept. rsch., 1969-72, dir. divsn. gastroenterology, 1972-96; prof. medicine, dir. divsn. gastroenterology Tex. A&M Coll. Medicine, 1978-96; adminstrv. dir. rsch. and edn. divsn., chief acad. officer Scott and White Meml. Hosp., Temple, 1996—; sr. assoc. dean Tex. A&M Coll. Medicine, 1996—. Mem. gen. medicine study sect. A NIH, 1973-77. Fellow ACP, Am. Coll. Gastroenterology; mem. AMA, Am. Fedn. Clin. Rsch., Am. Gastroenterology Assn., Am. Physiol. Soc., So. Soc. Clin. Investigation, Soc. for Exptl. Biology and Medicine, Am. Pancreatic Assn., N.Y. Acad. Scis. Office: Scott and White Hosp 2401 S 31st St Temple TX 76508-0002

DYCKMAN, RICHARD HARRIS, cardiologist; b. N.Y.C., June 28, 1960; s. Samuel and Florence Dyckman; m. Elizabeth Jane Hahn, Nov. 12, 1989; children: Rebecca Ariel, Rachel Hannah. BA, Yale U., 1981; MD, Cornell U., 1985. Diplomate in internal medicine and cardiovasc. disease Am. Bd. Internal Medicine, cert. in transthoracic, stress and transesophageal echocardiography Am. Bd. Echocardiography. Intern internal medicine N.Y. Hosp.-Cornell Med. Ctr., N.Y.C., 1985-86, resident internal medicine, 1986-88, fellow in cardiology, 1989-91; cardiology cons. Valley Cardiology Assocs., Bethlehem, Pa., 1991-97; dir. noninvasive cardiology St. Lukes Regional Med. Ctr., Bethlehem, 1995-97; assoc. dir. echocardiography St. Francis-The Heart Ctr., Roslyn, N.Y., 1997-2000, cardiology cons., 1997—, L.I. Cardiology Assocs., Patchogue, N.Y., 2000—. Instr. internal medicine Cornell Med. Coll., N.Y., 1986-88; asst. clin. prof. medicine Temple U., Phila., 1993-97, Columbia U., N.Y., 1998—. Editor The Yale Record, 1980. Fellow Am. Coll. Cardiology, Am. Soc. Echocardiography. Office: 285 Sills Rd Bldg 14 Patchogue NY 11772

DYCKMAN, THOMAS RICHARD, accountant, educator; b. Detroit, Feb. 25, 1932; s. Clovis E. and Wildarene A. (Andrus) Dyckman; m. Alice Ann Pletta, Nov. 4, 1955; children: Daniel, James, Linda, David. BA, U. Mich., 1954, MBA, 1955, PhD, 1961. Asst. prof. acctg. U. Calif., Berkeley, 1961-64; assoc. prof. Cornell U., Ithaca, NY, 1964-68, prof., 1968—, Ann Whitney Olin prof. bus., 1978—, assoc. dean Johnson Grad. Sch. Mgmt., 1985-95, acting dean, 1996-97, acting v.p. for info. tech., 1998-99. Cons. IBM, GTE, SNET, Fin. Acctg. Stds. Bd., mem. adv. com., 1984—88; chair audit com. bd. dirs. Galaxy Nutritional Foods. Author: (book) Topics in Cost Accounting and Decisions, 1963, Statistical Decision Theory, 1968, Algebra and Calculus for Business, 1975, Managerial Cost Accounting, 1971, 2d edit., 1976, Fundamental Statistics for Business and Economics, 1977, Efficient Capital Markets, 1975, 2d edit., 1986, Cases in Financial Accounting, 1987, 3d edit., 1989, Cost Accounting: Concepts and Managerial Applications, 1990, 2d edit., 1994, Intermediate Accounting, rev. edit., 1992, 5th edit., 2001. Mem. adv. com. Fin. Acctg. Found., 1990—93. With USNR, 1955—58. Recipient Gold medal award, AICPA, 1968, 1976. Mem.: Am. Acctg. Assn. (pres. 1981—82, dir. rsch. 1976—78, Outstanding Acctg. Educator award 1987). Home: 135 Eastlake Rd Ithaca NY 14850-9700 Office: Cornell U Sage Hall Ithaca NY 14853 E-mail: trd2@cornell.edu.

DYCUS, ELIZABETH RASMUSSEN, academic administrator; d. John Juergen Rasmussen and Elise Louise Leinhardt; m. J. Stephen Dycus, Sept. 21, 1968; children: Jamie Stephen, Anne Lee Dycus Shapiro. BA, So. Meth. U., 1962. Staff asst. Congressman Speedy O. Long, Washington, 1966—68; itinerary sec. Senator Elect Lloyd Bentsen, Houston, 1970; asst. to pres. Three Mile Island Commn., Hanover, Washington, 1979, Dartmouth Coll., Hanover, NH, 1980—83; dir. external rels. CLIPP, Dartmouth Coll., Hanover, NH, 1988—95; asst. dir. for recruitment IDE, Dartmouth Coll., Hanover, NH, 1999—2003; itinerary sec. sen.-elect Lloyd Bensten Hanvover, NH, 1970. Mem, chair Vt. State Bd. of Health, Burlington, 1988—2003; mem. exec. com. Vt. State Dem. Party, Vt., 1985—91. Democrat. Congregational. Office: Dartmouth Coll 1 McNutt Hall Hanover NH 03755

DYCUS, MARK, music educator; b. Paducah, Ky., Mar. 1, 1954; s. Ronald H. and Letha M. Dycus; m. Nancy Lou Farmer, Aug. 16, 1980; children: Teresa, Deeanna. B in Music Edn., Murray State U., 1977; M in Ch. Music, So. Bapt. Theol. Sem., 1981. Min. music Westmoreland Bapt. Ch., Huntington, W.Va., 1983—85, East Dayton (Ohio) Bapt. Ch., 1986—94; choral tchr. Calloway County H.S., Murray, Ky., 1995—. Composer: (choral anthem) Everlasting Arms, 1987. Mem.: NEA, Am. Choral Dirs. Assn., Music Educators Nat. Conf. Avocations: fishing, weight training. Office: Calloway County HS 2108 College farm Rd Murray KY 42071 Business E-Mail: mdycus@calloway.k12.ky.us.

DYDEK, MARGO, professional basketball player; b. Poland, Apr. 27, 1974; Profl. basketball player Poznzn Olympia, Poland, 1992—94, Fota Porta Gdynia, Poland, 1992—98, Valenciennes Ochies, France, 1994—96, Pool Getafe, Spain, 1996—98; mem. Polish Nat. Team, 1998—99; profl. basketball player Polpharma VBW Clima Gdynia, Poland, 2000—01, Lotos VBW Clima Gdynia, Poland, 2001—02, Utah Starzz, 1998—. Named MVP, Polish League Finals, 1999—2000, Best Basketball Player, Italian Sports Mag., La Gazetta dello Sport, Sport's Woman of Yr., Poland. Office: 301 W South Temple Salt Lake City UT 84101

DYE, ALAN PAGE, lawyer; b. Eustis, Fla., Apr. 4, 1946; s. Harlan Page and Maryse Jean (Tyre) D.; m. Rebecca Deen Comer, June 11, 1972; children: Katherine Ann, Andrew. AB in Econs., Duke U., 1968; JD, U. Fla., 1971; LLM, NYU, 1973. Bar: Fla. 1971, U.S. Ct. Claims 1974, U.S. Tax Ct. 1974, D.C. 1975, U.S. Ct. Appeals (10th cir.) 1975, U.S. Dist. Ct. D.C. 1976, U.S. Supreme Ct. 1976. Dir. Ea. Water Law Ctr., Gainesville, Fla., 1971—72; clk. U.S. Tax Ct., 1973—75; assoc. Webster, Chamberlain & Bean, Washington, 1975—79, ptnr., 1979—. Author: Association Legal Check List, 1983; contbr. articles to profl. jours. Bd. dirs. United Children's Fund, Washington, 1987—, Cancer Rsch. Found. and Prevention, Washington, 1986—, chmn., 1994-96, Capitol Hill Restoration Soc., Washington, 1975-79, Am. Franklin Friends Com., 1991-95, Lee-Fendall House, 1992-2003, Freedom House, 1996—, Barracks Row Mainstreet, 2000—. Capt USAR, 1972-80. Mem. ABA, Am. Coll. Tax Counsel, Federalist Soc. Republican. Presbyterian. Avocations: golf, skiing, tennis. Office: Webster Chamberlain & Bean Ste 1000 1747 Pennsylvania Ave NW Washington DC 20006-4693 E-mail: adye@wc-b.com.

DYE, DAVID RAY, tax accountant, financial advisor; b. Hobart, Ind., Aug. 4, 1951; s. Clifford C. and Lola May (Garrett) D.; m. Claudia Ann Forrester, June 20, 1974; children: Jason Charles, Eric David, Heather Ann. BBA in Acctg., Valparaiso U., 1973. CPA, Va., Ill., Ind.; lic. securities series 7, series 65, and health and life, Va., Ohio, N.C., Ind.; registered Renaissance advisor; cert. estate planner. From staff mem. to sr. mgr. Peat, Marwick, Mitchell, Chgo., 1973-81; dir. tax ops. Touche, Ross & Co., Richmond, Va., 1982-85; ptnr., prin. Womacke & Burke, Richmond, 1986-88; exec. v.p. Deaton Fin. Svcs., Inc., Richmond, 1988—; pres. DRD, Inc., Richmond, 1995—; assoc. H. Beck Inc., Richmond, 1990—. Pres. Paradigms for Client's, Inc.; registered advisor Renaissance, Inc.; founder Fin. Solutions. Mem. Rep. congl., nat. and life rep. orgns. and precinct coms., Hobart, Inc., 1978-83; mem. Save the Bay, Arbor Found., Neighborhood Housing Svcs. Bd. of Richmond. Named River Conservationist of Yr., Va. Wildlife Fedn., 1995. Mem. AICPA (tax com., personal fin. planning com.), Va. Soc. CPAs, Inc. Soc. CPAs, Ill. Soc. CPAs, Nat. Planned Giving Execs., Econ. Soc. Va. Planned Giving Study Group, U.S. Jaycees, Wilderness Soc., Audubon Soc., Lions, Omicron Epsilon, Sigma Tau Gamma. Home: 12511 Spring Run Rd Chesterfield VA 23832 Office: DRD Inc & Fin Solutions 7643 Hull Street Rd Ste 101 Richmond VA 23235-6445

DYE, JAMES LOUIS, chemistry educator; b. Soudan, Minn., July 18, 1927; s. Ray Ashley and Hildur Ameda Dye; m. Angeline Rosalie Medure, June 10, 1948; children: Roberta Rae, Thomas Anthony, Brenda Lee. AA, Virginia (Minn.) Jr. Coll., 1948; BA, Gustavus Adolphus Coll., 1949; PhD, Iowa State U., 1953; DSc (hon.), No. Mich. U., 1992. Rsch. assoc. Iowa State U., Ames, 1953; asst. prof. chemistry Mich. State U., East Lansing, 1953-60, assoc. prof., 1960-63, prof., 1963-94, chmn. dept. chemistry, 1986-90, prof. emeritus, 1994—. Vis. scientist Ohio State U., Columbus, 1968-69; cons. AT&T Bell Labs., Murray Hill, N.J., 1982-83. Author: Thermodynamics and Equilibrium, 1978; contbr. more than 220 articles to profl. jours. With U.S. Army, 1945-46. NSF fellow, 1961-62, Guggenheim fellow, 1975-76, 90-91, Fulbright scholar, 1975-76; recipient Disting. Alumni award Gustavus Adolphus Coll., 1969. Fellow AAAS; mem. NAS, Am. Acad. Arts and Scis., Am. Chem. Soc. (Inorganic Chemistry award 1997), Am. Inst. Chemists (Chem. Pioneer award 1990), Am. Phys. Soc., Materials Rsch. Soc., Phi Kappa Phi, Sigma Xi (rsch. awards 1968, 87), Golden Key (teaching award 1986). Lutheran. Avocations: fishing, golf. Home: 2698 Roseland Ave East Lansing MI 48823-3847 Office: Mich State Univ Dept Of Chemistry East Lansing MI 48824 E-mail: dye@msu.edu.

DYE, LINDA KAYE, elementary school educator; b. Shelbyville, Tenn., Dec. 26, 1962; d. John William Dye and Adeline Stewart Dye Adams. BS, David Lipscomb Univ., Nashville, 1985; postgrad., Middle Tenn. State U. Title I reading tchr. Bedford County Bd. Edn., Shelbyville, Tenn. Mem. NEA, Tenn. Edn. Assn., Nat. Coun. Tchrs. English, Bedford County Edn. Assn.

DYE, NANCY SCHROM, academic administrator, historian, educator; b. Columbia, Mo., Mar. 11, 1947; d. Ned Stuart and Andrea Elizabeth (Ahrens) Schrom; m. Griffith R. Dye, Aug. 21, 1972; children: Molly, Michael. AB,

Vassar Coll., 1969; MA, U. Wis., 1971, PhD, 1974. Asst. prof. U. Ky., Lexington, 1974—80, assoc. prof., 1980—88, prof., 1988, assoc. dean arts and scis., 1984—88; dean faculty Vassar Coll., Poughkeepsie, NY, 1988—92, acting pres., 1992—94; pres. Oberlin Coll., Oberlin, Ohio, 1994—. Author: As Equals And As Sisters, 1981; contbr. articles to profl. jours. Bd. mem. Pomona Coll. Mem.: Coun. Colls. of Art and Scis. (bd. dirs. 1980—91). Office: Oberlin Coll Cox Admin Bldg, Room 201 70 N Professor St Oberlin OH 44074-1090 Fax: 440-775-8937.

DYE, ROBERT HARRIS, retired manufacturing company executive; b. N.Y.C., Feb. 22, 1918; s. Abatha Agusta and Julia (Harris) D.; m. Tereseua Vergine, May 13, 1950; 1 child, Leslie Julie. BSEE, Purdue U., 1942. Engr. Gen. Elec. Co., Schenectady, 1942-43, 46-47, mgr. field engr. test group Key West, Fla., 1947-49, prog. mgr. Schenectady, 1949-53; divsn. chief guidance and control Dept. of Navy, Newport, R.I., 1953-56; sect. mgr. Gen. Precision Co., Little Falls, N.J., 1956-60; prog. mgr. missile Gen. Precision Co./Singer, Little Falls, 1960-87; ret. Lt. USNR, 1942—46. Mem. IEEE, Submarine Vet. WWII, NRA, Am. Legion. Republican. Achievements include development of procedures for mine field penetration by submarine. E-mail: bobtra@juno.com.

DYE, SHARON ELIZABETH HERNDON, speech pathologist; b. Springfield, Mo., June 14, 1952; d. Leonard Leroy and Virginia Louise (Kennard) Herndon; divorced children: Brian Keith Dye, Johnathan Paul Dye, Christopher Shawn Dye. BS, Marquette U., 1973, MS, 1975. Speech pathologist Milw. Pub. Schs., 1976-98; head start speech pathologist Peacé Action Milwaukee-Milwaukee, Inc., 1998—; speech pathologist Phillis Wheatley Elem. Sch., Milw., 1999—. Itinerant speech pathologist Wis. Speech Lang. Hearing Assn., 1998-99; speech pathologist North Divn. H.S. PTA, 1998—, mem. spl. edn. com., 2000-02. Author: (poetry) Wind Riders, 1996; guest host area cable TV program MATA. Vol. House of Correction, Franklin, Wis., 1993, glaucoma screenings, 1995, 96; mem. Jobs for Peace, 1994, 95; past mem. Progressive Milw., Jamie's Club Theatre, featured poet, 1999; mem. spl. edn. com. PTA, 2000-2003; commr. neighborhood perspective com. Fondy Neighborhood Bus. Assn., 2002-2003. Mem. NEA (del. rep. assembly 2000-03), Wis. Speech Lang. Hearing Assn., Wis. Edn. Assn. (del., rep. assembly), Nat. Assn. Black Speech, Lang. and Hearing, Milw. Tchrs. Edn. Assn. (parent tchr. cmty. partnerships com.), Marquette U. Alumni Assn. Baptist. Avocation: writing inspirational songs and poetry. also: PO Box 05498 Milwaukee WI 53205 E-mail: dyese@mail.milwaukeeK12.wi.us.

DYE, STUART S. lawyer; b. Ogden, Utah, 1939; BS cum laude with honors, U. Utah, 1961; LLB, U.Va., 1967. Bar: Va. 1967, D.C. 1967. Sec. Navy staff Deep Submergence Sys. Rev. Group Office of Legis. Affairs, 1963-64; spl. asst. on Law of the Sea matters internat. law divsn. Office of Judge Adv. Gen., 1965-66; ptnr. Holland & Knight, Washington. Adv. bd. Latin Am. Law and Bus. Report, 1994—. Mem. editl. bd. Va. Jour. Internat. Law, 1966-67; contbg. editor Oil and Gas Regulations Analyst, 1976-82. Mem. nat. adv. coun. U. Utah, 2001–. Lt. comdr. USNR. Mem. ABA (natural resources law sect., adminstrv. law sect.), Maritime Law Assn. (exec. com.), U.S., Maritime Adminstrv. Bar Assn., U.S.-Mex. C. of C. (chmn., bd. dirs. 1998—, chmn. transp. task force), Caribbean-Ctrl. Am. Action (bd. trustees, sec. 2003-), Phi Alpha Delta. Office: Holland & Knight LLP 2099 Pennsylvania Ave NW Washington DC 20006-6801 E-mail: sdye@hklaw.com.

DYE, THOMAS ROY, political science educator; b. Pitts., Dec. 16, 1935; s. James Clair and Marguerite Ann (Dewan) D.; m. Joan Grace Wohleber, June 29, 1957; children: Roy Thomas, Cheryl Price. BA, Pa. State U., 1957, MA, 1959; PhD, U. Pa., 1961. Asst. prof. polit. sci. U. Wis., Madison, 1962-63; asso. prof., head dept. polit. sci. U. Ga., Athens, 1963-68; prof., chmn. dept. govt. Fla. State U., Tallahassee, 1968-72, dir. policy scis., 1978-91, McKenzie prof. govt., 1991—98, prof. emeritus of polit. sci., 1998—; pres. Lincoln Ctr. for Pub. Svc., 1998—99. Vis. prof. polit. studies Bar Ilan U., Israel, 1972, U. Ariz., 1976 Author: Politics, Economics and the Public, 1966, Politics in States and Communities, 1969, 11th edit., 2003, The Irony of Democracy, 1970, 12th edit., 2003, The Politics of Equality, 1971, Understanding Public Policy, 1972, 10th edit., 2001, Power and Society, 1975, 9th edit., 2001, Who's Running America, 1976, Policy Analysis, 1976, Who's Running America-The Carter Years, 1979, Determinants of Public Policy, 1980, Who's Running America-The Reagan Years, 1983, Politics in the Media Age, 1983, 5th edit., 2003, Who's Running America-The Conservative Years, 1986, Power Elites and Organizations, 1987, Who's Running America-The Bush Era, 1990, American Federalism: Competition Among Governments, 1990, Politics in America, 1994, 5th edit., 2003, Who's Running America-The Clinton Years, 1994, Politics in Florida, 1998, Top Down Policymaking, 2000, Who's Running America: The Bush Restoration, 2002. 1st lt. USAF, 1961-62. Mem. Am. Polit. Sci. Assn. (sec. 1969-72), So. Polit. Sci. Assn. (v.p. 1974-75, pres. 1976-77), Phi Beta Kappa, Omicron Delta Kappa. Home: 651 Okeechobee Blvd P111 West Palm Beach FL 33401 E-mail: tomrdye@aol.com.

DYE, TIMOTHY DE VER, epidemiologist, anthropologist, educator; b. Syracuse, N.Y., July 1, 1964; s. Kenyon Milton and Phyllis Ann Dye; m. Theresa Elaine Davis-Dye, Aug. 16, 1986; children: Aleksandr Frederic, Lily Madeleine. BA, Syracuse U., 1985, MA, MPA, 1987; MS, SUNY, Buffalo, 1990, PhD, 1993. State maternal and child health epidemiologist W.Va. Bur. of Pub. Health, Charleston, 1990—92; perinatal epidemiologist Ctrs. for Disease Control and Prevention, Oklahoma City, 1992—93; asst. prof. SUNY Upstate Med. U., Syracuse, 1993—97; assoc. prof. U. Rochester, NY, 1997—. Grantee Costa Rica-US Cmty. Health Informatics Program, Fogarty Internat. Ctr., NIH, 1999—2004, Culture and Health in Antarctica, NSF, 2002-2005; Nat. Resource fellow in Hindi and South Asian Studies, US Dept. of Edn./Syracuse U., 1985-1987. Mem.: APHA, Am. Coll. of Epidemiology, Am. Anthrop. Assn. (Young Profl. award). Office: Univ Rochester 601 Elmwood Ave Box 324 Rochester NY 14642 Office Fax: 585-756-7656. E-mail: tim_dye@urmc.rochester.edu.

DYE, WILLIAM ELLSWORTH, lawyer; b. Detroit, Oct. 15, 1926; s. Edward Ellsworth and Elizabeth Esther (Bloom) D.; m. Joy Ann Kuehneman, Apr. 28, 1956 (div.); children: Constance, Elizabeth, William. BA, U. Wis., 1948, LLB, 1951. Bar: Wis. 1951. Assoc. John F. Thompson, Racine, Wis., 1951-75; ptnr. Heft, Dye, Paulson & Nichols, Racine, 1975-87, Foley, Dye, Foley and Tollaksen, S.C., Racine, 1987-92, Coates, Dye, Foley & Shannon, S.C., Racine, 1993-98, Dye, Foley, Krohn & Shannon, S.C., Racine, 1998—. Instr. U. Wis. Law Sch., 1970-71. Bd. visitors U. Wis., 1982-85. With U.S. Army, 1946-47. Mem. ABA, State Bar Wis. (bd. govs. 1972-78), Racine County Bar Assn. (pres. 1985-86), Racine Country Club, Somerset of Racine Club. Republican. Episcopalian. Home: 111 11th St Racine WI 53403-1966 Office: Dye Foley Krohn & Shannon 1300 S Green Bay Rd Racine WI 53406-4469 E-mail: dfkssc@amerilynk.com.

DYEKMAN, GREGORY CHRIS, lawyer; b. Ft. Collins, Colo., Aug. 2, 1955; s. Elmer Clifford and Patsy Joyce (Hill) D. BS with honors, U. Wyo., 1977, JD, 1980. Bar: Wyo. 1980, U.S. Dist. Ct. Wyo. 1980, U.S. Ct. Appeals (10th cir.) 1980, U.S. Tax Ct. 1981, U.S. Supreme Ct. 1988, U.S. Claims Ct. 1990. Assoc. Dray, Madison & Thomson, P.C., Cheyenne, Wyo., 1980-82, shareholder, 1983-96; Dray, Thomson & Dyekman, P.C., 1996—. Adj. prof. law U. Wyo., 1993, 98, 2000, 2002; chmn. law sch. liaison com., 1998—; bd. visitors Univ. Wyo. Coll. Arts and Scis., 1997—, vice chair, 1999-2001, chair, 2001—; ex-officio mem. U. Wyo. Coll. of Law Bd. Visitors, 2001—; mem. Leadership Wyo. Class of 2003. Editor-in-chief Land and Water Law Rev., 1978-79. Mem. dist. com. Boy Scouts Am., Cheyenne, 1980-83, 87-88, dist. chmn., 1987-88, fin. chmn., 1995-96; bd. counsel Symphony and Choral Soc. of Cheyenne, 1983-88; pres. Cheyenne Family YMCA, 1984-85, bd. dirs., 1982-88, YMCA Endowment Bd., 1993—; pres., elder 1st Presbyn. Ch., Cheyenne, 1983-85, treas., 1986—; bd. dirs. Meals on Wheels Found., 1993-99, 2002—, v.p., 1995, pres.-elect, 1996, pres., 1997-98; cabinet mem. United Way, 1997; trustee Long's Peak coun. Boy Scouts Am., 1998—, v.p. endowment; bd. dirs. Cheyenne Schs. Found., 2001—; mem. Leadership Wyo Class of 2003. Mem. ABA, Laramie County Bar Assn. (sec., treas. 1985-86), Wyo. Trial Lawyers Assn. (editor newsletter 1983—), Kiwanis Found. (bd. dirs. 1993-95, pres. 1995), Cheyenne Kiwanis Club (bd. dirs. 1998-2000). Republican. Avocations: music composition, sports, internet. Home: 5010 McCue Dr Cheyenne WY 82009-4815 E-mail: Greg.Dyekman@draylaw.com.

DYEN, ISIDORE, linguistic scientist, educator; b. Phila., Aug. 16, 1913; s. Jacob and Dena (Bryzell) D.; m. Edith Brenner, June 11, 1939 (dec. 1976); children— Doris Jane, Mark Ross. BA, U. Pa., 1933, MA, 1934, PhD in Indo-European Linguistics, 1939; postgrad. Slavic, Columbia, 1938-39, Yale, 1939-40. Faculty Yale U., 1942-84, prof. Malayan langs., 1957-58, prof. Malayopolynesian and comparative linguistics, 1958-73, prof. comparative linguistics and Austronesian langs., 1973-84, prof. emeritus, 1984—, dir. grad. studies Indic and Far Eastern langs. and lit., 1960-62, Indic and Southeast Asia, 1960-66, dir. grad. studies linguistics, 1966-68; adj. prof. linguistics U. Hawaii, 1985-89; linguist Coordinated Investigation Micronesian Anthropology, Truk, 1947, Sci. Investigation Micronesia, Yap, 1949. Vis. prof. U. Padjadjaran, Bandung, 1960-61, U. Auckland, summer 1969, Australian Nat. U., fall 1971, U. Philippines, spring 1972, Inst. Study of Langs. and Cultures of Asia and Africa, Tokyo U. for Fgn. Langs., 1982-83; coordinator linguistics sect. 10th Pacific Sci. Congress, Honolulu, 1961; asso. prof. U. Chgo. and Linguistic Soc. Am. Summer Inst., 1955; prof. U. Mich. and Linguistic Soc. Am. Summer Inst., 1957; dir. SE Asia Linguistics Program, 28th Internat. Congress Orientalists, Canberra, 1971; organizing com. Conf. Genetic Lexicostatistics, New Haven, 1971; organizer 1st Eastern Conf. Austronesian Linguistics, New Haven, 1973; adv. com. 1st Internat. Conf. Comparative Austronesian Linguistics, Honolulu, 1974; mem. adv. bd. Oceanic Linguistics. Author: Spoken Malay, 2 vols., 1945, The Proto-Malayo-Polynesian Laryngeals, 1953, A Lexicostatistical Classification of the Austronesian Languages, 1965, A Sketch of Trukese Grammar, 1965, A Descriptive Indonesian Grammar, 1967, Beginning Indonesian, 4 vols., 1967, Lexicostatistics in Genetic Linguistics: Proc. of Yale Conf., 1973, (with David Aberle) Lexical Reconstruction: The Case of the Athapaskan Kinship System, 1974, Linguistic Subgrouping and Lexicostatistics, 1975, (with Guy Jucquois) Lexicostatistics in Genetic Linguistics II, 1976, (with Joseph B. Kruskal and Paul Black) An Indoeuropean Classification: A Lexicostatistical Experiment, 1992. Research fellow Slavic Am. Council Learned Socs., 1938-40; Guggenheim fellow, 1949, 64; Tri-Instl. Pacific Program grantee, 1956-57; NSF grantee, 1960-77 Mem. Linguistic Soc. Am., Am. Oriental Soc. (v.p. 1965-66), Am. Anthrop. Assn., Current Anthropology, Société de Linguistique de Paris, Koninklijk Instituut voor Taal-, Land-, en Volkenkunde, New Haven Oriental Club (pres. 1963-64, 74-76) Office: Univ Hawaii Manoa Dept Linguistics Honolulu HI 96822 also: Yale U Dept Linguistics Hall Grad Studies New Haven CT 06520 *My aim has been to further linguistic science, particularly in comparative linguistics, by research in both Austronesian and Indoeuropean languages. In large part my work has been devoted to combining traditional and mathematico-statistical methods to improve subgrouping procedures. The different interlocking roles of theory, hypothesis, and methodology have been kept to the fore throughout. I hope my research will develop strong evidence regarding the Austronesian homeland.*

DYER, ARLENE THELMA, retail company owner; b. Chgo., Oct. 23, 1942; d. Samuel Leo Sr. and Thelma Arlene (Israel) Lewis; m. Don Engle Dyer, July 3, 1965 (div. 1970); 1 child, Artel Terren. Cert. in mgmt. effectiveness, U. So. Calif., 1987; cert. Ryan Designated Subjects, UCLA, 2000. Community resource rep. Calif. State Employment Devel. Dept., Los Angeles, 1975-76, spl. projects rep., 1976; employment services rep. Culver City, Calif., 1977; contract writer L.A., 1976-80; employment program rep., 1980—; pres. Yabba and Co., L.A., 1981-83; pres., designer, cons. Spiritual Ties Custom Neckwear, L.A., 1985—; pres. Dyer Custom Shirts, Blouses and Suits, Beverly Hills, Calif., 1988—; contr. writer L.A. Watts Times, 2002—. Founder self-evaluation seminar; pres. MYSELF, Inc., 1998. Author: Who Are You and What Are You All About?, 1994, Escaping to the Workplace, 1996, I Got the Job!. . .Now What?, 1998, You Got the Job?...Now What?, 1999; exhibited in fashion shows, Calif., 1984—; radio personality, 1995 Vol. Big Sister Gwen Bolden Found., L.A., 1986, Juvenile Hall, 1996; mem. Operation PUSH, Chgo., 1983, Mahogany Cowgirls & Co.; program chair Black Advs. in State Svc., 1987—; leader Girl Scouts U.S., L.A., 1982, L.A. Urban League; spirit team leader Calif. Special Olympics; mem. Big Sisters of L.A. Recipient IRWIN award, 1998. God's Leading Ladies, 2002. Mem. NAACP (Beverly Hills-Hollywood chpt.), Nat. Alliance Homebased Businesswomen (v.p., program chair 1987), NAFE, Nat. Spkrs. Assn. (Grtr. L.A. chpt.), Calif. State Employees Assn., Greater L.A. C. of C., Kiwanis Club (dir.), U. So. Calif. Alumni Assn., L.A. Urban League, Black Women's Forum. Democrat. Avocations: traveling, reading, bicycling, roller skating.

DYER, BARBARA F. retired accountant, writer; b. Rockland, Maine, May 19, 1924; d. Milton Earl and Elizabeth Ayoube Dyer. Grad., LaSalle Ext. U., 1967; student, U. Maine, Thomaston, 2001. Office mgr., acct. Camden (Maine) Shipbuilding Co., 1942—86; tchr. Adult Edn. Sch. Adminstrv. Dist. #28, Camden, 1987—93; freelance writer Camden, 1984—. Hist. lectr., 1984—2002; writer Village Soup.com. Author: Grog Ho, 1984, Vintage Views, 1987, History 1st Congregational Church, 1991, Images Camden-Rockport, 1995, Home Sweet Home, 1996, Vessels of Camden, 1998, More Memories of Camden, 1997; contbr. articles to publs. Bd. selectmen Town of Camden, 1992—95; ind. commr. Camden Pub. Libr., 1998—2002; mem. Camden War Meml. Com., 2003—; budget com. Town of Camden, 2003—; deacon First Congl. Ch., Camden, 1970—74, historian, 1985—2002, 2003—. Named Paul Harris fellow, Rotary Internat., Camden, 1995, Townsperson of Yr., Camden, Lincolnville, Rockport C. of C., Camden, 1996; recipient Disting. Personal Enrichment award, Maine Adult Edn. Assn., 1993, first place/weekly award, Maine Press Assn., 1993. Mem.: Camden H.S. Alumni Assn., Phi Theta Kappa. Republican. Avocations: knitting, crocheting, oil painting, swimming, dancing. Home: 11 Highland Ave Camden ME 04843-2119

DYER, CHARLES ARNOLD, lawyer; b. Blairstown, Mo., Aug. 29, 1940; s. Arnold and Mary Charlotte (West) D.; children: Kristine, Erin, Kathleen, Kerry. BJ, U. Mo., 1962; JD, U. Calif., 1970. Bar: Calif. 1971, U.S. Supreme Ct. 1976. Ptnr. Dyer & White, Menlo Park, Calif.; judge Pro Tem Mcpl. and SuperiorCt., San Mateo County, Calif., Pro Tem Superior Ct., Santa Clara County, Calif., arbitrator, mediator. Lectr. in field. Bd. dirs. Boys Club of San Mateo, 1971-83, pres., 1975; mem. exec. coun. Boys Clubs of Bay Area, 1977-83; mem. Dem. Nat. Fin. Com., 1978. Served to capt. USNR, 1963-93, ret. Mem. Calif. Bar Assn., San Mateo County Bar Assn., Santa Clara County Bar Assn., Palo Alto Bar Assn., Consumer Attys. Calif., Consumer Attys. San Mateo County, Assn. Atty. Mediators, Trial Lawyers Pub. Justice, Am. Bd. Trial Advs., Nat. Bd. Trial Advocacy. Roman Catholic. Office: Dyer & White 800 Oak Grove Ave Menlo Park CA 94025-4477

DYER, CHARLES RICHARD, law librarian, law educator; b. Richmond Heights, Mo., Aug. 20, 1947; s. Helmuth Kinner and Sue Anne (Stone) D.; m. Cecelia Ann Duncan, Dec. 20, 1969 (div. June 1982); m. Roberta Sharlyn Monroe, June 2, 1984; 1 child, Christina L. Floyd. BA, U. Tex., 1969; MA, Northwestern U., 1971; JD, U. Tex., 1974, MLS, 1975. Bar: Tex. 1974. Assoc. law libr., asst. prof. law St. Louis U., 1975-77; law libr., assoc. prof. U. Mo., Kansas City, 1977-87; dir. librs. San Diego County Pub. Law Libr., 1987—. Cons. in field. Editor Law Libr. Jour., 1972-74. Mem. Centre City adv. com. City of San Diego, 2000—02; chair relocation appeal bd. City of San Diego Redevel. Agy., 2001—. Mem. Am. Assn. Law Librs., Mid-Am. Assn. Law Librs (sec.-treas. 1976-78), Southwestern Assn. Law Librs. (v.p. 1981-82, pres. 1982-83), So. Calif. Assn. Law Librs. (mem. exec. bd. 1991-93), Coun. Calif. County Law Librs. (pres. 1998-2000). Democrat. Unitarian Universalist. Home: 2323 Montclair St San Diego CA 92104-5344 Office: San Diego County Pub Law Library 1105 Front St San Diego CA 92101-3904 E-mail: cdyer@sdcll.org.

DYER, CROMWELL ADAIR, JR., lawyer, international organization official; b. St. Louis, Sept. 9, 1932; came to The Netherlands, 1973; s. Adair and Tompie Leora (Giles) D.; m. Margaret Copeland Peickert, June 12, 1958 (div. Aug. 1976); children: Gretchen, Jack, Julie, Stephen; m. Susan Aynesworth, Aug. 20, 1977; stepchildren: Carol Godso, Amanda McDonough, Donnella Railsback. BA, U. Tex., 1954; JD, 1961; LLM, Harvard U., 1971. Bar: Tex. 1961, U.S. Dist. Ct. (no dist.) Tex. 1965, U.S. Dist. Ct. (ea. dist.) Tex. 1966, U.S. Dist. Ct. (we. dist.) Tex. 2003, U.S. Ct. Appeals (5th cir.) 1965, U.S. Ct. Appeals (11th cir.) 1982, U.S. Ct. Appeals (9th cir.) 1999. Law clk. FTC, Washington, 1960; assoc. Branscomb, Gary, Thomasson & Hall, Corpus Christi, Tex., 1961-62; staff atty. So. Union Gas Co., Dallas, 1962-64; assoc. Dedman & May, Dallas, 1964-65, White, McElroy & White, Dallas, 1965-67; sole practice, 1967-73; sec. Hague Conf. on Pvt. Internat. Law, The Hague, The Netherlands, 1973-78; 1st sec., 1978-93; dep. sec. gen., 1993-97; observer, cons. to intergovtl. orgns., 1976-97. Lectr. Asser Coll. Europe, 1992-96, Davis Sch. Law U. Calif. Davis, 1996, Brigitte M. Bodenheimer Meml. Lecture on the Family, 1996; ; moderator Common Law Jud. Conf. on Internat. Child Custody, Washington, 2000; condr. seminars. Honoree of symposium: Globalization of Child Law The Role of the Hague Conventions, 1999; co-author: Report on Trusts and Analogous Institutions, 1982; contbr. articles to profl. jours. Mem. adv. com., faculty internat. kidnapping program Nat. Jud. Coll., Reno, 2003; dir. studies Hague Acad., 1985, course on Unfair Competition in Pvt. Internat. Law, 1988, jury for award of Diploma in Internat. Law, 1980, 1984, 1985, 1986, 1987, 1991, 1994, 1995, 1996. Mem.: ABA (law sect. internat. law and practice, chair com. on internat. family law 2002—03, Leonard J. Theberge award for pvt. internat. law), Internat. Law Assn. (Am. br.), Inter-Am. Bar Assn., Internat. Bar Assn., Assn. Louis Chatin pour la Def. des Droits de l'Enfant (Paris), Internat. Soc. Family Law, Dallas Bar Assn., Travis County Bar Assn., Am. Fgn. Law Assn., Club du jeudi (The Hague) (pres. 1983—85). Office: PO Box 30020 Austin TX 78755-3020 Fax: 512-343-7299. E-mail: adyer@jump.net.

DYER, DORIS ANNE, nursing consultant; b. Washington, Jan. 14, 1944; d. William Edward and Helen Gertrude (Smith) Swain; m. Robert Francis Dyer, Jr., June 27, 1970; children: Robert Francis, William Edward, Anne-Marie Helen Sallie, Scott Robertson McGavin. RN cum laude, Sibley Nursing Sch., Washington, 1964; BS, Am. U., 1966, MEd, 1969. Mem. staff emergency medicine dept. George Washington U. Hosp., 1960-69, emergency specialist protective svcs. clinic, 1967-70, adminstrv. asst. to dir. clinic, 1970-78, nurse. cons., 1987—. Author: Say Ah, 1971; contbr. articles to profl. jours. Patron Sibley Meml. Hosp. Chapel, 1992. Trinity Coll. scholar, 1960; Lucy Webb Hayes scholar, 1964; recipient Martha Washington award Md. Soc. SAR, 1977, Cmty. Leaders award, 1979, Washington medal, 1984, disting. women of Washington award 1987; decorated Comdr. Order of St. Lazarus, 1984, medal of merit, 1989; created dame Order of Sovereign Mil. Order, 1980, dame comdr., 1992; named Dame Grand Cross, 1984, Dame Grand Officier, 1992. Mem. ANA, D.C. Nurses Assn., Am. Acad. Ambulatory Nursing Adminstrs., Washington Med.-Surg. Soc. Aux. (pres.), U. U. Grads. Assn., DAR, Washington Assembly, Colonial Hist. Soc., Washington Club, Annapolis Yacht Club, Kenwood Golf and Country Club. Address: 5608 Albia Rd Bethesda MD 20816-3303

DYER, FREDERICK CHARLES, writer, consultant; b. St. Louis, Feb. 17, 1918; s. George Leo and Katherine Mary (Dobson) D.; m. Lucrecia E. Herrera-Ibarguen, 1946; children: John R., Michael G., Lisa M. Dyer Fitzpatrick. BA, Holy Cross Coll., 1938; MBA, Dartmouth Coll., 1948. Ednl. writer, editor tng. publs. Bur. Naval Personnel, 1948-58, asst. for spl. projects, leadership staff, 1958-64; spl. asst. to Undersec. Navy U.S. Navy, 1964-66; asst. for spl. projects Office Civilian Manpower Mgmt., Dept. Navy, 1966-68; dir. program analysis div. Navy Publs. and Printing Service, Washington, 1968-74. Profl. lectr. George Washington U., 1956-60; adj. prof. Drexel Inst. Tech., 1962-67; profl. lectr. Am. U., 1967-73; adv. Ctr. for Applied Research in Apostolate, 1979-85. Author, co-author: Putting Yourself Over in Business, 1957, Executive's Guide to Handling People, 1958, Executive's Guide to Effective Speaking and Writing, 1962, Blueprint for Executive Success, 1964, Bureaucracy vs. Creativity, 1965, rev. edit., 1969, How to Make Decisions About People, 1966, The Petty Officer's Guide, 6 edits., 1952-66, The Enjoyment of Management, 1971, 82; contbr. more than 70 articles to profl. jours.; contbg. editor The Pope Speaks mag., 1954-64, Wall St. Rev. of Books, 1977-82. Mem. Town Council Somerset, Md., 1962-64; chmn. U.S. Civil Service Task Force on Mgmt. Edn. for Computers, 1965-66. Served with USNR, 1943-46; PTO; Navy Dept., 1948-52; ret. comdr., 1961 Mem. Authors Guild, Authors League Am., Columbia Country Club (Chevy Chase, Md.), Cosmos Club (Washington, fin. and hist. coms.), Nat. Press Club (Washington, libr. com.), Army and Navy Club (Washington). Home and Office: 4509 Cumberland Ave Bethesda MD 20815-5459

DYER, GARY ALDEN, dermatologist; b. St. Joseph, Mo., Dec. 7, 1939; s. Alden Oltman Dyer and Violet Lorraine Hinderks; m. Eileen Frances Meehan, Aug. 23, 1969; children: Jonathan Alden, Julie Anne Dyer Brokaw, Jared Thomas. AA, Graceland Coll., Lamoni, Iowa, 1959; BS in Edn., Ctrl. Mo. State U., 1961; MD, U. Mo., 1966. Diplomate Am. Bd. Dermatology, Am. Bd. Pathology with subspecialty in dermatopathology. Tchr. biology William Chrisman H.S., Independence, Mo., 1961—62; intern Kansas City Gen. Hosp. and Med. Ctr., Mo., 1966—67; resident in dermatology U. Mo. Health Scis. Ctr., Columbia, 1967—70; asst. prof. dermatology U. Mo., Columbia, 1972—74; pvt. practice dermatology and dermatopathology St. Joseph, Mo., 1974—. Founder, dir. Free Skin Cancer Detection Clinic, St. Joseph, 1985—; founder, dermatology rsch. fund Med. Sch. Found., Columbia, 1991, co-founder dermatology endowment fund, 1987. Maj. USAF, 1970—72. Recipient Disting. Svc. award, Mo. U. Med. Sch. Alumni Orgn., 2002, Faculty-Alumni award, U. Mo., 1990. Fellow: Am. Soc. Dermatopathology, Am. Dermatol. Assn., Am. Acad. Dermatology; mem.: Kansas City Dermatol. Soc. (pres. 1978), Mo. Dermatol. Soc. (pres. 1982—83), Mo. Med. Assn. (pres. 1990—91). Republican. Cmty. Of Christ Ch. Avocations: farming, genealogy, croquet, walking, Sherlock Holmes. Home: 802 N 25th St Saint Joseph MO 64506 Office: 1325 Village Dr Saint Joseph MO 64506

DYER, GREGORY CLARK, lawyer, mediator; b. Stanford, Calif., May 29, 1947; s. Allen Clayton (dec.) and Mary Louise (Sutter) D.; m. Karyne Lee Clough, June 28, 1980; children: Ash, Chelsea. BA, Stanford U., 1970, JD, 1971. Bar: Calif. 1972, U.S. Ct. Appeals (9th cir.) 1972, U.S. Dist. Ct. (no. dist.) Calif. 1972; cert. specialist estate planning, trust and probate law, Bd. Legal Specialization of State Bar of Calif. Pvt. practice, Marin County, Calif., 1972—. Referee, arbitrator, mediator Marin County Superior Ct. Bd. dirs. Legal Aid Soc., Marin, 1979-81; past coach Mill Valley Soccer Club; basketball coach YMCA, Cath. Youth Orgn.; mgr. Mill Valley Little League. Mem. Marin County Bar Assn. (bd. dirs. 1980-82, treas. 1985, pres. 1987), Rotary (pres. local club 1984-85, area rep. 1986-87, leader fgn. exch. team 1981, 87, dist. treas. 1991-92), Scott Valley Swim and Tennis Club (bd. dirs. 1976-80). Avocations: travel, tennis, scuba diving, photography. Office: 103 E Blithedale Ave Ste 3 Mill Valley CA 94941-2062

DYER, JAMES HARRISON, lawyer; b. Phoenix, Oct. 25, 1952; s. Harvey L. and Nonavie (Harman) D. BA, U. Ariz., 1975, JD, 1978. Bar: Ariz. 1978, U.S. Dist. Ct. Ariz. 1980. Assoc., Healy & Beal, P.C., Tucson, 1978-86; sole practice, Tucson, 1986—; instr. Ariz. State Bar, 1984-85; arbitrator Am. Arbitration Assn., 1980—; host monthly legal radio show Sta. KNST, Tucson. Chmn. for So. Ariz., Republican Commitment '80 campaign; mem. Ariz. Town Hall, 1981; pres. Tucson Sport Fishing Festival, 1983-85; surrogate speaker Reagan/Bush Campaign, 1984; founding mem., bd. dirs., sgt. at arms, chmn. environ. impact com. Tucson Horizons; sponsor Project Hospitality Homeless Shelter. Mem. ABA, Ariz. Bar Assn., Pima County Bar Assn., Assn. Trial Lawyers Am., Ariz. Trial Lawyers Assn., Blue Key, Phi Gamma Delta. Club: U. Ariz. Pres.'s, 20/30 Internat. Tucson (charter, bd. dirs. 1986-87, chmn. polo tournament 1986-87). Home: 2020 N Soldier Trl Tucson AZ 85749-9000 Office: 5255 E Williams Cir Ste 6000 Tucson AZ 85711-7717

DYER, JAMES MASON, JR., investment company executive; b. Corsicana, Tex., Sept. 22, 1928; s. James Mason Sr. and Tabby (Jackson) D.; m. Lorelle Wright, Dec. 29, 1954; children: James Mason IV, Diane Dyer Campbell. BBA, U. Tex., 1950. V.p. J. M. Dyer Co., Corsicana, 1954-77, pres., 1978-87; nmg. ptnr. J.M. Dyer Co., Corsicana, 1987—; pres. The Piccolo Co., Corsicana, 1988—. 1st lt. U.S. Army, 1952-54, ETO. Episcopalian. Office: JM Dyer Co PO Box 620 Corsicana TX 75151-0620

DYER, JOSEPH WENDELL, career officer; b. Murphy, N.C., Mar. 2, 1947; s. Joseph Wendell Sr. and Margaret (Kale) D.; m. Melda F. Goldfinch, Mar. 29, 1969. BSChemE, N.C. State U., Raleigh, 1969; MS in Fin. Mgmt., Naval Post Grad. Sch., Monterey, Calif., 1981. Commd. ensign USN, 1969, advanced through grades to vice admiral, 2000; pilot USN Naval Air Test Ctr, Patuxent River, Md., 1976-80; sys. integrator USN, China Lake, Calif., 1982-84, Commanding Officer Plant Rep. Office Melbourne, Australia, 1984-87, dep. program mgr. F/A-18 program Washington, 1988-90, AX airplane chief engr., 1990-91, exec. asst. to comdr. naval air sys. command, 1991-92, navy's chief test pilot Patuxent, Md., 1992-93, mgr. F/A 18 program Washington, 1993-97; comdr. Naval Air Warfare Ctr., Aircraft Divsn., 1997—2000; asst. comdr. for rsch. and engring. Naval Air Sys. Command, 1997-2000, comdr. naval air sys

command, 2000—. Contbr. articles to profl. jours. Recipient Acquisition Excellence award, U.S. Dept. Def., J.H. Doolittle award for outstanding tech./engring. achievement in aerospace tech., 2001. Fellow Soc. Exptl. Test Pilots; mem. Assn. of Old Crows. Achievements include first to includes leading DOD's first tactical data fusion effort; developed Navy's newest strike fighter, led DOD's Larjet acquisition. Avocation: sailing. Address: Naval Air Sys Command Ste 540 47123 Buse Rd Patuxent River MD 20670-1161 Personal E-mail: dyerjw@aol.com. Business E-Mail: dyerjd@navair.navy.mil.

DYER, L. KEITH, film company executive; b. Deland, Fla., May 9, 1963; s. Leslie Jay and Helen Frieda (Brock) Dyer. MusB, Fla. So. Coll., 1987; postgrad., Fla. State U., 1987-89. Tech. dir. Lake Junaluska (N.C.) Assembly, 1984-89; music mgr. Up With People, Denver, 1989-91, show mgr., 1991-92; stage technician Disney-MGM Studios, Lake Buena Vista, Fla., 1992-93; prodn. coord. Walt Disney Entertainment, Lake Buena Vista, 1993-94, prodn. mgr., 1994-2000, prodr., 2001—. Cons. Up With People, Denver, 1996. Mem.: Lambda Chi Alpha (High Alpha 1986—87, sr. leader 1987, Grad. scholar 1987), Omicron Delta Kappa, Pi Kappa Lambda, Order of Omega. Methodist. Avocations: travel, computers, films, reading.

DYER, NATALIE MARY, health products company executive, physician; b. Loniow, Kielce, Poland, Dec. 21, 1924; arrived in Can., 1930; came to U.S., 1996; d. Nicholas and Katherine (Szkutnicka) Staron; m. Allan Edwin Dyer, May 19, 1965; children: Lawrence, Brandon, Cherie, Cinda. MD, U. Toronto, Ont., Can., 1947. Jr. intern St. Michael's Hosp., 1947-48; resident anesthesiology Women's Coll. Hosp., Hosp. for Sick Children, 1949-50; resident in anesthesiology Toronto Western Hosp., 1950-51; anesthesiologist Humber Meml. Hosp., Weston, Ont., 1951-75; med. dir. birth control ctrs. Etobicoke (Ont.) Health Dept., 1975-80, Physicians Weight Control Ctrs., Toronto, 1980-85; v.p., med. dir. Vat-Tech Inc., Toronto, 1985-96, Vax-D Internat., Palm Harbor, Fla., 1996—. Contbr. articles to med. jours., including Can. Jour. Biochemistry and Physiology. Mem.: AMA, N.Y. Acad. Scis., Ont. Med. Assn., Coll. Physicians and Surgeons Ont., Can. Med. Assn., Can. Anesthesiologists Soc. Avocations: cooking, crafts, boating, skiing, snowmobiling. E-mail: vaxdcapo@vaxd.com.

DYER, ROSEMARY, musician; b. Denton, Tex., Aug. 6, 1935; d. Herschel O. and Mary H. Dyer; children: Mary Elizabeth, Allison Rose. Student, North Tex. U., 1953-54, U. Tulsa, 1954-55. Founder Prince Georges Opera Co., 1970-76; dir. Dimensions in Music Program Md.-Nat. Capital Park and Planning Commn., 1973; music dir. Washington Vocal Artists, Potomac United Meth. Ch. Musical dir. Burn Brae's 42nd Street; vocal coach Toby's Dinner Theater; music dir. Libr. Theatre, Young Columbians. Author: A Mirror of Ourselves (Am. Musical), 1991; Soloist Balt. Symphony. Fulbright scholar Rome Opera House. Mem. Arts Alliance Washington Met. Area (charter). Democrat. Episcopalian. Avocations: cooking, gardening, traveling. Office: Potomac United Meth Ch 9908 S Glen Rd Potomac MD 20854-4128

DYER, V. JEFFREY, educational administrator; b. Richardson, Tex., July 30, 1967; s. Van E. and Deborah L. Dyer; m. Robin Jane, Dec. 16, 1989; children: Drew Jeffrey, Abigail Marie. BS in Elem. Edn., Henderson St. U., 1989, MS in Elem. Adminstrn., 1995. Elem. tchr. Port Arthur Sch. Dist., Tex., 1989-91; mid. sch. tchr. Bryant Sch. Dist., Ark., 1991-92, elem. tchr., 1992-96; elem. asst. prin. Alma Sch. Dist., Ark., 1996—2001, Booneville Sch. Dist., Ark., 2001—. Area dir. Ark. Spl. Olympics, state tng. clinician, mem. games mgmt. team; coach World Summer Games Spl. Olympics, 1995, 99; Nat. Coach Team USA Special Olympics World Summer Games, Ireland, 2003, mem. Alma Vol. Fire Dept.; mem. Logan County Child Devel. Adv. Bd.; bd. dirs. South Logan County Boys and Girls Club, pres. of BGCSLC bd.; trustee Booneville United Meth. Ch.; apptd. Ark. Legis. Health Adequacy Adv. Com. Mem. NAESP, ASCD, Ark. Assn. Edn. Adminstrs., Henderson St. Alumni Bd., Saline Co. Henderson Alumni (charter, pres. 1993-95), Rotary Internat., Sigam Phi Epsilon. Avocations: golf, softball, reading, movies. Home: 980 E 6th St Booneville AR 72927 Office: 327 W 5th St Booneville AR 72927 E-mail: jdyer@bps.wsc.k12.ar.us.

DYER, VICTOR EUGENE, II, library administrator; b. Laconia, N.H., Jan. 26, 1950; s. Victor Eugene and Pauline Lucille (Truchon) D. BA, Boston Coll., 1972; MA, U. Chgo., 1975; cert. spl. studies in adminstrn. & mgmt., Harvard U., 1991. Cert. profl. libr. and sch. libr., Mass. Editor, searcher U. Chgo. Libr., 1974-76; cataloger Mcpl. Reference Libr., Chgo., 1976-77; libr. II Chgo. Pub. Libr., 1978-79; asst. dir. Abbot Pub. Libr., Marblehead, Mass., 1979-99; dir. Ipswich (Mass.) Pub. Libr., 1999—. Pres. Essex County Coop. Librs., Beverly, Mass., 1986-87, 88-89, 92-93; sec. Merrimack Valley Libr. Consortium, Andover, Mass., 2000—. Author: Prairie Avenue: An Annotated Bibliography, 1977. Vol. guide and rschr. Chgo. Archtl. Found., 1976 79; vol. guide Peabody Mus., Salem, Mass., 1984-91; vol. Brigham and Women's Hosp., Boston, 1996—. Mem. ALA, Pub. Libr. Assn., Mass. Libr. Assn., New Eng. Libr. Assn., Marblehead Hist. Soc. (dir. 1987-92, 94-98), Hyde Park Hist. Soc. (dir. 1978-79), Phi Beta Kappa. Democrat. Roman Catholic. Avocations: travel, reading, hiking, architecture. Home: 10 Pleasant St Lynn MA 01902-4401 Office: Ipswich Pub Libr 25 N Main St Ipswich MA 01938-2287 E-mail: victordyer@worldnet.att.net.

DYER, WAYNE WALTER, psychologist, writer, radio and television personality; b. Detroit, May 10, 1940; s. Melvin L. and Hazel I. (Vollick) D.; m. Marcelene Louise Dyer; children: Tracy, Stephanie, Skye, Sommer, Serena, Sands Jay, Saje Eykis. BS, Wayne State U., 1965, MS in Counseling and Ednl. Psychology, 1966, EdD in Counseling and Psychology, 1970. Tchr. and counselor Pershing H.S., Detroit, 1965-67; instr. counselor edn. Wayne State U., Detroit, summer, 1970, 71, 72, 73; dir. guidance and counseling Mercy H.S., Farmington, Mich., 1967-71; staff cons. and trainer guidance and sch. psychol. personnel Half Hollow Sch. Dist., Huntington, N.Y., 1973-75; staff cons. Drug Info. and Svc. Ctr., N.Y., 1972-74, Herman Kiefer Hosp., Detroit, 1974-75; mem. tchg. faculty North Shore U. Hosp. divsn. Cornell U. Med. Coll., Manhasset, N.Y., 1974-75; pvt. practice counseling and psychotherapy Huntington, N.Y., 1973—; asst. prof. counselor edn. St. John's U., Jamaica, N.Y., 1971-74; assoc. prof., 1974-77. Over 4000 appearances on TV and radio shows and programs including Phil Donohue Show, Tonight Show, Dinah Shore Show, Merv Griffin Show, Mike Douglas Show, Good Morning America, Canada A.M., Oprah Winfrey Show, numerous other talk shows in every state; radio host for: Kathryn Crosby Show, San Francisco, At Your Service program, Sta. KMOX, St. Louis.; Author: (with John Vriend) Counseling Effectively in Groups, 1973, Counseling Techniques That Work, 1974, 2d edit., 1977, Group Counseling for Personal Mastery, 1980, Your Erroneous Zones, 1976 (Literary Guild selection, Psychology Today Book Club selection, also 4 others), Pulling Your Own Strings, 1977, 1978 (Lit. Guild main selection, also 6 others), The Sky's the Limit, 1980 (Lit. Guild selection); novel Gifts from Eykis, 1983, What Do You Really Want for Your Children?, 1985, Happy Holidays, 1986, You'll See It When You Believe It, 1988, Real Magic, 1992, Everyday Wisdom, 1994, Your Sacred Self, 1995, Staying on the Path, 1995, A Promise is a Promise, 1996, Manifest Your Destiny, 1997, Wisdom of the Ages, There's A Spiritual Solution To Every Problem, 2000; cassette tape series The Wit & Wisdom of Dr. Wayne W. Dyer, 1977, How To Be a No-Limit Person, 1981, Secrets of the Universe, Choosing Your Own Greatness, What Do You Really Want for Your Children?, Transformation: You'll See It When You Believe It, The Awakened Life, others; contbr. chpts. on counseling to books on psychology, numerous articles on psychology to popular mags. and articles on counseling to profl. jours.; producer tape recordings on counseling techniques; audio cassette program Secrets of the Universe. Served with USN, 1958-62. Named Disting. Alumni of Yr., Wayne State U., 1980; recipient Golden Gavel award Internat. Toastmasters, 1987.

DYER, WILLIAM EARL, JR., retired newspaper editor; b. Kearney, Nebr., May 15, 1927; s. William Earl and Hazel Maud (Hosfelt) D.; m. Betty M. Meisinger, June 26, 1967; children: Lee Michael, Scott William. BA, U. Nebr., 1949. Reporter Nebr. City Daily News Press, 1943-44; reporter, copy editor The Lincoln Star, Nebr., 1948-50, city editor, 1951-60, exec. editor, 1960-92. Pres. Nebr. AP Editors, 1964. Author: Headline: Starkweather, 1993. Pres. Lincoln Unitarian Ch., 1962-63; state chmn. Nebr. We Shake Hands Indian Project, 1958-60; mem. Nebr. Adv. Com. on Indian Law Enforcement, 1960-62; mem. State Adv. Com. to Welfare Dept., 1970-73, 80-84. With AUS, 1945-46. Named hon. mem. Omaha Indian Tribe. Mem. Open Forum Club, Phi Beta Kappa, Sigma Delta Chi. Democrat. Home: 1115 Fall Creek Rd Lincoln NE 68510 4947 Office: Jour-Star Printing Co PO Box 81609 926 P St Lincoln NE 68508-3615 E-mail: dyers@inetnebr.com.

DYER-COLE, PAULINE, school psychologist, educator; b. Methuen, Mass., Aug. 20, 1935; d. F. Dewey and Rose Alma (Des Jardins) Dyer; m. Richard Grey, Aug. 1, 1964 (dec. 1977); children: Douglas Richard, Christopher Lachlan, Heather Judith; m. Malcolm A. Cole, July 23, 1983. BS in Edn. and Music, Lowell State Coll., 1957; MEd, Boston State Coll., 1961; EdD, Clark U., 1991. Lic. ednl. psychologist, Mass.; cert. sch. psychologist, Mass.; nat. cert. sch. psychologist. Supr. music and art Merrimac and W. Newburg (Mass.) Pub. Schs., 1957-59; music editor textbooks Allyn & Bacon, Inc., Boston, 1959-64; prof. music West Pines Coll., Chester, N.H., 1969-72; sch. psychologist Nashoba Regional H.S., Bolton, Mass., 1979—2001, chair SPED dept., 1995—2001, dir. SPED dept., 1998—2001; child study dept. Worcester (Mass.) Pub. Schs., 2001—. Vis. lectr., then vis. prof. Framingham (Mass.) State Coll., 1980—; dir. psychol. testing Nashoba Regional Sch. Dist., Bolton, Mass., 1980-94. Author: The Play Game Songbook, 1964. V.p., bd. dirs. Timberlane Devel. Ctr., Plaistow, N.H., 1970-73; founder Friends of Kimi Nichols Devel. Ctr., Plaistow, N.H., 1973; chmn. human svcs. St. Ann Parish, Southborough, Mass., 1974-77, active, 1973-85; citizen amb. del. People to People, China, 1995; active The Regional Lab., Andover, Mass., 1993-2001. Fellow Frances L. Hyatt fellow, Clark U., 1977—79. Mem. Nat. Assn. Sch. Psychologists (cert.), Mass. Assn. Sch. Psychologists, Mass. Tchrs. Assn., People to People Internat. Roman Catholic. Avocations: music, boating, swimming, reading, creative writing. Home: 43 Crowningshield Dr Paxton MA 01612-1253 Office: Child Study Dept 24 Chatham St Worcester MA 01609 E-mail: dyercole@charter.net.

DYER-RAFFLER, JOY ANN, special education diagnostician, educator; b. Stiltner, W.Va., Aug. 10, 1935; d. Ralph William and Hazel (Terry) Dyer; m. John William Raffler, Sr., Jan. 1, 1993; 1 child from a previous marriage, Keith Brian DeArmond. BA, U. N.C., 1969; MEd in Secondary Edn., U. Ariz., 1974, MEd in Spl. Edn., 1976. Cert. spl. edn.-learning disabilities, art edn., spl. edn.-emotionally handicapped. Art educator Tucson Unified Sch. Dist., Tucson, 1970-75, spl. edn. educator, 1975-89, spl. edn. diagnostician, 1989—. Den mother Cub Scouts Am., Raleigh, N.C., 1968-69. Recipient grant Tucson Unified Sch. Dist., 1977. Mem. NEA, CEC, Learning Disabilities Assn. Avocations: oil painting, snow skiing, bird watching, weight lifting, jogging. Home: 4081 N Kolb Rd Tucson AZ 85750-6127 Office: Rosemont Svc Ctr 750 N Rosemont Blvd Tucson AZ 85711-1229

DYESS, BOBBY DALE, lawyer; b. Waxahachie, Tex., Jan. 27, 1935; s. Robert Olin and Rubie Lee (Odom) D.; m. Janet Lee Hassell, Jan. 30, 1960 (dec. 1973); children: Robert Dale, Jonathan David, Julianna Whitfield; m. Sharon Erwin Saylor, June 6, 1974. BA, U. N. Tex., Denton, 1956; JD, So. Methodist U., 1959. Bar: Tex. 1959. Ptnr. Elliott, Churchill, Hansen, Dyess & Maxfield, 1965-82, DeHay & Blanchard, 1983-92, Payne & Blanchard, Dallas, 1992—. Chmn. bd. Rainbow Sound, Inc., 1975-85. Editor: Bests, Life and Health Ins. Edit., 1973-85. Mem. bd. mgmt. East Dallas YMCA, 1970, 1976, campaign chmn., 1976, chmn. bd. mgmt., 1977—79; chief Indian Guides, 1971; chmn. Cub Scout pack com. Boy Scouts Am., 1970; mem./sponsor Dallas Mus. Art; trustee Baylor Med. Ctr., Ellis County, 2002—; bd. dirs. Waxahachie Found., 1999—2003. Mem.: Am. Counsel Assn. (membership chmn. 1976, pres. 1979—80, sec.-treas. 1984—87, membership chmn. 1996—98), Coll. State Bar Tex. (dir. 1996—, chmn. 1999—2001), Scribes (bd. dirs. 1976), Am. Soc. Legal Writers, Dallas Bar Found. (charter), Tex. Bar Assn. Presbyterian. Home: 110 Magnolia Dr Waxahachie TX 75165 Office: Payne and Blanchard 500 N Tower Plz of America Dallas TX 75201 E-mail: bdyess@msn.com.

DYESS, JOSEPH DWIGHT, commercial banker; b. Hattiesburg, Miss., Dec. 18, 1949; s. Lonnie Jr. and Modena (Richardson) D.; m. Kathy Marlene Lee, Feb. 3, 1973; 1 child, Walker Lee. BSBA, Miss. State U., 1972, MS in Econs., 1980; postgrad., La. State U., 1979, U. Okla., 1980. V.p. Merchants and Farmers Bank, Starkville, Miss., 1975-81; fin. cons. Merrill Lynch, Jackson, Miss., 1982-87; cmty. bank pres. Bank of Miss., Starkville, 1987-91; pres. Pine Belt divsn. Bancorp South, Hattiesburg, Miss., 1991—2003, exec. v.p. external affairs, 2003—. Chmn. Area Devel. Partnership, Hattiesburg, 1996. Dir. Miss. Econ. Coun., Jackson, Miss., 1989—90, Miss. Power Found., Hattiesburg, Miss., 1991—94, Hattiesburg Area Edn. Foun.; chmn. SE Miss. Cert. Investment Corp., 1999—2003; dir. Forrest County Indsl. Park Commn., 1994—, vice chmn., 1998—; dir. Pearl River Coll. Workforce Adv. Coun. U. So. Miss. Found., 1996—2003; adv. The U. of So. Miss. Coll. Bus., Hattiesburg, 1992—2002; commr. Tourism Commn., Hattiesburg, 1992—2003; past pres. United Way SE Miss.; past pres Hattiesburg Downtown Assn.; civilian aide to sec. of Army for Miss.; bd. dirs. Camp Shelby Mil. Mus.; vestryman Trinity Episc. Ch., chmn. fin. com.; past bd. dir. Salvation Army So. Miss. Col. USAR, ret. Recipient Hub award, 2003; named Exec. of Yr. Sales and Mktg. Internat., 1997. Mem. Rotary Internat., Hattiesburg Civic Assn., Hattiesburg Country Club, M-L Pres.'s Club. Episcopalian. Fax: 601-545-5159. E-mail: dwight.dyess@bxs.com.

DYGERT, JAMES LLOYD, JR., music educator, musician; s. James Lloyd and Inez Orn Dygert; m. Patricia Marie Scott, June 23, 1962; children: Scott James, Holly Elizabeth Dygert Dreger. EdB (music), Hartt Sch. Music, Hartford, Conn., 1962; MAT, Conn. Coll., New London, Connecticut, 1974. Musician USN, 1954—58, U.S. Coast Guard, New London, Conn., 1962—86; second clarinet Ea. Conn. Symphony Orch., New London, Conn., 1966—2000; adj. music faculty Conn. Coll., New London, Conn., 1974—; asst. dir. U.S. Coast Guard Band, 1974—86; music instr. Thames Valley Music Sch., New London, Conn., 1986—. Woodwind coach Ea. Conn. Symphony Youth Orch., New London, Conn., 1966—71; baritone sax Dick Campo Big Band, 1996—. Master chief U.S. Coast Guard, 1962—86, New London, Connecticut. Mem.: Nat. Assn. Coll. Wind Percussion Instructors, Nat. Band Assn., Conn. Music Educators Assn. Home: 26 Skyline Drive Uncasville CT 06382-1504 Office: Connecticut College Box 5244 Mohegan Avenue New London CT 06320-4196

DYK, TIMOTHY BELCHER, federal judge, educator; b. Boston, Feb. 14, 1937; s. Walter and Ruth (Belcher) Dyk; m. Inga Shirer, June 18, 1960 (div. 1970); children: Deirdre, Caitlin; m. Sally Katzen, Oct. 31, 1981; 1 child, Abraham Benjamin. AB, Harvard U., 1958, LLB magna cum laude, 1961. Bar: DC, NY. Law clk. to Justices Reed and Burton U.S. Supreme Ct., Washington, 1961—62, law clk. to Chief Justice Earl Warren, 1962—63; spl. asst. to asst. atty. gen. U.S. Dept. Justice, Washington, 1963—64; assoc. Wilmer Cutler & Pickering, Washington, 1964—69, ptnr., 1969—90, Jones, Day, Reavis and Pogue, Washington, 1990—2000; cir. ct. judge U.S. Ct. of Appeals Fed. Cir., 2000—. Adj. prof. Georgetown U. Law Ctr., Washington, 1983, Washington, 86, Washington, 89, Washington, 91, U. Va. Law Sch., Charlottesville, 1984—85, Charlottesville, 1987—88, Yale U. Law Sch., 1986—87, 1989. Mem.: Harvard Law Rev., 1959—61; contbr. articles to profl. jours. Office: US Court Appeals Fed Cir 717 Madison Pl NW Ste 915 Washington DC 20439

DYKEMAN, ALICE MARIE, public relations executive; b. Fremont, Nebr., May 18; d. Cecil Victor and Dorothy Lillian (Sillik) Jansen; divorced; children: David Clair, Cinda Cecille Dykeman Nordgren. Feature writer Fremont (Nebr.) Guide and Tribune and Biloxi (Miss.) Daily Herald, 1950-55; adminstrv. asst. to v.p. sales promotion A. Harris & Co., Dallas, 1957-60; account exec. Contact Corp., Dallas, 1960-61; pub. relations dir. Meth. Hosp., Dallas, 1961-72; regional pub. info. officer Small Bus. Adminstrn., Dallas, 1972-74; owner Dykeman Assocs. Inc., Dallas, 1974—. Adj. prof. U. Dallas Grad. Sch. Mgmt., Irving, Tex. 1972-78; guest lectr. numerous Univs., and seminars; mem. pub. rels. com. Dallas/Ft. Worth Fed. Exec. Bd., 1973, mem. minority bus. opportunity com., 1974; mem. Gov.'s Coun. on Small Bus., Tex., 1980-81, 500, Inc., 1982-90; chmn. export coun. pub. affairs task force U.S. Dept. Commerce, 1980-83. Contbr. articles to bus., health care and pub. rels. jours. Mem. fgn. visitors com. Dallas Coun. on World Affairs, 1962-98, Dallas Pub. Health Bd., 1972-74, Dallas Urban Rehab. Stds. Bd., 1981-83, Econ. Devel. Adv. Bd., City of Dallas, 1983-86; pres. Concerned Citizens for Cedar Springs, 1982—; bd. dirs. Oak Lawn Forum, 1983-92; mem. exec. com. Oak Lawn Com., 1983-95. Recipient Matrix award Women in Comm., Dallas, 1968, 88. Fellow Pub. Rels. Soc. Am. (accredited, chmn. S.W. dist. 1971-72, bd. dirs. North Tex. chpt. 1966-72, pres. 1969, assembly del. 1970-73, 91); mem. North Dallas Fin. Forum (pres. 1991), Nat. Assn. Women Bus. Owners, S.W. Venture Forum, North Dallas C. of C. (bd. dirs. 1980-82, chmn. networking skills workshop 1990—), co-founder Breakfast Dallas 1994—, religion comm. coun. 1997—), Press Club Dallas (bd. dirs. 1981-83, headliner 4 times), SMU Mustang Club (bd. dirs. 1996-99), also others. United Methodist. Office: Dykeman Assocs Inc 4115 Rawlins St Dallas TX 75219-3661 E-mail: adykeman@airmail.net.

DYKEN, MARK ERIC, physician; b. Indpls., June 17, 1957; s. Mark Lewis and Beverly D.; children: Jennifer Lin, Mark Raymond. BA, Ind. U., 1979; MD, Ind. U., Indpls., 1984. Diplomate Am. Bd. Neurology; cert. clin. neurophysiology, sleep disorders medicine. Dir. dept. neurology U. Iowa Coll. Medicine Sleep Disorders Ctr., Iowa City, 1990—. Office: U Iowa Coll Medicine Iowa City IA 52242 E-mail: mark-dyken@uiowa.edu.

DYKES, ARCHIE REECE, financial services executive; b. Rogersville, Tenn., Jan. 20, 1931; s. Claude Reed and Rose (Quillen) D.; m. Nancy Jane Haun, May 29, 1953; children: John Reece, Thomas Mack. BS cum laude, East Tenn. State U., 1952, MA, 1956; EdD, U. Tenn., 1959. Prin., Church Hill (Tenn.) High Sch., 1955-58; supt. Greeneville (Tenn.) Schs., 1959-62; prof. edn., dir. U. Tenn. Ctr. for Advanced Grad. Study in Edn., Memphis State U., 1962-66; chancellor U. Tenn. at Martin, 1967-71, 1971-73, U. Kans., 1973-80; chmn., pres., chief exec. officer Security Benefit Group of Cos., Topeka, 1980-88; chmn. Capital City Holdings Inc., 1988—. Chmn. Pepsi Ams., Inc., Chgo., 2000—; bd. dirs. Fleming Cos., Inc., Dallas, Raytech Corp., Shelton, Midas, Inc., Chgo., The Employment Corp., Nashville; trustee Keene Industries Trust, N.Y.C., NY, Kans. U. Endowment Assn., Raytech Corp. Trust, N.Y.C., NY. Author: School Board and Superintendent, 1965, Faculty Participation in Academic Decision Making, 1968. Vice chmn. Commn. on Operation U.S. Senate, 1975-76; mem. Nat. Adv. Coun. Edn. Professions Devel., 1975-76; trustee Truman Libr. Inst., 1973-80, Menninger Found., 1982-88, Nelson Art Gallery, 1973-80, Dole Found., William Allen White Found.; chmn. bd. trustees U. Mid-Am., 1978-79; mem. adv. commn. U.S. Army Command. and Gen. Staff Coll., 1974-79, chmn., 1978-79; mem. consultative bd. regents U. Qatar, 1979-80; mem. bd. regents State of Kans., 1982-86. Ford Found. fellow, 1957-59; Am. Council on Edn. postdoctoral fellow U. Ill., 1966-67; named Outstanding Alumnus, E. Tenn. State U., 1970 Mem. Tenn. Coll. Assn. (pres. 1969-70), Am. Coun. Life Ins. (dir. 1981-86), Nat. Assn. State Univs. and Land Grant Colls. (coun. pres. 1971-80), Newcomen Soc. N.Am., Kans. Assn. Commerce and Industry (dir. 1975-82), Phi Kappa Phi. Home: 506 Belgrave Park Nashville TN 37215-2450

DYKES, KATHRYN A. community health nurse, educator, administrator, gerontological nurse practitioner; b. Racine, Wis., Sept. 11, 1951; d. Frank R. and Stella Korzilius; m. Herman J. Dykes, Apr. 2, 1977; children: Kathryn, Stephanie, John. BS, Coll. St. Teresa, Winona, Minn., 1973; MSN, U. Wis., Oshkosh, 1996. Cert. CPR, BLS, Emergency Response instr. trainer; cert. gerontol. nurse practitioner. Critical care staff nurse Milwaukee County Med. Complex, Milw.; case mgr./home health Vis. Nurse Assn., Milw.; staff., case mgmt. home health Vis. Nurses of Family Svc. Assn., Green Bay, Wis., staff devel. coord., dir. nursing; geriatric nurse practitioner Prevea Clinic, DePere, Wis., 1999 —. Mem. clin. faculty Alverno Coll., Milw.; mem. adj. nursing faculty U. Wis., Green Bay. Recipient Presdl. award Community Svc., 1990; named Vol. of Yr. Brown County, Wis., 1990, Outstanding Vol. Wis. Crisis Ctr., 1989. Mem. ANA, Am. Geriat. Soc., Wis. Dist. Nurses Assn. (pres.), Conf. Gerontol. Nurse Practitioners, Nat. Parish Nurses Assn. Office: Prevea Clinic 1686 Eisenhower Rd De Pere WI 54115-8145

DYKES, OSBORNE JEFFERSON, III, lawyer; b. L.A., Dec. 3, 1944; s. Osborne J. Jr. and Frances (Fox) D.; m. Ann Dennis, Dec. 29, 1973; children: Barbara Nell, Osborne J. IV. BA, Stanford U., 1966, MA, 1968; JD, U. Tex., 1972. Bar: Tex. 1973, U.S. Supreme Ct. 1977, U.S. Ct. Appeals (5th cir.) 1973, U.S. Ct. Appeals (11th cir.) 1981, U.S. Dist. Ct. (so. dist.) Tex. 1975, U.S. Dist. Ct. (ea. dist.) Tex. 1976, U.S. Dist. Ct. (no. dist.) Tex. 1994. Law clk. to Hon. Homer Thornberry U.S. Ct. Appeals 5th Cir., Austin, Tex., 1972-73; ptnr. Fulbright & Jaworski, Houston, 1973—. Contbr. articles to profl. publs. With U.S. Army, 1969-71. Fellow Am. Bar Found., Tex. Bar Found. (life), Houston Bar Found. (life); mem. ABA (chmn. property ins. law com. 1983-84, tort and ins. practice sect.), Fed. Bar Assn. (bd. dirs. South Tex. chpt. 2002), Energy Bar Assn., Bar Assn. of Fifth Fed. Cir., Am. Bd. Trial Advs., Tex. Assn. Civil Trial Specialists (pres. 2002-2003). Republican. Episcopalian. Avocations: tennis, bicycling. Home: 5135 Holly Terrace Dr Houston TX 77056-2125 Office: Fulbright & Jaworski 1301 Mckinney St Houston TX 77010-3031 E-mail: jdykes@fulbright.com.

DYKES, VIRGINIA CHANDLER, occupational therapist, educator; b. Evanston, Ill., Jan. 10, 1930; d. Daniel Guy and Helen (Schnedier) Goodman; children: Ron Lee, Chuch Lee Chandler, james R., Jr. BA in Art and Psychology, So. Meth. U., 1951; postgrad. in occupl. therapy, Tex. Women's U., 1953. Occupl. therapist Beverly Hills Sanitarium, Dallas, 1953-55; dir. occupl. and recreational therapy Baylor U. Med. Ctr., Dallas, 1956-60, 68-89; pvt. practice Dallas, 1989-92; dir. occupl. and recreational therapy Fla. Hosp., Orlando, 1962-65; staff therapist Parkland meml. Hosp., Dallas, 1965-68. Cons. Arthritis Found., 1974-89, benefactor; Fanny B. Vanderkodi lectr. Tex. Women's U., 1993—. Author: (manual) Lightcast II Splints, 1976; Adult Visual Perceptual Evaluation, 1981; contbr. articles to profl. jours. Sponsor Kimball Art Mus.; mem. coord. bd. allied health adv. com. Tex. Coll. and Univ. Sys., 1980—88; bd. dirs. Tex. Arthritis Found., chmn. patient svcs. com., 1985—89, exec. bd. sec.; bd. dirs. Dallas Opera, also women's bd.; bd. dirs. Dallas Arboretum, Theatre III, Fort Worth Opera, Baylor U. Med. Ctr. Found.; found. bd. Tex. Women's U.; chmn. adv. bd. healing environment program Baylor Med. Ctr.; pres. Diana Dean Head Injury Guild, 1992—93. Named Tex. Occupl. Therapist of Yr., 1985, Annual Virginia Dykes Leadership award named in her honor, Tex. Women's Univ. Mem. Tex. Occupl. Therapy Assn. (life mem. award), Am. Occupl. Therapy Assn. 9del. Fla. 1964, Tex. 1980-88), World Fedn. Occupl. Therapists (participant 8th Internat. Congress, Hamburg, Germany, 1982, del. to 10th European Congress on Rheumatology, Moscow 1983), Boomerang Club (dir. 1971-88), Les Femmes du Monde, Pierian Lit. Club. Home: 3203 Alderson St Dallas TX 75214-3059

DYKEWICZ, MARK STEVEN, physician; b. Flint, Mich., May 21, 1955; s. Richard Alfred and Evelyn Ellen Dykewicz. BS, U. Mich., 1977; MD, St. Louis U., 1981. Resident medicine Northwestern U. Med. Sch., Chgo., 1981-84, fellow allergy-immunology, 1984-86, asst. prof. medicine, 1986-90; asst. prof. internal medicine St. Louis U. Med. Sch., 1990—94, assoc. prof., 1994 –2002, prof., 2002—. Fellow ACP, Am. Coll. Chest Physicians, Am. Acad. Allergy-Immunology; mem. Am. Thoracic Soc. Office: St Louis U Med Sch 1402 S Grand Blvd #R209 Saint Louis MO 63104-1004

DYKHUIZEN, C. JEFFREY, child development psychologist, educator; b. Grand Rapids, Mich., Jan. 2, 1963; s. Charles E. and Sandy S. Dykhuizen; m. Akiko Ono, Apr. 6, 1991; children: Max, Jonah. PhD ednl. psychology, Kent State U., 1991—96, MA ednl. psychology; BA philosophy, psychology, Grand Valley State Coll. Japanese Language Proficiency Japanese Ministry of Edn. and The Japan Found., 1999. Peace corps vol. US Peace Corps, Kathmandu, Nepal, 1987—89; instr. of psychology and child devel. Delta Coll., Univ. Ctr., Mich., 2002—; asst. rschr. and tchg. fellow Kent State U., 1991—96; psychology program dir. Human Internat. U., Tokyo, 1997—99; curriculum developer and instr. Kent Gilbert's Gaigo Gakuen, Tokyo, 1989—91; asst. instr. of psychology and religion Lakeland Coll. Japan, Tokyo, 1999—2002. Cross-cultural tng. dir. ALC, Inc., Japan, 1996—97. Author various pofessional articles; translation editor (video series) Aikido and Tai Chi Chuan. Recipient Excellence in Tchg., Human Internat. U, 1999, Scholarship and Svc., Kent State U. 1996. Mem.: AAUP. Eclectic. Achievements include Second Degree Black Belt, Aikido; Language Proficiency, Nepali. Avocations: family, Aikido, travel, reading, recognizing beauty. Office: Delta College 1961 Delta Road University Center MI 48710 E-mail: jeffdykhuizen@alpha.delta.edu.

DYKLA, K.H.S. EDWARD GEORGE, retired social services administrator; b. Chgo., Apr. 13, 1933; s. Edward P. and Rose (Jedrzejczyk) D.; m. Loretta Gilski, Aug. 15, 1959; children: Michael, Mark. BA, Benedictine Coll. Tchr. Weber High Sch., Chgo., 1957-74. Chmn. bd. dirs. Polish Mus. Am., Chgo., 1986-98; bd. dirs. St. Joseph's Home, Chgo., 1986-92; trustee Felician Coll., Chgo., 1984-95; adv. bd., bd. govs. St. Mary's Nazareth Hosp., Chgo., 1988-2000; mem. devel. com. Resurrection Health Care; nat. pres. Polish Roman Cath. Union Am., Chgo., 1986-98, nat. pres. emeritus, amb., 1999—;

trustee Northeastern Ill. U., 1996—; trustee Pope John Paul II Cultural Ctr., Washington DC, 1997—; adv. bd. Ill. Tollway Commn., 1995-2003. With U.S. Army, 1953-55. Mem. Polish Am. Congress (treas. 1986-94, v.p. Ill. div. 1974—, nat. dir. 1994-99), Ill. Fraternal Congress (pres. 1984-86). Roman Catholic. Home: 733 Woodbridge Ct LBS Barrington IL 60010-3857

DYKSTRA, CLIFFORD ELLIOT, chemistry educator, researcher; b. Chgo., Oct. 30, 1952; s. Raymond and Vivian (Mishkutz) D.; m. Dana Ruth Stowers, July 29, 1988; children: Connor Thomas, Tracey Lauren. BS in Physics, BS in Chemistry, U. Ill., 1973; PhD, U. Calif., Berkeley, 1976. Mgmt. trainee Western Electric Co., Chgo., 1972; rsch. asst. U. Calif., Berkeley, 1973-77; asst. prof. chemistry U. Ill., Urbana, 1977-83, assoc. prof. chemistry, 1983-88, prof. chemistry, 1988-90, Ind. U.-Purdue U., Indpls., 1990-2001, assoc. dean of sci., 1992-96, Chancellor's prof., 2001—. Cons. Argonne Nat. Lab., Chgo., 1978-80; mem. editl. bd. Chem. Physics Letters, 1988—, Theoretical Chemistry Accounts, 1997—. Author: Calculation of Structures and Properties of Molecules, 1988, Quantum Chemistry and Molecular Spectroscopy, 1992, Physical Chemistry—A Modern Introduction, 1997; editor: Jour. Molecular Structure Theochem., 1993—. Beckman Rsch. fellow Ctr. for Advanced Study, 1986, Alfred P. Sloan Found. fellow, 1979; named Irwin Rsch. scholar, 2003. Mem. Phi Beta Kappa. Office: Ind Univ Purdue Univ Indpls Dept Chemistry 402 N Blackford St Indianapolis IN 46202-3217

DYKSTRA, DAVID ALLEN, corporate executive; b. Kalamazoo, Feb. 5, 1938; s. Alle and Elizabeth (VanderHorst) D. m. Kathryn Ann DeNio, Aug. 4, 1962 (div. Nov. 1985); children: Brian Thayer, Kristen Lee, Holly Beth. BBA, Western Mich. U., 1966. Pres. Dyco Corp., Portage, Mich., 1970—; realtor Crossroads Real Estate, Kalamazoo, 1994-96, Callander Woollam & Britigan Comml. Realtors, Portage, Mich., 1996-2000, Exit Gulder Real Estate, Naples, Fla., 2000—02, Naples Brokers Realty, 2002—. Cons. Waste Industry, Mich., 1976-82; owner Dairy World Yogurt Shops. Bd. dirs. Portage C. of C., 1980-83, mem. econ. devel. com.; alt. del. Rep. Conv., Mich., 1984; mem. Naples Lakes C. of C., adv. bd. Naples Christian Chamber. Mem.: Beacon Club, Ducks Unltd. (com. mem.), Safari Club Internat. Republican. Avocations: big game hunting, golf. Home: 2068 Crestview Way Naples FL 34119-3306 Office: 11983 N Tamiami Tr # 126 Naples FL 34110 E-mail: naplesdavid@juno.com.

DYKSTRA, DAVID CHARLES, management executive, consultant, accountant, author, educator; b. Des Moines, July 10, 1941; s. Orville Linden and Ermina (Dunn) Dykstra; m. Susan Ogden, Aug. 18, 2001; children from previous marriage: Suzanne, Karin, David S. BSChemE, U. Calif., Berkeley, 1963; MBA, Harvard U., 1966. CPA, Calif. Corp. controller Recreation Environs., Newport Beach, Calif., 1970-71, Hydro Conduit Corp., Newport Beach, 1971-78; v.p. fin. and adminstrn. Tree-Sweet Products, Santa Ana, Calif., 1978-80; pres., owner Dykstra Cons., Irvine, Calif., 1980-88, Marcer Island, Wash., 1998—. Pres. Easy Data Corp., 1981-88; pub. Easy Data Computer Comparisons, 1982-87; sr. mgr. Deloitte & Touche, Costa Mesa, Calif., 1988-90; prof. mgmt. info. sys. Nat. U., Irvine, 1984-90; pub. Dykstra's Computer Digest, 1984-90; pres., owner Golden West Pers., Long Beach, Wash., 1992-93; exec. v.p. Tegris Corp., Bellevue, Wash., 1994-98. Author: Manager's Guide to Business Computer Terms, 1981, Computers for Profit, 1983; contbr. articles to profl. jours. Chmn. 40th Congl. Dist. Tax Reform Immediately, 1977-80; mem. nat. com. Rep. Com.; vice-chmn. Orange County Calif. Rep. Assembly, 1979-80; bd. dirs. Corona Del Mar Rep. Assembly, 1980-94, v.p., 1980-87, pres., 1987-89; mem. Mercer Island Presbyn. Ch., 1998—. Mem. AICPA, Am. Mgmt. Assn., Calif. Soc. CPAs, Data Processing Mgmt. Assn., Am. Prodn. and Inventory Control Soc., Ind. Computer Cons. Assn., Internat. Platform Assn., Data Processing Mgmt. Assn., Orange County C. of C., Newport Beach C. of C., Harvard U. Bus. Sch. Assn. Orange County (bd. dirs. 1984-90, v.p. 1984-86, 87-88, pres. 1986-87, 91-92, chmn. 1993-94), Harvard U. Bus. Sch. Assn. So. Calif. (bd. dirs. 1986-87, 91-92, v.p. 1992-93), Harvard U. Bus. Sch. Assn. Puget Sound, Town Hall, Mercer Island Presbyn. Ch., Mercer Island Country Club, John Wayne Tennis Club, S. Cowichan Lawn Tennis Club, Lido Sailing Club, Columbia Tower Club, Rotary (bd. dirs. 1984-86). Home and Office: 3465 W Mercer Way Mercer Island WA 98040-3355

DYKSTRA, DENNIS DALE, physiatrist; b. Lakewood, Ohio, Feb. 21, 1950; s. Gerald and Grace Maire (Thomas) D.; m. Mary Louise Kerker, May 16, 1992; children: Dorothy, Perry, Caitlin, Patrick. AB in Zoology summa cum laude, Ohio U., 1972; MD, U. Cin., 1976; PhD, U. Minn., 1988, M in Health Adminstrn., 1999. Diplomate Am. Bd. Pediatrics, Am. Bd. Phys. Medicine and Rehab. Intern/resident Cin. Children's Hosp., 1976-81; instr. U. Minn., Mpls., 1981-88, asst. prof., 1988-92, assoc. prof. phys. medicine/rehab./pediatrics/urol. surgery, 1992—, head dept. phys. medicine/rehab., 1992—; assoc. chief staff for rehab. VA Med. Ctr., Mpls., 1994-97. Author: Krusen's Handbook of Phys. Medicine and Rehabilitation, 1991; contbr. articles to profl. jours. Med. advisor Minn. Spasmodic Torticolits Soc., Duluth, Minn., 1991—. Recipient Phys. Med. and Rehab. Investigator award Phys. Med. and Rehab. Rsch. Found., 1984, 85; Spinal Cord Soc. grantee, 1990. Fellow Am. Acad. Phys. Med. and Rehab. (chair edn. com. 1996—), Am. Acad. Pediatrics, Am. Assn. Electrodiagnostic Medicine. Achievements include 2 patents on method of apparatus for mechanical stimulation of nerves, method and device for pharmacological control of spasciticy. Office: Univ of Minn 420 Delaware St SE Box 297 Mayor Bldg Minneapolis MN 55455

DYKSTRA, PAUL HOPKINS, lawyer; b. Chgo., July 13, 1943; s. Paul C. and Frances Marie (Hopkins) D. Student, Exeter Coll. Oxford U., Eng., 1964; AB, Princeton U., 1965; LLB, Yale U., 1968. Bar: Ill. 1968, D.C. 1977. Assoc. Gardner, Carton & Douglas, Chgo., 1968-74, ptnr., 1975—2003, ptnr. Washington office, 1977-79, fin. ptnr., 1985-89, chmn., 1989-95; mem. Bell, Boyd & Lloyd LLC, Chgo., 2003—. Adj. prof. law Northwestern U. Sch. Law, 2001—. Contbr. articles to profl. jours. Trustee Chgo. Theatre Group, Inc. (Goodman Theatre), 1975—, pres., 1983-85, vice chmn., 1988-92, pres., 1992-97; mem. aux. bd. Art Inst. Chgo., 1973-77, 79-88, exec. com., 1976-77, 82-87, 2000—; chmn. Orange and Black Club of Princeton Club of Chgo., 1987-90; chmn. maj. gifts Princeton U. Class of 1965, 1982-85; mem. cultural affairs adv. bd. City of Chgo., 1990—, Blue Skies for Kids, Chgo. Cmty. Trust, Chgo. Pub. Libr. Bd., 1991-97, chmn. adminstrn. and fin. com., 1996—; trustee Chgo. Pub. Libr. Found., 1999—. Mem. ABA (fed. and regulation of securities com.), Chgo. Bar Assn. (sec. 1976-77), Chgo. Hist. Soc. (trustee 1999—, mem. Making History awards com. 1994—, chmn. 2000-2002), Econ. Club of Chgo. (reception com. 1982-85), Legal Club of Chgo., Law Club Chgo., Racquet Club of Chgo. (bd. govs., vice chmn. membership com. 1980-83), Chgo. Club (bd. dirs., sec. 1996-2000), Shoreacres, Chgo. Commonwealth Club, The Comml. Club of Chgo. (sec., mem. exec. com. 2001-03), Chgo. Coun. Fgn. Rels. (Chgo. com.). Episcopalian. Avocations: travel, golf, bicycling. Office: Bell Boyd & Lloyd LLC 70 W Madison St Chicago IL 60602-4207 Office Fax: 312-569-3112. E-mail: pdykstra@gcd.com.

DYKSTRA, ROBERT, retired education educator; b. Vesper, Wis., Feb. 26, 1930; s. John and Anna (Holstein) D.; m. Lou Ann Conselman, Oct. 6, 1956; children: S. Kim, Paul, Randall. BS in Elem. Edn., U. Wis., River Falls, 1957; MA in Ednl. Psychology, U. Minn., 1959, PhD in Ednl. Psychology, 1962. Cert. elem. edn. Elem. tchr. Cedar Grove (Wis.) Pub. Sch., 1954-55; asst. prof. U. Minn., Mpls., 1962-64, assoc. prof., 1965-69, prof., 1970-73, chair dept. curriculum and instrn., 1974-85, prof., 1986-93, ret., 1993. Co-author: Teaching Reading, 1974, Language Arts: Teaching and Learning Effective Use of Language, 1988; contbr. articles to profl. jours. With U.S. Army, 1952-54. Recipient Disting. Alumnus award U. Wis./River Falls, 1998; elected to Reading Hall of Fame, 1996; U.S. Office Edn. rsch. grantee, 1963, 65. Mem. Nat. Coun. Tchrs. of English (mem. exec. com. 1969-71), Nat. Conf. on Rsch. in English (pres. 1984-85), Twin City Area Reading Coun. (pres. 1990-91), Internat. Reading Assn. (mem. pub. com. 1975-77), Nat. Reading Conf. (mem. pub. com. 1978-80). Lutheran. Avocations: barbershop quartet singing, reading, golf. Home: 1998 16th St NW Saint Paul MN 55112-5555 E-mail: bobdykstra@prodigy.net.

DYKSTRA, VERGIL HOMER, retired academic administrator; b. Harrison, S.D., Feb. 1, 1925; s. Broer Doekeles and Nellie (Schippers) D.; m. Shirley Margaret Leslie, June 9, 1949 (div. July 1978); children: Leslie Fran, Lynne Meredith, Craig David, Kevin Scott; m. Wanda Rappaport, Feb. 10, 1980 (div. Apr. 1987). BA summa cum laude, Hope Coll., 1949; MA, U. Wis., 1950, PhD, 1953. Instr. philosophy U. Cin., 1953-54; instr. U. Oreg., 1954-56, asst. prof., 1957-60, assoc. prof., 1960-61; vis. lectr. U. Wis., 1956-57; postdoctoral fellow U. Mich., 1961-62; assoc. dean Harpur Coll., 1962-64; dean adminstrn. SUNY, Binghamton, 1964-65, v.p. adminstrn., 1965-69, prof. philosophy, 1969-73; pres. George Mason U., Fairfax, Va., 1973-77; ednl. cons., 1977-78; adminstrv. v.p. Montgomery Coll., Rockville, Md., 1978-89, ret., 1989. Contbr. articles to profl. jours. With USNR, 1943-46. Home: 10607 Norman Ave Fairfax VA 22030 E-mail: vergild@aol.com.

DYKSTRA, WILLIAM DWIGHT, business executive, consultant; b. Grand Rapids, Mich., June 15, 1927; s. John Albert and Irene (Staplekamp) D.; m. Ann McGuiness, Nov. 2, 1957 (dec. 1988); children: William Hugh, Mary Irene. AB, Hope Coll., 1949; MBA, Ind. U., 1951. Asst. mgr. Ply-Curves, Inc., 1950; originator magnesium metal furniture, 1951; pres. Dwight Corp., 1952-56, W.D. Dykstra Group, Grand Rapids, 1956—. Pres. Burton L. Norton Co., 1990, Tie Life Care, Inc.; bd. dirs. Sheldon Co., Orchard Machine Co. Author: Management and the 4th Estate, New Profits for Management. George F. Baker Scholar selector; elder Dutch Ref. Ch. Recipient Outstanding Furniture Merit award, 1955, Vehicle Color Design award, 1967, P.I.A. Graphic award, 1971, Am. Advt. Fedn. award, 1971, 73, 76, Disting. Entrepreneur Alumnus award Ind. U., 1983. Mem. Am. Econs. Assn., Am. Inst. Graphic Arts (Packaging award 1965, 67), Acad. Polit. Sci., Am. Mktg. Assn. (Mktg. Man of Yr. 1981), Engring. Soc. of Detroit, Soc. Packaging and Handling Engrs., Rotary, Phi Kappa Psi, Pi Kappa Delta. Republican. Home: 1145 Edison Ave NW Grand Rapids MI 49504-3919 Office: Old Tallmadge Grange Hall 01845 Leonard St NW Grand Rapids MI 49544-9510

DYKSTRA LYNCH, MARY ELIZABETH, library and information science educator; b. Philadelphia, Pa., May 21, 1939; arrived in Canada, 1964; d. Edward and Marietta R. (Kuiper) Heerema; m. Michael F. Lynch, Aug. 12, 1995; children from previous marriage: Mark Edward, Jeffrey Garth. BA, Calvin Coll., 1960; MLS, Dalhousie U., Halifax, N.S., 1970; PhD, Sheffield (Eng.) U., 1986. Head cataloguer Dalhousie U. Libr., 1970-74; asst. prof. Sch. Libr. Svc. Dalhousie U., 1974-78, assoc. prof., 1978-82, assoc. prof. Sch. Libr. and Info. Studies, 1983-86, prof., 1987-97, prof. emeritus, 1997—, dir. Sch. Libr. and Info. Studies, 1986-95. Sr. audiovisual libr. Nat. Film Bd. of Can., Montreal, 1982-83, cons. 1977-83; cons. Coun. Mins. Edn., Toronto, Ont., 1984-85, art history info. program J. Paul Getty Trust, Williamstown, Mass., 1988-94; mem. adv. bd. Sch. Health Records Sci., Halifax Infirmary, 1984-97, Libr. Technician Programme, Kings Regional Vocat. Sch., N.S., 1987-90; mem. Can. Commn. on Cataloguing, 1986-94; mem. working group on stds. for subject access Nat. Archives of Can., 1987-93; mem. Can. Adv. Com. for Internat. Orgn. for Standardization, Tech. Commn., Info. and Documentation, 1991—; mem. nat. info. highway adv. coun. of Can., 1994-95, 96-97; rsch. officer U. Sheffield (Eng.), 1996-97. Author: Access to Film Information, 1977, Precis: A Primer, 1985; editor 2 books, several film catalogues; editl. bd. Film Canadiana, 1982-84, Cataloging and Classification Quar., 1980-86, Expert Sys. for Info. Mgmt., 1990-93, Libr. and Info. Sci. Rsch., 1992-96; series editor, occasional papers Sch. Libr. and Info. Studies Dalhousie U., 1986-94; contbr. articles to profl. jours. Pres. Citadel North Neighbourhood Assn., Halifax, 1988; bd. dirs. CANARIE (Canadian Network for Advancement of Rsch., Industry & Edn.), 1996-98, internat. consultants com. World Info. and Comm. Report, UNESCO, Paris, 1998-99, Biblioteca nazionale centrale, Florence, Italy, 2001. Rsch. grantee Dalhousie U., 1976, 80, 90, 96, Social Scis. and Humanities Rsch. Coun., Ottawa, 1987-90. Mem. Can. Libr. Assn. (rep. Can. com. on cataloguing 1986-94), Nova Knowledge, Internat. Soc. for Knowledge Orgn. Office: Dalhousie Univ Sch Libr & Info Studies Halifax NS Canada B3H 4H8 E-mail: m.lynch@sheffield.ac.uk.

DYLAG, HELEN MARIE, healthcare administrator; b. Cleve., Oct. 14, 1950; d. Stanley John and Helen Agnes (Jarkiewicz) D. BSN, St. John Coll., Cleve., 1971; MS, Ohio State U., 1973. RN, Ohio. Nurse V.A. Adminstrn. Hosp., Brecksville, Ohio, 1971-72; clin. specialist, psychiat.-mental health nursing Marymount Hosp./Mental Health Ctr., Garfield Heights, Ohio, 1973-78, dir. consultation and edn. dept., 1978-84, dir. Ctr. for Health Styles, 1984-88; adminstrv. dir. Women's Healthcare Ctr./St. Luke's Hosp., Cleve., 1988-90; adminstrv. dir. dept. of psychiatry MetroHealth Sys, Cleve., 1990-97; pres. FarWest Ctr., Westlake, Ohio, 1997—. Contbg. author: Nursing of Families in Crisis, 1974, Distributive Nursing Practice: A Systems Approach to Community Health, 1977; producer and host "Health Styles" TV Talk Show, 1987-88; contbr. articles to profl. jours. Trustee The Stroke Assn. of Ohio, Cleve., 1990-91; mem. Women of Achievement com., Women's City Club, Cleve., 1989-91. Recipient award Greater Cleve. Hosp. Assn., 1981, Innovator award Am. Hosp. Assn./Ctr. for Health Promotion, 1985, Disting. Women Healthcare award Healthcare Monitor and Vis. Nurse Assn. Cleve., 2000. Mem. Assn. Mental Health Adminstrs., Am. Coll. Healthcare Execs., Healthcare Adminstrs. Assn. of Northeast Ohio, Sigma Theta Tau. Avocations: interior design, gardening, jazz, aerobic exercise, travel. Home: 5709 Onaway Oval Cleveland OH 44130-1642 Office: FarWest Ctr 29133 Health Campus Dr Cleveland OH 44145-5256

DYLAN, BOB (ROBERT ALLEN ZIMMERMAN), singer, composer; b. Duluth, Minn., May 24, 1941; Student, U. Minn., 1960; self-taught on guitar, piano, autoharp, harmonica; Mus.D. (hon.), Princeton U., 1970. Performer numerous tours and concerts, 1960—. Albums Bob Dylan, The Free Wheelin' Bob Dylan, The Times They Are a Changin', Another Side of Bob Dylan, Bringing It All Back Home, Highway 61 Revisited, Blonde on Blonde, John Wesley Harding, Nashville Skyline, Self Portrait, New Morning, Desire, Infidels, Empire Burlesque, Dylan, Planet Waves, (with The Band) Before the Flood, The Basement Tapes, Street Legal, Slow Train Coming, Knocked Out Loaded, 1986, Hard Rain, Blood on the Tracks, (5 record set) Biograph, 1960, Down In The Groove, 1988, (with Traveling Wilburys) Traveling Wilburys, 1988, (with Grateful Dead) Dylan and the Dead, Oh Mercy, 1989, (with the Grateful Dead) Under The Red Sky, 1990, (with Traveling Wilburys) Vol. 3, 1990 (Grammy award), The Bootleg Series, 1961, 1990, Good as I Been to You, 1992, World Gone Wrong, 1993, Unplugged, 1995, Time Out of Mind (Grammy award, 1998), appearances (films) Don't Look Back, Renaldo and Clara, Eat the Document, Pat Garrett and Billy the Kid, Concert for Bangla Desh, Hearts of Fire, 1987; composer: (songs) Blowin' in the Wind, Like a Rolling Stone, Lay, Lady, Lay, Subterranean Homesick Blues, Forever Young, Gotta Serve Somebody, Don't Think Twice, It's Alright, A Hard Rain's A-Gonna Fall, The Times They are A-Changin', Just Like a Woman, I'll Be Your Baby Tonight, I Shall Be Released, Mr. Tambourine Man, Simple Twist of Fate, Paths of Victory, others; author (numerous publs.): Tarantula, 1966, 1971, Writings and Drawings by Bob Dylan, 1973, The Songs of Bob Dylan from 1966-1975, 1976, Lyrics, 1985, Drawn Blank, 1994; interactive CD-ROM Highway 61 Revisited, 1995. Named to Rock and Roll Hall of Fame, 1988; recipient Grammy nomination (Best Rock Duo or Group Performance, 1994) for "My Back Pages", (with Roger McGuinn, Tom Petty, Neil Young, Eric Clapton, and George Harrison). Achievements include devising and popularizing folk-rock. Office: Columbia Records 550 Madison Ave New York NY 10022-3211

DYLEWSKI, GARY R. retired career officer; b. Erie, Pa., Nov. 22, 1952; m. Lynne Rousey; 2 children: Christopher, Matthew. BA in Biology, Kent State U., 1974; M in Mgmt., Troy State U., 1980; grad., Squadron Officer Sch., 1985, Air Command and Staff Coll., 1993, Air War Coll., 1993. Commd. 2d lt. USAF, 1975, advanced through grades to col., 1993; squadron weapons officer, flight examiner, instr. 425th Tactical Fighter Tng. Squadron, Williams AFB, Ariz., 1980-85; assignments officer, rated force mgr. for dep. chief staff Pers., Hdqs., Tactical Air Command, Langley AFB, Va., 1985-88; Air Force aide to Pres. Reagan The Pentagon, Washington, 1988-89; dir. tng. 21st Tactical Fighter Wing, Elmendorf AFB, Alaska, 1989-90; ops. officer 43d Tactical Fighter Squadron, Elmendorf AFB, 1990-91; comdr. 90th Tactical Fighter Squadron, Elmendorf AFB, 1991-92; joint dir. for ops. Alaskan Air Command, Elmendorf AFB, 1993-95; comdr. 33d Fighter Wing, Eglin AFB, Fla., 1996-97, 1st Fighter Wing, Langley AFB, 1997—, Space Warfare Ctr, Schriever AFB, CO, 1999—. Decorated Def. Superior Svc. medal, Meritorious Svc. medal with 3 oak leaf clusters. Office: SWC/USAF 730 Irwin Ave Ste 83 Falcon AFB CO 80912-7398

DYLINA, TIMOTHY JOSEPH, dentist, educator; b. Lewistown, Mont., May 30, 1948; s. Joseph John and Thelma Mary Dylina; m. Lisa Kaye Wilson, Mar. 23, 1983; children: Elizabeth Rayeann, Robert Joseph. DDS, U. of So. Calif., 1976—80. Dentist. Dir. No. Calif. Dawson/Pankey Study Club, Merced, Calif., 1996—2002. Contbr. articles to profl. jours. Pres. Mercy Hosp. Found. Bd., Merced, Calif., 2002—. Specialist 4 U.S. Army, 1970—72, South Vietnam. Decorated Vietnam svc. ribbon, combat infantryman's badge US Army. Fellow: Acad. of Gen. Dentistry and the Am. Osseointegration Soc. (licentiate); mem.: ADA, Yosemite Dental Soc. (licentiate; pres. 1998—99), Am. Acad. of Fixed Prosthodontics (licentiate), Am. Equilibration Soc. (licentiate). R-Consevative. Christian. Avocations: golf, travel, exercise, reading, embroidery. Home: 1573 EN Bear Creek Merced CA 95340 Office: Tim J Dylina DDS FAGD 360 E Yosemite Ave Merced CA 95340 Home Fax: 209-723-4823; Office Fax: 209-723-4823. Personal E-mail: timgolf2@aol.com.

DYM, CLIVE LIONEL, engineering educator; b. Leeds, Eng., July 15, 1942; came to U.S., 1949, naturalized, 1954; s. Isaac and Anna (Hochmann) D.; children: Jordana, Miriam; m. Joan Dym, June 28, 1998. BCE, Cooper Union, 1962; MS, Poly. Inst. Bklyn., 1964; PhD, Stanford U., 1967. Asst. prof. SUNY, Buffalo, 1966-69; assoc. professorial lectr. George Washington U., Washington, 1969; research staff Inst. Def. Analyses, Arlington, Va., 1969-70; assoc. prof. Carnegie-Mellon U., Pitts., 1970-74; vis. assoc. prof. TECHNION, Israel, 1971; sr. scientist Bolt Beranek and Newman, Inc., Cambridge, Mass., 1974-77; prof. U. Mass., Amherst, 1977-91, head dept. civil engring., 1977-85; Fletcher Jones prof. engring. design Harvey Mudd Coll., Claremont, Calif., 1991—, dir. Ctr. Design Edn., 1995—, chair dept. engring., 1999—2002. Vis. sr. rsch. fellow Inst. Sound and Vibration Rsch., U. Southampton, Eng., 1973; vis. scientist Xerox PARC, 1983-84; vis. prof. civil engring. Stanford U., 1983-84, Carnegie Mellon U., 1990; Eshbach vis. prof. Northwestern U., 1997-98; cons. Bell Aerospace Co., 1967-69, Dravo Corp., 1970-71, Salem Corp., 1972, Gen. Analytics Inc., 1972, ORI, Inc., 1979, BBN Inc., 1979, Avco, 1981-83, 85-86, TASC, 1985-86, D.H. Brown Assocs., 1991, Johnson Controls, 1996; vice chmn. adv. bd. Amerinex Artificial Intelligence, 1986-88. Author: (with I.H. Shames) Solid Mechanics: A Variational Approach, 1973, Introduction to the Theory of Shells, rev. edit. 1990, Stability Theory and Its Applications to Structural Mechanics, 1974, 2002, (with E.S. Ivey) Principles of Mathematical Modeling, 1980, (with I.H. Shames) Energy and Finite Element Methods in Structural Mechanics, 1985, (with R.E. Levitt) Knowledge-Based Systems in Engineering, 1990, Engineering Design: A Synthesis of Views, 1994, Structural Modeling and Analysis, 1997, (with P. Little) Engineering Design: A Project-Based Introduction, 1999, 2d edit., 2003, (with P.D. Cha and J.J. Rosenberg), Fundamentals of Modeling and Analyzing Engineering Systems, 2000; editor: (with A. Kalnins) Vibration: Beams, Plates, and Shells, 1977, Applications of Knowledge-Based Systems to Engineering Analysis and Design, 1985, Computing Futures in Engineering Design, 1997, Designing Design Education for the 21st Century, 1999, (with L. Winner) Social Dimensions of Engineering Design, 2001, Artificial Intelligence for Engring. Design Analysis and Mfg., 1986-96; contbr. articles and tech. reports to profl. publs. NATO sr. fellow in sci., 1973; Outstanding Engring. Educator award (first-runnerup), 2001. Fellow Acoustical Soc. Am., ASME, ASCE (Walter L. Huber research prize 1980); mem. Am. Assn. for Artificial Intelligence, Computer Soc. of IEEE, ASEE (Western Electric Fund award 1983, Fred Merryfield Design award 2002). Jewish. Office: Harvey Mudd Coll Engring Dept 301 E 12th St Claremont CA 91711-5901

DYMALLY, MERVYN MALCOLM, retired congressman, international business executive; b. Cedros, Trinidad, W.I., May 12, 1926; s. Hamid A. and Andreid S. (Richardson) D.; m. Alice M. Gueno; children: Mark, Lynn. BA in Edn., Calif. State U., 1954; MA in Govt., Calif. State U., Sacramento, 1970; PhD in Human Behavior, U.S. Internat. U., 1978; JD (hon.), Lincoln U., Sacramento, 1975; LLD (hon.), U. W. L.A., 1970, Calif. Coll. Law, L.A., City U., L.A., 1976, Fla. Meml. Coll., 1987, Lincoln U., San Francisco, 1984; HLD (hon.), Shaw U., N.C., 1981; PHD (hon.), Calif. Western. U., 1982. Cert. elem., secondary and exceptional children tchr. Tchr. L.A. City Schs., 1955-61; coord. Calif. Disaster Office, 1961-62; mem. Calif. Assembly, 1962-66, 2002—, Calif. Senate, 1967-74; lt. gov. Calif., 1975-79; mem. 97th-102nd Congresses from 31st Calif. dist., 1981-92; pres. Dymally Internat. Group Inc., Inglewood, Calif., 1992—. Mem. Com. on Fgn. Affairs and its subcoms. on Internat. Ops., chmn. subcom. on Africa, 1989-92; mem. Com. on D.C. and chmn. subcom. on judiciary and edn., 1981-92; chmn. Congl. Task Force on Minority Set Asides, 1987-92; chmn. Senate Majority Caucus, Senate Select Com. on Children and Youth; chmn. Senate coms. on mil. and vets. affairs, social welfare, elections and reapportionment, subcom. on med. edn. and health needs; chmn. joint coms. on legal equality for women, on revision of election code; chmn. assembly com. on indsl. rels.; current mem. Congl. Hispanic Caucus, Congl. Caucus Women's Issues, Congl. Human Rights Caucus, Congl. Black Caucus and chmn. of its task force on Caribbean; chmn. Caribbean Action Lobby, Caribbean Am. Rsch. Inst.; founder Congl. Inst. for Space, Sci. and Tech., chmn. adv. bd.; past chmn. Calif. Commn. Econ. Devel., Commn. of Califs. (U.S., Baja Calif., Calif. Sur, Mex.); past vice chmn., Nat. Conf. Lt. Govs.; former Gov.'s designee U.S. Border States Commn.; past mem. State Lands Commn., others; lectr. Claremont (Calif.) Grad. Sch., Golden Gate U., Sacramento, Pepperdine U., L.A., Pomona (Calif.) Coll., U. Calif., Davis, Irvine, Whittier (Calif.) Coll., Shaw U., Raleigh, N.C.; Disting. prof. Ctrl. State U.; mem. faculty Drew U. Medicine and Sci.; adj. prof. Compton Coll.; cons. to chancellor L.A. C.C. Author: The Black Politician-His Struggle for Power, 1971; co-auhtor: (with Dr. Jeffrey Elliot) Fidel Castro: Nothing Can Stop the Course of History, 1986, also articles; former editor:The Black Politician (quar.) Mem. L.A. County Water Appeals Bd.; advisor to Calif. Assembly Spkr. for Cmty. Congress; chmn. Calif. Black Leadership Roundtable, Caribbean Am. Coalition; chair select com. cmty. colls. Prof. Charles R. Drew U. Medicine Sci. Recipient numerous awards including Chaconia Gold medal Govt. Trinidad and Tobago, Adam Clayton Powell award Congl. Black Caucus, Dr. Solomon P. Fuller award Black Psychiatrists of Am., others from Golden State Med. Assn., United Tchrs. L.A., Bd. Suprs. L.A., L.A. City Coun., various univs., colls., orgns. Mem. AAUP, NAACP, Am. Acad. Polit. Sci., Am. Polit. Sci. Assn., Am. Acad. Polit. and Social Sci., ACLU, Urban League, Phi Kappa Phi, Kappa Alpha Psi Democrat. Office: Dymally Internat Group Inc 322 W Compton Blvd # 100 Compton CA 90220 Home: 223 S Acacia Ave # 206 Compton CA 90220 Fax: 310-764-4003. E-mail: mmdymally@yahoo.com.

DYMOND, LEWIS WANDELL, lawyer, mediator, educator; b. Lansing, Mich., June 28, 1920; s. Lewis Wandell and Irene (Parker) D.; m. Betty Louise Blood, Sept. 6, 1942; children: Lewis W., Jean Ann; m. Joann Surrey, Sept. 3, 1966; 1 son, Steven Henry. JD cum laude, U. Miami, 1956. Bar: Fla. 1957; cert. ct. mediator, Fla. With Nat. Airlines, Inc., Miami, Fla., 1938-62, mechanic, agt., sta. mgr., flight dispatcher, ops. mgr., pilot, v.p. ops., maintenance and engring., 1955-62; pres., chief exec. officer, dir. Frontier Airlines, 1962-79. Adj. prof. Sch. Bus. U. Miami, Coral Gables, Fla. Mem. U. Miami Alumni Club, Union League, Surf Club, Masons, Shriners, Phi Kappa Phi, Phi Alpha Delta. Home and Office: 6 E Belleview Way Greenwood Village CO 80121-1408

DYNARSKI, SUSAN MARIE, social studies educator; AB, Harvard U., 1987, MPP, 1995; PhD, MIT, 1999. Union organizer AFSCME, Cambridge, Mass., 1987—93; asst. prof. Harvard Kennedy Sch. Govt., 1999—. Fellow: Joint Ctr. Policy Rsch., Nat. Bur. Econ. Rsch. Office: Harvard Kennedy Sch Govt 79 JFK St Cambridge MA 02138

DYNES, ROBERT C. academic administrator; b. London, Ont., Can., Nov. 8, 1942; m. Frances Hellman. BS of Math. & Physics, U. Western Ont., 1964; MS of Physics, McMaster U., 1965, PhD of Phys., 1968. Postdoctoral fellow AT&T Bell Labs, Murray Hill, NJ, 1968—70, mem., technical staff, 1970—74, dept. head, semiconductor & chem. physics rsch., 1974—81, dept. head, solid state & physics of materials rsch., 1981—83, dir., chem. physics rsch., 1983—90; physics prof. U. Calif., San Diego, 1991—2003; chair, dept. physics U. Calif. San Diego, 1994—95; sr. vice chancellor, acad. affairs U. Calif., 1995—96, Chancellor, 1996—2003, U. Calif. System, Oakland, 2003—. Recipient Fritz London award Low Temp. Physics, 1990. Fellow: Can. Inst. Advances Rsch., Am. Phys. Soc.; mem.: Am. Acad. Arts & Scis., Nat. Acad. Scis. Office: Office of Pres U. Calif System 1111 Franklin St Oakland CA 94607-5200

DYNKIN, EUGENE B. mathematics educator; b. Leningrad, USSR, May 11, 1924; came to U.S., 1977, naturalized, 1983; s. Boris and Rebecca (Sheindlin) D.; m. Irene Pakshver, June 2, 1959; 1 child, Olga. BA, Moscow U., 1945, PhD, 1948, D.Sc., 1951; D Honoris Causa, U. Pierre and Marie Curie, Paris, 1997, Intermediate Moscow U. Asst. prof. Moscow U., 1948-49, assoc. prof.,

1949-54, prof., 1954-68; sr. research scholar Central Inst. Math. Econ. Acad. of Sci., Moscow, 1968-76; prof. math. Cornell U., Ithaca, N.Y., 1977—. Author: Theory of Markov Processes, 1960, Mathematical Conversations, 1963, Markov Processes, 1965, Mathematicl Problems, 1969, Markov Processes-Theorems and Problems, 1969, Controlled Markov Processes, 1979, Markov Processes and Related Problems of Analysis, 1982, An Introduction to Branching Measure-Valued Processes, 1994, Biography and Bibliography in the Dynkin Festschrift, Markov Processes and Their Applications, 1994, Selected Papers of E.B. Dynkin, 2000, Diffusion, Superdiffusions and Partial Differential Equations, 2002. Fellow: AAAS, Inst. Math. Stats.; mem.: NAS, Bernoulli Soc. Math. Stats. and Probability, Moscow Math. Soc. (hon. prize 1951), Am. Math. Soc. (Leroy P. Steele prize 1993). Home: 107 Lake St Ithaca NY 14850-3855 Office: Cornell U Dept Math Malott Hall Ithaca NY 14853 E-mail: ebd1@cornell.edu.

DYONIZIAK, ADAMA, health agency administrator; b. Bklyn., Dec. 10, 1966; d. Kazimierz and Marianna Barbara Dyoniziak. BA, U. Calif., San Diego, 1988; MPH, San Diego State U., 1992. Mgr. Watts Health Found., L.A., 1992-94; youth health edn. supr. Long Beach (Calif.) Dept. Health and Human Svcs., 1994-2000; L.A. regional program dir. Braille Inst., 2000—; prof. dept. health sci. Calif. State U., Long Beach, 2000—. Mem. Long Beach HIV Comprehensive Planning Group, 1996-2000. Mem.: APHA. Avocations: dancing, cross-stitch, reading. Home: 4540 Orange Ave #204 Long Beach CA 90807 Office: Braille Inst 741 N Vermont Ave Los Angeles CA 90029 E-mail: adamadyoniziak@hotmail.com.

DYREGROV, MICHAEL See BAKER, JOHN STEVENSON

DYRSTAD, JOANELL M. former lieutenant governor, consultant; b. St. James, Minn., Oct. 15, 1942; d. Arnold A. and Ruth (Berlin) Sletta; m. Marvin Dyrstad, 1965; children: Troy, Anika. BA, Gustavus Adolphus Coll., St. Peter, Minn., 1964; MA, Hamline U., 1996. Mayor City of Red Wing, Minn., 1985-90; lt. gov. State of Minn., 1991-94; now independent bus. and govt. cons. Ptnr. Corner Drugstore, Red Wing, 1968—; v.p. League Minn. Cities, 1990-91, Minn. Mayors Assn., 1989-90; mem. Nat. Conf. Lt. Gov.'s, 1991-94, chair, 1993-94. Trustee Gustavus Adolphus Coll., 1989-98, U. Minn. Found., 1993-99; dir. corp. bd. Fairview Health Sys.; dir. Fairview Red Wing Health Svcs., chair, 2002; dir. Minn. Hosp. Health Care Partnership, 1999—. Mem. AAUW (Citizen of yr. award 1985), LWV.

DYRUD, AMOS OLIVER, minister, educator; b. Newfolden, Minn., June 6, 1915; s. Petter Andrew and Marie (Hanson) D.; m. Ovidie Marie Evenson, June 15, 1948; children: Peter, Naomi, Rebecca, Samuel. BA, Augsburg Coll., 1949; postgrad. in Christian Theology, Luth. Free Ch. Theol. Sem., 1949; cert., L'Alliance Francaise, Paris, 1950. Ordained to ministry Free Luth. Ch., 1949. Pastor, missionary Luth. Free Ch., and Am. Luth. Ch., Madagascar, 1949-69; instr. Assn. Free Luth. Congregations Schs., Mpls., 1969—, dean theol. sem., 1971-81. Chmn. World Missions Com., Assn. Free Luth. Congregations, 1982-88. With USN, 1943. Home: 4509 Jersey Ave N Minneapolis MN 55428-5139

DYSART, BENJAMIN CLAY, III, consultant, conservationist, engineer; b. Columbia, Tenn., Feb. 12, 1940; s. Benjamin Clay and Kathryne Virginia (Thompson) D.; m. Nancy Elizabeth McDonald, Dec. 28, 1991. BE, Vanderbilt U., 1961, MS in San. Engring., 1964; PhD in Civil Engring., Ga. Inst. Tech., 1969. Staff engr. Union Carbide Corp., 1961-62, 64-65; from asst. prof. to prof. Clemson U., 1968-90, McQueen Quattlebaum prof. engring., 1982-83, dir. S.C. Water Resources Rsch. Inst., 1968-75, dir. water resources engring. grad. program, 1972-75, adj. prof., 1990-93; facility devel. mgr. Chem. Waste Mgmt., Inc., Marietta, Ga., 1990-91, regional facility devel. mgr. Memphis, 1991; dir. project planning and integration Waste Mgmt., Inc., Washington, 1991-92; pres. Dysart & Assocs., Inc., Atlanta, 1992—. Sci. advisor Office Sec. of Army, Washington, 1975-76; mem. EPA Sci. Adv. Bd., from 1983; sr. fellow The Conservation Found., 1985—; mem. adv. coun. Electric Power Rsch. Inst., 1989-95; mem., chief of engrs. environ. adv. bd. U.S. Army Corps Engrs., 1988-92; mem. Glacier Nat. Park Sci. Coun., Nat. Park Svc., 1988-91; mem. S.C. Gov.'s Wetlands Forum, 1989-90; sec. appointee Outer Continental Shelf Adv. Bd. and OCS Sci. Com. Dept. Interior, 1979-82; mem. S.C. Environ. Quality Control Adv. Com., 1980-90, chmn., 1980-81; mem. Sci. Panel to Rev. Interagy. Rsch. on Impact of Oil Pollution NOAA, Dept. Commerce, 1980; mem. Nuclear Energy Ctr. Environ. Task Force Dept. Energy-So. States Energy Bd., 1978-81; mem. Nonpoint Source Pollutant Task Force EPA, 1979-80; mem. civil works adv. com. Office Sec. Army-Young Pres.'s Orgn., 1975-76; mem. S.C. Heritage Adv. Bd., 1974-76; cons. on strategic environ. mgmt., corp. social responsibility and stakeholder involvement matters to industry and govt. agys. Editor: (with Marion Clawson) Managing Public Lands in the Public Interest, 1988, Public Interest in the Use of Private Lands, 1989; contbr. articles on math. modeling in water quality and environ. mgmt. and pub. involvement to profl. jours.; author numerous profl. papers, reports. Trustee Rene Dubos Ctr. for Human Environs., 1985-94, vice chmn., mem. exec. com., 1988-94; bd. visitors Kanuga Episcopal Conf. Ctr., 1988—. Recipient Tribute of Appreciation for Disting. Svc. EPA, 1981, 86, McQueen Quattlebaum Engring. Faculty Achievement award Clemson U., 1982, Order of Palmetto Gov. S.C., 1984; named Hon. Ky. Col., 1976. Mem. Trout Unltd. (trustee 1990-94), Nat. Wildlife Fedn. (bd. dirs. 1974-90, v.p. 1978-83, pres., chmn. bd. dirs. 1983-85), Assn. Environ. Engring. Profs. (bd. dirs. 1978-83, pres., chmn. bd. dirs. 1981-82), Water Environ. Fedn. (hon., bd. dirs. Rsch. Found. 1989-91), S.C. Wildlife Fedn. (bd. dirs. 1969—, pres., chmn. bd. dirs. 1973-74, S.C. Wildlife Conservationist Yr.), The Ga. Conservancy (bd. trustees 1994-97), Cosmos Club (Washington), Sigma Xi, Tau Beta Pi, Phi Kappa Phi, Chi Epsilon, Omega Rho, Sigma Nu. Episcopalian. Office: Dysart & Associates Inc 224 Broadland Ct NW Atlanta GA 30342-3601

DYSART, RICHARD A. actor; b. Brighton, Mass., Mar. 30, 1929; m. Kathryn Jacobi. BS, Emerson Coll., 1956, MS, 1983, LLD (hon.), 1988; PhD (hon.), U. Maine, 1992. Appeared off Broadway in Our Town, Six Characters in Search of an Author; on Broadway in A Man for All Seasons, The Little Foxes, A Place Without Doors, That Championship Season, Another Part of the Forest; (feature films) Petulia, The Lost Man, The Sporting Club, The Hospital, The Terminal Man, The Day of the Locust, The Hindenberg, Prophecy, Meteor, Being There, An Enemy of the People, The Thing, The Falcon and the Snowman, Mask, Pale Rider, Wall Street, Back to the Future Part III, Hard Rain; (TV movies) The Autobiography of Miss Jane Pittman, It Happened One Christmas, First You Cry, Bogie, The Ordeal of Dr. Mudd, Churchill and the Generals (BBC), Sandburg's Lincoln, People Vs. Jean Harris, Bitter Harvest, Last Days of Patton, Malice in Wonderland, Day One, Truman; (series) L.A. Law, 1986-94 (Supporting Actor TV-Series Emmy award 1992), L.A. Law Reunion Movie, 2002; (PBS spl.) Concealed Enemies; (mini-series) War and Remembrance. Trustee Gallaudet U., Washington, 1990—, Gould Acad., Bethel, Maine; founding mem. Am. Conservatory Theatre, San Francisco; active Native Am. Rights Fund. Mem.: Am. Judicature Soc. (bd. dirs., nat. exec. com. 1998—). Fax: 310-399-5330. E-mail: homerpilgrim@adelphia.net.

DYSON, ALLAN JUDGE, retired librarian; b. Lawrence, Mass., Mar. 28, 1942; s. Raymond Magan and Hilda D.; m. Susan Cooper, 1987; 1 child, Brenna Ruth. BA in Govt., Harvard U., 1964; MSLS, Simmons Coll., 1968. Asst. to dir. Columbia U. Librs., N.Y.C., 1968-71; head Moffitt Undergrad. Libr. U. Calif., Berkeley, 1971-79, univ. libr. Santa Cruz, 1979—2003, ret., 2003. Editor Coll. and Rsch. Librs. News, 1973-74; chmn. editl. bd. Choice mag., 1978-80, Am. Librs., 1986-89. CFO Cabrillo (Calif.) Music Festival, 1985-86; chmn. No. Calif. Regional Libr. Bd., 1986-88, 94-98, U. Calif. Librs. Group, 1998-2001. Lt. U.S. Army, 1964-66. Decorated Army Commendation medal; Coun. on Libr. Resources fellow, 1973-74. Mem. ALA, ACLU, Assn. Coll. and Rsch. Librs., Librs. Assn. U. Calif. (pres. 1976), Sierra Club.

DYSON, FREEMAN JOHN, physicist, educator; b. Crowthorne, Eng., Dec. 15, 1923; s. George and Mildred Lucy (Atkey) D.; m. Verena Haefeli-Huber, Aug. 11, 1950 (div. 1958); children: Esther, George; m. Imme Jung, Nov. 21, 1958; children: Dorothy, Emily, Mia, Rebecca. BA, Cambridge U., 1945. Operations research RAF Bomber Command, 1943-45; fellow Trinity Coll., Cambridge U., Eng., 1946-49; Commonwealth fellow Cornell U., Princeton, 1947-49; prof. physics Cornell U., 1951-53; prof. Inst. Advanced Study, Princeton, 1953-94; prof. emeritus, 1994—. Author: Disturbing the Universe, 1979, Weapons and Hope, 1984, Origins of Life, 1986, Infinite in all Directions, 1988, From Eros to Gaia, 1992, Imagined Worlds, 1997, The Sun, the Genome and the Internet, 1999. Recipient Enrico Fermi award U.S. Dept. of Energy, 1995, Templeton prize for Progress in Religion, 2000. Fellow Royal Soc. London; mem. NAS, Am. Phys. Soc. Home: 105 Battle Road Cir Princeton NJ 08540-4904 E-mail: dyson@ias.edu.

DYSON, TIM, public relations executive; Student, Loughborough U., Eng. CEO Text 100, London. Mem. U.K. Inst. Dirs., Inst. Pub. Rels., Pub. Rels. Soc. Am., Washington Software Assn. and Digital Media Alliance, Seattle C. of C. Office: Text 100 Ltd Network House Wood Ln London W12 7SL England

DYSON, WILLIAM R. state legislator, educator; b. Waycross, Ga., July 12, 1940; s. Edward James Jr. and Lula Lorene (William) D.; m. Rebecca Johnson, 1964; children: Sonia, Wilfred, Erick, Michael. BA, Morris Coll., 1962; postgrad., NYU, 1963-66, Howard U., 1970; MA, So. Conn. State U., 1976, diploma, 1981. Alderman, New Haven, Conn., 1976; mem. Dist. 94 Conn. Ho. of Reps., 1977—, asst. minority leader, mem. edn. com., chmn. appropriations com., mem. gov.'s child care study com.; tchr. Blackshear, Ga., 1967, Douglas, Ga., 1968-69, New Haven, Conn., 1970—. Mem. NEA, Conn. Edn. Assn., New Haven Edn. Assn., Masons. Address: 196 Mansfield St New Haven CT 06511-3539

DYTRYCH, DENISE DISTEL, lawyer; b. Chgo., June 20, 1961; d. Melvin John Distel and Patricia Loretta Blake. AA, Broward C.C., Coconut Creek, Fla., 1979; B in Associated Arts, Fla. Atlantic U., 1982; JD, Nova U., 1986. Bar: Fla. 1987; cert. Am. Coun. on Exercise, Lifestyle and Weight Mgmt. Cons.; cert. personal trainer, weight room instr. and advanced fitness practitioner Aerobic Fitness Assn. Am. Law clk. Panza, Maurer, Maynard, Ft. Lauderdale, Fla., 1984-86; asst. county atty. Palm Beach County Atty., West Palm Beach, 1986-94, exec. asst. county atty., 1994-96, county atty., 1996—. Author: Christmas Party Celebrations: 71 New and Exciting Party Plans for Holiday Fun, 1998. Auction com. mem. Am. Heart Assn., 1998—, advt. chmn. Heart Ball, 1999—. Recipient Up & Comers award Price Waterhouse, 1994; named Outstanding Young Women of Am., 1987. Mem. Fla. Bar (15th jud. at-large rep. govt. lawyer sect.), Palm Beach County Bar (com. mem. govt. lawyer sect.), Fla. Guild Cath. Lawyers, 15th Jud. Cir. Pro Bono Com. Roman Catholic. Avocations: reading, writing, health and fitness, golf. Address: Ofc Bd Cty Commrs PO Box 1989 West Palm Beach FL 33402-1989

DYYON, MARIO (LEROY FRAZIER), artist; b. Fort Myers, Fla., May 2, 1946; s. Sallie Frazier. Lectr., Westside Community Ctr., N.Y.C., 1971, Case Western Res. U., 1983. Group exhbns. include Cleve. Top Artists, Intown Club, Cleve., 1969, Art Inst. Akron, 1969-70, Mus. Modern Art, N.Y.C., 1970, Whitney Mus. Ann., 1972, Mus. Contemporary Hispanic Art, 1985; one-man show at Case Western Res. U., 1983; represented in permanent collections Mus. Modern Art, N.Y.C., Whitney Mus. Am. Art, N.Y.C., Case Western Res. U., Larry Aldrich Mus., Conn., various pvt. collections. Printmaker's Workshop scholar, 1982. Roman Catholic. Address: 155 W 73rd St New York NY 10023-2921 *Success is a love for your work. This may be too broad. Let me put a fine point on it. How to be successful really? In all your deeds, and in your dreams, try to make God smile. So, throw your vanity out the window and get to work. Be as the commen tern, on the move.*

DZAU, VICTOR JOSEPH, physician, scientist, educator; b. Shanghai, Oct. 23, 1945; MD, McGill U., 1972. Cert. in internal medicine, subspecialty in cardiovasc. disease. Intern N.Y. Hosp., 1972-73; resident in medicine Peter Bent Brigham Hosp., Boston, 1974-76, chief resident, 1976-78; fellow in rsch. Mass. Gen. Hosp., Boston, 1976-78, fellow in cardiology, 1979-80; chief divsn. vascular medicine and atherosclerosis Brigham & Women's Hosp., 1984-90; chief divsn. cardiovasc. medicine Stanford U. Sch. Medicine, 1990-96, dir. cardiovasc. rsch. ctr., assoc. chmn. dept. medicine, 1993-96, chmn. dept. medicine, 1995-96; dir. Am. Heart Assn.-Bugher Found. Ctr. for Molecular Biology, 1991-96; chmn. dept. med., dir. rsch. Brigham & Women's Hosp., 1996—. From asst. prof. medicine to assoc. prof. medicine Harvard Med. Sch., 1980-90; William G. Irvin prof. medicine Stanford U. Sch. Medicine, 1990-96, Arthur L. Bloomfield prof., chmn. medicine, 1995-96; Hersey prof. theory and practice of medicine Harvard Med. Sch., 1996—. Office: Harvard Med Sch-Brigham & Women's Hosp 75 Francis St Boston MA 02115-6110

DZHAFAROV, EHTIBAR N. mathematical psychologist; b. Baku, Azerbaijan, Nov. 4, 1952; s. Nuraddin and Adela Dzhafarov; m. Ivana Jirankova, June 19, 1973; children: Radomil, Damir. PhD in Psychology, Moscow State U., 1979. Prof. psychology Purdue U., West Lafayette, Ind., 1998—. Office: Purdue U 1364 Psychl Scis Bldg Lafayette IN 47907-1364 Business E-Mail: ehtibar@purdue.edu.

DZIADYK, BOHDAN, botany and ecology educator; b. Aschaffenburg, Germany, Mar. 26, 1948; came to U.S., 1950; s. Iwan and Maria (Jaroszuk) D.; m. Marietta Jay Johnston, Mar. 23, 1974; children: Jennifer Maria, Joseph Walter. BA, Southern Ill. U., 1970, MS, 1980; PhD, N.D. State U., 1982. From instr. to assoc. prof. botany and ecology Augustana Coll., Rock Island, Ill., 1980-96, prof., 1996—, co-dir. environ. studies program, 1981—, dir. coll. field stas., 1991—; chmn. biology dept., 1992-95. Bd. dirs. Quad Cities Bot. Ctr. Contbr. articles to profl. jours. Sgt. AUS, 1970-73. Pew Sci. Program researcher and grantee, 1988-94. Mem. Ecol. Soc. Am., Bot. Soc. Am., Ill. Native Plant Soc. (pres. Quad City chpt. 2003—), Ctr. for Plant Conservation, Ill. State Acad. Sci. (pres. 1993-95), Alpha Phi Omega (adv. and scouting coord. 1981—), Sigma Xi (pres. John Deere chpt. 1987-88). Office: Augustana Coll Dept Biology 639 38th St Rock Island IL 61201-2210 E-mail: bidziadyk@augustana.edu.

DZIEDUSZKO, JANUSZ WLADYSLAW, electrical engineer; b. Jaslo, Poland, Aug. 25, 1939; came to U.S., 1966; s. Wladyslaw and Waleria (Pankiewicz) D.; m. Lucyna Janina Ryba, Apr. 15, 1963; 1 child, Philip. MSEE, Acad. Mining and Metallurgy, Cracow, Poland, 1962. Sr. systems engr. Westinghouse Electric, Pitts., 1967-79, 86-90; mgr. hardware devel. BBC Brown Boveri, Pitts., 1979-84; mgr. power line comm. GE, Malvern, Pa., 1984-85; mgr. product devel. ABB Power Transmission & Distbn. Co., Coral Springs, Fla., 1990-97; exec. consulting R&D engineer ABB Electric Sys. Tech. Inst., Raleigh, N.C., 1997—. Contbr. papers to profl. confs. Mem. choir St. Michaels Roman Catholic Ch., Cary, N.C., 1997—. Mem. IEEE. Democrat. Achievements include 5 patents in digital data communication and data acquisition; significant contribution in data communication and microprocessor product design for electrical power industry. Home: 5412 Pine Dr Raleigh NC 27606-9589 Office: Electric Sys Tech Inst 1021 Main Campus Dr Raleigh NC 27606-5202 E-mail: janusz@ieee.org., januszdz@att.net.

DZIEDZIC, ZUZANNA, economist; b. Baczal Gorny, Poland, Mar. 27, 1948; d. Michat Wadas and Katarzyna (Pawlus) Wadas; m. Stanislaw Dziedzic, Aug. 27, 1967; 1 child, Joanna. MA, Acad. Econs., Jelenia, Gora, 1984. Fin. mgr. Building Co., Kowary, 1971-75; finance chief United Building Cos., Jelenia Gora, 1975-85; gen. dir. Lower Sileasian State Philharmonic, Jelenia Gora, 1985—. Avocations: music, tourism. Office: State Philharmonic ul Pilsudzkiego 60 58-500 Jelenia Gora Poland

DZIEWANOWSKA, ZOFIA ELIZABETH, neuropsychiatrist, pharmaceutical executive, researcher, educator; b. Warsaw, Nov. 17, 1939; came to U.S., 1972; d. Stanislaw Kazimierz Dziewanowski and Zofia Danuta (Mieczkowska) Rudowska; m. Krzysztof A. Kunert, Sept. 1, 1961 (div. 1971); 1 child, Martin. MD, U. Warsaw, 1963; PhD, Polish Acad. Sci., 1970. MD recert. U.K., 1972, U.S., 1973. Asst. prof. of psychiatry U. Warsaw Med. Sch., 1969-71; sr. house officer St. George's Hosp., U. London, 1971-72; assoc. dir. Merck Sharp & Dohme, Rahway, N.J., 1972-76; vis. assoc. physician Rockefeller U. Hosp., N.Y.C., 1975-76; adj. asst. prof. of psychiatry Cornell U. Med. Ctr., N.Y.C., 1978—; v.p., global med. dir. Hoffmann-La Roche, Inc., Nutley, N.J., 1976-94; sr. v.p. and dir. global med. affairs Genta Inc., San Diego, 1994-97; sr. v.p. drug devel. and regulatory Cypros Pharms. Corp., Carlsbad, Calif., 1997-99; pres., med. dir. New Drug Assocs., La Jolla, Calif., 1999—; sr. v.p. clin. and regulatory Maxia Pharms, San Diego, 2001—02; v.p. clin. rsch. Ligand Pharm, Inc., San Diego, 2002—. Lectr. in field. Contbr. articles to profl. publs. Bd. dirs Royal Soc. Medicine Found.; mem. alumni coun. Cornell U. Med. Ctr. Recipient TWIN Honoree award for Outstanding Women in Mgmt., Ridgewood (N.J.) YWCA, 1984. Mem. AMA, AAAS, Am. Soc. Pharmacology and Therapeutics, Am. Coll. Neuropsychopharmacology, N.Y. Acad. Scis., PhRMA. (vice chmn. steering com. med. sect., chmn. internat. med. affairs com., head biotech. working group), Royal Soc. Medicine (U.K.), Drug Info. Assn. (Woman of Yr. award 1994), Am. Assn. Pharm. Physicians. Roman Catholic. Achievements include original research on the role of the nervous system in the regulation of respiratory functions, research and development and therapeutic uses of many new drugs, pharmaceutical medicine and biotechnology; molecular biology derived as well as conventional products including antisense, interferon efficacy in cancer, virology and AIDS and drugs useful in cardiovascular, immunological, neuropsychiatric, infectious diseases, and others; impact of different cultures on medical practices and clinical research; drug evaluation and development management strategies of pharmaceutical industries; treatments against cardiac and brain ischemia, cytoprotection; speaker in field.

DZINDOLET, MARY TERESA, psychology educator; b. Framingham, Mass., July 16, 1962; d. Ricahrd Joseph and Patricia (Dowd) D.; m. George Lewis Porter, Aug. 9, 1987; children: Patricia, George. PhD, U. Tex., Arlington, 1992. Asst. prof. psychology Cameron U., Lawton, 1994-2001; prin. investigator Army Rsch. Lab., Ft. Sill, Okla., 1999—. Contbr. chpt. to book. Mem. APA. Fax: (580) 581-2623. E-mail: maryd@cameron.edu.

DZIORDZ, WALTER MICHAEL, priest; b. New Bedford, Mass., Oct. 20, 1951; s. Michael Raphael and Jane (Szczepanik) D. BA, U. Mass., 1977; MDiv, Washington Theol. Union, Silver Spring, Md., 1984; cert., Salem Inst., 1988; postgrad., Oblate Sch. Theology. Joined Soc. Marians, Roman Cath. Ch.; ordained priest; cert. in reality therapy. Asst. pastor St. Joseph's Cath. Ch., Pittsfield, Mass., 1984-85; pastor Our Lady of Grace Cath. Ch., Greensboro, N.C., 1988—; dir. vocation Marian Fathers-Province of St. Stanislaus Kostka, Stockbridge, Mass., 1986-87; dir. of resident/non resident candidates Marian Fathers Scholasticate, Washington, 1987-88, councilor 1st house, 1987-88. Superior local house Marian Community for Our Lady of Grace Parish, Greensboro, 1988—; 3d provincial councilor Congregation of Marians, Stockbridge, Mass., 1989—; del. provincial chpt. Marian Province of St. Stanislaus Kostka, Stockbridge, 1984, 90, elected provincial superior, 1993; chaplain pilgrimage Marian Helpers Ctr., Stockbridge, 1990. Sgt. U.S. Army, 1970-73; N.G., 1973-74. Mem. Washington Theol. Union Alumni Assn., KC (chaplain Greensboro chpt. 1988—, cert. appreciation 1989, 90). Republican. Home: 201 S Chapman St Greensboro NC 27403-1611 Office: Our Lady of Grace Cath Ch 2205 W Market St Greensboro NC 27403-1515

DZIUBA, HENRY FRANK, retired university official; b. Detroit, Feb. 16, 1918; s. Frank and Anna (Jarzynka) D.; m. Stella Madeline Walush, May 28, 1948; children: Kenneth John, Denise Susan. DDS, U. Detroit, 1942. With U. Detroit Sch. Dentistry, 1945—, prof. prosthetics, 1962-91, prof. emeritus, cons., 1991—, coord. clinics, 1962-63, asst. dean, 1962-66, dean, 1967, assoc. dean clin. affairs, 1977-92; ret., 1992. Recipient inter-prof. award Advocates, 1967, Prestigious Tower award, 1976; named Alumnus of Yr. U. Detroit, 1975 Fellow Am. Coll. Dentistry, Internat. Coll. Dentistry ; mem. ADA, Am. Prosthodontic Soc., Detroit Dist. Dental Soc., Mich. Dental Assn., Omicron Kappa Upsilon, Psi Omega. Home: 250 Claremont St Dearborn MI 48124-1368

DZIUK, PHILIP JOHN, animal scientist educator; b. Foley, Minn., Mar. 24, 1926; s. Edmund William and Ellen Catherine (Carlin) D.; m. Patricia Rosemary Weber, Sept. 29, 1951; children: Corinne, Constance, Rita, Catherine, Kenneth, Ronald, Carl. BS, U. Minn., 1950, MS, 1952, PhD, 1955. From rsch. asst. to rsch. assoc. U. Minn., Mpls., 1950-55; from asst. prof. to prof. U. Ill., Urbana, 1955-88, prof. emeritus, 1988—. Cons. Upjohn, Abbott, Eli Lilly, Am. Cynamid, Schering, Batelle, Advisys; reviewer of grants NIH, Bethesda, Md., 1982-86, USDA, Beltsville, Md., 1983-89. Contbr. peer reviewed publs. in sci. and profl. jours. With USN, 1945-46. Fellow Lalor Found., 1958, 61, Pig Industry Devel. Authority, Eng., 1961; recipient Achievement in Rsch. award Am. Fertility Soc., 1970, Sr. Scientist award Alexander von Humboldt Found., 1981, Pioneer award Internat. Embryo Transfer Soc., 2001, Outstanding Achievement award U. Minn., 2002. Mem. AAAS, KC, Am. Assn. Anatomist, Am. Soc. Animal Scis. (fellow 1987, Rsch. in Physiology award 1971), Soc. Study of Fertility, Soc. Study of Reproduction (dir., pres. 1987-88, Disting. Svc. award 1989), Lions Internat. (pres., sec. 1992-94), Farm House, Sigma Xi, Gamma Alpha, Phi Kappa Phi, Phi Zeta, Gamma Sigma Delta, Alpha Zeta. Avocations: woodworking, gardening, racquetball. Office: U Ill Dept Animal Scis 1207 W Gregory Dr Urbana IL 61801-4733

DZUIBLINSKI, GERARD ARTHUR, theatre educator, artistic director; b. Detroit, Sept. 23, 1954; s. Arthur Harold and Irene (Rogacki) D.; m. Anne Mansfield, Oct. 12, 1991; 1 chld, Illyana. BA in Comms. and Learning Environments, Antioch Coll., 1975; MA in Directing, Antioch U., 1991. Ednl. cons. Project Headline, Detroit, 1976; co-dir. Fantasy Theatre, Detroit, 1977-78; artistic dir. Exptl. Performing Arts Assn., Chira Twp., Mich., 1978—; theatre faculty Wayne County C.C., Detroit, 1979-87; dir. Theatre for Young Audiences, Henry Ford C.C., 1989—; children's theatre instr. Marygrove Coll., Detroit, 1982-96; TV acting faculty Detroit Bd. Edn., 1985-87; adj. theatre faculty Henry Ford C.C., Dearborn, Mich., 1987—, tech. dir., 1996—; drama dir. Crestwood H.S., Dearborn Hts., Mich., 1993-98; TV acting faculty Casablancas Model and Talent, Sterling Hts., Mich., 1996-99. Bd. dirs. Pathway Family Ctr. Author: (play) The Lion Roars, 1996; adaptor: (play) A Christmas Carol, 1995, Pinnochio, 1996; co-author: (handbook) Our New Family: Instructor's Guidebook, 1991, (Cable mini-series) The Gerry the Fool Show, 1986, (mime show) Only Fooling, 1983. Recipient Keystone award, and other awards for best prodn., scenic design, lighting design, tech. dir. and makeup design Dearborn Press and Guide. Mem.: ASCD, Network of Performing and Visual Arts Schs. Office: Henry Ford CC 5101 Evergreen Rd Dearborn MI 48128-2407 Personal E-mail: gdzub@hotmail.com.

DZUL, PAUL J. physician, medical journal editor; b. Milno, Ukraine, Oct. 14, 1921; came to U.S., 1949; s. John M. and Maria H. Dzul; m. Irene Dzul; children: Andrew I., George O. Grad., Lviv (Ukraine) Med. Inst., 1944, Med. U., Graz, Austria, 1945; MD, Med. U., Innsbruck, Austria, 1948; degree honoris causa, Odessa (Ukraine) Med. U., 1996, Lviv Med. U., 1998. Instr. Wayne State U., Detroit, 1960-62, asst. prof., 1962-66, assoc. prof., 1966-90, prof. emeritus, 1990—. Pres. Lakeshore Ear, Nose & Throat, St. Clair Shores, Mich., 1966-90. Editor in chief Jour. Ukrainian Med. Assns. N.Am., 1967—. Fellow ACS, Am. Acad. Otolrayngology-Head and Neck Surgery, World Fedn. Ukrainian Med. Assns. (pres. 1992—). Home: 21 Woodland Shores Dr Grosse Pointe MI 48236-2633 Office: World Fedn Ukrainian Med Assns PO Box 36305 Grosse Pointe MI 48236-0305 E-mail: pjdzulmd@aol.com.

DZVONIK, MICHAEL D. advertising executive; Exec. v.p. The Grizzard Agy., Atlanta, 1985-94, pres., 1994-97, chmn., CEO, 1997—. Office: The Grizzard Agy Ste 900 229 Peachtree St NE Atlanta GA 30303

DZWIK, LEIGH SETTLEMAIR, director; BS, Oakland U., 1998; MBA, Wayne State U., 2003. Human resources intern The Classic Cos., Troy, Mich., 1998; human resources adminstr. Automotive Composites Co., Sterling Heights, Mich., 1998—99, Textron Automotive Trim, Clinton Twp., Mich., 1999—2001; coord. faculty human resources Oakland U., Rochester, Mich., 2002—. Human resource adv. com. Oakland U., 2002—, mem. acad. affairs adminstrv. group, 2002—. Mem.: Soc. Human Resource Mgmt.

DZYALOSHINSKII, IGOR EKHIELIEVICH, physicist; b. Moscow, Feb. 1, 1931; s. Ekhiel Moiseevich and Maria Semionovna (Aseeva) D.; m. Elena Aronovna Lebedeva, Dec. 2, 1960; 1 child, Elena. MA in Physics, Moscow State U., 1953; PhD in Physics, Inst. for Phys. Problems, Moscow, 1957, DSc in Physics, 1962. Sr. rschr. Inst. for Phys. Problems, Moscow, 1957-65; head dept. magnetism Landau Inst. for Theoretical Physics, Moscow, 1965-91; prof. physics U. Calif., Irvine, 1992—. Author: Methods of Quantum Field, Theory in Statistical Physics (in Russian, English, Japanese and Chinese), 1962, 3d edit., 1975, 2d Russian edit., 1998. Decorated Order of Red Banner of Labour, Order of Honor, Medal of Vet. of Labour, Govt. of Russia; recipient State prize Govt. USSR, 1984. Fellow AAAS, Am. Phys. Soc.; mem. Russian Acad. Scis. (Lomonosov prize 1962, Landau prize 1989), Am. Acad. Art and Scis. (hon.

fgn. mem.). Achievements include research in theory of weak ferromagnetism; theory of van der Waals forces in condensed media; theory of one-dimensional metals. Office: Univ Calif Dept Physics Irvine CA 92697-0001

EABY, CHRISTIAN EARL, lawyer, small business owner; b. Reading, Pa., June 16, 1945; s. David Russell and Pearl Haller (Root) E.; m. Dace Rekis, Jan. 4, 1986. BA in Univ. Studies, U. N.Mex., 1976, JD, 1980. Bar: N.Mex. 1980, Pa. 1990, U.S. Dist. Ct. (ea. dist.) Pa. 1992. Tchr. Albuquerque Pub. Schs., 1976; ednl. dir. N.Mex. Pub. Employees Coun., 1977; tutor Am. Indian Law Ctr. U. N.Mex., 1978-79; pvt. practice Albuquerque, 1980-90; owner Eby Clock Co., New Holland, Pa., 1990-95; pvt. practice New Holland, 1990—. Past legal coun. N.Mex. Vietnam Vets. of Am. Contbr. articles to profl. jours. Bd. dirs. U. N.Mex. Cancer Ctr., 1984-92, Albuquerque United Artists Downtown Ctr. for Arts, Ea. Lancaster County Sch., 1990-93; pres. Coalition Albuquerque Neighborhoods, 1983-85, Nob Hill Neighborhood Assn., 1980-86; mem. task force Albuquerque Goals Com.; founding dir., sec. Nob Hill Main St., 1987; founding dir. Casa Esperanza Cancer Patients Homes, 1987. Mem. ABA, ATLA (product liability sect.), Am. Arbitration Assn., Am. Numismatic Assn., N.Mex. Bar Assn., N.Mex. Trial Lawyers Assn., Albuquerque Bar Assn., Pa. Bar Assn. (workers' compensation sect.), Lancaster Bar Assn., Pa. Trial Lawyers Assn. (auto law sect.), Nat. Assn. Watch and Clock Collectors, Berks County Bar Assn., Nat. Trust Hist. Preservation, Hist. Preservation Trust of Lancaster County, Lancaster Mennonite Hist. Soc., Lancaster Hist. Soc., Hist. Soc. of Cocalico Valley, Eby Family Assn. (pres. 1992—). Avocations: geneology, numismatics, horology, restoring 1727 family home. Home: 405 Peters Rd New Holland PA 17557-9389 Office: 1861 Charter Ln Ste 104 Lancaster PA 17601 Fax: 717-393-2559. E-mail: cee@eabylaw.com.

EADE, GEORGE JAMES, retired air force officer, research executive, defense consultant; b. Lockney, Tex., Oct. 27, 1921; s. George William and Isabel Theresa (Barnd) E.; m. Colette Eliane Cachelin, May 18, 1946 (dec. 1994); children: George Walter, Helen Marie-Louise (Mrs. Jean Oesch), Anne Catherine Eade Berry, Christine Colette, Dominique Frances. Commd. 2d lt. USAAF, 1942; advanced through grades to gen. USAF; pilot 37 combat missions in Europe World War II, 1942-46; pilot, squadron comdr., B-52 wing comdr.; airborne emergency action officer, sr. staff officer Strategic Air Command, Nat. Strategic Target Planning Staff, 1947-70; dep. chief of staff plans and ops. Hdqrs. USAF, Washington, 1971—72; dep. comdr.-in-chief U.S. Forces Europe, 1972-75; ret., 1975. Pres. Cath. Edn. Assn., Omaha, 1968—70. Decorated DSM with two oak leaf clusters, Legion of Merit, DFC, Air medal with five oak leaf clusters, Air Force Commendation medal with two oak leaf clusters; Order of Merit (France). Home: 1131 Sunnyside Dr Healdsburg CA 95448-3536 *Establish some general goals and lay plans to reach them. Neither be capricious nor struggle doggedly toward a goal no longer of interest. Above all follow your own plan, not what someone plans for you. The ultimate objective is to make a contribution to mankind and be happy in the process of so doing. Putting the two together is to discover the art of living and the meaning of life.*

EADES, RONALD WAYNE, law educator; b. Lexington, Ky., Sept. 6, 1948; s. Thomas William and Evelyn Louise (Smith) E.; m. Lillian Arpi Aivazian, July 2, 1971; children: Matthew Adrian, Emily Rachael. BA in English, Rhodes Coll., 1970; JD, U. Memphis, 1973; LLM, Harvard U., 1977. Bar: Tenn. 1974, Ky. 1984. Staff atty. Tenn. Valley Authority, Knoxville, Tenn., 1974-76; asst. prof. law U. Louisville, 1977-80, assoc. prof., 1980-82, prof. law, 1982—, disting. tchg. prof., 1991. Vis. prof. U. Leeds, England, 1993, Johannes Gutenburg U., Mainz, Germany, 1994, U. Turku, Finland, 2000, 03. Author: Wrongful Death Actions-The Law in Kentucky and supplements, 1981; author: (with Graham Douthwaite) Jury Instructions in Automobile Negligence Actions, 2d edit., 1991, 3d edit., 1996; author: Workers Compensation-The Law in Kentucky, 1989; author: (with John Palmore) Kentucky Jury Instructions, 1989; author: Products Liability Actions-The Law in Kentucky and supplements, 1981, Watson vs. Jones-The Walnut Street Presbyterian Church and the First Amendment, 1982, Kentucky Damages Law and supplement, 1985, 4th edit., 2003, Products Liability, Actions and Remedies, 1985, Kentucky Jurisprudence Evidence, 1987, Law for Asphalt Athletes, 1983, Jury Instructions on Products Liability, 3d edit., 1999, Kentucky Wrongful Death Actions, 1994, rev. edit., 2002, Kentucky Products Liability Law, 1994, Kentucky Law of Damages, 3d edit., 1996, Jury Instructions in Automobile Actions, 3d edit., 1996, Jury Instructions in Commercial Litigation, 1996, Jury Instructions on Medical Issues, 5th edit., 1997, Fights for Rights, 2000, Jury Instructions in Automobile Actions, 4th edit., 2001, Kentucky Workers Compensation, 4th edit., 2001, Jury Instructions in Commercial Litigation, 2d edit., 2002, Jury Instructions on Damages in Tort Actions, 5th edit., 2003. James R. Merritt fellow for disting. tchg., 1994-95; Disting. Univ. scholar, 1996—; CALI fellow in tort law, 2001; mem. Kentucky Evidence Rules Advisory Commn., 2001-. Mem. ABA, ATLA, Ky. Bar Assn., Louisville Bar Assn. Democrat. Presbyterian. Avocations: jogging, amateur radio. Office: U Louisville Sch Of Law Louisville KY 40292-0001

EADON, GEORGE A. scientist, administrator, educator; b. Islip, N.Y., Oct. 2, 1945; s. George and Elizabeth F. Eadon; married; children: George M, Geoffrey M. BS in Chemistry, MIT, 1967; PhD in Chemistry, Stanford U., 1971. Asst. prof. chemistry SUNY, Albany, 1971—77, assoc. prof., 1977—79, assoc. prof. Sch. Pub. Health, 1982—, chmn. dept. environ. health and toxicology, 1993—96; dir. Toxicology Inst. Wadsworth Ctr., Albany, 1979—82, dir. divsn. environ. disease prevention, 1982—. Contbr. over 50 articles to profl. jours. Grantee, NIH, Ctrs. for Disease Control, Am. Chem. Soc., Rsch. Found., Electric Power Rsch. Inst., 1971—2002. Home: 335 E High St Ballston Spa NY 12020 Office: Wadsworth Ctr Empire State Plz Albany NY 12201 Office Fax: 518-486-1505. Business E-Mail: eadon@wadsworth.org.

EADS, GEORGE CURTIS, economic consultant; b. Clarkesville, Tex., Aug. 20, 1942; s. Delbert Curtis and Eliza Mae (Hicks) E.; m. Margaret Helen Hall, Nov. 17, 1973; children: Geoffrey Thomas, Katherine Elizabeth. BA, U. Colo., 1964; MA, Yale U., 1965; MPhil, 1967; PhD, Yale U., 1968. Asst. prof. econs. Harvard U., Cambridge, Mass., 1968-69, Princeton U., 1969-71; spl. asst. antitrust div. Dept. Justice, Washington, 1971-72; assoc. prof. George Washington U., Washington, 1972-74; asst. dir. Council Wage and Price Stability, Washington, 1974-75; exec. dir. Nat. Commn. Supplies and Shortages, Washington, 1975-77; economist, research program dir. Rand Corp., Santa Monica, Calif., 1977-79, 81; mem. Pres.'s Council Advisors, Washington, 1979-81; prof. Sch. Pub. Affairs, U. Md., College Park, 1981-85, dean Sch. Pub. Affairs, 1985-86; v.p., chief economist GM, 1986-95; v.p. Charles River Assoc., Washington, Charles River Assocs., Washington, 1995—. Author: The Local Service Airline Experiment, 1972, Relief or Reform? Reagan's Regulatory Strategies, 1984. Mem. Am. Econ. Assn. Democrat. Home: 3718 Harrison St NW Washington DC 20015-1816 Office: Charles River Assoc Ste 700 1201 F St SW Washington DC 20004-1204 E-mail: geads@crai.com.

EADS, JOHN A. accountant; b. Dallas, Feb. 6, 1939; s. Arver A. and Nettie Mae (Dawson) E.; m. Joanna Y. Eads, Aug. 12, 1967; children: Leslie, Ashley, John Jr. BBA, U. Tex., 1966. CPA, Tex. Pvt. CPA practice, 1974-81; pres., mng. shareholder Eads, Hunter & Co., P.C., Dallas, 1981-98; tax shareholder Jackson & Rhodes, P.C., Dallas, 1998—2002; ptnr. Smith, Jackson, Boyer & Bovard, PLLC, Dallas, 2002—. Pres. Practice Mgmt. Group, Dallas, 1981, 2002; sec.-treas. Haemachem Rsch. Assocs., Inc., Dallas, 1983—. Author: Practice Continuation Agreements, 1992. Trustee Charlton Meth. Hosp., Dallas, 1988—, pres., chmn. bd. dirs., 1990; treas., bd. dirs. Citizens Devel. Ctr., Dallas, 1990-95; adv. coun. Dallas Meth. Hosp. Found., 1991—, Cmtys. Found. of Tex., 1988—, Dallas Found., 1998—; treas., bd. dirs., exec. com. DeSoto Ind. Sch. Dist. Found., 2000-. Served with USAF, 1960-66. Recipient Disting. Pub. Svc. Award for CPA, White House Office of Pvt. Sector Initiatives, 1987. Mem. AICPA (coun. governing body 1995-2001, Pub. Svc. award 1995), Tex. Soc. CPAs (bd. dirs., treas. 1991, pres. 1996-97, pres. Dallas chpt. 1989-90, Outstanding Chpt. Pres. award, CPA of Yr. 1988, Meritorious Svc. Acctg. in Tex. 2001), Dallas Estate Planning Coun. (bd. govs.), Internat. Assn. Lions Clubs (gov. 1985-86, state coun. chmn. 1986-87, chmn. Tex. endowment com. 1999—), Past Dist. Gov. Assn. Tex. (pres. 1993-94). Republican. Methodist. Avocations: golf, bird hunting. Office: 9400 NCX Ste 420 9400 N Central Expy Dallas TX 75231

EADS, ORA WILBERT, clergyman, church official; b. Mill Spring, Mo., Jan. 2, 1914; s. John Harrison and Effie Ellen (Borders) E.; m. Mary Ivaree Cochran, Mar. 25, 1944; children— Ora Wilbert, Wayne B., Carol Vernice, Janet Karen and Janice Inez (twins). JD, John Marshall Law Sch., Atlanta, 1940, LL.M., 1941; postgrad., Sch. Theology, St. Lawrence U., Canton, N.Y., 1947-48. Bar: Ga. bar 1940. Practiced in, Atlanta, 1940-46; ordained to ministry Christian Congregation, Inc., 1946; parish minister Sampson County, N.C., 1948-52; evangelist Charlotte, N.C., 1952-61; gen. supt. Christian Congregation, Inc., 1961—. Author numerous books of poetry, 1967— . Mem. Christian Congregation Ch. Home and Office: Christian Congregation Inc 812 W Hemlock St La Follette TN 37766 *A high school teacher asked her class, "What is our purpose on earth? Why are we here?" We students didn't know the answer. I now believe, some 65 years later, that the highest responsibility of any individual is to achieve his best potential.*

EADS, RONALD PRESTON, Christian management consultant; b. Greensboro, N.C., Oct. 17, 1948; s. Wayne Oather and Marcella (Tatarski) E.; m. Gail Senn, Feb. 8, 1975; children: Tanya, Michael, Shannon, Kevin. BBA, Roanoke Coll., 1970. Mgmt. trainee GE, Salem, Va., 1970-71; dept. mgr. Mauney Hosiery, Kings Mountain, N.C., 1971-72; v.p. Eads Mgmt. Devel. Assocs., Gastonia, N.C., 1972-82, pres., 1982—. Co-author: Let's Plan Management Future, 1983. Deacon, First Presbyn. Ch., Gastonia, 1986-88, elder, 1990—. Republican. Avocations: basketball, ballroom dancing. Home: 3548 Gardner Park Dr Gastonia NC 28054-4946 Office: Eads Mgmt Devel Assocs 2449 Redbud Dr Gastonia NC 28056-6555 E-mail: ron@eadsmanagement.com.

EAGAN, CLAIRE VERONICA, district court judge; b. Bronx, N.Y., Oct. 9, 1950; d. Joseph Thomas and Margaret (Lynch) E.; m. M. Stephen Barrett, Aug. 25, 1978 (div. 1984); m. Anthony J. Loretti, Jr., Feb. 13, 1988. Student, U. Fribourg, Switzerland, 1970-71; BA, Trinity Coll., Washington, 1972; postgrad., U. Paris, 1972-73; JD, Fordham U., 1976. Bar: N.Y. 1977, Okla. 1977, U.S. Dist. Ct. (no. dist.) Okla. 1977, U.S. Ct. Appeals (10th cir.) 1978, U.S. Supreme Ct. 1980, U.S. Dist. Ct. (we. dist.) Okla. 1981, U.S. Ct. Appeals (5th cir.) 1982, U.S. Dist. Ct. (ea. dist.) Okla. 1988, U.S. Ct. Appeals (Fed. cir.) 1990. Mem. Hall, Estill, Hardwick, Gable, Golden & Nelson, Tulsa, 1978-98, shareholder, 1981-98, also bd. dirs., exec. com.; magistrate judge U.S. Dist. Ct. (no. dist.) Okla., Tulsa, 1998—2001, dist. judge, 2001—. Mem. Jud. Conf. Com. on Defender Svcs., 2002—. Editor: Fordham Law Rev., 1975—76. Bd. dirs. Okla. Med. Rsch. Found., 2000—, Cath. Charities, Tulsa, 1983-98, Cystic Fibrosis Found., Tulsa, 1982-84; mem. Jr. League Tulsa, Inc., 1985—; trustee Gannon U., Erie, Pa., 1995-98; bd. dirs. Okla. Sinfonia, Tulsa, 1982-86; adj. settlement judge, Tulsa County, 1990-97. Fellow Am. Bar Found.; mem. Tulsa County Bar Assn., 10th Cir. Jud. Conf., Am. Inns of Ct. (chpt. pres. 1999-2000). Republican. Roman Catholic. Office: US Dist Ct No Dist Okla 333 W 4th St Ste 411 Tulsa OK 74103-3819

EAGAN, JAMES WILLIAM, JR., pathologist, educator; b. Bristol, Pa., Mar. 24, 1945; AB, Johns Hopkins U., 1967, MD, 1971. Diplomate Am. Bd. Pathology, Am. Bd. Anat. and Clin. Pathology. Intern in internal medicine Royal Victoria Hosp., Montreal, Can., 1971-72; resident in pathology Johns Hopkins Hosp., Balt., 1972-75, chief resident, 1976-77; Am. Cancer Soc. fellow in pathology Meml. Sloan-Kettering Cancer Ctr., N.Y.C., 1975-76; staff pathologist Balt. City Hosps., 1979-84, St. Joseph Med. Ctr., Balt., 1984-89, chmn. dept. pathology, 1989—; asst. prof. pathology Sch. Medicine Johns Hopkins U., Balt., 1979-97. Pres. St. Joseph Pathology Assocs., Balt., 1995—. Maj. USAF, 1977-79. Office: St Joseph Med Ctr Dept Pathology 7601 Osler Dr Baltimore MD 21204-7578

EAGAN, MARIE T. (RIA EAGAN), chiropractor; b. Rockville Ctr., N.Y., June 17, 1952; d. John F. and Mary (Ebner) E. BA, Goddard Coll., 1975; D in Chiropractic Medicine, N.Y. Chiropractic Coll., 1983. Pvt. practice chiropractic medicine, N.Y.C., 1983—. Chiropractic examiner N.Y. State Bd. Chiropractic, 1995. Mem.: Internat. Chiropractic Assn., Am. Chiropractic Assn. Democrat. Office: 231 W 21st St Apt B New York NY 10011-3116

EAGAN, WILLIAM LEON, lawyer; b. Tampa, Fla., Feb. 10, 1928; s. John Robert and Margaret (Williams) E.; m. Marjorie Young, Mar. 6, 1949; children: Barbara Anne, Rebecca Elizabeth, Laurel Lea. Student, U. Tampa, 1959; LLB, U. Fla., 1961. Bar: Fla. 1961, U.S. Dist. Ct. (mid. dist.) Fla. 1959, U.S. Dist. Ct. (so. dist.) Fla. 1962, U.S. Ct. Appeals (5th cir.) 1972; bd. cert. civil trial lawyer, Fla. Assoc. Dexter, Conlee & Bissell, Sarasota, Fla., 1961-62; ptnr., v.p. Arnold, Matheny & Fagan, P.A., Orlando, 1962—. Mem. Fla. Bar Ninth Circuit Grievance Com., 1982-84; mediator Family Law Mediation Program. Articles editor U. Fla. Law Rev., 1961. Chmn. bd. trustees First Bapt. Ch., Winter Park, Fla., 1970-72, chmn. bd. deacons, 1967-69; active Indsl. Devel. Commn. Mid-Fla., Orlando, 1979-84. Served to seaman 2d class USN, 1945-46. Mem. ATLA, Acad. Fla. Trial Lawyers, Lawyers Title Guaranty Assn., Orange County Bar Assn. (exec. coun.), Univ. Club, Order of Coif, Phi Alpha Delta, Phi Kappa Phi. Republican. Baptist and Methodist. Office: Arnold Matheny & Eagan PA 801 N Magnolia Ave Ste 201 Orlando FL 32803-3842 E-mail: Weagan@ameorl.com.

EAGAR, THOMAS WADDY, metallurgist, educator; b. Chattanooga, Jan. 9, 1950; s. Harry Douglas Sr. and Emily Clarkson (Thompson) E.; m. Pamela Dozier Garrett, Apr. 17, 1973; children: Matthew, Rebekah, Linda, Karen, James, Anna, Thomas. BS in Metallurgy, MIT, 1972, ScD in Metallurgy, 1975, postgrad., 1988, Lehigh U., 1975-76. Registered profl. engr., Mass. Rsch. engr. Homer Rsch. Labs. Bethlehem (Pa.) Steel Corp., 1974-76; asst. prof. materials engrng. MIT, Cambridge, 1976-80, assoc. prof., 1980-87, prof., 1987—, acting dept. head, 1989, Richard P. Simmons prof. materials engrng., 1990-93, Posco prof. materials engrng., 1993-99, Thomas Lord prof. engrng. systems, 2001—, dir. Materials Processing Ctr., 1990-93, dir. mfg. program, 1993-95, dept. head, 1995—2000. Liaison Scientist U.S. Office Naval Rsch., Tokyo, 1984-85; dir. metall. engrng. Simpson, Gumpertz and Heger, Inc., 1994; adv. bd. Edison Welding Inst., Columbus, Ohio, 1989-95; unit mfg. process rsch. com. Nat. Rsch. Coun., Washington, 1990-94, mem. nat. materials adv. bd., 1998—; tech. rev. bd. U.S. Army Rsch. Labs., 1993-95; cons. metallurgy and metall. failure analysis, 1976—; presenter and lectr. in field. Mem. adv. and tech. rev. bds. Materials Tech.; key reader Welding Jour.; contbr. over 190 articles to tech. publs.; patentee method of resistance welding, non-hygroscopic welding flux binders, large diameter stud and method and apparatus for welding same, laser instrument, age-hardenable sterling silver, emissivity independent multi-wavelength pyrometry, silver alloys of exceptional and reversilbe hardness; wear-resistant bond for abrasive tools, abrasive tool containing coated abrasive grain. Named Internat. Jr. Civitan of Yr., 1968; Dennison K. Bullens scholar, 1969-71, Foundry Edn. Fund scholar, 1970-71; grad. fellow NSF, 1972-74, Creativity Ext. award, 1988-90. Fellow AAAS, Am. Soc. Metals (Henry Marion Howe medal 1992), Am. Welding Soc. (hon. mem. Adams membership award 1979-83, Warren F. Savage award 1990, 96, Williams Sparagen award 1991, 94, Comfort A. Adams lectr., 1992, Charles H. Jennings Meml. medal 1983, 91, William Irrgang award 1993, Silver Quill award 2002); mem. AIME (metallurgy and metals prize Boston sect. 1972, Champion H. Mathewson Gold medal 1987, Henry Krumb lectr. 1987), Nat. Acad. Engrng., ASTM, ASME, Am. Ceramic Soc., Materials Rsch. Soc., Soc. Automotive Engrs., Soc. Mfg. Engrs., Welding Rsch. Coun. Internat. Inst. Welding (Am. coun. Houdremont lectr. 1990), Tau Beta Pi (bd. dirs. New England dist. 1977-80, chief advisor MIT chpt., disting. svc. award 1980), Phi Lambda Epsilon. Mem. Lds Ch. Office: MIT Rm 4-136 77 Massachusetts Ave Cambridge MA 02139-4307

EAGER, GEORGE SIDNEY, JR., electrical engineer, business executive; b. Balt., Sept. 5, 1915; s. George S. and Ada Elizabeth (Heinz) E.; m. Ruth Duff, Oct. 13, 1945; children: Robert W., John W., George S. III. BEE, Johns Hopkins U., 1936, PhD in Engring., 1941. Rsch. supr., asst. dir., assoc. dir. to dir. rsch. Gen. Cable Corp., Edison, N.J., 1945-80; pres. Barr Duff Corp., Upper Montclair, NJ, 1998—. Contbr. numerous articles to profl. jours. Author 35 patents elec. wires and cables. Lt. col. Signal Corps, U.S. Army, 1941-45, ETO. Fellow IEEE, Montclair Golf Club. Republican. Congregationalist. Home: 14 Bellegrove Dr Montclair NJ 07043-2527 E-mail: geager@earthlink.net.

EAGER, WILLIAM EARL, information systems corporation executive; b. Trenton, N.J., Dec. 22, 1946; s. Earl V. and Dorothy E. (Bowen) E.; m. Janice M. Kudlak, July 12, 1969; 1 child, Jason C. BA, Lycoming Coll., 1968; MBA, Gannon U., 1977; postgrad., Kent State U., 1984—. Cert. data processing. Systems supr. Gen. Electric Co., Erie, Pa., 1969-72; sr. cons. Touche Ross & Co., Detroit, 1972-74; mgmt. infor. systems dir. Limbach, Inc., Pitts., 1974-81; dir. sys. GenCorp, Inc., Akron, Ohio, 1981-87; sr. v.p. First Bancorp of Ohio, Akron, 1987-90, pres., CEO FBOH Svcs. Divsn., exec. v.p., 1991-94; sr. v.p. and CIO Cmty. Mut. Ins. Co., Cin., 1994-95; sr. ptrn. and E-bus. practice mgr. Computer Scis. Corp. Consulting, Boston, 1996-2000; mng. dir. Transition Ptnrs., Reston, Va., 2001—. Contbg. editor: Corp. Computing mag., 1992-93 Home: 8552 Egret Meadow Ln West Palm Beach FL 33412

EAGLE, JACK, commercial actor, comedian; b. N.Y.C., Jan. 15, 1926; s. Henry Eagle and Ida Mershon; children: Nikki, Jobbi, Ian; m. Susan M. Mohney, July 31, 1988 (div.); m. Susan Mohney, Aug. 6, 2001. Trumpet player Muggsy Spanier, Georgie Auld, Henry Jerome, Boyd Raeburn, 1943-55; comedian Eagle & Man, 1955-65; solo comedian and comml actor., 1965—; comml. actor, goodwill ambassador Xerox, 1975—. Comml. actor for numerous cos. including Xerox's "Broth Dominic" (Clio award 1976), Fleischman Margarine's "Mr. Cholesterol:, Carefree Chewing Gum's "Colombus's 1st Mate", Gillette's "The Perfect Face", N.Y. State Lottery "The Maize"; appeared in films New York Crossing, 1996, Step-Mom, 1997, Isn't She Great, 1998. Recipient Man of Yr. award Quick Print mag., Mr. Printing Week award Printing Industries. Mem. AFTRA, AGVA, Screen Actors Guild, Am. Fedn. Musicians. Avocations: drawing, collecting things. E-mail: jackeagle@usa.com.

EAGLE, KIM ALLEN, cardiologist; m. Darlene Eagle; 1 chid, Taylor. MD, Tufts U. Sch. of Medicine, Boston, 1979. Intern, resident Yale New Haven Hosp., 1979—82, chief resident, 1982—83; cardiology fellow Mass. Gen. Hosp., Boston, 1983, instr., 1986—88, asst. prof., 1988—94, assoc. prof., 1994; prof. medicine U. of Mich., Ann Arbor, 1994—. Editor: (book) Practice of Cardiology, 100 Years of Cardiology, (jour.) Current Jour. Rev. Fellow: Am. Coll. of Cardiology (life). Office: Univ of Mich Cardiovascular Ctr 300 N Ingalls 8B02 Ann Arbor MI 48109-0477

EAGLES, EUGENE, III, orthodontist; b. Newark, Oct. 27, 1940; s. Eugene Eagles Jr.; m. Jane Van Handel, June 11, 1966 (div. July 1994); children: Jeffrey T., Courtney Eagles Burke; m. Carroll Conklin, May 8, 1999. DMD, Tufts U., 1965; Cert. in Orthodontics, Boston U., 1969. Bd. cert. in orthodontics. Chief profl. svcs., prosthetic officer USAF Dental Clinic, Hunter AFB, Ga., 1965-67; pvt. practice Orthodontics, Bedford, Mass., 1969—; asst. clin. prof. dept. grad. orthodontics Tufts U. Sch. Dental Medicine, Boston, 1979—. Med. arts chmn. Citizens' Scholarship Found., Bedford, 1972-90, gen. chmn./pres., 1989, 90. Capt. USAF, 1965-67. Recipient Cert. of Merit, Am. Acad. Dental Medicine, 1965; named Bus. Person of Yr., Bedford C. of C., 1995. Mem. Omicron Kappa Upsilon. Congregationalist. Avocations: golf, tennis, sailboarding, cooking. Office: 50 Loomis St Bedford MA 01730-2208

EAGLES, SIDNEY SMITH, JR., judge; b. Asheville, N.C., Aug. 5, 1939; s. Sidney Smith Sr. and Mildred Truman (Brite) E.; m. Rachel Phillips, May 22, 1965; children: Virginia Brite, Margaret Phillips. BA, Wake Forest U., 1961, JD, 1964. Bar: N.C. 1964. Revisor Gen. Statutes Commn., Raleigh, N.C., 1967-70; asst. atty. gen. legis. drafting service Office Atty. Gen. N.C., Raleigh, 1970-74, dep. atty. gen. spl. prosecution divsn., 1974-76; counsel to speaker N.C. State Legislature, Raleigh, 1976-80; ptnr. Eagles Hafer & Hall, Raleigh, 1977-82; judge N.C. Ct. Appeals, Raleigh, 1983—, chief judge, 1998—. Adj. prof. Campbell U. Sch. Law, 1977—; chmn. N.C. Jud. Stds. Commn., 1994—96; mem. faculty Appellate Judges Sch. Law Sch. NYU, N.Y.C., 1993—99; mem. Uniform Laws Conf., 1968—83, 1992—, life mem., 2000. Co-author: North Carolina Criminal Procedure Forms, 1975, 3d edit., 1989; contbr. articles to profl. jours. V.p. Raleigh Jaycees, 1972-73; mem. Senatorial Dist. Dem. Com., 1979-81; bd. dirs. Wake County (N.C.) Symphony Soc., 1980-81, Women's Aid of Wake County, 1978—; bd. elders, bd. deacons, trustee, tchr. Sunday sch. Hillyer Meml. Christian Ch., 1980—, chmn bd., 1989; bd. visitors Wake Forest U. Sch. Law; vice chair bd. trustees Barton Coll., 1999, chair, 2002—. Served to capt. USAF, 1964-67; col., ret. 1991. Named Disting. Law Alumnus, Wake Forest U., 1981; N.C. Justice Found. fellow, 1972. Mem. ABA (chmn. appellate judges conf. 1993-94, mem. appellate jud. edn. com. 1994-98, ho. of dels. 1992—, mem. legal edn. 2002—), Am. Law Inst. (life), N.C. Bar Assn. (v.p. 1989-90), Wake county Bar Assn. (chmn. exec. com. 1975), N.C. State Bar, Execs. Club (pres. 1985), Kiwanis (disting. pres. Raleigh 1986-87, disting. lt. gov. 1995, Kiwanian of Yr. award 1989), Phi Delta Phi, Phi Alpha Delta (James Iredell award 1990). Avocations: politics, reading. Office: NC Ct of Appeals PO Box 888 Raleigh NC 27602-0888

EAGLES, STUART ERNEST, business executive; b. Saint John, N.B., Can., July 29, 1929; s. Ernest Lyle and Evelyn Gertrude (Feltmate) E.; m. Margaret Anne Gulliver, Sept. 30, 1952; children: James Stuart, Patricia Anne, Mark Edward. B.Sc., Acadia U., 1949, D.C.L. (hon.), 1992. Pres. Aegean Devel. Inc., Toronto, 1988—. Bd. dirs. AGF Trust Co., AGF Mgmt. Ltd., Hardit Corp., OPB Realty Inc.; past trustee, dir. Internat. Coun. Shopping Ctrs.; past pres. and dir. Can. Inst. Pub. Real Estate Cos. Gov. Jr. Achievement Can. Mem. Nat. Club (past pres.), Can. Club, Empire Club. Home: 24 Garfield Ave Toronto ON Canada M4T 1E7 E-mail: stuart.eagles@opb.on.ca.

EAGLESON, PETER STURGES, civil engineer, environmental engineer, educator; b. Phila., Feb. 27, 1928; s. William Boal and Helen (Sturges) E.; m. Marguerite Anne Partridge, May 28, 1949 (div.); children: Helen Marie, Peter Sturges, Jeffrey Partridge; m. Beverly Grossmann Rich, Dec. 27, 1974. BS in Civil Engring, Lehigh U., 1949, MS, 1952; Sc.D., MIT, 1956; D of Engring. (hon.), Lehigh U., 1998. Jr. engr. George B. Mebus (cons. engr.), Glenside, Pa., 1950-51; teaching asst. Lehigh U., 1951-52; research asst. Mass. Inst. Tech., 1952-54; mem. faculty MIT, 1954-93, prof. civil engring., 1965-93, head dept. civil engring., 1970-75, emeritus prof. civil and environ. engring., 1993—. Vis. asso. Calif. Inst. Tech., 1975-76; Fulbright sr. research scholar Commonwealth Sci. and Indsl. Research Orgn., Canberra, Australia, 1966-67 Author: (with others) Estuary and Coastline Hydrodynamics, 1966, Dynamic Hydrology, 1970, Ecohydrology, 2002. Served to 2d lt. C.E. AUS, 1949-50. Recipient Desmond Fitzgerald medal, 1959, Clemens Herschel prize, 1965 both Boston Soc. Civil Engrs., rsch. prize ASCE, 1963, William Bowie medal Am. Geophysical Union, 1994, Stockholm Water prize Stockholm Water Found., 1997. Fellow AAAS, Am. Meteorol. Soc. (hon.), Am. Geophys. Union (Robert E. Horton award 1979, Robert E. Horton medal 1988, pres. 1986-88, William Bowie medal 1994), Internat. Assn. Hydrological Scis. (Internat. Hydrology prize 1991); mem. NAE, European Geophys. Soc. (John Dalton medal 1999). Office: MIT Dept Civil & Environ Engring Room 48-335 Cambridge MA 02139

EAGLESON, WILLIAM BOAL, JR., banker; b. Phila., Dec. 10, 1925; s. William Boal and Helen (Sturges) E.; m. Catherine West McLean, May 28, 1960; children: Elizabeth E. Mackie, John McLean. BS, Lehigh U., 1949, LLD, 1983; MBA, U. Pa., 1951. With Fed. Res. Bank Phila., 1949-51; investment officer Girard Bank, Phila., 1951-61, v.p., 1961, exec. v.p., 1967; pres., dir. Girard Co., Girard Bank, 1970-80, chmn. bd., 1974-85, Mellon Bank Corp., 1983-85, chmn. emeritus, 1985—. Chmn. bd. Grant St Nat. Bank, 1988-95; trustee The Gen. Theol. Sem.; former mem. adv. bd. Yamaichi Internat. Am.; bd. dirs., chmn. exec. com. Gen. Accident Ins. Co.; advisor Tokai Bank Ltd.; hon. consul gen. Japan in Phila., 1991-99. Mem. Phila. City Planning Commn., 1970-74; mem. U.S. Treas. Govt. Borrowing Com., 1976-80, Fed. Adv. Council, 1978-80; bd. dirs. Nat. Alliance of Bus.; chmn. Gov.'s State Job Tng. Council, 1983-84; chmn. Pvt. Industry Council Phila., 1978-83; trustee Acad. Natural Scis., Phila., 1967-75; former trustee, chmn. fin. com. Lehigh U.; bd. dirs. Phila. Orch. Assn.; vice chmn. World Affairs Council of Phila.; mem. adv. council East Asian studies Princeton U. With USNR, 1944-46. Decorated Govt. Japan Order of Sacred Treasure with gold rays. Mem. Am. Philos. Soc. (chmn. fin. com.), Phila. Club, Gulph Mills Golf Club, Rolling Rock Club, Phi Beta Kappa. Episcopalian. Home: 1241 Denbigh Ln Radnor PA 19087-4646

EAGLET, ROBERT DANTON, electrical engineer, aerospace consultant, retired military officer; b. Cleve., Mar. 2, 1934; s. Albert Rudy and Dorothy Margaret (Beamer) E.; m. Sally Perry; children: Suzanne Carolyn, Allison Leigh, Kevin Robert. BSEE, U. Ariz., 1962; MSEE, U. So. Calif., 1968, PhD in Elec. Engring. and Physics, 1970. Commd. 2d lt. USAF, 1956, advanced through grades to maj. gen., 1986, forward air contr. in Vietnam, 1965-66, chief, classified program, space div., 1966-68, chief strategic def. div. hdqrs. Washington, 1970-74, mil. asst. to dep. undersec. def., 1974-75; dep. gen. mgr. NATO

airborne early warning program Brussels, 1975-79; dep. chief of staff devel. planning, sys. command USAF, Andrews AFB, Md., 1979-84, dep. comdr. armament divsn. Eglin AFB, Fla., 1984-86, dir. F-16 multinat. fighter program Wright Patterson AFB, Ohio, 1986-89; dep. asst. sec. of Air Force Pentagon, Washington, 1989-91; ret. USAF, 1991; pres. Eaglet Internat. Assocs., McLean, Va., 1992—. Decorated Disting. Svc. medal with oak leaf cluster, Legion of Merit with oak leaf cluster, Silver star, Disting. Flying Cross with oak leaf cluster, Bronze star with Valor device, Air medal with 24 oak leaf clusters, Purple Heart; named Outstanding Alumnus U. So. Calif. Mem. Air Force Assn., Nat. Def. Indsl. Assn. (v.p., tech. svcs. bd.), Assn. Old Crows, Assn. U.S. Army, Navy League, Belgian-Am. Assn. (bd. dirs.), French Am. Assn. Republican. Avocation: wind surfing. E-mail: eaglet@compuserve.com.

EAGLETON, EDWARD JOHN, lawyer; b. Tulsa, Jan. 22, 1932; s. William L. and Pauline (Dellinger) E.; m. Norma Lee, Oct. 6, 1956; children: Courtney Jean, Richard John. BA, Okla. U., 1954, JD, 1956. Bar: Okla. 1955, U.S. Dist. Ct. (ea., we. and no. dists.) Okla. 1956, U.S. Tax Ct. 1958, U.S. Supreme Ct. 1964; CPA, Tex., Okla. Acct. Peat Marwick Mitchell, Dallas, 1956-58; with IRS, Dallas and New Orleans, 1958-62; assoc. Houston & Klein, Tulsa, 1962-65; ptnr. Kothe & Eagleton, Tulsa, 1965-74, Houston & Klein Inc., Tulsa, 1974-94, Eagleton Eagleton & Harrison Inc., Tulsa, 1994—. Served with U.S. Army, 1956. Named one of Best Tax Lawyers in Am., Bar Register of Preeminent Lawyers, 1983—2001. Republican. Unitarian Universalist. Home: 3210 E 65th St Tulsa OK 74136-1225 Office: Eagleton, Eagleton & Harrison Inc 320 S Boston Ave Ste 1700 Tulsa OK 74103-4706

EAKELEY, DOUGLAS SCOTT, lawyer; b. Morristown, NJ, Mar. 2, 1946; m. Priscilla Van Tassel, June 2, 1973. BA, Yale U., 1968, JD, 1972; BA in Jurisprudence, MA in Jurisprudence, Oxford (England) U., 1970. Bar: N.Y. 1973, U.S. Ct. Appeals (2nd cir.) 1974, N.J. 1978, U.S. Ct. Appeals (3rd cir.) 1980, U.S. Supreme Ct. 1981. Law clk. to judge Harold R. Tyler, Jr. U.S. Dist. Ct. (so. dist.) N.Y., N.Y.C., 1972-73; assoc. Debevoise, Plimpton, N.Y.C., 1973-80; ptnr. Riker, Danzig, Scherer, Hyland & Perretti, Newark and Morristown, N.J., 1980-90, 91-94; first asst. atty. gen. State of N.J., 1990-91; ptnr. Lowenstein Sandler, PC, Roseland, N.J., 1994—. Chmn. Legal Svcs. N.J., North Brunswick, 1981-90, Legal Svcs. Corp., Washington, 1993-2003; pres. Legal Svc. Found. Essex County, Newark, 1981-90; chmn. N.J. Sentencing Policy Study Commn., 1992-93; trustee Practising Law Inst., N.Y.C., 1994—; trustee Boys and Girls Clubs of Newark, 1993-2003. Chmn. bd. editors N.J. Law Jour., 1984-90. Trustee N.J. Network Found., 1994—, N.J. Inst. for Social Justice, 1996—; pres. N.J. Shakespeare Festival, Madison, 1982-86. Rhodes scholar Oxford U., 1968. Fellow Am. Bar Found.; mem. ABA (John Minor Wisdom award, litigation sect. 1997), N.J. Bar Assn., Essex County Bar Assn., Fed. Bar Assn. N.J. (v.p. 1983-90), Urban League of Essex County (trustee 1987-88), Assn. Am. Rhodes Scholars (bd. dirs. 1995-2002), Phi Beta Kappa. Democrat. Office: Lowenstein Sandler PC 65 Livingston Ave Roseland NJ 07068-1725 E-mail: deakeley@lowenstein.com.

EAKEN, BRUCE WEBB, JR., lawyer; b. Cleve., Mar. 23, 1938; s. Bruce Webb and Kathryn (Peacock) E.; m. Wilhelmina Murray Martin, Oct. 23, 1971; children: Amanda, Webb. BA, Dartmouth Coll., 1960; JD, U. Mich., 1964. Bar: Ohio 1964, N.Y. 1965. Atty. Allied Chem. Co., N.Y.C., 1966-72; assoc. counsel U.S. Filter Corp., N.Y.C., 1972-81; prin. atty. N.Y. Power Authority, N.Y.C., 1981—95. Bd. dirs. East Harlem Little League, N.Y.C., 1970-73; pres. St. Bartholomews Players, N.Y.C., 1972-74; bd. dirs., treas. Media Ctr. for Children, N.Y.C., 1982-90. Mem. Assn. Bar City NY (adminstrv. law com. 1983-86, inter-Am. Affairs com. 1988-2001, corp. law dept. com. 1989-92, second century com. 1990-94, Africa affairs 2003—), UN Assn. NYC (v.p. 2000-2003, pres. 2003—), Dartmouth Alumni Assn. NYC (pres. 2000—). E-mail: eaken@aol.com.

EAKER, SHERRY ELLEN, entertainment newspaper editor; b. N.Y.C., Nov. 30, 1949; d. Ira and Lee (Eisenberg) E. BA, Queens Coll., 1971, MS, 1976. Tchr. art, English N.Y.C. Bd. Edn., 1971-76; editor-in-chief Back Stage, The Performing Arts Weekly, N.Y.C., 1977—, Editor, compiler: Handbook for Performing Artists: The How-to and Who-to-Contact Reference for Actors, Singers, Dancers, 1989, rev., 1991, 95, The Cabaret Artist's Handbook-Creating Your Own Act in Today's Liveliest Theatre Setting, 2000. Mem. Drama Desk (sec. 1984-87, v.p. 1987-91), Am. Theatre Critics Assn., Nat. Theatre Conf., League Profl. Theatre Women, N.Y. Coalition Profl. Women in Arts and Media (spl. adv.), advisory coun. Inst. of Outdoor Drama, Manhattan Assn. Cabarets. Avocations: theatre, cabaret. Office: Back Stage 770 Broadway New York NY 10003-9595

EAKIN, RICHARD RONALD, academic educator, mathematics educator; b. New Castle, Pa., Aug. 6, 1938; s. Everett Glenn and Mildred May (Hammerschmidt) E.; m. Jo Ann McGeehan, Aug. 23, 1960; children: Matthew Glenn, Maridy Lynn. AB in Math., Geneva Coll., Beaver Falls, Pa., 1960; MA in Math., Washington State U., 1962, PhD in Math., 1964. Asst. prof. math. Bowling Green (Ohio) State U., 1964-68, assoc. prof. math., 1968-87, asst. dean grad. sch., 1969-72, vice-provost student affairs, 1972-80, vice-provost instl. planning, 1979-80, exec. vice-provost budgeting and planning, 1980-83, v.p. budgeting and planning, 1983-87; chancellor, prof. math. East Carolina U., Greenville, 1987—2001, prof. ednl. leadership., 2001—. Editor revs. and evaluations sect. (jour.) The Math. Tchr., 1968-70. V.p. and mem. bd. dirs. Nat. Hemophilia Found., N.Y.C., 1983-84, chmn. bd., v.p. adminstrn. and fin., 1984-87; mem. bd. dirs. Ednl. Commn. for Fgn. Med. Grads., 2002—. NDEA fellow Wash. State U., Pullman, 1960-63, NSF fellow, 1963-64. Mem. Math. Assn. Am., So. Assn. Colls. and Schs. (commn. on colls.), Phi Kappa Phi, Omicron Delta Kappa. Office: East Carolina U Ragsdale Bldg Rm 219 Greenville NC 27858

EAKIN, THOMAS CAPPER, sports promotion executive; b. New Castle, Pa., Dec. 16, 1933; s. Frederick William and Beatrice (Capper) E.; m. Brenda Lee Andrews, Oct. 21, 1961; children: Thomas Andrews, Scott Frederick. BA in History, Denison U., 1956. Life ins. cons. Northwestern Mut. Life Ins. Co., Cleve., 1959-67; dist. mgr. Putman Pub. Co., Cleve., 1968-69; regional bus. mgr. Chilton Pub. Co., Cleve., 1969-70; dist. mgr. Hitchcock Pub. Co., Cleve., 1970-72; founder, pres. Golf Internat. 100 Club, Shaker Heights, Ohio, 1970—; pres TCE Enterprises, Shaker Heights, 1973—. Founder, pres. Ohio Humanitarian Hall of Fame, 2000—, Ohio Baseball Hall of Fame and Mus., 1976, Ohio Youth Sports Hall of Fame, 1996—, Tuscarawas County Sports Promotions Enterprises, 1987—, Ohio Sports Promotions Co., 1989, Ohio Sports Hall of Fame Promotional Enterprises, 1990—, Summit County Sports Promotion Enterprises, 1990—, Geauga County Hist. and Sports Traditions Enterprises, 1990—, Licking County Sports Stars Enterprises, 1990—, Lake County Cmty. Promotions Enterprises, 1990—, Trumbull County Sports Stars Publs., 1990—, Portage County Hist. and Sports Publs., 1990—, Cuyahoga County Promotion Co., 1990—, Ashtabula County Hist. and Sports Publs., 1990—, Ohio Pride in Cmty. Publs., 1990—, Mahoning County Sports Headlines Publs., 1990—, Ohio Fire Dept. Promotional Publs., 1990—, Ohio Law Enforcement Cmty. Publs., 1990—, Erie County Excellence in H.S. Sports Publs., 1990—, Ohio Sports Logo Creations, 1991—, Ohio Sports Stars Enterprises, 1991—, Ohio Sports Licensing Enterprise, 1991—, Huron County Sports Pub., 1995, Lucas County Baseball Pub., 1995, Winners of Wood County Pub., 1995, Harrison County Baseball Digest, 1998—, Belmont County Baseball League, 1998—, Ohio Promotions For Sports, 2000—, Ohio Baseball Digest Harrison County, 1998—; founder, chmn. twinsburg (Ohio) Cmty. Heritage Publs., Garrettsville (Ohio) Cmty. Svc. Publ., lectr. series Catch The Spirit, 2000—; founder, pub. Touching All the Bases, 1991; bd. dirs. New Hope Records, Hit and Run Records, Red Hour Records, Nat. William "Dummy" Hoy Baseball Com., 1995—; founder, dir. Cy Young Mus., 1975; mem. adv. bd. Sportsbeat, 1985—, sch. Calendar Co., Inc., 1984, 89, D & D Sports Prodn. and Mktg. Creations, 1990—, Damascus Steel Casting Co., 1987—, Advantage Sports Co., 1989—, Base Sports Co., 1989, M & M Publs., 1987—. Founder, pres., dir. Cy Young Mus., 1975-80, Ohio Baseball Hall of Fame, 1976—, Ohio Baseball Hall of Fame and Mus., 1980—, celebration, 1977-79, golf invitational, 1980—; founder, pres. Ohio Sports Hall of Fame, 1985—, Shaker Hts Sports Hall of Fame, 1989—, Ohio Sports Legends Found., 1991—, Toledo Baseball Bluecoats, 1984—, Tuscarawas County Sports Hall of Fame, 1980—, Tuscarawas County Am. Revolution Bicentennial Commn., exec. com. 1974-1976, Tuscarawas Valley Tourist Assn., 1979-81, Buckeye Baseball Lecture Series, 1989—, Cleve. Baseball Old Timers Assn., Ohio Sports Celebrity Golf Invitational, 1991—, 1991—, Midwest Sports Coun., Chesterland (Ohio) Hist. Found. Enhancement Fund, 1989—, Berea (Ohio) Hist. and Sports Fund, 1984—, Windham (Ohio) Cmty. Svc. Found., 1990—, Jefferson Hist. and Sports Found., 1986—, Ohio Sports Ednl. Coun., 1991—, Youth in Cmty. Svc. and Vols. are Winners Lecture Series, 1991—, Ohio Minor League Baseball Hall of Fame Assn., 1992—, U.S. Sports Hall of Fame, 1989—, Ohio Founders League, 1990—, Ohio Negro Baseball Hall of Fame Vets. Coun., 1991—, Ohio Women's Baseball Hall of Fame, 1998—, Alta Weiss Meml. award, 1998—, Ohio Baseball History Mus, 2002—; founder, chmn. Cy Young Centennial, 1967, Cy Young Golf Invitational; founder, chmn. Streetsboro (Ohio) Athletic Found., 1989—, Wickliffe (Ohio) Cmty. and Sports Fund, Madison (Ohio) Village Hist. Preservation Fund, Middlefield (Ohio) Fire Dept. Cmty. Promotions Fund, Burton Athletic Enhancement Fund, Fairview Pk. (Ohio) Cmty. Svc. Fund, Bath-Richfield Ohio Cmty. Fund, Independence Freedom Fund, 1988—, Aurora Hist. Preservation Fund, 1988—, Conneaut (Ohio) Cmty. Promotional Fund, 1991—; founder, dir. Target/Reach Youth, 1971—; pres. Tuscarawas County Old Timers Baseball Assn., 1985—; trustee Hiram House, 1989—, Nat. Jr. Tennis League, 1985—; hon. bd. dirs. Chautauqua Sports Hall of Fame, 1982—; bd. dirs. Greater Toledo Sports Hall of Fame; exec. sponsor, Ohio chmn. World Golf Hall of Fame, Pinehurst, N.C., 1979—; founder Famous Ohioans in Print Hall of Fame, 1994; mem. adv. bd. Portage County Sports Hall of Fame, 1983—, Cuyahoga Hills Boys Sch., Warrensville Hts., Ohio, 1971—, Camp Hope, Warrensville Hts., 1973—, Cleve. Sports Legend Found., 1988—, Great Ohioans Hall of Fame, 1988—, Solon Cmty. Promotional Fund, 1989—; mem. disting. citizens adv. bd. Am. Police Hall of Fame and Mus., 1987—; mem. career adv. bd. Denison U., 1990—, nom. com. Ohio Profl. and Amateur Athlete of Yr. Awards, 1990—; active Geauga County Hist. Soc., Summit County Sports Hall of Fame, Dunham Tavern Mus.; founder, chmn. Shaker Hts. Youth Hall of Fame, 1996; chmn. Ray Chapman Meml. com., 2000 and numerous others; assoc. Merrick Art Gallery. Served in AUS, 1956-58. Named to Order of Long Leaf Pine, N.C. State Senate, 1984, Hon. Order of Ky. Cols., 1986, Venerable Order Michael the Archangel, Am. Police Hall of Fame, 1989; Hon. Citizen, City of Memphis, 1986, City of Little Rock, 1986, Ohio Baseball Man of Yr., 1991, Ohio Baseball Hall of Fame, World Biographical Hall of Fame, 1984, Wis. Baseball Hall of Fame, 1998; founder, chmn. Moses Fleetwood Walker Baseball Meml. award, 1991, Phi Delta Theta; recipient Disting. Svc. award Hubbard, Ohio, 1986, Vermilion Kiwanis, 1996, Internat Friendship award Premier Ont., Can., 1985, Commr.'s award Trumbull County, 1985, Gov.'s citation State of Md., 1987, Hon. West Virginian award, 1987, J. Edgar Hoover award Am. Police Hall of Fame, 1991, Humanitarian award City of Cleve., 1991, Mayor's Volunteerism award, 1991, Vol. of Yr. award No. Ohio Live, 1991, Ohio Govs. award, 1978, Ohio Govs. award Cmty. Action, 1974, Sports Achievement award Dapper Dan Club of Upper Ohio Valley, 1993, Ohio Baseball Man of Yr. award Greater Youngstown Baseball Old Timers Assn., 1991, Sports Hero award Am. Ath. Assn. of Deaf, Inc., 1992, Ohio Profl. and Athlete of Yr. award, 1995, Lifetime Achievement award, 1995, 20th Century award Achievement Nat. Assn. Chiefs Police, 1998, A Spl. Friend award Blair County Spl. Olympics, 1998, Lifetime Achievement award Lake County Hist. Soc., 1998, Disting. Svc. award Rotary Club, Twinsburg, Ohio, 1998, Cmty. Svc. award Ohio Dr. Martin Luther King, Jr. Holiday Commn., 1999, Cmty. Builders award Flushing Ohio Masonic Lodge No. 298, 1998, Disting. Svc. award Solon Ohio Rotary Club, 1999, Comty. Svc. award Middlefield Fire Dept., 1999, Disting. Comty. Svc. award Lorain County Assn. Township Trustees and Clerks, 2001; commendation State of N.C. Senate, 1984, State of Pa. Senate, 1984, State of La., State of Ohio Senate and Reps., Greater Stark County Baseball Hall of Fame, 1994; Columbus (Ohio) City Coun., 1985, Cleve. City Coun., 1989; Thomas C. Eakin Day declared City of Cleve., 1974, N.Mex., 1987, others; world record holder Guinness Book of World Records, 1991; inducted Cy Young Tuscarawas County Old Timers Baseball Assn. Hall of Fame, 1993, Am. Athletic Assn. of Deaf Hall of Fame, 1992, Sports Hero Award, 1992, Chautauqua Sports Hall of Fame, 1983, City of Cleve. Vol. Hall of Fame, 1991, Ohio Record Holders Hall of Fame, 1989, Greater Akron Baseball Hall of Fame, 1993, Ohio Sr. Citizens Hall of Fame, 1995, Ohio Vets Hall of Fame, 1995, Old Time Ball Players Assn. of Wis. Hall of Fame, 1998, Rufus Putnam Disting. Svc. award Ohio Masons, 1999, medal of Honor Daughters of the Am. Revolution, 2000, Trumbull County Baseball Commendation Mahoning Valley Professional Baseball Assn., 2000; named Trustee of Yr. Nat. Jr. Tennis League, Cleve., 1996, Disting. Svc. Award, Solon Ohio Rotary, 1999, Cmty. Svc. Award, Middlefield Fire Dept., 1999, Paul Harris fellow Rotary Internat., 1999, Disting. Cmty. Svc. Award, Lorain County Assn. Township Trustees and Clerks, 2001, Ravenna Kiwanis Club honor award, 2001, Munroe Falls Kiwanis Club honor award, 2001, Commendation award Mahoning Valley Profl. Baseball Assn., 2002, Ellis Island Medal of Honor, 2002, The Am. Spirit award, 2002, U.S. Marine Corps Commendation, 2002, Cmty. Svc. award Copley Ohio Hist. Soc., 2002, Outstanding Spkr. award Stow-Munroe Falls Ohio C. of C., 2002, The Golden Legion of Phi Delta Theta, 2003, Baseball Achievement award, Greater Youngstown Old Timers Assn., 2003, and numerous others. Mem. U.S. Assn. Sports Halls of Fame, U.S. Hist. Soc., Soc. Am. Baseball Rsch., Nat. Trust Hist. Preservation, Ohio Hist. Soc., Ohio Assn. Sports Halls of Fame, Ohio Baseball Roundtable (founder, pres. 1991—), Ohio Assn. Old Time Baseball Players (founder, pres. 1990—), Ohio Racquetball Assn. (adv. bd. 1981-82), Old Time Ball Players Assn. Wis., Western Pa. Sports Hall of Fame, North Ohio Old Time Baseball Players Club (adv. bd. 1978—), Tuscarawas County Old Timers Baseball Assn. (hon. dir. 1972—, commendation 1970), Tuscarawas County Hist. Soc. (trustee 1978-81), Lawrence County Hist. Soc., Greater Youngstown Old Timers Baseball Assn. (inductee Hall of Fame, 1994), Madison Hist. Soc., Middlefield Hist. Soc. (adv. bd. 1986—), Clinton Hist. Soc. (hon. trustee 1987—), Windsor Hist. Soc. (adv. bd. 1987—), Solon Hist. Soc., Newcomerstown Hist. Soc., Shaker Hist. Soc. (trustee 1980-82), Greater Canton Amateur Sports Hall of Fame Assn. (commendation 1994), Barberton Sports Hall of Fame (founder, chmn. publs. 1989—), Holloway Old Timers Baseball Club (adv. bd. 1990—), Temperance House Mus., Negro Leagues Baseball Mus., Internat. Platform Assn., English Speaking Union (trustee 1994—), Denison U. Cleve. Men's Club, Gustave Courbet Soc., Western Res. Hist. Soc., Interact Club (adv. bd. Twinsburg chpt. 1981—, founder, dir. Shaker Heights chpt. 1971—), Exec. Club (Woodmere, Ohio chpt., Hall of Fame 1990), Univ. Sch. Tennis Club, Grandview Golf Club, PGA Nat. Golf Club (internat. mem.), Legend Lake Golf Club, Beachwood Athletic Club, Rotary (Svc. Above Self award Wickliffe chpt. 1991, Disting. Svc. award Swanton chpt. 1991, Outstanding Sports and Civic Svc. award Bellevue chpt., 1990, Spirit of Twinsburg award Twinsburg chpt. 1991, pres. Shaker Heights chpt. 1970-71), The Order of St. George (named Knight Commdr., 1994), Phi Delta Theta (exec. com. nat. Lou Gehrig award com. 1975—, charter inductee Ohio Iota Hall of Fame 1989, Outstanding Alumnus award 1989, Cleve. pres. 1970, Hall of Fame 1975, Disting. Alumnus award 1997, named to Internat. Fraternity Hall of Fame 1997), Ray Chapman Meml. Com. (chmn. 2000), Merrick Art Gallery (assoc.), Masons, Scottish Rite. Address: 2729 Shelley Rd Shaker Heights OH 44122

EAKINS, WILLIAM SHANNON, lawyer; b. Glen Cove, N.Y., July 22, 1951; s. William Shannon and Jean (Pickup) E.; 1 child, Amelia Moore. BA, Yale U., 1974; JD, Cornell U., 1977. Lawyer, trust adminstr. J.P. Morgan Bank, N.Y.C., 1977-81; counsel com. on taxation and investigations N.Y State Senate, Albany, 1981-84; assoc. Gelberg & Abrams, N.Y.C., 1981-84, Phillips, Nizer, Benjamin, Krim & Ballon, N.Y.C., 1984-88, ptnr., 1989-92, ptnr., chair trusts and estates dept. Olshan, Grundman, Frome & Rosenzweig, N.Y.C., 1993-98; ptnr. Forsythe, Patton, Ellis, Lipsett & Savage, N.Y.C., 1998—. Bd. dirs. Asphalt Green Inc.; mem. estate planning com. Arthritis Found. Contbr. articles to profl. jours. Vice chmn. N.Y. Rep. County Com., N.Y.C., 1985-89, exec. com., 1979-87, dist. leader, 1979-87; vice chmn. Manhattan Cmty. Bd. No. 8, N.Y.C., 1980-84, 93-97; Rep., Ind. Neighbors and Conservative candidate for N.Y. State Assembly, 1992; bd. dirs. Homecrest Cmty. Svcs., Inc.; sec. Hellgate Hill-Highgate Cmty. Assn.; elder, mem. session, mem. planned giving com. Brick Presbyn. Ch. Mem. N.Y. State Bar Assn., Assn. Bar City N.Y. (mem. com. on estate and gift taxation, mem. com. on N.Y. state legislation), Yale Club, St. Andrews Soc. State of N.Y. (bd. mgrs.). Republican. Presbyterian. Office: Forsythe Patton Ellis Lipsett & Savage 420 Lexington Ave New York NY 10170-0002 E-mail: wmeakins@rcn.com.

EAKLE, ARLENE HASLAM, genealogist; b. Salt Lake City, July 19, 1936; d. Thomas E. and Margaret (Mitchell) Haslam; m. Alma D. Eakle, Jr., Feb. 8, 1957; children: JoAnn, Richard, Linda, John. ADN, Weber State U.; MA in English history, PhD English history, U. Utah. Author: (with Linda Brinkerhoff) Family History for Fun and Profit-The Genealogy Research Process, 30th anniversary edit., 2003, Genealogy in Land Records, 1998, Migration Patterns of American Families, 1999; (with Johni Cerny) The Source: A Guidebook for American Genealogy, 1984, Ancestry's Guide to Research, 1985; editor: Research News, Immigration Digest; editor: Virginia Notebooks, N.Y. Rsch. Fellow Utah Geneal. Assn., 1987; recipient Award of Merit Fedn. Geneal. Soc., 1984, Julian Bickersteth medal Inst. Heraldic and Geneal. Studies, Eng. Mem. Am. Family Records Assn. (bd. dirs. 1990-2002), Assn. Profl. Genealogists (pres. 1980-82, Grahame Thomas Smallwood Jr. Award of Merit 1984), Md. Geneal. Soc., Utah Geneal. Assn., West Fla. Geneal. Soc. Office: Genealogical Inst 56 W Main St PO Box 129 Tremonton UT 84337-0129 E-mail: eakle@xmission.com., genealogy@utahlinx.com.

EAKMAN, KATE J. history educator; b. Somerset, Pa., Apr. 29, 1963; d. John R. and Betty J. James; m. Scott M. Eakman, July 5, 1997; children: Nathaniel Parker, Jeremy. BA, Okla. Christian U, 1992; MA in History, U N.C., 1994. Assoc. prof. of history Cascade Coll., Portland, Oreg., 1994—97, adj. history faculty, 1998—; social studies dept. chair Columbia Christian Schools, Portland, Oreg., 1998—. Mem.: Orgn. Am. Historians, 1st Oreg. Vol. Inf. Mem. Ch. Of Christ. Office: Columbia Christian Schools 413 NE 91st Portland OR 97220

EALY, CYNTHIA PIKE, artist, realtor; b. Eveleth, Minn., Apr. 13, 1932; d. Robert Sheldon Pike and Lila Mary Saari; m. Donald Rae Ealy, Dec. 14, 1952; children: Elizabeth, Dennis, Jonathan, Richard. Student, Coll. of Ams., Mexico City, 1950-52, U. So. Calif., 1952-53. Actress, Mexico City, 1950-52; owner Woodland World Travel, Tarzana, Calif., 1965-70; decorator Ridgewood, N.J., 1970-71; artist, 1972—; realtor, 1987—. Bd. dirs., pres. Rep. Women's club, Woodland Hills, Calif., 1964-69; active Internat. Sch. of Brussels, 1975-80; co-chmn. Reps. Abroad, Europe, 1978-82. Recipient Outstanding Svc. award Am. Women's Club of Brussels, 1984. Mem. Sierra Artists Network, Niguel Art Assn. of Orange County. Avocations: instructing French lang. and cuisine. Home: PO Box 6534 467 Driver Way Incline Village NV 89450 also: 27142 Paseo Del Este San Juan Capistrano CA 92675-4927

EALY, JONATHAN BRUCE, lawyer; b. L.A., Apr. 20, 1960; s. Donald Rae and Cynthia Howland (Pike) E. AB cum laude, Harvard U., 1982; JD, Duke U., 1985. Bar: Alaska 1986, U.S. Ct. Appeals (9th cir.) 1986. Clk. judge Karen Hunt Alaska Superior Ct., Anchorage, 1985-86; assoc. Taylor & Hintz, Anchorage, 1986-89, Heller, Ehrman, White & McAuliffe, Anchorage, 1989-93; gen. counsel Borisovich Internat., Inc., Anchorage, 1993—; of counsel Partnow, Sharrock & Tindall, Anchorage, 1995-2000; spl. counsel Heller Ehrman White and McAuliffe, Anchorage, 2000—. Bd. dirs. Borealis Brewing Co.; prin. Na'au, Inc., 1998—. Author: Third Story, 1998. Pres. Anchorage Youth Ct., 1993-94, legal advisor, 1989-92; bd. dirs. Kids Voting Alaska, Anchorage, 1993. Mem. Anchorage Bar Assn. (pres. 1994, v.p. 1993, pres. young lawyers sect. 1988-90). Office: 510 L St Ste 500 Anchorage AK 99501-1959

EAMES, ROBERT NEWTON, lawyer; b. Tyler, Tex., Oct. 18, 1945; s. Newton Lincoln and Helen Keith Eames; m. Phyllis Ann Prenevost, June 26, 1970; children: Erin, Brant. BA, Tex. Tech. U., 1967, JD, 1970. Bar: Tex. Felony prosecutor Dist. Atty.'s Office, Denton, Tex., 1971-72; ptnr. Griffin, Shelton & Eames, Denton, 1972-80; pres., shareholder Philips & Hopkins, PC, Denton, 1980-94, Philips, Hopkins, Eames, Cobb, Denton, 1994—. Contbr. scholarly articles to law jours. Bd. dirs. Little League Baseball, Denton, 1987-92. Mem. State Bar of Tex. (mem. dist. 14-B grievance com. 1993-95, chair dist. 14-B grievance com. 1995-96, pattern jury charge com. 1994-98), Tex. Acad. Family Law Specialists, North Tex. Family Law Specialists Assn. (dir. 1988-92), Denton Bar Assn. (pre.), Alliance Bar Assn. Avocations: golf, flying. Office: Philips Hopkins Eames & Cobb 525 N Locust St Denton TX 76201-4127 E-mail: eames@dentonlaw.com.

EARHART, EILEEN MAGIE, retired child and family life educator; b. Hamilton, Ohio, Oct. 21, 1928; d. Andrew J. and Martha (Waldorf) Magie; m. Paul G. Earhart; children: Anthony G., Bruce P., Daniel T. BS, Miami U., Oxford, Ohio, 1950; MA in Adminstrn. and Ednl. Services, Mich. State U., 1962, PhD in Edn., 1969; H.H.D. (hon.), Miami U., Oxford, Ohio, 1980. Tchr. home econs. W. Alexandria (Ohio) Schs., 1950-51; elementary tchr. Waterford Twp. Schs., Pontiac, Mich., 1958-65, reading specialist, 1965-67; prof., chmn. family and child ecology dept. Mich. State U., East Lansing, 1968-84; prof., head dept. home and family life Fla. State U., Tallahassee, 1984-89; ret., 1989. Author: Attention and Classification Training Curriculum; co-editor spl. issue of Family Relations, 1984; contbr. chpts. to profl. jours., books. Mem. adv. bd. Lansing Com. on Children's TV, Family/Sch./Cmty. Partnership Project, Tallahassee; bd. dirs. Women's Resource Ctr., Grand Rapids, Mich., Wesley Found., Fla. State U., 1989-99; mem. campus ministries bd. Fla. A&M U., 1995-98; Sunday sch. tchr. Haines City United Meth. Ch., 2001--; mem. Mich. Gov.'s Task Force on Youth. Mem. Nat. Coun. Family Rels. (pres. Assn. of Couns. 1987-88, bd. dirs. 1986-88, chair nat. meeting local arrangements 1992), Fla. Coun. Family Rels. (pres. elect 1985-86, pres. 1986-87), Nat. Assn. Edn. Young Children, Assn. Childhood Edn. Internat., Am. Home Econs. Assn. (named AHEA leader at 75th Ann. of Assn. 1984), Internat. Fedn. Home Econs., Mich. Home Econs. Assn. (pres. 1980-82), Fla. Home Econs. Assn. (chmn. scholarship com. 1986-88, dist. chmn. 1990-91, chmn. nominating com. 1991-92, co-chair ann. meeting 1995), Ednl. Rsch. Assn., Killearn United Meth. Ch., United Meth. Women (cir. chair 1993-97, pres. 1994), Phi Kappa Phi (pres. Fla State U. chpt. 1988-89), Delta Kappa Gamma, Omicron Nu, others. Home (Summer): 22 Oak Tree Ct Franklin NC 28734 Home: 2973 Chickasaw Dr Haines City FL 33844-8419 E-mail: emearhart@aol.com.

EARL, ANTHONY SCULLY, former governor of Wisconsin, lawyer; b. Lansing, Mich., Apr. 12, 1936; s. Russell K. and Ethlynne Julia (Scully) E.; children: Julia, Anne, Mary, Catherine. BS, Mich. State U.; JD, U. Chgo. Bar: Wis., Minn. Asst. dist. atty. Marathon County, Wausau, Wis., 1965-66; city atty. City of Wausau, 1966-69; mem. Wis. Assembly, Madison, 1969-74; mem. firm Crooks, Low & Earl, 1969-74; sec. Wis. Dept. Adminstrn., Madison, 1974-75, Dept. Nat. Resources, Madison, 1975-80; v.p. firm Foley & Lardner, Madison, 1980-82; gov. State of Wis., Madison, 1983-87; ptnr. Quarles and Brady, Madison, 1987—. Served as lt. USN, 1962-65. Democrat. Roman Catholic. Office: Quarles & Brady 1 S Pinckney St PO Box 2113 Madison WI 53701-2113

EARL, BOYD L. mathematician; b. Huntsville, Pa., July 20, 1927; BS in Math., Wilkes U., 1952; MA, Bucknell U., 1953; postgrad., Pa. State U., 1963. Tchr. h.s. math, Forty-Fort, Pa., 1952—56; math. prof. Bucknell U., 1956—63; prof. Wilkes Univ., Wilkes-Barre, Pa., 1963—92, prof. emeritus, 1992. Author: (textbook) Groups and Fields, 1962, Probability, 1963; co-author: (set of 12 soft cover math. textbooks) Stanford U., 1964—66. With USAF, 1946—48. Grantee 3 grants, NSF, 1961—63. Mem.: Nat. Math. Assn., Pi Mu Epsilon.

EARL, LEWIS HAROLD, economics and management consultant, lawyer; b. Guthrie, Tex., Dec. 17, 1918; s. Henry W. and Ruth (O'Neal) E.; m. Patricia Miller, Mar. 5, 1943 (dec. 1973); children: William Lee, Patricia Lewise, Robert Charles, James Michael; m. Meade Randolph Loomis, July 1, 1977 (div. 1979); m. Maxine Durrett Marks, Jan. 31, 1981. BA, Tex. Technol. Coll., 1939; student, U. Tex., 1939-40, Am. U., 1941-42, George Washington U., 1942-62; JD, Georgetown U., 1950. Bar: D.C. 1950, U.S. Supreme Ct. 1972, Tex. 1983. With Bur. Labor Statistics, Dept. Labor, 1940-42, 46-51; industry, commodity economist NPA Dept. Commerce, 1951-53; productivity specialist, economist, program analyst, asst. program officer U.S. Tech. Cooperation Program in Brazil, 1953-57; program officer U.S. Tech. Cooperation Program, Argentina, 1957-59, 1959—61; internat. relations officer AID, Washington, 1961-63; chief internat. research Office Manpower Automation and Tng., U.S. Dept. Labor, Washington, 1963-65; chief Fgn. manpower program staff Office Manpower Policy, Evaluation and Research, Dept. Labor, 1965-70; U.S. del. 8th meeting Am. mem. states ILO, Ottawa, Ont., Can., 1966, U.S. del. to chem. industries com. Geneva, 1969; tech. dir. Seminar for Ministry Labor Tng. Coordinators, OAS, Mexico City, 1970; asst. dir. for program devel. Ctr. for Human Resources U. Houston, 1970-75; manpower planning officer Gulf Coast CAMPS Secretariat, Mayor's Office, City of Houston, 1970-74; cons. Tex. Gov.'s Office Policy Coordination, Austin, 1974; asso. dir. human resources program, instr. econs. U. Mo.-Columbia, 1975-78; expert cons. Human Resources Devel., Bur. Internat. Labor Affairs, U.S. Dept. Labor and UN Devel. Program for Egypt, 1978-80; staff adv. Am. Productivity Center, Houston, 1980; program officer U.S. Operations Mission, El Salvador, 1966—69. Expert cons. UN Indsl. Devel.

Orgn., Cairo, Egypt, 1981; lectr. Coll. Bus. Adminstrn. Tex. Tech U., 1982-83; mgr. Post C. of C., 1984-87. Sec.-treas. Post Econ. Devel. Corp., 1984-90; bd. dirs. Tex. Common Cause, 1987—, legis. liaison, 1991, 93; mem. Lubbock-Garza County Pvt. Industry Coun., 1986-92, Friends of the Libr., Tex. Tech. U., Tex. Indsl. Devel. Coun.; chmn. Garza County Dem. Com., 1986-87, 91—; bd. dirs. Tex. Alliance for Edn. and the Arts, 1991-97, Maxine Durrett Earl Charitable Found., 1994—; founder Lewis and Maxine Earl Survey Rsch. Lab., Tex. Tech U., 2001; vol. ombudsman. Mem. ASTD, VFW, Am. Statis. Assn., Am. Acad. Polit. and Social Ssis., Acad. Polit. Sci., Tex. Hist. Assn., Houston Pers. Assn., South Plains Cmty. Action Assn., Soc. Internat. Devel., Nat. Planning Assn., Indsl. Rels. Rsch. Assn., Nat. Economist Club, Caprock Fin. (capital fin. com.), Garza County Trail Blazers (pres. 1994-97), Rotary, Lions (pres. 1996-97, 2001-02), Alpha Chi, Omicron Delta Epsilon, Pi Sigma Alpha, Sigma Iota Epsilon. Methodist. Home: 1929 Stoney Brook Houston TX 77063-1809 Office: PO Box 580 Post TX 79356-0580 *I believe that individuals will make the right decisions if they have full and adequate information and facts, and therefore, I have sought to find the truth that will make men free.*

EARL, MARTHA FRANCES, librarian, researcher; b. Washington, Aug. 18, 1956; d. Jefferson Davis Earl, Ruby Smith; m. Walter Robert Gawryla; 1 child, Frank Gawryla; m. Stephen Jack Cobert (div. Aug. 6, 1984). BS, U. Tenn., 1978, MS in Libr. Sci., 1985. Cert. seconary edn. Sci. tchr. First Assembly Christian Sch., Memphis, 1979—80; libr. clk. Memphis State U., 1980—81; sr. libr. asst. U. Tenn., Knoxville, 1981—87; reference libr. Meharry Med. Coll., Nashville, 1987—90; head of reference East Tenn. State U., Coll. Medicine Libr., Johnson City, Tenn., 1990—97; reference coord. U. Tenn. Med. Ctr., Knoxville, 1997—. Cons. Indian Path Hosp., Kingsport, 1990—94, N.E. Tenn. Rehab. Hosp., Johnson City, 1992—97, Morristown Hamblen Hosp., 1993—97, N.E. Tenn. Area Health Edn. Ctr., Greeneville, 1994—98, East Tenn. State U., Johnson City, 2001—; mem. adv. bd. Tenn. Adv. Coun. on Librs., Nashville, 1998—99. Author: (book) Bibkit #9: Managed Care: A Guide to Information Sources, 2000; contbr. chapters to books, revs. to publs., articles to profl. jours. Organizer Tenn. Libr. Legislative Day, 1999—2001; historian Alpha Phi Omega Svc. Fraternity, Knoxville, 1976—78; comm. team Ebenezer United Meth. Ch., Knoxville, 1998—2001; libr. First United Meth. Ch., Bristol, 1994—97, Holston Chapel United Meth. Ch., Knoxville, 1973—78, Sunday sch. tchr., 1972—78. Recipient Rsch. award, South Ctrl. Chpt. Med. Libr. Assn., 2001; grantee Grateful Med. Outreach grant, Nat. Libr. Medicine, 1990—92, Exhibit grant, Nat. Network Librs. Medicine, 1994, Nat. Network Librs. Medicine, 1996, Internet Tng. grant, Nat. Libr. Medicine, 1997—98, Access to Electronic Info. for the Pub. grant, NIH, 2001—02, Physicians Med. Edn. Resource Fund, 2001; scholar Nat. Alumni scholar, U. Tenn. Nat. Alumni Found., 1974—78, Roddy Mfg., 1974, 1978. Mem.: ALA (chpt. rels. coun. 1998—99), Med. Libr. Assn. (Brodman com. for excellence in acad. health scis. libr. 1995—97, So. chpt. rsch. com. chair 1997—98, So. chpt. sec. 1999—2000, program com. leadership and mgmt. sect. 2000—01, R&D and demonstration project jury chair 2000—01, Kronick jury chair 2001—02, So. chpt. comm. com. 2001—02), Assn. Coll. and Rsch. Librs. (state affiliate chair 1995—96), Knoxville Area Health Scis. Librs. Consortium (pres. 2001—02), East Tenn. Libr. Assn. (v.p. 2002—), Tenn. Adv. Coun. on Librs. (Tenn. electronic libr. subcom. 1998—99), Tenn. Health Scis. Librs. Assn. (membership chair 1998—2000), Tri-Cities Health Scis. Librs. Consortium (chair 1994), Tenn. Libr. Assn. (coll. and univ. librs. sect. chair 1996—97, Tenn. libr. editl. rev. bd. 1996—2000, pres. 1998—99, conf. com. program chair 1998—2000, assoc. pres. 1999, ad hoc com. on staffing 2000—01, chair strategic planning 2000—, Appreciation award 1999, 2002), Tennshare (chmn. long range planning 2002—), U. Tenn. Sch. Info. Sci. Alumni Bd. (mentoring subcom. and mem.-at-large 2001—). Methodist. Avocations: reading, walking, swimming, movies, travel. Office: Univ Tenn Med Ctr 1924 Alcoa Hwy Knoxville TN 37920 Office Fax: 865-544-9527. Personal E-mail: earlmartha@yahoo.com. Business E-Mail: mearl@utk.edu.

EARLE, ARTHUR PERCIVAL, textile company executive, airport executive; b. Montreal, Que., Can., Apr. 23, 1922; s. Arthur Percival and Bernadette (Gosselin) E.; m. Muriel Elizabeth Vining, June 1, 1946; children: Arthur Percival, Richard John, Janet Elizabeth. BEE, McGill U., Montreal, 1949; MMP, Harvard U., 1957. Registered profl. engr., Que., Ont. With Shawinigan Water & Power Co., 1949-63, asst. mgr. prodn. and plant; with Dominion Textile Inc., Montreal, 1963-90, chief engr., then group v.p. subs., 1970-78, sr. v.p. ops. svcs., 1978-87, sr. v.p., 1987-88, cons. corp. affairs, 1988-90. Bd. dirs. Stella Jones Inc., chmn., 1993; bd. dirs. Shermag Inc.; past pres. Lana Knit Ltd., Fireside Fabrics Ltd., Fiber-World Ltd., Elpee Yarns Ltd., Jaro Ltd., Esmond Mills Mtd.; past chmn. Pemans Ltd., Foresbec Inc., 1988-93; chmn. Aeroport de Montreal, 1989-96, bd. dirs., 1989-96, pres., 1989-90. Bd. dirs. Ecole de Technologie Superieure, U. Que., 1978-85, mem. exec. com., 1981-85; pres. Montreal Bd. Trade, 1980-81, chmn. bd. dirs., 1981-82; pres., exec. com. Phoenix Found., 1985-89; bd. dirs. Lakeshore Gen. Hosp., Pointe Claire, Que., 1987-94, vice chmn., 1989-94; chmn., Les Mercuriades Bus. Awards, 1985; chmn., bd. dirs. Aeroport De Montreal, 1989-96, pres., 1989-90; founding chmn. Can. Airports Coun., 1990-93, bd. dirs., 1990-96; chmn., pres. La Societe De Promotion Des Aeroport De Montrèal, 1987-96; hon. chmn. bd. Phoenix Ctr., 1991-96. Pilot RCAF, 1941-45. Named to Order of Can., 1996; recipient Award of Distinction, Concordia U., 1989, 125th Anniversary Can. Commemorative medal, 1992, Queen Elizabeth Jubilee medal, 2002. Fellow Engring. Inst. Can. (hon. treas. 1986-88, sr. v.p. 1988-89, pres. 1989-90); mem. IEEE (past sect. chmn.), Order Engrs. Que., Assn. Profl. Engrs. Ont., Am. Textile Managerial Engring. Soc., Que. C. of C. (pres. 1983-84, chmn., 1984-85), Royal Montreal Golf Club. Anglican.

EARLE, CLIFFORD JOHN, JR., mathematician; b. Racine, Wis., Nov. 3, 1935; s. Clifford John and Anne Elizabeth (Griffith) E.; m. Elizabeth Joan Deutsch, Dec. 27, 1960; children— Rebecca Ann, Susan Deborah. BA, Swarthmore Coll., 1957; MA, Harvard U., 1958, PhD, 1962. Instr. Harvard U., 1962-63, vis. lectr., 1968-69; mem. Inst. for Advanced Study, Princeton, N.J., 1963-65, 81; asst. prof. Cornell U., Ithaca, N.Y., 1965-66, assoc. prof., 1966-69, prof., 1969—, chmn. dept. math., 1976-79; vis. prof. U. Warwick, 1967; vis. lectr. Inst. Mittag-Leffler, 1972. Mem. geometric function theory program, Math. Scis. Rsch. Inst., Berkeley, Calif., 1986; hon. prof. U. Warwick, 1999—. Assoc. editor Duke Math. Jour., 1973-79; contbr. articles to math. rsch. jours. John Simon Guggenheim Meml. fellow, 1974-75 Mem. Am. Math. Soc. (editor Proc. 1989-97, mng. editor 1997-2001). Home: 314 Elmwood Ave Ithaca NY 14850-4812 Office: Cornell U Dept Math Ithaca NY 14853-4201 E-mail: cliff@math.cornell.edu.

EARLE, CRAIG CHRISTOPHER, oncologist, epidemiologist; b. Montreal, Que., Can., Dec. 5, 1965; came to U.S., 1998; BSc in Biochemistry, U. Ottawa, Ont., Can., 1989, MD, 1990, MSc in Epidemiology, 1998. Diplomate Am. Bd. Internal Medicine, Am. Bd. Med. Oncology. Med. oncologist Ottawa Regional Cancer Ctr., 1996-98, Dana Faber Cancer Inst., Boston, 1998—. Asst. prof. medicine, Harvard U. Med. Sch. Office: Dana Faber Cancer Inst 44 Binney St Ste 21-24 Boston MA 02115-6084 E-mail: craig_earle@dfci.harvard.edu.

EARLE, ELIZABETH DEUTSCH, biology educator; b. Vienna, Oct. 6, 1937; came to U.S., 1939; d. George F. and Sabina (Edel) Deutsch; m. Clifford J. Earle, Jr., Dec. 27, 1960; children: Rebecca A., Susan D. BA, Swarthmore Coll., 1959; MA, Radcliffe Coll., 1960; PhD, Harvard U., 1964. Rsch. fellow biology Harvard U., Cambridge, Mass., 1968-69; rsch. assoc. floriculture Cornell U., Ithaca, N.Y., 1970-74, rsch. assoc. plant breeding, 1975-78, sr. rsch. assoc. plant breeding, 1978-79, assoc. prof. plant breeding, 1979-86, prof. plant breeding, 1986—; vis. scholar biology Stanford (Calif.) U., 1986, chmn. plant breeding, 1993-2001. Mem. NSF Rev. Panel, Washington, 1979—82, USDA Rev. Panel, Washington, 1983—85; dir. Plant Tissue Culture FacilityC Cornell U., Ithaca, 1983—89; cons. on internat. biotech. issues. Editor Plant Cell Reports, 1986—. Trustee Cornell U., 2002—. Recipient predoctoral fellowship NSF, 1959-63, postdoctoral fellowship NIH, 1964-65; grantee NSF, USDA, Dept. Energy, Industry, 1978—. Mem.: Crucifer Genetics Coop., Am. Soc. Plant Biologists, Internat. Assn. Plant Tissue Culture, Phi Beta Kappa, Sigma Xi. Achievements include development of procedures for tissue culture and genetic manipulation of maize, sorghum, brassica, tomato, potato; development of improved cytoplasmic male-sterile and disease and insect-resistant lines of brassica vegetables. Office: Cornell U Dept Plant Breeding 514 Bradfield Hall Ithaca NY 14853-1901 E-mail: ede3@cornell.edu.

EARLE, J.D. physician; b. Pomona, Calif., Oct. 7, 1937; s. Clarence M. and Margaret E. E.; m. Sherrill A. Earle, Aug. 25, 1968; children: Eric A., Deborah J., Julie A. BA in Biology with honors, U. Oreg., 1959; MD, Stanford U., 1964. Assoc. dir. radiation oncology dept. Stanford U., 1970-76; Donner prof., chair radiation oncology Mayo Clinic, Rochester, Minn., 1976-96; prof., chair radiation oncology U. Calif. Davis, Sacramento, 1996—2001, Mayo Clinic Jacksonville, 2001—. Lt. comdr. USNR, 1968-70. Fellow Am. Coll. Radiology. Office: Mayo Clinic 4500 San Pablo Rd Jacksonville FL 32224 E-mail: earle.john@mayo.edu.

EARLE, JEAN BUIST, finance executve; b. Newton, N.J., Oct. 5, 1951; d. Richardson and Jean (Mackerly) Buist; m. Terry Dean Earle, Mar. 4, 1989; children: Morgan, Abigail. AB, Cornell U., 1973; MEd, Coll. William and Mary, 1974; MBA, U. Pa., 1987. Mgr. The Korman Corp., Jenkintown, Pa., 1975-77; v.p. ops. Community Assn. Mgmt. Co., Havertown, Pa., 1977-78; adminstrv. asst. Albert Einstein Med. Ctr., Phila., 1978-83; assoc. adminstr. Meml. Hosp. Burlington County, Mt. Holly, N.J., 1983-87; v.p. Overlook Hosp., Summit, N.J., 1987-95; exec. dir. Summit (N.J.) Child Care Ctrs., Inc., 1995-96; owner, ptnr. Computer Edn. Inst., Kenilworth, N.J., 1996—; CFO ECLC of N.J., Chatham, 1998—. Past pres. Family Link of Union and Essex Counties, 1994-96; chmn. Kirby Ctr. YMCA Family Coun., 1996-98. Fellow Am. Coll. Healthcare Execs; mem. Am. Hosp. Assn., U. Pa. Wharton Sch. Alumni Assn., Cornell Club, Ctr. for Enabling Tech. (trustee 1997—, treas. 1999—). Home: 37 Rose Ter Chatham NJ 07928-1826 Office: ECLC of NJ 21 Lum Ave Chatham NJ 07928 E-mail: jbearle@hotmail.com.

EARLE, MARY MARGARET, marketing executive; b. Newberry, Mich., June 26, 1947; d. William Loren and Naida Theresa (Ward) E. Student, St. Mary's Coll., Notre Dame, Ind., 1965-67. Cert. employment cons. Receptionist Western Girl World, San Francisco, 1968-69; receptionist, sec. Advanced Memory Systems, Sunnyvale, Calif., 1969-71; career cons. Qualified Personnel, Madison, Wis., 1972-75; VIP asst. Summit Sports Arena Grand Open, Houston, 1975, S. Petroleum Gp/OTC, Houston, 1976, Astrodomain Assn., Houston, 1976-77; bus. mgr. Mobile Colo TV Prodn., Houston, 1977-80; broadcast bus. affairs dir. G.D.L. & W. Adv., Houston, 1980-90; broadcast talent cons. Willis, Tex., 1990-93; mktg. cons., pvt. practice Marquette, Mich., 1993-95; pres. IXL Creative Mktg. Excellence, Marquette, Mich., 1996—; cable mktg. cons. Bresnan Comm., Marquette, 1998-2000, Charter Media, 2000—02. Modeling judge Page Parks Sch. Modeling, Houston, 1988-91; cons. industry/union rels. AFTRA/SAG, Houston, 1985-92. Houston mem. Fashion Group, 1989-90; sec. Bluebell Estates Assn., Willis, 1991, pres. 1992; pub. rels. vol. Women's Ctr. seminars, Houston, 1984-85; co-chair/treas. Art on the Rocks, 1999—; bd. dirs. Big Bros./Big Sisters; mem. exec. com. domestic Violence Coalition of Marquette County; bd. dirs. Marquette County Humane Soc. Named Disting. Salesman of Yr. Sales and Mktg. Execs., Madison, 1973, 74. Mem. Adminstrv. Mgmt. Soc. (cons. ofcl. panel 1974), Pers. Adminstrs. Soc., Am. Assn. Advt. Agys. (so. broadcast policy com.), Lake Superior Art Assn. (bd. dirs. 1996—), Ishpeming Art Faire Assn. (pres. 2000—), Rotary (pres. Ishpeming, Mich. 2002--). Avocations: walking, raising dogs. Home and Office: 612 County Road 480 Marquette MI 49855-9411 E-mail: mmearle@chartermi.net.

EARLE, SYLVIA ALICE, research biologist, oceanographer; b. Gibbstown, N.J., Aug. 30, 1935; d. Lewis Reade and Alice Freas (Richie) E. BS, Fla. State U., 1955; MA, Duke U., 1956, PhD, 1966, PhD (hon.), 1993, Monterey Inst. Internat. Studies, 1990, Ball State U., 1991, George Washington U., 1992, U. R.I., 1996, Plymouth State Coll., 1996; DSc (hon.), Ripon Coll., 1994, U. Conn., 1994. Resident dir. Cape Haze Marine Lab., Sarasota, Fla., 1966-67; research scholar Radcliffe Inst., 1967-69; research fellow Farlow Herbarium, Harvard U., 1967-75, researcher, 1975—; research assoc. in botany Natural History Mus. Los Angeles County, 1970-75; research biologist, curator Calif. Acad. Scis., San Francisco, from 1976; research assoc. U. Calif., Berkeley, 1969-75; fellow in botany Natural History Mus., 1989—; chief scientist U.S. NOAA, Washington, 1990-92, advisor to the adminstr., 1992-93; founder, pres., CEO, bd. dirs. Deep Ocean Engrs., Inc., Oakland, Calif., 1981-90; founder, chmn., CEO Deep Ocean Exploration and Rsch., Oakland, 1992—, bd. dirs., 1992—; advisor SeaWeb, 1996—. Bd. dirs. Dresser Industries, Oryx Energy, Inc.; explorer-in-residence Nat. Geog., 1998; dir., Natl. Geographic Sustainable Seas Expedition, 1998—. Author: Exploring the Deep Frontier, 1980, Sea Change, 1995; editor: Scientific Results of the Tektite II Project, 1972-75; contbr. 100 articles to profl. jours. Trustee World Wildlife Fund U.S., 1976-82, mem. coun., 1984—; trustee World Wildlife Fund Internat., 1979-81, mem. coun., 1981-95; trustee Charles A. Lindbergh Fund, pres., 1990-95; trustee Ctr. Marine Conservation, 1992—, Perry Found., chmn., 1993-95; mem. coun. Internat. Union for Conservation of Nature, 1979-81; corp. mem. Woods Hole Oceanographic Inst., trustee, 1996—; mem. Nat. Adv. Com. on Oceans and Atmosphere, 1980-94. Recipient Conservation Svc. award U.S. Dept. Interior, 1970, Boston Sea Rovers award, 1972, 79, Nogi award Underwater Soc. Am., 1976, Conservation Svc. award Calif. Acad. Scis., 1979, Order of Golden Ark Prince Netherlands, 1980, David B. Stone medal New Eng. Aquarium, 1989, Gold medal Soc. Women Geographers, medal Radcliffe Coll., 1990, Pacon Internat. award, 1992, Dirs. award Natural Resources Coun. Am., 1992, Washburn award Boston Mus. Sci., 1995, Charles A. and Anne Morrow Lindbergh award, 1996, Julius Stratton Leadership award, 1997, Kilby award, 1997, Bal de la Mar Found. Sea Keeper award, 1997, Sea Space Environment award, 1997; Environmental Global Zoo Awd., 1998; U.S. Environmental Hew Awd., 1998; named Woman of Yr. L.A. Times, 1970, Scientist of Yr., Calif. Mus. Sci. and Industry, 1981. National Women's Hall of Fame, 2000. Fellow AAAS, Marine Tech. Soc. (Compass award 1997), Calif. Acad. Scis., Calif. Acad. Sci., Explorers Club (hon., bd. dirs. 1989-94, Lowell Thomas award 1980, Explorers medal 1996); mem. Internat. Phycological Soc. (sec. 1974-80), Phycological Soc. Am., Am. Soc. Ichthyologists and Herpetologists, Am. Inst. Biol. Scis., Brit. Phycological Soc., Ecol. Soc. Am., Internat. Soc. Plant Taxonomists. Home and Office: 12812 Skyline Blvd Oakland CA 94619-3125

EARLE, TIMOTHY KEESE, anthropology educator; b. New Bedford, Mass., Aug. 10, 1946; s. Osborne and Eleanor (Clark) E.; m. Eliza Howe, June 14, 1969; children: Caroline, Hester. BA summa cum laude, Harvard U., 1969; MA, U. Mich., 1971, PhD, 1973. Rsch. archaeologist Bishop Mus., Honolulu, 1971-72; prof. anthropology UCLA, 1973-95, dir. Inst. of Archaeology, 1987-92; prof. anthropology Northwestern U., Evanston, Ill., 1995—, chair dept., 1995-2000. Author: Bronze Age Economics, 2002, How Chiefs Come to Power, 1997; co-author: Evolution of Human Society, 1987, 2nd edit., 2000; editor: Exchange Systems in Prehistory, 1977, Contexts for Prehistoric Exchange, 1982, Chiefdoms, 1991. Mem.: Soc. Econ. Anthrop., Soc. Am. Archaeology, Am. Anthrop. Assn. (pres. archaeology divsn. 1995—97, exec. bd. 1999—2002), Phi Beta Kappa. E-mail: tke299@northwestern.edu.

EARLE, VICTOR MONTAGNE, III, lawyer; b. NYC, June 13, 1933; s. Victor Montagne and Marian Jeanette (Litonius) E.; m. Lois MacKennan, Dec. 28, 1955 (div. Jan. 1980); children: Jane Stewart, Susan Elizabeth, Anne McCallum; m. Karen Peterson Howard, Aug. 24, 1985. AB, Williams Coll., 1954; LLB, Columbia U., 1959. Bar: NY 1960, US Supreme Ct. 1963. Law clk. to Hon. Leonard Moore, US Ct. Appeals (2nd cir.), 1959-60; assoc. Cravath, Swaine & Moore, NYC, 1960-68; gen. counsel KPMG, NYC, 1968-86, Peat, Marwick Internat., 1978-86; ptnr. Cahill, Gordon & Reindel, NYC, 1986-89; sr. v.p., gen. counsel Minet, NYC, 1989-93; gen. counsel KWELM Co. and KWELM Holdings, London, 1993—98, KWELM Co. and KWELM Holdings Ltd., NYC, 1993-98, sr. counsel, 1998-2000, KWELM Co. and KWELM Holdings, London, 1998—2000; of counsel O'Melveny & Myers, NYC, 2000—. Lectr. constl. and corp. law issues, U.S. and abroad. Contbr. articles to profl. jour. and popular mag. With US Army, 1954-56. Recipient Constitutional Law prize Columbia U. Assn. of Bar of City of NY (judiciary com. 1983-86), Am. Law Inst. (life), Legal Aid Soc. (bd. dir. 1980-86), Fund for Modern Ct. (bd. dir.), Columbia U. Alumni Assn. (bd. dir. 1982-87). Office: O'Melveny & Myers 153 E 53d St New York NY 10022-4611 E-mail: vearle@omm.com.

EARLES, KATHI AMILLE, pediatrician; b. Washington, Aug. 29, 1963; d. Lucius Chism III and Wilma Jean Earles; m. William Alexander Jackson Ross, July 17, 1993; children: William Alexander III Ross, Jordan Nicole Ross, Riley Marie Ross. BA, Howard U., 1986, MD, 1991; MPH, UCLA, 1998. Diplomate Am. Bd. Pediats. Physician CIGNA Healthcare, L.A., 1991—99; asst. clin. prof. Morehouse Sch. Medicine, Atlanta, 1999—, assoc. dir. pediat. residency, 1999—, faculty devel. preceptor, 1999—. Contbr. chpt. to book, article to med. jour. Trustee Zion Hill Bapt. Ch., Atlanta, 2002—. Named Leading African Am. Physician, Black Enterprise mag., 2001; grantee, NIH, Nat. Ctr. for Minority of Health Disparities Rsch., 2001—; scholar, Morehouse Sch. Medicine Dept., 2000—. Mem.: Ga. State Med. Assn., Am. Assn. Pediats., Assn. Pediat. Program Dirs., Atlanta Med. Assn., Nat. Health Execs. Assn., Nat. Med. Assn. (scholar 1992). Democrat. Achievements include research in effects of media on childhood obesity; effects of media on sexual behavior of youth; effects of media on alchol and tobacco consumption on youth; effects of the media violence on youth. Avocations: ceramics, basketball, jazz, reading, cooking. Office: Morehouse Sch Medicine Pediats Dept 720 Westview Dr SW Atlanta GA 30310-1495 Fax: 404-756-1357. E-mail: earlesk@msm.edu.

EARLEY, ANTHONY FRANCIS, JR., utilities company executive, lawyer; b. Jamaica, N.Y., July 29, 1949; s. Anthony Francis and Jean Ann (Draffen) E.; m. Sarah Margaret Belanger, Oct. 14, 1972; children: Michael Patrick, Anthony Matthew, Daniel Cartwright, Matthew Sean. BS in Physics, U. Notre Dame, 1971, MS in Engring., JD, U. Notre Dame, 1979. Bar: Va. 1980, N.Y. 1985, U.S. Ct. Appeals (6th cir.) 1981. Assoc. Hunton & Williams, Richmond, Va., 1979-85, ptnr., 1985; gen. counsel L.I. Lighting Co., Hicksville, N.Y., 1985-89, exec. v.p., 1988-89, pres., COO, 1989-94, also bd. dirs.; pres., COO The Detroit Edison Co. (now DTE Energy Co.), 1994—, also bd. dirs., chmn., CEO. Bd. dirs. Mutual Am. Contbr. articles to profl. jours. Mem. adv. coun. Coll. Engring., U. Notre Dame; Served to lt. USN, 1971—76. Mem.: ABA. Roman Catholic. Avocations: skiing, tennis, furniture restoration. Office: DTE Energy Co 2000 2ND Ave Detroit MI 48226

EARLEY, EDWARD JOSEPH, JR., studio musician, composer, copyist, trombonist; b. St. Louis, Mar. 16, 1952; s. Edward Joseph Earley Sr. and Frances (Hodges) May. Student, U. Mo., 1970-74, U. Mo., St. Louis, 1976-79. Copyist, musician, arranger Luther Ingram, St. Louis, 1978-80; musician, arranger, band leader Albert King Blues Band, N.Y.C., 1979-80, 83-87, 88—; musician Silver Cloud Blues Band, St. Louis, 1980-81, 87—; musician, songwriter, copyist, dir. child day-care YMCA, St. Louis, 1987—; performer Joe Louis Walker and the Boss Talkers, 1989-90. Substitute tchr. music St. Louis Bd. Edn., 1974, Normandy (Mo.) Pub. Schs., 1976-79; film extra Hilzar-Roche Casting-Paramount, Chgo., 1987; freelance studio musician and vocalist, 1978—; film extra Holzar-Roche Casting Paramount, Chgo., 1987; performer rec. with Elvin Bishop, Elvin Bishop Group, 1990—. Writer (song) The Game Goes On as recorded by Albert King on Phone Booth, 1984; musician Elvin Bishop Group. Active voter registration, St. Louis, 1976, Mo. Coalition for the Environment, St. Louis, 1987. Recipient Cert. Merit Am. Songwriters Festival, 1984, Cert. Merit N.Y. Pro/Am Songwriting Festival, 1985, Cert. of Merit Music City Songwriters Festival, 1987. Mem. ASCAP, Am. Fedn. Musicians, Internat. Trombone Assn., Omega Psi Phi. Avocations: art, music, softball, playing cards, soccer. Address: PO Box 1091 Larkspur CA 94977-1091

EARLEY, LAURENCE ELLIOTT, retired medical educator; b. Ahoskie, N.C., Jan. 23, 1931; s. Frank Claxton and Eleanor (Dilday) Earley; m. Joanne Frances Sinclair, Sept. 5, 1953; children: Laurence Elliott Earley Jr., Peter Hunter Earley. BS, U. N.C., 1953, MD, 1956; MA (hon.), U. Pa., 1978. Diplomate Am. Bd. Internal Medicine . Asst. prof. Harvard Med. Sch., Boston, 1967—68; assoc. prof. U. Calif. Sch. Medicine, San Francisco, 1968—69, prof., 1969—73, chief of nephrology, 1968—73; prof., chmn. dept. medicine U. Tex. Health Sci. Ctr., San Antonio, 1973—77; chmn. dept. medicine, Frank Wister Thomas Prof. U. Pa., Phila., 1977—90, chmn. dept. phys. medicine & rehab., 1987—90, Francis C. Wood prof., 1983—95, sr. assoc. dean., 1992—95; clin. prof. medicine U. N.C., Chapel Hill, 1995—2000; ret., 2001. Study sect. NIH, Bethesda, Md., 1969—77; chmn. Am. Bd. Internal Medicine, 1987—88. Editor: Diseases of The Kidney; contbr. articles to profl. jours. Chmn. sci. adv. bd. Nat. Kidney Found., N.Y.C., 1973—74. Sr. asst. surgeon USPHS, 1959—61. Recipient Kaiser award, U. Calif., 1972, Disting. Svc. award, U. N.C., 1976. Master: ACP; mem.: Assn. Am. Physicians (pres. 1988—89), Inst. Medicine, Am. Soc. Nephrology (pres. 1977—78), Am. Soc. for Clin. Investigation (pres. 1975—76), Assn. Profs. Medicine (pres. 1983—84), Alpha Omega Alpha, Phi Beta Kappa. Achievements include research in kidney disease, physiology. Avocations: photography, woodwork. Home: 5009 101st Avenue Ct NW Gig Harbor WA 98335-7051 E-mail: jseleech@aol.com.

EARLEY, MARK LAWRENCE, not-for-profit administrator, former state attorney general; b. Norfolk, Va., July 26, 1954; s. Whitmel Franklin and Ann Harris Earley; m. Cynthia Ellen Bteithaupt, June 5, 1982; children: Rachel, Justin, Mark, Jr., Mary Catherine, Franklin Edward, Anne Harris. BA in Religion, Coll. William and Mary, 1976, JD, 1982. Bar: Va. Ptnr. Tavss, Fletcher, Earley and King, P.C., Norfolk, 1982—97; senator Senate of Va., 1987—97; atty. gen. Commonwealth of Va., 1998—2002; pres. & CEO Prison Fellowship Ministries, 2002—. Senate Rep. Whip, 1993; mem. privelages and elections com. Va. State Senate, 1993—, cts. justice com., 1988—, local govt. com., 1988—, rehab. and social svcs. com., 1988—, chmn. local govt. charter subcom., 1992—; mem. Gov.'s Commn. Parole Abolition and Sentencing Reform, 1994, Gov.'s Commn. Champion Schs., 1994, State Water Commn., 1994, Commn. Preservation of Capitol, 1994, Adv. Commn. Welfare Reform, 1994, Commn. Youth's Juvenile Detention Task Force, 1994, Commn. Sentencing and Parole Policies and the Need to Establish Truth in Sentencing, 1993—, Quadrennial Rev. Panel for Child Support Guidelines, 1994, Poverty Commn., 1992—93, Chowan River Commn., 1988—, Commn. Youth's Task Force, 1992—94; mem. environ. quality and natural resources com. Southern Legis. Conf., 1994; mem. family ct. pilot project com. Supreme Ct. Va., 1989—93. Founding mem. Rep. Leadership Network; hon. chmn. Va. chpt. United Negro Coll. Fund, 1990; mem. Chesapeake Cmty. Svcs. Bd., 1985—87, Chesapeake Cmty. Corrections Resources Bd., 1985—87, vice-chmn., 1986—87; mem. Leadership Hampton Roads, 1990; del. Rep. Nat. Conv., 1988, 1992, mem. platform com., 1992; mem. Atlantic Shores Bapt. Ch.; bd. dirs. Comprehensive Health Investment Project, 1994, Va. CARES, Inc., 1993—, Tidewater Legal Aid, 1993—; Chesapeake bd. dirs. Commerce Bank, 1993—. Recipient Environ. award, Port Folio Mag., 1990, Appreciation award, Va. Crime Prevention Assn., Outstanding Alumnus and Disting. Pub. Svc. award, Presdl. Classroom for Young Ams., 1994; fellow Henry Toll, Coun. State Govts., 1994. Mem.: Norfolk-Portsmouth Bar Assn., Chesapeake Bar Assn., Va. Trial Lawyers Assn., Va. Bar Assn., Va. State Bar, Nat. Rep. Legislators Assn. (bd. dirs. 1990—97, Legislator of Yr. award 1997), Am. Trial Lawyers Assn., Tidewater Pro Bono Program, Great Bridge Sertoma Club, Rotary Club. Office: Prison Fellowship Ministries PO Box 1550 Merrifield VA 22116-1550

EARLL, JERRY MILLER, internist, educator; b. Hawarden, Iowa, Aug. 15, 1928; s. Harry Ezra and Magdalene Anna (Miller) E.; m. Faith Anne Allbaugh, Sept. 14, 1956; children: Leslie Anne, Nikki Lee, Holly Magdalene. BS, U. Nebr., 1950; MD, U. Iowa, 1958; postgrad., U. Calif., 1965-66. Diplomate Am. Bd. Internal Medicine, Am. Bd. Endocrinology, Am. Bd. Nuc. Medicine, Am. Bd. Geriat. Commd. 2d lt. U.S. Army, 1951, advanced through grades to col., 1972; intern Letterman Gen. Hosp., San Francisco, 1958, resident in internal medicine, 1959-62; chief endocrinology and metabolism William Beaumont Gen. Hosp., El Paso, 1963-65, Tripler Gen. Hosp., Honolulu, 1965-69, Walter Reed Army Inst. Rsch. and Walter Reed Army Hosp., Washington, 1969-76; chief dept. medicine Walter Reed Army Hosp., 1976-79; cons. endocrinology Office Surgeon Gen.; asso. prof. medicine U. Hawaii, 1967-69; clin. prof. medicine Georgetown U., 1976-79; prof. medicine, vice chmn. dept. medicine Uniformed Svcs. U. Health Scis., Washington, 1977-79; prof. and chief divsn. internal medicine Georgetown U., Washington, 1979-94, dir. geriatrics svc. dept. medicine, 1993—; med. dir. to v.p. med. affairs Washington Home, 1996, 97—. Decorated Legion of Merit, Army Commendation medal, Meritorious Service medal. Fellow ACP (regional laureate); mem. Am. Med. Dirs. Assn., Am. Diabetes Assn., Endocrine Soc., Am. Geriatric Soc. (Clinician of Yr. 2002, 03), Assn. Mil. Surgeons, Acad. Medicine of Washington. Achievements include research and publs. on pituitary and thyroid physiology. Home: 8529 Brickyard Rd Potomac MD 20854-4834 Office: Georgetown U Hosp 3800 Reservoir Rd NW Washington DC 20007-2113 E-mail: jearll@thewashingtonhome.org.

EARLOUGHER, ROBERT CHARLES, SR., petroleum engineer; b. Kans., May 6, 1914; s. Harry Walter and Annetta (Partridge) E.; m. Jeanne D. Storer, Oct. 6, 1937; children: Robert Charles, Jr., Janet Earlougher Craven, Anne Earlougher O'Connell. Grad., Colo. Sch. Mines, 1936. Registered profl. engr.,

Calif., Okla., Tex., Kans. Supr. core lab. The Sloan and Zook Co., Bradford, Pa., 1936-38; co-owner, cons. Geologic Standards Co., Tulsa, 1938-45; owner, cons. Earlougher Engring., Tulsa, 1945-73; chmn., cons. Godsey-Earlougher, Inc., Tulsa, 1973-76, Petroleum Cons. div. Williams Bros. Engring. Co., Tulsa, 1976-88, Reactivated Earlougher Engring., Inc., Tulsa, 1988. Patentee in field Mem. AIME (hon., Anthony F. Lucas Gold medal 1980), Am. Petroleum Inst. (chmn. mid-continent dist. 1961-62, citation for service 1964), Ind. Petroleum Assn. Am. (bd. dirs. 9 yrs.), Interstate Oil Compact Commn. (oil recovery com. 1947-96), Soc. Petroleum Engrs. (disting. svc. award 1973, disting. mem. award 1983, hon. mem. 1985, enhanced oil recovery pioneer 1992), Soc. Petroleum Evaluation Engrs. (hon. life award 1993), Summit Club, Petroleum Club, Southern Hills Country Club (Tulsa), Masons, Tau Beta Pi. Republican. Episcopalian. Home: Apt 235 Tulsa OK 74105-6546 Office: Ste 15 2250 E 49th St Tulsa OK 74105-8773

EARLS, JOY R. SHULMAN, professional society administrator; b. Weehawken, NJ, June 25, 1954; d. George and Mildred Shulman; m. Mark A. Earls, Apr. 1, 1981; children: Leland S., Carter J. BS, U. Mich., 1975; MPA, U. Mont., 1990. Surveyor Missoula (Mont.) County, 1979-82; engring. technician City of Missoula, 1982-88, dir. human resources, 1988-91, Ptnrs. in Home Care, Inc., Missoula, 1991-99; exec. dir. Mont. Assn. Home Health Agys., Inc., Missoula, 1999—. Chair Employers Adv. Job Svc., Missoula, 1991-98; adv. human resources issues, bd. dirs. YWCA, Missoula. Mem. Am. Assn. Execs., Soc. Human Resource Mgmt. Home: 3605 Snowdrift Ct Missoula MT 59808

EARLS, KEVIN GERARD, insurance company executive; b. N.Y.C., Mar. 24, 1952; s. Kevin Gerard and Geraldine Earls; m. Juliet Posner, Jan. 21, 1989; children: Tara, Sean. BS, Fordham U., 1974; MS, Columbia U., 1980. ChFC, CLU. Sales rep. Phoenix Home Life, N.Y.C., 1982-85, sales supr., 1985-87, asst. gen. mgr., 1987-90, assoc. gen. mgr., 1990-98; pres. Kevin G. Earls & Assocs., 1990-98; sr. v.p. fin. svcs. Hilb, Rogal & Hamilton Inc., N.Y.C., 1998—. Pres. HRH Securities Inc., 2000—. Contbg. author, illustrator: New Techniques in Rehabilitation, 1982. Mem. Nat. Assn. Life Underwriters, Am. Soc. Fin. Svcs. Profls., U.S. Judo Assn., U.S. Judo Fedn., Gen. Agts. and Mgrs. Assn. (bd. dirs. N.Y.C.), Am. Soc. Fin. Svc. Profls., U.S. Judo Inc., N.Y. Athletic Club (judo chmn. 1991-01, bd. govs. 2001—, chmn. athletics 2001—), Douglaston Club. Avocations: Judo, art, reading. Office: Hilb Rogal & Hamilton Inc 1211 Ave of AmericasFl 27 New York NY 10036-8701 E-mail: earls@hrh.com.

EARLY, ALEXANDER RIEMAN, III, judge; b. Phila., Sept. 22, 1917; s. A.R. Jr. and Elizabeth Frances (Dence) Early; m. Mary Celeste Worland, Aug. 15, 1959; children: A.R. IV, Lucia C. Stroh, Elizabeth V., John Drennan, V. BA, Cornell U., 1938; LLB, Harvard U., 1941. Bar: Calif. 1946. Pvt. law practice, L.A., 1946—50; sr. atty. Divsn. of Hwys., State of Calif., 1950-55; asst. U.S. atty. Lands divsn. U.S. Dept. Justice, L.A., 1955-57; asst. county counsel Los Angeles County, Calif., 1957-72; judge Superior Ct., L.A., 1972-87, chmn. Exec. Com., Rules Com., BAJI Com.; judge by assignment, 1987—; ret., 1987. Adj. prof. Southwestern Law Sch., L.A., 1970-79. Contbr. articles to profl. jours. Mgr. internat. fedn. rels. boxing venue 1984 Olympics. Comdr. USNR, 1941-46. Served U.S. Navy in Destroyers, Pacific (earned nine battle stars); dir. sinking I.J.N. sub. RO-38, 1943. Decorated comdr. Order Polonia Restituta (Poland); knight grand cross Order of Holy Sepulchre (Vatican), Law Enforcement medal SAR, 1981. Fellow: Samuel Victor Constant Soc.; mem.: Nat. Conf. State Tax Judges, Am. Bd. Trial Adv., Navy League, Aztec Club, U.S. Naval Inst. (hon. mem. crew USS Canberra), Md. Hist. Soc., Soc. Cincinnati, Soc. War of 1812 (v.p. gen., Disting. Svc. award), Calif. Soc. Colonial Wars (dep. gov. gen., Disting. Svc. medal), Calif. Soc. Sons of Revolution (pres., Disting. Svc. award). Roman Catholic. Avocations: American history, genealogy, camellia seedlings. Home: 3017 Kirkham Dr Glendale CA 91206-1127

EARLY, BERT HYLTON, lawyer, consultant; b. Kimball, W.Va., July 17, 1922; s. Robert Terry and Sue Keister (Hylton) E.; m. Elizabeth Henry, June 24, 1950; children— Bert Hylton, Robert Christian, Mark Randolph, Philip Henry, Peter St. Clair Student, Marshall U., 1940-42; AB, Duke U., 1946; JD, Harvard U., 1949. Bar: W.Va. 1949, Ill. 1963, Fla. 1981. Assoc. Fitzpatrick, Marshall, Huddleston & Bolen, Huntington, W.Va., 1949-57; asst. counsel Island Creek Coal Co., Huntington, W.Va., 1957-60, assoc. gen. counsel, 1960-62; dep. exec. dir. ABA, Chgo., 1962-64, exec. dir., 1964-81; sr. v.p. Wells Internat., Chgo., 1981-83, pres., 1983-85, Bert H. Early Assocs. Inc., Chgo., 1985-94, Early Cochran & Olson, Chgo., 1994-98, of counsel, 1999—. Dir. Am. Bar Found., Chgo., 1993-95; instr. Marshall U., Huntington, W.Va., 1950-53; legal search cons. and lectr. in field. Bd. dirs. Morris Meml. Hosp. for Crippled Children, 1954-60, Huntington Pub. Libr., 1951-60, W.Va. Tax Inst., 1961-62, Huntington Mus. Art, 1961-62; mem. W.Va. Jud. Coun., 1960-62, Huntington City Coun., 1961-62; bd. dirs. Cmty. Renewal Soc., Chgo., 1965-76, United Charities Chgo., 1972-80, Hinsdale (Ill.) Hosp. Found., 1987-93, Internat. Bar Assn. Found., 1987-89; bd. dirs. Am. Bar Endowment, 1983-95, sec., 1987-89, treas., 1989-91, v.p., 1991-93, pres., 1993-95, dir. emeritus, 1995-2000; mem. vis. com. U. Chgo. Law Sch., 1975-78; trustee Davis and Elkins Coll., 1960-63; mem. Hinsdale Plan Commn., 1982-85. 1st lt. AC, U.S. Army, 1943-45. Fellow Am. Bar Found., Ill. Bar Found. (charter); mem. ABA (ho. of dels. 1958-59, 84-93, chmn. young lawyers divsn. 1957-58, Disting. Svc. award young lawyers divsn. 1983), Am. Law Inst. (life), Internat. Bar Assn. (asst. sec. gen. 1967-82), Nat. Legal Aid and Defender Assn., Legal Aid Soc. Chgo., Am. Judicature Soc. (bd. dirs. 1981-84), Fla. Bar, W.Va. Bar Assn., Chgo. Bar Assn. Presbyterian. Office: Early Cochran & Olson LLC 401 N Michigan Ave Ste 2010 Chicago IL 60611-4206

EARLY, DELOREESE PATRICIA See REESE, DELLA

EARLY, JACK JONES, foundation executive; b. Corbin, Ky., Apr. 12, 1925; s. Joseph M. and Lela (Jones) E.; m. Nancye Bruce Whaley, June 1, 1952; children: Lela Katherine, Judith Ann, Laura Hattie. AB, Union Coll., Barbourville, Ky., 1948; MA, U. Ky., 1953, Ed.D. (So. scholar 1955-56), 1956; B.D., Coll. of Bible, Lexington, Ky., 1956; D.D., Wesley Coll., Grand Forks, N.D., 1961; LL.D., Parsons Coll., 1962, Iowa Wesleyan Coll., 1972; Litt.D., Dakota Wesleyan U., 1969; L.H.D., Union Coll., Barbourville, Ky., 1979; D.Adminstrn., Cumberland Coll., 1981. Ordained to ministry Methodist Ch., 1954; pastor Rockhold Circuit, Ky., 1943-44, Craig's Chapel and Laurel Circuit, London, Ky., 1944-47, Trinity Ch., Oak Ridge, summer 1945, Hindman Ch., Ky., 1947-52; dean of men Hindman Settlement Sch., 1948-51; assoc. pastor Park Ch., Lexington, Ky., 1952-54; asst. to pres., dean Athens Coll., Ala., 1954-55; v.p., dean of coll. Iowa Wesleyan Coll., Mount Pleasant, 1956 58; pres. Dakota Wesleyan U., 1958 69, Pfeiffer Coll., Misenheimer, N.C., 1969-71; exec. dir. Am. Bankers Assn., Washington, 1971-73; pres. Limestone Coll., Gaffney, S.C., 1973-79; exec. dir. edn. Combined Ins. Co. Am., Chgo., 1979-82, v.p., exec. dir. edn. and communications, 1982-84; pres. Ky. Ind. Coll. Fund, Louisville, 1984-93, pres. emeritus, 1993—; dir. edn., con. Napoleon Hill Found., Northbrook, Ill., 1997—. Pres. W Clement Stone PMA Communications, Inc., Chgo., 1987—. Active Boy Scouts Am.; mem. pres. adv. coun. North Pk. Coll.; mem. Felician adv. bd. Felician Coll.; mem. Ky. Ho. of Reps., 1952-54; bd. dirs. S.D. Found. Pvt. Colls., S.D. Meth. Found., Nat. Coun. on Youth Leadership, Ctr. for Citizenship Edn., YMCA, Motivational Inst., Mid-Am. chpt. ARC, 1980—, W. Clement and Jessie V. Stone Found., Northbrook Symphony Orch., Ky. Mountain Laurel Festival, 1990—, Internat. Coun. on Edn. for Teaching, 1990—; chmn. bd. Religious Heritage Am., 1989-92, Internat. Leadership Network, 1991—; Rep. nominee for Metro Mayor, Louisville, 2002. Recipient Spoke award Mitchell Jr. C. of C., 1959, Disting. Svc. award, 1960, Disting. Svc. award S.D. Jr. C. of C., 1960, Gaffney Jaycees, 1979, Chief Iron Eyes Cody medal of Peace, 1987, Outstanding Kentuckian award O'Tucks, 1990; named Outstanding Former Kentuckian, 1963; hon. fellow Wroxton Coll., Oxfordshire, Eng.; named to Disting. Alumni Hall of Fame, U. Ky., 1965, Union Coll. Hall of Fame, 2000. Mem. Am. Soc. Assn. Execs., Louisville C. of C., Blue Key, Masons (33d degree, chaplain Valley of Louisville chpt. 1990—), Rotary (pres. Louisville 1992-93, dist. 6710 gov. 1996—), Ky. Soc. Sons of the Am. Revolution (pres. 1998—), Soc. War of 1812 in the Commonwealth of Ky. (pres. 1997—), Huguenot Soc. of Ky. (pres. 1999—), Huguenot Soc.-Soc. of Manakin (Ky. br. pres. 1999—), Nat. Soc. Sons and Daus. of Pilgrims (gov. Ky. br. 2000—), Gen. for Pub. Rels.-Gen. Soc. of the War of 1812 (v.p. 1998—), Del. State Soc. of Cin., Nat. Sojourners Camp #134, Heroes of '76 (E.B. Jones Camp), Jamestowne Soc., Kappa Delta Pi, Phi Delta Kappa (bd. dirs. Northwestern U. chpt. 1980—), Kappa Phi Kappa, Alpha Psi Omega, Theta Phi, Pi Tau Chi. Republican. Home: 9002 Hurstwood Ct Louisville KY 40222-5716

EARLY, JAMES, education educator; b. Worcester, Mass., Apr. 19, 1923; s. Edward and Rose Shea Early; m. Ann McKenny, Sept. 20, 1949; children: Mark, Edward, Joanne. BA Bowdoin Coll., 1945; MA, Harvard U., 1949, PhD, 1953. Instr. Yale U., 1953—57; asst. prof. Vassar Coll., 1957—64; assoc. prof. SMU, 1964—66, prof., 1966—80, assoc. dean, 1971—77, dean, 1977—80, prof./prof. emeritus, 1980—. Mem., Tex. com. on the humanities Tex. Inst. of Letters, 1975—77. Author: (books) Romanticism and Am. Architecture, 1965, The Making of Go Down Moses, 1972, Colonial Architecture of Mex., 1994, Presidio, Mission, and Pueblo, 2003. Mem., coun. of planning/preservation City of Dallas, 1970—72. With U.S. Army, 1943—46, ETO. Mem.: Town and Gown Club of Dallas. Home: 7015 Lakeshore Dr Dallas TX 75214

EARLY, JAMES MICHAEL, electronics research consultant; b. Syracuse, N.Y., July 25, 1922; s. Frank J. and Rhoda Gray Early; m. Mary Agnes Valentine, Dec. 28, 1948; children: Mary Beth Early Dehler, Kathleen, Joan Early Farrell, Rhoda Early Alexander, Maureen Early Mathews, Rosemary Early, James, Margot Early. BS, N.Y. Coll. Forestry, Syracuse, N.Y., 1943; MS, Ohio State U., 1948, PhD, 1951. Instr., research assoc. Ohio State U., Columbus, 1946-51; dir. lab. Bell Telephone Labs., Murray Hill, N.J., 1951-64, Allentown, Pa., 1964-69; dir. research and devel. Fairchild Semicondr. Corp., Palo Alto, Calif., 1969-83, sci. advisor, 1983-86; research cons., 1987—. Contbr. over 20 papers to profl. jours. Served with U.S. Army, 1943-45. Fellow AAAS, IEEE (numerous coms., John Fritz Medal bd. of award); mem. IEEE Electron Device Soc. (J.J. Ebers award 1979), Am. Phys. Soc. Roman Catholic. Achievements include 14 patents; discovery of Space Charge Layer Widening effect (now called Early effect); invention of the high frequency bipolar transistor and intrinsic barrier transistor; developer of Telstar solar cells and transistors, of sealed junction beam lead integrated circuits; design theory of bipolar transistors; definition of fundamental speed-power limits in junction devices; first commercial use of ion implanter in semiconductor devices; first use of buried channel charge coupled devices, of traveling wave charge-coupled detectors, of high speed ECL and advanced CMOS; procurement of first practical commercial electron beam machine for maskmaking; proposing fastest bipolar circuit. Home and Office: 708 Holly Oak Dr Palo Alto CA 94303 4142 *Philosophy: Each experiment is inexact. Each theory has an assumption. Each miracle is doubted. Each person is free. Faith is a gift. Observations: Our lives tell our philosophies. Happiness is a habit. Proverbs are mostly true. Noble spirits are everywhere. Love and sacrifice give example and opportunity. Malice is rare. Ignorance and indifference make problems.*

EARLY, JOHN D. anthropologist, educator; b. Balt., Aug. 24, 1927; s. John Drennan and Florence Gallagher Early; m. Jacqueline Carpenter Early, Dec. 21, 1970; stepchildren: Grant, Robert, Mark Gelhardt. AB in Philosophy, St. Louis U., 1950, MA in Social Philosophy, 1952; MA in Theology, Woodstock Coll., 1958; MA in Sociology, Fordham U., 1961; PhD in Anthropology-Sociology, Harvard U., 1965. Instr. Latin and English St. Joseph's Prep., Phila., 1952—54; rsch. assoc. Georgetown U., Washington, 1965—66; asst. prof. behavioral sci. Woodstock (Md.) Coll., 1966—69; assoc. prof. anthropology Fla. Atlantic U., Boca Raton, 1969—82, prof. anthropology, 1982—93; ret., 1993. Cons. Peace Corps, Guatemala, 1965—70, Micatokla, Guatemala, 1965—70, Agy. for Internat. Devel., Guatemala, 1979. Author: The Demographic Structure & Evolution of a Peasant System, 1982, La Estructura y Evolucion Demografica, 2000; co-author: Population Dynamics of Mucajai Yanomama, 1990, Population Dynamics of a Philippine Rain Forest People, 1998 (Choice award, 1999), The Xilixana Yanomami, 2000; editor: Highland Guatemalan Historical Demography, 1982; contbr. chapters to books, articles to profl. jours. Grantee, Nat. Inst. Child Health and Devel., 1975, Ctr. for Disease Control, 1976, Sea Grant, 1979, Plumstock Found., 1990, LSB Leaky Found., 1994. Fellow: Am. Anthropol. Assn. Achievements include seminal descriptions of the population dynamics of preindustrial societies (foragers, tribals, traditional peasantry) and the impact of infanticide, malnutrition owing to land tenure systems; as well as the impact of mining and logging incursions on these groups. Avocation: woodworking. Home: 1000 SW 21st St Boca Raton FL 33486

EARLY, JUDITH K. social services director; b. Evansville, Ind., 1954; d. Forrest M. and Dorothea E. Early. BA, Brescia Coll., 1976; MS, So. Ill. U., 1985, PhD, 1991. Cert. vocat. evaluator; cert. family devel. specialist. Work activity supr. So. Ind. Rehab. Svcs., Inc., Boonville, 1976-78; vocat. evaluator Evansville Assn. for Retarded Citizens, 1978-85; vocat. evaluator Evaluation and Developmental Ctr., Carbondale, Ill., 1985-88; grad. asst., program evaluator So. Ill. U., Carbondale, 1988-90, rsch. and teaching asst., 1990-91; exec. dir. Albion Fellow Bacon Ctr., Evansville, Ind., 1991-93; family svcs. dir. Goodwill Family Ctr., Evansville, 1993-95, program evaluation dir., 1995-96, dir., 1996-2000; cmty. rels. dir. Evansville Goodwill Industries, Inc., 2000—. Contbr. articles to profl. publs. Bd. dirs. So. Ill. Ctr. for Ind. Living, Carbondale, 1990-91, Vanderburgh County Coun. Aging, 2000—, Southwestern Ind. Regional Coun. on Aging, 2002--; bd. dirs., youth worker 1st United Meth. Ch., Carbondale, 1989-91; v.p. Altrusa of Evansville, 1993-94; mem. Evansville Asbury United Meth. Ch., 1993—, treas., 1998—; bd. dirs. Youth as Resources, 1995-98, Transitional Svcs., Inc., Human Rights Com., 1992—; bd. dirs. Leadership Evansville, 1999-2002; bd. dirs. Family Resource Ctr., 1995-2002, v.p., 2000-2002. Mem. AAUW, Vocat. Evaluation and Work Adjustment Assn. (chmn. student affairs com. 1988-90, Student Lit. award 1987), Ill. Rehab. Assn. (bd. dirs. 1989-91), Ill. Vocat. Evaluation and Work Adjustment Assn. (chmn. mem. 1989-91, pres. 1991—, Disting. Svc. award 1989), Assn. Retarded Citizens, Altrusa Internat. of Evansville. Avocations: needlepoint, gardening, photography, cooking. Office: Evansville Goodwill Industries Inc 500 S Green River Rd Evansville IN 47715-7392

EARLY, STEPHEN BARRY, lawyer; b. South Gate, Calif., Apr. 8, 1945; s. Charles Nelson and Hilma Mae (Mumaw) E.; m. Janice Ann Webb, Aug. 20, 1966 (div. Feb. 1978); m. Susan Lippert Buzzotta, Dec. 28, 1996; children— Christian Webb, Jana Kay. B.A., Tex. Christian U., 1967; M.B.A., U. Dayton, 1970; J.D., So. Meth. U., 1975. Bar: Tex. 1975, Ky. 1982, U.S. Supreme Ct., various fed. cts. appeal and dist. cts.; CLU. Assoc. atty. Roberts, Harbour Smith, Harris, French & Ritter, Longview, Tex., 1975-77; sole practice, Longview, 1977-80; gen. counsel, sec., dir. Shakey's Inc., Dallas, 1980-81; v.p., gen. counsel Ky. Fried Chichken Corp., Louisville, 1981— . Served to capt. USAF, 1968-72. Mem. ABA, Tex. Bar Assn., Ky. Bar Assn., Soc. Mayflower Descs., SAR. Republican. Mem. Christian Ch. Avocations: running, flying. Office: Ky Fried Chicken Corp 1441 Gardiner Ln Louisville KY 40213-1914 Home: 4902 Fible Ln Crestwood KY 40014-9723

EARLY, TERI WILSON (DENISE WILSON), elementary education educator; b. Jacksonville, Ill., Sept. 3, 1952; d. Arthur Amos and LaVada Inez (Norton) Wilson (dec.); 1 child, Bill Duane (dec.). BS, No. Ill. U., 1973, MS, 1974. Tng. and tech. grad. asst. Head Start/No. Ill. U., DeKalb, 1973-74; tchr. 2d grade North Chicago (Ill.) Dist. 64, 1974-75; Head Start site adminstr. Archdiocese Bd. Edn., Chgo., 1975-76; Head Start tchr. Denver Pub. Schs., 1976-77; tchr., dir. day care lab. Met. State Coll., Denver, 1977; instr. Community Coll., Denver, 1980; toddler day-care dir. Denver Pub. Schs., 1977-80, tchr. 4th grade, 1980-81, kindergarten tchr., 1981-85; fin. rep. Equitable Fin. Svcs., 1985-86; Kindergarten tchr. San Diego Unified Sch. Dist., 1986-89; resource CRISD tchr., 1989-90, race and human rels. facilitator, 1991-92; project resource tchr. Keiller Mid. Sch., 1992-93; v.p. Garfield H.S., 1993-95. V.p. spl. assignment Sch. Cmty. Safety Network, grant coord. Race Human Rels. and Guidance Program, 1995-96; pres. African Am. Educators, 1997-98; v.p. Freese Elem. Sch., 1997-99; prin. Birney Elem. Sch., 1999—2002; del. People-to-People, China, 2001. Mem. Gov.'s Subcom. on Infants and Toddlers, State of Colo., 1979-80; bd. dirs. Big Sisters League, San Diego, 1994-96; peer coach Valencia Pk., 2002-03. Fellow San Diego Area Writing Project, 1987, Sci. Tchrs. Inst. U. Calif.-San Diego, 1988-90, Future Adminstrs. Academy-San Diego County; mem. Nat. Sci. Tchrs. Assn., Nat. Assn. Edn. Young Children, African Am. Educators, Nat. Coun. Negro Women, Assn. Calif. Sch. Adminstrs., ASCD, Alpha Kappa Alpha, Pi Lamba Theta, Phi Delta Kappa. Mem. African Methodist Episcopalian Ch. Home: 4937 Brighton Ave San Diego CA 92107-2519 Office: Valencia Park Elem 5880 Skyline Drive San Diego CA 92114 E-mail: tearly@mail.sandi.net.

EARLY, WILLIAM TRACY, journalist; b. Scurry County, Tex., Feb. 20, 1934; s. Willis Worley Jr. and Lillian Marian (Walton) E. BA, Baylor U., 1954; BDiv, Southeastern Bapt. Sem., 1958; ThD, Union Theol. Sem., 1963. Ordained minister So. Bapt. Conv, 1957. Pastor Urbanna (Va.) Bapt. Ch., 1964-68; editl. asst. World Coun. Chs., N.Y.C., 1968-69; freelance journalist N.Y.C., 1969—. Author: Simply Sharing, 1980. 1st lt., chaplain U.S. Army, 1957-59. Democrat. Home: 102 W 80th St Apt 31 New York NY 10024-6304

EARNER, WILLIAM ANTHONY, JR., naval officer; b. Pitts., Nov. 2, 1941; s. William Anthony and Marie Veronica (Ward) E.; m. Jennifer Elizabeth Laurence, Dec. 11, 1971; children: William Andrew, John Laurence. BS, U.S. Naval Acad., 1963; MS, U.S. Naval Postgrad. Sch., 1969; DBA, Harvard U., 1973. Commd. ensign USN, 1963, advanced through grades to vice adm., 1994, 1st lt. USS Blue, 1963-65, weapons officer USS Black San Diego, 1965-67, ops. officer River Sect. 534, 1967-68, weapons officer USS Dale, 1973-75, exec. officer USS Luce, 1975-77, prof. Naval War Coll. Newport, R.I., 1977-78, fellow strategic studies group, 1987-88, with Office Chief Naval Ops. Washington, 1978-81, comdg. officer USS Deyo, 1981-83, mil. asst. to dir. NET assesment Office of Sec. Def., 1983-85, comptr. naval air systems, 1988-90, comdr. Destroyer Squadron Four Charleston, S.C., 1985-87, comdr. naval Surface Group Mid-Pacific Pearl Harbor, Hawaii, 1990-92, budget officer Dept. Navy, 1992-94, dep. chief naval ops. (logistics), 1994-96, exec. v.p. Navy Fed. Credit Union, 1996-97, sr. exec. v.p. Navy Fed. Credit Union, 1998—. Instr. Harvard Grad. Sch. Edn., Cambridge, Mass., 1972-73; adj. prof. Bryant Coll., Smithfield, R.I., 1977-78; COO Navy Fed. Credit Union, 1998—; bd. dirs. Service Source, Inc. Chmn. George Mason dist. Boy Scouts, 2000—02. Decorated D.S.M., Legion of Merit, Bronze Star with V device. Mem. U.S. Naval Inst., Am. Soc. Mil. Comptrs., Credit Union Exec. Soc., U.S. Naval Acad. Alumni Assn., CUNA Govt. Affairs Com., Svc. Source, Inc. Avocations: running, gardening. Office: Navy Fed Credit Union PO Box 3000 Merrifield VA 22119-3000

EARNHARDT, DALE, JR., race car driver; b. Concord, N.C., Oct. 10, 1974; Co-owner, NASCAR Winston Cup Series No. 3 AC Delco-sponsored Chevrolet, 1998—. Named winner, Pontiac Excitement 400, 2000, DirectTV 500, 2000, 13th pl., NASCAR Busch Series event, Myrtle Beach, S.C. Avocations: water sports, computers. Office: Dale Earnhardt Inc 1675 Coddle Creek Hwy Mooresville NC 28115-8245

EARNHARDT, HAL J., III, automotive executive; b. Mar. 20, 1956; CEO, pres. Earnhardt's Motor Cos., Gilbert, Ariz., 1986. Office: Earnhardts Motor Cos 1301 N Arizona Ave Gilbert AZ 85233-1600*

EARNHARDT, KERRY, race car driver; b. Dec. 8, 1969; s. Dale Earnhardt; m. Rene Earnhardt; children: Bobby, Jeffrey, Blade. Racecar driver Goody's Dash Series, 1993, NASCAR, 1994—98, Doug Taylor Motorsports, 1999, Automobile Racing Club Am., 2000—. Recipient 1st pl., Pocono Raceway, 2000, Mich., 2001, Lowe's Motorspeedway, 2001, Atlanta, 2001. Mem.: Automobile Racing Club Am. Office: Fitz Bradshaw Racing 129 Bevan Dr Mooresville NC 28115

EARNHEART, FRANK JONES, lawyer; b. Salisbury, N.C., June 14, 1924; s. Hilbert F. and Fannie (Jones) Earnheart; m. Mildred Schulken, Aug. 15, 1946 (div. 1965); children: Laurie Jeanne, Gregory Steven, Barbara Susan; m. Sonia Keeble, May 6, 1967; 1 stepchild, Christopher Keeble. BA in Chemistry, U. N.C., 1947; postgrad. Law Sch., Duke U., 1947—48; JD, George Washington U., 1951. Bar: D.C. 1951, Ark. 1956, Ohio 1958, Pa. 1975. Assoc. Cushman, Darby & Cushman, Washington, 1948—52; asst. patent counsel Beaunit Mills Inc., N.Y.C., 1952—54; patent counsel Lion Oil divsn. Monsanto Chem. Co., El Dorado, Ark., 1954—56; chief patent counsel Gen. Tire & Rubber Co., Akron, Ohio, 1956—67; gen. mgr. Gen. Tire Internat. Co., 1967—69; v.p. adminstrn. Interpace Corp., Parsippany, NJ, 1969—71; asst. to pres., sec., corp. counsel Selas Corp. Am., Dresher, Pa., 1971—80, v.p., sec., gen. counsel, 1980—. Chmn. bd., spl. patent counsel Genitiruco, Zug, Switzerland, 1967—69; pres., dir. Interpace Found., 1969—71. Trustee N.J. Citizens Hwy Com., 1969—71; pres., counsel Plumstead Civic Assn., 1975—80. Lt. USNR, 1943—46. Fellow: Internat. Acad. Law and Sci.; mem.: ABA, Phila. Patent Law Assn., Am. Patent Law Assn., Delta Theta Phi. Republican. Lutheran. Home: Tall Trees Bergstrom Rd Doylestown PA 18901

EARNS, LANE ROBERT, academic administrator, historian, educator; b. Flint, Mich., May 8, 1951; s. Robert Lewis Earns and Shirley M. Earns (nee Martin). BA, Mich. State U., 1973; MA, U. Hawaii, 1977, PhD, 1987. Lectr. Kwassui Women's Jr. Coll., Nagasaki, Japan, 1977—79, 1984—86; asst. prof. U. Wis., Oshkosh, 1987—93, assoc. prof. history, 1993—97, prof. history, 1997—, John M. Rosebush prof., 2000, assoc. vice chancellor, 2002—. Co-founder., editor, writer Nagasaki Harbor Light, Nagasaki, 1985. Author: Nagasaki Kyoryuchi no seiyojin; co-author: Across the Gulf of Time: The International Cemeteries of Nagasaki; co-editor: Crossroads: A Jour. of Nagasaki History and Culture, 1993—98. Fellow, Fulbright Found., 1974—75; grantee, Japan Found., 1983, NE Asian Coun. Assn. Asian Studies, 1989, NEH, 1990—91. Mem.: Nagasaki Fgn. Settlement Rsch. Soc. (co-founder 2000), Midwest Conf. Asian Affairs (program chair 1992), Midwest Japan Sem. (chair 1992—94, exec. bd. mem. 1989—92). Home: 284C Campbell Rd Oshkosh WI 54902 Office: University of Wisconsin Oshkosh 800 Algoma Blvd Oshkosh WI 54901 Office Fax: 920-424-0247. E-mail: earns@uwosh.edu.

EASLEY, CHARLES D., JR., state supreme court justice; b. Port of Spain, Trinidad, Apr. 8, 1949; (parents Am. citizens); s. Charles D. and Doris B. Easley; m. Pamela Robinson; children: Christopher, Lindsey, Ali Mara. BBA, U. Miss., 1972, JD, 1979; MBA, Miss. State U., 1976. Asst. dist. atty. 3d Jud. Cir. Ct. Dist., 1980—83; pvt. practice Columbus, Miss., 1983—2000; prosecutor Caledonia, 1999, judge, 2000; assoc. justice Miss. Supreme Ct., 2001—. Mem.: AARP, ABA, Lowndes County Bar Assn., Miss. Mcpl. Judges Assn., NRA, Masons, Shriners. Office: Miss Supreme Ct Gartin Justice Bldg 450 High St Jackson MS 39201 also: PO Box 249 Jackson MS 39205

EASLEY, CHRISTA BIRGIT, nurse, researcher; b. Berlin, Apr. 30, 1941; came to U.S., 1966; d. Albert and Marianne (Uhlmann) Baldauf; m. Loyd Allen Easley, Oct. 23, 1964 (widowed Dec. 1993). Degree in nursing, Pawlow Coll. of Nursing, Aue, Fed. Republic of Germany, 1959; BS, NYU, Albany, 1978; MBA, Cen. Mich. U., 1979; EDS, Ctrl. Mo. U., 1983; PhD, Kensington U., Glensdale, Calif., 1983. With placement sect. Sembach, A.B., Fed. Republic of Germany, 1972-73, suggestion program mgr., 1973-74; adminstrv. clk. Lajes Field, A.B., Terceira, Acores, Portugal, 1975-78, incentive awards and suggestion program mgr., 1978-79; intern Cen. Mo. State U., Warrensburg, 1980-81; instr. in bus. overseas campus Cen. Tex. Coll./Yokota, A.B., Japan, 1983; instr. Tokyo Ctr. for Lang. and Culture, 1981-83; tchr. dept. of def. Yokota Dept. of Def., Yokota AFB, Japan, 1981-84; tax examiner IRS, Austin, Tex., 1984-86; sr. clin. rsch. coord. HealthQuest Rsch., Austin, 1987-96; v.p. Austin Clin. Rsch., 1996—. Treas. Am. Sch. System PTA, Acores, 1978-79; precinct chmn. Austin Rep. Com., 1988-96. Mem. Am. Acad. Allergy & Immunology, Am. Assn. Translators, AAUW, Sigma Tau Delta. Methodist. Avocations: rock hunting, flower gardens. Home: 12422 Deer Trak Austin TX 78727-5746 Office: Austin Clin Rsch Inc 12885 Research Blvd # 109 Austin TX 78750-3220

EASLEY, DAVID, economics educator; b. Lexington, Ky., Nov. 3, 1952; s. Alan Eugene and Jean (Ogden) E.; m. Maureen O'Hara, July 13, 1977; children: Megan, Casey. BA, U. Ky., 1974; PhD, Northwestern U., 1979. Asst. prof. econs. Cornell U., Ithaca, N.Y., 1979-84, assoc. prof., 1984-88, prof., 1988—, chmn. econs. dept., 1988-93, Henry Scarborough prof. econs., 1996—. Vis. prof. Calif. Inst. Tech., Pasadena, 1985-86; Overseas fellow Churchill Coll., Cambridge U., 1993-94. Contbr. articles to profl. jours. Recipient numerous grants NSF. Fellow Econometric Soc. Office: Cornell U Dept Econ Uris Hall Ithaca NY 14853 E-mail: dae3@cornell.edu.

EASLEY, GLENN EDWARD, lawyer; b. Vandalia, Mo., Mar. 6, 1952; s. Frank Edward and Betty Evalena (McCollum) E.; m. Mary Catherine Albrecht, May 26, 1978; children: Matthew Edward, Sarah Elaine. BA, U. Mo., 1974, JD, 1977. Bar: Mo. 1977, U.S. Dist. Ct. (we. dist.) Mo. 1977, U.S. Dist. Ct. (ea. dist.) Mo. 1978. Assoc. atty. Hyde, Purcell, Wilhoit, Edmundson & Merrell, Poplar Bluff, Mo., 1977-80, John Schwabe & Assocs., Columbia, Mo., 1980-97;

mediator State Mo., Divsn. Workers Compensation, Jefferson City, 1997—. Mem. Boone County Bar Assn., Cole County Bar Assn. Baptist. Home: 12501 S Rte N Columbia MO 65203-8836 Office: State Mo Divsn Workers Comp 3315 W Truman Blvd Jefferson City MO 65109-6805 E-mail: geasley691@aol.com.

EASLEY, JUNE ELLEN PRICE, genealogist; b. Chgo., June 7, 1924; d. Fred E. and Bernadette (Mailloux) Price; m. Raymond Dale Easley, Dec. 24, 1945. Student, McCormack Sch. Commerce, Englewood Jr. Coll., Chgo. Lic. genealogist Assn. Profl. Genealogists. Statis. clk. Arthur Andersen & Co., Chgo., 1968-74; corr. sec. ICG R.R., Chgo., 1974-86; self-employed genealogist-computers Arlington Heights, Ill., 1986-94, Mountain Home, Ark., 1994—2001, Springfield, Mo., 2001—. Editor, typist genealogical books, 1996—. Contbr. religion articles to Daily Herald, 1991; editor romance stories, 1990—, genealogy books, 1996—. Sec. Citizens for Clean Water, Mountain Home, Ark., 1996-98. Mem. AARP (sec. 1997-98), DAR (auditor-treas. Chgo. chpt. 1981-82, rec. sec. Chgo. chpt. 1982-88, Mountain Home ROTC 1995-97, publicity chmn. 1996-97), Huguenot Soc., Nat. Soc. R.R. Bus. Women (newsletter editor 1991-2002), Northwest Suburban Coun. Genealogists (pres. 1988-90, corr. sec. 1990-94), Daus. of War 1812, Daus. of Union Vets. (Civil War). Republican. Avocations: genealogy, writing, antiques, computers, travel. Home and Office: 2315 E Lark St Springfield MO 65804 E-mail: juneeasley@alltel.net.

EASLEY, MICHAEL F. governor; b. Rocky Mount, N.C., 1950; m. Mary Pipines; 1 child, Michael F., Jr. BA in Polit. Sci. cum laude, U. N.C., 1972; JD cum laude, N.C. Ctrl. U. Dist. atty. 13th Dist., N.C., 1982-91; pvt. practice Southport, N.C., 1991-93; atty. gen., 1993-2000; gov. State of N.C., 2000—. Contbr. numerous articles in field. Recipient Pub. Svc. award U.S. Dept. Justice, 1984. Pres. N.C. Conf. Dist. Attys.; mem. N.C. Dist. Attys. Assn. (past pres., legis. chmn.). Democrat. Avocations: hunting, sailing, woodworking. Office: Office of the Gov 20301 Mail Service Ctr Raleigh NC 27699-0303*

EASON, KAREN E. public health service officer, researcher; BSBA, Regis U., Denver, 1982; MPH, U. of No. Colo., 1994; DPH, U. Tex., Houston, 2000. Rsch. assoc. U. Tex., Houston, 2001—. Contbr. articles to profl. jours. Mem.: Delta Omega.

EASSON, WILLIAM MCALPINE, psychiatrist, educator; b. Evanston, Ill., July 3, 1931; s. Alexander and Anne Meldrum (Watson) E.; m. Gwendolyn Bowen, May 31, 1958; children: Anne, Jane, David, Michael. M.B., Ch.B., U. Aberdeen, Scotland, 1954, MD, 1967. Fellow in medicine and psychiatry Mayo Clinic, Rochester, Minn., 1956-59; resident in psychiatry U. Sask., 1959-60, instr. psychiatry, 1959-61; fellow in child psychiatry Menninger Clinic, Topeka, 1961-63, staff child psychiatrist, 1963-67; prof. psychiatry, chmn. dept. Med. Coll. Ohio, Toledo, 1967-72; prof., dir. div. child and adolescent psychiatry U. Minn. Med. Sch., Mpls., 1972-74; prof. psychiatry La. State U. Med. Ctr., New Orleans, 1974-96, head dept. psychiatry, 1974-82, prof. emeritus, 1996—. Vis. prof. psychiatry U. Garyounis Med. Sch., Benghazi, Libya, 1979; prof. grad. studies U. Riyadh, Saudi Arabia; U.S.-USSR health scientist, Moscow and Leningrad. Author: The Severely Disturbed Adolescent, 1969, The Dying Child, 2d edit., 1981, Psychiatry Exam. Rev., 5th edit., 1994, Psychiatry Patient Mgmt. Rev., 1977, (with N. Rock) Psychiatry Splty. Bd. Rev., 1991, The Management of the Severely Disturbed Adolscent, 1996; editor: Jour. Clin. Psychiatry, 1977-80. Carnegie fellow, 1956-58; Anderson fellow, 1956-58; WHO fellow, 1976 Fellow Am. Psychiat. Assn. (life). Home: 5218 Saint Charles Ave New Orleans LA 70115-4943

EAST, CHARLES E., JR., advertising and public relations executive; b. Baton Rouge, Dec. 5, 1949; s. Charles Elmo and Sarah (Simmons) E.; children: Rachel Elizabeth, Catherine Mae. BA in Journalism, La. State U., 1971. State desk copy editor, gen. assignment reporter-edn. writer Times-Picayune, New Orleans, 1971-73; co-founder, editor Gris-Gris, Baton Rouge, 1973; successively advt. and pub. rels. copywriter Weill/Strother, Inc., Baton Rouge, 1973-74, exec. v.p., 1974-79; ptnr. Weill/Stother/East, Inc., Baton Rouge, 1979-81, Weill & East, Inc., Baton Rouge, 1981-88, pres., 1984—88, The East Agy., Baton Rouge, 1988-89; advt. and pub. rels. cons., Baton Rouge, 1989-90; pres. East Advt. and Pub. Rels., Baton Rouge, 1990—. Recipient Telly award, 1991, 94, 96, 99. Mem. Am. Advt. Fedn. (treas. 7th dist. 1996-97, sect. 1997-98, lt. gov. 7th dist. 1998-00, gov.-elect 2000-01, gov. 2001-02, chmn. 2002-03, Pres. of Yr. award 7th dist. 1994), Pete Goldsby award 1996, Harry Hoile Former Gov.'s award 2003), La. Assn. Advt. Agys. (bd. dirs. 1983, v.p. 1984, pres. 1985), Advt. Fedn. Greater Baton Rouge (bd. dirs. 1991—, v.p. 1992-93, pres. 1993-94), La. State U. Manship Sch. Mass Comm. Alumni Assn. (exec. bd. pres-elect 2000-01, pres. 2001—), Rotary. Democrat. Home: 4436 Broussard St Baton Rouge LA 70808-1209 Office: 4436 Broussard St Baton Rouge LA 70808-1209

EAST, DON GAYLORD, computer engineer, archaeologist, writer; b. Carlisle, Ind., Mar. 7, 1935; s. Omer R. and Gladys A. (Jarrel) E.; m. Lillian M. Tim, Aug. 11, 1957; children: Donald A., Lynne M., Eric T. BS in Physics, BS in Engring. Physics, U. Ariz., 1970; cert. in field archaeology, Pima Coll., 1982. Cert. legal video specialist Nat. Ct. Reporters Assn. Field engr. IBM, Tucson, 1961-64, sr. assoc. engr. Poughkeepsie, N.Y., 1964-67, staff engr., 1967-70, adv. engr., 1970-74, sr. engr., 1974-78, Tucson, 1978-91; prin. Synchrony Co., Tucson, 1991—; dir. Xxotek Engring. Svcs. Inc., Tucson, 1992—. Cons. Ctr. for Archaeol. Field Studies, Tucson, 1988—; CEO Xxotek Engring. Svcs. Inc., Tucson; prin. Notesmith Midi Studio, Tucson, 1994—. Patentee in field. Bd. dirs. Tucson Assn. for the Blind, 1986-92, chmn. tech. com., 1990-92; mem. Ariz.-Sonora Desert Mus., Nature Conservancy; mem. adv. bd. Tucson Music Theatre. With USAF, 1957-61. Mem. IEEE (assoc.), Earthwatch, Found. for Field Rsch. Mem. Reformed Ch. Avocations: photography, music, mineral collecting, scuba.

EAST, JANETTE DIANE, marketing consultant; b. Phoenix, Jan. 5, 1950; d. Henry Melvin Clatterbuck and Dorothy (Eakin) Newman; m. John L. East, III, 2003. Student World Campus Afloat, Chapman Coll., 1967-68; BA in Anthropology and Archeology, Ariz. State U., 1972. CNA. Owner, mgr., buyer Walls Galore and Bath Decor, Corvallis, Oreg., 1977-84; mgr., trainer, buyer Bloomingdales, Dallas, 1984-85; mgr. Frederick and Nelson, Seattle, 1986-87; buyer The Bon Marché, Seattle, 1987-89; mktg. cons. Kinder-Harris, 1989-93; lectr., cons. merchandising and display, 1993—. Intern trainer Oreg. State U., 1981-83. Contbr. articles to profl. jours. Mem. Downtown Mchts. Assn., Corvallis, 1977-84, Oreg. Homebuilders Assn., Corvallis, 1977-84; vol. Make-A-Wish Found., Bailey-Boushay Hospice. Mem. Am. Business Woman's Assn. (Corvallis chpt.). Republican.

EAST, LARRY EUGENE, pharmaceutical researcher, minister; b. Rockwood, Tenn., Apr. 17, 1953; s. Carl and Wilma June East; m. Judy Leigh West, Sept. 18, 1982; children: Travis Hardin, Carla Lanham, Brett. BA in Microbiology with honors, U. Tenn., 1974. Microbiologist Baxter Travenol Labs., Cleveland, Miss., 1975—76, microbiology lab. supr., 1976—80; prodn. supr. small vol. parenterals Beecham Labs., Bristol, Tenn., 1980—85, sr. med. writer, 1985—90; sr. med. comm. assoc. Glaxo Inc., Research Triangle Park, NC, 1990—91, mgr. sci. info., 1991—92; asst. dir. clin. documentation Glaxo Wellcome, Inc., Research Triangle Park, 1992—96; assoc. dir. respiratory otc clin. devel. Glaxo Wellcome, plc, Research Triangle Park, 1996—97; mgr. med. publs. GlaxoSmithKline, Research Triangle Park, 1997—2001, mgr. clin. submissions, 2001—; min. Northside Christian Ch., Durham, NC, 2000—. Dir. Campus Christian Fellowship, Chapel Hill, NC, 1999—. Elder Northside Christian Ch., Durham, 1997—2002. Mem.: Am. Med. Writers Assn. Avocations: golf, reading, baseball. Office: GlaxoSmithKline 5 Moore Dr Research Triangle Park NC 27709

EASTAUGH, FREDERICK ORLEBAR, lawyer; b. Nome, Alaska, June 12, 1913; s. Edward Orlebar and Lucy Evelyn (Ladd) E.; m. Carol Benning Robertson, Aug. 8, 1942; children: Robert Ladd, Alison Benning Eastaugh Farnan. BA, U. Wash., 1937; D Humanities (hon.), U. Alaska, 1982. Bar: Alaska 1948, U.S. Ct. Appeals (9th cir.) 1956, U.S. Supreme Ct. 1958. With Alaska Steamship Co., Seattle, 1934-39; acct. Pan Am. Airways, Juneau, Fairbanks, Seattle and San Francisco, 1940-46; clk. Robertson, Monagle & Eastaugh, Juneau, 1946-48, ptnr., 1948-88, ret., 1988; Royal Norwegian Consul for Alaska, 1951-87; commr. Nat. Conf. Uniform State Laws, 1962-69; mem. Alaska Land Use Adv. Com., 1984-86; pres. Alaska-Dano Mines Co. Founder, bd. dirs. Develop Juneau, Inc.; pres. U. Alaska Found., Fairbanks, 1981-82; bd. dirs. Alaska Resource Devel. Council; trustee Pacific Legal Found., 1983-86. Named Citizen of Yr., Juneau C. of C., 1977. Fellow ABA Found.; mem. ABA, Alaska Bar Assn., Rocky Mt. Mineral Law Found., Alaska C. of C. (pres. 1955-56, named Outstanding Alaskan 1978). Republican. Episcopalian. Home: 12555 Auke Nu Dr PO Box 20589 Juneau AK 99802-0589

EASTAUGH, ROBERT L. state supreme court justice; b. Seattle, Nov. 12, 1943; BA, Yale U., 1965; JD, U. Mich., 1968. Bar: Alaska 1968. Asst. atty. gen. State of Alaska, 1968—69, asst. dist. atty., 1969—72; lawyer Delaney, Wiles, Hayes, Reitman & Brubaker, Inc., 1972—94; assoc. justice Alaska Supreme Ct., 1994—. Office: Alaska Supreme Ct 303 K St Anchorage AK 99501-2013*

EASTBURN, MARTIN HOWARD, engineer; b. Winston-Salem, N.C., Oct. 28, 1947; s. Lee Marvin and Lola Louise (Livermore) E.; m. Barbara Jean Bell, Sept. 2, 1965; 1 child, Sean. BS, Tex. A&M U., 1969, MS, 1972. Sr. adj. prof. electronics Tarrant County Jr. Coll., Ft. Worth, 1970-80; applications engr. Schlumberger, Austin, Tex., 1980-81, sr. applications engr., 1981-82, product specialist, 1982-85, product devel. specialist Simi Valley, Calif., 1985-87, technologist San Jose, Calif., 1987-95, sr. scientist, 1995-98; DRAM applications engring. mgr. Mitsubishi, Sunnyvale, Calif., 1999-2000; applications mgr. Internat. Microcircuits, Inc., Milpitas, Calif., 2000—01; staff applications engr. Cypress Semicondr. Inc., San Jose, 2001—. Mem. NRA (life, second amendment task force, Legion of Honor 1998), Order of De Molay (sr. De Molay, chaplin). Republican. Methodist. Achievements include patent for pattern generator with extended register programming. Home: 145 View Rd Felton CA 95018-9611 Office: Cypress Semicondr 3901 N 1st St San Jose CA 95134 E-mail: martin_eastburn@ieee.com.

EASTER, ARNOLD WAYNE, solicitor; m. Helen Easter; children: Kimberly, Jamie. DHL(hon.), UPEI, 1988. Parliamentary sec. Min. of Fisheries and Oceans; chair House Standing Com. on Fisheries and Oceans; solicitor gen. of Can., 2002—. Mem. exec. bd. Can.-European Parliamentary Assn.; adv. Trudeau Adminstrn. (fed. export agency); adv. to min. of agri. FAO Conf. in Rome, 1983; adv. and panelist Tri-nat. Exch. on Agrl., 1990; adv. and del. GATT, 1991; served as panelist Congressional Briefing on NAFTA in Wash., 1993. Pres., CEO Nat. Farmers Union. Recipient Gov. Gen. Can. 125 medal for cmty. svc., 1992. Office: Solicitor General 340 Laurier Ave W Ottawa On K1A 0P8 Canada

EASTER, SCOTT BEYER, lawyer; b. Seattle, Apr. 13, 1949; s. Frank Kenneth and Marjorie (Beyer) E.; m. Gay Lynn Garbe, Dec. 28, 1974; children: Renee Marie, Shane Barrett. BA in Econs. magna cum laude, U. Wash., 1971; JD, Stanford U., 1974. Bar: Wash. 1974, U.S. Dist. Ct. (we. dist.) Wash. 1978, U.S. Dist. Ct. (ea. dist.) Wash. 1994, U.S. Ct. Appeals (9th cir.) 1988. Dep. prosecutor King County Prosecutor, Seattle, 1974-76; assoc. King, Davidson & Dzeisler, Kirkland, Wash., 1976-79, Montgomery, Purdue, Blankinship & Austin P.L.L.C., Seattle, 1979-82, mem., 1983—. Lectr. U. Wash., Seattle. Mem. ABA (litigation sect. 1985—, health law sect. 1992—), Wash. State Bar Assn. (litigation sect. 1986—, health law sect. 1992—), Seattle-King County Bar Assn. (chair legal asst. com. 1985-87), Phi Beta Kappa. Avocation: skiing. Office: Montgomery Purdue Blankinship & Austin PLLC 701 5th Ave Ste 5800 Seattle WA 98104-7096 E-mail: easter@mpba.com.

EASTER, JR. WILLIE, artist, writer; b. York, Sc, Oct. 27, 1963; Employee FHS Supply Inc., Clover, SC, 2002—. Author: (book) Dawn of a New Age (Copyright award, 1998), Dawn of a New Age II: The Dragon People (Copyright award, 1999). Active connectional Lay Coun. Trinity A.M.E. Zion Ch., Gastonia, NC, 1991—92. Recipient Cert. Enrollment, Attendance, and Cooperation, Vocat. Bible Sch. Trinity A.M.E. Zion Ch., 1990. Home: 139 Quinn Road Apartment B-5 Clover SC 29710

EASTERBROOK, ELIOT KNIGHTS, chemist; b. Dudley, Mass., Oct. 28, 1927; s. Ralph Lewis and Hope Knights Easterbrook; m. Helena C. Daly, Feb. 9, 1957; children: Charlena Hope, Eliot Knights, Jr. BS, U. N.H., 1948, MS, 1950; PhD, Ohio State U., 1953. Sr. rsch. chemist Uniroyal Chem., Naugatuck, Conn., 1953, rsch. scientist, group leader, rsch. assoc., 1992. Rsch. group leader Uniroyal Chem. Author: (book chpt.) Rubber Technology, 1987. Pres. Jr. C. of C., Naugatuck, 1956—57; Coach YMCA Basketball, Naugatuck, 1970—71. Mem.: ACS, Rubber Divsn., Sigma Chi, Alpha Chi Sigma. Achievements include patents for EPDM related; Royalene. Avocations: gardening, golf, photography, sailing, nature walks.

EASTERBROOK, FRANK HOOVER, federal judge; b. Buffalo, Sept. 3, 1948; s. George Edmund and Vimy (Hoover) E. BA, Swarthmore Coll., 1970; JD, U. Chgo., 1973. Bar: D.C. Law clk. to Hon. Levin H. Campbell U.S. Ct. Appeals (1st cir.), Boston, 1973-74; asst. to solicitor gen. U.S. Dept. Justice, Washington, 1974-77, dep. solicitor gen. of U.S., 1978-79; asst. prof. law U. Chgo., 1978-81, prof. law, 1981—85, Lee & Brena Freeman prof., 1984-85; prin. employee Lexecon Inc., Chgo., 1980-85; sr. lectr. U. Chgo., 1985—; judge U.S. Ct. Appeals (7th cir.), Chgo., 1985—. Mem. adv. com. on tender offers SEC, Washington, 1983 Author: (with Richard A. Posner) Antitrust, 1981, (with Daniel R. Fischel) The Economic Structure of Corporate Law, 1991; editor Jour. Law and Econs., Chgo., 1982-91; contbr. articles to profl. jours. Trustee James Madison Meml. Fellowship Found., 1988—. Recipient Prize for Disting. scholarship Emory U., Atlanta, 1981 Mem. AAAS, Am. Law Inst., Mont Pelerin Soc., Order of Coif, Phi Beta Kappa. Office: US Ct Appeals Everett McKinley Dirksen Fed Bldg 219 S Dearborn St Ste 2746 Chicago IL 60604-1803*

EASTERDAY, BERNARD CARLYLE, veterinary medicine educator; b. Hillsdale, Mich., Sept. 16, 1929; s. Harley B. and Alberta M. Easterday D.V.M., Mich. State U., 1952; MS, U. Wis., 1958, PhD, 1961. Diplomate Am. Coll. Veterinary Microbiologists. Pvt. practice veterinary medicine, Hillsdale, Mich., 1952; veterinarian U.S. Dept. Def., Frederick, Md., 1955-61; assoc. prof., then prof. veterinary sci. U. Wis., Madison, 1961-94, prof. emeritus, 1994—, dean Sch. Vet. Medicine, 1979-94, dean emeritus, prof emeritus Sch. Vet. Medicine, 1994—. Mem., chmn. com. animal health Nat. Acad. Sci.-NRC, Washington, 1980-83, mem. com. on sci. basis meat and poultry inspection program, 1984-85; mem. tech. adv. com. Binat. Agrl. Research and Devel., Bet-Degan, Israel, 1982-84; mem. expert adv. panel on zoonoses WHO, Geneva, 1978-94; mem. tech. adv. com. on avian influenza USDA, 1983-85; mem. sec. USDA adv. com. on fgn. animal and poultry diseases, 1991-96. 1st lt. V.C., U.S. Army, 1952-54. Recipient Disting. Alumnus award Coll. Vet. Medicine, Mich. State U., 1975; named Wis. Veterinarian of Yr., Wis. Vet. Med. Assn., 1979, Disting. Alumni award Mich. State U., 1999. Mem. AVMA, Am. Assn. Vet. Med. Colls. (pres. 1975), Am. Assn. Avian Pathologists Office: U Wisconsin-Madison Sch Vet Medicine 2015 Linden Dr W Madison WI 53706-1100

EASTERLING, CHARLES ARMO, lawyer; b. Hamilton, Tex., July 22, 1920; s. William Hamby and Jennie (Arilla) E.; m. Irene A. Easterling, Apr. 25, 1943; children: Charles David, Danny Karl, Jan Easterling Petty. BBA, LLB, Baylor U., 1951, JD, 1969. Bar: Tex. 1950, U.S. Supreme Ct. 1954. Sr. asst. city atty. City of Houston, 1952-64; pvt. practice Houston, 1964-70; city atty. Pasadena, Tex., 1970-82; of counsel Easterling and Easterling, Houston, 1982—. Instr. So. Tex. Coll. Law, 1954-69. Lt. col. (ret.) USAFR. Mem. Houston-Harris County Bar Assn., Masons (33d degree, inspector gen. hon.), Shriners, Jesters, Arabia Temple Shrine (past potentate), Red Cross Constantine (past sovereign) Phi Alpha Delta. Democrat. Medthodist. Fax: 713-228-4072. E-mail: cae20@swbell.net.

EASTERLING, DAVID ROYER, climatologist; b. Chapel Hill, N.C., Nov. 25, 1955; s. William Ewart Jr. and Ellyn (Royer) E.; m. Kimberly O'Daniel, May 23, 1981; children: Hannah Marie, Katherine Ann. BA, U. N.C., 1979, MA, 1984, PhD, 1987. Asst. prof. Ind. U., Bloomington, 1987-90; rsch. meteorologist NOAA, Nat. Climatic Data Ctr., Asheville, NC, 1990-98, prin. scientist, 1999—2002, chief scientific svcs. divsn., 2002—. Adj. prof. dept. atmospheric scis. U. N.C., Asheville, 1996—; contbr. Intergovtl. Panel on Climate Change, 1999—. Contbr. articles to profl. jours. Recipient bronze medal U.S. Dept. Commerce, 1996, 2001. Mem. Am. Meteorol. Soc. (chair com. on applied climatology 1999—, com. on probability and stats. 1995-97, program chair), Assn. Am. Geographers. Episcopalian. Avocations: competitive swimming, golf. Office: Nat Climatic Data Ctr 151 Patton Ave Ste 120 Asheville NC 28801-5001 E-mail: david.easterling@nasa.gov.

EASTERLING, EDDIE JEAN, publisher; b. Norton, Va., Jan. 18, 1955; s. William Delmar Easterling and Betty Jean (Jordan) Whitaker; children: Jonathan, Micah, Emily. BS, Bluefield Coll., 1996. With USPS, Roanoke, Va., 1979—; owner Avenel Pub., Roanoke, 1995—. Author, photographer: In Search of A Golden Vault, 1995; cameraman, co-producer short film Dare to Care, 1977; guest spkr. BBC TV show, 1999; assisted in prodn. of segment featured on Mysterious Journeys, Travel Channel, 2002; actor The New Detectives, Discovery Channel, 2003, Critical Rescue, Discovery Channel, 2003; helped in prodn. of documentaries. Mem. Beale Cypher Assn. Avocations: treasure hunting, stained glass art, travel. Home: PO Box 7773 Roanoke VA 24019-0773 Office: Avenel Pub PO Box 7773 Roanoke VA 24019-0773

EASTERLING, WILLIAM EWART, JR., retired obstetrician, gynecologist; b. Raleigh, N.C., Nov. 8, 1930; s. William Ewart and Hannah Montgomery E.; m. Mary Ellyn Royer, June 7, 1952; children— William E. III, David R., John Wyatt, Robert Bryan, Jeffrey T. AB, Duke U., 1952; MD, U. N.C., 1956. Intern N.C. Meml. Hosp., 1956-57, resident in ob-gyn, 1957-61; instr. ob-gyn U. N.C. Sch. Medicine, 1960-61, asst. prof., 1964-67, assoc. prof., 1967-72, prof., 1972—, asst. dean, 1974-76, assoc. dean, 1976-77, vice dean, 1977-81, assoc. dean clin. affairs, 1981-89, assoc. dean continuing med. edn. and alumni affairs, 1989—; chief staff U. N.C. Hosp., Chapel Hill, 1974-89; ret., 1998. Mem. Council on Resident Edn. in Ob-gyn, 1972-80, chmn., 1978-80 Contbr. chpts. to textbooks; contbr. articles to profl. jours. Bd. dirs. Episcopal Home for Aging, Carol Woods Retirement Community, N.C. div. Am. Cancer Soc., chmn., 1976-77, pres., 1977-78. Capt. M.C. USAF, 1961-63; USPHS traniee 1963-64. Mem. ACOG, Am. Assn. Obstetricians and Gynecologists, Assn. Profs. in Gynecology and Obstetrics, Endocrine Soc., Soc. Gynecol. Investigation, Assn. Am. Med. Colls. (group on faculty practice, chair 1989-90, adminstrn. bd. 1992-95, steering com. interim chair, CME sect. 1996-97, group on edn. affairs), Coun. Acad. Socs., Soc. Med. Coll. Dirs. Continuing Med. Edn. (bd. dirs., pres. 1996-97).

EASTERLING, WILLIAM SAMUEL, structural engineering educator; b. Charlotte, NC, Mar. 7, 1959; s. William Stephen Easterling and Sue (Westmoreland) Hunt; m. Pamela Jo Dorinzi, June 20, 1981; children: Amanda Jo, Michael William. BS in civil engring., W.Va. U., 1981, MS, 1983; PhD in structural engring., Iowa State U., 1987. Reg. profl. engr., Va. Grad. rsch. tchg. asst. W.Va. U., Morgantown, 1981-83; grad. rsch. asst. Iowa State U., Ames, 1984-86, instr., 1986-87; asst. prof. civil engr. Va. Tech., Blacksburg, 1987-93, assoc. prof., 1993—2003, prof., 2003—. Cons. in field. Co-author: Composite Deck Design Handbook, 1997; editor: (book) Composite Construction in Steel and Concrete IV, 2002, Connections in Steel Structures IV, 2002. Recipient John Gundel award Steel Deck Inst., 1987, Outstanding Young Alumnus award Iowa State U., 1998, Profl. Progress in Engring. Award, Iowa State Univ., 2003. Mem. ASCE (outstanding svc. award 1988, co-recipient State-of-the-Art of Civil Engring. award 1996, 2000, Walter L. Huber Rsch. Prize, 1998), Internat. Assn. Bridge and Structural Engrs., Am. Inst. Steel Construction (composite construction com., T.R. Higgins award 2002), Structural Stability Rsch. Coun. (vice. chair). Home: 2015 Northside Dr Blacksburg VA 24060-2469 Office: Va Tech Dept Civil/Environ Engring Blacksburg VA 24061-0105 E-mail: seaster@vt.edu.

EASTERLY, SUSAN, music and humanities educator; b. St. Petersburg, Fla., Feb. 2, 1963; d. Kenneth Rudolph and Addeline Betty (Martin) E.; life ptnr. Sylvia Kay Fisher, Feb. 14, 1983; 1 child, Elise Dolores Easterly Fisher. AA, U. South Fla., 1983, BA, 1985, MusM, 1987; BA, Excelsior Coll., Albany, 1990; MA, Calif. State U., Dominguez Hills, 1991. Pvt. piano tchr., 1980—2002; gen.-vocal music tchr. Prince George's County Pub. Schs., Beltsville, Md., 1996-97. Adj. instr. Hillsborough C.C., Tampa, Fla., 1988-89, Polk C.C., Lakeland, Fla., 1989, Pasco-Hernando C.C., Brooksville and New Port Richey, Fla., 1989-93, Miami-Dade C.C., 1994, Stratford U., Falls Church and Woodbridge, Va., 1999-2001; piano tchr. Performer's Music Inst., Miami, Fla., 1994-95, Travelling Tchrs., Inc., Silver Spring, Md., 1995-96; accompanist Harmonic Dissidents, Tampa, 1993; pianist River Grove United Meth. Ch., 1987-88, Classical Ballet Ctr. of Tampa, 1988-89, Dove Ensemble, Tampa, 1991-92, Met. Cmty. Ch., Tampa, 1990-93, City of Gaithersburg Children's Chorus, 2000-01, others; accompanist, mem. prodn. com. Crescendo-The Tampa Bay Womyn's Chorus, 1991-93; mem. adv. rev. panelist Arts and Humanities Coun. of Montgomery County, 2001—. Contbr. articles to profl. publs. Recipient State Cmty. Svc. award Fla. State Music Tchrs.' Assn., 1981, Cmty. Svc. award, 1981, acad. scholarship Kiwanis Club of Seminole, 1981-82, talent grant U. S. Fla., 1982-85, others. Mem. AAUW, Cultural Alliance Greater Washington, Triangle Artists Group. Democrat. Unitarian Universalist. Avocations: visiting museums, concerts, plays, travel, reading.

EASTERSON, SAM, artist; b. Hartford, Jan. 24, 1972; BFA, Cooper Union Sch., 1994; MS, U. Minn., 1999. Instr. Art Inst. Minn., 1998—. Exhibited in group shows at Whitney Mus. Am. Art, N.Y.C., 1997, Walker Art Ctr., Mpls., 1998, New Mus., N.Y.C., 1998, Sanburg Inst., Amsterdam, 1998, Williams Coll. Mus. Art, 2001, Palm Beach Inst. Contemporary Art, 2001, others, Mass. Coll. Art, Boston, 1995, Grinnell Coll., Iowa, 1997. Recipient Book prize, RISD, 1990, Louis Comfort Tiffany prize, 1999; Creative Capital grantee, 2001. E-mail: anivegvideo@hotmail.com.

EASTHAM, ALAN WALTER, JR., foreign service officer, lawyer; b. Dumas, Ark., Oct. 16, 1951; s. Alan Walter and Ruth E. (Clayton) E.; m. Carolyn Laux, Aug. 2, 1974; children: Mark A., Michael S.G. BA, Hendrix Coll., Ark., 1973; JD cum laude, Georgetown U., 1982. Bar: D.C. 1982. Mgr. KDDA-AM Radio, Dumas, Ark., 1973-74; vice consul Am. Embassy, Kathmandu, Nepal, 1975-78; info. officer Dept. State, Washington, 1978-80, staff mem. office for combatting terrorism, 1980-82, desk officer Sri Lanka and Maldives, 1982-83, polit. officer for India, 1983-84; prin. officer Am. consulate, Peshawar, Pakistan, 1984-87; spl. asst. to under sec. polit. affairs Dept. State, 1987-89; counselor Am. Embassy, Nairobi, Kenya, 1989-92, Kinshasa, Zaire, 1992-94; consul gen. Bordeaux, France, 1994-95; counselor Am. Embassy, New Delhi, 1995-97, dep. chief of mission Islamabad, Pakistan, 1997-99; dep. asst. sec. of state for South Asian affairs Dept. of State, Washington, 1999—2001, spl. negotiator for conflict diamonds, 2001—02, dir. Cen. African affairs, 2002—. Methodist. Office: Dept of State AF/C Rm 4426 HST Washington DC 20520 E-mail: easthamaw@state.gov.

EASTHAM, DENNIS MICHAEL, advertising executive; b. Jacksonville, Ill., Dec. 18, 1946; s. Glenn R. and Ona M. (Camerer) E.; m. Dianne C. L. Watts; children: Susie, Brian, Brad. BA in Fin., U. Ill., 1968; MBA, U. Santa Clara, 1972. Asst. v.p. Crocker Bank, San Francisco, 1976-79; v.p. T & E Card div. Citicorp, L.A., 1979-81; exec. v.p. Barry Blau and Ptnrs. Inc., L.A., N.Y.C. and Chgo., 1981-87; pres. Barry Blau Worldwide, Deerfield, Ill., 1987—. Bd. dirs. Barry Blau and Ptnrs. Inc., Fairfield, Conn., 1985—. Mem. Direct Mktg. Assn. Home: 21835 Vernon Ridge Dr Mundelein IL 60060-5316 Office: BrannWorldwide 540 Lake Cook Rd Deerfield IL 60015-5289

EASTHAM, JOHN HOWARD, pharmacist, educator; b. San Luis Obispo, Calif., Sept. 2, 1969; s. Howard Ambrose and Linda Jane (Croft) E.; m. Lily Cheng, Aug. 7, 1993; children: Joseph David, Benjamin Samuel, Gabriela Grace. Student, Am. River Coll., 1987-90; D of Pharmacy, U. of the Pacific, 1994. Resident VA Med. Ctr., Long Beach, Calif., 1994-95; postdoctoral rsch. fellow U. Calif., San Diego, 1995-97; clin. pharmacist Naval Med. Ctr., San Diego, 1997—2002; clin. specialist Pomerado Hosp., Poway, Calif., 2002—. Mem. dean's adv. com. U. of Pacific, Sch. Pharmacy, Stockton, Calif., 1991-92; clin. asst. prof. Western U. Health Scis., Pomona, Calif., 1999—. Author: (with others) Clinical Geriatric Psychopharmacology, 1998; contbr. articles to profl. jours., chpt. to book. Pharmacy dir. Project Compassion, San Diego, 1995—, pharmacist, 1994—. Recipient Cert. of Appreciation, Project Compassion, 1998, 2000, 2003, Cert. Recognition, U.S. Assn. Mil. Surgeons, 1998, Letter of Appreciation, Comdr. Naval Med. Ctr., San Diego, 2001, Svc. and Dedication award, Project Compassion, 2002. Mem. Am. Coll. of Clin. Pharmacy, Christian Pharmacists Fellowship Internat., Am. Soc. of Health System Pharmacists, Calif. Soc. Health-Sys. Pharmacists, Acad. of Students of Pharmacy (rep. to

Calif. Pharmacists Assn. 1991-92, Outstanding Svc. 1992), Acad. of Students of Pharmacy (rep., Award 1992), others. Republican. Office: 11315 Rancho Bernardo Rd Ste 146 San Diego CA 92127 E-mail: john@projectcompassion.org.

EASTHAM, THOMAS, foundation administrator; b. Attelboro, Mass., Aug. 21, 1923; s. John M. and Margaret (Marsden) E.; m. Berenice J. Hirsch, Oct. 12, 1946; children: Scott Thomas, Todd Robert. Student English, Northwestern U., 1946-52. With Chgo. American, 1945-56, asst. Sunday editor, 1953-54, feature writer, 1954-56; news editor San Francisco Call Bull., 1956-62, exec. editor, 1962-65; exec. editor, then D.C. bur. chief San Francisco Examiner, 1965-82; dir. pub. info,press sec. to mayor of San Francisco, 1982-88; v.p., western dir. William Randolph Hearst Founds., 1988—. Active Nat. Trust Historic Preservation; mem. Pres.'s Roundtable, U. San Francisco. Pulitzer prize finalist, 1955, Disting Acheivement in Journalism award, Assn. Schs. of Journalism & Mass Comm., 1994. Mem. ACLU, Amnesty Internat., Am. Soc. Newspaper Editors, Inter-Am. Press Assn., Am., Internat. Press Insts., White House Corrs. Assn., Nat. Press Club, Ind. Sector, Coun. on Foundations, San Francisco Planning and Urban Rsch. Assn. Commonwealth Club, Marine Meml. Club, Peninsula Tennis Club, Sigma Delta Chi. Home: 1473 Bernal Ave Burlingame CA 94010-5559 Office: Hearst Found 90 New Montgomery St Ste 1212 San Francisco CA 94105-4596

EASTIN, KEITH E. lawyer; b. Lorain, Ohio, Jan. 16, 1940; s. Keith Ernest and Jane E. (Heimer) E. AB, U. Cin., 1963, MBA, 1964; JD, U. Chgo., 1967. Bar: Ill. 1967, Tex. 1974, Calif. 1975, U.S. Supreme Ct. 1975, D.C. 1983. Atty. Vedder, Price, Kaufman & Kammholz, Chgo., 1967-73; v.p., sec., gen. counsel Nat. Convenience Stores, Inc., Houston, 1973-79; ptnr. Payne, Eastin & Widmer, Houston, 1977-83; dep. under sec. U.S. Dept. Interior, 1983-86; prin. dep. asst. sec. USN, 1986-88; ptnr. Hopkins & Sutter, Washington, 1989-91; sr. v.p. Guy F. Atkinson Co., San Francisco, 1991-92; dir. environ. svcs. Deloitte & Touche, Washington, 1992-98. Sr. v.p., gen. counsel Guy F. Atkinson Co., 1991-92; bd. dirs. Nat. Money Orders Inc., Feast & Co., Inc., Kempco Petroleum Co., Bertman Drilling Co., Pacific Options, Inc., Del Rey Food Svcs., Inc., Stratford Feedyards, Inc., Pricewaterhouse Coopers; prin. Westec Environ., Inc., Reno, 1993—. Bd. dirs. Theatre Under the Stars, Houston, Statue of Liberty-Ellis Island Found.; mem. exec. com. Harris County Republican Party, 1976-83. Mem. ABA, Ill. Bar Assn., Tex. Bar Assn., D.C. Bar Assn., State Bar Calif., Knights Templar, Beta Gamma Sigma, Phi Delta Phi, Beta Theta Pi. Clubs: University (Houston); Capitol Hill (Washington). Home and Office: 101 Westheimer Rd Apt F Houston TX 77006-3360

EASTLUND, MARVIN EUGENE, physician; b. Breman, Ind., Apr. 25, 1944; s. Allen Edward and Ruth Mae (Barden) E.; m. Phyllis Diane Brower, June 4, 1966; children: Shelly Lynn, Kimberly Diane, Darcy Kay, John Bradley. AB, Manchester Coll., 1966; MD, Ind. U., 1970. Diplomate Am. Bd. Ob-Gyn. Intern St. Vincent Hosp., Indpls., 1970-71, resident in ob-gyn, 1971-74; practice medicine specializing in ob-gyn Ft. Wayne, Ind., 1976—. Mem. staff Ft. Wayne Ob-Gyn. Cons., 1976—; pres. Ft. Wayne Ob-Gyn, Inc., 1979—80; mem. staff Parkview Meml. Hosp., Ft. Wayne, Luth. Hosp., Ft. Wayne, Dupont Hosp., Ft. Wayne; med. dir. Dupont Women's Resource Ctr. With M.C., USN, 1974-76. Named Outstanding Young Man of Am., 1978. Fellow Am. Coll. Obstetricians and Gynecologists; mem. AMA, Ind. Med. Assn., Ft. Wayne Med. Soc., Ft. Wayne Ob-Gyn Soc., Am. Assn. Gynecologic Laparoscopists, Christian Med. Soc., Am. Fertility Soc., Am. Assn. Pro-Life Ob-Gyn. Home: 5204 Tatum Ct Fort Wayne IN 46835 Office: 1818 Carew Ste 300 Fort Wayne IN 46805

EASTMAN, ALAN DAN, chemist; b. San Francisco, Oct. 10, 1946; s. Dan M. and E. LaVelle (James) Eastman; m. Robyn Le Gillis (div. 2000); children: Daniel, Giselle, Krista, Evan, Jonathan; m. Vickie Muir Stewart, 2001. BA cum laude, U. Utah, 1971, PhD, 1975. Rsch. chemist Phillips Petroleum, Bartlesville, Okla., 1975—79, sr. rsch. chemist, 1979—81, mktg. rsch. specialist, 1981—83, mktg. rsch. sr. specialist, 1983—89, sr. rsch. chemist, 1990—; pres. Eco-Fuel Distbr., Ltd., 2002—. Named J. Gillie Citizen of Yr., 2002. Mem.: Internat. Chemometrics Soc., Soc. Applied Spectroscopy, Am. Chem. Soc., Lions, Phi Kappa Phi, Sigma Xi. Lds Ch. Achievements include patents in field of oxidation catalysts, hydrodesulfurization and hydrodenitrogenation catalysts, HF alkylation separation processes. Avocations: piano, organ, voice, carpentry. Office: 152 Petroleum Lab Bartlesville OK 74004-0001

EASTMAN, CAROLINE MERRIAM, computer science and engineering educator; b. Columbus, Ohio, Dec. 25, 1946; d. Robert Merriam and Kathryn Parmelee (Benedict) E.; m. Robin Michael Carter, Mar. 31, 1968. AB magna cum laude, Radcliffe Coll., 1968; MS in Computer Sci., U. N.C., 1974, PhD in Computer Sci., 1977. Asst. prof. dept. math. and computer sci. Fla. State U., Tallahassee, 1977-82; asst. prof. dept. computer sci. and engrng. So. Meth. U., Dallas, 1982-84, assoc. prof., 1984-85; program dir. NSF, Washington, 1984-85; assoc. prof. dept. computer sci. U. S.C., Columbia, 1986-91, prof., 1991-99, prof. dept. computer sci. and engrng., 2000—, dir. undergrad. studies, 1999—. Contbr. articles to profl. jours. Rsch. grantee NSF, Fla. State U., 1980-82, So. Meth. U., 1982-84, Air Force Office Sci. Rsch., Fla. State U., 1981-82, U. S.C., 2001—. Mem. AAAS (nominating com. sec. 1987-90, mem.-at-large sect. 1993-97, sect. chair 1998-99), Assn. Computing Machinery (v.p. N.W. Fla. chpt. 1978-79), Assn. Women in Computing (bd. dirs.-at-large 1979-83), Am. Soc. Info. Sci. Tech. Office: Dept Computer Sci/Engring Univ Of South Carolina Columbia SC 29208-0001 E-mail: eastman@cse.sc.edu.

EASTMAN, DONNA KELLY, composer, music educator; b. Denver, Sept. 26, 1945; d. Donald Lewis and Frances Marie (Smith) Kelly; m. John Bernard Eastman, July 1, 1973; children: Jonathan Kelly, James Alan; stepchildren: Barbara Kathleen, Sally Toye. B Music Edn., U. Colo., 1967; MA, U. Md., 1973, D in Mus. Arts, 1992. Pvt. studio tchr., coach, 1960—; choral dir. Dept. Def. Overseas Sch., Okinawa, Japan, 1970-72; dir. Choraleers Choral Ensemble, Stuttgart, Germany, 1974-76, Bangkok Music Soc. Ensemble and Madrigal Singers, Thailand, 1982-84; instr. in music No. Va. C.C., Alexandria, 1986-89. Creator, pianist, vocalist Am. Music Programs for U.S. Mission, Thailand, 1981-84; vis. asst. prof. Ill. Wesleyan U., Bloomington, 1994; vis. composer Sweet Briar (Va.) Coll., 1998, Grinnell (Iowa) Coll., 1999. Composer choral, orchestral, opera, vocal/instrumental solo and chamber, and electronic works; recs. include Capstone Records-Soc. of Composers, Inc. Series CPS 8632, 1996, and New Music for Flute and Piano, CPS 8664, 1999; Living Artist Recs.-Music from the Setting Century Series, Vol. 2, 1996; New Ariel Recordings-Contemporary American Eclectic Music for the Piano Series, AE002, 1996; Columbine Chorale Recs.--European Tour, 1999, Blue House Productions--Alone Into the Crowd, 2002; contbr. to jours. Recipient 6 Internat. Composition awards, Composer Guild, 1991—, Internat. Piano Composition award, Roodeport Internat. Eisteddfod, South Africa, 1991, Glad-Robinson-Youse Composition award, Nat. Fedn. Music Clubs, 1992, Internat. Choral Composition award, Florilège Vocal Tours, France, 1995, Keyboard award, Delius Composition Competition, 1997, Margaret Fairbank Jory Copying Assistance award, Am. Music Ctr., 1999, Nat. Music Composition Competition award, Nat. League of Am. Pen Women, 2000, Miriam Gideon award, Internat. Alliance for Women in Music Search for New Music, 2002; fellow, Charles Ives Ctr. for Am. Music, 1990; grantee, 1993, Ragdale Found., 1991, Va. Ctr. for Creative Arts, 1991—2002. Mem. Soc. for Electro-Acoustic Music in the U.S., Internat. Alliance for Women in Music (Miriam Gideon prize for new music 2002), Soc. of Composers, Inc. (life), Nat. Mus. Women in Arts (charter), Broadcast Music, Inc., Am. Composers Forum, Southeastern Composers League (pres.), Friday Morning Music Club Washington, Phi Kappa Phi, Pi Kappa Lambda, Sigma Alpha Iota. Avocations: travel, handicrafts, photography. Home: 6812 Dina Leigh Ct Springfield VA 22153-1019 E-mail: deastman@erols.com.

EASTMAN, HAROLD DWIGHT, retired social studies educator, journalist; b. Harbor Springs, Mich., Dec. 11, 1915; s. William Raymond and Edith Georgianna (Cross) Eastman; married, June 1, 1943; children: Danite Rae, Bruce Clyde, Jonathan Porter. BA, Sioux Falls Coll., 1941; MA, Coll. William and Mary, 1947; PhD, U. Iowa, 1954. Caseworker ARC, St. Paul, 1946-52; chief divsn. diagnosis and treatment Youth Conservation Comm., St. Paul, 1950-52; asst. prof. sociology Macalester Coll., St. Paul, 1947-50; assoc. prof. sociology Midland Coll., Fremont, Nebr., 1954-57; prof. sociology Carroll Coll., Waukesha, Wis., 1957-63; vis. prof. sociology U. Glasgow, Scotland, 1967-68; vis. lectr. Ottumwa Heights Coll., Ottumwa, Iowa, 1969-70; prof., head dept. sociology Parsons Coll., Fairfield, Iowa, 1963-71; head dept. sociology Truman State U., Kirksville, Mo., 1971-81, prof. emeritus Point Lookout, Mo., 1981—; guest prof. sociology Coll. of the Ozarks, Point Lookout, Mo., 1981-98, ret., 1998. Mem. Mayor's Com. Alcoholism, Mayor's Com. Juvenile Delinquency, Mayor's Com. Drug Abuse, 1963—70, Mayor's Study Com. Housing Needs for Impoverished Sr. Citizens, 1963—70. Author: poems; contbr. articles to profl. jours. Hospice creator, Kirksville, Mo., 1975; transport provider for terminally ill patients Branson, Mo.; pres. Waukesha County Coun. Social Agys., 1957—63; provost marshal 84th Divsn. Tng., Milw., 1957—63; chmn., co-founder N.E. Mo. Hospice Com., 1979—81; vol. Ozark Mountain Hospice, Branson, 1983—; chair com. Election of Hubert Humphrey for U.S. Senate, St. Paul, 1950; elected mem. Waukesha County Bd. Suprs., 1957—63; elder United Presbyn. Ch., 1971—; chmn. scholarship com. UNICO, Waukesha, 1957—63. Lt. col. U.S. Army, 1941—46. Mem.: Mark Twain Mental Health Assn. (bd. dirs. 1976—79), Am. Sociol. Assn., Am. Assn. Univ. and Coll. Profs., Ret. Officers Assn. (pres. 1987), Mo. Hospice Assn., Phi Kappa Phi, Kappa Delta Pi, Alpha Kappa Delta. Home: 15 Fleming Dr Columbia MO 65201-5418

EASTMAN, JOHN ROBERT, educator; b. San Diego, June 30, 1945; s. John Henry and Theresa (Wimberger) E. BA, Va. Poly. Inst. and State U., 1968; PhD, Julius-Maximilians U., Wuerzburg, 1985. Cert. tchr., Va. Tchr. So. H.S., Harwood, Md., 1968-69; instr. for English Dolmetscher Inst., Wuerzburg, 1976-83; bilingual tourist guide Arbeitsamt, Wuerzburg, 1976-85; summer sch. tchr. Archbishop Spalding H.S., Severn, Md., 1992; substitute tchr. Ft. Meade High Sch., 1990, Old Mill H.S. 1992, Anne Arundel Co., Md., 1987-97, Hampton (Va.) City Schs., 2001—; tchr. Peninsula Cath. H.S., Newport News, Va., 1997—2001; asst. prof. German Old Dominion U., Norfolk, Va., 2002—. Author: Papal Abdication in Later Medieval Thought, 1990; editor: Aegidius Romanus, De Renunciatione Pape, 1992; contbr. Internat. Medieval Bibliography, 1995—; contbr. articles to profl. jours. Mem. Am. Hist. Assn., Southeastern Medieval Assn., Nat. Coalition Ind. Scholars, Capital Area Ind. Scholars (sec.-treas. 1992-94, newsletter editor 1994-96), Am. Philol. Assn., Am. Cath. Hist. Assn., Am. Assn. Tchrs. German. Avocation: genealogy. Home: 11311 Winston Pl Apt 8 Newport News VA 23601-2238

EASTMAN, LESTER FUESS, electrical engineer, educator; b. Utica, N.Y., May 21, 1928; s. Howard Socrates and Mayme Lois (Fuess) E.; m. Anne Marie Gardner, Dec. 22, 1948; children: David Joel, Daniel Gardner, Laurie Suzanne. BEE, Cornell U., 1953, MS, 1955, PhD, 1957. Instr. Cornell U., Ithaca, N.Y., 1954-56, asst. prof., 1957-60, assoc. prof., 1960-66, prof. elec. engring., 1966-84; John L. Given Found. Chair prof. elec. engring., 1985—; founder, dir. joint services electronics program and research lab., 1977-87. Founding mem. Nat. Rsch. and Resource Facility for Submicron Structures, 1977—; laborator Chalmers Tech. U., Gothenburg, Sweden, 1960—61; mem. tech. staff RCA Rsch. Lab., 1964—65; founder, pres. Cayuga Assoc., Ithaca, 1971—72; mem. tech. staff MIT, Lincoln Lab., Lexington, Mass., 1978—79; dir. Cornell Rsch. Found., 1974—86; mem. U.S. Adv. Group Election Devices, 1978—85, 1986—88; vis. scientist IBM Watson Rsch. Lab., 1985—86; founder, chmn. bd. dirs. N.E. Semicondr., Inc., 1987—93; chmn. sci. adv. bd. Nova Crystals, 1998—; cons. to industry. Guest editor IEEE transactions, 1967, 78; Contbr. articles to profl. jours.; patentee in field. Served with USN, 1946-48. Recipient Welker medal and award Internat. Symposium Gallium Arsenide and Related Compounds, 1991, Aldert Van Der Ziel award, 1995, Prof. William Gould Dow Lectureship award U. Mich., 2002; Sperry Gyroscope fellow, 1953-54, GE fellow, 1956-57, Humboldt Sr. fellow, 1994—. Fellow IEEE (Grad. Educator award 1999, Third Millenium Medal, 2000, J.J. Ebers award 2002, Lester F. Eastman Biennial conf., 2002—), Am. Phys. Soc.; mem. NAE, Electromagnetics Acad., Sigma Xi, Eta Kappa Nu, Tau Beta Pi, Phi Kappa Phi. Presbyterian. Home: 61 Burdick Hill Rd Ithaca NY 14850-9760 Office: Cornell U 425 Phillips Hall Ithaca NY 14853-5401 E-mail: lfe@iiiv.tn.cornell.edu. *As a professor, I believe that my life contribution is through giving many students the opportunity to reach their full potential in the highest technology available.*

EASTMAN, W. DEAN, secondary school educator; b. Lawrence, Mass., Feb. 22, 1948; s. Weston D. and Harriett R. Eastman. BS in Social Sci. Edn., Drake U., 1970; MS in Edn., Springfield (Mass.) Coll., 1976, cert. advanced grad. adminstrn. studies, 1977; M in Liberal Arts, Harvard U., 2000. Coach track and field Springfield Coll. and U. Mass., Lowell, 1970-81; tchr. social sci. Beverly (Mass.) H.S., 1970—. Vis. prof. edn. Drake U., 1994-95. Contbr. articles to publs. including Scholastic Coach, Track Technique, Jour. Phys. Edn. and Recreation, Harvard Newsletter: Civil Perspective, Local History Mag. Common-Place; featured in (book) I Am a Teacher, 1990, (mags.) Tchg. Tolerance, Boston Mag.; featured for work with homeless students Today Show, NBC TV, 1991; host 10-part series on immigration Mass. Ednl. TV, 1992; features include (PBS series) Only a Teacher, 2001. Mem. ednl. steering com. Mass. Civil Liberties Union, Boston, 1990—. Christa McAuliffe fellow Mass. Dept. Edn., 1989, resident fellow Mass. Hist. Soc., 2001; recipient Outstanding Tchr. award John F. Kennedy Presdl. Libr., 1989, Am. Tchr. award Disney Channel, 1991, Alumni Achievement award Drake U., 1991, Derek Bok prize Harvard U., 2000; named one of Outstanding Young Men of Am., 1982. Mem. Nat. Assn. Scholars. Avocations: surf casting, poetry, harvard football games. Office: Beverly HS 100 Sohier Rd Beverly MA 01915-5533

EASTMENT, THOMAS JAMES, lawyer; b. N.Y.C., Mar. 3, 1950; s. George Thomas and Grace Anne (Manning) E. BChemE, Manhattan Coll., 1972; JD, U. Mich., 1975. Bar: N.Y. 1976, D.C. 1977. Assoc. Morton, Bernard, Brown, Washington, 1975-77, Baker Botts LLP, Washington, 1977-84, ptnr., 1985—. Mem. D.C. Bar Assn., Fed. Energy Bar Assn. Republican. Roman Catholic. Office: Baker Botts LLP The Warner 1299 Pennsylvania Ave NW Washington DC 20004-2400 E-mail: Tom.Eastment@BakerBotts.com.

EASTMOND-ROBINSON, JUNE PATRICIA, public health nurse; b. N.Y.C., June 21, 1938; d. Claude T. Eastmond and Olivia G. DeBello; m. Maroa W. Gikuuri, 1968 (div. 1978); children: Maroa L., Nyahiri Gikuuri-Bandele; m. Arthur L. Robinson, May 16, 1981; 1 stepchild, Randall. RN, Kings County Hosp. Sch. Nursing, Bklyn., 1958; BSN, NYU, 1964; MS Cmty. Health, L.I. U., Bklyn., 1974; EdD, Fla. Atlantic U., 1999. RN Fla. Bd. Nursing, 1978; cert. healing touch IIB Fla. Ctr. for Healing Touch. Staff nurse Kings County Hosp., Bklyn., 1958—59, dir. patient rels., 1974—78; pub. health nurse Dept. Health, Bklyn., 1961—63; pub. health nurse for pregnant teens Project Teen Aid, Bklyn., 1968—72; in svc. edn. coord. Medgar Evers Coll., Bklyn., 1972—74; dir. nursing Fla. Cmty. Health Ctrs., West Palm Beach, 1978—80; assoc. prof. Indian River C.C., Fort Pierce, Fla., 1980—2001, ret., 2001. Co-chair State of Fla. Sci. Taskforce, 1980—86; test cons. Nat. Coun. State Bds. Nursing, Atlanta, 1994, Atlanta, 97. Co-author: (textbook) Nursing Assistant Fundamentals, 1998. Active, past pres., publicity chair African-Am. Cultural Exposition for the Arts, Fort Pierce, Fla., 1983—; treas., actor Faces & Voices of St. Lucie County Inc.; v.p. region III Fla. Spl. Needs Assn., 1986—89; bd. dirs. Big Brothers Big Sisters, Fort Pierce, Fla., 2001—. Recipient cert. of appreciation, Nat. Coun. State Bd. Nursing, 1997, cert. acad. excellence award, Fla. Atlantic U., 1997. Mem.: NAACP, Fla. Nurse Assn. (treas. 2000—), Caribbean Nurses Assn. (bd. dirs. 1999—, gratitude award 2000), Assn. Practical Nurse Educators (pres., treas., bd. dirs.). Avocations: reading, exercising, organizing community activities, guest speaking on health issues, acting in community theater. Home: 5906 Papaya Dr Fort Pierce FL 34982 Home Fax: 772-466-0953. Personal E-mail: jeast_robinson@yahoo.com.

EASTON, CHARLES CLEMENT, JR., corporate executive; b. Allentown, Pa., July 14, 1930; s. Charles Clement and Harriet Ida (Williamson) E.; m. Priscilla Emma Herbert, Dec. 26, 1954; children: Joanne, Charles III, June, Jennifer. BS in Econs., Wharton Sch., 1952; MBA, Harvard U., 1956. CFP. Asst. to treas. Inmont Corp., N.Y.C., 1956-62, asst. treas., 1962-67, treas., 1967-80, Inmont Div./United Technologies, Clifton, NJ, 1980-84; dir. fin. planning Coatings and Inks Div./BASF Corp., Clifton, 1984-88; sr. rep. Excel Comms., Inc., Boca Raton, Fla. and Short Hills, N.J., 1995—. Trustee, bd. dirs. Comm. Agys. Corp., Newark, N.J., 1989—. 1st lt. USAF, 1952-54, Korea. Mem. Wyo. Club of Millburn, N.J., Racquets Club of Boca Raton, Alpha Chi Rho. Republican. Congregationalist. Avocations: tennis, bridge. E-mail: ceastonjr@myexcel.com.

EASTON, GLENN HANSON, JR., management and insurance consultant, federal official, naval officer; b. N.Y.C., Mar. 11; s. Glenn Herman and Cornelia Blanchard (Hanson) E.; m. Jeanne Milhall, June 15, 1944; children: Jeanne, Glenn Hanson III, Michelle, Carol. Assoc. in Bus. Adminstrn., U. Pa., 1949, BA in Econs., 1950; MBA, NYU, 1959. USCG lic. as 3d asst. engr. steam vessels of any horsepower, as 3d mate of steam and motor vessels of any gross tons upon the waters of oceans; CLU. Various positions to asst. traffic mgr. Keystone Shipping Co., Phila., 1940-54, Phila. Jr. C. of C., 1946-54; various positions to mgr. transp. econs. div. Standard-Vacuum Oil Co., White Plains, N.Y., 1954-59; various positions to cons. to pres. S.R. Guggenheim Found., N.Y.C., 1959-84; pres. Glenn Easton & Assocs. (mgmt. and ins. cons.), Port Chester, N.Y., 1970—; emeritus spl. agent Northwestern Mutual Life Ins. Co., 1974—; polit. appointee U.S. Dept. Labor, Washington, 1982-88; emeritus spl. agt. Northwestern Mut. Life Ins. Co., 1974—. Assoc. prof. mgmt. L.I. U., Brookville, N.Y., 1971-72 Rep. candidate for congressman, N.Y., 1972, 74, 80; pres. local Rep. Club, 1973-74; mem. Westchester County Rep. Com., 1972-83; Rep., Conservative and Ind. candidate for supr. Town of Rye, N.Y., 1973, 75, 79, 81, Rep. Candidate for councilman, 1977; vice chmn. Ind. Conservative Caucus, Westchester, 1977-83; exec. v.p. bd. trustees N.Y.-Phoenix Schs. Design, 1968-74; Eagle Scout with 4 Silver Palms. With Mainc N.G., 1936-38; served to comdr. USN, 1938-40, 43-46, 50-54, 70, PTO, ret., 1979. Mem. Soc. Naval Archs. and Marine Engrs. (life, Golden award), Navy Athletic Assn., Sr. Execs. Assn., Fed. Exec. Inst., Ret. Officers' Assn., C. of C., Am. Mgmt. Assn., Naval Res. Assn. (life, v.p. Westchester chpt.), Militia Assn. N.Y. (life), Westchester Organ Soc. (v.p.), Met. Organ Soc. Va., No. Va. Ragtime Soc., Am. Theatre Organ Soc., U.S. Capitol Hist. Soc., The Conservative Network (life), Am. Legion, Masons, Shriners, Kiwanis, Elks, Pi Gamma Mu, Sigma Kappa Phi, Phi Delta Theta (Golden Legionnaire). Avocations: swimming, reading, music, archery, numismatics. Home: 1385 Old Quincy Ln Reston VA 20194-1309 Office: 1537 Inlet Ct Reston VA 20190-4423 *Much hard work, a desire for knowledge, great integrity, persistence, enthusiasm, determination, and some vision are essential ingredients in the success formula. In addition, successful leaders must never shrink from responsibility! While it helps to be lucky, to have friends in the right places, or to be in the right place at the right time, it is more important in a man's quest for success to deal honestly and fairly with one's fellowman in order that when material success is achieved peace of mind and happiness come with it.*

EASTON, JILL JOHANNA, state official; b. Nassua County, N.Y., June 6, 1949; d. E. Paul and Thelma R. Easton. BA, U. So. Miss., 1971, MPA, 1986. Mgr. classified advt. Thibodeaux (La.) Daily Comet, 1971-73; on-air personality Sta. WNAT, Natchez, Miss., 1973-74; classified sales rep. Natchez Democrat, 1974; co-owner House of Pisces Pet Shop, Vidalia, La., 1974-75; employment interviewer Miss. Employment Svc., Gulfport, 1976-80; pub. relations rep. Miss. Dept. Health, Gulfport, 1980-83, health program rep., 1983-2000; COO Treble Hook Unltd.; free-lance outdoor writer, 2000—. Pres. J & K Ltd. Columnist: Sun Herald, contbg. writer: Today in Miss. Mem.: S.E. Outdoor Press Assn., Outdoor Writers of Am. Assn., So. Miss. Hist. and Geneal. Soc., Miss. Archaeology Assn. (bd. dirs.), Divers Alert Network. Lutheran. Avocations: scuba diving, hunting, fishing, painting, field archaeology. Home and Office: 206 Kuyrkendall Pl Long Beach MS 39560-3308 E-mail: jjeaston@worldnet.att.net.

EASTON, J(OHN) DONALD, neurologist, educator; b. Saskatoon, Sask., Can., Apr. 1, 1938; s. John and Winnifred J. (Small) E.; m. Carol Anne May, 1959 (div. 1984); children: Erin, John, Murray; m. K. Von Gunten, May 19, 1985; children: Andrew, Alexander. BS in Zoology, Wash. State U., 1960; MD, U. Wash., 1964. Cert. Am. Bd. Psychiatry and Neurology (examiner, dir. 1984-92). From asst. to assoc. prof. U. Calif., San Diego, 1970-73; from assoc. prof. to prof. So. Ill. U. Sch. Medicine, Springfield, 1974-77; prof., chair neurology dept. U. Mo. Sch. Medicine, Columbia, 1977-82, U. Tex. Health Sci. Ctr., San Antonio, 1982-86, Brown U. Sch. Medicine, Providence, 1986—. Pres. Neurology Found., Inc., Providence, 1990—. Author med. books; editor med. jours. Fellow Am. Heart Assn. Stroke Coun., 1971—, chmn., 1991-93, vol., Providence, 1986—. With USN, 1968-70. Fellow Am. Acad. Neurology; mem. Am. Neurol. Assn., Alpha Omega Alpha, Phi Beta Kappa. Presbyterian. Avocations: travel, computers, sports. Home: 7 Seaview Ave Jamestown RI 02835-1644 Office: RI Hosp Brown U 110 Lockwood St Providence RI 02903-4801 E-mail: j_easton@brown.edu.

EASTON, JOHN JAY, JR., lawyer; b. San Francisco, June 16, 1943; s. John Jay and Julia (Crawford) Easton; m. Donna Cecilia Ringger Startzel, May 4, 1996. BS, U. Colo., 1964; JD, Georgetown U., 1970. Bar: Va. 1970, Vt. 1971. Mktg. rep. Gen. Dynamics Corp., Washington, 1968-70; assoc. Paterson, Gibson, Noble & Brownell, Montpelier, Vt., 1970-72; ptnr. Davison & Easton, Stowe, Vt., 1972-75; asst. atty. gen., chief consumer protection Office Vt. Atty. Gen., 1975-78; dir. div. rate setting Vt. Agy. Human Services, 1978-80; atty. gen. State of Vt., 1981-85; pvt. practice, Burlington, Vt., 1985-86; v.p. Syn-Cronamics, Inc., Englewood Cliffs, NJ, 1986-87, Miller, Eggleston & Rosenberg, Ltd., 1987-89; asst. sec. Internat. Affairs and Energy Emergencies Dept. Energy, Washington, 1989-91, gen. counsel, 1991-92, asst. sec. Domestic and Internat. Energy Policy, 1992-93; pvt. practice, 1993-94; v.p. internat. programs Edison Elec. Inst., Washington, 1994—. Mem. product safety adv. coun. U.S. Consumer Product Safety Com., 1977—79; mem. industry sector adv. com. energy for trade policy matters, 1997—. Mem. Vt. Natural Resources Coun., 1976—89; Rep. nominee for gov. Vt., 1984. Served to capt. USAF, 1964—68. Mem.: VFW, ABA (ho. dels. 1979—84), Vt. Bar Assn. (del. 1980—84, chmn. coms. 1974—78, bd. mgrs. 1973—75), Am. Legion. Roman Catholic. Home: 5310 Saint Albans Way Baltimore MD 21212-3305 Office: Edison Elec Inst 701 Pennsylvania Ave NW Washington DC 20004-2696 E-mail: jeaston@eei.org.

EASTON, KELLY ANNE, writer, educator; b. Arcadia, Calif., Sept. 3, 1960; d. Robert William and Marilyn Eleanor Easton; children: Isabelle Easton Spivack, Isaac Robert Easton Spivack. MFA, U. Calif., San Diego, 1991. Lectr. U. N.C., Wilmington, 1994—2000; guest artist U. R.I., Kingstown, 2000—01; adj. prof. Roger Williams U., RI, 2002—. Instr. Inst. for Children's Lit. Author: (novels) The Life History of a Star, 2001 (Golden Kite Honor award, 2002, listed in Book Sense 76 Top Ten Books for Teens., 2002, ALA Popular Paperbacks for Teens), Trouble at Betts Pets, 2002, Canaries and Criminals: Trouble at Betts Pets, 2003; contbr. articles to profl. jours. Democrat. E-mail: eastonka@hotmail.com.

EASTON, LOIS BROWN, educational consultant; b. Detroit, Nov. 6, 1946; d. John Wallace and Christine Chambers Brown; 1 child, Lynn Denise. BA, Colo. State U., Fort Collins, 1966—70; MA, U. Ariz., Tucson, 1981—83, PhD, 1983—91. Tchr. & dept. chair Catalina Foothills Sch. Dist., Tucson, 1980—85; dir. curriculum and instrn. Ariz. Dept. of Edn., Phoenix, 1985—89, dir. curriculum & assessment planning, 1989—91; curriculum coord. & team leader Catalina Foothills Sch. Dist., 1991—92; dir. re-learning systems Edn. Commn. of States, Denver, 1992—94; dir. profl. devel. Eagle Rock Sch. & Profl. Devel. Ctr., Estes Park, Colo., 1994—; cons. in field. Author: (book) The Other Side of Curriculum: Lessons From Learners; editor: Powerful Designs for Professional Development, (journal) Ariz. Reading, 1982—83. Master: Assn. of State Coord of Eng/Lang Arts (founder and pres.), Ariz. English Tchrs. Assn. (pres. 1986—87, English Tchr. of Yr. 1984); mem.: Nat. Coun. Tchrs. of English (secondary steering com. mem. 1987—92), Phi Delta Kappa, ASCD (presenter & author 1970—2003), Nat. Staff Devel. Coun. (conf. co-chair 1999—2001), Phi Kappa Phi (life). Democrat. Unitarian Universalist. Avocation: international travel. Office: Eagle Rock School & Professional Develop P O Box 1770 Estes Park CO 80517-1770 Home Fax: 970-586-4805; Office Fax: 970-586-4805. E-mail: leaston@eaglerockschool.org.

EASTON, MICHELLE, foundation executive; b. Phila., Aug. 12, 1950; d. Glenn H. Jr. and Jeanne (Mulhall) Easton; m. Ron Robinson, Sept. 14, 1974; children: Ronald Jr., Daniel, Thomas. AA, BA, Briarcliff Coll., 1972; JD, Am. U., Washington, 1980. Bar: Va. 1981. Asst. to exec. dir. Young Ams. for Freedom, Sterling, Va., 1973-78; asst. to dir. pub. rels. Nat. Right to Work Com., Springfield, Va., 1978; legal asst. Nat. Right to Work Legal Def. Found., 1979; transition team mem. Office of Pres.-Elect, Equal Employment Opportunity Commn., Washington, 1980-81; atty. U.S. Dept. Justice, Washington, 1981; spl. asst. to gen. counsel U.S. Dept. Edn., Washington, 1981-83; pvt. vol. orgns. liaison officer, Africa Bur. Agy. for Internat. Devel., 1984; dir. Missing

Children's Program Office of Juvenile Justice and Delinquency Prevention, U.S. Dept. Justice, 1985-87; dir. intergovtl. affairs U.S. Dept. Edn., Washington, 1987-88, dep. under sec. for intergovtl. and interagy. affairs, 1988-91; dir. Office Pvt. Edn., Washington, 1991-93; pres. Clare Boothe Luce Policy Inst., 1993—. Apptd. by Gov. Allen to Va. State Bd. Edn., Richmond, 1994-98, bd. pres. 1996; bd. dirs. The Family Found., Richmond, Va., 1998-99; sec. Nat. Conservative Campaign Fund, 2000—. Mem.: Phila. Soc. (trustee 2000—02). Republican. Episcopalian.

EASTON, RICHARD ALLEN, electrical engineer; b. Ithaca, N.Y., Dec. 28, 1944; s. Hamilton Pratt and Anne Elizabeth Easton; m. Joyce Ardelle Englund, Oct. 9, 1971; children: Jay, Kjerstin. BSSE, Northwestern U., 1967; MSEE, Purdue U., 1968. Sr. staff engr. Hughes Aircraft Co., Fullerton, Calif., 1972-80; mgr. digital signal processing Northrop-Grumman, Anaheim, Calif., 1982-88; dir electronics Aerojet Gen. Corp., Azuza, Calif., 1988-94; mgr. video tech. Cohu Inc., San Diego, Calif., 1994—. Address: 23241 Tasmania Cir Dana Point CA 92629-3645

EASTON, ROBERT MORRELL, JR., optometric physician; b. Miami, Fla., Sept. 23, 1954; s. Robert Morrell Easton Sr. and Joan (Saxon) Faust; m. Gloria Rocio Flores, Mar. 19, 1983; children: Robert Morrell Easton III, Linda Easton. AA, Broward Community Coll., 1974; BS in Chemistry, U. Cen. Fla., 1977; OD, U. Houston, 1982. Bd. cert. Optometric physician, Fla. Extern Bascom Palmer Eye Inst., Miami; pvt. practice Ft. Lauderdale, 1982—. Apptd. by Fla. gov. Fla. Bd. Optometry, 1999—; apptd. Nat. Bd. Examiners in Optometry, 2001—, vice chair, 2000—; mem. examination com. Nat. Bd. Optometry, 2000—; adj. asst. clin. prof. Nova Southeastern Coll. Optometry. Mem. City of Oakland Park Code Enforcement Bd., 1999—2003. Named one of Top Optometrists in U.S., 20/20 Mag., 1991, Top Optometrists in Am., Consumers Rsch. Coun. of Am., 2001—; recipient Up & Cormer's award for health care, South Fla. Mag., 1993. Fellow Am. Acad. Optometry; mem. Fla. Optometric Assn. (pres. 1993-94), Am. Optometric Assn. (state rep. 1987-95, polit. action, profl. rels. com. 1994-95, bd. dirs., treas. AOA-PAC 1994—, chmn. 1999-2000), Fla. Pub. Health Assn. (charter, chmn. vision care sect. 1992-93), Broward County Optometric Assn. (past pres., Optometrist of Yr. 1985), Tower Forum (v.p. 1994-95, treas. 1999-2003), East Oakland Park Blvd. Bus. Assn. (charter pres. 1998-2003), Assn. Regulatory Bds. of Optometry (bd. dirs. 2003-2007), Leadership Broward Alumni Assn., Rotary (bd. dirs. Ft. Lauderdale 1986-89, svc. award 1989), Republican. Presbyterian. Avocations: physical fitness, hunting, fishing, surfing, martial arts. Office: 2708 E Oakland Park Blvd Fort Lauderdale FL 33306-1605 E-mail: eastonodreliv@msn.com.

EASTON, SUSAN DAWN, biochemist, educator; b. Harvey, Ill., Oct. 8, 1959; d. Dee Charles and Barbara Louise Shaffer. BS in Biol. Scis., Ill. State U., 1981. Med. rsch. technician Washington U. Sch. Medicine, St. Louis, 1981-83; biol. lab. technician VA Med. Ctr., Indpls., 1983-86; rsch. technician Ind. U., Bloomington, 1987-88, rsch. assoc., 1988-92; chemistry, microbiology, validation, document control, quality assurance mgr. Cook Imaging Corp., Bloomington, 1993-96, regulatory affairs mgr., 1996-99, tech. svcs., 1999—2001; tech. svcs. mgr. Baxter Pharm. Solutions, LLC, Bloomington, 2001—, mem. emergency response team, 2001—. Mem. emergency response team Cook Imaging Corp., Bloomington, 1995-2001; lectr. Ctr. Profl. Advancement, East Brunswick, N.J., 1996—, Internat. Soc. Pharm. Engrs., 2001—; lectr. Internat. Soc. for Pharm. Engrs., 2001. Author: Protein Expression and Purification, 1993. Named one of Outstanding Young Women of Am., 1983. Mem. Internat. Soc. Pharm. Engrs., Parenteral Drug Assn., Phi Sigma. Office: Baxter Pharm Solutions LLC PO Box 3068 Bloomington IN 47402-3068 Home: 3702 Stoney Brook Blvd Bloomington IN 47404

EASTON, SUSAN SHEARER, organizational development consultant, educator; b. Syracuse, N.Y., Oct. 19, 1950; d. Ralph Henry and Ellen Eva (Williams) Shearer; children: Justin, Darcy, Corrine. AAS, Auburn Community Coll., 1971; BA, Oswego State U., 1974; MS, Syracuse U., 1987; PhD, Fla. State U., 2000. Tchr. Ctrl. N.Y. Sch., Syracuse, 1974-84; orgnl. specialist GE Co., Syracuse, 1984-89; mgr. human resource devel. Emerson Electric Co., Sanford, Fla., 1989-90; pres. Easton and Assocs., Lake Mary, Fla., 1990—; prof. Rollins Coll., Winter Park, Fla., 2001—. Owner bus. offices, Atlanta and Belgium, 1991—; chair Internat. Conf. on Self Managing Teams, 1991; mentor coord. Fla. State U. Office Distributed and Distance Learning. Tutor writing Lake Mary Elem. Schs., 1991—; vol., cons. Hospice Assn., Orlando, Syracuse, 1991—; guest speaker local sch. systems, Fla., 1986—; sr. youth dir ch., 1991—. Mem. ASTD (nat. dir. mfg. industry group 1989-92, chair ctrl. Fla. chpt., editor newsletter 1990-91, Best of Conf. award 1989, 91), Fla. Communication Assn. (2d v.p.). Lutheran. Avocations: golf, swimming, racquetball, music. Home and Office: Easton and Assocs 149 Edgewater Circle Sanford FL 32773-6095 E-mail: Sueeaston@juno.com.

EASTTOM, CHUCK, computer scientist, educator; b. Bangkok, Oct. 5, 1968; m. Misty Dawn Baker, Oct. 15, 1994; 1 child, Andrew Jay (AJ). BA, 1997; M.Ed., Southeastern Okla. State U., 2000. Cert. Microsoft Certified Database Adminr. Microsoft, 2001, Microsoft Certified Systems Adminr. Microsoft, 2002, A+ Certified PC Technician CompTIA, 1998, Network+ CompTIA, 1999, Server + CompTia, 1999, I-Net+ CompTia, 2000, Linux+ CompTIA, 2001, A+ CompTIA, MCDBA Microsoft, 2002. Contract programmer/analyst Boeing Aerospace Ops., Midwest City, Okla., 1995—96; sr. software engr. Alegis Corp. Systems Group, N. Richland Hills, Tex., 1996—98; dir. ednl. tech. Southeastern Okla. State U., Durant, 1998—99; sr. software engr. DSSI, Richardson, 1999—2000; dept. chair for software info. systems dept Remington Coll. - Dallas Campus, Garland, Tex., 2000—. Author: (computer programming book) Learn Java Script, 2000; : Learn VB.Net, 2001, EJB Programming with JBuilder 7.0, 2002, Learn EJB with JBuilder 7.0, 2002, Fundamentals of C+ Programming, 2003, Computer Programming with C+, Fundamentals of C+ Programming, Learn VB.Net, Learn JavaScript, JFC Programming with JBuilder; : Learn VB.Net, 2001, (book) JFC and Jbuilder, 2002, (computer programming book) Learn EJB with JBuilder 7.0. With U.S. Army, 1987—91. Achievements include worked as a subject matter expert for the computer technology industry association in the development of their Server+ Certification test; worked as a subject matter expert for the computer technology industry association in the development of their Linux+ Certification test; worked as a subject matter expert for the computer technology industry association in the development of their Security+ Certification test. Home: 3605 Willow Creek Trail McKinney TX 75071 Personal E-mail: chuckeasttom@yahoo.com.

EASTUP, LAVONDA JO, writer, poet, songwriter; b. Valdasta, Tex., Aug. 29, 1931; d. Ira Albert and Maxine Lottie (Box) Greer; m. Admah C. Eastup, Jr., Dec. 12, 1948 (div. Oct. 1985); children: Lana Kay, Reggie Dale, Allen Ray, Debra Darlene. Grad. h.s. Author: Two Wheels to Glory--The Gentle Giant, 1982, Silver Teardrops and Golden Manna, Great Poems of the Western World, 1990, (with others) The World of Poetry Anthology, 1991, Who's Who in Poetry, Vol. III, 1991, Gold and Silver Poems, 1992, Poems that Will Live Forever, 1993, Great Poems of Our Time, 1993, Our World's Favorite Poems, Who's Who in Poetry, 1993, Outstanding Poets of 1994; contbr. poetry to books, including: On the Threshold of a Dream, Vol. 3, 1992, Selected Works of Our World's Best Poets, Best Poems of the 90's/Nat. Libr. Poetry, Letters From the Soul, 2002, The Best Poems & Poets of 2002, (CD-Cassette) The Sound of Poetry, 2002, Theatre of the Mind, 2003, 4 poems made into songs and released by Rainbow Records, 1991, 92, Theatre of The Mind, 2003. Recipient numerous awards and plaques for poetry; inducted to Internat. Poetry Hall of Fame Mus., 1996; published in book Best Loved Poems Nat. Libr. Poetry, Owings Mills, Md., 1997, 98; named Internat. Poetry Hall of Fame, 1996, 97, 98, 99, 2000. Mem. Little Black Book Poetry Soc. of Hunt County, Tex., Internat. Soc. Poets (hon.). Republican. Baptist. Avocations: gardening, raising cats and flowers.

EASTWOOD, CLINT, actor, film director, former mayor; b. San Francisco, May 31, 1930; m. Dina Ruiz. Student, Oakland Tech. High Sch.; attended, Los Angeles City Coll. Worked as lumberjack in Oreg. before being drafted into the Army; formed Malpaso Prodns., 1969. Chmn. AT&T/Pebble Beach Pro Am. Golf Tournament; owner, pres. Malpaso Records Co., Mission Ranch Resort, Carmel, Calif.; owner, co-ptnr. Prime Golf/Tehama Clothing Co., Prime Gold/Tehama Clothing Co.; owner Mission Ranch Resort, Carmel, Calif., Starred in TV series Rawhide, 1959-1966. Motion pictures include: (actor) Revenge of the Creature, 1955, Francis in the Navy, 1955, Lady Godiva, 1955, Tarantula, 1955, Never Say Goodbye, 1956, The First Travelling Saleslady, 1956, Star in the Dust, 1956, Away All Boats, 1956, Escapade in Japan, 1957, Ambush at the Cimmaron Pass, 1958, Lafayette Escadrille, 1958, A Fistful of Dollars, 1964, For a Few Dollars More, 1965, The Good The Bad and The Ugly, 1966, The Witches, 1967, Hang 'Em High, 1968, Coogan's Bluff, 1968, Where Eagles Dare, 1969, Paint Your Wagon, 1969, Two Mules for Sister Sara, 1970, Kelly's Heroes, 1970, The Beguiled, 1971, Dirty Harry, 1972, Joe Kidd, 1972, Magnum Force, 1973, Thunderbolt and Lightfoot, 1974, The Enforcer, 1976, Every Which Way But Loose, 1978, Escape from Alcatraz, 1979, Any Which Way You Can, 1980, City Heat, 1984, (dir. Amazing Stories TV) Vanessa in the Garden, 1985, Pink Cadillac, 1989, In the Line of Fire, 1993; (dir.) Breezy, 1973; (dir., actor) Play Misty For Me, 1971, High Plains Drifter, 1973, The Eiger Sanction, 1975, The Outlaw Josey Wales, 1976, The Gauntlet, 1977, Bronco Billy, 1980, The Rookie, 1990, A Perfect World, 1994, Absolute Power, 1996; (actor, prod.) Tightrope, 1984, The Dead Pool, 1988; (dir., prod.) Bird, 1988, Midnight in the Garden of Good and Evil, 1997; (dir., actor, producer) Firefox, 1982, Honky Tonk Man, 1982, Sudden Impact, 1983, Pale Rider, 1985, Heartbreak Ridge, 1986, White Hunter, Black Heart, 1990, Unforgiven, 1992 (Academy Award Best Director, Best Picture), The Bridges of Madison County, 1995, Absolute Power, 1997, True Crime, 1998, Space Cowboys, 2000, Blood Work, 2002; (exec. producer) Thelonious Monk-Straight, No Chaser, 1989, The Stars Fell on Henrietta, 1995; (cameo) Casper; singer (Midnight soundtrack album) Ac.cent.uate the Positive, 1997; (with Randy Travis) Smokin' the Hive; documentaries include Don't Pave Main St., 1994, Eastwood After Hours: A Night of Jazz. Mem. Nat. Coun. Arts, 1973; chmn. (Monterey) AT&T/Pebble Beach Pro-Am Golf Tournament. Office: c/o Leonard Hirshan 1680 Clearview Dr Beverly Hills CA 90210*

EASTWOOD, D(ANA) ALAN, author, publisher, consultant; b. Poughkeepsie, NY, June 1, 1947; s. Donald Edward and Edith Margaret (Davis) E.; m. Cynthia Carol Allen, Jan. 1, 1984; children: Athena Yvonne, Ashlee Lyn, Alysa Bryhn. Diploma, Am. Inst. Banking, Washington, 1980; diploma with highest honors, Paralegal Inst., Phoenix, 1983. Proprietor Eastwood Studio, Hyde Park, N.Y., 1965-70; credit rep. Bankers Trust of Hudson Valley, N.A., Poughkeepsie, 1970-73; installment loan supr. Poughkeepsie Savs. Bank, 1973-75, installment loan mgr., 1975-78, consumer loan officer, 1978-79, compliance officer, 1979-87, compliance officer, data security adminstr., 1987-89; compliance, community reinvestment act and loan rev. officer, 1989-91; pres. Modern Bus. Advisors of the Mid-Hudson, 1991-97. Editor/pub. Blue Knight Enterprises, 1997—; pres., chmn. bd. Consumer Credit Assn., Mid-Hudson Valley, Poughkeepsie, 1973-75; 1st v.p. Consumer Credit Group N.Y. State, N.Y.C., 1978-79; v.p. dist. 2 Internat. Consumer Credit Assn., N.Y. and N.J., 1978-79; mem. consumer credit com. Savs. Banks Assn. N.Y. State, N.Y.C., 1982-85; mem. supervisory com. Hudson Valley Fed. Credit Union, 1994-96. Author: Gravity Park, 1978, UFOmetry, 1997, Blue Rainbows, 1997, The Thirteenth Sign, 1999; editor The Right Banker, 1979-82; pub.: Mark of the White Wolf, 1999, The Hundredth Monkey, 2000, UFO's-A Selected Bibliography, 2001, Snowflakes on the Don, 2001; also painter of modern acrylic artworks. Consumer edn. adv. com. Dutchess County Coop. Extension Assn., Millbrook, N.Y., 1975-77. Recipient Award for Outstanding Leadership Consumer Credit Assn. Mid-Hudson Valley, Poughkeepsie, 1974, John C. Corliss Meml. award, 1977, Dedicated Service award Consumer Credit Group N.Y. State, N.Y.C., 1979. Fellow Soc. Cert. Credit Execs.; mem. Internat. Assn. for New Sci. Home and Office: 7 Carriage House Ct Hyde Park NY 12538-1505 E-mail: blue_knight_ent@hotmail.com.

EASTWOOD, DELYLE, chemist; b. Upper Darby, Pa., Nov. 19, 1932; d. Earl Vivian and Thelma Bernice Eastwood. MS in Phys. Chemistry, U. Chgo., 1955, PhD in Phys. Chemistry, 1964; MS in Mgmt. Sci., Rensselaer Poly. Inst., 1982. Postdoctoral rsch. fellow Harvard U., Cambridge, Mass., 1964-66; rsch. assoc. U. Wash., Seattle, 1966-69, Northeastern U., Boston, 1970-71; sr. scientist Baird Atomic Corp., Bedford, Mass., 1971-72; project chemist Bendix Rsch. Ctr., Southfield, Mich., 1972-73; rsch. chemist USCG Rsch. and Devel. Ctr., Groton, Conn., 1974-81; sr. staff scientist Brookhaven Nat. Lab., Upton, N.Y., 1981-83; Nat. Superfund design ctr. chemist U.S. Army Corps Engrs., Omaha, 1983-88; sr. staff scientist Lockheed Environ. Sys. and Tech. Co., Las Vegas, Nev., 1988-95; consulting scientist, 1996; sr. rsch. assoc. dept. engring. physics Air Force Inst. Tech., Wright-Patterson AFB, Ohio, 1996-99; rsch. prof. dept. chemistry and biochemistry U. S.C., Columbia, 2000-01; rsch. chemist Western Regl. Rsch. Ctr., Agrl. Rsch. Svc., USDA, Albany, Calif., 2001—. Adj. prof. physics U. Nev., Las Vegas, 1990-99. Editor books in field; contbr. articles to profl. publs., chpts. to books. Recipient Silver medal for Meritorious Svc. U.S. Dept. Transp., 1978. Fellow ASTM (chmn. subcom E13, exec. bd. 1983—, chmn. task force D19 1974—, E-13 Award of Merit, 1996, D-19 Stds. Devel. award 1991); mem. Soc. Applied Spectroscopy (chmn. Nev. chpt. 1988-90), Assn. Women in Sci. (facilitator, nat. contact So. Nev. chpt. 1989-94), Am. Chem. Soc., Am. Phys. Soc., Soc. of Photo Optical Instrumentation Engrs. Office: Western Regl Rsch Ctr Agrl Rsch Svc/USDA 800 Buchanan St Albany CA 94710 E-mail: delyle@pw.usda.gov.

EASTWOOD, GREGORY LINDSAY, academic administrator; b. Detroit, July 28, 1940; s. William Inwood and Kathryn (Bradley) E.; m. Lynn Marshall, June 19, 1964; children: Kristen, Lauren, Kara. AB, Albion Coll., 1962; MD, Case-Western Res. U., 1966. Diplomate: Am. Bd. Internal Medicine, Am. Bd. Gastroenterology. Resident in internal medicine Hosp. U. Pa., 1966—70; asst. prof. medicine Harvard U., Boston, 1974-77; assoc. prof. medicine U. Mass., Worcester, 1977-82, prof., 1982—89, dir. gastroenterology, 1977-89; dean Sch. Medicine Med. Coll. Ga., Augusta, 1989—92; pres. SUNY Upstate Med. U., Syracuse, 1993—. Chair biodef. coun., past chair bd. dirs. Assn. Acad. Health Ctrs. Fellow ACP. Office: SUNY Upstate Med U 750 E Adams St Syracuse NY 13210

EASTWOOD, SUSAN, medical scientific editor; b. Glens Falls, N.Y., Jan. 2, 1943; d. John J. and Della Eastwood; m. Raymond A. Berry. BA, U. Colo., 1964. Diplomate Bd. Editors in Life Scis. Adminstr. rsch. assoc. Depts. Psychol., Psychiat., Stanford (Calif.) U., 1965-68; prin., tchr. Colegio Capitan Correa, Arecibo, P.R., 1968-70; sr. editor dept. lab. medicine U. Calif., San Francisco, 1971-77, prin. analyst sci. publs. dept. neurol. surgery and Neurosurgical Rsch. Ctrs., 1977—. Cons. March of Dimes Calif. Birth Defects Monitoring Program, Oakland, 1988—; mem. QUOROM, CONSORT, coord., Asilomar Working Group on recommendations for reporting clinical trials, 1993-2001; chair, coun. Biology Editors task force for strategic planning, 1996-98, acad. networks, 1998—; co-chair, Liaison Task Force on Biomed. Authorship; conf. dir. Asilomar Conf., Am. Med. Writers Assn., 2002—. Collaborating editor: Current Neurosurgical Practice, 1984-91, Brain tumor biology and therapy, 1984; editor: Brain Tumors: A Guide, 1992; author: Guidelines on Research Data and Manuscripts, 1989, The Biomedical Publication Kit, 2003; author and editor: Biomedical Publication-A Program and Guide, 2000. Recipient Pres. award Am. Med. Writers Assn., Bethesda, Md., 1989, Chancellors Outstanding Achievement award U. Calif., San Francisco, 1989, 94, Cert. of award Nat. Brain Tumor Found., 1992, Am. Soc. Journalists and Authors, 1992, Harold Swanberg award disting. svc., 2003; Haas Found. co-grantee for devel. of U. Calif.-San Diego, U. Calif.-San Francisco clin. rsch. ethics program, Disting. Svc. award Coun. Sci. Editors, 2000. Fellow: Am. Med. Writers Assn. (Harold Swanberg Disting. Svc. award 2003); mem.: AAAS, Coun. Sci. Editors (v.p. 1995—96, pres. 1996—97), N.Y. Acad. Scis., Internat. Fedn. Sci. Editors, European Assn. Sci. Editors. Office: U Calif-San Francisco Dept Neurosurgery M-779 Box 0112 505 Parnassus Ave San Francisco CA 94122-2722

EASUM, DONALD BOYD, consultant, educator, former institute executive, diplomat; b. Ind., Aug. 27, 1923; m. Augusta Pentecost (dec.). BA, U. Wis., 1947; MPA, MA, Princeton U., 1950, PhD, 1953. Tchr., 1947-48; newspaper reporter, 1949; independent rsch., 1950-51, Buenos Aires, 1951-52; with U.S. Dept. of State, 1953-79; pers. officer Washington, 1953-54; econ.-labor officer, 1955—57; cons., econ. officer, 1957—59; exec. secretariat, 1959—61; exec. sec. ICA, 1961, AID, 1962-63; polit. officer Senegal, Gambia, Port Guinea, 1963-66; dep. chief mission, 1966—68; sr. sem. in fgn. policy Fgn. Svc. Inst., Washington, 1968-69, staff dir. NSC interdepartmental group for Latin Am., 1969—71; amb. to Upper Volta, 1971-74; asst. sec. state for African affairs, 1974-75; amb. to Nigeria, 1975-79; pres. African-Am. Inst., N.Y.C., 1980-88. Lectr. Princeton (N.J.) U., 1991; dir. World Space Found., Washington, 1997-98. Trustee The Rothko Chapel, Houston, Am. Sch. of Tangier; v.p. Global Bus. Access, Ltd., Washington; mem. Corp. Coun. for Africa, Washington; v.p., River Blindness Found., 1991-1995. With U.S. Army, 1943-45. Fellow Woodrow Wilson Nat. fellow, 1988—90, Paul Harris fellow, Rotary Internat., 1995, Stimson fellow, Yale U., 1999—. Address: 801 W End Ave Apt 3A New York NY 10025-5361

EATON, ALVIN RALPH, aeronautical and systems engineer, research and development administrator; b. Mar. 13, 1920; s. Alvin Ralph and Katherine (Hasel) E., m. Kathleen Steiner, Aug. 15, 1942 (div.); children: Eric Lloyd, Alan Ralph; m. Ellen Griffiths Phillips, Oct. 3, 1970. AB in Physics, Oberlin Coll.; MS in Aero. Engring., Calif. Inst. Tech. Rsch. asst. Calif. Inst. Tech., 1941-44; engr. So. Calif. Co-op Wind Tunnel, Pasadena, 1944-45; with The Johns Hopkins U. Applied Physics Lab., Silver Spring, Md., 1945-75, Laurel, Md., 1975—, mem. prin. profl. staff, 1950—, supr. aerodynamics, dynamics and guidance analysis groups, 1949-54, program supr. supersonic missile and weapon sys. programs, 1954-64, supr. missile sys. divsn., 1964-73, faculty evening coll. grad. sch., 1973-75, supr. fleet sys. dept., 1973-83, asst. dir. for tactical sys. Applied Physics Lab., 1973-79, asst. dir., 1979-86, assoc. dir., 1986-89, dir. spl. programs, 1989-2000, sr. fellow, 1989—. Mem. Johns Hopkins U. adv. bd. for Applied Physics Lab., 1963, 69-70, 73-89; chmn. Def. Sci. Bd. Task Force on Patriot Air Def. Sys., 1977-78, mem. task forces, 1979-83; cons. to under sec. def. for rsch. and engring., 1977-83, chmn. and mem. spl. NATO and U.S. task forces, 1977-92, mem. under sec. def. high energy laser rev. group, 1981-83, mem. under sec. def. durability of electronic countermeasures rev. group, 1983-86; mem. Navy planning and steering adv. Group for Surface Ship Security, 1979-82, chmn. and mem. subgroups, 1979-82; cons. to Asst. Sec. of Army for rsch., devel., and acquisition, 1969-74, 80-86, chmn., Asst. Sec. of Army ind. rev. panel for Patriot air def. sys., 1980-86; mem. Army Sci. Bd., 1980-86, 89-95; chmn. panel on adv. sys. test, 1980-81; dep. chmn. summer studies on sci. and engring. pers. and future devel. goals, 1982-83, mem. subgroup on ballistic missile def., 1984-86, 89; chmn. atmospheric scis. lab. effectiveness rev., 1985, chmn. panel on electromagnetic/electrothermal gun tech. devel., 1989-92; chmn. subgroup on Army tactical space sys., 1991-92; mem. rsch. and new initiatives issue group, 1991-95; mem. ad hoc study group on space sys. and airland ops., 1992; mem. summer study on future army missile programs, 1993; mem. ad hoc study group missile tech. shelf life, 1994; cons. army sci. bd., 2002—, mem.summer studies on future Army combat systems, 2002, 2003; chmn., asst. sec. army rsch., devel. and acquisition ind. rev. panel for anti-tactical missile programs, 1986-2002; chmn. high altitude theater missile def. sensor panel Army Strategic Def. Command, 1992-93; dep. chmn., exec. bd. Air Armaments Sys. Divsn. of Am. Def. Preparedness Assn., 1984-90 (life mem.). Mem. editl. bd. Jour. Def. Rsch., 1988-92, Johns Hopkins APL Tech. Digest, 1995—; inventor in field; contbr. articles to profl. jours. Trustee Howard County (Md.) Gen. Hosp., 1977-85, chmn. fin. com., treas., 1979-81, vice-chmn., 1981-83, chmn., 1983-85, chmn. Cmty. Rels. Coun., 1988-94. Recipient Meritorious Pub. Svc. award USN, 1957, Disting. Pub. Svc. award, 1975, Gov. Md. citation for leadership of Howard County (Md.) Gen. Hosp. Cmty. Rels. Coun., 1994, Patriotic Civilian Svc. award U.S. Army, 1995, Disting. Alumni award Morrison R. Waite H.S., Toledo, Ohio, 1995. Fellow Explorers Club; mem. Balt. Coun. on Fgn. Affairs, Rotary, Cosmos Club (Washington), Country Club of Hilton Head, Sigma Xi, Phi Beta Kappa. Methodist. Home: 6701 Surrey Ln Clarksville MD 21029-1605 Office: Johns Hopkins Rd Laurel MD 20723-6099 E-mail: alvin.eaton@jhuapl.edu.

EATON, AMOS JORGE, management consultant; b. Asuncion, Paraguay, Feb. 19, 1944; s. Robert James and Dorothy Iris Veronica (Kent) E.; m. Susan Yvonne Deslauriers, May 29, 1966 (div.); children: Amos Joseph, Catherine Veronica. BA in Econs. & Math., U. Vt., 1966. Sr. programmer, analyst Aetna Life & Casualty Co., Hartford, Conn., 1969-71; gen. prin. Bus. Start-Up & Turn-Around Svcs., Stoneham, Mass., 1970—; project leader Royal Typewriter Co. divsn. Litton Industries, Hartford, 1971-72; project mgr. Zayre Corp., Framingham, Mass., 1972-73; pres. Eaton-Turner, Inc., North Reading, Mass., 1974-83; exec. v.p., CFO Kevlar Comm., Inc., 1991-97; founding mem., bd. mem., 1st pres. Essex Aggie Found., 1993-94; chmn. Web Design Profls., 1999—, ProjectQuotes.com Corp., 1999—2002; acting CFO and CIO Am. Stockbrokers, Inc., Salem, Mass., 1984—90, Am. Discount Brokers, Inc., Salem, Mass., 1984—90. Chmn. Stoneham Rep. Town Com., 1988-90; chmn. CURE for the Commonwealth Com., 1990-95, Woburn Rep. City Com., 1994—; auditor, bd. dirs. Mass. Action Coalition, 1992-93; mem. Atty. Gen.'s Task Force to Abate Waste, Fraud and Abuse in the Workman Compensation Sys., 1993-95, Gov.'s Adv. Com. Info. Tech., 1994-98; founder, chmn. Changing Tide Com., 1996—; elected Rep. state committeeman 4th Middlesex Senatorial Dist., 2000. Served to 1st lt. U.S. Army, 1966-68. Mem. NRA (endowment), Mass. Chief Police Assn., Phi Delta Theta. Office: PO Box 80576 Stoneham MA 02180-0006

EATON, BARRY DAVID, retired city planner; b. Oakland, Calif., Dec. 1, 1937; s. J. Lloyd Eaton and Dorothy Ann Stockton; m. Paulette Elaine Eaton, 1962 (div. 1972); children: Colleen Ann, Cathleen Annissa (dec.); m. Susan Ann Eaton, 1977. AA, U. Calif., Berkeley, 1958, AB, 1960; MS, U. So. Calif., L.A., 1962. Planning dir. City Azusa, Calif., 1962-63, City of Stanton, Calif., 1964-65, City of Thousand Oaks, Calif., 1966-70; chief planner Boise Cascade Bldg. Co., L.A., 1970-71; cmty. devel. dir. City of Escondido, Calif., 1971-72; planning dir. VTN Inc., Irvine, Calif., 1973-74; chief planner City of Fullerton, Calif., 1975-95, ret., 1995. Pres. East Bluff Homeowners Assn., Newport Beach, Calif., 1998-2003; vice chair N.B. ENV Quality Adv. Com., Newport Beach, 1998—; v.p. Ret. Pub. Employees Assn., newport Beach, 1999-2002; dir. Airport Working Group, Newport Beach, 1999—; mem. Newport Beach Planning Commn., 2003—. Recipient Spl. Environ. award Thousand Oaks Escondidocom.s Forum, 1969, 71. Mem. Am. Inst. Cert. Planners, Am. Planning Assn., Assn. Environ. Profls., Nat. Assn. Environ. Profls., others. Avocations: travel, civic activities. Home: PO Box 802 Corona Del Mar CA 92625-0802 E-mail: eaton727@earthlink.net.

EATON, CANDACE JOHNSON, program director; b. Beverly, Mass., Apr. 3, 1952; d. George Andrew and Elizabeth Louise (Feltis) Johnson; m. Robert Norman Eaton, July 2, 1983. Student, Boston Archtl. Ctr., 1975-78, Northeastern U., Boston, 1975. Bookkeeper, data processor United Engrs. & Constructors, Inc., Boston, 1970-72; adminstr. Jackson & Moreland Internat., Inc., Boston, 1972-78; fin. dir. Downeast Health Svcs., Inc., Ellsworth, Maine, 1979—2003; program dir., cons. Hancock County Children's Coun., 1998—. Bd. dirs. Maine Children's Trust, 2000—; pres. Option One, Inc., Sullivan, Maine, 1982-2001; treas. Sullivan Woods, 1991-2001, Acoustic Energy, 1993-2001; cons. Hancock County Child Protection Coun., Ellsworth, 1987-98; bd. dirs. Hancock County Children's Coun.; cons. in field, 1987-98. Treas. Campaign to Elect Robert Eaton, Maine, 1987-88; treas. Sullivan Bicentennial Com., 1988-89; co-chair Sullivan 2000 Comprehensive Plan, 1989-91; mem. Prevent Child Abuse Maine, 1999-, bd. dirs., 1999-2001, Maine Children's Trust, 2002—. Mem. Maine Fedn. Bus. and Profl. Women (bd. dirs. 1985-93, co-editor jour. 1990-93, nominating chair 1990-91, corr. sec. 1989-90, del. to annual nat. convs. 1985, 86, 88, 90), Ellsworth Bus. and Profl. Women (bd. dirs. 1985—, del. to annual state cons. 1985-93, pres. 1985-87, fin. chair 1990-91, legis. chair 1988-90, Mem. of Yr. award 1988), Ellsworth C. of C., Women's Bus. Devel. Corp. Avocations: skiing, sailing, gardening, antiques. Office: Downeast Health Svcs Inc Christian Ridge Rd PO Box 1087 Ellsworth ME 04605-1087

EATON, CHARLES EDWARD, English language educator, author; b. Winston-Salem, N.C., June 25, 1916; s. Oscar Benjamin and Mary Gaston (Hough) E.; m. Isabel Patterson, Aug. 16, 1950. Student, Duke U., 1932-33; AB, U. N.C., 1936; postgrad., Princeton, 1936-37; MA, Harvard, 1940; DLitt (hon.), St. Andrews Coll., N.C., 1998. Instr. English U. Mo., 1940-42; prof. creative writing U. N.C., 1946-51; Am. vice-consul Rio de Janeiro, Brazil, 1942-46. Fellow Bread Loaf Writers Conf., 1941, Boulder Writers Conf., 1942. Author: (poems) The Bright Plain, 1942, The Shadow of the Swimmer, 1951, The Greenhouse in the Garden, 1956, Countermoves, 1963, On the Edge of the Knife, 1970, Colophon of the Rover, 1980, The Thing King, 1983, The Work of the Wrench, 1985, New and Selected Poems, 1942-87, 1985, New and Selected Poems, 1992, 2002, 2003, A Guest on Mild Evenings, 1991, The Country of the Blue, 1994, The Fox and I, 1996, The Scout in Summer, 1999, The Jogger By the Sea, 2000, Between the Devil and the Deep Blue Sea, 2002, (art criticisms)

Karl Knaths: Five Decades of Painting, 1973, Robert Broderson: Paintings and Graphics, 1975, (short stories) Write Me From Rio, 1959, The Girl from Ipanema, 1972, The Case of the Missing Photographs, 1978, New and Selected Stories: 1959-89, 1989, (novels) A Lady of Pleasure, 1993, (essays) The Man from Buena Vista. Selected Nonfiction, 1944-2000, 2001; contbr. anthologies including Best American Short Stories, 1952, American Literature: Readings and Critiques, 1961, Epoch Anthology, 1968, Best Poems of the Year, 1955-65, Best Poems of the Year, 1968-70, Best Poems of the Year, 1974-75, O. Henry Prize Stories, 1972, New Southern Poets, 1974, The Poet in Washington, 1977, Contemporary Poetry of North Carolina, 1977, Contemporary Southern Poetry, 1979, Anthology of Magazine Verse, 1980-81, Anthology of Magazine Verse, 1981, Anthology of Magazine Verse, 1985, 1980 Arvon Poetry Competition Anthology, The Direction of Poetry, 1988, The Courage to Grow Old, 1989, The Rough Ride Home, 1992, N.C. Poetry Soc. Anthology, 1992, Contemporary Authors Autobiographical Series, 1994, Anthology of Magazine Verse, 1997, anthologies, autobiographical/critical essays, New and Selected Nonfiction, 1999-2001. Mem. vis. com. Ackland Mus., U. N.C., 1987-98. Recipient Ridgely Torrence Meml. award, 1951, Gertrude Boatwright Harris award, 1955, Ariz. Quar. award, 1955, 56, 82, Roanoke-Chowan Poetry Cup, 1970, Oscar Arnold Young Meml. award, 1971, Golden Rose award New Eng. Poetry Club, 1972, Alice Fay di Castagnola award Poetry Soc. Am., 1974, Ariz. Quar. award, 1977, 79, Arvon Found. award London, 1980, Brockman award N.C. Poetry Soc., 1984, 86, Hollins Critic award, 1984, Roanoke-Chowan Poetry award, 1987, 91, Fiction award Kans. Quar./Kans. Art Commn., 1987, N.C. award for lit., 1988, Fortner award, 1993. Mem. Am. Acad. Poets, Poetry Soc. Am., New Eng. Poetry Club, N.C. Poetry Soc., N.C. Art Soc., North Caroliniana Soc., Phi Beta Kappa, Sigma Nu. Clubs: Harvard U.; Chancellors U. N.C. Address: 808 Greenwood Rd Chapel Hill NC 27514-3908 *I believe in the world seen through a temperament, and I am certain that it is always the main task of the writer to give us his personal vision of reality, objectively and subjectively explored.*

EATON, CLARA BARBOUR, retired librarian; b. Cleve., Oct. 24, 1930; d. George Willis and Lena Logan (Dulaney) Barbour; m. James Marvin Eaton, July 5, 1952 (div. July 1975); children: Jeffery George, Gary Lee. BS, Western Ky. U., 1952. Cert. librarian, Ky. Librarian Woodford County Schs., Versailles, Ky., 1952, Nortonville (Ky.) Sch., 1952-53, Anton (Ky.) Sch., 1953-54, Ea. Jr. High Sch., Owensboro, Ky., 1962-65, Emerson Elem. Sch., Owensboro, 1968-70, Owensboro Pub. Library, 1975-95. Mem. Ky. Libr. Assn., Green River Libr. Group (pres. 1984-86). Democrat. Episcopalian. Home: 621 Owen Ct Owensboro KY 42301-3641

EATON, DOREL, elementary school educator; b. Atlantic City, N.J., Sept. 08; d. Ethel Donovan Joyce; divorced; 1 child, Melissa Elizabeth Eaton-Midgley. BA in Edn., U. Fla.; MS, Barry U., 1973; Design degree, Sch. for Interior Design, Miami Shores, Fla., 1976. Cert. guidance counseling, elem. educator, Fla. Elem. edn. tchr. Dade County Pub. Sch., Miami. Art displayed in numerous galleries including The Curzon Art Gallery of Boca Raton (Fla.) Country Club, Bill Nessen's Showroom/Design Ctr. of the Americas, Dania, Fla.; contbr. Book Nat. Coalition Against Pornography. Vol. Ctr. Reclaiming Am. Named Outstanding Alumnus Barry U., 1996. Mem. MADD, Am. Family Assn., Nat. Coalition for Protection of Children and Families, U.S. Holocaust Meml. Mus. (charter mem.), Morality in Media, Inc., Prison Fellowship, Design Ctr. of the Ams., Physicians Com. for Responsible Medicine, Fla. Right to Life, Nat. Trust for Hist. Preservation. Avocations: writing, painting, reading, interior design, drama.

EATON, DORLA DEAN See KEMPER, DORLA DEAN EATON

EATON, EMMA PARKER, special education educator; b. Conway, N.C., June 21, 1945; BS in Special Edn., Norfolk State Coll., 1978; MA, Norfolk State U., 1995. Spl. edn. eduator Norfolk Pub. Schs., Va.

EATON, GARETH RICHARD, chemistry educator, university dean; b. Lockport, N.Y., Nov. 3, 1940; s. Mark Dutcher and Ruth Emma (Ruston) E.; m. Sandra Shaw, Mar. 29, 1969. BA, Harvard U., 1962; PhD, MIT, 1972. Asst. prof. chemistry U. Denver, 1972-76, assoc. prof., 1976-80, prof., 1980-97, dean natural scis., 1984-88, vice provost for rsch., 1988-89, John Evans prof., 1997—. Organizer Internat. Electron-Paramagnetic Resonance Symposium. Author, editor: 6 books, mem. editl. bd.: 4 jours.; contbr. articles to profl. jours. Lt. USN, 1962-67. Mem. AAAS, Am. Chem. Soc., Royal Soc. Chemistry (London), Internat. Soc. Magnetic Resonance, Soc. Applied Spectroscopy, Am. Phys. Soc., Internat. Electron Paramagnetic Resonance Soc. Office: U Denver Dept Chem/Biochem Denver CO 80208 E-mail: geaton@du.edu.

EATON, GARY DAVID, physician; b. South Bend, Ind., Oct. 20, 1952; s. William Joseph and Virginia Lee (Dreibelbis) E; children: Lynn, Heather, Brooke. AA in Fire Sci. Technology, Red Rocks C.C., Golden, Colo., 1978; BS in Biology, D Chiropractic Medicine, L.A. Coll. Chiropractic, Whittier, Calif., 1985; DO, U. Osteo. Med. and Health Sci., Des Moines, 1992. Diplomate Am. Acad. Disability Evaluating Physicans; bd. cert., Am. Bd. Phys. Medicine and Rehab.; cert. chiropractic physician, Utah, physician/surgeon, Mo. Firefighter, paramedic City of Aurora, Colo., 1976-82; chiropractic physician Pinehurst, Idaho, 1985-88; resident physician U. Ky., Lexington, 1992-94; staff physician, pvt. practice Tyler, Tex., 1994-95; resident U. Mo., Columbia, 1995-97; clin. fellow musculo skeletal medicine Rusk Rehab. Ctr., Columbia, 1997—98; pvt. practice, 1997—2002; med. dir. Spine and Pain Ctr. of Mo., Inc., 2002—03. Mem.: Internat. Spinal Injection Soc., Am. Bd. Phys. Medicine and Rehab. Republican. Avocations: photography, fly fishing, shotgun sports. Home: PO Box 30697 Columbia MO 65205-3697 E-mail: geaton@pol.net.

EATON, GORDON PRYOR, geologist, consultant; b. Dayton, Ohio, Mar. 9, 1929; s. Colman and Dorothy (Pryor) E.; m. Virginia Anne Gregory, June 12, 1951; children: Gretchen Maria, Gregory Mathieu. BA, Wesleyan U., 1951, Doctorate (hon.), 1995; MS, Calif. Inst. Tech., 1953, PhD, 1957; Doctorate (hon.), Colo. Sch. Mines, 2001. From instr. geology to asst. prof. Wesleyan U., Middletown, Conn., 1955-59; from asst. prof. to assoc. prof. U. Calif., Riverside, 1959-67, chmn. dept. geol. sci., 1965-67; with U.S. Geol. Survey, 1963-65, 67-81, 94-97; dep. chief Office Geochemistry and Geophysics, Washington, 1972-74; project chief geothermal geophysics Office Geochemistry Geophysics, Denver, 1974-76; scientist-in-charge Hawaiian Volcano Obs., 1976-78; assoc. chief geologist Reston, Va., 1978-81; dean Tex. A&M U. Coll. Geoscis., 1981-83; provost, v.p. acad. affairs Tex. A&M U., 1983-86; pres. Iowa State U., Ames, 1986-90; dir. Lamont-Doherty Earth Obs. Columbia U., Palisades, N.Y., 1990-94, U.S. Geol. Survey, Reston, Va., 1994-97; prin. Pac NW, SeaMountain Country, Tex., Wash., 1997—. Former mem. Com. on Internat. Edn., Am. Coun. Edn.; mem. bd. earth scis. and resources; ocean studies bd., and com. on formation of nat. biol. survey NRC, also mem. geophysics study com.; bd. dirs. Midwest Resources, Inc., Bankers Trust; mem., chair adv. com. U.S. Army Command and Gen. Staff Coll.; adv. bd. Sandia Nat. Lab. Geoscis. & Environ. Ctr.; adv. bd. Ohio State U. Ctr. Mapping. Mem. editl. bd. Jour. Volcanology and Geothermal Rsch., 1976-78; contbr. articles to profl. jours. Trustee Wesleyan U., 1995-98, Geol. Soc. Am. Found., 1999-2003; pres., bd. dirs. Iowa 4-H Found., 1986-90; mem. adv. bd. Sch. Earth Sci. Stanford (Calif.) U., 1995-2000; mem. U.S. del. sci. and tech. com. Gore-Chernomyrdin Commn., 1996-97; mem. vis. com. Colo. Sch. Mines; mem. water res. adv. com. Island Co., 2001—. Named Gordon P. Eaton Hall in his honor, Iowa State U., 2003; grantee, NSF, 1955—59; Standard Oil fellow, Calif. Inst. Tech., 1953. Fellow: AAAS, Geol. Soc. Am. Office: SeaMountain Country 705 N Snowberry Ln Ste O Coupeville WA 98239-3110 E-mail: geaton@whidbey.net.

EATON, HENRY FELIX, public relations executive; b. Cleve., Nov. 30, 1925; s. Henry F. and Stella (Simon) Eaton; m. Barbara Feder, Aug. 28, 1950; children: Deborah, Richard, David, Susan. BA, U. Chgo., 1947. Asst. advt. mgr. Kromex Corp., Cleve., 1947—48; editor Material Handling mag., Cleve., 1948—52; chmn. Dix & Eaton Inc., Cleve., 1952—2000, The Eaton Group, Cleve., 2000—. Vice chmn. bd. trustees Playhouses Sq. Found., Mus. Arts Assn., Cleve. With AUS, 1944—46. Mem.: Nat. Investor Rels. Inst., Pub. Rels. Soc. Am. (counselors sect.), Oakwood Country Club, Cleve. Racquet Club, Pepper Pike Club, Union Club. Home: 23690 Letchworth Rd Cleveland OH 44122-4110 Office: The Eaton Group 1301 E 9th St Ste 2700 Cleveland OH 44114-1882

EATON, JAMES ALONZA, humanities educator; b. Portsmouth, Va., Dec. 26, 1921; s. Lloyd Russell and Mary Louise Eaton; m. Bernice Freeman, Sept. 11, 1951 (div. Nov. 1955); 1 child, Christopher. AB, Va. State U., 1943; BD, Howard U., Washington, 1946; MA, Boston U., 1951; EdD, Columbia U., 1959. Acting chaplain Tuskegee (Ala.) Inst., 1955-56; asst. prof. psychology Ky. State Coll., Frankfort, 1957-58; prof. psychology Elizabeth City (N.C.) State Coll., 1959-63; program dir. Econ. Opportunity Authority, Savannah, Ga., 1965-67; dean grad. studies Savannah State U., 1968-81, prof. humanities, 1981-86, prof. emeritus, 1986—. Cons. Econ. Opportunity Authority, 1987—. Maj. U.S. Army, 1951-54, ETO. NEH fellow, 1980, 84. Mem. United Ch. of Christ. Avocations: photography, record collection. Home: 2323 South St Portsmouth VA 23704

EATON, JANET RUTH, lawyer, mediator; b. Cin., Dec. 25, 1947; d. Stanley Lee and Pettrila Grace (Ochs) E.; BMus Edn., Ind. U., 1969; JD, U. Cin., 1975. Bar: Ohio 1975, U.S. Dist. Ct. (so. dist.) Ohio 1975, U.S. Ct. Appeals (6th cir.) 1980; cert. master practitioner neurolinguistic programming. Staff atty. Legal Aid Soc., Cin., 1975-81; assoc. Dinsmore & Shohl, Cin., 1981-85; sole practice Cin., 1985—; assoc. Ctr. for Resolution Disputes, 1988—; adj. faculty Chase Law Sch. No. Ky. U., 1992—. Author: Your Day In Court and How To Prepare For It: Mental Health Professionals as Expert Witnesses, 1985. Trustee Mental Health Assn. Cin., 1976-87; mem. bus. relations com. Cin. Symphony Orch., 1983-86; active Cin. Symphony Assn., 1983-89. Am. Bar Found. grantee, 1972. Mem. Cin. Bar Assn., Acad. Family Mediators (practitioner). Democrat. Office: 2250 Kroger Bldg 1014 Vine St Cincinnati OH 45202-1141

EATON, JOE OSCAR, federal judge; b. Monticello, Fla., Apr. 2, 1920; s. Robert Lewis and Mamie (Gireadeau) E. AB, Presbyn. Coll., 1941, LLD (hon.), 1979; LLB, U. Fla., 1948. Pvt. practice law, Miami, Fla., 1948-51, 55-59; asst. state atty. Dade County, Fla., 1953; circuit judge Miami, 1954-55, 59-67; mem. Fla. Senate, 1956-59; mem. law firm Eaton & Achor, Miami, 1955-58, Sams, Anderson, Eaton & Alper, Miami, 1958-59; judge U.S. Dist. Ct. (so. dist.) Fla., 1967-83, chief judge, 1983-85, sr. judge, 1985—. Instr. law U. Miami Coll. Law, 1954-56 Served with USAAF, 1941-45; Served with USAF, 1951-52. Decorated D.F.C., Air medal. Mem.: Kiwanian. Methodist.

EATON, JOEL DOUGLAS, lawyer; b. Miami, Fla., Oct. 31, 1943; s. Joe Oscar and Patricia (MacVicar) E.; m. Mary Benson, June 24, 1967; children: Douglas, Darryl, David. BA, Yale U., 1965; JD, Harvard U., 1975. Bar: Fla. 1975, U.S. Dist. Ct. (so. dist.) Fla. 1976, U.S. Ct. Appeals (5th cir.) 1976, U.S. Supreme Ct. 1978, U.S. Ct. Appeals (11th cir.) 1981, U.S. Ct. Appeals (Fed. cir.) 1996. Ptnr. Podhurst Orseck, P.A. and predecessors, Miami, 1975—. With USN, 1965-71. Decorated Air medal with Bronze Star and numeral 14, Navy Commendation medal with 2 gold stars, Cross of Gallantry (Viet Nam). Mem. ABA, ATLA, Am. Law Inst., Acad. Fla. Trial Lawyers, Fla. Bar Assn. (appellate rules com. 1981-2002, chmn. 1989-90, jud. evaluation com. 1995-98, Fla. std. jury instn. com. 1998—), Am. Acad. Appellate Lawyers. Democrat. Office: Podhurst Orseck PA 25 W Flagler St Ste 800 Miami FL 33130-1720 E mail: jeaton@podhurst.com.

EATON, JOHN C. composer, educator; b. Bryn Mawr, Pa., Mar. 30, 1935; s. Harold C. and Fannie E. (Geer) E.; m. Nelda E. Nelson, May 31, 1973; children: Elizabeth Estela, Julian R.P. AB, Princeton U., N.J., 1957, MFA, 1959. Performing artist Columbia Artists, N.Y.C., 1961-65; prof. music Ind. U., Bloomington, 1970—, U. Chgo., 1991—. Composer-in-residence Am. Acad., Rome, Italy, 1975-76; lectr. Salzburg Seminar in Am. Studies, Austria, 1976; honored guest Soviet Composers Soc., 1977 Composer numerous operas, most recently: Myshkin, 1972 (Peabody award 1972), Danton and Robespierre, 1978, The Cry of Clytaemnestra, 1980, The Tempest, 1985 (Santa Fe Commn.), The Reverend Jim Jones, 1988, Peer Gynt, 1989, Let's Get This Show on the Road, 1993, Don Quixote, 1994, Golk, 1995, Travelling with Gulliver, 1997, Antigone, 1999, ...inasmuch, 2002, numerous chamber orchs. and elec. comps.; featured in numerous articles in profl. jours. Recipient Prix de Rome, Am. Acad., Rome, 1959-62; citation Am. Inst. Arts and Letters, 1972; plaque Ind. Arts Council, 1975; MacArthur award, 1990; Guggenheim fellow, 1962, 65 Achievements include being called the most interesting opera composer writing in America today. Office: U Chgo Dept Music Chicago IL 60637 E-mail: eat2@midway.uchicago.edu.

EATON, JOSEPH W. sociology educator; b. Nuremburg, Germany, Sept. 28, 1919; s. Jacob and Flora (Wechsler) E.; m. Helen Goodman, June 8, 1947; children: David, Seth, Debra, Jonathan. BS, Cornell U., 1940; PhD, Columbia U., 1948. Faculty Wayne State U., Detroit, 1947-56; lectr. then vis. prof. Sch. Social Welfare, U. Calif. at Los Angeles, 1956-60; prof. social work rsch. U. Pitts., 1960-70, dir. advanced program, 1966-69, prof. sociology in pub. health and social work research, 1970-73; prof. sociology in pub. health and social work rsch. Sch. Pub. and Internat. Affairs, 1974—, prof., later dir. program in econ. and social devel.; co-dir. U.S. Comparative Mgmt. Survey Title Ins., 1999—. Russell Sage Found. vis. prof. We. Res. U. (Med. Sch.), 1958-59; project dir. Conf. on Social Welfare Consequences of Migration and Residential Movement, 1969; dir. instn. bldg. program Interuniv. Rsch. Consortium, 1966-71; curriculum cons., later dir. social work and social adminstrn. program U. Haifa, Israel, 1970-74 USIA cons., lectr., Africa, 1979, Sweden, Fed. Republic Germany, 1982, 86, Romania, 1982, Abu Dhabi, Pakistan, Egypt, Sudan, Israel, 1986, Nepal, Pakistan, Egypt, Ethiopia, Iraq, 1988, Yugoslavia, USSR, 1989; Fulbright lectr. and cons., 1979, NAS. guest scholar in Poland and German Dem. Republic, 1980; co-dir. Jordan River Basin Water Resources Devel., U.S. Inst. Peace, 1992—; co-investigator search for inherited causes of schizophrenia in a genetically isolated cmty., 1997—; co-prin. investigator A Pub. Policy-Oriented Audit of Title Ins., 1999—. Author: (with Saul M. Katz) Research Guide on Cooperative Group Farming, 1942, Exploring Tomorrow's Agriculture, 1943, (with Albert Mayer) Man's Capacity to Reproduce, 1954, (with Robert J. Weil) Culture and Mental Disorders, 1955, (with Kenneth Polk) Measuring Delinquency, 1961, Stone Walls Not a Prison Make: The Anatomy of Planned Adminstrative Change, 1962, Prisons in Israel, 1964, (with Michael Chen) Influencing the Youth Culture: A Study of Youth Organization in Israel, 1970, The Rurban Village, 1980, Can Business Save South Africa, 1980, Card Carrying Americans: Security, Privacy and the National ID Card Controversy, 1986, (with Yuri Lvov) Capitalist Communism, 1991, The Privacy Card: A Low Cost Strategy to Combat Terrorism, 2003; also contbr. chpts. to books, articles to profl. jours.; editor: Institution Building and Development, 1972. Mem. cable svc. adv. com. City of Pitts. City Coun., 1994—, chmn., mem. cable comm. adv. com., 1996—. With AUS, 1941-46. Faculty Rsch. fellow Social Sci. Rsch. Coun., 1962 Mem. NASW (chmn. rsch. coun. 1968-71), Internat. Assn. Social Psychiatry (coun. 1969-72). Home: 1008 Summerset Dr Pittsburgh PA 15217-2535 Office Fax: 412-421-4288.

EATON, KATHERINE GIRTON, retired library educator; b. St. Paul, Mar. 9, 1924; d. John Frances and Mary Ahleen (Peck) Girton; m. Burt Elliott Eaton, Oct. 18, 1947; children: John Girton, Marilee Eaton Warkentin, David Elliott. BA in Journalism, U. Minn., 1944; MS in Journalism, U. Oreg., 1952, MLS, 1968. Reporter Bakersfield Calif., 1945 46; women's editor Rochester (Minn.) Post Bulletin, 1946-47; legal sec. Broady Law Offices, St. Paul, 1949-51; editor Oreg. State System Higher Edn., Eugene, 1952-53; cons. Oreg. State Libr., Salem, 1968-70; head pub. affairs libr. U. Oreg., Eugene, 1970-85, assoc. prof. emerita, 1985—. Author and editor rsch. reports. Chmn. Lane County Mental Health Bd., Eugene, 1964-88, Lane County Libr. Bd., 1981-85, Eugene City Budget Com., 1986-92, Citizens for Lane County Librs., 1980—, Human Resources Planning Project, Lane County, 1986-89, Oreg. Mental Health Svcs. Planning and Mgmt. Coun., 1988—, chmn., 1996-99; founding bd. dirs. Passages, Lane County substance abuse residential program for offenders, 1990-2001; pres. Wilani coun. Camp Fire Inc., 1967-68, nat. bd. dirs., 1966-70, N.W. regional chmn. 1966-70; adv. bd. Oreg. State Mental Health, 1989-2003, chmn. 1999-2003; mem. elections team LWV, Hungary, 1993; mem. U.S. State Dept. Bosnia Elections Supr., 1997, 2000; coord., convener Oreg. Women's Summit, 1996—. Named Outstanding Young Woman, Eugene Jaycettes, 1956, Outstanding Women of Yr., Lane County Orgns., 1974; recipient Gulick, Seaton, Hiitina awards Camp Fire, Inc., 1959, 66, 71, Outstanding Lib. Pub. award The Wilson Co., 1993, U. Oreg. Disting. Svc. award, 1997, Soroptimist Internat. Women of Distinction award, 1998, OASIS Sr. Role Model award, 1998, Adult Vol. of Yr. award J.C. Penney/United Way, 2000. Mem. AAUP (bd. dirs. U. Oreg. 1976-85, pres. 1977-78), ALA (coun. 1976-80), AAUW (del. NGO women's forum Kenya 1985, China 1995), Oreg. Libr. Assn. (hon. life, pres. 1973-74), Nat. Coun. Planning Librs. (pres. 1978-79, 88-89, Disting. Svc. award 1994), Pacific N.W. Libr. Assn. (editor, quar 1985-96, hon. life), Internat. Fedn. Univ. Women (coun. mem. 1983-85), Assn. Oreg. Faculties (state bd. dirs. 1981-89, v.p. 1983-85), AAUW (pres. Oreg. 1975-77, pres. nat. legal adv. fund 1981-85, nat. exec. v.p. 1981-85, Eugene-Lane branch pres. 1962-63), LWV Oreg. (1st v.p. 1989-91, pres. 1991-93, disting. svc. award 1995), LWV Lane County (pres. 1963-65, 97-99), Oreg. Women's Rights Coalition (pres. 1994-2001), Virginia Gildersleeve Internat. Fund (archival historian, bd. dirs. 1995—, 1st v.p. 1999-2002), Social Order of Beaucean (pres. 1993, 96). Democrat. Presbyterian. Avocations: beach combing, mystery reading, lobbying.

EATON, LARRY RALPH, lawyer; b. Quincy, Ill., Aug. 18, 1944; s. Roscoe Ralph and Velma Marie (Beckett) E.; m. Janet Claire Rosen, Oct. 28, 1978. BA, Western Ill. U., 1965; JD, U. Mich., 1968. Bar: Ill. 1968, U.S. Dist. Ct. (no. dist.) Ill. 1978, U.S. Ct. Appeals (D.C. cir.) 1984, U.S. Ct. Appeals (7th cir.) 1989, N.Y. 1997. Vol., instr. law U. Liberia Sch. Law, U.S. Peace Corps, Monrovia, 1968-70; lawyer Forest Park Found., Peoria Heights, Ill., 1970-71; asst. atty. gen. State of Ill., Springfield, 1971-75; ptnr. Peterson & Ross and predecessors, Chgo., 1975-94; founder Blatt, Hammesfahr & Eaton, Chgo., 1994-2000; sr. mem. Cozen O'Connor, Chgo., 2000—. Instr. environ. law Quincy Coll., Ill., 1973-75. Bd. dirs. Edgewater Cmty. Coun., Chgo., 2000—; pres. Lakewood Balmoral Residents' Coun., Chgo., 2000—02; bd. dirs. Near North Montessori Sch., 1989—95, vice chmn., 1992—95; bd. dirs., v.p. Edgewater Devel. Corp., 2000—, v.p., 0002—. Contbg. writer Chgo. Daily Law Bull., 1975-77; field editor Pollution Engring., 1976. Fellow: Ill. Bar Found. (charter); mem.: ABA (environ. ins. litig. task force 1990), Bar Assn. for 7th Jud. Cir., Chgo. Bar Assn., Ill. Bar Assn. (editor sect. newsletter 1972—77, coun. 1973—77, chmn. environ. control law sect. 1976—77, assembly 1980—86, 1989—92, coun. 1990—94, coun. jud. evaluation Cook County 2000—), Atticus Finch Inn of Ct., Lawyers Club Chgo., Law Club Chgo.

EATON, LEONARD JAMES, JR., aerospace executive; b. N.Y.C., Sept. 18, 1934; s. Leonard James and Alice Edna (Leach) E.; m. Patricia Pride, Nov. 30, 1957; children: Leslie, Pamela, Alexander. BA, Cornell U., 1956; postgrad., Harvard, 1971. With First Nat. City Bank, N.Y.C., 1956-71; exec. v.p. Bank of Okla. N.A. (formerly Nat. Bank of Tulsa), 1972-73, pres., 1973-78, chmn. bd., chief exec. officer, 1978-91, also dir.; dir. fin. The Nordam Group, 1993—2001; pres. World Travel Svc., Tulsa, 2001—. Regent Okla. State Regents for Higher Edn.; mem. adv. coun. Harry Ransom Humanities Rsch. Ctr. U. Tex. at Austin; bd. trustees Meadville/Lombard Theol. Sch. affiliated with U. Chgo.; dir. Okla. chpt. The Nature Conservancy. Mem. Met. Tulsa C. of C. (bd. dirs.). Office: World Travel Svc LLC 5727 S Lewis Ste 120 Tulsa OK 74105

EATON, LEONARD KIMBALL, retired architecture educator; b. Mpls., Feb. 3, 1922; s. Leo Kimball and Elizabeth (Barber) E.; m. Ann Valentine White, Dec. 24, 1979; children— Mark. R., Elisabeth K. BA, Williams Coll., 1943; MA, Harvard U., 1948, PhD, 1951. Mem. faculty U. Mich., Ann Arbor, 1950-89, prof. architecture, 1963-89. Author: New England Hospitals, 1790-1833, 1956, Landscape Artist in America, 1964, Two Chicago Architects and Their Clients, 1969, American Architecture Comes of Age, 1972, Gateway Cities and Other Essays, 1989, also numerous articles, revs.; book rev. editor Jour. Soc. Archtl. Historians, 1967-69 Democratic candidate for coun., City of Ann Arbor, 1957. With AUS, World War II, MTO. Decorated Bronze Star; recipient Finlandia award Finlandia Soc. Met. N.Y., 1965; Ford Found. faculty fellow, 1954-55 Mem. Soc. Archtl. Historians (bd. dirs. 1957-58), Phi Beta Kappa Clubs: Army-Navy (Washington). Home: PO Box 300 Otter Rock OR 97369-0300

EATON, MERRILL THOMAS, psychiatrist, educator; b. Howard County, Ind., June 25, 1920; s. Merrill Thomas and Dorothy (Whiteman) E.; m. Louise Foster, Dec. 23, 1942; children: Deirdre Ann, Thomas Anthony, David Foster. AB, Ind. U., Bloomington, 1941, MD, 1944. Diplomate: Am. Bd. Psychiatry. Intern St. Elizabeth's Hosp., Washington, 1944-45; resident Sheppard and Enoch Pratt Hosp., Towson, Md., 1948-49; pvt. practice medicine specializing in psychiatry Kansas City, Kans., 1949-60, Omaha, 1960-2000; dir. Nebr. Psychiat. Inst., 1968-85; assoc. in psychiatry Kans. U. Sch. Medicine, 1949-50, asst. prof., 1951-54, assoc. prof., 1954-60; assoc. prof. psychiatry U. Nebr. Coll. Medicine, 1960-63, prof., 1963-88, prof. emeritus, 1989—, chmn. dept. psychiatry, 1968-85; psychiatrist Immanuel Mental Health Ctr., 1986-88; pvt. practice cons. Omaha, 1989-2000. Author: Psychiatry, 1967, 5th edit., 1985, (with David Kentsmith) Treating Sexual Problems in Medical Practice, 1979. Served to capt. U.S. Army, 1945-47. Fellow ACP, Am. Psychiat. Assn., mem. Group for Advancement Psychiatry (chmn. com. on mental health services 1970-73, chmn. publ. bd. 1976-83, cons. pub. bd. 1983—, bd. dirs. 1984-86), Nebr. Med. Assn., Nebr. Psychiat. Soc. (pres. 1973-75).

EATON, MICHAEL CHRISTOPHER, accounting technician; b. Columbus, Ohio, Aug. 8, 1959; s. Ronald Andrew and Rosaleen Ann (Murnane) E.; m. Charlene Ann Gutmann, Nov. 6, 1993. AS, Burlington C.C., 1984. Contracting specialist Def. Supply Ctr., Columbus, 1996—. Active Feinstein Found. to Help Hunger. Sgt. USAF, 1980-86. Mem. K.C. (chancellor 1994—, 4th degree 1994, Dep. Grand Knight 1996-2000, Grand Knight 2001--, Sir Knight), DAV (life), AMVETS (life), Am. Legion, Cath. War Vets. Republican. Roman Catholic. Home: 720 E Mithoff St Columbus OH 43206-2956 Office: DSCC Columbus Ctr 3990 E Broad St Columbus OH 43218-2662

EATON, NANCY RUTH LINTON, librarian, university dean; b. Berkeley, Calif., May 2, 1943; d. Don Thomas and Lena Ruth (McClellan) Linton; m. Edward Arthur Eaton III, June 19, 1965 (div. 1980) AB, Stanford U., 1965; MLS, U. Tex., 1968, postgrad., 1969. From cataloger to asst. to dir. U. Tex. Libr., Austin, 1968-74; automation libr. SUNY, Stony Brook, 1974-76; head tech. svcs. Atlanta Pub. Libr., 1976-82; dir. libr. U. Vt., Burlington, 1982-89; dean libr. svcs. Iowa State U., Ames, 1989-97; dean univ. librs. Pa. State U., University Park, Pa., 1997—. Bd. dir. Ctr. for Rsch. Libr., 1988-92, chair, 1989-90; del. user's coun., mem. exec. com. Online Computer Libr. Ctr., Inc., Dublin, Ohio, 1980-82, 86-88, trustee, 1987-2002, chair bd. trustees 1992-96; mgr. Nat. Agrl. Text Digitalizing Project, 1986-92; bd. dir. New Eng. Libr. Network, 1987-89; chair steering com. Digital Libr. Fedn., 2000-2002; mem. adv. bd. Nat. Digital Info. Infrastructure and Preservation Program, 2001-2002. Co-author: Optical Information Systems: Implementation Issues for Libraries, 1988.; co-editor: A Cataloging Sampler, 1971, Book Selection Policies in American Libraries, 1972; contbr. articles to profl. jours. U.S. Office of Edn. post-master's fellow, 1969; Dept. Edn. Title II-C grantee, 1985, 87-88, Title II-D grantee, 1992-96. Mem. ALA, Libr. and Info. Tech. Assn. (pres. 1984-85, bd. dirs. 1980-86), Assn. Rsch. Librs. (bd. dirs. 1994-97), Digital Libr. Fedn. (exec. com. 1997-2003), Coalition for Networked Info. (steering com. 1999—). Democrat. Avocations: tennis, walking. Home: 441 Homan Ave State College PA 16801-6337 Office: Pa State Univ 510 Paterno Library University Park PA 16802-1812

EATON, PAULINE, artist, educator; b. Neptune, N.J., Mar. 20, 1935; d. Paul A. and Florence Elizabeth (Rogers) Friedrich; m. Charles Adams Eaton, June 15, 1957; children: Gregory, Eric, Paul, Joy. BA, Dickinson Coll., 1957; MA, Northwestern U., 1958. Lic. instr. Calif. Instr. Mira Costa Coll., Oceanside, Calif., 1980-82, Idyllwild Sch. Music and Arts, Calif., 1983—; instr. dept. continuing edn. U. N.Mex. Juror, demonstrator numerous art socs. One-woman shows include Nat. Arts Club, N.Y.C., 1977, Designs Recycled Gallery, Fullerton, Calif., 1978, 1980, 1984, San Diego Art Inst., 1980, Spectrum Gallery, San Diego, 1981, San Diego Jung Ctr., 1983, Marin Civic Ctr. Gallery, 1984, R. Mondavi Winery, 1987, exhibited in group shows at Am. Watercolor Soc., 1975, 1977, Butler Inst. Am. Art, Youngstown, Ohio, 1977—79, 1981, NAD, 1978, N.Mex Arts and Crafts Fair, 1994 (Best in Show award), Corrales Bosque Gallery, Represented in permanent collections Butler Inst. Am. Art, St. Mary's Coll., Md., Mercy Hosp., San Diego, Sharp Hosp., Redlands Hosp., Riverside; work featured in: book Watercolor, The Creative Experience, 1978, Creative Seascape Painting, 1980, Painting the Spirit in Nature, 1984, Exploring Painting (Gerald Brommer); author: Crawling to the Light, An Artist in Transition, 1987; author: (with Mary Ann Beckwith) Best of Watercolor Texture, 1997; contbr. chapters to books. Trustee San Diego Art Inst., 1977—78, San Diego Mus. Art, 1982—83. Recipient award, Hollywood (Calif.) Form Arts, 1986, Grumbacker award, Conf. 96 Hill Country Art Ctr., 2d award, Tex. Friends and Neighbors, Irving, 2000, award of excellence, Ariz. Aqueous, Tubac, 2002, Originals award, N.Mex. Women in Arts, Albuquerque Mus., 2003. Mem.: Soc. Layerists Multi-Media (bd. dirs. 1992—), Eastbay

Watercolor Soc. (v.p. 1988—90), W. Coast Watercolor Soc. (exhbns. chmn. 1983—86, pres. 1989—92), Western Fedn. Watercolor Socs. (chmn. 1983, 3d prize 1982, Grumbacher Gold medal 1983), N.Mex Watercolor Soc. (Grumbacker award, Wingspread award 1999), San Diego Artists Guild (pres. 1982—83), Artists Equity (v.p. San Diego 1979—81), San Diego Watercolor Soc. (pres. 1976—77, workshop dir. 1977—80), Marin Arts Guild (instr. 1984—87), Internat. Soc. Exptl. Artists (Nautilus Merit award 1992, 1998), Watercolor W. (Strathmore award 1979, Purchase award 1986), Rocky Mountain Watermedia Soc. (Golden award 1979, Mustard Seed award 1983), Nat. Watercolor Soc., Watercolor USA Soc. (hon. Veloy Vigil Meml. award 1986), Nat. Soc. Painters Acrylic an dCasein (hon.). Democrat. Home: 68 Hop Tree Trl Corrales NM 87048-9613 E-mail: pfeaton@earthlink.net.

EATON, RICHARD GILLETTE, surgeon, educator; b. Forty Fort, Pa., Dec. 3, 1929; s. Walter L. and Ruth (Shaw) E.; BA, Franklin and Marshall Coll., 1951; MD, U. Pa., 1955; m. Du Ree Hunter, June 13, 1954; children: Bradford (dec.), Holly, Hillary. Intern, U. Pa. Grad. Hosp., 1956; gen. surg. resident Peter Bent Brigham Hosp., Boston, 1957; orthop. resident Children's Hosp. Med. Center, Mass. Gen. Hosp. and Peter Bent Brigham Hosp., Boston, 1959-62; hand surgery fellow J.W. Littler, Roosevelt Hosp., N.Y.C., 1962, now attending orthop. surgery and reconstrn., chief hand surgery service, ret. 2002 emeritus; prof. emeritus clin. orthop. surgery Columbia Coll. Physicians and Surgeons, N.Y.C. Ruling elder Huguenot Presbyn. Ch., Pelham, N.Y. Capt., M.C., U.S. Army, 1957-59. NIH fellow, 1963-64. Diplomate Am. Bd. Orthop. Surgeons. Mem. Am. Acad. Orthop. Surgery, Am. Orthop. Assn., Am. Soc. Surgery of Hand, A.C.S., Interurban Orthop. Club, N.Y. Acad. Medicine, J.W. Littler Soc., N.Y. Soc. Surgery of Hand. Author: Joint Injuries of the Hand, 1971; contbr. articles to profl. jours. Home: 640 Ely Ave Pelham NY 10803-2402

EATON, SABRINA CATHERINE ELIZABETH, journalist; b. N.Y.C., Mar. 5, 1965; d. Barton Denis and Anne Elizabeth (Schaeffer) Eaton; life ptnr. Wendy Ann Rodgers; children: Isaac Nicholas, Gillian Elizabeth Rodgers Eaton. BA, U. Pa., 1985. Correspondent The Record, Hackensack, N.J., 1985-87; reporter Daily Record, Morristown, N.J., 1987-88; Washington correspondent States News Svc., Washington, 1988-90; metro reporter The Plain Dealer, Cleve., 1990-94, Washington correspondent Washington, 1994—. Mem. DAR, Nat. Press Club, Nat. Lesbian and Gay Journalists Assn., Investigative Reporters and Editors. Episcopalian. Office: The Plain Dealer Wash Bur 930 National Press Building Washington DC 20045-1928

EATON, SHIRLEY M. medical/surgical nurse; b. Charleston, SC; d. Benjamin W. Randall Sr. and Rena B. Randall; children: Everett Kennedy, Eran Margret Eaton Parker. MPH, So. Conn. U., 1997. RN Conn. Nurse, SC and Conn., 1960—; mem. staff ombudsman program Norwalk (Conn.) Social Svcs., 1996—. Mem. adv. coun. Area of Nursing, Norwalk, 1997—. Author: Handbook for Caregivers to the Elderly, 1998. Presbyterian. Avocations: singing, sewing, writing, travel, designing.

EATON, THOMAS, state legislator; b. Keene, N.H. children: Kristin, Tom Jr. Grad., New Eng. Inst. Anatomy. Pres., treas. Fletcher Funeral Home, Keene; mem. N.H. Senate from 10th Dist., Concord, 2000—, dep. majority leader, chmn. trans. com., 2000—, mem. fin., ways and means, environment coms., 2000—, mem. wildlife and recreation coms., 2000—, pres., 2002—. Bd. trustees Cheshire Med. Ctr., Cedarcrest, the Home Health & Cmty. Svcs. Bd., Cheshire County chpt. ARC, Cheshire County Crimestoppers; active Keene Family YMCA. Mem. Greater Keene C. of C., Lions, Elks, Masons, Shriner, Old Homestead Garden Club. E-mail: senate10Ajuno.com. Home: 27 Pheasant Hill Rd Keene NH 03431 Office: State House Rm 302 State House Bldg Concord NH 03301*

EATON, THOMAS R. state legislator, retired funeral director; b. Keene, NH, Nov. 23, 1949; BA, Upsala Coll., East Orange, N.J., 1971. Mem. Dist. 10 NH Senate, Concord, 1999; senate pres., 2002—. Mem. fin., fiscal, rules and enr. bills. Leadership positions with Cheshire Med. Ctr. Cheshire co. Red Cross, Keene Chamb. of Com. Named one of NH's "Ten Most Powerful" by Business NH Mag. Mem. Keene Lions Club, Keene Elks Club and Jerusalem Masonic Lodge. Office: State House Rm 302 Concord NH 03301

EATON, WILLIAM A. federal agency administrator; Degree magna cum laude, U. Va., 1978. Polit. and consular officer U.S. Dept. of State, Georgetown, Guyana, 1979—81, gen. svcs. officer Moscow, 1982—84; spl. asst. to asst. sec. adminstrn. U.S. Dept of State, 1984; spl. asst. to asst. sec. for diplomatic security U.S. Dept. of State, 1985—86; spl. asst. to under sec. state for mgmt. U.S. Dept. of State, 1986—87, adminstrv. officer, 1988—89, coord. in office of dep. sec. state, 1992—94, adminstrv. officer, 1993—94, adminstrv. counselor Ankara, Turkey, 1994—98, exec. dir. of bus. European affairs, 1998—2000, sr. adviser to under sec. for mgmt., 2001; asst. sec. state for adminstrn. U.S. Dept. State, Washington, 2001—; dir. internat. ops. Young Pres. Orgn., 1989—90, exec. dir., 1991—92. Former reporter, news editor Shenandoah Valley Herald, Woodstock, Va. Recipient Va. Press Assn. award. Office: US Dept of State Adminstrn 2201 C St NW Washington DC 20520-6310 Office Fax: 202-647-1558.

EATON, WILLIAM EDWARD, education educator; b. Cedar Rapids, Iowa, Feb. 19, 1943; s. Edward Loftus and Helen Christine (Carlson) E.; m. Judith Ann Kukarola, Mar. 30, 1964; children: Gregory Melville, Leslie Ann. BS in Edn., Ea. Ill. U., 1965; MS in Edn., So. Ill. U., 1968; PhD in Edn., Washington U., St. Louis, 1971. Tchr. Granite City (Ill.) High Sch., 1965-68; from asst. prof. to prof. dept. edn. adminstrn. So. Ill. U., Carbondale, 1971-85, prof., chmn. dept. edn. adminstrn. and higher edn., 1985—2000. Author: A.F.T.: History of the Movement, 1975, (with Lawrence Dennis) George S. Counts: Educator for a New Age, 1985, (with A. Lean) Education or Catastrophe, 1990; editor: Shaping the Superintendency, 1991. Mem. History of Edn. Soc., John Dewey Soc. Home: 26 Pinewood Dr Carbondale IL 62901-5200 Office: So Ill U Dept Adminstrn & Higher Edn Carbondale IL 62901-4606

EAVES, ALLEN CHARLES EDWARD, hematologist, medical agency administrator; b. Ottawa, Ont., Can., Feb. 19, 1941; s. Charles and Margaret E.; m. Connie Jean Halperin, July 1, 1975; children: Neil, Rene, David, Sara. BSc, Acadia U., Wolfville, N.S., Can., 1962; MSc, Dalhousie U., Halifax, N.S., 1964, MD, 1969; PhD, U. Toronto, Ont., Can., 1974. Intern Dalhousie U., Halifax, N.S., Can., 1968-69; resident in internal medicine Sunnybrook Hosp., Toronto, 1974-75, Vancouver Gen. Hosp., 1975-79; dir. Terry Fox Lab., Cancer Control Agy. B.C., Vancouver, Can., 1980—; asst. prof. medicine U. B.C., 1979-83, assoc. prof., 1983-88, head div. hematology, 1985—2003, prof., 1988—; pres. StemCell Technologies Inc., Vancouver, 1993—, Malachite Mgmt. Inc., 1996—, StemSoft Software Inc., 2000—. Treas. Found. for Accreditation of Hematopoetic Cell Therapy, 1995-2002. Fellow Royal Coll. Physicians (Can.), ACP; mem. Internat. Soc. Hematotherapy and Graft Engring. (pres. 1995-97), Am. Soc. Blood and Marrow Transplantation (pres. elect 1998-99, pres. 1999-2000). Home: 2705 W 31st Ave Vancouver BC Canada V6L 1Z9 Office: Terry Fox Lab 601 W 10th Ave Vancouver BC Canada V5Z 1L3 E-mail: aeaves@bccancer.bc.ca.

EAVES, GEORGE NEWTON, lecturer, consultant, research administrator; b. Athens, Tenn., Mar. 12, 1935; s. Felmont Farrell and Margaret Isobel (Dobson) E. BA, U. Chattanooga, 1957; MS, U. Tenn., 1959; PhD, Wayne State U. Sch. Medicine, 1962. Postdoctoral fellow Bryn Mawr Coll., Pa., 1963-65; postdoctoral fellow, guest investigator The Rockefeller U., N.Y.C., 1970-71; exec. sec. molecular biology study sect. NIH, Bethesda, Md., 1967-73; exec. sect. Nat. Heart and Lung Adv. Coun., NIH, Bethesda, 1973-74; assoc. staff dir. Pres.'s Biomed. Rsch. Panel, Washington, 1974-76; dep. dir. Divsn. Blood Diseases and Resources, NIH, Bethesda, 1976-83, dep. dir. Divsn. of Stroke and Trauma, 1983-94. Lectr. on tech. writing, grant applications and peer rev.; bd. dirs. Cyclotec Med. Industries, Inc.; asst. prof. Washington and Jefferson Coll., 1962-63. Cons. editor Procs. NAS, 1973-76; mem. editl. bd. Grants Mag., 1978-81, Nonprofit Mgmt. and Fin., 1981—; contbr. articles to tech. jours. and chpts. to sci. books. Mem. adv. coun. Park and Tree Commn., City of Savannah, 1994—. Recipient Citation for Profl. Achievement, McDonnell Douglas Corp., 1968, NIH Dir.'s award, 1976, 86, Sustained High Quality Performance award NIH, 1970, 74, 79, Spl. Achievement award HHS, 1989, Spl. Recognition award Pub. Health Svc., 1990. Mem. Sigma Xi. Republican. Anglican. Avocation: church organist. Home: 110 W Gordon St Savannah GA 31401-4909

EAVES, RONALD CLARK, special education educator; b. San Antonio, July 19, 1944; s. Andrew Jackson and Frances Louise (Wernette) E.; m. Judith Ann Dudek, May 6, 1964 (div. Aug. 1978); children: Tyson Brett, Tracy Jean; m. Ellis (Lisa) Bliss, Aug. 8, 1980; 1 child, Jackson Penn Kitchell. BA, U. Fla., 1967, MEd, 1968; PhD, U. Ga., 1974. Cert. tchr. emotionally disturbed, Ga., Pa., sch. psychologist, Pa. Tchr. Vanguard Sch., Ft. Lauderdale, Fla., 1968-71; asst. prof. Pa. State U., University Park, 1973-77; assoc. prof. Auburn (Ala.) U., 1977-83, prof., 1984—. Author: Recent Advances in Special Education and Rehabilitation, 1993; author (test): Slosson Full-Range Intelligence Test, 1993; contbr. to books, 1978, 91, 96, 98, also over 70 articles to profl. jours. Fellow U.S. Office Edn., U. Fla., 1967-68, U. Ga., 1971-73. Mem. Am. Assn. Ednl. Rsch., Coun. Exceptional Children (div. learning disabilities), Coun. Ednl. Diagnostic Svcs. Republican. Mem. Christian Sci. Ch. Avocations: horses, cars. Office: Auburn U 1228 Haley Ctr Auburn AL 36849

EAVES, SANDRA AUSTRA, social worker; b. Chgo., Aug. 30, 1960; m. Gerald Eaves, Oct. 7, 1989. BA, Northwestern U., 1982; MSW, Loyola U., Chgo., 1984. Social worker Chgo. Pub. Schs., 1982-83, Cook County Hosp., Chgo., 1983-84; pvt. practice, 1990—. Mem. NASW, Tex. Soc. for Clin. Social Work. Lutheran. Avocations: sports, pottery, classical piano.

EAVES, STEPHEN DOUGLAS, educator, vocational administrator; b. Honolulu, Aug. 30, 1944; s. Alfred Aldee and Phyllis Clarissa (Esty) E.; m. Sally Ann Winslow, Apr. 27, 1974; children: Trevor Bernard, Lindsay Douglas, Christian Francis. BA in Polit. Sci., U. Hawaii, 1967; MS in Bus. Mgmt., U. Ark., 1974; PhD in Edn. Adminstrn., Colo. State U., 1997. Cert. secondary tchr., prin., vocat. dir., post secondary bus. tchr., Colo. Commd. 2d lt. USAF, 1967, advanced through grades to lt. col., ret., 1989; aerospace sci. tchr. Adams County Sch. Dist. 50, Westminster, Colo., 1989-94, vocat. dir./prin., 1994—. Cons. Dept. of Edn., Colo., 1993—. Eucharistic min. Spirit of Christ Cath. Ch., Arvada, Colo., 1989—. Decorated Silver Star, DFC, Air medals, Commendation medals, Air Force Achievement medal; named Outstanding Tchr. Focus on Excellence Program, 1992, Outstanding Nat. Aerospace Sci. Tchr., 1994. Mem. ASCD, Coun. for Exceptional Children, Am. Vocat. Assn., Colo. Vocat. Assn., Colo. Assn. Vocat. Adminstrs., Colo. Assn. Sch. Execs., Am. Nat. Rose Soc., Royal Nat. Rose Soc., Lions (sec. Adams Centennial chpt. 1991-92, Lion of Yr. 1992), Elks, Phi Delta Kappa, Omicron Tau Delta. Avocations: snow skiing, rose gardening. Home: 8708 Independence Way Arvada CO 80005-1247 Office: Career Enrichment Park 7300 Lowell Blvd Westminster CO 80030-4821

EAVES, STEPHEN R. music educator; b. Nashville, Tenn., Aug. 9, 1963; s. Calvin Denton and Jo Ellen Eaves; m. Linda L. Stover, Jan. 6, 1996; children: Sam, Holly. B Music Edn., Union U., 1986; MusM, U. Miss., 1990; D of Conducting, U. S.C., 1999. Choral dir. Fayette-Ware H.S., Somerville, Tenn., 1986—88, Morton H.S., Morton, Miss., 1990—92; dir. choral activities Roane State C.C., Harriman, Tenn., 1992—99, McMurry U., Abilene, Tex., 1999—. Vol. YWCA, Abilene, 1999—, Zion Luth. Ch., Abilene, 1999—. Mem.: Tex. Music Educators Assn., Am. Choral Dirs. Assn. Avocations: travel, reading. Office: McMurry Univ S 14th St & Sayles Ave Abilene TX 79697

EBACHER, ROGER, archbishop; b. Amos, Que., Can., Oct. 6, 1936; Ordained priest Roman Cath. Ch., 1961; ordained bishop of Diocese of Baie-Comeau, Que., 1979; chevalier de Colomb de 4e degré, 1983; apptd. bishop Diocese of Gatineau-Hull, Que., 1988, archbishop, 1990—. Roman Catholic. Address: 180 Mont-Bleu Hull QC Canada J8Z 3J5 E-mail: archeveque@diocesegatineau-hull.qc.ca.

EBASHI, SETSURO, scientist, educator; b. Tokyo, Aug. 31, 1922; s. Haruyoshi and Hisaji (Watanabe) E.; m. Fumiko Takeda, May 20, 1956. MD, U. Tokyo, 1944, PhD, 1954. Prof. pharmacology U. Tokyo, 1959-83, prof. biophysics, 1971-83, prof. emeritus, 1983; prof. Nat. Inst. Physiol. Sci. (NIPS), Okazaki, Japan, 1983—86, dir.-gen., 1985—91, prof. Grad. U. Advanced Studies, 1988—91, prof. emeritus, 1993; pres. Okazaki Nat. Rsch. Inst., 1991-93. Vis. prof. U. Calif., San Francisco, 1963, Harvard U., Cambridge, Mass., 1974; pres. Internat. Union for Pure and Applied Biophysics, 1978-81, Internat. Union Pharmacology, 1990-94. Decorated grand cordon Order of the Sacred Treasure, Order Cultural Merit (Japan); recipient Asahi prize Asahi Newspaper Pub. Co., Tokyo, 1968, Imperial prize Japan Acad., 1972, Peter Harris award Internat. Soc. Heart Rsch., 1986, Internat. prize for Biology, 1999. Mem.: Japan Acad., Acad. Europaea, Acad. Nat. dei Lincei, Acad. Royal Medicine de Belgique, German Acad. Leopoldina, Royal Soc. (London), Am. Acad. Arts and Scis., Am. Soc. Biochemistry and Molecular Biology, NAS, Am. Physiol. Soc. (hon.). Home: 17-503 Nagaizumi Myodaiji Okazaki 444 0864 Japan Fax: 81-564-52-3719. E-mail: ebashi@nips.ac.jp.

EBATA, MASAKO, artist; b. Mito, Ibaraki, Japan; d. Yoshimi and Yukie Ebata; m. Naoki Muramatsu, June 24, 1998. BA, Ibaraki U., 1985; MFA, Sch. Visual Arts, N.Y.C., 1991. Illustrator, art dir., graphic designer, web designer. Recipient awards Am. Illustration, Tokyo Art Dirs. Club, Clio Awards. E-mail: info@ebata.com.

EBB, FRED, lyricist, librettist; b. N.Y.C., Apr. 8, 1936; s. Harry and Anna Evelyn (Gritz) E. BA, NYU, 1955; MA in English Lit., Columbia U., 1957; Hon. Degree in Theatre Arts, Emerson U., 1975; LittD (hon.), Niagra U., 1994. Lectr. in field. Lyricist (musical) Flora, The Red Menace, 1966, Cabaret, 1965 (Tony award best lyrics), Zorba, 1966, The Happy Time, 1968, 70, Girls, 70, 1971; co-author: (book) 70, Girls, 70, 1971; lyricist with Bob Fosse (book) Chicago, 1974, lyricist The Act, 1977, Woman of the Year, 1981 (Tony award best lyrics), The Rink, 1983, Kiss of the Spider Woman, 1990 (Tony award best lyrics, 1993, Drama Critics Circle award, 1993, Drama Desk award, 1993), And the World Goes Round, 1991, Chicago (revival), 1996, Steel Pier, 1997, Cabaret (revival), 1998, Curtains, 2002, The Skin of Our Teeth, 2003, (TV shows) Liza with a Z, 1967, Ole Blue Eyes is Back, 1972, Gypsy in My Soul, 1976, Goldie and Liza Together, 1980, Baryshnikov on Broadway, 1980, Liza at Radio City Music Hall, 1993 (Emmy award best music and lyrics, 1993), (films) Cabaret, 1970, Funny Lady, 1973, Lucky Lady, 1976, New York, New York, 1977, Stepping Out, 1991; author: Minelli on Minnelli, 1999; dir.: Minelli on Minnelli, 1999. Named Winner Outer Circle Critics Circle, 1990, honoree, Kennedy Ctr., 1998; named to Songwriters Hall of Fame, 1983, Theatre Hall of Fame, 1991, NYU Musical Theatre Hall of Fame, 1996; recipient Drama Desk award, Drama Critics Circle, 1967, 1968, Outer Circle award, Orgn. Writers on Theatre, 1968, 1969, George Foster Peabody award, Grady Sch. Journalism U. Ga., 1972, Drama Critics Circle award, 1967, Image award, NAACP, 1973, Ace award, Standing Room Only-Liza in London, Achievement award, B'nai B'rith, 1978, Christopher award, Cath. Soc., 1976, George Abbott award, Stage Dirs. and Choreographers Found., 1996, Helen Hayes award, 1999, Joseph Jefferson award, 2002, Golden Globe award, 2002. Mem. Dramatists Guild, Equity, Nat. Acad. TV Arts and Scis. (Emmy award 1972, 75, 76, 93), Am. Guild Authors and Composers, Acad. Motion Picture Arts and Scis.

EBBELS, BRUCE JEFFERY, physician, health facility administrator; b. N.Y.C., Dec. 26, 1924; s. Walter Jeffery and Mildred Christiana (Bruce) E.; m. Shirley Marie Cooley, July 3, 1950; children: Bruce Jeffery Jr., Cynthia, Stephanie, Leslie, David. Student, Colgate U., 1943-44; MD, N.Y. Med. Coll., 1948. Intern Hurley Med. Ctr., Flint, Mich., 1948-49; staff Mercy Hosp., Watertown, NY, 1954—88, Ho. of the Good Samaritan, Watertown, 1954—88; resident in internal medicine VA Hosp., Richmond, Va., 1951—54; pvt. practice gastroenterology and internal medicine Watertown, N.Y., 1954-90; med. dir. N.Y. Air Brake Co., Watertown, 1992-94; med. coord. VA Clinic, Watertown, N.Y., 1994-97; staff Genesis Healthcare, Watertown, NY, 1998-99; med. advisor Credo Cmty. Ctr. Addictions, Carthage, NY, 1992—. Chief medicine Mercy Hosp., Watertown, N.Y., 1975-78, House of the Good Samaritan Hosp., Watertown, 1978-83, pres. med. staff, 1978; cons. in internal medicine E.J. Noble Hosp., 1960-88, Lewis County Gen. Hosp., 1960-88, Carthage Area Hosp., 1966-88; cons. in field. Contbr. chpt. to book. Pres. Jefferson County Assn. for Mental Health, Watertown, 1969-70; bd. trustees Watertown (N.Y.) Savs. Bank, 1971—; bd. vestry Trinity Ch., Watertown, 1972-78, 2000—; med. advisor Credo-Cmty. Ctr. for Addicitons, 1992—. Capt. USNR, 1979—. Recipient John Philips Rice Svc. award Jefferson County Assn. for Mental Health, Watertown, 1970, Disting. Svc. award Jefferson County divsn. Am. Heart Assn. Fellow ACP (life), Am. Coll. Gastroenterology (sr.); mem. AMA (life), Med. Soc. State N.Y. (life), Med. Soc. Jefferson County (life; pres. 1979-80), Staplin Creek Soc. (past pres.). Republican. Episcopalian. Avocations: aquatic sports, scuba diving, writing, lecturing. Home: 283 Thompson Blvd Watertown NY 13601-4123 Office: Credo Cmty Ctr Addictions 410 State St Carthage NY 13619

EBBEN, JOY MARIE, human factors/ergonomics psychologist; b. Stanley, Wis., Nov. 11, 1952; d. Delton Joseph and Marie Elizabeth (Benzschawel) E. BA, U. Wis., Eau Claire, 1974, MS, 1977; MA, Calif. State U., Northridge, 1984; PhD, Claremont Coll., 1989. Diplomate Am. Bd. Psychol. Specialties; cert. profl. ergonomist, cert. human factors engrng. profl. Sch. psychologist Tucson Pub. Schs., Tucson, 1977-80; human factors specialist Hughes Aircraft Co., Canoga Park and Fullerton, Calif., 1982-93; ind. cons. Alto Loma, Calif., 1986-95; human factors and ergonomics specialist IAC Industries, Brea, Calif., 1993—; pres. JME Ergonomics, Tomahawk, Wis., 1996—2003; dir. human factors and ergonomics rsch. Ctr. for the Behavioral Scis., Tomahawk, 2000—; dir. Upward Bound and Talent Search, 2003—. Mem. APA, Human Factors and Ergonomics Soc., Am. Soc. Safety Engrs., Ergonomics Soc. Avocations: weightlifting, gardening, dogs.

EBBERS, LARRY HAROLD, education educator; b. Rockwell, Iowa, June 17, 1941; s. Harold Theodore and Gertrude Eleanor (Robeoltmann) E.; m. Barbara Ellen Smith, June 17, 1962; children: Lori Ann, Kimberly Jo. BS, Iowa State U., 1962, MS, 1968, PhD, 1971. Vocat. agrl. instr. Iowa Falls (Iowa) Sch., 1962-63, Spencer (Iowa) Schs., 1963-65; asst. dir. residences Iowa State U., Ames, 1965-72, asst. prof., 1972-75, assoc. prof., 1975-80, prof. edn., 1981—, dept. chair, prof. studies in edn., 1983-93, asst. to dean Coll. Edn., 1972-76, asst. dean Coll. Edn., 1976-83, assoc. dean, 1996-2000. Contbr. articles to profl. jours. Bd. dirs. Ames Parks and Recreation Commn., 1983-86, Iowa State U. Meml. Union, 1989-94; pres. Ctrl. Iowa Regional Substance Abuse Ctr., Ames, 1984-85, Meeker Sch. PTO, Ames, 1975-76; mem. task force on campus ministry Am. Luth. Ch., Des Moines, 1979-84; bd. regents Waldorf Coll., Iowa, 1999—. Recipient Outstanding Young Alumnus award, 1976, Outstanding Acad. Adv. award, 1977, Human Rels. award Human Rels. Commn., 1984, Human rels. award Student Affairs Divsn., 1985, Outstanding Faculty Citation award, 1991, Cardinal Key Leadership Hon., 1995, Golden Key Honor Soc., 1996, Pres.'s Disting. Svc. award, 1999, Regents award for faculty excellence, 2001, all from Iowa State U.; Rotary Found. fellow, Brazil, 1977; Fulbright scholar, Germany, 2000. Mem. Nat. Assn. Student Pers. Adminstrs. (dir. rsch. and program devel. 1979-81, chmn. Am. Coun. on Edn. Inst. 1984-86, editor jour. 1981-84, pres. 1987-88, v.p. Found. 1989-92, Disting. Svc. award 1990, Fred Turner award 1991, nat. conf. program chair 1992, chair Acad. Leadership & Exec. Effectivness, dir. acad. leadership & exec. effectiveness, 2002-, Robert Shaffer award for academic excellence as a grad. faculty mem. 1996), Kiwanis (Ames pres. 1977-78), Phi Delta Kappa, Phi Kappa Phi (pres. 1977-79, centennial medalist 1997). Lutheran. Avocations: athletics, spectator sports, jogging, mng. family farm. Home: 220 24th St Ames IA 50010-4832 Office: Iowa State U N226 N Lagomarcino Hl Ames IA 50011-0001

EBBS, GEORGE HEBERLING, JR., university executive; b. Sewickley, Pa., Sept. 20, 1942; s. George Heberling and Mae Isabelle (Miller) E.; m. Agnes Rak, 1989; children: Stacey Kirsten, Cynthia Lynn, George Heberling III, Alexandra Christine. BS in Engring., Purdue U., 1964; MBA, U. Wash., 1966; PhD in Bus., Columbia U., 1970. Sr. engr. Boeing Co., Seattle, 1966; assoc. Booz Allen & Hamilton, N.Y.C., 1969-72, sr. v.p., 1974-86; v.p. Fry Cons., N.Y.C., 1973; chmn., pres. The Canaan Group, Park City, Utah, 1986-98; pres. Embry-Riddle Aeronautical U., Daytona Beach, Fla., 1998—. Bd. dirs. Pinnacle Bank, NBAA-AMAC. Bd. dirs. Daytona Lively Arts; chmn. S.E. SATS Lab Consortium; mem. adv. bd. Aerospace Edn. Found., advisor. Bronfman fellow. Fellow: Royal Aero. Soc.; mem.: AIAA, Air Force Assn., Nat. Bus. Aviation Assn. (assoc. mem. adv. coun.), Purdue Old Masters, Iron Key, Wings Club (bd. govs.), Met. Opera Club, Aero Club of Washington, Oceanside Country Club, Prestwick Country Club, Beta Gamma Sigma, Omicron Delta Kappa. Presbyterian. Office: Embry-Riddle Aeronautical U 600 S Clyde Morris Blvd Daytona Beach FL 32114-3966

EBEL, DAVID M. federal judge; b. 1940; BA, Northwestern U., 1962; JD, U. Mich., 1965. Law clk. assoc. justice Byron White U.S. Supreme Ct., 1965—66; pvt. practice Davis, Graham & Stubbs, Denver, 1966—88; judge U.S. Ct. Appeals (10th cir.), Denver, 1988—. Adj. prof. law U. Denver Law Sch., 1987—89; sr. lectr. fellow Duke U. Law Sch., 1992—94. Mem.: Jud. Conf. U.S. (com. on codes of conduct 1991—98, co-chair 10th cir. gender bias task force 1994—99), Colo. Bar Assn. (v.p. 1982), Am. Coll. Trial Lawyers. Office: US Ct Appeals 1823 Stout St Rm 109L Denver CO 80257-1823 E-mail: david_m_ebel@ca10.uscourts.gov.

EBEL, THERON ARTHUR, physician; b. Ft. Wayne, Ind., May 12, 1941; s. Herman and Vada (Cheverton) E.; married; children: Kevin Bradley, Laura Amanda. BS, Butler U., 1963, MS in Pharmacology, 1966; MD, Ind. U., 1970. Diplomate Am. Bd. Internal Medicine, Am. Bd. Pulmonary Disease, Am. Bd. Critical Care Medicine. Med. dir. ICU VA Adminstrn. Hosp., Tampa, Fla., 1973-77, 78-79, asst. chief med. svc., 1974-77, staff physician, 1973-74; asst. prof. divsn. pulmonary diseases U. South Fla., Tampa, 1976-80, asst. dean, 1975-77, asst. prof., edn. coord., 1975-77, instr. medicine, 1973-75; dir. crit. care and progressive care Univ. Comm. Hosp., Tampa, 1984—; physician Fletcher Med. Ctr., Tampa. Contbr. articles to profl. jours. Mem. AMA, AAAS, ACP-Am. Soc. Internal Medicine, Am. Heart Assn., Am. Coll. Chest Physicians, Hillsborough County Med. Assn., Am. Thoracic Soc., Fla. Thoracic Soc., Fla. Med. Assn., Fla. Soc. Internal Medicine, Physicians for Social Responsibility, Soc. Critical Care Medicine, Alpha Omega Alpha. Office: Fletcher Med Ctr 3000 E Fletcher Ave Ste 270 Tampa FL 33613-4689 E-mail: theronebel@medscape.com.

EBELING, ARTHUR WILLIAM, mechanical engineer; b. Beloit, Wis., Aug. 31, 1926; s. Ernst E. and Ida (Lindeman) E.; m. Nancy M. Raes, July 9, 1951 (dec. Sept. 1989); children: Bertha, Mary, August. BSME, Rose Poly. Inst., Terre Haute, Ind., 1951. Area foreman Koppers Chem., Kobuta, Pa., 1951-53; field engr. Am. Bridge, Ambridge, Pa., 1953-61; engr. Griffin Wheel, Chgo., 1961-64; project engr. Armsted Rsch. Lab., Bensenville, Ill., 1964-69; dist. salesmgr. Beardley & Piper, Chgo., 1969; project engr. Kawecki Berylco, Reading, Pa., 1969-80; Midwest dir. ASME, Mt. Prospect, Ill., 1980-98; retired, 1998. Speaker in field. Mem. citizens adv. bd. Wilson H.S., Reading, 1978. Sgt. USAF, 1944-47. Fellow ASME (sect. officer Reading 1977-80, disting. lectr.); mem. Ky. Cols. Achievements include patents in steel industry. Home: 1074 Crimson Dr Wheeling IL 60090-5536

EBELING, BRIAN TERRY, family physician; b. Mpls., Apr. 7, 1946; s. Emerald William and Mildred L. (Arndt) E.; m. Miriam H. Schultz, Dec. 22, 1968; children: Patrick B., Michael W., Kristine E. BS, U. Minn., 1967, BA, 1968, MD, 1971. Diplomate Am. Bd. Family Practice, Am. Bd. Geriat. Medicine. Staff physician Quello Clinic Ltd., Mpls., 1974—; med. dir. Family Physicians/Quello Clinic Ltd., Mpls., 1980—, pres., 1990-98. Clin. asst. prof. U. Minn., Mpls., 1974-81, clin. assoc. prof., 1981-98, clin. prof., 1998—; v.p. med. affairs Araz Health Plan, Bloomington, Minn., 1981—; cons., com. mem. Share/Physician Health Plan/Allina/Medica Health Ptnrs., Mpls., 1981-98 (mem. Credentials Com. 1999), Health Partners, Preferred One, 1994-; bd. dirs. U. Care Minn. Med. Commn. Fellow Am. Acad. Family Physicians; mem. Am. Profl. Practice Assn., Am. Bd. Quality Assurance and Utilization Rev., Am. Bd. Quality Care Utilization Review Physicians, Minn. Med. Assn., Hennepin County Med. Soc. Home: 8125 Pennsylvania Cir S Bloomington MN 55438-1131 Office: Quello Clinic Ltd 7801 E Bush Lake Rd # 300 Minneapolis MN 55439-3120 E-mail: bebeling@quello.com.

EBELING, VICKI, marriage and family therapist, psychotherapist, educational therapist; b. Detroit, Nov. 18, 1948; d. Paul F. and Constance Jean Ebeling; m. James Robert Marchese, 1983; 1 child, Drew Ebeling Marchese. BA, Mich. State U., 1969; M of Sci., Marriage, Family & Child Counseling, Calif. State U., Dominguez Hills, 1990; PhD in Human Behavior, Newport U., 1999. Diplomate Am. Psychotherapy Assn.; cert. in child maltreatment and family violence; cert. parent effectiveness tng. instr.; cert. youth effectiveness

tng. instr.; bd. cert. ednl. therapist. With various TV and radio prodn. cos., Detroit, Lansing, Mich., 1969-74; TV and film prodn. cos. L.A., 1974-90; psychotherapist/marriage, family and child therapist Torrance, Calif., 1990—; ednl. therapist, 1994—. Author: Educating America in the 21st Century, 2002. Counselor South Bay Rape Crisis Ctr., 1988-92; mem. orientation team St. Peter's by Sea Presbyn. Ch., Palos Verdes Estates, Calif., 1993-95; vol. cons. 1736 Family Crisis Ctr., 1988, Calif. Spl. Olympics, 1990-91, pediat. ward UCLA-Harbor Hosp., 1991-92, Child Shelter Care, Los Angeles County Children's Ct., 1992-93, ARC Disaster Svc., 1995—. Named Adult Amateur Horsemanship Champion, Los Serranos Award Circuit, Rolling Hills, Calif., 1993. Mem. Calif. Assn. Marriage and Family Therapists (South Bay newsletter editor 1992-94), Assn. Ednl. Therapists. Office: 24586 Hawthorne Blvd # 7 Torrance CA 90505-6807

EBELL, C(ECIL) WALTER, lawyer; b. Baker, Oreg., June 26, 1947; s. Cecil John and Sylvia Jean (Malone) E.; m. Dianna Rae Gentry, June 2, 1980; children: Anne, Erik, Michael. BS, Oreg. State U., 1970; MS, U. No. Colo., 1973; JD, Lewis and Clark Coll., 1977. Bar: Oreg. 1977, Alaska 1978, U.S. Ct. Appeals (9th cir.) 1981, U.S. Supreme Ct. 1985, Wash. 1990. Pvt. practice, Portland, Oreg., 1977-78; ptnr. Hartig, Rhodes, Norman & Mahoney, Anchorage, 1978-84, Jamin, Ebell, Bolger & Gentry, Kodiak, Alaska, 1984-90, Seattle, 1990-2000, Jamin, Ebell, Schmitt & Mason, Anchorage, Alaska, 2000—. Press sec., Clay Myers for Gov. campaign, Oreg., 1974. Capt. USMC, 1970-73. Mem. ABA, Assn. Trial Lawyers Am., Rotary. Democrat. Avocations: photography, fishing, skiing. Office: Jamin Ebell Schmitt Mason 1007 W 3rd Ave Ste 201 Anchorage AK 99501 E-mail: webell@jesmanc.com.

EBELL, MARK HERBERT, physician, researcher; b. Montreal, Que., Can., Oct. 14, 1961; s. Herbert Otto and Hildegard (Franziska) E.; m. Laura Lee Bierema, June 30, 1990. BA, Kalamazoo Coll., 1983; MD, U. Mich., 1987, MS, 1995. Diplomate Am. Bd. Family Practice. Resident U. Mich. Hosps., Ann Arbor, 1987-90; family physician Colbert, Ga., 1990-94; asst. prof. Wayne State U., Detroit, 1994-96; assoc. prof. Mich. State U., East Lansing, 1996—. Author: Evidence-Based Diagnosis, 2001; mem. editl. bd. Med. Decision-Making, 1998—; editor Jour. Family Practice, 2000-02; co-editor: Essentials of Family Medicine, 1998; co-editor (newsletter) Evidence-Based Practice, 1998—; dep.-editor, Am. Family Physician (jour.); author (software) Info Retriever. Co-dir. Mich. Consortium for Family Practice Rsch., East Lansing, 1998-2000. Recipient generalist faculty physician scholar Robert Wood Johnson Found., 1998. Mem. Am. Acad. Family Physicians, Soc. for Med. Decision Making, Soc. Tchrs. Family Medicine, N.Am. Primary Care Rsch. Group. Avocations: biking, volleyball, computers. Office: Dept Family Practice B101 Clinical Center East Lansing MI 48824-1315 E-mail: ebell@msu.edu.

EBENEZER, JAZLIN V. adult education educator; m. Devairakkam L Ebenezer, Dec. 24, 1972; 1 child, Sudesh J. EdD, U.of British Columbia, 1987—91. Assoc. prof. U. of Man., 1991—2001, Wayne State U., 2001—. Math/sci. tchr. Seventh-day Adventist Sch. Sys., Abbotsford, Br. Columbia, Canada, 1979—87. Recipient Outstanding Students Honouring Outstanding teachers, U. of Man., 1994, Merit award in rsch., 1999, Rh award (rsch.), R & D, 2000; grantee Sci. Lesson Sequences Incorporating Students' Conceptions: A Collaborative Inquiry., Social Sciences and Humanities Rsch. Coun. of Can., 1994-1996, The validity and reliability of digraph: Assessing students' conceptual change in structural characteristic in sci., SSHRCC, 1996-1999, Sustainable Devel. Innovation Grant, Ministry of Edn., Man., 2001-2001, Sci. and Tech. for Sci. Teachers, Greater Cities Universities, 2001-2002. Mem.; NARST. Achievements include research in Science Education. Office: Wayne State University 5425 Gullen Mall Detroit MI 48226 Office Fax: 313-577-4091. E-mail: jebenezer@wayne.edu.

EBENSTEIN, JUDITH ANN, psychiatrist, educator; b. Peekskill, NY, Nov. 26, 1948; married; 2 children. AB cum laude, Radcliffe Coll., 1970; MD, Albert Einstein Coll. Medicine, 1974. Diplomate Am Bd Psychiatry and Neurology. Intern in medicine Montefiore Hosp. and Med. Ctr., Bronx, NY, 1974—75; resident in psychiatry Bronx Mcpl. Hosp. Ctr., 1975—78, chief psychiat. resident, 1977—78; inpatient fellowship NY Hosp./Westchester Divsn., White Plains, NY, 1978—79, acting unit chief, 1980; unit chief inpatient svc. Phelps Meml. Hosp. Ctr., North Tarrytown, NY, 1981—86, founder, dir. eating disorders program inpatient svc., 1984—87; clin. instr. psychiatry NY Hosp./Westchester Div., White Plains, 1988—91; pvt. practice Irvington, NY, 1979—. Lectr in field. Mem.: Depression After Delivery, Am. Anorexia Bulimia Assn. (Westchester task force coord. 1991—92, treas. 1993—2000), Am. Psychiat. Assn. Office: Irvington NY 10535-2019

EBER, KEVIN, science writer; b. Cleve., Aug. 14, 1958; s. Julius Louis and Winifred Ann (Hanf) E. BSChemE, Case Western Res. U., 1980; MA in Journalism, U. Colo., Boulder, 1990. Engr. Westinghouse Naval Reactors Facility/Idaho Nat. Engring Lab , Idaho Falls, 1980-82, Northeast Utilities, Berlin, Conn., 1982-87; tech. writer Stoller Corp., Boulder, 1988-89; sci. writer Brookhaven Nat. Lab., Upton, N.Y., 1989; journalism intern Boulder Daily Camera, 1990; sci. writer Nat. Renewable Energy Lab., Golden, Colo., 1991—. Asst. editor: Advances in Solar Energy, vol. 7, 1992; author, project leader various publs. on energy sources; writer, editor (e-mail newsletter) Energy Efficiency and Renewable Energy Network News, 1999—. Mem. Nat. Assn. Sci. Writers. Avocations: hiking, biking, backpacking, skiing, rollerblading. Office: Nat Renewable Energy Lab 1617 Cole Blvd Golden CO 80401-3305

EBER, LORENZ, aeronautical engineer, civil engineer, inventor; b. Bad Oldesloh, Germany, Jan. 30, 1963; came to U.S., 1980; s. Gerhard Clemens and Ursula Eber; m. Paula Susette Holmes, June 9, 1985; children: Anya C., Yvonne R. Student, Columbia U., 1981-83; BSCE, Northwestern U., 1986; postgrad., U. Tunis, Tunisia, 1986-87; MS in Aero. Engring., U. Wash., 2002. Registered profl. engr., Wash. Coop. engr. Harza Engring. Co., Chgo., 1985-86; civil engr. Howard Needles Tammen & Bergendoff, Chgo., 1988-90; project design engr. Andersen Bjornstad Kane Jacobs Inc., Seattle, 1990-93; owner, pres. Inventexx Co., 1993-97; engr. Boeing Aircraft Co., 1997—2000; engr., project mgr. City of Bainbridge Island, 2000—. Engring. vol. Navajo Indian Tribe, Window Rock, Ariz., 1984; product devel. cons. Ingenieur Büro Eber, Steinburg, Germany, 1983. Contbr. photographs to magazines, books. Pres. Winslow Park Condominiums, Bainbridge Island, Wash., 1990-92; v.p. Northwestern Outing Club, Evanston, Ill., 1984-86; pres. Olympic Terr. Assn., 1996-, v.p. World Bike for Breath. Recipient Boeing fellowship, 1996. Mem. AIAA, ASCE (treas. 1984-86), Inst. Transp. Engrs. Achievements include patent for surveying field book cover; invention of mechanical cable drum lifter, air cushion highway cleaning machine, novel airplaine wing structure, boundary layer airplane controls; planning, design and construction of a modern roundabout on Bainbridge Island. Home: 12106 Heron St NE Bainbridge Island WA 98110

EBERHARD, ANATOL, retired chemistry educator; b. Istanbul, Turkey, Nov. 13, 1938; came to U.S., 1948; s. Wolfram and Alide (Roemer) E.; m. Carolyn Veeder, Sept. 1, 1964. BA, U. Calif., Berkeley, 1959; MA, Harvard U., 1960, PhD, 1964. Postdoctoral assoc. zoology U. Calif., Berkeley, 1964-66; asst. prof. biology Harvard U., Cambridge, Mass., 1966-71; assoc. prof. chemistry Fairleigh Dickinson U., Teaneck, N.J., 1971-72; from assoc. prof. to prof. chemistry Ithaca (N.Y.) Coll., 1972—2002. Adj. prof. microbiology Cornell U., Ithaca, NY, 2002—. Contbr. over 20 articles to profl. jours. Fellow Woodrow Wilson Found., 1959. Mem. Phi Beta Kappa. Home: 2434 Coddington Rd Brooktondale NY 14817-9510 E-mail: ae57@cornell.edu.

EBERHARD, BARBARA ANNE, rheumatologist, researcher; d. Justus and Jeanie Eberhard; m. Mariusz Adam Neter, Mar. 17, 1962; children: Benjamin Neter, Andrew Neter. B Medicine B Surgery, Monash U., Melbourne, Australia, 1979. Diplomate Victoria, Australia, 1980. Staff rheumatologist Hosp. For Sick Children, Toronto, Canada, 1996—98; attending in rheumatology Children's Hosp., Boston, 1998—2001; chief pediat. rheumatology Schneider Children's Hosp., Manhasset, NY, 2001—. Recipient Young Investigator award, Am. Coll. of Rheumatology, 1991, McNeil award, 1991; fellow Clinician Scientist, Terry Fox, 1992—93; Fellowship, Med. Rsch. Coun. of Can., 1993—96. Fellow: Royal Australian Coll. Physicians, Royal Coll. of Physicians and Surgeons of Can.; mem.: Am. Acad. Pediat., Am. Coll. of Rheumatology. Achievements include research in Written Several Papers On Childhood Rheumatic Illness. Office: Schneider Children's Hosp 269-01 76th St Rm 197 New Hyde Park NY 11040

EBERHARD, FRANZ VALENTIN, association executive; b. St. Johann, Carinthia, Austria, Feb. 1, 1947; s. Johann and Theresia (Krušic) E.; m. Irmgard Kothmaier, Aug. 4, 1968; children: Christoph, Stephan. LLD, U. Vienna, Austria, 1970; D of Polit. Sci., U. Paris, 1973. Lectr. U. Vienna, 1970-82, U. Paris II, 1972-73; sec. Constl. Ct., Vienna, 1974-78; sec. gen. Austrian Rectors' Conf., 1978-82; dir. European Centre Higher Edn., UNESCO, Bucharest, Romania, 1982-86; sec. gen. Internat. Assn. U., Paris, 1987—2001; dir. Internat. U. Bur., UNESCO, Paris, 1987-2001, cons., 2001. Cons., 2002—. Editor in chief Higher Edn. in Europe, 1982-86; co-editor Adminstrv. Law and Adminstrv. Sci., 1976-82; pub. dir. Higher Edn. Policy, 1988-2001; contbr. articles to profl. jours.

EBERHARDT, H. ALFRED, retired manufacturing executive, retired mechanical engineer; b. East Lansdowne, Pa., June 7, 1924; s. Harry Alfred Eberhardt, Jr. and Ella A. Eberhardt; m. Nedra S. Simons, Feb. 4, 1947. BS in Mech. Engring., Pa. State U., 1948. Registered mech. engr., Pa. Mech. engr. Clark-Dresser, Olean, NY, 1948—51; design engr. Pa. Pump & Compressor, Easton, 1951—53; mgr. R&D Hale Products, Conshohocken, Pa., 1953—68, pres., CEO, 1968—92; ret., 1992. Capt. U.S. Army, 1942—47. Named Disting. Alumnus, Pa. State U., 1999. Mem.: Lely Classic Golf Club, Aronimink Golf Club.

EBERHART, RALPH E. career officer; BS in Polit. Sci., USAF Acad., 1968; grad., Squadron Officer Sch., 1973, Air Command and Staff Coll., 1974; MS in Polit. Sci., Troy State U., 1977; postgrad. studies, Nat. War Coll., Ft. Lesley J. McNair, Washington, 1987. Commd. 2d lt. USAF, 1968, advanced through grades to gen., 1997; forward air controller Tactical Air Support Squadron USAF, Plieka Air Base, S. Viet Nam, 1970; from instr. pilot to squadron hdqrs. comdr. 71st Flying Tng. Wing Air Tng. Command USAF, Vance AFB, Okla., 1970-74; flight commdr., instr. pilot 525th Tactical Fighter Squadron USAFs in Europe, Bitburg Air Base, Germany, 1975-77; instr. pilot, flight examiner, asst. chief evaluation 50th Tactical Fighter Wing, Hahn Air Base, Germany, 1977-78; action officer, chief exec. com. Air Force Budget team Hdqs. USAF, Washington, 1979-80; aide to comdr.-in-chief, comdr. Air Forces Ctrl. Europe USAF, Ramstein AFB, Germany, 1980-82; comdr. 10th tactical fighter squadron, asst. dep. comdr. ops. 50th tactical fighter wing USAF in Europe, Hahn Air Base, Germany, 1982—84; exec. officer to Air Force chief of staff Hdqs. USAF, Washington, 1984-86; vice comdr. to comdr. 363d tactical fighter wing Tactical Air Command USAF, Shaw AFB, S.C., 1987-90; dep. chief of staff, plans and ops. Hdqs. USAF, Washington, 1995-96; cmdr. U.S. Forces Japan, cmdr. 5th Air Force USAF, Yokota Air Base, Japan, 1996-97; vice chief of staff Hdqs. USAF, Washington, 1997—99; comdr. Air Combat Command, Langley AFB, Va., 1999—2000, Air Force Space Command, Peterson AFB, Colo., 2000—02; mgr. for manned space flight support ops. Dept. Def., Peterson AFB, Colo., 2000—02; comdr. in chief N.Am. Aerospace Def. Command and U.S. Space Command, Peterson AFB, Colo., 2000—02; comdr. U.S. Northern Command, Peterson AFB, Colo., 2002—. Numerous decorations include: Legion of Merit with Oak Leaf cluster, Disting. Flying Cross, Air medal with 11 Oak Leaf clusters, Vietnam Svc. medal with 3 svc. stars, Humanitarian Svc. medal with svc. star, Republic of Vietnam Gallantry Cross with Palm, Republic of Vietnam Campaign medal, The Grand Cordon of the Order of the Sacred Treasure, Japan, and many others. Mem. Coun. of Fgn. Rels.*

EBERHART, ROBERT CLYDE, biomedical engineering educator, researcher; b. Oakland, Calif., Apr. 17, 1937; s. George Perrin and Roberta Eberhart; m. Carol Eberhart, Aug. 4, 1960; 3 children. AB in Applied Physics, Harvard U., 1958; MS in Mech. Engring., U. Calif., Berkeley, 1960, PhD, 1965. Staff scientist Inst. Med. Scis., San Francisco, 1964-70, sr. scientist, 1970-75; assoc. prof. mech. engring. U. Tex., Austin, 1975-76; assoc. prof. surgery U. Tex. So. Med. Ctr., Dallas, 1976-86; chmn. biomed. engring. U. Tex. So. Med. Ctr. and U. Tex.-Arlington, 1983—2001; prof. engring. in surgery, chmn. biomed. engring. programs U. Tex. So. Med. Ctr. and U. Tex., Arlington, 1984—. Bd. dirs. Advanced Neuromodulation Systems, Inc.; bd. sci. advisors Tissue-Gen Inc., Andev, Inc.; cons. in field. Editor: Heat Transfer in Medicine and Biology, Vols. 1-2, 1985; assoc. editor Jour. Biomech. Engring., 1982-85; co-editor Biomaterials-Living Sys. Interactions, 1993-1998; mem. editl. bd. Jour. Applied Biomaterials, Jour. Biomaterials Sci.; contbr. articles to profl. jours., chpts. in books; patentee nonthrombogenic treatment for med. polymers, 1985. Recipient C.W. Hall Rsch. award So. Biomed. Engring. Conf., 1987, Career Achievement award Houston Symposium for Biomed. Engring., 1996. Fellow ASME, Am. Inst. Med. and Biol. Engring. (v.p. pub. policy 1996); mem. Am. Soc. Artificial Internal Organs (sec.-treas. 1992, pres.-elect 1993-94, pres. 1994-95), Biomed. Engring. Soc. (sr.), Soc. Critical Care Medicine (editl. bd. 1973-75), Biomaterials Soc., Found. for Sci. and Tech. of Portugal (chmn. pharmacology and biomaterials rev. panel), Harvard Club. Office: U Tex So Med Ctr Biomed Engring Program 5323 Harry Hines Blvd Dallas TX 75390-9130

EBERHART, WILLIAM COILE, apparel repair specialist, writer; b. Winter Haven, Fla., May 10, 1958; s. Marvin Dewitt and Thabetha June (Coile) Eberhart. Shoe repair tech. Cochran's Shoe Repair & Clothing, North Charleston, SC, 1983—84, Alps Shoe Repair, Athens, Ga., 1985—88, Marvin's Shoe Svc., 1985—97, Heel Quik, Inc., Atlanta, 1993; owner Cordova Svcs., Athens, 1994—97; shoe repair tech. Shoe Stop, Inc., Seattle, 1997—99; leather garment repair tech. Marvin's Shoe Svc., Athens, 2001—. Author: (booklet) Leather Plus! A Money Saving Guide to Leather Care, 2001. Publicity dir. Northeast Ga. Earth Day, Athens, 1990. Avocations: coin collecting, reading, writing, walking, hiking. Office: PO Box 669 Athens GA 30603

EBERLE, CHARLES EDWARD, paper and consumer products executive; b. St. Louis, Mar. 20, 1928; s. Charles Edward and Hazel (Williams) E.; m. Nancy Ellen Paddock, Aug. 1, 1953 (div. June 1995); children: Charles Edward, Richard Clay, Julia Lee; m. Denise S. Jackson, Apr. 12, 1997 (dec. Nov. 2002). BS in Chem. Engring., Washington U., St. Louis, 1949. Prodn. mgr. Procter & Gamble, St. Louis, 1949-55, plant mgr. Lexington, Ky., 1955-57, St. Louis, 1957-60, Sacramento, 1960-64, mgr. mfg. Cin., 1964-79, v.p. mfg., 1979-84, v.p. engring., 1984-85; pres. CEE Enterprises, Cin., 1985-88, Thomas & Eberle Assocs., Inc., Cin., 1986-88; v.p., James River Europe James River Corp., 1988-90, sr. v.p., group exec., 1990, exec. v.p. consumer products bus., 1990-91; pres. CEE Enterprises, Richmond, 1992—; chmn. exec. com. Richmond area TEC, Midlothian, Va., 1997-98; v.p. corp. devel. Lloyd Assocs., Inc., Richmond, 1999-2001. Mem. mfg. studies bd. NRC/NAS, 1984-89. Vice pres. bd. trustees Children's Hosp. Med. Ctr., Cin., 1975-78; mem. Cin. Council on World Affairs, 1979-89; v.p. Dan Beard coun. Boy Scouts Am., 1982-85. With U.S. Army, 1951-52. Recipient Engring. Alumni Achievement award Washington U., 1977 Mem. Commonwealth Club. E-mail: eberle@peoplepc.com.

EBERLE, DONALD CRAMER, lawyer, governmental relations consultant; b. Balt., Dec. 29, 1948; s. William Cramer and Margaret Elizabeth (Mullaney) E.; m. Patricia Ann Gorman Barry, Aug. 14, 1971. BA, U. Colo., 1970, JD, 1974; advanced studies Harvard, 1984. Bar: Colo., 1974. Asst. dean students U. Colo., Denver, 1970-72, dep. dist. atty., Denver, 1974-77; chief counsel Met. Econ. Crime Office, Denver, 1977-79; sr. appellate atty. Office of Denver Dist. Atty., 1979-80; state rep. Color. House of Reps., 1980-82; dir. legis. affairs gov. Colo., 1982-84; dir. external affairs regional gen. counsel MCI Telecomms. Corp., Denver, 1984-90; prin. Eberle & Assocs., 1991—; lectr. in field; chmn. State Bd. Equalization, 1985-93; bd. dirs. Capitol Complex Commn., 1983-85, Denver Civic Ventures, 1985-93, Colo. Dance Festival, 1986-89; chmn. exec. bd. U. Colo. Internat. Telecom Program, 1989—. Mem. DRCOG Clean Air Task Force, Colo., 1980-82; mem. adv. com. on Crime Reclassification, Colo., 1981-83; bd. dirs. Capitol Hill Community Ctr., Denver, 1981-82; chmn. Gov.'s. Task Force on the Homeless; chmn. The Denver Ptnrship. Com. on Homeless. Harvard scholar Gates Found., 1984; mem. Colo. Coun. on the Arts, 1993-96; bd. dirs., sec. CA:RE; chmn. Colo. Homeless Youth Adv. Com., 1992-96. Mem. ABA, Colo. Bar Assn., Nat. Dist. Attys. Assn., Colo. Dist. Attys. Assn. Democrat. Home: 379 Dahlia St Denver CO 80220-5713 Office: MCI Telecomms Corp 1760 Lafayette St Denver CO 80218-1117

EBERLE, TERRY R. editor, newspaper executive; With Chronicle-Tribune, Marion, Ind., 1975—90, mng. editor; with The Herald-Dispatch, Huntington, W.Va., 1971—75; editor The Times, Shreveport, La., 1990—92, North Hills News-Record, Pittsburgh, 1992—95, Valley News Dispatch, Pittsburgh, 1992—95; exec. editor The News-Press, 1995—2001; v.p., editor The Indianapolis Star, 2001—03; exec. editor Florida Today, Melbourne, Fla., 2003—. Office: Florida Today PO Box 419000 Melbourne FL 32941-9000*

EBERLE, WILLIAM DENMAN, international management consultant; b. Boise, Idaho, June 5, 1923; s. Julius Louis and Clare (Holcomb) E.; m. Jean Cilista Quick, Sept. 20, 1947; children— Jeffrey Louis, William David, Francis Quick, Cilista Clare. BA, Stanford U., 1945; MBA, Harvard U., 1947, JD, 1949; LLB (hon.), Gonzagua U., 1976. Bar: Idaho 1950. Ptnr. firm Richards, Haga & Eberle, Boise, 1950—57; mem. Idaho Ho. of Reps. from Ada County, 1953-61, majority leader, 1957, minority leader, 1959, speaker, 1961; dir. Boise Cascade Corp., 1959—66, v.p., 1961-66; pres., chmn., dir. Am. Standard, Inc., N.Y.C., 1966-71; U.S. trade rep., amb. Washington, 1971-75; exec. dir. Cabinet Council on Internat. Econ. Policy, 1974-75; mem. Pres.'s Econ. Policy Bd., 1974-75; pres., chief exec. officer Motor Vehicle Mfrs. Assn., 1975-77; chmn. Tertiary, Inc., Boise, 1978—80, Manchester Assocs. Ltd., Washington, 1977—. Bd. dirs. Ampco-Pitts. Corp., Am. Svc. Group; of counsel Kaye, Scholer, LLP, N.Y.C., Mid-States Plc. Chmn. Idaho Rep. Fin. Com., 1961-66; mem. nat. Rep. Fin. Com., 1961-66; trustee Stanford U., 1970—, Com. for Econ. Devel. Lt. USNR, 1944-46. Mem. ABA, Idaho Bar Assn., Coun. Fgn. Rels., Univ. Club (N.Y.C.), Met. Club (Washington). Episcopalian. Office: Manchester Assoc PO Box 1425 13 Garland Rd Concord MA 01742-2214 E-mail: wd.eberle@covad.net.

EBERLEY, HELEN-KAY, opera singer, classical record company executive, poet; b. Sterling, Ill., Aug. 3, 1947; d. William Elliott and P. (Conneely) E. MusB, Northwestern U., 1970, MusM, 1971. Chmn., pres., artistic coord. Eberley Inc., Evanston, Ill., 1973-92; founder H.K.E. Enterprises, 1993—, pres., 1993—; circulation libr. Evanston Pub. Libr., 1995-98. Founder EB-SKO Prodns., 1976-92, tchr., coach, 1976—; exec. dir., performance cons. E-S Mgmt., 1985-92; featured artist Honors Concert, Northwestern U., 1970, Alumni Concert, 1999, Master Class and guest lectr. various colls. and univs.; host Poetry in Process monthly seminar Barnes & Noble; music lectr. rep. Harvard Club, Chgo.; numerous TV and radio talk show appearances and interviews. Operatic debut in Peter Grimes, Lyric Opera, Chgo., 1974; starred in: Cosi Fan Tutte, Le Nozze Di Figaro, Dido and Aeneas, La Boheme, Faust, Tosca, La Traviata, Falstaff, Don Giovanni, Brigadoon, others; jazz appearances with Duke Ellington, Dave Brubeck and Robert Shaw; performing artist Oglebay Opera Inst., Wheeling, W.Va., 1968, WTTW TV/PBS, Chgo., 1968; solo star in: Continental Bank Concerts, 1981-89, United Airlines-Schubert, Schumann, Brahms, Mendelssohn, Faure, Mozart, Duparc/Wolf, Supersta. WFMT Radio, Chgo., 1982-90; featured artist with North Shore Concert Band, 1989; starring artist South Bend Symphony, 1990, Mo. Symphony Soc., 1990, Milw. Symphony, 1990; spl. guest artist New Studios Gala Sta. WFMT, 1995, West Valley Fine Arts Concert Series, Phoenix, 1999; prodr.-annotator Gentlemen Gypsy, 1978, Strauss and Szymanowski, 1979, One Sonata Each: Franck and Szymanowski, 1982; starring artist-exec. prodr. Separate But Equal, 1976, All Brahms, 1977, Opera Lady, 1978, Eberley Sings Strauss, 1980, Helen-Kay Eberley: American Girl, 1983, Helen-Kay Eberley: Opera Lady II, 1984; performed Am. and Can. nat. anthems for Chgo. Cubs Baseball Team, 1977-83, Chgo. Bears Football, 1977; also starred in numerous concert recital and symphony appearances, Europe, Can., U.S.; author: Angel's Song, 1994, The Magdaleva Poems, 1995, ChapelHeart, 1996, Desert Dancing, 1997, Canyon Ridge, 2000, Rivervoice, 2002. Docent, new mem. tour guide Art Inst. Chgo.; spl. events hotline vol. Art Inst. Chgo., Chgo. Christian Indsl. League, St. Joseph's Table of St. Peter's in the Loop, Chgo.; vol., facilitator City Yr. Chgo.-Urban Peace Corps; Chgo. Humanities Festival VIII of Ill. Humanities Coun., Evanston Shelter for Battered Women, Rape Victim Adv., Habitat for Humanity; Midwest Vol. Facilitator 1st Indsl. Realty Trust; mem. Mayor's founding com. Evanston Arts Coun., 1974-75; judge Ice-Skating Competition, Wilmette (Ill.) Park Dist., 1974-77, bd. dirs., 1973-77; bd. dirs. Ctr. for Voice, Chgo., 1994-96; vol. Saints-Usher Corps of Chgo., 1998-99. Recipient Creative and Performing Arts award Ind. Jr. Miss. and South Bend Jr. Miss, 1965, Milton J. Cross award Met. Opera Guild, 1968; prize winner Met. Opera. Nat. Auditions, 1968, 1st pl. prize for The Pond, Chicagoland Poetry Contest, 1997, 1st pl. prize and Best of the Best award for The Rose Garden, 1999; F.K. Weyerhauser scholar Met. Opera, 1967. Mem. People for Ethical Treatment of Animals, Am. Soc. for Prevention of Cruelty to Animals, Assisi Animal Found., Am. Guild Mus. Artists, Internat. Platform Assn., Whale Adoption Project, Amnesty Internat., Environ. Def. Fund, Doris Day Animal Found., Poets and Patrons, Humane Soc., Greenpeace, Physicians Com. for Responsible Medicine, Notre Dame Alumni Club, St. Mary's Acad. Alumnae Assn., Delta Gamma. Office: HKE Enterprises 1726 Sherman Ave Evanston IL 60201-5619

EBERLIN, RICHARD D. education educator; b. Erie, Pa., Sept. 28, 1947; s. Harry M. and Florence F. (Space) E.; m. Deanna A. Barron, Aug. 7, 1971; children: Richard D., Charles A. BS in Edn., Edinboro State Coll., 1969, MS in Edn., 1973. Tchr. Crawford Cen. Sch. Dist., Meadville, Pa., 1969-76, Millcreek Twp. Sch. Dist., Erie, Pa., 1976—, chair dept. sci., 1997—. Bd. dirs. Pa. State Edn. Assn., Harrisburg, 1996—, pres. N.W. region, 1998-2002, pers. com., 1999-2002; asst. scoutmaster Boy Scouts of Am., Erie, 1985-96. Mem.: NEA (bd. dirs. 2002—). Office: McDowell HS 3580 W 38th St Erie PA 16506-4021

EBERLY, HARRY LANDIS, retired communications company executive; b. Lancaster, Pa., Nov. 1, 1924; s. Chester Landis and Nola Marie (Clark) E.; m. Marion Ruth Royer, May 26, 1951; children: Jenny Ellen Eberly Holmes, Susan Lynn Eberly Patrick. BS in Chem. Engring., Pa. State U., 1945; postgrad., Lehigh U., 1947-48, Franklin and Marshall Coll., 1949. Engr. We. Electric, N.Y.C., 1945-49; mfg. engr. RCA, Lancaster, Pa., 1949-51, product devel. Harrison, N.J., 1951-64, mgr. mfg. Somerville, N.J., 1964-66, plant mgr. Palm Beach Garden, Fla., 1996-68, mgr. purchasing Palm Beach Gardens, Fla., 1968-72; v.p. Telex Computer Products, Inc., Tulsa, 1972-76, sr. v.p., 1976-77, pres. Communication Products div. Raleigh, N.C., 1977-83, exec. v.p., 1983-88, mem. exec. com. Tulsa, 1984-88, dir., 1982-84; exec. v.p. Memorex Telex Corp., 1988-90; COO, Novatel Comm., Ltd., Calgary, Can., 1991-92. Mem. bd. assocs. Meridith Coll., Raleigh, 1981—98, presdl. adv. coun., 1999—2002; mem. bd. assocs. Barton Coll. Global Focus Program, 1988—97; bd. dirs. Wake Tech. Cmty. Coll. Found., Raleigh, 1982—97, chmn., 1990—94; mem. N.C. State U. Engring. Found., Raleigh, 1984—87; exec. com. Edn. and Psychology Found., 1990—95; vice-chmn. Triangle East N.C., 1986—90, chmn., 1990—92; regional maj., gifts chmn. Campaign for Pa. State, 1986—90; chair Pa. State Grand Destiny Campaign Coll. of Edn., 1999—2003; bd. dirs., exec. com. Occoneechee Coun. Boy Scouts Am., 1989—95; bd. dirs. Raleigh Little Theatre, 1989—92, 1995—2003, Raleigh Housing Authority Scholarship Fund, 1993—98; bd. dirs., 1988 campaign chmn. United Way Wake County, 1980—89. Mem. IEEE (life), Wake County Edn. Found. (bd. dirs. 1990-92), Greater Raleigh C. of C. (bd. dirs. 1979-87), North Ridge Country Club, Masons, Shriners, Delta Gamma Delta. Methodist. Home: 7003 N Ridge Dr Raleigh NC 27615-7036

EBERLY, ROBERT EDWARD, foundation administrator; b. Greensboro, Pa., July 14, 1918; s. Orville Sebastian and Ruth Rhoda (Moore) E.; m. Elouise Ross Conn., Sept. 25, 1982; children: Robert E. Jr., Paul O., Mary Katherine Zickefoose, Sue C. Hudson, Thomas J. Conn, William H. Conn, Robert E. Conn. BA in Chemistry, Pa. State U., 1939; LittD (hon.), Calif. U. Pa., 1991, Waynesburg (Pa.) Coll., 1992; LLD (hon.), Slippery Rock U., 1994; D Pub. Svc. (hon.), Thiel Coll. Chemist Dept. Navy, 1940-45; pres., gen. mgr. Eberly Natural Gas Co., Uniontown, Pa., 1945—86, chmn., 1986—2000; pres., treas. GNB Corp., Uniontown, Pa., 1969-77, chmn. bd., 1977-85, Gallatin Nat. Bank, Uniontown, 1977-90, bd. dirs. Gen. mgr. Eberly Family Trust, 1983—; sec. treas. Eberly Found., 1963-88, pres., 1988—; chmn. Chalk Hill Gas, Inc., 1986-94, Greystone Resources, Inc., 1986—; pres. Fay-Penn Econ. Devel. Coun., 1991-2002, coun. mem., 2002-, vice chmn.; pres. Greystone Prodn. Co., 1995, Greystone Acquisition Corp., 1995, Greystone Oil and Gas Corp., 2001. Pres. bd. trustees Uniontown Hosp. Assn., 1968-70, trustee emeritus, 1978— ; bd. dirs. Penn's Southwest Assn., 1980—, trustee, 1978-95; bd. dirs., past pres. Uniontown Indsl. Fund, 1971; nat. chmn. alumni fund Pa. State U., 1972-74, mem. Found. Bd., mem. adv. bd. Fayette Campus Br., nat. treas. Campaign for Pa. State U., 1985-90, treas. Nat. Devel. Coun., 1991—; Penn State U. Libraries feasibility study, 1992-93; past sec. Uniontown Planning and Zoning Commn.; bd. dirs. Laurel Highlands, Inc., 1987—; active Westmoreland/Fayette coun. Boy Scouts Am.; bd. dirs. WQED-TV, 1990-94; chmn. Uniontown YMCA Pool Campaign, 1988-90, Uniontown Hosp. Found. Inc., 1990-91; Hist. Soc. Western Pa. (Blue Ribbon Comm.), 1992-95; Honorary Chmn. Fayette County

Columbus Quincentennial Celebration, 1992; hon. mem. Uniontown Area YMCA, 1995. Recipient Rockwell Recognition award, 1970, Jerusalem City of Peace award Fayette County Israel Bond Com., 1985, Silver Beaver award Boy Scouts Am., 1987, Eleanor Coldren award ARC-Uniontown Ch., 1993, Sheepskin award for disting. svc. to higher edn. Pa. Assn. Colls. and Univs., 1994, Libr. Citizien of Yr. award Pa. Citizens for Better Librs., 1993, Man of Yr. award B'nai B'rith, 1995, The Drake Well Found., The Col. Edwin L. Drake Legendary Oilman award, 2001; Melvin Jones fellow Lions Club Internat., 1993. Mem. Okla. Oil and Gas Assn., Okla. Ind. Petroleum Assn., Ohio Oil and Gas Assn., W.Va. Oil and Gas Assn., Pa. Oil and Gas Assn., Pa. Geol. Soc., Ind. Petroleum Assn., Greater Uniontown C. of C. (bd. dirs., past pres., named Man of Yr. 1968), Uniontown Country Club (past v.p., bd. dirs.), Rotary (past pres. Uniontown), Masons (past Master, hon. 33 degree), The Pa. Soc., Theta Chi. Office: Two W Main St Ste 600 Uniontown PA 15401-3448

EBERLY, WILLIAM SOMERS, financial consultant; b. Toledo, Sept. 25, 1921; s. Somers L. and Clara B. (Valentine) E.; m. Catharine L. Sloan (dec. Nov. 1979); children: Stephen, Michael; m. Elizabeth Eberly, Nov. 28, 1980. BBA, U. Toledo, 1943. Various positions Bklyn. Dodgers Nat. League Baseball team, 1944-52; bus. mgr. Milw. Braves Nat. League Baseball team, 1953-65; promotion mgr. Gladiux Corp., Toledo, 1966; fin. cons., sr. v.p. Salomon Smith Barney, 1967—. Spkr. on evolution of big league baseball, bus. Mem. adv. bd. U. Toledo Ctr. for Women, 1982—. Recipient Blue T award U. Toledo, 1992, Eli Lilly Pharm. award, 1996, New Eng. Deaconess Hosp. Diabetic Achievement award, 1997. Mem. U. Toledo Alumni Assn. (pres., 1972), Toledo Exch. Club (pres.). Home: 2521 Middlesex Dr Toledo OH 43606-3117 Fax: (419) 842-5370.

EBERSBERGER, ARTHUR DARRYL, insurance company executive, consultant; b. Balt., June 18, 1946; s. George Henry and Althea Ebersberger; m. Judith Simison, Nov. 18, 1982; 1 child, Leonard Darryl. BS in Mktg. and Mgmt., Susquehanna U., 1968; MBA, Loyola Coll., Balt., 1985; postgrad., Am. Coll., Bryn Mawr, Pa. CLU, ChFC; cert. ins. counselor; mem. Md. Bd. Architects. Owner Ebersberger & Assocs., Inc., Severna Park, Md., 1968-2000; pres. Ebersberger Consulting Inc., Severna Park, Md., 1986—. Pres. Anne Arundel Trade Coun., 1995-96, chmn., 1996-97; mem. Md. Bur. and Econ. Devel. Commn., 1995-99; mem. Md. Bd. Architects, 1993-99. Pres. Sheltered Workshop of Anne Arundel County, Glen Burnie, Md., 1978; pres., founder Leadership Anne Arundel, Inc., 1993-95, bd. dirs., 1995-96, chmn., immediate past pres., 1995-96, chmn. Exec. Series Program, 1997-99; mem. Anne Arundel County Planning Adv. Bd., 1996-99; chmn. v.p. Md. Conf. on Sml. Bus., 1989-90; grad. Leadership Md., 1993; bd. dirs. Ginger Cover Retirement Cmty, 1994-99, ASPIRE, 1995-99; trustee Anne Arundel Health Sys., Inc., 1997—, Anne Arundel C.C., 1998—. With USNR, 1960-71, Vietnam. Named Small Bus. Advocate of Yr., SBA, 1993. Mem. U.S. Jaycees (adv. bd. 1982, Outstanding Young Man Am. 1980-81, pres. Severna Park br. 1976), Assoc. Builders and Contractors (pres. 1986), Anne Arundel Life Underwriters (pres. 1981, life mem.), Million Dollar Round Table, CLU's (bd. dirs. Balt. chpt. 1981-83), Md. C. of C. (chmn. 1999-2001), Safari Club Internat. (pres. Chesapeake chpt. 1998-99), Profl. Liability Agts. Network (pres. 1985-86, exec. com. 1986-98), Chartwell Golf and Country Club (bd. dirs. 1981-83). Republican. Lutheran. Avocations: golf, fly fishing, hunting, exercise, tennis. Home: 51 Boone Trl Severna Park MD 21146-4501 Address: PO Box 959 Severna Park MD 21146-0959

EBERSOLE, BRIAN, former mayor; b. Tenn. BA, U. Tenn.; M in Ednl. Psychology, U. Conn. Tchr., counselor, adminstr. Tacoma Pub. Schs.; adminstr. Tacoma C.C., 1989-91; spkr. Wash. State Ho. of Reps.; state house majority leader; mayor City of Tacoma, 1995—2000; pres. Bates Tech. Coll., Tacoma, 2000—. Chair House Edn. Com., 1985-87; prime sponsor Omnibus Sch. Fin. Reform Act, 1987, Omnibus Drug Bill, 1989. Named Legislator of Yr. (6 consecutive yrs.), Assn. for Vocat. Edn., Legislator of Yr., Wash. State Firefighters Assn. and Wash. State Coun. of Policy Officers. Office: 1101 S Yakima Ave Tacoma WA 98405

EBERSOLE, CURT, music educator; b. Lancaster, Pa., Feb. 2, 1958; s. John C. and Helen L. Ebersole. MusB in Edn., Northwestern U., 1980, MusM, 1981; MFA, SUNY, 1996. Dir. of bands No. Valley Regional HS, Old Tappan, NJ, 1982—. Founder & coord. Bergen County Wind Conducting Symposium, Old Tappan, NJ, 1987—94. Musician: (plays) West Side Story, 1997 (Outstanding Overal Prodn. of the Yr. award Paper Mill Playhouse Rising Star, 1997), Phantom, 1998 (Outstanding Overal Prodn. of the Yr. award Paper Mill Playhouse Rising Star, 1998), Big, 2000 (Outstanding Overal Prodn. of the Yr. award Paper Mill Playhouse Rising Star, 2000); prodr.: (commission) El Jardin de Esperanza, by Timothy Broege; condr.: commission El Jardin de Esperanza, by Timothy Broege, musician. Named a J. Curtis Ebersole Day, Old Tappan, NJ. Mayor and Coun., 2002. Mem.: North Jersey Band Festival (sec. 1998—2002), Music Educators of Bergen County (treas. 1985—87). Avocations: cycling, fitness, travel, roller coasters. Home: 10 Stewart Place 2HE White Plains NY 10603 Office: Northern Valley Regional High School Central Avenue Old Tappan NJ 07675 Office Fax: 204-768-7724. Personal E-mail: jcebersole@ebernet.com. E-mail: ebersole@nvnet.org.

EBERSOLE, HELEN BROWNSBERGER, elementary school educator; b. Glendale, Ariz., Nov. 23, 1916; d. Albert Joseph Brownsberger and Estella Simmons; m. Walter Jennings Ebersole, Aug. 17, 1941; children: Brian, Susan, Joan. BA, LaVerne Coll., 1938; cert., UCLA. Tchr. Azusa Ctr., 1938—42, Bonita Unified Sch. Dist., LaVerne, Calif., 1956—77. Spkr. on traveling. Vol. ministries disaster child care Red Cross & Ch. of Brethren, 1980—90; vol., dir. song leader Camp LaVerne, Ch. Brethren, 1926—60. Mem.: DAR, AAUW, Traveler's Century Club. Republican. Protestant. Avocations: art, travel, reading, sports. Home: 3530 Damien Ave #198 La Verne CA 91750-3214

EBERSOLE, J. GLENN, JR., engineering, marketing, management and public relations executive; b. Lancaster, Pa., Feb. 8, 1947; s. J. Glenn and Marie Christine (Stoner) E.; m. Helen Walton, July 11, 1970. Student, Ohio No. U., 1965-67; BSCE, Pa. State U., 1970, M of Engring. Sci., 1973. Registered profl. engr., Pa. Vt., Md., Del., N.J. Rsch. tech. Pa. State U., University Park, 1968-70; civil engring. intern Pa. Dept. Transp., Harrisburg, 1970-71, asst. dist. design liaison engr., 1971, head rsch. & spl. studies Bur. Traffic Engring., 1971-76; asst. chief engr.-traffic Pa. Turnpike Commn., Harrisburg, 1976-78; chief transp. engr. Huth Engrs., Inc., Lancaster, 1978-81; exec. engr. GSGSB, Clarks Summit, Pa., 1981-82; founder, CEO J.G. Ebersole Asocs., Lancaster, Pa., 1982—, The Renaissance Group TM, Lancaster, Pa., 1983—; TAB cert. facilitator The Alternate Board TAB, 2001—. Part-time lectr. Pa. State U.; bus. agt. former NFL players; profl. mgr. & publicist for artists and authors; bd. dirs. Modern Transit Partnership. Contbr. articles to profl. jours. Past chmn. Rapho Twp. Planning Commn.; mem. regional devel. coun. Pa. State U.; active Pa. State legis. liaison program; ch. sch. tchr., lector, past chmn. brochure com. Ch. of the Apostles, past chmn. faith promise campaign, past mem. ch. coun., ch. steering com. for long range planning, past chmn. cable TV com.; bd. dirs., past pres. bd. trustees Actors Co. Pa.; past co-chmn. Le Cabaret Moulin Rouge Gala; past co-chmn. devel. com. Gt. Gatsby Gala; past chmn. fundraising campaign restoration project Mill Mus.; past trustee, past treas. bd. trustees Lancaster Found. Ednl. Enrichment; asst. sec., bd. dirs. Lancaster Indsl. Devel. Authority; bd. dirs. Ctrl. Pa. Friends Jazz; past bd. dirs. Lancaster Family YMCA; planning commn., econ. devel. task force, urban issues subcom. Lancaster County; bd. advisor Pa. State Harrisburg-The Capitol Coll.; chmn. bd. dirs. The First Tee of The Susquehanna Valley; bd. dirs. Modern Transit Partnership Bd. Mem. ASCE, NSPE, Am. Mktg. Assn. (dir., past Ctrl. Pa. chpt. pres.), Inst. Transp. Engrs., Lancaster C. of C. (govt. affairs com., chmn. golf com. 1985-87, long range transp. task force, local affairs com., mem. mktg./comm. coun., mem. transp. com., mem. mktg. coun.), Pa. Soc. Profl. Engrs., Pa. Soc., Pa. State Alumni Assn. (regional devel. coun.), Pa. State of Lancaster County (past pres., bd. dirs.), Pa. State Civil & Environ. Engring. Soc. (past pres., bd. dirs.), Pa. State Engring. Soc. (past bd. dirs.), Lancaster Country Club, Shriners, Masons (past master Mt. Joy, Pa. club, Royal Order of Jesters, Allentown, Ct.), Phi Eta Sigma, Alpha Sigma Phi. Home and Office: 1305 Wheatland Ave Lancaster PA 17603-4720 E-mail: jgeprman@aol.com.

EBERSOLE, MARK CHESTER, emeritus college president; b. Hershey, Pa., Nov. 3, 1921; s. Benjamin W.S. and Mary (Patrick) E.; m. Dorothy Baugher, June 26, 1943; children— Philip B., Stephen B. BS, Elizabethtown (Pa.) Coll., 1943, LL.D., 1969; B.D., Crozer Theol. Sem., 1946; MA, U. Pa., 1948; PhD, Columbia, 1952. UNRRA relief adminstr., Europe, 1946-47; asst. prof. religion and philosophy Elmira Coll., 1952-53; faculty Bucknell U., 1953-69, prof. religion, chmn. dept., chaplain of univ., 1958-61, asst. dean univ., 1961; dean Coll. Arts and Scis., 1961-62, v.p. acad. affairs, 1961-68, univ. provost, 1968-69; project specialist, spl. projects in edn. Ford Found., 1967-69, program adviser, 1969-71; dean Grad. Sch.; assoc. v.p. for acad. affairs Temple U., 1971-77; pres. Elizabethtown (Pa.) Coll., 1977-85, pres. emeritus, 1985—. Bd. dirs. Educators Mutual Life Ins. Co.; interim pres. Maryville Coll., 1992-93; ednl. cons., 1987—. Author: Christian Faith and Man's Religion, 1961; editor: Hail to Thee, Okoboji U. A Humor Anthology on Higher Education, 1992; contbr. articles to profl. jours. Trustee Linden Hall Sch., 1992—. J.P. Crozer Found. fellow, 1949-51 Mem. Pa. Soc., Cliosophic Soc. Home: 3001 Lititz Pike PO Box 5093 Lancaster PA 17606-5093

EBERSOLE, PATRICIA SUE, advertising executive, design educator; b. Poughkeepsie, N.Y., Nov. 6, 1952; d. Edward and Virginia Mae (Vanderof) E. AAS, Dutchess Community Coll., Poughkeepsie, 1974; student, Art Ctr. Coll. of Design, 1976-77; BS, SUNY, 1981; MA, Syracuse U., 1993. Cert. Distinction of Honorable Mention Printing Industries Am. Inc., 2002. Graphic artist So. Dutchess News, Wappingers Falls, N.Y., 1974; asst. illustrator Jarvis Studio, Westwod, Calif., 1975-78; freelance illustrator Poughkeepsie, N.Y., 1978—; graphic dir. Ulster County Coun. for the Arts, Kingston, N.Y., 1979; art dir. Diversified Creative Svcs., Kingston, 1979-80; graphic designer Advertiser's Graphic Svcs., Poughkeepsie, 1981-82; pres. Ebersole Graphiks, Poughkeepsie, 1982—. Adj. instr. Dutchess C.C., 1980-87. Recipient Recognition award IBM Corp., 1987, Cert. of Excellence Silver award Strathmore Graphics Gallery, 1988, 90, Desi award Graphic Design, 1984, 88, Excellence award Printing Industries of Am., 1988, Activities award Nat. Assn. for Campus Activities, 1985, Gold, Silver and Bronze awards Hudson Valley Area Mktg. Assn., Inc., 1989, 94, 95, 96, 97, Merit awards, 1994, Nat. Calendar Bronze award, 1991, Bronze award, 1995, Big Apple award, 1996, Communicator award of distinction, 1996, award of Excellence Am. Econ. Devel. Coun., 1992, Notable Merit award FPG Internat., 1992, Gold award Advt. Club of Westchester, 1996, Bronze award, 1997, Bronze award Westchester chpt. Women in Comms., Clarion award, 1997, 99, Bronze award Neenah Paper, 1998, Best of Show award Profl. Trade Shows, Inc., 1998, award of distinction, award of excellence, hon. mention The Communicator, 1999, 2000, cert. of merit Printing Industries Am. Inc., 2000, Gold award, Advertising Club of Westchester, 2001, Bronx Award, Advt. Club of Westchester, 2002. Mem. Greater So. Dutchess C. of C. Avocations: hunter equitation, scuba diving, photography, illustration. Office: Ebersole Graphiks 9 High Ridge Rd Hopewell Junction NY 12533-5560

EBERSTADT, NICHOLAS NASH, social sciences educator, researcher; b. N.Y.C., Dec. 10, 1955; s. Frederick and Isabel (Nash) E.; m. Mary Tedeschi, Oct. 24, 1987; children: Frederick William, Catherine Nash, Isabel, Alexandra. AB magna cum laude, Harvard U., 1976, MPA, 1979; MSc, London Sch. Econs., 1978; PhD, Harvard U., 1996. Vis. rsch. fellow Rockefeller Found., N.Y.C., 1979—80; vis. fellow Harvard Sch. Pub. Health, Cambridge, Mass., 1980—2002; vis. scholar Am. Enterprise Inst., Washington, 1985—99, Henry Wendt chair in polit. econ., 1999—. Mem. bd. advisers Nat. Bur. Asian Rsch., Seattle, 1996—; bd. dirs. Environ. Literacy Coun., Washington, U.S. Com. for Human Rights in North Korea, Washington; mem. publs. com. The Pub. Interest; mem. Adv. Com. for Vol. Fgn. Aid; mem. adv. bd. Nat. Ctr. for Health Stats.; cons. in field. Author: Poverty in China, 1979, The Poverty of Communism, 1988, Foreign Aid and American Purpose, 1989, A Critique of U.S. Foreign Aid Policy, 1990, The Tyranny of Numbers, 1995, Korea Approaches Reunification, 1995, The End of North Korea, 1999, Prosperous Paupers and Other Population Problems, 2000; co-author: The Population of North Korea, 1992; editor: Fertility Decline in the Less Developed Countries, 1981; co-editor: Comparing the Soviet and American Economies, 2000, Korea's Future and The Great Powers, 2001; contbr. articles to profl. jours. Mem. Cambridge Dem. City Com., 1974-77; founding mem. Com. for Free World, N.Y.C., 1981-90. Mem.: Coun. on Fgn. Rels., Harvard Club. Roman Catholic. Avocations: reading, exercising, travel. Office: Am Enterprise Inst 1150 17th St NW Washington DC 20036 E-mail: eberstadt@aei.org.

EBERSTEIN, ARTHUR, former biomedical engineering educator, researcher; b. Chgo., Apr. 23, 1928; s. Nathan and Sara (Estes) E.; m. Marion Apfel, Aug. 1, 1961; children— Sharon, Laura BS, Ill. Inst. Tech., 1950; MS, U. Ill., 1951; PhD, Ohio State U., 1957. Asst. mem. Inst. for Muscle Disease, N.Y.C., 1959-61; sr. scientist Am. Bosch Arma Corp., 1961-63; dir. biomed. engring. Lundy Electronics, Inc., Glen Head, N.Y., 1963-64; prof., dir. research dept. rehab. medicine NYU Med. Ctr, N.Y.C., 1964-96; rsch. coord. dept. rehab. medicine Kingsbrook Jewish Med. Ctr., Bklyn., 1997—2003. Co-author: Electrodiagnosis of Neuromuscular Disease, 1983 Served with U.S. Army, 1955-57 Fellow NSF, 1958, NIH, 1959 Mem. Am. Physiol. Soc., Biophys. Soc., Biomed. Engring. Soc. Am. Assn. Electrodiagnostic Medicine, Sigma Pi Sigma. Avocations: skiing; tennis.

EBERT, DARLENE MARIE, lawyer; b. Milw., Dec. 29, 1951; d. Frank James and Marie Antoinette (Ermenc) Leban; m. Lee Arthur Ebert, Dec. 30, 1972; children: Kristen Ann, Mark Alan. BA, U. Wis., 1973, MS, 1974, JD, 1977. Bar: Wis. 1977, Colo. 1977. Assoc. Lobato-Bleidt, Bleidt & Haight, Lakewood, Colo., 1978-79; asst. city atty. City of Denver, 1979-96; gen. counsel Denver Health and Hosp. Authority, 1997—. Mem. ABA, Colo. Bar Assn. (chmn. pub. coun. com., chmn. health law sect. 2003-04), Denver Bar Assn., Colo. Women's Bar Assn., Am. Health Lawyers Assn., Nat. Inst. Mcpl. Law Officers (chmn. pers. com. 1990-93), City Club (bd. dirs. 1991-94, pres. 1993), Beta Sigma Phi (pres. 1981-82, v.p. 1986-87, 89-90). Democrat. Roman Catholic. Home: 4015 S Niagara Way Denver CO 80237-2004 Office: Denver Health & Hosp Auth 660 Bannock St Fl 5 Denver CO 80204-4506

EBERT, DOROTHY ELIZABETH, retired county clerk; b. Beaver Dam, Wis., Apr. 16, 1941; d. Merlin Herman and Gertrude Elizabeth (Hupke) E. Grad. high sch., Beaver Dam. Sec., receptionist Household Fin. Corp., Beaver Dam, 1958—67; dep. county clk. Dodge County, Juneau, Wis., 1967—82, county clk., 1983—2003; ret., 2003. Past bd. dirs. Dodge County chpt. Am. Cancer Soc. Mem. Wis. County Clks. Assn. (historian 1994-95, treas. 1995-96, sec. 1996-97, v.p. 1997-98, pres. 1998-99). Republican. Lutheran. Avocations: bowling, golf, calligraphy, singing, bell choir.

EBERT, DOUGLAS EDMUND, corporate financial executive; b. Washington, Oct. 21, 1945; s. Edmund Francis and Lathelia Marie (Keesey) E.; m. Linda Sue Weick, June 24, 1994; children: Elizabeth Anne, Leslie Anne, Kevin Edward, Ashley Edward. BA, Williams Coll., 1968. Asst. sec. Mfrs. Hanover Trust Corp., N.Y.C., 1969-72, asst. v.p., 1972-73, v.p., 1973-76, sr. v.p., dep. gen. mgr., 1976-82, exec. v.p., 1982-85, sr. exec. v.p. investment banking sector, 1985-90; pres., CEO S.E. Bank N.A., Miami, 1990-91, also chmn. bd. dirs., 1990-91; with Lincoln Fin. Corp., Fort Wayne, Ind., 1992-93; pres., COO Mich. Nat. Bank, Farmington Hills, 1993-95; CEO Mich. Nat. Bank, Mich. Nat. Corp., 1995—2001; COO Cranbrook Ednl. Cmty., Bloomfield Hills, Mich., 2002—. Pres., chief exec. officer, S.E. Banking Corp., 1990-91, Miami, also bd. dirs.; bd. dirs. HomeSide Internat., Inc., Ind. One Capital Mgmt., Independence One Mortgage Corp., Detroit Renaissance, Detroit Symphony Hall, Detroit Regional C. of C., Detroit Econ. Club; trustee Cranbrook Inst. Sci. Bd. dirs. Cancer Research Ctr. Mem. Com. Econ. Devel., Bankers Assn. Fgn. Trade, U.S. Bus. Council, Bank Adminstrn. Inst., Assn. Res. City Bankers. Avocations: tennis, golf, bicycling, carpentry, reading. Office: 39221 Woodward Ave PO Box 801 Bloomfield Hills MI 48303*

EBERT, GERARD (GERRY EBERT), hypnotherapist, freelance/self-employed writer; b. Bklyn., June 14, 1956; s. George Thomas Ebert and Leonora Conway; m. Susan Anne Cabral-Ebert; 1 child, John. Cert. hypnotherapist, attention deficit disorder/attention defitit hyperactivity disorder. Price and order clk., sales mgr. D&S Chem. Co., 1982—89; with Hoffman LaRoche Maintenance, 0990—1992; hypnotherapist Belleville, NJ, 1993—98, Glendale, Calif., 1999—. Author: (poetry) Rage and Anger, 1998 (Achievement award, 1998), Little Girls, 1999 (Editors Choice award, 2000), Halloween Night, 2000 (Editors Choice award, 2000), The Hour is Late, 2000 (Achievement Award award, 2000), A Public Service Poem, 2001 (Poet of Merit award, 2002), Thoughts of a Man, 2002. Mem.: Acad. of Am. Poets (assoc.). Home: 3227 Cornwall Dr Glendale CA 91206-1420 Personal E-mail: GerryEbert@msn.com.

EBERT, ROBERT RAYMOND, economics educator; b. Cleve., June 15, 1943; s. Raymond Charles and Ellen Marie (Antalec) E.; m. Marcia Jo Maloch, July 15, 1967; 1 child, Sheryl Anne. BA in Econs., Baldwin Wallace Coll., 1965; MA in Econs., Western Reserve U., 1967; PhD in Econs., Case Western Reserve, 1974. Econs. educator Baldwin Wallace Coll., Berea, Ohio, 1967-84, Buckhorn econs. prof., 1984—. Cons. Associated Pipe Organ Builders Am.; trustee Fairview-Luth. Hosps. Contbr. articles to profl. jours. Mem. Am. Econs. Assn., Ohio Assn. Econs. Polit. Scientists (pres. 1983-84, treas. 1993-2002), Soc. Automotive Historians (bd. dirs.), Omicron Delta Epsilon (mem. exec. com.). Mem. United Church Christ. Avocations: church organist, antique cars, collecting music boxes. Home: 3300 Thomson Cir Cleveland OH 44116-3883 Office: Baldwin Wallace Coll 275 Eastland Rd Berea OH 44017-2088 E-mail: rebert@bw.edu.

EBERT, VIOLA ROTH, neuropsychologist, entrepreneur; b. McAlester, Okla., Feb. 1, 1938; d. Johann Maria and Irene Turnbow Roth; m. Robert Oliver Ebert (div. Dec. 2, 1992); children: Adrienne Ebert-LeBlanc, Cecile'. BA, U. N.C., 1972; MA, Wake Forest U., 1976; PhD, Heed U., 1979. Psychol. asst. Iredell County Mental Health Ctr., Statesville, NC, 1972—74; psychol. assoc. Bowman Gray Sch. of Medicine, Winston-Salem, NC, 1976—79, assoc. faculty mem., 1979—82; pvt. practice Biofeedback and Pain Control Clinic, Statesville, 1982—86; lectr./workshop leader USNAH, Inc., Statesville, 1982—2002; writer under pen name T. F. Sisters, Hendersonville, Tenn., 1998—2002; inventor KAH, Inc., Mooresville, NC, 1999—2002; artist mgr. SEM, Inc., Hendersonville, 1992—2002. Author: (book) DEADLY BREW She Loved Him to Death, 2002. Mem.: Nat. Assn. Women Writers, N.C. Psychol. Assn., Spiritual Frontiers Fellowship (life; dir. 1986—90), Bluegrass Yacht and Country Club. Avocation: fishing, off-road trekking,painting, designing jewelry, photography.

EBERWEIN, BARTON DOUGLAS, construction company executive, consultant; b. Balt., Aug. 19, 1951; s. Bruce George and Thelma Joyce (Cox) E. BS, U. Oreg., 1974, MBA, 1988. Sales mgr. Teleprompter of Oreg., Eugene, 1974-75; pres., owner Oreg. Images, Eugene, 1975-80; mktg. cons. Clearwater Prodns., Eugene, 1980—82; sales mgr. Western Wood Structures, Portland, Oreg., 1982-84, mktg. coordinator, 1984-85, mktg. dir., 1985-89; dir. bus. devel. Hoffman Constrn. Co., Portland, 1989-93, v.p., 1993—. Bd. dirs. N.W. Youth Corps, Eugene, 1984—, Police Activity League, 1991, Portland Arts and Lectrs., 1994—, Archtl. Found. Oreg.; vol. bd. dirs. Goodwill, Oreg. Symphony, Portland Inst. for Contemporary Art, 1997—, Cycle Oreg. Mem. AIA, Soc. Mktg. Profl. Svcs., Am. Mktg. Assn., Multnomah Athletic Club, Arlington Club, Archtl. Found. of Oreg. (bd. dirs.). Democrat. Presbyterian. Avocations: rare books, photography, outdoor recreation, architectural preservation. Home: 5225 SW Menefee Dr Portland OR 97239-2784 Office: Hoffman Constrn Co 805 SW Broadway Ste 2100 Portland OR 97205 E-mail: barte@hoffmancorp.com.

EBERWINE, JAMES, molecular biologist, educator; b. Newcastle, Ind., Mar. 10, 1956; s. Paul David and Mary Josephine Eberwine; m. JoanMarie Kienlen; children: Paul, Grace. BS, Yale U., 1978; PhD, Columbia U., 1984; M.Phil (hon.), U. of Pa, 1990. PhD Columbia Univ, 1984. Post-doctoral fellow Stanford U., Palo Alto, Calif., 1984—90; asst. prof. U. of Pa, Philadelphia, Pa., 1990—94, assoc. prof., 1994—96, prof., 1996—. Sci. founder molecular biology group Neurex Corp, Menlo Park, Calif., 1986—89; sci. founder Layton Biolscience, Menlo Park, Calif., 1991, LBS Technologies, Philadelphia, Pa.; sci. adv. bd. for 5 companies; cons. for various biotechnology and pharm. companies. Author: (two books) In Situ Hybridization: Applications to Neurobiology. Recipient MERIT Award, NIH, 2001, Disting. Investigator, NARSAD, 1996, Established Investigator, Am. Heart Assn., 1994. Achievements include first to Various Advances in Understanding the functioning of the CNS. Developed the techniques of Single Cell Molecular Biology; patents for 15 Patents Related To Biotechnology. Office: Univ of Pa Med Sch 36th and Hamilton Walk Philadelphia PA 19104 Office Fax: 215-573-2236. E-mail: eberwine@pharm.med.upenn.edu.

EBIE, WILLIAM D. museum director; b. Akron, Ohio, Feb. 7, 1942; s. William P. and Mary Louise (Karam) E.; m. Gwyn Anne Schumacher, Apr. 11, 1968 (div. Jan. 1988); children: Jason William, Alexandra Anne; m. Mary Teresa Hayes, June 10, 1989. BFA, Akron Art Inst., 1964; MFA, Calif. Coll. of Arts and Crafts, 1968. Graphic artist Alameda County Health Dept., Oakland, Calif., 1967-68; instr. painting Fla. A&M U., Tallahassee, 1968-69; instr. photography Lawrence (Kans.) Adult Edn. Program, 1969-70; asst. dir. Roswell (N.Mex.) Mus. & Art Ctr., 1971-87, dir., 1987-98, Millicent Rogers Mus., Taos, N.Mex., 1998—2002. Juror various art exhbns., 1971—; panelist N.Mex. Arts Divsn., Santa Fe, 1983-87; field reviewer Inst. for Mus. Svcs., 1988-90; mem. State Capitol Renovation Art Selection Com., Santa Fe, 1991-92; bd. dirs. State Capitol Found., Santa Fe, 1992-2002. Bd. dirs. Helene Wurlitzer Found., Taos, N.Mex., 1999—. Mem. Am. Assn. of Mus., Mountain Plains Mus. Assn., N.Mex. Assn. of Mus. Democrat. Avocations: photography, carpentry. E-mail: billebie@earthlink.net.

EBINER, ROBERT MAURICE, lawyer; b. L.A., Sept. 2, 1927; s. Maurice and Virginia (Grand) E.; m. Paula H. Van Sluyters, June 16, 1951; children: John, Lawrence, Marie, Michael, Christopher, Joseph, Francis, Matthew, Therese, Kathleen, Eileen, Brian, Patricia, Elizabeth, Ann, JD, Loyola U., L.A., 1953. Bar: Calif. 1954, U.S. Dist. Ct. (cen. dist.) Calif. 1954. Pvt. practice, West Covina, Calif., 1954—. Judge pro tem L.A. Superior Ct., 1964-66, 90—, arbitrator, 1979—; arbitrator San Bernardino Superior Ct., 1990—; judge pro tem Citrus Mcpl. Ct., 1966-70, 1990—, El Monte Mcpl. Ct., 1998—, Whittier Mcpl. Ct., 2001—, mediator, 2000-; mem. disciplinary hearing panel Calif. State Bar, 1968-75. Bd. dirs. West Covina United Fund, 1958-61, chmn. budget com., 1960-61; organizer Joint United Funds East San Gabriel Valley, 1962, bd. dirs., 1961-68; bd. dirs. San Gabriel Valley Cath. Social Svcs., 1969—, pres., 1969-72; bd. dirs. Region II Cath. Social Svc., 1970—, pres., 1970-74; trustee L.A. Cath. Welfare Bur. (now Cath. Charities), 1978—; charter bd. dirs. East San Gabriel Valley Hot Line, 1969-74, sec., 1969-72; charter bd. dirs. N.E. L.A. County unit Am. Cancer Soc., 1973-78, chmn. by-laws com., 1973-78; bd. dirs. Queen of the Valley Hosp. Found., 1983-89; organizer West Covina Hist. Soc., 1982—; active Calif. State Dem. Cen. Com., 1963-68; mng. meet dir. Greater La Puente Valley Spl. Olympics, 1985-88, Bishop Amat Relays, 1981-96; mem. MSAC Relays Com., 1978—; campaign mgr. Congressman Ronald B. Cameron, 1964. With U.S. Army, 1945-47. Recipient L.A. County Human Rels. Commn. Disting. Svc. award, 1978, Thomas A. Kiefer Humanitarian award, 1993; named West Covina Citizen of Yr., 1986, San Gabriel Valley Daily Tribune's Father of Yr., 1986. Mem. ABA, Calif. Bar Assn., L.A. County Bar Assn. (arbitrator 1975—), Fed. Ct. So. Dist. Calif. Assn., Consumer Attys. LA, Ea. Bar Assn. L.A. County (pres. Pomona Valley 1965-66), West Covina C. of C. (pres. 1960), Am. Arbitration Assn. (arbitrator 1965-98), KC, Bishop Amat H.S. Booster Club (bd. dirs. 1973-96, pres. 1978-80), Kiwanis (charter West Covina, pres. 1976-77, 2002-2003, lt. gov. divsn. 35 1980-81, Kiwanian of Yr. 1978, 82, Disting. Lt. Gov. 1980-81, bd. dirs. Cal-Nev-Ha Found. 1986-98, pres. 1994-96). Avocation: collector western U.S. historical olympic and political memorabilia. Office: 100 N Citrus St Ste 520 West Covina CA 91791-1694

EBISUZAKI, YUKIKO, retired chemistry educator; b. Mission City, B.C., Can., July 25, 1930; came to U.S., 1957; d. Masuzo and Shige (Kusumoto) E. BS with honors, U. Western Ont., London, Can., 1956, MS, 1957; PhD, Ind. U., 1962. Postdoctoral U. Pa., Phila., 1962-63; faculty rsch. assoc. Ariz. State U., Tempe, 1963-67; acting asst. prof. UCLA, 1967-75; assoc. prof. N.C. State U., Raleigh, 1975-99, assoc. prof. emeritus, 1999—. Contbr. articles to profl. jours. Ont. Rsch. Found. fellow Ont. Rsch. Coun., 1957-60, Gerry fellow Sigma Delta Epsilon, 1977-78. Mem. Am. Chem. Soc., Sigma Xi.

EBITZ, DAVID MACKINNON, art historian, educator; b. Hyannis, Mass., Oct. 5, 1947; s. Robert White Creeley and Ann (MacKinnon) Kucera; m. Mary Ann Stankiewicz, Jan. 1, 1983; children: Rebecca Aemilia, Cecilia Charlotte. BA, Williams Coll., 1969; AM, Harvard U., 1973, PhD, 1979. Teaching fellow, then head teaching fellow dept. fine arts Harvard U., Cambridge, Mass., 1975-78; asst. prof., then assoc. prof. dept. art U. Maine, Orono, 1978-87, interim dir. galleries, curator univ. art collection, 1986-87; head dept. edn. and acad. affairs J. Paul Getty Mus., Santa Monica, Calif., 1987-92; dir. John and Mable Ringling Mus. Art, Sarasota, Fla., 1992-2000; assoc. prof. art Pa. State U., University Park, 2000—. Vis. faculty Bangor (Maine) Theol. Sem., 1981;

lectr. in field; presenter workshops. Author exbhn. revs., book revs.; contbr. articles to arts publs., exhbn. catalogues. Heritage Found. fellow, 1968. Mem. Coll. Art Assn., Nat. Art Edn. Assn., Am. Assn. Museums (mus. edn. com.), Medieval Acad. Am., Internat. Ctr. Medieval Art, Phi Beta Kappa. Office: Penn State U 210 Patterson University Park PA 16802 E-mail: dme12@psu.edu.

EBITZ, ELIZABETH KELLY, lawyer; b. LaPorte, Ind., June 9, 1950; d. Joseph Monahan and Ann Mary (Barrett) Kelly; m. David MacKinnon Ebitz, Jan. 23, 1971 (div. 1981). AB with honors, Smith Coll., 1972; JD cum laude, Boston U., 1975. BAr: Maine 1979, Mass. 1975, U.S. Dist. Ct. Mass. 1976, U.S. Dist. Ct. Maine 1979, U.S. Ct. Appeals (1st cir.) 1976, U.S. Supreme Ct. 1982. Law clk. Boston Legal Assistance Project, 1973-75; law clk., assoc. Law Offices John J. Thornton, Boston, 1974-76; ptnr. Ebitz & Zurn, Northampton, Mass., 1976-79; assoc. Gross, Minsky, Mogul & Singal, Bangor, Maine, 1979-80; pres. Elizabeth Kelly Ebitz P.A., Bangor, 1980-92, Ebitz & Thornton, P.A., 1993—. Pres. Greater Bangor Rape Crisis Bd., 1983-85; bd. dirs., sec., legal counsel Bangor Area Homeless Shelter, 1985-92, 93-99; bd. dirs. Maine Women's Lobby, 1986-89, No. Maine Bread for the World, 1987-90; bd. dirs., sec. Machias River Clinic for Mental Health and Substance Abuse, 2000—; bd. dirs. Am. Heart Assn., Maine, 1989—, sec., 1989-91, chair, 1993-95; mem. various peace, feminist and hunger orgns., Bangor, 1982—. Named Young Career Woman of Hampshire County, Nat. Bus. and Profl. Women, Northampton, 1979. Mem. Maine State Bar Assn., Nat. Orgn. Social Security Claimants (rep. 1994—), Sigma Xi. Democrat. Roman Catholic. Home: 111 Maple St Bangor ME 04401-4031 Office: 329 Wilson St Brewer ME 04412-1504 E-mail: bgrlegal@aol.com.

EBLE, JOHN NELSON, pathologist, oncology researcher; b. Madison, Wis., Sept. 15, 1951; s. John Nelson and Jane Mildred (Brewer) E.; Kathy Marie Stelter, Sept. 30, 1972 (div. 1983); children: Nicholas, Benjamin, Elizabeth; m. Rosemarie A. Heltsley, May 25, 1985. BS, Ind. U., 1973, MBA, 1990; MD, Ind. U., Indpls., 1976. Diplomate in Anat. and Clin. Pathology, Am. Bd. Pathology, Am. Bd. Med. Mgmt. Intern Ind. U. Hosp., 1977, resident in pathology, 1978-80; asst. prof. pathology Ind. U., Indpls., 1980-82, asst. prof. pathology and exptl. oncology, 1982-85, assoc. prof., 1985-91, prof. pathology and exptl. oncology, 1991—, Nordschow prof. lab. medicine, 2000—. Chief pathologist VA, Indpls., 1982—, assoc. chmn. dept. pathology, 1985-90, chmn. dept. pathology and lab. medicine, 1999—; cons. pathologist Hawley Army Hosp., Ft. Benjamin Harrison, Ind., 1984-92; dep. coroner Marion County Coroner's Office, Ind.; chief pathologist Clarian Health Ptnrs. (Meth.-Ind. U.-Riley), Indpls., 1999—. Editor-in-chief Jour. Urologic Pathology, 1997-2000, Modern Pathology, 2000—; contbr. articles to profl. jours. Fellow Coll. Am. Pathologists, Am. Soc. Clin. Pathologists; mem. AMA, Am. Assn. Cancer Rsch., Arthur Purdy Stout Surgical Pathologists, Internat. Acad. Pathology, U.S. Acad. Pathology, Can. Acad. Pathology. Fellow: Royal Coll. Pathologists Australasia. Office: Dept Pathology and Lab Medicine 635 Barnhill Dr Indianapolis IN 46202-5126 E-mail: jeble@iupui.edu.

EBLER, MARILYN ANN, graphic designer, educator; b. Socorro, N.Mex., Mar. 9, 1955; d. Robert Gerald Ebler and Mary Eulala (Castillo) Barber; children: Manuel Anthony Anaya, Josephine Lynn Duke. Cert. Cosmetology, Lea County Beauty Coll., 1977; AAS, N.Mex. Jr. Coll., 1992; BS with honors, Ea. N.Mex. U., 1995; MS in Edn., Capella U., Mpls., 2001. Cosmetologist Glamour House, Hobbs, N.Mex., 1977—85, Linda's Styling Salon, Hobbs, N.Mex., 1985—91; staff graphic arts dept. N.Mex. Jr. Coll., Hobbs, 1991—92; computer lab. asst., office asst. Ea. N.Mex. U., 1993—94; graphic arts asst. N.Mex. Jr. Coll., Hobbs, 1994—95, prof. comml. graphic design, 1995—. Mem. faculty senate N.Mex. Jr. Coll., 1995—; attendee numerous confs. Contbr. graphic designs to profl. jours. Recipient numerous awards. Mem. Vocat. Indsl. Clubs Am. (advisor 1995-97), Kappa Pi (sec. 1993-94). Avocations: photography, water color, cross stitch, walking, crochet. Home: 1009 W Cain St Hobbs NM 88240-5612 E-mail: maebler@3dinet.com.

EBLIN, ROBERT L. lawyer; b. Columbus, Ohio, Apr. 21, 1963; AB cum laude, Harvard U., 1985; JD summa cum laude, Ohio State U., 1991. Bar: Ohio 1991, U.S. Dist. Ct. (so. dist.) Ohio 1991, U.S. Ct. Appeals (6th cir.) 1992, U.S. Supreme Ct. 1997. Assoc. Schwartz Warren & Ramirez, Columbus, 1991-96, Arter & Hadden LLP, Columbus, 1997-99, ptnr., 2000—03, Bailey Cavalieri LLC, Columbus, 2003—. Adj. prof. law Ohio State U., Columbus, 1997. Contbg. author: Looking at Law School, 3d edit., 1990, 4th edit., 1997, Liability of Corporate Officers and Directors, 6th edit., 1999, 7th edit., 2002. Mem. Ohio Human Rights Bar Assn. (trustee 1989-93, 99—, pres. 2000—), Profl. Liability Underwriting Soc., Order of Coif. Office: Bailey Cavalieri LLC 10 W Broad St Ste 2100 Columbus OH 43215 Office Fax: 614-221-0479. E-mail: Robert.Eblin@BaileyCavalieri.com.

EBNETER, STEWART DWIGHT, utility industry management consultant; b. Ledgewood, N.J., Oct. 10, 1933; s. William and Emily Ann (Burd) E.; m. Evadna Grace Custer, Dec. 28, 1957; children: Stewart D. Jr., Steven D., Scott D. BSEE, Tri-State U., 1959; MBA, Athens State Coll., 1971. Registered profl. engr., Calif. System engr. Boeing Co., Seattle, 1959-61; reliability dept. head Spaco, Inc., Huntsville, Ala., 1961-70, v.p. engring., 1971-73; div. dir. br. chief U.S. Nuclear Regulatory Commn., Atlanta, King of Prussia, Pa., 1973-87, dir. office spl. projects Washington, 1987-88, dir. div. radiation safety, regional adminstr., 1989-97; mgmt. cons. to utility industry, 1997—. Allocation com. United Way, Huntsville, 1970-73; scout leader Boy Scouts Am., Huntsville, 1970-73. Sgt. USAF, 1953-57. Mem. Am. Soc. for Quality Control (sr.), Am. Nuclear Soc. Home and Office: 107 Whitfield Run Peachtree City GA 30269-3313 E-mail: s.ebneter@attbi.com.

EBOMOYI, WILLIAM EHIGIE, epidemiologist; b. Benin, Edo, Nigeria, Dec. 19, 1949; came to the U.S., 1971; s. James and Igbinowan Ebomoyi; m. Josephine I. Orobor, Aug. 1, 1984; children: Carolyn, Pat, Uyi, Nosa. BA, Western Ill. U., 1975, MS, 1976; PhD, U. Ill., 1981; post-doctorate cert., USPHS NIH, 1990. Intern Tulane U. Med. Sch.; intern, resident Fed. Ministry Health, Lagos, Nigeria, 1977; sr. lectr. U. Ilorin (Nigeria) Med. Sch., 1982-88; rsch. fellow Tulane U. Med. Ctr., New Orleans, 1988-90, adj. asst. prof. pediat., 1992-96; program evaluator Boston Med. Ctr., 1990-91; sci. faculty Concordia U., New Orleans, 1996; assoc. prof. U. No. Colo., Greeley, 1996—2001, prof., 2002—. Cons. APHA, 1980—, Appeal for Charities and Good Will, Inc., Chgo., 1980—, The World Bank, Washington, 1993—, Weld County Dept. Pub. Health, Greeley, 1997—, Colo. Pub. Health Assn., 1999; adv. bd. vice chmn. Air Quality and Natural Resources, Greeley, 1999—. Author: Community Medicine: A Global Perspective, 1998, International Health: A Multi-cultural Approach, Public Health and Sustainable Development; contbr. articles to profl. jours. V.p. Edo Club, New Orleans br., 1992-96. Rsch. fellow Fogarty Internat., Bethesda, Md., 1988, Leadership fellow AAAS, 1990. Mem. AAHPERD, Am. Inst. for Health Promotion, Planetary Soc., Legacy Internat. Inc. (pres.), New Eng. Regional Genetic Group, Fedn. Am. Scientists, Greeley Writers Club. Avocations: bird watching, poetry, soccer, softball, chess. Home: 1739 28th Ave Greeley CO 80634-5764 Office: Univ No Colo Gunter 2280 501 20th St Greeley CO 80639-0001 E-mail: Webomoyi@hhs.unco.edu.

EBOZUE, BENSON OBIAN, financial analyst; b. Onitsha, Anambra, Nigeria, Nov. 14, 1960; came to U.S., 1984; s. Benjamen A. Ebozue and Regina A. Abanafo; m. Comfort N. Ndubisi, Feb. 16, 1994; children: Benson Onyeka Jr., Jesse Mezue Nna. Diploma in acctg., Sch. of Accountancy & Mgmt., Aba, Imo, Nigeria, 1982; BBA, Dallas Bapt. U., 1991; cert., U. Tex., Arlington, 1992. CPA, Tex.; cert. adminstrv. acct., U.K. Tutor Sch. of Commerce, Onitsha, 1980-81; sr. acctg. asst. Ekwenibe & Sons Trading Co., Onitsha, 1982-84; accounts payable asst. Makai Bros., Orlando, Fla., 1984-88, CompUsa, Dallas, 1989; loan auditor Mortgage Bankers Cons., Dallas, 1991-92; acctg. analyst Sunbelt Nat. Mortgage, Dallas, 1992—; default auditor FTB Mortgage Svcs., Dallas, 1992-97; pres., CFO, Home Health Care Response, Dallas, 1997-98; mgr., owner Diamond Shamrock (BCE Mart), Dallas, 1998—99; sr acct. Fed. Mgmt. System, Inc., Washington, 2000—; owner Benson O. Ebozue CPA, Cedar Hill, Tex., 2001—. Staff auditor Logan & Assocs., CPA, Cedar Hill, Tex., 1999—. Tutor Dallas Ind. Sch. Dist., 1991-92; vol. Boys Brigade, Onitsha, 1971-76. Mem. AICPA, Tex. Soc. CPAs (cert.). Avocations: soccer, table tennis. Home and Office: 219 Armstrong Dr Cedar Hill TX 75104-2348

EBRIGHT, RICHARD HIGH, molecular biologist; b. Reading, Pa., June 11, 1959; s. Richard Jerome and Jacqueline Katherine (Muth) Ebright; m. Yon Won, Dec. 39, 1985; children: Richard Yon, Katherine Yon. BA in Biology summa cum laude, Harvard U., 1981, PhD in Microbiology, Molecular Genetics, 1987. Jr. fellow Harvard U., Cambridge, 1984-87; asst. prof. dept. chemistry Rutgers U., New Brunswick, N.J., 1987-92, assoc. prof. dept. chemistry, 1992-95, prof. dept. chemistry, 1995—. Investigator Howard Hughes Med. Inst., Chevy Chase, Md., 1997—. Editor: Jour. Molecular Biology, 1997—; contbr. articles to scientific jours.; mem. editl. bd. Jour. Bacteriology, 1995-98; patentee in field (2). Searle scholar Searle Found., 1989; recipient Walter J. Johnson prize Acad. Press, 1995. Fellow Am. Acad. Microbiology; mem. Am. Soc. Biochem. Molecular Biology (Schering-Plough Sci. Achievement award 1995), Am. Chem. Soc., Am. Soc. Microbiology, AAAS, Biophys. Soc. Republican. Lutheran. Office: HHMI/Waksman Inst 190 Frelinghuysen Rd Piscataway NJ 08854-8020

EBY, CARL PETER, English educator; PhD, U. Calif., Davis, 1995. Lectr. Mich. State U., East Lansing, 1996-98; asst. prof. English U. S.C., Beaufort, 1998—, assoc. prof. english, 2003—. Author: Hemingway's Fetishism, 1999. Recipient Robert J. Stoller Found. Essay award for Psychoanalytic Rsch., 1996, John F. Kennedy Libr. Hemingway rsch. grant, 1996, S.C. Gov.'s Disting. Prof. award, 2001. E-mail: carlpeby@gwm.sc.edu.

EBY, CECIL DEGROTTE, English language educator, writer; b. Charles Town, W.Va., Aug. 1, 1927; s. Cecil and Ellen (Turner) E.; children: Clare Virginia, Lillian Turner. AB, Shepherd Coll., 1950; MA, Northwestern U., 1951; PhD, U. Pa., 1958. Instr., then asst. prof. English High Point Coll., 1955-57; asst. prof., then asso. prof. Madison Coll., 1957-60; mem. faculty Washington and Lee U., 1960-65; prof. U. Mich., 1965—; prof. English, chmn. dept. U. Miss., University, 1975-76. Fulbright prof. Am. lit. U. Salamanca, Spain, 1962-63; Fulbright prof. Am. studies U. Valencia, 1967-68; Fulbright prof. Am. lit. U. Budapest, 1981; prof. U. Szeged, 1988-89. Author: Porte Crayon: The Life of David H. Strother, 1960, The Siege of the Alcazar, 1965, (translations in Italian, German, Finnish, Dutch, Portuguese) Between the Bullet and the Lie: American Volunteers in the Spanish Civil War, 1969 (transl. in Spanish), That Disgraceful Affair: The Black Hawk War, 1973, The Road to Armageddon: The Martial Spirit in English Popular Literature, 1987, The War in Hungary: Civilians and Soldiers in World War II, 1998; editor: The Old South Illustrated, 1959, A Virginia Yankee in the Civil War, 1961. Served with USNR, 1945-46. Episcopalian. E-mail: cdeby@umich.edu.

EBY, JOHN WILMER, sociology educator; b. Lititz, Pa. s. Wilmer M and Arlene B. E.; m. Joyce R. Rutt, June 29, 1963; children: Carol L., Scott L. BA in Chemistry, Ea. Mennonite Coll., 1962; MS in Devel. Sociology, Cornell U., 1970, PhD in Devel. Sociology, 1972. Dir. voluntary svc. Ea. Mennonite Bd. Missions, Salunga, Pa., 1962-67; prof. sociology, chair sociology dept. Ea. Mennonite Coll., Harrisonburg, Va., 1970-74; sec. relief & svc. Mennonite Bd. Missions, Elkhart, Ind., 1974-79; country rep. Mennonite Ctrl. Com., Akron, Pa., 1979-82; prof. bus. & sociology, chair bus. dept. Ea. Mennonite Coll., 1982-89; acad. dean Goshen (Ind.) Coll., 1989-94; prof. sociology, dir. svc.-learning, chair sociology dept. Messiah Coll., Grantham, Pa., 1994—. Chair Ctr. Indsl. Tng., Silver Springs, Pa., 1999—, pres. CPARC. Co-author: Business Through the Eyes of Faith, 1990; editor: Service-Learning: Linking Academics and the Community, 1995. Mem. Am. Sociol. Assn., Am. Assn. Higher Edn., Phi Kappa Phi. Office: Messiah Coll Coll Ave Grantham PA 17027

EBY, LLOYD MARTIN, editor, writer, educator, filmmaker; b. Fayetteville, Pa., Feb. 9, 1943; s. Lloyd Arthur and Leona Ruth (Martin) E.; m. Susanna Mast, 1964 (div.); m. Anna Waisielwska, 1974 (div.); m. Pauline Pilote, Oct. 26, 1981; children: Jessica Anne, Christopher Lee, Stephanie Claire. AB, Washington U., St. Louis, 1967; MA, Fordham U., 1982, PhD, 1988. Lectr. in philosophy SUNY, Albany, 1969-70; mem. humanities faculty U. Md., U. Coll., College Park, 1990—; dir. of publics Internat. Cultural Found., N.Y.C., 1987-89; asst. sr. editor The World and I Mag., Washington, 1990—. Adj. lectr. in philosophy Unification Theol. Sem., Barrytown, N.Y., 1979-90; adj. prof. philosophy U. D.C., 1990-92; adj. lectr. bus. ethics Cath. U. Am., 2000; cons. Internat. Cultural Found., N.Y.C., 1980-84, New Ecumenical Rsch. Assn., Barrytown, N.Y. and N.Y.C., 1978-84; pres. Afghanistan Documentary Film Project, N.Y., 1987-88. Author/editor: (book) Art and Technology, 1986; author: Business and Professional Ethics, 1993, The World and I Mag., 1986—; contbr. articles to profl. jours. Fundraiser Rep. Party of N.Y., 1980; dist. leader Unification Ch. of Washington, Cheverly, 1996—97, mem. fin. com., 1998—. Nominated for Stanley Drazek award in tchg. U. Md. Univ. Coll., 1994. Mem. Am. Philos. Assn., Prof. World Peace Assn., Chesapeake Rifle and Pistol Club. Avocations: skeet and rifle shooting, photography, film and film studies, reading. Office: The World & I Mag 3600 New York Ave NE Washington DC 20002-1947 E-mail: leby@worldandimag.com.

EBY, MARTIN KELLER, JR., construction company executive; b. Wichita Falls, Tex., Apr. 19, 1934; s. Martin and A. Pauline (Kimbell) E.; m. Melodee Stanley, Aug. 20, 1955; children: Stanley, Suzanna, David. BS in Civil Engring. Kans. State U., 1956. Registered profl. engr., Kan. With Martin K. Eby Constrn. Co., Inc., Wichita, Kan., 1956—, engr., project mgr., v.p., 1956-67, pres., 1967-92, chmn., 1979—. Bd. dirs. Intrust Bank in Wichita, Intrust Fin. Corp., SBC Comms. Inc.; mem. engring. adv. coun. Kans. State U., Manhattan, 1970—. Bd. dirs. Kans. Pub. Policy Inst., chmn.; mem. Kans. State U. Coll. of Engring. Hall of Fame, 1989—; chmn. Constrn. Industry Polit. Action Com. of Kans., Topeka, 1978. Mem. ASCE, NSPE, Kans. Engring. Soc., Wichita Profl. Engring. Soc., Chief Execs. Orgn., Beavers (bd. dirs., pres. 1996-97), Moles (hon.). Congregationalist. Home: 624 N Longford Ln Wichita KS 67206-1818 Office: Martin Eby Constrn Co Inc PO Box 1679 610 N Main St Wichita KS 67203-3601

EBY, MICHAEL JOHN, marketing research and technology consultant; b. South Bend, Ind., Aug. 3, 1949; s. Robert T. and Eileen Patricia (Holmes) E.; m. Judith Alyson Gaskell, May 17, 1980; children: Elizabeth, Katherine. Student, Harvey Mudd Coll., 1969-70; BS in Biochemistry with high honors, U. Md., 1972, MS in Chemistry, 1977; postgrad., IMEDE, Lausanne, Switzerland, 1984. Product mgr. LKB Instruments Inc., Rockville, Md., 1976-79; mktg. mgr. LKB-Produkter AB, Bromma, Sweden, 1979-87; strategic planning mgr. Pharmacia LKB Biotech. AB, Bromma, 1987-88; dir. mktg. Am. Bionetics, Hayward, Calif., 1988-89; pres. PhorTech Internat., San Carlos, Calif., 1989—. Author: The Electrophoresis Explosion, 1988, Electrophoresis in the Nineties, 1990, DNA Amplification, 1993, Blotting and Hybridization, 1993, Capillary Electrophoresis, 1993, Densitometers and Image Analysis, 1995, Microplate Equipment, 1995, Synthetic Oligonucleotides, 1995, Electrophoretic Gel Media, 1995, Visualization Reagents, 1995, U.S. Laboratory Product Usage, 1996, Cell Biology Reagent Systems, 1996, Centrifugation, 1996, Molecular Biology Reagent Systems, 1997, DNA Diagnostics, 1997, DNA Amplification in Europe, 1998, Recombinant Protein Expression Systems, 1998, DNA Sequencing in Europe, 1998, Cytokines and Growth Factors, 1998, Molecular Biology Reagent Systems in the Far East, 1998, HPLC in the Life Sciences, 1998, Cytokines and Growth Factors, 1998, Cell and Tissue Culture, 1998, Monoclonal Antibodies, 1999, Microplate Instrumentation in Europe, 1999, DNA Sequencing, 1999, Worldwide Directory of Life Science Distributors, 2000, Global Laboratory Product Usage, 2000, DNA Amplification, 2000, DNA Sequencing, 2000, Electrophoretic Equipment and Reagents, 2001, Densitometers and Image Analysis in Europe, 2001, Molecular Biology Reagent Systems, 2001, DNA Sequencing in the Far East, 2001, DNA Amplification Instrumentation, 2002, DNA Amplification Regents and Methodology, 2002, Microplate Readers and Equipment, 2002, Global Laboratory Product Usage, 2002, Proteomics Research, Vol. 1, 2003, others; contbr. articles to profl. jours. Mem.: AAAS, Mktg. Rsch. Assn., Spirit of LKB Internat. Assn., The Electrophoresis Soc., Am. Soc. Cell Biology, Am. Chem. Soc., European Soc. Opinion and Mktg. Rsch., Am. Philat. Soc., Calif. Separation Sci. Soc., Am. Mensa, U. Md. Alumni Assn. Episcopalian. Avocations: astronomy, cheesemaking, photography, travel. Office: PhorTech Internat 238 Crestview Dr San Carlos CA 94070-1503 E-mail: mikeby@phortech.com.

EBY, RONALD K. polymer science educator, researcher; b. Reading, Pa., May 7, 1929; s. H. Elmer and Ruth (Kraft) E.; m. Barbara Leacock, July 19, 1952; children: Ronald, Douglas. ScB, Lafayette Coll., 1952; MS in Physics, Brown U., 1955, PhD in Physics, 1958. Physicist E.I. Du Pont, Wilmington, Del., 1957-63, Nat. Bur. Stds., Washington, 1963-67, chief polymer physics sect., 1967-68, chief polymers divsn., 1968-84; prof. materials sci. and engring. Johns Hopkins U., Balt., 1984-90; R.C. Musson prof. polymer sci., Ohio eminent scholar U. Akron, Ohio, 1990-2000, temp. mem. grad. faculty, 2000—01, rsch. prof., 2001—. Editor Polymer, 1976-98. Recipient medal for meritorious svc. Dept. Commerce, 1980, Alexander von Humboldt sr. prize A.V. Humboldt Stiftung, 1989; mem. NBS/NIST Disting. Scientists, Engrs. & Adminstrs., 2003. Fellow: N.Am. Thermal Analysis Soc., Soc. Plastics Engrs. (Internat. Rsch. award 1993), Acoustical Soc. Am., Am. Phys. Soc. (chmn. divsn .polymer physics 1972—73); mem.: ASTM D-20 Plastics (chmn. 1978—80, 1982—83), NBS/NIST Disting. Scientists, Engrs., Adminstrs., Am. Chem. Soc. (chmn. divsn. polymer chemistry 1980—83), Sigma Xi, Phi Beta Kappa. Office: U Akron Polymer Sci Dept Akron OH 44325-3909

ECABERT, PETER LEO, lawyer, accountant; b. Greenville, Ohio, Sept. 10, 1948; s. C.M. and Mary M. (Richard) E.; children: Christina Lynn, Angela Marie. BSBA in Acctg., Georgetown U., 1970; postgrad., Exeter (Eng.) U., 1973; JD with distinction, Ohio No. U., 1974; LLM in Taxation, Boston U., 1977. Bar: Ohio 1974, U.S. Dist. Ct. (ea. dist.) Ky. 1977, Ky. 1978, U.S. Tax Ct. 1979, U.S. Ct. Claims 1981; CPA, Ky. Tax sr. Deloitte Haskins & Sells, Boston, 1974-77, Lexington, Ky., 1977-79; assoc. Stites & Harbision, Lexington, Ky., 1979-81, ptnr., 1981-88; assoc. gen. counsel Deloitte Haskins & Sells, N.Y.C., 1988-90; mem. firm McBrayer, McGinnis, Leslie & Kirkland, Lexington, Ky., 1990-92; ptnr. Scoville, Cessna, Crawford & Ecabert, Lexington, Ky., 1992-95; pvt. practice Lexington, Ky., 1995—. Speaker in field. Mng. editor: Ohio No. U. Law Review, 1972-74. Mem. ABA, Ky. Bar Assn. (past chmn. taxation sect.), Ohio Bar Assn., Fayette County Bar Assn., Am. Inst. CPAs, Ky. Soc. CPAs, Am. Arbitration Assn., Willis Legal Hon. Soc., Phi Kappa Phi. Republican. Roman Catholic. Office: Chevy Chase Plz 836 E Euclid Ave Ste 207 Lexington KY 40502-1777 E-mail: pecabert@aol.com.

ECCARIUS, SCOTT, state official, eye surgeon; m. Alison Eccarius. Degree, U. S.D. Majority whip S.D. Ho. Reps., spkr. pro tempore, Spkr. of Ho. Dist. 34, 2001—. Mem.: State Affairs Com., Edn. Com. (chmn.), Taxation Com. (chmn.), Ho. Edn. Com. (past chmn.), Edn. and Legis. Procedures Com. (chmn.). Republican. Home: 4780 Carriage Hills Dr Rapid City SD 57702 Business E-Mail: NemoSD@aol.com.

ECCLES, DAVID FITZGERALD, conductor, educator; b. Portsmouth, Va., Dec. 13, 1963; s. Elizabeth Vaughan and George Franklin Eccles. MusB, Norfolk State U., 1991; MusM, U. Miami, 1996. Cert. music educator Fla., 1996. Dir. orch. activities Cypress Lake H.S. Ctr. for Arts, Ft. Myers, Fla., 2001—; music dir. S.W. Fla. Symphony Youth Orch., 2001—. Guest condr. Fla. State U., Tallahassee, 1998—. Dist. chmn. Fla. Orch. Assn., Miami, 1997—99. Scholar, U. Miami, 1994—96. Mem.: Fla. Music Educators Assn., Music Educators Nat. Conf., Alpha Kappa Mu, Phi Mu Alpha (frat. edn. officer 1984—85). Independent. Achievements include Principal creator of a music academy for training minority string musicians in orchestral performance practice. Avocations: golf, tennis, travel. Home: 2905 Winkler Ave Unit 710 Fort Myers FL 33916 Office: Cypress Lake Ctr for Arts 6740 Panther Ln Fort Myers FL 33919 Personal E-mail: eccello@yahoo.com. E-mail: davide@lee.k12.fl.us.

ECHEMPATI, RAGHU, mechanical engineering educator, consultant; b. Guntur, India, Oct. 6, 1948; came to U.S., 1979; s. Raja Gopal and Subhadra (Pratívadi) E.; m. Pankaja Karri, June 1, 1978; children: Sharwari, Aparna. BEng, Andhra U., Waltair, India, 1970; MTech, Indian Inst. Tech., Kharagpur, 1972, PhD, 1978. Registered profl. engr., Miss. Postdoctoral assoc. U. Fla., Gainesville, 1979-81; asst. prof. Indian Inst. Tech., New Delhi, 1977-87, Wash. State U., Pullman, 1988-90, Mich. Tech. U., Houghton, 1990-94, U. Miss., University, 1994-97; assoc. prof. Kettering U., Flint, Mich., 1997—, Bosch prof., 1997—. Cons. Batesville (Miss.) Am., Indian Railways, Lucknow, India, 1978-82, Greneda (Miss.) Elem. Sch., 1995, CMI-Schneible, Holly, Mich., 1998; dir. Indus Industries, India, 1987-97. Reviewer: Mechanics of Materials, 1996; contbr. articles to profl. jours., book chpts. Sec. Tech. Apt., New Delhi, 1983-87. Recipient Young Scientist award Dept. Sci. & Tech., India, 1984. Fellow ASME (chmn. Saginaw (Mich.) Valley chpt.); mem. Soc. Mfg. Engrs., Assn. Machines & Mechanisms (life), Soc. Automobile Engrs., Am. Soc. Engring. Edn. Office: Kettering Univ Flint MI 48504

ECHOHAWK, JOHN ERNEST, lawyer; b. Albuquerque, Aug. 11, 1945; s. Ernest V. and Emma Jane (Conrad) E.; m. Kathryn Suzanne Martin, Oct. 23, 1965; children: Christopher, Sarah. BA, U. N.M., 1967, JD, 1970. Bar: Colo. 1972, U.S. Dist. Ct. Colo. 1972, U.S. Appeals (8th cir.) 1976, U.S. Ct. Appeals (9th cir.) 1980. Research assoc. Calif. Indian Legal Services, Escondido, 1970, Native Am. Rights Fund, Berkeley Calif. and Boulder, Colo., 1970-72, dep. dir. Boulder, 1972-73, 1975-77, exec. dir., 1973-75, 1977—. Mem. task force Am. Indian Policy Rev. Commn., U.S. Senate, Washington, 1976-77; bd. dirs. Am. Indian Lawyer Tng. Program, Oakland, Calif., 1975—; bd. dirs. Assn. Am. Indian Affairs, 1980—, Nat. Com. Responsive Philanthropy, Washington, 1981-2000; mem. Clinton Adminstrn. Transition Team for Interior Dept., 1992-93. Presdl. appointee Western Water Policy Rev. Adv. Commn., 1995-97; Ind. Sector, Washington, 1986-92; mem. Natural Resources Def. Coun., N.Y.C., 1988—; bd. dirs. Nat. Ctr. Enterprise Devel., 1988—, Keystone Ctr., 1993-99, Environ. and Energy Study Inst., 1994—. Recipient Disting. Service award Ams. For Indian Opportunity, 1982, Pres. Indian Service award Nat. Congress Am. Indians, 1984, Annual Indian Achievement award Indian Council Fire, 1987; named one of most influential attys. Nat. Law Jour., 1988, 91, 94, 97, 2000. Mem. Native Am. Bar Assn., Colo. Indian Bar Assn. Democrat. Avocations: fishing, skiing. Office: Native Am Rights Fund 1506 Broadway St Boulder CO 80302-6217

ECHOLS, CAROL AVERY, music educator; b. Watford City, N.D., June 20, 1946; d. Harry C. Avery and Mary Florence Bulot; m. Wayne R. Echols, Sept. 9, 1966; children: Jason, Julie, Kelly, Karen, Leslie. AA, Mesa (Ariz.) C.C., 1967; BA, S.W. Mo. State U., 1995. Ind. music tchr. Music Founds., Monett, Mo., 1984—. Adj. faculty Drury U., Springfield, Mo., 1998—. Composer: Blessed is He, 1980; arranger: A Stranger from Galilee, 1982. Bd. dirs., v.p. Ozark Festival Orch., Monett, 1996-99, chair Young Artist Concert, 1999—. State Mo. scholar, 1993-94; Young Artist Concert grantee United Way, 1999—. Mem. Music Tchrs. Nat. Assn., Am. Coll. Musicians (adjudicator 1998—), Mo. Music Tchrs. Assn. (adjudicator 1998—), Mo. Fedn. Music Clubs (dist. chair 1991—, adjudicator 1998—, chmn. 1999—). Mem. Lds Ch. Avocations: boating, reading. Home: 405 Honeysuckle Ln Monett MO 65708-1061 Office: Drury U Dept Music 900 N Benton Ave Springfield MO 65802-3712

ECHOLS, M(ARY) EVELYN, travel consultant; b. LaSalle, Ill., Apr. 5, 1915; d. Francis Ira and Mary Irene (Coleman) Bassett; m. David H. Echols, Aug. 31, 1951 (dec.); children: Susan Echols O'Donnell, William. Grad. high. sch., Chgo. Founder Internat. Travel Tng. Courses, Inc., Chgo., 1962—; pres. Evelyn Echols Cons. Ltd., 1998. Bd. dirs. Conv. and Tourism Bur.; past pres. Pres. Reagan's Adv. Com. for Women's Bus. Ownership; v.p. United Cerebral Palsy Assn., Ptnrs. in Home Care; bd. dirs. Am. Cancer Soc., Gus Geordiano Jazz Dance Chgo., Little Sisters of the Poor; mem. Women's Internat. Forum. Named Entrepreneur of Yr. Women Bus. Owners N.Y., 1985, Bus. Woman of Yr. Nat. Assn. Women Bus. Owners, 1985, Crain's Chgo. Bus., 1993; named to Chgo.'s Hall of Fame, 1992. Mem.: Soc. Am. Travel Agts., Acad. TV Arts and Scis., Chgo. Execs. Club. Home and Office: # 403 155 N Harbor Dr Chicago IL 60601

ECHOLS, ROBERT L. federal judge; b. 1941; BA, Rhodes Coll., 1962; JD, U. Tenn., 1964. Law clk. to Hon. Marion S. Boyd US Dist. Ct. (we. dist.) Tenn., Nashville, 1965-66; legis. asst. Congressman Dan Kuykendall, 1967-69; ptnr. Baily, Ewing, Dale & Conner, Nashville, 1969-72, Dearborn & Ewing, Nashville, 1972-92; fed. judge US Dist. Ct. (mid. dist.) Tenn., Nashville, 1992—, chief judge, 1998—. Mem. Jud. Br. Com. US Jud. Conf. exec. com. 6th Cir. Jud. Coun.; mem libr. com. 6th Cir. Ct. Appeals; mem. ann. conf. planning com. 6th Cir.; mem. executive com. Federal Judges Assoc.; mem. Tenn. State-Fed. Jud. Count., mem. Tenn. State-Fed. Jud. Coun. With US Army, 1966; brig. gen. Tenn. Army N.G., 1969-2001 Mem. ABA, Am. Bar Found., Tenn. Bar Found., Tenn. Bar Assn., Nashville Bar Assn., Nashville Bar Found., Harry Phillips Am. Inn of Ct. Office: US Dist Ct 801 Broadway Ste 824 Nashville TN 37203-3868

ECHSNER, STEPHEN HERRE, lawyer; b. Columbus, Ind., Dec. 25, 1954; s. Herman Joseph and Virginia Blair (Lechleiter) E. BA, Marquette U., 1977; JD, St. Louis U., 1980. Bar: Fla. 1980, U.S. Dist. Ct. (no. dist.) Fla. 1980, U.S. Ct. Appeals (5th and 11th cirs.) 1980, U.S. Dist. Ct. (mid. dist.) Fla. 1988, U.S. Supreme Ct. 1988; bd. cert. in civil trial law Fla. Bar and Nat. Bd. Trial Advocacy. Assoc. Levin, Papantonio, Thomas, Mitchell, Echsner and Proctor, P.A., Pensacola, Fla., 1980—85, ptnr., 1985—. Mem. ABA, Assn. Trial Lawyers Am., Acad. Fla. Trial Lawyers. Roman Catholic. Home: 23 N Sunset Blvd Gulf Breeze FL 32561-4051 Office: Levin Papantonio et al PO Box 12308 Pensacola FL 32581-2308 E-mail: sechsner@levinlaw.com.

ECK, BERNARD JOHN, engineer; b. Springfield, Ill., May 2, 1928; s. Edward Franz and Pauline (Schafer) E.; m. Janice May Carlson, Apr. 7, 1956; children: William, Robert, John, James, Julie. BS, Mo. Sch. Mines, Rolla, 1950; postgrad., Columbia U., 1967. Technologist U.S. Steel, Chgo., 1950-57; dir., prodn. engr. Griffin Wheel Co., Chgo., 1957-88, sr. tech. advisor, 1988-91; dir. tech. svc. Amsted Industries Internat., Chgo., 1991-94; rlwy. engring. cons. Elmhurst, Ill., 1994. Chmn. Elmer A. Sperry Bd. of Award, N.Y.C., 1989. Contbr. articles to profl. jours. and chpt. to book. Past pres. Country Club Highland Homeowners Assn., Elmhurst, Ill, 1961; pres. St. Charles Borromeo Sch. Bd., Bensenville, Ill., 1975, past v.p. adv. bd. 1965; precinct committeeman Reps., Elmhurst, 1961-69. Sgt. U.S. Army, 1951-53, Korea. Recipient Commendation medal, U.S. Army, 1952, Bronze Star, 1953. Fellow ASME (chmn. Rail Transp. Div. 1984-85, sec.-treas. 1983-84, chmn. adv. com.); mem. ASTM (chmn. subcom.). Roman Catholic. Achievements include patent for wheel cooling. Home and Office: 155 Fairlane Ave Elmhurst IL 60126-3622

ECK, DAVID WILSON, minister; b. Pitts., Apr. 7, 1962; s. Herbert Walter Eck and Linda Joan (Pitrusu) Butera. BS in Chemistry, U. Pitts., 1984; MDiv, Luth. Theol. Sem., Gettysburg, Pa., 1988. Ordained to ministry Evang. Luth. Ch. in Am., 1988. Assoc. pastor Mt. Zion Luth. Ch., Conover, N.C., 1988-93; pastor Abiding Savior Luth. Ch., Asheville, N.C., 1993—. Mem. worship and mus. com. N.C. Synod, 1993-95, mem. AIDS Taskforce N.C. Synod, 1992, N.C. Synod Coun., 1995-98; bd. dirs. Coop Christian Ministry, Hickory, N.C., 1989; owner Twelvestring Pub., 1995—; worship and evangelism resource specialist ELCA, 1998—. Mem. editl. adv. bd. Soli Deo Gloria, 1990-97, also contbr. articles, poetry and music; singer, songwriter, music pub. Bd. dirs. Food for Fairview, 2001—. Recipient cert. of achievement Billboard Songwriting Contest, 1990. Democrat. Home: 110 Coleman Ave Asheville NC 28801-1304 Office: Abiding Savior Luth Ch 801 Charlotte Hwy Fairview NC 28730-9782 E-mail: twelstring@aol.com. *Creativity is the lifeblood of the human race. If we fail to dream, to generate new ideas, to look toward the future with great hope and enthusiasm, we will surely perish from the face of the earth.*

ECK, GEORGE GREGORY, lawyer; b. Evanston, Ill., Sept. 3, 1950; s. George F. and Dorothy E. (Frake) E.; m. Margaret K. Gorman, Sept. 1, 1973; children: Jessica Elizabeth, Michelle Margaret. BS, No. Ill. U., 1972; JD cum laude, U. Minn., 1977. Bar: Minn. 1977, U.S. Dist. Ct. Minn. 1977, U.S. Ct. Appeals (8th cir.) 1977. Assoc. Dorsey & Whitney, Mpls., 1977-83, ptnr., 1983—. Mem. editorial bd. U. Minn. Law Rev., 1977. With U.S. Army, 1972—74. Home: 6413 Mendelssohn Ln Hopkins MN 55343-8424 Office: Dorsey & Whitney 220 S 6th St Ste 2200 Minneapolis MN 55402-1498

ECK, ROBERT EDWIN, physicist; b. Ames, Iowa, Nov. 28, 1938; s. John Clifford and Helen (Behrendt) E.; m. Carolyn Jennie Vodicka, May 11, 1974; children: David Michael, Elizabeth Claire. BA in Physics, Rutgers U., 1960; MS in Physics, U. Pa., 1962, PhD in Physics, 1966; MA in Econs., U. Calif., Santa Barbara, 1973. Sr. rsch. scientist Ford Motor Co., Newport Beach, Calif., 1966-69; project engr. Santa Barbara Rsch. Ctr., Goleta, Calif., 1969-73, asst. mgr. infrared components, 1974-81, mgr. major program, 1982-84, dir. tech., 1985-88, dir./mgr. engring., 1989-95; new bus. devel. mgr. R.G. Hansen & Assocs., Santa Barbara, Calif., 1995-96; program mgr. Optoelectronics-Textron, Petaluma, 1996-2000; adminstrv. dir. Enhancement Inst., Houston, 2002—. Bd. dirs. Goleta Edn. Found. Mem. Goleta Noontime Rotary Club (pres. 1989-90). Achievements include patents on superconductors, infrared detector testing and magnetoresistor sensors.

ECK, ROBERT JOSEPH, lawyer; b. St. Louis, Mo., Mar. 10, 1939; s. Joseph A. and Virginia M. Eck; m. Carol J. Sawicki, May 21, 1966; children: Stephanie, Renee, Justin. BSCE, Washington U., St. Louis, 1961, JD, 1964. Bar: Mo. 1964, U.S. Supreme Ct. 1970, N.Y. 1981. Pvt. practice, St. Louis, 1964-71; assoc. gen. counsel Seven-Up Co., St. Louis, 1971-80; v.p., assoc. gen. counsel Philip Morris Mgmt. Corp. (now Altria Corp. Svcs., Inc.), Rye Brook, NY, 1980—. Mem. ABA, Internat. Bar Assn., Internat. Trademark Assn. (dir., pres. 1987-88), Met. St. Louis Assn. Protection of Indsl. Property, Inter-Am. Assn. Indsl. Property. Republican. Roman Catholic. Home: 245 Daybreak Rd Southport CT 06490-1011 Office: Altria Corp Svcs Inc 800 Westchester Ave Rye Brook NY 10573-1322 E-mail: robert.eck@altria.com.

ECK, RONALD WARREN, civil engineer, educator; b. Allentown, Pa., May 11, 1949; s. Warren Edgar and Viola (Ruth) E. BSCE, Clemson (S.C.) U., 1971, PhD, 1975. Registered profl. engr., W.Va. Asst. prof. civil engring. W.Va. U., Morgantown, 1975-80, assoc. prof. civil engring., 1980-84, prof. civil engring., 1984—, dir. rsch. coll. engring., 1994-96. Cons. in field. Contbr. articles to profl. jours. Chmn. City Traffic Commn., Morgantown, 1989—; mem. Region 3, U.S. DOT, Nat. Def. Exec. Res., 1982-94. Recipient Dow Outstanding Young Faculty award Am. Soc. Engring. Edn., 1980, W.Va. U. Found. Outstanding Tchr. award, 1988, others. Mem. NSPE, Am. Soc. Engring. Edn. (v.p., profl. interest coun., 1987-88), ASCE (pres. W.Va. sect. 1980), Inst. Transp. Engrs. (chmn. dept. 2 1987-90), Transp. Rsch. Bd. (chmn. com. on low volume rds. 1990-96), Am. Soc. Safety Engrs. Avocations: tennis, backpacking. Home: 609 Valley View St Morgantown WV 26505-2412 Office: West Virginia U PO Box 6103 Morgantown WV 26506-6103 E-mail: reck@wvu.edu.

ECKAUS, RICHARD SAMUEL, economist, educator; b. Kansas City, Mo., Apr. 30, 1926; s. Julius and Bessie (Finklestein) E.; m. Patricia L. Meaney; 1 child, Susan L. BS, Iowa State Coll., 1946; MA, Washington U., St. Louis, 1948; PhD, MIT, 1954. Instr., asst. prof., assoc. prof. Brandeis U., 1951-62; rsch. assoc. Ctr. Internat. Studies MIT, Cambridge, 1954-61, from assoc. prof. to prof., 1962—96, Ford internat. prof., 1977-96, head dept. econs., 1987-90, emeritus prof., 1996—2002. Vis. scholar Roxbury C.C., 1996—2002; nat. adv. coun. for environ. and tech. policy EPA; joint program sci. and policy climate change; mem. Bd. Econ. Advisors to Gov. Mass., 1963—65; cons. ADB, OECD, AID, World Bank, govts. of Jamaica, Portugal, Egypt, Sri Lanka, Chile, China, Mexico; vis. scholar Roxbury C.C., 1996—2002. Author: (with K. Parikh) Planning for Growth, 1968; editor: (with J. Bhagwati) Foreign Aid, 1970, Development and Planning, 1973, Basic Economics, 1972, Estimating the Returns to Education, 1973, Appropriate Technologies for Developing Countries, 1976; contbr. articles to profl. jours. Served with USNR, 1944-46. Guggenheim and Social Sci. Rsch. Coun.fellow, 1962; Ford Found. Faculty fellow, 1965. Mem. Am. Econ. Assn. Home: 131 Sewall Ave Apt 72 Brookline MA 02446-5336 Office: MIT Dept Econs 50 Memorial Dr Cambridge MA 02142-1347

ECKBERG, E. DANIEL, secondary education educator; b. Mpls., June 13, 1936; s. E.B.L. and Alvina H. (Sunde) E.; m. Mary Alice Banke, Dec. 27, 1962 (dec. Oct. 1982); children: David D. (dec.), Paul A. BA, St. Olaf Coll., 1958; BS, U. Minn., 1962, PhD, 1986. cert. tchr. econs., history, social studies, curriculum coord. K-12. Recording engr. WCAL-Radio, Northfield, Minn., 1954-58; recording engr., film editor TALC Divsn. TV, Radio and Film, St. Paul, Minn., 1958-62; tchr. Hopkins (Minn.) H.S., 1962-97, chmn. social studies dept., 1967-68; instr. Coll. Edn. U. Minn., Mpls., 1964-66; asst. dir. Hopkins (Minn.) Modular Curriculum Project, 1968-70; project dir. Demonstration Evaluation Ctr., Hopkins, 1970-73; coord. instr. svcs. Hopkins H.S., 1970-97; coord. dist. TV Hopkins Sch. Dist., 1982-97; ednl. cons., 1997—. Mem. social studies adv. com. Minn. State Bd. Edn., St. Paul, 1966-68; mem. European [illegible] and world cultures com. Coll. Entrance Exam. Bd., Princeton, N.J., 1970-81; mem. evaluation teams Nat. Coun. for Accreditation of Tchr. Edn., Va., Colo., Wis., 1974-82; mem. program [illegible] for media arts participation Minn. Sch. and Resource Ctr. of the Arts, 1987; curriculum writer [illegible] orgns. Producer: (TV program) All the Difference: Youth Svc. in Minn., 1988, A Gift of Yourself, 1990. Chmn. tng. com. viking coun. Boy Scouts of Am., Mpls., 1960-62, scoutmaster, 1962-74. Recipient Nat. Physics Hon. award Sigma Pi Sigma St. Olaf Coll., 1957, Outstanding Sr. Man award Coll. Edn. U. Minn., 1962, Program of Excellence award Commr. Edn. State of Minn., 1985, Exec. Dept. Commendation award Gov. State of Minn., 1988, 91. Mem. Nat. Coun. Social Studies (nom. com., curriculum com.), Minn. Fedn. Local Cable Programmers, Alliance for Cmty. Media, Phi Kappa Phi Nat. Grad. Student Honor Soc., Phi Delta Kappa. Office: 5211 Kellogg Ave Minneapolis MN 55424-1304

ECKBO, BJORN ESPEN ESPEN, economics educator; b. Oslo, Norway, June 2, 1952; came to Can., 1981; s. Per Leo Eckbo and Ranveig (Hoffgaard) Borsum; m. Sigrid Alsaker, June 20, 1975; children: Sigrid Camilla, Claus Espen, Hannah Cathrine. B.Commerce, Norwegian Sch. Econs., Bergen, 1975, MBA, 1977; MS, U. Rochester, 1980, PhD, 1981. Prof. econs. U. B.C., Vancouver, Can., 1981—; vis. prof. UCLA, 1985-86; cons. U.S. FTC, Washington, 1984, Consumer and Corp. Affairs Can., Ottawa, 1985. Contbr. articles to sci. jours. Fellow Norwegian Sch. Econs., 1979-81, U. Rochester, 1981, Batterymarch fellow, 1987-88; recipient Harry G. Johnson award Can. Econs. Assn., 1987. Mem. Am. Econ. Assn., Am. Fin. Assn., Can. Econ. Assn., European Fin. Assn. Avocations: music, lit., outdoors. Home: 4550 Langara Vancouver BC V6R 2A6 Canada Office: U BC Faculty Commerce Vancouver BC Canada V6T 1Y8

ECKEL, JAMES J. flight test engineer; b. Newark, Oct. 26, 1949; s. John Joseph and Margaret Agnes (Ellison) E.; m. Barbara Ann Stout Keeley, June 7, 1954. BEEE, Stevens Inst. Tech., 1971; MA, U. No. Colo., 1980. Officer USAF, 1972-80; asst. supt. Reynolds Elec. & Engring. Co., Las Vegas, 1980-84; sr. project engr. Northrop Grumman Corp., 1984—. Recipient nat. def. medal USAF, 1972, combat crew medal, 1979. Mem. AIAA, Assn. of Old Crows, Soc. Flight Test Engrs. Republican. Roman Catholic. Avocations: racquetball, model railroading, soaring, horseback riding. Home: 4514 Ripon Rd Crystal Lake IL 60012-2026 Office: Northrop Grumman Corp 600 Hicks Rd Rolling Meadows IL 60008-1015

ECKEL, JAMES ROBERT, JR., financial planner; b. Morley, Tenn., Nov. 3, 1927; s. James Robert and Jane Scott (Seymour) E. BE magna cum laude, U. Tenn., 1953, MS, 1957; JD, U. West L.A., 1974. CFP; enrolled agt.; registered patent agt. Instr. elec. engring. U. Tenn., 1953-57, U. Wis., 1957-62; sr. engr. Northrop Corp., L.A., 1962-66; staff engr. TRW Systems, L.A., 1966-69; sr. project engr. Hughes Aircraft Co., Culver City, Calif., 1969-89; fin. planner Culver City, 1989—. Real estate broker, Calif. With USN, 1946-49. Mem. IEEE, Am. Inst. Aeros. and Astronautics, Am. Soc. for Engring. Edn., Sigma Xi, Kappa Sigma, Omicron Delta Kappa, Phi Kappa Phi, Tau Beta Pi, Eta Kappa Nu, Phi Eta Sigma. Episcopalian. Home and Office: 5104 Copperfield Ln Culver City CA 90230-7501

ECKEL, KEITH WILLIAM, farmer; b. Scranton, Pa., Dec. 30, 1946; s. Frederick William Eckel and Dorothy Alice Boettger. Student, Dickinson Coll., 1964—66, student, 1967—68, Keystone Coll., 1966—67, Pa. State U., 1970—73. Ptnr. Fred W. Eckel Sons, Clarks Summit, Pa., 1971—; coord. flood relief Pa. Dept. Agrl., Harrisburg, 1973—74; pres. Eckel Farms, Inc., Clarks Summit, 1988—. Bd. dirs. Nationwide Mut. Ins., Columbus; chmn. bd. Allied Ins. Co., Des Moines, 1999—; mem. exec. com. Am. Farm Bur. Fedn., Park Ridge, Ill., 1986—96. Recipient Master Farmer award, Pa. State U., 1982, Outstanding Young Farmer award, U.S. Jaycees, 1983. Mem.: Pa. Vegetable Growers Assn. (dir. 2002—), Pa. Farm Bur. (pres. 1981—96). Republican. Methodist. Avocations: NASCAR, travel, reading. Home and Office: 1647 Falls Rd Clarks Summit PA 18411

ECKELMAN, RICHARD JOEL, engineering specialist; b. Bklyn., Mar. 25, 1951; s. Leon and Muriel (Brietbart) E.; m. Janet Louise Fenton, Mar. 21, 1978; children: Christie, Melanie, Erin Leigh, Alexandra. Student, Ariz. State U., 1988—. Sr. engr., group leader nondestructive testing Engring. Fluor Corp., Irvine, Calif., 1979-83; sr. engr. nondestructive testing McDonnell Douglas Helicopter Co., Mesa, Ariz., 1983-91; engring. specialist Convair div. Gen. Dynamics, San Diego, 1991-94; sr. tech. specialist McDonnell Douglas Techs., Inc., San Diego, 1994-96; scientist, engr. The Boeing Co., Mesa, Ariz., 1996-99, prin. engr., scientist Huntington Beach, Calif., 1999—. Mem. Am. Soc. Nondestructive Testing (nat. aerospace com. 1987—, sec. Ariz. chpt. 1987-88, treas. 1988—, sect. chmn. 1989—, sect. bd. dirs. 1990-91), Am. Soc. Quality Control, Soc. Mfg. Engrs., Lindbergh Yacht Club. Avocations: racquetball, sailing. Home: 3342 Hillrose Dr Los Alamitos CA 90720-4802

ECKELSON, ROBERT ALAN, orthodontist; b. Cleve., Feb. 2, 1947; s. Sam Robert and Frances (Kaplan) E.; m. Linda Goldstine, July 23, 1984. DDS, Ohio State U., 1971; postgrad., U. Ill., Chgo., 1971-73. Diplomate Am. Bd. Orthodontists. Pvt. practice, Boca Raton, Fla., 1973—. Mem. staff Boca Raton Community Hosp., 1978—. Bd. dirs. Boca Forum, Boca Raton, 1988-93, pres., 1992-93. Mem. So. Assn. Orthodontists, Fla. Dental Assn., Boca Raton Roundtable (pres. 1993-95), Rotary (pres. Boca Raton 1996-97, Paul Harris fellow), South Palm Beach County Dental Assn. (pres. 2000-01), Alpha Omega (pres. Palm Beach/Broward chpt. 1984-86). Avocation: flight instr. Office: 951 NW 13th St Ste 3B Boca Raton FL 33486-2337 also: 75 NE 6th Ave #212 Delray Beach FL 33483

ECKENHOFF, EDWARD ALVIN, health care administrator; b. Durham, N.C., Mar. 4, 1943; s. James Edward and Bonnie Lee E.; m. Judi G. Vicich, May 27, 1978 BA, Transylvania U., 1966, PhD (hon.), 2000; MA, U. Ky., 1968; MHA, Washington U., 1974. V.p., adminstr. Rehab. Inst. Chgo., 1976-82; pres., chief exec. officer Nat. Rehab. Hosp., Washington, 1982—; asst. prof. dept. community and family practice Med. Sch., Georgetown U., Washington, 1983-94; v.p. Medlantic Healthcare Group, 1987-99. V.p. Medlantic Healthcare Group, 1987-98; pres. Nat. Rehab. Services Corp., 1987-92; chmn. bd. NASCOTT, IBIS; instr. Med. Sch., Northwestern U., preceptor Grad. Sch. Bus.; mem. Ill. Commn. on Health Assistance Programs; mem. Ill. adv. com., chmn. exec. com. Internat. Yr. of Disabled; surveyor Commn. on Accreditation of Rehab. Facilities, bd. dirs., 1980-82; bd. dirs. Nat. Assn. Rehab. Facilities, 1982-83; mem. com. on accreditation and edn. Am. Phys. Therapy Assn.; mem. Healthcare Rsch. Devel. Inst.; bd. dirs. Am. Med. Rehab. Provider Assn., chmn. bd. dirs., 2000-01 Contbr. articles to profl. jours. Bd. dirs. Am. Occupl. Therapy Found., Easter Seal Soc., Boy Scouts Am., Chgo. Area Coun., Nat. Area, 1987-87, Operation ABLE Chgo., Access Living of Met. Chgo., Am. Chamber Symphony, Chgo. Named Washingtonian of the Yr., Washingtonian Mag., 1989; recipient Citation for Disting. Svc., AMA, 1990, Ann. Healthcare Leader award B'nai B'rith, 2003. Fellow Inst. Medicine Chgo., Am. Coll. Hosp. Execs.; mem. Am. Hosp. Assn. (chmn. governing coun. for rehab. hosps. 1985, trustee 1991-93, chmn. policy com. 1993, mem. exec. com. 1993), Am. Congress Rehab. Medicine (chmn. policy and devel. com.), Chgo. Hosp. Coun. (chmn. com. rehab. 1978-82, exec. com. 1983), Healthcare Devel. and Rsch. Inst., Am. Med. Rehab. Providers Assn. (chmn. bd. dirs. 2000-01), Nat. Orgn. on Disability (Medicare Coverage adv. commn. 1999—), DC Hosp. Assn. (DCHA) (bd. dirs. 2003-). Episcopalian. Office: Nat Rehab Hosp 102 Irving St NW Washington DC 20010-2949

ECKER, HOWARD, lawyer; b. N.Y.C., June 10, 1946; s. David and Sylvia (Goldstein) E.; children: David, Ashley. BA, U. Mich., 1967; JD, NYU, 1971. Bar: Nev. 1973, U.S. Dist. Ct. Nev. 1974, U.S. Ct. Appeals (9th cir.) 1976, U.S. Supreme Ct. 1976. Pub. defender Clark County Pub. Defender's Office, Nev., 1973-77; ptnr. Ecker & Standish, Chtd., Clark County, Nev., 1977—. Guest lectr. in field. Mem. Nev. Employee Mgmt. Rels. Bd., Las Vegas, 1990-94. Mem.: Am. Acad. Matrimonial Lawyers, Am. Inns of Ct. (barrister 1990—93, master 1993—), Nev. Trial Lawyers Assn. (bd. govs. 1977—89, pres. 1985—86), Clark County Bar Assn., State Bar Nev. (bd. govs. 1984—90), ATLA. Avocations: travel, golf, reading. Office: Ecker & Standish Chtd 300 S 4th St Ste 901 Las Vegas NV 89101-6025

ECKERSLEY, NORMAN CHADWICK, bank executive; b. Glasgow, Scotland, June 18, 1924; arrived in U.S., 1969; s. James Norman and Beatrice (Chadwick) E.; m. Rosemary J. Peters, May 23, 1986; 1 child, Anne. D Laws, Strathclyde U., Scotland. With Chartered Bank, London and Manchester, 194[illegible] Bombay, 1948-52, 1952-54, 1954-56, 1956-58, 1958-59, Hong Kong, 1959-60; asst. mgr. [illegible] 1960-62; mgr. Calcutta and Thailand, 1962-67; pres. Chartered Bank London, San [illegible] 1964-74, chmn., CEO, 1974-79; chmn. Std. Chartered Bancorp, 1978-82; dep. chmn. Union Bank, L.A., 1979-82; chmn., CEO The Pacific Bank, San Francisco, 1982-93; chmn. emeritus, 1993. Chmn. Diners Club (Asia), 1967-69, Devel. Bank Thailand, 1967-69, Scottish Am. Investment Com., U. Strathclyde Found.; chmn. Balmoral Fin. Corp., 1995-99; exec. Bank of the Orient, San Francisco, 1999-2003; cons. Digital Ventures (Asia) Ltd., 2001—, Las Vegas East Entertainment (Macau) Ltd.; exec. dir., cons. EW Internat. Ltd., 2001—; dir. Asia Pacific Devel. Holdings Ltd. With RAF, 1940-46. Decorated D.F.C., comdr. Order Brit. Empire. Mem. Overseas Banks Assn. Calif. (chmn. 1972-74), Calif. Coun. Internat. Trade, San Francisco C. of C., World Trade Assn., Hong Kong Assn. (San Francisco) (bd. dirs.), Royal and Ancient Club, St. Andrews (Scotland), Royal Troon Golf Club (Scotland), Royal Hong Kong Golf Club, World Trade Club, San Francisco Golf Club, Pacific Union Club (San Francisco). Mem. Ch. Of Scotland. Home: 11718 Saddle Rd Monterey CA 93940-6653

ECKERSLEY, RICHARD HILTON, graphics designer, educator; b. Warrington, Lancashire, Eng., Feb. 20, 1941; s. Tom and Daisy Eckersley; m. Dika Jacquette Helène Lagercrantz; children: Nell, Camilla, Sam. BA with honors, London Coll. Printing, 1966; MA, Trinity Coll., Dublin, Ireland, 1962. Asst. designer Percy Lund Humphries, London, 1966—68; freelance designer London, 1969—74; sr. designer Kilkenny (Ireland) Design Workshops, 1974—80, U. Nebr. Press, Lincoln, 1981—. Vis. lectr. London Coll. Printing, 1969—74, Cleve. Acad. of Arts, 1979—79; assoc. prof. Tyler Sch. Art, Phila., 1980; sr. critic Yale U. Sch. Design, New Haven, 1995—. Author: Glossary of Typesetting Terms, 1994. Named Royal Designer for Industry, Royal Soc. Arts, 1999; recipient award of excellence for book design, Assn. Am. U. Presses, 1982—2001, Am. Inst. Graphic Design, 1985—2001, Silver medal, Leipzig Book Fair, 1989, Carl Herzog prize, U. Tex., 1994. Mem.: Am. Inst. Graphic Arts. Home: 1345 Garfield St Lincoln NE 68502 Office: U Nebr Press 233 North 8th St Lincoln NE 68588-0255 Office Fax: 402-472-0308. Business E-Mail: reckersley1@unl.edu.

ECKERSLEY, RICHARD LAURENCE, accountant; b. Scranton, Pa., July 29, 1948; s. Robert Neal and Helen Elizabeth (Palmer) E.; m. Linda K. Forsythe, Feb. 11, 1967; children: Laura Lynnette, Tristan Dael, Travis Morgan. AB in English, U. Scranton, 1971, MA in History, 1993. CPA, Pa. Staff acct. Acctg. Svc. Assocs., Inc., Scranton, 1967-77; ptnr. Eckersley Acctg. Svc., Scranton, 1977-80, shareholder, pres. Eckersley and Eckersley, P.C., Scranton, 1980-86; ptnr. Eckersley and Ostrowski, LLP, Scranton, 1987—. Lectr. acctg. Keystone Jr. Coll., LaPlume, Pa., 1974-76. Asst. treas. The Real Bob Casey Com., Scranton, 1985-96; bd. dirs., officer Family Svc. Lackawanna County, Scranton, 1978-84, Planned Parenthood N.E. Pa., Trexlertown, Pa., 1981-86, 89-93; treas. Casey for Congress Com., 1998—. Mem. AICPA, Pa. Inst. Cert. Pub. Accts. Methodist. Avocations: reading, history, hunting, diving. Home: RR 3 Box 5 Dalton PA 18414-9528 Office: Eckersley and Ostrowski LLP 300 Gerard Bldg Scranton PA 18503

ECKERT, ALLAN WESLEY, writer; b. Buffalo, Jan. 30, 1931; s. Edward Russell and Ruth Rose (Roth) E.; m. Joan Dowling, 1955 (div.1975); children: Joseph Matthew, Julie Anne; m. Gail Greene, 1977 (div. 1978); m. Nancy Dent, 1978. Student, U. Dayton, 1951-52, Ohio State U., 1953-54; PhD (hon.), Bowling Green State U., 1985, Wright State U., 1998. Assoc. editor Nat. Cash Register Co. News, Dayton, Ohio, 1955-58; reporter, columnist Dayton Jour. Herald, Dayton, Ohio, 1958-60; free-lance writer, 1960—. Cons. LaSalle Extension U., Chgo. Writer over 200 TV scripts for NBC's Wild Kingdom; created courses article and short story writing Writer's Digest; author: The Great Auk, 1963, A Time of Terror, 1965, The Silent Sky, 1965, Wild Season, 1967, The Frontiersmen, 1967, Bayou Backwaters, 1967, The Dreaming Tree, 1967, The Crossbreed, 1968, Blue Jacket, 1968, The King Snake, 1968, Wilderness Empire, 1968, In Search of a Whale, 1969, The Conquerors, 1970, Incident at Hawk's Hill, 1971, The Court-Martial of Daniel Boone, 1973, The Owls of North America, 1973, The HAB Theory, 1976, The Wilderness War, 1978, The Wading Birds of North America, 1979, Savage Journey, 1979, Song of the Wild, 1980, Whattizzit?, 1981, Gateway to Empire, 1982, Johnny Logan: Shawnee Spy, 1982, The Dark Green Tunnel, 1983, The Wand, 1984, The Scarlet Mansion, 1985, Earth Treasures, 4 vols., 1987, Twilight of Empire, 1988, A Sorrow in Our Heart: The Life of Tecumseh, 1991, That Dark and Bloody River: Chronicles of the Ohio River Valley, 1995, The World of Opals, 1997, Return to Hawk's Hill, 1998, (outdoor drama) Tecumseh!, 1971, (screenplays) Kentucky Pioneers, 1969, The Legend of Koo-Tan, 1971, (playscript) Tecumseh!, 1974; editor: A Treasury of Tips for Writers, 1966; contbr. articles to popular and profl. publs. Trustee Dayton Museum Natural History, 1963-65; Founder, chmn. bd. Lemon Bay Conservancy, Englewood, Fla. Served with USAF, 1948-52. Recipient Ohioana Book award, 1968, Best Book award Friends of Am. Writers, 1968, Emmy award outstanding program achievement Nat. Acad. TV Arts and Scis., 1968-69, Newbury-Caldecott Honor Book award, 1972, George G. Stone/Claremont Colls. Recognition of Merit, 1974, Austrian Juvenile Book of Yr. award, 1976, Americanism award The Daniel Boone Found., 2d Ann. Silver Arrow Humanitarian award Scioto Soc., 1987, Internat. Readers Assn. Tchrs. Choice award, 1999; commd. Ky. Col. by Gov. State of Ky., 1987; finalist Spur award Western Writers Am., 1995; named Writer of Yr., Am. Culture Assn., 1997; nominated 7 times for Pulitzer prize; Allan W. Eckert Collection established at Mugar Meml. Libr., Boston U., 1965, at the Filson Club Hist. Soc., Louisville, Ky., 1993, named by Citizens of Ohio as favorite Ohio writer of all time, Ohioana Libr. Assn., 1999; Allan W. Eckert Nature Trail, Scioto County Commrs., Riverside Pk., 2001. Mem. Authors Guild, Dayton Soc. Natural History (life), Am. Soc. of Gem Cutters, Mazon Greek Project (life). Office: care Russell Galen Scoville Chichak and Galen 381 Park Ave S Rm 1020 New York NY 10016-8806 Office Fax: (212) 679-6710. E-mail: allaneck@charter.net., allan@allaneck.com.

ECKERT, CHARLES ALAN, chemical engineering educator; b. St. Louis, Dec. 13, 1938; s. Clarence Theodore and Mildred Hortense (Potlitzer) E.; children: Carolyn Helen, Theodore James; m. Susan Schneider, 1997. S.B., MIT, 1960, S.M., 1961; PhD, U. Calif.-Berkeley, 1964. Postdoctoral fellow CNRS, Paris, 1964-65; asst. prof. U. Ill., Urbana, 1965-69, assoc. prof., 1969-73, prof., 1973-89, head dept. chem. engring., 1980-86; J. Erskine Love prof. engring. Ga. Inst. Tech., Atlanta, 1989—, Inst. prof., 1994. Dir. Splty. Separations Ctr., 1991—; cons. numerous cos. Author several books, instructional computer programs Fellow NATO, 1964, Guggenheim Found., 1971 Fellow AIChE (Allan Colburn award 1973, William H. Walker award 1999): mem. NAE, Internat. Soc. for Advancement of Supercritical Fluids (v.p.) Am. Chem. Soc. (Ipatieff prize 1977, Murphree award 1995), Am. Soc. Engring. Edn. Home: 1053 Saint James Xing NE Atlanta GA 30319-1984 Office: Ga Inst Tech Sch Chem Engring Atlanta GA 30332-0001 E-mail: cae@che.gatech.edu.

ECKERT, JEAN PATRICIA, elementary education educator; b. Pitts., July 22, 1935; d. Homer Michael and Berdena Leona (Kessler) Canel; m. William L. Eckert, June 13, 1959; 1 child, Suzanne Mary. BS, Indiana U. Pa., 1957; postgrad., U. Pitts., 1958-59, U. San Diego, 1981. Cert. pub. instrn., Pa. Elem. tchr. Pine-Richland Sch. Dist., Gibsonia, Pa., 1957—60, substitute tchr., 1963—65; elem. tchr. Shaler Twp. Sch. Dist., Glenshaw, Pa., 1965—66, St. Scholastica Sch., Diocese of Pitts., Aspinwall, Pa., 1966—91, substitute tchr., 1991—, tutor, 1991—. Judge election 4th dist. Rep. Party, Aspinwall, 1962-65, 91—. Mem.: AAUW, Nat. Cath. Edn. Assn., Literacy Vols. Am., Ind. U. (Pa.) Alumni Assn., Delta Zeta (sec. 1955, pres. 1956). Roman Catholic. Avocations: travel, literature. Home: 210 12th St Pittsburgh PA 15215-1600

ECKERT, MICHAEL JOSEPH, television executive, media specialist; b. Chgo., Mar. 20, 1947; s. Stephen Michael and Mary Theresa (Kovacs) E.; m. Janis Lynn Kamps, Oct. 28, 1972; children: Eric, Jacob, Morgan. BS in Edn., No. Ill. U., 1969; postgrad., De Paul U., 1969-72. Tchr., coach St. Rita H.S., Chgo., 1969-73; account mgr. Sta. WDHF, Chgo., 1973; sales mgr. Sta. WAIT, Chgo., 1974-76; account exec. John Blair Co., Chgo., 1976-78, sales mgr., 1979-81; gen. sales mgr. Sta. WLAK, Chgo., 1978; v.p. sales The Weather Channel, Chgo., N.Y., 1982-85, pres., COO, Atlanta, 1985-90, CEO, 1990—99; CEO, The Travel Channel, Atlanta, 1992-93; pres., CEO Pathfire, Inc., Roswell, 2000—. Cons. Metomedia, Montreal, 1988—92; pres. Prime Time tonight, Atlanta, 1989, Landmark Comm. Broadcast and Video Enterprises Divsn., 1990—; bd. dirs. Pelmorex Inc., Toronto, Der Wetter Kanal, Dusseldorf, Beyond Z, 2001—, Cable TV Advt. Bur., 1989—, sec, 1993—94, treas., 1995—96, vice chmn., 1997—98; bd. dirs. Multichannel Advt. Bur.; pres. Landmark Comm.. Video Networks and Entrprises; chmn. World Cup Com.,

1991—95, Golden Cable Ace Award Com., 1992—95, Award Competition Com., 1996. Active United Way, Atlanta, 1987-88; bd. dirs. Atlanta Symphony Orch., 1996—. Recipient spl. leadership award ARC, Washington, 1985, 89; named man of achievement Phi Kappa Theta, 1994. Mem.: Cable TV Adminstrn. and Mgmt. Soc., Nat. Acad. Cable Programming (bd. dirs. 1985—2000), Nat. Cable TV Assn. (satellite programming com. 1983—2000), Atlanta Alliance Bus. and Edn., Dunwoody Country Club, Georgian Club, Vinings Club (bd. govs. 1993—96). Avocations: fly fishing, mountain trekking, skiing. Home: 1470 Masters Club Dr Atlanta GA 30350-4439 Office: Pathfire Inc 245 Membree Park Dr Roswell GA 30076

ECKERT, ROBERT A. manufacturing company executive; BSBA, U. Ariz., 1976; MBA in Mktg. and Fin., Northwestern U., 1977. Various mktg. positions Kraft Foods, 1977-87, v.p. strategy and devel. grocery products divsn., 1987-89, v.p. mktg. refrigerated products, 1989-90, v.p., gen. mgr. cheese divsn., 1990-97, pres., CEO, 1997-2000; chmn. bd., CEO Mattel, Inc., 2000—. Active adv. bd. J.L. Kellogg Grad. Sch. Mgmt., Northwestern U.; bd. dirs., mem. exec. com. Met. Family Svcs.; bd. dirs., chmn. govt. affairs coun. Grocery Mfrs. Am.; trustee Ravinia Festival Assn., Art Inst. Chgo.; nat. trustee Lake Forest Coll. Office: Mattel Inc 333 Continental Blvd El Segundo CA 90245-5012 Fax: 310-252-2179.*

ECKERT, ROGER E(ARL), chemical engineering educator; b. Lakewood, Ohio, Aug. 8, 1926; s. Elmer George and Elsie V. (Schwede) E.; children: Roger Earl, Rhonda Carol, Robyn Claire. BS, Princeton U., 1948; MS, U. Ill., 1949, PhD, 1951. Process devel. engr., indsl. and biochems. dept. E.I. duPont de Nemours & Co., Inc., Wilmington, Del., 1951-64, math. cons., 1956-60, sr. research engr., engring. research lab. and elastomers chems. dept., 1960-64; assoc. prof. Purdue U., West Lafayette, Ind., 1964-73; asst. head Sch. Chem. Engring., 1970-75, prof. chem. engring., 1973—. Vis. prof. U. Colo., 1971, U. Wis., 1981; Am. Soc. Engring. Edn.-NASA faculty fellow Case Western Res. U. and Lewis Research Center, 1966-67 Contbr. tech. articles to profl. jours. Served with U.S. Army, 1946-47. Mem. Am. Inst. Chem. Engrs., Phi Beta Kappa, Sigma Xi, Phi Lambda Upsilon, Pi Mu Epsilon, Alpha Chi Sigma. Presbyterian. Home: 153 Indian Rock Dr West Lafayette IN 47906-1255 Office: Sch Chem Engring Purdue U West Lafayette IN 47906

ECKFELD, WILLIAM GROVER, music educator, composer, musician; b. Cleveland, Ohio, June 19, 1951; s. Daniel Norman and Evelyn Bibbee Eckfeld; m. Rebecca Pettigrew, June 30, 1973; 1 child, Evan Alban. BM, Eastman Sch. of Music, Rochester, NY, 1973; MA, Lehman Coll., Bronx, NY, 1986. Teaching Certificate NY, 1973. Orchestral musician Rochester Philharm., Rochester, NY, 1969—73, Dallas Symphony Orch., Dallas, Tex., 1973—79; music educator Augustine Sch. of the Arts, Bronx, NY, 1980—86; organist St Philip Neri, Bronx, NY, 1983—; orch. condr./educator White Plains Pub. Schools, White Plains, NY, 1987—. Pres. Greater Westchester Youth Orchestras Assn, Westchester County, NY, 1999—; guest condr. Westchester All-County Elem. Orch., Westchester County, NY, 2000—00. Composer: (orchestral music) Requiem for Bosnia, September Threnody, (chamber music) Sonata for Viola and Piano. Recipient Jenkins Award, White Plains H.S. PTA, 2000. Mem.: Westchester County Sch. Music Assn, Music Educators Nat. Conf., Am. Fedn. of Musicians. Democrat-Npl. Methodist. Avocations: reading, foreign languages, foreign languages, fitness. Home: 43 Archer Ave White Plains NY 10603

ECKFORD, WENDEL, historian, educator; s. Bess Eckford. BArch, Prairie View A&M U. of Tex., 1988; MA in History and Hist. Preservation, Calif. State U., Carson, 1997; postgrad., Claremont Grad. U., 1997—, UCLA, 2002—. Profl. historian Register of Profl. Historians. Prin. educator Cultural Resource Mgmt., LLC, Pomona, Calif.; adj. prof. of history Chaffey Coll., Rancho Cucamonga, Calif., 1999—. Archtl. assoc., preservationist City of L.A., 1989—2001. Preservation plan, City of Arcadia Historic Resource Survey, Old Medina - Casablanca Restoration, City of San Fernando Historic Resource Survey, City of Ontario Historic Resource Survey; contbr. African Am. Biog. Dictionary; author: (book) Allison Davis: The History of Psychological Testing of African Americans. Big brother Big Bros. of Am., L.A., 1990—92. 1st lt. USAR, 1994—2002. Named Outstanding Mil. Historian, U.S. ROTC, 1994; recipient Mary Johnston acad. scholarship, Claremont Grad. U., 2001, UCLA Academic Grad. scholarship, UCLA, 2002. Mem.: Orgn. of Am. Historians, Am. Hist. Assn., Res. Officers Assn. (life), Prince Hall Masons, Phi Alpha Theta, Alpha Phi Alpha (Eta Gamma Joseph York Cmty. Svc. award 1984). Avocation: flying (pilot). Office: Cultural Resource Mgmt #305 281 S Thomas St Pasadena CA 91104 Office Fax: 909-622-6156. E-mail: crm@wedohistory.com.

ECKHARDT, AUGUST GOTTLIEB, retired law educator; b. Sylvan, Wis., Aug. 8, 1917; s. Levi and Euphemia (Hall) E.; m. Catherine Louise Henderson, June 26, 1942; children— James Henderson, Patricia Kay. Student, Nebr. State U. at Kearney, 1935-37; BA, U. Wis., 1939, LL.M., 1946, S.J.D, 1951; LL.B., George Washington U., 1942. Bar: D.C. bar 1941, Wis. bar 1946, Ariz. bar 1974. Sole practice, Merrill, Wis., 1946-47, 50-52; asst. prof. law George Washington U., 1947-49; prof. law U. Wis.-Madison, 1954-72, U. Ariz., Tucson, 1972-89, prof. emeritus, 1989—. Dir. Continuing Legal Edn. Wis., 1954-58, 63-67; labor arbitrator, 1955-89 Author: Eckhardt's Workbook for Wisconsin Estate Planners, 1961; author: (with others) 4th edit., 2003, supplement, 2003. Served with USNR, 1942-46. Mem. State Bar Ariz. (founder world peace through law sect. 1989). Home: 6231 N Montebella Rd Apt 445 Tucson AZ 85704 E-mail: akeckhardt@msn.com.

ECKHART, MYRON, JR., (MAX ECKHART), retired marine engineer; b. South Bend, Ind., Mar. 29, 1923; s Myron Lester and Neva (Whitmer) E.; m. Joan Elizabeth Daniels, June 29, 1946; children: Joan Theresa, Michael Thomas, Jeri Anne. BS, U.S. Naval Acad., 1945; BSEE, MIT, 1949; MSEE, George Washington U., 1967. Commd. ensign USN, 1945; advanced through grades to capt. U.S. Navy, 1966; stationed at Norfolk (Va.) Naval Shipyard, 1950-55; project officer Regulus Missile (Underwater Sound Lab.), 1955-60; chmn. elec. sci. U.S. Naval Acad., 1962-65; dir. ship design divsn. Hdqrs. USN, 1967-70; ret., 1970; mgr. advanced engring., chief scientist marine sys. divsn. Rockwell Internat., Anaheim, Calif., 1970-84, cons., 1985—. Contbr. articles to profl. jours. Mem. Soc. Naval Architects and Marine Engrs., Am. Soc. Naval Engrs., Am. Def. Preparedness Assn., U.S. Naval Inst. Achievements includes patent of fourier synthesis of complex waveforms; shipsinclude designs of Nimitz aircraft carriers, Trident strategic submarines, Los Angeles class submarines; prin. devel. roles include airborne radar to shipboard displays, radar-based landing control of aircraft, in-helmet radio communications link, REGULUS strategic missile guidance system. Home: 1211 Belle Vista Dr Alexandria VA 22307-2016 *Success depends upon figuring out the price associated with each of one's goals, and then being willing to pay that price with no assurance of reward.*

ECKHART, WALTER, molecular biologist, educator; b. Yonkers, N.Y., May 22, 1938; s. Walter and Jean (Fairnington) E. BS, Yale U., 1960; postgrad., Cambridge U., Eng., 1960-61; PhD, U. Calif.-Berkeley, 1965. Postdoctoral fellow Salk Inst., San Diego, 1965-69, mem., 1970-73, assoc. prof. molecular biology, 1973-79, prof., 1979—, dir., 1976—. Adj. prof. U. Calif.-San Diego, 1973— Contbr. articles on molecular biology and virology to profl. jours. NIH research grantee, 1967—. Mem. AAAS, Am. Assn. Cancer Rsch., Am. Soc. Microbiology, Am. Soc. Virology Home: 951 Skylark Dr La Jolla CA 92037-7731 Office: Salk Inst PO Box 85800 San Diego CA 92186-5800

ECKHOUT, JR. GIFFORD VAN, physician; s. Gifford Van and Velma Christine Eckhout; m. Marlise Marie Martin, July 17, 1990; children: Ellen Louise Eckhout, Austin Gifford Eckhout. BA, Colo. Coll., Colorado Springs, 1981; MD, St. Louis U., 1985; MBA, Weatherhead Sch. of Bus., Cleve., 2003. Diplomate Am. Bd. of Anesthesiology, 1991. Anesthesiologist Anesthesia Consultants, Enid, Okla., 1990—91, Franklin Anesthesia Consultants, Cleve., 1991—95, Westgate Med. Anesthesia Group, Cleve., 1995—2000; staff anesthesiologist Cleve. Clinic Found., Cleve., 2000—. Chair staff recruiting, dept. Gen. Anesthesiology Cleve. Clinic Found., 2001—; v.p. Ohio Soc. of Anesthesiologists, Columbus, 2002—. Contbr. articles to profl. jours. Mem.: AMA, Ohio Soc. of Anesthesiologists (v.p. 2002—03), Am. Soc. of Anesthesiologists (del. 2001—03). Avocations: sailing, skiing, golf, piano, hiking. Office: Cleve Clinic Found 9500 Euclid Ave/ E31 Cleveland OH 44195 Office Fax: 216-444-9247.

ECKL, WILLIAM WRAY, lawyer; b. Florence, Ala., Dec. 2, 1936; s. Louis Arnold and Patricia Barclift (Dowd) E.; m. Mary Lynn McGough, June 29, 1963; children: Eric Dowd, Lynn Lacey. BA, U. Notre Dame, 1959; LLB, U. Va., 1962. Bar: Va. 1962, Ala. 1962, Ga. 1964. Law clk. Supreme Ct. of Ala., 1962; ptnr. Gambrell, Harlan, Russell & Moye, Atlanta, 1965-68, Swift, Currie, McGhee & Hiers, Atlanta, 1968-82, Drew, Eckl & Farnham, Atlanta, 1983—. Served to capt. JAGC, USAR, 1962-65. Mem. Am. Bd. Trial Advocates, Trial Attys. Am., Lawyers Club of Atlanta, Brookwood Hills Club. Roman Catholic. Home: 348 Camden Rd NE Atlanta GA 30309-1513 Office: Drew Eckl & Farnham 880 W Peachtree St PO Box 7600 Atlanta GA 30357-0600

ECKLAND, JEFF HOWARD, lawyer; b. Warren, Ohio, Jan. 17, 1957; s. William Howard and Barbara Ann (Hirsch) E.; m. Deborah Pauline Causey, May 27, 1989. BA summa cum laude, U. Minn., 1979; JD, U. Chgo., 1982. Bar: Minn. 1982, U.S. Dist. Ct. Minn. 1982, U.S. Ct. Appeals (8th cir.) 1987, U.S. Ct. Appeals (9th cir.) 1990, U.S. Ct. Appeals (fed. cir.) 1993, U.S. Ct. Fed. Claims 1993, U.S. Supreme Ct. 1997. Ptnr. Faegre & Benson, Mpls., 1982—. Vol. Lawyer Network. Mem. ABA, Minn. Bar Assn., Hennepin County Bar Assn., Fund for the Legal Aid Soc., Nat. Contract Mgmt. Assn., Phi Beta Kappa. Avocations: sailing, tennis. Office: Faegre & Benson LLP 2200 Wells Fargo Ctr 90 S 7th St Ste 2200 Minneapolis MN 55402-3901 E-mail: jeckland@faegre.com.

ECKLER, PAUL EUGENE, chemist; b. Mexico, Mo., May 17, 1946; s. Paul Meridith and Frieda Louise (Blaue) E. BS in Chemistry, U. Mo., 1969; PhD in Chemistry, U. Oreg., 1975. Chemist Internat. Minerals & Chems., Terre Haute, Ind., 1975-89; dir. tech. svcs. Alcolac Inc., Balt., 1989-90, Rhone-Poulenc, Cranbury, N.J., 1990-96; staff scientist Bayer-Agfa, Somerville, N.J., 1997-99. Cons., 1996— Author: Chemistry of Dimethylolpropionic Acid, 1987, Complete Guide to Trimethylolethane, 1988. With U.S. Army, 1970-72. Mem. Am. Chem. Soc., Federated Coatings Soc., Powder Coatings Inst. (assoc. mem.). Achievements include 22 patents. Home and Office: 5 Wheatston Ct Princeton Junction NJ 08550-1936 E-mail: peckler@bellatlantic.net.

ECKLEY, WILTON EARL, JR., humanities educator, educator; b. Alliance, Ohio, June 25, 1929; s. Wilton Earl and Louise (Bert) E.; m. Grace Ester Williamson, Sept. 12, 1954; children: Douglas, Stephen, Timothy. BA, Mt. Union Coll., 1952, MA, Pa. State U., 1955; PhD, Case Western Reserve U., 1965; John Hay fellow, Yale U., 1961-62. Chmn. English Euclid (Ohio) Sr. High Sch., 1955-63; dir. tchr. tng. Hollins Coll., 1963-65; prof. English Drake U., 1965-84, chmn. dept. English, 1965-80; head dept. humanities and social scis. Colo. Sch. Mines, 1984-93, dir. honors program, 1989-92; prof. humanities Drake U., 1984—; prof. humanities and internat. studies Colo. Sch. Mines, 1994-99, prof. emeritus, 1999—. Fulbright prof. Am. lit. U. Ljubljana, Yugoslavia, 1972-73, U. Veliko, Turnovo, Bulgaria, 1981-82; vis. prof. Bilkent U., Ankara, Turkey, 1993-94. Chmn. bd. dirs. Colo. Endowment for the Humanities, 1989-91. Coe fellow Am. Studies, 1957— Mem. MLA, Circus Hist. Soc., AAUP, Phi Kappa Tau. Home: 636 Ridgeside Dr Golden CO 80401-5757

ECKLIN, ROBERT LUTHER, materials company executive; b. Lancaster, Pa., Sept. 26, 1938; s. Luther Joseph and Ella Frances (Smith) E.; m. Loretta Rohrer Stoner, Sept. 3, 1960; children: Robert Luther, Jr., Suzanne Beth, Kristina Ann, Stephanie Ann. B in Archtl. Engring., Chgo. Tech. Coll., 1961; postgrad., Dartmouth U., 1983, cert., 1984. With Corning Inc., N.Y.C., 1961—; pres. Corning Engring. Corning (N.Y.) Glass Works, 1982-86, corp. v.p. bus. devel., chmn. Corning Engring., 1986-88, sr. v.p., 1988-99, exec. v.p., 1999—. Chmn. Maklin Ltd., Stone-on-Trent, Eng., 1983-86; ptnr. Ecklin & Ecklin Investments, Lancaster, 1986—; bd. dirs. MacDermid, Inc., Waterbury, Conn., Alfred Ul. Tech. Resources, Pitts.-Corning Corp. Chmn. Com. of 50, Corning, 1985—; mem. rsch. adv. bd. N.Y. State U.; pres. Univ. Industry Pub. Partnership for Econ. Growth. Mem. Corning C. of C. Republican. Methodist. Home: 248 Cedar St Corning NY 14830 3128 Office: Corning Inc MP HQ E2 Riverfront Plz Corning NY 14831-0001 E-mail: ecklin@corning.com.

ECKLUND, CONSTANCE CRYER, French language educator; b. Chgo., Nov. 20, 1938; d. Gilbert and Electra (Papadopoulos) Cryer; m. John E. Ecklund, Mar. 22, 1975. BA magna cum laude, Northwestern U., 1960; PhD, Yale U., 1965. Asst. prof. Ind. U., Bloomington, 1964-66; asst. prof. French Southern Conn. State U., New Haven, 1967-70, assoc. prof., 1970-76, prof., 1976—2002. Speaker in field. Contbr. articles to profl. jours. Named Tchr. of Yr., So. Conn. State U., 2002. Mem. AAUP, Am. Coun. Teaching Fgn. Langs., Am. Assn. Tchrs. French, Modern Lang. Assn., Phi Beta Kappa. Republican. Avocations: piano, gardening, cooking, travel, graphic art. Home: 27 Cedar Rd Woodbridge CT 06525-1642

ECKLUND, JUDITH LOUISE, academic administrator; b. Baton Rouge, June 14, 1946; d. Norman Carl and Laverne (Borg) E. BA, U. Calif., Davis, 1968; MA, Cornell U., 1971, PhD, 1977. Adminstr. U. Calif., Berkeley, 1971-72, Cornell U., Ithaca, N.Y., 1976-78, Tulane U., New Orleans, 1980-90, v.p. devel. & alumni affairs, 1984-87, co-dir. internat. devel. ctr., 1987-90; dir. devel. The Carter Ctr., Atlanta, 1990-92; dir. internat. devel. UCLA, L.A., 1992—2002; dir. devel. and external rels. U. Calif., San Diego, 2002—. Mem. adv. coun. Cornell U., 1991—; mem. acad. adv. com. UCLA Ctr. for S.E. Asian Studies, 1999—. Fellow Am. Anthropology Assn.; mem. Assn. Asian Studies.

ECKLUND, RALPH EARL, property manager; b. Seattle, Jan. 29, 1930; s. Earl Frank and Ruby Frances (Bradshaw) Ecklund. AB in Design/Arch., Harvard U., 1952; postgrad., U. Wash., 1955. Asst. mgr. Liberty Ct. Apts., Seattle, 1957—68; dir. Lockhaven Apts., Seattle, 1958—. Author: Ripples newsletter, 1970. Sgt. U.S. Army, 1952—55. Mem.: Seattle Rhododendron Soc. (life), Seattle Men's Garden Club (sec.-editor 1963—70). Republican. Congregationalist. Avocations: photography, reading, genealogy, rhododendrons, collecting books. Home: 8321 32d Ave NW Seattle WA 98117-3922 Office: Lockhaven Apts 3040 NW Market St Seattle WA 98107

ECKMAN, FERN MARJA, journalist; b. N.Y.C., Aug. 27; d. Isidor Peter and Zara Nettie (Sloate) Friedman; m. Irving Eckman, June 21, 1957. BA, N.Y. U., 1957. Reporter N.Y. Post, 1944-78; assigned to UN, 1945-49, 60-65. Author: The Furious Passage of James Baldwin, 1967; contbg. editor Working Mother, 1981-91; feature writer for nat. publs., 1965-90. Recipient George Polk Meml. award for distinguished met. reporting, 1951, 55; Page One award for community service N.Y. Newspaper Guild, 1955, for best feature reporting, 1961; citation for community service Council Puerto Rican and Spanish-Am. Orgns., 1955; Lasker award for med. journalism, 1960; Front Page award for distinguished feature writing, News Women's Club N.Y., 1949, 51, 56, 64; for distinguished series (co-recipient), 1970; Cultural News award Newspaper Reporters Assn., N.Y.C., 1967; Empire State award for excellence in med. reporting, 1968 Home: 749 W End Ave New York NY 10025-6224

ECKMAN, MARK H. physician, educator; s. Sidney and Adeline Eckman; m. Margaret Fredrickson Fredrickson, Apr. 30, 1983; children: Laura Eliana, Nathaniel Benjamin. MD, Albany Med. Coll., 1981; MS, Northwestern U., 1977; BS, Trinity Coll., 1976. Medical Diplomate Am. Bd. of Internal Medicine, 1984. Asst. prof. of medicine Tufts U./New Eng. Med. Ctr., Boston, 1986—94, assoc. prof. of medicine, 1994—99. Chief, divsn. of gen. medicine Tufts U./New Eng. Med. Ctr., Boston, 1996—99; rsch. affiliate MIT, Cambridge, Mass., 1988—99; prof. of medicine Tufts U./New Eng. Med. Ctr., Boston, 1999—99; dir., divsn. of gen. internal medicine U. of Cin. Coll. of Medicine, Ohio, 1999—; dir., ctr. for clin. effectiveness Inst. for Health Policy and Health Services Rsch., U. of Cin. Med. Ctr., Cincinnati, Ohio, 1999—; pres. med. staff New Eng. Med. Ctr., Boston, 1996—98. Mem. United Way Vision Coun., Cincinnati, Ohio, 2000—03. Recipient Margaret Alice Posey Chair of Medicine, U. of Cin. Coll. of Medicine, 1999 - present. Fellow: Am. Coll. of Med. Informatics (Fellowship 1992), ACP (Fellowship 1990); mem.: Acad. Health, Am. Coll. of Physician Executives, Cin. Soc. of Internal Medicine (pres. 2002—03), Soc. of Gen. Internal Medicine, Soc. for Med. Decision Making (pres. 1999—2000, v.p., Lee Lusted Award 1986). Office: Univ Cincinnati 231 Albert Sabin Way PO Box 670535 Cincinnati OH 45267-0535 E-mail: mark.eckman@uc.edu.

ECKMAN, MATTHEW JAY, physiatrist, educator; b. Duluth, Minn., Jan. 19, 1940; s. Ralph Johan and Irene (Kennebrook) Eckman; m. Kay Sethre, July 31, 1971; children: Peter, Erik, Annalisa. BA, Gustavus Adolphus Coll., St. Peter, Minn., 1962; MD, U. Minn., 1966. Diplomate Am. Bd. Phys. Medicine and Rehab. Intern St. Mary's Hosp., Duluth, Minn., 1966-67; resident in phys. medicine and rehab. U. Minn. Hosp., Mpls., 1970-73; pvt. practice Polinsky Med. Rehab. Ctr., Duluth, 1973-80, med. dir., 1973-99; mem. med. staf St. Mary's-Duluth Clinic, 1981—. Med. cons. Minn. Svcs. for Children with Handicaps, 1973-90, Minn. Vocat. Rehab. and Svcs. for Blind, 1977—; clin. assoc. prof. U. Minn., Duluth and Mpls., 1974—; med. dir. Lakeshore Luth. Home, Duluth, 1987—; chief staff Miller-Dwan Med. Ctr., Duluth, 1980. Pres. ch. coun. 1st Luth. Ch., Duluth, 1996—98; bd. dirs. Residential Svcs., Duluth, 1986—92. Capt. M.C. U.S. Army, 1967—69, Vietnam. Fellow Am. Acad. Phys. Medicine and Rehab.; mem. AMA, Am. Spinal Injury Assn., Minn. Physiatrist Soc., Minn. Med. Assn., Lake Superior Med. Soc. Avocations: gardening, walking, music. Home: 1110 W Morgan St Duluth MN 55811 Office: Polinsky Med Rehab Ctr 530 E 2d St Duluth MN 55805 Fax: 218-786-3055.

ECKOLS, THOMAS AUD, lawyer, educator; b. Springfield, Ill., Oct. 3, 1950; s. Aud L. and Jean (Sutton) E.; m. Cynthia Marie Yontz, Aug. 19, 1973; children: Molly, Cally. BA, U. Iowa, 1972; JD, U. Ill., 1975. Bar: Ill. 1975, U.S. Dist. Ct. (cen. dist.) Ill. 1975, U.S. Supreme Ct., 1998. Assoc. Fleming, Messman & O'Connor, Bloomington, Ill., 1975-80; ptnr. Fleming, Messman, O'Connor & Eckols, Bloomington, Ill., 1980-81; sr. atty. State Farm Ins. Cos., Bloomington, Ill., 1981-85, asst. counsel, 1985-87, counsel, 1987—. Asst. prof. legal studies Ill. State U., Normal, 1984-92. Chmn. issues com. Sen. John Maitland, Ill., 1980-92; program chmn. McLean County Lincoln Club, Bloomington, 1978-80; legis. aid Rep. John Hirschfeld, Champaign, Ill., 1972-75; precinct committeeman, 1994—. Mem. ABA (commerce, banking and bus. subcom. 1985—, litigation sect. 1984—), Ill. Bar Assn., McLean County Bar Assn. (sec. 1977 78). Republican. Presbyterian. Avocations: swimming, running, golf. Home: RR 13 Bloomington IL 61704-9813 Office: State Farm Ins Cos Corp Law Dept One State Farm Plaza Bloomington IL 61710

ECKSTAT, ARTHUR GENE, consultant; b. N.Y.C., Feb. 11, 1943; s. Maurice and Sophie Rebecca E.; m. Barbara June Tausend, Feb. 1, 1964 (div. July 1986); 1 child, Tony. BSME, Detroit Inst. Tech., 1968; MBA, U. Phoenix, 1985; DBA, Nova Southeastern U., 2002. Test engr. Continental Aviation & Engring., Detroit, 1966—68; engring. specialist Allied Signal Aerospace, Phoenix, 1968—98; v.p. tng. & orgn. devel. Personal Bridges to Teamwork, Inc., Phoenix, 1996—2000, pres., 2000—, Global Turbine Specialists, Chandler, Ariz., 1998—. Honored as contbr. to aviation history, Smithsonian Nat. Air and Space Mus. Mem. Nat. Assn. Gender Diversity Trainers, Acad. Mgmt. Avocations: boating, male-female conflict management. Office: Global Turbine Specialists PO Box 130 Chandler AZ 85244-0130 Fax: 480-380-2551. E-mail: gtseckstat@qwest.net.

ECKSTEIN, JEROME, philosopher, educator; b. N.Y.C., June 28, 1925; s. Marcus and Blanche (Wohlberg) E.; m. Kathleen Sharon Hoisington; 1 stepchild, Mari O'Donnell Midurski; children: Esther Schwartz, Sandra Bellehsen, Michael. Student, Rabbi Isaac Elchanan Theol. Sem., 1943-45; BA, Bklyn. Coll., 1949; postgrad., New Sch. Social Research, 1949-50; PhD, Columbia U., 1961. Buyer antique silverware Blanche Eckstein Silverware, Bklyn., 1945-53; dir. edn. and youth activities, various Hebrew congregations, 1950-61; lectr. philosophy CCNY, 1955-56, Bklyn. Coll., 1955-60; instr. contemporary civilization and philosophy Columbia U., N.Y.C., 1960-63; asst. prof., then assoc. prof. philosophy, coordinator div. humanities Adelphi Suffolk Coll., Adelphi U., 1963-66; prof. philosophy of edn. SUNY-Albany, 1966-70, also first chmn. Judaic studies, 1970-74, prof. Judaic studies, 1970-97, prof. religious studies, 1990-97, prof. emeritus, 1997—. Participant Internat. Philosophy Yr., Brockport, N.Y., 1967, Conf. on Gerontology, U. Minn., 1978; vis. prof. philosophy Bar-Ilan U., Israel, 1978-79 Author: The Platonic Method: An Interpretation of the Dramatic-Philosophic Aspects of the Meno, 1968; The Deathday of Socrates, 1981, Metaphysical Drift: Love and Judaism, 1991, On Meanings or Life: Their Nature and Origin, 2002; also numerous articles. Fellow in logic CCNY, 1955-56; vis. scholar Va. Commonwealth U., Richmond, 1975; Am. Council Learned Socs. sr. fellow, 1973 Mem. Phi Beta Kappa

ECKSTEIN, JOHN ALAN, lawyer; b. Iowa City, Aug. 11, 1948; s. John William and Imogene B. (O'Brien) E.; m. Ledy R. Garcia, June 10, 1972; children: Cody Brien, Maria Alejandra. Student Grinnell Coll., 1966-67; BA, Iowa U., 1970; MA, Johns Hopkins U., 1972; JD, U. Va., 1975. Bar: Ind. 1975, U.S. Dist. Ct. (so. dist.) Ind. 1975, U.S. Tax Ct. 1975, Colo. 1981, U.S. Dist. Ct. Colo. 1981. Assoc. Ice, Miller, Donadio & Ryan, Indpls., 1975-81; assoc. Calkins, Kramer, Grimshaw & Harring, Denver, 1981-83, ptnr., 1983-89; ptnr. Kelly, Stansfield & O'Donnelly, 1989; ptnr., officer, dir. Jensen Byrne Parsons Ruh & Tilton, P.C., 1990—; lectr. internat. fin. Contbr. articles to profl. jours. Mem. Gov.'s Edn./Industry Mobilization Coun., 1987-90; mem. adv. com. Colo. Sec. Commr., 1987—; mem. Millenium Club Colo. Dems., 1984-88; chmn. elect Colo. Advanced Tech. Inst., 1990—. Mem. ABA, Fed. Bar Assn. (bd. dirs. 1982—, pres. Colo. chpt. 1986-87), Colo. Bar Assn., Denver Bar Assn., Denver C. of C., Colo. Assn. Commerce and Industry, Serra, Denver Athletic Club, Phi Delta Phi. Democrat. Roman Catholic. Home: 1737 Glencoe St Denver CO 80220-1342

ECKSTEIN, JOHN WILLIAM, physician, educator; b. Central City, Iowa, Nov. 23, 1923; s. John William and Ellen (Ellsworth) Eckstein; m. Imogene O'Brien, June 16, 1947; children: John Alan, Charles William, Margaret Ann, Thomas Cody, Steven Gregory. BS, Loras Coll., 1946; MD, U. Iowa, 1950; DSc (hon.), Ind. U., 1995. Asst. prof. internal medicine U. Iowa, Iowa City, 1956—60, assoc. prof., 1960—65, prof., 1965—92, prof. emeritus, 1993; assoc. dean VA Hosp. affairs, 1969—70, dean coll. medicine, 1970-91, dean emeritus, 1993. Chmn. cardiovasc. study sect. NIH, 1970—72, Nat. Heart, Lung and Blood Adv. Coun., 1974—78; mem. adv. com. to dir. NIH, 1990—95. Author papers and abstracts. Mem. VA Manpower Study Group, 1988—92. Served with USAF, 1943—45, served with U.S. Army Med. Corps., 1950—51. Named established investigator, Am. Heart Assn., 1958—63, in his honor, Eckstein Med. Rsch. Bldg., U. Iowa, 1988; recipient Rsch. Career award, USPHS, 1963—70, Dist. Alumni Svc. award, U. Iowa, 1994, Disting. Physicians, Dept. Vets. Affairs, 1995—98; fellow postdoctoral, Rockefeller Found., 1953—54, Am. Heart Assn. Rsch., 1954—55, spl. rsch., Nat. Heart Inst., 1955—56. Mem.: Assn. Acad. Health Ctrs. (mem. sci. policy study group 1988—93), Inst. Medicine, Assn. Am. Med. Colls. (exec. coun. 1981—82, administry. bd. 1980—82, 1985—86), Assn. Am. Physicians, Am. Clin. and Climatol. Assn., Am. Soc. Clin. Investigation, Ctrl. Soc. Clin. Rsch. (sec.-treas. 1965—70, pres. 1973—74), Am. Fedn. Clin. Rsch. (chmn. Midwestern sect. 1965), AMA (mem. health policy agenda panel 1982—86, mem. study sect. faculty and resh. 1985—86, governing. coun. sect. on med. schs. 1985—95, alt. del. Ho. of Dels. 1986—90, del. 1990—92, Disting. Svc. award 1992), Am. Heart Assn. (v.p. 1969, chmn. coun. on circulation 1969—71, pres. 1978—79). Home: 1415 William White Blvd Iowa City IA 52245-4443 Office: U Iowa Hosps & Clinics Iowa City IA 52242-1101 E-mail: john-eckstein@uiowa.edu.

ECKSTEIN, MARLENE R. vascular radiologist; b. Poughkeepsie, N.Y., Sept. 6, 1948; d. Marc and Lola (Charm) E. AB, Vassar Coll., 1970; MD, Albert Einstein Coll. Medicine, 1973. Diplomate Nat. Bd. Med. Examiners; cert. Am. Bd. Radiology. Intern in medicine Yale-New Haven Med. Ctr., 1973-74, resident in diagnostic radiology, 1974-77; asst. radiologist, chief vascular radiology sect. South Nassau Cmtys. Hosp., Oceanside, N.Y., 1977-78, assoc. radiologist, chief vascular radiology sect., 1978-81, asst. dir. dept. radiology, chief vascular radiology sect., 1981-83; asst. radiologist Mass. Gen. Hosp., 1983-87, assoc. radiologist, 1987—. Asst. prof. clin. radiology SUNY-Stony Brook Med. Sch., 1980-83; instr. radiology, Harvard Med. Sch., 1983-84, asst. prof., 1984—. Mem. exec. com. and hosp. chmn. United Jewish Appeal of Physicians and Dentists of Nassau County, N.Y., 1981-83. Fellow Am. Coll. Angiology, Soc. Cardiovasc. and Interventional Radiology; mem. AMA, Am. Coll. Radiology, Am. Inst. Ultrasound in Medicine, Am. Assn. Women Radiologists, Am. Med. Women's Assn., Mass. Radiol. Soc., Mass. Med. Soc.,

New Eng. Soc. Cardiovasc. and Interventional Radiology (pres. 1985-86), Radiol. Soc. N.Am. Achievements include design and development of line of vascular catheters. Home: 141 Fulton Ave Apt 312 Poughkeepsie NY 12603-2841 Office: Mass Gen Hosp Vascular Radiology Sect Boston MA 02114 E-mail: mreckstein@alum.vassar.edu.

ECKSTEIN, RUTH, artist; b. Nuremberg, Germany, May 11, 1916; came to the U.S., 1939; d. Nathan and Ida (Schiffer) Friedmann; m. George Gunther Eckstein, May 16, 1935; children: Margaret E. Loble, Susan E. Student, Art Students League, N.Y.C., 1953-57, Pratt Graphic Art Ctr., 1957-58, 68. One woman shows include Nassau County Mus., Roslyn, N.Y., Elaine Benson Gallery, Bridgehampton, N.Y., 1976, 81, Silvermine Guild, New Canaan, Conn., 1984, Anita Shapolsky Gallery, N.Y.C., 1985, Discovery Gallery, Glen Cove, N.Y., 1985, 91, St. Peter's Ch., N.Y.C., 1986, Great Neck (N.Y.) Libr., 1988, Suzuki Gallery, N.Y.C., 1994, Nese Alpan Gallery, Roslyn, N.Y., 1996, 98, 99, Heckscher Mus. at Bryant Libr., Roslyn, N.Y., 1998-99, Art Ctr., Great Neck, N.Y., 2000; exhibited in group shows at Neuberger Mus., Purchase, N.Y., 1989, Midge Karr Art Ctr., Old Westbury, N.Y., 1990, Andre Zarre Gallery, N.Y.C., 1991, Edwin Ulrich Mus. Art, Wichita, Kans., 1992, Silvermine Guild Galleries, New Canaan, Conn., 1992, 96, Suzuki Gallery, N.Y.C., 1993, Noyes Mus., Oceanville, N.J., 1994, Nassau C.C., Garden City, N.Y., 1994, S.W. Tex. State U., San Marcos, 1994, Nelson Atkins Mus. Art, Kansas City, Mo., 1995, James Howe Gallery, Keane Coll., Union, N.J., 1996, Westbeth Gallery, N.Y.C., 1996, Baruch Coll., N.Y.C., 1996, Nassau County Mus. Art, Roslyn, 1997, Fed. Res. Bank Hdqs., N.Y.C., 1997, Discovery Gallery, Sea Cliff, N.Y., 1998, Prince St. Gallery, N.Y.C., 1999, A.I.R. Gallery, N.Y.C., 2000, Hillwood Art Mus., L.I. U., Brookville, N.Y., 2000, Brooklyn Mus. of Art, Civic Ctr., Tulsa, Columbia U., Omni Gallery, Uniondale, N.Y., 2002, Martin Art Gallery, Muhlenberg Coll., Allentown, Pa., 2002, Swope Art Mus., Terre Haute, Ind., 2002. Recipient James R. Marsh award Audubon Artists, N.Y.C., 1977, Edna P. Stauffer award Audubon Artists, N.Y.C., 1978, Fairfield award Silvermine Guild, New Canaan, Conn., 1983, John Taylor Arms award Audubon Artists, N.Y.C., 1985. Mem. Silvermine Guild Artists (life), Am. Abstract Artists (hon.), Art Students League (life). Home: 5 Cricket Ln Great Neck NY 11024-1004 E-mail: rutheckstein@webtv.net.

ECONOMAKI, CHRIS CONSTANTINE (CHRISTOPHER ECONOMAKI), publisher, editor; b. Bklyn., Oct. 15, 1920; s. Christopher C. and Gladys Toomey (Burt) E.; m. Alvera H. Tomljanovic, May 29, 1946; children: Christine, Corinne. Student, Drake U. Sales rep. Divco Corp., 1946-49; editor, pub. emeritus Nat. Speed Sport News newspaper; pres. Kay Pub. Co., Harrisburg, N.C., 1949—; Color commentator Wide World of Sports ABC-TV, 1961-83, CBS-TV Sports, 1984-93. Served with AUS, 1942-46, ETO. Recipient Tom Marchese award for dedication to automobile racing, 1972, Henry McLemore award for excellence in broadcast journalism, 1973, Ken Purdy award Internat. Motor Press Assn., 1978, Ray Marquette Meml. award, 1981, Patrick Jacquemart award for service to motorsports, 1983, Dave Fritzlen Meml. award Outstanding Service to Chgo. Lathrop Boys Club, 1984, Walt Ader Meml. award, 1985, 1st Hugh Deery Meml. award for long service to automobile racing, 1985, Excellence award Nat. Assn. for Stock Car Auto Racing, 1990, Presdl. award U.S. Auto Club, 1992, Appreciation award svc. auto racing Charlotte, N.C. Motor Speedway, 1990, Chevy Proud award to Dean Am. Motorsports Journalism, 1990, Achievement award svc. racing Ford Motor Co., 1990, Dean Batchelor award Lifetime Achievement, 1996, Lifetime Media award NASCAR/ESPN, 1998; Economaki Award named in his honor Driver of Yr. Panel, 1991; Amb. Motorsports Time, Cleve., 1992; Lifetime Achievement award named in his honor; named to Stock Car Hall of Fame, Oceanside (Fla.) Rotary Club, 1993, Nat. Sprint Car Hall of Fame, Knoxville, Iowa, 1993, Motorsports Hall of Fame, 1994, Nebr. Auto Racing Hall of Fame, 1999, NASCAR's Buddy Shuman award for svc. to auto racing, 2000, Speedvision Lifetime Achievement award for motorposrts journalism, 2000; recipient 12th ann. Good Scout award Great Sauk Trail Coun., Boy Scouts Am., 2002, Lifetime Achievement award Ea. Motorsports Press Assn., 2003; Mayor Indpls. pronounces May 2, 2002 Chris Economaki Day. Mem. Am. Assn. Auto Racing Writers and Broadcasters (pres. 1969-71, Angelo Angelopolous Meml. award 2000), Nat. Motorsports Press Assn., Ea. Motorsports Press Assn., Oceanside Rotary, Order of Long Leaf Pine. Home: 9506 Charolais Ln Charlotte NC 28213-3741 Office: PO Box 1210 Harrisburg NC 28075-1210

ECONOMIDES, CHRISTOPHER GEORGE, pathologist; b. Alexandria, Egypt, Dec. 25, 1940; came to U.S., 1967; s. George and Tina E. MD, Alexandria U., 1966. Diplomate Am. Bd. Anatomic Pathology, Am. Bd. Clin. Pathology, Am. Bd. Cytopathology. Intern Alexandria U. Hosps., 1965-66, Balt. City Hosps., 1967-68; resident in anatomic pathology, then chief resident Jackson Meml. Hosp., U. Miami, Fla., 1968-70, resident in clin. pathology, 1970-71, 73-74, resident in ob-gyn., 1971-72, resident in anatomic pathology, 1972-73; pathologist Hialeah (Fla.) Hosp., 1974, chief dept. pathology, 1975—. Officer med. bd. Hialeah Hosp., 1975—, chief of staff, chmn. med. bd., 1980, 81, trustee, 1989-95, chmn. governing com., 1996—, mem. numerous coms.; med. and surg. clerkships Alexandria U. Hosp., Victoria Hosp., Scotland, Royal Salop Infirmary, England; mem. family planning program Broward County Health Dept., Fla., 1972-77; mem. courtesy staff North Shore Hosp., Miami, 1975, Palmetto Gen. Hosp., Hialeah, 1979-90; clin. asst. prof. pathology U. Miami, 1980-85; med. dir. SmithKline-Beechman Clin. Labs., 1983-99; bd. dirs. Immunopathology Labs., 1987-92, Ambulatory Ctr. of Hialeah, 1987-95, Dimension Health-PHO, 1993—. Trustee The Hialeah Found., 1989-91, Dade Community Found., 1992-94. Trustee The Hialeah Found., 1989-91, Dade Community Found., 1992—. Recipient Physician Recognition award AMA, 1971—, St. Marks Cross from His Holiness Patriarch Nicholaus I, 1981. Fellow Am. Soc. Clin. Pathologists, Coll. Am. Pathologists, Internat. Coll. Surgeons; mem. Am. Soc. Cytology, Internat. Acad. Pathology, Internat. Acad. Cytology, Fla. Med. Assn., Fla. Soc. Pathologists, South Fla. Soc. Pathology (pres. 1983, 84), Dade County Med. Assn., N.Y. Acad. Sci., Fisher Island Club (charter). Avocation: sailing. Office: Hialeah Hosp 651 E 25th St Hialeah FL 33013-3878

ECONOMOS, CORA MATHENY, librarian; b. Camden, Ark., July 15, 1921; d. Walter Stanton and Cora Smith Matheny. BS in Edn. summa cum laude, Centenary Coll. La., 1963; MS in Libr. Sci. (grad. fellow), U. Miss., 1965, PhD, 1973; postgrad., U. Okla., 1973. Tchr. pub. schs., Shreveport, La., 1963—64; dir. Pine Bluff and Jefferson County Pub. Libr., Pine Bluff, Ark., 1965—86, mem. bd. trustees, 1991—, libr. emerita, cons., 1987—. Bd. dirs. Pine Bluff Cmty. Art Ctr., 1966—67; mem. steering com. Pine Bluff-Jefferson County Am. Revolution Bicentennial Celebration, 1975—76. Mem.: Alpha Chi, Phi Delta Kappa, Kappa Delta Pi. Episcopalian. Home: 1305 W 35th Ave Pine Bluff AR 71603-6315

ECONOMOU-PEASE, BESSIE CARASOULAS, city planner, consultant; b. N.Y.C., Sept. 29, 1933; d. Alexander Stelianos and Maria (Trilivas) Carasoulas; m. Constantine J. Economou, Sept. 10, 1955 (div. May 1966); m. Robert Barnard Pease, Oct. 1, 1976; children: Robert W., Richard B. BA, Barnard Coll., 1955; postgrad., Columbia U., 1955-57, MS in Urban Planning, 1960. Med. researcher Coll. Physicians and Surgeons Columbia U., N.Y.C., 1955-60; planning and renewal cons. Brown & Anthony, Engrs. Planners, N.Y.C., 1960-62; dir. research, edn. ACTION Inc., N.Y.C., 1962-66; exec. asst. to adminstr. N.Y.C. Housing and Devel. Admin., N.Y.C., 1966-69; dep. dir., exec. asst. N.Y. State Urban Devel. Corp., N.Y.C., 1969-73; exec. v.p. Nat. Housing Conf., Washington, 1973-76; prin. Bessie C. Economou Assocs., Pitts., 1976—. Dir. ACTION Housing, Inc., Pitts., 1982-88, Nat. Housing Conf., Washington, 1973—, also exec. v.p. 1973-76, Health Systems Agy. Western Pa., Pitts., 1984-87; adj. prof. U. Pitts, 1986—; mem. adv. com. Bur. Census Housing, 1977-81. Mem. Am. Inst. Cert. Planners (cert.), Nat. Assn. Housing and Redevel. Officials, Lamda Alpha.

ECROYD, LAWRENCE GERALD, trade association administrator; b. Montreal, Que., Can., Sept. 14, 1918; s. George Smith and Marie (Guibord) E.; m. Dorothy Gertrude Howson, Dec. 26, 1949; children: Lynn (Mrs. Thomas Egan), Claire (Mrs. Lawrence Northway), Beverly, Bruce. Intermediate cert., U. London, Eng., 1960; MBA, Fla. Atlantic U., 1972. B.C. mgr. Can. C. of C., Vancouver, 1946-53; exec. dir. Mitchell Press Ltd., Vancouver, 1953-61; exec. v.p. Travel Industry Assn. Can., Ottawa, Ont., 1961-73; pres. Can. Inst. Plumbing and Heating, Toronto, 1973-84, cons., 1984—. Served to lt. comdr. Royal Can. Navy, 1941-45. Recipient Bota award tourism, 1973 Mem. Am. Soc. Assn. Execs. (Merit award 1971, Cert. Assn. Exec. 1974), Inst. Assn. Execs. (Can.). Home: 1510 Riverside Dr Apt 402 Ottawa ON Canada K1G 4X5

ECTON, DONNA R. business executive; b. Kansas City, Mo., May 10, 1947; d. Allen Howard and Marguerite (Page) E.; m. Victor H. Maragni, June 16, 1986; children: Mark, Gregory. BA (Durant Scholar), Wellesley Coll., 1969; MBA, Harvard U., 1971. V.p. Chem. Bank, N.Y.C., 1972-79, Citibank, N.A., N.Y.C., 1979-81; pres. MBA Resources, Inc., N.Y.C., 1981-83; v.p. adminstrn., officer Campbell Soup Co., Camden, N.J., 1983-89; chmn. Triangle Mfg. Corp. subs. Campbell Soup Co., Raleigh, N.C., 1984-87; sr. v.p., officer Nutri/System, Inc., Willow Grove, Pa., 1989-91; pres., CEO Van Houten N.Am., Delavan, Wis., 1991-94, Andes Candies Inc., Delavan, 1991-94; chmn., pres., CEO Bus. Mail Express, Inc., Malvern, Penn., 1995-96; COO PETsMART, Inc., Phoenix, 1996-98; chmn., pres., CEO EEI Inc., Phoenix, 1998—. Bd. dirs. H&R Block, Kansas City, Mo.; commencement spkr. Pa. State U., 1987. Bd. Overseers Harvard U., 1984-90; mem. Coun. Fgn. Rels., N.Y.C., 1987—; trustee Inst. for Advancement of Health, 1988-92. Named One of 80 Women to Watch in the 80's, Ms. mag., 1980, One of All Time Top 10 of Last Decade, Glamour mag., 1984, One of 50 Women to Watch, Bus. Week mag., 1987, One of 100 Women to Watch, Bus. Month mag., 1989; recipient Wellesley Alumnae Achievement award, 1987; Fred Sheldon Fund fellow Harvard U., 1971-72; Margaret Rudkin scholar Harvard U., 1969-71. Mem. Harvard Bus. Sch. Assn. (pres. exec. council 1983-84), N.Y.C. Harvard Bus. Sch. Club (pres. 1979-80), Wellesley Coll. Nat. Alumnae Assn. (bd. dirs., 1st v.p. 1977-80). Avocations: public speaking, art, gardening, reading, bicycling.

EDBERG, JUDITH FLORENCE, music educator; b. Royal Oak, Mich., Apr. 13, 1933; d. DeWitt and Florence (Machris) Patterson; m. Hugo Charles Edberg; children: Charles Eric, Christine Elisabeth. B Music, Wayne State U., 1954, M Music, 1971. Tchr. Royal Oak Pub. Sch. Sys., 1952-54; pianist, artist tchr. Edberg Music Studio, Royal Oak, 1950-71; prof. music U. Tampa, Fla., 1972—, pre-coll. music program exec. dir., 1981—. Pre-concert lectr. Fla. Orchestra, 1990—, mem. edn. com., 1998—; co-dir. Nicaragua Music Edn. Project, 1998—. Pianist recording Piano Works of Clark Eastham, 1987. Mem. governing bd. Tampa Bay Youth Orch., Tampa, 1990—; bd. dirs. Sarasota Music Archives, Tampa, 1995-98. Grantee Dana Found., 1987, 95; named Outstanding Musical Artist, Tampa Bay Chamber Orch., 1996. Mem. Nat. Guild Piano Tchrs. (chmn. Tampa chpt. 1994—, adjudicator 1997—), Fla. Music Tchrs. Assn., Music Tchrs. Nat. Assn. Democrat. Avocations: herbalist, couture sewing, photography. Office: U Tampa Music Dept Tampa FL 33606 E-mail: jedberg@ut.edu.

EDDEY, GARY ERWIN, physician, administrator, educator; b. Englewood, N.J., Dec. 10, 1951; s. Erwin Carnes and Emma (Bogart) E.; m. Ilene N. Eddey, July 31, 1976 (div.); children: John, AnnMichele, Emily. BS, U. Md., 1976; ScM, U. Pitts., 1978; MD, Cornell U., 1983. Diplomate Am. Bd. Pediats. Intern U. N.C., Chapel Hill, 1983-84; resident N.Y. Hosp.--Cornell, N.Y.C., 1984; chief resident in pediats. N.Y. Hosp.-Cornell U., N.Y.C., 1984; asst. prof. pediats. Cornell Med. Coll., N.Y.C., 1986-88; clin. asst. prof. pediats. Columbia U., N.Y.C., 1986-88; from clin. assoc. prof. to assoc. prof. pediats. N.J. Med. Sch., Newark, 1997—; assoc. med. dir. Matheny Hosp., Peapack, N.J., 1990—, dir. comprehensive continuum of care, 2001; med. dir. Matheny Ctr. Medicine and Dentistry, Peapack, 2002—. Bd. dirs. Lesch-Nyhan Coun., Matheny. Contbr. articles to profl. jours. Recipient Outstanding Pediatrician award Morris County Office Hispanic Affairs, 1993. Mem. Am. Acad. Pediats., Am. Acad. Devel. Medicine. Unitarian Universalist. Avocations: genealogy, history, creative writing, jazz, recording arts. Home: 22 Max Dr Apt 7A Morristown NJ 07960 Office: Matheny Hosp Main St Peapack NJ 07977

EDDINGTON, THOMAS L. human resources consultant; b. Westland, Mich., Mar. 10, 1960; s. William Thomas and Janet Lorraine (Woodard) E.; married; 2 children. BA in Bus. Psychology, Adrian Coll., 1982; MA in Orgnl. Dynamics, U. Pa., 1997. Employee benefits rep. Aetna Life Ins. Co., N.Y.C., 1982-84, Concord, N.H., 1984-86, account exec. Phila., 1986-90; mng. cons., owner Hewitt Assocs., Phila., 1990—98, mng. cons. St. Albano, 1998—2002. Mem. Pa. Employee Benefits Assn. Presbyterian. Office: Hewitt Assoc Embarkadero Ctr #1 Ste 1400 San Francisco CA 94111

EDDINS, JAMES WILLIAM, JR., marketing executive; b. Wadesboro, N.C., Dec. 22, 1944; s. James William and Mildred Ruth Eddins; m. Barbara Ann Nelson, Oct. 2, 1965 (div. 1986); 1 child, Christopher; m. Ann Manley McAdams, Sept. 25, 1988; 1 stepchild, Keith. AB, Pfeiffer Coll., 1966; M.Pub. Sch. Adminstrn., Appalachian State U., Boone, N.C., 1968; postgrad., U. N.C., 1969. Prin. Stanly County Bd. Edn., Albemarle, N.C., 1966-70; gen. sales mgr. ITT Continental Baking Co., Tampa, Fla., 1970-75; reg. sales mgr. Sunshine Biscuit Co., Tampa, 1975-81; nat. sales mgr. Beatrice Foods, Bakery div., Augusta, Ga., 1981-83; dir. sales/mktg. Bensons, Inc., Athens, Ga., 1983-86; reg. sales mgr. Sunshine Biscuit Co., Greenville, S.C., 1986-87; dir. sales, nat. accts. Christie-Brown and Co., Burlington, N.C., 1987—; dir., v.p. Atlas Mktg.-Food Broker, Charlotte, N.C., 1996—. Cons. in field. Active in past various charitable orgns. Named Oustanding Prin., Stanly County Bd. Edn., 1970. Mem. Biscuit Cracker Distbrs. Assn., Nat. Food Distbrs. Assn. Republican. Methodist. Avocations: tennis, basketball, travel. Home: 3230 Ardmore St Burlington NC 27215-8109 Office: Christie-Brown & Co PO Box 994 Burlington NC 27216-0994 E-mail: sbabille@msn.com.

EDDLEMAN, FLOYD EUGENE, retired English language educator; b. Mena, Ark., Dec. 3, 1930; s. Floyd Newton and Ruby Kate (Cannon) E. BSE, U. Cen. Ark., 1951; MA, U. Ark., 1955, PhD, 1961. Teaching asst. U. Ark., Fayetteville, 1953-55, 56-58; instr. U. Colo., Boulder, 1955-56; instr. English, Tex. Tech U., Lubbock, 1958-62, asst. prof., 1962-65, assoc. prof., 1965-75, prof., 1975-90, prof. emeritus, 1991—. Author: American Drama Criticism, 1976, 79, 84, 89, 92; co-editor: Almayer's Folly in the Cambridge Edit. of the Works of Joseph Conrad, 1994; contbr. articles to profl. jours. Sgt. U.S. Army, 1951-53. Democrat. Mem. Christian Ch. (Disciples Of Christ). Avocations: travel, collecting bison art objects. Home: 1309 Cole Ave Mena AR 71953-3722

EDDS, STEPHEN CHARLES, lawyer; b. Lexington, Ky., Apr. 28, 1949; s. William Harold and Ann Louise (Fisher) E.; m. Carole Brand. BA, U. Miss., 1971, JD, 1973. Bar: Miss. 1973, U.S. Dist. Ct. (no. and so. dists.) Miss. 1973, U.S. Ct. of Appeals (5th cir.) 1973, U.S. Supreme Ct. 1977. Ptnr. Gholson, Hicks and Nichols, Columbus, Miss., 1973-86, Heidelberg, Woodliff & Franks, Jackson, Miss., 1986-90, Ott, Purdy & Scott, Jackson, 1991—. Mem. editorial bd. Mag. Barrister, 1979-83, editor, 1981-83. Pres. Lowndes County Heart Assn., Columbus, 1981, Columbus Civic Arts Coun., 1984; v.p. Lowndes County Red Cross, Columbus, 1982; mem. Miss. Art Commn., Jackson, 1983—, chmn., 1985-88; mem. Leadership Jackson, 1990. Mem. Miss. Bar Assn. (young lawyers sect., sec. 1981, pres. 1984), ABA (young lawyers div. exec. coun. coord. 1983, budget dir. 1984, coun. mem. litigation sect. 1985-87, pres. fellows Miss. young lawyers sect. 1992), Golden Triangle Young Lawyers (pres. 1982), Am. Judicature Soc. (bd., dirs. 1984), Nat. Assn. Bond Lawyers, Miss. State Bar Assn. (chmn. ethics com. 1981, bd. bar commrs. 1985, 2d v.p. 1986), Omicron Delta Kappa, Phi Delta Phi. Home: 300 Sherborne Pl Flowood MS 39232-8959 Office: Ott Purdy & Scott PO Box 1079 Jackson MS 39215-1079

EDDY, CHARLES ALAN, chiropractor; b. Kansas City, Mo., Feb. 20, 1948; s. Sam Albert and Ella Louise (Gani) E.; m. Donna Darlene Perry, Oct. 23, 1971. Student, U. Mo., Kansas City, 1967; D in Chiropractic, Cleveland Chiropractic, Kansas City, 1970. Diplomate Nat. Bd. Chiropractic Examiners. Pvt. practice, Kansas City, 1970—. Peer rev. bd. Blue Cross and Blue Shield, Kansas City, 1972; pres. hon. bd. govs. Bapt. Hosp., Kansas City, 1993-94; cons. Quality Corp., Overland Park, Kans., 1988. Leader, profl. musician Chuck Eddy Band, Kansas City, 1964—; res. officer Kansas City Police Dept., 1970-77, sgt., 1977-82, capt., 1982-94; vice chmn. Citizens Assn., 1995-98, candidate for City Coun., Kansas City, 1995; mem. pub. improvement adv. com. City of Kansas City, 1997-98; city councilperson 6th Dist., chmn. bd. Mid Am. Reg. Coun., Kansas City, Mo., 1st v.p. 2001-02; bd. dirs. Econ. Devel. Coun., 1999-, 1st v.p. 2001-03, chair 2003-. Mem. Am. Chiropractic Assn., Mo. State Chriopractic Assn., Mo. Dist. II Chiropractic Assn. (bd. dirs., v.p. 1998-2003), Cleve. Chiropractic Coll. (trustee 1990, vice chmn. 1992—), Cleve. Chiropractic Alumni Assn. (v.p. 1995-97, pres. 1997-99, bd. dirs. 1990—, amb.'s soc. 1983—, chmn. 1990-96, 2001—, bd. mem. Truman Med. Ctr.), Optimist Club of Landing (pres. 1980, lt. gov. Mo. dist. 1982), South Kansas City C. of C. (Sml. Bus. of Yr. award 1998), Am. Lebanon Syrian Men's Club (pres. 1988-91, chmn. bd. 1992), St. Andrews Soc. (drummer in pipe band), DeMolay Legion Hon. (sec. 1988, treas. 1990, vice-dean 1991, dean 1992), Pipes and Drums of Ararat (treas. 1977-90, pres. 1985, dir. 1989, 90), Elks, Shriners (Potentate of Ararat shrine temple 1999, publicity chmn. 1991-92), Royal Order Jesters, Order Quetzalcoatl. Episcopalian. Avocations: photography, guns, stereo and video entertainment. Home: 406 W 109th St Kansas City MO 64114-4910 Office: 8301 State Line Rd Ste 108 Kansas City MO 64114-2019

EDDY, DARLENE MATHIS, poet, educator; b. Elkhart, Ind., Mar. 19, 1937; d. William Eugene and Fern (Paulmer) Mathis; m. Spencer Livingston Eddy, Jr., May 23, 1964 (dec. May 1971). BA, Goshen Coll., 1959; MA, Rutgers U., 1961, PhD, 1967. Instr., lectr. Douglass Coll. and Rutgers U., 1962-64, 66-67; asst. prof. English Ball State U., Muncie, Ind., 1967-70, assoc. prof., 1971-75, prof., 1975-99, poet-in-residence, 1989-93, prof. emerita, 1999, Whitinger lectr. Honors Coll., 1998-99; tchr., cons. numerous creative writing workshops; adj. prof. core program U. Notre Dame, 2001-; adj. prof. Eng. Goshen Coll., 2002-. Author: The Worlds of King Lear, 1968, Leaf Threads, Wind Rhymes, 1985, Weathering, 1991, Portraits, 1992; poetry editor Forum, 1985-89; contbg. editor Snowy Egret, 1988-89; cons. editor Blue Unicorn, 1995—; founding editor The Hedge Row Press, 1995; contbr. articles to English Lang. Notes, Am. Lit., other jours.; contbr. poetry to various publs. Mem. commn. on the status of women in the profession, Nat. coun. of Teachers of English, 1976-79; coord. Women's Studies program, 1976-82. Woodrow Wilson Nat. fellow, 1959-62, Notable Woodrow Wilson fellow, 1991, Rutgers U. grad. honors fellow, 1964-65; recipient numerous rsch., creative teaching and creative arts grants. Mem. AAUW, DAR, Soc. Mayflower Descs., Nat. League Am. Pen Women, League Women Voters. Home: 1840 Cobblestone Blvd Elkhart IN 46514

EDDY, DAVID MAXON, health policy and management administrator; BA, Stanford (Calif.) U., 1964, PhD with great distinction, 1978; MD, U. Va., 1968. Intern in gen. surgery Stanford U. Med. Ctr., 1968-69, resident, postdoct. fellow cardiovascular surgery, 1969-71, acting asst. prof., 1976-78; assoc. prof. Dept. Engring.-Econ. Systems, Stanford U., 1978-80, prof., 1980-81; J. Alexander McMahon prof. health policy and mgmt. Duke U., 1986-90, prof. health policy and mgmt., 1990-95; dir. WHO Collaborating Ctr. for Rsch. in Cancer Policy, 1984-95. Sr. advisor health policy, mgmt. Kaiser Permanente So. Calif. Region, 1991—; columnist Jour. of the AMA, 1990—; spl. govt. employee Hillary Rodham Clinton's Health Care Task Force, 1993; expert adv. panel on cancer WHO, 1981-96; cons. numerous cos., orgns. and assns. Author: A Manual for Assessing Health Practices and Designing Practice Policies, 1992, FAST*PRO: Software for Meta-Analysis by the Confidence Profile Method, 1992, The Synthesis of Statistical Evidence: meta-Analysis by the Confidence Profile Method, 1992, Common Screening Tests, 1991, Screening for Cancer: Theory, Analysis and Design, 1980, (Lanchester Prize, 1981), Clinical Decision Making: From Theory to Practice, 1996; contbr. articles to profl. jours. Recipient Sci. and Technol. Achievement award EPA, 1993, FHP Prize Internat. Soc. of Tech. Assessment in Health Care, 1991, USQA Quality Algorithm award, 1995, Novartis Outcomes Leadership award, 1997, Founders award Am. Coll. Med. Quality, 1998. Mem. Inst. of Medicine, Nat. Acad. Scis.

EDDY, DON, artist; b. Long Beach, Calif., Nov. 4, 1944; s. Myron and Ruth (Chase) Eddy King; m. Nancy Walker, June 12, 1967 (div. 1976); 1 child, Sarah. B.F.A., U. Hawaii, 1967, M.F.A., 1969. Artist, N.Y.C. Subject of monographs: Don Eddy: The Resonance of Realism in the Art of Post War America, Virginia Anne Bonita, Internet Publ.; Conversations with Don Eddy, interviewer Lela Compellin, Pub. Cleup Scarl, Padua, Italy; Don Eddy: The Art of Paradox, Donald Kuspit, 2002. One-man shows include Galerie Petit, Paris, 1973, Nancy Hoffman Gallery, N.Y.C., 1974, 1976, 1979, 1983, 1986, 1990, 1992—94, 1996, 1998, 2000, 2002, Mitch Shaheen Gallery, Cleve., 1994, Molly Barnes Gallery, L.A., 1970, 1971, French & Co., N.Y.C., 1971, Huntington (W.Va.) Mus., 1996, Duke U. Mus. Art, 2000, Boca Raton Mus. Art, 2000, New Orleans Contemporary Art Ctr., 2000; exhibited in group shows U.S. and Europe; Represented in permanent collections Akron Art Inst., Cleve. Mus. Art, Fogg Art Mus., Harvard U., Utrecht Mus. Belgium, Whitney Mus. Am. Art, others.

EDDY, DONALD DAVIS, English language educator; b. Norfolk, Va., Apr. 19, 1929; s. Clarence Ford and Rebekah (Proctor Davis) E.; m. Edith Ann Quattlebaum, Dec. 20, 1954; children: Edith Evelyn, Elizabeth Nelson. BA, Dartmouth Coll., 1951; MA, PhD, U. Chgo.; MA (Munby fellow), Cambridge (Eng.) U., 1978. Prof. English Cornell U., Ithaca, N.Y., 1961-96, head dept. rare books univ. libr., 1968-89, prof. emeritus, 1996—. Works include A Bibliography of John Brown, 1971, Samuel Johnson: Book Reviewer in the Literary Magazine, 1979, Samuel Johnson, LL.D., 1983, Bibliography of Richard Hurd, 1999; editor John Brown, Essays on the Characteristics, 1969, Samuel Johnson and Periodical Literature, 16 vols., 1978-79, Sale Catalogues of the Librs. of Samuel Johnson, Hester Lynch Thrale (Mrs. Piozzi) and James Boswell, 1993. Served with USN, 1952-55. Mem. MLA, Bibliog. Soc., Oxford Bibliog. Soc., Cambridge Bibliog. Soc., Bibliog. Soc. Am., Bibliog. Soc. U. Va. Clubs: Grolier; Athenaeum (London); The Johnsonians. Episcopalian. Home: 240 Renwick Dr Ithaca NY 14850-2142 E-mail: dde2@cornell.edu.

EDDY, ELSBETH MARIE, retired government official, statistician; b. Buffalo, Apr. 8, 1934; d. Willy and Wilhelmine (Hartman) Gnueg; m. Leonard John Eddy, Feb. 5, 1956; children: John, Bruce, Lisa. Student, schs. in Md., Va., N.C.; spl. courses, U.S. Dept. Agriculture Grad. Sch.; cert. in mgmt., Prince Georges Coll., 1976. With fgn. trade div. U.S. Bur. Census, Washington, 1967-90, chief metals and minerals, 1980-90. Recipient Cert. of Appreciation, USAF, 1973. Republican. Avocations: swimming, gardening, growing orchids, oil painting, mineral and gem collecting. Home: 601 Collins St Sebastian FL 32958-4413

EDDY, HEATH ROBERT, urban planner; b. Oconto, Wis., May 8, 1971; s. Curtiss Edward and Kathleen Kathryn Eddy; m. Kristy J. Deischer, June 13, 1993; 1 child, Deidre Linette. BA, Northwestern U., 1993; M in Urban and Regional Planning, Ball State U., 1995. Planner I Monroe County Planning Dept., Bloomington, Ind., 1995-98; sr. zoning planner City of Bloomington, 1998-99, sr. environ. planner, 1999-2001; sr. cmty. planner Chester County Planning Commn., West Chester, Pa., 2001—. Recipient Land Use Planning award So. Ind. Devel. Project, 1997. Mem. Am. Inst. Cert. Planners (cert.), Am. Planning Assn., Ind. Planning Assn. (sec. 1998-2000), Pa. Planning Assn. (vice chair S.E. sect. 2003—). Avocations: music, astronomy, urban growth issues, politics. Home: 536 Summercroft Dr Exton PA 19341-3047 Office: 601 Westtown Rd West Chester PA 19382-4958 E-mail: heddy@chesco.org.

EDDY, JOHN JOSEPH, diplomat; b. Lakewood, Ohio, Jan. 8, 1933; s. John Ezekiel and Pauline Edna (Ryan) E.; m. Armonia Badenes, Feb. 14, 1967; children— John Louis, Christopher Robert, William Francis, Isabel Ann (dec.) AB, Boston Coll., 1960; MA, Fletcher Sch. of Law and Diplomacy, 1961; student, Nat. Def. U., 1979-80. Joined Fgn. Service, Dept. State, 1966; asst. comml. attache Am. Embassy, Caracas, Venezuela, 1966-69, comml. attache San Salvador, El Salvador, 1970-71, first sec., comml. attache Bogota, Colombia, 1971-74, counselor for econ. and comml. affairs Nairobi, Kenya, 1974-77, dep. chief of mission Bridgetown, Barbados, 1977-79; dir. Office Regional Econ. Policy, Bur. Inter-Am. Affairs, Dept. State, 1980-81; consul gen. Am. consulate gen., Dhahran, Saudi Arabia, 1983-87, Am. Consulate Gen., Bombay, 1987-90; sr. spl. asst. to dir. gen. Fgn. Svc., Dept. State, Washington, 1991-92; sr. insp. Dept. State, 1992-94, ret., 1994, cons., 1994—. Served with USAF, 1952-56, Korea. Roman Catholic. Office: Dept State Oig Isp Rm 6817 Washington DC 20520-0001

EDDY, JULIA VERONICA, educator; b. Phila., Pa., May 25, 1950; d. Horace Charles and Pearl Marie (Houser) E. BA in Liberal Arts, Rutgers U., 1973; MA in History Edn., SUNY, Stony Brook, 1974, MA in L.Am. History, 1979, postgrad., 1974—. Cert. secondary tchr. Social studies dir. Community Voyage Sch., Phila., 1976-79; edn. mgr. Project 70001, Phila., 1979-82, Am. Bus. Inst., Phila., 1982-84; vis. lectr. C.C. Phila., Pa., 1984-87; mgr. Pvt. Industry Coun., Phila., 1988-92, Tradeswomen of Phila. in Non-Traditional Work, Inc., Pa., 1991-93; founder Eddy & Assoc., Phila., 1993—; tchr. tech. studies Sch. Dist. Phila., Pa., 1994—; computer specialist cons., 1997—; lead tchr. Victory Charter Schs., Ga., 2001. Cons. Jr. Achievement of Am., 1996—, WAWA Teen

Parenting, Phila., 1995-96, Top/Win, Inc., Phila., 1991-92, Sch. for Exec. Secs., Newark, 1984, Voyage House, Inc., Phila., 1980, Advantage Schs., Pa. and Ga., 1999—; workshop presenter. Editor, contbr: Women in Technology & Trades, 1992; contbg. editor: JTPA/PIC Case Management, 1991; editor: Unions/Apprenticeship in Pennsylvania, 1991. Bd. dirs. New Birth, Inc., Phila., 1993—; founder, pres. Mentor, Phila., 1993—; mem. Doris Day Animal League, Washington, 1989—; with advantage schs. Pa., Ga., 1999—. Recipient PIC Excellence award Pvt. Industry Coun., 1988, Phila. Sch. Dist. Mentor award, 1998; Samuel Robinson fellowship Lincoln U., 1970. Mem. Tutor Roundtable (treas. 1986), Am. Hist. Assn., Lamba Kappa Mu, Inc. (workshop presenter 1993, Community Svc. award 1993). Democrat. Roman Catholic. Avocations: amateur radio, cats, puzzles. Home and Office: Eddy & Assocs 1907 September Way Douglasville GA 30135 E-mail: JuliaEddy555@juno.com.

EDDY, MARK JAMES, healthcare industry executive; b. Detroit, June 17, 1958; s. James Joseph and Sharon Lou (Nelson) E.; m. Wendy Mary Kohler, Aug. 8, 1980; 1 child, Matthew Mark. Student, U. Mich., Ann Arbor, 1976-78; BBA, Ea. Mich. U., Ypsilanti, 1980. CPA, Tenn. Intern Karpus & Karpus, Detroit, 1979; staff auditor, internal audit dept. HCA, Nashville, 1980-81, sr. auditor, 1981-82, audit supr., 1982-84, sr. audit supr., 1984-85, corp. and constrn. audit mgr., 1985-87; audit mgr. HealthTrust, Inc., Nashville, 1987-93, dir. internal audit, 1994-95, HCA, Nashville, 1995-97, asst. v.p. cons. and audit svcs., 1997—2000, v.p. internal audit, 2000—. Bd. dirs. Spl. Olympics Tenn., 2001—, treas., 2002—, chmn. elect, 2003—. Mem. Am. Inst. CPAs, Tenn. Soc. CPAs, Am. Mgmt. Assn., Healthcare Compliance Assn., Assn. Healthcare Internal Auditors. Avocations: sports, travel, reading, antiques. Home: 413 Benton Ln Franklin TN 37067-4404

EDDY, MELISSA JANE, small business owner; b. Dec. 27, 1951; d. ERnest DeRhone and Jane Anne (Lose) Eddy; m. Tracy Schiemenz, Jan. 17, 1981. BA magna cum laude, Kalamazoo Coll., 1974; MA with honors, Western Mich. U., 1976. Psychologist Battle Creek (Mich) Cmty. Mental Health Clinic, 1976—77; coord. program svcs. Ctr. for Battered Women, Austin, Tex., 1978—81; pvt. practice counseling and cons. Austin, 1982—; owner women's bridal and formal-wear consignment bus., 1985. Mem. alcohol svcs. adv. com. Mental Health/Mental Retardaton, 1980—83; mem. adv. com. Austin Family Violence Diversion Network, 1980—84; program assoc. Tex. Coun. on Family Violence, Austin, Tex., 1984—87, tng. dir., 1987—88, comms. dir., 1988—92; owner arts adminstrn. bus., 2000—. Pres. Dispute Resolution Ctr. of Travis County, 1984—86; exec. dir. Austin Civic Chorus, Inc., 1993—2000; trustee Arts Ctr. Stage, 1997—; campaign vol. Dem. candidates, 1980—82; bd. dirs. Tex. Coun. on Family Violence, 1978—85, Dispute Resolution Ctr. of Travis County, 1983—89. Mem.: Tex. Counseling Assn., Assn. for Psychol. Type (founder Austin area br., bd. dirs. 1989—95), Tex. Coun. Famiy Violence, Chorus Am., Alpha Lambda Delta, Phi Beta Kappa. Achievements include research in on burnout among family-violence workers, treatment programs for spouse abusers. E-mail: proartsmgt@aol.com.

EDDY, ROGER L. state representative; b. Ottawa, Ill., May 8, 1958; m. Rebecca Eddy; children: Matt, Lisa, Brenda, Beth, Jessica. BA, Northern Ill. Univ., 1981; MA, Eastern Ill. Univ., 1986, Specialist, 1996. State Rep. House of Representitves, Dist. 109, Ill., 2002—; supt. Hutsonville Sch. Dist. #1, 1996—; prin. Watseka HS, 1991—96, Hutsonville HS, 1988—91, tchr., 1981—88. Mem. Local Town Bd., 1986—88. Mem.: Elem. & Secondary Ed. Comm., Legis. Comm., Ill. Assoc. of Sch. Admin., 1996-present, Computer Tech. Comm., Agr. & Conservation Comm., Appropriations: Elem., Secondary, Higher Ed., Elks, 1987-present. Republican. Efca. Office: Capitol 222-N Stratton Office Bldg Springfield IL 62706 also: District 108 South Main PO Box 125 Hutsonville IL 62433*

EDDY, WILLIAM BAHRET, psychology educator, university dean; BS, Kans. State U., 1955, MS in Indsl. Psychology, 1957; PhD in Indsl. Psychology, Mich. State U., 1963. From asst. prof. to prof. U. Mo., Kansas City, 1962-99, dir., Ctr. for Mgmt. Devel., 1966-69, prof., dir. pub. adminstrn., 1972-77, assoc. dean, 1981-86, dean and Harzfeld prof. Bloch Sch. Bus. and Pub. Adminstrn., 1986-99, asst. to chandellor for urban affairs Adminstrv. Ctr., 1999—2001, interim provost, vice chancellor acad. affairs, 2000-01; ret., 2001. Bd. dirs. Metcalf Bank; prof., assoc. dir. Fed. Exec. Inst., Charlottesville, Va., 1971-72; lectr. Woodrow Wilson Dept. Govt. and Fgn. Affairs, U.Va., 1972; presenter in field. Author: Public Organization and Development, 1981, The Manager and the Working Group, 1985, Hiking Kansas City, 1989, 4th edit., 2001, others; contbr. articles to profl. jours.; co-editor Adminstr. and Soc., 1980-86. Chmn. nat. bd. trustees Shepherd's Ctrs. of Am., 1991-96; founding bd. dirs., pres. Kansas City Consensus, 1985-86; pres. bd. Greater Kansas City Mental Health Found., 1987-88; pres. Helzberg Entrepreneurial Mentoring Program. Fellow APA; mem. Gold Key, Psi Chi, Phi Kappa Phi, Beta Gamma Sigma, Delta Sigma Pi, Alpha Tau Omega. Home: 611 E 54th St Kansas City MO 64110-2411

EDEAWO, GALE SKY, publishing company executive, writer; b. Detroit, Mar. 22, 1946; d. John Bryd Martin and Minerva Lee Dubrey; m. Robert Judkins, Jan. 23, 1965 (div. Jan. 1979); children: Consuella Judkins. AA, L.A. City Coll., 1977; student, Calif. State U., L.A., 1977-78. Telecom. PBXtra Placement, L.A., 1979-98; owner, mgr., writer Sky Publs., Savannah, Ga., 1998—; pvt. real estate investor, 2000—. Travel cons. Alwayz Travel, Inglewood, Calif., 1989-92. Peer counselor Rosa Parks Rape Crisis Ctr., L.A., 1990—98, Rape Crisis Ctr., Savannah, Ga., 1999—2001, bd. dirs., 2000—; jail, prison activist, 2000—; AIDS activist, contbg. writer Project Azuka, Savannah, 1998—2000, AIDS Project L.A., 1997—; cmty. outreach, spkr. Alzheimer's Assn., L.A., 1996—97; bd. dirs. Alcoholism Ctr. Women, L.A., 1992—94; leader writer's workshops for youth at risk Dept. Family and Children's Svcs., Savannah, 1999—; founder re-entry program for incercerated women Project Welcome Home, 2001—; mem. adv. bd. Regional Youth Detention Ctr., 2001—; local storyteller, 2001—. Mem. Am. Legion Women's Aux. (mem. pub. rels. 1986, historian 2000), Am. Corrections Assn., Nat. Coun. Negro Women, Fraternal Order Police. Democrat. Methodist. Avocations: traveling, writing, cats, reading, researching the south. Office: Sky Publs 12511 Largo Dr Savannah GA 31419-2601 Fax: 912-961-9076.

EDEBO, RALPH BERTIL, engineer, economist; b. Eskilstuna, Sweden, June 11, 1932; s. Fritz N. and Swea (Ohrn) E.; m. Anne-Charlotte Hoflund, 1958; children: Camilla, Fredrik; m. Nancy Carter, Nov. 6, 1982. MScME, Royal Inst. Tech., Stockholm, 1955; MBA, Stockholm Sch. of Econs., 1958. Mgr. corp. devel. Atlas Copco AB, Stockholm, 1958-70; mktg. dir. Statsforetag AB, Stockholm, 1971-77; chief exec. officer Berol Nobel AB, Stenungsund, Sweden, 1978-90; sr. v.p. Nobel Industries, Stockholm, 1990-92, ret., 1992. Contbr. articles to profl. jours. Mem. Royal Acad. Engring. Sci. Home: 516 Braemar Ranch Ln Santa Barbara CA 93109-1064

EDEL, ABRAHAM, philosophy educator; b. Pitts., Dec. 6, 1908; s. Simon and Fannie (Malamud) E.; m. May Mandelbaum, Jan. 30, 1934 (dec. May 1964); children: Matthew (dec.), Deborah; m. Elizabeth Flower, May 11, 1973 (dec. June 1995); m. Sima Szaluta, Apr. 20, 1997. BA, McGill U., 1927, MA, 1928; BA, Oxford U., 1930; PhD, Columbia U., 1934. Mem. faculty dept. philosophy CCNY, 1931-73, prof., 1962-73, prof. emeritus, 1973—; Disting. prof. Grad. Sch. CUNY, 1970-73; emeritus City U. N.Y. Grad. Sch., 1973—; rsch. prof. philosophy U. Pa., 1974—2001, rsch. prof. emeritus, 2001—. Vis. appointments instns. including Columbia U., U. Calif., Berkeley, Swarthmore Coll., U. Pa., Case Western Res. U., SUNY, Downstate Med. Ctr., others. Author: The Theory and Practice of Philosophy, 1946, Ethical Judgment, 1955, 2d edit. with new intro., 1995, Science and the Structure of Ethics, 1961, 2nd edit., 1998, with new intro., Method in Ethical Theory, 1963, with new intro., 1994, Aristotle, 1967; co-author: (with May Edel) Anthropology and Ethics, 1959, rev. edit., 1971, 2000, Analyzing Concepts in Social Science, 1979, Exploring Fact and Value, 1980, Aristotle and His Philosophy, 1982, with new intro., 1996, Interpreting Education, 1985, (with Elizabeth Flower and Finbarr O'Connor) Morality, Philosophy and Practice, 1988, Relating Humanities and Social Thought, 1990, The Struggle for Academic Democracy, 1990, In Search of the Ethical, 1993, (with others) Critique of Applied Ethics, 1994; (with Yervant H. Krikorian) Contemporary Philosophic Problems, 1959; editor: (with May M. Edel) The Chiga of Uganda, 1996, Ethical Theory and Social Change: The Evolution of John Dewey's Ethics, 1908-32, 2001. Assoc. Nat. Humanities Ctr., 1978-79; sr. fellow Ctr. for Dewey Studies, 1981-82. Recipient Butler Silver medal Columbia U., 1959; Guggenheim fellow, 1944-45; Grantee, Rockefeller Found., 1952-53, NSF, 1959-60. Mem. Am. Philos. Assn. (v.p. Ea. div. 1972), Metaphys. Soc., Am. Soc. Polit. and Legal Philosophy, Am. Soc. Value Inquiry (pres. 1984), Internat. Assn. Philosophy Law and Social Philosophy (v.p. Am. sect. 1971-73, pres. 1973-75, hon. pres. 1997), Philosophy Edn. Soc., Soc. for Advancement Am. Philosophy.

EDELBAUM, PHILIP R. lawyer; b. Bklyn., June 2, 1936; s. Maurice and Selma (Samuels) E.; m. Corinne Edelbaum, May 29, 1960 (div. Mar. 1974); children: Stacey K. Boretz, Evan Mark. BA, Adelphi U., 1957; LLB, NYU, 1960. Bar: N.Y. 1961, U.S. Dist. Cts. (so. and ea. dists.) N.Y. 1962, U.S. Ct. of Appeals (2d cirs.) 1964, (3d cir.) 1977, U.S. Supreme Ct. 1965. Atty. criminal div. Legal Aid Soc., N.Y.C., 1961-63; pvt. practice N.Y.C., 1963—. Faculty Nat. Inst. Trial Advocacy-N.E. Region, Nat. Inst. Trial Advocacy-N.E. Master Advocates, Hempstead, N.Y., 1985—, Cardozo Law Sch. intensive trial advocacy program, 1993—, ABA/USTA Trademark Trial Advocacy Inst., 1993—, Widener U. Sch. Law intensive trial advocacy program, 1995—; faculty trial techniques program Hofstra U. Sch. of Law, Hempstead, 1985—. Chmn. pool feasibility com. Town of Eastchester, N.Y., 1971-72. Mem. Nat. Def. Lawyers Criminal Cases, N.Y. Criminal Bar Assn., Assn. Bar City N.Y. (com. on criminal cts. op. and budget 1988-92, chmn. com. on criminal advocacy 1995-98, mem. coun. criminal justice 1992-98, 2001—, com. to study alts. to incarceration and probation 1993-94, CLE com. 1998-2001, numerous sub-coms. on criminal justice 1988-98, chair com. on criminal cts. 2001—). Avocations: classical music, bird watching, N.Y. Mets, cooking. Home: 345 E 93d St New York NY 10128-5515 Office: 39 Broadway Rm 1440 New York NY 10006-3003

EDELCUP, NORMAN SCOTT, management and financial consultant; b. Chgo., May 8, 1935; s. Irving L. and Pauline (Bolz) E. BS in Bus. Adminstrn, Northwestern U., 1957. C.P.A., Fla., Ill. Sr. accountant Arthur Andersen & Co., Chgo., 1957-62; sec.-treas. Acme Printing Ink Co., Chgo., 1962-65; accountant, asst. to chmn. Commonwealth Edison Co., Chgo., 1965-68; sr. v.p., vice-chmn. bd. Keller Industries, Miami, Fla., 1968-76; v.p., treas. Avatar Holdings (formerly GAC Corp.), 1976-80, exec. v.p., treas., chief fin. officer, dir., mem. exec. com., 1980-83; pres., treas., dir. Avatar Properties Inc. (formerly GAC Properties, Inc.), 1976-83, Avatar Properties Credit (formerly GAC Properties Credit, Inc.), 1976-83; vice chmn., chief operating officer Nat. Banking Corp. Fla., Miami, 1983-84; chmn. treas. Scroll Casual Inc., 1983-84; chmn. Fla. Powder Coatings, Inc., Confidata Corp., 1983-87; chmn., treas. First United Leasing Corp., 1983-86; ptnr. E&H Assocs., 1983-91; chmn. Item Processing Am. Inc., Miami, 1987-98. Sr. v.p., dir., Fla. Savs. Bancorp, Pinecrest, Fla., 2001—; bd. dirs. Valhi Inc., Baron Asset Fund. Commr. City of Sunny Isles, Fla., 2001. With AUS, 1958—60. Mem. Am. Inst. CPA's, Fla. Inst. CPA's, Ill. Inst. CPA's, Greater Miami C. of C. (trustee 1979-83). Lodges: Kiwanis. Home: 17395 North Bay Rd North Miami Beach FL 33160 Office: Fla Savs Bancorp 8181 SW 117th St Miami FL 33156

EDELHEIT, LEWIS S. research physicist; b. Chgo., Aug. 24, 1942; m. Susan Wershkoff, 1965; children: David, Dena. BS, U. Ill., 1964, MS, 1965, PhD in Physics, 1969. Physicist GE R&D Ctr., Schenectady, NY, 1969—76; mgr. Applied Sci. & Diagnostic Imaging Lab. GE Med. Sys., Milw., 1976—80; mgr. computed tomography prodn. engring. GE Corp. R&D, Schenectady, 1980—82, gen. mgr. dept. engring., 1982—83, gen. mgr. dept. computed tomography programs, 1983—85; pres., CEO Quantum Med. Sys., 1985—91, 1985—91; mgr. electronics sys. rsch. ctr. GE Corp. R&D, Schenectady, 1991—92, sr. v.p., 1992—. Mem.: NAE, Indsl. Rsch. Inst., Am. Physics Soc., Sigma Xi. Achievements include research in medical imaging systems, computerized imaging systems. Office: GE Corp R&D Ctr Bldg K1 Rm 5A1 One Rsch Cir Niskayuna NY 12309

EDELIN, KENNETH CARLTON, physician; b. Washington, Mar. 31, 1939; s. Benedict and Ruby (Goodwin) E.; m. Barbara Evans, Aug. 5, 1978; children— Kenneth Carlton, Kimberly Cybele, Joseph Evans, Corrine Ruby-Elizabeth. B.A., Columbia Coll., 1961; M.D., Meharry Med. Coll., 1967. Intern, Wright-Patterson AFB Hosp., Ohio, 1967-68; resident Boston City Hosp., 1971-74; instr. ob-gyn sch. Medicine, Boston U., 1974-76, asst. prof., 1976, assoc. prof., 1977-78, prof. ob-gyn, dept. chmn., 1978— ; asst. dir. ob-gyn Boston City Hosp., 1974-76, asso. dir., 1977-78, dir., 1978— ; gynecologist-in-chief Univ. Hosp., 1978— ; med. dir. Boston Family Planning Project; pres. Roxbury Comprehensive Community Health Ctr., Inc. Pres., New Eng. com. NAACP-Legal Def. Fund, Inc. Served to capt. USAF, 1968-71. Fellow Am. Coll. Obstetricians and Gynecologists, Obstetrical Soc. Boston; mem. Planned Parenthood Fedn. Am. (tru- stee) 1974, Nat. Med. Assn., New Eng. Med. Soc., Am. Fertility Soc., Assn. Profs. Ob-Gyn, Assn. Gynecologist Laparoscopists, Sigma Pi Phi. Office: 80 E Concord St Boston MA 02118-2307

EDELMAN, ALAN IRWIN, lawyer; b. Poughkeepsie, N.Y., June 14, 1958; s. Edwyn Herman and Shirley Frances (Kandel) E.; m. Erica Joy Schwartz, Aug. 16, 1981; children: Leah Hanit, Avram Natan, Samuel Aaron. BA, Cornell U., 1980; JD, Boston U., 1983. Bar: D.C. 1983, U.S. Dist. Ct. D.C. 1985, U.S. Supreme Ct. 1991. Atty. enforcement div. SEC, Washington, 1983-86, atty. Office of Gen. Counsel, 1986-87; counsel U.S. Senate Permanent Subcom. on Investigations, Washington, 1987-97, U.S. Senate Com. on Govtl. Affairs, 1997-99; trial atty. divsn. enforcement Commodity Futures Trading Commn., Washington, 1999—. Edward F. Hennessy scholar Boston U., 1983. Mem. ABA, Fed. Bar Assn. Office: Commodity Futures Trading Commn Three Lafayette Centre 1155 21st St NW Washington DC 20581-0001

EDELMAN, ALVIN, lawyer; b. Chgo., Dec. 12, 1916; m. Rose Marie Slossy, Sept. 22, 1940; children: Marilyn Frances Edelman Snyder, Stephen D., Leon F. BS in Law, Northwestern U., 1938, JD, 1940. Bar: Ill. 1940. Practiced in Chgo., 1940—; pres. Edelman & Edelman, Chartered and predecessors, 1973—; gen. counsel Internat. Coll. Surgeons. Lectr. Internat. Mus. Surg. Sci. and Hall of Fame; chmn. wills and gifts com. Medinah Temple of Masonic Shrine, Chgo., 1975-79; pres. Lawyers Shrine Club of Medinah Temple, 1971-73. Contbr. articles to profl. jours. Fellow Am. Coll. Trust and Estate Counsel; mem. ABA, Ill. Bar Assn., Chgo. Bar Assn. (chmn. grievance com. 1971-72), Phi Beta Kappa (pres. Chgo. area assn. 1975-85), Phi Beta Kappa Fellows (bd. dirs. 1985—, nat. v.p. 1986-95, nat. pres. 1996-2001), Elks (past exalted ruler). Office: 100 W Monroe St Chicago IL 60603-1967

EDELMAN, DANIEL JOSEPH, public relations executive; b. N.Y.C., July 3, 1920; s. Selig and Selma (Pfeiffer) Edelman; m. Ruth Rozumoff, Sept. 3, 1953; children: Richard, Renee, John. Grad., Columbia U., 1940; MS, 1941. Reporter Poughkeepsie (N.Y.) newspapers, UPI, 1941—42; news writer CBS, 1946—47; staff mem. Edward Gottlieb & Assocs., 1947; pub. rels. dir. Toni Co., Chgo., 1948—52; founder, chmn. 44 offices Daniel J. Edelman, Inc. (Edelman Pub. Rels. Worldwide P.R. 21, Blue Advt., Strategy One Rsch., Edelman Interactive Svcs.), Chgo., 1952—. Chmn. vis. com. U. Chgo. Libr., 1976; chmn. sustaining fellows individual campaign Chgo. Art Inst., 1982; bd. dirs. Lyric Opera, Chgo.; dir. Comm. for Econ. Growth of Israel, The Chgo. Project for Violence Prevention. With U.S. Army, 1942—46. Named Pub. Rels. Profl. of Yr., Pub. Rels. News, 1993; named to Chgo. Bus. Hall of Fame, Jr. Achievement, 1998, Entrepeneurship Hall of Fame, U. Ill., Chgo., 2001; recipient Disting. Alumnus award, Columbia U., 1988, John Jay award, 1990, Agy. of Yr., Inside PR Mag., 1993, Lifetime Achievement All-Star award, 1998, Tom Mosser award, St. Bonaventure U., 1998, First award, China Pub. Rels. Assn., 1999, First Lifetime Achievement award, Publicity Club Chgo., 2003. Fellow: Pub. Rels. Soc. Am. (past chmn., counselor sect., Top Gun Career Achievement award 1998, Gold Anvil award for outstanding contbns. to pub. rels. profession 1999, 35 Silver Anvil awards, Atlas Internat. Leadership award 2003); mem.: Pub. Rels. Seminar, Arthur Page Soc. (Hall of Fame 1997), Chief Execs. Orgn., Young Pres. Orgn. (chmn. Chgo. chpt. 1963), Casino Club, Chgo. Club, Mid-Am. Club, Harmonie Club, Std. Club, Phi Beta Kappa (dir. fellows). Jewish. Home: 1301 N Astor St Chicago IL 60610 Office: Edelman Aon Ctr 200 E Randolph Dr Chicago IL 60601-6436 E-mail: dan.edelman@edelman.com.

EDELMAN, DAVID JOEL, urban planning executive; b. N.Y.C., Aug. 3, 1946; BA in History, U. Rochester, 1968; MRP in Urban Planning and Devel., Cornell U., 1974, PhD in Policy Planning/Regional Analysis, 1978. Tchr. English as a Fgn. Lang. Internat. Sch. of English, Tokyo, 1971; planning cons. Village of Watkins, Glen, N.Y., 1972; analyst EPA, N.Y.C., 1973, Fed. Energy Adminstrn., Washington, 1974; various positions Cornell U., N.Y.C., 1974-76; Lady David Rsch. fellow in policy planning Technion-Isreal Inst. of Tech., Haifa, 1976-77; sr. assoc. Planning Rsch. Corp. Energy Analysis Co., McLean, Va., 1978-80; energy cons. Orgn. of Am. States, Washington, 1980-81; mgr., renewable energy programs Syscon Corp., Washington, 1981; staff energy cons. Asian Devel. Bank, Manila, 1981-82; sr. econ. devel. cons. The Futures Group, Washington, 1982-83; sector modeling cons. UN Food and Agrl. Orgn., Rome, 1983; chief planner, economist Motor-Columbus Cons. Engrs. Inc./Holinger Ltd., Baden, Switzerland, 1984-92; assoc. prof. energy planning and policy Asian Inst. of Tech., Bangkok, Thailand, 1990-92; prin. planner Werkstatt für Architektur and Planung AG, Zurich, Switzerland, 1992-93; chmn. dept. Housing and Urban Devel. Studies Wageningen U., The Netherlands, 1993-98, dir. Ctr. Urban Environment, 1993-98; prof. planning, dir. Sch. of Planning U. Cinn., 1998—. Sci. tchr. N.Y. Bd. Edn., 1968; social worker Suffolk County, 1968; internat. adv. bd. Ctr. for Urban Environ., Rotterdam, 1998—. Contbr. chpts. to books and articles to profl. jours. Exec. bd. Cin. Kharkiv Sister City Program, 1999—. Merchant marine USCG. Mem.: Fedn. Europeanne Assn. Nat. Engrs., Royal Dutch Inst. of Engrs. (registered planner), Swiss Assn. of Engrs. and Architects (registered planner), Am. Inst. of Cert. Planners (cert.). Jewish. Avocations: movies, books, languages, basketball, running, swimming, city walks. Office: Sch of Planning Coll of Design U Cin PO Box 210016 Cincinnati OH 45221-0016

EDELMAN, ERIC STEVEN, ambassador; m. Patricia Davis; children: Alexander, Stephanie, Terrence, Robert. BA in History and Govt., Cornell U., 1972; PhD in U.S. Diplomatic History, Yale U., 1981. With U.S. Fgn. Svc., U.S. Middle East Delegation to West Bank/Gaza Autonomy Talks, 1980-81, watch officer State Dept. Ops. Ctr., 1981-82, staff officer Secretariat Staff, 1982, spl. asst. to Sec. of State George P. Shultz, 1982-84; mem. Office of Soviet Affairs Dept. of State, Moscow, 1984-86, head external polit. sect., 1987-89, spl. asst. to Under Sec. of State for Polit. Affairs, 1989-90; asst. dep. under sec. def. for Soviet/East European Affairs Office of Sec. of Def., 1990-93; dep. to Strobe Talbott, spl. advisor Sec. of State Dept. of State, 1993, dep. chief of mission, 1994-96, exec. asst. to dep. Sec. of State, 1996-98, amb. to Finland, 1998—2001; prin. dep. asst. to Vice Pres. Richard B. Cheney. for national security affairs Washington, 2001—03; amb. to Turkey Dept. of State, Ankara, 2003—. Recipient Sec. of Def. award for disting. Civilian Svc., 1993, Superior Honor award State Dept., 1989, 90, 95. Office: American Embassy PSC 93 Box 5000 APO AE 09823 Ankara Turkey*

EDELMAN, GERALD MAURICE, biochemist, neuroscientist, educator; b. N.Y.C., N.Y., July 1, 1929; s. Edwin and Anna (Freedman) Edelman; m. Maxine Morrison, June 11, 1950; children: Eric, David, Judigh. BS, Ursinus Coll., 1950, Sc.D., 1974; MD, U. Pa., 1954, D.Sc., 1973; PhD, Rockefeller U., 1960; MD (hon.) (hon.), U. Siena, Italy, 1974; DSc (hon.) (hon.), Gustavus Adolphus Coll., 1975, Williams Coll., 1976; DSc Honoris Causa (hon.), U. Paris, 1989; LSc Honoris Causa (hon.), U. Cagliari, 1989; DSc, Georgetown U., 1989; DSc Honoris Causa (hon.), U. degli Studi di Napoli, 1990, Tulane U., 1991, U. Miami, 1995, Adelphi U., 1995, U. Bologna, 1998, U. Minn., 2000. Med. house officer Mass. Gen. Hosp., 1954—55; asst. physician hosp. of Rockefeller U., 1957—60, mem. faculty, 1960—92, assoc. dean grad. studies, 1963—66, prof., 1966—74, Vincent Astor disting. prof., 1974—92; mem. faculty and chmn. dept. neurobiology Scripps Rsch. Inst., La Jolla, Calif., 1992—. Mem. biophysics and biophys. chemistry study sect. NIH, 1964—67; mem. Sci. Council Ctr. for Theoretical Studies, 1970—72, assoc., sci. chmn. Neurosciences Research Program, 1980—, dir. Neuroscis. Inst., 1981—; mem. adv. bd. Basel Inst. Immunology, 1970—77, chmn., 1975—77; non-resident fellow, trustee Salk Inst., 1973—85; bd. overseers Faculty Arts and Scis. U. Pa., 1976—83; rustee, mem. adv. com. Carnegie Inst., Washington, 1980—87; bd. govs. Weizman Inst. Sci., 1971—87, mem. emeritus; researcher structure of antibodies, molecular and devel. biology. Author: Neural Darwinism, 1987, Topobiology, 1988, The Remembered Present, 1989, Bright Air, Brilliant Fire, 1992, A Universe of Consciousness: How Matter Becomes Imagination, 2000. Trustee Rockefeller Bros. Found., 1972—82. Capt. M.C. U.S. Army, 1955—57. Recipient Spencer Morris award U. Pa., U. Pa., 1954, Ann. Alumni award, Ursinus Coll., 1969, Nobel prize for physiology or medicine, 1972, Albert Einstein Commemorative award, Yeshiva U., 1974, Buchman Meml. award, Calif. Inst. Tech., 1975, Rabbi Shai Shacknai meml. prize, Hebrew U.-Hadassah Med. Sch., Jerusalem, 1977, Regents medal Excellence, N.Y. State, 1984, Hans Neurath prize, U. Wash., 1986, Sesquicentennial Commemorative award, Nat. Libr. Medicine, 1986, Cécile and Oskar Vogt award, U. Dusseldorf, 1988, Disting. Grad. award, U. Pa., 1990, Personnalité de l'année, Paris, 1990, Warren Triennial Prize award, Mass. Gen. Hosp., 1992, C.V. Ariens-Kappers medal, 1999, medal of the Presidency of the Italian Republic, 1999, medaille de la Ville de Paris, 2002, Cátedra Santiago Grisolia Prise, Spain, 2003, Caiamello Internat. award, INNS, 2003, Calabria award, Italy, 2003. Fellow: AAAS, N.Y. Acad. Medicine, N.Y. Acad. Scis.; mem.: NAS, Am. Chem. Soc. (Eli Lilly award biol. chemistry 1965), Century Assn., Coun. Fgn. Rels., Soc. Developmental Biology, Acad. Scis. of Inst. France (fgn.), Am. Soc. Cell Biology, Japanese Biochem. Soc. (hon.), Pharm. Soc. Japan (hon.), Am. Acad. Arts and Scis., Harvey Soc. (pres. 1976—77), Genetics Soc. Am., Am. Assn. Immunologists, Am. Soc. Biol. Chemists, Am. Philos. Soc., Cosmos Club, Alpha Omega Alpha, Sigma Xi, Phi Beta Kappa. Office: Scripps Rsch Inst Dept Neurobiol SBR-14 10550 N Torrey Pines Rd La Jolla CA 92037-1000

EDELMAN, HARRY ROLLINGS, III, engineering and construction company executive; b. Pitts., Aug. 16, 1928; s. Harry Rollings, Jr. and Marian A. (Crooks) E.; m. Nancy Jane McCune, Aug. 26, 1950; children: Lisa E. Turbeville, Harry Rollings IV, John Reed, Amy E. Carrick. BS, U. Pitts., 1950. CEO, chmn. CCL-X Mgmt. Inc., Pitts., 1993—. Chmn. Heyl & Patterson, Inc., Heylpat Techs., Inc., Bridge & Crane Inspection, Inc., ForeTesting Labs., Inc. Author papers in engring., constrn., religion and mgmt. Past bd. dirs. Allegheny Health Edn. and Rsch. Found., Allegheny Gen. Hosp., Allegheny U. Med. Scis.; past pres. Christian Assn. S.W. Pa.; past chmn. Allegheny Neuropsychiat. Inst., Vocat. Rehab. Ctr. Allegheny County, Allegheny Singer Rsch. Inst., Med. Coll. Pa.; chmn. Presbyn. SeniorCare; past chmn. Allegheny U. Hosp. East; past moderator Pitts. Presbytery; pres. Presbyn. Scholarship Fund. With AUS, 1952-54. Recipient Regional Ecumenism award, 1985, Allegheny Disting. Svc. award, 1997. Mem. World Pres.'s Orgn., Duquesne Club, Pitts. Field Club, The Club at Seabrook Island. Office: CCL-X Mgmt Inc PO Box 36 Pittsburgh PA 15230-0036

EDELMAN, HENDRIK, library and information science educator; b. Wageningen, Netherlands, Nov. 27, 1937; came to U.S., 1967; s. Cornelis Hendrik and Johanna (van Werkhoven) E.; m. Antoinette M. Kania; children: Stijn Willem, Mark Bastiaan, Kees Maarten. MLS, George Peabody Coll., 1969. With Martinus Nijhoff (Pubs. & Booksellers), Netherlands, 1958-65, D. Reidel Pub. Co., Netherlands, 1965-67; bibliographer Vanderbilt U., 1967-70; asst. dir. Cornell U. Libraries, Ithaca, N.Y., 1970-78; libr. Rutgers-State U. N.J., New Brunswick, 1979-85, prof. libr. and info. sci., 1985—. Adj. prof. Palmer Sch. Libr. and Info. Sci., L.I. U., 2002—; chmn. bd. Ctr. Book Rsch., U. Scranton, 1983-88; chmn. bd. Rsch. Libr. Group, Inc., 1982-83; bd. dirs. Book Industry Study Group, 1977-84; USIA/ALA Libr./Book fellow, U. Surinam, 1992-93; editl. mktg. cons. Am. European pubs. (booksellers); acad. libr. cons.; chmn. edn. com. Netherland Am. Found., 1993-2002; chmn. adv. bd. Rutgers Inst. Jazz Studies, 2001—. Author: The Dutch Language Press in America, 1986, Libraries and Information Science in the Electronic Age, 1986, A History of Religious Publishing and Bookselling in the United States and Canada, 1640-1985, 1987, Marketing to Libraries for the New Millennium, 2002, The Netherland Club of New York, An Illustrated History, 2003; contbr. articles, revs. to profl. jours. Mem. ALA, Soc. for Scholarly Pub., Bibliog. Soc. Am., Am. Antiquarian Soc., Grolier Club, Beta Phi Mu. Office: 138 Colton Ave Sayville NY 11782-3108 E-mail: hedelman@scils.rutgers.edu.

EDELMAN, ISIDORE SAMUEL, biochemist and medical educator; b. Bklyn., July 24, 1920; Student, Bklyn. Coll., 1937-39; BA, Ind. U., Bloomington, 1941; MD, Ind. U., Indpls., 1944; DSc (honoris causa), Columbia U., 2001. Resident Montefiore Hosp., Bronx, N.Y., 1947-48; AEC postdoctoral fellow Harvard Med. Sch., 1948-49; research fellow Am. Heart Assn. Brigham Hosp., Boston, 1950-52; asst. prof. medicine U. Calif., San Francisco, 1952-54, assoc. prof. medicine, 1954-60, prof. medicine, 1960-78, assoc. dir. cardiovascular research inst., 1960-69, prof. biophysics, Samuel Neider rsch. prof. medicine,

1967-78; chief med. service San Francisco Gen. Hosp., 1956-58; chmn. dept. biochemistry and molecular biophysics Columbia U., N.Y.C., 1978-88, Robert Wood Johnson Jr. prof. biochemistry, 1978-90, prof. emeritus, 1990—. Dir. Columbia Genome Ctr., 1995—2000. Contbr. articles to profl. jours. Served to capt. M.C., U.S. Army, 1945-47. Recipient Homer W. Smith award N.Y. Heart Assn., 1980, Mayo H. Soley medal We. Soc. Clin. Rsch., 1980, Disting. Svc. award Columbia U., 1993, A.N. Richards Disting. Rsch. award Internat. Soc. Nephrology, 1999; Calif. Inst. Tech. sr. rsch. fellow, 1958-59. Fellow AAAS; mem. NAS, Inst. Medicine, Am. Acad. Arts and Scis., Assn. Am. Physicians, Biophys. Soc., Endocrine Soc. (Eli Lilly Lectureship award 1969, Robert H. Williams Disting. Leadership award 1996), Harvey Soc. (pres. 1989-90), Am. Soc. Biochem. and Molecular Biology. Achievements include established investigator Am. Heart Assn., 1952-57. Home: 464 Riverside Dr New York NY 10027-6801 E-mail: ise1@columbia.edu.

EDELMAN, JANICE, artist, educator; b. Phila., Apr. 13, 1933; d. Samuel and Anna (Finkelstein) Fishman; 1 child, Susan Helfrich. Degree, Art Inst. Phila., 1956; studied with, Henry Hensche, Provincetown, Mass., 1957, Boris Blai, Phila., 1979-80. Cert. art tchr., Pa. Advt. illustrator John Wanamaker, Phila., 1954-66; advt. art dir. Strawbridge & Clothier, Phila., 1967-76; comml. art instr. Hussian Sch. of Art, Phila., 1976-77; head of art dept. Montgomery County Vocat. Sch., Upper Moreland, Pa., 1978-79; watercolor instr. Woodmere Art Mus., Phila., 1991—. Docent Woodmere Art Mus., 1989-91; judge juror Glassboro State Coll., N.J., 1992, Norristown Art League, 1999; bd. dirs. Friends of Moore Coll. of Art, Phila., 1977; workshop leader Pa. Acad. Fine Arts; lectr. in field. Exhibited in group shows at Fashion Group of Phila., 1955 (Fine Arts Gala award, 1955, 1st prize, 1957), 1957, Phila. Club Advt. Women 12th Ann., 1966, 1967 (1st prize for layout, 1966, for art-layout, 1967), 13thAnn., 1974 (1st prize for art-layout, 1974, 1975), Artist Guild of Delaware Valley 25th Ann., 1975 (Bronze award, 1975), Art Dirs. Club of Phila. 39th Ann., 1979 (2 awards for excellence, layout design, 1979), Am. Coll., 1985, Phila. Water Color Club 67th Ann., 1985, 70th Ann., 1988, 71st Ann., 1989, 74th Ann., 1992, 75th Ann., 1993 (award of excellence, 1988, show chmn., 1992), Watercolor Soc. Ala. 45th Ann., 1986, Oreland Art Ctr. Ann., 1986 (1st prize in watercolor, 1986), Artilleries Gallery, 1987, Perkiomen Valley Retirement Cmty., 1987, Charlotte Watercolor Soc., 1987, Woodmere Art Mus. 47th Ann., 1987, 48th Ann., 1988, 49th Ann., 1989, 52d Ann., 1992, 56th Ann., 1996, Abington Art Ctr. Ann., 1988, Pa. Watercolor Soc. 10th Ann., 1988, 11th Ann., 1989 (Grumbacher award, 1988), 20th Ann., 1999, Salmagundi Club 11th Ann., N.Y., 1988, 16th Ann., 1993 (Merit award, 1988), Yellow Spring Art Show, 1989, Art Inst. Phila., 1989, Phila. Art Show, 1989, 1990, Balt. Watercolor Soc., 1990, Susquehanna Art Soc. 84th Biennial, 1990, Barn Studio Gallery, 1990, Greater Harrisburg (Pa.) Arts Coun., 1993, Springfield Art League 74th Nat., 1993, Artist Guild Nat., Scottbluff, Nebr., 1993, Batavia (N.Y.) Soc. Artists 9th Nat., 1993, Watercolor Art Soc., Houston, 1994, W.Va. Water Color Soc., 1994, Watercolor West XXVI Ann., Brea, Calif., 1994, Main Line Arts Festival, Haverford, Pa., 1994, Nat. Watercolor Soc., Calif., 1995, Pitts. Watercolor Soc. Ann., 1995, Bald Eagle Art League Nat., 1995, N.W. N.Mex. Arts Coun., 1997 (award), Woodmere Art Mus., 2003, one-woman shows include, Phila., 1997, Phila. Water Color Club 98th juried exhbn., 1998, Pa. Watercolor Soc. Ann., 1999, Atlantic City Art Mus., 1999, Krasdale Gallery, N.Y., 1999—2003, Beth Or Congregation, Springhouse, Pa., 2003, Represented in permanent collections Woodmere Art Mus., Two Watercolors, Woodmere Art Must. Chmn. art study group, exec. sec. Ret. Execs. and Profls., Cheltenham, Pa., 1999—; juror Norristown Art League, 1999, art lectr., 1999—2003; mem. mus. com. Keneseth Israel Congregation. Mem. Am. Watercolor Soc. (assoc.), Nat. Watercolor Soc. (assoc.), Pa. Watercolor Soc., Phila. Watercolor Soc., Art Dirs. Club Phila. (pres. 1978-80), Phila. Water Color Club (v.p. 1993-94, lectr. and slide presenter on art and artists, 2000-2003). Jewish. Avocations: painting, traveling, reading, creative cooking. Home: 3505 Hale Rd Huntingdon Valley PA 19006-3230 E-mail: jan.e@erols.com.

EDELMAN, JOEL, medical center executive; b. Chgo., Mar. 24, 1931; s. Maurice B. and Ethel J. (Newman) E.; m. Beth L. Sommers, July 31, 1955; children: Peter J., Ann Elizabeth, Deborah S. BA in Spl. Edn., U. Mich., 1952; JD, DePaul U., 1960. Bar: Ill. 1961. Program dir. Chgo. Heart Assn., 1955-61; staff atty. Michael Reese Hosp. and Med. Center, Chgo., 1961-70, exec. v.p., 1971-73; dir. Ill. Dept. Pub. Aid, 1973-74; exec. dir. Ill. Legis. Adv. Com. on Pub. Aid, 1974-77; pres. Rose Med. Ctr., Denver, 1979-95; prin., sr. v.p. Frontier Holdings, Inc., Englewood, Colo., 1995—. Asst. prof. dept. preventive medicine U. Colo.; U.; dir. office legal affairs Am. Hosp. Assn., 1970 Contbr. articles to profl. jours. Served with AUS, 1955. Mem. Soc. Hosp. Attys. (charter) Home: 3156 S Hills Ct Denver CO 80210-6830

EDELMAN, JUDITH H. architect; b. Bklyn., Sept. 16, 1923; d. Abraham and Frances (Israel) Hochberg; m. Harold Edelman, Dec. 26, 1947; children: Marc, Joshua. Student, Conn. Coll., 1940-41, NYU, 1941-42; BArch, Columbia U., 1946. Designer, drafter Huson Jackson, N.Y.C., 1948-58; Schermerhorn traveling fellow, 1950; pvt. practice, 1958-60; ptnr. Edelman & Salzman, N.Y.C., 1960-79, Edelman Partnership (Architects), N.Y.C., 1979—2002, Edelman, Sultan, Knox, Wood /Architects LLP, N.Y.C., 2002—. Adj. prof. Sch. Architecture CUNY, 1972-76, vis. lectr. grad. program in environ. psychology, 1977, 77; vis. lectr. Washington U., St. Louis, 1974, U. Oreg., 1974, MIT, 1975, Pa. State U., 1977, Rensselaer Poly. Inst., 1977, Columbia U., 1979; First Claire Watson Forrest Meml. lectr. U. Oreg., U. Calif., Berkeley, U. So. Calif., 1982. Prin. works include Restoration of St. Mark's Ch. in the Bowery, N.Y.C., 1970-82, Two Bridges Urban Renewal Area Housing, 1970-96, Jennings Hall Sr. Citizens Housing, Bklyn., 1980, Goddard Riverside Elderly Housing and Cmty. Ctr., N.Y.C., 1983, Columbus Green Apartments, N.Y.C., 1987, Chung Pak Bldg., N.Y.C., 1992, Child Care Ctr., Queens, N.Y., 1999. Recipient Bard 1st honor award City Club N.Y., 1969, Bard award of merit, 1975, 82, award for design excellence HUD, 1970, 1st prize Nat. Trust for Hist. Preservation, 1983, award of merit Mcpl. Art Soc. N.Y., 1983, Pub. Svc. award Settlement Housing Fund, 1983, Women of Vision award NOW, 1989, 1st prize for design excellence C. of C., Borough of Queens, N.Y., 1989, Best in Srs.' Housing award Nat. Assn. Home Builders, 1993, Hamilton-Madison House Cmty. Svc. award, 1997. Fellow AIA, dir. N.Y. chpt., chmn. commn. on archtl. edn. 1971-73, chmn. nat. task force on women in architecture 1974-75, v.p. N.Y. chpt. 1975-77, chmn. ethics com. 1975-77, Residential design award 1969, Pioneer in Housing award 1990, N.Y. State Assn. Architects-AIA Honor award 1975); mem. Alliance of Women in Architecture (founding, mem. steering com. 1972-74), Architects for Social Responsibility (mem. exec. com. 1982-85), Columbia Archtl. Alumni Assn. (bd. dirs. 1968-71). Home: 37 W 12th St New York NY 10011-8502 Office: Edelman Sultan Knoxwood 100 Lafayette St 6th Fl New York NY 10013 E-mail: judithedelman@mac.com., jedelman@edelmansultan.com.

EDELMAN, LAUREN B. law educator, sociologist, educator; d. Murray J. and Bacia Edelman. JD, Boalt Hall, 1986; PhD, Stanford U., 1986. Asst. to assoc. prof. U. Wis., Madison, 1986—96; prof. U. Calif., Berkeley, 1996—. Fellow, Guggenheim Found., 2000. Mem.: Am. Sociol. Assn. (chair, sociology of law sect. 1993—94, Dist. Scholarship award 1995), Law and Soc. Assn. (pres. 2002—03). Achievements include research in analyses of relationship between employment law and organizational governance. Office: JSP Program/ UC Berkeley 2240 Piedmont Ave Berkeley CA 94720-2150 Office Fax: 510-642-2951. E-mail: ledelman@law.berkeley.edu.

EDELMAN, MARIAN WRIGHT (MRS. PETER B. EDELMAN), lawyer; b. Bennettsville, S.C., June 6, 1939; d. Arthur J. and Maggie (Bowen) Wright; m. Peter B. Edelman, July 14, 1968; children: Joshua, Jonah, Ezra. Merrill scholar, Univs. Paris, Geneva, 1958-59; BA, Spelman Coll., 1960; LLB (J.H. Whitney fellow 1960-61), Yale U., 1963, LLD (hon.), Smith Coll., 1969, Lowell Tech. U., 1975, Williams Coll., 1978, Columbia U., U. Pa., Amherst Coll., St. Joseph's Coll.; DHL (hon.), Lesley Coll., 1975, Trinity Coll., Washington, Russell Sage Coll., 1978, Syracuse U., Coll. New Rochelle, 1979, Swarthmore Coll., 1980, SUNY Old Westbury, Northeastern U., 1981, Bard Coll., 1982, U. Mass., 1983, Hunter Coll., U. So. Maine, SUNY, Albany, 1984, Columbia U., U. Pa., Yale U., 1985, Rutgers U., Bates Coll., Maryville Coll., Bank St., 1986, Claremont Grad Sch., Lincoln U., Georgetown U., Chgo. Theol. Coll., 1987, Wheaton Coll., Tulane U., Grinnell Coll. Brandeis U., Wheelock Coll., Dartmouth Coll., U. S.C., U. N.C., Grad. Ctr. CUNY, U. Wis. Milw., 1988, Interdenom. Theol. Ctr., Hofstra U., Tufts U., Borough Manhattan Community Coll., Wesleyan U., Calif. State U. L.A., Dillard U., U. Md., U. Miami, 1989, Howard U., Beloit Coll., Queens Coll., Am. U., New Sch. of Social Rsch., Coll. of Notre Dame, DePaul U., 1990, Beaver Coll., Fordham U., Simmons Coll., Hamline U., Clark U., Harvard U., Union Coll., 1991, Tuskegee U., Washington U. St. Louis, Hood Coll., Duke U., Mercy Coll., 1992, Princeton U., U. Ill., Calif. State U. San Francisco, Wittenberg (Ohio) Coll., Shaw U., So. Meth. U., 1993, Brown U., U. Balt., Ea. Conn. State U., U. Notre Dame, 1994. Bar: D.C., Miss., Mass. Staff atty. NAACP Legal Def. and Ednl. Fund, Inc., N.Y.C., 1963-64, dir. Jackson, Miss., 1964-68; Congl. and fed. liaison Poor People's Campaign, summer 1968; partner Washington Research Project of So. Center for Pub. Policy, 1968-73; dir. Harvard U. Center for Law and Edn., 1971-73; pres., founder Children's Def. Fund, 1973—. Author: The Measure of Our Success: A Letter To My Children and Yours, 1992, Families in Peril, 1987. Mem. exec. com. Student Non-Violent Coordinating Com., 1961-63; mem. adv. coun. Martin Luther King Jr. Meml. Libr.; mem. adv. bd. Hampshire Coll.; mem. Presdl. Commn. on Missing in Action, 1977, Presdl. Commn. on Internat. Yr. of Child, 1979, Presdl. Commn. on Agenda for 80's, 1980; bd. dirs. NAACP Legal Def. and Ednl. Fund; trustee Spelman Coll., Carnegie Coun. on Children, 1972-77, Martin Luther King Jr. Meml. Ctr.; mem. Yale U. Corp., 1971-77, Aetna Found., Nat. Commn. on Children, 1989—; bd. dirs. Aetna Life Casualty Found., Citizens for Constitutional Concerns, US. com. UNICEF, Robin Hood Found., Aaron Diamond Found., Nat. Alliance Business, City Lights, Leadership Conf. Civil Rights, Skadden Fellowship Found., Parents as Tchrs. Nat. Ctr., Inc.; U.S. rep. UNICEF; active U.S. Olympic Com. Named one of Outstanding Young Women of Am., 1966; recipient Mademoiselle mag. award, 1965, Louise Waterman Wise award, 1970, Washington of Yr. award, 1979, Whitney M. Young award, 1979, Profl. of Yr. award Black Ent., 1979, Leadership award Nat. Women's Polit. Caucus, 1980, Black Womens Forum award, 1980, medal Columbia Tchrs. Coll., Barnard Coll., 1984, Eliot award Am. Pub. Health Assn., John W. Gardner Leadership award of Ind. Sector, Pub. Svc. Achievement award Common Cause, Compostela award Cathedral St. James, 1987, MacArthur prize fellow, 1985, Albert Schweitzer Humanitarian prize Johns Hopkins U., 1987. Philip Hauge Ahelson award AAAS, 1988, Hubert Humphrey Civil Rights award, AFL-CIO award, 1989, Radcliffe Coll. medal, 1989, Fordham Stein prize, 1989, Gandhi Peace award, 1990, M. Carey Thomas award, Robie award for humanitarianism, Essence award, numerous others; hon. fellow U. Pa. Law Sch. Mem. Phi Beta Kappa (hon.), Inst. Medicine. Address: Children's Def Fund 25 E St NW Washington DC 20001-1522

EDELMAN, MARTIN JOSEPH, medical educator, oncologist, researcher; b. N.Y.C., Jan. 28, 1959; s. Daniel Bernard and Norma Joan (Wilbur) E.; m. Sherri Marlene Miller, Mar. 12, 1983. BS in Biology, Rensselaer Poly. Inst., 1982; MD, The Albany Med. Coll., 1982. Internal medicine intern US Naval Hosp., San Diego, 1982-83; med. officer U.S.S. Duluth, 1983-84; resident in internal medicine U.S. Naval Hosp., San Diego, 1985-86, head dept. internal medicine Twenty Nine Palms Hosp., 1986-87; fellow hematology-oncology USN Med. Corps., San Diego, 1987-90; asst. prof. medicine U. Calif.-Davis Med. Ctr., Sacramento, 1993-99; chair hematology-oncology VA No. Calif., Martinez, 1994; assoc. prof. medicine U. Md., Balt., 1999—. Contbr. over 100 articles, abstracts to profl. jours., chapters to books. Mem. Am. Soc. Clin. Oncology, Internat. Assn. Study Lung Cancer. Avocations: gardening, skiing. Office: U Md Greenbaum Cancer Ctr 22 S Greene St Baltimore MD 21201-1544

EDELMAN, NORMAN HERMAN, medical educator, university dean and official; b. N.Y.C., May 21, 1937; s. Irving H. and Pearl Ruth (Solomon) E.; m. Ida Nadel, June 1959; children: David, Ruth, Deborah. AB, Bklyn. Coll., 1957; MD, NYU, 1961. Diplomate Am. Bd. Internal Medicine, Am. Bd. Pulmonary Diseases. Intern NYU Med. Sch., N.Y.C., 1961-62, resident, 1962-63; rsch. fellow NIH, Balt., 1963-65; vis. fellow Columbia U., Presbyn. Med. Ctr., N.Y.C., 1965-67; rsch. assoc. Michael Reese Med. Ctr., Chgo., 1967-69; asst. prof. medicine U. Pa. Sch. Medicine, Phila., 1969-72; prof. medicine, chief pulmonary medicine Robert Wood Johnson Med. Sch., U. Medicine and Dentistry of N.J., New Brunswick, N.J., 1972-95, dean, 1988-95; prof. medicine and physiology and biophysics SUNY, Stony Brook, 1996—, v.p. health sci. ctr., dean Sch. Medicine, 1996—. Cons. for sci. Am. Lung Assn., N.Y.C., 1984—; mem. pulmonary disease adv. com. NIH, 1984-88. Contbr. articles, abstracts to profl. jours., chpts. to med. textbooks; mem. editorial bd. Jour. Applied Physiol., Am. Rev. Respiratory Diseases. Served as surgeon USPHS, 1963-65. Fellow AAAS; mem. Assn. Am. Physicians, Am. Soc. Clin. Investigation, Am. Thoracic Soc., Am. Physiol. Soc.

EDELMAN, PAUL STERLING, lawyer; b. Bklyn., Jan. 2, 1926; s. Joseph S. and Rose (Kaminsky) E.; m. Rosemary Jacobs, June 15, 1951; children: Peter, Jeffrey. AB, Harvard U., 1946, JD, 1950. Bar: N.Y. 1951, U.S. Dist. Ct. (so. and ea. dists.) N.Y. 1954, U.S. Ct. Appeals (2d cir.) 1965, U.S. Supreme Ct. 1967. Ptnr. Kreindler & Kreindler, N.Y.C., 1953-95, counsel, 1996—. Legal advisor Andrea Doria TV show, 1984, QE2 TV show, 1995; cons. Slave Ship TV Program, April, 2001. Author: Maritime Injury and Death, 1960; editor: Maritime Law Reporter, 1987-99, Marine Laws, 1993, 94; columnist N.Y. Law Jour. With U.S. Army, 1944-46. Fellow N.Y. Bar Found.; mem. ABA (past chmn. admiralty com., toxic and hazardous substances litigation com., mem. long range planning com. 1982-84, mem. TIPS coun. 1984-88, Soviet-Am. lawyers conf. Moscow 1987, 94, TIPS lawyer conf. Russia 1993), ATLA (past chmn. admiralty coms.), Maritime Law Assn. (rep. to law of the sea seminar Moscow 1994), N.Y. State Bar Assn. (TICL award 1980, 90, 93, chmn. INCL sect. 1982-83, editor Ins. Jour. 1973—), Maritime Law Assn. (sec. maritime personnel com.), Hastings Hist. Soc., Oliver Wendell Holmes Soc. of Harvard Law Sch., Supreme Ct. Hist. Soc., World Peace Through Law Ctr., Hudson Valley Tennis Club, Hastings on Hudson (past chmn., planning bd.), Supreme Ct. Hist. Soc., Hastings Hist. Soc. Democrat. Jewish. Home: 57 Buena Vista Dr Hastings On Hudson NY 10706-1103 Office: 100 Park Ave New York NY 10017-5516 E-mail: pedelman@kreindler.com.

EDELMAN, RICHARD WINSTON, public relations executive; b. Chicago, Ill., June 15, 1954; s. Daniel J. and Ruth Ann (Rozumoff) Edelman; m. Rosalind Ann Walrath, May 17, 1986. BA, Harvard U., 1976, MBA, 1978. Mgr. N.Y. office Daniel J. Edelman, Inc., N.Y.C., pres. U.S. opers.; pres., chief oper. officer Daniel J. Edelman, Inc. (now Edelman Worldwide), N.Y.C., 1989—96; CEO Edelman Worldwide, N.Y.C., 1996—, pres., CEO, 1996—. Rep. in crisis mgmt. Great Lakes Dredge and Dock Co., Time Warner, E.F. Hutton, CBS vs. Westmoreland trial, Star-Kist. Bd. dirs. Young Profls. for Gov. Jim Thompson, Chgo., 1978, Young People for Ed Koch, N.Y.C., 1985, Planned Parenthood Fedn. Am., 1980—81, The Jewish Mus.; active polit. campaign Robert Abrams, N.Y. State Atty. Gen. for Senate. Mem.: Pub. Rels. Soc. Am. (Silver Anvil award 1981), Harmonie Club (N.Y.C.), Harvard Club. Jewish. Avocations: squash, history. Office: Edelman Worldwide 1500 Broadway Ste 504 New York NY 10036-4048

EDELMANN, CAROLYN FOOTE, writer, poet, editor, photographer; Studied with Theodore Weiss, Galway Kinnell, Stanley Plumly, Princeton U. Author: (poetry) Gatherings, 1987, Between the Dark and the Daylight, 1997, (anthologies) Cool Women Vol. I, 2001, Cool Women Vol. II, 2002; appearances include (TV) People Are Talking, Phila., (radio) Pub. Radio, Manhattan, WDVR, Sergeantsville, N.J., poetry readings Princeton Univ. Store, Princeton (N.J.) Pub. Libr., Grounds for Sculpture, Hamilton, N.J., Mary Jacobs Libr., Rocky Hill, Beaver Pond Poetry Forum, New Hope, Pa., Micawber Books, Princeton, Barnes & Noble; writer, photographer: nature/travel/history series USI Newspaper and West Windsor Plainsboro News, The Packet Publs., lectr. with slides:, book reviewer, lectr.:. Founder Cool Women Poets' Group, Princeton. Recipient William Carlos Williams prize, Paterson Pub. Libr., 1977, N.J. Poetry Monthly prize, 1978, Delaware Valley Poets prize, 1992, 2001, ie Press prize, 1997, 1st prize, N.J. Very Spl. Arts Wordsmith Contest, 1999, 2000, 2001.

EDELSBERG, SALLY COMINS, physical therapy educator and administrator; b. Rowno, Poland, Aug. 6, 1937; came to U.S., 1949; d. Joseph Luria and Chana (Bebczuk) Comins; m. Warde C. Pierson, Oct. 8, 1968 (div. 1978); m. Paul Edelsberg, Feb. 2, 1979; 1 child, Tema. BS in Phys. Medicine, U. Wis., 1963; MS, Northwestern U., 1972. Lic. phys. therapist. Staff and supervisory phys. therapist Hines VA Hosp., Maywood, Ill., 1963-67; program dir. Health Careers Council of Ill., Chgo., 1967-70; instr., clin. edn. coord. Programs in Phys. Therapy, Northwestern U. Med. Sch., Chgo., 1970—72, dir., assoc. prof., 1972—99, dir. devel. and alumni rels., 1999—2003. Pres. Phys. Therapy Ltd., Chgo., 1986-95; v.p. World Confedn. Phys. Therapy, 1995-99, exec. com., 1991-95. Mem.: Am. Phys. Therapy Assn. (bd. dirs. 1975—78, 1979—82, Ill. pres. 1972—76, Catherine Worthingham fellow 1999). E-mail: s-edelsberg@northwestern.edu.

EDELSON, EDWARD HAROLD, research chemist; m. Judith Linda Miller, Mar. 28, 1970; children: Erica, Mindy. BS, CUNY, 1973; PhD, Rensselaer Poly. Inst., 1977. Rsch. assoc. Ames Rsch. Ctr. NASA, Moffet Field, Calif., 1977-79; instr., rsch. asst. U. So. Calif., L.A., 1979-80; rsch. chemist Exxon Rsch. and Engring. Co., Baytown, Tex., 1980-85; sr. rsch. chemist Mobil Rsch. and Devel. Corp., Paulsboro, N.J., 1985-93; analytical lab. mgr. Royal Lubricants, Inc., East Hanover, N.J., 1993—. Author: (with others) COSPAR Life Sciences and Space Research, 1980, 1980 McGraw-Hill Yearbook of Science and Technology, 1980, Origin of Life, 1981; contbr. articles to profl. jours. Mem. SAE, Am. Chem. Soc. (chmn. symposium 1978, 80), Soc. Tribologists and Lubrication Engrs. Avocations: classical guitar, photography. Office: Royal Lubricants Inc PO Box 518 East Hanover NJ 07936-0518

EDELSON, GILBERT SEYMOUR, lawyer; b. N.Y.C., Sept. 15, 1928; s. Saul and Sarah (Sunshine) E.; m. Jane Barbara Levin, Sept. 6, 1953; children: Martha Jane, Paula Topal, Dorothy Rachel. BS, NYU, 1948; LLB, Columbia U., 1955. Bar: N.Y. 1955, U.S. Dist. Ct. (so. dist.) N.Y. 1959, U.S. Ct. Appeals (2nd cir.) 1959, U.S. Dist. Ct. (ea. dist.) N.Y. 1960, U.S. Ct. Appeals (9th cir.) 1995. Assoc. Rosenman Goldmark Colin & Kaye, N.Y.C., 1955-63; ptnr. Rosenman & Colin, N.Y.C., 1963-97, counsel, 1997—2002, Katten Muchin Zavis Rosenman, NYC, 2002—. Adminstrv. v.p., counsel Art Dealers Assn. Am., N.Y.C., 1985—. Editor Columbia Law Rev., 1955. Bd. dirs. Coll. Art Assn. Am., N.Y.C., 1969-88, High Five Tickets for the Arts, N.Y.C., 1999-2001; sec., trustee Am. Fedn. Arts, N.Y.C., 1984-94; trustee Internat. Found. for Art Rsch., 1986-99, N.Y. Studio Sch., 1989—, Archives Am. Art, N.Y.C., 1989—. With U.S. Army, 1950-52, JLC. Mem. ABA, N.Y. Bar Assn., Assn. Bar of N.Y.C. (chmn. com. on art law 1992-95), Columbia U. Law Sch. Alumni Assn. (bd. dirs. 1981-84), Century Assn. Jewish. Avocation: collecting art. Home: 580 W End Ave New York NY 10024-1723 Office: Katten Muchin Zavis Rosenman 575 Madison Ave New York NY 10022-2585 E-mail: gilbert.edelson@kmzr.com.

EDELSON, IRA J. venture banker, trade finance executive; b. Chgo., Dec. 30, 1946; s. Alvin L. and Naomi Edelson; m. Starr Gramaila, Feb. 11, 1973; children: Jason Avrum, Megan Anne. BS, DePaul U., 1968. Spl. advisor to chmn. Chgo. Housing Authority, 1983; acting dir. revenue City of Chgo., 1984; ptnr.-in-charge bus. svcs. dept. Deloitte, Haskins & Sells, Chgo., 1979-87; ptnr.-in-charge corp. fin. Deloitte & Touche-U.S. Partnership, Chgo., 1987-91; pres. Transcap Assocs. Inc., Northbrook, Ill., 1991—. Fin. and policy advisor to mayor City of Chgo., 1984-85; former instr. Northwestern U. Kellogg Sch. Mgmt.; cons., speaker in field. Co-chmn. Chgo. Sports Stadium Commn., 1985. Mem.: AICPA, Fgn. Trade Assn., TMA, Nat. Contract Mgmt. Assn., Comml. Fin. Assn., Ill. Soc. CPAs. Office: Transcap Assocs Inc 900 Skokie Blvd Ste 210 Northbrook IL 60062-4031

EDELSON, MARSHALL, retired psychiatry educator, psychoanalyst; b. Chgo., May 31, 1928; s. George I. E. and Ida (Bernstein) Riskind; m. Zelda Sarah Toll, Dec. 27, 1952; children: Jonathan Toll, Rebecca Jo, David Jan. Ph.B., U. Chgo., 1946, PhD, 1954, MD, 1955; AB, Stanford U., 1949; MA hon., Yale U., 1976. Diplomate: Nat. Bd. Med. Examiners. Intern Presbyterian Hosp., Chgo., 1955-56; resident in psychiatry Sheppard and Enoch Pratt Hosp., Towson, Md., 1956-59; asst. prof. psychiatry U. Okla., Oklahoma City, 1961-63; staff psychiatrist Austen Riggs Ctr., Stockbridge, Mass., 1964-68; assoc. prof. psychiatry Yale U., New Haven, 1968-76, prof. psychiatry, 1976-97, prof. emeritus, psychiatry, 1998—. Dir. research outpatient div. Yale's Conn. Mental Health Ctr., 1983-88; ednl. cons. Western New Eng. Inst. Psychoanalysis, 1973-97. Author: Sociotherapy and Psychotherapy, 1970, Language and Interpretation in Psychoanalysis, 1975, Hypothesis and Evidence in Psychoanalysis, 1984, Psychoanalysis: A Theory in Crisis, 1988, (with David N. Berg) Rediscovering Groups: A Psychoanalyst's Journey Beyond Individual Psychology, 1999. Served to capt. U.S. Army, 1959-61. Recipient Heinz Hartmann award N.Y. Psychoanalytic Inst., 1973; NIMH Career Tchr. fellow, 1962, Founders Tchg. prize Western New England Psychoanalytic Soc., 2002. Fellow APA (life); mem. AMA, Am. Psychoanalytic Assn. (cert., Edith Sabshin Tchg. award 2001), Internat. Psychoanalytic Assn., Western New Eng. Inst. Psychoanalysis and Psychoanalytic Soc.

EDELSTEIN, DAVID SIMEON, historian, educator; b. NYC, Jan. 19, 1913; s. William and Clara (Brener) E.; m. Frances Fisher, June 4, 1939 (dec. Jan. 1990); children: Helen Freedman, Henry, Daniel Louis; m. Gertrude Bernstein, Jan. 5, 1997. BA, CCNY, 1932; MA, Columbia U., 1933, PhD, 1949. Cert. elem. tchr., N.Y. Tchr., adminstr. various sch., NYC, 1934-67; lectr. in-svc. courses Bd. Edn., NYC, 1946-65; lectr. History CCNY, 1947-67; lectr. Edn. U. Colo., 1960, Yeshiva U. Grad. Sch. Edn., 1960-61, Hunter Coll., 1964-65; prof. Edn. Western Conn. State U., Danbury, 1967-83; adj. assoc. prof. History Fordham U., Bronx, NY, 1967-70; instr. in-svc. course Stamford Bd. Edn., Conn., 1970-71; adj. assoc. prof. History CUNY, 1970-75; adj. prof. History Western Conn. State U., Danbury, 1984-85. Lectr. in field. Author: Joel Munsell, Printer and Antiquarian, 1950; author: (with others) M. Stern: editor: Publishers for Mass. Entertainment in the Nineteenth Century, 1980; contbr. biog. sketches Nat. Am. Biography, 1999; contbr. articles to profl. jours. Mem. AAUP, Am. Assn. Sch. Adminstrs., Am. Hist. Assn., Conn. Edn. Assn., Nat. Assn. of Elem. Sch. Prins., N.Y.C. Elem. Sch. Prins. Assn. (life), Nat. Coun. of Local Adminstrs. of Vocat. Edn., Social Studies Coun., Coun. of Chmn. of Acad. Subjects, Nat. Soc. for the Study of Edn., New Eng. Hist. Assn., New Eng. Assn. of Tchr. Educators, Phi Alpha Theta, Phi Delta Kappa. Democrat. Jewish. Home: 118 Rosedale Rd Yonkers NY 10710-3033 Office: Western Conn State U 181 White St Danbury CT 06810-6826

EDELSTEIN, JOAN ERBACK, physical therapy educator; b. East Orange, N.J., Mar. 28, 1935; d. Frank William and Sadie Edith (Levine) Erback; m. Haskell Edelstein, Jan. 19, 1964; children: David, Benjamin. BS magna cum laude, NYU, 1956, MA, 1958. Lic. phys. therapist, N.Y. Chief phys. therapist children's div. Rusk Inst. (formerly Inst. Phys. Medicine & Rehab.), N.Y.C., 1956-59; instr. U. Wis., Madison, 1959-61; clin. asst., prof., sr. rsch. scientist NYU, N.Y.C., 1961-91; assoc. prof. clin. phys. therapy Columbia U., 1991—2001, dir. program in phys. therapy, 1992—2001, spl. lectr., 2002—. Organizer and condr. seminars nationwide and worldwide. Author: Prosthetic and Orthotic Educational Aids, 1987, Orthotics: Comprehensive Clinical Approach, 2002; contbr. numerous articles to profl. jours.; mem. editl. bd. Jour. Assn. Children's Prosthetic-Orthotic Clinics, 1983—91; Jour. Rehab. R&D, 1984—, Archives Phys. Medicine and Rehab., 1991—95; mem. editl. bd.: Phys. Occupl. Therapy Geriatrics, 1985. Nat. Found. for Infantile Paralysis grantee, 1959. Fellow Internat. Soc. for Prosthetics and Orthotics (sec., treas. 1979-88, vice chmn. 1988-91); mem. Am. Phys. Therapy Assn., Am. Congress of Phys., Medicine and Rehab., Nat. Flute Assn. (performance health com. 1991—). Home: 340 E 69th St New York NY 10021-5706

EDELSTEIN, ROSEMARIE (ROSEMARIE HUBLOU), medical/surgical nurse, educator, medical and legal consultant; b. Drake, N.D., Mar. 3, 1935; d. Francis Jerome and Myrtle Josephine (Merbach); m. Harry George Edelstein, June 22, 1957 (div.); children: Julie, Lori, Lynn, Toni Anne. BSN, St. Teresa of Avila Coll., Winona, Minn., 1956; MA in Edn., Holy Names Coll., Oakland, Calif., 1977; EdD, U. San Francisco, 1982, postgrad., 1987, U. Ariz., 1985—; cert. pub. health nurse, U. Calif., Berkeley, 1972. Dir., clin. supr. San Francisco Sch. for Health Professions, 1971-74, Rancho Arroyo Sch. of Vocat. Nursing, Sacramento, 1974-75; intensive care nurse Kaiser-Permanente Hosp., San Rafael, Calif., 1976-77; dir. insvc. edn. Ross Hosp., Calif., 1977-78; dir. nursing edn. St. Francis Meml. Hosp., San Francisco, 1978-85; med.-legal nursing cons., med.-surg. staff nurse met. hosps., San Francisco, 1985-90, St. Luke's Hosp., Duluth, Minn., 1990-91, St. Charles Hosp., New Orleans, 1992, U. Tex. Med. Br., Galveston, 1992-94; staff nurse family medicine faculty practice, 1995; med.-surg. nurse St. Anthony of Padua Hosp., Oklahoma City, 1994-95; nurse Northgate Conv. Hosp., San Rafael, 1995—. Night charge nurse Creekside Conv. Hosp., Santa Rosa, Calif., 1996; charge nurse medications, treatment and Alzheimer's Unit Fallon Conv. Ctr., Nev., 1996; charge nurse Medicare unit White Pine Conv. Ctr., Ely, Nev., 1997; emergency rm., ICU nurse Battle Mt. Gen. Hosp., Nev., 1997; nurse supr. Medicare-Med. Seaview Care Ctr. Sun

Corp., Eureka, Calif., 1997—98; mem. staff Walker Post Manor Oxford, NE Lantis Corp., 1998, The Lincoln Ambassador, 1999, Rapid City (S.D.) Care Ctr. Beverly Enterprises, 2000—01, Houghton County Med. Care Facility, Hancock, Mich., 2000—, Norlite Nursing Ctr., Marquette, Mich., 2001—02, Whidbey Island Manor, Oak Harbor, Wash.; mem. staff Medicare unit Everett (Wash.) Rehab. and Care Ctr., 2002, St. Joseph Care Ctr., Spokane, 2003; invited mem. People to People Nursing Edn. and Adminstrn.; candidate to East Asia Philosophy, 1985; postgrad. candidate U. Zurich, Switzerland, 1988; staff Everett Rehab. and Care Ctr., 2002, Whidbey Island Manor, Oak Harbor, Wash., 2003, St. Joseph's Care Ctr., Spokane, Wash., 2003. Author: The Influence of Motivator and Hygiene Factors in Job Changes by Graduate Registered Nurses, 1977; Effects of Two Educational Methods Upon Retention of Knowledge in Pharmacology, 1981; co-author: (with Jane F. Lee) Acupunture Atlas, 1974. Candidate U.S. Senate Inner Circle, 1988, 89. Lt. col. USAR Med. Res. Mem. Am. Heart Assn., Calif. Nurses Assn., Sigma Theta Tau. Roman Catholic.

EDELSTEIN, TERI J. art history educator, art administrator; b. Johnstown, Pa., June 23, 1951; d. Robert Morten and Hulda Lois (Friedhoff) E. BA, U. Pa., 1972, MA, 1977, PhD, 1979; cert., NYU, 1984. Lectr. U. Guelph, Ont., 1977-79; asst. dir. for acad. programs Yale Ctr. Brit. Art, New Haven, Conn., 1979-83; dir. Mt. Holyoke Coll. Art Mus., South Hadley, Mass., 1983-90, Skinner Mus., 1983-90, mem. faculty dept. art, 1983-90; dir. Smart Mus. Art U. Chgo., 1990-92, sr. lectr. dept. art, 1990-2000. Dep. dir. Art Inst. Chgo., 1992—99, mus. con., 1999—; mem. adv. bd. Sculpture Chgo., 1991—96, Mus. Loan Network, Knight and Pew Founds., 1994—96. Office: 1648 E 50th St # 6B Chicago IL 60615-3166 Fax: 773-241-9992.

EDELSTEIN, TILDEN GERALD, university official, history educator; b. N.Y.C., June 11, 1931; s. Theodore and Nettie (Strusser) E.; m. Rose Ann Stargardter, Nov. 1, 1970; children: Jordan, Russell. BS, U. Wis., 1953; PhD, Johns Hopkins U., 1961. From instr. to assoc. prof. Simmons Coll., Boston, 1957-67; from adj. assoc. prof. to prof. history Rutgers U., New Brunswick, N.J., 1967-89, chmn. history dept., grad. dir., 1974-81, assoc. dean social sci. and humanities, faculty personnel, 1981-84, dean faculty arts and scis., 1984-89; prof. history, provost, acad. v.p. SUNY, Stony Brook, 1989-93, prof. history, provost, exec. v.p. for academic affairs, 1992-94; v.p. for acad. affairs Wayne State U., Detroit, 1995-98, prof. history, 1998—. Hist. cons. Columbia Pictures, Hollywood, Calif., 1978-80, NBC, N.Y.C., 1980-89; chair Sponsors Bd. The Thomas A. Edison Papers Project, 1980-89. Author: Strange Enthusiasm, 1968, 2d edit., 1970; co-editor: The Black Americans, 1975. Commr. Housing Authority, Highland Park, N.J., 1977-89; Einstein Archives Adv. Com. Hebrew U., 1993-94; mem. adv. bd. Cohen/Haddow Ctr. for Jewish Studies, Mich. Civil War Regimental Round Table. Mem. Orgn. Am. Historians, Prismatic Club Detroit. Office: Wayne State U Coll Liberal Arts Dept of History Detroit MI 48202 E-mail: aa1768@wayne.edu.

EDEMEKA, UDO EDEMEKA, surgeon; b. Ndon Eyo, Akwa Ibom, Nigeria, Sept. 11, 1944; came to U.S., 1973; s. Buddie Udo and Dinah Buddie (Ekwere) E.; m. Iboro Udo David Akpan, May 18, 1973; children: Ubong, Dinah, Idara, David, Dennis, Donald. MB and BS, U. Ibadan, Nigeria, 1970; diploma in anesthesia, U. Lagos, 1972. Diplomate Am. Bd. Surgery, Am. Bd. Emergency Physicians. Instr. surgery Downstate Med. Ctr., Bklyn., 1974-80; attending physician Kings County Hosp. Ctr., Bklyn., 1980-91, Meth. Hosp., Bklyn., 1988—. Leverhulme Exchange scholar Lever Bros. U. Coll. Hosp., London, 1969. Fellow N.Y. Acad. Scis., Internat. Coll. Surgeons, Am. Coll. Emergency Physicians. Office: Meth Hosp 506 6th St Brooklyn NY 11215-3645

EDEN, ALVIN NOAM, pediatrician, author; b. Bklyn., Mar. 21, 1926; s. Emanuel M. and Rae (Taran) Edelstein; m. Elaine R. Jaffe, Nov. 20, 1952; children: Robert, Elizabeth. BA, Columbia Coll., 1948; MD, Boston U., 1952. Intern Bellevue Hosp., N.Y.C., 1952-53; resident in pediat. Univ. Hosp., N.Y.C., 1953-55; pvt. practice specializing in pediat. Forest Hills, N.Y., 1955—. Assoc. clin. prof. pediat. NYU Sch. Medicine, 1960-84; chmn., dir. dept. pediat. Wyckoff Heights Med. Ctr., Bklyn., 1959—; lectr. SUNY-Downstate Med. Ctr., Bklyn., 1984-86, assoc. clin. prof. pediat., 1986-90; assoc. clin. prof. pediat. Cornell Med. Coll., 1990-99, clin. prof., 1999—. Author: Growing Up Thin, 1975, Handbook for New Parents, 1978, Positive Parenting, 1980, Dr. Eden's Healthy Kids, 1987; contbr. articles to profl. jours.; author text and reference materials. Mem. med. adv. com. YMCA of U.S., 1987—. With USMC, 1944-46. Mem. N.Y. Pediatric Soc. (pres. 1980-81), Queens Pediatric Soc. (pres. 1972-73), N.Y. Acad. Medicine (chmn. pediatric sect. 1985-89), Am. Acad. Pediatrics (chmn. nutrition com. chpt. 2 1985-89). Avocation: tennis. Home: 710 Park Ave New York NY 10021-4944 Office: 10721 Queens Blvd Forest Hills NY 11375-4451 E-mail: babydoceden@hotmail.com.

EDEN, BARBARA JANIECE, commercial and residential interior designer; b. Inpls., Oct. 14, 1951; d. Justin January and Marjorie May (Miller) E.; m. Stephen A. Bowman, Oct. 25, 1975; children: Christopher Eden Bowman, Jessica Eden Bowman. BA, Purdue U., 1973. Interior design dir. Bohlen, Meyer, Gibson & Assoc., Indpls., 1973-78; interior designer, sole propr. Barbara Eden Design, Indpls., 1978-85; pres., prin. designer Eden Design Assocs., Inc., Carmel, Ind., 1985-97, Carson Design Assocs. Design/Project Mgmt./ Mktg., Carmel, Ind., 1997—. Past mem. accreditation team Found. for Interior Design Edn. Rsch. (FIDER); past mem. adv. bd. Purdue U. Interior Design Dept.; bd. dirs. Hamilton County Intercultural Svcs. Prin. projects include wheelchair accessible bathroom Kohler (Wis.) Design Ctr., United Airlines, Indpls. Maintenance Ctr., N.Am. hdqrs. Brightpoint, Inc., Plainfield, Ind., Peabody Retirement Ctr., North Manchester, Ind., Oakwood Inn, Syracuse, Ind., Resort Condominiums, Internat., Carmel, Ind., Merchants' Pointe, Carmel, restaurant, retail & office devel., arch., interior design; also corp., healthcare, schs., univs., librs., sr. living and residential interior design, space planning and project mgmt. Mem. Internat. Facility Mgrs. Assn., Internat. Interior Design Assn., Illuminating Enging. Soc., Carmel Clay C. of C. (mem. exec. bd., chair edn. com., Small Bus. Person of Yr. 1993). Avocations: hiking, horseback riding, traveling. Office: Carson Design Assocs 11590 N Meridian St Ste 104 Carmel IN 46032-6955 E-mail: edenbj@carsondesign.com.

EDEN, F. BROWN, artist; b. Jericho Center, Vt., Oct. 10, 1916; d. Arthur Castle and Eva Merita (Lowrey) Brown; m. Edwin Winfield Eden, Sept. 4, 1937; m. Allan L. Day, July 11, 1994; children: Donna Jean, Sandra Elizabeth, Kathy Lynn. Student, U. Fla. Extension, 1955-59, U. Mich., 1963. Art instr. Ann Arbor (Mich.) City Club, 1962-63; tchr., oil painting, printmaking Jacksonville (Fla.) Art Mus., 1963-68. One-woman shows include The Fox Galleries, Atlanta, 1986, Harmon Galleries, Sarasota, 1987, 1989—90, 1992—93, Gallery Contemporanea, Jacksonville, Artist Assocs. Gallery, Atlanta, 1965—90, The Hodgell Gallery, Sarasota, 1997—2002, The Center, Ponte Vedra, Fla., 1998, Kent Campus Gallery, Fla. C.C., Jacksonville, 1999, Represented in permanent collections Fed. Res. Bank Atlanta, Bank Am., Coca-Cola, So. Bell, Sheraton Corp., AT&T, Trust Co. Ga., Shell Oil Co., Touche Ross, Cooper and Lybrand, Delta Airlines "Crown Rm.", 5th Dist. Ct. Appeals Bldg., Daytona Beach, Fla., Edwin and Ruth Kennedy Mus. Am. Art, U. Ohio, Athens, exhibited in group shows at Ala. Nat. Watercolors, Fla., Ga., nationally, exhibitions include Am. Painters in Paris, 1975—76, Painters in Casein and Acrylics, N.Y.C. Chmn. area VI Fla. artist group Jacksonville Mus. Art, 1979—89. Recipient Painting of Yr. award, Mead Co., 1962—63, First award, Fla. Artist Group, 1971, 1979, Fla. Artists, 1969, The Painting award, Maj. Fla. Artists, 1979, others. Mem.: Fla. Crown Treasures, Fla. Artists Jacksonville, Jackson Coalition of Visual Artists, Ala. Watercolor Soc., Ga. Watercolor Soc., Fla. Watercolor Soc. (Signature artist), So. Watercolor Soc., Nat. Mus. of Women in Arts (charter), Am. Women Artists. Avocation: playing organ. Home: 5375 Sanders Rd Jacksonville FL 32277-1333

EDEN, JAMES GARY, electrical engineer, educator, physicist, researcher; b. Washington, Oct. 11, 1950; s. Robert Otis and Joyce (West) Eden; m. Carolyn Sue Thomas, June 10, 1972; children: Robert Douglas, Laura Ann, Katherine Joy. BS, U. Md., 1972; MS, U. Ill., 1973, PhD, 1976. Teaching asst. elec. engring. dept. U. Ill., Urbana, Jan.-June 1972, rsch. asst., 1972-75, asst. prof. elec. engring. dept., 1979-81, assoc. prof., 1981-83, prof. elec. engring. dept. and rsch. prof. Coordinated Sci. Lab, 1983—, dir. Lab. for Optical Physics and Engring., 1995—, assoc. vice-chancellor for rsch., 2000—03, assoc. dean Grad. Coll., 1994-96, rsch. prof. Microelectronics Lab., 2000—, mem. physics grad. rsch. faculty, asst. dean Coll. Engring., 1992-93; postdoctoral rsch. assoc. NRC, Washington, 1975-76; rsch. physicist U.S. Naval Rsch. Lab., Washington, 1976-79. Mem. tech. adv. bd. Anvik Corp., Hawthorne, NY, Caviton, Inc., Urbana; assoc. mem. Ctr. Advanced Study U. Ill., 1987—88; mem. program com. Conf. Lasers and Electro-Optics, 1982, 83, 88, 89, 1994—97; founder, chmn Engring. Found. Conf. Ultraviolet Lasers, 1987, co-chair, 90, 94; program chair ann. meeting IEEE Lasers and Electro-Optics Soc., 1990, conf. chair, 92, mem. program com., 1988—2003; program vice chmn Interdisciplinary Laser Sci. Conf. V, 1989; program chair ILS V, 1990; conf. chair ILS VII, 1992; mem. adv. bd. Chem. Vapor Deposition, 1995—, CRC Handbook Series Laser Sci. and Tech., 1996—; cons. Wilson, Sonsini, Goodrich and Rosati, Palo Alto, Calif., 1996—2003, Morrison & Foerster, Palo Alto, 1998—2000, Smart and Biggar, Ottawa, Canada, 1999—2000, Morrison and Foerster, Alexandria, Va., 2003—, San Francisco, 2003—. Author: (book) Photochemical Vapor Deposition, 1992, Gas Laser Technology, 2000; editor: IEEE Jour. Quantum Electronics, 1996—2002; assoc. editor: Photonics Tech. Letters, 1988—94; contbr. chapters to books, more than 170 articles to profl. jours. Recipient Rsch. Publ. award, Naval Rsch. Lab., 1978, Beckman Rsch. award, U. Ill., 1988, IBM Rsch. award, 1994, Faculty Outstanding Tchg. award, Dept. Elec. and Computer Engring., U. Ill., 2000; James F. Towey Univ. scholar, U. Ill., 1996—99. Fellow: IEEE (3d Millennium medal 2000), Am. Phys. Soc., Optical Soc. Am.; mem.: IEEE Lasers and Electro-Optic Soc. (bd. govs. 1991—93, v.p. tech. affairs 1993—95, pres. 1998, Disting. Svc. award 1996, Disting. Lectr. 2003—), Phi Kappa Phi, Eta Kappa Nu, Tau Beta Pi, Sigma Xi. Achievements include patents for 17 inventions. Avocation: archaeology. Home: 314 County Rd 2650 N Mahomet IL 61853-9579 Office: U Ill Everitt Lab 1406 W Green St Urbana IL 61801-2918

EDEN, JOHN, ophthalmologist; b. Germany, Apr. 30, 1933; came to U.S., 1938; s. Eric and Trudy (Geck) E. BA, NYU, 1953; MD, George Washington U., 1957. Diplomate Am. Bd. Ophthalmology. Intern Temple U. Med. Ctr., Phila., 1957-58, resident ophthalmology, 1958-61; attending ophthalmologist St. Lukes Roosevelt Med. Ctr., 1961-88, 88—, Columbia Presbyn. Coll. Physicians & Surgeons, N.Y.C., 1961-88, attending ophthalmologist emeritus, 1988—. Author: The Eye Book, 1978 (PEN award 1978), The Physicians Guide to Cataracts, Glaucoma and Other Eye Problems, 1994. Office: PO Box 173 Sagaponack NY 11962-0173

EDEN, MURRAY, electrical engineer, emeritus educator; b. Bklyn., Aug. 17, 1920; s. Emanuel and Rae (Taran) Edelstein; m. Patricia Warnock, Sept. 16, 1962; stepchildren— Shirley Hartle McDaniel, John W. Hartle; children by previous marriage— Abigail, Susanna, Mark D. BS, CCNY, 1939; MS, U. Md., 1944, PhD, 1951. Physic. chemist Nat. Bur. Standards, 1943 49; biophysicist Nat. Cancer Inst., 1949-53; spl. fellow math. USPHS, Princeton, 1953-55; biophysicist Nat. Heart Inst., 1955-59; prof. elec. engring. MIT, 1959-79, prof. emeritus, 1979—; adj. prof. elec. engring. Johns Hopkins U., 1979-81; guest prof. Ecole Federale Polytechnique de Lausanne (Switzerland), 1983, 87; dir. bioengring. and instrumentation program NIH, 1976-94, scientist emeritus, 1994—. Lectr. preventive medicine Harvard Med. Sch., 1960-74, Am. U., 1949-50; adj. prof. environ. health Sch. Pub. Health, Boston U., 1999—; cons. for rsch. to dir. gen. WHO, 1963-74. Author: (with David Rutstein) Engineering and Living Systems, 1970; editor: (with Paul Kolers) Recognizing Patterns, 1968, (with Henry S. Eden) Microcomputers in Patient Care, 1981, (with John W. Boretos) Contemporary Biomaterials for Clinical Care, 1983, (with Leonid Yaroslavsky) Fundamentals of Digital Optics, 1996; editor-in-chief: Information and Control, 1961-84; editor: Methods of Information in Medicine, 1961-82; mem. editl. bd.: Med. Rsch. Engring., 1964-80, Internat. Jour. Health Care Tech. Assessment, 1986-92, Real Time Imaging, 1994-2000; adv. editl. bd.: Linguistic Inquiry, 1970-85. Chmn. U.S. Nat. Com. Engring. in Medicine and Biology, 1967-73. Recipient Med. Soc. medal WHO, 1983, Dirs. award NIH, 1993. Fellow IEEE (chmn. adminstrv. com. group engring. in medicine and biology 1964-66, 87-90, mem. editl. bd. Spectrum 1990-92, mem. press bd. 1993-2001, mem. publs. adv. bd. 1998-2003, Centennial medal 1984), AAAS, Am. Inst. for Med. Biol. Engring. (founding fellow); mem. Am. Physiol. Soc., Biophys. Soc., Am. Soc. for Engring. Edn., Cosmos Club, Sigma Xi, Tau Beta Pi. Home and Office: 148 University Rd Brookline MA 02445-4546

EDEN, NATHAN E. lawyer; b. Key West, Fla., Mar. 24, 1944; s. Delmar M. and Lois (Archer) E.; m. Cindy Pike, Jan. 4, 1964 (div. Mar. 1984); 1 child, Jennifer S. BA, U. Fla., 1966; JD magna cum laude, Stetson U., 1969. Bar: Fla. 1969, U.S. Dist. Ct. (so. and mid. dists.) Fla. 1969, U.S. Ct. Appeals (5th cir.) 1969, U.S. Ct. Appeals (11th cir.) 1982. Assoc. Nelson, Stinnett, Surfus, et al, Sarasota, Fla., 1969; ptnr. Feldman & Eden & predecessors, Key West, 1970-84; pvt. practice Key West, 1984—99, 2002—; of counsel Lazzara and Paul, P.A., Tampa, 1982—; ptnr. Browning, Eden, Sireci & Klitenick, 1999—2002. Bd. atty. Utility Bd. of Key West, 1974—; asst. pub. defender State of Fla., Key West, 1970, county solicitor State of Fla., Key West, 1970-72; chief asst. state atty State of Fla., Key West, 1972-74; U.S. magistrate, U.S. Dist. Ct. (so. dist.) Fla., 1974-78. Mem. jud. nominating com. 16th Jud. Cir. State of Fla., 1995, bd. dirs. Hospice Monroe County, Hospice-VNA of Fla. Keys, 1998—. Mem. Acad. Trial Lawyers, Fla. Acad. Trial Lawyers, Nat. Assn. Criminal Def. Lawyers, Fla. Bar Assn. (bd. govs. 1976-80), North Am. Hunt Club, NRA. Democrat. Avocations: hunting, softball, jogging, basketball. Office: 402 Applerouth Ln Key West FL 33040-6535 also: Lazzara and Paul PA 606 E Madison St Ste 2001 Tampa FL 33602-4017

EDEN, ROBERT ELWOOD, lawyer; b. Freeport, Ill., Mar. 8, 1947; s. Bert Richard and Glades Kathryn (Randecker) E.; m. Kathryn Sue Martin, Aug. 7, 1976; children: Angela, Rebecca, Andrew. BA, Luther Coll., 1969; MA, U. Iowa, 1976, JD, 1979. Bar: Iowa 1979, Ill. 1979, U.S. Dist. Ct. (no. dist.) Ill. 1980. Tchr. Kee H.S., Lansing, Iowa, 1969-75; tchr. supr. U. Iowa, Iowa City, 1975-76; prin. Plager, Hasting & Krug, Freeport, Ill., 1979-83, dir., asst. sec., 1984-88; pvt. practice Freeport, Ill., 1989—. Mem. ATLA, Ill. Trial Lawyers Assn., Iowa State Bar Assn., Ill. State Bar Assn., Stephenson County Bar Assn. (sec. 1980-81, pres. 1995), Shannon C. of C., Lena Bus. & Profl. Club, Lions, Phi Delta Kappa. Lutheran. Office: 722 Santa Fe Dr Freeport IL 61032-2924 also: 156 W Main St Lena IL 61048-7906 also: 106 E Market St Shannon IL 61078-9340

EDENFIELD, CYNTHIA SMITH, education educator; d. Paul Preston Smith and Joyce; m. Jerry Edenfield, Mar. 24, 1979; children: Nathaniel R., Alena Marceia Aviles. BS, Ga. Southern U., Statesboro, Ga., 1987, M, 1993, EdS, 1998. Owner, dir. Little Land Daycare Ctr., Twin City, Ga., 1983—87; tchr. Carver Elem. Sch., Wadley, Ga., 1987; instr. Swainsboro Tech. Coll., Swainsboro, Ga., 1991—. Dir. Swainsboro Tech. Child Devel. Ctr., Swainsboro, Ga., 1991—; early head start policy coun. Emanuel County Early Head Start, Swainsboro, Ga., 2002—; adv. bd. Emanuel County and Johnson County, 2002—. Author: (article) GSU Ednl. Forum, 1996. Recipient Com. Educator of the Yr., Ga. Com. En. Assoc., 1997, Kappa Delta Pi, 1993—. Mem.: Ga. Assn. on Young Children, Nat. Assn. for Edn. of Young Children, Kappa Delta Pi. Avocations: writing, reading, painting, childre's lit.. Office: Swainsboro Tech Coll Gen Edn Dept 346 Kite Rd Swainsboro GA 30401-5700 E-mail: cedenfield@swainsborotech.org.

EDENS, BETTY JOYCE, reading recovery educator; b. Hillsboro, Tex., Oct. 20, 1944; d. Edward Alton and Mary Alma (Pendley) Harbin; m. Eugene Cliett Edens, May 29, 1964; children: Michael Eugene, Anne-Marie DeWitt, Kristen Babovec. BEd, Ind. U., 1985; MS, Tex. A&M of Commerce, 1995. Cert. elem. tchr., reading tchr., Tex. 1st grade tchr. Monday Primary, Kaufman, Tex., 1986-93, Franklin Elem., Hillsboro, Tex., 1993-96, reading recovery tchr., 1994-98, 99-00, 2nd grade tchr., 1998-99; reading recovery tchr. Hillsboro Elem. Sch., 1999—. Mem. early literacy com. TSRA, 1998, Susan G. Komen Found. Mem. Reading Recovery Coun. of N.Am., Internat. Reading Assn., Tex. Reading Assn., Monday Rev. Club. Republican. Mem. Ch. of Christ. Avocations: recreational reading, walking, computers.

EDENS, DONALD KEITH, oil company executive; b. Salt Lake City, Aug. 3, 1928; s. Roger Edward and Elsie Vera (Johnson) E.; m. Elizabeth Adele Mays, Dec. 29, 1950; children: Karen Elizabeth, Donald Edward, Douglas Mays. BS in Bus. Adminstrn, U. Utah, 1951. With Phillips Petroleum Co., 1953-72; mng. dir. Phillips Petroleum Ltd., London, 1964-68; v.p. Coastal Corp., Houston, 1972-74; pres., chief exec. officer Union Petroleum Corp., subsidiary Costal Corp., Revere, Mass., 1974-78; sr. v.p. Oasis Petroleum Corp., also pres. Gulf Coast and Eastern region, 1979-82; v.p. Barrick Petroleum Corp., Toronto, Ont., Canada, 1983-85, Barrick Petroleum (USA) Inc., Houston, 1983-85; cons. to petroleum industry, 1985—. Served with AUS, 1946-48; Served with USAAF, 1951-53. Recipient Chmn.'s Cup award Phillips Petroleum Co., 1971 Mem. 25 Yr. Club of Petroleum Industry, UN Assn., Beta Theta Pi. Clubs: Champions Golf, Houston. Lodges: Masons. Home: 6110 Rolling Water Dr Houston TX 77069-2546

EDENS, GARY DENTON, broadcasting executive; b. Asheville, N.C., Jan. 6, 1942; s. James Edwin and Pauline Amanda (New) E.; m. Hannah Suellen Walter, Aug. 21, 1965; children: Ashley Elizabeth, Emily Blair. BS, U. N.C., 1964. Account exec. PAMS Prodns., Dallas, 1965-67, Sta. WKIX, Raleigh, N.C., 1967-69; gen. mgr. Sta. KOY, Phoenix, 1970-81; sr. v.p. Harte-Hanks Raido, Inc., Phoenix, 1978-81, pres., CEO, 1981-84; chmn., CEO Edens Broadcasting, Inc., 1984-95. Dir. Citibank Ariz., 1986—, Inter-Tel, Inc., 1994—; chmn. The Hanover Cos., Inc., 1995—; chair fin. seminar Chief Execs. Orgn./World Pres. Orgn., N.Y.C., 1998. Bd. dirs. Valley Big Bros., 1972-80, Ariz. State U. Found., 1979—, COMPAS, 1979—, Men's Arts Coun., 1975-78. Named one of Three Outstanding Young Men, Phoenix Jaycees, 1973; entrepreneurial fellow U. Ariz., 1989; inducted into Ariz. Broadcasters Assn. Hall of Fame, 2000. Mem. Phoenix Execs. Club (pres. 1976), Nat. Radio Broadcasters Assn. (dir. 1981-86), Radio Advt. Bur. (dir. 1981—), Young Pres. Orgn. (chmn. Ariz. chpt. 1989-90), Chief Execs. Orgn., Ariz. Pres. Orgn. Republican. Methodist. Office: 5112 N 40th St Ste 102 Phoenix AZ 85018-2142 E-mail: edens@hanover.com.

EDER, ELAINE ANNMARIE, lawyer; b. Chgo., Apr. 25, 1953; d. Kurt Eduard and Violet Alvy (O'Malley) E.; m. Alfred Ernest Moreau, Oct. 9, 1982; children: Elizabeth, Andrew, Eileen. BA, Northwestern U., Evanston, Ill., 1973; JD, Emory U., 1975. Bar: Ga. 1976, Mass. 1977. Law clk. Mass. Land Ct., Boston, 1976-77; atty., advisor Army Armament Material Readiness Command, Rock Island, Ill., 1977-80; atty. Gen. Svcs. Adminstrn., Chgo., 1980-83; trial atty. procurement law, chief counsel USCG, Washington, 1983-95, chief trial atty., chief office of procurement law, 1995—, ADR coord. Cross program, 1998—. Mem. alumni admissions coun. Northwestern U., No. Va., 1988—; founding bd. dirs., vice-chair Our Kids Inc. USCG, Washington, 1991-93. Apptd. mem. Early Childhood Edn. Adv. Com., Arlington, Va., 1993-95, Arts Edn. Adv. Com., Arlington, 1995—99; vol. Kennedy Ctr., Washington, 1995—01; active Arlington PTA. Mem. Fed. Bar Assn. (pub. contract law sect.), Bds. of Contract Appeals Bar Assn. (v.p.), State Bar Ga. E-mail: eeder@comdt.uscg.mil.

EDER, HOWARD ABRAM, physician, education educator; b. Milw., Sept. 23, 1917; s. Samuel and Rebecca (Abram) Eder; m. Barbara Straus, July 15, 1954 (dec. Nov. 1997); children: Rebecca, Susan, Michael. AB, U. Wis., 1938; MD, Harvard U., 1942, MPH, 1945; MD (hon.), U. Linkoping, Sweden. Intern Peter Bent Brigham Hosp., Boston, 1942—43, asst. resident, 1943—44; research fellow in medicine Harvard Med. Sch., 1943—44, research fellow in biochemistry, 1945—46; asst. in medicine, asst. physician Rockefeller U. Hosp., 1946—50; asst. prof. medicine Cornell U. Med. Coll., N.Y.C., 1950—53; mem. staff Nat. Heart Inst., Bethesda, Md., 1953—55; assoc. prof. medicine State U. N.Y., Downstate Med. Coll., Bklyn., 1955—57, Albert Einstein Coll. Medicine, 1957—60, prof., 1960—88, prof. emeritus, 1989—. Chmn. lipid metabolism adv. com. Nat. Heart, Lung and Blood Inst., 1978—80, mem. bd. sci. counselors, 1986—90, chmn., 1989—90; mem. diabetes and heart disease rev. panel NIH, 1995—96. Editl. bd. Am. Jour. Physiology, 1968—71, 1979—82, Jour. Lipid Rsch., 1964—, Am. Jour. Medicine, 1976—80. Mem.: Am. Diabetes Assn., Am. Heart Assn. (mem. coun. on arteriosclerosis, Disting. Accomplishment award 1985, Spl. Recognition award 1993), Am. Physiol. Soc., Am. Soc. Biol. Chemists, Am. Soc. Clin. Investigation, Assn. Am. Physicians, Inst. Medicine NAS, Interurban Clin. Club (pres. 1971—72), Alpha Omega Alpha, Phi Beta Kappa. Home: 4465 Douglas Ave Bronx NY 10471-3525 Office: Albert Einstein Coll Medicine 1300 Morris Park Ave Bronx NY 10461-1926 E-mail: eder@aecom.yu.edu.

EDER, RICHARD GRAY, newspaper critic; b. Washington, Aug. 16, 1932; s. George Jackson and Marceline (Gray) E.; m. Esther Garcia Aguirre, Apr. 21, 1955; children: Maria, Ann, Claire, Michael, Luke, Benjamin, James. BA, Harvard U., 1954. Fgn. corr. N.Y. Times, various countries in Europe and Latin Am., 1962-77, 80-82, book critic, 1999—, theater critic, 1977-79; book critic L.A. Times, 1982-99, L.A. Times and Newsday, 1992-99. Vis. lectr. Bard Coll., 1983, Boston U., 1986-87; lectr. MIT, 1997. Ferris Fellow Princeton U., 1984-85, 95-96; recipient Pulitzer prize for criticism, 1987. Mem. Nat. Book Critics Circle (citation for reviewing 1987). Roman Catholic. Office: NY Times 2 Faneuil Hall Marketplace Boston MA 02109

EDERLE, DOUGLAS RICHARD, investment adviser; b. St. Louis, Aug. 10, 1962; s. Richard Joseph and Mary Ellen (Gorman) E.; m. Virginia Foss Mara, June 5, 1988; children: Ryan Douglas, William Gorman, Samuel Mara, Katherine Rose. BS in Acctg. magna cum laude, U. Ill., 1984; JD, Harvard U., 1987. Bar: Tex. 1987, Mass. 1989. Assoc. Hughes & Luce, Dallas, 1987-88; ptnr. Testa, Hurwitz & Thibeault, Boston, 1989-98; sr. v.p., mng. dir. Pell, Rudman Trust Co., N.A., Boston, 1998—2002; mng. dir. SCS Fin., Boston, 2002—. Bd. advisors Project Gurnet and Bug Lighthouses, Little Angels Fund, Bay Farm Montessori Acad.; former treas. Duxbury Edn. Found.; bd. trustees Duxbury Youth Basketball. Mem. ABA, Tex. Bar Assn., Mass. Bar Assn., Boston Bar Assn. Roman Catholic. Avocations: golf, basketball, tennis. Home: 100 Powder Point Ave Duxbury MA 02332-4421 Office: SCS Financial 610 Lincoln Street Waltham MA 02451 E-mail: dederle@scsfinancial.com.

EDESKUTY, FREDERICK JAMES, engineer, consultant; b. Minneapolis, Minn., Sept. 29, 1923; s. Joseph and Alcestis St. Clair Edeskuty; m. Jeanette Bergen Edeskuty, July 3, 1947; children: Sharman Lee, Celeste Jean, Janet Anne, Frederick James Edeskuty, Jr. BChE, U. Minn., Minneapolis, MN, 1944, PhD, 1950. Staff mem. Los Alamos Sci. Lab, Los Alamos, N.Mex., 1950—53; engr. J.V. Edeskuty Associates, Minneapolis, Minn., 1953—54; staff mem. Los Alamos Nat. Lab, Los Alamos, N.Mex., 1954—89, assoc. group leader, 1954—89, assoc. cons., 1989—; cons. Edeskuty Engring., Los Alamos, N.Mex., 1982—. Lectr. N.Mex Acad. Sci., N.Mex., 1967—93. Author: (book) Safety in Handling Cryogens; contbr. articles to profl. jours. Presenter safety courses, Various Places, 1979—2002; lectr. safety UCLA Ext. Divsn., Los Angeles, Calif., 1988—95. T-4 US Army, 1944—46. Lutheran. Avocations: travel, photography. Office: Edeskuty Engineering 913 Tewa Loop Los Alamos NM 87544 E-mail: edeskuty7@cs.com.

EDGAR, GREGORY T. author; b. Hartford, Conn., Nov. 22, 1951; s. David A. and Dorrit G. Edgar; m. Rosemary Farley, Aug. 19, 1972; children: Laura, Dylan, Suzanne. BA, U. Conn., 1973. Presenter to elem. schs. on Am. Revolutionary War. Author: Liberty Or Death, 1994, Campaign of 1776, 1996, Reluctant Break with Britain, 1997, The Philadelphia Campaign, 1777-1778, 1998, (young adult hist. fiction) Are the Yankees Cowards Now?, 1995, Gone to Meet the British, 1996, Patriots, 2000. Home: 131 Pinnacle Rd Ellington CT 06029-3526 E-mail: Gregory_Edgar@hotmail.com.

EDGAR, JAMES MACMILLAN, JR., management consultant; b. N.Y.C., Nov. 7, 1936; s. James Macmillan Edgar and Lilyan (McCann) E.; m. Judith Frances Storey, June 28, 1958; children: Suzanne Lynn Randolph, James Macmillan III, Gordon Stuart. B in Chem. Engring., Cornell U., 1959, MBA with distinction, 1960. CPA; cert. mgmt. cons. New product rep. E.I. duPont Nemours, Wilmington, Del., 1960-63, mktg. svcs. rep., 1963-64; with Touche Ross & Co., 1964-78, mgr., 1966-68, ptnr. in charge, mgt. svcs. ops. for No. Calif. and Hawaii San Francisco, 1971-78, ptnr. Western regional mgmt. svcs., 1978; sr. ptnr. Edgar, Dunn & Co., San Francisco, 1978-2000; ind. mgmt. cons., 2000—. Bd. dirs. Oreg. Industries Svcs. Corp.; ptnr. Global Brand Positioning, 2001—; owner We. Sport Shop, San Rafael and Santa Rosa, Calif. Patentee nonwoven fabrice. Active San Francisco Mayor's Fin. Adv. Com., 1976-2001, exec. com., 1978-2001, Blue Ribbon com. for Bus., 1987-88, Alumnae Resources adv. bd., 1986-94, San Francisco Planning and Urban Rsch. Bd., 1986-89, adv. bd., 1989-93; alumni exec. coun. Johnson Grad. Sch. Mgmt. Cornell U., Cornell Coun., 1970-73; steering com. Bay Area Coun., 1989-95, program adv. com., 1996-2001, bd. dirs., 1999-2001; chmn. San Francisco Libr. Found., 1989-96; bd. dirs. Rosenberg Found., 1996—, chmn. bd. dirs., 2001-02; bd. dirs. Harding Lawson Assoc. Group, 1996-2000, Golden Gate U., 1997-99; mem. San Francisco Com. on Jobs, 1994-2000. Recipient Merit award for outstanding pub. svc. City and County of San Francisco, 1978, Honor award for

outstanding contbns. to profl. mgmt. Johnson Grad. Sch. Mgmt., Cornell U., 1978. Mem. AICPA, Assn. Corp. Growth (v.p. membership San Francisco chpt. 1979-81, v.p. programs 1981-82, pres. 1982-83, nat. bd. dirs. 1983-86), Calif. Soc. CPAs, Inst. Mgmt. Cons. (regional v.p. 1973-80, bd. dirs. 1975-77, v.p. 1977-80), San Francisco C. of C. (bd. dirs. 1987-89, 91—, mem. exec. com. 1988-89, 91-95, chmn. mktg. San Francisco program 1991-92, membership devel. 1993, chmn. bd. dirs. 1994, dir. emeritus 1995—), Pacific Union Club, Marin Rod and Gun Club, Tau Beta Pi. Home: 10 Buckeye Way San Rafael CA 94904-2602 Office: James Edgar Mgmt Cons 10 Buckeye Way Kentfield CA 94904-2602 E-mail: jedgarconsulting@aol.com., jedgar7777@aol.com.

EDGAR, JANELLE DIANE WARD, financial services executive; b. Albany, Ga., Aug. 27, 1955; d. John David and Margaret Irene (Curtis) Ward; m. James Curtis Edgar, July 7, 1973; children: Lauren Marie, William Robert. BA, Marymount U., 1989. Treas. specialist Fed. Home Loan Mortgage Corp., Washington, 1977-81; mgr. cash acctg. Pentagon Fed. Credit Union, Alexandria, Va., 1981-84; mgr. bus. devel. Fin. Technologies, Inc., Alexandria, 1984-85; v.p. ops. Continental Fed. Savs. Bank, Fairfax, Va., 1985-88; v.p. corp. ops. and info. svcs. Md. Nat. Bank/Am. Security Bank, Washington, 1988-89; dir. mktg. NRC, McLean, Va., 1990-91; dir. mktg. cash mgmt. div. Fin. Mgmt. Svcs. Dept. U.S. Treasury, 1991-98; dir. bus. devel. Diversinet Corp., McLean, Va., 1998—. Mem. tech. and ops. com. Internet, Inc., Reston, Va., 1986-88. Adv. The Women's Ctr. of No. Va., Vienna, 1987; deacon Little Falls Presbyn. Ch. Mem. Washington Cash Mgmt. Assn., Mid-Atlantic Clearing House Assn. (rep. Va. League Savs. to bd. dirs. 1987-88), Bank Adminstrn. Inst. (bd. dirs. 1989-90), Nat. Corp. Cash Mgmt. Assn., Nat. Automated Clearing House Assn. (rules and ops. com.). Republican. Presbyterian. Avocations: ice skating, reading, kayaking, kick-boxing. Office: Diversinet Corp 8201 Greensboro Dr Ste 1000 Mc Lean VA 22102-3840

EDGAR, JIM, former governor; b. Vinita, Okla., July 22, 1946; m. Brenda Smith; children: Brad, Elizabeth. Grad., Eastern Ill. U., 1968; postgrad., U. Ill., Sangamon State U., 1971-74. Legis. intern pres. pro tem Ill. Senate, 1968; key asst. to speaker ho. Ill. Ho. of Reps., 1972-73; aide to pres. Ill. Senate, 1974, to Ho. minority leader, 1976; mem. Ill. Ho. of Reps., 1977-79; dir. legis. affairs Ill. Gov., 1979-80; sec. state State of Ill., 1981-91; gov. State of Ill., 1991-98; disting. fellow Inst. Govt. and Publs. U. Ill., Urbana, 1999—. Co-lead gov. Nat. Gov.'s Assn. Transp. Com., 1995-96; chair Edn. Commn. of States, 1993-94; chair Nat. Gov.'s Assn. Com. on Econ. Devel. and Commerce, 1992-93; pres. Coun. State Govts., 1992-93; chair Gov.'s Ethanol Coalition, 1992-93; chair Nat. Gov.'s Assn. Com. on Econ. Devel. and Tech. Innovation, 1991-92. Precinct committeeman, treas. Coles County Rep. Com., 1974; dir. state svc. Nat. Conf. State Legislatures, 1975, 76; mem. campaign com. Ill. Ho. of Reps.; pres. Nat. Assn. Secs. of State, 1988; exec. com. Coun. State Govts., 1988, v.p. exec. com., 1991, pres., 1992-93; bd. dirs. Nat. Commn. Against Drunk Driving, 1989; chmn. Ill. Literacy Coun., 1989; chmn. Edn. Commn. of the States, 1993-94; chmn. Gov.'s Ethanol Coalition, 1992-93; pres. Bd. Coun. State Govts. Mem. Nat. Govs. Assn. (chmn. econ. devel. and commerce com. 1992-93, strategic planning rev. task force 1991—, past chmn. task force on edn., mem. edn. goals panel, chair com. econ. devel. and technol. innovation 1991-92, edn. commn. of states 1993-94, co-lead gov. transp. com. 1995-96), Coles County Hist. Soc. (pres. 1976-79). Baptist. Office: U Ill Inst Govt and Pub Affairs 1007 W Nevada St # MC-037 Urbana IL 61801-3812

EDGAR, MARILYN RUTH, marriage and family therapist; b. Springfield, Mo., Oct. 2, 1948; d. Donald LaVerne Sr. and Ruth Elenor (McClellan) Wilson; m. Robert Stephen Edgar, June 23, 1979 (dec. July 1998); stepchildren: Terri, John, Shawna (dec. 1995). BA in Psychology, Calif. State U., Sacramento, 1983, MS in Counseling, 1987. Lic. marriage, famiy therapist, Calif. Counselor Sacramento Life Ctr., 1983-91; marriage and family therapist New Horizons Counseling Ctr., Carmichael, Calif., 1987—, exec. dir., supr. intern counselors, 1993—. Mem. Warehouse Ministries of Sacramento, 1978—; mem. Arthritis Found., 1996. Mem. Am. Assn. Christian Counselors, Calif. Assn. Marriage and Family Therapists (Valley chpt. 1992—), Capital City Motorcycle Club (pub. rels. officer 1994, sec., bd. mem. 1996-97, 99—). Republican. Office: New Horizons Counseling Ctr 3300 Walnut Ave Carmichael CA 95608-3240 E-mail: pshnwnd@msn.com.

EDGAR, R(OBERT) ALLAN, federal judge; b. Munising, Mich., Oct. 6, 1940; s. Robert Richard and Jean Lillian (Hansen) E.; m. Frances Gail Martin, Mar. 30, 1968; children: Amy Elizabeth, Laura Anne. BA, Davidson Coll., 1962; LLB, Duke U., 1965. Bar: Tenn. 1965. From assoc. to ptnr. Miller & Martin, Chattanooga, 1967-85; judge U.S. Dist. Ct. (ea. dist.) Tenn., Chattanooga, 1985—. Mem. com. ct. adminstrn. and case mgmt. Jud. Conf. of the U.S. Mem. Tenn. Ho. of Reps., Nashville, 1970-72, Tenn. Wildlife Resources Commn., Nashville, 1979-85. Served to capt. U.S. Army, 1966-67, Vietnam. Decorated Bronze Star, 1967. Mem. Fed. Bar Assn., Chattanooga Bar Assn. Episcopalian. Office: US Dist Ct PO Box 1748 960 Georgia Ave Chattanooga TN 37402-2220

EDGAR, RUTH R. retired educator; b. Great Falls, S.C., Jan. 7, 1930; d. Robert Hamer and Clara Elizabeth (Ellenberg) Rogers. AA, Stephens Coll., Columbia, Mo., 1949; BS, So. Meth. U., 1951; MA, Appalachian State U., Boone, N.C., 1977; postgrad., Limestone Coll., Gaffney, S.C., 1971. Lic. real estate salesman, broker. Home economist Lone Star Gas Co., Dallas, 1951-53, So. Union Gas Co., Austin, Tex., 1953-56, Southwestern Pub. Svc. Co., Amarillo, Tex., 1956-57; with Peeler Real Estate, 1970-71, Burns High Sch., Lawndale, N.C., 1971-73, Cen. Cleveland Mid. Sch., Lawndale, 1973-77, Burns Jr. High Sch., Lawndale, 1977-88; resource tchr. South Cleveland Elem. Sch., Shelby, N.C., 1988-90, Elizabeth Elem. Sch., Shelby, 1990-94, Washington Elem. Sch., Waco, N.C., 1990-92; ret., 1994. Mem. supts. adv. coun., Cleveland County, 1971-75, Cleveland County Art Soc., 1972-73, Cen. United Meth. Ch. Home: 401 Forest Hill Dr Shelby NC 28150-5520

EDGAR, THOMAS FLYNN, chemical engineering educator; b. Bartlesville, Okla., Apr. 17, 1945; s. Maurice Russell and Natalie (Flynn) E.; m. Donna Jean Proffitt, July 15, 1967; children: Rebecca, Jeffrey. BS in Chem. Engring., U. Kans., 1967; PhD in Chem. Engring., Princeton U., 1971. Registered profl. engr., Tex. Process engr. Conoco, Balt., 1968-69; prof. chem. engring. U. Tex., Austin, 1971—, chmn. dept., 1985-93, Abell chair, 1991—, assoc. dean engring., 1993-96, assoc v.p. acad. computing, 1996-2001; prof. chem. engring. U. Calif., Berkeley, 1978. Pres. CACHE Corp., Austin, Tex., 1981-84, exec. officer, 2000--; pres. Am. Automatic Control Coun., Chgo., 1990-91; chair Coun. for Chem. Rsch., Washington, 1992-93. Author: Coal Processing and Pollution Control, 1983; co-author: Real Time Computing, 1982, Optimization of Chemical Processes, 1988, 2d edit., 2000, Process Dynamics and Control, 1989, 2d edit., 2003; editor: Chemical Process Control, 1981, In Situ (Marcel Dekker), 1977-89; also jours. Recipient Edn. award Am. Automatic Control Coun., 1992. Fellow AIChE (Outstanding Counselor award 1975, Colburn award 1980, Computing in Chem. Engring. award 1995, editl. bd. jour. 1983-85, chmn. cast divsn. 1986, bd. dirs. 1989-92, v.p. 1996, pres. 1997, chair bd. dirs. Found. 2000—); mem. Am. Soc. Engring. Edn. (Westinghouse award 1988, Meriam-Wiley Disting. Author 1990, Chem. Engring. Divsn. Leadership award 1996), Instrument Soc. Am. (Eckman Edn. award 1993), Am. Chem. Soc., Tau Beta Pi, Phi Lambda Upsilon, Omicron Delta Kappa, Phi Kappa Phi (Joe King award U. Tex. 1989, U. Kans. Disting. Engring. Svc. award 1990). Democrat. Methodist.

EDGAR, WALTER BELLINGRATH, historian, educator; b. Mobile, Ala., Dec. 10, 1943; s. Ernest, Jr. and Amelia E.; m. Elizabeth Giles, Aug. 6, 1966; children: Eliza, Amelia. AB, Davidson Coll., (N.C.), 1965; MA, U. S.C., 1967, PhD, 1969; LLD (hon.), Coker Coll., 1999; HLD (hon.), Coastal Carolina U., 2001; LLD (hon.), Davidson Coll., 2003. From asst. prof. to prof. history U. S.C., Columbia, 1974—, dir. Inst. So. Studies, 1980—, Neuffer prof. so. studies, 1995—, George Washington Disting. prof. history, 1999—. Author: History of Santee Cooper, 1984, South Carolina in the Modern Age, 1992, South Carolina: A History, 1998, Partisans and Redcoats, 2001; editor: The Letterbook of Robert Pringle, 1972, A Southern Renascence Man: Views of Robert Penn Warren, 1984. Served to capt. U.S. Army, 1969-71; col. Res. Decorated Bronze Star, Legion of Merit; Nat. Hist. Publs. Commn. fellow, 1971-72. Mem. The Hist. Soc., So. Hist. Assn., S.C. Hist. Assn. (pres. 1982-83), S.C. Hist. Soc. (bd. mgrs. 2000—), South Caroliniana Soc. (pres. 1984-87), Blue Key, Omicron Delta Kappa, Phi Alpha Theta. Home: 1731 Hollywood Dr Columbia SC 29205-3215 Office: U SC Inst So Studies Columbia SC 29208-0001

EDGAR, WILLIAM JOHN, philosophy educator; b. Charlottesville, Va., Jan. 20, 1933; s. William John and Frances (Ring) E.; m. Stacey Lynn Walter, June 20, 1962; children: Michael Kent, Stephen Scott, Elizabeth Anne, Chandra Lynn. BA, Cornell U., 1959; MA, Syracuse U., 1966, PhD, 1972. Systems analyst Advanced Electronics Ctr., Ithaca, N.Y., 1959-62, Electronics Lab., Syracuse, N.Y., 1962-65; asst. prof. philosophy SUNY-Geneseo, 1969-74, assoc. prof., 1974-79, disting. teaching prof., chmn. dept., 1979—. Author: Evidence, 1980, The Problem Solver's Guide to Logic, 1983, The Elements of Logic, 1989; contbr. articles to profl. jours. Served to 1st lt. U.S. Army, 1952-56. Recipient Chancellor's award for excellence in teaching, 1974, 76, Excellence award State of N.Y. and UUP, 1991; fellow NDEA Title IV Syracuse U., 1965-68. Mem. Am. Philos. Assn. Home: 5722 Logan Rd RD 1 Mount Morris NY 14510 Office: SUNY Dept Philosophy Geneseo NY 14454 E-mail: edgarb@geneseo.edu.

EDGE, DANIEL, education educator, artist, consultant; b. Norfolk, Va., June 6, 1940; s. Emmett and Emma Joy (Goddard) Edge. BA, Old Dominion Coll., 1965; BFA, Yale U., 1967, MFA, 1969. Adj. asst. prof. CUNY, 1970—82; adj. assoc. prof. No. Va. C.C., Annandale, Va., 1983—2000; adj. prof. of fine arts Tex. State U. System-srsu, Alpine, Tex., 2001—. Exhibitions include Va. Ann. Exhibit (best-in-show, 1969), Julian Pretto, 1978. Va. Mus. Fine Arts fellow, 1966—67, 1967—68, Tiffany fellow, 1970, Nat. Endowment for the Arts fellow, 1975, Guggenheim fellow, 1978. Mem.: The Mind Assn. Home: 1010 South Yale Ave Pobox 822 Marfa TX 79843-0822 Office: Dan Edge Studio #8 Officers' Row Marfa TX 79843-0822 Personal E-mail: dedge@christophers.net. E-mail: dedge@christophers.net.

EDGE, JAMES EDWARD, health care administrator; b. Anacortes, Wash., Apr. 29, 1948; s. Edward and Carol Marie (Lian) E.; m. Nellie Ruth Horton, Mar. 21, 1970; children: Elissa Marie, Gina Dawn. BS in Pharmacy, U. Wash., 1971; MPH, U. Hawaii, 1979. Registered pharmacist. Commd. USPHS, 1969-2000, advanced through grades to capt.; staff pharmacist USPHS Indian Hosp., Albuquerque, 1971-73; chief pharmacy, lab/x-ray S.W. Indian Poly. Inst., Albuquerque, 1972-73, Neah Bay Indian Health Ctr., Wash., 1973-75; svc. unit dir. Neah Bay Svc. Unit, Indian Health Svc., 1975-78, Western Oreg. Service Unit, Indian Health Svc., Salem, 1980-2000; mgr. policy unit Office of Med. Assistance Programs, State of Oreg., Salem, 2000—02; asst. state Medicaid dir. State of Oreg., 2003—. Cons. in field. Active Combined Fed. Campaign, Salem, 1985-2000. John Quick Pharmacy scholar, U. Wash., 1967, Health Professions scholar, 1969. Mem. APHA, Am. Coll. Healthcare Adminstrs., Am. Acad. Med. Adminstrs., Assn. Mil. Surgeons U.S., Mensa, Res. Officers Assn., Commd. Officer USPHS, Wash. Pharm. Assn., nat. Coun. Svc. Unit Dirs. (chmn. 1986-88). Avocations: running, sculling. Office: PO Box 932 Salem OR 97308

EDGE, J(ULIAN) DEXTER, JR., lawyer; b. Newport News, Va., June 7, 1942; s. Julian Dexter and Mildred (Castellow) E.; m. Carol Kinsley Browning, May 30, 1964; children— Julian Dexter III, Kinsley, Richard. B.S.I.M., Ga. Inst. Tech., 1964; J.D., Emory U., 1973; M.B.A., Ga. State U., 1977. Bar: Ga. 1973, D.C. 1977. Assoc., Henkel & Lamon, Atlanta, 1973-77, ptnr., 1977-81; ptnr. Henkel, Hackett, Edge, & Fleming, Atlanta, 1981-85, Troutman Sanders, Atlanta, 1985—, lectr. to bus., profl. meetings. Mng. editor Emory Law Jour., 1972-73. Co-chmn. DeKalb County Govt. Study Com., Ga., 1977; mem. DeKalb County Govt. Reorgn. Commn., 1979; chmn. DeKalb County Select Com. on Property Appraisals, 1982; mem. Ga. Republican Exec. Com., 1977-79; Ga. Rep. fin. chmn., 1977-79; treas. Bob Bell for Gov. Ga., 1981-82; Ga. Rep. counsel for Fourth Dist., 1981-86; mem. Mattingly Fin. Com., 1983-86; mem. adv. bd. DeKalb Community Coll., 1982-88. Served to lt. USN, 1964-70; Vietnam. Decorated Air medal, Navy Commendation medal. Mem. State Bar Ga. (sect. taxation), D.C. Bar (div. taxation), ABA (sect. taxation), Atlanta Bar Assn., Decatur DeKalb Bar, Lawyers Club Atlanta, Nat. Assn. Bond Lawyers, Order of Coif, Omicron Delta Kappa. Home: 1775 Redd Rd Alpharetta GA 30004-3146 Office: Troutman Sanders 600 Peachtree St NE Ste 5200 Atlanta GA 30308-2216

EDGE, RONALD DOVASTON, physics educator; b. Bolton, Eng., Feb. 3, 1929; came to U.S., 1958, naturalized, 1968; s. James and Mildred (Davies) E.; m. Margaret Skulina, Aug. 14, 1956 (div. 1989); children: Christopher James, Michael Dovaston; m. Gertrude Hansen, Dec. 31, 1992. BA, Cambridge U., 1950, MA, 1952, PhD, 1956. Research fellow Australian Nat. U., Canberra, 1954-58; asst. then assoc. prof. physics U. S.C., Columbia, 1958-63, prof., 1964-94, disting. prof. emeritus, 1994—. Rsch. assoc. Yale U., New Haven, 1963-64; vis. prof. Stanford U., Calif. Tech. Inst., U. Munich, U. Sussex, U. Witwatersrand, U. Aarhus, Oak Ridge Nat. Lab., Los Alamos Nat. Lab.; leader 1st Am. team Internat. Physics Olympiad, 1986; judge Internat. Young Physicists Tournament, 1999, 2001. Author: Physics in the Arts, 1973, String and Sticky Tape Experiments, 1978; contbr. articles to profl. jours. Recipient Russell award U. S.C., Guy And Rebecca Forman award tchg. Physics, Vanderbilt U., 1998. Fellow Am. Phys. Soc. (James B. Pegram award 1979), Am. Assn. Physics Tchrs. (apparatus award 1973, v.p. 1995, pres. elect 1996, pres. 1997). Unitarian (past pres. Columbia fellowship) Home: 220 Jadetree Dr Hopkins SC 29061-9347 Office: U SC Physics Dept Columbia SC 29208-0001 E-mail: redge@sc.rr.com.

EDGELL, KARIN JANE, reading specialist, special education educator; b. Rockford, Ill., July 17, 1937; d. Donald Rickard and Leona Marquerite (Villard) Williams; m. George Paul Edgell III, May 6, 1960; 1 child, Scott. Student, Rollins Coll., 1955-57; BS, U. Ill., 1960, MEd, 1966; MA, Roosevelt U., 1989; adminstrv. endorsement, U. Va., 2001. Tchr. Alexandria (Va.) City Pub. Schs., 1963-79; asst. to dir. Reading Ctr. George Washington U., Washington, 1979-80; tchr. Winnetka (Ill.) Pub. Schs., 1982-89, Arlington County (Va.) Pub. Schs., 1989—. Mem. NEA, ASCD, Nat. Coun. Tchrs. Eng., Internat. Reading Assn., Va. Edn. Assn., Va. Reading Assn., Greater Washington Reading Coun., Coun. Exceptional Children, Phi Delta Kappa. Presbyterian. Home: Landmark Mews 6275 Chaucer View Cir Alexandria VA 22304-3546 E-mail: Karinedgell@mindspring.com.

EDGELL, STEPHEN EDWARD, psychology educator, statistical consultant; b. Inglewood, Calif., June 20, 1947; s. Stephen F. and Evelyn L. (Humborg) E.; m. Donna M. Grassello, Aug. 17, 1974. AA in Math., El Camino Jr. Coll., Gardena, Calif., 1968; AB in Psychology, Calif. State U., Long Beach, 1970; PhD in Math. Psychology, Ind. U., 1974; MA in Math., U. Louisville, 1987. Tchg. and rsch. asst. Ind. U., Bloomington, 1971-72, rsch. asst., computer sys. programmer, 1972, fellow, 1972-73, assoc. instr., 1973-74; asst. prof. psychology U. Louisville, 1974-80, assoc. prof., 1980-85, prof., 1985—, dir. exptl. psychology program, 1983, 88-91. Mgr. software devel. Shelton Metrology Lab., Paducah, Ky., summer 1979; cons. on statis. analysis and exptl. design, product design, customer profile analysis, discrimination, computer software sys.; presenter in field at confs. and profl. meetings. Contbr. articles to profl. jours. Fellow NIMH, 1970-71. Mem. Soc. for Judgment and Decision Making (sec.-treas. 1986-89, newsletter editor 2000-02), Soc. for Med. Decision Making, Soc. for Math. Psychology, Am. Statis. Assn., Psychometric Soc., Psychonomic Soc., Cognitive Sci. Soc., Sigma Xi. Achievements include research on judgment, decision making and choice with emphasis on using mathematical models, artificial neural network models, artificial intelligence and computer simulation of decision making, including Bayesian methods, development of statistical techniques, medical decision making. Home: 10604 Grassy Ct Louisville KY 40241-2011 Office: U Louisville Dept Psychol and Brain Scis Louisville KY 40292-0001 E-mail: edgell@louisville.edu.

EDGEMAN, RICK LEE, statistics educator, consultant; b. Pueblo, Colorado, Nov. 28, 1954; s. Howard Curtis and Eunice Marie (Stucker) E.; m. Lisa Anne (Allen), Aug. 12, 1978; children: Emily, Grant, Stephen. BS in Exptl. psychology, U. So. Colo., 1977; MS in Rsch. and statis. methodology, U. No. Colo., 1979; PhD in stats., U. Wyo., 1983. Lectr. in stats. U. Wyo., Laramie, Wyo., 1981-83; asst. prof. bus. Bradley Univ., Peoria, Ill., 1983-85; study design and analysis mgr. Bausch and Lomb, Rochester, NY, 1985; asst. prof. stats. Rochester Inst. Tech., NY, 1985-86; asst. prof. mgmt. sci. U. North Tex., Denton, 1986-88; assoc. prof. computer info. sys. Colo. State U., 1988-93, prof. computer info. sys., 1993-2001, dir. SABER Inst. for self-assessment and bus. excellence rsch., 1988-2001; QUEST tchg. prof. U. Md., 2001—, exec. dir. QUEST program, 2001—. Stats. cons. Eastman-Kodak, Rochester, N.Y., 1985-86; Mobil Chem., Macedon, N.Y., 1985-86; Hewlett-Packard, Ft. Collins, 1988-89; Colo. Dept. Social Svc., Denver; vis. prof. quality and innovation, Aarhus Sch. Bus., Denmark, 1997-98; exec. dir. Multinational Alliance for the Advancement of Orgnl. Excellence, 1998-2002; vis. prof. divsn. quality and environ. mgmt. Luleå U. Tech., Sweden, 2000; invited prof. U. Versailles, France, 2000—; mem. adv. coun. ETQM Coll., Knowledge U., Dubai, United Arab Emirates, 2002—. Editor: Measuring Business Excellence, 2000-03; contbg. some 150 articles to profl. jour. Pres. Colo. Citizens for Decency, Ft. Collins, Colo., 1989-91; dir. Jesus Video Project Ft. Collins Colo.; Campus Crusade for Christ, 1993-94. Named one of 21 Voices of Quality for the 21st Century, Quality Progress, 2000; Caterpillar Tractor Co. Rsch. fellow Caterpiller Rsch. Found., Peoria, 1983-84. Mem. IEEE (reliability soc., higher edn. com.); Am. Soc. for Quality (editor Quality Progress 1991-94); Am. Stats. Assn. (pres. Rochester N.Y. chpt. 1985-86); Sigma Xi. Ind. Avocations: baseball coach, writing, pub. speaking, hiking, religious tchg.. Home: 30 Tindal Springs Ct Montgomery Village MD 20886 Office: U Md Robert H Smith Sch Bus Decision Info Tech Dept Van Munching Hall College Park MD 20742-1815 Fax: 801-681-9470. E-mail: rick_edgeman@rhsmith.umd.edu.

EDGERLY, WILLIAM SKELTON, banker; b. Lewiston, Maine, Feb. 18, 1927; s. Stuart and Florence (Skelton) E.; m. Lois Stiles, June 12, 1948; children: Leonard Stuart, Stephanie Lois. BS in Econs. and Engring., MIT, 1949; MBA, Harvard U., 1955. With Eastman Kodak Co., 1949-50; with Cabot Corp., Boston, 1952-75, fin. v.p., 1969-75, also dir.; chief exec. officer State St. Corp., 1975-91, chmn., 1992, chmn. emeritus, 1993—. Chmn. Found. for Partnerships, 1992—; bd. dirs., former chmn. Met. Boston Housing Partnership; bd. dirs. Fed. Res. Bank Boston, Depository Trust Co., N.Y.C., Arkwright-Boston Ins. Co.; life mem. emeritus MIT Corp. Bd. fellows Harvard Med. Sch.; bd. dirs. Jobs for Mass., former pres.; dir. Boston Pvt. Industry Coun., former chmn.; bd. dirs. Inst. for Fgn. Policy Analysis and Pioneer Inst.; trustee Com. Econ. Devel., The Gen. Hosp. Corp.; former mem. fed. adv. coun. Fed. Res. Bd., Washington. With USNR, 1945-46, 50-52. Fellow Am. Acad. Arts and Scis.; mem. MIT Alumni Assn. (pres. 1973-74), Harvard Bus. Sch. Assn., Assn. Res. City Bankers, Boston Econ. Club, Somerset Club, Cambridge Boat Club. Office: 124 Mount Auburn St Cambridge MA 02138-5758

EDGERTON, BRADFORD WHEATLY, plastic surgeon; b. Phila., May 8, 1947; s. Milton Thomas and Patricia Jane (Jones) E.; children: Bradford Wheatly Jr., Lauren Harrington; m. Louise Dungan Edgerton; stepchildren: Catherine Kelleher, Robert Kelleher. BA in Chemistry, Vanderbilt U., 1969, MD, 1973. Diplomate Am. Bd. Plastic Surgery, Am. Bd. Hand Surgery. Intern U. Calif., San Francisco, 1973-74; resident U. Va., Charlottesville, 1974-78; resident in plastic surgery Columbia-Presbyn., N.Y., 1979-81; fellow in hand surgery NYU, 1981-82, clin. instr. plastic surgery, 1981-89; ptnr. So. Calif. Permanente Med. Group, L.A., 1989—; assoc. prof. clin. plastic surgery U. So. Calif., L.A., 1989—. Trustee Harvard-Westlake Sch., L.A., 2001—; pres. Edgerton Found., Beverly Hills, Calif, 2001-. Mem. Am. Assn. Hand Surgery, Am. Soc. Plastic and Reconstructive Surgery, Am. Soc. Surgery of Hand, L.A. Tennis Club. Episcopal. Home: 494 S Spalding Dr Beverly Hills CA 90212-4104 Office: 6041 Cadillac Ave Los Angeles CA 90034-1702

EDGERTON, DEBRA, artist, educator; b. Junction City, Kans., Mar. 15, 1958; d. Hughes and Tamie E.; m. Terry Baxter, Apr. 13, 1991; children: Noah Hunter, Jesse Dylan. Student, Am. Acad. Art, Chgo., 1979; BFA, U. Kans., 1980. Artist Hallmark Cards, Kansas City, Mo., 1981-86; freelance artist Flagstaff, Ariz., 1986—. Instr's. asst in printmaking U. Kans., Lawrence, 1987, instr. painting Lawrence Art Ctr., 1991-93, Sr. Citizen Ctr., Lawrence, 1992, No. Ariz. U., Flagstaff, 1993—. Exhibited in group shows Tex. Watercolor Soc., Ann. Allied Artists of Am. 86th Ann. Exhbn., Midwest Watercolor Soc. Ann. Transparent Exhbn., Am. Watercolor Soc.'s Ann. Exhbn., Nat. Watercolor Soc.'s Ann. Exhbn. Mem. Round Table for Arts, Lawrence, 1991-92; mayoral appointee Lawrence Art Commn., 1992-93; pres. Lawrence Art Guild Assn., 1992. Recipient Excellence award Geary County Sch. Dist., 1991, Merit award Ariz. Aqueous, 1994; Profl. Devel. grantee Kans. Art Commn., 1992, Tech. Asst. grantee Lawrence Arts Commn., 1992; Dolan Found. scholar, 2001; San Francisco Art Inst. Grad. fellow, 2001. Mem. Am. Watercolor Soc., Nat. Watercolor Soc., Allied Artists Am., Midwest Watercolor Soc. (life). Office: No Ariz U PO Box 6020 Flagstaff AZ 86011-0001

EDGERTON, ROBERT BRECKENRIDGE, anthropologist, educator; b. Maywood, Ill., Nov. 28, 1931; s. Robert Alfred and Marjorie Adelaide (Close) E.; m. Karen Ito. PhD, UCLA, 1960. Faculty dept. psychiatry UCLA, 1962—, prof., 1996—. Author: The Cloak of Competence, 1967, Rules, Exceptions and Social Order, 1985, Sick Societies, 1992, Death or Glory, 1999, Hidden Heroism, 2001. Sgt. USAF, 1951-54. Am. Assn. on Mental Deficiency Rsch. awardee, 1976; recipient Career Rsch. award Acad. Mental Retardation, 1995. Fellow AAAS, Am. Assn. Arts and Scis.; mem. Soc. for Med. Anthropology (pres. 1976-77), Soc. for Psychol. Anthropology (pres. 1985-86). Office: UCLA Dept Psychiatry Los Angeles CA 90024

EDGERTON, WILLIAM B. foreign language educator; b. Winston-Salem, N.C., Mar. 11, 1914; s. Paul Clifton and Annie Maude (Benbow) E.; m. Jewell Mock Conrad, June 6, 1935 (dec. Dec. 1993); children: Susan, David. BA, Guilford Coll., 1934; MA, Haverford Coll., 1935; PhD, Columbia U., 1954. Tchr. French. German, Spanish, English in secondary schs., U.S. and France, 1935-39; faculty French and Spanish Guilford Coll., 1939-47; faculty Russian lit. Pa. State U., University Park, 1950-56, U. Mich., Ann Arbor, 1954-55, Columbia U., N.Y.C., 1956-58; prof. Slavic langs. and lits. Ind. U., Bloomington, 1958-83, prof. emeritus, 1983—, chmn. Slavic dept., 1958-65, 69-73, acting dir. Russian and East European Inst., 1981-82. Cons. Ford Found., 1952-61; mem. joint com. on Slavic studies Am. Coun. Learned Socs., 1951-62, chmn. 1958-61; vis. rsch. scholar USSR Acad. of Sci., 1963-64, 78, 87, 88, 89, 90, Bulgarian Acad. Scis., 1986, 88. Editor, co-author: Quaker Profiles, 1995; gen. editor: Columbia Dictionary of Modern European Literature, 1980; translator, editor: Satirical Stories of Nikolai Leskov, 1969, Memoirs of Peasant Tolstoyans in Soviet Russia, 1993; editor: Ind. Slavic Studies, III, 1963, Ind. Slavic Studies, IV, 1967, Am. Contributions to the Fifth Internat. Congress of Slavists, 1963; contbr. articles to profl. internat. jours. Bd. dirs. Am. Friends Svc. Com., 1956-59; trustee Guilford Coll., 1969-86; mem. vis. com. for Slavic Studies Harvard U., 1967-77; mem. adv. com. Nat. Humanities Ctr., 1978—; war relief work Am. Friends Svc. Com. Yugoslav refugee camp, Egypt, 1944-45, dir., lectr. internat. student seminars U.S., 1948, 51, Geneva, 1949, Vienna, 1956, Leningrad, 1960; organizing search fgn. child victims Nazis, Germany, 1945-46, Quaker relief work, Poland, 1946, internat. missions Yugoslavia, Greece, 1950, USSR, 1955, Poland, 1957. Recipient Josef Dobrovsky medal Czechoslovak Acad. Sci., 1968; Am. Council Learned Socs. fellow, 1948-50; Guggenheim fellow, 1963-64 Mem. MLA (exec. council 1962-65), Am. Assn. Advancement Slavic Studies (pres. 1961), Am. Com. Slavists (1958-78), Internat. Com. Slavists (Am. rep., 1958-78, hon. mem 1978—). Mem. Soc. Of Friends. Home: 1801 E Maxwell Ln Bloomington IN 47401-5208 Office: Ind U 502 Ballantine Rd Bloomington IN 47401-5018

EDGERTON, WINFIELD DOW, retired gynecologist; b. Caruthersville, Mo., Nov. 8, 1924; s. Winfield Dow and Anna Kathryn (Hale) E.; m. Rose Marie Cahill, June 24, 1945; 1 child, Winfield Dow Student, Central Coll., Fayette, Mo., 1942-44; MD, Washington U., St. Louis, 1947. Intern St. Luke's Hosp., St. Louis, 1947-48; resident Chgo. Lying-In Hosp., 1948-49, Free Hosp. for Women, Brookline, Mass., 1951, U.S. Naval Hosp., Chelsea, Mass., 1951-53; practice medicine specializing in obstetrics and gynecology Davenport, Iowa, 1955-87; clin. asst. prof. obstetrics and gynecology U. Iowa Coll. Medicine, 1971-78, clin. assoc. prof., 1979-82, clin. prof., 1982—; ret., 2000. Mem. staff, med. dir. Maternal Health Ctr. St. Luke's Hosp. (name changed to Edgerton Women's Health Ctr.), 1972-2000. Contbr. articles to med. jours. and texts Served to lt. M.C., USN, 1949-55 Fellow Am. Coll. Obstetricians and Gynecologists (past chmn. Iowa sect.), Royal Soc. Medicine; mem. Central Assn. Obstetricians and Gynecologists, Am. Fertility Soc., Am. Assn. Gynecologic Laparoscopists (past trustee), Gynecologic Laser Soc., AMA, Iowa Med. Soc., Scott County Med. Soc. (past pres.) Republican. Congregationalist. Home: 4 Lombard Ct Davenport IA 52803-2348

EDGETT, WILLIAM MALOY, lawyer, labor arbitrator; b. Balt., Feb. 26, 1927; s. Eugene Albert and Priscilla Ruff (Streett) E.; m. Bronwen Winifred Reese, Nov. 25, 1950. AA, Towson State Coll., 1949; BA, U. Md., 1951, JD, 1959; LL.M., Georgetown U., 1970. Bar: Md. bar 1959. Asst. personnel mgr. Am. Sugar Refining Co., Balt., 1951-55; supr. indsl. relations Westinghouse Electric Co., Balt., 1955-61; sr. labor relations specialist Martin Co., Balt., 1961-64; asst. mgr. indsl. relations Md. Shipbuilding and Drydock Co., Balt., 1964-67; pvt. practice law, 1967—. Asst. prof. Towson State U., 1971-72 Mem. Md. Commn. Nursing, 1974-76; chmn. pub. law bds Nat. Mediation Bd., 1971— ; neutral mem. Nat. R.R. Adjustment Bd., 1971— . Served to staff sgt. USAAF, 1944-46. Mem. ABA. Nat. Acad. Arbitrators, Am. Arbitration Assn., Am., Roster Arbitrators Fed. Mediation and Conciliation Service. Home: 3 Beechmere Ln Cockeysville Hunt Valley MD 21030-1101 Office: PO Box 203 Cockeysville Hunt Valley MD 21030-0203

EDGEWORTH, EMILY, retired insurance agency executive-antique dealer; b. Brilliant, Ala., July 12, 1927; d. James Allen and Cara Margie (Mayes) Addison; m. Billy Pate, Oct. 8, 1947 (div. July 1968); m. William Edgeworth, Sept. 24, 1972. Student, Ala. Bus. Coll., 1952; grad. life underwriters tng. coun. U. Ala., 1976. Med. aide, receptionist Office Dr. A.M. Walker, Tuscaloosa, Ala., 1952-58; credit mgr. Busch Jewelry Co., Tuscaloosa, 1958-66; purchasing clk. Avco Fin. Corp., Tuscaloosa, 1966-71; sec. Ala. Farm Bur. Ins. Co., Tuscaloosa, 1971-73; multilines saleswoman Farm Bur. Ins. Co., Tuscaloosa, 1973-76; owner, salesman Emily Edgeworth Ins. Co., Tuscaloosa, 1976-86; owner, mgr. Rural Relics, Tuscaloosa, 1986-89; ret., 1989. Contbr. poetry and short stories to various publs., including Best Poems of 1996 and 1997, Journey of the Mind, 1994, Growing Up on a Two Mule Farm, 1996. Active Heritage Found., Washington, Meals on Wheels, Tuscaloosa, 1980's, Unity Bapt. Ch., Tuscaloosa; active Tuscaloosa Rep. Com., Nat. Rep. Com. Mem. Internat. Soc. Poets (disting. mem.). Avocations: writing poetry and short stories, collecting depression era farm items. Home: 6103 41s St Tuscaloosa AL 35401

EDGINGTON, THOMAS S. pathologist, educator, molecular biologist, vascular biologist; b. LA, Feb. 10, 1932; BA in Biol. Scis., Stanford U., 1953, MD, 1957. Diplomate Am. Bd. Pathology, spl. cert. immunopathology. Intern Hosp. Univ. Pa., Phila., 1957—58; resident Ctr. Health Scis. UCLA, 1958—60; sr. postdoctoral fellow immunology Scripps Clinic & Rsch. Found., La Jolla, Calif., 1965—68, assoc. mem. dept. exptl. pathology, 1968—71; founder, head dept. anatomic pathology and lab. medicine Scripps Clinic and Rsch. Found., La Jolla, 1968—74, prof. depts. immunology and vascular biology, 1971—; asst. prof., surg. pathologist dept. pathology UCLA Sch. Medicine, 1962—65; assoc. adj. prof. pathology U. Calif., San Diego, La Jolla, 1968—75, adj. prof. 1975—. Cons. Centocor, 1993—95, Eli Lilly, 1982—85, Becton-Dickinson, 1977—80; founder, bd. dirs. Corvas Internat., NuVas. Contbr. numerous articles to profl. jours. Recipient Coll. de France medal, 1981, John A. Lynch Molecular Biology award, U. Notre Dame, 1992, Rous-Whipple prize, Am. Soc. Investigative Pathology, 1995, Disting. Career award, Internat. Soc. Thrombosis and Hemostatis, 1995. Fellow: AAAS; mem.: Inst. of Medicine of NAS, Thrombosis Inst. (bd. sci. govs. 1995—), Internat. Soc. Thrombosis and Hemostasis, Fedn. Am. Socs. Exptl. Biology (pres. 1990—91, chmn. bd. 1990—91). Office: The Scripps Rsch Inst C-204 10550 N Torrey Pines Rd # C204 La Jolla CA 92037-1000 E-mail: tsedgington@hotmail.com.

EDGINTON, JOHN ARTHUR, lawyer; b. Kingsburg, Calif., July 23, 1935; s. Arthur George and Pochantas Clementina (Ball) E.; m. Jane Ann Simmons, June 25, 1960. AA, U. Calif., Berkeley, 1955, AB in Econs., 1957, JD, 1963. Bar: Calif. 1964, No. Marianas 1969, U.S. Ct. Claims 1969, U.S. Ct. Appeals (9th cir.) 1969, U.S. Supreme Ct. 1969. Assoc. Graham & James, San Francisco, 1964-71, ptnr., 1971-94, Dezurick Edginton & Harrington LLP, Emeryville, Calif., 1994-98, Booth Banning LLP, San Francisco, 1999-2000; pvt. practice Point Richmond, Calif., 2000—. Author: Maritime Bankruptcy, 1989, Benedict on Admiralty, vol. 3B and 3C; editor-in-chief Maritime Practice and Procedure, vol. 29 Moore's Federal Practice, 1997, Benedict's Maritime Bull., 2003; editor Maritime Desk Reference, Benedict on Admiralty, vol. 8, 2001; contbr. articles to profl. jours. With USN, 1957—60. Disting. U. Calif. alumni Order of Golden Bear. Mem.: East Bay Model Engrs. Soc. (bd. dirs. 1996—2002, pres. 2000—02), Swedish-Am. C. of C. (bd. dirs. 1971—, pres. Western Nat. 1988—90, nat. vice chmn. 1988—90, pres. Western Nat. 1998—2000, bd. dirs. 1998—, CFO 1999—2000, corp. sec. 2000—), Maritime Law Assn. (chmn. practice and procedure com. 1991—95, bd. dirs. 1993—96), Golden State Model R.R. Mus. (corp. sec., bd. dirs. 1995—), Sierra Club (nat. outing com. 1964—, chmn. ins. com. 1991—, internat. trips 1992—95, outing governance com. 1992—). Democrat. Methodist. Avocations: mountaineering, hiking, photography, model railroads. Office: Law Office of John A Edginton 124 Washington Ave Ste A-1 Point Richmond CA 94801 3979 Fax. (510) 235-4427. E mail: jedginton@edg-law.com.

EDGMON, GARY MARTIN, orthodontist; b. Nashville, Nov. 25, 1952; s. Deward Thomas and Jeanne (Woodell) E.; m. Janice Lynn McPherson, May 5, 1975; children: Lisa Renee, Lorina Lyn, Sherri Lea. BA in Biology, So. Adventist U., Collegedale, Tenn., 1976; DDS, Loma Linda U., 1980, MS in Orthodontics, 1987. Diplomate ADA, Am. Assn. Orthodontists. Dentist ADA, Calhoun, Ga., 1980—, Ga. Dental Assn., Calhoun, 1980—, N.W. Dist. Dental Soc., 1980—, Calif. Dental Assn., Hemet, Calif., 1985-87, ADA, Hemet, Calif., 1985-87, Pacific Coast Dental Soc., Hemet, Calif., 1985-87; orthodontist Am. Assn. Orthodontists, Calhoun, Ga., 1987—, So. Assn. Orthodontists, Calhoun, Ga., 1987—, Ga. Assn. Orthodontists, Calhoun, Ga., 1987—, Am. Assn. Orthodontists, Dalton, Ga., 1998—, So. Assn. Orthodontists, Dalton, Ga., 1998—, Ga. Assn. Orthodontists, Dalton, Ga., 1998—. Co-founder Regall Residence-Intermediate Health Care, Calhoun, Ga. Author: Comparison of Bond Strengths, 1987. Vice chmn. Downtown Devel. Authority, Calhoun; chmn./vice chmn. Sch. Bd., Calhoun; Pres., pres.-elect, bd. dirs. Rotary, Calhoun, 1999— (GRSP award); pres./v.p. Am. Cancer Soc., Calhoun, 1983-85, Gordon County Dental Soc., 1984-85; Apalacian H.S.A. rep., Ga. Dental Assn., N.W. Ga., 1982-85. Mem.: Calhoun C. of C., Dalton Dental Study Club (pres.). Conservative. Adventist. Avocations: skiing, cycling, camping. Office: Orthodontics/Dentofacial Orthopedics 300 S Piedmont St Calhoun GA 30701-2422

EDGREEN, ROBERT J. equity company executive; b. Coudersport, Pa., May 23, 1946; s. Howard J. and Lucille (Leete) E.; m. Sherian J. Campbell, Aug. 23, 1969; children: Kristen, Gregory. BS in Aerospace Engring., Pa. State U., 1968; MBA, U. Va., 1972. V.p. Merrill Lynch Capital Markets, N.Y.C., 1975-81; 1st v.p. E.F. Hutton & Co., N.Y.C., 1981-86; pres. Integrated Resources Acquisitions, N.Y.C., 1986-89; chmn. Learjet Corp., Wichita, Kans., 1987-89; pres. K.D. Equities, N.Y.C., 1989-92; mng. ptnr. Value Added Capital, LLC, N.Y.C., 1993—. Chmn. Kane Magnetics Internat, Kane, Pa., 1995—, Omni Facility Resources, South Plainfield, N.J., 1998-2000. Mem. Yale Club N.Y.C. Presbyterian. Avocations: biking, tennis, skiing. E-mail: edgreen@valueaddedcapital.com.

EDGREN, GRETCHEN GRONDAHL, magazine editor; b. Portland, Oreg., Mar. 17, 1931; d. Jack W. and Alice Belle (Wells) Grondahl; m. James McNeese, Oct. 22, 1955 (div. Nov. 1974); children: Amy, Terence James; m. Alvin H. Edgren, Dec. 14, 1984. BJ, U. Oreg., 1952. Staff writer The Oregonian, Portland, 1952-61; editor Sunday mag. The San Juan (P.R.) Star, 1963-65; inventory and info. specialist USAF and U.S. Army Recruiting Command, San Antonio and Chgo., 1965-67; assoc. editor VIP mag. Playboy Clubs, Chgo., 1967-69, mng. editor, 1969-70; assoc. editor Playboy mag., Chgo., 1970-74, sr. editor, 1974-92, contbg. editor, 1992—. Author: The Playboy Book, 1994, The Playmate Book, 1996, Inside the Playboy Mansion, 1998; editor: New Credit Rights for Women, 1976; contbr. articles to mags. Adv. bd. Old Oreg. Alumni mag. U. Oreg., Eugene, 1988-96; bd. dirs. Civic Arts Coun., Oak Park, Ill., 1976-84, pres., 1979-80, Village Players, Oak Park-River Forest (Ill.) Symphony Assn., Oak Park Concert chorale, 1975-91; mem. Oak Park Cable TV Commn., 1984-86; active Anna Maria Island (Fla.) Cmty. Chorus, 1992—, Anna Maria Island Turtle Watch, 1992—. Mem. Confrerie des Vignerons de St. Vincent Mâcon (maitresse du chpt. 1988-92), Webfoot Soc. U. Oreg., Phi Beta Kappa, Delta Delta Delta. Episcopalian. Avocations: singing, travel, loggerhead turtle rescue, wines.

EDIGER, MARK D. chemistry educator; b. Newton, Kans., July 26, 1957; BA in Chemistry and Math., Bethel Coll., 1979; PhD in Phys. Chemistry, Stanford U., 1984. Asst. prof. dept. chemistry U. Wis., Madison, 1984-90, assoc. prof., 1990-94, prof. dept. chemistry, 1994—, Grantee Chemistry Program, 2000—, Polymers Program, NSF, 2001—, Am. Chem. Soc., 2002—. Fellow Am. Phys. Soc.; mem. Am. Chem. Soc. Office: Univ Wis Dept Chemistry 1101 University Ave Madison WI 53706-1322

EDIGER, MARLOW, education educator; b. Inman, Kans., Oct. 10, 1927; BS in Edn., Kans. State Tchrs. Coll., 1958, MS in Edn., 1960; EdD, U. Denver, 1963. Tchr. Sandcreek Sch., rural Newton, Kans., 1951-52; English tchr. Mennonite Sch., Jericho, 1952-53; tchr. English and geography Friends Boys Sch., Ramallah, Jordan, 1953-54; tchr. Countryside Sch., Lehigh, Kans., 1955-57; tchr., prin. Lincolnville Grade Sch., Kans., 1957-61; prof. edn. Truman State U., Kirksville, 1962—92. Spkr. in field at over 200 nat., internat. tchr. edn. convs.; evaluator over 135 PhD theses at numerous univs. in India including Kerala U., Mother Teresa U., U. Madras, Utkal U., Sambalpur U., Alagappa U.; mem. editl. bd. Experiments in Edn. Jour., India, Jour. Karnataka State Edn. Fedn., India, Reading Improvement, Education, Jour. English Lang. Tchg. in India, The Progress of Edn. in India, Edutracks (India); v.p. NMSU-AAUP, 1974-75, pres., 1975-76. Author: Relevancy in the Elementary Curriculum, 1975, 2nd edit., 1991, The Elementary Curriculum, A Handbook, 1977, 2nd edit., 1988, Social Studies Curriculum in the Elementary School, 5th edit., 2000, Language Arts Curriculum in the Elementary School, 1983, 92, 2nd edit., 1988, revised, 1994, The Modern Elementary School, 1997, Teaching Math in the Elementary School, 1997, Improving the Teaching of Elementary School Mathematics, 1999, The Holy Land, 1998, Teaching Science in the Elementary School, 2nd edit., 2000, Teaching Science Successfully, 2001, Teaching Social Studies Successfully, 2001, Philosophy and the Curriculum, 2003; Psychology and the Curriculum, 2003; Teaching Language Arts Successfully, mem. editl. bd. The Edn. Rev., The Math Tchr., Jour. English Lang., also Edn.; publ. more than 2,400 manuscripts on six continents; co-author: Teaching Reading Successfully, 2000, Teaching Mathematics Successfully, 2000, Language Arts Curriculum, 2003, Improving School Administration, 2003, Elementary Curriculum, 2003, Philosophy and the Curriculum, 2003, Teaching Mathematics in the Elementary School, 2003; contbr. articles to profl. jours. Treas. Marion County Kans. Tchrs. Assn., 1958-59, pres., 1959-60; mem. adv. coun. Himalayan Jour. Edn. R&D, India; mem. nat. coun. social studies com. Religion in the Schs.; chmn. Marion County Curriculum Com., 1960-61chr. Sunday sch., 1950-52, 54-58, 64-99. Mem. ASCD, NSTA (com. tchr. edn.), NEA (life, Mo. chpt., core competencies and key skills com., higher edn. com., com. on pub. rels. 2000-01), Internat. Reading Assn. (sub com. evaluating literacy standards), Nat. Coun. Social Studies (adv. coun. rural schs. and social studies, ethics com., pub. rels. curriculum com., archives com.), Nat. Coun. Tchrs. English (vice chmn. rural lang. arts com., lang. and learning across the curriculum com., tracking in the pub. schs. com.), Mo. Coun. Social Studies (bd. control), Sci. Tchrs. Mo. (bd. dirs.), Mo. Geog. Alliance, Phi Delta Kappa. Office: 201 W 22nd PO Box 417 North Newton KS 67117-0417 E-mail: mediger2@cox.net.

EDIGER, ROBERT IKE, botanist, educator; b. Hutchinson, Kans., Apr. 2, 1937; s. Peter F. and Martha (Friesen) E.; m. Patricia L. Dickerson, Feb. 7, 1981; children: Madeline, Maureen, Alan, Shelly. BA, Bethel Coll., 1959; MS, Emporia State U., 1964; PhD, Kans. State U., 1967. Tchr. public schs., Ford, Kans., 1959-62, Hays, Kans., 1962-63; teaching and research asst. Kans. State U., 1964-67; asst. prof. dept. biol. scis. Calif. State U., Chico, 1967-71, asso. prof., 1971-74, prof., 1975-99, chmn. dept. biol. scis., 1974-77, dir.Eagle Lake field sta., 1967-73; ret., 1999. Mem. Am. Soc. Plant Taxonomists, Orgn. Biol. Field Stas. (pres. 1975), Calif. Bot. Soc., Calif. Native Plant Soc. Methodist. Home: 5359 Royal Oaks Dr Oroville CA 95966-3837 Office: Calif State U Dept Biol Scis Chico CA 95929-0001 E-mail: bpediger@aol.com.

EDIL, TUNCER BERAT, civil and environmental engineering educator; b. Konya, Turkey, July 25, 1945; came to U.S., 1962; s. Halil and Ismet Edil; m. Berrin Inci Demircioglu, Sept. 26, 1969; children: Barish H., Banu E. BS in Civil Engring., Robert Coll., Istanbul, Turkey, 1967, MS in Civil Engring., 1969; PhD in Civil Engring., Northwestern U., 1973. Registered profl. engr., Wis. Bridge design engr. Ministry of Village Affairs, Istanbul, 1969; ptnr. Mono Engring. Firm, Istanbul, 1967-69; engr. Mirza Engring. Co., Chgo., 1970; lectr. Northwestern U., Evanston, Ill., 1973; asst. prof. U. Wis., Madison, 1973-77, assoc. prof., 1977-80, prof., 1980—, assoc. chmn. dept. civil engring., 1990—2000, chmn. dept. geol. engring., 2002—. Retained cons. Warzyn Engring., Inc., Madison, 1985-89; geotech. cons. engring. firms., govt. bodies Wis., Minn., Ill., Ariz., Wash., Turkey, 1974—; expert witness law firms, Wis., Ill., Penn.., Nebr., 1977—; tech. cons. Vets. Meml. Park, Minn., 1989, Bender Pk., Wis., 2001, Madison Met. Sewerage Dist. Sludge Lagoon Capping, Wisc., 2002. Editor-in-chief ASCE Jour. Geotech. Engring., 1984-88; contbr. articles to profl. jours. Nat. bd. dirs. U.S. Univs. Coun. on Geotech. Engring. Rsch., 1991-94, pres., 1993-94. Recipient Team award for electonic pulse tech., U.S. Army Constrn. Engr. Res. Lab., 2000. Mem. ASTM (Standard Devel. award 1992, 96, Spl. Svc. award 1997, 2001), ASCE (pres. Madison br. 1989-90, bd. dirs. Wis. sect. 1992-93, v.p. 1995-96, pres. 1997-98, Geo Inst. chair internat. activities coun. 2000—, Young Civil Engr. award 1977, Merit for Ind. Achievement award Wis. sect. 1988, Outstanding Civil Engr. award S.W. br. 1999), Internat. Soc. Soil Mechanics and Found. Engring., Am. Soc. Engring. Edn. (Dow Outstanding Young Faculty award 1980), U. Wis. Polygon Engring. Soc. (Outstanding Instr. award 1992). Avocations: international travel, world history, soccer. Home: 3100 Lake Mendota Dr Apt 303 Madison WI 53705-1458 Office: U Wis 1415 Engring Dr Madison WI 53706-1691

EDINGER, LEWIS JOACHIM, political science educator; b. Frankfort, Germany, Feb. 1, 1922; came to U.S., 1936; s. Mark A. and Dora (Meyer) E.; m. Hanni Blumenfeld, Sept. 11, 1950; children: Monica Ruth, Susan Yvonne. AB, Wabash Coll., 1943; PhD, Columbia U., 1951. Instr. NYU, 1947-49; vis. asst. prof. Sweet Briar Coll., 1950-51; vis. lectr. Vassar Coll., 1951-52; vis. asst. prof. U. N.C., 1952-53; assoc. prof. Air War Coll., 1953-57; asst. prof.to prof. Mich. State U., East Lansing, 1957-63; Fulbright prof. Free U. Berlin, 1959-60; prof. Washington U., St. Louis, 1963-67; Fulbright prof. U. Bonn, 1964-65; prof. govt. Columbia U., N.Y.C., 1967-92, prof. emeritus, 1992. Co-adj. prof. Rutgers U., 1975; vis. Fulbright prof. U. Bonn, Fed. Republic Germany, 1980-81; vis. fellow Nuffield Coll., Oxford U., 1981; vis. prof. U. Bonn, 1988, U. Florence, Italy, 1989. Author or co-author: West German Armament, 1955, German Exile Politics, 1956, Germany Rejoins the Powers, 1959, 73, Kurt Schumacher: A Study in Personality and Political Behavior, 1965, France, Germany, and the Western Alliance, 1967, Political Leadership in Industrialized Societies, 1967, 76, Politics in Germany, 1968, Politics in West Germany, 1977, West German Politics, 1986, From Bonn to Berlin: German Politics in Transition, 1998. Ford Found. fellow, 1956-57; Social Sci. Research Council grantee, 1958, 59-63, NSF grantee, 1971-73; Guggenheim Found. fellow, 1973-74 Mem. Hemlock Soc. Office: 420 W 118th St New York NY 10027-7213

EDINGER, STANLEY EVAN, clinical chemist; b. Bklyn., Aug. 9, 1943; s. Louis and Lenore (Danenberg) E. BS in Chemistry cum laude, CUNY, 1964; MS in Phys. Chemistry, NYU, 1969, PhD in Phys. Chemistry, 1970. Cert. clin. chemistry lab. dir. N.Y.C., N.Y. State; cert. chemist, Nat. Cert. Commn. for Chemists and Chem. Engrs. From tchg. fellow to asst. rsch. N.Y.U., 1964-70; translator, editor N.Y.C., 1970-71; clin. chemist Mt. Sinai Med. Ctr., N.Y.C., 1971-76; sr. scientist bur. quality assurance USPHS, 1976-78; sr. scientist health standard and quality bureau U.S. Health Care Fin. Adminstrn., Balt., 1978-86, scientist dir., asst. to dir. OSC, 1986-87; scientist dir. Nat. Inst. on Drug Abuse, Pres. Initiative on Drug Testing in Work Place, Rockville, Md.; scientist dir. Office Program Assessment and Info. U.S. Health Care Fin. Adminstrn., Rockville, Md., 1988; USPHS rep. to com. on energy and commerce, Congl. fellow U.S. Ho. of Reps., Washington, 1989; sr. health policy analyst Agy. for Health Care Policy and rsch. office of forum for quality and effectiveness in health care USPHS, Rockville, 1990-93; spl. asst., chmn. subcom. on oversight and investigation U.S. Ho. of Reps. Com. on Energy & Commerce, Washington, 1991-94; sr. legis., adv., adminstr. Agy. for Healthcare Policy and Rsch., 1993-94, sr. sci. advisor Ctr. Info. Tech., 1994-98, sr. sci. advisor Ctr. Quality Measurement and Improvement, 1998-99; sr. sci. advisor Agy. for Health Care Rsch. and Quality Ctr. for Quality Improvement and Patient Safety, 2000—. Sr. legis. adv. Office of Surgeon Gen., 1995-96; project officer HHS, Washington, 1977-80; sr. scientist bur. com. health svcs. and delivery systems, 1989-90; mem. U.S. Surgeon Gen.'s Scientist Profl. Adv. Com., Rockville, 1986-90, adv. com., 1984-87; commr. Nat. Cert. Commn. Chemistry and Chem. Engring., Bethesda, Md., 1987—; mem. U.S. Health Care Fin. Adminstrn. AIDS Task Force, Washington, 1986-90, Profl. Exam Svc., Inc., N.Y.C., 1974-76, Nat. Com. Clin. Lab. Stds. subcom. on cost acctg. and wellness testing, and com. on quality of care, materials coms. on computer record sys., med. records and clin. lab. data sys.; mem. quality of care task forces HHS, 1998—; chief staffer for quality work group Nat. Ctr for Vital Health Stats., 1999-2003, mem. staff for quality workgroup and populations suybcom., 2003—; mem. mentor program NYU; mem. Nat. Cert. Commn. in Chemistry and Chem. Engring., 1986—. Author: The Chemistry of Gypsum and its Dehydration Products, 1975, Infection Control As Health Care Facilities, 1977, Statistics for Laboratory Surveyors; co-author: The Federal Regulation of Clinical Laboratories Quality Assurance Standards and Technological Change, 1986; contbr. articles to profl. jours. Sr. scientist USPHS, 1976-77, comdr., 1976-86, capt., 1986—. N.Y. State Regents scholar, 1960-64, N.Y. State Scholar Incentive award, 1964-68. Fellow Am. Inst. Chemists (chmn. membership com. N.Y. sect. 1974-76, chmn. nat. coun. for health lab. svcs., 1988-92, govt. affairs com. 1993—, bd. dirs. 1996-98, 2000—), Washington Acad. Scis.; mem. ASTM (com. computer records sys., med. records, clin. lab. data), Am. Assn. for Clin. Chemists (legis. com. 1989, advisor to legis. com. 1990—), Am. Chem. Soc., N.Y. Acad. Scis., Assn. of Mil. Surgeons U.S., Soc. Armed Forces Mil. Lab. Scientists, Commd. Officers Assn. U.S., APHA (lab. sect. legis. com., chmn. membership com., planning com., action bd. 1984-96, joint policy com. 1993-96), U.S. Naval Sailing Assn., Annapolis Naval Acad. Sailing Assn., Bklyn. Coll. Chemistry Alumni (dir. 1970-86), Bklyn. Coll. Alumni Assn., NYU Alumni Assn., Sigma Xi. Clubs: Washington Ski. Democrat. Jewish. Achievements include development of legislation and regulations to assure quality of clinical laboratory and drug abuse testing, oversight legislative initiatives to improve quality, access and financing of American health care system. Home: 5901 Montrose Rd 1400 South Rockville MD 20852 Office: Agy for Health Care Rsch and Quality Ctr for Qual Improvement/Patient Safety 540 Gaither Rd Ste 300 Rockville MD 20852 Office Fax: 301-427-1341. E-mail: stanedinger@earthlink.net., sedinger@arh4.gov.

EDINGTON, MARK DAVID WHEELER, clergyman, educational administrator; b. East Lansing, Mich., Mar. 15, 1961; s. Edgar D. Jr. and Patricia C. E. AB summa cum laude in Philosophy and Polit. Sci., Albion (Mich.) Coll., 1983; MDiv, Harvard U., 2000. Ordained deacon Episcopal Ch., 2000; priest, 2001. Adminstrv. asst. house minority leader Mich. Ho. of Reps., Lansing, 1984; sr. rsch. assoc., dir. publs. Inst. for Fgn. Policy Analysis, Cambridge, Mass., 1985-96; cons. editor Daedalus, Cambridge, 1996—2001; sr. adminstr. Ctr. for the Study of World Religions, Harvard U., Cambridge, 2001—; Epps fellow, chaplain Harvard Coll., The Meml. Ch., Cambridge, 2000—. Mem. Boston com. on Fgn. Rels., 1990—; co-founder, 1st pres. Am. Coms. on Fgn. Rels., Washington; mem. Coun. on Fgn. Rels., N.Y., 1996—; lectr. in field. Active Boston Athenaeum, Boston, Hardwick Farmers' Coop.; vestryman St. John's Episcopal Ch., Newtonville, Mass., 1985 93, sr. warden, 1898-91; seminarian Meml. Ch., Harvard U., 1998-2000, min., 1999-2000, 02; chaplain intern Beth Israel Deaconess Med. Ctr., 1997-98; direct svc. vo. Hospice of the Good Shepherd, Newton, Mass., 1994-97; dir. Partakers, Inc. Mem. Clericus Club of Boston, Signet Club, Odd Volumes Club, Phi Beta Kappa. Office: The Meml Ch Harvard Yard Cambridge MA 02138 Fax: 617-496-9166.

EDINGTON, PATRICIA ANN, social services administrator; b. Chgo., July 3, 1941; d. Michael Joseph and Bernice Ruth (Reifon) Nobilio; m. Richard Fredrick Edington, Sept. 21, 1963; children: Mark Michael, Jill Mariette. BS in Social Scis., Loyola U., 1963. Dir. welfare svcs. Hanover Twp., Bartlett, Ill., 1974-92; phone bank coord. Medina County (Ohio) Rep. Party, 1992; councilwoman Village of Westfield Ctr., Ohio, 1992—, fin. co-chair, 1993—, chair social com., 1992—, mem. tree com., 1999—, mem. twp. pk. com., 2000—, ins. com., 2002—. Mem. Govs. Gen. Assistance Adv. Coun., State of Ill., Springfield, 1985-87; svc. rep. Salvation Army, 1985-92; instr. Gen. Assistance Tng. Inst., State of Ill., 1990-92. Columnist: Ill. County and Twp. Ofcl., 1989-92; editor Medina County Rep. Newsletter, 1992-95. Mem. Stray's Halfway House, Hoffman Estates, Ill., 1982-92, Medina County Com. for Homeless, 1993-95, Medina County Human Svcs. Coalition, 1993-96, Medina County Fedn. Rep. Women, 1992-94, sec. 1993; camp com. YMCA, Schaumburg, Ill., 1984-86; bd. councilors Alexian Bros. Med. Ctr., Elk Grove, Ill., 1984-92; judge Paddock Publs. Young Women of Yr. Program, Arlington Heights, Ill., 1987-92; mem. Medina County Planning Commn., 1997—; membership chair LeRoy United Meth. Ch., 1995—, treas. Women's Fellowship, 1993-99, pres., 1999-2002, fin. com., 1999, chair, 2000-01, lay spkr., 1999—; del.-at-large ann. conf. Wooster dist. Meth. Ch., 2003—; marshall Meml. Day Parade, 1997. Recipient award of appreciation Stray's Halfway House, Hoffman Estates, 1987. Mem. Community Econ. Devel. Assn. (bd. dirs., vice chmn. 1984-85, sec. 1988-90), Suburban Primary Health Care Coun. N.W. Suburban Coun. for Community Svcs., Twp. Ofcls. of Ill. (edn. and publs. com. 1986-92), Cook County Twp. Social Workers (pres. 1988-92), Ill. Twp. Social Workers (pres. 1988-92), Cloverleaf Women's Club (pres. 1998-99, editor newsletter 1994—). Avocations: crafts, reading, sewing. Home: PO Box 821 Westfield Center OH 44251-0821

EDIS, GLORIA TOBY, pediatrician; b. N.Y.C., Dec. 6, 1939; d. Murray Alvin and Anna G. (Goldstein) E.; m. Myron Royal Schoenfeld, June 14, 1959; children: Bradley, Glenn, Dawn, Melody. BA, Cornell U., 1960; MD, NYU, 1963. Intern Montefiore Hosp., N.Y.C., 1963-64; pediatric resident Columbia Presbyn. Med. Ctr., N.Y.C., 1966-68; pediatrician Scarsdale (N.Y.) Pediatric Assocs., 1977—; pediatric attending Albert Einstein Med. Coll., Bronx, 1968-70; pediatrician Barsky Med. Group, N.Y.C., 1970-80. Fellow Am. Acad. Pediatrics; mem. AMA, Westchester County Med. Soc., Cornell Alumni Assn. Avocations: hiking, cycling, reading, weight training, theater. Office: Scarsdale Pediatric Assn 2 Overhill Rd Scarsdale NY 10583-5323

EDISEN, CLAYTON BYRON, physician; b. Chgo. s. Byron Parker and Elsie Elinor (Mielkie) E.; m. Adele Uskali, 1948 (div. 1968); children: Laura, Glenn, Lynn; m. Barbara S., Dec. 1968 (dec. 2000). PhB, U. Chgo., 1949, MD, 1953. Diplomate Am. Bd. Neurology and Psychiatry. Various positions in field to psychiatrist The Monroe (La.) Area Guidance Ctr., 1956-58, med. dir., psychiatrist, 1957-58; instr. psychiatry Tulane U. Sch. Medicine, New Orleans, 1956-57; staff cons. Children's Bur., New Orleans, 1958-60; staff psychiatrist The Guidance Ctr., New Orleans, 1957-59; staff cons. Crippled Children's Divsn./La. State Dept. Health, 1959; with New Orleans Psychoanalytic Tng. Ctr., 1958-61; pvt. practice New Orleans, 1957—; apptd. in psychiatry De Paul Hosp., New Orleans, 1957 -. Adj. full prof. exptl. comms. design, Tulane U., New Orleans, 1973-74; courtesy staff Coliseum Med. Ctr., New Orleans, 1974—; fellow Scientific Coun. of the Internat. Coll. of Angiology, 1972; del. Internat. Congress on Drug Edn., Montreux, Switzerland/World Psychiat. Assn., 1973, others; vis. faculty lectr. Sch. of Social Work, Tulane U., 1958-60; asst. vis. physician Charity Hosp. of La., New Orleans, 1954-56; vis. staff psychiatrist Touro Infirmary, New Orleans, 1958-72; temporary dir. De Paul Hosp., New Orleans, 1960; lectr. to Annual Life Inst., Jewish Fedn. New Orleans, 1961, others; panelist/lectr. in field. Contbr. numerous articles to profl. jours. and publs. Sgt. U.S. Army, 1945-47, ETO. Fellow Am. Geriatric Soc., Interam. Coll. Physicians and Surgeons, Royal Soc. Health/London; mem. AMA (Physicians Recognition awards), Am. Group Psychotherapy Assn., La. Group Psychotherapy Soc. and Inst., La. State Med. Soc. (numerous offices), Orleans Parish Med. Soc., Am. Psychiat. Assn., So. Med. Assn., New Orleans Psychiat. Forum, 2nd Dist. Med. Soc., La. Dist. Br. APA, New Orleans Area Psychiat. Soc., La. Psychiat. Assn., Pan Am. Med. Assn., World Psychiatric Assn., Assn. Am. Physicians and Surgeons, Am. Heart Assn., N.Y. Acad. Scis., Sigma Xi, others. Republican. Avocations: golf, bridge. Office: 2900 Hessmer Ave Metairie LA 70002-5820 E-mail: cedisenmd@aol.com.

EDISON, ALLEN RAY, electrical engineer, educator; b. Plainview, Nebr., Sept. 21, 1926; s. Arthur and Lela (Johnson) E.; m. Betty Jean Broer, Dec. 27, 1949; children— Karl Arthur, Kathryn Johannah. BS, U. Nebr., 1950, MS, 1957; D.Sc., U. N.M., 1962. Engr. Silas Mason Co., Burlington, Iowa, 1950-53; instr. U. Nebr., Lincoln, 1953-57, prof. elec. engring., 1957-89, prof. emeritus, 1989—, chmn. dept. elec. engring., 1964-70. Served with USNR, 1944-46. Mem. I.E.E.E. (past sect. chmn.), Sigma Xi, Sigma Tau, Eta Kappa Nu. Home: 511 S 54th St Lincoln NE 68510-2006 E-mail: aedison@alltel.net.

EDISON, BERNARD ALAN, retired retail apparel company executive; b. Atlanta, 1928; s. Irving and Beatrice (Chanin) Edison; m. Marilyn S Wewers, Apr. 26, 1975. BA, Harvard U., 1949, MBA, 1951. With Edison Bros. Stores Inc., St. Louis, 1951—, asst. v.p., 1957-58, v.p. leased depts., 1958-67, v.p., asst. treas., 1967-68, pres., 1968-87, chmn. fin. com., 1987-89, dir. emeritus, 1989-96. Bd dirs Anheuser-Busch Cos, Inc. Office: Edison Founds 220 N Fourth St Ste A Saint Louis MO 63102

EDISON, JONATHAN E. assistant principal, motivational speaker; b. Detroit, Sept. 8, 1973; AA, Wayne County C.C., 1995; BS in Edn., Wayne State U., 1996, MS in Leadership and Supervision, 1998, student in Ednl. Policy Studies, 2001—. Tchr. Detroit (Mich.) Pub. Schs., 1998—2000, asst. prin., 2001—. Prin., owner Jonathan Edison Prodns., Inc., Detroit; spkr. in field. Office: Jonathan Edison Productions Inc 250 East Harbor Tower Dr Ste 808 Detroit MI 48207

EDISON, THOMAS ROBERT, management educator, retired military officer; b. Aberdeen, Wash., Aug. 24, 1945; s. Karold Sigurd and Agnes Cecilia Edison; m. Judith Edison, June 21, 1969; children: Thomas Robert Edison, Jr., Dana Edison Varga, Merriddith. BS, Stanford U., 1967, BA, 1968; MEdn, Chapman U., 1977; MS, Air Force Inst. Tech., Dayton, Ohio, 1978. Cert. total quality mgmt. UCLA, profl. logistician Sole of Internat. Logistics, quality engr. Am. Soc. Quality. Commd. 2nd lt. USAF, 1968, advanced through grades to lt. col., 1984, ret., 1993; quality mgr. Modern Techs. Corp., Beavercreek, Ohio, 1993—98; logistics mgr. Titan Corp., San Diego, 1998—2001; prof. mgmt. Def. Acquisition U., San Diego, 2001—. Cons. USAF, Edwards AFB, Calif., 1993—98. Home and Office: 503 Fifth St Coronado CA 92118

EDLES, GARY JOEL, lawyer; b. N.Y.C., Feb. 27, 1941; s. Allen Irving and Helen (Hurowitz) E.; m. Nadine Cohen, Feb. 15, 1973. BA, Queens Coll., 1962; JD, NYU, 1965; LLM, George Washington U., 1966, DJuridical Sci., 1975. Bar: N.Y. 1966, U.S. Ct. Appeals (D.C. cir.) 1970. Staff atty. Civil Aeronautics Bd., Washington, 1967-75, assoc. gen. coun., 1975-77, dep. gen. coun., 1977-80; dir. office of procs. Interstate Commerce Commn., Washington, 1980-81; administrv. appeals judge Nuclear Regulatory Commn., Washington, 1981-87; gen. coun. Administrv. Conf. U.S., Washington, 1987-95; fellow Am. U., 1995—. Faculty Dept. Justice Legal Edn. Inst., 1982-97; vis. prof. U. Sheffield, Eng., 1994, U. Hull, Eng., 1997—. Co-author: Federal Regulatory Process, 2d edit., 1989; contbr. articles to profl. jours. Mem. ABA, Fed. Bar Assn. (chmn. administrv. law sect. (1989-91). Home: 10 Keldgate Beverley HU17 8HY England E-mail: G.J.Edles@hull.ac.uk., Gedles@wcl.american.edu.

EDLICH, RICHARD FRENCH, biomedical engineering educator; b. N.Y.C., Jan. 19, 1939; MD, NYU, 1962; PhD, U. Minn., 1973. From instr. to assoc. prof. U. Va. Sch. Medicine, Charlottesville, 1971-76, prof. plastic surgery and biomed. engring., 1976-82, disting. prof. plastic and maxillofacial surgery and biomed. engring., 1983-96, Raymoon F. Morgan prof. plastic surgery and disting. prof. biomed. engring., 1996—2001. Dir. Emergency Med. Svc. and Burn Ctr., 1974-85; physician tech. adviser Bur. Emergency Svc., HEW, 1974-79; cons. Divsn. Health Manpower and Nat. Ctr. Health Svc. Rsch., 1977-79. Editor-in-chief: Jour. Long-Term Effects of Med. Implants. Recipient outstanding teaching award U. Va., 1989, Thomas Jefferson award, 1991, outstanding faculty award Commonwealth of Va. Coun. Higher Edn., 1989, 5th Ann. David Boyd Lectr. in Emergency Medicine, 2001. Mem. ACS, Soc. Univ. Surgeons, Am. Assn. Surg. Trauma, Am. Burn Assn. (Harvey Stuart Allen award 2000), Univ. Assn. Emergency Medicine, Am. Soc. Plastic and Reconstructive Surgeons, Soc. of Acad. Emergency Medicine, Coll. Emergency Physicians, Am. Surg. Assn. Achievements include research in the biology of wound repair and infection. Home and Office: 16155 New Jenne Lake Ct Beaverton OR 97006

EDLOW, KENNETH LEWIS, securities brokerage official; b. Washington, July 27, 1941; s. Ellis and Leonora (Kraft) Edlow; m. Mary Glanzrock, Dec. 19, 1970; children: Elizabeth, Brian. BS in Econ., U. Pa., 1963. Stockbroker Ferris & Co., Washington, 1963-69; various positions Bear, Stearns & Co., Inc., N.Y.C., 1969—; corp. sec. Bear Stearns Cos. Inc., 1987—. Pres Monterey Fund Inc; vp, secy Edlow Family Fund, Inc. Trustee Congregation Emanu-El, New York, NY, 1994—. Mem.: Am Numismatic Soc (trustee 1993—, treas. 2000). Avocations: fishing, numismatics. Home: 35 E 85th St New York NY 10028-0954 Office: Bear Stearns & Co Inc 383 Madison Ave New York NY 10179 E-mail: kedlow@bear.com.

EDLUND, LENA, finance educator; b. Seoul, Republic of Korea, June 5, 1967; m. Marcus Asplund, June 2, 1999. PhD, Stockholm Sch. Econ., 1996. Assoc. prof. Columbia U., NYC, 2002—. Office: Columbia U 420 W 118th St New York NY 10027

EDLUND, TIMOTHY WENDELL, management educator, consultant, researcher; b. Niagara Falls, N.Y., May 28, 1930; s. Sidney Wendell and Mary (Garlichs) E.; m. Patricia Johannsen, June 10, 1952; children: S. Rebecca, Stephen W. BSME, Cornell U., 1952; MS in Engring. Administrn., Case Inst. Tech., 1960; MBA, Boston U., 1984, D of Bus. Adminstrn., 1986. Registered profl. engr., N.Y., Ind., Wis. Field engr., rsch. engr. The Warner & Swasey Co., Cleve., 1955—61; facilities engr. Otis Elevator Co., Yonkers, NY, 1961—68; sr. assoc. Mfg. Sys., Milw., 1968—70; asst. to mfg. v.p. Perfex Inc., Milw., 1970—72; mgr. mfg. engring. Madison Industries, Smithfield, RI, 1972—75; chief mfg. engr. Energy Products Divsn. Gulf & Western, Warwick, RI, 1975—78; chief mfg. engr. Atwood & Morrill, Salem, Mass., 1978—81; vis. asst. prof. U. N.H., Durham, 1985—86; asst. prof. Loyola Coll., Balt., 1986—91; assoc. prof. strategic mgmt. Morgan State U., Balt., 1991—. Contbr. articles to profl. jours. Lt. j.g. USN, 1952-55. Recipient rsch. grant Thomas Walter Ctr., 1993, tchg. grant Shriver Ctr. of U. Md., 1996, rsch. grant Nat. Transp. Ctr., 1998, sabbatical rsch. grant, 2000. Fellow The Case Assn. (pres. 1991-93); mem. N.Am. Case Rsch. Assn. (v.p. 1996-97, pres.-elect 1997-98, pres. 1998-99, sec.-treas. 2001-02), Acad. Mgmt., Internat. Assn. for Bus. and Soc. (charter), World Assn. for Case Rsch. and Analysis. Mid - Atlantic Planning Assn. Episcopalian. Avocations: sailing, singing. Home: 16 Coldwater Ct Baltimore MD 21204-2443 Office: Morgan State U 1700 E Cold Spring Ln Baltimore MD 21251-0002 E-mail: tim.edlund@toad.net.

EDMARK, DAVID STANLEY, communications director; b. Oklahoma City, Aug. 2, 1951; s. Carl Bernard and Dorothy (Stacy) E. BJ, U. Mo., 1973; MA, U. Ark., 1993. Reporter Springdale (Ark.) News, 1974-78, State Jour.-Register, Springfield, Ill., 1978-79, Ark. Gazette, Little Rock, 1979-81; asst. dir. info. U. Ark., Fayetteville, 1981-84; city editor The Morning News, Springdale, Ark., 1984-95; comm. dir. Food Safety Consortium, U. Ark., 1995—. Mem. Coun. for Advancement and Support of Edn., 1981-84; bd. dirs. Fayetteville Open Channel TV, 1986-90, pres. bd., 1988. Named Ark. Journalist of Yr., Council for Advancement and Support of Edn., 1989. Mem. Sigma Delta Chi Soc. Profl. Journalists (pres. Ozarks chpt. 1977, 82), Agrl. Communicators in Edn., Pub. Rels. Soc. Am. (N.W. Ark. chpt. bd. dirs., accredited), Fayetteville Evening Lions Club. Presbyterian. Avocations: guitar, travel, reading, golf. Home: 220 E Cleburn St Fayetteville AR 72701-2109 Office: U Ark 110 Agriculture Bldg Fayetteville AR 72701 E-mail: dedmark@uark.edu.

EDMISTON, CHERYL LEE, educator, clergywoman; b. Newport, R.I., May 21, 1947; d. John Edward and Virginia Theresa (Fleming) E. BA, Wheaton Coll., 1969; MS, George Williams Coll., 1973; PhD, Christian Bible Coll., Rocky Mount, N.C., 1986. Cert. tchr., Ill.; ordained to ministry Full Gospel Ch., 1990. Tchr. Cmty. Consol. Sch. Dist. 59, Elk Grove Village, Ill., 1969—2003. Founder, dir. Children of King Ministries, Elk Grove Village, 1978—; hostess, producer TV show Lift Jesus Higher, 1980—, radio show A Vision for Our Children, 1982—; lectr. in field. Author: He Owns the Cadillacs on a Thousand Hills, 1978, A Vision for our Children, 1980, 3rd edit., 1994, Bring Them into His Courts, 1985, 2d edit., 1995, Breaking Spiritual Dullness, 1986, A Vision for Children: Spanish edit. Una Visan Para Nuestros Niños, 1988; producer edn. videos, LP record albums. Founder dir. Father's House for Inner City Children, 1988—. Recipient Angel award Religion in Media, 1988-91, 93, Silver Angel award, 1992, 94-2000, Silver Angel award in radio, 1998, 99. Office: Children of King Ministries PO Box 92073 Elk Grove Village IL 60009-2073

EDMISTON, MARK MORTON, publishing company executive; b. Yonkers, N.Y., July 9, 1943; s. Marcus Morton and Josephine (Brown) E.; m. Lisa Mary Pustorino, Aug. 28, 1965; children: Ann Kathleen, Laura Mary. BA, Wesleyan U., 1966. Circulation mgr. Life mag., N.Y.C., until 1969, circulation and mktg. dir. Tokyo, 1969-70; circulation dir. Saturday Rev., Inc., 1971-73; circulation dir. internat. edits. Newsweek, Inc., 1973-76, pub., 1976-78, pres., 1978-79, corp. exec. v.p., 1979-81, chmn. and pres., 1981-86; pres. TVSM Inc., N.Y.C., 1987-91; exec. v.p. Times Mirror Mag., N.Y.C., 1991-92; co-chmn. The Jordan Edmiston Group Inc., N.Y.C., 1992—99; mng. dir. Admedia Ptnrs., Inc., N.Y.C., 1998—99. Founder Civilization: The Mag. of the Libr. of Congress, Univ. Bus. Mag. Trustee emeritus Wesleyan U.; trustee Children's Aid Soc. of N.Y., Cmty. Svc. Soc. N.Y. Office: Admedia Ptnrs 444 Madison Ave New York NY 10022-6903

EDMO, JEAN UMIOKALANI, artist, poet; b. L.A., Apr. 12, 1942; d. Lemuel Kanekikawaiola Cutter and Nancy James Watson; m. Edward McCleary Edmo, Mar. 17, 1984 (dec. Mar. 1996); 8 stepchildren. Grad., Comml. Art Sch., San Francisco, 1963. Author: (poetry) Songs of Life and Love, 2000, rev. edit., 2002, (short stories) Some Passions Never Die, 2002; one-woman shows include nine oil, acrylic and mixed media landscapes., Photographs in One Woman Shows, Chile, 1962; Nat. Photo Book. Nominee Poet of Yr., Internat. Poetry Guild, 2001; recipient Editors award, 2002, Outstanding Achievment cup, Internat. Soc. Poets, Merit Award medal. Green Party. Episcopalian. Avocation: walking, gardening, making craft wreaths, birdwatching.

EDMONDS, ALBERT J. career officer; b. Columbus, Ga., Jan. 17, 1942; m. Jacquelyn Y. McDaniel; children: Gia, Sheri, Alicia. BS Chemistry, Morris Brown Coll., 1964, DSc (hon.), 1990; MA Counseling Psychology, Hampton U., 1969; grad., Air War Coll., 1980. Data systems officer Keesler AFB, Miss., 1966; inspection team chief, dir. emergency mission support Pacific Comm. Area Hickam AFB, Hawaii, 1969; chief ops. 2083d Comm. Squadron Takhli Royal Thai AFB, Thailand, 1969-72; action officer Directorate Command, Control and Comm. Hdqs. USAF, Washington, 1973; head Commercial Comm. Policy Office Defense Comm. Agy., Washington, 1975; dir. comm. electronics Strategic Air Command's 3d Air divsn., commander 27th comm. squadron Andersen AFB, Guam, 1977; chief joint matters group, Directorate Command, Control, Telecom. Office Dep. Chief Staff Plans and Ops. Hdqs. USAF, Washington, 1980-83, dir. plans and prgrams for asst. chief info. systems, 1983; asst. dep. chief staff comm. and electronics, vice commander Tactical Comm. divsn. Hdqs. Tactical Air Command Langley AFB, 1983-84; dep. chief staff comm.-computer systems, commander Tactical Comm. divsn. AF Comm. Command Langley AFB, 1985-88; dir. Command and Control, Comm. and Computer Systems Directorate, U.S. Ctrl. Command MacDill AFB, Fla., 1988; asst. chief staff, systems for command, control, comm. and computers AF Hdqs., Washington, 1989-90, dep. chief staff, command, control, comm. and computers, 1990-91, vice dir. command, control, comm. and computer systems directorate, dep. dir. Defense-Wide C4 support, 1991; lt. gen., dir. command, control, comm., computer systems directorate Joint Staff Dept. Defense, Washington, 1993; dir. Def. Info. Sys. Agy. and mgr. Nat. Comm. Sys., Arlington, Va., 1994—98; chmn & CEO Electronic Data Systems, Plano, Tex., 1998—. Recipient Defense Superior Svc. medal, Legion of Merit, Meritorious Svc. medal with two oak leaf clusters, AF COmmendation medal with three oak leaf clusters. Mem. Kappa Alpha Psi, Kappa Delta Pi, Armed Forces Comm. and Electronics Assn. (life). Office: Electronic Data Systems 5400 Legacy Dr Plano TX 75024

EDMONDS, ANNE CAREY, librarian; b. Penang, Malaysia, Dec. 19, 1924; d. William John and Neil (Carey) E. Student, U. Reading, England, 1942-44; BA, Barnard Coll., 1948; MSLS, Columbia U., 1950; MA, Johns Hopkins U., 1959; postgrad., Western Res. U., 1960-61; LHD, Mount Holyoke Coll., 1994. With War Damage Commn., London, 1944-46; children's asst. Enoch Pratt Free Libr., Balt., 1948-49; reference libr. Sch. Bus. Adminstrn., CCNY, 1950-51; reference libr. then asst. libr. readers' svcs. Goucher Coll., Balt., 1951-60; exchange reference libr. European svcs. libr. BBS, London, 1955; instr. Sch. L.S., Syracuse U., summer 1960; libr. Douglass Coll., Rutgers U., New Brunswick, N.J., 1961-64, instr., summer 1962, fall 1963; libr. Mt. Holyoke Coll., 1964-94. Vis. libr. U. North, Turfloop, South Africa, 1976-77; mem. libr. vis. com. Wheaton Coll., Norton, Mass., 1978-92; mem. local systems adv. group Online Computer Libr. Ctr., Inc., 1984-87, mem. adv. com. on coll. and univ. librs., 1988-89. Author: A Memory Book: Mount Holyoke College, 1834-1987, 1988 (with Gai Carpenter and others) Computing Strategies in Liberal Arts Colleges, 1992. Mem. South Hadley (Mass.) Bicentennial Com., 1975—76; mem. accreditation teams Middle State Assn. Colls. and Secondary Schs., 1963—94, New Eng. Assn. Schs. and Colls., 1986—94; exec. com. New Eng. Libr. Info. Network, 1974—76, 1979—85, chmn., 1982—84; mem. Adv. Commn. Historic Deerfield, 1975—81, 1986—94; trustee Ctr. for Maine Contemporary Art, Rockport, Maine, 2001—; bd. dirs. U.S. Book Exch., 1973—76, 1980—83. Mem. AAUW (bd. dirs. main chpt. 1998—), ALA, Assn. Coll. Rsch. Librs. (pres. 1970-71, chmn. constn. and bylaws com. New Eng. chpt. 1975-76, pres. New Eng. chpt. 1983-84). E-mail: ACE13@midcoast.com.

EDMONDS, DEAN STOCKETT, JR., physicist, educator, director; b. N.Y.C., Dec. 24, 1924; s. Dean Stockett and Mary Watkins (Arms) Edmonds; m. Mary Louise Wilson, July 28, 1951 (dec. May 1978); children: Dean Stockett III, Louis Round Wilson, Ann Helene Edmonds Mahoney, Elizabeth V. Casey; m. Wendy Nickerson Adams, Nov. 7, 1993. BS, MIT, 1950, PhD, 1958; MA, Princeton U., 1952. Co-founder, v.p., dir. Nuclide Corp., 1958-65; asst. prof. physics Coll. Liberal Arts Boston U., 1961-67, assoc. prof. physics, 1967-83, prof. physics, 1983-91, prof. emeritus, 1991—; co-founder, pres., chmn. Tachisto Laser Sys., Inc., 1971-85; dir., chief sci. adv. bd. Gen. Ionex Inc., 1974-85; regional v.p., dir. Nat. Aeronautic Assn., 1988—. Vis prof physics Univ Western Ont, London, 1972—74; research fellow Harvard Univ, Cambridge, Mass., 1959—61; guest physics dept MIT, Cambridge, Mass., 1959—61. Author: (book) Novel Experiments in Physics II, 1975; author: (with B Cioffari) Experiments in College Physics, 6th ed, 1978, Cioffari's Experiments in College Physics, 7th ed, 1983, Cioffari's Experiments in College Physics, 10th ed, 1997; co-editor: Experiments in Physics for General Physics Courses Without Calculus, 1968, Experiments in Physics for General Physics Courses With Calculus, 1968; contbr. articles to profl jours. Master sgt U.S. Army, 1943—47, ETO, PTO. Mem.: IEEE, Am. Assn. Physics Tchrs. (Spec Merit Award), Am Phys. Soc., Cosmos Club Washington. Achievements include research in molecular beams leading to cesium atomic clock, the present internat. time standard; development of the racetrack microtron accelerator for cancer therapy. Avocations: amateur radio, restoring antique aircraft and sports cars, sport flying, opera, building high fidelity systems. Home: 1019 Spyglass Ln Naples FL 34102-7734 Office: Boston U Dept Physics 590 Commonwealth Ave Boston MA 02215-2521

EDMONDS, IVY GORDON, writer; b. Frost, Tex., Feb. 15, 1917; s. Ivy Gordon and Delia Louella (Shumate) E.; m. Reiko Mimura, July 12, 1956; 1 dau., Annette. Student pub. schs. Pub. rels. mgr. Northrop Corp., Anaheim, Calif., 1968-79, indsl. editor, Hawthorne, Calif., 1979-86. Freelance writer; author books including: Solomon In Kimono, 1957, Ooka the Wise, 1961, The Bounty's Boy, 1963, Hollywood RIP, 1963, Joel of the Hanging Gardens, 1966, Trickster Tales, 1966, Taiwan-the Other China, 1971, The Possible Impossibles of Ikkyo The Wise, 1971, The Magic Man, 1972, Mao's Long March, 1973, Motorcycling for Beginners, 1973, China's Red Rebel: Mao Tse-Tung, 1973, Micronesia, 1974, Pakistan, Land of Mystery, Tragedy and Courage, 1974, Automotive Tuneups for Beginners, 1974, Ethiopia, 1975, The Magic Makers, 1976, The Shah of Iran, 1976, Allah's Oil: Mid-East Petroleum, 1976, Second Sight, 1977, Motorcycle Racing for Beginners, 1977, Islam, 1977, The Mysteries of Troy, 1977, Big U Universal in the Silent Days, Buddhism, 1978, D.D. Home, 1978, Bicycle Motocross, 1979, Hinduism, 1979, Girls Who Talked to Ghosts, 1979, The Magic Brothers, 1979, (with William H. Gebhardt) Broadcasting for Beginners, 1980, (with Reiko Mimura) The Oscar Directors, 1980, The Mysteries of Homer's Greeks, 1981, The Kings of Black Magic, 1981, Funny Car Racing for Beginners, 1982, The Magic Dog, 1982; author textbooks: (with Ronald Gonzales) Understanding Your Car, 1975, Introduction to Welding, 1975; also author pulp and soft cover fiction and nonfiction under names of Gene Cross and Gary Gordon and publishers house names. With USAAF, 1940-45, USAF, 1946-63. Decorated D.F.C., Air medals, Bronze Star. Home: 5801 Shirl St Cypress CA 90630-3326

EDMONDS, JAMES PATRICK (JIM EDMONDS), professional baseball player; b. Fullerton, Calif., June 27, 1970; Grad., H.S., Calif. Outfielder Calif. Angels (now Anaheim Angels), 1993—99, St. Louis Cardinals, 2000—. Named to All-Star Team, Am. League, 1995. Office: St Louis Cardinals 250 Stadium Plz Saint Louis MO 63102-1722

EDMONDS, MARY PATRICIA, biological sciences educator; b. Racine, Wis., May 7, 1922; d. Millard Samuel and Sarah (Gibbons) E. BA, Milw.-Downer Coll., 1943; MA, Wellesley (Mass.) Coll., 1945; PhD, U. Pa., 1951; DSc (hon.), Lawrence U., 1983. Instr. Wellesley Coll., 1945-46; postdoctoral fellow U. Ill., Urbana, 1950-52, U. Wis., Madison, 1952-55; rsch. assoc. Montefiore Hosp., Pitts., 1955-65; asst. prof. U. Pitts., 1965-71, assoc. prof., 1971-76, prof., 1976—92, prof. emeritus, 1992—. Mem. molecular biology study sect. NIH, Bethesda, Md., 1974-78. Contbr. articles to profl. jours. Recipient Woman of Yr. in Sci. award Chatham Coll., 1986; Rsch. Career Devel. award NIH, 1962-71, rsch. grantee, 1962-91. Mem.: NAS, Am. Soc. Biochemistry and Molecular Biology. Office: U Pitts Dept Biol Sci Pittsburgh PA 15260

EDMONDS, MICHAEL DARNELL, music educator, educator; b. May 19, 1960; s. William Thomas and Virginia (Haskins) E.; m. Janet Denise Wyche. BS, Norfolk State U., 1987. Minister of music Christian Charities Deliverance, Wakefield, Va., 1980-92; sale specialist B.D. Laderberg and Son, Inc., Suffolk, Va., 1989-91; sales specialist T.J. Maxx, Chesapeake, Va., 1991-97; reporter Maxxline for T.J. Maxx, Chesapeake, 1991-98; customer svc. rep. Apac Telesvcs., Newport News, Va., 1996-99; customer care Nextel Comms. Hampton Rds., Hampton, Va., 1999—2001, TeleTech Holdings-Nextel Comms., Hampton, 2001—. Music dir. First Calvary Handbell Choir, Norfolk, Va., 1982-83, Norfolk State U. Gospel Choir, 1984-85, Little Gilfield Bapt. Ch. Gospel Choir, Ivor, Va., 1988; music min. Full Gospel Ch. of Deliverance, Norfolk, 1986-87; singer with I. Sherman Greene Chorale, Norfolk, 1984-88, Covenant Presbyn. Choir, 1984-85, 87-88, The Brown Delegation of Ivor, 1987-89; mem. Norfolk State U. Concert Choir and Chamber Emsemble, 1983-87; mus. dir. pageant Shiloh Bapt. Ch., Zuni, 1988; founder, dir. Interdenominational Singers, Norfolk, 1984-85, New Horizon Singers of Ivor, 1987-89; choir, vocal coach, tchr. piano Ctr. State Theatre, Norfolk, 1985-87; performer sixth ann. Am. Negro Spiritual Festival; tchg. asst. Jr. Music Program Norfolk State U., 1983-84; sales specialist So. Food Stores, Windsor, Va., 1988-89; tchr. asst. specialist Southampton Sch. Sys., 1987-89; customer svc. rep. T.J. Maxx, Jallal and Norfolk, Va., 1985-87. Editor Chrisitn Charity Newsletter, Wakefield, 1980-90, composer choral gospel arrangements. Mem. Choir of Joy, Suffolk, Va., 1991; mem. Crusade choir St. Mark Ch. of Deliverance, Portsmouth, Va., 1993, sr. sunday sch. asst. tchr., 1991-92, club staff mem., praise and worship leader; mem. Norfolk State U. Chamber Ensemble; mem. nat. nomination com. Outstanding Young Women of Am., 1997, Outstanding Young Men of Am., 1998. Mem. Music Educators Nat. Conf., Intercollegiate Music Assn. Avocations: photography, computers. Home: 1038 Cherokee Rd Apt H Portsmouth VA 23701-1858 Office: Tele Tec Holdings-Nextel Comms 400 Butler Farm Rd Hampton VA 23666-1577 E-mail: mike7edmonds@yahoo.com.

EDMONDS, THOMAS ANDREW, legal association administrator; b. Jackson, Miss., July 5, 1938; BA, Miss. Coll., 1962; LL.B., Duke U., 1965. Bar: Fla. 1965, Va. 1981. Pvt. practice law, Orlando, Fla., 1965-66; assoc. prof. law U. Miss., Oxford, 1966-70; assoc. prof.law Fla. State U., Tallahassee, 1970-74, prof., 1974-77; dean Sch. Law, U. Richmond (Va.), 1977-87, U. Miss. Sch. Law, University, 1987-89; exec. dir. Va. State Bar, Richmond, 1989—. Vis. assoc. prof. Duke U., 1968-69; vis. prof. McGeorge Sch. Law of the Univ. of the Pacific, 1975-76. Served with USMC, 1957-60. Office: VA State Bar 707 E Main St Ste 1500 Richmond VA 23219-2800

EDMONDS, VELMA MCINNIS, nursing educator; b. NYC, Feb. 17, 1940; d. Walter Lee and Eva Doris (Grant) McInnis; children: Stephen Clay, Michelle Louise. Diploma, Charity Hosp. Sch. Nursing, New Orleans, 1961; BSN, Med. Coll. Ga., 1968; MSN, U. Ala., Birmingham, 1980; D of Nursing Sci., La. State U., 2001. Staff nurse Ochsner Found. Hosp., New Orleans, 1961-63, 1987—, clin. educator, 1987-89; staff nurse Suburban Hosp., Bethesda, Md., 1963-65; asst. DON svc., dir. staff devel. Providence Hosp., Mobile, Ala., 1967-70; staff nurse MICU U. So. Ala. Med. Ctr., Mobile, 1980-82, clin. nurse specialist, nutrition/metabolic support, 1982-84; instr., coord., BSN completion program Northwestern State U. Coll. Nursing, Pineville, La., 1984-86; head nurse So. Bapt. Hosp., New Orleans, 1986-87; instr. nursing La. State U. Health Sci. Ctr., New Orleans, 1989-91, asst. prof. nursing, 1991—; clin. coord. Transitional Hosp. Corp., 1994-95; cons., vis. prof. U. of Guam Coll. of Nursing and Health Scis., 2002—. Gov.-apptd. mem. La. Bd. Examiners in Dietetics and Nutrition, 1990-98, sec.-treas., 1996-97; cons. on internat. health and nursing edn., 1992—; rschr. with recently immigrated Honduran women; cons., faculty U. Guam, 2002—; presenter in field. Advisor Hispanic C. of C., New Orleans; adv. bd. Cmty. Vietnamese Outreach Program, Meth. Hosp., New Orleans; chmn. Silent Auction, New Orleans Dollars for Scholars Found., 2000; founding bd. dirs., edn. coord. Orgn. Health and Med. Profession Women. Recipient Excellence in Nursing group award Ochsner Fedn. Hosp., New Orleans, 1987, cert. Merit Tuberculosis Assn. Greater New Orleans, 1961. Mem. ANA, Nat. Soc. Nutrition Edn., La. State Nurses' Assn. (dist. 7), Am. Soc. Parenteral and Enteral Nutrition, La. State Soc. Parenteral and Enteral Nutrition (program and edn. coms.), Mobile Area Nonvolitional Nutrition Support Assn. (past pres.), Transcultural Nursing Soc., Soc. Nutrition Edn., Orgn. Health & Med. Profl. Women (Guam & We. Pacific region founding bd. dirs., edn. coord.), Sigma Theta Tau. Office: LSU Health Scis Ctr Sch of Nursing 1900 Gravier St New Orleans LA 70112 E-mail: vedmonds@ite.net.

EDMONDS, WILLIAM FLEMING, retired engineering and construction company executive; b. Birmingham, Ala., June 11, 1923; s. Henry M. and Mary (Fleming) E.; m. Joan McCoy, Aug. 7, 1953; children: Henry Morris, Bryson Glass BSCE, Va. Mil. Inst., 1948; DSc (hon.), U. Ala., Birmingham, 1986. Former registered profl. engr., Ala., Ark., Calif., Fla., Ga., Ind., Mich., N.C., Tenn., Va. Project mgr. Rust Engring. & Harbert Constrn., Birmingham, 1953-58; v.p., chief engr. Rust Engring. Co., Birmingham, 1958-66, sr. v.p. Pitts., 1969-72; pres. Coppee-Rust, Brussels, Belgium, 1967-69; pres., chief exec. officer BE&K Inc., Birmingham, 1972-83, chmn., 1983-89; ret. Chmn., bd. dirs. Presbyn. Retirement Homes; former trustee Ala. Symphony, Birmingham, 1982-93; bd. dirs. So. Rsch. Inst., Alys Stephens Ctr.; hon. mem. pres.'s coun. U. Ala., Birmingham, 1980-92, pres., 1985, former bd. dirs. Rsch. Found., Energen, Regions Bank. Capt. U.S. Army, 1943-46, 51-53, ETO, PTO, Korea. Decorated knight Order of Crown (Belgium); named Engr. of Yr., Engring. Coun., Birmingham, 1983, So. Profl. Engrs., Montgomery, Ala., 1983, Citizen of Yr., Young Men's Bus. Club Birmingham, 1988; inducted into Ala. Engring. Hall of Fame, 1992, Ala. Acad. Honor, 1991; recipient Disting. Eagle Scout award, 1996. Fellow ASCE, Newcomen Soc.; mem. NSPE. Lodges: Rotary, Redstone. Republican. Presbyterian. Avocations: golf, skiing, tennis. Home: 2600 Arlington Ave S Apt 60 Birmingham AL 35205-4160

EDMONDSON, FRANK KELLEY, retired astronomer; b. Milw., Aug. 1, 1912; s. Clarence Edward and Marie (Kelley) E.; m. Margaret Russell, Nov. 24, 1934 (dec. Jan. 1999); children: Margaret Jean Olson, Frank K. Jr. AB, Ind. U., 1933, A.M., 1934; PhD, Harvard U., 1937. Lawrence fellow Lowell Obs., 1933-34, research asst., 1934-35; Agassiz fellow Harvard Obs., 1935-36, asst., 1936-37; instr. astronomy Ind. U., Bloomington, 1937-4O, asst. prof., 1940-45, assoc. prof., 1945-48, prof., 1949-83, prof. emeritus, 1983—, dir. Kirkwood Obs., 1945-78; dir. Goethe Link Obs., 1948-78, chmn. astronomy dept., 1944-78; research asso. McDonald Obs., 1944-83. Observations of asteroids in cooperation with Internat. Astron. Union's Minor Planet Center; statistical adviser to Prof. Alfred Kinsey for gall wasp and human sex behavior rsch., 1939-56; program dir. for astronomy NSF, 1956-57; acting dir. Cerro Tololo Inter-Am. Obs., 1966; lectr. astron. socs.; mem. adv. bd. Lowell Obs., 1988-2000. Author: AURA and its US National Observatories, 1997; contbr. numerous papers to Am., Brit., German astron. jours. Decorated Order of Merit Chile, 1964; recipient Meritorious Pub. Service award NSF, 1983, Disting. Alumni Svc. award Ind. U., 1997; honored with Daniel Kirkwood (1814-95) in Ho. Resolution No. 58 adopted by Ind. 109th Gen. Assembly, First Session, 1995. Fellow AAAS (chmn. sect. D, v.p. 1962); mem. Assn. Univs. Research in Astronomy (v.p. 1957-61, pres. 1962-65, dir. 1957-83, cons./historian 1983—), Can. Astron. Soc., Am. Astron. Soc. (treas. 1954-75, 70 yr. attendance award

2001), Astron. Soc. Pacific, Internat. Astron. Union (chmn. U.S. nat. com. 1963-64, v.p. commn. minor planets, comets and satellites 1967-70, pres. 1970-73), Ind. Acad. Science, Am. Mus. Natural History (corr. mem.), Friends of Ctr. for History of Physics (exec. com. 2001—), Explorers Club, Phi Beta Kappa, Sigma Xi. Home: 716 S Woodlawn Ave Bloomington IN 47401-4936 Office: Ind U Dept Astronomy 319 Swain Hall West 727 E 3rd St Bloomington IN 47405-7105 *President Calvin Coolidge was right when he said: "Nothing in the world can take the place of persistence.".*

EDMONDSON, FRANK KELLEY, JR., lawyer, legal administrator; b. Newport, R.I., Aug. 27, 1936; s. Frank Kelley Sr. and Margaret (Russell) E.; m. Christiane Semirot, Mar. 5, 1959 (div. Sept. 1969); children: Mylene Anne, Yvonne Marie, Catherine May; m. Elaine Sueko Kaneshiro, Aug. 17, 1970 (div. June 1992); m. Karen Louise Bishop, Feb. 27, 1993 (div. Feb. 1996). BBA, Ind. U., 1958; MBA, So. Ill. U., 1978; JD, U. Puget Sound, 1982. Bar: Wash. 1982, U.S. Dist. Ct. (we. dist.) Wash. 1983. Commd. 2d lt. USAF, 1959, advanced through grades to maj., 1969, ret., 1979; contracts specialist Wash. State Lottery, Olympia, 1982-85, asst. contracts adminstr., 1985-87; contracts officer 1989 Washington Centennial Commn., 1987-90; fin. svc. officer Office of the Adminstr. for the Cts., 1990-92; contracts officer, office of adminstr. for the cts. State of Wash. Supreme Ct., Olympia, 1992-99. Mem. Seattle U. Sch. Law, Law Alumni Soc. Nat. Coun., 1997—, scholarship com. Wash. State Employees Credit Union, 1995-2001. Bd. dirs. Friends of Chambers Creek, Tacoma, 1981-90; mem. pro bono panel Puget Sound Legal Assistance Found., Olympia, 1985-90; mock trial program com. Youth and Govt. YMCA, 1994-96. Mem. Wash. State Bar Assn. (spl. dist. counsel 1993-95), Thurston County Bar Assn., Ind. U. Soc. Advanced Study, Govt. Lawyers Bar Assn. (sec. 1985-86, 1st v.p. 1986-87, pres. 1987-89, liaison to Wash. State Bar Assn. 1989-93), Beta Gamma Sigma, Coll. Club. Home: 6600 Miner Dr SW Tumwater WA 98512-7282 E-mail: fkedmon@aol.com.

EDMONDSON, JACQUELINE, education educator; b. Harrisburg, Pa., Jan. 11, 1967; d. James Russell and Betty Jane Zehring; m. Michael Clarence Edmondson, Apr. 27, 1991; children: Jacob Ellsworth, Luke Michael. BS in Elem. and Kindergarten Edn., Pa. State U., 1989, MS in Ednl. Psychology, 1996, PhD in Curriculum and Instrn., 1999. Cert. Elem. Tchr. Pa. State U., 1989, Reading Specialist Pa. State U., 1996. Asst. prof. edn. U. of Minn., Morris, 1998—2000; asst. prof. edn., lang. and literacy edn. Pa. State U., 2000—. Author: (book) America Reads: A Critical Policy Analysis, Prairie Town: Redefining Rural Life in the Age of Globalization. Mem.: Nat. Reading Conf., Am. Ednl. Rsch. Assn., Nat. Coun. of Tchrs. of English, Internat. Reading Assn. Office: Pa State U 265 Chamber Bldg University Park PA 16802

EDMONDSON, JAMES LARRY, federal judge; b. Jasper, Ga., July 14, 1947; s. James George and Ruth (Holcomb) Edmondson; m. Eugenia Dettelbach (div. 1992); children: Kelley Eugenia, Alexandra Lisa. BA, Emory U., 1968; JD, U. Ga., 1971; LLM in Jud. Process, U. Va., 1990. Bar: Ga. 1971. Law clk. to Hon. Sidney O. Smith U.S. Dist. Ct. (no. dist.), Gainesville, Ga., 1971—73; instr. in trial practice U. Ga. Sch. Law, Athens, 1975—84; assoc. Webb, Fowler, Tanner & Edmondson, Lawrenceville, Ga., 1973—76, ptnr., 1976—81; mem. Tennant, Davidson & Edmondson, PC, Lawrenceville, 1982—86; judge U.S. Ct. Appeals (11th cir.), Atlanta, 1986—2002; chief judge, 2002—. Instr. U. Ga. Sch. Law, 1975—84. Contbr. articles to profl. jours. Trustee Inst. Continuing Legal Edn., 1980—84. Mem.: Fellows Ga. Bar Found. (charter), Gwinnett County Bar Assn (pres. 1980—81), State Bar Ga. (bd. govs. 1982—86), Old War Horse Lawyers Club, Order of Barristers, Pi Sigma Alpha. Episcopalian. Office: US Ct Appeals 11th Circuit 56 Forsyth St NW Rm 416 Atlanta GA 30303-2205*

EDMONDSON, JOANNE HOLT, counselor, educator; b. Byron, Ga., Oct. 1, 1940; d. William Joseph and Frances Orelia Holt; m. Gerald Gelon Edmondson, Aug. 23, 1958; children: Sheree, Gerald G. Jr. BS, Tift Coll., 1969; MEd, North Ga. Coll., 1980; PhD, Ga. State U., 1993. Tchr. Bibb County (Ga.) Bd. Edn., Macon, 1969-73; migrant edn. tchr./coord. North Ga. Migrant Edn. Services, Dahlonega and Canton, 1973-80; tchr. 4th grade Lumpkin County Elem. Sch., Dahlonega, 1980-85; sch. counselor Lumpkin County Mid. Sch., Dahlonega, 1985-2000; counselor Cornerstones Counseling Ctr., Cleveland, Ga., 2000—. Adj. prof. North Ga. Coll. and State U., Dahlonega, 1994—, Ga. State U., Atlanta, 1999—; cons. Family Connection, Dahlonega, 1990-2000, Interagy. Coun., Dahlonega, 1992-2000, Big Rock Clinic, Suches, Ga., 1998-2001, Adolescent and Family counseling Svcs., Gainesville, 2000—. Author: The Effects of Tutoring and Counseling At-risk Students, 1993; contbr. articles to profl. jours. Mem. Am. Counseling Assn., Am. Sch. counselor Assn., Am. Assn. Christian Counselors, Ga. Sch. Counselor Assn., Kappa Delta Pi, Chi Sigma Iota. Baptist. Avocations: piano, walking, gardening, cooking, family. Home: 365 Cloudland Rd N Dahlonega GA 30533

EDMONDSON, JOHN RICHARD, lawyer, pharmaceutical manufacturing company executive; b. N.Y.C., Mar. 1, 1927; s. Richard Emil and Josephine (Schroeter) E.; m. Rozanne Hume, Oct. 30, 1954; children: Lisa M., Kate H., Timothy H., Nicholas D., Julia N. AB, Georgetown U., 1950; LL.B., Columbia U., 1953. Bar: N.Y. 1953. Assoc. atty. Winthrop, Stimson, Putnam & Roberts, N.Y.C., 1953-59; with Bristol-Myers Co., N.Y.C., 1959—; asst. sec. Bristol-Myers Squibb Co., N.Y.C., 1960-69, sec., 1969-74, v.p., 1974-80, gen. counsel, 1977-89, sr. v.p., 1980-92; cons., 1992-94; ret., 1994. Served with AUS, 1945-47. Mem. ABA, Assn. Bar City N.Y., Univ. Club, Lake Waramaug Country Club, Longboat Key Club, Honourable Co. of Edinburgh Golfers. Home: 43 Old Stilson Hill Rd New Milford CT 06776-5413 E-mail: caux@aol.com.

EDMONDSON, KEITH HENRY, retired chemical company executive; b. Wheaton, Ill., May 16, 1924; s. Edwin Ray and Mildred Lorraine (Henry) E.; m. Peggy Eleanor Wood, Sept. 22, 1945; children— Robert Earl, Kris E., John David, Keith Clark. BS, Purdue U., 1948, MS, 1949. With Upjohn Co., Kalamazoo, Mich., 1949-86, exec. v.p. internat. div., 1962-67, v.p., gen. mgr. chem. div., 1967-86; exec. dir. Stryker Ctr., 1986-90; prof. Kalamazoo Coll., 1986-90; dir. Career Devel. Ctr., Kalamazoo Coll., 1990-94; retired, 1994—. Mem. Kalamazoo Bd. Edn., 1958-62, pres., 1962. Served to 1st lt. USAAF, 1942-45. Decorated D.F.C. with oak leaf cluster, Air medal with 6 oak leaf clusters. Mem. Internat. Isocyanate Inst. (pres. 1976), Kalamazoo C. of C. (v.p. 1973), Kalamazoo Mgmt. Assn. (pres. 1957), Am. Inst. Chem. Engrs., Am. Chem. Soc., Tau Beta Pi, Sigma Xi, Phi Lambda Upsilon. Republican. Methodist. Home: 8565 W H Ave Kalamazoo MI 49009-7516 Office: Kalamazoo Coll 1200 Academy St Kalamazoo MI 49006-3268 E-mail: edmond@iserv.net.

EDMONDSON, LINDA LOUISE, optometrist; b. Wyandotte, Mich., Dec. 11, 1947; d. Richard Eugene and Mildred Louise (Horste) Weaver; m. William Edmondson II, June 1, 1969. BA, Ohio Wesleyan U., 1969; AM, Ind. U., 1971; BS, Pa. Coll. Optometry, 1975, OD, 1977. Assoc. instr. Ind. U., Bloomington, 1967-72; editor biol. abstracts Biosis Info. Svcs., Phila., 1972-73; pvt. practice pvt. practice, Bluefield, W.Va., 1977-84; prof. Northeastern State U. Coll. Optometry, Tahlequah, Okla., 1984—. Referee Jour. of Am. Optometric Assn., 1988—, Optometry and Vision Sci., 1990—. Editor: Eye and Vision Conditions in the American Indian, 1990; contbr. articles to profl. jours. Approved arranger Sweet Adelines Internat.; active Okla. Jubilee Chorus. Mem. Am. Acad. Optometry, Am. Optometric Assn., Okla. Profl. Country Dance Assn., Sweet Adelines Internat., Cherokee County Soc. for Prevention of Cruelty to Animals, Beta Sigma Kappa. Avocations: piano, arranging barbershop music, computer music. Home: PO Box 871 Tahlequah OK 74465-0871 Office: NSU Coll of Optometry Tahlequah OK 74464

EDMONDSON, MICHAEL HERMAN, secondary school educator; b. Lafayette, Ala., Aug. 9, 1954; s. Herman L. and M. Ruth (Hurley) E. BSEd in Chemistry and, Edn., Columbus (Ga.) Coll., 1978, MS in Gen. Sci., 1986, Specialist in Edn., Sci., 1990; PhD in Sci. Edn., Auburn U., 2001. Cert. tchr. sci. edn. T-7, chemistry, tchr. support, curriculum and adminstrn. L-7. Tchr. sci., chemistry and physics William H. Spencer H.S., 1980-94; tchr. phys. sci., chemistry and physics Hardaway H.S., Columbus, Ga., 1995, 1997—2002; lead tchr. sci. tech., chair dept. Carver H.S.; lead flight dir. Ga. Space Sci. Ctr.; lead sci. tchr., engring. magnet coord. Northside H.S., 2002—. Staff devel. instr. computer course Muscogee County Sch. Dist., 1987-90; part-time lab. instr. Columbus Coll., summers, 1988, 89, organizer, tchr. summer chemistry program for h.s. students, summer 1989, part-time instr., 1990-93, Ext. in LaGrange, 1994; instr. Columbus Coll. Youth Acad., 1993; instr. KIDS Club, Ga. Inst. Tech., 1993, Workshop for Middle Sch. Tchrs., Auburn U., 1993, 94, summer programs for engring. students Ga. Inst. Tech., 2002—; project reviewer chemistry and physics edn. NSF, Washington, 1990; head tchr. sci./tech. Magnet Sch. Program, Carver H.S. Planning Team, 1991; advisor sci., math., integrated tech. magnet sch. program Dimon Elem. Sch., 1993; developer chemistry camp ages 11-14 Columbus Coll. Continuing Edn. Ctr., 1994; tchr. rep. Muscogee County Sch. Dist.; inst. Columbus State U., part-time 1998—; lead flight dir. Coca-Cola Space Sci. Ctr., 1994-97; planner magnet program Carver H.S., 1990-92; planner engring. and architecture magnet program Northside H.S., 2002. Co-author: Atomic Structure and the Periodic Table: A Resource Book for Teachers, 1987, Chemistry for the Health Sciences, Part 1: Inorganic chemistry, 1988, Part 2: Organic Chemistry, 1988; contbr. numerous articles to profl. jours.; writer numerous sci. curriculums; contbr. to America Online Edn. Librs., Compuserve's Education+ and Science/Math+ Forums' Librs., FCClient Bull. Bd. Svc.: Education, Debates and Hypercard Librs., 1994, lectr. in field. Vol. Ft Benning Inf. Mus., 1984; reader's adv. coun. Ledger-Enquirer newspapers, 1989, chmn., 1986-89; bd. dirs. Springer Theater Co., 1986-87, 88-90, Springer Children's Theatre, 1986-89, sec., 1987-89, mailing list organizer, 1986-89, nominating com., 1988; participant Alzheimer's Memory Walk, 1994; originator Christmas Stocking and Coloring Book project for Housing Project Day Care Ctr. Children, Easter Egg project; actor Springer Theatre, 1982—; bd. dirs. Edn. Excellence Found., 2003—. Recipient cert. of excellence NSF Summer Inst., 1985, Page One award, 1987, cert. of appreciation Nat. Honor Soc. Spencer H.S., 1988, 89, 92, Gov.'s tech. award for Muscogee County, 1988, cert. of recognition Key Club Spencer H.S., 1989, Outstanding Southeastern Educator award Optical Soc. Am., 1989, Presdl. award for excellence in sci. and math. tchr., Ga., 1989, Outstanding Physics Tchr. award Am. Assn. Physics Tchrs., 1990, Swift Textiles Outstanding Educator award, 1990, Tchr. of Yr. award Muscogee County Sch. Dist., 1990, 93, Ga. Secondary Schs., 1989; Tandy Tech. scholar, 1990; grantee NSF, Muscogee County Sch. Dist.; sci.-math. fellow Coun. for Basic Edn., 1995; finalist Christa McAuliffe fellowship, 1994. Mem. Nat. Sci. Tchrs. Assn., Ga. Sci. Tchrs. Assn. (Dist. VI Sci. Tchr. Yr. 1989, Ga. Secondary Schs. Sci. Tchr. of Yr. 1989), Am. Chem. Soc., Valley Area Sci. Tchrs. (v.p. 1989, Valley Area Sci. Tchrs. pres. 1993-94, 2000-2001), Optical Soc. Am., Assn. Presdl. Awardees for Excellence in Sci. Teaching, Nat. Sci. Tchrs. Assn., Phi Delta Kappa (Secondary Schs. Tchr. of Yr. 1993), Kappa Delta Pi. Avocations: reading, computers, walking, photography, cooking. Home: 4913 River Rd Columbus GA 31904-5836 Office: Northside HS 2002 American Way Columbus GA 31909

EDMONDSON, ROBERT CAMPBELL, retired hematologist, oncologist, internal medicine educator; b. Waukesha, Wis., Feb. 16, 1930; BA, U. Wis., 1951, MD, 1954. Diplomate of Am. Bd. Internal Medicine, Am. Bd. Med. Oncology, Am. Bd. Hematology. Intern Phila. Gen. Hosp., 1954-55; resident in pathology Boston City Hosp., 1957-58; resident in internal medicine Cleve. Clinic, 1958-60; fellow in hematology U. Utah, Salt Lake City, 1960-61; mem. staff Woodland (Calif.) Meml. Hosp., 1961-95; ret., 1995. Clin. prof. internal medicine U. Calif., Davis. Fellow ACP; mem. AMA, Am. Soc. Clin. Oncology, Am. Soc. Hematology, Western Trauma Assn. E-mail: edsmails@earthlink.net.

EDMONDSON, WILLIAM ANDREW, state attorney general; b. Washington, D.C., Oct. 12, 1946; m. Linda Larason; children: Mary Elizabeth, Robert Andrew. BA in Speech Edn., Northeastern State U., Tahlequah, Okla., 1968; JD, U. Tulsa, 1978. Mem. Okla. Legislature, 1974—76; intern Office Dist. Atty., Muskogee, Okla., 1978—, asst. dist. atty., 1979, chief prosecutor, 1982—, dist. atty., 1982—92; pvt. practice atty. Muskogee, 1979—82, Green & Edmondson, 1992—94; atty. gen. State of Okla., 1994—. With USN, 1968—72. Named Outstanding Dist. Atty., State of Okla., 1985. Mem.: Okla. Dist. Attys. Assn. (pres. 1983—85), Okla. Bar Assn. Democrat. Office: Office Atty Gen 2300 N Lincoln Blvd Rm 112 Oklahoma City OK 73105-4894

EDMONDSON, WILLIAM BROCKWAY, retired foreign service officer; b. St. Joseph, Mo., Feb. 6, 1927; s. Harold and Anna Laura (Sherman) E.; m. Donna Elizabeth Kiechel, Oct. 6, 1951; children: Barbara Elizabeth Edmondson Schneider, Paul William. AB with high distinction, U. Nebr., 1950; MA, Fletcher Sch. Law and Diplomacy, 1951; student African area studies, Northwestern U., 1957-58. Joined U.S. Fgn. Service, 1952; fgn. affairs officer Bur. UN Affairs, State Dept., 1951-52; adviser U.S. delegation 11th session UN Trusteeship Council, 1952; vice consul Dar es Salaam, Tanganyika, 1952-55; 3d sec., then 2d sec. embassy Bern, Switzerland, 1955-57; research analyst, then acting chief W. Africa div. Office Research and Analysis for Africa, State Dept., 1958-61; 2d sec., then 1st sec. and consul, polit. sect. chief Am. embassy, Accra, Ghana, 1961-64; officer charge Ghanaian affairs Bur. African Affairs, State Dept., 1964-65; counselor of embassy, dep. chief of mission Lusaka, Zambia, 1965-68; chargé d'affaires ad interim, 1968-69; assigned Nat. War Coll., 1969-70; dep. dir. African programs Bur. Ednl. and Cultural Affairs, Dept. State, 1970, dir. Office African Programs, 1971-74; minister-counselor, dep. chief mission Am. embassy, Pretoria, South Africa, 1974-76; dep. asst. sec. for African affairs State Dept., 1976-78; ambassador to South Africa Pretoria, 1978-81; sr. fgn. service insp., 1981-82; dep. insp. gen., 1982-86. Served to 1st lt. AUS, 1944-48. Mem. Am. Fgn. Svc. Assn. Diplomatic and Consular Officers Ret. (past pres., hon. life gov.), DACOR Bacon House Found. (past pres., trustee), Phi Beta Kappa. Address: 4900 28th St N Arlington VA 22207-2712 *Persistent hard work, sincerity, broad intellectual curiosity and a strong touch of idealism in striving for a better world are qualities I admire and try to emulate.*

EDMONSON, PHYLLIS DENTY, artist; b. Hope, Ark., Feb. 27, 1935; d. Nathaniel Wynne and Dell (McRae) Denty; m. Frank Alonzo Edmonson, Jan. 29, 1956; children: Frank Jr., Kathryn Dell. BS in Edn., Henderson State U., 1956. Exhibitions include Texarkana Regional Arts & Humanities Coun. Ann. Exhbn., 1989, 1992—93, 1995—2000, Cottey Coll., Nevada, Mo., 1991, 1992, Old Washington State Park, Ark., 1992, Little River County Courthouse, Ashdown, 1992, Niagara Frontier Watercolor Soc. Nat. Exhbn., Lockport, N.Y., 1992, Tom Peyton Meml. Arts Festival, Alexandria, La., 1993, 1998, 1999, 2000, 2001, 2002, 2003, Mid-Southern Watercolorists Ann. Exhbn., 1997, 2001, Ark. Gov.'s Office, Little Rock, 1994, Okla. Art Workshop Nat. Exhbn., Tulsa, 1995, Henderson State U., Arkadelphia, Ark., 1996, Art Ctr. of the Ozarks, Springdale, Ark., 1997, 2002, Ark. Arts Ctr., Little Rock, 1997, Nat. Watercolor Okla. Ann. Exhbn., 2000, 2002, 2003, Internat. Soc. Exptl. Artists Ann. Exhbn., 2000, 2002, Houston Ann. Internat. Exhbn. Watercolor Art Soc., 2001, Hilton Head Art League An. Nat. Exhbn., 2001, Fort Smith (Ark.) 51st Ann. Art Competition, 2001, North East Watercolor Soc. 25th Ann. Internat. Exhbn., 2001, Audubon Artist, Inc. 59th Ann. Exhbn. Salamagundi Club, N.Y.C., 2001, Southwestern Watercolor Soc. 39th Ann. Exhbn., 2002, Western Fedn. Ann. Watercolor Soc., 2002, Western Fedn. 27th Ann. Watercolor Soc., 2003, Ga. Ann. Nat. Exhbn., 2002, 2003, Watercolor, Houston, 2003, one-woman shows include Southwestern Elec. Power Co. Bldg., Texarkana, 1992, Cantrell Gallery, Little Rock, 1994, 1998, Texarkana Regional Arts and Humanities Coun. Mus., 1999, Sen. Blanche Lincoln's Little Rock Offices, 2003—, exhibited in group shows at The Carousel Studio, Ashdown, 1992, Magee's Cafe & Coffee House, Hot Springs, Ark., 1993, Am. Art Gallery, Hot Springs, 1994, Small Works on Paper Annual Tour, Ark., 1996, 1998, Cantrell Art Gallery, Little Rock, Ark., 1996, 2000, 2002, Assoc. Artists of Winston-Salem Nat. Competition Untitled-Non-Objective Art, 1997, Arts & Sci. Ctr., Pine Bluff, Ark., 1998, Represented in permanent collections Ark. Arts Ctr., Little Rock, Southeast Ark. Arts and Sci. Ctr. V.p. Little River Arts Coun., Ashdown, Ark., 2003. Recipient 2d pl. award Texarkana Regional Arts and Humanities Coun. Ann. Exhbn., 1995, Purchase award, Ark. Arts. Coun., 1996, Corp. Purchase award, Henderson State U., 1996, First Place Mid-So. Watercolorists, Little Rock, 1997, Finalist The Artist's Mag. Art Competition, 1999, Merit award Tom Peyton Meml. Arts Festival, 2001,2002, Neiman Marcus award Ga. Watersolor Soc. XXIII Exhbn., 2002, Merchandise award, Nat. Watercolor Okla. 28th Ann. Exhbn., 2002 Mem.: Little River Arts Coun., Mo. Watercolor Soc., Ga. Watercolor Soc., Nat. Collage Soc., Audubon Artist, Inc., Southwestern Watercolor Soc., Ark. Arts Ctr., Internat. Soc. Exptl. Artists, Nat. Mus. Women in the Arts, Texarkana Regional Arts and Humanities Coun., Mid-So. Watercolorists, PEO Internat. Sisterhood (treas. 1980—82, v.p. 1982—83, chaplain 1988—90, corr. sec. 1996—98). Baptist. Avocations: gardening, photography. Home: 210 Highway 32 West Ashdown AR 71822-8792 Office: The Carousel Studio 410 W Main St Ashdown AR 71822-2752

EDMONSON-NELSON, GLORIA JEAN, freelance writer; b. Nowata, Okla., Oct. 7, 1938; d. Cornelius Edmonson and Virginia (Cole) E.; m. Forest Nelson, Oct. 7, 1996; children: Vincent Ross, Victor Ross, Vernon Ross. AA, Labette C.C., Parsons, Kans., 1959; BS in Mgmt., U. San Francisco, 1979. Adminstr. Far West Lab for Ednl. R&D, San Francisco, 1969-81; reporter The Doctor's Co. Med. Malpractice, Emeryville, Calif., 1986-89. Cons. arbitrator NASD, San Francisco, 1992-2000. Author: How to Start a Medical Collecting Agency, 1990, Recognizing Abuse--Reclaiming Your Birthright, 1998, Recognizing Child Abuse and Domestic Violence, 1998, Prayer Works, 2003, (screenplays) What Would God Think?, 2002. Telephone interviewer United Way, 1989-91, voter registrar, 1990-91. Recipient various poetry awards. Mem.: NAFE, West Angeles COGIC, Am. Assn. Ret. Persons, Nat. Assn. Securities Dealers. Avocations: writing poetry, travel, jazz. Address: PO Box 45770 Los Angeles CA 90045-0770 E-mail: GEdmon1800@aol.com.

EDMONSTON, WILLIAM EDWARD, JR., publisher, educator; b. Balt., Nov. 20, 1931; s. William Edward and Helen (Mallonee) E.; m. Nellie Jane Kerley, Aug. 3, 1957; children: Kathryn Nell, Rebecca Jane, Owen William. BA, Johns Hopkins U., 1952; MA, U. Ala., 1956; PhD, U. Ky., 1960. Diplomate: Am. Bd. Psychol. Hypnosis. Instr., asst. prof. Washington U., St. Louis, 1960-64; mem. faculty Colgate U., Hamilton, N.Y., 1964-93, dir. neurosci. program, 1972-93, prof. psychology, 1973-93, prof. emeritus, 1993—, chmn. dept. psychology, 1971-81; Gast prof. U. Erlanger, Nürnberg, Fed. Republic Germany, 1982. Pub. Edmonston Pub., Inc., Hamilton Author: Hypnosis and Relaxation: Modern Verification of an Old Equation, 1981, The Induction of Hypnosis, 1986, Unfurl the Flags: Remembrances of the American Civil War, 1989, The Strange Case of Mr. Nobody, 2000; editor: Am. Jour. Clin. Hypnosis, 1968-76; contbr. articles to profl. jours. Served with U.S. Army, 1952-54. Sloan Found. fellow, 1967, 69, Fulbright Found. fellow, 1982, U. Wash. sr. fellow, 1971; recipient Bernard E. Gorton award, 1961, grant USPHS, 1964-65, Prof. of Yr. award CASE N.Y. State, 1988. Mem. Sigma Xi. Home: 1841 Preston Hill Rd Hamilton NY 13346-9522 *By being born to intelligent parents, I started with the genetic potential for success and was reared in a social atmosphere in which hard work, honesty, thrift and accomplishment were highly regarded. I later recognized perseverance, even in the face of apparent failure, and a compulsive attention to (but not an obsession with) details as fundamental to accomplishment. Perseverance is by far the most regnant, for without tenacity one's genetic potential and early social learnings will lie fallow. There is a time for action and a time for reflection. Choosing the appropriate time for each is the secret of happiness and success.*

EDMUND, NORMAN WILSON, educational researcher; b. Feb. 27, 1916; Cert., U. Pa., 1939. Founder, pres. Edmund Sci. Co., Barrington, N.J., 1942-75; ednl. rschr. Ft. Lauderdale, Fla., 1989—. Author: The General Pattern of the Scientific Method, 1994, The Scientific Method Today, 2000. Office: 407 NE 3rd Ave Fort Lauderdale FL 33301-3233 E-mail: nwe@scientificmethod.com.

EDMUNDS, JANE CLARA, communications consultant; b. Chgo., Mar. 16, 1922; d. John Carson and Clara (Kummerow) Carrigan; m. William T. Dean, Aug. 30, 1947 (div. 1953; dec. July 1984); 1 son, John Charles; Edmund S. Kopacz, Sept. 24, 1955 (div. 1973); children: Christine Ellen, Jan Carson. Student in chemistry and math., Northwestern U. Chemist Mars Inc., Oak Park, Ill., 1942-47; with Cons. Engr. Mag., Maujer Pub. Co., St. Joseph, Mich., 1953-58, 69-74; sr. editor Cons. Engr. Mag. Tech. Pub. Co., Barrington, Ill., 1975-77, exec. editor, 1977-82, editorial dir., 1983-86; asst. editor women's pages rewrite desk News-Palladium, Benton Harbor, Mich., 1967-68; freelance journalist St. Joseph, 1959-68; communications cons. Schaumburg, Ill., 1987—. Chmn. Berrien County (Mich.) Nat. Found. March of Dimes, 1968; mem. campaign com. Rep. Party, 1954. Recipient award Bausch & Lomb, 1940, award Nat. Found. Service, 1969, Silver Hat award Constrn. Writers Assn., 1986, honor mem. 2000, Chmn.'s award Profl. Engrs. in Pvt. Practice div. NSPE, 1987; grantee AID, 1979 Assoc. fellow Soc. Tech. Communication (chmn. St. Joseph chpt. 1972 Disting. Tech. Communication awards); mem. Am. Soc. Bus. Press Editors (past bd. mem.), Constrn. Writers Assn., Smithsonian Instn., Chgo. Art Inst. Assocs., Field Mus. Assocs. Republican. Episcopalian.

EDMUNDS, JOHN SANFORD, lawyer; b. L.A., Jan. 3, 1943; s. Arthur Edmunds and Sarah Bernadine (Miles) E.; m. Virginia Maejan Ching, Nov. 30, 1975; children: Laura, Shauna. AB, Stanford U., 1964; JD, U. So. Calif., 1967. Bar: Hawaii 1972, U.S. Dist. Ct. Hawaii, U.S. Ct. Appeals (9th cir.), U.S. Supreme Ct. Chief dep. pub. defender State of Hawaii, 1970-72, spl. dep. atty. gen., 1974-75; acting chief justice Supreme Ct., Republic of Marshall Islands, 1980-81; ptnr. Edmunds & Verga, Honolulu, 1981-97, Edmunds, Maki, Versa and Thorn, Honolulu, 1997—. Adj. prof. law U. Hawaii, 1976-77, 85-89; counsel Hemmeter Investment Co., Obayashi Corp., Shell Oil Co., Nestle, U.S.A., Inc., Bank of Am. Bd. dirs. Legal Aid Soc. Hawaii, 1974-75; vice-chair selection commn. Hawaii State Jud., 2000-. Fellow Internat. Acad. Trial Lawyers, Am. Coll. Trial Lawyers (state chmn. 1991-92, nat. com. legal ethics and profl. responsibility 1994), Internat. Soc. Barristers, Am. Bar Found.; mem. ABA, ACLU (bd. dirs. 1969-73, pres. 1971-73, adv. counsel 1974-75), Hawaii Bar Assn., Assn. Trial Lawyers Am., Hawaii Acad. Plaintiffs Attys (bd. govs. 1995—), Master of Bench, Am. Inns. of Ct. Office: Edmunds Maki Verga & Thorn 841 Bishop St Ste 2104 Honolulu HI 96813-3921 E-mail: jedmunds@emut.com.

EDMUNDS, KENNY (BABYFACE), popular musician; b. Inpls., Apr. 10, 1959; Co-songwriter Lucky Charm, 1988, The Lover In Me, Love Saw It, Every Little Step, Dial My Heart, 1988, It's No Crime, Whip Appeal, Tender Lover, Ready or Not, My Kinda Girl, Can't Stop, Lovers, 1989, Giving You the Benefit, I'm Your Baby Tonight, My, My, My, 1990, On Our Own, A Closer Look, 1991, For the Cool in You, 1993, The Day, 1996, soundtrack Ghostbusters II, 1989, The Bodyguard, 1992, Waiting to Exhale, 1995, singles This is For the Lover in You, 1996; exec. prodr.: Have Plenty, 1998. Nominee Grammy (Best Rhythym & Blues Male Vocal) for "For All the Cool in You", 1994; recipient Soul Train Music Award, 2000, Grammy award for prodr. of the year, 1995, 1996, 1997. Office: Solar Epic Recordings Sony Music Distbr 550 Madison Ave New York NY 10022-3211*

EDMUNDS, LOWELL (ARTHUR LOWELL EDMUNDS), philology educator; b. Franklin, NH, Oct. 11, 1938; s. Arthur Lowell and Ruth Harriet (Humphrey) E.; m. Susan Dain Trafton, June 22, 1966; children: Hannah, Leah. AB, Harvard U., 1960, PhD, 1970; MA, U. Calif., Berkeley, 1965. From asst. to assoc. prof. Harvard U., Cambridge, Mass., 1970-78; assoc. prof. Boston Coll., Chestnut Hill, Mass., 1978-83; prof., chmn. dept. Johns Hopkins U., Balt., 1983-88; prof. Rutgers U., 1988—, chmn. dept., 1990-96. Author: Chance and Intelligence in Thucydides, 1975, Oedipus: A Folklore Casebook, 1983, 2d edit., 1995, Oedipus: The Ancient Legend and its Later Analogues, 1985, Approaches to Greek Myth, 1989, From a Sabine Jar: Reading Horace, Odes 1.9, 1991, Myth in Homer: A Handbook, 1992, 2d edit., 1993, Theatrical Space and Historical Place in Sophocles' Oedipus at Colonus, 1996; Martini, Straight Up: The Classic American Cocktail, 1998, Intertextuality and the Reading of Roman Poetry, 2001. Mem. Am. Philol. Assn., Assn. Ancient Historians. Avocations: yoga, recorder-playing. Business E-Mail: edmunds@rci.rutgers.edu.

EDMUNDS, NANCY GARLOCK, federal judge; b. Detroit, July 10, 1947; m. William C. Edmunds, 1977. BA cum laude, Cornell U., 1969; MA in Teaching, U. Chgo., 1971; JD summa cum laude, Wayne U., 1976. Bar: Mich. 1976. With Plymouth Canton Public Schools, 1971-73; law clk. Barris, Sott, Denn & Driker, 1973-75; law clk. to Hon. Ralph Freeman U.S. Dist. Ct. (ea. dist.) Mich., 1976-78; with Dykema Gossett, Detroit, 1978-84, ptnr. litigation sect., 1984-92; apptd. judge U.S. Dist. Ct. (ea. dist.) Mich., 1992—. Commr. 21st Century Commn. on Cts., 1990; mem. faculty, bd. mem. Fed. Advocacy Inst., 1983-91. Editor in chief Wayne Law Review. Mem. com. of visitors Wayne Law Sch., Detroit; mem. com. on defender svcs. Nat. Jud. Conf.; mem. Nat. Coun. Jewish Women; bd. gov.'s Cranbrook Schs.; bd. dirs. Mich. Mems. of Stratford Festival; bd. trustees Stratford Shakespearean Festival of Am., Temple Beth El, 1990-97, Hist. Soc. U.S. Dist. Ct. (ea. dist.) Mich., 1993-98. Mem. ABA, FBA (exec. bd. dirs. 1989-92), Am. Judicature Soc., Fed. Judges Assn., State Bar Mich. (chair U.S. cts. com. 1990-91). Avocations: skiing, reading. Office: US Dist Ct US Courthouse #211 231 W Lafayette Blvd Detroit MI 48226-2700 E-mail: karen_hillebrand@mied.uscourts.gov.

EDMUNSON, JAMES L. political organization administrator; b. Eugene, Oreg., 1951; m. Ellen Edmunson; 2 children. BS, Oreg. State U.; JD, U. Oreg., 1983. Chmn. Oreg. Dem. Party, Portland, 2001—; rep. 39th dist. State of Oreg., 1987—95; lawyer, appellate counsel Malagon, Moore & Johnson; pvt. practice Eugene, Oreg. Office: Democratic Party Oregon 232 NE 9th Ave Portland OR 97232-2915 Fax: 503-224-5335.*

EDRINGTON, SUE ELLEN, critical care nurse; b. Noblesville, Ind., Sept. 14, 1955; d. Donald Mur and Edna Irene (Carraway) E. BS in Secondary Edn., Bob Jones U., 1978, BSN, 1982; MS in Adult Health, Clemson U., 1994. RN, S.C., Ind., Mo.; cert. med.-surg. nurse. Staff nurse ICU, med.-surg. emergency rm. St. Francis Hosp., Greenville, S.C., 1982-95, asst. head nurse ICU, head nurse ICU, acute dialysis, staff devlop. post coronary; spl. projects coord.; CNS Intensive Care Svcs. St. Francis Med. Ctr., Cape Girardeau, Mo., 1995-96; CNS Critical Care Svcs. Piedmont Med. Ctr., Rock Hill, S.C., 1997-2000; pediatrics care coord. Riverview Hosp., Noblesville, Ind., 2000—02; emergeny dept. RN Cmty. Hosp. North, Indpls., 2002—. Mem. AACN, Sigma Theta Tau. E-mail: suellen@indy.net.

EDSALL, THOMAS BYRNE, reporter; b. Cambridge, Mass, Aug. 22, 1941; s. Richard Linn and Katharine (Byrne) E.; m. Mary Deutsch, Aug. 22, 1965; 1 child, Alexandra Tileston Victor Eckall. BA, Boston U., 1966. Reporter Providence Jour., 1965; vol. VISTA, Balt., 1966-67; reporter Balt. Sun, 1967-81, Washington Post, 1981—. Regents lectr. U. Calif., San Diego, 1991; lectr. Nutfield Coll. Oxford U., 1995. Author: The New Politics of Inequality, 1984, Power and Money, 1988, (with Mary D. Edsall) Chain Reaction: The Impact of Race, Rights and Taxes on American Politics, 1991; co-editor: The Reagan Legacy, 1988; contbr. articles to NY Rev. of Books, Atlantic, Am. Prospect, popular jour. Chmn. Standing Com. of Corr. US Congress, 1982. Recipient Front Page award, Bill Pryor Meml. award Washington-Balt. Newspaper Guild, 1981, Carey McWilliams award Am. Polit. Sci. Assn., 1994; Woodrow Wilson found. fellow, 1996-97, Hoover Instn. media fellow, Stanford U., 1997, 2001, 03. Home: 19 2nd St NE Washington DC 20002-7301 Office: Washington Post 1150 15th St NW Washington DC 20071-0002

EDSBERG, LAURA E. research scientist, consultant; b. Rochester, N.Y., Jan. 3, 1964; d. Robert L. and Amina Edsberg. BS, Cornell U., 1986; MS, PhD, SUNY, Buffalo, 1994. Dir. biomed. rsch. lab. Sisters of Charity Hosp., Buffalo, 1995—98; dir. Natural and Health Scis. Rsch. Ctr. Daemen Coll., Amherst, NY, 1998—. Contbr. articles to profl. jours. Mem.: Wound Healing Soc. Office: Daemen Coll 4380 Main St Amherst NY 14226 Personal E-mail: leedsberg@aol.com.

EDSON, ANDREW STEPHEN, public relations executive; b. N.Y.C., Jan. 8, 1946; s. Herbert and Frances (Bauling) E.; m. Marilyn Borer, July 22, 1972; children: Garrett Matthew, Gregory Todd. BA, Fairleigh Dickinson U., 1967; MA, Memphis State U., 1969. Staff writer Memphis Press-Scimitar, 1968-69; account exec. Harshe-Rotman & Druck, Inc., Memphis, 1969-70, Ruder & Finn, Inc., N.Y.C., 1970-73; asst. dir. corp. pub. relations Anaconda Co., N.Y.C., 1973-74; pub. affairs mgr. Citicorp, N.Y.C., 1974-78; sr. account exec. Padilla & Speer Inc., N.Y.C., 1978-79, v.p., 1979-86, sr. v.p., 1986, Padilla Speer Beardsley Inc., N.Y.C., 1986-94; pres., COO Anreder and Co., N.Y.C., 1994-96; pres. Andrew Edson & Assocs., Inc., N.Y.C., 1996—; sr. counselor, corp. and fin. rels. Manning, Selvage & Lee, Inc., N.Y.C., 1996-2001. Adj. asst. prof. NYU, 1983-87; sec., bd. dirs. The Worldcom. Group, Inc., N.Y., 1988-96; pres. bd. dirs. Finch Apt Corp., N.Y.C. Mem.: Nat. Investor Rels. Inst., Jericho Pub. Libr. (trustee 1998—99). Republican. Avocations: tennis, skiing, bicycling. Office: Andrew Edson & Assoc 79 Madison Ave Fl 3 New York NY 10016-7802 E-mail: andrew@edsonpr.com.

EDSON, CHARLES LOUIS, lawyer, educator; b. St. Louis, Dec. 14, 1934; s. Harry G. and Mildred (Solomon) E.; m. Susan Kramer, Mar. 29, 1959; children: Richard, Nancy, Margaret. AB, Harvard U., 1956, LLB, 1959. Bar: Mo. 1959, U.S. Supreme Ct. 1966, D.C. 1967. Assoc. Lewis, Rice, Tucker, Allen & Chubb, St. Louis, 1959-65; chief ops. officer Legal Svc. Program, OEO, Washington, 1966-67; gen. counsel Pres.'s Commn. on Postal Orgn., Washington, 1967-68; chief pub. housing sect. Officer of Gen. Counsel, HUD, Washington, 1968-70; ptnr. Lane and Edson, P.C., Washington, 1970-89, Kelley, Drye & Warren, Washington, 1989-93, Peabody & Brown, Washington, 1993-99, Nixon Peabody LLP, Washington, 1999—, ptnr., sr. counsel, 2002—. Adj. prof. law Georgetown U. Law Sch., Washington, 1970-76, 2000—; HUD coord. Pres. Carter's Transition Staff, 1976-77. Co-author: A Practical Guide to Low and Moderate Income Housing, 1972, A Leased Housing Primer, 1975, A Section 8 Deskbook, 1976, Guide to Federal Housing Programs, 1982, Secondary Mortgage Market Guide, 1985, HDR Affordable Seniors Housing Handbook, 2002. Councilman Town of Somerset, Md., 1976-78; trustee Md. Hist. Trust, 1995—, vice chair, 2000—. With USNR, 1953-61. Alt. White House fellow, 1965. Mem. ABA (chmn. forum com. on affordable housing and comm. devel. 1991-93, chmn. spl. housing and urban devel. 1987-90), Harvard U. Law Sch. Assn. D.C. (pres. 1972-73), Cosmos Club (Washington). Home: 5802 Surrey St Chevy Chase MD 20815-5419 Office: 401 9th St NW Ste 900 Washington DC 20004-2134 E-mail: cedson@nixonpeabody.com., granchuck@aol.com.

EDSON, HERBERT ROBBINS, retired foundation and hospital executive; b. Upper Darby, Pa., Dec. 26, 1931; s. Merritt Austin and Ethel Winifred (Robbins) E.; m. Constance Anne Lowell, May 20, 1961 (div. Nov. 8, 1967); m. Rose Anne McGowan, July 25, 1970; children: Patricia Anne, David William, Merritt Austin III, Herbert Robbins Jr. BA, Tufts U., 1955; MBA, U. Pa., 1972. Commd. 2d lt. USMC, 1955, advanced through grades to major, 1967, adminstr., mgr., supr. various orgns., 1955-72, controller III Marine Amphibious Force and 3d Marine Div., 1972-73, dir. acctg. Marine Corps Supply Activity Phila., 1973-75, ret., 1975; cons. acctg. Ardmore, Pa., 1975-77; CFO Mercy Meml. Hosp. Corp., Monroe, Mich., 1977-92, Mercy Meml. Hosp. Found., Monroe, 1986-92, Monroe Health Ventures Inc., 1986-92, Monroe Community Health Svcs., 1989-92, Byerly Hosp., Hartsville, S.C., 1992-95, Byerly Found., Hartsville, S.C., 1995-97; ret., 1997. Assoc. Quorum Health Resources, Inc., Brentwood, Tenn., 1992-95. Co-pres. Custer Elem. Sch. Parent Tchr. Orgn., Monroe, 1985-87; v.p., trustee Christ Evang. Luth. Ch., Monroe, 1981-86; dir. Monroe County C. of C., 1982-84; treas., chmn. Taylor Endowment Fund com. St. Paul's Evang. Luth. Ch., Ardmore, Pa., 1974-76, trustee, chmn. property com., 1976. Decorated Purple Heart, Navy Commendation medal, Combat Action ribbon. Mem. NRA (life), U.S. Naval Inst. (life), Marine Corps Assn. (life), 1st Marine Div. Assn. (life), Edson's Raiders Assn. (hon. life 1st Marine Raider Bn.), Ret. Officers Assn. (life), Am. Assn. Ret. Persons, Nat. Geog. Soc., Edson Geneal. Assn., Marines Meml. Club, Army and Navy Club. Democrat. Lutheran. Home: PO Box 569 Ellenton FL 34222-0569

EDSON, MARGARET, playwright; b. Washington, July 4, 1961; life ptnr. Linda Merrill. BA, Smith Coll., 1983; MA, Georgetown U., 1992. Tchr., elementary D.C. public schools, 1992—98; tchr. kindergarten John Hope Elem. Sch., Atlanta, 1998—. Author: (play) Wit. Recipient Drama League of NY playwright award, 1993, LA Drama Critics Circle award, 1996, Berrilla Kerr Found. playwrights award, 1998, Fellowship of Southern Writers drama award, 1999, Pulitzer prize for drama, 1999.

EDSON, WAYNE E. retired dentist, consultant; b. Marinette, Wis., July 4, 1947; s. E.J. Edson and Anita (Pearson) Edson Sebero; m. Linda Mary Hullison, Apr. 3, 1971; children: William Earl, Erin Hullison, Thomas John. BS, U. Wis.-Madison/Milw., 1973; DDS, Northwestern U., 1977. Gen. practice dentistry, Winnetka, Ill., 1982-97, ret., 1996 . Pres. Kenilworth United Fund, 1983-84, bd. dirs., 1981-85; com. mem. Kenilworth Baseball, 1978-83; troop leader Boy Scouts Am., Kenilworth, 1994—. . Served with USN, 1965-72. Mem. Chgo. Dental Soc., Ill. State Dental Soc., ADA. Roman Catholic. Avocations: hunting; fishing, curling. Clubs: John Evans of Northwestern U., G.V. Black Soc. of Northwestern U., Kenilworth. Home: 624 Exmoor Rd Kenilworth IL 60043-1021

EDSON, WILLIAM ALDEN, electrical engineer, researcher; b. Burchard, Nebr., Oct. 30, 1912; s. William Henry and Pearl (Montgomery) E.; m. Saralou Peterson, Aug. 23, 1942; children: Judith Lynne, Margaret Jane, Carolyn Louise. BS (Summerfield scholar), U. Kans., 1934, MS, 1935; D.Sc. (Gordon McKay scholar), Harvard U., 1937. Mem. tech. staff Bell Telephone Labs., Inc., N.Y.C., 1937-41, supr., 1943-45; asst. prof. elec. engring. Ill. Inst. Tech., Chgo., 1941-43; prof. physics Ga. Inst. Tech., Atlanta, 1945-46, prof. elec. engring., 1946-51, dir. sch. elec. engring., 1951-52; vis. prof., research asso. Stanford U., 1952-56, cons. prof., 1956; mgr. Klystron sub-sect. Gen. Electric Microwave Lab., Palo Alto, Calif., 1955-61; v.p., dir. research Electromagnetic Tech. Corp., Palo Alto, 1961-62, pres., 1962-70; sr. scientist Vidar Corp., Mountain View, Calif., 1970— 71; asst. dir. Radio Physics Lab., SRI Internat., Menlo Park, Calif., 1971-77; sr. prin. engr. Geosci. and Engring. Ctr., SRI Internat., 1977-2001; ret., 2001. Cons. high frequency sect. Nat. Bur. Standards, 1951-64; dir. Western Electronic Show and Conv., 1975-79 Author: (with Robert I. Sarbacher) Hyper and Ultra-High Frequency Engineering, 1943, Vacuum-Tube Oscillators, 1953. Life fellow IEEE (chmn. San Francisco sect. 1963-64, com. standards piezoelectricity 1950-67); mem. Am. Phys. Soc., Sigma Xi, Tau Beta Pi, Sigma Tau, Phi Kappa Phi, Eta Kappa Nu, Pi Mu Epsilon. Home: 23350 Sereno Ct Unit 29 Cupertino CA 95014-6543

EDSTROM, PAM, public relations executive; b. 1954; Pvt. practice, 1968-74; with Fred Meyer Savings and Loan, Portland, Oreg., 1974-77, Tektronix, Inc., Beaverton, Oreg., 1977-81, Microsoft Corp., Redmond, Wash., 1982—84; sr. v.p. Waggener Edstrom, Inc., Portland, 1984—2000, exec. v.p., 2000—. Office: Waggener Edstrom Inc 3 Center Pointe Dr Ste 300 Lake Oswego OR 97035

EDWARD, DAVID ANDREW, environmental engineer; b. Sierra Vista, Ariz., Nov. 24, 1962; s. Edmond Stricklan and Jeanne Clark (Herbert) E.; m. Paula Elizabeth Woods; children: Paul David, Stephen Seth, Elizabeth Rachelle, Luke Andrew, Peter Elijah, Ethan Thomas. BS in Petroleum Engring., West Va. U., Morgantown, 1986; MBA, U. Louisville, 1991. Registered profl. engr., Ky., Ind., Va., Ill., Ga., Ohio. Commd. 2nd. lt. U.S. Army, 1985; advanced through grades to capt., 1992; exec. officer A Co. 3/81st Armor Regiment, Ft. Knox, Ky., 1987-88; asst. adjutant 1st Armor Tng. Brigade, Ft. Knox, Ky., 1988-89; adj. 4/13th Armor Regiment, Ft. Knox, Ky., 1989-90; platoon leader, exec. officer A Troop 5/12 Cavalry Regiment, Ft. Knox, 1990; ops. mgr. Earth Sci. Techs., Inc., Louisville, 1990-92; project engr. Commonwealth Tech., Inc., Lexington, Ky., 1992-93; project mgr., 1993-97, The Evergreen Group, Inc., Crestwood, Ky., 1997-98; sr. project mgr. Advanced Techs. Intl. Inc., 1998-99; pres. PSE Engring., 1999—. Chmn. various coms. Alpha Phi Omega Svc. Fraternity, W.Va. U., Morgantown, 1981-86; post mgr. Army Emergency Relief Fund Drive, Ft. Knox, 1988; Sunday sch. tchr. Beulah Presbyn. Ch., Louisville, 1988, 92; com. mem. Goals for Greater Louisville, 1992; mem. citizens adv. com. Jefferson County (Ky.) Pub. Schs., 1992; mem. Bluegrass Tomorrow Regional Devel. Com., 1992; mem. adv. com. Ohio River Corridor Master Plan, 1994; mem. Jefferson County Comprehensive Land Use Adv. Com., 1994; mem. Ky. Profl. Engrs. Disaster Response Com., 1993, 94, chmn., 199699; den leader Cub Scouts, Louisville, 1995—; youth soccer, basketball, field hockey and T-ball coach N.E. Louisville YMCA, 1995—. Named Ky. Col., State of Ky., 1989. Mem. ASCE, NSPE, Am. Acad. Environ. Engrs., Soc. Petroleum Engrs., Soc. Am. Mil. Engrs., Hazardous Materials Mgrs. (Ky. chpt.), Nat. Ground Water Assn., Am. Assn. Cost Engrs., Air and Waste Mgmt. Assn., Louisville C. of C. (chmn. water com. 1996-98), Kentuckiana Post-Soc. Am. Mil. Engrs. (membership chmn. 1997-98), U. Louisville Alumni Assn., Scottish-Am. Mil. Soc., W.Va. U. Alumni Assn., Nat. Eagle Scout Assn., Tau Beta Pi. Home: 4507 Deepwood Dr Louisville KY 40241-1006 E-mail: kyedward@aol.com.

EDWARDS, ANN CONCETTA, human resources director; b. Bklyn., Feb. 15, 1941; d. Joseph T. and Anna R. Lazzarino; m. Andrew F. Edwards, Jan 14, 1967; children: Alison, Jacqueline. BA, U. S.C., 1961; MA, St. John's U., Jamaica, N.Y., 1963. Cert. sr. profl. human resources. From asst. to mgr. human resources Lab-Volt Sys., Inc., Wall Township, N.J., 1982-97, human resources mgr., 1997—2001, human resources dir., 2002—. Writer Shore News, Sea Girt, N.J., 1970-75; cons. Edwards Assocs., Sea Girt, 1975-82. Recipient Govs. Certificate of Achievement award N.J. Sch. to Careers Sys., 1997-98. Mem.: NAFE, Jersey Shore Assn. Human Resources (area 1 rep. 1990—92), Soc. for Human Resource Mgmt. (dir. 1994—, found. chair 1997—2001, high tech. net 1998—, sch.-to-work chair 2002—, trustee Garden State coun.). Avocation: writing. Office: Lab-Volt Systems Inc PO Box 686 Farmingdale NJ 07727-0686 E-mail: aedwards@labvolt.com.

EDWARDS, ANTHONY, actor; b. Santa Barbara, CA, July 19, 1962; Student, Royal Acad. of Dramatic Art, London, 1980. Films include: Fast Times at Ridgemont High, 1982, Heart Like a Wheel, 1982, Revenge of the Nerds, 1984, The Sure Thing, 1985, Gotcha!, 1985, Top Gun, 1985, Summer Heat, 1987, Revenge of the Nerds II: Nerds in Paradise, 1987, Mr. North, 1988, Miracle Mile, 1989, How I Got Into College, 1989, Hawks, 1989, Downtown, 1990, Pet Sematary II, 1992, The Client, 1994, Playing by Heart, 1998; television movies include: The Killing of Randy Webster, 1981, High School U.S.A., 1983, Going for the Gold: The Bill Johnson Story, 1985, El Diablo, 1990, Hometown Boy Makes Good, 1990, In Cold Blood (TV), 1996, Playing by Heart, 1998, Don't Go Breaking My Heart (also prodr.), 1998, Jackpot, 2001, Northfork, 2003; series include: It Takes Two, 1982-83, Northern Exposure, 1992-93, ER, 1994-2002, Rock Story, 2000; dir. (TV series) ER, 1996, 98, Charlies Ghose Story, 1994; prodr. Us Begins with You, 1998; guest appearance Monday Nigh Clive, 1999, Strangers, 1996; producer of film Die, Mommie, Die, 2003, (TV films) Border Line, 1999, N.Y.H.C., 1999, My Louisiana Sky, 2001. Recipient SAG award, 1996, 98, 99, Golden Globe, 1998.*

EDWARDS, ARDIS LAVONNE QUAM, retired elementary education educator; b. Sioux Falls, S.D., July 30, 1930; d. Norman and Dorothy (Cade) Quam; m. Paul Edwards, Apr. 18, 1953 (dec. Sept. 1988); children: Kevin (dec. 1980), Kendall, Erin, Sally, Kristin, Keely. Tchg. credentials, Augustana Luth. Coll., Sioux Falls, 1949; provisional tchg. credentials, San Jose State Coll., 1953, student, 1953-57. Lic. pvt. pilot, FAA. Mgr. The Cottage Restaurant, Sioux Falls, 1943-50; one-room sch. tchr. Whaley Sch., Colman, S.D., 1949-50; one-room sch. tchr. 8 grades East Sioux Sch., Sioux Falls, 1950-51; recreation dir. City of Albany, Calif., 1951-52; first grade tchr. Decoto (Calif.) Sch. Dist., 1952-58; ret., 1958. Author Health Instrn. Unit Study Packet for Tchrs. Treas. PTA, Hayward, Calif., 1959; chmn. Our Savior Luth. Ch. Blood Bank, 1968—; officer Healthy Cmtys., Healthy Youth; mem. Am. Heart Assn., March of Dimes, Am. Cancer Soc., Arthritis Found.; rm. mother Chadbourne Grammar Sch.; team mother Fremont Little League; Brownie leader, den mother; bible sch. tchr., Sunday sch. tchr. East Side Luth. Ch., Sioux Falls, SD, 1945—51; charter mem. Our Savior Luth. Ch., Fremont, Calif., 1964—, mem. choir, transition task force, Christian Week Day Sch. tchr., 1970, 1987, ch. historian, 1986—; other offices; pres. Luth. Women's Missionary League, 1976; edn. officer, fraternal communicator, respecteen officer Luth. Brotherhood. Recipient Spl. Svc. award Girl Scouts U.S., 1971, Arthritis Found., Fremont, 1974-75, Spl. Commendation March Fong Eu, 1954. Mem. NAFE, AARP, Republic Airlines Ret. Pilots Assn., Ret. Airline Pilots Assn., N.W. Airlines Ret. Pilots Assn., Aircraft Owners and Pilots Assn., S.W. Airways Pilots Wives Assn., Concerned Women for Am., World Affairs Coun., Mission Swim Club, Philomathian Lit. Soc., Tri-Cities Assn. Evangelicals, Washington Twp. Hist. Soc. Republican. Avocations: bible study, grandchildren, flying, history, antiques. *My greatest sense of fulfillment is in being a Christian, wife, mother, teacher and writer...in that order.*

EDWARDS, BERT TVEDT, accountant; b. Washington, Aug. 23, 1937; s. Archie Campbell and Geniana (Rasmussen) Edwards; m. Susan Elizabeth Dye, July 18, 1964; children: Christopher Andrew, Stacey E. Leonard. BA, Wesleyan U., 1959; MBA, Stanford U., 1961. CPA D.C. With Arthur Andersen LLP, Washington, 1961-69, 70-94, mgr., 1965-69, 70-71, ptnr., 1971-94, cons., 1994—98, 2001, ret. ptnr., 1994; fin. v.p. Leisure Time Industries, Inc., 1969-70; CFO, asst. sec. U.S. Dept. State, 1998-2001; exec. dir. office hist. trust acctg. U.S. Dept. Interior, 2001—. Mem. U.S. Comptr. Gen. Auditing Stds. Adv. Coun., 1985—88, 2000—02. Mem. spl. adv. commn. for indsl. and comml. devel. D.C. City Coun., 1972—74; mem. D.C. Mayor's Commn. Budget and Fiscal Priorities, 1989—91, 1993—95, D.C. Tax Rev. Commn., 1996—98; bd. dirs. Children's Nat. Med. Ctr. Rsch. Inst., 2002—, Com. Capital City, 1995—98, 2001—02; trustee Barker Found., 1968—78, 1994—96, treas., 1968—71, 1st v.p., 1971—72, pres., 1972—75; trustee, treas. Population Reference Bur., Inc., 1975—98, 2001—, vice chmn., 1993—94; bd. dirs. Jr. Achievement Met. Washington, Inc., 1973—87, treas., 1973—74, 2d v.p., 1974—75, 1st v.p., 1975—77, pres., 1977—78, chmn., 1978—80; bd. dirs., treas. Heritage Walk Homes Corp., 1975—80; chmn. JA Nat. Bus. Leadership Conf., 1978, Metro Washington Boys and Girls Clubs Ann. Congl. Dinner, 1993, dinner com. mem., 1992—98, found. bd., treas., 1995—; mem. Nat. Com. Pub. Employees Pension Sys., 1993—98, treas., 1995—98; bd. dirs., treas. Bethany West Recreation Assn., 1994—98; bd. dirs. D.C. Appleseed Found. Ctr. Law and Justice, 1995—98, 2001—, treas., 1998; mem. cmty. rels. bd. Sta. WAMU, 1994—97, CFO coun., chmn. stds. com., 1998—2001. Mem.: AICPA (govt. acctg. and auditing com. 1981—84, fed. govt. audit subcom. 1981—84, ad hoc task force univ. audit 1985—87, govt. acctg. and auditing com. 1985—88, author single audit course 1985—92, task force on quality of govt. audits 1986—87, govt. acctg. and auditing com. 1989—92, task force on quality of fed. program audits 1991—94, author single audit course 1994—96), Govt. Fin. Officers Assn. Met. Washington (co-founder, bd. dirs. 1984—91, Outstanding Svc. award 1993), Assn. Govt. Accts. (Andy Barr Lifetime Achievement award 1993), Md. Govt. Fin. Officers Assn. (bd. dirs. 1992—94), Orgn. Am. States (chmn. bd. external auditors 2000—02), Govt. Fin. Officers Assn. (co-chmn. ann. conf. 1987), Am. Acctg. Assn. (vice chair govt. nonprofit sect. 1993—94), Inst. Mgmt. Accts., Va. Soc. CPAs, Assn. Govt. Accts. Edn. and Rsch. Found. (chmn. bd. dirs. 1993—95), Greater Washington Soc. CPAs (chmn. membership com. 1973—74, chmn. SEC com. 1974—75, chmn. govt. acctg. com. 1979—81, chmn. rels. with D.C. govt. com. 1995—98, bd. govs. 1999—, Lifetime Pub. Svc. award 1997), Hist. Soc. Washington (bd. dirs. 2002—, chmn. fin. com. 2003—), Univ. Club (mem. bd. admissions 1976—82, chmn. 1980—82, bd. govs. 1982—85), Wesleyan U. Alumni Club Washington (pres. 1969—71). Methodist. Home: 309 Casey Ln Rockville MD 20850-4733 E-mail: BertTEdwards@aol.com.

EDWARDS, BLAINE DOUGLASS, lawyer; b. Borger, Tex., Sept. 30, 1961; s. Charles Afton and Harriett (Hauser) E.; m. Jill Summers Hendrickson. Sept. 1, 1984; children: Audrey Summers, Cole Douglass. BBA in Acctg. and Fin., Tex. A&M U., 1984; JD magna cum laude, St. Mary's U., 1990. Bar: Tex. 1990, U.S. Dist. Ct. (so., no., and ea. dists.) Tex. 1991, 96, U.S. Ct. Appeals (5th and 11th cirs.). Oil and gas/real estate lending officer InterFirst Bank, San Antonio, 1984-87; participating assoc. Fulbright & Jaworski, LLP, Houston, 1990-95; ptnr. Shook, Hardy & Bacon, LLP, Houston, 1995—. Adj. prof. law South Tex. Coll. Law, Houston. Co-author: Texas Environmental Law Handbook, 1990, 92; editor St. Mary's Law Jour., 1989-90; contbr. articles to profl. jours. Mem. Phi Delta Phi. Avocations: reading, snow skiing, golfing. Office: Shook Hardy & Bacon Ste 1600 600 Travis St Houston TX 77002

EDWARDS, BOB (ROBERT ALAN EDWARDS), radio news anchor; b. Louisville, May 16, 1947; s. Joseph Richard and Loretta Bernardine (Fuchs) E.; m. Sharon Ann Kelly, May 14, 1979; children: Brean, Susannah, Eleanor. BS in Commerce, U. Louisville, 1969; MA in Communication, Am. U., 1972; D.Pub. Svc. (hon.), U. Louisville, 1985; LHD (hon.), Grinnell Coll., 1991, Spalding U., 1998, Albertson Coll., 2001. News dir., program dir. Sta. WHEL-AM, New Albany, Ind., 1968-69; news anchor Sta. WTOP-AM, Washington, 1972; corr., night editor Mut. Broadcasting Sys., Washington, 1972-73; assoc. producer Nat. Pub. Radio, Washington, 1974, co-host All Things Considered, 1974-79, host Morning Edit., 1979—. Author: Fridays with Red, 1993. Served in U.S. Army, 1969-71, Korea. Named to Esquire Register, Esquire mag., 1986, Ky. Journalism Hall of Fame, 2003; recipient Oral Comm. award, L.I.U., 1980, Unity award in media, Lincoln U., Jefferson City, Mo., 1983, Edward R. Murrow award, Corp. for Pub. Broadcasting, 1984, Fleur-de-Lis award, Louisville Forum, 1985, Gabriel award, Cath. Assn. Broadcasters, 1987, 1990, Oak award, Ky. Advs. for Higher Edn., 1991, Alumni Recognition award, Am. U., 1991, Alumni fellow, U. Louisville, 1994, duPont Columbia award, Silver Baton, 1995, George Foster Peabody award, Coll. Journalism and Mass Comm. U. Ga., 1999, Alumni Achievement award, Am. U., 2001, Douglas Edwards award, St. Bonaventure U., 2002. Mem. AFTRA (nat. v.p. 1988—), Radio-TV Corrs. Assn., Soc. Profl. Journalists, U. Louisville Alumni Assn., St. Xavier HS Alumni Assn. Avocations: softball, genealogy, tennis. Office: Nat Pub Radio 635 Massachusetts Ave NW Washington DC 20001-3753

EDWARDS, BRIAN FRANCIS PEREGRINE, science educator; b. Kamloops, B.C., Can., Jan. 4, 1947; m. Lana Lee; children: David, Sarah. BS, U. B.C., 1969; AM, Harvard U., 1971, PhD, 1975. Rsch. assoc. U. Alberta, Edmonton, 1975-77, profl. assoc., 1977-80; asst. prof. to prof. Wayne State U., Detroit, 1980-89, prof., 1989—. Mem. Am. Chem. Soc., Can. Fedn. Biol. Socs., Am. Cystallographic Assn., Biophys. Soc., Am. Soc. Biochemistry and Molecular Biology, Protein Soc. Office: Wayne State U Biochemistry 540 E Canfield St Detroit MI 48201-1928

EDWARDS, BRUCE GEORGE, retired ophthalmologist, naval officer; b. Idaho Springs, Colo., Apr. 6, 1942; s. Bruce Norwood and Evelyn Alice (Kohut) Edwards. BA, U. Colo., 1964; MD, U. Colo., Denver, 1968. Diplomate Am. Acad. Ophthalmology. Commd. ensign USN, 1964; advanced through grades to capt. U.S. Naval Hosp., 1980, intern, 1968-69; USN med. officer USS Long Beach (CGN-9), 1969-70; gen. med. officer U.S. Naval Hosp., Taipei, Taiwan, 1970-72, U.S. Naval Dispensary Treasure Island, San Francisco, 1972-73; resident in ophthalmology U.S. Naval Hosp., Oakland, Calif., 1973-76, U. Calif., San Francisco, 1973-76; mem. ophthalmology staff Naval Hosp., Camp Pendleton, Calif., 1976-83, ophthalmologist, chief of med. staff Naples, Italy, 1983-85; ophthalmology head Camp Pendleton Naval Hosp., 1985-97, dir. surg. svcs., 1990-92, physician advisor quality assurance, 1985-86, ret., 1997. Vol. Internat. Eye Found., Harar, Ethiopia, 1975. Fellow Am. Acad. Ophthalmology (diplomate); mem. AMA, Calif. Med. Assn., Calif. Assn. Ophthalmologists, Am. Soc. Contemporary Ophthalmologists, Assn. U.S. Mil. Surgeons, Pan Am. Assn. Ophthalmology, Order of DeMolay (Colo. DeMolay of Yr. 1961, Idaho Springs Chevalier, Colo. State sec. 1961-62). Republican. Methodist. Avocations: piano, camping, hiking, biking, travel.

EDWARDS, C. KAREN, consultant company executive; b. Washington, Dec. 2, 1949; d. Charles Frederick and Christine (Oakley) Edwards; m. James Walker Pearce, Apr. 5, 1980; children: Ryan Christopher, Loren McKenzie. BA, U. Tenn., 1970; postgrad., George Washington U., 1971-72. Russian linguist Dept. of Def., Washington, 1971-74; pers. specialist AEC, Oak Ridge, Tenn., 1975-78; labor rels. specialist Dept. Energy, Oak Ridge, 1978-82, supervisory pers. mgr., 1982-91, directives/stds. mgr., 1991-96; pres. Pegasus Cons. Corp., Lenoir City, Tenn., 1996—. Cons. Dept. Energy and Dept. Energy contractors, Oak Ridge and Washington, 1996— Author: A Practical Guide to Work Smart Standards, 1997. Bd. dirs. Oak Ridge Civic Music Assn., 1976-80; pres. bd. dirs. Knox Arabian Horse Club, Knoxville, 1982-87; vol. Spanish tchr. Woodland Elem. Sch., Oak Ridge, 1996-97. Recipient Hammer award Vice Pres. Gore, Washington, 1996. Mem. Internat. Arabian Horse Assn., Arabian Horse Registry, Soc. Fed. Labor Rels. Profls., Beefmaster Breeders Universal, Phi Beta Kappa. Avocations: horses, farming, art, creative writing, reading. Office: Pegasus Consulting Corp 254 Babbs Rd Lenoir City TN 37771-3616 E-mail: edwardskc@pegasustech.com., webmaster@sss-mag.com.

EDWARDS, CARL NORMAN, lawyer; b. Norwood, Mass., Jan. 22, 1943; s. Wilfred Carl and Cecile Marie-Anne (Pepin) E.; m. Mary Louise Buyse, Jan. 22, 1982. MEd, Suffolk U., 1969; postgrad., Harvard U.; JD, Boston Coll., 1998; PhD, U. So. Calif., 1997. Cons. dept. social rels. Harvard U., Cambridge, Mass., 1966-69, rsch. fellow, 1969-71, lectr. social rels., 1971-72; cons. rsch. psychologist Cambridge Computer Assocs., Mass., 1966—; rsch. social psychologist Tufts-New Eng. Med. Ctr., 1969—; assoc. clin. prof. psychiatry Tufts U. Sch. Medicine, 1971—. Dir. Four Oaks Research Inst., Norfolk, Mass., 1974—; sr. assoc. for policy planning and research Justice Resource Inst., 1971—; field faculty grad. program Goddard Coll., Plainfield, Vt., 1972-82; chmn. bd. dirs. MEDx Systems, Ltd., Dover, Mass., 1985—; chmn. bd. trustees Ctr. for Birth Defects Info. Services, Inc., Dover, 1984—; tchr. seminars; cons. to major corps., govt. agys. and pub. instns. in human dynamics and pub. policy; lectr., thesis adviser, program devel. cons. schs., colls., insts. Author: Responsibilities and Dispensations: Behavior, Science and American Justice, 2001; contbr. articles to profl. jours., monographs, revs. Mem. USNG, 1963-64. Mem. ABA, APA, Mass. Psychol. Assn. (bd. dirs.), Am. Acad. Forensic Scis., Nat. Trust for Historic Preservation, Harvard Club, Appalachian Mt. Club, Norfolk Hunt Club, Blue Ridge Hunt Club. Home: Four Oaks PO Box 1776 Dover MA 02030-0279

EDWARDS, CHARLES, neuroscientist, educator; b. Washington, Sept. 22, 1925; s. James Moses and Lola (Rosenthal) Edlavitch; m. Lois Bender, Aug. 12, 1951; children: Jan, James, Sally, David. AB, Johns Hopkins U., 1945, MA, 1948, PhD, 1953. Found. Infantile Paralysis postdoctoral fellow, asst. lectr.

Univ. Coll., London, 1953-55; instr., asst. prof. physiol. optics Johns Hopkins U., Balt., 1955-58; asst. prof. physiology U. Utah, Salt Lake City, 1958-60; assoc. prof. physiology U. Minn., Mpls., 1960-65, prof., 1965-67; prof. biol. scis., dir. neurobiology rsch. ctr. SUNY, Albany, 1967-84, prof. emeritus biol. sci., 1986—; spl. asst. to sci. dir. Nat. Inst. Diabetes and Digestive and Kidney Diseases, NIH, 1984-88; prof. physiology, assoc. dean rsch. and grad. affairs U. South Fla. Coll. Medicine, Tampa, 1988-91. Grass lectr. CIEA del IPN, Mexico City, 1966; vis. prof. Karolinska Inst., 1975, 79, 84; mem. physiology study sect. NIH, 1971-75. Mem. editorial bd. Am. Jour. Physiology, 1967-73, Gen. Physiology Biophysics, 1983-95, Neurosci., 1979-92, Neurosci. Rsch., 1984-94. Mem. ACLU, Md. chpt., 1956-58, Utah chpt., 1959-60; mem. citizen adv. com. Sarasota Bay Nat. Estuary Program, 1994—. Lalor fellow, 1957, Lederle fellow, 1959-60; Nat. Acad. Scis. Czechoslovak Acad. Sci. Exchange fellow, 1980, 82, 84, 87, Japan Soc. Promotion of Sci. fellow, 1981, Naito Found.fellow, 1985; named to Johns Hopkins Univ. Soc. Scholars, 1987. Fellow AAAS; mem. AAUP (mem. coun. 1972-75), Am. Physiol. Soc., Marine Biol. Lab., Biophys. Soc., Physiol. Soc. Japan (hon.), Soc. Gen. Physiology (sec. 1971-73), Neurosci. Soc.

EDWARDS, CHARLES ARCHIBALD, lawyer; b. Lumberton, N.C., Sept. 19, 1945; s. Charles Edwin and Elizabeth Gertrude (Gooden) E.; m. Judy Carol Griffin, Aug. 14, 1966; children: Lee McNeill, Caroline Averitt Clark. AB, Davidson Coll., 1967; JD, U. N.C., 1970. Bar: Ga. 1970, U.S. Supreme Ct. 1974, D.C. 1981, N.C. 1987. Assoc. Connerat, Dunn, Hunter, Houlihan, Maclean & Exley, Savannah, Ga., 1970-71, ptnr., 1972-76, Constangy, Brooks & Smith, Atlanta, Ga., 1976-82, Greene, Buckley, Derieux & Jones, Atlanta, 1982-86, Graham & James, Raleigh, N.C., 1986-94, Womble Carlyle Sandridge & Rice, PLLC, Raleigh, 1994—. Author: Georgia Employment Law, 1983; contbr. articles to profl. publs. Mem. Warrenton Town Council, 2001—. Mem. N.C. Bar Assn., Fed. Bar Assn., Atlanta Bar Assn. (chmn. labor law sect. 1983-84). Republican. Episcopalian. Office: Womble Carlyle Sandridge & Rice PO Box 831 2100 1st Union Capitol Ctr Raleigh NC 27602 E-mail: cedwards@wcsr.com.

EDWARDS, CHARLES CORNELL, surgeon, research administrator; b. Overton, Nebr., Sept. 16, 1923; s. Charles Busby and Lillian Margaret (Arendt) Edwards; m. Sue Cowles Kruidenier, June 24, 1945; children: Timothy, Charles Cornell, Nancy, David. Student, Princeton U., 1941—43; BA, U. Colo., 1945, MD, 1948; MS, U. Minn., 1956; LLD (hon.), Phila. Coll. Pharmacy and Sci.; LHD (hon.), Pa. Coll. Podiatry; LHD (hon.), U. Colo., 1993. Diplomate Am. Bd. Surgery. Intern St. Mary's Hosp., Mpls., 1948—49; resident surgery Mayo Found., 1950—56; pvt. practice medicine specializing in surgery Des Moines, 1956—61; mem. surg. staff Georgetown U., Washington, 1961—62; also cons. USPHS; dir. div. socio-econ. activities AMA, Chgo., 1963—67; v.p., mng. officer health and sci. affairs Booz, Allen & Hamilton, 1967—69; commr. FDA, Washington, 1969—73; asst. sec. for health HEW, Washington, 1973—75; sr. v.p., dir. Becton, Dickinson & Co., 1975—77; pres. Scripps Clinic and Research Found., La Jolla, Calif., 1977—91; pres., CEO Scripps Insts. Medicine and Sci., La Jolla, 1991—93. Bd. dirs. Bergen Brunswig Corp., No. Trust Bank, IDEC Pharms., Materia, Inc., Scripps Health Sys. Bd. regents Nat. Libr. Medicine, 1981—85; mem. Nat. Leadership Commn. on Health Care, 1986—; bd. govs. Hosp. Corp. Am., 1986—89; trustee Scripps Insts. Medicine & Sci., Scripps Found.; Scripps Rsch. Inst.; chmn. bd. dirs., trustee San Diego Hospice; trustee San Diego, YMCA. Lt. M.C. USNR, 1942—46. Recipient Disting. Svc. award, HEW, Disting. Alumnus award, Mayo Found., 1986, Humanity award, Nat. Conf., 1994, Lifetime Achievement in Corp. Governancy award, Corp. Dirs. Forum, 2001. Mem.: Nat. Acad. Scis., Inst. Medicine, Am. Hosp. Assn. (hon.), La Jolla Beach and Tennis Club, La Jolla Country Club, Princeton Club. Office: Scripps Rsch Inst 10666 N Torrey Pines Rd La Jolla CA 92037-1027

EDWARDS, CHARLES MUNDY, III, financial consultant; b. N.Y.C., Jan. 30, 1935; s. Charles Mundy Jr. and Nancy Blow (Rawls) E.; m. Janice Elaine Petty, Oct. 22, 1966; children: Melanie LeMoyne, Meghan Elizabeth Adams. AB, Princeton U., 1957; postgrad., NYU, 1959-63. With Shearson Lehman Bros., Inc., N.Y.C., 1959-85, assoc., asst. v.p., v.p., sr. v.p.; prin. Grumman Hill Assocs., Inc., Westport, Conn., 1985—. Cons. Lynch & Mayer, Inc., N.Y.C., 1994; bd. dirs. EOMG, Inc., Virginia Beach, Va. Treas. fund for Ednl. Advancement, Newark, 1985-87, pres., 1988-90, v.p., 1990-97, trustee, 1985—; trustee Family Svc. Assn. of Summit, 1987-91; pres., adminstrv. bd. United Meth. Ch., Summit, 1987-94, trustee, 1990-94; mem. City Planning Bd., Summit, 1989-91; mem. adminstrv. bd. Mt. Bethel United Meth. Ch., Marietta, Ga., 1995—, mem. fin. com., 1995—, chmn. endowment com., 1997—; bd. advisors Thurston Arthritis Rsch. Ctr., Chapel Hill, N.C., 1999-2002. 1st lt. USMCR, 1957-59. Mem. Princeton Quadrangle Club, Beacon Hill Club (pres. 1987-88, v.p. 1986-87, treas. 1985-86), Chattahoochee Plantation Tennis Club. Republican. Methodist. Home: 495 Atlanta Country Club Dr Marietta GA 30067-4684

EDWARDS, CHARLES RICHARD, entomology and pest management educator; b. Lubbock, Tex., Jan. 22, 1945; s. Troy B. and Jeanette E. E.; m. Claudia Frances Henderson, Dec. 21, 1966; children: Cecily Elizabeth, Celeste Elaine. BS, Tex. Tech. U., 1968; MS, Iowa State U., 1970, PhD, 1972. Bd. cert. entomoloist. Prof. Entomology Purdue U., West Lafayette, Ind., 1972—. Cons. Consortium for Internat. Crop Protection, Corvallis, Oreg., 1985—. Food and Agr. Orgn. UN, 1995—; USAID Integrated Pest Mgmt. Collaborative Rsch. Support Program, 1993—; adj. prof. St. István U., Gödöllo, Hungary. Contbr. articles to profl. jours. Mem. Entomol. Soc. Am. (Ext. Achievement award 1984, award of merit 1985), Royal Entomol. Soc. London, Sigma Xi, Alpha Zeta, Gamma Sigma Delta. Avocations: running, woodworking. Office: Purdue U 1158 Smith Hall 901 W State Street West Lafayette IN 47907-2089 E-mail: rich_edwards@entm.purdue.edu.

EDWARDS, CHET, congressman; b. Corpus Christi, Tex., Nov. 24, 1951; m. Lea Ann Wood. BA, Tex. A&M U., 1974; MBA, Harvard U., 1981. Legislative and dist. aide to Rep. Teague, 1974-77; assoc. Trammell Crow Ptnrs., 1981—85; pres. Edwards Communications Corp.; state senator, 1983—91; chmn. Tex. Sunset Commn.; mem. U.S. Congress from 11th Tex. dist., Washington, 1991—; Dem. chief dep. whip; mem. appropriations and policy coms., co-chmn. house army caucus and impact aid coalition. Mem. Nat. Security Com., ranking min. mem. vets. affrs. subcom. on hosp. and health care. Democrat. Office: US House of Reps 2459 Rayburn HOB Washington DC 20515-0001*

EDWARDS, CHRISTINE ANNETTE, retired lawyer, securities firm executive; b. Ft. Monmouth, N.J., Aug. 30, 1952; d. Harry W. Jr. and Elizabeth Power; m. John H. Edwards, Aug. 24, 1974; children: Lindsey, John. BA, U. Md., College Park, 1974; JD with honors, U. Md., Balt., 1983. Bar: Md. 1983, D.C. 1984, Ill 1990. With Sears, Roebuck and Co., Md., 1971-81, sr. paralegal, staff asst., 1981-83, atty. govt. affairs, 1983-87; asst. v.p., dir. govt. affairs Dean Witter Fin. Svcs. Group, Washington, 1987-88, v.p., gen. counsel Lincolnshire, Ill., 1988-89, sr. v.p., 1989-91, exec. v.p., sec., chief legal officer N.Y.C., 1991-97; exec. v.p., chief legal officer, corp. sec. Morgan Stanley Dean Witter & Co. (merger Dean Witter Discover & Co. with Morgan Stanley & Co. Inc.), N.Y.C., 1997—99; legal dept. ABN AMRO, 1999—2000; v.p., gen. counsel Bank One Corp., 2000—03. Mem. bd. Fin. Svcs. Coun., Washington, 1990—; bd. trustees Nat. Found. for Consumer Credit Counseling Svcs., Silver Spring, Md., 1990-92; mem. Women in Housing and Fin., Washington, 1982—, SAI Letigation Com., 1995—, N.Y. Stock Exchange Legal Adv. Com., 1992-95; bd. dirs. Chgo. Bd. of Options Exchange, SPS Transaction Svcs. Inc.; exec. v.p., chief legal officer, corp. sec. CLO Roundtable, 1995—. Recipient Disting. Mem. award Women in Housing and Fin., Washington, 1988; named 1 of 50 Top Women Lawyers Nat. Law Journal, 1998. Mem. ABA, Securities Industry Assn. (mem. fed. regulation com. 1990—).

EDWARDS, CHRISTOPHER LEVON, medical association administrator; PhD, U. Ky., 1997. Dir. Duke U. Med. Ctr., Chronic Pain Mgmt. Program, Durham, NC, 2001—03. Dir. Duke U. Med. Ctr., Neurobehavioral Cognitive Assessment Lab., 2001—. Orgnl. devel. Bridges Point Found., Inc., Durham, 2000—03. Grantee Fin., Nat. Alliance for Rsch. on Schizophrenia and Depression, 1. Mem.: APA (assoc.), Soc. of Behavioral Medicine. Achievements include research in race and pain; race and diabetes; prostate cancer and african am. men; Alzheimer's Disease and african ams; genetics and Alzheimer's Disease. Office: Duke U Med Ctr 932 Morreene Rd Rm 170 Durham NC 27705 Office Fax: 919-668-2811. E-mail: christopher.edwards@duke.edu.

EDWARDS, CLIFFORD HENRY COAD, law educator; b. Jamalpur, Bihar, India, Nov. 8, 1924; s. George Henry Probyn and Constance Ivy (Coad) E.; m. Kathleen Mary Faber, Jan. 6, 1951; children: Jeanette Marie, John Philip, Michael Hugh, Margaret Susan. LLB with 1st class honors, U. London, 1945. Sr. lectr. Kumasi Coll., Chana, 1956-58; assoc. prof. law U. Man., Winnipeg, 1958-64, prof., dean Sch. Law, 1964-79, dean emeritus, 1986—; pres. Man. Law Reform Commn., 1979—. Queen's coun., 1980. Recipient Stanton Tchg. Award for Excellence, U. Man., 1994. Mem. Soc. Internat. Ministries (chmn. 1984-90), Can. Bar Assn., Man. Bar Assn. (Disting. Svc. award 1995). Baptist. Office: Univ of Manitoba Fort Garry Campus Robson Hall Winnipeg MB Canada R3T 2N2

EDWARDS, D. M. retail, wholesale distribution and commercial real estate investment executive; b. Tyler, Tex., Apr. 12, 1953; s. Welby Clell and Davida (Mount) E.; m. Susan Alicia Pappas, 1984 (div. 1986). AA cum laude, Tyler Jr. Coll., 1974; BBA, Baylor U., 1976. Ordained deacon Bapt. Ch. Corp. coord. Dillard Dept. Stores, Inc., Ft. Worth, 1976-77; exec. v.p. W.C. Supply Co., Tyler, 1977-83; pres., owner Walker Auto Spring, Inc., Shreveport, La., 1978-88, Edwards & Assocs., Inc., 1984—96; v.p. W.C. Square, Inc., 1976-92; CEO, chmn. bd. dirs. Pruitt Co. Inc., Houston, 1988—; chmn. bd., CEO Odessa Spring Brake & Axle, Inc., 1991—; pres., owner Shreveport Spring, Brake & Axle, Inc., 1998—; v.p., prin. owner CountryMedic, Inc., Ft. Worth, 2001—. Comml. real estate investor, Shreveport, La., Houston, Odessa, and Tyler, Tex.; gen. ptnr. ESE Properties, Tyler, 1991—; mng. gen. ptnr. Heritage Dr. Plz. Office Stes., 1992-95. Mem. planning com. Tyler Heritage Tour, 1982-83; originator Designer Show-Case, Tyler, 1983; founder, chmn. Rose Garden Trust Fund, 1981-87; bd. dirs. Carnegie History Ctr., 1984-85; chmn. merger com. Smith County Hist. Soc. and Carnegie History Ctr. merger, 1993-94; pres. Smith County Youth Found., 1986-87, mem., bd. dirs., 1984-91; pres. East Tex. State Fair, 1991-94; bd. assocs. East Tex. Bapt. U., Marshall, 1988—, v.p. bd. assocs., 1990-91, pres. bd. assocs., 1991-93; mem. exec. com. bd. trustees, vice chmn. bd. trustees, 2001—, East Tex. Bapt. U., Marshall, 1996—; mem. exec. com. East Tex. State Fair, 1990—; v.p. Camp Fannin Assoc., 1992-97, Tyler, 1992—; trustee Timberline Bapt. Camp and Conf. Ctr., 1987-90, 2001—, treas., 1989-90; mem. Smith County Hist. Commn., 1984-85, 991-94; chmn. stewardship com. First Bapt. Ch., Tyler, 195-96, mem. fin. com., 1987—, mem. long range planning com., 1999-2003; v.p. Camp Fannin Assn., 2001—; treas. Timberline Bapt. Camp and Conf. Ctr., 2002-03. Mem. Tyler Area C. of C., Smith County Hist. Soc. (chmn. bd. govs. 1984-85, 87-88, pres. 1984-85, bd. govs. 1991-94), Hist. Tyler, Inc., Tyler Jaycees (v.p. 1982-83, bd. dirs. 1982-85), Nat Trust for Hist. Preservation, SCV (treas. camp 124, 1979-83), Rotary Club of Tyler (bd. dirs. 1998—, pres. 2000—, pres. found. 2002—), Rotary Internat. (Paul Harris fellow 1998), Willow Brook Country Club (stockholder), Hollytree Country Club, East Tex. Baylor Club (chair scholarship com. 1997—, pres. 2001-02), Camp Ford Hist. Assn. (bd. dirs. 1999—, v.p. 2000, pres. 2001-03). Baptist. Home: 3600 Jill Cir Tyler TX 75701-8619 Office: PO Box 929 Tyler TX 75710-0929 also: Mountwood Ranch RR 17 Box 30 Tyler TX 75704-9817

EDWARDS, DALE LEON, communications educator; b. Nampa, Idaho; s. Wayne Martin and Thelma Lucile Edwards; m. Julie Ann Rosa, Aug. 19, 1975; children: David, Corey, Stephen, Lisa, Russell. BA, Brigham Young U., 1980, M of Libr. and Info. Sci., 1990; MS, Utah State U., 2001. Program dir., announcer Sta. KSUB, Cedar City, Utah, 1977-80; news dir. Sta. KRPX, Price, Utah, 1980-84; news writer Sun Advocate Newspaper, Price, 1984-86; dir. Learning Resource Ctr., Price Libr., Price, 1986-90; dir. libr. svcs. Treasure Valley C. C., Ontario, Oreg., 1990—2002; comm. prof. U. NC, Chapel Hill, 2002—. Legis. com. mem. Utah Libr. Assn., Salt Lake City, 1986-90. Recipient Excellence in Reporting award Utah Sch. Bds. Assn., 1985. Mem. ALA, Oreg. Libr. Assn., Oreg. C.C. Libr. Assn. (pres. 1993-94), Oreg. Edn. Assn. (legis. com. 1990-2002), East Oreg. Libr. Assn. (pres. 1997-99), Pacific N.W. Libr. Assn., Broadcast Edn. Assn.,Treasure Valley Chorale (pres. 1991-93), Phi Kappa Phi, Beta Phi Mu. Mem. Lds Ch. Avocations: music, dancing, sports. Office: U NC at Chapel Hill Sch Journalism and Mass Communication CB #3365 Chapel Hill NC 27599

EDWARDS, DANIEL WALDEN, lawyer; b. Vancouver, Wash., Aug. 7, 1950; s. Chester W. Edwards and Marilyn E. Russell; m. Joan S. Heller, Oct. 18, 1987; children: Nathaniel, Matthew, Stephen, Alexander. BA in Psychology magna cum laude, Met. State Coll., Denver, 1973, BA in Philosophy, 1974; JD, U. Colo., 1976. Bar: Colo. 1977, U.S. Dist. Ct. Colo. 1977. Dep. pub. defender State of Colo., Denver, 1977-79, Littleton, 1979-81, Pueblo, 1981-86, head office pub. defender Brighton, 1987-89, mem. jud. faculty, 1988-91; sole practitioner Denver, 1991-93; magistrate Denver Juvenile Ct., 1993-99; sole practice law Denver, 1999—. Instr. sch. of law U. Denver, 1988-91, adj. prof., 1991—, coach appellate advocacy team, 1991-99; adv. coun. Colo. Legal Svcs., 1989—; adj. mem. Colo. Supreme Ct. Grievance Com., 1991-95. Author: Basic Trial Practice: An Introduction to Persuasive Trial Techniques, 1995, Principles of Persuasion: Basic Appellate Advocacy Techniques, 1999. Mem. visual arts com. City Arts III, 1989-90, com. chmn., mem. adv. coun., 1991; bd. dirs. Metropolitan State Coll., Alumni Assn., 1991-92; vol. lectr. CSE Thursday Night Bar Pro Se Divorce Clinic, 1991-95. Named Pub. Defender of Yr. Colo. State Pub. Defender's Office, 1985, Outstanding Colo. Criminal Def. Atty., 1989. Mem. ABA, Assn. Trial Lawyers Am., Colo. Bar Assn., Adams County Bar Asss., Denver Bar Assn., Met. State Coll. Alumni Assn. (bd. dirs. 1991-94). Home: 2335 Clermont St Denver CO 80207-3134 Office: 1733 High St Denver CO 80218-1320 E-mail: edwards_dan_atty@msn.com.

EDWARDS, DARREL, psychologist; b. San Francisco, July 9, 1943; s. Darrus and Rose Pearl (Sannar) E.; children: Alexander High, Peter David, James Royce. BS in Psychology and Philosophy, Brigham Young U., 1965, MS in Psychology and Philosophy, 1967, PhD in Clin. Psychology and Philosophy, 1968. Diplomate Am. Bd. Profl. Psychology. Postdoctoral fellow in psycholinguistics Pa. State U., 1969; commd. lt. (j.g.) USN, 1970, advanced through grades to lt. comdr., 1978; dir. psychologist Tri Community Svc. Systems, San Diego, 1973-78; prof. Calif. Sch. Profl. Psychology, San Diego, 1971-78; dir. Grid Rsch., San Diego, 1978-83; pres. The Edwards Assoc., San Diego, 1983—. Pres. Strategic Vision, 1987—; cons. strategist for govt. and pvt. sector, U.S., Eng., France, Germany, Italy, Mex., Brazil, Argentina, Russia, Republic of China, Japan, Can., 1978—; ; established Inst. for Value-Centered Life, 1999; cons. in field. Co-inventor in field; contbr. articles to profl. jours. Cons., researcher U.S., U.K., France, Germany, Hungary, Japan, Brazil, Argentina, Mexico, Colombia, Kenya, Central America, India, Italy, Republic of China, Russia, numerous other countries, 1986—. Mem. Am. Psychol. Assn. Achievements include creation of Values Centered research and consulting procedures, The Inst. for Value Centered Life, Training Value Centered Vision of principles of excellence; total quality measures for the automotive industry; total customer experience measures for 30 product and service categories, Values in America bi-annual survey; four fold principles of motivation; ValueCentered theory, clinical interview, and intervention; quality research in medicine service delivery and outcomes; founder Inst. for a Value Centered Life for evaluating, reporting, and honoring Value Centered lives, products, and services. Office: The Edwards Assocs PO Box 420429 San Diego CA 92142-0429 E-mail: DrDarrelE@aol.com.

EDWARDS, DARRELL, orchestra executive; Exec. dir. Buffalo Philharmonic Orch., Buffalo, N.Y., Charleston Symphony Orch., Charleston, S.C. Office: Charleston Symphony Orch 14 George St Charleston SC 29401-1524

EDWARDS, DAVID ALLEN, internist, educator, researcher; b. Port Jervis, N.Y., Apr. 18, 1946; s. George Shevlin and Dorothea (Ratcliffe) E.; divorced; children: Ryan, Alexis, Erin. BA with honors, Transylvania U., Lexington, Ky., 1968; MD, Creighton U., 1972; DH in Homeopathy, Brit. Inst., London, 1995. Diplomate Am. Bd. Internal Medicine, Am. Bd. Chelation Therapy. Intern internal medicine Creighton U. Affiliated Hosps., Omaha, 1972-73, resident internal medicine, 1973-75; pvt. practice Reno, Nev., 1975—; clin. instr. phys. diagnosis U. Nev., Reno, 1975-77, clin. asst. prof. medicine, 1978—. Med. dir. Internat. Biomed. Rsch. Inst., Reno, Nev.; staff physician internal medicine St. Mary's Hosp., Reno, 1975-88, chmn. cardiac care unit, 1976-78, chmn. dept. medicine, 1979-80; staff physician internal medicine Washoe Med. Ctr., Reno, 1975-88; med. advisor Planned Parenthood, Reno, 1977-79; preceptor summer program U. Calif., San Diego, 1978; mem. concurrent rev. Nev. PSRO, 1979-80; dir. Nev. Nuclear Diagnostic Ctr., Reno, 1983-88; mem. courtesy staff St. Mary's Hosp., Reno, 1988-97; ambulatory care physician Reno VA Hosp., 1989-91; med. dir. Internat. Biomed. Rsch. Inst., Reno, 1993—. Contbr. articles to profl. jours. Fellow ACP, Brit. Inst. Homeopathy, Am. Coll. Preventive Medicine; mem. Am. Acad. Acupuncture, Am. Coll. Advancement in Medicine, Am. Acad. Neural Therapy, Internat. Biooxidative Medicine Found., Nev. Med. Soc. (med.-legal screening panel 1978-82), Nev. Homeopathic and Integrative Medicine Assn., Washoe County Med. Soc. (ethics com. 1977-78), N.Y. Acad. Scis. (life). Office: 6490 S McCarran Blvd Ste 24 Reno NV 89509

EDWARDS, DONALD MERVIN, biological systems engineering educator, university dean, emeritus; b. Tracy, Minn., Apr. 16, 1938; s. Mervin B. and Helen L. (Halstenrud) E.; m. Judith Lee Wilson, Aug. 8, 1964; children: John, Joel, Jeffrey, Mary. BS, S.D. State U., 1960, MS, 1961; PhD in Agrl. Engring, Purdue U., 1966. Registered profl. engr. With soil conservation svc. U.S. Dept. Agr., Marshall, Minn., 1957-62; teaching, rsch. asst. S.D. State U. and Purdue U., 1960-66; assoc. prof. agrl. engring. U. Nebr., Lincoln, 1966-71, prof., 1971-80, asst. dean Coll. Engring and Architecture, 1970-73, assoc. dean, dir. Engring Rsch. Ctr., Coll. Engring and Tech., 1973-80, dir. Energy Rsch and Devel. Ctr., 1976-80; prof. and chmn. dept. agrl. engring Mich. State U., East Lansing, 1980-89; prof. biol. systems engring., dean Coll. Agrl. Scis. and Natural Resources U. Nebr., Lincoln, 1989-00, spl. projects, 2000-01, emeritus prof. biol. sys. engring., 2001—, emeritus dean Coll. Agrl. Scis. and Natural Resources, 2001—. Mem. Engring. Accreditation Bd. Engring. and Tech.; collaborator, cons. to numerous industries and agys., 1966—. Contbr. numerous articles on irrigation, water pollution, remote sensing, energy, agrl., natural resources and engring. edn. to profl. jours. Active Boy Scouts Am., Am. Field Svc., 4-H; past bd. dirs. Nat. Safety Coun.; past chmn. bd. dirs. Lincoln Transp. System. Recipient Massey-Furguson award Am. Soc. of Agriculture Engineers, 1994, Outstanding Tchr. award U. Nebr. Fellow Am. Soc. Engring. Edn., Am. Soc. Agrl. Engrs.; mem. AAAS, NSPE (nat. bd. dirs., nat. v.p.), Profl. Engrs. Nebr., Mich. Soc. Profl. Engrs., Coun. for Agrl. Sci. and Tech., Farmhouse Fraternity, Sigma Xi, Alpha Gamma Rho, Triangle. Home: 11420 Wenzel Dr Lincoln NE 68527-9484 E-mail: dedwards1@unl.edu.

EDWARDS, E. STEPHEN, medical association administrator; b. Spring Hope, N.C. m. Sylvia Edwards; 3 children. Postgrad., Davidson Coll., Duke U. Sch. Medicine, Emory U. Pres. Rex Hosp. Med. Staff; mng. prtnr., pediat. practice Raleigh Children and Adolescent Medicine; clin. prof., pediat. U.N.C.; v.p. AAP, past pres., N.C. chpt., bd. dirs., pres., 2002—. Chair Wake County Drug Awareness Com. Avocations: golf, poker. Office: 141 Northwest Point Blvd Elk Grove Village IL 60007

EDWARDS, EDGAR O. economist; b. Foxboro, Mass, Dec. 20, 1919; s. John and Winifred (Roberts) E.; m. Jean E. Lotz, Apr. 27, 1946; children: Kathryn L., Carolyn J., Douglas J. AA, Green Mountain Coll., Poultney, Vt., 1939; AB, Washington and Jefferson Coll., Pa., 1947; MA, Johns Hopkins U., 1949, PhD, 1951. Controller Telescope Folding Furniture Co., Granville, NY, 1939-41; lectr. to assoc. prof. Princeton U., NJ, 1950-59; Hargrove prof. econ. Rice U., Houston, 1959-69, chmn. dept. econs., 1959-65; advisor Govt. of Kenya, Nairobi, 1966-68, 74-84; econ. advisor Asia prog. Ford Found., NYC, 1969-74; pres. Edgar O. Edwards, Inc., Poultney, Vt., 1989—. Cons. USAIDX, 1987, 89, 2003; econ. cons. Ministry Fin. and Devel. Planning, Gaborone, Botswana, 1990-95. Author: The Theory of Measurement of Business Income, 1961, Accounting for Economic Events, 1980; contbr. articles to profl. jour. Recipient Disting. Alumni award Washington and Jefferson Coll., 1962, Green Mountain Coll., 1980; named Elder Order of the Burning Spear Govt. Kenya, 1984; named to Acctg. Hall of Fame, 2003. Mem. Phi Beta Kappa. Address: PO Box 198 Poultney VT 05764-0198

EDWARDS, EDITH MARTHA, lawyer; b. Great Neck, N.Y., Mar. 7, 1945; d. Paul Walter and Alice Matilda (Hansen) Steen; m. Thomas Murray Edwards Sr., Dec. 27, 1966; children: Janice Audrey, Thomas Murray Jr. BS, Coker Coll., 1967; JD, Olgethorpe U., 1981. Bar: Ga. 1982, U.S. Dist. Ct. (no. dist.) Ga. 1983, U.S. Supreme Ct. 1986. Atty. Ga. Legal Svcs., Nashville, 1983-84; asst. dist. atty. Alapaha Cir., Ga., 1984-86; asst. dist. Cherokee Jud. Cir., Ga., 1987; atty. pvt. practice, Valdosta, Ga., 1988—. Mem.: AAUW. Republican. Episcopalian. Avocation: art. Home and Office: 508 Gornto Rd Valdosta GA 31602-1602

EDWARDS, ELEANOR MATTIASICH, singer, voice educator; b. Mt. Vernon, N.Y., May 14, 1938; d. Anton Casimir and Eleanor (Gallessich) Mattiasich; m. Peter L. Edwards, Sept. 4, 1960; 1 child, Jonathan Anthony. MusB, Oberlin Coll., 1960; MusM, New Eng. Conservatory, Boston, 1963; Sommer Akademie cert., Das Mozarteum, Salzburg, Austria, 1959. Soprano soloist Temple Israel, Brookline, Mass., 1964—76, Trinity Ch., Boston, 1966—80, Boston Pops Orch., 1965, 1974. Presented by Concert Artists Guild in Recital Town Hall, N.Y.C., 1967; voice tchr. pvt. studio, 1972—, South Shore Conservatory, Hingham, Mass., 1978—86; owner Music for Sale purchasing svc.; soprano soloist major choral orgns. in Boston area; soloist numerous chs., temples; recitalist Isabella Stewart Gardner Mus., other New Eng. locations; soloist European Choral Symposium, Salzburg and Linz, Austria, 1980; former chmn. voice dept. Thayer Acad., Braintree, Mass.; voice tchr. Stonehill Coll., Oliver Ames H.S.; instr. quilting and needlework guilds. Bd. trustees, choir mem. Old South Union Ch. (Congregational), South Weymouth, Mass., 1980—. Recipient 2d place award, Met. Opera Auditions, Boston, 1966. Mem.: Nat. Assn. Tchrs. of Singing (bd. dirs. Boston chpt., pres. 6 yrs.), Fedn. Internat. Luge Ofcls. (ofcl. 2002 Olympics), Pi Kappa Lambda. Democrat. Avocations: needlecrafts, old house restoration, hockey, luge, Camp Dudley. Address: 779 Main St South Weymouth MA 02190-1659

EDWARDS, EPHRAIM ZENO, retired anesthesiologist; b. St. Lucia, W.I., 1926; BS, Howard U., 1947, MD, 1952. Diplomate Am. Bd. Anesthesiology. Pvt. practice, Laurinburg, N.C., 1952-59, Shelby, N.C., 1959-69; intern Springfield Hosp. Med. Ctr., 1969-70; resident Hartford Hosp., 1970-73; chief of staff Noble Hosp., Westfield, Mass., 1977-83, chief anesthesiology divsn., 1982-86; ret., 1986. Mem. Am. Soc. Anesthesiologists.

EDWARDS, FRANCES LAVINIA, city official; b. Phila., Sept. 12, 1948; d. Harry Donaldson and Anna Louise (McColgan) Edwards; children: Frances Lavinia Papapietro, David Allen Winslow Jr. BA, Drew U., 1969, MA, 1971; M Urban Planning, NYU, 1974, PhD, 1978. Cert. in hazardous material mgmt.; cert. emergency mgr. Adminstrv. asst. Borough of Florham Park, N.J., 1970-73; instr. Kean Coll., Union, N.J., 1973-75; adminstrv. analyst Irvine (Calif.) Police Dept., 1984-86; coord. emergency svcs. City of Irvine, 1986-91; dir. emergency svcs. City of San Jose, Calif., 1991—, acting asst. fire chief, 1993—94; dir. San Jose Met. Med. Task Force, 1997—. Instr. U. Calif., Irvine, 1990—91, Berkeley, 1996—98, Santa Cruz, 1997—2001; adj. prof. San Jose State U., 1999, Santa Clara U., 2002; mem. Calif. Seismic Safety Commn., 1991—95, Calif. Hosp. Bldg. Safety Bd., 1994—95; mem. exec. session on domestic preparedness Kennedy Sch., Harvard U., 1999—; vice chair Collaborative for Disaster Mitigation, 2000—; met. med. response sys. rev. com. NAS/Inst. Medicine, 2000—02; rsch. assoc. Mineta Transp. Inst., 2001—; mem. U.S.-Germany Counter Terrorism project Stanford U., 2002—, biol. warfare working group, 1998—; mem. air monitoring project NAS, 2002; mem. radiol. edn. project CDC, 2003—; cons. in field. Editor: NCEER Workshop Procs., 1990, 1992, others; contbr. chpts. in books and articles to profl. jours.; panelist BioWar series on Nightline, 1999, guest (TV series) Live Response, 2001; author (columnist): ASPA On-Line, 2001—. Vice pres. San Diego Chaplain's Wives, 1976-79; treas. Girl Scouts U.S.A., Yokohama, Japan, 1980-81, Camp Pendleton Officer's Wives Club, 1982-83, pres., 1983-84; vice-chmn. curriculum ARC Disaster Acad., 1989-90, chmn., 1991; cmty. disaster preparedness com. ARC, 1992-97; del. Internat. Assn. Emergency Mgrs., 1990—; bd. dirs. Calif. Earthquake Safety Found., 1997—; bd. dirs. Vol. Ctr. Silicon Valley, 2002—, emergency svc. com., 2002—; active Copertino Gen. Plan Task Force, 2003—. Recipient Vol. Svc. award Navy Relief Soc., 1984; Lasker Found. fellow, 1972; named one of Women of Distinction, Soroptimists Internat., 1991; named Pub. Adminstr. of Yr., Governing Mag., 2002, named to Silicon Valley Power 100, San Jose Mag., 2002. Mem. ASPA (program chmn. Orange County 1984-85, chmn. criminal justice sect. award com. 1988-92, Santa Clara County bd. dirs., 1992—, co-chmn. mini-conf. 1993, sec. 1994-95, pres. 1995-98, bd. dirs.

1993—, chair sect. emergency mgmt. 1999-2002, nat. policy com. 1995-99, nat. membership chair 1996-97, nat. coun. 1998-2000, chpt. awards chair 1993-98, 2000-01, mem. editl. bd. Pub. Adminstrn. Rev. 2003—), Am. Planning Assn. (regional conf. planning com. 1989-90), Internat. City Mgrs. Assn., Assn. Police Planning and Res. Officers (past ec., v.p. Orange County 1984-90), Creekers Club (pres. 1985-88), San Jose Mgmt. Assn. (bd. dirs. 1992-98), Portofino Villas Homeowners Assn. (v.p. 1995-2001, 2003—, bd. dirs. 1995—), Calif. Emergency Svcs. Assn. (conf. program com. 1992, 95, 98, 2001, legis. chair 1997-98, Platinum award 1998, Gold award 1998, John Fetz Meml. award 2000), Santa Clara County Emergency Mgrs. Assn. (sec. 1995, v.p. 1996, pres. 1997), Yokohama Internat. Women's Club (v.p. for social svcs. 1979-81). Republican. Methodist. Avocations: amateur radio, music, reading, biking, swimming. Home: PO Box 2753 Cupertino CA 95015-2753 Office: City of San Jose OES 855 N San Pedro St # 404 San Jose CA 95110-1718 E-mail: KC6THM@yahoo.com., frances.winslow@ci.sj.ca.us.

EDWARDS, FRANKLIN R. economist, educator, consultant; b. Palmerton, Pa., May 5, 1937; s. Franklin Richard and Mary Edytha (Morgan) E.; m. Linda Nasif, June 9, 1968; children— Rebecca, Jarett BA in Econs., Bucknell U., 1958, MA in Econs., 1960; PhD in Econs., Harvard U., 1964; JD, NYU, 1968. Economist Bankers Trust Co., N.Y.C., 1961; economist Fed. Res. Bd., Washington, 1962, 63-64; sr. economist Office of Comptroller of Currency, Washington, 1964-66; asst. prof. Bus. Sch. Columbia U., N.Y.C., 1966-68, assoc. prof. Bus. Sch., 1968-74, prof. Bus. Sch., 1974—, vice dean acad. affairs, 1979-81, dir., prof. Columbia Futures Ctr., 1980—. Vis. scholar Am. Enterprise Inst., Washington, 1994-95; vis. prof. Inst. des Sci. Economique, Ctr. Rsch. Interdisciplinaires Droit-Economie, U. Cath., Louvain, Belgium, 1969-70. Assoc. editor Jour. of Futures Markets; editor Jour. Fin. Svcs.; contbr. articles to profl. jours. Mem. adv. bd. Futures Industry Assn. Bd., 1981-88; nominating com. Am. Stock Exchange, 1988-90; mem. bus. conduct com. N.Y. Merc. Exchange, 1989-92. Mem. Am. Econ. Assn., Am. Fin. Assn., Soc. Royale D'Economie Politique Belgique (hon.), Shadow Fin. Regulations Com., Fin. Economists Roundtable. Home: 25 Fairview Rd Scarsdale NY 10583-2137 Office: Columbia U Dept Fin Uris Hall 625 3022 Broadway New York NY 10027-6945

EDWARDS, FRED L., JR., writer consultant; b. Muskogee, Okla., Oct. 3, 1932; s. Fred L. Edwards Sr. and Mary Jane (Stewart) Johnson; m. Wilma Pauline Utter, Nov. 10, 1950; children: Fred Curtis, Jerri Jane. BA in Sociology summa cum laude, Park U., 1971; postgrad., U. S. Fla., 1980-82. Enlisted USMC, 1949, advanced through grades to lt. col., 1973, ret., 1979; pres. F.L. Edwards & Co., St. Petersburg, Fla., 1979-87; exec. asst. to pres. EXAMCO Inc., Kenner, La., 1990-92; gen. ptnr. Fred Edwards Writer-Cons., St. Petersburg, 1987—; mil. corr. Armed Forces News, 2000—. Free-lance writer, St. Petersburg, 1979-87; writer cons. Sea Sch., St. Petersburg, 1986-88, Houston Marine Tng. Svcs., Kenner, 1989-90; tech. cons. Sailors' Gazette, St. Petersburg, 1986-88. Author: Sailing as a Second Language, 1988, Charter Your Boat for Profit, 1989, Making Money with Boats, 1996, The Bridges of Vietnam, 2000. Bd. dirs. Vol. Action Com., St. Petersburg, 1980; mem. mayor's adv. com. South Pasadena, Fla., 1992—; mem. city charter rev. com., 1992; mem. city fin. com., 1996—2001. Decorated Legion of Merit, Meritorious Svc. medal; recipient George Washington hon. medal Freedom's Found. Mem. Ret. Officers Assn. (chpt. pres. 1996-97, chmn. legis. affairs state coun. 1996-99, v.p. state coun. 1998-2000, pres. state coun. 2000-2002, nat. bd. dirs. 2002—), Pinellas County Vets. Liaison Coun. (v.p. 1996—). Office: Ste 607 7979 Sailboat Key Blvd S Saint Petersburg FL 33707-6356

EDWARDS, GARY THOMAS, historian, educator; b. Murfreesboro, Tenn., Aug. 13, 1965; s. Preston and Martha Cleo Edwards; m. Michelle Eileen Eckhart, Oct. 7, 1988. BA, Abilene Christian U., 1993, MA, 1996; PhD, U. Memphis, 2004. Adj. prof. history U. Memphis, 1997—. Cons. askahistorian.com, Tempe, Ariz., 2000—; creator, advisor Conf. African Am. History, Memphis. Contbr. book, reference; sr. assoc. editor: So. Historian/U. Ala, 1999—2002. Judge Nat. History Day, Memphis, 1998—2002; docent Miss. River Mus., Memphis, 1997—97. Ruth and Harry Woodbury/So. History fellow, U. Memphis, 2001—02, Jesse E. Wills fellow, Tenn. Hist. Soc., 2002. Mem.: Orgn. Am. Historians (assoc.), Soc. History Edn. (assoc.), So. Hist. Assn. (assoc.), Am. Hist. Assn. (assoc.), Phi Alpha Theta (assoc.). Avocations: camping, hiking, singing. Office: Univ Memphis 100 Mitchell Hall Memphis TN 38152 Office Fax: 901-678-2720.

EDWARDS, GEOFFREY HARTLEY, newspaper publisher; b. Liverpool, Eng., Mar. 28, 1936; s. James S. and Edith (Ellison) E.; m. Pamela Duncan, Oct. 9, 1965; children: Robert James, Alistair Duncan. HNC Mech. Engring., Merseyside Tech. Coll., Birkenhead. Plant mgr. Inverest Paper Group, Derbyshire, Eng., 1962-65; gen. mgr. Liverpool Web Offset Ltd., 1965-68; asst. gen. mgr. Liverpool Daily Post & Echo, 1968-71, dir., gen. mgr., 1971-77; pub. Jour. Newspapers, Inc., Washington, 1977-91, Army Times, Washington, 1991-93; pub., CEO Current Newspapers, Washington, 1993-94; v.p. Washington Times, 1994—. Bd. dirs. Greter Washington Bd. Trade, Cultural Alliance Greater Washington, pres., 1984-86; mem. kennedy Ctr. Cmty. & Friend Bd., 1987—; campaign chmn. United Way of Nat. Capital Area, 1989, pres., 1998-2000. Mem. Brit. Newspaper Soc. (coun. 1974-77), Indsl. Rels. Newspaper Soc. (vice chmn. 1974-77).

EDWARDS, GEORGE CHARLES, III, political science educator, writer; b. Rochester, N.Y., Jan. 3, 1947; s. George Charles Jr. and Mary Elizabeth (Laing) E.; m. Carmella Rose Pierce, May 22, 1981; 1 child, Jeffrey Allan. BA, Stetson U., 1969; MA, U. Wis., 1970, PhD, 1973. Asst. prof. polit. sci. Tulane U., New Orleans, 1973-78; assoc. prof. polit. sci. Tex. A&M U., College Station, 1978-81, prof., 1981-90, disting. prof., 1990—, Jordan prof. in liberal arts, 1991—, dir. Ctr. for Presdnl. Studies, 1991—. Vis. asst. prof. U. Wis.-Madison, 1976; vis. prof. U.S. Mil. Acad., West Point, N.Y., 1985-88, Peking U., Beijing, 1993, Hebrew U., Jerusalem, 1997; John Adams fellow U. London, 2003; pres. Presidency Rsch. Group, 1984-85; lectr. U.S. Info. Svc., Europe, 1985, 89, U.S., 1988, 92, Brazil, 1988; cons. NSF, Washington, 1977—, Internat. Rep. Inst., Moscow, 1994, Ctr. for Strategic and Internat. Studies, Washington, 1990-91, Nat. Acad. Pub. Adminstrn., Washington, 1987-88; bd. dirs. Roper Ctr. Pub. Opinion Rsch.; bd. advisors Stetson U., Transition to Governing Project; bd. acad. advisers Ctr. for Congl. and Presdl. Studies; exec. com. White House Interview Program; mem. Coun. on Fgn. Rels., 2002— Author: On Deaf Ears, 2003, Presidential Approval, 1990, At the Margins, 1989, Government in America, 1989, 91, 94, 96, 97, 98, 99, 2000, 01, Presidential Leadership, 1985, 90, 94, 97, 99, 2001, The Public Presidency, 1983, Presidential Influence in Congress, 1980, Implementing Public Policy, 1980, The Policy Predicament, 1978; editor: Reinventing the Presidency, 2001, Researching the Presidency, 1993, National Security and the U.S. Constitution, 1988, The Presidency and Public Policy Making, 1985, Studying the Presidency, 1983, Public Policy Implementation, 1984, Perspectives on Public Policy-Making, 1975, Reinventing the Presidency, 2000; editor Presdl. Studies Quarterly; mem. editl. bd. Am. Jour. Polit. Sci., 1985-87, 94—, Jour. Politics, 1997—, Am. Politics Quar., 1981-87, Presdl. Studies Quar., 1978—, Congress and the Presidency, 1981—, Policy Studies Jour., 1981-83, Am. Rev. Politics, 1994—; contbr. articles to profl. jours. Pres. Greenfield Plaza Condominium Assn., Bryan, Tex., 1980-81; mem. East Tex. 2000 Commn., 1980. Capt. USAR, 1971-79. Decorated for Disting. Civilian Svc. U.S. Army, 1960; Woodrow Wilson fellow, 1969-70, Ford fellow, 1970-73, John Adams fellow U. London, 2003. Mem.: Coun. on Fgn. Rels., Ctr. Study of Presidency (bd. dirs. 1978—), Policy Studies Assn., Midwest Polit. Sci. Assn., So. Polit. Sci. Assn. (Pi Sigma Alpha award 2001), Am. Assn. Pub. Opinion Rsch., Am. Polit. Sci. Assn. (sect. pres. 1984—85), Phi Beta Kappa, Phi Kappa Phi, Phi Alpha Alpha, Phi Alpha Theta, Pi Sigma Alpha. Avocations: collecting art, skiing, tennis, scuba diving, sailing. Home: 2910 Coronado Dr College Station TX 77845-7716 Office: Texas A&M Univ Dept of Polit Sci 4348 TAMU College Station TX 77843

EDWARDS, GEORGE HENRY, retired aeronautical engineer; b. Hammond, Ind., Feb. 19, 1932; s. Samuel Finley and Eula Gertrude (Gruber) E.; m. Marian Joan Weiss, May 24, 1958; children: Susan, Judith, Sandra. BA in Math., Am. U., 1959. Engr. Cook Rsch. Lab., Washington, 1959—62; sr. prin. engr. Amecom Litton Sys., Inc., College Park, Md., 1962—73; sr. engr. Vitro Labs., Silver Spring, Md., 1973-76; mem. tech. staff Rockwell Internat., Anaheim, Calif., 1976-81; dep. program mgr. Lockheed Aircraft Svcs., Ontario, Calif., 1981-83; program mgr. Flight Systems Inc., Newport Beach, Calif., 1983-87; engring. mgr. Litton Applied Tech., San Jose, Calif., 1987-89; broker Edwards Real Estate, San Jose, 1989-91; tech. writer San Jose, 1991-93; computer network engr. San Jose, Surfside Beach, S.C., 1993-97; real estate broker-assoc. Surfside Beach, 1997—2001; ret., 2001. Pres. Presidents' Assn. Prince George's County, 1971—72; bd. dirs. various civic assns., 1970—73; v.p. Toastmasters, Olney, Md., 1974; pres. Mission Club, Assn. Old Crows, Orange County, Calif., 1982—83, bd. dirs., 1983—84; founder, facilitator San Jose Dist. 8 Cmty. Leaders Assn., 1994; mem. planning coms. tree preservation, buffers, landscaping, sign control Horry County, SC, 1998—2002; founder, webmaster Growth Income Action Com., 2002. Mem. Mensa. Achievements include co-invention of electronic counter-counter measure system. Home: 1439 Windwood Xing Surfside Beach SC 29575-5376 E-mail: georgehe@earthlink.net.

EDWARDS, HAROLD MORTIMER, mathematics educator; b. Champaign, Ill., Aug. 6, 1936; s. Harold Mortimer and Marian Bell (Scarlett) E.; m. Betty Rollin, Jan. 21, 1979. BA, U. Wis., 1956; MA, Columbia U., 1957; PhD, Harvard U., 1961. Instr. Harvard U., 1961-62; rsch. assoc. Columbia U., 1962-63, asst. prof., 1963-66, N.Y. U., N.Y.C., 1966-69, assoc. prof., 1969-79, prof. math., 1979—2002, prof. emeritus, 2002—. Vis. sr. lectr. Australian Nat. U., 1971. Author: Advanced Calculus, 1969, Riemann's Zeta Function, 1974, Fermat's Last Theorem, 1977, Galois Theory, 1984, Divisor Theory, 1990, Linear Algebra, 1995. Guggenheim fellow, 1981-82 Mem. Am. Math. Soc. (Steele prize 1980), Math. Assn. Am., N.Y. Acad. Scis. Home: 67 Park Ave New York NY 10016-2557 Office: 251 Mercer St New York NY 10012-1110

EDWARDS, HARRY LAFOY, lawyer; b. Greenville, SC, July 29, 1936; s. George Belton and Mary Olive (Jones) E.; m. Suzanne Copeland, June 16, 1956; 1 child, Margaret Peden. *Third Great Grandfather, Judge Thomas Edwards, Revolutionary War soldier with Washington at Yorktown, Probate, County and District Judge and Member of South Carolina Legislature from Greenville County, married Mary Ann McClanahan, niece of Mary Marshall, Aunt of Chief Justice John Marshall. Great Great Grandfather, Francis, Edwards, War of 1812 soldier, married Laodicea, daughter of Captain Daniel Bailey, Revolutionary war soldier at Kings Mountain and Cowpens. Great Grandfather, Thomas Edwards, was with Lee at Appomattox. Grandfather William Francis Edwards was a farmer. Father was President of the family real estate company. Mother was a descendant of the Aiken and Peden families.* LLB, U. S.C., 1963, JD, 1970. Bar: S.C. 1963, U.S. Dist. Ct. S.C. 1975, U.S. Ct. Appeals (4th cir.) 1974. Assoc. Edwards and Edmunds, Greenville, 1963; v.p., sec., dir. Edwards Co., Inc., Greenville, 1963-65; atty. investment legal dept. Liberty Life Ins. Co., Greenville, 1965-67, asst. sec., asst. v.p., head investment legal dept., 1967-70; asst. sec. Liberty Corp., 1970-75; asst. v.p. Liberty Life Ins. Co., 1970-75; sec. Bent Tree Corp., CEL, Inc., 1970-75; sec., dir. Westchester Mall, Inc., 1970-75; asst. sect. Libco, Inc., Liberty Properties, Inc., 1970-75; pvt. practice, Greenville, 1975—. Editor U. S.C. Law Rev., 1963. Com. mem. Hipp Fund Spl. Edn., Greenville County Sch. Sys.; mem. Boyd C. Hipp II Scholarship Com., Wofford Coll. Spartanburg, S.C.; scholarship com. Liberty Scholars, U. S.C., 1984, 86-2003. With USAFR, 1957-63. Mem. ABA, S.C. Bar Assn., Greenville County Bar Assn., Phi Delta Phi, Greenville Lawyers, Poinsett Club (Greenville). Baptist. Home: 106 Ridgeland Dr Greenville SC 29601-3017 Office: PO Box 10350 Greenville SC 29603-0350 E-mail: hle106@aol.com.

EDWARDS, HARRY T. judge; b. N.Y.C., Nov. 3, 1940; s. George H. Edwards and Arline Ross Lyle; m. Pamela Carrington; children: Brent, Michelle. BS, Cornell U., 1962; JD, U. Mich., 1965. Assoc. firm Seyfarth, Shaw, Fairweather & Geraldson, Chgo., 1965—70; prof. law U. Mich., 1970—75; vis. prof. law Harvard U., 1975—76, prof., 1976—77; judge U.S. Ct. Appeals (D.C. cir.), Washington, 1980—; vis. prof. Free U. Brussels, 1974; dir. AMTRAK, 1977—80, chmn. bd., 1979—80; disting. lectr. law Duke U., 1983—89; lectr. law Georgetown Law Ctr., 1985—86; chief judge U.S. Ct. Appeals (D.C. cir.), Washington, 1994—2001; prof. law U. Mich., 1977—80. Adj. prof. law NYU Law Sch., 1989—; lectr. Harvard Law Sch., 1982—88, Mich. Law Sch., 1988—89; mem. Adminstrv. Conf. of U.S., 1976—80. Co-author: Labor Relations Law in the Public Sector, 1974, 1979, 1985, Lawyer as a Negotiator, 1977, Collective Bargaining and Labor Arbitration, 1979, Higher Education and the Law, 1979. Mem.: ABA (sec. sect. labor law 1976—77), Am. Law Inst., Am. Arbitration Assn. (dir. 1979—80), Am. Acad. Arts and Scis., Nat. Acad. Arbitrators (dir. 1975—80, v.p. 1978—80), Order of Coif. Office: US Ct Appeals 333 Constitution Ave NW Washington DC 20001-2866

EDWARDS, HELEN THOM, physicist; b. Detroit, May 27, 1936; d. Edgar Robertson and Mary (Milner) Thom; m. Donald A. Edwards. BS in Physics, Cornell U., 1957, MA in Physics, 1963, PhD in Physics, 1966. Rsch. assoc. Cornell U., Ithaca, N.Y., 1966-70; assoc. head booster Fermi Nat. Accelerator Lab., Batavia, Ill., 1970-71, staff physicist, M.R., 1971-75, head switchyard extraction group, 1975-78, leader tevatron design group, 1978-79, dep. head saver div., 1980-81, dep. head accelerator div., 1981-86, head accelerator div., 1987-88; head accelerator constrn. div. SSC/URA, Dallas, 1989-90, tech. dir., 1990-91. Recipient Achievement in Accelerator Physics and Tech. U.S. Summer Sch. on Particle Accelerator Prize, 1985, Ernest O. Lawrence award Dept. of Energy, 1986, Nat. Medal Tech., 1989; MacArthur Found. Chgo. fellow, 1988. Fellow Am. Phys. Soc.; mem. NAE.

EDWARDS, HERMAN, professional football coach; b. Monmouth, N.J., Apr. 27, 1954; Student, Monterrey Peninsula J.C., San Diego State, 1987—89. Profl. football player Eagles, 1977—85, L.A. Rams, 1986, Atlanta Falcons, 1986; scout, asst. coach Kansas City Chiefs, 1990—95; asst. head coach, defensive backs coach Buccaneers, 1996—2000; profl. football head coach N.Y. Jets, 2001—. Office: NY Jets Ticket Office 1000 Fulton Ave Hempstead NY 11550-1099 Office Fax: 516-560-8198.

EDWARDS, HOWARD LEE, retired petroleum company executive, lawyer; b. Baker City, Oreg., June 10, 1931; s. Elmer L. and Bernice (Stringham) E.; m. Carolyn Bagley, Mar. 19, 1954; children: Bryant B., H. McKay, Mitchell L., Paul S. BS, Brigham Young U., 1955; postgrad., Stanford U., 1955-56, U. Utah, 1956-57; JD, George Washington U., 1959. Bar: Utah 1959, Colo. 1981, Alaska 1982, Calif. 1987. Legal asst., atty. US Dept. Interior, Washington and Salt Lake City, 1957-61; ptnr. Van Cott, Bagley, Cornwall & McCarthy, Salt Lake City, 1961-68; asst. gen. counsel Anaconda Co., NYC, 1968, asst. to chmn. bd., 1969, v.p., sec., 1970-77; gen. atty. Denver, 1977-82, Anchorage, 1982-83; corp. sec. Atlantic Richfield Co., LA, 1984-95; ret., 1995. Bd. dirs. Dynatronics Corp., 1996—. Trustee Rocky Mountain Mineral Law Found., 1968-87; mem. nat. adv. coun. Brigham Young U. Sch. Mgmt., 1972-85; mem. nat. adv. coun. Dixie State Coll., St. George, Utah, 1987—, chmn., 1994-95; bd. visitors J. Reuben Clark Law Sch., 1980-83; bd. dir. LA region NCCJ, 1987-94, Ettie Lee Homes for Youth, 1989-96, Kostopoulos Dream Found., 1997-2002, Deseret Found.; chmn. cmty. adv. coun. Heart and Lung Rsch. Found.; mem. exec. bd. Verdugo Hills coun. Boy Scouts Am., 1992-95, Verdugo Hills Hosp. Found., 1992-95; honorary bd. Utah Symphony, 2002—. Recipient Disting. Citizen award, Dixie State Coll., St. George, Utah, 2000. Mem. Am. Mining Congress (chmn. pub. lands com. 1970-84, Disting. Svc. award 1983), Coun. on Fgn. Rels., Pacific Coun. on Internat. Policy, Brigham Young U. Alumni Assn. (bd. dir. 1974-83, pres. 1980-81), Econ. Round Table, Rotary. Republican. Mem. Lds Ch. Home: PO Box 680934 Park City UT 84068-0934 E-mail: howardledwards@hotmail.com.

EDWARDS, IRENE ELIZABETH (LIBBY EDWARDS), dermatologist, educator, researcher; b. Winston-Salem, N.C., Mar. 17, 1950; d. Robert Dixon Edwards and Irene Octavia (Temple) Fisher; m. Clayton Samuel Owens, Apr. 19, 1985; 1 child, Sarah Tay. BS magna cum laude, Wake Forest U., 1972; MD, Bowman Gray Sch. Medicine, 1976; postgrad., N.C. Bapt. Hosp., 1979, U. Ariz., 1981, 84. Diplomate Nat. Bd. Med. Examiners, Am. Bd. Internal Medicine, Am. Bd. Pediatrics, Am. Bd. Dermatology. Intern N.C. Bapt. Hosp., Winston-Salem, 1976-78, resident in pediatrics, 1978-79; resident in internal medicine U. Ariz. Health Scis. Ctr., Tucson, 1979-81, resident in dermatology, 1982-84; instr. dermatology U. Ariz. Coll. Medicine, Tucson, 1984-85, asst. prof. dermatology, 1985-90; chief section dermatology Tucson VA Med. Ctr., 1984-90; chief dermatology Carolinas Med. Ctr., Charlotte, N.C., 1990—; clin. assoc. prof. dermatology, clin. rsearcher Wake Forest U., Winston-Salem, 1993—; clin. assoc. prof. dermatology, clin. researcher U. N.C., Chapel Hill, 1993—. Nat. lectr. in field. Author: Dermatology in Emergency Care, 1997; co-author: Genital Dermatology, 1994; contbr. chpts. to books, numerous articles to profl. jours. Reynolds scholar, 1969-72. Fellow Am. Acad. Dermatology, Am. Acad. Pediatrics; mem. Soc. Pediatric Dermatology, Internat. Soc. Tropical Dermatology, Women's Dermatologic Soc., Internat. Soc. for Study of Vulvovaginal Disease (sec.-gen.), Charlotte Dermatological Soc., Phi Beta Kappa, Alpha Epsilon Delta. Home: 2409 Cuthbertson Rd Waxhaw NC 28173-8110

EDWARDS, JACK, former congressman, lawyer; b. Birmingham, Ala., Sept. 20, 1928; s. William Jackson and Sue (Fuhrman) E.; m. Jolane Vander Sys, Jan. 30, 1954; children: Mrs. Richard Weavil, Richard Arnold. BS in Commerce and Bus. Adminstrn., U. Ala., 1952, LLB, 1954. Bar: Ala. 1954, D.C. 1983. Practice, Mobile, 1954-64; mem. 89th-98th Congresses from 1st Dist. Ala., 1965-85; mem. com. appropriations; mem. def. and transp. subcom.; vice chmn. Ho. Rep. Conf.; with Hand Arendall L.L.C., Mobile, Ala., 1985—. Bd. dirs. ret. The Southern Co., Holnam Inc., Northrop Grumman Corp., Aerospace Corp., Dravo Corp., QMS, Inc. Trustee U. Ala. Served with USMC, 1946-48, 50-51. Mem. ABA, Ala. Bar Assn., Mobile Bar Assn. (sec. 1956), Mobile Jr. Bar Assn. (pres. 1957), D.C. Bar Assn., Mobile Area C. of C. (chmn. bd. 1986), Kappa Alpha (pres. 1951-53), Omicron Delta Kappa. Presbyterian. (elder). Office: Am South Bank Bldg 107 Saint Francis St Ste 3000 Mobile AL 36602-3330 E-mail: jedwards@handarendall.com.

EDWARDS, JAMES BENJAMIN, accountant, educator; b. Atlanta, Apr. 27, 1935; s. James T. and Frances L. (McEachern) E.; m. Virginia Ann Reagin, Feb. 21, 1958; children: James Benjamin II, Chad Reagin, Calli Ann, Judy Clair. BBA in Fin., U. Ga., 1958, MBA, 1962, PhD in Bus. Adminstrn., 1971. CPA Tenn., Ga., S.C.; cert. mgmt. acct.; cert. internal auditor; cert. in data processing; cert. cost analyst. Contr. Better Maid Dairy Products, Inc., Athens, Ga., 1958-62; staff acct. Max M. Cuba & Co., Atlanta, 1962-63; mng. ptnr. Wilson, Edwards and Swang, accts., Nashville, 1964-66; ptnr. Q.F. Lester & Co., Athens, 1967-68; v.p., chmn. bd. dirs. Gen. Data Svc. Inc., Athens, Ga., 1970-71; internal cons. J.W. Hunt and Co., CPAs, Columbia, 1983-84; v.p. Integrated Cost Mgmt. Systems Inc., Arlington, Tex., 1990-91; instr. David Lipscomb Coll., Nashville, 1963-66; instr. Nashville Ctr. U. Tenn., 1964-66; instr. acctg. U. Ga., Athens, 1966-71; asst. prof. U. S.C., Columbia, S.C., 1971-73, assoc. prof., 1973-77, prof., 1977—, fellow Bus. Partnership Found., 1977-90, William W. Bruner Disting. Faculty fellow, 1990—. Instr. staff tng. program local C.P.A. firms, Nashville, 1963-66 Editor: (ann. publs. Warren, Gorham & Lamont, Inc.) Emerging Practices in Cost Management and, Activity-Based Mnagment, Handbook of Cost Management for Service Industries, 1997—; contbr. articles on mgmt. acctg. to profl. publs. Coach Little League Baseball, Columbia, 1972-76; bd. dirs. Atlanta Bible Camp, Inc.; bd. dirs. Ga. Christian Found., Inc., pres., 1968-69; bd. dirs. Spring Valley Edn. Found., 1983-93, v.p., 1983-85, treas., 1985-93. Recipient 8 nat. awards for contbns. to acctg. lit. Mem. Am. Acctg. Assn., Am. Inst. CPAs, Inst. Internal Auditors, Planning Execs. Inst. (asst. editor nat. mag. 1971-77), Am. Inst. Decision Scis. (v.p. Southeastern sect. 1975-76), Inst. Mgmt. Accts. (pres. Columbia chpt. 1973-74, nat. rsch. com. 1974-75, nat. edn. com. 1977-80, 95—, nat. dir. 1975-77, pres. Carolinas coun. 1976, nat. v.p. 1980-81), S.C. Soc. CPAs, S.C. Assn. Acctg. Instrs. (founding pres. 1972-73), Omicron Delta Epsilon, Beta Alpha Psi, Delta Sigma Pi, Sigma Chi. Mem. Ch. of Christ. Clubs: Five Points Optimist of Athens, Spring Valley Band Boosters. Office: c/o U SC Sch Acctg Darla Moore Sch 1705 College St Columbia SC 29208-0001

EDWARDS, JAMES DALLAS, III, consulting company executive; b. Harriman, Tenn., Aug. 9, 1937; s. James Dallas Jr. and Helen Louise (Milburn) E.; m. Louisa Diane Fultz, July 15, 1961. BBA, U. Tenn., 1959. Customer service supr. Aluminum Co. Am., Alcoa, Tenn., 1964-67, staff product planner Pitts., 1967-70, traffic mgr., 1970-74; plant mgr. Soundesign Corp., Santa Claus, Ind., 1974-78; v.p., gen. mgr. Thermwood Corp., Dale, Ind., 1978-81; pres., chief exec. officer Spencer Plastic Products Corp. (name now Spencer Industries), Dale, 1981-92, also bd. dirs.; pres. Edwards & Assocs., Santa Claus, Ind., 1992—. Chmn. bd. dirs. So. Ind. Rehab. Services, Boonville, 1977-82; bd. dirs. Southwest Ind. Pvt. Industry Coun., 1989—, Ind. Small Bus. Coun.; mem. Santa Claus Indsl. Park Bd., Santa Claus, 1978—; pres. Licolnland Econ. Devel. Corp. Named Ind. Small Bus. Person of Yr., 1989, Ind. Entrepeneur of Yr., 1989, recipient Ind. Global Competitiveness award, 1989. Mem. Am. Prodn. and Inventory Control Soc. (bd. dirs. 1970-72), Soc. Plastics Engrs., Soc. Mfg. Engrs., Naval Res. Assn. (pres. 1967-71), SBA (Ind. adv. coun. 1989—), Res. Officers Assn., Ind. C. of C. (dir.), Dale C. of C., Rolling Hills Country Club, Kiwanis, Elks, Optimist. Presbyterian. Avocations: golf, reading. Home: 826 Balthazar Dr Santa Claus IN 47579 Office: PO Box 372 Santa Claus IN 47579-0372 E-mail: jdedwards@psci.net.

EDWARDS, JAMES MALONE, lawyer; b. Champaign, Ill., Aug. 15, 1931; s. Harold Mortimer and Marion Bell (Scarlett) E.; m. Veronica Marianne Greeven, Mar. 2, 1968; children: Nina Scarlett, Philip Mortimer. BA, U. Ill., 1953; postgrad., Inst. des Sci. Politiques, 1955; LLB, Yale U., 1960. Bar: N.Y. 1961. Law clk. to justice Charles E. Whittaker U.S. Supreme Ct., Washington, 1960-61; assoc. Cravath, Swaine & Moore, N.Y.C., 1961-69, ptnr., 1969—. 1st lt. USAF, 1955-56.

EDWARDS, JAMES RICHARD, lawyer; b. Long Beach, Calif., Apr. 14, 1951; s. Nelson James and Dorotny June (Harris) E.; m. Joan Marie Carriveau, Sept. 24, 1988. BS, Colo. State U., 1973; JD, U. San Diego, 1977. Bar: Calif. 1977, U.S. Dist. Ct. (so. dist.) Calif. 1977, U.S. Dist. Ct. (cen. dist.) Calif. 1978. Atty. Downtown Sr. Ctr., San Diego, 1977-78, Getty Oil Co., L.A., 1978-80, Logicon Inc., Torrance, Calif., 1980-85, sec., 1982-85, gen. counsel, 1981-85; ptnr. Mirassou, Nyznyk & Edwards, 1985-87; v.p., gen. counsel, sec. Gen. Atomics, San Diego, 1987-2000, Vapotronics Inc., 2000—. Lawyer; b. Long Beach, Calif., Apr. 14, 1951; s. Nelson James and Dorothy June (Harris) E.; m. Joan Marie Carriveau, Sept. 24, 1988. BS, Colo. State U., 1973; JD, U. San Diego, 1977. Bar: Calif. 1977, U.S. Dist. Ct. (so. dist.) Calif., 1977, U.S. Dist. Ct. (cen. dist.) 1978. Atty., Downtown Sr. Ctr., San Diego, 1977-78, Getty Oil Co., Los Angeles, 1978-80; atty. Logicon, Inc., Torrance, Calif., 1980-85, sec., 1982-85, gen. counsel, 1981-85; ptnr. Mirassou, Nyznyk & Edwards, 1985-87; v.p., gen. counsel, sec. Gen. Atomics, San Diego, 1987—. Recipient championship medals U.S. Parachute Assn., 1977, 79, 80. Mem. ABA, State Bar Calif., San Diego County Bar Assn., Am. Corp. Counsel Assn. Recipient championship medals U.S. parachute Assn., 1977, 79, 80. Mem. ABA, State Bar Calif., San Diego County Bar Assn., Am. Corp. Counsel Assn. Office: Vapotronics Inc 12555 High Bluff Dr Ste 330 San Diego CA 92130

EDWARDS, JAMES ROBERT, religious educator; b. Colo. Springs, Oct. 28, 1945; s. Robert Emery and Mary Eleanor (Callison) E.; m. Mary Jane Pryor, June 22, 1968; children: Corrie, Mark. BA, Whitworth Coll., Spokane, Wash., 1967; MDiv, Princeton (N.J.) Seminary, 1970; PhD, Fuller Seminary, Pasadena, Calif., 1978. Youth min. First Presbyn. Ch., Colo. Springs, 1971-78; prof. religion Jamestown (N.D.) Coll., 1978—97, Whitworth Coll., Spokane, Wash., 1997—. Speaker in field. Author: (with others) The Layman's Overview of the Bible, 1987, Commentary on Romans, 1992, The Divine Intruder, 2000, Commentary on Gospel of Mark, 2002; contbr. articles to profl. jours. Recipient several tchg. awards. Mem. Soc. Bibl. Lit. Office: Whitworth College Dept Religion Spokane WA 99251

EDWARDS, JENNIFER J. county official; d. Vernon Jones and Barbara Gregg; m. Ronald Gene Edwards, Apr. 18, 1992; 1 child, Kristen Gayle Indriago. M in Bus. Edn., Ea. Ky. U.; B in Bus. Edn., U. Ky. Bus. edn. instr. Laurel County H.S., London, Ky., 1974—77; asst. sch. food svc. dir. Clay County Pub. Sch. Sys., Manchester, Ky., 1977—79; auditor Ky. Dept. Edn., Frankfort, 1979—81, acct., 1982—84; sr. staff auditor Bank Fla., Naples, 1984—85; coord. bus. edn. distributive edn. Collier County Pub. Sch., Naples, 1985—86; analyst budget and mgmt. Collier County Govt., Naples, 1987—91, asst. to county mgr., 1991—96, human resources dir., 1996—2000; supr. elections Collier County, Fla., 2000—. Bd. dirs. United Way, Collier County, Fla., 2002—. Mem.: LWV, AAUW, Fla. Assn. Supr. Elections, Kiwanis. Office: Supr of Elections 3301 Tamiami Trail East Naples FL 34112 Office Fax: 239-774-9468.

EDWARDS, JEROME, lawyer; b. N.Y.C., July 5, 1912; s. Philip and Anna (Hollinger) E.; m. Mildred Kahn, Dec. 7, 1941 (dec.); children: Susan, Bruce (dec.). BS, NYU, 1931, JD, 1933. Bar: N.Y. State 1934, Calif. 1975. Asso. firm

T.J. Lesser, 1934-36; pvt. practice N.Y.C., 1936-42; sr. partner Phillips, Nizer, Benjamin, Krim & Ballon, N.Y.C., 1942-62; v.p., gen. counsel 20th Century Fox Film Corp., N.Y.C. and Los Angeles, 1962-77; of counsel Kaplan, Livingston, Goodwin, Berkowitz & Selvin, Beverly Hills, Calif., 1977-81, Musick, Peeler & Garrett, Los Angeles, 1982-83, Phillips, Nizer, Benjamin, Krim & Ballon, Los Angeles, 1985-89. Mem. ABA, Am. Film Mktg. Assn. (arbitrator panel), Am. Arbitration Assn. (nat. pnel neutral arbitrators 1960-2000). Fax: 310-475-6328. E-mail: JerEdwards1903@aol.com.

EDWARDS, JESSE EFREM, physician, educator; b. Hyde Park, Mass., July 14, 1911; s. Max and Nellie (Gordon) E.; m. Marjorie Helen Brooks, Nov. 12, 1952; children— Ellen Ann Villa, Brooks Sayre. BS, Tufts Coll., 1932, MD, 1935; DSc (hon.), Georgetown U., 1990. Diplomate Am. Bd. Med. Examiners, Am. Bd. Pathology. Resident Mallory Inst. Pathology, Boston, 1935-36, asst., 1937-40; intern Albany (N.Y.) Hosp., 1936-37; instr. pathology Boston U., 1938; instr. pathology, bacteriology, surgery Tufts Med. Coll., 1939-40; research fellow Nat. Cancer Inst. USPHS, 1940-42; cons. sect. pathologic anatomy Mayo Clinic, 1946-60; asst. prof. grad. sch. U. Minn., Mpls., 1946-51, asso. prof., 1951-54, prof. pathologic anatomy, clin. prof. med. sch., prof. pathology grad. sch., 1960—96; chief pathologist United Hosp. (formerly Chas. T. Miller Hosp.), St. Paul, 1960-80; cons. pathologist Hennepin County Hosp., Mpls., 1964—; cons. dept. pathology Mpls. Vets. Hosp., 1966—90; cons. pathologist St. Paul Ramsey Hosp., 1967-80; dir. registry of cardiovascular disease United Hosp., St. Paul, 1980-87, sr. cons. registry of cardiovascular disease, 1987—, also sr. cons. Jesse E. Edwards Registry of Cardiovascular Disease, 1987—. Pres. World Congress Pediatric Cardiology, 1980; mem. pathology study sect. USPHS, 1957-62; civilian cons. surgeon gen. AUS, 1947-69 Author: Atlas Acquired Diseases of Heart and Great Vessels, 1961, (with T.J. Dry and others) Congenital Anomalies of the Heart and Great Vessels, 1948, (with others) An Atlas of Congenital Anomalies of the Heart and Great Vessels, 1954, (with R.S. Fontana) Congenital Cardiac Disease, 1962, (with J.R. Stewart, O. Kincaid) An Atlas of Vascular Rings and Related Malformations of the Aortic System, 1963, (with C.A. Wagenvoort, D. Heath) Pathology of Pulmonary Vasculature, 1963, (with others) Correlation of Pathologic Anatomy and Angiocardiography, 1965, Coronary Arterial Variations in the Normal Heart and in Congenital Heart Disease; 1975, Coronary Heart Disease, 1976, (with Brooks S. Edwards) Jesse E. Edwards Synopsis of Congenital Heart Disease, 2000; Editor: (with others) Circulation; Contbr. (with others) articles to profl. jours. Served from capt. to lt. col. M.C. AUS, 1942-46. Recipient Distinguished Tchr. award Minn. Med. Found., 1974; Gold Heart award Am. Heart Assn., 1970; Gifted Tchr. award Am. Coll. Cardiology, 1977 Mem. AMA, Minn. Med. Assn., Soc. Exptl. Biology and Medicine, Am. Heart Assn. (pres. 1967-68), Minn. Heart Assn. (pres. 1962-63), Internat. Acad. Pathology (pres. 1955-56), Am. Assn. Pathologists and Bacteriologists, World Congress Pediat. Cardiology, Coll. Am. Pathologists, Am. Soc. Exptl. Pathology, Sigma Xi, Alpha Omega Alpha. Home: 1565 Edgcumbe Rd Saint Paul MN 55116-2304 Office: United Hosp Saint Paul MN 55102

EDWARDS, JOANN LOUISE, human resources executive; b. Lebanon, Pa., June 15, 1955; d. Harold Eugene and Kathryn Faye (Smith) E. AA in Human Svcs. with honors, Harrisburg Area C.C., 1975; BS with honors, Pa. State U., 1981; MA in Indsl. Rels./Human Resources Mgmt., St. Francis Coll., 1994. Cert. sr. profl. mgmt. Residential program worker Pan Am. Corp., Hershey, Pa., 1975-80, residential program supr., 1981-82, intensive behavior shaping supr., 1982-83; program mgr. Devel. Resources, Inc., Harrisburg, Pa., 1983-85, dir. minimum supervision, 1985-86, dir. human resources, 1986-96, Northwestern Human Svcs., Inc. of Ctrl./Western Region, Harrisburg, Pa., 1996—, corp.v.p. human resource exec., 2002—. Mem. New Directions for Progress Pers. Com., Harrisburg, 1988-96; instr. Mt. Aloyusius Coll., 2000—; adj. prof. human resources mgmt. St. Francis U., 2001. Mem. Christian Chs. United Pers. Com., Harrisburg, 1989-90. Mem. Harrisburg Area SHRM (past pres.), Soc. Human Resource Mgmt. Avocations: theater, classical music, antiques. Office: Northwestern Human Svcs 620 Germantown Pike Lafayette Hill PA 19444-

EDWARDS, JOHN CARVER, retired archivist; b. Charleston, SC, Dec. 8, 1939; s. John Pelham and Elizabeth Carver Edwards; m. Judith Brina Task, Jan. 29, 2002; children: Leigh Carver, John Spann, Liam Morgan Quinlan, Kelly Harris Quinlan. BA with honors, Wofford Coll., 1964; MA, U. Ga., 1966, Ph.D, 1975. Head, manuscripts divsn. Ga. Dept. of Archives and History, Atlanta, 1970—72; records officer U. Ga., Athens, 1972—77, univ. archivist, 1977—93, spl. projects archivist, 1993—2000, emeritus, 2000—. Program codirector, exhibit preparator conf. and exhibit Deliver them from Evil: A commemoration of America's Role in the Global War Against Fascism, 1941-1945, 1994; regular history and biography book reviewer libr. jour., N.Y.C., 1996—. Author: (history) Patriots In Pinstripe: Men Of The National Security League, 1982, Berlin Calling: American Broadcasters in Service to the Third Reich, 1991, Airmen Without Portfolio: U.S. Mercenaries In Civil War Spain, 1997; contbr. 3 essays, two one hour radio broadcast (Best Documentary award Soc. of Profl. Journalists, The Pub. Radio News Directors Inc., Ga. Assn. of Broadcasters, 1994), (Hon. Mention award, 1999), articles to profl. publs. Active various polit. campaigns, Cleveland, Ga., 2002—03. Mem.: Acad. Cert. Archivists (cert., charter mem.), Soc. Am. Archivists, Delta Tau Kappa (assoc.), Pi Gamma Mu (assoc.), Phi Alpha Theta (assoc.), Phi Kappa Phi (assoc.). Independent. Episcopalian. Avocations: military modeling, reading, walking, baseball, fishing. Home: 1475 Highway 255 South Cleveland GA 30528 Personal E-mail: carver@linkamerica.net.

EDWARDS, JOHN DAVID, investment executive; b. Gallipolis, Ohio, Apr. 14, 1958; s. Vernard David and Virginia Isabelle (Tate) E. Student, Rio Grande Coll., 1976-78. V.p. VD Edwards Ins. Agy., Inc., Pomeroy, Ohio, 1979-85, pres., 1985-86, CLC Ltd. Gold and Silver, Inc., Athens, Ohio, 1987-88; presiding ptnr. NXS Investment Club, Pomeroy, 1988—. Mem. High Frontier, Va., 1987; chmns. advisor U.S. Congl. Adv. Bd., Washington, 1987; charter mem. Ronald Reagan Trust, Washington, 1988; mem. Rep. Presdl. Task Force, Washington, 1988. Recipient Medal of Honor, High Frontier, 1987. Mem. Am. Def. Preparedness Assn. (life), U.S. Naval Inst., Assn. of U.S. Army, Am. Numismatics Assn., Am. Film Inst., Nat. Geog. Soc., Players Club Internat. (charter mem.), Single Action Shooting Soc. Methodist. Avocations: coins, photography, target shooting, reading, civil war mementos. Home: 100 Union Ave Pomeroy OH 45769-1000

EDWARDS, JOHN DAVID, university educator; b. Middlesbrough, Yorkshire, Eng., May 5, 1938; arrived in France, 1961; s. Cyril David Edwards and Dorothy Greenhough. BA with honors, Leeds (Eng.) U., 1960, EdD, 1961; licence es lettres, U. Lille, France, 1963; DLitt, U. Lille, 1973, Doctorat d'Etat, 1983. Reader U. Lille, France, 1961—64; asst. and assoc. prof. U. Paris, 1968—85, full titular prof., 1985—. Lectr. Inst. d'Etudes Politiques, Paris, 1964—82; vis. prof. CUNY, 1981—96; pres. Inter U. Mission for Franco-Am. Exch., Paris, 1984—88; spl. envoy Ministry Edn. France U.S. Acad. Rels., Paris, 1998—; rep. to U.S. French U. Agy., 2001—; lectr. in field. Contbr. articles to profl. jours. Mem. founding body U. Paris VIII, 1968—90, bd. dirs., 1981—2001. Named hon. prof., Queens Coll., N.Y., 1998; recipient Knight of the Order of Acad. Palms, 1994, Officer of the Order of Acad. Palms, 1999; scholar, Leverhulme Trust, London, 1966. Mem.: Jean de La Fontaine Soc. Am. (pres.), Internat. Assn. Univ. Profls. English, Soc. Univ. Profs. English, Andiron Club. Avocations: music, gardening, travel, gastonomy. Home: 7 Rue Bachaumont 75002 Paris France Office: MICEFA 26 rue du Fug Saint Jacques 75014 Paris France

EDWARDS, JOHN DUNCAN, law educator, librarian; b. Louisiana, Mo., Sept. 15, 1953; s. Harold Wenkle and Mary Elizabeth (Duncan) E.; m. Beth Ann Rahm, May 21, 1977; children: Craig, Martha, Brooks. BA, Southeast Mo. State U., 1975; JD, U. Mo., Kansas City, 1977; MALS, U. Mo., Columbia, 1979. Bar: Mo. 1978, U.S. Dist. Ct. (we. dist.) Mo. 1978. Instr. legal research and writing U. Mo., Columbia, 1978, dir. legal research and writing, librarian, 1979-80; pub. svcs. librarian Law Sch., U. Okla., Norman, 1980-81, assoc. librarian, 1981-84, adj. instr. sch. library sci., 1983-84; prof. law, dir. law library law sch. Drake U., Des Moines, 1984—. Adj. instr. Columbia Coll., 1979-80; cons. Cleveland County Bar Assn., 1984. Editor: Emerging Solutions in Reference Services: Implications for Libraries in the New Millennium, 2001, Iowa Legal Research Guide, 2003; contbr. articles to profl. jours. Cons. Friends Drake U. Libr., 1985—; coach, mgr. Westminster Softball Team. Des Moines, 1987 94; pres. Crestview Parent-Tchr. Coun., Des Moines, 1988-90; trustee Westminster Presbyn. Ch., Des Moines, 1988-89, treas., 1990, pres., 1991; mem. Clive City Coun., 1995—, mayor pro tem, 1998—; trustee Des Moines Metro Transit Authority, 1996—, chmn. bd. dirs., 1997-98, 2003—, sec.-treas., 1996, 2001-02. Recipient Presdl. award Drake U. Student Bar Assn., 1987; named Outstanding Vol., Crestview Elem. Sch., 1989-90. Mem. Am. Assn. Law Librs. (chmn. awards com. 1987-88, chmn. grants com. 1996-97, chmn. scholarship com. 1998-99), Mid-Am. Assn. Law Librs. (chmn. resource sharing 1986-93, v.p. 1994-95, pres. 1995-96), Mid-Am. Law Sch. Librs. Consortium (pres. 1986-88), Delta Theta Phi, Beta Phi Mu. Avocations: softball, tennis. Office: Drake U Libr Law Sch 27th & Carpenter Sts Des Moines IA 50311

EDWARDS, JOHN RALPH, retired chemist, educator; b. Streator, Ill., Feb. 27, 1937; s. Ralph E. and Ruth M. Edwards; m. Margaret E. Smith, July 15, 1961; children: Peter J., Sharon E., Susan D. BS, Ill. Wesleyan U., 1959; PhD, U. Ill., 1964. NIH postdoctoral fellow Tufts U., Boston, 1964-66; asst. prof. chemistry Villanova (Pa.) U., 1966-73, assoc. prof., 1973-80, prof., 1980—, chmn. dept. chemistry, 1980-90, asst. chmn., 1996—2002, ret., 2002. Contbr. articles to profl. jours. Grantee, NIH, 1970—76. Mem. Am. Soc. Biochemistry and Molecular Biology, Am. Chem. Soc., U.S. Orienteering Fedn., Sigma Xi, Phi Kappa Phi Office: Villanova U Dept Chemistry Villanova PA 19085 E-mail: John.Edwards@Villanova.edu.

EDWARDS, JOHN REID, senator, lawyer; b. Seneca, S.C., June 10, 1953; s. Wallace R. and Catherine Edwards; m. Mary Elizabeth Anania; children: Lucius Wade (dec.), Catharine, Emma Claire, Jack Atticus. BS with high honors, N.C. State U., 1974; JD with honors, U. N.C., 1977. Bar: N.C. 1977, Tenn. 1978, U.S. Dist. Ct. (ea. dist.) N.C. Assoc. Dearborn & Ewing, Nashville, Tenn., 1978-81, Tharrington Smith & Hargrove, Raleigh, N.C., 1981-83, ptnr., 1984-92, Edwards & Kirby, LLP, Raleigh, 1993-99; U.S. senator from N.C., 1999-. Bd. dirs. Urban Ministries, Raleigh, 1996—97; soccer coach Capital Area Soccer League, Raleigh, 1985—97; v.p. Challenge Soccer League, Raleigh; youth basketball coach YMCA Salvation Army, Raleigh; founding trustee Wade Edwards Found., 1996—; mem. adv. bd. Frank Porter Graham Child Devel. Ctr., Chapel Hill, 2000—; visionary com. Edenton St. United Meth. Ch. Recipient Steven J. Sharp Pub. Svc. award, 1997; named Lawyer of Yr. Lawyers Weekly, 1996. Fellow Am. Coll. Trial Lawyers; mem. ABA, ATLA, Inner Circle of Advocates, Am. Bd. Trial Advocacy, Chief Justice Susie M. Sharp Inns of Ct. (master), N.C. Acad. Trial Lawyers (v.p., bd. govs.), N.C. Bar Assn., Tenn. Bar Assn., So. Trial Lawyers Assn., U. N.C. Law Sch. Alumni Assn. (bd. dirs. 1993-99), Order of Coif, Phi Kappa Phi. Democrat. Office: US Senate Senate Office Bldg 225 Dirkson Washington DC 20510-0001

EDWARDS, JOHN WESLEY, II, lawyer; b. Williamsport, Pa., Nov. 29, 1948; s. Robert Wesley Edwards and Jean Eleanor (Seitzer) Leprohon; m. Lee Ellen Berliner, May 22, 1971; children: Wesley David, Katherine Lee, Meredith Jean. BA, Colgate U., 1970; JD, Duke U., 1974. Bar: Ohio 1974, Calif. 2001, U.S. Dist. Ct. (no. dist.) Ohio 1974, U.S. Dist. Ct. (no. dist.) Calif. 2001, U.S. Ct. Appeals (6th cir.) 1974, U.S. Ct. Appeals (9th cir.) 2001. Assoc. Jones, Day, Reavis & Pogue, Cleve., 1974-82, ptnr., 1982—. Served to cpl. USMCR, 1970-76. Mem. Cleve. Bar Assn. (Fed. ct. com.), Order of Coif, Phi Beta Kappa. Clubs: Mayfield Country (Lyndhurst, Ohio). Republican. Presbyterian. Office: Jones Day 2882 Sand Hill Rd Ste 240 Menlo Park CA 94025 Home: 1272 San Raymundo Rd Hillsborough CA 94010-6653

EDWARDS, JOHN WESLEY, JR., urologist; b. Ferndale, Mich., Apr. 9, 1933; s. John W. and Josephine (Wood) E.; m. Ella Marie Law, Dec. 25, 1954; children: Joella, John III. Student, Alma Coll., 1949-50; BS, U. Mich., 1954; postgrad., Wayne State U., 1954-56; MD, Howard U., 1960. Internship Walter Reed Gen. Hosp., 1960-61, surg. resident, 1962-63, urol. resident, 1963-66; asst. chief urology Tripler Army Med. Ctr., 1966-69; comdr. 4th Med. Battalion, 4th Infantry Div., Vietnam, 1969; chief profl. svcs., urology 91st Evacuation Hosp., Vietnam, 1969-70; urologist Straub Clinic, Inc., 1970-74; pvt. practice, 1974-97; v.p. med. staff. svcs. Queen's Med. Ctr., Honolulu, 1993-94; v.p. physician rels. Queen's Health Sys., Honolulu, 1994-96; acting adminstr. Diagnostic Lab. Svcs., Inc., Honolulu, 1995-96, pres., 1996—. Chief dept. surgery Straub Clinic and Hosp., 1973; asst. chief dept. srgery Queen's Med. Ctr., 1977-79, chief, 1989-93; cons. in urology; chief det. cln. svcs. Kapiolani Women's and Children's Med. Ctr., 1981-83; clin. assoc. prof. U. Hawaii Sch. of Medicine; chmn. task force on phys. hosp. collaboration The Queens Health System, 1993—. Contbr. articles to profl. jours. Bd. dirs. Hawaii Med. Svc. Assn., Honolulu, 1979—85, Hawaii Heart Assn., Honolulu, 1977—79, Hawaii Assn. for Physician's Indemnification, Honolulu, 1980—86; commr. City and County of Honolulu, Honolulu, 1990—91; Bd. dirs. Mediation Ctr. of the Pacific, Inc., 1995—2001, Queens Devel. Corp., 1999—2000, Kahala Sr. Living Cmty., Inc., 2000—01. Recipient Howard O. Gray award for Professionalism, 1988, Leaders of Hawaii award, 1983; named Hawaii African-Am. Humanitarian of the Yr. by Hawaii chpt. Links, Inc., 1991. Fellow: ACS (gov. at large from Hawaii 1986—92, sec.-treas. Hawaii chpt. 1991); mem.: NAACP, AMA, Surgicare of Hawaii (v.p. 1983—86), Hawaii Med. Assn., Hawaii Urol. Assn., Am. Urol. Assn. (gen. chmn. Western sect. 56th ann. meeting 1980, exec. com. 1983—84, del. dist. 1 1985—86, gen. chmn. 63d ann. meeting 1987, pres. 1989—90, nom. com. 1990—93, alt. del. Western sect. 1991—92, chmn. nom. 1992—93), Alpha Omega Alpha, Chi Delta Mu, Alpha Phi Alpha. Office: Diagnostic Lab Svcs 650 Iwilei Rd Ste 300 Honolulu HI 96817-5319 E-mail: jedwards@dls.queens.org.

EDWARDS, JOHN WOMER, aerospace systems engineer; b. Sharon, Pa., Aug. 12, 1958; s. John Roy and Doris Ellen (Womer) E. AA in Math, Cochise Community Coll., 1977; BS in Physics, Math., U. Ariz., 1979, MS in Systems Engring., 1982. Cons. Computerland, Tucson, 1980-82; systems engr. Rockwell Internat., Anaheim, Calif., 1982-85, Tex. Instruments, Dallas, 1985-87; sr. engr. Garrett Controls, Tucson, 1987-88; supr. engring. computing and computer network div. Garrett Controls (name changed to Ai Rsch. Tucson div. Allied-Signal Aerospace Co.), Tucson, 1988-90. Cons. Starfyre Software, Brea, Calif., 1982—87, Arnell Audio/Visual Prodns., Tucson, 1980—, Pers. Computer Cons. Assocs., 1990—93; pres. Renaissance Music and Entertainment, Inc., 1994—2002, Renaissance Records, Inc., 1995—, Discs Online, LLC, 2002—; dir., found. chmn. Popular Recs. Internat. Music Archive, 2002—. Author: (with others) The Rock Record, 1987, The Encyclopedia of Rock and Roll Music, 1960-1990, 1990, Who's Who In Rock and Roll: The 1960s, 1991, The 1970s, 1992; mng. editor Rockstreet mag.; pub., mng. editor Country Sounds mag., 1992-94. Mem. Nat. Card Collectors Assn., Am. Assn. of Recording Arts and Sciences, Plantary Soc. Republican. Presbyterian. Avocations: baseball card collecting, music, baseball, basketball, the family dogs. Home and Office: PO Box 30547 Tucson AZ 85751-0547 Office Fax: 520-885-9738. E-mail: john81258@aol.com.

EDWARDS, JOYCE PERRY, language educator; b. Durham, NC, Dec. 24, 1944; d. Lawrence Pryor and Artelia Marsh Perry; m. Murray L. Edwards, Mar. 12, 1988. BA, NC Coll., Durham, 1966; MA, NC Ctrl. U., 1978; MEd, NC State U., 1971, PhD, 1983. Cert. tchr. NC, curriculum specialist NC, prin. NC, supt. NC. English tchr. Somerset County Schs., Princess Anne, Lynchburg (Va.) City Schools, 1966—68; sch. counselor Wake County Pub. Sch. Sys., Raleigh, NC, 1971—76, guidance supr., 1976—81, asst. supt., 1981—86; exec. dir. of student services and instrn. Durham (NC) City Schools, 1988—91, supt. of schools, 1991—92, assoc. supt., 1992—93; asst. supt. Edgcombe County Schools, Tarboro, NC, 1993—96; assoc. prin. for instrn. Moore County Schools, Southern Pines, NC, 1996—99, prin. Southern PInes, NC, 1999—2001; assoc. prof. of edn. Pfeiffer U., Misenheimer-Charlotte, NC, 2001—; supt. of schools Halifax County Schools, Halifax, NC. Workshop leader, adminstr. in Cchristian edn. AME Zion Ch., NC, 1990—2003. Named Outstanding Black North Carolinian, Ea. Region of Zeta Phi Beta Sorority, Inc., 1987, Citizen of Yr., Tau Beta Beta chpt., Omega Psi Phi Frat., 1987, Woman of the Yr., Durham chpt., Nat. Coun. of Negro Women, 1992; recipient Outstanding Svc. award, Nat. Coun. of Negro Women, 1984, Citizen of Yr., James E. Shepard Sertoma Club of Durham, 1992; Action Rsch./ Edn. of the Learning Disabled grantee, U.S. Dept. of Edn., 1986. Mem.: NC ASCD, ASCD. African Methodist Episcopal Zion. Office: Pfeiffer U US Hwy 52N Misenheimer NC 28109 E-mail: jedwards@pfeiffer.edu.

EDWARDS, JUNE CAROLINE, retired education educator; b. Oklahoma City, Okla., Mar 5, 1934; d. Ralph Eldon and Katharine Louetta (Rose) Kirkhuff; m. Richard Alan Edwards, Sept. 3, 1958 (div. Oct. 1992); children: Jennifer, Emily, Jonathan. BA, U. Okla., 1955; MEd, Va. Poly. Inst. and State U., 1974, EdD, 1977. Jr. high sch. tchr. Markham (Ill.) Sch. Dist., 1960-62, 66-68; mid. sch. tchr. Greenville (Pa.) Sch. Dist., 1968-72; lectr., Sch. of Edn. Va. Polytechnic Inst. and State U., 1974-77; asst. prof. dept. of English Marquette U., Milw., 1985-87; asst. prof. dept. of edn. Nat.-Louis Univ., Evanston, Ill., 1987-89; assoc. prof. dept. of edn. SUNY, Oneonta, 1992—2000, prof., 2000—02, prof. emerita, 2003—. Author: Opposing Censorship in Public Schools: Religion, Morality and Literature, 1998, Women in American Education, 1820-1955: The Female Force and Educational Reform, 2002; contbr. articles to profl. jours. Bd. dirs. ACLU, Milw., 1990-92, Catskill Choral Soc., Oneonta, 1994—. Mem. Phi Delta Kappa (pres. Catskill area 1994-96, Marquette U. chpt. 1988-89, v.p. 1987-88, G. Read travel fellowship). Democrat. Unitarian Universalist. Avocations: singing, travel, writing.

EDWARDS, KATHLEEN, real estate broker, former educator; b. Grundy, Va., Nov. 13, 1929; d. Cornelius and Vallie Mae (Wallace) Lester; m. George Perry Bailey, July 18, 1950; children: Shearer, George, Craig; m. Richard C. Edwards, June 10, 1967; 1 child, Richard Cornelius; stepchildren: Randall, Mark, Ashley. BA, Radford (Va.) U., 1950; MEd, U. Va., 1965. Cert. tchr., Va.; lic. real estate broker. Tchr. pub. elem. schs., Va., 1950-71, 1971-73, dir., owner Fireside Sch., Va., 1973-81; real estate broker, pres., owner View Properties Inc., Va., 1977—. Mem.: DAR (regent Harmony Hall chpt. 1999—2001), Nat. Assn. Realtors. Avocations: oil and pastel painting, travel, grandchilren.

EDWARDS, KATHRYN INEZ, educational technology consultant; b. L.A., Aug. 26, 1947; d. Lloyd and Geraldine E. (Smith) Price; 1 child, Bryan. BA in English, Calif. State U., L.A., 1969; supervision credential, 1974, adminstrn. credential, 1975; MEd in Curriculum, UCLA, 1971; PhD, Claremont Grad. Sch., 1979. Tchr. L.A. Pub. Schs., 1969—78, adv. specially funded programs, 1978—80, advisor librs. and learning-resources program, 1980—81, instructional specialist, 1981—84; cons. instructional media L.A. County Office of Edn., Downey, Calif., 1984-90; coord. ednl. media and tech. Pomona (Calif.) Unified Sch. Dist., 1990-92; cons. edn. tech. Apple Computer, Inc., 1992-96; client mktg. rep. IBM; sales devel. mgr. SUN Microsys., 1999—2000; dir. mktg. Vinendi Universal Interactive Pub., 2000—02; mgr. strategic urban initiatives Apple Computer, 2002—. Cons. Walt Disney Prodns., Alfred Higging Prodns., others; mem. distance lng. think tank U.S. Office Edn., 1997. Author guides and curriculum kits. Apptd. by assembly spkr. Willie Brown to Calif. Ednl. Tech. Com., 1990-92, Calif. State Assembly Resolution from Gwen Moore, 1988, Edn. Coun. for Tech. in Learning, 1993-96; mem. spl. com. Cable Access Corp. co-owners, 1991-92. Recipient cert. commendation Senator Diane Watson, 1988, Mabel Wilson Richards scholar, 1968, Calif. Congress Parents and Tchrs. scholar, 1968, UCLA fellow, 1968; named Outstanding Woman of Yr. L.A. Sentinel, 1987. Mem. ASCD, Nat. Assn. Minority Polit. Women, Internat. Reading Assn. (spkr. nat. conv. 1988), L.A. Reading Assn. (pres.), Calif. Assn. Tchrs. of English (conf. del. 1982), Calif. Media and Libr. Educators Assn. (state conf. co-chair 1989, v.p. legal divsn. 1992—), Nat. Assn. Media Women (Media Woman of Yr. 1987), Alpha Kappa Alpha. Democrat. Roman Catholic. Avocations: reading, gardening, travel. Office: IBM Corp 400 N Brand Blvd Glendale CA 91203-2311 E-mail: Kathryne1@attbi.com.

EDWARDS, KEITH B. airport administrator; Mgr. Massena Internat. Airport. Office: Massena Internat Airport Richards Field Seaway Valley Aviation LLC 90 Aviation Rd Massena NY 13662-3255

EDWARDS, KENNETH NEIL, chemical engineering executive; b. Hollywood, Calif., June 8, 1932; s. Arthur Carl and Ann Vera (Gomez) E.; children: Neil James, Peter Graham, John Evan. BA in Chemistry, Occidental Coll., 1954; MS in Chem. and Metall. Engring., U. Mich., 1955. Prin. chemist Battelle Meml. Inst., Columbus, Ohio, 1955-58; dir. new products rsch. and devel. Dunn-Edwards Corp., L.A., 1958-72; sr. lectr. organic coatings and pigments dept. chem. engring. U. So. Calif., L.A., 1976-80; CEO Dunn-Edwards Corp., 2001—. Bd. dirs. Dunn-Edwards Corp., L.A.; co-chair indsl. adv. coun., mem. pres.'s cir. Calif. Poly. U., San Luis Obispo. Contbr. articles to sci. jours. Recipient Judo Masters belt (6th dan), Korean Judo Assn., 2000. Mem. Am. Chem. Soc. (chmn. divisional activities 1988-89, exec. com. divsn. polymeric materials sci. and engring. 1963—, chair divsn. 1970, mem. devel. adv. com. 1996-99, Disting. Svc. award 1996, chair Disting. Svc. award selection 1997—, chair So. Calif. local sect. 1999), Alpha Chi Sigma (chmn. L.A. profl. chpt. 1962, counselor Pacific dist. 1967-70, grand profl. alchemist nat. v.p. 1970-76, grand master alchemist nat. pres. 1976-78, nat. adv. com. 1978—). Achievements include patents for air-dried polyester coatings and application, for process and apparatus for dispensing liquid colorants into a paint can, fluidic fillers, and for mechanical mixers. Home: Bottle Bay Rd Sagle ID 83860 also: 2926 Graceland Way Glendale CA 91206-1331 Office: Dunn Edwards Corp 136 W Walnut Ave Monrovia CA 91016-3444 E-mail: KNEatDE@aol.com.

EDWARDS, KIRK LEWIS, medical services company executive; b. Berkeley, Calif., July 30, 1950; s. Austin Lewis and Betty (Drury) E.; m. Randi Edwards, Feb. 14, 1998; children: Elliott Tyler, Jonathan Bentley. BA in Rhetoric and Pub. Address, U. Wash., Seattle, 1972; postgrad., Shoreline Coll., 1976. Cert. bus. broker. From salesperson to mgr. Rede Realty, Lynnwood, Wash., 1973-77; br. mgr. Century 21/North Homes Realty, Lynnwood, Wash., 1977-79, Snohomish, Wash., 1979-81; pres., owner Century 21/Champion Realty, Everett, Wash., 1981-82, Champion Computers, Walker/Edwards Investments, Everett, 1981-82; br. mgr. Advance Properties, Everett, 1982-87; exec. v.p. Bruch & Vedrich Better Homes & Garden, Everett, 1987-88, dir. career devel., 1988-90; pres., CEO Century 21/Champion Realty, Everett, 1991-95, KR Bus. Brokers, Kirkland, Wash., 1995-2001; pres. Exec. Med. Svcs., Bellevue, Wash., 2001—. Named Top Business Broker In Washington Investment Brokers Assn., 1994-96. Mem. Snohomish County Camano Bd. Realtors (chmn. 1987-88), Snohomish County C. of C., Hidden Harbor Yacht Club, Mill Creek Country Club. Republican. Avocations: travel, water skiing, scuba diving. Office: KR Business Brokers 2285 116th Ave NE # 100 Bellevue WA 98004 E-mail: mrbzns@hotmail.com.

EDWARDS, LARRY CECIL, management consultant; b. Monroe, N.C., July 27, 1949; s. Tommy Cecil and Frances (Hinson) E.; m. Thelma Dolores Edwards, June 28, 1947; 1 child, Tonya Dennise. Student, Ga. State U. Cert. mgmt. cons. Svc. mgr. Newport Datsun, Newport News, Va., 1971-74; svc. dir., v.p. Hickman Nissan, Atlanta, 1974-79; cons. Net Profit, Inc., Birmingham, Ala., 1979-81; pres. Edwards Dodge, Montgomery, Ala., 1981-86, Creative Advt., Ft. Myers, Fla., 1986-89; v.p. Automotive Svc. Cons., Birmingham, 1989-94; pres. Edwards & Assos. Cons., Charlotte, N.C., 1994—. Contbr. articles to profl. jours. With USN, 1968-70, Vietnam. Republican. Baptist. Avocation: races vintage datsun 510s in historic road racing. Office: Edwards & Assocs 5615 Harrisburg Indsl Park Harrisburg NC 28075 E-mail: EdwardsAssociates@compuserve.com.

EDWARDS, LARRY DAVID, internist, educator; b. Macomb, Ill., June 20, 1937; s. Richard Marshall and Anna Louise (Hare) Edwards; m. Ann Leanor Will, Mar. 31, 1959; children: Elliott, Sharon, Beth. Pre-Med, U. Ill., 1961, MD, 1965. Diplomate Am. Bd. Internal Medicine, Am. Bd. Infectious Disease, Am. Bd. Geriatric Medicine, Nat. Bd. Med. Examiners, Am. Bd. Med. Mgmt., Am. Coll. Healthcare Execs; cert. physician exec., healthcare exec. Rotating intern USPHS Hosp., Staten Island, N.Y., 1965-66, resident in internal medicine, 1966-68; fellow in infectious diseases Rush-Presbyn.-St. Luke's Med. Ctr., Chgo., 1968-70; instr. dept. internal medicine U. Ill. Coll. Medicine, Chgo., 1968-70; asst. prof. depts. internal medicine, preventive medicine, microbiology Rush Med. Coll., Chgo., 1972-74; assoc. prof. internal medicine U. Ill. Coll. Medicine, Rockford, 1974-80, prof., 1980-81; prof. internal medicine Oral Roberts U. Sch. Medicine, Tulsa, 1981-90; dir. div. infectious diseases Rockford Sch. Medicine, 1974-81, dep. head dept. biomed. scis., 1980-81; prof. internal medicine U. Va., Charlottesville, 1991-92; chief of staff VA Med. Ctr., Salem, Va., 1990-92; assoc. dean for acad. affairs VA, U. Va., Charlottesville, 1991-92. Adj. assoc. prof. epidemiology U. Ill. Sch. Pub. Health, 1977—81; affiliate dept. medicine Abraham Lincoln Sch. Medicine, U. Ill., Chgo., 1977—81; dir. divsn. infectious diseases Oral Roberts U., 1981—84; assoc. dean clin. affairs Oral Roberts Sch. Medicine, 1981, 84, vice chmn. dept. internal medicine, 1981—83, chmn., 1983—86, chmn. preventive and internat. medicine, 1987—88, dean, 1984—90, v.p. for health affairs, 1987—90; COO City of Faith Med. & Rsch. Ctr., 1989—90; med. dir. Cen. Bapt. Home for Aged, Norridge, Ill., 1968—74, Columbia County Homes, Wyocena, Wis., 1974—80; asst. dir.

infectious diseases, hosp. epidemiologist, dir. infectious disease research Rush-Presbyn.-St. Luke's Hosp., Chgo., 1972—74, asst. sci. dept. microbiology, 1970—74; asst. med. dir. Mcpl. Contagious Disease Hosp., Chgo., 1970—74; cons. infectious diseases numerous other hosps. and med. ctrs.; med. dir. City of Faith Hosp., Tulsa, 1984—87, chmn. bd., 1989—90; bd. dirs. City of Faith Clinic, Tulsa, 1985—87; pres. Infectious Diseases Cons. Svcs., Inc., Barnhart, Mo., 1993—2001; med. dir., missionary Bible Basics Internat. Contbr. numerous articles to med. jours. Advisor resource com. Sch. Health Coalition of N.W. Ill., 1979-81; med. adv. com. State of Ill. Refugee Health Services Program, 1980-81; Ill. health svcs. task force State Ill. Dept. Pub. Health, 1980-81; infectious disease adv. com. Tulsa City-County Health Dept., 1981-88; physician manpower adv. com. Okla. Bd. Regents, 1984-88; Titan scholarship bd. Oral Roberts U., 1985-87; v.p. World-Wide Med. Missions, Oral Roberts Evangelistic Assn., 1986-88, pres. 1989-90; active Leadership Roanoke Valley, 1991-92; dir. Strategic Tchg. and Reaping; med. dir. Bible Basics Internat.; Bible tchr., missionary in Russia, Dominican Republic, Chile, Honduras. With U.S. Army, 1955-58, with USPHS, 1965-70, lt. col. USAR, 1985, col. 1990-97, ret., 1997. Smith, Kline and French fellow for study in Ethiopia, 1964; named Outstanding Faculty Mem. of Yr. Oral Roberts U. Sch. Medicine, 1982-83. Fellow: ACP, Am. Coll. Healthcare Execs. (ret.), Am. Coll. Physician Execs., Infectious Diseases Soc. Am. (emeritus). Avocations: reading, writing.

EDWARDS, LEIGH HOLLADAY, literature educator; d. Steve and Helen Carothers Edwards. BA, Duke U., 1992; MA, U. Pa., 1993, PhD, 1999. Asst. prof. English Fla. State U., Tallahassee, 2001—. Spkr. Am. Studies Colloquia Fla. State U., Tallahassee, 1998; inst. faculty and plenary spkr. Dartmouth/NEH Inst., Hanover, NH, 2000; mem. planning com. for conf. So. Am. Studies Assn., Tallahassee, 2002—03. Editl. asst.: Am. Lit., 1991—92; contbr. articles to profl. jours. Scriptwriter ednl. CD-ROM Forest Fever Fla. Dept. Forestry and Interactive Tng. Media, Inc., 2001. Nat. Mellon fellow, Mellon Found., 1992—97, Angier B. Duke Meml. scholar, Duke U., Durham, N.C., 1988—92, First Yr. Asst. Prof. Rsch. grantee, Fla. State U., 2002, Rsch. and Creative Activity Award grantee, 2002. Mem.: MLA, Am. Studies Assn., Phi Beta Kappa. Avocations: writing, film and media studies, sports. Office: Dept English Fla State Univ Tallahassee FL 32306-1580

EDWARDS, LEISL MARIE BAUM, interior designer; b. Camp Hill, Pa., Aug. 4, 1970; d. Paul Edwin and Norma Kay (Fink) B. BS, Va. Poly. Inst. and State U., 1992. Cert. NCIDQ. Asst. designer Interior Merchandising Group, Gt. Falls, Va., 1993-94; sr. interior designer Marriott Internat., Washington, 1994-2000, Interiors by Design, Inc., 2000—02, MS Interiors/Merchandising East, 2002; interior design mgr. Marriott Internat., Washington, 2002—. Mem. Am. Soc. Interior Designers (profl.). Home: 832 Elmcroft Blvd Rockville MD 20850 E-mail: leisl.edwards@marriott.com.

EDWARDS, LILLIE JOHNSON, history educator; b. Columbus, Ga., Dec. 11, 1952; d. Allen and Laverna (Williams) Johnson; m. Paul Bryant Edwards; Sept. 20, 1982; children: Paul Johnson, Nia Molliene. BA, Oberlin Coll., 1975; MA, U. Chgo., 1976, PhD, 1981. Asst. prof., coord. African-Am. studies Earlham Coll., Richmond, Ind., 1981-83; asst. prof. U. N.C., Chapel Hill, 1983-87, DePaul U., Chgo., 1987-89, assoc. prof., 1989—, dir. Am. studies, 1990-92; prof., dir. African-Am. studies Drew U., Madison, N.J., 1992—. Cons., lectr. NEH Summer Inst., Trenton, N.J., 1987, N.J. State Grants, Trenton, 1986; cons. N.J. Higher Edn., Trenton, 1985-87, Exxon Found., N.Y.C., 1983. Mem. exec. bd. Oberlin Coll. Alumni Coun., Ohio, 1987-88; music dir. St. Matthews Ch., Chgo., 1987—; v.p. Oberlin Coll. Class of 1975, 1986-89. Rockefeller fellow, 1986-87. Mem. Orgn. Am. Historians, Am. Hist. Soc., Am. Studies Assn., Assn. Black Women Historians (nominating com. 1986-87, 89-90, nat. dir. 2000-01), Assn. for Study Afro-Am. Life and History (program com. 1987, 90), NJ Amistad Comm., 2002-. Democrat. Methodist. Office: Drew U Dept History Madison NJ 07940 E-mail: ledwards@drew.edu.

EDWARDS, LINCOLN PAUL, pharmacologist, educator; b. St. Catherine, Jamaica, Sept. 17, 1960; s. Enos George and Linnette Edwards; m. Sandra Young; children: Alex, Ross-Andre, Alexa. BSc, U. W.I., Jamaica, 1985; PhD, Loma Linda U., 1998. Rsch. assoc. Case Western Res. U., Cleve., 1998—2001; asst. prof. physiology and pharmacology Loma Linda U., Calif., 2001—. Contbr. chapters to books, articles to profl. jours. Elder Temple of Praise Ch., Cleve., 1999—2001, Redlands (Calif.) Seventh-Day Adventist Ch., 2001, Jones Ave. Ch., Spanish Town, Jamaica, 1981—91. Mem.: N.Y. Acad. Scis., Am. Physiology Soc., Am. Soc. Pharmacology and Therapeutics. Achievements include demonstration that imidazoline receptors are couled to protein kinase C and MAP kenose pathways. Office: Loma Linda U Loma Linda CA 92350-0001

EDWARDS, LINDA NASIF, economics educator; b. San Diego, Aug. 26, 1942; m. Franklin R. Edwards; 2 children. BA in Math., U. Pa., 1963; PhD with distinction, Columbia U., 1971. Rsch. asst. Nat. Bur. Econ. Rsch., Inc., N.Y.C., 1964-65; teaching asst. in stats. Columbia U., N.Y.C., 1966-67; rsch. economist Chem. Bank N.Y. Trust Co., N.Y.C., 1967; rsch. fellow U. Catholique de Louvain, Inst. des Scis. Economiques, Belgium, 1969-70; lectr. econs. Queens Coll., CUNY, 1970-71, asst. prof., 1971-77, assoc. prof. Queens Coll. and the Grad. Ctr., 1978-82, acting chair dept. econs., 1987-88; exec. officer, prof. PhD program in econs. CUNY, 1995-99; assoc. provost CUNY Grad. Ctr., 1999—. Rsch. assoc. Nat. Bur. Econ. Rsch., 1976-80. Contbr. numerous articles to profl. jours. Pres.'s fellow Columbia U., 1967-68, Perkins fellow, 1965-66. Mem. Am. Econs. Assn. (bd. dirs. com. for status of women in econs.). Office: CUNY Grad Ctr 365 Fifth Ave New York NY 10016

EDWARDS, SIR LLEWELLYN ROY, company executive; b. Aug. 2, 1935; s. Roy Thomas and Agnes Dulcie Gwendoline Edwards; m. Leone Sylvia Burley, 1958 (dec.); 3 children; m. Jane Anne Brumfield, 1989. MB, BChir, U. Queensland, 1965, LLD (hon.), 1988; D (hon.), Griffith U., Australia, 1996. Qualified electrician; qualified med. practitioner. RMO, registrar surgery Ipswich Hosp., 1965-68; gen. practice Ipswich, 1968-74; MLA Ipswich Queensland Parliament, 1972-83; min. health Queensland, 1974-78; dep. premier, treas., 1978-83; dep. med. supt. Ispwich Hosp., 1984; exec. cons. Jones Lang, Brisbane, 1989—, chancellor, 1992—, The U. Queensland, Australia. Mem. senate U. Queensland, 1984—; chmn., CEO World Expo 88 Authority, 1984—89, Australian Coachline Holdings Ltd., 1992—96; bd. dirs. Westpac Banking Corp., James Hardle Industies Pty. Ltd., T.N.Z. (Aust) Pty. Ltd., R.T. Edwards & Sons Pty. Ltd., Uniseed Pty. Ltd.; chmn. Pacific Film and TV Corp., UQ Holdings, Pty. Ltd. Fellow Royal Australian Coll. Med. Adminstrs., Australian Inst. Mgmt. Avocations: tennis, walking, music, rugby. Office: U Queensland 8 Ascot St Saint Lucia 4072 Australia

EDWARDS, LOUISE WISEMAN, career counselor, educator; b. Greeley, Colo., Feb. 20, 1932; d. Hunter R. and Sarah L. (Spencer) Wiseman; m. Jasin W. Edwards (div. 1975); children: Mark Hunter, Kathleen Margaret. BA, U. Colo., 1953; MA, U. N.Mex., 1983. Lic. profl. clin. counselor. Asst. dir. pub. info. Mills Coll., Oakland, Calif., 1956-57; ESL tchr. Peace Corps, Santiago, Chile, 1963-64; career counselor U. N.Mex. Career Svcs., Albuquerque, 1980-84, supr. career counseling, 1984-87, asst. dir., 1987-98, interim dir., 1992-93; pvt. counselor, 1998—. Presenter U. N.Mex. Law Sch., 1982-95, Nat. Assn. Med. Schs. Admissions and Registrations Conv., 1993; instr. Anderson Sch. Mgmt. U. N.Mex., 1983-95. Active Dem. Women of N.Mex., 1970-80. Mem. N.Mex. Career Devel. Assn. (bd. dirs., George Keppens award 2002), Rocky Mt. Placement Assn. (co-chair conf. 1980—). Avocations: singing with univ. chorus, hiking, cross country skiing, docent. Home: 2821 Tennessee St NE Albuquerque NM 87110-3707

EDWARDS, MARIE D. social services administrator; b. Cin., Sept. 17, 1943; d. George Junior Denning and Lola Dortheia Jackson; children: Daniel J., Grayson G.; m. Terrance Anthoney Edwards Sr., July 24, 1982; stepchildren: Terrance A. Edwards, Troy Edwards, Heather Kraus. Owner, mgr. Greendale Grill, Lawrenceburg, Ind., 1980-86, M.E. & Assocs. Realtors, Vevay, Ind., 1986-93; mgr. Coldwell Banker, Lawrenceburg, 1993-98; exec. dir. Dearborn Adult Ctr., Lawrenceburg, 1998—. Bd. dirs. Southea. Ind. Econ. Opportunity Ctr., 1995—; chairperson I Love Lawrenceburg com., 1999—, Bicentennial City of Lawrenceburg, 2001—. Named Cmty. Leader 2000, Lawrenceburg C. of C., 2001; recipient Dearborn County award for svc. and humanitarian effort, 2001. Mem. Dearborn County C. of C. (gov.'s com. transp., Cmty. Leader of Yr. 2001, 02), Southea. Women's Network (pres. 2000-2001), Southea. Bd. Realtors (treas. 1990), Order Ea. Star (assoc. matron). Democrat. Methodist. Avocation: gardening. Office: Dearborn Adult Ctr Inc 311 W Tate St Lawrenceburg IN 47025 E-mail: maedwards@seidata.com.

EDWARDS, MARK BROWNLOW, lawyer; b. Asheville, N.C., Nov. 14, 1939; s. Mark and Sarah Juanita (Whitaker) E.; m. Doris Julian Reynolds, June 26, 1966; children: Mark Brownlow Jr., Elizabeth Reynolds. AB, Duke U., 1961, JD, 1963. Bar: N.C. 1963. Ptnr. Poyner & Spruill, L.L.P., Charlotte, N.C., 1988-98, of counsel, 1998—. Author: North Carolina Probate Handbook, 1994, What You Need to Know About Wills, Trusts, Estates in North Carolina, 1994. Vice chmn. The Meth. Home, Inc., Charlotte, 1980-94, chmn., 1994-99. Fellow Am. Coll. Trust and Estates Counsel, Order of Coif., Phi Beta Kappa. Methodist. Avocations: music, pub. speaking, writing. Office: Poyner & Spruill 301 S College St Ste 2300 Charlotte NC 28202

EDWARDS, MARVIN RAYMOND, investment counselor, economic consultant; b. N.Y.C., June 29, 1921; s. Albert H. and Blanche (Gans) E.; m. Helene C. Sirota, Mar. 20, 1955; children: Jeffrey Randall, Douglas Lee, Carolyn Beth. BS, NYU, 1947. Pres. White Star Sales Corp., Jacksonville, Fla., 1947-58; pres. Edwards & Edwards, Inc., Jacksonville, 1958—. Interviews on investments and the economy have appeared in numerous publs. including Bus. Week, Scrap Age, Miami Herald, Tampa Tribune, The Market Chronicle, Fla. Trend Mag., others; polit. columnist Folio Weekly, 1996—; subject of interview ABC World News Tonight, 1993, 94, 2002. Exec. v.p., bd. dirs. Greater Jacksonville Taxpayers Assn., 1965-71; pres., bd. dirs. Better Schs. Citizens Com, Jacksonville, 1959-65, Community Service Planning Council, Jacksonville, 1955-58; v.p., b.d dirs. Jacksonville Humane Soc., 1953-56, Jacksonville Safety Council, 1948-50; bd. dirs. North East Fla. Kidney Found., Jacksonville, 1971-73; mem. Office Strategic Svcs. Lt. USAF, 1943-46, ETO. Decorated Air medal; recipient Outspoken Citizen's award Jacksonville Southside Bus. Men's Club, 1993. Mem. Jacksonville Fin. Analysts Soc. (pres., bd. dirs. 1977-78, 87-88), Econ. Roundtable Jacksonville (pres., bd. dirs. 1975-77, 90-91, 95—), Assn. for Investment Mgmt. and Rsch., Nat. Assn. Bus. Economists, Nat. Economists Club, Soc. Profl. Journalists, Nat. Press Club of Washington, The O.S.S. Soc., Inc., Mosquito Aircrew Assn. Eng., Smithsonian Nat. Air and Space Mus., Am. Mus. Natural History, Nat. Space Soc., Planetary Soc. Home: 1345 Riverbirch Ln Jacksonville FL 32207-7540 Office: Edwards & Edwards Inc 1345 Riverbirch Ln Jacksonville FL 32207-7540 E-mail: eandeinc@earthlink.net.

EDWARDS, MATTHEW E. physicist, educator; b. Snow Hill, N.C., Mar. 3, 1947; s. Offie Collin and Calena Edwards; m. Glenda R. Edwards, Dec. 29, 2001; m. Mary E. Ferrell, June 10, 1966 (div.); m. Cheri Y. White, July 17, 1993 (div.); children: Natasha M., Matthew E. Jr. BS in Engring Physics, N.C. State U., 1969; MS in Physics, Howard U., 1975, PhD in Physics, 1977. Lectr. D.C. Tchrs. Coll., 1975—77; asst. prof. physics Howard U., 1977; assoc. prof. physics U. Ark., Pine Bluff, 1977—81; assoc. prof. physics, dir. MBRS program Fayetteville State U., NC, 1981—96; assoc. prof. physics, dir. IDS course Spelman Coll., Atlanta, 1996—2001; prof. physics Ala. A & M U., Normal, 2002—. Adj. prof. physics U. Pitts., 1992—94, vis. rsch. prof., 1995—2001, co-founder rsch. for undergrads. program; vis. rsch. prof. Spelman Coll., 2002—. Contbr. articles to profl. jours. Recipient Presdl. award Excellence Tchg., Spelman Coll., 2001; grantee, NASA Goddard Space Flight Ctr., 2002—, NSF, 2002—. Fellow: AICE (assoc.); mem.: Soc. Indsl. and Applied Math., Soc. Photo-Optical Instrumentation Engrs., Nat. Soc. Black Physcists (assoc.), Am. Math. Soc. (assoc.), Am. Phys. Soc. (assoc.), Sigma Pi Sigma Physics (life). Home: 156 RiverWalk Trail New Market AL 35761 Office: Ala A & M U PO Box 1268 Normal AL 35762 Office Fax: 256-851-5622. Personal E-mail: edwar4@aol.com. E-mail: edwardsm@aamu.edu.

EDWARDS, MICHAEL AUBREY, writer, foundation executive; b. Liverpool, Eng., June 29, 1957; s. David Arthur and Millicent Elizabeth (Heathcote) E.; m. Cora Anne Castro. BA summa cum laude with honors, U. Oxford, U.K., 1978, MA, 1981; PhD, U. Coll. London, 1982. Rschr., tutor U. Coll. London, 1978-82; devel. officer Vol. Svc. Overseas, London, 1982-84; regional rep. OXFAM-UK, Zambia, Malawi, 1984-88; dir. Prasad Found., India, 1988-90; head rsch. Save the Children Fund, London, 1990-96; pres. Edwards Assocs., London, 1996-98; sr. adviser The World Bank, Washington, 1998-99; dir. Governance and Civil Soc., Ford Found., N.Y.C., 1999—. Sr. cons. UNCHS, Nairobi, Kenya, 1989—; assoc. Inst. for Devel. Policy and Mgmt., Manchester, U.K., 1992—; advisor Commn. on Future of Vol. Sector, London, 1995-96; advisor to numerous charities in over 20 countries, 1995—. Author: Future Positive, 1999, Civil Society, 2003; co-editor: Making a Difference, 1992, Beyond the Magic Bullet, 1995, Too Close for Comfort, 1997, Global Citizen Action, 2000, Earthscan Reader on NGO Management, 2002; contbr. articles to profl. jours. Del. World Bank-Ngo Com., Washington, 1993-96; chair Internat. Childrens Rights Info. Network, Paris, 1995; mem. Nexus Network, U.K., 1996—. Recipient Rsch. fellowship Leverhulme Trust, London, 1995-96, Simon Indsl. and Profl. fellowship U. Manchester, 1996. Mem. Brit. Labour Party. Avocations: reading, travel, soccer, meditation. Home: 250 W 89th St Apt 7 E New York NY 10024 E-mail: m.edwards@fordfound.org.

EDWARDS, MICHAEL GERARD, physician; b. Duluth, Minn., Apr. 27, 1956; s. Charles and Cecelia Edwards; m. Patricia Ann Roedl; children: Matthew, Conor, Anne. BA, U. Notre Dame, 1978; MD, Creighton U., 1982. Resident in radiology SUNY, Buffalo, 1983-86; fellow William Beaumont Hosp., Royal Oak, Mich., 1986-87, staff radiologist, 1987-92, Providence Hosp., Southfield, Mich., 1992—. Address: 1825 Pine St Birmingham MI 48009 E-mail: medwards02@comcast.net.

EDWARDS, MICHAEL STEVEN BRENT, b. Sept. 7, 1945; MD, Tulane U., New Orleans, 1970. Diplomate Am. Bd. Neurol. Surgeons. Intern Tulane U. Affiliated Hosps., New Orleans, 1970-71; resident in neurosurgery Tulane U. VA Hosp., New Orleans, 1971-72; resident in gen. surgery Oschner Found. Hosps., New Orleans, 1972-73, resident in neurosurgery, 1973-75; chief resident neurosurgery Tulane U., VA Hosp., New Orleans, 1975-76, Charity Hosp., New Orleans, 1976-77; neuro-oncology fellow U. Calif. Sch. Medicine, San Francisco, 1977-78, clin. instr. neurol. surgery, 1977-78, asst. prof. in residence, 1978-83, assoc. prof. in residence, 1983-87, assoc. prof. in residence pediatrics, 1983-87, dir. divsn. pediatric neurosurgery, 1987-95, prof. in residence neurol. surgery and pediatrics, 1988-95, vice chair dept. neurol. surgery, 1992-95, clin. prof. neurol. surgery and pediatrics, 1995-99. Attending neurosurgeon Moffitt Hosp., U. Calif. San Francisco, 1977-99; cons. neurosurgery VA Med. Ctrs., Reno, Nev., 1977-95, VA Hosp., San Francisco, 1978-98; attending neurosurgeon San Francisco Gen. Hosp., 1978-98, Ralph K. Davies Hosp., San Francisco, 1980-95, Mt. Zion Hosp., San Francisco, 1982-98, Shriners Hosps. for Crippled Children, Sacramento, 1982—, Washoe Med. Ctr., Reno, 1983—, St. Mary's Regional Med. Ctr., Reno, 1983—, CPMC/CMS Childrens Hosp., San Francisco, 1983—, Sutter Med. Ctr., Sacramento, 1995; dir. pediatric neurosurgery Sutter Med. Ctr., Sacramento, 1995-97, dir. pediatric neuroscis., 1997—; dir. Gamma Knife Program Sutter Health Sys., Sacramento, 1998—; dir. Sutter Neurosci. Inst., 2002; vis. prof. dept. neurosurgery various univs., 1983, 84, 86, 87, 88, 89, 90, 95—; mem. study com. Childrens Cancer Group, 1992—; mem. med. adv. bd. No. Calif. Hydrocephalus Assn., 1984—; mem. med. adv. bd. rsch. founds. Guardians of Hydrocephalus, 1984—; mem. med. adv. bd. No. Calif. Spina Bifida Assn., 1985—; mem. med. adv. bd. Hydrocephalus Found., 1992—; mem. profl. adv. bd. Nat. Tuberous Sclerosis Assn., 1990—; mem. med. adv. bd. Nat. Neurofibromatosis Found., Inc., 1992—; bd. dirs. Nat. Neurofibromatosis Found., 1995; sci. reviewer rsch. proposals Hydrocephalus Rsch. Found., 1995—; presenter various symposia and workshops. Asst. editor Clin. Neurosurgery, 1981-84; editl. bd. Neurosurg. Consultations, 1989—, Jour. Radiosurgery, 1998—; reviewer Surgery Gynecology and Obstetrics, 1979-91, Neurosurgery, 1979—, Pediatrics, 1980—, Jour. Neuro-oncology, 1985—, Pediatric Neurosurgery, 1985—; contbr. articles to profl. jours. Recipient rsch. grant in cellular biology Am. Cancer Soc., 1965, jr. faculty clin. fellowship Am. Cancer Soc., 1977-80, tchr. investigator devel. award, 1980-85, Preuss award Congress Neurol. Surgeons, 1987, cert. of appreciation Assn. for Care of Children's Health, 1992; grantee U. Calif., San Francisco, 1981—, NIH, 1992, 94. Mem. ACS (chmn. neurosurgery sect. No. Calif. chpt. 1981-83), Am. Acad. Cerebral Palsy and Devel. Medicine, Am. Acad. Neurol. Surgery, Am. Acad. Pediatrics, Am. Assn. Neurol. Surgeons (membership com. pediatric sect. 1982—, Donald Matson award com. 1982—, Am. Soc. Pediat. Neurosurgery (edn. com. 1984—), Am. Soc. Clin. Oncology, Calif. Assn. Neurol. Surgeons (profl. rels. and peer rev. com. 1983—), Calif. Med. Assn., Congress Neurol. Surgeons (chmn. publs. sect. com. on nervous sys. tumors 1984-89), Fedn. Western Socs. Neurol. Sci., Internat. Soc. Pediatric Neurosurgery, Neurosurg. Soc. Am., Pediatric Oncology Group/Childrens Cancer Group, Rsch. Soc. Neurol. Surgeons, Sacramento-El Dorado Med. Soc., Sacramento Pediatric Soc., San Francisco Med. Soc., Soc. Neurol. Surgeons, Sutter Neurosci. Inst., Western Neurosurg. Soc. (program dir. 1993, 94), Phi Delta Kappa. Office: Complex Pediat and Adult Neurosurgery 2800 L St Ste 340 Sacramento CA 95816-5616 E-mail: EdwardM@Sutterhealth.org.

EDWARDS, OTIS CARL, JR., theology educator; b. Bienville, La., June 15, 1928; s. Otis Carl and Margaret Lee (Hutchinson) E.; m. Jane Hanna Trufant, Feb. 19, 1957; children: Carl Lee, Samuel Adams Trufant, Louise Reynes BA, Centenary Coll., 1949; postgrad., Duke U., 1949-51; STB, Gen. Theol. Sem., 1952; postgrad., Westcott House, Cambridge, Eng., 1952-53; STM, So. Meth. U., 1962; MA, U. Chgo., 1963, PhD, 1971; DD, Nashotah House, 1976. Ordained priest Episcopal Ch., 1954. Curate Episcopal Ch., Baton Rouge, 1953-54, vicar Abbeville, La., 1954-57, Waxahachie, Tex., 1960-61, rector Morgan City, La., 1957-60, priest in charge Chgo., 1961-63; instr. Wabash Coll., 1963-64; asst. prof. Nashotah House, Wis., 1964-69, assoc. prof., 1969-72, prof., 1972-74, sub-dean, 1973-74, acting dean, 1973-74; dean Seabury-Western Theol. Sem., Evanston, Ill., 1974-83, prof., 1983-93, prof. emeritus, 1996; chaplain, scholar in residence Coll. Preachers. Chmn. Coun. for Devel. of Ministry, Episcopal Ch., Coun. Sem. Deans; mem. Bd. for Theol. Edn.; mem. Gen. Bd. Examining Chaplains; vis. prof. Notre Dame, 1986—, Duke U., 1996; rsch. assoc. The Newberry Libr.; interim priest Episcopal Ch., Asheville, N.C. Author: How It All Began, 1973, The Living and Active Word, 1975 (with Robert Bennett) The Bible for Today's Church, 1979, Luke's Story of Jesus, 1981, (with John Westerhoff) A Faithful Church: Issues in the History of Catechesis, 1981, Elements of Homiletic, 1982, How Holy Writ Was Written, 1989; book rev. editor Anglican Theol. Rev., 1971-76, v.p. of corp., 1975-85; contbr. articles and book revs. to various jours. and mags. Chmn. campus affairs com.; trustee Kendall Coll.; sec. Commn. on Faith and Order Nat. Coun. Chs.; bd. dirs., Native Am. Theol. Assn., U. N.C. at Asheville Found.; exec. com. Nat. Coun. Chs. in the USA; v.p. bd. dirs. Coll. for Srs./U. N.C., Asheville; program com. Kanuga Confs., Inc., Friends of St. Benedict. Recipient Spl. award Mystery Writers Am., 1965; grantee The Conant Fund, Pew Foun., St. Paul's Ministry and Mission Found., Indpls. Mem. Soc. Bibl. Lit., Cath. Bibl. Assn., Am. Acad. Religion, Chgo. Soc. Bibl. Rsch., Acad. Homiletics, (pres.), Societas Homiletica (exec. coun., treas.), Coll. of Preachers (long-range planning com.), Mystery Writers of Am. Democrat. Home: 115 Murphy Hill Rd Weaverville NC 28787-8630 E-mail: janeoce@aol.com.

EDWARDS, PATRICK ROSS, former retail company executive, lawyer, management consultant; b. Montreal, Que., Can., Mar. 17, 1940; came to U.S., 1952; s. Claude Victor and Edith May Peace (Wyatt) E.; m. Gracelyn Regina LaSala, July 2, 1961; children— Pamela Lynn, Jennifer Anne BA, Kenyon Coll., 1962; JD, Columbia U., 1965. Bar: N.Y. 1967. Staff atty. Allied Stores Corp., N.Y.C., 1965-69, asst. to pres., 1970-74, v.p. adminstrn., 1974-83, sr. v.p. ops. and adminstrn., 1983-85; pres., chief operating officer Genovese Drug Stores, Inc., Melville, N.Y., 1985-86; exec. v.p., chief operating officer Am. Trim Products, Inc., 1987-88, pres., chief exec. officer, 1988-89; prin. The Rosse Co., 1990—. Sr. v.p. sys. svcs. North Shore--L.I. Jewish Health Sys., 1996-2000. Trustee Northshore U. Hosp., Manhasset, N.Y., 1984-93, spl. asst. to pres., 1993-96; mem. exec. coun. Inner City Scholarship Fund, N.Y.C., 1983-93; mem. deans adv. coun. SUNY Sch. Bus., Albany, 1984-86; mem. Ea. regional panel Pres.'s Commn. on White House Fellowships, N.Y.C., 1984-86. Mem. Kenyon Coll. Alumni Assn. Clubs: Strathmore Vanderbilt Country (Manhasset). Roman Catholic.

EDWARDS, PAUL ANDREW, vitreo-retinal surgeon, ophthalmologist; b. New Gardens, Jamaica, June 27, 1954; s. Harold Julian and Iris Maud (Blair) E.; m. Jennifer Marie Jones Edwards, Dec. 3, 1977; children: Nikeisha Ayanna, Tiffany Aisha, Paul Andrew II. MB, BS, U. W.I., Kingston, Jamaica, 1979. Diplomate Am. Bd. Ophthalmology. Intern Univ. Hosp. of W.I., Kingston, Jamaica, 1979-80; resident in surgery Washington Hosp. Ctr., 1980-82; rsch. fellowship in ophthalmology Nat. Eye Inst., Bethesda, Md., 1984-89; resident in ophthalmology Henry Ford Hosp., Detroit, 1989-92, vitreo-retinal fellow, 1991-93, divsn. head of ophthalmology for Mercy Divsn., 1992-96; divsn. head ophthalmology HFH Med. Ctr., 1996—; interim chair dept. eye care svcs. Henry Ford Health System, 2001—; chair dept. of opth. Henry Ford Health Sys., 2002—. Vis. prof. ophthalmology U. W.I., 1994—. Fellow ACS, Am. Acad. Ophthalmology. Office: Henry Ford Health Sys One Ford Pl #5A Detroit MI 48202 E-mail: pedward2@hfhs.org.

EDWARDS, PAUL BEVERLY, retired science and engineering educator; b. Ridge Spring, S.C., Nov. 12, 1915; s. Paul Bee and Chloe Agnes (Watson) E.; m. Sarah Dee Barnes, Apr. 10, 1943 (dec. July 1999); 1 child, Susan Dee Edwards Von Suskil. BS, U. Tampa, 1937; EdM, Harvard U., 1958; EdD, George Washington U., 1972. Owner, operator Edwards' Hobbies, Tampa, Fla., 1938-54; tchr. math. Hillsborough High Sch., Tampa, 1955-60; head dept. math. King High Sch., Tampa, 1960-63; coord. Grad. Ctr., supr. edn. and tng. Johns Hopkins U. and Applied Physics Lab., Balt. and Laurel, Md., 1963-75, dir. Grad. Ctr., supr. edn. and tng., 1975-81. Contbr. articles to profl. jours. Mem. Sun City Ctr. Voters League, 1989—, Community Assn., Sun City Ctr., 1987—; mem. Greenbriar Property Owners Assn., Sun City Ctr., 1987—. Lt. comdr. USNR, 1942-46. Named Meritorious Tchr., State of Fla., 1962; recipient various fellowships. Mem. Ret. Officers Assn., Naval Res. Assn., Golf and Racquet Club. Avocations: swimming, computing, photography. Home: 1843 Wolf Laurel Dr Sun City Center FL 33573-6422

EDWARDS, PAUL N. science educator; BA, Wesleyan U., 1980; postgrad., U. Paris VIII, 1980—81; PhD in History of Consciousness, U. Calif., Santa Cruz, 1988. Rsch. analyst EcoPlan Internat., Paris, 1981; acting asst. prof., lectr. program in sci., tech. and soc. and dept. computer sci. Stanford U., 1994—97, dir. info. tech. and soc. project, 1995—97, sr. rsch. scholar, lectr. program in sci., tech. and soc., 1997—98; assoc. prof. Sch. Info., chair sci., tech. and soc. program Residential Coll., U. Mich., 1999—. Recipient Guggenheim fellowship, 2003, student fellowship, Wesleyan Ctr. for Humanities, 1979, Silicon Valley Rsch. Group rsch. grant, U. Calif., Santa Cruz, 1985, Regent's fellowship, 1981, 1985, Peace Studies Program/MacArthur Found. rsch. grant, Cornell U., 1991—92, NSF Profl. Devel. fellowship, 1993—94, Sloan Found. Rsch. grant, 1997—2000, NSF rsch. grant, 1997—2001, W. K. Kellogg Found. Rsch. grant, 2001; fellow, Inst. on Global Conflict and Coop. Summer Seminar on Global Security and Arms Control, La Jolla, Calif., 1987, Inst. on Global Conflict and Coop. Summer Seminar on Global Security and Arms Control, Sussex, Eng., 1988. Office: U Mich Sch of Info 301 D West Hall Ann Arbor MI 48109-1092*

EDWARDS, PETER, educator, writer; b. Kalgoorlie, Australia; m. Susan Christine Maslowski, Feb. 1, 1985; children: Lance, Michael, Diana, Tania, Dean, Monique. BA, U. West Australia, Perth, 1964, BEd, 1968; MA, U. B.C., Vancouver, Can., 1972, EdD, 1974. Cert. tchr., West Australia, B.C., VA. Tchr. Edn. Dept. West Australia, Perth, 1957-68, Edn. Dept. B.C., Vancouver, 1968-71; lectr. edn. U. B.C., 1974-75; sr. lectr. Monash U., Melbourne, Victoria, Australia, 1976-89; adj. instr. Saginaw (Mich.) Valley State U., 1989-90; assoc. prof. Clarion (Pa.) U. Pa., 1990-92; prof. SUNY, Plattsburgh, 1992-98, VA Edn. Dept., 1998-2001, SUNY, New Paltz, 2001—. Cons. Tchrs.' Resource Ctr., Canberra, Australia, 1976, Aboriginal Affairs, Melbourne, 1977, 80, Commonwealth of Australia, Canberra, 1980-83. Author: Reading Problems, 1981, Edwards Diagnostic Reading Test, 1981, Seven Keys to Successful Study, 1991, 2d edit., 1996, Literacy Techniques, 1995, 2d edit., 2002; (with others) Reading Education, 1981, Special Education, 1981; (simulation game) Successful Negotiation, 1984; (computer program) Reading and Study Skills, 1988; (video) Creative Responses to Reading, 1991, Reading Showcase, 1992; contbr. articles to ednl. publs. Mem.: Am. Fedn. Tchrs., United Univ. Professions, Internat. Reading Assn., Ulster County Reading Coun., Kappa Delta Phi. Avocations: creative writing, traveling. Office: OMB 223 SUNY New Paltz NY 12561

EDWARDS, PETER S. executive management/computer consulting; b. Staten Island, N.Y., June 7, 1966; s. Theodore Peter and Gertrude Edwards; m. Teresa S. Robinson, Aug. 28, 1993; children: Tess, Will children: Ben. BS in computer sci., Villanova U., 1985—89. Sr. mgmt. Application Consulting Group, Mor-

ristown, NJ, 1990—2000, ceo, 2001—. Mem.: Data Warehousing Inst. (assoc.). Home: 15 Stonehenge Rd Morristown NJ 07960 Office: Application Consulting Group 121 Headquarters Plaza Morristown NJ 07960 Office Fax: 973-898-9054. E-mail: pedwards@acgi.com.

EDWARDS, PHILLIP MILTON, retired import-export company executive; b. Borger, Tex., Feb. 24, 1933; s. Aaron Moses and Ada Elsie (Feist) E.; m. Mildred M. L. Weber, Aug. 18, 1956 (dec. Sept. 22, 2001); m. Arlene Irvine Davis, Jan. 4, 2002. BA, Okla. U., 1958. Polit. officer U.S. Embassy, Jedda, Saudi Arabia, 1961-64; vice consul U.S. Consulate Gen., Dhahran, Saudi Arabia, 1965-67; sr. advisor Dept. of Army, Vinh Long, Vietnam, 1968-70; publs. mgr. DOT Systems, Incorp., Vienna, Va., 1971-77; v.p. Transcontinental Trade Corp., Washington, 1978-81; sr. writer, editor Sci. Applications Internat. Corp., McLean, Va., 1981-87; v.p. Security Support Svcs., Washington, 1981-92; mem. profl. staff Alderson Reporting Co., Washington, 1992-97; ret., 1997. Freelance writer, editor, 1997—. Contbr. articles to profl. jours. Recipient Silver medal SAR, 1979. Presbyterian. Avocations: flying, photography, mountain climbing, tennis. Home: 1917 Aubrey Place Ct Vienna VA 22182-1976 E-mail: pedwa666@aol.com.

EDWARDS, PRISCILLA ANN, paralegal, business owner; b. Orlando, Fla., Sept. 28, 1947; d. William Granville and Bernice Royster; m. Charles R. King, Apr. 2, 1981. Paralegal cert., U. Calif., Berkeley, 1994. Paralegal Charles R. Garry Esquire, San Francisco, 1989-90; owner, mgr. Fed. Legal Resources, San Francisco, 1991—. Speaker Sonoma State U., Santa Rosa, Calif., 1993. Publisher: (book) Zero Weather, 1981. Recipient Wiley W. Manuel award for pro bono legal svcs. Bd. Govs. State Bar of Calif., 1994, 95, 96, 97, 98. Episcopalian. Avocations: horseback riding, mountain biking.

EDWARDS, RALPH M. librarian; b. Shelley, Idaho, Apr. 17, 1933; s. Edward William and Maude Estella (Munsee) E.; m. Winifred Wylie, Dec. 25, 1969; children: Dylan, Nathan, Stephen. BA, U. Wash., 1957, M.Library, 1960; D.L.S., U. Calif.-Berkeley, 1971. Libr. N.Y. Pub. Libr., N.Y.C., 1960-61; catalog libr. U. Ill. Libr., Urbana, 1961-62; br. libr. Multnomah County Libr., Portland, Oreg., 1964-67; asst. prof. Western Mich. U., Kalamazoo, 1970-74; chief of the Central Libr. Dallas Pub. Libr., 1975-81; city librarian Phoenix Pub. Libr., 1981-95, ret., 1996—. Author: Role of the Beginning Librarian in University Libraries, 1975. U. Calif. doctoral fellow, 1967-70; library mgmt. internship Council on Library Resources, 1974-75 Mem. ALA, Pub. Library Assn. Democrat. Home: 2884 Spring Blvd Eugene OR 97403-1662 E-mail: wedwards@efn.org.

EDWARDS, RICHARD ALAN, banker; b. Minot, N.D., Apr. 26, 1957; s. Duane LaVoy Sr. and Virginia Ione (Lyson) E.; m. Deon Rae Schmidt, June 3, 1989. BBA, Minot State Coll., 1979. Bank teller Norwest Bancorp., Minot, 1977-80; bank examiner N.D. Dept. Banking, Fargo, 1980-85; loan adminstrn. officer Banks of Iowa, Inc., Des Moines, 1985-88, asst. v.p. loan adminstrn., 1988-90, v.p. loan rev., 1990-91; v.p. credit adminstrn. Firstar Corp. of Iowa, Des Moines, 1991-92, 1st v.p. credit adminstrn., 1992-95, sr. v.p. credit adminstrn., 1995—2000; sr. v.p. credit approval mgr. US Bank, 2000—. Mem. Am. Inst. Banking, Robert Morris Assocs., Sigma Tau Gamma. Meth. Avocations: bowling, jogging, softball, waterskiing, music collecting. Home: 2820 Eula Dr Des Moines IA 50322-4258

EDWARDS, RICHARD ALAN, retired lawyer; b. Portland, Oreg., June 28, 1938; s. Howard A. and Kay E. (Sheldon) E.; m. Renee Rosier, June 18, 1960; children: Teri Edwards Obye, Lisa Edwards Smith, Steve. BS, Oreg. State U., 1960; JD summa cum laude, Willamette U., 1968. Bar: Oreg. 1968, U.S. Dist. Ct. Oreg. 1968, U.S. Ct. Appeals (9th cir.) 1969. Various positions 1st Interstate Bank of Oreg., Portland, 1960-65; assoc. Miller, Nash, Wiener, Hager & Carlsen, Portland, 1968-74, ptnr., 1974—, mng. ptnr., 1991-96. Editor Willamette Law Jour., 1967-68. Mem. ABA (litigation sect. 1972), Oreg. State Bar (chairperson debtor-creditor sect. 1981-82, mem. various coms.). Republican. Presbyterian.

EDWARDS, RICHARD LANSING, lawyer; b. Wilmington, Del., Apr. 16, 1944; s. Robert Wilson Jr. and Eleanor (Inscho) E.; m. Betsey Ann Barney, Aug. 24, 1980; children: Beth, Melissa, Jeffrey, Jason, Karen. BS in Indsl. Engring., Lehigh U., 1966; JD, Northeastern U., 1980. Bar: Mass. 1980, U.S. Dist. Ct. Mass. 1981, U.S. Ct. Appeals (1st cir.) 1983, U.S. Supreme Ct. 1985, U.S. Dist. Ct. Conn. 1998. Lawyer Craig & Macauley, Boston, 1980-83; lawyer, shareholder Campbell, Campbell, Edwards & Conroy P.C., Boston, 1983—. Faculty Internat. Assn. Def. Counsel Trial Acad., 1994, ABA TIPS Nat. Trial Acad., 2000. Contbr. articles to profl. jours. Capt. USAF, 1966—70. Decorated Bronze star. Mem. ABA (tort and ins. practice and litigation sect. 1984—, faculty torts and ins. sect. Nat. Trial Acad. 2000), Mass. Bar Assn. (civil litigation sect. 1983—), Def. Rsch. Inst. (bd. dirs. 1999-2002, products liability com., chmn. 1997-99, chmn. duty to warn and labeling subcom. 1985-88, steering com. 1988—), Internat. Assn. of Def. Counsel (chmn. advocacy practice and procedure com. 1993-95, faculty Trial Acad. 1994), Mass. Def. Lawyers Assn., Product Liability Adv. Coun., Boston Bar Assn. Office: Campbell Campbell Edwards & Conroy PC One Constitution Plaza Boston MA 02129 E-mail: redwards@campbell-trial-lawyers.com.

EDWARDS, RICHARD WALTON, JR., law educator; b. Columbus, Ohio, June 2, 1935; s. Richard Walton and Jessamal Brophy Edwards; m. Margaret Alice Witzeman, Aug. 30, 1958; children: Evelyn Evangeline Edwards Loughman, Kenneth Brophy. BA, Cornell U., 1957, JD in Internat. Affairs, 1959. Bar: DC 59, NY 60, U.S. Supreme Ct. 64. Asst. to exec. dir. Am. Soc. Internat. Law, Washington, 1961—67, asst. dir., 1967—70; asst. dean Coll. of Law U. Toledo, 1970—73, assoc. prof. law, 1970—75, prof. law, 1975—90, prof. law emeritus, 1990—. Cons. Dana Fund for Internat. and Comparative Legal Studies, Toledo, 1978—87. Author: International Monetary Collaboration, 1985 (award, 86); contbr. articles to profl. jours.; asst. editor: Internat. Legal Materials, 1962—67; editor, 1967—70. Mem. nat. bd. dirs. A Christian Ministry in the Nat. Parks, Freeport, Maine, 1992—. Mem.: Antique Tribal Art Dealers Assn. (mem. legal com. 1998—), Am. Soc. Internat. Law (mem. exec. coun. 1984—86, chmn. ann. meeting 1990, Francis Deak award 1977, hon. mention ann. award 1986). Republican. Mem. Christian Ch. (Disciples Of Christ). Avocations: collecting Plains Indian art, hiking, bird study. Office: U Toledo Coll Law 2801 W Bancroft St Toledo OH 43606

EDWARDS, ROBERT, professional football player; b. Oct. 2, 1974; Student, U. Ga. Running back New Eng. Patriots, 1998—2001, Miami Dolphins, 2002—. Office: New England Patriots 60 Washington St Foxboro MA 02035-1388

EDWARDS, ROBERT HAZARD, retired college president; b. London, May 26, 1935; s. Arthur Robinson and Marjorie Hazard (Mayes) E. (father Am. citizen); m. Blythe Morton Bickel, Nov. 5, 1988; children from previous marriage: Elizabeth, Daphne, Nicholas. AB, Princeton U., 1957; BA, Cambridge (Eng.) U., 1959, MA (hon.), 1977; LLB, Harvard U., 1961; LHD (hon.), Carleton Coll., 1986, Bowdoin Coll., Colby Coll., 2001. Bar: Fed. 1961. Fellow Ford Found., 1961—63; with UN polit. affairs Dept. State, 1963—65, Ford Found., 1965—77; rep. for Pakistan, 1968—72; head Middle East and Africa, 1973—77; pres. Carleton Coll., Northfield, Minn., 1977—86; head social welfare dept. Secretariat of the Aga Khan, Paris, 1986—90; pres. Bowdoin Coll., Brunswick, Maine, 1990—2001. Mem. bd. visitors U. Maine. Trustee Aga Khan U. Mem. Coun. on Fgn. Rels. N.Y.C., Maine Math. and Sci. Alliance (chmn.), Am. Acad. Arts & Sci.*

EDWARDS, ROBIN MORSE, lawyer; b. Glens Falls, N.Y., Dec. 9, 1947; d. Daniel and Harriet Morse; m. Richard Charles Edwards, Aug. 30, 1970; children: Michael Alan, Jonathan Philip. BA, Mt. Holyoke Coll., 1969; JD, U. Calif., Berkeley, 1972. Bar: Calif. 1972. Assoc. Donahue, Gallagher, Thomas & Woods, Oakland, Calif., 1972—77, ptnr., 1977—89, Sonnenschein, Nath & Rosenthal, San Francisco, 1989—, mgmt. com., 1998—. Bd. dirs. Temple Sinai, 1997-2002. Mem. ABA, Calif. Bar Assn., Alameda County Bar Assn. (bd. dirs. 1978-84, v.p. 1982, pres. 1983), Alameda County Bar Found. (bd. dirs. 1998-2000). Jewish. Avocations: skiing, cooking. Office: Sonnenschein Nath Rosenthal 685 Market St 6th Flr San Francisco CA 94105-4202 E-mail: redwards@sonnenschein.com.

EDWARDS, RYAN HAYES, baritone; b. Columbia, S.C. m. Leila Scelonge; 1 child, Geoffrey. MusB, U. Tex.; MusM, Tex. Christian U. Artistic cons. Marquee Theatre Co., Evanston, Ill., Internat. Opera Acad., Rome, master tchr. Scholar Julliard Am. Opera Ctr., N.Y.C., debut, N.Y.C. Opera, Hollywood Bowl, N.Y. Philharm., L.A. Philharm., Chgo. Symphony, London Symphony, Boston Symphony, San Francisco Opera Co., Teatro del Liceo, Barcelona, Royal Festival Hall, London, Metropolitan Opera; radio debut, O.R.T.F., Paris; films and recs. include Caterina Cornaro, I Pagliacci, Maid of Orleans, Mahler Symphony No. 8 others; author: The Verdi Baritone: Studies in Development of Dramatic Character, Verdi & Puccini Heroines: Dramatic Characterization in Great Soprano Roles, A.K.A. Doc: Oral History of a New Orleans Street Musician. Named awardee Nat. Opera Inst.; Rockefeller grantee, Nat. Opera Inst. grantee, Edwin H. Mosler Found. grantee, William Mathews Sullivan Mus. Found. grantee. Mem. Nat. Opera Assn. (pres.), Am. Guild Musical Artists, Actors Equity, Phi Mu Alpha, Lambda Chi Alpha, Pi Kappa Lambda. Achievements include winning San Angelo Symphony competition, Nat. Radio Auditions for Acad. Vocal Arts, Phila., Internat. Verdi competition, Busseto, Italy. *I was a totally American trained and prepared artist. Hopefully this fact will be of inspiration to other young American singers who, for too many years, have had to try to impress European smaller companies before becoming worthy to have any sort of career here in their own country. America is finally coming to acknowledge its own native operatic talent.*

EDWARDS, SIR SAMUEL FREDERICK, physicist, educator; b. Swansea, Wales, Feb. 1, 1928; m. Merriell Bland, 1953; 4 children. Ed., Cambridge U., Harvard U.; DSc (hon.), U. Bath, U. Edinburgh, U. Loughborough, U. Salford, U. Birmingham, 1976, U. Strasbourg, 1986, U. Wales, 1987, U. Sheffield, 1989, U. Dublin, 1991, U. Leeds, U. Swansea, 1994, East Anglia, 1995, U. Cambridge, Eng., 2001; DSc (hon.), U. Mainz, 2002. Mem. Inst. Advanced Study, Princeton, N.J.; rsch. fellow U. Birmingham; prof. U. Manchester; emeritus Cavendish prof. physics Cavendish Lab.; pro vice chancellor Cambridge U., 1992-95; fellow, pres. Gonville and Caius Coll. Vis. prof. U. Calif., San Diego, 1980-81; dir. Lucas Industries, 1981-93; chmn. Sci. Rsch. Coun. U.K., 1973-77, Def. Sci. Adv. Coun., 1977-80; chief sci. advisor U.K. Dept. Energy, 1983-88; program dir. ITP U. Calif., Santa Barbara, 1997; hon. prof. chemistry Beijing U. Contbr. articles to profl. jours. Recipient Sci. pour l'Art prize Louis Vuitton Moet Hennessy, 1993, Boltzmann medal Internat. Union Pure and Applied Physics, 1995. Fellow Royal Soc. (Davy medal 1985, Royal medal 2001), Inst. Physics (Maxwell medal, Guthrie medal, Keller Meml. Polymer medal 2001), Royal Soc. Chemistry, Inst. Math. (Gold medal 1986), Am. Phys. Soc. (High Polymer Physics prize), Brit. Assn. Advancement of Sci. (chmn. 1977-82, pres. 1988-89), Brit. Soc. Rheology (Gold medal 1991), French Acad. Scis. (fgn. assoc.), NAS (fgn. assoc.), French Phys. Soc. (hon.), European Phys. Soc. (hon.); mem. Athenaeum Club. Home: 7 Penarth Pl Cambridge CB3 9LU England Office: Cavendish Lab Cambridge CB3 OHE England E-mail: sfe11@phy.cam.ac.uk.

EDWARDS, SAMUEL HOLLIS, lawyer, urban/regional planner; b. Lebanon, Tenn., Apr. 13, 1950; s. Hollis Elverton and Aggie Rhea Edwards; m. Debra Joyce Edwards, Aug. 19, 1972; children: Rebecca Joyce Sellars, Samantha Leigh Granstaff. BS, Mid. Tenn. State U., 1972; MPA, U. Tenn., 1976; JD, Nashville Sch. Law, 1991. Bar: Tenn., 1991, U.S. Dist. Ct. (middle dist.), Tenn., 1992. Transp. planner Dept. Transp., Nashville, 1972-76; planning dir. Wilson County/Lebanon Planning Office, 1977-86; dep. exec. dir. Greater Nashville Regional Coun., 1986—, legal counsel, 1991—. Mem. ABA, Am. Inst. Cert. Planners, Am. Planning Assn., Tenn. Bar Assn., Nashville Bar Assn. Home: 208 Oakdale Dr Lebanon TN 37087 Office: Greater Nashville Regional Coun 501 Union St 6th Fl Nashville TN 37219 E-mail: sedwards@gnrc.org.

EDWARDS, SAMUEL ROGER, internist; b. Santa Barbara, Calif., Aug. 11, 1937; s. Harold S. and Margaret (Spaulding) E.; m. Marcia Elizabeth Dutton, June 17, 1961; children: Harold S. II, Charles Dutton. BA, Harvard U., 1960; MD, U. So. Calif., 1964. Intern Presbyn. Hosp., Phila., 1964-65; resident in internal medicine U Calif., San Francisco, 1968-70; fellow in cardiology Pacific Presbyn. Med. Ctr., San Francisco, 1970; pvt. practice specializing in internal medicine Santa Paula, Calif., 1971-94; med. dir. Santa Paula Convalescent, Twin Pines Convalescent Hosps., 1974-95; pres. med. staff Ventura (Calif.) County Med. Ctr., 1979-80, med. dir., 1983-95; hosp. adminstr. Ventura (Calif.) County Med. Ctr., 1995—2002. Mem. clin. faculty UCLA Sch. Medicine, 1980-95; bd. dirs. Citizens State Bank of Santa Paula, 1975-97, chmn., 1994-97; bd. dirs. Limoneira Co., 1985—, chmn., 2003—; bd. dirs. Santa Barbara Bank and Trust, 1999—; chief dept. medicine Ventura County Gen. Hosp., 1975; chief med. staff Santa Paula Meml. Hosp., 1977. Lt. Comdr. USNR, 1966-68. Recipient Disting. Svc. award Ventura County Heart Assn., 1974. Fellow: ACP; mem.: AMA, Am. Coll. Hosp. Execs. Episcopalian. Home: 19789 E Telegraph Rd Santa Paula CA 93060-9693 Office: 243 March St Santa Paula CA 93060-2511

EDWARDS, SARAH ANNE, radio, cable TV personality, clinical social worker; b. Tulsa, Jan. 7, 1943; d. Clyde Elton and virginia Elizabeth Glandon; m. Paul Robert Edwards, Apr. 24, 1965; 1 son, Jon Scott. BA with distinction, U. Mo., Kansas City, 1965; MSW, U. Kans., 1974. Cmty. rep. OEO, Kans. City Regional Office, 1966-68; social svc./parent involvement and resource specialist Office of Child Devel., HEW, Kansas City, Kans., 1968-73; dir. tng. social svcs. dept., children's rehab. unit U. Affiliated Facility, U. Kans. Med. Ctr., Kansas City, 1975-76; co-dir. Cathexis Inst. S., Glendale, Calif., 1976-77; pvt. practice psychotherapy, tng. and cons. personal and interpersonal, orgnl. behavior, Sierra Madre, Calif., 1973-80; sys. operator CompuServe Info. Svc., 1983-98. Prodr., co-host radio show Working From Home, on Bus. Talk Radio, 1988-01; co-host cable show Working from Home Scripp's Howard Home and Garden Cable TV Network, 1995-97; commentator CNBC, 1996-99, NPR Marketplace, 1996-97. Columnist for Home Office Computing Mag., 1988-97, Your Home Office, L.A. Times Syndicate, 1997-99, Entrepreneur's Home Office, 1998—, Price CostCo Connection, 1994—, Inc-Com., 2000—; co-author: How to Make Money with Your Personal Computer, 1997, Getting Business to Come to You, 1998, Working From Home, rev. edit., 1999, Secrets of Self-Employment, 1996, Finding Your Perfect Work, 1996, Teaming Up, 1997, Home Businesses You Can Buy, 1997, Cool Careers for Dummies, 1998, Making Money in Cyberspace, 1998, Best Home Business for the 21st Century, 1999, Working From Home, 1999, The Practical Dreamer's Handbook, 2000, Home-Based Business for Dummies, 2000, Changing Directions without Losing Your Way, 2001, Entrepreneurial Parent, 2002, Sitting with the Enemy, A Novel, 2002, Why Aren't You Your Own Boss?, 2003. Dir. nature-guided counseling programs Pine Mountain Inst., 2001. Address: Box 6775 2624 Teakwood Ct Pine Mountain CA 93222 E-mail: sedwards@frazmtn.com.

EDWARDS, SHARON JANE, nurse; b. Staten Island, N.Y., Aug. 15, 1967; BSN, Oral Roberts U., 1990; MSN, St. Louis U., 1998, PhD in Nursing, 2002. Nurse extern City of Faith Hosp., Tulsa, 1989-90; nurse Loma Linda (Calif.) U., 1990-93, George Washington U. Med. Ctr., Washington, 1993, Walter Reed Army Med. Ctr., Washington, 1994-96, Jefferson (Mo.). Meml. Hosp., 1997, Belleville Meml. Hosp., Ill., 1997-98; pres. Advanced Practice Nursing Svcs., Inc., St. Louis, 1998—2002; vis. asst. prof. Coll. of Nursing U. South Fla., Tampa, 2002—

EDWARDS, SHEILA M. banker, educator; b. Arab, Ala., Aug. 10, 1960; d. Raymond O'Neal and Nellie Marie Moody; m. Justion Kyle Edwards, Dec. 17, 1976; children: Melissa LaAnn, Justina Marie. AS, Jefferson State U., Pinson, Ala., 1982; student, Am. Inst. Banking, Birmingham, Ala., 1992, 93. Asst. head teller Leeth Nat. Bank, Cullman, Ala., 1982-83; loan asst. v.p. Regions Bank, Oneonta, Ala., 1987-93; br. mgr. Valley Fin., Guntersville, Ala., 1993-95; adminstrv. mgr. Lowe's, Cullman, 1995-96; comml. lending SouthTrust Bank, Guntersville, 1996-99; v.p. EvaBank, Cullman, 1999—; tchr. fin. Am. Inst. Banking-Wallace State, Cullman, 1999—; br. mgr. Colonial Bank, Locust Fork, Ala., 2001—03; v.p. risk mgmt. Cmty. Bank, 2003—. Trainer/spkr., pres. trainer/seminars in fin., career success, customer svc. Edwards Profl. Svc. Troop leader Girls Scouts U.S., Blountsville, Ala., coord., 1984—91. Mem.: Bount W Bus. and Profl. Women (pres. 2002—), Cullman Bus. and Profl. Women (pres. 2001—), Ala. Bus. Women (bd. dirs.), Bus. and Profl. Women (v.p. 2000, pres. 2001—), Fin. Women Internat. (pres. Mountain Valley group 1999—2000, state officer 2001—, Ala. v.p. 2002—03, Ala. state officer of edn., tng., state pres. 2003—), C. of C. Office: PO Box 177 Locust Fork AL 35097 E-mail: jsedward@urisp.net.

EDWARDS, STEPHEN ALLEN, lawyer; b. Battle Creek, Mich., July 12, 1953; s. Louis Ward and Elizabeth Yvonne (Stahl) E.; m. Alice Veronica; children: Amelia Hatfield, Nathaniel Gordon. BA with high honors, U. Mich., 1975, JD cum laude, 1978. Bar: Wis. 1978, U.S. Dist. Ct. (ea. and we. dists.) Wis. 1978, Mich. 1980, Pa. 1980, Ga. 1999. Assoc. Godfrey & Kahn S.C., Milw., 1978-80, Pepper, Hamilton & Scheetz, Phila., 1980-82, Morgan, Lewis & Bockius, Phila., 1982-87, ptnr., 1987-98, Kilpatrick Stockton LLP, Altanta, 1998—. Author: Arbitrage, 1990; exec. editor: The Issuer's Guide to Tax-Exempt Finance, 1994, Municipal Leasing, 2002. Mem. ABA (tax sect.), Wis. Bar Assn., Mich. Bar Assn., Ga. Bar Assn., Phila. Bar Assn., Pa. Bar Assn., Nat. Assn. Bond Lawyers (chmn. arbitrage seminar 1990, edn. com. 1990-91, bd. dirs. 1991-94, treas. 1994-95), Bond Attys. Workshop (panelist 1984-95, steering com., chmn. arbitrage 1986-87), Pa. Soc. SR (bd. dirs. 1991-94), Phila. Club. Republican. Episcopalian. Avocation: cycling. Office: Kilpatrick Stockton LLP Peachtree St Ste 2800 Atlanta GA 30303-1303 Home: 360 Cannady Ct Atlanta GA 30350-5622

EDWARDS, STEVE, attorney, former political organization executive; Staff atty. Office of the Gen. Counsel, Reagan Adminstrn., Washington, polit. cons. Sen. Jeremiah Denton Re-election campaign, Ala., 1986; dep. assoc. dir. presdl. personnel for Pres. Bush Washington, 1989; chief legal counsel Nat. Rep. Congrl. Com., Washington, 1989-91; chief of staff for Senator James Inhofe Tulsa, Okla., 1991—; Chair. Okla. Rep. Party, 1999—2001. Office: 453 Russell Senate Bldg Washington DC 20510-3603

EDWARDS, SYLVIA ANN, artist; b. Boston, Jan. 30, 1937; d. Junius Griffiths and Sylvia Emma (Mailloux) E.; m. Sadredin M. Golestaneh (div.); children: Shirin, Nader, Leila. Diploma, Mass. Coll. of Art, Boston, 1957, Boston Mus. of Fine Arts, 1958; postgrad., Modern Art Studies, London, 1980-81. One-woman shows include CCA Gallery, Oxford, Eng., 1996, Munson Gallery, Chatham, Mass., 1992, Jaeshke Gallery, Braunschweig, Germany, 1991, Natalie Knight Gallery, Johannesburg, South Africa, 1991, Bankamura, Tokyo, 1991, Gallery K. Hyazaki Perfecture, 1991, The Berkeley Sq. Gallery, London, 1991, CCA Gallery, 2003, numerous others, exhibited in group shows at Cadogan Contemporary Art, London, 1996, Berkeley Sq. Gallery, Korea Art Expo, Seoul, 1996, 2002, N.Y. Art Expo, N.Y.C., 1994, Lond Internat. Contemporary Art Fair, 1989, The Bath Arts Festival, Eng., 1988, Paris Art Salon, 1986, 1987, 1988, Sarasota Visual Art Ctr., numerous others, Represented in permanent collections Nat. Mus. for Women in the Arts, Washington, Boston U. Spl. Collections, Cape Mus Fine Arts, Dennis, Mass, Mus. Fine Arts, Alexandria, Egypt, Governorate of Alexandria, Mass. Gen. Hosp., Boston, Chelsea Westminster Hosp., London, Midwest Mus. Am. Art, Elkhart, Ind., Tate Gallery, London, publs., Valley of Sils, Lithograph, 1982, N.Mex. Watch, lithograph, 1982, covers, Arts Rev., 1982, 1985, others, numerous, UNICEF cards, Greenpeace publs., World Wildlife/U.K., book covers, reference and art books, others, monograph, Pallas Athere, London, 2003. Mem. U.K. UNICEF Com. Mem. London Royal Acad., World Watercolor Soc., Chelsea Arts Club/London. Avocations: writing, theatre, travel, swimming, reading. Studio: 14 Cadogan Square London SW1X 0JU England

EDWARDS, TERRI LYN WILMOTH, education educator; b. Bremerton, Wash., June 18, 1959; d. Marvin Earl and Beverly Joanne Wilmoth; m. Eddie Lee Edwards, Sr., Nov. 4, 1988; children: Eddie Lee Jr., Clint, Sparky, Jaime. AAS, Rogers State Coll., Claremore, Okla., 1986; BABS in Edn., Langston U., 1988; MEdn., Northeastern State U., Tahlequah, Okla., 1996; postgrad. in Edn. Psychology PhD program, Okla. State U., Stillwater, 1996—. Nat. Bd. Cert. Tchr. Elementary sch. tchr. Coweta (Okla.) Pub. Schs., 1988—2001; Great Expectations instr. Northeastern State U., Tahlequah, 1999—; prof. edn. U. Phoenix, Tulsa, 1999—; asst. prof. elem. edn. Bacone Coll., Muskogee, Okla., 2001—. Spkr. Shurley English, Ark., 1998—2001, Nat. Bd. Profl. Tchg. Stds., 1999—. Named State Sci. Tchr. of Yr., Nat. Conservation Dists., Oklahoma City, 2000; recipient Fulbright Found. award, 2000. Mem.: Assn. Supervision and Curriculum Devel., Nat. Bd. Profl. Tchg. Stds., Delta Kappa Gamma. Democrat. Baptist. Avocations: continued learning, golf. Home: 1515 Bowden Pl Ft Gibson OK 74434 Office: Bacone Coll 2299 Old Bacone Rd Muskogee OK 74403 E-mail: edwardst@bacone.edu.

EDWARDS, TRACI VAN ARSDALE, drug company official; b. L.A., July 16, 1957; d. Larry Anderson and Jo Ann (Horst) Van Arsdale; m. Thomas Wayne Edwards, Dec. 10, 1951; 1 child, Barry Ryan. BS in Microbiology, S.D. State U., 1979; MBA, Golden Gate U., 2000. Cert. quality auditor and quality engr. Microbiologist Shaklee Corp, Norman, Okla., 1979-88; auditor Johnson & Johnson, New Brunswick, N.J., 1988-90, Genentech, South San Francisco, Calif., 1990-91; quality mgr. Syntex, Palo Alto, Calif., 1991-94; dir. quality InSite Vision, Alameda, Calif., 1994-97; cons., 1997-99; dir. quality and regulatory AeroGen, Sunnyvale, Calif., 1999—. Vis. mem. stds. com. Internat. Stds. Orgn., 1994—; sr. examiner Malcolm Baldrige Nat. Quality Award, Nat. Inst. Stds. and Tech., 1996—. Mem. Am. Soc. for Quality (cert. bd. 1996-98, cert. quality auditor and quality engr., conf. com. 1998-2001). Avocation: writing. Home: 7282 Valley View Ct Pleasanton CA 94588-3766

EDWARDS, VICKI ANN, elementary school principal; b. Fremont, Nebr., Dec. 19, 1947; d. Howard Carl and Donna Marie (Earleywine) Schneider; m. Charles Douglas Edwards, May 27, 1977; 1 child, Janci. BS in Edn., Midland Luth. Coll., Fremont, 1972; MA in Edn., Ariz. State U., 1979, No. Ariz. U., 1986, EdD in Curriculum and Instrn., 1988. Lang. arts tchr. Arlington (Nebr.) Pub. Schs., 1972-76, Glendale (Ariz.) Elem. Sch. Dist., 1977-80; reading specialist Deer Valley Sch. Dist., Phoenix, 1980-92, asst. prin., 1992-2000, prin., 2000—. Recipient award of achievement U.S. West Comm., Ariz., 1992, Mountain Shadows PTSA Outstanding Educator award, 2001. Mem. Internat. Reading Assn., Assn. for Supervision and Curriculum Devel. Nat. Coun. Tchrs. English, Nat. Assn. Elem. Sch. Prins., Ariz. Sch. Adminstrs., Phi Kappa Phi, Phi Delta Kappa. Democrat. Avocations: reading, needlework, music. Home: 2336 W Laurel Ln Phoenix AZ 85029-3423 Office: Mountain Shadows Elem Sch 19602 N 45th Ave Glendale AZ 85308-7339 E-mail: vedwards@ms.dvusd.org.

EDWARDS, VICTOR HENRY, chemical engineer; b. Galveston, Tex., Oct. 17, 1940; s. Philip Lacey and Margaret Ruth (Hopkins) E.; m. Mary Margaret Litzmann, June 10, 1963; children: Henry L., Mary E. BA, Rice U., 1962; PhD in Chem. Engring., U. Calif., Berkeley, 1967. Registered profl. engr., Tex. Asst. prof. chem. engring. Cornell U., Ithaca, NY, 1967-73; mgr. adv. tech. U.S. Nat. Sci. Found., Washington, 1971-72; rsch. fellow Merck, Sharp, Dohme Rsch., Rahway, NJ, 1973-76; supr. rsch. engring. United Energy Resources, Houston, 1976-79; vis. prof. environ. engring. Rice U., Houston, 1979-80; sr. process engr. Fluor Engrs. and Constructors, Houston, 1980-82; southwest editor Plant Services mag., Chgo., 1982-85; project engr. Allstates/BE&K, Inc., Houston, 1984-90, lead process engr., 1990-93, process engring. mgr., 1993-94, prin. engr. process and environ., 1994-95, process dir. Aker Kvaerner, Houston, 1995—. Tech. adv. com. Mary Kay O'Connor Process Safety Ctr., Tex. A&M U., 1995—. Contbr. articles to profl. jours. Organizing com. Woodlands (Tex.) Harvest Festival, 1979-86; chmn. industry adv. coun. dept. chem. engring. Prairie View A&M U., 1991-94. Recipient Disting. Svc. award Prairie View A&M U., 1992, 94, Shield of Irenee award E.I. duPont de Nemours & Co., 1994, 98, 2001, Environ. Excellence award, 1994, Safety, Health, and Environ. Excellence award, 1996, Svc. award Mary Kay O'Connor Process Safety Ctr., 2002. Fellow: AIChE (chmn. Process Plant Safety Symposium 1992, exec. position 1 1993, program co-chmn. 1994, chmn. 1995, South Tex. sect. chmn. 2nd internat. plant ops. and design conf. 1997, Disting. Svc. award 1991); mem.: NSPE, AAAS, Engrs. Coun. Houston (councilor 1987—92), Rice U. Alumni Assn. (class of '62 reunion com. 1982, 1987, 1992, 1997, co-chmn. fundraising drive 1998, class of '62 reunion com. 2002), Am. Chem. Soc. (chmn. Ithaca sect. 1969, councilor divsn. biochem. and microbial tech. 1970—77), N.Y. Acad. Scis. (life). Methodist. Avocations: reading, tennis, sailing, golf. Business E-Mail: vic.edwards@akerkvaerner.com.

EDWARDS, VIRGINIA DAVIS, music educator, concert pianist; b. Syracuse, N.Y., Jan. 8, 1927; d. Leslie Martz and Elsie (Gannon) Davis; m. William B. Edwards, Jan. 12, 1954. BA magna cum laude, Marshall U., 1948; MusB, MusM, Cin. Conservatory of Music, 1950; postgrad., U. Chgo., 1950-56, U. Calif., Berkeley, 1963. Pianist, young artists series Conservatory of Music, Cin., 1949-50, piano instr. Evanston, Ill., 1955-56; music instr. Harvard Sch. for Boys, Chgo., 1954-55; pianist Opera Studios of Dimitri Onofrei/Bianca Saroya, Chgo., 1957-61; piano instr. Community Music Ctr., San Francisco, 1962-63;

v.p. Gold Rush Gun Shop, Benet Arms Co. Imports, San Francisco, 1963-68, Afton, Va., 1968—; pvt. practice Afton, Va., 1978—; instr. piano Mary Baldwin Coll., Staunton, Va., 1988—. Soloist Marshall U. Symphony Orch., 1948, Chgo. Pops Concert Orch., Duluth, Minn., 1961; recitalist Curtis Hall, Chgo., 1961, Legion of Honor, San Francisco, 1966, Sta. WRFK-FM, Richmond, Va., 1979; prodr., performer Presbyn. Hunger Program series, 1984-87, St. John's Cath. Ch., Waynesboro, Va., 1985, Basic Meth. Ch., 1989, Augusta Hosp. Corp. Benefit, 1989; author: Conspiracy of 30 -- Their Misuse of Music from Aristotle to Onassis, 1994. Mem. AAUW, DAR, Va. Museum Soc. Unitarian Universalist. Home: 6049 Howardsville Tpke Afton VA 22920-2509

EDWARDS, WALLACE WINFIELD, retired automotive company executive; b. Pontiac, Mich., May 9, 1922; s. David W. and Ruby M. (Nutting) E.; m. Jean Austin Wolfe, Aug. 24, 1944; children: Ronald W., Gary R., Ann E. BS in Mech. Engring, Gen. Motors Inst., 1949; MBA, Mich. State U., 1966. With GMC Truck & Coach div. Gen. Motors Corp., Pontiac, Mich., 1940-78, truck service mgr., 1961-62, head engine design, 1962-64, dir. reliability, 1964-66, dir. prodn. control and purchasing, 1966-70, dir. engring., 1970-78; dir. Worldwide Truck Project Center, Warren, Mich., 1978-80; gen. dir. Worldwide Truck and Transp. Sys. Center, 1980-81; v.p. G.M.O.D.C., 1980-81; group mgr. small and light truck and van ops. Truck and Bus. Group, Gen. Motors Corp., 1981-82, mgr. internat. staff, 1982-84, gen. dir. mil. vehicle ops. Power Products and Def. Group, 1984-86. Bd. dirs. Crystal Mountain Resort, Thompsonville, Mich., 1991—. Past pres., mem. exec. com. Clinton Valley coun. Boy Scouts Am.; dir. Grand Traverse Regional Land Conservancy, 1991—, chmn. 1996-98; regent Nat. Eagle Scout Assn. (life). Served with USNR, 1944-46. Mem. Soc. Automotive Engrs., U.S. Navy League, Tau Beta Pi, Beta Gamma Sigma. Office: 5089 Crystal Dr Beulah MI 49617-9617

EDWARDS, WARREN CHAPPELLE, military career officer; b. Franklin, Va., June 3, 1947; m. Diane Dorsey; 1 child, Joel. BS in English, U. Richmond; MA in Nat. Security, U.S. Naval War Coll.; M in Mil. Arts and Scis., U.S. Army Command & Gen. Coll.; grad., Army Command & Gen. Staff Col., Naval War Coll. Commd. 2nd lt. U.S. Army, advanced through grades to maj. gen., 1998, comdr. 4th Squadron, 7th Cavalry, comdr. 5th Squadron, 17th Cavalry, 2nd Infantry Divsn., comdr. 10th Aviation Brigade, 10th Mountain Divsn., chief ops. divsn., ops. directorate Office Joint Chiefs; chief of staff U.S. Army Aviation Ctr., Ft. Rucker, Ala.; asst. divsn. comdr. 2nd Infantry Divsn. U.S. Army, Korea; dep. commanding gen. Fifth U.S. Army, 1997-99, Third U.S. Army, 1999—. Decorated Def. Superior Svc. medal, Legion of Merit with 2 oak leaf clusters, Meritorious Svc. medal with oak leaf cluster, 10 air medals, Army Commendation medal. Office: Fifth US Army Fort Mcpherson GA 30330

EDWARDS, WILLIAM BENNETT, firearms industry consultant, gun dealer; b. Auburn, N.Y., Nov. 10, 1927; s. John Bowen and Virginia Hampton (Bean) E.; m. Virginia Jane Davis, Jan. 12, 1954. Fed. firearms dealer, U.S.A. Pvt. practice, Afton, Va., 1963—; prin., owner Benet Arms Co., various, 1947—; technical dir. Mars-Centennial Arms Co., Chgo., 1955-62; prin., owner Gold Rush Gun Shop, various, 1964—; artistic creator Pastimes LTD, Staunton, Va., 1985-92. Cons. Saddam Hussein, 1990-91, Pres. Clinton, 1993. Author: The Story of Colt's Revolver, 1953, Civil War Guns, 1962, 2d edit., 1997; editor Conspiracy Press, 1994—; editor, founder GUNS Mag., 1955; inventor. With USNG, 1949-51. Mem. NRA, Sons of Confederate Veterans, Va. Arms Collectors Assn. Republican. Unitarian Universalist. Avocation: observation of jesuit plans. Home and Office: PO Box 47 Waynesboro VA 22920-2509

EDWARDS, WILLIAM DEAN, pathologist; b. Wichita, Kans., Nov. 12, 1948; BA in Chemistry, U. Kans., 1970, MD, 1974. Diplomate Am. Bd. Anatomic Pathology. Resident in anatomic pathology U. Kans. Med. Ctr., Kansas City, 1974-76; resident in cardiovasc. pathology United Hosps.-Miller Divsn., St. Paul, 1976-77; cons. in pathology Mayo Clinic, Rochester, Minn., 1980—, prof. pathology, 1988—. Fellow Am. Coll. Cardiology; mem. AMA, Soc. Cardiovasc. Pathology. Baptist. Office: Mayo Clinic 200 1st St SW Rochester MN 55905-0002 E-mail: edwards.william@mayo.edu.

EDWARDS, WILLIAM JAMES, broadcasting executive; b. Birmingham, Ala., Mar. 30, 1915; s. Perron Austin and Eugenia (Evans) E.; m. Julia M. Stacey, May 15, 1937; children: Julia Beverly, Linda J. Edwards Riley. Student, Birmingham-Southern Coll., 1935-37; LLD (hon.), Birmingham So. Coll., 2001, Saginaw Valley State U., 1994, Northwood U., 1995. Announcer, Sta. WBRC, Birmingham, 1933-34; program dir. Sta. WMBR, Jacksonville, Fla., 1934; announcer Sta. WLW, Cin., 1938; comml. mgr. Storer Broadcasting, Fairmont, W.Va., 1939-42; news commentator Sta. KMTR (now KLAC), Hollywood, Calif., 1944-45; exec. Sta. WIBC, Indpls., 1942-44; founder, pres. Lake Huron Broadcasting Corp., Saginaw, Mich., 1947—. Pres. G.C.C. Communications of Houston, Inc., Suncoast Stereo Corp., St. Petersburg, Fla.; (Stas. KRBE-FM & AM, Houston, WQYK, Tampa-St. Petersburg); dir. Design Craftsmen, Inc., Midland, Mich.; Co-chmn. Saginaw chpt. ARC, 1951, gen. fund chmn., 1952 Pres. Saginaw Symphony Orch. Assn., 1954; pres. United Fund Saginaw County, 1960-62, Saginaw Community Chest, 1960-62; chmn. YWCA Adv. com., 1955-68; mem. Saginaw Libr. Commn., 1952-70, Am. Coun. United Funds, 1965-66; bd. of fellows Saginaw Valley State U., 1968-75; trustee Alvin M. Bentley Found., Owosso, Mich., 1969—, Birmingham-So. Coll., Ala., 1989—; pres. Julia M. and William J. Edwards Found.; gen. ptnr. Edwards Family Partnership, chmn. bd. govs., 1994; chmn. bd. govs. Northwood U., West Palm Beach, Fla., 1991—, bd. trustees, Midland, Mich., 1993—. With Armed Forces Radio Svc., USN, 1945-46. Recipient Disting. Svc. award Jaycees, 1951, Outstanding Bus. Leaders award Northwood U., West Palm Beach, Fla., 1991; named Saginaw Man of Yr., 1950 Mem. Birchwood Golf and Country Club, USN League (chpt. dir.), Govs. Club of Palm Beaches, Ballen Isles Country Club, City Club of Palm Beaches, Palm Beach Round Table (bd. dirs. 1994), Masons, Shriners, Rotary (pres. Saginaw club 1959-60). Republican. Methodist. Home: 1275 S Ocean Blvd Palm Beach FL 33480-5008 Office: Birchwood Farms Estate 840 US Hwy 1 Ste 315 North Palm Beach FL 33408

EDWARDS, WILLIAM THOMAS, JR., lawyer, consultant; b. Eglin AFB, Fla., Feb. 8, 1956; s. William Thomas and Josephine (Fabian) E.; children: Jennifer, Ali. BA, Fla. State U., 1977, JD, 1980. Bar: Fla. 1980, U.S. Dist. Ct. (mid. dist.) Fla. 1981, U.S. Ct. Claims 1981, U.S. Tax Ct. 1981, U.S. Ct. Appeals (11th cir.) 1983. Assoc. William T. Lassiter Jr., P.A., Jacksonville, Fla., 1980-82; sole practice Middleburg, Fla., 1982-93, 95-98, The Edwards Law Firm, P.A., Orange Park, Fla., 1999—; owner Edwards Internat., Orange Park, 1994—. Pres. Middleburg Bus. Coun., 1985, 87, v.p., 1984. Mem. Am. Acad. Estate Planning Attys., Fla. Bar Assn., Clay County Bar Assn., Jacksonville Bar Assn., Clay County C. of C. (bd. dirs. 1985, 87-90, chmn. film liaison com. 1990-91, chmn. mil. affairs com. 1990, v.p. membership svcs. 1990), Cath. Lawyers Guild, KC. Republican. Roman Catholic. Avocations: travel, reading, walking.

EDWARDS-LEBOEUF, RENEE CAMILLE, public relations professional, logistics engineer; b. Falls Church, Va., Aug. 6, 1961; d. Walter Thomas and Elizabeth Ann Holt. BS, George Mason U., Fairfax, 1983; MS, Central Mich. U., Merrifield, 1988; grad. program mgmt. course, Def. Systems Mgmt. Coll., 1990. Cert. contracting officer's rep. Logistics analyst The BDM Corp., McLean, Va., 1983-85; deputy program mgr. COMARCO/IBS, Arlington, Va., 1985-88; logistics mgr., speaker, briefer SWL, Inc., Arlington, Va., 1988-89; mem. profl. staff Def. Systems Mgmt. Coll., Ft. Belvoir, Va., 1989-92; dir. computer-aided acquisition and logistics support tng. and edn. Office Asst. Sec. of Def. Prodn. and Logistics, Falls Church, Va., 1992-93; dir. pub. affairs U.S. Dept. Commerce, Nat. Tech. Info. Svc., Springfield, Va., 1993—. Co-chmn. computer aided acquisition Logistics Systems Rsch. Group. Contbr. articles to profl. jours. Bd. dirs. Woodwalk Condominium, Burke, Va., 1987-96, mem. indsl. tech. adv. com., 1997-99. Named Best Speaker Toastmasters, McLean, 1985, Best Evaluator Toastmasters, McLean, 1985; recipient Excellence award Dept. Def., 1993, Outstanding Svc. award Dept. Commerce, 1996. Mem. Soc. of Logistics Engrs., Pub. Rels. Soc. Am. Republican. Avocations: racquetball, cycling, embroidery, guitar. Office: US Dept Commerce NTIS 5285 Port Royal Rd Springfield VA 22161-0001

EDWARDS-MITCHUM, LILLIAN (RED THE POET), secondary school educator, writer; d. Richard and Kathrine Edwards; m. Lawrence Joseph Mitchum, Apr. 11, 1977 (div. 1993); children: Lawrence Joseph Mitchum Jr., Lance Alexander Mitchum. AAS, Harold Washington, Chgo., 1990; BS in Behavioral Sci., Nat. Louis U., Chgo., 2000. Cert. tchr. Bd. of Ed./Ill. Adminstr. Cook County Hosp., Chgo., 1972—2002; tchr. Bd. Edn., Chgo., 2003—. Author: Bold From the Soul Spiritual Healing, 2003; contbr. poetry to anthology. Domestic violence advocate Chgo. Woman Abuse, 2001—02; mem. bldg. and ground com. Deliverance Bapt. Ch., Chgo., 2003.

EDWARDSON, JOHN ALBERT, security firm executive; b. Terre Haute, Ind., July 23, 1949; s. John Albert and Mildred Ruth (Anderson) E.; m. Catharine Orr, June 11, 1971; children: Laura, Anne, Shelley. BS in Indsl. Engring., Purdue U., 1971; MBA in Fin. and Internat. Bus., U. Chgo., 1972. Comml. banking officer First Bank-St. Paul, 1972-77; v.p., treas. Ferrell Cos. Inc., Kansas City, Mo., 1977-83, sr. v.p. fin. services group, 1983-85; exec. v.p. fin., chief fin. officer Northwest Airlines Inc. and NWA Inc., St. Paul, 1985-88; exec. v.p., chief fin. and adminstrv. officer Internat. Minerals and Chems. Corp., Northbrook, Ill., 1988-90; chief fin. officer United Airlines Employees Acquisition Corp., Chgo., 1990; exec. v.p., chief fin. officer Ameritech, Chgo., 1991-94; pres., COO UAL Corp., Elk Grove Village, Ill., 1994—; chmn., pres. & CEO Burns Internat. Svcs Corp, Chgo., 1999—2000; chmn., CEO CDW, Vernon Hills, Ill., 2001—. Trustee, pres. Ravina Festival Assn., Highland Park, Ill. Recipient Disting. Engring. Alumnus award Purdue U., 1988. Presbyterian. Avocations: sailing, hiking, bicycling. Office: CDW 200 N Milwaukee Ave Vernon Hills IL 60061*

EDWARDS-TATE, LAURIE ELLEN, human services administrator, educator; b. San Diego, June 3, 1951; d. Donald Morgan and Doral (Erickson) Hurd; m. William James Tate Jr., Jan. 1, 1995. Student, Calif. Poly. State U., 1977; BA, Nat. U., San Diego, 1978; MS, Chapman Coll., 1986. Instr. bus. local C.C., 1979—91; founder, owner Am. Med. Claims, La Jolla, Calif., 1981-86; pres., founder At Your Home Svcs., San Diego, 1985—, Familycare, 1996—; founder The Learning Acad. Mem. Rancho Bernardo Chamber; edn. co-chair San Diego Coun. Aging, North County Providers Coun., South Bay Providers Coun. Mem.: NAFE, Nat. Assn. Homecare, San Diego Regional Home Care Coun. (edn. com.), North County Inland Providers, East County Providers Coun. (health com., aging and indp. svcs.), Calif. Assn. Health Svcs. at Home (past bd. dirs., steering com., providers co-chair Long Term Care Integration Project, adv. bd., governance com.), Soft-Coated Wheaten Club So. Calif. Avocations: photography, travel, dog fancier. Office: At Your Home Familycare 6540 Lusk BlvdSte C-266 San Diego CA 92121 E-mail: familycare@ayhs.cncdsl.com.

EELLS, WILLIAM HASTINGS, retired automobile company executive; b. Princeton, N.J., Mar. 30, 1924; s. Hastings and Amy (Titus) E.; 1 child, Jonathan William. BA, Ohio Wesleyan U., 1946; MA, Ohio State U., 1950; DHL (hon.), Kent State U., 1983; D of Pub. Svc., Bowling Green State U., 1983. Asst. to dir. Inst. Practical Politics Ohio Wesleyan U., 1948-50, dir., 1953-57, instr. dept. polit. sci., 1952-59; instr. polit. sci. Mt. Union Coll., 1950-51; mem. Ohio Gov.'s Cabinet, 1957-59; coord. Atomic Devel. Activities State of Ohio, 1957-59; Midwest regional mgr. civic and govtl. affairs Ford Motor Co., Columbus, 1959-87. Author: (book) Your Ohio Government, 1953 (6 edits.); contbr. numerous articles to profl. jours. Mem. Nat. Coun. on Arts, NEA, 1976-82; chmn. bd. Blue Cross of Northeast Ohio, 1963-72, Blossom Music Ctr., Cleve., 1968—; chmn. bd. govs. Gov.'s Coun. on Rehab., 1966-68; mem. exec. com. Met. Opera's Nat. Coun., 1967-81; pres. Nat. Coun. High Blood Pressure Rsch., 1974-79; chmn. Ohio Pub. Expenditure Coun., 1981-84, Gov.'s Task Force on State Ops., 1984-85; vice chmn. Ohio Northwest Bicentennial Com., 1986-87; bd. dirs. Am. Heart Assn., 1974-79, Columbus Mus. Art, 1982-88, Opera/Columbus, 1984-86, Columbus Ballet, 1985-86, Nat. Coun. French Am. Scholarship Found., 1985-87; trustee Cleve. Orch., 1964—, Hist. Morven Found., Princeton, N.J., 1988-96, Ednl. TV, Cleve., 1965-75, Cleve. Playhouse, 1965-82, Cleve. Ballet, Cleve. Zoo, 1965-76, Ohio Arts Coun., Columbus Symphony, Cleve. Luth. Hosp., 1966-76, Mt. Union Coll., 1984—, Ohio Wesleyan U., 1988—; trustee Franklin U., 1987—, Columbus Assn. Performing Arts, 1978—, Ohio Found. Ind. Colls., 1986—, Grady Meml. Hosp., 1987-94, Riverside Hosp. Found., 1990-96; hon. chmn. Del. Arts Ctr., 1989—; life trustee Fairview Health Cleve., 1980—; trustee, v.p. Oak Grove Cemetery, 1983—; chmn. Ohio Commn. for Son of Heaven Imperial Arts of China, 1988; mem. Ohio Humanties Coun., 1993-95; patron Morgan Libr., N.Y.C., 1995—; trustee Del. County Dist. Libr. Bd., 1994—; mem. Ohio Bicentennial Commn., 1997—; trustee Columbus Zoo Assn., 1998—; mem. Friends Princeton U. Libr., 1997—. Recipient USCG Disting. award, 1965, Silver medal Royal Life Saving Soc., Ohio State U. Devel. award, 1967, award for disting. svc. Am. Heart Assn., 1979, Ohio Arts Coun. award, 1979, Ohio Theatre Alliance award, 1981, Gov. award, 1985, Alumni Achievement award Ohio State U., 1987, Silver medal Japanese Red Cross Soc. Republican. Presbyterian (elder). Home: Honeystone 54 Elmwood Dr Delaware OH 43015-1617 *Parents, teachers and friends can do just so much, you have to do the rest. God helps those who help themselves, and being in the right place at the right time does help.*

EERNISSE, GLENN P. music educator; b. Sheboygan, Wis., Feb. 2, 1957; s. Jess Earl and June Josephine Eernisse; m. Florence Susan Freeman, Aug. 26, 1976; children: Melody, Jessica. A in Fine Arts, Anderson Coll., 1977; MusB, Berry Coll., 1979; M of Ch. Music, So. Bapt. Theol. Sem., 1981, D of Music Ministry, 1994. Min. of music Northside Bapt. Ch., Ruskin, Fla., 1981—83, Brunswick, Ga., 1983—87, First Bapt. Ch., Cedartown, Ga., 1987—95; prof. Brewton-Parker Coll., Mt. Vernon, Ga., 1995—. Bd. dirs. Creator Mag., Healdsburg, Calif. Contbr. articles to profl. jours.; composer: numerous songs. Mem.: ASCAP (Std. award 2001—03), Internat. Trombone Assn., Mus. Educators Nat. Conf. Office: Brewton-Parker Coll Hwy 280 Mount Vernon GA 30445 Office Fax: 912-583-2997. Business E-Mail: geernisse@bpc.edu.

EFAW, CARY ROSS, manufacturing executive; b. Waynesburg, Pa., Dec. 26, 1949; s. William C. and Julia M. (Whitfield) Efaw; m. Kathleen E. Dunkle, July 21, 1973; children: Dawn, Heather, Nathan. BS in Acctg./Econs., Waynesburg Coll., 1975; MBA, Youngstown State U., 1989. CPA Pa., cert. mgmt. acct.; fin. mgmt., bus. mgmt. Sr. acct. Ernst & Young LLP, Pitts., 1975-79; staff acct. Equitable Resources, Pitts., 1979-81; sr. fin. analyst Joy Mfg. Co., Pitts., 1981-82; owner, cons. Efaw Enterprise, Pitts., 1982—; mgr. gen. and cost acctg. Cooper Energy Svcs., Grove City, Pa., 1987-98; ptnr. Ruddy & Assocs. CPAs, Wexford, Pa., 1999-2000; divsn. contr. GenSystems, Inc., Callery, Pa., 2000—; ind. contractr/cons., 2000—; contr. Chelsea Bldg. Products, 2001—. Cons. Hodor Assocs., Eighty-Four, Pa., 1979—85, Lindley Enterprise, Washington, 1981—85, Zelienople, 2000—; bd. dirs., advisor 8r Electronics, Houston, 1980—87. Contbr. articles to profl. jours. V.p. S.V. Track Boosters; chmn. bd. dirs. Grove City Area Fed. Credit Union, 1999—; advisor state rep., Upper St. Clair, Pa., 1981—84; Sunday sch. tchr. Westminster Ch., Upper St. Clair, 1982—85; elder, chmn. long range planning com., co-chmn. bldg. fund campaign Calvin Ch., Zelienople. With USMC, 1969—71, Vietnam. Named Competent Toastmaster, 1980. Mem.: VFW, AICPA, DAV (life), Assn. Profls. Bus. Mgmt., Nat. Assn. Accts. (assoc. dir. 1977—78), Assn. MBA Execs., Assn. Inst. Mgmt. Accts. (bd. dirs. Pitts. chpt. 1999—2001, pres., regional dir. 2001—02, pres. coun. 2002—), Pa. Inst. CPAs (contrs. conf. com.), Steel Town Corvettes Club (treas. 1977—80), Masons, Am. Legion, Alpha Kappa Psi. Presbyterian. Avocations: auto racing, golf, softball, running, weightlifting. Home: 1 Zelie Dr Zelienople PA 16063-9707

EFAW, DAVID SCOTT, surgeon; b. Bloomington, Ill., May 22, 1965; s. Larry and Barbara Efaw; m. Dana Efaw, Oct. 25, 1997. DDS, U. Iowa, 1990; MD, U. Conn., 1993. Diplomate Am. Bd. Oral and Maxillofacial Surgery. Head/neck anatomy instr. U. Conn., Farmington, 1994; surg. fellow N.W. Facial Surgery, Seattle, 1995-97; pvt. practice Bloomington, 1997—. Mem. craniofacial team U. Conn., Farmington, 1990-95; mem. cancer com. Bromenn/St. Joseph, Bloomington, 1998—. Author: (with others) Scar Revision, 1997. Recipient Pub. Health award McLean County Bd. of Health, 1998, Fenton award U. Iowa, 1990, 1923 award, 1990, Am. Scholarship award, 1986. Mem. AMA, ADA, Am. Assn. Oral and Maxillofacial Surgeons. Republican. Presbyterian. Avocations: pierce-arrow motor cars, scuba, golf. Office: 109 N Regency Dr Bloomington IL 61701-4365

EFFEL, LAURA, lawyer; b. Dallas, May 9, 1945; d. Louis E. and Fay (Lee) Ray; m. Marc J. Patterson, Sept. 19, 1992 (dec. July 30, 2002); 1 child, Stephen Patterson. BA, U. Calif., Berkeley, 1971; JD, U. Md., 1975. Bar: N.Y. 1976, U.S. Dist. Ct. (so. and ea. dists.) N.Y. 1976, U.S. Ct. Appeals (2d cir.) 1980, U.S. Supreme Ct. 1980, D.C. 1993, N.C. 1998, Va. 2001. Assoc. Burns Jackson Miller Summit & Jacoby, N.Y.C., 1975-78, Pincus Munzer Bizar & D'Alessandro, N.Y.C., 1978-80; v.p., sr. assoc. counsel Chase Manhattan Bank, N.A., N.Y.C., 1980-96; counsel Baker & McKenzie, N.Y.C., 1996-99; gen. counsel Garban Cos., 1999-2000; counsel Flippin Densmore Morse & Jessee, Roanoke, Va., 2000—02, ptnr., 2002—. Bd. dirs. Blue Ridge Pub. TV, 2001—. Treas. Workforce Devel. Com., New Century Tech. Coun.; bd. dirs. Bklyn. Legal Svcs. Corp. A, 1992-2000. Mem.: ABA (com. pretrial practice 2000—03, litig. sect. co-chair, subcom. atty. client privilege), Roanoke Bar Assn., Va. Bar Assn., NC Bar Assn., Am. Corp. Counsel Assn. (dir. emeritus, pro bono svc. award 1989). Office: Flippin Densmore Morse & Jessee Drawer 1200 Roanoke VA 24006 E-mail: effel@flippindensmore.com.

EFFNER, MARSHA GAY, retired employee development officer; b. Denver, Mar. 15, 1937; d. Eugene Blaine and Mary Louise (Marshall) Sparks; m. Lee Effner, Mar. 17, 1957 (dec.); children: Michael Lee, Scott Allan. Student, Colo. State U., 1955-57. Cert. quality improvement team leader, facilitator, instr., Fla. Light and Power Qual-tech. Data control coord. Black & Veatch Eng., Ft. Collins, 1980-82; sec. Platte River Power Authority, Ft. Collins, 1982-92, employee devel. officer, 1992-99. Tng. cons. sexual harrassment Markley Motors, Saturn, USDA-Epidemeology, Internat. Assn. Exec. Women, Poudre R-1 Sch. Dist., City of Ft. Collins, Town of Estes Park, High Plains Libr. Assn., 1st Presbyn. Ch. Ft. Collins, 1993-94; quality improvement instr. City of Ft. Collins and Platte River, 1990-99, conflict resolution instr., 1987-99, diversity trainer, facilitator Air Quality Adv. Bd., Ft. Collins, 1996. Vol. Harmony House, Ft. Collins, 1997—99; VIPS coord. Poudre R-1 Schs., Ft. Collins, 1990—99; adult literacy tutor Ft. Collins, 1969—99; election judge, 2002. Mem. ASTD, NAFE, Ft. Collins C. of C. (com. mem. 1994), Delta Zeta (chmn. scholarship com. 1956).

EFFRON, ANDREW S. federal judge; b. 1948; BA, Harvard U., 1970, JD, 1975; student, JAG's Sch. U.S. Army, 1976, 84. Legis. aide to mem. Ho. of Reps., 1970-76; with Office of staff Judge Adv., Ft. McClellan, Ala., 1976-77; atty.-advisor Office of Gen. Counsel, Dept. Def., 1977-87; counsel, gen. counsel and minority counsel Senate Armed Svcs. Com., Washington, 1987-96; judge U.S. Ct. Appeals for the Armed Forces, Washington, 1996—. Office: 450 E St NW Washington DC 20442-0001

EFFRON, DAVID LOUIS, conductor, music director; b. Cin., July 28, 1938; s. Sigmund and Babette Jane (Holstein) E.; children: Michael, Daniel. MusB, U. Mich., 1960; MusM, Ind. U., 1962. Asst. condr., condr. N.Y.C. Opera, 1964-82; asst. condr. Nat. Ballet, Washington, 1969-70; music dir. Central City (Colo.) Opera, 1972-76; condr. Curtis Inst. Music, Phila., 1970-77; music dir. Eastman Philharm., Eastman Sch., Rochester, NY, 1977-98, Youngstown (Ohio) Symphony Orch., 1987-96, Heidelberg (Fed. Republic Germany) Castle Festival, 1980-92, Chautaugua Instn. Music Sch. Festival Orch., 1990-96; artistic dir., prin. condr. Brevard (N.C.) Music Ctr., 1996—; prof. instrumental conducting Ind. U., Bloomington, 1998—. Guest condr. numerous assignments Europe, Far East, U.S. Condr. recs. Schwantner Aftertones, 1983, Schuman Judith, 1984, Benita Valente, 1986, Mahler & Berlioz with Jan deGaetani, 1989. Recipient Grammy award, 1984, Best Contemporary Rec. award Ovation Mag., 1988. Office: Brevard Music Center PO Box 312 Brevard NC 28712-0312

EFFRON, SETH ALAN, editor, journalist; b. July 23, 1952; m. Nancy G. Thomas; children: Rebecca, Eve. BA in Polit. Sci. with honors, U. N.C., 1974. Asst. to editor Fayetteville (N.C.) Times (now Fayetteville Observer), 1974—75, reporter, 1975—77, Tallahassee Dem., 1977—80, Wichita (Kans.) Eagle-Beacon (now Wichita Eagle), 1980—82, 1983—85, coord. legis. coverage, 1982; state govt. and polit. reporter Greensboro (N.C.) News & Record, 1985—93; editor, founder the insider, N.C. State Govt. News Svc., Raleigh, 1993—96; exec. editor on-line content Nando Media, Nando Times, Raleigh, 1996—99; account exec. Capital Strategies, Raleigh, 2000—01; dep. curator Nieman Found. for Journalism, 2001—02, spl. projects dir., 2002—. NEH summer fellow Williams Coll., 1979; lectr. Freedom Forum Media Studies Ctr. Columbia U., N.Y.C., 1995; lectr. Annenberg Washington program Northwest U., 1995; lectr. Ctr. for Pub. TV U. N.C., fellow, 1993; lect. Inst. for Polit. Leadership, 1994; lectr. Salzburg (Austria) Seminar, 1994, Human Svcs. Automation Conf., 1994. Author: 100 Proof Pure Old Jess: Jesse Helms Quoted, 1993, Coachspeak: Triangle ACC Men's Basketball Coaches Quoted, 1995, North Carolina Almanac of Government and Politics, 1995—96; contbr. articles. Mem. adv. panel Z. Smith Reynolds Found., 1988—91; mem. area edn. adv. bd. Broughton HS, 1996—2001; v.p. Fred A. Olds Elem. Sch. PTA, 1994—95, pres., 1995—96; bd. dirs. Edenton St. United Meth. Ch. Child Devel. Ctr., 1986—88, 1993—94. Recipient Nieman fellow, Harvard U., 1991—92, Cert. of Merit, Am. Acad. Trial Lawyers, 1975, Pub. Svc. award, N.C. Press Assn., 1976, News Enterprise award, William Allen White Found., 1985, 2nd Pl. awards, N.C. Press Assn., 1987, 1989, 3rd Pl. awards, 1990. Home: 29 Sherman St Cambridge MA 02138 Office: Nieman Found Harvard U One Francis Ave Cambridge MA 02138 E-mail: effron@fas.harvard.edu.

EFIRD, JAMES MICHAEL, theology educator; b. Kannapolis, N.C., May 30, 1932; s. James Rufus and I. Z. (Christy) E.; m. Vivian Lee Poythress, Mar. 7, 1975; 1 child, Whitney Michelle; 1 stepchild, Anthony Kevin Crumpler. AB, Davidson Coll., 1954; MDiv, Louisville Presbyn. Theo. Sem., 1958; PhD, Duke U., 1962. Ordained to ministry Presbyn. Ch., 1958. Asst. prof. Duke Div. Sch., Durham, N.C., 1962-68, assoc. prof., 1958-85, prof., 1985—, dir. acad. affairs, 1971-75. Interim min. Glenwood Presbyn. Ch., Greensboro, N.C., 1989-91, Mebane Meml. Presbyn. Ch., Roxboro, N.C., 1991-92, Hillsborough Presbyn. Ch., 1993, Little River Presbyn. Ch., 1995-98, Jonesboro Presbyn. Ch., 1998-2000, First Bapt. Ch., Hillsborough, N.C., 2002—. Author: How To Interpret the Bible, 1984, Marriage and Divorce, 1985, End-Times: Rapture, Anti-Christ, and Millennium, 1986, Revelation for Today, 1989, A Grammar For New Testament Greek, 1990. Duke U. scholar, 1958-62. Mem. Soc. Bibl. Lit., Phi Beta Kappa. Home: 6101 Bent Oak Dr Durham NC 27705-9115 Office: Duke Div Sch Durham NC 27708-0967 E-mail: jefird@div.duke.edu.

EFIRD, JIMMY THOMAS, statistician; BA, UCLA, Los Angeles, CA, 1979; MSC, Calif. State U., Hayward, 1985; PhD, Stanford Sch. of Medicine, Palo Alto, CA, 2003. Pres. Applied Stats. Corp., Palo Alto, Calif., 1986—2002. Mem.: Am. Statis. Assn., Bay Area SAS Users Group (chmn.), Disting. Statistician Filming Com. Home: PO Box 303 Palo Alto CA 94302-0303

EFROS, ALEXEI L. physics educator, researcher; b. Leningrad, Russia, Aug. 11, 1938; came to U.S., 1989; s. Lev S. and Natalia N. (Melteva) E.; m. Irina A. Zdanovitch Efros, Dec. 13, 1994; m. Natalia J. Feldman Efros, Dec. 31, 1973 (div. Sept. 10, 1994); children: Alexei, Daniil. MS, Poly. U., Leningrad, Russia, 1961; PhD, Ioffe Inst., Leningrad, Russia, 1962; DSc, 1972. Scientist Ioffe Inst., Leningrad, Russia, 1961-85; prin. scientist, 1985-89; part time prof. physics Electrotech. Inst., Leningrad, Russia, 1985-89; vis. prof., disting. scholar U. Calif. Riverside, 1989-91; prof. physics U. Utah, 1991-94, Disting. prof. physics, 1994—. Author: Physics and Geometry of Disorder, 1982, Electronic Properties of Doped Semiconductors, 1984; editor: International Journal Solid State Communications, 1987—. Recipient Landau award Acad. Sci., USSR, 1986, Humboldt award Humboldt Com., Germany, 1997, Forehheimer, Professorship in Israel, 1997. Fellow Am. Phys. Soc. Office: Dept of Physics University of Utah Salt Lake City UT 84112

EFROS, ELLEN ANN, lawyer; b. N.Y.C., Jan. 18, 1950; d. Edwin David and Judith (Breitman) E.; m. Fritz R. Kahn, June 26, 1983. BA, Case Western Res. U., 1971; MA, St. John's U., 1973; JD, Hofstra U., 1978. Bar: D.C. 1978, N.Y. 1979, Md. 1990, U.S. Ct. Appeals (5th cir.) 1978, U.S. Ct. Appeals (2d, 7th and D.C. cirs.) 1979, U.S. Ct. Appeals (Fed. cir.) 1993, U.S. Dist. Ct. D.C. 1981, U.S. Ct. Claims 1986, U.S. Supreme Ct. 1989. Trial atty. ICC Gen. Counsel, Washington, 1978-79; assoc. Verner & Liipfert, Washington, 1979-81; ptnr. Vorys, Sater, Seymour & Pease, Washington, 1981-97; hearing officer, office dispute resolution NASD Regulation, Inc., Washington, 1997-2000; ptnr. Rader, Fishman & Grauer, Washington, 2000—. Asst. editor Antitrust Law Jour., 1987-90. Mem. ABA (sects. intellectual property and litigation), D.C. Bar Assn., N.Y. Bar Assn., Md. Bar Assn. Office: Rader Fishman & Grauer 1233 20th St NW Ste 501 Washington DC 20036-2365 E-mail: eae@raderfishman.com.

EFROS, LEONID, computer software scientist and developer; b. Balhash, Kazakhstan, USSR, Apr. 16, 1943; arrived in U.S., 1991; s. Boris and Anna (Taraseiskey) E.; m. Svetlana Efros; children: Daniel, Olga. MS in Quantum Electronics, Leningrad (Russia) Inst., 1965; PhD in Computer Scis., Acad. Scis. USSR, Novosibirsk/Moscow, 1974 Chief rsch. lab., project leader, rschr. Acad. Scis. USSR, Novosibirsk Academcity, 1965-88; sr. sys. rschr. Acad. Scis., Vilnius, Lithuania, 1988-91; software engr., rschr. & developer NView Corp., Newport News, Va., 1992-93; cons., computer software developer Old Dominion U. Rsch. Found., Norfolk, Va., 1993-94; sr. project and sys. analyst Allied Signal, Inc./Aerospace, Goddard Corporate Pk., Lanham, Md., 1994-97; sr. computer software rschr. and system analyst SpaceTec, Inc., Hampton, Va., 1997-98; beam physics software scientist Thomas Jefferson Nat. Accelerator Facility-Jefferson Lab., Newport News, Va., 1998-99, 2000—; pres. Needsoft, LLC, Newport News, 1999—. Contbr. articles to profl. jours. Recipient prize Coun. Ministers of USSR, 1983. Mem. N.Y. Acad. Scis. Achievements include research in real-time and large-scale software project design and implementation, software/hardware integration and software technology; parallel programming, network-oriented applications. Avocations: classical music, travel.

EFRUSSY, ALAN MAURICE, urban planner; b. Chgo., May 6, 1937; s. Benjamin and Rose E.; m. Linda Louise, Mar. 25, 1973; children: Joel Brian, Jill Ellen. BA in Liberal Arts and Scis., U. Ill., 1959; MA in Urban Studies with honors, Roosevelt U., 1973. Chief planner Freese & Nichols, Austin, Tex., 1983-84; coord. comprehensive planning program City of Richardson, Tex., 1984-87; dir. planning, cmty. devel. City of McKinney, 1987-94, City of Rowlett, Tex., 1994—. Contbg. author: Guide to Urban Planning in Texas Communities, 2000. With U.S. Navy, 1960-62. Recipient Profl. Merit award Am. Planning Assn., 1984-85, 90. Mem. Am. Inst. Cert. Planners (charter). Avocations: fly fishing, model trains. Office: Planning Dept City of Rowlett 3901 Main St Rowlett TX 75088

EFTEKHARI, NASSER, physiatrist; b. Aug. 15, 1940; MD, U. Tehran, 1965. Diplomate Am. Bd. Phys. Medicine and Rehab. Intern Greater Balt. Med. Ctr., 1967-68; resident in phys. medicine and rehab. Temple U. Sch. Med., Phila., 1968-70, Hahneman Med. U., Phila., 1970-71; rsch. fellow SUNY, Bklyn., 1971-72; chief dept. phys. medicine and rehab. Shafa Rehab. Hosp., Tehran, Iran, 1973-75; dean Coll. of Rehab. Scis., Tehran, 1973-79; phys. med. and rehab. cons. Golestan Clinic, Mehr Hosp., Tehran, 1980-84; staff physician VA Hosp., Miami, Fla., 1985—, Mercy Hosp., 1989—, Cedars Med. Ctr., 1989—, Bapt. Health Sys. Hosp. South Fla., Miami, 1996—; chief phys. med. and rehab. svc. VA Hosp., Miami, 1997—. Clin. asst. prof. orthopedics, rehab. U. Miami Sch. Med., 1989—. Fellow Am. Assn. Electrodiagnostic Medicine; mem. Fla. Soc. Phys. Medicine and Rehab., AMA, Am. Acad. Phys. Medicine and Rehab. Office: VA Med Ctr PMR-117 1201 NW 16th St Miami FL 33125-1624

EFTIMOFF, ANITA KENDALL, educational consultant; b. Granite City, Ill., May 3, 1927; d. David Harlow and Ollie Lorena (Galloway) Kendall; m. Vasil Eftimoff, June 14, 1959; 1 child, James Kendall. BA, Washington U., St. Louis, 1949; MA, So. Ill. U., Edwardsville, 1978, EdD, 1983. Cert. in multiple gen. edn., spl. edn., Ill. Spl. edn. instr. Community Unit 9, Granite City, 1968-83; ednl. cons. Efti Enterprises, Granite City, 1982—; program dir. At-Risk Presch. Grant, Granite City, 1986—. Del. NDEA Conf. Ea. Mich. U., Ypsilanti, 1968, Gifted Edn. Conf. Ill. Office of Edn., Springfield, 1975-77; adminstrv. intern Ill. State Bd. Edn., Springfield, 1981. Editor: Symphony Youth Orch. Newsletter, 1991—, Symphony Vol. Key Notes Newsletter, 1991-93. Bd. dirs. Ill. Gov.'s Adv. Coun. on Women's Affairs, Springfield, Rape Crisis and Sexual Abuse Ctr., So. Ill. U., 1978—, Family Resource Ctr.; chmn. adopt-a-friend St. Louis Ambs., 1982-84, co-chmn. Vets. Day, 1984-86; chmn. St. Louis Symphony Youth Orch., 1985—, St. Louis Symphony Young Artists Competitions, 1993—; mem. aux. St. Louis Children's Hosp., 1980; v.p. mus. activities St. Louis Symphony Vol. Assn.; bd. pres. Ill. Ctr. for Autism, 1993. At-risk presch. grantee Ill. Bd. Edn., 1986—. Mem. World Coun. for Gifted and Talented Children, Nat. Assn. for Gifted Children, Assn. for the Gifted, Ill. Council for the Gifted, Asthma and Allergy Found. Southeastern Mo., Am. Lung Assn. St. Louis, Women's Assn. (bd. dirs. 1961—, pres. 1989-91), St. Louis Symphony Women's Assn., AAUW, Delta Kappa Gamma, Phi Delta Kappa. Lodges: Daus. of Nile, Rotary-Anns. Avocations: performing arts, classical music. Home: 2800 Michigan Ave Granite City IL 62040-3536 Office: At-Risk Presch Program 2300 W 25th St Granite City IL 62040-2025

EGAN, CHARLES JOSEPH, JR., lawyer, greeting card company executive; b. Cambridge, Mass., Aug. 11, 1932; s. Charles Joseph and Alice Claire (Ball) E.; m. Mary Bowersox, Aug. 6, 1955; children: Timothy, Sean, Peter, James. AB, Harvard U., 1954; LLB, Columbia U., 1959. Bar: N.Y. 1960, Mo. 1973. Assoc. Donovan, Leisure, Newton & Irvine, N.Y.C., 1959-62; ptnr. Hall, McNicol, Marett & Hamilton, N.Y.C., 1962-68; v.p., gen. counsel Thomson & McKinnon Securities, N.Y.C., 1969-70, Hallmark Cards, Inc., Kansas City, Mo., 1972—. Bd. dirs. Am. Multi Cinema, Inc., Kansas City, Mo. Trustee Notre Dame de Sion Sch., Kansas City, 1973-77, Pembroke Country Day Sch., Kansas City, 1976-82, Kansas City Art Inst., 1995—; bd. dirs. Kansas City YMCA, 1976-80; mem. dean's coun. Columbia Law Sch., 1991—; vice chmn. Harvard Coll. Fund, 1994-99, co-chmn., 2000—. Served to 1st lt. USMC, 1954-56. Mem. Mo. Bar Assn., Kansas City Lawyers Assn., Harvard Alumni Assn. (pres. 1989-90, exec. com. 1987—), Century Assn., Somerset Club, Harvard Club of N.Y., Harvard Club of Kansas City (pres. 1985-87). Roman Catholic. Office: Hallmark Cards Inc 2501 Mcgee St Kansas City MO 64108-2600

EGAN, CORRINE HALPERIN, management consultant; b. Providence, Feb. 8, 1936; d. Barney and Rose Ruth (Bilsky) Gordon; m. Leo William Egan, Nov. 28, 1986 (dec.); children: Karen Halperin Shor, Michael Jay, Amy Marlene. BA, Mercyhurst Coll., 1980. Exec. dir. Coun. Vols. Erie County, Pa., 1971-78, YWCA, Erie, Pa., 1978-81; unit dir. Am. Cancer Soc., Erie, 1982; adj. faculty, dir. cmty. edn. Mercyhurst Coll., 1982-84, dir. spl. events, 1984-85; program dir. Northwest Pa. Area Labor Mgmt. Coun., Erie, 1985-86, exec. dir., 1986-97; orgnl. devel. cons., pres. Sys. Group Cons., Erie, 1997—. Mem. Pa. Commn. Women, 1990—96, N.W. Regional Pa. Planning Commn., 1992—2002. Home and Office: 3294 Georgian Ct Erie PA 16506-1174 E-mail: SGCCOR@aol.com.

EGAN, DENISE, home health nurse; b. Boston, Dec. 29, 1954; d. Walter A. and Frances Sullivan; children: Colleen, Edward Jr., Jason. Diploma LPN, Boston Pub. Schs. LPN Program, 1976; BSN, Curry Coll., Milton, Mass., 1986; postgrad. in Enterostomal Therapy, Wicks Harrisburg Program, 1997; MS, U. Mass., 2002. RN, Mass. Supr. Hyde Park Convalescent Home, Hyde Park, Mass., 1986-88; staff nurse/prenatal nurse Roslindale Med. and Dental Ctr., Roslindale, Mass., 1988-90; pediatric home care nurse STAFF Builders Agy., Boston, 1990, cmty. health nurse, 1991—98; asst. dir. nursing Presentation Manor Nursing Home, Brighton, Mass., 1990—91; nurse reviewer divsn. med. assistance Commonwealth of Mass., Boston, 1999—2002, mgr., care coord. divsn. med. assistance, 2002—. Cmty. health nurse, South Shore Vis. Nurse Assn. Home: 39 Farnum Rd Pembroke MA 02359-3602 E-mail: degan76997@aol.com.

EGAN, EDWARD M. cardinal; b. Oak Park, Ill., Apr. 2, 1932; s. Thomas J. and Genevieve (Costello) Egan. PhB, St. Mary of Lake, Mundelein, Ill., 1954; STL, Gregorian U., Rome, 1958, JCD, 1963; PhD (hon.), St. John's U., N.Y., Thomas More Coll., N.H., Western Conn. State U. Ordained priest Roman Catholic Ch., 1957. Sec. to Albert Cardinal Meyer Archdiocese of Chgo., 1958—60, sec. to John Cardinal Cody, 1966—68, co-chancellor, 1969—72; faculty Pontifical N.Am. Coll., Vatican City, 1960—65; judge Sacred Roman Rota, Vatican City, 1972—85; aux. bishop, vicar for edn. Archdiocese of N.Y., N.Y.C., 1985—88; bishop of Bridgeport Conn., 1988—2000; archbishop of N.Y. N.Y.C., 2000—; cardinal Roman Cath. Ch., 2001—. Mem. Pontifical Coun. for the Family and Pontifical Coun. for Fin. and Adminstrv. Affairs of the Holy See, 2000—; chmn. bd. Bishop Curtis Homes, Fairfield County, Conn., 1988—2000; adminstrv. bd. U.S. Cath. Conf., 1991—94, 1996—99; chmn. bd. govs. Pontifical N.Am. Coll., Vatican City, 1991—95; mem. Supreme Tribunal of the Apostolic Signatura, 2002—, Coun. of Cardinals for the Study of Orgnl. and Econ. Problems of the Apostolic See, 2001—, Pontifical Coun. of the Family, 2001—, Prefecture of the Econ. Affairs of the Holy See, 2002—, Pontifical Commn. for the Cultural Goods of the Ch., 2002—; chmn. com. sci. and human values Nat. Conf. Cath. Bishops, com. Canonical Affairs, com. nat. collections, com. edn., com. nominations. Trustee Cath. U. Am., Washington, 2000—; bd. trustees Ratisbonne Inst., Jerusalem, 2000—, Thomas More Coll., Merrimack, NH, 1995—, Nat. Shrine Immaculate Conception, Washington, Cath. U. Am., Washington, Ave Maria Sch. Law, Ann Arbor, Mich.; chmn. bd. trustees St. Joseph Med. Ctr., Stamford, Conn., 1988—96; chmn. Inner-City Found. for Edn. and Charity, Fairfield County, Conn., 1992—2000; chmn. bd. trustees Sacred Heart U., Fairfield, Conn., 1988—2000, bd. trustees. Mem.: Cath. Neareast Welfare Assn. (chmn. 2000—). Roman Catholic.

EGAN, FRANK T. writer, editor; b. N.Y.C., May 1, 1933; s. Frank X. and Ann M. (Hatton) E.; m. Helen Birmingham, June 5, 1954; children: Patricia, Thomas, Barbara, Richard, Maureen. Student, Drexel Inst. Tech., 1955-56, N.Y. U., 1956-60. Editor, Mc-Graw-Hill Pub. Co., N.Y.C., 1956-65, Hayden Pub. Co., Rochelle Park, N.J., 1965-71, Cahners Pub. Co., Boston, 1971-76, Hearst Bus. Media, Garden City, N.Y., 1976— ; author: Ideas for Design, 1970. Served with USN, 1951-55. Home: 35 Coneflower Ln Princeton Junction NJ 08550-2410 Office: Hearst Bus Pub 645 Stewart Ave Garden City NY 11530-4709

EGAN, JOHN FREDERICK, retired electronics executive; b. Council Bluffs, Iowa, Feb. 25, 1935; s. Frederick Emerson and Ruth Pauline (Russell) E.; m. Anne B. Patterson, June 14, 1958; children: John Jr., James Michael. BA in Physics with honors, Grinnell Coll., 1957; MSEE, Northwestern U., 1958, PhD in Elec. Engring., 1961. Tech. dir. computer systems, Electronics Systems div. USAF, Bedford, Mass., 1964-67; sr. staff specialist intelligence Office Dir. Def., Research and Engring., Washington, 1967-71; chief scientist command support Office Chief Naval Ops., Washington, 1971-73; group dir. fed. systems Sanders Assocs., Inc., Nashua, N.H., 1973-77; v.p. Sanders Assoc., Inc., Nashua, N.H., 1977-87; group v.p. Lockheed Corp., 1987-93; corp. v.p. corp. devel. Lockheed Martin Corp., Bethesda, Md., 1993-98. Mem. exec. panel Chief Naval Ops., Washington, 1971—; mem. naval studies bd. NRC, 1990-98. Trustee Grinnell Coll., 2002—, Daniel Webster Coll., 1998—, Hunt Cmty., 2002—. With USAF, 1961-64. Mem. IEEE, AIAA, AAAS, Sigma Xi. Home: 7 Beverlee Dr Nashua NH 03064-1674 E-mail: ergwatt@hotmail.com.

EGAN, KENNETH J. dermatologist; b. N.Y.C., Feb. 2, 1956; m. Marcia Beth Robins, May 23, 1982; children: Heather, Daniel, Brian. BA, Franklin and Marshall Coll., 1978; MD, N.Y. Med. Coll., 1982. Bd. cert. Am. Acad. Dermatology. Resident internal medicine North Shore Univ. Hosp./Meml. Sloan-Kettering Hosp., Manhasset, N.Y., 1982-85; resident dermatology Albert Einsten Coll. Medicine, N.Y.C., 1985-88; pvt. practice Ridgefield, Conn., 1988—. Fellow Am. Acad. Dermatology; mem. AMA, Am. Soc. for Laser Medicine, Fairfield County Med. Assn. Avocation: golf. Office: 38B Grove St Ridgefield CT 06877-4667

EGAN, KEVIN JAMES, lawyer; b. Chgo., June 24, 1950; s. Raymond Basil and Harriet Olene (Landbo) E.; children: Ryan, Daniel. BA, U. Ill., 1972; JD, Northwestern U., 1975. Bar: Ill. 1975, U.S. Dist. Ct. (no. dist.) Ill. 1975, U.S. Ct. Appeals (7th cir.) 1976, U.S. Ct. of Customs and Patent Appeals 1978. Law clk. to judge U.S. Dist. Ct. (no. dist.) Ill., Chgo., 1975-77; assoc. Pattishall, McAuliffe & Hofstetter, Chgo., 1977-78; asst. U.S. atty. No. Dist. of Ill., 1978-82; assoc. Winston & Strawn, Chgo., 1982-84, ptnr., 1984-93, Sonnenschein, Nath & Rosenthal, Chgo., 1993-98, Foley & Lardner, Chgo., 1998—. Article editor Jour. Criminal Law and Criminology, 1974-75. Bd. trustees Village of Frankfort, 1991—. Mem. ABA, Chgo. Bar Assn. (com. mem.), Bar Assn. of 7th Cir., Prestwick Country Club (Frankfort, Ill.). Roman Catholic. Avocation: hockey. Home: 904 Huntsmoor Dr Frankfort IL 60423-8747 Office: Foley & Lardner 321 N Clark St Ste 2800 Chicago IL 60610

EGAN, MARSHA CHRISTINE, school psychologist; b. Schenectady, N.Y., Oct. 8, 1946; d. Edwin G. and Doris (Brownell) E.; m. Kurt Patrick Riesenberg. BA in Liberal Arts and Social Scis., Buffalo State Coll., 1968; MS in Elem. Edn., Syracuse U., 1981, postgrad.; MS, cert. advanced study sch. psychology, SUNY, Oswego, 1988. Cert. in edn. and sch. psychology, N.Y. Tchr. elem. edn. Liverpool (N.Y.) Schs., 1968-69, St. Rose of Lima Sch., North Syracuse, N.Y., 1981-83; tchr. Tappan (N.Y.) Elem. Sch., South Orangetown Sch. Dist., 1969-71; sch. psychologist Liverpool Ctrl. Schs., 1988—. Cons., evaluator Learning Disabilities Assn., Syracuse; presenter Nat. Coun. for Family Rels. Conf., Milw., 1998, Ann. Conf. Nat. Assn. for Edn. of Young, Rochester, N.Y., 1999. Columnist Ptnrs. in Parenting, Syracuse Herald Jour., 1998—. Avocations: stained glass work, newspaper writing on children and families. Home: 6050 Bannister Dr Cicero NY 13039-8309 Office: Liverpool Ctrl Schs Donlin Drive Elem Sch Liverpool NY 13039

EGAN, MICHAEL JOSEPH, retired lawyer, state legislator; b. Savannah, Ga., Aug. 8, 1926; s. Michael Joseph and Elise (Robider) E.; m. Donna Cole, Apr. 14, 1951; children: Moira Elizabeth, Michael Joseph, Donna, Cole, Roby, John Patrick. BA, Yale U., 1950; LL.B., Harvard U., 1955. Bar: Ga., D.C. Assoc. Sutherland, Asbill & Brennan, Atlanta, 1955-61, ptnr., 1961-77, 79-97, ret. ptnr., 1998; mem. Ga. Ho. of Reps., 1966-77, minority leader, 1971-77; assoc. atty. gen. U.S. Dept. Justice, Washington, 1977-79; mem. Ga. Senate, 1989-2001. Served with U.S. Army, 1945-47, 50-52. Mem. ABA, Atlanta Bar Assn., State Bar Ga., Am. Law Inst., Am. Coll. Trust and Estate Counsel. Republican. Roman Catholic. Home: 3145 Argonne Dr NW Atlanta GA 30305-1949 Office: Sutherland Asbill & Brennan 999 Peachtree St NE Atlanta GA 30309-3915 also: 1275 Pennsylvania Ave NW Washington DC 20004-2404

EGAN, PATRICIA JANE, foundation executive, former university development director, writer; b. San Francisco, Aug. 7, 1951; 1 child, Kathryn Michele. AB, U. Calif., Berkeley, 1978; postgrad., N.J. Inst. Tech., 1996—. Cert. fund raising exec. Grants officer The Mus. Modern Art, N.Y.C., 1979-81; assoc. devel. officer grants Whitney Mus. Am. Art, N.Y.C., 1981-84; assoc. dir. devel. Columbia Bus. Sch., Columbia U., N.Y.C., 1984-86; mgr. major gifts New York Bot. Garden, N.Y.C., 1987-88; dir. devel. N.Y.C. Partnership, 1989-91; dir. devel. Cal Performances U. Calif., Berkeley, 1991-92; cons., 1992—. Cons. to various cultural and environ. orgns., N.Y., N.J., Calif., 1983—; co-prodr. distance learning course proposal writing N.J. Inst. Tech., 1997—. Prodr., program host including Terpsichore, KUSF-FM, 1978-79. Bd. dirs. Universala Esperanto Asocio/N.Y., 1980-83, Dance Perspectives Found., N.Y.C., 1985-2002, treas. 1987-91, found. officer, treas.; trustee Riverside Ch., N.Y.C., 1986-87. Fellow Nat. Endowment Arts, 1977. Mem. Soc. for Tech. Comm. (Bernard J. Goodman Meml. award N.Y. Metro chpt. 1998), Women in Comm., Internat. Assn. Bus. Communicators, Esperanto League of N.Am., Jr. League of San Francisco, Churchill Club, Alpha Epsilon Lambda. Avocations: art and technology, ballet, modern dance, martial arts. Office: PO Box 194391 San Francisco CA 94119-4391

EGAN, SHIRLEY ANNE, retired nursing educator; b. Haverill, Mass. d. Rush B. and Beatrice (Bengle) Willard Diploma, St. Joseph's Hosp. Sch. Nursing, Nashua, N.H., 1945; BS in Nursing Edn., Boston U., 1949, MS, 1954. Instr. sci. Sturdy Meml. Hosp. Sch. Nursing, Attleboro, Mass., 1949-51, Peter Bent Brigham Hosp. Sch. Nursing, Boston, 1951-53, ednl. dir., 1953-55, assoc. dir. Sch. Nursing, 1955-59, med. surg. coord., 1971-73, assoc. dir. Sch. Nursing, 1973-79, dir., 1979-85; cons. North Country Hosp., Newport, Vt., 1985-86; infection control practitioner, 1986-87; contract instr. Natchitoches Area Tech. Inst., 1988-90, Sabine Valley Tech Inst., 1990-91; coord. quality assurance Evangeline Health Care Ctr., 1991-92, asst. dir. nursing, 1992-93, coord. quality assurance, 1994-96, retired, 1996. Nurse edn. adviser AID (formerly ICA), Karachi, Pakistan, 1959-67; prin. Coll. Nursing, Karachi, 1959-67; dir. Vis. Nurse Service, Nashua, N.H., 1967-70; cons. nursing edn. Pakistan Ministry of Health, Labour and Social Welfare, 1959-67; adviser to editor Pakistan Nursing and Health Rev., 1959-67; exec. bd. Nat. Health Edn. Com., Pakistan; WHO short-term cons. U. W.I., Jamaica, 1970-71; mem. Greater Nashua Health Planning Council. Contbr. articles to profl. publs. Bd. dirs. Matthew Thornton health Ctr., Nashua, Nashua Child Care Ctr.; vol. ombudsman N.H. Council on Aging; mem. Nashua Service League. Served as 1st lt., Army Nurse Corps., 1945-47. Mem. Trained Nurses Assn. Pakistan, Nat. League for Nursing, Assn. for Preservation Hist. Natchitoches, St. Joseph's Sch. Nursing Alumnae Assn., Boston U. Alumnae Assn., Brit. Soc. Health Edn., Cath. Daus. Am. (vice regent ct. Bishop Malloy), Statis. Study Grads. Karachi Coll. Nursing, Sigma Theta Tau. Home: 729 Royal St Natchitoches LA 71457-5716

EGAN, WESLEY WILLIAM, former ambassador; b. Madison, Wis., Jan. 21, 1946; s. Wesley William and Ruth (Skeuse) E.; m. Virginia Warren, Aug. 15, 1967; children: Wesley Matthew, Kimberly Katherine. BA with honors, U. N.C., 1968. Vice consul Am. Consulate Gen., Durban, South Africa, 1972-74; spl. asst. to sec. state Dept. State Washington, 1974-77; 1st sec. Am. embassy, Portugal, 1977-79, dep. chief mission, 1979-82; ambassador to Republic of Guinea-Bissau, 1983-85, Chief of Staff to Dep. Sec. of State, 1985-87; Dep. Chief of Mission Am. Embassy, Lisbon, Portugal, 1987-90, Cairo, Egypt, 1990-93; amb. Hashemite Kingdom of Jordan, 1994-98; dep. insp. gen. Dept. of State, Washington, 1998-2000. Mem.: Assn. for Diplomatic Studies and Training (bd. mem.), Middle East Inst., Washington Inst. Fgn. Affairs. Episcopalian.

EGBERT, EMERSON CHARLES, retired publisher; b. Los Angeles, Nov. 30, 1924; s. Charles Barnes and Ethel Annette (Feader) E.; m. Kathryn Eleanor Tressel, Apr. 6, 1947; children— Susan Ann, John Charles, James Emerson, Michael Warren, Patricia Ann. Ed., Pasadena Jr. Coll., Woodbury Bus. Coll. Distbn. mgr. Newsstand Distbrs., 1947-49; dist. sales mgr. So. Calif., Pocket Books, Inc., 1949-59, sales mgr. Eastern div., 1959-61, v.p., circulation dir., 1961-71; pres. Pocket Books Distbn. Corp., N.Y.C., 1971-81; sr. v.p. Silhouette Books div. Simon & Schuster, 1981-85, sr. v.p. trade pub. group, 1985-89; ret., 1989; pres. B/K Book Cons. Svcs. Inc., Rockville Ctr., N.Y., 1990-93, Madison, Conn., 1993-97; ret., 1997. Past dist. commr. Boy Scouts Am.; bd. dirs. 25 Yr. Club; bd. dirs. YMCA, Westbrook, Conn.; mem. vestry com. St. Andrew's Episcopal Ch., Madison. With USNR, 1942-45. Decorated D.F.C., Air Medal with 4 oak leaf clusters. Mem. Ind. Newsstand Circulation Execs. Assn. (past chmn.), Internat. Periodical Distbrs. Am. (chmn.), Bur. Ind. Pubs. and Distbrs. (past chmn. book com.), Anti-Defamation League. Republican. Home: 287 Legend Hill Rd Madison CT 06443-1864

EGBERT, PETER ROY, ophthalmologist, educator; b. Indpls., Dec. 6, 1941; BA magna cum laude, DePauw U., Greencastle, Ind., 1963; MD, Yale U., 1967. Diplomate Nat. Bd. Med. Examiners, Am. Bd. Ophthalmology. Intern Cleve. Met. Gen. Hosp., 1967—68; resident in ophthalmology Yale U., New Haven, 1968—69; acting asst. prof. surgery (ophthalmology Stanford (Calif.) U., 1973—74, dir. Ophthalmic Pathology Lab., 1973—, asst. prof. surgery, 1974—81; acting head divsn. ophthalmology Stanford U. Med. Ctr., 1980—82, assoc. prof. surgery, 1981—88, prof. ophthalmology, 1988—, chmn. dept. ophthalmology, 1992—97; resident in ophthalmology Yale U., New Haven, 1971—73. Vis. prof. ophthalmology Govt. Hosp., San Pedro Sula, Honduras, 1974, Noor Eye Hosp., Kabul, Afghanistan, 1975, U. West Indies Med. Sch., Kingston, Jamaica, 1976, Princess Marina Hosp.-The Ctrl. Govt. Hosp., Gadorone, Botswana, 1978, Grenfell Regional Health Avcs., St. Nathony, Nfld., Canada, 1981, Govt. Hosp. Western Samoa, 1982, Project Orbis, Ismir, Turkey, 1985, Bamako, Mali, 1983, San Jose, Costa Rica, 1986, Port-au-Prince, Haiti, 1987, King Khaled Eye Hosp., Rihayd, Saudi Arabia, 1985, Korle-bu Tchg. Hosp., U. Ghana, Accra, 1987—2002, Leicester Royal Infirmary, England, 1987, Esperanca Hosp., Santarem, Brazil, 1987, Chinese Med. Sch., Hong Kong, 1988, Inst. Ophthalmology, Canton, 1988, Peking Med. Coll., Beijing, 1988, Nepal-Trilovan Tchg. Hosp., 1990; vis. prof. ophthamology COVA Eye Hosp., Tegucigalna, Honduras, 2000—. Recipient Bordon prize, DePauw U., 1960. Mem.: Verhoeff Ophthalmic Pathology Soc., Peninsula Eye Soc., Michael Hogan Eye Pathology Soc., Am. Intra-Ocular Implant Soc., Am. Assn. Ophthalmic Pathologists, Am. Acad. Ophthalmology, Phi Beta Kappa, Alpha Omega Alpha. Office: Stanford U Sch Medicine 300 Pasteur Dr Stanford CA 94305-5308

EGBERT, RICHARD COOK, retired banker; b. N.Y.C., June 23, 1927; s. Lester D. and Beatrice (Cook) E.; m. Anne Merrill Becker, Sept. 11, 1954; children: Allison Huntting (Mrs. Roberts Wyckoff Brokaw III), Anne Merrill (Mrs. Thomas Hamilton Grape), Richard Cook Jr. BA, Yale U., 1950. With Chase Nat. Bank, 1950-53; with Estabrook & Co., N.Y.C., 1954-68, ptnr., 1963-68; v.p. Spencer Trask & Co., Inc. (and successor cos.), N.Y.C., 1968-79, Bankers Trust Co., N.Y.C., 1979-84, Hamilton, Johnson & Co., Inc., N.Y.C., 1984-87, ret., 1987. Mem. Blue Hill Troupe, Ltd., N.Y.C., 1951—, pres., 1961-62; v.p., dir. 1030 Fifth Ave. Corp., 1968-72 Trustee, former treas. and chmn. finance com. W. Side Day Nursery, N.Y.C., 1957— ; adv. bd. Nat. Choral Council, 1981— . Served with USNR, 1945-46. Mem. Soc. Colonial Wars, Colonial Order of Acorn, St. Nicholas Soc. N.Y., Pilgrims U.S., Chi Phi. Episcopalian. Home: 250 Old Church Rd Greenwich CT 06830-4823

EGDAHL, RICHARD HARRISON, surgeon, medical educator, health science administrator; b. Eau Claire, Wis., Dec. 13, 1926; s. Harry I. and Rebecca (Ball) Egdahl; m. Cynthia Taft, Apr. 1983; children from previous marriage: Scott, David, Bruce, Julie. MD, Harvard U., 1950; PhD, U. Minn., 1957. Intern U. Minn. Hosp., 1950—51, resident, 1956—57; prof. surgery Med. Coll. Va., 1957—64; prof., chmn. surgery Boston U. Med. Ctr., 1964—73, dir., 1973—96, Health Policy Inst., Boston U.; Alexander Graham Bell prof. health care entrepreneurship Boston U. Trustee Pioneer Family of Mut. Funds. Past mem. editl. bd.: Am. Jour. Surgery, New Eng. Jour. Medicine. Trustee Boston Med. Ctr. Lt. USNR, 1952—55. Mem.: ACS, Am. Soc. for Clin. Investigation, Internat. Assn. Endocrine Surgeons (pres. 1981—83), Inst. Medicine NAS, Endocrine Soc. (CIBA award 1961), Soc. Med. Adminstrs., Boston Surg. Soc. (pres. 1977), Am. Surg. Assn. (1st v.p. 1980), Soc. Univ. Surgeons (pres. 1970—71), The Registry Resort, Badminton and Tennis Club, Algonquin Club, Brookline Country Club, Comml. Club, Alpha Omega Alpha, Phi Beta Kappa. Home: 333 Commonwealth Ave Apt 23 Boston MA 02115-1931 Office: Boston U Healthcare Entrepreneurship Program 53 Bay State Rd Boston MA 02215-2101 E-mail: regdahl@bu.edu.

EGELSTON, ROBERTA RIETHMILLER, writer; b. Pitts., Nov. 20, 1946; d. Robert E. and Doris (Bauer) Riethmiller; m. David Michael Egelston, Oct. 10, 1975; 1 child, Brian David. BA in Bus. Adminstrn., Thiel Coll., 1968; MLS, U. Pitts., 1974. Bus. mgr. Pitts. Pastoral Inst., 1968-70; adminstrv. asst. Coun. Alcoholism and Drug Abuse, Lancaster, Pa., 1970-72; dir. career planning libr. U. Pitts., 1974-78; writer, 1978—; libr. Pitts. Inst. Mortuary Sci., 1991—2001, instr. bus. English, 1992-98; mem. site-based mgmt. team Fox Chapel Area H.S., 1999-2001. Instr. beginning genealogy, 1991-98; book reviewer Coll. Placement Coun., Bethlehem, Pa., 1977-78; cons. State Affiliated Colls. and Univs., 1976; group leader Johns-Norris Assocs., Pitts., 1975-76. Author: Career Planning Materials, 1981, Credits and Careers for Adult Learners, 1985. Bd. dirs. Lauri Ann West Libr., Pitts., 1983-84; active PTA, 1985-88; mem. peace and justice com. Fox Chapel Presbyn. Ch., 1994-2000, deacon, 1995-98, mem. libr. com., 2000-02; mem. spiritual life com. East Liberty Presbyn. Ch., 2002-. Mem. AAUW (bd. dirs. Fox Chapel Area br. 1980-91, 2001-03), Les Lauriers (sr. women's hon. at Thiel Coll.), Western Pa. Geneal. Soc. (libr. rsch. com. 1990-94, edn. com. 1992—), Beta Phi Mu. Avocations: hiking, reading, gourmet cooking.

EGENES, THOMAS ARTHUR, ancient language educator; s. Harold Rolfe and Mary Elizabeth Egenes; m. Linda Alice Egenes, Feb. 24, 1981. PhD, U. Va., 1985. Assoc. prof. Sanskrit Maharishi U. Mgmt., Fairfield, Iowa, 1985—. Author: (textbook) Introduction to Sanskrit, Part One, Part Two, Learning the Sanskrit Alphabet, (book) All Love Flows to the Self, Eternal Stories from the Upanishads.

EGENOLF, ROBERT F. lawyer; b. San Francisco, Jan. 23, 1946; s. John D. and Virginia (Kirkland) Butler; m. Judy Wish, Jan. 23, 1970; children: Cristi Michelle, Jonah Wish. BA, U.S. Internat. U., San Diego, 1970; JD, Calif. Western U., San Diego, 1973; LLM, U. Miami, Fla., 1974. Bar: Calif. 1973, U.S. Tax Ct. 1974. Assoc. Blum & Blum, Oakland, Calif., 1974-75; ptnr. Westwick & Collison, Santa Barbara, Calif., 1976-80, Egenolf & Moore, Santa Barbara, 1980-94. Pres., founder Calif. Exchange Corp., Santa Barbara, 1984-90, Santa Barbara Exch. Corp., 1984-90, 97—, First Exch. Corp., Santa Barbara, 1988-90, Amherst Exch. Corp., Santa Barbara, 1989—; instr., lectr. Santa Barbara City Coll., 1987—; lectr. in real estate exch. seminars Lawyers Throughout the U.S., 1987—. Bd. dirs. Tri Counties Devel. Disabilities Bd., Santa Barbara, 1977-78, Child Abuse Listening Mediation, Santa Barbara, 1979-80, Ensemble Theatre Project, Santa Barbara, 1981-83, Santa Barbara City Coll. Theatre Group, 1983-84; dir., Anti-Defamation League, Santa Barbara, 2000-; trustee Laguna Blanca Sch., 1997-2003; dir. Am. Inst. Food and Wine, 1991-93, Santa Barbara Wine Auction, 1993-94, Semana Nautica Masters Volleyball Tournament, 1993-97; mem. polit. action com. Planned Parenthood, 1995; mem. fin. devel. steering com. Santa Barbara Contemporary Arts Forum, 1995-96; dir. Santa Barbara bd. ACLU, 2002—. With USN, 1963-69. Recipient Disting. Cmty. Svc. award, Anti-Defamation League, 2002.

Mem. Calif. Bar Assn. (co-chair joint tax subsect. 1990-95), Santa Barbara Bar Assn. (bd. dirs. 1978, 95-2001, pres. 2000), Barristers Santa Barbara (pres. 1976-77). Avocations: pilot, volleyball, sailing. Office: Egenolf Assocs LLP 130 E Carrillo St Santa Barbara CA 93101-2111 E-mail: egenolf@egenolf.com.

EGER, JOSEPH, conductor, music director; b. Hartford, Conn., July 9, 1925; s. Abraham and Clara (Ellovich) E. Grad., Curtis Inst., Berkshire Music Center; studied with, Monteux, Stokowski, Steinberg, Lert, Rudolf, Kahne. Faculty Aspen (Colo.) Music Festival, 1952-57; mem. faculty Peabody Conservatory, 1962-65, New Sch., 1971-72; condr. Greater Hollywood Philharm., 2001—; lectr. Fla. Atlantic U., 2003. Creator Harlem Music Project (published by Schirmer's, Consol. Music Pubs.); condr. seminar Smithsonian Instn., 1979; faculty, dir. internat. concert/seminar Salzburg Seminars, 1980. First horn N.Y. Philharm., L.A. Philharm., Israel Philharm., other major orchs.; solo rec. artist: RCA Victor, (albums) Joseph Eger Retrospective Series, 1978, also for motion picture, TV and radio; French horn soloist world concert tours, 1956; lectr., music dir. Eger Players; founder, condr. Camera Concerti Chamber Orch., 1958, Westside Symphony Orch., 1961, N.Y. Orch. Soc., 1963-73; condr. Midland (Mich.) Symphony, 1962-64, Town Hall series, 1962-63, Carnegie Hall, 1964-71, Philharm. Hall, 1965-72, Athens Festival, young people and teenage concerts, (concert series) UN, 1980, N. Miami Beach Symphony, 1997; guest condr. Royal Philharm., London Philharm, Moscow State Symphony, Lithuania State Symphony, New Philharmonia, Sinfonia of London, Pitts. Symphony Orch., Dallas Symphony, Cin Symphony Orch., Balt. Symphony Orch., Am. Symphony Orch., Vienna Radio Orch., Dessoff Choir, Haifa, Nat. Symphony Costa Rica, Shanghai Philharmonic Orch., Nat. Symphony Cuba, Nat. Symphony South Africa, Nat. Symphony Ireland, Bucharest Philharm. Orch., 1997, Romanian Orch., 1997, others; assoc. condr. to Leopold Stokowski, 1967-70; composer: (recs.) Life mag., 1966, Westminster Record Co., 1967; (film score) Carolina, 1970, Hidden Fears; music dir. Indian Hill, 1967, N.Y. Symphony Premiere Performance, 1968, N.Y. Concertante, Symphony for UN, 1975—, UN Singers, 1975, Bklyn. Heights Symphony, 1978-82, S.W. Fla. Symphony, 1986-90, Champlain Islands Symphony, 1988—; founder, music dir. Symphony of N.Y., Aware, N.Y., 1971-74, Internat. Yoga Symphony, Can. and N.Y., 1973; founder Crossover; apptd. prin. guest condr. Ctrl. Symphony, Beijing, People's Republic of China; contbg. author: UNESCO Cultures, author: (guest editorials) Newsweek mag., 1980, Christian Sci. Monitor, 1981, N.Y. Times, 1982; editor: Citibank AWARE Playbill; exec. producer: (TV film/music video) Ode to Joy, 1988. Chmn. UN Coord. Com. for Nongovtl. Orgns., 1990—; elected chmn. cultural com. City of Pompano Beach, 1999. Served to staff sgt. USAAF. Recipient Eleanor Roosevelt Man of Vision award, 1994, N.Y.C. Mayor's award, 1975, Internat. Music Therapist award, 1993; Maestro Joseph Eger Day in his honor, Pompano Beach, 1999. Mem. Nat. Assn. Am. Condrs. and Composers (program chmn. 1965-67), Acad. Ind. Scholars Home: 3200 NE 7th Ct Apt 205A Pompano Beach FL 33062-4506 E-mail: suneger@aol.com.

EGER, MARILYN RAE, artist; b. Offett AFB, Nebr., Jan. 2, 1953; d. John W. Shaver and Joyce Faye (Carpenter) Shaver (dec.), stepmother Myrle I. Masoner (dec.); m. Darrell W. Masoner, Feb. 28, 1971 (div. Sept. 1977); children: William Matthew Masoner, Melissa Rae Masoner Hurt; m. Gerard J. Eger, Jan. 30, 1982. BA, Calif. State U., Turlock, 1987. Cert. art tchr. 1990, Calif., lang. devel. specialist, 1993. Freelance artist oil painting Gibson Greetings Inc., Cin., 1992-97; tchr. art, A.P. art, advanced art Bear Creek High Sch., Stockton, Calif., chmn. dept. art, 1994-99, mentor tchr., 1998-99; pvt. art tchr. One-woman shows include Stockton Fine Arts Gallery, 1984-88, Accurate Art Gallery, Sacramento, 1989-90, Sharon Gile Gallery, Isleton, Calif., 1988-91, Le Galerie, Stockton, 1989-91, Masterpiece Gallery, Carmel, Calif., 1991-95, Alan Short Gallery, Stockton, 1991, Lodi Art Ctr., 1997; exhibited in group shows Calif. State U. Stanislaus Gallery, Turlock, 1999; represented by Iona's Gallery, Stockton, 1995-96, Heart of the Arts Gallery, Stockton, 1996-2000, C's Floral Gallery, Stockton, 1995-98, Lodi Art Ctr., 1984— (award of excellence, 1st pl. in graphics Membership Show 1999, 1st pl. in collage 2001, 1st pl. in oil in graphics Haggin Mus.), feature artist, 1985—, S.A.L. Else May Goodwin Gallery, 2001-03, Tidewater Gallery, Stockton, 2002, San Joaqin Delta Coll., Stockton, Calif., 2003; represented in permanent collections Gulf Oil Chems., Kaiser Permanente, Masterpiece Gallery, U. Calif. Davis Med. Ctr.; prints pub. in Mus. Edits. West. Bd. dirs. Lodi Art Ctr., 1988-91, chmn. 1989. Recipient Award of Excellence Unitarian Fall Art Festival, 1990, Award of Excellence in Oils, 1992, Ben Day Meml. award, 1993, Bank Stockton award and H.M. Haggin Mus., 1989, U.S. Nat. Collegiate Art Merit award, 1988, Lodi 31st Ann., 1st Oils, 1988, Award of Excellence in Pastel Haggin Mus., 1992, 1st Oils and Don Morrell Meml. award CCAL Gallo Show, 1993, Art of Calif. Bronze Discovery award, 1993, 1st pastel Lodi Art Ann., 1995, Hon. mention, 1998, award of merit Haggin Mus., 1997, 3rd in graphics Unitarian Fall Art Festival, 1998, 3rd Graphics award Lodi Art Ann., 1998, Mabel Myers award Haggin Mus., 1999, numerous others; Mellon grantee, 1994. Mem. Calif. Art Edn. Assn., Stockton Art League, Nat. League Am. Pen. Women, Lodi Art Ctr. Republican. Methodist. Avocations: sculpting, gardening, vineyards, painting, travel. Home: 1295 E Peltier Rd Acampo CA 95220-9652 Office: 1295 1/2 E Peltier Rd Acampo CA 95220-9652 E-mail: meger@lodinet.com.

EGERER, KAREN ANN, association executive; b. Chgo., Jan. 15, 1947; d. Carl F. and Lillian (Rottinger) Egerer; m. Richard Johnson, Aug. 5, 1995; 1 child, Paul Augustine. BA, DePaul U., 1968. Tchr. St. Teresa Sch., Chgo., 1968-74; program dir. World Without War Coun., Chgo., 1974-77, co-dir., 1977-80; program dir. Mid-Am. Com. Internat. Bus. and Govt. Cooperation, Chgo., 1981-83; coord. internat. programs U. Ill., Chgo., 984-88; program cons. John D. and Catherine T. MacArthur Found., Chgo., 1988-89; founder, dir. Heartland Internat., Chgo., 1989—. Founding mem. Silver Iris Photography, 2003. Editor: Salt II: Facts, Values, Choices, 1977. Co-founder Alliance Cath. Laity, Chgo., 1976-80, Chgo. Call to Action, 1977-80. Recipient community svc. award Assn. Chgo. Priests, Chgo., 1979. Mem.: Soc. for Internat. Devel. E-mail: kegerer@heartlandinternational.org.

EGERMEIER, ROBERT PAUL, retired engineer, retired lawyer; b. Oklahoma City, Dec. 25, 1927; s. Paul Fred Egermeier and Dorothy Laura Kluber; m. Virginia T. Kotte, Mar. 2, 1952; children: John Carl, Paul William. BS in Engring. Physics, U. Okla., 1951; MSME, N.Mex. State U., 1957; LLB, La Salle U., 1977. Registered profl. engr., N.Mex., Tex., Utah, Calif.; bar: Calif. 1977. Asst. prof. N.Mex. State U., Las Cruces, 1952—62; engring. mgr. Aerospace Corp., San Bernardino, Calif., 1962—67, RCA West Coast Divsn., Van Nuys, Calif., 1967—69; sr. scientist Hughes Aircraft, Canoga Park, Calif., 1969—79, chief scientist radar labs., 1981—89; patent atty. Alberi & Radke, Canoga Park, 1979—81; cons. Teledyne Systems, Newbury Park, Calif., 1990—93; engring. dir. Sci. & Applied Tech., Canoga Park, 1994—96. Mem., chmn. ethics and practice com. N.Mex. Soc. Profl. Engrs., 1958—62. Contbr. Ethics for Engineers, 1960. Advisor Explorer Scout Post Canoga Park H.S., 2002—; chancellor, vestry mem. Episcopal Ch., Canoga Park, 1967—84. Served with U.S. Army, 1951—53. Fellow, Inst. Advancement of Engring., 1970. Fellow: AIAA (assoc.; tactical missile adv. com., bd. dirs.); mem.: AAAS, ASME (faculty advisor), Calif. State Bar, Inst. Elec. and Electronic Engrs. (sr. life, sect. chmn.). Avocations: deep sea fishing, Explorer Scouts. Home: 22354 Malden St Canoga Park CA 91304 E-mail: bobeger@earthlink.net.

EGERTON, CHARLES PICKFORD, anatomy and physiology educator; b. Toronto, Ont., Can., Mar. 17, 1939; (parents Am. citizens); s. Matthew Davis and Margaret Swain (Pickford) E.; m. Carol Anne Carlson, Dec. 16, 1976; children: Matthew, Andrew, Victoria. BA in Zoology, Duke U., 1962; BS in Medicine, U. Okla., Oklahoma City, 1978; MS in Sci. Edn., U. So. Miss., 1981, PhD in Sci. Edn., 1991, MPH in Health Edn., 1994. Cert. physician asst. Nat. Commn. on Cert. Physician Assts. Commd. 2d lt. USAF, 1962, advanced through grades to maj., 1980, ops. officer, 1962-76, primary care med. officer, 1978-88; ret., 1988; instr. anatomy and physiology Miss. Gulf Coast C.C., Gautier, 1992—. Mem. Miss. Health Adv. Coun., Jackson, 1990—; guest lectr. dept. physician asst. studies U. South Ala. Author: Student Study Guide for Anatomy and Physiology; editor: Physician Assistant Handbook, 1995, Principles of Anatomy and Physiology, 9th edit., 2000; contbr. articles to profl. jours. Lectr. Miss. Inst. Drug-Free Sch., Hattiesburg, 1992; lectr. single parent-displaced spouse, Guatier, 1994-97; dir. smoking cessation Keesler AFB Med. Ctr., 1986-88; lay reader St. Luke's Anglican Ch., Gulfport, Miss., 1986-94. Mem. Am. Assn. Anatomists, Am. Acad. Physician Assts., Human Anatomy and Physiology Soc., Miss. Acad. Scis., Miss. Sci. Tchrs. Assn., Phi Delta Kappa, Eta Sigma Gamma. Democrat. Avocation: boating. Home: 6008 E Moreton Pl Ocean Springs MS 39564-2725 Office: Miss Gulf Coast CC PO Box 100 Gautier MS 39553-0100 E-mail: charles.egerton@mgccc.edu., egerton@cableone.net.

EGGAN, HUGH MELFORD, retired accountant; b. Velva, N.D., Feb. 24, 1930; s. Elmer M. and Esther (Guernsey) E.; m. Dorothy L. Rowland, June 3, 1949; children: Kathleen Eggan Davis, Gary, Laurie Eggan Berry Ward. BA magna cum laude, U. Wash., 1956. CPA, Wash., N.C. Mem. staff Deloitte Haskins & Sells (now Deloitte & Touche), Seattle, 1956-64, Washington, 1964-67, ptnr., 1967-68, with exec. office N.Y.C., 1968-72, ptnr. in charge Cleve., 1972-78, ptnr. in charge So. region Atlanta, 1978-85; ret., 1985. Contbr. to Jour. Accountancy. Former chmn. Pacific (Wash.) Town Planning Comm.; former officer Calvary Luth. Ch., Federal Way, Wash.; former bd. trustees Citizens League Cleve.; adminstrv. sec., coun. mem., pres. Emmanuel Luth. Ch., Vienna, Va.; former bd. trustees Luth. Planning Coun. Met. Washington; treas., bd. dirs. D.C. Inst. Mental Hygiene, 3d St. Music Sch., N.Y.C.; former bd. dirs. Goodwill Industries, Atlanta. Mem. AICPA, Country Club Asheville, Phi Beta Kappa, Beta Alpha Psi.

EGGEBRAATEN, GARY BRUCE, software engineer, consultant; b. Oct. 21, 1958; s. Bradley Delaine and Pearl Ottilee (Roberts) E.; m. Debra Yvonne Sloneker, July 26, 1980. BA in Math., BS in Math. Edn., Fla. State U., 1979; MBA, Duke U., 1991. Student programmer Fla. State U., Tallahassee, 1980—81, computer sys. analyst, 1981—84, mgr. tech. svc. CSII, 2001—; part-time tchr. Lincoln High Sch., Tallahassee, 1983—84; mem. tech. staff Found. Computer Sys., Cary, NC, 1984—85; sr. software engr. No. Telecom, Inc., Raleigh, NC, 1985—87, mgr. tech. automation, 1987—93; UNIX supr. South Fla. Water Mgmt. Dist., West Palm Beach, Fla., 1993—96, project mgr., 1996—97; mgr. opers. Sensormatic Electronics, Boca Raton, Fla., 1997—98, dir. IT, 1998—2001; mgr. tech. svc. Fla. State U., Tallahassee, 2001—. V.p. comm. Project Mgmt. Inst., Tallahassee, 2002—. Co-author: computer software KEY2DISK, 1983. Mem.: Help Desk Inst. Democrat. Methodist. Avocations: softball, baseball, music. Home: 505 Waverly Rd Tallahassee FL 32312-2855 E-mail: geggebra@csit.fsu.edu.

EGGENBERGER, ANDREW JON, federal agency administrator; b. Harlowton, Mont., May 8, 1938; s. Andrew D. and Gladys F. Eggenberger. BS, Carnegie Mellon U., 1961, PhD, 1967; MS, Ohio State U., 1963. Prof. U. S.C., Columbia, 1967-72; project mgr. D'Appolonia Cons. Engrs., Pitts., 1972-84; program dir. NSF, Washington, 1984-89; vice chmn. Def. Nuclear Facilities Safety Bd., Washington, 1989—. Fellow Marshall Space Flight Ctr., Huntsville, Ala., 1969, Lewis Rsch. Ctr., Cleve., 1967, 68; rsch. engr. Boeing Co., Seattle, 1961-63. Recipient Ralph R. Teetor award Soc. Automotive Engrs., 1968. Mem. AIAA, Am. Nuclear Soc., Earthquake Engring. Rsch. Inst., Sigma Alpha Epsilon. Lutheran. Avocations: auto racing, flying. Office: Def Nuclear Facilities Safety Bd 625 Indiana Ave NW Ste 700 Washington DC 20004-2901

EGGER, M. DAVID, neurobiology educator; b. Bakersfield, Calif., June 21, 1936; s. Henry and Ida Egger; m. Ellen M. Egger, Sept. 4, 1958 (dec. Jan. 1983); children: Daniel, Rachel, Gideon; m. Audrey Agin Egger, June 2, 1985. BS, Stanford U., 1958; MS, Yale U., 1960, PhD, 1962. Asst. prof., then assoc. prof. Yale U. Sch. Medicine, New Haven, 1965-74; assoc. prof. neurobiology U. Med. and Dentistry N.J.-Robert Wood Johnson Med. Sch., Piscataway, 1974—78, prof., vice chmn. dept. neurosci. and cell biology, 1979—. Mem. rsch. scientist devel. rev. com. NIMH, Washington, 1975-79; mem. neurobiology rev. group NIH, Washington, 1982-83; mem. presdl. young investigator awards program NSF, Washington, 1985; mem. sci. panel, sect. chmn. U.S. Civilian R & D Found., Washington, 1996, 97, 2000, 01, 03. Contbr. articles to sci. jours., including Jour. Physiology, Brain Rsch., Jour. Comparative Neurology. Recipient R.W. Wood prize Optical Soc. Am., 2000; Fulbright fellow, Hamburg, Germany, 1958-59; rsch. career grantee NIMH, 1969-74. Fellow AAAS, APA, Am. Psychol. Soc.; mem. Soc. for Neurosci. Democrat. Jewish. Achievements include patent for scanning laser confocal microscope. Office: UMDNJ-Robert Wood Johnson Med Sch 675 Hoes Ln Piscataway NJ 08854 E-mail: egger@umdnj.edu.

EGGER, TERRANCE C.Z. publishing executive; V.p. adv. Tucson Newspapers; gen. mgr. Post-Dispatch, 1996—; pub. St. Louis Post-Dispatch, LLC, 1999—, pres., 2000—. Holder mktg. positions, adv. positions Copley Newspapers; tchr. coll. comm. courses, Calif. Office: St Louis Post Dispatch 900 N Tucker Blvd Saint Louis MO 63101 Business E-Mail: tegger@post-dispatch.com.*

EGGERS, ALFRED JOHN, JR., research corporation executive; b. Omaha, June 24, 1922; s. Alfred John and Golden May (Meyers) E.; m. Elizabeth Ann Hills, Sept. 9, 1950; children— Alfred John III, Philip Norman BA, U. Nebr.-Omaha, 1945; MS, Stanford U., 1951, PhD, 1957. Aerospace scientist, asst. dir. NASA Ames Research Ctr., Mountain View, Calif., 1944-64; dep. assoc. adminstr., asst. adminstr. for policy NASA, Washington, 1964-71; Hunsaker prof. MIT, Cambridge, 1969-71; asst. dir. NSF, Washington, 1971-77; dir. Lockheed Research Lab., Palo Alto, Calif., 1977-79; chmn. bd., chief exec. officer RANN, Inc., Palo Alto, Calif., 1979—. Mem. sci. adv. bd. USAF, Washington, 1958-72, Aerospace Engring. Bd., NAE, Washington, 1973-77; mem. adv. bd. Solar Energy Rsch. Inst., Golden, Colo., 1985-89; chmn. A.J. Eggers & Co., Atherton, Calif., 1981—. Author: Hypersonic Flow, 1962; contbr. articles to profl. jours.; patentee in field. Vice chmn. Sch. Community Devel. Com., Los Altos Hills, Calif., 1963-64; mem., chmn. troop com. Boy Scouts Am., Arlington, Va., 1968-75; mem. safety com. ARC, Arlington, 1975-77. Served to lt. (j.g.) USN, 1943-46 Recipient Arthur S. Flemming award USJCC, 1956, TOYM award USJCC, 1957, Exceptional Svc. medal NASA, 1971, Disting. Svc. medal NSF, 1975, Disting. Svc. medal Pres. of U.S., 1977, commendation Nat. Sci. Bd., 1977. Fellow AAAS, AIAA (founder, bd. dirs. 1962-66, Sylvanus Albert Reed award 1961), Am. Astron. Soc.; mem. NAE (long-range planning and devel. com. 1983-85), Am. Wind Energy Assn., Washington Golf and Country Club, Sigma Xi, Tau Beta Pi. Republican. Avocations: swimming; golf; skiing. Home: 23 Fair Oaks Ln Atherton CA 94027-3808 Office: RANN Inc 744 San Antonio Rd Ste 26 Palo Alto CA 94303-4624 *Success in life is always burdened by achieving competence and working hard at what you do. Happiness is the unique reward for enjoying what you do.*

EGGERS, GEORGE WILLIAM NORDHOLTZ, JR., anesthesiologist, educator; b. Galveston, Texas, Feb. 22, 1929; s. George William Nordholtz and Edith (Sykes) E.; m. Mary Futrell, Dec. 30, 1955; children: Carol Ann, George William. BA, Rice U., Tex., 1949; M in anesthesiology, U. Tex., 1953. Diplomate Am. Bd. Anesthesiology. Instr. dept. anesthesiology, U. Tex., Galveston, Tex., 1956-59; asst. prof. dept. anesthesiology, U. Tex., Galveston, Tex., 1959-61; assoc. prof. dept. anesthesiology, U. Mo., 1961-67; prof. dept anesthesiology U. Mo., 1967—94, acting chmn. dept. anesthesiology, 1969, chmn. dept. anesthesiology, 1970-94, prof. emeritus, 1994—2001. Vis. instr. USAF Hosp., Lackland AFB, San Antonio, 1956-61; vis. rsch. prof. dept. anesthesiology Northwestern U. Med. Sch., Chgo., 1968-69; rsch. assoc. Space Sci. Rsch. Ctr., U. Mo., 1965-66. Contbr. over 50 articles to profl. jours. Recipient Ashbel Smith Disting. Alumnus Award U. Tex., 1993. Mem. Am. Soc. Anesthesiology (bd. dirs. 1979-86, v.p. 1986-89, 1st v.p. 1990, pres. elect 1991, pres. 1992), Am. Coll. Anesthesiology (bd. govs., 1965-74, chmn. bd. govs., 1973), Soc. Acad. Anesthesiology Chmn. (pres. 1971), Assn. Am. Med. Colls. (adminstrv. bd. coun. acad. socs. 1976-79), Mo. Soc. Anesthesiologists (pres. 1970, Disting. Svc. Award 2001), Tex. Gulf Coast Anesthesiology Soc. (v.p. 1960), Boone County Med. Soc. (pres. 1988), Am. Bd. Anesthesiology (assoc. examiner 1968, joint coun. with Am. Soc. Anesthesiology on in-tng. exams.), Acad. Anesthesiology (pres. 1994, Citation of Merit 1997), Accreditation Coun. Grad. Med. Edn. (mem. residency rev. com. for anesthesiology 1989-94), Anesthesia Found. (trustee 1993—), Alpha Omega Alpha, Mu Delta, Sigma Xi. Republican. Roman Catholic. Avocations: hunting, astronomy, magic, photography, shooting. Home: 1509 Woodrail Ave Columbia, MO 65203-0931 Office: U Mo Dept Anesthesiology 1 Hospital Dr Dept Columbia MO 65201-5276

EGGERS, JAMES WESLEY, executive search consultant; b. Des Moines, Feb. 7, 1925; s. Paul William and Opal Imo (Cardiff) E.; m. Marjorie Mardell Freel, Aug. 2, 1947; children: James S., Barbara Bucher, Mark D. Grad., Knoxville High Sch., 1943. Farmer, Knoxville, Iowa, 1948-55; sales rep. Iowa Power & Light Co., Des Moines, 1953-60, Cedar Rapids, Iowa, 1960-62; sales exec. Thomas D. Murphy Co., Red Oak, Iowa, 1962-67; pres., owner Eggers Cos., Omaha, 1967—. Bd. dirs. Nebr. State Bank, Omaha; owner, mgr. Exec. Realty and Mgmt. Co., Omaha, 1979—. Bd. dirs. local Meth. Ch., Nebr. Meth. Hosp. Found.; chmn. local dist. George Bush for Pres. campaign, Nebr., 1988; chmn. State of Nebr. Merit Coun., Lincoln, 1979-83; mem. nat. adv. cabinet Guideposts, Pawling, N.Y.; chmn. and mem. various civic bds. Mem. Nebr. Assn. Pers. Cons. (pres. 1974-75), Nat. Assn. Pers. Cons. (mem. nat. com. 1979-83, cert.), Omaha C. of C. (bd. dirs. 1980-83), Rotary (bd. dirs. Omaha chpt. 1983—, sgt.-at-arms 1986-90), Masons, Shriners. Republican. Avocations: reading, travel, religious study, walking. Office: Eggers Cons Co Inc Eggers Plz 11272 Elm St Omaha NE 68144-4788 E-mail: admin@eggersconsulting.com.

EGGERT, JAMES EDWARD, economics educator, writer; b. Chgo., Feb. 3, 1943; s. Robert John and Alice Elizabeth (Bauer) E.; m. Patricia Ellen Stock, May 8, 1971; children: Anthony, Leslie. BA in Econs., Lawrence U., 1967; MA in Econs., Mich. State U., 1968. Tchr. econs. U. Wis.-Stout, Menomonie, 1968—, emeritus, 2001—. Vis. prof. No. Ariz. U., Flagstaff, 1978. Author: Low-Cost Earth Shelters, 1982, Invitation to Economics, 2d edit., 1991, What is Economics?, 4th edit., 1997, Song of the Meadowlark, 1999. Vol. Peace Corps, Kenya, East Africa, 1964-66; adviser GreenSense Environment Club, 1991-2002; advisor planning comm. Town of Colfax, Wis. Mem. Astron. Soc. Pacific, Wis. Environ. Edn, Sierra Club, Thoreau Soc. Avocations: photography, music, tennis, astronomy, botany. Home: E-9001 Hwy N Colfax WI 54730 Office: U Wis Stout Harvey Hall 319A Menomonie WI 54751

EGGERT, ROBERT JOHN, SR., economist; b. Little Rock, Dec. 11, 1913; s. John and Eleanora (Fritz) Lapp; m. Elizabeth Bauer, Nov. 28, 1935 (dec. Dec. 1991); children: Robert John, Richard F., James E.; m. Annamarie Hayes, Mar. 19, 1994. BS, U. Ill., 1935, MS, 1936; candidate in philosophy, U. Minn., 1938; LHD (hon.), Ariz. State U., 1988; D Econ. Forecast, Lincoln Coll., 2002. Research analyst Bur. Agrl. Econs., U.S. Dept. Agr., Urbana, Ill., 1935; sec. War Meat Bd., Chgo., 1942-45, prin. marketing specialist, 1943; rsch. analyst U. Ill., 1935-36, U. Minn., 1936-38; asst. prof. econs. Kans. State Coll., 1938-41; asst. dir. mktg. Am. Meat Inst., Chgo., 1941-43, economist, assoc. dir., 1943-50; mgr. dept. mktg. rsch. Ford divsn. Ford Motor Co., Dearborn, Mich., 1951-53, mgr. program planning, 1953-54, mgr. bus. rsch., 1954-57, mgr. mktg. rsch. mktg. staff, 1957-61, mgr. mktg. rsch., mem. div. op. com., 1961-64, mgr. internat. mktg. rsch. mktg. staff, 1964-65, mgr. overseas mktg. rsch. planning, 1965-66, mgr. mktg. rsch. Lincoln-Mercury div., 1966-67; dir. and founder first agribus. programs Mich. State U., 1967-68; staff v.p. econ. and mktg. rsch. RCA Corp., N.Y.C., 1968-76; pres., chief economist Eggert Econ. Enterprises, Inc., Sedona, Ariz., 1976—. Founder, editor emeritus Blue Chip Econs. Ind.; lectr. mktg. U. Chgo., 1947-49; chmn. Fed. Statistics Users Conf., 1960-61; adj. prof. bus. forecasting No. Ariz., 1976-79; mem. econ. adv. bd. U.S. Dept. Commerce, 1969-71, mem. census adv. com., 1975-78; mem. panel econ. advisers Congl. Budget Office, 1975-76; interim dir. Econ. Outlook Ctr. Coll. Bus. Adminstrn. Ariz. State U., Tempe, 1985-86, cons., 1985—; mem. Econ. Estimates Commn. Ariz., 1979-03; apptd. Ariz. Gov.'s Commn. Econ. Devel., 1991-95, vice chmn. investment adv. coun. Ariz. State Retirement System, 1993-98; trustee Marcus J. Lawrence Med. Ctr. Found., 1992-96, Flagstaff Inst.; chmn. market rsch. com. Gov.'s Strategic Partnership for Econ. Devel.; co-chmn. Ariz. Sr. Industries Cluster, 1995-97. Contbr. articles to profl. lit.; founder, editor emeritus: monthly Blue Chip Econ. Indicators, 1976—; exec. editor Ariz. Blue Chip, 1984—, Western Blue Chip Econ. Forecast, 1986—, Blue Chip Job Growth Update, 1990—, Mexico Consensus Econ. Forecast, 1993—, Red Rock Sales Tax Collections, 1998—, National Consensus Forecast of Labor Employment, Compensation and Productivity, 2000-01; guest appearances on CNN, Wall Street Week, NBC's Today show. Mem. long range planning com. Ch. of Red Rocks, 1998-2001. Recipient Econ. Forecast award Chgo. chpt. Am. Statis. Assn., 1950, 60, 68; Seer of Yr. award Harvard Bus. Sch. Indsl. Econ., 1973, Golden Gloves Boxing award, U. Ill., 1935, Participation in Genetics of Human Longevity Study, 2002, Proclamation signed by Gov. Ariz., 2003. Fellow Am. Statis. Assn. (chmn. bus. and econ. stats sect. 1957—, pres. Chgo. chpt. 1948-49), Nat. Assn. Bus. Economists (coun. 1969-72); mem. Coun. Internat. Mktg. Rsch. and Planning Dirs. (chmn. 1965-66), Am. Mktg. Assn. (dir., v.p. mktg. mgmt. divsn. 1972-73, nat. pres. 1974-75), Fed. Stats. Users Conf. (chmn. trustees 1960-61), Conf. Bus. Economists (chmn. 1972-73), Am. Quarter Horse Assn. (dir. 1966-73), Ariz. Econ. Roundtable, Am. Econs. Assn., Phoenix Econ. Club (hon.), Ariz. C. of C. (bd. dirs. 1991-95), Alpha Zeta. Republican. Office: Eggert Econ Enterprises Inc PO Box 4313 West Sedona AZ 86340-4313 Fax: (928) 282-2128. E-mail: eee@sedona.net. *I have always strived to be a person of greater value. My modest success has resulted largely from the manifold contribution of others. For example, my AG teacher, Ralph K. Morray at Lincoln, Ill., obtained a four year scholarship for me at the University of Illinois in 1931. In fact, the only true measure of my accomplishments will unfold in the future. What the future will be is difficult to foretell, but it always has been a challenge to maximize productivity and to look ahead, and to dream of things that never were and say—why not? My motto is "Aiming for Excellence in Economic Forecasting".*

EGGERT, RUSSELL RAYMOND, lawyer; b. Chgo., July 28, 1948; s. Ralph A. and Alice M. (Nischwitz) E.; m. Patricia Anne Alegre, 1998. AB, U. Ill., 1970, JD, 1973; postgrad., Hague Acad. Internat. Law, The Netherlands, 1972. Bar: Ill. 1973, U.S. Supreme Ct. 1979. Assoc. U. Ill., Champaign, 1973-74; asst. atty. gen. State of Ill., Chgo., 1974-79; assoc. O'Conor, Karaganis & Gail, Chgo., 1979-83; legal counsel to Ill. atty. gen., Chgo., 1983-87; ptnr. Mayer, Brown, Rowe & Maw, Chgo., 1987—. Contbr. articles to profl. jours. Mem. ABA. Democrat. Office: Mayer Brown Rowe & Maw 190 S La Salle St Chicago IL 60603-3441 E-mail: reggert@mayerbrownrowe.com.

EGGERTSEN, JOHN HALE, lawyer; b. Ann Arbor, Mich., Jan. 7, 1947; s. Claude Andrew and Nita (Wakefield) E.; m. Claire Chenoweth, July 19, 1969 (div. 1987); children: Melissa Anne, Helen Emma; m. Sharon Ingram, June 13, 1987 (div. 1994); children: Alexandria, Andrea; m. Robin Rich, Sept. 23, 1995; 1 child, Brendon Hale. BA, U. Mich., 1968; JD cum laude, U. Toledo, 1974; LLM in Taxation, NYU, 1975. Bar: Ohio 1974, Mich. 1975. Instr. Highland Park (Mich.) Sch. Dist., 1968; claims adjuster State Farm Mutual Ins. Co., Ann Arbor, Mich., 1968-70; ptnr. Honigman Miller Schwartz and Cohn, Detroit, 1975-2000. Adj. prof. Wayne State U. Law Sch., Detroit, 1980-94; active Mich. Employee Benefits Conf., Detroit, 1980—. Contbr. articles to profl. jours. Bd. dirs. Neighborhood Svcs. Orgn., Detroit, 1992-2000, pres., 1994-97. Rsch. grantee NYU, 1974-75; Gerald Wallace scholar NYU, 1974-75. Mem. ABA (taxation sect., employee benefits com.), State Bar Ohio, State Bar Mich. Democrat. Mem. Lds Ch. Avocations: softball, bowling, reading. Home: 6369 Munger Ypsilanti MI 48197 Office: Eggertsen & Assocs PC Ste 107 5340 Plymouth Rd Ann Arbor MI 48105 Office Fax: 734-794-7104. Business E-Mail: john@jhelaw.com.

EGGINTON, EVERETT, educational administrator; b. N.Y.C., Apr. 6, 1943; s. Hersey Benner and Mary Florence (Twining) Egginton; m. Wynn Meagher, Sept. 27, 1986; 1 child from previous marriage, William Everett. BA in Econs., Colgate U., 1965, MA in Social Sci. Edn., 1968; MS in Comparative Edn., Syracuse U., 1971, PhD in Edn. Founds., 1974; EdD (hon.), U. Francisco Gavidia, San Salvador, El Salvador, 1990. Asst. prof. U. Louisville, 1974-78, acting dir. Internat. Ctr., 1978-79, assoc. prof., 1978-84, prof. edn., 1984—2002, dir. L.Am. Edn. Ctr., 1986—2002, chair ednl. founds., 1989-2000, dir. Internat. Ctr., 1996—2002; vice provost Internat. and U.S.-Mex. Border Programs N.Mex. State U., Las Cruces, N.Mex., 2003—. Sr. policy analyst U.S. Dept. Health and Human Svcs., Washington, 1980—81; pres. Consortium of Ctrl. Am. Univs., 1990—96, sec.-gen., 1991—98; cons. Ministry of Edn. El Salvador and Honduras; cons. World Bank, U.S. AID, 1992—; mem. exec. com. Commn. on Internat. Programs Nat. Assn. State Univs. and Land Grant Colls., 2000—. Contbg. editor: U.S. Libr. of Congress, 1980—88, Handbook of Latin Am. Studies; contbr. revs. and articles to profl. publs. and encys. Recipient Fulbright Rsch./Lectr. award, El Salvadaor, 1999—2000; Fulbright/Hays fellow, 1973—74, Fulbright/Stanford fellow, U. Santiago Compostela Spain, 1977, HEW fellow, 1979—80. Home: 5371 Redman Rd Las Cruces NM 88011 Office: New Mexico State Univ MSC 3567 PO Box 30001 Las Cruces NM 88003-8001 E-mail: egginton@nmsu.edu.

EGGINTON, WILLIAM EVERETT, humanities educator; b. Syracuse, N.Y., Mar. 24, 1969; s. Everett Egginton and Margaret L. Maguire; m. Bernadette M. Wegenstein, July 3, 1999; children: Alexander Everett, Charlotte Elisabeth. AB, Dartmouth U., 1991; MA, U. Minn., 1994; AM, Stanford U., 1996, PhD, 1999. Asst. prof. U. Buffalo, 1999—. Author: (scholarly book) How the World Became a Stage; editor: (book) The Pragmatic Turn in Philosophy; translator: Borges: The Passion of an Endless Quotation. Fellow, Stanford Humanities Ctr., 1996—97, Inst. for Human Scis., Vienna, Austria, 2002. Mem.: MLA. Democrat. Roman Catholic. Avocations: travel, cooking, tennis. Office: Univ Buffalo North Campus Buffalo NY 14260-4620 Office Fax: 716-645-5981. Personal E-mail: bill@egginton.org.

EGGLESTON, CLAUD HUNT, III, company executive, venture capitalist; b. Buffalo, June 21, 1954; s. Claud Hunt Jr. and Arlene (Shank) E.; m. Ann Pendleton, Feb. 14, 1988; children: Brett Andrew, Blake Edward Hunt. BA, Union Coll., 1976; MS, MEd, Columbia U., 1979. Pres. Checo Electronics, Schenectady, N.Y., 1974-78; chief fin. officer, bus. mgr. performing arts divsn. Smithsonian Inst., Washington, 1978—79; staff mgr. long lines AT&T, Washington, 1980—81, dist. mgr. strategy and product devel. Morristown, NJ, 1981-82, divsn. mgr. venture devel. consumer products, 1982— 84, br. mgr., 1984-85; v.p., gen. mgr. Asia Internat., Morristown, 1985-87; exec. dir. new ventures U.S. West Inc., Denver, 1987-88, v.p. mergers and acquisitions, 1988-90; v.p. bus. devel. and mktg. Corel/Ventura Software Inc., San Diego, 1990-92; mng. dir. Crest Tech. Ventures, Inc., Poway, Calif., 1992—; pres. Tech. Trends Technology Focus, Inc., San Diego, 1992-2000; CEO, pres. Basic4 Broadband, Inc., San Diego, 1999—. Editor: Financing Independent Education, 1978. Recipient Young Entrepreneur award Schenectady C. of C., 1975; Klingenstein fellow Columbia U., 1977-78. Mem. Am. Mgmt. Assn., Met. Club (Denver). E-mail: huntegg@hotmail.com.

EGGLESTON, G(EORGE) DUDLEY, management consultant, publisher; b. Buffalo, June 11, 1936; s. George Staub and Betty (Ball) E.; m. Susan Michaels, June 4, 1960 (div. Sept. 1987); children: George Dudley Jr., Michele Blair; m. Linda Stephens, Mar. 31, 1990 (div. Sept. 1996). BE, Vanderbilt U., 1960; MBA, Ga. State U., 1979. Product mgr. Exxon Chem., N.Y.C., 1960-71; sales mgr. Exxon Chem. Sweden, Stockholm, 1968-69; real estate agt. Woodward & Assocs., Atlanta, 1971-74; v.p. JFK Land Co., Atlanta, 1974-75; pres. Dudley Eggleston Co., Atlanta, 1975—, Maids Unique, Atlanta, 1976-81, Eggleston Cons. Internat., Atlanta, 1981—. Pub. revenue-producing Web site eggcon-.com., compensation reports for sr. real estate execs. Pres. Fanwood-Scotch Plains, N.J., Jaycees, 1968. Capt. USMC, 1960-63. Mem. Urban Land Inst., Beta Gamma Sigma. Republican. Episcopalian. Avocations: boating, skiing, hiking. E-mail: dudley@eggcon.com.

EGGLETON, ARTHUR C. former Canadian government official, member of Parliament; b. Toronto, Ont., Can., Sept. 29, 1943; 1 child, Stephanie. Acct., up to 1969; mem. Toronto City Coun., Met. Toronto Coun., 1969-91, city budget chief, 1973-80; mayor City of Toronto, 1980-91; mem. from York Centre in City of North York Parliament of Can., 1993—, pres. treasury bd., minister for infrastructure, 1993-96; min. international trade Can., 1996-97, min. nat. def., 1997—2002. Mem. Bd. Fedn. Can. Mcpls.; chmn. Internat. Programs Com.; co-chmn. Nat. Action Com. Race Rels., apptd. Minister for Internatl. Trade, 1996, apptd. pres. of treas. bd. and Minister, Infrastructure, 1993, appointed Minister of Natl. Defense, 1997, vice chmn. of cabinet com. on Econ. Policy. Mem. Met. Toronto Police Comm., Bd. Can. Nat. Exhbn. Recipient Civic Award of Merit, City of Toronto, 1992. Mem. York Centre for City of Toronto. Office: York Centre 845 Wilson Ave M3K1E6 Downsview ON Canada also: House of Commons 365 W Block Ottawa OT Canada

EGGLETON, PATRICK J. mathematician, educator; b. Mich. s. Charles R. and Sallye J. Eggleton; m. Dawn J. Fitzgerald, Aug. 17, 1991; children: Nathan, N. Timothy, Elizabeth A. BS, U. South Fla., 1987, MEd, 1991; PhD, U. Ga., 1995. Math. tchr. Pasco Comprehensive H.S., Dade City, Fla., 1987—91; asst. prof. math. edn. Berry Coll., Mount Berry, Ga., 1995—99; assoc. prof. math. Huntington (Ind.) Coll., 1999—. Cons. Huntington County Schools, 2002—. Christian edn. dir. Huntington Bapt. Ch., 2002—03. Named Forrester Lectr., Huntington Coll., 2002. Mem.: Nat. Coun. Tchrs. Math., Ind. Coun. Tchrs. Math. (pres. 2002—). Office: Huntington Coll 2303 College Ave Huntington IN 46750

EGHBAL, MORAD, geologist, lawyer; b. Tehran, Iran, June 7, 1952; s. Mohammad Ali and Fari Eghbal; m. Niloofar Sadjadi, July 17, 1983; children: Elaheh, Aria. BA, George Washington U., 1975, MA, 1977; JD, Howard U., 1989; LLM, U. Pacific, 1991. Asst. George Washington U., Washington, 1972; asst. to dir. Smithsonian Instn., Washington, 1972-75; spl. advisor to dir. Georgetown U., Washington, 1975; cons. Leo A Daly, Washington, 1975, Kodak, Rochester, N.Y., 1976; ofcl. del. 2d Circum-Pacific Energy and Mineral Resources conf., Honolulu, 1978; CEO MERE Enterprises, Washington, 1976—87; fgn. assoc. Pestalozzi, Gmuer & Heiz, Zurich, 1989; law clk. to Hon. William B. Bryant, US Dist. Ct. DC, Washington, 1990-91; trustee, CFO Riess Inst., Washington, 1983—. Dir., pres. The Grail Corp., 1983—; dir., v.p. exploration GASCO, Inc.; judge oral arguments and memls. regional and internat. semi-finals, finals Jessup competition Internat. Law Students Assn., 1990—2003, past mem. bd. dirs.; adj. prof. legal and ethical studies U. Balt., 1994—95, adj. prof. law, 1995—99, adj. prof. internat. mgmt., 1998—99, vis. asst. prof. law, internat. mgmt. and legal, ethical and hist. studies, 1999—2001, asst. dir. Ctr. for Internat. and Comparative Law, 2000—, vis. assoc. prof. law, 2001—; mng. editor Iu Genttum, 2003—, Internt. Legal Theory, 2003—; guest spkr. in field. Rschr. The Divining Hand (E.P. Dutton), 1973-79; keynote spkr. symposium Dickinson Sch. Law, Carlisle, Pa., 1991, 1st Conf. Expeditionary Learning/Outward Bound, Greenbelt, Md., 2000; author: 1995 Philip C. Jessup Internat. Law Moot Ct. Competition Problem, 1995. Trustee Capital City Pub. Charter Sch., 2000—03. Recipient Cert. Achievement, Circum-Pacific Energy & Mineral Resources conf., 1978, Ga. U., 1980, 2d Place Nat. Roscoe Hogan Environ. Law Essay contest award ATLA, 1988, Outstanding Student Adv. award Met. Trial Lawyers Assn., 1989, Citizen Citation City and mayor of Balt., 2000, Spirit of Excellence award U. Balt. Alumni Assn., 2002, John May Award for Teaching Excellence and Svc. to the Univ., SBA- Univ. of Balt., 2003. Mem. ABA, Nat. Bar Assn., Internat. Law Assn., Am. Assn. Petroleum Geologists (founding mem. energy minerals divsn.), Geol. Soc. Am., Soc. Econ. Paleontologists and Mineralogists, Potomac Appalachian Trails Club, Nat. Capital Area Paralegal Assn., Internat. Law Students Assn. (past mem. bd. dir.), Nat. Lawyers Club, US Japan Trade Coun., Am. Inns Ct. (Prettyman/Leventhal chpt.), Phi Delta Phi. Office: Riess Inst 9555 Friendship Station Washington DC 20016-9555 E-mail: eghbal@riess.org.

EGIELSKI, RICHARD, illustrator; b. N.Y.C., July 16, 1952; s. Joseph and Caroline (Rzepny) Egielski; m. Denise Saldutti, May 8, 1977. Student, Pratt Inst., Bklyn., 1970—71, Parsons Sch. Design, N.Y.C., 1971—74. Illustrator (children's books) Moonguitars, 1974, The Porcelain Pagoda, 1976, The Letter, the Witch and the Ring, 1976, I Should Worry, I Should Care, 1979, Finders Weepers, 1980, Louis the Fish, 1980, Getting Even, 1982, It Happened in Pinsk, 1983 (Plaque award, 1985), Lower! Higher! You're a Liar!, 1984, The Little Father, 1985, Amy's Eyes, 1985, Hey, Al, 1986 (Caldecott medal, 1987), Friends Forever, 1988, Bravo Minski, 1988, The Tub People, 1989, Oh, Brother, 1989, A Telling of Tales: Five Stories, 1990, Christmas in July, 1991, The Lost Sailor, 1992, Ugh, 1992, The Tub Grandfather, 1993, Fire! Fire! Said Mrs. McGuire, 1995, Call Me Ahnighito, 1995, Buz, 1995 (Best Illustrated Book of 1995 by N.Y. Times), The Gingerbread Boy, 1997. Recipient Cert. of Merit, Soc. of Illustrators, N.Y.C., 1978, 1981, 1984, 1985. Avocation: playing the mandolin. Office: care Farrar Straus & Giroux 19 Union Sq W New York NY 10003-3304

EGILMEZ, NEJAT K. science educator; b. Istanbul, Turkey, Feb. 23, 1958; arrived in U.S., 1976; s. Ahmet Nurettin and Sukran Egilmez; m. Samina Z. Raza-Egilmez, June 24, 1988; 1 child, Aral. BS, U. Minn., 1980; MA, SUNY, Buffalo, 1983, PhD, 1986. Post-doctoral fellow La. State U. Med. Ctr., New Orleans, 1986—88; asst. prof. Bogazici U., Istanbul, 1989—93; cancer rsch. scientist Roswell Park Cancer Inst., Buffalo, 1994—2001; asst. prof. SUNY, Buffalo, 2001—. V.p. Therapyx, Inc., Buffalo, 2001—. Contbr. articles to profl. jours. Grantee, NIH, 2000—03, 2001, 2002, Nat. Cancer Inst., 2001, DOD Breast Cancer Program, 2001—. Mem.: AAAS, Soc. for Biol. Therapy. Achievements include patents pending for methods and products for tumor immunotherapy. Office: SUNY Buffalo Dept Microbiology 138 Farber Hall 3435 Main St Buffalo NY 14214

EGINTON, CHARLES THEODORE, surgeon, educator; b. Staples, Minn., 1914; m. Sally Eginton; children— William C., Julie Ann, Mark Theodore, C. William, Nancy Elizabeth. BA, Macalester Coll., 1935; BS, U. Minn., 1937, M.B. with distinction, 1938, MD, 1939, MS in Surgery, 1942. Diplomate: Am. Bd. Surgery. Intern Ancker Hosp., St. Paul, 1938-39; fellow in surgery Mayo Found., Rochester, Minn., 1939-42; asst. in surgery Mayo Clinic, 1941-42; practice medicine specializing in surgery St. Paul, 1946-67; chief surg. svc. VA Hosp., Fargo, N.D., 1967-71, chief of staff, 1971-78, chief surg. svcs., 1978-87, ret. surg. svcs., 1987—. Clin. prof. surgery U. N.D., 1970— ; adj. prof. pharmacy N.D. State U., 1970—. Served to maj., M.C. AUS, 1942-46. Fellow ACS, Internat. Coll. Surgeons; mem. AMA, Phi Beta Kappa, Alpha Omega Alpha. Home: 509 1/2 N Shore Dr Detroit Lakes MN 56501-4411

EGINTON, WARREN WILLIAM, federal judge; b. Bklyn., Feb. 16, 1924; AB, Princeton U., 1948; LLB, Yale U., 1951. Bar: N.Y. 1952, Conn. 1954. Assoc. Davis Polk & Wardwell, N.Y.C., 1951-53; ptnr. Cummings & Lockwood, Stamford, Conn., 1954-79; judge U.S. Dist. Ct., Bridgeport, Conn., 1979—. Editor-in-chief Products Liability Law Jour., 1988-93. Mem. ABA, Am. Judicature Soc., Am. Bar Found., Am. Law Inst., Conn. Bar Assn., Fed. Bar Coun., Fed. Bar Assn., Ins. Jud. Adminstrn., Jud. Leadership Devel. Coun., Internat. Jud. Acad., Fgn. Policy Assn., Raymond E. Baldwin Am. Inn of Ct. (founder, pres.). Office: US Dist Ct 915 Lafayette Blvd Ste 335 Bridgeport CT 06604-4765

EGLEE, CHARLES HAMILTON, television and movie writer, producer; b. Boston, Nov. 27, 1951; s. Donald Read and Nancy (Hamilton) E.; m. Madeline Dalton, Feb. 29, 1984; children: Blythe Dalton, Eli Hamilton. BA in English, Yale U., 1974. Teaching asst. Yale U., New Haven, 1976; producer, writer for film Deadly Eyes Warner Bros., L.A., 1982; story editor for TV series St. Elsewhere MTM Prodns., Studio City, Calif., 1984-86; exec. story cons. for TV series Moonlighting ABC Circle Films, L.A., 1986-87, producer for TV series Moonlighting, 1987-89; exec. producer 20th Century Fox TV, 1989-91; writer, co-exec. producer "Civil Wars" Steven Bochco Prodns., 1991-93; writer L.A. Law, 1992; co-creator, exec. producer The Byrds of Paradise (Steven Bochco Prodns.), 1993-94; co-exec. producer N.Y.P.D. Blue (Steven Bochco Prodns.), 1994-95; co-creator, exec. prodr. Murder One (Steven Bochco Prodns.), 1995 97, Total Security (Steven Bochco Prodns.), 1997-98; co-creator, exec. prodr. TV series Dark Angel Cameron-Eglee Prodns., 1999—2002; cons. prodr. The Shield, FX, 2003—04. Story editor (St. Elsewhere episode) Bye George, 1985 (Humanitas prize); co-writer (St. Elsewhere episode) Haunted, 1986 (Emmy nomination, Salute to Excellence Award nominee NAACP 1986), (Moonlighting episode) I Am Curious. Maddie, 1987 (Emmy nomination), N.Y.P.D. Blue, 1994 (Emmy award for best drama), Murder One, 1996 (People's Choice award for best new drama, Emmy nomination, best writing in one hour drama, pilot episode 1996, Golden Globe nomination 1996, best fgn. drama Brit. Acad. Film and TV, 1996), Dark Angel, 2001 (People's Choice award for best new drama 2001). Nominee Best Drama award Writers Guild Am., 1996. Mem. Acad. TV Arts and Scis., Writers Guild Am., Yale U. Alumni Fund, Mory's Assn. (New Haven). Democrat. Avocations: sailing, skiing, Am. art pottery, gardening.

EGLEY, THOMAS ARTHUR, computer services executive, accountant; b. Aberdeen, S.D., June 23, 1945; s. Ralph Joseph and Cora Ellen (Wade) E.; m. Cecelia K. Kuskie, Feb. 22, 1985. BBA, U. Mont., 1967, postgrad., 1973-75. CPA, Mont. Programmer, analyst Comml. Data, Missoula, Mont., 1973-77; data processing mgr. John R. Daily, Inc., Missoula, 1977-78; ptnr. Egley & White CPA's, Missoula, 1978-84, Egley & White Computer Services, Missoula, 1978-85; pres. Able Fin., Inc., Missoula, 1984—, PC Software, Inc., 1987—, E & W Computer Services, Inc., 1983—; owner Bitterroot Stables, LLC, 1994—, Homeland Security Inst., LLC, 2002—. Lectr., Missoula, 1973—. Bd. dirs. Missoula Children's Theater, 1975-82. Served to sgt. U.S. Army, 1968-71. Mem. Am. Inst. CPAs, Mont. Soc. CPAs, Phi Sigma Kappa Alumni Club (pres. 1973—). Lodges: Elks. Republican. Lutheran. Avocations: fishing, photography, travel. Home and Office: E&W Computer Svcs Inc PO Box 1180 Florence MT 59833-1180

EGLIT, HOWARD CHARLES, educator, lawyer, arbitrator; b. Chgo., Sept. 20, 1942; s. Nathan Norman and Grace (Wiener) E.; m. Barbara Weiner, July 1, 1973; children: Daniel, Michael, Susan. BA, U. Mich., 1963, JD, 1967. Bar: Ill. 1967, D.C. 1971, U.S. Dist. Ct. (no. dist.) Ill. 1973, U.S. Ct. Appeals (7th cir.) 1973, U.S. Supreme Ct. 1973. With office of gen. counsel U.S. Office Econ. Opportunity, Washington, 1968-69; legis. asst. rep. William F. Ryan, Washington, 1969-71; counsel Com. on Judiciary, U.S. Ho. of Reps., Washington, 1971-73; legal dir. ACLU, Chgo., 1973-75; prof. Ill. Inst. Tech./Chgo.-Kent Coll. Law, 1975—; dir. Nat. Conf. on Constl. and Legal Issues Relating to Age Discrimination, Chgo., 1981; mem. bd. dirs. Buehler Ctr. on Aging, Mcgaw Sch. Medicine, Northwestern Univ., 1991—. Author: Age Discrimination, vols. 1-4, 1982, ann. supplements 1983—, 2d edit., 1994. Contbr. articles to profl. jours. Order of Coif, Phi Beta Kappa, Phi Kappa Phi. Office: Ill Inst Tech Chgo Kent Coll Law 565 W Adams St Chicago IL 60661-3613 E-mail: heglit@kentlaw.edu.

EGLOFF, FRED ROBERT, manufacturers representative, writer, historian; b. Evanston, Ill., Nov. 30, 1934; s. Edward Gottfried and Pearl Elizabeth (Fischrupp) E.; m. Sharon Lee Geyer, June 30, 1962. BS in Commerce, Loyola U., 1956. Asst. adv. mgr. The Englander Co., Chgo., 1956-57; indsl. film svc. Accurate Cinema Svc., Chgo., 1960-62; indsl. sales The EMF Co., Chgo., 1962-69, Avery Internat., Azusa, Calif., 1969-77, The Stanley Works, Hartford, Conn., 1977-78; mfg. rep. ARTCO, Chgo., 1979-99. V.p., bd. dirs. Westerners Internat., Oklahoma City, 1982-2002, pres. 1997-99; cons. ALA, Chgo., 1982-2002; tchr. New Trier Extension, Wilmette, Ill., 1985—; adv. bd. Western Outlaw-Lawman History Assn., 1999—. Author: El Paso Lawman, 1982; editor Westerners Brand Book, 1986-96. Bd. dirs. Wilmette Hist. Soc., 1973-77; hist. cons. Wilmette Hist. Mus., 1978; com. mem. Save the Depot Preservation, Wilmette, 1974; sec. Wilmette Sailing Assn., 1974; vis. com. D'Arcy McNickle Ctr. for Am. Indian History, Newberry Libr., 1999-02. Recipient Don Russell Meml. award, 1998, Wola award for most outstanding contbns. to western history, 1999. Mem. Western History Assn., Western Writers Am., Soc. Midland Authors, Chgo. Corral the Westerners (sheriff 1978-80, sidewinder 1984), Windy City BMW Car Club Am. (pres. 1976, Big Wheel 1972, Founders Recognition award 1997), Vintage Sportscar Club (sec. 1972-80, top competitor award 1970, 97), Nat. Cowboy Hall Fame, Soc. of Automotive Historians, Am. Legion. Republican. Roman Catholic. Avocations: vintage sports cars, photography, skiing, horseback riding, books. Office: ARTCO 2035 Greenwood Ave Wilmette IL 60091-1439

EGNER, JOHN DAVID, electrical engineer; b. New Castle, Pa., June 30, 1957; s. John David Enger and Ann Irene (Nevin) Parta; m. Ann E. Willgrube, Dec. 21, 2001; 1 child, Travis J. BS in Elec. Engring., U. Vt., 1979. Devel. engr. Hewlett-Packard Co., Sunnyvale, Calif., 1979—82, Apple Computer, Inc., Cupertino, Calif., 1982—86; analog engr. Next Computer, Inc., Redwood City, Calif., 1986—93; compliance engring. mgr. Fire Power Sys., Inc., Menlo Park, Calif., 1993—96; sr. sys. engr. Microsoft, Inc., Redmond, Wash., 1996—. Mem.: IEEE, Tau Beta Pi. Home: 22109 NE 27th Pl Sammamish WA 98074 Office: Microsoft Inc One Microsoft Way Redmond WA 98052-6399 E-mail: degner@microsoft.com.

EGNOR, JOANNE MCCLELLAN, psychology educator; b. Williamson, W.Va.; d. Ernest Edward and Thelma Isabel (Chafin) McC.; children: Michael Edward, Sherry Beth, William Mark. BS in Psychology, U. North Fla., 1987; MS in Mental Health Counseling, Nova U., 1992. Adj. prof. psychology and human growth and devel. Fla. C.C., Jacksonville. Mem. adv. com. Clay County Health and Human Svcs., Orange Park, Fla., 1996-98; mem. adv. coun. Calvary United Meth., Orange Park, 1996—; presenter in field. Author (booklet) AAD Doesn't ADD UP, 1996, Crispy Piffles, Thirty Years at a Two Year College, 2000. Stalker Alert, 2003; author, pub.: Care and Feeding of the Chronologically Gifted (Older) Brain, 1999; contbr., pub. (monthly newsletter) FCCJ FACC Facts, 1996-98. Princess Ct. of Queen Sylvia, Mountain State Forest Festival; bd. dirs. Quigley Ho. Shelter Abused Women. Mem. DAR (chair Constitution Week Jacksonville chpt. 1999—, treas. Jacksonville chpt. 2000-2002), Fla. Assn. C.C's (rep., sec. Learning Resources Commn. 1998—, pub., editor FCCJ chpt. newsletter 1996-98, 99—, winner career employees commn. writing contest 1997, chair instnl. effectiveness 1999—), Marshall U. Alumni Assn., U. North Fla. Alumni Assn., Nova U. Alumni Assn., Cummer Mus. (Jacksonville), Nat. Soc. DAR (rec. sec. Jacksonville chpt. 1998—, chair Constitution Week 1999—), Sigma Kappa.

EGOLF, JAMES EDWARD, history educator, secondary school educator; b. Lewistown, Pa. s. John LeRoy and Anna Barbara E.; m. Aileen Janice, June 6, 1966 (div. Feb. 1982) ; children: James E. Jr., Sonya L. Jordan; m. Dolores T. Starnes, Nov. 13, 1984. BEd, Clarion State Coll., 1966; MA, Duquesne U., 1970. Cert. secondary sch. tchr., Fla. Grad. tchg. asst. Duquesne U., Pitts., 1967-69; instr. history South Coll. (Patrick Henry), Monroeville, Ala., 1975-83; tchr. Christian Bros., Kansas City, Mo., 1983-84; tchr. history Okeechobee (Fla.) High Sch., 1990—; instr. history Indian River C.C., Ft. Pierce and Okeechobee, Fla., 1986—. Mem. Kiwanis (adv. Key Club 1990-95, 99—, 5-yr. plaque 1995). Home: 9730 NE 16th St Okeechobee FL 34974-8268 Office: Indian River C C 2229 NW 9th Ave Okeechobee FL 34972-4342

EGOYAN, ATOM, film director; b. Cairo, July 19, 1960; arrived in Can., 1962; s. Joseph and Shushan (Devletian) E.; m. Arsinee Khanjian; 1 child, Arshile. BA in Internat. Rels. with honours, U. Toronto, Ont., Can., 1982; Phd (hon.), Trinity Coll., U. Toronto and U. Victoria. Dir. Ego Film Arts, Toronto, 1982—. Films shown at internat. film festivals of Sydney, Birmingham, Melbourne, Valladolid, Picadilly, Cleve., Berlin, Hong Kong, Locarno, Melbourne, Jerusalem, London, LA, Miami, Turin, Cairo, Antwerp, Montreal, Uppsala, Ghent, Chgo., Chgo., Sao Paulo, NYC, Edinburgh, San Francisco, Rotterdam, also others. Writer, dir., prodr. (feature films) Next of Kin, 1984 (Gold Ducat award Mannheim Internat. Film Week 1984), Family Viewing, 1987 (Internat. Critics award 1988, Best Feature Film award Uppsala, Priz Alcan, Festival du Nouveau Cinema, Montreal), Speaking Parts, 1989 (best screenplay prize Vancouver Internat. Film Festival), The Adjuster, 1991 (spl. prize of jury Moscow Film Festival, Golden Spike award Valladolid Film Festival), Calendar, 1993 (prix Berlin Internat. Film Festival), Exotica, 1994 (Internat. Film Critics award Cannes Film Festival 1994, Prix de la Critique award for best foreign film 1994, Acad. award nominee), Salome Canadian Opera Co., 1996, 2002, Houston Grand Opera, 1997, The Sweet Hereafter, 1997 (Grand Prix, Internat. Critics prize Cannes Film Festival 1997, Acad. award nominee), Elsewhereless, 1998, Dr. Ox's Experiment, 1998, Felicia's Journey, 1999, Ararat, 2002, Special Recognition for freedom of Expression, Nat. Bd. of review, 2002; Genie for Best Motion Picture, Acad. of Can. cinema and TV, 2002; Samuel Beckett's Krapp's Last Tape, 2000. Recipient Officer Order Can., other numerous awards and nominations for awards. Avocation: classical guitar. Office: Ego Film Arts 80 Niagara St Toronto ON Canada M5V 1C5 E-mail: questions@egofilmarts.com.

EGSMOSE, RAGNA KOPP, cultural sociologist, researcher; b. Copenhagen, Apr. 24, 1924; d. Jorgen and Else Margrethe (Rump) Holm-Jorgensen; m. Tage Egsmose; children: Lisbeth, Charlotte, Mark. RN, Bispebjerg Hosp., Denmark, 1947; BS, Minn. U., 1952; BA, Copenhagen U., 1975, MA, 1987. Pub. health nurse Danish Red Cross, Germany, 1948; escort nurse Internat. Refugee Org., Italy and Australia, 1949-50; health instr. UNICEF, Ecuador, 1950-51; tuberculosis rschr. WHO, Asian countries, 1953-55; pvt. health worker Kenya, Nigeria, 1958—67; rsch. advisor WHO, Denmark, 1976-77; educator Muslim youth Copenhagen Coun. Youth Edn., Denmark, 1977-86; rschr. Ctr. for Devel. Rsch., Denmark, 1987-92; semi-ret., 1994—. Rsch. cons. Copenhagen U., 1970-72; rsch. assoc. Nairobi U., Kenya, 1989-92, Kenyatta U., 1980-82; conf. spkr. Free U., Holland, 1992, Internat. Assn. Devel. Rsch., Norway, 1983. Contbr. articles to profl. jours. including Women & Agrl. Prodn. Grantee Danish Agy. Devel. Aid. 1980-89, Nordic Africa Inst., Sweden, 1984, 88, 92. Mem. Danish Assn. Master's and PhDs, Nordic Assn. for the Study of Edn. in Developing Countries, Nordic Youth Rsch. Avocations: painting, travel, reading, swimming, art museums. Home: Klockersvej 23 2820 Gentofte Denmark E-mail: R.Kopp@Ofir.dk.

EGUCHI, YASU, artist; b. Japan, Nov. 30, 1938; came to U.S., 1967; s. Chihaku and Kiku (Koga) E.; m. Anita Phillips, Feb. 24, 1968. Student, Horie Art Acad., Japan, 1958-65. Exhibited exhbns., Tokyo Mus. Art, 1963, 66, Santa Barbara Mus. Art, Calif., 1972-74, 85, Everson Mus. Art, Syracuse, N.Y., 1980, Nat. Acad. Art, N.Y.C., 1980—; one-man shows include Austin Gallery, Scottsdale, Ariz., 1968-87, Joy Tash Gallery, Scottsdale, 1989-99, Greystone Galleries, Cambria, Calif., 1969, 70, 72, Copenhagen Galleries, Calif., 1970-78, Charles and Emma Frye Art Mus., Seattle, 1974, 84, 98, Hammer Galleries, N.Y.C., 1977, 79, 81, 93, 2001, 2002, City of Heidenheim, Germany, 1980, Artique Ltd., Anchorage, 1981—, Heidenheim Mus. Art, 2000; pub. and pvt. collections, Voith Gmbh, Germany, City of Giengen and City of Heidenheim, Germany, represented, Deer Valley, Utah, Hunter Resources, Santa Barbara, Am. Embassy, Paris, Charles and Emma Frye Art Mus., Seattle, Nat. Acad. Art; author: Der Brenz Entlang, 1980; author: Yasu Eguchi, Kunstmuseum Heidenheim, 2000; contbr. to jours in field. Active Guide Dogs for the Blind, San Raphael, Calif., 1976, City of Santa Barbara Arts Coun., 1979, The Eye Bank for Sight Restoration, NY, 1981, Anchorage Arts Coun., 1981, Santa Barbara Mus. Natural History, 1989, Kinder & Kunst Artist Projecti, Heidenheim. Recipient Selective Artist award Yokohama Citizen Gallery, 1965; recipient Artist of Yr. award Santa Barbara Arts Council, 1979, Hon. Citizen award City of Heidenheim, 1980, The Adolph and Clara Obrig prize NAD, 1983, Cert. of Merit NAD, 1985, 87. Home: PO Box 30206 Santa Barbara CA 93130-0206

EGYUD, RALPH DAVID, JR., music educator; b. Dayton, Ohio, July 26, 1954; s. Ralph David and Doris Jane Egyud; m. Susan Jane Christopher, June 12, 1976; children: David, Rebecca. BA in Music, SUNY, Stony Brook, 1976. Cert. tchr. Pa. Music tchr. Conneaut Lake H.S., Pa., 1993—. Worship leader Ch. of the Firstborn, Internat., Conneaut Lake, 1981—. Composer: (various worship songs and cantatas) By His Stripes, Carry Me Away, 2002. Former overseer Crawford County Pomona Grange; former state dep. Pa. State Grange; former coach Little League; founder, dir. Christian Choir of the Lakes, 1991—98; mem. Lakeland String Quartet, 1996—; chmn. Zoning Hearing Bd., Conneaut Lake, 1995—. Mem.: Pa. Music Educators Assn., Kiwanis (pres. 2001—). Democrat. Avocations: harp & bowl praise and intercession, travel, auctions. Home: PO Box 319 Conneaut Lake PA 16316 Personal E-mail: rsegyud@toolcity.net. E-mail: regyud@conneaut.iu5.org.

EHDE, AVA LOUISE, librarian, educator; b. Buffalo, Feb. 11, 1963; d. Louise and Robert Andrew Kinn(Stepfather), Henry Emil Nonnenberg. BA in History and German, SUNY, Buffalo, 1995, MLS, 1997. Cert. pub. libr. N.Y. Intern libr. Niagara Falls (N.Y.) Pub. Libr., 1996—97, local history libr., 1997—98; reference libr. Trocaire Coll., Buffalo, 1998—99, libr. dir., 1999; libr. Buffalo & Erie County Pub. Libr., 1999—2002; head reference, sys. coord. D'Youville Coll. Libr., Buffalo, 1999—2002; adj. faculty SUNY Sch. Informatics, Buffalo, 2001—; adult svcs. reference libr. Manatee County Pub. Libr. Sys., Bradenton, Fla., 2002—. Co-chair Western N.Y. Reference Discussion Group, Buffalo, 2000—02; mem. Regional Automation Com., Buffalo, 2000—02. Co-author (workshop): Networking and Operating Systems for Librarians, 2001—. Reader Niagara Frontier Radio Reading Svc., Cheektowaga, NY, 1999—2002. Named Alberta Riggs Meml. scholar, Sch. Info. and Libr. Studies, 1997; recipient Dr. Marie Ross Wolcott Meml. award, 1997; grantee, NYLA Reference and Adult Svcs. Sect. Continuing Edn., 2002; Profl. Devel. grant, Western N.Y. Libr. Resources Coun., 2001—02. Mem.: AAUP (v.p., exec. com. 2001—02), ALA, Assn. Coll. and Rsch. Librs., Libr. and Info. Tech. Assn., Beta Phi Mu. Avocations: bicycling, hiking, reading, scuba diving, cooking. Home: 401 Clark Lane Holmes Beach FL 34217 Office: Manatee County Libr Sys Ctrl Libr 1301 Barcarrota Blvd W Bradenton FL 34205 Fax: 941-749-7155. E-mail: librarianava@hotmail.com., ava.ehde@co.manatee.fl.us.

EHINGER, ALBERT LOUIS, JR., securities trader; b. Lansing, Mich., May 20, 1927; s. Albert Louis and Irene B. (Cavanaugh) E.; m. Anita Jean Gay, Feb. 9, 1963; 1 child, Andrew. BA, Mich. State U., 1950; MBA, U. Pa., 1954. Researcher Nat. Bur. Econ. Research, N.Y.C., 1954-55; bond portfolio mgr. Nat. City Bank, Cleve., 1955-57, Chem. Bank, N.Y.C., 1957-61; bond dept. mgr. Parabas Corp., N.Y.C., 1962-64; bond investment officer SwissRe Corp., N.Y.C., 1964-70; bond trader Wood, Struthers & Winthrop, Inc., N.Y.C., 1970-74; mng. ptnr. Albert Ehinger & Ptnrs., N.Y.C., 1974—; sr. ptnr.

Fieldsend, Ehinger & Co., N.Y.C., 1986—. Pres. Albert and Anita Ehinger Found., N.Y.C., 1983—; trustee Robert R. Livingston Masonic Library, N.Y.C., 1987—. Served with USNR, 1945-46. Mem. Money Marketeers N.Y.U. (bd. dirs. 1987—), Soldiers, Sailors and Airmen's Club, Catherine Lorilard Wolfe Art Club (hon. male mem. 1986—), Union Club, St. George's Soc. N.Y., Masons. Episcopalian. Avocations: sailing, art collecting. Home: 444 E 82nd St New York NY 10028-5903 Office: One World Fin Ctr 200 Liberty St New York NY 10281-1003

EHLE, JOHN MARSDEN, JR., writer; b. Asheville, N.C., Dec. 13, 1925; s. John M. and Gladys (Starnes) E.; m. Gail Oliver, Aug. 30, 1952 (div. Apr. 1967); m. Rosemary Harris, Oct. 22, 1967; 1 child, Jennifer Anne. BA, U. N.C., 1949; DFA (hon.), N.C. Sch. Arts, 1981; LHD (hon.), Berea Coll., 1986, U. N.C., Asheville, 1987; DLitt (hon.), U. N.C., Chapel Hill, 1990. Faculty U. N.C., Chapel Hill, 1951-63; spl. asst. to Gov. Terry Sanford, Raleigh, N.C., 1963-64; program officer Ford Found., N.Y.C., 1964-65. Spl. cons. Duke U., 1976-80; co-founder N.C. Gov.'s Sch., N.C. Sch. Arts, N.C. Sch. Sci. and Maths. Author: (novels) Move Over, Mountain, 1957, Kingstree Island, 1959, Lion on the Hearth, 1961, The Land Breakers, 1964, The Road, 1967, Time of Drums, 1970, The Journey of August King, 1971, The Changing of the Guard, 1975, The Winter People, 1981, Last One Home, 1983, The Widows Trial, 1989, (biographies) The Free Men, 1965 (Mayflower Soc. cup), The Survivor, 1968, Shepherd of the Streets, 1960, Dr. Frank, Living with Frank Porter Graham, 1993, (non-fiction) The Cheeses and Wines of England and France, with Notes on Irish Whiskey, 1972, Trail of Tears: The Rise and Fall of the Cherokee Nation, 1988; pub. also in several fgn. countries; (screenplay) The Journey of August King, 1996. Apptd. by Pres. Johnson to White House Group for Domestic Affairs, 1964-66, Nat. Coun. Humanities, 1966-70; mem. exec. com. Nat. Book Com., N.Y.C., 1972-75, N.C. Sch. Arts Found., Winston-Salem, 1970-75; mem. awards commn. State of N.C., 1982-93, Mary Reynolds Babcock Found., Winston-Salem, 1985-89. With AUS, 1944-46. Recipient Walter Raleigh prize for fiction N.C. Dept. Cultural Affairs, 1964, 67, 70, 75, 84, State of N.C. award for Lit., 1972, Gov.'s award for Disting. Meritorious Svc., 1978, Lillian Smith prize Southern Regional Coun., 1982, Disting. Alumnus award U. N.C., Chapel Hill, 1984, Thomas Wolfe Meml. award Western N.C. Hist. Assn., 1984, W.D. Weathertord award Berea Coll., 1985, Caldwell award N.C. Humanities Coun., 1995; named to N.C. Lit. Hall of Fame, 1997. Mem. PEN, Authors League, Century Club (N.Y.C.). Democrat. Methodist. Home: 125 Westview Dr NW Winston Salem NC 27104

EHLEN, TIMOTHY JOHN, music educator, musician; b. Boston, Oct. 16, 1962; s. Arlis John and Dayna Leah Ehlen. MusB, U. So. Calif., 1985, MMus, 1987; DMA, Cleve. Inst. of Music-Case Western Res. U., 1999. Instr. of piano Cleve. Inst. of Music, 1996—97, Youngstown St. U., Ohio, 1996—99; vis. asst. prof. piano Kent St. U., Ohio, 1997—99; asst. prof. of piano U. of Okla., Norman, 1999—2001, U. of Ill., Champaign-Urbana, 2001—. Performances heard on Nat. Publ. Radio, WFUZ, NYC, WXXI, Rochester, WFMT, Chgo., WGVC, Cin., KUSC and KMZT, LA; internat. jury World Piano Competition, Cin., 1998-99, adjudicator for numerous competitions; Recordings on the Crystal, Nemus, and Felia Mundi labels. Musician: (performance) solo recital in Weill Hall at Carnegie Hall, 1997, solo recital debut Alice Tully Hall Lincoln Ctr., 1988, (performances) Internat. Franz Liszt Festival in Munster, France; Stadtteater in Fuerth, Germany; the festival Rencontres Internat. de Piano en Alsace. Recipient Gold medal, Am. Music Scholarship Assn., 1987. Mem.: Music Teachers Nat. Assn., Coll. Music Soc. Avocation: FAA licenced private pilot, piano tuning and temperaments, chess. Home: 1506 Maywood Dr Champaign IL 61821 Office: U Ill Music Bldg 1114 W Nevada Urbana IL 61801 Business E-Mail: tehlen@uiuc.edu.

EHLERMAN, PAUL MICHAEL, motorcycle and recreational batteries manufacturing company executive; b. Montgomery, Ala., 1938; BBA, U. Notre Dame, 1960. With GE, 1960-65, U.S. Gypsum, Chgo., 1965-68, Northwest, Inc., Chgo., 1968-75, Gen. Battery, Exide Corp., Reading, Pa., 1975-91; vice chmn., CEO Yuasa, Inc., Reading, 1991-2000; chmn., CEO Yuasa Battery, Inc., 2000—. Mem. exec. com., bd. dirs. Greater Berks Devel. Fund; bd. dirs. Sovereign Bancorp and Sovereign Bank; mem. Berks Econ. Partnership Bd., Our City Reading Bd. Bd. dirs., chmn. Berks County Conv. Ctr. Authority; bd. dirs. Reading Hosp. and Med. Ctr., Berks County Cmty. Found. Office: Yuasa Battery Inc PO Box 14715 Reading PA 19612-4715

EHLERS, DEBORAH LAYNE, educator, dramaturg, director; b. Lincoln, Nebr., Dec. 29, 1950; d. Joseph Buddy Plessel and Ellen Janet (McDonald) Lesoing; m. Christian H. Ehlers, Apr. 7, 1973; children: Jeff, Matt, Brian, Zack. BA, Nebr. Wesleyan U., 1973; MA, U. Nebr., 1987, PhD, 1995. Instr. U. Northern Iowa, Cedar Falls, 1988; grad. tchr. asst. U. Nebr., Lincoln, 1986-92, adj. instr., 1993-96, dir. theatre camp, 1995-97; dir. theatre, asst. prof. Bethany (W.Va.) Coll., 1997—2001, Bacone Coll., Okla., 2001—, chmn. Divsn. Humanities, 2003—. Investigator opera houses Nebr. State Hist. Soc., Lincoln, 1987-88; news letter editor Assn. for Theatre in Higher Edn., 1987-94; festival coord. Region V Kennedy Ctr. Am. Coll. Theater Festival, 1990-91, 94-95, mem. selection com., 1996, 1999-2000, region II preliminaries judge, 1999; focus group conf. planner Playwrights Program, 2003—. Workshop developer A Little Feelgood Magic, 1987; makeup designer A Little Night Music, 1988; playwright Harry's Bar, 1989 (crawford hon. mention); dir. Blind Harassment, 1999, The Futz Theatre, 1996, Muskogee Little Theatre, 2002— (Newcomer of Yr. award 2002-03), Brooke Hills Playhouse, 1999-2000, Inherit The Wind Show of the Yr., 2002-03; editl. adv. bd. Collegiate Press, 1999.; contbr. to articles to profl. jours. Den leader Cub Scouts, 1989; merit badge counselor Boy Scouts, 1994—; children's coord. Calvary United Meth., Lincoln, 1987-91; Saratoga Sch. Parents Orgn. Travel grant rsch. Day Found., U. Nebr., 1990, 91. Mem.: Pi Kappa Delta, Theta Alpha Phi, Alpha Psi Omega. Avocations: trivia, old movies, museums and nat. parks. Home: 219 North P St Muskogee OK 74403 Office: Bacone Coll 214 Barnett 2299 Old Bacone Rd Muskogee OK 74403

EHLERS, KATHRYN HAWES (MRS. JAMES D. GABLER), physician; b. Richmond Hill, N.Y., Aug. 22, 1931; d. Albert and Edna (Hawes) E.; m. James D. Gabler, Dec. 5, 1959; children— Jennifer K., Emily E. AB, Bryn Mawr Coll., 1953; MD, Cornell U.; MD (Hannah E. Longshore Meml. Med. scholar 1953-57, Elsie Strang L'Esperance scholar 1956-57), 1957. Diplomate: Am. Bd. Pediatrics, Am. Bd. Pediatric Cardiology. Intern N.Y. Hosp., 1957-58, asst. resident pediatrics, 1958-60; fellow in pediatric cardiology Cornell U. Med. Coll., N.Y.C., 1960-64, instr. pediatrics, 1964-66, asst. prof., 1966-70, asso. prof. pediatrics, 1970-75, prof., 1975-96, prof. emeritus, 1996—, vice-chmn. pediat., 1988-96; practice medicine specializing in pediat. cardiology N.Y.C., 1958-96. Contbr. articles to profl. jours. Research trainee N.Y. Heart Assn., 1960-62, Am. Heart Assn., 1962-64. Fellow Am. Coll. Cardiology; mem. N.Y. Heart Assn., Am. Heart Assn., Harvey Soc., Am. Pediatric Soc., Am. Acad. Pediatrics, Alpha Omega Alpha. Home: 1035 Park Ave New York NY 10028-0912

EHLERS, VERNON JAMES, congressman; b. Pipestone, Minn., Feb. 6, 1934; m. Johanna Meulink, 1958; children: Heidi, Brian, Marla, Todd. Student, Calvin Coll.; AB, U. Calif., Berkeley, 1956, PhD in Physics, 1960. Tchg. asst. U. Calif., Berkeley, 1956-57, rsch. asst., 1957-60, lectr. in physics, 1960-66; prof. physics Calvin Coll., 1966-83; mem. Mich. State Ho. of Reps., 1983-85, Mich. State Senate, 1985-94, pres. pro tem, 1991-94; mem. U.S. Congress from 3d Mich. dist., 1994—; chmn. Joint Com. Libr. Congress; mem. transp. and infrastructure com., sci. com., edn. and workforce com., house adminstrn. com. Mem. Gov. Milliken's Task Force on Environ. Problems, 1977, Kent County Rep. Exec. Com., Kent County Bd. Commrs., 1975-83, chmn., 1979-82, Mich. Toxic Substance Control Commn., 1982; asst. floor leader Mich. State Ho. of Reps., 1983-85 Contbr. articles to profl. jours. NATO Rsch. fellow U. Heidelberg, Germany, 1961-62, Sci. Faculty fellow NSF, Joint Insts. for Lab. Astrophysics, U. Colo. 1971-72, fellow Calvin Coll. Ctr. for Christian Scholar, 1977-78. Mem. AAAS, Am. Phys. Soc., Am. Assn. Phys. Tchrs. Mem. Christian Reformed Ch. Home: 1848 Morningside Dr SE Grand Rapids MI 49506-5121 Office: 1714 Longworth House Ofc Bldg Washington DC 20515-2203 also: Federal Bldg 110 Michigan St Grand Rapids MI 49503-2313*

EHLINGER, RALPH JEROME, lawyer; b. Oconto, Wis., Mar. 22, 1941; s. Jerome Nicholas and Margaret Ann (Otradovec) E.; m. Nancy L. McKinley, Dec. 26, 1966 (div. Oct. 1986); children: Nicholas Joseph, Martha Johanna; m. Mary Verstegen, Sept. 25, 1987; children: Autumn V., Andrea V., Jessa V., Jenna V. BA in Philosophy, St. Paul Sem., 1963; JD, Georgetown U., 1968. Bar: Wis. 1968, U.S. Dist. Ct. (ea. dist.) Wis. 1969, U.S. Dist. Ct. (we. dist.) Wis. 1977, U.S. Ct. Appeals (7th cir.) 1983, U.S. Supreme Ct. 1986, D.C. 1988, U.S. Ct. Appeals (4th cir.) 1988. Ptnr. Meissner, Tierney, Ehlinger & Whipp, Milw., 1968-86; pvt. practice Milw., 1986-87; counsel Casson, Harkins & LaPallo, Washington, 1987-88; pres. Ehlinger & Krill, SC, Milw., 1988-99, Ehlinger Law Office, Milw., 2000—; adj. prof. law Marquette U. Law Sch., 1999—. Dir. Milw. Bar Assn., 1990-93. Articles editor: The Georgetown Law Jour., 1967-68 (Outstanding Editor 1968); editor-in-chief: The Milwaukee Lawyer, 1982-84. Trustee Wis. Sch. Profl. Psychology, Milw., 1990-93; bd. pres. Grand Ave Club, Milw., 1990-92, Mental Health Assn., Milw., 1992-93; dir. Centro Legal Por Derechos Humanos, 1996-2001; mem. planning commn. Town of Richfield, 2002—. Mem. Am. Judicature Soc., Milw. Bar Assn. Found. (pres. 1994-97), Nordic Ski Club (life), Milw. Bar Assn. (Lawyer of Yr. award 1997). Democrat. Roman Catholic. Avocations: instrumental and vocal music, cross-country skiing, backpacking, canoeing, poetry. Office: Ehlinger Law Office W175 N 11117 Stonewood Dr Germantown WI 53022 E-mail: ehlinger@execpc.com.

EHLKE, BRUCE FREDERIC, lawyer; b. Two Rivers, Wis., Aug. 31, 1942; s. Roland W. and Mary E. (Mueller) E.; m. Darlene Carol Erickson (div.); children— Stephen, Kara, Christopher; m. Jacqualine Caren Andersen, Aug. 20, 1977; 1 son, John. BA, U. Wis.-Milw., 1965; JD, U. Wis., 1968. Bar: Wis. 1968, U.S. Dist. Ct. (we. dist.) Wis. 1968, U.S. Dist. Ct. (ea. dist.) Wis. 1971, U.S. Tax Ct. 1978, U.S. Ct. Appeals (7th cir.) 1971, U.S. Ct. Appeals (fed. cir.) 2002, U.S. Supreme Ct. 1979, U.S. Ct. Vets. Appeals 1993. With Wis. Local Affairs and Devel. Dept., Madison, 1968; shareholder Lawton & Cates, S.C., Madison, 1968-94; ptnr. Shneidman, Myers, Dowling, Blumenfield, Ehlke, Hawks & Domer, Madison, 1995-2001; shareholder Shneidman, Hawks & Ehlke, SC, 2001—. Mem. Wis. State Bar, Wis. Acad. Trial Lawyers, Dane County Bar Assn. (pres. 1995-96). Lutheran. Home: 605 Hilltop Dr Madison WI 53711-1358 Office: Shneidman Hawks & Ehlke SC PO Box 2155 Madison WI 53701-2155

EHMANN, ANTHONY VALENTINE, lawyer; b. Chgo., Sept. 5, 1935; s. Anthony E. and Frances (Verweil) E.; m. Alice A. Avina, Nov. 27, 1959; children: Ann, Thomas, Jerome, Gregory, Rose, Robert. BS, Ariz. State U., 1957; JD, U. Ariz., 1960. Bar: Ariz. 1960, U.S. Tax Ct. 1960, U.S. Supreme Ct. 1968; CPA, Ariz.; cert. tax specialist, trusts and estates specialist. Spl. asst. atty. gen., 1961-68; mem. Ehmann and Hiller, Phoenix, 1969—. Rep. dist. chmn. Ariz., 1964; pres. Grand Canyon coun. Boy Scouts Am., 1987-89, mem. exec. com., 1981—, v.p. western region, 1991-99; bd. dirs. Nat. Cath. Com. on Scouting, 1995—. Recipient Silver Beaver award Boy Scouts Am., 1982, Bronze Pelican award Cath. Com. on Scouting, 1981, Silver Antelope award Boy Scouts Am., 1994. Fellow Am. Coll. Trusts and Estate Counsel; mem. State Bar Ariz. (chmn. tax sect. 1968, 69), Ctrl. Ariz. Estate Planning Coun. (pres. 1968, 69), KC (grand knight Glendale, Ariz. 1964, 65), Serra Internat. (pres. Phoenix 1992-93, dist. gov. ariz. 1993-95), Knight of Holy Sepulchre, Knight of Malta, Legatus. Republican. Roman Catholic. Office: Ehmann & Hiller 2525 E Camelback Rd Ste 720 Phoenix AZ 85016-4229 E-mail: ehmann@ehpclaw.com.

EHMANN, NANCY GALLAGHER, civic worker; b. Milw., Mar. 29, 1932; d. Edwin John and Adelaide (Erwin) Gallagher; m. William Donald Ehmann, July 16, 1955; children: William James, John Michael, James Thomas, Kathleen Elizabeth. BS in Elem. Edn., Edgewood Coll., Madison, Wis., 1954. Elem. tchr. Lincoln Sch., West Allis, Wis., 1954-55, Colfax Sch., Pitts., 1955; kindergarten tchr. Mother Goose Nursery Sch., Pitts., 1956-57; substitute tchr. Joliet (Ill.) Pub. Schs., 1957-58, Sayre Elem. Sch., Lexington, Ky., 1958-59. Coord. Meals on Wheels, Lexington, 1982—; tutor Operation Read, Lexington, 1988-93; sec. Fayette County Commn. on Aging, Lexington, 1985-87; precinct capt. Lexington Rep. Com.; vol. usher U. Ky. Fine Arts Ctr., 1980-85; mem. Cardinal Hill Hosp. Aux. Recipient Outstanding Vol. of Yr. award in Fayette County, Vol. Action Ctr., 1987. Mem. Nat. Assn. Meals on Wheels Programs (state rep.), Cen. Ky. Assn. Vol. Adminstrs. (sec. 1985-87, treas. 1987-88), Lexington Woman's Club (scholarship chmn. 1982-86, chmn. pub. affairs dept. 1982-86), U. Ky. Woman's Club. Roman Catholic. Avocations: reading, needlework, travel. Home: 769 Zandale Dr Lexington KY 40502-3371 Office: Meals on Wheels 1530 Nicholasville Rd Lexington KY 40503-1435

EHNTHOLT, DANIEL JAMES, chemist; b. Manchester, N.H., Sept. 19, 1945; s. Daniel James Dolores (Donohue) E.; m. Eileen Marie Dunne, Aug. 14, 1971; children: Kimberly, Amy, Christopher. BS, Fordham U., 1966; PhD, SUNY, Stony Brook, 1971. Postdoctoral fellow Brandeis U., Waltham, Mass., 1971-72; asst. prof. Boston U., 1972-77, Worcester (Mass.) State Coll., 1977-78; cons. Arthur D. Little, Inc., Cambridge, Mass., 1978-84, unit mgr., 1984-91, v.p., 1991—2002; dir. Nat. Security Programs, TIAX, LLC, Cambridge, Mass., 2002—. Contbr. articles to profl. jours. Commr. Conservation Commn., Hudson, Mass., 1974-79; mem. Bd. Health, Hudson, 1981-88, 91—, chmn. 1995-98, 2000—. N.Y. State Regents fellow, 1962-70, German Acad. Exchange fellow Max Planck Inst., Mülheim an der Ruhr, 1974. Mem. ACS (Petroleum Rsch. fellow 1970), Am. Inst. Chemists, Nat. Sci. Tchrs. Assn., Phi Lambda Upsilon. Roman Catholic. Office: TIAX LLC 15 Acorn Park Cambridge MA 02140-2301 E-mail: ehntholt.d@tiax.biz.

EHREN, CHARLES ALEXANDER, JR., lawyer, educator; b. N.Y.C., Dec. 13, 1932; s. Charles Alexander and Alma Elise (Holmstrom) E.; m. Joan Anne Bansemer, Sept. 4, 1954. AB, Columbia U., 1954, JD, 1956. Bar: N.Y. bar 1956. Asso. firm LeBoeuf, Lamb and Leiby, N.Y.C., 1958-67; Reginald Heber Smith fellow U. Pa. Sch. Law at Legal Aid Soc. of Westchester County (N.Y.), White Plains, 1967-68, dir. soc., 1975-77; dir. curriculum Nat. Inst. Edn. in Law and Poverty, Northwestern U., 1968-70; asso. prof. law U. Denver, 1970-74, prof., 1974-75; dean, prof. Pace U. Sch. Law, 1975-76; vis. scholar Columbia U. Sch. Law, 1976-77; dean Valparaiso U. Sch. Law, 1977-82, prof., 1977-96, prof. emeritus, 1996—. Trustee Ind. Continuing Legal Edn. Found., Ind. Bar Found., 1977-82; dir. Westchester Legal Services, 1975-77 Author: (with others) Electricity and the Environment, The Reform of Legal Institutions, 1972. Served with U.S. Army, 1956-58. Mem. Ind. State Bar Assn. (ho. of dels. 1977-82), Assn. Bar City N.Y. (exec. dir. spl. com. on electric power and environment 1971-73), ABA, N.Y. State Bar Assn., Fed. Energy Bar Assn., Soc. Am. Law Tchrs. Democrat. Lutheran. Home: 16 High Point Rd East Hampton NY 11937-1059

EHRENBERG, RONALD GORDON, economist, educator; b. N.Y.C., Apr. 20, 1946; s. Seymour and Judith G. E.; m. Randy Ann Birch, June 29, 1967; children: Eric L., Jason H. BA in Math. cum laude, SUNY, Binghamton, 1966; MA, PhD, Northwestern U., 1970. Instr. econs. Northwestern U., Evanston, Ill., 1970; asst. prof. econs. Loyola U., Chgo., 1970-71, U. Mass., Amherst, 1971-72, assoc. prof. econs., 1972-75; assoc. prof. econs. and labor econs. Cornell U., 1975-77, chmn. dept. labor econs., 1976-81, prof. econs. and labor econs., 1977-85; dir. rsch. N.Y. State Sch. Indsl. and Labor Rels., 1979-95; Irving M. Ives prof. indsl. and labor rels. and econs. Cornell U., 1985—, v.p. for acad. programs, planning and budgeting, 1995-98. Rsch. assoc. Nat. Bur. Econ. Rsch., 1981—; dir. Cornell Inst. Labor Mktg. Policies, 1990-98, dir. Cornell Higher Edn. Rsch. Inst., 1998—; staff Coun. Econ. Advisors, 1970; cons. in field. Author: Fringe Benefits and Overtime Behavior: Theory and Econometric Analysis, 1971, The Demand for State and Local Government Employees: An Economic Analysis, 1975, The Regulatory Process and Labor Earnings, 1979, (with R. Smith) Modern Labor Economics: Theory and Public Policy, 1982, 8th edit., 2003, (with others) Economic Challenges in Higher Education, 1991, Labor Markets and Integrating National Economics, 1994, Contemporary Policy Issues in Education, 1995, The American University: National Treasure of Endangered Species, 1997, Gender and Family Issues in the Workplace, 1997, Tuition Rising: Why College Costs So Much, 2000; contbr. articles to profl. jours. Endowment study advisors bd. Nat. Assn. Coll. and Univ. Bus. Officers, 2001—. Rsch. grantee NSF, U.S. Dept. Labor, various pvt. founds.; NDEA fellow, 1969; Woodrow Wilson Nat. Fellowship Found. Dissertation Yr. fellow, 1970. Mem. AAUP (chmn. com. on econ. status of the profession 2002—), Am. Econ. Assn. (exec. com. 1996-98), Indsl. Rels. Rsch. Assn., Am. Fin. Assn., Soc. Labor Economists (pres. 2002), Nat. Acads. (assoc.), Nat. Acad. Edn. Office: Cornell Higher Edn Rsch Inst 256 Ives Hall Ithaca NY 14853-3901 E-mail: rge2@cornell.edu.

EHRENFELD, DAVID WILLIAM, biology educator, writer; b. N.Y.C., Jan. 15, 1938; s. Irving and Anne Ehrenfeld; m. Joan Gardner, June 28, 1970; children: Kate, Jane, Jonathan, Samuel. BA, Harvard Coll., 1959; MD, Harvard Med. Sch., 1963; PhD, U. Fla., 1966. From asst. prof. biology to assoc. prof. biology Barnard Coll. Columbia U., N.Y.C., 1967-74; prof. biology Cook Coll. Rutgers U., New Brunswick, N.J., 1974—. Author: Biological Conservation, 1970, Conserving Life on Earth, 1972, The Arrogance of Humanism, 1978, Beginning Again: People and Nature in the New Millennium, 1993, 1995, Swimming Lessons: Keeping Afloat in the Age of Technology, 2002; founder, editor Conservation Biology, 1987—93, consulting editor, 1994—, bd. editors Ecosys. Health, 1994—, columnist (mag.) Orion, 1989—2002; contbg. editor: (mag.) Orion, 2003—; contbr. articles to profl. and popular publs.; co-author (with C.K. Mack): (novels) The Chameleon Variant, 1980. Trustee E.F. Schumacher Soc., Great Barrington, Mass., 1979-2002, bd. founders, 2003—; bd. trustees Caribbean Conservation Corp., Gainesville, Fla., 1980—, Ednl. Found. Am., Westport, Conn., 1987-93, 98-2002. Fellow AAAS; mem. Ecol. Soc. Am., Internat. Union for the Conservation of Nature, Marine Turtle Specialist Group. Jewish. Home: 44 N 7th Ave Highland Park NJ 08904-2931 Office: Rutgers U Cook Coll New Brunswick NJ 08901-8551

EHRENFELD, ELLIE (ELVERA EHRENFELD), health science association administrator; b. Phila., Mar. 1, 1942; m. Donald F. Summers. BA cum laude, Brandeis U., 1962; PhD in Biochemistry, U. Fla., 1967; postdoctoral student, Albert Einstein Coll. Medicine, 1967—74. Asst. to assoc. prof. dept. cell biology Albert Einstein Coll. Med.; from assoc. prof.to prof. biochemistry and biology U. Utah, 1974—92; dean sch. biol. scis. U. Calif., Irvine, 1992—97; dir. ctr. scientific rev. Dept. Health and Human Svcs., Bethesda, Md., 1997—. Mem. various coms. including rsch. adv. panel Walter Reed Army Inst. Rsch., exptl. virology study sect. NIH; mem. bd. sci. counselors Nat. Inst. Allergy and Infectious Diseases; cons. immunopathology lab. Scripps Inst. Med. Rsch. Recipient Bill Joklik Lectureship award, Am. Soc. Virology; scholar Nat. Sci., Brandeis U. Office: Rockledge II Bldg 6701 Rockledge Dr Rm 3016 Bethesda MD 20892-0001

EHRENFELD, PHYLLIS RHODA, editor, playwright, book reviewer; b. Montreal, Que., Can., Sept. 28, 1932; came to U.S., 1954; d. Carl and Thelma (Azeff) S.; m. Sylvain Ehrenfeld, May 29, 1955; children: David, Temma. BA in Psychology, Sir George Williams Coll., Montreal, 1952; BSW, McGill Sch. of Social Work, Montreal, 1953; postgrad. in lit., Columbia U., 1954-57. Social worker Jewish Family Welfare, Baron de Hirsch Inst., Montreal, 1952-54; tchr., program dir. Jack & Jill Day Care Ctr., Landing, N.J., 1956—; editor-in-chief, sr. editor Am. Anorexia Bulimia Assn. Newsletter, N.Y.C., 1980-93. Playwright five plays; book reviewer No. N.J. NOW Newsletter, 1987-88, New Directions for Women, 1989—; editor, book reviewer: Ethical Culture Review of Books. Publicity chmn. Ethical Culture Soc. of Bergen County, Teaneck, 1987-88, producing artistic dir. The Superfluous Lover, 1996, tchr. adult edn. programs, 1999; drama coord. Garden State Playwrights, Teaneck, 1989-90; UN rep. for Nat. Svc. Conf. Am. Ethical Union, 2001—. Recipient Arnold Gingrich award for Fiction, N.J. State Council on the Arts, 1980-81. Mem. Am. Anorexia Bulimia Assn. (bd. dirs. 1981-89, sec. 1981-87, rec. sec. 1990-91), Inst. for Ethical Edn. (chmn., program com.), Ethical Culture Soc. Bergen County (program chmn. 1992-94, co-chmn. 1997-98, co-chair Inst. Ethical Edn. 2000-2001). Avocations: hiking, gardening. Home: 276 Grove St Teaneck NJ 07666-3214

EHRENFRIED, GEORGE, photographic physicist, educator; b. Boston, Oct. 1, 1913; s. Albert and Grace (Waterman) E. BA, Harvard U., 1935. Photographic chemist Eastman Kodak Co., Rochester, N.Y., 1936-42; electronic physicist MIT Radiation Lab., Cambridge, Mass., 1942-45; photographic physicist Polaroid Corp., Cambridge, Mass., 1946-83; tchr. photography, geology and Icelandic sagas Cambridge Ctr. for Adult Edn., 1948-96. Contbr. articles to profl. jours.; patentee in field. Mem. Cambridge Conservation Commn., 1988-98; bd. dirs. New Eng. Trail Conf., 1978-81; active several local natural-area protection campaigns in eastern Mass. Mem. Photographic Soc. Am., Soc. Imaging Sci. and Tech., Nat. Assn. Geology Tchrs., Optical Soc. Am., Boston Browning Soc., Scandinavian Forum, Appalachian Mountain Club, Genesee Valley Hiking Club, Sub Sig Outing Club, Boston Grotto Caving Club, Boston Camera Club, Boston Mineral Club, Boston Bay Group, Brookline Bird Club, Mosaic Outdoor Mountain Club. Democrat. Jewish. Avocations: hiking, canoeing, nature study, photography, geology. Home: 102 Aberdeen Ave Cambridge MA 02138-4624

EHRENHAFT, PETER DAVID, lawyer; b. Vienna, Aug. 16, 1933; came to U.S., 1940, naturalized, 1945; s. Bruno B. and Ann J. (Polacek) E.; m. Charlotte Kennedy, May 4, 1958; children: Elizabeth Ann, James Bruno, Daniel Parker. AB with honors, Columbia Coll., 1954; LLB, M Internat. Affairs with honors, Columbia U., 1957. Bar: (N.Y.) 1958, (D.C.) 1961. Motions law clk. to U.S. Ct. Appeals (D.C. cir.), 1957—58; sr. law clk. to Chief Justice U.S. Supreme Ct., 1961—62; assoc. Cox, Langford & Brown, Washington, 1962—66, ptnr., 1966—68, Fried, Frank, Harris, Shriver & Kampelman, Washington, 1968—77; dep. asst. sec., spl. counsel tariff affairs U.S. Dept. Treasury, Washington, 1977—79; ptnr. Hughes Hubbard & Reed, Washington, 1980—83, Bryan Cave, Washington, 1984—95; mem. Ablondi, Foster, Sobin & Davidow, P.C., Washington, 1995—2001, Miller & Chevalier, Chartered, Washington, 2001—. Professorial lectr. law George Washington U., 1965-72, U. Pa., 1980-85; mem. faculty Salzburg (Austria) Seminar in Am. Studies Law Session, 1973; mem. Fed. Jud. Ctr. Study Group on Workload of Supreme Ct., 1971-74; mem. adv. com. U.S. Ct. Appeals (fed. cir.), 1992-96; mem. industry sector adv. com. on trade in svcs. Dept. Commerce and U.S. Trade Rep., 1999—. Contbr. articles and revs., primarily on internat. trade, to law jours.; mem. adv. bd. Jour. Law and Policy in Internat. Bus., 1967—, Patent, Trademark and Copyright Jour., 1970—; mem. editl. bd. Internat. Legal Materials, 1977-87. Pres. bd. trustees Nat. Child Rsch. Ctr., Washington, 1976-77; mem. adv. coun. George Washington U. Med. Ctr., 1990-96. With USAF, 1958-61, USAFR, 1962-88; judge Ct. Mil. Rev., 1987-88. Mem.: ABA (mem. coun. internat. law sect. 1983—85, 1989—97, chmn. task force on legal svcs. in Japan 1991—98, liaison to Gen. Agreement on Tariffs and Trade 1992—94, vice chair 1993—94, internat. legal scholar 1994—97, vice chair transnat. practice com. 1998—, commn. on multijurisdictional practice 2000—02), Am. Arbitration Assn. (corp. counsel com. 1993—), Washington Fgn. Law Soc. (bd. govs. 1982—92, pres. 1986—87), Am. Soc. Internat. Law, Am. Law Inst. (mem. various cons. coms.). Home: 2510 Virginia Ave NW Washington DC 20037-1904 Office: Miller & Chevalier Chartered 655 15th St NW Washington DC 20005-5701 E-mail: pehrenhaft@milchev.com.

EHRENKRANTZ, DAVID, medical researcher, researcher; b. New Haven, Aug. 26, 1952; s. Harold Louis and Katherine (Russo) E. BA magna cum laude, U. Hartford, 1979; MSW, Adelphi U., 1982; MPH, N.Y. Med. Coll., 1987; ScD, U. Pitts., 1991. Cert. social worker, N.Y. Rsch. asst. U. Conn. Sch. Medicine, 1985; med. rsch. affiliate Genentech Corp., San Francisco; fellow in psychiatry Mt. Sinai Med. Ctr., N.Y.C., 1996—98; disabilities epidemiologist dept. health State of Kans., Bur. Health Promotion, 1999—2001; asst. rsch. prof. Sch. Medicine U. Kans.; rsch. dir. Logicon ROW Scis., Rockville, Md., 2001—02; maternal and child health epidemiologist State of Maine Bur. of Health, Augusta, 2002—; asst. rsch. prof. dept. applied med. scis. U. So. Maine, 2002—. Rschr. AIDS, Alzheimer's disease. Contbr. rsch. articles on pediat. lead poisoning, endocrine investigation of retardive disorders to sci. jours. Mem. Alpha Chi. Home: 25 2d St Apt 225 Hallowell ME 04347 Office: 11 State House Sta Key Bank Plz 4th Fl Augusta ME 04333-0011

EHRENKRANZ, GIL, lawyer; b. Bklyn., Sept. 27, 1959; s. Louis Richard and Eleanor Ehrenkranz; m. Anne Bial, May 19, 1985; children: Rebecca Carrie, Naomi Rose. BA, Hunter Coll., 1981; JD, Georgetown U., 1984. Assoc. Hiscock & Barclay, Syracuse, NY, 1984-86; staff counsel Deak Internat., Inc., N.Y.C., 1986-88; asst. counsel-cable ops. Cablevision Systems Corp., Woodbury, NY, 1988-93; asst. gen. counsel Cablevision Industries Corp., Liberty, NY, 1993—96; v.p. legal affairs Discovery Comm., Inc., Silver Spring, Md., 1997—. Counsel Sullivan County Shields, Liberty, 1995; recording sec. Congregation Ezras Israel, Rockville, Md., 1998. Recipient Appreciation cert. Sullivan County Shields, 1995. Mem. Fed. Comm. Bar Assn., Am. Corp. Counsel Assn. Office: Discovery Comm Inc One Discovery Pl Silver Spring MD 20910-3354

EHRENKRANZ, JOEL S. lawyer; b. Newark, Mar. 25, 1935; s. George J. and Hilda (Schreiber) E.; m. Anne Bick, June 9, 1963; children: Alissa, John, Jeanne. BS in Econs., U. Pa., 1956, MBA, 1957; LLB, NYU, 1961, LLM in Taxation, 1964. Bar: N.Y. 1961; CPA, N.Y. Acct. Peat, Marwick, Mitchell & Co., N.Y.C., 1957-62; sr. ptnr. Ehrenkranz & Ehrenkranz, N.Y.C., 1962—. Trustee, distbn. com. Fedn. Jewish Philanthropies, N.Y.C., 1979—83, United Jewish Appeal/Fedn. Jewish Philanthropies, N.Y.C., 1982—92, pres., 1987—92; trustee Archives Am. Art, 1973—, pres., 1984—86; trustee Whitney Mus. Am. Art, 1973—, v.p., 1973—, pres., 1998—2002, chmn. investment com., 2000—; trustee NYU Law Sch., 1992—; grad. bd. Wharton Sch. U. Pa., 1985—; trustee, vice chmn., mem. exec. com. Mt. Sinai Med. Ctr., NYC, 1987—92, chmn. fin. budgets and accts. com., 1992—95; trustee NYU, 1998—2001; bd. overseers Calif. Inst. Arts, 2001—. Mem. Century Club (White Plains, N.Y.). Office: 375 Park Ave New York NY 10152-0002 also: Keeler Ln North Salem NY 10560 also: Mayfly Dr Wilson WY 83014

EHRENREICH, HENRY, physicist, educator; b. Frankfurt, Germany, May 11, 1928; came to U.S., 1940, naturalized, 1945; s. Nathan and Frieda (Rosenstein) E.; m. Tema P. Hasnas, Feb. 1, 1953; children: Paul, Beth Herst, Robert. Student, Columbia U., 1950-51; BA, Cornell U., 1950, PhD, 1955; MA (hon.), Harvard U., 1963. Theoretical physicist Gen. Electric Research Lab., Schenectady, N.Y., 1955-63; vis. lectr. Harvard U., 1960-61, Gordon McKay prof. applied physics, 1963-82, Clowes prof. sci., 1982—2001, Clowes rsch. prof., 2001—02; vis. prof. Brandeis U., 1969, U. Paris, 1969, U. Pa., 1976; univ. ombudsman Harvard Univ., Cambridge, Mass., 2002—. Mem. def. scis. rsch. coun. Advanced Rsch. Projects Agy., U.S. Dept. Def., 1972-2002; sec. solid state commn. Internat. Union Pure and Applied Physics, 1978-81; mem. solar photovoltaic energy adv. com. Dept. Energy, 1980-83; dir. Harvard Materials Rsch. Lab., 1982-90; cons. White House Office Sci. and Tech., 1991. Contbr. articles to profl. jours.; bd. editors Phys. Rev. 1965-67; co-editor: Solid State Physics, 1966—; asst. editor Annals of Phys., 1984-2002. Trustee Dibner Inst. for History of Sci. and Tech., 1992-98; cons. Wolf Found., 1997-99. Fellow AAAS, Am. Acad. Arts and Scis., Am. Phys. Soc. (chmn. div. solid state physics 1969, chmn. study group on solar energy 1977-81, chmn. panel on pub. affairs 1990-91); mem. Phi Beta Kappa, Sigma Xi. Office: Harvard U Divsn Engring and Applied Scis and Physics Dept Cambridge MA 02138 E-mail: ehrenreich@deas.harvard.edu.

EHRENREICH, ROBERT MARC, archaeologist, materials scientist, museum administrator; b. Schenectady, N.Y., May 8, 1960; m. Carmel Rafaella McGill, Apr. 14, 1991; children: Deborah Niamh, Nathan Patrick, Rianna Sophie. AB with honors, Harvard U., 1982; PhD in Archaeology, Oxford U., 1985. Computer database specialist Harvard U. Peabody Mus., 1983, 84-85; postdoctoral rsch. fellow Smithsonian Instn., Washington, 1985-87; sr. program mgr. Nat. Materials Adv. Bd., NRC, Washington, 1987-99; assoc. rsch.prof. George Washington U., Washington, 1994-95; dir. univ. programs divsn. Ctr. for Advanced Holocaust Studies U.S. Holocaust Meml. Mus., Washington, 1999—. Rsch. assoc. Smithsonian Instn., 1990-94; archaeometall. expert Roanoke (N.C.) Lost Colony excavations, 1992-96; mem. ASM Internat. Hist. Landmarks award selection com., 1994-96; mem. first Brit. Coun. Archaeol. Acad. Exch. with No. Ireland, 1989; rsch. assoc. Materials Rsch. Lab., U. Ill., 1987. Editor: Archeomaterials, 1991-94; cons. editor Jour. Archaeol. Method and Theory, 1994—; coord. editor JOM, 1994—; mem. editl. rev. bd. ARD, 1997—; contbr. numerous articles and book revs. to profl. jours.; lectr. in field. Recipient Egyptian Antiquity Orgn. grant to attend 1st Internat. Symposium on the Gt. Sphinx, Cairo, 1992, 3 Meyerstein awards for Oxford U. Archaeology Grad. Students, 1982-85, CETS Sr. Program Mgr. Achievement award Nat. Rsch. Coun., 1998, Achievement awards U.S. Holocaust Meml. Mus., 2000-02. Fellow Am. Anthropol. Assn.; mem. Am. Rsch. Ctr. in Egypt, Am. Soc. for Materials Internat., Hist. Metallurgy Soc., Soc. for Anthropology of Europe, Soc. for Am. Archaeology, Soc. for Archaeol. Scis. Office: US Holocaust Meml Mus 100 Raoul Wallenberg Pl SW Washington DC 20024-2126

EHRENSTEIN, GERALD, retired biophysicist; b. N.Y.C., Sept. 27, 1931; s. Irving and Adele (Holzer) E.; m. Deborah Ploscowe, Dec. 17, 1960; children: Ruth, David, Steven. BEE, Cooper Union, 1952; MA, Columbia U., 1958, PhD, 1962. Engr., Arma Corp., N.Y.C., 1952; rsch. physicist, NIH, Bethesda, Md., 1962-75, chief biophysics sect., 1975—2002, ret., 2002. Corp. mem. Marine Biol. labs., Woods Hole, Mass., 1970-86 . Mem. editl. bd. Biophys. Jour., 1980-83; editor Methods of Exptl. Physics-Biophysics, 1982. Lt. (j.g.) USCG, 1952-54. Mem. Biophys. Soc. (mem. program com. 1981-84, 1992-93, coun. mem. 1992-95, mem. pub. policy com. 1991-96), Am. Phys. Soc., Sigma Xi. Avocation: birdwatching. E-mail: debandger@earthlink.net. Home: 7502 Nevis Rd Bethesda MD 20817-4742 E-mail: debandger@earthlink.net.

EHRENWERTH, DAVID HARRY, lawyer; b. Pitts., Apr. 22, 1947; s. Ben and Beatrice Lee (Schwartz) E.; m. Judith B. Ehrenwerth; children: Justin Reid, Lindsey Royce. BA, U. Pitts., 1969; JD, Harvard U., 1972. Bar: Pa. 1972, U.S. Dist. Ct. (we. dist.) Pa. 1972, U.S. Ct. Appeals (3d cir.) 1976. Asst. atty. gen. Commonwealth of Pa., Pitts., 1972-74; assoc. Kirkpatrick & Lockhart LLP, Pitts., 1974-79, ptnr., 1979—. Pres. Pitts. chpt. Am. Jewish Com., 1988-90, nat. bd. govs., 1991-95, 2001—, chmn. Pitts. chpt., 1996-98; mem. nat. adv. coun. Fed. Nat. Mortgage Assn., 1984-85; bd. dirs. Pa. Bd. Vocat. Rehab., Harrisburg, 1983-88, United Jewish Fedn., Pitts., 1991-93, Presbyn. U. Hosp., Pitts., 1993-94, Riverview Ctr. for Jewish Srs., 1991-93, U. Pitts. Cancer Inst., 1995-99, Pitts. Symphony, 2001—; bd. mem. Am. Israel Pub. Affairs Com., 1995-99, 2001—; bd. dirs. Montefiore Hosp., Pitts., 1985-93, treas., 1989, vice chmn., 1990-92, chmn., 1992-93; bd. govs. Pa. Econ. League, Western Region, 1999—. Recipient Human Rels. award Am. Jewish Com., 1999; named Pittsburgher to Watch Pitts. Mag., 1980. Mem. Pa. Bar Assn. (chmn. real estate fin. com. 1985-87), Allegheny County Bar Assn. (Bar fellow, 2000—, chmn. real property sect. 1989), Harvard U. Law Alumni Assn. Western Pa. (pres. 1986-87), Concordia Club, Westmoreland Country Club, Heinz Fifty-Seven Club (chmn. 1974-91), Duquesne Club, Phi Beta Kappa. Jewish. Avocations: tennis, golf. Home: 413 Windmere Dr Pittsburgh PA 15238-2440 Office: Kirkpatrick & Lockhart LLP 1500 Oliver Building Bldg Pittsburgh PA 15222-2312 E-mail: dehrenwerth@kl.com.

EHRET, JOSEPHINE MARY, microbiologist, researcher; b. Roswell, N.Mex., Feb. 26, 1934; d. Edward and Glenna (Memmer) E. BS, U. N.Mex., 1955. Med. technologist U. Colo. Health Scis. Ctr., Denver, 1956-75, rsch. microbiologist, 1956—, Denver Dept. Health and Hosps., 1980—; instr. sch. medicine U. Colo., 1985—. Contbr. articles to profl. publs. Mem. Am. Soc. for Microbiology, Am. Soc. Med. Technologists (cert.), Am. Venereal Disease Assn., Calif. Assn. Continuing Med. Lab. Edn. Democrat. Avocations: reading, birding. Home: 1344 S Eudora St Denver CO 80222-3526 Office: Denver Pub Health Dept 605 Bannock St Denver CO 80204-4505

EHRHARDT, MARGARET WRIGHT, retired librarian; b. Orangeburg, S.C., Sept. 17, 1918; d. Harry Alison and Florence Olive (Black) Wright; B.A., Duke U., 1939; B.A.L.S., Emory U., 1949; postgrad. Furman U., 1970, U. S.C., 1978, U. Pitts., 1978; m. Benedict Groseclose Ehrhardt, Oct. 27, 1951; 1 son, Benedict Glen. High sch. librarian, library supr. Orangeburg (S.C.) Public Schs., 1945-51; children's librarian Richland County (S.C.) Public Library, Columbia, 1952-58; asst. order librarian U. S.C., Columbia, 1960 64; order librarian Wofford Coll., 1964-65; library cons. S.C. Dept. Edn., Columbia, 1965-87. Mem. ALA, Southeastern Library Assn., S.C. Library Assn. (sec. 1971-72, pres. 1977), Delta Kappa Gamma. Lutheran. Editor: Media Services Newsletter, 1965-77, contbr. articles, revs. to S.C. Librarian, Media Center Messenger. Home: 227 Lawand Dr Columbia SC 29210-7557

EHRHART, JOSEPH EDWARD, retired television broadcast engineer; b. Monterey Park, Calif., Dec. 27, 1933; s. Theophile George and Catherine Louise (Spaulding) E.; m. Mary Frances Bos, Nov. 30, 1957; children: James Edward and Teresa Louise. AA in Electronics, Pasadena City Coll., 1954. 1st class lic. radiotelephone, FCC. Child actor MGM, RKO, United Artists, Republic, Warner Bros., 20th Century Fox, Universal, Hollywood, Calif., 1939-54; TV broadcast engr. Sta. KOAT-TV, Albuquerque, 1957, Sta. KOB-TV, Albuquerque, 1958, Sta. KHJ-TV, Hollywood, Calif., 1959, ABC, Hollywood, 1960-93; videotape supr. Sta. KABC-TV, Hollywood, 1987-93, ret., 1993. Scoutmaster Boy Scouts of Am., Montrose, Calif., 1970-72; choir dir., Holy Redeemer Cath. Ch., Montrose, 1967-75, mem. Am. Assn. of Variable Star Observers, 1973-78; inspector County of San Diego Registrar of Voters, 1998—. Served in USNR, 1954-56. Mem. Soc. Motion Picture and TV Engrs., Cath. Press Coun., Mensa, Pacific Pioneer Broadcasters, Soc. for Preservation and Encouragement of Barber Shop Quartet Singing in Am., L.A. Astron. Soc., Am. Legion. Lodges: KC, Order of the Alhambra, (Illustrious Supreme Vizier, 2003—). Avocations: church choir, instrumental music. Home: Apt 333 1255 N Broadway Escondido CA 92026-2865

EHRHART, WILLIAM DANIEL, writer, poet; b. Roaring Spring, Pa., Sept. 30, 1948; s. John Harry and Evelyn Marie (Conti) E.; m. Anne Gulick, June 27, 1981; 1 child, Leela. BA, Swarthmore (Pa.) Coll., 1973; MA, U. Ill., 1978; PhD, U. Wales, Swansea, U.K., 2000. Tchr. George Sch., Newtown, Pa., 1981-83, Germantown Friends Sch., Phila., 1986-89; vis. prof. U. Mass., Boston, 1990; poet-in-residence Detroit YMCA, 1996; dir., summer writers workshop LaSalle U., Phila., 1997-2000; rsch. fellow U. Wales, Swansea, 1997—2002; tchr. Haverford (Pa.) Sch., 2002—. Author: Beautiful Wreckage, 1999, Busted, 1995, Passing Time, 1986, Vietnam-Perkasie, 1983. Sgt. USMC, 1966-69. Arts fellowship Pew Charitable Trusts, 1993, Pa. Coun. on the Arts, 1981, 88; grantee Mary Roberts Rinehart Found., 1980. Avocations: jogging, cycling, swimming.

EHRHORN, RICHARD WILLIAM, electronics company executive; b. Marshalltown, Iowa, Jan. 21, 1934; s. Theodore Raymond and Zelda Elizabeth (Axtell) E.; m. Marilyn Patrick, Aug. 1, 1959; children: Scott Patrick, Kimberlee Dawn. BSEE, U. Minn., 1955; MSEE, Calif. Inst. Tech., 1958. Sr. engr. Gen. Dynamics Corp., Pomona, Calif., 1956-60; sr. rsch. engr. Calif. Inst. Tech. Jet Propulsion Lab., Pasedena, 1960-63; mgr. advanced devel. lab. Electronic Communications Inc., St. Petersburg, Fla., 1963-68; gen. mgr. Signal/One div., 1968-70; chmn., CEO Ehrhorn Tech. Ops., Inc., Colorado Springs, Colo., 1970-95; vice chmn. ASTeX/ETO, Inc., Colorado Springs, 1996-99; regent Liberty U., 1995—; chmn., CEO Alpha/Power, Inc., Longmont, Colo., 1996-2000. Author: (with others) Principles of Electronic Warfare, 1959; patentee in field. Mem. IEEE (sr. life), Am. Radio Relay League, Quar. Century Wireless Assn. Home and Office: PO Box 6249 Breckenridge CO 80424-6249

EHRICH, FELIX FREDERICK, technical consultant; b. N.Y.C., Oct. 19, 1919; s. Harry and Henrietta (Brenner) E.; m. Ceceil Rinder, July 26, 1953; children: Anne, Elisabeth, Margaret. BS, CCNY, 1939; MS, State U. Iowa, 1940; PhD, U. Md., 1942. Rsch. chemist E.I. Dupont, Newark, 1946-58, rsch. supr., 1958—70, tech. dir. Mexico City, 1970-72, mgr. colors internat. devel., tech. mgr. colors mktg. Wilmington, Del., 1972-82; tech. cons. numerous cos., 1982-98. Cons. numerous cos., 1982—; cons. organic pigment colors, expert witness Connolly, Bove, Lodge, Hutz for Bayer, Inc., 1991-95; arbitrator Better Bus. Bur. of Del., 1983—. Inventor, patentee in field quinacridones, phthalocyanines. Lt. U.S. Army, 1942-46. Mem. Am. Chem. Soc., Sigma Xi. Home: 706 Sudbury Rd Wilmington DE 19803-2212

EHRINPREIS, MURRAY NORMAN, gastroenterologist, educator; b. Detroit, May 30, 1946; s. Jacob and Anna Frieda Ehrinpreis; m. Alice Fellman, Apr. 12, 1970; children: Andrew Bernard, Jeffrey Lawrence. BA, U. Mich., 1968; MD, NYU, 1972. Diplomate Am. Bd. Internal Medicine, Am. Bd. Gastroenterology. Intern Bronx (NY) Mcpl. Hosp. Ctr., 1972—73, resident, 1972—75; fellow in gastroenterology Albert Einstein Coll. Medicine, Bronx, 1975—77; from asst. prof. to prof. Wayne State U., Detroit, 1972—2000, prof., 2000—, gastrointestinal fellowship dir., 2000— . Contbr. articles to profl. jours. Fellow: Am. Coll. Gastroenterology (bd. govs. 1992—98); mem.: Am. Gastroenterol. Assn., Mich. Gastroent. Assn. (pres. 1985—86, 1996—98), Am. Soc. Gastrointestinal Endoscopy, Am. Assn. Study Liver Disease. Avocations: violin, tennis, golf, literature. Office: Harper U Hosp 3990 John R Detroit MI 48201

EHRLE, WILLIAM LAWRENCE, lawyer, association executive; b. Colorado City, Tex., Dec. 11, 1932; s. Frank Lawrence and Mary Elma (Hinds) E.; m. Sandra Faye Luckey, Aug. 3, 1963; children— Sharon Elaine, William Lawrence, Rhonda Kay. B.A., McMurry Coll., 1953; J.D., U. Tex., 1961. Bar: Tex. 1961. Asst. gen. counsel Lone Star Gas Co., Dallas, 1961-67; pres. Coaches Life Ins. Co., El Paso, Tex., 1967-70; sole practice, Austin, Tex., 1970-78; pres., gen. counsel Tex. Manufactured Housing Assn., Austin, 1978— ; dir. Nat. Manufactured Housing Fedn., Washington, 1978— ; mem. adv. council Fed. Nat. Mortgage Assn., Dallas, 1983-84. Mem. Tex. Ho. of Reps., 1957-63. Served as 1st lt. USMC, 1953-56. Office: Tex Manufactured Housing Assn PO Box 14428 Austin TX 78761-4428

EHRLICH, ANNE HOWLAND, research biologist, b. Des Moines, Nov. 17, 1933; d. Winston Densmore and Virginia Lippincott (Fitzhugh) Howland; m. Paul Ralph Ehrlich, Dec. 18, 1954; 1 child: Lisa Marie Daniel. Student, U. Kans., 1952-55; LLD (hon.), Bethany Coll., 1990; doctorate (hon.), Oreg. State U., 1999. Technician Dept. Entomology U. Kans., Lawrence, 1955; rsch. asst. Dept. Biol. Scis. Stanford (Calif.) U., 1959-72, rsch. assoc., 1972-75, sr. rsch. assoc., 1975—; assoc. dir. Ctr. for Conservation Biology Stanford U., 1987—. Bd. dirs. Pacific Inst., Ploughshares Fund. Author: (with others) Ecoscience: Population, Resources, Environment, 1977, The Golden Door, 1979, Extinction, 1981, Earth, 1987, The Population Explosion, 1990, Healing the Planet, 1991, The Stork and the Plow, 1995, Betrayal of Science and Reason, 1996; contbr. articles to profl. jours. Named to Global 500 Roll of Honour for Environ. Achievement, UN, 1989, UNEP-Sasekawa prize, 1994, Heinz award, 1995, Tyler prize, 1998. Fellow Am. Acad. Arts & Scis., Calif. Acad. Scis. (hon.); mem. Am. Humanists Assn. (hon. life, Disting. Svc. 1985, Raymond B. Bragg award 1985). Avocations: flyfishing, hiking, reading. Home: Pine Hill Stanford CA 94305 Office: Stanford U Dept Biol Scis Stanford CA 94305

EHRLICH, AVA, television executive; b. St. Louis, Aug. 14, 1950; d. Norman and Lillian (Gellman) Ehrlich; m. Barry K. Freedman, Mar. 31, 1979; children: Alexander Zev, Maxwell Samuel. BJ, Northwestern U., 1972, MJ, 1973; MA, Occidental Coll., 1976. Reporter, asst. mng. editor Lerner Newspapers, Chgo., 1974-75; reporter, news editor Sta. KMOX, St. Louis, 1976-79; producer Sta. WXYZ, Detroit, 1979-85; exec. producer Sta. KSDK-TV, St. Louis, 1985—. Guest editor Mademoiselle mag., N.Y.C., 1971; freelance writer, coll. prof. Detroit, Chgo., St. Louis, 1987; adj. faculty mem. Washington U., St. Louis, 1994—. Trustee CORO Found., St. Louis, 1976-77, 86—, St. Louis Jewish Light, 1999—, Crown Ctr., 2000; bd. dirs. Nat. Kidney Found., St. Louis, 1987, Crowne Ctr., 2000—. Named Outstanding Woman in Broadcasting, Am. Women in Radio & TV, 1983, Among 18 Most Influential Women in the Region St. Louis Dispatch, 2000; recipient Journalism award Am. Chiropractic Assn., 1989, AP award Ill. UPI, 1989, Illuminator award AMC Cancer Rsch., 1994, Women in Comms. Nat. award, 1988, Emmy award, 1995, Virginia Betts award for Contbns. in Journalism, 1999; CORO Found. fellow in pub. affairs, 1975-76. Mem. NATAS (com. mem. 1986—, bd. dirs. 1994—, 18 local Emmy awards 1986—), Women in Comms., Inc. (sec. 1978-79, Clarion award 1989, Best in Midwest Feature award 1989), Soc. Profl. Journalists. Democrat. Jewish. Home: 8002 Walinca Ter Saint Louis MO 63105-2565 Office: Sta KSDK-TV 1000 Market St Saint Louis MO 63101-2011 E-mail: aehrlich@ksdk.gannett.com.

EHRLICH, BERNARD HERBERT, lawyer, association executive; b. Washington, Apr. 3, 1927; s. Samuel Zachary and Elsie (Klein) E.; m. Edna Kraft, June 17, 1951 (div.); children— Vivian Rose, Beverly Denise, Brenda Susan, Lisa Jean. AB, George Washington U., 1946, LLB, 1949, MA, JD, 1950. Bar: D.C. 1949. Pvt. practice, Washington; gen. counsel numerous corps., industries, 1947-89; mgr., gen. counsel Inst. Indsl. Launderers, Washington, 1947-89; counsel KEX Nat. Assn., 1960-94. Counsel Nat. Home Study Coun., 1947-89, Nat. Assn. Cosmetology Schs., 1967-83; mem. adv. panel employee recruitment and job devel. U.S. C. of C., 1967-84; mem. Pres.'s Com. on Employing the Handicapped, 1975—; gen. counsel KEX Nat. Assn., 1960-95; Accrediting Bur. Health Edn. Schs., 1965-92, Commn. Accredited Truck Driving Schs., 1985-92, Nat. Assn. Trade and Tech. Schs., 1968-86. Bd. dirs. Washington B'nai B'rith Hillel Found., 1997-2000. With USN, 1943-45. Recipient svc. plaque Am. Inst. Launderers, 1966, svc. plaque Nat. Assn. Trade and Tech. Schs., 1967, svc. plaque Nat. Home Study Coun., 1970, svc. plaque Accrediting Bureau of Health Edn. Schs., 1992, svc. plaque Commn. Accredited Truck Driving Schs., 1992, N.F. Cimaglia award Melody Pub. Co., 1985. Mem. ABA, Bar Assn. D.C., Am. Soc. Internat. Law, Am. Hist. Assn., Am. Soc. Assn. Execs., Soc. Am. Travel Writers, Am. Polit. Sci. Assn., Nat. Assn. Trade and Tech. Schs. (hon.), KEX Nat. Assn. (hon.), Inst. Indsl. Launderers (hon.), Am. Forestry Assn. (life), Phi Beta Kappa, Nu Beta Epsilon, Phi Delt Pi. Jewish. Home and Office: 4907 Lakescene Pl Sarasota FL 34243

EHRLICH, CHARLES DAVID, physicist; b. Miami, Fla., Sept. 10, 1951; s. Maurice Lee and Bena Zeva (Shechtman) E.; m. Susan Rae Morris, June 2, 1974; children: Rebecca, Gabriel. BS, U. Miami, 1973; PhD, U. Pa., 1979. Physicist R&D Varian Assocs. Extrion Div., Gloucester, Mass., 1979-83, mgr. batch process product devel., 1984; staff physicist Nat. Bureau of Standards, Gaithersburg, Md., 1984-87; group leader, pressure group Nat. Inst. Standards & Tech., Gaithersburg, Md., 1987-94, program analyst, 1994-95, sr. program analyst, 1995-96, dep. chief, tech. stds. activities program, 1996-99, nat. measurement and stds. needs assessment coord., 1999-2000, chief tech. stds. activities program, 2000—01, leader Internat. Legal Metrology Group, 2002—. U.S. rep. Internat. Orgn. Legal Metrology, 2000—; workshop organizer Nat. Inst. Stds. and Tech., 1987-89; instr. 1990-94; co-chmn. to Internat. Sts. Orgn. Tech. Adv. Group 4 on Metrology; invited conf. procs. author Proceedings of 4th Italy-U.S. Bilateral Seminar, 1992. Contbr. articles to profl. jours. Boy scout asst. patrol leader Boy Scouts Am., Gaithersburg, 1991-94, cub scout den leader Cub Scouts Am., Gaithersburg, 1989 91. Recipient Bronze Medal award U.S. Dept. Commerce, 1992, Best Paper award Nat. Conf. Standards Labs., 1997, Andrew J. Woodington award for Professionalism in Metrology Measurement Sci. Conf., 1999. Mem.: Am. Nat. Stds. Inst. Exec. Stds. Coun., Internat. Joint Com. Guides for Metrology, Intrinsic Derived Sts. Com., Nat. Conf. Stds. Labs. (chmn. 1989—98), Internat. Bur. Weights and Measures, Am. Vacuum Soc., Am. Soc. Testing & Materials (vice chmn 1986—90), Internat. Orgn. Legal Metrology (U.S. rep.), Sigma Xi (NIST chpt. pres.-elect 2002—03, pres. 2003—). Achievements include invited keynote speaker IMEKO World Congress, Turin, Italy, 1994; invited speaker Shanghai and Beijing, China, 1994, Bratislava, Slovakia, 1991 explained measured equilibration time constants in helium permeation leaks. Milestones in Metrology Congress, Maastricht, The Netherlands, 2003. Home: 9804 Darcy Forest Dr Silver Spring MD 20910-1176 E-mail: charles.ehrlich@nist.gov.

EHRLICH, DAVID GORDON, film director, educator; b. Elizabeth, N.J., Oct. 14, 1941; s. Max and Jeannette (Gordon) E.; m. Marcela Josepha Rydlova, July 17, 1975. BA in Govt., Cornell U., 1963; sculpture cert., Madras Sch. Fine Arts, India, 1964; MA in Dramatic Art, U. Calif., Berkeley, 1966; MFA in Film, Columbia U., 1975. Artist-in-residence Vt. Coun. on Arts, Montpelier, Vt., 1978—, N.H. Coun. on Arts, Concord, N.H., 1986—; vis. prof. film studies Dartmouth Coll., Hanover, N.H., 1993—. Lectr. art U. Vt., 1977-82; adj. asst. prof. interdisciplinary arts SUNY, Purchase, 1971-75; instr. animation summer session U. Calif., Berkeley, yearly 1988-93, summer session U. Hawaii, Honolulu, yearly 1991-98, Mongolia Coll. Art, Ulan, Baatar, Mongolia, CAS Sch., Karachi, Pakistan, 1993; mem. adv. bd. ADA Animation Inst., Shanghai, 1988—; vis. prof. film MRDH Coll., Volda, Norway, 1990-91; art therapy cons. Manhattan State Hosp., 1975-76; hon. pres. Ottawa Internat. Animation Festival, 2002; presenter various internat. confs. and festivals. Author: The Bowel Book, 1981; dir., animator: (animated short films) Metamorphosis, 1975, Album Leaf, 1976, Vermont Etude, 1977, Robot, 1977, Vermont Etude, No. 2, 1979, Robot Two, 1979, Precious Metal, 1980, Fantasies. Animation of Vermont Schoolchildren, 1981, Dissipative Dialogues, 1982, Precious Metal Variations, 1983, Point, 1984, Dissipative Fantasies, 1986, Pixel, 1987, Dryads, 1988, Academy Leader Variations, 1987, Animated Self-Portraits, 1989, A Child's Dream, 1990, Dance of Nature, 1991, Genghiz Khan, 1993, Etude, 1994, Interstitial Wavescapes, 1995, Robot Rerun, 1996, Asifa Variations, 1997, Radiant Flux, 1999, Color Run, 2001, Taking Color for a Walk, 2001, Current Events, 2002; mem. editl. bd. Animation Jour., 1991—; contbr. articles to profl. jours.; films in collections at MOMA, Pacific Film Archive, Berlin ASIFA Animation Archive, Tokyo Internat. Animation Libr., Montreal Cinematheque Quebecoise, Moscow Film Archive; film retrospectives include Ottawa Internat. Animation Festival, 2002, Ballargues Animation Festival, France, 1998, Balt. Film Forum, Cinanima Animation Festival, Portugal, 1990, N.W. Film & Video Study Ctr., 1989, Pacific Film Archives, Shanghai Animation Festival, 1988, Mus. Modern Art, Varna World Animation Festival, Bulgaria, Belgrade Film Inst., Yugoslavia, 1987, Sinking Creek Film Celebration, Vienna Art Acad., 1986, Mus. Moving Image, 1985, Turin (Italy) City Hall, Cakovec Cultural Ctr., Yugoslavia, 1984, SUNY at Plattsburgh, Bradford Coll., 1982, Animators Gallery, N.Y.C., 1982, BVAU Gallery, Boston, Umwelt Galerie, Stuttgart, Germany, 1979; subject of book David Ehrlich: Citizen of the World, 2002. Recipient awards Cannes Film Festival, Chg. Film Festival, San Francisco Film Festival, Am. Film Festival, Krakow Film Festival, Cinanima Film Festival, Houston Film Festival, WorldFest, Charleston Film Festival, Roshd Film Festival, Iran, Murcia Film Festival, Spain, ASIFA-East Animation Festival, Sinking Creek Film Celebration, Black Maria Film Festival, N.Y. Filmmakers' Expo, Athens Film Festival, New Eng. Film Festival, ASIFA Spl. award, 2002; travel grantee Arts Internat., N.Y.C., 1992-93, Am. Film Inst. grantee, 1988, Holographic Film Found grantee, 1978, 83, 84; Fulbright fellow, 1963-64. Mem. Nat. Expressive Therapy Assn. (cert. expressive therapist), Internat. Animation Assn. (exec. bd. 1988-2000, v.p. 1991-97), Soc. Animation Studies (mem. steering com. 1999-2000), Asian Cinema Studies Soc., Vt. Coun. on Arts (filmmaking grantee 1978, 79, 84, 86, 89, 90, 91), Mongolia Soc., Miagmar Animation Workshop (bd. dirs. 1992—). Avocations: composing music, painting, sculpture, dancing, travel. Office: Dartmouth Coll Film Studies Wilson Hall Hanover NH 03755

EHRLICH, GARTH DAVID, molecular biologist; b. Plattsburgh, NY, July 9, 1956; s. Robert Elias and Evelyn Gertrude (Talvitie) E.; children: Ian S.G., Nathan E.G. BA, Alfred U., 1977; PhD, Syracuse U., 1987. Rsch. microbiologist Bethesda Rsch. Labs., Md., 1980-81; rsch. specialist Syracuse U., NY, 1981-83; rsch. scientist C indsl. divsn. Bristol Meyers, 1981-83, rsch. scientist B, 1983-84; tech. specialist I SUNY Health Sci. Ctr., Syracuse, NY, 1984-86, rsch. instr., 1988-89, rsch. asst. prof., 1989-90; tech. specialist II SUNY Rsch. Found., Syracuse, NY, 1986-88; asst. prof., dir. PCR facility U. Pitts., Pa., 1990-97; chief microbiology, virology and infectious diseases sect. molecular diogostics divsn. U. Pitts. Med. Ctr., Pa., assoc. prof., 1995-97; vis. prof. Cleve. Clin., 1992. Cons. Teltech, Inc., 1990—, Kodak, Rochester, NY, 1991-95, Oncogenetics, Phoenix, 1993-95; Visible Genetics, 1997-99, CL Sci., 1997-99, Quest Diagnostics, 1998-99; invited participant NCI Symposia, 1989, NMMS Symposia, 1989, NIAID Symposia, 1991, NILD Coun., 1995, NILC Symposium, 2000; adj. mem. Ctrl. Blood Bank Pitts., 1992—; lectr. Heritage Found. Cross Cancer Ctr., Edmonton, Can.; Feinstein lectr. Alfred U., 1995; invited participant Internat. Chromosome 10 Workshop, Crete, Greece; invited guest spkr. Mexican Infection Disease Soc. Ann. Meeting, 1995; exec. dir. Ctr. for Genomic Sci., Allegheny Singer Rsch. Inst., 1997—; prof. otolaryngology and human genetics Drexel Univ. Coll. of Med., vice-chmn. dept. human genetics, 1998—; hon. prof. med. genetics West China U. of Med. Sci., Chengdu, Sichuan, 1999—; invited spkr. World Congress of Pediat. Infectious Disease, Acapulco, Mex., 1996, Bicor Conf. on Antiinfective Agents, Leipzig, Germany, 1996, Case Western Res. U., 1997; lectr. Kaiyuon Bioengring., Xian, China, 1997, Chinese U. Hong Kong, 1999; hon. lectr. West China U. Med. Sci., 1999; keynote spkr. Nat. Conv. of Dir. of Clin. Labs., Health Ministry of China, 1998; Keynote speaker, Assoc. of Indian Medical Microbiol. silva Justice Meeting, New Delhi, India, 2001; organizer symposia in field, 1995-1997, 2000, 2003; mem. numerous NIH grant rev. coms. Author, editor: PCR-Based Diagnostics in Infectious Disease, 1994; contbr. numerous articles to profl. jours., chpts. to books, editls. to med. jours. Mem. gifted edn. adv. bd. Syracuse City Sch. Dist., 1989-90; lectr. on AIDS to secondary sch. children, sci. to elem. sch. children, 1989—. Recipient Disting. Alumni citation Alfred U., 1995, Feinstein Lectureship Alfred U., 1995, 4 NIH grants, 2000. Mem. Soc. for Leukocyte Biology, Assn. for Rsch. in Otolaryngology, Assn. Med. Lab. Immunologists, Acad. Clin. Lab. Physicians and Scientists, Am. Soc. for Microbiology, Assn. Molecular Pathology (co-chair infectious diseases sect.), Sigma Xi, Phi Kappa Phi. Address: Allegheny General Hosp Ctr Genomic Sci 320 E North Ave Pittsburgh PA 15212-4756 E-mail: gehrlich@wpahs.org.

EHRLICH, GEORGE EDWARD, rheumatologist, international pharmaceutical consultant; b. Vienna, July 18, 1928; came to U.S., 1938, naturalized, 1944; s. Edward and Irene (Elling) E.; m. Gail S. Abrams, Mar. 30, 1968; children: Charles Edward, Steven L. Abrams, Rebecca Sayles. AB cum laude, Harvard U., 1948; MB, MD, Chgo. Med. Sch., 1952. Intern Michael Reese Hosp., Chgo., 1952; resident Francis Delafield Hosp., N.Y.C., 1955, Beth Israel Hosp., Boston, 1956, New Eng. Center Hosp., Boston, 1957; fellow rheuma-

tology NIH, Bethesda, Md., 1958, Hosp. for Spl. Surgery, N.Y.C., 1959-61, asst. attending physician, 1960-64; spl. fellow Sloan Kettering Inst., 1960-61; instr. medicine Cornell U., 1960-64; dir. Arthritis Center, chief rheumatology Albert Einstein Med. Center and Moss Rehab. Hosp., Phila., 1964-80; asst. prof. medicine Temple U., 1964-67, asso. prof. medicine, 1967-72, prof. medicine, 1972-80, asso. prof. rehab. medicine, 1964-74, prof., 1974-80; vis. lectr. U. Pa., 1964-80; prof. medicine, dir. div. rheumatology Hahnemann U., Phila., 1980-83; v.p. Anti-Inflammatory/Endocrine CIBA-Geigy Pharmaceuticals, Summit, N.J., 1983-86; head med. affairs CIBA-Geigy Ltd., Switzerland, 1987-88; pres. George E. Ehrlich Assocs., pharmaceutical cons. Adj. prof. clin. medicine NYU Med. Ctr., 1984—; lectr. in medicine U. Pa., 1989-91, adj. prof. medicine, 1992—; expert advisor, cons. Diabetes and Other Noncommunicable Diseases unit WHO, 1990-98, Chronic Disease Mgmt., 1998—; chmn. Internat. Low Back Pain Initiative; rep. of pres. Internat. League Assns. Rheumatology for Soft Tissue Rheumatisms, 1993-97, exec. com.; liaison to WHO, 1997—; mem. arthritis adv. com. FDA, 1993-96, chmn., 1993-96; expert, FDA, 1997-99; mem. coun. Chairs, FDA, 1996—; chmn. sci. adv. bd. Hochrheininstitut (Rheumatic Disease and Rehab. Rsch. Inst. of Upper Rhine in Germany, France and Switzerland for Treatment, Tchg., and Rsch.), 1993—; bd. dirs. Greenwich Inst. Am. Edn., 1994—; chmn., U.S. mem. Expert Adv. Panel on Chronic Degenerative Diseases, WHO, 1996—; bd. dirs. sci. adv. bds., several U.S. and internat. socs. Author: Differential Diagnosis of Rheumatoid Arthritis, 1972, Oculocutaneous Manifestations of Rheumatic Diseases, 1973; editor: Total Management of the Arthritic Patient, 1973, Rehabilitation Management of Rheumatic Conditions, 1980, 2d edit., 1986; editor: (with J. Fries) Prognosis, 1981; editor: (with H.E. Paulus) Controversies in the Clinical Evaluation of Analgesic-Anti-Inflammatory-Antirheumatic Drugs, 1981; editor: (with P. Utsinger, N. Zvaifler) Rheumatoid Arthritis, 1985; editor: (with W. Simon) Medicolegal Consequences of Trauma, 1992; editor: (with N. Khaltaev) Low Back Pain, 2000; editor: (with W. Simon A. Sadwin) Conquering Chronic Pain After Injury, 2002; editor: Jour. Albert Einstein Med. Ctr., 1966—71, Arthritis and Rheumatic Diseases Abstracts, 1968—71; mem. editl. bd.: Inflammation, 1974—88, Psychosomatics, 1977—83, Sexual Medicine Today, 1977—84, Jour. Rheumatology, 1982—, Internat. Jour. Immunotherapy, 1984—, Immunopharmacology, 1985—, Med. Problems Performing Artists, 1985—92, Brazilian Jour. Rheumatology, 1992, 1996—99, Italian Jour. Rheumatic Diseases, 1999—; contbr. articles to profl. jours. Pres. Ed. Pa. chpt. Arthritis Found. 1970-72; mem. Phila. Mayor's Sci. and Tech. Adv. Coun., 1972-81; chmn. ad hoc adv. com. Bur. Drugs, FDA, 1971; mem. subcom. on redefinition of disability Social Security Adminstrn., 1982-86. Served to comdr. M.C. USNR, 1953-55; Res. to 1975, ret. Recipient citations City Phila., 1969, 74, Distinguished Alumnus award Chgo. Med. Sch., 1969; decorated Cavaliere Order of Star of Italian Solidarity. Fellow ACP, Royal Coll. Physicians Edinburgh, Phila. Coll. Physicians, Am. Coll. Rheumatology (elected master, 1994, com. for publ. Arthritis and Rheumatism, 1977-79, mem. editl. bd. 1980-83), Rheumatism Socs. Ecuador, India (hon.); mem. AMA (editl. bd. Jour. 1972-82), Am. Soc. Clin. Pharmacology and Therapeutics, Assn. Mil. Surgeons (Philip Hench award 1971), Brit. Assn. Rheumatology and Rehab. (overseas mem., editl. bd. 1979-82), Internat. Soc. for Behcet's Disease (hon. life pres.), Alpha Omega Alpha. Clubs: Harvard (Boston, N.Y.C.). Home: 38 Holly Dr Beach Haven NJ 08008-6119 Office: 1 Independence Pl Ste 1101 Philadelphia PA 19106-3731 E-mail: g2e@mindspring.com. *Respect for the ideas of others, but ultimately responsible for my own ideas, thus, a liberal philosophy in a conservative setting. Like Brecht's Galileo, I should like to be remembered as a lover of old wines and new ideas.*

EHRLICH, GERALDINE ELIZABETH, management consultant; d. Joseph Vincent and Agnes Barbara (Campbell) McKenna; m. S. Paul Ehrlich, Jr.; children: Susan Patricia, Paula Jeanne, Jill Marie. BS, Drexel Inst. Tech. Nutrition cons. hypertension rsch. team U. Calif. Micronesia, 1970; regional sales mgr. Marriott Corp., Bethesda, Md., 1976-78; dir. sales and profl. svcs. Coll. and Health Care divsn. Macke Co., Cheverly, Md., 1978-79, v.p. ops. divsn., 1979-80, pres. Health Care divsn., 1980-81; regional v.p. Custom Mgmt. Corp., Alexandria, Va., 1981-83, v.p. mktg., 1983-87; v.p. mktg. and healthcare sales Morrison's Custom Mgmt., Mobile, Ala., 1987-88; v.p. sales ARA Svcs., Phila., 1988-93; v.p. bus. devel. ARAMARK, Phila., 1993-95; exec. dir. The Resource Group, Phila., 1995—2001; healthcare mktg. cons., 2001—. Cons. mktg. The Green House, Tokyo, 1987-88; chmn. bd. Mktg. Matrix, Falls Church, Va., 1984—. Mem. Health Systems Agy. No. Va., 1976-77; chmn. Health Care Adv. Bd., Fairfax County, Va., 1973-77; vice chmn. Fairfax County Cmty. Action Com., 1973-77; treas. Fairfax County Dem. Com., 1969-73; trustee Fairfax Hosp., 1973-77; bd. dirs. Tennis Patrons, Washington, 1984-88, Phila. Singers, 1993-98, Physicians for Peace, 1993-98; mem. adv. bd. Nat. Mus. Women in the Arts, 2000—. Mem. NAFE, AAUW, Internat. Women's Assn., Am. Mgmt. Assn., Soc. Mktg. Profls., Gulfstream Club, Rotary Club. Home: 1132 Seaspray Ave Delray Beach FL 33483 E-mail: gehrlich@profserve.com.

EHRLICH, GERT, science educator, researcher; b. Vienna, June 22, 1926; came to U.S., 1939; s. Leopold and Paula Maria (Kucera) E.; m. Anne Vogdes Alger, Apr. 27, 1957. AB with honors in Chemistry, Columbia U., 1948; AM, Harvard U., 1950, PhD, 1952. NIH postdoctoral fellow Harvard U., Cambridge, Mass., 1951-52; research assoc., Dept. Physics U. Mich., Ann Arbor, 1952-53; mem. research staff GE Rsch. Lab., Schenectady, N.Y., 1953-68; prof. materials sci. Coordinated Sci. Lab. U. Ill., Urbana-Champaign, 1968—. Former mem. editorial adv. bd. Chem. Physics Letters, Jour. Chem. Physics, Jour. Vacuum Sci. & Tech., Surface & Colloid Sci., Progress in Surface & Membrane Sci.; contbr. numerous articles on molecular behavior at crystal surfaces and on properties of individual atoms and atom clusters. Served to cpl. U.S. Army, 1945-47, ETO. Guggenheim fellow, 1985. Fellow Am. Phys. Soc., N.Y. Acad. Scis.; mem. Nat. Acad. Scis., Am. Chem. Soc. (Kendall award 1982), Am. Vacuum Soc. (Medard W. Welch award 1979), Alexander von Humboldt Found. (Humboldt-Preis 1992), Sigma Xi, Phi Beta Kappa. Office: U Ill Materials Rsch Lab 104 S Goodwin Ave Urbana IL 61801-2985

EHRLICH, HENRY LUTZ, biology educator; b. Stettin, Pommerania, Germany, Aug. 31, 1925; came to U.S., 1940; s. Max and Gerda (Tannenwald) E. BS cum laude, Harvard Coll., 1948; MS, U. Wis., 1949, PhD, 1951. From asst. prof. to prof. biology Rensselaer Poly. Inst., Troy, N.Y., 1951-94; prof. emeritus, 1994. Cons. in field. Author: Geomicrobiology, 1996, 3d edit., 1995, 4th edit., 2002; author, co-editor: Workshop on Biotechnology for the Mining, Metal Refining and Fossil Fuel Processing Industries, 1986; co-author, co-editor: Microbial Mineral Recovery, 1990; editor-in-chief Geomicrobiology Jour., 1983-95; mem. editl. bd. Applied and environ. Microbiology, Applied Microbiology and Biotech. Mem. interdisciplinary com. World Cultural Coun., Monterrey, Mex. Am. Acad. Microbiology fellow. Fellow AAAS; mem. Symposia for Environ. Biogeochemistry (former v.p., treas.), Am. Soc. Microbiology, Soc. Indsl. Microbiology, Am. Inst. Biol. Scis., Sigma Xi. Jewish. Achievements include research on microbial manganese oxidation and reduction; microbial chromate reduction; microbial bauxite weathering; bioleaching. Home: 2423 21st St#3 Troy NY 12180-1826 Office: Rensselaer Polytech Inst Biology Dept 110 8th St Troy NY 12180-3590 E-mail: ehrlih@rpi.edu.

EHRLICH, IRA ROBERT, mechanical engineering consultant; b. Washington, Sept. 1, 1926; s. Abraham Moses and Anna (Garonzik) E.; m. Sheila Lenor Kaminsky, June 11, 1950; children: Richard Mark, Heather Maureen Ehrlich Reiser BS, U.S. Mil. Acad., 1950; MS, Purdue U., 1956; PhD, U. Mich., 1960; MS (hon.), Stevens Inst. Tech., 1982. Registered profl. engr., Mich., N.J. Supr. ITT, Paramus, N.J., 1960-62; mgr. transp. research group Stevens Inst. Tech., Hoboken, N.J., 1962-74, dean research, 1974-83, head dept. mech. engring., 1979-83, v.p. research, 1983-85, v.p. acad. affairs, 1984-85, prof. emeritus, 1988—; pres. I. Robert Ehrlich P.A., Teaneck, N.J., 1988—. Chmn. sci. adv. com. U.S. Army Tank-Automotive Rsch. and Devel. Command, 1970-77; cons. to industry; mem. N.J. Motor Vehicle Insp. Sta. Rev. Commn., chmn. safety com., 1977-80. Asso. editor Tire Sci. and Tech, 1972-80. Served to capt. U.S. Army, 1950-60. Themis grantee, 1967-72 Fellow Soc. Automotive Engrs., Internat. Soc. Terrain-Vehicle Systems (gen. sec. 1967-78, v.p. 1978-81, pres. 1981-84); mem. ASME, NSPE, ASTM, Nat. Safety Coun., Nat. Assn. Profl. Accident Reconstructionists (bd. dirs. 1997-99), B'nai Brith (chpt. pres. 1967-68). Jewish. Home and Office: 859 Columbus Dr Teaneck NJ 07666-6612 E-mail: rehrlich@bellatlantic.net. *Make the most of your scraps of time.*

EHRLICH, ISAAC, economist, educator, economist, department chairman;, naturalized, U.S., 1964; s. Haim and Malka Ehrlich; m. Chaya Choresh Ehrlich. BA cum laude, Hebrew U., Jerusalem, 1963; PhD with distinction, Columbia U., 1970; Doctorate (hon.), U. Orleans, France, 2002. Instr. bus. econs. U. Chgo., 1969—70, asst. prof. bus. econs., 1970—74, assoc. prof. bus. econs., 1974—78; prof. econs. SUNY, Buffalo, 1977—, Melvin H. Baker prof. Am. enterprise, 1981—, leading prof. econs., 1985—, UB disting. prof., 2002—, chair dept. econs., 1997—. Lectr. econs. Tel-Aviv U., 1971—72; vis. assoc. prof. law and econs. U. Va., 1973; vis. prof. econs. Hong Kong U. Sci. and Tech. Sch. Bus. and Mgmt., 1992—94; hon. prof. City U. Hong Kong, 1999—; rsch. analyst Nat. Bur. Econ. Rsch., 1969, rsch. assoc., 1970—76, sr. rsch. assoc., 1977, mem. conf. on rsch. in income and wealth, 1984—; mem. U.S. Presdl. Health Policy Adv. Group and Pres. Reagan's Transition Team on Health Policy, 1980—81; mem. health svcs. com. Hong Kong Govt., 1993—94, mem. expert subcom. on grant applications and awards, 1993—94; assoc. mem. Inst. for Policy Analysis U. Toronto, Canada, 1992—; mem. bd. advisors Hong Kong Ctr. Econ. Rsch., 1993—; dir. Inst. for the Study of Free Enterprise Sys. SUNY, Buffalo, 1987—92; cons. Ctr. for Naval Analysis, 1970—71. Editor: National Health Policy: What Role for Government, 1982; contbr. articles to profl. jours. Mem.: Mont Pelerin Soc., Am. Econ. Assn. Office: State Univ NY Buffalo 415 Fronczak Hall Buffalo NY 14260

EHRLICH, JEFFREY, data processing company executive; married; 1 child. BSEE, U. R.I.; MS in Tech. Mgmt. and Computer Sci., Rensselaer Polytechnic Inst.; postgrad., GE Mgmt. Inst., Crotonville, N.Y. Formerly CIO GE Med. Syss. Bus., Milw.; chief tech. officer Nat. Data Corp., Atlanta, 1995—. Office: Nat Data Corp 5 National Data Plz NE Atlanta GA 30329-2087

EHRLICH, JEROME HARRY, lawyer; b. Bklyn., Jan. 22, 1937; s. Harvey I. and Jeanne S. (Bayer) E.; m. Deena Rosenfeld, Feb. 15, 1987. BBA, CCNY, 1958; LLB, NYU, 1962. Bar: N.Y. 1962, U.S. Dist. Ct. (ea. and so. dists.) N.Y. 1964, U.S. Ct. Appeals (2nd cir.) 1965, U.S. Ct. Mil. Appeals 1966, U.S. Supreme Ct. 1966. Ptnr. Jaspan, Ginsberg, Ehrlich, Schlesinger & Hoffman, Garden City, N.Y., 1964-91, Ehrlich, Frazer & Feldman, Garden City, N.Y., 1992—; arbibrator U.S. Dist. Ct. (ea. dist.). Mem. panel mediators and fact-finders Nassau County Pub. Employment Rels. Bd., Mineola, N.Y., 1969—; mem. adv. bd. Little Village Sch. for Handicapped Children, Garden City, N.Y., 1979—, N.Y. State Sch. Music Assn., 1987—. Staff sgt. USAR, 1962-68. Fellow N.Y. State Bar Found.; mem. ABA, N.Y. State Bar Assn., N.Y. State Sch. Attys. Assn. (pres. 1983), Nassau County Bar Assn. (chair edn. law com. 1994-96), Theodore Roosevelt Am. Inns of Ct. Office: Ehrlich Frazer & Feldman 1415 Kellum Pl Garden City NY 11530-1695

EHRLICH, JOHN GUNTHER, writer; b. Berlin, Apr. 6, 1930; s. Walter Frederick and Henrietta (Fletch) E.; m. Frances Hendrika Vernon, Nov. 17, 1952 (div. Nov. 1978); children: Timothy Walter, Lisa Frances Gaffney; m. Karen Ann Carr, Dec. 31, 1982. BJ, Syracuse U., 1952; JD, Bklyn. Law Sch., 1962. Bar: N.Y. 1962; Federal, 1962; U.S. Dist. Ct. (so. dist., ea. dist.), 1962. Reporter Newsday, Huntington, N.Y., 1955-60; exec. asst. Suffolk County Rep. Com., Blue Point, N.Y., 1960-63; bur. chief Suffolk County Dist. Atty., Hauppauge, N.Y., 1963-90; writer Little River, S.C., 1990—. Author: (as Jack Ehrlich) Revenge, 1959, Court Martial, 1960, Parole, 1961, Slow Burn, 1961, Cry, Baby, 1962, The Girl Cage, 1967, Close Combat, 1969, The Drowning, 1970, The Chatham Killing, 1976, The Fastest Gun in the Pulpit, (German, French, Swedish transl., movie script from novel), 1972, Bloody Vengeance, 1973, The Laramie River Crossing, 1973, Rebellion at Cripple Creek, 1979, Command Influence, 2000; contbr. short stories, non-fiction articles to mags. Capt. USAF, 1952-54. Recipient Investigative Reporting award Nat. Home Builders, 1958, Edgar Allan Poe award Mystery Writers, N.Y.C., 1970, Cert. Appreciation, Suffolk County Police Benevolent Assn., 1989. Republican. Episcopalian. Avocations: golf, gardening, music, horseback riding. Office: PO Box 62 Little River SC 29566-0062 also: Theron Raines 103 Kenyon Rd Medusa NY 12120-2507

EHRLICH, KENNETH JAMES, television producer; b. Cleve., May 11; s. Arthur A. and Lucile Ehrlich; m. Harriet Stromberg, Feb. 19, 1967; children: Mathew, Dori. BS in Journalism, Ohio U., 1964. Pres. Comminique, Chgo., 1970-72; dir. devel. Sta. WTTW-TV, Chgo., 1972-76; pres. Ken Ehrlich Prodns., Los Angeles, 1976—. Exec. producer (series) Showtime Coast to Coast, numerous spls. with Paul Simon, Stevie Wonder, Phil Collins, Elton John, Shania Twain, Faith HIll, Celine Dion, others; producer Grammy Awards Show, 1980—, Blockbuster Awards, 1995-2001, Latin Grammys, Alma Awards; producer Soundstage (creator), 1974-83, Fame, 1983-85, Nelson Mandela Freedom Fest, 1988. Recipient Golden Rose of Montreaux (Switzerland) Montreax Film Fest, 1975, Golden Globe award Hollywood Fgn. Press Assn., Los Angeles, 1983, Emmy award Acad. of TV Arts and Scis., Los Angeles, 1984, Emmy award nominations, 1986, 88. Mem. Nat. Assn. Cable TV (bd. dirs.). Avocations: golf, music, writing. Office: Ken Ehrlich Prodns 17200 Oak View Dr Encino CA 91316-4014

EHRLICH, M. GORDON, lawyer; b. Springfield, Mass., Sept. 28, 1930; s. Robert and Ida (Gordon) E.; m. Eleanor Fradkin, Sept. 1, 1956; children: Kenneth, Virginia, Sarah, Alexandra. BS, Yale U., 1951; LLB, Harvard U., 1954. Bar: Mass. 1954. Atty. Bingham, McCutchen, Boston, 1957—. Former chmn. Boston Tax Forum; chmn. Boston Estate and Bus. Planning Coun.; lectr. Harvard U. Law Sch. Contbr. articles to profl. jours. Former pres. Chestnut Hill Assn.; bd. overseers Beth Israel Deaconess Hosp., Boston. Mem. ABA (tax sect.), Am. Law Inst. Office: Bingham McCutchen 150 Federal St Fl 14 Boston MA 02110-1745

EHRLICH, MORTON, international finance executive; b. N.Y.C., Dec. 1, 1944; s. Milton and Anne (Tannenbaum) E.; children from previous marriage: Bruce, Ellen, Wendy; m. Paula Ehrlich, Feb. 25, 1991. BBA cum laude, CCNY, 1960; PhD in Econs. (Ford Found. fellow), Brown U., 1965. Economist Fed. Res. Bank of N.Y., 1965-67, Nat. Indsl. Conf. Bd., N.Y.C., 1967-68; v.p. Eastern Airlines, Miami, 1968-76, sr. v.p. planning, 1976-85; exec. v.p. Transworld Airlines, N.Y., 1985-88. Also bd. dirs.; pres. LIFECO Svcs. Corp., 1988-91; chmn., CEO Integrated Mgmt. Corp., 1991-96, NSE, Inc., 1998—; trustee AETNA Mut. Funds; bd. dirs. Nat. Bur. Econ. Rsch., IBM/AFEC. Author: Discretionary Income, 1967, A Weekly Index of Business Activity, 1967, U.S. Foreign Trade, 1968, Computer Application in the Allocation of Airline Resources, 1975, An Integrated System for Airline Planning and Management Information, 1977, An Integrated Strategic Plan for Network Marketing, 1996, Paradigm Shift Syndrome, 1997. With U.S. Army, 1953-56. Mem. Am. Econ. Assn., Nat. Assn. Bus. Economists, U.S. C. of C. Office: A Privileged LIfestyle Inc 1000 Venetian Way Ste 1702 Miami FL 33139-1009 E-mail: lifestyle2@bigplanet.com.

EHRLICH, PAUL RALPH, biology educator; b. Phila., May 29, 1932; s. William and Ruth (Rosenberg) E.; m. Anne Fitzhugh Howland, Dec. 18, 1954; 1 child, Lisa Marie. AB, U. Pa., 1953; AM, U. Kans., 1955, PhD, 1957. Research assoc. U. Kans., Lawrence, 1958—59; asst. prof. biol. scis. Stanford U., 1959—62, assoc. prof., 1962—66, prof., 1966—, Bing prof. population studies, 1976—, dir. grad. study dept. biol. scis., 1966—69, pres. Ctr. for Conservation Biology, 1988—, dir. grad. study dept. biol. scis., 1974—76. Cons. Behavioral Rsch. Labs., 1963—67; corr. NBC News, 1989—92. Author: How to Know the Butterflies, 1961, Process of Evolution, 1963, Principles of Modern Biology, 1968, Population Bomb, 1968, Population Bomb, 2d edit., 1971, Population, Resources, Environment: Issues in Human Ecology, 1970, Population, Resources, Environment: Issues in Human Ecology, 2d edit, 1972, How to Be a Survivor, 1971, Global Ecology: Readings Toward a Rational Strategy for Man, 1971, Man and the Ecosphere, 1971, Introductory Biology, 1973, Human Ecology: Problems and Solutions, 1973, Ark II: Social Response to Environmental Imperatives, 1974, The End of Affluence: A Blueprint for the Future, 1974, Biology and Society, 1976, Race Bomb, 1977, Ecoscience: Population, Resources, Environment, 1977, Insect Biology, 1978, The Golden Door: International Migration, Mexico, and the U.S., 1979, Extinction: The Causes and Consequences of the Disappearance of Species, 1981, The Machinery of Nature, 1986, Earth, 1987, The Science of Ecology, 1987, The Birder's Handbook, 1988, New World/New Mind, 1989, The Population Explosion, 1990, Healing the Planet, 1991, Birds in Jeopardy, 1992, The Birdwatchers Handbook, 1994, The Stork & the Plow, 1995, Betrayal of Science and Reason, 1996, World of Wounds, 1997, Human Natures, 2000, Wild Solutions, 2001; contbr. Co-recipient Crafoord prize in population biology and conservation biol. diversity, 1990; recipient World Wildlife Fedn. medal, 1987, Volvo Environ. prize, 1993, World Ecology medal, Internat. Ctr. Tropical Ecology, 1993, UN Sasakawa Environ. prize, 1994, Heinz prize for the environment, 1995, Tyler Environ. prize, 1998, Heineken prize for environ. sci., 1998, Blue Plant prize, 1999; fellow MacArthur Prize fellow, 1990—95. Fellow: AAAS, Entomology Soc. Am., Am. Philos. Soc., Am. Acad. Arts and Scis., Calif. Acad. Scis.; mem.: NAS, Lepidopterists Soc., Am. Mus. Natural History (hon.), Am. Mus. Natural History (life), Brit. Ecol. Soc. (hon.), Am. Soc. Naturalists, Soc. Systematic Biology, Soc. for Study of Evolution, Ecol. Soc. Am. (Eminent Ecologist award 2001). Office: Stanford U Dept Biol Scis Stanford CA 94305

EHRLICH, ROBERT L., JR., governor, former congressman; b. 1957; Law clk. H. Russell Smouse, Esq., 1981; assoc. Ober, Kaler, Grimes, and Shriver, 1982-92, of counsel, 1992-94; mem. Md. Ho. of Dels., 1987-94, mem. Ho. Jud. Com., Joint Legis. Ethics Com., Gov.'s Coun. Child Abuse & Neglect, Gov.'s Adv. Panel for Justice Adminstrn., mem. Gov.'s Select Panel on Drug-Addicted Newborns, Gov.'s Select Panel on the Hickey Sch., also Ho. co-chmn. Joint Com. on Md.'s Procurement Laws; mem. U.S. Ho. of Reps., Washington, 1995—2003, mem. commerce com., subcom. finance & hazardous waste, energy & power, telecomm., trade & consumer protection, mem. budget com.; mem. Banking & Fin. Svcs. Com., subcoms. Fin. Insts. and Commercial Credit, Housing and Fin. Svcs., Spkrs. Spl. Adv. Com. on Corrections, U.S. Ho. of Reps., 104th Congress; asst. majority whip, Nat. Security Working Group, House Commerce Com. U.S. Ho. of Reps., 106th Congress; Governor, 2003—. Mem. house com. on energy and commerce, subcom. on environ. and hazardous waste, subcom. on telecomm. and internet, subcom. on health; co-chair congressional biotech. caucus, 2000-03. Named Guardian of Small Bus. Nat. Fedn. Ind. Bus., 1987-90, Legislator of Yr. Md. State's Attys. Assn., 1989, Fraternal Order of Police Md. State Lodge, 1994, Nat. Conf. for Prevention of Child Abuse, 1994, Outstanding Young Marylander Md. Jaycees, 1995, Outstanding Rep. Male Md. Rep. State Ctrl. Com., 1995, Disting. Svc. award German Soc. Md., 1997, Legislator of Yr. Nat. Assn. Mortgage Brokers, 1997; recipient Spirit of Enterprise award U.S. C. of C., 1996, 97, Thomas Jefferson award Food Distbrs. Internat., 1996, Congl. Tax Fighter award Nat. Tax Limitation Com., 1996, Taxpayer Hero award Citizens Against Govt. Waste, 1997. Republican. also: 1407 York Rd Ste 304 Lutherville MD 21093-6054 Office: Office of the Governor 100 State Circle Annapolis MD 21401*

EHRLICH, S(AUL) PAUL, JR., physician, consultant, former government official; b. Mpls., May 4, 1932; s. Sol P. and Dorothy E. (Fiterman) E.; m. Geraldine McKenna, June 20, 1959; children: Susan P., Paula J., Jill M. BA, U. Minn., 1953, BS, 1955, MD, 1957; M.P.H., U. Calif., 1961. Diplomate: Am. Bd. Preventive Medicine. Intern USPHS Hosp., S.I., N.Y., 1958; resident epidemiology U. Calif., 1961-63; mem. grants and tng. br. Nat. Heart Inst., Bethesda, Md., 1959-60; chief field and tng. sta. div. chronic diseases Heart Disease Control Program, San Francisco, 1961-65, asst. chief program devel. Arlington, Va., 1966-67; dep. chief Heart Disease Control Program of Nat. Center Chronic Disease Control, Arlington, 1967; asso. dir. bilateral programs Office Internat. Health of USPHS, Washington, 1967; dep. dir. Office of Internat. Health, Office of Sec., HEW, Washington, 1968-69, acting dir., 1969-70, dir., 1970-77; also acting surgeon gen. USPHS, 1973-77, dep. surgeon gen., 1976-77; v.p. Am. Insts. Research, Washington, 1978-79; dep. dir. Pan Am. Health Orgn., Washington, 1979-83; sr. adviser Am. Assn. World Health, 1984-86; health cons., 1984—. Adj. prof. internat. health U. Tex.; U.S. rep. exec. bd. WHO, 1969-72, 73-76, chmn., 1972 Contbr. articles to profl. jours. Bd. regents Uniformed Services U. Health Scis. Served to lt. USCG, 1958-59. Fellow Am. Coll. Preventive Medicine, Am. Pub. Health Assn.; mem. Assn. Mil. Surgeons (pres. 1977), Assn. Tchrs. Preventive Medicine, Nat. Coun. Internat. Health. Home: 1132 Seaspray Ave Delray Beach FL 33483-7140 E-mail: spehrlich@webtv.net.

EHRLICH, STACY WHEELER, school fundraiser, administrator; b. Austin, Tex., May 30, 1969; d. Robert Green and Sandria Eberhardt Wheeler; m. James Charles Ehrlich, June 11, 1994; 1 child, Megann Simms. BS in Advt., U. Tex., 1991; postgrad., U. Tex. Pan Am., Edinburg, 1995; MA in Human Svcs., St. Edwards U., 1996. Cert. fund raising exec. Asst. account exec. Meyer, Griffin and Wright, Houston, 1992-93; dir. devel., pub. rels. With Love Found., Houston, 1993; freshman counselor U. St. Thomas, Houston, 1993-94; dir. corp. found. giving Marine Mil. Acad., Harlingen, Tex., 1994-95; devel. assoc. major gifts U. Tex., Austin, 1995-96; dir. devel. Austin Waldorf Sch., Austin, 1996—. Cons. Non-Profit Mgmt. Assistance Program, Austin, 1997. Oscar night sponsor party co-chair Child and Family Svc., Austin, 1997. Mem. Jr. League of Austin, Nat. Soc. of Fund Raising Execs. (v.p. membership 1998-99), U. Tex. Ex-Students Assn., Zeta Tau Alpha. Roman Catholic. Avocations: volunteer work, church activities, self development tasks. Office: Austin Waldorf Sch 8700 S View Rd Austin TX 78737-1241

EHRLICH, STANLEY LEONARD, acoustical engineer, consultant; b. Newark, Jan. 7, 1925; s. Henry Max and Mary (Lichtenstein) Ehrlich; m. Louise Dorothy Waldfogel, June 19, 1949; children: Barbara Ellen, Stephen Mark, Michael Alan. BS, Brown U., 1944, MS, 1945; postgrad., MIT, 1945—48, U. Conn., 1951—53. Physicist USN Underwater Sound Lab., New London, Conn., 1948—53; sr. engr., submarine signal divsn. Raytheon Co., Boston, also Newton, Wayland, Mass., 1953—59, sect. mgr. Waltham, Mass., 1959—62, Portsmouth, RI, 1959—62, prin. engr., 1962—70, cons. engr., 1970—91; prin. acoustical cons. Stan Ehrlich Assocs., Newport, RI, 1992—. Assoc. editor Jour. Oceanic Engring., 1975—81, editor, 1982—88; assoc. editor Jour. Acoustical Soc. Am., 1981—2002. Translator (with F. Pordes): Fundamentals of Electroacoustics, 1955; patentee in field. City of Waltham chmn. Brown U. Ann. Fund, 1956—60, head class agt. Class of 1945, 1970—, 1940's decade chmn., 1980—82, class sec., 1990—; team capt. Newport Hosp. Bldg. Fund, 1967; Norman Bird Sanctuary, 1968—; mem. Brown U. Cmty. for Learning in Retirement, 1991—; mem. curriculum com. Salve Regina U. Cir. of Scholars, 1997—; mem. facilities mgmt. com. Middletown Pub. Schs.; mem. Middletown Devel. Adv. Com., Middletown (R.I.) Rep. Town Com., 1981—89, 2000—; bd. dirs. R.I. Arts Found. at Newport; sec. RI. Arts Found. at Newport, 1977—79; bd. dirs. Soc. Friends of Touro Synagogue, Newport, 1975—78. Recipient Freemen award, Providence Engring. Soc., 1976, Brown Engring. Alumni medal, 1998, 1st Mira Paul Meml. award as Internationally Renowned Acoustician Gold medal, Acoustical Found. for Edn. and Charitable Trust, presented at Vellore, India, 2001. Fellow: Am. Nat. Stds. Inst. (com. S1-acoustics, individual expert 1983—), Internat. Orgn. Standardization, Am. Phys. Soc., Oceanic Engring. Soc. (adminstrv. com. 1983—90), Acoustical Soc. Am. (chmn. Narragansett chpt. 1965—66, chmn. com. on regional chpts. 1976—85, chmn. 95th mtg. 1978, chmn. com. on engring. acoustics 1979—81, tech. coun. 1979—81, exec. coun. 1986—89, chmn. com. on medals and awards 1991—93, v.p.-elect 1992—93, v.p. 1993—94, chmn. com. on societal governance 1993—96, pres.-elect 1995—96, pres. 1996—97, past pres. 1997—98, Disting. Svc. citation 1986), Ultrasonics, Ferroelectrics, and Frequency Control Soc. (chmn. piezomagnetic tech. com. 1984—); mem.: IEEE (vice chmn. piezoelec. and ferroelec. crystals com. 1962—66, mem. coun. on oceanic engring. adminstrv. com. 1981—82, chmn. 1988—, stds. coord. com. 14.5 letter symbols for acoustics 1997—, stds. coord. com. SCC 14.5, life sr., Centennial award 1984), N.Y. Acad. Scis., Acoustical Soc. India (life), Newport Hist. Soc., Friends of the Middletown Pub. Libr., Newport Preservation Soc., Newport Hist. Soc., Middletown Hist. Soc., Friends of the Middletown Pub. Libr. (life), Middletown Hist. Soc. (life), Brown Club of Newport County (pres. 1969—71), B'nai B'rith (pres. Waltham 1957—58), Tau Beta Pi, Sigma Xi, Sigma Pi Sigma. Home: 1 Acacia Dr Middletown RI 02842-7001 Office: PO Box 3684 Newport RI 02840-0305

EHRLICH, SUSAN PATRICIA, banking executive; b. Long Beach, Calif., July 23, 1966; d. Clifford John and Patricia Marie E. BA, Brown U., 1988; MBA, Harvard U., 1993. Asst. v.p. Citibank NA, N.Y.C., 1995-97, Citibank Mastercard/Visa, Long Island City, N.Y., 1997-2000; v.p., dir. electronic bill payment c2it by Citibank, N.Y.C., 2000—. Mem. Congl. Country Club, Harvard Club. Roman Catholic. Avocations: golf, travel, sailing, wine. Office: Apt 2208 41 River Terr New York NY 10282 E-mail: susan.ehrlich@citicorp.com.

EHRLICH, THOMAS, law educator; b. Cambridge, Massachusetts, Mar. 4, 1934; s. William and Evelyn (Seltzer) E.; m. Ellen (Rome), June 18, 1957; children: David, Elizabeth, Paul. AB, Harvard U., Cambridge, Mass., 1956, LLB, 1959; LLD (hon.), Villanova U., 1979, Notre Dame U., 1980, Pa. State U., 1987. Bar: Wis., 1959. Law clk. Judge Learned Hand U.S. Ct. Appeals 2d. Cir., 1959-60; spl. asst. to legal adviser U.S. State Dept., 1962-64, spl. asst. to under-sec., 1964-65; assoc. prof. law Stanford U., Stanford, Calif., 1965-68; prof. Stanford U., Stanford, Calif., 1968-75; dean Stanford U., Stanford, Calif., 1971-75, Richard E. Lang dean and prof., 1973-75; pres. Legal Services Corp., Washington, 1976-79; dir. Internat. Devel. Coop. Agy., Washington, 1979-81; provost, prof. law U. Penn., Phila., 1981-87; pres., prof. law Ind. U., Bloomington and Indpls., Ind., 1987-94; vis. prof. Duke U., Durham, NC, 1994; disting. Univ. scholar U. Calif., San Francisco, 1995-2000. Vis. prof. Stanford Law Sch., 1994-99; sr. scholar, Carnegie Found. for Advancement of Tchg., 1997—. Author: (with Abram Chayes and Andreas F. Lowenfeld) The Internat. Legal Process, 3 vols., 1968; (with Herbert L. Packer) New Directions in Legal Edn., 1972, Internat. Crises and the Role of Law, Cyprus, 1958-67, 1974; editor: (with Geoffrey C. Hazard Jr.) Going to Law School?, 1975; (with Mary Ellen O'Connell) Internat. Law and the Use of Force, 1993, The Courage to Inquire, 1995, Philanthropy and the Nonprofit Sector in a Changing Am., 1998, Civic Responsibility and Higher Edn., 2000; (with Jane V. Wellman) How the Student Hour Shapes Higher Education: The Tie that Binds, 2003; (with others) Educating Citizens: Preparing America's Undergraduates for Lives of Moral and Civic Responsibility, 2003. Office: Carnegie Found Advancement Tech 555 Middlefield Rd Menlo Park CA 94025-3443

EHRLING, SIXTEN, orchestra conductor; b. Malmö, Sweden, Apr. 3, 1918; came to U.S., 1963; s. Gunnar and Emilia (Lundgren) E.; m. Gunnel Lindgren, Sept. 19, 1947; children: Elisabeth, Ann-Charlotte. Student, Royal High Sch. Music, Stockholm, 1936-40. Head conducting and orch. dept. Juilliard Sch., N.Y.C., 1973-88, Manhattan Sch. of Music, N.Y.C., 1993—. Condr. Royal Opera House, Stockholm, 1940-53, 90; prin. condr., music dir., 1953-60, condr., music dir. Detroit Symphony Orch., 1963-73; mus. advisor, prin. guest condr. Denver Symphony, 1978-89, music advisor, 1989—; guest condr. Met. Opera, N.Y.C., U.S., Europe, Japan, Australia, South Am., Vienna State Opera.

EHRMAN, JOACHIM BENEDICT, mathematics educator; b. Nuremberg, Germany, Nov. 12, 1929; emigrated to U.S., 1938, naturalized, 1943; s. Fritz Sally and Ilse (Benedict) E.; m. Gloria Jeanette Gould, Jan. 24, 1961; 1 son, Carl David. AB, U. Pa., 1948; A.M., Princeton, 1949, PhD, 1954. Research physicist N.Am. Aviation, Inc., Downey, Calif., 1951-53; instr. physics Yale, 1954-55; research physicist U.S. Naval Research Lab., Washington, 1955-68; prof. dept. applied math. U. Western Ont., Can., 1968—. Asso. prof. physics George Washington U., 1956-57; lectr. U. Md., 1963-64; vis. research staff Plasma Physics Lab., Princeton, 1975-76 Contbr. profl. jours. Mem. Phi Beta Kappa. Jewish. Office: U Western Ont Dept Applied Math London ON Canada N6A 5B7 E-mail: jehrman@uwo.ca.

EHRMAN, LEE, geneticist, educator; b. N.Y.C., May 25, 1935; m. Richard Ehrman, 1955; children: Esther, Judith. BS, Queens Coll., 1956; MS, Columbia U., 1957, PhD in Genetics, 1959; DSc (hon.), CUNY, 1989. Mem. faculty Barnard Coll., 1956-58; postdoctoral fellow in genetics Columbia U., N.Y.C., 1959-61, assoc. seminar on population biology, 1981—; mem. faculty SUNY-Purchase, 1970—, prof. div. natural scis., 1972—; Disting. prof. biology SUNY, Purchase, 1995—; mem. spl. study sect. NIH, NIMH, 1979-80. Vis. disting. prof. U. Miami, Coral Gables, Fla., 1981; vis. lectr. U. Puerto Rico, Rio Piedras, 1987; coordinator, panelist workshops, programs in field; mem. panels NIH, 2003—. Author: Behavior Genetics and Evolution, 2d edit., 1981, 2 other books; assoc. editor Evolution; assoc. editor for genetics and cytology Am. Midland Naturalist; co-editor: Behavior Genetics; assoc. editor, exec. com. Soc. Am. Naturalists, 1977-85, pres.-elect 1990; contbr. more than 500 articles to profl. jours. Recipient Lit. Soc. Found. medal in German, 1956; Shirley Farr postdoctoral fellow, 1961-62; USPHS postdoctoral fellow, 1959-61; faculty exch. scholar, 1974—; NSF grantee, 1979-84; Sr. Scientist awardee Whitehall Found., 1987, 93; NIH gen. med. scis. grantee, 1987—; SUNY travel grantee, 1988, 93, 96; Merck rsch. support grantee, 2000—. Fellow AAAS (Rsch. Support award Merck/AAAS, 2001), Inst. Soc. Ethics and Life Scis; mem. AAUW (life), Am. Soc. Naturalists (pres. 1990), Behavior Genetics Assn. (pres. 1978, Dobzhansky award for lifetime rsch. 1988), Soc. for Study of Evolution (exec. council 1986—), Phi Beta Kappa, Sigma Xi Home: 2 Jennifer Ln Rye Brook NY 10573-1916 Office: SUNY Div Natural Scis Purchase NY 10577 Fax: (914) 251-6635.

EHRMAN, MADELINE ELIZABETH, federal agency administrator; b. N.Y.C., July 4, 1942; d. Donald McKinley and Marie Madeleine (Brandeis) Ehrman. BA summa cum laude, Brown U., 1964, MA, 1965; M of Philosophy, Yale U., 1967; PhD, The Union Inst., 1989. Sci. linguist U.S. Dept. State, Washington, 1969-73; regional land. supr. U.S. Embassy, Bangkok, Thailand, 1973-75; lang. tng. supr. U.S. Dept. State, Washington, 1975-84, curriculum and tng. specialist, 1984-85, acting chmn. dept. Asian and African Langs., 1985, chmn. dept. Asian and African Langs., 1986-88, acting assoc. dean Sch. Lang. Studies, 1987-88, dir. rsch., evaluation and devel., 1989—. Sr. assoc. Nat. Fgn. Lang. Ctr., 2001—. Author: The Meanings of the Modals in Present Day American English, 1966, Contemporary Cambodian, 1975, Indonesian Fast Course, 1982, Communicative Japanese Materials, 1984, Ants and Grasshoppers, Badgers and Butterflies: Qualitative and Quantitative Exploration of Adult Language Learning Styles and Strategies, 1989, Understanding Second Language Learning Difficulties, 1996, Interpersonal Dynamics in Second Language Education, 1998, (CD-ROMS) Out and About in Bangkok, Beijing, Moscow, 2000; mem. editl. bd. Jour. Psychol. Type, 1991—. Mem. ESOL/HILT Citizen's Adv. Coun., Arlington County, Va., 1985-89; psychotherapist Meyer Treatment Ctr. Washington Sch. Psychiatry, 1989-94. Recipient Meritorious Honor award, U.S. Dept. State, 1972, 1983, 1998, 1999, 2001. Fellow Nat. Fgn. Lang. Ctr.; mem. Am. Psychol. Assn., Tchrs. of English to Spkrs. of Other Langs., Am. Assn. for Applied Linguistics, Assn. for Psychol. Type, Phi Beta Kappa, Psi Chi. Avocations: reading, computers, gardening. Office: Fgn Svc Inst 4000 Arlington Blvd Arlington VA 22204-1586

EHRMANN, SUSANNA, foreign language educator, writer, photographer; b. Detroit, Oct. 17, 1944; d. Frederick Michael and Stephanie (Fiala) Ehrmann. Student, Universite Laval, summer 1965; BA, Antioch Coll., 1966; MAT, U. Chgo., 1968. Cert. tchr., Ill., Tex. Tchr. fgn. lang. U. Chgo. Lab. Schs., 1967-74, Maimonides Sch., Brookline, Mass., 1975-76, North Shore Country Day Sch., Winnetka, Ill., 1977-78, Copenhagen Internat. Jr. Sch., 1978-79, Houston C.C., 1979-81, 84, Kinkaid Sch., Houston, 1980-82, Alief Ind. Sch. Dist., Houston, 1982-85, Houston Ind. Sch. Dist., 1990-91; pvt. instr., 1986—; freelance rschr., editor, 1986—; writer, photographer, 1993—. Mem. North Cen. evaluating teams, Chgo., Rockford, 1971; mem. MAT coordinating com. on Romance langs., U. Chgo., 1971-74. Creator German Grammar Game, 1982. Reader for the blind, Chgo., 1972-74. NDEA fellow, 1966-68; Goethe Inst. grantee, summer 1983. Mem. MLA, Am. Assn. Tchrs. of French, Am. Assn. Tchrs. of German. Home: 3001 Landwehr Rd Northbrook IL 60062-7517 E-mail: fiala3@juno.com.

EHRNSCHWENDER, ARTHUR ROBERT, former utility company executive; b. Cin., Oct. 3, 1922; s. Arthur Michael and Lydia Carol (Widmer) E.; m. Grace Scholl Popplewell, Oct. 19, 1950; children: Barry N., Scott A. ME, U. Cin., 1948, BS in Commerce, 1959; MBA, Xavier U., 1959; D in Tech. Letters (hon.), Cin. Tech. Coll., 1980. Registered profl. engr., Ohio, Ky. Field engr. SKF Bearing Co., Cin., 1948-49; Chevrolet field rep. GM, Cin., 1949-50; with Cin. Gas and Electric Co., 1952-84, former sr. v.p. Bd. dirs. Porter Precision Products, Cin.; vice chmn., bd. dirs. OKI Supply Co., Cin.; past chmn. The Hwy. Rental Co., Cin. Electric Co. Past pres. Goodwill Industries, Cin., 1961-85; trustee Cin. Assn. for Blind, 1965—, Hamilton county YMCA, 1974—; chmn. bd. trustees Deaconess Hosp., Cin., 1970— . Capt. U.S. Army, 1943-46, 1950-52. Decorated Bronze Star, 1952; named Disting. Alumnus U. Cin., 1974, Xavier U. Mem. Soc. Automotive Engrs. (sect. chmn.), Engring. Soc. Cin., Edison Electric Inst. (divsn. chmn.), Am. Gas Assn. (sect. chmn.), Queen City Club, Cin. Country Club, The Club Pelican Bay, Naples Yacht Club, Stumps Boat Club, Masons (hon. 33d degree). Republican. Presbyterian. Home: 1201 Edgecliff Pl Apt 1083 Cincinnati OH 45206-2853 Home (Winter): 5954 Pelican Bay Blvd Naples FL 34108-8153

EHSANI, MEHRDAD (MARK EHSANI), electrical engineering educator, consultant; naturalized, 1980; s. Heshmat and Didar (Ahmadi) Ehsani; m. Zohreh Khadem; children: Evan Mancil, Nathaniel William. MS, U. Tex., 1974; PhD, U. Wis., 1981. Registered profl. engr., Tex. Rsch. engr. Fusion Rsch. Ctr. U. Tex., Austin, 1974-77; rsch. engr. Argonne (Ill.) Nat. Lab., 1977-81; prof. elec. engring. Tex. A&M U., College Station, 1981, Halliburton prof. elec. engring., 1992, Dress Industries prof., 1994, dir. Tex. Applied Power Electronics Ctr., 1999, dir. advanced vehicle systems rsch. program, Dow Chem. fellow Coll. Engring., 2001—02. Lectr. in field. Author: Converter Circuits for Superconductive Magnetic Energy Storage, 1988, Modern Electrical Drives, 2000; co-author: ANSI/IEEE Standards 936, 1987; contbr. over 300 articles to profl. jours.; 23 patents in field. Named Outstanding Young Engr., Tex. Soc. Profl. Engrs., 1984, Disting. Lectr., IEEE-Industry Applications Soc., Inds. Elecs. Soc., Dow Chem. fellow, Coll. Engring., Tex. A&M U., 2001. Fellow IEEE (Undergrad. Tchr. award 2003); mem. Power Electronics Soc. of IEEE (adminstrv. com. 1990-96), Industry Applications Soc. of IEEE (exec. coun. 1989-93, Disting. lectr.), IEEE Vehicular Tech. Soc. (bd. govs., bd. dirs., assoc. editor, James R. Evans Avant Garde award, 2001). Baha'I. Office: Tex A&M U Dept Elec Engring College Station TX 77843-0001 E-mail: ehsani@ee.tamu.edu.

EIBEL, ANDREW H. lawyer; b. N.Y.C., Sept. 3, 1950; s. A. Isadore and Cecele (Wainstein) E.; m. Nancy Roberta Stenzler Friedrich, June 22, 1987. AB, Columbia Coll., 1971; JD, Hofstra U., 1976. Bar: N.Y. 1977. Staff atty. criminal appeals bur., parole revocation def. Legal Aid Soc., N.Y.C., 1976-79, staff atty. criminal def. div. Bklyn., 1979-89, supervising atty. criminal def. div., 1989—98, 2002—, tng. coord. crim. def. divsn., 1998—2002. Adj. prof. legal writing program N.Y. Law Sch., 1996-99. Mem. Nat. Assn. Criminal Def. Lawyers, Nat. Legal Aid & Defender Assn., N.Y. State Assn. Criminal Def. Attys., N.Y. State Defender Assn., Kings County Bar Assn., N.Y. County Lawyers' Assn., Assn. of Bar of City of N.Y., N.Y. Criminal Bar Assn. Democrat. Avocations: fencing, reading, travel. Home: 140 8th Ave Apt 5A Brooklyn NY 11215-1729 Office: Legal Aid Suc Criminal Def 111 Livingston St Brooklyn NY 11201 E-mail: aeibel@legal-aid.org.

EIBEN, ROBERT MICHAEL, pediatric neurologist, educator; b. Cleve., July 12, 1922; s. Michael Albert and Frances Carlysle (Gedeon) E.; m. Anne F. Eiben; children: Daniel F., Christopher J., Thomas M., Mary, Charles G., Elizabeth A. BS, Western Res. U., 1944, MD, 1946. Diplomate Am. Bd. Pediatrics. Intern medicine Univ. Hosp., Cleve., 1946-47; asst. resident pediatrics and contagious diseases City Hosp., Cleve., 1947, asst. med. dir. div. contagious diseases, 1949-50, visitant in pediatrics, 1949-50, acting dir. dept. pediatrics and contagious diseases, 1950-52; asst. resident pediatrics Babies and Children's Hosp., Cleve., 1948, clin. fellow pediatrics, 1948-49; practice medicine specializing in pediatrics Cleve., 1949-90; asst. dir. dept. pediatrics and contagious diseases Cleve. Met. Gen. Hosp., 1952-60; med. dir. Respiratory Care and Rehab. Center, 1954-60, pres. med. staff, 1958-60, pediatric neurologist, 1963-90, acting med. dir. comprehensive care program, 1966-67, med. dir., 1968-73, mem. med. exec. com., 1974-76, acting dir. dept. pediatrics, 1979-80; USPHS fellow in neurology U. Wash., 1960-63; acting chief, sect. on clin. investigations and therapeutics Developmental and Metabolic Neurology br. Nat. Inst. Neurol. and Communicative Disorders and Strokes, NIH, Bethesda, Md., 1976-77; clin. instr. pediatrics Western Res. U., 1949-50, instr. pediatrics, 1950-51, asst. clin. prof., 1951-54, asst. prof., 1954-65, asst. prof. neurology, 1964-72, assoc. prof. pediatrics, 1965-75, assoc. prof. neurology, 1972-85, prof. pediatrics, 1975-90, prof. neurology, 1985-90, prof. emeritus pediatric neurology, 1991—. Cons., project site visitor Nat. Found. Birth Defects Center Programs, 1961-66; mem. adv. com. on grants to train dentists to care for handicapped Robert Wood Johnson Found., 1975-80; marshall emeriti faculty Case Western Reserve U., 1994—. Mem. coun. Bratenahl Village-County of Cuyahoga, 1982-98. Recipient Presdl. award Internat. Poliomyelitis Congress, Geneva, 1957, Clifford J. Vogt Alumni Svc. award Case Western Res. U., Cleve., 1985; established Annual Robert M. Eiben, M.D. vis. professorship in child neurology MetroHealth Med. Ctr. Dept. Pediat., 1991. Mem.: Child Neurology Soc. (chmn. tng. program com. 1976—77, sec.-treas. 1978—81, pres. 1983—85), Innominatum Soc., No. Ohio Pediat. Soc., Am. Epilepsy Soc., Am. Pediat. Soc., Am. Soc. Human Genetics, Am. Acad. Neurology (chmn. residence exam. com. 1989—93), Am. Acad. Pediat., Case Western Res. U. Med. Alumni Assn. (pres. 1979), Pasteur Club. Home: 2 Oakshore Dr Bratenahl OH 44108-1118 Office: MetroHealth Med Ctr 2500 Metrohealth Dr Cleveland OH 44109-1900

EIBENSTEINER, RON, political organization administrator, venture capitalist; Co-founder, CFO Arden Med. Sys., 1983-87; pres., CEO, chmn. Mirror Techs., Inc., 1988-92, 94—, chmn., 1992-94; pres. Wyncrest Captial; dir. IntraNet Solutions, Inc., 2003—; chmn. OneLink Comm., Inc., 2003—, KidsFirst Scholarship Fund Minn., Inc., 2003—; dir. Ctr. Am. Experiment, 2003—. Co-founder Diametrics, OnHealth Network; chmn. Prodea Software. Chmn. Minn. Reps., 1999—; chair Minn. Rep. Party, 1999-. Mem.: Republican Nat. Conv. (com. on call 2000), Midwestern State Chmn.'s Assn. Office: Rep Party Minn 480 Cedar St Ste 560 Saint Paul MN 55101-2240*

EIBERGER, CARL FREDERICK, lawyer; b. Denver, Jan. 17, 1931; s. Carl Frederick and Madeleine Anastasia (Ries) E.; children: Eileen, Carl III, Mary, James. BS in Chemistry magna cum laude, U. Notre Dame, 1952, JD magna cum laude, 1954; MBA, Denver U., 1959. Sole practice, 1954-55; ptnr. Rovira, DeMuth & Eiberger, Denver, 1957-69, Eiberger, Stacy, Smith & Martin, Denver, 1979-96; prin. Carl F. Eiberger & Assocs., Denver, 1996—. Chmn. CBA/DBA/Econs. of Law Practice Coms.; co-founder CBA/Steering Com. Labor Law Com., Denver; arbitrator Am. Arbitration Assn.; asst. bar examiner, 1963-68; lectr. on continuing legal edn. Contbr. articles to legal jours. Bd. dirs. Colo. Assn. Commerce and Industry; pres. Prospect Recreation and Park Dist.; founder Applewood Athletic Club, Jefferson County; gen. counsel Denver Symphony Orch. Recipient merit award Jefferson County Commrs., merit cert. Jefferson County Homeowners, McCafferty Disting Svc. award U. Notre Dame Law Sch.; named Man of the Yr. Notre Dame Club of Denver, Vol. of Yr. Channel 9TV, Denver., Citizen of Yr., Lions Club Internat; Prospect Dist. Pk. named in his honor. Mem. ABA, Colo. Bar Assn. (bd. govs.), Denver Bar Assn. (nominated pres.), Notre Dame Law Assn. (bd. dirs. 1965—, exec. com. 1998—), Gov. Adv. Coun. to Colo dept. of labor, Notre Dame Club (pres., bd. dirs.), Athletic Club (Denver). Roman Catholic. Home: 14330 Fairview Ln Golden CO 80401-2050 Office: 14330 Fairview Ln Golden CO 80401-2050

EICHBERG, RODOLFO DAVID, physician, educator; b. Pforzheim, Germany, July 26, 1937; came to the U.S., 1965; s. Julio and Ilse (Schonfarber) E.; m. Yvette Salama, May 21, 1965; children: William Amadeo, Matias David. Baccalaureate, St. Andrews Scots Sch., Argentina, 1955; MD, U. Buenos Aires, 1963. Intern, resident Grace Hosp. Wayne State U., Detroit, 1965-67; orthopedic surgeon Mar Del Plata, Argentina, 1968-73; resident physical medicine NYU, 1973-75; pvt. practice Rehab. and Electro Diagnosis Assocs., P.C., Tampa, 1975-96, 98—; asst. prof. U. So. Fla., Tampa, 1975-93, clin. assoc. prof., 1994—; chief spinal cord injury rehab. Tampa Gen. Hosp., 1984-96; chief phys. medicine & rehab. VA Med. Ctr., New Orleans, 1997 98; med. dir. Meml. Hosp. Ctr. for Comprehensive Rehab., 1998—. Mem. state adv. coun. Head Spinal Cord Injuries, Tallahassee, 1976-96; clin. assoc. prof. La. State U. Sch. Medicine, 1997-98; physician advisor State of Fla. Athletic Commn., 1998-99; mem. advisor State of Fla. Agy. for Healthcare Adminstrn., 2001—. Contbr. articles to profl. jours. Bd. trustees Congregation Schaaraizedek, Tampa, 1980-82. Recipient Honors award City of La Paz, Bolivia, 1994, Physician of Yr. award Tampa Bay Latin Am. Med. Soc., 1997. Mem. AMA, Am. Acad. Phys. Medicine and Rehab. (health policy legis. com. 1990-95), Am. Spinal Injury Assn. (internat. rels. rep. S.C. 1990-95), Assn. Med. Latino Americana de Rehab., Colombian Phys. Medicine Rehab. Soc. (corr.), Argentine Soc. Rehab. Medicine (corr.), Fla. Med. Assn., Fla. Soc. Phys. Medicine Rehab. (pres. 1994-96), Hillsborough County Med. Assn. (exec. coun. 2001-03), So. Soc. Phys. Medicine and Rehab. (pres. 1999-2000). Jewish. Avocations: boating, tennis, travel. Office: Rehab and Electro Diag Assocs PA 2914 N Boulevard Tampa FL 33602-1208 E-mail: eichberg@tampabay.rr.com.

EICHBERGER, LEROY CARL, mechanical engineer, consultant, stress analyst; b. Chgo., Oct. 26, 1927; s. Roy George and Phyllis Zena (Goss) E.; m. Mary Ann Teresa Bronars, Sept. 10, 1955; children: Charles David, David Paul, Scott Thomas. BSME, U. Ill., 1951, MS, 1955, PhD, 1959. Registered profl. engr., Tex. Assoc. prof. U. Houston, 1959-77; mgr. engring. Weatherford Lamb USA, Houston, 1977-80; mgr. R&D Atlas Bradford, Houston, 1980-89; ind. cons. Houston, 1989—. Tech. cons. Reed Roller Bit Co., Houston, 1959-61, Exxon Co. USA, Houston, 1968-77; staff cons. H.O. Mohr Rsch. and Engring., Houston, 1989-2001, Mohr Engring. and Testing, 2001-03, mohr engring divsn., 2003— . Author monographs on methods for dynamic calibration of pressure transducers. With USCG, 1946-47. Recipient Arthur Lubinski award of excellence Offshore Tech. Conf., Houston, 1984. Mem. ASME, Soc. Exptl. Stress Analysis. Christian Scientist. Home and Office: 5310 Dumfries Dr Houston TX 77096-5107

EICHEL, EDWARD WILLIAM, psychotherapist, painter; b. Bklyn., June 8, 1932; s. Martin and Elizabeth (Shapiro) Eichelbaum. BFA, Sch. Art Inst. Chgo., 1958; MA, NYU, 1984; LHD (hon.), Med. U. of Americas, Nevis, W.I., 2003. Cert. experiential psychotherapist. Psychotherapist in pvt. practice, N.Y.C., 1969—; group therapy leader Aureon Inst., N.Y.C., 1968 70; founder, dir. Creativity Labs., Inc., 1971-84; pres. Marriage Sci., Inc., N.Y.C., 2001—. Instr. art Ea. Mich. U., Ypsilanti, 1965-66, Queens (N.Y.) Coll., 1966, L.I. U., Bklyn., 1967, St. Vincent's Hosp., N.Y.C., 1967-69, Hartford (Conn.) Art Sch., 1981-83; health educator Medgar Evers Coll., Bklyn., 1984, Flushing (N.Y.) Boys Club, 1985-86; counselor AIDS Hotline, N.Y.C. Health Dept., 1990; faculty 1995 Nat. Clin. Conf., Am. Acad. Clin. Sexologists. Artist: The Glass Cage: The Jerusalem Trial (of Adolf Eichmann), 1962 (original drawings on loan to Dallas Meml. Ctr. for Holocaust Studies), Israel Sketchbook, 1962, The Beast Book (by Jan Wahl), 1964; author: Kinsey, Sex and Fraud: The Indoctrination of a People, 1990, The Perfect Fit: How to Achieve Mutual Fulfillment, 1992; prodr. (video) The Coital Alignment Technique, version 1.1, 2002; contbr. articles to profl. jours. With USCG, 1951-54. Recipient award Oskar Kokoschka Acad., Salzburg, Austria, 1959, medal of merit Painters and Sculptors Soc. N.J., 1968; Louis Comfort Tiffany Fond. grantee for painting, 1967; George D. and Isabella A. Brown Fgn. Travel fellow, 1958. Mem. Soc. for Sci. Study of Sex (com. on sci. and profl. affairs 1986-87), Am. Assn. Sex Educators, Counselors and Therapists, Fedn. Modern Painters and Sculptors (v.p.), Nat. Expressive Therapy Assn. (hon. life; bd. dirs. 1979-83).

EICHEL, PAUL HERMAN, electrical engineer; b. Dayton, Ohio, Mar. 28, 1956; s. Herman Joseph and Margaret Ann (Ens) E.; m. Catherine Jean (Jones) Eichel, Oct. 13, 1979; children: Carl, Daniel, Julia. BE, Vanderbilt U., 1978; MS, Stanford U., 1979; PhD, U. Mich., 1985. Mem. tech. staff Bell Labs., Holmdel, N.J., 1978-81; disting. mem. tech. staff Sandia Nat. labs., Albuquerque, 1985—. Instr., lectr. SAR Edn. Assocs., Albuquerque, 1996—. Author: Spotlight-Mode Synthetic Aperture Radar: A Signal Processing Approach, 1996; patentee in field. Recipient R&D 100 award R&D mag., 1990. Mem. IEEE. Office: Sandia Nat Labs MS 1207 Albuquerque NM 87185 E-mail: eichel@ieee.org.

EICHELBERGER, CHARLES BELL, retired career officer; b. LaGrange, Ga., Nov. 19, 1934; s. Charlie Wirt and Sybil Peavy (Johnson) E.; m. Jaqueline Ann Wood, July 17, 1955; children: Susan Christie Eichelberger Benator, Terrie Lynn Eichelberger Safranca. Cert. in Liberal Arts, Ga. Mil. Coll., 1955, BS in Law Enforcement, U. Nebr., 1971; MEd, Pepperdine U., 1977. Commd. 2d lt. U.S. Army, 1957, advanced through grades to lt. gen., 1989; comdr. U.S. Army Field Station, Berlin, 1978-80; div. chief Reconnaissance, Intelligence, Surveillance and Electronic Warfare Div., dep. chief of staff for ops. and plans, Dept. of Army, Washington, 1980-82; dep. comdt. U.S. Army Intelligence Ctr. and Sch., Ft. Huachuca, Ariz., 1982-84; dir. of intelligence (J-2) U.S. Cen. Command, MacDill AFB, Fla., 1984-86; dep. chief of staff for intelligence U.S. Army Europe, Heidelberg, Fed. Republic Germany, 1986-88, Dept. of Army, Washington, 1988-91; ret., 1991. Contbr. articles to profl. jours. Decorated D.S.M. with oak leaf cluster, Nat. Intelligence D.S.M. (CIA), Master Parachutist badge. Mem. Assn. Old Crows, Assn. U.S. Army, Ret. Officers' Assn. Home: 124 Sweetwater Oaks Peachtree City GA 30269-2110 E-mail: ceichelber@aol.com.

EICHENBERG, DAVID JAMES, artist, educator; b. Toledo, Mar. 21, 1972; s. Donald James Eichenberg and Loralie Marie Hughes; m. Stephanie Ann Burger. BFA, U. Toledo, 1997. Visual coord. It's Reigning Frogs, Toledo, 2001—02; tech. asst. Astist Jack Schmidt, Toledo, 2000—01. Instr. Toledo Mus. Art, 1996—2003; art tech. U. Toledo, 2002—03. Pub. collections, Corpus Christi Parish, Toledo, 1998, commd. design, U. Toledo, 1997, didactic display, Toledo Mus., Tampa Mus., 1996. Com. bd. mem. One Percent for the Arts, U. Toledo, 1996—97. Avocations: painting, sculpting, travel, reading, Tai Jitsu. Home: 2642 Scottwood Ave Toledo OH 43610 Personal E-mail: molten@buckeye-express.com.

EICHENBERG, PETER THOMPSON, state agency administrator; s. Paul Lawrence Eichenberg and Patricia Ann Thompson; married, June 2, 1982; children: Cory Franklyn, Pete L. AS, BS, U. Albuquerque, 1986. Juvenile probation officer 2d Jud. Dist. Ct., 1974—75; security officer Fed. Protection Svc., 1975—76; fraud investigator, owner Albuquerque Investigation Svc., 1977—91; patrol operator, owner Peter Thompson & Assoc., 1978—80; recreation aide KAFB Youth Ctr., N.Mex., 1980—82, asst. dir., 1982—84; spl. dep. Sandoval County Sheriff's Dept., 1983—84; investigator litigation unit City Atty.'s Office, 1985—86; fraud investigator N.Mex. Workers' Compensation Adminstrn., 1991—2000; cons. Peter Eichenberg & Assocs., 2000—02; gaming auditor N.Mex. Gaming Control Bd., N.Mex., 2002—. Instr., coach Youth Sports Assn., 1981—; dir. N.Mex. Respite Assn., Inc., 2002—. Contbr. articles to profl. jours. Driver Catholic Charities of N.Mex.; sponsor Christian Found. for Children and Aging, Kansas City, Kans. With U.S. Army, 1965—71. John Robert Meml. scholar, 1986. Mem.: VFW, Nat. Notary Assn., Nat. Police and Firefighters Assn., Delta Epsilon Sigma. Democrat. Roman Catholic. Avocations: reading, fishing, softball, running. Mailing: PO Box 11671 Albuquerque NM 87192 Home: 11800 Elvin NE Albuquerque NM 87112 Office: NMex Gaming Control Bd 6400 Uptown Blvd NE Ste 100-E Albuquerque NM 87110

EICHENBERGER, JERRY ALAN, lawyer; b. Columbus, Ohio, Apr. 16, 1947; m. Candace R. Roberson, Jan. 17, 1971; 1 child, Sara Marie. BS, Ohio State U., 1970; JD, Capital U., 1975. Bar: Ohio 1975, U.S. Supreme Ct. 1978, U.S. Dist. Ct. (no. and so. dists.) Ohio 175, U.S. Ct. Appeals (6th cir.) 1976. Ptnr. Martin & Eichenberger, Columbus, 1975-90, Crabbe, Brown, Jones, Potts & Schmidt, Columbus, 1990-2000, Eichenberger & Assocs., Columbus, 2001—. Adj. prof. aviation law Ohio State U., Columbus, 1988-90. Author: General Aviation Law, 1990, 2d edit., 1998, Your Pilot's License, 1998, Cross Country Flying, 1996, Handling In-Flight Emergencies, 2001; contbr. articles to bus. and comml. aviation jours. Lt. col. CAP, chief check pilot 1980-84, legal officer, 1986-90. Named Ky. Col. Commonwealth Ky., 1972. Mem. ABA, Lawyer-Pilots Bar Assn., Ohio State Bar Assn., Aviation Ins. Assn., Aircraft Owners and Pilots Assn., Exptl. Aircraft Assn., Gen. Aviation Operators Assn., Columbus Maennerchor Club, Masons, Shriners. Republican. Baptist. Avocations: aviation, bicycling. Office: Eichenberger & Assocs 6099 Frantz Rd Columbus OH 43017 E-mail: JEichenberger@ehlawyers.com.

EICHENWALD, HEINZ FELIX, physician; b. Switzerland, Mar. 3, 1926; came to U.S., 1936, naturalized, 1945; s. Ernst M. and Stella E.; m. Linda E. Moragné, July 20, 1995; children: Kathryn S., Eric C., Kurt A., Michael M. BA in Biochem. Scis. magna cum laude, Harvard U., 1946; MD, Cornell U., 1950. Successively intern, sr. asst. resident, sr. resident pediatrician N.Y. Hosp., 1950-51; asst. in pediatrics Cornell U. Med. Sch., 1951-53, instr., then asst. prof., 1955-58, assoc. prof., then prof. pediatrics, 1958-64; USPHS instr. pediatrics Emory U. Med. Sch., 1953-55; also vis. physician Grady and Crawford Long hosps., Atlanta; mem. staff N.Y. Hosp., 1958-65, attending pediatrician, 1963-65; vis. asst. prof. Albert Einstein Med. Sch., 1956-58; cons. Hosp. Spl. Surgery, N.Y.C., 1956-64, Patterson (N.J.) Gen. Hosp., 1958-64; prof. pediatrics, chmn. dept. U. Tex. Southwestern Med. Sch., Dallas, 1964-83; chief-of-staff Children's Med. Ctr., Dallas, 1964—; chief pediatrics Parkland Meml. Hosp., Dallas, 1964—. Cons. St. Paul, Irving Community, Presbyn. hosps., Dallas; chief hepatitis investigation unit, epidemiology br. USPHS, 1954-55; Richard Bruce Miller lectr. Harvard U. Med. Sch., 1960; lectr. Columbia U. Tchrs. Coll., 1960-64; chmn. Internat. Rsch. Confs. Mental Retardation, 1965-66; chmn. panel anti-infectives NAS-NRC, 1966-69; vis. prof. U. Saigon Med. Sch., 1968-72; Vanuxem lectr. Princeton U., 1970; bd. dirs. Dallas Free Clinic, 1970-74, Children's Devel. Ctr., Dallas, 1974— ; mem.

bd. maternal and child health NIH, 1974-78; cons. in field, mem. numerous profl. coms. Assoc. editor Pediatric Therapy, 1974; editor Practical Pediatric Therapy, 1985, Current Therapy in Pediatrics, 1989, Pediatric Therapy, 1993; mem. editorial bd. profl. jours.; contbr. numerous articles in profl. publs. Bd. dirs., chmn. exec. com. Lamplighter Sch., Dallas, 1971—; bd. dirs. Winston Sch., 1974. Recipient Career Rsch. award NIH, 1963-65, Alexander von Humboldt prize Govt. of Germany (then Fed. Republic Germany), 1979, Weinstein-Goldeson award United Cerebral Palsy Found., 1980; Markle scholar med. sci., 1953. Mem. Harvey Soc., Soc. Pediatric Rsch., Am. Pediatric Soc., Infectious Disease Soc. Am., N.Y. Acad. Scis., Tex. Pediatric Soc., Phi Beta Kappa, Sigma Xi, Alpha Omega Alpha. Office: 5323 Harry Hines Blvd Dallas TX 75390-7208 E-mail: echo18@prodigy.net.

EICHER, DONALD E., III, lawyer; b. Vicksburg, Miss., July 26, 1969; s. Donald E. Jr. and Rosemary E. Eicher; m. Amy Christine Carlson, May 30, 1998. BBA cum laude, U. Miss., 1991, JD, 1994. Bar: Miss. 1994, U.S. Dist. Ct. (no. and so. dists.) Miss. 1994, U.S. Ct. Appeals (5th cir.) 1994, Ala. 1996, U.S. Dist. Ct. (ctrl. dist.) Ala. 1999, U.S. Ct. Appeals (11th cir.) 1999. Assoc. McTeer Assocs., Greenville, Miss., 1994-96, William L. Bambach, Columbus, Miss., 1996; atty. Malone Law Firm PLLC, Ridgeland, Miss., 1996-97; assoc. McDavid Noblin & West PLLC, Jackson, Miss., 1997—. Mem. ABA, Miss. Oil and Gas Lawyers Assn., Hinds County Bar Assn. Home: 204 Barkley Ln Brandon MS 39047-7664 Office: McDavid Noblin West PLLC 248 E Capitol St Ste 840 Jackson MS 39201-2505 E-mail: eicher@mnwlaw.com.

EICHER, THEO STEFAN, economist; b. Dusseldorf, Germany, Aug. 22, 1966; arrived in U.S., 1989; s. Theobald and Carin Eicher; m. Regina Mary Lyons. BA, Grinnell Coll., 1988; PhD in Econs., Columbia U., 1994. Assoc. prof. U. Wash., Seattle, 2000—. Fellow Ctr. for Econ. Studies, Munich, 1999—. Recipient grant, Humboldt Found., Bonn, Germany, 1999. Mem.: Am. Econ. Assn. Office: Univ Wash Dept Econs PO Box 353330 Seattle WA 98195

EICHHOLZ, ALEXANDER A. physiology researcher, consultant; b. Zagreb, Yugoslavia, Dec. 12, 1926; came to U.S., 1951; s. Alexander A. and Helen M. E.; m. Susanne R. Hilker, Dec. 26, 1990. BA, Blackburn Coll., 1954; MS, PhD, U. Ill., Chgo., 1960. Rsch. assoc. Rush Med. Coll., Chgo., 1962-63; asst. prof. Chgo. Med. Sch., 1963-65; prof. Med. Sch. Rutgers U., Piscataway, N.J., 1965-87, prof. emeritus, 1987—. Cons., translator Moscow State U. Med. Sch., 1993—; cons. Pavlov Inst. Physiology, St. Petersburg, Russia, 1994. Co-author: Methods in Enzymology, 1970; contbr. articles to profl. jours. Recipient Rsch. award Chgo. Med. Sch. Bd. Trustees, 1965. Avocations: boating, travel. Home: PO Box 39044 Sarasota FL 34238 E-mail: eichholzaa@yahoo.com.

EICHHORN, ARTHUR DAVID, music director; b. St. Louis, Oct. 13, 1953; s. Arthur Louis and Adele (Stankunas) Eichhorn. BA, Concordia U., River Forest, Ill., 1975, MA, 1976, Webster U., 1986; EdD, Calif. Coast U., 1997. Cert. elem. tchr., Mo. Dir. music St. John Luth. Ch., Mt. Prospect, Ill., 1974-76, Our Savior Luth. Ch., Springfield, Ill., 1976-81, Holy Cross Luth. Ch., St. Louis, 1981-91, Timothy Luth. Ch., St. Louis, 1991—. Part-time instr., dir. St. Louis extension site Concordia U., Wis. Mem.: Assn. Luth. Ch. Musicians, Am. Guild Organists, Choristers Guild (pres. local chpt. 1990—92). Republican. Home: 7116 Mardel Ave Saint Louis MO 63109-1123 Office: Timothy Luth Ch 6704 Fyler Ave Saint Louis MO 63139-2239 E-mail: timothy@sbcglobal.net., aeich53024@aol.com.

EICHHORN, FREDERICK FOLTZ, JR., retired lawyer; b. Gary, Ind., Oct. 16, 1930; s. Frederick Foltz and Adele D. (DeLano) E.; m. Julia Abel, Aug. 27, 1955; children: Jill, Thomas, Timothy, Linda. BS, Ind. U., 1952, JD, 1957. Bar: Ind. 1957, U.S. Ct. Appeals (7th cir.) 1957, U.S. Dist. Ct. (no dist.) Ind. 1957, U.S. Supreme Ct. 1973. Assoc. Gavit, Eichhorn, Gary, 1957-62; ptnr. Eichhorn, Eichhorn & Link, and predecessor firm, 1963-76; sr. ptnr. Eichhorn, Eichhorn & Link and predecessor firm, 1977-96; ret., 1996. Mem. Ind. Sesquicentennial Commn.; chmn. Lake County Cmty. Devel. Com., 1984; commr. Conf. Uniform State Law; bd. dirs. Gary Housing Authority, 1972—75, Planned Parenthood, Gary Police Civil Svc. Commn., 1975—82; bd. dirs., founder Miller Citizens Corp., 1971; bd. dirs. N.W. Ind. Symphony; trustee Ind. U., 1990—, bd. pres., 2002—; chmn. N.W. Ind. Forum, World Affairs Coun., Gary Regional Airport Task Force, 1989—94. With USAF, 1952—54. Fellow: Ind. Bar Found., Am. Bar Found.; mem.: ABA (membership chmn. for Ind. ho. of dels.), Ind. Soc. Chgo. (trustee 1989—92), Midwest Gas Assn. (legal affairs sect. 1982), Am. Gas Assn. (state rate litigation com. 1982, regulation of gas supplies com., state regulatory matters com.), Ind. Bar Assn. (inst. chmn. white collar crime 1979, treas. 1977—78, bd. mgr. 1979—80, v.p. 1983—84, pres. 1985—86), Delta Tau Delta, Phi Delta Phi.

EICHHORN, GUNTHER LOUIS, chemist, researcher; b. Frankfurt am Main, Germany, Feb. 8, 1927; s. Fritz David and Else Regina (Weiss) E.; m. Lotti Neuhaus, June 25, 1964; children: David Mark, Sharon Julie. AB in Chemistry, U. Louisville, 1947; MS, U. Ill., 1948, PhD, 1950. From asst. prof. to assoc. prof. chemistry La. State U., 1950-57; commd. officer USPHS, 1954-57; assoc. prof. chemistry Georgetown U., 1957-58; guest scientist Naval Med. Rsch. Inst., 1957-58; chief sect. molecular biology Gerontology Rsch., NIH, Balt., 1958-78, chief lab. cellular and molecular biology and head sect. inorganic biochemistry, 1978-94; scientist emeritus NIH, 1994—. Counsellor La. State U. Hillel Found., 1952—54; pres. Nat. Inst. Child Health and Human Devel. Assembly of Scientists, 1972—73; mem. panel nickel NRC, 1974; organizer Am. Chem. Soc. Symposium on Function of Metal Ions in Biol. Processes, NY, 1961; disting. lectr. Mich. State U., 1972; lectr. Internat. Conf. on Biology and the Future of Mankind, Paris, 1974, Internat. Conf. on Coord. Chemistry, São Paulo, Brazil, 1977, Symposium on Coord. Chemistry and Cancer Chemotherapy, Toulouse, France, 1978; Watkins vis. prof. Wichita State U., 1983; organizer symposium Internat. Conf. Bioinorganic Chemistry, Netherlands, 1987; lectr. Internat. Conf. Molecular Mechanisms of Metal Toxicity and Carcinogenicity, Urbino, Italy, 1988, Bailar Symposium, Houston, 1992, G.L. Eichhorn Symposium on Metals, Nucleic Acids, Transcription and Aging, 1995; acting sci. dir. Nat. Inst. Aging, 1988; Henry Lardy lectr. S.D. U.; lectr. Metal Ion Nucleic Acid Interactions Conf., Amsterdam, 1991; organizer, presenter and lectr. in field; lectr. Internat. Conf. on Coord. Chemistry, Sao Paulo, Brazil, 1997. Editor: Inorganic Biochemistry, 1973; co-editor: Advances in Inorganic Biochemistry, 1978—; contbr. articles to profl. jours. Gen. Aniline and Film Co. grantee, 1949; Ohio State U. fellow, summers 1951-52; recipient Woodcock medal U. Louisville, 1947, Md. Chemist award, 1978, NIH Dir.'s award, 1979, Sr. Exec. Svc. bonus award, 1982, 88. Fellow AAAS, Am. Inst. Chemists, Gerontol. Soc. (fin. com. 1980-82, research and edn. com. 1982-83); mem. Am. Chem. Soc., N.Y. Acad. Scis., Am. Inst. Biol. Chemists, Biophys. Soc. Achievements include reseach in metal-ion induced stabilization and destabilization of DNA double helix, mechanism of RNA degradation by metal ions, nucleic acid conformational changes induced by metal ions; structural basis by which RNA polymerase produces fidelity in transcription (of DNA to RNA), catalysis of double bond cleavage by metal ions, discovery of Schiff base tautomers in vitamin B6-metal complexes; molecular age changes involving metal ions, proteins and nucleic acids. Home: 10500 Rockville Pike Rockville MD 20852-3350 Office: NIH NIA Gerontology Rsch Ctr 5600 Nathan Shock Dr Baltimore MD 21224-6825 E-mail: eichhorngl@juno.com.

EICHINGER, MARILYNNE HILDEGARDE, museum administrator; children: Ryan, Kara, Julia, Jessica, Talik. BA in Anthropology and Sociology magna cum laude, Boston U., 1965; MA, Mich. State U., 1971. With emergency and outpatient staff Ingham County Mental Health Ctr., 1972; founder, pres., exec. dir. Impression 5 Sci. and Art Mus., Lansing, Mich., 1973-85; pres. Oreg. Mus. Sci. and Industry, Portland, 1985-95; bd. dirs. Portland Visitors Assn., 1985-95; pres. Informal Edn. Products Ltd., 1995—, 1995—. Bd. dirs. N.W. Regional Edn. Labs., 1991-97; instr. Lansing (Mich.) C.C., 1978; ptnr. Eyrie Studio, 1982-85; condr. numerous workshops in interactive exhibit design, adminstrn. and fund devel. for schs., orgns., profl. socs. Author: (with Jane Mack) Lexington Montessori School Survey, 1969, Manual on the Five Senses, 1974; pub. Mich. edit. Boing mag. Founder Cambridge Montessori Sch., 1964; bd. dirs. Lexington Montessori Sch., 1969, Mid-Mich. South Health Sys. Agy., 1978-81, Cmty. Referral Ctr., 1981-85, Sta. WKAR, 1981-85; active Lansing "Riverfest" Lighted Boat Parade, 1980; mem. state health Coordinating Coun., 1980-82; mem. pres.'s adv. coun. Portland State U., 1986—90, mem. pres.' adv. bd., 1987-91; bd. dirs. Portland Visitors Assn., 1994-97, Friends of Tryon Creek State Pk., 2001—. Recipient Diana Cert. Leadership, YWCA, 1976-77, Woman of Achievement award, 1991, Community Svc. award Portland State U., 1992. Mem. Am. Assn. Mus., Oreg. Mus. Assn., Assn. Sci. and Tech. Ctrs. (bd. dirs. 1980-84, 88-93), Mus. Store Assn., Direct Mktg. Assn., Zonta Lodge (founder, bd. dirs. East Lansing club 1978), Internat. Women's Forum, Portland C. of C. Office: Informal Edn Products Ltd 2517 SE Mailwell Dr Milwaukie OR 97222

EICHMAN, CHARLES MELVIN, school counselor, career assessment educator; b. Ft. Hays, Kans., June 16, 1950; s. Melvin Joseph and Barbara Ann (Bennett) E. BA, U. No. Colo., 1972; MA, Fuller Theol. Sem., 1974; grad., U. Mo., 1991, Idaho State U., 2002. Cert. vocat. evaluator, career guidance specialist, sch. counselor, job devel. specialist, secondary sch. tchr, sch. admin. K-12, vocational admin. Youth activity coord. YMCA, Glendale, Calif., 1972-74; counselor U. Colo., Colorado Springs, 1975-76; resident hall advisor U. No. Colo., Greeley, 1976-77; secondary tchr., coach Jefferson County Dist. R-1, Lakewood, Colo., 1978-80; pres., owner Big Sky C.F.M. and Mgmt. Resources, Rock Springs, Wyo., 1980-85; secondary tchr. Boulder (Colo.) Valley Dist. RE-2, 1986-88; vocat. evaluator and dir. Platte County Dist. RE-111 Vocat. Evaluation Ctr., Platte City, Mo., 1988-92; pres., owner Career Assessment Svcs., Arvada, Colo., 1992-94; sch. counselor, head dist. elem. at-risk student program Albany Schs. Re-1, Laramie, Wyo., 1993-94; sch. counselor, dir. dist. model Kids at Risk program Franklin Jr. H.S. and New Horizons Alt. H.S., Pocatello, 1994—; developer counseling program New Horizons Alt. H.S., Pocatello, 1994—. Contbr. articles to profl. jours. Mem. ACA (one of 25 nat. legis. inst. participants 2000), Am. Vocat. Assn., NEA, Nat. Assn. Vocat. Edn. Spl. Needs Pers. (region III com. chair 1989-90, cert. of recognition 1990), Am. Sch. Counselors Assn., Am. Assn. Marriage and Family Therapy, Vocat. Evaluation and Work Adjustment Assn. (Wyo. rep. 1993-94, conf. presenter 1991), Mo. Vocat. Spl. Needs Assn. (exec. v.p. 1990-92, spkr. 1989-92, Outstanding Achievement award 1990-91, certs. of appreciation 1988-91), Mo. Sch. Counselors Assn. (spkr. 1989-91), Mo. Vocat. Assn. (spkr. 1992), Idaho Edn. Assn. (assembly del. 2001-03, state legis. del. 2002), Idaho Sch. Counseling Assn., Idaho Counseling Assn. (chair pub. policy and legislation com. 1999-2002, conf. presentor, exec. bd. dirs. legislative bill writing), Idaho Assn. Marriage and Family Therapy, Idaho Vocat. Guidance Assn. (com. chair 1997), Idaho Assn. Career Devel., Kiwanis. Avocations: handball, skiing, outdoor adventure trips, creative arts activities, swimming. Office: PO Box 4931 Pocatello ID 83205-4931 E-mail: CMEichman@aol.com.

EICHMAN, PATRICIA, retired interior designer; b. Detroit, Mich., Dec. 12, 1938; d. Stanley Z. Pasierbek and Annette T. (Rogusz) Spindler; m. Richard R. Bourassa, 1957 (div. 1978); children: Robert, Jeffrey, Lori; m. John W. Eichman Jr., 1983 (div. 1992); m. John Walters, 1995. Grad. H.S., Detroit. Cert. interior designer, Calif. Sales designer Ethan Allen Store, Phoenix, 1974-79; interior designer Lou Regester Furniture, Phoenix, 1979-84, VJ Lloyds Furniture, San Diego, 1985-94; pvt. practice Patricia Eichman Interiors, San Diego, 1994—2003; ret., 2003. Treas. Friends of Downtown San Diego, 1993, bd. dirs., 1993-94, 97, co-chair charities, 1994, 97, 2d v.p., 1995, 97, bd. dirs. Design Alliance to Combat AIDS, San Diego, 1990-91. Recipient Sam award Bldg. Industry Assn., San Diego, 1993, Grand Orchid award Orchid & Onions, San Diego, 1993, Best Master Bedroom Suite award Street of Dreams, San Diego, 1991; featured in ASID Kitchen and Bath Showcase and San Diego Home & Garden Mag., 1995. Mem. Internat. Soc. Interior Designers (pres. San Diego chpt. 1992, treas. 1987-89, bd. dirs. 1989-93), Am. Soc. Interior Designers, Internat. Interior Design Assn. Avocations: sewing, gardening, cooking, reading. Home: 2452 Carriage Cir Oceanside CA 92056-3603

EICHNER, KAY MARIE, mental health nurse; b. Des Moines, Apr. 28, 1955; d. Earl C. and Rachel L. (Martens) E. BSN, Grand View Coll., 1979. Staff nurse U. Iowa Hosp., Iowa City, 1979-80; staff nurse, supr. nursery Oasis Day Care Ctr., Indianola, Iowa, 1985-86; staff nurse Iowa Meth. Med. Ctr., Des Moines, 1980-83, 87-96, Iowa Luth. Hosp., Des Moines, 1996-98, mem. accessible med. staff, 1999-2000; staff nurse Heritage Health Care and Rehab. Ctr., 2000. Spkr. in field. Mem. Nat. Nurses Soc. on Addictions. Republican. Mem. Christian Ch. Home: 3208 Fairlane Dr Des Moines IA 50315-7726

EICHOLD, SAMUEL, medical educator, medical museum curator; b. Mobile, Ala., May 27, 1916; s. Bernard H. and Myra (Solomon) E.; m. Charlotte Hartsig, Feb. 26, 1943; children: Beth, Alice, Bert. BS, Tulane U., 1937, MD, 1940; LLD (hon.), Spring Hill Coll., 1991. Intern Touro Infimary, 1941; resident in internal medicine City Hosp. Mobile, 1941; pvt. practice medicine specializing in internal medicine Mobile, 1946-72; prof. medicine dept. internal medicine U. South Ala., Mobile, 1973-84, prof. emeritus, 1984—; hon. prof. Universidad Francisco Marroquin, 1985—; dir. continuing edn. U. South Ala., Mobile, 1975-82, perceptor history of medicine, 1976, perceptor rural and tropical medicine in developing nation, 1976—; med. dir. Central Plaza Towers Med. Ctr., 1981-98, Allen Meml. Home, 1973—, Cogburn Nursing Home, 1975-81, Hillhaven-Mobile, 1980-85, Mercy Med. Hosp., 1985-94; med. advisor Ala. Dept. Corrections, 1987—. Bd. dirs. Mercy Med., 1989-98, vice chmn. Old Mobile Restoration; bd. trustees Spring Hill Coll., 1991-2000; pres. Mobile Revolving Fund for Hist. Properties, 1992-96. Author: Without Malice-100 Year History of Comic Cowboys of Mobile; mem. editorial bd. ADA Forecast mag., 1987-91, Ala. Treasure Forest Gulf Coast Hist. rev.; contbr. articles to profl. jours. Asst. county health officer Mobile County; bd dir. Preventable Disease, 1974-75; active Josiah C. Nott Found., 1980; founder, curator Heustis Med. Mus.; established Camp Seale Harris for Diabetic Children, 1947; sec./treas. Mobile Imfirmary, 1967-68; officer Mobile Tree Commn., 1968-73, chmn., 1973; bd. dirs. Mobile Symphony, Mobile Chamber Music Soc., Inc., 1952-75, Mobile Opera Assn., Hist. Mobile Preservation, 1977-84, Mobile chpt. ARC, 1951, Fine Arts Mus. of South, 1975-81, Mobile Mus., 1975-81, Mobile Hist. Mus., 1994—, Mobile Mus. Art, 1995—, Cmty. Found. S.W. Ala., 1998—, Friends Magnolia Cemetery, 1999—; active adv. bd. Ala. Hist. Commn., 1974—; pres. Mobile Hist. Devel. Found., 1973-75, bd. dirs., 1973-76; mem. council, chmn. regents Spring Hill Coll., 1984, trustee, 1991—. With USNR, 1941-69, comdr. ret. Recipient M.O. Beale Scroll of Merit award, 1951, 56, 59, Doc E award ADA, 1975, Ruth E. Hanson award 1978, Dept. Internal Medicine Faculty award, 1979, Comic Cowboy of Yr. award, 1982, Joe Treadwell award Ala. affiliate ADA, 1990; named Hon. Fellow Mobile Coll., 1977; named Mobilian of Yr. Mobile Civitan Club, 1989. Mem. AMA, ACP, Am. Assn. Diabetes Educators, Med. Soc. Mobile County (recognition award 1975), So. Med. Assn., Am. Diabetes Assn. (citation Mobile chpt. 1980, Becton Dickinson award 1981), Am. Soc. Internal Medicine, Ala. Diabetes Assn., Mobile County Physicians, Franklin Soc. (pres. 1975), Mobile Area C. of C. Clubs: Country of Mobile, Mobile Yacht. Lodges: Masons, Shriners, Kiwanis. Republican. Jewish. Home: 300 Chatham St Mobile AL 36604-3107

EICHSTADT, CRAIG MARTIN, lawyer; b. Huron, S.D., Aug. 1, 1951; s. Martin Edward and Edith Marie (Scheibe) E.; m. Gail Lynn Carlson, June 1, 1975; children: Anne Elizabeth, Neil Craig, Carl Martin. BA, S.D. State U., 1973; postgrad., Ohio U., 1973-74; JD, U. S.D., 1978. Bar: S.D. 1978, U.S. Dist. Ct. S.D. 1979, U.S. Ct. Appeals (8th cir.) 1984, U.S. Supreme Ct. 1986, U.S. Ct. Appeals (D.C. cir.) 1987. Law clk. S.D. Supreme Ct., Pierre, 1978-79, U.S. Dist. Ct. S.D., Pierre, 1979-80; assoc. Bantz, Gosch & Cremer, Aberdeen, S.D., 1980-81; ptnr. Steele & Eichstadt, Plankinton, S.D., 1981-84; asst. atty. gen. State of S.D., Pierre, 1984-90; dep. atty. gen., head appellate div. Office Atty. Gen. State of S.D., Pierre, 1991—. W.W. French scholar U. S.D., 1977-78, Dean Marshall, Alice and Frances McCusick scholar U. S.D., 1976-77. Mem. S.D. Bar Assn. (com. criminal pattern jury instructions 1983-88, com. on adminstrv. law 1988-91, 92—), Phi Kappa Phi, Delta Phi Alpha. Lutheran. Avocations: furniture refinishing, coin collecting, reading. Home: 412 N Van Buren Ave Pierre SD 57501-2665 Office: Office Atty Gen State Capitol Bldg 500 E Capitol Ave Pierre SD 57501-5070 E-mail: cmeace1@pie.midco.net., craig.eichstadt@state.sd.us.

EICKELMANN, NANCY SUE, research scientist; b. Booneville, N.Y., Oct. 16, 1951; BS, San Diego State U., 1988, MBA, 1992; MS, U. Calif., Irvine, 1994, PhD, 1997. Staff rschr. Hughes Rsch. Lab., Malibu, Calif., 1992-97; sr. mem. tech. staff Microelectronics Computer Tech. Corp., MCC, Austin, TEx., 1997-98; rsch. assoc. Software Rsch. Lab. NASA/W.Va., Fairmount, W.Va., 1998-2000; rsch. scientist Motorola Labs., Schaumburg, Ill., 2000—. Contbr. articles to profl. publs. Evaluator, litaracy tutor Read San Diego Pub. Libr., 1986-88. Hughes Aircraft fellow, 1995—; Calif. state scholar, 1992. Mem. IEEE, Assn. Computing Machinery, INFORMS. Address: Motorola 1303 E Algonquin Rd Schaumburg IL 60196-4041 Fax: 847-576-3280. E-mail: Nancy.Eickelmann@motorola.com.

EICKHOFF, JOHN R. (JACK EICKHOFF), business executive; BA in Bus. Adminstrn. and Acctg., St. Cloud State U. Various acctg. and fin. planning positions Ceridian Corp., Mpls., 1963-82, v.p. corp. svcs., 1983, v.p., contr. fin. plans and controls, comml. credit, 1983, v.p., contr. fin. plans and controls, fin. and bus. svcs., 1985, v.p., contr. fin. plans and controls, computer sys. group, 1986, v.p., contr. fin. plans and controls computer products group, 1988, v.p., corp. contr., 1989, exec. v.p., CFO, 1995—. Mem. retirement com. Ceridian Corp.; bd. dirs. Norstan Inc. Mem. Fin. Execs. Inst., Fin. Execs. Inst. (Twin Cities chpt.). Office: Ceridian Corp 3311 E Old Shakopee Rd Minneapolis MN 55425-1640

EICKHOFF, THEODORE CARL, epidemiologist; b. Cleve., Sept. 13, 1931; s. Theodore Henry and Clara (Strasen) E.; m. Margaret Heinecke, Aug. 24, 1952; children: Stephen, Mark, Philip. BA, Valparaiso U., 1953; MD, Case Western Res. U., 1957. Diplomate: Am. Bd. Internal Medicine. Intern, then resident Harvard Med. Services, Boston City Hosp., 1957-59; fellow in medicine Harvard Med. Sch.-Boston City Hosp., 1961-64; epidemiologist Center for Disease Control, 1964-67; prof. medicine U. Colo. Med. Ctr., 1975—, head div. infectious disease, 1967-80; vice chmn. dept. medicine U. Colo. Med. Center, 1976-81; dir. internal medicine Presbyn./St. Luke's Med. Ctr., 1981-92; dir. medicine Denver Gen. Hosp., 1978-81. Cons. FDA, Ctrs. for Disease Control, Am. Hosp. Assn.; mem. nat. commn. orphan diseases HHS, 1986-90, mem. vaccines adv. com., 1995-99. Contbr. articles to med. jours. Served with USPHS, 1959-67. Recipient Commr.'s Spl. Citation, FDA, 1990, Trustee's award Am. Hosp. Assn., 1993. Mem. ACP (Disting. Internist award Colo. chpt. 1995), Am. Fedn. Clin. Rsch., Am. Soc. Clin. Investigation, Assn. Am. Physicians, Infectious Diseases Soc. Am. (sec. 1978-82, pres. 1983-84, Finland Lectureship award 1995), Am. Epidemiol. Soc. (pres. 1985-86). Home: 15 S Franklin Cir Greenwood Village CO 80121-1245 Office: Univ Colo Health Sci Ctr Div Infectious Disease B 168 Denver CO 80262-0001 E-mail: theodore.eickhoff@uchsc.edu.

EIDE, JOEL SYLVESTER, art consultant, appraiser; Dir. No. Ariz. U. Art Mus. and Galleries, 1975-98; prof. fine art No. Ariz. U., Flagstaff, 1970—98; fine art cons. Clarkdale, Ariz., 1999—. Home: 1926 N Crescent Dr Flagstaff AZ 86001-1114 Office: PO Box 82 Sycamore Canyon Rd Clarkdale AZ 86324 E-mail: eideart@bmol.com.

EIDELHOCH, LESTER PHILIP, physician, educator, surgeon; b. N.Y.C., Jan. 7, 1932; s. Abraham David Eidelhoch and Ella (Sarah) Lovinger; m. Cecily Ruth Rosenberg, Apr. 28, 1963; children: Alison Marc, Arthur Mark, Meredith Marc. BA, Columbia U., 1952; MD, NYU, 1956. Diplomate Am. Bd. Med. Examiners. Intern Strong Meml. Hosp., Rochester, N.Y.; resident Harvard Surg. div. Boston City Hosp., 1958-62; pvt. practice New Hartford, N.Y., 1965—. Med. dir. Walsh Med. Ctr., Rome, N.Y., 1991—; mem. faculty SUNY. Bd. dirs. Jewish Fedn., Utica (N.Y.) Symphony, Charles T. Sitrin Home. Lt. comdr. USN, 1962-64. Recipient Lindner Surg. award NYU. Fellow ACS, Royal Coll. Medicine; mem. N.Y. Cen. Soc. Surgeons, Cen. N.Y. Acad. Medicine, Oneida County Med. Soc. Republican. Avocations: skiing, sailing. Home and Office: 6 Old Willow Rd New Hartford NY 13413-2419

EIDEM, BENJAMIN WALTER, cardiologist; b. St. Paul, July 31, 1964; s. Daniel Eldon Eidem and Susan Jane Duckstad; m. Debra Louise Eidem; 1 child, Katherine Lynn. BS, Bob Jones U., 1987; MD, Wayne State U., 1991. Diplomate Am. Bd. Pediatrics, Am. Bd. Pediatric Cardiology, Nat. Bd. Med. Examiners. Pediatrics resident Baylor Coll. Medicine, Houston, 1991-94, chief resident in neonatology, 1993; fellow in pediatric cardiology Mayo Grad. Sch. Medicine, Rochester, Minn., 1994-97; attending physician dept. pediatrics Loyola U. Med. Ctr., Maywood, Ill., 1997—, pediatric cardiologist, 1997—, asst. prof. pediatrics divsn. pediatric cardiology, dir. Pediatric Echocardiography Lab. Cons. physician dept. pediatrics West Suburban Med. Ctr., Oak Park, Ill., 1997—, Ctrl. DuPage Hosp., Winfield, Ill, 1997—, Edward Hosp., Naperville, Ill., 1997—, Rush-Copley Med. Ctr., Aurora, Ill., 1997—, Alexian Bros. Med. Ctr., Elk Grove Village, Ill., 1998—, Elmhurst Hosp., Ill., 1998—, Resurrection Med. Ctr., Chgo., 1999—, St. Francis Hosp., Evanston, Ill., 1999—; spkr. in field. Contbr. articles to profl. jours. Fellow Am. Acad. Pediatrics, Am. Coll. Cardiology; mem. Am. Heart Assn., Am. Soc. Echocardiography, Soc. Pediatric Echocardiography, Alpha Omega Alpha. Avocations: golf, basketball. Office: Loyola U Med Ctr Dept Pediatrics 2160 S 1st Ave Maywood IL 60153-3304

EIDMAN, VERNON ROY, agricultural economist, educator; b. Mascoutah, Ill., Aug. 24, 1936; s. Roland Gerhard and Cora Marie (Doelling) E.; m. Bonnie Jean Klingelhoefer, Dec. 28, 1958; children: James, Patricia, Keith. BS in Agr., U. Ill., 1958, MS in Agrl. Econs., 1961; PhD in Agrl. Econs., U. Calif., Berkeley, 1965. Rsch. economist U. Calif., Berkeley, 1963-64; asst. prof. agrl. econs. Okla. State U., Stillwater, 1964-68, assoc. prof. agrl. econs., 1968-71, prof. agrl. econs., 1971-75; prof. agr. and applied econs. U. Minn., Mpls., 1975—, head applied econs., 1998—. Mem. editorial coun. Am. Jour. Agrl. Econs., 1972-74, '84-87, So. Jour. Agrl. Econs, 1969-72; vis. prof. Swedish Agrl. Coll. Uppsala, Sweden, 1973, U. Md., Coll. Park, 1989-90. Co-author: (with others) (book) Farm Management, 1984; contbr. numerous articles to profl. jours., presented numerous papers at profl. seminars, meetings, etc. 1st lt. U.S. Army, 1958-59. Recipient Outstanding Tchr. award Okla. State U. Alumni Assn., 1970, Disting. Teaching award, U. Minn. Coll. Agr., 1988. Mem. Am. Agrl. Econs. Assn. (exec. bd. 1989-92, pres. 1995-96, Best article in Jour. Farm Econs. 1968), Western Agrl. Econs. Assn. (Outstanding Published Rsch. award 1969), So. Agrl. Econs. Assn. (v.p. 1975-76), Am. Econs. Assn., Soc. of Farm Mgrs. and Rural Appraisers. Methodist. Home: 90 Mid Oaks Ln Saint Paul MN 55113-5647 Office: U Minn Dept Applied Econs 1994 Buford Ave Saint Paul MN 55108-6038

EIDSVOLD, GARY MASON, physician, public health officer, medical educator; b. Morris, Minn., Sept. 28, 1938; s. Lyman Woodrow and Julia Magdalene (Mason) E. BA, St. Olaf Coll., 1960; MD, U. Minn., 1964; MPH, Johns Hopkins U., 1966. Diplomate Am. Bd. Preventive Medicine. Rotating intern Long Island Coll. Hosp., Bklyn., 1964-65; resident in preventive medicine Johns Hopkins U. Sch. Pub. Health, Balt., 1965-68; asst. prof. Haile Selassie U., Gondar, Ethiopia, 1967-68; dir. Indian Health Svc. Hosp., Tuba City., Ariz., 1968-70; South Bronx health officer N.Y.C. Health Dept., 1970-73, North Bklyn. health officer, 1973-74, Bronx and Staten Island dir., 1974-78; N.Y.C. med. dir. N.Y. State Health Dept., 1978-97, amb. care program dir., 1978-85, home health and HMO program dir., 1978-85, Medicaid program dir., 1978-95, alternative delivery sys. program dir., 1995, managed care program dir., 1995-97, family health managed care program dir., 1997-2000. Clin. asst. prof. dept. preventive medicine N.Y. Med. Coll., N.Y.C., 1971-73; asst. prof. SUNY Health Sci. Ctr., Bklyn., 1973-2000; lectr. Columbia U. Sch. Pub. Health, N.Y.C., 1973-2000; faculty New Sch. Social Rsch., N.Y.C., 1974-75. Contbr. articles to profl. jours. Con. and com. chmn. Trinity Ch. in the City of N.Y., 1972-76, St. John's Evang. Luth. Ch., N.Y.C., 1988-2002, Surgeon, USPHS, 1968-70. Recipient Outstanding Leadership award East N.Y. Health Coalition, Bklyn., 1973. Fellow Am. Coll. Preventive Medicine, Am. Tchrs. Preventive Medicine; mem. Am. Pub. Health Assn. (chmn. Health Adminstrn. Sect. 1979-81), Pub. Health Physicians Assn. N.Y.C. (pres. 1973-76), Pub. Health Assn. N.Y.C. (bd. dirs. 1975-81), Nat. Assn. County Health Officers (bd. dirs. 1975-78), Lutheran Soc. Svcs. Metro N.Y. (bd. dirs. 1991-94), Norwegian Am. Hist. Soc. (life). Democrat. Lutheran. Avocations: Norwegian language, genealogy, cooking, gym, music. Home: 71 Grand St New York NY 10013-2219

EIDT, JACOB IVAN, language educator; s. Jacob William and Amanda Rodriguez (Fonseca) Eidt. BA, U. Miss., 1993; MA, Cath. U. Eichstat, Germany, 1997; PhD, U. Tex., 2003. Instr. English, Eurosprachen Inst., Ingzolstadt, Germany, 1994—97; asst. instr. German, U. Tex., Austin, 1998—; instr. English, Tex. Inst. English Proficiency, Austin, 2001—. Interpreter, translator St. Francis Assisi Acad., Eichstatt, 1995—97. Translator: Dimension 2, 2003. European Travel grantee, Erasmus Inst., 2000, June and Helmut Rehder

Found. scholar, 2000, Summer fellow, U. Tex. Austin, 2000. Mem.: MLA, Am. Assn. Tchrs. German, Am. Comparative Lit. Assn., Hispanic Family Staff Assn. Roman Catholic. Avocations: chess, dancing.

EIFLER, MARK ANTHONY, historian, educator; b. Louisville, Jan. 30, 1956; s. Waller Davenport and Virginia Marie (Livingston) Judy; m. Karen Elizabeth Perlenfein, Oct. 10, 1987; 1 child, Conor. PhD, U of CA, Berkeley, CA, 1985—92. Asst. prof. U of NE, Kearney, Nebr., 1992—98; assoc. prof. U of Portland, Portland, Oreg., 2000—. Author: (novels) (history) Gold Rush Capitalists. Office: U of Portland 5000 N Willamette Blvd Portland OR 97203-7803 Home: 4902 N Amherst Portland OR 97203

EIFRIG, DAVID ERIC, ophthalmologist, educator; b. Oak Park, Ill., Jan. 4, 1935; m. Kathryn Caufield; children: David Jr., Elizabeth A. Heitala, Catherine C. Ulrich, Charles W.G. BA, Carleton Coll., Northfield, Minn., 1956; MD, Johns Hopkins U., 1960. Diplomate Am. Bd. Ophthalmology. Mem. liaison svc. Johns Hopkins U. Hosp., Balt., 1957, mem. dept. pathology, 1958, mem. dog lab. dept. surgery, 1959-60; intern, then asst. resident Halsted Surg. Svc. Johns Hopkins U. Hosp., Balt., 1960-62, resident in ophthalmology Wilmer Eye Inst., 1964-67; retinal fellow Jules Stein Eye Inst., UCLA, 1967-68; asst. prof. dept. ophthalmology U. Ky. Sch. Medicine, Lexington, 1968-70, U. Minn. Sch. Medicine, Mpls., 1970-73, assoc. prof., 1973-77; prof. dept. ophthalmology U. N.C. Sch. Medicine, Chapel Hill, 1977—, Sterling A. Barrett prof., 1980-2000, chmn. dept. ophthalmology, 1977-2000, chmn. emeritus ophthalmology, 2000—. Z80 com. Am. Nat. Stds. Inst., 1980-97, chmn. 1985-97; mem. Med. Devices Stds. d., 1986-98; mem. Internat. Stds. Orgn., 1986-97; adv. bd. Am. Coll. of Surgeons, 1994—. Contbr. articles to profl. jours.; lectr. to profl. confs. With M.C., USNR, 1962-64. Recipient Schwentker medal for rsch. Johns Hopkins U., 1967. Fellow ACS; mem. AMA, Am. Acad. Ophthalmology, Assn. Rsch. in Vision and Ophthalmology, Assn. Univ. Profs. in Ophthalmology (trustee, pres. 1994-95), Durham-Orange County Med. Soc., Johns Hopkins Med. and Surg. Assn., N.C. Med. Soc., N.C. Soc. Ophthalmology, Retina Soc., Gov.'s Com. Diabetes, Mensa, Order Ky. Cols. Home: 128 New Castle Dr Chapel Hill NC 27517-6545 Office: U NC Sch Medicine Dept Ophthalmology CB#7040 617 Clinical Scis 229H Chapel Hill NC 27599-7040 E-mail: David_Eifrig_Sr@med-unc.edu.

EIG, BLAIR MITCHELL, pediatrician; b. Washington, Jan. 26, 1956; s. Blaine H. and Elizabeth Eig; m. Kaethe Enos, Aug. 5, 1979; children: Sarah, Joshua, Steven. BA in Biology and Biochemistry, MA in Biochemistry, Brandeis U., 1977; MD, Harvard U., 1983. Diplomate Am. Bd. Pediat., Nat. Bd. Med. Examiners. From intern to chief resident Children's Nat. Med. Ctr., Washington, 1983-87, pres. med. staff, 1998-2000; pvt. practice Cohen, Eig & Madden, LLC, Silver Spring, Md., 1987-01; sr. v.p. med. affairs, chief med. officer Holy Cross Hosp., Silver Spring, Md., 2001—; clin. prof. of pediatrics George Washington Univ. Co-chmn. lab. adv. com. State of Md., 1993—; chmn. med. adv. bd. Treatment and Learning Ctr., Rockville, Md., 1996; chmn. instnl. rev. bd. Holy Cross Hosp., Silver Spring, 1999-01. Contbr. chpt. to book Bridging the Family-Professional Gap, 1999. Student activity theater sponsor Montgomery County Pub. Schs., Md., 1993—. Fellow Am. Acad. Pediat.; mem. Med. and Chirurgical Faculty Md., Montgomery-Prince Georges Pediat. Soc. (pres. 1992-93), Phi Beta Kappa. Avocations: opera, animation, roller coasters. Office: Holy Cross Hosp 1500 Forest Glen Rd Silver Spring MD 20910

EIG, NORMAN, investment company executive; b. Passaic, N.J., Mar. 9, 1941; s. Edward H. and Mary (Friedman) Eig; m. Barbara Minkin, Feb. 1, 1964; children: Andrew, Alissa, Karin. BS, Ohio State U., 1963; MBA, Columbia U., 1965. Asst. contr. Silver Burdett Co., Morristown, NJ, 1965; controller Juliet Footwear, East Paterson, NJ, 1965-68; security analyst Brimberg and Co., N.Y.C., 1968; portfolio mgr. EFC Mgmt., N.Y.C., 1968-69, Scherl, Egener and Co., N.Y.C., 1970-71; exec. v.p. Internat. Rsch. and Devel., Princeton, NJ, 1971-72; pres. Rotunda Advisors, Princeton, 1972-73; ptnr. Oppenheimer and Co., N.Y.C., 1973-82; mng. dir. Lazard LLC, N.Y.C., 1982—2002; CEO, Lazard Asset Mgmt. LLC, N.Y.C., 2003—. Chmn. bd. dirs. Lazard Funds Inc.; bd. dirs. PK Ops., Inc. Mem. corp. adv. bd. Sch. Social Work, Columbia U., N.Y.C., 1986—90; mem. bd. overseers Columbia Bus. Sch., N.Y.C., 1994; bd. dirs. Damon Runyon Cancer Rsch. Found.; trustee NYU Sch. Medicine Found. Mem.: Bear's Club (Jupiter, Fla.), Secession Golf Club (Beaufort, S.C.), Hamilton Farm Golf Club (Gladstone, N.J.), Mountain Ridge Country Club, Columbia Club N.Y. Jewish. Avocations: golf, tennis, jazz, non-fiction reading. Office: Lazard Asset Mgmt LLC 30 Rockefeller Plz Fl 58 New York NY 10112-0002

EIGEL, EDWIN GEORGE, JR., mathematics educator, retired university president; b. St. Louis, June 4, 1932; s. Edwin George and Catherine (Rohan) E.; m. Marcia Jeanne Duffy, May 30, 1959; children: Edwin George III, Mary Marcia. BS, MIT, 1954; postgrad., U. Marburg, Germany, 1954-55; PhD, St. Louis U., 1961; DHL (hon.), U. Bridgeport, 1999. Lectr. math. George Washington U., 1961; asst. prof. math. St. Louis U., 1961-64, assoc. prof., 1964-69, asst. to dean Grad. Sch., 1965-67, prof., 1969-79, dean Grad. Sch., 1967-71, assoc. acad. v.p., 1971-72, acad. v.p., 1972-79, exec. v.p., 1973; assoc. prof. math. U. Bridgeport, Conn., 1979-82, prof., 1982—2002, Univ. prof., 1995—, v.p. acad. affairs, 1979-91, provost, 1981-91; pres., 1991-95; pres. emeritus U. Bridgeport, Conn., 1995—. Mem. adv. com. on accreditation Conn. Dept. Higher Edn., 1989—92. Commr. McDonnell Planetarium, St. Louis, 1972-79; mem. Conn. Disting. Citizens Task Force on Quality Tchg., 1982-83; acting exec. dir. Bridgeport Area Consortium Colls. and Univs., 1989; bd. dirs. Bridgeport Pub. Edn. Fund, 1993-97, Bridgeport Regional Bus. Coun., 1994-95, United Way Ea. Fairfield County, 1994-98, Univ. Bridgeport, 1995—. Mem. Am. Math. Soc., Math. Assn. Am., Rotary (bd. dirs. Bridgeport 1994-97), Phi Beta Kappa, Phi Beta Kappa Fellows, Sigma Xi, Pi Mu Epsilon, Phi Kappa Phi, Beta Gamma Sigma, Upsilon Pi Epsilon, Sigma Beta Delta. Achievements include: research in math. applications of computers. Home: 33 Pepperbush Ln Fairfield CT 06824-4036 E-mail: egeorgee@optonline.net.

EIGEL, JAMES ANTHONY, environmental engineer; b. St. Louis, Mar. 1, 1939; s. Edwin George and Catherine Margaret (Rohan) E.; m. Carolyn Margaret Sudheimer, June 10, 1972 (div. 1990); 1 child, Christine. BS, St. Louis U., 1961, postgrad. Ordained to ministry Episcopal Missionary Ch., 1998. Rsch. chemist Falstaff Brewing Corp., St. Louis, 1965-67; rsch. chemist water divsn. City of St. Louis, 1967-71; rsch. chemist Continental Telephone, Hickory, N.C., 1971-75; mgr. main analysis labs. Hoechst Celanese, Spartanburg, S.C., 1975-85; dir. pretreatment/lab. svcs. Macon-Bibb County (Ga.) Water Authority, 1985-89; mgr. tech. svcs. Pima County Wastewater Mgmt., Tucson, Ariz., 1989—. Contbr. articles to profl. jours. Mem. Am. Chem. Soc., Am. Water Works Assn., Water Environ. Fedn., Lions (pres. 1988-89). Mem. Am. Anglican Ch. Achievements include patent for electrical insulation protector. Office: Pima County Wastewater Mgmt 2600 W Sweetwater Dr Tucson AZ 85705 E-mail: jameseigel@clicksouth.net.

EIGEL, MARCIA DUFFY, editor; b. Denver, July 15, 1936; d. Eugene and Margaret (Foley) Duffy; m. Edwin G. Eigel Jr., May 30, 1959; children: Edwin III, Mary. BA, Webster U., 1958. Editor, writer corp. hdqrs. GE, Fairfield, Conn., 1985-92, copy editor, 1996-2000; dir. comms. Girl Scouts of Housatonic Coun., Bridgeport, Conn., 1994-97; editor Blue Cross of Northeastern Pa., 2001—. Instr. in bus. writing So. Conn. State U., New Haven, 1986, U. Bridgeport, 1990. Writer, editor newsletter Customer Fin. Svcs. News, 1987-92, Woman Traveler, 1990—; contbr. articles and poetry to profl. jours. Bd. trustees Greater Bridgeport (Conn.) Symphony, 1998—. Mem.: AAUW, U. Bridgeport Women's Forum. Home and Office: 33 Pepperbush Ln Fairfield CT 06424-4036

EIGEN, HOWARD, pediatrician, educator; b. N.Y.C., Sept. 8, 1942; s. Jay and Libbie (Kantrowitz) E.; children: Sarah Elizabeth, Lauren Michelle. BS, Queens Coll., 1964; MD, Upstate N.Y. Med. Ctr., Syracuse, 1968. Diplomate Am. Bd. Pediatrics, Am. Bd. Pediatric Pulmonology, Am. Bd. Critical Care Medicine, Nat. Bd. Med. Examiners (mem. pediatric test com. 1986-90). Resident in pediatrics Upstate Med. Ctr., Syracuse, 1968-71; fellow in pediatric pulmonology Tulane U., New Orleans, 1973-76; asst. prof. pediatrics Ind. U., Indpls., 1976-84, prof., 1984-96, Billie Lou Wood Prof. pediatrics, 1996—. Assoc. chmn. of Pediatrics for Clin. Affairs, dir. pediatric intensive care, pulmonology sect. Riley Hosp. for Children, med. dir. ambulatory care, 1989— Co-editor: Respiratory Disease in Children: Diagnosis and Management; assoc. editor Pediatric Pulmonology, 1984-91; contbr. articles to profl. jours. Served to maj. U.S. Army, 1971-73. Fellow Am. Acad. Pediatrics (pres. chest sect. 1983-85, pulmonology 1986—), Am. Thoracic Soc., Am. Bd. Pediatrics, Am. Lung Assn. (pres. Ind. 1984-85). Avocation: tennis. Office: Ind U Dept Pediatrics 702 Barnhill Dr Rm 2750 Indianapolis IN 46202-5128

EIGEN, MANFRED, physicist; b. Bochum, Germany, May 9, 1927; s. Ernst E. and Hedwig (Feld) Eigen; m. Elfriede Müller; children: Gerald, Angela. PhD, Georg-August U., Göttingen, 1951; studies in physics and chemistry, hon. degrees, U. Göttingen, Germany, U. Chgo., Washington U., St. Louis, Nottingham U., Bristol U., U.K., Hebrew U., Jerusalem, Cambridge U., U.K., Debrecen U., Techn. U., Munich, Bielefeld U., Utah State U. Sci. asst. Inst. Phys. Chemistry U. Göttingen, 1951-53; mem. staff Max Planck Inst. Biophys. Chemistry (formerly known as Max Planck Inst. for Phys. Chemistry), Göttingen, 1953—, sci. mem., 1958—, head, dept. chem. kinetics, 1962—, dir., 1964—. Author tech. papers. Co-recipient Nobel prize in chemistry, 1967, Max-Planck-Forschungs-Preis, Alexander von Humboldt-Stiftung, 1994, Paul Ehrlich award, 1996. Mem. Bunsen Soc. Phys. Chemistry (Bodenstein Preis 1956), Faraday Soc., NAS, Royal Soc. (fgn. mem., Paul Ehrlich award 1996). Achievements include studying evolution of biol. macromolecules; research on control of enzymes. Office: Max Planck Inst 37077 Göttingen Germany*

EIGENBERGER, MARTIN E, education educator; b. Plymouth, Wis., Nov. 25, 1947; s. Warren A Eigenberger and Rosemary G Nigh. BS in philosophy, U. of Wisconsin-Oshkosh, 1976—79; PhD, U. of Wyo., 1989—96. Adj. prof. No. Ariz. U., 1997—99; asst. prof. U. of Wisconsin-Parkside, 1999—. Office: University Of Wisconsin-Parkside 600 Wood Rd Kenosha WI 53141

EIGER, RICHARD WILLIAM, retired publisher; b. N.Y.C., May 11, 1933; s. William and Helen M. (Fetten) E.; m. Ruth B. Engelke; 1 child, Keith R. BFA, Pratt Inst., 1955; MBA, NYU, 1960. With Western Pub. Co., N.Y.C., 1958-80, pub. dir., 1968-74, v.p. pub., 1975-80; pres. Macmillan Ednl. Co., N.Y.C., 1980-91; sr. v.p. Macmillan Pub. Co., N.Y.C., 1980-91; v.p. K-III Reference Corp. (now PRIMEDIA Reference Corp.), Mahwah, N.J., 1991-93; pub. The World Almanac, 1993-98; ret., 1998. Cons. Langenscheidt Pub. Co., 2002—, VirtuelEd., Inc., 2000—; prof. pub. Pratt Inst. Sch. Info. and Libr. Sci., 2003—. Bd. dirs. alumni bd. The Pratt Inst., N.Y.C., 1986—, trustee, 1992—, mem. exec. com., 1995—, sec. 1996—, chmn. devel. com., 1997—; mem. pub. com. Brandeis U., Waltham, Mass., 1993-2000; trustee The Katharine Gibbs Sch., Montclair, N.J., 1995-2001, Piscataway, N.J., 1996-2001, Hist. Soc. Princeton, NJ, 2002—. Lt. U.S. Army, 1956-57. Home: 6 Otter Creek Rd Skillman NJ 08558-2364

EIGLER, DONALD MARK, physicist; b. L.A., Mar. 23, 1953; s. Irving Baer and Evelin Muriel (Baker) E.; m. Roslyn Winifred Rubesin, Nov. 2, 1986. BA, U. Calif., San Diego, 1975, PhD in Physics, 1984; D (hon.), Delf U. Tech., 2002. Rsch. assoc. U. Köln (Fed. Republic Germany), 1975-76, U. Calif., San Diego, 1977-84, postdoctoral rsch. assoc., 1984, assoc. rsch. physicist dept. physics, 1986; postdoctoral mem. tech. staff AT&T Bell Labs., Murray Hill, N.J., 1984-86; rsch. staff mem. IBM, San Jose, Calif., 1986-93, IBM fellow, 1993—. Alexander M. Cruickshank lectr. in phys. sci. (Gordon Rsch. Confs.), 1994; Alvin Weinberg lectr. Oak Ridge (Tenn.) Nat. Labs., 2001; Regents lectr. UCLA, 2001; Hubert James lectr. Purdue U., 2002. Co-winner 1993-94 Newcomb Cleveland prize AAAS; recipient Dannie Heineman prize Göttingen Acad. Scis., 1995, Outstanding Alumnus award U. Calif. San Diego alumni Assn., 1998, Nanoscience prize Conf. on Atomically Controlled Interfaces and Surfaces, 1999. Fellow AAAS, Am. Phys. Soc. (Davisson-Germer prize 2001). Office: IBM Almaden Rsch Ctr 650 Harry Rd San Jose CA 95120-6099

EIGNER, WILLIAM WHITLING, lawyer; b. Dover, Ohio, Feb. 4, 1959; s. Stanley Spencer and Jeraldine (Lippy) E.; m. Jeanne Beach, May 24, 1987. BA, Stanford U., 1981; JD, U. Va., 1986. Bar: Calif. 1986, U.S. Dist. Ct. (so. dist.) Calif. 1986. Jud. intern U.S. Supreme Ct., Washington, 1981; assoc. Higgs, Fletcher & Mack, San Diego, 1986-89, Procopio, Cory, Hargreaves & Savitch, LLP, San Diego, 1989-95, ptnr., 1995—. Mem. bd. advisors QuantumThink Group, Inc. (QThink), Concerto Networks, Inc., Sky River Comms., Inc.; mem. San Diego Venture Group; mem. San Diego Telecom Coun. and chmn. policy com. Contbr. articles to profl. jours. Trustee, La Jolla (Calif.) Town Coun., 1988-92. chmn. land use com., 1988-90; bd. trustees La Jolla Country Day Sch. Recipient spl. commendation San Diego City Coun. Mem. ABA, State Bar Calif., San Diego County Bar Assn. (bus. sects.), Greater San Diego C. of C. (bd. dirs. 1998-2001, 03—, chmn. bus. recognition and awards com. 1989-98, chmn. emerging bus. com. 1998-2000, energy com., pub. policy com.). Republican. Jewish. Avocations: tennis, civil war history. Office: Procopio Cory Hargreaves & Savitch LLP 530 B St Ste 2100 San Diego CA 92101-4496 E-mail: wwe@procopio.com.

EIGO, FRANCIS AUGUSTINE, theology studies educator; b. Smithville, N.J., Dec. 10, 1925; d. James Joseph and Cherry Bartlet (Applegate) Eigo. BA, LaSalle U., 1948; lic. in sacred theology, Cath. U., Washington, 1964, MA, 1965, PhD in Sacred Theology, 1969. Tchr. Camden (N.J.) Cath. H.S., 1947—58, Austin Prep., Reading, Mass., 1964—66; prof. theology Villanova (Pa.) U., 1966—. Chmn. theology Villanova U., 1972—77, 1980—90, dir. Theology Inst., 1972—, editor Inst. Publ., 1972—. Mem.: N.Am. Acad. Ecumenists, Am. Acad. Religion, Soc. for Sci. Study of Religion, Coll. Theology Soc., Cath. Theol. Soc. Am., Phi Kappa Phi. Avocations: reading, music, collecting. Office: Villanova Univ St Thomas Monastery Villanova PA 19085

EIGSTI, ROGER HARRY, retired insurance company executive; b. Vancouver, Wash., Apr. 17, 1942; s. Harry A. and Alice E. (Huber) E.; m. Mary Lou Nelson, June 8, 1963; children: Gregory, Ann. BS, Linfield Coll., 1964. CPA, Oreg., Wash. Staff CPA Touche Ross and Co., Portland, Oreg., 1964-72; asst. to controller Safeco Corp., Seattle, 1972-78, controller, 1980, Safeco Life Ins. Co., Seattle, 1978-80; pres. Safeco Credit Co., Seattle, 1980-81, Safeco Life Ins. Co., Seattle, 1981-85; exec. v.p., CFO Safeco Corp., Seattle, 1985, CEO, chmn., 1985-2001. Bd. dirs. Ind. Colls. of Wash., Seattle, 1981-87, bus. dir. Seattle Repertory Theatre, 1981—, bd. dirs. 1981—. Mem. Am. Inst. CPA's, Life Office Mgmt. Assn. (bd. dirs. 1983—), Seattle C. of C. (chmn. metro budget rev. com. 1984—). Clubs: Mercer Island (Wash.) Country (treas., bd. dirs. 1981-84); Central Park Tennis. Republican. Home: 1503 Parkside Dr E Seattle WA 98112-3719

EIKLEBERRY, CAROL, psychologist, writer; b. Iowa City, Mar. 18, 1955; d. William Francis and Lois (Schillie) E.; m. Robert Ronald Pagano, Sept. 12, 1989; 1 child, Robert Schillie Pagano. BA in English Lit., Stanford U., 1977; MA in English Lit., U. Va., 1980; PhD in Counseling Psychology, U. Wash., 1988. Lic. psychologist Colo. Staff psychologist U. Pitts., 1990—96; pvt. practice, 1996—. Psychologist Poudre Sch. Dist., Ft. Collins, Colo., 2000—. Author: The Career Guide for Creative and Unconventional People, 1995, 2d edit., 1999. E-mail: carol@creativecareers.com.

EILAND, GARY WAYNE, lawyer; b. Houston, Apr. 25, 1951; s. William N. and Louise A. (Foltin) E.; m. Sandra K. Streetman, Aug. 4, 1973; children: Trina L. Wuensche, Peter T. BBA, U. Tex., 1973, JD, 1976. Bar: Tex. 1976, U.S. Ct. Claims 1977, U.S. Ct. Appeals (5th cir.) 1978, U.S. Ct. Appeals (11th cir.) 1981, U.S. Supreme Ct. 1989. Assoc. Wood, Lucksinger & Epstein, Houston, 1976-81, ptnr., 1981-91, Vinson & Elkins L.L.P., Houston, 1991—; ptnr., co-chair health industry group, 1996—. Lectr. Aspen Health Care Industry seminars, Aspen Pubs., Inc., Rockville, Md., 1978-89, HLO Health Care seminars, 1990-91; charter mem. health law exam. commn. Tex. State Bd. Legal Specialization, 2002—. Mem. Tex. Bar Assn. (chmn. health law sect. 1991-92), Am. Acad. Healthcare Attys. (bd. dirs. 1991-97, pres. 1996-97), Am. Health Lawyers Assn. (past pres., exec. com. 1997-98), Healthcare Fin. Mgmt. Assn. (pres. Tex. Gulf Coast chpt. 1992-93, Region 9 chpt. liaison rep. 1994-95, compliance officers forum adv. coun. 2000-02, Founders medal of honor 1999), Assn. Am. Med. Colls., Houston Ctr. Club, Bentwater Yacht and Country Club. Home: 23319 Holly Hollow Tomball TX 77377-3684 Office: Vinson & Elkins LLP 1001 Fannin St Ste 2300 Houston TX 77002-6760 E-mail: geiland@velaw.com.

EILEN, HOWARD SCOTT, lawyer, mediator; b. N.Y.C., Mar. 28, 1954; m. Sharon R. Kornbluth, Oct. 21, 1979; children: Michael, Jeffrey. BA summa cum laude, MA, CUNY, 1975; JD, St. John's U., 1979. Bar: N.Y. 1980, U.S. Tax Ct. 1980, U.S. Dist. Ct. (so., ea. dists.) N.Y. 1980, U.S. Dist. Ct. (ea. dist.) Mich. 1982. Assoc. Bloom & Tese, N.Y.C., 1980-83; ptnr. Bloom & Eilen, N.Y.C., 1983-86, 87-94; of counsel Spengler, Carlson, Gubar, Brodsky & Frischling, N.Y.C., 1986-87; ptnr. Lehman & Eilen, Uniondale, N.Y., 1994—. Arbitrator Nat. Assn. Securities Dealers, Inc., Nat. Futures Assn., Am. Arbitration Assn., U.S. Arbitration and Mediation, Inc., N.Y. Stock Exch., Inc.; mediator Nat. Assn. Securities Dealers, Inc.; spl. master N.Y. Supreme Ct.; mem. faculty securities arbitration program Practising Law Inst.; lectr. securities arbitration program Nassau Acad. Law. Contbg. editor Futures Tribune Mag., Japan, Securities Arbitration, Practising Law Inst., 1993-2003. Mem. N.Y. County Lawyers Assn. (com. on securities and exchs. 1983—, chmn. subcom. on commodities regulation, com. on arbitration and conciliation 1990—), Nassau County Bar Assn. (securities law com.). Office: Lehman & Eilen LLP Ste 505 50 Charles Lindbergh Blvd Uniondale NY 11553-3650 E-mail: heilen@lehmaneilen.com.

EILER, JASON E, music educator; b. Warsaw, Ind., Aug. 13, 1965; s. L Dean and E Ann Eiler; m. Patricia Ward, Dec. 29, 1992; children: Kaisa J, Ian M, Logan S, Aiden L. AA, Ea. Ariz. Coll., Thatcher, Arizona, 1983—85; MusB Edn., Idaho State U., Pocatello, Idaho, 1993—98. Dir. of bands The Pride of Holbrook Bands, Holbrook, Ariz., 1999—. Band chair NE Ariz. Region. R-Consevative. The Church Of Jesus Christ Of Latter-Day Saints. Avocations: husband, father. Office: Holbrook High School PO Box 640 Holbrook AZ 86025

EILERS (BOWERS), BETTY SUE, elementary school educator, writer; b. Beaver County, Okla., May 5, 1947; d. Charles Donovan and Mabel Ann Bowers; m. Lowell Dean Eilers, May 2, 1947; children: Christy Lynn Poston, Justin Paul Eilers, Jeremy Donovan Eilers. BS, Northwestern Okla. State U., Alva, 1970, 5th and 6th grade tchr. pub. schs., Woodward, Okla., 1971—72; elem. tchr. Ft. Supply Pub. Schs., Ft. Supply, Okla., 1987—. Mem.: Ft. Supply Edn. Assn. (treas. 2001—), Town and Country Club (assoc.; v.p. 2002—03). Republican. Avocations: writing, songwriting, playing the piano, sewing. Home: 1006 Countryside Dr Mooreland OK 73852

EILTS, HERMANN FREDERICK, international relations educator, former diplomat; b. Weissenfels Saale, Germany, Mar. 23, 1922; came to U.S., 1926; naturalized, 1930; s. Friedrich Alex and Meta Dorothea (Pruser) E.; m. Helen Josephine Brew, June 12, 1948; children: Conrad Marshall, Frederick Lowell. BA, Ursinus Coll., 1942, LLD, 1960; MA, Johns Hopkins U., 1947; postgrad., U. Pa., 1950-51. Joined Fgn. Svc., Dept. State, 1947; 3d sec., vice consul Tehran, Iran, 1947-48, Jidda, Saudi Arabia, 1948-50; consul prin. officer, 1951-53; 2d sec., consul, 1951-53; 2d sec., consul, chief polit. sect. Bahdad, Iraq, 1954-56; officer in charge Baghdad Pact affairs Dept. State, Washington, 1957-59, officer in charge Arabian Peninsula affairs, 1959-61; 1st sec. Am. Embassy, London, 1962-64, counsellor, dep. chief of mission Tripoli, Libya, 1964-65; amb. to Saudi Arabia, 1965-70; dep. commandant for internat. affairs, diplomatic adviser U.S. Army War Coll., Carlisle Barracks, Pa., 1970-73; amb. to Egypt Cairo, 1973-79; Disting. Univ. prof. internat. rels. Boston U., 1979—, chmn. dept. polit. sci., 1982-87, chmn. dept. internat. rels., 1989-93, acad. coord., mil. edn. div., 1990-93, prof. emeritus, 1993—. 1st lt. M.I., AUS, 1942-45. Decorated Purple Heart, Bronze Star; recipient Arthur Flemming award, 1958, Disting. Civilian Honor award Dept. Army, 1973, Disting. Honor award Dept. State, 1979, Joseph C. Wilson award, 1979, Disting. Alumnus award Johns Hopkins U., 1980, All-Pa. Coll. Alumni Assn. citation, 1987, Am. Foreign Svc. cup Dept. State, 1992; named Disting. Fellow U.S. Army War Coll., 1991. Fellow Royal Geog. Soc., Royal Asiatic Soc.; mem. Am. Fgn. Svc. Assn., Middle East Inst., Royal Cen. Asian Soc. Mem. Evang. Reformed Ch. Address: 67 Cleveland Rd Wellesley MA 02481-2434

EILTS, MICHAEL DEAN, research meteorologist, manager; b. La Chapelle, France, Aug. 22, 1959; (parents Am. citizens); s. Leonard Gene and Arlys Mamie (Ziegler) E. BS in Meteorology, U. Okla., 1981, MS in Meteorology, 1983, MBA in Fin. and Human Resource Mgmt., 1991. Rsch. asst., rsch. meteorologist Coop. Inst. for Mesoscale Meteorol. Studies, Norman, Okla., 1981-84; rsch. meteorologist Nat. Severe Storms Lab., Norman, 1984-87, mgr. weather hazards to aviation project, 1987-91, chief forecast applications rsch. group, 1991-93, asst. dir., chief stormscale rsch. and applications divsn., 1993-2000; pres., CEO Weather Decision Techs., Inc., 2000—. Mem. exptl. forecast facility mgmt. group, 1991-95; mem. Cleveland County YMCA Program Com., 1991-93; spl. mem. adj. faculty U. Okla. Sch. Meteorology, Norman, 1989—; mem. Okla. Mesonet Steering Com.; coun. mem., fellow Coop. Inst. Mesoscale Meteorol. Studies. Contbr. articles to profl. jours. Grantee FAA, 1987-99, NASA, 1990-91, 96-97, Nat. Weather Svc., 1991-99, Ga. Emergency Mgmt. Agy., 1999; recipient Dist. Authorship award Environ. Rsch. Labs., 1991, Adminstrs. award NOAA, 1998. Mem. Am. Meteorol. Soc. Lutheran. Avocations: golf, volleyball, softball. Home: 3405 S Bryant Ave Moore OK 73160-8401 Office: Weather Decision Technologies Inc Bldg D Ste 228 1818 W Lindsey St Norman OK 73069 E-mail: eilts@wdtinc.com.

EIMER, NATHAN PHILIP, lawyer; b. Chgo., June 26, 1949; s. Irving A. and Charlotte Eimer; m. Kathleen L. Roach; children: Micah Jacob, Noah Joseph, Daniel Jordan, Anna Beatrice. AB in Econs. magna cum laude, U. Ill., 1970; JD cum laude, Northwestern U., 1973. Bar: Ill. 1973, U.S. Supreme Ct. 1978, N.Y. 1985, Tex. 1998. Assoc. Sidley & Austin, Chgo., 1973-80, ptnr., mem. exec. com., 1980—2000; founding ptnr. Eimer Stahl Klevorn & Solberg, Chgo., 2000—. Adj. prof. Law Sch., Northwestern U., Chgo., 1989-96. Note and comment editor Northwestern U. Law Rev., 1972-73. Bd. dirs. Chgo. Lawyers Com. for Civil Rights, 1991—, pres., 1993-94; bd. dirs. UNICEF, 1992-93, Infant Welfare Soc., Chgo., exec. v.p., 1992-96, pres., 1996-98; mem. adv. bd. Children & Family Justice Ctr., Northwestern U. Legal Clinic, 1996—. Mem. ABA, Univ. Club. Office: Eimer Stahl Klevorn & Solberg Ste 1100 224 S Michigan Ave Chicago IL 60604 E-mail: neimer@eimerstahl.com.

EIMERS, JERI ANNE, retired therapist; b. Berkeley, Calif., Jan. 20, 1951; d. Alfred D. Wallace and Marjorie E. (Nordheim) Stevens; m. Roy A. Neiman, June 12, 1969 (div. Aug. 1977); children: Lorien, Arwen; m. Richard A. Eimers, Mar. 2, 1996. AA, Palomar Jr. Coll., 1977; BA in Psychology with distinction, Calif. State U., Long Beach, 1979, MA in Psychology with distinction, 1981; postgrad. Human Sexuality Program, UCLA, 1991-92. Lic. marriage, family, child therapist, Calif.; cert. community coll. instr., counselor; cert. sex therapist. Rsch. asst. Calif. State U., 1978-82; tchr. Artesia (Calif.)-Bellflower-Cerritos Unified Sch. Dist., 1982-83; dir. Am. Learning Corp., Huntington Beach, Calif., 1983-85; social worker Los Angeles County Children's Protective Svcs., Long Beach, 1986-88; sr. social worker Orange County Social Svc. Agy., Orange, Calif., 1988-90; therapist Cypress Mental Health, Cypress, Calif., 1988—, cons., 1990—. Cons., 1990—; group chair, leader Adults Abused as Children, Los Altos Hosp., Long Beach, 1991—, Coll. Hosp., Cerritos, 1993—; speaker, presenter in field. Mem. Child's Sexual Abuse Network, Orange, 1988—; mem. legis. com. Child Abuse Coun. of Orange County, 1988. Women's League scholar, 1980-81. Mem. AAUW, Am. Assn. Marriage, Family Therapists, Calif. Assn. Marriage, Family Therapists, Am. Profl. Soc. for Abused Children, Calif. Profl. Assn. for Abused Children, Phi Kappa Phi, Psi Chi. Republican. Methodist. Avocations: writing, theater, classical and jazz music, swimming.

EIN, DANIEL, allergist; b. Liege, Belgium, Nov. 26, 1938; arrived in U.S., 1941; s. Max Motel and Sabine (Toeman) E.; m. Marion Hess, June 25, 1961 (div. 1978); children: Mark David, Jon Spencer; m. Marina Wallach, Apr. 10, 1988; stepchildren: Jacqueline A. Newmyer, Tory Newmyer. AB, Columbia U., 1959; MD, Albert Einstein Coll. Medicine, 1964. Diplomate Am. Bd. Internal Medicine, Am. Bd. Allergy and Immunology. Intern Bronx Mcpl. Hosp., N.Y.C., 1964-65; staff assoc. Nat. Cancer Inst., Washington, 1965-67, clin. assoc., 1967-68; asst. resident Mass. Gen. Hosp., Boston, 1968-69; sr. investigator Nat. Cancer Inst., Washington, 1969-71; pvt. practice Washington, 1971—. Clin. prof. medicine George Washington U., Washington, 1984—; founder, pres. Capital Physicians Network, 1994-99. Contbr. articles to profl. jours. and newspapers. Fellow ACP, Am. Acad. Allergy (AMA del. 1994), Am. Coll. Allergy (bd. dirs. 2000—); mem. Joint Coun. of Allergy (pres. 1998-2000), Med. Soc. of D.C. (pres. 1991), Greater Washington Allergy Soc. (pres.

1979), Cosmos Club. Jewish. Achievements include discovery of OZ factors on human immunoglobulin light chains. Home: 4636 Kenmore Dr NW Washington DC 20007-1924 E-mail: dein1@bellatlantic.net.

EINACH, CHARLES DONALD, advertising and publishing executive; b. Buffalo, July 1, 1929; s. Joseph and Esther Riva (Liner) E.; m. Elen Simon, Mar. 15, 1971. BA, U. Buffalo, 1951; MA, Syracuse U., 1953. Broadcast dir. The Rumrill Co. Inc., Buffalo, 1954-60; dir. advt. J. Nelson Prewitt Inc., Rochester, N.Y., 1960-63; account supr., v.p. Grey Advt. Inc., N.Y.C., 1963-71; exec. v.p. Nadler & Larimer Inc., N.Y.C., 1971-84; sr. v.p. Mandelbaum, Wolf, Wiskowski Inc., Jersey City, 1986-87; pres. Headwork Svcs. Cons., N.Y.C., 1985-94; chief editor mut. fund. publs. Value Line Publ., Inc., N.Y.C., 1994—. Co-chmn. Citizens for Sane Residential Zoning, N.Y.C., 1984-85. Mem. Nat. Acad. TV Arts and Scis., Internat. Wine Soc. Clubs: Les Amis du Vin (N.Y.C.). Avocation: enology. Home: 301 E 66th St New York NY 10021-6216 Office: Value Line Publs Inc 220 E 42d St New York NY 10017-5891

EINAUDI, LUIGI ROBERTO, diplomat, educator; b. Cambridge, Mass., Mar. 1, 1936; s. Mario and Manon (Michels) E.; m. Carol Peacock, Aug. 26, 1958; children: Maria, Elisabeth, Mario, Peter. AB cum laude, Harvard Coll., 1957; postgrad., Harvard U., 1959-61, PhD, 1966. Tchg. fellow Harvard U., 1960-61; instr. Wesleyan U., 1961-62; with social sci. dept. Rand Corp., 1962-73; vis. prof. U. Calif., L.A., 1964-73; mem. policy planning staff Dept. State, Washington, 1974-77, dir. inter-Am. regional planning office, 1977-89, sr. adviser policy planning staff, 1993-97, acting dir., 1994; U.S. rep. with rank of amb. Orgn. of Am. States, 1989-93, spl. rep. of sec. gen. for Honduras and Nicaragua, 1999-2000, asst. sec. gen., 2000—. Mem. Coun. on Fgn. Rels.; mem. internat. coun. Inst. Conflict Analysis and Resolution, George Mason U., 1991—; U.S. spl. envoy for Ecuador-Peru peace talks, 1995-98; mem. sci. com. Luigi Einaudi Found., Turin, Italy, 1995—; sr. fellow multilateral govt. and conflict resolution Inter-Am. Dialogue, Washington, 1997-2000; adj. prof. Georgetown U., 1998, 99; mem. edn. adv. bd. U.S. Army, 1998-2000. Author: Beyond Cuba, 1974; contbr. numerous articles to profl. jours. With U.S. Army, 1957-59. Bartels World Affairs fellow Cornell U., 1993; recipient Disting. Exec. Presdl. Rank award, 1987, Robert C. Frasure Meml. award, 1997, Disting. Honor award Sec. of State, 1997, Gran Cruz, Orden "el Sol del Peru", 1999, Gran Cruz, Orden "Nacional al Merito", Ecuador, 1999. Mem. Acad. Am. Diplomacy. Office: Orgn Am States 17th St and Constitution Ave NW Washington DC 20006

EINHORN, CARL MURRAY, psychologist; b. N.Y.C., Oct. 21, 1922; s. Albert H. and Florence (Spiegel) E.; m. Ruth Anna Hollander, July 22, 1946; children: Freda B. Rhodes, Susan R., Michael L. BA, Yeshiva Coll., 1945; MA, U. Mich., 1950, PhD, 1955. Diplomate Am. Bd. Profl. Psychology, Am. Bd. Forensic Examiners, Am. Bd. Forensic Medicine, Am. Bd. Psychol. Splties. Assoc. prof. Lawrence Inst. Tech., Detroit, 1947-52; supervisory psychologist VA Hosp., Lyons, N.J., 1958-69; unit psychologist VA Med. Ctr., Lyons, N.J., 1970-83, ret., 1983; dir. Ctrl. Jersey Biofeedback & Stress Control Ctr., Inc., South Plainfield, 1984-89; cons. psychologist N.J. Divsn. of Disability Determinations, Newark, 1992-94; exec. dir. Ctr. for Health Psychology, Inc., South Plainfield, 1994-99; dir. Ctr. for Psychol. Svcs., East Brunswick, 1994—; adj. prof. Union for Experimenting Colls. and Univs., Cin., 1994—; consulting psychologist East Brunswick Dept. Pub. Safety, 1974-99. Adj. prof. Fairleigh Dickinson U., 1960-65; adj. prof. Newark State (Kean) Coll., 1964-69, dir. psychol. svcs. and counseling, 1969-70; cons. psychologist Lab. of Psychol. Studies, Stevens Inst. Tech., Hoboken, N.J., 1958-69; indsl. and mgmt. cons. Sci. Resources Assocs., 1969-72; dir. psychol. svcs. New Brunswick Rehab. Ctr., 1975-77; dir. Ctr. for Human Rels., Inc., East Brunswick, N.J., 1977-88. Recipient Disting. Sr. Contbr. to Counseling Psychology award Divsn. of Counseling Psychology, Am. Psychology Assn., 1990, Psychologist Recognition award N.J. Acad. Psychology, 1982. Mem. Am. Psychol. Assn. (emeritus), N.J. Psychol. Assn. (emeritus). Home: 44 Yorktown Rd East Brunswick NJ 08816-3325 E-mail: cmephsycserv@aol.com.

EINHORN, DAVID ALLEN, lawyer; b. Bklyn., Dec. 11, 1961; s. Harold and Jane Ellen (Wiener) Einhorn. BA in Computer Sci. magna cum laude, Columbia U., 1983, JD, 1986. Bar: N.Y. 1987, DC 1988, U.S. Dist. Ct. (so. and ea. dists.) N.Y. 1989, U.S. Ct. Appeal (fed. cir.) 1992, U.S. Dist. Ct. (no. dist.) Calif. 1994, U.S. Dist. Ct. Conn. 2003. Assoc. Kaye, Scholer, Fierman, Hays & Handler, N.Y.C., 1986-89; ptnr. Anderson Kill & Olick, PC, N.Y.C., 1989—. Lectr. Am. Conf. Inst.; arbitrator Nat. Arbitration Forum, 2002—. Co-author: (2-vol. treatise) Patent Licensing Transactions; editor-in-chief: Intellectual Property for the New Millenium, 1997—; contbr. articles to profl. jours.; columnist: Grapevine. Lt. col. JAGC, N.Y. Guard, 1987—. Named to Order of Merit, Les Amis du Vin, 1982; recipient Nat. prize, Nathan Burkan Copyright Essay Competition, 1985, Off Off Broadway Rev. award for producing Ionesco Fest.; Harlan Fiske Stone scholar, Columbia U., 1985. Mem.: ABA (chmn. software patent subcom. 1988—91, software licensing subcom. 1991—95, software copyright subcom. 1995—96, chmn. broadcasting, sound recordings, and performing artists com. 2000—02, chmn. com. trademarks and internet 2002—), Licensing Execs. Soc. (computer law sect.), DC Bar Assn. (computer law sect.), Internat. Trademark Assn., N.Y. Intellectual Property Law Assn., Am. Intellectual Property Law Assn. (chmn. software copyright subcom. 1999—), Intellectual Property Owners Assn. (chmn. cybersquatting com. 2003—), Untitled Theater Co. #61, Ltd. (chmn. bd. dirs., producing dir., treas. 1994—, vice chair cybersquitting com.), Tasters Guild (v.p., bd. dirs. 1997—), N.Y. Soc. Mil. and Naval Officers (v.p. 1995—). Democrat. Jewish. Avocations: tennis, racquetball, wine tasting, theater. Home: 2373 Broadway Apt 802 New York NY 10024-2835 Office: Anderson Kill & Olick PC 1251 Ave of the Americas New York NY 10020-1182 E-mail: deinhorn@andersonkill.com.

EINHORN, JERZY, internist, endocrinologist, consultant; b. Sosnowiec, Poland, Mar. 17, 1919; s. Oskar Einhorn and Karola (Birman) Mazurkiewicz; m. Jadwiga Piaskowski, Mar. 17, 1946 (div. Apr. 1968); children: Janusz Richard, Robert Krzysztof, Ewa Krystyna; m. Ruth Mary Gregor, May 23, 1968; 1 child, Edward William. MD, Poznan (Poland) Med. Acad., 1951; PhD, Silesia Med. Acad., Katowice, Poland, 1963. Dir. State Endocrinology Consulting Ctr., Katowice, 1954-66; assoc. prof. 3rd Dept. Internal Medicine, Katowice, 1962-66; endocrine rschr. Royal Postgrad. Med. Sch., London, 1965, 67; assoc. prof. U. Pitts. Med. Sch., 1971-94; dir. Hazelwood & Greenfield Cmty. Health Ctrs., Pitts., 1971-84; dir. thyroid screening program U. Pitts. Med. Sch., 1976-93. Author: Recollections of the End of an Era, 2000; contbr. over 35 rsch. articles to profl. jours. Maj. Polish Light Horse Artillery, 1939 Polish Underground Army, 1940—44 Warsaw Uprising, 1944. Recipient Silver Cross of Merit, 1957, Endocrine rsch. awards Polish Endocrine Soc., 1962, 63, 1st Class prize Min. Health, 1967; recipient mil. awards Virtuti Militari, 1939, Cross of Valour, 1944, Cross of the Warsaw Uprising, 1944. Avocations: woodworking, photography, horseback riding. Home: 415 Summit Dr Pittsburgh PA 15228-2617

EINHORN, MARTIN B. physics educator; b. Dayton, Ohio, Aug. 14, 1942; s. Aaron Howard and Rosalind (Rosen) E.; m. Vibeke Gjoe Geleff, Feb. 18, 1967; children: Michael, Linda. BS (hons.), Calif. Inst. Tech., 1965; PhD, Princeton U., 1968. Post-doctoral fellow Stanford (Calif.) Linear Accelerator Ctr., 1968-70, Lawrence Berkeley (Calif.) Lab., 1970-72, Fermi Nat. Accelerator Lab., Batavia, Ill., 1972-73, staff physicist, 1973-76; assoc. rsch. scientist U. Mich., Ann Arbor, 1976-79, assoc. prof., 1979-83, prof. physics, 1983—. Chair adv. bd. Theoretical Advanced Study Inst., Boulder, Colo., 1984-91, dep. dir. Inst. for Theoretical Physics, U. Calif., Santa Barbara, 1990-92. Contbr. 75 articles to profl. jours. Mem. high energy physics adv. panel Dept. of Energy, Washington, 1983-87. John Simon Guggenheim Meml. Found. fellow, 2003—. Fellow Am. Phys. Soc.; mem. AAUP, AAAS.

EINHORN, THOMAS ALFRED, orthopaedic surgeon; b. Newark, Nov. 9, 1950; s. Harvey Paul and Patricia Irene (Kalb) E.; m. Kyle Rickel, Aug. 9, 1975; children: Emily, Zachary. AB, Rutgers U., 1972; MD, Cornell Med. Coll., 1976. Diplomate Nat. Bd. Med. Examiners, Am. Bd. Orthopaedic Surgery. Intern, gen. surgery Hosp. of U. Pa., Phila., 1976-77; resident, orthop. surgery St. Luke's-Roosevelt Hosp. Ctr., N.Y.C., 1978-81; asst. attending orthop. surgeon Kings County Hosp., Bklyn., 1982-86; asst. prof. orthop. surgery SUNY Health Sci. Ctr., Bklyn., 1982-86; assoc. prof. orthop. surgery Mt. Sinai Sch. Medicine, N.Y.C., 1982-86, prof. orthop. surgery, 1992-97, dir. orthop. rsch., 1988-97; prof., chair orthop. surgery Boston U. Sch. Medicine, 1997—. Adv. med. panel Paget's Disease Found., N.Y.C., 1991—. Contbr. articles to Jour. Orthopaedic Rsch., Jour. Bone Joint Surgery, Clin. Orthopaedics. Hon. surgeon N.Y.C. Transit Police Dept., 1984-97; trustee Nat. Osteoporosis Found. Metabolic Bone Disease fellow, Hops. Spl. Curgery, 1981-82, ABC Traveling fellow, Am. Orthopaedic Assn., 1989; recipient S. Oakley Van Der Poel Chemistry award, 1972, Philip D. Wilson award, 1982, Career Devel. award, 1986, Kappa Delta award, 1999, Marshall R. Urist award, 2002. Mem. Internat. Soc. Fracture Repair (bd. dirs. 1990-2000, newsletter editor 1990-95), Orthopaedic Rsch. Soc. (bd. dirs. 1988—. sec. 1991-93), Phi Beta Kappa. Achievements include patent for Einhorn Bone Biopsy System; development of widely used expiremental fracture model, identification of circulating osteogenic factor during fracture healing, identification of role of neutral proteases in regenerating bone. Office: 720 Harrison Ave Boston MA 02118

EINISMAN, MYRON SACHAR, publisher; b. Chgo., Mar. 13, 1940; s. William and Ada Joyce (Brenner) E.; m. Margaret Movius Boland, Sept. 26, 1977. BA in Liberal Arts, U. Chgo. Coll., 1962; MBA, U. Chgo., 1963; JD, U. Louisville, 1966. Atty. NLRB, L.A., 1966-67; devel. officer U. Chgo., 1967-71; cons. Charles R. Feldstein & Co., Chgo., 1971-73; dir. devel. and pub. rels. United Charities of Chgo., 1973-76; chief cons. I.D.C. Corp., Chgo., 1976-82; v.p. mktg. OMG/Publs., Chgo., 1982-94; pres., pub. OMG/Philanthropy Publ. Founding chmn. student/alumni theatre com. U. Chgo., 1992-96. Author syndicated articles on charitable fin. planning, 1990—; pub., project editor: (audiotapes) Masterpieces of Legal Fiction, 1997; co-pub. reprints of artists' drawings used in origianl Sherlock Holmes mag. stories, 1988. Student editor, chmn. U. Louisville Law Sch. Brandeis Lecture Series, 1963-65; paid con. to varitety of charitable groups in health, edn., arts, 1967-86; cons., advisor Recovery, Inc., 1986-87; coll. reunion co-chmn. U. Chgo. Coll., 1992; donated major audiotape collectionto Union League Libr., 1997; chmn. Friends of Union League. Recipient Outstanding Alumni Svc. award U. Chgo. Theatre Alumni, Chgo., 1994. Mem. Union League Club of Chgo., Club of Chgo. Libr. Avocations: collector of autographed mystery books, mystery writing, admirer of wife's gardening, sports. Home: 477 Green Bay Rd Highland Park IL 60035-4935

EINODER, CAMILLE ELIZABETH, retired secondary education educator; b. Chgo., June 15, 1937; d. Isadore and Elizabeth T. (Czerwinski) Popowski; m. Joseph X. Einoder, Aug. 5, 1978; children: Carl Frank, Mark Frank, Vivian Einoder, Joe Einoder, Tim Einoder, Sheila Einoder, Jude Eindoer. Student, Fox Bus. Coll., 1954; BEd in Biology, Chgo. Tchrs. Coll., 1964; MA in Analytical Chemistry, Gov.'s State U., 1977; MA in Adminstrn. and Supervision, Roosevelt U., 1986; postgrad., 1992—. Sec., Chgo., 1955-64; tchr. biology Chgo. Bd. Edn., 1964-1975, tchr. biology and agr., 1975-81, tchr. biology, agr. and chemistry, 1981-2000, ret., 2000. Human rels. coord. Morgan Park High Sch., Chgo., 1980—, tchr. biology Internat. Studies Sch., 1983—, adv. bd., 1989—; owner Einoder Masonry, 1997—, Einoder Antiques, 1996—; career devel. cons. for agr. related curriculum; internat. baccalaureate tchr., Chgo. pub. schs. consulting tchr., 1997; edn. cons. Neighborhood Coun., 1974; rep. Chgo. Tchrs. Union, 1969; exec. bd. dir. The Lira Ensemble, 1996—; mem. Renaissance Circle, DePaul U.; edn. com. Polish-Am. Initiative of Chgo. Cmty. Trust, 1999—; owner Einoder Masonry, 1998—; antique dealer, 1995—. Bd. dirs., founding mem., author constn. Cmty. Coun., 1970—; bd. dirs., edn. cons. Neighborhood Coun., 1974; rep. Chgo. Tchrs. Union, 1969; exec. bd. dirs. The Lira Ensemble, 1996—. Mem. AAAS, NSTA, Polish Inst. for Arts and Sci., Am. Chem. Soc., Am. Biology Tchrs. Assn., Nat. Assn. Women Bus. Owners, Found. Women Contractors, Copernicus Found., Kosciuszko Soc., Polish Arts Club, Phi Delta Kappa, Iota Sigma Pi. Home: 10637 S Claremont Ave Chicago IL 60643-3101 E-mail: camilleein@aol.com.

EINREINHOFER, NANCY ANNE, art gallery director; b. Paterson, N.J., Sept. 8, 1944; d. John Edward and Nora (Niland) Gleason; m. Robert Einreinhofer, Nov. 26, 1966; 1 child, Robert. BA in Art, William Paterson Coll., 1976, BA in English, 1977, MA in Visual Arts, 1978; cert. in supervisory mgmt., Rutgers U., 1986; PhD in Mus. Studies, Leicester U., England, 1993. Art critic N.J. News, 1973-76; gallery curator O.K. Harris Works of Art, N.Y.C., 1978; dir. gallery William Paterson U., Wayne, N.J., 1979—. Bd. dirs. Mus. Council of N.J., 1984—; cons. Sussex County Arts Council, N.J., 1987. Author: The American Art Museum: Elitism and Democracy, 1997; contbr. articles to profl. jours. Recipient grant Nat. Endowment for Arts, 1979, NEH, 1984-85, 87-88, N.J State Ccouncil Arts, 1984-85, 85-86, 87-88, 2000—. Mem. Am. Assn. Mus., Internat. Council Mus., Mid Atlantic Assn. Mus., Assn. Coll. and U. Mus. Galleries, Mus. Council of N.J. (exec. bd. 1984-88). Home: 1 Cheyenne Trl Sparta NJ 07871-2924 Office: William Paterson U Ben Shahn Galleries Wayne NJ 07470 E-mail: EinreinhoferN@WPUNJ.edu.

EINS, STEFAN, painter, conceptual artist, sculptor, arts curator; b. Prague, Bohemia; came to U.S., 1967; s. Stefan and Daisy (Ganghofer) Schmid. MA in Theology, U. Vienna, 1965; BA in Sculpture, Akad. Bildenen Kuenste, Vienna, 1967. Founder, exec. dir. 3 Mercer St, N.Y.C., 1972-79, Fashion Moda, N.Y.C., 1978-84, 88-93; painter, 1980—. Sculptor: prin. works include Variables, 1966, Liquid Steel/Life, NYC, 1972, Project Vertebrae, Austria, 1994. Co-founder chpt. The Audubon Soc., N.Y.C., 1979. Grantee, NEA, 1980, 1987, NY Found. for the Arts, 2002. Mem. Collaborative Projects, Inc. (pres. 1988-89, 2001—). Achievements include research on liquids formation; discovery of formation process of vertebrae, 1985; uncovered stone age artifacts in Austria, 1987-94. Home: PO Box 33 New York NY 10013-0033 E-mail: oneins@hotmail.com.

EINSEL, DAVID WILLIAM, JR., retired army officer and consultant; b. Tiffin, Ohio, Nov. 4, 1928; s. David William and Naomi Dorothy (Williams) E.; m. Elva yates Aylor, June 16, 1956; children: Susan Vagnier, Mary Kost. BA, MA in Chemistry, Ohio State U., 1950; MSc, U. Va., 1956. Commd. 2d lt. U.S. Army, 1950, advanced through grades to maj. gen., 1980; staff officer Orgn. of the Joint Chiefs of Staff, Washington, 1968-70; comdr. Harry Diamond Labs., Adelphi, Md., 1970-75; chief nuclear-chem. officer hdqrs. Dept. of the Army, Washington, 1975-76; dep. commanding gen. U.S. Army Armament R&D Command Picatinny (N.J.) Arsenal, 1976-80; asst. to sec. of def. Office of the Sec. of Def., Washington, 1980-85; officer Nat. Intelligence Coun., Washington, 1985-89; ret. U.S. Army, 1985; cons. Tiffin, Ohio, 1989—. Author: International Military Encyclopedia, 1991; contbr. article to Jour. Analytical Chemistry. Decorated Silver Star, Bronze Star, Purple Heart; named to U.S. Army Chem. Corps Hall of Fame, 1993; recipient Profl. Achievement award Ohio State U., 1998. Mem. AAAS, Assn. of the U.S. Army, Am. Def. Preparedness Assn., Kiwanis, Masons (33d degree), Phi Beta Kappa, Sigma Xi. Republican. Methodist. Achievements include patent in automatic electrolytic apparatus for determining acid prodn. rates. Home and Office: 594 S Washington St Tiffin OH 44883-3320

EINSELEN, KENNETH LEE, civil engineer; b. Peru, Ind., Nov. 5, 1954; s. John Harold and Carolyn (Agness) E.; m. Cynthia Jean Bateman, Dec. 27, 1980; children: John Michael, Mark Andrew, Lisa Marie, Lydia Anne, Matthew David. BSCE, Purdue U., 1976, MSCE, 1977. Registered profl. engr., Ind. Airport engr. A & E Engring., Indpls., 1977-82; transp. engr. Mid-States Engring., Indpls., 1982-83; county hwy. engr. County of Miami, Peru, 1984—. Active Wabash River Heritage Corridor commn., 1992—. Mem. ASCE, United Meth. Men (pres. McGrawsville chpt. 1990-91). Office: Miami County Rm 101 County Courthouse Peru IN 46970 E-mail: ken_einselen@juno.com.

EINSPRUCH, BURTON CYRIL, psychiatrist; b. N.Y.C., June 27, 1935; s. Adolph and Mala (Goldblatt) E.; m. Barbara Standen Traeger, Oct. 9, 1960; children: Julia E. Lewis, Alexander Louis, Robert Sands. BA, So. Meth. U., 1956, ScB, 1958; MD, Southwestern Med. Sch., Dallas, 1960. Diplomate Am. Bd. Psychiatry and Neurology (examiner 1974—). Intern Montefiore Hosp., N.Y.C., 1960-61; resident Nat. Hosp. Inst. Neurology, London, 1962; resident, fellow U. Tex., Dallas, 1961—64; chief resident Parkland Meml. Hosp., Dallas, 1964; instr. psychiatry U. Pa., 1964-66; pvt. practice psychiatry Dallas, 1966—. Staff Presbyn. and Parkland Hosps., Timberlawn Psychiat. Hosp.; clin. asst. prof. U. Tex., Health Sci. Center, Dallas, 1966-70, dir. Southwestern Adult Psychiat. Clinic, Dallas, 1966-74; dir. psychiat. service Dallas Geriatric Research Inst., 1974-80; adj. prof. sociology N. Tex. State U., Denton, 1975-82; cons. staff Baylor U. Hosp., Golden Acres Hosp.; clin. assoc. prof. psychiatry U. Tex. Health Scis. Ctr., Dallas, 1971—; prof. psychiatry U. Tex. Southwestern Med. Ctr., Dallas, 1971—; bd. dirs., founder Dallas Nat. Bank; clin. assoc. prof. psychiatry NYU Med. Ctr., N.Y.C., 1990; adj. prof. dept. Occupl. and Environ. Med. UT Med. Ctr., Tyler, Tex., Devel. Psych. and Communcations, UTD, Dallas; chmn. bd. dirs. Planned Behavioral Health Care, Inc., Dallas; affiliate Tex. Inst. Rsch. and Edn. on Aging, Health Sci. Ctr. Fort Worth; mem. editl. bd. Tex. Medicine Bd., 1991-2002 dirs. Mental Health Assn. Dallas, 1960-69; Jewish Family Service, 1969-71, 73-75; bd. dirs. Am. Svc. Group. Contbr. articles to profl. jours. Trustee Evans Fedn., N.Y.C., 1986—, U. Tex., Dallas, 1987—, St. Mark's Sch. Tex., 1987—, chmn. holocaust studies program bd., 1998—; mem. exec. bd. libr. So. Meth. U., 1992—; adv. dir. Leonhardt Fedn., N.Y.C., 1990, Children of Alcoholics Fedn., 1991, 1995; arbitrator, N.Y. and Am. Exchs., N.Y.C., 1984; bd. dirs. Wyndham Internat., 1997-2000 Lt. comdr. M.C., USNR, 1964-66. Fellow Am. Psychiat. Assn. (disting. life, Am. Coll. Psychiatrists, Am. Soc. Adolescent Psychiatry, N. Tex. Soc. Adolescent Psychiatry (past pres.); mem. Royal Coll. Psychiatry London, AMA, Tex. Med. Assn. Home: 3505 Lindenwood Ave Dallas TX 75205-3229 Office: 8330 Meadow Rd Ste 117 Dallas TX 75231-3750

EINSPRUCH, NORMAN GERALD, physicist, engineering educator; b. N.Y.C., June 27, 1932; s. Adolph and Mala (Goldblatt) E.; m. Edith Melnick, Dec. 20, 1953; children— Eric, Andrew, Franklin. BA in Physics, Rice U., 1953; MS in Physics, U. Colo., 1955; PhD in Applied Math, Brown U., 1959. Mem. tech. staff, central research labs. Tex. Instruments, Inc., Dallas, 1959-62, mgr. electron transport physics br., central research labs., 1962-68, dir. advanced tech. lab., central research labs., 1968-69, dir. tech., chem. materials div., 1969-72, dir. central research labs., 1972-75, asst. v.p., 1975-77, mgr. corp. devel., 1975-76, mgr. tech. and planning consumer products, 1976-77; prof. dept. elec. and computer engrng. Coll. Engring. U. Miami, Coral Gables, Fla., 1977—, dean Coll. Engring., 1977-90, sr. fellow in sci. and tech., 1990—, chmn. dept. indsl. engring., 1994-99. Vis. prof. Rensselaer Poly. Inst., 2001-02; chmn. panel on thin film microstructure sci. and tech. NRC, 1978-79, mem. panel on impact of Dod bery high speed integrated crcts. program, 1980-81, panel on edn. and utilization of the engr., 1981-82; bd. dirs. Covanta Energy Corp, Zinc Matrix Power, Inc. Author: Electronic Genie: The Tangled History of Silicon, 1998 editor: (series) VLSI Electronics: Microstructure Science, 24 vols., VLSI Handbook, 1985; contbr. articles to profl. jours. Recipient George Washington Honor medal Freedoms Found. Valley Forge. Fellow Am. Phys. Soc., Acoustical Soc. Am., IEEE, AAAS; mem. Golden Key, Iron Arrow, Sigma Xi, Omicron Delta Kappa, Tau Beta Pi, Eta Kappa Nu, Phi Kappa Phi, Alpha Pi Mu, Tau Sigma Delta. Home: 1415 Trillo Ave Miami FL 33146-2312 Office: U Miami Coll Engring PO Box 248581 Coral Gables FL 33124-8581 E-mail: neinspruch@miami.edu.

EINSTEIN, CLIFFORD JAY, advertising executive; b. L.A., May 4, 1939; s. Harry and Thelma (Bernstein) E.; m. Madeline Mandel, Jan. 28, 1962; children: Harold Jay, Karen Holly. BA in English, UCLA, 1961; PhD, DFA, Otis Coll. Art and Design, 2002. Writer Norman, Craig and Kummel, N.Y.C., 1961-62, Foote, Cone and Belding, L.A., 1962-64; ptnr. Silverman and Einstein, L.A., 1965-67; pres., creative dir. Dailey and Assos., L.A., 1968-93, chmn., CEO, 1994—, also bd dirs. Dir. Campaign '80, advt. agy. Reagan for Pres., 1980; lectr. various colls.; founder First Coastal Bank; bd. dirs. The Jewish Cmty. Found. Contbr. articles to Advertising Age; prodr.: (play) Whatever Happened to Georgie Tapps, L.A. and San Francisco, 1980; film appearances include Real Life, Modern Romance, Defending Your Life, Face/Off, 1997; T.V. appearance in Bizarre, Super Dave Show. Bd. dirs. Rape Treatment Ctr., Santa Monica Med. Ctr., Discovery Fund for Eye Rsch.; vice-chmn. bd. Mus. Contemporary Art, L.A., 1994—; trustee Otis Coll ARt & Design. With U.S. Army, 1957. Recipient Am. Advt. award, 1968, 73, 79, Clio award, 1973, Internat. Broadcast Pub. Svc. award, 1970, 85, Nat. Addy award, 1979, Gov.'s award, 1987; named Creative Dir. of the West, Adweek Poll, 1982, Exec. of West, 1986, Western States Assn. Advt. Agys. Leader of Yr., 1992, Leader of the West, Am. Advt. Fedn., 2002. Mem. AFTRA, ASCAP, SAG, Dirs. Guild Am., Hillcrest Country Club, Calif. Club. Office: Dailey & Assocs 8687 Melrose Ave West Hollywood CA 90069-5701

EINSTEIN, ERIC BRANDT, internal medicine physician; b. Boston, Mar. 16, 1951; s. Robert Maier (dec.) and Hope Susan (Rosen) E.; m. Claudia Beth Gruss, June 12, 1977; 1 child, Joshua Adam. BSc in Chemistry, Brown U., 1973; MD, Yale U., 1978. Diplomate Nat. Bd. Med. Examiners; cert. Am. Bd. Internal Medicine. Intern and resident in internal medicine R.I. Hosp., Providence, 1979-81; teaching fellow in medicine Brown U., 1979-81; emergency physician Meml. Hosp., Pawtucket, R.I., 1981-82; pvt. practice Georgetown (Conn.) Med. Assocs. (now Arbor Med. Group LLC), 1982—; med. dir. Honey Hill Care Ctr., Norwalk, Conn., 1996—; med. staff Meadow Ridge Health Ctr., Redding, Conn., 2002—. Sr. attending physician Norwalk (Conn.) Hosp.; med. dir. Fairfield Manor Health Care Ctr., Norwalk, 1985-2000; med. staff Wilton Meadows Health Care Ctr., Wilton, Conn., 1988—. Mem. Region 9 Bd. Edn., Easton-Redding, Conn., 1993-2001. Mem. Am. Geriatrics Soc., Am. Med. Dirs. Assn., Conn. State Med. Soc. (com. on geriatrics), Fairfield County Med. Assn., Georgetown C. of C. (pres. 1991-94), Sigma Xi. Republican. Office: Arbor med Group LLC PO Box 270 73 Redding Rd Georgetown CT 06829

EINSTEIN, STEPHEN JAN, rabbi; b. LA, Nov. 15, 1945; s. Syd C. and Selma (Rothenberg) E.; m. Robin Susan Kessler, Sept. 9, 1967; children: Rebecca Yael, Jennifer Melissa, Heath Isaac, Zachary Shane. AB, UCLA, 1967; BHL, Hebrew Union Coll., L.A., 1968, DHL, 1995, DD (hon.), 1996; MAHL, Hebrew Union Coll., Cin., 1971. Ordained rabbi. Rabbi Temple Beth Am, Parsippany, N.J., 1971-74; rabbi Temple Beth David, Westminster, Calif., 1974-76, Congregation B'nai Tzedek, Fountain Valley, Calif., 1976—. Co-author: Every Person's Guide to Judaism, 1989; co-editor: Introduction to Judaism, 1983. Pres., trustee Fountain Valley (Calif.) Sch. Bd., 1984—90; chmn. pers. commn. Fountain Valley Sch. Dist., 1991—; pres. Retinoblatoma Internat., 2000—01; chaplain Fountain Valley Police Dept.; pres. Greater Huntington Beach Inter-Faith Coun., 2001—02; active Anti Defamation League, Am. Jewish Com.; co-chmn. Commn. on Outreach and Synagogue Cmty., 1999—; regional bd. dirs. Nat. Conf. Cmty. and Justice, 2001—. Honored for Maj. Contributions to Jewish Learning, Orange County (Calif.) Bur. Jewish Edn., 1986; recipient Micah Award for Interfaith Activities, Am. Jewish Com., 1988. Mem.: Inst. for Character Edn. (exec. adv.bd.), Clergy for Choice, Orange County Bur. Jewish Edn. (v.p. 1982—84, 1992—94, pres. 1994—97), Jewish Educators Assn. Orange County (pres. 1979—81), Orange County Bd. Rabbis (pres. 1976—79, 1997—98), Pacific Assn. Reform Rabbis (exec. bd. 1987—91, 1998—2002, pres. 2002—03), Ctrl. Conf. Am. Rabbis (exec. bd. 1989—91, ethics com. 1993—98), Alzheimers Assn. (religious adv. com.), Am. Cancer Soc. (v.p. West Orange County dist. 1994—98), Phi Beta Kappa. Democrat. Office: Congregation Bnai Tzedek 9669 Talbert Ave Fountain Valley CA 92708 E-mail: rebgiraffe@aol.com.

EINSTEIN, STEVEN HENRY, investment banker, lawyer, accountant; b. N.Y.C., Aug. 14, 1954; s. Ralph Gunther and Beatrice (Katz) E.; children: Theodore Aaron, Peter Raymond, Hannah Louise. BS, Lehigh U., 1976; JD, Seton Hall U., 1979; LLM in Taxation, NYU, 1985. Lic. CPA, N.Y., N.J.; Bar: N.J. 1979, N.Y. 1985, U.S. Dist. Ct. N.J. 1979, U.S. Tax Ct. 1982, U.S. Ct. Appeals (3d cir.) 1983, U.S. Supreme Ct. 1985. Judicial law clk. to presiding justice Superior Ct., Hackensack, NJ, 1979—80; assoc. Wacks, Hirsch, Ramsey & Berman Esqs., Morristown, NJ, 1980—81; sr. tax mgr. Touche Ross & Co., Newark, 1981—86; v.p., investment banking, mergers & acquisitions dept. PaineWebber Capital Mkts., N.Y.C., 1986—88; v.p., merchant banking/pvt. equity Kluge, Subotnick, Perkowski & Co., N.Y.C., 1988—90; mng. dir. Price WaterhouseCoopers Corp. Fin. Group, N.Y.C., 1991—98; ptnr. & mng. dir. PricewaterhouseCoopers Securities LLP, N.Y.C., 1998—99, ptnr., chmn.'s office, global leader, corp. devel., 1999—. Mem. editl. bd. Corp. Taxation Mag.; contbr. articles to profl. jours. Mem. ABA, AICPAs, N.J. State Bar Assn., N.Y. State Bar Assn., Essex County Bar Assn. (taxation divsn.), N.J. Soc. CPAs, Beta Gamma Sigma, Phi Eta Sigma. Jewish. Home: 174 Carter St New Canaan CT 06840-5007 Office: PricewaterhouseCoopers LLP 1177 Avenue of the Americas New York NY 10036-2714

EINZIG, STANLEY, pediatric cardiologist, researcher; b. Bklyn., July 25, 1942; s. Louis and Sally (Weiser) E.; m. Gloria Einzig (div.); children: Deborah, Dana, David. MD, UCLA, 1967; PhD, U. Minn., 1977. Diplomate Am. Bd. Pediatrics, sub.-bd. Pediatric Cardiology. Intern, then resident dept. pediatrics U. Minn., Mpls., 1967-70, from instr. to assoc. prof., 1977-90; prof. physiology and pediatrics, chief pediatric cardiology W.Va. U., Morgantown, 1990—2001; with children's cardiac ctr. Newark Beth Israel Md. Ctr., 2001—. Contbr.

numerous articles to profl. jours. Lt. comdr. USN, 1971-73. NIH fellow, 1974, 75. Fellow Am. Coll. Cardiology; mem. Am. Phys. Soc., Soc. for Pediatric Rsch., Alpha Omega Alpha. Achievements include discovery of blood flow and antioxidant effects of anisodamine. Office: Childrens Cardiac Ctr 201Lyons Ave at Osborne Terr Newark NJ 07112

EIRICH, FREDERICK ROLAND, chemist, educator; b. Vienna, May 23, 1905; came to U.S., 1947, naturalized, 1953; s. Otto George and Hermine (Perlhefter) E.; m. Maria Dorothea Dehne, Feb. 1, 1936; children-Ursula D., Richard S. Moeller, Susan H, PhD, U. Vienna, 1929, Dr. Phil. habil., 1938; MA, U. Cambridge, Eng., 1939. Research asso., lectr. U. Vienna, 1934- 38, U. Cambridge, 1939-47; mem. faculty Poly. Inst., Bklyn., 1948—, prof., 1952—; distinguished prof., 1969—; dean research, 1967-70. Vis. prof. U. Uppsala, 1950; Unilever prof. U. Bristol, 1965; vis. scientist Lab. Chem. Evolution, U. Md., 1985— ; cons. Govt. Com. Chems., Plastics and Rubber Industry. Author, editor numerous books and research papers. Recipient A. Humboldt Found. award, 1980; Bingham Medal, 1983, M. Huggins award, 1985, H.F. Mark medaille, 2000. Fellow N.Y. Acad. Sci. (chmn. chem. sect. 1952-53), Faraday Soc., Internat. Inst. Fracture Mechanics (hon.); mem. Am. Chem. Soc. (chmn. colloid div. 1960, Distinguished Service award 1975, Merit award Rubber Div. 1978), AAAS (chmn., councillor Gordon Confs. 1959-65), Soc. Rheology (pres. 1972-73), Am. Phys. Soc. (gov. bd. 1970-74), Sigma Xi (research award 1970) Home: Meadow Lks Apt 45-01 Hightstown NJ 08520-3354 Office: Poly U Bklyn Campus 6 Metrotech Ctr Brooklyn NY 11201-3840

EISCH, JOHN JOSEPH, chemist, educator, writer, consultant; b. Milw., Nov. 5, 1930; s. Frank Joseph and Gladys (Riordan) E.; m. Joan Terese Scheuerell, Sept. 5, 1953; children: Margaret (dec.), Karla, Paula, Joseph, Amelia. BS summa cum laude, Marquette U., 1952, PhD, 1956; P&G fellow, Iowa State U., 1956; DS honoris causa (hon.), Marquette U., 2002. Postdoctoral Union Carbide fellow Max Planck Inst. für Kohlenforschung, Mülheim, Germany, 1956-57; rsch. assoc. European Rsch. Assocs., Brussels, 1957; mem. faculty St. Louis U., 1957-59; faculty U. Mich., 1959-63, Cath. U. Am., Washington, 1963-72; chmn. dept. chemistry SUNY, Binghamton, 1972-78, prof., 1972—, disting. prof., 1983—. Sr. rsch. fellow Japan Soc. for Promotion of Sci., 1979, Alexander von Humboldt Found., Germany, 1993-96; cons. in field, 1957—; legal expert witness. Author: The Chemistry of Organometallic Compounds, 1967, (with R. B. King) Organometallic Syntheses, Vol. I, 1965, Vol. II, 1981, Vol. III, 1986, Vol. IV, 1988; contbr. over 335 articles to profl. publs.; patentee in field. Mem. Am. Chem. Soc., Am. Inst. Chemists, Sigma Xi, Phi Lambda Upsilon, Phi Kappa Phi. Republican. Roman Catholic. Achievements include research and publs. on the synthesis and properties of organometallic compounds (those with carbon-metal bonds) and heterocycles, with emphasis on the kinetics and stereochemistry of carbon-metal bond and hydrogen-metal bond additions to olefins, acetylenes; radical-anion, nonbenzenoid aromatic studies, photochemistry of organometallics; catalytic processes of carbocyclization, oligomerization and polymerization of carbon pi-bonded molecules and prebiotic organic synthesis. Home: 212 Sheedy Rd Vestal NY 13850-5905 Office: SUNY Binghamton Dept Chemistry Binghamton NY 13902-6000 Fax: 607-777-4865. E-mail: jjeisch@binghamton.edu.

EISDORFER, CARL, psychiatrist, health care executive; b. Bronx, N.Y., June 20, 1930; BA, NYU, 1951, MA, 1953, PhD, 1959; MD, Duke U., 1964; postgrad. in health systems mgmt., Harvard U., 1981. Lectr. in psychology Duke U. Med. Ctr., Durham, N.C., 1959-72, intern in medicine, 1964-65, psychiat. trainee, 1964-67, dir. tng., research coordinator Ctr. for Study Aging and Human Devel., 1965-70, prof psychiatry and med. psychology, 1968-72, dir. med. studies behavioral scis. program, 1970-72, head div. med. psychology dept. psychiatry, 1970-72, dir. Ctr. for Study Aging and Human Devel., 1970-72; founding dir. Inst. on Aging, U. Wash., Seattle, 1977-79, prof., chmn. dept. psychiatry and behavioral scis. Sch. of Medicine, adj. prof. psychology, 1972-81; sr. scholar in residence Inst. Medicine, Nat. Acad. Scis., Washington, 1979-80; prof. psychiatry and neurosci. Albert Einstein Coll. Medicine, N.Y.C., 1981-85; chief exec. officer Montefiore Med. Ctr., N.Y.C., 1981-85; prof., chmn. dept. psychiatry U. Miami, Fla., 1986—; chief div. mental health Jackson Meml. Med. Ctr., 1986—. Coordinator Community Mental Health Services, Halifax County N.C., 1969-70; vis. prof. architeture U. Calif.-Berkeley, 1969-70; H.T. Dozer vis. prof. geriatrics and psychiatry Ben Gurion U., Negev, Israel, 1980; cons. NIH, Bethesda, Md., Robert Wood Johnson Found., numerous others. Editor in chief Ann. Rev. Gerontology and Geriatrics, 1978; mem. editl. bd. Alzheimers Disease and Related Disorders-Internat. Jour., Aging and Human Devel., Western Jour. Medicine, Neurobiology of Aging: Exptl. and Clin. Rsch.; contbr. articles to profl. jours and books. Served with U.S. Army, 1954-56 Recipient Kesten award Ethel Percy Andrus Gerontology Ctr., U. So. Calif., 1976, Potamkin prize, 1982, Disting. Alumnus award Duke U. Sch. of Medicine, 1985, Allid Signal award, 1991. Fellow Soc. Behavioral Medicine, N.Y. Acad. Medicine, Am. Psychol. Assn. (chmn. div. adult devel. and aging 1970-71, task force on aging 1971-73, award for disting. contbns. 1981, award for contbns. on aging research 1985), Gerontol. Soc. Am. (pres. 1971-72, Robert W. Kleemeier award 1969, Donald P. Kent award, 2002, Joseph Freeman award div. clin. medicine 1979), Am. Geriatrics Soc. (Edward B. Allen award 1974, Edward Henderson Meml. award 1988), Am. Psychiat. Assn. (Jack Weinberg Meml. award 1984), Am. Coll. Psychiatrists, Am. Coll. Physicians (Menninger award 1990), AAAS; mem. Am. Soc. Aging (pres. 1980-82), Am. Fed. Aging Res. (pres. 1986-88), Sigma Xi, Alpha Omega Alpha, Phi Beta Kappa. Office: U Miami Sch Medicine Dept Psychiatry D-28 PO Box 16960 Miami FL 33101-6960 E-mail: ceisdorf@med.miami.edu.

EISELE, ROBERT HENRY, screenwriter, producer, playwright, educator; b. Altadena, Calif., June 9, 1948; s. Lawrence C. and Helen (Klimek) E.; m. Diana G. Ryterband, June 21, 1975; children: Nicholas A., Marissa C. BA cum laude, UCLA, 1971, MFA, 1974. Screenwriter, playwright, Los Angeles, 1975-86; assoc. prof. theater arts Rio Hondo Coll., Whittier, Calif., 1976-86; story editor Crime Story New World TV, Los Angeles, 1986-87; co-producer The Equalizer Universal TV, Los Angeles, 1987-88, supervising producer The Equalizer, 1988-89; writer, producer Warner Bros. TV, 1989-91, Universal Studios, 1991-94, Paramount Studios, 1994-97. Author: (plays) Animals Are Passing From Our Lives, 1974 (Donald Davis Dramatic Writing award 1974), West Coast Plays, vol. 3, 1979, A Dark Night of the Soul, 1979, The Murder of Einstein, 1980, (episodes for TV series) (Cagney and Lacey) Ordinary Hero, 1985 (Humanitas prize Human Family Inst. 1986, Imagen award Hispanic Task Force, NCCJ 1986), Schedule One, 1986, (Crime Story) Torello on Trial, 1987, The Pinnacle, 1987, Ground Zero, 1987, (The Equalizer) Suspicion of Innocence, Shadow Play, The Rehearsal, No Place Like Home, 1987-88, Day of the Covenant, The Visitation, Starfire, Prisoners of Conscience, 1988-89, (Resurrection Blvd.) El Baile, 2000, La Gran Pelea, 2001, Nino de Polvo, 2002 (Writers Guild award nominee 2002), (pilots) Cain, 1991, Darkman, 1992, (cable TV features) Last Light, 1993 (Showtime, Writers Guild award nominee 1993), Vanishing Son: The Klansman, 1994, Vanishing Son, Dragon Head, 1994, Vanishing Son: Ancestors, 1994, Lily in Winter, 1995 (Writers Guild award nominee 1995, PEN Literary award nominee 1996); also poems and short stories; exec. producer The Osiris Chronicles, 1996, Resurrection Blvd., 2000-01. Recipient Samuel Goldwyn Writing award, 1973; Oscar Hammerstein Playwriting fellow, 1974, Am. Conservatory Theatre fellow, 1975-76, Alma award, 2001. Mem. Writers Guild Am. West, Dramatists Guild, Screen Actors Guild, Actors Equity Assn. Democrat. Avocations: martial arts, skiing, fishing, back-packing. Office: care Bruce Vinokour Creative Artists Agy 9830 Wilshire Blvd Beverly Hills CA 90212-1804

EISELT, MICHAEL HERBERT, optics scientist; b. Oldenburg, Germany, Jan. 25, 1963; s. Theodor and Ursula (Eiselt) Wuerdemann; m. Renate Viktoria Marianne Helm, Aug. 21, 1992; children: Susanna Marie Helm Eiselt, Elisabeth Viktoria Helm Eiselt. Diploma in elec. engring., U. Hannover, Germany, 1989; DEng, Tech. U. Berlin, 1994. Rsch. staff Heinrich-Hertz Inst., Berlin, 1989-97; prin. tech. staff mem. AT&T Labs Rsch., Red Bank, N.J., 1997-2000; prin. architect Celion Networks, Tinton Falls, N.J., 2000—. Vis. rschr. AT&T Bell Labs Rsch., 1995-96. Patentee in field. With German Army, 1982-83. Mem.: IEEE (sr.). Office: Celion Networks 1 Sheila Dr Ste 2 Tinton Falls NJ 07724 Fax: 732-747-9986. E-mail: eiselt@celion.com.

EISEN, ARRI, biologist, educator; b. Lafayette, Ind., Mar. 6, 1963; s. Eugene J. and Jacqueline Serxner Eisen; m. Lisa Lee Hoveland, Aug. 11, 1990; children: Gabriel Conlan, Micah Charles. BS, U. N.C., Chapel Hill, 1985; PhD, U. Wash., Seattle, 1990. Lectr. Emory U., Atlanta, sr. lectr., 1996—. Dir. Emory Coll. Program in Sci. & Soc., Atlanta, Sci., Ethics, and Soc. Initiative; Emory Ctr. for Ethics, Atlanta, 1999—; tchg. coord. Fellowships in Rsch. and Sci. Tchg., Atlanta, 1999—. Author: (textbook) The Living Staircase; contbr. articles to profl. jours. including:. Grantee Rsch. Experience for Undergrads., NSF, 1999-2002, Healing, Health, and Religion, Ctr. for Theology and the Natural Sciences, 2002-2003, An Undergrad. Lab in Devel. Biology, NSF, 1994. Democrat. Jewish. Avocations: reading, long-distance running, creative writing. Office: Dept of Biology Emory University Atlanta GA 30322 E-mail: aeisen@emory.edu.

EISEN, EDWIN ROY, lawyer; b. Bklyn., May 25, 1932; s. Edward and Cecile (Kurland) E.; m. Elaine Sollar, Feb. 15, 1963; 1 child, Marc. A.B., Colby Coll., 1954; LL.B., Cornell U., 1957. Bar: N.Y. 1958, U.S. Dist. Ct. (ea. and so. dists.) N.Y. 1963, U.S. Ct. Appeals (2d cir.) 1963. Ptnr., Tenzer, Greenblatt, Fallen & Kaplan, N.Y.C., 1973-74, Eisen & Fishman, N.Y.C., 1979-81; ptnr. Eisen & Schulman, P.C., 1974-78, 81— . Clubs: Brae Burn Country (exec. com.) (Purchase, N.Y.); City Athletic (bd. dirs) (N.Y.C.). Office: Eisen & Schulman PC 575 5th Ave New York NY 10017-2422

EISEN, ERIC ANSHEL, lawyer; b. N.Y.C., Apr. 9, 1950; s. Morton and Victoria (Goldstein) E.; m. Claire L. Shapiro, Jan. 6, 1979; children: Rebecca, Jennifer, Melissa. AB, U. Mich., 1971, JD magna cum laude, 1975. Bar: Alaska 1976, D.C. 1977, Md. 1988. Law clk. to presiding justice Alaska Supreme Ct., Fairbanks, 1975-76; assoc. Covington & Burling, Washington, 1976-81, Birch, Horton, Bittner, Washington, 1981-85, ptnr., 1985-93, Eisen Law Offices, Bethesda, Md., 1993—. Prin. speaker various seminars and colloquia on energy and bus. matters. Contbr. articles to legal publs. Pres. Wildwood Hills Citizens Assn., Bethesda, Md., 1987—; sec. N. Bethesda Cong. Citizens Assns., 1989-90. Mem. ATLA, Energy Bar Assn. (antitrust com.), D.C. Bar Assn., Montgomery County Bar Assn. (chmn. bus. sect., mem. intellectual property and litig. sects.), Toastmasters, Order of Coif. Avocation: woodworking. Office: Eisen Law Offices 10028 Woodhill Rd Bethesda MD 20817-1218 also: 1101 30th St NW Ste 500 Washington DC 20007-3708

EISEN, GLENN PHILIP, management consultant, teacher; b. Chgo., Feb. 8, 1940; s. Sol Eisen and Lorraine (Winsberg) Lukinsky; m. Devera Arne Chiz, May 7, 1961 (div. 1974); children: Julia, Steven; m. Barbara Baxter McNear, June 7, 1987. BS in Indsl. Mgmt., Ill. Inst. Tech., 1972. Cert. mgmt. cons.; registered EMT, Conn., Calif. Prodn. supr. Intercraft Industries, Chgo., 1961-64; sr. buyer Simoniz Co., Chgo., 1964-65; purchasing/packaging mgr. Paper Mate div. Gillette, La Grange Park, Ill., 1965-69; assoc. The Packaging House Inc., Chgo., 1969-73; cons. Israel Inst. of Packaging, Tel Aviv, 1973-74; prin. The Emerson Cons., N.Y.C., 1975-80, Arthur Andersen & Co., Chgo., 1980-87; chief exec. officer The Eisen Group, Wilton, Conn., 1987-96; prin. The Omega Cons., LLC, 1996-2000. Internat. comml. arbitrator Am. Arbitration Assn., N.Y.C., 1985—2003; bd. fin. Wilton, Conn., 2001-02; lectr., mgr. mfg. industry edn. Arthur Andersen Ctr. for Profl. Edn., 1980-83; lectr., seminar leader Am. Mgmt. Assn., 1967-99; clin. instr. UCLA Ctr. Prehospital Care, 2003—; counselor Svc. Corps. Ret. Execs., 2003—. Author: Purchasing Negotiations, 1983, Group Buying in Health Care, 1985, Supply Market Management, 1989, Maximizing Your Value When Using Management Consultants, 1992, Ethical Practices and Conflicts of Interest Benchmark Study, 1994, Procurement Best Practices, 1997, Maintenance Planning and Management Best Practices, 1998; mem. editl. bd.: In Bound Logistics Mag., 1990. Active Westport Emergency Med. Svc. 2000-02; disaster med. assistance team Los Angeles County, 2002—; CPR and 1st aid instr. ARC, 1999—, Am. Heart Assn.; mem. western nat. med. response team U.S. Dept. Homeland Security, 2003—. With U.S. Army, 1958-61. Mem. Kiwanis Internat. Jewish. Home and Office: 1860 Homewood Dr Altadena CA 91001

EISEN, HERMAN NATHANIEL, immunology researcher, medical educator; b. Bklyn., Oct. 15, 1918; m. Natalie Aronson, 1948; 5 children. AB, NYU, 1939, MD, 1943. Asst. in pathology Coll. Physicians and Surgeons, Columbia U., N.Y.C., 1944—46; NIH fellow Coll. Medicine, NYU, 1947—48, fellow in chemistry, 1948—49, asst. prof. indsl. medicine, 1949—53, assoc. prof., 1953—55; prof. medicine Sch. Medicine, Washington U., St. Louis, 1955—61; dermatologist-in-chief Barnes Hosp., St. Louis, 1955—61; prof. microbiology, head dept. Sch. Medicine Washington U., St. Louis, 1961—73; prof. MIT, Cambridge, 1973—82, Whitehead Inst. prof. immunology, 1982—89; prof. emeritus, 1989—. Mem. adv. bd. Mass. Gen Hosp., Yale Med. Sch., Harvard Sch. Pub. Health, Children's Hosp., Boston, Merck, Sharpe, Dohme Rsch. Labs., Roche Inst. for Molecular Biology, Howard Hughes Med. Inst. (Behring-Heidelberger award 1993); chmn. Nat. Inst. Health Study, 1962—66; bd. of sci. counselors Nat. Inst. of Arthritis and Metabolic Dis., 1971—75; chmn. World Health Orgn. Sci. Group on Regulation of Immune Responses, 1969; lectr. Harvey Soc., N.Y., 1964, Phillips lectr. Haverford Coll., 1971; Burroughs & Wellcome vis. lectr. Med. Coll. So. Carolina, 1979; Culpepper Found. lectr. State Univ. of N.Y., Stonybrook, 1981; Lowry lectr. Washington Univ., St. Louis, 1989. Recipient Outstanding Investigator award, Nat. Cancer Inst., NIH, 1986—93, Dupont award, Clin. Ligand Soc., 1987, Med. Sci. Achievement award, NYU, 1978, others. Mem.: Am. Assn. Immunologists (pres. 1968), Am. Acad. Arts and Scis., Inst. Medicine, Am. Assn. Physicians, Nat. Acad. Sci. (editl. bd. Proceedings of the NAS). Office: MIT Ctr Cancer Rsch E17-128 77 Massachusetts Ave Cambridge MA 02139-4307 E-mail: hneisen@mit.edu.*

EISEN, HOWARD JOEL, physician, researcher; b. Forest Hills, N.Y., May 25, 1956; s. Ezra Michael and Gertrude Margaret (Schmidt) Eisen; m. Judith Ellen Wolf, June 26, 1983; children: Johnathan Ezra, Miriam Sarah. BA in Biology, Cornell U., 1977; MD, U. Pa., 1981. Diplomate Am. Bd. Med. Examiners, Am. Bd Internal Medicine, Am. Bd. Cardiovascular Diseases. Med. intern Hosp. U. Pa., Phila., 1981—82, resident in medicine, 1982—84; fellow in cardiology Washington U. Sch. Medicine-Barnes Hosp., St. Louis, 1984—87; asst. prof. medicine U. Pa., Phila., 1990—93; assoc. prof. medicine and physiology Temple U., Phila., 1993—97, prof. medicine and physiology, 1997—, dir. heart failure care unit, 1993—99, med. dir. cardiac transplant program, 1993—99, assoc. dir. Gen. Clin. Rsch. Ctr., 1995—, med. dir. Cardiomyopathy and Transplant Ctr., 1999—, med. dir. advanced heart failure and transplant program, 1999—. Mem. cryptosporidiosis adv. com. Dept. Pub. Health, Phila., 1995—. Fellow: Am. Heart Assn. (clin. coun. 1995—, mem. rsch. com. 1995—, chmn. peer-review com. 1996—, established investigatorship award 1996—), Am. Coll. Cardiology, ACP; mem.: Internat. Soc. Heart and Lung Transportation, Am. Fedn. Clin. Rsch (mem. nat. coun. 1992—95, H. Christian award 1993), Phi Beta Kappa, Alpha Omega Alpha. Avocations: reading, rowing, classical music, running, e-mail. Home: 507 Shortridge Dr Wynnewood PA 19096-1609 Office: Temple U Sch Medicine 3401 N Broad St # 9pp Philadelphia PA 19140-5103 E-mail: eisenh@tuhs.temple.edu

EISEN, RICH, reporter; b. N.Y.C., June 24, 1969; BA in Comms., U. Mich., 1990; MS in Broadcast Journalism, Northwestern U., 1994. Staff writer S.I. Advance, 1990-93; stringer pub. h.s. football and basketball Chgo. Tribune, 1993-94; prodn. asst. CBS Evening News with Dan Rather and Connie Chung, 1994; corr. Medill News Svc., Washington, 1994; sports anchor/reporter Sta. KRCR-TV, Redding, Calif., 1994-96; anchor/reporter SportsCenter ESPN, 1996—. Office: c/o ESPN ESPN Plz 935 Middle St Bristol CT 06010-1001

EISEN, STEVEN JEFFREY, lawyer; b. Nashville, May 14, 1958; s. Harvey and Ann Eisen; m. Gay Lisa Levine, June 26, 1988. BA in Econs., Northwestern U., 1979; MBA, Vanderbilt U., Nashville, 1983; JD, Vanderbilt U., 1983. Bar: Tenn 1983, U.S. Dist. Ct. (mid. dist.) Tenn., U.S. Ct. Appeals (6th cir.). Assoc. Bone, Langford & Armistead, Nashville, 1983-87; ptnr. Baker, Donelson, Bearman & Caldwell, Nashville, 1988—. European Inst. scholar, 1980, Owen scholar, 1979. Mem. ABA, Tenn. Bar Assn., Nashville Bar Assn. Avocations: tennis, boating. Office: Baker Donelson Bearman & Caldwell 211 Commerce St Ste 1000 Nashville TN 37201

EISENBERG, ADI, chemist; b. Breslau, Germany, Feb. 18, 1935; emigrated to U.S., 1951; s. Oscar and Helene E.; m. Sandra M. Kloner, June 9, 1957 (div. 1985); 1 son, Elliot; m. Katia Chantal Wegliszewski, Sept. 1, 2002; 3 children by previous marriage. BSc, Worcester Poly. Inst., 1957; MA, Princeton U., 1959, PhD, 1960. Postdoctoral fellow U. Basel, Switzerland, 1961-62; asst. prof. chemistry UCLA, 1962-67; assoc. prof. chemistry McGill U., Montreal, Que., Can., 1967-74, prof., 1975—; dir. Polymer McGill, 1991-99, Otto Maass Prof. Chemistry, 1993—. Cons. in field. Author 7 books in field; contbr. articles to profl. jours. NATO fellow, 1961-62, Killam Research fellow, 1987-88; recipient E.W.R. Steacie award, 1998. Fellow Am. Phys. Soc. (chmn. div. high polymer physics 1975-76), Chem. Inst. Can. (Macromolecular Sci. and Engring.-Dunlop award 1988, E.W.R. Steacie award 1998); mem. Am. Chem. Soc. Achievements include patents in field. Office: McGill University 801 Sherbrooke St W Montreal QC Canada H3A 2K6

EISENBERG, ALAN, professional society administrator; b. N.Y.C., Apr. 15, 1935; s. Arthur and Mollie (Novak) E.; m. Claire Copley, May 23, 1982; children: Mollie Copley, Emma Copley. AB, U. Mich., 1956; LLB, NYU, 1959. Bar: N.Y., Va., D.C. Assoc. Booth. Lipton & Lipton, N.Y.C., 1960, Hirson & Bertini, N.Y.C., 1960-64; atty. NLRB, Washington and Chgo., 1964-68; assoc. Seligman & Seligman, N.Y.C., 1968-72; ptnr. Eisenberg & Paul, Arlington, Va., 1972-81; exec. dir. Actors' Equity Assn., N.Y.C., 1981—. Vis. prof. theatre adminstrn. Yale U. Sch. Drama, New Haven, 1982—; adj. faculty Sch. of Arts Columbia U., 1995-98. Gen. v.p. dept. for profl. employees AFL-CIO; dir. Actors's Equity Found., Non Traditional Casting Project, Inc., Career Transition for Dancers, Times Square Bus. Improvement Dist.; trustee Equity League Pension and Health Funds, Actors' Fund of Am.; trustee, v.p. Broadway Cares, Equity Fights AIDS. Office: Actors' Equity Assn 165 W 46th St Fl 15 New York NY 10036-2500 E-mail: aeisenberg@actorsequity.org.

EISENBERG, ALBERT CHARLES, senior government official; b. Jersey City, Oct. 15, 1946; s. Albert Simon and Henrietta (Kirschner) E.; m. Sharon Eileen Davis, Jan. 10, 1976; children: Matthew Davis, Alexander Davis. BA, U. Richmond, Va., 1968; MA, Hampton (Va.) U., 1971. Tchr. intern Nat. Tchr. Corps, Hampton, 1969-71; tchr. Chesapeake (Va.) City Schs., 1970-74; campaign dir. Robert Richards for Congress, Norfolk, Va., 1974; legis. asst. Office of U.S. Senator Harrison A. Williams, Jr., Washington, 1975-79; staff dir. U.S. Senate Subcom. on Housing and Urban Affairs, Washington, 1979-82; dir. fed. legis. affairs AIA, Washington, 1982-96; dep. dir., cons. Nat. Pks. and Conservation Assn., Washington, 1996-98; dep. asst. sec. for transp. policy U.S. Dept. of Transp., Washington, 1999-2001, chmn. Global Climate Change Ctr., 1999-2001, Sec.'s designee adv. coun. on historic preservation and White House cmty. empowerment bd., 1999—2001; sr. policy advisor Va. Senate Dem. Caucus, Richmond, 2001; pub. policy cons., 2001; adminstrv. asst. to U.S. Rep. John J. LaFalce, 2002; v.p. for govt. rels. Greater Washington Bd. Trade, 2002—. Chmn. Miss. Delta Region Initiative Task Force, 1999-2001; chmn. 9-11 Meml. Task Force, Arlington County, 2002; mem. Va. Transp. Safety Bd., 2003 –. Mem. Arlington (Va.) County Bd., 1984 99, chmn., 1987, 90, 95, 99, vice chmn., 1986, 89, 94, 98; mem. Lyon Pk. and Ashton Heights Civic Assns., 1983—; co-chmn. Arlington County Affordable Housing Task Force, 1999; mem., chmn. No. Va. Transp. Commn., Arlington, 1998; mem. Washington Met. Govts. Transp. Planning Bd., 1992-99, chmn. pub. safety policy com., 1984-86, chmn. land use and met. devel. policy coms., 1992-93; mem. No. Va. Transp. Coordinating Coun., Fairfax, 1992-99, No. Va. Planning Dist. Commn., 1984-99, 2001—, chmn., 1995-97; commr. Va. Housing Devel. authority, Richmond, 1991-96, Arlington Tenant-Landlord Commn., 1977-79; mem. Arlington County Cmty. Devel. Citizens Adv. Commn., 1977-79; chmn. Arlington United Way Social Planning Com., 1981-83; mem. Arlington County Bicentennial Commn., 2000; co-founder, convenor No. Va. Housing Coalition, Fairfax, 1986-99; co-founder, vice chmn. Washington Area Housing Partnership, 1991-95; various offices Arlington County Dem. Com., 1975-99, Va. Young Dems.; mem., sec. 10th Dist. Dem. Com., Arlington, 1981-84; mem. Va. State Dem. Ctrl. Com., Richmond, 1981-84; del. Va. State Dem. Conv., 1972, 76, 79, 84, 85, 89, 92, 93, Dem. Nat. Conv., N.Y.C., 1992; sec. Norfolk (Va.) Dem. Com., 1972-73; candidate Va. HO. of Dels., 2003. Named Citizen of Yr., Arlington-Fairfax Elks, 1990, Citizen Ptnr. of Yr., Arlington Housing Corp., 1990; named to Housing Hall of Fame, Arlington Housing Corp., Inc., 2001; recipient Bronze Good Citizenship medal, Nat. Soc. SAR, 1986, Elizabeth and David Scull Pub. Svc. award, Washington Met. Coun. Govts., 1992, Recognition of Leadership award, Arlington Heritage Alliance, 1995, Human Rights award, Arlington County Human Rights Commn., 2002. Mem.: NAACP, Arlington C. of C., Arlington Hist. Soc. (v.p. 2002—). Jewish. Avocations: civil war research and memorabilia, political activities. E-mail: alsharon@erols.com.

EISENBERG, ANDREW LEWIS, lawyer; b. Nov. 28, 1949; s. Eugene Robert and Shirley (Helman) Eisenberg; children: Benjamin Samuel, Lauren Beth. AB, Brown U., 1971; JD, Columbia U., 1974. Bar: Mass. 1974, U.S. Dist. Ct. Mass. 1975, U.S. Ct. Appeals (1st cir.) 1979, U.S. Supreme Ct. 1980. Assoc. Herrick & Smith, Boston, 1974—81, ptnr., 1982—84, Goldstein & Manello, Boston, 1984—89, Palmer & Dodge, Boston, 1989—2002, Seyfarth Shaw, Boston, 2002—. Pres. SNCR Corp. Dir., mem. exec. bd. Combined Jewish Philanthropies, Boston, 1983—94, vice chmn., 1987—89; trustee, dir. Hebrew Coll., Brookline, Mass., 1983—2001, vice chmn., 1987—89; pres. Jewish Cmty. Ctr. Greater Boston, 1991—94; dir. Jewish Cmty. Ctrs. Assn. of N.Am., 1987—; bd. dir. Jewish Cmty. Rels. Coun., Boston, 1985—87, Jewish Cmty. Ctr., Newton, Mass., 1985—, v.p., 1986—87, pres., 1987—89; dir. Jewish Vocat. Svc., Boston, 1983—87. Recipient Young Leadership award, Combined Jewish Philanthropies, 1986. Home: 75 Clarendon St Apt 409 Boston MA 02116-6051 Office: Seyfarth Shaw World Trade Ctr E Boston MA 02210

EISENBERG, BURTON L. surgeon; b. Hartford, Conn., Oct. 28, 1948; s. Samuel and Ruth (Herman) E.; m. Vickie Eisenberg; children: Jamie, Corey. BA, U. Conn., 1970; MD, U. Tenn., 1974. Intern USAF Med. Ctr., San Antonio, 1974-75, resident in gen. surgery, 1975-79; resident in surg. oncology M.D. Anderson Hosp., Houston, 1978; fellow in surg. oncology Meml. Sloan-Kettering Cancer Ctr., N.Y.C., 1979-81; clin. asst. prof. surgery U. Tex. Health Sci. Ctr., San Antonio, 1981-87; clin. assoc. prof. U. Health Scis., Bethesda, Md., 1987—. Chief surg. oncology USAF Med. Ctr., 1981-87; cons. to Surgeon Gen. in Surg. Oncology, 1981-87; acting chmn. dept. surgery Fox Chase Cancer Ctr., 1990-91, staff surgeon, 1987—, fellowship dir., 1991—, chmn. dept. surg. oncology, 1991—; assoc. prof. surgery Temple U. Sch. Medicine, Phila., 1987-92, chief sect. surg. oncology, 1991—, prof., 1992—. Contbr. articles to profl. jours.; reviewer Jour. Clin. Oncology, Jour. Cancer Rsch., Cancer Jour., Cancer; mem. editl. bd. numerous profl. jours. Fellow ACS; mem. Assn. for Acad. Surgery, Soc. Air Force Clin. Surgeons, Phila. Acad. Surgery, Soc. Surg. Oncology, Am. Soc. Clin. Oncology, Pa. Oncologic Soc., Soc. Head & Neck Surgery, Soc. for Surgery of Alimentary Tract, Am. Assn. for Cancer Rsch., Am. Radium Soc., Alpha Omega Alpha. Office: Fox Chase Cancer Ctr 7701 Burholme Ave Ste 2 Philadelphia PA 19111-2497

EISENBERG, CAROLA, psychiatry educator; b. Buenos Aires, Sept. 15, 1917; came to U.S., 1945; d. Bernardo and Teodora (Kahan) Blitzman; m. Manfred Guttmacher, Oct. 11, 1946 (dec. 1966); m. Leon Eisenberg, Aug. 31, 1967; children: Laurence, Alan. M of Social Work, Liceo de Senoritas; MD, U. Buenos Aires, 1945. Resident in psychiatry U. Md., 1946-48; fellow in child psychiatry Johns Hopkins Hosp., 1948-50, asst. prof. psychiatry and pediatrics, 1960-67; psychiatrist MIT, Boston, 1967-72, dean of students, 1972-78; dean student affairs Harvard Med. Sch., Boston, 1978-90, dir. internat. programs for students, 1990-92, lectr. psychiatry, 1970-92, lectr. social medicine, 1992—. Co-chmn. women in biomed. careers workshop Office on Women's Health, NIH, 1992, mem. adv. com. on rsch. and women's health, 1995-98; mem. com. on human rights ACP; mem. com. on women in sci. and engring. NAS, 1992-95. V.p. Physicians for Human Rights, Boston, 1987—; pres. Examiners Club, Boston, 1993-2003. Recipient Morani Renaissance Woman award, Found. for History of Women in Medicine, 2003. Fellow Am. Psychiat. Assn. (Disting. life fellow 2003, mem. Coun. Internat. Affairs, com. on human rights), Am. Orthopsychiat. Assn. (life); mem. AAUP. Avocations: traveling, music, reading. Home and Office: 9 Clement Cir Cambridge MA 02138-2205

EISENBERG, DANIEL, filmmaker; Instr. in film Collective For Living Cinema, NY, 1978, Boston Film/Video Found., 1979; asst. prof. film Mass. Coll. Art, Boston, 1979—82, 1993—94, instr. video, 1987; spl. instr. in film and photography U. R.I., Kingston, 1984; vis. artist in film San Francisco Art Inst., 1993; asst. prof. film, chair dept. filmmaking Sch. Art Inst. Chgo., 1994—97, assoc. prof. film, chair dept. filmmaking, 1998—. Editor various works WGBH, Boston, 1981—90; presenter in field. One-man shows include Collective for Living Cinema, N.Y.C., 1981, 1989, MIT, Cambridge, 1984, Sch. Mus. Fine Arts, Boston, 1986, Boston Film/Video Found., 1987, Montserrat Sch. Art, Beverly, Mass., 1987, Brattle Theatre, Cambridge, 1988, Art Cinema, Binghamton, N.Y., 1988, Mass. Coll. Art, Boston, 1988, San Francisco Cin-

ematheque, San Francisco, 1988, Pacific Film Archive, Berkeley, 1988, Kino Arsenal, Berlin, 1988, 1991, Am. Mus. Moving Image, N.Y., 1988, Inst. Contemporary Arts, Boston, 1989, Mus. Modern Art, Cineprobe, N.Y., 1989, 1998, Harvard U., Grad. Sch. Design, 1990, Boston Film/Video Found., 1991, London Filmmakers Coop, 1991, Hochschule der Kunst, Berlin, 1991, Braunschweig, 1991, Musée du Cinema, Brussels, 1991, Kommunales Kino, Hannover, 1991, Kiel, 1991, De Unie, Rotterdam, 1992, 't Hoogt, Utrecht, 1992, Filmmuseum, Frankfurt, 1992, Filmmuseum, Munich, 1992, Musee Nat. d'Art Moderne, 1992, Calif. Coll. Arts and Crafts, Oakland, 1993, Davis Mus., 1994, U. Iowa, Iowa City, 1996, L.A. Film Forum, 1997, Pacific Film Archive, Berkeley, Calif., 1997, Rocky Mountain Film Ctr., Boulder, Colo., 1998, Boston U., 1998, Harvard Film Archive, Cambridge, 1998, others, exhibited in group shows at Viper, Lucerne, Switzerland, 1995, Sydney Internat. Film Festival, 1997, Vue Sur Les Docs Festival, Marseilles, 1998, Goethe Inst., Chgo., 1999, numerous others, Represented in permanent collections; filmmaker : Matrice, 1975; Film Studies, 1979, 1990; To A Brother in Asia, 1983; Persistence, 1997; others; dir.: The Conjuror, 1983;, editor numerous films. Named Berlin artist-in-residence, Deutscher Akademischer Austauschdienst, 1991, 1997; recipient Outstanding Film award, New Eng. Film Festival, 1981, CEBA awards for excellence, 1988, Hon. Mention, New Eng. Film Festival, 1988, Grand prize, Black Maria Film and Video Festival, 1988—89; fellow New Eng. Regional fellow, Nat. Endowment Arts, 1982, in film, Mass. Artists Found., 1982, artist fellow, The MacDowell Colony, 1990, fellow in film, Mass. Artists Found., 1991, John Simon Guggenheim Meml. Found. fellow, 1999—; grantee Mass. Prodns. grantee, Mass. Coun. on Arts, 1986—88, Media Arts grantee, Nat. Endowment Arts, 1989—92, Sch. Art Inst. Faculty Enrichment, 1995, 1997.

EISENBERG, DAVID SAMUEL, molecular biologist, educator; b. Chgo., Mar. 15, 1939; s. George and Ruth E.; m. Lucy Tuchman, Aug. 25, 1963; children: Jenny, Nell. AB, Harvard U., 1961; Phil.D., Oxford U., Eng., 1964. NSF postdoctoral fellow Princeton U., 1964-66; research fellow chemistry Calif. Inst. Tech., Pasadena, 1966-69; asst. prof. UCLA, 1968-71, assoc. prof., 1971-76, prof. chemistry, biochemistry, 1976—, assoc. dir. Molecular Biology Inst., 1981-85; dir. UCLA-DOE Ctr. for Genomics and Proteomics, 1993—; investigator Howard Hughes Med. Inst., 2001—. Author: (with W. Kauzmann) Structure and Properties of Water, 1969, (with D.M. Crothers) Physical Chemistry with Applications in the Life Sciences, 1979. Chmn. Citizens for the West L.A. Veloway, 1977—2001; bd. dirs. Westlake Sch., 1983—89, Harvard-Westlake Sch., 1990—91. Recipient USPHS Career Devel. awardee, 1972-77; Rhodes scholar, 1961-64; Guggenheim fellow, 1985, Stein & Moore award, 1996, Repligen award, 1998. Fellow Biophys. Soc.; mem. NAS, Am. Acad. Arts and Scis., Am. Soc. Biol. Chemists, Am. Crystallographic Assn., Biophys. Soc. (councillor 1977-80), The Protein Soc. (pres. 1987-89, councillor 1989-94). Office: UCLA-DOE Ctr for Genomics and Proteomics PO Box 951570 Los Angeles CA 90095-1570

EISENBERG, DOROTHY, federal judge; b. 1929; LLB, Bklyn. Law Sch., 1950. Bar: N.Y. 1951, U.S. Dist. Ct. (ea. and so. dists.) N.Y., U.S. Ct. Appeals (2nd cir.), U.S. Supreme Ct. Assoc. Otterbourg, Stiendler, Houston & Rosen, N.Y.C., 1950-51, Goldman, Horowitz & Cherno, Mineola, N.Y., 1970-80; pvt. practice Garden City, N.Y., 1981; ptnr. Shaw, Licitra, Eisenberg, Esernio & Schwartz, P.C., Garden City, 1981-89; bankruptcy judge ea. dist. U.S. Bankruptcy Ct., N.Y., 1989—. Mem. Com. on Character and Fitness, Appellate divsn, 2nd Dept., 1983-89; panel trustee U.S. Bankruptcy Ct. (so. dist.) N.Y., 1975-89, U.S. Bankruptcy Ct. (ea. dist.) N.Y., 1979-89. Fellow: Am. Bar Found.; mem.: ABA, Am. Bankruptcy Inst., N.Y. State Women's Bar Assn. (Nassau County chpt.), Nat. Assn. Women Judges. Office: LI Fed Courthouse 290 Federal Plz Central Islip NY 11722-4437

EISENBERG, GARY JULIUS, writer, musician, printmaker; s. Harold and Myra Eisenberg; m. Maria Elena Hernandez. Musician, writer, printmaker (musical recordings) Caravana Cubana (Grammy Nomination, 1999), writer (articles on wine and spirits) Many articles for regional and trade magazines, printmaker (printed and pub.of) many etchings, noted artists. Personal E-mail: eisegary@pacbell.net.

EISENBERG, HOWARD EDWARD, physician, psychotherapist, consultant, medical educator, writer; b. Montreal, Que, Can, Aug. 5, 1946; s. Harold and Elsie (Goldbloom) Eisenberg; m. Susan Doelman; children: Taryn Noelle, Jory Michael, Meredith Kate, Tessa Chloe. BS Psychology(hon.), McGill U., Montreal, 1967, MS in Psychology, 1971; internship, Sunnybrook Med. Ctr., U of Toronto, Toronto, Can., 1972—73; MD, McGill U., Montreal, 1972. Lic. LMCC Med. Coun. Can., cert. Province of Ont., 1973, Province of Brit. Columbia, 1980, State of Vt., 1988. Rsch. asst. psychology dept. McGill U., 1966-69, rsch. asst. gerontology unit Alan Meml. Inst. Psychiatry, 1968; intern Sunnybrook Med. Ctr. U. Toronto, Canada, 1972—73; lectr. Ctr. Continuing Edn. York U., 1973-78, supr. individual directed study Faculty Environ. Studies, 1975; clin. fellow Clarke Inst. Psychiatry U. Toronto, 1973, lectr. dept. interdisciplinary studies, 1975, instr. ind. studies program Innis Coll., 1975-78, lectr., 1976-81, spl. conf. coord., 1977-79, 88-89, lectr. Sch. Continuing Studies, 1977-89; pvt. practice Mind/Body Med., Toronto, 1973—91; lectr. Sheridan Coll., Oakville, 1974-76; lectr. Sch. Adult Edn. McMaster U., 1980—89; assoc. staff dept. family practice Drs. Hosp., Toronto, 1987—92; cons. staff dept. med.-psychiatry Copley Hosp., Morrisville, Vt., 1990—96; lectr. continuing edn. U. Vt., 1990—92, assoc. prof. Coll. Medicine, 1993—99; pvt. practice Mind/Body Med., Stowe Wellness Ctr., Vt., 1991—98; clin. assoc. prof. Dept. of Family Practice, Coll. of Med., Univ. of Vt., 1993—99; pvt. practice Mind/Body Med., Toronto, 1999—. Assoc. dir. edn. and growth opportunities program York U., 1975—76, dir. E.G.O. program, 1976—78; lectr. Sch. Adult Edn. McMaster U., 1980—89; instr. profl. and mgmt. devel. Humber Coll., 1982—85; pvt. practice psychotherapy and behavioral medicine, Toronto, 1973—91, Toronto, 1999—, Stowe, Vt., 1991—98; assoc. prof. dept. family practice Coll. Med. U. Vt., 1993—99; cons. staff dept. medicine Copley Hosp., Vt., 1990—96; pres. Synectia Cons., Inc., Toronto, 1980—84, Syntrek, Inc., Montpelier, Vt., 1989—2000, Toronto, 1974—; co-founder Healthcare Knowledge Mgmt. Consortium, 1998. Author: (book) Inner Spaces, 1977, The Tranquility Experience, 1987, Stress Mastery for the Real World, 2d edit., 1995, Fundamentals of High Performance Teamwork, 1995, Creative Thinking Tools for Innovation, 2d edit., 1997; contbr. articles to profl. jours.; prodr.: (presentation) VI World Congress of Psychiatry, Max Planck Inst. of Psychiatry, Langley-Porter Neuropsychiatric Inst., UCLA Neuropsychiatric Inst., Sci. Coun. of Can., Allan Mem. Inst. of Psychiatry, Acad. of Organ. & Occupl. Psychiatry. Fellow McGill Scholar, 1966—67, Earle C. Anthony, 1967—68; scholar Que., 1967—68, Med. Rsch. Coun. Can., 1977. Mem.: Ont. Med. Assn. (former chmn. sect. ind. physicians). Achievements include co-founder of Health Care Knowledge Mgmt. Consortium, 1998-2000. Office: Syntrek Inc 7 B Pleasant Blvd Ste 1008 Toronto ON Canada M4T 1K2 E-mail: howard@syntrek.com.

EISENBERG, HOWARD MICHAEL, neurosurgeon; b. N.Y.C., N.Y., May 4, 1939; s. Monroe L. and Regina (Fish) Eisenberg; children: Nancy M. Hoy, John A. BA, Syracuse U., 1960; MD, SUNY, N.Y.C., 1964. Diplomate Am. Bd. Neurol. Surgery. Intern N.Y. Hosp., N.Y.C., 1964-65; resident, fellow Cornell U. Med. Sch., N.Y.C., 1964-66; resident in neurosurgery Peter Bent Brigham Hosp., Boston, 1966-70; surgery instr. Harvard U., Boston, 1972-75; assoc. prof. U. Tex. Med. Br., Galveston, 1975-80, prof., chief neurosurgery, 1980-92; chmn. divsn. neurosurgery U. Md., Balt., 1992-96, dir. med. svcs. Shock Truama Ctr., 1992-96, prof. chair dept. neurosurgery, 1996—, R.K. Thompson prof., 2000—. Chmn. neurology A study sect. NIH, Bethesda, Md., 1980—87; numerous vis. professorships and guest lectureships. Mem. editl. bd. Jour. Neurosurgery, 1989—99, chair, 1997—99; editor: (book) The Cerebral Microvasculature, 1980, Neurobehavioral Recovery from Head Injury, 1987, Mild Head Injury, 1989, Neurosurgery Clinics of North America-Mangement of Head Injury, 1991, The Frontal Lobes, 1991; contbr. articles to profl. jours. Mem. devel. bd. Houston Grand Opera, 1989—92. Lt. comdr. USN, 1970—72. Recipient William Savernes award, Nat. Head Injury Found., 1994, Wakeman award, 1990; numerous grants in field. Mem.: ACGME (mem. residency rev. com. neurosurgery 2001—02, v.p.), ACS (chair neurosurgical adv. coun.), Am. Surg. Assn., Acad. Neurol. Surgeons (v.p.), Soc. Neurol. Surgeons (v.p., pres.-elect, pres.), Am. Bd. Neurol. Surgery (bd. dirs., sec.-treas., bd. dirs. 1990—95, chmn. 1995—96), N.Y. Yacht Club (mem. seamanship com.), Cruising Club Am., Annapolis Yacht. Club, Cosmos Club. Office: U Md Med Systems Dept Neurosurgery 22 S Greene St Ste S12D Baltimore MD 21201-1544

EISENBERG, JAY LYNN, marketing research professional; b. Mpls., Mar. 28, 1943; s. Benjamin Gene and Blanche (Goldfetter) E.; m. Gabriela Hubert, Aug. 17, 1975. BA, U. Minn., 1966, MA, 1970. Jr. project dir. Gen. Mills Inc., Mpls., 1968-70; mktg. rsch. analyst Green Giant Co., Bloomington, Minn., 1970-72; project mgr. Am. Guidance Svc., Circle Pines, Minn., 1973-80; mgr. mkt. rsch. Nash Finch Co., Mpls., 1981—, sr. market rsch. mgr., 1999—. Co-author: Peabody Picture Vocabulary Test-Revised Technical Supplement, 1981; contbr. articles to profl. and popular publs. Co-coord. family coun. Sholom West Nursing Home, St. Louis Park, Minn., 1993-97. Grantee U. Minn. Computer Ctr., 1968; recipient Bronze award 40th Pacific Internat. Philatelic Exhb., 1980, others. Mem. Am. Mktg. Assn. (Minn. chpt.), Am. Philat. Soc., Am. Topical Assn., Classic Corvettes Minn., Chesstamp Rev. (charter). Achievements include development of Store Insight Assessment Model. Office: Nash Finch Co PO Box 355 7600 France Ave S Minneapolis MN 55435-5920

EISENBERG, JONATHAN LEE, lawyer; b. Hornell, N.Y., Jan. 10, 1955; s. Louis and Marcia E.; m. Jill Levenson, May 22, 1976; children: Samuel David, William Mayer. BA summa cum laude, Macalester Coll., 1976; JD, Yale U., 1979. BAr: Minn. 1979, U.S.Ct. Appeals (8th cir.) 1979, U.S. Dist. Ct. Minn. 1980. Law clk. to assoc. justice Minn. Supreme Ct., St. Paul, 1979-80; assoc. Pepin, Dayton, Herman, Graham & Getts, Mpls., 1980-84, ptnr., 1985-86; litigation atty. Pillsbury Co., Mpls., 1986-90; shareholder Briggs & Morgan, Mpls., 1990-95; sr. legal counsel Medtronic, Inc., Mpls., 1995—. Mem. ABA, Am. Corp. Counsel Assn., Minn. State Bar Assn., Hennepin County Bar Assn., Macalester Coll. Alumni Assn. (bd. dirs. 1982-84). Office: Medtronic Inc 710 Medtronic Pky NE Minneapolis MN 55432-3576

EISENBERG, JOSEPH MARTIN, psychologist, consultant; b. Bklyn., June 19, 1944; s. David and Dora (Levine) E.; m. Susan Joan Kahn, Aug. 16, 1980; children: Ian, Lara, Jason, Davida. BA in Psychology magna cum laude, C.W. Post Coll., 1966; MA in Psychology, U. Alta, 1969, PhD in Psychology, 1971. Cert., lic., Md.; cert. clin. hypnotherapist, Negotiation Inst. Psychol. diagnostician, counselor dept. psychology U. Alta, Can., 1969-70; field rschr. Dept. Youth Alta, 1969-70; assoc. dir. Toronto (Ont.) YMCA Ctr. for counselling and Human Rels., 1970-71; chief psychologist Salvation Army House of Concord, Toronto, 1971-72; dir. outpatient svc. St. Vincent Hosp. Cmty. Mental Health Ctr., Erie, Pa., 1972-73; dir. Erie County Ctr. for Learning Disabilities, 1973-74; pvt. practice psychology Erie and Balt., 1972—; v.p. in charge personnel and comm. Bridge Energy Corp., Balt., 1981—, Reason House, Balt., 1981-97. Spl. cons. Md. Children and Family Svcs., Inc.; mem. profl. adv. bds. Balt. Assn. children with Learning Disabilities; cons. Mormac Ltd., 1979-97; forensic cons. Howard County/Balt. County/Carroll County, Office of Pub. Defendeers and Balt. City Solicitor's Office, 1977—. Co-author computer software; contbr. articles to profl. jours. Chmn. Carroll County Child Abuse Consultation Com., 1978-80; dir. Psychol. Svcs. for the Metabolic Nutrition Program, 1986-89; mem. profl. adv. bd. Catonsville Group Home, 1980-81. Recipient Richard P. Runyon award, 1966. Mem. Am. Psychol. Assn., Md. Psychol. Assn., Am. Bd. Profl. Disability Cons., Am. Bd. Cert. Managed Care Providers, Psi Chi, Phi Theta. Office: 1402 York Rd Ste 207 Lutherville MD 21093-6031

EISENBERG, LEE B. communications executive, author; b. Phila., July 22, 1946; s. George M. and Eve (Blonsky) E.; m. Linda Reville, June 7, 1986; children: Edmund George, Katherine Eve. AB, U. Pa., 1968; MA, Annenberg Sch. Communications, 1970. Assoc. editor Esquire Mag., N.Y.C., 1970-72, sr. editor, 1972-74, mng. editor, 1974-75, editor, 1976-77, v.p. devel., 1980-84, editor-in-chief, 1987-90; founding editor-in-chief Esquire, U.K., London, 1990-91; founding ptnr. The Edison Project, Knoxville, Tenn., 1992-95; editor creative devel. Time Mag., N.Y.C., 1995-99; exec. v.p., creative dir. Lands' End, Dodgeville, Wis., 1999—. Cons. N.Y. Times Co., 1977-78, Warner Bros., Los Angeles, 1978-79; founder Eisenberg, McCall & Okrent, N.Y.C., 1978-81. Author: Sneaky Feats, 1974, Atlantic City, 1978, Ultimate Fishing Book, 1981, Breaking Eighty, 1997. Founder Rotisserie League Baseball, N.Y.C., 1980—. Recipient One Show award Art Dirs. Club, 1976, Gold Cindy award Assn. Visual Comms., 1984, various nat. mag. awards, 1984-90. Office: Lands' End 1 Lands End Ln Dodgeville WI 53595-0001

EISENBERG, LEON, psychiatrist, educator; b. Phila., Aug. 8, 1922; s. Morris and Elizabeth (Sabreen) E.; m. Ruth Harriet Bleier, June 11, 1948 (div. 1967); children: Mark Philip, Kathy Bleier; m. Carola Blitzman Guttmacher, Aug. 31, 1967; children: Laurence, Alan. AB, U. Pa., 1944, MD, 1946; MA (hon.), Harvard U., 1967; DSc (hon.), U. Manchester, Eng., 1973, U. Mass., 1991. Diplomate: in child psychiatry and psychiatry Am. Bd. Psychiatry and Neurology. Intern Mt. Sinai Hosp., N.Y.C., 1946—47; instr. physiology U. Pa., 1947-48; resident psychiatry Sheppard-Pratt Hosp., Towson, Md., 1950-52; with Johns Hopkins, 1952-67, prof. child psychiatry Med. Sch., 1961-67; psychiatrist-in-charge children's psychiat. service Harriet Lane Home, 1958-67; prof. psychiatry Harvard U. Med. Sch., Boston, 1967—, Maude and Lillian Presley prof. psychiatry, 1975-80, chmn. exec. com. dept. psychiatry, 1973-80, Maude and Lillian Presley prof. social medicine, 1980-93, chmn. dept., 1980-91, prof. of social medicine emeritus, 1993—; psychiatrist-in-chief Mass. Gen. Hosp., 1967-74, mem. bd. consultation, 1974—; sr. assoc. in psychiatry Children's Hosp., Boston, 1974—; prof. emeritus, 1993—. Paley lectr. Cornell U., 1983; Schilder lectr. NYU, 1984; Eli Robins lectr. Washington U., St. Louis, 1985; plenary session lectr. Internat. Pediat. Assn., Amsterdam, 1998; lectr. Italian Psychiat. Soc., Bologna, 1998; Alpha Omega Alpha lectr. U. Rochester, 1999; plenary lectr. World Psychiat. Assn., Athens, 1999; vis. lectr. Yale U., 1987, John Peters lectr., 2002; R.W. Johnson vis. prof. U. Rochester, 1987; Carolyn Voorsanger lectr. Stanford U. Med. Sch., 1989; Willard Sears Simpkins lectr. Johns Hopkins U., 1989; William Potter lectr. Thomas Jefferson U., 1992; vis. prof. McMaster U., Canada, 1991, Charles U., Prague; psychiat. cons. Crownsville (Md.) State Hosp., 1954—58, Rosewood State Tng. Sch., Owings Mills, Md., 1957—60, Balt. City Hosp., 1959—62, Children's Guild, Balt., 1954—61; cons. Sinai Hosp., Balt., 1963—67; Mapother-Lewis ann. lectr. Maudsley Hosp., London, 1977; Baan Meml. lectr. Netherlands Psychiat. Soc., Amsterdam, 1978; Royal Soc. Medicine vis. prof., London, 83; mem. subcom. psychiat. nomenclature com. vital stats. USPHS; chmn. WHO Conf. Devel. Regulation, 1964—67; mem. Joint Commn. Mental Health of Children; cons. divsn. mental health WHO, 1974—, chmn. sci. group on evaluation of psychiat. treatment, 1989; mem. adv. com. to dir. NIH, 1977—80; lectr. Can. Royal Coll. Psychiatry, 1993, Italian Soc. for Biol. Psychiatry, Cagliari, Sardinia, 1994; Richard Goldbloom lectr. Dalhousie U., Halifax, N.S., Canada, 1995; Wolfe Adler lectr. Sheppard-Pratt Hosp. Sys., Balt., 1995; spl. lectr. Health of the Child of the Eve of the Yr. 2000, Bologna, Italy, 1995; plenary lectr. Royal Australian & New Zealand Coll. Psychiatry, 1999, World Congress of Psychiatry, Hamburg, 1999, XII World Congress of Psychiatry, Yokohama, Japan, 2002. Editor Am. Jour. Orthopsychiatry, 1963-73; editorial bd.: Culture, Medicine and Psychiatry, Psychol. Medicine, Jour. Psychiat. Research. Capt. M.C., U.S. Army, 1948-50. Recipient Theobald Smith award Albany Med. Coll., 1979, Orton award Orton Soc., 1980, Disting. Alumnus award U. Pa., 1992, Presdl. Commendation Am. Psychiat. Assn., 1992, Agnes Purchell McGavin award, 1994, Camille Cosby World of Children award Judge Baker Children's Ctr., 1994, Salmon medal N.Y. Acad. Medicine, 1995, Mumford award and lecture, 1996, Walshe McDermott Medal, Inst. of Medicine, 2003. Fellow: AAAS, Royal Soc. Medicine, Soc. Rsch. Child Devel. (award for contbns. to policy for children 2003), Royal Coll. Psychiatrists (hon.; Eli Lilly lectr. 1986), Am. Psychiat. Assn. (life; trustee 1973—76, Disting. Svc. award 2003), Am. Orthopsychiat. Assn. (life Ittleson Meml. award 1996); mem.: I.O.M. (chair com. on planned childbearing 1993—95, chair com. bridging the brain, behavioral and clin. scis. 1999—2000), AAUP (past pres. Johns Hopkins chpt.), Mass. Med. Soc., Soc. Neurosci., Psychiat. Rsch. Soc. (past pres.), Am. Acad. Arts and Scis. (comm. sec. 1995—2002), Md. Psychiat. Soc. (past pres.), Ecuadorean Soc. Neurosci. (hon.), Greek Soc. Neurology and Psychiatry (hon.), Am. Psychopath. Assn., Assn. Rsch. Nervous and Mental Disease, Can. Pediat. Soc. (Queen Elizabeth II lectr. 1986), Am. Pediat. Soc., Am. Acad. Pediat. (Dale Richmond lectr. 1989, Aldrich award 1980), Inst. Medicine NAS (coun. 1975—77, program and membership coms. 1979—82, bd. on health sci. policy 1989—91, Rhoda and Bernard Samat prize in mental health 1996), Johns Hopkins Soc. Scholars, Alpha Omega Alpha (lectr. Jefferson Med. Coll. 1994), Sigma Xi, Phi Beta Kappa (chpt. pres. 1958, vis. scholar 1994—95). Home: 9 Clement Cir Cambridge MA 02138-2205 Office: Harvard U Med Sch Dept Soc Med Boston MA 02115 E-mail: Leon_Eisenberg@HMS.Harvard.edu.

EISENBERG, MARVIN JULIUS, art history educator; b. Phila., Aug. 19, 1922; s. Frank and Rosalie (Julius) E. BA, U. Pa., 1943; M.F.A., Princeton, 1949, PhD, 1954; D.Litt. (hon.), St Andrews, 2003. Mem. faculty U. Mich., Ann Arbor, 1949-89, prof. art history, chmn. dept., 1960-69, Collegiate prof., 1974-75, prof. emeritus, 1989—; mem. Inst. for Advanced Study, Princeton, N.J., 1970. Vis. prof. Stanford U., 1973; mem. adv. com. Center for Advanced Study in Visual Arts, Nat. Gallery, Washington, 1981-84; mem. vis. com. dept. fine arts, Harvard U., 1975-81, Freer Gallery Art, Washington, 1970-96, Commn. on Preservation and Access, Washington, 1991-94, Ga. Mus. Art, 1997—; disting. Berg prof. Colo. Coll., 1990, 93, 95, 97, 2000, 2002; Hooker disting. vis. prof. McMaster U., 1993; Saunders lectr. St Andrews U., 1998. Author: Lorenzo Monaco, 1989; co-author: The Confraternity Altarpiece by Mariotto di Nardo, 1998; contbr. articles on early Italian painting to profl. jours. Served with AUS, 1943-46. Recipient Star of Solidarity II Italy, 1966; Coll. Art Assn. Disting. Teaching of Art History award, 1987; Guggenheim fellow, 1959. Fellow Japan Soc. for Promotion of Sci.; mem. Coll. Art Assn. Am. (dir. 1965-70, v.p. 1966-67, pres. 1968-69), Royal Soc. Arts (Benjamin Franklin fellow 1969), Phi Beta Kappa, Phi Kappa Phi. Home: 2200 Fuller Ct Apt 1201 Ann Arbor MI 48105-2307

EISENBERG, MELVIN A. law educator; b. N.Y., Dec. 3, 1934; s. Max and Laura (Wallance) E.; m. Helen Garlitz, Feb. 5, 1956; children: Bronwyn, David Abram (dec. 1997). AB, SCL, Columbia U., 1956; LLB, SCL, Faye Diploma in Law, Harvard U., 1959; LLD (hon.), U. Milan, 1998. Bar: N.Y. 1960. Assoc. Kaye Scholer Fierman Hays & Handler, 1959-63, 64-66; corp. counsel City of N.Y., 1966; acting prof. U. Calif.-Berkeley, 1966-69, prof. law, 1969-83, Koret prof. law, 1983—. Vis. prof. Harvard U., 1969-70, vis. prof. law Columbia U., 1998—; asst. counsel Pres. Commn. on Assassination Pres. Kennedy, Warren Commn., 1964; counsel mayor's task force on reorgn N.Y.C. govt., 1966; mem. mayor's task force on N.Y.C. transp. reorgn., 1966; mem. mayors' task force on mcpl. collective bargaining, 1966; reporter Am. Law Inst., principles of corporate governance: analysis and recommendations, 1980-84, chief reporter, 1984-94, Ammi Cutter chair, 1991-93; adviser, restatement 3d of agy. 1996—; adviser, restatement 2d of restitution, 1998—; prof.-in-residence, Cologne U., 1984, U. Milan, 1992; mem. ABA com. on corp. laws, 1992—; U. Iowa inaugural lectr., 1987, Roy R. Ray lectr. So. Meth. U., 1993, Robert L. Levine Distg. lectr., Fordham U., 1993; chmn. AALS contracts sect., 1989, AALS contracts workshop, 1986; chmn. AALS bus. assns. sect., 1998; visitor-in-residence U. Murdoch, U. Western Australia, 1992, McGill U., 1981; Sobeloff lectr. U. Md., 1994; Freehill, Hollingsdale and Page vis. fellow U. New South Wales, Australia, 1994. Author: The Structure of the Corporation, 1977 (Coif Triennial Book award honorable mention 1980), The Nature of the Common Law, 1988, (with L. Fuller) Basic Contract Law, 2001, Cases and Materials on Corporations and Other Business Organization, 2000; also numerous articles. Pres. Queen's Child Guidance Ctr., 1963-66. Guggenheim fellow, 1971-72, Canterbury vis. fellow U. Canterbury, New Zealand, 1988, Kimber fellow York U., Toronto, 1989, Rabin fellow Yale Sch. Law; Fulbright Sr. scholar, Australia, 1987, Disting. Mellon scholar U. Pitts., 1989, Manuel F. Cohen vis. scholar George Washington U. Sch. Law; Cooley lectr. U. Mich., 1985; Baron de Hirsch Meyer lectr. U. Miami Sch. Law, 1983, Wythe lectr. William and Mary Law Sch., 1999, TePoel lectr. Creighton U. Sch. Law, 1982; recipient Faye Diploma Harvard U. Law Sch., Rudder Outstanding Tchg. award Boalt Hall Law Sch., 2002, Disting. Tchg. award U. Calif., Berkeley, 1990, 2002. Fellow AAAS; mem. ABA (com. on corp. law 1992--), Am. Law Inst., Am. Assn. Law Schs. (chair contracts sect. 1989, chair bus. assns. sect. 1999), Phi Beta Kappa. Home: 1197 Keeler Ave Berkeley CA 94708-1753 Office: U Calif Sch Law 331 Boalt Hl Berkeley CA 94720-0001 also: 201 E 79th St New York NY 10021-0830 also: Columbia U Law Sch 435 W 116th St New York NY 10027-7201 E-mail: eisenberg@law.berkeley.edu.

EISENBERG, MEYER, lawyer; b. Bklyn., Dec. 15, 1931; s. Samuel and Bella Eisenberg; m. Carolyn Schoen, Dec. 26, 1954; children— Julie S., Ellen M. BA, Bklyn. Coll., 1953; LLB, Columbia U., 1958. Bar: N.Y. 1960, D.C. 1970, U.S. Supreme Ct. 1963. Law clk. to Chief Justice William McAllister Supreme Ct. Oreg., Salem, 1958-59; atty. SEC, Washington, 1959-70, counsel spl. study securities markets, 1962-64, asst. gen. counsel, 1966-68, exec. asst. to chmn., 1968-69, assoc. gen. counsel, 1969-70; with firm Lawler, Kent & Eisenberg, Washington, 1970-79, Rosenman, Colin, Freund, Lewis & Cohen, Washington, 1980-87, Ballard, Spahr, Andrews & Ingersoll, Washington, 1987-93, Kramer, Levin, Naftalis & Frankel, Washington, 1994-98; dep. gen. coun. sec. SEC, Washington, 1998—. Adj. prof. law George Washington U., 1972-75, Georgetown U. Law Sch., 1988-90; vis. prof. law U. Calif., Berkeley; dir. Nat. Ctr. Fin. Svcs., 1985-86; mem. exec. com. Calif. Securities Regulation Inst.; cons. in field. Contbr. articles to profl. publs. Mem. internat. bd. govs. B'nai B'rith, 1978-92; mem. nat. exec. com. Anti-Defamation League, 1980—, nat. vice chmn., 1994—, chmn. Nat. Civil Rights Com., 1992-94, Nat. Legal Affairs Com., 1980-92. Mem. ABA (chmn. com. on devels. in investment svcs. 1981-86, chmn. com. on long-range issues affecting bus. law practice 1986-90, coun. sect. bus. law 1990-94, chmn. com. on internat. tech. assistance 1994—, sec. bus. law), Fed. Bar Assn. (chmn. securities law com. 1984-85). Home: 8216 Lakenheath Way Potomac MD 20854-2740 Office: SEC Office of Gen Counsel 450 5th St NW Washington DC 20549-0001 E-mail: eisenbergm@sec.gov.

EISENBERG, PABLO SAMUEL, non-profit organization executive; b. Paris, July 1, 1932; came to U.S. 1939; s. Maurice and Paula (Halpert) E.; m. Helen Leone Cierniak, June 5, 1960; 1 child, Marina. BA, Princeton U., 1954; BLitt, Oxford U., Eng., 1957. Fgn. svc. officer USIA, 1960-63; program dir. Operation Crossroads Africa, N.Y.C., 1963-65; coord. Pa. Office Econ. Opportunity, 1965-67; dep. dir. Rsch. and Demonstration Office, Office of Econ. Opportunity, Washington, 1967-68; asst. dir. Nat. Urban Coalition, Washington, 1968-73; ind. cons. Washington, 1973-75; pres. Ctr. for Cmty. Change, Washington, 1975-98; sr. fellow, cons. Georgetown Pub. Policy Inst., Washington, 1998Y. Contbr. articles to profl. jours., chpts. to book; columnist Chronicle of Philanthropy. Mem. exec. com. Nat. Com. for Responsive Philanthropy, Washington, 1976—; pres. Friends of VISTA, Washington, 1980—; vice chmn. Nat. Neighborhood Coalition, Washington, 1976-98; bd. dirs. Environ. Support Ctr., Coll. Pub. Svc. and Citizenship, Tufts U., 1993-2000, Milton Eisenhower Found., Citizens Funds. Recipient John Gardner Leadership award, 1998; German Marshall Fund of U.S. travelling fellow, 1988. Democrat. Jewish. Avocations: tennis, antique books, movies, sports. Home: 3729 Massachusetts Ave NW Washington DC 20016-5004 Office: Pub Policy Inst Georgetown U 3240 Prospect St NW Washington DC 20007-3214

EISENBERG, PAUL DAVID, philosophy educator; b. Worcester, Mass., July 7, 1939; s. Alfred Herbert and Sophie (Kleinberg) E.; m. Lana Kay Ruegamer, Feb. 10, 1942; stepchildren: Vivienne Venderley, William Tam; 1 child, Charles Eisenberg. BA summa cum laude, Clark U., 1961; MA, Harvard U., 1965, PhD in Philosophy, 1967. Teaching fellow Harvard U., 1963-66; asst. prof. Ind. U., Bloomington, 1966-70, assoc. prof., 1970-78, prof. Philosophy, 1978—, adj. prof. Jewish Studies, 1989—. Part-time instr. MIT, 1964; vis. asst. prof. U. Ill., 1970; vis. adj. prof. U. Mass., 1980. Editorial bd. Nigerian Philosophical Journal; contbr. numerous articles to profl. jours. Recipient Harvard U. fellowships, 1961-64. Mem. Am. Philos. Assn., Ind. Philos. Assn. (pres 1969-70, 92-93), Soc. for Ancient Greek Philosophy, Hegel Soc. Am., N. Am. Nietzsche Soc., Am. Assn. Tchrs. Philosophy (exec. bd. 1991—), Phi Beta Kappa (pres. Ind. U. chpt. 1992-93). Avocation: book collecting. Office: Ind U Sycamore Hall #026 Bloomington IN 47405

EISENBERG, PAUL RICHARD, cardiologist, consultant, educator; b. Rome, Mar. 9, 1955; came to U.S., 1956; s. David Marvin and Sonia Maria (Benesdetti) E.; m. Patricia Lynn Goodman, Apr. 25, 1982; 1 child, Jamie. BS, Tulane U., 1975, MPH, 1980; MD, N.Y. Med. Coll., Valhalla, 1980. Diplomate Am. Bd. Internal Medicine, Am. Bd. Cardiology. Intern in internal medicine Barnes Hosp., St. Louis, 1980-83, fellow in cardiology, pulmonary medicine, 1983-85, asst. dir. CCU, 1986-91, dir. CCU, 1991-98; asst. prof. Washington U., St. Louis, 1985-91, assoc. prof., 1991-97, prof., 1997-98; med. dir. cardiovasc therapeutics Eli Lilly & Co., Indpls., 1998-2000, exec. dir. cardiovasc discovery, 2000—01, v.p. med., 2001—02, v.p. global drug safety, 2003—. Asst. editor: Medical Management of Heart Disease; contbr. over 100 articles to

profl. jours. Fellow Am. Heart Assn. (clin. cardiology), Am. Coll. Chest Physicians, Am. Coll. Cardiology; mem. Am. Fedn. Clin. Rsch., Internat. Soc. Thrombosis and Haemostasis. Office: Lilly Rsch Labs Lily Corp Ctr Drop Code 0520 Ctr Indianapolis IN 46285-0001

EISENBERG, R. NEAL, restoration company executive, b. Newark, July 15, 1936; s. William C. and Elsie G. (Greenfield) E.; m. Barbara J. Mayer, Dec. 18, 1966; children: Michael S., Elissa P. Student, Stevens Inst. of Tech., 1954-55; postgrad. Coll. Engring., NYU, 1955-57, BS in Acctg., 1960. Sr. acct. Puder & Puder (now Deloitte Touche), Newark, 1958-60, J.H. Cohn & Co., Roseland, N.J., 1960-63; ptnr. Universal Engring. and Waterpoofing Svc., Newark, 1963-69; pres. Universal Restoration and Waterproofing Svc., Inc., West Orange, N.J., 1970—; v.p. Universal Restoration, Inc., Washington, 1967-69, pres., CEO, 1993-96; v.p. Restoration Svcs., Inc., Washington, 1967-69; pres. Vitrifix of N.Am., Inc., Washington, 1986-87; chmn. Universal Family Group, West Orange, 1987—; pres. Universal Waterproofing Svc., Inc., West Orange, 1969—. Cons. and expert in structural restoration. Co-inventor Dekosit/Permo-Bond Restoration Method. Recipient Second Biennial Design award Gen. Svcs. Administrn., 1967. Mem. Constrn. Specifications Inst., Nat. Assn. Waterproofing Contractors, Nat. Trust Hist. Preservation, N.J. Bus. and Industry Assn., Masons. Office: Universal Waterproofing Svc 623 Eagle Rock Ave Ste 377 West Orange NJ 07052-2948

EISENBERG, RICHARD MARTIN, pharmacology educator; b. Weehawken, N.J., May 15, 1942; s. Herbert and Evelyn (Stecker) E.; m. Marsha Eisenberg, July 3, 1966; children: Marla, Aaron, Shana. BA, UCLA, 1963, MS, 1967, PhD, 1970; postdoc., U. Rochester, 1970-71. Asst. prof. pharmacology U. Minn., Duluth, 1971-76, assoc. prof., 1976-77, assoc. prof., acting dept. head, 1977-80, assoc. prof. dept. head, 1980-85, prof., dept. head, 1985—. Author-developer: (computer software) Mac Pharmacology, Mac MedVirology, Mac BrainLesion; presenter in field; contbr. articles to profl. jours. Recipient numerous rsch. grants Nat. Inst. Drug Abuse, 1978—, other instns., 1975—. Mem. Am. Soc. Pharmacology and Exptl. Therapeutics, Assn. Med. Sch. Pharmacology (treas. 1994-98, pres. 1998-2000), Endocrine Soc., Western Pharmacology Soc., Coll. on Problems of Drug Dependence. Avocations: cabinet making, microcomputers, photography. Office: U Minn Duluth Sch Medicine Dept Pharmacology 10 University Dr Duluth MN 55812-2403

EISENBERG, ROBIN LEDGIN, religious education administrator; b. Passaic, N.J., Jan. 10, 1951; d. Morris and Ruth (Miller) Ledgin. BS, West Chester State U., 1973; M Edn., Kutztown State U., 1977. Administrv. asst. Keneseth Israel, Allentown, Pa., 1973-77; dir. edn. Cong. Schaarai Zedek, Tampa, Fla., 1977-79, Kehilath Israel, Pacific Palisades, Calif., 1979-80, Temple Beth El, Boca Raton, Fla., 1980-99, 2003—, Levis Jewish Cmty. Ccn., Boca Raton, 1999—2003. Contbr. Learning Together, 1987, Bar/Bat Mizvah Education: A Sourcebook, 1993, The New Jewish Teachers Handbook, 1994. Chmn. edn. info., Planned Parenthood, Boca Raton Fla. 1989. Recipient Kamiker Camp award Nat. Assn. Temple Educators, Pres.'s award for adminstrn., 1990; Mandel fellow in Jewish Edn., Levis Jewish Cmty. Ctr., 2001-2003. Mem. Nat. Assn. Temple Educators (pres. 1990-92, chair UAHC-CCAR-NATE commn. on Jewish edn. 1997-99, accreditation chair 2000—, conf. daytime program co-chair 2002, 2003), Coalition Advancement of Jewish Edn. (chair strategic planning com. 2003—), Assn. Jewish Ctr. Profls. (Profl. of Yr. award 2003). Avocation: photography. Home: 2428 NW 35th St Boca Raton FL 33431 Office: Temple Beth El 333 SW 4th Ave Boca Raton FL 33432 E-mail: robledeise@aol.com., robine@bocafed.org.

EISENBERG, SONJA MIRIAM, artist; b. Berlin, June 10, 1926; arrived in U.S., 1938, naturalized, 1947; d. Adolf and Meta Cecilie (Bettauer) Weinberger; m. Jack Eisenberg, Mar. 31, 1946; children: Ralph, Lynn, Lauren. Student, Queens Coll., 1943—46, Middlebury Coll., 1945, NYU, 1952—54, BA, 1954; postgrad., Nat. Acad. Sch. Fine Arts, 1961. Artist-in-residence Cathedral of St. John the Divine, N.Y.C.; apptd. art dir. Hermes Media B.V., Amsterdam, 1992. One-woman shows include Bodley Gallery, N.Y.C., 1970, 1973, 1975, 1980, Galerie Art du Monde, Paris, 1973, Buyways Gallery, Sarasota, Fla., 1973—75, 1978, Galerie de Sfinx, Amsterdam, Netherlands, 1974, Huntsville (Ala.) Mus. Art, 1974, Anglo-Am. Art Mus., Baton Rouge, 1974, Comara Gallery, L.A., 1974, Palm Spring (Calif.) Desert Mus., 1975, Fordham U., N.Y.C., 1976, Omega Inst., New Lebanon, NY, 1979, Am. Mus., Hayden Planetarium, N.Y.C., 1980, Avila Graphics, Ltd., 1981, YWCA, N.Y.C., 1981, Cathedral of St. John the Divine, 1983, 1985, The Millbrook Gallery, NY, 1989, 1994, Christopher Leonard Gallery, N.Y.C., 1993, Park Hotel, Vitznau, Switzerland, 1994, The Burgenstock (Switzerland) Hotels, 1995, Wainscott Gallery, NY, 1997, Galerie Dussmann, Kulturkaufhaus, Berlin, 1998, Horton Gallery, Phila., 2001, exhibited in group shows at Mus. Fine Arts, St. Petersburg, Fla., 1973, Am. Watercolor Soc., 107th, 108th Exhbn., 1974—75, Galerie Frederic Gollong, St. Paul de Vence, France, 1978, Betty Parson's Gallery, N.Y.C., 1981, Foster Harmon Galleries of Am. Art, Sarasota, Fla., 1988, Tokyo Met. Art Mus. 14th Internat. Art Friendship Exhbn., 1989, Galerie Herbert Leidel, Munich, Germany, 1991, Park Ave. Armory, N.Y.C., 1996, Akim-USA, 1996, Represented in permanent collections Archives Am. Art, Smithsonian Inst., Jewish Mus., N.Y.C., Fordham U. Mus., Palm Springs Desert Mus., Omega Inst., Cathedral of St. John the Divine; designer WFUNA cachet for UN Water Power Conf., 1977, UN Internat. Yr. of Disabled Persons, 1981, commd. commemorative painting Crystal Night for Telecom Telefon Karte, Munich, 1993, completed project Seeing the Gospel According to St. John (text and 41 paintings) for Cathedral of St. John, 1987; author: From Here to There and Back Again, 2001, Poems and Paintings, 2002, The Red Painted House, 2002. Regent Cathedral of St. John the Divine, 1990. Recipient Gold medal for artistic merit, Internat. Parliament for Safety and Peace, 1983, Palma D'Oro Europe, 1986. Mem.: Accademia Italia delle Arti e del Lavoro (Gold medal 1981). Home and Office: 1020 Park Ave New York NY 10028-0913 *When you focus your mind, you may break through the Known with its borders of words and ideas, and get a glimpse of the "nothing" that is so creative.*

EISENBERG, SUSAN MARY, retired employment representative; b. Duquesne, Pa., July 24, 1929; d. John and Maria (Sokolovsky) Boronkay; m. Jack Cleon Seidling, Sept. 18, 1949 (wid. Feb. 1979); children: Cheryl Susan Seidling Lindsey, Janet Marie Seidling Kelly, David John Seidling; m. Ronald John Eisenberg, Sept. 26, 1992. Student, LaSalle Inst., 1947-48; fin., N.Y. Inst. of Fin., 1964. Lic. ins. agt. Pa., stockbroker. Paralegal A.J. Rosenbleet, McKeesport, Pa., 1949-51, Stokes & Lurie, Clairton, Pa., 1952-56; asst. mgr. Bernstein & Co., McKeesport, 1963-64; stockbroker Chaplin McGuiness Co., Pitts., 1965-66; account exec. Bache & Co., Pitts., 1966-75; employee rep. Dept. of Labor and Industry, McKeesport, 1975-91. Author/editor: (newsletter) Sr. Ams. Newsletter, 1981—. Girl Scout leader Girl Scouts U.S., West Mifflin, Pa., 1956-61, troop cons., 1957-58; telephone reassurance vol. Contact Pitts., Inc., N. Versailles, Pa., 1995; vol. Eye & Ear Hosp., Pitts., 1995-96; eucharistic minister, N. Versailles, 1993-96; founder, travel chair ALPS, Inc., v.p. 1982-83, founder, pres. Sr. Ams. Club, Inc., 1981-91. Recipient Senatorial citation Pa. Senate, 1988, Lt. Gov.'s proclamation Sate of Pa., 1988, People Who Care award Pa. Sec. of Labor, 1990. Mem.: VFW Aux. (life; parliamentarian, trustee 1997—), Polish Legion of Am. Vets. (historian 2001—), Am. Legion Aux. (pres., v.p., membership chair 1980—84), Tri-County Computer Users Group (recording sec. 2002), St. Stephens Ladies Guild (pres. 1983—84). Avocations: playing organ, reading, dancing, gardening, charitable volunteering. Home: 3035 Fairway Dr Fort Pierce FL 34982-4319

EISENBERG, TED STEVEN, plastic and reconstructive surgeon; b. Phila., June 21, 1952; s. Martin John and Mitzi (Singer) E.; m. Joyce Janet Kirschner, Sept. 1, 1973; children: Ben, Samantha. BS, Pa. State U., 1972; DO, Phila. Coll. Osteo. Medicine, 1976. Diplomate Nat. Bd. Examiners for Osteo. Physicians and Surgeons; Bd. cert. in Osteo. Plastic Surgery, Laser Surgery, Gen. Surgery; lic. physician, N.Y., Pa. Intern North Miami Beach Osteo. Gen. Hosp., 1976-77; resident in gen. surgery Met. Hosp., Phila., 1977-81; resident in hand surgery Hand Rehab. Ctr./Jefferson U., Phila., 1981; preceptee in plastic surgery Rolling Hill and Albert Einstein Med. Ctrs., Phila., 1983-85; practice plastic and reconstructive surgery Phila. area, 1985—; assoc. prof. Phila. Coll. Osteo. Medicine, 1991—. Attending staff physician Grad. Hosp., John F. Kennedy Hosp., Northeastern Hosp., Suburban Genl. Hosp., others; cons. staff physician Delaware Valley Med. Ctr., Springfield Hosp.; lectr. in field. Contbr. numerous articles to profl. jours. Recipient numerous awards for sci. exhibits and publs. Fellow Am. Coll. Osteo. Surgeons; mem. Am. Acad. Aesthetic and Restorative Surgery (charter), Am. Osteo. Assn., Jefferson Hand Club (charter), Pa. Osteo. Med. Assn., Philadelphia County Osteo. Soc., Phila. Coll. Osteo. Medicine Alumni Assn. (life), Lambda Omicron Gamma (v.p. 1993-94). Office: Ste 102 2375 Woodward St Philadelphia PA 19115

EISENBUD, DAVID, mathematics educator; b. N.Y.C., Apr. 8, 1947; s. Leonard and Ruth-Jean (Rubinstein) E.; m. Monika Margarete Schwabe, June 3, 1970; children: Daniel, Alina. BS, U. Chgo., 1966, MS, 1967, PhD, 1970. Lectr. Brandeis U., Waltham, Mass., 1970-72, asst. prof., 1972-76, assoc. prof., 1976-80, prof., 1980—97, chmn. dept. of math., 1982-84; prof. U. Calif., Berkeley, 1997—. Vis. prof. U. Bonn, Fed. Republic of Germany, 1979-80, MSRI, Berkeley, 1986-87, Harvard U., 1987-88; mem. adv. panel in maths. NSF, 1978-81; dir. Math. Sci. Res. Inst., Berkeley, 1997—. Editor: Procs. of Am. Math. Soc., 1978-82, Asterisque, 1983-88, (book series) Wadsworth Advanced, 1985-92, Jour. Algebraic Geometry, 1990—, Annals of Math, 2001-2004, Springer Algorithms and Computation in Math.; contbr. numerous articles to profl. jours. Alfred P. Sloan Found. fellow, 1973-75; NSF grantee, 1970—. Mem. Am. Math. Soc. (coun., pres. 2003—), SIAM, AWM, MAA. Avocations: flute, vocalist, juggling. Office: MSRI 17 Gauss Way Berkeley CA 94720

EISENDRATH, CHARLES RICE, journalism educator, manufacturer, farmer, consultant; b. Chgo., Oct. 9, 1940; s. William Nathan and Erna Sarah (Rice) E.; m. Julia Cardozo, Jan. 28, 1967; children: Benjamin Cardozo, Mark William. BA, Yale U., 1962; MA, U. Mich., 1965. Reporter Post-Dispatch, St. Louis, 1962, 64, Evening Sun, Balt., 1966-68; corr. Time Mag., Washington, London, Paris, bur. chief Buenos Aires, 1968-73; prof. U. Mich., Ann Arbor, 1975—. Propr. Overlook Farm, East Jordan, Mich., 1972—; chmn. Grillworks, Inc., Ann Arbor, 1978—; cons. Midland Bank of London, Pfizer, W.K. Kellogg Found.; mem. Pulitzer Prize Jury, 2002—03. Contbr. articles to profl. jours.; inventor in field. Dir. Knight-Wallace Journalism Fellows, 1986—; founding dir. Livingston Awards, Ann Arbor, 1980—; judge nat. barbecue contest, 1994—; pres. task force journalism Columbia U., 2002-03. NEH Mich. Journalism fellow, 1974-75. Mem. Coun. Fgn. Rels., Century Assn. (N.Y.C.), Soc. Profl. Journalists, Com. of Concerned Journalists (founding), Project on the State of the Am. Newspaper (founding bd. dirs. 1998-2000), Landsdowne Club (London), Phi Kappa Phi. Jewish. Office: Wallace House 620 Oxford Rd Ann Arbor MI 48104-2623 E-mail: drath@umich.edu.

EISENHOWER, JOHN SHELDON DOUD, former ambassador, author; b. Denver, Aug. 3, 1922; s. Dwight David (34th Pres. of U.S.) and Mamie (Doud) E.; m. Barbara Jean Thompson, June 10, 1947 (div. 1986); children: Dwight David II, Barbara Anne, Susan Elaine, Mary Jean; m. Joanne Thompson, Apr. 9, 1990. BS, U.S. Mil. Acad., 1944; MA in English Lit., Columbia, 1950; LHD (hon.), Northwood Inst., 1970. Commd. 2d lt. U.S. Army, 1944, advanced through grades to lt. col., 1963; assigned 1st Army, Europe, 1945, Army of Occupation, Europe, 1945-47, Korean War, 1952-53, Army Gen. Staff, 1957-58, White House Staff, 1958-61; resigned, 1963; brig. gen. USAR, 1974; engaged in writing, 1965-69; U.S. amb. to Belgium, Am. Embassy, Brussels, 1969-71. Cons. to the Pres.; also chmn. Interagency Classification Review Com., 1972-73; chmn. bd. Acad. Life Ins. Co., Atlanta; mem. adv. council Nat. Archives, 1974-77; chmn. President's Adv. Com. on Refugees, 1975; mil. editor Algonguin Books of Chapel Hill. Author: The Bitter Woods, 1969, Strictly Personal, 1974; editor: Letters to Mamie, 1978, Allies, 1982, So Far From God, 1989, Intervention!, 1993, Agent of Destiny, 1997, Yanks, 2001, General Ike, 2003. Mem. diplomatic coun., bd. govs. USO, 1983-85; trustee Alumni Fedn. Columbia U., 1976-80. Decorated Legion of Merit, Bronze Star, Combat Inf. badge, grand cross Order of Crown Belgium, Chungmu Disting. Service medal (Korea); recipient Grad. Faculties Alumni award for excellence Columbia U., 1970. Mem. Diplomatic and Consular Officers Ret., Capitol Hill Club.

EISENHUTH, JOHN C. training professional; b. Wyo. s. Harold P. and Mary A. Eisenhuth; m. Diane M. Eisenhuth, Oct. 1988; 1 child, Spencer A. AB, Brown U.; MBA, U. R.I.; MSFS (Master of Scis.), Am. Coll., 1997. CLU; ChFC. Sales mgr. N.Y. Life, Providence, tng. mgr. Portland, Maine, dir. N.Y.C., 1995—, asst. v.p., 1999. Mem. Toastmasters Internat. (rec. sec.). Avocation: fishing. Office: NY Life 51 Madison Ave Rm 809 New York NY 10010-1603 E-mail: jeisenhuth@ft.newyorklife.com.

EISENMAN, PETER DAVID, architect, educator; b. Newark, Aug. 11, 1932; s. Herschel I. and Sylvia H. (Heller) E.; m. Elizabeth Henderson, 1963 (div. 1990); children: Julia, Nicholas; m. Cynthia Davidson, 1990; 1 child, Samuel Chapin. B.Arch. (Charles G. Sands Meml. medal 1955), Cornell U., 1955; MS in Architecture (Alumni tuition scholar 1959, William Kinne fellow 1960-61), Columbia U., 1960; MA, Cambridge (Eng.) U., 1962, PhD, 1963. Prin. firm Eisenman/Robertson Architects, N.Y.C., 1980-88, Eisenman Architects, N.Y.C., 1988—. Founder Inst. Architecture and Urban Studies, N.Y.C., 1967, dir., 1967-82; mem. faculty Cambridge U., 1960-63, Princeton U., 1965-67; faculty Cooper Union, 1970—, adj. prof., 1975-86, Irwin Chanin Disting. prof. 1986—; architect-in-residence Am. Acad. Rome, 1976; Kea prof. U. Md., 1978; Charlotte Davenport prof. Yale U., 1980, Louis I. Kahn prof. arch., 2001—; Arthur Rotch prof. Harvard U., 1982-85, Eliot Noyes vis. critic, 1993; Louis H. Sullivan rsch. prof. architecture U. Ill., Chgo., 1987-93; vis. prof. Ohio State U., 1991-93; John Williams prof. architecture U. Ark., 1997. Author: Diagram Diaries, Choral Works, (with Jacques Derrida) Blurred Zones; editor: Oppositions Books, House X Rizzoli, Houses of Cards; prin. works include pvt. residences Princeton, N.J., Hardwick, Vt., Lakeville and Cornwall, Conn., 1968-76; others Housing Koch-Friedrichstrasse, Berlin, 1980-86, Wexner Ctr. for Visual Arts, Columbus, Ohio, 1983-89, U. Cin. Coll, Design, Art, Architecture and Planning, 1988-96, Columbus (Ohio) Conv. Ctr., 1988-93, Koizumi Sangyo Bldg., Tokyo, 1989-90, Nunotani Office Bldg., 1990-92, Emory U. Art Ctr., 1991-95, Rebstock Pk., Frankfurt, Germany, 1991-95, U.S. Pavilion, Venice Biennale, 1991, Max Reinhardt Haus, Berlin, 1992—, Haus Immendorff, Dusseldorf, Germany, 1993-94, Staten Island Inst. Arts and Scis., 1997—, Holocaust Meml., Berlin, Germany, 1998—, City of Culture, Santiago de Compostela, Spain, 1999—, Multi-Purpose Stadium, Glendale, Ariz., 1999—. Served with U.S. Army, 1955-57. Fellow Graham Found., 1966; Guggenheim Found., 1976; grantee Princeton U., 1964, 66; recipient Arnold W. Brunner Meml. prize in architecture Am. Acad. and Inst. Arts and Letters, 1984 Fellow AIA; mem. Am. Acad. Arts and Scis., Am. Acad. Arts and Letters, Archtl. League N.Y. (v.p. 1970), Conf. Architects Study Environ. (co-founder 1964) Clubs: Century Assn. (N.Y.C.). Office: Eisenman Architects 41 W 25th St New York NY 10010-2021

EISENSHTAT, SIDNEY HERBERT, architect; b. New Haven, June 6, 1914; s. Morris and Ella (Sobole) E.; m. Alice D. Brenner, Dec. 19, 1937 (dec. Feb. 2001); children: Carole Oken, Abby Robyn. BArch, U. So. Calif., 1935. Registered architect, Calif. Prin. Sidney Eisenshtat & Assocs. FAIA, Beverly Hills, Calif., 1941—. Mem. architects panel Union Am. Hebrew Congregations; bd. dirs. Internat. Tech. Coop. Ctr., Tel Aviv; pres., chmn. bd. dirs. Beth Jacob Congregation; v.p. L.A. Assn. Jewish Edn.; chmn. bd., pres. West Coast Talmudical Sem.; co-chmn. Nat. Conf. Religious Architecture; cons. Great Synagogue, Jerusalem, Israel; chmn. bd. Torah U. (now Yeshiva of L.A.). Prin. works include House of the Book, Brandeis, Calif., 1970 (Landmark award 1979), Sinai Temple, Los Angeles, 1959 (25 yr. Landmark award 1984), Knox Presbyn. Ch., 1965 (Los Angeles Beauty award 1975), Wells Fargo Bldg., 1975 (Beverly Hills award 1978), Union Bank Bldg., 1960, Beverly Hills, Exec. Life Bldg., 1966, Beverly Hills, Hughes Aircraft Satellite Testing and Computer Ctr., El Segundo, Calif., Friars Club, Los Angeles, 1961, Marlton Sch. for Deaf, Los Angeles, 1968, Sven Lokrantz School for Handicapped, Univ. Judaism Master Plan & Bldgs., Los Angeles, 1977, B'nai Zion Temple, El Paso, Tex., 1983, Temple Mt. Sinai, El Paso, 1962, Ctrl. Jewish Community Ctr., L.A., Bnai David Synagogue, Southfield, Mich., Hillel House, U. So. Calif.; whole body of archtl. work in permanent collection at U. So. Calif., Arts and Architecture Libr. as core collection of Jewish Architecture in America. Chmn., charter agy. pres. Bur. Jewish Edn. Greater L.A.; v.p., lifetime bd. mem. Jewish Fedn. Coun.; bd. dirs. Hebrew Immigration Soc.; v.p. Coun. Pres. Affiliated Orgns.; vice chmn. R-1 Commn., City of Beverly Hills. Recipient Nat. Sch. Adminstrs. award, 1966, Pub. Svc. award City of Beverly Hills, Nat. Disting. Svc. award Union Orthodox Jewish Congregations; honoree Bur. Jewish Edn. 60th Anniversary Celebration, Beth Jacob Congregation Banquet, 2001. Fellow AIA (honor award 1960, 66). Home and Office: 2736 Motor Ave Los Angeles CA 90064-3413 *When a sanctuary succeeds in helping the congregation to feel that it stands in the presence of God, its architect has received his lifetime award. For one who has been so rewarded a few times.*

EISENSTADT, G. MICHAEL, diplomat, writer, educator, researcher; b. Free City of Danzig (now Gdansk, Poland), Nov. 16, 1928; s. Isidor and Edith (Lange) E.; 1 child, Judith Luzann. BA, Queens Coll., 1951; MS, U. Wis., 1952; postgrad., Russian Inst. Columbia U., 1954-56, Fgn. Svc. Inst., 1982-83. Instr. history Queens Coll., Flushing, N.Y., 1955-60; jr. officer Am. Embassy, Belgrade, Yugoslavia, 1960-61; cultural officer Am. Consulate Gen., Guayaquil, Ecuador, 1962-63; asst. cultural affairs officer Am. Embassy, Belgrade, Yugoslavia, 1963-67, cultural attaché Warsaw, Poland, 1968-71, br. pub. affairs officer Bonn, Fed. Republic of Germany, 1973-76, counselor for pub. affairs Budapest, Hungary, 1977-80, dep. counselor for pub. affairs Bonn, 1983-84, counselor for pub. affairs Belgrade, 1984-88; dep. policy officer Voice of Am., Washington, 1971-73; dir. Office Internat. Visitors USIA, Washington, 1980-82; mem. sr. seminar State Dept., Washington, 1982-83; dir. Office European Affairs USIA, Washington, 1988-89; diplomat-in-residence NYU, 1989-90; dir. N.Y. Reception Ctr. USIA, 1990-92; sr. rsch. scholar Inst. East Cen. Europe Columbia U., 1992-94. Cons. on the Balkans, Ea. and Ctrl. Europe, countries of the former Soviet Union; chmn. coordinating com., chmn. drafting com. Conf. on Peace and Tolerance, Istanbul, 1994; chmn coordinating com. Conflict Resolution Conf., Vienna, 1995; election observer OSCE in Serbia, 1997; coord. Peace and Tolerance Conf. on Kosovo, Vienna, 1999; election observer Appeal of Conscience Found. in Russia, 1999. Sec. Appeal of Conscience Del. to Switzerland, 1997; dir. internat. programs Appeal Conscience Found; coord. Appeal of Conscience Found. Conf., Ohrid, Macedonia, 2003. With U.S. Army, 1952-54. Mem. Internat. Conf. and Seminar Assn. (pres.). Home: 880 5th Ave Apt Phe New York NY 10021-4951 E-mail: gme1@earthlink.net.

EISENSTADT, PAULINE DOREEN BAUMAN, investment company executive, state legislator; b. N.Y.C., Dec. 31, 1938; d. Morris and Anne (Lautenberg) Bauman; m. Melvin M. Eisenstadt, Nov. 20, 1960; children: Todd Alan, Keith Mark. BA, U. Fla., 1960; MS, U. Ariz., 1965; postgrad., U. N.Mex. Tchr., Ariz., 1961—65, 1972—73; adminstrv. asst. Inst. Social Rsch. U. N.Mex., 1973—74; founder, 1st exec. dir. Energy Consumers N.Mex., 1977—81; chmn. consumer affairs adv. com. Dept. Energy, 1979—80; v.p. tech. bd. Nat. Ctr. Appropriate Tech., 1980—; pres. Eisenstadt Enterprises, investments, 1983—; mem. N.Mex. Ho. of Reps., 1985—92, chairwoman majority caucus, chair rules com., 1987—, chair sub. com. on children and youth, 1987; mem. N.Mex. State Senate, 1996—2000; mem. senate fin. com., com. higher edn., com. econ. devel., sci. & tech., water & natural resources, electric deregulation com., chair conservation co; mem. senate fin. com., com. higher edn., com. econ. devel., sci. & tech., water & natural resources, electric deregulation com.; chair conservation com. Mem. exec. com., vice chair pvt. coun. Nat. Conf. State Legislators, 1987; vice chmn. Sandoval County (N.Mex.) Dem. Party, 1981—; mem. N.Mex. Dem. State Ctrl. Com., 1981—; N.Mex. del. Dem. Nat. Platform Com., 1984, Dem. Nat. Conv., 1984. Host (TV program) N.Mex. Today and Tomorrow, 1992—, exec. prodr., host Tech Talks, 2001—; author: Corrales, Portrait of a Changing Village, 1980. Pres. Anti Defamation League, N.Mex., 1994—95; mem. N.Mex. First; pres. Sandoval County Dem. Women's Assn., 1979—81, vice chmn. N.Mex. Dem. Platform Com., 1984—; mem. Sandoval County Redistricting Task Force, 1983—84, Rio Rancho Ednl. Study Com., 1984—. Recipient Gov.'s award Outstanding N. Mex. Women, Commn. on the Status of Women and Gov. Bruce King, 1992; grantee, NSF, 1965. Mem.: Rio Rancho Rotary Club (pres. 1995—, Rotarian of Yr. 1995), Kiwanis (1st woman mem. local club). Home: PO Box 658 Corrales NM 87048-0658 E-mail: peisenstad@aol.com.

EISENSTAT, THEODORE ELLIS, colon and rectal surgeon, educator; b. N.Y.C., Sept. 24, 1942; m. Sharon Diane Leonard, July, 1966; children: Maren Elise, Loren Aline. BA, Vanderbilt U., 1964; MD, N.Y. Med. Coll., 1968. Diplomate Am. Bd. Surgery, Am. Bd. Colon and Rectal Surgery, Nat. Bd. Med. Examiners. Rotating intern St. Vincent's Hosp., Worcester, Mass., 1968-69; resident in surgery Thomas Jefferson U. Hosp., Phila., 1969-71; chief resident in surgery Pa. Hosp., Phila., 1971-73, fellow in colon and rectal surgery Muhlenberg Hosp.-Robert Wood Johnson Sch. Medicine, N.J., 1977-78; dir. surg. endoscopy U. Md., 1975-80, dir. colon & rectal svc., 1976-80; asst. prof. surgery U. Md. Sch. Medicine, 1975-80; sr. attending surgeon Muhlenberg Regional Med. Ctr., Plainfield, N.J., 1979—, John F. Kennedy Med. Ctr., Edison, N.J., 1979—; clin. assoc. prof. surgery U. Medicine and Dentistry of N.J., Newark, 1981—, clin. prof. surgery Robert Wood Johnson Med. Sch. New Brunswick, N.J., 1979-91, clin. prof. surgery, 1991—, dir. colon and rectal residency program, 1993—. Cons. surgeon Lock Raven VA Hosp., Balt., 1975-80, U.S. Army, Kimbrough Army Hosp., Ft. Meade, Md., 1975-80; bd. dirs., ACS rep. Am. Bd. Colon and Rectal Surgery, 1990-96, pres., 1995-96; attending surgeon Robert Wood Johnson U. Hosp., New Brunswick, N.J., 1984—; exhibitor and presenter in field; vis. prof. U. Md. Sch. Medicine, 1983, Abington (Pa.) Meml. Hosp., 1985, York (Pa.) Hosp., 1990, Pa. Hosp., Phila., 1990, others. Contbr. articles to profl. jours. Maj. U.S. Army, 1973-75. Fellow ACS (adv. coun. colon and rectal surgery), Am. Soc. Colon and Rectal Surgeons (Walter A. Fansler award 1977, Purdue Frederick fellow 1977, 1st prize sci. exhibit 1979); mem. AMA, Soc. for Surgery of Alimentary Tract, Assn. for Acad. Surgery, Soc. Am. Gastrointestinal Endoscopic Surgeons (founder 1981, bd. govs. 1986-89), Am. Soc. Gastrointestinal Endoscopy, N.Y. Soc. Colon and Rectal Surgeons (mem. coun. 1983-85, sec.-treas. 1986-87, v.p. 1988-89, pres. 1990-92, 1st prize film 1978), Pa. Soc. Colon. and Rectal Surgeons, N.J. Soc. Colon and Rectal Surgeons (sec.-treas. 1983-85, pres. 1989-90), N.J. Soc. Gastroenterology, N.J. Soc. Gastrointestinal Endoscopy, Assn. Mil. Surgeons U.S., Soc. Surgeons N.J., Crohn's and Colitis Found. Am.

EISENSTEIN, ELIZABETH LEWISOHN, historian, educator; b. N.Y.C., Oct. 11, 1923; d. Sam A. and Margaret V. (Seligman) Lewisohn; m. Julian Calvert Eisenstein, May 30, 1948; children: Margaret, John (dec.), Edward. AB, Vassar Coll., 1944; MA, Radcliffe Coll., 1947, PhD, 1953; LittD (hon.), Mt. Holyoke Coll., 1979. From lectr. to adj. prof history Am. U., Washington, 1959-74; Alice Freeman Palmer prof. history U. Mich., Ann Arbor, 1975-88, prof. emerita, 1988—. Scholar-in-residence Rockefeller Found. Ctr., Bellagio, Italy, June 1977; mem. vis. com. dept. history Harvard U., 1975-81, vice-chmn., 1979-81; dir. Ecole des Hautes Etudes en Sciences Sociales, Paris, 1982; guest spkr., participant confs. and seminars; I. Beam vis. prof. U. Iowa, 1980; Mead-Swing lectr. Oberlin Coll., 1980; Stone lectr. U. Glasgow, 1984; Van Leer lectr. Van Leer Fedn., Jerusalem, 1984; Hanes lectr. U. N.C., Chapel Hill, 1985 first resident cons. Ctr. for the Book, Libr. of Congress, Washington, 1979; mem. Coun. Scholars, 1980-88; pres.'s disting. visitor Vassar Coll., 1988; Pforzheimer lectr. N.Y. Pub. Libr., 1989, Lyell lectr. Bodleian Libr., Oxford, 1990, Merle Curti lectr. U. Wis., Madison, 1992, Jantz lectr. Oberlin Coll., 1995, Clifford lectr. Austin, Tex., 1996; vis. fellow Wolfson Coll., Oxford, 1990; sem. dir. Folger Inst., 1999. Author: The First Professional Revolutionist: F. M. Buonarroti, 1959, The Printing Press as an Agent of Change, 1979, 2 vols. paperback edit., 1980 (Phi Beta Kappa Ralph Waldo Emerson prize 1980), The Printing Revolution in Early Modern Europe, 1983 (reissued as Canto Book, 1993), Grub Street Abroad, 1992; mem. editorial bd. Jour. Modern History, 1973-76, 83-86, Revs. in European History, 1973-86, Jour. Library History, 1979-82, Eighteenth Century Studies, 1981-84; contbr. articles to profl. jours., chpts. to books. Bd. dirs. Folger Shakespeare Libr., 2000—. Belle Skinner fellow Vassar Coll., NEH fellow, 1977, Guggenheim fellow, 1982, fellow Ctr. Advanced Studies in Behavioral Scis., 1982-83, 92-93, Humanities Rsch. Ctr. fellow Australian Nat. U., 1988. Fellow Am. Acad. Arts and Scis., Royal Hist. Soc.; mem. Soc. French Hist. Studies (v.p. 1970, program com. 1974), Am. Soc. 18th Century Studies (nominating com. 1971), Soc. 16th Century Studies, Am. Hist. Assn. (com. on coms. 1970-72, chmn. Modern European sect. 1981, coun. 1982-85, Scholarly Distinction award 2003), Renaissance Soc. Am. (coun. 1973-76, pres. 1986), Am. Antiquarian Soc. (exec. com., adv. bd. 1984-87), Phi Beta Kappa. Office: U Mich Dept History Ann Arbor MI 48109 E-mail: eisenst@mindspring.com.

EISENSTEIN, HESTER, sociology educator; b. N.Y.C., Oct. 14, 1940; d. Myron and Ruth (Richards) E.; m. Michael David Tanzer; stepchildren: David, Kenneth J., Charles. BA, Harvard U., 1961; MA, Yale U., 1962, PhD, 1967. Instr., asst. prof. Yale U., New Haven, 1966-70; coord. exptl. studies program Barnard Coll., Columbia U., 1970-80; sr. officer, assoc. dir. Equal Opportunity in Pub. Employment, Sydney, Australia, 1980-86; leader EEO unit Dept. Edn.,

Sydney, 1986-88; vis. prof. SUNY, Buffalo, 1988-90, prof. Am. studies, 1990-96; prof. Sociology Queens Coll., Grad. Sch. & Univ. Ctr. CUNY, 1996—, dir. women's studies Queens Coll., 1996-2000. Author: Contemporary Feminist Thought, 1983, Gender Shock, 1991, Inside Agitators: Australian Femocrats and the State, 1996. Office: The Grad CtrCUNY PhD Program in Sociology 365 Fifth Ave New York NY 10016

EISENSTEIN, SAM, pediatric dentist; b. Montreal, Que., Can., Jan. 12, 1936; came to U.S., 1964; s. Isaac and Eva (Katz) Eisenstein; children: Sandra Toby, Lana Rachel, Jeffrey Joshua. BSc, Sir George Williams Coll., 1957; MSc, McGill U., 1959, PhD, 1963; DMD cum laude, Tufts U., 1973. Rsch. asst. Royal Victoria Hosp., Montreal, 1962-64; postdoctoral trainee Wistar Inst., Phila., 1964-65; rsch. assoc. Albert Einstein Med. Ctr., Phila., 1965-66, Variety Children's Rsch. Found., Miami, Fla., 1966-69; dental resident Children's Hosp., Boston, 1973-75; pediatric dentistry fellow Harvard U. Sch. Dental Medicine, 1974-75; pvt. practice pediatric dentistry South Weymouth, Mass., 1975-81, Miami, 1981—; clin. asst. in pedodontics Boston Children's Hosp., 1976-80; clin. instr. Harvard Sch. Dental Medicine, Boston, 1978-80, Tufts Sch. Dental Medicine, Boston, 1980-81; mem. attending staff Miami Children's Hosp., 1982—. Mem. ADA, Am. Soc. Dentistry for Children (cert. of merit 1973), Am. Acad. Pediatric Dentistry, Sigma Xi, Alpha Omega Delta, Omicron Kappa Epsilon, Dental Hon. Soc. Jewish. Avocations: photography, model railroading, stamp collecting. Home: 203 Dunwoody Lane Hollywood FL 33021-2907 Office: 12333 NW 18th St Ste 4 Pembroke Pines FL 33026-4386 E-mail: sameisenstein@cs.com.

EISENSTEIN, TOBY K. microbiology educator; b. Phila., Sept. 15, 1942; d. Edward and Sylvia (Mandel) Karet; m. Bruce A. Eisenstein, Sept. 8, 1963; children: Eric, Andrew, Ilana. BA, Wellesley Coll., 1964; PhD, Bryn Mawr Coll., 1969. Instr. Med. Sch. Temple U., Phila., 1969-71, asst. prof., 1971-79, assoc. prof. microbiology and immunology Med. Sch., 1979-84, prof., 1984—, acting chair, 1990-92, co-dir. Ctr. Substance Abuse Rsch., 1992—. Mem. bacteriology and mycology study sect., NIH, 1976-80, 88-92, Drugs of Abuse and AIDS study sect., 1994—. Contbr. articles to profl. jours. NIH fellow, 1965-69; USPHS grantee, 1971—, Fellow Am. Acad. Microbiology; mem. AAAS, Am. Soc. Microbiology (pres. Ea. Pa. br. 1982-86, coun. policy com. 1993-96, chair membership bd. 2003—), Am. Assn. Immunologists, Soc. Leukocyte Biology (sec. 1998-2000), Internat. Endotoxin Soc., Soc. Neuroimmune Pharmacology (Jospeh Wybran award), Psychoneuroimmunology Rsch. Soc., Coll. on Problems of Drug Dependence, Sigma Xi, (pres. Temple U. chpt. 1981-83). Office: Temple U Sch Medicine Dept Microbiology and Immunology 3400 N Broad St Philadelphia PA 19140-5104

EISENTHAL, KENNETH B. physical chemistry educator; b. N.Y.C., Mar. 23, 1933; s. Benjamin and Sarah (Schafer) E.; children: Julia, Jessica, Andrew. BS, Bklyn. Coll., 1954; MA, Harvard U., 1957, PhD, 1959. NIH postdoctoral fellow UCLA, 1959-61; rsch. scientist Aerospace Corp., El Segundo, Calif., 1961-63; rsch. assoc. UCLA, 1963-64; rsch. scientist, head of phys. scis IBM, San Jose, Calif., 1964-75; prof. Columbia U., N.Y.C., 1975—, chair dept. chemistry, 1996—. Cons. IBM, Yorktown Heights, N.Y., 1985—. Author (editor): Picosecond Phenomena, 1982, Ultrafast Phenomena IV, 1984, Picosecond Specification to Chemistry, 1984; contbr. ; mem. editl. adv. bd. Chem. Physics Letters, 1987—, Jour. Chem. Physics, 1985—87, Laser Chemistry, 1985—, Jour. Phys. Chemistry, 1980—83, Molecular Physics, 1992, Chem. Phys. Chemistryy, 2001. Guggenheim fellow, 1984-85; recipient Bryce Crawford award in Spectroscopy, 1995' Oxford U. Hinshelwood lectr., 1996. Fellow Am. Phys. .Soc. (chmn. div. chem. physics 1993); mem. Am. Chem. Soc. (Arthur W. Adamson award 1998), Nat. Acad. Scis., Phi Beta Kappa, Sigma Xi. Jewish. Avocations: reading, handball, biking. Office: Dept Chemistry Columbia Univ 3000 Broadway Mail Code 3107 New York NY 10027

EISER, ARNOLD ROBERT, internist, bioethicist, nephrologist; b. Newark, N.Y., Jan. 2, 1949; s. Harold H. and Anne Eiser; m. Barbara Joyce Andrews, June 15, 1975; 1 child, Arielle Veronica. BA magna cum laude, U. Pa., 1970; MD, Northwestern U., 1974. Intern Pa. Hosp., 1974-75; resident Med. Coll. Pa., 1975-77; fellow Hahnemann U., 1977-79; nephrologist Elmhurst (N.Y.) Hosp. Ctr., 1979-95, assoc. chief nephrology, 1993-95, dir. ambulatory care, 1995-97, dir. med. residency program, 1996-97; chief sect. gen. internal medicine U. Ill., Chgo., 1997—, prof. medicine, 1997—. Assoc. prof. medicine Mt. Sinai Sch. Medicine, N.Y.C., 1986-97; adj. assoc. Hastings Ctr., Briarcliff Manor, N.Y., 1994-98. Contbg. author: The Kidney in Collagen Vascular Diseases, 1993, Violence Against Women: Philosophical Perspective, 1998; contbr. articles to profl. jours. Fellow: ACP, Inst. Medicine Chgo. (pres.-elect Chgo. clin. ethics program, sec., treas.); mem.: AMA, Soc. Gen. Internal Medicine, Coll. Physician Execs. Avocations: travel, jogging. Office: MC 718 840 S Wood St Chicago IL 60612-7317 Fax: 312-413-8283. E-mail: aeiser@uic.edu.

EISERER, LEONARD ALBERT CARL, publishing executive; b. Polar, Wis., June 3, 1916; s. Herman Frederick and Anna Elizabeth (Schnieder) E.; m. Lorraine Elizabeth Hickey, June 28, 1941; children: Carol Jean, Elaine Roberta, Leonard Arnold, Beverly Arlene. BA, Roosevelt U., Chgo., 1937; MS in Journalism, Northwestern U., 1939. Editor Am. Aviation Publs., Inc., Washington, 1939-51, v.p., gen. mgr., 1952-57, exec. v.p., sec., 1958-62; pres., pub. Sports Age, Inc., Washington, 1962-63; chmn., CEO Bus. Pubs., Inc., Silver Spring, Md., 1963—. Chmn. Carol Jean Cancer Found., Inc.; bd. dirs. U. N.C. at Greensboro Excellence Found.; pres., dir. Eiserer-Hickey Found., Inc.; dir. Univ. Club of Washington Found. Lt. USN, 1942-46. Named to Hall of Fame Newsletter Pubs. Found., 1994, Man of Yr. Univ. Club of Washington, 1995; inductee Hall of Achievement, Northwestern U. Medill Sch. Journalism, 1997. Mem. Air and Waste Mgmt. Assn., Water Environ. Fedn., Soc. Profl. Journalists, Nat. Press Club, Univ. Club, Newsletter Pubs. Assn. Home: 9101 Sligo Creek Pky Silver Spring MD 20901-3360 Office: Bus Pubs Inc 8737 Colesville Rd Silver Spring MD 20910-4400

EISERT, EDWARD GAVER, lawyer; b. N.Y.C., May 26, 1948; s. Israel Jay and Bess (Gaver) E.; div.; children: Carolyn B., Stephen J. AB, Cornell U., 1969; JD, NYU, 1973. Bar: N.Y. 1974. Law clk. to Judge Charles L. Brieant U.S. Dist. Ct. (so. dist.) N.Y., N.Y.C., 1973-74; assoc. Simpson Thacher & Bartlett, N.Y.C., 1974-76, Schulte Roth & Zabel, N.Y.C., 1976-80, ptnr., 1981—2002; sr. v.p., gen. corp. counsel Fiduciary Trust Co. Internat., N.Y.C., 2002—. Bd. dirs. N.Y. Small Bus. Venture Fund LLC., 1998—. Note and comment editor NYU Law Rev., 1972-73. Mem. ABA (com. on fed. regulation of securities 1983—, subcom. on ann. rev. fed. regulation of securities 1983-89, subcom. on mcpl. and govtl. obligations 1984-92, subcom. on investment cos. and investment advisors 1992—), Internat. Bar Assn., N.Y. Stat Bar Assn., Assn. Bar City N.Y., Univ. Club N.Y.C. Home: 302 Church St White Plains NY 10603-3525 Office: Fiduciary Trust Co International 600 Fifth Avenue New York NY 10020

EISLER, MILLARD MARCUS, financial executive; b. Toledo, Ohio, Mar. 31, 1950; s. Joseph R. and Marilynn (Gross) E. BS, Ind. U., 1972; MBA, Cornell U., 1977. CPA, Ill., Mass., N.H. Auditor Arthur Andersen & Co., Boston, 1977-79; mgr. internat. acctg. Wheelabrator-Frye, Inc., Hampton, N.H., 1979-81; mgr. ops. analysis and audit GCA Corp., Bedford, Mass., 1981-85; mgr. cost acctg. and fin. analysis Precision Sci., Inc., Chgo., 1985-86, contr., chief fin. officer, 1986-89; tax preparer H&R Block, Inc., Chgo., 1989-92, Lincoln, Nebr., 1993, quality control mgr., 1994, franchise dir., dist. mgr. Madison, Wis., 1994-98; tax preparer H.R. Block, Madison, Wis., 1999—; fin. mgmt. cons. CUNA Mutual Group, Madison, 1998—. Bd. dirs. Franklin Software Co., Arvada, Colo.; lectr. Northeastern Ill. U., Chgo., 1986-88. Mem. Ind. U. Alumni Assn., Cornell U. Alumni Assn. of Wis. Democrat. Jewish. Home: 834 S Gammon Rd Madison WI 53719-1381 Office: CUNA Mutual Group 5910 Mineral Point Rd Madison WI 53705-4498

EISLER, ROBERT DAVID, engineer; b. N.Y.C., June 7, 1952; s. Leo and Lillian (Gottlieb) E.; m. Fern Robin Eisler, Aug. 1, 1982; children: Lee William, Neal Alan. BA, Colgate U., 1974; BS, Columbia U., 1980, MS, 1981, profl. engrng. degree, 1982; MBA, UCLA, 1998; Postgrad. Cert. in Med. Product Devel., U. Calif., Irvine, 2001. Cert. engr., N.Y. Respiratory therapist Norwalk (Conn.) Hosp., 1970-76; pres., gen. mgr. Fillow Flower Co., Inc., Westport, Conn., 1976-78; biomed. rsch. assoc. Norwalk (Conn.) Hosp., 1978-80; rsch. assoc. Columbia U. Guggenheim Inst. for Flight Structures, N.Y.C., 1980-82, Argonne Nat. Lab., Idaho Falls, 1980; program mgr., prin. investigator McDonnell Douglas Astronautics Co., Huntington Beach, Calif., 1982-85; leader applied mechanics and material scis. group Mission Rsch. Corp., Laguna Hills, Calif., 1985—. U.S. del. to NATO for close combat ops.; mem. Joint Army Navy NASA Air Force Com. Design and Analysis of Composite Rocket Motor Cases. Contbr. articles to profl. jours. Recipient McDonnell Douglas Corp. award for contbns. to the Strategic Def. Initiative, 1982; Dept. of Energy fellow Argonne Nat. Lab., 1980. Mem. AIAA (sr.), ASME (exec. com. 1983-86), Soc. Advancement of Materials and Process Engrng., Materials Rsch. Soc., Internat. Assn. Wound Ballistics, Mil. Ops. Rsch. Soc.

EISMA, JOSE A. physician; b. Jolo, Sulu, Phillipines, Oct. 18, 1939; came to U.S., 1964, naturalized, 1973; s. Marcelo L. and Rosa A. (Albarracin) E.; m. Lenora Womack, Sept. 14, 1977; children: Joseph Alan, John Mitchell, Gregory Mitchell, Teresa Lyn, Lorell Elizabeth, Julia Dawn. AA, Silliman U., Philippines, 1958; MD, U. Santo Tomas (Manila), 1963. Diplomate Am. Bd. Family Practice. Rotating intern Wilson Meml. Hosp., Johnson City, N.Y., 1964-65, med. resident, 1965-67, Kingsbrook Jewish Med. Ctr., Bklyn., 1967-68; gen. internist Reynolds Army Hosp., Ft. Sill, Okla., 1971-73; resident in pulmonary disease Brooke Army Med. Ctr., Ft. Sam Houston, Tex., 1973-74; chief of medicine, med. dir. respiratory therapy dept. West (Tex.) Cmty. Hosp., 1976—2001; bd. dirs. West (Tex.) Community Hosp., 1986. Bd. dirs. West Hosp. Auth., 1986—. Contbr. article to profl. publ. in field. Served to col. M.C., 1975-2000, Army N.G.; surgeon Army N.G. State, 1991-93. Fellow Am. Acad. Family Physicians; mem. A.C.P., Res. Officers Assn., Tex. N.G. Assn., Assn. U.S. Army, Assn. Mil. Surgeons of U.S. Home: 1406 N Reagan St West TX 76691-1022 Office: 401 Meadow Dr West TX 76691-1033

EISMAN, AUDREY WALDO, psychologist; b. Phila., Sept. 2, 1934; d. Irving and Claire Brockmon Waldo; m. Larry Eisman, July 25, 1953; children: Dayl Gibson, Robin Peterse. BS in Mental Health Tech., Hahneman U., 1975; MEd in Counseling Psychology, Temple U., 1981. Lic. psychologist Pa., cert. Nat. Bd. Cert. Counselors, Nat. Bd. Geriatric Counselors. Activities therapist Phila. Geriatric Ctr., 1975—76; mental health technologist Hahnemann U./JFK CMH/MR, Phila., 1976—80; mental health worker Consortium CMH/MR, Phila., 1980—82; psychologist CATCH CMH/MR, Phila., 1982—99, Einstein, Phila., 2001—02, Care Connection, Phila., 2002—. Editor: (poetry publ.) The Phila. Poetry and Literary Forum, 2002, author poetry. Mem.: Phila. Soc. for Clin. Hypnosis, Am. Soc. for Clin. Hypnosis. Avocations: art, crafts, swimming, writing, poetry. Home: 8106 Cadwalader Ave Elkins Park PA 19027

EISMANN, DANIEL T. state supreme court justice; b. Eugene, Oreg. m. Sheila Wood, 1982; 1 child, Matthew stepchildren: Catherine Richardson, Christine Putz. Grad. cum laude, U. Idaho, 1976. Magistrate judge Owyheee County, 1986—95; dist. judge Fourth Jud. Dist., 1995—98; adminstrv. dist. judge Id. State Supreme Ct., Boise, 1998—2000, Supreme Ct. justice, 2001—. Mem. Ada County Domestic Violence Task Force, Region III Coun. for Children and Youth; judge Ada County Drug Ct. With USAR. Decorated 2 Purple Hearts. Mem.: Inns of Ct. (Boise Chpt.), Id. Bar Assn. (mem. Bar Exam Preparation Com.). Office: Supreme Ct PO Box 83720 Boise ID 83720*

EISNER, ALAN BRADLEY, entrepreneur; b. Chgo., June 29, 1967; s. Marvin M. and Gail A. (Leon) E.; m. Helaine Korn, 1995. BS, Cornell U., 1989, M Engrng., 1992; PhD, NYU, 1997. Sys. analyst Mobil Oil Corp., Valley Forge, Pa., 1989-90; engr. United Techs. Carrier, Syracuse, N.Y., 1990-92; cons. Health Plus of Mich., Flint, 1992; investor Eisner Investments, N.Y.C., 1993—; prin. Hydra Techs., N.Y.C., 1994-95; asst. prof. Lubin Sch. Bus. Pace U., N.Y.C., 1997—2002, assoc. prof. grad. program, mgmt. chair Lubin Sch. Bus., 2003—. Advisor NSF project Edgar on the Internet, N.Y.C., 1994; cons. in field. Author various conf. presentations; contbr. articles to profl. jours. M Engrng. fellow United Techs., Syracuse, 1990-92, doctoral fellow NYU, N.Y.C., 1992-97. Mem. Acad. Mgmt., Inst. Mgmt. Sci., Strategic Mgmt. Soc., Inst. Indsl. Engrs. Avocations: raquetball, internet surfing. Office: 1 Martine Ave White Plains NY 10606

EISNER, ALVIN, optics scientist; b. Bklyn., Sept. 20, 1950; s. Nathan and Anne Eisner; m. Carla Jean Burmeister, Mar. 5, 1994; 1 child, Brian. BS in Math. summa cum laude, SUNY, Stony Brook, 1972; MA in Math., U. Calif., La Jolla, 1975, MA in Psychology, 1976, PhD in Psychology, 1979. Postdoctoral fellow U. of Fla., Gainseville, U. of Calif., Berkeley and San Francisco, 1980—81, U. of Chgo., 1981—82; from asst. to assoc. scientist Legacy Health Sys./Good Samaritan Hosp., Portland, Oreg., 1982—98; assoc. scientist Oreg. Health & Sci. U., Beaverton, 1998—. Advisor carotenoids in age-related eye disease study U. of Wis., Madison, 2000—02; grant reviewer NIH, Besthesda, MD. Mem. editl. bd.: Jour. Glaucoma, 1991—94; contbr. articles to profl. jours. Grantee, Nat. Eye Inst., 1984—96, 1999—, Oreg. Cancer Ctr., 1999—2000. Mem.: AAAS, Optical Soc. Am., Assn. for Rsch. in Vision and Ophthalmology (Travel grantee 1978). Avocations: swimming, bicycling, hiking, photography, reading. Office: Oregon Health & Sci U 505 NW 185 Ave Beaverton OR 97006 Office Fax: 503-418-2501. Business E-Mail: eisnera@ohsu.edu.

EISNER, CAROLE SWID, artist; b. N.Y.C., Oct. 30, 1937; d. David and Selma (Claar) Swid; m. Richard Alan Eisner, May 7, 1961; children: Joseph, Susan, Michael, Douglas, Hallie. AB, Syracuse U., 1958; studies with Schwabacher, N.Y.C., 1963; studies with Marge Walzer, Westport, Conn., 1969-78; postgrad., Internat. Sch. Photography, 1976-78. Solo shows include Silvermine (Conn.) Ctr. for Arts, 1977, 84, Lubin House Gallery, N.Y.C., 1979, 82, Segal Gallery, N.Y.C., 1984-85, 86, Jill Youngblood Gallery, L.A., 1985, Jack Gallery, N.Y.C., 1987, 88, First Women's Bank, N.Y.C., 1988, New Inst. of Contemporary Art, London, 1988, David Findlay Galleries, N.Y.C., 1990, Gallery Tanishima, Tokyo, 1992, Gallery Sagan, Tokyo, 1992; group shows include Segal Gallery, N.Y.C., 1985, 86, Guggenheim Mus., N.Y.C., 1986, Images Gallery, Norwalk, Conn., 1986, Jack Gallery, N.Y.C., 1987, Inst. of Contemporary Art, London, 1988, many others; represented in permanent collections at Guggenheim Mus., Syracuse U., Nat. Assocs., Inc., S.E. Banking Corp., Northstar Reins. Co., Knoll Internat., FMC Corp., Skadden, Arps, Meager & Flom, Orion Bank, Ltd., Goldmark Ptnrs., Inc., MBS Multi Mode, Inc., Bill Silver Assocs.; sculptures exhibited at The River Park Atrium, Norwalk, Conn., 1997-98, Chesterwood, Stockbridge, Mass., 1998, Burlington County Coll. Sculpture Garden, Pemberton, N.J., 1998, Veterans Park, Norwalk, 1999, Peninsula Park, Jersey City, 1999, Cranbury Park, Norwalk, 1999, City Hall, Norwalk, 1998-99, Fordham U., 2000, Lock Bldg., Norwalk, 2001, Heritage Park, Norwalk, 2002, Silvermine Guild, Norwalk; created stage design for four Off-Broadway plays at Theater XII, 1978. Recipient Award for Sculpture Merchants Bank and Trust Co., 1975, Champion Internat. Corp., 1980, Rosenthal Award for Outdoor Sculpture, 1978; named among ten outstanding young women Mademoiselle Mag., 1962; finalist Nat. Sculpture Competition, 1980. Home and Office: 1107 5th Ave New York NY 10128-0145 Fax: 212-828-4415.

EISNER, DAVID GEORGE, retired surgeon; b. N.Y.C., Sept. 22, 1912; s. Adolph and Regina (Freier) E. AB, Case Western Res. U., 1934, MD, 1937. Diplomate Am. Bd. Surgery. Intern Cleve. City Hosp., 1937-38, resident in surgery, 1939-40, Madigan Gen. Hosp., Tacoma, 1947-48, Brooke Gen. Hosp., San Antonio, 1948-49; fellow thoracic surgery Letterman Gen. Hosp., San Francisco, 1950—51; fellow in surgery Tripler Gen. Hosp., Honolulu; pvt. practice surgery. Clin. dir. surgery R.E. Thomason Gen. Hosp., El Paso, Tex., 1971-74; assoc. prof. surgery Tex. Tech. Health Scis. Ctr., El Paso, 1974-76, adj. prof. surgery, 1976-88, clin. prof. surgery, 1988-2000. With M.C., U. S. Army, 1940-71. Fellow ACS; mem. AMA, Tex. Med. Assn., El Paso County Med. Soc. Jewish. Address: Apt A11 252 Shadow Mountain Dr El Paso TX 79912-4720

EISNER, DIANA, pediatrician; b. Houston, May 7, 1951; d. Elmer and Edith (Dubow) E. BA in Biology cum laude, Brandeis U., 1973; MD, Southwestern Med. Sch., 1977. Diplomate Am. Bd. Pediatrics. Intern, resident Baylor Coll. Medicine, Houston, 1977-80; pvt. practice Houston, 1981—. Chmn. dept. pediat. Meml. N.W. Hosp., Houston, 1990. Recipient Commendation award Children's Protection Com. Tex. Children's Hosp., 1978, Physician's Recognition award AMA, 1983. Mem. Am. Acad. Pediatrics, Tex. Med. Assn., Tex. Pediatric Soc., Houston Pediatric Soc. (treas. 2001-02, sec. 2002-), Harris County Med. Soc. Avocations: ballet, swimming, walking. Office: 2030 North Loop W Ste 125 Houston TX 77018-8132

EISNER, ELEANOR, social worker; b. Keokuk, Iowa, Dec. 1, 1928; d. Curtis W. and Marie Andrea (Johnson) Wiberg; m. Henry Eisner, Aug. 13, 1958; children: Benjamin, Elizabeth. BA, U. Nebr., 1950; MS, Smith Coll., 1953. Caseworker, guidance counselor Child Study Inst. Bryn Mawr Coll., Bryn Mawr, Pa., 1980-85; coord. day care for frail elderly INTERAC, Phila., 1985-86; Preferred Alternative Treatment Homes coord. Children's Aid Soc., Norristown, Pa., 1986-94; behavior specialist/therapist Ctrl. MH/MR, Norristown, Pa., 1994-96.

EISNER, GAIL ANN, artist, educator; b. Detroit, Oct. 17, 1939; d. Rudolph and Florence (White) Leon; m. Marvin Michael Eisner, June 14, 1959 (dec. Feb. 1993); 1 child, Alan. Student, Art Student League of N.Y.; BFA, Wayne State U. Alan prof. Pace U., N.Y.C. (one-woman shows) The Starkweather Art Cultural Ctr., Romeo, Mich., Shiawassee Arts Ctr., Owosso, Mich., Worthington Art Ctr., Ohio, OK Harris/David Klein Gallery, Birmingham, Mich., Sinclair Coll., LRC Gallery, Dayton, Ohio, U. Mich. Hosps., Ann Arbor, Collin County Coll., Plano, Tex., 1997, Art Ctr. Mt. Clemens, (group shows) Islip Art Mus., East Islip, N.Y., Columbia (Mo.) Coll., Tubac (Ariz.) Ctr. of Arts, Ft. Wayne (Ind.) Mus. of Art, C.W. Post Coll., Brookville, N.Y., NAWA, Jacob K. Kavits Ctr., N.Y.C., Schoharie County Coun. of Arts, Cobbleskill, N.Y., ARC Gallery, Chgo., McPherson (Kans.) Coll., Med. Coll. Ga., Augusta, Heckscher Mus. Art, Huntington, Nassau County Mus. Art, Roslyn, N.Y., Guild Hall, East Hampton, N.Y., Castle Gould, Sands Point, N.Y., Pastel Soc. Am., N.Y.C., Carrier Found., Belle Meade, N.J., Hill Country Arts Found., Ingram, Tex., Cunningham Meml. Art Gallery, Bakersfield, Calif., Henry Hicks Gallery, Bklyn. Hts., U. N.D., Grand Forks, Nassau C.C., Garden City, N.Y., Trenton (N.J.) State Coll., Wenatchee Valley (W.Va.) Coll., Del Mar Coll., Corpus Christi, Tex., Minot (N.D.) State U., Ctrl. Mo. State U., McNeese State U., Lake Charles, La., Worthington Art Ctr., Ohio, Art Ctr., Mt. Clemens, Mich., Oakland C.C., Krasl Art Ctr., St. Joseph, Mich., Fontana Concert Soc., Kalamazoo, Mich., Art Ctr. Battle Creek, Mich., Ctrl. Mich. U., Mt. Pleasant, Birmingham (Mich.) Bloomfield Art Assn., Cmty. House, Birmingham, Sch. Art Inst., Chgo., Cheekwood Mus. Art, Nashville, Grand Rapids (Mich.) Mus. Art, Flint (Mich.) Inst. Arts, Ariana Gallery, Royal Oak, Mich., Judith Paul Gallery, Medford, Oreg., The Art Collector, San Diego, Gwenda Jay Gallery, Chgo., Columbia Greens Coll., Hudson, N.Y., Worthington (Ohio) Art Ctr., Holland Area Arts Coun., Mich., The Art Source, Santa Barbara, Calif., Outside The Line Gallery, Grosse Ile, Mich., (permanent collections) Rabobank, Chgo., Resurrection Hosp., Kauai (Hawaii) Hotel, Jules Joyner Designs, Royal Oak, Mich., The Lumber Store, Chgo., others, (also pvt. collections). Recipient Adriana Zahn award Pastel Soc. Am., Heckscher Mus. award, Our Visions: Women in Art award Oakland C.C., 1995, Beatrice G. Epstein meml. award, 1997. Mem. Nat. Assn. Women Artists (Sara Winston Meml. award 1992), N.Y. Artist Equity Assn., Art Student League N.Y. (Sidney Dickinson Meml. award), Birmingham Bloomfield Art Assn. Studio: Ste 108 27600 Farmington Rd Farmington Hills MI 48334-3365

EISNER, HENRY WOLFGANG, advertising agency executive; b. July 3, 1920; came to U.S., 1940, naturalized, 1943; s. Walter M. and Elsa J. Eisner; m. Harriet Sauber, July 11, 1943; children: Nancy, Steve C. Student, U. Zurich, 1938-39, London Poly. U., 1939-40, Georgetown U., 1943, Johns Hopkins U., 1946-49. Editor European story dept. 20th Century Fox, 1939; copywriter Balt. News Am., 1940-42; prodn. mgr. S.A. Levyne Co., Balt., 1946-48, copywriter, 1948-52, account mgmt. supr., 1952-60, exec. v.p., 1960-65; pres. Eisner Comms., Balt., 1965-85, chmn., 1986—91, chmn. emeritus, 1991—. Bd. dirs. The Associated Jewish Cmty. Fedn. Balt.; trustee, mem. sr. adv. coun. Park Sch., Jewish Family Svcs.; chmn. Levering Hall adv. com. Johns Hopkins U.; mktg. adv. dept. cardiology, John Hopkins. Mem. Am. Assn. Advt. Agys., Suburban Club of Baltimore County (pres.). Home: 3623 Anton Farms Rd Baltimore MD 21208-1705 Office: Eisner Comms 509 S Exeter St Baltimore MD 21202-4344 E-mail: Hwolfgange@aol.com.

EISNER, HOWARD, engineering educator, engineering executive; b. N.Y.C., Aug. 8, 1935; s. Samuel Eisner and Mary Wegodner; m. Joan Arlene Knopfer, Feb. 9, 1957(div. 1994); children: Seth Eric, Susan Rachel, Oren David; m. June B. Linowitz, Nov. 8, 1995. BEE, CCNY, 1957; MS, Columbia U., 1958; DSc, George Washington U., 1966. Teaching asst. Columbia U., 1957; lectr. dept. physics Bklyn. Coll., 1957-59; lectr., asst. professorial lectr. George Washington U., 1961-67; prof. U. Maryland, 1987-89; various engring. positions ORI, Inc., Rockville, Md., 1959-68, v.p., 1968-71, exec. v.p., 1971-84, corp. exec. v.p., 1984-85, also dir.; pres. Intercon Systems Corp. subs. ORI, Group, Inc., Rockville, 1985-89, Atlantic Research Services Corp., Alexandria, Va., 1987-89; Disting. rsch. prof. George Washington U., Washington, 1989—. Author: Advanced Algebra, 1960, Computer-Aided Systems Engineering, 1988, Essentials of Project and Systems Engineering Management, 1997, Reengineering Yourself and Your Company: From Engineer to Manager to Leader, 2000; contbr. articles in field. Fellow IEEE, N.Y. Acad. Scis.; mem. AIAA, INFORMS, Sigma Xi, Tau Beta Pi, Eta Kappa Nu, Omega Rho. Avocations: personal computers, tennis, choral singing, writing. Office: George Washington U Rm 157 SEAS-EMSE 1776 G St NW Washington DC 20052 E-mail: heisner@seas.gwu.edu.

EISNER, LAWRENCE BRAND, lawyer, real estate developer; b. New Haven, Sept. 27, 1951; s. Robert Raphael and Anita Stanton (Brand) E.; m. Anne Levine, Apr. 16, 2000; children: Benjamin, Anna, Julia. B.A., Union Coll., 1973; J.D., Georgetown U., 1976. Bar: Conn. 1976, D.C. 1978, Mass. 1982. Atty., adviser Commodity Futures Trading Commn., Washington, 1977-79; treas. Continental Lumber Co., West Haven, Conn., 1979-85; pres. Eisner Devel. Group, Hamden, Conn., 1985—. Mem. Conn. Bar Assn., D.C. Bar Assn., Phi Beta Kappa. Democrat. Jewish. Home: 44 Valley Rd Bethany CT 06524-3410 Office: Corp Counsel HSS Inc 2321 Whitney Ave Hamden CT 06518

EISNER, MICHAEL DAMMANN, entertainment company executive; b. Mt. Kisco, N.Y., Mar. 7, 1942; s. Lester and Margaret (Dammann) E.; m. Jane Breckenridge; children: Breck, Eric, Anders. BA, Denison U., 1964. Began career in programming dept. CBS; asst. to nat. programming dir. ABC, 1966-68, mgr. spls. and talent, dir. program devel.-East Coast, 1968-71, dir. program devel. East Coast, 1968-71, dir. feature films and program devel., 1969, v.p. daytime programming, 1971-75, v.p. program planning and devel., 1975-76, sr. v.p. prime time prodn. and devel., 1976; pres., chief operating officer Paramount Pictures, 1976-84; chmn., CEO Walt Disney Co., Burbank, Calif., 1984—; founder The Eisner Found. Governor Mighty Ducks of Anaheim, 1993; mem. bus. steering com. Global Business Dialogue on Electronic Commerce. Author: (book) Work in Progress. Trustee Denison U., Calif. Inst. Arts; bd. dirs. Am. Hosp. of Paris Found., UCLA Exec. Bd. for Med. Sci. Office: Walt Disney Co 500 S Buena Vista St Burbank CA 91521-0006*

EISNER, PETER NORMAN, journalist, author, news agency executive; b. Jersey City, Aug. 27, 1950; s. Bernard and Lorraine (Gropper) Eisner; m. Musha Salinas, Aug. 27, 1981; children: Isabel, Marina. BA, Rutgers U., 1972. Reporter Hudson (N.Y.) Register-Star, 1974-75, Poughkeepsie (N.Y.) Jour., 1975-76; newsman AP, Columbus, N.Y.C., 1978-1979, Brazil corr. Brasilia, 1979-81, Venezuela bur. chief. Caracas, 1982, news editor, Mex., Cen. Am. Mex. City, 1982-83; dep. fgn. editor Newsday, N.Y.C., 1984-85, sr. editor fgn. news, 1985-89, sr. corr., 1989-94; mng. dir. NewsCom, Coral Gables, Fla., 1994-98, Ctr. for Pub. Integrity, Washington, 1999—2001; dep. fgn. editor Washington Post, 2003. Author editor, translator: Death Beat, 1994, America's Prisoner, 1997. Mem bd advisors Ctrl. Am Jounalists Program, 1989—93. Mem.: Interamerican Press Asn (freedom of press comt 1988—94, bd dirs 1988—94). E-mail: peisner@verizon.net.

EISNER, RICHARD ALAN, accountant; b. N.Y.C., Feb. 25, 1934; s. Joseph and Helen (Cohen) E.; m. Carole Swid, May 7, 1961; children: Joseph, Susan, Douglas, Michael, Hallie. BA, Yale U., 1956; MBA, Harvard Bus. Sch., 1958. CPA, N.Y. Acct. Eisner & Lubin, N.Y.C., 1959-63; mng. ptnr. Eisner LLP N.Y.C., 1963—. Mem. new sch. adv. bd. Columbia Sch. Pub. Health. Chmn audit com. UJA of N.Y.; bd. trustees Jewish Fund for Justice, N.Y.C, Beth Israel Hosp., Legal Aid Soc.; hon. bd. trustees Horace Mann Sch., Bronx, N.Y.C. Mem. Harmonie Club, Yale Club. Democrat. Avocations: reading, classical music, tennis, chess. Office: Eisner LLP 750 3rd Ave New York NY 10017-2597

EISNER, SIGMUND, retired English language educator; b. Red Bank, N.J., Dec. 9, 1920; s. Victor and Helene Eisner; m. Nancy Fereva Eisner, June 15, 1949; children: Kirpal Singh, Charles, Nicholas, Victoria, Halley, Cassandra. BA in English, U. Calif., Berkeley, 1947, MA in English, 1949; PhD in English, Columbia U., 1955. Instr., asst. prof. Oreg. State Coll., Corvallis, 1954—58; Fulbright fellow Inst. for Advanced Studies, Dublin, 1958—59; asst. prof. English Alameda (Calif.) State Coll., 1960; asst. and assoc. prof. English Dominican Coll. San Rafael, Calif., 1960—66; prof. English U. Ariz., Tucson, 1967—95, prof. emeritus English, 1995—. Vis. assoc. prof. English U. Ariz., Tucson, 1966—67. Author: (book) A Tale of Wonder: A Source Study of "The Wife of Bath's Tale", 1957 (U. Chgo. Folklore prize, 1958), The Tristan Legend: A Study in Sources, 1969, The Kalendarium of Nicholas of Lynn, 1980, The Variorum Edition of Chaucer's Treatise on the Astrolabe, 2002; contbr. articles to profl. jours. With U.S. Army, 1942—45. Recipient faculty rsch. support in humanities grant, Grad. Coll. of U. Ariz., 1972, Sabbatical award for study, London, 1972—73, Oxford, Eng., 1980—81, Spring Sabbatical award, 1989. Democrat.

EISNER, SUSAN PAMELA, communications executive, management consultant, educator; b. N.Y.C., Apr. 19, 1950; d. Nathaniel Julius and Frances Rochelle (Linick) Eisner. Student, Smith Coll., 1968-69; BA, Wellesley Coll., 1971; MPA, Kennedy Sch. Govt., Harvard U., 1974. Mem. staff HEW, Washington, 1971; asst. to dir. comm. Dem. Nat. Com., Washington, 1972; nat. coord. press ops. McGovern Presdl. Campaign, Washington, 1972; dir. communications Dem. Nat. Com. Telethons II and III, Washington, N.Y.C., L.A., 1973-74; creative dir. Ways and Means, Inc., Louisville, 1974; producer, writer Sta. WNET-Thirteen TV, N.Y.C., 1975-79, asst. dir. broadcasting, 1979-81, dir. acquisitions, scheduling and spls., 1981, dir. broadcasting, 1981-83, spl. advisor to sr. v.p., 1983; pres., mgmt. and comm. cons., project devel. production Susan Eisner Assocs., N.Y.C., 1983—; staff intern to Senator Javits U.S. Senate, Washington, 1970. Mem. adj. faculty NYU, N.Y.C., 1994—, glocalization adv. bd., 1994-95; asst. prof. mgmt. Ramapo Coll., N.J., 1995-99, assoc. prof. mgmt., 1999—; acad. reviewer Irwin/McGraw Hill, Simon & Schuster, Southwestern, 1997—; profl. connection advisor Harvard U., 1998—; presenter in field. Folk singer, Boston, 1969-71; dir. broadcasting various TV programs and mini series including Cinema Thirteen, Classics Showcase, Star Movie, Viewer's Choice, Gala of Stars, Astaire, Hepburn, Years of Darkness, The American Worker, Black History, Celebrate Dance, Chanukah.Christmas, Disarmament, Remember the Holocaust, A Salute to Britain, First Person Reports, others; exec. producer and producer various TV specials, spots, reports, segments including Listening to You (Nat. Assn. Ednl. Broadcasters Graphics and Design award 1978), Masterpiece Theatre Quotes Montage (Nat. Assn. Ednl. Broadcasters Graphics and Design award 1978), Haven't Stopped Dancin' Yet (Nat. Assn. Fdn. Broadcasters Graphics and Design award 1979), Window on the World (Nat. Assn. Ednl. Broadcasters Graphics and Design award 1979), Everything Beautiful At the Ballet (Nat. Assn. Ednl. Broadcasters Graphics and Design award 1979), Making Poldark--Location (Nat. Assn. Ednl. Graphics and Design award 1979), Work in Progress--Dance in America (Nat. Assn. Ednl. Graphics and Design award 1979), Cavett Conversation with Baryshnikov-Gregory, I Claudius/Poldark/Duchess of Duke Street/Upstairs-Downstairs Farewells, Masterpiece Theatre's Tenth Anniversary Party, On location--Dance Grand Finale, Thirteen: The First Twenty Years, Newsline, Artists at Work, Culture Spots, Eliot Feld audition, Lenoni, Metro Minutes, Preview, You're the Top: Empire State, Be There, Go Public, The Next Twenty Years, People and Programs, Think Again, Think Thirteen, We Are You, Where Every Minute County, others; creator, The Premier Way, 1984; dir. communications various nat. multimedia prodns. for March of Dimes including Witness to Conquesta, A Tribute to Jonas Salk (cabinet and congl. wives' dinner), Mommy Don't (prenatal care campaign), Beautiful Babies: Right from the Start, Journey to Birth; Nat. Communications Adv. Com. Symposiums on Drug Use and Pregnancy and Environ. Risks and Pregnancy, Nat. Vol. Leadership Conf., Nat. Program Tng. Conf., various nat. pub. svc. announcements and campaigns, nat. promotional and instl. campaigns; internatl. cons. various spl. events inclusding Fiftieth Anniversary, Nat. Telethons. Cons. pre-publ. rsch. for book on Bill Cosby, 1987. Creator, Mediasmarts, 1993. Writer contemporary folk songs, 1969-75; author of speeches, presentations, reports, press, ednl., instl. and promotional materials; rsch. on various topics. Dir. comm. March of Dimes Birth Defects Found., N.Y., 1985-87; spl. cons. to exec. dir. Nat. Urban League, 1969-71; tutor MIT, 1972 Recipient award for Citizenship Am. Legion, 1965, Mayor's award for Young Citizenship Mayor of New Rochelle, N.Y., 1965, Thomases award for faculty excellence, 1999, Outstanding Tchr. award SAB, 1998, 2003, Best Paper award Internat. Bus. and Econ. Rsch. Conf., 2001; named one of Outstanding Young Women Am., U.S. Jayvees, 1981; Durant scholar Wellesley Coll., 1971; Harvard U. Kennedy Sch. adminstrn. fellow, 1971-75; SBR grantee, 1997, Ramapo Coll. Found. grantee, 1997, FIPSE grantee, 1997, Sanyo grantee, 1995, 98, Pres. award for excellence in tchg., 1999. Mem. AAUW (mem. conv. planning com. 1999, BD minority scholar program mentor 1999, 2000), NAFE, Soc. Advancement of Mgmt (mem. editl. rev. bd. 2000—), Nat. Bus. Edn. Assn., Acad. Mgmt., Assn. Bus. Comm., Omicron Delta Kappa, Delta Mu Delta (hon.). Office: Ramapo Coll 505 Ramapo Valley Rd Mahwah NJ 07430-1623 E-mail: seisner@ramapo.edu.

EISNER, THOMAS, biologist, educator; b. Berlin, June 25, 1929; s. Hans Edouard and Margarete (Heil) E.; m. Maria Lobell, June 10, 1952; children: Yvonne, Vivian, Christina. BA, Harvard U., 1951, PhD, 1955; DSc (hon.), U. Würzburg, Germany, 1982, U. Zürich, Switzerland, 1983, U. Göteborg, Sweden, 1989, Drexel U., 1992. Postdoctoral fellow Harvard U., 1955—57; asst. prof. biology Cornell U., Ithaca, NY, 1957—62, assoc. prof., 1962—66, prof., 1966—76, Jacob Gould Schurman prof. chem. ecology, 1976—, dir. Cornell Inst. for Rsch. in Chem. Ecology, 1992—; sr. fellow Cornell Ctr. for the Environment, 1994—. Vis. scientist dept. entomology Sch. Agr., Wageningen, The Netherlands, 1964—65; vis. scientist Smithsonian Tropical Rsch. Lab., Barro Colorado Island, C.Z., 1968; sr. vis. scientist Max Planck Inst. fur Verhaltensphysiologie, Seewiesen, Germany, 1971, Divsn. Entomology, CSIRO, Canberra, Australia, 1972—73; Rand fellow Marine Biol. Labs., Woods Hole, Mass., 1974; vis. rsch. prof. U. Fla., Gainesville, 1977—78; chief scientist Biodiversity IMAX Film, 1996—2001; mem. internat. adv. bd. INBio, 1997—98, FUNDAQUIM U. de la Republica, Uruguay, 1997—, Butterfly Discovery Pk., 1997—2001; rsch. assoc. Archbold Biol. Sta., 1973—; vis. prof. Stanford U., 1979—80, U. Zürich, 1980—81. Co-author: Animal Adaptation, 1964, Life on Earth, 1973, 7 other books; mem. editl. bd.: Sci., 1970—71, Am. Naturalist, 1970—71, Jour. Comparative Physiology, 1974—80, Jour. Chem. Ecology, 1974—, Behavioral Ecology and Sociobiology, 1976—97, Sci. Yr. World Books, 1979—82, Human Ecology Forum, 1981—85, Living Bird Quar., 1982—88, Experientia, 1982—96, Quar. Rev. Biology, 1983—87, Chemoecology, 1997—; co-editor: Explorations in Chemical Ecology Series, 1987—; contbr. articles to profl. jours. Recipient Archie F. Carr medal, 1983, Procter prize, Sigma Xi, 1986, Karl Ritter von Frisch medal, 1988, Centennial medal, Harvard U., 1989, Tyler Environ. Achievement prize, U. So. Calif., 1990, Esselen award, 1991, Silver medal, Internat. Soc. Chem. Ecology, 1991, Nat. medal sci., 1994, NWF Nat. Conservation Achievement award, 1997, Green Globe award, 1997, John Wiley Jones award, 1999, Iscal Dist. Environ. Lectr. award, 2000; Guggenheim fellow, 1964—65, 1972—73. Fellow: Entomol. Soc. Am., Animal Behavior Soc., Royal Soc. Arts, Am. Acad. Arts and Scis.; mem.: AAAS (chmn. biology sect. 1980—81, com. on sci. freedom and responsibility 1980—87, chmn. subcom. sci. and human rights 1981—87), NAS (rsch. opportunity in biology com. 1985, film com. 1986—, com. on human rights 1987—90), Ency. of Biodiversity (internat. adv. bd. 1997—2000), Ctr. of Biodiversity Conservation Am. Mus. Natl. History (adv. com. 1995—2000), Nat. Mus. Natural History (adv. com. 1996—2001), Xerces Soc. (sci. adv. com. 1990—, pres. 1992—), Union Concerned Scientists (bd. dirs. 1993—), Com. Concerned Scientists (nat. sponsor 1988—), World Resources Inst. (adv. coun. 1988—95), Monell Chem. Senses Ctr. (adv. coun. 1988—95), Am. Soc. Naturalists (pres. 1989—90), Mo. Botanical Garden Ctr. Plant Conservation (adv. bd. econ. potential rare and threatened plants 1992), Am. Inst. Biol. Sci. (task force for 90s 1990—), Ctr. on Consequences Nuclear War (steering com. 1983—90), Fedn. Am. Scientists (coun. mem. 1977—81), Nat. Audubon Soc. (bd. dirs. 1970—75), Zero Population Growth (bd. dirs. 1969—70), Acad. Europaea, Am. Philos. Soc., World Wildlife Fund (sci. adv. coun. 1983—91), Nature Conservancy (nat. sci. adv. coun. 1969—74), Deutsche Acad. Naturforscher Leopoldina, Explorers Club. Office: Cornell U W347 Seeley Mudd Hall Dept Neurobiology & Behavior Ithaca NY 14853 *I am a naturalist, interested primarily in field exploration and discovery. My research deals with the behavior and chemical ecology of insects, and with the photographic and cinematographic documentation of little known aspects of the life of these animals. My chief goal in life is to relate my findings to the cause of wildlife and wilderness preservation.*

EISNER, WILL, publishing company executive; b. N.Y.C., Mar. 6, 1917; s. Samuel and Fannie (Ingber) E.; m. Ann Louise Weingarten, June 15, 1950; children: John David, Alice Carol (dec.). Student, Art Student's League, N.Y.C., 1935. Pres. Am. Visuals Corp., 1949—, N.Am. Newspaper Alliance, 1962-64, Ednl. Supplements Corp., 1965-72; exec. v.p. Koster-Dana Corp., 1962-64; chmn. bd. Croft Ednl. Services Corp., 1972-73. Mem. faculty Sch. Visual Arts, N.Y.C., 1973-95. Author, cartoonist (syndicated newspaper feature) The Spirit, 1940-52; pub.: Eisner-Arnold Comic Group; editor: U.S. Army Ordnance. 1942-45 (recipient award comic book artist of yr. Nat. Cartoonist Soc., N.Y. 1967, Best artist award 1968-69, Best Comic Book Story cartoonist 1979, ann. award for quality of art in comic books Soc. Comic Art Rsch., 1968, Internat. Cartoonist award Angouleme, France, 1974); author: America's Combat Weapons, 1960, America's Space Vehicles, 1961, Contract with God, 1978, Gleeful Guides Series, 1980, Life on Another Planet, 1982, Big City, 1983 (graphic novel), Life Force, 1984, Comics and Sequential Art, 1985, To the Heart of the Storm, 1991, Invisible People, 1993, Dropsie Avenue, 1995, Graphic Storytelling, 1996, A Family Matter, 1998, Last Day in Vietnam, 1999, Minor Miracles, 2000, Name of the Game, 2001, Fagin the Jew, 2003. Trustee Internat. Mus. Cartoon Art, 1994. Recipient Life Work award Barcelona Internat. Comic and Illustration Conv., Spl. Lifetime Achievement award Lucca Internat. Salon, 1986, Best Comic Book Artist award Nat. Cartoonists Soc., 1967-68, 79, 88, 89, Spl. Career Achievement award U.K. Comic Art Awards, 1994, Max and Mortiz Life-Work Achievement award, Erlangen, Germany, 1994, San Diego Comic Conv. Humanitarian award, 1994, Lifetime Achievement award Nat. Cartoonist Soc., 1995, Grand Prize Yellow Kid award, Rome, 1997, Reuben award Nat Cartoonists Soc., 1998, Lifetime Achievement award Nat. Found. Jewish Culture, 2002; inducted into Hall of Fame, Cartoon Art Mus., 1989. Mem. Illustrators Soc. N.Y.C., Internat. Mus. Cartoon Art (trustee), Scottish Cartoonist Soc. (hon. pres.), Svenska Serieaka demins Goteborg (diplomate), Princeton Club (N.Y.C.). Home and Office: 8333 W Mcnab Rd Ste 131 Fort Lauderdale FL 33321-3203

EISSENBERG, DAVID MARTIN, retired engineering executive; b. Bklyn., Aug. 5, 1929; s. Samuel William and Anne Ida Eissenberg; m. Ethel Mae Mikula, Aug. 23, 1953; children: Joel, Judith, Sara Carpenter, Michael, Thomas. BS in Physics, Coll. William and Mary, 1950; BSChemE, MIT, 1952; MSChemE, U. Tenn., 1963, PhD in Chem. Engring., 1972. Registered profl. engr., Tenn. R&D engr., group leader Oak Ridge Nat. Lab., Tenn., 1952—91; pres. Valvision Inc., Cambridge, NY, 1991—98. Cons. Met. Water Dist., L.A., 1993—97, AquaGen Inc., Laguna Hills, Calif., 1998—2001. V.p. Washington County Lit. Vols., 2001—03; chmn. Washington County Covered Bridge Adv. Com., NY, 1998—2003. Lt. USN, 1955—58. Avocation: travel. Home: 1555 State Rte 313 Cambridge NY 12816 Personal E-mail: eissenbd@sover.nct.

EISSMANN, ROBERT FRED, retired manufacturing engineer; b. Bklyn., Jan. 17, 1924; s. Fred Arno and Katherine Elizabeth (Petersohn) E.; m. June I. Vreeland, Dec. 29, 1950; 1 child, Roy Norman. Student, Pratt Inst., 1942-43, 46. Wireman Western Electric Co., Kearney, N.J., 1946-49; assembler Indsl. TV, Clifton, N.J., 1949-51; leadman Bogue Electric, Paterson, N.J., 1951-60, 65-68, wireman, engring. asst. Kearfott, Gen. Precion, West Paterson, N.J., 1960-65; assembler-wireman Henderson Industries, Fairfield, N.J., 1968-72; prodn. mgr. Mipco Inc., West Caldwell, N.J., 1972-80, plant mgr. Fairfield, 1980-84, product support mgr., 1984-85, value engr., 1985-86; advance product design engr., 1986-87; design engr. indsl., elec. products Amerace Corp., 1987-90; ret., 1990. Staff mem. Russellstoll divsn. Midland Ross Corp., Livingston, N.J., 1980-83. Mem. freight contrainer stds. com. Elec. Task Force. With Signal Corps, U.S. Army, 1943-46. Methodist.

EISSMANN, WALTER JAMES, consulting company executive; b. Newark, N.J., Apr. 20, 1939; s. Walter Curt Eissmann and Alice Delice (Irving) Clark; m. Dorothea Ann Donaldson, June 1, 1963; children: Patricia Helene Ridenhour, Walter William. BS in Indsl. Engring., Rutgers U., 1962. Account mgr. Gen. Electric, Engelwood Cliffs, N.J., 1962-67; regional sales mgr. Tymshare, Engelwood Cliffs, 1968-71, Buffalo, N.Y., 1971-73, v.p. mktg. svc. divsn. Cupertino, Calif., 1974-79, divsn. v.p., 1980-84; sr. v.p. McDonnell Douglas Corp., Cupertino, 1984-86; gen. ptnr. Archer Assocs., Cupertino, 1985-92; pres., chmn. bd. Walter J. Eissmann Inc., Napa, Calif., 1989—. Bd. dirs. NSF Corp., Nutri/system Franchisee Corp.; chmn. bd. businesswise Inc., 1992-93; mng. gen. ptnr. Grand Tyme Partnership, 1992-98. Lead singer: Soc. for Preservation and Encouragement of Barber Shop Quartet Singing in Am., 2001. Bd. dirs. Saratoga Little League, Calif., 1976-81, Saratoga Boosters, 1981-84; active Vienna Theatre Players, Va., 1973; mem. Church Men's Choir, Saratoga, 1980-82. Named to President's club Tymshare, Golden Circle, Nutri/system Master of the Keys. Mem. Pi Tau Sigma. Republican.

EISWERTH, BARRY NEIL, architect, educator; b. Williamsport, Pa., Sept. 16, 1942; s. Eugene Lewis and Mary Jane (Winters) E.; m. Anne Caroline Essl, Apr. 8, 1967; children: Jason Andreas, Brendan Eugene. BArch., Pa. State U.-University Park, 1965. Registered architect, Pa. Assoc. H2L2 Architects/Planners, Phila., 1967-77, ptnr., 1977-88, sr. ptnr., 1988—; pres. H2L2 Design Co., Phila., 1980—; asst. prof. archtl. design Drexel U., 1975-81; mem. faculty, thesis advisor Phila. Coll. Art. Archtl. works include Children's Hosp., Phila., bldgs. Phila. '76 Bicentennial, Phila. Bourse Bldg., Cypress Sq. Townhouse Complex Phila. (recipient Design award Old Phila. Devel. Corp., Preservation Alliance award for Design Offices and Montgomery McCracken Warker & Rhodes), Constitutional Pavillion for We The People 200, Master Plan and New Classroom Adminstrn. Bldg. Cairo Am. Coll., Engring. and Computer Sci. Campus-Am. U. Cairo, Master Plan Am. Internat. Sch., Tel Aviv, Master Plan and New Classroom Bldgs. Am. Embassy Sch., New Delhi, Master Plan and Design new campus Am. Sch. of Warsaw, Brit. Internat. Sch., Cairo; Master Plan and Expansion Am. Sch. Paris; design of hdqrs. Arab Bank, Cairo. Trustee curator Phila. City Inst.; bd. dirs. Marymount Internat. Sch., Paris; bd. mem. World Affairs Coun., Penverdel Coun. Recipient awards for archtl. designs, Alumni Achievement award Pa. State U., 2000. Mem. AIA, Pa. Soc. Architects, Nat. Acad. Design, Phila. Club. Democrat. Roman Catholic. Office: H2L2 Architects/Planners 714 Market St 6th Fl Philadelphia PA 19106-2372

EITAN, TONY See FIORINO, ANTHONY

EITINGON, DANIEL BENJAMIN, insurance company executive, consultant; b. NYC, Nov. 20, 1950; s. Mark and Aimee Brigitte (Berline) E. BBA, Hofstra U., 1977, PhD, LaSalle U., Mandeville, La., 1997. CPCU; ACE; ACD; assoc. in risk mgmt.; assoc. in underwriting; accredited customer svc. rep.; accredited advisor in ins.; cert. ins. counselor. Dir. mktg. BHK&R Inc., Mpls., 1982-89; v.p., broking exec. Alexander & Alexander, Inc., Mpls., 1990-95; pres., CEO Outsource Ins. Svcs., Ltd., Mpls., 1995—. Adj. prof. bus. Mpls. Cmty. and Tech. Coll., 1997—. Mem. Soc. CPCUs (Minn. chpt. media contact com.), Soc. Ins. Trainers and Educators, Twin Cities Ins. Club. Democrat. Jewish. Avocations: piano playing, walking, classical music, travel, speaking french. Home: 3782 Kipling Ave South Minneapolis MN 55416-4848 Office: Outsource Ins Svcs Ltd 5115 Excelsior Blvd # 328 Minneapolis MN 55416-2906 E-mail: drdanny@prodigy.net.

EITNER, JAMES WILLIAM, physician, medical consultant, administrator; b. Phoenix, Mar. 12, 1957; s. Henry C. Jr. and Patty Ann (Lee) E. BS in Biology, BA in Chemistry, Ariz. State U., 1979, BA in Secondary Edn., 1980, MEd, 1982; DO, Coll. Osteo. Medicine Pacific, 1987. Lic. osteo. physician and surgeon, Ariz.; cert. Am. Coll. Osteo. Family Practitioners. Gen. mgr. Cave Creek Rd. Rentals, Phoenix, 1971-79; substitute tchr. various schs., 1979-81, 86-87; student tchr. biology, advanced biology, microbiology Moon Valley H.S., Phoenix, 1980; instr. chemistry and gen. sci. Shadow Mountain H.S., Phoenix, 1981-83; adj. instr. Ariz. State U. Portal Sch. Program, Tempe, 1983-84; intern then resident Phoenix Gen. Hosp., 1987-89; with Bell Rd. Med., Phoenix, 1989-90; osteopath Jay Bernstein, D.O., P.C., Phoenix, 1990-93; med. cons. Phoenix, 1994—; med. dir. Cmty. Hospice, Phoenix, 1996, Integra Hospice and Home Health, Phoenix, 1996; dir. clin. svcs. preventive med. svcs. Maricopa County Dept. Pub. Health, 1998—2001; prin. investigator MDS Pharma Svcs., Phoenix, 2002—. Bd. dirs. Ariz. Sch. Health Assn., 1981-83, treas., 1988-95 (Outstanding Svc. award); asst. team physician Paradise Valley H.S., 1987-89, team physician, 1989-90; chmn. teen pregnancy, sexuality, and sexually transmitted disease com. Ariz. Adolescent Health Coalition, 1991—; preceptor nurse practitioner program Ariz. State U., 1993—; assoc. prof. family practice U. Osteo. Medicine and Health Scis., 1989—. Counselor, camp physician, health and safety com., Camp Geronimo chmn. Boy Scouts Am., 1975-94; chmn. health and edn. subcom. Gov's Adv. Com. on Tobacco Free Ariz., 1989-90; bd. dirs. Lakeside HOA, Gilbert, Ariz., 1994-96, Valvista Lakes C.A., Gilbert, 1995—; vol. Spl. Olympics, 1984—; mem. Phoenix Gen. Hosp. and Ctr. for Sports Medicine and Orthopedics Sports Medicine Clinics, 1979-95; team physician North H.S., Phoenix, 1997—; host KKLT/KTAR radio show on Ariz. youth and tobacco, 1990. Home: 1841 E Bay Tree Cir Gilbert AZ 85234-4935 E-mail: Aquadoc@pol.net.

EITNER, LORENZ EDWIN ALFRED, art historian, educator; b. Brunn, Czechoslovakia, Aug. 27, 1919; came to U.S., 1935, naturalized, 1943; s. Wilhelm and Katherina (Thonet) E.; m. Trudi von Kathrein, Oct. 26, 1946; children: Christy, Kathy, Claudia. AB, Duke U., 1940; MFA, Princeton U., 1948, PhD, 1952. Research unit head Nuremberg War Crimes Trial, 1946-47; from instr. to prof. art U. Minn., Mpls., 1949-63; chmn. dept. art, dir. mus. Stanford U., Calif., 1963-89. Organizer exhbn. works of Gericault for museums of Los Angeles, Detroit and Phila., 1971-72 Author: The Flabellum of Tournus, 1944, Gericault Sketchbooks in the Chicago Art Institute, 1960, Introduction to Art, 1951, Neo-Classicism and Romanticism, 1969, Gericault's Raft of the Medusa, 1972, Gericault, His Life and Work, 1983 (Mitchell prize 1984, C.R. Morey award 1985), An Outline of 19th Century European Painting from David through Cezanne, 1987, Nat. Gallery, Washington, French Nineteenth Century Paintings, 2000; (with others) The Arts in Higher Education, 1963, Stanford Mus. Art, The Drawing Collection, 1993; contbr. articles to profl. jours. Mem. Regional Area Arts Coun. San Francisco Bay Area. Officer OSS, AUS, 1943-46; sect. head ministries divsn. Nuremberg War Crimes Trial, 1946-47. Fulbright grantee, Belgium, 1952-53; Guggenheim fellow, Munich, Federal Republic Germany, 1956-57; recipient Gold Medal for Meritorious Service to Austrian Republic, 1990. Mem. AAAS, Am. Acad. Arts and Scis., Coll. Art Assn. Am. (bd. dirs., past v.p.), Phi Beta Kappa Home: 684 Mirada Ave Stanford CA 94305-8475 Office: Stanford U Art Dept Stanford CA 94305

EITTREIM, RICHARD MACNUTT, lawyer; b. Neptune, N.J., Feb. 10, 1945; s. Wilbur Lawrence and Leta Blanch (MacNutt) E.; m. Margaret Anne Nolan, June 11, 1967; children: Theodore Scott, Elisabeth Marie, Samantha Leta. AB, Yale U., 1967; JD, U. Va., 1973. Bar: N.J. 1973, U.S. Dist. Ct. N.J. 1973, U.S. Ct. Appeals (3d cir.) 1984, (11th cir.) 1996, U.S. Supreme Ct. 1998. Assoc. McCarter & English, Newark, N.J., 1973-80, ptnr., 1980—. Trustee Children's Psychiat. Ctr., Eatontown, N.J., 1977-87, Riverview Hosp. Found., Red Bank, N.J., 1988-93. Mem. ABA, N.J. State Bar Assn., Essex County Bar Assn., Phi Alpha Delta, Sea Bright Lawn Tennis and Cricket Club (pres. 2000—, bd. govs. 1994—), Monmouth Boat Club (treas. 1983-86), Essex Club, Yale Club (pres. 1986-87). Democrat. Presbyterian. Home: 100 Woodland Dr Fair Haven NJ 07704 Office: McCarter & English 4 Gateway Ctr 100 Mulberry St Newark NJ 07102-4004 E-mail: reittreim@mccarter.com.

EITZEN, DAVID STANLEY, sociologist, educator; b. Glendale, Calif., Aug. 4, 1934; s. David Donald and Amanda Emma (Heidebrecht) E.; m. Florine Kay Voran, May 29, 1956; children: Keith, Michael, Kelly. AB in History, Bethel Coll., 1956; MS, Emporia State U., 1962; MA in Sociology, U. Kans., 1966, PhD in Sociology, 1968. Recreational therapist Menninger Found., Topeka, Kans., 1956-58; tchr. Galva (Kans.) High Sch., 1958-60, Turner (Kans.) High Sch., 1960-65; asst. prof. sociology U. Kans., 1968-72, assoc. prof., 1972-74; prof. sociology Colo. State U., Ft. Collins, 1974-95, prof. emeritus, 1995—. Author: Social Structure and Social Problems, 1974, Sociology of American Sport, 1978, In Conflict and Order: Understanding Society, 1978, Sport in Contemporary Society, 1979, Social Problems, 1980, Elite Deviance, 1981; Criminology: Crime and Criminal Justice, 1985, Diversity in American Families, 1987, Society's Problems: Sources and Consequences, 1989, Crime in the Streets and Crime in the Suites: Perspectives on Crime and Criminal Justice, 1989, The Reshaping of America: Social Consequences of the Changing Economy, 1989, Paths to Homelessness, 1994, Solutions to Social Problems: Lessons from Other Societies, 1997, Fair and Foul: Beyond the Myths and Paradoxes of Sport, 1999, Experiencing Poverty: Voices from the Bottom, 2003; editor Social Sci. Jour., 1978-84; contbr. articles to profl. jours. NDEA fellow, 1965-67 Mem. Internat. Sociol. Assn., Am. Sociol. Assn., Midwest Sociol. Soc., Soc. Study Social Problems, Western Social Sci. Assn., Southwestern Social Sci. Assn., Internat. Com. for Sociology Sport., N.Am. Soc. for Sociology of Sport (pres. 1986-87). Democrat. Mennonite. Home: 924 Breakwater Dr Fort Collins CO 80525-3345 Office: Colo State U Dept Sociology Fort Collins CO 80523-0001

EIZENBERG, JULIE, architect; BArch, U. Melbourne, Australia, 1978; MArch II, UCLA, 1981. Lic. architect, Calif., reg. architect, Australia. Principal, architect Koning Eizenberg Architecture, Santa Monica, Calif., 1981—. Instr. various courses UCLA, MIT, Harvard U.; lectr. in field; jury member P/A awards. Exhbns. incl. Koning Eizenberg Architecture 3A Garage, San Francisco, 1996, "House Rules" Wexner Ctr., 1994, "The Architect's Dream: Houses for the Next Millenium" The Contemporary Arts Ctr., 1993, "Angels & Franciscans" Gagosian Gallery, 1992, Santa Monica Mus. Art, 1993, "Broadening the Discourse" Calif. Women in Environmental Design, 1992, "Conceptional Drawings by Architects" Bannatyne Gallery, 1991, Exhbn. Koning Eizenberg Projects Grad. Sch. Architecture & Urban Planning UCLA, 1990; prin. works include Digital Domain Renovation and Screening Room, Santa Monica, Lightstorm Entertainment Office Renovation and Screening Room, Santa Monica, Gilmore Bank Addition and Remodel, L.A., 1548-1550 Studios, Santa Monica, (with RTA) Materials Rsch. Lab. at U. Calif., Santa Barbara, Ken Edwards Ctr. Cmty. Svcs., Santa Monica, Peck Park Cmty. Ctr. Gymnasium, San Pedro, Calif., Sepulveda Recreation Ctr., L.A. (Design award AIA San Fernando Valley 1995, Nat. Concrete and Masonry award 1996, AIA Calif. Coun. Honor award 1996, L.A. Bus. Coun. Beautification award 1996, AIA Los Angeles Chpt. Merit Award, 1997), PS # 1 Elem. Sch., Santa Monica, Farmers Market, L.A. Additions and Master Plan (Westside Urban Forum prize 1991), Stage Deli, L.A., Simone Hotel, L.A. (Nat. Honor award AIA 1994), Boyd Hotel, L.A., Cmty. Corp. Santa Monica Housing Projects, 5th St. Family Housing, Santa Monica, St. John's Hosp. Replacement Housing Program, Santa Monica, Liffman Ho., Santa Monica, (with Glenn Erikson) Electric Artblock, Venice (Beautification award L.A. Bus. Coun. 1993), 6th St. Condominiums, Santa Monica, Hollywood Duplex, Hollywood Hills (Record Houses Archtl. Record 1988), California Ave. Duplex, Santa Monica, Tarzana Ho. (Award of Merit L.A. chpt. AIA 1992, AIA Calif. Coun. Merit Award, 1998, Sunset Western home Awards citation 1993-94), 909 Ho., Santa Monica (Award of Merit L.A. chpt. AIA 1991), 31st St. Ho., Santa Monica (Honor award AIACC 1994, Nat. AIA Honor award 1996), others. Recipient 1st award Progressive Architecture, 1987; named one of Domino's Top 30 Architects, 1989. Mem. L.A. County Mus. Art, Westside Urban Forum, Urban Land Inst., Architects and Designers for Social Responsibility, Mus. Contemporary Art, The Nature Conservancy, Sierra Club. Office: Koning Eizenberg Architecture 1454 25th St Santa Monica CA 90404-3008

EIZENSTAT, STUART ELLIOT, ambassador, lawyer; b. Chgo., Jan. 15, 1943; m. Fran Eizenstat; children: Jay, Brian. AB cum laude, U. N.C., 1964; LLB, Harvard U., 1967; LLD (hon.), Yeshiva U., 1998, Weizmann Inst. Sci., 1999, U. N.C., 2000, Jewish Theol. Sem., 2000, Hebrew Coll., 2000, Brandeis U., 2001, Fla. Atlantic U., 2002. Bar: Ga. 1967, D.C. 1981. Mem. White House staff, 1967-68; mem. nat. campaign staff Hubert H. Humphrey, 1968; law clk. U.S. Dist. Ct. No. Dist. Ga., 1968-70; ptnr. Powell, Goldstein, Frazer & Murphy, Washington, 1970-77, vice chmn., 1981-93; asst. to Pres. U.S. for domestic affairs and policy, 77-81, dir. White House Domestic Policy Staff, 1977-81; amb. to European Union Brussels, 1993-96; spl. envoy Dept. State Property Claims in Ctrl. Europe, 1995-2001; undersec. for internat. trade Dept. Commerce, Washington, 1996-97; envoy Pres. of U.S. for Promotion of Democracy in Cuba, 1996-97; undersec. of state for econ., bus. and agrl. affairs Dept. State, Washington, 1997-99; alt. gov. World Bank, 1998-99, Regional Devel. Banks, 1998-99; dep. sec. Dept. Treasury, 1999-2001; dir. Kead Internat. Trade and Fin., Covington and Burling, Wash., 2001—. Spl. rep. of Pres. and Sec. of State on Holocaust Issues, 1999-2001; adj. lectr. J.F. Kennedy Sch. Govt., Harvard U., 1981-92; guest scholar Brookings Inst., Washington, 1981;

mem. Energy Coord. Coun., Econ. Policy Group, 1977-81, Pres. Bush task force on U.S. Internat. Broadcasting, 1991; head U.S. del. CSCE Econ. Forum, 1994; lectr. coll., bus. and civic groups. Author: Imperfect Justice: Slave Labor, Looted Assets and the Unfinished Business of World War II, 2003; co-author: Andrew Young: The Path to History, 1973;Environmental Auditing Handbook, 1984; co-editor: The American Agenda: Report to the 41st President of the United States, 1988, reprint, 1989; contbr. articles to profl. jours. and newspapers. Vice-pres. Jewish Publ. Soc., 1981-85; chmn. Inst. U.S. Jewish-Israeli Relations, 1982-86; bd. dirs. Woodrow Wilson Center for Internat. Scholars, 1978-87, Jerusalem Found., 1992-93, Eurasia Found., 1993; pres. Greater Washington Jewish Community Ctr., 1989-91; mem. exec. com. Ctr. for Dem. Policy, 1982-93; bd. visitors U. N.C., Chapel Hill, 1987-90; co-dir. The American Agenda (with Pres. Ford and Pres. Carter), 1991; trustee Jerusalem Inst. Mgmt., 1987-93; mem. coun. Harvard Law Sch. Assn., 1988-92, Gov.'s Commn. on Fed. Funding, Commonwealth of Va., 1986, Com. on Federalism and Nat. Purpose, 1984-85; chmn. Econ. and Budget Strategy Com., Montgomery County Coun., 1986; v.p., bd. dirs. Am. Assocs., Ben-Gurion U. of the Negev. N.Y.C., 1981-89; trustee Washington Inst. for Jewish Leadership and Values, 1988—, Brandeis U., 1991—; commr. Commn. on Jewish Edn. in N.Am., 1988-90; v.p. Atlanta Bur. Jewish Edn., 1973-76; mem. exec. com. Atlanta Jewish Community Center, 1970-76; mem. B'nai Brith Youth Commn., Washington, 1981-82; bd. dirs. United Synagogues Am., 1981-84.; internat. bd. dir. Weizmann Inst., 1989-93; active in Dem. party and political campaigns. Pub. policy scholar Woodrow Wilson Ctr. Internat. Scholars, 2001; recipient Man of Yr. award Nat. Capital Assn., State Dept. award for Public Svs., 1996. B'nai B'rith Lodges, 1982, Outstanding Svc. to Summer Youth Program U.S. Dept. Labor, 1980, Outstanding Svc. award Hebrew Aid Immigration Soc., 1980, Outstanding Svc. award Opportunities Industrialization Ctrs., 1979, award Washington Internat. Bus. Coun., 1978, award Nat. Coalition Involved People, 1977, Young Man of Yr. award Am. Assn. Jewish Edn., 1973-74, Leadership award Acad. Jewish Religion, 1989, Tree of Life award Hadassah, Boston, 1989, Myrtle Wreath award Fla. Atlantic Region Hadassah, 1991, Benjamin Cardozo Professionalism award Atlanta Jewish Fedn., 1992, Export Finance award Coalition for Employment Through Exports, 1993, award for pub. svc. Sec. of State, 1996, Moral Statesman award Anti-Defamation League, 1997, Phillip Klutznick B'Nai B'Rith award for Outstanding Pub. Svc., 1996, award for transatlantic svc. European Inst., 1997, Myrtle Wreath award Hadassah, 1997, 98, Transatlantic Svc. award European Inst., 1997, award for courage and conscience Israeli Knesset, 1998, Leadership award Sec. of State, 1999, B'nai B'rith Leadership award, 2000, Auschwitz Holocaust Ctr. award, 2000, Washington Inst. Jewish Leadership and Values, 2001, award for leadership Sec. of State, 1999, Alexander Hamilton award Sec. of Treasury, 2001, Humanitarian award Inst. Leadership and Values, 2001, knight comdr.'s cross Fed. Rep. Germany, 2002, Leadership award United Jewish Cmtys., 2002, Great Negotiator award Harvard Negotiation Group, 2003, French Legion of Honor, 2003. Fellow Nat. Acad. Pub. Adminstn., Ctr. for Excellence in Govt.; mem. ABA (spl. com. on lawyers in govt., mem. com. govt. standards 1992-93), Atlanta Bar Assn., D.C. Bar Assn., Ga. Bar Assn., U.S. C. of C. (Internat. Policy Com. 1982-89), Nat. Fgn. Trade Coun. (Internat. Trade Com.), Washington Policy Coun. (Internat. Mgmt. and Devel. Inst.), Phi Beta Kappa, Phi Eta Sigma. Democrat. Jewish. Home: 9107 Brierly Rd Chevy Chase MD 20815-5654 Office: Covington & Burding 1201 Pennsylvania Ave NW Washington DC 20004

EJIMOFOR, CORNELIUS OGU, political scientist, educator; b. Owerri, Nigeria, Oct. 10, 1940; came to U.S., 1963; s. Osuji and Helen Domaonu (Atashia) E.; m. Priscilla Loveth Amaugo, Mar. 10, 1966; children: Cornelia, Caroline, Cornelius Jr., Priscilla, Ebere. AA, Warren Wilson Coll., 1965; BA in Polit. Sci., Wilberforce U., 1966; MPA, U. Dayton, 1967; MA, PhD, U. Okla., 1971. Tchr. Cath. Mission Schs., Emekuku, Nigeria, 1959-63; rsch. asst. U. Dayton, Ohio, 1966-67; instr. polit. sci. Edward Waters Coll., Jacksonville, Fla., 1967-68, prof. polit. sci., 1992—, chmn. divsn. arts and scis., 1992-93; grad. asst. U. Okla., Norman, 1968-70; asst. prof. William Paterson Coll., Wayne, N.J., 1970-72; from assoc. prof. to prof. Tuskegee (Ala.) U., 1972-80, dept. head polit. sci., 1972-77; sr. lectr., reader U. Nigeria, Nsukka, 1980-91, prof. polit. sci., 1991-92. Coord., head, prof. sub-dept. pub. adminstrn. and local govt. U. Nigeria, 1990-92, coord. local govt. tng. programs, 1990-92. Author: British Colonia Objectives and Policies in Nigeria, 1987, Management of Human Resources: A Generic Approach, 1992. Mem. AAUP (sec. Fla. chpt., sec. Edward Waters Coll. chpt.), Am. Soc. Pub. Adminstrn., Am. Polit. Sci. Assn., KC. Democrat. Roman Catholic. Avocations: swimming, reading and writing, discussing civics. Home: 157 Lamson St Jacksonville FL 32211-8066 E-mail: cejimofor@ewc.edu.

EK, ALAN RYAN, forester, educator; b. Mpls., Sept. 5, 1942; BS in Forestry, U. Minn., St. Paul, 1964, MS, 1965; PhD, Oreg. State U., Corvallis, 1969. Rsch. officer Can. Dept. Forestry and Rural Devel., Sault Ste Marie, Canada, 1966-69; from asst. prof. to assoc. prof. forestry U. Wis., Madison, 1969-77; from assoc. prof. to prof. U. Minn., St. Paul, 1977—, head dept. forest resources, 1984—. Mem. forestry rsch. adv. com. USDA, 1994—96, 1998—99, chair, 1998—99; cons. in field. Contbr. chapters to books, articles to profl. jours. Fulbright scholar, Finland, 1997. Fellow: Soc. Am. Foresters (various coms., chmn forest sci. and tech. bd. 1989—90); mem.: AAAS, Am. Soc. Photogrammetry and Remote Sensing, Am. Statis. Assn., Nat. Assn. Profl. Forestry Schs. and Colls. (chmn. rsch. com. 1993—95, 1999—2002), Sigma Xi, Gamma Sigma Delta, Xi Sigma Pi. Avocations: reading, sports. Home: 4744 Kevin Ln Saint Paul MN 55126-5849 Office: U Minn Dept Forest Resources Saint Paul MN 55108

EK, JON MERRILL, music educator; b. Trimont, Minn., Jan. 18, 1954; s. Leland Richard and Marilyn Dean Ek; m. Suzanne Kay Ek; children: Kari Elizabeth, Jason Matthew. BA in Vocal Music Edn., Augustana Coll., 1976; MusM in Music Edn., Mankato State U., 1988. Music Teacher K-12 State of Minn., 2003. Tchr. vocal music Renville (Minn.) Pub. Schools, 1976—81, Maple River Schools, Mapleton, Minn., 1982—. Choir dir. United Ch. of Mapleton, 1983—, St. John Luth. Ch., 2002—. Mem.: Minn. Music Educators Assn. (assoc.), Edn. Minn. (assoc.). Lutheran. Achievements include development of Self-Paced Music Reading Program for Elem. Music Students; Independent Study-Based Music Theory Curriculum for H.S. Students. Avocations: travel, genealogy, stamp collecting, golf. Home: 503 5th Avenue NE Mapleton MN 56065 Office: Maple River Schools 101 6th Avenue NE Mapleton MN 56065 Personal E-mail: jonek@hickorytech.net.

EKANGER, LAURIE, retired state official, contractor; b. Salt Lake City, Mar. 4, 1949; d. Bernard and Mary (Dearth) E.; m. William J. Shupe, Nov. 6, 1973; children: Ben, Robert. BA in English, U. Oreg., 1973. Various pos. Mont. State Employment & Tng. Divsn., Helena, 1975-80, dep. adminstr., 1980-82; adminstr. Mont. State Purchasing Divsn., Helena, 1982-85, Mont. State Personnel Divsn., Helena, 1985-93; labor commr. Mont. Dept. Labor & Ind., Helena, 1993-97; dir. Mont. Dept. Pub. Health and Human Svcs., 1997-2000. Council chair State Employee Group Benefits Coun., 1985-93; bd. dirs. Pub. Employee Retirement Bd., 1988; mem. various state adv. couns. for health and human svcs. Home: 80 Pinecrest Rd Clancy MT 59634-9505

EKBATANI, GLAYOL, English as second language educator, program director, writer; b. Tehran, Iran; d. Saed and Parvin (Sohai) E. PhD, U. Ill., 1981. Dir., prof. English 2d lang. program U. Maine, Orano, 1987-90; dir. English 2d lang., bilingual programs C.C. Phila., 1990-92; dir., prof. English 2d lang. programs St. John's U., Jamaica, N.Y., 1992—. Rschr. Georgetown U., Washington, 1986-87. Author: Learner Directed Assessment, 1999; contbr. articles to profl. jours. Mem. Nat. Assn. Fgn. Students Washington, Tchrs. English to Spkrs. of Other Langs. (pres. 1991-92). Home: 301 E 79th St Apt 16 New York NY 10021-0951 Office: St John's U 8000 Utopia Pkwy Rm 377 Jamaica NY 11432-1343

EKBERG, JAN, retired pharmaceutical company executive; Chmn. Pharmacia & Upjohn Inc., Stockholm, Sweden, 1995-98; bd. dirs. Pharmacia & Upjohn Inc., Stockholm, 1995-98. Office: Pharmacia & Upjohn Inc 67 Anna Rd Windsor Berkshire SL4 3MD England

EKDAHL, JON NELS, lawyer, association executive; b. Topeka, Nov. 15, 1942; s. Oscar S. and Dorothy O. (Ekdahl) M.; m. Marcia Opp, May 24, 1975; children: Kirsten, Erika, Kristofer. AB magna cum laude, Harvard U., 1964, LLB, 1968; MS in Econs., London Sch. Econs., 1965. Bar: Ill. 1969, U.S. Ct. Appeals (7th cir.) 1981, U.S. Supreme Ct. 1981. Assoc. Sidley & Austin, Chgo., 1968—73, ptnr., 1973—75; mng. ptnr., gen. counsel Andersen Worldwide SC, Chgo., 1975—2000; sr. v.p., gen. counsel AMA, Chgo., 2001—. With USAR, 1968-74. Mem. ABA, Chgo. Bar Assn., Mid-Am. Club, Chgo. Club. Office: Am Med Assn 515 N State St Chicago IL 60610 E-mail: jon_ekdahl@ama-assn.org.

EKELMAN, DANIEL LOUIS, lawyer; b. Cleve., May 1, 1926; s. William Harry and Edna Mae (James) E.; m. Ann Jane Farnacy, Aug. 5, 1950 (dec. June 1993); children: Sally, Karen, Barbara, Beth; m. Phyllis E. Patton, Oct. 18, 1997. BA, Ohio Wesleyan U., 1950; LLB, Case Western Res. U., 1952. Bar: Ohio 1952, U.S. Dist. Ct. (no. dist.) Ohio 1953, U.S. Tax Ct. 1955. Assoc. Calfee, Halter & Griswold, Cleve., 1952-59, ptnr., 1959-77, mng. ptnr., 1977-85, sr. ptnr., 1985-95; ret., 1996. Gen. ptnr. Sawmill Creek Resort, Huron, Ohio, 1968-80. Trustee Brentwood Hosp., Cleve., 1960-94, Greater Cleve. Hosp. Assn., 1975-78 (Outstanding Trustee award 1992), Case Western Res. Law Sch., 1984-87, Merridia South Pointe Hosp., 1995, Brentwood Found., 1995-99. With USN, 1944-46, PTO. Fellow ABA; mem. Ohio Bar Assn., Cleve. Bar Assn., Soc. Benchers, Order of the Coif, The Country Club (Pepper Pike, Ohio, trustee 1988-91), Union Club, Jupiter Hills Club (Jupiter, Fla.). Republican. Home: 22029 Douglas Rd Shaker Heights OH 44122

EKERN, PAUL C. retired meteorologist; b. Ardmore, Okla., July 2, 1920; s. Paul C. and Sallie Mays (McCoy) Ekern; m. Claire Lamson, June 5, 1950 (dec. Apr. 1951); 1 child, Sallie; m. Nancy Oakes, June 20, 1956; children: Christina, Carrie, Mollie. BA, Westminster Coll., 1942; cert. meteorologist, U. Chgo., 1943. Asst. prof. U. Wis., Madison, 1950—55; soil physicist Pineapple Rsch. Inst., Honolulu, 1955—64; prof. U. Hawaii, Honolulu, 1969—87, prof. emeritus, 1987—. 1st lt. USAF, 1942—46. Avocation: Bromeliad culture. Home: 3133 Huelani Pl Honolulu HI 96822

EKEY, CARRIE RAE, elementary education educator; b. North Platte, Nebr., July 6, 1947; d. Chester O. and Alice A. (Johnson) Florom; m. Glenn W. Ekey, Mar. 22, 1970; children: Brian, Todd. BA in Elem. Edn. and Math., U. No. Colo., 1969; MA in Curriculum and Instrn., U. Colo., Denver, 1990. Cert. elem. tchr., Colo. 3d grade tchr. Jefferson County, Lakewood, Colo., 1969-73, 4th-6th grade tchr. Wheatridge, Colo., 1981-85, 1st-2d grade tchr. Arvada, Westminster, Colo., 1985-97, staff developer Lakewood, Colo., 1997—2002. Instr. Regis U., Denver, 1989—, curriculum coord. Masters in Whole Learning program, 1994—; cons. various sch. dists., Colo., Ohio, Hong Kong, Tokyo, 1989—. Mem. Nat. Coun. Tchrs. English, Nat. Coun. Tchrs. Math., Internat. Reading Assn., Assn. for Supervision and Curriculum Devel., Colo. Coun. Tchrs. English, Colo. Reading Assn. Avocations: reading, golfing, gardening, walking. E-mail: cekey@jeffco.k12.co.us.

EKLOF, PAUL C. mathematician, educator; b. Bklyn., Dec. 28, 1942; s. Eric G. and Helen Mathiesen Eklof; m. Sharon E. Kintner, Sept. 16, 1972; children: Katharine Spink, Alice. AB, Columbia Coll., 1964; PhD, Cornell U., 1968. Gibbs instr. in math. Yale U., New Haven, 1968—70; asst. prof. math. Stanford U., Palo Alto, Calif., 1970—73; assoc. prof. math. U. Calif., Irvine, 1973—78, prof. math., 1978—. Author: (book) Almost Free Modules, rev. edit., 2002, Almost Free Modules: Set-theoretic Methods, 1990; editor: Abelian Groups and Modules, 1999. Mem.: Assn. Symbolic Logic (exec. com. 2002—), Am. Math. Soc. E-mail: peklof@math.uci.edu.

EKLOF, SVEA CHRISTINE, ballet dancer; b. L.A., May 31, 1951; d. Theodore Herman and Christiane (Simonpietri) E.; m. Michel Rahn, Aug. 27, 1976 (div. Jan. 1986); m. John Michael Grey, Jan. 29, 1986; 1 child, Georgina Germaine. Student, U. N.C., 1969-70. Mem. corps de ballet Pa. Ballet Co., Phila., 1970-71; soloist Ballet Classico de Mex., Mexico City, 1971-73, Ballet Du Grand Theatre, Geneva, Switzerland, 1973-74, Netherlands Dance Theatre, Den Haag, The Netherlands, 1974-75; prin. dancer Ballet Du Grand Theatre, Geneva, Switzerland, 1975-76, N.C. Dance Theatre, Winston-Salem, 1976-79, Alta. Ballet Co., Edmonton, 1979-83; soloist Royal Winnipeg Ballet, Man., 1983-85; prin. dancer Royal Winnipeg Ballet Co., Man., 1985-89. Guest tchr. N.C. Sch. Arts, Winston-Salem, 1976-79, 89, Edmonton Sch. Ballet and Alta. Ballet Sch. Ballet, 1979-83, Nat. Ballet Sch., Toronto, 1989-93, W.Va. Dance Festival, 1992-96; guest coach Royal Winnipeg Ballet Sch.; prin. tchr. Dancespace, Toronto, 1991-94; artistic dir. Profl. Sch. of Toronto Ballet Ensemble, 1994—; judge new choreography on Dora Maria Moore awards panel, 1989-90; classical coach Ballet Jörgen, 1989-91; coach for applicants of IV Internat. Ballet Competition, Jackson, Miss.; tchr. Ont. Ballet Theatre Co., 1989-90, 90-93. Guest appearances include Chgo. Ballet, 1976-77, Ballet Galaxie, Taiwan, 1981, New World Ballet, Miami, Fla., 1982, W.Va. Ballet, 1979-81, Edmonton Symphony Orch., 1987-90; prin. ballerina Internat. Opera Festival, 1989, Memphis Concert. Ballet, 1989. Guest tchr. ballet W.Va. Dance Festival, 1992-94, 96; accessor Ont. Arts Coun., 1993—, Met. Toronto Arts Coun., Canada Coun., 1996. Mem. Alta. Ballet Co. (adv. bd. 1986—), Manitoba Dance Assn. (ajudicator dance festival 1994), Can. Dance Tchrs. Assn. (guest tchr. 1995). Avocation: speaking fluent french and spanish. Office: 27 Sackville Pl Toronto ON Canada M4X 1X5

EKLUND, CARL ANDREW, lawyer; b. Aug. 12, 1943; s. John M. and Zara (Zerbst) E.; m. Nancy Jane Griggs, Sept. 7, 1968; children: Kristin, Jessica, Peter. BA, U. Colo., 1967, JD, 1971. Bar: Colo. 1971, D.C. 2001, Colo. (U.S. Dist. Ct.) 1971, (U.S. Ct. Appeals (9th cir.)) 1975, (U.S. Ct. Appeals (10th cir.)) 1978, (U.S. Supreme Ct.) 1978. Dep. dist. atty. Denver Dist. Attys. Office, 1971-73; ptnr. DiManna, Eklund, Ciancio & Jackson, Denver, 1975-81, Smart, DeFurio, Brooks & Eklund, Denver, 1982-84, Roath & Brega, P.C., Denver, 1984-88, Faegre & Benson, Denver, 1988-94, LeBoeuf, Lamb, Greene & MacRae LLP, Denver, 1994—. Mem. local rules com. Bankruptcy Ct. D.C., 1979-80; reporter Nat. Bankruptcy Conf., 1981-82; lectr. ann. spring meeting Am. Bankruptcy Inst., Rocky Mountain Bankruptcy Conf., Continuing Legal Edn. Colo., Inc., Colo. Practice Inst., Colo. Bar Assn., Nat. Ctr. Continuing Legal Edn., Inc., Profl. Edn. Sys., Inc., Comml. Law Inst. Am., Law Edn. Inst., Inc., Bur. Nat. Affairs, Inc., Practising Law Inst., So. Meth. U. Sch. Law, Continuing Edn. Svcs., Law Seminars Internat., Lorman Bus. Ctr., Inc. Author: The Problem with Creditors' Committees in Chapter 11: How to Manage the Inherent Conflicts without Loss of Function; contbg. author: Collier's Bankruptcy Practice Guide, Representing Debtors in Bankruptcy, Letters Formbook and Legal Opinion, Advanced Chapter 11 Bankruptcy Practice, mem. adv. bd. ABI Law Rev., 1993-2000; contbr. to law jours. Fellow Am. Coll. Bankruptcy; mem. ABA (bus. law and corp. banking sect. 1977—, bus. bankruptcy com. 1982—, subcom. on rules 1981—), Colo. Bar Assn. (bd. govs. 1980-82, corp. banking and bus. law sect. 1977—, ethics com. 1981-82, subcom. bankruptcy cts.), Am. Bankruptcy Inst. (dir. Rocky Mountain Bankruptcy Conf.), Denver Bar Assn. (trustee 1983-86). Office: LeBoeuf Lamb Greene & MacRae LLP 633 17th St Ste 2000 Denver CO 80202-3620

EKLUND, THOR IGNATIUS, aeronautical engineer, consultant; b. Phila., Oct. 21, 1946; s. Thor and Mary (Vitti) E.; m. Mary Tobin, Mar. 22, 1980; children: Robert, Andrew. BSE, Princeton U., 1968; MSc, Brown U., 1973, PhD, 1975. Aerospace engr. Naval Air Propulsion Ctr., Phila., 1969-70; mech. engr. Arthur D. Little, Cambridge, Mass., 1973; project engr. FAA, Pomona, N.J., 1975, suprv. engr., program mgr., mgr. Fire Rsch. br., 1997; pres. Eklund Cons. Svcs., Haddonfield, N.J., 1997—. Sponsor NRC Aircraft Materials study, Aircraft Fuel Safety study; mem. FAA com. on reinventing rsch. infrastructure; cons. Nat. Materials Adv. Bd., Washington, 1997; ind. advisor Office Sec. of Def., 1997—; cons. Boeing Comml. Airplane Group, 2000-02; mem. ind. rev. panel NIST, 2001-; cons. NATO Rsch. and Tech. Agy., 2002-03. Inventor and patentee in field; contbr. numerous articles and studies to profl. jours. Mem. Spl. Aviation fire and Explosion Reduction com.; lectr. Aviation Fire Safety, 1998—. Mem. ASME, AIAA, Soc. Automotive Engrs. Avocations: fishing, reading, water gardening, pottery, bird watching. Home and Office: Eklund Cons 119 North Dr Haddonfield NJ 08033-2739

EKMAN, PETER ERIK, urologist, educator; b. Umea, Sweden, Oct. 23, 1943; s. Erik Wilhelm and Margareta Emma Hildegard (Duse) Ekman; m. Amelie Margareta Sundblad, May 4, 1968 (div. Jan. 1991); children: Johan, Kristoffer, Niklas, Jenny; m. Soili Annikki Kupiainen, Sept. 2, 2000; 1 child, Alexandra Anna Margareta. MD, Karolinska Inst., 1969, PhD, 1978. Resident surgery Sabbatsberg, Stockholm, 1972-75; resident urology Karolinska Inst., Stockholm, 1975-79, assoc. prof., 1980-90, prof., dept. chair, 1991—. Co-dir. WHO G.U. Cancers, Stockholm, 1991—. Contbr. chpts. in books, articles to profl. jours. Lt. Swedish Marine Corps, 1969-86. Recipient Fogarty Rsch. award NIH, 1981. Mem. Am. Assn. Genito Urinary Surgeons, Am. Urology Assn., European Assn. Urology. Avocations: choir singing, skiing, swimming, sports. Home: Odengatan 52 S 11351 Stockholm Sweden Office: Karolinska Hosp Dept Urology S 17176 Stockholm Sweden

EKMAN, RICHARD, association executive, educator; b. NYC, Oct. 1, 1945; s. Sheldon Victor and Judith (Saturen) E.; m. Caroline Read, June 15, 1975; children: Nathaniel Paul, Peter Sheldon Read. AB magna cum laude, Harvard U., 1966, AM, 1967, PhD, 1972. Asst. to provost U. Mass., Boston, 1971-73; dep. dir. div. edn. programs NEH, Washington, 1973-78, dir. div. edn. programs, 1982-85, dir. div. rsch. programs, 1985-91; v.p., dean of coll. Hiram Coll., Ohio, 1978—82; sec. of found. Andrew W. Mellon Found, NYC, 1991-99; v.p. for programs Atlantic Philanthropies, 1999-2000; pres. Coun. Ind. Coll., 2000—. Mem. nat. adv. com. Yale-New Haven Tchrs. Inst., 1984—, Johns Hopkins U. Press. Mem. Harvard Grad. Sch. Alumni Coun., 1997—. Mem. Harvard Club N.Y.C., Cosmos Club. Home: 180 Highland Ave Ridgewood NJ 07450-4002 Office: Coun Ind Colls One Dupont Cir Ste 320 Washington DC 20036

EKNOYAN, GARABED, medical educator, researcher; b. Aleppo, Syria, Apr. 14, 1935; s. Peter and Armenouhie Eknoyan; m. Sybil Hunter, Feb. 22, 1937; children: Gregory Winston, Byron Armen, Donald Armen. MD, Am. U. of Beirut, Lebanon, 1961. Diplomate Am. Bd. of Internal Medicine, 1974. Asst. prof. medicine U. of Cin. Sch. of Medicine, 1966—68; prof. medicine Baylor Coll. of Medicine, Houston, 1974—. Editor: (book) History of Nephrology (Medal of Excellence, 2000). Pres. Nat. Kidney Found., N.Y.C., 1998—2000. Recipient Pres.'s Award, Nat. Kidney Found., 1996, Chairman's award, 1999, Medal of Excellence, Am. Assn. of Kidney Patients, 2000. Fellow: Am. Coll. of Physicians (life). Office: Baylor Coll of Medicine One Baylor Plz Houston TX 77030 Office Fax: 713-790-0681. E-mail: geknoyan@bcm.tmc.edu.

EKSTROM, JOHN EDWARD, mathematician, educator; b. Boston, Mar. 28, 1949; s. Elisabeth Ann and John Olaf Ekstrom; m. Beverly Ann Solimini, July 9, 1953; 1 child, Victoria Maria. BA in Math., Stonehill Coll., 1971; MA in Tchg. Math., Bridgewater State Coll., 1976; MS in Math., Northeastern U., 1980; EdD in Math., Boston U., 1987. Cert. secondary math. edn. Commonwealth of Mass., 1998. Tchr. math. Archbishop Williams H.S., Braintree, Mass., 1971-75, Medfield Jr H.S., 1975—76; chmn. math. Xaverian Bros. H.S., Westwood, 1976—93, Scituate Pub. Schs., 1995—. Math. assessment com. Mass. Dept. Edn., Malden, 1999—; vis. assoc. prof. Bridgewater State Coll., 1980—94. Author: (educational software) XBHS - Administrative Software. Named Outstanding Tchr., Tufts U., 1995, 1996, 2000, MIT, 2002; recipient Harvard Book award Excellence Edn., Harvard U., 1993. Mem.: Math. Assn. Am. (assoc.). Roman Catholic. Office: Scituate Pub Schs 606 Chief Justice Cushing Hwy Scituate MA 02066 Personal E-mail: dokeks@attbi.com. E-mail: jekstrom@shs.scit.org.

EKSTROM, RUTH BURT, psychologist; b. July 2, 1931; d. Ralph Amos and Bertha Paisley (Lambert) Burt; m. Lincoln Ekstrom, Nov. 9, 1957. AB, Brown U., 1953; EdM, Boston U., 1956; EdD, Rutgers U., 1967; LLD (hon.), Brown U., 1988. Pub. sch. tchr., Beverly, Mass., 1953-57; sr. rsch. asst. Ednl. Testing Svc., 1957-64, dir. documentation svcs., 1964-68, rsch. scientist, 1968-80, sr. rsch. scientist, 1980-91, acting dir. edn. policy rsch. divsn., 1992-94, prin. rsch. scientist, 1991-98. Vis. lectr. Rutgers U., 1958-60. Co-author: Education and American Youth: The Impact of the High School Experience, 1988; co-editor: Kit of Factor-Referenced Cognitive Tests, 1976, Assessing Individuals with Disabilities, 2002; editor: Measurement, Technology and Individuality in Education, 1983; mem. editl. bd.: Psychology of Women Quar., 1978—86, Jour. Counseling and Devel., 1982—85, Measurement and Evaluation in Counseling and Devel., 1989—91, 2002—; contbr. articles. Pres. Bennington (Vt.) Hist. Soc., 1999—2001; trustee Bennington Mus., 2000—; mem. corp. (governing bd.) Brown U., 1972—88, trustee, 1972—77, fellow, 1977—88, sec. corp., 1982—88, co-chmn. joint com. on testing practices, 1994—98. Fellow APA (com. on psychol. tests and assessment 1996-98), AAAS, Am. Psychol. Soc.; mem. ACA (rsch. award 1994, extended rsch. award 1996), Am. Ednl. Rsch. Assn. (chmn. rsch. on women and edn. 1984-85, publ. com. 1995-98), Assn. for Study of Higher Edn. (program com. 1993), Assn. for Assessment in Counseling (chair com. on test use 1991-93, exec. coun. 1992-95), Nat. Coun. Measurement Edn. Home: 78 Westerly Rd Princeton NJ 08540-2621 Office: Ednl Testing Svc Princeton NJ 08541-0001 E-mail: rekstrom@ets.org.

ELAARAG, HALA, adult education educator; b. Alexandria, Egypt, Mar. 15, 1967; d. Ahmed ElAarag and Aida Sheta; m. Mohamed Abdel-Aty, Sept. 16, 1989; children: Yassmeen Abdel-Aty, Ahmad Abdel-Aty. PhD, U. of Ctrl. Fla., 1996—2001. Tchg. asst. Alexandria U., Egypt, 1989—91; post grad. rsch. engr. U. of Calif. at Davis, 1993—94; grad. tchg. asst. U. of Ctrl. Fla., 1996—97, grad. rsch. asst., 1997—99; grad. rschr. Ctr. For Advanced Transp. Simulation Systems, Orlando, 2000—00; post doctorate rschr. Inst. for Simulation and Tng., Orlando, 2002—02; asst. prof. Stetson U., DeLand, Fla., 2002—. Contbr. articles in profl. jours. Additions vol. Orange County Pub. Schools, Orlando, 1997; mem., sch. adv. coun. Lawton Chiles Elem., Orlando, 2000—00. Grantee UCF Grad. Merit Fellowship, U. of Ctrl. Fla., 2001. Mem.: IEEE Women in Engring., IEEE, UPE Honor Soc. in the Computing Sciences, Phi Kappa Phi. Office: Stetson University 421 N Woodland Blvd DeLand FL 32723 E-mail: helaarag@stetson.edu.

ELACHI, CHARLES, aerospace engineer; b. Apr. 18, 1947; BS, U. Grenoble, France, 1968; MS, Calif. Inst. Tech., 1969, PhD in Elec. Sci., 1971; MBA, U. So. Calif., 1978; MS, UCLA, 1983. Rsch. fellow Calif. Inst. Tech., Pasadena, 1971-74, leader Radar Remote Sensing Team, 1974-80, asst. lab. dir. space and sci. instruments, 1987-95, sr. scientist Jet Propulsion Lab., 1971-74, sr. rsch. scientist Jet Propulsion Lab., 1981—, dir. space and earth sci. programs Jet Proplusion Lab., 1995—2000, Watson lectr., 1983—, dir., 2000—. Prin. investigator NASA, 1973-87, mem. Solar Sys. Exploration Com. Coun., 1988—, Astrophysics Coun., 1988—; mem. Electromagnetic Acad., 1990-95. Contbr. over 200 articles to profl. jours.; patentee in field. Recipient Prof. R.W.P. King award for outstanding contbrn. in field of electromagnetics, 1973. Mem. AIAA (Dryden Lecturship in Rsch., 2000), NAE, IEEE (Geosensing and Remote Sensing Disting. Achievement award 1987, Engring. Excellence medal 1992), Am. Astronautical Soc., Electromagnetic Soc., Am. Geophys. Union, Planetary Soc., Sigma Xi. Office: Jet Propulsion Lab MS 180-704 4800 Oak Grove Dr Pasadena CA 91109-8001*

ELAHI, DARIUSH, physiologist, researcher; PhD, Dalhousie U., 1970—74. Physiologist Mass. Gen. Hosp., 1996. Dir., geriat. rsch. lab. Mass. Gen. Hosp., Boston, 1996—. Author original rsch. pubs. Office: Massachusetts Gen Hosp 55 Fruit St Boston MA 02114 Office Fax: 617-726-2334. E-mail: delahi@partners.org.

ELALI, TAAN, engineering and computer science educator; b. Soor, Lebanon, Mar. 13, 1963; s. Saeed Taan ElAli and Shandoukha Ali AlAwad; m. Salam ElZaher, Jan. 6, 1997; children: Zayd T., Ali T., Nusayba T. BS, Ohio State U., 1987; MS, Wright State U., 1989, U. Dayton, Ohio, 1991; PhD, U. Dayton, 1993. Prof. engring. and computer sci. Wilberforce (Ohio) U., 1994—. Adj. prof. U. Dayton, 1994—. Author: Continuous Signals and Systems with Matlab, Discrete Signals and Systems with Matlab, Introduction to Engineering with C programming and Matlab; contbr. articles to profl. jours. Mem. Islamic Soc. of Greater Dayton, 1996—. Mem.: AAUP. Moslem. Achievements include research in new approach to system identification. Avocations: swimming, running, reading, writing. Office: Wilberforce U Bicket Rd Wilberforce OH 45384 Personal E-mail: telali@wilberforce.edu. E-mail: telali@wilberforce.edu.

ELAM, FRED ELDON, retired career army officer; b. Seminole, Okla., July 10, 1937; s. Jack Eldon Elam and Maye (Gaskill) E.; m. Judy Teller, Feb. 21, 1959; children: Jacqueline Marie Elam Kabat, Justin Eldon. BS, U. Ark., 1960; MBA, Mich. State U., 1964; grad. strategy mgmt. and naval ops., Naval War Coll., 1977; grad., Harvard Grad. Sch. Bus. Admin., 1998. Commd. 2d lt. U.S. Army, 1960, advanced through grades to maj. gen., 1986, with Div. G-4, 101st Airborne (Air Assault), 1976-77, comdr. Materiel Support Ctr. Waegwan, Republic of Korea, 1977-79, dir. programs and evaluation Army Materiel Command Alexandria, Va., 1979-82; comdg. gen. 19th Support Command,

Taegu, Republic of Korea, 1982-84; dir. mgmt. Hdqrs. Dept. Army, Washington, 1984-85; chief U.S. Army Transp., Hdqrs. Transp. Ctr. Fort Eustis, Va., 1985-88; comdr. Joint U.S. Mil. Mission for Aid to Turkey Ankara, 1988-90; asst. dep. chief of staff for logistics, Dept. Army Washington, 1990-93; v.p. profl. tech. svcs. Advancia Corp., Arlington, Va., 1993—2002. Mem. lifetime staff and faculty Army Logistics Mgmt. Ctr., Fort Lee, Va., 1971—, Va. Mil. Commn., 1986-88; disting. mem. Transp. Corps Rgt., U.S. Army; counselor Sr. Corps. Ret. Exec.; mem. bd. dirs. Advancia Corp. Decorated D.S.M., Def. Superior Svc. medal, Legion of Merit, Bronze Star with two oak leaf clusters, Meritorious Svc. medal with two oak leaf clusters, Air medal, Army Commendation medal with three oak leaf clusters, Armed Forces expeditionary medal, Vietnam Svc. medal with four oak leaf clusters, Overseas Svc. ribbon with "4" device, Republic of Vietnam campaign medal, Republic of Korea Svc. medal, Medal of Merit of Turkish Armed Forces, Meritorious Svc. medal. Mem. Assn. U.S. Army, Air Traffic Control Assn., Soc. of 173d Airborne Brigade, Nat. Def. Transp. Assn., Res. Officers Assn., Am.-Turkish Friendship Assn., Sr. Corps of Ret. Execs., Beta Gamma Sigma. Avocations: running, reading, military history. E-mail: fred.elam@advancia.com.

ELAM, JOHN RICHARD, mortgage company executive; b. Kansas City, Mo., Dec. 4, 1945; s. Jonnie Elam; m. Kathy Elam, Aug. 1996; 1 child, MacKenzie. BS, Auburn U., 1967; MA, U. Ga., 1973; MBA, Harvard U., 1985, Golden Gate U., 1986. With Sallie Mae, Tampa, Fla., 1988-92; divsn. supt. Chase Manhattan Mgmt., Tampa, 1992-96; gen. mgr. CIS, Champaign, Ill., 1996-98; CIO ops. N.Am. Mortgage Co., Santa Rosa, Calif., 1998—. Col. U.S. Army, 1968-88. Avocations: running, weight lifting, golf, reading. Office: N Am Mortgage Co 3883 Airway Dr Santa Rosa CA 95403 Home: 16104 Condover Ct Tampa FL 33647-1042 E-mail: jaelam@namc.com.

ELAM, LESLIE ALBERT, retired museum administrator; b. Balt., May 12, 1938; s. Albert and Mary (Walker) E.; m. Judith Anne Clark, Apr. 4, 1964; children— Jennifer Helen, Jeffrey Walker. BA, Lehman Coll., City U. N.Y., 1973. Editor J.J. Augustin, Inc. Pub., Locust Valley, N.Y., 1958-61; editorial asst. Am. Numis. Soc., N.Y.C., 1963-66, editor, 1966-89, adminstrv. officer, 1966-69, sec., 1969-99, dir., 1972-97, exec. dir., 1997-99; cons., 1999-2000. Editor: Am. Numis. Soc. Museum Notes, 1966-89. Served with AUS 1961-63. Mem. Phi Beta Kappa. Home: 36 Lord Brook Rd Rindge NH 03461-4126 E-mail: LAElam@aol.com.

ELAM, LLOYD CHARLES, psychiatrist, educator; b. Little Rock, Oct. 27, 1928; s. Harry and Ruth (Davis) Elam; m. Clara Carpenter, Feb. 16, 1957; children: Gloria, Laurie. BS, Roosevelt U., 1950, LHD (hon.), 1974; MD, U. Wash., 1957; postgrad., U. Ill., 1957-58, U. Chgo., 1957-61; LLD (hon.), Harvard U., 1973. Staff psychiatrist Billings Hosp., Chgo., 1961, Hubbard Hosp., Nashville, 1961, asst. prof., chmn. dept. psychiatry, 1961-63, prof., chmn. dept. psychiatry, 1963; interim dean Meharry Med. Coll., Nashville, 1966, 6th pres., 1968-81, chancellor, 1981-82, Disting. Svc. prof. psychiatry, 1983-95, prof. emeritus, chmn. emeritus dept. psychiatry and behavioral scis., 1996—2000; ret. Mem. Frontiers of Am., Nashville. Recipient Eleanor Roosevelt Key award Roosevelt U., 1972, Bus. and Profl. Leader of Yr. award Heritage of Am., 1974. Mem. AMA, Am. Psychiat. Assn., Nat. Med. Assn., Inst. Medicine, Nashville Acad. Medicine, R.F. Boyd Med. Soc. Office: Meharry Med Coll Dept of Psychiatry 1005 D B Todd Blvd Nashville TN 37208

ELANAYAR, SUNIL K. research and development engineer; arrived in U.S., 1986; s. Sivadasan Arangott and Komalam Sivadasan; m. Seema S. Nair, Dec. 27, 1996; 1 child, Adira Nair. B Tech, ITT Delhi, Delhi, India, 1986; MS, Univ. Ala., Tuscaloose, Ala., 1988; PhD, Purdue Univ., W. Lafayette, Ind., 1993. Rsch. fellow Purdue Univ., W. Lafayette, Ind., 1993—94; sr. engr. Computer-vision, Pune, India, 1994—96; dir. Gentech Corp., Tokyo, 1996—98; sr. rsch. engr. Caice Corp., Tampa, Fla., 1998—2000; sr. engr. Knowledge Tech., Lexington, Mass., 2000—. Fellow David Ross Found., W. Lafayette, Ind., 1991—93. Contbr. scientific papers. Achievements include research in neural networks in mfg. process monitoring knowledge based engring. Avocations: travel, tennis, photography. Home: 14 Royal Crest Dr #6 Nashua NH 03060 Office: Knowledge Tech 10 Maguire St 232 Lexington MA 02421

ELANDER, RICHARD PAUL, consultant, retired pharmaceutical executive; b. Worcester, Mass., Sept. 17, 1932; s. Arthur Waldemar and Edith Alma Louise (Engstrand) E.; m. Barbara Ann Sudz, Feb. 8, 1958; children: Tracy, Richard, Ronald. BS with honors, U. Detroit, 1955, MS, 1956; PhD, U. Wis., 1960; postdoctoral, U. Minn., 1965-66. Rsch. scientist Eli Lilly and Co., Indpls., 1960-67; assoc. dir. Wyeth Labs., West Chester, Pa., 1967-72, Smith Kline and French, Phila., 1972-75; dir. fermentation devel. Bristol-Myers Squibb Co., Syracuse, N.Y., 1975-80, sr. dir. biotech. and rsch. devel., 1980-83, v.p. biotech., 1983-97; cons. to biotech./pharm. industry, 1997—. Lectr. Butler U., Indpls., 1965-66, Rensselaer Poly. Inst., 1983-88; rsch. prof. Syracuse U., 1983-97; biotech. adv. bd., Dartmouth, MIT, Cornell; mem. adv. bd. Coll. Agr. and Life Scis., Cornell U., 1998. Mem. editl. bd. Biotech. Letters, 1985-97, Jour. Indsl. Microbiology, 1985-94, Applied and Environ. Microbiology, 1974-83; contbr. articles to profl. jours., also chpts. to books in field; patentee in field. Recipient Charles Thom award Soc. Indsl. Microbiology, 1984. Fellow Am. Acad. Microbiology, Am. Inst. Chemists, Soc. Indsl. Microbiology (sec. 1968, pres. 1974); mem. AAAS, Am. Soc. Microbiology (chmn. div. 1977), Am. Chem. Soc., Lions (bd. dirs. 1970-73), Sigma Xi (v.p. Syracuse chpt. 1991, pres. Syracuse chpt. 1992). Republican. Avocations: music, skiing, gardening, writing. Home and Office: 318 Gravilla St La Jolla CA 92037-6006

ELARABY, NABIL A. Egyptian diplomat; b. Cairo, Mar. 15, 1935; m. Nadia Teymour; children: May, Marwan, Hisham. Licencie en Droit, Cairo U., Egypt; LLM in Internat. Law, JSD, NYU, U.S.A. Legal advisor to Egyptian del. UN Mid. East Peace Conf., Ministry of Fgn. Affairs, Geneva, 1973-75; counsellor to mission from Egypt UN, Geneva, 1974-76, amb., dep. permanent rep. of Egypt N.Y.C., 1978-81, 91-99, amb. extraordinary and plenipotentiary, permanent rep. of Egypt Geneva, 1987-91, permanent rep. N.Y.C., 1991—; legal advisor, dir. legal and treaties dept. Ministry of Fgn. Affairs, Geneva, 1976-78, 83-87; Egyptian amb. India, 1981-83; arbitrator (Suez Canal dispute) ICC Internat. Ct. of Arbitration, Paris, 1989; judge Jud. Tribunal Orgn. Arb Petroleum, 1990. Commr. UN Compensation Commn.; ptnr. Zaki Hashon & Ptnrs., Attys. at Law; rep. Egypt in UN orgns. including The Gen. Assembly, Security Coun., Econ. and Social Coun., Human Rights Commn., 1966—; head Egyptian Del. UN Conf. on Disarmament, 1987—91; leader Egyptian Delegation to Egyptian-Israeli Arbitration Tribunal Taba Talks, 1986—89; former chair numerous UN coms. and working groups; pres. Security Coun., 1996; mem. Internat. Ct. of Justice, The Hague, 2001—; lectr. The Hague acad. of Internat. Law, Columbia U., NYU, Duke U., Yale U., The Egyptian Soc. Internat. Law, Am. Soc. Internat. Law, many others. Contbr. to profl. jours. and internat. law publs. Adlai Stevenson fellow UN Inst. for Tgn. and Rsch., 1968, Spl. fellow, 1973. Mem. Egyptian Soc. Internat. Law (bd. dirs.), Am. Soc. Internat. Law, Internat. Law Assn. (am. br.), Inst. World Affairs (bd. dirs.). Address: 23 Kasr El Nil St Cairo 11211 Egypt

ELARBA, NAGIB A. mechanical engineer, consultant; b. Maturin, Venezuela, Nov. 3, 1956; s. Badih and Marie Elarba; children: Erika, Patty, Badih, Nagib. BS, Tex. A&M U., Kingsville, TX, 1980. Registered profl. engr., Tex. Tech. asst. Venauum, Venezuela, Venezuela, 1980—83; project engr. Chgo. Bridge and Iron, Venezuela, 1984—87; project mgr. Venauum, Venezuela, 1987—92; plant superintendant Secoinca, Venezuela, 1993—96; plant engr. Smith Tank & Equipment, Tyler, Tex., 1997—98; cons. Rimrus Consulting Group, Houston, Tex., 1998—. Mem.: Tex. Assn. Accident Reconstruction Specialist, Assn. Energy Engrs., Am. Indoor Air Quality Coun., Nat. Soc. Profl. Engrs. Office: Rimrus Consulting Group 555 N Carancahua suite 1050 Corpus Christi TX 78413 Office Fax: 361-883-5983. E-mail: ntonye@yahoo.com.

ELARDO, ROBERT ANTHONY, secondary school educator, financial analyst; b. Buffalo, Feb. 3, 1945; s. Robert Joseph and Marie Margaret Elardo; m. Rosalie Germain DeReu, Aug. 3, 1968; children: Jason, Justin. BA in History, Canisius Coll., 1967, MS in Edn., 1971; MA in History, St. Louis U., 1969. H.s. social studies tchr. Buffalo Pub. Sch., 1969—2002; womens soccer coach Medaille Coll., Buffalo, 2002—. Secondary social studies methods instr. U. Buffalo, Amherst, NY, 1991—93; instr. Buffalo State Coll., 1999—2001; fin. analyst Primerica Fin. Svcs., West Seneca, NY, 1995—; cons. in field. Campaign adv. Rep. Party, Hamburg, NY, 1997. Mem.: N.Y. State Coun. on Social Studies. Avocations: photography, backpacking. Home: 4580 Kennison Pkwy Hamburg NY 14075 Office: South Park HS 150 Southside Pkwy Buffalo NY 14220-1595

ELBAUM, CHARLES, physicist, educator, researcher; b. May 15, 1926; married; 3 children. MASc, U. Toronto, 1952, PhD in Applied Sci., 1954; MA (hon.), Brown U., 1961. Rsch. fellow in metal physics U. Toronto, 1954-57, Harvard U., 1957-59; asst. prof. applied physics Brown U., Providence, 1959-61, assoc. prof. physics, 1961-63, prof. physics, 1963—, chmn. dept. physics, 1980-86, also Hazard prof. physics, 1991—. Cons. to industry. Fellow Am. Phys. Soc.; mem. AIME, AAAS, Soc. Neurosci. Office: Brown U Dept Physics PO Box 1843 Providence RI 02912-1843 E-mail: elbaum@physics.brown.edu.

ELBAUM, MAREK, electro-optical sciences executive, researcher; b. Kovel, U.S.S.R., May 8, 1941; came to U.S., 1969; s. Isaak Elbaum and Maria Rajbenbach; m. Lia Krusin, Jan. 2, 1969; 1 child, Martin Krusin-Elbaum. MSc, Warsaw (Poland) Tech. U., 1966; PhD, Columbia U., 1977. Rsch. assoc. Polish Acad. Sci., Warsaw, 1966-68; mem. rsch. staff Riverside Rsch. Inst., N.Y.C., 1969-79, mgr. electro-optics div., 1979-82, rsch. dir., 1982-90; pres., CEO Electro-Optical Scis., Irvington, N.Y., 1990—. Contbr. more than 60 articles to profl. jours. Recipient Award Christopher Columbus Found., 1998. Achievements include development of novel holographic technique, novel techniques for tracking space object in the visible and infrared, theory for direct detection laser radars; first demonstration of frequency diversity technique for laser speckle reduction and ultrasound applications; development of multi-spectral lesion imaging method for automatic early detection of melanoma; development digital fiber optics transillumination for detection of early caries. Office: Electro Optical Scis 1 Bridge St Irvington NY 10533-1543 E-mail: elbaum@eo-sciences.com.

EL-BAZ, FAROUK, science administrator, educator; b. Zagazig, Egypt, Jan. 1, 1938; came to U.S., 1967, naturalized, 1970; s. El-Sayed Mohammed and Zahia Abul-Ata (Hammouda) El-B.; m. Catherine Patricia O'Leary, 1963; children: Monira, Soraya, Karima, Fairouz. BSc, Ain Shams U., 1958; MS, U. Mo., 1961; PhD, U. Mo. and MIT, 1964; DSc (hon.), New England Coll., 1989. Demonstrator geology dept. Assiut U., Egypt, 1958-60; lectr. Mineralogy-Petrography Inst., U. Heidelberg, Germany, 1964-65; geologist exploration dept. Pan Am.-UAR Oil Co., Egypt, 1966; supr. lunar exploration Bellcomm and Bell Tel. Labs., Washington, 1967-72, rsch. dir. Center for Earth and Planetary Studies, Nat. Air and Space Mus., Smithsonian Instn., Washington, 1973-82; v.p. sci. and tech. Itek Optical Sys., Litton Industries, Lexington, Mass., 1982-86; cons. geology, prof. geology and geophysics U. Utah, 1975-77; prof. geology Ain Shams U., Egypt, 1976-81, 95—; sci. adviser Pres. Anwar Sadat of Egypt, 1978-81; sr. advisor Nat. Rsch. Inst. for Astronomy and Geophysics, Helwan, Egypt, 1996—; dir. Ctr. for Remote Sensing Boston U., 1986—. Author: Say It in Arabic, 1968, Astronaut Observations from the Apollo-Soyuz Mission, 1977, Egypt as Seen by Landsat, 1979, The Geology of Egypt: An Annotated Bibliography, 1984; co-author: Coprolites: An Annotated Bibliography, 1968, Glossory of Mining Geology, 1970, The Moon as Viewed by Lunar Orbiter, 1970, Apollo Over the Moon: A View from Orbit, 1978; co-editor: Apollo Soyuz Test Project Summary Science Report: Earth Observations and Photography, 1979, Desert Landforms of Southwest Egypt: A Basis for Comparison with Mars, 1982, Physics of Desertification, 1986, Remote Sensing and Resource Exploration, 1989, Sand Transport and Desertification in Arid Lands, 1990, The Gulf War and the Environment, 1994, Atlas of State of Kuwait from Satellite Images, 2000; editor: Deserts and Arid Lands, 1984; contbr. articles to profl. jours. Decorated Order of Merit 1st class Egypt; recipient certificate merit U.S. Bur. Mines, 1961, Exceptional Sci. Achievement medal NASA, 1971, Alumni Achievement award U. Mo., 1972, Honor citation Assn. Arab-Am. U. Grads., 1973, Outstanding Contbns. to Sci. and Space Tech. award Am.-Arab Anti-Discrimination Com., 1995, Achievement award Egyptian-Am. Profl. Soc., 1995, Human Needs award Am. Assn. Petroleum Geologists, 1996. Fellow: AAAS (Pub. Understanding of Sci. and Tech. award 1992), Geol. Soc. Am. (cert. commendation 1973), Royal Astron.; mem.: Nat. Acad. Engring., Internat. Inst. of Boston (Golden Door award 1992), World Aerospace Edn. Orgn. (Cert. of Merit 1973), Explorers Club, Sigma Xi. Office: Boston U Ctr Remote Sensing 725 Commonwealth Ave Boston MA 02215-1401 E-mail: farouk@bu.edu.

ELBEIK, TAREK ALI, research scientist; b. Benghazi, Cyrenaica, Libya, Dec. 11, 1958; s. Ali Hassan Elbeik and Emma Charlotte Gurtner. BSc(hon.), Monmouth Coll., Long Branch, N.J., 1981; PhD, Georgetown U., Washington, D.C., 1986. Dir. clin. microbiology rsch. lab. U. of Calif., San Francisco, 1997—, protocol microbiologist, tb rsch. unit, 2001—02, founder and co-dir. hiv-1 virology core lab., 1988—97; protocol virologist, adult aids clin. trials group NIH, Bethesda, Md., 1988—97, protocol virologist, pediatric aids clin. trials group, 1988—97; protocol virologist Cmty. Programs for Clin. Rsch. on AIDS, San Francisco, 1995—. Infectious disease cons. Profl. Habitat Design, San Francisco, 1998—, Bill Rosen Consulting, San Francisco, 1995—, Bayer Diagnostics, Nucleic Acid Divsn., Berkeley, Calif., 1999—, Chiron Corp., Emmeryville, Calif., 1990—; lectr. in field. Contbr. Grantee Rsch. and Honorarium grantee, Bayer Diagnostics, Nucleic Acid Divsn., 1999—2002, Rsch. and Honorarium grant, Chiron Corp., 1990—99, Rsch. and Honorarium grantee, Roche Molecular Systems, 1999—2002, Rsch. grantee, Applied Biosystems, 2000—02, Honorarium grantee, VaxGen, 2001, Rsch. grantee, ViroLogic, 2001. Mem.: Am. Assn. for Microbiology (mem. 1988—2002, None None). Democrat-Npl. Moslem. Achievements include research in on the in-vivo development of HIV-1 resistance in patients during drug treatment success (viral load less than 50 copies/ml); first to design an HIV-1 viral load assay cost engine to determine labor and supply cost differentials between different brand assays; development of of an HIV diagnostic and monitoring infrastructure survey for health care centers in developing countries to elucidate the needs and specifications directly from respondents. Avocations: cooking, weightlifting. Office: University of California Bldg NH Rm 2M35 1001 Potrero Ave San Francisco CA 94110 Office Fax: 415-206-3045. E-mail: elbeik@itsa.ucsf.edu.

ELBER, RON, computer science educator; b. Rehovot, Israel, Mar. 28, 1957; s. Yair and Rachel Neter Elber; m. Victoria Buch, Aug. 1983 (div. Aug. 1996); 1 child, Dassi; m. Virginia Yip, 2000; children: Nurit, Nis. BSc, Hebrew U., 1981, PhD in Chemistry and Physics, 1984. Postdoctoral Harvard U., Boston, 1984-87; asst. prof. chemistry U. Ill., Chgo., 1988-91, assoc. prof. chemistry, 1992-94; assoc. prof. chemistry and biology Hebrew U., Jerusalem, 1994-96, prof. chemistry and biology, 1996-98; prof. computer sci. Cornell U., Ithaca, N.Y., 1999—. Cons. Tera Computers, Israel, 1996-98, Peptor, Israel, 1996—; acting dir. NIH Resource for Parallel Computing, Ithaca, 1999—; organizer numerous scientific meetings. Editor: Recent Development in the Theoretical Studies of Proteins, 1996. Sgt. Israel Def. Forces, 1978-81. Scholar U. Ill., 1990-92; recipient Alon fellow State of Israel, 1992; recipient numerous grants. Mem. AAAS, N.Y. Acad. Sci., ACS, Israel Chem. Soc., Soc. Indsl. and Aplied Maths. Avocations: chess, hiking. Office: Cornell U 4130 Upson Hall Ithaca NY 14853-7501 E-mail: ron@cs.cornell.edu.

ELBERGER, RONALD EDWARD, lawyer; b. Newark, Mar. 13, 1945; s. Morris and Clara (Denes) Elberger; m. Rena Ann Brodey, Feb. 15, 1975; children: Seth, Rebecca. AA, George Washington U., 1964, BA, 1966; JD, Am. U., 1969. Bar: Md. 1969, D.C. 1970, Ind. 1971, U.S. Ct. Appeals (7th cir.) 1971, U.S. Supreme Ct. 1973. Atty. Balt. Legal Aid Bur., 1969-70; chief counsel Legal Services Orgn., Indpls., 1970-72; ptnr. Elberger & Stanton, Indpls., 1974-76; assoc. Bose, McKinney & Evans, LLP, Indpls., 1972—74, ptnr., 1976—; asst. sec. Chip Ganassi Racing Teams, Inc., 1998—. V.p. Worldwide Slacks, Inc., 1984—92, Cardboard Shoe Prodns., Inc., 1989—93; asst. sec., v.p., litig. counsel Emmis Comm. Corp., 1986—2002. Mem., v.p. Med. Licensing Bd., Ind., 1982—98; pres., chmn. bd. dirs. Ind. Civil Liberties Union, Indpls., 1972—77, bd. dirs., 1972—77, 1980—82; mem. nat. coun. media and pub. affairs George Washington U., 2000—; bd. dirs. Jewish Cmty. Rels. Coun., 1997—2000, ACLU, N.Y.C., 1972—77; trustee Children's Mus. Indpls., 1994—2003, Disting. advisor, 2003—; bd. dirs. Flanner Ho. Indpls., Inc., 1999—. Fellow Reginald Heber Smith, U. Pa., 1969—71. Fellow: Ind. Bar Found., Indpls. Bar Found.; mem.: ABA, Ind. Bar Assn. Democrat. Jewish. Avocations: fishing, music, gardening. Office: Bose McKinney & Evans LLP 2700 First Indiana Pla 135 N Pennsylvania St Indianapolis IN 46204-2400

ELBERT, CHARLES STEINER, lawyer; b. St. Louis, May 18, 1950; s. Harold I. and Carol B. (Steiner) E.; m. Karen Berry, Dec. 9, 1979; children: Matthew Berry, Lisa Beth. AB, Washington U., 1972; JD cum laude, St. Louis U., 1976. Bar: Mo. 1976, Ill. 1977, U.S. Dist. Ct. (ea. and we. dists.) Mo. 1977, U.S. Ct. Appeals (8th cir.) 1977, U.S. Supreme Ct. 1985. Assoc. Kohn, Shands, Elbert, Gianoulakis & Giljum, LLP, St. Louis, 1976-81, ptnr., 1982—. Spl. rep. 22d Jud. Bar Com., St. Louis, 1978-88; spk. labor and employment law CLEs. Contbr. articles to profl. jours. Trustee Clayton Gardens Neighborhood Assn., Mo., 1983-84, 85-86, pres., 1984-85; bd. dirs. St. Louis chpt. Am. Diabetes Assn., 1998—, St. Louis chpt. Am. Jewish Com., 1984-97, mem. nat. legal com., 1997--; sec., 1994-97; v.p. Nursery Found., St. Louis, 1988-89, bd. dirs., Mo. Coalition Against Censorship, 1986-92, sec., 1988-92; mentor Dunbar Sch., 1995-2001. Mem. ABA (labor law sect. 1984—, corp. banking and bus. law sect. 1987—), Mo. Bar Assn. (labor law com. 1977—), Ill. State Bar Assn., Bar Assn. Met. St. Louis (labor law com. 1977—, grievance com. 1978-87, Clayton Hockey Club (pres. 2001-02). Jewish. Home: 8137 University Dr Saint Louis MO 63105-3726 Office: Kohn Shands Elbert et al Ste 2410 One US Bank Plaza Saint Louis MO 63101 E-mail: celbert@ksegg.com.

ELBERT, JAMES PEAK, independent insurance agent, minister; b. Pampa, Tex., Feb. 5, 1937; s. James Monteen and Nannie Pearle (Harwell) E.; m. Jean Coburn, June 25, 1960 (div. Jan., 1983); children: James Michael, Steven Lawrence; m. Ann English Smith, Apr. 23, 1983; 1 child, Jennifer English Aberle. BA, Southwestern U., Georgetown, Tex., 1959; MDiv, So. Meth. U., 1962. Minister First Meth. Ch., Glen Flora, Tex., 1962-65, Falvey Meml. Meth. Ch., Wells, Tex., 1965-67; assoc. minister First United Meth. Ch., Orange, Tex., 1967-69; minister of edn. Trinity United Meth. Ch., Beaumont, Tex., 1969-70; minister First United Meth. Ch., Murchiston, Tex., 1970-71; campus minister Henderson County Jr. Coll., Athens, Tex., 1970-71; v.p., owner Elbert Insur. Agy., Lake Jackson, Tex., 1971-76, Bennett-Elbert Co., Lake Jackson, 1976-83; v.p., gen. mgr. Jahn-Austin Insur., Galveston, Tex., 1983-96; prin., owner Brazoria (Tex.) Ins. Agy., 1998—. Pres. Galveston Ins. Bd., 1986-88; Elbert Ins. Agy., Lake Jackson, Tex., 1995—, pres., Insurco, Inc., 1997— ; apptd. to Windstorm Study com. Tex. Dept. Ins., 1992, liaison to Tex. Dept. Ins. bldg. code study com., 1992—; supernumerary Tex. Conf. United Meth. Ch. Bd. dirs. Jr. Achievement of Brazoria County, 1980 81; active Lake Jackson Little League, 1974-77, Lake Jackson Teenage League, 1978-79, Lake Jackson Babe Ruth League, 1980; sec. Galveston Windstorm Action Com., 1988—; pres. Galveston Housing Fin. Corp., 1993-95, City of Galveston Property Fin. Authority, Inc., 1993-95; v.p. Bay Area coun. Boy Scouts Am., 1988—; pres. Ball H.S. Band Boosters, Galveston, 1991-92; mem. Mayor's Roundtable on Housing, City of Galveston, 1993-95; chmn. com. on ministries Moody Meml. First United Meth. Ch., 1994-95. Recipient Merit award Bay Area Coun. Boy Scouts Am. Quintana Dist., Lake Jackson, 1979, Silver Beaver award Bay Area Coun. Boy Scouts Am., Galveston, 1985. Mem.: Tex. Assn. Ins. Agts. (liaison to Tex. Windstrom Pool Assn. 1993—95, bd. dirs. 1995—98, Chmn. of the Yr. 1993—94), Tex. Windstrom Ins. Assn. (bd. dirs. 1998—, Tex. fair plan governing com. 2002—), Ind. Ins. Agts. Tex. (chmn. com. 1991—95), Cert. Ins. Counselors (pres. Tex. chpt. 1992, edn. com. 2002, cert.), Brazosport C. of C. (mem. bd. 1980—81), Galveston C. of C. (bd. dirs. 1992—95), Rotary of Galveston Island (pres. 1993—94, Rotarian of Yr., Paul Harris fellow 1990, Bd. Mem. of Yr. 1991), Phi Delta Theta. Avocations: family camping, gardening. Home: 7754 Beaudelaire Cir Galveston TX 77551-1625 Office: Elbert Ins Agy PO Box 4009 107 W Way Ste 21 Lake Jackson TX 77566-2409 also: Brazoria Ins Agy 100 E Hwy 332 PO Box 1240 Brazoria TX 77422-1240 E-mail: eia_james@elbertinsurance.com.

ELBERY, KATHLEEN MARIE, lawyer, accountant, cartoonist; b. Boston, Nov. 30, 1959; d. Norman F. and June E. (Ramsay) E. BSBA with high honors, Northeastern U., 1983; JD cum laude, Suffolk U., 1990. Bar: Mass. 1990, U.S. Ct. Appeals (1st cir.) Mass. 1991, U.S. Dist. Ct. Mass. 1991; CPA, Mass. 1986. CPA, supr. Gately & Assocs., P.C., Wellesley, Mass., 1983-87; sr. tax mgr. and multi-state income and franchise tax practice leader KPMG Peat Marwick LLP, Boston, 1988-96; tax mgr. state taxes Arthur Andersen LLP, Boston, 1996—98; pvt. practice Boston, 1998—. Mem. Mass. Dept. Revenue Practitioner Liaison Com.; instr., panel mem. state taxation seminars and profl. devel. courses; spkr. in field. Creator: Funny Bone Cartoons; Funny Bone Cartoons; creator Funny Bone Cartoons. Merit scholar Northeastern U., 1978; recipient Outstanding Achievement award in Appellate Brief Writing, 1988. Mem. AICPAs, ABA, Mass. Soc. CPAs (chair multi-state tax sub-com. 1996-97), Mass. Bar Assn., Beta Alpha Psi (elected recording sec. 1981-82), Beta Gamma Sigma, Phi Kappa Phi, Phi Delta Phi.

ELBIN-SCHELL, CAROL GERTRUDE, television promotion manager; b. Sept. 30, 1937; d. Harry C. and Gertrude I. (Simms) Elbin; 1 child, Karen Denise Schell. BFA, Cin. Coll.-Conservatory, 1959; student, Foley Modeling Sch., 1961; postgrad., Tidewater C.C., 1976-77. Promotion mgr. Sta. WAVY-TV, Norfolk, Va., 1975-76; promotion pub. svc. mgr. Sta. WNYS-TV (now WIXT), Syracyse, N.Y., 1962-71; asst. promotion dept. Sta. KRCA (now KNBC-TV), Hollywood, Calif., 1959; asst. promotion-pub. svc. mgr. Sta. WCPO-TV, Cin., 1956-59, 60-61; promotion-pub. svc. mgr. Sta. KUSK-TV, Prescott, Ariz., 1982-83; promotion mgr. Sta. KMIR-TV, Palm Springs, 1984; sta. mgr., promotion mgr. Gt. S.W. Broadcasting, Bakersfield, Calif., 1987-88; freelance writer Prescott, 1983—. Writer Videoview Mag., Phoenix, 1985; gen. mgr. Prescott Cmty. Access Channel, 1988-91; supr. personal appearances: Mike Douglas, Jack LaLanne, Vic Morrow, others, 1961-83; personal appearance coord., publicist to Elizabeth Taylor-Warner, 1977-78; exec. prodr., writer, editor TV series, spls., 1962-91. Author: Great Hospital Connection, 1976, Self Signs, 1976. Campaign coord. Sen. John W. Warner of Va., 1977-78; campaign worker Sen. Barry Goldwater of Ariz., 1980. Recipient Gabriel award Office of Cath. Dioceses, Washington, 1971. Mem. Women in Comms., Am. Women in Radio and TV, Broadcast Promotion Assn., Am. Film Inst., Delta Omicron. Republican. Methodist.

ELCANO, MARY S. lawyer; BA cum laude, Lynchburg Coll., 1971; JD, Cath. U., Washington, 1976. Litigation atty. Balt. Legal Aide Bur., 1976; staff atty. Office Solicitor Dept. Labor, 1979; gen. trial and appellate atty. Office Labor Law U.S. Postal Svc., 1982, exec. dir. Office EEO, 1984, regional dir. human resources N.E. region, 1987, sr. v.p., gen. counsel, 1992-99, exec. v.p., gen. counsel, 1999-2000; ptnr. Sidley Austin Brown & Wood LLP, Washington, 2000—03; gen. counsel, corp. sec. ARC, Washington, 2003—. Office: ARC 2025 E St NW Washington DC 20006 E-mail: ElcanoM@usa.redcross.org.

ELCHERT, KENNETH CLARENCE, aerospace engineer; b. Delaware, Ohio, Aug. 3, 1949; s. Franklin Clarence and Marie Margaret Elchert; m. Celia Berumen, Oct. 27, 1979; children: John, Marissa, Amanda. BA in Math. and Physics, St. Joseph Coll., Rensselaer, Ind., 1971; BS in Aero. and Astro. Engring., Ohio State U., 1973. Engr., space shuttle separation Rockwell Internat., Downey, Calif., 1974—81, lead engr., space shuttle, 1981—87, launch vehicle systems engr., 1987—97; advanced launch vehicle engr. Boeing, Huntington Beach, Calif., 1997—2002, missile def. systems engr. Anaheim, Calif., 2002—. Contbr. articles to profl. publs. Troop scoutmaster Boy Scouts Am., Covina, Calif., 1988—94; coach Am. Youth Soccer, Covina, 1989—91. Mem.: AIAA, KC (officer, recorder, Glendora, Calif. chpt. 1983—88). Roman Catholic. Achievements include successfully analyzed separation systems for space shuttle launch vehicle; successfully integrated flight sequencing requirements for Delta IV launch vehicle; successfully provided systems engineering for missile defense qualification tests. Avocation: model rocketry. Home: 353 E Carter Dr Glendora CA 91740 Office: Boeing 3370 Miraloma Ave Anaheim CA 92803

ELCIK, ELIZABETH MABIE, fashion illustrator; b. Bklyn., Sept. 16, 1933; d. Cornelius Peter and Anna Julia (Cunningham) Mabie; m. John Joseph Elcik, Apr. 20, 1963. Grad., Jamesine Franklin Sch. Profl. Arts, N.Y.C., 1954; student in painting, NYU; student life class, Art Students League, N.Y.C., Alliance of Queens Artists, 2003. Fashion illustrator Vogue patterns Conde Nast Publs., 1954-59; freelance illustrator various clients, N.Y.C., 1960-74; fashion illustrator Butterick Fashion Mktg. Co., N.Y.C., 1974-82, McCall Pattern Co., N.Y.C.,

1982—2001. Monitor monitor profl. sketch classes, N.Y.C., 1962—79. Scholar N.Y.C Art, 1951, Jamesine Franklin Sch., 1952. Mem.: Women's Studio Ctr. Inc., Nat. Mus. Women in Arts. Roman Catholic. Avocation: travel.

ELDADA, LOUAY A. fiber optic engineer; b. Oct. 3, 1966; s. Chafic and Adela (Salam) E.; m. Katharina Hannelore Haegi, June 28, 1991; 1 child, Seraina Adela. BSEE, Columbia U., 1989, MSEE, 1991, MPhil in Elec. Engring., 1993, PhD in Elec. Engring., 1994. Staff engr. Allied Signal, Inc., Morristown, NJ, 1994—97, sr. staff engr., 1997—99, prin. engr., 1999—2000; mgr. device devel. Corning, Inc., 2000; chief tech. officer Telephotonics, Inc., Wilmington, Mass., 2000—02, DuPont Photonics, 2002—. Author: Photonic Integrated Circuits, 1994, Future Trends in Microelectronics, 1998, WDM Components, 1999, Optoelectronic Interconnects, Integrated Circuits and Packaging, 2002, The Encyclopedia of Optical Engineering, 2002,Photonic Integrated Systems, 2003; contbr. articles to profl. jour. Mem. IEEE (sr.), Internat. Soc. for Optical Engring., Optical Soc. Am., Lasers and Electro-Optics Soc., Communications Soc. Achievements include 30 patents in the area of fiber optics. Office: 100 Fordham Rd Wilmington MA 01887-2154

ELDEFRAWI, AMIRA TOPPOZADA, medical educator, toxicologist, pharmacologist, neuroscientist; b. Giza, Cairo, Egypt, Feb. 10, 1937; came to U.S., 1968; d. Hussein Khairy Toppozada and Fadila Arif; children: Mosen M., Mona D. Hoff, Mohab M. BS, U. Alexandria, Egypt, 1957; PhD, U. Calif., Berkeley, 1960. Asst. prof. U. Alexandria, 1960-68; rsch. assoc. prof. Cornell U., Ithaca, N.Y., 1968-76; from rsch. assoc. prof. to rsch. prof. U. Md. Sch. Medicine, Balt., 1976-88; prof. U. Md., Balt., 1988—. Cons. U.S. State Dept., U.S. Environ. Protection Agy., Washington, 1982—, Nat. Inst. Environ. Health Sci. Rev. Com., Research Triangle Park, N.C., 1987-91, ad-hoc, 1991—, EPA Sci. Adv. Panel, 1997—; scholar-in-residence Queen's U. Sch. Medicine, Kingston, Ont., Can., 1985. Author: Resistance of Insects to Insecticides, 1966; editor Myasthenia Gravis, 1983; assoc. editor Membrane Biochemistry, 1987-93; mem. editorial bd. Pesticide Biochemistry & Physiology, 1987-99, Jour. Toxicology and Environ. Health, 1987—, Environ. Rsch., 1995—, Jour. Pesticide Management and Environ., 1996—; publ. scientific papers and revs. in field. Grantee NIH, 1975—, NATO, 1986-89, U.S. Army, 1995-98. Mem. Am. Soc. Pharmacology and Exptl. Therapeutics, Soc. Toxicology (pres. neurotoxicology splty. sect. 1996-97). Office: U Md Sch Medicine 655 W Baltimore St Baltimore MD 21201-1509 E-mail: aeldefra@umaryland.edu.

ELDEN, GARY MICHAEL, lawyer; b. Chgo., Dec. 11, 1944; s. E. Harold and Sylvia Arlene (Diamond) E.; m. Phyllis Deborah Mandler, Apr. 20, 1975; children: Roxanna Mandler, Erica Mandler. BA, U. Ill., 1966; JD, Harvard U., 1969. Bar: Ill. 1969, U.S. Dist. Ct. (no. dist.) Ill. 1969, U.S. Ct. Appeals (7th cir.) 1973, U.S. Supreme Ct. 1973, U.S. Dist. Ct. (ea. dist.) Mich. 1985, U.S. Ct. Appeals (8th cir.) 1988, U.S. Ct. Appeals (6th and 10th cirs.) 1990, U.S. Dist. Ct. (ea. dist.) Wis. 1992. Ptnr. Kirkland & Ellis, Chgo., 1969-78, Reuben & Proctor, Chgo., 1978-86, Isham, Lincoln & Beale, Chgo., 1986-88, Grippo & Elden, Chgo., 1988—. Contbr. articles to profl. jours. Fellow Am. Coll. Trial Lawyers; mem. ABA, Chgo. Bar Assn. (sec. com. appellate procedures 1975-77), Chgo. Coun. Lawyers, Appellate Lawyers Assn. (bd. dirs. 1975-77), Met. Club. Home: 3750 N Lake Shore Dr Chicago IL 60613-4238 Office: Grippo & Elden 227 W Monroe St Ste 3600 Chicago IL 60606-5098

ELDER, CHRISTIAN, race car driver; b. Mpls. Race car driver Elko Speedway, Minn., NASCAR Busch Series. Achievements include winner of 1999 Daytona Season Opener. Avocations: skydiving, scuba diving, skiing, hunting, fishing. Office: c/o Akins Motor Sports 400 Akins Dr Concord NC 28027

ELDER, FRED KINGSLEY, JR., physicist, educator; b. Coronado, Calif., Oct. 19, 1921; s. Fred and Ethel S. (Tait) E.; m. Elinor Jean Goertz, July 5, 1947; children: Nancy Elisabeth Elder Backus, Jessie Custer Elder James, Jacqueline Lesesne Elder Shafer, Elinor Tait Elder Powell, Lydia Jean Elder Archer, Robert Abraham, Mary Grace Elder Graham, John Philip. BS in Physics, U. N.C., 1941; MS in Physics, Yale U., 1943, PhD, 1947. Instr., Yale U., 1943-44; instr. U. Pa., 1947-49; physicist Nat. Bur. Standards, summer 1949; asst. prof. U. Wyo., 1949-50; sr. physicist applied physics lab. Johns Hopkins U., 1950-53; assoc. prof. physics Wabash Coll., Crawfordsville, Ind., 1953-55; prof., chmn. physics dept. and div. natural scis. and math. Belhaven Coll., Jackson, Miss., 1955-59; research physicist U.S. Naval Ordnance Lab., White Oak, Md., summers 1957-59; head research br. antisubmarine warfare lab. U.S. Naval Air Devel. Center, Johnsville, Pa., 1959-65; prof. physics Rochester Inst. Tech., N.Y., 1965-91, prof. emeritus, 1991—, head dept., 1965-72. Scientist Physics Research Labs., Eastman Kodak Co., summer 1982; hon. vis. lectr. physics Aston U., Birmingham, Eng., 1985-86; vis. research fellow Lanchester Poly., Coventry, Eng., 1985-86 Scoutmaster, Nat. Capital Area council Boy Scouts Am., 1950-53; Scoutmaster Central Indiana council, 1953-55; trustee Westminster Theol. Sem., Phila., 1960-99, hon. trustee, 1999—, sec. bd. trustees, 1981-83, mem. exec. com., 1965-78; trustee Presbyn. Guardian Pub. Corp., 1958-79; bd. dirs. Presbyn. Jour. Corp., 1979-87, mem. exec. com., 1979-84, mem. editorial com., 1984-87, mem. various denominational bds.; coms. gen. assembly Orthodox Presbyn. Ch., 1952— ; trustee Great Commn. Publs., 1975-99, v.p., 1975-76, 77-78, pres. 1978-79, 86-87, 90-91, 92-93. Served to lt. comdr. USNR, 1944-46; physicist U.S. Naval Research Lab. Washington. Mem. Am. Assn. Physics Tchrs. (vice chmn. N.Y. State sect. 1976-78, chmn. 1978-82), Netherlands, Am. phys. socs., Am. Geophys. Union, Am. Soc. for Engring. Edn., Inst. Physics (Gt. Britain), Franklin Inst., U.S. Naval Inst., Phi Beta Kappa, Phi Kappa Phi, Sigma Pi Sigma, Sigma Xi. Orthodox Presbyterian (ruling elder 1952—). Research, publs. on physics of fluids, physics edn. Home: 341 Barrington St Rochester NY 14607-3304 Office: Rochester Inst Tech Physics Dept Rochester NY 14623

ELDER, GENE WESLEY, artist; b. Dallas, July 4, 1949; s. James Monroe and Billie Mae Elder. BA, Trinity U., San Antonio, 1973. Owner/mgr. San Antonio Country, 1973—74; studio coord. Blue Star Arts Complex, San Antonio, 1985—93; archives dir. HAPPY Found., San Antonio, 1988—. Bd. dirs. Blue Star Art Space, San Antonio, 1988—90; curator San Antonio Mus. Contemp. Art, San Antonio, 1992—, Time Capsule, Samoa, 1984; curator Power to the Pulp, 89; curator Yard Art Exhibits, 82; prin., owner MUDgallery, 1976—78; founder MUDunderground, 1978—; curator Artist As Administrator Locus Gallery, San Antonio, 1987. Author: Murder By Collage With Found Objects: A Q-bist Ficto-Reala, 2000; Exhibited in group shows at Blue Star Art Space, 1989. Founder MUD Underground; mayoral candidate, The Party Party artists' polit. ticket City of San Antonio, 1979. Mem.: Knights of the Isosceles Triangle (Green Knight). Mailing: 142C Armour San Antonio TX 78212 Office: HAPPY Found 411 Bonham San Antonio TX 78205 E-mail: elder4tomato@bigfoot.com.

ELDER, JAMES CARL, lawyer; b. Detroit, Mar. 11, 1947; s. Carl W. and Alta M. (Bradley) E.; m. Margaret Ford, Apr. 6, 1974; children: James B., William J., Michael L., Samuel F. BA, U. Okla, 1969, JD, 1972. Bar: Okla. 1972, U.S. Dist. Ct. (we. dist.) Okla. 1972. Ptnr., dir. Crowe & Dunlevy, Oklahoma City, 1972-82; dir., mem. Mock, Schwabe, Waldo, Elder, Oklahoma City, 1982-96, 98—; ptnr. Gable Gotwals Mock Schwabe Kihle Gaberino, 1996-98. Nat. coun. rep. Last Frontier Coun. Boy Scouts Am., 1989—, pres., 1997-99; trustee Norman (Okla.) Pub. Sch. Found., 1988-97, pres., 1995-97; elder Meml. Presbyn. Ch., Norman, clk. of session, 1992-95; dir. Cmty. Coun. Ctrl. Okla., 1999-2003, v.p., 2002-03. Capt. 95th Inf. Div. USAR, 1972—78. Recipient Silver Beaver award Boy Scouts Am., Oklahoma City, 1989, Silver Antelope award, 1999. Fellow Okla. Bar Found. (life), Baden Powell World Fellowship; mem. ABA (mem. title ins. com. real property, probate and trust law sect. 1993—, chmn. closing issues subcom. 1995—), Rotary, Beta Theta Pi Corp. of Okla. (trustee, v.p., chpt. counselor 1975-86, 95—, pres. 1995-2002). Avocations: scouting, skiing, reading. Office: Mock Schwabe Waldo et al 211 N Robinson 2 Leadership Sq 14th Fl Oklahoma City OK 73102

ELDER, JAMES PERRY, management consultant; b. Burlington, N.C., Oct. 27, 1939; s. James P. and Elizabeth (Miller) E. AB, Elon Coll., 1960; MA, U. N.C., 1963, PhD, 1970. From asst. prof. to prof. Elon (N.C.) Coll., 1963-73; dep. dir. Folger Libr., Washington, 1973-82; pres. James P. Elder & Co., Washington, 1982—. Mem. exec. bd. Social Sci., 1980-90, Shakespeare Quar., 1978-84; contbr. articles to numerous scholarly revs. and jours. Bd. dirs. N.C. Sch. Arts, Winston-Salem, 1994—. Mem. Nat. Tropical Botanical Gardens (chmn. coun. of fellows 1995—); mem. Acad. of Sacred Music (chmn. 1993-95), Shakespeare Guild (bd. dirs.). Democrat. Presbyterian. Avocations: travel, cooking, reading. Office: 300 M St SW Ste 315 Washington DC 20024-4008

ELDER, JOAN ELIZABETH, music educator, consultant; b. June 15, 1954; d. Lonnie Carl and Edith Elizabeth (Ellis) Bartee; m. Charles Roy Elder, June 30, 1973; children: Angela Marie, Charles Jeffrey. AA with hons., Miami Dade Jr. Coll., 1972; BME magna cum laude, Fla. State U., 1975. Cert. tchr. Fla.; ordained minister. Exec. sec. Rose Printing Co., Tallahassee, 1975-76; music dir. First Presbyn. Ch. of Havana, Fla., 1975-80; tchr., music dir. Gadsden Christian Acad., Havana, 1979-86; state dir. Sunburst U.S.A. Beauty Pageant, Inc., Tenn., Pa., 1984-86; music dir. Whispering Pine Camp, Havana, 1980. 84, Faith Christian Fellowship, Quincy, Fla., 1982-83, Quincy Chpt. Aglow Fellowship, Quincy, 1983-84; co-owner, sec., treas. Integrity Automotive Svc., Inc., Quincy, 1989—. Cons. BeautiControl Image, 1987; minister and spkr., 2001—. Co-organizer, music dir. Cmty. Christmas Program, Havana, 1978; video tape min. Kenneth Copeland Ministries, 1982-84; organizer, mem. bd. Shekinah Christian Ctr., Havana, 1979-83; organizer, dir. Cmty. Youth Group, 1976; dir. winning choir Nat. Teen Talent Competition, 1986. Recipient Small Bus. of Yr. Personal Svc. award Tallahassee C. of C., 1990; selected to Top Shop of S.E., Undercar Digest, 1992. Office: 2461 Greer Rd Tallahassee FL 32308-4201

ELDER, KARL CURTIS, writer, educator; b. Beloit, Wis., July 7, 1948; s. Amos Ted Leautellus and Anna Mae Greife E.; m. Brenda Kay Olson, Aug. 23, 1969; children: Seth, Wade. BSEd, No. Ill. U., 1971, MSEd, 1974; MFA, Wichita (Kans.) State U., 1977. Instr. S.W. Mo. State U., Springfield, Mo.; Fessler prof. creative writing Lakeland Coll., Sheboygan, Wis., 1979—, poet in residence, 2002—. Writing program coord. Lakeland Coll., Sheboygan, 1990—, basic studies coord., 1984-2002. Author: Can't Dance An' It's Too Wet To Plow, 1975, RUN, 1978, The Celibate, 1982, Phobophobia, 1987, What is the Future of Poetry?, 1991, A Man in Pieces, 1994, Earth As It Is In Heaven, 2001, The Geocryptogrammatist's Pocket Compendium of the United States, 2001; editor Seems mag., 1978—, poetry editor, 1973-78; contbr. poetry to mags. Advancement chmn. Boy Scouts of Am. Troop 828, Howards Grove, Wis., 1989—; mem. Order of the Arrow Awase Lodge 61, Neenha-Menasha, Wis., 1989-2000. With U.S. Army, 1971-73. Recipient Eagle Scout Boy Scouts Am., 1963, Vigil Honor Order of the Arrow Nee Schoock Lodge 143, 1966, Lucien Stryk award, 1975, Ill. Arts Coun. award, 1976, Pushcart prize, 2001, Mikrokosmos poetry prize, 2002. Mem. Associated Writing Programs. Avocations: book collecting, order of the arrow insignia collecting, jogging and walking, rose gardening. Home: 1117 Robin Rd Howards Grove WI 53083-1468 Office: Lakeland Coll PO Box 359 Sheboygan WI 53082-0359 Fax: 920-565-1206. E-mail: kelder@excel.net., elderk@lakeland.edu.

ELDER, MARY LOUISE, librarian; b. Ann Arbor, Mich., Sept. 7, 1937; d. John Dyer and Elsie (Phelps) E. BA, St. Louis U., 1959; MA, U. Chgo., 1962; postgrad., U. Calif., Berkeley, 1965-69. Libr. U. Chgo., 1961-63; rare book cataloger U. Kans., Lawrence, 1963-65; rare books libr. St. Louis Pub. Libr., 1969-74; rare book cataloger Duke U., Durham, N.C., 1979-84, Smithsonian Inst., Washington, 1984-91, Libr. Congress, Washington, 1991—2002. Mem. ALA, Am. Printing History Assn., Bibliog. Soc., Bibliog. Soc. Am., Cath. Libr. Assn., Soc. History Authorship, Reading and Publishing, Alpha Sigma Nu.

ELDER, RICHARD BRUCE, artist, writer; b. Hawkesbury, Ont., Can., June 12, 1947; s. David Murdoch and Edrie Maud (Campbell) E.; m. Kathryn LeRoy, Sept. 4, 1970. Student, McMaster U., 1969; MA, U. Toronto, 1970; B of Applied Arts in Media Studies, Ryerson Poly. Inst., 1976. Curator film programs for Can. Coun., 1982, Can. Images, 1982, 83, Festival of Festivals, 1984, Art Gallery Ont., 1986, 89, Internat. Exptl. Film Congress, 1989. Prodr. (films) The Book of All the Dead, 1975-94. The Book of Praise, 1997—; works exhibited at Mus. Modern Art, Millennium, N.Y.C., San Francisco Cinematheque, Hood Mus., Atlanta, Kino Arsenal, Berlin, Festival of Festivals, Ctr. Georges Pompidou, George Eastman House, Albright-Knox Gallery, Munich Stadtmuseum, Cineteca, Bologna, Italy, Le Fresnoy, France; retrospectives of film work Art Gallery Ont., 1985, Cinémathèque Québecoise, 1986, Anthology Film Archives, 1988, 95, Senzatitolo, Treno, Italy, 1996, Images '97, Toronto, The Antechamber, Regina, Can., 2000; author: Image and Identity: Reflections on Canadian Film and Culture, 1989, The Body in Film, 1989, Stan Brakhage: A Retrospective, 1977-95, 1995, A Body of Vision, 1997; author: The Films of Stan Brakhage in the American Tradition of Ezra Pound, Gertrude Stein, and Charles Olson, 1998; contbr. articles to profl. jours. Recipient Can. Film award for best exptl. film, 1976, L.A. Film Critics Circle award for best ind. exptl. film, 1980, Auswortiges Amt. F.G.R. study tour, 1986; grantee Can. Coun., Ont. Arts Coun., Social Scis. and Humanities Rsch. Coun. Can.; Sarwan Sahoto Disting. scholar Ryerson Poly. U., 2000. Address: Unit 5 692 St Clarens Ave Toronto ON Canada M6H 3X1 E-mail: elderb@acm.org.

ELDER, STEWART TAYLOR, dentist, retired naval officer; b. Darlington, Pa., Aug. 6, 1917; s. William Carl and Olive Gertrude (Taylor) E.; m. Loretta Tersa Vitlo, Apr. 23, 1946; children: Donna Lou, Susan Loretta. BS, Mt. Union Coll., 1940; DDS, Ohio State U., 1945; postgrad., Naval Dental Sch., Nat. Naval Med. Center, Bethesda, Md., 1952-53. With Deming Pump Co., Salem, Ohio, 1935-36, prodn. mgr., 1952-53; commd. lt. (j.g.) U.S. Navy, 1945; advanced through grades to capt. Dental Corps, 1960; prosthetics officer 50th Field Hosp., Paris, 1946-47; asst. dental officer Norfolk Naval Shipyard, Portsmouth, Va., 1948-50, U.S.S. Wisconsin, 1950-52; postgrad. resident in prosthodontics Naval Weapons Plant, Washington, 1953-54; prosthetics officer Norfolk Naval Shipyard, Portsmouth, 1954-55, 57-60; dental officer, prosthetics officer U.S.S. Vulcan, 1955-57; prosthetics officer, exec. officer Naval Dental Clinic, Guantanamo Bay, Cuba, 1960-62; prosthetics officer Naval Dental Clinic Marine Corps Base, Camp Pendleton, Calif., 1962-66; comdg. officer 11th Dental Co., Republic of Vietnam, 1966-67; chief dental service Naval Hosp., Camp Pendleton, 1967-71; exec. officer Naval Dental Clinic, Washington, 1971-73, comdg. officer, 1973-75, Naval Regional Dental Center, Washington, 1975-76, Nat. Naval Dental Center, Bethesda, Md., 1976-79; lectr., instr. Navy Dental Corps Continuing Edn. Program, 1963—, Dental Intern and Postdoctoral Fellowship Programs, 1967—. Practice gen. dentistry, Salem, Ohio, 1947-48, lectr. and condr. clinics in field Mem. ADA (life), Am. Prosthodontic Soc. (life), Fedn. Prosthodontic Orgns. (life). Home: 1436 Patriot Dr Melbourne FL 32940-6818

ELDERKIN, CHARLES EDWIN, retired meteorologist; b. Seattle, Aug. 6, 1930; s. Andrew Charles and Hilda Olena E.; m. Mary DuPriest, May 28, 1959; 1 child, Christopher Charles. BS, U. Wash., 1953, PhD, 1966. Meteorologist Gen. Electric Co., 1959-65; mgr. atmospheric physics sect. Battelle Pacific N.W. Lab., Battelle Meml. Inst., Richland, Wash., 1965-72, assoc. mgr. atmospheric scis. dept., 1972-79, program mgr. wind characteristics program element of fed. wind energy program, 1976-79, mgr. atmospheric scis. dept., 1979-82, assoc. mgr. geoscis. research and engring. dept., 1982-84, mgr. Hanford environ. oversight office, 1984-85, assoc. mgr. earth scis. dept., 1985-86, sr. program mgr. earth and environment scis. ctr., 1986-92. Sci. dir. multi-lab. rsch. program Atmospheric Studies in Complex Terrain, Dept. Energy, 1989-92. Served with USAF, 1954-55. Recipient E.O. Lawrence award U.S. Energy Rsch. and Devel. Adminstrn., 1975. Mem.: Sigma Xi. Home: 531 Holly St Richland WA 99352-1822

ELDERKIN, HELAINE GRACE, lawyer; b. New Rochelle, N.Y., Sept. 18, 1954; d. EllsworthJay and Madelyn A. (Roberts) E.; m. Stefan Shrier, Feb. 23, 1985. BA, Fla. Atlantic U., 1975; JD, George Mason U., 1985. Bar: Va. 1985, U.S. Ct. Appeals (4th cir.) 1985, U.S. Ct. Fed. Claims 1994. Aide Carter/Mondale Presdl. Campaign Com., Atlanta, 1976, Presdl. Transition Staff, Washington, 1976-77; spl. asst. Agy. Internat. Devel. U.S. Dept. State, Washington, 1977; spl. asst. U.S. Dept. Def., Washington, 1977-79; mem. tech. staff System Planning Corp., Arlington, Va., 1980-83; dir. corp. rsch. Analytics, Inc., McLean, Va., 1983-85, v.p., gen. counsel Fairfax, Va., 1985-91; of counsel Feith and Zell, P.C., Washington, 1986-91; dep. gen. counsel Computer Scis. Corp., 1991—. Mem. Army Sci. Bd., 1994-98. Fellow Mil. Ops. Rsch. Soc.; mem. ABA (mem. coun. sect. pub. contract law 2001--). Democrat. Home: 624 1/2 S Pitt St Alexandria VA 22314-4138 Office: Computer Scis Corp 3170 Fairview Park Dr Falls Church VA 22042-4516

ELDRED, GERALD MARCUS, retired performing arts association executive; b. Cambridge, Ont., Can., Oct. 5, 1934; s. Albert Harold and Ethel Emily Hope (Bardwell) E.; m. Marjorie Christine Kidd, Aug. 4, 1956; 1 child, Peter Marcus (dec.). Diploma, Nat. Theatre Sch., Montreal, 1965. Adminstr. Nat. Ballet Can., Toronto, 1972-79; adminstrv. dir., acad. prin. Nat. Ballet Sch., Toronto, 1979-82; exec. dir. Stratford Festival, (Ont.), 1982-86; dir. fin. and ops. Harbourfront Corp., 1987-97. Cons. in field; mem. arts adv. com. The Laidlaw Found., 1980-90. Stage producer, dir., adminstr. Canadian Players, Toronto, 1965-66, Man. Theatre Centre, Winnipeg, 1966-72, Shaw Festival, Niagara-on-the-Lake., Ont., 1967, Expo '67, Montreal, 1967, Rainbow Stage, Winnipeg, 1968, Kawartha Summer Festival, Lindsay, Ont., 1966, producer commd. opera for Nat. Arts Centre, Ottawa, 1969— . Mem. adv. com. program in art York U., 1982-90; mem., officer, bd. dirs. The Theatre Mus. Corp., 1988-2001, The Pleiades Theatre, Toronto, 1996. Mem. Can. Actors Equity Assn., Assn. Cultural Execs., Can. Coun. (adv. arts panel 1970-72, adv. bd. touring office 1983-85). mem. bd. dir. Waterloo Regional Arts Found., 2002. Home: 5-260 Deer Ridge Dr Kitchener ON Canada N2P 2M3 E-mail: gm.eldred@sympatico.ca.

ELDRED, HEATHER ANN, librarian; b. Racine, Wis., Sept. 4, 1942; d. Sverre S. and Fern (Fulton) Elsmo; m. John Walter Eldred, Feb. 26, 1966. BA, U. Wis., 1964, MLS, 1965. Cert. libr., Wis. Children's libr. Cudahy (Wis.) Pub. Libr., 1966; cataloger/acting dir. Marquette U. Law Sch. Libr., Milw., 1966-70; cataloger Holy Redeemer Coll., Union Grove, Wis., 1970-72; cons. Wis. Valley Libr. Svc. Wausau, Wis., 1972-75, system administrator, 1975-83, dir., 1983—. Mem. ALA, Wis. Libr. Assn. (v.p. to pres.-elect 1987, pres. 1988, past pres. 1989, Muriel Fuller award 1995). Methodist. Avocations: family and neighbors, reading, writing, travel. Office: Wisconsin Valley Libr Svc 300 N 1st St Wausau WI 54403-5405

ELDRED, KENNETH MCKECHNIE, acoustical consultant; b. Springfield, Mass., Nov. 25, 1929; s. Robert Moseley and Jean McKechnie (Ashton) E.; m. Helene Barbara Koerting Fischer, May 31, 1957; 1 dau., Heidi Jean. BS, MIT, 1950, postgrad., 1951-53, UCLA, 1960-63. Engr. in charge vibration and sound lab. Boston Naval Shipyard, 1951-54; supervisory physicist, chief phys. acoustics sect. U.S. Air Force, Wright Field, Ohio, 1956-57; v.p., cons. acoustics Western Electro-Acoustics Labs., Los Angeles, 1957-63; v.p., tech. dir. sci. services and systems group Wyle Labs., El Segundo, Calif., 1963-73; v.p., dir. div. environ. and noise control tech. Bolt Beranek and Newman Inc., Cambridge, Mass., 1973-77, prin. cons., 1977-81. Dir. Ken Eldred Engring.; mem. exec. stds. coun. Am. Nat. Stds. Inst., 1979-89, vice-chmn., 1981-85, chmn., 1985-87, bd. dirs., 1983-87; bd. dirs., Ince Found.; mem., past chmn. Acoustical Stds. Bd.; mem. com. hearing, bioacoustics and biomechanics NRC, 1963-88; chmn. Internat. Stds. Orgn. Tech. Com. TC108 Mechanical Shock and Vibration, 1994-99; bd. dirs., treas. Earcraft Tech. Inc., 1999-2003. Served with USAF, 1954-56. Fellow Acoustical Soc. Am. (stds. dir. 1987-93, past chmn. coordinating com. environ. acoustics, Silver Medal in Noise 1994); mem. NAE, Inst. Noise Control Engring. (pres. 1976, bd. dirs. 1987-91), Soc. Naval Architects and Marine Engrs., Boothbay Harbor Yacht Club, Blue Water Sailing Club, Down East Yacht Club. Home: Meadow Cove East Boothbay ME 04544 Office: PO Box 501 East Boothbay ME 04544-0501 E-mail: keldred@alum.mit.edu.

ELDREDGE, CHARLES CHILD, III, art history educator; b. Boston, Apr. 12, 1944; s. Henry and Priscilla Marion (Bateson) E.; m. Jane Allen MacDougal, June 11, 1966; children: Henry Gifford, Janann Bateson. BA, Amherst Coll., 1966; PhD, U. Minn., 1971. Curator asst. Minn. Hist. Soc., St. Paul, 1966-68; mem. edn. dept. Mpls. Inst. Arts, 1967-69; teaching assoc. art history U. Minn., 1968-70; asst. prof. art history, curator collections Spencer Mus. Art, U. Kans., Lawrence, 1970-71, dir. mus., 1971-82, assoc. prof., 1974-80, prof., 1980-82; dir. Nat. Mus. Am. Art, Washington, 1982-88; Hall disting. prof. of Am. art and culture U. Kans., Lawrence, 1988—. C.H. Hynson vis. prof. U. Tex., Austin, 1985; trustee Watkins Cmty. Mus., Lawrence, 1972-76, Assn. Art Mus. Dirs., 1982, 87, Reynolda House Mus. Am. Art, 1986-88, Amherst Coll., 1987-93, trustee Georgia O'Keeffe Found., 1989-95, Amon Carter Mus., 2003—; rsch. assoc. Smithsonian Instn., 1988—; founder Smithsonian Studies in Am. Art, 1987. Author: Marsden Hartley: Lithographs and Related Works, 1972, Ward Lockwood, 1894-1963, 1974, American Imagination and Symbolist Painting, 1979, Charles Walter Stetson, Color and Fantasy, 1982, Pacific Parallels: Artists and the Landscape in New Zealand, 1991, Georgia O'Keeffe, 1991, Georgia O'Keeffe: American and Modern, 1992, The College on the Hill, 1996, Reflections on Nature: Small Paintings by Arthur Dove, 1997, The Floor of the Sky: Artists and the North American Prairie, 2000; co-author: The Arcadian Landscape: 19th Century American Painters in Italy, 1972, Art in New Mexico, 1900-1945, 1986, Georgia O'Keeffe and The Calla Lily in American Art, 2002; gen. editor: The Register of Mus. Art, 1971—82; mem. editl. bd. Am. Studies, 1974—77, Am. Art, 1996—. Fulbright scholar N.Z., 1983; Smithsonian Instn. fellow Nat. Collection Fine Arts, 1979, Found. Visitor fellow U. Auckland, 1993, Smithsonian fellow Nat. Mus. Am. Art, 1995, Kemper Teaching fellow, U. Kans., 2003; recipient Outstanding Alumnus award U. Minn., 1986, Ctr. for Tchg. Excellence award U. Kans., 2000. Mem. Coll. Art Assn. Am., Am. Studies Assn., Am. Assn. Mus., Assn. Art Mus. Dirs. (hon.). Office: U Kans Dept Art History 209 Spencer Mus Art 1301 Mississippi St Lawrence KS 66045-0001 E-mail: cce@ku.edu.

ELDREDGE, JONATHAN DEFOREST, medical librarian, educator; s. LeRoy Lincoln and Elizabeth Belding Eldredge; m. Regina Wolfe Vigil, Nov. 19, 1994; children: Nicolas-Etienne, Gabriela Regina. BA cum laude, Beloit Coll., 1976; MLS, U. Mich., 1978; PhD, U. N.Mex., 1993. Acad. Health Info. Profls. Med. Libr. Assn., 1989. Libr. dir. Ea. N.Mex U., Clovis, 1981—83; asst. prof., chief Collections and Info. Resources Devel. U. N.Mex, Albuquerque, 1986—2000, asst. prof., acad. and clin. svcs. coord., 2001—. Oversight com. Nat. Libr. Medicine, Bethesda, Md., 2001—. Jour. rev. editor: Jour. AMA, 1994—2000, mem. adv. bd.: New Eng. Jour. Medicine, 2001—; contbr. articles to profl. jours. Sec., bd. mem. Friends Librs., N.Mex., Albuquerque, 1995—2003; pres. Serendipity Day Sch. PTA, Albuquerque, 1999—2000. Mem.: Med. Libr. Assn. (Louise Darling medal for disting. achievement in collection devel. in health scis. 1999), ALA (life). Unitarian Universalist/Buddhist. Achievements include one of the main founders of the international Evidence-Based Librarianship movement. Avocations: alpine skiing, surfing, mountain biking, hiking, travel. Office: Univ NMex Health Sci Lib and Informatics Ctr Albuquerque NM 87131-5686 Home Fax: 505-272-5350; Office Fax: 505-272-5350. Personal E-mail: jeldredge@salud.unm.edu. E-mail: jeldredge@salud.unm.edu.

ELDREDGE, LINDA GAILE, psychologist; b. Tex., 1959; BS, Howard Payne U., 1980; MA, Tex. Woman's U., 1981; EdD, Baylor U., 1989. Lic. psychologist, Tex.; cert. tchr. hearing impaired, sch. counselor, spl. edn. counselor, Tex.; cert. verbal self def. trainer. Tchr. hearing impaired Waco (Tex.) Ind. Sch. Dist., 1982-85, spl. edn. sch. counselor, cons. hearing impaired, 1986-87; doctoral teaching fellow Baylor U., Waco, 1985-87; dir. regional alcohol and drug abuse svcs. Heart of Tex. Coun. Govts., Waco, 1987; psychotherapist Houston, 1989-91; psychologist, 1991—, Tex. Sch. for the Deaf, Austin, Tex., 1993-95. Mem. APA, Am. Deafness and Rehab. Assn., Am. Assn. of the Deaf-Blind, Gentle Art of Verbal Self-Defense Trainers Network, Internat. Soc. for the Study of Subtle Energies and Energy Medicine. Avocations: collecting minerals and seashells, world music, reading, art, water sports. Office: Bldg 4 Ste 200 4601 Spicewood Springs Rd Austin TX 78759

ELDREDGE, PEGGY, oncological nurse; b. Russell, Kans., Nov. 20, 1953; d. Anthony J. and Beverly J. (Osburn) Rizzo; m. Donald Eldredge, Aug. 28, 1993; children: Jennifer, Nicholas. BS in Nursing, Avila Coll., 1987; LPN, Kans. City (Mo.) Bd. Edn., 1973; ADN, Pa. Valley Community Coll., 1976; MS, U. Kans., 1992. LPN, staff RN, head nurse, clin. dir. Trinity Luth. Hosp., Kansas City, Mo.; clin. nurse specialist in hematology and oncology svcs. U. Kans. Med. Ctr., Kansas City, Kans. Mem. Am. Cancer Soc. (speakers bur.), ONS, Sigma Theta Tau. Office: U Kans Med Ctr 3901 Rainbow Blvd Kansas City KS 66160-7820 E-mail: peldredge@kumc.edu.

ELDREDGE, ROBERT JOHN, social services administrator, psychologist; b. Salt Lake City, Apr. 20, 1947; s. John Eugene and Blythe Vivian (Wright) E.; m. Pamela Ellen Waterman, Sept. 9, 1969; children: Hilary Elizabeth, Christopher Robert, Eric Michael. BS, Brigham Young U., 1971, MA, 1973; PhD, UCLA, 1984. Lic. psychologist; nat. cert. sch. psychologist; cert. sch. psycholo-

gist, S.D. Psychologist Dist. 251, Ribgy, Idaho, 1973-76, Bonneville Dist. 93, Idaho Falls, Idaho, 1976-78, S.D. Devel. Ctr., Redfield, 1983-87; lic. psychologist Northeastern Mental Health Ctr., Aberdeen, SD, 1987—2003; clin. dir. Dakota House, Aberdeen, 1990—2003; psychologist Aberdeen Sch. Dist., 2003—, Adj. instr. No. State U., Aberdeen, 1996, 99-2000, 01—; mem. adv. com. autism and related disorders program U. SD Sch. Medicine; mem. adv. com. master's degree in counseling program No. State U. High councilor, Fargo (N.D.) Stake, LDS Ch., 1990-96, bishop, 2002—, troop com. Boy Scouts Troop 81, Aberdeen, 1996-2000, 02--. Grad. sch. scholar Brigham Young U., Provo, Utah, 1972; univ. grantee UCLA, 1978, Chancellor's grantee UCLA, 1979; predoctoral fellow U.S. Dept. Edn., 1978-83. Mem. APA, Nat. Assn. Sch. Psychologists. Republican. Avocations: flyfishing, early christian and mormon history, playing keyboards and electric guitar, tennis, bicycling. Office: Aberdeen Sch DIst 314 S Main St Aberdeen SD 57401

ELDRIDGE, AMY HELENE, clinical social worker, academic dean; b. Chgo., May 10, 1953; d. Stanley Howard and Barbara Mae Lader; m. Howard Earl Eldridge, Aug. 18, 1973 (div. Dec. 1998); children: Brian Howard, Elizabeth Ashley. BA, U. Ill., 1977; MSW, Loyola U., Chgo., 1981; PhD, Inst. for Clin. Social Work, 1992. Diplomate, lic. clin. social work. Clin. staff Juvenile Protective Assn., Chgo., 1981-86, co-dir. infant devel. project, 1986-87; clin. staff Josselyn Ctr. for Mental Health, Northfield, Ill., 1987-90, coord. case assignment, 1990-93, dir. treatment, 1993-94; acad. dean, chief adminstrv. officer Inst. for Clin. Social Work, Chgo., 1997—. Adj. prof., lectr. Loyola U., 1990-97; cons. Lawrence Hall Youth Svcs., Chgo., Ravinia Nursery Sch., Highland Park, Ill., 1993-99. Author: (with others) Progress in Self Psychology, 1997; contbr. articles to profl. jours. Former mem. Child Welfare Coun. of Highland Park, Highwood, Ill., 1990-92, Profl. Connection Group for Learning Disabilities, Highland Park, 1995-99, Adolescent Issues com. PTA Edgewood Sch., Highland Park, 1995-97. Mem. Ill. Soc. for Clin. Social Work (bd. dirs. 1991, 95-98), Alumni Assn. Inst. for Clin. Social Work, Coun. on Social Work Edn., Ill. Assn. of Deans and Dirs. in Social Work. Avocations: biking, hiking, gardening. Office: Ste 1E 565 Vine Ave Highland Park IL 60035 E-mail: Leld@aol.com.

ELDRIDGE, DAVID CARLTON, art appraiser; b. Lansing, Mich., July 15, 1949; s. Carlton Brady and Blythe (Axford) E.; m. Suzanne Hamrick, Dec. 12, 1970; 1 child, Morgan Worth B.F.A., Ill. Wesleyan U., 1971; postgrad., U. Denver, 1972-73; M.F.A., So. Ill. U., 1974. Curator exhibits Nature Sci. Park, Winston Salem, N.C., 1974; curator exhibits Tenn. State Mus., Nashville, 1974-80; exec. dir. Mus. Arts and Scis., Macon, Ga., 1980-82; dir. Eldridge Appraisals, Naples, Fla., 1982—. Mem. Am. Soc. Appraisers (sr.), Appraisers Assn. Am. Office: 1839 Imperial Golf Course Blvd Naples FL 34110-8140

ELDRIDGE, JOHN COLE, judge; b. Balt., Nov. 13, 1933; s. Arthur Clement and Bertha Jean (Klitch) E.; m. Dayne S. Worsham, July 15, 1961; children: Kathryn Chandler, John Cole. BA, Harvard U., 1955; LL.B., U. Md., 1959. Bar: Md. 1960, D.C. 1961. Law clk. to chief judge U.S. Ct. Appeals 4th Circuit, 1959-61; trial atty. appellate sect., civil div. Dept. Justice, 1961-67, asst. chief appellate sect., 1967-69; chief legis. officer, counsel Staff of Gov. of Md., 1969-74; judge Ct. Appeals Md, Annapolis, Md., 1974—. Chmn. Md. Adv. Bd. Correction, 1969-70; dir. Annapolis Fine Arts Found., 1974-77 Mem. Anne Arundel County Bar Assn., Annapolis Yacht Club. Democrat. Methodist. Office: Ct Appeals Md Robert Murphy Cts Appeal Bldg 361 Rowe Blvd Annapolis MD 21401-1672*

ELDRIDGE, RICHARD MARK, lawyer; b. Okmulgee, Okla., June 20, 1951; s. H.G. and Marcheta (Barnes) E.; m. Nellene Jane Mark, Aug. 20, 1971; children: Richard Mark Jr. (dec.), Christopher Bryan, Ryan Matthew, Michael Jonathan. BA, Okla. State U., 1973; JD, U. Tulsa, 1975. Bar: Okla. 1976, U.S. Dist. Ct. (no. dist.) Okla. 1976, U.S. Dist. Ct. (ea. dist.) Okla. 1989, U.S. Ct. Appeals (10th cir.) 1977, U.S. Dist. Ct. (we. dist.) Okla. 1991, U.S. Dist. Ct. (ea. dist.) Ark. 2001. Ptnr. Jacobus, Green & Eldridge, Tulsa, 1976-78; spl. judge Dist. Ct., Tulsa, 1979-81; ptnr. Rhodes, Hieronymus, Jones, Tucker & Gable, Tulsa, 1981—2001, Eldridge Cooper Steichen & Leach, PLLC, Tulsa, 2001—. Adj. prof. Oral Roberts U., Tulsa, 1985. Tchr. Couples for Christ, Asbury United Meth. Ch., Tulsa, 1979—; pres., sec. Christian Businessmen's Com., Tulsa, 1981-93; chmn. Asbury Presch. Bd., Tulsa, 1985-95; trustee Metro. Christian Acad., 1998—, 1st v.p., 2001-02, chmn., 2002-03. Recipient Cert. of Achievement, Am. Acad. Jud. Edn., 1979. Mem.: ABA, Okla. Assn. Def. Coun., Am. Judicature Soc., Def. Rsch. Inst., Tulsa County Bar Assn., Okla. Bar Assn. Republican. Avocation: coaching baseball and basketball. Home: 2985 E 45th Pl Tulsa OK 74105 Office: Eldridge Cooper Steichen & Leach PLLC 110 W 7th St Ste 200 Tulsa OK 74119

ELDRIDGE, TRUMAN KERMIT, JR., lawyer; b. Kansas City, Mo., July 27, 1944; s. Truman Kermit and Nell Marie (Dennis) E.; m. Joan Ellen Jurgeson, Feb. 9, 1965; children: Christina Joanne, Gregory Truman. AB, Rockhurst Coll., 1966; JD, U. Mo., Kansas City, 1969. Bar: Mo. 1969, U.S. Dist. Ct. (we. dist.) Mo. 1969, U.S. Ct. Appeals (8th cir.) 1977, (10th cir.) 1995, U.S. S. Ct., 1992, U.S. Dist. Ct. Kans. 1998. Assoc. Morris, Foust, Moudy & Beckett, Kansas City, 1969-70, Dietrich, Davis, Dicus, Rowlands & Schmitt, Kansas City, 1971-74, ptnr., 1975, Armstrong, Teasdale, LLP, Kansas City, 1989-2000; sr. counsel Schlee, Huber McMullen & Krause, 2001—. Author: (with othrs) Missouri Environmental Law Handbook, 1990, 2d edit., 1993, 3d edit., 1997; contbr. articles to profl. jours. Chmn. bd. dirs. Loretto Sch., Kansas City, 1981-83; mem. Energy and Environ. Commn. City of Kansas City, 1990-91, 1994, bd. dirs. Sheffield Pl., 1997—, vice chair, 1998-99, chair, 1999-2000. Master Ross T. Roberts Inn of Ct.; mem. ABA, Def. Rsch. Inst., Mo. Bar Assn., Kansas City Met. Bar Assn. (fed. ct. com., vice chair 1989-90, chair 1990-91), Am. Arbitration Assn. (arbitrator), Nat. Arbitration Forum (arbitrator), Kansas City Club (athletic com. 1990—2001, chair 199-2001, house com. 1993-96, 98-99, long range planning com. 1993-97, bd. dirs. 1997-2001). Roman Catholic. Avocations: sailing, reading, photography, raquetball. Home: 448 W 68th Ter Kansas City MO 64113-1933 Office: PO Box 32430 4050 Pennsylvania Ste 300 Kansas City MO 64171-5430 E-mail: truman_eldridge@hotmail.com., teldridge@schleehuber.com.

ELDRIDGE, WILLIAM BUTLER, lawyer; b. Greensboro, N.C., Jan. 26, 1931; s. James Eiffel and Clara Mae (Butler) E.; m. Barbara Jeanette Galloway, June 15, 1957; children— David Mark, Julia Claire. A.B., Duke U., 1953, J.D., 1956. Bar: Mo. 1956. Assoc., Coburn & Croft, St. Louis, 1956-57; research adminstratr. Am. Bar Found., Chgo., 1960-65, asst. exec., 1966-68; dir. research Fed. Jud. Ctr., Washington, 1969— . Author: Narcotics and the Law, 1967; co-author: Second Circuit Sentencing Study, 1974; contbr. articles to chptrs. in books and profl. jours. Served to cpt. U.S. Army, 1957-60. Home: 11209 Old Post Rd Rockville MD 20854-2533 Office: Fed Jud Ctr Rsch Thurgood Marshall Fed Jud Bldg 1 Columbus Cir NE Washington DC 20002-8000

ELEDGE, JEAN DOROTHY, French language educator, administrator; b. Bristol, Va., Apr. 14, 1949; d. James Willis and Dorothy Dale Honaker; m. William W. Eledge, Aug. 21, 1971; 1 child, Eric. EdD, U. Tenn., 1995 Tchr. French and English Chickamauga (Ga.) City Schs., 1971—73; interim tchr. French Lee Coll., Cleveland, Tenn., 1978—79; music dir. Calhoun (Tenn.) 1st Bapt. Ch., 1979—; tchr. French and English McMinn County H.S., Athens, Tenn., 1981—82, Cleveland (Tenn.) H.S., 1982—91; prof. French and edn. Lee U., Cleve., Tenn., 1990—, chmn. dept. English and modern lang., 1997—. Music dir. McMinn-Meigs Bapt. Assn. Evanglism Confs., Athens, Tenn., 1998-2002. Named Tenn. Tchr. of Yr., 1989, S.E. Dist. Tchr. of Yr., 1989. Mem. Am. Assn. Tchrs. Fgn. Langs., Am. Coun. Tchrs. Fgn. Langs., Kappa Delta Pi. Avocations: music, sports.

ELENKO, STUART S. historian, educator; b. June 6, 1934; m. Carole Rothgans; children: David, Robin. BA in History, Hunter Coll., 1957; M. Edn. and History, NYU, 1960; PhD in Humane Letters (hon.), Hebrew Coll., Mass., 1998. Tchr. history Bronx (N.Y.) H.S. Sci., 1964-91; ret.; founder, dir. one of 1st The Holocaust Mus. in U.S., Bronx, 1977-99. Adj. asst. prof. history CUNY, 1960-74; lectr. on The Holocaust, The Grad. Ctr. of CUNY, 1986-88; lectr. on the Holocaust to instns., profl. meetings, gatherings, cmty. groups, 1976-99; cons. N.Y.C. Mus. Jewish Heritage, 1984-90, Nat. Holocaust Mus., Washington, 1982-88; expert hist. autographed materials, 1969-. Mem. sr. editl. bd. The Holocaust Libr., 1983-88; contbr. biography of Eli Wiesel to Dictionary Lit. Biography (1st biography in U.S.), 1986. Bd. dirs. The Anti-Defamation League Holocaust Ctr., 1986-88; advisor on Holocaust curriculum N.Y. State Dept. Edn., 1983. Recipient multiple resolutions for Outstanding Tchg. and Pioneer Work in field of human rights, N.Y. State Senate, State Assy. and N.Y.C. Coun., 1982-99; recipient 1st Anne Frank Educator award N.Y. State Gov.'s spl. commendation, 1996, Yavner award for outstanding tchg. of The Holocaust, N.Y. State Regents, 1984, Torch of Freedom award Anti-Defamation League; named Outstanding Tchr., U. Chgo., 1980, 85; Cornell Univ. Elenko 4-yr scholarship created for tchg. excellence, 1990, Eagle Scout. Mem. MENSA. Home: 3965 Sedgwick Ave 5C Bronx NY 10463-3135 E-mail: sse59@aol.com.

ELEQUIN, CLETO, JR., retired physician; b. Antique, Philippines, Oct. 18, 1933; s. Cleto and Enriqueta (Tengonciang) E.; m. Nancy Johnson, May 14, 1958; children: Tracy, Thomas Kyle, Stuart Scott MD, Far Eastern U., Philippines, 1957. Rotating intern Good Samaritan Hosp., Lexington, Ky., 1957-58; gen. practice resident Central Bapt. Hosp., Lexington, 1958-59; psychiat. resident State Hosp., Danville, Pa., 1959-60, 61-62, psychiat. resident with child psychiatry New Castle, Del., 1962-63; staff physician Eastern State Hosp., Lexington, 1960-61, dir. Fayette County Project, dir. intensive treatment service, 1964-67, supt., 1969-71; dep. commr. Dept. Mental Health, State Ky., 1967-69; practice medicine, specializing in family practice Pecos, Tex., 1971-72, Austin, Tex., 1974-89; ret. Cons. psychiatrist Texas Youth Commn., Peyote, Tex., Permian Basin Cmty. Mental Health-Mental Retardation, Odessa, Tex., Prude Ranch for Emotionally Disturbed Children and Adolescents, Ft. Davis, Tex., Dept. Mental Health Mental Retardation State of Tex.; vis. lectr. in medicine and psychiatry Am. U. of the Caribbean, Plymouth, Montserrat; asst. dep. commr. Tex. Dept. Mental Health and Mental Retardation, Austin, 1973-74, dep. commr. mental health, 1974; pvt. practice family practice and psychiatry, Austin, 1974-85; mem. attending staff Brackenridge Hosp., St. David Med. Ctr., Seton Med. Ctr., Shoal Creek Hosp.; med. dir. Mary Lee Sch. and Found., 1974-80, bd. trustees, 1980-85; attending psychiatrist U. Ky. Med. Ctr., 1964-71, Good Samaritan Hosp., 1969-71, Ctrl. Bapt. Hosp., 1966-71; cons. psychiatrist U. Ky. Student Health Svc., 1965-71, Peace Corps, 1966-68, Bur. Rehab. State Ky., 1965-71, Blue Grass Cmty. Care Ctr., 1967-71, Covington (Ky.) Cmty. Care Ctr., 1969-71, Hazard Cmty. Care Ctr., 1969-71, Danville (Ky.) Cmty. Ctr., 1969-71, Maysville (Ky.) Cmty. Care Ctr., 1969-71; clin. instr., asst. clin. prof. dept. psychiatry U. Ky. Med. Ctr., 1964-69, assoc. clin. prof., 1969-71; cons. psychiatrist Tex. Youth Commn. Tex. Dept. of MH-MR, State of Tex.; pvt. practice in psychiatry, Austin, 1974-85; mem. attending staff Brackenridge Hosp., St. David Med. Ctr., Seton Med. Ctr., Shoal Creek Hosp.; med. dir. Mary Lee Sch. and Found., 1974-80, mem. bd. trustees, 1980-85, Mem. Profl. Adv. Coun. Community Mental Health-Retardation Ctr., Lexington, 1967-71; mem. Lexington Hosp. Coun., 1969-71. Mem. AMA, Am. Psychiat. Assn., Am. Acad. Family Physicians (life), Assn. Med. Supts. Mental Hosps., Tex. Med. Assn., Travis County Med. Soc., Austin Psychiat. Soc. Home: 10101 Jupiter Hills Dr Austin TX 78747-1322 E-mail: c1nelequin@aol.com.

ELEUTERIO, MARIANNE KINGSBURY, retired genetics educator; b. Cassopolis, Mich., Aug. 7, 1929; d. Manning Marion and Marion Salina (Orr) Kingsbury; m. Herbert Souza Eleuterio, June 12, 1951; children: Susan, Kathi, Thomas, Mary Beth, John, Daniel. BS, Mich. State U., 1950; PhD, U. Del., 1971. Postdoctoral student Temple U. Sch. Medicine, Phila., 1971-72; post doctoral student U. Del., Newark, 1972-73; asst. prof. West Chester (Pa.) U., 1973-76, assoc. prof., 1976-88, prof., 1988-97; rsch. scientist Ctr. for Natural Products Rsch. Nat. U., Singapore, 1997—98. Inst. for Molecular and Cell Biology Nat. Univ. Singapore, 1998—2001; with Lab. Mycobacteria and Drug Design IMCB, 2000—01; lectr. Acad. Life Long Learning U. Del. Contbr. articles to profl. jours.; contbr. to book: Catalog of Chromosomal Variants and Anomalies, 1984. Mem. Am. Soc. for Microbiology, Am. Soc. Human Genetics, Sigma Xi, Phi Kappa Phi, Tau Sigma. Democrat. Roman Catholic. Home: 513 Ivydale Rd Wilmington DE 19803-4329

ELEUTERIUS, NANCY LEA, health administrator; b. Biloxi, Miss., Aug. 19, 1943; d. Leo and Mary (Cochran) E.; m. Nick Cefalu, Sept. 9, 1961 (div. Oct. 1975); children: Deborah, Cindy. Student, Thomas Nelson Coll., 1972-73, Ind. U., 1975-76, Va. Wesleyan Coll., 1986-87. Dir. patient adminstrv. svcs. Riverside Hosp., Newport News, Va., 1970-80; dir. adminstrv. svcs. Sentara Norfolk (Va.) Gen. Hosp., 1980-86; COO, Sentara Health Sysm., Norfolk, 1986-89; pres. Sentara Mental Health Mgmt., Virginia Beach, Va., 1989—. Workshop leader Ea. Va. Med. Sch., Norfolk, 1981. Contbr. articles to profl. jours. Bd. dirs. local unit Am. Cancer Soc., 1979-80, Jackson Field Homes, 1991-93, Virginia Beach Health Clinic, 1991-93, Cmty. Alliance Drug Rehab. and Edn., 1991—. Named Hampton Roads Bus. Woman of Yr., 1997 Mem. Nat. Assn. Hosp. Admitting Mgrs. (accredited; regional facilitator 1984, regional rep. to edn. com. 1983—), Tidewater Assn. Hosp. Admitting Mgrs. (pres., founder 1979, bd. dirs. 1979—, v.p. 1981—), Va. Hosp. Assn. (prin. spkr. 1980), Am. Hosp. Assn., Norfolk Gen. Hosp. Vols. Roman Catholic. Avocations: music, theatre, sailing. Home: 1024 Saw Pen Point Trail Virginia Beach VA 23455-5638 Office: Sentara Mental Health Mgmt 4417 Corporation Ln Ste 250 Virginia Beach VA 23462-3162

ELEVITCH, MORTON D. writer, editor; b. Duluth, Minn., July 23, 1925; s. Herman and Evelyn (Blehart) E.; m. Carol Kageff, Aug. 27, 1956 (separated 1981); children: Nikolas, Ilena, Kathrin. BA summa cum laude, U. Minn., 1949, MA, 1950. Instr. English George Washington U., Washington, 1956-57; editor fiction Audience Lit. Jour., Cambridge, Mass., 1959-60; co-founder, dir. info. Assn. of Lit. Mags. Am., N.Y.C., 1961-64; co-founder, dir. Writers Roundtable, Rockland Ctr. for Arts, Rockland County, N.Y., 1978-79; seismology asst. Lamont Doherty Earth Obs., Columbia U., Palisades, N.Y., 1989-95; instr. writing SUNY Inst. Sr. Edn., Suffern, 1997-98. Editl. cons. Chelsea Lit. Jour., 1974-76, Humerus, 1988-90, The Pushcart Prize Yearly Anthology, 1977-2000; advisor, mentor Young Writers Inst., Hartford, Conn.; contbr. fiction and nonfiction to lit. jours., anthologies, newspapers. Author: Grips or Efforts to Revive the Host, 1972, Americans at Home, 1976, Single for Tonight (also known as Green Eternal Go), 1990, Dog Tags Yapping: The WWII Letters of a Combat GI, 2003; editor, pub. First Person: Travel Memoirs Humor, 1960-61. Pfc U.S. Army, 1943—45, ETO. Fellow Yaddo, 1975-76, Va. Ctr. for Creative Arts, 1986, Atlantic Ctr. for the Arts, 1987; recipient award in fiction Pacific Coast Jour., 1996. Mem. Pen Am. Ctr., Poets and Writers, Phi Beta Kappa. Avocations: cartooning, biking. Home: PO Box 604 Palisades NY 10964

ELEWSKI, BONI ELIZABETH, dermatologist, educator; b. Cleve., Aug. 7, 1953; d. John Stanley and Alberta (Gulish) E.; married. BA summa cum laude, Miami U., Oxford, Ohio, 1975; MD cum laude, Ohio State U., 1978. Intern U. N.C., Chapel Hill, 1978-79, resident, 1979-82; staff dermatologist Akron (Ohio) Clinic, 1982-88; prof. dermatology Univ. Hosps. of Cleve., Case Western Res. U., 1988-99; prof. U. Alabama, 1999—. Author chpts. to books; editor: Cutaneous Fungal Infections, 1992, 2d edit., 1998; contbr. articles to profl. jours. Fellow Cleve. Dermatology Soc. (sec. bd. dirs., chair skin cancer screening program 1988—, pres. 1994), Am. Acad. Dermatology (bd. dirs. 1996-2000, v.p. elect, 2000, v.p. 2001, pres.-elect 2003—); mem. Am. Dermatol. Assn., Women's Dermatology Soc. (sec.-treas., pres.-elect 1999, pres. 2000), Dermatology Found. (trustee 1987-91). Roman Catholic. Home: PO Box 430037 Birmingham AL 35243 Office: U Alabama Birmingham Dept Derm 700 18th St S Birmingham AL 35233-1856 Fax: 205-934-5766. E-mail: BEElewski@aol.com.

ELEY, LYNN W. political science educator, former mayor; b. Zearing, Iowa, Oct. 23, 1925; s. Wilbur Charles and Myrtle (Wolford) E.; m. Elizabeth Sherwood Hill, Aug. 25, 1950 (div. 1970); children— Thomas Wendell, David Matthew, Mary Sherwood; m. Janet Burdy, Aug. 26, 1971; children— Benjamin Charles, Margaret Burdy. BA, Harvard U., 1949; MA, U. Iowa, 1951; PhD, 1952. Orgn. and methods analyst Dept. Agr., Washington, 1952-55; research assoc., supr. Lansing Office, Inst. Pub. Adminstrn., 1955-58; assoc. dir. Extension Service; assoc. prof. polit. sci. U. Mich., 1959-64; dean Sch. Continuing Edn., and Summer Sch.; assoc. prof. polit. sci. Washington U., St. Louis, 1964-68; asst. chancellor U. Wis., Milw., 1968-72, prof. dept. govtl. affairs, 1972-91, prof. emeritus govtl. affairs, 1991—, chmn. dept., 1985-91. Editorial asst. com. on appropriations U.S. Ho. of Reps., 1953; instr. U.S. Dept. Agr. Grad. Sch., 1954-55; mayor City of Mequon, Wis., 1980-86 Author: The Executive Reorganization Plan: A Survey of State Experience, 1967, The Regionalization of Business Services in the Agricultural Research Service, 1967, Local Ombudsmen in America, 1973, An Ombudsman for Milwaukee? 1974; with others Representation of the Poor in Milwaukee's War on Poverty, 1977, A Guide to Citizen Participation in Government: Administrative Rule Making, 1979, 80; Sr. editor: with others The Politics of Fair-Housing Legislation: State and Local Case Studies, 1968, Wisconsin Government and Politics, 4th edit., 1987; mem. editorial bd.: Pub. Adminstrn. Rev, 1969-72. Sec. Gov.'s Adv. Com. Reorgn. State Govt. Mich., 1958-62; city councilman Ann Arbor, Mich., 1961-63; mem. Milw. Model Cities Policy Commn., 1970-75; bd. dirs. Wis. Congress on Aging, 1979-82, N.W. Gen. Hosp., Milw., 1990-94; exec. dir. Mid-Moraine Mcpl. Assn., 1986-95; pres. Riveredge Nature Ctr., Newburg, Wis., 1993-95; mem. planning and zoning commn. City of Bisbee, Ariz., 1998-99; pres. Unitarian-Universalist Ch., Sierra Vista, Ariz., 1999-2000. With USNR, 1944-46. Ellis L. Phillips Found. Postdoctoral intern in acad. adminstrn., 1963-64 E-mail: jeley@theriver.com.

ELEY, RANDALL ROBBI, lawyer; b. Portsmouth, Va., Jan. 29, 1952; s. Melvin Clyde and Florence Beatrice (Lomax) E.; m. Beverly Joyce Gibson, Feb. 5, 2000. BA, Yale U., 1974; JD, U. Chgo., 1977. Bar: U.S. Dist. Ct. Nebr. 1977, D.C. 1986. Ptnr. Kutak, Rock & Campbell, Omaha, 1977-86, The Edgar Lomax Co., Springfield, Va., 1986—. Avocation: stock investments. Office: The Edgar Lomax Co Ste 310 6564 Loisdale Court Springfield VA 22150-1812

ELEY, RICHARD ROBERT, science educator; s. Robert Martell and Eva Maxine Eley; m. Suzanne Sterling, May 7, 1966; children: Dale Robert, Anne Elizabeth Scott, Mary Kathleen Crow, Paul Richard, John Mark. PhD, Kent State U., 1973; Post-doctoral fellowship, Georgetown U., 1973. Asst. prof. U. S. Naval Acad., Annapolis, Md., 1973—75; sr. scientist ICI Paints, Strongsville, Ohio, 1975—. Adj. prof. U. of Del., 1993—. Contbr. articles to profl. jours. Recipient Roon award, Fedn. of Societies for Coatings Tech., 1986, 1988, 2001, Mattiello lectureship, 1994, Disting. lectr., 1995—2002, ICI Polymer Sci. Lectr., U. of Akron, 1997. Mem.: Soc. of Plastics Engineers, Applied Rheology SIG, Soc. of Rheology, Am. Chem. Soc., Cleve. Soc. for Coatings Tech. (life), Fedn. of Societies for Coatings Tech. (life). Office: ICI Paints 16651 Sprague Rd Strongsville OH 44136

EL-FAYOUMY, J. P. QUINN, writer, poet, teacher; b. L.I., N.Y., Oct. 7, 1930; d. Thomas Joseph and Helen Veronica (Foster) Quinn; m. Saad G.A. El-Fayoumy, Sept. 8, 1963 (dec. 1989). BA, Barnard Coll., 1952; MA, Columbia U., 1964. Copy trainee, sec. J. Walter Thompson & Co., N.Y.C., 1952-55; sec. BBDO, N.Y.C., 1956-57; pub. relations asst., writer Helena Rubenstein Inc., N.Y.C., 1957-59; asst., writer Bob Taplinger Assocs., N.Y.C., 1959-60; adminstrv. asst. Protestant Coun. of City of N.Y., 1964-67; instr. Norfolk (Va.) State U., 1967-74, asst. prof., 1974-88, ret., 1988. Rsch. guest lectr. U. Jordan, Amman, 1986-87; numerous poetry readings. Author of poetry in various anthologies; editor: New Accounting Systems, 1984, New Budgeting Systems, 1984, (with Saad El-Fayoumy for Agrl. Bank of Sudan/World Bank) Agricultural and Commercial Banking, 1984. Founding mem. Coptic Orthodox Ch. N. Am., 1964; sec. Am. Arab Anti-Discrimination Commn., Hampton Roads, Va., 1990. Recipient award Tidewater Writers Conf., 1st prize Poetry Soc. Va., 1994; honoree Irene Leach Meml. Contest. Mem. AAUW (leader 1967-70), Arab Am. Assn. Va. (founding mem. 1973-80), World Affairs Coun. (dir. 1970-72), Poetry Soc. Va. (first prize 1993), Acad. Am. Poets, Nat. Mus. Women, Cape Cod Writers Ctr., Twelve O'Clock Scholars. Republican. Coptic and Roman Orthodox. Avocations: writing poetry, reading, lecturing on art of writing, volunteering, gardening. Home: 440 Starboard Ln Osterville MA 02655-1432

ELFENBEIN, GERALD JAY, physician, educator; b. Norristown, Pa., Mar. 4, 1945; s. Robert Lawrence and Edna (Ungerleider) E.; m. Dianne Strobel, June 22, 1968; children: Daniel, Johanna. AB, Harvard U., 1966; MD, Johns Hopkins U., 1970; med. intern, 1970-71; rsch. assoc., Lab. of Immunology, NIH, Allergy/Infect. Disease, 1971-73; med. resident, Johns Hopkins Hosp., 1973-74; fellow, med. oncology, Johns Hopkins Oncology Ctr., 1974-76. Diplomate Am. Bd. Medical Oncology, Am. Bd. Internal Medicine. Asst. prof. medicine Johns Hopkins U., Balt., 1976-81; investigator Howard Hughes Med. Inst., Balt., 1977-80; assoc. prof. medicine U. Fla., Gainesville, 1981-89, assoc. prof. immunology and med. microbiology, 1981-89; med. dir. bone marrow transplant unit, mem. staff Shands Tchg. Hosp., Gainesville, 1981-89; prof. medicine U. South Fla., Tampa, 1989—98; dir. bone marrow transplant divsn. Bone Marrow Transplant Program, H. Lee Moffitt Cancer Inst., Tampa, 1989—98; dir. blood and marrow transplant program Roger Williams Med. Ctr., Providence, 1998—; dir. Decof Cancer Ctr., Roger Williams Med. Ctr., Providence, 1998—; prof. medicine Boston U., 2000—. Cons. Gainesville Va. Med. Ctr., 1981-89. With USPHS, 1971-73. Fellow ACP; mem. Internat. Soc. Exptl. Hematology, Am. Soc. Clin. Oncology, Am. Assn. Immunologists, Am. Soc. Hematology. Office: Roger Williams Med Ctr 825 Chalkstone Ave Providence RI 02908

ELFERS, WILLIAM, retired investment company director; b. N.Y.C., June 6, 1918; s. Herman and Katherine (Evers) E.; m. Ann Rice, Dec. 8, 1944; children: William Rice, Joanne, Jane Fuller (Mrs. Herbert C. Muther III). Student, Hotchkiss Sch., 1933-37; BA, Princeton U., 1941; MBA, Harvard U., 1943; LHD (hon.), Northeastern U., 1989. Advt. mgr. Modern Materials Handling, Boston, 1946-47; staff assoc. Am. Research and Devel. Corp., Boston, 1947-50, asst. v.p., 1950-52, v.p., 1952-65; gen. ptnr. Greylock and Co., Boston, 1965-79, Greylock Investors and Co., 1973-76, ltd. partner, 1977-85; pres. Greylock Mgmt. Corp., Boston, 1965-76, chmn. exec. com., 1977-87. Ltd. ptnr. Greylock Capital Ltd. Partnership, 1987-97, Greylock Ventures Ltd. Partnership, 1984-95, Greylock Ltd. Partnership, 1990-96, and subsequent Greylock venture partnerships.. Trustee emeritus Northeastern U. Boston, Hotchkiss Sch., Lakeville, Conn.; hon. trustee Mus. Fine Arts, Boston. Lt. USNR, 1943-46. Mem.: Commercial, Algonquin (Boston); Longwood Cricket (Chestnut Hill, Mass.); Wellesley Country; Princeton, River (N.Y.C.). Episcopalian. Home: 70 Greylock Rd Wellesley MA 02481-1323 Office: Greylock Mgmt Corp 880 Winter St Ste 200 Waltham MA 02451-1465

ELFERS-MABLI, LINDA M. educational consultant, educator; d. Henry J. and Lillian A. Elfers; m. Gerard M. Mabli, Aug. 14, 1982; 1 child, Peter H. Mabli. MA, Montclair State U., Upper Montclair, NJ; BA, Fairleigh Dickinson U., Teaneck, NJ. Teacher of English NJ, 1979. Sr. lectr./English Fairleigh Dickinson U., Teaneck/ Hackensack, NJ, 1999—; adj. instr./English Teaneck/Hackensack, NJ, Montclair State U., Upper Montclair, NJ, 1985—90, Bergen C.C., Paramus, NJ, 1989—99. Pres./ednl. tech. cons. The Ednl. Web Design Group, LLC, Ridgewood, NJ, 1999—; academic web page designer, 1996—. Fellow Full Grad. Fellowship, Montclair State U. Roman Catholic. Achievements include first to Integrating technology into university-level courses. Avocations: travel, web page design, distance learning course developer, online magazine publisher, writing. Personal E-mail: linda@edwebdesign.com.

ELFIN, MEL, magazine editor; b. Bklyn., July 18, 1929; s. Joseph and Bess (Margolis) E.; m. Margery Lesser, June 21, 1953; children: David, Dana. AB, Syracuse U., 1951; MA, Harvard U., 1952; postgrad., New Sch. Social Research, 1955-58; LHD, Ill. Wesleyan U., 1997. Copywriter Marvin and Leonard, Boston, advt. staff, 1953-54; successively reporter, travel editor, asst. city editor L.I. Daily Press, Jamaica, N.Y., 1954-58; mem. staff Newsweek mag., 1958—, gen. editor, 1964-65; chief Washington bur., 1965-85, sr. editor, 1985-86; editor spl. projects U.S. News and World Report, 1986-97; editor emeritus U.S. News Coll. Guides, 1997—. TV panelist; cons. Ednl. Facilities Lab., N.Y.C. Author: (with others) Bricks and Mortarboards, 1963; editor America's Best Colleges, 1987-97, Guide to America's Best Graduate Schools, 1987-97, Triumph Without Victory, 1992; contbr. articles to various publs. Served as officer SAC, USAF, 1952-53. Recipient George Polk Meml. award reporting, 1957, N.Y. Newspaper Guild Page One award, 1957; award Edn. Writers Assn., 1966 Mem. Phi Beta Kappa Home: 4515 30th St NW Washington DC 20008-2126 E-mail: melfin@aol.com.

EL-FISHAWY, SAAD SAMUEL, lawyer; b. Tanta, Egypt, Feb. 20, 1924; arrived in U.S., 1957; s. Samuel Athanasious Bistawrous and Regina Youssef Ekdawy; m. Mona Youssef Milad, Sept. 15, 1960; children: Sani, Karim, Paul. BA with honors, U. Cairo, 1944, MA in Civil Law with honors, 1949, MA in Econs. with honors, 1950; LLD, U. Chgo., 1959. Bar: Egypt, U.S. Ct. Appeals (D.C. cir.). Dist. atty. Minisry of Justice, Luxor, Egypt, 1945; ptnr. Saba Habashy Law Firm, Cairo, 1946-53, Maksoud El-Fishawy Law Firm, Cairo, 1953-57; atty. World Bank, Washington, 1959-63; gen. counsel Kuwait Fund for

Arab Econ. Devel., 1963-66; sr. counsel legal dept. World Bank, Washington, 1966-74, sr. adviser fin. sect., 1974—, spl. adviser to pres., 1976-87. Counsel Aren Fox Law Firm, Washington, 1987-92, G. William Miller & Co.-Merchant Banking, Washington, 1987—. Author: Freedom of Belief in Egypt, 1954. Mem. supreme com. Nat. Party, Egypt, 1946-57. Recipient Distinction prize, Islamic Law. Mem. Egyptian Bar Assn., D.C. Bar Assn., Cosmos Club. Avocations: swimming, tennis, chess. Home: 4155 27th St N Arlington VA 22207-5211 Office: G William Miller & Co 1215 19th St NW Washington DC 20036-2401 E-mail: saadel@earthlink.net.

ELFMAN, ERIC MICHAEL, lawyer; b. Phila., Oct. 24, 1954; s. Isaac Selig and Mae (Kline) E.; m. Barbara Cecile Feldstein, Oct. 9, 1982; children: Elizabeth, Bradley, Todd. BS in Econs., U. Pa., 1975, MS in Acctg., 1976; JD, George Washington U., 1980. Bar: Calif. 1980, U.S. Tax Ct. 1981, Mass. 1986; CPA, Pa. Acct. Peat, Marwick, Mitchell and Co., Phila., 1976-77; assoc. Pettit & Martin, San Francisco, 1980-83; assoc. office of tax legis. counsel U.S. Dept. of Treas., Washington, 1983-85; ptnr. Ropes & Gray, Boston, 1985—. Mem. ABA (chair corporate tax com. 1996-97, taxation sect.), AICPA, Mass. Soc. CPAs, Boston Bar Assn. Home: 19 Gypsy Trl Weston MA 02493-1607 Office: Ropes & Gray LLP One Internat Pl Boston MA 02110-2624 E-mail: eelfman@ropesgray.com.

ELFMAN, JENNA, actress; b. L.A., Sept. 30; m. Bodhi Rice Elfman. Studied with Milton Katselas, L.A. Actress in Dharma & Greg Moore Metavoy, L.A., 1997—2002. TV appearances include Townies, The Single Guy; guest appearances include Roseanne, Murder One, NYPD Blue, Almost Perfect; TV films include Her Last Chance, Obsessed, 2002; films include Grosse Point Blank, Krippendorf's Tribe, Can't Hardly Wait, 1998, (voice) Dr. Dolittle, 1998, EdTV, 1999, Keeping the Faith, 2000, Town & Country, 2001; starred in many music videos including Antrax video for Crossroads Films. Recipient TV Guide award, 1999, 2000. Avocation: performing ballet.

ELFNER, ALBERT HENRY, III, retired mutual fund management company executive; b. Boston, Oct. 6, 1944; s. Albert Henry and Nellie May (Stewart) E.; m. Norma Elfner (div.); 1 child, Nicholas Stewart; m. Jane Colgrove, Oct. 10, 1980; 1 child, Kimberly Ann Druker. AB, Middlebury Coll., 1966; postgrad., Harvard U., 1993; D of Comml. Sci. (hon.), Merrimack Coll., 1999. CFA. Investment analyst Bank of Boston, 1966-69; portfolio mgr. Keystone Custodian Funds, Inc., Boston, 1969-81, pres., 1983-91; chmn. Keystone Investment Mgmt. Corp., Boston; pres. Keystone Group, Boston, 1990-95, pres., CEO, 1995—; CEO Keystone Investments, 1995. Bd. dirs. Keystone Funds, Keystone Investments, Inc., NGM Ins., Unitil Corp., Hampton, N.H. Trustee Anatolia Coll., Middlesex Sch., Optimum Q Funds, Cambridge, Mass., Trustees of the Donations, Boston. Mem. Boston Soc. Security Analysts, Union Boat Club (bd. dirs., pres. 1983-86), Somerset Club, Boston Econs. Club, The Country Club (Brookline, Mass.), Ausable Club. Republican. Episcopalian. Avocations: skiing, squash, golf, gardening. Home: 53 Chestnut St Boston MA 02108-3506 E-mail: chipelfner@aol.com.

ELFVIN, JOHN THOMAS, federal judge; b. Montour Falls, N.Y., June 30, 1917; s. John Arthur and Lillian Ruth (Dorning) E.; m. Peggy Pierce, Oct. 1, 1949. B.E.E., Cornell U., 1942; JD, Georgetown U., 1947. Bar: D.C. 1948, N.Y. 1949. Confidential clk. to U.S. Circuit Ct. Judge E. Barrett Prettyman, 1947-48; asst. U.S. atty., Buffalo, 1955-58; U.S. atty. Western Dist. N.Y., 1972-75; with firm Cravath, Swaine & Moore, N.Y.C., 1948-51, Dudley, Stowe & Sawyer, Buffalo, 1951-55, Lansdowne, Horning & Elfvin, Buffalo, 1958-69, 70-72; justice N.Y. Supreme Ct., 1969; judge U.S. Dist. Ct., Buffalo, 1975—, now sr. judge. Mem. bd. suprs. Erie County, N.Y., 1962-65, mem. bd. ethics, 1971-74, chmn., 1971-72; mem., minority leader Buffalo Common Council Delaware Dist., 1966-69. Mem.: Tech. Socs. Niagara Frontier (pres. 1960—61), Engring. Soc. Buffalo (pres. 1958—59), Erie County Bar Assn., Am. Judicature Soc., Saturn Club, Cornell Club (pres. 1957—58), Phi Kappa Tau. Republican. Office: US Dist Ct 716 US Courthouse 68 Court St Buffalo NY 14202-3405

ELFVING, DON C. horticulturist, educator; b. Albany, Calif., June 20, 1941; BS in Botany, U. Calif., Davis, 1964, MS in Horticulture, 1966; PhD in Plant Physiology, U. Calif., Riverside, 1971. From asst. prof. to assoc. prof. pomology Cornell U., Ithaca, N.Y., 1972-79; rsch. scientist Hort. Rsch. Inst. Ontario, Simcoe, Can., 1979-91, mgr. rsch. programs Vineland, Can., 1991-93; supt. tree fruit rsch. and extension ctr. Wash. State U., Wenatchee, 1993-97, horticulturist, prof., 1997—. Cons. U.S. AID, 1977; cons. Internat. Agrl. Devel. Svc., Ark., 1981-82. Author: Training and Pruning of Apple and Pear Trees, 1992. Recipient U.P. Hedrick 1st Pl. award Am. Pomological Soc., 1992. Mem. Am. Soc. for Hort. Sci. (bd. dirs. 1993-95, chair publs. com. 1993-95), Internat. Dwarf Fruit Tree Assn. (R.F. Carlson Disting. lectr. 1993). Office: Tree Fruit Rsch & Ext Ctr 1100 N Western Ave Wenatchee WA 98801-1230

EL-GALLEY, RIZK, urologist, educator; b. Oct. 13, 1959; s. El-Seadawi El-Galley and Anhar Fahmey Hawash; m. Christine Anderson, July 10, 1992; children: Salma Rizk, Mohamed Rizk, Suzanne Rizk. B Medicine, B Surgery, Cairo U., 1983. Diplomate Am. Bd. of Urology. Urology resident El-Sahel Tchg. Hosp., Cairo, 1986—89; surg. registrar Edinburgh, Scotland, 1990—93; resident Emory U., Atlanta, 1995—2000; asst. prof. of urology/surgery U. Ala., Birmingham, 2000—. Assoc. scientist Nat. Comprehensive Cancer Network. Recipient Scholars in Urology award, Pfizer Pharms., 1999, Sam Graham Rsch. award, Emory U., 1998. Fellow: Royal Coll. Surgeons Ediburgh, Royal Coll. Surgeons; mem.: Am. Urologic Assn. (Montigue Boyd award 1999). Achievements include invention of oplog surgical computer software; patents pending for surgical laparscopic tourniquet; surgical laparoscopic needle holder; surgical foot switch. Office: U Ala FOT 1138 1530 3rd AVE S Birmingham AL 35294-3296 Office Fax: 205-934-4933. E-mail: rizk.el-galley@ccc.uab.edu.

ELGAMAL, AHMED, geotechnical and structural engineering educator; BSc, Cairo U., 1977; MA, Princeton U., 1982, PhD, 1984. Rsch. fellow, lectr. Calif. Inst. of Tech., Pasadena, 1985—86; asst. prof. Rensselaer Poly. Inst., Troy, NY, 1986—92, assoc. prof., 1992—96, Columbia U., N.Y.C., 1996—97; prof. structural engring. U. Calif. San Diego, La Jolla, 1997—, chair dept., 2003—. Thrust area leader Pacific Earthquake Engring. Rsch. Ctr. NSF, U. Calif., Berkeley; coordination com. mem. U.S./Japan seismic rsch. initiative NSF. Contbr. articles to profl. jours. Named Presdl. Young Investigator, NSF, 1990—95; recipient Shamsher Prakash Rsch. award, Shamsher Prakash Found., 1996; grantee Lilly Tchg. fellow, 1991—92, NSF, 2000—03; Info. Tech. Rsch. grantee, 2002—07, NSF grantee, 2002—. Mem.: ASCE (mem. editl. bd. Jour. Geotech. and Geoenviron. Engring. 1997—2003). Office: U Calif-San Diego 0085 SERF Rm 255 Dept of Structural Engring La Jolla CA 92093-0085 Office Fax: 858-822-2260. E-mail: elgamal@ucsd.edu.

ELGART, LARRY JOSEPH, orchestra leader; b. New London, Conn., Mar. 20, 1922; s. Arthur M. and Bessie (Aisman) E.; m. Lynn Walzer, June 28, 1963; children by previous marriage: Brock, Brad. Altosaxophonist, formed Les and Larry Elgart Orch., 1947, rec. artist for Decca, RCA, Victor, MGM, Columbia labels. Recipient Billboard award, 1959, Downbeat Most Played Band award Disc Jockey poll, 1959, Downbeat, Cashbox and Billboards awards in popularity polls, Gold record album for Hooked on Swing, 1982, Platinum, 1984.

ELGART, MERVYN L. dermatologist, educator; b. Bklyn., Aug. 12, 1933; s. Jacob and Sally R. E.; m. Sheila Ruth Cliff, June 13, 1954; children— Brian, George, Paul, Adam, James. AB, Bklyn. Coll., 1953; MD, Cornell U., 1957. Intern Buffalo Gen. Hosp., 1957-58; resident in dermatology Walter Reed Gen. Hosp., Washington, 1960-63; chief dermatology Andrews AFB Hosp., Washington, 1964-66; mem. faculty George Washington U. Med. Sch., 1967-97, prof. dermatology, 1974-97, chmn. dept., 1975-97, prof. pediatrics, 1974-97, prof. medicine, 1974-97; clin. prof. dermatology, medicine and pediatrics Univ. Dermatology Assocs., Washington, 1997—2002, emeritus prof. dermatology, 2002—. Mem. med. adv. com. Nat. Orgn. Rare Diseases, 2000—. Served as officer M.C. USAF, 1958-66. Fellow Am. Acad. Dermatology; mem. AMA, So. Med. Assn., Internat. Soc. Dermatology, Washington Dermatol. Soc., Am. Dermatol. Assn., Phi Beta Kappa, Alpha Omega Alpha. Roman Catholic. E-mail: mervynelgart@sprintmail.com.

ELGAVISH, ADA, molecular and cellular biologist; b. Cluj, Romania, Jan. 23, 1946; came to U.S. 1979; d. David and Malca (Neuman) Simchas; m. Gabriel A. Elgavish. Dec. 28, 1968; children: Rotem, Eynav. BSc, Tel-Aviv U., 1969, MSc, 1972; PhD, Weizmann Inst. Sci., Rehovot, Israel, 1978. Postdoctoral vis. fellow NIH, Balt., 1979-81; instr. U. Ala. Sch. Medicine, Birmingham, 1981-82, rsch. assoc., 1982-84, rsch. asst. prof. pharmacology, 1984-89, from asst. prof. to assoc. prof. comparative medicine, 1989—2002, assoc. prof. genetics, 2002—. Scientist Cell Adhesion and Matrix Rsch. Ctr., Birmingham, 1995—, Clin. Nutrition Rsch. Ctr., 2001—, Ctr. Metabolic Bone Cisease, Ctr. for Aging, 1996; mem. Cancer Ctr.; founder Diacell, Inc., 1998. Grantee Cystic Fibrosis Found., 1986—90, Am. Lung Assn., 1987—92, NIH, 1989—2000, Interstitial Cystitis Assn., 1998, Am. Inst. Cancer Rsch., 2000, Pfizer, 2000—03. Mem.: AAAS, Am. Assn. Cancer Rsch., Soc. for Basic Urol. Rsch., Am. Physiol. Soc., Sigma Xi. Office: U Ala Sch Medicine Dept Genetics Birmingham AL 35294-0019 E-mail: aelgavis@aub.edu.

ELGAVISH, GABRIEL ANDREAS, physical biochemistry educator; b. Budapest, Hungary, July 29, 1942; arrived in Israel, 1957, came to U.S., 1979; s. László and Katalin Barbara (Szentmiklóssy) Schwarcz; m. Ada Stephanie Simcas, Dec. 28, 1967; children: Rotem László Abraham, Eynav Elgavish. BSc, Hebrew U., Jerusalem, 1967; MSc, Tel-Aviv U., 1972; PhD, Weizmann Inst. of Sci., 1978. Vis. fellow NIH, Balt., 1979-81; asst. prof. U. Ala., Birmingham, 1981-87, assoc. prof., 1987-95, prof., 1995—. Contbr. articles to profl. jours. 1st lt. Israeli Army, 1961-64. Mem. Am. Chem. Soc., Am. Soc. for Biochemistry and Molecular Biology, Am. Heart Assn./Basic Sci., Soc. Magnetic Resonance in Medicine. Jewish. Achievements include patents on Contrast Agents for Nuclear Magnetic Resonance Imaging; research in biomedical nuclear magnetic resonance spectroscopy. Office: U Ala THT 336 1900 University Blvd Birmingham AL 35294-0006 E-mail: gabi@uab.edu.

ELGEE, NEIL JOHNSON, retired internist, educator, retired endocrinologist, educator; b. Oxford, N.S., Can., Apr. 3, 1926; arrived in U.S., 1946, naturalized, 1955; s. William Harris and Lucile (Nevers) Elgee; m. Leona Victoria Karlsson, Aug. 18, 1951; children: Joan, Susan, Laurie, Steven, Karen. BSc, U. N.B., Can., 1946, MD, U. Rochester, 1950, Intern Peter Bent Brigham Hosp., Boston, 1950—51; resident Strong Meml. Hosp., Rochester, NY, 1951—52; fellow in endocrinology U. Wash., 1952—54, co-chief resident in medicine, 1954—55, clin. prof. medicine, 1968—93, emeritus clin. prof. medicine, 1993—; practice medicine specializing in endocrinology Seattle, 1957—93; retired, 1993. Founder, pres. Ernest Becker Found., 1993—. Capt. USAF, 1955—57. Master: ACP (gov. for Wash. and Alaska 1965—71, regent 1974—78); mem.: Inst. Medicine, Endocrine Soc. Home: 3621 72nd Ave SE Mercer Island WA 98040-3330 E-mail: nelgee@u.washington.edu.

ELGER, WILLIAM ROBERT, JR., accountant; b. Chgo., Mar. 20, 1950; s. William Robert and Grace G. (LaVaque) E.; m. Kathryn Michele Johnson, July 10, 1971; children: Kimberly, William, Kristin, Joseph. AS in Applied Sci., Coll. of DuPage, Glen Ellyn, Ill., 1970; BS magna cum laude, U. Ill.-Chgo., 1972. CPA, Ill. Staff acct. Ernst & Whinney, Chgo., 1973, in-charge acct., 1973-74, sr. acct., 1974-78, mgr., 1978-82, sr. mgr., 1982-88; chief fin. officer U. Ill. Eye and Ear Infirmary, 1988-89; CFO U. Mich. Med. Sch., Ann Arbor, 1989-99, exec. dir. adminstrn., CFO, 2000—. Chair fin. controls frame work task force U. Mich.; presenter various confs. in field. Author, developer: (tng. course) Auditing Third Party Reimbursement, 1986, 87. Active Union League Civic and Arts Found., Chgo., 1982-89, Union League Found. for Boys and Girls Clubs, Chgo., 1982-89; treas. Newport Assn., Carol Stream, Ill., 1982-83; coach Tri-City Soccer Assn., St. Charles, Ill., 1984, 87, Saline Soccer Assn., 1990, 91, 93, 94, 95, Saline H.S. Soccer Club, 1996, 97. Mem. AICPA, Healthcare Fin. Mgmt. Assn. (advanced mem., acctg. and reimbursement com. 1982-87, chpt. task force com. 1986, 87, auditing com. 1986, 87, Spl. Recognition award 1986, Follmer Bronze Merit award 1999), Ill. Soc. CPAs (mem. long term healthcare com. 1983, hosps. com. 1988-89), Nat. Coun. Univ. Rsch. Adminstrs., Assn. of Univ. Technology Mgrs., Med. Group Mgmt. Assn., Assn. Am. Med. Colls. Group on Bus. Affairs (chair Midwest region). Methodist. Avocation: golf. Office: 1301 Catherine St PO Box 624 Ann Arbor MI 48106-0624

EL-GHAZALY, SAMIR, electrical engineering educator; b. Luxor, Egypt, July 1, 1959; came to U.S., 1986; s. M. E. El-Ghazaly; m. Siham A. Abdel-Naby, June 27, 1985; children: Sarah, Hada, Amal. BS, Cairo U., Egypt, 1981, MSc, 1984; PhD, U. Tex. at Austin, 1988. Asst. lectr. Faculty of Engring. Cairo (Egypt) U., 1981-84; rschr. U. Lille, France, 1982-83; rschr., teaching asst. U. Ottawa, Ontario, Can., 1984-85; rsch. asst., postdoctoral rsch. assoc. U. Tex., Austin, 1986-88; asst. prof. Ariz. State U., Tempe, 1988-93, assoc. prof., 1993-98, prof., 1998—2002; head elec. and computer engring. dept. U. Tenn., Knoxville, 2002—. Cons. Superconductor Tech., Inc., Santa Barbara, Calif., 1990-92; summer faculty fellow Jet Propulsion Lab., Pasadena, Calif., 1994. Contbr. over 75 articles to profl. jours. Mem. Commn. D, Internat. Union of Radio Scis., Washington, 1988, Commn. A, Geneva, 1994; sec. U.S. Nat. Com. of URSI Commn. A, 1996-99, vice-chmn. 1999-2000, chmn. 2000-02; gen. chair Internat. Microwave Symposium, Phoenix, Ariz., 2001, editor in chief Microwave and wireless components letters, 2001—; chmn. U.S. Nat. Com. of URSI Comm. D, 2003—. Recipient Young Scientist award Internat. Union Radio Sci., 1990, Teaching Excellence award Ariz. State U., 1992. Fellow IEEE (internat. chpt. funding coord. 1993-96, chmn. Phoenix chpt. 1992-93, chmn. chpt. activities 1997), Microwave Theory and Techniques Soc. Avocations: tennis, sight seeing, travel. Office: Dept Electrical and Computer Engring U Tenn 414 Ferris Hall Knoxville TN 37996-2100

ELGIN, GITA, psychologist; came to U.S., 1968, naturalized, 1987; d. Serafin and Regina (Urizar) Elguin; m. Bart Bödy, Oct. 23, 1971; children: Dio Christopher Karoly, Alma Ilona Raia Julia. PsyD summa cum laude, U. Chile, Santiago, 1964; PhD in Counseling Psychology, U. Calif., Berkeley, 1976. Lic. psychologist, Chile, Calif. Clin. psychologist Barros Luco-Trudeau Gen. Hosp., Santiago, 1964-65; co-founder, co-dir. Lab. for Parapsychol. Rsch. Psychiat. Clinic, U. Chile, Santiago, 1965-68; rsch. fellow Found. Rsch. on Nature of Man, Durham, N.C., 1968; rschr. psychol. correlates of EEG-Alpha waves U. Calif., Berkeley, 1972-76; originator holistic method of psychotherapy "Psychotherapy for a Crowd of One", 1978; co-founder, clin. dir. Holistic Health Assocs., Oakland, Calif., 1979-2000, Cardiff by the Sea, Calif., 2001—, Montclair Mediation Group, Oakland, 1994; psychol. cons. The Wellness Ctr., Escondido, Calif., 2000—01. Lectr. holistic health Piedmont (Calif.) Adult Sch., 1979—80; lectr. homeopathy Calif. Naturopathic Coll., 2001, lectr. holistic psychology, 01; hostess Holistic Perspective, Sta. KALW-FM, Nat. Pub. Radio, 1980; creator Holistic Renewal, The Elgin Process of Creative Self Mastery. Author (with Bart Bödy): Sing Your Own Song, Dance Your Own Dance: Holistic Psychology, the Art and Science of Personal Transformation and Healing; author: (video documentary) Taking the Risk: Sharing the Trauma of Sexual and Ritualistic Abuse in Group Therapy, 1992; contbr. articles in clin. psychology and holistic health to profl. jours. and local periodicals. Chancellor's Patent Fund grantee U. Calif., 1976; NIMH fellow, 1976. Mem.: APA, Montclair Health Profls. Assn. (co-founder, pres. 1983—85), Calif. State Psychol. Assn., San Diego Psychol. Assn., Holistic Village (co-founder, pres. 1997), Am. Holistic Psychol. Assn. (founder 1995), U. Calif. Alumni Assn. Offices in Cardiff by the Sea and Escondido, Calif. E-mail: DrGitaElgin@yahoo.com.

EL-GUEBALY, LAILA AHMED, nuclear engineer; b. Bani Sweaf, Egypt, Sept. 23, 1947; came to U.S., 1980; d. Fatma (Ahmed) El-Adawi; m. Mohamed El-Sayed Sawan, Aug. 17, 1969; children: Mohamed, Ahmed. BS in Nuclear Engring., U. Alexandria, Egypt, 1970, MS in Nuclear Engring., 1973, BS in Physics, 1976, PhD in Nuclear Engring., 1979. Registered profl. engr., Egypt. Asst. prof. U. Alexandria, 1979-81; rsch. assoc. U. Wis., Madison, 1981-83, project assoc., 1983-84, asst. scientist, 1984-87, assoc. scientist, 1987-91, sr. scientist, 1991—. Author: Fusion Engineering and Design, 2003, Fusion Science and Technology, 2003. Mem. Am. Nuclear Soc. Moslem. Office: Fusion Tech Inst 1500 Engineering Dr Madison WI 53706-1609

ELIAS, ALAN, physician, educator; MD, U. of Calcutta, India, 1969. Medical diplomate U. of Calcutta, 1970. Prof., medicine U. of Calif., Irvine, Calif., 1989—. Achievements include patents for Oral Insulin, Thioureylenes In Psoriasis.

ELIAS, ANTONIO L. science administrator; b. Mar. 3, 1949; married, 1972; 4 children. BS, EAA, PhD Aeronautics, Astronautics, MIT. Rschr., staff mem. Space Guidance & Nav. Divsn., CS Draper Lab., 1972—80; asst. prof. aeronautics and astronautics MIT, 1980—86, sr. v.p. engring., 1986—93, sr. v.p. adv. project group, 1993—96; sr. v.p., chief tech. officer Orbital Sci. Corp., Fairfax, Va., 1996—; now exec. v.p. Advanced Programs, Fairfax, Va. Contbr. numerous articles to sci. jours.; patentee in field. Recipient Nat. Medal Tech., 1991, Aircraft Design award, Am. Inst. Aeronautics and Astronauts, 1991. Fellow: AIAA, Am. Astron. Soc.; mem.: Nat. Acad. Engring. Office: 21939 Atlantic Blvd Dulles VA 20166-6801 E-mail: ae@orbital.com.

ELIAS, CARLOS ENOC, music educator, conductor; b. San Salvador, El Salvador, Sept. 4, 1966; arrived in U.S., 1986; s. Carlos and Alma Vera Elias; m. Andrea Ana Arese; children: Briana Elizabeth, Melissa Beatriz. MusB, Biola U., La Mirada, CA, 1990; MusM, U. of Cin., 1993; diploma, Duquesne U., Pitts., PA, 1998. Prof. of violin Nat. Ctr. for the Arts, San Salvador, El Salvador, 1990—91; asst. concertmaster El Salvador Symphony, 1990—91; first violin Sendai Philharm. Orch., Sendai, Japan, 1993—97; assistantship Duquesne U., Pitts., 1997—98; dir. of strings/orch. Mesa State Coll., Grand Junction, Colo., 1999—; concertmaster Grand Junction Symphony Orch., 1999—. Dir. Music at Mesa Guest Artists Series, Grand Junction, Colo., 2001—. Musician: Elias Duo Recital, 2002, Biola U. Concerto Competition (First Prize award, 1988), World Philharm. Orch. Concert, El Salvador Nat. Violin Competition (Second Prize award, 1985), Portland Youth Philharm. 60th Anniversary Concert; conducting debut: Pleven Philharm. Orch., 2003. Mem.: Conductor's Guild, Am. String Tchr. Assn. (advisor 2001—), Music Educators Nat. Conv. Avocations: travel, swimming, soccer. Home: 591 Maxwell Dr Grand Junction CO 81504 Office: Mesa State College 1100 North Avenue Grand Junction CO 81501 E-mail: celias@mesastate.edu.

ELIAS, DONALD FRANCIS, environmental consultant; b. Cleve., Aug. 8, 1949; s. Richard Joseph and Marie Terese (Sievers) E. BS in Chemistry with honors, U. S.C., 1971; cert. in meteorology, St. Louis U., 1972; MS in Environ. Engring., Wash. State U., 1977. Chemist S.C. Dept. of Health and Environ. Control, Columbia, 1974-75; rsch. asst. Wash. State U., Pullman, 1975-77; sr. assoc. scientist I.I.T. Rsch. Inst., Chgo., 1977-78; mgr. USEPA Air Pollution Tng. Inst. Northrop Svcs., Research Triangle Park, N.C., 1978-80; prin. Dames & Moore, Houston and Bethesda, Md., 1980-82; mgr. Camp, Dresser & McKee, Denver and Edison, N.J., 1982-86; founding prin. Research Triangle Park Environ. Assocs., Inc., Green Brook, N.J., 1978-86, pres., prin., 1986—, pres., 1990-92, chmn. bd. dirs., 1992—, CEO, 2002—; ptnr. Waverly Properties. Founding ptnr. Waverly Properties, Columbia, S.C., 1994—; CEO, bd. dirs. Haztraacht, LLC, 1996—. Contbr. articles to profl. jours. Mem. Martinsville (N.J.) Rescue Squad, 1984—, lt., 1984-90, pres., 1991-95, 2002, del. 5th dist., 1998-2000, trustee, 2000-02; eucharistic min., lectr. Blessed Sacrament, Martinsville, 1986—; mem. Green Brook Rescue Squad, 1988-93; mem. ptnrs. coun. Habitat for Humanity. Lt. USAF, 1971-74. Mem. Am. Chem. Soc., Am. Meteorol. Soc., Natural Resources Def. Coun., Assn. Energy Engrs. (sr.), Air and Waste Mgmt. Assn. (vice chmn. waste source group 1989-94), Environ. Def. Fund, Amnesty Internat., Consumer's Union (life), Sierra Club (life), Nat. Arbor Soc., Humane Soc. U.S., ASPCA. Avocations: golf, tennis, reading. Office: RTP Environmental Assoc Inc 239 US Highway 22 Green Brook NJ 08812-1916

ELIAS, G.D. ONDITI, radiologist, educator; b. Nairobi, Kenya, Sept. 19, 1955; s. Elias Joseph Ndekwe and Getruda Muyonga Ogoba; m. Jane Amanya Kadima, July 1980 (div. 1995); 8 children. MB ChB, Nairobi U., 1980, MMed, 1986. Diplomate Am. Bd. Radiology, Am. Bd. Gen. Medicine. Intern Provincial Hosp., Kakamega, Kenya, 1980-81, med. officer, 1981-82, Dist. Hosp., Busia, Kenya, 1982; resident Kenyatta Nat. Hosp., Nairobi, 1983-86, cons. radiologist, 1987-90, Provincial Hosp., Nyeri, Kenya, 1986-87; lectr. Nairobi U., 1987-88; vis. assoc. U. Iowa, Iowa City, 1988-89; sr. lectr. Moi U., Eldoret, Kenya, 1990—. Author: Manual of Diagnostic Ultrasound, 1996. Mem. staff assn. Uasian Gishu Meml. Hosp., 1999, mem. med. adv. com., 2000. Recipient 1st prize Kenya Med. Women's Assn., 1986, gold medal 4th All Africa Games Organizing Com., 1987; 3d prize for slide photography Nairobi Photographic Soc., 1990. Mem. Kenya Med. Assn. (chmn. Eldoret Div. 1997-98), Kenya Assn. Radiologists (1st prize 1985), Red Cross Soc. Kenya (life). Avocations: photography, wildlife, travel, sight seeing, music. Home: Kipkarren Rd PO Box 7337 Eldoret North Rift Kenya Office: MOI Tchg & Referral Hosp Nandi Rd PO Box 4606 Eldoret North Rift Kenya E-mail: Onditielias@yahoo.com., mufhs@net2000ke.com.

ELIAS, JOHN SAMUEL, lawyer; b. Lawrence, Mass., May 2, 1951; s. Fred G. and Evon (Erban) E.; m. Cynthia Lee Eppley, Jan. 29, 1979; children: Daniel, Allison. AB summa cum laude, Dartmouth Coll., 1973; MA, Oxford U., Eng., 1975; JD, Harvard U., 1979; LLM in Taxation, NYU, 1982. Bar: Ill. 1979, Ohio 1980, U.S. Tax Ct. 1980, N.Y. 1981, Mass. 1982. Law clk. Ohio Supreme Ct., Columbus, 1979-81; assoc. Goodwin, Proctor & Hoar, Boston, 1982-84; ptnr. Sutkowski & Washkuhn Assocs., Peoria, Ill., 1984-89, Keck, Mahin & Cate, Peoria, 1989-96, Elias, Meginnes, Riffle & Seghetti, P.C., Peoria, 1996—. Lectr. Ill. Inst. CLE, Springfield, 1984—; lectr. law edn., 1990—. Contbr. articles to legal jours. Reynolds Meml. scholar Oxford U., 1974. Mem. ABA, Ill. State Bar Assn. (chmn. fed. tax sect. coun. 1991, corp. and securities law sect. coun.), Peoria County Bar Assn., Peoria County Club, Rotary, Phi Beta Kappa. Roman Catholic. Office: Elias Meginnes Riffle & Seghetti PC 416 Main St Ste 1400 Peoria IL 61602-1611 E-mail: jelias@emrslaw.com.

ELIAS, MERLE, writer, consultant; b. N.Y.C., June 1, 1958; d. Pincus and Helen Elias. Student, SUNY, Stony Brook, 1977—79, NYU, 1980—83. Exec. asst. to Dustin Hoffman, N.Y.C., 1982—85, Billy Joel, N.Y.C., 1986—89, Quincy Jones, L.A., 1992—94, Michael Crichton, L.A., 1994—96; freelance project mgr., writer Merle Elias Inc., L.A., 1996—. Author: Los Angeles First Class, 2001. Mem.: Ind. Writers So. Calif., PEN West. Home and Office: 4040 Farmdale AVe Studio City CA 91604

ELIAS, PAUL S. marketing executive; b. Chgo., July 5, 1926; s. Maurice I. and Ethel (Tieger) E.; m. Jennie Lee Feldschreiber, June 28, 1953; children— Eric David, Stephen Mark, Daniel Avrum. BS, Northwestern U. Sch. Bus., 1950; hon. degree, N.Y. U. Sch. Continuing Edn., 1972. Buyer Mandel Bros., Chgo., 1950-53; salesman Internat. Latex Corp., Chgo., 1953-56; v.p. Hy Zeiger & Co., Milw., 1957-59; exec. v.p. K-Promotions, Inc., Milw., 1960-78, pres., 1979-80; chief exec. officer, pres. consumer promotions Carlson Mktg. Group, Mpls., 1981-84, chief exec. officer promotions div. Milw., 1985-86; pres. K-Promotions Div. Carlson Promotion Group, 1987-88, Giftmaster Div. Carlson Promotion Group, 1989—, Elias Mktg., Inc., 1989—. Officer, dir. Milw. Jewish Community Center; pres. regional bd. Anti-Defamation League; pres. Regional Bd. Jewish Nat. Fund, 1993-96. Served with USAAF, 1945-46. Mem. Am. Jewish. Achievements include developing inflight mail order mktg. programs for airlines. Office: Elias Mktg Inc 10134 N Gettysburg Ct Mequon WI 53092

ELIAS, ROBERT ALAN, political science educator; b. N.Y.C., Aug. 22, 1950; s. August Charles Elias and Madeline Theresa Foran; 1 child from previous marriage, André-Jacques P.; m. Jennifer Ellen Turpin, June 3, 1993; children: Madeleine Rachel, Jack Anders BA, U. Pa., 1972; MA, Pa. State U., 1974, PhD, 1980; cert. in internat. human rights, U. Strasbourg, France, 1982. Instr. Pa. State U., University Park, 1976-77; rsch. assoc. Vera Inst. Justice, N.Y.C., 1978; asst. prof. U. Md., College Park, 1979-80; assoc. prof. Tufts U., Medford, Mass., 1980-84, 85-86; rsch. assoc. Inst. for Def. and Disarmament Studies, Brookline, Mass., 1984-85; vis. scholar U. Calif., Berkeley, 1986-88; prof., chair U. San Francisco, 1989—. Mem. adv. bd. Calif. Hist. Soc., San Francisco, 2001—; cons. UN, N.Y.C., 1989—, UN U. for Peace, San Jose, Calif., 1984—; Davies prof. U. San Francisco, 1998, NEH chair NEH/U. San Francisco, 1990. Author: (books) Victims of the System, 1983, Politics of Victimization, 1986, Victims Still, 1993; editor: (books) Rethinking Peace, 1994, Baseball and the American Dream, 2001, (jour.) Peace Rev., 1989—; mem. editl. bd. Internat. Rev. Victimology, 1990—. Mem. Dem. Socialists of Am., N.Y.C., 1984—, Amnesty Internat., London, 1985—; active Green Party, San Francisco, 1989-. Recipient Tchg. award Fulbright Found., 1987; Writing grantee MacArthur Found., 1990, 91. Mem. Internat. Peace Rsch. Assn., Am. Fedn. Tchrs., Am. Polit. Sci. Assn., Caucus for a New Polit. Sci. (editl. bd. 1991—), Peace Studies

Assn., Soc. for Am. Baseball Rsch., Am. Soc. Criminology. Home: 60 Ryan Ave Mill Valley CA 94941 Office: U San Francisco Politics Dept 2130 Fulton St San Francisco CA 94117 E-mail: eliasr@usfca.edu.

ELIAS, SALWA EMIL GHABRIAL, allergist, immunologist, pediatrician; b. Cairo, Dec. 24, 1955; MD, U. Ain Shams, Egypt, 1978. Diplomate Am. Bd. Allergy and Immunology, Am. Bd. Pediat. Intern Beth Israel Hosp., Newark, resident, 1990-93; fellow Cornell U., 1993-95; staff Beth Israel Med. Ctr., Newark, St. Barnabas Med. Ctr., Livingston, N.J., Trinitas Hosp.; staff physician Morristown (N.J.) Meml. Hosp., St. Barnabas Med. Ctr.; pvt. practice Morris Plains, N.J., 1995—. Office: Medical Arts Plaza 2839 Rte 10 Ste 202 Morris Plains NJ 07950-1200 Fax: 973-912-0689.

ELIAS, THOMAS SAM, botanist, author; b. Cairo, Ill., Dec. 30, 1942; s. George Sam (dec.) and Anna (Clanton) E.; m. Barbara Ana Boyd (dec.); children: Stephen, Brian; m. Hiromi Nakaoji, 2000. BA in Botany, So. Ill. U., 1964, MA in Botany, 1966; PhD in Biology, St. Louis U., 1969; PhD (hon.), Russian Acad. Scis., Moscow, 2003. Asst. curator Arnold Arboretum of Harvard U., Cambridge, Mass., 1969-71; adminstr., dendrologist Cary Arboretum, N.Y. Botanical Garden, Millbrook, 1971-73, asst. dir., 1973-84; dir., CEO Rancho Santa Ana Bot. Garden, Claremont, Calif., 1984-93; chmn., prof. dept. botany Claremont Grad. Sch., 1984-93; dir. U.S. Nat. Arboretum, Washington, 1993—. Lectr. in extension Harvard U., 1971; adj. prof. Coll. Environ. Science and Forestry, Syracuse, N.Y., 1977-80; coord. U.S.A/U.S.S.R. Botanical Exch., Program for U.S. Dept. of Interior, Washington, 1976—, U.S.A./China Botanical Exch., Program for U.S. Dept. of Interior, 1988-94; sr. exec. svc. USDA, 1993—. Editor: Extinction is Forever, 1977 (one of 100 Best Books in Sci. and Tech. ALA 1977), Conservation and Management of Rare and Endangered Plants, 1987; author: Complete Trees of North America, 1980 (one of 100 Best Books in Sci. and Tech. ALA 1980), Field Guide to Edible Wild Plants of North America (one of 100 Best Books in Sci. and Tech. ALA 1983). Recipient Cooley award, Am. Soc. Plant Taxonomists, 1970, Disting. Alumni award, So. Ill. U., 1989, Presdl. Rank award, 2000, Writer's Artist and Photographer's award, Bonsai Clubs International, 2001. Home: 6276 15th Rd N Arlington VA 22205 Office: US Nat Arboretum 3501 New York Ave NE Washington DC 20002-1958 E-mail: tselias@msn.com.

ELIAS, W. JEFFREY, neurosurgeon; b. Durham, N.C., Apr. 16, 1968; s. William S. and Adele J. Elias. BA in Chemistry, Wake Forest U., 1990; MD, U. Va., 1994. Resident Neurosurgery U. Va., Charlottesville, 1994—2001; fellow Functional Neurosurgery Oreg. Health Scis. U., Portland, 2001—02; asst. prof. Neurosurgery U. Va. Health Scis. Ctr., Charlottesville, 2002—. Office: Univ Va Neurosurgery Dept PO Box 800212 Charlottesville VA 22908

ELIASHBERG, YAKOV, mathematician, educator; arrived in U.S., 1988; Doctorate, Leningrad U., 1972. Assoc. prof. Syktyvkar U., Russia, 1972—75, chair dept. math., 1975—79; head computer software group Russia, 1981—87; with Math. Scis. Rsch. Inst., Berkeley, Calif., 1988—89; prof. Stanford U., Calif., 1989—. Recipient Oswald Veblen prize, Am. Math. Soc., 2001; Guggenheim fellow, 1995. Mem.: NAS. Office: Dept Math Bldg 380 Stanford U Stanford CA 94305-2125*

ELIASI, JENNIFER REBECCA, dietician, consultant; b. Long Island, NY, July 21, 1975; d. Hooshang Henry and Mahin May Eliasi; m. Jonathan Teich, Nov. 23, 2003. BA, Queens Coll., CUNY, 1993—97; MSc, Tufts U., Sch. of Nutrition Sci. and Policy, 1997—99; Registered Dietitian, Frances Stern Nutiriton Ctr. at the New Eng. Med. Ctr., 1997—99. Cert. Dietitian Nutritionist NY, 2002. Nutrition intern God's Love We Deliver, N.Y.C, 1996—97; AIDS rsch. vol. New Eng. Med. Ctr., Boston, 1998—99; rsch. asst. Frances Stern Nutrition Ctr., Boston, 1997—99; nutrition counselor The Bklyn AIDS Task Force, NY, 2001—02; dir. of nutrition services Program for AIDS Treatment and Health at Bklyn Hosp., NY, 1999—; nutrition cons. Millennium Biotechnologies, Bernardsville, NJ, 2001—. Sec. Bklyn AIDS Task Force Treatment Adeherence Com., NY, 1999—; team leader Bklyn Hosp. World AIDS Day Team, NY, 1999—; cons. MTI Biotech, Inc., Ame, Iowa, 2000—, Agouron-Pfizer Pharmaceuticals, N.Y.C, NY, 2000—. Contbr. articles to profl. jours. Recipient Campus Ministries award for Promoting Racial Harmony, Queens Coll., CUNY, 1997, Dietetics Svc. award, 1997, Recognized Young Dietitian of the Yr., Am. Dietetic Assn., 2003; scholar NY State Dietetic Assn. scholarship, NY State Dietetic Assn., 1998. Mem.: Am. Dietetic Assn. Nutrition Entrepreneurs (mem.), Am. Dietetic Assn. HIV/AIDS Dietetic Practice Group (quality mgmt. chair 2002—03, chair elect 2003—), Nutritionists In AIDS Care (co-chair 2000—). Independent. Jewish. Achievements include research in relationship of testosterone deficiency and side effects; effect of steroids, nutrition and exercise in HIV/AIDs. Avocations: walking, travel, writing. Office: Programs for AIDS Treatment and Health 100 Parkside Ave 5th Floor Brooklyn NY 11226 Personal E-mail: jenneliasi@aol.com.

ELIASON, JAMES FREDERICK, hematology and oncology researcher; b. Detroit, July 17, 1947; s. Paul George and Mary Emily (Harder) E.; m. Maria Elisabeth Baracskai, Apr. 25, 1974; 1 child, Antonia Lillian. BA, Coll. Wooster, 1969; MS in Chemistry, U. Chgo., 1973, PhD in Biochemistry, 1978. Rsch. technician Argonne Cancer Rsch. Hosp., Chgo., 1970-72; vis. fellow Paterson Labs., Manchester, U.K., 1978-79; vis. rschr. Radiobiol. Inst. TNO, Rijswijk, The Netherlands, 1980-82; assoc. mem. Swiss Inst. for Experimental Cancer Rsch., Lausanne, 1982-88; project leader oncology F. Hoffmann-LaRoche, Basel, Switzerland, 1988-91; sect. head oncology Nippon Roche Rsch. Ctr., Kamakura, Japan, 1991-95; assoc. prof. Karmanos Cancer Inst., Wayne State U., Detroit, 1995—, dir. rsch. resources, 1999—; v.p. Asterand, Inc., 2000—03, CSO, 2003—. Vis. scientist Ludwig Inst. for Cancer Rsch., Sao Paulo, Brazil, 1986; organizer European Stem Cell Club, Lausanne, 1983; adj. prof. dept. biophysics U. Debrecen, Hungary, 1995-96. Mem. editl. bd. Experimental Hematology, 1984-89; contbr. articles to profl. jours. Recipient Nat. Rsch. Svc. award NIH, 1980-82. Mem. Internat. Soc. Experimental Hematology, Am. Assn. for Cancer Rsch., Swiss Soc. for Molecular and Cell Biology, Am. Soc. Hematology, AAAS, Detroit Soc. Immunology, Sigma Xi. Office: Karmanos Cancer Inst 4100 John Rd Detroit MI 48201-1312 E-mail: eliasonj@karmanos.org.

ELIASON, JON TATE, electrical engineer; b. Menominee, Mich., Mar. 23, 1938; s. Edwin Adolph and Irene Albertyn (Longlais) E.; m. Barbara Ann Love, July 2, 1960 (div. Dec. 1980); children: Ellen Artimese, Eric Alan, Eileen Amber; m. Kathleen Ann Vitell, May 25, 1996. BS in Sci. Engring., U. Mich., 1960; MS in Physics, Oreg. State U., 1966. Registered profl. engr., Ala. Engr. Vallecitos Nuclear Lab. GE, Pleasanton, Calif., 1964—66; sr. staff engr., engring. cons. Sperry Rand Corp., Huntsville, Ala., 1966—76; sr. staff engr. Martin Marietta Corp., Denver, 1976—84; master program engr., group engr. Sundstrand Corp., Rockford, Ill., 1984—92; engr. Insight Industries, Inc., Platteville, Wis., 1993—96, Insight Info. Inc., Platteville, Wis., 1996; project engr. electronic sys. Smiths Aerospace (formerly known as Barber-Colman Co.), Rockford, 1996—2003; founder Eliason Applied Engring., Rockford, 2003—. Recipient New Tech. award NASA, 1973, 75; Regents/Alumni scholar U. Mich., 1956-60. Mem. IEEE, AIAA, Am. Phys. Soc., Sigma Pi Sigma, (chpt. pres. 1963-64). Achievements include patents in field. Avocations: amateur radio, private pilot. Office: PO Box 7231 Rockford IL 61126-7231 E-mail: jteliason@worldnet.att.net.

ELIASON, RUSSELL ALLEN, judge; b. Mpls., Jan. 28, 1944; s. Walter Joseph and Hazel Agnes Pearl (Jensen) Eliason; m. Karen L. Stevens; children: Nathaniel, Heidi, Justine, Danielle. At, U. Minn., 1964—65, JD, 1970; BA, Yale U., 1967; at, Wake Forest Law Sch., 1967—68. Bar: Minn. 1970, Iowa 1971, Nebr. 1975, U.S. Dist. Ct. (no. dist.) Iowa 1971, U.S. Dist. Ct. (mid. dist.) N.C. 1974, U.S. Dist. Ct. Nebr. 1975, U.S. Ct. Appeals (8th cir.) 1971, U.S. Ct. Appeals (4th cir.) 1976. Law clk. to judge U.S. Ct. Appeals (8th cir.), 1970—71; asst. U.S. atty. Dept. Justice, Sioux City, Iowa, 1971—72; law clk. to judge U.S. Dist. Ct. (mid. dist.) N.C., 1972—74; assoc. Ryan, Scoville & Uhlir, South Sioux City, Iowa, 1974—75; asst. U.S. atty. Dept. Justice, Greensboro, NC, 1975—76; U.S. magistrate judge U.S. Dist. Ct. (mid. dist.) N.C., Winston-Salem, NC, 1976—. Lectr. in field; active law sch. skills programs. Trumpeter Salem Band, Old Salem Band. Mem.: ABA, Nebr. Bar Assn., Minn. Bar Assn., Forsyth County Bar, N.C. Bar Assn., Sons of Norway, Phi Alpha Delta. Mem. Moravian Ch. Office: 224 Fed Bldg 251 N Main St Winston Salem NC 27101-3914

ELIASOPH, PHILIP, art historian, gallery director; BA, Adelphi U., 1972; MA, SUNY, Binghamton, 1975; PhD, SUNY, 1979; studied with, Kenneth C. Lindsay. From instr. to prof. art histry and art criticism Fairfield (Conn.) U., 1975-77, chmn. fine arts dept., 1984-90, dir. Thomas J. Walsh Art Gallery, 1990-96, prof. art history, 1984-87; dir. open visions forum, public affairs series, 1997—. Ednl. cons. TV series Art of the Western World PBS, 1987—; judge numerous art exhbns. Author: Paul Cadmus: Yesterday and Today, 1981, Robert Cottingham: Rolling Stock, 1992, Mark Balma: Drawing From Tradition, 1993; contbr. Bd. dirs. The Discovery Mus.; dir., host Open Visions Forum, 1997—. Recipient Golden Eagle award, CINE, 1986. Mem.: Internat. Assn. Art Critics, Coll. Art Assn. Am. Office: Fairfield U Art History Program Canisius Hall Fairfield CT 06824 Fax: (203) 254-4076. E-mail: pieliasoph@fair1.fairfield.edu.

ELIASSEN, JON ERIC, retired utility company executive; b. Omak, Wash., Mar. 10, 1947; s. Marvin George and Helen Grace (Meyer) E.; m. Valerie A. Foyle, Aug. 14, 1971; 1 child, Michael T. BA in Bus., Wash. State U., 1970. Staff acct. Wash. Water Power Co., Spokane, 1970-73, tax acct., 1973-76, fin. analyst, 1976-80, treas., 1980-86, v.p. fin., CFO, 1986-96; sr. v.p., CFO Avista Corp., Spokane, 1996—2003; ret., 2003. Bd. dirs. Itron Corp. Trustee Wash. State U. Found., Pullman, 1987-99, NW Mus. Art & Culture, 1998-2003; treas. Wash. State U. Found., 1995-97; trustee Spokane Symphony, 1989-95, treas., 1990-95, mem. endowment bd., pres. symphony 2002-03; pres. Spokane Intercollegiate Rsch. & Tech. Inst. Found., 1996-2000, bd. trustees, Spokane Symphony, 2000--; mem. Western Energy Inst. (bd. dirs., chair 2001-02); mem. bd. Wash. Tech. Ctr., 2002—, Wash. State U. Rsch. Found., 2002—. Mem. Fin. Exec. Inst. (Inland N.W. chpt. 1983—). Episcopalian. Avocations: skiing, traveling, bicycling, photography. Office: Avista Corp PO Box 3727 Spokane WA 99220-3727

ELIASSON, JAN K. Swedish ambassador; b. Goteberg, Sweden, Sept. 17, 1940; s. John H. and Karin (Nilsson) E.; m. Kerstin E. Englesson; children: Anna, Emilie, Johan. Grad., Swedish Naval Acad., Stockholm, 1962; MA, Sch. of Econs., Goteborg, 1965; Doctorate (hon.), Am. U., 1994, Goteborg U., 2001. Attaché Ministry of Fgn. Affairs, Stockholm, 1965-67, dir., 1977-80, dep. undersec., 1980-82, undersec. for polit. affairs, 1983-87; 2d sec. Embassy of Sweden, Bonn, Fed. Republic of Germany, 1967-70, 1st sec. Washington, 1970-74; advisor Prime Minister's office, Stockholm, 1982-83; amb., permanent rep. to UN, N.Y.C., 1988-92, under-sec.-gen. for humanitarian affairs, 1992-94; amb., chmn. Minsk Conf. on Nagorno-Karabach, 1993—94; state sec. fgn. affairs Govt. of Sweden, 1994—2000; amb. to U.S., 2000—. V.p. UN Econ. and Social Coun., 1991-92; pers. rep. to Sec.-Gen. of UN on Iran-Iraq matters, 1988-92; chmn. UN Trust Fund for South Africa, 1988-92; bd. dirs. Inst. for East-West Security Studies, N.Y., 1988-92, Internat. Peace Acad., N.Y., 1988-2001; vis. prof. dept. peace and conflict rsch. Uppsala (Sweden) U., 1994—; lectr. on fgn. policy and diplomacy. Served to comdr. Swedish Mil. Reserves. Recipient decorations from France, Netherlands, Germany, Egypt, Brazil, Portugal, Luxembourg, Denmark, Estonia, Latvia, Austria, Ukraine, Italy. Lutheran. Home: 3900 Nebraska Ave Washington DC 20016 Fax: 202-467-2699. E-mail: jan.eliasson@foreign.ministry.se.

ELIAZ, NOAM, materials engineer, researcher; b. Petach Tikva, Israel, June 18, 1970; s. Mordechai Yakobovitch and Meira Eliaz. BS in Materials Engring. with honors, Ben-Gurion U., Beer Sheva, Israel, 1991, MBA magna cum laude, 1998, PhD Materials Engring. summa cum laude, 1999. Officer Metall. Lab., Israel Air Force, 1992—95; postdoctoral assoc. H.H. Uhlig Corrosion Lab., MIT, Cambridge, Mass., 1999—2001; sr. lectr. dept. solid mechanics, materials and sys. Tel-Aviv U., Israel, 2001—, supr. grad. students, 2001—; rsch. affiliate H.H. Uhlig Corrosion Lab., MIT, Cambridge, 2001—. Chmn. sci. com. IMEC-10, Dead Sea, 2002. Contbr. articles to profl. jours. Com. mem. Israel Basketball Assn., Tel-Aviv, 1994. Capt. Israel Air Force, 1991—95. Postdoctoral fellow Fulbright Found., Israel, 1999-2000, Rothschild Found., Jerusalem, 1999-2000; recipient Eshkol scholarship Israel Min. of Sci., Jerusalem, 1995-99, Provost prize for Outstanding Grad. Student of 1998, Ben-Gurion U., 1999, Dan David prize Tel-Aviv U., 2002. Mem. NACE Internat., Am. Soc. Metals Internat., Minerals, Metals and Materials Soc., Electrochem. Soc., Sigma Xi. Avocations: pianist, magician, basketball referee. Office: Rm 235 Tel-Aviv U Ramat Aviv Tel Aviv 69978 Israel Business E-Mail: neliaz@eng.tau.ac.il.

ELIAZ, ROM EZER, chemical engineer, educator; b. Beer-Sheva, Israel, May 16, 1971; s. Joseph Arie and Bruria (Moskovitch) E.; married Yael Rozenberg, Mar. 18, 1997; 1 child, Kinor. BSChemE, BSc in Biotech., Ben-Gurion U. Negev and Weizmann Inst. Scis., Beer-Sheva, Israel, 1993, MSc (hon.), 1995, MBA, 1997, PhD, 1998. Cert. chem. engr. Israeli Engring. Assn., 1993. Rschr. Ben-Gurion U., Beer-Sheva, 1993-94; project coord., process engr. UPS Techs. Ltd., Beer-Sheva, 1994-95; process engr. Baran Group Ltd., Beer-Sheva, 1995-96; rschr. Ben-Gurion U., Beer Sheva, 1993-94. Postdoctoral fellow, asst. prof. U. San Francisco, 1998-2001. Contbr. numerous articles to profl. jours.; patentee pharmacetics, 1996, 2000, 2001. Concert musician. Recipient Sixth Internat. Tumor Necrosis Factor Outstanding Rsch. award, The Nagai Found. Tokyo Grad. Student award Controlled Release Soc., 1996, Post-doctoral award, 2000, Rothschild Post-doctoral Fellowship Honorarium award Rothschild Found., 1998, Cancer Rsch. Coordinating Com. Post-doctoral fellowship U. Calif. San Francisco, 1998-99. Mem. AAAS, Am. Assn. Gene Therapy, Controlled Release Soc., Israel Polymers Assn., Israel Soc. Polymers and Plastics. Avocations: basketball, diving, music. Office: U Calif Dept Biopharm Sci PO Box 0446 San Francisco CA 94143 also: 513 Parnassus Ave San Francisco CA 94143-0446 E-mail: eliaz@itsa.ucsf.edu.

ELIBOL, TARIK, gastroenterologist, educator; b. Sept. 1, 1939; s. Ismail Cemal and Nuriye (Tutkun) E.; m. Eileen Elibol, Aug. 30, 1997; children: Kimberly, Lisa, David, Adam, John. MD, U. Istanbul, 1964. Resident in internal medicine E.J. Meyer Hosp. U. Buffalo, 1964-66; fellow in gastroenterology Cleve. Clinic, 1966-68; clin. asst. prof. medicine U. Buffalo, 1975—; practice medicine specializing in digestive diseases Buffalo, 1969—. Former chief of staff DeGraff Meml. Hosp.; mem. staff Erie County Med. Center. Fellow ACP, Am. Coll. Gastroenterology; mem. Am. Soc. Internal Medicine, Am. Soc. Gastrointestinal Endoscopy, N.Y. State Med. Soc., Erie County Med. Soc., Western N.Y. Soc. Gastrointestinal Endoscopy (past pres.), Western N.Y. Gastrointestinal Liver Soc. (pres. 1980—), Western N.Y. Physician Found. (pres. 1980—). Home: 55 Leicester Rd Buffalo NY 14217-2111 Office: 2949 Elmwood Ave Kenmore NY 14217-1356

ELIE, JEAN ANDRÉ, investment banker; b. Montreal, Que., Can., Oct. 8, 1943; s. Jean-Paul and Violet (Trempe) E.; m. Josée Langevin. BA, Coll. Jean de Brébeuf, 1962; BCL, McGill U., 1965; MBA, U. Western Ont., 1968. Bar: Que. 1966. With Rolland Inc., Montreal, 1968-81, sec., 1974-81, counsel, 1974-81, v.p. administrn., 1978-81; dir. corp. services Burns Fry Ltd., Montreal, 1981-88; v.p., dir. corp. and govt. svcs. Burns Fry Lte., Montreal, 1988-94; fin. cons. Birinco Holdings Internat., Inc., Montreal, 1994—. Mem. adminstrv. coun. Coopers & Lybrand, 1996; mng. dir. Corp. and Investment Banking, Can., Soc. Générale, 1998; bd. dirs. Procrea Bioscis. Inc., Alimentation Couchetard, Inc.; pres. Jelinco Internat., 2003--. Bd. dirs. Montreal Symphony Orch.; bd. dirs., v.p. Found. Hosp. Notre Dame. Mem. Can. Bar Assn., Que. Bar Assn., Investment Dealers Assn. Can. (exec. com., bd. dirs.), Mt. Royal Club, St. Denis Club. Roman Catholic. Home: 1929 Laird Blvd Mount Royal QC Canada H3P 2V2 Office: 1929 Laird Blvd Mount Royal QC Canada H3P2V2

ELIEL, ERNEST LUDWIG, chemist, educator; b. Cologne, Germany, Dec. 28, 1921; came to U.S., 1946, naturalized, 1951; s. Oskar and Luise (Tietz) E.; m. Eva Schwarz, Dec. 23, 1949; children: Ruth Louise, Carol Susan. Student, U. Edinburgh, Scotland, 1939-40; degree in phys.-chem. sci., U. Havana, Cuba, 1946; PhD, U. Ill., 1948; DSc (hon.), Duke U., 1983, U. Notre Dame, 1990, Babes-Bolyai U., Cluj, Romania, 1993. Mem. faculty U. Notre Dame, South Bend, Ind., 1948-72, prof. chemistry, 1960-72, head dept., 1964-66; W.R. Kenan Jr. prof. chemistry U. N.C., Chapel Hill, 1972-93, prof. emeritus, 1993—. Le Bel Centennial lectr., Paris, 1974; Sir C.V. Raman vis. prof. U. Madras, India, 1981; Geoffrey Coates lectr. U. Wyo., 1989; Smith, Kline & French lectr. U. Ill., 1990; Richard and Doris Arnold lectr. U. So. Ill., 1997. Author: Stereochemistry of Carbon Compounds, 1962, Elements of Stereochemistry, 1969, From Cologne to Chapel Hill, 1990; co-author: Conformational Analysis, 1965, Stereochemistry of Organic Compounds, 1994, Basic Organic Stereochemistry, 2001; co-editor: Topics in Stereochemistry, vols. I-XXI, 1967-94. Pres. Internat. Rels. Coun., St. Joseph Valley, Ind., 1961-63; chmn. bd. U.S.-Mex. Found. for Sci., 1994-96. Recipient Coll. Chem. Tchrs. award Mfg. Chemists Assn., 1965, Laurent Lavoisier medal French Chem. Soc., 1968, Amoco Teaching award U. N.C., 1975, Thomas Jefferson award U. N.C., 1991, N.C. award in Sci., 1986, Chirality medal Internat. Symposium on Chiral Discrimination, 1996; NSF sr. rsch. fellow Harvard U., 1958, Calif. Inst. Tech., 1958-59, E.T.H. Zurich, Switzerland, 1967-68, Guggenheim fellow Stanford U., Princeton U., 1975-76, Duke U., 1983-84; named One of Top 75 Disting. Contbrs. to Chem. Enterprise, Chem. and Engring. News, 1998. Fellow AAAS (chmn. chemistry sect. 1991-92), Royal Soc. Chems.; mem. NAS (award for chemistry in svc. to society 1997), AAUP (chpt. pres. 1971-72, 78-79), Am. Acad. Arts and Scis., Am. Chem. Soc. (chmn. St. Joseph Valley sect. 1960, councillor 1965-73, 75—, chmn. com. publs. 1972, 76-78, dir. 1985-93, chmn. bd. dirs. 1987-89, pres. 1992, Morley medal Cleve. sect. 1965, Harry and Carol Mosher award Santa Clara Valley sect. 1982, Herty medal Ga. sect. 1991, So. Chemist award Memphis sect. 1991, Madison Marshall award North Ala. sect., 1993, George C. Pimentel award in Chem. Edn. 1995, Priestley medal 1996), Coun. Sci. Soc. Pres.'s (pres. 1996), Royal Spanish Chem. Soc. (hon.), Argentine Chem. Assn. (hon.), Peruvian Chem. Soc. (corr.), Mex. Chem. Soc. (hon.), Mex. Acad. Scis. (corr.), Chilean Chem. Soc. (hon.), Cuban Chem. Soc. (hon.), Sigma Xi (pres. U. Notre Dame chpt. 1968-69), Phi Lambda Upsilon, Phi Kappa Phi. Home: 345 Carolina Meadows Villa Chapel Hill NC 27517-7519 E-mail: eliel@email.unc.edu.

ELIKANN, LAWRENCE S. (LARRY ELIKANN), television and film director; b. N.Y.C., July 4, 1923; s. Harry and Sadye (Trause) E.; m. Corinne Corky Schuman; Dec. 6, 1947; children— JoAnne Jarrin, Jill Barad. BA, Bklyn. Coll., 1943; E.E., Walter Harvey Coll., 1948. Tech. dir. NBC-TV, N.Y.C., 1948-64; comml. dir. VPI-TV, N.Y.C., 1964-66, Filmex-TV, N.Y.C., 1966-68, Plus two TV, N.Y.C., 1968-70. Dir. mini-series Last Flight Out, The Great L.A. Earthquake, The Big One, The Inconvenient Woman, Fever, Story Lady, One Against the Wind, Bonds of Love, I Know My First Name is Steven, Hands of a Stranger, Kiss of a Killer, God Bless the Child, Out of Darkness, Menendez—A Killing in Beverly Hills, Tecumseh—The Last Warrior, A Mother's Prayer, Blue River, "Unexpected Family", Lies He Told. Mem. Mus. Contemporary Art of L.A., L.A. County Mus.; mem. rsch. coun. Scripps Clinic and Rsch. Found. With Signal Corps, U.S. Army, 1943-46. Recipient Emmy award, 1978-79, 89, Golden Globe award, 1989, 91, 94, Christopher award 1973-76, 77, 78-79, 91, Chgo. Internat. Film Festival award 1977, Internat. Film and TV Festival of N.Y. award, 1977, Dir. of Yr. award Am. Ctrs. for Children, 1978; Humanitas prize, 1988, 94, 96. Mem. NATAS (gov. 1961-63), Dirs. Guild Am., Am. film Inst., Nat. Hist. Preservation Soc., Smithsonian Inst., Scripps Inst. (bd. dirs.), Acad. TV Arts and Scis.

ELIKANN, PETER TODD, writer, lawyer, commentator; b. N.Y.C., May 6, 1953; s. Gerald Arthur and Leonore Rita (Reiser) E. BS in Journalism magna cum laude, Boston U., 1975; JD, Western New England Sch. Law, 1980. Bar: Mass. 1981, U.S. Dist. Ct. Mass. 1981, U.S. Ct. Appeals (1st cir.) 1982, Conn. 1993, U.S. Dist. Ct. Conn. 1993. Asst. nat. press sec. Fred Harris for U.S. Pres., 1975-76; corr. The Hartford (Conn.) Courant, 1976-78; assoc. Nathan & Clayman, Bloomfield, Conn., 1980; asst. reporter jud. decisions Conn. Supreme Ct., Hartford, 1981-82; investigative legal reporter TV Channel Twelve, Norwalk, Conn., 1982-84; reporter news WRC-TV NBC, Washington, 1984-86; criminal def. atty. Boston, 1986—; network commentator Ct. TV, N.Y.C., 1997—. Instr. Western New England Coll., Springfield, Mass., 1981-82, Baypath Jr. Coll., Longmeadow, Mass., 1982. Author: The Boston Tenant's Guide to Housing, 1975, The Tough on Crime Myth: Real Solutions to Cut Crime, 1996, Superpredators: The Demonization of Our Children By The Law, 1999; mem. editl. bd. Mass. Law Rev. Mem. ABA (corrections and sentencing com.), Mass. Assn. Criminal Def. Lawyers, Mass. Bar Assn. (corrections and sentencing com., chmn. criminal justice sect. 1997-99, vice chmn. individual rights sect. 2001-03, ho. of dels. 2001—), Boston Bar Assn. Jewish. Avocations: dogsledding, opera, writing, mountain climbing. Office: 93 Beacon St Boston MA 02108-3397

ELIN, RONALD JOHN, pathologist, educator; b. Mpls., Apr. 14, 1939; s. John Matthew and Helen Sophia (Lind) E.; m. Susan May Krogh, June 14, 1969; children: Derek, Justin. BA, U. Minn., 1960, BS, 1962, MD, 1966, PhD, 1969. Diplomate Am. Bd. Pathology, Am. Bd. Clin. Chemistry. Intern U. Hosp. Calif., San Diego, 1969-70; commd. med. officer USPHS, 1970, advanced through grades to med. dir., 1975; staff assoc. Nat. Inst. Allergy and Infectious Diseases NIH, Bethesda, Md., 1970-73, resident clin. pathology dept., 1973-74, chief clin. pathology dept., 1975-97, chief chemistry svc., 1977-97; vice chmn. pathology U. Louisville, Ky., 1997—2001, chmn. dept. pathology and lab. medicine, 2002. Clin. prof. Uniformed Svcs. U. of Health Scis., Bethesda, 1978-97; initiator, first chmn. Gordon Rsch. Conf. on Magnesium in Biomed. Processes and Medicine, 1978. Contbr. more than 200 articles to profl. jours. Decorated Commendation medal USPHS, 1980, Meritorious Svc. medal USPHS, 1984. Fellow Am. Coll. Nutrition, Coll. Am. Pathologists, Am. Soc. Clin. Pathologists; mem. Am. Assn. Pathologists, Am. Assn. Clin. Chemistry (Outstanding Contbns. to Clin. Chemistry in a Selected Area of Rsch. award 1994), Acad. Clin. Lab. Physicians and Scientists (sec.-treas. 1985-87, pres. 1990-91, Gerald T. Evans award 1995). Lutheran. Achievements include research on magnesium metabolism, properties of endotoxin. Office: U Louisville Hosp Dept Pathology and Lab Medicine 512 S Hancock St Rm 203 Louisville KY 40202-1675 E-mail: rjelin01@gwise.louisville.edu.

ELINSON, HENRY DAVID, artist, language educator; b. Leningrad, USSR, Dec. 14, 1935; came to U.S., 1973; s. David Moses and Fraida Zelma (Ufa) E.; m. Ludmila Nicholas Tepina, Oct. 7, 1955; 1 child, Maria Henry. Student, Herzen State Pedagogical U., Leningrad, 1954-57; BA, Pedagogical Inst., Novgorod, USSR, 1958; MA, Pedagogical Inst., Moscow, 1963. Cert. educator. Spl. edn. tchr. Leningrad Sch. Spl. Edn., 1961-64; supr. dept. speech therapy Psychoneurological Dispensary, Leningrad, 1964-73; instr. Russian lang. Yale U., New Haven, Conn., 1975-76, Def. Lang. Inst., Presidio of Monterey, Calif., 1976-94. One-man shows include The Light and Motion Transmutation Galleries, N.Y.C., 1974, Thor Gallery, Louisville, 1974, Monterey (Calif.) Peninsula Art Mus., 1977, U. Calif. Nelson Gallery, Davis, 1978, Nahamkin Gallery, N.Y.C., 1978, Nahamkin Fine Arts, N.Y.C., 1980, Gallery Paule Anglim, 1981, 85, 87, Gallery Paule Anglim, San Francisco, 1991, 93, 96, 99, 2000, Dostoevsky's Mus., St. Petersburg, Russia, 1992, Mus. Art Santa Cruz, Calif., 1994, Duke U. Mus. Art, 1996, Mead Art Mus, 1998, Mus. of Non Conformist Art, St. Petersburg, Russia, 2000; exhibited in group shows at Bklyn. Coll. Art Ctr., 1974, CUNY, 1974, Galleria Il Punto, Genoa, Italy, 1975, New Art From the Soviet Union, Washington, 1977, Gallery Hardy, Paris, 1978, Mus. of Fine Art, San Francisco, 1979, Santa Cruz Mus. Fine Arts, 1994, V. Morlan Gallery Transylvania U., Lexington, Ky., 1995, Art Gallery, Adirondack C.C., Queensbury, N.Y., 2002, A.P.E. Gallery, Northampton, Mass., 2003; numerous others; represented in permanent collections Mus. Fine Arts, San Francisco, Yale U. Art Gallery, Monterey Mus. Art, U. Calif. Art Mus., Berkeley, Bochum Mus., Germany, Check Point Charlie Mus., Berlin, State Russian Mus., Leningrad, Zimmerly Art Mus., Rutgers U., N.J., Duke U Mus. Art, 1996, Mead Art Mus., 1998, The Russian State Mus., St. Petersburg, 2001-2002, Mus. of St. Petersburg History, Mus. Non Conformist Art, State Hermitage, St. Petersburg,2000, Visual Arts Gallery Adirondack Cmty. Coll. N.Y., A.P.E. Gallery, Northampton, Mass., others. Mem. Underground Anti-Soviet Govt. Students' Orgn., 1957. Recipient Gold medal Art Achievement City of Milan, 1975. Avocations: travel, writing essays and short stories. Home: 997 Benito Ct Pacific Grove CA 93950-5333

ELINSON, JACK, sociology educator; b. N.Y.C., June 30, 1917; s. Sam and Rebecca (Block) Elinson; m. May Gomberg, July 5, 1941; children: Richard, Elaine, Mitchell, Robert. BS, CCNY, 1937; MA, George Washington U., 1946, PhD, 1954. Social sci. analyst Dept. Def., Washington, 1942-51; sr. study dir. Nat. Opinion Research Center, 1951-56; asst. prof. sociology U. Chgo., 1954-56; assoc. prof. adminstrv. medicine Columbia U., N.Y.C., 1956-64, prof. adminstrv. medicine, 1964-68, prof. sociomed. scis. and sociology, 1968-86, prof. emeritus, 1986—; Service fellow Nat. Center Health Stats., 1977-81; vis. prof. behavioral scis. U. Toronto, 1969-77; Disting. vis. prof. Inst. Health Care Policy, Rutgers U., 1986-89, Disting. sr. scholar, 1990—; vis. prof. Robert Wood Johnson Med. Sch. (formerly Rutgers Med. Sch.), Univ. Medicine and Dentistry of N.J., 1986—; dir. program evaluation dept. patient care Harlem Hosp. Ctr., 1966-71. Bd. dirs. Med. and Health Rsch. Assn., N.Y.C., 1977—89,

Bergen County N.J. Tb and Health Assn., 1960—65; mem. adminstrv. bd. Bur. Applied Social Rsch. Columbia U., 1970—75; co-dir. health care orgn. and adminstrn. track Program for Master's in Pub. Health Rutgers U.-U. Medicine and Dentistry of N.J., 1983—92. Co-author (with R.E. Trussell): Chronic Illness in a Rural Area, 1959; co-author: (with J.J. Williams and R.E. Trussell) Family Medical Care Under Three Types of Health Insurance, 1962; co-author: (with E. Padilla and M. Perkins) Public Image of Mental Health Services, 1967; editor (with A.E. Siegmann): Sociomedical Health Indicators, 1979; editor: (with A. Mooney and A. Siegmann) Health Goals and Health Indicators: Policy, Planning and Evaluation, 1977; editor: (with N.K. Wenger, M.E. Mattson and C.D. Furberg) Assessment of Quality of Life in Clinical Trials of Cardiovascular Therapies, 1984. Named Jack Elinson Sociomed. Scis. Libr., Columbia U. Sch. Pub. Health, 1998; recipient Nat. Merit award, Delta Omega Soc., 1982, Festschrift, spl. issue of Social Sci. and Medicine, 1989. Fellow: APHA (1st award Assn. Social Scis. in Health 1984), Am. Assn. Pub. Opinion Rsch. (pres. 1979—80, Exceptionally Disting. Achievement award 1993), Am. Sociol. Assn. (chmn. med. sociology, Leo G. Reeder award 1985), AAAS; mem.: Med. and Health Rsch. Assn. N.U.C. (bd. dirs.), N.J. Pub. Health Assn. (exec. bd., Dennis J. Sullivan award 1990), N.Y.C. Pub. Health Assn. (bd. dirs.), Inst. Medicine NAS. Office: Columbia U Sch Pub Health Dept Sociomed Scis 600 W 168th St New York NY 10032-3722 E-mail: je7@columbia.edu., jelinson@juno.com.

ELIOPOULOS, BARBARA J. health facility administrator, medical/surgical nurse; b. Columbus, Ga., July 6, 1945; d. Elie Joseph Simard and Helen Louise Scanlin; m. Paul C. Eliopoulos, Sept. 19, 1972; children: Janice, Earl, Suzanne, Dawn, Sabrina. LPN, Boston City Hosp. Sch. Nursing, 1977; residential care adminstrn., Kennebec Valley Tech. Coll., 1995, RCSI trainer, 1998; PSS trainer, Behavioral Health Sci. Inst., Augusta, Maine, 2003. Office: Sebasticook Cmty Home RR 3 Box 1400 Pittsfield ME 04967

ELIOT, ALEXANDER, author, mythologist; b. Cambridge, Mass., Apr. 28, 1919; s. Samuel Atkins, Jr. and Ethel (Cook) E.; m. Jane Winslow Knapp, May 3, 1952; children: May Rose, Jefferson, Winslow. Student, Black Mountain Coll., 1936-38, Boston Mus. Sch., 1938-39. Dir. Pinkney St. Artists Alliance, Boston, 1940-41; asst. to producer March of Time newsreel, 1941-42; asst. dir. films Office of War Info., 1942-43; editor films Office of Coord. Inter-Am. Affairs, 1943-45; art editor Time mag., 1945-60. Prof. emeritus program Hampshire Coll., 1977. Editor Parabola mag., 1995-96; contbg. editor Harvard mag., 1988-95; author: Proud Youth, 1953, Three Hundred Years of American Painting, 1957, Sight and Insight, 1959, Earth, Air, Fire and Water, 1962, Greece, 1963, Love Play, 1966, Creatures of Arcadia, 1967, Socrates, 1967, A Concise History of Greece, 1972, Myths, 1976, Zen Edge, 1979, (with Jane Winslow Eliot) Fisher's Guide to Greece, 1984, Abraham Lincoln, 1985, The Universal Myths, 1990, The Global Myths, 1993, The Timeless Myths, 1996; (film with Jane Winslow Eliot) The Secret of Michelangelo, Every Man's Dream, 1968. Guggenheim fellow, 1960; Japan Found. sr. fellow, 1975 Mem. Century Assn., Dutch Treat Club (N.Y.C.). Home: 105 Paloma Ave Venice CA 90291-2572 *The moon, the planets, pass around my heart. The sun shines into me, and in me as well. Yet what am I? A goose-pimpled crazy on a skewed glass bicycle, continually crashing into scribbled walls. And this moment, this being is the thing.*

ELIOT, CHARLES WILLIAM JOHN, former university president; b. Rawalpindi, Pakistan, Dec. 8, 1928; s. William Edmund and Ann Catherine (McDougall) E.; m. Mary Williamson, Sept. 2, 1954; children: Charles, Sophia (dec.), Nicholas, Johanna, Luke. BA, U. Toronto, Ont., Can., 1949, MA, 1951, PhD, 1961; DCL, King's Coll., 1988; DLitt, St. Mary's, 1999. Lectr., asst. prof., assoc. prof., prof. U. B.C., Vancouver, Can., 1957-71; prof. archaeology Am. Sch. Classical Studies, Athens, Greece, 1971-76; prof. classics Mount Allison U., Sackville, N.B., Can., 1976-85, acad. v.p., 1981-83; pres. U. P.E.I., Charlottetown, Can., 1985-95, pres. emeritus, 1996—. Mem. Acad. Panel of the Social Scis. and Humanities Rsch., 1978-82, chmn., 1980-81. Author: Coastal Demes of Attika, 1962, Campaign of the Falieri and Piraeus in the Year 1827; or a Journal of a Volunteer, 1992. Contbr. revs. and articles to profl. jours. Mem. Sch. Bd. Dist. 14 N.B., 1983-85 Mem. Order of Can., 1994; scholar Am. Sch. Classical Studies, 1952-54, Can. Coun., 1965-66, Dumbarton Oaks, 1980, Social Scis. and Humanities Rsch. Coun. Can., 1984-85. Mem. Classical Assn. Can. (pres. 1992-94). Anglican. Avocation: works of john galt. E-mail: wmeliot@pei.sympatico.ca.

ELIOT, THEODORE LYMAN, JR., international consultant; m. Patricia P. Peters. BA, Harvard U., 1948, M.P.A., 1956; LL.D., U. Nebr., Omaha, 1975. With U.S. Fgn. Svc., 1949-78; spl. asst. to under sec. of state; to sec. treasury; country dir. for Iran Dept. State; exec. sec. State Dept.; also spl. asst. to sec. of state Dept. State; ambassador to Afghanistan; insp. gen. Dept. State., Washington; dean Fletcher Sch. Law and Diplomacy, Tufts U., 1979-85; exec. dir. Ctr. for Asian Pacific Affairs Asia Found., San Francisco, 1985-87. Bd. dirs. Neurobiol. Tech., Fiberstars, Cornell Lab. of Ornithology. Trustee emeritus Asia Found. Mem. Am. Acad. Diplomacy, Univ. Club (San Francisco).

ELISEEV, PETR GEORGIEVICH, physicist, researcher; b. St. Petersburg, Russia, Feb. 3, 1936; s. Georgy Petrovich and Elena Kharitonovna Eliseev; m. Elena Iosifovna Naiditch, 1963; children: Georgy, Anna, Olga Diploma in physics, Moscow State U., 1959; Cand Sci, P.N. Lebedev Physics Inst., Moscow, 1965, DSc, 1974. Jr. rschr. Moscow State U., 1959-63; sr. rschr., then prin. rschr., head lab. P.N. Lebedev Physics Inst., 1963—; physicist, rsch. prof. Ctr. for High Tech. Materials, U. N.Mex., Albuquerque, 1995—. Author: Semiconductor Lasers, 1976, Introduction into Physics of Injection Lasers, 1983, Reliability Problems of Semiconductor Lasers, 1991. Mem.: IEEE, Russian Acad. Natural Scis., Optical Soc. Am. Office: U NMex Ctr for High Tech Materials 1313 Goddard SE Albuquerque NM 87106 Fax: 505-272-7801. E-mail: eliseev@chtm.unm.edu.

ELIX, DOUGLAS THORNE, computer company executive; b. Adelaide, Australia, July 27, 1948; s. David Llewellyn and Margaret Thorne (Martin) E.; m. Robin Claire Wallace; children: Claire, Penelope, David, Sarah. Dir. banking region IBM Australia Ltd., 1987-89; dir. fin. industry IBM Asia Pacific, Tokyo, 1990-91; dir. of ops. IBM Australia Ltd., 1991-92, gen. mgr. fin. svcs., 1992-93, asst. mng. dir., CEO, 1993-96; pres., CEO Integrated Sys. Solution Corp., Somers, N.Y., 1996-97; gen. mgr. IBM Global Svcs., N.A., 1997-98, IBM Global Svcs. Ams., 1998-99; sr. v.p., group exec. IBM Global Svcs., 1999—. Bd. dirs. Royal Bank of Can., IBM Global Svcs. Australia Ltd., Bus. Coun. Australia. Chmn. Roseville Coll. Found., Sydney, 1994—. Fellow Australian Inst. Mgmt. Office: IBM Global Svcs M/D 4305 Rt 100 Somers NY 10589

ELIZABETH, HER MAJESTY, II, (ELIZABETH ALEXANDRA MARY), Queen of United Kingdom of Great Britain and Northern Ireland, and her other Realms and Territories, head of the Commonwealth, Defender of the Faith; b. Apr. 21, 1926; d. King George VI (formerly Duke of York) and Queen Elizabeth (formerly Duchess of York); m. Prince Philip, Duke of Edinburgh, Nov. 20, 1947; children: Charles Philip Arthur George, Anne Elizabeth Alice Louise, Andrew Albert Christian Edward, Edward Antony Richard Louis. Succeeded to throne following death of father, Feb. 6, 1952; crowned Queen, June 2, 1953. Address: Buckingham Palace London SW1A 1AA England*

ELIZONDO, HECTOR, actor; b. N.Y.C., Dec. 22, 1936; s. Martin Echevarria and Carmen Medina (Reyes) E.; m. Carolee Campbell, Apr. 13, 1969; 1 son, Rodd. Student, CCNY, 1955-56, Ballet Arts Co. of Carnegie Hall. Appearances include (plays) The Price (Broadway), Drums in the Night, Steambath, 1970 (OBIE award), Prisoner of Second Avenue, 1974, The Great White Hope, 1977, Sly Fox (Dr. Desk-Nun award), Medal of Honor Rag, American Playhouse; (movies) Report to the Commissioner, 1975, The Taking of Pelham-1-2-3, 1975, Cuba, 1978, American Gigolo, 1979, The Fan, 1979, Young Doctors in Love, 1983, The Flamingo Kid, 1984, Nothing in Common, 1985, Leviathan, Pretty Woman, 1990 (Golden Globe nominee best supporting actor), Chains of Gold, Paydirt, Necessary Roughness, Frankie and Johnny, 1991, Being Human, 1992, Exit to Eden, 1993, Getting Even with Dad, 1993, Beverly Hills Cop III, 1993, Safe House, 1996, Turbulence, 1996, Dear God, 1996, Romy & Michelle, 1996, The Other Sister, 1998, Runaway Bride, 1998-99, The Princess Diaries, 2001, Tortilla Soup, 2001, How High, 2001; (TV series) Popi, 1976, Freebie and the Bean, Foley Square, 1985, Great Performances, WCET, 1987, The Impatient Heart, All in the Family, Chicago Hope, 1994-2000, The West Wing, 2002; (TV films) Casablanca, 1983, Medal of Honor Rag, 1982, Mrs. Cage (Emmy nominee for best supporting actor), 1992, The Dain Curse, 1978, Courage, 1986, Honey Boy, 1982, Out of the Darkness, 1985, Natica Jackson, 1987, Addicted to His Love, 1988, Your Mother Wears Combat Boots, 1989, The Amnesty File, 1990, The Burden of Proof, (winner Emmy best supporting actor), 1992, Borrowed Hearts, 1997, Fidel, 2002. Recipient Lifetime Achievement Image award, 1997, ALMA award for best actor, 1998, Best Actor in Drama Series, 2000, Latin Legends award, N.Y.C., 2000, Lifetime Achievement IMPACT award, 2002. Mem. Amnesty Internat., The Creative Coalition. Roman Catholic.*

ELJABIRI, OSAMA M. education educator, director; s. Husseini; m. Nuha Hattab, Jan. 16, 1990; children: Anas, Yazan. Masters, N.J.Inst. Of Tech., 1999—2001. Software engring. instr. N.J. Inst. Of Tech., Newark, 1999—2001, spl. lectr., dir. sr. project capstone course, 2001—. Exec. mgr. United Indsl. Group Corp., Madaba, Jordan, 1993—97. Author: (jour. paper) Jour. of Sys. and Info. Tech., (conf. paper) Reengring. Bus. in the E-Bus. Age: A Field Study, An Effective Taxonomy for Software Process Models, Factors Influencing Design Quality and Assurance in Software Development: An Empirical Study, Drivers For Software Process Modeling Evolution, Toward a Comprehensive Framework for Software Process Modeling Evolution, Specialized sys. devel. Scholar Scholarships, N.J. Inst. of Tech., 1999—2000. Mem.: IEEE, Assn. for Info. sy., Assn. for Univ. Profs., ACM, N.J. Inst. of Tech. Sigma Chpt. of Alpha Epsilon Lambda. Office: NJ Inst of Tech Univ Heights Newark NJ 07102 Office Fax: 973-596-5777. Personal E-mail: eljabiri@optonline.net. E-mail: oe2@njit.edu.

EL-JACK, MOHAMMED S. urologist; b. Khartoum, Sudan, Jan. 1, 1968; s. Sid Ahmed El-Jack and Saadia Ahmed Younis; m. Nazik Abdallah Abdel Rahman, Apr. 10, 1994; children: Khalid, Waleed H. M.B.B.S., U. Khartoum, 1991. Intern Faculty of Medicine, U. Khartoum, 1991—92; resident Royal Coll. Surgeons Ireland, Wexford/Kilkenny, 1992—95, resident in urology Dublin, 1995—2000; fellow in urology/transplant Cleve. Clinic Found., Cleve., 2000—02; urol. surgeon Bay Area Med. Ctr., Marinette, Wis., 2002—. Contbr. Recipient Univ. prize in biochemistry and physiology, Faculty of Medicine, U. Khartoum, 1985—86, Univ. prize in pathology, microbiology, forensic medicine, 1987—92. Fellow: Royal Coll. Surgeons in Ireland; mem.: Am. Urol. Assn. Avocations: fishing, car racing, drawing. Office: Bay Area Medical Ctr 3130 Shore Dr Marinette WI 54143

ELKES, TERRENCE ALLEN, communications executive; b. N.Y.C., Apr. 28, 1934; s. Sidney and Beatrice (Sachnin) E.; m. Ruth Jerkowsky, June 14, 1959; children: Steven Andrew, David Adam, Daniel Arthur. BA cum laude, CCNY, 1955; JD, U. Mich., 1958. Bar: N.Y. 1959. Atty. Prentice Hall, Inc., 1958-59; counsel internat. div. Norwich Pharmacal Co., 1959-65; corp. counsel, also v.p., sec. Parsons & Whittemore, Inc., 1965-72; corp. counsel Black Clawson Co., 1965-72; treas. Prince Albert Pulp Co. Ltd., 1966-72; v.p., sec., gen. counsel Viacom Internat., Inc., N.Y.C., 1972-76, exec. v.p., 1976-78, pres., 1978-87, chief exec. officer, 1984-87; prin. Apollo Ptnrs., LLC-NY, N.Y.C., Conn., 1987—. Bd. dirs. IDC Svcs. Corp., Doane Agrl. Svcs., Inc., The Tennis Channel, 2001—; mng. dir. Apollo Radio, Ltd., 1989-96; chmn. Compact Video Corp., 1991-93, Internat. Post Ltd., 1994-97; chmn. Video Svcs. Corp., 1997-2000; dir. The Tennis Channel, 2002—. Trustee U. Mich. Law Sch., 1992, mem. pres. adv. group U. Mich., 1992, mem. investment adv. group & tech. transfer group, 1992. Home: 12 Trails End Rye NY 10580-2227 Office: Apollo Ptnrs LLC 500 5th Ave New York NY 10110-0002

EL KHADEM, HASSAN SAAD, chemistry educator, researcher; b. Cairo, Mar. 24, 1923;, naturalized, 1975; s. Saad S. and Nimet (Zulficar) El K.; m. Nadia M. Said, Sept. 6, 1951 (dec. 2002); children: Samiha, Saad. DSc Tech., ETH Zurich, Switzerland, 1950; PhD, Imperial Coll., London, 1952; DSc, U. London, 1967; BSc with honors, Cairo U., 1946; DSc, U. Alexandria (Arab Republic of Egypt), 1963. Lectr. Alexandria U., 1952-58, asst. prof., 1958-64, prof. organic chemistry, 1964-71; prof. chemistry Michigan Tech. U., Houghton, 1971-74; head dept. chemistry and chem. engring. Mich. Tech. U., Houghton, 1974-80, pres. prof. chemistry, 1980-84; Isbell prof. chemistry The Am. U., Washington, 1984-93, Isbell prof. chemistry emeritus, 1993—. Mem. editorial bd. Carbohydrate Rsch., 1966-92; contbr. over 170 articles on carbohydrates and medicinal chemistry to profl. jours.; author 15 books including Carbohydrate Chemistry: Monosaccharides and their Oligomers, Synthetic Methods for Carbohydrates, Anthracycline Antibiotics; patentee in field. Fulbright scholar U.S. Dept. State, Ohio State U., Columbus, 1963-64; recipient Phys. Sci. award Washington Acad. Sci., 1992. Mem. AAAS, Am. Chem. Soc. (chmn. carbonhydrate div. 1984-85, Melville L. Wolfrom award 1989), Sigma Xi. Achievements include discovery of a lost Greek manuscript by Zosimos (300 A.D.) translated to Arabic in a twelveth century Alchemy book (donated to the Libr. of Congress). Home: 4948 Sentinel Dr Apt 101 Bethesda MD 20816-3586 Office: Am U Dept Chemistry Beeghly Bldg 4400 Massachusetts Ave NW Washington DC 20016-8001 *One reason why many students stop asking questions in class is that they do not get satisfying answers.*

ELKHADEM, SAAD ELDIN AMIN, foreign language and literature educator, writer, editor, publisher; b. Cairo, May 12, 1932; emigrated to Can., 1968, naturalized, 1974; s. Amin Saad and Zahra Amin (Tharwat) E.; m. Madiha Mahmoud, July 16, 1962; 1 child, Sherifa. PhD, U. Graz, 1961. Press attache Egyptian Govt., Berne, 1962-65; dir. Office for Cultural Relations, Cairo, 1965-67; asst. prof. U. N.D., Grand Forks, 1967-68; assoc. prof. German U. N.B., Fredericton, Can., 1968-74, prof. dept. German and Russian, 1974-95, prof. emeritus, from 1995. Author: Sechs Essays ueber den deutschen Roman, 1969, Ajniha Min Rasas, 1972, Zur Geschichte des deutschen Romans, 1974, Tajarib Laylah Wahidah, 1975, Dictionary of Literary Terms, 1976, The York Press Style manual, From Travels of the Egyptian Odysseus, 1979, The York Companion to Themes and Motifs of World Literature, 1981, History of the Egyptian Novel, 1985, Ulysses' Hallucinations or the Like, 1985, The Ulysses Trilogy, 1988, The Plague, 1988, Canadian Adventures of the Flying Egyptian, 1990, Chronicle of the Flying Egyptian in Canada, 1991, The Concise Dictionary of Greek, Roman, Norse and Egyptian Mythology, 1991, Crash Landing of the Flying Egyptian, 1992, Wings of a Lead: A Modern Egyptian Novella, 1994, Five Innovative Egyptian Short Stories, 1994, An Egyptian Satire about a Condemned Building, 1996, The Blessed Movement: An Egyptian Micronovel, 1997, The Great Egyptian Novel, 1998, Creative Writing, 1999, Brief Definitions of All Essential Literary Terms, 2000, One Night in Cairo, 2001, On Egyptian Fiction: Five Essays, 2001; editor Internat. Fiction Rev., 1974-96; editor, gen. mgr. York Press, (also transl.) Life is Like a Cucumber: Colloquial Egyptian Proverbs, 1993, The Sayings of the Prophet Muhammad, 1994; gen. editor Authoritative Studies in World Literature; contbr. articles to profl. jours. Can. Council grantee, 1974-75; recipient Min. of State multiculturalism awards, 1989, 90. Mem. MLA. Home: Toronto, Canada. Died Feb. 25, 2003.

ELKIN, LOIS SHANMAN, business systems company executive; b. Cin., Oct. 31, 1937; d. Jerome David and Mildred Louise (Bloch) Shanman; m. Alan I. Elkin, May 6, 1962; children: Karen A., Jeffrey R. BA in Math., Goucher Coll., 1959. Sys. engr. ea. region IBM, Balt. and Columbia, S.C., 1959-61, mgr. Computer Test Ctr. ea. region, 1961-64; exec. v.p. Advance Bus. Sys., Balt., 1964—, A&L Real Estate, Balt., 1970—; pres. Our World Gallery, Inc., Balt., 1995—. Mentor for math. and bus. Goucher Coll., Balt., 1982—86; co-owner ATMS, Balt., 1994—2002; guest lectr. MBA program Loyola Coll. Md., Balt., 1993—94, Towson U., 1999; steering com. Loyola Ctr. Closely Held Cos., Balt., 1993—; conducted seminars Towson U. Leadership Group, 1999; bd. dirs. Hunt Valley Bus. Forum, Balt.; ptnr. Enable Technologies, Balt., 2001—. Vol. House of Ruth, Balt., 1990—, Image Recovery Ctr., Union Meml. Hosp., Balt., 1995—96; exec. bd. dirs. Pride of Balt. II, 1994—2000; co-chair Multiple Sclerosis Class of '98 fundraiser, 1998; exec. bd. Md. chpt. Nat. Multiple Sclerosis Soc., 2000—; sponsor maj. fundraising event Johns Hopkins Children's Ctr., Balt., 2002; bd. dirs. Hearing and Speech Agy., Balt., 1996—2001. Named Entrepreneur of Yr., Ernst and Young, 2001; named one of Top 500 Women-Owned Businesses in U.S., Working Woman Mag., 1998—2001, Mds. Top 100 Women, 1999, 2001; recipient AAA Torch award for ethics in bus., 1997, honoree, Chimes Ann. Hall of Fame Tribute, 2002. Mem.: Women's Bus. Club (founder 2002—), Nat. Assn. Women Bus. Owners (Woman of the Yr. award Balt. chpt. 1985). Avocation: collecting art. Office: Advance Bus Sys 10755 York Rd Cockeysville Hunt Valley MD 21030-2114

ELKIN, LYNNE OSMAN, science historian, educator; b. NYC, June 10, 1946; d. Henry and Beatrice (Abramson) Osman; m. Edward Lawrence (div. Dec. 19, 1978). BA, U. Rochester, NY, 1967; PhD, U. Calif., Berkeley, 1973. Lectr. Calif. State Hayward, 1971—72, asst. prof., 1973—76, prof., 1978—2004, prof. emeritus, 2004—. Cons. Biology Media, Berkeley, Calif., 1973—78; spkr. AAAS, Boston, 2002, Denver, 03, Am. Chem. Soc., 2003—. Prodr., author (multi-media slide shows) Photosynthesis, Energy and Life, 1973—78; contbr., articles to profl. jours. including Physics Today. Mem.: AAAS, Assn. Women in Sci. Democrat. Jewish. Avocation: biol. photography. Home: 2690 Mountaingate Way Oakland CA 94611 E-mail: lelkin@csuhayward.edu.

ELKIN, NORMAN, urban planner; b. Chgo., Mar. 25, 1924; s. Louis B. and Fannie (Ovrutsky) E.; m. Betty Gene Lee, Nov. 1, 1959; children: Karen Ruth, Laurie Sue, Vicki Ann. AA, Wright Jr. Coll., Chgo., 1943; postgrad., DePaul U., 1946; MA, U. Chgo., 1949. Asst. to Alderman R.E. Merriam City Coun. City of Chgo., 1951, staff dir. com. on housing, 1952-54; rsch. dir. Citizens for Merriam, Chgo., 1955; rsch. supr. Leo Burnett Advt. Agy., Chgo., 1955-56; asst. exec. sec. Neighborhood Redevel. Commn. City of Chgo., 1957, dir. coordination divsn. Dept. City Planning, 1958-59, dir. cmty. renewal program, 1959-60; sr. planner Jack Meltzer Assocs., Chgo., 1960-64; v.p. urban planning Leo J. Shapiro & Assocs., Chgo., 1964-68; dir. projects Lemberg Ctr. for Study of Violence Brandeis U., Waltham, Mass., 1968-69; exec. dir. Gov.'s Commn. on Urban Area Govt. State of Ill., 1969-71; v.p., planning dir. Urban Investment & Devel. Co., Chgo., 1971-85; v.p. new bus. devel. JMB Realty Corp., Chgo., 1986-91; prin. Norman Elkin Planning Cons., Chgo., 1991—. Instr. urban and rural soc. U. Chgo., 1950-51, lectr. polit. sci., 1954, 56, 57; instr. Am. history and soc. Wright Jr. Coll., 1956-57. Contbr. articles to profl. jours. Past mem. Gov.'s Rural Devel. Cabinet, State of Ill., Governing Bd. Planning Com. St. Joseph Hosp., Chgo., fin. com. Earl & Esther Johnson Fund, U. Chgo., Mayor's Task Force to Restore the Blvd. Sys. of Chgo., Ill. Landmarks Preservation Coun.'s Blue Ribbon Com. to Save Chgo. Theatre, Mayor's Citizens Adv. Com. on New Ctrl. Libr., Chgo.; mem. planning com. Cosmopolitan C. of C., Chgo., Landmarks Preservation Coun. of Ill., Friends of the Pks., Chgo., Friends of Downtown, Chgo., Chgo. Arch. Found., Chgo. Hist. Soc.; past bd. dirs. Civic Fedn. Chgo., New Trier Twp. H.S., Winnetka, Ill., 1983-89; past chmn. long range planning com., mem. exec. com. redevel. com. Greater State St. Coun., Chgo. With USN, 1943-46, PTO. Recipient cert. of merit New Trier Twp. Bd. Edn., 1989, appreciation award City of Chgo. Dept. Planning and Greater State St. Coun., 1990, Lifetime Achievement award Friends of Downtown, 1996, Exceptional Leadership award Greater State St. Coun., 1997, Honoree of Yr. award Greater State St. Coun., 1999. Mem. Am. Inst. Cert. Planners, Am. Planning Assn., The Cliff Dwellers, Phi Beta Kappa. Jewish.

ELKIN, STEPHEN LLOYD, political science educator; b. N.Y.C., Mar. 1, 1941; s. Max and Mildred (Miller) E.; m. Diana Muriel Wilson, Mar. 26, 1967. BA, Alfred U., 1961; MA, PhD, Harvard U., 1969. Fellow Joint Ctr. for Urban Studies Harvard U.-MIT, 1965-66; lectr. Smith Coll., 1966-68; dir. Masters of Pub. Policy program Wharton Sch. U. Pa., 1973-75; prof., dir. honors, dept. govt. and politics U. Md., 1985—. Vis. fellow Australian Nat. U., summer 1993, 2000; vis. lectr. politics and adminstrn. Beijing U., 1989; vis. scholar Derryfield Sch., Manchester, N.H., 1988, 89; co-founder, co-chair Conf. Group on Polit. Economy, 1978-90; co-founder, co-chair, mem. exec. com. Com. on the Polit. Economy of the Good Soc., 1988—; co-prin. The Democracy Collaborative, 2000—; co-dir. Md. Seminar in Polit. Theory and Polit. Economy, 1986-89; co-organizer First Ind. Conf. Polit. Economy of the Good Soc., Yale U., 1991; co-organizer Politics as Politics conf., Brookings Instn., 1982; cons. Fels Inst., U. Pa., 1971, Regional Sci. Rsch. Inst., Phila., 1976-77, dept. legis. ref. State of Md., 1979-80, Pub. Interest Law Ctr., Phila., 1983-84. Mem. editl. bd. Policy Scis., 1986—; mem. adv. editl. bd. Theories of Instl. Design, 1993—; author: Politics and Land Use Planning: The London Experience, 1974, City and Regime in the American Republic, 1987; co-editor, co-author: The Democratic State, 1985, The New Constitutionalism, 1993; author: (with others) Comparative Public Policy: A Cross National Bibliography, 1978, National Resources and Urban Policy, 1980, The Democratic State, 1985, The Politics of Urban Development, 1987, Handbook of Political Theory and Policy Science, 1987, The New Constitutionalism, 1993, An Heretical Heir of the Enlightenment: Studies in the Thought of C.E. Lindblom, 1993, Encyclopedia of the American Presidency, 1993, The Constitution of Good Societies, 1996, Citizen Competence and Democracy, 1999; editor: The Good Society; contbr. articles, book revs. to profl. jours. Recipient Theodore Lowi Best Paper award Policy Studies Jour., 1985; grantee Smith, Amherst, Mt. Holyoke, and U. Mass., 1967, Am. Philos. Soc., 1969-70, Social Sci. Rsch. Coun., 1969-70, Ford Found., 1969-70, Ctr. for Environ. Studies, 1971, NSF, 1971, NSF-RANN, 1974, U. Md., 1977, 78, 88, Yale U., 1990, Bauman Found., 1992-93, Ams. Talk Issues Found., 1993-94; Leverhulme fellow U. Leicester, 1969-70, Lehrman Inst. fellow, 1980-81, U. Md., 1993-94; grantee Ams. Talk Issues Found., 1993, J.M. Kaplan Found., 1994-98, MacArthur Found., 1997. Mem. ASPA, Am. Polit. Sci. Assn. (sect. chair 1985, Best Book in Urban Theory Assn., 1985-89), Internat. Polit. Sci. Assn., Southwestern Social Sci. Assn. Office: U Md Dept Govt And Politics College Park MD 20742-0001

ELKIND, DAVID, psychology educator; b. Detroit, Mar. 11, 1931; s. Peter and Bessie (Nelson) E.; children: Paul Steven, Robert Edward, Eric Allen. BA, UCLA, 1952, PhD, 1955; DSc (hon.), R.I. Coll., 1987; DHL (hon.), Mitchell Coll., 2000. Diplomate: Am. Bd. Profl. Examiners in Psychology. Research asst. to David Rapaport, Austen Riggs Ctr., Stockbridge, Mass., 1956-57; staff psychologist Beth Israel Hosp., Boston, 1957-59; asst. prof. Wheaton Coll., Norton, Mass., 1959-61; asst. prof. med. psychology U. Calif. Med. Sch., Los Angeles, 1961-62; assoc. prof., dir. Child Study Ctr., U. Denver, 1962-66; prof., dir. grad. tng. in developmental psychology, dept. psychology U. Rochester, N.Y., 1966-78; chmn. Eliot Pearson dept. child devel. Tufts U., Medford, Mass., 1978-83; prof. child devel. sr. resident scholar Lincoln Filene Ctr. Eliot Pearson dept. child study Tufts U., Medford, Mass.; research dir. World of Inquiry Evaluation-NSF, 1970; project dir. Tng. of Early Childhood Specialists, U.S. Office Edn., 1970; psychol. cons. VA, 1962-74, Rochester Mental Health Center, 1966-74, Rochester Family Ct., 1967-73; headmaster Mt. Hope Sch., Rochester, 1974-77. Seamus Heany lectr. U. Coll., Dublin, 2000; co-host Lifetime TV series "Kids These Days". Author: (with H.J. Flavell) Studies in Cognitive Development, 1969, Children and Adolescents, 1974, A Sympathetic Understanding of the Child, 1974, (with I. Weiner) Child Development: A Core Approach, 1972, (with others) Psychology: An Introduction, 1973, Child Development and Education, 1976, (with D. Hetzel) Readings in Human Development: Contemporary Perspectives, (with I. Weiner) Development of the Child, 1978, The Child's Reality: Three Developmental Themes, 1978, The Child and Society, 1979; The Hurried Child, 1981, All Grown Up and No Place to Go, 1984, Miseducation: Preschoolers at Risk, 1987, Grandparenting: Understanding Today's Children, 1988; editor: Perspectives in Early Childhood Education, 1991, Parenting Your Teenager in the Nineties, 1993, Images of the Young Child, 1993, Understanding Your Child, 1994, A Sympathetic Understanding of the Child Birth to Sixteen, 1994, Ties that Stress: The New Family Imbalance, 1994, Reinventing Childhood, 1998. Recipient Great Friends to Kids award Assn. Youth Mus., 2001, Dale Richmond award Child and Adolescent Divsn. Am. Acad. Pediat.; NSF Sr. Postdoctoral fellow Geneva, 1964-65. Fellow Am. Psychol. Assn. (recipient Nicholas Hobbs Award div. 26), AAAS, Nat. Assn. Edn. of Young Children (pres. 1986-88). Home: 7 Lloyd Ln East Sandwich MA 02537-1225 Office: Tufts U Dept Child Devel Medford MA 02155 E-mail: delkind995@aol.com., delkind@emerald.tufts.edu.

ELKIND, MORT WILLIAM, business consultant; b. N.Y.C., Sept. 10, 1925; s. Samuel William and Leah Fannie (Meschen) E.; m. Mary Johanna Ruggiero, June 10, 1962; children: Lori Ann, Susan Marie, Edward William. BS in Chemistry summa cum laude, U. S.W. La., 1949; MS Analytical Chemistry, La. State U., 1951; postgrad., Georgetown U. Inst. Lang. & Linguistics, 1952, UCLA, 1954-55, Berkeley Coll., 1991-92. Intelligence officer CIA, Washington, 1952-53; head waiter Scaroon Manor Hotel, Schroon Lake, N.Y., 1956-57; copywriter J. B. Rundle; Sanders & Lowen; Cayton, Inc., N.Y.C., 1959-65; dir. profl. rels. Kings County Rsch. Labs., Bklyn., 1965-67; copywriter L.W. Frohlich, N.Y.C., 1967-74; sr. copywriter William Douglas McAdams, N.Y.C., 1974-76; copy supr. Kallir, Philips, Ross, Inc., N.Y.C., 1976-85; cons. Chestnut Ridge, N.Y., 1965—; co-founder Photocell Corp. of Am., 1965, Screen Features, Inc., 1966; founder, prin. MWE Assocs. Advt., 1970; co-founder Quadrisec, Inc., 1980, Modular Exports, Inc., 1988; v.p. mktg. Am. Investor Note Paper Corp., N.Y.C., 1985-86; dir. mktg. Air Baby, Inc., Blauvelt, N.Y.,

1990-91. Author: Internecine, 1957; editor: McNeil Psychiatric Calendar, 1978-83; writer, producer: (TV series) Billy Bang-Bang, 1966-68; creator: (film) The Internecine Project, 1974, (TV series) Bringing Up Kids, 1989 (Disting. mem. Internat. Soc. Poets 1994). Polit. cons. N.Y. State Senator, Rockland County and Albany, N.Y., 1978-80. Sgt. C.E., U.S. Army, 1943-46, ETO. Named to U. S.W. La. Athletic Hall of Fame, 1978; recipient Andy award N.Y. Advt. Club, 1979. Mem. Internat. Soc. Poets (Disting. mem.), Blue Key, Phi Kappa Phi, Phi Lambda Upsilon. Avocations: reading, writing, math problem solving. E-mail: melkind@earthlink.net.

ELKINS, ALFRED DAVID, insurance company administrator; b. N.Y.C., Sept. 16, 1946; s. Nathaniel and Emily Elkins; m. Ethel Lehman Elkins, Sept. 24, 1978. *Alfred Elkins' mother, Emily Elkins, was a successful schoolteacher in the New York City public school system. Before that, during the Depression, she was in the Works Progress Administration and wrote the manual on remedial reading in elementary schools. His father, Nathaniel Elkins, was a musician and interior designer. His father-in-law, the deceased Richard Lehman, was a longtime and successful real estate broker in Greenwich Village.* AB, Herbert H. Lehman Coll., 1969. Corp. proofreader Mut. of Am., N.Y.C., 1985-96, documents file adminstr., 1996—. *In 1989, Alfred Elkins read a historical essay at the Triumph of the American Revolution Symposium. The Symposium was held at Keene State College, in New Hampshire. The essay was entitled "The Constitution: Conservative or Radical?" It was later read "with interest" by the retired Chief Justice of the Supreme Court of the United States, Warren Burger, who said that he would have it published if he could.* Recipient Golden Poet Trophy World of Poetry, 1991, Editor's Choice award Nat. Llbr. of Poetry, 1994. Mem. Am. Hist. Assn., Poetry Soc. of Am., Acad. Am. Poets, Poets House. Avocations: writing poetry, reading history, listening to music. Home: 2145 Matthews Ave Bronx NY 10462-2028

ELKINS, DAN, small business owner, educator; b. Bisbee, Ariz., Jan. 19, 1947; AA, Cochise Coll., 1967; BA, Lowell State Coll., 1975; MBA, Lowell U., 1980. Cert. secondary and bilingual edn. tchr., Mass. Seaman USN, 1967, commd. lt. jr. grade, 1979, advanced through grades to lt. comdr., 1986, res. intelligence program officer Naval Air Facility Detroit, 1980-83, staff officer hqrs. U.S. So. Command Quarry Heights, Panama, 1984-87, manpower officer hqrs. Naval Intelligence Command Washington, 1987-90, instr. Joint Mil. Intelligence Tng. Ctr., 1990-94; ret., 1994; grad. asst. Lowell (Mass.) U., 1979-80; fin. analyst Simplex Time Recorder Co., Gardner, Mass., 1980; proprietor DWE Enterprises, Alexandria, Va., 1995—. Dir. DWE Inst., Alexandria, 1998—; cons. Cmty. Mgmt. Staff, Washington, 1996-97, Hdqs. U.S. Naval Security Group Command, Ft. Meade, Md., 2000, Litton TASC, Rosslyn, Va., 1997-98, MITRE Corp., Vienna, Va., 1999. Author: ref. manuals. Vol. tutor Draper Elem. Sch., Washington, 1988—. Recipient Exemplary Svc. award DC Pub. Schs., 1992; named Instr. of Quarter Def. Intelligence Coll., 1991. Mem. Naval Res. Assn. (life), Lowell U. Alumni Assn. (chmn. fin. com. 1980), U. Mass. Lowell Alumni Assn. Avocations: tennis, crossword puzzles, chess, bowling. Office: DWE Enterprises PO Box 4514 Alexandria VA 22303-0514

ELKINS, DONALD MARCUM, dean, agronomy educator; b. Woodville, Ala., Sept. 15, 1940; s. Lotus Marcum and Una (Troup) E.; m. Earline Mizell, Feb. 16, 1963; children: Mark Willis, Daniel Joseph. BS, Tenn. Polytech. Inst., 1962, MS, Auburn U., 1964, PhD, 1967. Rsch. asst., NASA fellow Auburn (Ala.) U., 1965-67; asst. prof. So. Ill. U., Carbondale, 1967-71, assoc. prof., 1971-74, prof., 1974-95, assoc. dean for acad. programs, 1985-95; dean Coll. Agr. and Human Ecology Tenn. Technol. U., Cookeville, Tenn., 1995—. Advisor Agr. Students Adv. Coun., 1985-95; chmn. North Ctrl. Region Deans and Dirs. Resident Instrn., 1990-91. Author: (with others) Growth Regulating Chemicals, 1982; co-author Crop Production Principles and Practices, 4th edit., 1980; author: Crop Science Laboratory Studies, 1990; contbr. articles to jours. in field. Fellow Am. Soc. Agronomy (resident edn. award 1981, fellow award 1987); mem. Nat. Assn. Colls. and Tchrs. Agr. (Outstanding Tchr. award 1978), Agbassadors Club (advisor 1986-95), Agr./Human Ecology Ambs. Club (advisor 1995—), Sigma Xi, Phi Kappa Phi, Alpha Zeta, Alpha Gamma Rho (hon.), Omicron Delta Kappa (faculty sec. 1996—), Lambda Alpha Sigma (advisor 1996-97), others. Mem. Ch. Of Christ. Office: Tenn Tech U Coll Agr and Human Ecology Box 5165 Cookeville TN 38505 Home: 1335 Buckingham Pl Cookeville TN 38501-0734 E-mail: delkins@tntech.edu.

ELKINS, FRANCIS CLARK, history educator, university official; b. Scranton, Ark., Feb. 24, 1923; s. Frank and Auby (Moore) E.; m. Norma Trice, Aug. 18, 1946; 1 dau., Annette. BA, U. Cen. Ark., 1943; MA, U. Ark., 1947; PhD, Syracuse U., 1953; postdoctoral, U. Minn., 1956. From instr. to prof., chmn. div. social sci. Henderson State U., Arkadelphia, Ark., 1946-61; pres. Chadron (Nebr.) State Coll., 1961-67, N.E. Mo. State Coll., Kirksville, 1967-69; coordinator Univ. Coll., Ark State U., 1969-70, v.p. instrn., 1970-78, v.p. univ. rels., 1979-80; v.p. univ. rels. and devel. No. Ariz. U., Flagstaff, 1980—88, prof. history, 1980-88, president's coord. univ. rels., 1983-88. Edn. cons., 1988—; mem. exec. com. Rocky Mountain Edn. Lab., 1965-67; examiner North Cen. Assn. Colls. and Schs.; examiner, cons. Nat. Council Accreditation Tchr. Edn., chmn. visitation and appraisal com., 1963-68; mem. Nebr. Ednl. TV Council Higher Edn., 1966-67, Ark. Council Econ. Edn., 1970-81. Mem. adv. coun. Mo. 4-H Found., 1968-69; mem. Ark Adv. Coun. on Career Edn.; bd. dirs. United Way, 1980-88. Served with USAAF, 1943-45. Decorated D.F.C., Air medal with four oak leaf clusters, Unit citation with 1 star; recipient John Vaughn Excellence in Edn. award, North Ctrl. Assn. Colls. and Schs. Commn. on Schs., 1988, Disting. Svc. award, Chadron (Nebr.) State Coll., 1989. Mem. NEA (life), Am. Assn. Colls. for Tchr. Edn. (dir. 1968-71, state liaison rep. 1974-77), Assn. Orgns. Tchr. Edn. (adv. coun.), Ark. Hist. Assn., Ark. Edn. Assn. (life), Ark. Assn. Colls. for Tchr. Edn. (charter pres. 1973-75), Flagstaff C. of C. (dir. 1980-88), Craighead County Hist. Assn. (life), Elks, Rotary Internat. (Paul Harris fellow), Phi Delta Kappa, Kappa Delta Pi, Phi Alpha Theta, Alpha Chi, Phi Kappa Phi, Sigma Tau Gamma, Sigma Nu. Methodist. Home and Office: 3004 Hillridge Cv Jonesboro AR 72401-5937

ELKINS, GLEN RAY, retired service company executive; b. Winnsboro, Louisiana, May 23, 1933; s. Ceicel Herbert and Edna Mae (Lewallen) E.; m. Irene Kay (Hildebrand), Aug. 25, 1951; children: Steven Breen, Douglas Charles, Karen Anne, Michael Glen; m. Diane (Hodgson), Mar. 2, 1992. AA in Indsl. mgmt., Coll. San Mateo, 1958. Successively mgr. prodn. control, mgr. logistics, plant mgr., asst. v.p. ops. Aircraft Engring. and Maintenance Co., 1957-64; from mgr. field ops. to pres. Internat. Atlas Svc. Co., Princeton, NJ, 1964-85; sr. v.p. Atlas Corp., Princeton, NJ; chmn., CEO, dir. Global Assoc., 1973-85; pres. Global Assoc. Internat. Ltd., 1975-84; pres., CEO Triad Am. Svc. Corp., 1985-2000; pres. Pacific Mgmt. Svc. Corp., TASC Enterprises Inc., dba, Gottschall Engraving Co., 1993-2000; ret., 2000. Area chmn. Easter Seals drive, 1974; bd. dir. Utah Children's Mus.; served in USN, 1950-54. Mem. Nat. Mgmt. Assn.; Electronic Industries Assn.; Lakeview Club; Willow Creek Country Club (past pres.). Home: 1445 Harvard Ave Salt Lake City UT 84105-1917 Personal E-mail: grelkinsut@aol.com.

ELKINS, JAMES ANDERSON, JR., banker; b. Galveston, Tex., Mar. 24, 1919; s. James Anderson and Isabel (Mitchell) E.; m. Margaret Wiess, Nov. 24, 1945; children— Elise, James Anderson III, Leslie K. BA, Princeton U., 1941. With First City Nat. Bank, Houston, 1941—, v.p., 1946-50, pres. then chmn. bd., 1950-82; dir. First City Bancorp., Houston, 1982-88. Bd. dirs. Central Houston Inc. Bd. dirs. Houston Grand Opera; trustee Tex. Children's Hosp., Tex. Med. Ctr., 1991; chmn. bd. trustees Baylor Coll. Medicine, 1970—; trustee Menil Found.; mem. vestry Christ Ch. Cathedral. Episcopalian. Address: 1001 Fannin St Ste 1166 Houston TX 77002-6708

ELKINS, JAMES ANDERSON, III, investment professional; b. Houston, May 21, 1952; s. James Anderson Jr. and Margaret K. (Wiess) E.; m. Mary Virginia Arnold, Dec. 8, 1984; children: Margaret Wiess, James Anderson IV, Buck Arnold, John Caldwell, Harry Carothers, Samuel Hill, Lucy Gray. BA, Princeton U., 1974; MBA, U. Tex., 1976. Asst. treas. Morgan Guaranty Trust Co., N.Y.C., 1976-79; exec. v.p. First City Tex., Houston, 1979-93; chmn. Houston Trust Co., 1994—. Bd. govs. Rice U., Houston, 1982—; chmn. Tex. Children's Hosp., Houston, 1997—, trustee, 1989—; trustee Children's Mus., Houston, 1988—, Houston Mus. Natural Sci., 1993—, Houston Zoo Inc., 1993—, Baylor Coll. Medicine, 2001—, The Meth. Hosp., Houston, Tex., 2003—; bd. advisors U. Tex. Health Sci. Ctr., Houston, 1990; vice chmn. Salvation Army, 1990—; treas. Houston Parks Bd. Mem. Am. Bankers Assn. (exec. bd. corp. council), Houston Club, Tex. Bankers Assn., Forum Club. Methodist. Office: Houston Trust Co 1001 Fannin St Ste 700 Houston TX 77002-6707

ELKINS, KEN JOE, retired broadcasting executive; b. Prenter, W.Va., Oct. 12, 1937; s. Ernest Eugene Elkins and Gay (Avis) Dodrill; married; children: James, Diana. Student, Nebr. U., 1966-69. Engr. Sta. KETV-TV, Omaha, 1960-67, asst. chief engr., 1967-70, ops. mgr., nat. sales, gen. sales mgr., 1972-75, gen. mgr., 1975-80; chief engr. Sta. KOUB-TV, Dubuque, Iowa, 1970-71, gen. mgr., 1971-72, Sta. KSDK-TV, St. Louis, 1980-81; v.p., CEO Pulitzer Broadcasting Co., St. Louis, 1981-84, pres., CEO, 1984-99; ret., 1999. Bd. dirs. Commerce Bank St. Louis, Maximum Svc. Telecasters, Washington; chmn. BMI; pres. Nebr. Broadcasters, Omaha, 1979-80; chmn. NBC Affiliate Bd. Govs. Bd. dirs. BJC Health Sys. With USAF, 1957-61. Inducted into Nebr. Broadcasters Hall of Fame, 1990. Mem. Nat. Assn. Broadcasters (1st amendment com. Washington chpt. 1986-91, 1st amendment com. 1986, bd. dirs.), Found. Broadcasters Hall of Fame (bd. dirs., trustee 1990), TV Operators Caucus, Algonquin Club. Avocations: golf, water sports. Home: 720 Twin Fawns Dr Saint Louis MO 63131-4722 E-mail: kelkins@stlnet.com.

ELKINS, LLOYD EDWIN, SR., petroleum engineer, energy consultant; b. Golden, Colo., Apr. 1, 1912; s. Edwin and Beulah M. (Feltch) E.; m. Virginia L. Crosby, May 27, 1934; children: Marylou, Barbara Lee, Lloyd Edwin Jr. Degree in Petroleum Engring., Colo. Sch. Mines, 1934; PhD in Sci., U. Ozarks. With Amoco Prodn. Co., 1934-77; successively field engr., petroleum engr. Tulsa gen. office, sr. petroleum engr., petroleum engring. supr., asst. chief prodn. engr., chief prodn. engr., mgr. prodn. rsch., 1949-77; energy cons., 1977-97. Contbr. articles to profl. jours. Named to Engring. Hall of Fame Okla. State U., 1961; recipient Distinguished Service medal Colo. Sch. Mines, 1961; named to Engring. Hall of Fame U. Tulsa. Mem. Am. Assn. Petroleum Geologists, Am. Petroleum Inst. (chmn. mid-continent dist. div. prodn. 1948-49, chmn. adv. com fundamental research on occurrence and recovery petroleum 1941), Am. Inst. Mining, Metall. and Petroleum Engrs. (hon., v.p. 1953-59, pres. 1962, Anthony F. Lucas gold medal 1966), Nat. Acad. Engring., Tulsa Geol. Soc., Australian Inst. Mining and Metallurgy (hon.) Clubs: Engineers (Tulsa) (pres. 1950-51), Petroleum (Tulsa), Tulsa Country (Tulsa). Methodist. Home and Office: 5 Primrose Pl Amarillo TX 79106-4000

ELKINS, STANLEY MAURICE, historian, educator; b. Boston, Apr. 27, 1925; s. Frank and Frances (Reiner) E.; m. Dorothy Adele Lamken, June 22, 1947; children: Susan Roselyn, Robert Joel, Barbara Marion, Sara Ann. AB, Harvard, 1949; MA, Columbia, 1951, PhD, 1959. Tchr. Fieldston Sch., N.Y.C., 1951-54; asst. prof. history U. Chgo., 1955-60; faculty Smith Coll., Northampton, Mass., 1960—, prof. history, 1964-69, Sydenham Clark Parsons prof. history, 1969—94; fellow Inst. for Advanced Study, 1970-71, 76-77. Author: Slavery: A Problem in American Institutional and Intellectual Life, 1959, The Age of Federalism, 1993 (Bancroft prize Soc. Cin. Book Prize 1995). Served with AUS, 1943-46. Social Sci. Research Council fellow, 1963-64; Rocketeller fellow, 1954-55; Guggenheim fellow, 1976-77 Mem. Orgn. Am. Historians, Am. Hist. Assn., Soc. of Am. Historians. Home: 126 Vernon St Northampton MA 01060 2905 E-mail: s-elkins@mediaone.net.

ELKINS, STEVEN PAUL, architect; b. Ephrata, Wash., Feb. 18, 1949; s. Hugh Kyle Elkins and Fern Irene (Vining) Johnson; m. Linda Louise Harris, Aug. 6, 1977; children: Andrea Rouleau, Michael Rouleau, Jennifer. BArch, Wash. State U., 1972. Registered arch., Wash., Oreg., Utah. Designer, draftsman Eng & Wright Architects, Vancouver, B.C., Can., 1972-73, Harthorne-Hagen-Gross, Inc., Seattle, 1973-75, Leo A. Daly Co., Seattle, 1975-77; architect Lawrence Campbell & Assocs., Kent, Wash., 1977-81; prin. Steven P. Elkins Architects, Inc., Seattle, 1981—. Mem. community adv. com. Auburn (Wash.) Gen. Hosp., 1985—, mem. planning and bldg. com. Campus Way Covenant Ch., Federal Way, Wash., 1985—. Recipient Award of Excellence Wash. Precast Concrete Industry Assn., 1985, 86, Appreciation award Vocat. Indsl. Clubs Am., Wash., 1985, 86., Superintendant of Pub. Instrn., Auburn Sch. Dist., 1987. Mem. AIA (corp.), Nat. Trust for Hist. Preservation. Clubs: Washington Athletic. Democrat. Protestant. Avocations: golf, hiking, sailing, skiing. Home: 1326 183d Ave NE Bellevue WA 98008-3440 Office: 2630 116th Ave NE Ste 200 Bellevue WA 98004 E-mail: steve@spe-architects.com.

ELKINS, TONI MARCUS, artist, art association administrator; b. Tifton, Ga., Feb. 22, 1946; m. Samuel M. Elkins, 1968; children: Stephanie Elkins Sims, Eric Marcus. Student, Boston U., 1965; ABJ, U. Ga., 1968; postgrad., Columbia (S.C.) Coll., Athens, 1980-82; postgrad. photography/silk screening, Columbia (S.C.) Coll. Owner, designer Designs by Elkins, Columbia, 1986—. Water color artist, 1983—; supt. fine art S.C. State Fair Art Exhbn., 1987-96. Works include watercolors All American Things, And the Good Ones Look Alike, And the Good Ones with Lace. Auction chair The Elegant Egg McKissick Mus., Columbia, 1994; bd. dirs. Trustus Theatre, 1994-96; chmn. S.C. Playwright's Festival, 1994—. Recipient Best of Show award 18th Internat. Dogwood Festival, 1991, So. Water Color Assn. Pres.'s award, 1992, Purchase award Anderson County Arts Coun. 17th Ann. Exhibit, 1992, Meyer Hardware award Rocky Mountain National, 1992, Howard B. Smith award S.C. Watercolor Ann., 1992, Women of Distinction award Girl Scouts of Congaree Area, Inc., 2000. Mem. Nat. Watercolor Soc. (1st v.p., 2003—), Watercolor U.S.A., S.C. Watercolor Soc., Nat. Watercolor Okla., Penn. Watercolor Soc., Ga. Watercolor Soc., Rocky Mountain Nat. Watercolor Soc., Cultural Coun. of Richland & Lexington Counties (exec. bd. sec. 1990-93), Ctrl. Carolina Cmty. Found. (chmn. devel. 2000-01), Southeastern Art and Craft Expn. (adv. bd. 1993-94, Elizabeth O'Neill Verner award for the arts 1999), Columbia Coll. Com. of 150. Avocations: roller blading, reading, swimming, collecting porcelain, S.C. art and rare books. Home: 1511 Adger Rd Columbia SC 29205-1407

ELKINS-ELLIOTT, KAY, law educator; b. Dallas, Nov. 21, 1938; d. William Hardin and Maxidine (Sadler) E.; m. Michael Gail Hodgson, July 7, 1960 (div. Dec. 1974); children: Michael Brett, Ashley Kim, Samantha; m. Frank Wallace Elliott, Aug. 15, 1983. AA with honors, Stephens Coll., 1958; JD, U. Okla., 1964; LLM, So. Meth. U., 1984; MA, U. Tex., Dallas, 1990. Bar: Okla. 1964, Tex. 1982, U.S. Dist. Ct. (no. dist.) Tex. 1982, U.S. Supreme Ct. 1984, U.S. Dist. Ct. (we. dist.) Okla. 1989. Assoc. Ben Hatcher and Assocs., Oklahoma City, Okla., 1964-65; dir., gen. counsel Take-A-Tour Swaziland, Mbabane, Swaziland, 1966-74; atty. Dept. Health and Human Svcs., Dallas, 1975-80; hearing officer EEOC, Dallas, 1980-84; atty. pvt. practice, Dallas, 1984-92; vis. assoc. prof. Tex. Wesleyan U. Sch. Law, Dallas, 1992-95; arbitrator State Farm Ins., Dallas, 1991-96. Adj. prof. Wesleyan U. Sch. Law, 1995—, coach nat. ABA champion negotiation team, 1998; mediator pvt. practice, Dallas, Granbury, 1991—; coord. cert. in conflict resolution program Tex. Woman's U., 1996—; coach internat. champion negotiation team ICOD, 2002-; coach internat. champion online dispute resolution competition; cons. in field. Author: (with others) West Texas Practice, 1995; (with Frank Elliott) State Bar of Texas ADR Handbook, 2003. Dir. diversity tng. State Bar Tex. 9/11 project. Mem. ABA (negotiation and tng. coms., alternative dispute resolution sect.), Tex. Bar Assn. (ADR sect. coun. mem. 1998-2001, chair publs. com.), Tex. Bar Found., Tex. Initiatives for Mediation in Edn. (founder, planning com. 1993-95), Assn. for Conflict Resolution (pres. Dallas region 1995-97), Tex. Assn. Mediators, Dallas Bar Assn. (coun. mem. 1993-94), Inst. for Responsible Dispute Resolution (charter), Granbury C. of C. and Historic Merchants Assn., Toastmasters (v.p. 1993-94, pres. 1996-97), Optimist Internat. Avocations: singing, public speaking. Home: 2120 N Rough Creek Ct Granbury TX 76048-2903 Office: 2401 Turtle Creek Blvd Dallas TX 75219-4712 E-mail: k4mede8@swbell.net.

EL KODSI, BAROUKH, gastroenterologist, educator; b. Cairo, Aug. 24, 1923; arrived in U.S., 1957, naturalized, 1963; s. Moussa and Zohra (Aslan Cohen) El Kodsi; m. Marie Menasha, Mar. 26, 1960; children: Sylvia, Robert, Karen. MD, Cairo U., 1945. Intern Univ. Hosp. Cairo Sch. Medicine, 1946; resident in gen. medicine Jewish Hosp., Cairo, 1947—50, attending physician, 1950—57; intern Miriam Hosp., Providence, 1958; resident in internal medicine Boston City Hosp., 1959—61, chief resident, 1961—62, fellow in gastroenterology, 1962—64; asst. dir. medicine Union Hosp., Framingham, Mass., 1964—65; assoc. dir. medicine Maimonides Med. Ctr., Bklyn., 1965—67, dir. gastroenterology, 1968—; chief gastroenterology Coney Island Hosp., N.Y.C., 1967—68. Instr. Boston City Hosp., 1962—65; instr. Downstate Med. Ctr., SUNY, Bklyn., 1965—69, asst. prof. medicine, 1969—76, assoc. prof., 1976—. Contbr. articles to profl. jours. Named one of Best Drs. N.Y., New Yorker, 1966—67, 1968—89, NY Mag., 1996—2002. Fellow: ACP, Am. Coll. Gastroenterology; mem.: AMA, N.Y. Gastroent. Assn. (pres. 1985—86), Am. Soc. Study of Liver Disease, Am. Soc. Gastrointestinal Endoscopy, Am. Gastroent. Assn., Am. Fedn. Clin. Rsch., Ostomy Club (mem. exec. coun.). Home: 118 Girard St Brooklyn NY 11235-3010 Office: 925 48th St Brooklyn NY 11219-2919

ELKOWITZ, LLOYD KENT, dental anesthesiologist, dentist, pharmacist; b. Bklyn., Jan. 26, 1936; s. Paul and Lillian (Applebaum) E.; m. Deanna A. Weinger; children: Sheryl, Andrew, Marc. BS in Pharmacy, Columbia U., 1956; DDS, Case Western Res. U., 1960, postgrad., 1961. Diplomate Am. Dental Bd. Anesthesiology, Am. Soc. Dentist Anesthesiologists. Resident in anesthesiology U. Ctr Hosp, Pitts., 1961, fellow in anesthesiology, 1966; anesthesiologist Walson Army Hosp., Fort Dix, N.J., 1962-64; pvt. practice Great Neck, N.Y., 1964— Dir. divsn. dental anesthesiology dept. dentistry Nassau County Med. Ctr., East Meadow, L.I., 1975—; chmn. dept. dental anesthesiology Flushing (N.Y.) Hosp. Med. Ctr., 1989-95; pres. dental adv. coun. Adelphi U., Tufts U., Garden City, N.y., 1986—; adj. prof. dental biology Adelphi U., 1982—. Trustee Kings Point (N.Y.) Civic Assn., 1978-95. Capt. U.S. Army, 1962-64. Recipient Callahan Meml. award Ohio State Dental Assn., 1960. Fellow Am. Coll. Dentists, Am. Dental Soc. Anesthesiology, Acad. Gen. Dentistry (diplomate), Am. Soc. Dentist Anesthesiologists, Am. Soc. for Advancement of Anesthesia in Dentistry (pres. 1995-2000), Internat. Coll. Dentists; mem. ADA, Am. Pharm. Assn., N.Y. State Dental Assn., Queens Dental Assn., Queens County Dental Soc. (trustee 1995), Internat. Anesthesia Rsch. Soc., Am. Soc. Dentistry for Children, Queens Inst. for Continuing Dental Edn. (charter), Alpha Zeta Omega, Alpha Omega, Alpha Epsilon Delta. Avocations: piano, snow skiing, sailing, boating, tennis. Office: 107 Northern Blvd Great Neck NY 11021-4309

ELKOWITZ, SHERYL SUE, radiologist; b. N.Y.C., Apr. 20, 1962; BS in Biology summa cum laude, Adelphi U., Garden City, N.Y., 1982; MD, Wayne State U., Detroit, 1986. Diplomate Am. Bd. Radiology; lic. physician, N.Y. Intern internal medicine L.I. Jewish Hillside Med. Ctr., New Hyde Park, N.Y., 1986-87, resident diagnostic radiology, 1987-91; fellow pediatric radiology, chief fellow L.I. Jewish Hillside Med. Ctr., Schneider Children's Hosp., New Hyde Park, 1991-92; staff attending dept. diagnostic radiology L.I. Jewish Hillside Med. Ctr., New Hyde Park, 1992-96; asst. prof. radiology Albert Einstein Coll. Medicine, Yeshiva U., Bronx, N.Y., 1992—. Presenter various orgns. Contbr. articles to profl. jours. Mem. AMA, Soc. Pediatric Radiology, Radiol. Soc. N.Am., Am. Coll. Radiology, Am. Roentgen Ray Soc., Am. Assn. Women in Radiology (bylaws com. 1995), N.Y. Met. Pediatric Radiology Group, Neuhauser Soc., N.Y. State Radiol. Soc. Home: 3 Phaeton Dr Melville NY 11747-2019 Office: Good Samaritan Hosp Med Ctr 1000 Montauk Hwy West Islip NY

ELKUS, HOWARD FELIX, architect; b. San Francisco, Apr. 12, 1938; s. Eugene S. and Felice (Kahn) E.; m. Lorna Wheatley, Apr. 25, 1971. BS in Mech. Engring., Stanford U., 1959, MArch with distinction, Harvard U., 1963. Registered architect, Ariz., Calif., Conn., Fla., Ill., Ky., Maine, Mass., N.J., N.Y., Ohio, R.I., Vt., Wis., U.K. With Wagner & Martinez, Palo Alto, Calif., 1957, A.B. Atomenergi, Stockholm, 1958, Wilsey, Ham & Blair, San Mateo, Calif., 1960, Fry Drew & Ptnrs., London, 1961; prin., v.p. The Architects Collaborative, Cambridge, Mass., 1962-88; ptnr. Elkus/Manfredi Architects Ltd., Boston, 1988—. Prin. works include major mixed use devel. in Dallas (Victory), Boston, Providence, Hartford and Santa Ana, AOL Time Warner Ctr. retail and pub. galleries, N.Y., 33 Arch St., Boston, Intercontinental Hotel and Residence, Boston, City Place West Palm Beach, Fla., 730 N Michigan Ave. and Peninsula Hotel, Chgo., The Paramount, San Francisco, 28 State renovation, Boston, Pacific Place, Seattle, EF Centre N. Am. hdqr. bldg., Cambridge, Mass., Putnam Investments Hqtrs. Offices, Boston, Am. Express Bldg., Providence, Limited, Inc., World Hdqs., Columbus, Ohio, Office and Distbn. Complex, Reynoldsburg, Ohio, Henri Bendel, other store designs, U.S., Nat. Coun. of Archtl. Registration Bds. Hdqrs., Washington, At the Archs. Collaborative, the Near West Campus Stanford U., The Taubman Bldg., Kennedy Sch. of Harvard U., Copley Pl. (Urban Land Inst. excellence award 1988), Boston, Heritage on the Garden, Boston (Boston Soc. Architects Hon. award 1989), Flagship Wharf, Charlestown Navy Yard, Boston, Johnson Wax Hdqrs. Complex Expansion, Racine, Wis., Liberty Ctr. Pitts., AIA Hdqrs. Bldg., Washington, Limited Hdqrs., Columbus, Ohio, GSIS Hdqrs. and Fin. Ctr., Manila, The Philippines; maj. mixed use devels., Dallas, Hartford, Boston, Providence, Santa Ana. Recipient Prestressed Concrete Inst. award, 1983, citation, Engring. News Record, 1982, Constrn. Man of Yr. award, 1982, White House citation for contbn. to energy efficient environment, 1983, Passive Solar Design award, 1982, Owens-Corning Energy Conservation award, 1982, Nat. Landscape award, 1986, Progressive Arch. Urban Design award, 1987. Fellow: AIA (honor award 1966, 1974, citation 1973); mem.: Nat. Trust for Hist. Preservation, Urban Land Inst. (Award of Excellence 1988, 1996, 1998, Sadi award 2002), Boston Soc. Architects, Mass. Assn. Architects, Royal Inst. Brit. Architects. Office: Elkus/Manfredi Architects Ltd 530 Atlantic Ave Boston MA 02210-2218

ELKUS, RICHARD J., JR., electronics company executive; b. San Francisco, Feb. 25, 1935; s. Richard J. and Ruth (Kahn) E.; m. Helen Morrison, Aug. 17, 1956; children: Miriam Lyster, Richard M., Kevin J. BA, Stanford U., 1957; MBA, Dartmouth Coll., 1959. Prodn. control mgr. Ampex Corp., Redwood City, Calif., 1959-64, asst. to pres., 1968-71, mem. ops. bd., 1969-71, gen. mgr. ednl. and indsl. products divsn., 1969-72; pres., CEO, dir. Eyrle Co., Santa Clara, Calif., 1964-67; gen. mgr. Gould Med. systems, Santa Clara, Calif., 1973-74; exec. v.p., gen. mgr. Geometrics, Inc., Sunnyvale, Calif., 1974-80. Bd. dirs., chmn. bd. Integrated Systems, Inc., Santa Clara, 1985-92; bd. dirs. KLA-Tencor, San Jose, Calif., Lam Rsch., Fremont, Calif., SOPRA, Paris, Virage Logic, Fremont, Calif.; CEO Voyan Tech., Santa Clara. Mem. coun. on competitiveness, chmn. panel High Defination products and systems, NSF; mem. adv. bd. Ctr. Strategic and Internat. Studies Inst., 1990-96, Sch. Engring., Ga. Inst. Tech., 1996-98. Capt. USAR, 1957-65; bd. dirs. Nat. Sci. and Tech. Medals Found.; turstee Palo Alto Med. Found., Scripps Rsch. Ints.; pres. bd. sci. and innovation U. Calif. Mem. Am. Mgmt. Assn. (pres.'s coun.), Am. Electronics Assn. (bd. dirs., co-chmn. task force high resolutin systems), Electronics Assn. Calif. (vice chmn. nat. medal tech. nomination evaluation com. 1992-94, chmn. 1994-97), Econ. Strategy Inst. (adv. bd.), Foothills Tennis and Swim Club (Palo Alto, Calif.), Menlo Circus Club (Atherton, Calif.). Office: Voyan Tech 2700 Augustine Dr # 145 Santa Clara CA 95054

ELKUS, ROBERT MICHAEL, general surgeon; b. Detroit, Jan. 19, 1957; s. Philip Leonard and Estelle Elkus; m. Robin Lee Riley, May 27, 1990; children: Nathan Todd, Russell Wiley. BS, U. Mich., 1979, MD, 1983. Intern, then resident Med. Coll. Pa., Phila., 1983-88, staff physician, 1988-90, Henry Ford Hosp., Detroit, 1990—. Patentee in field. Achievement include patent for suture passer. Office: Henry Ford Hosp Divsn Gen Surgery 2799 W Grand Blvd Detroit MI 48202-2689 also: Henry Ford Hosp 6777 W Maple Rd West Bloomfield MI 48322-3013

ELL, TRAVIS EUGENE, electronics engineer; b. Minot, N.D., Oct. 3, 1951; s. Walter Joseph and Irene Dorthy (Ruby) E.; m. Deborah LouAnn Sorensen, Aug. 23, 1975 (div. June 1985); children: Joshua Michael, Jacob Matthew, John Thadeus; m. Sonia Ovsep Yazgulian. BSEE, N.D. State U., 1974, MSEE, 1978. Tchg. asst. N.D. State U., Fargo, 1974-77; servo engr. IBM Corp., Rochester, Minn., 1977-94; engring. mgr. Micropolis Corp., Chatsworth, Calif., 1994-96; servo engr. Lumonics Corp., Oxnard, Calif., 1996-97, Seagate Tech., Inc., Moorpark, Calif., 1997—. Recipient IBM Market-Driven Quality award, 1993. Mem. IEEE (chmn. N.D. State U. student br. 1993-94), Sigma Phi Delta (sec. 1993-94). Unitarian-Universalist. Achievements include patent for data disk drive velocity estimator. Home: 2609 Dante Ct Austin TX 78748 Office: Oak Technology 7000 W William Connor Dr Bldg One Ste 120 Austin TX 78735 E-mail: t.e.ell@att.net.

ELLEBY, GAIL, management consultant; b. Seattle, Sept. 15, 1949; d. William Lee and Marie (Davis) E.; 1 child, Courtney Champion. BA, U. Wash., 1973, MPA, 1975; MSA in Sports Adminstrn., Ohio U., 1980. Cert. ISSATF Ofcl. Adminstrn. specialist Mayor's Office, City of Seattle, 1986-87; adminstr. asst. Seattle 1990 Goodwill Games, 1987-88; adminstr. Met. Enrichment Ctr., San Francisco, 1988-90, assoc. v.p. United Way of the Bay Area, San Francisco,

1990-93; cons., pres. Gail Elleby & Assocs., Daly City, Calif., 1993—. Orgnl. and program devel., cmty. devel., collaboration tng., non-profit founds., corp. programs; dir. Even Start San Francisco Unified Sch. Dist., 1997-98, mgmt. and tng. specialist Western Ky. U., 1998—. Mem. San Mateo County Child Care Coun., 1992-97; mem. San Mateo County Commn. on Status of Women, 1994-98. Mem. SAMCEDA, Cons. Group (founder). Mem. Ch. of Christ. Avocations: music, sports, reading, cooking, collecting dolls. Home: 111 Timber Springs Way Lawrenceville GA 30043 Home Fax: 770-338-5849. Personal E-mail: gewku@aol.com.

ELLEDGE, GLENNA ELLEN TUELL, journalist; b. Welch, W.Va., Aug. 2, 1931; d. William Jackson and Ellen Annabelle (Jackson) Tuell; div.; children: Carl Gene, Jerry Elwood, Ernest Everett. Certificate in comptometer, Capital City Coll., 1949; student, Wytheville (Va.) C.C., S.W. Va. C.C., Richlands, Va. Intermont Coll. Accounts clk. Household Fin. Corp., Charleston, W.Va., 1951-52; with incest divsn. FBI, Washington, 1953; asst. bookkeeper and acctg. clk. Ft. McNair Officers Open Mess, Washington, 1953-54; stat. analyst Office Strategic Intelligence, Washington, 1954-55; stock control 836th Supply Squadron, Langley AFB, Va., 1957-59; acct., office asst. Comml. Contracting, Troy, Mich., 1970-71; office svcs. asst. Southwestern State Hosp., Marion, Va., 1971-95; staff writer, photographer Saltville (Va.) Progress, 1977-81, Saltville News-Messenger, 1981-93, Family Cmty. Newspapers, Marion, 1993-2000, Saltville Progress, 2000—. Fire brigade Southwestern State Hosp., Marion, 1986-93, instr. CPR, 1986-89, adv. bd., 1986-93. Editor, keyboardist Grandma's Favorite Recipes, 2000, Lucy's Secret, 2001-02. Vol. Air Force Family Svcs., 1956-69, den mother Cub. Scouts Am., 1962-67; bd. dirs. Smyth County Crisis Ctr., Marion, 1971-81; sec., pres. Smyth Coun. Santa's Elves, Marion, 1974-78, Family Oriented Group Home parent Group Home Juveniles 28th Juvenile Domestic Rels. Ct., Abingdon, Va., 1978-81; EMT, instr. Am. Heart Assn., Smyth, Wise, Grayson Counties, 1986-89; mem. and former sunday sch. tchr., supr. Laural Springs United Meth. Ch.; chairperson Mayor's promotional com., Marion, 1994-95; mem. Surry County (N.C.) Hist. Soc., Grayson County (Va.) Hist. Soc. Mem. Nat. Fedn. Press Women (del. 1978, awards), Va. Press Women (del. 1978, awards), Va. Press Assn. (awards), Nat. Press Assn., Nat. Soc. DAR, Nat. Soc. Col. Dames XVII Century. Jamestowne Soc. Republican. Avocations: writing, reading, gardening, camping, traveling. Office: PO Box 901 Marion VA 24354-0901 E-mail: ellglen@hotmail.com.

ELLEGARD, ROY WHITNEY, appraiser; b. Hartford, Conn., Sept. 16, 1957; s. Roy Taylor and Jeanette (Whitney) E.; m. Bernadette O'Brien, May 22, 1999. BA in Econs., U. Richmond, 1980. Appraiser Stone & Webster, Inc., N.Y.C., 1980-82; cons. Arthur Andersen & Co., N.Y.C., 1983; sr. cons. Arthur D. Little, Inc., Metro Park, N.J., 1984-87; nat. dir. machinery and equipment valuation advisors Ernst & Young LLP, N.Y.C., 1987-98; mng. dir. corp. value consulting Pricewater House Coopers LLP, 1998—2001, Standard & Poor's, 2001—. Mem. Am. Soc. Appraisers (sr., pres. Princeton chpt. 1992-93, 98-99), Kappa Alpha Alumni Assn. (treas. Princeton chpt. 1990-92), Princeton Club N.Y. Republican. Episcopalian. Home: 175 E 96th St Apt 8K New York NY 10128-6204 Office: Standard & Poor's 1177 Avenue Of The Americas New York NY 10036-2714 Home: 211 Kent Rd Kent CT 06757

ELLEGOOD, DONALD RUSSELL, publishing executive; b. Lawton, Okla., June 21, 1924; s. Claude Jennings and Iva Claire (Richards) E.; m. Bettie Jane Dixon, Dec. 11, 1947; children— Elizabeth Nemi, Francis Hunter, Kyle Richards, Sarah Helen. BA, U. Okla., 1948, MA, 1950. Asst. editor U. Okla. Press, 1950-51; editor Johns Hopkins Press, 1951-54; dir. La. State U. Press, 1954-63, U. Wash. Press, Seattle, 1963—96. Contbr. articles to profl. jours. Served to 1st lt. USAAF, 1943-46. Decorated Air medal, D.F.C. Mem. Am. Univ. Pubs. Group London (dir.), Am. Assn. Univ. Presses (pres.), Phi Beta Kappa. Home: 17852 49th Pl NE Seattle WA 98155-4312 Office: U Wash Press PO Box 50096 Seattle WA 98145-5096 E-mail: DREedit@aol.com.

ELLEN, JANE, composer, music educator, researcher; b. San Pedro, Calif., May 11, 1956; d. Annabel M. Quesnel. BA, U. N.Mex., 1992, postgrad., 1992-93. Cert. music tchr., N.Mex. Freelance composer, Albuquerque, 1986—. Parish organist Our Lady of Annunciation, Albuquerque, 1994—98; admissions dir. Signa Alpha Iota Am. Composers Bur., 1999—; contract prof. ElderHostel, U. N.Mex., 1996—2001; resident instr. OASIS, 1996—. Composer (more than 300 works including): Dancing in Deep Heaven for chamber orch., 1991; composer: Elegy for the Children of Sarajevo, woodwind quintet, 1992; composer: (with text by Ann Cragg) Phantom Lost for voice, oboe and piano, 1999; composer: Images of Rome for piano, 2000; composer: (with text by Claire Roth) The Eternal Ring for SATB choir, 2001; : commns. include NEA/NMAD; composer: MTNA state composer New Music Across Am., Canossian Daus. of Charity, Am. Guild Organists Dist. VII Conf., 1993, N.Mex. Quincentenary Commn., N.Mex. Women Composers Guild, (with text by Roth) Per La Grazia di Dio for SATB choir, 2001; composer: (with text by Roth) Per La Grazia di Dio for SATB choir, 2001. Recipient 1st place award Nat. League Am. Pen Women, 1996, 1st, 2d and 3d place awards, 1998. Mem. ASCAP (grantee 1990—), Internat. Alliance for Women in Music, Music Tchrs. Nat. Assn. (profl. cert.), N.Mex. Music Tchrs. Assn. (cert.), Albuquerque Music Tchrs. Assn. (1st v.p. 1998-00), Phi Beta Kappa, Phi Kappa Phi, Sigma Alpha Iota (Ruby Sword of Honour award 1992). Roman Catholic. Avocations: reading, studying italian, writing poetry and prose, watching old films, researching civil war music. Home: 2226 B Wyoming NE 182 Albuquerque NM 87112-2620 E-mail: Jane@JaneEllen.com.

ELLENBERGER, DIANE MARIE, nurse, consultant; b. St. Louis, Oct. 5, 1946; d. Charles Ernst and Celeste Loraine (Neudecker) E. RN, Barnes Hosp., St. Louis, 1970; BSN, St. Louis U., 1976; MSN, U. Colo., 1977. Bd. cert. legal nurse cons.; cert. clin. nurse specialist. Staff nurse hosps., clin. nurse, St. Louis, 1973-76; nurse clinician Sedalia, Mo., 1977-78; nurse clinician, educator Bothwell Hosp., Sedalia, 1977-78; clin. nurse specialist, coord. perinatal outreach edn. Cardinal Glennon Meml. Hosp. Children, St. Louis, 1978-80; instr. McKendree Coll., Lebanon, Ill., 1980; asst. prof. Maryville Coll., St. Louis, 1982-85; nurse cons. Carr, Korein, Tillery, Attys. at Law, East St. Louis, Ill., 1986—97; owner, nurse cons. The Med-Legal Advantage, San Anselmo, Calif., 1997—. Owner, operator Diane Designs Needlepoint, St. Louis, 1981-96. Contbr. articles to profl. jours. Mem. Divine Sci. Ch. With Nurse Corps, USAF, 1970-72. Mem. ANA (Calif. affiliate bd. dirs. 1998-2002), AACN, Am. Assn. Legal Nurse Cons. (Bay Area bd. dirs. 1999-2003), Nat. Perinatal Assn., Assn. Women's Health, Obstetric and Neonatal Nurses, Mo. Nurses Assn. (bd. dirs. 1995-97, bylaws chair 1990-2001, del. to ANA 1996, 3d dist. pres. 1993-96), Mo. Perinatal Assn. (v.p. 1980), Sigma Theta Tau. Office: PO Box 1638 San Anselmo CA 94979-1638 E-mail: mladvntg@pacbell.net.

ELLENBERGER, JACK STUART, law librarian; b. Lamar, Colo., Sept. 5, 1930; s. Emmert C. and Ruby F. (Overstreet) E. BS, Georgetown U., 1957; M.L.S., Columbia U., 1959. Law libr. HEW, 1957; libr. Carter, Ledyard & Milburn, N.Y.C., 1957-60, Jones, Day, Reavis & Pogue (and predecessor firm), Cleve., 1960, Bar Assn. of D.C., Washington, 1961-63, Covington & Burling, Washington, 1963-78, Shearman & Sterling, N.Y.C., 1978-93, law libr. emeritus, 1994-95; ret., 1995. Editor: (with Mahar) Legislative History of the Securities Act of 1933 and the Securities Exchange Act of 1934, 1973. Served with USAF, 1951-54. Mem. Am. Assn. Law Libraries (pres. 1976-77, M.G. Gallagher Disting. Svc. award 1994), Spl. Libraries Assn.

ELLENBERGER, WILLIAM JOSEPH, retired engineering consultant; b. Nashville, Jan. 14, 1908; s. William Penn and Birdie Eliza (Brown) E.; m. Barbara Marie Larsen, Aug. 3, 1940 (dec. May 1977); children: Katherine Brown, Joseph Larsen; m. Eleanor Hinman Brown, May 20, 1978 (dec. Nov. 1988). BS in Elec. Engring., George Washington U., 1930, BS in Mech. Engring., 1934. Registered profl. engr., D.C. Engr. Potomac Electric Power Co., Washington, 1928-30, 32-42; rsch. assoc. Nat. Bur. Stds., Washington, 1930-31, plant supt., 1946-51; sr. engr. Dept. of Army, Washington, 1954-68; engr. cons. self employed, Washington, 1968-75, Escondido, Calif., 1985—. Co-author, co-editor AIEE Manual on Indsl. Power systems. Col. U.S. Army, 1935-68.d Sch. Assn., Washington, 1948-57; Masonic visitor Vets. Hosp., Washington, 1950-80. Mem. ASME (life), IEEE (life sr.; chmn. Washington sect. 1955), Washington Soc. Engrs. (pres. 1969), Masons. Republican. Congregationalist. Achievements include seven volumes of Recollections of a Professional Engineer. Home: 15234 Sky High Rd Escondido CA 92025-2401 E-mail: wmjellenberger@aol.com.

ELLENBOGEN, ELISABETH ALICE, retired accountant; b. Lemberg, Ukraine, Sept. 10, 1940; d. Joseph and Leah Karolina (Wiener) E. B in Humanities, cert. acctg., Pa. State U.; student, Elizabethtown Coll. Cert. civil servant. Buyer McCrory Corp., York, Pa., 1959-65; account mgr. WT Grant Co., York, Pa., 1965-70; various acctg. civil svc. positions Commonwealth of Pa., Harrisburg, 1970-89. Contract mgr. health and human svcs. Commonwealth of Pa., 1989-99. Author: Bill of Rights for Citizens Facing the End of Life, 1997, (bulletin) Out Cry!, 1975; author policies/procedures Constitutional Rights for Handicapped Citizens, 1975—. Bd. dirs. ACLU, Pa., 1978—, disability rights adv., 1978—; convenor Ecumenical Coalition to Abolish the Penalty of Death, Pa., 1985—; activist Harrisburg Rape Crisis, 1973-77; counselor Women's Ctr., Harrisburg, 1975-79. Mem. NOW, Prime Time Group (women's consciousness raising support 1973-77). Democrat. Jewish. Avocation: to declare constitutional rights as guaranteed in the preamble of the americans with disabilities act. Home and Office: 298 Colonial Rd # 4 Harrisburg PA 17109-1556 E-mail: handicaprights@webtv.net.

ELLENBOGEN, GEORGE, poet, educator; b. Montreal, Que., Can., Nov. 19, 1934; came to U.S., 1966; s. Moses and Jenny (Borenstein) E.; m. Karia Doris Feinzig, Dec. 18, 1960 (div. 1984); children: Sara Rachel, Adam. BA, McGill U., Montreal, 1955; MA, U. Montreal, 1962; PhD, Tufts U., 1969. Mem. faculty Bentley Coll., Waltham, Mass., 1965—, prof. English, 1980—, chmn. dept., 1980-85, dir. Forum for Creative Writing, 1987—; poetry editor Boston Today, 1978-81. Vis. prof., writer-in-residence U. Siegen, Germany, 1996. Author: Winds of Unreason, 1957, The Night Unstones, 1971, Along the Road from Eden, 1989, The Rhinogate Poems, 1996, La Porte aux rhinos et autres poemes (bilingual edit.), 1997; Winterfischer, 2002; subject of German documentary film produced by Wolfgang Lippke George Ellenbogen: A Canadian Poet in America; contbr. numerous articles and poems to mags. and anthologies. Recipient award Karolyi Meml. Found., 1986, Va. Ctr. for Creative Arts, 1987, 92, 93, 2000, 02, 03, Montalvo Assn., 1987, Whiting Found., 1994; grantee Can. Internat. Cultural Rels., 1997, Gesellschaft for Kanada Studies, 1998, Can. Dept. Fgn. Affairs, 2003. Mem. AAUP, MLA, Coll. English Assn., Nat. Council Tchrs. of English Home: 21 Wren St West Roxbury MA 02132-2625 E-mail: gellenbogen@bentley.edu.

ELLENBOGEN, LEON, nutritionist, pharmaceutical company executive; b. N.Y.C., May 3, 1927; s. Martin and Bella (Zalesnick) E.; m. Roslyn Barban, June 30, 1951; children: Kenneth Alan, Richard Glen, Cheryl Sue. BS, CCNY, 1949; MS, NYU, 1951; PhD, Ind. U., 1954. Technician and med. corpsman USN, 1945-47; rsch. technician Columbia U., N.Y.C., 1949-51; teaching asst. gen. chemistry and biochemistry Ind. U., Bloomington, 1951-53; rsch. biochemist Lederle Labs., Am. Cyanamid Co., Pearl River, N.Y., 1953-59, sr. rsch. biochemist, group leader, 1959-77, chief nutritional sci., sr. assoc. dir. med.. pharm. devel., 1977-95; asst. v.p. nutritional scis. Lederle Consumer Health divsn. Whitehall Robins Health Care, Am. Home Products, Madison, N.J., 1995-97; ret., 1997. Adj. prof. nutrition in medicine Cornell U. Med. Coll., 1978—; adj. prof. nutrition N.Y. Med. Coll., 1981—; adj. prof., adv. com. intrinsic factor Nat. Formulatory Com.; mem. sci. affairs com. Proprietary Assn., 1980-89. Contbr. numerous articles to profl. jours., tech. books; author, presenter abstracts and papers profl. meetings; editor Contemporary Issues in Clin. Nutrition, 1980—, guest editor vols. 2 and 12; editor Drug Nutrient Interactions, 1982-91; cons. editor Biochemistry, Jour. AMA, Am. Jour. Clin. Nutrition, Sci., The Med. Letter, Nutrition Reports Internat., Thrombosis Rsch., Jour. Medicinal Chemistry, Archives Biochem. and Biophys., Annals Internal Medicine, Jour. Biol. Chemistry, Biochem. Pharmacology. Pharmacists mate USN, 1945-47. Recipient Steuben apple for contbns. to sci. rsch. Coun. for Responsible Nutrition. Fellow Am. Soc. Nutritional Scis., N.Y. Acad. Scis. (steering com. biochem. pharmacology discussion group 1973-77); mem. Am. Heart Assn., Am. Soc. Hematology, Am. Inst. Nutrition (nomenclature com.), Am. Soc. Clin. Nutrition, Am. Soc. Biol. Chemists, Am. Soc. Pharmacology and Exptl. Therapeutics, Am. Chem. Soc. (chmn. biochem. discussion group N.Y. sect. 1959, counselor divsn. biol. labs. 1977-79), Soc. Exptl. Biology and Medicine (editor proc. 1961-62), U.S. Pharmacopeia (com. on revision 1990-95, subcom. for nonprescription drugs and nutritional supplements 1995-2000, U.S. Pharmacopia Nutrition and Electrolytes Expert Com., expert com. on rbioavailability and nutrient absorption of U.S. pharmacopia 2000—), Sigma Xi, Phi Lambda Upsilon. Avocation: sports. Home: 16 Morris Dr New City NY 10956-4652 Office: Wyeth Consumer Whithall Robins Healthcare Madison NJ 07940-0871 E-mail: ellenbl@wyeth.com., ellenblr@aol.com.

ELLENBROOK, EDWARD CHARLES, county official, small business owner; b. Lawton, Okla., Aug. 12, 1938; s. Edward Charles Ellenbrook and Lera Belle (Pair) Becker; m. Carolyn Kay Baker, Apr. 13, 1968; 1 child, Margaret Elizabeth. BA, Okla. Bapt. U., 1964. Social worker Dept. Human Svcs., Lawton, 1964-73; dir. Comanche County Juvenile Bur., Lawton, 1973-98; author, owner, pub. In-The-Valley-Of-The-Wichitas, Lawton, 1983—. Trustee Inst. of the Great Plains of the Mus. of the Great Plains, 1995—. Author: Outdoor & Trail Guide to the Wichita Mountains, 1983, Endless Encounters, 1988; outdoors/nature columnist Lawton-Constitution-Wichita Mountains Field Notes newspaper, 1989. Bd. dirs. Lawton Heritage Assn., 1989, Southwestern Okla. Hist. Soc., Lawton, 1970, Okla. Ornithol. Soc., Ada, Okla., 1990, Friends of the Wichitas, Lawton, 1989, City of Lawton's Model Cities Com., 1968, Teen Ct., Inc.; mem. Mayor's Centennial Task Force, Lawton Centennial Book Com.; mem. criminal adv. bd. Cameron U. With U.S. Army, 1962-64. Mem. N.Am. Butterfly Assn. Avocations: hiking, backpacking, nature, illustration/book design, arts. Home: 1603 NW Keystone Dr Lawton OK 73505-2445 Office: In Valley of Wichitas PO Box 6741 Lawton OK 73506-0741 E-mail: ecebrook@sirinet.net.

ELLENS, J(AY) HAROLD, philosopher, educator, psychotherapist, pastor; b. McBain, Mich., July 16, 1932; s. John S. and Grace (Kortmann) E.; m. Mary Jo Lewis, Sept. 7, 1954; children: Deborah, Jackie, Dan, Beckie, Rocky, Brenda, Brett. AB, Calvin Coll., 1953; BD, Calvin Sem., 1956; ThM, Princeton Sem., 1965; PhD, Wayne State U., 1970; M in Divinity, Calvin Seminary, 1986; MA, U. Mich., 2000, PhD, 2002. Ordained to ministry Christian Reformed Ch., 1956; ordained theologian and pastor Presbyn. Ch., 1978. Pastor Newton (N.J.) Christian Reformed Ch., 1961-65, North Hills Ch., Troy, Mich., 1965-68, Univ. Hills Ch., Farmington Hills, Mich., 1968-78, Westminster Presbyn. Ch., 1980-84, Erin Presbyn. Ch., 1986-88, Cherry Hill Presbyn. Ch., 1994-96, White Lake Presbyn. Ch., 1998-2000, Troy Presbyn. Ch., 2000—01, Mt. Clemens 1st Presbyn. Ch., 2001—02; pvt. practice psychotherapy Farmington Hills, 1967—. Religious broadcaster TV, weekly, 1970-74, periodically to date; lectr. humanities and classics Wayne State U., John Wesley Coll., 1970—, Oakland U., 1970-90, Wayne C.C., Oakland C.C., Calvin Sem.; vis. lectr. Princeton Theol. Seminary, 1977-79; with Inst. for Antiquity and Christianity, Claremont U.; lectr. U.S. and abroad. Author: Program Format in Religious Television, 1970, Models of Religious Broadcasting, 1974, Chaplain (Major General) Gerhart W. Hyatt: An Oral History, 1977, (with others) Internat. Standard Bible Encyclopedia, 1979-89, Eternal Vigilance, 1980, God's Grace and Human Health, 1982, Life and Laughter, 1983, Psychology in Worship, 1984, (with others) Baker's Encyclopedia of Psychology, 1984, 1995, Psychotherapy: Key Issues, 1986, (with others) Psychotherapy in Christian Perspective, 1987, (with others) Christian Counseling and Psychotherapy, 1987, Love, Life and Laughter, 1988, (with others) Psychology and Religion, 1988, (with others) The Church and Pastoral Care, 1988, (with others) Moral Obligation and the Military, 1988, (with others) God se genade is genoeg, 1989, (with others) Counseling and the Human Predicament, 1989, (with others) Turning Points in Pastoral Care, (with others) Christian Perspectives on Human Development, 1992, The Ancient Library of Alexandria and Early Christian Theological Development, 1993, 95, Alexander The Great and Hellenistic Culture, 1997, Human Disfunction, 1998, (with others) Humanistic Psychology, 1998, (with others) Dictionary of Pastoral Care and Counseling, 1990, (with others) The Interpretation of the Bible, 1998, three books in Portuguese and one in Spanish; editor: CAPS Internat. Directory vols. II-V, 1976-87, Ethical Reflections, 1977, The Beauty of Holiness, 2d edit., 1985, God's Grace in Free Verse, 1987, (with others) Eerdmans Dictionary of the Bible, 2000, with others; editor in chief Jour. Psychology and Christianity, 1975-88; contbr. 150 articles to profl. jours. Served to col. AUS, 1956-61, ret., 1992. Created knight, Queen Juliana, The Netherlands, 1974. Mem. Christian Assn. Psychol. Studies (now exec. dir. emeritus), Soc. Bibl. Lit., Mil. Chaplain Assn., Ret. Officers Assn., Archeol. Inst. Am., Mil. Order World Wars. Home and Office: 26705 Farmington Rd Farmington MI 48334-4329 Office: 1150 Delaney Ave Orlando FL 32806-1264 E-mail: jharoldellens@juno.com. *Secular and religious communities alike tend continually to shift their focus toward some orthodoxy or other, usually in the form of according ultimate authority to an aspect of the community's traditional thought or behavior, thus imposing constraints upon the quest for growth and for truth which are not responsive to reality or authenticity or relevant and wholesome freedom. Orthodoxy is always, therefore, a form of idolatry; it is a psychological phenomenon; it is the posture of arrogance in those who see themselves as "the chosen" or the elect; it is lunge for security vs. growth; it is designed to guard against the destablizing effect of change; it is, therefore inherently imperialistic, arbitrary, propagandist, and abusive.*

ELLENWOOD, CHRISTIAN KENT, music educator; b. Lincoln, Nebr., Mar. 7, 1970; s. Sandra K. and Robert B. Ellenwood; m. Elisabeth Marie Deussen, June 20, 1970. MusB, Eastman Sch. Music, 1992; MusM, Ind. U., 1993; D Musical Arts, U. N.C.-Greensboro, 1996. Assoc. prof. clarinet U. of Wis.-Whitewater, Whitewater, Wis., 1996—; faculty leave replacement U. N.C.-Greensboro, 1995—96; artist, tchr. clarinet Rocky Ridge Music Ctr., Estes Park, Colo., 2001, New Eng. Music Camp, Sidney, Maine, 1997—99. Musician: (performances) Solo, Chamber and Orchestral. Music clinician, Wis., 1996—2002. Recipient W.P. Roseman Award for Excellence in Tchg., U. of Wisconsin-Whitewater, 2001, Coll. Excellence in Tchg. Award, UW-Whitewater Coll. of Arts and Communication, 2000, Nat. Finalist, MTNA Collegiate Competition, Music Teachers Nat. Assn., 1997, Who's Who Among America's Teachers, Who's Who, 1998, 2000, Award for Excellence in Tchg., Phi Eta Sigma, 1999; fellow Grad. Fellowship, Univ. of North Carolina-Greensboro, 1993-1996, Ind. U., 1992-1993; scholar Edith Babcock Scholarship, Eastman Sch. of Music, 1989-1992, George Eastman Scholarship, 1988-1992. Mem.: NACWPI, Coll. Music Soc., Internat. Clarinet Assn., Phi Eta Sigma (Excellence in Tchg. 1999), Pi Kappa Lambda. Avocations: visual arts-drawing/painting, sea kayaking, hiking. Home: N7285 Woodfield Ln Whitewater WI 53190 Office: Univf Wisconsin-Whitewater 800 West Main St Whitewater WI 53190 E-mail: ellenwoc@mail.uww.edu.

ELLER, WARREN BERNSON, retired insurance company executive; b. Alpena, Mich., Apr. 8, 1931; s. William Carl and Rachel Bernson Eller; m. Marilyn Walling, Oct. 30, 1954 (div. 1983); children: Marc William, Brian Theodore, Cynthia Marie; m. Dolton Rosilda Missick, Sept. 29, 1983; children: Dawson Romano, Anthea Tinburn Missick. Student, U. Mich., 1954—55, Wayne State U., 1955—56. Agt. Northwestern Mut. Life Ins. Co., 1957—59, asst. mgr. Occidental Life of Calif., 1959; founder, pres. Warren B. Eller Agy., Inc., Farmington, Mich., 1959—93; ret., 1993. With USAF, 1950—54, Korea. Mem.: Risk Appraisal Forum (founder), Life Underwriter Polit. Action Com. (trustee 1970), Detroit Assn. Life Underwriters (pres. 1967—68), Nat. Assn. Life Underwriters. Lutheran. Office: PO Box 4101 Sarasota FL 34230-4101

ELLERBUSCH, FRED, environmental engineer; b. Germany, Mar. 5, 1951; BSCE in Environ. Engring., N.J. Inst. Tech., 1973, MS in Environ. Engring., 1980; MPH, U. Medicine Dentistry N.J., 2000. Registered profl. engr., N.J.; diplomate Am. Acad. Environ. Engrs.; cert. hazardous materials mgr. Staff engr. Elson T. Killam Assocs., Inc., Millburn, N.J., 1973-74; staff environ. engr. Indsl. Environ. Rsch. Lab. U.S. EPA, Edison, N.J., 1974-77; environ. systems engr. METREK div. MITRE Corp., McLean, Va., 1977-78; regulatory conformance coord. Bristol-Myers Products div. Bristol-Myers Squibb Co., Bridgewater, N.J., 1978-83, mgr. regulatory compliance and govt. affairs, 1983-85, dir. safety, security and environ. affairs, 1985-89; dir. corp. environ. affairs Rhone-Poulenc Inc. affiliate Rhone-Poulenc SA, Monmouth Junction, N.J., 1989-95, dir. environ. affairs and remediation, 1995-96, dir. health, safety, environ. affairs, 1996-98; pres. Systemsthink, LLC, Warren, N.J., 1998—; sr. rsch. fellow Nat. Environ. Policy Inst., 1999; acting dir. Ctr. Policy Studies, 1999-2001. Adj. prof. environ. engring. grad. divsn. N.J. Inst. Tech., Newark, 1980-83; seminar leader divsn. continuing edn. N.J. Inst. Tech., Newark, 1977-90; chair unified environ. statute sector Nat. Environ. Policy Inst., 1995-99; lect. N.J. Inst. Tech., 1998—, U. Medicine Dentistry N.J. Sch. Pub. Health, 2001—; dir. tech. N.J. Inst. Tech., Newark, 2001—. Co-author: Electrotechnology Applications in Manufacturing, Vol. 2, 1978, Industrial/Hazardous Waste Impoundment, 1979, Biomass Applications and Technology, 1980; co-editor: Carbon Adsorption Handbook, 1978, Guide for Industrial Noise Control, 1982; contbr. articles to profl. pubs. Mem. nat. panel consumer arbitrators Better Bus. Bur. Mem. Acad. Hazard Control Mgmt., Acad. Hazardous Materials Mgmt. (bd. examiners 1984-85), Am. Indsl. Health Coun. (govt. affairs com. 1987, sci. policy com. 1988—, vice chmn. 1989.), Am. Sci. Affiliation, Chem. Mfrs. Assn. (mem. various coms.), N.Y. Acad. Scis., Soc. for Risk Analysis, N.J. Water Control Assn., N.J. Inst. Tech. (indsl. adv. bd. 1986—), Nat. Environ. Tng. Assn., N.J. Acad. Scis., Pharm. Mfrs. Assn. (environ. control resource com. 1985-89), APHA, AAUP, others. Home: PO Box 4225 Warren NJ 07059-5501 Office: SystemsThink LLC PO Box 4225 Warren NJ 07059-0225 E-mail: fred@systemsthink.com., fred.ellerbusch@njit.edu.

ELLERBY, JAMES EDWARD, JR., judge; b. Valhalla, N.Y., May 27, 1959; s. James Edward Sr. and Harriet Ellerby. BA cum laude, Columbia Coll., 1981, MS, 1984, JD, 1986. Bar: N.Y. 1987, U.S. Dist. Ct. (so. and ea. dists.) N.Y. 1992, U.S. Ct. Appeals (2d cir.) 1993. Adj. instr. Hudson County C.C., Jersey City, 1986-88; asst. counsel Mayor's Office of Midtown Enforcement City of N.Y., 1986-88; litigation assoc. Fennel & Minkoff, N.Y.C., 1988-89; of counsel Law Firm of Gail Butler, N.Y.C., 1989-92; adminstrv. law judge Environ. Control Bd., N.Y.C., 1992-93; adj. instr. John Jay Coll. Criminal Justice CCNY, 1992-93; of counsel McCarthy & Sullivan, N.Y.C., 1984-95; pvt. practice James Edward Ellerby, Jr., Esq., N.Y.C., 1995; adminstrv. law judge N.Y. State Dept. Social Svc., N.Y.C., 1995—. Mem. Assn. Bar of City of N.Y. Home: James Ellerby Esq 80 Longdale Ave White Plains NY 10607

ELLERIN, THELMA RUTH, psychiatric social worker; b. Gloucester, Mass., Oct. 22, 1926; d. Isidor Ralph and Eva (Davis) Tarlow; m. Saul W. Ellerin, July 12, 1959; children: Steve, Judith. BS, U. Mass., 1948; MS, Simmons Sch. Social Work, 1951. Cert. social worker. Social worker Presbyn. Hosp., N.Y.C., 1951-52, Boston City Hosp., 1952-54, VA Regional Office, Boston, 1954-56, VA Hosp., Jamaica Plains, Mass., 1956-59, VA, Manchester, N.H., 1959-60; psychiat. social worker Mental Health Assn. Greater Manchester (N.H.), 1960—95. Mem. NASW, Hadassah. Avocations: tennis, aerobics. Home: Apt 204 300 River Rd Manchester NH 03104-2401

ELLERKMANN, RICHARD MARCUS, gynecologist, educator, surgeon, educator; b. N.Y.C., Nov. 20, 1962; s. Richard Ellerkmann and Hildegard Ryals; m. Ariane K. Cometa, July 15, 2000; 1 child, Sophia. BA, Oberlin Coll., 1985; postgrad., Bryn Mawr Coll., 1989—90; MD, Dartmouth U., 1994. Physician dept. ob-gyn. Maine Med. Ctr., Portland, 1994—98, Greater Balt. Med. Ctr., 1998—; physician, asst. prof. Johns Hopkins Hosp., Balt., 1999—, assoc. residency dir. dept. ob-gyn., 2000—. Mem. gynecol. adv. com. dept. ob-gyn. Greater Balt. Med. Ctr., 2001—. Mem. edit. bd.: Jour. Pelvic Medicine and Surgery, 2001—; contbr. chapters to books, articles to profl. jours. Grantee German-Am. scholar for German studies, Oberlin Coll., 1984. Fellow: ACOG; mem.: Physicians for Social Responsibility, Med. Soc. Md., Am. Urogynecologic Soc., Monterey Land Trust. Episcopalian. Avocations: mountain climbing, woodworking. Office: Greater Balt Med Ctr 6569 N Charles Dt Baltimore MD 21204

ELLETT, ALAN SIDNEY, real estate development company executive; b. Seven Kings, Essex, Eng., Jan. 6, 1930; came to U.S., 1974, permanent resident, 1974; s. Sidney Walter and May (Fowler) E.; children: Denise, Michelle, Wayne. BSc in Bldg. Constrn., 1951, MBA. Mng. dir. Gilbert Ash Structures, 1960-68; dir., gen. mgr. Lyon Group (real estate), 1968-70; mng. dir. (pres.) Gilbert Ash Ltd., 1970-72; dir. Bovis Ltd.; chief exec. Bovis Property divsn. Audley Properties Ltd., 1972-74; chmn. bd. Forest City Dillon, Inc., 1974-88; exec. v.p., dir. Forest City Enterprises, Inc., Cleve., 1974-89; chmn. Forest City Rental Properties, 1982-89; chmn., pres. Forest City Comml. Constrn. Co., Inc., 1987-89; exec. v.p., COO Am. Malls Internat., Washington, 1997—2000; pres. Intercontinental Devel. and Investment Corp., 1997—. Contbr. articles to profl. jours. Fellow Inst. Builders, Inst. Dirs. Mem. Conservative Party. Mem. Church of England. (London).

ELLETT, JOHN SPEARS, II, retired taxation educator, accountant, lawyer; b. Richmond, Va., Sept. 17, 1923; s. Henry Guerrant and Elizabeth Firmstone (Maxwell) E.; m. Mary Ball Ruffin, Apr. 15, 1950; children: John, Mary Ball, Elizabeth, Martha, Henry. BA, U. Va., 1948, JD, 1957, MA, 1961; PhD, U.

N.C., 1969. CPA, Va., La.; bar: Va. 1957. Lab. instr. U. Va., Charlottesville, 1953-58; instr. Washington and Lee U., 1958-60; asst. prof. U. Fla., 1967-71; assoc. prof. U. New Orleans, 1971-76, prof. taxation, 1976-94, prof. emeritus, 1994—. Trainee Va. Carolina Hardware Co., Richmond, 1948-51; acct. Equitable Life Assurance Soc., Richmond, 1951-52; staff acct. Musselman & Drysdale, Charlottesville, 1952-54; staff acct. R.M. Musselman, Charlottesville, 1957-58; mem. U. New Orleans Oil and Gas Acctg. Conf., 1973-92; bd. dirs., publicity chmn. U. New Orleans Energy Acctg. and Tax Conf., 1993-94, bd. dirs. publicity com.; pres. Maxwelton Farm and Timber Corp., 1994—; treas. U. New Orleans Estate Planning Seminar, 1975-78, lectr. continuing edn.; CPCU instr. New Orleans Ins. Inst., 1975-78. Author books; contbr. articles to profl. jours. Served with AUS, 1943-46. Mem. AICPA (40 yr. hon. mem. 2000—), Am. Acctg. Assn., Am. Assn. Atty.-CPAs (chmn. ptnrship. taxation continuing edn. com. 1989, ptnrship. taxation com. 1990, organized La. chpt., v.p. 1991-93), Va. Soc. CPAs, Soc. La. CPAs, Va. Bar Assn. (40 yr. hon. mem. 2000—). Democrat. Episcopalian. Home: 177 Maxwelton Rd Charlottesville VA 22903-7859

ELLICKSON, BRYAN CARL, economics educator; b. Bklyn., Feb. 12, 1941; s. Raymond Thorwald and Loene (Gibson) E.; m. Phyllis Lynn Rutter, June 19, 1965; 1 child, Paul Bryan. BA, U. Oreg., 1963; PhD, MIT, 1970. From asst. prof. to assoc. prof. UCLA, 1968-83, prof., 1983—, chair econs. dept., 1996-99. Cons. Rand, Santa Monica, Calif., 1970—. Author: Competitive Equilibrium, 1993; contbr. articles to profl. jours. Rsch. grantee HUD, 1979-81, NSF, 1982-87. Mem. Am. Econ. Assn., Econometric Soc. Avocation: scuba diving. Home: 18409 Wakecrest Dr Malibu CA 90265-5620 Office: UCLA Dept Econs 405 Hilgard Ave Los Angeles CA 90095-1477 E-mail: ellickson@econ.ucla.edu.

ELLICKSON, ROBERT CHESTER, law educator; b. Washington, Aug. 4, 1941; s. John Chester and Katherine Heilprin (Pollak) Ellickson; children: Jenny, Owen. AB, Oberlin Coll., 1963; LLB, Yale U., 1966. Bar: D.C. 1967, Calif. 1971. Atty. adviser Pres.'s Com. Urban Housing, Washington, 1967-68; mgr. urban affairs Levitt & Sons Inc., Lake Success, N.Y., 1968-70; prof. law U. So. Calif., L.A., 1970-81; prof. Stanford U., Calif., 1981-85, Robert E. Paradise prof. natural resources law, 1985-88; Walter E. Meyer prof. property and urban law Yale U., New Haven, 1988—, dep. dean, 1991-92. Author: (with Tarlock) Land-Use Controls, 1981, Order Without Law, 1991 (Triennial award Order of the Coif), (with Rose & Ackerman) Perspectives on Property Law, 3d edit., 2002, (with Been) Land Use Controls, 2d edit., 2000. Mem. Am. Acad. Arts and Scis., Am. Law and Econs. Assn. (pres. 2000-01), Am. Law Inst. Office: Yale U Law Sch PO Box 208215 New Haven CT 06520-8215 E-mail: robert.ellickson@yale.edu.

ELLICOTT, JOHN LEMOYNE, lawyer; b. Balt., May 26, 1929; s. Valcoulon LeMoyne and Mary Purnell (Gould) Ellicott; m. Mary Lou Ulery, June 19, 1954 (dec. Jan. 1995); children: Valcoulon, Ann; m. Beatrice Berle Meyerson, Sept. 14, 1996. AB summa cum laude, Princeton U., 1951; LLB cum laude, Harvard U., 1954. Bar: D.C. 1957, U.S. Supreme Ct. 1959. Assoc. Covington & Burling, Washington, 1958-65, ptnr., 1965-98, chmn. mgmt. com., 1986-90, sr. counsel, 1998—. Pres. Fairfax County Fedn. Citizens Assn., Va., 1964; mem. governing bd. Nat. Cathedral Sch., Washington, 1973—80, 1989—90, chmn., 1978—79; trustee Landon Sch., Bethesda, Md., 1972—76; bd. dirs. Protestant Episc. Cathedral Found., Washington, 1980—88. Mem.: ABA (sect. internat. law and practice), Washington Inst. Fgn. Affairs, Am. Bar Found. (life), Phi Beta Kappa. Democrat. Home: 5117 Macomb St NW Washington DC 20016-2611 Office: Covington & Burling 1201 Pennsylvania Ave NW Washington DC 20004

ELLIES, DEBRA L, biologist; d. Brian A and Nicole Ellies; life ptnr. John E Holt, May 30, 1965. BSc (hon.), Kings Coll. London, 1996; MA, Kings Coll., 1997, PhD, 1999. Icsi Jaques Cohen, 1995. Post doctoral fellow Stowers Inst. for Med. Rsch., Kansas City, Mo., 2000—; student Kings Coll. London, England, 1996—99; icsi lab setup Ottawa Civic Hosp., Ottawa, Canada, 1995—96; student LOEB Rsch. Inst., Ottawa, Canada, 1993—95; rsch. technitian Marine Gene Probe Lab, Halifax, Canada, 1991—93. Contbr. articles. Mem.: Soc. for Devel. biology (assoc.), FASEB (assoc.). Achievements include patents pending for Role of novel WNT modulators; development of Method for Nucleic acid purification. Office: Stowers Inst Med Rsch 1000 E 50 St Kansas City MO 64119 Personal E-mail: dle@stowers-institute.org.

ELLIG, BRUCE ROBERT, personnel director; b. Manitowoc, Wis., Oct. 15, 1936; s. Robert Louis and Lucille Marie (Westphal) Ellig; m. Janice Reals; 1 child from previous marriage, Brett Robert. BBA, U. Wis., 1959, MBA, 1960. With Pfizer, Inc., N.Y.C., 1960-96, mgr. compensation and pers. rsch., 1968-70, corp. dir. compensation and benefits, 1970-78, v.p. compensation and benefits, 1978-83, v.p. employee rels., 1983-85, v.p. pers., 1985-95, v.p. employee resources; ret., 1996. Spkr. in field; mem. standing coms. Pfizer, 1985—96; corp. edn. Employee Compensation and Mgmt. Devel., Retirement Plan, Retirement Plan Assets, Savs. and Investment, Corp. Adv. Coun., 1996—2001; cons. Orgn. Resources Counselors Inc., 1996—2001; bd. dirs. Headway Corp. Resources, Inc., 1997—2001; adv. panel Career Ctrl., wave adv. bd.; bd. dirs. First2.learn.com, 2000—. Author: (book) Compensation and Benefits: Analytical Strategies, 1978, Executive Compensation: A Total Pay Perspective, 1982, Compensation and Benefits: Design and Analysis, 1985, Future Focus: Human Resources in the 21st Century, 1998, The Complete Guide to Executive Compensation, 2002; contbg. author: Encyclopedia of Professional Management, 1978, Handbook of Business Administration, 1984, Tomorrow's Human Resources Management, 1997, cons. editor: Compensation and Benefits Rev., mem. adv. bd.: Jour. Compensation and Benefits, adv. bd.: Executive Compensation Reports, 1999—2002; contbr. more than 70 articles to profl. jours. Mem. Mayor's Adv. Pay Commn., N.Y.C., 1977—78, chmn., 1980; mem. Presdl. Quadrennial Pay Commn., 1976; mem. merit pay task force U.S. Civil Svc. Commn., 1979; mem. sector staff Coun. Wage and Price Stability, 1979—80; mem. Ctr. Advanced Human Resource Studies Cornell U., 1985—95; adv. bd. Ky. Ednl. TV, 1987—90, Global Remuneration Orgn. Named Person of the Yr., U. Wis. Alumni Club N.Y., 1995, Human Resources Exec. of the Yr., Human Resource Exec. Mag., 1995; recipient Am. Compensation's Keystone award, 1999; fellow Aresty, Wharton Bus. Sch. Fellow: Wharton's Aresty Inst., Employer Benefits Rsch. Inst., Nat. Acad. Human Resources (life); mem.: Sr. Execs. Forum, Human Resources Roundtable Group, Bus. Roundtable Conf. Bd. (adv. coun. human resource mgmt.), Soc. Human Resource Mgmt. (life; chmn. bd. dirs. 1996, faculty staff 1996—, Lifetime Achievement award 1999), Am. Compensation Assn. (life; cert. program developer 1996—), Pers. Round Table (life), N.E. Sr. Human Resources Exec. Mtg. Group, N.Y. Pers. Mgmt. Assn. (past pres.), Am. Mgmt. Assn., N.Y. Assn. Compensation Adminstrs. (charter pres.), U. Wis. Bus. Sch. Alumni (bd. dirs. emeritus), Wharton/Spencer Stuart Dir. Inst., N.Y. C. of C., Wall of Fame, Ind. C. of C. (human resource com.), U. Ill. Ctr. Human Resource Mgmt. (past ptnr.), U. So. Calif. Ctr. Effective Orgns. (adv. bd. emeritus), Phi Beta Kappa, Phi Eta Sigma, Beta Gamma Sigma. Republican. Roman Catholic.

ELLIMAN, DONALD, magazine company executive; Exec. v.p. Time Inc. Office: Time Inc Time & Life Bldg 1271 Avenue Of The Americas New York NY 10020-1300

ELLIMAN, DONALD M., JR., magazine publisher and executive; b. Bronxville, N.Y., Sept. 4, 1944; s. Donald M. Elliman; m. Mary Elliman; children: Kristin, Lindsay, Anderw, Mack. BA, Middlebury Coll., 1967. With mktg. svc. dept. Time, N.Y.C., 1967-70, mem. advt. staff, assigned to London, circulation dir. People mag., 1976-78, pub. People, 1985-88; circulation dir. Time Internat., N.Y.C., 1978-81; pres. Time Distbn. Svcs., Inc., N.Y.C., 1981-82; advt. sales dir. Time Internat., N.Y.C., 1982-85, pub. dir., 1985; exec. v.p. mktg. for mags. Time Inc., N.Y.C., 1988-91, responsible for People and Entertainment Weekly mags., 1988-91, group pub., 1990-92, pres. sales and mktg. div., 1991-92, pres., pub. Sports Illustrated, 1992-93, pres. Sports Illustrated, 1992-98, exec. vice vres., communications NYC, 1988-99; pres., Ascent Sports (Denver Nuggets, CO Avalanch, Pepsi Center) Ascent Ent. Group Inc., Denver, 2000—. Bd. dirs. Operation Sail; trustee N.Y. Yacht Club, Jimmie Heuga Ctr; hon. chmn. United Hosp. Fund. N.Y. Avocations: skiing, sailing. Office: The pepsi Center 1000 Chopper Cir Denver CO 80204-5809

ELLIN, MARVIN, lawyer; b. Balt., Mar. 6, 1923; s. Morris and Goldie (Rosen) E.; children: Morris, Raymond, Elisa; m. Marta I. Quintana, Aug. 15, 2001. JD, U. Balt., 1953. Bar: Md. 1953, U.S. Supreme Ct. 1978; diplomate Am. Bd. Forensic Examiners. Practice law, Balt., 1953—; mem. firm Ellin & Baker, 1957—; specialist in med. malpractice law. Cons. on med. and legal trial matters; lectr. ACS, U. Md. Law Sch., U. Balt. City, Yale U. Sch. Medicine, Johns Hopkins Hosp., U. Calif., San Francisco, U. N.J.; former mem. chmn.'s adv. coun. com. on judiciary U.S. Senate. Mem. editl. adv. bd.: Ob/Gyn Malpractice Prevention; contbr. chpts. on med. malpractice to various profl. publs. including Radiation Therapy of Benign Diseases. Fellow Internat. Acad. Trial Lawyers; mem. ABA, Am. Soc. Law and Medicine. Home: 13414 Longnecker Rd Glyndon MD 21136-4839 Office: 1101 Saint Paul St Baltimore MD 21202-2662 E-mail: EllinLaw@aol.com.

ELLINGHAUS, WILLIAM MAURICE, communications executive; b. Balt., Apr. 19, 1922; m. Erlaine Dietrich, May 30, 1942; children: Marcia A. Barone, Eric J., Douglas A., Barbara E. Gurne, Raymond W., Mark D., Christopher C., Jonathan P. LLD, Iona Coll., 1974, Pace U., 1976, St. John's U., 1976, Poly. Inst. N.Y., 1976; LL.D., W.Va. Wesleyan Coll., 1981; L.H.D., Manhattan Coll., 1975, Union Coll., 1982; D.B.A, Curry Coll., 1978; D.Sc. (hon.), Washington Coll., 1979; D.Sc., NYU, 1981. With Bell System, 1940-84; comml. mgr. Chesapeake & Potomac Tel. Co. Md., Balt., 1950-51; pub. office mgr. Chesapeake & Potomac Tel. Co. Va., Norfolk, 1951-52, dist. comml. mgr. Culpeper, 1952-55; from gen. comml. supr. to v.p. dir. Chesapeake & Potomac Tel. Co. W.Va., Charleston, 1955-62; from v.p. accts. to v.p. pers. Chesapeake & Potomac Tel. Cos., Washington, 1962-65; from asst. v.p. planning to exec. v.p. AT&T, N.Y.C., 1965-70, exec. v.p., 1970, vice-chmn. bd., 1976-79, pres., also bd. dirs., 1980-84, pres., 1970-76. Pres. N.Y. Telephone Co., 1970-76; exec. vice chmn. bd dirs. N.Y. Stock Exchange, 1984-86; 1st chmn. N.Y. Mcpl. Assistance Corp., 1975; mem. N.Y. Emergency Fin.Ctrl. Bd., 1975-76. Trustee Lawrence Hosp.; hon. trustee Mt. Sinai Med. Ctr. With USNR, 1943-45. Mem. Am. Soc. Corp. Execs., Monroe County Telecomm. Authority, Sovereign Order Knights of Malta, Equestrian Order Holy Sepulchre of Jerusalem. Home: Apt 3-H Stoneleigh 2 Bronxville NY 10708 E-mail: wme419@aol.com.

ELLINGS, RICHARD JAMES, political and economic research institution executive; b. Santa Barbara, Calif., Jan. 7, 1950; s. George MacMachan and Barbara Marie (Kollin) E.; m. Marta Anna Korduba; children: Katherine Nicole, John William, Julia Victoria, Ruric George. AB, U. Calif., Berkeley, 1973; MA, U. Wash., 1976, PhD, 1983. Lectr. Calif. Poly. State U., San Luis Obispo, 1980-81, U. Wash., Seattle, 1982-83, assoc. dir. Henry M. Jackson Sch. Internat. Studies, 1986-89; legis. asst. U.S. Senate, Washington, 1984-85; dir. Nat. Bur. Asian Rsch., Seattle, 1989-99, pres., 1999—. Dir. George E. Taylor Fgn. Affairs Inst., Seattle, 1986-89; lectr. USIA, 1992, 97; cons. in field. Author: Embargoes and World Power, 1985; co-author: Private Property and National Security, 1991, (monograph) Asia's Challenge to American Strategy, 1992; editor: Americans Speak to APEC: Building a New Order with Asia, 1993, MFN Status, Human Rights and U.S.-China Relations, 1994, Access Asia: A Guide to Specialists and Current Research, 1994—, NBR Analysis, 1990—, Southeast Asian Security in the New Millenium, 1996, Korea's Future and the Great Powers, 2001, Strategic Asia: Power and Purpose, 2001, Asian Aftershocks, 2002. Del. Rep. Party State Conv., Tacoma, 1988. Grantee Dept. Def., 1990-95, 97, 98, 2000—, Dept. State, 1994, Henry M. Jackson Found., 1989—, Japan Found. Ctr. for Global Partnership, 1995-98, Lynde and Harry Bradley Found., 1998-99, 2000-02, USIA, 1992, 97. Mem. Internat. Studies Assn., Pacific Coun. on Internat. Policy. Avocations: hiking, skiing, tennis. Home: 1615 85th Ave NE Clyde Hill WA 98004-3346 Office: Nat Bur Asian Rsch 4518 University Way NE Ste 300 Seattle WA 98105-4535

ELLINGSEN, MICHAEL O. music educator, theater educator; b. Two Harbors, Minn., June 16, 1953; s. Esther L Ellingsen; m. Susan P Amundson, July 2, 1977; children: Andrew, Katherine. BS magna cum laude, Bemidji State U., 1975; MusM, Mankato State U., 1984. Cert. K-12 music tchr. Minn. Vocal and instrumental music East Chain Pub. Schools, Blue Earth, Minn., 1975—80; vocal music and drama tchr. grades 7-12 Blue Earth Area HS, 1980—. Singer: (vocal ensemble) Nova Cantabile, 1990—; actor: (musical theater) The Secret Garden, 1998 (Archibald Craven), You're a Good Man Charlie Brown, 1999 (Charlie Brown), Into the Woods, 1996 (Jack). Treas. Blue Earth Town and Country Players, Blue Earth, Minn., 1984—2002; dir. Trinity Luth. Sr. Choir, Blue Earth, Minn., 1980—2002. Recipient East Chain Pub. Sch. Tchr. of the Yr., 1979—80, Golden Apple Award, Ashland Oil Co., 1984, Blue Earth Area Sch. Tchr. of the Yr., 2001—02. Mem.: NEA, Minn. Music Educators Assn. (choral v.p. 1992—94), Am. Choral Directors Assn. (life). Lutheran. Avocations: quilting, bicycling, music, theater. Home: 312 North Holland Blue Earth MN 56013-1231 Office: Blue Earth Area HS 1125 Highway 169 North Blue Earth MN 56013 Office Fax: 507-526-3260. Personal E-mail: musician@bevcomm.net. E-mail: mellingsen@blueearth.k12.mn.us.

ELLINGSON, JILL EVELYN, psychologist, educator; b. Mpls., Sept. 2, 1972; d. George Warren and Evelyn Wherry Sonnichsen; m. Christopher John Ellingson, Dec. 30, 1994. BA, U. Minn., 1994, PhD, 1999. Undergrad. rsch. asst. U. Minn., Mpls., 1991—93; project mgr. Devel. Resources, Mpls., 1993; NSF trainee U. Minn., Mpls., 1993—94, grad. rsch. asst.; rsch. project mgr. ProStaff Pers. Svcs., Mpls., 1995—97; instr. U. Minn., Mpls., 1995—96; asst. prof. Ohio State U., Columbus, 1999—. Mem. tech. rev. bd. Avert, Inc., Ft. Collins, Colo., 2001—; exec. coach Limited, Inc., Columbus, 2001—; cons. Marathon Ashland Petroleum, Findley, Ohio, 2002—. Contbr. Named Most Published Female Author, Indsl./Orgnl. Psychologist, 2000; fellow dissertation fellow, Human Resource Rsch. Orgn., 1998. Mem.: APA, Acad. Mgmt., Phi Beta Kappa. Methodist. Achievements include research in faking a personality assessment is less detrimental than previously thought; multi-predictor composites are a key way to alleviate ethnic group differences on intelligence tests; temporary employees are a heterogeneous population and yet their performance is homogenous. Avocations: interior design, hiking, classical music, skiing. Office: Ohio State U 734 Fisher Hall 2100 Neil Ave Columbus OH 43210 Office Fax: 614-292-7062. E-mail: ellingson@cob.osu.edu.

ELLINGTON, CHARLES RONALD, lawyer, educator; b. Cuthbert, Ga., Sept. 3, 1941; s. Charles Bartlett and Annie Claire (Moore) E.; m. Jean Alice Spencer, Apr. 29, 1967; children— Gregory Spencer, Alicia Nicole. AB summa cum laude, Emory U., 1963; LL.B., U. Va., 1966; LL.M., Harvard U., 1978. Bar: Ga. 1967, D.C. 1967. Assoc. firm Sutherland, Asbill and Brennan, Atlanta, 1966-69; mem. law faculty U. Ga. Law Sch., 1969—, prof. law, 1977—, Thomas R.R. Cobb prof. law, 1983-93, dean, 1987-93, J. Alton Hosch prof. law, 1993-99, A. Gus Cleveland prof. legal ethics and professionalism, 1999—. On leave as scholar in residence U.S. Dept. Justice, Washington, 1979-80; reporter Standards of the Profession Com., State Bar of Ga., mem. formal adv. opinion bd. Harvard U. fellow in law and humanities, 1973-74. Mem. Am. Law Inst. Avocation: hiking. Office: Univ Ga Sch Law Herty Dr Athens GA 30602

ELLINGTON, HOWARD WESLEY, architect; b. Anthony, Kans., Mar. 2, 1938; s. John Wesley and Cressie May (Wilson) E.; m. Nelda Lee Newlin, Sept. 5, 1959; children: Howard Wesley II, Eric John, Craig Alan, Amy Lee. BArch, U. Kans., 1961. Registered architect, Kans., N.Mex., Mo., Ohio. Prin. Howard W. Ellington, AIA, Architect, Wichita, Kans., 1979—; co-owner Gallery Ellington, Wichita, 1978-97. Founding trustee Kans. Cultural Trust, Wichita, 1985—, exec. dir. 1993—; mem. bldg. and grounds com. Wichita Ctr. for Arts, trustee, 1995-97, treas., 1997, acting exec. dir., 1997-98, exec. dir. 1998—; bd. dirs. arts com. Ulrich Mus., Wichita, 1992-97; founding trustee, exec. dir. Allen-Lambe House Found., Wichita, 1990—; mem. Wichita Wayfinding Design Adv. Group, 1997. Editor: The Prairie Print Makers, 1984. Mem. aesthetic rev. team Wichita City Mgrs., 1992-99; trustee Wichita Ctr. for the Arts, 1995-97; bd. dirs. Wichita-Sedgwick County Arts & Humanities Coun., 1996—, Wichita Pub. Arts Adv. Bd., 1996-99, Wichita Art and Design Bd., 1999—. Recipient Kans. Preservation award, 1993, Pedestal award Wichita Hist. Preservation Bd., 1996. Mem. Friends of Wichita Art Mus., Western Penn. Conservation, Nat. Trust for Hist. Preservation, Chgo. Archtl. Found., Frank Lloyd Wright Home and Studio Found., Birger Sandzen Meml. Gallery. Republican. Episcopalian. Avocation: art collecting.

ELLINGTON, JAMES WILLARD, retired mechanical engineer; b. Richmond, Ind., May 26, 1927; s. Oscar Willard and Leola Lenora (Sanderson) E.; m. Sondra Elaine Darnell, Dec. 6, 1952 (dec. Jan. 1997); children: Ronald, Roxanna; m. Vada M. Jellsey, Oct. 10, 1998. BSME summa cum laude, West Coast U., L.A., 1978. Designer NATCO, Richmond, Ind., 1954-67; design engr. Burgmaster, Gardena, Calif., 1967-69; sr. mfg. engr. Xerox Co., El Segundo, Calif., 1969-84, cons. mem. engring. staff Monrovia, 1984-87; staff engr. Photonic Automation, Santa Ana, Calif., 1987-88; sr. mech. engr. Optical Radiation Co., Azusa, Calif., 1988; sr. staff engr. Omnichrome, Chino, Calif., 1988-96, ret., 1996. With USN, 1945-52. Mem. Soc. Mfg. Engrs. (sec. 1984). Republican. Baptist. Avocation: gardening.

ELLINGTON, KAREN RENAE, secondary education resource specialist; b. Turlock, Calif., Oct. 19, 1965; d. Edward Ray and Barbara Janet (Rafatti) E. BS, Calif. Poly., 1989; postgrad., Chapman U., 1994-96. Tchg. credentials include multiple subject, agr., bus., spl. edn.-learning handicapped; cert. resource specialist; cert. crosscultural, lang. and acad. devel. specialist. Asst. mgr. House of Fabrics, San Luis Obispo, Calif., 1985-88, Macy's, Sacramento, 1988-90; clk. Raley's, Modesto, Calif., 1990-93; substitute tchr. Merced & Stanislaus Counties, Calif., 1993; resource specialist Los Banos (Calif.) H.S., 1994—. Computer instr. ARBOR, Modesto and Merced, 1994-97. Leader 4-H, Merced County, 1990—, dir. 1998—; mem. Calif. State Citizenship Coun., 1999—. Mem. NEA, Calif. Tchrs. Assn., Los Banos Tchrs. Assn., Coun. for Exceptional Children, Calif. Ag. Tchrs. Assn. (assoc.), Internat. Dyslexia Assn. Avocations: traveling, stitchery, photography, athletics. Office: Los Banos HS 1966 S 11th St Los Banos CA 93635-4812 E-mail: karenellington@hotmail.com., kellington@losbanosusd.k12.ca.us.

ELLINGTON, MILDRED L. librarian; b. Marion, Ohio, June 7, 1921; d. Edward J. and Julia Ellen (Oiler) E. BA, Olivet Nazarene Coll., Kankakee, Ill., 1943; MA in French, Ohio State U., 1952; MA in English, Bowling Green (Ohio) U., 1964; MLS, Rosary Coll., River Forest, Ill., 1976. English and French tchr. Morral (Ohio) High Sch., 1944-49, Reddick (Ill.) High Sch., 1949-55; English tchr. Bremen Community High Sch., Midlothian, Ill., 1955-58, Bloom Twp. High Sch., Chicago Heights, Ill., 1958-60, Willowbrook High Sch., Villa Park, Ill., 1960-66; English tchr., then library dir. Addison (Ill.) Trail High Sch., 1966-82; reference librarian Maywood (Ill.) Pub. Library, 1982—. Sunday sch. supt. Elgin (Ill.) Ch. of the Nazarene, 1985-92. Mem. Ill. Library Assn. Democrat. Mem. Ch. of the Nazarene. Avocations: opera, singing, genealogy, travel. Office: Maywood Pub Libr 121 S 5th Ave Maywood IL 60153-1307

ELLINGWOOD, BRUCE RUSSELL, structural engineering researcher, educator; b. Evanston, Ill., Oct. 11, 1944; s. Robert W. and Carolyn L. (Ehmen) E.; m. Lois J. Drager, June 7, 1969; 1 son, Geoffrey D. BSCE, U. Ill., 1968, MSCE, 1969, PhD, 1972. Profl. engr., D.C. Structural engr. Naval Ship Rsch. and Devel. Ctr., Bethesda, Md., 1972—75; rsch. structural engr., leader structural engring. group Ctr. Bldg. Tech., Nat. Bur. Standards, Washington, 1975—86; prof. civil engring. Johns Hopkins U., Balt., 1986—2000, chmn. dept., 1990—97; chmn. sch. civil and environ. engring. Ga. Inst. Tech., Atlanta, 2000—02, prof. civil engring., 2002—. Lectr., cons. Editor Jour. Structural Safety; mem. editl. bd. Engring. Structures, Probabilistic Engring. Mechanics; contbr. articles to profl. jours. Recipient Dural Research prize U. Ill., 1968, Nat. Capital award for Engring. Achievement D.C. Joint Council Engring. and Archtl. Socs., 1980, Walter L. Huber prize ASCE, 1980, Silver medal U.S. Dept. Commerce, 1980, Markwardt Rsch. prize Forest Products Rsch. Soc., 1988; named Engr. of Yr. of U.S. Dept. Commerce, Nat. Soc. Profl. Engrs., 1986. Mem. ASCE (pres. Md. sect. 1998-99, State of Art in Civil Engring. award 1983, 88, Norman medal 1983, 98, Moisseiff award 1988, Walter P. Moore award 1999), Am. Concrete Inst., Am. Nat. Stds. Inst., Am. Inst. Steel Constrn. (T.R. Higgins lectureship 1988), Nat. Acad. Engring., Sigma Xi, Chi Epsilon, Tau Beta Pi. Presbyterian. Achievements include administered the secretariat of American National Standard Committee A58 on minimum design loads from 1977-84 and was responsible for coordinating and directing revisions to the A58 Standard that culminated in the publication of ANSI A58.1-1982 (now ASCE Standard 7), the first load standard in the U.S. to contain probability-based load combinations for limit states. Such load combinations now are used in Canada, the U.S. and in the Eurocodes now being developed in the common market. Was instrumental in the move by the steel industry toward limit states design. Office: Ga Inst Tech Sch Civil and Environ Engring Dept Civil Engring Atlanta GA 30332-0355

ELLIOT, CAMERON ROBERT, lawyer; b. Portland, Oreg., Jan. 6, 1966; s. James Addison and Dianne Louise (Youngblood) Elliot. BS, Yale U., 1987; JD, Harvard U., 1996. Bar: Calif 1996, DC 1999. Jud. clk. U.S. Dist. Ct., Reno, 1996-98; atty. civil divsn. U.S. Dept. Justice, Washington, 1998—2001; asst. U.S. atty. So. Dist. Fla., 2001—. Editor-in-chief: jour Harvard Environ Law Rev, 1995—96. Mem Reno Environ Bd, 1996—97. Lt USN, 1987—92. Home: 1717 N Bayshore Dr Apt 1250 Miami FL 33132 Office: US Atty's Office 99 NE 4th St Miami FL 33132 E-mail: cameron@justice.com.

ELLIOT, DAVID CLEPHAN, historian, educator; b. Larkhall, Scotland, Sept. 17, 1917; came to U.S., 1947, naturalized, 1954; s. John James and Edith Emily (Bell) E.; m. Nancy Franelle Haskins, Dec. 3, 1945 (dec.); children: Enid Frances, John Clephan (dec.), Nancy Elizabeth. MA, St. Andrews U., 1939; A.M., Harvard U., 1948, PhD, 1951; MA, Oxford U., 1956, postgrad. (Ford fellow), 1956-57. With Indian Civil Service, 1941-47; teaching fellow Harvard U., 1948-50; asst. prof. history Calif. Inst. Tech., Pasadena, 1950-53, asso. prof., 1953-60, prof., 1960-86, prof. emeritus, 1986—; chmn. Calif. Inst. Tech. (75th Anniversary), 1965-67, exec. officer for humanities and social scis., 1967-71. Trustee Westridge Sch., 1970-90, trustee emeritus, 1992—, pres., 1976-78. With Royal Arty., 1940. NATO fellow, 1980 Mem. Inst. Current World Affairs (gov. 1964-70, chmn. 1969-70, trustee 1979-82, hon. trustee 1992—). Home: 1251 Inverness Dr Pasadena CA 91103-1115 Office: Calif Inst Tech Div Humanities & Social Scis 1200 E California Blvd Pasadena CA 91125-0001 E-mail: DCE@HSS.Caltech.edu.

ELLIOT, DAVID HAWKSLEY, geologist, educator; b. Chilwell, Eng., May 22, 1936; came to U.S., 1966; m. Ann Elliot, 1963. BA, Cambridge U., Eng., 1959; PhD, Birmingham U., 1965. Mem. faculty Ohio State U., Columbus, 1969—, prof. dept. geol. scis., 1979—, dir. Byrd Polar Reseach Ctr. (formerly Inst. Polar Studies), 1973-89. Mem. Geol. Soc. Am., Geol. Soc. London, Ohio Acad. Sci., Am. Geophys. Union, Sigma Xi. Office: Ohio State Univ Dept Geol Scis Columbus OH 43210 E-mail: elliot.1@osu.edu.

ELLIOT, GERRI, information technology executive; married; 2 children. BA in Polit. Sci., NYU. V.p. distbn. sector IBM, Tokyo, IBM Americas Group; corp. v.p. industry solutions group Microsoft, Redmond, Wash. Avocations: restoring homes, coaching & playing basketball, step aerobics, travel. Office: One Microsoft Way Redmond WA 98052-6399

ELLIOT, JEFFREY M. political science educator, author; b. L.A., June 14, 1947; s. Gene and Harriet (Sobsey) E. BA, U. So. Calif., 1969, MA, 1970; ArtsD in Govt., Claremont Grad. Sch., 1978; LittD (hon.), Shaw U., 1985; LLD (hon.), City U. L.A., 1986; cert. in grantsmanship, Grantsmanship Tng. Ctr., 1980; cert. in internat. trade and devel., N.C. Ctrl. U., 1995; cert. in conflict resolution, Ctr. for Peace Edn., 1997. Rsch. asst. U. So. Calif., 1969-70; instr. polit. sci. Glendale Coll., 1970-72, Cerritos Coll., 1970-72; asst. prof. history and polit. sci. U. Alaska-Anchorage C.C., 1973-74; asst. prof. history and polit. sci., dean curriculum Miami-Dade C.C., 1974-76; asst. prof. polit. sci. Va. Wesleyan Coll., Norfolk, 1978-79; sr. curriculum specialist Edn. Devel. Ctr., Newton, Mass., 1979-81; prof. polit. sci., dir. grad. studies, dir. internat. progs. N.C. Ctrl. U., 1981—. Disting. advisor fgn. affairs Congressman Mervyn M. Dymally (Dem. Calif.), 1985-94. Author: 150 books, including Keys to Economic Understanding, 1976, Science Fiction Voices, 1979, Literary Voices, 1980, Analytical Congressional Directory, 1981, Deathman Pass Me By: Two Years on Death Row, 1982, Tempest in a Teapot: The Falkland Islands War, 1983, Kindred Spirits, 1984, Black Voices in American Politics, 1985, Urban Society, 1985, The Presidential-Congressional Political Dictionary, 1985, Fidel Castro: Nothing Can Stop the Course of History, 1986, The State and Local Government Political Dictionary, 1986, The Third World, 1987, The Arms Control, Disarmament, and Military Security Dictionary, 1988, Dictionary of American Government, 1988, Fidel, 1988, Conversations with Maya Angelou, 1988, Voices of Zaire: Rhetoric or Reality?, 1990, Brown & Benchmark Reader in American Government, 1991, Brown and Benchmark Reader in International Relations, 1991, The Trilemma of World Oil Politics, 1991, Starclimber: The

Autobiography of Raymond Z. Gallon, 1991, Adventures of a Free-Lancer: The Autobiography of Stanton A. Coblentz, 1991, The Work of Jack Dann: An Annotated Bibliography and Guide, 1991, The Work of George Zebrowski: An Annotated Bibliography and Guide, 1991, Brown & Benchmark Reader in American Government, 1992, Brown & Benchmark Reader in International Relations, 1992, The Third World, 1992, Into the Flames: The Life Story of a Righteous Gentile, 1992, After All These Years: Sam Moskowitz On His Science Fiction Career, 1992, The Encyclopedia of African-American Politics, 1994, The Work of Raymond Z. Gallun: An Annotated Bibliography and Guide, 1994, Fidel By Fidel, 1994, The African-American Historical Atlas, 1994, The Historical Dictionary of OPEC, 1995, The Dictionary of State and Local Government, 1995, The Historical Dictionary of the Third World, 1995, The Work of Pamela Sargent: An Annotated Bibliography and Guide, 1996, The Work of George Zebrowski: An Annotated Bibliography and Guide, 1996, The Work of Jack Dann: An Annotated Bibliography and Guide, 1997; contbr. 550 articles and revs. to profl. and popular jours.; contbg. editor Negro History Bull., 1976-80, West Coast Writers' Conspiracy, 1978-80, Trumphet of Conscience, 2000—. Mem. cmty. svcs. adv. coun. Miami (Fla.) Comty. Svcs., 1974-76; mem. Los Angeles Mayor's Adv. Com., 1971-72; speechwriter, rsch. asst., campaign strategist U.S. Sen. Howard W. Cannon of Nev., 1969— ; cons. Calif. Clean Environment Act, 1970-72; commr. Human Rels. Commn., Durham, N.C., 1999—; co-chmn. Sister Cities Program, Durham, 1999—; bd. dirs. Justice Policy Ctr., Durham, 1999—, N.C. Student Rural Health Projec, 1999—. Recipient 100 literary and scholarly awards including Fair Enterprise Medallion award, 1965, Outstanding Polit. Sci. Scholar citation, 1970, Outstanding Tchr. award, 1971, Outstanding Am. Educator citation, 1975, Disting. Svc. Through Community Effort award, 1976, Outstanding Rsch. prize, 1987, 91, Disting. Scholarship award, 1987, Outstanding Rsch. Prize, 1991, Nancy Susan Reynolds award, 1991, Disting Svc. award Acad. Help Ctr., 1992, Gen. News, Election Analysis Associated Press award, 1993, Documentary Profile Cmty. TV award, 1994, Excellence award, Soc. Internat. Develop., 1995, meritorious contributions for Human and Civil Rights award, City of Durham, NC, 2002. Mem. AAUP, ASCD, Cmty. Coll. Social Sci. Assn. (dir. 1970-77, pres. 1975-77), So. Assn. Coll. and Sch. (accreditation team 1974-76), Am. Polit. Sci. Assn., Nat. Coun. for Social Studies, Rocky Mountain Social Sci. Assn., Soc. Internat. Devel. Coun. Fgn. Affairs, Internat. Studies Assn., Assn. Third World Studies, Am. Hist. Assn., Pi Sigma Alpha, Phi Delta Kappa. Home: 511 N Water's Edge Dr Durham NC 27703-6722 Office: NC Cen Univ Dept Polit Sci Durham NC 27707 E-mail: jmelliot@aol.com. *I have attempted to live those ideals which inspire me to fight for a more humane world love, honor, courage, integrity, and truth. I have also taken to heart the wisdom of the prophets who implore us to live and love as though life and love were one. Although this is a difficult and frustrating task, it is the only way to live. And finally, I have come to recognize that what matters most, after everything is said, are people-close family and friends who reach out and say in a host of ways, "I care.".*

ELLIOT, RALPH GREGORY, lawyer; b. Hartford, Conn., Oct. 20, 1936; s. K. Gregory and Zarou (Manoukian) E. BA, Yale U., 1958, LLB, 1961. Bar: Conn. 1961, U.S. Dist. Ct. Conn. 1963, U.S. Ct. Appeals (2d cir.) 1966, U.S. Ct. Appeals (Fed. cir.) 1993, U.S. Ct. Appeals (1st cir.) 1997, U.S. Supreme Ct. 1967. Law clk. to assoc. justice Conn. Supreme Ct., Hartford, 1961-62; assoc. Alcorn, Bakewell & Smith, Hartford, 1962-67, ptnr., 1967-83, Tyler, Cooper & Alcorn, Hartford, 1983—. Adj. prof. law U. Conn., Hartford, 1973—; sec. Superior Ct. Legal Internship Com., Conn., 1971—; chmn. Superior Ct. Legal Specialization Screening Com., Conn., 1981—, U.S. Dist. Ct. Panel Spl. Masters, Hartford, 1983-88. Chmn. bd. editors Conn. Law Tribune, 1986-87. Chmn. Constn. Bicentennial Commn., Conn., 1986-91; mem. Criminal Justice Commn. Conn., 1991-95. Recipient Fenton P. Futtner award Conn. Reps., 1993, Pub.'s award Conn. Law Tribune, 2003. Conn. Law Tribune Pub. Award, 2003, Fellow Am. Bar Found.; mem. ABA (standing com. on ethics and profl. responsibility 1989-95, standing com. on profl. discipline 1998-2001, ho. of dels. 1983-87), Conn. Bar Assn. (officer, bd. govs. 1971-79, 83-87, pres. 1985-86, John Eldred Shields Disting. Profl. Svc. award 1993), Am. Law Inst., Yale Law Sch. Assn. (pres. 1988-90, chmn. exec. com. 1990-92), Yale Club (pres. 1977-79, Nathan Hale award 1984, Betty McCallip Meml. award 1991), Hartford, Grad. Club (New Haven), Phi Beta Kappa. Republican. Episcopalian. Home: 27 Brookline Dr West Hartford CT 06107-1265

ELLIOTT, ARTHUR Y. microbiologist, administrator; b. Tyler, Tex., Feb. 8, 1936; s. Arthur Oits and Thelam Ora (York) E.; m. Pamela Irene Rose, June 17, 1978; children: Laurie Elliott Stavros, David Michael. BA in Biology, North State U., Denton, Tex., 1957, MS in Microbiology, 1958; PhD in Virology/Biochemistry, Purdue U., 1969. Rsch. asst. M.D. Anderson Hosp., Houston, 1960-62; sr. rschr. Pitman Moore divsn. Dow, Zionsville, Ind., 1962-70; assoc. prof. microbiology and surgery U. Minn. Sch. Medicine, Mpls., 1970-78; exec. dir. bio. ops. Merck and Co. Inc., West Point, Pa., 1978-94; sr. v.p. ops., COO N.Am. Vaccine, Beltsville, Md., 1994-98, acting pres., 1998; pres. Biol. Cons., Lansdale, Pa., 1999—. Contbr. chpts. to books. Named Disting. Alumnus, Purdue U. Sch. of Sciences, 2003; named to Outstanding Young Men in Am., U.S. Jaycees, 1966; USPHS fellow, 1958—59. Mem. Am. Soc. for Microbiology, Internat. Soc. for Pharm. Engring., Parenteral Drug Assn., Pharm. Rsch. and Mfrs. Assn. Republican. Presbyterian. Avocations: golf, art collecting, reading. Home: 2586 Cold Spring Rd Lansdale PA 19446-6066 Office: Biological Consultant 2586 Cold Spring Rd Lansdale PA 19446-6066 E-mail: drayelliott@aol.com.

ELLIOTT, BARBARA JEAN, librarian; b. Bluffton, Ind., Oct. 2, 1927; d. Dale A. and Gwendolyn I. (Long) E.; m. Robert J. Elliott, June 13, 1949; 1 son, Michael Roger. BS with honors, Ind. U., 1949, MLS, 1979. Dir. tech. info. svcs. uranium divsn. Mallinckrodt Chrms., St. Louis, 1949-59; rsch. libr. Petrolite Corp., Webster Groves, Mo., 1961-63; head tech. svcs. St. Frances Coll., Ft. Wayne, Ind., 1974-76; dir. Bluffton-Wells County Pub. Libr., 1976-95, ret., 1995. Pres. Wells County Found., 1996—97, Friends of the Wells County Libr., 1997—99; sec. Wells County Coun. on Aging, 1996—2001; pres. Ch. Women of Wells County, Family Centered Svcs., 1999—2002. Mem. ALA, LWV of Ind. (state sec. 1981-83, chmn. health care 1983-89, 3d v.p. 1985-86), Ind. Libr. Assn. (fed. legis. coord.), Ind. Bus. and Profl. Women (pres. 1987-88, dist. dir. 1988-93), Wells County Hist. Soc. (pres. 1997-2000), Bluffton Garden Club (pres.) Home: 6831 SE State Rd 116 Bluffton IN 46714-9420 E-mail: belliott@parlovcity.com.

ELLIOTT, BILL, race car driver; b. Dawsonville, Ga., Oct. 8, 1955; Named winner, Daytona 500, 1985, 1987, Coca-Cola 500, 1985, Winston 500, 1985, Budweiser 500, 1985, 1988, Van Scoy 500, 1985, Miller 400, 1985, 1986, 1989, Pocono 500, 1985, Champion Spark Plug 400, 1985, 1986, 1987, So. 500, 1985, 1988, Atlanta Jour. 500, 1985, 1987, The Winston, 1986, AC Delco 500, 1987, Oakwood Home 500, 1987, Talledaga 500, 1987, Busch Clash, 1987, Del 500, 1988, Summer 500, 1988, Firecracker 400, 1988, 1991, Valleydale 500, 1988, Autoworks 500, 1989, AC Spark Plug 500, 1989, Peak 500, 1990, Pepsi 400, 1991, GM Goodwrench 500, 1992, Pontiac Excitement 400, 1992, Motorctaft Quality PArts, 1992, Tran South 500, 1992, Hooters 500, 1992, So. 500, 1994, Winston Cup Champion, 1988.

ELLIOTT, BRADY GIFFORD, judge; b. Harlingen, Tex., Nov. 26, 1943; s. Clyde Andres Elliott and Mildred (Parker) Bounds; m. Rhea Elizabeth Ricks, May 15, 1967; children: Adrian Winthrope, Jason Lawrence. BBA, McMurray Coll., 1970; JD, South Tex. Coll. Law, 1973. Bar: Tex. 1973, U.S. Dist. Ct. (so. dist.) Tex. 1974, U.S. Tax Ct. 1974, U.S. Ct. Appeals (5th cir.) 1974, U.S. Supreme Ct. 1979, U.S. Ct. Appeals (11th cir.) 1981. Asst. sec., asst. treas., asst. gen. counsel Gordon Jewelry Corp., Houston, 1970-79; sec., gen. counsel Oshman's Sporting Goods, Inc., Houston, 1979-82; sole practice, Sugar Land, Tex., 1982-88; legal counsel Ft. Bend C. of C., Sugar Land, Tex., 1982-88; mcpl. judge Missouri City, Tex., 1983-88; judge 268th Dist. Ct., Fort Bend County, Tex., 1988—. Bd. dirs. Ft. Bend chpt. Texans' War on Drugs, Sugar Land, 1981-94; bd. dirs. Ft. Bend Boys Choir, 1984-94. Mem. ABA, Houston Bar Assn., Fort Bend County Bar Assn., Masons, Rotary (treas. 1983-85). Republican. Methodist. Office: County Ct House Richmond TX 77469

ELLIOTT, BRIG (CHIP), network scientist; b. Hartford, Conn., Dec. 9, 1954; AB, Dartmouth Coll., 1976. Software mgr. Dartmouth Coll., Hanover, N.H., 1976-83, vis. lectr., 1990-92; v.p. True Basic, Inc., Hanover, 1983-88; prin. scientist Bolt Beranek and Newman, Cambridge, Mass., 1992—. Vis. prof., Indian Inst. Tech., Kanpur, 1979-80; instr., Tunghai U., Taichung, Taiwan, 1986-87; chief designer nat. and comml. satellite networks, comm. sys. for U.S., Can., U.K.; cons. in field. Author: PL/I Runtime, 1978, True BASIC, 1984, 3-d Scientific and Business Graphics, 1984—88, Statistics Graphics, 1989, Wilmos Goes to Heaven, 1989, Paperflow, 1990, Video Team, 1993, Iris, 1995, NTDR, 1997, Bowman, 2000, Quantum Cryptography, 2002; creator software; contbr. Bd. dirs. Naval Studies Bd. NAS, Army Sci. Bd., Def. Sci. Bd.; mem. ARDA Tech. Experts panel. Recipient Nat. Merit scholar, Bausch & Lom; scholar Rufus Choate scholar. Mem. IEEE (sr.).

ELLIOTT, BRUCE ROGER, secondary education educator, artist; b. N.Y.C., Aug. 3, 1938; s. Bruce Irving and Elizabeth (Barrus) E. BS, SUNY, Buffalo, 1960; MA in Art, U. Md., 1969. Tchr. art Kings Park (N.Y.) H.S., 1961-67; asst. prof. art R.I. Coll., Providence, 1969-71, Coll. of Holy Cross, Worcester, Mass., 1971-77; tchr., chmn. art dept. Germantown Acad., Ft. Washington, Pa., 1980—. Illustrator: Digging the Past, 1979; contbr. articles to art publs.; numerous juried exhbns., U.S. Avocation: photography. Home: 331 Green St Lansdale PA 19446-3672 Office: Germantown Acad PO Box 287 340 Morris Rd Fort Washington PA 19034-2096

ELLIOTT, CANDICE K. interior designer; b. Cedar Rapids, Iowa, Aug. 29, 1949; d. Charles H. and Eunice A. (Long) Goodrich; m. John William Jr. Elliott, Jan. 27, 1973 (div.); 1 child, Brandon Christian; m. Timothy G. Kling, Sept. 14, 2002; 1 stepchild, John William III, Andrew Timothy, Nathan David. BA, U. Iowa, 1971. Interior designer Dayton's, Mpls., 1971-76, Candice Interior Space Planning and Design, Guilford, Conn., 1981-87; owner, interior designer Sofa Works, King of Prussia, Pa., 1987-90; interior designer Jerrehians's Home Furnishings, West Chester, Pa., 1990-92; dir. sales and visual merchandising Sheffield Furniture, Malvern, Pa., 1992-95; owner Candice Interior Space Planning and Design, Wayne, Pa., 1996-97, Mt. Vernon, Iowa, 1997-2000, Kill Devil Hills, NC, 2000—01, Kitty Hawk, NC, 2001—. Bd. dirs. The Old Capitol Restoration Com., Iowa City, 1970-76; curator Guilford Keeping Soc., 1983-88; cons. Zion Episcopal Ch., North Branford, Conn., 1985-88; mem. planning and zoning bd. City of Mt. Vernon, Iowa, 1997-99. Mem. Am. Soc. Interior Designers (bd. dirs. Conn. chpt., profl. mem.). Republican. Avocations: golf, needlepoint, gardening. Home and Office: 1016 Creek Rd Kitty Hawk NC 27949

ELLIOTT, CAROL C. career officer; BS in Internat. Rels. and Polit. Sci., Iowa State U., 1972; disting. grad., Officer Tng. Sch., 1973, Squadron Officer Sch., 1977; MBA in Aviation, Embry-Riddle Aero. U., 1984; disting. grad., Air Command and Staff Coll., 1987; student, Nat. War Coll., 1992. Commd. 2d lt. USAF, 1973, advanced through grades to brig. gen., 1998; intelligence analyst 432d Tactical Fighter Wing, Udorn Royal Thai AFB, Thailand, 1974-75, USAF, Clark Air Base, The Philippines, 1975-76; chief target intelligence br. 388th Tactical Fighter Wing, Hill AFB, Utah, 1976-79, 52d Tactical Fighter Wing, Spangdahlem Air Base, W. Germany, 1979-82; target intelligence officer Armed Forces Air Intelligence Ctr., Lowry AFB, Colo., 1983; chief target devel. br. then target studies br. Hdqs. USAF Europe, Ramstein Air Base, W. Germany, 1983-86, directorate intelligence applications, dep. chief staff intellegence, 1983-86; various assignments Hdqs. USAF, Pentagon, Washington, 1987-91, 97, vice dir. intelligence J2 joint staff, 1997—; chief collection mgmt. div., asst. chief staff intelligence Hdqs. U.S. Forces Korea, Yongsan, S. Korea, 1992-94; dep. dir. intelligence Air Combat Command, Langley AFB, Va., 1994-95; comdr. 692d Intelligence Group, Hickam AFB, Hawaii, 1995-96; dir. intelligence Hdqs. Pacific Air Force Base, Hickam AFB, 1996-97; dep. dir. intelligence, surveillance and reconnaissance Hdqs. USAF, Washington, 1997, dep. chief staff for Air & Space Ops., 1997; vice dir. intelligence J2 Joint Staff, Washington, 1997-99; vice comdr. Air Intelligence Agy., Kelly AFB, Tex., 1999—. Decorated Legion of Merit. Office: Kelly AFB SAALC / CV 100 Moorman Ste 1 Kelly A F B TX 78241-5800

ELLIOTT, DANIEL WHITACRE, surgeon, retired educator; b. Greenville, Ohio, Aug. 5, 1922; s. James Scott and LaVirge (Whitacre) E.; m. Elizabeth Lucille Wolff, Aug. 11, 1961; children: James Calvin, Lisa Ann. Student, Ohio State U., 1942-43, M.Med. Sci., 1956; MD, Yale, 1949. Diplomate: Am. Bd. Surgery. Intern surgery Columbia Presbyn. Hosp., N.Y.C., 1949-50; surgery resident Ohio State U. Hosp., 1951, 53-57; mem. faculty Ohio State U. Sch. Medicine, 1957-64; prof. surgery U. Pitts. Sch. Medicine, 1965-76; Chief surgery Pitts. VA Hosp., Pitts., 1971-76; staff Presbyn., Western Pa., Shadyside, Children's hosps., Pitts., to 1976; mem. staff Kettering Meml., Miami Valley, Good Samaritan, St. Elizabeth's, VA hosps., all Dayton, Ohio; chmn. dept. surgery Wright State U. Sch. Medicine, 1976-88. Contbr. numerous articles to profl. jours. Pres. Ctrl. Surgical Assn. Found., 1993. Served with AUS, 1943-45; as capt. M.C. USAF, 1951-53. Fellow ACS; mem. Am. Surg. Assn., Cen. Surg. Assn. (pres. 1988), Western Surg. Assn., Internat. Surg. Assn., Am. Burn Assn., Soc. Univ. Surgeons, Assn. Acad. Surgery, Am. Gastroenterology Assn., Soc. Surgery Alimentary Tract, Sigma Xi., Alpha Kappa Kappa, Alpha Omega Alpha. Home: 5917 Yarmouth Dr Dayton OH 45459-1449 Home Fax: 937-208-2105.

ELLIOTT, DAVID DUNCAN, III, science research company executive; b. L.A., Aug. 4, 1930; s. David Duncan Elliott II and Mildred B. (Young) Mack; m. Arline L. Leckrone, Aug. 18, 1962; children: Lauren, Elliott Croft. BS, Stanford U., 1951; MS, Calif. Inst. Tech., 1953, PhD, 1959. Mem. tech. staff Lockheed Rsch. Lab., Palo Alto, Calif., 1959-61; postdoctoral fellow U. Paris., 1962; dept. head Aerospace Corp., El Segundo, Calif., 1962—70; sci. advisor Nat. Aeronautics and Space Coun., Washington, 1970-72; sr. staff mem. exec. office of pres. NSC, Washington, 1972-77; v.p. SRI Internat., Menlo Park, Calif., 1977-86; sr. v.p. Sci. Applications Internat. Corp., San Diego, 1986-91, Syst Control Tech., Palo Alto, Calif., 1991-94; corp. v.p. Sci. Applications Internat. Corp., Palo Alto, Calif., 1994-95; cons., 1995-99; cons. prof. Ctr. Internat. Security & Coop., Stanford U., Calif., 1999—. Mem. Army Sci. Bd., The Pentagon, Washington, 1982-89; cons. NRC, NAS, 1988—; mem. bd. visitors U. Calif., Davis, 1997—. Mem. editorial bd. Jour. Def. Rsch., 1988—. Recipient Outstanding Civilian Svc. award U.S. Army, 1989. Mem. AIAA, AAAS, Am. Phys. Soc., Am. Geophys. Union. Home: 2434 Sharon Oaks Dr Menlo Park CA 94025-6829 Office: CISAC Encina Hall Stanford CA 94305-6165

ELLIOTT, DAVID LEROY, mathematician, educator, engineering educator; b. Cleve., May 29, 1932; m. Kiyoko Akaeda, Mar. 24, 1956 (div. 1980); children: Marguerite, Philip David; m. Pauline Wei-Ying Tang, Oct. 31, 1984. BA, Pomona Coll., 1953; MA, U. So. Calif., 1959; PhD, UCLA, 1969. Mathematician U.S. Naval Ocean Systems Ctr., Pasadena, Calif., 1955-69; lectr. UCLA, 1969-71; mem. faculty Washington U., St. Louis, 1971—, prof. dept. systems sci. and math., 1980-94, prof. emeritus, 1994—; with NSF, Washington, 1987-89. Vis. prof. Brown U., Providence, 1979, UCLA, 1987; vis. rsch. scientist U. Md., 1992—; sr. rsch. scientist NeuroDyne, Inc., 1993-99. Editor: Neural Systems for Control, 1997. Fellow IEEE; mem. Am. Math. Soc., Soc. Indsl. Applied Math., Math. Assn. Am., Sigma Xi. Avocations: music, science fiction. E-mail: delliott@isr.umd.edu.

ELLIOTT, DENNIS DAWSON, communications executive; b. Evansville, Ind., Jan. 30, 1945; s. Thomas Ira and Mary Pauline (Dawson) Elliott; m. Rebecca Lynn Robinett, Jan 28, 1967 (div. Oct. 1987); children: Jodi Suzanne, Dawn Denise; m. Catherine A. Canfield, Feb. 24, 1996. AB in Journalism, Ind. U., 1969. From bus. intern to advt. mgr. pharm. divsn. Mead Johnson & Co., Evansville, 1967-80, dir., devel. affairs pharm. divsn., 1980-85; advt. dir. Bristol-Myers U.S.P. & G., Evansville, 1985-89; exec. v.p. Campus Group Cos., Tuckahoe, N.Y., 1989-92; pres. Interactive Edn., N.Y.C., 1992—; v.p. bus. devel. CME, Inc., Santa Ana, Calif., 1993-94; sr. dir. Scienta Healthcare Edn., Durham, N.C., 1994-97; v.p. mktg. Campus Group Cos., Tuckahoe, N.Y., 1997-2001; sr. v.p., mng. dir. S.G. Madison, Irving, Tex., 2001. Bd. dirs. So. Ind. Region Sports Car Club of Am., Evansville, 1970s. Recipient news photography award AP, 1967, Ernie Pyle scholarship Ind. U. Sch. Journalism, Bloomington, 1967. Mem. Med. Mktg. Assn., Pharm. Advt. Coun., Ind. U. Alumni Assn. (life, pres. 1969-79, sec.-treas., bd. dirs. Vanderburgh County), Sigma Delta Chi. Methodist. Avocations: photography, sports car racing, bicycling, writing. Home: 1416 Stone Lakes Dr Southlake TX 76092

ELLIOTT, EDWARD, investment executive, financial planner; b. Madison, Wis., Jan. 11, 1915; s. Edward C. and Elizabeth (Nowland) Elliott; m. Letitia Ord, Feb. 20, 1943 (div. Aug. 1955); children: Emily, Ord; m. Melita Uihlein, Jan. 1, 1958 (dec.); 1 child, Deborah; m. Sally Dodds Combs, Jan. 5, 2002. BS in Mech. Engring, Purdue U., 1936. Engr. Gen. Electric Co., Schenectady, 1936-37; with. Pressed Steel Tank Co., Milw., 1937-41, 46-58; v.p. sales Cambridge Co. div. Carrier Corp., Lowell, Mass., 1958-59; mgr. indsl. and med. sales Liquid Carbonic div. Gen. Dynamics Corp., Chgo., 1959-61; v.p. Haywood Pub. Co., Chgo., 1961-63; pres. Omnibus, Inc., Chgo., 1963-67; gen. sales mgr. Resistoflex Corp., Roseland, N.J., 1967-68; investment exec. Shearson, Hammill & Co., Inc., Chgo., 1968-74; v.p. McCormick & Co., Inc., 1974-75, Paine Webber, Inc., Naples, Fla., 1975-91, ret., 1991. Mem. pres.' coun. Purdue U. Lt. col. USAAF, 1941-46. Decorated officer Order Brit. Empire; inducted Indiana Basketball Hall of Fame. Mem.: ASME, Air Force Assn., Rotary, Family Club (San Francisco), Naples Yacht Club, Royal Poinciana Golf Club, Hole-in-Wall Golf Club, Naples Athletic Club, Phi Delta Theta. Episcopalian. Home: 122 Moorings Park Dr Apt G701 Naples FL 34105-2116

ELLIOTT, ELEANOR THOMAS, foundation executive, civic leader; b. N.Y.C., Apr. 26, 1926; d. James A. and Dorothy Q. (Read) Thomas; m. John Elliott, Jr., July 27, 1956. BA, Barnard Coll., 1948; DHL (hon.), Duke U., 2002. Assoc. editor Vogue mag., 1948-52; asst. dir. research and speech writing div. N.Y. State Republican Com., 1952; social sec. to Sec. of State and Mrs. John Foster Dulles, 1952-55; dir. James Weldon Johnson Community Centers, N.Y.C., 1955-60; bd. dirs. Celanese Corp., 1974-87, CIT Fin. Corp., 1978-81, INA Life Ins. Co. of N.Y., 1983-1998. Author: Glamour Magazine Party Book, 1966. Trustee Barnard Coll., 1959—, chmn. bd., 1973-76; bd. dirs. Maternity Center Assn., 1960-70, pres., 1965-69; bd. govs. N.Y. Hosp., 1972—, v.p., 1979— ; bd. dirs. Found. for Child Devel., N.Y.C., 1969—, chmn., 1972-79, 1973— ; bd. dirs. United Way Greater N.Y., 1977-86, NOW Legal Def. and Edn. Fund, 1983-90, Catalyst Inc., 1978-83, Am. Women's Econ. Devel. Corp., 1980-86, Woodrow Wilson Nat. Fellowship Found, 1983—, chmn. 1993-1999, co-chair, Nat. Adv. Coun., 2000—, Edna McConnell Clark Found., 1984-93, Coun. on Women's Studies, Duke U.; overseer Cornell U. Med. Coll., 1995—. Recipient Alumni medal, Columbia U., 1977, medal of distinction, Barnard Coll., 1979, Red Cross Humanitarian award, 1986, Extraordinary Woman of Achievement award, NCCJ, 1978, Disting. Trustee award, United Hosp. Fund., 1991, Disting. Cmty. Svc. award, 1994, award for disting. svc. to City of New York, St. Nicholas Soc., 2002. Mem.: Colony Club of N.Y.C. Episcopalian. Home: 1035 5th Ave New York NY 10028-0135 Fax: (212)472-6506.

ELLIOTT, ELIZABETH MARIE, education educator; b. Fairfield, Calif., Sept. 28, 1954; d. Shirley M. Elliott; m. Charles R. Barksdale, July 25, 1995. AA, Manatee C.C., Bradenton, FL, 1991; BA, MA, U. South Fla., 1995; PhD, U. Tenn., 2001. Asst. prof. early childhood edn. Fla. Gulf Coast U., Ft. Myers, 2001—, dir. family resource ctr. Ft. Myers, 2001—. Bd. dirs. John Maxwell Biasco Found., Naples, Fla., 2002—03. Mem.: Coun. Exceptional Children. Republican. Avocation: travel. Office: Fla Gulf Coast U 10501 FGCU Blvd S Fort Myers FL 33965 Home Fax: 239-590-7801; Office Fax: 239-590-7801. Personal E-mail: eelliott@fgcu.edu. E-mail: eelliott@fgcu.edu.

ELLIOTT, EMERSON JOHN, education consultant, policy analyst; b. Ann Arbor, Mich., Nov. 13, 1933; s. Clarence Hyde and Ella Ruth (Kohl) E.; m. Joyce Ann Dodge, Aug. 19, 1956; children— Douglas, Stuart, Susan BA, Albion Coll., Mich., 1955; M.P.A., U. Mich., 1957. Chief edn. br. OMB, Washington, 1967-70, dep. chief human resources programs div., 1970-72; dep. dir. Nat. Inst. Edn., Washington, 1972-77; dir. ednl. staff seminar Inst. for Ednl. Leadership, Washington, 1977-79; dir. sch. fin. study U.S. Dept. Edn., Washington, 1979-81, dir. planning and evaluation, 1981-82, dir. issues analysis, 1982-84; head Nat. Ctr. for Edn. Stats., Washington, 1984-92; com. of edn. stats., 1992-95; dir. spl. projects Nat. Coun. Accreditation Tchr. Edn., Washington, 1995—. Recipient Disting. Alumnus award Albion Coll., 1975; Dirs. Superior Service award Nat. Inst. Edn., 1979; Presdl. Rank awards for Meritorious Service U.S. Govt., 1983, 91. Disting. Service U.S. Govt., 1987. Office: Nat Coun Accred Tchr Edn Ste 500 2010 Massachusetts Ave NW Washington DC 20036-1012

ELLIOTT, EMORY BERNARD, English language educator, educational administrator; b. Balt., Oct. 30, 1942; s. Emory Bernard and Virginia L. (Ulbrick) E.; m. Georgia Ann Carroll, May 14, 1966; children: Scott, Mark, Matthew, Laura, Constance. AB, Loyola Coll., Balt., 1964; MA, Bowling Green State U., 1966; PhD, U. Ill., 1972. Instr. Cameron Coll., Lawton, Okla., 1966-67, U.S. Mil Acad., West Point, N.Y., 1967-69; from asst. prof. to prof. English, Princeton U., N.J., 1972-89, chmn. Am. studies program, 1976-82, master Lee D. Butler Coll., 1982-86, chmn. English dept., 1987-89; Pres.'s chair English U. Calif., Riverside, 1989-91, disting. prof., 1992—, univ. prof., 2001—; dir. Ctr. for Ideas and Soc., 1996—. Writing cons. Bell Labs., Holmdel, N.J., 1975-79, RCA, Princeton, 1980-81; edn. cons. Western Electric Corp. Edn. Ctr., Hopewell, N.J., 1974-79 Author: Power and the Pulpit in Puritan New England, 1975, Puritan Influences in American Literature, 1979, Revolutionary Writers: Literature and Authority in the New Republic, 1982, The Literature of Puritan New England in The Cambridge History of American Literature, Vol. 1, 1994, The Cambridge Introduction to Early American Literature, 2002; editor: Dictionary of Literary Biography, 3 Vols., 1606-1810, 1983-84; editor: Columbia Literary History of the United States, 1988 (Am. Book award 1988), American Literature: A Prentice Hall Anthology 3 Vols., 1990, Columbia History of The American Novel, 1991, The Jungle, 1991, Wieland, 1994, Huckleberry Finn, 1998, Aesthetics in a Multicultural Age, 2002; series editor Am. Novel Series, 1985—, Critical Studies in Contemporary Am. Fiction, 1987—; mem. editorial bd. Am. Quar., 1976-80, PMLA, 1990-92, Am. Lit., 1995—98, Modern Fiction Studies, 1993—, Ill. Studies Lang. Lit., 1993—, Studies in Am. Puritan Spirituality, 1991—; mem. adv. com. Gale Bibliography of Am. Lit., 1981—; editor-at-large Am. Studies Internat., 1993—. Served to capt. U.S. Army, 1966-69. Fellow Woodrow Wilson Found., 1971-72, Am. Coun. Learned Socs., 1973, Guggenheim Found., 1976, Nat. Humanities Ctr. 1979-80, NEH, 1986-87, Inst. for Rsch. in the Humanities, 1991-92, Ford Found., 1998-99, 2000-2003, 2002—, Rockefeller Found., 2000—03; Richard Stockton preceptor Princeton U., 1975-78. Mem. MLA (chmn. Early Am. lit. div., Am. lit. div. 1991, regional del.). Office: U Calif Dept English Riverside CA 92521-0001 E-mail: Emory.Elliott@ucr.edu.

ELLIOTT, FRANCES CARANO, lawyer, educator; b. Carovilli, Italy, Aug. 17, 1950; d. Remo Marino and Angelia (Elia) Carano; m. G. Mark Elliott, Sept. 23, 1972; children: Cara, Adrienne. BS in Phys. Therapy, Ohio State U., 1972; JD cum laude, U. Akron, 1983; postgrad., John Marshall Sch. Law, Chgo., 1998—. Bar: Ohio, U.S. Dist. Ct. Ohio; cert. phys. therapist. Dir. phys. therapy Ohio Rehab. Clinic, Columbus, 1972-76; rsch. asst. U. Akron Sch. Law, 1980, adj. prof., 1984-85; prodr., legal advisor Feedback Series: Legal Questions, WEAO Pub. TV, Kent, Ohio, 1989-94; ind. contractor West Group, Inc., 1998—; sole practitioner Hudson, Ohio, 1983—. Legal advisor WEAO Pub. TV, 1989-94; lectr. in field. Pres., Hudson Music Assn., 1990-94; mem. cabinet, legal divsn. United Way, Akron, 1987; publicity dir. Hudson Bicentennial Commn., 1995-97. Mem. Ohio State Bar Assn., Ohio Bar Coll., Akron Bar Assn. (publicity dir.), Hudson C. of C. (bd. dirs. 1986-88). Republican. Roman Catholic. Avocations: gardening, trading in the stock market, reading, travel. Home: 83 Sussex Rd Hudson OH 44236-1650 Office: Law Offices of Frances Elliott 118 W Streetsboro St # 140 Hudson OH 44236-2711 E-mail: eeefce@yahoo.com.

ELLIOTT, FRANK NELSON, retired college president; b. Dunkirk, N.Y., Mar. 18, 1926; s. Warren D. and Ima M. (Wilson) E.; m. Mary Elizabeth Neish, July 26, 1952; children: Robert Frank (dec.), Susan Marie, Ann Neish. BA cum laude with dept. honors, Alfred U., 1949, LL.D., 1972; MA, Ohio U., 1950; PhD, U. Wis., 1956; LLD (hon.), Rider U., 1994. Grad. asst. Ohio U., 1949-50; Draper fellow Wis. Hist. Soc., 1951-52, field rep., field supr., 1952-56; curator history, asst. prof. history Mich. State U., 1956-61; asso. dean Sch. Gen. Studies, Columbia U., 1961-64, acting dean, 1964; dir. div. arts and scis. State U. N.Y. Coll. at Cortland, 1964-65, acting dean, 1965-66; v.p. Hofstra U., Hempstead, N.Y., 1966-69; pres. Rider Coll., Lawrenceville, N.J., 1969-90. Contbr. articles to profl. jours. Mem. adv. coun. N.J. State Libr., 1972-87; bd. dirs. N.J. Coun. for Humanities, 1972-76, Deleware Valley United Way, 1986-92, Presbyn. Homes N.J., 1990-96, Granville Acad., Trenton, N.J., 1990-94; bd. dirs. Mercer Med. Ctr., 1980-97, chmn., 1992-95; trustee Alfred U., 1964-69; elder Presbyn. Ch. With AUS, 1944-46, PTO. Mem. Am. Assn.

State and Local History (coun. 1960-62), Mich. Hist. Soc. (trustee 1959-61, award for TV lectures 1960), Mercer County C. of C. (dir. 1975-88, Citizen of Yr. 1990). Home: 425 Ramsey Rd Yardley PA 19067-4642

ELLIOTT, FRANK WALLACE, lawyer, educator; b. Cotulla, Tex., June 25, 1930; s. Frank Wallace and Eunice Marie (Akin) E.; m. Winona Trent, July 3, 1954 (dec. 1981); 1 child, Harriet Lindsey; m. Kay Elkins, Aug. 15, 1983. Student, N.Mex. Mil. Inst., 1947-49; BA, U. Tex., 1951, LLB, 1957. Bar: Tex. 1957, U.S. Supreme Ct. 1962, U.S. Ct. Mil. Appeals 1974, U.S. Dist. Ct. (no. dist.) Tex. 1987, U.S. Ct. Appeals (5th cir.) 1988. Asst. atty. gen. State of Tex., 1957; briefing atty. Supreme Ct. Tex., 1957-58; prof. U. Tex. Law Sch., 1958-77; dean, prof. law Tex. Tech U. Sch. Law, 1977-80; pres. Southwestern Legal Found., 1980-86; ptnr. Baker, Mills & Glast, Dallas, 1987-88; of counsel Ramirez & Assocs., 1988—; dean Dallas/Ft. Worth Sch. Law, 1989-92; dean Sch. Law Tex. Wesleyan U., 1992-94, prof., dean emeritus, 1994—. Parliamentarian Tex. Senate, 1969-73; dir. rsch. Tex. Constl. Revision Commn., 1973 Author: Texas Judicial Process, 2d edit., 1977, Texas Trial and Appellate Practice, 2d edit., 1974, Cases on Evidence, 1980, West's Texas Forms, 20 vols., 1977—, West's Texas Practice, vol. 11, 1990, vol. 14, 1996. Served with U.S. Army, 1951-53, 73-74. Decorated Purple Heart. Mem. ABA, Judge Advs. Assn., Am. Judicature Soc., Am. Bar Found., Tex. Bar Found., Dallas Bar Found., Am. Law Inst., N.Mex. Mil. Inst. Alumni Hall of Fame. Home: 2120 N Rough Creek Ct Granbury TX 76048-2903 Office: 1515 Commerce St Fort Worth TX 76102-6572 E-mail: felliott@law.txwes.edu.

ELLIOTT, FRANKLYN, psychologist; b. Bklyn., Oct. 30, 1926; s. Bernard Neufeldt and Lulu Michaels; m. Esther Belle Levine, Dec. 26, 1983 (dec.); children: Marc Edward, Pamela Ruth, Lisa Ann(dec.). BA, CCNY-Bklyn., 1949, MA, 1952. Cert. sch. psychologist N.Y., 1968, lic. psychologist N.Y., 1959, speech pathologist N.Y., 1976, cert. diplomate Am. Bd. Disability Analysts, 1995, registered Nat. Directory Health Providers in Psychology, 1978, cert. psychologist Nat. Assn. Master Psychologists, 1995. Speech therapist Kings County Med. Ctr., Bklyn., 1950—52; instr. Speech, supr. Speech Clinic Adelphi U., Garden City, NY, 1953—56; speech therapist North Shore Schs., Sea Cliff, NY, 1956—69; sch. psychologist Mineola Pub. Schs., NY, 1969—93; psychologist Levittown, NY, 1959—. Psychotherapist Family Svc. Assn., Hempstead, NY, 1980—85; co-dir. Midwood Theater Workshop, Bklyn., 1996—98. Tech. sgt. U.S. Army, 1943—46. Grantee, Nat. Assn. Handicapped Children and Adults, 1952. Mem.: APA, Nassau County Psychol. Assn. (pres. 1981—82), N.Y. State Psychol. Assn. (ethics com. mem. 1978—79), Kappa Delta Pi. Jewish. Avocations: archaeology, photography. Home and Office: 6 Old Hill Ln Levittown NY 11756

ELLIOTT, GEORGE ALGIMON, pathologist, toxicologist, veterinarian; b. Trappe, Md., June 6, 1925; s. George A. and Mattie Tileston (Sullivan) E.; m. Marguerite Van Zandt Hammond, Aug. 15, 1949; children: Kathleen, Elizabeth, Jennifer. DVM, U. Ga., 1953; MSc in Vet. Pathology, U. Pa., 1957. Diplomate Am. Coll. Vet. Pathologists. From instr. to asst. prof. U. Pa. Sch. of Vet. Medicine, Phila., 1955-60; asst. prof. comparative pathology Vanderbilt U. Sch. of Medicine, Nashville, 1960-62; rsch. scientist (sr. vet. pathologist, toxicologist) The Upjohn Co., Kalamazoo, Mich., 1962-90. Contbr. articles to profl. jours. With U.S. Navy, 1945-46 PTO. Mem. Am. Vet. Medicine Assn., Phi Kappa Phi, Sigma Xi. Democrat. Mem. Reformed Ch. of Am. Avocation: orchids. Home: 4430 Romence Rd Portage MI 49024-3834

ELLIOTT, GEORGE ARMSTRONG, III, artist, journalist; b. Wilmington, Del., July 24, 1929; s. George Armstrong Elliott Jr. and Amy Lewis (Rupert) Thomas; m. Shirley Barbara Henin, Oct. 16, 1965. BA, Colgate U., 1951; cert. in journalism, Columbia U., N.Y.C., 1964. Reporter, copy editor, corr. local and nat. newspapers and news agys., 1950-66, Balt. Sun, 1955-62, N.Y. Herald Tribune, 1964, New York Daily News, 1965-66; adminstrv. asst./press sec. Spiro T. Agnew, Baltimore County Exec., Towson, Md., 1962-65, campaign press mgr., 1962; campaign press sec., speechwriter Spiro T. Agnew, Gov. of Md., 1966; pub. affairs dir. Md. State Rds. Commn., Balt., 1967-69; legis. asst. U.S. Congresswoman from Mass. Margaret M. Heckler, Washington, 1969-71; spl. asst. U.S. Sec. of Commerce Peter G. Peterson, Washington, 1972; campaign writer John H. Chafee for U.S. Senator, Providence, 1972; speechwriter Chmn. of FTC Lewis Engman, Washington, 1973; dir. nat. campaign for 55 m.p.h. speed limit U.S. Dept. Transp., Washington, 1976-77; spl. asst., speechwriter U.S. Congressman from Minn. Albert H. Quie, Washington and Mpls.-St. Paul, 1978; press sec. Rep. Margaret M. Heckler, Washington, 1979-81; prin. writer Nat. Alcohol Fuels Commn., Washington, 1980; writer Nat. Commn. on Air Quality, Washington, 1980-81; internat. pub. rels. counsel A. F. Sabo Assocs., Washington, 1981; Washington and East Coast corr. Jet Cargo News, Washington, 1984-93; profl. Chinese brush painting artist, 1993—. Writer former Md. Gov. Theodore R. McKeldin for Mayor, Balt., 1963; writer for numerous congrl. and local polit. campaigns, 1962-63. Exhibitions include M-Pac Fine Arts Shows, Sugarloaf Mt. Works Shows, Towson, Md., Invitational Art Exhibit, Waterford, Va., Art Mart and Garden tour, Wilmington, Brandywine Arts Festival, Sydney (NSW, Australia) Internat. Art Soc., 1996, Internat. Salon de Haute-Loire, Puy-en-Velay, France, 1997, 99, 7th St. Internat., Washington, 1997, 99, Lalit Kala Nat. Acad. Art, New Delhi, 1998, 99-2000, 2002, Overseas Chinese Culture and Art Festival, Wash., 2000, Internat. Cultural Union, Haifa, 2000-2001, Balt. City Hall Courtyard Galleries, 2000, Marlboro Gallery., Largo, Md., 2000, Mus. Contemporary Art, Wash., 1996, 2001, 03, Russian Cultural Centre, Wash., 2002, Acad. Arts and Design, Tsinghua U., Beijing and Capital Normal U., Beijing, 2002, The Warehouse, Washington, 2003, Gorohavaya 6 Gallery, St. Petersburg, Russia, 2003. With U.S. Army, 1951-54. Ford Found. fellow in advanced internat. reporting Grad. Sch. Journalism, Columbia U., 1963-64. Mem. Nat. Assn. Govt. Communicators, Overseas Press Club Am., Washington Ind. Writers, Montgomery County Art Assn., Internat. Artists Support Group (pres. 1999-2001), Sumi-e Soc. Am., Weekend Art Group. Address: 5826 Bradley Blvd Bethesda MD 20814-1128

ELLIOTT, GORDON JEFFERSON, retired English language educator; b. Aberdeen, Wash., Nov. 13, 1928; s. Harry Cecil and Helga May (Kennedy) E.; m. Suzanne Tsugiko Urakawa, Apr. 2, 1957; children: Meiko Ann, Kenneth Gordon, Nancy Lee, Matthew Kennedy. AA, Grays Harbor Coll., 1948; BA, U. Wash., 1950; Cert. Russian, Army Lang. Sch., Monterey, Calif., 1952; MA, U. Hawaii, 1968. Lifetime credential, Calif. Community Coll. System. English prof. Buddhist U., Ministry of Cults, The Asia Found., Phnom Penh, Cambodia, 1956-62; English instr. U. Hawaii, Honolulu, 1962-68; dir., orientation English Coll. Petroleum and Minerals, Dhahran, Saudi Arabia, 1968-70; asst. prof., English/linguistics U. Guam, Mangilao, 1970-76; tchr., French/English Medford (Oreg.) High Sch., 1976-77; instr., English Merced (Calif.) Coll., 1977-98, ret., 1998. Cons. on Buddhist Edn., The Asia Found., San Francisco, Phnom Penh, Cambodia, 1956-62; cons. on English Edn., Hawaii State Adult Edn. Dept., Honolulu, 1966-68; conf. on English Edn. in Middle East, Am. U., Cairo, Egypt, 1969; vis. prof. of English, Shandong Tchrs. U., Jinan, China, 1984-85. Co-author: (textbooks, bilingual Cambodian-English) English Composition, 1962, Writing English, 1966, (test) Standard English Recognition Test, 1976; contbr. articles to profl. jours. Mem. Statue of Liberty Centennial Commn., Washington, 1980-86, Heritage Found., Washington, Rep. Presdl. Task Force Founders' Wall, 2001, Lincoln Inst., Am. Near East Refugee Aid, Washington, Rep. Presdl. Task Force, 2001. Sgt. U.S. Army Security Agy., Kyoto, Japan, 1951-55. Tchr. Fellowship, U. Mich., Ann Arbor, 1956; recipient summer seminar stipend, Nat. Endowment For Humanities, U. Wash., Seattle, 1976, travel grants, People's Rep. of China, Beijing, 1984-85. Mem. NRA, Collegiate Press (editorial adv. bd.), Merced Coll. Found., Am. Assn. Woodturners, Elks. Republican. Avocations: swimming, woodturning, classical guitar, stamp/coin collecting, travel. Home: 680 Dennis Ct Merced CA 95340-2410 Office: Merced Coll 3600 M St Merced CA 95348-2806 E-mail: gjelliott@aol.com.

ELLIOTT, GRAHAM, science educator; b. Sydney, NSW, Australia, Apr. 2, 1965; s. Christine Elliott. PhD, Harvard U., 1994. Prof. U. Calif.-San Diego, La Jolla, 1994—. Achievements include research in I develop statistical methods for evaluating data that grows over time. Office: U California - San Diego 9500 Gilman Dr San Diego CA 92109 Office Fax: 858-534-7040.

ELLIOTT, HOMER LEE, lawyer; b. Madison, Ind., Aug. 3, 1938; s. William A. and Mabel E. (Talbot) E.; children: Homer, Charles, Jane. AB, Ind. U., 1960; postgrad., Princeton U., 1960-61; JD, Coll. William and Mary, 1969. Bar: Va. 1969, D.C. 1970, Pa. 1977, U.S. Supreme Ct. 1973, U.S. Tax Ct. 1971. Assoc. Steptoe & Johnson, Washington, 1969-77; ptnr. Drinker, Biddle & Reath, Phila., 1977-98, Duane, Morris & Heckscher, Phila., 1998—. Contbr. articles to profl. jours. With U.S. Army, 1961-65. Mem. ABA, Pa. Bar Assn., D.C. Bar Assn., VA State Bar, Princeton Club (Phila.), Phi Beta Kappa. Home: 1326 Spruce St Unit 2701 Philadelphia PA 19107 Office: Duane Morris & Heckscher LLP One Liberty Pl Philadelphia PA 19103-7396 E-mail: elliothl@aol.com., hlelliott@duanemorris.com.

ELLIOTT, HOWARD, JR., lawyer, gas distribution company executive; b. St. Louis, July 4, 1933; s. Howard and Ruth Ann (Thomas) E.; m. Susan Jane Spoehrer, Sept. 2, 1961; children: Kathryn Elliott Love, Elizabeth Elliott Niedringhaus. Student Brown U., 1956; JD, Washington U., St. Louis, 1962. Bar: Mo. 1962. Assoc. Boyle, Priest, Elliott & Weakley, St. Louis, 1962-65, ptnr., 1965-67; mem. Mo. Pub. Svc. Commn., 1967-70, U.S. Postal Rate Commn., 1970—73; assoc. gen. counsel Laclede Gas Co., St. Louis, 1973-77, v.p. adminstrn., 1977-92, sr. v.p. adminstrn., 1992-93, cons., 1993-94, atty., counselor, 1994—. Mem. com. on electricity and nuclear energy Nat. Assn. Regulatory Utility Commrs., 1968-70, mem. exec. com., 1971-73. Charter mem. Com. of 30 for Adoption St. Louis and St. Louis County Jr. Coll. Dist., 1962. With U.S. Army, 1956-58. Mem.: ABA, Bar Assn. Met. St. Louis, Mo. Bar, Loblolly Golf Club (Hobe Sound, Fla.), Chevy Chase (Md.) Club, St. Louis Country Club, St. Louis Club. Republican. Presbyterian. Home: 46 Clermont Ln Saint Louis MO 63124-1351 also: 6820 SE Wood Lark Ln Hobe Sound FL 33455-8048 E-mail: aceelliott@aol.com.

ELLIOTT, INGER MCCABE, designer, textile company executive, design consultant; b. Feb. 23, 1933; arrived in U.S., 1941, naturalized, 1946; d. David and Lova (Katz) Abrahamsen; m. Osborn Elliott, Oct. 20, 1963; children from previous marriage: Kari McCabe, Alexander McCabe, Marit McCabe. AB in History with honors, Cornell U., 1954; postgrad., Harvard U., 1955; AM, Radcliffe Coll., 1957. Photographer Photo Rschrs., 1960—98; pres. China Seas, Inc., N.Y.C., 1972—80, Gifted Textile Collection to L.A. County Mus. Art, 1991—. Textile Exhibit L.A. County Mus. Art, 1996—96; cons. Sotheby's Inc., 1992—; mem. Coun. Fgn. Rels. Author: A Week in Amy's World, A Week in Henry's World, Batik: Fabled Cloth of Java, 1985, Exteriors, 1992; contbr.: photographic essays to Esquire, Vogue, Life, Newsweek, N.Y. Times, Infinity, House & Hargen. Mem. East Asia vis. com. Harvard U.; trustee The Asia Soc., Am. Scandinavian Found. Recipient Roscoe awards, 1978—. Mem.: Am. Women's Econ. Devel. Corp., Am. Soc. Mag. Photographers, Com. of 200, Ellis Island Yacht Club (lt. comdr.), Cosmopolitan Club, Phi Beta Kappa. Home: 84 Water St Stonington CT 06378

ELLIOTT, JACK, folk musician; Albums Bull Durham Sacks and Railroad Tracks, Young Brigham, Me & Bobby McGee, South Coast, 1995 (Grammy award, 1995), Ramblin' Jack, 1996, Kerouac's Last Dream, 1997, Friends of mine, 1989, Long Ride, 1999. Recipient Bill Graham Lifetime Achievement award Bay Area Music Awards, 1996, Nat. Medal of Arts award, Pres. Clinton, 1998. Address: Hightone Records 220 4th St Ste 101 Oakland CA 94607-4335

ELLIOTT, JAMES A. oceanographer, researcher; b. Pierceland, Sask., Can., Feb. 24, 1941; s. James John and Dorothy (Spear) E.; m. Gillian Hope, May 13, 1967; children: Rebecca Jean, Jonathan James Patrick. BSc, U. Sask., 1962; MSc, U. B.C., 1965, PhD, 1970. Rsch. sci. Bedford Inst. Oceanography, Dartmouth, N.S., Can., 1962-78, rsch. mgr., 1979-85, rsch. dir., 1985-97, project dir., 1998, emeritus scientist, 1999—. Contbr. numerous articles to oceanographic jours. Dir. A.G. Huntsman Found., 1980-98. Office: Bedford Inst Oceanography PO Box 1006 Dartmouth NS Canada B2Y 4A2

ELLIOTT, JAMES WARD, lawyer; b. Norwich, N.Y., Mar. 4, 1954; m. Susan Talbot, Dec. 22, 1979; children: Shawn, Chris. BA, SUNY, Oneonta, 1976; JD, Union U., Albany, N.Y., 1979. Bar: N.Y. 1980, Va. 1991, Tenn. 2002, U.S. Dist. Ct. (no. dist.) N.Y. 1980, U.S. Dist. Ct. (ea. dist.) Tenn. 2002, U.S. Ct. Mil. Appeals 1980. Procurement and govt. contracts counsel Grumman Aerospace Corp., Bethpage, N.Y., 1986-89; corp. counsel McDermott, Inc. subs. BWX Techs., Inc., Lynchburg, Va., 1989-2000; mng. atty., gen. counsel BWXT Y-12 LLC, Oak Ridge, Tenn., 2000—. With JAGC, U.S. Army, 1980-86; lt. col. USAR. Mem. Nat. Security Indsl. Assn. (subcom. law), Am. Arbitration Assn. (panel of arbitrators). E-mail: xel@y12.doe.gov.

ELLIOTT, JEAN ANN, librarian emeritus; b. Martinsburg, W.Va., Jan. 18, 1933; d. Howard Hoffman and Dorothy Jean (Horn) E. AB in Edn., Shepherd Coll., Shepherdstown, W.Va., 1954; MS in Libr. Sci., Syracuse U., 1957; MS, Shippensburg (Pa.) U., 1974. Asst. libr. Fairmont (W.Va.) State Coll., 1957-60; reference asst. U. Pitts., 1960-61; acting libr. Shepherd Coll., 1961-62; coord. libr. sci., 1962-97. Compiler Jefferson County Hist. mag., 1990. Nat. treas. Palatines of Am., Columbus, Ohio, 1986-88. Mem. ALA, AAUW, DAR (W.Va. treas. 1980-83, 86-89, 95-98, state regent 1998-2001, hon. state regent 2001—), W.Va. Libr. Assn. (election chmn. 1988-90), Jefferson County Hist. Soc., Nat. Soc. Daus. Am. Colonies (nat. libr. 1991-94, hon. state regent 1991—), Nat. Soc. Daus. 1812 (nat. libr. 1994-96), W.Va. Soc. Daus. 1812 (state pres. 1991-94, hon. state pres. 1994—), Nat. Soc. Daus. Colonial Wars (state pres. 2001—), Alpha Beta Alpha (nat. exec. sec. 1968-76), Phi Kappa Phi. Presbyterian. Avocations: genealogy, travel, knitting, computers. Home: PO Box 1649 Shepherdstown WV 25443-1649 E-mail: jaelliot@ix.netcom.com.

ELLIOTT, JOHN, JR., advertising agency executive; b. N.Y.C., Jan. 25, 1921; s. John and Audrey Neilson (Osborn) E.; m. Eleanor Lansing Thomas, July 27, 1956. AB, Harvard U., 1942. Copywriter Batten, Barton, Durstine & Osborn, 1945-49, account exec., 1949-60, v.p., 1956-60, dir., 1958-60; sr. v.p., dir. Ogilvy, Benson & Mather, 1960-65; chmn. Ogilvy & Mather (U.S.), N.Y.C., 1965-75, Ogilvy & Mather Internat., N.Y.C., 1975-82, chmn. emeritus, 1982—. Dir. Fireman's Fund Am. Life Ins. Co. N.Y., 1972-82. Author: Inventing Christmas, 2002. Trustee, pres. Alumni Assn. Browning Sch., 1950-60; trustee St. Paul's Sch., 1978-81, Internat. House, 1967—, Wildlife Conservation Soc., 1979—, Park Assn., N.Y.C., 1956-60, Sta. WNET/Channel 13, 1983—; v.p. Mus. City of N.Y., 1956-65; gen. chmn Red Cross Campaign for Mems. and Funds, N.Y.C., 1970-71; TV advisor Rep. Party, 1950-53; bd. overseers Meml. Sloan-Kettering Cancer Care Center, 1980-84; bd. dirs. Advt. Ednl. Found., 1984-99, Ctr. for Communication, 1982-90; pres. Scottish Nat. Trust Golden Jubilee Found., 1980-93; mem. President's Adv. Council Pvt. Sector Initiatives, 1983-85, Pres.'s Adv. Bd., 1985-89. Served to maj. USMCR, 1942-45. Mem. Am. Assn. Advt. Agys. (chmn. 1974-75), Advt. Council (dir. 1972—, vice chmn. 1979-84, chmn. 1984-85), Advt. Hall Fame (elected 1983). Clubs: Bedford Golf and Tennis, Harvard (N.Y.C.), Century Assn., Hon. Company Edinburgh Golfers, Grolier. Office: Ogilvy & Mather 309 W 49th St Fl 12 New York NY 10019-7316

ELLIOTT, JOHN GREGORY, aerospace design engineer; b. Soerabaya, Dutch East Indies, Nov. 9, 1948; came to U.S., 1956; s. Frans Jan and Charlotte Clara (Rosel) E.; m. Jennifer Lee Austin, May 7, 1988. AA, Cerritos Coll., 1974; BS, Calif. State U., Long Beach, 1978. Design engr. Boeing Airplane Co., Long Beach, 1978-82, lead engr., 1983-89, sect. mgr. elect. installations group, 1989—. With USN, 1969-73. Mem. So. Calif. Profl. Engring. Assn., The Boeing Co. Tennis Club, The Boeing Co. Surf Club, The Boeing Co. Mgmt. Club. Republican. Presbyterian. Avocations: sailing, guitar, reading, remote-control gliders, painting. Office: Boeing Aircraft Co Long Beach Divsn Internal Mail Code 800 6 Long Beach CA 90846-0001 E-mail: john.g.elliott@boeing.com.

ELLIOTT, JOHN MICHAEL, lawyer; b. Girardville, Pa., July 8, 1941; s. John T. and Clair C. E.; children: John P., Heather D., Kirwan B., Kyle M. AB in Econs. magna cum laude, St. Vincent Coll., 1963, LL.D. (hon.), 1985; LL.B. cum laude, Georgetown U., 1966. Bar: Pa. 1966, U.S. Dist. Ct. (ea., we. and mid. dists.) Pa. 1967, U.S. Ct. Appeals (3d cir.) 1967, U.S. Supreme Ct. 1968,. Chmn. Elliott, Reihner, Siedzikowski & Egan, Phila., 1990—. Pa. counsel Del. River Port Authority, 1987-95; mem. Phila. Coal Rail Task Force, Rockefeller Commn., White House Coal Adv. Commn., 1980; bd. dirs. James A. Finnegan Fellowship Found., 1976-90; bd. dirs. Irish Edn. Devel. Found., Inc., chmn., 2002; mem. Pa. Citizens Adv. Coun. Dept. Environ. Resources, 1970-78, chmn. urban com.; mem. environ. quality bd. Commonwealth of Pa., 1970-78; commr. Del. River Port Authority; rep. auditor Gen. Robert P. Casey; mem. Phila. City Planning Commn., 1970-75, Del. Valley Citizens Coun. for Clean Air; chmn. Disciplinary Bd. Supreme Ct. Pa., 1985-86, vice chmn., 1985, chmn. rules com., 1982, Pa. Bar Inst., 1988-94; mem. Commn. on Security and Coop. in Europe Conf. on the Human Dimension, Paris, 1989, Conf. on Dem. Instns., Oslo, 1991; mem. coun. of advisors Sch. of Humanities and Fine Arts, Georgetown U., 2002. Contbr. articles to profl. jours. Bd. dirs. Mann Music Ctr., 1988-91, Walnut St. Theatre, 1988-93, Internat. League for Human Rights, 1988-95; mem. adv. coun. Arts and Humanities, 2002—. Recipient St. Patrick's Coll. Maynooth Ireland Salamanaca Archives Dedication, Cahal B. Cardinal Daly, 1995, Gold medal St. Patrick Desmond Cardinal Connell Dublin, 2001; Williston rsch. fellow, 1965. Fellow Pa. Bar Found.; mem. ABA (lectr. on trial practice), Pa. Bar Assn. (ho. of dels. 1983-91, task force on civil ct. rules), Pa. Bar Inst. (bd. dirs. 1987-93, course planner, faculty), Am. Law Inst. (ABA appelate practice program), Nat. Inst. Trial Advocacy (lectr.), Phila. Bar Assn., Nat. Lawyers Com. for Civil Rights Under Law, Braehon Law Soc., Mil. History Soc. Ireland. Home: 1202 Penllyn Blue Bell Pike Blue Bell PA 19422-2108 Office: Elliott Reihner Siedzikowski & Egan 925 Harvest Dr Blue Bell PA 19422-1956

ELLIOTT, KATI MARIE, communications company official; b. Fridley, Minn., July 20, 1965; d. James F. and Barbara (Swanson) E. AA, Rochester (Minn.) C.C., 1985; BA in Pub. Rels., Winona State U., 1986-89. Asst. to quadrapalegic, Winona, Minn., 1986-87; waitress Brass Lantern, Rochester, 1987-89; tchr. Aldridge Presch., Rochester, 1989-90; office mgr. Gold Crown Limousine, Rochester, 1990-91; mng. editor Curriculum Product News, Stamford, Conn., 1991-94; account exec. Connors Comm., N.Y.C., 1994-95, sr. account exec. Mpls., 1995-98; pres. KEH Comm., Md., 1998—. Presenter on pub. rels. for schs. Fla. Ednl. Tech. Confs., Orlando, 1995. Contbr. articles on edn. tech. to profl. publs. Mem. Cmty. Vols. in Action, Conn., 1992-94, Corp. Vols. in Action, Stamford, 1993-95; participant Habitat for Humanity, Conn., 1993-95. Mem. Internat. Bus. Communicators Assn. (presenter, conf. com. 1996—), Pub. Rels. Soc. Am., Minn. Software Assn. (edn. com. 1995—). Avocations: aerobics, running, biking, rock climbing, volleyball. Office: KEH Comm 524 Bowline Rd Severna Park MD 21146-3316 Office Fax: 410-975-9639.

ELLIOTT, LARRY PAUL, cardiac radiologist, educator; b. Manhattan, Kans., Oct. 16, 1931; s. Leonard Paul and Mary Elizabeth (Myers) E.; m. Betty Lou Hawkins, June 23, 1956; children: Laurie Lou, Mary Elizabeth, Larry Paul. BS, U. Fla., 1954; MD, U. Tenn., 1957. Intern John Gaston Hosp., Memphis, 1957-58; resident in pediat. and pediat. cardiology U. Fla. Hosp., 1958-61; resident in cardiac pathology and cardiovasc. radiology U. Minn. Hosp., 1961-65; assoc. prof. cardiac radiology Washington U. Med. Sch., St. Louis, 1966-67; prof. cardiac radiology U. Fla. Med. Sch., 1967-76; prof. radiology, dir. divsn. cardiac radiology U. Ala. Med. Sch., Birmingham, 1976-81; prof., chmn. dept. radiology Georgetown U. Sch. Medicine, 1981—, clin. prof., chmn. emeritus, 1996—; clin. prof. radiology Emory U. Med. Ctr., Atlanta, 1997—, Med. U. S.C., 1999—. Chmn. Fac. Practice Group, 1989—; clin. prof. Med. U. S.C., 1999—. Author: The X-Ray Diagnosis Heart Disease, 1968, 79; editor: Radiology, 1967—, Cardiovascular and Interventional Radiology, 1979—, The Fundamentals of Cardiac Imaging in Infants, Children and Adults, 1990; assoc. editor cardiovasc. sect. Taveras Radiology, 1986; contbr. articles to med. jours. Recipient Disting. Alumnus award U. Fla., 1981, Outstanding Alumnus award U. Tenn. Med. Sch., 1993; grantee cardiac radiology Nat. Heart Inst., 1968-76, Allied Health Profl. Act, 1970. Fellow N.Am. Soc. Cardiac Radiology (pres. 1977-78), Am. Coll. Cardiology; mem. Radiol. Soc. N.Am., Soc. Cardiac Angiography, Am. Heart Assn., Soc. Thoracic Radiology (founding mem., pres. faculty practice group 1989-93). Home: 3 Ocean Point Dr Isle Of Palms SC 29451-3852 *In my own success, I have found 5 key ingredients. (1) A mentor who ignited the switch or literally turned me on. (2) Superb training, especially in sound fundamental principles. (3) An obsessive enthusiasm, a prime feature I look for in all postgraduate students. (4) An element of discipline, which has prevented succumbing to the siren song of private practice. (5) Reward, the only fountain of youth that exists - a close association with each generation of students.*

ELLIOTT, LUELLA LEE, retired women's health nurse, educator; b. Trafalgar, Ind., Jan. 10, 1937; d. James Arnold and Gladys Maudaline (Pitcher) Greer; m. John R. Elliott, Nov. 29, 1959 (div. Mar. 1986); children: Lisa L. Elliott, John R. Elliott II, Lora L. Elliott, James R. Elliott; m. Floyd Elbert Thomas, Apr. 20, 1991 (div. Apr. 2001). BSN, Ball State U., Muncie, Ind., 1959; MSN, Ind. U., 1976. RN, Ind., Fla. Staff nurse Cmty. Hosp., Indpls., 1959-70, 1992-94; asst. prof. U. Indpls., 1970-87; svc. area mgr. Wishard Meml. Hosp., Indpls., 1987-89; staff nurse Favorite Nurses, Indpls., 1989-92, Columbia Easpointe & Gulf Coast Hosp., Ft. Myers, Fla., 1995-96; women's educator Columbia Gulf Coast Hosp., Ft. Myers, 1996-99; case mgr. Healthy Start Program Lee County Health Dept., 1999-2000; ret. Instr. Maternity Family League, Indpls., 1987-89, ARC, Indpls., 1982-86. Sec., bd. dirs. Cmty. Outreach Ministries Eastside, Indpls., 1986-88; mem. outreach com. Old Bethel United Meth. Ch., Indpls., 1986-89; mem. Good Citizen Group, 1996—. Mem. Am. Diabetes Assn. Avocations: golf, reading. Home: 319 Pioneer Pl Fort Myers FL 33917-4040 E-mail: imluthomas@aol.com.

ELLIOTT, LUKE ALEXANDER, family practice physician; b. Detroit, Feb. 15, 1960; s. Kevin Michael and Margaret Katherine (Skinner) E.; m. Susanna Zapalski, June 20, 1987; 1 child, Noah James. BS, Wheaton Coll., 1982; MS, Wayne State U., 1985, MD, 1989. Diplomate Am. Acad. Family Physicians; cert. advanced trauma life support provider. Surg. asst. animal rsch. lab. William Beaumont Hosp., Royal Oak, Mich., summers 1974-75; surg. rsch. asst. animal lab. Wayne State U., Detroit, 1982-85; resident family practice Bon Secours Hosp., Grosse Pointe, Mich., 1989-92; family physician Shorepointe Family Physicians, Grosse Pointe, 1992-94, 96, Bon Secours Hosp.-Shorepointe Family Physicians, Grosse Pointe Farms, Mich., 1996—, co-dir. primary care office, 1996. Vol. faculty Bon Secours Hosp., Grosse Pointe, 1992—, chmn. med. records com., 2000—, chmn. family practice dept., 2001-02; vol. clin. asst. prof. dept. family medicine Wayne State U., Sch. Medicine, Detroit, 1996—; physician Bon Secours Nursing Home, St. Clair Shores, Mich., 1992-94; emergency room physician Bon Secours Hosp., Grosse Pointe, 1992-94, 94-96; physician Tri-County Urgent Care, Clinton Twp., Mich., 1995-96; presenter and cons. in field. Contbr. articles to profl. jours. Bd. mem. Detroit Rescue Mission Ministries, Detroit, 1985—, chmn. med. com., 1993—; mem. Christian Business Men's Com., Detroit, 1992—. Recipient Soc. Tchrs. Family Medicine Resident Tchr. award, 1992; named one of top 9 primary care doctors in Mich., Town and Country Mag., 2000; Burroughs Wellcome Family Practice scholar, 1991. Fellow Am. Acad. Family Physicians; mem. Christian Med. and Dental Soc. R.publican. Presbyterian. Office: Shorepointe Family Physicians Bon Secours Hosp 22646 E 9 Mile Rd Saint Clair Shores MI 48080-1951 E-mail: luke1252@comcast.net.

ELLIOTT, OSBORN, journalist, educator, urban activist, former dean; b. N.Y.C., Oct. 25, 1924; s. John and Audrey N. (Osborn) E.; m. Deirdre M. Spencer, May 8, 1948 (div. Dec. 1972); children: Diana, Cynthia, Dorinda; m. Inger McCabe, Oct. 20, 1973; stepchildren: Kari, Alexander, Marit. Grad., St. Paul's Sch., 1942; AB, Harvard U., 1946; LHD (hon.), Mich. State U., 1972; LittD (hon.), Marlboro Coll., 1996; LHD (hon.), Marymount Manhattan Coll., 1998. Reporter N.Y. Jour. Commerce, 1946-49; contbg. editor Time mag., 1949-52, assoc. editor, 1952-55; sr. bus. editor Newsweek mag., 1955-59; mng. editor Newsweek, 1959-61, editor, 1961-69, 72-75, editor-in-chief, vice chmn., pres., CEO, chmn. bd., 1969-76; former dir. Washington Post Co., A.S. Abell Co. (Balt. Sun); dep. mayor econ. devel. City of NY, 1976—77; dean Grad. Sch. Journalism, Columbia U., N.Y.C., 1979-86, George Delacorte prof., 1986-94, pub. Columbia Journalism Rev., 1979-86. Author: Men At the Top, 1959, The World of Oz, 1980; editor: The Negro Revolution in America, 1964. Bd. overseers Harvard Coll., 1965—71; trustee N.Y. Pub. Libr., 1968—72, 1977—79, St. Paul's Sch., 1969—73, Am. Mus. Natural History, 1958—80, Lincoln Ctr. Theater, 1987—92, Pulitzer Prize Bd., 1979—86; judge Livingston Journalism Awards; chmn. China Seas, Inc., 1973—90, Bernstein Book award N.Y. Pub. Libr.; chmn. bd. dirs. Citizens Com. for N.Y.C., 1975—79, 1990—; bd. dirs. New Yorkers for Children, 1999—; organizer 250,000 person Save Our Cities! Save Our Children! March on Washington, 1992. With USNR, 1944—46. Named to Hall of Fame, N.Y.C. Deadline Club, 2000; recipient Carr Van Anda award, Ohio U., 1969, Frederick Douglass award, N.Y. Urban League, 1993, Editor's Hall of Fame award, Am. Soc. Mag. Editors, 1996,

Creative Spirit award, Black Alumni Pratt Inst., 1997, Browning Sch. Alumni award, 2001. Fellow Am. Acad. Arts and Scis.; mem. Coun. Fgn. Rels., Asia Soc. (1966-93, life trustee 2003—), Harvard Club, Century Assn., Ellis Island Yacht Club (commodore). Home: 84 Water St Stonington CT 06378

ELLIOTT, PETER R. retired athletic organization executive; b. Bloomington, Ill., Sept. 29, 1926; s. Joseph Norman and Alice (Marquis) E.; m. s. Joan Connaught Slater, June 14, 1949; children: Bruce Norman, David Lawrence. BA, U. Mich., 1949. Asst. football coach Oreg. State U., 1949-50, U. Okla., 1951-55; head football coach Nebr. U., 1956, U. Calif., Berkeley, 1957-59, U. Ill., 1960-66, U. Miami, Fla., 1973-74, dir. athletics, 1974-78; asst. football coach St. Louis Cardinals, 1978; exec. dir. Pro Football Hall of Fame, Canton, Ohio, 1979-96, ret., 1996. Served with USNR, 1944-45. Named to Mich. Sports Hall of Fame, 1983, Coll. Football Hall of Fame, 1994. Mem. Am. Football Coaches Assn. (Region 8 Coach of Yr. 1958, Region 5 Coach of Yr. 1963). Presbyterian. Home: 3003 Dunbarton Ave NW Canton OH 44708-1818

ELLIOTT, RALPH H. educator; b. Danville, Va., Mar. 2, 1925; s. Earl A. and Consuela (Arnn) E.; m. Virginia Ellen Case, Oct. 14, 1945; children: Virginia Lee, Beverly A. AB, Carson Newman Coll., 1949; BD, Southern Bapt. Theol. Sem., 1952, ThD, 1956; LHD (hon.), Cen. Philippines U., 1987; DD (hon.), Alderson Broaddus Coll., 1989; LHD (hon.), Hebrew Coll., 1999. Ordained to ministry Bapt. Ch., 1945. Prof. Old Testament Crozer-Midwestern Southern Bapt. Sems., 1956-64; sr. pastor Emmanuel Bapt. Ch., Albany, N.Y., 1964-71, 1st Bapt. Ch., White Plains, N.Y., 1971-77, North Shore Bapt. Ch., Chgo., 1977-89; v.p. acad. life, dean of faculty Colgate Rochester Div. Sch., Rochester, N.Y., 1989-91; interim sr. min. First Bapt. Ch., Rochester, N.Y., 1992-93; interim pres. Andover Newton Theol. Sch., Newton Centre, Mass., 1993-94; interim sr. min. First Bapt. Ch., Worcester, Mass., 1994-96, 1st Bapt. Ch., White Plains, NY, 2000—01. Trustee U. Chgo. Div. Sch., 1978—; vis. prof. U. Melbourne, Australia, 1992. Author: The Message of Genesis, 1961, Reconciliation and the New Age, 1973, Church Growth that Counts, 1982, The Genesis Controversy and Continuity in Southern Baptist Chaos--A Eulogy for a Great Tradition, 1992; contbr. articles to profl. jours. Served with U.S. Infantry, 1943—45. Recipient Courage award, William H. Whitsitt Bapt. Heritage Soc., 1994, Murray I. Rothman award for contbns. toward advancement of Jewish-Christian understanding, 1995. Mem. Internat. Bonhoeffer Soc. Home: 41 Waterford Cir Rochester NY 14618-5422

ELLIOTT, RICHARD HOWARD, lawyer; b. Astoria, N.Y., Apr. 30, 1933; m. Judith A. Kessler, Dec. 26, 1956; children: Marc Evan, Jonathan Hugh, Eve; m. 2d, Diane S. Schaefer, Nov. 18, 1978; children: Alexis, Sara Jane, Benjamin, David. BS, Lehigh U., 1954; JD cum laude, U. Pa., 1962. Bar: U.S. Dist. Ct. (ea. dist.) Pa. 1962, Pa. Supreme Ct. 1962, U.S. Ct. Appeals (3d cir.) 1963, U.S. Dist. Ct. (mid. dist.) Pa. 1976. Assoc. Clark, Ladner, Fortenbaugh & Young, Phila., 1962-69, ptnr., 1970-75, Elliott & Magee, Doylestown, Pa., 1976—. Moderator Permanent Jud. Commn., Presbytery of Phila.; v.p., dir. Bucks County Soc. Prevention Cruelty to Animals; former pres., dir. Pa. Soc. for Prevention of Cruelty to Animals; gen. counsel, dir. Fedn. Humane Socs. Pa., adj. faculty Bucks County Cmty. Coll.; mem. Pa. Navigation Commn., 1977-80. Lt. USN, 1954-59. Mem. ABA, Pa. Bar Assn., Phila. Bar Assn., Bucks County Bar Assn. Republican. Home: 1205 Victoria Rd Warminster PA 18974-3923 Office: Elliott & Magee 11 Duane Rd PO Box 885 Doylestown PA 18901-2837 E-mail: relli59360@aol.com.

ELLIOTT, ROBBINS LEONARD, consultant; b. Can., Aug. 12, 1920; s. Malcolm Robertson and Jean Steadman (Haley) E.; m. Myfanwy Esther Millward, Sept. 9, 1950; children: Michael, Wendy, Ruth, Malcolm. BA, Acadia U., 1941; MA in Econs., U. Toronto, 1947. With Can. Fed. Govt., Ottawa, 1947-58, 63-76; exec. dir. Royal Archtl. Inst. Can., Ottawa, 1958-63; dir. planning and ops. Centennial Adminstrn., 1963-68; exec. v.p. Royal Archtl. Inst. Can., 1976-81; pres. Robbins Elliott Assos. Ltd., Ottawa, 1981-83; exec. dir. Can. Housing Design Council, 1982-86. Trustee Ottawa Bd. Edn., 1974-76; vice chmn. Ont. Heritage Found.; dir. Ont. Bicentennial Adv. Commn.; chmn. Wolfville Cent. Com., 1990-93; adv. com. on comms. Nat. Capital Commn.; Wolfville town councillor, 1994-97. Served to capt. Can. Army, World War II. Recipient Vet. Affaris Ministerial Commendation. Mem. Archaeol. Inst. Am. Progressive Conservative. Baptist. Home: 9 Balcom Dr Apt 3 Wolfville NS Canada B4P 2N8

ELLIOTT, ROBERT LLOYD, lawyer, educator; b. Lexington, Ky., Oct. 22, 1949; s. James Nathan and Lloyd (Lanier) E.; m. Jane Webb Higgins, June 25, 1971; children: James Kenneth, Lloyd Blair. BA, Centre Coll., Danville, Ky., 1971; JD, U. Ky., 1974. Bar: Ky. 1974, U.S. Dist. Ct. (ea. dist.) Ky. 1974, U.S. Ct. Appeals (6th cir.) 1982. Assoc. Harbison, Kessinger, Lisle & Bush, Lexington, 1974-78; ptnr. Harbison, Kessinger, Lyle & Bush, Lexington, 1978-82; assoc. Turley, Savage & Moore, Lexington, 1982-84; ptnr. Savage, Garmer & Elliott, P.S.C., Lexington, 1984— ; adj. prof. litigation skills U. Ky. Coll. Law, Lexington, 1981— ; dir. Central Ky. Legal Services, Inc., Lexington. Mem. Mayor's Adv. Com. on Cable TV, 1978— ; bd. dirs. Lexington Humane Soc., Metro Group Homes. Mem. ABA, Ky. Bar Assn. (Continuing Legal Edn. Commn. 1984—, admissions com. 1983—), Fayette County Bar Assn. (sec. 1975-76, bd. dirs. 1976-78, 83-84, v.p. 1985), Centre Coll. Alumni Assn. (bd. dirs.). Democrat. Episcopalian. Lodge: Optimists. Avocations: coaching youth baseball, basketball, tennis, jogging. Home: 4711 Iron Works Rd Georgetown KY 40324-9490 Office: Savage Garmer & Elliott PSC 141 N Broadway Lexington KY 40507-1240

ELLIOTT, RODNEY GORHMAN, urologist; b. Middleburg, Ky., June 27, 1935; s. James Lloyd and Myra (Taylor) E.; m. Ann Walker, June 21, 1958; children— Karen Gregory, Rodney Bain. B.S., Coll. of William and Mary, 1957; M.D., Med. Coll. Va., 1961. Diplomate Am. Bd. Urology. Intern USPHS Hosp., Seattle, 1961-62; resident in urology USPHS Hosp., Staten Island, N.Y., 1962-66; dep. chief urology USPHS Hosp., Seattle, 1966-69; practice medicine specializing in urology, Memphis, 1969— ; assoc. clin. prof. urology U. Tenn. Coll. Medicine. Adv. med. bd. Planned Parenthood; chief staff Bapt. Hosp. East, 1985. Mem. AMA, Am. Urol. Assn. (S.E. sect.), Memphis Urol. Soc., Phi Beta Kappa, Omicron Delta Kappa, Alpha Omega Alpha. Unitarian. Contbr. articles to profl. jours. Home: 1958 Old Lake Pike Memphis TN 38119-5516 Office: 995 S Yates Memphis TN 38119

ELLIOTT, ROY FRASER, lawyer, holding and management company executive; b. Ottawa, Ont., Can., Nov. 25, 1921; B.Comm., Queen's U., Kingston, Ont., Can., 1943; LLB, Osgoode Hall Law Sch., 1946; grad., Harvard U. Sch. Bus. Adminstrn., 1947. Bar: Ont. 1946, Que. 1948; created queen's counsel. Ptnr. Stikeman, Elliott, Toronto, Ont., 1952—. Bd. dir. CAE Inc., Toronto; lectr. co. law McGill U., Montreal, 1951. Contbg. author, editor: Que. Corp. Manual, 1948-53; co-editor: Doing Business in Canada. Mem. Montreal Bar Assn., Can. Bar Assn., Law Soc. Upper Can. Home: 22 St Thomas St Ste 17B Toronto ON Canada ON M5S 3E7 Office: Commerce Ct W Ste 5300 Toronto ON Canada M5L 1B9 E-mail: felliott@stikeman.com.

ELLIOTT, SCOTT, lawyer, seminarian; b. San Jose, July 26, 1957; s. Roland Meredith and Sandra Gale (Deem) E.; m. Nancy Marie Oller, Apr. 6, 1979; children: Tristan Robin, Jordan Brook, Robin Sage, Forest Dream. BA in Drama magna cum laude, Calif. State U. Stanislaus, Turlock, 1979; JD, U. Oreg., 1987. Bar: Oreg. 1987, U.S. Dist. Ct. Oreg. 1988, U.S. Ct. Appeals (9th cir.) 1992. Assoc. Larry O. Gildea, Eugene, Oreg., 1987-88, Thorp, Dennet, Purdy & Golden, Springfield, Oreg., 1988; law clk. U.S. Dist. Ct. Nev., Las Vegas, 1988-89; ptnr. Green & Elliott, Lincoln City, Oreg., 1989-95; assoc. Thorp, Purdy, Jewett, Urness & Wilkinson, Springfield, Oreg., 1995-96, Wine, Weller, Ehrlich and Green, Lincoln City, 1996-98; pvt. practice Lincoln City, 1998—; seminarian Eden Theol. Sem. Founder, artistic dir. Cmty. Family Players, 1997—2003; mem. choir Congl. Ch., 1997—2003. Recipient Commitment to Excellence in Art award, 4Cs, 2001; grad. tchg. fellow, U. Oreg. Theatre, 1979—80. Mem. Kiwanis. Mem. Congl. Ch. Avocations: family, theology, gardening, theatre, singing. Office: 2137 NW Highway 101 Ste B Lincoln City OR 97367-4214 also: Lincoln City Congl Ch 1760 NW 25th St Lincoln City OR 97367-4151 E-mail: lawyer_elliott@yahoo.com.

ELLIOTT, SCOTT DEAN, public relations executive; b. Lebanon, Pa., Sept. 25, 1957; s. Douglas R. and Suzanne Solt E. BS in TV Prodn., Kutztown U., 1979; MA in Comm., U. Wash., 1991. Field producer KATU-TV, Portland, 1984-85; news editor, coord. KIRO-TV, Seattle, 1985-86; corp. TV producer, editor The Boeing Co., Seattle, 1986; freelance TV producer, editor Octopus Video, Seattle, 1987-93; grad. teaching asst. U. Wash., Seattle, 1990-93, 93-94; rschr., primary book author IT Cons., Portland, 1995; press sec. Commonwealth Pa., Harrisburg, 1996—2002; sr. assoc. Bravo Group, Harrisburg, 2002—. Author: Wireless Communications for Intelligent Transportation Systems, 1995; primary author: Information Technology. Recipient Timothy O'Reilly award, 1980, Iris award, 1985, Silver Reel award, 1986, 88, Rsch. Article award Soc. Motion Picture & Television Engrs., 1991, Nat. Videographer award, 2002; Dale Carnegie Highest award for achievement, 2000; grantee Kaltenborn Found., 1990; Annenburg Washington fellow, 1993, Pub. Policy fellow, 1993. Avocations: hiking, weight lifting, travel. Home: 518 Cumberland St Lebanon PA 17042 Office: Bravo Group 20 N Market Square Ste 800 Harrisburg PA 17101 Fax: 717-214-2205. E-mail: elliott@thebravogroup.com.

ELLIOTT, SCOTT EMORY, reporter; b. West Point, N.Y., Apr. 30, 1968; s. Emory Bernard and Georgia Ann Elliott; m. Jennifer Marie Emmerich, June 26, 1993; children: Claire, Kate, Abby. BA, U. Dayton, 1990. Publs. editor Woolpert Cons., Dayton, Ohio, 1990-91; editor New Carlisle (Ohio) Sun, 1991-93; city editor Eaton (Ohio) Register-Herald, 1993; news editor Troy (Ohio) Daily News, 1993-96; reporter Springfield (Ohio) News-Sun, 1996-98, Dayton Daily News, 1998—. Mem. Soc. Profl. Journalists, Edn. Writers Assn. Roman Catholic. Office: Dayton Daily News 45 S Ludlow St Dayton OH 45402

ELLIOTT, SEAN P. pediatrician, infectious disease specialist; b. Balt., Oct. 18, 1967; s. Jan A. and Sandra J. Elliott; m. Kim Gayton, Jan. 19, 1958; 1 child, Meghan Kristine. BA, U. Chgo., 1989; MD, Columbia U., 1993. Diplomate pediat. Am. Bd. Pediat., 1996, pediat. infectious diseases Am. Bd. Pediat., 2001. Pediatric resident Northwestern U. Sch. Medicine, Chgo., 1993—96; fellow pediatric infectious diseases Washington U. Sch. Medicine, St. Louis, 1996—2000; faculty dept. pediat. U. Ariz. Coll. Medicine, Tucson, 2000—. Pediatric infectious diseases specialist U. Ariz. Coll. Medicine, Tucson, 2000—. Contbr. articles to profl. jours. Recipient Kenny Meml. award in Pediat. Rsch., Midwest Soc. for Pediat. Rsch., 1997; fellow, Nat. Found. for Infectious Diseases, 1998—99; Deans' Tchg. scholar, U. Ariz. Dept. Ednl. Devel., 2000—01. Mem.: Am. Acad. Pediat., Infectious Diseases Soc. Am., Pediatric Infectious Diseases Soc. (mem. tng. programs com. 2002—). Avocations: camping, running, carpentry, piano, guitar. Office: Arizona Health Scis Ctr 1501 N Campbell Ave Tucson AZ 85724-5073 E-mail: selliott@peds.arizona.edu.

ELLIOTT, STANLEY B. chemist, researcher; s. Louis Alexander Elliott and Nellie Cecilia Bennett; m. Elizabeth Marie Seitz, Aug. 2, 1958. Student, Wittenberg Coll., 1935—36; BA, Case Western Reserve U. Analytical chemist Harshaw Chem., Cleve., 1936—38, rsch. chemist, 1938—41, Ferro Corp. and U.S. O.S.R.D., Cleve., 1941—45, chem. engr., 1941—45; v.p. Ferro Chem., 1945—48, pres., 1948—55; rsch. self-employed, Walton Hills, Ohio, 1955—. Author (A.C.S. Monograph No. 103): Metallic Soaps; contbr. articles. Mem.: Sigma Xi, N.Y. Acad. of Sci., Am. Chem. Soc. Achievements include patents in field of Practical electrical superconductors of high temperature power and performance. Office: Management/Research 7125 Conelly Blvd Walton Hills OH 44146

ELLIOTT, SUSAN SPOEHRER, information technology executive; b. St. Louis, May 4, 1937; d. Charles Henry and Jane Elizabeth (Baur) Spoehrer; m. Howard Elliott Jr., Sept. 2, 1961; children: Kathryn Elliott Love, Elizabeth Elliott Niedringhaus. AB, Smith Coll., 1958. Systems engr. IBM, St. Louis, 1958-66; founder, chmn., CEO, SSE (Sys. Svc. Enterprises, Inc.), St. Louis, 1966—; systems analyst Mo. State Dept. Edn., Jefferson City, Mo., 1967-70; systems coord. Bank of Am. (formerly Boatmen's Nat. Bank), St. Louis, 1979-83. Bd. dirs., mem. exec. com. Mo. Automobile Club; class C dir., dep. chmn. Fed. Res. Bd., St. Louis, 1996-98, chmn., 1999-2000; dir. St. Louis Zoo, 1990-96; dir. Angelica Corp., Regional Bus. Coun., 2000—; bd. dirs. St. Louis Regional Commerce and Growth Assn., sec. bd. dirs., 1991-94; bd. dirs. AAA Mo. Trustee, vice chmn. Mary Inst., St. Louis, 1976-89, Webster U., 1987-96; commr., vice chmn. St. Louis Civil Svc. Commn., 1985-86, Mo. Lottery Commn., Jefferson City, 1985-87; bd. dirs. St. Louis Sci. Ctr., 1995—; mem. pres.'s adv. coun. area coun., mem. techn. com. Girl Scouts U.S.; chair women bus. owner's com. United Way, 1996-97. Mem. Internat. Women's Forum. Republican. Presbyterian. Avocations: golf, fitness. Office: SSE (Sys Svc Enterprises Inc) 77 West Port Plz Ste 500 Saint Louis MO 63146-3126 E-mail: sselliott@SSEinc.com.

ELLIOTT, THOMAS MICHAEL, retired association executive, educator, consultant; b. Evansville, Ind., Aug. 4, 1942; s. Thomas Ira and Pauline (Dawson) E.; m. Susan M. Spiers, July 8, 1967 (div. Aug. 1975); 1 son, Christopher Michael; m. Loretta S. Glaze, Jan. 28, 1976. AB in Zoology, Ind. U., 1965, MS in Higher Edn., 1967, EdD, 1970. Asst. to pres. Purdue U., West Lafayette, Ind., 1972-73, asst. provost, 1973-74; exec. dir. Nat. Commn. United Meth. Higher Edn., Nashville, 1974-77; ptnr. Planning Mgmt. Services Group, Washington, 1976-82; dep. commr. Mo. Dept. Higher Edn., Jefferson City, 1977-79; exec. dir. Ark. Dept. Higher Edn., Little Rock, 1979-82; exec. dir., CEO IEEE Computer Soc., Washington, 1982-2000; ret., 2001—. Cons. numerous colls. and univs. Author: Computer Simulation System, 1975; contbr. articles to profl. jours. Bd. dirs., mem. exec. com. So. Regional Edn. Bd., Atlanta, 1980-82; mem. Cabinet of Gov. Bill Clinton and Gov. Frank White, State of Ark., 1979-82. Mem. IEEE (sr.), IEEE Computer Soc., State Higher Edn. Exec. Officers Assn., Am. Soc. Assn. Execs., Am. Mgmt. Assn., Assn. Computing Machinery. Home: 1735 Q St NW Washington DC 20009-2407

ELLIOTT, TOMMY, secondary school educator; b. Memphis, Tenn., Nov. 22, 1971; s. Martha R. and Betty Jean Wallace; m. Kenya M. Elliott; 1 child, Shirlesa Rushawn. MEd, Cambridge Coll., Cambridge, MA, 2001; BS in Edn., U. Tenn., Martin, 1995. Educator, counselor Youth Villages, Memphis, 1995—96; spl. edn. tchr. Memphis City Schools, 1996—99; tchr. Memphis City Schs., 1999—2001; educator DeKalb County Sch. Sys., Decatur, Ga., 2002—. Mentor, trainer U. Memphis, 1998—2001. Author: (educator's guide) Strategies for Behavior Modification. Rep. Memphis Beautiful Commn., Memphis, Tenn., 1998. Nominee Disney's Am. Tchr. award, 1999—2000; recipient Congl. Recognition for Meritorious Achievement, US Govt., 1998, Contbn. to Cmty. award, Memphis City Coun., 2000. Mem.: NEA, Assn. for Supervision and Curriculum Devel., Ga. Assn. Educators, Nat. Fedn. of State H.S. Assns., Alpha Phi Alpha. Avocations: coaching, writing, music, playing basketball, church activities. Personal E-mail: t2elliott@teacher.com.

ELLIOTT, VIRGIL IRL, JR., artist, writer; b. St. Louis, Aug. 30, 1944; s. Virgil Irl Elliott Sr. and Dollye Cleo McAlister; m. Lillian Rose Peiffer, 1963 (div. 1966); 1 child, Steven Christopher; m. Victoria Anne Lore, Sept. 3, 1988. Student, U. Mo., Kansas City, 1965, U. Mo., St. Louis, 1966, Washington U., 1967-68. Cert. Am. Portrait Soc. Freelance musician, 1969—; artist, 1966—; freelance comml. artist, 1976-82; art instr., 1985—; art instr., dir. Penngrove, Calif., 1993—; art instr. Coll. Marin, Ignacio, Calif., 1995-98. Mem. artists adv. panel Calif. State Fair Art Show, Sacramento, 1987. Contbr. articles to profl. jours; art represented in pvt. and pub. collections. With U.S. Army, 1963-66. Mem. ASTM (com. artists' materials 1998—), Am. Soc. Portrait Artists (Signature award 1996), Am. Soc. Classical Realism. Avocation: music. Studio: 111 Goodwin Ave Penngrove CA 94951-8660 E-mail: VirgilElliott@aol.com.

ELLIOTT, VIRGINIA F. HARRISON, retired anatomist, kinesiologist and educator, investment advisor, publisher, philanthropist; b. St. Louis, Mar. 15, 1918; d. George Benjamin and Florence Gertrude (McManus) H.; m. William Hector Marsh, Dec. 1, 1963 (dec. Dec. 1986); m. George William Elliott, Oct. 27, 1991; stepchildren: Carolyn Frances Roberts, George William II, Robert Bonner (dec. Apr. 1995), Cathrine Susan Dimino. BS, U. Wis., 1940, PhD, 1959; MA, Columbia U., 1944. Lectr. Columbia U., N.Y.C., 1943-46; asst. prof. Mary Washington Coll. of U. Va., Fredericksburg, 1946-48, Oreg. State U., Corvallis, 1948-50, assoc. prof., 1950-59; instr. Army Med. Acad./Brooks Army Med. Ctr., San Antonio, 1959-60, assoc. prof., 1960-64; lectr. U. Tex. Med. Sch., Galveston, 1962-64, Hadassah Med. Sch., Hebrew U. of Jerusalem, 1965; lectr. grad. sch. U. Wis., Madison, 1964; pvt. practice stock market investment lectr. Washington, 1969-84; pub. stock market letter, 1969-84; ret., 1984. Fashion model, 1936-47, with John Robert Powers Schs., Phila., Pitts., N.Y.C., 1943-47; cons. U. Tex. Med. Sch., 1962-64, U.S. Pentathlon Team, San Antonio, 1960-64, Dentists for Treatment of Pain from Muscular Tension, San Antonio, 1960-64; vis. prof. grad. sch. U. Wash., Seattle, 1961; lectr. in field. Contbr. articles to profl. jours. Mem. bd. visitors Sch. Edn., U. Wis., Madison, 1992-95, now emeritus; mem. Washington com. Nat. Coun. on Women's Giving. Recipient Civilian Meritorious Svc. award U.S. Civil Svc., 1965; Amy Morris Homans fellow, 1958; hon. fellow U. Wis., 1956, 58, 59. Fellow AAHPERD, Tex. Acad. Sci.; mem. Am. Alliance Health, Physical Edn., Recreation and Dance, Am. Assn. Anatomists divs. Fedn. Am. Socs. for Exptl. Biology (emeritus) Avocations: designing clothing, furniture, landscaping and boats, sculpting, painting. Home: 6333 Cavalier Corridor Falls Church VA 22044-1301

ELLIOTT, WARREN G. lawyer; b. Pueblo, Colo., Jan. 3, 1927; s. Wallace Ford and Hazel (Ellsworth) E.; m. Martha McCabe, June 20, 1953 (div. Sept. 1980); children: Mark, Winthrop, Carolyn, Byron. Student, U. Nebr., 1944-45, U. Colo., 1947-49, AB, 1973; JD, U. Mich., 1952. Bar: Colo. 1952, Conn. 1976, D.C. bar 1978. Asst. city mgr., city atty., Pueblo, 1952-55; adminstrv. asst., legislative counsel U.S. Senator Gordon Allott, 1956-61; asst. gen. counsel Life Ins. Assn. Am., Washington, 1961-68; gen. counsel Aetna Life & Casualty Co., Hartford, Conn., 1968-78; mem. firm Hedrick & Lane, Washington, 1978-79; ptnr. Nossaman, Guthner, Knox & Elliott, Washington, 1979-85, of counsel, 1986—, Epstein, Becker & Green, P.C., Washington, 1986—. Bd. dirs. Friends of the Hopkins Ctr.; trustee Opera North. Served with USAAC, 1944-46. Mem. ABA, Fed. Bar Assn., Phi Gamma Delta, Phi Alpha Delta. Office: 3703 Magnolia Ln Santa Barbara CA 93105 E-mail: warrengelliott@hotmail.com.

ELLIOTT-MOSKWA, ELAINE SALLY, psychologist, researcher; b. St. Louis; d. Walter Leonard and Helen (Krelo) E.; m. Alexander Moskwa Jr.; 1 child, Katherine. BA in Psychology, U. Mo., 1973; MA in Psychology, San Diego State U., 1977; PhD in Psychology, U. Ill., 1980. Vis. rsch. assoc. Lab. Human Devel., Harvard U., Cambridge, Mass., 1980-81; lectr. dept. psychology Brandeis U., Waltham, Mass., 1981; fellow Ctr. for Cognitive Therapy, U. Pa., Phila., 1982-83; cons. Presbyn. U. Pa. Med. Ctr., Phila., 1984-85; pvt. practice Newton Centre, Mass., 1985-92; dir. Ctr. for Cognitive Therapy Greater Boston, Newton Centre, 1988-92; pvt. practice Princeton, N.J., 1992—. Instr. Med. Sch. Harvard U., 1989-99; asst. dir. tng., cognitive therapy and rsch. program Mass. Gen. Hosp., 1991-92, cons. depression rsch. program, 1992-99. Author: chpt. Carmichael's Handbook of Child Psychology, 1983, Advances in Psychology, 1989. Nat. Inst. on Aging grantee Brandeis U., 1988. Mem. Am. Psychol. Assn., Assn. for Advancement Behavior Therapy. Office: 20 Nassau St Ste 507 Princeton NJ 08542-4505

ELLIOTT-SCHEINBERG, WENDY, history educator, genealogist; b. Delano, Calif., Oct. 14, 1939; d. Alva Thomas Bebout and Rena Leon Hill; m. Sy Scheinberg, Jan. 3, 1998; m. Bruce Alan Elliott, Nov. 27, 1957 (div.); children: Brian Keith, Bradley Kent, Beth Kathleen, Brent Kevin, Katrina Diane, Kyle Darren. AA, Fullerton City Coll., 1983; BA, Calif. State U., 1987, MA, 1991; PhD, Claremont Grad. U., 2001. Cert. genealogist Bd. for Cert. of Genealogists. V.p. Lineages Inc., Salt Lake City, 1985—90; prof. history Calif. State U., Fullerton, 1996—. Editor, author: book The Library: A Guide to the LDS, 1988 (ALA Book of Yr., 1988); author: Printed Sources, 1999 (ALA Book of Yr., 2000); contbr. articles to profl. jours. Advisor, cons. Japanese Am. Nat. Mus., L.A., 1999—2002; pres. YMCA Youth Orgn., North Orange County, Calif., 1976—80; v.p. Fedn. Geneal. Soc., Austin, Tex., 2000—02; pres. Calif. State Geneal. Alliance, Calif., 1991—98. Recipient Disting. Svc. award, Fedn. Geneal. Soc., 1995, Calif. State Geneal. Alliance, 1998, Outstanding Svc. award, YMCA, 1979. Mem.: S.W. Oral History Assn. (pres. 2002—03). Democrat. Avocations: needlework, baking. Home: 1060 Magnolia Ave Placentia CA 92870-4423 Office: Calif State U 800 N State College Blvd Fullerton CA 92834

ELLIOTT-ZAHORIK, BONNIE, nurse, administrator; b. Algona, Iowa; AAS, Coll. Lake County, Grayslake, Ill., 1979; student, U. Iowa; BS, U. St. Francis, Joliet, Ill., 1988; MS, Nat. Louis U., Evanston, Ill., 1989; grad., Northwestern U., 2001. Cert. nurse adminstr.-advanced; cert. critical incident stress debriefing provider. Dir. med./surg. units across the life span Vista Health/Victory Meml. Hosp., Waukegan, Ill., 2000—; chair managerial coun. Vista Health, 1998—2002, chair coordinating coun., 2002. Preceptor/mentor Graceland U., Parkside and St. Xavier U.; fellow, doctorate pgm, adminstrn Walden U., 1995—96. Contbr. articles to profl. jours. Co-chair Victory Healthcare Svcs. Combined Appeal Campaign, 1997; mem. combined appeal com., Am. Heart Assn. vol., 1996—; designer and vol. Festival of Trees fundraiser, 1992—2001. Mem.: AACN, Ill. Orgn. Nurse Leaders (bd. dirs. 1991—, pres. 1998, past pres., state chmn. bylaws com. 1998—99, pres.-elect region 2-B 2000, strategic planning com. 2000—, pres. IONL region 2-B 2001, ballot pres.-elect IONL state 2001), Ill. Coalition for Nurse Resources (legis. funding com. 2001—, pres. 2004, exec. bd.), Ill. Coun. Nurse Mgrs. (past pres. Region 2B), Am. Orgn. Nurse Execs.

ELLIS, ALBERT, clinical psychologist, educator, author; b. Pitts., Sept. 27, 1913; s. Henry Oscar and Hettie (Hanigbaum) E. BBA, CCNY, 1934; MA, Columbia U., 1943, PhD, 1947. Diplomate: Am. Bd. Profl. Psychology; in clin. hypnosis Am. Bd. Psychol. Hypnosis; Am. Bd. Med. Psychotherapists, Am. Bd. Sexology. Free-lance writer, 1934-38; personnel mgr. Distinctive Creations, 1938-48; sr. clin. psychologist N.J. State Hosp., Greystone Park, 1948-49; instr. psychology Rutgers U., 1948-49, adj. prof., 1971-83; instr. psychology N.Y. U., 1949; adj. prof. Union Grad. Sch., 1971-77, U.S. Internat. U., 1974-80, Pittsburg State U., 1978—; chief psychologist N.J. State Diagnostic Center, Menlo Park, 1949-50, N.J. Dept. Instns. and Agys., Trenton, 1950-52; pvt. practice psychotherapy and marriage and family therapy N.Y.C., 1943-68; exec. dir. Albert Ellis Inst. for Rational Emotive Behavior Therapy, N.Y.C., 1959-89; pres., 1989—. Cons. clin. psychology VA, 1961-67 Author: An Introduction to the Principles of Scientific Psychoanalysis, 1950, The Folklore of Sex, 1951, (with A.P. Pillay) Sex, Society and the Individual, 1953, The American Sexual Tragedy, 1954, Sex Life of the American Woman and the Kinsey Report, 1954, New Approaches to Psychotherapy Techniques, 1955, (with Ralph Brancale) The Psychology of Sex Offenders, 1956, How to Live With a Neurotic, 1957, Sex Without Guilt, 1958, What Is Psychotherapy, 1959, The Place of Values in the Practice of Psychotherapy, 1959, The Art and Science of Love, 1960, (with Robert A. Harper) A Guide to Successful Marriage, 1961, (with R.A. Harper) A Guide to Rational Living, 1961, (with Albert Abarbanel) The Encyclopedia of Sexual Behavior, 1961, Reason and Emotion in Psychotherapy, 1962, The Intelligent Woman's Guide to Manhunting, 1963, If This Be Sexual Heresy, 1963, Sex and the Single Man, 1963, The Origins and the Development of the Incest Taboo, 1963, Nymphomania, A Study of the Over-Sexed Woman, 1964, Homosexuality, 1965, Suppressed: Seven Key Essays Publishers Dared Not Print, 1965, The Case for Sexual Liberty, 1965, The Search for Sexual Enjoyment, 1966, (with others) How to Raise an Emotionally Healthy, Happy Child, 1966, (with Roger O. Conway) The Art of Erotic Seduction, 1967, Is Objectivism a Religion, 1968, (with John M. Gullo) Murder and Assassination, 1971, (with others) Growth Through Reason, 1971, Executive Leadership: A Rational Approach, 1972, The Civilized Couple's Guide to Extramarital Adventure, 1972, How to Master Your Fear of Flying, 1972, The Sensuous Person: Critique and Corrections, 1972, (with others) Sex and Sex Education: A Bibliography, 1972, Humanistic Psychotherapy: The Rational-Emotive Approach, 1973, (with Robert A. Harper) A New Guide to Rational Living, 1975, Sex and the Liberated Man, 1976, Anger How to Live With and Without It, 1977, (with Russell Grieger) Handbook of Rational-Emotive Therapy, 1977, (with W. Knaus) Overcoming Procrastination, 1977, (with E. Abrahms) Brief Psychotherapy in Medical and Health Practice, 1978, (with J.M. Whiteley) Theoretical and Empirical Foundations of Rational-Emotive Therapy, 1979, The Intelligent Woman's Guide to Dating and Mating, 1979, (with I. Becker) A Guide to Personal Happiness, 1982, (with M. Bernard) Rational-Emotive Approaches to the Problems of Childhood, 1983, (with M. Bernard) Clinical Applications of Rational-Emotive Therapy, 1985, Overcoming Resistance, 1985, (with Russell Grieger) Handbook of Rational-Emotive Therapy, Vol. 2, 1986, (with Windy Dryden) The Practice of Rational-Emotive Therapy, 1987, (with others) Rational-Emotive Treatment of Alcoholism and Substance Abuse, 1988, How To Stubbornly Refuse to Make Yourself Miserable About Anything-Yes Anything!, 1988, (with others) Rational-Emotive Couples Therapy, 1989, (with R. Yeager) Why Some Therapies Don't Work: The Dangers of Transper-

sonal Psychology, 1989, (with Windy Dryden) The Essential Albert Ellis, 1990, (with Patricia Hunter) Why Am I Always Broke: How to Be Sane about Money, 1991, (with Windy Dryden) A Dialogue with Albert Ellis: Against Dogma, 1991, (with Emmett Velten) What To do When AA Doesn't Work For You: Rational Steps to Quitting Alcohol, 1992, (with Lidia Dengelegi and Michael Abrams) The Art and Science of Rational Eating, 1992, (with Arthur Lange) How to Keep People from Pushing Your Buttons, 1994, (with Michael Abrams) How to Cope with a Fatal Illness, 1994, Reason and Emotion in Psychotherapy Revised, 1994, Better, Deeper and More Enduring Brief Therapy, 1996, (with Jack Gordon, Michael Neenan and Stephen Palmer) Stress Counseling: A Rational Creative Behavior Therapy Approach, 1996, (with R.A. Harper) A Guide To Rational Living, 1997, (with R.C. Tafrate) How to Control Your Anger Before It Controls You, 1997, (with Catherine MacLaren) Rational Emotive Behavior Therapy: A Therapist's Guide, 1998, How to Control Your Anxiety Before It Controls You, 1998, (with Shawn Blau) The Albert Ellis Reader, 1998, Optimal Aging: How to Get Over Growing Older, 1998, How to Make Yourself Happy and Remarkably Less Disturbable, 1999, (with Marcia Grad Powers) The Secret of Coping With Verbal Abuse, 2000, (with S.L. Nielsen and Brad Johnson) Counseling and Psychotherapy With Religious Persons: A Rational Emotive Behavior Therapy Approach, 2001, Feeling Better, Getting Better, Staying Better, 2001, Overcoming Destructive Beliefs, Feelings, and Behaviors, 2001, (with Ted Crawford) Intimate Connections, 2001, (with Robert A. Harper) Dating, Mating, and Relating: How To Build a Healthy Relationship, 2001, (with Jerry Wilde) Case Studies in Rational Emotive Behavior Therapy with Children and Adolescents, 2001, (with Stevan Nielsen and W. Brad Johnson) Counseling and Psychotherapy with Religious Persons: A Rational Emotive Behavior Therapy Approach, 2001, Overcoming Resistance: A Rational Emotive Behavior Therapy Integrative Approach, 2002, (with Ira L. Reiss) From The Dawn of The Sex Revolution, 2002, Anger: How To Live With and Without It, 2003, Ask Albert Ellis, 2003, (with W. Dryden), Best Ellis, Life!, 2003. Fellow APA (pres. divsn. cons. psychology 1961-62, exec. com. divsn. psychotherapy 1969-73, coun. reps. 1963-64, 72-74), AAAS, Am. Assn. Marriage and Family Therapists (exec. com. 1957-59), Soc. Sci. Study Sex (exec. com. 1957-58, pres. 1958-60), Am. Orthopsychiat. Assn., Am. Sociol. Assn., Am. Assn. Applied Anthropology; mem. ACA, Am. Assn. Sex Educators, Counselors and Therapists (bd. dirs. 1981-82), Nat. Acad. Practice, Soc. Psychotherapy Rsch., N.Y. Assn. Clin. Psychologists in Pvt. Practice (chmn. 1952-54), N.Y. Joint Coun. Psychologists on Legislation (exec. com. 1951-53), Am. Group Psychotherapy Assn., Am. Acad. Psychotherapists (exec. com. 1954-64, v.p. 1962-64), Mensa, Am. Assn. Advancement Psychotherapy, N.Y. State Psychol. Assn., Soc. Exptl. and Clin. Hypnosis. Office: Albert Ellis Inst 45 E 65th St New York NY 10021-6508 E-mail: aiellis@aol.com. *I now see that I have given up any addiction to MUSTurbation many years ago—to thinking that I must do well; that others must treat me considerately or fairly; and that the world must provide me with the things I want easily and quickly. I now almost always think that it would be better or nicer if I did well, others treated me fairly, and the world proved easy and pleasant. But it doesn't have to turn out those ways—and that makes quite a difference!*

ELLIS, ALFRED WRIGHT (AL ELLIS), lawyer; b. Cleve., Aug. 26, 1943; s. Donald Porter and Louise (Wright) E.; m. Kay Genseke, June 1965 (div. 1976); 1 child, Joshua Kyle; m. Sandra Lee Fahey, Feb. 11, 1989. BA with honors, U. Tex., Arlington, 1965; JD, So. Meth. U., 1971. Bar: Tex., U.S. Dist. Ct. (no., so., ea. and we. dists.) Tex., U.S. Ct. Appeals (5th cir.), U.S. Supreme Ct.; cert. personal injury and civil trial lawyer, Best Lawyers in Am. 2003-04. Atty. Woodruff, Kendall & Smith, Dallas, 1972; ptnr. Woodruff & Ellis, Dallas; pvt. practice Dallas, 1983-96; of counsel Howie & Sweeney, 1996—2003, Sommerman, Moore, & Quesada, 2003—. Instr. So. Meth. U. Law Sch. Trial Advocacy; past pres. Law Focused Edn., Inc. Past mem. City of Dallas Urban Rehab. Standards Bd., Dallas Assembly, Salesmanship Club, Dallas; bd. dirs. Dallas Habitat for Humanity, 1998-2002; trustee Hist. Preservation League, 1992-94; tournament dir. Dallas Regional Golden Gloves Tournament, 1976-96; pres., bd. dirs. Dallas Coun. on Alcoholism, 1980. Capt. U.S. Army, 1965-69, Dallas All Sports Assn. (pres. 1980). Fellow Roscoe Pound Found.; named one of Outstanding Young Mem of Am., 1977, named Boss of Yr. Dallas Assn. Legal Secs., 1978; recipient Certs. of Recognition (8) D.I.S.D., 1971-83, Wall St. Jour. award So. Meth. U. Law Sch., 1972, Hayward McMurray award Dallas Jaycees, 1975-76, Spl. Recognition award All Sports Assn., 1977, Cert. of Appreciation for Exceptional and Disting. Vol. Svc. Gov. Mark White, 1983, Community Spirit award Dallas Bus. Jour., 1993, Disting. Svc. award Dallas All Sports Assn., 1993, award Nancy Garms Meml. for Outstanding Contr. to Law Focus Edn., 1996-, Leon Jaworski award, Al Ellis award Dallas Minority Bar Assn. 2002, D Mag., Best Lawyers in Dallas (personal injury) 2003. Fellow Tex. Bar Found. (sustaining life, Dan R. Price Meml. award 2003), Dallas Bar Found., Dallas Assn. Young Lawyers Found. (life); mem. ATLA, Internat. Acad. Trial Lawyers, Am. Bd. Trial Advocates (diplomate, sec.-treas. Dallas chpt. 1998, pres. 1999), Am. Coll. Legal Medicine (assoc.), Million Dollar Advocates Forum, Legal Svcs. of North Tex. (bd. dirs., Outstanding Svc. award 1990), State Bar Tex. (lectr. seminars, bd. dirs. 1991-94, Excellence in Diversity award 1994, Outstanding 3d Yr. Dir. award, Judge Sam Williams Local Bar Leadership award), Internat. Acad. Trial Lawyers, Dallas Bar Assn. (bd. dirs. 1978, chmn. bd. dirs. 1986, v.p. 1987-88, pres. 1990), Dallas Trial Lawyers Assn. (pres. 1977, Disting. Cmty. Svc. award 1990), Tex. Trial Lawyers Assn., Tex. Equal Access to Justice Found. (bd. dirs. 1994-96), Am. Coll. Barristers, Coll. State Bar of Tex. (bd. dirs. 1997-1999), Tex. Commn. Lawyer Discipline, Tex. Ctr. for Legal Ethics and Professionalism (bd. dirs. 1999—, chmn. 2002—), Tex. Legal Svcs. Ctr. (bd. dirs. 1999-2002), William Mac Taylor Inn of Ct. Avocations: tennis, skiing. Office: 3232 McKinney Ste 1160 Dallas TX 75204

ELLIS, ANDREW JACKSON, JR., lawyer; b. Ashland, Va., June 23, 1930; m. Dorothy L. Lichliter, Apr. 24, 1954; children: Elizabeth E. Attkisson, Andrew C., William D. BA, Washington and Lee U., 1951, LLB, 1953. Bar: Va. 1952. Ptnr. Campbell, Ellis & Campbell, Ashland, 1955-70, Mays, Valentine, Davenport & Moore, Richmond, Va., 1970-88, Mays & Valentine, Richmond, 1988-96, sr. counsel, 1998—2002, Troutman & Sanders, Richmond, 2002—. Substitute judge County of Hanover (Va.) Ct., 1955—63, 15th Jud. Dist., 1990—96; commr. chancery cir. ct. Hanover County, 1955—96; commonwealth atty., 1963—70; county atty., 1970—78; judge 15th Dist. Juvenile and Domestic Rels. Ct., 1996—98; capital adv. bd. NationsBank Va., 1960—93. Mem. Ashland Town Coun., 1956—63; mayor Town of Ashland, 1958—63; trustee J. Sargent Reynolds CC, 1972—80. 1st lt. U.S. Army, 1953—55. Fellow: Va. Law Found., Am. Coll. Trial Lawyers; mem.: S.R., Hanover Bar Assn. (past pres.), 15th Jud. Cir. Bar Assn. (past pres.), Richmond Bar Assn., Va. Trial Lawyers Assn., Va. State Bar (coun. 1968—74), Va. Bar Assn., Kiwanis. Episcopalian. Home: 15293 Old Ridge Rd Beaverdam VA 23015-1610 Office: PO Box 1122 Richmond VA 23218-1122

ELLIS, ANNE ELIZABETH, fundraiser; b. Orngestad, Aruba, Aug. 21, 1945; d. Thomas Albert and Anne Elizabeth (Belis) Wolfe; m. Earl Edward Ellis, Feb. 14, 1970. BS, La. State U., 1967. Fashion coord., Baton Rouge, 1962-67; textile researcher La. State U., Baton Rouge, 1965-67; buyer I.H. Rubensteins., Baton Rouge, 1967-68; fashion distbr. J.C. Penney, Inc., Arlington, Tex., 1969-70, asst. buyer Dallas, 1970-73; exec. dir. Nassau County Mus. Fine Art Assn., Roslyn, N.Y., 1985-88. Speaker C.W. Post U., Greenvale, N.Y., 1988—; cons. in field. Chmn., editor: (cookbook) Specialities of the House, 1981-83. Bd. dirs., com. chmn. Congregational Ch., Manhasset, N.Y., 1975-96; exec. v.p., bd. dirs., com. chmn. Jr. League Internat.; benefit gala chmn., com. chmn. Grenville Baker Boys & Girls Club, Locust Valley, N.Y., 1983-91; pres. bd., vice-chmn. cmty. outreach, benefit gala chmn. Tilles Performing Art Ctr. L.I. U., Greenvale, N.Y., 1985—; bd. dirs., benefit co-chmn. Nassau County Family Assn. Svcs., Hempstead, 1988-96; benefit vice-chnn. Glen Cove/North Shore Cmty. Hosp., 1989-93; mem. exec. bd., exec. v.p., trustee WLIW, L.I. Pub. TV, 1990-2001, chmn. bd. dirs., 1997-99; trustee Cmty. Found. of Oyster Bay, 1991-94; trustee Dowling Coll., Oakdale, N.Y., 1993-98, exec. bd., 1997-98; adv. bd. Westbury (N.Y.) Gardens, 1993-97; chmn. adv. bd. Long Island chpt. Save the Children, 1995-2001; trustee L.I. U., 1998—. Recipient Vol. of Yr. award Jr. League L.I., 1984, 85, Outstanding Vol. Svcs. and Commitment award County of Nassau, 1989, Juliette Low award Nassau County Girl Scouts, L.I., 1991, Disting. Leadership award, L.I., 1991, Outstanding Community Vol. award Jr. League of L.I., 1991-92, Disting. Svc. medal L.I. State Parks Found., 1999, Women of Achievement award Jr. League L.I., 2000. Mem. P.E.O. (pres. 1985-87), The Creek Inc., Meadowbrook Club Inc., Nat. Arts Club, Lost Tree Club, Forest Creek Club, Kappa Kappa Gamma (alumna pres. 1971-72). Republican. Congregationalist. Avocations: golf, gardening, needlepoint.

ELLIS, ANTHONY JOHN, education educator; b. Scunthorpe, Eng., June 15, 1945; came to U.S., 1990; s. Jack and Nancy Doreen (Read) E.; m. Maureen Anne Twomey, July 16, 1966 (div.); children: Katherine, Seonaid; m. Alice Anne Findlay, Sept. 4, 1980; 1 child, Bridget Anne. BA, Kings Coll., London, 1967, MA, 1968. From lectr. to sr. lectr., dept. chmn. U. St. Andrews, Scotland, 1971-90; prof. Va. Commonwealth U., Richmond, 1990—. Contbr. articles to profl. jours.; editor: Philosophical Books, 1985—. U. Wollongong fellow, Australia, 1989; recipient Fulbright Travel award, 1989. Mem. Am. Philos. Assn., Royal Inst. Philosophy, Aristotelian Soc. Avocation: music. Office: Va Commonwealth Univ PO Box 842025 Richmond VA 23284-2025

ELLIS, BARNES HUMPHREYS, lawyer; b. Boston, Jan. 21, 1940; s. Raymond Walleser and Eleanor (Gwin) E.; m. Beatrice Cleland, Aug. 25, 1962; children: Cynthia, Barnes, Mary, Joy, Heidi, Curtis. BA, Yale U., 1961; postgrad., Stanford U., 1962; LLB, Harvard U., 1964. Bar: Oreg. 1964, Wash. 1983, U.S. Dist. Ct. Oreg. 1964, U.S. Dist. Ct. (we. dist.) Wash. 1983, U.S. Ct. Appeals (1st cir.) 1968, U.S. Ct. Appeals (9th cir.) 1971, U.S. Supreme Ct. 1968. Assoc. Stoel, Rives, Boley, Jones & Grey, Portland, Oreg., 1964-70, ptnr., 19770—, White House fellow U.S. Dept. Justice, Washington, 1967-68. Chmn. Met. Pub. Defender Svcs. Inc., Portland, 1975-2000; chmn. Oreg. Commn. on Jud. Br., Salem, 1979-83; chmn. Oreg. Pub. Def. Svcs. Commn., 2000—. Fellow Am. Coll. Trial Lawyers; mem. ABA, Oreg. State Bar Assn., Wash. State Bar Assn., Multnomah Bar Assn. Republican. Home: 410 Bergis Rd Lake Oswego OR 97034-6250 Office: Stoel Rives LLP 900 SW 5th Ave Ste 2300 Portland OR 97204-1229 E-mail: bhellis@stoel.com.

ELLIS, BARTON DEE, music educator; b. Klamath Falls, Oreg., Mar. 28, 1960; s. Arnold Dee and Janice Ann Ellis. BS, Western Oreg. U., Monmouth, OR, 1982; MM, U. Idaho, Moscow, ID, 1987. Dir. bands Josephine County Sch. Dist., Cave Junction, Oreg., 1982—85; band dir. Kelso Sch. Dist., Kelso, Wash., 1987—88; music instr. Oreg. Inst. Tech., Klamath Falls, Oreg., 1988—90; dir. bands N Clackamus Sch. Dist., Milwaukie, Oreg., 1991—93, Bethel Sch. Dist., Eugene, Oreg., 1993—. Lutheran. Home: 1766 N Park Avenue Eugene OR 97404 E-mail: bellis@bethel.k12.or.us.

ELLIS, BERNICE, financial planning company executive, investment advisor; b. Bklyn. d. Samuel and Clara H.; m. Seymour Scott Ellis; children: Michele, Wayne. BA, Bklyn. Coll.; MS, Queens Coll., 1970. Cert. fin. planner, N.Y. 1987, elem. educator, N.Y.C. Elem. tchr. L.I. Sch. Dists., Merrick, N.Y.; tchr. reading N.Y.C. Bd. of Edn., Bklyn., 1972-73; coordinator Reading is Fundamental, Lawrence, N.Y., 1973-75; pres., founder N.Y. State Assn. for the Gifted and Talented, Valley Stream, N.Y., 1974-87; pres. Ellis Planning, Valley Stream, N.Y., 1984—. Cons. Nassau County Bd. Coop. Ednl. Svcs., Westbury, N.Y., 1973-74; adminstrv. intern region II U.S. Office Edn., 1977-78; adj. asst. prof. Nassau C.C., Garden City, N.Y., 1975-91, adj. assoc. prof., 1991-94, adj. full prof., 1995—; fin. commentator Money Talk radio program WHPC FM; arbitrator NASD, 1996. Contbr. articles to profl. jours and fin. newsletters. Mem. adv. com. Ams. for Ams. for Hope, Growth and Opportunity, 1998; mem. Nat. Rep. Party, Valley Stream Rep. Party, N.Y. State Rep. Party. Recipient Ednl. Professions Devel. Act fellow CUNY Inst. for Remediations Skills for Coll. Personnel, Queensborough Community Coll., 1970-73; named Business Person of Yr. by NRCC, 2003. Mem. AAUW (North Shore bd., chmn. Money Talk 1991—), Nat. Assn. Securities Dealers (arbitrator 1996), Nat. Alliance of Sales Execs., Inst. for CFPs, Inst. for CFPs of L.I. (bd. dirs.), Internat. Assn. Fin. Planners (legis. com. L.I. chpt. 1986-87), N.Y. State Reading Assn., Adj. Faculty Assn. Nassau C.C., L.I. C. of C., Rotary, Womens Nat. Republic Club. Avocations: reading, swimming. Office: Ellis Planning Inc 628 Golf Dr Valley Stream NY 11581-3594

ELLIS, BERNICE ALLRED, personnel executive; b. Lincoln, Ala., Mar. 15, 1932; d. Bernard Bobo and Lucille (Hogue) Allred; m. Marvin Leonard Ellis; 1 child, Jeffrey Craig Canada. Student, Ala. A&M U., 1990, U. Ala., Huntsville, 1990, Gadsden State C.C., Ala., 1993. Personnel staffing specialist Bd. of U.S. Civil Svc. Examiners, Anniston, Ala., 1957-66; personnel mgmt. specialist Dept. of Army, Anniston, 1966-73, tech. svcs. officer, 1973-74, personnel mgmt. specialist, 1974-79; supervisory personnel mgmt. specialist U.S. Army Europe, Mannheim, Fed. Republic of Germany, 1979-83, tech. svcs. officer Darmstadt, Fed. Republic of Germany, 1983-86; supervisory personnel mgmt. specialist Dept. of Army, Fort Ritchie, Md., 1986-87; ret., 1987; tax preparer H&R Block, Gadsden, Ala., 1994, 95. Tax preparer H&R Block, Gadsden, 1994-95, Etowah Chem., Gadsden, 1995-96. Vol. Huntsville Bot. Gardens, 1989-92; mem. local group Master Gardeners, Huntsville, 1990, Huntsville Wildflower Assn, 1990-92, State and Local Master Gardeners Assn., 1990-93. Mem. Huntsville Bot. Soc. (vol.), Ala. Master Gardeners Assn. (local and state vol.), Huntsville Wildflower Assn. Avocations: reading, square dancing, walking, bicycle riding, music. Home: 82 Ty Pl Ohatchee AL 36271-9231

ELLIS, BRADFORD GRAHAM, Spanish language educator, literature educator; b. Bellefonte, Pa., Jan. 20, 1968; s. William Grenville and Nancy Kempton Ellis; m. Diane Jean Mulroney, Sept. 18, 1994. BA, Bates Coll., 1990; MA, U. Wis., 1992, PhD, 2000. Teaching asst. U. Wis., Madison, 1990—96; asst. prof. Aquinas Coll., Grand Rapids, Mich., 1997—2002, St. Norbert Coll., De Pere, Wis., 2002—. Chair dept. modern & classical langs. Aquinas Coll., 2001—02. Mem.: AAUP, Cervantes Soc. Am., Midwest Modern Lang. Assn., Modern Lang. Assn. Am. Office: St Norbert Coll 100 Grant St De Pere WI 54115 Fax: 920-403-4086. E-mail: brad.ellis@snc.edu.

ELLIS, CAROLYN TERRY, lawyer; b. N.Y.C., Apr. 20, 1949; D. Francis Martin and Sarah Baker (Ames) E. m. H. Lake Wise, Feb. 27, 1982; children: Carolyn Campbell Wise, Burke Ames. BA, U. Chgo., 1971; JD, NYU, 1974. Bar: N.Y. 1975. Rsch. analyst Dept. Justice, N.Y.C., 1973-74; from assoc. to ptnr. Lord, Day & Lord, N.Y.C., 1974-86; ptnr. Coudert Bros., N.Y.C., 1986-98; pres., gen. counsel Bklyn. (N.Y.) Cmty. Housing & Svcs., Inc., 1998—2003; asst. atty. gen. Charities Bur. N.Y. State Office Atty. Gen., 2003—. Instr. Bklyn. Law Sch., 1980-82. Mem. Assn. of Bar of City of N.Y. (antitrust and trade regulation com. 1989-92, internat. trade com. 1993-95).

ELLIS, CHARLES NORMAN, professor, researcher; b. Mich. MD, U. Mich., 1977. Diplomate Am. Bd. of Dermatology. Prof., assoc. chair dept.f dermatology U. Mich. Med. Sch., Ann Arbor, 1981—. Cons. Pharm. Industry, 1985—. Contbr. articles to profl. jours. Office: U Mich Med Sch 1910 Taubman Ctr Ann Arbor MI 48109-0314

ELLIS, CLAUD M. BUDDY, diversified financial services company executive; b. Oklahoma City, July 2, 1950; s. Charles and Cloal Marie (Shirley) E.; 1 child, Carla Mohler. BA in Polit. Sci. and Mktg., Columbia U., 1970; MBA in Internat. Banking and Econs., London Sch. Econs., 1972. Dir. govt. rels. and pub. policy Aero Comdr. divsn. Rockwell Internat. Corp., Seal Beach, Calif., 1973-83; White Ho. fellow V.P. George Bush, Washington, 1984-85; pres., CEO Banco Resources Ltd., London, 1985—. Office: Banco Resources Ltd 18 Trafalgar St London England Home: PO Box 721658 Oklahoma City OK 73172-1658 E-mail: bancor@swbell.com.

ELLIS, COURTENAY, lawyer; b. Cottingham, Eng., Jan. 4, 1946; came to the U.S., 1970; BA, Oxford U., Eng., 1967, MA, 1974; LLM, George Washington U., 1972. Bar: D.C. 1973; cert. solicitor, Eng. Solicitor's articled clk. Field, Fisher & Co., London, 1968-69; solicitor Farrer & Co., London, 1970; assoc. atty. Covington & Burling, Washington, 1972-76, Akin, Gump, Strauss, Hauer & Feld, 1976-78, ptnr., 1979-98, Oppenheimer Wolff Donnelly Bayh, Washington, 1998-99, Murphy Ellis Weber, 2000—. Bd. dirs. The Episcopal Ctr. for Children, Washington, 1986-92. Mem. ABA, Law Soc. London, Brit. Am. Bus. Assn. (bd. dirs., program chair 1997-98, pres. 1999-2001), Washington Fgn. Law Soc. (bd. govs., membership coord. 1993-95, program coord. 1995-96, pres. 1997-98), Fed. Bar Assn. (internat. law sect., chair 1996-98), Globalscot, The Law Soc., London, Met. Club, Annapolis Yacht Club. Office: Murphy Ellis Weber Ste 1200 818 Connecticut Ave NW Washington DC 20006 E-mail: cellis@murphyellisweber.com.

ELLIS, CYNTHIA BUEKER, musician, educator; b. Santa Monica, Calif., Dec. 3, 1958; d. Robert Arthur and Patricia June Bueker; m. Tony Lyle Ellis, June 18, 1983. B Music, Calif. State U., 1981, M Music, 1983. 2nd flutist Pasadena (Calif.) Chamber Orch., 1981—84; piccoloist Pacific Symphony Orch., Santa Ana, Calif., 1979—; prin. flutist Opera Pacific Orch., Costa Mesa, Calif., 1995—; lectr. Calif. State U., Fullerton, 1985—; applied flute instr. Pomona Coll., Claremont, Calif., 1990—92. Adj. faculty Claremont Grad. Sch., 1996—97; mem. faculty Pacific Symphony Inst., 1993—; flute instr. Pomona Coll., 1990—92. Contbr. articles to profl. jours.; musician: (songs) (for motion pictures) Twilight, 1998, Kissing a Fool, 1998, Pentagon Wars, 1998, She's So Lovely, 1997, First Time Felon, 1997, Campfire Tales, 1996, Breaking Commandments, 1996, Baby's Day Out, 1994, Pochahontas, 1994, Stayed Tuned, 1992, Wind, 1992; numerous others. Family coord. Southern Calif. Labrador Retriever Rescue, 1999—. Mem.: Music Tchrs. Assn. Calif., Nat. Flute Assn. (chamber music competition 1st place award 2000), Mu Phi Epsilon, Phi Kappa Phi, Pi Kappa Lambda. Republican. Methodist. Avocations: fitness, cooking. Home: 1192 Beechwood Dr Brea CA 92821

ELLIS, DAVID DALE, lawyer; b. Columbus, Ga., Dec. 22, 1952; s. Audie Stammattee and Eva Grace (Thomas) E. BA cum laude Mercer U., Macon, Ga., 1974; JD, Drake U., 1976, MPA, 1977. Bar: Iowa 1977, Ga. 1978, U.S. Dist. Ct. (no. dist.) Ga. 1979, U.S. Ct. Appeals (11th cir.) 1979, U.S. Supreme Ct. 1983, U.S. Dist. Ct. (so. dist.) 1985, Tex. 1986. Instr. Grad. Sch., Drake U., Des Moines, 1977; claims adjuster Farm Bur. Ins. Co., Des Moines, 1977; assoc. firm Cotton, White & Palmer, Atlanta, 1978-82; mng. atty. Hyatt Legal Svcs., Marietta and Smyrna, Ga., 1982-84, regional ptnr., Houston, 1984-86; sr. ptnr. Hughes & Hilbert P.C., 1986-87; sr. ptnr. Jeffers & Ellis, P.C., Houston, 1987-88; pvt. practice, 1988—. Contbr. articles to profl. jours. Career awareness chmn. Houston coun. Boy Scouts Am., 1984-85; instr. project bus., legal advisor Jr. Achievement, Houston, 1984-85; mem. Houston Bankruptcy Conf. Mem. Iowa Bar Assn., Ga. Bar Assn., State Bar Tex., Am. Soc. Tng. and Devel., Atlanta Jaycees (chmn. Empty Stockings Fund 1982, v.p. individual devel. 1983-84; Officer of Yr. 1984), U.S. Jaycees (life, ambassador award 1985, named JCI senator), Houston Jaycees (exec. v.p. 1986—, chmn. govt. affairs 1984-85, pres. 1987—), Tex. Jaycees (legal counsel 1985-87), ABA (chmn. bankruptcy com. 1985-87, co-chmn. 1987, chmn. 1987—), Atlanta Bar Assn., Houston Bar Assn., Houston Young Lawyers Assn., Tex. Young Lawyers Assn., Assn. Trial Lawyers of Am., Ga. Trial Lawyers Assn., Fed. Bar Assn., Masons. Office: PO Box 130447 Houston TX 77219-0447

ELLIS, DAVID WERTZ, retired museum director; b. Huntingdon, Pa., Feb. 8, 1936; s. Calvert Nice and Elizabeth Oller (Wertz) E.; m. Marion Elizabeth Schmitt, June 24, 1961; children: Kathryn Dana, Lorna Beth, Audrey Heather. BA with honors in Chemistry, Haverford Coll., 1958; PhD in Chemistry, MIT, 1962; LLD (hon.), Lehigh U., 1979, Lafayette Coll., 1990; DSc (hon.), Susquehanna U., 1982, Ursinus Coll., 1985; LHD (hon.), Juniata Coll., 1989; DCL (hon.), U. of the South, 2000; DSc (hon.), Northeastern U., 2002. Asst. prof. chemistry U. N.H., 1962-67, assoc. prof., 1967-78, acting asst. dean Grad. Sch., 1967, asst. dean Coll. of Tech., 1968, assoc. acad. v.p., 1968-71, vice provost, v.p. acad. affairs, 1971-78; pres. Lafayette Coll., Easton, Pa., 1978-90; pres., dir. Mus. of Sci., Boston, 1990—2002, pres. emeritus, 2003—. Mem. Adv. Com. for The Directorate on Edn. and Human Resources, NSF, 1998-2001, chmn., 2000-01. Author: (with others) Calculations of Analytical Chemistry, 7th edit., 1971; contbr. articles to profl. jours. Bd. dirs. Giant Screen Theater Assn., 1992-94, 96-98, chmn. mktg. com., 1992-94, mem. liaison com., 1994-98, chmn. liaison com., 1996-98; bd. dirs. Assn. Sci. Tech. Ctrs., 1992-93, 95—2002, v.p., 1997-99; convener Nat. Health Scis. Consortium, 1994-96, bd. dirs. Sci. Mus. Exhibits Collaborative, 1990—2002, sec.-treas., 1992-93, chmn., 1993-95; bd. dirs. Elderhostel, 1983-87, 89-2000, chmn., 1990-95, 96-2000; bd. dirs. Mus. Film Network, 1990—2002, chmn., 1993-97; bd. dirs. Sta. WGBH, pub. broadcasting, 1990-2000, mem. exec. com., 1992-2000, chmn. audit com., 1993-2000, mem. tech. com., 2000—; mem. bd. overseers Tufts U., Colls. of Arts and Sci., 1995-2001; bd. dirs. U. N.H. Found., 1997—, vice chmn., 1999-2002; mem. Am. Coun. on Edn. commn. on leadership devel., 1988-90; mem. bd. visitors U. Maine, Machias, 2001—; bd. advisors Whitehead Inst., 1996—, Flaschner Inst., 2000—, Rappaport Inst., 2001—, Lemelson Ctr., 2003--, Smithsonian Instn., 2003--. Dupont fellow, 1960-61. Fellow: The Boston Found. (sr.); mem. AAAS, Am. Chem. Soc., Am. Assn. Mus., Assn. Sci. Mus. Dirs., Nat. Assn. Ind. Colls. and Univs. (vice chmn. 1987-88, chmn. 1988-89), The Mus. Group, Harvard Club. Mem. United Ch. of Christ. Home: Thomas Graves' Landing 6 Canal Park # 710 Cambridge MA 02141-2211

ELLIS, DONALD LEE, lawyer; b. Oct. 2, 1950; s. Truett T. and Rosemary (Tarrant) Ellis; children: Angela Nicole, Laura Elizabeth, Natalie Dawn, Donald Lee II. BS, U. Tulsa, 1973; JD, Okla. City U., 1976. Bar: Tex. 1979, Okla. 1977, U.S. Dist. Ct. (ea. dist.) Tex. 1978, U.S. Dist. Ct. (we. dist.) Okla. 1978, U.S. Ct. Appeals (5th cir.) 1984, U.S. Ct. Appeals (11th cir.), U.S. Supreme Ct. 1984. Spl. agt. FBI, Washington, 1976—78; asst. dist. atty. Smith County, Tyler, Tex., 1979—80; mem. firm Barron & Ellis, Tyler, 1980—85; pvt. practice, 1985—. Bd. dir. Mental Health Assn. Mem.: Lawyers-Pilot Bar Assn., FBI Agents Assn., Tex. Trial Lawyers Assn., Soc. Former Spl. Agts. FBI, Smith County Bar Assn., Okla. Bar Assn., Tex. Bar Assn., Assn. Trial Lawyers Am. Home: PO Box 131221 Tyler TX 75713-1221 Office: 217 W Houston St Tyler TX 75702-8137

ELLIS, DORSEY DANIEL, JR., lawyer, educator; b. Cape Girardeau, Mo., May 18, 1938; s. Dorsey D. and Anne (Stanaland) E.; m. Sondra Wagner, Dec. 27, 1962; children: Laura Elizabeth, Geoffrey Earl. BA, Maryville Coll., 1960; JD, U. Chgo., 1963; LLD, Maryville Coll., 1998. Bar: N.Y. 1967, U.S. Ct. Appeals (2d cir.) 1967, Iowa 1976, U.S. Ct. Appeals (8th cir.) 1976. Assoc. Cravath, Swaine & Moore, N.Y.C., 1963-68; assoc. prof. U. Iowa, Iowa City, 1968-71, prof., 1971-87, v.p. fin. and univ. svcs., 1984-87, spl. asst. to pres., 1974-75; dean Washington U. Sch. Law, St. Louis, Mo., 1987-98, prof. law, 1998-99; disting. prof. law, 1999—. Vis. mem. sr. common room Mansfield Coll., Oxford U., Eng., 1972-73, 75; vis. prof. law Emory U., Atlanta, 1981-82, Victoria U., New Zealand, 1999; vis. sr. rsch. fellow Jesus Coll. Oxford U., Eng., 1998; bd. dirs. Maryville Coll., 1989-98, 99—, vis. scholar U. Va., 2003. Contbr. articles to profl. jours. Trustee Mo. Hist. Soc., St. Louis, 1995-2000. Nat. Honor scholar U. Chgo., 1960-63; recipient Joseph Henry Beale prize, 1961, Alumni award Maryville Coll., 1988. Mem. ABA, Am. Law Inst., Bar Assn. Metro St. Louis, Mound City Bar Assn., Iowa Bar Assn., AALS Acad. Resource Corps., Order of Coif. Home: 6901 Kingsbury Blvd Saint Louis MO 63130 Office: Box 1120 1 Brookings Dr Saint Louis MO 63130-4862 E-mail: ellis@wulaw.wustl.edu.

ELLIS, EDWARD R. career officer; BS in Bus. Mgmt., Va. Polytechnic Inst. and State U., 1968; MA in Bus. Stats., U. Ala., 1970; grad., Squadron Officer Sch., 1975, Air Command and Staff Coll., 1984, Air War Coll., 1986, Nat. War Coll., 1991. Commd. 2d lt. USAF, 1971, advanced through grades to brig. gen., 1998; instr. pilot then flight examiner 29th Flying Tng. Wing, Craig AFB, Ala., 1973-77; F-4E pilot, asst. flight comdr. 18th Tactical Fighter Squadron, Elmendorf AFB, Alaska, 1977-80; sect. comdr., ops. officer for dir. student ops. Squadron Officer Sch., Maxwell AFB, Ala., 1980-83, exec. officer to comdt., 1980-83; F-4E pilot, asst. ops. officer then ops. officer 36th Tactical Fighter Squadron, Osan Air Base, S. Korea, 1984-86; exec. officer to comdr. 51st Tactical Fighter Wing, Osan Air Base, 1984-86; faculty instr., comdr. 3823rd Air Command and Staff Coll. Student Squadron, Maxwell AFB, 1986-88; comdr. 35th Flying Tng. Squadron, Reese AFB, Tex., 1988-90; chief Caribbean Basin br. then chief We. Hemisphere div. Strategic Plans and Policy, Joint Staff, Pentagon, Washington, 1991-94; chief flying tng. div. Hdqs. Air Edn. and Tng. Command, Randolph AFB, Tex., 1994-95; comdr. 71st Flying Tng. Wing, Vance AFB, Okla., 1995-97; comdt. Squadron Officer Sch., Maxwell AFB, 1997; comdr. Air Force Accession and Tng. Schs., Maxwell AFB, 1997-99; dep. comdr. 5th Allied Tactical Air Force, Vicenza, Italy, 1999, Combined Air Ops. Ctr. Seven, Larissa, Greece, 2000—. Decorated Legion of Merit.

ELLIS, ELDON EUGENE, surgeon; b. Washington, Ind., July 2, 1922; s. Osman Polson and Ina Lucretia (Cochran) E.; m. Irene Clay, June 26, 1948 (dec. 1968); m. Priscilla Dean Strong, Sept. 20, 1969 (dec. Feb. 1990); children: Paul Addison, Kathe Lynn, Jonathan Clay, Sharon Anne, Eldon Eugene, Rebecca Deborah; m. Virginia Michael Ellis, Aug. 22, 1992. BA, U. Rochester, 1946, MD, 1949. Intern in surgery Stanford U. Hosp., San Francisco, 1949-50, resident and fellow in surgery, 1950-52, 55; Schilling fellow in pathology San Francisco Gen. Hosp., 1955; ptnr. Redwood Med. Clinic, Redwood City, Calif., 1955-87, med. dir., 1984-87; semi-ret. physician, 1987—; med. dir. Peninsula Occupl. Health Assocs., San Carlos, Calif., 1991-94, physician, 1995-99, Sequoia Med. Clinic, Redwood City, Calif., 1999—. Asst. clin. prof. surgery Stanford U., 1970-80; dir. Sequoia Hosp., Redwood City, 1974-82. Pres.

Sequoia Hosp. Found., 1983-92, bd. dirs.; pres., chmn. bd. dirs. Bay Chamber Symphony Orch., San Mateo, Calif., 1988-91; mem. Nat. Bd. Benevolence Evang. Covenant Ch., Chgo., 1988-93; mem. mgmt. com. The Samarkand Retirement Cmty., Santa Barbara, Calif., 1991-2000; past pres. Project Hope Nat. Alumni Assn., 1992-94, bd. dirs., 1994—; med. advisor Project Hope, Russia Commonwealth Ind. States, 1992. With USNR, 1942-46, 50-52. Named Outstanding Citizen of Yr., Redwood City, 1987. Mem.: AMA, Calif. Thoracic Soc., Cardiovasc. Coun., San Mateo Individual Practice Assn. (treas. 1984—97), Stanford Surg. Soc., San Mateo Surg. Soc., San Mateo County Comprehensive Health Planning Coun. (v.p. 1969—70), San Mateo Med. Soc. (pres. 1969—70), San Mateo County Heart Assn. (pres. 1961—63), Calif. Heart Assn. (pres. 1965—66), Am. Heart Assn. (v.p. 1974—75), Am. Coll. Chest Physicians, Calif. Med. Assn. Republican. Mem. Peninsula Convenant Ch. Home: 2305 Wooster Ave Belmont CA 94002-1549 Office: Sequoia Med Clinic 633 Veterans Blvd Redwood City CA 94063-1408 E-mail: eldonellis@hotmail.com.

ELLIS, ELLA THORP, writer, retired educator; b. L.A., July 14, 1928; d. William Dunham and Marian (Yates) Thorp; m. Leo Herbert Ellis, Dec. 17, 1949; children: Steven, David, Patrick. Student, U. Cordoba, Argentina, 1961-62; BA in English and History, UCLA, 1966; MA in English and Writing, San Francisco State U., 1975. Instr. creative writing U. Calif. Ext., Berkeley, 1972-77, lectr., instr. fiction, 1986-94; lectr. creative writing San Francisco State U., 1975-80; lectr. lit. Univ. Women Internat., Buenos Aires, 1981-85. Author: (novels) Roam the Wild Country, 1967, Riptide, 1969, Celebrate the Morning, 1972, Where the Road Ends, 1974, Hallelujah, 1976, Sleepwalker's Moon, 1980, Hugo and the Princess Nena, 1983, Swimming with the Whales, 1995, The Year of My Indian Prince, 2001, also fgn. and paperback edits. Recipient 6 Am. Libr. Honor Book awards, 1 Jr. Lit. Guild Book of Month award, also state awards. Mem. Authors Guild, Soc. Childrens Book Writers, Soc. Woman Geographers, Opera Guild, Sierra Club, Amnesty Internat. Democrat. Episcopalian. Avocations: travel, gardening, opera, reading. Home: 1438 Grizzly Peak Blvd Berkeley CA 94708-2202

ELLIS, ELMO ISRAEL, broadcast executive, consultant, columnist; b. Birmingham, Ala., Nov. 11, 1910; s. Samuel B. and Bertha F. (Seletz) Israel; m. Ruth M. Ballinger, Dec. 26, 1944; children: Janet Faye, William Bryan. AB, U. Ala., 1940; MA, Emory U., 1948; postgrad., Am. Mgmt. Assn., 1959, Emory U., 1965; LittD (hon.), Oglethorpe U., 1995. Dir. publicity, prodn. mgr. Sta. WSB-AM-FM, Atlanta, 1940-42; writer, prodr. "We The People" and other network radio programs CBS, 1946-47; prodn. mgr. Sta. WSB-TV, 1948-52; instr., radio-tv Emory U., 1948—52, Ga. State U., 1956—60; mgr. programming Sta. WSB-AM-FM, 1952-63, v.p., gen. mgr., 1963—; v.p. Cox Broadcasting Corp., 1969-82. Former chmn. Radio Advt. Bur.; syndicated radio commentator Jacor Communications, Inc., 1982-87; syndicated columnist Neighbor newspapers, 1982—; former chmn. NAFMB, NBC Radio Affiliates, Radio Code Bd. Nat. Assn. Broadcasters; former instr. in radio-TV Emory U., Ga. State U.; lectr. Oglethorpe U., bd. trustees, 1975—; bd. visitors Coll. Comm., U. Ala., 1997; mem. journalism adv. bd. Emory U., 1997—; pres. Elmo Ellis Prodns., 1982—. Co-author: Radio Station Management, 1960; author: Sleepy Hollow Poems, 1942, Removing the Rust from Radio, 1954, Happiness is Worth the Effort, 1970, Opportunities in Broadcasting Careers, 1986, 5th edit., 1999, The Youthful Option, 1997, The Phoenix-Civil War Centennial Pageant, 1961, Power of the South and other comml. films, articles, poems, TV and radio commercials; contbg. author: Diagnosis and Prognosis in Journalism, 1962, A Forward Look for Communications, 1967, Business and the Media, 1979. Pres. Ga. Safety Coun., 1981-82; past chmn. S.E. regional adv. bd. Anti-Defamation League, B'nai B'rith, hon. life mem. nat. adv. commn., 1983; chmn. Atlanta Christmas Seals Drive, 1977, 78; asst. to dir. Dem. Nat. Convs., 1952, 56, 60, 64; bd. dirs. Atlanta Landmarks, Inc.; chmn. Friends of the Libraries, Emory U., 1985-90; past mem. exec. com., bd. dirs. Peach Bowl; founder Elmo Ellis Profl.-in-Residence Fund U. Ala., 1987; former trustee, mem. adv. bd. Multiple Sclerosis Soc., Ga., Ga. State . Coll. Bus. Adminstrn.; bd. visitors Emory U., Clark Coll. Comms. Dept., Ctr. for Holocaust Studies, Washington, Girl Scouts Greater Atlanta, Boy Scouts Metro Atlanta, Am. Jewish Com., Ga., Consumer Credit Svcs., Ga. Coun. on Child Abuse, Gerontology Ctr. Ga. State U., Jr. Achievement Greater Atlanta. Capt. USAAF, 1942-46. Recipient Ga. Libr. Assn. award, 1965, Silver Medal award Atlanta Advt. Club, 1965, Peabody awards, 1954, 66, Alfred P. Sloan award, 1966, Sch. Bell award Ga. Edn. Assn., 1967, Citizen of Yr. award Ga. Assn. Broadcasters, 1965, Southeastern Father of Yr. award, 1978, Natl. Media Cancer Awd., 1976, Thomas Alva Edison award, 1966, Red Cross Disting. Svc. award, 1968, 25 yr. Svc. Awd., 1967, Big Drop Awd., 1979, Abraham Lincoln awards So. Bapt. Radio-TV Commn., 1972, 77, Silver Beaver award Boy Scouts Am., 1972, Pioneer Broadcaster Ga. award Phi Gamma Kappa, 1972, Meritorious Svc. award Am. Heart Assn., 1970, Disting. Alumnus award U. Ala., 1971, Gavin Disting. Broadcaster award, 1971, 72, 84, Disting. Svc. award Nat. Safety and Gas Safety Coun., 1973, 79, George Washington Honor medals and Disting. Svc. awards Freedom's Found., 1973-99, Abe Goldstein award Anti-Defamation League, 1975, Gold Boot award March of Dimes, 1975, George Erwin award Ga. Assn. Realtors, 1975, 76, 77, 78, Humanitarian award Nat. Jewish Hosp., 1979, Mass Media award Protestant Radio-TV Ctr., 1981, Emory Univ., Disting. Svc. award, 1985, 2001, Nat. Bronze award Jr. Achievement, 1985; 1st appointee to Atlanta chpt. U. Ala. Hall of Fame, 1987; named one of Atlanta's Leaders of Tomorrow Time mag. 1951; Disting. Svc. award Arthritis Found., 1966, news and editl. awards AP, UPI, SDX; U.S. Presdl. Commendation, 1970, Heroes, Saints and Legends award Wesley Woods Found., 1995; Ga. Music Hall of Fame, 1995, U. Ala. Coll. of Comm., Hall of Fame, 1999; Georgian of the Century award, Ga. Trend Mag., 2000; named lt. col. Aide-de-Camp Gov.'s Staff State of Ga., 1990, Hugo Black Award, U. of Alabama, 2000. Mem. NARAS (Hall of Fame elections com. 1987-95), Broadcast Pioneers, Internat. Radio-TV Soc., Ga. Assn. Broadcasters (bd. dirs., past pres., Hall of Fame 1987), Am. Values Inc. (nat. adv. bd. 1987—), Soc. Profl. Journalists (past pres., Ralph McGill award 1993), U. Ala. Alumni Assn. (Disting. Alumnus award 1993), Commerce Club, Phi Beta Kappa, Phi Eta Sigma, Tau Kappa Alpha, Omicron Delta Kappa. Home: 6345 Aberdeen Dr NE Atlanta GA 30328-4208 Office: Elmo Ellis Prodns 6345 Aberdeen Dr NE Atlanta GA 30328 *Just look around at the unfinished work of the world, and you can see our reason for being.*

ELLIS, EMORY LEON, former biochemist; b. Grayville, Ill., Oct. 29, 1906; s. Walter Leon and Bertha May (Forman) W.; m. Marion Louise Faulkner, Sept. 17, 1930 (dec. Aug. 1994). BS, Calif. Inst. Tech., 1930, MS in Chemistry, 1932, PhD in Biochemistry, 1934. Registered profl. engr., Calif. Chemist U.S. FDA, L.A., 1934-35; rsch. assoc. CalTech, Pasadena, 1935-43; dept. head U.S. Navy Ordnance Test Sta., China Lake, Calif., 1943-54; dir. ordnance plan Rheem Ordnance Lab, Downey, Calif., 1954-57; project leader Inst. for Def. Analysis, Washington, 1957-63; cons. U.S. Navy Weapons Ctr., China Lake, 1966-68. Ptnr. Devcom, La Habra, Calif., 1965-68. Contbr. chpt. in books and articles to profl. jours. Recipient Naval Ordnance Devel. award USN, 1945, Alumni Disting. Svc. award Calif. Inst. Tech., 1970; Paul Harris fellow Rotary Internat., 1993. Mem. AAAS, Am. Chem. Soc., Tau Beta Pi, Sigma Xi. Avocations: writing essays, travel. Home: 1405 E Main St # 407 Santa Maria CA 93454

ELLIS, EUGENE JOSEPH, cardiologist; b. Rochester, N.Y., Feb. 23, 1919; s. Eugene Joseph and Violet (Anderson) E.; m. Ruth Nugent, July 31, 1943; children: Eugene J., Susan Ellis Renwick, Amy Ellis Miller. AB, U. So. Calif., L.A., 1941; MD, U. So. Calif., 1944; MS in medicine, U. Minn., 1950. Diplomate Am. Bd. Internal Medicine and Cardiovascular Diseases. Intern L.A. County Hosp., 1944, resident, 1946; fellowship Mayo Clinic, Rochester, Minn., 1947-51; dir. dept. cardiology St. Vincent's Hosp., L.A., 1953-55, Good Samaritan Hosp., L.A., 1955-84, ret., 1984; prof. emeritus medicine U. So. Calif., 1984—. Mem. Med. Bd. of Calif., 1984-91; pres., 1988; pres. Div. of Med. Quality, State of Calif., 1985-89; exec. com. trustees U. Redlands, 1976-86. Lt. USN, 1944-46. Contbr. articles to profl. jours. Bd. dirs. Cancer Found. Santa Barbara, Casa Dorinda Retirement Facility, Alcohol Coun. Santa Barbara; trustee Sansum-Santa Barbara Clinic, 2002-, Santa Barbara Mus. Natural History. Lt. USN, 1944-46. Mem. L.A. Country Club, Birnam Wood Golf Club (bd. dirs. 1994-95), Valley Club of Montecito. Republican. Avocations: golf, fly fishing. Home: 450 Eastgate Ln Santa Barbara CA 93108-2248

ELLIS, F. HENRY, JR., surgeon, educator; b. Washington, Sept. 20, 1920; s. Franklin Henry and Katherine (McClintock) E.; m. Mary Jane Walsh, Dec. 2, 1978; children: Katherine de Saulles (Mrs. Robert Manoff), Elizabeth Dunston (Mrs. Joseph Browning), Franklin Henry III, Margot McClintock, Laura Lawson (Mrs. David Milliken), Marie-Armide Longer (Mrs. Charles Storey), Hedrick Watson, Michael Garrison. AB, Yale U., 1941; MD, Columbia U., 1944; PhD, U. Minn., 1951. Diplomate: Am. Bd. Surgery, Am. Bd. Thoracic Surgery. Intern Bellevue Hosp., N.Y.C., 1944-45; fellow surgery Mayo Clinic, 1945-46, 48-52, fellow thoracic surgery, 1952-53, asst. to surg. staff, 1952-53, cons. surgery, 1953-70; mem. faculty Mayo Grad. Sch. Medicine, 1952-70, prof. surgery, 1964-70, chmn. thoracic surg. sect., 1966-70; chief cardiovascular surgery Lahey Clinic Found., Boston, 1970-75; chief thoracic and cardiovascular surgery Lahey Clinic Med. Ctr., 1975-86, sr. cons., 1986-90; chmn. dept. thoracic and cardiovascular surgery New Eng. Deaconess Hosp., Boston, 1971-90; lectr. surgery Harvard Med. Sch., 1970-74, asso. clin. prof. surgery, 1974-80, clin. prof. surgery, 1980-91, prof. emeritus, 1991—. Served with USNR, 1946-48. Mem. AMA (Billings Gold medal 1955), ACS, Am. Assn. Thoracic Surgery, Internat. Soc. Surgery, Boston Surg. Soc. (pres. 1985-86), New Eng. Surg. Soc., Soc. Clin. Surgery, Soc. Vascular Surgery (pres. 1971), Soc. Thoracic Surgeons (pres. 1977), Assn. Cardiothoracic Surgeons Gt. Britain and Ireland (hon.), Am. Surg. Assn., European Assn. Cardiothoracic Surgery, European Soc. Thoracic Surgeons (corr.), Internat. Soc. Diseases of Esophagus (hon.). Home: 21 Fairmount St Brookline MA 02445-5905 Office: BI-Deaconess Med Ctr 110 Francis St Ste 2A Boston MA 02215-5501 Fax: 617-632-7562.

ELLIS, FRANK HALE, English literature educator; b. Chgo., Jan. 18, 1916; s. Frank Hale and Gay (Shepherd) E.; m. Constance Dimock, Dec. 20, 1940; 1 dau., Gay. BS with honors, Northwestern U., 1939; PhD, Yale U., 1948. Mem. faculty U. Buffalo, 1941-42; mem. faculty Yale U., 1945-51; with Dept. State, Washington, 1951-54; mem. faculty Smith Coll., 1958-86, Mary Augusta Jordan prof. English lit., 1974-86. Author: Swift's Discourse, 1967, Twentieth Century Interpretations of Robinson Crusoe, 1969, Poems on Affairs of State, 1697-1714, 2 vols., 1970, 75, Swift vs. Mainwaring, 1985, Sentimental Comedy: Theory and Practice, 1991, John Wilmot Earl of Rochester: The Complete Works, 1994, The ABC of Criticism, 2003; contbr. articles to profl. jours. and Oxford New Dictionary of Nat. Biography. Served with AUS, 1942-45, ETO and PTO. Decorated Bronze Star; Morse fellow, 1950-51; Huntington Library fellow, 1975 Mem. Cum Laude Soc., Conn. Acad. Arts and Scis., Phi Beta Kappa. Clubs: Elizabethan, Lawn (New Haven). Home: 64 Gothic St # 201 Northampton MA 01060-3042

ELLIS, FRANK RUSSELL, retired pathologist; b. Celina, Ohio, Oct. 19, 1915; s. Frank Luzerne and Elsie Wickersham Ellis; m. Gertrude Klaver, June 21, 1941; children: Kevin R., Merrie E. Brownson, Thomas K., Brian J. MD, U. Mich., 1943. Diplomate in anatomic, clin. and blood banking Am. Bd. Pathology. Intern Henry Ford Hosp., Detroit, 1943-44; resident in pathology VA Hosp., Salt Lake City, 1946-47, Salt Lake County Hosp., 1947-48; rsch. fellow U. Wash., Seattle, 1949-50; pvt. practice pathology Wenatchee, Wash., 1950-52; pathologist DePaul Hosp., Cheyenne, Wyo., 1952-54; clin. pathologist Wayne County Gen. Hosp., Eloise, Mich., 1954-67; dir. blood svc. S.E. Mich. Red Cross, Detroit, 1965-72, St. Louis Red Cross, 1976-89; assoc. med. dir. blood svc. ARC, Washington, 1973-76; ret., 1989. Co-author/contbr.: Transfusion Therapy, 1985, Director of Memorials Honoring the 70th Infantry Division, 1999. Col. Med. Corps U.S. Army, 1939-69, ETO. Fellow Am. Soc. Clin. Pathologists; mem. AMA, Am. Assn. Blood Banks, 70th Inf. Divsn. Assn. (v.p. west region 1998-2002). Avocations: antique automobiles, preservation of military artifacts and history. Home: 6716 E Clinton St Scottsdale AZ 85254-5254

ELLIS, GEOFFREY ERNEST, landscape architect; b. Feb. 24, 1967; BA, U. Utah, 1990; MLA, Utah State U., 1996. Owner Oakcrest Design, Ogden, Utah, 1996—; exec. dir. Weber Pathways, Ogden, 1999—. Home: 763 1st Ave Salt Lake City UT 84103 Office: PO Box 972 Ogden UT 84402-0972 E-mail: gellis@xmission.com.

ELLIS, GEORGE EDWIN, JR., chemical engineer; b. Beaumont, Tex., Apr. 14, 1921; s. George Edwin and Julia (Ryan) E. BSChemE, U. Tex., 1948; MS, U. So. Calif., 1958, MBA, 1965, MS in Mech. Engring., 1968, MS in Mgmt. Sci., 1971, Engr. in Indsl. and Systems Engring., 1979. Rsch. chem. engr. Tex. Co., Port Arthur, 1948-51, Houston and Long Beach, Calif., 1952-53, Space and Info. Divsn., N.Am. Aviation Co., Downey, Calif., 1959-61, Magna Corp., Anaheim, Calif., 1961-62; chem. process engr. AiResearch Mfg. Co., L.A., 1953-57, 57-59; chem. engr. Petroleum Combustion & Engring. Co., Santa Monica, Calif., 1957, Jacobs Engring. Co., Pasadena, Calif., 1957, Sesler & Assocs., L.A., 1959; rsch. specialist Marquardt Corp., Van Nuys, Calif., 1962-67; sr. project engr. Conductron Corp., Northridge, Calif., 1967-68; info. systems asst. L.A. Dept. Water and Power, 1969-92. Instr. thermodynamics U. So. Calif., L.A., 1957. With USAAF, 1943-45. Mem. ASTM, ASME, AIChE, Nat. Assn. Purchasing Mgmt., Nat. Contract Mgmt. Assn., Am. Inst. Profl. Bookkeepers, Am. Soc. Safety Engrs., Am. Chem. Soc., Am. Soc. Materials, Am. Electroplaters and Surface Finishers Soc., Nat. Assn. Corrosion Engrs., Inst. Indsl. Engrs., Am. Prodn. and Inventory Control Soc., Am. Soc. Quality, Am. Indsl. Hygenists Assn., Steel Structure Painting Coun., Soc. Plastics Engrs., Inst. Mgmt. Accts., Soc. Mfg. Engrs., L.A. Soc. Coating Tech., Assn. Finishing Processes, Soc. Tribologists and Lubrication Engrs., Soc. Human Resources Mgmt., Soc. Energy Mgmt. Systems, Pi Tau Sigma, Phi Lambda Upsilon, Alpha Pi Mu. Home: 1344 W 20th St San Pedro CA 90732-4408

ELLIS, GEORGE FITZALLEN, JR., retired energy services company executive; b. Salisbury, N.C., May 4, 1923; s. George F. and Lena (Ramsay) E.; m. Rachael Trexler, Oct. 27, 1945 (dec. Jan. 1995); children: Susan Ellis Snyder, George F. III; m. Carol Andrews, July 19, 1997. BS, U.S. Naval Acad., 1944; MS, Rensselaer Poly. Inst., 1957. Commd. ensign U.S. Navy, 1944, advanced through grades to rear adm., 1972; comdr. South Atlantic Force, U.S. Atlantic Fleet, 1975-76; staff supreme Allied Command Europe, 1974-75; ret. U.S. Navy, 1976; dir. internat. bus. Babcock & Wilcox Co., Lynchburg, Va., 1976-78, dir. govt. relations Washington, 1978-79; v.p. govt. ops. McDermott Internat., Inc., Washington, 1979-88; bd. dirs. John Hanson Savs. Bank, Beltsville, MD., 1989-90. Trustee Am. U., 1982-91; trustee Ch. of the Covenant, Arlington, Va., 1981-82. Decorated Legion Merit with 4 clusters. Mem. Army-Navy Club (Washington), Vero Beach (Fla.) Yacht Club, Annapolis Yacht Club, Naval Acad. Faculty Club. Home: 1824 Milvale Rd Annapolis MD 21401-5923 also: 3554 Ocean Dr Vero Beach FL 32963-1673 E-mail: botbro@aol.com.

ELLIS, GEORGE HATHAWAY, retired banker and utility company executive; b. Orono, Maine, Jan. 29, 1920; s. Milton Ellis and Carrie (Voadecia) White; m. Sylvia Poor, Aug. 18, 1946; children— Rebecca Anne, George Milton, Randall Poor, Deborah Josephine BA, U. Maine, 1941, LLD, 1962; MA, Harvard U., 1948, PhD, 1950; LLD, Nasson Coll., Springvale, Maine, 1961, Bates Coll., Univ. Mass., 1968; DCS, Western NE Coll., 1968. Pres. Fed. Res. Bank Boston, 1961-68; pres., chief exec. officer Keystone Funds, Boston, 1968-74, Home Savs. Bank, Boston, 1975-85; chmn. bd. Cen. Maine Power Co., Augusta, 1983-90, ret., 1990. Editor, contbg. author: The Economic State of New England, 1954; contbr. articles to profl. jours. Trustee Econ. Edn. Coun. Mass.; mem. devel. coun. U. Maine, Orono, 1960-84; corp. mem. Univ. Hosp., Boston, 1978-84; bd. dirs. Greater Boston Community Devel., 1979-86; chmn. bd. trustees United Ch. of Christ Pension Bds., N.Y.C., 1985-90. Maj. inf. U.S. Army, 1941-45; PTO. Nat. honoree Beta Gamma Sigma, U. Mass., 1968 Fellow Am. Acad. Arts and Scis.; mem. Phi Beta Kappa, Phi Kappa Phi Congregationalist. Home: PO Box 250 Andover ME 04216-0250

ELLIS, GEORGIANA KEHR, internist; b. Buffalo, Jan. 25, 1947; MD, U. Wash., 1982. Diplomate Am. Bd. Internal Medicine. Intern U. Wash. Affiliate, Seattle, 1982-83, resident in internal medicine, 1983-85, fellow in med. oncology, 1985-88; asst. prof. U. Wash., Seattle. Office: U Wash Cancer Ctr Cancer Ctr PO Box 356043 Seattle WA 98195-6043

ELLIS, GLEN EDWARD, JR., insurance agent, financial planner; b. Austin, Tex., Sept. 7, 1960; s. Glen Edward and Virginia Lee (Walter) E.; m. Sherry Kay Testolin, Aug. 8, 1992. BS, Stanford U., 1983. ChFC. Registered rep., sr. field underwriter, fin. planner ING Fin. Advisers, LLC, Hartford, Conn., 1987—; fin. planner Aetna Investment Svcs., LLC., Hartford, Conn., 1996—. Mem. Fin. Planning Assn., Million Dollar Round Table, Nat. Assn. Ins. and Fin. Advisors (Nat. Sales Achievement award 1989-90, 93-95, 97-2001, Nat. Quality award 1990-2001), Soc. Fin. Svc. Profls. Avocations: hiking, fishing. Office: ING Fin Advisers Ste 1300 8911 N Capital of Texas Hwy Austin TX 78759-7200

ELLIS, GREG EVAN, investment sales executive, consultant; b. South Bend, Ind., Mar. 4, 1953; s. George Frank and Anna Evelyn (Johnson) E.; s. Christine Jo Ellis, May 24, 1975 (div. Aug. 1998); children: William Scott, Matthew Steven. BS in Math., Ball State U., 1975, MA in Actuarial Sci., 1977. Registered rep.; cert. fund specialist. Asst. actuary Travelers Ins., Hartford, Conn., 1977-79; assoc. actuary Travelers Pension Svcs., Hartford, Conn., 1979-82; pension svcs. mgr. Nationwide Life Ins., Columbus, Ohio, 1982-85, dir. pension ops., 1985-87; sr. cons. Coopers & Lybrand, Cleve., 1987-93; regional pension sales mgr. Nationwide Fin., Chgo., 1993-98; sr. v.p. Morley Fin., Lake Oswego, Oreg., 1998-2000, Villanova Capital, Columbus, Ohio, 2000—. Mem. pension com. Midwest Pension Conf., Cleve., 1987-93. Bd. dirs., pres. Civil Svc. Commn., Gahanna, Ohio, 1986-87; bd. dirs. Hudson (Ohio) Baseball Assn., 1989-97. Mem. Soc. Actuaries (assoc.), Stable Value Assn. (spkr., writer 1998-99), Internat. Assn. Fin. Planners, Internat. Found. Employee Benefit Plans, Life Office Mgmt. Assn. (pension com. 1985-87). Avocations: golf, fishing, coaching baseball, travel, family. Office: Villanova Capital 1 Nationwide Plz # Na-0301 Columbus OH 43215-2220

ELLIS, HAROLD DONALD, auto repair company executive, consultant; b. Lynwood, Calif., Aug. 10, 1946; s. Lloyd Ellis and Gladys Worthington. BA in Sociology, Roosevelt U., 1970. Mgr. student svcs. M-W Edn. Corp., Chgo., 1973-79; from mgr. customer svc. to v.p. Midas Internat., Chgo., 1981—99, v.p. franchise support svcs., 1999—2001; pvt. practice cons. Chgo., 2001—. Chmn. Motorist Assurance Program, Washington, 1994—2002; pres. Chgo. Aquarium & Pond, Chgo., 1981—. Mem. Automotive Maintenance and Repair Assn. (chmn. 1994-97). Avocations: water gardening, collecting koi.

ELLIS, HARRIETTE ROTHSTEIN, editor, writer; b. Memphis, Feb. 29, 1924; d. Samuel and Edith (Brodsky) Rothstein; m. Manuel J. Kaplan, June 1, 1944 (div. Jan. 1970); children: Deborah Elise Kaplan-Wyckoff, Claire Naomi Kaplan, Amelia Stephanie Kaplan; m. Theodore J. Ellis, Aug. 22, 1970 (div. Jan. 1992). Student, Memphis State U., 1941-42, Memphis Art Acad., 1940-43; BA, U. Ala., Tuscaloosa, 1944; postgrad., UCLA, 1949-50, Chouinard Art Inst., L.A., 1948. Advt. art/copy retail industry, New Orleans, Albuquerque, L.A., 1944-49; writer, graphic artist for newspapers and mags., L.A., 1944-49; editor Jewish Fedn. News, Long Beach, Calif., 1969-81; editor, writer Calif. Fashion Publs., L.A., 1982-86; editor Valley Mag., Granada Hills, Calif., 1987; pub. rels. Joan Luther & Assocs., Beverly Hills, Calif., 1988-90; editor Jewish Cmty. Chronicle, Long Beach, 1990—; dir. corp. comms. Startel Corp., Irvine, Calif., 1981-82. Active on com. to help implement infusion of fluoridated water in city water sys., Long Beach; cmty. interfaith com.; bd. dirs. Hillel, 1999—, Camp Komaroff, 1994—2001, Jewish Cmty. Ctr., Long Beach, Temple Israel, Long Beach. Named Woman of Yr., Temple Israel, Pioneer Women; recipient awards, Coun. Jewish Fedns. Mem.: AAUW, Am. Jewish Press Assn. (exec. com.), Calif. Media Profls. (pres. 1997—2002, bd. dirs., treas., v.p., Newspaper awards), Women of Reform Judaism (bd. dirs.), Nat. Fedn. Press Women (Newspaper awards), Sierra Club. Avocations: theater, music, travel, archaeology. Office: 3801 E Willow St Long Beach CA 90815-1734 E-mail: jchron@surfside.net.

ELLIS, HELENE RITA, social worker; b. St. Paul, Sept. 20, 1935; d. Moe and Cele (Sidletsky) Weisman; m. Bernard M. Ellis, Sept. 30, 1956; children: Miriam, Arienne, Elia, Evie. BS, U. Minn., 1956; MSW, Loyola U., 1974; PhD, Inst. Clin. Social Work, Chgo., 1996. Lic. clin. social worker, Ill.; bd. cert. diplomate. Tchr. Roosevelt High Sch., Mpls., 1957-58, Barrington (Ill.) High Sch., 1958-59; social worker Dist. #39 Schs., Wilmette, Ill., 1974—2003. Adj. assoc. prof. Loyola U. of Chgo., 1996—; chairperson Dist. 39 Health and Safety Curriculum Project, Wilmette, 1987-92. Named Ill. Sch. Social Worker of Yr., Ill. Assn. Sch. Social Workers, 1997-98. Mem. NASW, Am. Orthopsychiatric, Sch. Social Work Assn. Am., Am. Group Psychotherapy Assn., Ill. Assn. Sch. Social Workers (Social Worker of Yr. 1997-98), Pi Lambda Theta, Phi Beta Kappa, Alpha Sigma Nu. Home: 2530 Wellington Ct Evanston IL 60201-4975 Office: 3330 Old Glenview Rd Wilmette IL 60091

ELLIS, JAMES ALVIS, JR., lawyer; b. Lubbock, Tex., Mar. 19, 1943; s. James Alvis and Myrle Alice (Peden) E.; m. Sandra Gay Gillespie, June 18, 1966; children: Claire Ellis Gentry, James Alvis III. BA, Tex. Tech U., 1965; JD, U. Tex., 1968. Bar: Tex. 1968, U.S. Dist. Ct. (no., so., ea. and we. dists.) Tex. 1969, U.S. Ct. Appeals 1970, U.S. Supreme Ct. 1980; cert. in civil trial law Tex. Bd. Legal Specialization. Law clk. to presiding judge U.S. Dist. Ct. (we. dist.) Tex., 1968—69; assoc. Carrington, Coleman Sloman & Blumenthal, Dallas, 1970—74; ptnr. Carrington, Coleman Sloman & Blumenthal, LLP, Dallas, 1975—. Pres. Dallas Jr. Bar Assn., 1972. Fellow Tex. Bar Found., Dallas Bar Found.; mem. ABA, State Bar Tex., Dallas Bar Assn. Clubs: Crescent. Presbyterian. Office: Carrington Coleman Sloman & Blumenthal LLP 200 Crescent Ct Ste 1500 Dallas TX 75201-1848 E-mail: Jellis@CCSB.com.

ELLIS, JAMES D. communications executive, corporate lawyer; b. 1943; BBA, U. Iowa, 1965; JD, U. Mo., 1968. Bar: Mo. 1968, U.S. Ct. Appeals (D.C. cir.) 1977, Tex. 1980. Atty. AT&T, 1972-74, AT&T Long Lines, 1974-77; atty. gen. depts. AT&T, 1977-79; gen. atty. Southwestern Bell Telephone Co., San Antonio, 1979-83; v.p., gen. counsel Bellcore, 1983-84, Southwestern Bell Telephone Co., Tex., 1984-86, v.p., gen. counsel, sec., 1986-88; sr. v.p., gen. counsel Southwestern Bell Corp., 1988-89; sr. exec. v.p., gen. counsel SBC Comm., San Antonio, 1989—. With U.S. Army, 1968-72. Office: SBC Communications Inc 175 E Houston St San Antonio TX 78205-2255

ELLIS, JAMES HENRY, lawyer, management consultant; b. Hartford, Conn., May 6, 1933; s. Robert Isaac and Eve (Alperin) E.; m. Linda Abess, Feb. 22, 1959; children: James Arthur, Nancy Jean, Arthur Ungar. BS, U. Conn., 1955; MBA, Harvard U., 1957; JD, U. Miami, 1968. Bar: Fla. 1968, D.C. 1969, N.Y. 1975. V.p., sec. Fed. Fire & Casualty Co., Miami, Fla., 1959-68; atty. SEC, Washington, 1968-70; exec. v.p., sec., gen. counsel CNA Mgmt. Corp. and 5 related mut. funds, N.Y.C., 1970-79; pres., gen. counsel Mut. Fund Cons. Group, Scarsdale, N.Y., 1979—. Founder, pres. Sentry Savs. and Loan Assn., Stamford, Conn., 1983-90; chmn. edn. com., assocs. div. No. Load Mut. Fund Assn., 1986-89. Contbr. numerous articles to profl. jours.; prodr. of several off-broadway shows; prodr. (short film) Italian Lessons (best narrative short film Westchester N.Y. Film Festival 2000). Bd. dirs., v.p. White Plains (N.Y.) Symphony Orch., 1975-87; bd. dirs. Stanford Ctr. for the Arts, 1994—; pres., bd. dirs. Parsons Dance Found., 1998—. Mem. ABA, N.Y. State Bar Assn. (chmn. theater and performing arts com. 2001--), Harvard Club (N.Y.C.). Democrat. Jewish. Home: 36 Butler Rd Scarsdale NY 10583-2214 E-mail: jhellis@cyburban.com.

ELLIS, JAMES IRA, network technician; b. Osceola, Ark., July 7, 1974; s. Ira Edwin and Elizabeth Stratton Ellis. BS in Math., MusB in Edn., Culver-Stockton Coll., 1996. Resnet and network support coord. Culver-Stockton Coll., Canton, Mo., 1997—. Network cons., support Canton R-V Pub. Schs., 1998—. Mem.: Music Educators Nat. Conf., Nat. Eagle Scout Assn. Baptist. Office: Culver-Stockton Coll One College Hill Canton MO 63435 Office Fax: 217-231-6610. Personal E-mail: jellis774@hotmail.com.

ELLIS, JAMES O., JR., military officer; m. Paula Matthews; children: Lauren, Patrick. BS, U.S. Naval. Acad., 1969; MS in Aerospace Engring., Ga. Inst. Tech.; MS in Aero. Sys., U. West Fla.; grad., U.S. Navy Test Pilot Sch., 1975; grad. in U.S. naval nuc. power tng., 1987; grad. sr. officer program in nat. security strategy, Harvard U., 1989. Commd. ensign USN, 1969, advanced through grades to adm., 1999; various assignments; designated naval aviator, 1971; insp. gen. U.S. Atlantic Fleet, 1993; mem. staff of comdr.-in-chief, 1993; comdr. Carrier Group Five/Battle Force Seventh Fleet USS Independence (CV 62), 1995; dep. chief of naval ops., plans, policy and ops., 1996-98; comdr.-in-chief allied forces So. Europe U.S. Naval Forces, 1998—2001; pilot fighter squadron 92 USS Constellation (CV-64); pilot fighter squadron 1 USS Ranger (CV-61); exptl., operational test pilot; navy office legis. affairs; F/A 18 program coord., dep. chief naval ops. (airwarfare); dep. comdr., chief staff joint task force

Five U.S. Pacific Command Counter Narcotics Force; commdg. officer strike fighter squadron 131, F/A 18 Hornet USS Coral Sea (CV-43), 1985, XO USS Carl Vinson (CVN-70), 1988; commdg. officer USS LaSalle (AGF 3), 1989—90, USS Abraham Lincoln (CVN 72), 1991—93; insp. gen. U.S. Atlantic Fleet, 1991, staff comdr. in chief, 1993; dir. ops. plans and policy (N3N5); comdr.-in-chief U.S. Naval Forces and Allied Forces So. Europe, 1998; comdr. U.S. Strategic Command, 2001. Decorated Navy D.S.M., Legion of Merit with 3 oak leaf clusters, Def. Meritorious Svc. medal with oak leaf cluster, Def. Disting. Svc. medal with oak leaf cluster, Meritorious Svc. medal, Navy Commendation medal; grand officer Order of Merit (Italy).

ELLIS, JAMES REED, retired lawyer; b. Oakland, Calif., Aug. 5, 1921; s. Floyd E. and Hazel (Reed) E.; m. Mary Lou Earling, Nov. 18, 1944 (dec.); children: Robert Lee, Judith Ann (dec.), Lynn Earling, Steven Reed. BS, Yale, 1942; JD, U. Wash., 1948; LLD (hon.), Lewis and Clark U., 1968, Seattle U., 1981; PSD (hon.), Whitman Coll., 1992. Bar: Wash. 1949, D.C. 1971. Ptnr. Preston, Thorgrimson, Horowitz, Starin & Ellis, Seattle, 1952-69, Preston, Thorgrimson, Starin, Ellis & Holman, Seattle, 1969-72, Preston, Thorgrimson, Ellis, Holman & Fletcher, Seattle, 1972-79; sr. ptnr. Preston, Thorgrimson, Ellis & Holman, Seattle, 1979-90, Preston, Thorgrimson, Shidler, Gates & Ellis, Seattle, 1990-92; of counsel Preston, Gates & Ellis, Seattle, 1992—2002; chmn., CEO Wash. State Convention and Trade Ctr., Seattle, 1986—2002. Dep. pros. atty. King County, 1952; gen. counsel Municipality of Met. Seattle, 1958-79; dir., mem. exec. com. Key Bank of Wash., 1969-94, KIRO, Inc., 1965-95; dir. Blue Cross of Wash. and Alaska, 1989-98. Mem. Nat. Water Commn., 1970-73; mem. urban transp. adv. council U.S. Dept. Transp., 1970-71; mem. Wash. Planning Adv. Council, 1965-72; mem. Washington State Growth Strategies Commn., 1989-90; pres. Forward Thrust Inc., 1966-73; chmn. Mayors Com. on Rapid Transit, 1964-65; trustee Ford Found., 1970-82, mem. exec. com., 1978-82; bd. regents U. Wash., 1965-77, pres., 1972-73; trustee Resources for the Future, 1983-92; mem. council Nat. Mcpl. League, 1968-76, v.p., 1972-76; chmn. Save our Local Farmlands Com., 1978-79, King County Farmlands Adv. Commn., 1980-82; pres. Friends of Freeway Park, 1976-99; bd. dirs. Nat. Park and Recreation Assn., 1979-82; trustee Lewis and Clark U., 1988-94; pres. Mountains to Sound Greenway Trust, Inc., 1991—; trustee Henry M. Jackson Found., 1992—. 1st lt. USAAF, 1943-46. Recipient Bellevue First Citizen award, 1968, Seattle First Citizen award, 1968, Nat. Conservation award Am. Motors, 1968, Distinguished Service award Wash. State Dept. Parks and Recreation, 1968, Distinguished Citizen award Nat. Municipal League, 1969, King County Distinguished Citizen award, 1970, La Guardia award Center N.Y.C. Affairs, 1975, Environ. Quality award EPA, 1977, Am. Inst. for Public Service Nat. Jefferson award, 1974, State Merit medal State of Wash., 1990, Nat. Founders award Local Initiatives Support Corp., 1992, Henry M. Jackson Disting. Pub. Svc. medal, 1998, U. Wash. Alumnus Summa Laude Dignatus award, 1999. Fellow: Am. Bar Found.; mem.: ABA (ho. dels. 1978—82, past chmn. urban, state and local govt. law sect.), AIA (hon.), Acad. Pub. Adminstrn., Am. Judicature Soc., D.C. Bar Assn., Seattle Bar Assn. (Pres.'s award 1993), Wash. Bar Assn., Nat. Assn. Bond Lawyers (com. stds. of practice), Mcpl. League Seattle and King County (past pres.), Coun. Fgn. Rels., Rainier Club (Seattle), Order of Coif (hon.), Phi Gamma Delta, Phi Delta Phi. Home: 903 Shoreland Dr SE Bellevue WA 98004-6738 Office: 925 4th Ave Seattle WA 98104-1158 Fax: (206) 623-7022.

ELLIS, JOANNE HAMMONDS, computer consultant; b. Rome, Ga., Aug. 15, 1946; d. James Randolph and Louise Hammonds; m. James H. Ellis Jr.; 1 child, Stephanie Louise Cantrell Ellis. BS, AB, Jacksonville (Ala.) State U., 1968; MBA, Ga. State U., 1979, MPA, 1981. With GSA, 1969-82, computer systems analyst, 1985-87; dir. mgmt. svc., dir. prodn. svcs. divsn. NARDAC, 1989—91; dir. info. resources mgmt. Food and Nutrition Svcs. USDA, Alexandria, Va., 1991—2000; dir. info. resources mgmt. divsn Nat Fin. Ctr. USDA, New Orleans, 2000—. Mem. Office Mgmt. & Budget's Info. Tech. Resources Bd.; bd. dirs. Info. Resources Mgmt. Coun. Contbr. articles to profl. jours. Named Fed. Exec. of Yr, New Orleans Fed. Exec. Bd., 1998; recipient Meritorious Svc. medal, USN, 1991. Mem. Assn. Women in Computing, Federally Employed Women, Atlanta Assn. Fed. Execs., NAFE, Dept. of Def. Exec. Leadership Devel. Program, Beta Sigma Phi. Methodist. Home: PO Box 208 Centre AL 35960

ELLIS, JOE MIKE, reclamation scientist; b. Linton, Ind., Feb. 3, 1953; s. Herbert Josiah and Margaret Beatrice (Isenogle) E.; m. Jennifer Marie Woods, Sept. 26, 1992; children: Claire Marie, Melissa Anne. BS, Purdue U., 1975. Cert. profl. erosion and sediment control specialist; lic. real estate broker, securities rep., ins. salesman. Asst. plant mgr. Pioneer Seed Co., Worthington, Ind., 1975-77; reclamation supr. Peabody Coal Co., Jasonville, Ind., 1977-79, reclamation mgr., 1979-87, mgr. environ. affairs Henderson, Ky., 1987-88, mgr. permits, 1988-92, permits supr., 1992-94, Lynnville, Ind., 1994-98; sr. reclamation splst. Lynnville/Sq. Creek (Ind.) Bus. Unit, 1996-98; environ. scientist Am. Enviro-Svcs. Inc., Newburgh, Ind., 1999-2001, mgr. environ. health and safety, 2001—, Ferro Corp., Evansville, Ind., 2002. Editor Report Tree Planting, 1990. Named Jaycee of Yr. Ind. Jaycees, Linton, 1985. Mem. Linton Jaycees (pres. 1985-86), Purdue Club of Evansville (pres. 1990-92), Masons, Shriners, Scottish Rite, Elks. Methodist. Home: 10866 Millersburg Rd Chandler IN 47610-9330 Office: Ferro Corp 5001 Ohara Dr Evansville IN 47711 Business E-Mail: ellisj@ferro.com.

ELLIS, JOHN, small business owner; b. Amherst, Ohio, Sept. 15, 1929; s. Edward Pierson and Jean (Scott) E.; m. Carolyn Elizabeth Collier, Dec. 29, 1951; children: Linda Ellis Wieand, Jeanine Ellis Klausing, Jeanette Ellis Hale, John Edward. BS, Bowling Green State U., 1953; MA, Case Western Res. U., Cleve., 1958; EdD, Harvard U., 1964. Tchr. pub. schs., Lorain, Ohio, 1953-54, prin., 1957-61, from asst. supt. to supt. schs. Massillon, Ohio, 1963-66, supt. schs. Lakewood, Ohio, 1966-71, Columbus, Ohio, 1971-77; exec. dep. commr. edn. U.S. Office Edn., Washington, 1977-80; supt. schs. pub. schs., Austin, Tex., 1980-90; commr. N.J. Dept. Edn., 1990-92; owner Ellis Broadcasting Corp., Wimberley, Tex., 1992-2000; cons. Wimberley, Tex., 2000—. Adj. prof. edn. adminstrn. Ohio State U., Columbus, 1971-77. Elder local Presbyn. Ch. With USAF, 1947-49, 54-57. Recipient Massillon Young Man of Yr. award, 1965; named to Saturday Rev. Honor Roll, 1977. Mem. Rotary, Phi Delta Kappa, Pi Kappa Alpha, Phi Alpha Theta, Kappa Delta Pi, Gamma Theta Upsilon. Home: 500 Leath Hollow Dr Wimberley TX 78676-5207

ELLIS, JOHN, urban designer; BA, MA, Cambridge Univ., Eng. He has over 28 years architectural experience, 20 of them in the US. Ptnr. Solomon, ETC, San Francisco, 1996—99, prin., 2000—02; dir. of Urban design Solomon ETC, San Francisco, 2002—. Adj. prof. Calif. Coll. of Arts and Crafts, San Francisco, 1984; cont. writer Arch. Rev., London, 1984. Mem.: RIBA, AIA. John has been responsible for most of the large scale urban and campus planning work in the office, including the UC Berkeley Sector Plan. Prior to joining Solomon, John was a Sr. Designer to Kaplan McLaughlin Diaz in San Francisco where he was responsible for the design of several large-scale commercial projects including the one million square foot Oakland Fed. Build., Plaza Pk. Tower in Sacramento, the Reno Fed. Courthouse, and the renovation of the hist. Flood Build. in San Francisco. He designed the first new Single Room Occupancy Hotel project in San Francisco, the Canon Kip project for 105 units completed in 1992. He was also employed at the San Francisco office of Anshen + Allen where he designed a mixed-use high-rise in Shanghai, China. Office: Solomon ETC 1328 Mission St 4th Fl San Francisco CA 94103*

ELLIS, JOHN DAVID, data processing executive; b. Tyler, Tex., Dec. 24, 1949; s. James Wade Ellis and Betty Jean (Arnold) Ellis Hughes; m. Sherry Lyn Welch, Jan. 3, 1952; children: Brandon Heath, Christopher Shawn. AA, Tyler Jr. Coll., 1975; student, Sam Houston State U., 1968-69, U. Tex., Tyler, 1976-77; BBA, LeTourneau U., 2002. From computer operator to mgr. computer ops. Brookshire Grocery Co., Tyler, 1974-82; sr. systems programmer/analyst Buford TV, Inc., Tyler, 1982-87, mgr. corp. data processing, 1987-90, v.p. mgmt. info. systems, 1992—99, Classic Cable, Tyler, 1999—. Mem. adv. council for computer sci. Tyler Jr. Coll., 1986-87. Served with U.S. Army, 1970-72. Republican. Methodist. Home: 5703 Regents Row Tyler TX 75703-4542 Office: Classic Cable PO Box 9200 Tyler TX 75711-9090

ELLIS, JOHN MARTIN, German literature educator; b. London, May 31, 1936; came to U.S., 1966, naturalized, 1972; s. John Albert and Emily (Silvey) E.; m. Barbara Stephanie Rhoades, June 28, 1978; children: J. Richard, Andrew W., Katherine M., Jill E. BA with 1st class honours, U. London, 1959, PhD, 1965. Tutorial asst. German Univ. Coll., Wales, Aberystwyth, 1959-60; asst. lectr. U. Leicester, Eng., 1960-63; asst. prof. U. Alta., Edmonton, Can., 1963-66; mem. faculty U. Calif., Santa Cruz, 1966—, prof. German, 1970-94, prof. emeritus, 1994, dean grad. div., 1977-86. Vis. prof. U. Kent, Canterbury, Eng., 1970-71 Author: Schiller's Kalliasbriefe and the Study of His Aesthetic Theory, 1969, Kleist's Prinz Friedrich von Homburg: A Critical Study, 1970, Narration in the German Novelle, 1974, The Theory of Literary Criticism: A Logical Analysis, 1974, Heinrich von Kleist: Studies in the Character and Meaning of His Writings, 1979, One Fairy Story Too Many: The Brothers Grimm and Their Tales, 1983, Against Deconstruction, 1989, Language, Thought and Logic, 1993, Literature Lost: Social Agendas and the Corruption of the Humanities, 1997 (Peter Shaw Meml. award). Served with Brit. Army, 1954-56. Fellow Guggenheim Found., 1970-71; Fellow NEH, 1975-76, 92. Mem. NAS, ACLA, Am. Assn. Tchrs. German, Internat. Assn. Germanic Studies, Assn. Lit. Scholars and Critics (sec.-treas. 1994-2002). E-mail: john.ellis@earthlink.net.

ELLIS, JOSEPH NEWLIN, retired distribution company executive; b. Tenn., Oct. 19, 1928; s. Richard M. and Pearl A. (Fuqua) E.; m. Barbara Harpster, Sept. 17, 1955; 1 child, Patricia Anne. BS, Northwestern U., 1954. Co-founder LaSalle-Deitch Co., Inc., Elkhart, Ind., 1963, exec. v.p., 1969-72, pres., chief exec. officer, 1972-89, chmn. of the bd., chief exec. officer, 1989-94. With U.S. Army, 1950-52. Home: 1160 Benders Ferry Rd Gallatin TN 37066-5703

ELLIS, JUNE B. human resource consultant; b. Portland, Ind., June 17, 1921; children: Kenneth G., Reyn K. BS, Mary Washington Coll., 1942; MSW, Tulane U., 1953; PhD, Internat. U., 1977. Asst. dir. social services East La. State Hosp., Jackson, 1960-62; instr. Tulane U. Sch. Social Work, New Orleans, 1962-63, asst. prof. dept. psychiatry, Sch. Medicine, 1963-68; exec. dir. Family Service-Travelers Aid, Ft. Smith, Ark., 1967-71; pres. Child and Family Cons., Ft. Smith, 1971—. Dir. Human Resource Devel. Ctr., Ft. Smith; mem. adv. bd. Suspect Child Abuse and Neglect; cons. Volvo Health Care, Goteborg, Sweden, 1974-92, Kontura Personal, 1974-92, Christian Counseling Ctr., Vellore, India, 1974—; mem. Tulane Alumni Bd., 1978-88; mem. continuing profl. edn. com. Tulane Univ. Sch. Social Work, 1996—. Author: TA Tally, 1974, TA Talk, terms and references in transaction, 1976, BEING, 1982. Mem. Ark. Gov.'s Commn. on Status of Women, 1970-73, Ark. Gov.'s Com. Drug Abuse Prevention; cons. Cuban Resettlement Program, Ft. Chaffee, Ark., 1980; del. leader to China, 1984; mem. adv. bd. Jr. League Am.; mem. scholarship selection com. Whirlpool Corp.; bd. mem. Ctr. for Long Life Learning, Tulane U.; coord. Western Ark. Health Advocacy Svc., 1995—; mem. adv. bd. Ctr. for Long Life Living, Tulane U., 1996, 1st emeritus adv. bd. mem., 2000; cons. gerontology, Tulane U., 1998—; judge Odyssey of the Mind, Tex. Sch. Sys., 1998—; appointee rehab. adv. coun. Presbyn. Hosp. of Dallas, 2000—; apptd. Univ. Libr. Bd.; charter mem. Friends of the Libr., 2001. Named Outstanding Alumni, Tulane U., 1984. Mem. ASTD, AAUS, AAUW, Am. Acad. Psychotherapists, Am. Group Psychotherapy Assn., Am. Orthopsychiat. Assn., Acad. Cert. Social Workers, Western Ark. Mental Health Assn. (adv. bd.), Conf. for Advancement of Pvt. Practice in Social Work, Am. Assn. Ret. Persons, Am. Assn. of Individual Investors, Park Cities Club. Episcopalian. Office: 4242 Lomo Alto Dr N76 Dallas TX 75219

ELLIS, KEM BYRON, public library administrator; b. Greensboro, N.C., Apr. 4, 1953; s. Laynelle Zenetues and Bernice (Godley) E.; m. Lelia Joanne Turner, June 4, 1977; children: Joseph Byron, Sarah Kathryn. AB in History and Polit. Sci., High Point (N.C.) U., 1975; MLS, U. N.C., Greensboro, 1977. Cert. librarian, N.C. Libr. asst. High Point Pub. Libr., 1972-77, head of gen. rsch., 1977-84, head of bus. rsch., 1984-88, head of rsch. svcs., 1988-92, dir., 1992—. Vol. C. of C., High Point; mem. Leadership High Point 1987—; bd. dirs. Cmtys. in Schs., 1998—, chmn., 2001—; vol. United Way, High Point, 1986—. Named Vol. of Yr., Gov. of N.C., 1987. Mem. ALA, N.C. Libr. Assn., Pub. Libr. Assn., N.C. Pub. Libr. Dirs. Assn. (pres. 2000), High Point Rotary Club (sec. 1988—, Paul Harris fellow 1992). Methodist. E-mail: kem.ellis@ci.high-point.ne.us.

ELLIS, LARRY R. military officer; m. Jean Williams; 2 children: Deborah, Renee. BS, Morgan State U., 1969; MS, Ind. U., 1975; grad., Armed Forces Staff Coll., Army War Coll. Commd. 2d lt. U.S. Army, 1969, advanced through grades to lt. gen., 1999; various assignments worldwide; dep. dir. strategic planning and policy Hdqrs. U.S. Pacific Command, Camp H.M. Smith, Hawaii; asst. divsn. comdr. 2d Inf. Divsn., Camp Casey, Republic of Korea; asst. chief of staff UN Command/Combined Forces Command, Republic of Korea; comdr. gen. 1st Armored Divsn., 1997-99; dep. chief staff for ops. and plans Hdqrs. Dept. of Army, Washington, 1999—.

ELLIS, LAURA RENEE, music educator; b. Albert Lea, Minn., Dec. 11, 1963; d. Leon Ray and Annette leNoir (Christianson) E. BA, Luther Coll., 1986; MusM, U. Kans., 1989, D Musical Arts, 1991. Asst. prof. U. of the Ozarks, Clarksville, Ark., 1991-96; prof. music McMurry U., Abilene, Tex., 1996—. Parish organist Ch. of the Heavenly Rest, Abilene, 1996—. Performer CD recording Legacy: Laura Ellis Plays Organ Works of Jeanne Demessieux, 1996. Dial Corp. faculty enrichment grantee, 1994; winner Gruenstein Meml. Organ Competition, Chgo. Club of Women Organists, 1988. Mem. Am. Guild Organists (dean), Music Tchrs. Nat. Assn., Tex. Music Educators, Phi Beta Kappa, Pi Kappa Lambda. Lutheran. Avocation: golf. Home: 3525 Rolling Green Dr Apt 1023 Abilene TX 79606-2657 Office: McMurry U PO Box 698 Abilene TX 79604-0698

ELLIS, LEE, social sciences educator; b. Iola, Kans., Mar. 1, 1942; s. Lee Ellis, Sr. and Dorothy Ellis; children: Lasha, Holly. BA, Pittsburg (Kans.) State U., 1966, MS, 1970; PhD, Fla. State U., 1981. Prof. sociology Minot (N.D.) State U., 1976—. Author (with Anthony Walsh): Criminology: A Global Perspective, 2000; author: Research Methods in the Social Scis., 2d edit., 2003; author: (with foreword by Hans J. Eysenck) Theories of Rape: Inquiries into the Causes of Sexual Aggression, 1989; editor (with L. Ebertz, foreword by Milton Diamond): Males, Females, and Behavior: Toward Biological Understanding, 1998; editor: (with L. Ebertz, foreword by Brian Gladue) Sexual Orientation: Toward Biological Understanding, 1997; editor: (foreword by Robert Retherford) Social Stratification and Socioeconomic Inequality, Volume II: Reproductive and Interpersonal Aspects of Dominance and Status, 1994; editor: Research Methods in the Social Sciences: Workbook and Reader, 1994; editor: (forward by Lionel Tiger) Social Stratification and Socioeconomic Inequality, Volume I: A Comparative Biosocial Analysis, 1993; editor: (with Harry Hoffman, foreword by Larry Siegal) Crime in Biological, Social and Moral Contexts, 1990; contbr. over 100 articles to profl. jours., chapters to books. Office: Minot State U 500 University Ave Minot ND 58707 Business E-Mail: ellis@minotstateu.edu.

ELLIS, LESTER NEAL, JR., lawyer; b. Washington, Aug. 1, 1948; s. Lester Neal and Marie (Brooks) E. BS, U.s. Mil. Acad., 1970; JD, U. Va., 1975. Bar: Va. 1975, U.S. Ct. Appeals (5th cir.) 1977, D.C. 1978, U.S. Ct. Appeals (4th and D.C. cirs.) 1979, U.S. Ct. Appeals (11th cir.) 1982, N.C. 1985, U.S. Supreme Ct. 2000, U.S. Dist. Ct. (ea., mid., we. dists.) N.C., U.S. Dist. Ct. (ea., we. dists.) Va., U.S. Ct. Claims. Trial atty. litigation divsn. Office of JAG, U.S. Dept. Army, Washington, 1975-78; assoc. Hunton & Williams, Richmond, Va., 1978-84, ptnr. Raleigh, 1984—. Maj. U.S. Army, 1970-78, col. USAR, 1993-99. Recipient Judge Paul Brosman award U.S. Ct. Mil. Appeals, 1975. Mem.: D.C. Bar Assn. (Wake County bd. elections 1986—93, chmn. 1987—93, ct. rules com.), Va. Bar Assn. (spl. issues com. 1982), ABA (chair tort and trial practice steering com., editor-in-chief Tort Source, chair comml. torts commn., chair trial techniques com., tort and ins. practice sect., editor-in-chief Tort and Ins. Law Jour., coun. mem.), Phi Kappa Phi. Republican. Episcopalian. Home: 1116 Wagon Ridge Rd Raleigh NC 27614 Office: Hunton & Williams One Hanover Sq PO Box 109 Raleigh NC 27602-0109

ELLIS, LLOYD H., JR., emergency physician, art historian; b. Denver, Apr. 7, 1936; s. Lloyd Harris and Lura Lou (Wallace) E.; m. Nancy Kay Greenamyre, June 4, 1962 (div. June 1979); children: Peter, Amanda Hunt Thurber; m. Eva Marie Bevan, Sept. 1, 1984; children: Gwendolyn Ruth, David Bevan. BA, Yale U., New Haven, Conn., 1960, MA, 1961; MD, Case Western Reserve U., Cleve., 1970; MA, Case Western Reserve U., 1990, PhD, 2002. Diplomate Am. Bd. Emergency Medicine. Farm mgr., Hastings, Nebr., 1961-62; vice consul Dept. of State, Lourenco Marques, Mozambique, 1963-64, intelligence analyst Washington, 1965-66; dir. emergency dept. Univ. Hosps., Cleve., 1976-84, emergency physician, 1985-94, Emergency Profl. Svcs., Wooster, Ohio, 1995-96, Chardon, Ohio, 1997, Warren, Ohio, 1998. Instr. in surgery Case Western Reserve U., Cleve., 1976-78, asst. prof. surgery, 1979-94; mng. ptnr. Ellis Family Ltd. Partnership, 1992—. Med. dir. Cleve. Emergency Svc., 1976-94; pres. Jeffrey Wallace Ellis Found., Hastings, 1993—; sr. warden Good Shepard, Lyndhurst, Ohio, 1985-86; jr. warden St. Christopher's, Gates Mills, 1998, sr. warden, 1999, Diocesan Coun., 1999-2002; trustee Lynn Lou Wallace Ellis Trust, 1992—. 1st Lt. Armor, 1956-59. Recipient Ford scholar Ford Found., New Haven, 1952-55. Mem. Am. Coll. Emergency Physicians, Am. Acad. Emergency Medicine. Republican. Episcopalian. Home and Office: 32250 Woodsdale Ln Cleveland OH 44139-1335

ELLIS, LYNN WEBSTER, management educator, telecommunications consultant; b. San Mateo, Calif., Feb. 27, 1928; s. Lynn Webster Sr. and Mary Eleanor (Barstow) E.; m. Eileen Mary Gallagher; children: Lynn W. Jr., Margaret, Katherine. BEE, Cornell U., 1948; MS, Stevens Inst. Tech., 1954; D Profl. Studies in Mgmt., Pace U., 1979. Exec. ITT Corp., 1948-79; v.p. engring. Bristol Babcock Co., Waterbury, Conn., 1980-82; cons. Lynn W. Ellis Assocs., Westport, Conn., 1982-85; prof. U. New Haven, West Haven, Conn., 1985-94, scholar-in-residence, 1994-97, prof. emeritus, 1997—. Author: Evaluating R&D Processes, 1996, Financial Side of Industrial Research Management, 1984; contbr. and co-contbr. over 50 articles to profl. jours.; patentee in field. Chmn. adv. com.Dept. Commerce, Washington, 1973-75; mem. five panels and coms. NRC, Washington, 1970-95. Capt. U.S. Army, 1948-52. Fellow IEEE (internat. communication award 1983), AAAS. Home: 1301 Gulf Blvd Apt 115 Clearwater FL 33767-2803 Office: U New Haven 300 Orange Ave West Haven CT 06516-1916

ELLIS, MARK CARLTON, music educator; s. Robert Wayne and Jean LaVonne Ellis; m. Pamela Kodger, May 21, 1991; children: Dana Lynne Cummings, Miles Robert. BA, U. No. Iowa, 1969; MMus, Mankato State U., 1975; PhD, U. Iowa. Prof. and asst. dean Ohio State U., Mansfield, Ohio, 1986—; instr. U. No. Iowa, Cedar Falls, 1980—86. Author: (rsch.) Jour. Rsch. in Music Edn., Contbns. to Rsch. in Music Edn., Psychology of Music, Bull. of Coun. of Rsch. in Music Edn., Dialogues in Music Edn., Motor and Perceptual Skills. Specialist 5: spl. bandsman U.S. Army, 1969—72. Recipient Outstanding Tchg. Award, Ohio State U., 1998, Outstanding Rsch. Award, 1992, Pres.'s Award, Am. Fedn. of Musicians, Local 159, 1998. Home: 3463 Needham Rd Lexington OH 44904 Office: Ohio State University 1680 University Dr Mansfield OH 44907 Office Fax: 419-755-4241. E-mail: ellis.10@osu.edu.

ELLIS, MARK E. school librarian; b. Owosso, Mich., Sept. 24, 1950; s. Jack E. and Lorraine M. Ellis; m. Kathleen Q. Quinn, Dec. 16, 1982; children: Travis J., Corinne A. M. Mich. State U., 1975—78, Fla. State U., 1991—93. Librarian 5B Ga., 2004. Libr. Albany State U., Albany, Ga., 1994—. Prodr.: (multi-media presentation) From Harper's Ferry to Appomattox Court House; author: (library reference) Historical Dictionary of the Gilded Age. Office: Albany State University 504 College Dr Albany GA 31705 Office Fax: 229-430-4803. E-mail: mellis@asurams.edu.

ELLIS, MARY LOUISE HELGESON, retired insurance company executive, business consultant; b. Albert Lea, Minn., May 29, 1943; d. Stanley Orville and Neoma Lois (Guthier) Helgeson; m. David Readinger, Nov. 5, 1994; children from previous marriage: Christopher, Tracy. BS in Pharmacy, U. Iowa, 1966; MA in Pub. Adminstrn., Iowa State U., 1982, postgrad., 1982—83. Faculty Duquesne U., Pitts., 1977; cons. in pharmacy Colville, Wash., 1978—79; dir. pharmacy Mt. Carmel Hosp., Colville, 1978—79; clin. pharmacist Iowa Vets. Home, Marshalltown, Iowa, 1980—81; instr. Iowa Valley C.C., Marshalltown, 1981—83; dir. Iowa Dept. Substance Abuse, Des Moines, 1983—86, State of Iowa Pub. Health; dir. Iowa Dept. Pub. Health, Des Moines, 1986—90; spl. cons. health affairs Blue Cross/Blue Shield of Iowa, 1990—91; v.p. Blue Cross/Blue Shield of Iowa and S.D., 1991—2000; ret., 2000; bus. cons., 2001—. Chair Iowa Health Data Commn., Des Moines, 1986—90; bd. dirs. Health Policy Corp. Iowa, 1986—90; adj. asst. prof. U. Iowa, Iowa City, 1984—; commd. officer U.S. FDA, 1989—90; mem. alumnae bd. dirs. U. Iowa Coll. of Pharmacy, 1989—; chair Nat. Commn. Accreditation of Ambulance Svcs., 1992—. Mem. Iowa State Bd. Health, 1981—83, v.p., 1982—83; mem. adv. coun. Iowa Valley C.C., 1983—85. Recipient Woman of Achievement award, Des Moines YWCA, 1988. Mem.: APHA, Iowa Pub. Health Assn. (bd. dirs., Henry Albert award 1990), Iowa Pharmacists Assn., Pi Sigma Alpha, Phi Kappa Phi, Alpha Xi Delta. Republican. Home: 2912 Caulder Ave Des Moines IA 50321-2637

ELLIS, MICHAEL DAVID, aerospace engineer; b. Sacramento, July 13, 1952; s. John David and Priscilla Agnes (Tupper) E.; m. Virginia Katherine Hanlon, Mar. 27, 1976; children: Gwendolyn Dawn, January Marie, Jennifer Noel. BS in Space Sci., Fla. Inst. Tech., 1975. With satellite ops., orbit analyst Western Union, Sussex, N.J., 1976-77; with satellite ops., 3 axis RCA Americom, Sussex, N.J., 1977-78; with satellite ops., Land Sat ATS-6 Goddard Space Flight Ctr., Greenbelt, Md., 1978-79; with Voyager System Lead Jet Propulsion Lab., Pasadena, Calif., 1979-82; STS ground ops. analyst Applied Rsch. Inc., El Segundo, Calif., 1982-83; mission ops. Aerospace Corp., El Segundo, Calif., 1983-88; space sta. mission ops. Johnson Spaceflight Ctr., Houston, 1988—2002, ISS med. ops., 2002—. Mem. troop asst. San Jacinto Girl Scouts U.S., Houston, 1988-94; Confraternity Christian Doctrine tchr. St. Bernadette, Clear Lake, 1990; Clear Lake Drill Team support Starlettes, 1989-95, Clear Lake Flares, 1995-96. Mem.: AIAA (chmn. 1972—75), Soc. Automotive Engrs. (chmn. spacecraft com. 1986—87). Personal E-mail: mdellis@swbell.net. Business E-Mail: mellis@ems.jsc.nasa.gov.

ELLIS, MICHAEL EUGENE, documentary film producer, writer, director, marketing executive; b. Murphysboro, Ill., Aug. 1, 1946; s. Robert Eugene and Lula May (Williams) E. BS, So. Ill. U., Carbondale, 1971. Asst. to pres. So. Ill. U., 1970; asst. dir. Ill. Info. Svc., Springfield, 1971-72; mgr. press rels. Ill. Ho. of Reps., Springfield, 1973-77; dep. dir. com. Rep. Nat. Com., Washington, 1977; pres. Lincana Corp., Springfield, 1978-80; mgr. mktg. presentations Ill. Dept. Commerce, Springfield, 1980-91; dir. devel. and comms. Sparc Inc., Springfield, 1993—2002; pres. Assocs. and Ellis, Springfield, 2002—; dir. advancement Coll. Applied Arts and Scis., So. Ill. U., Carbondale, 2003—. Co-author: Work and the College Student, 1975; author: Elements of Political Public Relations, 1977; editor: Springfield Eats, 1996; author film scripts, 1983—. Dir. comm. Pres. Ford Com. in Ill., Chgo., 1976; mem. Ill. Rep. Com., Springfield, Rep. Presdl. Task Force, Washington, Sangamon Rep. Found., Springfield. Recipient Gold Award Advt. Assn., Springfield, Ill., 1987-89. Mem.: Ill. Soc. Assn. Execs. (bd. dirs. 1998—2000, Excellence in Comms. award 1998, 2000, 2001), Nat. Soc. Fund Raising Execs. (bd. dirs. 1998—2003), World Affairs Coun., Assn. Multi Image Internat., Am. Film Inst., Internat. Comms. Industry Assn. Avocations: writing, gardening, photography. Home: 627 Witherspoon Dr Springfield IL 62704-1424 E-mail: ellisspringfield@aol.com.

ELLIS, PATRICIA WEATHERS, small business owner, retired electronic technician; b. Shelby, N.C., June 21, 1941; d. William Roy and Lucille Elzora (Allen) Weathers; m. Donald Eugene Ellis, Nov. 16, 1957; children: Dana Michelle, Lisa Maria. Student, Gaston Coll., Gastonia, N.C., 1970, 82. Tel. operator So. Bell, Greensboro, N.C., 1959-61, Gastonia, N.C., 1961-63, dial clk., 1963-68, frame technician, 1968-79, test technician, 1980-84, maintenance adminstr., 1984-85, toll test technician, 1985-87; electronic technician Bell-South, Gastonia, 1987-91, Charlotte, N.C., 1991-2000, electronic technician toll rm. Gastonia, 2000—02; store mgr. Ellis Carpet and Floor Ctr., Inc., 2002—, 2002—. Store mgr. Ellis—Bowen Carpet Svc., Gastonia, 1969-70. Commr. Gaston County, Gastonia, 1992-96; bd. dirs. Gaston County Health Dept., Airport Com., Gaston Mus. Art and History, 1992-96, Gaston County Dept. Social Svcs.; alt. Ctrl. Lina Coun. Govts., 1994-95; mem. Nat. Rep. Party, NC Rep. Party, NC Rep. Women of Gaston County, Gaston Good Neighbor Courthouse Dedication Com.; com. mem. Right-Sizing County Govt. Mem. Tel. Pioners Am., Home Builders Assn. Gaston County, Inc., Woman's Aux. Fedn. Postal Clks. (charter; pres. Gastonia 1966, State v.p. 1966-69). Republican. Avocations: art, writing poems and songs, collecting dolls and stam[illegible]

ELLIS, BROTHER PATRICK (H. J. ELLIS), academic administrator; b. Balt., Nov. 17, 1928; s. Harry James and Elizabeth Alida (Evert) E. AB, Cath. U. Am., Washington, 1951; AM, U. Pa., 1954, PhD, 1960; postgrad., Barry Coll., 1963-64, Inst. Catholique, Paris, 1958; LHD (hon.), Assumption Coll., 1982, La Salle U., 1992; HHD (hon.), King's Coll., 1987; LLD (hon.), U. Scranton, 1988, C.C. Phila., 1992, Quincy U., 1993; PdD, Manhattan Coll., 1993; DEd, Anna Maria Coll., 1993, Loyola U., 1997; LHD (hon.), Villa Julie Coll., 2002. Joined Bros. of Christian Schs., Roman Cath. Ch., 1946. Tchr. English dept. West Cath. High Sch. for Boys, Phila., 1951-60, chmn. English dept., 1956-58, guidance dir., 1959-60; dir. practice teaching, sch. prin. St. Gabriel's Hall, Phoenixville, Pa., summers 1960-61, 65-66; asst. prof. English La Salle U., Phila., 1960-62, assoc. prof., 1968-73, prof., 1973—, dir. housing, 1961-62, dir. honors program, 1964-69, dir. devel., v.p., 1969-76, pres., 1977-92; prin. La Salle HS, Miami, Fla., 1962—64; pres. Cath. U. Am., Washington, 1992-98. Author: Called To Teach: Persons Are Forever, 2001; condr.: series for How To Read Gt. Books, U. of the Air, WFIL-TV, Phila., 1961, 65; Contbr. articles to profl. publs. Trustee Manhattan Coll., N.Y.C., Calvert Hall H.S., Balt., to 2001; bd. dirs. Phila. Cath. Charities, 1986-92, Greater Phila. Urban Coalition, Police Athletic League, Phila., Free Libr. Phila., 1991-92, Del. Valley Citizens Crime Commn., Fed. City Coun., D.C. Econ. Club, D.C. Bd. Trade; former trustee Cmty. Leadership Seminars, BBB; mem. recognition com. Coun. for Higher Edn. Accreditation, 1999-2001. Recipient Lindback award for disting. teaching LaSalle Coll., Phila., 1965 Mem. Sunday Breakfast Club (Phila.), Phila. Club, Univ. Club (Washington), Phi Beta Kappa, Knights of Holy Sepulchre. Home and Office: Calvert Hall HS 8102 La Salle Rd Baltimore MD 21286-8022 E-mail: brotherpatrickellis@erols.com.

ELLIS, RANDALL POOR, economist, educator; b. Newton, Mass., 1954; s. George Hathaway and Sylvia (Poor) E.; m. Joyce H. Huber; children: Richard G., Scott R., Karina J. B.A., summa cum laude, Yale U., 1976; M.S., London Sch. Econs., 1977; Ph.D., M.I.T., 1981. Asst. prof. econs. Boston U., 1981-89, assoc. prof., 1989-95, prof., 1995—; sr. scientist DxCG, Inc. Mem. APHA, Am. Econ. Assn., Econometric Soc., Internat. Health Econ. Assn., Assn. for Health Svcs. Rsch., Phi Beta Kappa. Office: Boston U Dept Econs 270 Bay State Rd Boston MA 02215-1403

ELLIS, RICHARD, artist, writer; b. N.Y.C., Apr. 2, 1938; s. Robert Butler and Sylvia Diana (Levy) E.; m. Anne Kneeland, Sept. 25, 1963 (div. 1982); children: Elizabeth Tiffany, Timothy Kneeland. BA, U. Pa., 1959. Designer Acad. Natural Sciences, Phila., 1964-65; designer Mus. Natural History, N.Y.C., 1965-66; pres. Mus. Planning Inc., N.Y.C., 1966-72; artist, writer N.Y.C., 1972—. Trustee Am. Cetacean Soc., L.A., 1979—, Oceanic Soc., Washington, 1987—; v.p. Soc. Animal Artists, N.Y.C., 1968—. Author: The Book of Sharks, 1976, The Book of Whales, 1980, Dolphins and Porpoises, 1982, Men and Whales, 1991; (with John McCosker) Great White Shark, 1991, Monsters of the Sea, 1994, Deep Atlantic, 1996, Imagining Atlantis, 1998, Search for the Giant Squid, 1998, Encyclopedia of the Sea, 2000, Aquagenesis: The Origin and Evolution of Life in the Sea, 2001, The Empty Ocean, 2003. Del. Internat. Whaling Commn., Washington, 1980-90. With U.S. Army, 1959-61. Mem. Soc. for Marine Mammalogy, Century Assn., Explorers Club. Avocations: photography, diving, book collecting, travel. Home and Office: 17 E 16th St New York NY 10003-3116

ELLIS, RICHARD SALISBURY, astronomer, educator; b. Colwyn Bay, Wales, May 25, 1950; s. Arthur (dec.) and Marion (Davies) E.; m. Barbara Williams, July 28, 1972; children: Hilary Rhona, Thomas Marc. BSc with honors, U. Coll., London, 1971; PhD, Oxford U., 1974; DSc (hon.), Durham U., 2002. From sr. demonstrator to lectr. in astronomy Durham U., 1974-83, prof. astronomy, 1985-93; prin. rsch. assoc. Royal Greenwich Obs., 1983-85; Plumian prof. astronomy Cambridge U., U.K., 1993-99; dir. Inst. Astronomy, Cambridge, 1994-99; prof. astronomy Calif. Inst. Tech., 1999—2002; dir. Palomar Obs., Pasadena, Calif., 2000—02; Steele prof. astronomy Calif. Inst. Tech., 2002—; dir. Caltech. Optical Obs., 2002—. Vis. prof. Princeton U., 1992, Calif. Inst. Tech., 1991, 97. Sr. Rsch. fellow Sci. and Engring. Rsch. Coun., 1989-94, Professorial fellow Magdalene Coll., Cambridge, 1994-99; fellow Univ. Coll., London. Fellow AAAS, Royal Astron. Soc., Inst. of Physics, Royal Soc. London; mem. Am. Astron. Soc., Astron. Soc. Pacific. Avocations: travel, skiing. Office: Calif Inst Asronomy MS 105-24 1200 E California Blvd Pasadena CA 91125 E-mail: rse@astro.caltech.edu.

ELLIS, RICHARD W. lawyer; b. Raleigh, N.C., Apr. 20, 1942; AB, U. N.C., 1964, JD with high honors, 1969. Bar: N.C. 1969. Mem. Ellis & Winters, Raleigh. Assoc. editor N.C. Law Rev., 1968-69. With USNR, 1964-66. Mem. Am. Coll. Trial Lawyers, Interant. Assn. Def. Counsel, Def. Rsch. Inst., N.C. Assn. Def. Attys., Order of Coif. Office: Ellis & Winters LLP PO Box 33550 Raleigh NC 27636 E-mail: dick_ellis@elliswinters.com.

ELLIS, ROBERT WILLIAM, materials engineer, consultant; b. Richmond, Va., Oct. 16, 1939; s. Robert William and Odessa (Thompson) Ellis; m. Donna Lee Bell, Mar. 22, 1960; children: Robert William III, Richard Berkeley, John Stephen, Donna Elaine. BS, Va. Poly. Inst., 1962, MS, 1963, PhD, 1966. Registered profl. engr., Mich. Materials engr., engr. polyscience divsn. Litton Industries, Blacksburg, Va., 1962-63; Nat. Def. fellow engring. Va. Poly. Inst., 1962-65; asst. prof. engring. U. S. Fla., Tampa, 1965-66, assoc. prof., 1967-68, asst. dean engring., 1969-71, asst. v.p. acad. affairs, 1971-72; dean Sch. Bus. Fla. Internat. U., Miami, 1972-74, dean Sch. Tech., 1972-78, provost North Miami campus, 1977; exec. v.p. Detroit Inst. Tech., 1978-80, pres., 1980-81; sr. engr. U.S. Army Tank Automotive R & D Ctr., Warren, Mich., 1981-84; lectr. mech. engring. Lawrence Inst. Tech., 1981-84, dean Sch. Engring., 1984-89; provost Lawrence Tech. U., 1989-94, prof. mech. engring., 1994-99; pvt. cons., 1999—. Cons. Gen. Dynamics Corp., 1984—89; tech. adv. bd. Fla. Solar Energy Ctr.; bd. govs. Nat. Inst. Cert. Engring. Tech., 1994—2000, chmn., 1997. Mem. economy task force Met. Dade County Planning Adv. Bd.; vice chmn. Metro Dade County Constrn. Licensing Bd.; bd. dirs. Fla. State U. Sys. Inst. Oceanography. Recipient Nat. Faculty Svc. award, Nat. Univ. Ext. Assn., 1977; NASA fellow, 1969. Fellow: Mich. Soc. Profl. Engrs. (pres. Detroit chpt. 1987, pres. state soc. 1990, Engr. of the Yr. in Mich. 1987), Engring. Soc. Detroit; mem.: NSPE (vice chmn. ctrl. region profl. engrs. edn.), Soc. Automotive Engrs. (engring. edn. bd. 1987—90, chmn. scholarship com. 1989—91), Am. Soc. Engring. Edn. (bd. dirs. coll. industry coun. 1975—78, chmn. southeastern sect. tech. divsn. 1976, chmn. divsn. rels. with industry 1990—91), Sigma Xi, Alpha Sigma Mu, Sigma Lambda Chi, Tau Beta Pi, Sigma Pi Sigma, Phi Kappa Phi, Omicron Delta Kappa. Home: Box 603 Hartland MI 48353 E-mail: ellis300@hotmail.com.

ELLIS, SARAH ELIZABETH, librarian; b. Vancouver, Can., May 19, 1952; d. Joseph Walter and Ruth Elizabeth (Steabner) E. BA, U. B.C., Vancouver, 1973, MLS, 1975; MA, Simmons Coll., 1980. Children's librarian Vancouver Pub. Libr., 1976-81, North Vancouver Dist. Libr., 1981—; lectr. U. B.C., 1982—. Author: The Baby Project, 1986, Next-Door Neighbors, 1989, Putting Up with Mitchell, 1989, Pick-up Sticks, 1991, Out of the Blue, 1994, Back of Beyond, 1996, The Young Writer's Companion, 1999, From Reader to Writer, 2000, Next Stop, 2000, A Prairie as Wide as the Sea, 2001, Big Ben, 2001, The Several Lives of Orphan Jack, 2003. Mem. Writers Union Can., Can. Soc. Children's Authors, Illustrators and Performers, PEN. Home: 4432 Walden St Vancouver BC Canada V5V 3S3 Office: North Vancouver Dist Libr 1280 E 27th St North Vancouver BC Canada V7J 1S1

ELLIS, SCOTT, theatrical director; Grad., Goodman Sch. of Drama, Chgo. Dir. plays 1776 (Drama Desk, Outer Critics Circle and Tony nominations), Steel Pier (Drama Desk, Outer Critics Circle and Tony nominations), Company, She Love Me (Tony nomination, Outer Critics Circle award Best Dir., Best Revival, Olivier award), Picnic (Outer Critics Circle nomination), A Month in the Country, Dark Rapture, The World Goes Round: The Music of Kander and Ebb (Drama Desk, Outer Critics Circle awards Best Director, Best Musical Revue), Flora, the Red Menace, 110 in the Shade, A Little Night Music (Drama Desk award Best Director, Best Revival), Sondheim: A Celebration at Carnegie Hall. Office: Nederlander Producing Co Am 1450 Broadway Fl 6 New York NY 10018-2201

ELLIS, SHARON HENDERSON, arbitrator, mediator; b. Wenatchee, Wash., May 31, 1944; d. Marvin T. and Nola Henderson; m. Alfred D. Ellis, Aug. 1972. BA, U. Wash., 1967; JD, Suffolk U., 1975. Adminstrv. law judge Mass. Labor Rels. Commn., Boston, 1978-81; arbitrator, mediator Brookline, Mass., 1982—. Adj. prof. New Eng. Sch. Law, 2002—. Contbg. author: (book) Labor and Employment Arbitration, 1988. Vol. II, tchr. U.S. Peace Corps, Tunisia, 1967-69. Mem. Am. Arbitration Assn., Nat. Acad. Arbitrators (regional chair 1997-99), Mass. Bar Assn. (sect. co-chair 1999-2000), Assn. for Conflict Resolution. Home: 36 Salisbury Rd Brookline MA 02445-2105 E-mail: sharonhendersonellis@rcn.com.

ELLIS, STEVEN GEORGE, public relations/corporate communication executive; b. Mar. 14, 1949; s. George G. and Betty (Chew) E.; m. Sylvia Regina Ellis; children: Steven Adnrew, Christopher John, Katharine Marie. BA, U. Ga., 1971. V.p. Burson-Marsteller, Washington, 1976-83; v.p., gen. mgr. Earle Palmer Brown Pub. Rels., Bethesda, Md., 1983-84, pres., 1987-88; v.p. corp. comms. RKO Gen. Co. subs. GenCorp, Inc., N.Y.C., 1984-86; pres. Steve Ellis Comms. Inc., 1988-95; sr. v.p. Jefferson-Waterman Internat., Washington, 1995-98; dir. corp. comms. SAGA Software, Inc., 1998-2000; v.p. global corp. comm. Metiom, Inc., N.Y.C., 2000-01; sr. dir. global corp. comm. Think Tools AG, Zurich, Switzerland, 2001—02; prin. Ellis Internat. Comm., 2003—. Mem. adv. bd. Henry W. Grady Coll. Journalism and Mass Comm. Recipient Gold Key award Pub. Rels. News, 1985, 86.

ELLIS, SUSAN GOTTENBERG, psychologist; b. N.Y.C., Jan. 24, 1949; d. Sam and Sally (Hirschman) Gottenberg; m. David Roy Ellis, July 23, 1972; children: Sharon Rachel, Dana Michelle. BS, Cornell U., 1970; MA, Columbia U., 1971, Hofstra U., 1975, PhD, 1976. Instr. health edn. Nassau C.C., Garden City, N.Y., 1971-73; sch. psychologist pub. schs., Somerville, N.J., 1976-77, clin. psychologist Pinellas County, Fla., 1977-78; instr. St. Petersburg (Fla.) Jr. Coll., 1978; clin. psychologist Largo, Fla., 1977—. Cons. Fla. Dept. Health and Rehab. Services, Med. Center Hosp., Largo, Morton Plant Hosp., Clearwater, Fla., 1978-79, N.Y. State Regents scholar, 1966-71; adj. prof. Eckerd Coll. St. Petersburg, 1988. Author: Interpret Your Dreams, 1987, A Dream Primer, 1988, Makes Sense of Your Dreams, 1988. Mem. Am. Psychol. Assn., Fla. Psychol. Assn., Pinellas Psychol. Assn. (treas. 1978, polit. action chmn. 1979), Cornell U. Suncoast Club (v.p. 1979-80), Kappa Delta Pi. Office: 3233 E Bay Dr Ste 100 Largo FL 33771-1900

ELLIS, SYLVIA D. HALL, development and library education consultant; b. Kewanee, Ill., June 21, 1949; d. Martin Orrill and Elizabeth Jean (Boase) Dunn; m. J. Theodore Ellis, Dec. 24, 1990. BA, Rockford Coll., 1971; MLS, U. N. Tex., 1972; MA, U. Tex., San Antonio, 1975; PhD, U. Pitts., 1985. Libr. Holding Inst., Laredo, Tex., 1972-73; dist. coord. San Antonio Pub. Librs., 1973-76; divsn. libr. Corpus Christi Pub. Librs., Tex., 1976-78; asst. dir. So. Tier Libr. System, Corning, N.Y., 1978-81; devel. officer Pitts. Regional Libr. Ctr., 1981-85; dir. librs. Rocky Mountain Coll. of Art and Design, Denver, 1992-93; asst. prof. Sam Houston State U., Huntsville, Tex., 1993-96; devel. officer Region 1 Edn. Svc. Ctr., Edinburg, Tex., 1995-97; dir devel. Mid-Continent Regional Ednl. Lab., Aurora, Colo., 1997-98; mng. ptnr. 886, Inc., 1998—. Dir. Tech. Prep of Rio Grande Valley, Inc., Harlingen, Tex., 1995—; cons. States of Colo., Mont., Iowa, S.D., Tex., Pa., 1981—; prof. U. Denver, 2000—, Emporia (Kans.) State U., 2000—, San Jose State U., 2002—. Author: Grant Writing for Small Libraries and School Library Media Centers, 1999, Grants for School Libraries, 2003; contbr. articles to profl. jours. Democrat. Episcopalian. Mailing: PO Box 61048 Denver CO 80206-1048 Office: 2135 E Wesley Ave Ste 107 Denver CO 80208-4709 E-mail: shellis@bigplanet.com.

ELLIS, WALTER LEON, minister; b. McKinney, Tex., Oct. 22, 1941; s. Erwin Ballard and Mary Edra (Bray) E.; m. Susan Elizabeth Elder, Nov. 23, 1960; children: Bruce Walter, David Anthony, Patrick Durward. BA, U. North Tex., 1964, MA, 1966; MDiv, Va. Sem., 1977; DMin, Austin Presbyn. Theol. Sem., 1993. Ordained to ministry Episc. Ch., 1977. Vicar St. Michael & All Angels', Longview, Tex., 1977-79, St. Mark's, Gladewater, Tex., 1977-79; rector St. Michael & All Angel's, Longview, Tex., 1979-82, St. Christopher, League City, Tex., 1982-2001, Ch. of the Ascension, Houston, 2001—. Dean Galveston Convocation, League City, 1989-97; mem. Diocesan Standing Com., Houston, 1996-99, pres., 1998; Order of St. Luke Chaplain, 1996-2001, Diocesan E xec. Bd., 1998-2001, Cursillo Secretariat, 1997-99; trustee St. James House, Baytown, Tex., 1983-84, 90-93, Camp Allen, Navasota, Tex., 1987-90, Bishop Quin Found., Houston, 1991-97, St. Vincent's House, Galveston, 1996-99, 2000-01; chmn. dept. environment Diocese of Tex., 1993-95; b.d dirs. Interfaith Caring Ministries, League City, 1993-94; stewardship cons. Episcopal Ch. Ctr., N.Y.C., 1990-95. Contbr. articles to profl. jours. Bd. dirs. pres. Parents Anonymous, Longview, 1980; mem. exec. bd. Bay Area coun. Boy Scouts Am., Tex., 1983-86; pres. Rotary Club, League City, 1989-90. Paul Harris fellow Space Ctr. Rotary Club, Houston, 1989. Mem. West Houston Assistance Ministry. Office: 10915 Chevy Chase Houston TX 77042 E-mail: rector@ascensionchurch.org. *You have been blessed by God through others. Find something you admire in each person you meet. Then bless those people by telling them what you admire in them.*

ELLIS, WILLIAM BEN, environmental educator, retired utility executive; b. Vicksburg, Miss., July 4, 1940; s. Conrad Ben and Viola Elizabeth (Stigall) E.; children by previous marriage: Bradford, Katherine, Emily, Ben; m. Elaine Klutsavage, July 10, 1988; children: John, David. BS, Carnegie Mellon U., 1962; PhD, U. Md., 1966. Rsch. asst. Olin Mathieson Chem. Corp., West Monroe, La., 1958, Comml. Solvents Corp., Sterlington, La., 1959; engr. Procter & Gamble Co., Cin., 1961; process engr. Standard Oil N.J., Baton Rouge, 1962-67; assoc. McKinsey & Co., Inc., Washington, 1969-75, prin., 1975-76; exec. v.p., cfo Northeast Utilities and Subs., Hartford, Conn., 1976-78, pres., cfo, 1978-80, pres., coo, 1980-83, chmn., ceo, 1983-93, chmn., 1993-95. Sr. fellow Yale U. Sch. of Forestry and Environ. Studies, 1995—; trustee Northeast Utilities, Hartford, Conn., 1977-95; bd. dirs. Mass. Mutual Life Ins. Co., Catalytica Energy Sys., Inc., numerous others. Bd. dirs. Smithsonian Natural History Mus., 1999-2002, Pew Ctr. Global Climate Change. With U.S. Army, 1967-69. Mem. Metro Hartford C. of C. (bd. dirs. 1978—, chmn. 1985).

ELLIS, WILLIAM GENE, neuropathologist; b. Cin., June 12, 1932; s. Richard Karl and Lucile E.; m. Arlene Lois Kaslow, June 12, 1960; children: David Karl, Heidi Beth. BA, Iowa Weslyan Coll., 1953; MD, U. Iowa, 1957. Diplomate Am. Bd. of Neurology, 1965, Am. Bd. of Neuropathology, 1976. Staff neurologist Hines (Ill.) VA Hosp., 1965-66; asst. neuropathologist Langley Porter Neuropsychiat. Inst., San Francisco, 1966-72; prof. U. Calif., Davis, 1972—; dir. neuropath. Cons. Napa (Calif.) State Hosp, Sonoma Devel. Ctr., Eldridge, Calif. Contbr. articles to profl. jours. Capt. U.S. Army, 1961-63. Fellow Am. Acad. Neurology; mem. Am. Assn. Neuropathologists, Royal Soc. Med., U.S. and Can. Acad. Pathology. Office: UC Davis Med Ctr Dept Pathology 2315 Stockton Blvd Sacramento CA 95817

ELLIS, WILLIAM GRENVILLE, academic administrator, management consultant; b. Teaneck, N.J., Nov. 29, 1940; s. Grenville Brigham and Vivian Lilian (Breeze) E.; m. Nancy Elizabeth Kempton, 1963; children: William Grenville, Bradford Graham. BS in Bus. Adminstrn., Babson Coll., 1962; MBA, Suffolk U., 1963; MEd, Westfield State Coll., 1965; EdD, Pa. State U., 1968; MS, Concordia U., 1991; MLE (Sears Roebuck Found. scholar), Harvard U., 1980; postgrad., U. Chgo., 1983, MIT, 1984, Harvard U., 1988, 96. Asst. prof. bus. Rider U., 1968-69; div. dir., assoc. prof. Castleton (Vt.) State Coll., 1969-72; exec. v.p., prof. St. Joseph Coll. in Vt., Rutland, 1972-73; acad. v.p., dean grad. sch. Thomas Coll., Waterville, Maine, 1973-82; pres. Wayland Acad., Beaver Dam, Wis., 1982-95, New Eng. Coll., Henniker, N.H., 1995-97; dean Sch. Bus. and Legal Studies, Concordia U. Wis., Mequon, 1997—. Mem. adv. bd. CFX Bank, 1996-97; corporator 1st Consumers Savs., 1974-81, Maine Savs., 1981-82. Author: The Analysis and Attainment of Economic Stability, 1963, The Relationship of Related Work Experience to the Teaching Success of Beginning Business Teachers, 1968, Marketing for Educational Administrators, 1991, A Gunner's Moon, 1997; contbr. numerous articles and abstracts to profl. jours. Trustee C.C. Vt., 1972-73, Marian Coll., 1988-91, Wayland Acad., 1982-95, New Eng. Coll., 1995-97; auditor Town of Castleton, 1969-71; pres. Kennebee Valley Youth Hockey, Augusta, Maine, 1975-77; pres. Beaver Dam C. of C., 1985, 86, Midwest Classic Athletic Conf., 1989, Wis. Assn. Ind. Schs., 1984-86; chair bd. dirs. Beaver Dam Cmty. Hosp., 1985-95; dir. North Ctrl. Assn. Colls. and Secondary Schs., 1991-94, Ind. Schs. Ctrl. States, 1991-95; dir. N.H. Coll. and Univ. Coun., 1995-97; dir. Ozaukee County Indsl. Devel. Corp., 2003—. Recipient Cmty., Svc. award Rutland C. of C., 1973, Disting. Svc. citation Wayland Acad., 1995, Excellence in Edn. award Pa. State U., 2001; named Cons. of Yr., SBA, 1975, 77, Prof. of Yr. Concordia U. Wis., 1999. Mem. APA, Nat. Assn. Intercollegiate Athletics (cert. of merit 1979), Soc. for Advancement of Mgmt., Cum Laude Soc., Pheasant City Club, Rotary, Alpha Chi, Pi Omega Pi, Alpha Delta Sigma, Delta Pi Epsilon, Phi Delta Kappa. Home: 8655 N Regent Rd Fox Point WI 53217-2362 Office: Concordia U Sch Bus & Legal Studies 12800 N Lake Shore Dr Mequon WI 53097-2418 E-mail: william.ellis@cuw.edu.

ELLIS, WILLIAM GRENVILLE, JR., marine biologist, educator; b. Waterbury, Conn., Aug. 4, 1964; s. William Grenville and Nancy (Kempton) E.; m. Lola Eustis-Hogeman Ellis, July 1, 1989; 1 child, Anna West. AB, Bowdoin Coll., 1986; PhD, U. R.I., 1992. Rsch. assoc. U. Md., College Park, 1992-94; postdoctoral fellow U. R.I., Kingston, 1994-96; asst. prof. Maine Maritime Acad., Castine, 1996-2000; asst. coach men's and women's varsity cross county Maine Maritime Acad. (NCAA Divsn. III), 1997-99, head coach men's and women's varsity cross country, 1999-2000; coord. upward bound math-sci. program U. Maine, Orono, 2000—02, coop. asst. prof. marine scis., 2000—, asst. dir. upward bound math-sci. program, 2002—. Mem. Maine Com. for Global and Geog. Edn., Augusta, 1998. Contbr. articles to profl. jours. V.p. alumni exec. bd. U. R.I., 1994-96. Mem. Am. Geophys. Union. Achievements include determination of sources of selenium in the atmosphere; research on the transport of Saharan dust in the atmosphere, on ozone chemistry in the atmosphere. Office: U Maine Upward Bound Math-Sci Program 5713 Chadbourne Hall Rm 226 Orono ME 04469-0001

ELLISON, BETTY D. retired elementary educator; b. Meriwether County, Ga., Jan. 28, 1950; d. Haywood Sr. and Mary Susan (Green) Daniel; m. Darthus Ellison, Jr., June 25, 1972; children: Darthus III, Keith Brandon. BA, Morris Brown Coll., 1972; MA, Atlanta U., 1975. Cert. tchr. Tchr. Meriwether County Bd. Edn., Greenville, Ga.; reading specialist Talbot County Bd. Edn., Talbotton, Ga. Advisor Nat. Jr. Honor Soc.; owner, operator Ellison's Tutorial Svc. Ga. State Tchrs. scholar; named County Star Tchr., 1991. Mem. NEA, Internat. Reading Assn., Ga. Assn. Educators, Zeta Phi Beta, Pi Delta Phi. Home: 88 Johnson Ave Manchester GA 31816-1602

ELLISON, BOBBIE DILWORTH, retired music educator, composer; b. San Antonio, Apr. 06; m. Rothchild Ellison, Dec. 24, 1958; 1 child, Arnold. BS, EdM, Prairie View A/M U; additional studies, W TX State U, Canyon, TX. Cert. administration TX A&I U. Tchr.: third grade Brockman Elem. Sch., Monahans, Tex., 1958—61, Hilltop Elem. Sch., Amarillo, Tex., 1963—70; tchr. Alice Landercin Elem. Sch., Amarillo, Tex., 1970—71, Belmar Elem. Sch., Amarillo, Tex., 1971—74, T.G. Allen Elem. Sch., Corpus Christi, Tex., 1975—98. Composer: (songs) Secret Closet, 1999; author: The Healing Heart. Home: 3525 Crestdale Corpus Christi TX 78415-3703

ELLISON, CYRIL LEE, literary agent, retired publisher; b. N.Y.C., Dec. 11, 1916; m. Anne N. Nottonson, June 4, 1942 (dec. June 2000). Assoc. pub., v.p. Watson-Guptill Publs., 1939-69, v.p., advt. dir., 1939-69, assoc. pub. Am. Artist mag.; exec. v.p. Communication Channels, Inc., N.Y.C., 1969-88; pub. emeritus Fence Industry, Access Control, Pension World, Trusts & Estates, Nat. Real Estate Investor, Shopping Center World; pres. Lee Comms., 1980—; assoc. Kids Countrywide, Inc., 1987-94; literary agent, 1994—. Pub. cons., book rep., advt. and mktg. cons., 1987-94; assoc. Mark Clements Rsch. N.Y., Inc., 1994—; pub. cons. Mag. Rsch. Co., 1994—. Served with USAAF, 1942-46, PTO. Named Gray-Russo Advt. Man of Year Ad Men's Post Am. Legion, 1954; recipient Hall of Fame award Internat. Fence Industry Assn., 1985. Mem. Am. Legion (life, comdr. advt. men's post 1954, 64). Home: 6839 N 29th Ave Phoenix AZ 85017-1213 Office: Lee Communications 5060 N 19th Ave Phoenix AZ 85015-3210

ELLISON, DAVID CHARLES, special education educator; b. Agana, Guam, Apr. 20, 1957; s. Leo Charles and Joan Ruby (Hendrickson) E.; m. Teresa Josephine Vos, Dec. 20, 1980; children: Johanna Marie, Matthew David. BAA in Social Sci., U. Minn., Duluth, 1980. Tchr. spl. edn. ISD #94, Cloquet, Minn., 1981—; spl. edn. adminstr. ISD # 94, Cloquet, Minn., summers 1991-99. Head coach Cloquet Lumberjacks Spl. Olympics, 1981—; girls varsity hockey asst. coach Cloquet Lumberjacks. Recipient Transition Excellence award Dept. Children, Families and Learning in Minn., 1997. Democrat. Roman Catolic. Avocations: fishing, camping, hunting, family outings. Home: 705 Jasper St Cloquet MN 55720-1212 Office: ISD # 94 Cloquet Sr H S 1000 18th St Cloquet MN 55720-2438

ELLISON, EARL OTTO, computer scientist; b. Elizabeth, N.J., Apr. 26, 1938; s. Thorleif and Reidun E. (Anderson) Ingeborg; m. Judith Roque Impoc, Feb. 2, 1997; children: Reidun Impoc, Arnfinn Alejandro. BS, Am. U., Washington, 1964, postgrad., 1964-66. Head supplies and equipment at Pentagon C & P Telephone Co. (now Bell Atlantic), Arlington, Va., 1956-62; tax acct. Trust Dept. Nat. Bank of Washington, 1964-65; methods analyst Automation Industries, Consol. Am. Svcs. Mgmt. Cons. Subs., Washington, L.A., 1965; mgmt. instr. fed. supply svc. GSA, Washington, 1965-67, contract negotiator info. tech. svc., 1967-77, computer sys. contracting officer, 1977-97; pres. Teledesic Svcs., Inc., Washington, 1997—. Author: Revenue Code of 1962: Effects on the Multi-National Firm, 1965. Judge ballroom dancing U.S. Ballroom Dancing Assn., Eastern seaboard, 1986—; swimming and diving coach Pike Br. Swim and Tennis Club, Alexandria, Va., 1966-2001. With USNR, 1961-62. Mem. The Beethoven Soc. Am. (exec. bd. 1993—), Norwegian Soc., Sons of Norway (prin. bldg. fund 1985—, Washington chpt. pres. 1994, 95, counselor 1993—, investment adv. 1979—, internat. del. to conv. 1988, trustee 2002-). Presbyterian. Avocations: swimming, diving, ballroom dancing. Home: 6324 Telegraph Rd Alexandria VA 22310-2969 Office: 710 W Peachtree St NW Atlanta GA 30308-1139 also: Rosfjord 4580 Lyngdal Norway

ELLISON, EDWIN CHRISTOPHER, physician, surgeon; b. Columbus, Ohio, Jan. 10, 1950; s. Edwin Homer and Molly (Scheeler) E.; m. Mary Pat Borgess, Dec. 23, 1978; children: Jonathan Scott, Eric Christopher. BS, U. Wis., 1972; MD, Med. Coll. Wis., 1976. Diplomate Am. Bd. Surgery. Resident surgery Ohio State U., Columbus, 1976—83, asst. prof. surgery, 1983—93, assoc. prof., 1993—99, prof., 1999—; chief divsn. gen. surgery, bd. dirs. Ohio Digestive Disease Inst., Columbus, 1987—93; chief of staff Ohio State U. Med. Ctr., Columbus, 1999—2000, vice chmn. dept. surgery, 1996—99, 1interim chair surgery, 0999—2000, chmn. surgery, 2000—, assoc. v.p. health sci., 2002—, vice dean clin. affairs, 2002—. Fellow ACS. Office: 327 Means Hall 1654 Upham Dr Columbus OH 43210-1240

ELLISON, HARLAN JAY, author, screenwriter; b. Cleve., May 27, 1934; s. Louis Laverne and Serita (Rosenthal) E.; m. Charlotte Stein, 1956 (div. 1959); m. Billie Joyce Sanders, 1961 (div. 1962); m. Lory Patrick, 1965 (div. 1965); m. Lori Horwitz, 1976 (div. 1977); m. Susan Toth, Sept., 1986. Student, Ohio State U., 1953-55. A founder Cleve. Sci.-Fiction Soc., 1950; pub. mag. Sci.-Fantasy Bull. (later retitled Dimensions); editor Rogue Mag., Chgo., 1959-60, Regency Books, Chgo., 1960-61; lectr. colls. and univs.; book critic Los Angeles Times, 1969-82. Editl. commentator Canadian Broadcasting Co., 1972-78; pres. Kilimanjaro Corp., 1979— ; instr. Clarion Writers Workshop, Mich. State U., 1969-77, 1984; TV spokesman Chevrolet GEO Imports, 1988-89; on-screen TV actor for numerous shows including Babylon 5 and Psi-Factor. Actor: Cleveland Playhouse, part-time 1944-49; scriptwriter: TV series Alfred Hitchcock Hour, Outer Limits, The Man From U.N.C.L.E., others, 1962-77; writer 7 scripts for Burke's Law; creator (under pseudonym Cordwainer Bird) The Starlost, NBC-TV series; scenarist 2-hour NBC spl. The Tigers Are Loose, 1974-75; writer motion pictures The Dream Merchants, The Oscar, Nick the Greek, Best by Far, Harlan Ellison's Movie; scenarist I, Robot, 1978, Bug Jack Barron, 1982-83; writer Nebula winning novella-into-film A Boy and His Dog, 1975 (Hugo award for film adaptation 1976); author: 75 books including Web of the City, 1958, The Sound of a Scythe, 1960, Gentleman Junkie, 1961, Memos from Purgatory, 1961, Spider Kiss, 1961, Ellison Wonderland, 1962, Paingod (translated into French, Japanese, German, Spanish), 1965, I Have No Mouth & I Must Scream (translated into Japanese, French, Italian, Spanish, German), 1967, From the Land of Fear, 1967, Love Ain't Nothing But Sex Misspelled, 1968, The Beast that Shouted Love at the Heart of the World, 1969, Over th[illegible] Edge, 1970, Alone Against Tomorrow, 1971, Partners in Wonder, 197[illegible] Approaching Oblivion, 1974, Deathbird Stories, 1975, No Doors, No Window[illegible] 1976, Strange Wine, 1978, All The Lies That Are My Life, 1980, Shatterda[illegible] 1980, Stalking the Nightmare, 1982, Sleepless Nights in the Procrustean Be[illegible]

1984, An Edge in My Voice, 1985, Medea: Harlan's World, 1985, The Essential Ellison, 1987 (Bram Stoker award Horror Writers Am. 1988), Night and the Enemy, 1987, Angry Candy, 1988 (World Fantasy award for best short story collection, 1989, Major Works in Am. Lit. award 1988), Harlan Ellison's Watching, 1989 (Bram Stoker award Horror Writers Am. 1990), The Harlan Ellison Hornbook, 1990, Harlan Ellison's Movie, 1990, Dreams with Sharp Teeth, 1991, Mefisto in Onyx (Bram Stoker award Horror Writers Am. 1994), (with artist Jacek Yerka) Mind Fields (Morpheus), 1994, The City on the Edge of Forever, 1995, Edgeworks: The Collected Ellison, Vol 1 & Vol 2, 1996, Edgeworks, Vols. 3 and 4, 1997, Slippage, 1997, Repent, Harlequin!, 1997, The Essential Ellison (A 50 Year Retrospective), 2001, Troublemakers (young adult collection), 2001; editor, compiler: anthology Dangerous Visions (transls. French, German, Japanese, Italian, Spanish, U.K. edits.), 1967, 35th Anniversary Edit., 2002, Again, Dangerous Visions, 1972; author 4 books on juvenile delinquency; writer weekly TV column The Glass Teat, L.A. Free Press, 1968-71, pub. in 2 vols., 1970, 75, weekly column Harlan Ellison Hornbook, L.A. Free Press, 1972-73, An Edge in My Voice, Future Life, 1980-81, L.A. Weekly, 1982-83, pub. in 1 volume, 1985; on-camera commentator, critic cable Sci-Fi channel, 1993-98; host radio series, 2000, Nat. Pub. Radio, 2000—; creator (with Larry Brody) weekly series The Dark Forces, NBC-TV, 1986, (with Ben Bova) series Brillo, ABC-TV, 1974, computer game based on I Have No Mouth and I Must Scream for Cyberdreams, 1995, creative cons., writer, dir. The Twilight Zone, CBS-TV, 1984-85, Cutter's World, 1987, 88; conceptual cons. Babylon 5, Warner Bros., 1993—; creator, editor series Harlan Ellison Discovery Series of 1st novels for Pyramid Books, 1973-77; voiceovers for animated cartoons; audio collection of stories, The Voice From the Edge: I have no Mouth and I Must Scream, 1999, The Voice from the Edge: Midnight in the Sunken Cathedral, 2001; various works credited as inspiration for The Terminator (1984, Orion Pictures). With AUS, 1957-59. Recipient Hugo awards World Sci.-Fiction Conv., 1966, (2) 67, 68, 73, 74, 76, 77, 86, Spl. Achievement awards, 1968, 72, Certificate of Merit Trieste Film Festival, 1970, Edgar Allan Poe award Mystery Writers Am., 1974, 88, Am. Mystery award, 1988, 6 Bram Stoker Awards Inc., Lifetime Achievement, 1988, VIRA award for best vintage TV, The Outer Limits: Demon with a Glass Hand, 2 Audie Awards Audio Publishers Assn., 1999, George Méliès awards for cinematic achievement, 1972, 73, Jupiter award Instrs. Sci. Fiction in Higher Edn., 1974, 77, award for journalism PEN Internat., 1982, Americana Ann. award, 1989, Disting. Skeptic award Com. for Sci. Investigation of Claims of the Paranormal; inducted to Swedish Nat. Encyclopedia, 1992; honored by PEN for continuing commitment to artistic freedom and battle against censorship, 1990; selection of short story The Man Who Rowed Christopher Columbus for inclusion in The Best American Short Stories, 1993; Ray Bradbury award for drama series. Mem. SAG, Writers Guild Am. (Most Outstandign Scripts awards 1965, 67, 73, 86, screen bd., mem. West coun. 1971-72, 85-87), Sci. Fiction Writers Am. (co-founder, Nebula awards 1965, 69, 77, v.p. 1965-66). Address: PO Box 55548 Sherman Oaks CA 91413-0548 *The two most common elements in the universe are hydrogen and stupidity.*

ELLISON, HERBERT JAY, historian, educator; b. Portland, Oreg., Oct. 3, 1929; s. Benjamin F. and Esther (Anderson) Ellison; m. Alberta M. Moore, June 13, 1952; children: Valery, Pamela. BA, U. Wash., 1951, MA, 1952; PhD (Fulbright fellow), U. London, 1955. Instr. history U. Wash., 1955-56, prof. Russian and Eastern European studies, 1968—, dir. divsn. internat. programs, 1968-72, vice provost for ednl. devel., 1969-72, dir. Inst. Comparative and Fgn. Area Studies, 1973-78, chmn. Russian and East European studies, 1979-83; asst. prof. U. Okla., 1956-62; assoc. prof. history, chmn. Slavic studies program U. Kans., 1962-67, prof., 1965-68, dir. NDEA Lang. and Area Ctr. Slavic Studies, 1965-67, assoc. dean faculties internat. programs, 1967-68; sec. Kennan Inst. Advanced Russian Studies, Washington, 1983-85. Trustee Nat. Coun. Russian and E. European Rsch., 1983—87; dir. Russian rsch. Nat. Bur. Asian Rsch., 1990—, bd. dirs., 1993—; chmn. bd. dirs. Internat. Rsch. and Exchs. Bd., 1992—98; dir. new Russia in Asia rsch. and conf. project, 1993—96; chmn. acad. coun. Kennan Inst. Advanced Russian Studies, 1997—2001; bd. govs. Blakemore Found., 1998—. Author: (book) History of Russia, 1964, Sino-Soviet Conflict, 1982, Soviet Policy Toward Western Europe, 1983, Japan and the Pacific Quadrille, 1987; co-author: Twentieth Century Russia, 1999; contbr. articles to profl. jours.; chief cons., exec. dir. (TV series) Messengers from Moscow, 1995, Yeltsin, 2000. Mem.: AAUP, Am. Assn. Advancement Slavic Studies, Am. Hist. Assn., Univ. Club. Home: 12127 SE 15th St Bellevue WA 98005-3821 Office: Univ Wash Jackson Sch Internat Study PO Box 353650 Seattle WA 98195-3650 E-mail: hellison@u.washington.edu.

ELLISON, JEFFREY ALAN, educator; b. Bronx, Nov. 7, 1951; s. Eli Robert and Estelle (Appelbaum) E.; m. Rebecca Sporn (div. Sept. 1994); children: Erin, Felicia. BA in History and Art History, Lake Forest Coll., 1973; MA in Anthropology, Wash. State U., 1977; EdD, Fla. Atlantic U., 2002. Rschr. Field Mus. Natural History, Chgo., 1977-78; tchr. Chgo. Latin Sch., 1979-85; mgr. Spornette Internat., Homewood, Ill., 1985-90; tchr. Benjamin Sch., Palm Beach Gardens, Fla., 1990-93; tchr., chair dept. social studies Bernard Zell Anshe Emet Day Sch., Chgo., 1994—, coach chess team. Ill. state scholar, 1969, Travelling scholar, 1977. Mem. Nat. Coun. Social Studies Tchrs. Avocations: reading, chess, tennis. Home: 602 Green Bay Rd Glencoe IL 60022-2606 Office: 3760 N Pine Grove Ave Chicago IL 60613-4103

ELLISON, JOHN VOGELSANGER, retired engineer; b. Cape Girardeau, Mo., Aug. 7, 1919; s. Floyd Anderson and Clara (Vogelsanger) Ellison; m. Louise Ruby Day, Dec. 15, 1949; children: Elizabeth Louise Marks, Barbara Henley Stalker; m. Virginia Klutz Ellison, June 1940 (div. July 1949); children: Andrea Lee Keebler(dec.), Victoria Sue. BA, S.E. Mo. State U., 1940; grad. study, State U. Iowa, Ill. Inst. Tech., Mass. Inst. Tech. Registered profl. engr., DC, 1952, electrical engr./electronics, DC, 1959. Tchr. physics and biology Fornfelt Mo. Pub. Sch., 1939—40, Sikeston Mo. Pub. Sch., 1940—41; grad. asst. Ill. Inst. Tech., Chgo., 1941; dean of instrs. Am. TV Labs., Chgo., 1941—43; staff mem. divsn. of war rsch. Columbia U., New London, Conn., 1943—45; staff mem. radiation lab. Mass. Inst. Tech., Cambridge, Mass., 1945; scientist U.S. Naval Rsch. Lab., Washington, 1945—59; mgr. reconnaissance lab, McDonnell Aircraft Co. McDonnell Douglas Corp., St. Louis, 1959—83. Mem.: OBP (sec., v.p., pres. 1966—71), 10-10 Internat. (head, Gateway chpt. 1975—84), Acoustical Soc. of Am. Episcopalian. Achievements include invention of underwater telephone for submarines; mine and torpedo detectors; design of sonar displays; patents in field. Avocations: ham radio, photography. Home: Apt 4149 1010 Wiggins Pkwy Mesquite TX 75150

ELLISON, LAWRENCE J. computer company executive; b. 1944; BS. With Amdahl, Inc., Santa Clara, Calif., 1967—71, systems architect; pres. systems divsn. Omex Corp., 1972—77; CEO Oracle Corp., Redwood, Calif., 1978—, pres., 1977—96, chmn., 1990—92, 1995—, bd. dirs. Recipient Disting. Info. Scis. award, Assn. Info. Tech. Profls., 1996. Office: Oracle Corp 500 Oracle Pkwy MSC 5OPCEO Redwood City CA 94065-1675*

ELLISON, LUTHER FREDERICK, oil company executive; b. Monroe, La., Jan. 2, 1925; s. Luther and Gertrude (Hudson) E.; m. Frances Williams, July 18, 1948 (dec.); children: Constance Elizabeth, Carolyn Williams; m. Patsy Hunter, Nov. 23, 1996. Student, Emory U., 1943-44; BS in Petroleum Engring., Tex. A&M U., 1949, BS in Geol. Engring., 1950. Registered profl. engr., Tex., La. Jr. petroleum engr. Sun Prodn. Co., Kilgore and McAllen, Tex., 1950-52, area petroleum engr. Garcia Field, Tex., 1952-54, Delhi (La.) unit engr., 1954-60, asst. region supt., 1960-62, dist. drilling engr. Corpus Christi, 1962-63, dist. engr. McAllen, 1963-65, supr. engring. Dallas, 1965-66, div. chief petroleum engr., 1966-70, regional mgr. engring., 1970-75, region mgr., 1975-78, dir. devel., 1978-80, v.p. devel., 1980-84; div. v.p., dir. Sun Exploration and Prodn. Co., 1984-86, pres., bd. dirs., 1986—; pres., chief exec. officer Oil & Gas Experts, Inc., Dallas, 1986—, Am. Energy Enterprises Inc., Dallas, 1988—. Pres., dir., mem. exec. com. Nabors-Sun Drilling Co.; dir., mem. exec. com. East Tex. Salt & Water Disposal Co.; CEO, pres. Oil & Gas Experts Inc., 1986; speaker in field. V.p. Northwood Jr. High Sch. PTA, Dallas, 1967-68, pres., 1968-69; elder, trustee Preston Hollow Presbyn. Ch. Found.; bd. dirs. Glen Lakes Assn. With USNR, 1943-46. Mem. Tex.-Mid-Continent Oil and Gas Assn. (Outstanding Achievement award 1964, chmn. area 1964-65, mgr. north region, operating com., Outstanding Performance award 1985—), Am. Petroleum Inst., Soc. Petroleum Engrs., Dallas Engrs. Club, Petroleum Engrs. Club, Dallas Petroleum Club, Park City Club, Northwood Club (Dallas), Lions Club, Premier Club (Dallas), Parents League, Sigma Alpha Epsilon (pres. 1944-45). Home: 526 Preston Trail Loop Kerrville TX 78028-6406 Office: PO Box 1119 Tijeras NM 87059

ELLISON, MARCIA A. anthropologist, researcher; PhD, U. of Calif. Postdoctoral rsch. fellow Harvard Med. Sch., Boston, 2000—. Contbr. articles to profl. jours. Recipient Excellence in Women's Health award, Harvard Med. Sch., 2000; fellow, NIH, 2000—. Mem.: Am. Anthropology Assn., Soc. of Psychol. Anthropology, Soc. of Med. Anthropology. Office: Massachusetts General Hospital 55 Fruit Street Bartlett Hall Ext 5 Boston MA 02114

ELLISON, MICHAEL SCOTT, former financial executive, sailing coach; b. Chgo., Jan. 2, 1951; s. Harold Charles and Royal Soxie Ellison; m. Cynthia Marie Feller. BSME, U.S. Naval Acad., 1973; MSBA, U.S. Naval Postgrad. Sch., 1978. EIT Pa. Commd. ensign USN, 1969, advanced through grades to lt. comdr., 1978; sr. cons. Kurt Salmon Assocs., Atlanta, 1979—82, gen. mgr. Deansgate Clothing, New Orleans, 1982—84, Houston Marine Inc., New Orleans, 1984—86; v.p. fin. and adminstrn. Anheuser Busch Inc., New Orleans, 1986—96; ops. mgr. Tanaka Constrn., Okinawa, Japan, 1996—98; v.p. Landersman Assocs., San Diego, 1998—2001; varsity offshore sailing coach U.S. Naval Acad., Annapolis, Md., 2001—. Navigator tall ship Pilgrim of Newport, 1998. Recipient Osaka Cup, Offshore Sailing Race, 1996. Mem.: USN Sailing Assn. (bd. dirs. 2001—02), USN Sailing Found. (bd. dirs. 2001—02), Shrine, Masons (pres. La. lodge 102 1996). Avocations: offshore sailing, scuba diving, running, collecting books. Home: 2930 Garfield St NW Washington DC 20008-3536 E-mail: ellisonms@hotmail.com.

ELLISON, NICHOLAS HOWELL, literary agent; b. N.Y.C., Mar. 18, 1948; s. William and Virginia (Howell) Soskin; children: Gustave Nicholas, Catherine Hannah. BA, Boston U., Sorbonne, 1969. Sr. editor Thomas Y. Crowell Pub. Co., N.Y.C., 1972-76; sr. editor Harper & Row Pubs., N.Y.C., 1976-79; editor-in-chief Delacorte Press, N.Y.C., 1979-81; pres. Nicholas Ellison, Inc., 1983—. Prof. writing Fairfield U., 1980— ; dir. Verreaux Enterprises. Editor numerous books. Pres. Bell Island Assn., Rowayton, Conn., 1972. Recipient Outstanding Achievement award Folio Mgmt. Tng. Seminars, 1979 Mem.: Shore and Country (Norwalk, Conn.). Congregationalist. Home: 92 Mather Rd Stamford CT 06903-3026 Office: 55 5th Ave New York NY 10003-4301

ELLISON, PATRICIA LEE, lawyer; b. Elizabeth, N.J., Oct. 17, 1943; d. Harry C. and Leila D. Ellison. Student, U. Paris, France, 1963-64; BA, Denison U., France, 1965; MA, U. Calif., Riverside, 1967; JD cum laude, U. San Diego, 1973. Bar: Calif. 1973, N.Y. 1983. Fin. analyst NASA, Greenbelt, Md., 1967-68; rsch. atty. Dist. Atty.'s Office, San Diego, 1973-74; assoc. atty. Butler Ruff & Harrigan, San Diego, 1974-75; ptnr. Ellison Eichten & Bell, San Diego, 1975-82; pvt. practice Kingston, N.Y., 1983—. Bd. dirs. Ulster County YWCA, Kingston, 1988-91, pres. bd. dirs., 1992; chair Dem. Com. Town of Shandaken, N.Y., 1993—; mem. Ulster County Youth Bd., 2002—; mem. panel surrogate decision-making com. N.Y. State Commn. on Quality of Care, 2001— . Recipient Internat. Acad. Trial Lawyers Advocacy award, 1973. Mem. Alpha Chi Omega. Avocations: piano, gardening. Office: 175 Clinton Ave PO Box 1717 Kingston NY 12402-1717

ELLISON, ROBERT W. sculptor; b. Detroit, Dec. 13, 1946; s. Owen and Mary Ellison. BFA, Mich. State U., 1969, MFA, 1971. Sculpture design instr. Mich. State U., Lansing, 1970-71, Kentfield, Calif., 1972-77. Steel sculptures include Untitled, 1969, Borbourygmi, 1979, Contest, 1990, Mr. Zebra and Friends, 1999, Spin, 2002, Know Way, 2002. Recipient 1st pl. award 21st Annual All Calif. Juried Show. Mem. Cultural Arts Coun. Sonoma. Avocation: growing cactus and succulents. Home and Office: Ellison Studio 6480 Eagle Ridge Rd Penngrove CA 94951-9574

ELLISON, WILLIAM THEODORE, marine engineer; b. Wilmington, N.C., Nov. 30, 1941; s. Robert Jay and Marie Catherine (Robinson) E.; m. Annelise Manecky, Dec. 18, 1987; children: Britt Kirsten, Hans Salter, Katerina Astri-Marie. BS, U.S. Naval Acad., 1963; MSME, MIT, 1968, PhD, 1970. Scientist, v.p. Cambridge (Mass.) Acoustical Assn., Inc., 1974-83; pres., CEO Marine Acoustics, Inc., Newport, R.I., 1983—. Contbr. articles to profl. jours. Capt. USNR, ret. Named Disting. Alumni of Yr. The Breck Sch., 2001. Fellow Explorers Club; mem. Acoustical Soc. Am., Tau Beta Pi, Sigma Xi. Achievements include designing passive acoustical whale tracking system for population assessment of endangered species in the Arctic; pioneering work in impact of underwater sound on marine resources, breakthrough tech. in handheld voice translation sys. Address: PO Box 340 Litchfield CT 06759

ELLIS-SCRUGGS, JAN, theater arts educator; b. Phila., Apr. 7, 1951; d. Roger C. and Greta M. Ellis; m. William Marquis Scruggs, Aug. 8, 1970; children: William Marcus Jr., Christopher Michael. BA, Cheyney U., 1987; MA, Villanova U., 1991. Lectr., instr. U. Conn., Storrs, 1989-90; theatre arts instr. Delaware County C.C., Media, Pa., 1994-95; asst. prof. theatre arts Cheyney (Pa.) U., 1993-94, 97—; actor, singer, dir., theater educator, adminstr. U.S. and London. Assoc. prodr., Citeaux, Inc., London, 1979-83; dir. Cheyney U., 1997—. Mem. editl. adv. bd., Collegiate Press, San Diego, 1999—. Missionary, Mother Bethel African Meth. Episc. Ch., Phila., 1994—. Mem. AFTRA, SAG (Screen Actors Guild), Actors Equity Assn., Alpha Psi Omega. Home: 7942 Cedarbrook Ave Philadelphia PA 19150 Office: Cheyney U of Pa Marian Anderson Music Ctr Cheyney PA 19319 E-mail: jebs267@aol.com.

ELLISTON, KRISTINE, not-for-profit fundraiser; d. R. Wayne and Joelle Elliston. BS in bus. adminstrn., Union Coll., Lincoln, Nebr., 1997; MBA, West Tex. A&M U., Canyon, Tex., 2000. Dir. devel. Platte Valley Acad., Shelton, Nebr., 1998—2001; assoc. dir. devel. Adventist World Radio, Silver Spring, Md., 2001—. Mem.: Assn. of Fundraising Profls.

ELLIS-VANT, KAREN MCGEE, elementary and special education educator, consultant; b. La Grande, Oreg., May 10, 1950; d. Ellis Eddington and Gladys Vera McGee; m. Lynn F. Ellis, June 14, 1975 (div. Sept. 1983); children: Megan Marie, Matthew David; m. Jack Scott Vant, Sept. 6, 1986; children: Kathleen Erin, Kelli Christine (dec.). BA in Elem. Edn., Boise State U., 1972, MA in Spl. Edn., 1979; postgrad. studies in curriculum/instrn., U. Minn., 1985-86. Tchr. learning disabilities resource rm. New Plymouth Joint Sch. Dist., 1972-73, Payette Joint Sch. Dist., 1973; diagnostician project SELECT, 1974-75; cons. tchr. in spl. edn. Boise Sch. Dist., 1975-90, tchr. 1-2 combination, 1990-91, team tchr. 1st grade, 1991-92, 95—, site based leadership team, 1997-99. Chpt. 1 program cons., 1992-95, mem. Idaho Mgmt. Change Project, 1997-99, Learning for the 21st Century project, 1999—; mem. profl. Stds. Commn., 1983-86. Contbr. articles to profl. jours.; editor, author ednl. texts and comminique; conductor of workshops, leadership tng. coop. learning and frameworks. Bd. dirs. Hotline, Inc., 1979-82; mem. Idaho Coop. Manpower Com., 1984-85; mem. First United Meth. Ch., childcare bd., 1998-2000, mem. diversity com., 2001-02, mem. leadership team Many Hands One Spirit, 2002—03; bd. dirs. Idaho Coun. for History Edn., 2001—02; FUMC, 2002. Recipient Disting. Young Woman of Yr. award Boise Jaycettes, 1982, Idaho Jaycettes, 1983; Coffman Alumni scholar U. Minn., 1985-86. Mem. NEA (mem. civil rights com. 1983-85, state contact for peace caucus 1981-85, del. assembly rep. 1981-85), NSTA, ASCD, Internat. Reading Assn. (v.p. Boise chpt. 1996-97), NCTE, NCHE, Internat. Coop. Learning Assn., Idaho Edn. Assn. (bd. dirs. region VII 1981-85, pres. region VII 1981-82), Boise Edn. Assn. (v.p. 1981-82, 84-85, pres. 1982-83), Nat. Coun. Urban Edn. Assn., World Future Soc., Coun. for Exceptional Children (pres. chpt. 1978-79), Nat. Coun. Tchrs. English, Minn. Coun. for Social Studies, Calif. Assn. for Gifted, Assn. for Grad. Edn. Students, Phi Delta Kappa. Office: Highlands Elem 3434 Bogus Basin Rd Boise ID 83702-1507

ELLMAN, NORMAN KENNETH, psychologist, psychoanalyst; b. Yonkers, N.Y., June 29, 1932; s. Sidney Lionel and Sadelle (Volan) E.; children: Deborah, Sharon, Douglas; m. Donna E. Ellman, May 20, 1995; stepchildren: Cheryl Graybush, Christina Graybush. BSin Edn., SUNY, New Paltz, 1954; MEd, Queens Coll., N.Y.C., 1958; M.Psychology, Yeshiva U., 1967; PhD, NYU, 1972. Lic. psychologist, N.J., Fla.; cert. tchr.; cert. in psychoanalysis; diplomate Am. Bd. Psychoanalysis in Psychology. Tchr. 6th grade Malverne (N.Y.) Pub. Schs., 1956-57, East Williston (N.Y.) Pub. Schs., 1957-59; sch. psychologist Brentwood (N.Y.) Pub. Schs., 1959-62, Wantagh (N.Y.) Pub. Schs., 1962-67; pvt. practice psychotherapy Oakland, N.J., 1967—; co-dir. North Jersey Mental Health Assocs., 1972-83, Counseling and Psychotherapy Svcs., Oakland, 1983—, North Jersey Mental Health Assocs., 1972-83. Chief psychologist, dir. child study team Glen Rock (N.J.) Pub. Schs., 1967-72, psychol. cons., 1972-82; head counselor and dir. day camp Long Beach, N.Y., 1959-67; tchr. N.J. Inst. Psycholotherapy, Teaneck, N.J., part-time, 1975; adj. faculty psychology Nassau C.C., Hempstead, N.Y., 1966, Paterson (N.J.) State Tchrs. Coll., 1969; staff therapist Lynbrook (N.Y.) Cons. Ctr., Bi-County Cons. Ctr., Amityville, N.Y., 1963-67. With U.S. Army, 1954-56. Mem. APA, N.J. Psychol. Assn., Bergen County Psychol. Assn., Assn. Advancement of Psychology, Nat. Assn. Advancement of Psycholoanalysis, Am. Bd. Psychoanalysis in Psychology, Acad. Psychoanalysis. Avocations: baseball, softball, chess, piano. Home and Office: 60 Tidy Island Blvd Bradenton FL 34210-3302 E-mail: donnorm@earthlink.net.

ELLMANN, DOUGLAS STANLEY, lawyer; b. Detroit, July 15, 1956; s. William Marshall and Sheila Estelle E.; m. Claudia Joan Roberts, Feb. 16, 1985. AB, Occidental Coll., 1978; JD, U. Mich., 1982. Bar: Mich. 1982, U.S. Dist. Ct. (ea. dist.) Mich. 1982, U.S. Ct. Appeals (6th cir.) 1982. Prin. Ellmann & Ellmann, P.C., Ann Arbor, Mich., 1989—. Spl. asst. atty. gen., 1986; trustee U.S. Panel, 1989-, U.S. panel trustee, 1989—; sec. bankruptcy trustee assoc. U.S. Bankruptcy Ct. (ea. dist.) Mich., 1993—. Author: Selected Issues in Asset Protection, 1994, My Advice: Next Time Go Solo, 1994, LWUSA; co-author: Winning Labor Arbitrations, 1987. Mem. U. Mich. Law Sch. Fund, 1986-87. Mem. ABA (vice chair bankruptcy com. 1995—), Mich. Bar Assn. (rep. assembly 1983-89, 90-92, 98—, exec. counsel young lawyers sect. 1985-87, mem. client security fund com. 1987-95), State Bar Mich. (mem. manditory CLE com. 1989-96, chmn. 1995-96, judicial qualifications com. 2000—), Washtenaw County Bar Assn. (chmn. banking, bus., bankruptcy com. 1995-2000). Office: 308 W Huron St Ann Arbor MI 48103-4204

ELLMANN, SHEILA FRENKEL, investment company executive; b. Detroit, June 8, 1931; d. Joseph and Rose (Neback) Frenkel; m. William M. Ellmann, Nov. 1, 1953 (dec. Jan. 16, 2002); children: Douglas Stanley, Carol Elizabeth, Robert Lawrence. BA in English, U. Mich., 1953. Dir. Advance Glove Mfg. Co., Detroit, 1954-78; v.p. Frome Investment Co., Detroit, 1980-96, pres., 1996—. Mem. U. Mich. Alumni Assn., Nat. Trust Hist. Preservation, VFW Aux. Home: 28000 Weymouth Dr Farmington Hills MI 48334

ELLNER, JOSEPHINE HELENE, art educator; b. N.Y.C., Apr. 5, 1940; d. Angelo Edward and Ann (Ballentoni) Bilello; m. Michael William Ellner, Aug. 24, 1957; children: Eileen Lorraine, Deborah Lynn, Laurence Steven. AA in Art, San Jose City Coll., 1972; BA with great distinction, San Jose State U., 1974, MA, 1976, postgrad, 1976-77, U. Calif., Santa Cruz, 1980-81, U. Calif., San Francisco, 1985. Cert. secondary art tchr., community coll. art tchr., Calif., learning handicapped life tchr., resource specialist life tchr., adminstrv. credential. Art and English tchr. John Muir Jr. High Sch., San Jose, 1975-80, tchr. art, humanities, gifted, 1981-82; spl. edn. tchr. Pioneer High Sch., San Jose, 1982-84, chair art dept., 1984-91; visual arts coord., dept. chair A. Lincoln AVPA Magnet High Sch., San Jose, 1991-97; Saturday Acad. San Jose Unified Sch. Dist., 1996—; prof. art San Jose City Coll., 1996—. Mentor tchr. San Jose Unified Sch. Dist., 1984-88; cons. Coll. Bd., San Jose, 1989-97; advisor Nat. Art Honor Soc., San Jose, 1984—; co-convenor Lincoln H.S. Magnet Curriculum Coun., San Jose, 1991-97; intern advisor Casa Program, San Jose, 1991—; guest curator MACLA Gallery, San Jose, Genesis Gallery, San Jose, San Jose Art League; curator Egyptian Mus. Art Gallery, San Jose, New World Gallery, San Jose, Visions Gallery, San Jose, 1970—. Paintings included in numerous pub. collections including Coll. Bd., San Jose, Calif., Foot Mus., Long Beach, Calif.; mural grant Rose Garden Assn., San Jose, 1996, exhibited in over 200 group and one-person shows; executed 6 cmty. murals; curator more than 100 art exhbns.; represented inseveral art books on painting, sculpture and poetry. Recipient award San Jose Adminstrn. Assn., 1984; grantee San Jose Found., 1985, Calif. Tchrs. Instrnl. Incentive Program, 1986, Nat. League Am. Pen Women, 1994-99, program awards Nat. Blue Ribbon Sch., 1998, Magnet Sch. Am., 1991-93, Calif. Dist. Sch. award, 1992, 96, Golden Bell award, 1994, Kennedy Ctr. award for the arts, 1995, Excellence in Edn. award City of San Jose, 2000, Youth Focus award, 1999; inductee Calif. State Senate Youth Mentor's Hall of Fame, 1999. Mem. Nat. Art Edn. Assn., Calif. Tchrs. Assn., NEA, San Jose Tchrs. Assn., Artists Alliance Calif., Cmty. Partnership Santa Clara County, San Jose Inst. Contemporary Art (open studios South Bay artists steering com., Anti-Graffit Program, Phi Kappa Phi. Avocations: art, painting, muralist, sculpture, jewelry design. Home: 1429 Scossa Ave San Jose CA 95118-2456

ELLNER, MICHAEL WILLIAM, art educator; b. N.Y.C., Apr. 1, 1938; s. Charles and Sylvia May (Golub) E.; m. Josephine Helene Bilello, Aug. 24, 1957; children: Eileen Lorraine, Deborah Lynn, Laurence Steven. AA in Engring., San Jose City Coll., 1963, AA in Art, 1966; BA, Coll. Notre Dame, 1970; MA, San Jose State U., 1971, postgrad., 1973-74, U. Calif., Santa Cruz, 1980. Cert. secondary art tchr., c.c. art tchr., Calif. Chair art dept. John Muir Jr. High Sch., San Jose, Calif., 1973-80; assoc. prof. art San Jose State U., 1974; chair art dept. Willow Glen Edn. Park, San Jose, 1980-91; visual arts coord. A. Lincoln AVPA Magnet High Sch., San Jose, 1991-96. Cons. Coll. Bd., San Jose, 1989-97, San Jose Unified Sch. Dist., Saturday Acad., San Jose, 1996—; prof. art San Jose City Coll., 1996—; advisor Nat. Art Honor Soc., San Jose, 1991—; intern advisor Casa Program, San Jose, 1991—; co-convenor Lincoln HS Magnet Curriculum Coun., San Jose, 1991-96; mentor tchr. San Jose Unified Sch. Dist., 1985-94. Paintings included in more than 200 collections including San Jose Mus. Art, Calif., De Saisset Mus., Santa Clara, Calif., Foot Mus., Long Beach, Calif., Coll. Notre Dame, Belmont, Calif.; guest curator Egyptian Mus. Art Gallery, San Jose, Calif., New World Gallery, San Jose, Calif., San Jose Art League, Calif.; guest curator Macla Gallery, San Jose, Calif., Genesis Gallery, San Jose, Calif., 1970—; exhibited in more than 300 group and one-person shows; created 21 cmty. murals; curator over 100 art exhbns.; represented in several art books on painting, and murals and poetry. Past pres. San Jose Art League; past treas. Cambrian Art League; mem. Anti-Graffiti Program, San Jose. Recipient Program Stds. award Nat. Art Edn. Assn., 1993, 94, 95, 96, Art grant City of San Jose, 1994, Mural grant Rose Garden Assn., San Jose, 1996, grant Nat. League Am. Pen Women, 1996, 97, 98, 99, Program awards Nat. Blue Ribbon Sch., 1998, Magnet Sch. of Am., 1991, 92, 93, Calif. Disting. Sch. award, 1992, 96, Golden Bell award, 1994, Kennedy Ctr. award for the arts, 1995, State Farm Good Nieghbor award Nat. Art Edn. Assn., 1996; inductee Calif. State Senate Youth Mentor's Hall of Fame award, 1999, Excellence in Edn. award City of San Jose, 2000, Youth Focus award, 1999; named Tchr. of Yr., Willow Glen Edn. Park PTA, 1985, San Jose Shrine, 1986. Mem. Calif. Tchrs. Assn., NEA, San Jose Tchrs. Assn., San Jose Inst. Contemporary Art, Artists Alliance Calif., South Bay Artists Assn. (adv. com.), Cmty. Partnership Santa Clara County, San Jose Art League (past pres.), Cambrian Art League (past treas.), Phi Kappa Phi. Avocations: painting, poetry, murals. Home: 1429 Scossa Ave San Jose CA 95118-2456

ELLNER, PAUL DANIEL, clinical microbiologist; b. N.Y.C., May 2, 1925; s. George and Cele (Weis) E.; m. Estelle Ziswasser, 1948 (div. 1960); 1 child, Diane; m. Cornelia Johns, Jan. 15, 1965; children— David, Jonathan BS, L.I. U., 1948; MS, U. So. Calif., 1952; PhD, U. Md., 1956. Diplomate Am. Bd. Med. Microbiology; cert. clin. lab. dir. N.Y.C. Dept. Health. Clin. bacteriologist Los Angeles hosps., 1948-52; rsch. asst. Mt. Sinai Hosp., N.Y.C., 1952-53; instr. microbiology U. Fla. Coll. Medicine, 1956-60; asst. prof. U. Vt. Coll. Medicine, 1960-63, Columbia U. Coll. Physicians and Surgeons, N.Y.C., 1963-66, assoc. prof., 1966-70, prof. microbiology, 1971-78, prof. microbiology and pathology, 1978-89, prof. emeritus, 1989, dir. clin. microbiology service, 1971-89; assoc. microbiologist Presbyn. Hosp., N.Y.C., 1966-70, attending staff, 1971-89. Cons. in field; vis. prof. N.Y. Med. Coll., Valhalla, 1979; ASM Latin Am. vis. prof., Medellín, Colombia, 1982; Am. Bur. Med. Advancement in China vis. prof., Taiwan, 1982; regional coordinator Nat. Disaster Med. System; v.p. Am. BioSci. Cons. Author: Current Procedures in Clinical Bacteriology, 1978, Understanding Infectious Disease, 1992; editor: Infectious Diarrheal Diseases: Current Concepts and Laboratory Procedures, 1984; mem. editorial bd. Sexually Transmitted Diseases, 1982-84, European Jour. Clin. Microbiology, 1985-89; contbr. chpts. to books, numerous articles to profl. jours. With AC, USN, 1943-44; to capt. USPHS Res.; health project officer USCG, 1982-91. Rsch. fellow USN, 1954-56. Fellow Am. Acad. Microbiology, Assn. Clin Scientists,

N.Y. Acad. Medicine (assoc.), Infectious Diseases Soc. Am.; mem. AMA (spl. affiliate), Am. Soc. Microbiology (chmn. clin. divsn. 1980-81, Sonnenwirth Meml. award 1992), Acad. Clin. Lab. Physicians and Scientists, Am. Venereal Disease Assn., Sigma Xi. Republican. Jewish. Avocations: fishing, gardening, photography. E-mail: pdel@columbia.edu. *The greatest satisfaction for the scientist is recognition by his peers for honesty and integrity in his studies, fairness and impartiality to his colleagues, and guidance and encouragement to his students.*

ELLOIAN, PETER, artist, educator; b. Cleve., Apr. 20, 1936; s. Oscar Elloian and Haigouhi Minasian; m. Carolyn Ann Autry, May 27, 1966; 1 chld, Cybele Justine. BFA, Cleve. Inst. Art, 1962; MFA, U. Iowa, 1965. Instr. art Toledo Mus. Art Sch. Design, 1966-87; prof. art U. Toledo, 1987-2001. Vis. artist, tchr. Lacoste (France) Sch. of Arts, fall 1984, summer and fall 1987. Exhibited in group shows Portsmouth (Va.) Arts Ctr., 1980, Rutgers U., 1981, Yugoslav Portrait Gallery, Bosnia, 1982, 86, Biella, Italy, 1982, 87, House of Humor and Satire, Bulgaria, 1995, 97, 99, Bitola Inst., Mus. and Gallery, Rep. of Macedonia, 2000; Master exhbn., Minsk Rep. of Belarus, 2002. With U.S. Army, 1957-59, West Germany. Recipient Gascar award, Bulgaria, 1995, award Hunterdon Nat. Print Exhbn., N.J., 1992. Mem. Soc. Am. Graphic Artists, Boston Printmakers. Home: 26114 W River Rd Perrysburg OH 43551-9128

ELLROY, JAMES, writer; b. L.A., Mar. 4, 1948; s. Geneva (Hillaker) E.; m. Mary Doherty, 1988. Author: (novels) Brown's Requiem, 1981, Clandestine, 1982, Blood on the Moon, 1984, Because the Night, 1984, Killer on the Road (formerly Silent Terror) 1986, Suicide Hill, 1986, The Black Dahlia, 1987, The Big Nowhere, 1988 (Prix Mystere award 1990), L.A. Confidential, 1990, White Jazz, 1992, Hollywood Nocturnes, 1994, Dick Contino's Blues, American Tabloid, 1995, My Dark Places, 1996, Crime Wave, 1999, The Cold Six Thousand, 2001, Destination Morque, 2003; contbr.: Fallen Angels: Six Noir Tales Told for Television, 1993; contbr., editor: Best American Mysteries, 2002. Office: care Warner Books Publicity Dept 1271 Ave of Americas New York NY 10020*

ELLSAESSER, HUGH WALTER, retired atmospheric scientist; b. Chillicothe, Mo., June 1, 1920; s. Charles Theobald and Louise Minerva (Bancroft) E.; m. Lois Merle McCaw, June 21, 1946 (dec. May 1998); children: Corbin Donald, Adrienne Sue; 1 adopted child, Robin Keith. AA, Bakersfield (Calif.) Jr. Coll., 1941; SB, U. Chgo., 1943, PhD, 1964; MA, UCLA, 1947. Commd. 2d lt. USAF, 1943, advanced through grades to lt. col., 1960, weather officer, 1942-63; ret., 1963; physicist Lawrence Livermore (Calif.) Nat. Lab., 1963-86, guest scientist, 1986-97. Ind. atmospheric cons., 1997—. Editor: Global 2000 Revisited, 1992; contbr. numerous articles to profl. jours. Mem. Am. Meteorol. Soc., Am. Geophysics Union. Republican. Presbyterian. Avocation: languages. Home and Office: 4293 Stanford Way Livermore CA 94550-3463

ELLSTROM-CALDER, ANNETTE, research consultant; b. Duluth, Minn., Dec. 19, 1952; d. Raymond Charles Ellstrom and Ruth Elaine (Bloomquist) Larson; m. Jeffrey Ellstrom-Calder, July 30, 1982; children: Hannah, Ian. BA in Social Work, Psychology, Sociology, Concordia Coll., 1974; MSW, U. Wis., 1978. Group therapist N.D. State Indsl. Sch., 1973; social worker Fergus Falls (Minn.) State Hosp., 1974, Jackson County Dept. Social Services, Black River Falls, Wis., 1975-77; sr. clin. social worker U. Wis. Hosp., Madison, 1979-90, clin. instr. medicine, 1989—; mktg. mgr. Med. Media Assocs., Madison, 1990-97. Cons. Waupun (Wis.) Meml. Hosp., 1979-84, lectr. grad. sch. social work U. Wis., Madison, 1979-82, prin. investigator in rsch. U. Wis. Hosp., Madison, 1985—. Editor: A Guide to Patients and Families, 1984; mem. editl. bd. Advances in Renal Replacement Therapy; contbr. articles to profl. jours. Del. trustee, bd. dirs. Nat. Kidney Found., N.Y.C., 1983-91, chmn. bd. dirs., Milw., 1985-87, vice chmn., 1983-85, sec., 1982-83, chmn. patient svcs. com., 1981-82, bd. dirs., 1981—, chmn. nat. tng. and edn. com., mem. nat. patient svcs. com., N.Y.C., 1987-91, mem. pers. com., bd. dirs. Madison chpt., 1979-80; bd. dirs. Combined Health Appeal Wis., 1990-97, sec., 1992-97; mem. nat. rsch. com. Am. Assn. Spinal Cord Injury Psychologists and Social Workers, N.Y.C., 1988-95. Recipient Health Advancement award Nat. Kidney Found. Wis., 1985, Vol. Yr. award Nat. Kidney Found. Wis., 1984, Vol. Service award Nat. Kidney Found. Wis., 1983, Nat. Nephrology Social Worker of Yr. Merit award Nat. Kidney Found. and Council of Nephrology Social Workers, 1987; hon. adoptee Winnebago Indian Tribe, 1978; named Outstanding Young Wisconsinite Wisc. Jaycees, 1988. Mem. Council Nephrology Social Workers (nat. v.p. 1984-86, nat. exec. com. 1984-86, Nat. Nephrology Social Worker Yr. award 1987, mem. Nat. Rsch. Rev. com. 1996—), Nat. Assn. Social Workers, Pi Gamma Mu. Democrat. Avocations: travel, camping, skiing, gardening, swimming.

ELLSWEIG, PHYLLIS LEAH, retired psychotherapist; b. Irvington, N.J., Apr. 19, 1927; d. Sumar and Jeanette (Geffner) Schwartz; m. Martin Richard Ellsweig, Dec. 25, 1947; children: Bruce, Steven. BS, East Stroudsburg U. (Pa.), 1947; EdM, Lehigh U., 1966, EdD, 1972. Tchr. Stroud Union High Sch., 1963-66; guidance counselor East Stroudsburg (Pa.) Schs., 1966-68; asst. prof. edn. East Stroudsburg U., 1968; staff psychologist, outpatient supr. Mental Health Center Carbon, Monroe and Pike Counties, Stroudsburg, Pa., 1968-80; pvt. practice in psychotherapy and clin. hypnosis Stroudsburg, 1969-87. Mem. staff Pocono Hosp., 1968—80; pub. spkr. in field; cons. to schs. and pvt. orgns.; tchr. adult edn., Palm Beach County, Pa. Mem. Am. Soc. Clin. Hypnosis, Internat. Soc. Hypnosis, NOW (profl. cons. 1973—). Home: 2584 NW 12th St Delray Beach FL 33445-1353

ELLSWORTH, BOB See WISE, ROBERT ELLSWORTH JR.

ELLSWORTH, FRANK L. business executive; b. Wooster, Ohio, May 20, 1943; s. Clayton Sumner and Frances (Fuller) E.; 1 child, Kirstin Lynne. BA, Western Res. Coll., 1965; MEd, Pa. State U., 1967; MA, Columbia U., 1969; PhD, U. Chgo., 1976; LLD, Pepperdine U., 1997. Asst. dir. devel. Columbia Law Sch., 1968-70; dir. spl. projects, prof. lit. Sarah Lawrence Coll., N.Y., 1971; asst. dean Law Sch., U. Chgo., 1971-79, instr. social sci. collegiate div., 1975-79; pres., prof. polit. sci. Pitzer Coll., Claremont, Calif., 1979-91; pres. Ind. Colls. So. Calif., L.A., 1991-97; v.p. Capital Rsch. & Mgmt. Co., 1997—. Pres. Endowments, Inc. Author: The Foundation of the 21st Century, 2002, Law on the Midway, 1977, Student Activism in American Higher Education; contbr. articles to profl. jours. Trustee, chmn., exec. com. Japanese Am. Nat. Mus., Pitzer Coll., Ind. Colls. So. Calif., Southwestern U.; chmn. Am. Sch. Internat. Studies, Seattle, Global Ptnrs. Inst., Can. Global Ptnrs., Ctr. for the Preservation of Democracy. Recipient Disting. Young Alumnus award Case Western Res. U., 1981, True of Life award United Jewish Fund, 1991. Mem. History of Edn. Soc., Coun. for Advancement of Secondary Edn., Young Pres.'s Orgn., Ukiyo-e Soc., Asia Soc. Home: 254 La Mirada Rd Pasadena CA 91105-1019 Office: The Capital Group 333 S Hope St 33d Fl Los Angeles CA 90071-1406

ELLSWORTH, FREDERICK LEE, music educator; b. Erie, Pa., Apr. 8, 1952; m. Bennett Lee Martin, Aug. 23, 1975; children: Seth, Clark. BS, Clarion U. of Pa, 1974; MEd, Pa. State U., 1986. Cert. music tchr. Pa. Band dir. Tuscarora Jr. H.S., Mifflintown, Pa., 1974—77, East Juniata H.S., Cocolamus, Pa., 1977—86, North East (Pa.) Intermediate Elem., 1986—88, North East H.S., 1988—. Choir dir. First Bapt. Ch., Mifflintown, 1978—86, North East, 1988—91, pianist, Ripley, NY. Mem.: Pa. Music Educators Assn., Kappa Kappa Psi (v.p. 1973—74), Phi Beta Mu (v.p. 2001—). Republican. Baptist. Avocation: hunting.

ELLSWORTH, JOHN DAVID, lawyer; b. Clarion, Iowa, Nov. 13, 1944; s. John Alfred and Marjorie Eileen (Smith) E.; m. Jane Porteous, July 9, 1975; children: John P., Charles G. AB, Carleton Coll., 1966; JD, Harvard U., 1969; LLM, Georgetown U., 1974. Bar: Nebr. 1969, D.C. 1972, U.S. Ct. Appeals (8th cir.) 1972. Law clk. to judge U.S. Ct. Appeals (8th cir.), St. Louis, 1971-72; atty., advisor SEC, Washington, 1972-74; from assoc. to ptnr. Ober, Kaler, Grimes & Shriver, Washington, 1974-80; ptnr. Kutak, Rock & Campbell, Omaha, 1980-81; pvt. practice Omaha, 1981-90; prin. Lieben, Whitted, Houghton, Slowiaczek & Cavanagh, Omaha, 1990—. Pres. Broker-Dealer Communications Ltd., Omaha, 1983—. Author: How to Register the DPP Broker-Dealer, 1982, How to Operate the DPP Broker-Dealer, 1984, Real Estate Syndication Handbook, 1984. Capt. USAR, 1970—78. Mem. Real Estate Securities and Syndication Inst. (chmn. various coms.), Nat. Assn. Securities Dealers (real estate com.), Nebr. Environ. Trust, Audubon Soc. Nebr., Nebr. Land Trust, Happy Hollow Club. Presbyterian. Avocations: hunting, fishing. Office: 2027 Dodge St Ste 100 Omaha NE 68102-1229 E-mail: jellsworth@liebenlaw.com.

ELLSWORTH, JOSEPH CORDON, real estate executive, lawyer; b. Washington, Aug. 13, 1955; s. Richard Grant and Betty (Midgley) E.; m. Rebecca Ann Moss, Nov. 2, 1979; children: Lindsey, Stephanie, Brian, Brittney. Grad., Brigham Young U., 1980; JD, Calif. Western U., 1983. Bar: Utah 1984, U.S. Dist. Ct. Utah 1984. Asst. legal counsel Meadow Fresh Farms, Inc., Salt Lake City, 1983; mgr. property and leasing Equitec Properties Co., Atlanta, 1984-85; sr. mgr. real estate and adminstrn. MCI Telecom. Corp., Atlanta, 1985—94; with MCI Worldcom, Englewood, Colo., 1994—2001; v.p. real estate, gen. counsel Pameco Corp., Golden, 2001—03; corp. realtor Johns Manville, Denver, 2003—. V.p. Rebecca's Sunnybrook Yogurt, Inc., Atlanta, 1985-90. Mem. Corenet Global, Nat. Assn. Corp. Real Estate Execs. Internat., B.Y.U. Alumni Assn. (chmn. Atlanta region 1988-94), Phi Alpha Delta. Republican. Avocations: sports, outside business ventures. Office: Pameco Corp 651 Corporate Circle Ste 200 Golden CO 80401

ELLSWORTH, MYRNA RUTH, accountant; b. Port Arthur, Tex., May 13, 1948; d. Joseph Curry and Ada Ruth (Pate) Meyer; m. Alfred Wells Ellsworth, May 25, 1973; children— Gordon Wells, Carleton Curry. BBA, Lamar U., 1977. CPA, Tex. Mem. acctg. dept. Port Iron and Supply Co., Inc., Port Arthur, 1970-76; acct. Wathen Deshong & Co., CPAs, Beaumont, Tex., 1977-79; prin. Myrna R. Ellsworth, CPA, Port Arthur, 1980-81; mgr. acctg. and data processing depts. Hayes Enterprises, Port Arthur, 1981-83; acct. Alan Hefty, CPA, Beaumont, Tex., 1983-89; CPA Sweatt & Ellsworth, Beaumont, 1989, ptnr. 1989—. Mem. AICPA, Tex. Soc. CPAs (pres. SE Tex. chpt.), Am. Women's Soc. CPAs, Lamar U. Ex-Students Assn., Mensa, Beaumont Spindletop Bus. and Profl. Woman's Club, Delta Sigma Pi. Home: 3175 Sandalwood Dr Port Neches TX 77651-6019 Office: 2370 Eastex Fwy Beaumont TX 77703-4626

ELLSWORTH, OLIVER BRYANT, music educator, writer; s. Edward Bryant and Phyllis Stephens Ellsworth. Ph.D., U. of Calif., Berkeley, CA, 1965—69, M.A., 1961—63, B.A., 1959—61. Prof. emeritus U. of Colo., Boulder, Colo., 2002—, prof., 1994—2002, assoc. prof., 1977—94, asst. prof., 1970—77, instr., 1969—70; part-time instr. U. of Calif., Berkeley, Calif., 1967—68. Author: (book) Johannes Ciconia, Nova Musica and De Proportionibus, The Berkeley Manuscript. First lt. U.S. Army, 1963—65, Kirch Goens, Germany. Mem.: Am. Musicological Soc. Democrat-Npl. Unitarian. Avocation: philately. Office: College of Music University of Colorado Ucb 301 Boulder CO 80309-0301

ELLSWORTH, RICHARD GERMAN, psychologist; b. Provo, Utah, June 23, 1950; s. Richard Grant and Betty Lola (Midgley) E.; m. Carol Emily Osborne, May 23, 1970; children: Rebecca Ruth, Spencer German, Rachel Priscilla, Melanie Star, Richard Grant, David Jedediah. BS, Brigham Young U., 1974, MA, 1975; PhD, U. Rochester (N.Y.), 1979; postgrad., UCLA, 1980-84; PhD, Internat. Coll., 1983. Cert. Am. Bd. Med. Psychotherapy, (fellow), Am. Bd. Sexology. Instr. U. Rochester, 1976-77; asst. prof. Chapman U., 1995—2002; rsch. assoc. Nat. Tech. Inst. for Deaf, Rochester, 1977; instr. West Valley Coll., Saratoga, Calif., 1979-80, San Jose (Calif.) City Coll., 1980; psycholinguist UCLA, 1980-81, rsch. assoc., 1982-85; psychologist Daniel Freeman Meml. Hosp., Inglewood, Calif., 1981-84, Broderick, Langlois & Assocs., San Gabriel, Calif., 1982-86, Beck Psychiat. Med. Group, Lancaster, Calif., 1984-87, Angeles Counseling Ctr., Arcadia, Calif., 1986-89, Assoc. Med. Psychotherapists, Palmdale, Calif., 1988-2001; prof. Chapman Univ., 1995—2002; pvt. practice Lancaster, Calif., 2001—; adj. prof. Calif. State U., Bakersfield, Calif., 2000—. Cons. LDS Social Svcs. Calif. Agy., 1981—, Antelope Valley Hosp., 1984—, Palmdale Hosp., 1984-96, Treatment Ctrs. of Am. Psychiat. Hosps., 1985-86, Hollywood Cmty. Hosp., 1994-01, Lancaster Cmty. Hosp., 1996—; commr. Calif. State Bd. Psychology, 1994—2000. Contbr. articles to profl. jours. Scoutmaster, Boy Scouts Am., 1976-79. UCLA Med. Sch. fellow in psychiatry, 1980-81. Mem.: APA, Am. Soc. Clin. Hypnosis, Assn. Mormon Counselors and Psychotherapists (editor AMCAP jour. 2000—), Am. Assn. Sex Educators, Counselors and Therapists, Psi Chi. Office: 1672 W Ave J Ste 207 Lancaster CA 93534

ELLSWORTH, ROBERT FRED, investment executive, former government official; b. Lawrence, Kans., June 11, 1926; s. W. Fred and Lucile (Rarig) E.; children: Robert William, Ann Elizabeth; m. Eleana L. Biscoe, July 14, 2002 BS, U. Kans., 1945; JD, U. Mich., 1949. Bar: D.C., Mass., Kans., U.S. Supreme Ct. Mem. 87th to 89th Congresses from 2d and 3d Dist., Kans., 1961-67; asst. to Pres. of U.S., Washington, 1969; U.S. ambassador to NATO, 1969-71; gen. ptnr. Lazard Freres & Co., N.Y.C., 1971-74; asst. sec. for internat. security affairs U.S. Dept. Def., Washington, 1974-75, dep. sec. Def., 1975-77. Bd. dirs. Price Comm. Corp.; chmn. Hamilton Tech. Ventures, L.P. Lay reader Episcopal Ch. Knight Honor Johanniterorden. With USNR, 1944-46, 50-53. Recipient Presdl. Nat. Security medal, 1977. Mem. Coun. Fgn. Rels., Internat. Inst. Strategic Studies (v.p.), Atlantic Coun. of the U.S. (dir.), Am. Coun. on Germany (dir.), Coun. of Am. Amb. Home: 3900 Cathedral Ave NW Washington DC 20016-5201 Office: 12526 High Bluff Dr Ste 260 San Diego CA 92130

ELLWANGER, THOMAS JOHN, lawyer; b. Summit, N.J., Feb. 26, 1949; s. James Warren and Lorean (Nicholson) E.; children: James Hunter, Margaret Lorean. BA, Northwestern U., 1970; JD, U. Fla., 1974. Bar: Fla. 1975, U.S. Dist. Ct. (mid. dist.) Fla. 1976, U.S. Ct. Appeals (11th cir.) 1976, U.S. Dist. Ct. (so. dist.) Fla. 1977, U.S. Tax Ct. Mem. Fowler, White, Gillen, Boggs, Villareal & Banker P.A. (now Fowler, White, Boggs, Banker P.A.), Tampa, Fla., 1975—. Instr. law U. Fla., Gainesville, 1975; adj. prof. Stetson U. Coll. Law, 1997-2000. Editor: Gadsden County Times, 1970-72. Pres. Neighborhood Housing Services Hyde Park, Tampa, 1978. Fellow Am. Coll. Trust and Estate Counsel, Fla. Bar (cert. tax lawyer), Hillsborough County Bar Assn. (chmn. com. probate liaison 1985-86, real property probate and trust law sect. 1987-89), Tampa Bay Estate Planning Counsel (pres. 1994-95). Democrat. Avocations: music. lit., sports. Office: Fowler White Boggs Banker PA 501 E Kennedy Blvd Ste 1700 Tampa FL 33602-5239 E-mail: tellwang@fowlerwhite.com.

ELLWOOD, DAVID TABOR, public policy educator; b. Mpls., Sept. 16, 1953; s. Paul and Ann Ellwood; m. Marilyn Rymer. AB in Econs. summa cum laude, Harvard U., 1975; PhD in Econs., 1981. Rsch. asst. to prof. Martin S. Feldstein Harvard U., Cambridge, Mass., 1974-75, 77; rsch. assoc. health policy program U. Calif., San Francisco, 1975-76; tchg. fellow labor econs. Harvard U., Cambridge, 1977-79; rsch. asst. Nat. Bur. Econ. Rsch., Cambridge, 1978-80; asst. prof. pub. policy John F. Kennedy Sch. Govt., Harvard U., Cambridge, 1980-84, assoc. prof. pub. policy, 1984-88, prof. pub. policy, 1988-92, Malcolm Wiener prof. pub. policy, 1992-98, Lucius N. Littauer prof. polit. economy, 1998—; co-dir. Malcolm Wiener Ctr. Pub. Policy, Harvard U., Cambridge, 1992-93; acad. dean John F. Kennedy Sch. Govt. Harvard U., Cambridge, 1992-93, 95-97; asst. sec. planning and evaluation HHS, Washington, 1993-95. Rsch. assoc. Nat. Bur. Econ. Rsch., 1984-93; faculty mem. retreat U.S. House Ways and Means com.; panel mem. Work and Welfare Demonstration Manpower Demonstration Rsch. Corp., 1985-93, 95—; bd. overseers panel study income dynamics, 1986-88; dir. domestic strategy group The Aspen Inst., 1998—; bd. dirs. Abt Assocs.; cons. in field. Author: Poor Support: Poverty and the American Family, 1988 (notable books N.Y. Times Book Review 1988, outstanding book 1988 Policy Studies Orgn.); co-editor Welfare Policies for the 90s; co-author Welfare Realities: From Rhetoric to Reform, 1994; contbr. numerous articles, book reviews to profl. jours. Panel Com. Status Black Ams., NAS, 1986-91; adv. bd. Children's Program Edna McConnell Clark Found., 1989-93; mem. Nat. Forum Future Children and Their Parents, Nat. Rsch. Coun., 1988-91; mem. Task Force Poverty and Welfare Mario Cuomo, gov. State N.Y., 1986-87, Project Welfare Families Bruce Babbitt, gov., State Ariz., 1986-87. Recipient George Kershaw award Assn. Pub. Policy Analysis and Mgmt.; Lehman fellow Harvard U. Fellow Am. Acad. Arts and Scis.; mem. NAS (panel poverty and family assistance), Phi Beta Kappa. Office: Harvard U John F Kennedy Sch Govt 79 John F Kennedy St Cambridge MA 02138-5801

ELLWOOD, EDITH MUESING, free-lance writer; b. Manhattan, N.Y., Sept. 18, 1947; d. Carl Earl and Elsbeth Helen (Bushbeck) Muesing; m. William Adonis Ellwood, Sept. 15, 1980; children: Jeanie, Colin, Caroline. BA, Fordham U., 1969; MA, NYU, 1971; adult tng. cert., Katharine Gibbs Sec. Sch., 1978; cert. in news editing, U. So. Calif. Rschr. Acad. Rsch. Group, Rutherford, N.J., 1975-78, 80-82; pres. Colin Press, Bklyn., 1984-88; editor Ellwood Editing Svc., Bklyn., 1990-93; free-lance writer, editor Bushkill, Pa., 1993—. Distbr. symposium paper Soc. Philosophy and Tech., The Netherlands. Author: The Alternative to Technological Culture, 1986, U.S. Dem. Myth vs. Reality, 1985, Dragonfly, 1985 (Reader's Best of Issue award 1985); contbr. articles to profl. jours.; author numerous poems. Social concerns com. St. Johns. Mem. AAUW, Women in Scholarly Pub. (writer, editor newsletter 1990-93), Interstitial Cystitis Assn., Acad. Am. Poets, St. John's Women's Guild (writer, editor newsletter, sec.), Pocono Writers and Poets. Democrat. Roman Catholic. Avocations: painting, sketching, antiques, poetry. Home: RR 1 Box 178 Bushkill PA 18324-9801 E-mail: edithmellwood@earthlink.net.

ELLWOOD, PAUL MURDOCK, JR., health policy analyst, consultant; b. San Francisco, July 16, 1926; s. Paul and Rebecca May (Logan) Ellwood; divorced; children: David, Cynthia, Deborah. BA, Stanford U., 1949, MD, 1953. Dir. Kenny Rehab. Inst., Mpls., 1962—63; exec. dir. Am. Rehab. Found., Mpls., 1963—73; dir. Inst. Interdisciplinary Studies, Mpls., 1970—73; pres. InterStudy, health policy analysis Excelsior, Minn., 1973—85; pres. Paul Ellwood & Assocs., Excelsior, 1985—87; chmn. bd., pres. InterStudy, 1987—92; pres. Jackson Hole Group, Teton Village, Wyo., 1992—; founding dir. Found. for Accountability/Quality Measure for Healthcare, Portland, Oreg., 1997—. Dir., mem. exec. com. Jackson Hole Ski Corp., Wyo., 1972—87; clin. prof. phys. medicine and rehab., neurology and pediat. U. Minn. Med. Sch.; cons. in health and delivery systems. Co-author: Assuring the Quality of Health Care, 1973; co-editor: Handbook of Physical Medicine and Rehabilitation, 1971. Served with USNR, 1944—46. Named Disting. fellow, Am. Rehab. Found., 1973; recipient award, Ministry Pub. Health, Republic Argentina, 1957, 1st award sci. exhibit, Am. Acad. Neurology, 1958, citation, Pres.'s Com. Employment Handicapped, 1962, Gold Key award, Am. Congress Rehab., 1971. Mem.: Group Health Assn. Am. (dir. 1975—76), Assn. Rehab . Ctrs. (pres. 1960—61, U.S. Healthcare Quality award 1991), Nat. Health Coun. (dir. 1971—76), Inst. Medicine NAS. Home: PO Box 165 Bondurant WY 82922-0165 Office: Jackson Hole Group PO Box 270 Bondurant WY 82922-0270

ELLWOOD, SCOTT, lawyer; b. Boston, July 8, 1936; s. William Prescott and Doris (Cook) E.; m. Suzanne M. Timble; children: Victoria, William Prescott II, Marjorie. Student, Williams Coll., 1954-56; AB, Eastern Mich. U., 1958; LLB, Harvard U., 1961. Bar: Iowa 1961, Ill. 1961, U.S. Dist. Ct. (no. dist.) Ill., 1961. Assoc. McBride & Baker, Chgo., 1961-67, ptnr., 1968-84, McDermott, Will & Emery, Chgo., 1984-99. Pres. Miller Investment Co., 1975-93, bd. dirs.; pres. SMI Investment Corp., 1978—. Pres., bd. dirs. 110 N Wacker Dr Found., 1974-84, Northfield Found., 1978-84, Leadership Found., 1979-84, Woodbine Found., 1980-84, The Cannon River Found., 1982-84, L.M. McBride Found., 1982-84, Bellarmine Found., 1982-84, Mark Morton Meml. Fund, 1982—. Mem. Iowa Bar Assn., Ill. State Bar Assn., Harvard Law Soc. Ill. (bd. dirs. 1983-98, treas. 1987-88, sec. 1988-89, v.p. 1989-93, pres. 1993-95), Harvard Club Chgo. (bd. dirs. 1993-95), Monroe Club (bd. dirs. 1988-98), Skokie Country Club (Glencoe, Ill.). Republican. Episcopalian. Home: 1296 Hackberry Ln Winnetka IL 60093-1606 Office: McDermott Will & Emery 227 W Monroe St 58th Fl Chicago IL 60606-5096

ELM, DAWN RAE, business educator; b. Seattle, Nov. 3, 1957; d. Arthur Lewis and Elizabeth Mower (Stevens) Lomker; m. Chance Raymond Elm, Oct. 17, 1981; children: Courtney Meryl-Lomker, Kendra Daneille-Lomker. BSChemE, U. Mass., 1980; PhD in Strategic Mgmt., U. Minn., 1989. Project mgr. The Procter & Gamble Co., Cin., 1980—84; prof. U. St. Thomas, St. Paul, 1989—; mgmt. concentration dir. grad. programs U. St. Thomas Coll. Bus., St. Paul, 1998—. Mem. editl. bd.: Jour. Bus. Ethics, 1997—; contbr. articles to profl. jours. Mem.: Internat. Assn. Bus. and Soc., Acad. Mgmt. (program chair SIM divsn. 1998—99, chair elect SIM divsn. 1998—99, chair/pres. SIM divsn. 2000—01). Avocation: ballroom dancing. Office: U St Thomas Coll Bus Mail #TMH343 1000 Lasalle Ave Minneapolis MN 55403

ELMA, BAYANI BORJA, physician; b. Manila, Philippines, Nov. 3, 1942; s. Medardo Romero and Hiwaga Rada Borja E.; m. Maria Mercado Chavez-Elma, July 4, 1971; children: Michael Anthony, Mary Anne. Degree in Preparatory Medicine, U. Philippines, 1963; MD, U. of the East, Quezon City, Philippines, 1968. Diplomate Am. Bd. Quality Assurance, Utilization Review Physicians. Vice-chief of staff Md. Gen. Hosp., Balt., 1985-90, dir., trustee, 1988-95, chmn., prof. affairs com., 1992-95. Mem. panel editl. advisers Internal Medicine for the Specialist, Livingston, N.J., 1990—; editl. bd. Md. Med. Jour., Balt., 1993-96; pres. Assn. of Philippine Physicians in Md., 1997-99. Pres. U. East Med. Alumni Assn., 1992-94; dir., trustee U. East Med. Alumni Found, 1994—; vice-chmn. Govs. Commn. on Asian-Pacific Am. Affairs, Balt., 1992—; alt. del. House Del. Balt. City Med. Soc., 1997-99; vice-chmn. bd. trustees U. East Med. Alumni Found., 1998-2003, chmn. bd. trustees U. East Med. Found., U.S.A., Inc., 2003—; trustee Found. for Aid to Philippines, Inc., 2002--. Named One of the Twenty Outstanding Filipino Am. U.S. and Can. Filipino Image mag., 1998-99. Mem.: Am. Coll. Physician Execs. Republican. Roman Catholic. Avocations: reading, writing, traveling. Home: 10907 Tony Dr Lutherville MD 21093-3618 E-mail: bbelmamd@radicus.net.

ELMAN, GERRY JAY, lawyer; b. Chgo., Oct. 7, 1942; s. Earl Samuel and Lucille Paulyne Elman; m. Lois Suzanne Bermet Levine; children: Jason Farrel, Floren Haley. BS, U. Chgo., 1963; MS in Chemistry, Stanford U., 1964; JD, Columbia U., 1967. Bar: N.Y. 1967, Pa. 1969, U.S. Dist. Ct. (so. and ea. dists.) N.Y. 1971, U.S. Dist. Ct. (ea. dist.) Pa. 1973, U.S. Dist. Ct. (mid. dist.) Pa. 1974, U.S. Ct. Appeals (Fed. cir.) 1987, U.S. Ct. Appeals (3d cir.) 1989, U.S. Patent Office, 1967, U.S. Supreme Ct. 1973, U.S. Dist. Ct. Colo. 2002. Assoc. Hubbell, Cohen & Stiefel, N.Y.C., 1967-68; patent atty., enzymes and health products Rohm and Haas Co., Phila., 1968-72; dep. atty. gen. Pa. Dept. Justice, Harrisburg, 1972-76; trial atty. Mid. Atlantic office antitrust divsn. U.S. Dept. Justice, Phila., 1976-82; pvt. practice Phila., 1982-83; mem. Elman Assocs., Phila., 1984-88, Lipton, Famiglio & Elman, Media, Pa., 1988-89, Elman Wilf & Fried, Media, 1990-95, Elman & Fried, Media, 1995-96, Elman & Assocs., Media, 1996—2002, Elman Tech. Law, P.C., Swarthmore, Pa., 2002—. Instr. short course in computer law Temple U., Phila., 1984; mem. faculty in intellectual property mgmt. U. Phoenix Online Campus, 1995-98. Contbg. author: Lawyers' Microcomputer Users Group Jour., 1985-88; editor: Columbia Jour. Transnat. Law, 1966-67; mem. adv. bd. Jour. Computer Law Reporter, 1983-90; mem. editl. bd. Jour. Trademark Reporter, 1968; founder, editor in chief legal jour. Biotech. Law Report, 1982—; mem. adv. bd. BNA Spl. Reports Biotech., 1989-90, The Licensing Jour., 1998—; mem. bd. advisors Santa Clara Computer and High Tech. Law Jour., 1994—; mem. Global CyberLaw Network, 1997—, World Tech. Network, 2001-. Chmn. Three Steps Nursery Sch., Phila., 1977; arbitrator Phila. Ct. Common Pleas, 1971-72, 83-88, U.S. Dist. Ct. (ea. dist.) Pa. 1983—, Am. Arbitration Assn., 1987-96, Delaware County Ct. Common Pleas, Pa., 1993—, Forum Sysop, CompuServe online svc., 1994-99. Mem. ABA, Licensing Execs. Soc., Am. Intellectual Property Law Assn., Phila. Bar Assn. (chmn. jurimetrics com. 1975-77), Phila. Intellectual Property Law Assn. (chmn. biotech. subcom. 1982-86, continuing legal edn. com. 1995-97), Delaware County Bar Assn., Computer Law Assn., Benjamin Franklin Am. Inn of Ct. Home: 406 Yale Ave Swarthmore PA 19081-2024 Office: Elman Tech Law PC 406 Yale Ave PO Box 209 Swarthmore PA 19081-0209 E-mail: elman@elman.com.

ELMAN, NAOMI GEIST, artist, producer; b. Chgo. d. Harry and Rita (Goldstein) Geist; m. Murray Elman, May 29, 1946 (dec. Dec. 1965); 1 child, Margaret (Peggy) Gillespie. Student, Hamilton Inst. for Girls, Nat. Acad. of Design, Art Students League. Personal mgr. in performing arts, prodr. concerts in, N.Y.C. and Hawaii, N.Y., 1968-80. One-woman shows include Churchill Gallery, 1962, Pen and Brush Club, 1986, Neuwirth Gallery, Phoenix, 1994; exhibited in group shows; represented in a permanent collection Tchrs. Coll. N.Y.C. Alumni Assn. Vol. nurses aid pvt. and army hosps., ARC, 1939-45; v.p. N.Y. Diabetes Assn., 1955-58; mcpl. chmn. Dem. Club, Tenafly, N.J., 1958; Dem. com. woman, 1959-61; bd. dirs. Nat. Children's Cardiac Home, N.Y.C., 1940-49, Bergen County Dem. Club, 1958-60. Recipient Margareet Sussman award, 1985, Salamagundi award, 1987, Julia Lucille award, 1988. Mem. Internat. Platform Assn., Soc. Mil. Widows, Retired Officers Club (life), Disabled Am. Vets., Artists Equity, Kent Art Assn. Democrat. Address: 500 E 77th St New York NY 10162-0025

ELMENDORF, DOUGLAS WILLIAM, economist; b. Mt. Kisco, N.Y., Apr. 16, 1962; s. William R. and Gertrude L. (Schutt) E.; m. Karen E. Dynan, Apr. 17, 1993; children: Caroline Marie, Laura Patrice. AB, Princeton U., 1983; AM, Harvard U., 1985, PhD, 1989. Asst. prof. dept. econs. Harvard U., Cambridge, Mass., 1989-94; analyst Congrl. Budget Office, U.S. Congress, Washington, 1993-95; economist Fed. Res. Bd., Washington, 1995-98; sr. economist Coun. Econ. Advisors, Exec. Office of Pres., Washington, 1998-99; dep. asst. sec. U.S. Treasury Dept., Washington, 1999-2000; sr. economist Fed. Res. Bd., Washington, 2001—02, section chief, 2002—. Grad. fellow NSF, 1983. Mem. Phi Beta Kappa.

ELMENDORF-LANDGRAF, MARY LINDSAY, retired anthropologist; b. Ruby, S.C., Apr. 13, 1917; d. James Calvin Lindsay and Ana Eugenia MacGregor; m. John van Gaasbeek Elmendorf, Dec. 27, 1937 (dec. Feb. 1980); children: Calvin Lindsay, Susan Elmendorf Roberts; m. John L. Landgraf, Nov. 27, 1981. AB in Psychology, U. N.C., 1937, MA in Social Work and Pub. Adminstrn., 1940; PhD in Anthropology, Union Grad. Sch., 1972, U. N.C., 1987, PhD (hon.), 1994. Rsch. fellow Ford Found., N.Y.C., Mex., 1972-73; cons. anthropologist UNITAR/AAAS, Washington, 1975—, USAID, Washington, 1980-85, Internat. Devel. Rsch. Ctr., Ottawa, Calif., 1980-90, World Bank, Washington, 1975-95; ret., 1996—. Instr. Putney (Vt.) Sch., 1941—43; dir. AFSC Spanish Refugee Program, France, 1945—46; dir. CARE de Mex., 1952—60; coord. off-campus studies Brown U., 1962—65, New Coll., U. Fla., 1965—69; vis. assoc. prof. anthropology Hampshire Coll., Amherst, Mass., 1973, Semester at Sea, 1974—75; mem. part-time faculty Goddard Coll., Vt., 1973; adj. prof. anthropology U. Fla., 1992—; mentor New Coll., U. Fla., 1987—; advisor Union Inst., 1990—; cons. World Bank/UNDP Water and Sanitation Program, 1978—96, UNICEF, WHO, FAO, IDRC, others, IRC, WASH; lectr. in field. Author: The Mayan Woman and Change, 1972, La Mujer Maya y el Cambio, 1973, Nine Mayan Women: A Village Faces Change, 1976, The Socio-Cultural Aspects of Excreta Disposal, 1980, The International Drinking Water and Sanitation Decade and Women's Involvement, 1990, Priorities, Challenges and Strategies: A Feminine Perspective, Women, Water and UNIFEM, 2001, Water is Life at Hannover, Germany, 2002, Rights, Resources, Culture and Conservation in Maya Communities of Yucatan, Mexico: Studies Inspired by the Work of Mary Elmendorf, 2003; contbr. ; collection papers Smathers Libr., U. Fla., Nat. Anthrop. Archives, Smithsonian Instn. Recipient with other Quaker vols. Nobel Peace Prize, 1947; recipient Margaret Mead award, 1982, Disting. Alumna award U. N.C., 1997. Fellow: Soc. Applied Anthropology, Am. Anthrop. Assn.; mem.: UNIFEM, AAUW, Sister Cities, AAAS, UN Assn./USA, Internat. Drinking Water Commn. (Ad Hoc Com. 2003—). Democrat. Mem. Soc. Of Friends. Avocations: gardening, swimming, playing with grandchildren. Home: 535 S Blvd Of Presidents Sarasota FL 34236-2014 also: San Miguel Allende Mexico E-mail: maryelmendorf17@aol.com.

ELMER, BRIAN CHRISTIAN, lawyer; b. Washington, Apr. 18, 1936; s. Arthur Christian and Kathryn Aleen (O'Brien) E.; m. Sonja Kay Glass, Sept. 3, 1966; children: Mark Christian, Kimberly Kay, Robin Ann. BA in Arts and Sci., Cornell U., 1960; JD, U. Mich., 1962. Bar: D.C. 1963. Law clk. U.S. Ct. Appeals for D.C. Cir., Washington, 1962-64; ptnr. Jones, Day, Reavis and Pogue, Washington, 1964-79, Crowell and Moring, LLP, Washington, 1979—. Author: Fraud in Government Contracting, 1985; contbr. articles to profl. jours. Mem. ABA, D.C. Bar Assn., Met. Club. Office: Crowell & Moring LLP 1001 Pennsylvania Ave NW Washington DC 20004-2595 E-mail: belmer@crowell.com.

ELMER, MICHAEL BENDIK, legal administrator; b. Feb. 26, 1949; life ptnr. Annette Andelsen. Cand. jur., U. Copenhagen, 1973. Civil servant Min. of Justice, 1973-76, 77-82, head of divsn., 1982-87, 88-91; dep. judge Hillerød, 1976-77; high ct. judge Eastern High Ct., Copenhagen, 1987-88; v.p. a.i. Maritime and Comml. Ct., Copenhagen, 1988; dep. permanent sec. for justice, head of cmty. law and human rights dept., 1991-94; advocate gen. EC Ct. of Justice, Luxembourg, 1994—97; v.p. Maritime & Comml. Ct., Copenhagen, 1998—. Assoc. prof. U. Copenhagen, 1975-85; asst. pub. prosecutor, 1980-81; part time judge Ct. of Ballerup, 1981-82; external examiner Danish law schs., 1985—; internat. comml. arbitrator, 2000—; chmn., mem. numerous govt. and internat. orgns. Author of several books and articles, especially on property law, cmty. law and penal law. Recipient Grand Cross, Order of Merit, Luxembourg, Knight of the Order of Dannebrog, Denmark. Mem.: UNIDROIT (governing coun.), European Acad. of Law (governing coun.), Assn. of European Competition Law Judges (London) (3d v.p.). Home: Skovalléew 16 DK-2880 Bagsvaerd Denmark Office: Maritime & Comml Ct Bredgade 70 DK-1260 Copenhagen Denmark E-mail: michael@elmer.as.

ELMES, DAVID GORDON, psychologist, educator; b. Newton, Mass., Feb. 15, 1942; s. Leslie and Ruth (Adams) E.; m. Anne Louise Lawrence, June 7, 1963; children: Matthew David, Jennifer Anne. BA, U. Va., 1964; MA, U. Va., 1966; PhD, U. Va., 1967. Mgmt. trainee C & P of Va., 1963; asst. prof. psychology Washington and Lee U., Lexington, Va., 1967-71, assoc. prof., 1971-74, prof., 1975—, head dept. psychology, 1990-2000, co-dir. cognitive sci., 1987-2000. Rsch. assoc. Human Performance Ctr., U. Mich., 1973-74; vis. fellow Univ. Coll., Oxford (Eng.) U., 1987. Author: Readings in Experimental Psychology, 1978, Experimental Psychology, 2004, Research Methods in Psychology, 2003; contbr. articles to profl. jours. Bd. dirs. Rockbridge Mental Health Clinic, 1968-73. Fellow Am. Psychol. Soc.; mem. Psychonomic Soc., Va. Acad. Sci., Coun. on Undergrad. Rsch. (past pres.), Phi Beta Kappa. Office: Washington and Lee U Dept Psychology Lexington VA 24450-0303 E-mail: elmesd@wlu.edu.

ELMETS, HARRY BARNARD, retired osteopath, dermatologist; b. Des Moines, Apr. 22, 1920; s. William and Sara Charlotte (Ginsberg) E.; m. Charlotte Irene Musin, Dec. 9, 1945; children: Craig Allan, Steven Kent, Douglas Gregory BA, U. Iowa, 1942; DO with distinction, Coll. Osteo. Medicine and Surgery, Des Moines, 1946; DSc (hon.), U. Osteo. Medicine/Health Sci., 1994. Intern Des Moines Gen. Hosp., 1946-47; resident in dermatology Coll. Osteo. Medicine, Des Moines, 1947-52; practice osteo. medicine specializing in dermatology Des Moines, 1952-2000; ret. Chief of dermatology Iowa Methodist Med. Ctr., Iowa Lutheran Hosp., Broadlawns Polk County Med. Ctr., Mercy Hosp. Med. Ctr.; clin. prof. dermatology U. Osteo. Medicine and Health Scis., 1947-99; vis. prof. dermatology Kirksville Coll. Osteo. Medicine; guest lectr. Coll. Medicine U. Iowa; cons. dermatology VA Med. Ctr., Knoxville, Iowa, Iowa Dept. Health re tanning bed regulations; mem. Iowa Task Force Venereal Disease Editorial referee Jour. Am. Osteo. Assn.; editorial bd. CUTIS, 1982— Trustee, bd. dirs. Coll. Osteo. Medicine and Surgery, Des Moines Ctr. Sci. and Industry; co-chmn. Des Moines-Polk County Immunization Program; mem. adv. com. Iowa Dept. Pub. Health, Sci. Ctr. (hon.). Named Alumnus of Yr., Coll. Osteo. Medicine and Surgery, 1980; recipient Life Svc. award Iowa Osteopathic Med. Assn., 1997, Disting. Bd. Serv. award Des Moines U., 2001. Fellow Am. Osteo. Coll. Dermatology (pres. 1963, 71, Lifetime Achievement award); mem. Am. Osteo. Bd. Dermatology (chmn. 1962-89), Am. Osteo. Assn. (life), Iowa Soc. Osteo. Physicians and Surgeons (life), Polk County Osteo. Assn. (past pres.), Iowa Acad. Sci., Am. Social Health Assn. (bd. dirs. 1968-77), Am. Venereal Disease Soc., Am. Acad. Dermatology (life), Iowa Dermatol. Soc., Missouri Valley Dermatol. Soc., Minn. Dermatol. Soc., Nat. Assn. VA Dermatologists (charter), Wakonda Country Club, Des Moines Club, Embassy Club, Masons, Shriners. Republican. Jewish. Home: 4238 Park Hill Dr Des Moines IA 50312-2530

ELMORE, CENIETH CATHERINE, music educator; b. Wilson, N.C., July 4, 1930; d. Thomas Onestrus Elmore and Effie Lee Morris. MusB in Theory, U. N.C., Greensboro, 1953; MusM in Composition, U. N.C., 1962, MA in Musicology, 1963, PhD in Musicology, 1972. Piano tchr. pub. sch., Fuquay Springs, NC, 1953—57, Louisburg, NC, 1957—60; grad. asst. piano tchr. U. N.C., Chapel Hill, 1960—63; music prof. Campbell U., Buies Creek, NC, 1963—94, prof. emeritus, 1994—. Lectr. in field. Author. Active Franklin County Arts Coun., Louisburg, NC, 1970—, Franklin County Person Place Preservation Soc., Louisburg, 1980—, Perry's Chapel Bapt. Ch., Franklinton, NC, 1948—. Named Artist of Yr., Franklin County Arts Coun., 1995. Mem.: N.C. Music Tchrs. Assn., Am. Musicological Soc., Raleigh Piano Tchrs. Assn. (first v.p. 1996—98, 2000—02, pres. 2002—), Current Lit. Book Club. Republican. Avocations: painting, reading, gardening, travel, internet. Home: 981 Perys Chapel Church Rd Franklinton NC 27525-8263

ELMORE, EDWARD WHITEHEAD, lawyer; b. Lawrenceville, Va., July 15, 1938; s. Thomas Milton and Mary Norfleet (Whitehead) E., m. Gail Harmon, Aug. 10, 1968; children: Mary Jennifer, Edward Whitehead Jr. BA, U. Va.-Charlottesville, 1959, JD, 1962. Bar: Va. 1962. Assoc. firm Hunton & Williams, Richmond, Va., 1965-69; staff atty. Ethyl Corp., Richmond, 1969-78, asst. gen. counsel, 1978-79, gen. counsel, 1979-80, gen. counsel., sec., 1980-83, v.p., gen. counsel, sec., 1983-94, spl. counsel to exec. com., corp. sec., 1994-97; sr. v.p., gen. counsel, sec. Albemarle Corp., Richmond, 1994-2001, exec. v.p., sec., 2001—02, exec. v.p., 2002—. Served to capt. AUS, 1962-65. Decorated Army Commendation medal Mem. ABA, Va. Bar Assn., Internat. Bar Assn., Va. State Bar, Am. Corp. Counsel Assn., Bar Assn. Richmond, Am. Soc. Corp. Secs., Raven Soc., Phi Beta Kappa Office: Albemarle Corp 330 S 4th St Richmond VA 23219-4350

ELMORE, GARLAND CRAFT, information science educator; b. Bluefield, W.Va., May 3, 1946; s. Garland C. and Helen M. (Sutherland) E.; m. Jean Anne Schans; 1 child, Martha Erin. BA, Concord Coll., 1968; MA, Marshall U., 1971; PhD, Ohio U., 1979. Teaching asst. Marshall U., Huntington, W.Va., 1969-71; instr. So. West Community Coll., Logan, W.Va., 1971-74; teaching asst. Ohio U., Athens, 1974-75; asst. prof. So. W.Va. Community Coll., Logan, 1975-76; assoc. faculty Ind. U., Indpls., 1976—77, resident lectr., 1977—79, from asst. to assoc. prof., dir. telecommunications, 1979—89, assoc. dean faculties, dir. office of learning techs., 1989—92, exec. dir. integrated techs., 1992—94, assoc. vice chancellor for info. techs., 1992—97, assoc. v.p. tchg. and learning info. techs., dean, 1997—, founding faculty mem. New Media Sch. Informatics, 1997. Pres. faculty, chmn. faculty senate So. W.Va. Community Coll.; mem. numerous coms. at Ind. U., also nat. profl. assns. and cmty. orgns. Author: Communication Media in Higher Education: A Directory of Academic Programs and Faculty in Radio-Television-Film and Related Media, 1987, The Communication Disciplines in Higher Education, 1990, 2d edit., 1993, 3rd edit., 1995; contbr. articles to profl. jours. Served to sgt. U.S. Army, 1966-72. Mem. Educause Ctr. for Applied Rsch., Midwestern Higher Edn. Commn., Coalition for Networked Info., Am. Assn. Higher Edn., Nat. Learning Infrastructure Initiative, Assn. Assn. for Computing Machinery, Educause, Assn. for Commn. Adminstrn., Educause. Office: Ind U Office of VP for Info Tech ES 2129 902 W New York St Indianapolis IN 46202-5157

ELMORE, JAMES WALTER, architect, retired university dean; b. Lincoln, Nebr., Sept. 5, 1917; s. Harry Douglas and Marie Clare (Minor) E.; m. Mary Ann Davidson, Sept. 6, 1947; children: James Davidson, Margaret Kay. AB, U. Nebr., 1938; MS in Architecture, Columbia U., 1948. Mem. faculty Ariz. State U., 1949-86, prof. architecture, 1959-86, founding dean Coll. of Architecture, 1964-74. Cons. architect, 1956— Trustee Heard Museum, Phoenix, 1968-79; bd. dirs. Valley Forward Assn., 1969-89, pres., 1985; bd. dirs. Central Ariz. chpt. Ariz. Hist. Soc., 1973-89; bd. dirs. Ariz. Architects Found., 1978-86, Rio Salado Devel. Dist., 1980-87. Served to col., C.E. U.S. Army, 1940-46. Decorated Bronze Star. Fellow AIA; mem. Ariz. Acad. Home: 6229 N 29th Pl Phoenix AZ 85016-2251

ELMORE, JOANN GRACE, medical researcher, medical educator, physician; m. Bruce Ransom; 1 child, Cole Ransom. MD, Stanford U Sch. of Medicine, Calif., 1982—87; MPH, Yale U Sch. of Epidemiol. and Pub. Health, New Haven, CT, 1990—92. MD Wash. Asst. prof. Dept. of Internal Medicine, Yale U, New Haven, 1993—95; asst. dir. Robert Wood Johnson Clin. Scholars Program, Yale U, New Haven, 1995; asst. prof. Dept. of Medicine, Divsn. of Gen. Internal Medicine, U of Wash., Seattle, 1996—98; adj. asst. prof. Dept. of Epidemiol., U of Wash., Seattle, 1996—98; assoc. prof. Dept. of Medicine, Divsn. of Gen. Internal Medicine, U of Wash., Seattle, 1998—; adj. assoc. prof. Dept. of Epidemiol., U of Wash., Seattle, 1998—; assoc. dir. Robert Wood Johnson Clin. Scholars Program, U of Wash., Seattle, 1999—; sect. head of gen. internal medicine Harbor View Med. Ctr., U of Wash., Seattle, 2000—. External rev. for devel. tech. for early detection of breast cancer Inst. of Medicine, 2000—; nat. discussion group com. mem. NIH, Office of Med. Applications of Rsch., 2000—; faculty award nat. adv. com. mem. Robert Wood Johnson Generalist Physicians, 2001—. Author: (textbook) Epidemiol., Biostatistics, Preventive Medicine, (jour. article) Jour. of the Am. Med. Assoc., (journal article) New Eng. Jour. of Medicine, Annals of Internal Medicine, (jour. article) Jour. of Gen. Internal Medicine, Jour. of the Nat. Cancer Inst., Jour. of Women's Health. Grantee Rsch. Devel., Am. Cancer Soc., 1991—92, Found. Award-Generalist Faculty Scholar, Robert Wood Johnson Found., 1994—99, Pilot Funds, Nat. Institutes on Aging, 1995—97, Rsch. Project Grant, Am. Cancer Soc., 1997—99, RO1, Agy. for Health Rsch. Quality/Nat. Cancer Inst., 2000—, Gift, AVON Products Found., 2000—.

ELMORE, MATTHEW BRET, radio, television announcer; b. San Francisco, Oct. 26, 1951; s. Jack Prentis and Margaret Hanna (Turnquist) E.; m. Marcia Marquez, July 14, 1973; 1 child, Nicholas Bret. Student, Coll. San Mateo, 1975-77. Announcer Sta. KCSM-TV-FM, San Mateo, Calif., 1975-81; freelance camera operator, film and video narrator San Francisco Bay Area, 1977-82, 88—, San Luis Obispo, Calif., 1982-87; announcer, program dir. Sta. KCBX-FM, San Luis Obispo, 1982-87; relief announcer Sta. KKAL, Arroyo Grande, Calif., 1984-86; staff announcer Sta. KQED-FM, San Francisco, 1987—, Sta. KQED-TV, San Francisco, 1991—; relief announcer Sta. KQED-TV/KQEC-TV, San Francisco, 1988-91. Bd. dirs. San Luis Obispo County Jazz Fedn., 1985-90. Recipient Disting. Tech. Comm. award Soc. for Tech. Comm., 1985, mem. Broadcast Legends, 2001—. Mem. AFTRA (bd. dirs. 1999-2003, bd. dirs. San Francisco chpt. 1995—), NATAS, Nat. Assn. Broadcast Employees and Technicians (alt. mem. bd. 1996—). Office: Sta KQED-FM 2601 Mariposa St San Francisco CA 94110-1426 E-mail: melmore@kqed.org.

ELMORE, WALTER A. electrical engineer, consultant; b. Bartlett, Tenn., Oct. 2, 1925; s. Walter Alcorn and Lucile (Tapp) E.; m. Jane Ann Huey, June 3, 1950; children: Robin, Jamie, Laura. BSEE, U. Tenn., 1949. Registered profl. engr., Fla. Mgr. cons. engring. sect. Protective Relay div. Westinghouse Elec. Corp., Newark, 1951-79, Protective Relay div. ABB Power T & D Co., Coral Springs, Fla., 1979-89; mgr. cons. engring. sect. protective relay divsn. ABB Power T&D Co., Coral Springs, Fla., 1989-94, cons. engr. high voltage protection, 1994-96, ret., 1996. Author: (with others) Applied Protective Relaying, 1976, Protective Relaying Theory and Application, 1994, Pilot Protective Relaying, 1999. Fellow IEEE (chmn. IEEE/PES tech. coun. 1988-89, Gold medal for engring. excellence 1989); mem. NAE, Tau Beta Pi, Eta Kappa Nu, Phi Kappa Phi Republican. Home: 104 Macgregor Dr Blue Ridge VA 24064-1526

ELMQUIST, JOHN GUNNAR, plastic surgeon, general surgeon; b. Redlands, Calif., July 24, 1936; s. Frans Gunnar and Dagmar Caroline E.; m. Carol Jean Grindahl, Aug. 11, 1962 (div. Apr. 1980); children: Karin, Jon, Thomas; m. Regina Barbara Gatto Allen, Dec. 27, 1992 (div. Oct. 2001). AA, North Park U., 1956; BA, Northwestern U., 1958, MD, 1961. Diplomate Am. Bd. Surgery, Am. Bd. Plastic Surgery. Pvt. practice, W. Palm Beach, Fla., 1971-96; ret., 1996. Capt. U.S. Army, 1966-68. Fellow ACS; mem. Am. Soc. Plastic Surgeons, Am. Soc. Aesthetic Plastic Surgery. Republican. Lutheran. Avocations: travel, golf. Home: 1281 Crown Point Wellington FL 33414-7931 E-mail: elmquist1@msn.com.

ELMS, BEN, actor, director; b. Syracuse, N.Y., July 1, 1935; s. Benjamin Charles and Sarah Mildred (Nourse) E. BA, Syracuse U., 1957. Appeared in TV shows including Unsolved Mysteries, 1990; films include Man Who Knew Too Much, 1985, The Judgement, 1990; musicals include The Fantasticks, 1987, Jesus Christ Superstar, 1987, Phantom, 1997, Hello Dolly, 1998; plays include Death of a Salesman, 1989, Foxfire, 1991, Noises Off, 1996, Hamlet, 1997, Our Town, 1999, Julius Caesar, 2000, The Diary of Anne Frank, 2001, The Miracle Worker, 2002, Joseph & The Amazing Technicolor Dreamcoat, 2002, The Crucible, 2002, Jekyl & Hyde, 2003, Alice in Wonderland, 2003, Midsummer Night's Dream, 2003; dir. plays including Butterflies Are Free, 1978, Extremities, 1987; also commls. Capt. U.S. Army, 1958-60. Mem. SAG, Actors Equity Assn. Republican. Roman Catholic. Home: 60 Presidential Plz Syracuse NY 13202-2292

ELMUSTAFA, ABDELMAGEED AHMED, senior research scientist; b. Khartoum North, Khartoum, Sudan, June 10, 1960; s. Ahmed Elhaj and Noor Mohamed Elmustafa; m. Widad Ibrahim Elmahboub; 1 child, Mohamed. BS in engring., U. Khartoum, Sudan; MSCE, SD State U., Brookings, 1990; MS in mech. engring., U. Wis., Madison, 1993, PhD in Materials Sci. and Engring., 1999. Rsch. asst. U. Wis., Madison, 1994—99; prog. mgr. & prin. investigator Piezomax Technologies Inc., Madison, 1999—2000; sr. rsch. scientist CONITS NASA, Hampton, Va., 2000—. Structural engr. Pierce & Harris Consulting Engineers, Huron, SD, 1990—90; rsch. asst. U. of Wisconsin-Madison, 1994—99, rsch. assoc., 1999—2000; tech. reviewer NSF, 10 jours. Contbr. articles to more than 15 prof. jours. Mem.: Heat Treating Progress Material Today. Achievements include invention of Nanopositioners for Nano and Micro Scratch Test. Office: 4 Langley Blvd NASA LaRc Bldg 1230 Hampton VA 23681

ELNAKIB, HESHAM MOUSSA, diplomat; b. Cairo, Sept. 2, 1961; s. Moussa Morsi Elnakib and Kariman Radwan. BA in Polit. Sci., Am. U., Cairo, Egypt, 1984; Diploma in Polit. Sci., Inst. of Diplomacy, Berlin, 1986; M in Internat. Rels., The Internat. Inst. of Pub. Adminstrn., Paris, France, 1987; D in Polit. Sci., Inst. of Oriental Studies of the Russian Acad. Sci., Moscow, 2000. Diplomatic attache Egyptian Diplomatic Inst., Cairo, 1985—86; third sec. The Cabinet of the Min. of Fgn. Affairs, Cairo, 1987—88, Embassy of Egypt, Vienna, 1988—89; rsch. analyst The UN Devel. Program, N.Y.C., 1989—90; second sec. Office of the Polit. Dir. of the Egyptian President's Bur. (Dr. Osama El Baz), Cairo, 1990—92; first sec. Embassy of Egypt, Washington, 1992—97; dir. (first sec.) North Am. Dept., Ministry of Fgn. Affairs, Cairo, 1997—99; dir. (counselor) Cabinet of the First Undersec. to the Min. of Fgn. Affairs, Ministry of Fgn. Affairs, Cairo, 1999—2001; dir. (press counselor and head of office) Press and Info. Bur., Embassy of Egypt, Washington, 2001—. Lectr., guest spkr. Participant youth com. Nat. Dem. Party, Cairo, 1982—85. Recipient Wall of Tolerance, Nat. Campaign for Tolerance, 2002; Honor Scholarship, Am. U., 1986. Mem.: Nat. Press Club, Acad. of Polit. Sci. in NY, Bd. of Diplomatic Club, Cairo (dep. pres. 1999—2000). Office: Egyptian Press and Info Bur 1666 Connecticut Ave NW Suite 440 Washington DC 20009 Office Fax: 202-234-6827. E-mail: egyprsinfo@aol.com.

ELOFSON, NANCY MEYER, retired office equipment company executive; b. Glencoe, Ill., Jan. 27, 1923; d. Bernard Francis and Agnes (Ulbrich) Meyer; m. Carl L. Elofson, Nov. 27, 1946 (dec. Dec. 1991); 1 child, Peter Carl. BA, Western Coll., 1944; postgrad., SUNY, Jamestown, 1960-80. Sales corr. Scott, Foresman Pub., Chgo., 1944-46; sec., treas. Office Machines and Equipment Co., Jamestown, 1948-86; ret., 1986—. Mem. coun. camp com. Girl Scouts U.S.A., Jamestown, 1962-66, mem. alumnae archives com., 1992—; candidate Chautauqua County Legis., 1979; mem. choir 1st Congl. United Ch. of Christ, Jamestown, 1948—, moderator, 1978-79, ch. clk., 1995, mem. ch. coun., 1990-95, chmn. 175th anniversary com., 1990-91, mem. ch. growth com., mem. long range planning com., 1993-95, trustee, 1996—; mem. ch. and ministry com. Western area N.Y. conf. United Ch. of Christ, 1997—; founder, pres. bd. dirs. Chautauqua Adult Day Care Ctrs., Inc., Jamestown, 1981-91, bd. dirs., 1981—; pres. bd. dirs. YWCA, Jamestown, 1983-85, trustee, 1987—; mem. exec. bd./com. United Way, Jamestown, 1991-96, allocations chmn., 1991-95, chmn. planning com., 1996; active Chautauqua County Domestic Violence Guidance Team, 1994; pres. Inter-Club Coun., 1997—; apptd. Chautauqua County Commn. on Women's Issues, 2000. Named Chautauqua County Caregiver of Yr., Chautauqua County Office of Aging, 1988, Vol. of Yr., United Way, 1992, Woman of 1996 Yr., Jamestown, 1997; recipient Caregiver's award N.Y. State Office of Aging, 1988, Women Making a Difference award Jamestown Post Jour., 1991. Mem. AAUW (sec. 1948), WJamestown Audubon Soc., The Fortnightly, Jamestown Koinonia, Roger Tory Peterson Inst., Lucille Ball Little Theatre Jamestown, The Fortnightly, Allied Arts. Avocations: human and elder svcs., gardening, music. Home: 81 Gordon St Jamestown NY 14701-1641

ELOUBEIDI, MOHAMAD ALI, gastroenterologist, internist; b. Beirut, Lebanon, Lebanon, Sept. 4, 1967; m. Rana al-Khatib; children: Dala, Samih. MD degree, Am. U. of Beirut, Beirut, Lebanon, 1989—93. Doctor of Medicine Am. Univ. of Beirut, 1993. Fellow in tng. Duke U., Durham, NC, 1996—99, Med. U. of SC., Charleston, SC, 1999—2000; resident in internal medicine Duke Univ. Med. Ctr., Durham, NC, 1993—96; faculty Univ. of Ala. at Birmingham, Birmingham, 2000. Dir., endoscopic ultrasound program U. of Ala., Birmingham, Ala., 2000. Author journal articles. Pres. AANA, chapel Hill, NC, 1997—99. Not attended Not attended. Recipient Haskel Schiff Award, Duke U. Med. Ctr., 1996. Mem.: ASGE, ASIM-ACP, AGA, Am. Coll. of Gastroent. Home: 6121 Crowne Falls Pkwy Hoover AL 35244 Office: Univ of Ala at Birmingham 408 Lhrb 1530 3rd Ave S Birmingham AL 35294 Home Fax: 205-975-6381; Office Fax: 205-975-6381 Personal E-mail: meloubeidi@uabmc.edu. E-mail: meloubeidi@uabmc.edu.

ELPERIN, LOUIS SOLOMON, physician; b. LA, June 8, 1958; s. Harry and Dina (Budgor) E.; m. Beth Ann Cyrlin, June 27, 1982; children: Dina Tiffany and Jason Michael. BA in Biology magna cum laude, UCLA, 1980; MD, Loma Linda U., 1986. Diplomate Am. Bd. Internal Medicine. Intern Loma Linda (Calif.) U. Med. Ctr., 1986-87, resident, 1987-89; attending physician Kaiser Permanante, Woodland Hills, Calif., 1989—. Mem. pharmacy and therapeutics com. Kaiser Permanete, Woodland Hills, 1990—, med. records com., 1991—, internal medicine compensation com. 1992—, internal medicine residency program coord., 1993—; chmn. peer rev. com., clin. instr. medicine UCLA. Contbr. articles to profl. jours. Mem. Temple Aliyah, Mulwood Homeowners' Assn., Woodland Hills, 1995. Mem. ACP, Phi Eta Sigma, Alpah Omega Alpha. Democrat. Avocations: bicycling, photography. Office: Kaiser Permanente 5601 De Soto Ave Woodland Hills CA 91367-6798 E-mail: lelperin@pol.net.

ELPERS, KATHLEEN MARGARET, social work educator; b. Evansville, Ind., Jan. 30, 1950; d. Aemilian B. and Matilda M. (Will) E.; m. Ward Eugene Harbin. BA in Psychology, St. Joseph Coll., 1972; MSW, Rutgers U., 1977; EdD in Leadership Edn., Spalding U., 2001. Cert. ACSWT; lic. clin. social worker; lic. marriage and family thepist. Caseworker Cath. Charities, Evansville, Ind., 1972-75; clin. therapist So. Hills Counseling Ctr., Tell City, Ind., 1977-86; assoc. prof. social work U. So. Ind., Evansville, 1987—, Cons. St. Mary's Counseling Ctr., Evansville, 1988-98, Ohio Valley Hospice, Evansville, 1989-92, Vanderburgh Divsn. Family and Children, Evansville, 1989-94. Bd. dirs. Dept. Pub. Welfare, Tell City, 1979-84, Cath. Charities, Evansville, 1996-98, Youth as Resources, Evansville, 1990-92, Health Professions Bur., Indpls., 1993-95. Named Ky. Col. Gov. of Ky., 1990, Sagamore of the Wabash Gov. of Ind., 1990. Mem. NASW (bd. mem. com. on inquiry 1995—, Social Worker of Yr. 1991), Coun. Social Work Edn., Am. Assn. Marriage and Family Therapists. Roman Catholic. Avocations: antiques, travel, reading. Office: U So Ind 8600 University Blvd Evansville IN 47712-3534

ELROD, BEN MOODY, academic administrator; b. Rison, Ark., Oct. 13, 1930; s. Benjamin Searcy and Frances Othello (Sadler) E.; m. Betty Lou Warren, Aug. 7, 1951; children: Cynthia Lou, William Searcy. BA, Ouachita Baptist U., 1952; ThD, Southwestern Bapt. Theol. Sem., 1962; EdD, Ind. U., 1975. Ordained to ministry Baptist Ch., 1950; pastor First Bapt. Ch., Atkins, Ark., 1951-53, Tioga, Tex., 1955-57, Marlow, Okla., 1957-60, South Side Bapt. Ch., Pine Bluff, Ark., 1960-63; pres. Oakland City (Ind.) Coll., 1968-70, Georgetown (Ky.) Coll., 1978-83, Ind. Colls. of Ark., 1983-88; v.p. devel. Ouachita Bapt. U., Arkadelphia, Ark., 1963-68, 70-78, pres., 1988-97, chancellor, 1998—. Commr. Ark. Econ. Devel. Commn., 2002—08; vis. lectr. in field; cons. in higher edn. Contbr. articles to religion jours. Page U.S. Ho. of Reps., 1946-47; trustee Clark County (Ark.) Hosp., 1973-77, chmn., 1975-77; trustee Ark. Bapt. Med. System, 1978, 1989-2001. Mem. Nat. Assn. Ind. Colls. and Univs. (chmn. tax policy commn. 1993), Ark. State C. of C. (bd. dirs. 1990-98), Assn. So. Bapt. Colls. and Schs. (pres. 1996-97), Consortium for Global Edn. (chmn. bd. dirs. 1997-99, mem. exec. com. bd. dirs. 1997-2002). Home: 1008 Village Dr Arkadelphia AR 71923-2922 Office: Ouachita Bapt Univ Ouachita Sta Arkadelphia AR 71923-3221

ELROD, EUGENE RICHARD, lawyer; b. Roanoke, Ala., May 14, 1949; s. James Woodrow and Selma Fromer (Steinbach) E. AB, Dartmouth Coll., 1971; JD, Emory U., 1974. Bar: Ga. 1974, D.C. 1976, U.S. Ct. Appeals (D.C. cir.) 1985, U.S. Ct. Appeals (5th cir.) 1987, U.S. Dist. Ct. D.C. 1987, U.S. Ct. Appeals (11th cir.) 1987, U.S. Supreme Ct. 1987, U.S. Ct. Appeals (10th cir.) 1997. Trial atty. Fed. Power Com., Washington, 1974-76; atty.-advisor Fed. Energy Adminstrn., Washington, 1977; assoc. Sidley & Austin, Washington, 1977-80, ptnr., 1981—. Mem. adv. bd. The Keplinger Cos., Houston. Mem. selection com. for Woodruff scholars Emory U. Law Sch., Dartmouth '71 Exec. Com. Mem. ABA, D.C. Bar Assn., Ga. Bar Assn., Energy Bar Assn. (chmn. oil

pipeline com. 1982-83, tax com. 1980-81, 92-95, liaison with adminstrv. law judges 1986-87, ethics com. 1997-2001, bd. dirs. 2000-03), Dartmouth Club (exec. com. class of 1971), Book Club of Calif. Avocations: running, book collecting, gardening. Home: 4300 Hawthorne St NW Washington DC 20016-3571 Office: Sidley Austin Brown & Wood 1501 K St NW Ste 900 Washington DC 20005 E-mail: eelrod@sidley.com.

ELROD, LINDA DIANE HENRY, lawyer, educator; b. Topeka, Kans., Mar. 6, 1947; d. Lyndus Arthur Henry and Marjorie Jane (Hammel) Allen; divorced; children: Carson Douglas, Bree Elizabeth. BA in English with honors, Washburn U., 1969, JD cum laude, 1971. Bar: Kans. 1972. Instr. U. S.D., Topeka, 1970-71; research atty. Kans. Jud. Council, Topeka, 1972-74; asst. prof. Washburn U., Topeka, 1974-78, assoc. prof., 1978-82, prof. law, 1982-93, disting. prof., 1993—, dir. Children and Family Law Ctr. Vis. prof. law U. San Diego, Paris Summer Inst., 1988, 90, Washington U. Sch. Law, St. Louis, 1990, 98, summer 1991, 93, Fla. State U. Law Sch., spring, 2000. Author: Kansas Family Law Handbook, 1983, rev. edit., 1990, supplement, 1993, Child Custody Practice and Procedure, 1993, supplements, 1994-97, 99, 2000, 01, 02; co-author: Principles of Family Law, 1999, 5th edit., 2003, Kansas Family Law Guide, 1999, supplement, 2000, 01, 02; editor Family Law Quar., 1992—; contbr. articles to profl. jours. Pres. YWCA, Topeka, 1982-83; vice-chair Kans. Commn. on Child Support, 1984-87, Supreme Ct. Commn. on Child Support, 1989—; chair Kans. Cmty. Svc. Orgn., 1986-87; adv. bd. CASA, 1997—; bd. dirs. Appleseed, 2000—. Recipient Disting. Service award Washburn Law Sch. Assn., 1986; named YWCA Woman of Distinction, 1997. Mem. ABA (coun. family law sect. 1988-92, sec. 1998, vice-chair, 1999, chair-elect 1999-2000, chair 2000-01, chair Schwab Meml. Grant Implementation 1984-87, co-chair Amicus Curiae com. 1987-92, ch-chair pro bono child custody project adv. bd. 2001—, steering com. on unmet legal needs of children 2002—), Topeka Bar Assn. (sec. 1981-85, v.p. 1985-86, pres. 1986-87), Kans. Child Support Enforcement Assn. (bd. dirs. 1988—, Child Support Hall of Fame 1990), Kans. Bar Assn. (sec.-treas. 1988-89, com. ops. and fin. 1988, pres. family law sect. 1984-86, Disting. Svc. award 1985), NONOSO, Phi Kappa Phi, Phi Alpha Delta Alumni Assn. (justice 1976-77), Phi Beta Delta, Kappa Alpha Theta (pres. alumnae chpt. 1995-97). Presbyterian. Avocations: bridge, reading, quilting. Office: Washburn U Law Sch 17th and College Topeka KS 66621 E-mail: linda.elrod@washburn.edu.

ELROD, LU, music educator, actress, author; b. Chattanooga, Tenn., Apr. 23, 1935; d. John C. Elrod and Helen Pauline (Kohn). MusB, Ga. State U., 1960; M in Music Edn., U. Ga., 1970, EdD, 1971; PhD, U. London, 1975. Prof. music, music coach U. Md., Balt., 1972-78, Calif. State U., L.A., 1978—. Singer with Dallas (Tex.) Opera, 1957. Appeared in movies Charly, 1969, Brewster's Millions, 1986, Major Pettigrew and Me, 1976, Seduction of Joe Tynan, 1977, Atlanta Child Murders, 1985, Children Don't Tell, 1986, For Love or Money, 1986, High School High, 1996, Wag the Dog, 1997, The Big Lebowski, 1998, Primary Colors, 1998, Lloyd the Ugly Kid, 1999, Beautiful, 1999, Glory Days, 2001, Freaky Friday, 2003; appeared on TV in Lazarus Syndrome, 1980, Hill Street Blues (Emmy award), 1988, Superior Court, 1988, TV Bloopers, 1989, Beakman's World (Emmy award), Dream On, 1993, Misery Loves Company, 1995, Caroline in the City, 1995, Louie, 1996, George and Alana, 1996, Maggie, 1998, Two Guys and a Girl, 2000, Glory Days, 2001; appeared in TV commls. Recipient Leadership Devel. award Ford Found., 1967, Leadership Fellows award Ford Found., 1968; Tift Coll. voice scholar, 1953, Baylor U. voice scholar, 1956; Lu Elrod scholarship named at Calif. State U., L.A., 1989. Mem. AAUP, AFTRA, SAG, Am. Guild Variety Artists, Calif. Faculty Assn., Coll. Music Soc. Avocations: philanthropy, fundraising. Office: Calif State Univ 5151 State University Dr Los Angeles CA 90032-4226 E-mail: lelrod@calstatela.edu.

ELROD, STEPHEN ROY, theater educator; b. Trion, Ga., May 3, 1957; s. Roy Elrod and Mary Elrod Derby. BA in Comm./Theatre, Reed-Hardeman U., 1981; MA in Theatre, Abilene Christian U., 1988. Tchr. Adairsville (Ga.) HS and Mid. Sch., 1988—91; prof. Faulkner U., Montgomery, Ala., 1991—. Office: Faulkner Univ Dept Theatre 5345 Atlanta Hwy Montgomery AL 36109-3323

ELS, THEODORE ERNEST, professional golfer; b. Kempton Park, South Africa, Oct. 17, 1969; s. Cornelius and Hester E. Diploma, Jan de Klerk Tech. Coll. Mem. nat. teams Dunhill Cup, 1992, 93, 94, 95, 96, 97, 98, 99, 2000, World Cup, 1992, 93, 96, 97, Pres.'s Cup, 1996, 98, 2000. Winner numerous matches, including U.S. Open 1994, World Match Play Championship, 1994-96, Buick Classic, 1996-97, U.S. Open, 1997; named PGA European Player of Yr., 1994; South African Sportsman of the Yr., 1994, winner Bay Hill Invitational, 1998, Nissan Open, 1999, Alfred Dunhill PGA Championship, 1999, Million Dolar Challenge, 1999, 2000, Nedbank Golf Challenge, 1999, 2000, Loch Lamand Invitational, 2000, The Internat., 2000. Mem. Ocean Club (Paradise Island, The Bahamas). Avocations: squash, movies. Address: c/o PGA European Tour Wentworth Dr Virginia Water Surrey GU25 4LX England

ELSASSER, GLEN ROBERT, journalist; b. Marion, Ohio, Oct. 18, 1935; s. Glen Robert and Mary Louise (Hogan) E.; m. Katharine Macy Kersting, Sept. 8, 1973; 1 child, Daniel. BA, Ohio State U., 1957; MS, Columbia U. Sch. Journalism, 1961. Reporter UPI, Louisville, 1957-58; reporter, writer Indpls. Star, 1961-63; reporter, writer, editor Chgo. Tribune, Chgo., N.Y.C., Washington, 1963—. With U.S. Army, 1958-60, Kansas City, Mo. Recipient Gavel award ABA, 1979. Home: 319 C St NE Washington DC 20002-5709 Office: Chgo Tribune 1325 G St NW Ste 200 Washington DC 20005-3129

ELSAYED, ELSAYED ABDELRAZIK, industrial engineer, educator; b. Talkha, Egypt, Dec. 29, 1947; came to U.S., 1976; s. Abdelrazik E. and Rawhya (Bayoumi) E.; m. Linda Elaine Gungle, Nov. 8, 1975; children: Aladdin, Amena, Amira, Amardean. BSc, Cairo U., 1969, MSc, 1973; PhD, U. Windsor, Can., 1976. Registered profl. engr., Can. Rsch. and tchg. assoc. U. Utah, Salt Lake City, 1976-77; asst. prof. indsl. enging. Rutgers U., Piscataway, NJ, 1977-81, assoc. prof., 1981-85, prof., 1985—, chmn. dept., 1983—2001, dir. Ctr. for Quality and Reliability Engring. Cons. AT&T Bell Labs., AT&T Comm., Ingersoll Rand Personal Products, Bell Comm. Rsch., Ethicon, Inc. Author: (with Thomas Boucher) Analysis and Control of Production Systems, 1985, 2d edit., 1994, Reliability Engineering, 1996 (Book of Yr. award 1997); co-author: Quality Engineering in Production Systems, 1989 (Book of Yr. award 1990). Grantee NSF, 1980-81, 90-94, 97—, Material Handling Inst., 1979-82, Sea-Land Svc. Inc., 1979-81, EPA, 1980-85, NJDHE, 1986-87, FAA 1988-89, 91—, N.J. Commn. on Sci. and Tech., 1999-2001, Office Naval Rsch., 2001-02. Fellow Inst. Indsl. Engrs. (editor Trans. 1993-2001); mem. ASME, Am. Soc. Engring. Edn., Sigma Xi, Tau Beta Pi. Moslem. Home: 11 Center Ln East Brunswick NJ 08816-2911 Office: Rutgers U Sch Engring 96 Frelinghuysen Rd Piscataway NJ 08854-8018 E-mail: elsayed@rci.rutgers.edu.

EL-SAYED, KHALIL MOHAMAD, aerospace engineer; b. Zahleh, Lebanon, July 9, 1950; arrived in U.S., 1976; s. Mohamad Hassan and Hadia Yussef (Ali Ahmed) El-Sayed; m. Wilma Beatriz Ramirez, Oct. 11, 1976; children: Mohamad Omar, Marie Joumana, Ramzi Khalil, Sami Omar. BS in Engring. Tech., Northrop U., 1983; BSBA, U. Phoenix, 1983, MBA, 1986; BT2, Ecole des arts et mètiers, Beirut, 1972. Aircraft A&P mechanic Mid. East Airlines, Beirut, 1972-76; aircraft mechanic Steward Davis Inc., Long Beach, Calif., 1976-77; airframe and power plant mechanic Aircraft Tank Svc., Burbank, Calif., 1977-78; leadman, devel. mechanic Northrop Corp., Hawthorne, Calif., 1978-81, mfg. engr., 1981-83, sr. mfg. engr., 1983-88, sr. structural design engr., 1988-90, project engr., 1990—; gen. mgr. El-Sayed Pubs., Hawthorne, 1990-97; airbus programs team leader Honeywell Aerospace, Torrance, Calif., 1997-98, ECS rep. in Europe, 1998—2001, air quality mgmt. team leader, 2001—03, tech. planning mgr. engines, sys. and svcs., 2003—. Author, pub.: book Arabic as Spoken in Lebanon, 1983, 2d edit., 1990, The Visitor's Guide to America, 1990, Arabic as Spoken in Saudi Arabia and Kuwait, 1991. Active Los Angeles County Youth Motivation Task Force, 1986—97. Mem.: AIAA, Young Astronauts Program (chpt. establisher, advisor 1986), Robotics Internat., Soc. Mfg. Engrs., Aircraft Owners and Pilots Assn. Republican. Moslem. Avocations: flying, reading, camping, bicycling, ping pong. Home: 12061 Smokie Ln Cerritos CA 90703 E-mail: kal.el-sayed@honewell.com.

EL-SAYED, OSAMA MOHAMED, cardiologist; b. Bilqas, Egypt, June 19, 1965; arrived in U.S., 1996; s. Mohamed Mohsen El-Sayed and Nawal Imam Mohamed; m. Rehab Rabiae Abdel-Fattah, Nov. 18, 1998; children: Rana, Hania. MD, Alexandria (Egypt) Faculty Medicine, 1991. Diplomate Am. Bd. Internal Medicine. Intern Alexandria Faculty Medicine, 1992—93; emergency dr. Egyptian Mil., 1993—96; med. resident Mt. Sinai Sch. Medicine, Jersey City, 1997—2000, fellow in cardiology, 2000—01, Ohio State U., Columbus, 2001—. Sgt. Egyptian mil., 1993—96. Fellow: AMA; mem.: ACP, Egypt Med. Soc. Avocations: reading, fishing. Home: 1170 Chambers Rd Columbus OH 43212 Office: Ohio State U HLRI 2d Fl 12th Ave Columbus OH 43210 E-mail: oelsayed@hotmail.com.

ELSBACH, PETER, physician, medical educator; b. Zeist, The Netherlands, Nov. 9, 1924; came to U.S., 1953; s. Louis and Mary Judith Catharina (Kalff) E.; m. Patricia Ruth Mosberg, Jan. 25, 1959; children: Jan Kees, Bart Lodewijk. MD, U. Amsterdam, The Netherlands, 1950; DMS cum laude, U. Leiden, The Netherlands, 1964; MD (hon.), U. Lund, Sweden, 1993. Rotating intern Amsterdam U. Hosp., 1951-53; asst. resident med. divsn. NYU-Bellevue Hosp., 1953-55, chief resident, 1955-56; rsch. assoc., asst. physician Rockefeller U., N.Y.C., 1956-59; instr. dept. medicine Sch. Medicine NYU, 1959-61, asst. prof., 1961-68, assoc. prof., 1968-72, prof., 1972—. Attending physician Univ. Hosp., N.Y.C.; vis. physician Bellevue Hosp.; sr. rsch. fellow N.Y. Heart Assn., 1959-64; Burroughs Wellcome vis. prof. Marian Coll., Fond du Lac, Wis., U. Wis., Milw., 1992; mem. study panel on metabolism of rev. com. Health Rsch. Coun., City of N.Y., 1970-75; vice chmn. Gordon Rsch. Conf. on Phagocytes, 1985, chmn., 1987; cons. NIH, VA, NSF. Mem. editorial bd. Jour. Lipid Rsch., 1967-85, assoc. editor, 1977-79; mem. editorial bd. Infection and Immunity, 1981-87., Procs. of Soc. Exptl. Biology, 1974-80; contbr. or co-contbr. articles to sci. publs. Recipient Career Scientist award Health Rsch. Coun., City of N.Y., 1964-75, Merit award NIH, 1987; Josiah Macy Jr. Found. faculty scholar, 1975-76. Fellow N.Y. Acad. Scis.; mem. Am. Assn. Physicians, Am. Soc. Clin. Investigation, Am. Physiol. Soc., Am. Fedn. Clin. Rsch., Am. Soc. Microbiology, N.Y. Lipid Rsch. Club (chmn. 1971-72), Royal Dutch Acad. Scis. (corr.), Harvey Soc. Office: NYU Sch Medicine Dept Med 550 1st Ave New York NY 10016-6402 E-mail: elsbap01@popmail.med.nyu.edu.

ELSBERG, JOHN WILLIAM, editor-in-chief; b. N.Y.C., Aug. 4, 1945; s. John Christian and Paula Hutter E.; m. Constance Waeber, June 17, 1967; 1 child, Stephen John. BA in History magna cum laude, Columbia Coll., 1967; BA in History with honors, Cambridge U., 1969, MA in History, 1973. Editor U.S. Army Ctr. Mil. History, Washington, 1974-80, acting chief editl. br., 1981, chief editl. br., 1982, editor-in-chief, 1983, chief prodn. svcs. divsn., 1987—. Judge numerous writing competitions; lectr. Manassas campus Am. history and We. civilization No Va. C.C., 1974-75, 75-76; freelance rschr. bicentennial project Nat. Pub. Affairs Ctr. T.V., 1974; adj. prof. European div. U. Md., 1970-73; counselor, adminstr. residential Upward Bound program Columbia U., 1965-67. Editor: Gargoyle, 1977—80, Bogg: A Jour. Contemporary Writing, 1980—, author numerous poems, fifteen books and chapbooks of poetry; contbr. articles to profl. jours. MC poetry readings, chair various pub. panel discussions The Writer's Ctr., Bethesda, Md; mem. poetry com. Folger Shakespeare Libr., Washington. Kellett fellow U. Cambridge. Fellow Va. Ctr. Creative Arts; mem. Coun. Lit. Mags. and Pubs., Poets and Writers, Columbia U. Club Washington, Phi Beta Kappa. Avocations: bicycling, hiking, traveling, raising dogs. Home: 422 N Cleveland St Arlington VA 22201 Office: US Army Ctr Mil History 103 Third Ave Washington DC 20319

ELSE, CAROLYN JOAN, retired library director; b. Mpls., Jan. 31, 1934; d. Elmer Oscar and Irma Carolyn (Seibert) Wahlberg; m. Floyd Warren Else, 1962 (div. 1968); children: Stephen Alexander, Catherine Elizabeth. BS, Stanford U., 1956; MLS, U. Wash., 1957. Cert. profl. libr. Wash. Libr. Queens Borough Pub. Libr., N.Y.C., 1957—59, U.S. Army Spl. Svcs., France, Germany, 1959—62; info. libr. Bennett Martin Libr., Lincoln, Nebr., 1962—63; br. libr. Pierce County Libr., Tacoma, 1963—65, dir., 1965—94; ret., 1994. Wellness cons. Nikken, Inc., 1994—. Mem. Higher Edn. Coun., South Puget Sound, 1988—92; mem. study commn. Wash. State Local Governance, 1985—88; bd. dirs. Campfire, Tacoma, 1984—92, Cmty. Health Care, 1997—. Mem.: Pacific N.W. Libr. Assn. (sec. 1969—71), Wash. Libr. Assn. (v.p. 1969—71), ALA, Tacoma Rotary #8 Club (bd. dirs. 1995—97), City Club (Tacoma). Personal E-mail: carolyn.else@stanfordalumni.org.

ELSEN, SHELDON HOWARD, lawyer; b. Pitts., May 12, 1928; m. Gerri Sharfman, 1952; children: Susan Rachel, Jonathan Charles. AB, Princeton U., 1950; AM, Harvard U., 1952, JD, 1958. Bar: N.Y. 1959, U.S. Supreme Ct. 1971. Ptnr. Orans, Elsen & Lupert LLP, N.Y.C., 1965—. Adj. prof. law Columbia U. Law Sch., 1969—; chief counsel N.Y. Moreland Act Commn. on UDC, 1975-76; asst. U.S. atty. So. Dist. N.Y., 1960-64; cons. Pres.'s Commn. Law Enforcement Adminstrn. Justice, 1967; mem. faculty Nat. Inst. Trial Advocacy, 1973; panel chair 1st dept. disciplinary com. N.Y., 1992-96. Contbr. articles to profl. jours. Fellow Am. Coll. Trial Lawyers; mem. Assn. of Bar of City of N.Y. (v.p. 1988-89, chmn. com. on fed. legislation 1969-72, chmn. com. on fed. cts. 1983-86, chmn. nominating com. 1986-87, chmn. com. amenities in land use process for N.Y.C. 1987-88), Am. Law Inst. (adviser Transnat. Rules of Civil Procedure 1999—), Phi Beta Kappa. Office: 1 Rockefeller Plz New York NY 10020-2102 Office Fax: 212-765-3662. Business E-Mail: selsen@oellaw.com.

ELSENER, G. DALE, lawyer; b. Frederick, Okla., Mar. 26, 1951; s. Gordon Lee and Anita Lois (Vaughan) Elsener; children: Hayley Lynn, Garrett Dale. BS, Okla. State U., 1973; JD, Okla. U., 1976. Bar: Okla. 1976, U.S. Dist. Ct. (ea. and we. dists.) Okla. 1984. Assoc. Richard S. Roberts, Wewoka, Okla., 1976-78; ptnr. Roberts & Elsener, Wewoka, 1979-86; sole practice, 1986-90. City atty. City of Wewoka, 1986—. Chmn. bd. trustees Seminole County Law Libr., 1986; chmn. Seminole County Econ. Devel. Adv. Com., 1986; bd. dirs. Rural Water Dist. 3, Cromwell, Okla., 1982—90; mem. Seminole Econ. Devel. Coun., 1997—2000. Mem.: Seminole County Bar Assn., Okla. Bar Assn. (real property and mineral law sects.), Seminole State Coll. Edn. Fund (bd. dirs.), Seminole C. of C. (pres. 1998). Office: Elsener & Cadenhead PO Box 2067 Seminole OK 74818-2067 E-mail: delsener@swbell.net.

ELSEY, GEORGE MCKEE, retired foundation administrator; b. Palo Alto, Calif., Feb. 5, 1918; s. Howard McKee and Ethel May (Daniels) E.; m. Sally Phelps Bradley, Dec. 15, 1951; children: Anne Kranz, Howard McKee. AB, Princeton U., 1939; A.M., Harvard U., 1940; L.H.D., Am. Internat. Coll., 1982. Mem. staff The White House, 1947-53; with ARC, 1953-61, v.p., 1958-61; with various divs. Pullman Inc., 1961-65, asst. to chmn. and pres., 1966-70; pres. Am. Nat. Red Cross, 1970-82, pres. emeritus, 1983—. Bd. dirs. Security Storage Co. Suburban Health Found., chmn., 1996-98; mem. Washington adv. bd. MNC Fin., 1991-93; bd. dirs. The White House Hist. Assn., pres., 1990-95. Pres. Meridian House Internat., Washington, 1961-66, vice chmn., 1967-68, counselor, 1971—; trustee Brookings Instn., 1971-83, George C. Marshall Rsch. Found., 1973-83, Harry S. Truman Libr. Inst., 1973-95, PCC Charitable Found., 1997—; mem. Nat. Archives Adv. Coun., 1974-79, mem. com. on presdl. librs., 1988-95; trustee emeritus Nat. Trust Hist. Preservation, 1976—; fin. chmn. League Red Cross and Red Crescent Socs., Geneva, 1977-87; mem. adv. bd. Nature's Best Found., 1999—; bd. dirs. U.S. Capitol Hist. Soc., 1993-95. Comdr. USNR, 1941-47. Decorated Legion of Merit, Order Brit. Empire, medals from Red Cross Socs. Finland, Korea, Greece, Netherlands, Fed. Republic Germany, Can. and Magen David Adom (Israel), comdr. Order of St. John; recipient Disting. Pub. Svc. medal Dept. Def. Internat. Humanitarian award Am. Red Mogen David for Israel, Henry Dunant medal Internat. Red Cross and Red Crescent, 1989. Mem. Hist. Soc. Washington, Nat. Geog. Soc. (trustee 1977-93), Nat. Alliance for Mentally Ill, Princeton Club (N.Y.), Met. Club (Washington), City Tavern Club (Washington), White House Mil. Aides Assn. (hon. chmn. 1998—), Phi Beta Kappa. Presbyterian. Home: 5351 Macarthur Blvd NW Washington DC 20016-2539

ELSEY, JAMES KEVIN, vascular surgeon, educator; b. Bethesda, Md., Jan. 11, 1953; s. William Thomas and Patricia (Rea) E.; m. Beth Reddick, Dec. 5, 1992; children: Jennifer, Michelle. BS, U. Ga., 1975; MD, Med. Coll. Ga., 1979. Diplomate Am. Bd. Med. Examiners, Am. Bd. Surgery, Am. Bd. Vascular Surgery. Resident in internal medicine Emory U. Sch. Medicine, Atlanta, 1979-80, resident in gen. surgery, 1981-84, fellow in vascular surgery, 1985-86; chief vascular surgery Upson Regional Med. Ctr., 1986—. Chief of surgery Upson Regional Med. Ctr, 1993-94, chief of staff, 1991; instr. surgery Emory U. Sch. Medicine, 1987—, Mercer U. Sch. Medicine, 1994—; chief of staff 117th MASH Army N.G. Contbr. articles to profl. jours. Bd. dirs. Upson County Coun. on Child Abuse, 1988—, pres., 1990-91; bd. dirs. Ga. Coun. on Child Abuse, 1990-92, Assn. Retarded Citizens, Upson County, 1991-92, Upson County Emergency Shelter, 1991—, Upson Bd. Pub. Health, 1991—; pres. Harbor House Emergency Shelter for Abused Children, 1995; del. Ga. State Rep. Conv., 1996; co-chmn. Upson County Ednl. Project, 1996; Olympic torch bearer Upson County, 1996; commr. dist. 2 Upson County, 1997—. Fellow ACS (Ga. coun. on trauma 1993—, sec. Ga. chpt. 2002, Ga.'s Young Surgeon award 1993); mem. AMA, Internat. Coll. Surgeons, Am. Assn. Mil. Surgeons, Southeastern Surg. Congress, So. Assn. Vascular Surgery, Med. Assn. Ga., Ga. Assn. of Trauma (bd. dirs. 1994—), Ga. Surg. Soc., Internat. Soc. Cardiovascular Surgery, Internat. Soc. Endovascular Surgery, Upson County Med. Soc. (pres. 1991), Upson County C. of C. (bd. dirs. 1992-93, 94-95, chmn. com. on health 1991-92, Membership award 1991), Emory Vascular Soc. (pres. 2000—), Atlanta Vascular Soc., Alpha Omega Alpha. Avocations: mountaineering, hiking, travel. Office: 600 Professional Dr Ste 250 Lawrenceville GA 30286

EL SHAHAWY, MAHFOUZ, internist, cardiologist, educator; b. Cairo, Aug. 1, 1936; came to U.S., 1967, naturalized U.S. citizen; married; 2 children. Diploma Medicine summa cum laude, U. Vienna, Austria, 1962, diploma cardiovasc. dis., 1966; MSc in Medicine and Cardiovasc. Diseases, U. Minn., Rochester, 1971. Diplomate Am. Bd. Internal Medicine, Am. Bd. Cardiovasc. Disease; cert. Can. Bd. Internal Medicine. Resident in medicine and cardiology U. Vienna-Algemeines Krankenhaus, 1962-67; rotating intern Flushing (N.Y.) Hosp. and Med. Ctr., 1967-68; fellow in medicine Mayo Clinic, Rochester, 1968-70, rsch. fellow in medicine and cardiovasc. disease, 1970-71; fellow, tchg. fellow, instr. cardiology Med. Coll. Ga., Augusta, 1971-73; asst. prof. medicine and cardiology U. Fla., Gainesville, 1973-75, mem. clin. professorial faculty, 1976—, clin. prof. medicine; pvt. practice, Sarasota, Fla., 1976—. Dir. adult cardiac catheterization lab., dir. heart sta. Shands Tchg. Hosp.-U. Hosp., 1973-74, dir. CCu, 1974-75; mem. staff Sarasota Meml. Hosp., 1975-83, Columbia-HCA Doctors Hosp., Sarasota, 1975—; chief medicine Doctors Hosp., Sarasota, 1980-81, trustee, 1986-90, vice chmn. bd., 1987-88, chmn. bd. 1988-89, med. dir. cardiac catheterization lab., 1995—; asst. clin. prof. medicine and cardiology U. South Fla., Tampa, 1976-78; chmn. long term investment com. Sarasota County Pub. Hosp., 1991-92, trustee, 1990-92; pres. Cardiovasc. Inst. Sarasota, 1989-95, Cardiovasc. Inst. Sarasota Found. for Edn. and Rsch., 1995—; mem. Rehab. Inst. Sarasota, 1986—; presenter to nat. and internat. meetings, 1971—; organizer, dir. nat. and internat. cardiovasc. symposia, 1988—. Contbr. articles and abstracts to med. jours., including Chest, Circulation, Jour. Fla. Med. Assn., Brit. Heart Jour., Cardiovasc. Rsch. Jour., Am. Heart Jour., Jour. Med. Assn. Ga., Jour. AMA, Lancet, Circulation Rsch. Supplement, Clin. Rsch. Bd. dirs. YMCA, Ringling Mus., Selby Gardens, Sarasota Opera Soc., New Coll. Libr. Assn., Boys Club Sarasota, Sarasota County Pub. Health Clinic, Sun Coast Heart Assn. United Arab Republic scholar, 1962-67. Fellow ACP, Am. Coll. Chest Physicians (coun. on critical care), Am. Coll. Cardiology, Am. Soc. Echocardiology; mem. AMA, Am. Heart Assn. (fellow coun. on clin. cardiology), Internat. Soc. for Holter and Non-Invasive Electrocardiology, Am. Med. Soc. Vienna (life), Fla. Med. Assn., Sarasota County Med. Soc., N.Y. Acad. Scis., Mayo Clinic Cardiovasc. Alumni Assn., Sarasota County C. of C. (bd. dirs.) Century Club Meml. Hosp., Longboat Key Club. Office: Cardiovasc Ctr Sarasota 1851 Arlington St Ste 206 Sarasota FL 34239-3517 Fax: 941-366-2781. E-mail: mshahawy@cardiologycenter.net.

EL-SHERIF, MAHMOUD A. electrical engineering educator; b. Cairo, July 7, 1942; came to U.S., 1981; s. Abd-El-Rahman E. and Hakmat Kaleb (El-Saied) E.; m. Jeylan Talaat El-Mansoury, Mar. 15, 1950; children: Dina, Dalia, Mohamed. BSc in Comm. Engring., Cairo U., 1966; Diploma in Electronic Engring., Alexadria (Egypt) U., 1977, MSc in Electro-Physics, 1980; MSEE, U. Pa., 1983; PhD in Elec. Engring., Drexel U., 1987. Engr. The Egyptian Telecom. Orgn., Cairo, 1966-67; radar instr. Air Def. Inst., Alexandria, 1967-77, radar dept. chmn., 1977-81; dean engring. edn. Air Def. Coll., Alexandria, 1987-89; rsch. prof. Drexel U., Phila., 1989-94, dir., founder Fiber Optics and Photonics Lab., 1994—, dir., founder Fiber Optics and Photonics Mfg. Engring. Ctr., 1997—. Prin. investigator NASA Lewis Rsch. Ctr., 1991-95, Dept. Def., 1990—; pres. Photonics, Inc., Wilmington, Del. and Phila., 1990—; cons. David Sarnoff Rsch. Ctr., Princeton, 1996—. Mem. laser tech. delegation U.S. Citizen Ambassador Program, Spokane, Wash., 1996—. Recipient 1st Class Medal of Disting. Performance Pres. of Egypt, Pres. of Egypt, 1971, Medal and cert. of Appreciation, Egyptian Engring. assn., 1987, Am. medal of Honor, 2001. Fellow Optical Soc. Am.; mem. IEEE, Am. Ceramic Soc., Internat. Soc. Optical Engrs., Soc. for Advancement of Material and Processing Engrs. Achievements include research in on optical fibers as active devices; invention of first fiber-optic modulator, coupler, switch and multiplexers; novel structure of Bragg optical fibers; novel process for manufacturing of sapphire optical fibers (core, clad, jacket) for IR transmission and application up to 1700 degress centegrade; design of and devel. of intelligent, smart structures with fiber optic sys. embeddded in composites, ceramic, metallic materials for in-situ real-time characterization/health monitoring structures; development of smart soldier's uniform with embedded fiber optic biological sensors for automatic detection of battle field biological threats; of smart parachutes with embedded fiber optic strain sensors for remote sensing of stresses during air drop. Avocations: chess, history, movies, classical music. Home: 1117 Hillcrest Rd Narberth PA 19072-1223 Office: Drexel Univ Dept Material Engring 32d and Chestnut Sts Philadelphia PA 19104

ELSHTAIN, JEAN BETHKE, social and political ethics educator; b. Windsor, Colo., Jan. 6, 1941; d. Paul G. and Helen L. Bethke; m. Errol L. Elsthain, Sept. 3, 1965; children: Sheri, Heidi, Jenny, Eric. BA in History, Colo. State U., 1963; MA in History, U. Colo., 1965; PhD in Politics, Brandeis U., 1973; LLD (hon.), Gonzaga U., 1996; DHL (hon.), Valparaiso U., 1996, Grinell Coll., 1997, Maryville U., 1997, Messiah Coll., 1999, Carthage Coll., 2000, Lake Forest Coll., 2001, Siena Coll., 2002, North Park Coll., 2002. Prof. polit. sci. U. Mass., Amherst, 1973-88, Vanderbilt U., Nashville, 1988-94; vis. prof. Haryard U., Cambridge, Mass., 1994; prof. ethics U. Chgo., 1995—. Author: Public Man, Private Woman: Women in Social and Political Thought, 1982, 2d edit., 1992 (Top Choice acad. book), Czech transl., 1999, Ukrainian transl., 2002, Women and War, 1987, Japanese translation, 1994, Power Trips and Other Journeys, Essays on Feminism as Civic Discourse, 1990, Meditations on Modern Political Thought: Masculine/Feminine Themes Luther to Arendt, 1992, Democracy on Trial, 1995 (N.Y. Times Notable Book 1995), Augustine and the Limits of Politics, 1996; co-author: But Was It Just? Reflections on the Morality of the Gulf War, 1992; editor: The Family in Political Thought, 1982, Just War Theory, 1991; co-editor: Women, Militarism and War, 1990, Politics and the Human Body, 1995, Promise to Keep, Decline and Renewal of Marriage in America, 1996, Real Politics, Political Theory and Everyday Life, 1997, New Wine in Old Bottles: International Politics and Ethical Discourse, 1998 (Top Choice acad. book), Who are We? Critical Reflection, Hopeful Possibilities, 2000 (Named Best Acad. Book, Am. Theol. Booksellers Assn. 2000), Jane Addams and the Dream of American Democracy, 2002; editor: The Jane Addams Reader, 2002, Just War Against Terror: The Burden of American Power, 2003. Trustee Inst. for Advanced Study, 1994-99, Nat. Humanities Ctr., N.C., 1996—; chair Coun. on Civil Soc., N.Y.C. and Chgo., 1995—, Coun. on Families in Am., N.Y.C., 1995—; bd. dirs. Nat. Endowment for Democracy, 2002--. Fellow AAAS; mem. Am. Polit. Sci. Assn. (v.p. 1998-99, Goodnow award for lifetime svc. 2002), Am. Soc. Polit. and Legal Philosophy (v.p. 1996-97). Avocations: movies, reading. Home: 4010 Wallace Ln Nashville TN 37215-2308 Office: U Chgo Div Sch 1025 E 58th St Chicago IL 60637-1509 E-mail: jbelshta@uchicago.edu.

ELSILA, DAVID AUGUST, editor; b. Detroit, Feb. 2, 1939; s. Edward J. and Sylvia (Mikkola) E.; m. Kathlyn Deutch, July 17, 1965; children: Mikael, Jamie and Kari (twins). BA, Eastern Mich. U., 1960, postgrad., 1962. Tchr. pub. schs., Livonia, Mich., 1960-64; editor-in-chief Livonia Observer, 1964-65; dir. publs., editor Am. Tchr., also, Changing Edn., Am. Fedn. Tchrs., Washington, 1965-76; editor UAW Solidarity, 1976—98; asst. dir. pub. rels. and publs. dept. UAW, 1976-98; sr. editor Working USA, 1997—. Editor ofcl. publs. ACLU, Ill., 1964—67, Mich., 1964—67; del. Greater Washington Ctrl. Labor Coun., AFL-CIO; mem. adv. bd. (TV show) We Do The Work, 1992—2001; instr. Labor Studies Ctr., Wayne State U., 1999—2003, Nommos Ednl. Svcs., 1999—2001. Co-author: Union Town: A Labor History Guide to Detroit, 1980; contbg. author: Working Detroit, 1986, The New Labor Press, 1992. Nat. sec. Workers Edn. Local 189, 1978—86, Great Lakes bd. mem., 1986—88, Mich. chpt. bd. mem., 1992—99, exec. bd., 1994—99; co-chair Detroit Laborfest, 1997—; coord. Mich. Labor Legacy Project, Inc., 2001—; trustee Cranbrook Peace Found., 2001—; treas. SE Mich. Jobs. with Justice, 2002—. Recipient

Page 1 award, Chgo. Newspaper Guild, 1967, 1st awards in journalism, Internat. Labor Comm. Assn., 1968—69, 1972—73, 1975—76, 1983—97, Ednl. Press Assn. Am., 1968—76, Joady award, Film Arts Found., 1991, Pollic award, Am. Assn. Polit. Cons., 1992, Max Steinbock award, Saul Miller award, Internat. Labor Comm. Assn., 1996, Eugene V. Debs award, Dem. Socialists Am., 1998, Solidarity award, UAW, 1998, Communicator of Yr. award, Met. N.Y. Labor Comm. Coun., 2000, Eugene V. Debs award, Midwest Labor Press Assn., 2000, Journalism award, Mich. Labor Press, 2001, Spl. award, Matrix Theatre Co., 2001. Mem. Washington-Balt. Newspaper Guild (mem. exec. bd. 1970-71), Detroit Newspaper Guild, Ednl. Press Assn. Am. (pres. Washington chpt. 1971), Internat. Labor Comms. Assn. (v.p. 1983-89, sec.-treas 1990-91), ACLU (mem. exec. bd. Detroit chpt. 1993—, sec. 1999—), Phi Delta Kappa. Home: 1411 Three Mile Dr Grosse Pointe Park MI 48230-1125 E-mail: davelsi@aol.com.

ELSMAN, JAMES LEONARD, JR., lawyer; b. Kalamazoo, Sept. 10, 1936; s. James Leonard and Dorothy Isabell (Pierce) E.; m. Janice Marie Wilczewski, Aug. 6, 1960; children— Stephanie, James Leonard III. BA, U. Mich., 1958, JD, 1962; postgrad., Harvard Div. Sch., 1958-59. Bar: Mich. 1963. Clk. Mich. Atty. Gen.'s Office, Lansing, 1961; atty legal dept. Chrysler Corp., Detroit, 1962-64; founding ptnr. Elsman, Young, O'Rourke, Bruno & Bunn, Birmingham, Mich., 1964-72; pvt. practice Elsman Law Firm, Birmingham, 1972—. Owner Radio Sta. WOLY, Battle Creek, Mich. Author: The Seekers, 1962; screenplay, 1976, 200 Candles to Whom?, 1973; contbr. articles to profl. jours.; Composer, 1974, 76; talk show host Citizen's Court, TV-48, Detroit. Mem. Regional Export Expansion Coun., 1966-73, Mich. Ptnrs. for Alliance for Progress, 1969-80; cand. U.S. Senate, 1966, 76, 94, 96, U.S. Ho. of Reps., 1970. Rockefeller Bros. Found. fellow Harvard Div. Sch., 1959. Mem. ABA, Am. Soc. Internat. Law, Econ. Club Detroit, World Peace Through Law Center, Full Gospel Businessmen, Bloomfield Open Hunt Club, Pres. Club (U. Mich.), Circumnavigators Club, Naples Bath and Tennis, Rotary. Republican. Mem. Christian Ch. Home: 4811 Burnley Dr Bloomfield Hills MI 48304-3781 Office: 635 Elm St Birmingham MI 48009-6768 *Christianity is not a religion. It is knowing Jesus, i.e. God, personally. It does not hinge on man's works or effort. Christianity is the only way to God, as Christ is the only Mediator between God and man. Choose! You can be sincerely wrong and still go to Hell eternally. Just a country lawyer in a big city, representing the common man in mass tort and class actions and other litigation, whose priority client is Jesus.*

ELSON, ALEX, lawyer, educator, arbitrator; b. nr. Kiev, Russia, Apr. 17, 1905; came to U.S., 1906, naturalized, 1913; s. Jacob and Rebecca (Brodsky) E.; m. Miriam Almond, July 6, 1933; children: Jacova Silverthorne (dec.), Karen O'Neil. PhB, U. Chgo., 1925, JD, 1928. Bar: Ill. 1928. Bill drafter Legislative Reference Bur., Springfield, Ill., 1929; atty. Legal Aid Bur., Chgo., 1929-34; assoc. atty. Tolman, Chandler & Dickinson, 1934-38; regional atty. Wage-Hour Div., Chgo., 1938-41; regional atty., asst. gen. counsel OPA, 1941-45; sr. ptnr. Elson, Lassers & Wolff, 1952—79. Of counsel Rosenthal & Schanfield, 1979-99; lectr. U. Chgo., intermittently 1933-48, 79-99, Yale Law Sch., 1946, seminar-labor rels. Northwestern U. Sch. Law, 1961-65; seminar constl. law Ariz U., 1971 Author: Civil Practice Forms, 1934; co-author: Civil Practice Forms, Illinois-Federal, 1952, rev., 1965; contbr.: articles to profl. jours., also to Ency. Brit. Former pub. mem. Regional War Labor Bd.; former chmn. Chgo. Rent Commn.; pres. Fund for Justice, 1972-76; former chmn. Ill. divsn. ACLU (hon. mem. bd. dirs. Ill. divsn.); former vice chmn. Ill. Commn. on Children; former chmn. Bd. Mental Health Commns. State Ill., 1960-69; v.p. Law in Am. Soc. Found.; pres. Nat. Acad. Arbitrators Rsch. and Edn. Found., 1987-90; bd. govs. Orthogenic Sch., U. Chgo.; mem. instnl. rev. bd. divsn. social sci. U. Chgo., 1994-97; cons. Ford Found., 1963-68; bd. dirs. Hull House Assn., 1955-65. Fellow Am. Bar Found., Emeritus fellow Coll. of Labor and Employment Lawyers, 1998—; mem. ABA, Ill. Bar Assn., Chgo. Bar Assn. (bd. mgrs.), Am. Law Inst. (life), Nat. Acad. Arbitrators (hon. life mem., v.p. 1983-85), Inst. Psychoanalysis (pres. 1976-79) Home: 5550 South Shore Dr Chicago IL 60637

ELSON, BEVERLY LYNN, art educator; d. Edward L.R. and Helen Louise Elson; m. Frank Madison Gray, May 15, 1976. AA, Colby-Sawyer Coll., 1961; BA, Am. Univ., 1964, MA, 1971; MBA, Southeastern U., DC, 1989; PhD, U. Md., 1981. Prof. Southeastern U., DC, 1975—. Curator art collection Am. Embassy, Stockholm, 1982; curator art exhbn. Am. Embassy to UN, Geneva, 1995—96. Faculty advisor Kiwanis Club. Grantee, NEH, 1985, 1989, 1992, Fulbright grant, State Dept., 1966—67, 1967—68. Mem.: Soc. Archtl. Historians, Coll. Art Assn., Nat. Soc. Arts Letters, Cosmos Club, Washington Club. Home: 1903 S Street NW Washington DC 20029 Office: Southeastern U 501 I St SW Washington DC 20024 Personal E-mail: belson2382@aol.com.

ELSON, CHARLES MYER, law educator; b. Atlanta, Nov. 12, 1959; s. Edward Elliott and Suzanne (Goodman) E.; m. Aimee F. Kemker, Dec. 18, 1993; children: Caroline Kemker, Charles MacKenzie. AB magna cum laude, Harvard U., 1981, postgrad., 1981—82; JD, U. Va., 1985. Bar: N.Y. 1987, D.C. 1988, U.S. Dist. Ct. (so. and ea. dists.) N.Y. 1987, U.S. Ct. Appeals (11th cir.) 1987. Law clk. to judge U.S. Ct. Appeals (11th cir.), Atlanta, 1985-86; assoc. Sullivan & Cromwell, N.Y.C., 1986-90; asst. prof. Stetson U. Coll. Law, St. Petersburg, Fla., 1990-93, assoc. prof., 1993-96, prof., 1996-2001; Edgar S. Woolard Jr. prof. corp. governance U. Del., 2000—, dir. John L. Weinberg Ctr. for Corp. Governance, 2000—. Vis. prof. law U. Ill., Champaign-Urbana, 1995, Cornell U. Law Sch., Ithaca, N.Y., 1996, U. Md. Law Sch., Balt., 1998; cons. Holland & Knight, 1995—, Towers, Perrin, 1998; bd. dirs. Alderwoods Group, Inc., Auto Zone, Inc., Nuevo Energy Co., Investor Responsiblity Rsch. Ctr. Bd. dirs. Big Apple Circus, Ltd., N.Y.C., 1987-93, Circon Corp., 1997-99, Sunbeam Corp., 1996-2002; trustee Talladega Coll., 1994-2001, Tampa Bay Performing Arts Ctr., 2000—, Tampa Mus. Art, 1993-99, Del. Mus. Natural History, 2003—. Salvatori fellow Heritage Found., 1993-94. Mem.: ABA (vice chair com.on corp. governance, mem. com.on corp. laws), Nat. Assn. Corp. Dirs. (commn. dir. compensation 1995, commn.dir. professionalism 1996, com.on securities litig. reform and fraud detection 1997, adv. coun. 1997—, com.on succession planning 1998, com. on audit coms. 1999, com on role of bd. in strategic planning 2000, com. on dir. evaluation 2001, com. on exec. compensation 2003, com. on compensation coms. 2003—), Assn. of Bar of City of N.Y., Am. Law Inst., Univ. Club N.Y.C., Down Town Assn., Harvard Club N.Y.C., Chevaliers du Tastevin. Home: 906 Cecil Rd Wilmington DE 19807 Office: U Del Coll Bus and Econs Alfred Lerner Hall Newark DE 19716 E-mail: elson@lerner.udel.edu.

ELSON, EDWARD ELLIOTT, diplomat; b. N.Y.C., Mar. 8, 1934; s. Harry and Esther (Cohn) E.; m. Suzanne Wolf Goodman, Aug. 24, 1957; children: Charles Myer, Louis Goodman, Harry Elson II. Grad., Phillips Acad., 1952; BA in Polit. Sci. with honors, U. Va., 1956; JD, Emory U., 1959; DHL (honoris causa), Talladega Coll., 1995; JD (hon.), Brenau U., 1997. With Atlanta News Agy., Inc., 1959-86, pres., 1967-82, chmn. bd. dirs., pres., 1982-85, chmn. bd. dirs., 1985-86; pres. Airport News Corp., Atlanta, 1961-82, chmn. bd. dirs., 1982-85; pres. Elson's, Atlanta, 1963-82, chmn. bd. dirs., 1982-86; chmn. Gordon County Bank, 1979-83; chmn. bd. dirs. W.H. Smith & Son Holdings, PLC, 1985-88; amb. to Denmark Dept. State, 1993—. Bd. dirs. NationsBank of Ga., Citizens and So. Ga. Corp., Atlantic Am. Corp., Citizens and So. Trust Co., Inc., Genesco Inc., Specialty Coffee Holdings Inc., Mitre Sports Internat. Ltd., RF & P Corp., New & Lingwood Holdings Ltd., Thorkild Kristensen AG, Köllmann AG, Hamton Investment Funds; chmn. W.H. Smith Group PLC, 1986—, Majestic Wine Corp., 1988; hon. pres. Am. Club, Copenhagen, 1993-98; mem. hon. com. European Assn. for Jewish Studies' 5th Cong., 1993—; vis. prof. Aalborg (Denmark) U. Mem. publs. com. Commentary Mag., 1967—, chmn., 1975-80. Dir., Am. Coun. Ambs.; bd. dirs. Southern Regional Coun., 1966—, exec. com., 1986—; bd. govs. Am. Jewish Com., 1966—, trustee, 1977—, chmn. bd. trustees, 1986-89, v.p., 1982-84, treas., 1984-86; v.p. Nat. Found. Jewish Culture, 1990—; mem. Presdl. Commn. on Obscenity and Pornography, 1967-71, Nat. Adv. Commn. Pub. Edn. and Desegregation, 1976-77; mem. funds appeals rev. bd. City of Atlanta, 1971-73, Atlanta-Fulton County Recreation Authority, 1973-80, vice chmn., 1975-80; adv. com. to US Commn. on Civil Rights, State of Ga., 1974—, chmn., 1974-82; chmn. bd. dirs. Nat. Pub. Radio, 1977-80, chmn., 1992—; chmn. Nat. Pub. Radio Found.; chmn. so. regional adv. com. to US Commn. on Civil Rights, 1978, U. Va. Bayley Mus., 1986—; pres.'s coun. Brandeis U., 1967—, dir. Reading is Fundamental program, 1975-86, fellow, 1979; trustee Am.-Skandanavian Found., 1998—; bd. visitors U. Va., 1984-92, rector, 1990-92, exec. com. Health Sci. Coun., 1989—, chmn. Real Estate Found., 1990-92; bd. visitors Clark Coll., 1973-, chmn. bd. vis., 1982; trustee Brown U., 1988—, U. Va. Med. Ctr., 1987—, exec. com., 1987—; trustee Am. Friends of Brit. Mus., Talladega Coll., 1973—, U. Mid-Am., 1979-82, Am. Fedn. Arts, 1985—, Brenau Coll., 1986—, Hampton Inst., 1986—, Hebrew Union Coll., 1992—, Spellman Coll., 1992—, Jewish Mus., 1992—, Glyndebourne Assn. Am., 1992—; mem. alumni coun. Phillips Acad., Andover, Mass., 1973-76, charter trustee, 1997; pres. coun. Agnes Scott Coll., 1973-82, chmn., 1975-82; mem. coun. White Burkett Miller Ctr. Pub. Affairs, 1990—; dean's adv. bd. Columbia U. Sch. Internat. Affairs and Pub. Affairs; chmn. adv. bd., bd. dirs. Southeastern Ctr. for Contemporary Art, 1976—; chmn. bd. vis. Emory U. Mus. Art and Archaeology, 1985-92; resource planning com. Nat. Gallery, Washington, 1986—, trustee's coun., 1990—, dir. Coun. of Am. Ambs.; chmn. U. Va. Real Estate Found., 1990-92; presdl. del. returning Crown of Stephen to Hungary, 1978; exec. com. U. Va. Health Sci. Coun., 1989-; gov. J.C. Brown Libr., R.I., 1989—; bd. dirs. Acad. for Corp. Governance, Fordham U., 1991—; chmn. bd. trustees Jeffersonian Restoration, 1992—; trustee Nat. Symphony Orch., 1992—; hon. pres. Copenhagen Theatre Cir., 1993-98; exec. com. Assn. Friends of Hans Christian Andersen Mus., 1993-98; active Internat. Inst. Strategic Studies, 1995—; assoc. dir. The Met. Opera, 2000—; dir. Am. Coun. Ambassadors. Recipient Robert B. Downs award Grad. Sch. Library Sci., U. Ill., 1971, Human Relations award Am. Jewish Com., 1975, Disting. Service award Nat. Pub. Radio, 1979, Inst. Human Relations award, 1982, Merkonom award, 1997, Outstanding Alumnus award Emory U. Law Sch., 2002; Guggenheim fellow, 1994. Mem. Ga. Bar Assn., L.Q.C. Lamar Soc. (v.p. 1973-74, chmn. bd. dirs. 1974-80), Jewish Publ. Soc. (trustee 1974-82, 85—, v.p. 1986-87, pres., 1987-90, chmn. 1990—), Asia Soc. (trustee exec. com. 1999—), Am. Jewish Hist. Soc. (exec. com. 1980—, v.p. 1982-85), Am. Scandinavian Found. (vice chmn. 1998—), coun. St. George's Ho., Muscular Dystrophy Assn. Am. (v.p. 1972-73, mem. corp. 1973-74), U. Va. Alumni Assn. (bd. mgrs. 1982-84), Assn. Governing Bds. Univs. and Colls. (bd. dirs. 1992—), Nat. Peace Garden Found. (dir. 1998—), Inst. Study of Europe (co-chair 1999—), European Assn. Jewish Studies (hon. com. 5th congress 1993-98), Coun. Fgn. Rels., St. George's House, Royal Copenhagen Shooting Soc. and Danish Brotherhood, Farmington Country Club, Univ. Club (N.Y.C.), Century Assn., Palm Beach Country Club, Sailfish Club (Palm Beach, Fla.) Fax: 561-833-5044.

ELSON, HANNAH FRIEDMAN, biologist, researcher; b. Lublin, Poland, July 10, 1943; came to U.S., 1949; m. Edward C. Elson; 2 children. BA, Vassar Coll., 1964; PhD, MIT, 1970. Arthritis Found. postdoctoral fellow Med. Rsch. Coun. Lab Molecular Biology, Cambridge, Eng., 1970-72; asst. prof., then asst. rsch. biologist U. Calif.-San Diego, La Jolla, 1972-79; rsch. sci. MEDSAT Rsch. Co., Bethesda, Md., 1986-90, 94-00; sr. resident rsch. assoc. Nat. Rsch. Coun. Walter Reed Army Inst. Rsch., Washington, 1988-90; sr. staff fellow Nat. Heart, Lung, Blood Inst. NIH, Bethesda, 1990-92, expert Nat. Cancer Inst., 1992-94; pres. Kenwood Park Citizens Assn., Inc., Bethesda, 1995-99; prin. investigator, sci. mgr. McKesson BioSvcs., Rockville, Md., 2000—. Contbr. articles to sci. jours. Bd. dirs. Kenwood Park Citizens Assn., 1995—, editor newsletter, 1998—. Mem.: AAAS, Am. Chem. Soc., MIT Club Washington (bd. dirs. 2000—), Sigma Xi (treas. D.C. chpt. 1996—). Achievements include research on protein synthesis, membrane changes during development of skeletal muscle, membrane fusion by HIV, and gene therapy.

ELSON, JAMES MARTIN, retired historic foundation director; b. N.Y.C., Nov. 25, 1932; s. John James and Elizabeth Jane (Slights) E.; m. Joan Mary Scott Elson, Aug. 21, 1965 (dec. Feb. 15, 1991); children: Elizabeth Joan Elson, Christina Marie Elson, James Scott Elson; m. Karen Sue Porter Elson, Aug. 22, 1992. BA, U. Tenn., 1955; MS, The Juilliard Sch., 1961; Mus. AD, W.Va. U., 1970. Chmn. vocal dept. Dana Sch. Music, Youngstown (Ohio) State U., 1962-68; grad. asst. Creative Arts Ctr., W.Va. U., Morgantown, 1968-70; chmn., vocal dept. Sch. Music, Winthrop U., Rock Hill, 1970-72; chmn., dept. visual and performing arts Huntingdon Coll., Montgomery, Ala., 1972-76; chmn., dept. fine arts High Point (N.C.) U., 1976—83; exec. dir. Acad. of Music Theatre, Lynchburg, Va., 1984-88; exec. v.p. Patrick Henry Meml. Fdn., Brookneal, Va., 1988-2000, exec. v.p. emeritus, 2000—. Performing arts critic High Point (N.C.) Enterprise, 1977-83. Author: Academy of Music, Lynchburg, VA: The Golden Age of Live Performance, 1993; author, editor: Patrick Henry Essays, 1994, Patrick Henry and Thomas Jefferson, 1997; editor Lynch's Ferry mag., 2000—; contbr. articles to profl. jours. 1st lt. U.S. Army, 1955-57. Fulbright grant Fulbright Commn., 1961-62. Mem. Coll. Music Soc. (life), Res. Officers Assn. (life), Kappa Sigma (life). Episcopalian. Home: 34 N Princeton Cir Lynchburg VA 24503-1547 Fax: (434) 845-1117. E-mail: jelson@inmind.com.

ELSON, MIRIAM, social work educator; b. Chgo., July 21, 1909; d. David and Elizabeth (Elson) Almond; m. Alex Elson, July 6, 1933; children: Jacova Miller (dec.), Karen O'Neil. BA, Northwestern U.; AM in Social Svc. Adminstrn., U. Chgo. Researcher Jewish Children's Bur., Chgo., 1939-42; supr. adoptions Ill. Children's Home and Aid Soc., Chgo., 1945-53; chief psychiat. social worker student mental health unit U. Chgo., 1956-79, lectr. Sch. Social Svc. Adminstrn., 1979-94; emeritus lectr., 1994—. Author: Self Psychology in Clinical Social Work, 1986; editor: Vulnerable Youth, Adolescent Psychiatry, 1980, Kohut Seminars: On Self Psychology and Psychotherapy with Late Adolescents and Young Adults, 1987. Fellow Am. Orthopsychiat. Assn.; mem. NASW (life, cert.). Home: 5642 S Dorchester Ave Chicago IL 60637-1722 E-mail: melson@midway.uchicago.edu.

ELSON, SARAH LEE, art historian and consultant; b. Valley Forge, Pa., Oct. 1, 1962; d. John Everett and Ione (Coker) Lee; m. Louis Goodman Elson, Aug. 26, 1989; children: Isabel Coker Elson, Everett Esther Elson, Edward Lee Elson. BA, Princeton U., 1984; MA, MPhil in Art History, Columbia U., 1992. Prof. English Beijing Normal U., 1984-85; pub. affairs asst. Guggenheim Mus., N.Y.C., 1985-87; lectr. Met. Mus. Art, N.Y.C., 1990-92; freelance lectr. Nat. Gallery, London, 1994-98; founder Galatea Contemporary Art Advisors, London, 1998—. Rschr. Met. Mus., 1990-92, Tate Gallery, London, 1992-93; fellow The Frick Collection, N.Y.C., 1990—. Author catalogs. Nat. Endowment for Arts fellow, 1988, Pres.'s fellow Columbia U., 1988-90, Luce Travel grant, 1992. Mem. Woolnoth Soc. in the City of London. Democrat. Home: 2 Kensington Gate London W8 5NA England E-mail: galateaArt@aol.com.

ELSON, SUZANNE GOODMAN, community activist; b. Memphis, Oct. 17, 1937; d. Charles F. and Isabel (Ehrlich) Goodman; m. Edward Elliott Elson, Aug. 24, 1957; children: Charles Myer, Louis Goodman, Harry II. Student, Randolph-Macon Women's Coll., Lynchburg, Va.; BA, Agnes Scott Coll., 1959. Sec. Nat. Coun. Jewish Women, N.Y.C., 1977-79; pres. Nat. Mental Health Assn., 1980-82; trustee emeritus Randolph Macon Women's Coll., 1988-98, 99. Chmn. Am. Craft Coun., 1989-92, honorary chmn., 1992-94, hon. trustee, 1994—; bd. dirs. Rosalynn Carter Inst., 1990—, Nat. Coun. Medicine Emory U., 1990-95; trustee Va. Mus. of Fine Art., 1992-96, High Mus. Fine Art, 1972-92, Am. Craft Mus., 1999—; bd. regents U. System of Ga., 1993-97; adv. bd. Breast Cancer Rsch. Found., 1998—; bd. dirs. Friends of Art and Preservation in Embassies, 1999— (trustee 1998); bd. govs. Mus. of Art and Design, 1998—. Home: 180 Cocoanut Row Palm Beach FL 33480-4121

ELSORADY, ALEXA MARIE, secondary education educator; b. San Francisco, Jan. 4, 1946; d. Willard John and Helen Mary (Bardmess) Saunders; m. R.M. Elsorady, Nov. 24, 1972; children: Tarik, Alexander. BA, San Jose State U., 1967, MA, 1976. Cert. secondary and cmty. coll. tchr. Tchr. biology, integrated sci., English, and social studies Fremont Union High Sch. Dist., San Jose, Calif., 1970—. Mem. Workforce Silicon Valley Leadership Inst., summers 1996, 98, 99, 2000, 01; instr. School-Within-a-School sci. team Lynbrook H.S., 1994-2000; mem. task force com. Calif. Health Occupations Resource Ctr. Mission Coll., 1998-99; mem. Lynbrook Leadership Team, 1997—, chmn., 2000-01. Named English Mentor Tchr., State of Calif., 1987-88, Sci. Mentor, 1993-94; grantee Superschs. Found. Sci.-Math.; fellow NSF, 1992, Evolution and Nature of Sci. Inst., San Jose State U., 1993, Mayor Susan Hammer's San Jose Edn. Network Tech. Inst., summer 1994. Mem.: Nat. Sci. Tchrs. Assn., Calif. Acad. Scis. (mem. biology forum 1990—), San Jose State U.alum (life), Calif. Sci. Tchrs. Assn. (life), Phi Alpha Theta (life), Phi Kappa Phi (life), Kappa Alpha Theta (life). Home: 1233 Redmond Ave San Jose CA 95120-2745 Office: Lynbrook High Sch 1280 Johnson Ave San Jose CA 95129-4199

ELSTER, J. ROBERT, lawyer; b. Mar. 10, 1938; m. Suzan Douglas, July 9, 1960; children: John Robert Jr., Mary Douglas Peters. BA in History, Rice U., 1959; JD, Duke U., 1964. Bar: N.C. 1964, U.S. Dist. Ct. N.C. 1964, U.S. Ct. Appeals (4th cir.) 1964, U.S. Supreme Ct. 1972. Assoc. Petree & Stockton, Winston-Salem, N.C., 1964-70; ptnr. Kilpatrick Stockton LLP (formerly Petree & Stockton), 1970—. Adj. prof. law Wake Forest U., 1995-96. Contbr. articles to profl. publs. Bd. dirs. YMCA, 1978-80, Summit Sch., Winston-Salem, 1978-81, Forsyth Country Day Sch., Winston-Salem, 1981-83; bd. trustees Centenary United Meth. Ch., 1988-91. Capt. USMC, 1959-61. Master Inns of Ct.; mem. Am. Coll. Trial Lawyers (trial comp. com. 1987-92, trial advocacy com. 1992—), N.C. Assn. Def. Attys. (pres. 1978-79), Forsyth County Bar Assn. (sec. 1966-67), N.C. Bar Assn. (bd. govs. 1987-90, mem. ethics and grievance com. 1986-89, endowment com. 1990-2000, chair professionalism com. 1996-99, v.p. 2001--), Rotary (bd. dirs. 1984-89, pres. 1987-88). Republican. E-mail: belster@kilpatrickstockton.com.

ELSTER, SAMUEL KASE, college dean, medical educator, physician; b. N.Y.C., Dec. 6, 1922; s. Morris and Rebecca (Post) E.; m. Maxine Lefkowitz, June 17, 1945; 1 child, Charles BS, CCNY, 1942; MD, NYU, 1946. Diplomate Am. Bd. Internal Medicine, Cardiovascular Diseases. Intern Mt. Sinai Hosp., 1946-47, resident, 1950-52; asst. in pathology NYU Sch. Medicine, N.Y.C., 1947-48; instr. medicine Columbia U. Coll. Physicians and Surgeons, N.Y.C., 1959-66; clin. prof. medicine Mount Sinai Sch. Medicine, CUNY, N.Y.C., 1974-97, clin. prof. emeritus medicine, 1997—, dean Page and William Black Postgrad. Sch. of Medicine, 1976-85, dean emeritus, 1985—, dean emeritus for continuous edn., 1985—. Contbr. articles in field to profl. jours. Mem., pres. bd. edn., Tenafly, N.J., 1968-73. Served to capt., M.C. U.S. Army, 1948-50. Fellow Am. Coll. Cardiology, ACP, N.Y. Acad. Medicine; mem. Am. Heart Assn. (mem. council in clin. cardiology), Assn. Am. Med. Colls. Democrat. Jewish. Office: Mt Sinai Med Ctr Box 1030 1 Gustave Levy Pl New York NY 10029

ELSTON, MICHAEL JAMES, lawyer, educator; b. Rockford, Ill., Feb. 7, 1969; s. James L. and Barbara Emanuel; m. Julie Ann Bohardt, Dec. 11, 1999. BA in Polit. Sci., Drake U., 1991; JD with high honors, Duke U., 1994. Bar: Ill. 1994, Mo. 1997, Kans. 1998, Va. 2002, U.S. Ct. Appeals (10th and 11th cirs.) 1997, U.S. Ct. Appeals (7th and 8th cirs.) 1995, U.S. Ct. Appeals (4th cir.) 2002, U.S. Supreme Ct. 1997. Law clk. to Hon. Pasco. M. Bowman U.S. Ct. Appeals (8th cir.), Kansas City, Mo., 1994-96; assoc. Shughart Thomson & Kilroy, P.C., 1997-99; asst. U.S. Atty. No. Dist. Ill., 1999—2002; spl. counsel to asst. atty. gen. Office of Legal Policy, 2001—02; asst. U.S. Atty., chief appellate sect. Ea. Dist. Va., 2002—. Adj. prof. law U. Mo., Kansas City, 1995-99. Co-author: Grand Jury Law & Practice, 1997. Office: 2100 Jamieson Ave Alexandria VA 22314 E-mail: michael.j.elston@usdoj.gov.

ELTRINGHAM, DANA KRISTIN, writer; b. Santa Monica, Calif., Apr. 28, 1974; d. Lee Gordon and Gail Ann (Minett) Eltringham. B in English, Goucher Coll., 1996; MFA in Creative Writing, George Mason U., 2003. Sr. tech. writer Lockheed Martin, Arlington, Va., 1998-2000; mgr. methods and procedures Nextel Comm., Reston, Va., 2000—01; documentation team lead, sr. tech. writer ATS, Inc., McLean, Va., 2001—. Writer, Alexandria, Va., 1996—; adj. instr. in English NOVA CC, 2001 -02. Contbr. articles to profl. jours. Mem.: Associated Writing Programs. Avocations: oil painting, yoga. Home: 68 Fremont St Providence RI 02906 E-mail: danaeltringham@hotmail.com.

ELTRINGHAM, THOMAS JAMES GYGER, telecommunications professional; b. Riverside, Calif., Nov. 4, 1943; s. Thomas Lamar and May Katharyn (Gyger) E.; m. Hana Libuse Strachen, Jan. 21, 1966 (Feb. 1978); m. Lydia Rose Boss, Oct. 4, 1980; children: Glenn Alexander, Eric Douglas. HSST, Hubbard Coll., Copenhagen, 1969. Ordained to ministry. Minister Ch. of Scientology, L.A. and Clearwater, Fla., 1961-83; installations mgrs. Am. Sun, Inc., Commerce, Calif., 1984-86; v.p. ops. Power Ins. Inc., Santa Fe Springs, Calif., 1986-90; dir. L.D. Svcs., Inc., Santa Fe Springs, Calif., 1990-98; CEO GCC Telecomm. Inc., 1991-98; ret., 1998. Contbr. articles to profl. jours.; developer drug rehab. program, L.A., 1966. Chmn. bd. trustees Eltringham Family Found. Mem. Internat. Assn. Scientologists. Republican. Avocations: tennis, skiing, reading, computers, golf. E-mail: guyelt@earthlink.net.

ELVERUM, GERARD WILLIAM, JR., retired electronic and diversified company executive; b. Mpls., Sept. 29, 1927; m. Mary Jean Proverbs, Dec. 28, 1948. Student, U. Nebr., 1945, S.D. State U., 1945; B in Physics, U. Minn., 1949. Engr. Jet Propulsion Lab., Pasadena, Calif., 1949-59; sect. head, mgr. dept. Space Tech. Lab., El Segundo, Calif., 1959-62; dir. lab. Systems Group TRW, Redondo Beach, Calif., 1963-66, mgr. ops. Def. and Space Systems Group, 1969-81, v.p., gen. mgr. Applied Tech. Div./Space and Tech. Group, 1981-91, ret., 1991. Mem. adv. panel NASA/Aerospace Safety Bd., Washington, 1982-91; mem. NASA Access to Space Panel, 1995-2001; mem. Space Studies Bd., NRC, 1996-99; mem. space transp. subcom. NASA adv. coun., 1996-2002. Contbr. articles to profl. jours.; patentee in field. Commr. Commn. on Engring. and Tech. Systems, Nat. Rsch. Coun., 1991-94. Served with USAF, 1944-46. Recipient Spl. Achievement award ASME, 1971; named Outstanding Engr. Inst. Advancement Engring., 1972. Fellow AIAA (James H. Wyld Propulsion award 1973); mem. Am. Def. Preparedness Assn., Nat. Acad. Engring. Personal E-mail: jerryelverum@earthlink.net. *Preparation, perseverance, patience with others, and absolute integrity will create the career opportunities that many will simply attribute to being at the right place at the right time.*

ELWAY, JOHN ALBERT, retired professional football player; b. Port Angeles, Wash., June 28, 1960; s. Jack Elway; m. Janet Elway; children: Jessica Gwen, Jordan Marie. BA in Econs., Stanford U., 1983. Quarterback Denver Broncos, 1983—98; ret., 1998. Played Super Bowl XXI, 1986, XXII, 1987, XXIV, 1989. Mem. Mayor's Coun. on Phys. Fitness City of Denver; chmn. Rocky Mountain regional Nat. Kidney Found. Named to Sporting News Coll. All-Am. team, 1980, 1982, Sporting News NFL All-Pro team, 1987, Pro Bowl team, 1986, 1987, 1989, 1991, 1993, 1994.

ELWELL, BARBARA LOIS DOW, community organizer; b. Purcell, Okla., Feb. 15, 1933; d. Henry Kenneth and Leah Maude (Caldwell) Dow; m. Robert G. Elwell, Apr. 7, 1956 (div. July 1977); children: David Robert, Kenneth Dow. Student, Endicott Coll., 1950-51, Jackson Von Ladau Sch. Design, 1952-54. Dir. Alternative House, Inc., Lowell, Mass., 1976-84; mem. staff Encode Tech., Inc., Nashua, NH, 1984-87; staff asst. Harvard Smithsonian Ctr. Astrophys., Cambridge, Mass., 1987-99; pvt. asst. Smithsonian Astrophys. Obs., 1999—. Founder Alternative House, Lowell, 1978; founding mem. Mass Coalition of Battered Women Svc. Groups, Boston, 1976, steering com., 1976-84, adv. bd. 1978-80. Recipient Outstanding Achievement award, Mass. Coalition of Battered Women Svc. Groups, 1976. Avocations: woodworking, antique collecting, miniatures, gardening, painting. Home: 142 Graniteville Rd Chelmsford MA 01824-1122

ELWELL, HOWARD ANDREW, safety engineer; b. Wichita, Kans., July 21, 1940; s. Howard Andrew and Mary Helen (Uncapher) E.; m. Landis Elain Kerr, Sept. 10, 1965. BSME, Purdue U., 1963. Exptl. engr. Pratt and Whitney, West Palm Beach, Fla., 1968-75, performance analysis engr., 1975-78, system safety engr., 1978-81, asst. project engr., 1981-87, project engr., 1987-92; v.p. Elwell & Assoc., Jupiter, 1992—. Safety cons. Gary Robinson, Inc., Jupiter, Fla., 1988—; v.p. Profl. Safety, Inc., Royal Palm Beach, Fla., 1988—; sys. safety mgr. CCTT program Dynamics Rsch. Corp./IBM, 1992-93. Lt. USN, 1963-68. Mem. Sys. Safety Soc., World Safety Orgn. (affiliate), Am. Soc. Safety Engrs. (profl.), Soc. Risk Analysis, Soc. Automotive Engrs., Human Factors Ergonomics Soc., Vets. of Safety. Home and Office: 12454 184th Ct N Jupiter FL 33478-2035

ELWELL, MARK W. writer; b. San Diego, May 29, 1958; BA, U. Wis., Green Bay, 1993. Author: (book) Catching the Last Train, 2002. Home: Apt 815 304 N Adams Green Bay WI 54301

ELWIN, JAMES WILLIAM, JR., lawyer; b. Everett, Wash., June 28, 1950; s. James William Elwin and Jeannette Georgette (Zichy-Litscheff) Sherman; m. Regina K. McCabe, Oct. 25, 1986. BA, U. Denver, 1971, MA, 1972; JD, Northwestern U., 1975. Bar: Ill. 1975, U.S. Dist. Ct. (no. dist.) Ill. 1975, U.S. Ct. Appeals (7th cir.) 1977, U.S. Supreme Ct. 1980, U.S. Ct. Fed. Claims 1989.

Trial atty. antitrust divsn. U.S. Dept. Justice, Chgo., 1975-77; asst. dean Sch. Law Northwestern U., Chgo., 1977-82, assoc. dean, 1982-2000; dir. profl. devel. and tng. Shearman & Sterling, N.Y.C., 2000—. Exec. dir. Corp. Counsel Ctr., 1984-2000; planning dir. Corp. Counsel Inst., Garrett Corp. and Securities Law Inst., Chgo., 1983-2000; dir. Short Course for Pros. Attys., 1981-2000, Short Course for Def. Lawyers in Criminal Cases, Chgo., 1979-2000. Bd. dirs. Legal Assistance Found. of Chgo., 1985-97; vice chmn. Gov.'s Adv. Coun. on Criminal Justice Legis., 1986-91. Fellow German Acad. Exch. Svc., 1986; Fulbright scholar, Germany, 1990. Mem. Chgo. Coun. Fgn. Rels. (mem. Chgo. com.), Chgo. Bar Assn. (bd. mgrs. 1983-85), Chgo. Bar Found. (bd. dirs. 1985-93, pres. 1989-91), Ill. Inst. Continuing Legal Edn. (bd. dirs. 1978-90, chmn. 1987-88), Am. Law Inst., Legal Club (pres. 1991-92), Univ. Club, Law Club City of Chgo., Phi Beta Kappa, Pi Gamma Mu. Office: Shearman & Sterling 599 Lexington Ave Ste N721 New York NY 10022-6030

ELWOOD, WILLIAM NORELLI, medical educator; b. East Orange, NJ, Aug. 21, 1962; s. William Rogers and Frances Emma Nuñez (Norelli) E. BS in Comm., U. Fla., 1985; MA in Human Comm., U. South Fla., 1989; PhD in Human Communication, Purdue U., 1992. Grad. teaching asst. U. South Fla., 1988-89; grad. teaching instr. Purdue U., 1989-91; asst. prof. Auburn (Ala.) U., 1992-94; rsch. assoc. Affiliated Systems Corp., Houston, 1994-96; adj. asst. prof. Ctr. for Health Promotion Rsch. and Devel. U. Tex. Sch. Pub. Health, Houston, 1996—2000; rsch. asst. prof. U. Miami (Fla.) Sch. Medicine, 2000, registrar Campus South, 2001—02, dir. Safeport programs, 2002—03; dir. R&D Guidance Clinic of the Keys, Inc., 2003—. Co-prin. investigator Nat. Inst. on Drug Abuse, 1994-2000; sr. rsch. scientist NOVA Rsch. Co., Bethesda, Md., 1995-2000. Author: Rhetoric in the War on Drugs, 1994, Public Relations Inquiry as Rhetorical Criticism, 1995, Power in the Blood: A Handbook on AIDS, Politics and Communication, 1999; contbr. articles to profl. jours. Chmn. Grove St./Blossom Brook Neighborhood Improvement Project, Sarasota, Fla., 1990-92; poll sheriff Tippecanoe County, Ind. State Elections, 1990; precinct capt. Sarasota County, Fla., 1986-89; local chairperson Office of Nat. Drug Control Policy/Houston Partnership; v.p. Lovett Sq. Civic Assn., 1999-2000; mem. Houston Crackdown Com. on Treatment and Rsch., Tex. Drug Epidemiology Workgroup, U.S.-Mex. Border Drug Epidemiology Workgroup, City of Houston HIV Prevention Cmty. Planning Group. Recipient Alan H. Monroe Disting. Grad. scholar, and teaching award, 1990-91; rsch. grantee, Auburn U., 1993, Nat. Inst. Drug Abuse, 1997, 99, Tex. Commn. on Alcohol and Drug Abuse, 1998-99, Tex. Commn. Alcohol and Drug Abuse, 1997, 99. Mem.: APHA (sec. alcohol, tobacco and other drugs sect. 1999—). Home: 3355 Donald Ave Key West FL 33040-4488

ELWOOD-AKERS, VIRGINIA EDYTHE, retired librarian, archivist; b. L.A., Nov. 9, 1938; d. George Henry and Eileen Edythe Elwood; m. Roy Stanley Akers, Apr. 12, 1980. BA, UCLA, 1964; MLS, U. Oreg., 1972; MA in Mass. Comm., Calif. State U., Northridge, 1981. Editor UCLA, L.A., 1970-71, writer, 1971-72; libr., archivist Calif. State U., Northridge, 1972—2001, ret., 2001. Reader Huntington Libr., San Marino, Calif., 1990—. Author: Women War Correspondents in the Vietnam War, 1988; contbr. articles to profl. jours. Calif. State U. Found. grantee, Northridge, Calif. State U. Libr. grantee. Mem. Calif. Acad. & Rsch. Librs., Western Assn. Women Historians, Soc. Calif. Archivists. Democrat. Episcopalian. Avocations: travel, musical theater.

ELY, DAVID (DAVID E. LILIENTHAL JR.), writer; b. Chgo., Nov. 19, 1927; s. David Eli and Helen Marian (Lamb) Lilienthal; m. Margaret Anne Jenkins, Aug. 7, 1954; children: Michael, Pamela, David, Margaret. AB, Harvard U., 1949. Author: (novels) Trot, 1963, Seconds, 1963, The Tour, 1967, Poor Devils, 1970, Walking Davis, 1972, Mr. Nicholas, 1974, A Journal of the Flood Year, 1992, (short stories) Time Out, 1968, Always Home, 1991. Home: PO Box 1387 East Dennis MA 02641-1387

ELY, DONALD J(EAN), clergyman, secondary school educator; b. Frederick, Md., July 15, 1935; s. George Kline and Jennie Mabel (Boyer) E. m. Lois Jean Kirkpatrick, Aug. 27, 1967; children: Kathleen Rose, Stephen David, Yvonne Elaine. AB, Gettysburg Coll., 1955; BD, Lancaster Sem., 1958; MEd, Bloomsburg State U., 1972. Ordained to ministry Evang. and Reformed Ch., 1958. Pastor St. John Evang. and Reformed Ch., Riegelsville, Pa., 1958-61, Zion's Reformed Ch., Ashland, Pa., 1961-64, Augusta Reformed Parish, Sunbury, Pa., 1964-74, Salem United Meth. Ch., Middleburg, Pa., 1974-79, Salem Ind. Brethren Ch., Middleburg, Pa., 1979-83; tchr. social studies Shikellamy High Sch., Sunbury, Pa., 1966-98; ret., 1998. Bd. dirs. Sunbury Area YMCA, 1966—, sec., 1973-80, 88-2000; bd. dirs. Greater Susquehanna Valley YMCA, 1993—, sec. 1999—; bd. dirs. Northumberland County unit Am. Cancer Soc., 1971-74, Snyder County unit, 1974-84; rep. candidate state legis., 1982; vice chmn. Govt. Study Commn. of City of Sunbury, 1989-91; mem. Northumberland County Rep. com., 1987—, state committeeman, 1992—. Mem.: SAR (chaplain 1971—, chpt. pres. 1981—86, 1992), Greater Susquehanna Valley C. of C., Federalist Soc., Commonwealth Found., Intercollegiate Studies Inst., Am. Conservative Union, Hist. Soc. Evang. and Ref. Ch., Northumberland County Hist. Soc. (life; trustee 1972—83), Snyder County Hist. Soc. (life; pres. 1980—83), Union County Hist. Soc., Hereditary Register of U.S., Rolls Royce Owners' Club, Susquehanna Valley Country Club, Antique Auto Club Am., Masons. Home and Office: PO Box 765 Sunbury PA 17801-0765 Fax: 570-286-4444.

ELY, DUNCAN CAIRNES, non profit/human services executive, civic leader; b. Phila., Apr. 3, 1951; s. Donald and Barbara Dercum (Mifflin) E.; m. Elizabeth Caroline Wickenberg, June 14, 1984; 1 child, Penn Wickenberg Ely. BA, U. Ariz., 1974; MDiv, Gen. Theol. Sem., N.Y.C., 1988; cert. mentor Edn. for Ministry, U. of South, 1985. Cert. in clin. pastoral edn. Bapt. Med. Ctr., 1985; cert. human svcs. adminstrn. Human Svcs. Inst., 1991. Nat. exec. dir. Assn. for Independence of Disabled, Inc., Tucson, 1974-77; exec. dir. Frat. of Alpha Kappa Lambda, Inc., Indpls., 1977-79; asst. St. Stephen's Episcopal Ch., Phila., 1979-80; exec. dir. The Youth Alternatives Camps, Inc., Tucson, 1980-83, Crisis Assistance Clothing Ministry, Charlotte, N.C., 1989-93, N.C. Harvest, Inc., Charlotte, 1993-96, Spartanburg (S.C.) Cmty. Events, Inc., 1996-98; dir. Camp Gravatt, Aiken, S.C., 1998—. Chmn. bd. advisors Expanded Foods and Nutrition Edn. Program N.C. State U., 1989-96; mem. foster care rev. bd. child protective svcs. Dept. Social Svcs., Charlotte, 1991-96. Author, editor: The Truth and the Word, 1978; also numerous articles in books, jours., mag. and newspapers. Past pres. Ely Assn., Inc., N.Y.C.; trustee Wildlife Guard, Inc., 1973—, past nat. pres., also past chmn. bd. advisors The Relatives, Inc., Charlotte, 1989-96, Ret. Sr. Vol. Program, Charlotte, 1990-96, Vol. Ctr. Charlotte, 1990-96; bd. dirs. Charlotte Emergency Housing, Inc., 1989-96, Met. Music Ministries, Inc., 1993-96, Piedmont Area Girl Scouts, Inc., 1997—, S.C. Inst. Nonprofit Leadership, Share the Vision resource com. City of Spartanburg, 1997—; mem. Vol. Leadership Devel. Program, Charlotte, 1991; grad. class XIII, Leadership Charlotte, 1991; grad. class III Carolinas Leadership Program, 1994; grad. class I Leadership N.C., 1995; chmn. bd. dirs. Spartanburg Caregivers, Inc., 1996—; grad. class 17 Leadership Spartanburg, 1997; grad. class 19 Leadership S.C., 1998; commr. for nat. and cmty. svc. State of N.C.; mem. N.C. Gov.'s Commn. on Nat. and Cmty. Svc.; mem. christian formation steering com. Episcopal Diocese Upper S.C., 1998—, mem. mission and outreach steering com., 1998—, mem. peer ministry conf., 1998. Recipient gold pin Phila. State Hosp., 1973, One of Nine Who Care award Sta. WSOC-TV and United Way, Charlotte, 1991, 94. Mem. S.R., Internat. Festivals and Events Assn., Nat. Soc. Am. Royal Descent, Barorial Order Magna Charta, Colonial Order of the Crown, Soc. Mayflower Descendants, Am. Mgmt. Assn., Am. Soc. Assn. Execs., Nat. Christian Counselors Assn. (lic. pastoral counselor), Metrolina Assn. for Vol. Adminstrn. (past pres.), N.C. Assn. Vol. Adminstrs. (past v.p.), S.C. Festival Assn., Penn Laurel Poets, Soc. Nonprofit Execs., Soc. Cin., Pen and Pencil Club, Alpha Kappa Lambda (past pres.), Alpha Phi Omega (past pres.), Theta Kappa Psi (past pres.), Theta Omega (past pres.), Psi Chi (past pres.), Country Club of Spartanburg, Piedmont Club, Fripp Island Club (S.C.), numerous others. Republican. Episcopalian. Avocations: arts, genealogy, historic preservation horticulture, reading, sports and outdoor activities. Home: Skidaway 605 Crystal Dr Spartanburg SC 29302-2716 Office: Camp Gravatt 1006 Camp Gravatt Rd Aiken SC 29805-8730 E-mail: DuncanEly@Hotmail.com.

ELY, GARY G. utilities company executive; Grad., Brigham Young U.; postgrad., U. Idaho, Stanford U., Edison Elec. Inst. Leadership. With Avista Corp., Spokane, 1967—, v.p. mktg., 1986-91, v.p. natural gas, 1991-95, sr. v.p., 1996-97, pres., CEO, 1997—. Mem. State Bldg. Code Coun. Mem. Pacific Coast Gas Assn. (chmn. gas mgmt. exec. com., chmn. mktg. exec. com., bd. dirs.), N.W. Electric Light and Power Assn. (bd. dirs.), Spokane Valley C. of C. (exec. bd.), N.W. Gas Assn. (bd. dirs.). Office: Avista Corp 1411 E Mission Ave Spokane WA 99220-3727

ELY, HIRAM, III, lawyer; b. Lexington, Ky., May 14, 1951; s. Hiram and Buena E. (Wright) E.; m. Deborah A. Johnson, Oct. 22, 1977. B.A., Centre Coll. Ky., 1973; J.D., Washington and Lee U., 1976. Bar: Ky. 1976, U.S. Dist. Ct. (we. dist.) Ky. 1976, U.S. Dist. Ct. (ea. dist.) Ky. 1979, U.S. Supreme Ct. 1979, U.S. Ct. Appeals (6th cir.) 1979, U.S. Ct. Claims, 1979, U.S. Tax Ct. 1984. Clk. to presiding justice U.S. Dist. Ct. Va., Roanoke, 1976-77; assoc. Ewen, MacKenzie & Peden, P.S.C., Louisville, 1977-81; assoc. Greenebaum, Doll & McDonald, Louisville, 1981-84, ptnr., 1984—. Chmn. Ky. Atty. Gen.'s Task Force on Election Reform, 1987-88; vice-chmn. policy com. Downtown Action Plan for Louisville; fund raiser profl. div. Metro United Way, Louisville, 1983-85; bd. dirs. Goodwill Industries, 1985—, Louisville C. of C., 1985—. Legal Research Assn. grantee, 1974; named among Top Ten Outstanding Kentuckians, Ky. Jaycees, 1969. Mem. Young Lawyers Club (v.p. 1982-83, pres. 1983-84), Louisville Bar Found. (chmn. continuing legal edn. sect. 1985—, bd. dirs. 1986—), Louisville Bar Assn. (mem. litigation, internat. law, fed. practice sects.) Ky. Bar Assn., ABA (discovery com. litigation sect. 1981-84), Ky. Acad. Trial Atty's., Ky. Def. Counsel, Def. Research Inst., Sigma Chi. Club: Jefferson, Harmony Landing Country (Louisville). Office: Greenebaum Doll & McDonald 3300 First Nat Towers Louisville KY 40202

ELY, JAMES WALLACE, JR., law educator; b. Rochester, NY, Jan. 20, 1938; s. James Wallace and Edythe (Farnham) E.; m. Ruth Buell MacCameron, Aug. 27, 1960; children: A. Elizabeth, Kimberly Farnham, Suzanne B., James W. AB, Princeton U., 1959; LLB, Harvard U., 1962; PhD, U. Va., 1971. Bar: N.Y. 1962, U.S. Dist. Ct. (we. dist.) N.Y. 1963. Assoc. Harris, Beach and Wilcox, Rochester, 1962-67; instr. U. Va., 1970; from instr. to asst. prof. U. Richmond, Va., 1970-73; asst. prof. law Vanderbilt U., Nashville, 1973-75, assoc. prof., 1975-78, prof., 1978—, Milton R. Underwood prof. law, 1999—. Vis. prof. law. U. Leeds, Eng., 1981-82; Chapman disting. vis. prof. U. Tulsa, 1985. Author: The Crisis of Conservative Virginia: The Byrd Organization and the Politics of Massive Resistance, 1976, The Guardian of Every Other Right: A Constitutional History of Property Rights, 1992, 2d edit., 1998, The Chief Justiceship of Melville W. Fuller 1888-1910, 1995, Railroads and American Law, 2001; co-author (with Bruce): Modern Property Law: Cases and Materials, 1984, 5th edit., 2003, The Law of Easements and Licenses in Land, 1988, rev. edit., 1995, 2001; co-editor (with Bodenhamer): Ambivalent Legacy: A Legal History of the South, 1984, The Bill of Rights in Modern America: After 200 Years, 1993; co-author (with Brown): Legal Papers of Andrew Jackson, 1987; co-author: (with Hall) An Uncertain Tradition: Constitutionalism and the History of the South, 1989; editor: Property Rights in American History, 6 vols., 1997—, A History of the Tennessee Supreme Court, 2002; co-editor (with Hall, Grossman, Wiecek): The Oxford Companion to the Supreme Court, 1992; co-editor: (with Hall, Clark, Grossman, Hull) The Oxford Companion to American Law, 2002; mem. editl. bd.: Am. Jour. Legal History, 1987—99. Mem. Am. Soc. Legal History (treas. 1980-81, 82-83, 84-85), Orgn. Am. Historians, So. History Assn. Office: Vanderbilt U Sch Law 21st Ave S Nashville TN 37240-0001

ELY, JOE, singer, songwriter; b. Feb. 9, 1947; With Flatlanders Band, Joe Ely Band; albums include Joe Ely, 1977, Honky Tonk Masquerade, 1978, Down on the Drag, 1979, Live Shots, 1980, Musta Notta Gotta Lotta, 1981, Hi-Res, 1984, Lord of the Highway, 1987, Milkshakes & Malts, 1988, Dig All Night, 1988, Live at Liberty Lunch, 1990, Love and Danger, 1992, From Chippy, 1994, Letter to Laredo, 1995, Twistin' in the Wind, 1998, Los Super Seven, 1999 (Grammy 1999), Live at Antone's, 2000, Best of Joe Ely, 2001, Poet, A Tribute to Townes Van Zandt, 2000 (Grammy nominee), Now Again (The Flatlanders, 2002), Streets of Sin, 2003. Address: LC Media Attn: Lance Cowan PO Box 965 Antioch TN 37011-0965

ELY, JOHN HART, lawyer, university dean; b. N.Y.C., Dec. 3, 1938; s. John H. and Martha Foster (Coyle) E.; children: John Duff, Robert Allan Duff, m. Gisela Cardonne, 2002. AB summa cum laude, Princeton U., 1960; LL.B. magna cum laude, Yale U., 1963, MA (hon.), 1971, Harvard U., 1973; LLD, U. San Diego, 1988, Ill. Inst. Tech., 1991. Bar: D.C. 1965, Calif. 1967. Atty. Warren Commn., 1964; law clk. to Chief Justice Warren, 1964-65; Fulbright scholar London Sch. Econs., 1965-66; atty. Defenders, Inc., San Diego, 1966-68; asso. prof., then prof. law Yale U. Law Sch., 1968-73; prof. Harvard U. Law Sch., 1973-1982, Ralph S. Tyler, Jr. prof. constl. law, 1981-1982; Richard E. Lang prof. law Stanford U. Law Sch., Calif., 1982-87, dean, 1982-87; Robert E. Paradise prof. Stanford (Calif.) U. Law Sch., 1987-96; Richard A. Hausler prof. U. Miami (Fla.) Law Sch., 1996—. Gen. counsel U.S. Dept. Transp., 1975-76 Author: Democracy and Distrust, 1980, War and Responsibility, 1993, On Constitutional Ground, 1996. Served with USAR, 1963-69. Fellow Woodrow WIlson Internat. Ctr. scholars (1978-79), Am. Acad. Arts and Scis., Coun. on Fgn. Rels. Office: U Miami Law Sch PO Box 248087 Coral Gables FL 33124-8087

ELY, JOHN P. lawyer; b. Lubbock, Tex., Apr. 21, 1945; s. John O. and Laverne (Barton) Ely; m. Julie McCall Sherman, Dec. 27, 1967. BA, U. N.H., 1967; JD, Boston U., 1976. Bar: Mass. 1977, U.S. Dist. Ct. Mass. 1977, U.S. Dist. Ct. Conn. 1980, U.S. Supreme Ct. 1980. Sole practice, Agawam, Mass., 1977-78; assoc. Laming, Smith, et al., Springfield, Mass., 1978-80; jr. ptnr. Auchter, Bozenhard & Socha, Springfield, 1980-83, ptnr., 1984-85, Bozenhard, Socha, Ely & Kolber, Springfield, 1985-92, Bozenhard, Socha & Ely, Springfield, 1992—. 1st lt. USMC, 1968—71. Mem.: Mass. Conveyancers Assn., Hampden County Bar Assn., Mass. Bar Assn., West Springfield C. of C. (bd. dirs. 1990—96, 2003—), 3d Marine Divsn. Assn., Marine Corps Assn. Office: Bozenhard Socha & Ely 1252 Elm St Ste 12 West Springfield MA 01089 E-mail: bsejpe@aol.com.

ELY, KATHRYN R. crystallographer; b. Omaha; BA, Clarke Coll., 1966; PhD, U. Utah, 1981. Scientific asst./assoc. Argonne (Ill.) Nat. Lab., 1966-76; instr. to assoc. prof. of biology U. Utah, Salt Lake City, 1976-88; staff scientist La Jolla (Calif.) Cancer Rsch. Found., 1988-93, prof., 1993—, dir. structural biology, 1992—2002, dir. sci. advancement, 2002—. Mem. Cancer Ctr. rev. com., Nat. Cancer Inst., Washington, 1994-2000.; mem. U.S. Commn. on Crystallography, 2001—. Mem. AAAS, Protein Soc., Am. Soc. Biochem. Molecular Biology, Am. Crystallographic Assn. Office: The Burnham Inst 10901 N Torrey Pines Rd La Jolla CA 92037-1062

ELY, LAURENCE DRIGGS, III, theoretical Christian astrologer; b. N.Y.C., Feb. 3, 1945; s. Laurence D. Ely Jr. and Winifred F. (Forgit) Ewing; m. Tamson Myers, Mar. 14, 1970; children: Nicholas Myers, Alexander Nash. AB with honors, Princeton U., 1967. Rsch. chemist Monsanto, Springfield, Mass., 1968-69; dir., tchr. Demeter Inst., Amherst, Mass., 1973—. Author: True Solar and Lunar Progressions, 1982, (anthology) Astrology's Special Measurements: Toward a General Theory of Rectification, 1994. Organizer Prison Visitors Chess Club, Boston, 1970-72; mem. choir South Congl. Ch., 1995-2002, chair arts com., 1998-2003; active Friends of Rudolf Steiner. With Peace Corps, 1967, USNG, 1969-72, conscientious objector discharge, 1972. Avocations: classical music, chess, choir, tennis. E-mail: ldely@crocker.com.

ELY, LAWRENCE ORLO, retired surgeon; b. Guthrie Center, Iowa, Dec. 13, 1919; s. John Ermerson and Luella Mabel (Knapp) E.; m. Dorothy Maxine Jenkins, Aug. 23, 1942; children: Patricia Anne, Lawrence Orlo, Stephen Craig, Bennett Knapp, Carolyn Elizabeth. BA, State U. Iowa, 1942, MD, 1943, MS, 1948, PhD, 1950. Diplomate Am. Bd. Gen. Surgery. Intern Mt. Carmel Mercy Hosp., Detroit, 1943-44; instr. dept. physiology Med. Sch., State U. Iowa, Iowa City, 1946-48, resident, instr. dept. surgery, 1948-52; pvt. practice gen. surgery Des Moines, 1952-85. Mem. staff Iowa Luth. Hosp., Des Moines, 1952-85, Mercy Med. Ctr., Des Moines, 1952-85, Iowa Meth. Med. Ctr., Des Moines, 1952-86; cons. Iowa Blue Cross-Blue Shield, 1985-86, Iowa Found. for Med. Care, 1985-86. Sect. head United Campaign, Des Moines, 1958-60; mem. Des Moines Opera Bd., 1973—, pres., 1973-78; mem. Health Planning Coun. of Iowa Med. Corp., 1970-78; bd. dirs., pres. Ramsey Home, 1988-94; bd. dirs. Civic Music Assn. Des Moines, 1984-98; mem. steering com. Friends of the Arts, Drake U., Des Moines. Capt. M.C., U.S. Army, 1944-46. Fellow ACS; mem. AMA, Iowa Med. Soc., Polk County Med. Soc. Republican. Mem. Christian Ch. (Disciples Of Christ). Avocation: singing. Home: 3500 Fleur Dr Des Moines IA 50321-2650

ELY, MELVIN PATRICK, historian, writer, educator; b. Richmond, Va., June 11, 1952; s. Clarence Patrick and Vivien King Ely; m Naama Zahavi, Sept. 14, 1983; children: Oren N.Z., Kinneret K.S. AB, Princeton U., 1973, MA, 1982, PhD, 1985; MA, U. Tex., 1978. Postdoctoral fellow Carter G. Woodson Inst. U. Va., Charlottesville, 1985-86; asst. and assoc. prof. history and African Am. studies Yale U., New Haven, 1986-95; assoc. prof and prof. history and Black studies Coll. William and Mary, Williamsburg, Va., 1995—. Fulbright prof. Am. studies Hebrew U., Jerusalem, 1998-99. Author: The Adventures of Amos 'n' Andy: A Social History of an American Phenomenon, 1991 (Notable Book N.Y. Times Book Rev, 1991, 2d pl. award Theatre Libr. Assn. 1992), 2d edit., 2001; co-translator, The Handicap Principle: A Missing Piece of Darwin's Puzzle, 1997; bd. dirs. U. Va. Press, Charlottesville, 1999—. Recipient Heyman prize for outstanding scholarly publ. and rsch. Yale Coll., 1992, prize for tchg. excellence, 1989. Mem. AAUP, Am. Hist. Assn., Va. Hist. Soc. Methodist. Avocations: fishing, travel, foreign languages. Office: Dept History Coll of William and Mary PO Box 8795 Williamsburg VA 23187

ELY, PARRY HAINES, dermatologist, educator; b. Washington, Sept. 19, 1945; s. Northcutt and Marica (McCann) E.; m. Elizabeth Magee, June 24, 1969 (div. June 1998); children: Sims, Rebecca, Meredith, Tess. AB, Stanford U., 1967; MD, U. So. Calif., 1971. Diplomate Am. Bd. Dermatology, Am. Bd. Pathology; lic. dermatologist, Calif. Intern in medicine U. So. Calif.-L.A. County Med. Ctr., 1971-72, resident in dermatology, 1972-75; clin. prof. dermatology U. Calif., Davis, 1975—. Bd. dirs. Nevada City Wineries Mem. editl. bd. Calif. Physician, 1994—; manuscript reviewer Archives of Internal Medicine, 1988—, Annals of Internal Medicine, 1980—, Archives of Dermatology, 1977—; contbr. articles to med. jours. Fellow Am. Acad. Dermatology (asst. editor jour. 1988-94, manuscript reviewer 1994—), Am. Soc. Dermatopathology; mem. AMA, Internat. Soc. for Tropical Dermatology, Am. Fedn. for Clin. Rsch., Am. Soc. for Dermatologic Surgery, N.Am. Clin.. Dermatologic Soc., Calif. Med. Assn. (alt. del. 1995—, rep. to Calif. Telehealth/Telemedicine coord. project planning com. 1996—), Pacific Dermatologic Soc. (Nelson Paul Anderson Meml. Essay 1st pl. award 1979, Mini Presentation of Yr. award 1984), Noah Worcester Dermatol. Soc., Cutaneous Therapy Soc., Soc. Investigative Dermatology, Sacramento Valley Dermatol. Soc. (pres. 1990-91), Placer Nev. Med. Soc. (bd. dirs. 1978-79, 91-93, v.p. 1994, pres. 1995), Skin Cancer Found. (med. coun. 1987—), Tri-County Am. Cancer Soc. (bd. dirs. 1978-79, 91-92), Royal Soc. Medicine (London), Dermatology Found., Space Dermatology Found. (founding mem.), Shivas Irons Soc. (founding mem.) Office: Brunswick E # 7 10565 Brunswick Rd Grass Valley CA 95945-9053

ELY, PAUL C., JR., electronics company executive; b. McKeesport, Pa., Feb. 18, 1932; s. Paul C. and Jean C. E.; m. Barbara Sheiry, Apr. 3, 1953 (dec. May 2000); children: Paul C., Glenn E. m. Geri Cherem, Sept. 25, 2000. BSEE, Lehigh U., 1953; MSEE, Stanford U., 1964. Research and devel. engr. Sperry Rand Corp., Great Neck, N.Y. and Clearwater, Fla., 1953-62; research and devel. sect. mgr., engring. mgr. microwave div. Hewlett-Packard Co., Palo Alto, Calif., 1962-73, gen. mgr. data systems div., 1973-74, gen. mgr. computer group, 1974-76, v.p., 1976-80, exec. v.p., also bd. dirs., 1980-85; chmn., chief exec. officer Convergent Technologies (name now Unisys), San Jose, Calif., from 1985; exec. v.p. Unisys Corp., San Jose, 1989; gen. ptnr. Alpha Ptnrs. Venture Capital, 1989-98. Bd. dirs. Parker-Hannifin Corp., Tektronix, The Sabre Group, Travelocity.com Chmn. Cupertino United Fund, 1976, Bay Area Sci. Fair, 1969; regent U. Santa Clara; mem. Calif. Econ. Devel. Commn., 1976. Mem. IEEE, Am. Electronics Assn. (bd. dirs., exec. com. 1985-89).

ELY, ROBERT EUGENE, lawyer, author, educator; b. Ft. Wayne, Ind., Aug. 18, 1949; s. Virgil Eugene and Alberta Irene (Steiner) E.; m. Jackline Sue Meyer, Apr. 14, 1973; 1 child, Elizabeth Vanessa. BA, Manchester Coll., 1971, MA, 1975; JD, Ind. U., 1983. Bar: Ala. 1985, U.S. Dist. Ct. (mid. dist.) Ala. 1988. Sales promotion cons. Lincoln Nat. Corp., Ft. Wayne, 1971-73; asst. dir. humanities Manchester Coll., North Manchester, Ind., 1973-75; assoc. instr. English Purdue U., West Lafayette, Ind., 1975-77; instr. English Ala. State U., Montgomery, 1977-81, dir. honors, 1984-86, asst. v.p., 1984-85, assoc. prof. English, 1986—; pvt. practice law Montgomery, 1985—. Communications cons. Cummins Internat., Columbus, Ind., 1982; adj. prof. paralegalism Auburn (Ala.) U., 1990-95. Author: The Humanities, 1979, Mose T.'s Slapout Family Album (children's verse), 1996 (Shaw-Montgomery prize for poetry 1985), Encanchata, 2001; contbr. articles to profl. jours. Summer inst. fellow NEH, 1981; rsch. fellow Ala. State U., 1978; Mobil Found. fellow for Islamic studies in Turkey, 1999; Henry Luce Found. fellow for East-West studies U. Hawaii, 2000, Fulbright fellow 2002; named to Order of Reyes del Monte do Gozo. Mem. ABA, Ala. Bar Assn., Montgomery County Bar Assn., Am. Acad. Poets, Nat. Coun. Tchrs. English, Lower Audubon Brook Soc., Coventry Motoring and Aviation Soc., The Writs. Democrat. Presbyterian. Avocations: serious and light verse, fishing, folk art, sports cars. Home: 3212 LeBron Rd Montgomery AL 36106-2334 Office: 659 S Hull St Montgomery AL 36104-5807 E-mail: relylaw@juno.com.

ELY, STANLEY E. language educator, writer; b. Dallas, Nov. 9, 1932; s. Henry and Rebecca (Shapiro) Ely. BA, Northwestern U., 1953; B of Fgn. Trade, Am. Inst. Fgn. Trade, 1957; MA, Hunter Coll., 1972. Acct. exec. Young and Rubicam, N.Y.C., 1957—60, Dorothy Gray Ltd., N.Y.C., 1960—69; French and Spanish tchr. New Rochelle (N.Y.) H.S., 1969—89; French and Spanish tutor N.Y.C., 1989—. Author: In Jewish Texas: A Family Memoir, 1998, Perfect Mondays, 2002. Bd. dirs. Collen-Lorde Health Ctr., N.Y.C., 1988—2002; steering com. Pub. Triangle, N.Y.C., 1991—2002. Sgt. U.S. Army, 1954—56, Korea. Home: Apt 3C 117 E 77th St New York NY 10021 Personal E-mail: firstely@msn.com.

ELYN, MARK, retired opera singer, educator; b. Seattle, Feb. 4, 1932; s. Isadore and Goldie Elyn; m. Jaclyn Rendall, 1956. Student, U. Wash., 1948-51, Seattle U., 1951-52; student of Robert Weede. Bd. mem. Bel Canto Inst., NY. Debut, N.Y.C. Opera, 1956, leading roles, San Francisco Opera, NBC Opera, Phila. Lyric Opera, leading bass, Cologne, Munich, Hamburg, Stuttgart, Vienna, Monte Carlo, Geneva, Barcelona; roles include: Don Giovanni, Sarastro in The Magic Flute, Philip II in Don Carlo, Figaro in The Marriage of Figaro; prof. music, U. Ill., Urbana, 1977—, chmn. voice dept., 1990-98, prof. emeritus, guest lectr., 1998—. Mem. Am. Guild Mus. Artists, Deutsche Buehnengenossenschaft, Nat. Assn. Tchrs. of Singing. Home: 1238 10th Ave E Seattle WA 98102-4324

ELY-RAPHEL, NANCY, diplomat; b. N.Y.C, Feb. 4, 1937; d. Thomas Clarkson and Margaret (Merritt) Halliday; widowed; children: John Duff Ely, Robert Duff Ely, Stephanie Joyce Raphel. AB, Syracuse U., 1957; JD, U. San Diego, 1968. Bar: Calif. 1968, U.S. Supreme Ct. 1976. Dep. city atty. City of San Diego, 1969—70; asst. U.S. atty. So. Dist. Calif., 1970—71; assoc. Tyler, Cooper, Grant, Bowerman and Keefe, New Haven, 1971—72; from asst. to assoc. dean Sch. Law Boston U., 1972—75; atty.-advisor U.S. Dept. State, Washington, 1975—77; spl. atty. Boston Strike Force U.S. Dept. Justice, 1977—78; asst. legal advisor African Affairs U.S. Dept. State, Washington, 1978—87, asst. legal advisor Nuclear Affairs, 1988—89; dep. asst. Sec. of State Bur. Democracy, Human Rights and Labor Affairs, Washington, 1878—83, prin. dep. asst., 1993—95; Balkan coord. Bur. European and Can. Affairs, Washington, 1995—98; U.S. amb. to Slovenia, Am. Embassy, Ljubljana, 1998—2001, sr. advisor to sec., 2001—03; counselor on internat. law, 2003—. Mem. Coun. on Fgn. Rels., 1990—. Recipient Outstanding Alumni award U. San Diego Law Sch., 1979, Superior Honor award U.S. Dept. State, Washington, 1983, 84, Presdl. Meritorious Svc. award U.S. Govt., Washington, 1986, 94, 98, Presdl. Disting. Svc. award, 1992, Author Hughes Career Achievement award, 2001. Home: 1304 30th St NW Washington DC 20007-3343 Office: US Dept State Office of Legal Adviser 2201 C St NW Washington DC 20520-6419 E-mail: nancyelyraphael@earthlink.net.

ELZA, BETTY ANN, retired librarian; b. Wymer, W.Va., Feb. 27, 1944; d. Floyd and Gertrude (Snyder) E. BS, Clarion U., 1966, MSLS, 1971, postgrad., 1971—, U. Dundee, Scotland, Summer 1969. Libr. Brookville (Pa.) Area Sch. Dist., 1966—97, mem. steering com. for self study for evaluation, 1976—77;

ret, 1997. Presenter workshop on parliamentary procedure Tall Tree Coun. Boardmanship Tng., Clarion Holiday Inn, June 1991; mem. task force Pa. Guidelines for Media Programs, 1975-76; chairperson joint rev. com. Pa. Libr. Master Plan Report, 1975; vis. faculty Clarion U. Pa., 1972-73; inst. adviser U. Pitts., 1976. Contbr. articles to profl. publs. Organizer parish libr. Immaculate Conception Ch., Brookville, 1968-69, First Bapt. Ch., Brookville, 1976-77; mem. steering com. for strategic planning Brookville Sch. Dist., 1994-95; mem. capital stewardship campaign Immaculate Conception, Brookville, 2002; bd. trustees Summerville Pub. Libr., 1997-2003. Mem. NSDAR, Pa. Sch. Librs. Assn. (chairperson profl. stds. com. 1974-76), Embroiderers' Guild Am. (Nydill chpt.), Alpha Delta Kappa. Roman Catholic. Avocations: crafts, reading, travel, photography. Home: 618 Simpson Rd Corsica PA 15829-9409

EL-ZAWAHRY, M. A. MONEIM, epidemiologist, tropical medicine specialist; b. Hehia, Sharkyia, Egypt, Jan. 17, 1926; s. M. A. El-Karim and Sany'ia M. (Aly) El-Zawahry; m. Grace Ellen Ransdell, Dec. 31, 1956; 1 child, A. Sabry. MD, Cairo U., 1952; MPH, U. N.C., 1957; MPH, PhD, Johns Hopkins U., 1959. Resident in internal medicine Kings Hosp., Cairo, 1952-53; chief med. officer Rural Tng., Demonstration and Rsch. Ctrs., Cairo, 1953—57; pediatrician cardiac clinic Johns Hopkins Hosp., Balt., 1957-59; demonstrator, lectr., assoc. prof., chair prof. epidemiology High Inst. Pub. Health, Alexandria (Egypt) U., 1957-73; sec., med. rsch. coun. Ministry of Rsch., Egypt, 1961—68; WHO prof. Inst. Medicine, Rangoon, Burma, 1968-75; WHO reg. advisor SEARO, New Delhi, 1975-79; WHO rep. Jakarta, Indonesia, 1979—86; WHO sr. health adviser to UNICEF Hdqs., N.Y.C., 1988; sec. W.H.O./UNICEF Joint Com. Health Policy, Geneva. Cons. primary health care UN Devel. program and WHO, 1986—87; WHO and UN cons. in Yemen, Egypt, Morocco, Ethiopia, Switzerland, U.S., India, Indonesia, Burma, Thailand, Nepal, Saudi Arabia, and Mongolia, 1987—96; WHO cons. on HIV/AIDS, EMRO, 1990—93; guest lectr. internat. health Coll. Medicine and Pub. Health & Children Hosp. Ohio State U., Columbus, 1987—2003; spokesperson Child Immunization Coalition, 1997—2002; lectr. HIV/AIDS Ohio U., Chillicothe, 2001—; cons. to voluntary health projects, Chillicothe, 1986—2003; presenter in field; mem., chair numerous adv. & rsch. com. W.H.O. & several countries. Co-editor: Egyptian Jour. Pub. Health, 1960—68; contbr. over 146 articles to sci. reports and W.H.O. documents;, author 68 publ. and 25 W.H.O. publ. Panelist Global Health Forum Ohio State U., Columbus, 2001—; chmn. Polio-Plus and World Cmty. Svcs. Com., Rotary, Chillicothe, 1986—2001; cons. AIDS Task Force, Ross County, Ohio, 1995—2003; mem. bd. dirs. Family Healthcare, Inc., Chillicothe, Ohio, 1999—. Recipient honors and awards, U.S. Internat. Coop. Adminstrn., Johns Hopkins U., Rockefeller Found., Burma Med. Assn., Govt. Indonesia, WHO, U. N.C., Rotary, APHA, Govt. Saudi Arabia, Egyptian Med. Syndicate, Family Healthcare, Inc., others. Mem.: APHA (hon. life, awards), New Eng. Jour. Med., Mass. Med. Soc., Burma Med. Assn. (hon., life), Johns Hopkins Med. and Surg. Assn. (hon. life), Egyptian Family Planning Assn., Egyptian Assn. of Tuberculosis and Chest Diseases, Egyptian Pub. Health Assn. (governing coun. 1960—68), Tropical Medicine Soc., Egyptian Med. Syndicate (awards), others, U. N.C. Alumni Assn. (life), Johns Hopkins U. Alumni Assn. (life), Chillicothe Rotary (Paul Harris fellow 1986—2003). Avocations: classical music, nature photography, fishing. Home: 72 N Courtland Dr Chillicothe OH 45601-2149

ELZAY, RICHARD PAUL, retired dental school administrator; b. Lima, Ohio, Dec. 6, 1931; s. Paul William and Edna Virginia (Moyer) E.; 1 child, Mark S. BS, Ind. U., Indpls., 1957, DDS with honors, 1960, MS in Dental Surgery, 1962. Diplomate Am. Bd. Oral Maxillofacial Pathology. Gen. practice dentistry, Brownsburg, Ind., 1960-62; instr. dept. oral pathology Med. Coll. Va. Sch. Dentistry, Richmond, 1962-64; asst. prof. Sch. Dentistry Med. Coll. Va., Richmond, 1964-66, assoc. prof., 1966-69, prof., chmn. dept. oral pathology, 1969-86, asst. dean acad. affairs, 1970-74; prof., dep. v.p. for health scis., dean Sch. Dentistry U. Minn., Mpls., 1986-96.

ELZINGA, KENNETH GERALD, economics educator; b. Coopersville, Mich., Aug. 11, 1941; s. Clarence Albert and Lettie (Albrecht) E.; m. Barbara Ann Brunson, June 17, 1967 (dec. 1978); m. Terry M. Maguire, Aug. 9, 1981. BA, Kalamazoo Coll., 1963; MA, Mich. State U., 1966, PhD, 1967; LHD, Kalamazoo Coll., 2000. Rsch. economist Senate Antitrust and Monopoly Subcom., 1964; asst. instr. Mich. State U., 1965-66; asst. prof. U. Va., Charlottesville, 1967-71, assoc. prof., 1971-73, prof., 1973—; fellow in law and econs. U. Chgo., 1974; vis. prof. econs. Trinity U., 1984; Thomas Jefferson fellow Cambridge U., 1990, Cavaliers Disting. Tchg. Professorship, 1992-97. Spl. econ. advisor to asst. atty. gen., antitrust divsn. Dept. Justice, 1970-71; trustee Hope Coll., 1983-90, Inter-Varsity Christian fellowship, 1992-2000; mem. editl. bd. Antitrust Bull., 1977—. Author: (with others) The Antitrust Penalties, 1976, The Fatal Equilibrium, 1985, Murder at the Margin, 1993, A Deadly Indifference, 1995, The Antitrust Casebook, 3rd edit. 1996. Recipient Thomas Jefferson award U. Va., 1992, Commonwealth of Va. Outstanding Faculty award, 1992, Kenan Enterprise award for tchg. econs., William R. Kenan Jr. Charitable Trust, 1996, Templeton Honor Roll award for Edn. in a Free Soc. John Templeton Found., 1997, Disting. Alumni award Mich. State U., 1999; named Tchr. of the Yr. Phi Eta Sigma, 1992. Mem. ABA, Am. Econs. Assn., Mystery Writers of Am., Am. Law and Econs. Assn., So. Econ. Assn. (pres. 1991), Internat. J.A. Shumpeter Soc., Industrial Orgn. Soc. (pres 1979). Presbyterian. Avocations: water skiing, travel. Office: U VA Dept Econs PO Box 400182 Charlottesville VA 22904-4182

ELZUFON, JOHN A. lawyer; b. Newark, N.Y., Nov. 1, 1946; s. Milton Harold and Muriel (Albert) E.; m. Lena Janis Jacobs, Mar. 22, 1981. B.S.Ch.E., Rose Hulman Inst. Tech., 1968; J.D., Georgetown U., 1974. Bar: Del. 1974, U.S. Dist. Ct. Del. 1975, U.S. Ct. Appeals (3d cir.) 1977. Assoc., Killoran & Van Brunt, Wilmington, Del., 1974-76; assoc. Tybout, Redfearn, Casarino & Pell, Wilmington, 1976-82; sole practice, Wilmington, 1982-83; ptnr. Elzufon & Bailey, Wilmington, 1983-84, dir. Elzufon & Bailey, P.A., 1984— ; of counsel Del. Claims Assn., 1984. Co-author: New Member's Manual to U.S. Ho. of Reps., 1974. Served to 1st lt. U.S. Army, 1969-70, Vietnam. Decorated Bronze Star. Mem. Am. Trial Lawyers Assn. (assoc.), Def. Research Inst., Del. Trial Lawyers Assn. Democrat. Jewish. Club: Toastmasters (Wilmington, pres. 1984). Home: 512 Ruxton Dr Wilmington DE 19809-2830

EMAMI, BAHMAN, oncologist, educator, radiologist; arrived in US, 1971; s. Bagher and Fatemeh Emami; m. Loba Emami, Oct. 16, 1977; children: Behrad, Barzin. MD, Tehran U., Iran, 1968. Asst. prof. Tufts U. Sch. Med., Boston, 1978—81; from. asst. prof. to prof. radiology Washington U., St. Louis, 1981—97, prof. otolaryngology, 1995—96, Loyola U. Med. Ctr., Maywood, Ill., 2000—, chmn. radiation oncology, 1997—. Contbr. articles to profl. jours. Fellow: ACR. Office: Loyola Univ Med Ctr 2160 S First Ave 105-293 Maywood IL 60153

EMAN DELMAR, EVELYN (EVELYN EMAN DELMAR), communications executive; b. N.Y.C., Dec. 31, 1949; d. John and Gay (Simon) Eman; m. Larry E. Delmar. Student, NYU, 1975—76, Baruch Coll., 1981—82. Asst. mgr. Vanderbilt Athletic Club, N.Y.C., 1967—68; pub. rels. mgr. DEC Enterprises, Inc., 1968—73; exec. interviewer Dun & Bradstreet, Inc., 1974; pub. rels. rep. Parsons & Whittemore, Inc., 1974—77; corp. mgr. pub. rels. NEC Am., Inc., Melville, 1977—82; pres. Perception Plus, Colorado Springs, Colo., 1982—87; v.p. L. C. Williams & Assocs., Inc., Chgo., 1987—90; assoc. editor First Draft, 1989—90, editor-in-chief, 1991—92; pvt. practice pub. rels. cons., 1991—94; exec. dir., pres. bd. dirs. Children Remembered, Inc., Northbrook, 1994—2002, now bd. dirs. Pub. rels. cons. ARK Celebrity Classic, 1986—87, World Cycling Championships, 1986; writer and spkr. in adoption field. Composer: Face Another Day, 1973, Songbird, 1973, There's the Man, 1973, Hey Mister, 1974, In the Morning, 1974, It's Never Been Like This, 1974; contbg. editor: PR Essay, 1976—77; editor: Women's Exch. Network Newsletter, 1983; contbr. articles to mags. Bd. dirs. Hear My Voice/Protecting Our Nations Children, Ill., 1996—2001, Hear My Voice/Protecting Our Nations Children, Mich., 1998—2001. Recipient cert. of merit, Publicity Club N.Y., 1976—77. Mem.: Women in Comm. (Women of Achievement award 1986), Pub. Rels. Soc. Am., Pikes Peak Advt. Fedn. (Addy award 1986, 1987), Promoters (dir. 1983—84, pres. 1984—85, chmn. 1985—86), Internat. Assn. Bus. Communicators (editor Exec. Forum FOCUS 1988, 1989, Gold Nuggets award 1984—86, Silver Quill 1986, Spectra award 1989), Colorado Springs Press Assn. (pres. S. Colo. 1985—86, Gridiron award 1986, 1987), Colorado Springs C. of C. Office: PO Box 234 Northbrook IL 60065-0234

EMANOUILIDIS, EMANUEL V. computer scientist, educator; b. Karpathos, Greece, May 6, 1962; arrived in U.S., 1974; s. Vasilios and Kaliopi Emanouilidis; m. Evdoxia Kanakis Emanouilidis, July 23, 1989. BS in Computer Sci., MS in Computer Sci., NJ Inst. Tech., 1985. Spl. lectr. NJ Inst. Tech., Newark, 1985—88; asst. prof. Kean U., Union, NJ, 1988—2001, assoc. prof., 2001—. Office: Kean U Morris Ave Union NJ 07083

EMANUEL, RAHM, congressman; b. Chgo., Ill., Nov. 29, 1959; m. Amy Emanuel; children: Zachariah, Ilana, Leah. BA, Sarah Lawrence Coll., 1981; MA in Speech and Comm., Northwestern U., 1985. With Ill. Pub. Action; sr. advisor, chief fundraiser Richard M. Daley Campaign for Mayor, 1989; mng. dir. Dresdner Kleinwort Wasserstein; top advisor Pres. Bill Clinton; congressman 5th Dist. Ill. U.S. Ho. Reps., 2003—. Democrat. Office: 1319 Longworth House Office Bldg Washington DC 20515 also: 3742 W Irving Park Rd Chicago IL 60618*

EMANUEL, WILLIAM JOSEPH, lawyer; b. Oct. 31, 1938; s. Lawrence John and Henrietta (Moser) Emanuel; m. Elizabeth Wolfe, Mar. 14, 1964; children: Christina, Michael, Steven. AB, Marquette U., 1960; JD, Georgetown U., 1963. Bar: Nebr. 1963, Calif. 1965, U.S. Supreme Ct. 1976. Assoc. Musick, Peeler & Garrett, L.A., 1963—70, ptnr., 1970—76, Morgan, Lewis & Bockius, L.A., 1976—97, Jones, Day, Reavis & Pogue, L.A., 1998—. Mem. labor rels. com. Am. Hosp. Assn., also mem. spl. subcom. to analyze report of Nat. Commn. on Nursing, Comparable Worth Task Force; mem. adv. com. NLRB, 1994—. Author (with Michael L. Wolfram): California Employment Law, A Guide to California Laws Regulating Employment in the Private Sector, 1989; contbr. articles to profl. jours. Mem.: ABA (com. on devel. of law under Nat. Labor Rels. Act, sect. on labor and employment law), State Bar Nebr., Am. Soc. Hosp. Attys., So. Calif. Labor Law Symposium (founding chmn. 1980, 1981), Los Angeles County Bar Assn. (chmn. labor law sect. 1983—84, exec. com. 1974—86), State Bar Calif. (labor and employment law sect.). Home: 345 17th St Santa Monica CA 90402 Office: Jones Day 555 W 5th St Ste 4600 Los Angeles CA 90013-1025

EMANUEL-SMITH, ROBIN LESLEY, special education educator; m. Allen Weston Smith, Apr. 14, 1983; children: David, Ariel, Weston. BS in Engring., U.S. Mil. Acad., 1981; BS in Health-Phys. Edn. summa cum laude, Cameron U., Lawton, Okla., 1992; M Spl. Edn., Coll. of St. Rose, Albany, 1995. Cert. spl. edn., health and phys. edn. tchr., N.Y. Enlisted U.S. Army, 1974-76, commd. 2nd lt., 1981, advanced through grades to capt., 1984, resigned, 1990; tchr. spl. edn. Ulster County Bd. Coop. Ednl. Svcs., Port Ewen, N.Y., 1992—. Roman Catholic. Avocations: weightlifting, coaching and officiating youth soccer, softball and baseball. Office: Ulster County Bd Coop Ednl Svs Rt 32 New Paltz NY 12561

EMANUELSON, JAMES ROBERT, retired insurance company executive; b. Hammond, Ind., Sept. 12, 1931; s. Clarence Harry and Ethel Janet (Anderson) E.; m. Dolores Patricia Fordyce, Aug. 10, 1957; children: James Robert, John Thomas, Karen Lynn. BS, Denison U., 1953. With Midland Mut. Life Ins. Co., Columbus, Ohio, 1953-67, mgr. gen. accounting, 1957-62, dir. cost accounting, 1962-67; with Columbus Mut. Life Ins. Co., 1967—, comptroller, 1969—, apptd. v.p., 1970-76, v.p., elected officer, 1976-91, v.p., comptroller, treas., 1991-93, ret., 1993—. Mem. Ins. Acctg. and Statis. Assn. (chpt. pres. 1954-69, pres. 1966-67, mem. interco. fin. rev. com. 1972-82, chmn. com. 1978-82, mem. fin. planning and control coun. 1978-91, cost acctg. com. 1982-91), Sigma Chi. Republican. Home: 3635 Cedar Circle Powell OH 43065-9148

EMBER, CAROL R. anthropology educator, author; b. Bklyn., July 7, 1943; d. Hy and Elsie (Kardonsky) Ruchlis; m. Lawrence Baldwin, 1963 (div. 1969); m. Melvin Ember, Mar. 21, 1970; children: Katherine Ann, Julie Beth. BA, Antioch Coll., 1965; postgrad., Cornell U., 1965-66; PhD, Harvard, 1971. Lectr. Hunter Coll. CUNY, 1970-71; from asst. prof. to assoc. prof. CUNY, 1971-80; prof. Hunter Coll., 1981-97; exec. dir. Human Rels. Area Files Yale U., New Haven, 1997—. First author (sr author/editor): Anthropology, 1973, 10th edit., 2002, Cultural Anthropology, 1973, 11th edit., 2002, (with M. Ember) Marriage, Family, and Kinship: Comparative Studies of Social Organization, 1983; sr. co-author: Anthropology: A Brief Introduction, 1991, 5th edit., 2003, (with Burton Pasternak and M. Ember) Sex, Gender, and Kinship: A Cross-Cult Perspective, 1997; sr. co-author: Cross-Cultural Research Methods, 2001; co-editor: Cross-Cultural Research for Social Science, 1998, Portraits of Culture, 1998; sr. co-author: Research Frontiers in Anthropology, 1998; co-author: Countries and Their Cultures, 2001, Encyclopedia of Urban Culture, 2002; sr. co-author: New Directions in Anthropology, 2003. Woodrow Wilson Fellow, 1965-66, predoctoral fellow NIMH, 1969-70; rsch. grantee NSF, 1983-84, 86-98, U.S. Inst. Peace, 1990-92. Mem. Am. Anthrop. Assn., Soc. for Cross-Cultural Rsch. (pres. 1985), Soc. for Psychol. Anthropology, Human Behavior and Evolution Soc. Office: Yale U Human Rels Area Files 755 Prospect St New Haven CT 06511-1225

EMBER, MELVIN LAWRENCE, anthropologist, educator; b. NYC, Jan. 13, 1933; s. Martin William and Ida F. (Trebuchovskaya) E.; m. Irma Stalberg, July 11, 1954 (div. Jan. 1970); children: Matthew, Rachel; m. Carol Lee Ruchlis, Mar. 21, 1970; children: Katherine, Julie. BA, Columbia Coll., 1953; PhD, Yale U., 1958. Postdoctoral fellow Yale U., New Haven, 1958-59; rsch. anthropologist NIH, Bethesda, MD, 1959-63; from asst. to assoc. prof. anthropology Antioch Coll., Yellow Springs, Ohio, 1963-67; assoc. prof. Hunter Coll., CUNY, 1967-70, prof., 1971-87; pres. Human Rels. Area Files, Inc., Yale U., New Haven, 1987—. Chmn. dept. anthropology Hunter Coll., CUNY, 1968-73, exec. officer PhD program in anthropology Grad. Sch., 1973-75. Co-author: Anthropology, 1973, Cultural Anthropology, 1973; : 10th edit., 2002, Marriage, Family and Kinship, 1983, Anthropology: A Brief Introduction, 1992, 5th edit., 2003, Sex, Gender and Kinship: A Cross-Cultural Perspective, 1997, Cross-Cultural Research Methods, 2001; co-editor: Portraits of Culture, 1998, Research Frontiers in Anthropology, 1998, Cross-Cultural Research for Social Science, 1998, Encyclopedia of Cultural Anthropology, 1996, American Immigrant Cultures: Builders of a Nation, 1997, Cultures of the World, 1999, Countries and Their Cultures, 2001, Encyclopedia of Prehistory, 2001—02, Encyclopedia of Urban Cultures, 2002, Archaeology: Original Readings in Method and Practice, 2002, Physical Anthropology: Original Readings in Method and Practice, 2002; editor: Cross-Cultural Rsch.: The Jour. of Comparative Social Sci., 1982—. Fellow AAAS, Am. Anthrop. Assn.; mem. Soc. for Cross-Cultural Rsch. (pres. 1981-82). Office: Yale U Human Rels Area Files Inc 755 Prospect St New Haven CT 06511-1225

EMBERGHER, MARY LOUISE, elementary educator; b. Bklyn., July 22, 1943; d. Joseph and Anna Buonfiglio E. BS in Elem. Edn., St. John's U., 1964; MS in Elem. Edn., Bklyn. Coll. U. of N.Y., 1966. Cert. elem. tchr., Fla. Tchr. N.Y.C. Pub. Schs., Ozone Park, 1964-68, Broward County Pub. Schs., Pembroke Pines, 1968—. Adminstr. summative for master tchr. program State of Fla., Pembroke Pines, 1984-87; mem. tchr. rep. Broward county Quality Incentive coun. Broward County Pub. Sch. Bd., Ft. Lauderdale, 1983-84, peer tchrs., coach for new tchrs. Broward County Pub. Schs., Pembroke Pines, 1980-98; supr. tchr. for intern tchrs., 1970-98. Publicity chmn. Greater Hollywood Young, Fla., 1969; sec. Reps., 1970. Named Outstanding Young Educator Pembroke Pines Jaycees, 1973, Fla. Master Tchr. State of Fla., 1984-87; recipient Achievement in Edn. award Pembroke Pines Optimist Club. Mem. Women Educators (chpt. pres. 1980-82), Delta Kappa Gamma (yearbook chair 1972-73, chpt. 1st v.p. 1978-80). Republican. Roman Catholic. Avocations: traveling, reading, music, politics, working with children. Office: Lakeside Elem Sch 900 NW 136th Ave Pembroke Pines FL 33028

EMBLETON, TOM WILLIAM, horticultural science educator; b. Guthrie, Okla., Jan. 3, 1918; s. Harry and Katherine (Smith) E.; m. Lorraine Marie Davidson, Jan. 22, 1943; children: Harry Raymond (dec.), Gary Thomas, Wayne Allen, Terry Scott, Paul Henry. BS, U. Ariz., 1941; PhD, Cornell U., 1949; Diploma de Honor al Ingeniero Agronomo, Coll. Engring. Agronomy, Santiago, Chile, 1991. Jr. sci. aide Bureau Plant Industry USDA, Indio, Calif., 1942, horticulturist Bureau Plant Industry, 1942, 1946; asst. horticulturist Wash. State Coll., Prosser, 1949-50; asst. horticulturist to prof. hort. sci. U. Calif., Riverside, 1950-86, prof. hort. sci. emeritus, 1987—. Cons. in field, 1973—. Contbr. numerous articles to profl. jours. Scoutmaster, coun. committeeman, pack com. Riverside Boy Scouts of Am., 1952-74. Recipient Citrograph rsch. award Citrograph mag., 1965, Chancellor's Founders' award U. Calif., 1990, Salter award Calif. Citrus Contol Coun., 1999, Celebration of Citrus, Past, Present, and Future award U. Calif.-Riverside, 2000. Fellow AAAS, Am. Soc. Hort. Sci. (Wilson Popenoe award 1985, chmn. western region 1958-59); mem. Internat. Soc. Horticultural Sci., Internat. Soc. Citriculture (hon., exec. bd. 1984-96), Am. Soc. Agronomy (honor award 1993), Soil Sci. Soc. Am., Western Soc. Soil Sci., Calif. Avocado Soc. (life, honor award 1987), Coun. Soil Testing and Plant Analysis, Coun. Agrl. Sci. and Tech., Lemon Men's Club (Honor award 1987, life), U. Calif. Riverside Faculty Club (pres. 1958), Sigma Xi (pres. Riverside chpt. 1981-82), others. Achievements include research on use of leaf analysis as guide for citrus and avocado fertilization; on providing a means of substantially reducing nitrate pollution of ground-waters from citrus fertilization. Home: 796 Spruce St Riverside CA 92507-3039 Office: U Calif Dept Botany Plant Scis Riverside CA 92521-0001 E-mail: tomlorraine@hotmail.com.

EMBLETON, TONY FREDERICK WALLACE, retired Canadian government official; b. Hornchurch, Essex, Eng., Oct. 1, 1929; emigrated to Can., 1952; s. Frederick William Howard and Lucy Violet Muriel (Wallace) E.; m. Eileen Loraine Blackall, Nov. 14, 1953; 1 dau., Sheila. B.Sc. with honours, U. London, 1950, PhD in Physics, 1952, D.Sc., 1964. Postdoctoral fellow NRC, Ottawa, Ont., Can., 1952-53, asst. research officer, 1954-57, asso. research officer, 1957-62, sr. research officer, 1962-74, prin. research officer, 1974-90, ret., 1990. Vis. lectr. U. Ottawa, 1959-69, MIT, 1964, 67, 72; John Wiley Jones award lectr.Rochester Inst. Tech., 1976; adj. prof. Carleton U. 1977-90. Patentee in field; contbr. articles to profl. jours. Mem. Rockcliffe Park Pub. Sch. Bd., 1966-69; bd. dirs. Youth Sci. Found., 1967-72. Recipient Arch T. Coldwell award Soc. Automotive Engrs., 1974 Fellow Acoustical Soc. Am. (assoc. editor jour., exec. coun., v.p. 1977-78, pres. 1980-81, stds. dir. 1993-97, Biennial award 1964, Silver medal in Noise 1986, Gold medal 2002), Royal Soc. Can. (hon. treas. 1982-85); mem. NAE (fgn. assoc.), Can. Acoustical Assn. (founding sec. 1961-64, founding editor jour. 1971-74), Inst. Noise Control Engrng. (dir. tech. group 1983 87, editl. bd. jour. 1983-93), Internat. Inst. of Noise Control Engrng. (bd. dirs. 1992-2003, v.p. devel. 1998-2002). Home: PO Box 786 80 Sheardown Dr Nobleton ON Canada L0G 1N0

EMBODY, DANIEL ROBERT, biometrician; b. Ithaca, N.Y., July 10, 1914; s. George Charles and Mary Madeline (Riceman) E.; m. Margaret Constance Gran, Mar. 21, 1946 (dec. Mar. 1961); children: James Michael, Daniel Robert, David Richard. BS, Cornell U., 1938, MS, 1939, postgrad., 1939-42, N.C. State Coll., summer 1940. Instr. limnology Cornell U., Ithaca, N.Y., 1940-42; sr. math. analyst Arnold Bernard & Co., N.Y.C., 1947-48; statistician Wash. Water Power Co., Spokane, 1949-53; head statistics sect. E.R. Squibb & Sons-Olin, New Brunswick, N.J., 1953-57, mgr. electronic data processing svc. ctr., 1958-63, coord. sci. computations, 1964-65; math. statistician Bur. Ships, Navy Dept., Washington, 1965-67; biometrician Dept. Agr., Beltsville, Md., 1967-72, staff biometrician animal and plant health inspection svc. Hyattsville, Md., 1972-87; sr. ptnr. EIC Assocs., Hyattsville, 1981—. Cons. Idaho Fish and Game Dept., 1950-60, U.S. Geol. Survey, 1953-58, N.J. Dept. Fish and Game, 1953-60. Contbr. articles to profl. jours. Lt. comdr. USNR, 1942-46, ETO. Mem. IEEE, NRA, Am. Statis. Assn., Biometric Soc., Entomol. Soc. Am. (cert.; emeritus), N.Y. Acad. Scis., Assn. Computing Machinery, Am. Legion, Am. Fisheries Soc., Sigma Xi, Gamma Alpha. Home and Office: 7414 Jefferson St Hyattsville MD 20784-1758

EMBREE, AINSLIE THOMAS, history educator; b. N.S., Can., Jan. 1, 1921; came to U.S., 1958, naturalized, 1965; s. Ira Thomas and Margaret (Langley) E.; m. Suzanne Helene Harpole, May 24, 1947; children: Ralph Thomas, Margaret Louise. BA, Dalhousie U., Halifax, N.S., 1941; BD, Pine Hill Theol. Sem., Halifax, 1946; MA, Union Theol. Sem., 1947, Columbia U., 1955, PhD, 1960; LLD (hon.), Juniata Coll., 1982. Prof. history Indore (India) Christian Coll., 1948-58; asst. prof., assoc. prof. history Columbia U., 1958-69, prof., 1972-91, prof. emeritus, 1991; assoc. dean Sch. Internat. Affairs, 1972-78, chmn., 1982-85, acting dean, 1989-90. Prof. Duke U., 1969-72; counsellor for cultural affairs Am. Embassy, New Delhi, 1978-80, cons., 1994-95; vis. disting. prof. Brown U., 1996-97, vis. prof. Sch. Advanced Internat. Studies, Johns Hopkins U., 2002-2003. Author: Charles Grant and British Rule in India, 1962, India, 1967, India's Search for National Identity, 1971; editor: The Hindu Tradition, 1966, Alberuni's India, 1971, Pakistan's Western Borderlands, 1978; editor in chief The Encyclopedia of Asian History, 4 vols., 1988, Imagining India, 1989, Utopias in Conflict, 1990. Served with RCAF, 1942-45. Recipient Van Doren award, 1985, Bancroft award, 1991, T. Das award, 1999, Tannenbaum award, 1999; Can. Council fellow, 1953-54; Am. Council Learned Socs. fellow, 1967; Am. Inst. Indian Studies fellow, 1968-69, 85-86; NEH fellow, 1977. Fellow AAAS; mem. Council Fgn. Relations, Assn. Asian Studies (pres. 1982-83), Am. Hist. Assn., Am. Inst. Indian Studies (pres. 1970-73), Cosmos Club. Home: 10450 Lottsford Rd Apt 1008 Mitchellville MD 20721-2745 E-mail: atembree@aol.com.

EMBREE, MARY EVELYN, retired secondary school educator; b. Columbus, Ohio, May 10, 1940; d. Francis Marion and Mary Edith (Howdyshell) E. BFA, Ohio U., 1962; MS, Nova Southeastern U., 1982; postgrad., Oxford U., Eng., 1987—96. English tchr. Chillicothe (Ohio) Pub. Schs., 1962-67, Columbus (Ohio) Pub. Schs., 1967-74, Palatka (fla.) H.S., 1974—99, chair dept., 1994—99. Coach acad. competition Palatka H.S., 1996-97; adj. faculty mem. St. Johns River C.c., Palatka, 1990-94. Mem. Sch. Improvement Team, Palatka, 1990-92. Tchrs. as Advisors grantee State of Fla., 1989-91. Mem.: Putnam Fedn. Tchrs., Nat. Coun. Tchrs. English, Pi Lambda Theta, Alpha Delta Kappa (internat. dist. officer 1994—96). Democrat. Methodist. Avocations: world study courses, travel, writing. Office: Palatka HS 302 Mellon Rd Palatka FL 32177-4018

EMBREE, ROBERT ARTHUR, retired psychologist, minister; b. Anselmo, Nebr., Sept. 11, 1927; s. Ernest N. and Elmina F. (Cantrell) E.; m. Valda J. Franz, Aug. 23, 1950; children: Marlowe C., Rodney C. BA, York (Nebr.) Coll., 1951; MDiv, United Theol. Sem., Dayton, Ohio, 1954; MA, U. Omaha, 1957; PhD, U. Denver, 1964. Ordained to ministry, United Meth. Ch.; emeritus diplomate Am. Bd. Sexology. Minister Evang. United Brethren Ch., Omaha, 1954-57, Presbyn. Ch., Waterloo, Nebr., 1957-58; instr. psychology Teikyo Westmar U. (formerly Westmar Coll.), LeMars, Iowa, 1958-93, prof. emeritus, 1993—; ret. Former bd. dirs. Found. for Sci. Study of Sex. Contbg. editor: The American Board of Sexology: An Outline of Sexology, 1993 (study guide); contbr. articles to books and profl. jours. Trustee, Westmar Coll. Endowment Trust, LeMars, 1990-96; charter bd. dirs. Plains Area Mental Health Ctr., LeMars. With U.S. Army, 1946. Fellow Soc. for Sci. Study of Religion; mem. APA, Soc. for Sci. Study of Sex (bd. rep. 1985-88, pres. Mid-continent region 1990-91), Am. Assn. of Sex Educators, Counselors and Therapists, Iowa Psychol. Assn. Achievements include development of personal beliefs scale. Home: 926 3rd Ave SE Le Mars IA 51031-2650 E-mail: rembree@frontiernet.net.

EMBRY, C B, JR., state representative; b. Louisville, Ky, July 29, 1941; m. Wanda Lou Embry; children: Lauraann, CB III, Barbara Ann. Attended, Univ. of Louisville, 1992, Univ. of Ky., Inst. of Econ. Devel., 1986; BS, W. Ky. Univ., 1963. State Rep. House of Rep., Dist. 17, 2002—; gen. mgr. Hughes and Coleman (Regional Firm), 1996—2000; CTO Ky. Justice Cabinet, 1991—96; Judge/exec. Ohio County Gov., 1982—89; pres. The Embry Newspapers, Inc., 1974—89; owner Retail property, 1963—95; tchr. Ohio County Sch. Sys. Mayor City of Beaver Dam, 1970—73. Decorated George Washington Medal for Patriotism; recipient Outstanding Young Man, Beaver Dam, 1970—72, Outstanding Young Rep. in the Nation, 1975, Ohio Co. Citizen of the Yr., 1982; fellow Christian Athletes. caucuses: Vice chair, GRADD Transport. Comm., 1982-1983; Mem. Ten Commandments Defense Fund Comm., 2002-present; mem., WKU Coll. of Ed. Devel. Comm., 1982-1984. Republican. Baptist. Office: Dist PO Box 463 Caneyville KY 42721 also: Dist PO Box 1215 Morgantown KY 42261 also: Capitol Capitol Annex rm 351E Frankfort KY 40601*

EMBRY, MICHAEL DALE, writer, editor; b. Louisville, Oct. 30, 1948; s. G.T. Dale and Dolores Lorraine (Colburn) E.; m. Mary Elizabeth Frederick, Aug. 7, 1971; children: Justin Michael, Sean Russell. AB in journalism, Ea. Ky. U., 1975. Sports editor Messenger, Madisonville, Ky., 1975-77; sports writer Lexington (Ky.) Herald, 1977-80; newsman AP, Louisville, 1980-82, sports writer N.Y.C., 1982-83, state sports editor Milw., 1983-85, corr. Lexington,

1985—98; editor Ky. Mo., 1998—. Mem. adv. bd. Ea. Ky. U. Dept. Comms., 1990-93, Ea. Ky. Progress, 1990-93. Author: Basketball in the Bluegrass State, 1983, March Madness, 1985, The Touch, 1999, Baron of the Bluegrass, 2000, A Long Highway, 2001; contbr. articles to profl. publs. With USAF, 1969-73. Recipient Writing award Ky. chpt. Am. Cancer Soc., 1986-87, 89-90, 93, Ea. Ky. U. Comms. Alumni of Yr. 1983, DeDe award Ky. Devel. Planning Coun., 1988. Mem. AARP, Nat. Sportscasters and Sportswriters Assn., Blue Grass Soc. Profl. Journalists (pres. 1985-86),, Ky. Writers Coalition, Ky. Romance Writers, Romance Writers of Am., Amnesty Internat., U.S. Basketball Writers Assn., Milw. chpt. Basketball Writers Assn. (pres. 1983), Milw. Pen and Mike Club (2nd v.p. 1985), Sierra Club, Friends of Paul Sawyer Libr., Hon. Order of Ky. Cols. Avocations: tennis, music, reading, hiking, travel, writing. Home: 152 Skyview Dr Frankfort KY 40601-9154 E-mail: membry@fewpb.net.

EMBRY, STEPHEN CRESTON, lawyer; b. Key West, Fla., Feb. 13, 1949; s. Jewell Creston and Julia Martine (Taylor) E.; m. Priscilla Mary Brown, Aug. 21, 1971; children: Nathaniel, Julia, Jessamyn. BA, Am. U., 1971; JD, U. Conn., 1976. Bar: Conn. 1976, U.S. Dist. Ct. Conn. 1976, U.S. Ct. Appeals (2d, 5th and 9th cirs.). Staff aide to Pres. The White House, Washington, 1969-72; assoc. Turner & Hensley, Great Bend, Kans., 1976, O'Brien, Shafner, Bartinik, & Stuart, Groton, Conn., 1976-85, Embry and Neusner, Groton, Conn., 1985—. Editor: Longshore and Harborworkers Textbook; mem. editl. bd. Matthew Bender, BRB Reporter; contbr. articles to profl. publs. Mem. Groton Rep. com., 1976-83, North Stonington Rep. com., 1984-88; chmn. Groton Housing Authority, 1979-80; mem. dean's adv. coun. Am. U. Sch. Internat. Svc., 2002—. Mem. ATLA (chair workers compensation sect. 1984-85, bd. dirs. workplace injury litigation group, sec. 1999-2000, pres.-elect 2001-02, pres. 2002-03), Maritime Claimants Attys. Assn. (bd. dirs.), Conn. Trial Lawyers, Conn. Bar Assn. (exec. bd.), Thames Club, Grange. Democrat.

EMBURG, KATHRYN MARIA, social worker, writer; b. Nurnburg, Republic of Germany, Oct. 13, 1959, d. Richard Macmillian and Carol Ann (Duvall) Hohenberger; m. Edwin Kenneth Emburg, Feb. 14, 1987; children: Leann Maria, Kaitlyn Ashley, Tabitha Clara, Damion Chandler. BA in English, Rutgers U., 1981. Office mgr. IHI, Inc., NYC, 1985-87; bookseller Waldenbooks, Sacramento, 1987-90; eligibility worker Sacramento County, Calif., 1990-93, social worker, 1993—99. Child protective svc. liaison Sacramento County, 1991-93; foster parent Sacramento County, 1988-93, foster parent Sacramento County, 1988-93, Atkinson youth Svc., 1998- Author: The Whispering Belltower, 1993, Recipe for Love, 1995; The Lang. of Love, 1996; co-author: The Adventures of Susan Slut, 1990, vol.2, 1991, vol. 3, 1993, The Girls' Series Companion, 1990, 2d edit., 1994; editor The Whispered Watchword mag., 1985—. Mem. Soc. Phantom Friends (pres. 1985—), Sierra Doll Discov. Club. United Meth. Avocation: doll collecting. Home and Office: PO Box 1437 North Highlands CA 95660-1437

EMCH, GERARD GUSTAV, mathematics and physics educator; b. Geneva, July 21, 1936; came to U.S., 1964; s. Martial Désiré and Violette Marie (Cornaglia) E.; m. Antoinette S. Dériaz, July 25, 1959; children: Florence Christiane, René-Didier Guillaume. PhD, U. Geneva, 1963. Asst. in theoreticlal physics. U.Geneva, 1959-63; chef des travaux in math. physics U. Geneva, 1963-64; research assoc. Princeton U., 1964-65; research assoc. dept. applied math. U. Md., 1965-66; asst. prof. math. and physics. U. Rochester, N.Y., 1966-71, assoc. prof., 1971-78, prof., 1978-86; prof., chmn. dept. math. U. Fla., 1986-88, prof. math, 1988—. Vis. prof. U. Nijmegen, U. Brussels, EPF-Lausanne, U. Bielefeld, U. Geneva, U. Sao Paulo, U. Vienna, U. Paris 7; Gauss prof. Akademie der Wissenschaften zu Göttingen, 1985; vis. fellow All Souls Coll., Oxford, 2004. Author: Algebraic Methods in Statistical Mechanics and Quantum Field Theory, 1972, Mathematical and Conceptual Foundations of 20th-Century Physics, 1984; author: (with C. Liu) The Logic of Thermostatistical Physics, 2001; editor: On Klauder's Path, 1994, Selected Works of E.P. Wigner, vol. 6, 1994; contbr. chpts., numerous articles to profl. publs. Mem. Internat. Assn. Math. Physics (treas. 1988-94), Am. Phys. Soc., Am. Math. Soc., Am. Math. Assn. (hon.), Phi Beta Kappa. Presbyterian. Office: U Fla Dept Math Gainesville FL 32611 E-mail: gge@math.ufl.edu.

EMEAGWALI, GLORIA THOMAS, humanities educator; b. Trinidad, West Indies, Feb. 6, 1950; came to U.S., 1991; BA, U. W.I., 1973; edn. dipl., London U., 1975; MA, Toronto U., 1976; PhD, Ahmadu Bello U., Zaria, Nigeria, 1986. Asst. prof. Ahmadu Bello U., Zaria, Nigeria, 1979-86; assoc. prof. Nigerian Def. Acad., 1986, Ilorin U., Nigeria, 1986-89; vis. prof. U. W.I., Trinidad, 1989, Oxford U., U.K., 1990-91; assoc. prof. history and African studies Conn. State U., New Britain, 1991-96, tenured prof. history and African studies, 1996—. Vis. prof. Internat. Devel. Ctr., Oxford (Eng.) U., spring 2000; mem. editl. bd. Review of African Political Economy, U.K., chief editor Africa Update, CCSU.; mem. adv. bd. Encyclopedia of the History of Science, Technology and Medicine, Hampshire Coll., Amherst. Keynote speaker, Third World Foundation, Chicago March 2001. Keynote Speaker, Southern cntrl and East African Libr. assn. SCESAL, 2002. Editor: Historical Development of Science and Technology in Nigeria, 1992, Science and Technology in African History, 1992, African Systems of Science Technology and Art, 1993, Women Pay the Price: Structural Adjustment in Africa and the Caribbean, 1995, African Civilization, 1997. Recipient UNESCO award, 1999; Oxford U. fellow, 1990; grantee Old Dominion U., 1986, 88. Mem. AAUP (Conn. state award 1992, 97, 2002), Internat. Soc. for Study of Comp. Civilization (mem. governing body, exec. com. 1992—), World Anthrop. Soc., World Archeaol. Congress, Am. Hist. Assn., African Studies Assn. Avocations: keyboard playing, table tennis. Office: Cen Conn State U History/African Studies Dept New Britain CT 06050

EMEK, SHARON HELENE, risk management consultant; b. Bklyn., Oct. 23, 1945; d. Hyman Sampson and Cynthia Gertrude (Roth) Rabinowitz; children: Aleeza Judith, Joshua Michael, Elana Yael. BA, CCNY, 1967; MA, Bklyn. Coll., 1970; EdD, Rutgers U., 1977. Cert. ins. counselor. Dir. preliminary program for small coll. Bklyn. Coll., 1969-71, 73-74; dir. Am. Ctr. Reading Skills, Tel Aviv, 1972; asst. prof. Brookdale C.C., Lincroft, N.J., 1975-77, Rutgers U., New Brunswick, N.J., 1977-82; pres. The Emek Group, Inc., N.Y.C., 1980-98, CEO Metro Ptnrs., Inc., N.Y.C., 1998—2001; dir. CBS Coverage Group, Inc., 2001—. Spkr. profl. meetings. Author: Answers for Managers, 1986, Dealing Successfully with Key Management Issues, 1986; contbr. articles to profl. jours. Mem. Mayor's Small Bus. Adv. Bd., N.Y.C., 1998—2001, Small Bus. Rsch. and Tech. Adv. Coun. IBM, 1998—2000, Ctr. for Women's Bus. Rsch. adv. bd., 2000—; mem. adv. coun. Women's Fin. Network at Siebert, 2000—02; founding bd. dirs. Nat. Mus. Women's History, 1997—2002; bd. dirs. Family Bus. Coun. Greater N.Y., 1997—98; bd. dirs., v.p. N.Y. Women's Agenda, 2000—; chair, bd. dirs. Inst. for Student Achievement, N.Y.C., 1999—; bd. dirs. Women's Econ. Devel. Task Force, N.Y.C., 1999—2001; mem. Women's Leadership Exch. adv. bd., 2002—. Recipient Promising Rsch. award Nat. Coun. Tchrs. English, 1978, Woman of Power and Influence award NOW, N.Y.C., 1999, Mem. Profl. Ins. Agts. Assn., Nat. Assn. Women Bus. Owners (bd. dirs., pres. 1997-98, Mem. of Yr. 1997), Ind. Ins. Agts. and Brokers of Am. (bd. dirs. 2000—), Ins. Fedn. N.Y., Ins. Brokers Assn. N.Y., Coun. Ins. Brokers Greater N.Y., Nat. Assn. Ins. Women (Helen Garvin Outstanding Achiever in Ins. Industry award 1999), Assn. Profl. Ins. Women, Women's Pres. Orgn., Emily's List (majority coun.), Coun. Ins. Brokers Greater N.Y. Avocations: writing, reading, jogging, tennis, travel. E-mail: semek@cbsinsurance.com.

EMELY, CHARLES HARRY, trade association executive, consultant; b. Phila., Oct. 30, 1943; s. Charles Walter and Jane Beatty (Stott) E.; m. Susan Elizabeth Lawton, June 18, 1966 (dec. Mar. 1977); 1 child, Charles Walter II; m. Mary Ann Horvath, Sept. 1, 1979; 1 stepchild, Wendy A. Vellrath. Student, Drexel Inst. Tech., 1961-62; BA, Temple U., 1967; MA, Fairfield U., 1974; postgrad., NYU, 1974-76; PhD, Calif. Western U., 1978; postgrad., Ohio U., 1981-82. Adminstrv. asst. City of Phila., 1966-68; nat. rep. ARC, Washington, 1968-70; exec. dir., chief exec. officer Bridgeport, Conn., 1970-77; pres., chief exec. officer Comprehensive Bus. Cons., Ft. Washington, Pa., 1977-86; exec. v.p., chief exec. officer Adhesive & Sealant Council, Washington, 1987-88; pres., CEO Comprehensive Bus. Cons., Inc., Fairfax, Va., 1988—; exec. dir., CEO Internat. Assn. Law Firms, 1988—; exec. dir., COO Am. Soc. Hort. Sci., Alexandria, Va., 1994-97; CEO Am. Railway Engring. and MOW Assn., Landover, Md., 1998—. Chmn. Cmty. Cons. Corps, Ft. Washington, 1980—; sr. cons. Philippine Nutrition Ctr., Manila, 1980; adj. faculty Ohio U., Athens, 1982-83, bd. dirs. ICM Internat., Inc.; comunications officer, U.S.A. Nat. Disaster Med. Sys., 1992—. Mem. bd. mgrs. YMCA, Fairfield, Conn., 1971-75; bd. dirs. Hope Ctr., Inc., Bridgeport, 1972-76, Comprehensive Health Planning Agy., Bridgeport, 1973-74, Found. for Internat. Meetings; mem. Mayor's Energy Adv. Com., Bridgeport, 1973-74, Fayetteville (N.Y.) United Meth. Ch., 1985; trustee, v.p. Mental Health Assn. Conn., 1973-77; mem. adminstrv. bd. Nichols United Meth. Ch., Trumbull, Conn., 1975-77; adv. com. campaign coun. Rep. Nat. Com.; mem. Patriots Soc. Germantown Acad., Ft. Washington, 1978-80; pres. Ambler (Pa.) Symphony Orchestra, 1979-80; mem. Pvt. Industry Council, Ambler, 1979-80, Zanesville, Ohio, 1981-83; mem. parents council Hartwick Coll., Oneonta, N.Y., 1987. Mem.: Associated Pub. Safety Comm. Officers, Found. for Internat. Meetings, Am. Railway Engring. and Maint. of Way Assn. (CEO 1998—), Nat. Assn. Corp. Dirs. (sec./treas. Washington chpt.), Am. Soc. Assn. Execs. (cert. assn. exec. 1977), Adminstrv. Mgmt. Soc., Am. Mgmt. Assn., Heritage Found. (exec. com.), Officers Club Nat. Naval Med. Ctr. (Bethesda), U. Conn. Alumni Assn. (life), Mensa, Officers Club Marine Corps Base Quantico, Renewable Natural Resources Found. (bd. dirs.), Armed Forces Comms. and Electronics Assn., Aircraft Owners and Pilots Assn., Am. Radio Relay League, Rep. Nat. Com. Campaign Coun., Rotary, Nat. Assn. Execs. Club, City of Washington Club, Univ. Club, Vesper Club, Phila. Aviation Country Club, Rep. Nat. Com. Pres.'s Club, Elks, Shriners, Masons. Avocations: music, amateur radio, aviation, philately, travel. Home: 7 Beaver Ridge Rd Stafford VA 22556-6677 Office: Comprehensive Bus Cons Inc PO Box 545 Garrisonville VA 22463-0545 E-mail: chemely@cbc.org.

EMELY, MARY ANN, association executive; b. Bridgeport, Conn., Aug. 10, 1947; d. John and Stefanie Maria (Hutta) Horvath; m. Timothy Vellrath, Sept. 7, 1968 (div. Mar. 1975); 1 child, Wendy Amethyst Vellrath Delbrook; m. Charles H. Emely, Sept. 1, 1979. BA, U. Conn., 1969; postgrad., U. Bridgeport, 1975-76, Ohio U., 1982-83. Adminstrv. asst. ARC, Bridgeport, 1973-78; dir. mem. svcs. Comprehensive Assn. Cons., Ft. Washington, Pa., 1978-81; exec. dir. Muskingum County Respiratory Disease, Zanesville, Ohio, 1981-83; assoc. exec. dir. The Vol. Ctr., Syracuse, N.Y., 1984-86; dir. mem. programs NEA, Rockville, Md., 1986-91; dir. mem., mktg. Am. Geophys. Union, Washington, 1991-93; sr. dir. membership Coun. for Exceptional Children, Reston, Va., 1993-94; dep. exec. dir. Spl. Librs. Assn., Washington, 1994-95; exec. dir. Fedn. Govt. Info. Processing Couns., Fairfax, Va., 1995-99; mng. dir. Nat. Assn. Profl. Employer Orgns., Alexandria, Va., 2000—01; v.p. ops. Am. Coun. Engring. Cos., 2001—. Cons. Comprehensive Assn. Cos., Garrisonville, Va., 1991—. Editor Husky P.A.W. Print, 1995-96, Fedn. Facts, 1995-99; columnist Female Exec., 1994-95. Bd. dirs. Pub. Employees Roundtable, Washington, 1995-99; mem. Nat. Rep. Coalition for Choice, Washington, 1993—, Jr. League of Washington, 1986—. Mem. NAFE, Am. Soc. Assn. Execs. (cert., mentor diversity programs 1994-95), Am. Radio Relay League, Greater Washington Soc. Assn. Execs., Found. for Internat. Meetings, Mercedes Benz Club of Am., U. Conn. Alumni Assn. (Washington chpt., pres. 1996-99, nat. bd. dirs. 2002-, nat. fundraising com. 2001-), Kappa Alpha Theta. Methodist. Avocations: gardening, flower arranging, reading, travel. Home: PO Box 96 Garrisonville VA 22463-0096 Office: 1015 15th St NW Washington DC 20005

EMENHISER, JEDON ALLEN, political science educator, academic administrator; b. Clovis, N.Mex., May 19, 1933; s. Glen Allen and Mary Opal (Sasser); m. Patricia Ellen Burke, Jan. 27, 1954; 1 child, Melissa Mary Emenhiser Westerfield. Student, Am. U., 1954; BA, U. Redlands, 1955; PhD, U. Minn., 1962. Cert. community coll. adminstr., Calif. Instr. to prof. polit. sci. Utah State U., Logan, 1960-77, acting dean, 1973-74; prof. Humboldt State U., Arcata, Calif., 1977—, dean, 1977-86, acting v.p., 1984; chair Social Sci. Rsch. and Instrnl. Coun. Calif. State U., 1994-95; prof. Jr. Statesmen Summer Sch., Stanford U., 1989—. Vis. instr. U. Redlands, Calif., 1959—60; vis. prof. U. Saigon, Vietnam, 1964—65; asst. dean Colgate U., Hamilton, NY, 1972—73; staff dir. Utah Legislature, Salt Lake City, 1967, cons., 1968—77; dir. Bur. Govt. and Opinion Rsch., Logan, 1965—70; cons. USCG, McKinleyville, Calif., 1982; v.p. Exch. Bank, New Franklin, Mo., 1970—76; reader advanced placement exam. U.S. Govt. Coll. Bd., 1990—98; vis. fellow govt. divsn. Congl. Rsch. Svc., Libr. of Congress, 1996; vis. fellow Nat. U. Ireland, Galway, 2002; vis. prof. U. Mons-Hainaut, Belgium, 2002; vis. prof. Am. studies Royal Libr., Belgium, 2003. Author: Utah's Governments, 1964, Freedom and Power in California, 1987; editor, contbr. Dragon on the Hill, 1970, Rocky Mountain Urban Politics, 1971; producer, dir. TV broadcasts The Hawks and the Doves, 1965-66; contbr. articles to profl. jours. Sec. Cache County Dem. Party, Logan, 1962-63; chmn. Mayor's Commn. on Govt. Orgn., Logan, 1973-74; campaign mgr. various candidates and issues, Logan, 1965-75; bd. dirs. Humboldt Connections, Eureka, Calif., 1986-96, pres., 1989-92; elder Presbyn. ch. Sr. Fulbright-Hays lectr. Com. Internat. Exch. of Persons, Vietnam, 1964-65; Adminstrv. fellow Am. Coun. Edn., Colgate U., 1972-73; Paul Harris fellow Rotary Internat.; Fulbright prof., Belgium, 2003. Mem. Am. Polit. Sci. Assn., Western Polit. Sci. Assn., Am. Studies Assn., Phi Beta Kappa, Omicron Delta Kappa. Presbyterian. Avocations: gardening, photography, travel. Home: PO Box 250 Bayside CA 95524-0250 Office: Humboldt State U Dept Polit Sci Arcata CA 95521 E-mail: jae1@humboldt.edu.

EMENS, J. RICHARD, lawyer; b. Jackson, Mich., May 3, 1934; s. John R. and Aline (Brainerd) E.; m. Mary Francis, July 31, 1957 (div. Aug. 1980); children: Anne, John D., Alaine, Elizabeth; m. Beatrice Wolper, Aug. 31, 1983; children: Renee, Jennifer. BA, DePauw U., 1956; JD, U. Mich., 1959. Bar: Mich. 1959, Ohio 1964. Ptnr. McInally, Rosenfeld & Emens, Jackson, 1959-64, Emens and Ashworth, Marion, Ohio, 1964-68; dir. Emens, Kegler, Brown, Hill & Ritter, Columbus, Ohio, 1968-97, mng. dir., 1984-95; ptnr. Chester, Willcox & Saxbe LLP, Columbus. Trustee Ea. Mineral Law Found., pres., 1982-83. Co-author: Family Business Basics: The Guide to Family Business Financial Success; contbr. articles to law jours. Co-founder Emens scholars program Ball State U. Muncie, Ind., 1977—; trustee, chmn. bd. trustees Franklin U., Columbus, 1995-96; past chmn. fin. com. Franklin County Rep. Com.; former trustee and pres. Friends of Librs. Ohio State U. Mem. Internat. Bar Assn., Ohio Audubon (pres.), Rotary, Phi Beta Kappa. Avocations: travel, reading, fishing. Office: Chester Willcox & Saxbe Llp 65 East State St Ste 1000 Columbus OH 43215

EMERICK, JOHN L. library director; b. Fleetwood, Pa., Apr. 26, 1937; s. Leo J. and Rachael E. Emerick; divorced; 1 child, Michael J. BS in Libr. Sci., Kutztown U., 1959; MLS, Villanova U., 1965; media cert., Temple U., 1969. Librarian, English tchr. Daniel Boone Sch. Dist., Birdsboro, Pa., 1959-62; English tchr. Fleetwood Area Sch. Dist., 1962-65; librarian, head dept. Muhlenberg Sch. Dist., Laureldale, Pa., 1965-72; dir. sch. libs. Boyertown (Pa.) Area Sch. Dist., 1972-93; dir. sch. libr. media svcs. Pa. Dept. Edn., Harrisburg, 1993—. Mem. adv. bd. dept. libr. sci. Kutztown U., 1984—; cons. Phila. Sch. Dist., 1994-95, Ctrl. Bucks Sch. Dist., Doylestown, Pa., 1992-94. Contbr. articles to profl. jours. Pres. Berks County (Pa.) Sch. Librarians, 1982-84, Berks County Libr. Assn., 1990-92; mem. sch. bd. Oley (Pa.) Valley Sch. Dist., 1984-90; supr. Ruscomb Manor Twp., Fleetwood, 1983-87, Mem. ALA (mem. com. 1976-80), Am. Assn. Sch. Librarians (mem. com. 1982-86), Pa. Assn. for Ednl. Comms. and Tech. (chmn. com. 1989-91, award 1997), Pa. Sch. Librarians (chmn. com. 1990-93, award 1999), Pa. Ednl. Tech. (planning com. 1993—, Spl. Svc. award 1997). Democrat. Lutheran. Avocations: travel, swimming, reading, biking, camping. Home: 315 Charleston Ln Wyomissing PA 19610 Office: Pa Dept Edn 333 Market St Harrisburg PA 17126 E-mail: jemerick@state.pa.us.

EMERICK, NORMAN COOPER, consulting engineer; b. Springfield, Ill., Nov. 26, 1921; s. Athal Elder and Hazel Frances (Cooper) E.; m. Charlotte Lorraine Thompson, Feb. 19, 1950 (dec. Dec. 1996); children; Bruce Clay Cooper, Ingrid Anne. BS in Civil Engring., U. Ill., 1949, MS, 1950. Registered profl. engr., Md., Va., Del. Consulting engr., Balt., 1960—. Co-founder, founding pres. Mid-Atlantic Germanic Soc., 1982—. With U.S. Army, 1942—47, WWII, PTO. Fellow ASCE; mem. Chi Epsilon. Avocations: genealogy, hunting, fishing, biking. Office: 132 W 25th St Baltimore MD 21218-5006

EMERICK, ROBERT EARL, sociologist, educator; b. Cleve., Mar. 17, 1942; s. Merl Lowell and Virginia Melissa (Newmyer) E.; m. Carol Ann Carter, Nov.24, 1963; children: Laura Lee, Lynn Lee Emerick Hall. BA, U. Calif., Santa Barbara, 1964; PhD, Northwestern U., 1971. Prof. sociology San Diego State U., 1968—, chmn., dept. sociology, 2000—. Contbr. numerous articles to profl. jours. Home: 3829 Albatross St San Diego CA 92103-3017 Office: San Diego State U Dept Sociology San Diego CA 92182 E-mail: remerick@mail.sdsu.edu.

EMERLING, CAROL G(REENBAUM), consultant; b. Cleve., Sept. 13, 1930; d. Bernard and Florence A. Greenbaum; m. Norton Harvey Noll, Oct. 1, 1950 (dec. July 1951); m. Stanley Justin Emerling, May 2, 1953 (div. Aug. 1971); children— Keith S., Susan C.; m. Jerrold A. Fadem, Aug. 24, 1974 (div. Oct. 1977). Student, Vassar Coll., 1948-49, Case Western Res. U., 1949-50; LL.B. summa cum laude, Cleve. State U., 1955. Bar: Ohio 1955, Calif. 1975, N.Y. 1982, N.Y. Supreme Ct. 1975. Instr. Cleve. Coll., 1956-59; from staff atty. to atty.-in-charge Legal Aid Defenders Office, Cleve., 1962-70; regional dir. FTC, Cleve., 1970-74, L.A., 1974-78; sec. Am. Home Products Corp., N.Y.C., 1978-96; chmn. bd. Global Health Coun., 1998—2002. Adv. com. criminal rules Supreme Ct. Ohio, 1970-73; chmn. Cleve. Fed. Exec. Bd., 1973; internat. health policy cons.; bd. chair Global Health Coun., 1998-2002; nat. adv. com. Cleve. State U. Law Sch. Co-author: The Allergy Cookbook, 1969; contbr. articles to legal jours. Founder Pepper Pike (Ohio) Civic League, 1959; sec. Pepper Pike Charter Commn., 1966. Recipient Claude E. Clarke award Legal Aid Soc., 1967, Disting. Service award FTC, 1972. Mem. State Bar Calif., State Bar Ohio. E-mail: cgemerling@earthlink.net.

EMERSON, ALICE FREY, political scientist, educator emerita; b. Durham, N.C., Oct. 26, 1931; d. Alexander Hamilton and Alice (Hubbard) Frey; divorced; children: Rebecca, Peter. AB, Vassar Coll., 1953; PhD, Bryn Mawr Coll., 1964; LLD (hon.), Wheaton Coll., 1986, Middlebury Coll., 1998; DHL (hon.), Trinity Coll., 1992. Tchr., Newton (Mass.) High Sch., 1956-58; mem. faculty Bryn Mawr (Pa.) Coll., 1961-64, U. Pa., Phila., 1966-75, asst. prof. polit. sci., 1966-75, dean of women, 1966-69, dean of students, 1969-75; pres. Wheaton Coll., Norton, Mass., 1975-91, pres. emerita, 1991—; sr. fellow Andrew Mellon Found., N.Y.C., 1991-98, sr. advisor, 1998—2002. Bd. dirs. AES Corp.; mem. adv. bd. HERS Mid-Am. Mem. World Resources Inst., Szburg Seminar, Nantucket Hist. Assn., [illegible] Address: PO Box 206 Siasconset MA 02564-0206 E-mail: afe@alum.vassar.edu.

EMERSON, ALTON CALVIN, retired physical therapist; b. Webster, N.Y., Sept. 29, 1934; s. Homer Douglas and Pluma (Babcock) E.; m. Nancy Ann Poarch, Dec. 20, 1955 (div. 1972); children: Marcia Ann, Mark Alton; m. Barbara Irene Stewart, Oct. 6, 1972. BS in Vertibrate Zoology, U. Utah, 1957; cert. phys. therapy, U. So. Calif., 1959. Staff phys. therapist Los Angeles County Crippled Children's Services, 1958-65; pvt. practice phys. therapy Los Angeles, 1966-98; ret., 1998. Cons. City of Hope, Duarte, Calif., 1962-72; trustee Wolcott Found. Inc., St. Louis, 1972-86, chmn. bd. trustees, 1980-85. Recipient Cert. of Achievement, George Washington U., Washington, 1986. Mem. Masons (pres. Temple City High Twelve Club 1971, master Camellia 1973 (Hiram award Conejo Valley Lodge 2001), pres. Calif. Assn. High Twelve Clubs 1986, internat. pres. High Twelve 1990-91, mem. High Twelve Internat., Pasadena Scottish Rite Bodies, Venerable Master, Lodge of Perfection 1998, KCCH, Legion Merit, coroneted 33, 2001), Royal Order Scotland, Al Malaikah Tmeple, Ancient Arabic order Nobles Mystic Shrine, DeMolay Legion of Honor, Order of DeMolay (hon. internat. supreme coun.), Conejo-Westlake Shrine Club (pres. 1996, 2002), Conejo Valley High Twelve Club 2000 (pres.), Divan 2000, Sigma Phi Epsilon. Home and Office: 287 W Avenida De Las Flores Thousand Oaks CA 91360-1808

EMERSON, ANDI (MRS. ANDI EMERSON WEEKS), sales and advertising executive; b. N.Y.C., Nov. 1, 1932; d. Willard Ingham and Ethel (Mole) E.; m. George G. Fawcett, Jr. (div.); children: Ann Fawcett Ambia, George Gifford III, Christopher Babcock; m. Kenneth E. Weeks (div.); 1 child, Electra Ingham. Student, Barnard Coll. Successively v.p. Eugene Stevens, Inc., N.Y.C.; pres., dir. Emerson Mktg. Agy., Inc., N.Y.C., 1960—. Pres., dir. Mail Order Operating Co. Ltd., N.Y.C. and London, 1976-88, Ingham Hall, Ltd., 1977-83; chmn. bd. dirs. Sonal World Mktg. Ltd., N.Y.C. and Delhi, India, 1983-87; instr. NYU, 1960-65, 87—; internat. lectr., seminar conductor Buenos Aires, Argentina, 1995—, Manila, Philippines, 1996. Vol. children's ward Meml. Hosp., 1964-66, Hosp. for Spl. Surgery, 1967; mem. adv. com. African Students League, 1965-67; bd. dirs. Violet Oakley Meml. Found., Phila., 1964-81; founder, pres., chmn. John Caples Internat. Awards, 1977—; elected N.Y. State Del. to White House Conf. on Small Bus., 1986. Inducted into Silver Apple Hall of Fame, 1985. Mem. N.Y. Acad. Scis., Direct Mktg. Assn. (Hall of Fame selection comn. 1989-91), Soc. Profl. Writers, Direct Mktg. Creative Guild (Andi Emerson award 1991, pres. 1975-81, bd. dirs. 1975-93), Direct Mktg. Club of N.Y. (treas. 1960-61), N.Y. Acad. Scis. Home: 16 E 96th St New York NY 10128-0753 Office: Emerson Mktg Agy Inc 636 Broadway Rm 1000 New York NY 10012-2624

EMERSON, ANN PARKER, dietitian; b. Twin Lakes, Fla., Dec. 3, 1925; d. Charles Dendy and Gladys Agnes (Chalker) Parker; m. Donald McGeachy Emerson, Sept. 22, 1950; children: Ann Mary, Donald McGeachy, Charles Parker, William John. BS, Fla. State U., 1947; MS, U. Fla., 1968. Rsch. dietition U. Chgo., 1948—50; adminstrv. rsch. dietitian U. Fla. Coll. Medicine, Gainesville, 1962—68, dir. dietetic edn., 1968—74, dir. dietetic internship program, 1968—75, dir. program in clin. and comty. dietetics, 1974—83; ret. Mem. Commn. on Dietetic Registration, 1974—77, Commn. in Accreditation, 1980—83. Recipient VA Allied Health Manpower grant, 1974—81, HEW Allied Health Manpower grant, 1975—78, 1978—81. Mem.: Fla. Dietetic Assn., Am. Dietetic Assn., Altrusa Internat. (Gainesville chpt. 1977—78), Jr. League. Republican. Roman Catholic.

EMERSON, CARTER WHITNEY, lawyer; b. Oak Park, Ill., Mar. 18, 1947; s. Garner P. and Daisy M. (Carter) E.; m. Susan D. Emerson, June 28, 1969. BS in Fin., Miami U., Oxford, Ohio, 1969; JD magna cum laude, Northwestern U., 1972. Law clk. to judge U.S. Dist. Ct. (no. dist.) Ill., 1972-73; assoc. Kirkland & Ellis, Chgo., 1974-78, ptnr., 1978—. Mem. ABA (business corps. and banking sect.), Order of Coif. Clubs: Mid-Am. (Chgo.). Office: Kirkland & Ellis 200 E Randolph St Fl 54 Chicago IL 60601-6636

EMERSON, DANIEL EVERETT, retired communications company executive; b. Passaic, N.J., Oct. 22, 1924; s. Daniel T. and Jennie (VanBeveren) E.; m. Patricia Thorston, June 14, 1947; children— Patricia Sue, Nancy Ellen, Pamela Thorston. B.E.E., Cornell U., 1949; postgrad., George Washington U., Boston U., N.Y. U., 1951-56, Dartmouth Coll., 1956, U. Pa., 1959-60. With A.T.&T., 1949—, v.p. fed. relations, 1968-74; v.p. network ops. N.Y. Telephone, N.Y.C., 1974-75, v.p. ops. analysis and methods, 1975-76, exec. v.p. corp. devel., dir., 1976-83; exec. v.p. NYNEX Corp., 1983-86; chmn. bd. NYNEX Mobile Communications Co., 1983-86, NYNEX Info. Resources Co., 1983-86. Bd. dirs. Adams Express Co., Petroleum and Resources Corp., bd. trustees, chmn. YMCA of the USA FUnd., Inc. Former mem. bd. dirs., chmn. YMCA U.S.A.; former dir. trustee YMCA of Greater N.Y.; former trustee, pres. Kent Pl. Sch., Summit, N.J. 1st lt. USAAF, 1943-45. Decorated Air medal. Mem. U.S. C. of C. (communications com. 1972-74), Canoe Brook Country Club (Summit), Vero Beach (Fla.) Country Club, Cornell Club (N.Y.C.), Vero Beach Yacht Club, Tau Beta Pi, Eta Kappa Nu, Theta Xi.

EMERSON, JAMES LARRY, beverage company executive; b. Garrett, Ind., Jan. 23, 1938; s. George Cary and Ellen A. (Bennett) E.; m. Madalyn Carol Brown, June 24, 1962; children: Todd Jeffrey, Kiersten Christine, Leisel Renee. Student in pre-vet medicine, Purdue U., 1958, MS, 1964, PhD, 1966; DVM, Ohio State U., 1962. Diplomate Am. Coll. Vet. Pathologists. Rsch. assoc. Norwich Pharmacal Co., Norwich, NY, 1966—69; sr. rsch. specialist dept. pathology and toxicology Dow Chem. Co., Indpls., 1969-76; assoc. faculty Ind. U., Purdue U., Indpls., 1972-76; mgr. pathology Abbott Labs., North Chicago, Ill., 1976-79; mgr. life scis. Coca-Cola Co., Atlanta, 1979-81, assoc. dir. external tech. affairs, 1981-82, dir. sci. and regulatory affairs, 1982-99, sr. sci. fellow sci. and regulatory affairs, 1999-2001, asst. v.p., 2001—. Chmn. saccharin tech. com. Internat. Life Scis. Inst., Washington, 1984—2000, mem. editl. bd., 1983—99; trustee Health and Environ. Scis. Inst., 1990—2001; hon. prof. Kirov Med. Inst., Russia, Salvador U., Buenos Aires. Sci. lay review com., mgmt. adv. bd. Juvenile Diabetes Rsch. Found., 1998—. Fellow Royal Soc. Medicine; mem. AVMA, Indsl. Vet. Assn., Soc. Toxicology, Internat. Acad. Pathologists, Flavor and Extract Mfrs. Assn. (bd. govs. 1987-97, chmn. sec. com. 1984-2001, pres. 1994-95, bd. dirs. calorie control coun. 1998-2000),

Internat. Orgn. Flavor Industries (bd. dirs. 1999—). Methodist. Home: 290 Landfall Rd NW Atlanta GA 30328-1826 Office: Emerson Cons Internat 290 Landfall Rd NW Atlanta GA 30328 E-mail: foodchain@hotmail.com.

EMERSON, JO ANN, congresswoman; b. Sept. 16, 1950; d. Ab and Sylvia Hermann; m. Bill Emerson, 1975 (dec.); children: Victoria, Katharine; m. Ron Gladney, 2000; stepchildren: Elizabeth, Abigail, Alison, Jessica, Stephanie, Sam. BA in Polit. Sci., Ohio Wesleyan U., 1972, DHL (hon.), Westminster Coll., Fulton, Mo. Mem. 105th-108th Congress from 8th Mo. dist., 1997—; appropriations com. 106th Congress, 1998—. Sr. v.p. Am. Ins. Assn.; dir. state rels. and grassroots programs Nat. Restaurant Assn.; dep. dir. comm. Nat. Rep. Congl. Com.; mem. Sub-Com. Agriculture, Transp. Energy & Water Devel. Mem. PEO Womens's Svc. Group (FY chpt.), Cape Girardeau; mem. adv. com. Children's Inn, NIH; mem. adv. bd. Arneson Inst. Practical Politics and Pub. Affairs, Ohio Wesleyan U.; trusteearry Truman Scholarship Found.; hon. and life trustee Westminster Coll. Mem. Copper Dome Soc. Republican. Presbyterian. Office: 2440 Rayburn HOB Washington DC 20515-2508*

EMERSON, R. CLARK, priest, business administrator; b. L.A., Mar. 9, 1945; s. George Heins and Irma Furney (Sorter) E.; m. Katharine Ann Lawrence, June 27, 1980; children: Cynthia, Holly, Angela, William, Richard. BA, San Jose State U., 1966; MDiv, Ch. Div. Sch. of Pacific, 1972. Ordained deacon Episcopal Ch., 1972, ordained priest, 1973; cert. secondary tchr., Calif. Comml. tchr. Middletown (Calif.) High Sch., 1967-69; asst. to rector St. Francis Ch., Palos Verdes, Calif., 1972-76; adminstr. Power Transistor Co., Torrance, Calif., 1977-85; priest assoc. St. John's Ch., L.A., 1976-85; adminstr. Richard B. Belli Accountancy, San Jose, Calif., 1988-96; priest assoc. St. Luke's Ch., Los Gatos, Calif., 1985—. Contr. St. John's Well Child Ctr., L.A., 1985. Republican. Episcopalian. Avocations: steam railroading, antique automobiles, hot air ballooning.

EMERSON, RICHARD B. marketing company executive; Past positions in copywriting, pub. rels. and sales promotions; past v.p., past acct. supr. Cabot Advt.; founding ptnr., pres., CEO, acct. supr. Sperry Top Sider, Fidelity Investments, Marriott Corp., Stop & Shop, Thom McAn Emerson Lane Forkino, 1981-91; COO intergrated divsns., sr. accts. mgr. Century 21, The Hartford, Stop & Shop (merged with Arnold Advt.), 1991; mng. ptnr., COO Arnold Comm., Inc., Boston. Past pres. Leukemia Soc. Am., Mass. Mem. 4A's (past chmn. New England bd. govs.), Ad Club (chmn. bd. dirs.). Address: Arnold Fortuna Lawner Cabot 101 Huntington Ave Fl 2300 Boston MA 02199-7603

EMERSON, RICHARD P. information technology executive; B of Econs., M of Econs., Stanford U.; MBA, Dartmouth Coll. With T.J. Watson Rsch. Lab., IBM; with Corp. R&D Lab., GE; with Lazard and Morgan Stanley, San Francisco and N.Y.C.; mng. dir., co-head tech. and telecom. adv. svcs. Microsoft, Redmond, Wash., 2000, sr. v.p. corp. devel. strategy. Bd. trustees Calif. Acad. Scis.; mem. Bus. Leadership Team, Microsoft. Office: Microsoft One Microsoft Way Redmond WA 98052-6399

EMERSON, SHARON B. biology researcher and educator; b. Santa Monica, Calif., July 14, 1945; BA, U. Calif., Berkeley, 1966; MS, U. So. Calif., 1968, PhD, 1971. Rsch. assoc. Field Mus. Natural History, Chgo.; rsch. prof. Dept. Biology U. Utah. Recipient excellence in environ. health rsch., Lovelace Inst., Albuquerque, 1995; fellow John D. and Katherine T. Mac Arthur fellowship, 1995. Mem.: Am. Soc. Zoology (chair divsn. vertebrate morphology). Office: U Utah Dept Biology 257 S 1400 E Salt Lake City UT 84112-0840

EMERSON, STEPHEN G. hematologist, educator, oncologist; b. N.Y.C., Oct. 21, 1953; BA, Haverford Coll., 1974; MSc, Yale U., 1976, PhD, MD, Yale U., 1980; MA (hon.), U. Pa., 1994. Intern, resident Mass. Gen. Hosp., Boston, 1980—82; fellow Brigham & Women's Hosp., Dam-Farber Cancer Inst., Children's Hosp., Boston, 1982—86; asst. to assoc. prof. medicine U. Mich., Ann Arbor, 1986—94; prof. medicine U. Pa., Phila., 1994—, chief hematology & oncology, 1994—. Founder Astrom Biosci., Inc., Ann Arbor, 1989—. Contbr. articles. Recipient Career Achievement award, Rolex Corp., 1999; scholar, Leukemia Soc. Am., 1987—92. Fellow: ACP; mem.: Internat. Clin. Club, Am. Assn. Physicians. Office: Univ Pa Maloney Bldg 36th & Spruce Sts Philadelphia PA 19104 E-mail: emersons@mail.med.upenn.edu.

EMERSON, STERLING JONATHAN, lawyer; b. Pasadena, Calif., July 2, 1929; s. Sterling H. and Mary Foote (Randall) E.; m. Virginia Beabes, July 3, 1954; children: Margaret Ellen, Henry Rollins, Peter Randall. BA in Econs. with honors, U. Calif., Berkeley, 1955; JD, U. Mich., 1957. Bar: Pa. 1958, U.S. Dist. Ct. (ea. dist.) Pa. 1958, U.S. Ct. Appeals (3d cir.) 1958. Assoc. Montgomery, McCracken, Walker & Rhoads, Phila., ptnr., 1966-97; pvt. practice Media, Pa., 1998—. Asst. editor Law Rev. U. Mich., 1957. With U.S. Army, 1950—52, Korea. Fellow Am. Coll. Trust and Estate Counsel; mem. ABA, Fiduciary Law Soc., Pa. Bar Assn., Phila. Bar Assn. (former bd. govs., former chmn. sect. on probate and trust law), Delaware County Bar Assn. Avocations: tennis, gardening, travel. Home: 16 Oberlin Ave Swarthmore PA 19081-1512 Office: Monroe Profl Bldg 117 N Monroe St Media PA 19063-3037

EMERSON, WILLIAM ALLEN, retired investment company executive; b. Columbia, Tenn., July 13, 1921; s. Henry Houston and Mabel N. (Allen) E.; m. Jane Stannard, Oct. 5, 1944; children: Marshal Henry, Shelley, Stacey, Kimberly. AA, St. Petersburg Jr. Coll., 1941; BSBA, U. Fla., 1946. With Merrill Lynch, Pierce, Fenner & Smith, Inc., 1947-87, dir. gen. services div., 1968-72, Southeast regional dir., corp. dir. Atlanta, 1972-81, sr. v.p., nat. sales dir., 1981-86; dir. Merrill Trust Co. Past vice chmn. bd. trustees St. Joseph-St. Anthony Health Sys. Trustee Oglethorpe U., Atlanta, Mus. Fine Arts, St. Petersburg, Salvadore Dali Mus., St. Petersburg; trustee, past pres. U. Fla. Found. Pilot with USMC, 1942-45. Named Emerson Alumni Hall at U. Fla. in his honor, 2003. Mem.: Feather Sound Country Club (St. Petersburg), St. Petersburg Yacht Club, Capital City Club, Masons. Republican. Baptist. Home: 3050 82nd Way N Saint Petersburg FL 33710-2220 E-mail: ladyjane1@webtv.net. *I believe that what you give away returns to bless you in many ways, and that what you have left is worth more than before the gift.*

EMERSON, WILLIAM HARRY, lawyer, retired, oil company executive; b. Rochester, N.Y., Jan. 13, 1928; s. William Canfield and Alice Sarah (Adams) E.; m. Jane Anne Epple, Dec. 27, 1956; children: Elizabeth Anne, Carolyn Jane. BA, Cornell U., 1951, LLB, 1956. Bar: Ill. 1974. Atty. Amoco Corp., 1956-91; sec., dir. Amoco Gas Co., 1979-91. Pres., dir. Undercroft Montessori Sch., Tulsa, 1965-67, Tulsa Figure Skating Club, 1969; bd. dirs. Lake Forest (Ill.) Found. for Hist. Preservation, 1983-2001; mem. vestry Ch. Holy Spirit, Lake Forest, 1988-91. Home: 593 Greenvale Rd Lake Forest IL 60045-1526

EMERSON, WILLIAM KARY, engineering company executive; b. Enid, Okla., July 15, 1941; s. Kary Cadmus and Mary Rebecca (Williams) E.; m. Marcie Louise Stogner, Mar. 13, 1965; children: Rebecca A., Phillip W. BS, Okla. State U., 1965, MS, 1974; diploma, Command and Gen. Staff Coll., 1979, Defense Systems Mgmt. Coll., 1980. Commd. 2d lt. U.S. Army, 1965, advanced through grades to lt. col., 1985; prin. program mgr. Honeywell, Inc., Minnetonka, Minn., 1985-90; sr. program mgr. Alliant Techsystems, Inc., Minnetonka, 1990-92; dep. dir. engring. Teledyne Brown Engring. Co., Huntsville, Ala., 1992-96, dir. advanced engring., 1996-97; sr. program mgr. PEI Electronics, Huntsville, Ala., 1997-2001; pres. Emerson Consulting, Inc., 2001—. Disting. guest lectr. Def. Sys. Mgmt. Coll., 1997; pres., bd. dirs. Non Profit Counseling Ctr., 2000-02. Author: Chevrons, 1983, Encyclopedia of Insignia, 1995; contbr. articles to profl. jours. and ency. Mem. adv. com. Dist. 281 Sch. Bd., Minn., 1986-88, mem. summer sch. concept com., 1988-89; mem. Huntsville Land Trust, 1994—; chmn. recycling com. N. Ala. Sierra Club, 1994-98; citizen mem. City of Huntsville Ordinance Rewrite Com., 1995-97; lay leader Asbury Meth. Ch., 1997-00, chair adminstrv. bd., 2000-02; bd. mgmt. Anne S.K. Browne Collection, Brown U., Providence, 1998—. Decorated Legion of Merit, Bronze Star with V and one oak leaf cluster, Purple Heart with two oak leaf clusters; inducted into Madison County (Ala.) Hall of Heros, 1996; recipient Lit. award Orders and Medals Soc. Am., 1998, Silver medal, 2000, 02. Fellow Co. Mil. Historians (bd. dirs. 1983-86, 2000—, editor 1986-92, pres. 2003—, Miller award 1977); mem. VFW (life), Am. Soc. Mil. Insignia Collectors (editor jour. 1993—, Best Nat. Display award 1984), Am. Def. Preparedness Assn., Assn. U.S. Army, Am. Assn. Mil. Uniform Collectors (Writing award 1999, 2000, Achievement medal 2002), Orders and Medals Soc. Am. (bd. dirs. 2003—, chmn. publs. 2003—), Mil. Order Purple Heart, Heritage Club, Sierra Club (local chmn. recycling com.). Methodist. Avocations: running, fishing, racquetball. Office: Emerson Cons Inc 124 Kensington Dr Madison AL 35758

EMERT, GEORGE HENRY, former academic administrator, biochemist; b. Tenn., Dec. 15, 1938; s. Victor K. Emert and Hazel G. (Shultz) Ridley; m. Billie M. Bush, June 10, 1967; children: Debra Lea Lipp, Ann Lanie Taylor, Laurie Elizabeth, Jamie Marie. BA, U. Colo., 1962; MA, Colo. State U., 1970; PhD, Va. Tech. U., 1973. Registered profl. chem. engr. Microbiologist Colo. Dept. Pub. Health, Denver, 1967-70; post doctoral fellow U. Colo., Boulder, 1973-74; dir. biochem. tech. Gulf Oil Corp., Merriam, Kans., 1974-79; prof. biochemistry, dir. biomass rsch. ctr. U. Ark., Fayetteville, 1979-84; exec. v.p. Auburn (Ala.) U., 1984-92; pres. Utah State U., Logan, 1992—2000, pres. emeritus, porf. biochemistry, 2001—. Adj. prof. microbiology U. Kans., Lawrence, 1975-79. Editor, author: Fuels from Biomass and Wastes, 1981; author book chpt.; contbr. articles to profl. jours.; poet. Mem. So. Tech. Coun., Raleigh, N.C., 1985-92; dir. Ala. Supercomputer Authority, Montgomery, 1987-92, Blue Cross Blue Shield Utah, 1996—, Utah Partnership Econ. Devel.; trustee, adv. bd. First Security Bank. Capt. U.S. Army, 1963-66, Vietnam. Named to Educators Hall of Fame, Lincoln Meml. U., 1988. Fellow Am. Inst. Chemists; mem. Rotary (Paul Harris fellow, pres., v.p. 1989-90), Phi Kappa Phi, Sigma Xi. Republican. Achievements include patent for method for enzyme reutilization. Office: Utah State U 0300 Old Main Logan UT 84322

EMERT, JOHN WESLEY, mathematician, musician; s. Howard Mitchell and Dorthia Mae Emert; m. Elizabeth Joan Jared. PhD, U. of Tenn., 1989. Prof. math Ball State U., Muncie, Ind., asst. chmn. Dept. Math. Scis. Composer songs; contbr. articles to profl. jours. Office: Ball State University Department of Mathematical Sciences Muncie IN 47306-0490 E-mail: emert@bsu.edu.

EMERTON, ROBERT WALTER, III, lawyer; b. Hanover, Pa., Feb. 4, 1950; s. James Leonard and Dorothy (Davenport) E.; m. Sharon Whitaker, June 9, 1973 (div. Mar. 1982); children: Chad, Ryan. BA, U. Fla., 1972, JD, 1975. Bar: Fla. 1975, U.S. Dist. Ct. (mid. dist.) Fla. 1976, U.S. Ct. Appeals (11th cir.) 1981, U.S. Supreme Ct. 1982. Asst. pub. defender State of Fla., Tampa, 1975-76; litigation counsel Jim Walter Corp., Tampa, 1976-79, sr. litigation counsel, 1979-82, asst. v.p., 1982-88, v.p., gen. counsel, sec., 1988—; bd. dirs. Asbestos Claims Facility, Inc., Celotex Corp.; legal cons. Com. for Equitable Compensation, Washington, 1982—. Spl. award Ctr. for Pub. Resources, 1985. Mem. Hillsborough County Bar Assn. (corp. counsel subcom. 1977—). Republican. Home: 928 W Cimmeron Dr Tampa FL 33603-1728 Office: Jim Walter Corp 4010 W Boy Scout Blvd Tampa FL 33607-5727

EMERY, ALAN ROY, museum executive; b. Trinidad, West Indies, Feb. 21, 1939; s. Roy W. and Ruth I. (Jackson); m. Frances D. Ruttan, June 23, 1962; children: Katherine, Timothy. BSc with honors, U. Toronto, Ont., Can., 1962; MSc, McGill U., Montreal, Que., Can., 1964; PhD, U. Miami, 1968. Rsch., teaching asst., Toronto and Montreal, 1959-65; rsch. asst. Inst. of Marine Scis., Miami, Fla., 1965-68; rsch. scientist Ont. Ministry of Natural Resources, Maple, 1968-72; from rsch. assoc. to assoc. curator Royal Ont. Mus., Toronto, 1969-80, curator, Ichthyology and Herpetology, 1980-83; assoc. prof. U. Toronto, 1976-83; pres. Can. Mus. Nature, Ottawa, 1983-96, KIVU Nature Inc., 1997—. Bd. dirs. Ctr. Traditional Knowledge, sec.-treas., 1993—2000; pres. Kivu Nature, Inc., 1997—; sr. v.p. mktg. Emery Internat. Devels. Ltd., 2001—; CEO, chmn. of the bd. Free Impressions, Inc., 2002—03; cons. in field. Author: The Coral Reef, 1981; contbr. articles to profl. jours. Recipient Citation Sports Fishing Inst., Washington, Marine Environ. award Found. for Ocean Rsch., Toronto, 1986, Reconocimiento de honor Fundacian Cultural Banesto, Spain, 1992. Mem. World Conservation Union (pres. nat. com. Can. 1995-98), Assn. Systematics Collections (pres. 1987-89), Royal Can. Inst. (pres. 1983), Am. Soc. Ichthyologists and Herpetologists (editor, bd. govs. 1976-86). Avocations: photography, writing, music.

EMERY, FRANK EUGENE, publishing executive; b. Wichita, Kans., May 14, 1934; s. Frank A.C. and Nellie Mae (Bloss) E.; m. Sara Manette Marble, Nov. 3, 1956 (div. 1983); children: Frank Michael, Mark W., Timothy T., Todd A.; m. Sandra Kay Adamson, June 28, 1988. BA, U. Kans., 1955, MD, 1959. Diplomate Am. Bd. Orthopedic Surgery, Nat. Bd. Med. Examiners. Intern U. Kans. Med. Ctr., Kansas City, 1959-60, resident radiology, 1960-61, resident gen. surgery, 1961-62; resident orthopedic surgery U. Tex. Med. Br., Galveston, 1968; fellow Orthopedic Rsch. and Edn. Found. U. Edinburgh, Scotland, 1968; pvt. practice specializing in orthopedic surgery Springfield, Mo., 1969-73; asst. prof. surgery, orthopedics U. Tex. Med. Br., Galveston, 1973-77, assoc. prof. surgery, orthopedics, 1977-78, dir. Arthritis Minimal Care Unit, 1975-76; pub. Ft. Scott (Kans.) Tribune, 1980—; pres. Tribune Monitor Co., Ft. Scott, 1982—. Bd. dirs. Tribune Monitor Co., Ft. Scott, Gateway Comm., Wichita; gen. ptnr. Hotel Ptnrs., I, II, III, IV, Wichita. Contbr. articles to med. publs. V.p. Mo. and Ark. River Basins Assn., 1984-86; co-chmn. Gov.'s Task Force Pub. Sector Funding, Kans., Main St. Program, Topeka, 1985-86; chmn. basin adv. com. Kans. Water Authority, Topeka, 1986-90; bd. dirs. Kans. C. of C. and Industry, Topeka, 1990-91. Lt. comdr., surgeon USPHS, 1961-63. Pediatric psychiatry fellow NIH, 1957; fellow United Cerebral Palsy Found., 1967-68. Fellow Am. Acad. Orthopedic Surgeons; mem. Kans. Press Assn., Inland Press Assn., Am. Soc. for Surgery of the Hand, Sigma Xi, Nu Sigma Nu, Delta Upsilon. Avocations: boating, swimming, hiking, mountain climbing. Home: 4559 E Creeksbend Ln Springfield MO 65809-3395 Office: Fort Scott Tribune 6 E Wall St Fort Scott KS 66701-1423

EMERY, HENRY ALFRED, petroleum engineer; b. Northfield, N.H., Feb. 9, 1926; s. Henry A. and Ruth (Trask) Emery; children: Trask, Timothy, Ptarmigan. BA, U. Maine, 1950; diploma in petroleum engring., Colo. Sch. Mines, 1956; MBA, U. Denver, 1966. Registered profl. engr., Colo. With Mobil Pipeline Co., 1950-53, Portland Montreal Pipeline Co., 1956-59; maintenance design engr., planning supr., engring. supt., project mgr. Pub. Svc. Co., Colo., 1959-72; pres. Computer Graphics Co., Denver, 1972-78; divsn. mgr. Kellogg Corp., Littleton, Colo., 1978-82; chmn., CEO Emery DataGraphic Inc., Englewood, Colo., 1982-86; pres. Emery DataGraphic divsn. Harris-McBurney Co., 1987-93, Emery & Assoc., Inc., Greenwood Village, Denver, 1993—. Mem.: Am. Water Works Assn., Urgan Regional Info. Sys. Assn., Geospatial Info. Tech. Assn. (past pres.), Tau Beta Pi. Democrat. Home and Office: 11 S Adams St #701 Denver CO 80209 E-mail: emery@ecentral.com.

EMERY, JAMES PATRICK, composer, musician; b. Youngstown, Ohio, Dec. 21, 1951; s. Alva Vincent and Rosemary E.; m. Colleen Marie McEvoy, Aug. 1, 1980; 1 child, Hannah Louise. Guitar and composition instr. Creative Music Studio, Woodstock, NY, 1975—81; guitarist, composer String Trio of NY, N.Y.C., NY, 1977—; guitarist, composer, bandleader James Emery Ensemble, Warwick, NY, 1980—; chmn. Sound Directions Inc., Warwick, 1985—. Pres. Jamem Pub. Co., Warwick, 1980—2003; adj. prof. post-grad. guitar studies Aaron CoplandSch. Music QueensColl., N.Y.C., 1985—86. Composer, guitarist (CD) Transformations (Music for 3 Improvisers and Orchestra), Octagon, An Outside Job, Intermobility, Turbulence, TimeNever Lies, Ascendant, (LP) Exo Eso, (CD) String Trio of NY & Jay Clayton, Natural Balance, Rebirth of a Feeling, Gut Reaction, (LP) Artlife, (CD) Common Goal, Area Code 212, First String, Fourth World, Luminous Cycles (Top Ten CDs of 2001, Downbeat Mag., Jazz Times, allaboutjazz.com, 2001), Faze Phour: A Twenty Year Retrospective, Spectral Domains, String Trio of New York with Anthony Davis, Standing on a Whale Fishing for Minnows (Top CDs of 1996, The Tracking Angle, Jazziz Mag., 1997), Blues.?. Dir., lectr. Village Coll., Warwick, 2001—03. Music Composition Fellowship, Guggenheim Found., 1995, Jazz Performance fellow, NEA, 1985, 1994, Music Composition fellow, NY Found. Arts, 1986, 1990, 2000, Rec. grant, Mary Flagler Cary Charitable Trust, 1991, Mary Flagler Cary Charitable Trust, 1996, Mary Flagler Cary Charitable Trust, 1999, Music Composition Commn. grant, 2000, Meet the Composer/Rockefeller/AT&T program, 1987, Va. Coun. Art, 1988, Meet the Composer/Lila Wallace Jazz Program, 1994, Meet the Composer's Commissions USA Program, 1997. Mem.: ASCAP (assoc. spl. awards 1980—2002), Chamber Music Am. (assoc.). Home: 18 Woodside Dr Warwick NY 10990 Home Fax: 845-987-8484. Personal E-mail: jamem@warwick.net.

EMERY, KITTY FRANCES, curator, educator; d. Alan R. and Frances H. Emery. BSc, Trent U., Peterborough, Ont., 1986; MA, U. of Toronto, 1989, Cornell U., 1993, PhD, 1997. Postdoctoral scholar Royal Ont. Mus., Toronto, Canada, 1997—98; prof. of anthropology SUNY, Potsdam, NY, 1998—2001; curator of environ. archaeology Fla. Mus. of Natural History, Gainesville, Fla., 2001—. Fellow, Social Scis. and Humanities Rsch. Coun. of Can., 1992—96, Cornell U., 1992—96, Social Scis. and Humanities Rsch. Coun. of Can., 1998—2000; grantee, Sigma Xi, 1994, Wenner-Gren Found., 1995—96. Mem.: Am. Anthrop. Assn., Soc. for Am. Archaeology, Soc. for Archaeological Sci., Internat. Coun. of Zooarchaeology, Assn. of Environ. Archeology, Lambda Alpha (life), Sigma Xi (life), Phi Kappa Phi (life). Office: Florida Museum of Natural History Dickinson Hall Box 117800 Gainesville FL 32611-7800 Office Fax: 352-392-3698.

EMERY, LIN, sculptor; d. Cornell and Jean (Weill) E.; m. Shirley Brooks Braselman, Aug. 17, 1962, 1 child, Brooks. Certificat, Sorbonne U., Paris, 1949; studies with Ossip Zadkine, Paris, 1949-50. Vis. critic architecture Tulane U., New Orleans, 1969-70; vis. artist Newcomb Sch. Art, New Orleans, 1980; lectr., vis. artist various including U. Tex., Ga. Coll., Art Acad. Cin., U. New Orleans, LaGrange Coll., 1980-86; vis. artist U. Maine, 1988. Adv. New Orleans Art com., 1987-88, Nat. Sculpture Conf.; Works by Women, Cin., 1986-87; chair studio sessions Coll. Art Assn., N.Y.C., 1979, conf. Nat. Sculpture Ctr., Lawrence, Kans., 1976; chair Internat. Sculpture Conf., Phila., 1992. Prin. works include meml. column, fountain New Orleans Civic Ctr., 1966, 70, kinetic sculptures Lawrence Civic Ctr., 1982, fed. bldg. Houma, La., 1977, state library, Baton Rouge, 1982, various pub., corp. commns. Singapore, Chgo., Osaka (Japan), Washington, various pub. art commns. City of Va. Beach, 1988, Oxnard, Calif., 1989, Melbourne, Fla., 1990, Tallahassee, Fla., 1990, Hofstra U., 1992, Daytona Airport, 1993, Sterling Drug Rsch. Ctr., Pa., 1993; one-woman shows include New Orleans Mus. Art, 1962, 64, Sculpture Ctr., N.Y.C., 1962, 67, Tenn. Fine Arts Ctr., Nashville, 1962, Mus. N.Mex., Santa Fe, 1966, Centennial Art Mus., Corpus Christi, Tex., 1967, Lauren Rogers Mus., Laurel, Miss., 1977, Hunter Mus., Chattanooga, 1985; solo gallery exhibits Max Hutchinson, Kouros, N.Y.C., Arthur Roger, New Orleans. Mem. Internat. Sculpture Ctr., Hamilton, NJ, 2000—; bd. mem. NY Sculpture Ctr., New York, NY, 1990—92, Contemporary Arts Ctr., New Orleans, La., 1994—2000; advisor Arts Coun., New Orleans, La., 1997—2003. Va. Ctr. Creative Art fellow, 1981; recipient mayor's award City of New Orleans, 1980, "Sweet-art" award Contemporary Arts Ctr., New Orleans, 1987, Lazlo Aranyi Honor award for Pub. Art, 1990, Gov.'s Arts award, La., 2001; named Woman of Achievement, State of La., 1984, Disting. La. Artist, New Orleans Ctr. for Creative Arts, 1988. Mem. Internat. Sculpture Ctr. (bd. dirs. 1973-79, 88-89), Sculptors Guild, New Orleans PerCent for Art Com., N.Y. Sculpture Ctr. (bd. mem. 1989-91). Democrat. Achievements include 22 museum collections:National Collection of American Art; Walter Chrysler Museum; Sofia Museum of Foreign Art; etc; 52 solo exhibitions: U.S.; Kyoto, Paris, London, Canada. Avocations: archaeology, metallurgy. Home: 7520 Dominican St New Orleans LA 70118-3738 E-mail: lin@linemery.com

EMERY, NANCY BETH, lawyer; b. Shawnee, Okla., July 9, 1952; d. Paul Dodd Finefrock and Kathryn Jo (Saling) Hutchens; m. Lee Monroe Emergy, May 18, 1974. BA with highest honors, U. Okla., 1974; JD, Harvard U., 1977. Bar: D.C. 1981. Atty. advisor Office Gen. counsel, USDA, Washington, 1977-79; legal advisor Fed. Energy Regulatory Commr. Matthew Holden, Jr., Washington, 1979-81; assoc. Pierson, Ball & Dowd and predecessor Sullivan & Beauregard, Washington, 1981-83, Paul Hastings, Janofsky & Walker, Washington, 1983-87, ptnr., 1987-93, Sutherland, Asbill & Brennan, Washington, 1993-97; v.p., gen. counsel, corp. sec. Calif. Ind. Sys. Operator Corp., 1997-99; ptnr. Hopkins & Sutter, Washington, 1999-2001, Ballard, Spahr, Andrews & Ingersoll, LLP, Washington, 2001—. Nat. adv. bd. USAID Tng. Program, 1994—98. Bd. dirs., sec. Park Place Condominium Assn., Inc., Washington, 1982—84; page Continental Congress DAR, 1978—82, chpt. del., 1981, 1984; bd. dirs. New Hope Housing, Inc., Alexandria, Va., 2001—, chmn. strategic planning com., 2002—. Mem.: ABA (natural resources energy and eviron. law sect. 1990—98, bd. editors Natural Resources & Environment 1990—98, pub. utility law sect., vice chmn. electricity com. 1998—, chmn. program com. 2000—01, chmn. mem. com. 2001—02, chmn. strategic planning com. 2001—02, chmn. cmty. outreach com. 2002—, mem. coun. 2002—, chmn. cmty. involvment 2002—), Soc. Profl. Journalists, Fed. Energy Bar Assn. (chair tax com. 1986—87, chair FERC ops. and adminstrn. com. 1991—93, chair elec. utility regulation com. 1995—97, chair program com. 1997—98), Mortar Bd., Phi Beta Kappa. Democrat. Office: Ballard Spahr Andrews & Ingersoll LLP 601 13th St NW Washington DC 20005 E-mail: bemery@ballardspahr.com.

EMERY, PAUL EMILE, psychiatrist; b. Montreal, May 2, 1922; arrived in U.S., 1951; s. Esdras Fernand and Julia (Benoit) E.; m. Virginia Olga B. Kennick, July 27, 1979. BA, U. Montreal, 1942, MD, 1948. Diplomate in gen. psychiatry and forensic psychiatry, Am. Acad. Experts in Traumatic Stress. Staff psychiatrist Austen Riggs Ctr., Stockbridge, Mass., 1958-60; chief mental hygiene VA, Bridgeport, Conn., 1960-62, staff psychiatrist, chief of psychiatry Manchester, NH, 1988-99; pvt. practice Concord, NH, 1962-85, 99—; clin. dir. Ctr. for Stress Recovery, Brecksville, Ohio, 1985-87, dir., 1987-88. Med. dir. forensic unit N.H. Hosp., Concord, 1980-82; cons. VA med. Ctr., Manchester, 1962-64, 82-85, pub. health State of N.H., Concord, 1962-71, St. Paul's Sch., Concord, 1971-78; mem. faculty Dartmouth Coll. Med. Sch., 1971—, Western Res. Sch. Medicine, 1985—. Contbr. articles to profl. jours.; author: Trauma Psychology Model of the Mind, 1993. Sec. adv. commn. health and welfare State of N.H., Concord. Capt. U.S. Army, 1953-55. Recipient Salutation plaque N.H. Program on Alcoholism, 1971, cert. honor for scholarly achievement Internat. Assn. Psychohistory, 1998. Fellow Am. Psychiat. Assn. (life, disting., founder N.H. dist. br. 1972, chair ethics com.), Am. Acad. Experts in Traumatic Stress; mem. N.H. Med. Soc. (cert. commendation 1972), Mass. Psychiat. Soc. (pres. 1965), N.H. Psychiat. Soc. (pres. 1980). Office: 15 Buckingham Dr Bow NH 03304-5207

EMERY, ROBERT FIRESTONE, economist, educator; b. Kenton, Ohio, Jan. 18, 1927; s. Clayton Sprague and Sarah Webster (Firestone) E.; m. Phyllis Eileen Swanson, June 29, 1957; children: Ross David, Ann Elaine, Hope Roberta. BA, Oberlin (Ohio) Coll., 1951; MA, U. Mich., 1952, PhD, 1956. Fellow U. Mich., 1954-55; economist Fed. Res. Bd., Washington, 1955-92; adj. prof. econs. Southeastern U., Washington, 1960-88, chmn. dept. fin. adminstrn., 1963-65, dean sr. div., 1965-68, prof. emeritus, 1988; internat. econ. cons., 1992—. Author: The Financial Institutions of Southeast Asia, 1971, The Japanese Money Market, 1983, The Money Markets of Developing East Asia, 1991, The Bond Markets of Developing East Asia, 1997, Korean Economic Reform: Before and Since the 1997 Crisis, 2001. Admstrv. bd. Chevy Chase (Md.) United Meth. Ch., 1978-80. Served as midshipman U.S. Mcht. Marine Cadet Corps, 1945-47. Horace H. Rackham Grad. fellow U. Mich., 1952-53; Fulbright Grad. Research student U. Rangoon, Burma, 1953-54. Mem. Soc. Govt. Economists (treas. 1976-78), Internat. Economists' Club (pres. 1977-92). Republican. Presbyterian. Avocations: golf, piano, classical music. Home: 3421 Shepherd St Chevy Chase MD 20815-3223

EMERY, SANFORD EMIL, orthopedic surgeon; b. Albany, N.Y., Feb. 19, 1956; s. Charles M. and Betty June Emery; m. Gwen Arens; children: Nathaniel, Lindsay, Eric. AB, Dartmouth Coll., 1978; MD, Duke U., 1982; MBA, Weatherhead Sch. Mgmt., Cleve., 2003. Bd. cert. Orthopedic Surgery. Asst. prof. orthopedic surgery Case We. Res. U., Cleve., 1988—97, assoc. prof. orthopedic surgery, 1997—; prof., chmn. Dept. of Orthopaedics W. Va. U., Morgantown, 2003—. Co-editor (textbook): Surgery of the Cervical Spine, 2003. Pres. Shaker Youth Soccer Assn., Shaker Heights, Ohio, 1995—99. Mem.: Scoliosis Rsch. Soc. (chair program com. 1997—98, Russell Hibbs award 1992), Cervical Spine Rsch. Soc. (chair rsch. com. 2001—, co-author Outstanding Resident award 1993). Office: West Virginia Univ Chmn Dept of Orthopaedics Morgantown WV 26506-9196 E-mail: semery@hsc.wvu.edu.

EMERY, VICKI MORRIS, school library media administrator; b. Kansas City, Mo., Sept. 7, 1948; d. Arthur Paul and Merna Alva (Powell) Morris; m. Harvey William Emery Jr., July 19, 1974. BS in Edn., Emporia (Kans.) State U., 1970; M in Urban Affairs, Va. Poly. Inst. and State U., 1980; MS in Libr. Sci., Cath. U. Am., 1995; postgrad. student in ednl. leadership, U. Va., 1997—. Tchr. St. Pius X Sch., Mission, Kans., 1970-72, Shawnee Mission (Kans.) Pub. Schs., 1973-74; editing supr. CTB/McGraw-Hill, Monterey, Calif., 1975-76; sch. libr.

media specialist Fairfax County (Va.) Pub. Schs., 1995-99, sch. libr. adminstr., 1999—. Mem. adv. bd. Fairfax County Sch. Bd., 1996-99. Contbr. revs. and articles to profl. jours. Pres. PTA Sangster Sch., Springfield, Va., 1994-95, 96-98, scholarship chair Fairfax County Coun. PTAs, 1995-99; pres., bd. dirs. Spring-Mar Coop. Presch., Springfield, 1989-90. Recipient Outstanding Svc. award Va. Coop. Presch. Coun., 1991. Mem. ALA, Am. Assn. Sch. Librs. (mem. pres.'s program com. 1998), Assn. Supervision and Curriculum Devel., Va. Ednl. Media Assn., Va. Soc. Tech. Edn., Va. Congress Parents and Tchrs. (hon. life mem.), Beta Phi Mu (local chpt. sec. 2000—). Office: Lake Braddock Secondary Sch 9200 Burke Lake Rd Burke VA 22015-1682

EMERY, VIRGINIA OLGA BEATTIE, psychologist, researcher; b. Cleve., Apr. 9, 1938; d. W. Joseph P. and Antoinette Pauline (Misjack) Kennick; m. Paul Hamilton Beattie Sr., 1960 (div. 1975); children: Tamsan Beattie Tharin, Paul Hamilton Beattie Jr.; m. Paul E. Emery, 1979. BA, U. Chgo., 1962, PhD, 1982; MA, Ind. U., 1973. Diplomate Am. Bd. Disability Analysts, Am. Acad. Traumatic Stress; lic. psychologist, N.H., Ohio; cert. brief therapist Nat. Acad. Brief Therapists; cert. cognitive therapist Nat. Bd. Behavioral Therapists, cert. domestic violence counselor endorsement; cert. expert traumatic stress, cognitive therapist. Asst. prof. psychology Case Western Res. U., Cleve., 1986-89, asst. clin. prof. psychiatry, 1986-89; sr. faculty assoc. Ctr. on Aging and Health, Concord and Hanover, N.H., 1986-89, dir., 1989—; adj. clin. asst. prof. psychiatry Dartmouth Med. Sch., Lebanon, 1983-85, clin. assoc. prof., 1989—. Mem. com. human devel. NIMH, Adult Devel. & Aging Traineeship, U. Chgo., 1974-76; sub-project dir. Case Western Res. U. Sch. Medicine, 1986-90; sec. women's faculty assn. Case Western Res. U., 1987-89; cons. Vets. Affairs Med. Ctr., Manchester, N.H., 1989—; sub-project dir. NIMH Mental Health Clin. Rsch. Ctr. Grant, Case Western Res. U. Sch. Medicine, 1986-90; mem. Dartmouth Coll. and Dartmouth Med. Sch. Neurosci. Group, 1990—; lectr. on medicine Harvard U. Faculty of Medicine, 1996—; Paul Janssen lectr. U. Goteberg, Sweden, 1997; invited lectr. Inst. for Health of Elderly, Newcastle-upon-Tyne, Eng., 1999. Author: Language and Aging, 1985, Pseudodementia: A Theoretical and Empirical Discussion, 1988, Language Impairment in Dementia of the Alzheimer Type: A Hierarchical Decline, 2000, Interface between Vascular Dementia and Alzheimer Syndrome: Nosologic Redefinition, 2000; editor: Dementia: Presentations, Differential Diagnosis, and Nosology, 1991, 2d edit., 2003; contbr. chapters to books, articles to profl. jours. Bd. dirs. Frontiers of Knowledge Civic Trust, Concord, N.H., 1990—, pres. 1990-95. Recipient Adult Devel. and Aging grant/traineeship NIH/NIMH, 1974-76, Rsch. prize Am. Aging Assn., 1983, Havighurst prize for aging rsch. U. Chgo., 1984; named Frontiers of Knowledge Atlee Zellers lectr., 1994, Paul Janssen Med. Inst. lectr., 1997; rsch. grantee Western Res. Coll., 1986-87, NIMH Mental Health Clin. rsch. grantee, 1986-89. Fellow Gerontol. Soc. Am. (Disting Creative Contbn. award 1989; clin. medicine membership com. state liaison 1998—; lectr. Boston, 2002), Am. Psychol. Assn., N.H. Psychol. Assn. (bd. dirs. 1991-93, chair com. acad. rsch. interests 1992-94, sec. 1994—, Riggs Disting. Contbn. award 1991, chmn. Women and Minorities com. 2001—), APA (student rsch. award 1984), Am. Acad. Experts in Traumatic Stress; mem. AAAS, AAUW, Internat. Psychiat. Rsch. Soc., Internat. Psychogeriatric Assn. (Pfizer lectr. 1997, 2d place award for rsch. paper 1995, 2nd Pl. Rsch. award in psychogeriatrics for paper 1995, IPA/Bayer Rsch. award in psychogeriatrics 1995), Boston Soc. Gerontol. Psychiatry, Acad. Psychosomatic Medicine, N.Y. Acad. Scis., Am. Acad. Experts in Traumatic Stress, Assn. Alzheimer's Disease Scientists, Am. Mensa Ltd. Home: 15 Buckingham Dr Bow NH 03304-5207 Office: Dartmouth Med Sch Dept Psychiatry Box HB 7750 Lebanon NH 03756 Fax: 603-625-8199.

EMHARDT, CHARLES DAVID, lawyer; b. Indpls., Feb. 13, 1931; s. John William and Martha Jack (Macdougall) Emhardt; m. Ann Devaney, Nov. 12, 1954; children: John D., Frederick D., Martha A., Lucy E. BSME, Purdue U., 1952, AS in Elec. Engring., 1966; LLB, Harvard U., 1955. Bar: D.C. 1955, Ind. 1958, U.S. Patent Office 1955. Patent atty. We. Electric Co., Washington, Balt., 1955—57; assoc. Harold B. Hood, Indpls., 1957—59, Lockwood, Woodard, Smith & Weikart, Indpls., 1959—64; ptnr. Woodard, Emhardt, Naughton, Moriarty & McNett (former firm Woodard, Weikart, Emhardt & Naughton), Indpls., 1964—. Precinct committeeman Rep. Com., 1965—70. With Nat. Guard U.S. Army, 1955—66. Mem.: ABA, Indpls. Bar Assn. (bd. dirs. 1979—81, chmn. ethics com. 1982—83), Ind. State Bar Assn. (chmn. patent sect. 1967—68), Lawyers Club, Optimists, Shriners, Masons, Indpls. Athletic Club, Woodstock Club. Home: 4801 Fauna Ln Indianapolis IN 46234 Office: Woodard Emhardt Moriarty McNett & Henry 37400 Bank Once Ctr 111 Monument Cir Indianapolis IN 46204-5137

EMILSON, HENRY BERTIL, artist; b. Sundals-Ryr, Dalsland, Sweden, June 1, 1933; came to U.S., 1951; s. Harry Cristoffer Emilsson and Hanna (Nilsson) Svensson. BFA, Okla. U., 1960; MFA, Inst. Allende San Miguel, Mexico, 1967. Dir. U.S. Army Arts and Crafts Recreation Svcs., U.S. and overseas, 1962-88; artist Bollungsnas, Bralanda, Sweden, 1988—. Exhibited in one-man shows in Erlangen, Germany, 1979, Bad Windsheim, Germany, 1981, Gothenburg, Sweden, 1990, Vanersborg, Sweden, 1994, also others; represented in nat. and internat. pub. and pvt. collections. With USAF, 1952-56. Office: Bollungsnas 460 65 Bralanda Sweden

EMISON, EWING RABB, JR., lawyer; b. Vincennes, Ind., Feb. 3, 1925; s. Ewing and Tuley (Sheperd) E.; m. Kathleen M. Crowley, Nov. 28, 1952; children: Susan, Anne Emison Wishard. AB, DePauw U., 1947; LLB, Ind. U., 1950. Bar: Ind. 1950. Of counsel Emison Doolittle Kolb & Roellgen, Vincennes; dep. atty. gen. State of Ind., 1968-69. Lectr. CLE seminars, ABA Nat. Conf. for Diversity, 2002. Contbg. columnist Res Gestae, Ind. State Bar mag., 1987—. Mem. Wabash Valley Interstate Commn., 1959-62, Ind. Flood Control and Water Resources Commn., 1961-65; mem. bd. visitors Ind. Univ. Sch. Law, 1984-87. With USN, 1943-46, 52-53. Mem. ABA (sects. on litigation, econs. of law practice, Spirit of Excellence award commn. on racial and ethnic diversity in the profession 2003), Nat. Bar Assn., Ind. State Bar Assn. (bd. of mgrs. 1975-77, chmn. ho. of dels. 1979, pres. 1986-87), Columbia Club, Phi Delta Phi, Phi Kappa Psi. Republican. Presbyterian. Avocations: golf, assistance to minority law students, military history. Office: Emison Doolittle Kolb & Roellgen PO Box 215 8th and Busseron Sts Vincennes IN 47591

EMISON, JAMES WADE, petroleum company executive; b. Indpls., Sept. 21, 1930; s. John Rabb and Catherine (Stanbrough) E.; divorced; children: Catherine Emison Stoick, Elizabeth Ann, Thomas Weston, William Ash; m. Jane Bale Larson, Feb. 14, 1983. BA, DePauw U., 1952, HHD, 2003. Gen. mgr. C&C Oil Co. Inc., Huntington, Ind., 1954-59; pres. May Petroleum Co. Inc., Lima, Ohio, 1959-61; sales mgr. Oskey Bros. Petroleum Corp., St. Paul, 1961-66; v.p. mktg. Nfld. Refining Co. Ltd., N.Y.C., 1965—69; v.p. Oskey Gasoline & Oil Co., Mpls., 1969-76; pres. Western Petroleum Co. (successor to Oskey Gasoline & Oil Co.), Mpls., 1977—. Pres. Western Internat. Trading Co., Eden Prairie, Minn., 1981—; bd. dirs. Hydrocarbon Trading & Transport Co., Houston, Community Bank Group, Inc., Eden Prairie, Minn.; ptnr. Bellwood Ptnrs., City Ctr. East and Riverview Bus. Pl. Trustee DePauw U., Greencastle, Ind., 1981—, former vice chair bd. trustees, co-founder Ctr. for Mgmt. and Entrepreneurship; trustee USMC Marine Corps U. Found. Inc., Quantico, Va., 1984—95; past chair bd. trustees Phi Kappa Psi Endowment Found. Capt. USMC, 1952—54. Recipient Old Gold Goblet, DePauw U., 1987. Mem.: Nat. Assn. Scholars, Nat. Petroleum Coun., Assn. Governing Bds. of Univs. and Colls. (bd. dirs. 1993), Marine Corps Assn. (bd. govs. 1981—84), Minn. Petroleum Assn., Am. Petroleum Inst., Ind. Acad. (hon.), Nat. Soc. Sons of Am. Revolution, DePauw U. Alumni Assn. (bd. dirs. 1975—81, pres. 1979—81), Army and Navy Club (Washington), Woodhill Country Club, Spring Hill Country Club, Tralee Golf Club, Ballybunion Golf Club, Monterey Peninsula Country Club, The Minikahda Club, Sagamore of the Wabash, Am. Legion. Republican. Avocations: golf, fly fishing. Home: 3340 Hill Ln Wayzata MN 55391-2602 Office: Western Petroleum Co 9531 W 78th St Ste 102 Eden Prairie MN 55344-3897

EMISON, JANE BALE LARSON, interior designer; b. Dickinson, N.D., Sept. 30, 1946; d. Stanley Walter and Hazel Eleanor (Bartow) Bale. BS, N.D. State U., 1968. Cert. interior designer Minn. Home fashion coord. Montgomery Wards, Mpls., 1968—69; staff interior designer McClain, Hedman & Schultz, St. Paul, 1969—72; design mgr. Dayton's Contract Interiors, Mpls., 1972—73; v.p., contract mgr. Contemporary Designs, Inc., Mpls., 1973—79; pres., owner J.B. Larson Assocs., Inc., Mpls., 1979—, Jane Larson-Emison Designs, Deephaven, Minn., 1983—85. Mem. adv. bd. design dept. U. Minn. Coll. Home Econs., 1982—84. Mem. Gov.'s Residence Coun., 1993—97, WAMSO (Minn. Orch. Vol. Group), 1991—, chair decorations for symphony ball, 1995; mem. patron com. Friends of Mpls. Inst. Art, 1998—2000; mem. Minn. Hist. Soc., Harvard Mus. Natural History; hostess China benefit Minn. Internat. Ctr., 1993, chair decorations U.K. benefit, 2002; chair, Art in Bloom Mpls. Inst. Arts; trustee Boys and Girls Clubs of the Twin Cities, 1986—; chmn. bd. dirs. Boys and Girls Club of Mpls., 1993—95, co-chair $10M endowment campaign, 1996—98; bd. dirs. Boys and Girls Clubs of Twin Cities Found., 1996—; nat. Midwest trustee, mem. strategic planning com. Boys and Girls Clubs of Am., 1998—; mem. devel. com. Kidsfirst Scholarship Fund, 2000—. Recipient Merit award, Minn. Soc. AIA, 1979, Architecture Minn. Pubs. Design award, 1980, Architecture Minn. Advt. award excellence, 1981. Mem.: U.S. Golf Assn., Fashion Group, Mpls. C. of C. (cultural activities com. 1980), Inst. Bus. Designers, Ballybunion Golf Club (Ireland), Springhill Golf Club, Woodhill Country Club, Monterey Peninsula Country Club, The Minikahda Club, Lake Minnetonka Garden Club, PGA Tour Ptnrs. Club. Avocations: gardening, golf, travel, collecting antique and contemporary art glass. Home and Office: 3340 Hill Ln Wayzata MN 55391-2602

EMLEN, WARREN METZ, computer-related services company owner; b. Elizabeth, N.J., Oct. 12, 1932; s. Andrew Arnberg and Dorothy Emma (Metz) E.; m. Carol Ringold Taylor, Sept. 28, 1958; children: Deborah Emlen Baker, David Taylor, Anne Emlen Donohue. BS in Forestry, U. Calif., Berkeley, 1955; BSEE, Pa. State U., 1963; MS in Systems Mgmt., U. So. Calif., 1973; MA in Pub. Adminstrn., U. N.Mex., 1980. Jr. forester U.S. Forest Service, Klamath, Calif., 1955-56; electronic engr. USAF, Griffiss AFB, N.Y., 1967-87; cons. forester, ptnr. L&E Environ. Cons., Rome, N.Y., 1965-87; v.p., adminstrv. asst. BPLW Architects & Engrs., Inc., Albuquerque, 1988-94; adminstrv. asst. Lovelace Health Systems, 1994-95; adminstrv. coord. Molzen-Corbin & Assocs. P.A., 1995-96; cons. in field; sole propr. Bus. Solutions and Svcs., 1998-2001. Trustee DEDANE Trust, ANDOREM Trust; co-chmn. Industry Looks at Rome Air Devel. Ctr., Griffiss AFB, 1981; sec. Def. Intelligence Tech. forum, Washington, 1981-86; automated data processing cons., 1987-88, 96-97; adminstrv. asst., v.p. BPLW Architects& Engrs., Inc., Albuquerque, 1988-94; adminstrv. coord. Molzen-Corbin & Assocs., P.A., 1995-96. Contbr. numerous articles to profl. jours. Served to capt. USAF, 1956-67. Mem. IEEE (sr., chmn engring. mgmt. group Mohawk Valley sect. 1975-76), Armed Forces Comm. and Electronics Assn. Republican. Methodist. Avocations: stamp and coin collecting, investments, hiking, reading. Home and Office: 4871 Quail Ct Frederick CO 80504-5553

EMMA, LYNNE ANNE, healthcare administrator; b. Bethpage, N.Y., July 12, 1954; d. Charles P. and Evelyn M. (Calone) E. BSN, Tex. Christian U., 1976; MPH, UCLA, 1983. CCRN. Staff and charge nurse, critical care UCLA Med. Ctr., 1976-83; study nurse coord., vascular specialist VA Med. Ctr., West Los Angeles, Calif., 1983-86; nurse educator Hollywood Presybn. Med. Ctr., L.A., 1986-88, clin. nurse specialist, 1988-92; clin. dir. Good Samaritan Hosp., L.A., 1992-93; dir. case mgmt. and social svcs. HealthCare Ptnrs. Med. Group, L.A., 1993-96, v.p. population health, 1996-97; dir. med. ops. Cedars-Sinai Med. Network Svcs., Beverly Hills, Calif., 1997—2002; svc. line mgr. divsn. cardiology Cedars-Sinai Med. Ctr., L.A., 2002—. Mem. AACN, sigma Theta Tau.

EMMANOUILIDES, GEORGE CHRISTOS, physician, educator; b. Drama, Greece, Dec. 17, 1926; came to U.S., 1955; s. Christos Nicholas and Vassiliki (Jordanopoulos) E.; married; children: Nicholas, Elizabeth, Christopher, Martha, Sophia. MD, Aristotelion U., 1951; MS in Physiology, UCLA, 1963. Diplomate Am. Bd. Pediatrics (pediatric cardiology and neonatal-perinatal medicine). Asst. prof. UCLA, 1963-69, assoc. prof., 1969-73, prof., 1973-95, prof. emeritus, 1995—. Chief divsn. pediatric cardiology Harbor UCLA Med. Ctr., Torrance, Calif., 1963-95. Co-author: Practical Pediatric Electrocardiography, 1973; co-editor: Heart Disease in Infants, Children and Adolescents, 2d edit., 1977, Moss' Heart Disease in Infants, Children and Adolescents, 3d edit., 1983, 4th edit., 1989, 5th edit., 1995, Neonatal Cardiopulmonary Distress, 1988; contbr. more than 70 articles in field to profl. jours. Served as 2d lt. M.C., Greek Army, 1953-55. Recipient Sherman Mellincoff award UCLA Sch. Medicine, 1982, several rsch. awards Am. Heart Assn., 1965-83. Fellow Am. Acad. Pediatrics (cardiology sect., chmn. 1978-80, Founders award 1996), Am. Coll. Cardiology; mem. Am. Pediatric Soc., Soc. for Pediatric Rsch., Hellenic-Am. Med. Soc. (pres.), Acad. of Athens (corr. mem.). Clubs: Hellenic Univ. (Los Angeles) (bd. dirs.). Democrat. Greek Orthodox. Avocation: gardening. Home: 4619 Browndeer Ln Rolling Hills Estates CA 90275-3911 Office: Harbor-UCLA Med Ctr 1000 W Carson St Torrance CA 90502-2004 E-mail: gemmanou@ucla.edu.

EMMANUEL, JORGE AGUSTIN, chemical engineer, environmental consultant; b. Manila, Aug. 28, 1954; came to U.S., 1970; s. Benjamin Elmido and Lourdes (Orozco) E.; 1 child, Andres Layanglawin. BS in Chemistry, N.C. State U., 1976, MSChemE, 1978; PhD in Chem. Engring., U. Mich., 1988. Registered profl. engr., Calif., environ. profl.; cert. hazardous materials mgr. Process engr. Perry Electronics, Raleigh, N.C., 1973-74; rsch. asst. N.C. State U., Raleigh, 1977-78; rsch. chem. engr. GE Corp. R & D Ctr., Schenectady, N.Y., 1978-81; Amoco rsch. fellow U. Mich., Ann Arbor, 1981-84; sr. environ. analyst TEM Assocs., Inc., Emeryville, Calif., 1988-91; pres. Environ. & Engring. Rsch. Group, Hercules, Calif., 1991—. Environ. cons. to the Philippines, UN Devel. Program, 1992, 94; rsch. assoc. U. Calif., Berkeley, 1988-90. Contbr. articles to profl. jours. Mem. Assn. for Asian Studies, Ann Arbor, 1982-88; sec. Alliance for Philippine Concerns, L.A., 1983-91; assoc. Philippine Resource Ctr., Berkeley, 1988-92; bd. dirs. ARC-Ecology, San Francisco, 1990—, Asia Pacific Ctr., Washington, 1995-2000; bd. advisors Urban Habitat, 1995-2002; chmn. bd. Filipino-Am. Coalition for Environ. Solutions, 2001-03. N.C. State U. grantee, 1976, Phoenix grantee U. Mich., 1982. Mem. NSPE, AAAS, Air and Waste Mgmt. Assn., Calif. Acad. Scis., N.Y. Acad. Sci., Filipino-Am. Soc. Architects and Engrs. (exec. sec. 1989-90, Svc. award 1990). Avocations: classical guitar, ethnomusicology, asian studies. Office: The Environ & Engring Rsch Group 628 2nd St Rodeo CA 94572-1111

EMMANUEL, RAHM, former federal official, investment banker; Asst. to Pres., polit. affairs div., dep. dir. comms. Polit. Affairs Office, Washington, 1993-99; mng. dir. Wasserstein & Perella, Chgo., 1999—. Office: Wasserstein & Perella Ste 5700 3 1st National Plaza Chicago IL 60602

EMMEL, BRUCE HENRY, retired secondary education mathematics educator; b. St. Cloud, Minn., Jan. 8, 1942; s. Henry Joseph and Mary Ann Emily (Kangas) E.; m. Phyllis Wanda Campbell, Aug. 29, 1982; children: Debra Lynn Huber, Kathi Marie, Brent Boyd, Daniel Henry Huber, Brandi Rose, Joseph Skye Olson. BS, St. Cloud State U., 1967; MA in Edn., Ball State U., 1973; PhD, Univ. N.D., 2002. Cert. vocat. tchr., Minn. Tchr. Lincoln Jr. High Sch., Hibbing, Minn., 1967-70, West Concord (Minn.) High Sch., 1970-72; vocat. tchr. Moorhead (Minn.) Tech. Coll., 1972-90; tchr. Moorhead Pub. Schs., 1984-2000, ret. Mem. Dist. Math. Com., Moorhead, 1978-2000. Comdr. Fargo (N.D.) CAP, 1984-86, 89, 94-96; dir. pub. affairs N.D. CAP, Mandan, 1986-89; precinct chmn. Dem. Com., Moorhead, 1968-90. Mem. Phi Delta Kappa, Kappa Delta Pi. Congregationalist. Avocations: flying, aircraft builder, hunting, walking, traveling. Home: 1121 3rd St S Moorhead MN 56560-4015

EMMELUTH, BRUCE PALMER, investment company executive, venture capitalist; b. L.A., Nov. 30, 1940; s. William J. and Elizabeth L. (Palmer) E.; children: William J. II (dec.), Bruce Palmer Jr., Carrie E.; m. Canda E. Samuels, Mar. 29, 1987. Sr. investment analyst corp. fin. dept. Prudential Ins. Co. Am., L.A., 1965-70; with Seidler Amdec Securities, Inc., 1970-90, sr. v.p., mgr. corp. fin. dept., 1974-90, also bd. dirs.; gen. ptnr. VK Ventures, VK Capital, 1990—2000; exec. v.p., sr. mng. dir., mgr. corp. fin. dept., mem. exec. com., mem. mgmt. com., bd. dirs. Wells Fargo Van Kasper, LA, 2000—01; exec. v.p., sr. mng. dir. investment banking Van Kasper & Co., L.A., 1990—99, First Security Van Kasper, 1999—2000, Wells Fargo Securities, 2001—03. Pres., bd. dirs. SAS Capital Corp., venture capital subs. Seidler Amdec Securities, 1977-90; bd. advisors Entrepreneurial Studies Program, Anderson Grad. Sch. Mgmt. UCLA, 1985. Active Calvary Ch., Pacific Palisades, Calif. With U.S. Army N.G., 1965-71. Home: 16 Augusta Lane Santa Barbara CA 93108

EMMER, BARBARA LOUISE, librarian, consultant; b. Charleroi, Pa., Apr. 11, 1947; d. William John and Helen Martha (Radzik) E. BS in Edn., Clarion U. Pa., 1969, cert. advanced studies, 1989; MLS, U. Pitts., 1978. Libr. dir. Pa. State U., DuBois, 1984-89; libr. Ridgway (Pa.) Area Sch. Dist., 1969-84, Brockway (Pa.) Area Sch. Dist., 1989—. Sec. Riverview Libr. Consortium, Shippenville, Pa., 1990-93, chmn., 2001-03; reviewer, cons. Choice 1985-89. Pres. Friends of the Libr., DuBois, 1989-91; mem. hosp. aux. DuBois Regional Med. Ctr., 1985—. Mem. AAUW (bd. dirs. 1979—, legis. chair 1990—, Woman of Yr. 1991), NEA, ALA (chair off-campus libr. svcs. 1988-89), Pa. State Edn. Assn., Pa. Sch. Librs. Assn. (regional rep. 1996—), Brockway Area Edn. Assn. (sec. 1991-93), DuBois Area Coun. on the Arts, DuBois Hist. Soc. (print libr. and property com. 1994—), Delta Kappa Gamma Soc., Beta Phi Mu. Home: 526 1st St Du Bois PA 15801-3059 Office: Brockway Schs 100 Alexander St Brockway PA 15824-1016

EMMERICH, KAROL DENISE, foundation executive, daylily hybridizer, former retail executive; b. St. Louis, Nov. 21, 1948; d. George Robert and Dorothy (May) Van Houten; m. Richard James, Oct. 18, 1969; 1 son, James Andrew. BA, Northwestern U., 1969; MBA, Stanford U., 1971. Nat. divsn. account officer Bank of Am., San Francisco, 1971-72; fin. analyst Dayton Hudson Corp., Mpls., 1972-73, sr. fin. analyst, 1973-74, mgr. short term financing, 1974-76, asst. treas., 1976-79, treas., 1979—, v.p., 1980-93; exec. fellow U. St. Thomas Grad. Sch. Bus., 1993—; pres. Emmerich Found., Edina, Minn., 1993—. Bd. dirs. Slumberland. Bd. dirs. Hemerocallis Soc. Minn., Royal Treasure. Mem. Minn. Women's Econ. Roundtable. Home and Office: 7302 Claredon Dr Edina MN 55439-1722

EMMERICH, WERNER SIGMUND, physicist, educator; b. Dusseldorf, Germany, June 3, 1921; s. Adolph and Julia (Frank) E.; m. Eva G. Pauson, June 13, 1953; children— Fay Lillian, Ralph Austin, Bertram Frank BS, Ohio State U., 1949, MS, 1950, PhD, 1953. Research physicist Westinghouse Research and Devel. Ctr., Pitts., 1954-57, adv. physicist, 1957-64, mgr. arc and plasma research, 1964-73, dir. applied physics, 1973-75, dir. corp. research, 1975-79, dir. power systems, 1979-83, dir. corp. and comml. research, 1983-86; retired, 1986. Author: Fast Neutron Physics, 1963; patentee in field Served with AUS, 1942-46, ETO Fellow Am. Phys. Soc.; mem. AAAS (life), Sigma XI, Phi Beta Kappa, Zeta Beta Tau Home: 1883 Beulah Rd Pittsburgh PA 15235-5004

EMMERMAN, MICHAEL N, financial analyst; b. Bklyn., Oct. 7, 1945; s. Leon and Ida E.; m. Janet Louise Goldman, Dec. 20, 1969 (div. Apr. 1978); children: Daniel Blake, Karen Stacey; m. Patricia Anne Stockhausen, Sept. 9, 1995; 1 child, Thomas Justin Stockhausen Emmerman. BBA, Pace U., 1966; MBA, L.I. U., 1967. Bd. cert. forensic examiner; diplomate Am. Bd. Forensic Examiners. Security analyst Standard & Poor's Inc., N.Y.C., 1965-68; sr. security analyst Arnhold & S. Bleichroeder Inc., N.Y.C., 1968-69; dir. managed accounts Lombard, Nelson, McKenna & Paganucci, N.Y.C., 1970-72; pres. Dominick Mgmt. Co., N.Y.C., 1972-74; mng. dir., money mgr. Neuberger Berman L.L.C., N.Y.C., 1974—. Co-founder, bd. dirs. Kentek Info. Sys. Inc., Boulder, Colo., 1980-97. Author: Flying and Diving: A New Look, 1987; contbr. articles to jours. in med. and underwater sci. fields. Vice chmn. Fed. Drug Agts. Found., Inc.; hon. dep. chief N.Y.C. Police Dept.; advisor N.Y. Police Dept. Harbor Unit Scuba Team; hon. battalian chief Fire Dept. N.Y.; govt. liaison officer ARC; trustee Long Island U. Fellow Fin. Analysts Fedn., Explorers Club; mem. N.Y. Soc. Security Analysts (accredited sr. security analyst), Undersea and Hyperbaric Med. Soc., Am. Acad. Underwateer Scis., Nat. Assn. Underwater Instrs. (life), Profl. Assn. Diving Instrs. (instr. 1986—), Princeton Club. Avocations: underwater exploration, squash, music. Office: Neuberger Berman LLC 605 3d Ave 38th Fl New York NY 10158-3698

EMMERSON, ARCHIE ALDIS (RED EMMERSON), sawmill owner; b. 1929; Mgr. R.H. Emmerson & Son, 1949—52, 1954—69; pres. now Sierra Pacific Industries, Redding, Calif. Office: Sierra Pacific Industries 19794 Riverside Ave Redding CA 96007 also: PO Box 496028 Redding CA 96049-6028*

EMMERT, GILBERT ARTHUR, engineer, educator; b. Merced, Calif., June 2, 1938; s. Allan Valentine and Mildred (Vanderbilt) E.; m. Nancy Sue Johnson, June 12, 1964; children: David Allan, Daniel Andrew. BS, U. Calif., Berkeley, 1961; MS, Rensselaer Poly. Inst., Troy, N.Y., 1964; PhD, Stevens Inst. Tech., Hoboken, N.J., 1968. Analytical engr. United Tech. Corp., East Hartford, Conn., 1961-64; asst. prof. U. Wis., Madison, 1968-72, assoc. prof., 1972-79, prof., 1979—, dept. chair, 1992-01. Contbr. articles to profl. jours. Mem. AIAA, Am. Physical Soc., Am. Nuclear Soc. Office: U Wis Dept Engring Physics 1500 Engineering Dr Madison WI 53706-1609 E-mail: emmert@engr.wisc.edu.

EMMERT, RICHARD EUGENE, retired industrial and professional association executive; b. Iowa City, Iowa, Feb. 23, 1929; s. Frank Thomas and Okie Leona (Seydel) E.; m. Marilyn Ruth Marner, June 19, 1949; children: Debra Sue Emmert Warrington, Andrea Gale Emmert Mazzuca, Lisa Alison Emmert Grant. BS, U. Iowa, 1951; MS, U. Del., 1952, PhD, 1954; DSc (hon.), Manhattan Coll., 1992. Supt. mfg. textile fibers dept. E.I. du Pont de Nemours & Co., Martinsville, 1966-67, mgr. engring. tech. and materials rsch. Wilmington, 1969-73, dir. rsch. and devel. pigments dept., 1973-75, dir. instrument products, photo products dept., 1975-77, dir. electronic products, photo products dept., 1977-79, gen. mgr. textile fibers dept., 1979-80, v.p. corp. plans, 1980-83, v.p. electronics dept., 1984-87; exec. dir. AIChE, N.Y.C., 1988-96, ret., 1996. Trustee U. Del. Rsch. Found., Newark, 1987—, pres., 1994-2000; commencement spkr. Coll. Engring., U. Iowa, 1995. Author: Gas Absorption and Solvent Extraction, 1963; contbr. articles to profl. jours. Vice chmn. Stanton Sch. Bd., Del., 1961-64; chmn. adv. bd. Coll. Engring., U. Iowa, Iowa City, 1974-80; chmn. adv. bd. dept. chem. engring. U. Calif., Berkeley, 1978-87, chmn., 1982-83; co-chmn. adv. bd. dept. chem. engring. U. Del., Newark, 1984-88, mem. Coll. Engring. adv. coun., 1995—; trustee Christiana Care Health Sys., Wilmington, 1983—; pres. Del. Found. for Phys. Edn. (now Del. Tennis Found.), Wilmington, 1984-86. With U.S. Army, 1954-56. Recipient 1st Disting. Engring. Alumni award U. Del., 1984, Medal of Distinction, U. Del., 1993, Disting. Alumni award U. Iowa, 1988, Kenneth Andrew Roe award Am. Assn. of Engring. Socs., 1996, Disting. Engring. Alumni Acad. award U. Iowa, 1996. Fellow AIChE (Van Antwerpen award 1998); mem. Nat. Acad. Engring., Del. Tennis Assn. (pres. 1982-83), United Engring. Found. (trustee 1988-2001), Chem. Heritage Found. (dir. 1998—), Tau Beta Pi, Sigma Xi, Phi Eta Sigma. Republican. Presbyterian. Avocation: tennis. Home: 24 Brandywine Falls Rd Wilmington DE 19806-1002

EMMETT, JOHN COLIN, retired inventor, consultant; b. Bradford, Yorkshire, Eng., Apr. 27, 1939; BS, PhD, London U. Former rsch. team leader SmithKline Beecham Corp.; cons. Euromedica Ltd. Co-inventor over 100 patents in field. Office: Nat Inventors Hall of Fame 221 S Broadway St Akron OH 44308-1505

EMMETT, MICHAEL, physician, educator; b. Linz, Austria, Oct. 29, 1945; arrived in U.S., 1949; s. Issac and Pearl (Gladstone) E.; m. Rachel Kozuch, Aug. 2, 1969; children: Mira, Daniel, Joshua. BS, Pa. State U., 1967; MD, Temple U., 1971. Diplomate Am. Bd. Internal Medicine, Am. Bd. Internal Medicine, Nephrology. Intern, then resident Yale U. Med. Ctr., New Haven, 1971-74; nephrology fellow Hosp. U. of Pa., Phila., 1974-76; clin. asst. prof. medicine U. Tex. Southwestern Med. Sch., Dallas, 1976-80, clin. assoc. prof. medicine, 1980-85, clin. prof. medicine, 1985—; Ralph Tompsett prof. medicine Baylor U. Med. Ctr., Dallas, 1986—, dir., nephrology/metabolism, 1986-96, dir. nephrology endocrinology labs, 1986—, chief of medicine, 1996—. Cons. physician Parkland Hosp., Dallas, 1976—, Presbyn. Hosp., Dallas, 1976—. Contbr. articles to profl. jours. Fellow ACP; mem. Am. Fedn. Clin. Rsch., Dallas County Med. Soc., Tex. Med. Assn., So. Med. Soc., Am. Soc. Nephrology, Internat. Soc. Nephrology. Avocations: tennis, skiing. Office: Baylor U Med Ctr 3500 Gaston Ave Dallas TX 75246-2096 E-mail: m.emmett@baylorhealth.edu.

EMMETT, RITA, professional speaker; b. Chgo., Apr. 12, 1943; d. Thomas Henry Dorney and Helen Fischer; m. Bruce Karder, May 21, 1994; children: Robb Sean, Kerry Shannon. BA in English, Northeastern Ill. U., 1979; MS in Adult and Cont. Edn, Nat. Louis U., Evanston, Ill., 1985. Coord. edn. programs Leyden Family Svc., Franklin Park, Ill., 1977-95; pres. Emmett Enterprises, Inc., Des Plaines, 1994—. Adj. faculty Triton Coll., River Grove, Ill., 1977-99,

Wright Coll., Chgo., 1985-99; presenter in field. Author: The Procrastinator's Handbook: Mastering the Art of Doing It Now; The Procrastinating Child: A Handbook for Adults to Help Children Stop Putting Things Off; Great Speakers Anthology; contbr. articles to newspapers and mags. Pres. Parent's Club, River Grove, 1987-88; keynote spkr. Gov.'s Mansion, Springfield, Ill. Mem. Bus. and Profl. Women (Achievement award 1986), Assn. Consultation and Edn. (sec.), Ill. Prevention Network, Century Club, Nat. Spkrs. Assn., Profl. Spkr.'s of Ill. (bd. dirs. 1995-96, 2002-03). Roman Catholic. Avocations: reading, writing, travel, friends. E-mail: rita@ritaemmett.com.

EMMONS, ROBERT DUNCAN, diplomat; b. Los Angeles, Mar. 1, 1932; s. Richard Norman and Margaret Houston (Kelly) E.; m. Susan Mary Likeman, Aug. 23, 1958; 1 child, Robert Campbell; m. Carolyn Elizabeth Kingsley, Sept. 27, 1995. BA, UCLA, 1954, LL.B., 1957. Contract adminstr. N.Am. Aviation, Inc., Los Angeles, 1958-60, 62-63; contract adminstr. Litton Industries, Los Angeles, 1961; fgn. service officer Dept. State, Washington, 1963-88; vice consul, 3d sec. Am. embassy, Beirut, 1963-65; consul Am. consulate, St. John, N.B., Can., 1966-68; program officer AID, Saigon, Vietnam, 1968-70; sr. watch officer Dept. State, Washington, 1970-71; chief consular sect. Am. embassy, Warsaw, Poland, 1972-74, counselor of embassy Copenhagen, 1974-76, consul gen. Kingston, Jamaica, 1976-78; office dir. Dept. State, Washington, 1978-80; chief immigration br. Am. embassy, London, 1980-84; consul gen. Am. consulate gen., Tijuana, Mex., 1984-87; retired, 1988. Recipient Vietnam award, Dept. State, 1969. Mem.: Calif. State Bar.

EMMONS, WILLIAM MONROE, III, business educator, consultant; b. Atlanta, Nov. 6, 1959, s. William Monroe Jr. and Frances Belle (Cook) E. AB, Harvard U., 1981, MBA, 1985, PhD, 1989. Rsch. asst. Mgmt. Analysis Ctr., Inc., Cambridge, Mass., 1981-83; with Harvard U., Boston, 1984-99, instr. Bus. Sch., 1987, 89, asst. prof. Bus. Sch., 1989-94, assoc. prof. Bus. Sch., 1994-99; assoc. prof. McDonough Sch. Bus. Georgetown U., Washington, 2000—. Regional screening dir. Am. Field Svc., 1989-95; bd. dirs. New Opera Theatre Ensemble, Boston, 1989-98, GLSEN, 1998—; bd. dirs. Coro Allegro, 1998—, pres., 2000—. Baker scholar Harvard U., 1985, dean's doctoral fellow, 1985-88. Mem. Am. Econs. Assn., Phi Beta Kappa. Avocations: singing, photography. Home: 144 W Canton St Boston MA 02118-1216 Office: Georgetown U MSB G-4 Old North Washington DC 20057 E-mail: wme@georgetown.edu.

EMMONS JR. CHARLES N. music educator; s. Charles N Emmons Sr. and Dorothy H Emmons; m. Carol Ann Blachley, June 13, 1964; children: Philip Shin Emmons, Benjamin Tae Emmons. MusB, So. Meth. U., Dallas, 1964, MusM, 1965. Cert. tchg. Tx, Ks, Il, 1965. Band and orch. tchr. Wichita Pub. Sch.-Roosevelt Jr. High, Wichita, Kans., 1965—67; music and drama dept. chair and dir. of instrumental music Wichita H.S. West, Wichita Pub. Schools, Wichita, Kans., 1967—78; dir. of orchestral activities New Trier West H.S., Sch. Dist. #203, Winnetka, Ill., 1978—79, Deerfield and Highland Pk. H.S., Sch. Dist. #113, Highland Pk., Ill., 1979—2001; dir. of string music edn. VanderCook Coll. of Music, Chgo., 2002—; band dir. Trinity Internat. U., Deerfield, Ill., 2002—03. Stage mgr., adminstrv. coord., band and orch. dir. Interlochen Ctr. for the Arts, Interlochen, Mich., 1962—91; dist. and state orch. chairperson Kans. Music Educators Assn., Wichita, Kans., 1972—77; dist. vii orch. chairperson Ill. Music Educators Assn., LaSalle, Ill., 1981—85; dist. vii pres. Ill. Music Educators Assn. Bd. of Directors, LaSalle, Ill., 1985—88; orch. divsn. v.p. Ill. Music Educators Assn. Bd. of Dir., LaSalle, Ill., 1988—92; program task force chairperson Am. String Teachers Assn., Montgomery, Ill., 2001—. Dir.(orchestra and jazz band director): (Nat. Band Assn. Citation for Excellence, 1976, Quinlan and Fabish Outstanding Chicagoland Pub. Sch. Tchr., 1992, Am. String Teachers Assn. Outstanding Pub. Sch. Tchr., 1995);, musician (member of the focus on the arts music). Mem. of the youth commn. Wilmette Village Bd., Wilmette, Ill., 1983—85; chair or staff parish rels. Trinity United Meth. Ch., Wilmette, Ill., 1986—88, chair of the adminstrv. bd., 1994—96, chair of the stewardship com., 1997—97, mem. of the organ com., 1999—2002. Airman first class Tex. Air N.G., 1960—66, Grand Prarie, TX. Recipient Pi Kappa Lambda, So. Meth. U., 1965; scholar Music Performance Scholarship, So. Meth. U., Meadows Sch. of the Arts, 1959-1965. Mem.: Am. String Teachers Assn. with NSOA (program task force chair 2001—03, Outstanding Pub. Sch. Teachers 1995), Music Educators Nat. Conf. (il dist. vii pres. and il orchestral divsn. v.p. 1988—92), NEA (life), Phi Mu Alpha, SInfonia (life; delta upsilon pres. and sec. 1962—64). Meth. Avocations: travel, golf, reading, games. Home: 445 Pine Manor Dr Wilmette IL 60091 Office: VanderCook Coll Music 3140 S Federal St Chicago IL 60616-3731 Personal E-mail: c.emmons@comcast.net. E-mail: cemmons@vandercook.edu.

EMOND, LIONEL JOSEPH, management consultant; b. Winnipeg, Man., Can., May 31, 1932; s. Henri R. and Anastasia E.; m. Elisabeth Boelen, Sept. 9, 1957; children: Catherine, Pierre, Marise, Robert. B in Comerce, McGill U., 1953, MBA, 1957. Chartered acct., Can. Pvt. practice auditing, 1953-55; with Shell Oil Co. of Can., Montreal, 1955-58; mgr. fiscal dept. Can. Chem. & Cellulose Co., 1958-60; asst. corp. contr. Kruger Pulp & Paper Co., 1960-62, contr., 1962-65; mgr. fin. Dominion Bridge Co., Montreal, 1965-68; asst. gen. mgr. Churchill Falls Project, 1968-70; sr. fin. cons. Acres Internat., 1970-71; v.p. fin. Can. Gen. Ins. Co., 1971-75; v.p., treas. United Coops. of Ont., Toronto, 1976-80; v.p. fin. svcs. The S.N.C. Group, Montreal, 1980-83; ptnr. Guerra Emond Internat. Mgmt. Cons., 1983-85; pres., sec. L.J. Emond Cons., Inc., Eastman, Can., 1986—. Lectr. fin. Concordia U.; lectr. project mgmt. U. Helsinki. Mem. editl. bd. Cost. and Mgmt., 1965—; contbr. articles to profl. jours. Pres. Etobicoke Rate Payers Assn., 1978-80; bd. mgmt. Etobicoke Olympium, 1977-80; exec. com. Canadian Coop. Credit Soc., 1977-80; bd. dirs. Richardson Hosp. Ctr., 1996—, Ctre for Literacy, Que., 1999-, Knowlton Playhouse, 2001-02. Recipient citation Can. Coop. Credit Soc., 1980. Mem. Fin. Exec. Inst. (pres. 1986-87), Inst. Chartered Accts., Soc. Mgmt. Accts., Am. Assn. Cost Engrs., Montreal Amateur Athletic Assn., Les Artisanats Centre-ville Montreal (pres. 1984-90), Rotary Vieux Montreal (pres. 1995-96, Dist. Svc. award 1997). Roman Catholic. Home and Office: PO Box 261 583 Rt 112 Eastman QC Canada J0E 1P0

EMORY, LEE (WHITNEY EDEN), writer; b. Eureka, Calif., Dec. 5, 1943; d. James Oliver Emory and Doris Jean Walls; m. Richard G Rosengreen, Sr., Sept 8, 1990; children from previous marriage: Nicholas A. Stivers, Callie Anne Cribbs. At, South Seattle C. C., U. Wash, Seattle. Buyer The Boeing Co., Seattle. Tech. writer The Boeing Co., Seattle, tech. editor. Author: (novels) A Call to Magic, Gatekeeper's Promise, Gatekeeper's Challenge, Hot Rod's Law, Love Donor, Counselor at Large, Last Act of Grace. Hon. co-chmn. Nat. Rep. Party, Washington, 2003; mem. Ariz. congressional com. Recipient Business-woman of the Year. Fax: 520-458-5618.

EMORY, SAMUEL THOMAS, retired educator; b. Durham, N.C., June 22, 1933; s. Samuel Thomas and Mary (Dortch) E.; m. Sylvia Callaway; children: Samuel Thomas III, Greer Callaway. AB, U. N.C., 1954, MA, 1959; PhD, U. Md., 1964. With Mary Washington Coll., Fredericksburg, Va., 1959—, assoc. prof., 1965—68, prof., 1968—88, disting. prof., 1988—98. Adj. prof. Va. Commonwealth U., Richmond, 1960—91, USMC Staff and Command Coll., 1975—80, U. Richmond, 1968—78; faculty rep. to bd. visitors Mary Washington Coll., Fredericksburg, Va., 1988—89; mem. Faculty Senate of Va., Richmond, 1989—90; pres. Sammy T's Inc., 1987—. Contbr. articles to profl. jours. Cpl. USAR, 1953—61. Fellow: Am. Geographical Soc.; mem.: Assn. Am. Geographers, Kappa Sigma. Republican. Episcopalian. Home: 608 Hawke St Fredericksburg VA 22401-3645

EMPERADO, MERCEDES LOPEZ, librarian; b. Manila, Aug. 9, 1941; came to U.S., 1969; d. Evaristo Villasor and Marina (Gallardo) Lopez; m. Conrado Emperado, June 30, 1968; children: Joshua Caleb, Marita Eve. BS in Elem. Edn., Philippine Normal Coll., 1963; MLS, Cath. U. Am., 1974. Libr. math. and computation lab. Fed. Preparedness Agy., Washington, 1976-79; libr. Fed. Emergency Mgmt. Agy., Washington, 1979—. Mem. ALA, Am. Soc. Info. Sci., Spl. Librs. Assn., Nat. Coordinating Coun. on Emergency Mgmt. Baptist. Home: 6303 Elm Way Clinton MD 20735-3928 Office: Fed Emergency Mgmt Agy Libr 500 C St SW Washington DC 20024-2523

EMPEY, GENE F. real estate executive; b. Hood River, Oreg., July 13, 1923; BS in Animal Husbandry, Oreg. State U., 1949; M. of Tech. Journalism Iowa State U., 1950; m. Janet Halladay, Dec. 27, 1950; children: Stephen Bruce, Michael Guy. Publs. dir. U. Nev., Reno, 1950-55; mgr. Zephyr Cove Lodge Hotel, Lake Tahoe, Nev., 1955-65; owner Empey Co., real estate agy., Carson City and Tahoe, Nev., 1964—; land developer, owner investment and brokerage firm . Mem. Nev. Planning Bd., 1959-72, chmn., 1961-66; mem. Nev. Tax Commn., 1982—; participant People to People Program, China, 1996, Egypt, Jordan, 1997. Capt., inf. U.S. Army, 1943-47; PTO. Grad. Realtors Inst. Mem. Nat. Assn. Realtors, (cert. comml. investment mem.; pres. Nev. chpt.), Tahoe Douglas C. of C. (pres. 1962, dir.), Carson City C. of C., Carson-Tahoe-Douglas Bd. Realtors, Capital City Club, Rotary, Heavenly Valley Ski (pres. 1968) Club, The Prospector's Club (Reno). Republican. Home: PO Box 707 Zephyr Cove NV 89448-0707 Office: 512 S Curry St Carson City NV 89703-4614

EMPEY, KERRY MCGARR, pharmacist; d. Scott Elliot and Charlene McGarr; m. Philip Earle Empey, Sept. 2, 2000. PharmD, U. of RI, 1999; PhD candidate, U. of Ky., 2002—. Cert. Pharmacy Practice Residency U. of Ky., 2000, Profl. Tchg. cert. U. of Ky., 2001. Clin. pharmacy practice resident U. of Ky. Hosp., Lexington, 1999—2000, clin. infectious diseases splty. resident, 2000—01, clin. infectious diseases pharmacist, 2001, hosp. pharmacist, 1999—; clin. pharm. sciences phd candidate U. of Ky., Lexington, 2001—. Pharmacist for pharmacy benefits mgmt. co. ProMark, Wakefield, RI, 1996 97; retail pharmacist CVS Pharmacy, Greenville, RI, 1998—99. Author many pharmacy/med. jours. Mem. Am. Assn. Health-Sys. Pharmacists, ASHP, Balt., 1996. Fellow Infectious Diseases Splty. Residency Funding, Wyeth Ayerst, 2001. Mem.: ACCP (assoc.), ASHP (assoc.). Achievements include research in Improve infectious diseases outcomes. Office Fax: 859-323-2049.

EMRICH, EDMUND MICHAEL, lawyer; b. N.Y.C., Apr. 12, 1956; s. Edmund and Mary Ann (Picarella) E. BA, SUNY, Albany, 1978; JD, Hofstra U., 1981. Bar: N.Y. 1982, U.S. Dist. Ct. (so. and ea. dists.) N.Y. 1982, U.S. Ct. Appeals (2d cir.) 1987. Law clk. to presiding justice U.S. Bankruptcy Ct. (ea. dist.) N.Y., Westbury, 1982-83; assoc. Levin & Weintraub & Crames, N.Y.C., 1983-90, Kaye, Scholer, Fierman, Hays & Handler, N.Y.C., 1990-92, ptnr., 1993—. Local rules com. U.S. Bankruptcy Ct. (ea. dist.) N.Y., 1985-86; mem. local rules drafting subcom. U.S. Bankruptcy Ct. (so. dist.) N.Y., 1985-86, 95-98. Mem. Hofstra U. Law Rev., 1981-82. Mem. ABA, N.Y. State Bar Assn., Am. Bankruptcy Inst. Avocations: golf, tennis, wine collecting. Home: 300 E 85th St New York NY 10028-4500 Office: Kaye Scholer LLP 425 Park Ave New York NY 10022-3506 E-mail: eemrich@kayescholer.com.

EMRICH, JEANNE ANN, poet, artist; b. Mpls. d. George Jacob Emrich and Janis Virginia (Elstone) Emrich Erickson; m. Glenn Merle Eriksen, Jan. 17, 1981; children: Stephanie, Anthony. BA in Art History, U. Minn., 1969. Pub., founder Lone Egret Press, Mpls., 1996—2003; founder. first editor HAIGA Online, Mpls., 1998—2001; tchr. The Loft Lit. Ctr., Mpls., 1998—2000. Author (editor): (book) The Haiku Habit, 1996, Barely Dawn, 1999, Berries and Cream: Contemporary Haiga in North America, 2000, Reeds: Contemporary Haiga, 2003. Bd. dirs. Bloomington Art Ctr., 1994—98. Recipient H.G. Henderson award, Haiku Soc. Am., 1995, 2001. Mem.: Nat. League of Am. Penwomen (pres. br. and state assn. Minn. chpt. 1998-2000), Minn. Artists Assn. (pres. 1988-90), Minn. Watercolor Soc. (co-founder, first pres. 1983-86), Minn. Haiku Soc. (co-founder 2003), Rendezvous Minn. (co-founder, first pres. 1993-94). Avocations: nature study, painting. E-mail: jemrich@aol.com.

EMRICK, DONALD DAY, chemist, consultant; b. Waynesfield, Ohio, Apr. 3, 1929; s. Ernest Harold and Nellie (Day) E.; B.S. cum laude, Miami U., Oxford, Ohio, 1951; M.S., Purdue U., 1954, Ph.D., 1956 Grad. teaching asst. Purdue U., Lafayette, Ind., 1951-55; with chem. and phys. research div. Standard Oil Co. Ohio, 1955-64, research asso., 1961-64; cons., sr. research chemist research dept. Nat. Cash Register Co., Dayton, Ohio, 1965-72, chem. cons., 1972—. Mem. AAAS, Am. Chem. Soc., Phi Beta Kappa, Sigma Xi. Patentee in Field. Contbr. articles to profl. jours. Home: 4240 Lesher Dr Dayton OH 45429-3042

EMSLEY, SARAH LOUISE BAXTER, critic, educator; b. Edmonton, Alberta, Can., Sept. 8, 1973; d. John and Lorraine Baxter; m. Jason Emsley, Aug. 16, 1995. BA with honors, U. Alberta, 1995; MA, Dalhousie U., 1996, PhD, 2002. Lectr. Dalhousie U., Halifax, Canada, 1996—98. Author: St. Paul's in the Grand Parade, 1749, 1999. Doctoral fellow, Social Sci. Humanities Rsch. Coun. Can., 1998—2002, postdoctoral fellow, 2002—, doctoral fellow, Izaak Walton Killam Meml. Trust, 1999—2002, postdoctoral fellow, Rothermere Am. Inst., U. Oxford, 2002—. Mem.: MLA, Edith Wharton Soc., Assn. Can. Coll. and Univ. Tchrs. English, Jane Austen Soc. N.Am., Harvard Neighbors (bd. dirs. 2002—). Home: One Emerson Pl Apt 10F Boston MA 02114 Office: Rothermere Am Inst 1A S Parks Rd Oxford OX1 3TG England Personal E-mail: semsley@fas.harvard.edu. E-mail: sarah.emsley@rai.ox.ac.uk.

EMSLIE, WILLIAM ARTHUR, electrical engineer; b. Denver, Oct. 30, 1947; s. William Albert and Hazel Esther (Niles) E.; m. Tracey Jane Palmer, Feb 22, 1975; children: David Barrett, Andrew Niles, Charles William, Alexis Claire. BSEE, U.S. Naval Acad., 1971; MSEE, Mich. State U., 1972. Registered profl. engr., Colo. Commd. ensign USN, 1971, advanced through grades to capt., 1997; commdg. officer 6 naval res. units USNR, 1978—2001; energy conversion engr. Pub. Svc. Co. of N.Mex., Albuquerque, 1978-79; mgr. engr. Horizon Tech., Ft. Collins, Colo., 1979-80; staff engr. Platte River Power Authority, Ft. Collins, 1980-85, planning supr., 1985-89, mgr. quality improvement, 1989-92, exec. engr., 1992-95, supr. engring. svcs., 1995-97, bus. planning mgr., 1997-2001, sr. project engr., constrn. mgr. GE Combustion Turbines, 2001—02. Mem. renewable task force Electric Power Rsch. Inst., Palo Alto, Calif., 1982-85, mgt. com. Western Energy Supply and Transmission Assocs., Albuquerque, 1991-2000, vice chair, 1994-95, chair, 1996—; chmn. Am. Pub. Power Assn. Demonstration of Energy Efficient Devels. Bd., Washington, 1992-94; project engr. installation three Gen. Electric 7 EA combustion turbines Platte River Power Authority's Rawhide Energy Sta. Chmn. campaign Ft. Collins Area United Way, 1986, pres. bd. dirs., 1988; chmn. Sch. Mill Levy Tax Com., Ft. Collins, 1988. Grantee State of Colo., Am. Public Power Assn./Demonstration of Energy Efficient Devels., Western Energy Supply and Transmission Assocs., U.S. Dept. Energy, City of Colorado Springs, 1986-90. Mem. IEEE, Foothills Rotary of Ft. Collins (pres. 1995-96). Achievements include research in photovoltics which provided a solar insolation assessment that is more accurate than the typical meterological year and a comprehensive evaluation of the effectiveness of 4 types of photovaltic systems. Home: 825 E Pitkin St Fort Collins CO 80524-3839 Office: Platte River Power Auth 2000 E Horsetooth Rd Fort Collins CO 80525-5721

EMSWILLER, JULIE L. not-for-profit developer; d. Frank R. and Linda K. Emswiller. BA, Purdue U., 1997. Credit reporter Crosby Sq. Credit & Collections, Inc., Frankfort, Ind., 1992—97; coord. devel. Wesley Manor Retirement Cmty., Inc., Frankfort, Ind., 1997—2000; devel. dir. Ind. Assn. Cities and Towns, Inc., Indpls., 2000—01, Janus Devel. Svcs., Inc., Noblesville, Ind., 2001—. Mem. Hamilton County Leadership Acad., Hamilton County, Ind., 2002—03. Mem.: Purdue Alumni Assn., Women of Moose, Kappa Alpha Theta Alumni Assn. Republican. Avocations: auto racing, golf, puzzles, board games. Office: Janus Developmental Services 1555 Westfield Road Noblesville IN 46060

ENAM, SYED ATHER, neurosurgeon, researcher; b. Sindri, Bihar, India, Nov. 21, 1961; s. Syed Enamul Haque and Razia Enam; m. Kishwar Fakhar, Jan. 1, 1989; children: Syed Faaiz, Syed Zayd, Syed Usman. MBBS, Dow Med. Coll., Karachi, Pakistan, 1987; PhD, Northwestern U., 1991. Diplomate Am. Bd. Neurol. Surgeons. Resident in gen. surgery SUNY, Buffalo, 1991-92; resident in neurosurgery Henry Ford Hosp., Detroit, 1992—97, chief resident in neurosurgery, 1997—98, chief Neurosurgery Assocs. of Macomb, 1998—2003; vice chmn. Dept. Neurosurgery Henry Ford Hosp., 2001—03; attending neurosurgeon William Beaumont Hosp., 2001—03, Oakwood Hosp. Med. Ctr., 2001—03; dir. clin. rsch. St. Joseph Mercy of Macomb Hosp., Mich., 2003; dir. neurosurg. svcs. William Beaumont Hosp., Troy, Mich., 2003; head, divsn. neurosurgery Aga Khan U., Karachi, Pakistan, 2003—. Contbr. chpts. to textbooks, articles to profl. jours. Recipient: Physician of the Year award St. Joseph's Mercy of Maycomb Hosp, 2002; Outstanding Resident award Henry Ford Med. Assn., 1998, 1st prize Midwest Soc. Electron Microscopists, 1991; Am. Health Assn. Found. fellow, 1990, Northwestern U. Dean's fellow, 1987; Quaid-e-Azam scholar/medal Bd. of Edn., Punjab, 1977. Fellow: Royal Coll. Surgeons Ireland, Royal Coll. Physicians and Surgeons Can.; mem.: Congress of Neurol. Surgeons, Rsch. Soc., World Fedn. Neurology, Am. Assn. Neurol. Surgeons, Soc. Neurosci., Sigma Xi (Grad. Rsch. Symposium award). Muslim. Achievements include research on cell biology of Alzheimer's Disease, neuron interaction and neuronal development, cell biology of brain tumor invasion; Immunotherapy for brain tumors. Home: E-138 Block 7 Gulshan Iqbal Karachi Pakistan Office: Henry Ford Hosp Dept Neurosurgery 2799 W Grand Blvd Detroit MI 48202-2689 Home: 5957 Teakwood Dr Troy MI 48085

ENARSON, HAROLD L. retired academic administrator; b. Villisca, Iowa, May 24, 1919; s. John and Hulda (Thorson) E.; m. Audrey Pitt, June 7, 1942; children: Merlyn Pitt Prentice, Elaine, Lisa. BA, U. N.Mex., 1940, L.H.D., 1981; MA, Stanford U., 1946; PhD, Am. U., 1951; L.H.D., Kent State U., 1972, U. Detroit, 1975, Ohio State U., 1981; D.P.S., Bethany Coll., 1975; LL.D., Miami U., Oxford, Ohio, 1978, U. Akron, 1981, Central State U., 1981; Dr. Pub. Service (hon.), U. W. Fla., 1986; LLD (hon.), SUNY, 1987; LHD (hon.), Cleve. State U., 1990, U. Nebr., CCNY, 1993; HHD, No. Mich. U., 1993. Teaching asst., research asst. Stanford U., 1940-41, asst. prof., 1949-50; examiner Bur. Budget, Washington, 1942-43, 46-49; asst. prof. Whittier Coll., 1949; exec. sec. Steel Industry Bd., summer 1949; cons. Nat. Security Resources Bd., summer 1950; spl. asst. White House, Washington, 1950-52; pub. mem. WSB, 1952-53; asst. dir. commerce City Phila., 1953; exec. sec. mayor Phila., 1954; exec. dir. Western Interstate Commn. Higher Edn., 1954-60, sr. advisor, 1981-99; adminstrv. v.p. U. N.Mex., 1960-61, acad. v.p., 1961-66, past project dir.; Internships in Latin Am.; pres. Cleve. State U., 1966-72, Ohio State U., Columbus, 1972-81, pres. emeritus, 1981—; Carl Hatch chair pub. adminstrn. U. N.Mex., 1982-83; Regents' prof. U. Calif., San Francisco, spring 1984. Carnegie Corp. adminstrs. fellowship, 1958; mem. Nat. Dental Research Council, 1958-62, surgeon gen.'s cons. group on med. manpower, 1960; cons. Ford Found., Egypt, 1960, C.Am., 1961-63, AID, 1965; dir. edn. svcs. Office Human Resources and Social Devel., 1963-64; nat. adv. health coun. USPHS, 1964-68, task force on reorgn., 1967, Nat. Com. on U.S.-China Rels., 1976—, Nat. Commn. for Coop. Edn., 1968-78, adv. com. U.S. Army Command and Gen. Staff Coll., 1975-78; planning com. Coun. for Fin. Aid to Edn., 1977-81; panelist nat. identification program for advancement women in higher edn. Am. Coun. on Edn., 1977-80, commn. on internat. edn., 1965-67, past mem. commn. on acad. affairs, coun. overseas liaison com., 1977-80, bd. dirs., 1970-73, 79-82; chmn. Inter-Univ. Coun. Ohio, 1979-80; sr. cons. Kellogg Nat. Fellows program W.K. Kellogg Found., 1981-85; pub. mem. U.S. Med. Licensing Exams., 1991-94. Trustee Am. Coll. Testing Program, 1979-82; mem. Nat. Coun. on Ednl. Rsch., 1980-81; mem. nat. sponsors com. Coun. for Internat. Exch. of Scholars, 1981-84; co-chmn. Com. on Future of SUNY, 1984; bd. visitors Air U., 1968-70; chmn. bd. dirs. Acad. Ind. Scholars, 1984-88. With AUS, 1943-46. Recipient Disting. Svc. award Pub. Sector, Assn. of Governing Bds. of Univs. and Colls., 1992. Mem. Nat. Assn. State Univs. and Land-Grant Colls. (chmn. internat. affairs com., mem. com. on financing higher edn., commn. on arts and scis. 1978, chmn. assn. and exec. com. 1980-81), Coun. of Presidents (chmn. 1978-79, mem. exec. com. 1978-79), Nat. Acad. Pub. Adminstrn., Assn. Urban Univs. (pres. 1971-72), Assn. Am. Univs. (health policy joint com. 1978-88), Am. Optometric Assn. (coun. on optometric edn. 1984-88), Rotary. Home: 2994 Nogales Ct Boulder CO 80301-1518

ENBYSK, H. MONTE, writer, editor; b. Oct. 22, 1953; BS in Journalism, U. Oreg., 1975, MS in Journalism, 1978. Reporter, editor Eastside Jour., Bellevue, Wash., 1984-95; mng. editor Wash. CEO Mag., Seattle, 1995-97; copy editor, writer MSN Money Ctrl., Redmond, Wash., 1997-98; comms. specialist Microsoft Corp., Redmond, Wash., 1998-2000; news editor, columnist Microsoft bCentral, Redmond, Wash., 2000—02, editor, 2002—. Office: One Microsoft Way Redmond WA 98052 E-mail: montee@microsoft.com.

ENCEL, SOLOMON, education educator, consultant; b. Warsaw, Mar. 3, 1925; arrived in Australia, 1929; s. Gustav and Ethel (Kutner) E.; m. Diana Helen, June 23, 1949; children: Vivien, Deborah, Daniel, Sarah. BA, U. Melbourne, 1949, MA, 1952, PhD, 1960. Lectr. U. Melbourne, Victoria, Australia, 1952-55; reader Australian Nat. U., Canberra, 1956-66; prof. U. New South Wales, Sydney, Australia, 1966-90, emeritus prof., 1990—. Commr. Edn. Commn. New South Wales, 1980-83; mem. Higher Edn. Bd. New South Wales, 1981-83; mem. Australian Sci. and Tech. Council, 1975; mem. Nat. Health and Med. Rsch. Coun., 1991-94; mem. com. on aging N.S.W., 1993-97. Author: Equality and Authority, 1970, Women and Society, 1974, Cabinet Government in Australia, 1974, The Japanese Connection, 1989, Ageing and Social Policy in Australia, 1997, Continuity, Commitment and Survival, 2003. With Australian Air Force, 1944-45. Fellow Australian Acad. Social Scis., Sociol. Assn. Australia (pres. 1969-71). Mem. Australian Labor party. Jewish. Club: U. New South Wales. Avocations: walking, music, wine. Office: Univ New South Wales Sydney NSW 2052 Australia E-mail: S.Encel@UNSW.edu.au.

ENDE, ARLYN RUTH, textile artist, arts administrator; b. New Orleans, Oct. 6, 1932; d. Harry Gerhard Ende and Ruth Wilhelmina Anderson; 1 child, Mark William Lovett; m. Jack B. Hastings, Sept. 17, 1987. Student, La. State U., 1949-51, Tulane U., 1951, The Art Inst. Chgo., 1951-52. Co-founder Dodge/Ende Assocs., N.Y.C., 1959-62; asst. to dir. urban design Boston Redevel. Authority, 1961-64; co-owner, designer Fogeater Art Wearables, Tucson and Block Island, R.I., 1967-72; exec. dir. The Arts Ctr., Woodbury, Tenn., 1991-95; textile designer, 1972—; dir. art gallery U. of the South, Sewanee, Tenn., 2000—. Craft coord. Rural Area Devel. Com., Woodbury, Tenn., 1989-92; tchr., adj. instr. Mid. Tenn. State U., Murfreesboro, 1986; workshop instr. Appalachian Ctr. for Crafts, Smithville, Tenn., 1994—. Nat. Fiber Forum, Nashville, 1996; mem. adv. bd. Tenn. Assn. Craft Artists, 1995-97. Prin. works include 11 elevator lobby wall textiles Vanderbilt U. Med. Ctr., 1985 (Design Competition winner), atrium textile Provident Life and Accident Ins. Co., Chattanooga, 1990, 3 maj. textiles Mid. Tenn. State U. Recreation Ctr., Murfreesboro, 1995. Recipient Grand Prize, Am. Craft Awards, 1989, Best of Show award Fiber Arts in the 90s, 1990. Mem. Am. Craft Coun., Surface Design Assn., Tenn. Assn. Craft Artists. Avocations: playing cello, making collages, monotypes. Home: 464 Wildwood Ln Sewanee TN 37375-3016

ENDE, MILTON, internist; b. N.Y.C., Dec. 9, 1918; s. Abraham S. and Elsie Ende; children: Frederick L., Mark. BS, U. Richmond, Va., 1940; MD, Med. Coll. Va., Richmond, 1943. Diplomate Am. Bd. Internal Medicine. Intern Med. Coll. Va., Richmond, 1944; resident Kennedy VA Hosp., Memphis, 1947—50, asst. chief of hematology and medicine, 1950; pvt. practice internal medicine Petersburg, Va., 1950—. Staff mem. Southside Regional Med. Ctr., Petersburg, chief of medicine, chief of staff, chief of renal unit, dir. pre-hosp. mobile coronary care unit; instr. cardio-pulmonary resuscitation; past dir. chem. dependency unit Poplar Springs Hosp.; lectr. in field. Contbr. articles. With U.S. Army, 1945—46. Mem.: ACP (life), Am. Fedn. Clin. Rsch. (sr.), Phi Beta Kappa. Achievements include research in umbilical cord blood. Home: 1865 Westorer Ave Petersburg VA 23805 Mailing: Ende Medical Practice LLP 121 S Market St Petersburg VA 23803

ENDERS, ALLEN COFFIN, anatomy educator; b. Wooster, Ohio, Aug. 5, 1928; s. Robert Kendal and Abbie Gertrude (Crandell) E.; m. Alice Hay, June 15, 1950 (div. Dec. 1975); children: Robert H., George C., Richard S., Gregory H.; m. Sandra Jean Schlafke, Aug. 5, 1976. AB, Swarthmore Coll., 1950; AM, Harvard U., 1952, PhD, 1955. From asst. prof. to assoc. prof Rice Inst., Houston, 1954-63; from assoc. prof. to prof. Washington U., St. Louis, 1963-75; prof., chmn. dept. human anatomy U. Calif., Davis, 1976-86, prof. cell biology and human anatomy, 1986—. Cons. NIH, Bethesda, Md., 1964-68, 70-73, 76-80, 83-93. Author: (with others) Bailey's Microscopic Anatomy, 1984; editor: Delayed Implantation, 1964; contbr. numerous articles on anatomy and reproduction to profl. jours. Nat. pres. Perinatal Research Soc., 1981. Grantee NIH, 1959-99. Fellow AAAS; mem. Am. Assn. Anatomists (v.p. 1980-82, pres. 1983-84), Soc. Study Reprodn., Am. Soc. Cell Biology. Home: 39707 Barry Rd Davis CA 95616-9415 Office: U Calif Sch Medicine Cell Biology & Anatomy Davis CA 95616

ENDERS, ELIZABETH MCGUIRE, artist; b. New London, Conn., Feb. 18, 1939; d. Francis Foran and Helen Cuseck (Connolly) McGuire; m. Anthony Talcott Enders, June 9, 1962; children: Charles Talcott, Alexandra Eustis, Camilla, Ostrom II. BA, Conn. Coll., 1962; MA, NYU, 1987. Trustee Artists Space, N.Y.C., 1986-95, Conn. Coll., New London, 1988-93; assoc. dept. prints and illustrated books Mus. Modern Art, 1993—, Lyman Allyn Art Mus., 1994—. One-woman shows include Paul Schuster Gallery, Cambridge, Mass., 1966, Ulysses Gallery, N.Y.C., 1992, 94, Lyman Allyn Art Mus., New London, Conn., 1994, Charles Cowles Gallery, N.Y.C., 1995, Norbert Considine Gallery,

Princeton, N.J., 1997, Artists Space, N.Y.C., 2001; exhibited in group shows at Boston Symphony Orch., 1982, NYU, 1983, Conn. Conn., 1988, Bronx Coun. on Arts, 1990-91, Addison Gallery Am. Art, 1993, Angel Art, L.A., 1993, Lyman Allyn Art Mus., New London, Conn., 1994-95, 98, 99, So. Alleghenies Mus. Art, Loretto, Pa., 1994, Artists Space Multiple, 1995, New Mus. Contemporary Art, N.Y.C., 1995, Denise Bibro Fine Art, N.Y.C., 1995, 99, N.Y. Studio Sch., N.Y.C., 1995, 2002, Divine Design '95, L.A., Spring Benefit Raffle, Sculpture Ctr., N.Y.C., 1996, 97, 98, 2000, 03, Charles Cowles Gallery, N.Y.C., 1996, 98, 2000, 01, 02, 03, Fax Art Week, Copenhagen, Assn. Danish Graphic Artists, 1996, Open Studio, Downtown Arts Festival, N.Y.C., 1997, 98, Dieu Donne Papermill, 1997, 99, 2001, Robert Brown Gallery, Wash. D.C., 1999, 2001, 02, New York Acad. of Art Benefit Auction, 1999, Cooley Gallery, Old Lyme, Conn., 1999, 2002, (Benefit for the Nature Conservancy), Nielsen Gallery, Boston, 2001, Artwalk, Coalition for the Homeless, 2001; traveling group show Artists Space, 1992, 94, Southeastern Ctr. Contemporary Art, Winston-Salem, N.C., 1993, Allentown (Pa.) Art Mus., 1994, Cleve. Ctr. Contemporary Art, 1994, Salt Lake Art Ctr., Salt Lake City, 1995, Kemper Ctr. Contemporary Art and Design, Kansas City, Mo., 1996, Bass Mus. of Art, Miami Beach, Fla., 1997, Flint (Mich.) Inst. Arts, 1998, Blaffer Gallery, U. Houston, TX, 1998, Contemporary Art Ctr., Va. Beach, 1998, Tampa Mus. of Art, 1998-99, Art Mus. of Southeast Tex., 1999, Fresno Metropolitan Mus., Calif., 2000, www.sfnbotanicalart.com, 2003; represented in permanent collections at Addison Gallery of Am. Art, Andover, Mass., Graham Gund, Cambridge, Dow Jones, N.Y.C., Agnes Gund, N.Y.C., Lyman Allyn Art Mus., Conn. Coll., New London. Recipient Citation of Appreciation, Conn. Coll., 1990, medal, 1993. Mem. The Bklyn. Mus., Contemporary Art Coun. Home: 530 E 86th St New York NY 10028-7535

ENDICOTT, JENNIFER JANE REYNOLDS, education educator; b. Oklahoma City, Oct. 17, 1947; d. M. Ector and Jessie Ruth (Carter) Reynolds; m. William George Endicott, June 2, 1969 (dec. Sept. 1976); 1 child, Andrea A. BA History, U. Okla., 1969, MEd Adminstrn., 1975, PhD, 1987. Cert. secondary edn. tchr.: history, govt., geography, econs., adminstr., Okla. Mid. sch. tchr. Norman (Okla.) Pub. Schs., 1970-77, adminstr. elem. edn., 1977-80; grad. asst. U. Okla., Norman, 1984-88; adj. lectr. U. Ctrl. Okla., Edmond, 1988-90, asst. prof., 1990-94, assoc. prof., 1995-98, prof., 1999—. Mem. adv. bd. The Annual Editions Series, Guilford, Conn., 1994—; editor Okla. Assn. Tchr. Educators Jour., 1997-2001, mem. editl. bd., 2002—; reviewer Action in Teacher Education ATE Jour.; contbr. articles to profl. jours. Bd. dirs. Cleveland County Hist. Soc., Norman, 1980-88, Arts and Humanities Coun., Norman, 1982-88; bd. dirs. Jr. League, Inc., Norman, 1982-90; bd. dirs. Assistance League, Norman, 1982-90, pres. 1988-89. Recipient Harriet Harvey Meml. award U. Okla. Found., 1984; named Norman Cmty. Family of the Yr. Finalist, LDS Ch., Norman, 1985; named to The Educator's Leadership Acad., The Outstanding Profs. Acad., 1999-2000. Mem. ASCD, Okla. Assn. for Supervision and Curriculum Devel., Okla. Assn. Tchr. Educators (bd. dirs. 1994—, pres. 1996-97, exec. sec. 2001-03), Am. Assn. Tchr. Educators, Soc. for Philosophy and History of Edn., Nat. Soc. Study of Edn., Am. Ednl. Rsch. Assn., Philosophy of Edn. Soc., Kappa Delta Pi (univ. sponsor 1991-96), Phi Delta Kappa (bd. dirs. Mid. State chpt. 1993-99, v.p. 1997-99, Svc. Key 1998). E-mail: jendicott@ucok.edu.

ENDICOTT, JOHN EDGAR, international relations educator; b. Cin., Aug. 9, 1936; s. Charles Lafayette and Alice Willa (Campbell) E.; m. Mitsuyo Tiffani Kobayashi, Aug. 24, 1959; children: Charlene Nobel, John Edward. BA, Ohio State U., 1958; MA in History, Omaha U., 1968; MA in Internat. Rels., Tufts U., 1972, MALD, PhD, Tufts U., 1973; student, Natl. War Coll., 1982, Air Command Staff Coll., 1978, Air War Coll., 1976, Squadron Officer Sch., 1963. Commd. USAF, advanced through grades to col.; dep. head polit. sci. and philosophy dept. USAF Acad., 1969-71, 73-78; dep. Air Force rep. mil. staff com. UN Security Coun., 1979-81; dir. internat. affairs divsn. Air Force Plans, The Pentagon, 1978-81; assoc. dean Nat. War Coll., 1981-83; dir. rsch. directorate Nat. Def. U., 1983-86; dir. Inst. Nat. Strategic Studies, Dept. Def., 1986-89; prof. Sam Nunn Sch. Internat. Affairs Ga. Inst. Tech., Atlanta, 1989—, founding dir. Ctr. Internat. Strategy Tech. and Policy, 1989—; apptd. Olympic attache Mongolian Olympic Com., Ulaan Bataar, 1995-96. Co-chair Coun. U.S.-Japan Security Rels.; bd. dirs. Nat. Def. U. Found.; cons. Dept. Def., Chmn. Joint Chiefs Staff, Process for Accreditation of Joint Edn. Program, NRC of NAS, Office Internat. Affairs, Def. Task Force, Inst. Def. Analysis, others; chmn. interim secretariat Agy. for Ltd. Nuclear Weapons-Free Zone for N.E. Asia, 1996—; mem. rev. group Funabashi Commn. U.S.-Japan Alliance and Disarmament, 1999—; bd. dirs. UN Assn., Atlanta, 1998-2000; mem. Task Force on U.S. Policy in Korea, 2003. Mem. editl. bd. The Japan Digest, Small Wars and Insurgencies, New South Mag.; author: Japan's Nuclear Option, 1975; co-editor, contbr.; American Defense Policy, 1977, Regional Security Issues, 1991; co-author: Politics of East Asia, 1978; contbr. articles to profl. jours. Mem. bd. advisors Atlantic Coun. for Internat. Rels., 2003—. Decorated Def. Superior Svc. medal, Legion of Merit, Bronze Star, Meritorious Svc. medal, Air medal with oak leaf cluster, Air Force Commendation medal with oak leaf cluster; Vietnam Svc. Medal with 2 bronze stars; Natl. Defense Svc. Medal, Rep. of Vietnam gallantry cross with device; Rep. of Vietnam Campaign Medal; Dept. of the Army Exceptional Civilian Svc. Medal; W. Alton Jones rsch. grantee Ploughshares Found.; rsch. grantee Carnegie Corp., 2d Chance Found., MacArthur Found. Nat. Security Seminar Series. Fellow Internat. Inst. Strategic Studies; mem. Internat. Studies Assn., Assn. Asian Studies, Army and Navy Club, Ga. Polit. Sci. Assn., Japan-Am. Soc. Ga. (recipient Mike Mansfield award 1996, exec. com., bd. dirs.), S.E. Korea-Am. Friendship Soc. (charter, bd. dirs., exec. vice chmn. 2000—), Georgian Club, Phi Beta Kappa. Avocations: tennis, French horn, writing, language study. Office: Ga Inst Tech Ctr Internat Strategy Atlanta GA 30332-0001 E-mail: john.endicott@inta.gatech.edu.

ENDICOTT, KIRK MICHAEL, anthropologist, educator; b. Seattle, Aug. 6, 1942; s. Charles Walker and Margaret Irene Endicott; m. Karen Ann Lampell, June 30, 1974; children: Evan Aaron, Britt Kathryn, Brendan Samuel; m. Anne-Mette Jacobsen, Aug. 6, 1966 (div. Apr. 26, 1974). BA, Reed Coll., 1965; BLitt, U. of Oxford, 1969; PhD, Harvard U., 1974; DPhil, U. of Oxford, 1976. From lectr. to instr. Calif. State U., Northridge, Calif., 1967—69; asst. lectr. U. of Malaya, Kuala Lumpur, Malaysia, 1972—73; vis. asst. prof. Cornell U., Ithaca, NY, 1973—74; rsch. and tchg. fellow Australian Nat. U., Canberra, Australia, 1974—81; from asst. prof. to prof. Dartmouth Coll., Hanover, NH, 1982—93, prof., 1993—, dept. chair, 2000—03. Vis. lectr. U. Toronto, 1988. Author: An Analysis of Malay Magic, 1970, Batek Negrito Religion, 1979; co-author: Malaysia and the Original People, 1997; co-editor: Taking Sides: Clashing Views on Controversial Issues in Anthropology, 2001—03; editor: Orang Asli Studies Newsletter, 1982—95. Co-coord. Orang Asli Assistance Fund, Cambridge, 1997—2002. Fellow Fulbright-Hays fellow, U.S. Govt., 1990. Mem.: Assn. for Asian Studies, Am. Anthrop. Assn. Democrat. Avocations: woodworking, fishing, hiking. Office: Dartmouth College Anthropology 6047 Silsby Hall Hanover NH 03755-3547 Office Fax: 603-646-1140.

ENDICOTT, WILLIAM F. journalist; b. Harrodsburg, Ky., Aug. 26, 1935; s. William O. and Evelyn E.; m. Mary Frances Thomas, Dec. 27, 1956; children: Gene, Fran, Greg. Student, Am. U., 1955; BA in Polit. Sci., Transylvania U., 1957. With Lexington (Ky.) Leader, 1957; sports writer Louisville Courier-Jour., 1958-62; reporter Tulare (Calif.) Advance-Register, 1963; reporter, city editor Modesto (Calif.) Bee, 1963-66; city editor Sacramento Union, 1966-67; with Los Angeles Times, 1968-85; Capitol bur. chief Sacramento Bee, 1985-95, asst. mng. editor, 1995-98, dep. mng. editor, 1998-2000, ret. Hearst vis. profl. U. Tex., 1993. Served with USMCR, 1957-58. Recipient various journalism awards Disting. Alumnus award Transylvania U., 1980 Episcopalian.

ENDIEVERI, ANTHONY FRANK, lawyer; b. Syracuse, N.Y., May 21, 1939; s. Santo and Anne Rose (Zeolla) Endieveri; m. Arlene Rita McDonald, May 20, 1967; children: Anne C., Steven A. BA, Syracuse U., 1961, LLB, 1965, JD, 1968. Bar: N.Y. 1967, U.S. Dist. Ct. (no. dist.) N.Y. 1967, U.S. Ct. Appeals (2d cir.) 1969, U.S. Supreme Ct. 1970; cert. civil trial lawyer Nat. Bd. Trial Advocacy. Assoc. Ronald Crowley, Atty., North Syracuse, NY, 1965-67, Love, Balducci & Scacciz, Syracuse, 1967; pvt. practice law Camillus, NY, 1968—; appellate counsel Hiscock Legal Aid, Syracuse, 1968-70; asst. corp. counsel, housing code prosecutor City of Syracuse, 1970-74. Participant Nat. Coll. Advocacy, 1981-83, 86; lectr. Melvin Belli seminar, San Francisco, 1987, 93, Kansas City, Mo., 1988, Boston, 1989, San Diego, 1990; spkr. in field. (spkr.) in field. Mem. ministry program Syracuse Diocese Pre-Deacon Study, 1980-82. Maj. USMCR, 1972-88, ret. Mem. ATLA (spkr. nat. conv. 1990, seminar 1990, ultimate trial advocacy course 1 991), Assn. Trial Lawyers Am. Coll. Advocacy, N.Y. State Bar Assn., Onondaga County Bar Assn., N.Y. Trial Lawyers Assn., Nat. Brain Injury Assn., N.Y. Brain Injury Assn, Phi Delt Phi. Democrat. Roman Catholic. Home: 205 Emann Dr Camillus NY 13031-2009

ENDRENYI, JANOS, research engineer, educator; b. Budapest, Hungary, Nov. 9, 1927; came to Can., 1957; s. Sandor and Lilly (Szegvari) E.; m. Edith Bernat, Dec. 5, 1956. Diploma in Engring., Tech. U., Budapest, 1951; MASc, U. Waterloo, Ont., Can., 1965; PhD, U. Toronto, Ont., 1972. Registered profl. engr., Ont., Can. Instr. Tech. U., Budapest, 1949-52; rsch. engr. Rsch. Inst. for Electric Power, Budapest, 1952-56; engr. Toronto Hydro, 1957-59; rsch. engr. rsch. divsn. Ont. Hydro, Toronto, 1959-79, head reliability and stats. sect., 1979-90, prin. rsch. engr., 1990-92, prin. scientist emeritus, 1992—. Lectr. U. Toronto, 1972-80, adj. assoc. prof., 1980-83, adj. prof., 1983—; spkr. at seminars worldwide. Author: Electric Shock Prevention (in Hungarian), 1956, Reliability Modeling in Electric Power Systems, 1978 (translated into Russian and Chinese); contbr. papers to profl. jours. Mem. Music Toronto, 1995—2001. Fellow IEEE; mem. Toronto Mozart Soc. (pres. 2001—). Home: 80 Front St E Apt 201 Toronto ON Canada M5E 1T4 Office: Kinectrics Inc 800 Kipling Ave Toronto ON Canada M8Z 6C4 E-mail: john.endrenyi@kinectrics.com.

ENDRESEN, LISA CASTRO, curatorial assistant; b. Ft. Hood, Tex., Oct. 31, 1969; d. Albert Charles Castro and Sandra Lynne Moore-Pope. BA in Art History, U. Md. European Divsn., Heidelberg, Germany, 1997; postgrad., U. Tex., San Antonio, 2002—. Adminstrv. asst. U. Md. Euorpean Divsn., Heidelberg, 1988-93, adminstv. asst. grad. programs, 1993-98; art auction coord. Sta. KLRN Pub. TV, San Antonio, 1998-99; curatorial asst. McNay Art Mus., San Antonio, 1999—. Advisor Predls. Scholarship Com., Heidelberg, 1995-98. One-woman shows include Hanau Exhbn., 1996. Elected advisor Dems. Abroad, Heidelberg, 1995-97. Mem. Urban 15, Art History Webmasters Assn. Democrat. Avocations: painting, writing, dance, travel. Office: McNay Art Mus 6000 N New Braunfels Ave San Antonio TX 78209-4618 Fax: 210-824-0218.

ENDRIZ, JOHN GUIRY, electronics executive, consultant; b. Oak Park, Ill., Jan. 10, 1942; s. John Daniel and Florence (Guiry) E.; m. Sally Jean Doubleday, July 19, 1975. BSEE, MSEE, MIT, 1965; PhD in EE, Stanford U., 1970. Guest rschr. Linkoping (Sweden) U., 1970-72; project mgr. R.C.A. Rsch. Lab., Princeton, N.J., 1972-77; engring. mgr. Varian Assocs., Palo Alto, Calif., 1977-88; v.p. engring. S.D.L., Inc., San Jose, Calif., 1988-97, v.p. power delivery bus. unit, 1997-99. Contbr. 53 articles to profl. jours.; patentee more than 30 inventions. Mem. IEEE, S.P.I.E., Soc. Information Display. Home: 5 Heritage Ct Belmont CA 94002-2944

ENDRUSICK, ROSE MARIE, educator; b. Creighton, Pa., Feb. 11, 1929; d. Paul Anthony and Ann Catherine Fricioni; m. Stanley Endrusick, June 19, 1950; children— Anne, Scott. B.S., Drexel Inst. Tech., 1950; M.A., Calif. State U.-Los Angeles, 1970; cert. Culinary Inst. Am., 1973. Tchr. home econs., Springdale, Pa., 1950-53, Glendale, Calif., 1953-55, Arcadia (Calif.) Unified Sch. Dist., 1955-83; designer antique doll clothes. Named Outstanding Tchr. in Arcadia, So. Calif. Industry-Edn. Council, 1968. Mem. Am. Home Econs. Assn., Calif. Tchrs. Assn., NEA, Arcadia/San Gabriel PTA (hon. life), Doll Collectors Gallery Calif. (v.p. 1981-83). Republican. Roman Catholic. Office: 301 S 1st Ave Arcadia CA 91006-3802

ENDSLEY, DANIEL STEVEN, public administrator; b. Palo Alto, Calif., Mar. 25, 1954; s. Daniel Steven Sr. and Susan (Tolnay) E. AB, U. Calif. Berkeley, 1976, MCP, 1985. Exec. dir. Rochdale Housing, Santa Barbara, Calif., 1980-82; sr. analyst City of Berkeley, 1986-90; head fin. dept. City of Woodside, Calif., 1990-93; city mgr. City of Del Rey Oaks, Calif., 1993-98; dir. planning and fin. Fort Ord Reuse Authority, Marina, Calif., 1998—. Adj. instr. Monterey (Calif.) Inst. Internat. Studies, 2001—; pres. Sustainable Base Reuse Inst., 2000—. Author, editor: Outline of American History, 1977, Outline of American Economics, 1978. Mem. ASPA (Contbr. of Yr. award San Francisco chpt. 1990), Am. Planning Assn. Democrat. Avocations: mountain biking, soccer. Office: Fort Ord Reuse Authority 100 12th St Bldg 2880 Marina CA 93933 E-mail: steve@fora.org.

ENDSLEY, MEREDITH NELSON, lawyer; b. Jan. 28, 1946; d. Kenneth Meredith and Margaret (Ihling) N.; m. Harry Barclay, May 28, 1971; children: Alexis Christine, Victoria Caroline. BA, Duke U., 1968; JD, U. Mich, 1971. Bar: Calif. 1972, D.C. 1987. Fgn. assoc. Anderson,Mori & Rabinowitz, Tokyo, 1973-75; assoc. Thelen, Marrin, Johnson & Bridges, San Francisco, 1971-72, 76-78; sr. counsel Matson Nav. Co., San Francisco, 1978-81; asst. gen. counsel, 1983—. Panelist 15th Inst. of Law Office Mgmt. and 17th Denver, Mpls. dir. Community Disputes Service, Am. Arbitration Assn., San Francisco, 1980-82. Mem. ABA, San Francisco Bar Assn. (chmn. corp. law dept. sect. 1983, exec. com. 1980-84, exec. com. law office mgmt. com. 1994—), Am. Corp. Counsel Assn. Office: Matson Nav Co PO Box 7452 San Francisco CA 94120-7452

ENDYKE, DEBRA JOAN, data communications marketing professional; b. Manchester, N.H., July 24, 1955; d. Paul Ronald and Theresa Joan (Smith) Cote; m. Michael Thomas Pidgeon, May 15, 1976 (div. Aug. 1984); m. Thomas Allen Endyke, Sept. 21, 1985. BS in Computer Sci., N.H. Coll., 1984. Mktg. specialist Bedford (N.H.) Computer Corp., 1981-84; sales and mktg. dir. electronic services program First Software Corp., Lawrence, Mass., 1984-86; account exec. Genesys Software Systems, Inc., Lawrence, 1986-87; group sales mgr. N.E. data communications div. Panasonic Co., Secaucus, N.J., 1987-88; sr. account exec. Bus. Systems Sales Group Gen. DataComm, Inc., Middlebury, Conn., 1988-89; sr. cons. Hollis (N.H.) Info. Assocs., 1989-90; applications engr. Octocom Systems, Inc., Wilmington, Mass., 1989-94; sr. sys. product mgr. Microcom Inc., Norwood, Mass., 1995-99; sr. product line mgr. Nortel Networks, Billerica, Mass., 1999—; dir. product mgmt. voice divsn. Unisphere Solutions, Burlington, Mass., 1999—. Republican. Roman Catholic. Avocations: golf, fishing, reading, theatre. Home: 41 Naticook Ave Litchfield NH 03052-8036 Office: Unisphere Solutions 10 Technology Park Dr Westford MA 01886-3140

ENEGESS, DAVID NORMAN, chemical engineer; b. Winchester, Mass., Aug. 25, 1946; s. Norman Leonard and Shirley Mildred (Lewis) E.; m. Jane Deborah Enegess, June 20, 1970; children: Deborah Marie, Christine Kerry. BSChemE, Tufts U., 1968, MSChemE, 1971. Registered profl. engr., Conn., Mich. Nuclear systems engr. Combustion Engring. Inc., Windsor, Conn., 1972-75, supr. radwaste systems devel. and design, 1975-77; project engr. Hazardous Waste Systems Group, WP Corp., Ramsey, N.J., 1977-79, mgr. projects, 1979-80, gen. mgr., 1980-82; co-founder, v.p. Waste Chem. Corp., Paramus, N.J., 1982-88, Envirogen, Inc., Princeton, N.J., 1988—. Mem. EPA Bioremediation Action Adv. Com., Washington, 1990—, Waste Mgmt. Symposia Tech. Program Com., Tucson, 1980-88, Oak Ridge (Tenn.) Nat. Lab. Waste Form Adv. Com., 1988-90; adviser Tufts U. Career Adv., Medford, Mass., 1990—; mem. Tufts Alumni Admissions Program, 1996—; bd. dirs. Vapex Corp, CVT America. Contbr. articles to profl. jours. Mem. Wyckoff (N.J.) Environ. Commn., 1986-88, Com. on Extended Learning, Wyckoff, 1984-85; mem., co-chair High Sch. Music Program Fund Raising, Wyckoff, 1987-90; coach Jr. Soccer League, Wyckoff, 1981-82; mem. Tufts U. Alumni Admissions Program, 1996—. 1st lt. U.S. Army, 1969-72. NSF fellow, 1968-69. Mem. ASME (mem. radwaste systems com. 1978-85), Am. Inst. Chem. Engrs., Atomic Indsl. Forum (rep. 1976-77), Am. Nuclear Soc., Hazardous Materials Control Rsch. Inst., Applied Biotreatment Assn. (dir. 1989-90). Achievements include patents for a static device for separations of gas mixtures into individual components, system using membrane device for radwaste processing, and process involving thin-film evaporation for radioactive wastewaters. Office: Envirogen Inc 4100 Quakerbridge Rd Lawrenceville NJ 08648-4702

ENELOW, ALLEN JAY, psychiatrist, educator; b. Pitts., Jan. 15, 1922; s. Isadore M. and Rose (Kasdan) E.; m. Mary Cleveland, July 21, 1946 (div. Sept. 1965); children: David, James, Susan, Margaret, Patience, Abigail; m. Sheila Kearns, Oct. 1, 1966; stepchildren: Lauren, Lisa. AB, W.Va. U., 1942; MD, U. Louisville, 1944. Intern Michael Reese Hosp., Chgo., 1944-45; resident psychiatry Winter VA Hosp., Topeka, 1947-49; mem. staff Menninger Found. and Asso. Hosps., 1947-52; practice medicine specializing in psychiatry Beverly Hills, Calif., 1952-58, Pacific Palisades, Calif., 1956-64; faculty U. So. Calif., Los Angeles, 1960-67; prof., chmn. dept. psychiatry Mich. State U., East Lansing, 1967-72; prof. psychiatry U. of Pacific, 1972-78; chmn. dept. psychiatry Pacific Med. Center, San Francisco, 1972-82; clin. prof. psychiatry U. Calif., 1977-82, U. So. Calif., 1982-89, clin. prof. emeritus, 1989—. Cons. NIMH, VA, others; pres. VISTAS Lifelong Learning, Inc., Santa Barbara, Calif., 1999-2001. Author: Psychiatry in the Practice of Medicine, 1966, Interviewing and Patient Care, 1972, 3d edit., 1985, 4th edit., 1996, Elements of Psychotherapy, 1977; contbr. numerous articles to profl. jours. Served with M.C. AUS, 1945-47. Fellow Am. Psychiat. Assn. (life), ACP. Office: 1532 Anacapa St Santa Barbara CA 93101-1929

ENENBACH, MARK HENRY, community action agency executive, educator; b. Chgo., July 28, 1949; s. Joseph Henry and Antonette Regina (Kasko) E.; children: Joy Elizabeth, Erin Regina; m. Kai Lindquist Bergin, Sept. 28, 1985; 1 child, Faith Marie. BA in Polit. Sci. with honors, Loyola U., Chgo., 1971, MA in Urban Studies with honors, 1973. Cmty. resource specialist Model Cities, Chgo., 1974-79; grad. prof. Govs. State U., Park Forest South, Ill., 1977-89; dir. energy program City of Chgo., 1980-83; prof. St. Augustine's Coll., Chgo., 1981-82; coord. cmty. svcs. Dept. Human Svcs., Chgo., 1984-91; prof. urban planning and pub. adminstrn. DePaul U., Chgo., 1987—; dir. cmty. svcs. block grant programs Cmty. and Econ. Devel. Assn. Cook County, Inc., Chgo., 1992-96, v.p./COO, 1997—; CEO CEDA Neighborhood Devel. Corp., Chgo., 2000—. Mem. adv. bd. City Colls. Chgo., 1984-88; spkr. Nat. Headstart Assn., Washington, 1995; mem. task force Ill. Dept. Commerce and Cmty. Affairs, Springfield, 1996—; spkr. Nat. Assn. Cmty. Action Agys., 1996-2000, Nat. Assn. State Cmty. Svcs. Programs, 2000. Pres. Lincoln Park Interagy. Coun., Chgo., 1986-91; mem. adv. bd. Salvation Army, Chgo., 1987-91. Grad. rsch. fellow Loyola U., 1972-73. Mem. Nat. Assn. Cmty. Action Agys., Ill. Assn. Cmty. Action Agys. Avocations: urban research, writing and travel in over 30 countries. Office: Cmty and Econ Devel Assn 208 S Lasalle St Ste 1900 Chicago IL 60604-1119 E-mail: menebach@cedaorg.net.

ENFIELD, D(ONALD) MICHAEL, insurance company executive; b. LA, Jan. 24, 1945; s. Fred Donald Jr. and Suzanne Arden (Hinkle) Enfield; children: Susan Ann, Michael David, Peter Christian. BA in Polit. Sci., U. San Francisco, 1967. Mgmt. trainee Marsh & McLennan, Inc., San Francisco, 1967-70, acct. exec., 1970-77, asst. v.p., 1977-79, v.p., 1979-81, sr. v.p., 1981-82, mng. dir., 1982-89; chmn., CEO Frank B. Hall & Co. of No. Calif., San Francisco, 1989-92; founder, chmn., CEO Metro/Risk, Inc., San Francisco, 1992—. Cons. in field. Contbr. articles to profl. jours. Bd. dirs. Ronald McDonald Ho., San Francisco, 1989—92, Philharmonica Baroque Orch., San Francisco, 2003—; chmn. bd. dirs. Midsummer Mozart Festival, San Francisco, 1985—90; trustee Lamplighters Music Theater, 1996—2003. Mem.: Wine Adv. San Francisco (founder), San Francisco C. of C. (dir. bus./arts coun. 1987—93), Club des Oenophiles Gastronome de Paris (dep. pres. 2000—), Olympic Club San Francisco, City Club of San Francisco, Lotus Club N.Y., Soc. Calif. Pioneers (county v.p. 1974—). Avocation: classical music. Office: Metro/Risk Inc 153 Townsend St San Francisco CA 94107

ENFIELD, SUSAN ANN, secondary school educator; b. San Francisco, May 30, 1968; d. D. Michael and Julia Ann (Bettencourt) Enfield. Student, York (Eng.) U., 1988-89; BA in English, U. Calif., Berkeley, 1990; MEd, Stanford U., 1993, Harvard U., 2002. Editl. asst. Jossey-Bass, Inc. Pubs., San Francisco, 1990-92; tchr. Homestead HS, Cupertino, Calif., 1993-97; tchr. English Sir Francis Drake HS, San Anselmo, Calif., 1997-99; HS support provider U. Calif. Berkeley Tchg. and Learning Alliance, 1999—2001; bur. dir. curriculum and academic svcs. Pa. Dept. Edn., Lancaster, 2003—. Co-author: (book) When Tutor Meets Student. Named Outstanding Tchr., Tufts U., 1994, Carleton Coll., 1995, Coll. Wooster, 1996, U. Calif., Santa Barbara, 1997, U. Ariz., 1997. Mem.: ASCD, Phi Delta Kappa.

ENG, CATHERINE, health care facility administrator, physician, medical educator; b. Hong Kong, May 20, 1950; came to U.S., 1953; d. Doi Kwong and Alice (Yee) E.; m. Daniel Charles Chan; 1 child, Michael B. BA, Wellesley Coll., 1972; MD, Columbia U., 1976. Diplomate Am. Bd. Internal Medicine, Am. Bd. Gastroenterology; cert. added qualifications geriatrics. Intern in internal medicine Presbyterian Hosp./Columbia, Presbyterian Med. Ctr., 1976-77, resident in internal medicine, 1977-79; fellow in gastroenterology/hepatology N.Y. Hosp./Cornell U. Med. Coll., 1979-81; instr. medicine Cornell U. Coll. Medicine, N.Y.C., 1980-81; staff physician On Lok Sr. Health Svcs., San Francisco, 1981-86, supervising physician, 1986-91, med. dir., 1992—. Asst. clin. prof. dept. family and cmty. medicine U. Calif., San Francisco, 1986-95, asst. clin. prof. dept. medicine, 1992-95; assoc. clin. prof. dept. medicine, U. Calif., San Francisco, 1995-2001, clin. prof. medicine, 2001—; primary care specialist Program of All-inclusive Care for the Elderly, San Francisco, 1987-94; asst. chief dept. medicine Chinese Hosp., San Francisco, 1993-98, chmn. com. credentials, 1994—. Instr. BLS Am. Heart Assn., San Francisco, 1988-92; mem. nominating com. YWCA of Marin, San Francisco, San Mateo, 1991-95; mem. mgmt. com. YWCA-Chinatown/North Beach, San Francisco, 1989-95; bd. dirs. Chinatown Cmty. Children's Ctr., San Francisco, 1987-90. Durant scholar Wellesley Coll., 1972. Fellow ACP; mem. Am. Geriatrics Soc., Am. Soc. Aging, Am. Gastroent. Assn., Calif. Med. Assn. (assoc.), San Francisco Med. Soc. (assoc.), Sigma Xi, Alpha Omega Alpha. Avocations: reading, hiking. Home: 130 Dorchester Way San Francisco CA 94127-1110 Office: On Lok Sr Health Scvs 1333 Bush St San Francisco CA 94109-5691 E-mail: cathy@onlok.org.

ENG, LAWRENCE FOOK, biochemistry educator, neurochemist; b. Spokane, Wash., Feb. 19, 1931; s. On Kee and Shee (Hue) E.; m. Jeanne Leong, Aug. 30, 1957; children: Douglas, Alice, Steven, Shirley. BS in Chemistry, Wash. State U., 1952; MS in Chemistry, Stanford U., 1954, PhD in Chemistry, 1962. Chief chemistry sect. path. and lab. med. svc. PAVA Health Care Sys., Palo Alto, Calif., 1961—; rsch. assoc. dept. pathology Sch. Medicine Stanford (Calif.) U., 1966-70, sr. scientist dept. pathology Sch. of Medicine, 1970-75, adj. prof., 1975-82, prof. dept. pathology Sch. of Medicine, 1982—. Mem. ad hoc neurol. sci. study sect. and neurology B study sect. NIH, 1976-79, mem. neurol. sci. study sect., 1978-83; mem. adv. bd. VA Office of Regeneration Rsch. Program, 1985-89; mem. VA Merit Rev. Bd. for Neurobiology, 1987-90; mem. Nat. Adv. Neurol. Disorders and Stroke Coun., 1991-94. Mem. editorial bd. Neurobiology, 1970-75, Jour. of Neurochemistry, 1978-85, Jour. of Neuroimmunology, 1980-83, Molecular and Chem. Neuropathology, 1982-98, Glia, 1987-2001, Jour. for Neurosci. Rsch., 1991—, Neurochemical Rsch., 1993-2000. Capt. USAF, 1952—57. Mem. Am. Soc. for Neurochemistry (coun. 1979-83, 85-87, 93—, sec. 1987-93), Am. Soc. Biochemistry and Molecular Biology, Internat. Soc. for Neurochemistry, Soc. for Neurosci. Office: VAPA Health Care System Path & Lab Med Svc 3801 Miranda Ave Palo Alto CA 94304-1207 E-mail: lfeng@stanford.edu.

ENG, MAMIE, librarian; b. Oceanside, N.Y., May 21, 1954; d. Yen Wah and Hong Lew (Lum) E. BA in History and Edn., Vassar Coll., 1976; MS in Libr. Sci., Columbia U., 1977, MA in Ednl. Psychology, 1979. Asst. dir. Henry Waldinger Meml. Libr., Valley Stream, N.Y., 1979—. Editor, salary schedules and pers. benefits publ., 2001- Mem. ALA, hon. life mem. N.Y. Libr. Assn., Nassau County Libr. Assn. (editor assn. newsletter 1985-88, 89-92, 94—, div. pres. 1986-87, 99, media svcs. div. pres, 2002, bd. dirs. 1988-89, v.p./pres. elect 1992, pres. 1993), Suffolk County Libr. Assn., Internat. Reading Assn. (bd. dirs., Manhattan Coun. 1985-90), Phi Delta Kappa, Reading Reform Found. Avocations: flower arranging and related crafts, reading, flowers. Office: Henry Waldinger Meml Libr 60 Verona Pl Valley Stream NY 11580-5468

ENG, ON-YUEN See LONG, HARRY

ENGBER, CHERYL ANN, language educator, linguist; b. East Chicago, Ind., Oct. 12, 1945; d. James Ward and Beryl Ann (Crowe) Biddle; m. Michael David Engber, Nov. 25, 1967; children: Sara Ann, Kimberly Sue. BA in Spanish with honors, Ind. U., 1967, PhD in Linguistics, 1992, MA in Spanish, 1974; MA in Tchg. ESL, Ball State U., 1979. Instr. Spanish Anderson (Ind.) U., 1979-82; assoc. instr. intensive English program Ind. U., Bloomington, 1983-86, adminstrv. asst. com. for R & D, 1989-91, instr. semi-intensive English program, 1991-93; assoc. prof. linguistics Truman State U., Kirksville, Mo., 1993—, Instr. ESL Ind. U., Kuala Lumpur, Malaysia, 1985—86; grader for Test of Written English Edn'l. Testing Svc., Princeton, NJ, 1989—98, reader for AP exams, 2001—; asst. to editor Studies in Second Lang. Acquisition Ind. U.,

1987—89; spkr. in field. Contbr. Understanding English: A Listening Approach to ESL, 1983; contbr. articles to profl. jours. Founder Muncie (Ind.) Internat. Ctr., 1974; vol. tchr., founder internat. summer workshops for children, Muncie, 1977; deacon, elder, mem. com. First Christian Ch., Bloomington, Ind., 1987-92. Ind. U. fellow, 1982; Truman State U. grantee, 1994, 2001. Mem. Linguistic Soc. Am., Tchrs. ESL, Am. Assn. for Applied Linguistics, Phi Beta Kappa, Phi Kappa Phi. Avocations: travel, gardening, gourmet cooking. Office: Truman State Univ Divsn Lang and Lit McClain Hall 310 Kirksville MO 63501 E-mail: cengber@truman.edu., cmengber@att.net.

ENGDAHL, TODD PHILIP, editor; b. Jamestown, N.Y., Feb. 8, 1950; s. George Philip and Janice Marie (Wallin) E.; m. Caroline C.N. Schomp, Dec. 29, 1973; children: Anders Justus Schomp, Mats Philip Schomp. BA, Pomona Coll., 1971; MS, Northwestern U., 1972. Reporter Oregonian, Portland, 1972-75; reporter Denver Post, 1975-80, asst. city editor, 1980-83, night city editor, 1983-85, Sunday editor, 1985-86, city editor, 1986-90, exec. city editor, 1990-95; editor DenverPost.com, 1995—2003; perspective editor Denver Post, 2003—. Lectr. journalism Portland State U., 1974. Democrat. Lutheran. Avocations: reading, gardening, woodworking. Office: Denver Post PO Box 1709 Denver CO 80201-1709 E-mail: tengdahl@denverpost.com.

ENGEBRETSON, ANDREW, lawyer; b. Starbuck, Minn., Aug. 21, 1932; s. Herman Ferdinand and Agnes Serina (Knutson) E.; m. Fay Louise Amundson, Nov. 28, 1959 (div. Apr. 1970); children: Peter, Sarah; m. Rachel Wayne Warrick, June 16, 1970; 1 child, Margaret. BA cum laude, St. Olaf Coll., 1954; JD, U. Minn., 1959. Assoc. Rudolph L. Swore, Alexandria, Minn., 1959, Ernest H. Steneroden, St. Paul, 1962—69; ptnr. Engebretson Law Offices, St. Paul, 1969-94, pvt. practice, 1995—. Conv. del. Ramsey County Republicans, St. Paul, 1974-90, congrl. candidate, St. Paul, 1976. With U.S. Army, 1955-56. Mem. ABA, Minn. Bar Assn., Minn. Trial Lawyers Assn., Am. Trial Lawyers Assn., Mason. Republican. Lutheran. Avocations: fishing, chess, fgn. lang. studies, non-fiction books. Office: Engebretson Law Offices 5 N 3d Ave W Ste 300 Duluth MN 55802

ENGEBRETSON, DOUGLAS KENNETH, architect, interior designer; b. Dawson, Minn., Nov. 5, 1946; s. Melvin Kenneth and Mary Louise (Jackson) E.; m. Kathleen Stella Jefferies, June 14, 1969; children: Leif Erik, Kristin Ann. BArch, U. Ariz., 1969. Registered arch., Mass., Vt., N.H., Conn., N.Y., R.I., Maine. Draftsman William B. Tabler, FAIA, N.Y.C., summer 1969, Wheeler Petterson Coffeen, Tucson, 1968-69; assoc. Alderman & MacNeish, West Springfield, Mass., 1970-78; pres. Tessier Assocs., Springfield, 1978 —. Mem. Mass. Bd. Registration Archs., 1996—, chair, 2002—; dir. Nat. Coun. Archtl. Registration Bds., 2000-2003, nat. sec., 2003—; corporator Chicopee (Mass.) Savs. Bank, trustee, 2000. Works include Putnam Vocat. Tech. Sch., Springfield, Mass., Palmer H.S. and Elem. Schs., Cmty. Savs. Bank, South Hadley, Mass., Ring Nursing Home, Springfield, Mt. Everett Regional Sch., Sheffield, Mass., Heritage Bank Hdqrs., Holyoke, Mass.; co-author: Norway, 1978. Mem. Zoning Bd. Appeals, Southampton, Mass., 1976-84, Pers. Policy and Procedures Bd., 1983-85; trustee Bay Path Coll., Longmeadow, Mass., 1991—, Brightside for Families and Children, West Springfield, 1992-96, Sta. WGBY-TV, Springfield, 1992-2001, Colony Club, 2001—, bd. govs., 2002—. With USAF, 1969-73. Recipient Group Study Exch. award to Norway, Rotary Internat., Evanston, Ill., 1978, Philanthropist of Distinction award Nat. Soc. Fundraising Execs., Hampden County, 1996. Fellow AIA (nat. dir. 1986-89, nat. sec. 1991-92, pres. New Eng. regional coun. 1985-86, Richard Upjohn fellow 1992); mem. Western Mass. Chpt. AIA (pres. 1980-82), Mass. State Assn. Archs. (pres. 1982-83), Rotary (pres. 1985-86). Republican. Lutheran. Home: 6 Madison Ave Southampton MA 01073-9520 Office: Tessier Assoc Inc Tower Sq Ste 250 1500 Main St PO Box 15169 Springfield MA 01115-5169

ENGEBRETSON, ERIK JOHN, music educator, director; b. Kalispell, Mont., June 20, 1960; s. Rik and Marcia Engebretson; m. Jeanne Arnott, July 21, 1984; children: Kristen, Peter, Elizabeth. BA, Luther Coll., 1982; MS, Univ. of Ill., 1986. Cert. tchr. Office of Pub. Instrn., 2002. Band dir. Wolf Point (Mont.) Sch. Dist., 1982—85, Malta (Mont.) HS/Jr. High, 1986—. Del. ELCA Nat. Conv., Denver, 1999. Mem.: Mont. Bandmaster Assn. (pres. 1996—98). Lutheran. Office: Malta High School 1 High School Lane Malta MT 59538 Office Fax: 406-654-2226.

ENGEBRETSON, MARK JEROME, science educator, researcher; b. Decorah, Iowa, Dec. 4, 1946; s. Oscar Edwin Engebretson and Irene Octavia Engebretson (Lembke); m. Lynette Sue Brown, June 29, 1974; children: David Michael, John Mark, Julie Lynn Helps. PhD, U. of Minn., 1972—76; MDiv, Luther Theol. Sem., 1968—72; BA, Luther Coll., 1964—68. Asst. pastor Luth. Ch. of the Master, Edina, Minn., 1972—74; postdoctoral rsch. assoc. U. of Minn., 1976—77; asst. prof. Augsburg Coll., 1976—84, assoc. prof., 1984—89; vis. scientist Applied Physics Lab., Johns Hopkins U., 1985—86; prof. of physics Augsburg Coll., 1989—; fulbright sr. scholar Tech. U. of Braunschweig, Germany, 1997—97. Author: (space physics rsch. articles) Jour. of Geophys. Rsch.; editor: (book in geophys. monograph series) Solar Wind Sources of Ultra-Low-Frequency Waves. Edn. award com. chair Am. Geophys. Union, Washington, 1998—2000. Lutheran. Home: 2905 Dakota Ave St. Louis Park MN 55416 Office: Augsburg College 2211 Riverside Ave Minneapolis MN 55454 Office Fax: 612-330-1649. E-mail: engebret@augsburg.edu.

ENGEL, ALBERT JOSEPH, retired federal judge; b. Lake City, Mich., Mar. 21, 1924; s. Albert Joseph and Bertha (Bielby) Engel; m. Eloise Ruth Bull, Oct. 18, 1952; children: Albert Joseph III, Katherine Ann, James Robert, Mary Elizabeth. Student, U. Md., 1941—42; AB, U. Mich., 1948, LLB, 1950. Bar: Mich. 1951. Administrative asst. to U.S. Rep. Ruth Thompson, 1951; ptnr. firm Engle & Engel, Muskegon, Mich., 1952—67; judge Mich. Circuit Ct., 1967—71; judge U.S. Dist. Ct. Western Dist. Mich., 1971—74; circuit judge U.S. Ct. Appeals, 6th Circuit, Grand Rapids, Mich., 1974—88, chief judge, 1988—89, sr. judge, 1989—2002; ret., 2002. With U.S. Army, 1943—46, ETO. Fellow: Am. Bar Found.; mem.: FBA, ABA, Am. Judicature Soc., Grand Rapids Bar Assn., Cin. Bar Assn., Mich. Bar Assn., Grand Rapids Torch Club, Am. Legion, Phi Delta Phi, Phi Sigma Kappa. Episcopalian.

ENGEL, ANDREW GEORGE, neurologist; b. Budapest, Hungary, July 12, 1930; s. Alexander and Alice Julia (Gluck) E.; m. Nancy Jean Brombacher, Aug. 15, 1958; children: Lloyd William, Andrew George. BSc, McGill U., 1953, MD, 1955. Diplomate: Am. Bd. Internal Medicine, Am. Bd. Psychiatry and Neurology. Intern Phila. Gen. Hosp., 1955-56; sr. asst. surgeon, clin. asso. USPHS, NIH, Bethesda, Md., 1958-59; fellow in neuropathology Columbia U., N.Y.C., 1962-64; with Mayo Clinic, Rochester, Minn., 1956-57, 60-62; cons. Rochester, Minn., 1965—; prof. neurology Mayo Med. Sch., Rochester, 1973—, William L. McKnight-3M prof. neurosci., 1984—; disting. investigator Mayo Clinic, 1995—. Mem. sci. adv. com. Muscular Dystrophy Assn., 1973-99; mem. rev. com. NIH, 1977-81. Mem. editl. bd. Neurology, 1973-77, Annals Neurology, 1978-84, 90-95, Muscle and Nerve, 1978-97, 2000—, Jour. Neuropathology, 1981-83, 1996-2000, European Neurology, 1989—, Jour. Neuroimmunology, 1991-98, Molecular Neurobiology, 1997—; contbr. over 300 articles to med. jours. Served with USPHS, 1957-59. Mem. Am. Acad. Neurology, Am. Neurol. Assn., Am. Soc. Cell Biology, Soc. Neurosci., AAAS. Home: 2027 Lenwood Dr SW Rochester MN 55902-1051 Office: Mayo Clinic 200 1st St SW Rochester MN 55905-0002

ENGEL, BERNARD THEODORE, psychologist, educator; b. Chgo., Apr. 18, 1928; s. Marvin I. and Hannah (Hollander) E.; m. Rae Goldberg, Mar. 10, 1951; children: Sandra E., Jeffrey P., Lauren C. BA, UCLA, 1954, PhD, 1956. Jr. rsch. psychologist UCLA, 1956; rsch. psychologist Inst. Psychosomatic and Psychiatric. Research and Tng., Michael Reese Hosp., Chgo., 1957-58; lectr. med. psychology, mem. sr. staff Cardiovasc. rsch. Inst., Sch. Medicine U. Calif., San Francisco, 1959-67; chief behavioral physiology sect., chief Lab. Behavioral Scis. Gerontology Research Center, Nat. Inst. Aging, NIH, Balt., 1967-95; assoc. prof. behavioral biology Johns Hopkins Sch. Medicine, Balt., 1970 82, prof., 1982—. Bd. dirs. Insts. for Behavioral Resources, Inc.; adj. prof. psychiatry and behavioral scis. Duke U. Sch. Medicine, Durham, N.C., 1999—. Contbr. 175 articles to sci. jours.; editorial bds. Applied Psychophysiology and Biofeedback, Jour. of Behavioral Medicine. Served U.S. Army, 1950—52. Recipient award Pavlovian Soc., 1979; cert. of Appreciation, N.C. State Hwy. Patrol, 2003. Fellow AAAS, Gerontol. Sci.; mem. Soc. Psychophysiol. Rsch. (pres. 1970-71), Assn. Applied Psychophysiology and Biofeedback (pres. 1981-82, Disting. Scientist award 2001), Am. Psychosomatic Soc. (sec.-treas. 1981-85, pres. 1985-86, Patricia R. Barchas award in sociophysiology 1999), Gerontol. Soc. Am., Acad. Behavioral Medicine Rsch., Sigma Xi. E-mail: btere@aol.com.

ENGEL, CHARLENE STANT, artist, art historian; b. Norfolk, Va., Nov. 5, 1946; d. Vernon Earl Sr. and Mary Elizabeth (Rawles) Stant; m. Wilson F. Engel III, May 11, 1969; children: Grace Elizabeth, Wilson F. IV. BFA, Old Dominion U., 1968; MA, U. Wis., 1974, PhD, 1976. Asst. prof., curator art collection, dir. gallery Moravian Coll., Bethlehem, Pa., 1979-84; artist, art historian Newport News, Va., 1984-97. Vis. asst. prof. Coll. William and Mary, 1991-94, lectr. Christopher Wren Assn. Coll. William and Mary, 1994-97; guest curator, lectr. San Diego Museum of Art, 1997-2001; lectr. Riverside Art Mus., 1998-2001; curator Hyde Gallery, Grossmont Coll., 1999-2000; vis. lectr. Mira Costa Coll., 1999-2000. Solo exhbns. at Ea. Va. Med. Sch., 1988, 92, Crestar Bank Gallery, 1988, Thomas Nelson Coll., 1977-89, Twentieth Century Gallery, Williamsburg, 1989, Peninsula Fine Art Ctr., 1991, Williamsburg Regional Libr., 1992, Peninsula Fine Arts Ctr., 1996, Gallerie Lafayette, 1998, Tex. Tech. U., 1999; contbr. articles to profl. jours. and exhbn. catalogues. Recipient Cert. of Appreciation, Maine State Legislature, 1991; Hermitage Found. Mus. fellow, 1965, Va. Mus. fellow, 1964, 67, Kress fellow, 1975. Mem. Coll. Art Assn., San Diego Watercolor Soc., San Diego Art Inst., Women's Caucus for Art. Home: 45 Green Needles Rd Littleton MA 01460

ENGEL, DAVID ANTHONY, lawyer; b. Albany, N.Y., Mar. 5, 1951; s. Herbert and Rose Helen (Fink) E.; m. Cynthia Ann White, Nov. 2, 1975; children: Leslie Ruth, Jeffrey Aaron. BA, Union Coll., Schenectady, N.Y., 1972; JD, Albany Law Sch., 1975. Bar: N.Y. 1976, U.S. Dist. Ct. (no. dist.) N.Y. 1976, U.S. Ct. Appeals D.C. 1984. Asst. atty. N.Y. State Dept. Agr. and Markets, Albany, 1975-77, staff atty., 1977; sr. atty. N.Y. State Dept. Environ. Conservation, Albany, 1977-79, energy counsel, 1979-84, asst. counsel for enforcement, 1984-86, dep. dir. Environ. Enforcement Div., 1986-87, dir., 1987-88; atty. Herzog, Engstrom, Burke, Koplovitz & Cavalier, P.C., Albany, 1988-90; ptnr. Burke, Cavalier, Lindy & Engel, P.C., Albany, 1990-92, Harris, Beach & Wilcox, Albany, 1992—. Mem. Chmn.'s Com. Handgun Control, Inc., Washington, 1983-84, County Dem. Com., Schenectady, 1983-87. Recipient Merit award Catskill Ctr., Arkville, N.Y., 1988. Mem. ABA (nat. resources, pub. utility law sects.), N.Y. State Bar Assn. (exec. com. environ. law sect.), Fed. Energy Bar Assn., Sierra Club (wilderness guardian 1983), So. Poverty Law Ctr . Democrat. Jewish. Avocations: skiing, travel, reading. Home: 1246 Viewmont Dr Niskayuna NY 12309-1220 Office: Harris Beach & Wilcox 20 Corporate Woods Blvd Ste 2 Albany NY 12211-2349

ENGEL, DAVID LEWIS, lawyer; b. N.Y.C., Mar. 31, 1947; s. Benjamin and Selma (Fruchtman) Engel; m. Edith Greetham Smith, June 9, 1973; children: Richard William, Jonathan Martin. AB in Gen. Studies in Econ. cum laude, Harvard U., 1967, JD magna cum laude, 1973; Disting. Naval grad., U.S. Naval Officer Candidate Sch., 1969. Bar: Mass. 1975. Law clk. to Judge Henry J. Friendly U.S. Ct. Appeals (2d cir.), N.Y.C., 1973-74; assoc. Goodwin, Procter & Hoar, Boston, 1974-76, 79-80; asst. prof. law Stanford U., Calif., 1976-79; ptnr. Berman, Dittmar & Engel, P.C., Boston, 1980-84, Bingham McCutchen LLP, Boston, 1984—. Pres. Harvard Law Rev., 1972—73. Mem. bd. visitors Stanford U. Law Sch., 1982—84; bd. dirs. Project Joy, 1995—2001. Lt. j.g. USNR, 1969—71. Recipient Sears prize, 1968, John Bingham Hurlbut award, 1979; John Harvard scholar, Harvard Coll. scholar, Nat. Merit scholar, 1964—67. Mem.: ABA, Boston Bar Assn. (working group of task force on revision of Mass. corp. statute 1987—2001), Phi Beta Kappa. Office: Bingham McCutchen LLP 150 Federal St Boston MA 02110-1713 E-mail: david.engel@bingham.com.

ENGEL, DAVID WAYNE, lawyer, federal official; b. Salisbury, Md., Nov. 29, 1956; s. Robert Peter Engel and Joan (King) Bradshaw; m. Laura Marie Tuck, June 25, 1983; children: Michael Andrew, Jennifer Lynn, Matthew Alan. AB, William & Mary Coll., 1978; JD, Washington & Lee U., 1981; LLM, Judge Advocate Gen.'s Sch., Charlottesville, Va., 1988. Bar: Va. 1981, U.S. Dist. Ct. (ea. and we. dists.) Va. 1981, U.S. Ct. Mil. Appeals 1981, U.S. Ct. Appeals (4th cir.) 1981, U.S. Tax Ct. 1982, U.S. Ct. Appeals (5th cir.) 1985, Tex. 1985, U.S. Dist. Ct. (we. dist.) Tex. 1985, U.S. Supreme Ct. 1988, U.S. Ct. Appeals Vets. Claims 1990, U.S. Ct. Appeals (Fed. cir.) 1991, U.S. Ct. Appeals (10th cir.) 1998, U.S. Dist. Ct. (no. dist.) Okla. 1998. Capt. U.S. Army, 1981-89, active duty, 1989, USAR, 1989-97; appellate litigation atty. U.S. Dept. Vets. Affairs, Washington, 1989-92, spl. asst. to acting asst. gen. counsel, 1992-93; deputy asst. Gen. Coun., 1993-97; U.S. adminstrv. law judge Social Security Adminstrn., Office Hearings & Appeals, Tulsa, Okla, 1997—; col. USAF Res., 1997—; hearing office chief judge, 2002—. Office: Office of Hearings & Appeals Social Security Adminstrv 5110 South Yale Ste 204 Tulsa OK 74135-7481 E-mail: david.engel@ssa.gov.

ENGEL, ELIOT L. congressman; b. N.Y.C., Feb. 18, 1947; s. Philip and Sylvia (Bleend) E. BA, CUNY, 1969, MS, 1973. Counselor, advisor N.Y. Urban Corps, 1968; tchr., dept. chmn. N.Y. Bd. Edn., 1969-76; guidance counselor N.Y. Pub. Schs., 1973-75; mem. N.Y. State Assembly, 1977-89, U.S. Congress from 17th N.Y. dist., 1989—; mem. econ. and ednl. opportunity com., energy and commerce com.; mem. internat. rels. com. Columnist Co-op City News, 1972. V.p. Park-East Ind. Dem. Club, N.Y., 1970-71; del. Bronx Com. for Dem. Voters, 1971-76, v.p., 1975-76; del., mem. steering com. Youth Caucus, Dem. Nat. Conv., 172; v.p. Ind. Dems. of Co-op City, 1972-73, pres., 1974-75; committeeman Bronx County Dem. Com., N.Y., 1972—; mem. exec. coun. N.Y. State New Dem. Coalition, 1973-75; founder New Dem. Club Co-op City, 1975, pres., 1975-76; jud. del. N.Y. Supreme Ct. Conv., 1st Jud. Dist., 1975-76, dist. leader, 1976—. Recipient Man of Yr. award FDR Ind. Dem. Club, 1976. Mem. United Fund Tchrs., Ams. for Dem. Action (bd. dirs. N.Y. 1974—), Zionist Orgn. Am., K.P. Democrat. Jewish. Office: US Ho of Reps 2264 Rayburn Hob Washington DC 20515-0001*

ENGEL, JOEL STANLEY, telecommunications executive; b. N.Y.C., Feb. 4, 1936; s. Fred and Pauline (Bienstock) E.; m. Marian Myers, Feb. 1, 1959; children: Stewart Allen, Mark Edward, Amy Ruth. BEE, CCNY, 1957; MSEE, MIT, 1959; PhD in Elec. Engring., Poly. Inst. Bklyn., 1964. Rsch. staff instrumentation lab. MIT, Cambridge, 1957-59; mem. tech. staff Bell Labs., Holmdel, NJ, 1959-64, supr., 1967-73, dept. head, 1975-83; mem. tech. staff BellComm, Washington, 1964-65; R & D mgr. Page Communications, Washington, 1965-67; div. mgr. AT&T, N.Y.C., 1973-75; v.p. Satellite Bus. Systems/MCI, McLean, Va., 1983-87, Ameritech, Chgo., 1987-97; pres. JSE Consulting, 1997—. Exec. adv. coun. Internat. Comms. Forum, Chgo., 1990—; bd. dirs. Syracuse (N.Y.) Rsch. Corp. Contbr. numerous articles to profl. jours.; patentee in field. Recipient Nat. Medal of Tech., 1994. Fellow IEEE (guest editor Transactions on Comm./Vehicular Tech. Jour. 1973, Alexander Graham Bell medal 1987); mem. Nat. Acad. Engring. Office: JSE Consulting 5 Hemlock Hollow Pl Armonk NY 10504-3016 E-mail: jsecons@worldnet.att.net.

ENGEL, JOHN CHARLES, lawyer, lobbyist; b. Milw., Aug. 24, 1955; s. Russell Bernard Glen and Helen Marie (Poh) E.; m. Debra Ann McCall, Apr. 17, 1982; children: Stephanie, Jacqueline, Elizabeth, Thomas. BA, U. Wis., Milw., 1982, MLS, 1983; JD, Marquette U., 1986. Bar: Wis. 1986, U.S. Dist. Ct. (ea. dist.) Wis. 1986, U.S. Dist. Ct. (we. dist.) Wis. 1987, U.S. Supreme Ct. 1989. Staff atty. Wis. Credit Union League, Pewaukee, Wis., 1986-93, mgr. tech. dept., 1993-94, sr. mgr. tech. dept., 1994-96, staff atty. compliance, rsch. and publs., 1996-99, sr. compliance counsel, 1999—2002, dir. legal affairs, 2002—. Bd. dirs. Outpost Natural Foods Coop., pres., 1991, sec., 1992-93. Active Mil. Dems. Mem. ACLU, ABA, Wis. Bar Assn., Wis. Pub. Interest Rsch. Group, Phi Alpha Theta. Roman Catholic. Avocation: genealogy. Home: 2359 S 78th St West Allis WI 53219-1857 Office: Wis Credit Union League N25 W23131 Paul Rd Pewaukee WI 53072-5734 E-mail: jcengel@wcul.org.

ENGEL, JOHN JACOB, communications executive; b. N.Y.C., June 9, 1936; s. Stewart I. and Beatrice (Schapiro) E.; m. Miriam Jarman, Aug. 17, 1986; children by previous marriage: Susan Lisa, Mark Alan; stepchildren: Alan Brett, Amy Ruth. BA, Adelphi U., Garden City, N.Y., 1957; MS, Boston U., 1959. Program dir. Sta. WLAD FM, Danbury, Conn., 1954-57; account exec. Sta. WBRY AM, Waterbury, Conn., 1959-62, Sta. WNHC AM, New Haven, 1962-63, N.Am. Precis Syndicate, Inc., N.Y.C., 1963-68, exec. v.p., prin., bd. dirs., 1968—. Guest lectr. Publicity Club of N.Y., 1971. Mem. Manalapan Englishtown Bd. Edn., N.J., 1971-77, pres., 1975-77; treas. Rosegate Condominium Assn., Old Bridge, N.J., 1986-2002. Mem. Pub. Rels. Soc. Am., Publicity Club of N.Y. (bd. dirs.), B'nai B'rith (pres. 1967-69). Home: 5200 Brittany Dr S Saint Petersburg FL 33715 E-mail: mirajon2@aol.com.

ENGEL, PAUL BERNARD, lawyer; b. Balt., Feb. 6, 1926; s. Robert and and Ida (L) E.; m. Lorraine Goodman, Sept. 7, 1947; children— Seena Engel Kling, Cindy Engel Dubansky, Lon Craig. AA, U. Balt., 1947, JD, 1950. Bar: Md.1950, DC 1950. Ptnr. Engel and Engel P.A., Balt., 1950—. Bd. govs. Boca Highland Ctr. Assn., gov., 1992-, also treas., pres., chmn. legal com.; v.p. Aberdeen Arms Condos. With AUS, 1944-45. With USAR, 1944—45. Mem. ABA, Md. Plaintiffs Bar Assn., Balt. City Bar Assn., Bonnie View C. of C. (bd. dirs. 1964-67, 69-72). Clubs: Bonnie View Country (bd. dirs.). Lodges: Masons. Home: 3409 Deep Willow Ave Baltimore MD 21208-3116 Office: 11 E Lexington St Ste 200 Baltimore MD 21202-1733 E-mail: pb.e2626@aol.com.

ENGEL, RALPH MANUEL, lawyer; b. N.Y.C., May 13, 1944; s. Werner Herman and Ruth Fredericke (Friedlander) E.; m. Diane Linda Weinberg, Aug. 10, 1968; children— Eric M., Daniel C., Julie R. BA in Econs. with highest honors, NYU, 1965, JD, 1968. Bar: N.Y. 1968, U.S. Supreme Ct. 1972. Assoc. Gilbert, Segall and Young, N.Y.C., 1968—71, Trubin Sillcocks Edelman & Knapp, N.Y.C., 1971—76; assoc., then ptnr. Summit Rovins & Feldesman and predecessor firms, N.Y.C., 1976—91; ptnr. Rosen & Reade, LLP, N.Y.C., 1991—2001, Sonnenshein Nath & Rosenthal, LLP, N.Y.C., 2001—. Lectr. Sch. Law, Fordham U., 1990-91. Contbr. articles to legal and other publs.; editor-in-chief The Commentator, NYU, 1968 Mem. Planning Com., Larchmont, N.Y., 1992—. Fellow Am. Coll. Trust and Estate Counsel; mem. N.Y. State Bar Assn. (trust and estate law sect. com. on practice and ethics 1991—, elder law sect., com. on guardianships and fiduciaries 1991-97, com. on estates and tax planning 1997—), Assn. Bar City of N.Y. (com. on estate and gift taxation 1992-95, chmn. subcom. on splitting and combining trusts 1994-95, chmn., subcom. on spousal rights 1994-95, com. on trusts, estates and surrogate's cts. 1997-2000), Estate Planning Coun. Westchester County (bd. dirs. 1985-91). Home and Office: 6 Rockwood Dr Larchmont NY 10538-2537 Office: Sonnenschein Nath & Rosenthal 1221 Ave of the Americas New York NY 10020 Personal E-mail: engelesq@yahoo.com. Business E-Mail: rengel@sonnenschein.com.

ENGEL, RICHARD L. career officer; b. L.A., July 2, 1946; s. Richard Leroy and Margret Ellen (Wilson) E.; m. Connie Jean Ricks, Sept. 8, 1973; children: Lindsey, Jennifer, Shelly. BS in Mech. Engring., Tex. A&M U., 1968; MS in Indsl. and Sys. Mgmt. Engring., Ariz. State U., Tucson, 1975; student, Air Force Test Pilot Sch., 1976-77, Armed Forces Staff Coll., 1981; M in Nat. Security Strategic Studies, Naval War Coll., 1988. Commd. 2d lt. USAF, 1968, advanced through grades to maj. gen., 1996, pilot spl. ops., 1970-71, instr. pilot, 1971-74; air staff officer Hdqs. Air Tng. Command, Randolph AFB, Tex., 1974-76; advanced simulator rsch. flight test officer Air Force Human Resources Lab., Williams AFB, 1978-81; chief of acads. Air Force Test Pilot Sch., Edwards AFB, Calif., 1981-83; dep. dir. F-16 LANTIRN Test Program, Edwards AFB, 1983-85; comdr. F-16 and LANTIRN Combined Test Forces, Edwards AFB, 1985-87; divsn. chief weapons sys. divsn. Office of Legis. Liaison for Sec. of Air Force, Washington, 1988-89; comdr. 3246th Test Wing, Air Force Devel. Test Ctr., Eglin AFB, Fla., 1989-92, 412th Test Wing, Edwards AFB, 1992-93, Air Force Flight Test Ctr., Edwards AFB, 1993-98; commandant Indsl. Coll. of the Armed Forces, Ft. McNair, 1998—. Decorated Legion of Merit, D.F.C. with two oak leaf clusters, Air medal with nine oak leaf clusters, Air Force Commendation medal. Mem. AIAA, Soc. Exptl. Test Pilots. Office: Indsl Coll of the Armed Forces 408 4th Ave Washington DC 20319-5062

ENGEL, ROBERT, chemist, educator, dean; b. Pitts., Aug. 30, 1942; s. Ralph Emil and Clara Elizabeth (Schmidt) Engel; m. Elizabeth Ella Neidigh, Oct. 1, 1966 (dec. May 22, 2002); children: Cheryl Noel, Erik Michael. BS, Carnegie Inst. Tech., 1963; PhD, Pa. State U., 1966. Prof. chemistry Queens Coll. CUNY, Flushing, NY, 1968—, dean rsch. and grad. study Queens Coll., 1998—. Author: 10 Books; contbr. over 120 articles to profl. jours. Capt. U.S. Army, 1966—68. Fellow, NATO, 1975, Rohm & Haas Co., 1986. Mem.: Am. Chem. Soc., Royal Soc. Chemistry, Internat. Coun. Main Group Chemistry (exec. sec. 1997—, treas. 1997—). Achievements include patents in field. Office: Queens College CUNY 65 30 Kissena Blvd Flushing NY 11367 Fax: 718-997-5198. E-mail: robert_engel@qc.edu.

ENGEL, TALA, lawyer; b. N.Y.C. d. Volodia Vladimir Boris and Risia (Modelevska) E.; m. James Colias, Nov. 22, 1981 (dec. Nov. 1989). AA, U. Fla., 1952; BA in Russian and Spanish, U. Miami, 1954; JD, U. Miami, Coral Gables, 1957; postgrad., Middlebury Coll., 1953. Bar: Fla. 1957, D.C. 1982, U.S. Dist. Ct. (so. dist.) Fla. 1957, Ill. 1962, U.S. Dist. Ct. (no. dist.) Ill. 1962, U.S. Supreme Ct., 1965. Pvt. practice, Miami, Fla., 1957—61, Chgo., 1966—86, Washington, 1987—89, Chgo., 1990—93, Washington, 1993—2002, Miami, Fla., 2002—. Atty. Immigration and Naturalization Svc., Chgo., 1961-62; parole agt. Ill. Youth Commn., Chgo., 1963-66. Editor The Lawyer, 1956; mem. editl. bd. Miami Law Quar., 1955-57, 10 ML Q 110 Criminal Law, 10 ML Q 608 Ins. Law, 1955-56. Bd. dirs. Cordi-Marian Settlement, Chgo., 1977-93. Named One of 2000 Outstanding Women of 20th Century, Dictionary Internat. Biography, 2000. Mem.: Fla. Bar Assn., Fed. Bar Assn., Chgo. Bar Assn. (devel. of law com. 1985—87, entertainment com. 1971—72), Ill. Bar Assn. (gen. assembly 1984—86), Chgo. Bar Found. (life), Nu Beta Epsilon, Alpha Lambda Delta. Avocations: travel, theater, singing, Russian and Spanish languages. Address: PO Box 221432 Hollywood FL 33022 E-mail: talaengel@aol.com.

ENGEL, WALBURGA See VON RAFFLER-ENGEL, WALBURGA

ENGELAGE, JAMES ROLAND, business executive; b. Springfield, Mo., Dec. 5, 1945; s. Roland C. and Dorothy (Deeds) E.; m. Marcia Cooley, July 5, 1968. BS, SW Mo. State U., 1965; MS, Troy U., 1968; MA, Cen. Mich. U., 1978; PhD, St. Louis U., 1977. Dept. chmn. Montgomery (Ala.) Pub. Schs., 1968-69; asst. prin. Francis Howell Sch. Dist., St. Charles, 1969-74, asst. supt., 1974-75; adj. faculty Command & Gen. Staff Coll., Ft. Leavenworth, Kans., 1976-93; dean Randolph Macon Acad., Front Royal, Va., 1993-94; CEO JAMARC Mgmt. Corp., Winchester, Va., 1994—. Evening dir. Temple Schs., Silver Spring, Md., 1982-84; adj. prof. Park Coll., Ft. Myer, Va., 1980-82. Editor: Operation Desert Shield, 1992; contbr. articles to publs. Served to col. U.S. Army, 1975-93. Recipient legion of merit award Dept. Army, Washington, 1993. Mem. Res. Officers Assn. (pres. Chgo. chpt. 1992, Louisville chpt. 1993), Civil Air Patrol (capt. 1973-74), Lions Club (charter 1970-71), Civitans. Republican. Methodist. Avocations: computers, aviation. Home: 411 Windsor Ln Winchester VA 22602-2333 Office: JAMARC Mgmt Corp 2021 S Pleasant Valley Rd Winchester VA 22601-7001

ENGEL-ARIELI, SUSAN LEE, physician; b. Chgo., Oct. 7, 1954; d. Thaddeus S. Dziengiel and Marion L. (Carpenter) Kasper; m. Udi Arieli. BA, Northwestern U., 1975; MD, Chgo. Med. Sch., 1982. Diplomate Am. Bd. Gen. Practice, Am. Bd. Ambulatory Medicine. Med. technician G.D. Searle, Skokie, Ill., 1972, 73, assoc. dir., 1983-84, dir. U.S. Regional Clin. Support, 1984-86; rsch. editorial asst. U. Chgo., 1974; rsch. assoc. Loyola U., Maywood, Ill., 1977-78; intern Rush Presbyn. St. Lukes Hosp., Chgo., 1982-83; resident U. Chgo., 1983; mgr. hosp. products div. Abbott Labs., Abbott Park, Ill., 1986-87. Bd. govs., dep. gov. Am. Biog. Inst. Rsch. Assn., 1988; vis. prof. Rush Presbyn.-St. Luke's Hosp., Chgo., 1985, faculty assoc., 1985; assoc. investigator, asst. prof. medicine King Drew Med. Ctr., UCLA, 1985-90; practical cardiology panel experts, 1988; Med. World News Rev. panel, 1988; bd. dirs. Am. Soc. Handicapped Physicians, acting v.p.; bd. dirs. fundraising, chmn. Vestibular Disorders Assn. Author: How Your Body Works, 1994, C-D Rom version, 1995; contbr. articles to profl. and scholarly jours. Bd. govs. Art Inst. Chgo., 1985—, mem. aux. bd., 1988—, mem. multiple benefit coms., 1984—, vice chmn. Capital Campaign, 1984-85; mem. pres. com. Landmark Preservation Coun., Chgo., 1984-90, chmn. multiple coms. polit. candidates, 1986; bd. dirs. Marshall unit Chgo. Boys Clubs, 1984—; mem. benefit com. Hubbard St. Dance Co. 10th Gala, 1988, Victory Garden's Theatre Ann. Benefit, 1988. Recipient Gold award, 1995, Nat. Health Info. award, 1995; Internat. Coll. Surgeons fellow, 1982. Mem. AMA, ACP, Am. Fedn. for Clin. Rsch., Southern Med. Assn., Ill. State Med. Soc., Chgo. Med. Soc., Am. Acad. Med. Dirs., Nat.

Acad. Arts and Scis., Am. Soc. Handicapped Physicians (bd. dirs., v.p.), Vestibular Disorders Assn. (bd. dirs., pub. rels. com., co-chmn. fundraising). Avocations: german language, organ playing, composing music, writing.

ENGELBRECHT, RUDOLF, electrical engineering educator; b. Atlanta, Apr. 18, 1928; s. Walter and Dorothea E.; m. Christel M. Kluth, Sept. 10, 1950; children— Richard, Rolf, Erika. B.S., Ga. Inst. Tech., 1951, M.S. in Elec. Engring., 1953; Ph.D. in Elec. Engring., Oreg. State U., 1979. Mem. tech. staff Bell Labs., Whippany, N.J., 1953-60, supr., Murray Hill, N.J., 1961-63, dept. head, 1964-69; dir. RCA Tech. Ctr., Somerville, N.J., 1970-72; group leader RCA Labs., Zurich, Switzerland, 1972-77; assoc. prof. Oreg. State U., Corvallis, 1977-93. Co-author: Microwave Devices, 1969; contbr. articles to profl. jours.; patentee in field. Named to Oreg. State U. Engring. Hall of Fame, 1998. Fellow IEEE (life, Centennial award 1984, Third Millenium medal 2000); mem. Sigma Xi. Office: Oreg State U Dept Elec Computer Eng Corvallis OR 97331

ENGELHARD, ARTHUR WILLIAM, research scientist, consultant; b. Dayton, Ohio, Apr. 9, 1928; s. Paul George and Luisa Emma Engelhard; children: Eric Andrew, Lisa Diane, Arthur William. BS, Ohio U., 1950; MS, Yale U., 1952; PhD, Iowa State Coll., Ames, 1955. Grad. asst. Iowa State Coll., Ames, 1952—55; asst. plant pathologist Ill. State Natural History Survey, Urbana, 1955—56. Rsch. biologist E.I. DuPont de Nemours & Co., Wilmington, Del., 1956—64; sr. sales rsch. biologist E.I. Du Pont de Nemours & Co., Bradenton, Fla., 1964—65, sr. rsch. biologist, Wilmington, Del., 1965—66; assoc. prof. U. Fla., Bradenton, 1966—77, prof. plant pathology, 1977—92, prof. emeritus, Gainsville, 1992—; cons. floral industry, Fla., 1970—95. Author: Index of Hosts to Verticillium, 1957, Management of Diseases with Macro and Micro Elements, 1989; contbr. articles to profl. jours. Com. chairmanships Boy Scouts of Am., Bradenton, Fla., 1967—82; chair several coms. Hernando De Soto Hist. Soc., Bradenton, Fla., 1972—88; mem., chair spl. com. Manatee County Sch. Bd., Bradenton, Fla., 1976. Recipient Outstanding Paper, Fla. Hort. Soc., 1968, Medal of Merit, Ohio U., 1983, Outstanding Paper, Fla. Hort. Soc., 1970, 1972. Mem.: Am. Phytopatological Soc. (com. chairmanships 1960—90), Antique Car Clubs, three (pres. of each club 1975—2001). Achievements include patents for for control of Arachnids; research in Management of Fusarium Wilt with an Integrated Lime Nutrent and Chemotherapy Regime. Avocations: antique cars, antique furniture, snow skiing, scuba diving. Home: 5306 7th Avenue Drive West Bradenton FL 34209 Office: University Florida 5007 60th Street East Bradenton FL 34205

ENGELHARDT, ALBERT GEORGE, physicist; b. Toronto, Ont., Can., Mar. 17, 1935; came to U.S., 1957, naturalized, 1965; s. Samuel and Rose (Menkes) E.; m. Elzbieta Szajkowska, June 14, 1960; children— Frederick, Leonard, Michael. BASc., U. Toronto, 1958; MS, U. Ill., 1959, PhD (grad. fellow), 1961. Research asst. elec. engring. U. Ill., Urbana, 1958-61; staff research and devel. center engr. Westinghouse Electric Co., Pitts., 1961-70, mgr., 1966-69, fellow scientist, 1969-70; sr. research scientist, group leader Hydro-Que. Research Inst., Varennes, Can., 1970-74; mem. staff Los Alamos Sci. Lab., 1974-86; adj. prof. elec. engring. Tex. Tech. U., Lubbock, 1976—; pres., chief exec. officer, founder Enfitek, Inc., Los Alamos, N.Mex., 1982—. Vis. prof. U. Que., 1970-77 Contbr. articles to profl. jours. Group leader Boy Scouts Can., 1972-74. Mem. IEEE Nuclear and Plasma Scis. Soc., Am. Phys. Soc. Home and Office: 549 Bryce Ave Los Alamos NM 87544-3607 E-mail: agengelhardt@mailaps.org. *Since 1959 my basic research interest has been plasma physics and concomitantly nuclear fusion. The importance of the latter is that it shows great promise for providing us with renewable energy resources with acceptably small environmental and ecological perturbation.*

ENGELHARDT, IRL F. coal company executive; b. Oct. 19, 1946; m. Suzanne C.; children: Joel, Erin, Evan. BS in Acctg., U. Ill., 1968; MBA, So. Ill. U., 1971. From mem. staff to pres., CEO Peabody Energy, St. Louis, 1979-90, pres., CEO, 1990—, now chmn., CEO. Bd. dirs. U.S. Bank N.A., St. Louis. Mem. Nat. Mining Assn. (bd. dirs., chmn. 1995-96), Nat. Coal Assn. (chmn. 1995-96), Internat. Energy Agy. (coal industry adv. bd., chmn., special com. mem.), Nat. Assn. Mfrs. (bd. dirs.), Coal Utilization Rsch Group (co-chmn.), Coal Based Stockholders Group (co-chmn.), St. Louis Arts and Edn. Council, St. Louis Area Council (exec. bd.), Boy Scouts of Am. Office: Peabody Energy 701 Market St Saint Louis MO 63101 Fax: 314-342-7797. E-mail: lengelhardt@peabodyenergy.com.*

ENGELHARDT, JOHN HUGO, lawyer, banker; b. Houston, Feb. 3, 1946; s. Hugo Tristram and Beulah Lillie (Karbach) E.; m. Jasmin Inge Nestler, Nov. 12, 1976; children: Angelique D., Sabrina N. BA, U. Tex., 1968; JD, St. Marys U., San Antonio, 1973. Tchr. history Pearsall H.S., Tex., 1968-69; pvt. practice New Braunfels, Tex., 1973-75, 82—; examining atty. Comml. Title Co., San Antonio, 1975-78, San Antonio Title Co., 1978-82. Adv. dir. M Bank Brenham, Tex., 1983-89. Fellow Coll. State Bar Tex.; mem. ABA, Pi Gamma Mu. Republican. Roman Catholic.

ENGELHARDT, LEROY A. retired paper company executive; b. Saginaw, Mich., Mar. 15, 1924; s. Herman J. and Alma (Engelhard) E.; m. Arlene L. Papineau, July 12, 1947; children— Richard C., Kay C., Douglas R. BBA, U. Mich., 1949, MBA, 1950. Plant, div. or subsidiary controller Chrysler Corp., 1950-60; mgmt. controls cons. Diehl K.G., Nuremberg, Germany, 1960-63; sec. Genesee Brewing Co., Rochester, N.Y., 1963-67; v.p. fin. Consol. Papers, Inc., Wisconsin Rapids, Wis., 1967-89, also ret. dir. Served with AUS, 1943-46. Home: 444 Two Mile Ave Wisconsin Rapids WI 54494-6559 E-mail: arlroy@wctc.net.

ENGELHARDT, REGINA, cosmetologist, artist, small business owner; b. Kiwerce, Poland, Oct. 1, 1928; came to U.S., 1949; d. Marian and Maria (Wardach) Engelhardt; m. Gerard Edward Twardon, May 30, 1953 (div. 1961); children: Miriam Teresa Twardon Bielski, Elizabeth Maria Twardon Israel, Renee Marie Twardon Gilchrist. Grad., Laski Inst. Tech., 1951; lic. cosmetologist, Hamtramck Beauty Sch., 1960; art student, Mercy Ctr., 1980-84. Sec. Am. Savs., Detroit, 1950-55; cosmetologist Magic Touch Salon, Oak Park, Mich., 1960—. Owner Regina's Fine Arts, Detroit, 1986—, Art Restorations, 1986—; art tchr. Farmington Activity Ctr., Farmington Hills, Mich., 1993—; spkr. in field. Artist lithographs; represented in permanent collection at Althorp Mus., Eng., 1998, also pvt. collections in U.S., Can., Poland, Eng., India, The Philippines. Mem. Dem. Nat. Com., 1996—; mem. nat. com. to preserve social security and medicare, 1993—. Recipient Gold and Silver medals Internat. Art Challenge, 1987-88, 90, Kubinski award Friends of Polish Arts, 1989, First and Fourth awards Mich. State Exhibit, 1988. Mem. Sculptores Guild of Mich., Four Octave Club, Farmington Artists Club (6 Popular Vote awards 1985, 86, 97, merit award local art exhibit 1997, two merit awards 1998), Sierra Club, Internat. Platform Assn., Nature Conservancy. Roman Catholic. Avocations: music, needlework, dance, reading. Home: 17345 Wildemere St Detroit MI 48221-2722 E-mail: reginaart@webtv.net.

ENGELHARDT, SARA LAWRENCE, organization executive; b. Phila., Aug. 23, 1943; d. Ruddick Carpenter and Barbara (Dole) Lawrence; m. Dean Lee Engelhardt, June 20, 1970; children: Barbara Elizabeth, Margaret Ann. BA, Wellesley Coll., 1965; MA, Tchrs. Coll., Columbia U., 1970. Staff asst. Carnegie Corp., N.Y.C., 1966-70, asst. sec., 1972-74, assoc. sec., 1974-75, sec., 1975-87; exec. v.p. Found. Ctr., N.Y.C., 1987-91, pres., 1991—. Free-lance editor and writer, Storrs, Conn., 1970-72. Bd. dirs. Nat. Charities Info. Bur., 1984-2000, chair, 1987-91; trustee Found. Ctr., 1984-87; bd. dirs. Trust for Philanthropy AAFRC, 1989-98; trustee Consortium for Advancement of Pvt. Higher Edn., 1989-93, chair, 1992-93; mem. bd. overseers Ctr. Rsch. on Women, Wellesley Coll., 1979-88; nat. bd. dirs. Girls Inc., 1992-98, Ind. Sector, 1992-98, Coun. Ind. Colls., 1993-94; bd. dirs. NOW Legal Def. and Edn. Fund, 1994-2001, Amigos de las Americas, 1995-2001, Nat. Coun. for Rsch. on Women, 2001—, Rsch. Found. of Metro N.Y. Better Bus. Bur., 2002—. Home: 173 Riverside Dr New York NY 10024-1615 Office: Foundation Ctr 79 5th Ave Fl 2 New York NY 10003-3076

ENGELHARDT, THOMAS ALEXANDER, editorial cartoonist; b. St. Louis, Dec. 29, 1930; s. Alexander Frederick and Gertrude Dolores (Derby) E.; m. Katherine Agnes McCue, June 25, 1960; children— Marybeth, Carol Marie, Christine Leigh, Mark Thomas. Student, Denver U., 1950-51, Ruskin Sch. Fine Arts, Oxford (Eng.) U., 1954-56, Sch. Visual Arts, N.Y.C., 1957. Free-lance cartoonist, comml. artist, N.Y.C., 1957-60, Cleve., 1961-62, asst. editorial cartoonist, Newspaper Enterprise Assn., Cleve., 1960-61; editorial cartoonist St. Louis Post-Dispatch, 1962-97; freelance cartoonist, 1998—; one-man exhbns. of cartoons at Fontbonne Coll. Art Gallery, St. Louis, 1972, Old Courthouse (Jefferson Nat. Meml.), St. Louis, 1981, Mark Twain Bank, Frontenac, Mo., 1989; group exhbns. Washington U., St. Louis, 2000, Nat. Press Club, Washington, 2001, St. Louis Artists Guild, 2001. Served with USAF, 1951-53. Recipient Ethical Humanist of Yr. award St. Louis Ethical Soc., 1986, Kay and Leo Drey Environ. Leadership award Mo. Coalition for Environment, 1999. Roman Catholic. Office: 7830 Lafon Pl Saint Louis MO 63130-3805

ENGELHARDT, THOMAS FRANCIS, lawyer, consultant; b. May 24, 1926; s. William Fredrick and Norma Agnes Engelhardt; m. Elizabeth Lina Blais, Sept. 24, 1954. BA, U. Wis., Madison; JD, George Washington U., 1958. Bar: Va. 1959, U.S. Dist. Ct. D.C. 1963, U.S. Ct. Appeals (D.C. cir.) 1963, U.S. Supreme Ct. 1964. Intelligence officer CIA, Washington, 1952—59; chief trial counsel AEC, Washington, 1959—65, chief counsel, 1966—74; chief dept. contract law Westinghouse Electric, Pitts., 1965—66; dep. legal dir. Nuclear Regulatory Commn., Washington, 1974—82; cons. Sun City, Ariz., 1982—2000, Peoria, Ariz., 2000—. Chmn. adv. com. Battelle Meml. Inst., Columbus, Ohio, 1983—86. Pres. Sun City United Way, Sun City Cmty. Coun., Montgomery Cmty. Assn., Montgomery County, Md., 1976, Sumner Cmty. Assn., Bethesda, Md., 1982; v.p. Cath. Social Svc. Ariz. Served with U.S. Army, 1944—46. Recipient Disting. Svc. award, Nuclear Regualatory Commn., 1980. Mem.: D.C. Bar Assn., Va. Bar Assn. Roman Catholic. Home and Office: 20554 N 101st Ave Apt 2018 Peoria AZ 85382-5501

ENGELKING, ELLEN MELINDA, pattern company executive, real estate broker, manufacturing company; b. Columbus, Ind., May 12, 1942; d. Lowell Eugene and Marcella (Brane) E.; children: Melissa Claire Fairbanks John David Prohaska, Ellen Margaret Brunner. Student, Sullins Coll., 1961, Franklin Coll., 1961-62, Ind. U., 1963. Chmn., CEO Engelking, Inc., Columbus, Ind. Founder The FlexCell Group. Sec. Bartholomew County Rep. Party, 1976-80; chmn. bd. dirs. Jr. Achievementm 1996—; chmn. Pvt. Industry Coun. South Ctrl. Ind.; protocol hostess Pan Am. Games X, Indpls., 1987. Bd. dirs. Ind. Humanities Coun., 1997—, United Way, 2000—. Recipient Franklin Coll. Alumni Citation, 1994, Athena award Oldsmobile Inst. Am. Bank C. of C., 1995. Mem. Columbus Area C. of C. (vice chmn. bd. dirs. 1990, bd. dirs. 1997—), Centra Credit Union (bd. dirs.), Delta Delta Delta. Roman Catholic. Avocation: study and present adaptation of shaker work ethic. Office: Engelking Inc PO Box 607 Columbus IN 47202-0607

ENGELL, JAMES THEODORE, English educator; b. Danville, Pa., Sept. 6, 1951; s. Frederick Jacob and Ruth Louise Engell; m. Ainslie Sheridan Brennan, June 2, 1984; children: Marleny Brennan, Alexander E. BA, Harvard Coll., 1973; PhD, Harvard U., 1978. Asst. prof. Harvard U., Cambridge, Mass., 1978-80, assoc. prof., 1980-83, prof. English and comparative lit., 1983—2000, Gurney prof. English, prof. comparative lit., 2000—, chair degree program in history and lit., 1988-93, dir. undergrad. studies in English, 1995-97. Author: The Creative Imagination, 1981 (Thomas Wilson prize 1982), Forming the Critical Mind, 1989, The Committed Word: Literature and Public Values, 1999; editor: Coleridge: The Early Family Letters, 1994; co-editor: Coleridge, Biographia Literaria, 1983; editor, contbr.: Johnson and His Age, 1984, Teaching Literature: What Is Needed Now, 1988; editl. advisor Jour. History of Ideas, 1986—, Coll. Lit., 1990—, 1650-1850 Ideas, Aesthetics, and Inquiries in the Early Modern Era, Eighteenth-Century Thought, Literature and Religion. Corporator Emerson Hosp. and Health System, Concord, Mass., 1989-94. Recipient Levenson Tchg. prize, 1995, Roslyn Abramson Tchg. award, 1997, Coun. for Advancement and Support Edn. Gold award, 1999, Phi Betta Kappa Tchg. award, 2002, John Marquand Advising prize, 2003; Ford Found. grantee, 1978; Cabot fellow, 2001. Mem. MLA, Am. Soc. 18th Century Studies, Johnsonians (chair 1990-91), Assn. Lit. Scholars and Critics (pres. 2001-2002, sec. 2002—), Friends of Coleridge. Avocations: travel, sports, music. Office: Harvard U Barker Ctr Dept English 12 Quincy St Cambridge MA 02138-3804

ENGELMAN, KARL, physician; b. N.Y.C., June 23, 1933; s. Samuel and Lillian (Wachs) E.; m. Elaine Kaufman, June 10, 1956; children— Harold Kent, Ross Mitchell, Jeffrey Steven. BS, Men's Coll. Arts and Scis., Rutgers U., 1955; MD, Harvard U., 1959; MA (hon.), U. Pa., 1971. Diplomate Am. Bd. Internal Medicine. Intern, asst. resident, resident in medicine Mass. Gen. Hosp., Boston, 1959-64; clin. asso., sr. investigator, attending physician Nat. Heart Inst., NIH, Bethesda, Md., 1961-70; assoc. prof. medicine and pharmacology Sch. Medicine U. Pa., Phila., 1971-95; chief hypertension sect., dir. clin. research center Sch. Medicine U. Pa. Cons. physician Phila. VA Hosp., 1971-95, Children's Hosp., Phila., 1971-95; clin. prof. medicine Med. U. of S.C., 1996—; cons. Beaufort-Jasper Comprehensive Health Svcs., 1996—. Patentee in field. Med. staff Vols. in Medicine, 2002--. Served with USPHS, 1961-63. Mem. ACP, Am. Coll. Clin. Pharmacology, Internat. Soc. of Hypertention (sci. coun. on hypertension), U.S. Pharmacopeia and Nat. Formullary (adv. coun.), Coun. for High Blood Pressure Rsch. (adv. bd.), Am. Heart Assn., Phila. Doctors Golf Assn., Sea Pines Club. Jewish. Home: 20 Turnberry Ln Hilton Head Island SC 29928-4108

ENGELMAN, MELVIN ALKON, retired dentist, business executive, scientist; b. Waterbury, Conn., July 27, 1921; s. Herman B. and Marion (Halpern) E.; m. Muriel Phillips, Aug. 27, 1949; children: Curtis Land, Suzanne Ruth. AB, Ohio U., 1942; DDS, Western Res. U., 1944. Diplomate: Am. Bd. Oral Electrosurgery. Pvt. practice dentistry, Wappingers Falls, N.Y., 1949-89; chmn. oral diagnosis and oral pathology sect., dir. oral diagnostic ctr. St. Francis Hosp., Poughkeepsie, N.Y., 1963-77, attending dentist, 1963-89, dir. dept. dentistry, 1967, 71-74, 78, hon. staff, 1989—; pres. Di-Equi Dental Products Inc., 1980-99, Dentifax Internat. Inc., 1982-99. Observer Meml. Hosp. Cancer and Allied Diseases, N.Y.C., 1962-66; mem. adv. bd. Dutchess Community Coll., 1963-69, lectr. dental assts. program, 1960-63; dir. 1st regional sci. fair, Dutchess County, N.Y., 1960-61; project dir. USPHS community cancer demonstration project, St. Francis Hosp., 1963-66; asst. chief med. officer Dutchess County N.Y. CD, 1963-68; cons. Nat. Cancer Inst., mem. clin. cancer tng. com., 1968-71, Profl. edn. com. for cancer control, 1972-73; attending dentist Central Dutchess Nursing Home, 1970-85; cons. VA Hosp., Castle Point, N.Y., 1976-77, Lactona Corp., div. Warner Lambert, 1976-80; internat. lectr. on fixed prosthodontics, premedication, oral cancer, metallurgy. Co-author: Oral Cancer Examination Procedure, 16 edits., 1967-83; contbr. articles to profl. jours.; patentee for feeder bar, spruing assembly, sprue pin, and hollow movable reservoir. Chmn. Wappinger Red Cross Fund Drive, 1956; committeeman Troop 6, Boy Scouts Am., Chelsea, N.Y., 1963-67; pres. Dutchess County unit Am. Cancer Soc., 1969-71. From ensign to lt. comdr. Dental Corps, USNR, FMF PAC, 1942-46; lt. comdr. ret., 1986. Fellow AAAS (life), Royal Soc. Health (Eng.), Am. Pub. Health Assn., Acad. Gen. Dentistry; mem. ADA (life), Internat. Assn. Dental Research, Assn. Mil. Surgeons (life mem.), 9th Dist. Dental Soc. (life mem.), Dutchess County Dental Soc. (pres. 1965), Am. Acad. Dental Electrosurgery (pres. 1983), Wappinger Conservation Assn. (v.p. 1970-71), Wappingers Falls C. of C. (pres. 1952-54), Alpha Omega. Clubs: Masons (32 deg.), Shriners, B'nai B'rith (pres. So. Duchess lodge 1963-64). Address: 5720 Cottonwood St Bradenton FL 34203-8806 E-mail: mur4545@aol.com.

ENGELMANN, PAUL VICTOR, plastics engineering educator; b. Ann Arbor, Mich., Jan. 15, 1958; s. Manfred David and Patricia (Park) E.; m. Sarah C. Sanford, Oct. 24, 1998; children: Thomas, David. AS in Geology, Lansing (Mich.) C.C., 1980; BS in Indsl. Edn., Western Mich. U., 1982, MA in Vocat. Edn., 1984, EdD in Ednl. Leadership, 1988. Owner H.L. & S. Auto Restoration & Fabrication, Lansing, Mich., 1977-82; from tchg. asst. dept. engring. tech. to prof. dept. indsl. and mfg. engring. Western Mich. U., Kalamazoo, 1982—2000, prof. Indsl. and Mfg. Engring. Dept., 2000, asst. chmn. dept., 2001—02, chmn. dept., 2002—. Prin. investigator Rsch. and Tech. Inst., Grand Rapids, Mich., 1988-97; prin. investigator Right Place, Grand Rapids, 1997—; rschr. Robert Morgan & Co., Battle Creek, Mich., 1990-94; prin. investigator Copper Devel. Assn. Inc., 1995—; cons. plastics Parker Hannafin Corp., Ostego, Mich., 1990-97; v.p. Western Mich. SPE Edn. Found., 1994-97. Author: Manufacturing Technology, 1989; contbr. 50 articles to profl. jours.; patentee in field. Pres. Plainwell (Mich.) Hist. Preservation Soc., 1990-91, 97-99; pres. bd. dirs. Pipp Found., 1992—, sec. 1992—; chmn., bd. trustees 1st United Meth. Ch., Plainwell, 1996-97, vice chmn. bldg. com., 1997-00. Presdl. scholar, 1982; recipient Protective Package of the Yr. award Children's Hosp. of Birmingham, 1990, Teaching Excellence award Western Mich. U., 1990. Mem. Soc. Plastics Engrs. (sr., past pres. 1992-93, pres. 1991-92, pres.-elect 1990-91, v.p. Western Mich. sec. 1989-90, sec. 1988-89, edn. chmn. 1985-88, Sectional award 1986, 87, 88, Best Paper award 1993, 99, 2000, Outstanding Mem. award 1994). Methodist. Avocations: antique auto restoration, old house preservation, environmental preservation. Home: 311 E Chart St Plainwell MI 49080-1703 Office: Western Mich U Dept Indsl and Mfg Engring MailStop5336 Kalamazoo MI 49008-5336 E-mail: paul.engelmann@wmich.edu.

ENGELMANN, RUDOLPH HERMAN, electronics consultant, writer; b. Hewitt, Minn., Mar. 5, 1929; s. Herman Emil Robert and Minna Louise (Kniep) E.; children: Guy Robert, Heidi Louise. BA, U. Minn., 1953. Electronic designer Lawrence Livermore (Calif.) Lab., 1959-61; cons. Atlantic Rsch. Corp., Manchester, N.H., 1961-64, Gen. Radio Co., West Concord, Mass., 1963-69, Possis Engring., Mpls., 1970—, 3M Co., St. Paul, 1977-78, Pako Photo, Mpls., 1977-78, Litton Microwave, Mpls., 1977-79. Presenter papers at confs., 1988-89, 89-90. Author: The Emperor's Last Man, 2000, Father Fathers Day, 2000; contbr. articles to profl. jours. 1st lt. USAF, 1946-53. Achievements include developments and patents in gigahertz digital frequency scalers and counters and time interval meters, touchtone telephone for U.S. Army, automatic photographic focus control, automatic temperature monitor and control for grain and petroleum storage safety and volume correction, optical character recognition, high efficiency battery charging systems, end-of-charge detector, rudderless flight control, ultra lightweight muscle prostheses, flight controls, power management, stealth penetrating radar, high efficiency shape memory alloy modulation and linear circuitry, high-efficiency electronic orthetic muscle, digitally variable 90db A.C. power source, raster scanning microscope, linear wave blood pump.

ENGELS, BEATRICE ANN, retired real estate company executive, poet, artist; b. N.Y.C., Oct. 1, 1925; d. Sydney and Marguerite Agnes (Carroll) Jonap; m. James J. Engels, May 10, 1944 (dec.); children: James J. Jr.(dec.), Edward R., Marguerite Mary McHale. Brokers degree, Dowling Coll., Oakdale, N.Y., 1970. Real estate sales agt. Kathleen Hart Real Estate, Bayport, NY, 1969—70; real estate broker, pres. Beatrice A. Engels Realty, Patchogue, NY, 1970—76, Blue Point, NY, 1976—95; dir., pres. Beatrice A. Engels Art Gallery, Patchogue, 1970—76, Petite Pallette Art Gallery, Bayport, 1989—91; ret., 1995. Mem. real estate bd. Suffolk County, 1970—80, ecology adv., Blue Point, 1974—94; columnist LI Advance, Patchogue, NY, 1971—75; columnist Suffolk County News The Long Island Advance, Patchoque, NY, 0197—1976. Author: Morning Song, 1996 (Editor's Choice award, 1996), Sea Sonnets and Other Poems, 1997, Endless Skies of Blue (Editor's Choice award, 1997), Best Poems of 1997, Celebration of Poets, 1997, Outstanding Poets of 1998 (Editor's Choice award, 1998), Best Poems of 1998; author, illustrator: Marguerite, The Story of a Dolly, 2003, songwriter: Best Christmas Present, 1998; artist numerous mediums. Mem. Blue Point Rep. Club, 1970—88. Mem.: Rosary Soc. (pres.), Internat. Soc. Poets (life), Wet Paints Studio Group (life). Roman Catholic. Achievements include ecological efforts that helped to save the wetlands near Blue Point, N.Y. Home Fax: 954-783-9725. E-mail: beabysea@bellsouth.net.

ENGELS, LAWRENCE ARTHUR, retired metals company executive; b. Darlington, Wis., Sept. 26, 1933; s. Henry Morris and Nell Ellen (O'Connor) E.; m. Marilyn Rae Stellick, Sept. 6, 1958; children: Laurie, Michael, Thomas, Stephen. BBA, U. Wis., 1959; MBA, Northwestern U., 1970. Dist. credit mgr. U.S. Steel Corp., Chgo., 1959-69; asst. treas. Nat. Can Corp., Chgo., 1969-77; corp. treas. Comml. Metals Co., Dallas, 1977—, chief fin. officer and treas., 1979—, v.p., treas., chief fin. officer, 1981-99, retired, 1999. Served with USN, 1952-55. Fellow Nat. Inst. Credit; mem. Cash Mgmt. Practitioners Assn. (Chgo. sec. 1975), Chgo. Midwest Credit Mgmt. Assn. (dir. 1973-75), Chgo. Midwest Credit Service Corp. (dir. 1975), Fin. Execs. Inst., Nat. Assn. Corp. Treas.

ENGELS, PATRICIA LOUISE, lawyer; b. Joliet, Ill., July 2, 1926; d. Fred Bridges and Loretta Mae (Fisk) B.; m. Henry William Engels, Feb. 1, 1947; children: Patrick Henry, Michael Bruce, Timothy William. BS in Edn., Olivet Nazarene Coll., 1970, MEd, 1971; JD, John Marshall Law Sch., 1979. Bar: Ill. 1979, Ind. 1979; cert. elem. and high sch. tchr., edn. adminstrn., Ill. Tchr. Bourbonnais (Ill.) and Momence (Ill.) Unit Schs., 1970-76; instr. Kankakee (Ill.) Community Coll., 1975; sole practice Ind. and Ill., 1979—. Qualified divorce mediator, 1991—. Active Lake Village (Ind.) Civic Assn., 1980—; edn. coord. St. Augusta Ch., Lake Village, 1985-89. Avocations: exercise, swimming, sewing, country dancing, reading. Mem. ABA, Ind. Bar Assn., Ill. Bar Assn., Pub. Defender Bar Assn., Theta Chi Sigma, Kappa Delta Pi. Roman Catholic. Avocations: exercise, swimming, sewing, dancing, reading. Home and Office: 33 Brittany Ln Bourbonnais IL 60914-1640

ENGELS, THOMAS JOSEPH, sales executive; b. New Orleans, May 24, 1958; s. Ronald Henry and Sally (Jacobsen) E.; m. Tamara Lewis Engels, May 29, 1982; children: Kristen, Danielle. BS in Gen. Mgmt., Purdue U., 1980. Sales rep. Johnson & Johnson, New Brunswick, N.J., 1980-82, mgr., 1982-83; dist. sales mgr. Pepsi Cola U.S.A., Somers, N.Y., 1983-87; regional sales mgr. Rich Sea Pak Corp., St. Simons Island, Ga., 1988-89; cen. regional mgr. food svc. div. Sara Lee Bakery, Chgo., 1990-93; area mgr. Ctrl. Zone Sara Lee Bakery Food Svc., 1993-94, divsn. promotion mgr. East, 1995-96; no. zone mgr. food svc. Land O'Lakes, Inc., 1996-2000, dir. sales No. U.S.; v.p. sales, food svc Aurora Foods Co., St. Louis, 2000—. Roman Catholic. Avocations: tri-athlons, golf, basketball, coaching soccer. E-mail: engs3x5@aol.com.

ENGEN, D(ONALD) TRAVIS, diversified telecommunications company executive; b. Pasadena, Calif., June 27, 1944; s. Donald Davenport and Mary (Baker) E.; m. Anne Elizabeth Erickson, June 4, 1967; 1 child, Leigh Elizabeth. BS in Aeronautics and Astronautics, MIT, 1967. Dir. electronics mktg. Bell Aerospace, Niagara Falls, N.Y., 1965-76; dir. mktg. Republic Electronic Industries Corp., Melville, N.Y., 1976-79; dir. govt. avionics Bendix Avionics divsn. Bendix Aircraft Systems Co., Ft. Lauderdale, Fla., 1979-83, v.p., gen. mgr., 1983-85; pres., gen. mgr. avionics divsn. ITT Corp., Nutley, N.J., 1985-87, sr. v.p. Washington, 1987-91; pres., chief exec. officer ITT Def., Washington, 1987-91; exec. v.p. ITT Corp., N.Y.C., 1991-95; chmn., CEO ITT Industries Inc., 1994-2000. Avocations: triathlons, vintage car racing. Office: Alcan Inc PO Box 6090 Montreal QC Canada H3C 3A7 Office Fax: 514-848-8115.

ENGEN, JOHN SCOTT, academic administrator, consultant; b. Seattle, Feb. 8, 1956; s. John K. and Muriel K. Engen; life ptnr. Mary Lisa Spahr. BA in Bus Adminstrn., Wash. State U., 1978, BS in Psychology, 1979; MA in Social Sci., Pacific Luth. U., 1981. CFRE Internat./VA, 1993. Therapist Comprehensive Mental Health Ctr., Tacoma, 1980—81; case mgr. Treatment Alternatives to St. Crime, Tacoma, 1980—85; dir. Project CHOICE, Tacoma, 1985—86; planner, devel. dir. Pierce County Alliance, Tacoma, 1986—89; exec. dir. Wash. State 4-H Found., Puyallup, 1990—95, Ariz. 4-H Youth Found., Tucson, 1995—99; dir. U. Ariz., Tucson, 1996—2002; v.p., dir. of devel. Biosphere 2 Ctr. Columbia U., Oracle, Ariz., 2002—03; assoc. v.p. for devel. Fla. Internat. U., Miami, 2003—. Regional rep. Nat. 4-H Coun., Chevy Chase, 1993—94. Prodr.: (video) 4-H Then and Now (Nat. Communicator Award, 1995). Bd. dirs. Habitat for Humanity, Tucson, 1996—2003, 100th ho. campaign chair, 1997—98; social sciences adv. bd. Tacoma C.C., Tacoma, 1992—95; bd. dirs. Operation Nightwatch, Tacoma, 1986—90. Mem.: Nat. Soc. Fund Raising Executives (program chair 1994—95), Assn. Fundraising Profls. (cert. chair 1997—98, treas. 1998—2000, mentorship dir. 2000—01, profl. devel. chair 2001—02), So. Ariz. Rescue Assn., Nat. Ski Patrol (Sr. OEC 2000), Psi Chi (assoc.), Phi Kappa Phi (assoc.), Beta Gamma Sigma (assoc.). Office: Fla Internat U Univ Pk MARC 552 LI 200 SW 8th St Miami FL 33199

ENGEN, LEE EMERSON, retired savings and loan executive; b. Clark, S.D., Sept. 8, 1921; s. Harold O. and Esther V. (Heig) E.; m. Elizabeth M. Eaton, Oct. 29, 1943; children: Barry Lee, Rodney Kent, Timothy Ray. BS, S.D. State U., 1947; postgrad., Ind. U., 1961. Furrier Norris Furs, Sioux Falls, S.D., 1947-50; with Home Fed. Savs. and Loan Assn., Sioux Falls, 1953-86, pres., 1970-86; chmn. bd. Home Fed. Fin. Corp. and Home Fed. Savs. Bank, 1991-96; ret. Treas. Sioux Empire United Way, 1968-73, campaign chmn., 1976, pres., 1982-83; bd. dirs. Sioux Valley Hosp., 1972-81; pres. Family Practice Ctr., 1977-78; treas. Children's Care Hosp. and Sch., 1975-95, pres., 1983-84; pres. Jr. Achievement, 1971-72, Crippled Children Hosp. and Sch. Found., 1989-90, Sioux Falls H.S. Found., 1968-96; sec. Sioux Falls Cmty. Hotel Corp., 1975-85;

mem. Sioux Falls City Planning Commn., 1968-76; treas. Sioux Falls H.S. Found., 1973-89, Mary Chilton Dar Found., 1991-94; chmn. Sioux Valley Hosp. Found., 1984-86, bd. dirs., 1984-87; pres. Nordland Fest, 1987-88, also bd. dirs., 1983-90; bd. dirs. MinnIaKota coun. Girl Scouts U.S., 1985-89, Nordland Heritage Found., 1992-98, pres., 1996-98. Served with AUS, 1943-46, U.S. Army, 1950-53. Decorated Bronze Star with 2 oak leaf clusters, Purple Heart; named Boss of Yr., Sioux Falls Jaycees, 1967, Bus. Citizen of Yr., Sioux Falls Area C. of C. and Sioux Falls Sales and Mktg. Execs., 1985, Boss of Yr., Am. Bus. Womens Assn., 1986; recipient Bronze Leadership award Jr. Achievement, 1978, Silver Leadership award, 1985, Disting. Svc. award Sioux Falls Cosmopolitan Club, 1981. Mem. Sioux Falls Area C. of C. (pres. 1973-74), Minnehaha Country Club, Masons, Shriners. Mem. United Ch. of Christ. Home: 3201 Woodcrest Way Sioux Falls SD 57105-4261

ENGER, EDWARD HENRY, JR., retired editor, writer; b. Mpls., Mar. 16, 1930; s. Edward Henry Sr. and Anastasia (Barber) E.; m. Carolyn Sue Bush, June 1, 1964. BS in Edn., U. Minn., 1952. Cert. tchr., Calif. Tchr. Downers Grove (Ill.) Pub. Sch., 1956-58; editor Harper & Row, Evanston, Ill., 1958-62, author NYC, 1975—78; editor Silver Burdett Co., Morristown, N.J., 1962-68, Dell Pub. Co., N.Y.C., 1968-75; author Nat. Textbook Co., Chgo., 1979-81; editl. dir. Amsco Sch. Publs., N.Y.C., 1982-97; ret., 1997. Author: Writing by Doing, 1981, (textbook series) Language Basics, 1975-78. Served to cpl. U.S. Army, 1954-56, Korea. Mem. Nat. Council Tchrs. English. Democrat. Avocations: gardening, cooking, hiking, jogging.

ENGERRAND, DORIS DIESKOW, business educator; b. Chgo., Aug. 7, 1925; d. William Jacob and Alma Wilhelmina (Cords) Dieskow; m. Gabriel H. Engerrand, Oct. 26, 1946 (dec. June 1987); children: Steven, Kenneth, Jeannine. BS in Bus. Adminstrn., N. Ga. Coll., 1958, BS in Elementary Edn., 1959; M. Bus. Edn., Ga. State U., 1966, PhD, 1970. Tchr., dept. chmn. Lumpkin County H.S., Dahlonega, Ga., 1960-63, 65-68; tchr. Gainesville, Ga., 1965; asst. prof. Troy (Ala.) State U., 1969-71; asst. prof. bus. Ga. Coll. and State U., Milledgeville, 1971-74, assoc. prof., 1974-78, prof., 1978-90, chmn. dept. info. sys. and comms., 1978-89; retired, 1990. Contbr. articles on bus. edn. to profl. publs. Named Outstanding Tchr. Lumpkin County Pub. Schs., 1963, 66; Outstanding Educator bus. faculty Ga. Coll., 1975, Exec. of Yr. award, 1983. Fellow Assn. for Bus. Communication (v.p. S.E. 1978-80, 81-84, 89-92, bd. dirs.), Nat. Bus. Edn. Assn., Ga. Bus. Edn. Assn. (Postsecondary Tchr. of Yr. award 10th dist. 1983, Postsecondary Tchr. of Yr. award 1984), Am. Vocat. Assn., Ga. Vocat. Assn. (Educator of Yr. award 1984, Parker Liles award 1989), Profl. Secs. Internat. (pres. Milledgeville chpt. 1996-97), Ninety-nines Internat. (chmn. N. Ga. chpt. 1975-76, named Pilot of Yr. N. Ga. chpt. 1973). Methodist. Home: 1674 Pine Valley Rd Milledgeville GA 31061-2465

ENGERRAND, KENNETH G. lawyer, law educator; b. Atlanta, June 30, 1952; s. Gabriel H. and Doris A. (Dieskow) E.; m. Anne Walts, Mar. 16, 1985; children: Caroline Elizabeth Turner, Catherine Anne Denton. BA, Fla. State U., 1973; JD, U. Tex., 1976. Bar: Tex. 1976, U.S. Dist. Ct. (so. dist.) Tex 1977, U.S. Ct. Appeals (5th cir.) 1978, U.S. Supreme Ct. 1980, U.S. Ct. Appeals (11th cir.) 1981, U.S. Dist. Ct. (ea. dist.) Tex. 1987. Assoc. Royston, Rayzor, Vickery & Williams, Houston, 1976-80, Brown, Sims & Ayre, Houston, 1980; v.p., gen. counsel Huthnance Offshore Corp., Houston, 1980-86; ptnr. Brown, Sims, Wise & White, Houston, 1986-2000, Brown Sims PC, Houston, 2000—. Adj. prof. law S. Tex. Coll. Law, 1978-93; columnist The Reporter, 1984-87; contbr. articles to profl. jours.; faculty advisor to spl. maritime edits. S. Tex. Law Jour., 1981-86. Fund drive vol. Houston Grand Opera, 1985-93, trustee, 1986-93; trustee Judge John R. Brown Scholarship Found., 1994—. Recipient outstanding contbn. to cmty. award Houston Jaycees, 1983. Mem. ABA (vce chmn. admiralty and maritime law com., tort and ins. practice sect. 1986-89), Def. Rsch. Inst., Maritime Law Assn., Coll. of State Bar Tex., Order of Coif, Phi Beta Kappa, Phi Delta Phi. Republican. Episcopalian. Avocations: legal writing, cultivating roses. Home: 3511 Durness Way Houston TX 77025 Office: Brown Sims PC 1177 West Loop S STE 1000 Houston TX 77027-9083 E-mail: kengerrand@brownsims.com.

ENGHETA, NADER, electrical engineering educator, researcher; b. Tehran, Iran, Oct. 8, 1955; came to U.S. 1978; s. Abdollah and Meymanat (Mesghali) E.; m. Susanne Hoshyar, Oct. 15, 1983; children: Alex Cameron, Sarah Katherine. BSEE, U. Tehran, 1978; MSEE, Calif. Inst. Tech., 1979, PhD in Elec. Engring., 1982. Grad. rsch. asst. Calif. Inst. Tech., Pasadena, 1979-82, postdoctoral rsch. fellow, 1982-83; sr. rsch. scientist Dikewood Divsn. Kaman Scis. Corp., Santa Monica, Calif., 1983-87; asst. prof. elec. engring. U. Pa., Phila., 1987-90, assoc. prof. elec. engring., 1990-95, prof. elec. engring., 1995—, UPS Found. Disting. Educator chair, 1999-2000. Grad. group chmn. elec. engring. U. Pa., 1993-97; gen. chmn. Benjamin Franklin Symposium, Phila., 1990-91; vis. lectr., UCLA, spring 1986; condr. seminars in field; IEEE Antennas and Propagation Soc. Disting. lectr., 1997-99. Guest editor spl. issue Jour. Electromagnetic Waves and Applications on Wave interaction with chiral and complex media, Vol. 6, No. 5/6, 1992, mem. editl. bd., 1993—, guest editor Jour. Franklin Inst. on Antennas and Microwaves, 13th Ann. Benjamin Franklin Symposium, Vol. 332B, No. 5, 1995, assoc. editor Radio Sci., 1991—96, IEEE Trans. on Antennas and Propagation, 1996—2001; contbr. over 60 articles to profl. jours., chpts. to books; co-guest editor (journal) Wave Motion, on Electrodynamics in Complex Environments, vol. 34, No. 3, 2001. NSF Presdl. Young Investigator, 1989; AT&T Spl. Purpose grantee, 1988; U. Pa. Rsch. Found. grantee, 1988, 90, 93; recipient Engring. Tchg. Excellence award W.M. Keck Found., 1995, Fulbright Naples Chair award for Italy, 1998, Guggenheim Fellowship award 1999. Fellow IEEE (chmn. antennas and propagation/microwave theory and technique Phila. chpt. 1990-91, 3d millennium medal 2000), Optical Soc. Am.; mem. AAAS, Am. Phys. Soc., Internat. Union of Radio Sci. (commn. B and D of USNC), Sigma Xi. Achievements include six patents (with others) for method of measuring chiral parameters of chiral materials, novel electromagnetic shielding reflection and scattering control using chiral materials, waveguides using chiral materials; printed-circuit antenna using material, rodomes using chiral materials, method of using polarization differencing to improve vision; patents pending (with others) for electromagnetically non-reflective material, novel antenna arrays using chiral materials, novel lenses using chiral materials; research on applied and theoretical electromagnetics, optics, complex unconventional electromagnetic materials, electromagnetic chiral materials, microwave, biologically-inspired polarization-difference imaging, waveguide theory, role of fractional calculus and fractional paradigm in electrodynamics; patentee in field. Office: Univ of Pa 200 S 33rd St Philadelphia PA 19104-6314 E-mail: engheta@ee.upenn.edu.

ENGIBOUS, THOMAS JAMES, electronics company executive; b. St. Louis, Jan. 31, 1953; s. James C. and Emma E. (Buck) E.; ; m. Wendy; children: Ryan T., Mandie, Christopher Megan. B of Elec. Engring., Purdue U., 1975, M of Elec. Engring., 1976, D of Engring. (hon.), 1997. Design engr. SCG, Tex. Instruments, Dallas, 1976-80, dept. mgr., 1980-86, v.p., 1986-91, sr. v.p., 1991-93; exec. v.p., pres. semi-condr. group Tex. Instruments, Dallas, 1993-96; pres., CEO Tex. Instruments Inc., Dallas, 1996-98, chmn., pres., CEO, 1998—. Mem. vis. com. Purdue U. Engring., 1995—; bd. dirs. J.C. Penny Co., Catalyst, U.S.-Japan Bus. Coun., Nat. Ctr. for Ednl. Accountability. Mem. Dallas Citizens Coun., 1996—; trustee So. Meth. U. Mem. IEEE, Bus. Roundtable, Bus. Coun. Roman Catholic. Avocations: boating, water sports, snow skiing.

ENGLAND, ANTHONY WAYNE, electrical engineering and computer science educator, astronaut, geophysicist; b. Indpls., May 15, 1942; s. Herman U. and Betty (Steel) E.; m. Kathleen Ann Kreutz, Aug. 31, 1962. SB, MIT, 1965, PhD, 1970, SM, 1965. With Texaco Co., 1962; field geologist Ind. U., 1963; scientist-astronaut NASA, 1967-72, 79-88; with U.S. Geol. Survey, 1972-79; crewmember on Spacelab 2, July, 1985; adj. prof. Rice U., Houston, 1987-88; prof. elec. engring. and computer sci. U. Mich., Ann Arbor, 1988—, prof. atmospheric, oceanic and space sci., 1989—, assoc. dean Rackham Grad. Sch., 1995-98. Mem. space studies bd. NRC, 1992-98. Assoc. editor Jour. Geophys. Rsch. Recipient Antarctic medal, Spaceflight medal NASA, Spaceflight award Am. Astron. Soc., Outstanding Scientific Achievement medal NASA. Fellow IEEE; mem. Am. Geophys. Union. Home: 7949 Ridgeway Ct Dexter MI 48130-9700 Office: U Mich Dept Elec Engring-Comp Sci Ann Arbor MI 48109-2122

ENGLAND, DAN BENJAMIN, accountant; b. Duncan, Okla., Aug. 23, 1955; s. Haskell Thomas and Lillian Lucille (Rouw) E.; m. Mary Elizabeth Metcalf, May 24, 1980; 1 child, Stuart Benjamin. BA, Southeastern Okla. State U., 1977, BS, 1982; MBA, Lincoln U. of the U.S.A., 2000. CPA, Okla. Br. mgr. Curtis Distbg. Co., Durant, Okla., 1978-79; dist. agt. Prudential Ins. Co., Durant, 1980-82; acct. Reedrill Inc., Sherman, Tex., 1982; mgr. Williams and Co. CPAs Inc., Durant, 1983-85; v.p. England Enterprises Inc., Durant, 1985—. Pvt. practice acctg., Durant, 1985—; adj. instr. Southeastern Okla. State U., Durant, 1985-86; investment advisor rep., 1993—. Bd. dirs. Red River Arts Coun., Durant, 1986-94. Mem. Nat. Assn. Tax Practitioners, Okla. Soc. CPAs, Durant Jaycees (bd. dirs. 1985), Durant C. of C. Republican. Mem. Ch. of Christ. Lodge: Kiwanis (treas. Durant, 1985, sec. 1986, v.p. 1988, pres. 1989). Avocations: golf, tennis, music, art. Office: 206 N 10th Ave Durant OK 74701-4328

ENGLAND, DOUGLAS M. pathologist; b. Watertown, S.D., Feb. 17, 1939; s. Sigfrid T. and Fern D. (Hanson) E.; m. Beverly A. Thorson, Dec. 28, 1962; children: Cheryl Ann, Thomas M., Todd D. BS, U. Wis., 1963, MS, 1968; MD, Chgo. Med. Sch., 1973. Intern in pathology Mayo Clinic, Rochester, Minn., 1973—74, resident in pathology, 1974—77; pathologist USAF Hosp., Wiesbaden, Germany, 1977—80; asst. chmn. dept. pulmonary pathology AFIP, Washington, 1980—82; chief, surg. pathologist Middleton Meml. Vets. Hosp., Madison, Wis., 1983—88; surg. pathologist Meriter Hosp., Madison, Wis., 1998—2003; clin. prof. pathology and medicine U. Wis., Madison, 1983—; ret., 2003. Staff pathologist, v.p. Wis. Pathologists, S.C., Madison, 1988-2003. Contbr. articles to profl. jours. Mem. adv. com. Nehemiah Corp., Madison, 1993—; mem. stewardship com. Bethel Luth. Ch., Madison, 1994-2003. Served to lt. col. USAF, 1960-82. Fellow Am. Coll. Chest Physicians, Internat. Acad. Pathology; mem. Sigma Xi, Alpha Omega Alpha. Avocations: fishing, boating.

ENGLAND, GARY ALAN, television meteorologist; b. Seiling, Okla., Oct. 3, 1939; s. Leslie Elwood and Hazel Wanda (Stong) E.; m. Mary Helen Carlisle, Aug. 27, 1961; 1 child, Molly Michelle. BS in Math. and Meteorology, U. Okla., 1965. Profl. meteorologist. V.p. mktg. Southwestern Weather Svc., Oklahoma City, 1965-67; cons. meteorologist A.H. Glenn & Assocs., New Orleans, 1967-71; v.p. mktg. England & May, Oklahoma City, 1971-74; v.p. meteorology U.S. Weather Corp., Oklahoma City, 1974-78; pres. The Gary Co., Oklahoma City, 1978-93, Weather Designs, Inc., Oklahoma City, 1994—; dir. meteorology Griffin TV, Oklahoma City, 1971—; chief meteorologist Storm Signal, LLC, 1999—. Cons. meteorologist Techrad, Okla., 1977-78; forensic meteorologist legal field, Okla., 1971—. Author: Oklahoma Weather, 1975, United States Weather, 1976, Those Terrible Twisters, 1987, Weathering the Storm, 1996. Fundraiser The Christmas Connection, Oklahoma City, 1982-98, Harvest Fund Drive, Oklahoma City, 1982-97. With USN, 1957-61. Named to Western Okla. Hall of Fame Western Okla. Hist. Soc., 1983, Dewey County Hall of Fame Dewey County Hist. Soc., 1989, Best Meteorologist Okla., 1984—, Outstanding Young Men of Am., 1976; recipient Ptnrs. for Excellence award Okla. Sch. Pub. Rels. Assn., 1989, Emmy for Best Weather Anchor, Heartland divsn. NATAS, 1994, Emmy Lifetime Achievement Heartland divsn., 1997, Golden Viddey award Nat. Acad. Profl. Journalists, 1997, Best Spot Weather-The Metro Tornado award Okla. Assn. Broadcasters, 1998, Best Spot Weather-The Metro Tornado award Okla. Soc. Profl. Journalists, 1998, Govs. Humanitarian award, Oklahoma City, 1999, Edward R. Murrow award, 1999, Meritorious Svc. award Oklahoma City, 1999, VFW, 1999, Best Spot News award '99 Tornado, Okla. Soc. Profl. Journalists, 2000, Soc. Profl. Journalists 2000, SilverCir. award NATAS, 2000, Lifetime Achievement award Am. Women in Radio and TV, 2002, others; named to Okla. Assn. Broadcasters Hall of Fame, 2002. Mem. AAAS, Am. Meteorol. Soc., N.Y. Acad. Scis. Mem. Christian Ch. Achievements include initiation of development with Enterprise Electronics Corp. of the world's first comml. Doppler radar; first person to use Doppler radar for direct warnings to the public; developed an automated weather warning system called First Warming; developed an automated severe weather tracking and projection computer system called Storm Tracker, now in use nation wide; co-developer storm signal computer warning sys., 1999. Office: Sta KWTV PO Box 14159 Oklahoma City OK 73113-0159

ENGLAND, GORDON R. civilian military employee; BS in Elec. Engring., U. Md., 1961; MBA, Tex. Christian U., 1975. With Gen. Dynamics, 1966—2001; v.p., pres., land systems Gen. Dynamics Corp., Falls Church, Va., 1986—91; pres. aircraft sys. Ft. Worth divsn., exec. v.p. Gen. Dynamics, 1991; exec. v.p. General Dynamics Corp., Falls Church, Va., 1991—93; pres. Lockheed Ft. Worth Gen. Dynamics, 1993-95; owner consulting co., 1995-97; exec. v.p. combat sys. group Gen. Dynamics, Falls Church, Va., 1997—2001; sec. U.S. Navy, Dept. Def., Washington, 2001—03, 2003—; dep. sec. Dept. Homeland Security, Washington, 2003. Mem. Def. Sci. Bd. Vice-chmn. Goodwill Internat.; bd. govs. USO; bd. visitors TCU. Recipient award, Boy Scouts Am., Nat. Def. Indsl. Assn., Nat. Mgmt. Assn., Centennial award, IEEE, inductee, Aviation Hall of Fame. Mem.: Beta Gamma Sigma, Omicron Delta Kappa, Eta Kappa Nu. Office: Dept Def Sec of Navy The Pentagon Rm 4E686 Washington DC 20350*

ENGLAND, JOHN DAVID, neurologist, educator; b. Clarksburg, W.Va., Jan. 20, 1954; s. John Draper and Imogene Lucille (Alexander) E.; m. Cathy Ann Drummond, Nov. 22, 1975. BA in Chemistry, W.Va. U., 1976, MD, 1980. Diplomate Nat. Bd. Med. Examiners, Am. Bd. Psychiatry and Neurology, Am. Bd. Electrodiagnostic Medicine; lic. physician, S.C., Pa., Colo., La. Intern Med. U. S.C., Charleston, 1980-81, resident in neurology, 1981-84; clin. neuromuscular fellow dept. neurology Hosp. of U. Pa., Phila., 1984-85, postdoctoral rsch. fellow dept. neurology, 1985-87; asst. prof. neurology U. Colo., Denver, 1987-92; assoc. prof. neurology La. State U., New Orleans, 1992-98, prof. neurology and neurosci., 1998-2001; attending physician U. Colo. Health Scis. Ctr., Denver, 1987-92, dir. electromyography lab., 1987-92; attending physician Med. Ctr. La., New Orleans, 1992-2001; prof. neurology and neurosci. La. State U., New Orleans, 1998-2001, dir. MDA clinic, 1998-2001; chmn. neurology, dir. neurosci. Deaconess Billings Clinic, Billings, Mont., 2001—. Lectr. in field. Contbr. numerous articles to profl. jours.; editl. cons. Muscle and Nerve, 1987—, Ann. Neurol., 1990—, Brain, 1993—; mem. editl. bd. Muscle & Nerve, 2000—. Recipient Koehler award in chemistry, Handbook award Chem. Rubber Co., Whitehall award of dept. chemistry; W.Va. U. Bd. Regents scholar, Masonic scholar, others; grantee Muscular Dystrophy Assn., 1985-87, NIH, 1987-88, Nat. Inst. Neurol. Disorders and Stroke, 1988-93, Nat. Inst. Aging, 1991-94, La. State U. Neurosci. Ctr. for Excellence, 1993-94, Dept. Def., 1993—. Mem. AMA, Am. Neurol. Assn., Am. Assn. Electrodiagnostic Medicine (profl. practice com. 1988-91, liaison rep. 1991-92, spl. interest group com. 1992-93, tng. program com. 1993-96, program com. 1996—, bd. dirs.), Am. Acad. Neurology (21st Century Leader in Neurology 2003), Am. Neurol. Assn., N.Y. Acad. Scis., Am. Soc. Neurol. Investigation, Soc. for Neurosci., Am. Acad. Clin. Neurophysiology (pres. 2002-2003, Disting. Svc. award 2003) 21st century leader in Neurology selected by Am. Acad. of Neurology, 2003; Distinguished Serv. award from Am. Acad. of clin. Neurophysiology, 2003, W.Va. U. Alumni Assn., Alpha Omega Alpha, Phi Kappa Phi, Phi Lambda Upsilon, Phi Beta Kappa. Democrat. Methodist. Avocations: skiing, running, hiking, reading. Office: Deaconess Billings Clinic Dept Neurology 2825 8th Ave N PO Box 37000 Billings MT 59107-7000

ENGLAND, JOHN HENRY, JR., judge; b. 1947; BS, Tuskegee U.; JD, U. Ala., 1974. Pvt. practice, Tuscaloosa; former assoc. justice Supreme Ct. State of Ala., Montgomery; now cir. court judge Sixth Jud. Cir. Court, Tuscaloosa County. Mem. Tuscaloosa City Coun. Office: Sixth Jud Cir Ct 225 Tuscaloosa County Cthse Tuscaloosa AL 35401

ENGLAND, JOHN MELVIN, lawyer, clergyman; b. June 29, 1932; s. John Marcus and Frances Dorothy (Brown) E.; m. Jane Cantrell, Aug. 2, 1953; children: Kathryn Elizabeth, Janette Evelyn, John William, Kenneth Paul, James Andrew, Samuel Robert. Student, Ga. State U., 1951-53; JD, U. Ga., 1956; BD magna cum laude with honors Theology, Columbia Theol. Sem., Decatur, Ga., 1964. Bar: Ga. 1959, U.S. Dist. Ct. (no. dist.) Ga. 1967, U.S. Ct. Mil. Appeals 1976, U.S. Ct. Appeals (5th cir.) 1967, U.S. Ct. Appeals (11th cir.) 1981, U.S. Supreme Ct. 1977, U.S. Dist. Ct. (mid. dist.) Ga. 1986, U.S. Dist. Ct. (so. dist.) Ga. 1991, U.S. Dist. Ct. (no. dist.) Tex. 1991; ordained to ministry Presbyn. Ch., 1964. Spl. agt. FBI, Washington, 1956-57, Indpls., 1957-59, Charlotte, N.C., 1959, Greenville, S.C., 1959-60; student supply pastor Bethel and Buford Presbyn. Chs., Atlanta, 1960-63; pastor Mullins (S.C.) Presbyn. Ch., 1964-67; asst. dist. atty. Fulton County, Ga., 1967-75; sr. ptnr. England and Weller, Atlanta, 1975-88, England, Weaver & Kytle, 1988-94, England & McKnight, 1994-2000, England & England, 2000—. Legal seminar lectr. and spkr. throughout the country under auspices of Christian orgns.; spl. pros. for gov. Ga., 1976-79; spl. cons. on appellate reform Supreme Ct. Ga., 1979-80; state bar rep. to Superior Ct. Uniform Rules Com. Coun. Superior Ct. Judges, 1984, Uniform Rules Com. State Bar Ga., 1993—. Elder, tchr., evangelism coord. Presbyn. Ch. USA; chmn. Christian Bus. Men's Coms. of U.S.A., Atlanta, 1971-73, chmn. internat. conv., Atlanta, 1979, bd. dirs., 1971-81. Mem. ABA, ATLA, State Bar Ga., Atlanta Bar Assn., Lawyers Club Atlanta, Ga. Trial Lawyers Assn., Nat. Assn. Criminal Def. Lawyers, Ga. Assn. Criminal Def. Lawyers, North Fulton Bar Assn. Office: England & England 201 Bombay Ln Roswell GA 30076 E-mail: england_england_11p@hotmail.com.

ENGLAND, LYNNE LIPTON, lawyer, speech pathologist, audiologist; b. Youngstown, Ohio, Apr. 11, 1949; d. Sanford Y. and Sally (Kentor) Lipton; m. Richard E. England, Mar. 5, 1977. BA, U. Mich., 1970; MA, Temple U., 1972; JD, Tulane U., 1981. Bar: Fla. 1982, U.S. Dist. Ct. (mid. dist.) Fla. 1982, U.S. Ct. Appeals (11th cir.) 1982; cert. clin. competence in speech pathology and audiology. Speech pathologist Rockland Children's Hosp., N.Y., 1972-74, Jefferson Parish Sch., Gretna, La., 1977-81; audiologist Rehab. Inst. Chgo., 1974-76; assoc. Trenam, Simmons, Kemker, Scharf, Barkin, Frye & O'Neill, Tampa, Fla., 1981-84; asst. U.S. atty. for Middle Dist. Fla. Tampa, 1984-87; asst. U.S. trustee, 1987-91; ptnr. Stearns, Weaver, Miller, Weissler, Alhadeff & Sitterson, P.A., 1991-94, Prevatt, England & Taylor, Tampa, Fla., 1994-99; pvt. practice Brandon, Fla., 1999—. Editor Fla. Bankruptcy Casenotes, 1983. Recipient clin. assistantship Temple U., 1972-74. Mem. ATLA, Comml. Law League, Am. Speech and Hearing Assn., Tampa Bay Bankruptcy Bar Assn. (dir. 1990-95), Am. Bankruptcy Inst., Fla. Bar Assn., Hillsborough County Bar Assn., Order of Coif. Jewish. Avocations: tennis, golf, playing french horn and piano. Office: 1463 Oakfield Dr Ste 125 Brandon FL 33511-0802 E-mail: englandlawoffice@aol.com.

ENGLAND, RICHARD JAY, retired chemist; b. Springfield, Ill., Aug. 5, 1926; s. James Clyde and Hazel Vera (Jay) England; m. Elsie Margaret Landes, May 19, 1951; children: Mark, James, Janet. AS, Springfield Jr. Coll., 1948, St. Louis U., 1949; BS in chemistry, Bradley U., Peoria, Ill., 1951. Cert. in chemistry Am. Chem. Soc., 1951. Rsch. and devel. officer U.S. Air Force, Dayton, Ohio, 1951—53; process chemist E.I. DuPont, Gibbstown, NJ, 1953—56, rsch. chemist Martinsburg, W.Va., 1956, Richmond, Va., 1957, Kinston, NC, 1957—59, sr. rsch. chemist Circleville, Ohio, 1959—87, cons., 1987—92; ret., 1987. Contbr. articles to profl. jours. With USNR, 1944—46, 1st lt. USAFR, 1951—53. Roman Catholic. Achievements include patents in field. Avocations: ham radio, music, electronics, photography, computers. Home: 370 Meadow Ln Circleville OH 43113

ENGLAND, ROBERT STOWE, writer; b. York, S.C., Jan. 14, 1944; s. Hershel Stowe and Myrtle Lorene (Deal) E. BA in English, Duke U., 1967. Reporter Hartford (Conn.) Times, 1967-68; editor, pub. Washington, A Tabloid Rev., 1973-76; editor Del. Valley Bus. Mag., Phila., 1976-77; sr. editor Ingersoll-Rand Co. Corp. Mag., Washington, N.J., 1977-79; editor Metro Newark Mag., 1982-84; writer Insight Mag., Washington, 1985-88; ind. writer bus., fin. and polit. mags., Arlington, Va., 1988—. Adj. fellow, dir. rsch. for global aging initiative, Ctr. for Strategic and Internat. Studies, Washington, 1999—. Author: The Fiscal Challenge of an Aging Industrial World, 2002 (One of the 25 Best Books, World Future Soc., 2002), Global Aging and Financial Markets: Hard Landings Ahead?, 2002, The Macroeconomic Impact of Global Aging: A New Era of Economic Frailty?, 2002. Pres. Harsimus Cove Neighborhood Assn., Jersey City, 1982-84. Recipient Blue Smoke and Mirrors award Insight mag., Washington, 1986. Mem. Washington Ind. Writers. Episcopalian. Avocations: piano, genealogy. Home: 3116 Military Rd Arlington VA 22207-4136

ENGLANDER, TOM, business owner; b. Presov, Czechoslovakia, June 3, 1946; came to U.S., 1947; s. Eugene and Gisela Englander; m. Carol Stephenson. BS, U. Wash., 1968; MBA, Tex. Christian U., 1973; M in Mgmt. Sci., U. Tex. at Dallas, 1981. Fin. mgr. Fox & Jacobs Inc., Carrollton, Tex., 1973-76; controller Omnicon Med. Corp., Farmers Branch, Tex., 1977-78; controller, personnel mgr. Austin Bridge Co., Dallas, 1978-86; mgr. orgn. devel. Austin Industries Inc., Dallas, 1986-88; owner Englander & Assocs., Farmers Branch, 1988—. Mem. adv. bd. Tex. A&M U. Ctr. Constrn. Edn., College Station, 1986-88; mem. human resource forum So. Meth. U., Dallas, 1986-88. Cons. I Have a Dream, Dallas, 1986-88; precinct chmn. Farmers Branch, 1986-92; pro bono instr. Jr. Achievement, Dallas, 1987-89; mem. Leadership Metrocrest, Carrollton, 1989—; bd. dirs. Metrocrest Area Rehab. Ctr. Capt. U.S. Army, 1969-72. Slumberger fellow Tex. Christian U., 1972. Mem. Internat. Assn. Outplacement Profls. (pres. Dallas chpt.), Metrocrest C. of C. (bd. dirs.), Brookhaven Bus. Assn. (bd. dirs.), Brookhaven Men's Golf Assn. (bd. dirs.), Internat. Assn. Career Mgmt. Profls. (treas.).

ENGLAR, KENNETH G. aerospace engineer; BS in Engring., Columbia U. Mem. Manhattan Project, Los Alamos, N.Mex.; chief engr., chief design engr. Delta Launch Vehicle McDonnell Douglas Corp.; engring. cons. Aerospace Safety Adv. Panel NASA, Washington, chief engr. lab. vehicle U.S. Air Force Manned Orviting Lab. Cons. Aerospace Safety Adv. Panel, 1995, mem., 96. Office: NASA Hdqrs Aerospace Safety Adv Panel 300 E St SW Washington DC 20546

ENGLE, CAROLE RUTH, aquaculture economics educator; b. Harrisburg, Pa., July 7, 1952; d. Morris Mumma Engle and Mildred Evelyn (Orris) Wambold; m. Nathan Mayhew Stone, May 30, 1981; children: Reina, Eric, Cody. BA, Friends World Coll., 1975; MS, Auburn U., 1978, PhD, 1981. Vis. prof. U. Centroamericana, Managua, Nicaragua, 1981-83; fisheries economist Inter-Am. Devel. Bank, Santiago, Panama, 1984-85; asst. prof. econs. Auburn U., Montgomery, Ala., 1985-88; assoc. prof. aquaculture econs. U. Ark., Pine Bluff, 1988-94, prof., 1994—; dir., Aguacultural Fisheries Ctr., U. Ark., Pine Bluff, 1989—. Aquaculture coord. U. Ark., Pine Bluff, 1989—; cons. FAO, Rome, 1986, 88. Contbr. articles to profl. jours.; editor conf. proceedings. Mem. World Aquaculture Soc., Am. Fisheries Soc., Am. Assn. Agriculture Econs., So. Agriculture Econs. Assn., Ark. Acad. Scis. Avocations: gardening, reading, swimming. Office: U Ark PO Box 108 1200 University Dr Pine Bluff AR 71601-2799

ENGLE, DONALD EDWARD, retired railway executive, lawyer; b. St. Paul, Mar. 5, 1927; s. Merlin Edward and Edna May (Berger) E.; m. Nancy Ruth Frank, Mar. 18, 1950; children: David Edward, Daniel Thomas, Nancy Ann. BA, Macalester Coll., St. Paul, 1948; JD, U. Minn., 1952, BSL., 1950. Bar: Minn. 1952, Mo. 1972. Law clk., spl. atty. Atty. Gen.'s Office Minn., 1951-52; atty., asst. gen. solicitor, asst. gen. counsel G.N. Ry., St. Paul, 1953-70; asso. gen. counsel Burlington No., Inc., 1970-72; v.p., gen. counsel S.L.-S.F. Ry., St. Louis, 1972-80, v.p. law, sec., 1979-80; v.p. law Burlington No., Inc., St. Paul, 1980-81, Burlington No. Ry., St. Paul, 1981-83, sr. v.p. law and govt. affairs, sec., 1983-86, also dir.; ptnr., chmn., chief exec. officer Oppenheimer, Wolff & Donnelly, 1986-93, chmn., chief exec. officer, 1991-93, of counsel, 1993—. Continuing edn. lectr. U. Minn.; bd. dirs. Regions Hosp. Found., 2001—. Bd. dirs. YMCA, St. Paul, 1981-84, ARC, 1981-84; bd. dirs. Boy Scouts Am., 1991—. Mem. ABA, Mo. Bar Assn., Minn. Bar Assn., Ramsey County Bar Assn., St. Louis Bar Assn., St. Paul C. of C. (bd. dirs. 1994-97), North Oaks Golf Club, Phi Delta Phi. Republican. Lutheran. Home: 9 W Bay Ln Saint Paul MN 55127-2601

ENGLE, FRED ALLEN, JR., economics educator, author; b. Louisville, Nov. 14, 1929; s. Fred Allen and Susan Kathryn (Johnson) E.; m. Mary Jean Purves, May 25, 1953; children: Susan E. McCool, Allen D., F. Bruce. B.S., Eastern Ky. U., 1951; M.B.A., U. Ky., 1954, Ed.D., 1966. Mgr., Gen. Electric Co., Lexington, Ky., 1955-57; prof. Coll. William and Mary, Williamsburg, Va., 1957-59; prof. econs. Eastern Ky. U., Richmond, 1959-98, ret. 1st lt. U.S. Army, 1951-53. Recipient Cert. of Recognition, Phi Delta Kappa, 1970, 80. Mem. SAR, Ky. Econs. Assn. (mem. labor com.). Republican. Baptist. Lodge: Masons. Author: (with others) Madison's Heritage, 1985. Contbr. weekly column on local history and periodic columns on econs. to Richmond Register. Home: PO Box 182 Richmond KY 40476-0182

ENGLE, HOWARD A. retired pediatrician; b. Wis., Sept. 11, 1919; married; three children. BS, U. Wis., 1939, MS, 1941, MD, 1943. Diplomate Am. Bd. Pediatrics. Intern Michael Reese Hosp., Chgo., 1943, resident in pediatrics, 1943-44; pvt. practice Miami Beach, Fla., 1947—; assoc. clin. prof. U. Miami Sch. of Medicine, assoc. prof. pediatrics emeritus. Sr. cons., past chmn. dept. pediatrics, Mount Sinai Med. Ctr., Miami Beach; com. mem., operation newborn U. Miami Sch. of Medicine; instr. dept. pediatrics U. Fla. Sch. of Nursing; pediatric preceptor Fla. Internat. U. Sch. Nursing; sr. cons. pediatrics Mount Sinai Med. Ctr.; courtesy staff Miami Childrens Hosp.; sr. attending pediatrics Jackson Mem. Hosp.; cons. Fla. Atlantic U. Dept. Spl. Edn., neuropediatrics, Childrens Home Soc. of Fla.; cons., lectr. Dupont de Nemours Found., State Miss.; cons. pediatric neurology Hope Sch.; dir. Symposium Cerebral Palsy, Miami; med. rep. Symposia Cerebral Palsy, State of Tex.; lectr. in field. Contbr. articles to profl. jours. Com. mem. Edn. and Therapy for the Handicapped, Dade County Sch. Bd.; past med. dir. United Cerebral Palsy of Miami; cons. neuropediatrics United Cerebral Palsy of Fla.; past. mem. clin. adv. bd. United Cerebral Palsy; nat. del. World Commn. on Cerebral Palsy, Copenhagen, 1963; med. cons. divsn. exceptional student edn. Miami-Dade County Sch. Bd. Recipient Ralph Hawley award for 50 yrs. svc. to medicine and the cmty. U. Wis., 1993. Mem. Am. Acad. Pediat., Child Neurology Soc., Am. Acad. Cerebral Palsy (exec. com.), Am. Acad. Neurology, Am. Assn. on Mental Retardation, Am. Population and Reproduction Assn. (pres., founder), Fla. Rehab. Assn., Internat. Soc. for Rehab. of Crippled and Disabled, Am. Acad. Phys. Medicine and Rehab., Internat. Soc. for Cerebral Palsy, Internat. Child Neurology Assn. (assoc.), Japanese Soc. Child Neurology, Dade County Med. Assn., Fla. Med. Assn., Fla. Pediatric Soc., Miami Pediatric Soc. (past pres.), Southeastern Med. Assn., European Paediatric Neurology Soc., World Med. Assn., Internat. Population and Reproduction Com. (chmn. edn. programs, bd. dirs., past pres. 1981-82), Alpha Omega Alpha, Sigma Sigma.

ENGLE, JAMES BRUCE, ambassador; b. Billings, Mont., Apr. 16, 1919; s. Bruce Wilmot and Verbeaudah Margaret (Morgan) E.; m. Priscilla Joyce Wright, June 10, 1950; children: Stephen, Judith, Philip, Susan, John, Peter. Diploma, Burlington (Iowa) Jr. Coll., 1938; BA, U. Chgo., 1940, postgrad., 1940-41, 46; diploma, Grad. Sch. Bus. Adminstrn., Harvard, 1945; Honours BA (Rhodes scholar), Exeter Coll., Oxford (Eng.) U., 1950, Honours MA, 1954; diploma, U. per Stranieri, Perugia, Italy, 1949; Fulbright scholar, Istituto Italiano Studi Storici, Naples, 1950-53; postgrad., Am. U., Washington, 1956-58; diploma, Goethe Institut, Germany, 1958; postgrad., King's Coll., Cambridge (Eng.) U., 1958-59. Dept. State liaison officer with Bd. Econ. Warfare, Washington, 1941-42; vice consul Quito, Ecuador, 1942-44, Rio de Janeiro, Brazil, 1946-47, Naples, 1951-53; 2d sec. Am. embassy, Rome, 1953-54; Italian desk officer Dept. State, Washington, 1955-58; 1st sec. Am. embassy, London, 1958-59; consul Frankfurt, Germany, 1959, Duesseldorf, Germany, 1959-60; labor attache Am. embassy, Bonn, Germany, 1960-61, 1st sec. Accra, Ghana, 1961-62, acting dep. chief mission, 1962-63, charge d'affaires, 1963; dep. chief mission, counselor embassy Managua, Nicaragua, 1963-67; charge d'affaires, 1967; mem. sr. seminar in fgn. policy Dept. State, Washington, 1967-68; dep. chief reports and analysis div. CORDS, Mil. Assistance Command, Saigon, Vietnam, 1968; province sr. advisor Phu Yen mil. region II, Tuy Hoa, Vietnam, 1969-70; dir. Vietnam working group Dept. State, sec. Nat. Security Council com. on Indochina, Washington, 1970-71; spl. advisor to ambassador-at-large on trade and currency negotiations, 1971-72; diplomatic advisor to sec. of treasury, 1972; spl. asst. to U.S. ambassador to North Atlantic Council, Brussels, Belgium, 1972; exec. sec. spl. interdepartmental task force on Indochina Dept. State, Washington, 1972-73; consul gen. Nha Trang, Vietnam, 1973; dep. chief mission, counselor of embassy Phnom Penh, Cambodia, 1973-74; charge d'affaires, 1974; ambassador to People's Republic of Bénin (Dahomey), Cotonou, 1974-76; polit. advisor with rank of ambassador to U.S. Comdr.-in-Chief Atlantic and Supreme Allied Comdr. Atlantic, 1976-78; sr. fgn. service insp. Dept. State, Washington, 1978-82; cons. on war gaming, 1983-84; dir. U.S. representation U.S.—Saudi Arabian Joint Commn. on Econ. Cooperation Riyadh, Saudi Arabia, 1984-85; Joint Commn. Advisor to Sr. Level Coms. U.S. and Saudi Arabian govts., 1985-87; cons. on fgn. affairs, 1987—; pres. Vermont Coverts: Woodlands for Wildlife, 1991-96, chmn. bd., 1996—. Mem. Vt. Forestry Communications Coun., 1991-95. Mem. Vt. Citizens Adv. Com., No. Forest Lands Coun., 1992-94, U. Vt. Extension Adv. Coun., 1993—. Served to lt. (j.g.) USN, 1944-46; mil. govt. officer Japan, 1945-46. Recipient Rockefeller Pub. Service award, 1958; named Tree Farmer of Yr. Caledonia County, Vt., 1997, Vt. Tree Farmer of Yr., 2001. Mem. The Oxford Union, Phi Beta Kappa. Congregationalist. Achievements include leading 11 U.S. Andean expdns. in Ecuador, 1942-43. Home: PO Box 64 Peacham VT 05862-0064

ENGLE, JANE, research nurse, artist; b. L.A., June 15, 1942; d. John Dean and Florence (Updike) E. BA with honors, U. N.C., 1965; BSN, Cornell U., 1970; MS in Nursing, U. Ill., Chgo., 1974; MDiv magna cum laude, Wesley Theol. Sem., 1988. RN. Tchr., vol., trainer Peace Corps, Afghanistan, 1965—68; pub. health nurse Tufts Delta Health Ctr., Mound Bayou, Miss., 1969; coord. pub. health nursing Ill. Cmty. Clinic, Chgo., 1970—72; nursing cons. rsch. edn. Dept. Pub. Health, Chgo., 1974—78; rsch. nurse AIDS, NIH, Bethesda, Md., 1989—97; abstract artist and paper maker, 1997—; hosp. chaplain, 2002—. Mem. AIDS task force Interfaith Conf. Met. Washington, 1988-90. Author: Outcome Measures in Home Care, 1987, Immune-Based Therapy for HIV, 1996; contbr. article to profl. jours. Vol. homeless agys.; v.p. women's bd. Episcopal Ch., Washington, 1981—82; mem. bd. deacons Nat. Presbyn. Ch., Washington, 1982—86; mem. Mayor's Task Force on Standards, Washington, 1985—87, Foundry Gallery, Washington, 2001. Wesley Theol. Sem. Biblical scholar, 1988; named Person of Week Washington Times, 1992; recipient award for excellence in painting, 2000, The Ethel Lorraine Bernstein Meml. award for excellence in painting Corcoran Coll. Art and Design, 2000. Mem. ANA (pres. local chpt. 1976-78), Assn. Nurses in AIDS Care, Phi Beta Kappa, Sigma Theta Tau. Democrat. Home: 4831 Sedgwick St NW Washington DC 20016-2323

ENGLE, JEANNETTE CRANFILL, medical technologist; b. Davie County, N.C., July 7, 1941; d. Gurney Nathaniel and Versie Emmaline (Reavis) Cranfill; m. William Sherman Engle (div. 1970); children: Phillip William, Lisa Kaye. Diploma, Dell Sch. Med. Tech., 1960; BA, U. N.C., Asheville, 1976; MS in Biomed. Sci.-Genetics, Marshall U., 1999. Instr. Dell Sch. Med. Tech., Asheville, 1960-67; rotating technologist Meml. Mission Hosp., Asheville, 1967-68, asst. supr. hematology, 1968-71; supr. Damon Subs. Pvt. Clinic Lab., Asheville, 1971-73; chemistry technologist VA Med. Ctr., Durham, N.C., 1973-74, 75-76, supr., 1974-75, asst. supr. microbiology Salem, Va., 1976-79; supr. rsch. Med. Svc. Lab., Salem, 1979-90; flow cytometrist VA Med. Ctr., Huntington, W.Va., 1990-92, cons. to clin. lab. flow cytometry dept., 1992—. Reviewer Jour. Club, Roanoke-Salem, Va., 1980-90. Author: (poem) Reflections on a Comet, 1984; contbr. numerous articles and abstracts on med. tech. to profl. jours., 1982—. Mem. The Acting Co. Ensemble. Democrat. Episcopalian. Avocations: reading, flower arranging, interior design, art, music. Home: 4775 Green Valley Rd Huntington WV 25701-9793 E-mail: jeaengle@aol.com.

ENGLE, LARS, language educator; b. NYC, June 4, 1953; s. Alan William and Jessie Ann Engle; m. Holly Laird, May 27, 1989; children: Carl Joseph Engle-Laird, Sage Menglian Engle-Laird. AB (magna cum laude), Harvard Coll., 1974; MA in English, Cambridge U., 1976; PhD in English, Yale U., 1983. Lectr. U. Stellenbosch, South Africa, 1977—79; asst. prof. Yale U., New Haven, 1982—86, U. Tulsa, Okla., 1988—92, assoc. prof., 1993—, chair English, 2003—. Author: Shakespearean Pragmatism: Market of His Time; editor: (norton anthology) English Renaissance Drama. Fellow Henry Kendall fellow, U. Tulsa, 1995, Mellon fellow, U. Va., 1986—88. Mem.: MLA, U.S. Tennis Assn., Shakespeare Assn. Am., Cole's Black Belt Club, Phi Beta Kappa. Avocations: tennis, singing, martial arts. Office: English University of Tulsa 600 S College Avenue Tulsa OK 74104

ENGLE, LINDA JANE, molecular biologist; b. Summit, N.J., Nov. 5, 1960; d. Thomas Edward and Patricia E.; m. John Edward Landers, Aug. 8, 1998. BS, Rutgers U., 1982; PhD, U. Pa., 1995. Sr. rsch. assoc. Children's Hosp. Phila., 1982-87; postdoctoral rsch. fellow Harvard Med. Sch., Boston, 1995-99; rsch. fellow McLean Hosp./Mass. Gen. Hosp., Boston, 1995-99; v.p., dir. rch. & devel., co-founder PolyGenyx, Inc., Worcester, Mass., 1999—. Cons. neurobiologist Nathan Kline Rsch. Inst. NYU Med. Sch., 1997-2000; cons. CytoMatrix, Cambridge, Mass., 1997-98, U. Pa., Phila., 1993-94. Grantee NIH, 1999-2000. Avocations: classical pianist, tennis, hiking, horticulture, creative writing. Home: Polygenyx One Innovation Dr Worcester MA 01605 E-mail: lengle@polygenyx.com.

ENGLE, MARY ALLEN ENGLISH, physician; b. Madill, Okla., Jan. 26, 1922; d. Russell C. and Vera (Apperson) English; m. Ralph Landis Engle, Jr., June 7, 1945 (dec. Oct. 2000); children: Ralph Landis III (dec.), Marilyn Elizabeth. AB cum laude, Baylor U., 1942; MD, Johns Hopkins U., 1945; D.Sc. (hon.), Iona Coll., 1982. Diplomate: in pediatric cardiology Am. Bd. Pediatrics. Intern pediatrics Johns Hopkins Hosp., 1945-46, asst. dir. pediatrics out-patient dept., 1946-47, fellow pediatric cardiology, 1947-48; instr. pediatrics Johns Hopkins U., 1946-48; asst. resident Sydenham Hosp. Contagious Diseases, Balt., 1946, N.Y. Hosp., 1948-49, asst. attending pediatrician, 1952-60, assoc. attending pediatrician, 1960-62, attending pediatrician, 1962-92, hon. staff, 1992—; fellow in pediatrics Cornell U., N.Y.C., 1949-50, mem. faculty, 1950-92, prof., 1969-92, prof. emeritus, 1992—, Stavros S. Niarchos prof. pediatric cardiology, 1979-92, emeritus, 1992—. Med. dir. Insts. in Care Premature Infant, 1952-55, dir. pediatric cardiology, 1963-92. Recipient Spence-Chapin award for contbns. to pediatrics, 1958, award of merit Philoptochos Soc. N. and S. Am., 1978, Woman of Conscience award Nat. Council Women, 1979, citation Nat. Bd. Med. Coll. Pa., 1979, Disting. Achievement award Baylor U., 1981, Disting. Alumna award Baylor U., 1988, Maurice Greenberg Disting. Svc. award N.Y. Hosp.-Cornell Med. Ctr., 1991; hon. fellow Cornell U. Med. Coll. Alumni, 1984; Mary Allen Engle Div. Pediatric Cardiology, N.Y. Hosp.-Cornell U. Med. Coll. dedicated in her honor, 1992, Johns Hopkins U. Soc. Scholars award, 1992, Alumni Assoc. Detlev Bronk award, 1993, Disting. Alumna award, 2002. Mem. Am. Acad. Pediat. (charter mem. sect. cardiology, Founder's award cardiology sect. 1983), Am. Clin. and Climatological Assn. (recorder 1992-2000, pres.-elect 2002), Am. Heart Assn. (bd. dirs. 1975-78, award of merit 1975, Helen B. Taussig award 1976), N.Y. Heart Assn. (bd. dirs. 1980-86), N.Y. Acad. Medicine, N.E. Pediatric Cardiology Soc., Harvey Soc., Soc. Pediatric Rsch., Assn. European Pediatric Cardiologists (corr.), Royal Soc. Medicine (bd. dirs. Found. 1983-92, hon. bd. dirs. 1992-2000), Am. Coll. Cardiology (master tchr. 1969, 73, 76, trustee 1974-79, bd. govs. 1990-94, pres. N.Y. State chpt. 1991-92, Theodore and Susan Cummings Humanitarian award 1973, 76), Am. Pediatric Soc., Pediatric Cardiology Soc. Greater N.Y., N.Y. Cardiology Soc. (bd. dirs., pres. 1986-87), Soc. Scholars, Phi Beta Kappa, Alpha Omega Alpha. Presbyterian. Home: 2451 Brickell Ave Ph A Miami FL 33129-2472 also: 27213 Baileys Neck Rd Easton MD 21601-8503

ENGLE, REED LAURENCE, landscape architect; b. Upper Darby, Pa., Jan. 4, 1944; s. Alexander Reed and Alice Lucille (Pickell) E.; m. Dolores Gill Dyson, Dec. 21, 1946; children: Elizabeth Gresham, Louisa Jefferis. BA, Lafayette Coll., Easton, Pa., 1967; MA in Am. History, Lehigh U., Bethlehem, Pa., 1977; M of Landscape Arch., U. Pa., 1986. Archtl. historian John M. Dickey, Media, Pa., 1976-83; hist. architect Nat. Park Svc., Phila., 1983-88, regional hist. landscape architect, 1988-89; chief cultural resources Gettysburg (Pa.) Nat. Mil. Park, 1989-94; cultural resource specialist Shenandoah Nat. Park, Luray, Va., 1994—. Author: Everything Was Wonderful: The C.C.C. in Shenandoah National Park, 1933-1942, 1999, In The Light of the Mountain Moon: An Illustrated History of Skyland, 1853-2003, 2003; co-author: Story Behind the Scenery, 1998; author 22 books/hist. structure reports; contbr. numerous articles to profl. jours. Mem. Am. Soc. Landscape Architects (preservation com. 1986—). Achievements include managed restoration of over 20 historic houses and landscapes in Pennsylvania, Delaware and Virginia. Avocations: gardening, reading, travel. Home: PO Box 44 Boston VA 22713-0044

ENGLE, RICHARD VICTOR, publishing executive; b. Chgo., Oct. 7, 1961; s. Frank J. and Margaret Anne Wenglewski; m. Denise Marie Denning, July 23, 1985; 1 child, Destiny René. AD, Christ for the Nations Inst., Dallas, 1983. Commr. of archives and records State of Okla., 1998—; pub. Mid-Del News and Harrah News, Midwest City, Okla., 1999-2000, BellWest Am. Bethany/WarrAcres and Nichols Hills/Quail Creek Telephone Directories, 2000—. Mem. City Coun., City of Bethany, Okla., 1998—2002; pres. Nat. Fedn. Rep. Assemblies; chmn. Okla. Fedn. Young Reps., 1997—2001; alt. del. Rep. Nat. Conv., 1996, del., mem. nat. rules com., 2000; bd. dirs. N.W. dist. coun. YMCA of Greater Oklahoma City, 1999—. Mem. Okla. Press Assn. (legis. affairs com. 1998-2001). Republican. Charismatic Christian. Avocation: cross country bicycling. Home and Office: 1705 N Oakhill Rd Bethany OK 73008-5619 E-mail: engle@MrGOP.com.

ENGLE, ROBERT IRWIN, music educator, musician, composer, writer, translator; b. New Kensington, Pa., Feb. 11, 1945; s. Dale Clair Engle and Rosalyn Imogene (Timblin) Erickson. BS in Music Edn., U. Cin., 1967; postgrad., Stanford U., 1967-68, Ind. U., 1969, U. So. Calif., 1969-71; MA in Music, U. Hawaii, 1973, cert. in Samoan, 1986; PhD in Music, U. Wash., 1994. Cert. tchr. music grades K-12, Calif. Choral instr. Terminal Island Prison, San Pedro, Calif., 1969-71; choral music tchr. Palos Verdes (Calif.) High Sch., 1968-72; dir. music Makiki Christian Ch., Honolulu, 1978-84, 1st United Meth. Ch., Honolulu, 1986-88; tchr. music and French Redemption Acad., Kailua, Hawaii, 1988-91; dir. music Kapiolani Community Coll., Honolulu, 1975-99; dir. choral activities U. Hawaii, Hilo, 1995-96; asst. dir. music Hilo First Samoan Assembly of God, 1995-96; dir. music Good Samaritan Samoan Ch., Honolulu, 1997-98, Tacoma, 1999-2001, San Diego, 2001—02; chair music dept. Northwest Coll., Kirkland, Wash., 1999-2001; choral music tchr. Mt. Carmel H.S., San Diego, 2001—03; artistic dir. San Diego Men's Chorus, 2002—03. Cons. Performing Arts Abroad, Kalamazoo, 1979-99, Pacific Basin Choral Festival in Hawaii, Berkeley, Calif., 1989, Gateway Music Festivals, 1997-99; tchr. music theory, piano S. Seattle C.C., 1993-94; choral music tchr. Inglemoor H.S., Bothell, Wash., 1994; prof. Polynesian music and dance U. Pitts., summer 1996; spkr. Internat. Soc. Music Edn. Convention, Tampa, Fla., 1994, Pretoria, South Africa, 1998; spkr. nat. conf. Soc. Ethnomusicology, L.A., 1995, Music Educators Nat. Conf., Kansas City, 1996; spkr. in field.; accompanist Honolulu Boy Choir, 1996; coord. summer course in Tahitian dance and music, Papeete, Tahiti, 1998. Author: Taking Note of Music, 1988, Piano is My Forte, 1989; editor: Pacific Island Choral Series, 1995—99; composer: Tatalo A Le Alii, 1984 (3d pl. state competition); composer, rec. artist Pese Pa'ia, 1988, (rec.) Music at Northwest, 2000, '01 In the Spirit, 2001, profl. rec. Christmas Aloha, dir., composer of new repertoire New Samoan Ch. Choir Repertoire Project, Am. and Western Samoa, 1997; contbr. articles to profl. jours. Founder E Himeni Kakou Colls. Choral Festival, Honolulu, 1976-99; founder, dir. Maile Aloha Singers, Honolulu, 1973-92, Carols at the Centerstage Festival, Honolulu, 1989-99, Lokahi Choral Festival, Honolulu, 1989-99, Aloha, America! Invitational Choral Festival, Honolulu, 1995; dir. Northwest Singers, Kirkland, 1999-2000, Northwest A Cappella, 2000-01; founder Wash. Collegiate Choral Festival, Seattle, 1999-2001, CANTATE! Mid. Schs. Honor Choir, 2002.. Dir. mus. group representing Hawaii, Cultural Office for Territorial Activity, Papeete, Tahiti, 1982, World U. Games, 1983, Casa De La Cultura, Southeastern Mex., 1984, La. World EXPO, 1984, EXPO '86, Vancouver, Hawaiian Airlines, 1987, Goodwill Tour Am. Samoa, 1989, Artists in the Schs. Auckland, N.Z., 1991, Paris, 1999, Detroit, 2000; dir. mus. group representing U.S.A., U.S. Dept. State, EXPO '85, Tsukuba, Japan, 1985; Dir. award 2d pl. group Collegiate Showcase, Chgo., 1988, Dir. award 1st place Choral Groups All Am. Festival, Orlando, Fla., 1994, 7 NW States H.S. Honor Choir, 2000. Mem. AAUP, Am. Choral Dirs. Assn. (Hawaii chpt. 1978-99, editor newsletter 1987-89, 97-99, state pres. 1989-91, state sec. 1997-99, ethnic music chair NW divsn.), Samoa Fealofani Club, Delta Tau Delta (life). Republican. Mem. Pentecostal Ch. Avocations: languages, weightlifting, polynesian dance, drumming, translating. Home: 3980 8th Ave Ste 209 San Diego CA 92103 E-mail: drrobertengle@hotmail.com., bengle@hawaii.edu.

ENGLE, STEVE EUGENE, artist; b. Honolulu, Dec. 27, 1950; BFA in Sculpture, Santa Barbara Art Inst., 1973; MFA in Sculpture, Ind. U., 1980; postgrad., Pa. Acad. Fine Art, 1982-84. One person shows include Lisa Harris Gallery, Seattle, 1990, 92; exhibited in group shows Santa Barbara (Calif.) Art Inst., 1973, Ind. U., Bloomington, 1980, Contemporary Arts Ctr., Honolulu, 1981, Honolulu Acad. Art, 1982, Shreveport (La.) Art Guild, 1984, Woodmere Art Mus., Phila., 1985, U. Del., Newark, 1986, Roger Lapelle Gallery, Phila., 1987, Phila. City Hall, 1988, Bellevue (Wash.) Art Mus., 1988, 92, U. Wash. Med. Ctr., Seattle, 1990, Port Angeles (Wash.) Fine Arts Ctr., 1990, Seattle Ctr., Modern Art Pavillion, 1990, Alt. Mus., N.Y.C., 1991, Whatcom Mus., Bellingham, Wash., 1991, 92, Honolulu Advt. Gallery, 1991, Microsoft Corp., Redmond, Wash., 1992, WestOne Bancorp, Wash., Oreg., and Idaho, 1992, Seattle Ctr. Pavillion, 1993, The Contemporary Mus., Honolulu, 1996, Davis/Cline Gallery, Ashland, 2000, Thorndike Gallery, So. Oreg. U., Ashland, 2001, Hypotenuse Gallery, Sinclair C.C., Dayton, Ohio, 2001; represented in permanent collections WestOne Bancorp, Boise, Microsoft Corp., Redmond, Wash. State Arts Commn. Collection, Sch. Dist. Lacey, Wash., Seattle Arts Commn., Portable Works Collection, 1st Hawaiian Bank, Honolulu, Linda and Robert Kanter, Seattle, Hirschl Adler, N.Y.C., Contemporary Arts Ctr., Honolulu, Laila and Thurston Twigg-Smith, Honolulu, Jonson Gallery, U. N.Mex., Albuquerque, 1999, others; works included in publs. Jour. Am., The Herald, Seattle Times, Alt. Mus. Exhbn. Catalog, The Weekly, Artweek, Star-Bull, Impact Weekly, Dayton, Ohio, Sunday Jour., Albuquerque, Contemporary Mus. News, Honolulu.. Recipient Betty Bowen Meml. Recognition award Seattle Art Mus., 1989, Juror award Bellevue Art Mus., 1992, Best of Category award Paris Gibson Sq. Mus. Art, 1993, Anita Chadwick award Chautauqua Ctr. Visual Arts, N.Y., 1997; tuition scholar Santa Barbara Art Inst., 1972-73; Ford grantee N.Y. Sch. Painting, Drawing and Sculpture, 1979, Nat. Endowment for Arts visual artists fellowship grantee in sculpture, 1990; Seattle Artists project grantee Seattle Arts Commn., 1990. E-mail: sengleart@yahoo.com.

ENGLE, STEVEN B. biotechnology company executive; BSEE, MSEE, U. Tex. Mgmt. cons. Strategic Decisions Group, 1979—84, SRI Internat., 1979—84; v.p. mktg. and divsnl. gen. mgr. Micro Power Systems, 1984—87; CEO Quantum Mgmt. Co., 1987—91; v.p. mktg. Cygnus Inc., 1991—93; exec. v.p., COO La Jolla Pharm. Co., San Diego, 1993—94, pres., dir., sec., 1994—95, CEO, 1995—, chmn. bd., CEO, 1997—. Chmn. BIOCOM; dir. CareLinc Corp. Office: La Jolla Pharmaceutical Co 6455 Nancy Ridge Dr San Diego CA 92121-2249

ENGLE, SUSAN ANN, chemist; b. Hershey, Pa., Nov. 16, 1956; d. Harold Glenn Jr. and Doris Jane (Hovis) Engle; m. Scott Vincent Carney (div. Dec. 1993); children: Kristin, David; m. I. Michael Zulak, Feb. 21, 1999. BS in Chemistry, Lebanon Valley Coll., 1978; MBA, Temple U., 1985, PhD, 1995. Lab. asst. Lebanon Valley Coll., Annville, Pa., 1976-78; rsch. technician Hershey Foods, Inc., 1976-78; technician Pitman-Moore, Inc., Washington Crossing, N.J., 1978-80, chemist, 1980-81, methods devel. chemist, 1981-83, supr. methods and analysis lab., 1983-85; group leader analytical control Rorer, Inc., Fort Washington, Pa., 1987-89; sr. supr. stability Rhone-Poulenc Rorer, Inc., Fort Washington, 1989-91, quality assurance mgr., 1991-93, quality control mgr., 1993-95, acting dir. plant quality assurance and control, 1995-96; dir. quality assurance Novartis Consumer Health N.Am., Inc., Lincoln, Nebr., 1996-2000, ALZA Corp., Vacaville, Calif., 2000—01, v.p. quality assurance, 2001—. Mem. choir Jarrettown United Meth. Ch., 1991-97. Recipient Scientisic German award, 1978, Rhone Poulenc Rorer award for advancement/devel. of women, 1994; scholar Nat. Honor Soc., 1978. Mem. Am. Chem. Soc. (Phila. sect.), Am. Assn. Pharm. Scientists, Consumer Health Products Assn. (mfg. controls com.). Republican. Methodist. Avocations: golf, swimming, skiing. Office: ALZA Corp 700 Eubanks Dr Vacaville CA 95688-9470

ENGLEHART, JOAN ANNE, consultant; b. Susquehanna, Pa., Sept. 15, 1940; d. George Louis and Muriel Elois (Washburn) Wanatt; m. Dale John Englehart, Nov. 24, 1958. AAS, Broome C.C., 1981; BS in Cultural Studies, Empire State Coll., 1984; postgrad., SUNY, Binghamton, 1984; PhD in Bus. Adminstrn., Century U., 1994. Office mgr., coord. sales Bush Transformer Corp., Endicott (N.Y.), Boston, 1959-65; mgr., cons. Snelling & Snelling, Binghamton, Endicott, 1965-71; mgr., tchr. Can. Acad., Kobe, Japan, 1971-72; owner Typewriting, Endicott, 1980-85; exec. v.p. Tioga County C. of C., Owego, N.Y., 1985-87, pres., 1988-99; exec. v.p. Chamber Found., 1987-99. Cons. specializing in non-profit orgns., 1999—. Mem. scholarship com. Civic Club Binghamton, 1984-87; adv. bd. Broome and Tioga County Health Fairs, 1985-87; sec.-treas. Tioga County C. of C. Found., 1987-99; chmn. sustaining membership com. Broome United Way, Binghamton, 1986-87; planning process com. Broome-Delaware-Tioga BOCES vocat. edn. coms., 1989, 92; bd. dirs. NYPENN Health Sys. Agy., 1989-91, Pvt. Industry Coun., 1994-99, Sch. to Careers, 1997-98, Tioga County Rural Ministry, 1992-97, chmn., 1993-97; pres. Tioga County divsn. Am. Heart Assn., 1994-99; active Tioga County Tourism Coun., 1994-99, County Comprehensive Plan, 1994-97; v.p. Tioga County Revitalization Task Force, 1997-98; adv. com. So. Tier Rail, 1997; active Binghamton Met. Transp. Study, 1997; media and pub. rels. specialist So. Tier chpt. Alzheimer's Assn., 1999-2000; pub. rels. coord. So. Tier SeniorNet, 2002-, ch. coun. mem and pub. rels. coord., Holy Nativity Luth. Ch., 2003-. Recipient award Boy Scouts Am., 1979, Evening Student Assn., 1991, Friends Binghamton Libr., 1982, ATHENA award C. of C., 1986; named Woman of Achievement Broome County Status of Women Coun., 1978. Mem. AAUW (life, pres. 1986-87), So. Tier World Commerce Assn. (bd. dirs. 1992-99), Nat. Assn. Women in C. of C.'s (charter mem., Nat. Achievement award 1993, com. chmn. 1994-96), Am. C. of C. Execs., N.Y. State C. of C. Execs. (bd. dirs. 1991), Zonta (pres. Tioga County area club 1985-89, mem. internat. bd. dirs., gov. dist. II 1982-84, Woman of Achievement 1985-88). Republican. Lutheran. Avocations: reading, interior design, music, photography, sports car activities. Home and Office: 4 Lancaster Dr Endicott NY 13760-4320 E-mail: jenglehar@stny.rr.com.

ENGLEHART, ROBERT WAYNE, JR., cartoonist; b. Ft. Wayne, Ind., Nov. 7, 1945; s. Robert Wayne Englehart, Sr. and Shirley Rose (Rogers) Bowers; m. Judith Ann King (div. 1986); children: Mark, Sherri; m. Patricia Ann McGrath, Mar. 16, 1947; 1 stepchild, Brian Loftus. Student, Am. Acad. Art, Chgo. Cartoonist, illustrator Chgo. Today, 1966-72; freelance artist, editorial cartoonist Jour. Gazette, Ft. Wayne, 1972-75; editorial cartoonist Jour. Herald, Dayton, Ohio, 1975-80, Hartford (Conn.) Courant, 1980—. Syndicated L.A. Times-Washington Post News Svc. Author: Never Let Facts Get In The Way of A Good Cartoon, 1979, A Distinguished Panel of Experts, 1985; illustrator (children's book) 1,2,3 I Can Count, 1972; cartoons have appeared in Time, Newsweek, N.Y. Times, Washington Post, Playboy; cartoons exhibited at Widener Gallery Trinity Coll., Hartford, 1988; prodr. (video comic strip) Out There with Englehart, Conn. Pub. TV, 1986-91, (New Eng. Emmy award 1989, 90, 1st Pl. award Conn. AP Broadcasters Assn. 1988, 89); prodr. (sports video comic strip) Last Row With Englehart & McGrath, 1991-95; appeared in Broadway polit. comedi rev. Raucous Caucus, 1992. Finalist Pulitzer Prize, 1979; recipient H.L. Mencken award Free Press Assn., 1979, various awards Overseas Press Club, UN Population Inst., John Fischetti Contest, Planned Parenthood Conn. Mem. Assn. Am. Editorial Cartoonists, Nat. Cartoonists Soc. Office: Hartford Courant Co 285 Broad St Hartford CT 06115-3785 E-mail: englehart@courant.com.

ENGLEMAN, DENNIS EUGENE, electrical engineer, author, photographer, musician; b. Falls City, Nebr., July 24, 1948; s. Eugene Adolf and Mary Alice (Franklin) E.; m. Deborah Faye Paulson, May 4, 1985; children: John Nicholas, Lily Eugenia, Mary Victoria. Student, U. Nebr., 1966-70; B in Engring. Tech., Wichita State U., 1982. Ordained to ministry Holy Order of Mans, 1977, ordained acolyte/reader Ea. Orthodox Ch., 1988. Minister various parishes, 1977-81; elec. technician Kans. Gas & Elec. Co., Wichita, 1981-82; elec. engr. Boeing Mil. Airplane Co., Wichita, 1982; design engr. Nat. Data Corp., Atlanta, 1983, Raymond Carousel Corp., Atlanta, 1984; elec. designer Cons. & Designers, Inc., Atlanta, 1984; from project engr. to engring. supr. Nordson Corp., Norcross, Ga., 1984-92, sr. engring. supr., 1992-94; project engr. ACE group, 1994-98; engr. Skaltek, 1999—2002; pres. Holy Mountain Imports, Atlanta, 1987-93, Engleman Photography Internat., Atlanta, 1989—, Liberty Imports, Atlanta. Editor Catacomb Press, 2000-02. Author: Ultimate Things, 1995, Beautiful America's Atlanta, 1996, The Saint Nicholas Secret, 1999, Pilgrimage to Paradise, 2000, How to Find Your Own Pot of Gold Trading Stock Options, 2000, Conversations with Angels, 2000, The Soul of Sarov, 2000, The Art of Revolution, 2000, A Childrens' Christian Primer, 2000, A Rumor of War, 2001; exhibitor Sacred Space Atrium Gallery Hartsfield Atlanta Internat. Airport, 2003; editor Catacomb Press, 2000-02; co-editor: Tree of Life, 1992-97; prodr. programming People TV, Pub. Access TV, 1990-93; singer, songwriter, arranger, 1992, Pristine Records, 1993; prodr. various slide shows; writer, prodr. folk opera; contbr. over 100 articles to profl. publs. Dir. St. Cyril's Village Orch., 1987-91; mem. Atlanta Balalaika Soc. Orch., 1984-87; mem.

Atlanta Mandolin Soc. Orch., 1994-96; pres. Christian Cmty. Atlanta, 1985-87; performer Dahlonega's Mountain Music and Medicine Show, 2001--. Republican. Orthodox Christian. Avocations: folk music, photography. E-mail: Englemania@aol.com.

ENGLEMAN, ELLEN G. federal agency administrator; BA in Eng. and Comm., Ind. U., 1983, JD, 1987; MPA, Harvard U., 1993. Bar: Ind. 1987, U.S. Dist. Ct. (no. and so. dists.) 1987. Pub. affairs exec. GTE, 1987—92; pres., CEO Electricore, Ind., 1994—2001; adminstr. rsch. and spl. programs adminstrn. U.S. Dept. Transp., Washington, 2001—03; mem., chmn. Nat. Transp. Safety Bd. (NTSB), Washington, 2003—. Dir. Corporate & Govt. Affairs, Direct Relief Internat., 1993—94. Bd. dirs. Direct Relief Internat., dir. corp. & govt. affairs. With USNR, 2000. Mem.: Pub. Rels. Soc. Am. (cert. pub. rels.). Office: NTSB Headquarters 490 L'Enfant Plaza SW Washington DC 20594 Office Fax: 202-366-3666.*

ENGLEMAN, EPHRAIM PHILIP, rheumatologist; b. San Jose, Calif., Mar. 24, 1911; s. Maurice and Tillie (Rosenberg) E.; m. Jean Sinton, Mar. 2, 1941; children— Ephraim Philip, Edgar George, Jill. BA, Stanford U., 1933; MD, Columbia U., 1937. Intern Mt. Zion Hosp., San Francisco; resident U. Calif., San Francisco, Jos. Pratt Diagnostic Hosp., Boston; research fellow Mass. Gen. Hosp., Boston, 1937-42; practice medicine specializing in rheumatology San Francisco, 1948—; mem. faculty U. Calif. Med. Center, San Francisco, 1949—, clin. prof. medicine, 1965—; dir. Rosalind Russell Arthritis Center, 1979—. Mem. staff U. Calif., Mills Meml., Peninsula hosps.; Chmn. Nat. Commn. Arthritis and Related Diseases, 1975-76 Author: The Book on Arthritis: A Guide for Patients and Their Families, 1979; also articles, chpts. in books. Served to maj. M.C. USMCR, 1942-47. Recipient medal of Honor, U. Calif., San Francisco, 1999; Nat. Inst. Arthritis grantee; recipient citation Arthritis Found., 1973; Ephraim P. Engleman Disting. Professorship in Rheumatology established in his honor U. Calif., San Francisco, 1991. Fellow ACP; mem. Internat. League Against Rheumatism (pres. 1981-85), Am. Coll. Rheumatology (founding fellow, master, pres. 1962-63, Presdl. Gold medal 2002), Nat. Soc. Clin. Rheumatologists, AMA, Am. Fedn. Clin. Research; hon. mem. Japanese Rheumatism Soc., Spanish Rheumatism Soc., Uruguay Rheumatism Soc., Australian Rheumatism Assn., Chinese Med. Assn., French Soc. Rheumatology, Internat. League against Rheumatism, Gold-Headed Cane Soc. (U. Calif., San Francisco), Family Club (San Francisco). Republican. Jewish. Office: U Calif Rosalind Russell Med Rsch Ctr Arthritis 350 Parnassus Ave Ste 600 San Francisco CA 94117-3608 Business E-Mail: ephraim@itsa.ucsf.edu.

ENGLER, BRIAN DAVID, association executive; b. Palmerton, Pa., Oct. 9, 1947; s. David James and Doreen Estelle (Sheldon) E.; m. Margaret Mary Hurlock, Dec. 31, 1969 (div. Apr. 1981); children: Donna, David; m. Maxine Sue Richard, May 24, 1981; children: Rachel, Stacey. BS with merit, U.S. Naval Acad., 1969; MS in Ops. Rsch., Naval Postgrad. Sch., Monterey, Calif., 1978; MBA in Fin., Acctg., Marymount U., 1986. Commd. ensign USN, 1969, advanced through grades to comdr., 1983, naval flight officer, mission comdr., ops. analyst, 1969-89, ret., 1989; ops. analyst, project leader Systems Planning and Analysis., Alexandria, Va., 1989-90, asst. program mgr., 1990-91, program mgr., 1991-2000; exec. v.p. Mil. Ops. Rsch. Soc., 2000—. Assoc. editor (alumni newsletter) O.R. News, 1976-78. Mem. Big Bros./ Big Sisters of Balt., Annapolis, Md., 1968-69; sec.-treas. bd. dirs. Gov.'s Sq. Homeowners Assn., Williamsburg, Va., 1989-97. Decorated Navy Commendation medals (2), Meritorious Svc. medal; recipient Juvenile Decency award Kiwanis Club, 1965, Cert. of Proficiency, Civil Air Patrol, 1963, Best Cadet award Temple U., 1965. Mem. Am. Soc. Assn. Execs., Greater Washington Soc. Assn. Execs., Mil. Ops. Rsch. Soc. (bd. dirs. 1991—, sec. treas. 1993-94, v.p. for adminstrn. 1994-95, v.p. fin. and mgmt. 1999-00), VFW (post comdr.), Am. Legion, Mil. Applications Soc., Inst. for Ops. Rsch. and Mgmt. Sci., Washington Inst. for Ops. Rsch. and Mgmt. Sci., Delta Epsilon Sigma. Avocations: running, sailing, reading, music, fencing, bowling. Home: 5918 Clermont Landing Ct Burke VA 22015-2565 Office: Mil Ops Rsch Soc Ste 450 1703 N Beauregard St Alexandria VA 22311-1717 E-mail: brian@mors.org.

ENGLER, EVA KAY, dental and veterinary products company executive; b. Czechoslovakia, May 7, 1927; m. Alfred Engler (dec. 1979); children: Raya, Michael David. Pres., founder med. and dental mfg. co. Engler Engring. Corp., Hialeah, Fla., 1964—. Avocations: languages, painting. Office: Engler Engring Corp 1099 E 47th St Hialeah FL 33013-2139 Fax: 305-685-7671.

ENGLER, JOHN, governor; b. Mt. Pleasant, Mich., Oct. 12, 1948; s. Mathias John and Agnes Marie (Neyer) E.; m. Michelle; children: Margaret Rose, Hannah Michelle, Madeleine Jenny; B.S. in Agrl. Econs., Mich. State U., 1971; J.D., Thomas M. Cooley Law Sch., 1981. Mem. Mich. Ho. of Reps., 1971-78; mem. Mich. Senate, 1979-90, Republican leader, 1983, majority leader, 1984-90; ; state senator, 1979-90; gov., 1991-2003. Del. White House Conf. on Youth, 1972; U.S. Trade Reps.' Intergovernmental Policy Adv. com., 1988, Intergovernmental Adv. Coun. on Edn., 1988; chmn. Presdl. Scholars, 1991-92; One of 5 Outstanding Young Men of Mich., Mich. Jaycees, 1983, Governing Magazine Public Official of the Yr.. pres. Gerald R. Ford Found.; mem. Nat. Gov.'s Assn. (welfare reform task force 1993—, edn. goals panel 1993—, chair 2001-02). Republican. Roman Catholic.

ENGLER, ROBERT, political science educator, author; b. N.Y.C., July 12, 1922; s. Isidore and Esther (Haber) E.; m. Rosalind Elowitz, May 16, 1946 (div. June 1960); children: Richard J., Elise P.; m. Inea Bushnaq, Sept. 5, 1968; 1 dau., Nadya Kate. BSS., CCNY, 1942; MA, U. Wis., 1946, PhD, 1947. Mem. faculty U. Wis., 1946-47, Syracuse U., 1947-50, Columbia U., 1959-63; prof. polit. sci. Queens Coll., CUNY, 1964-69, Grad. Sch. and Bklyn. Coll., CUNY, 1969-91, prof. emeritus, 1991—; prof. polit. sci. Sarah Lawrence Coll., 1951-71; mem. faculty New Sch. Social Research, 1961-64; chair, vis. prof. world politics of peace and war Princeton U., 1988-89. Vis. prof. U. P.R., 1961, U. Sask., 1973, Ctr. for Rsch. in Rural and Indsl. Devel., India, 1992, 2001, U. Havana, 1987, 92, 93; disting. vis. scholar Indian Coun. Social Sci. Rsch., 2001-02; disting. vis. prof. Am. U., Cairo, 1978; assoc. fellow Inst. for Policy Studies, Washington, 1979-80. Author: The Politics of Oil: Private Power and Democratic Directions, 1961, The Brotherhood of Oil; Energy Policy and the Public Interest, 1977; also articles, reviews; contbg. author: The Dissenting Academy, 1968, Winning America, 1988; editor: America's Energy: 100 Years of Struggle for the Democratic Control of Our Resources, 1980. Asst. to pres. Nat. Farmers Union, Washington, 1950-51; dir. Encampment for Citizenship, N.Y.C., 1961, 63. Served with AUS, 1943-46, ETO. Recipient Sidney Hillman Found. prize award polit. writing, 1955. Home: 444 Central Park W Apt 12F New York NY 10025-4358 Office: CUNY Grad Ctr 365 5th Ave New York NY 10016-4309

ENGLER, ROBERT L. retired cardiologist; b. Chicago, Ill., Mar. 8, 1945; s. Hershel and Zoe M Engler; children: Eric H, Matthew L. MD, Georgetown U., 1970; BS, U. of NC, Chapel Hill, 1966. Internal Medicine ABIM, 1973, Cardiology ABIM, 1975. Prof. of medicine, emeritus U. of Calif., San Diego, Calif., 1975—. Founder, dir. Collateral Therapeutics, Inc, San Diego, 1995—2002; faculty Inst. for Biomedical Engring., Calif. Author 104 scientific pubs. Dir. Nat. Assn. of VA Rsch. and Edns. Founds., 1997—2000. Fellow: Am. Soc. for Clin. Investigation, Am. Heart Assn. Avocations: golf, biking, back packing, skiing. Home: 14801 Vista del Oceano Del Mar CA 92014

ENGLERT, HELEN WIGGS, writer; b. Nashville, June 1, 1927; d. Lawrence Raymond and Frances Eloise (Smith) Wiggs; m. Roy Theodore Englert Sr., Sept. 25, 1948; children: Lee Ann Englert Regan, Roy Theodore Jr. AA, Ward Belmont Coll., Nashville, 1948; AB, George Washington U., Washington, 1954, postgrad., 1969-71. Lectr. Weight Watchers, Washington & Va., 1972-84. Author: Hey, Wait a Minute! Dealing with Feelings and Weight Control, 1992, We Hold These Values...What is Uniquely American about Being an American, 2002. Elder Old Presbyn. Meeting House, Alexandria, Va., 1982—; bd. mem. Sr. Citizens Employment & Svcs. Inc., Alexandria, 1994-97. Mem. George Washington U. Club, Campagna Ctr. (Alexandria), Nat. Mus. Women in Arts, Phi Theta Kappa. Avocations: walking, travel, tennis, grandchild, geneology. Home: 12183 Cathedral Dr Lake Ridge VA 22192-2227

ENGLERT, ROY THEODORE, lawyer; b. Nashville, Sept. 11, 1922; s. Roy T. and Ruth Rowe (Tindall) E.; m. Helen Frances Wiggs, Sept. 25, 1948; children: Lee Ann, Roy Jr. BA, Vanderbilt U., 1943; JD, Columbia, 1951; LLM, George Washington U., 1953. Bar: Tenn. 1951, U.S. Dist. Ct. D.C. 1951, U.S. Supreme Ct. 1955, Internat. Trade 1975. Asst. counsel Office Comptroller of Currency, U.S. Treasury Dept., 1951-58, chief counsel, 1958-62, asst. gen. counsel of dept., 1962-66, dep. gen. counsel, 1966-73; sole practice Washington, 1973-96. Bd. dirs., sec. Walker/Potter Assocs., Inc., Washington, 1973 96; mem. Sr. Seminar in Fgn. Policy, Dept. State, 1963-64, U.S. Assay Commn., 1975; lectr., writer on banking law. Contbr. articles to profl. jours. Judo tech. ofcl. Atlanta Olympics; bd. dirs. Westminster Ingleside Found. Lt. USNR, 1943—46. Recipient Exceptional Service award U.S. Treasury, 1972, Gen. Counsel's award, 1973; named US Track Nat. Masters Champion 10,000 meter run, 1998. Mem. ABA, Tenn. Bar Assn. Presbyterian. Home: 12183 Cathedral Dr Woodbridge VA 22192-2227 Office: 6720 Bellamy Ave Springfield VA 22152-3023

ENGLES, GREGG L. food company executive; Chmn. bd., CEO various predecessors Suiza Foods, Dallas, chmn. bd., CEO, 1994—. Bd. dirs. Evercom, Inc., Tex. Capital Bankshares. Office: Suiza Foods 2515 Mckinney Ave Ste 1200 Dallas TX 75201-1945

ENGLESMITH, TEJAS, actor, producer, curator; b. London, Nov. 28, 1941; came to U.S. 1957; s. George and Lydia Julia (Johnson-Briet) E. Student in art history, U. St. Thomas, Houston, 1959-63. Asst. dir. Whitechapel Gallery, London, 1963-69; curator Contemporary Art Jewish Mus., N.Y.C., 1969-70; dir. Leo Castelli Gallery, N.Y.C., 1970-76, Max Hutchinson Gallery, Houston, 1976-78; pvt. art cons. Houston, 1978-80; auction mgr. Sta. KUHT-TV, Houston, 1980-84, exec. prodr., 1980-86, assoc. dir., devel. managing editor Public Times, 1984-86; prodr., announcer Sta. KUHF-FM, Houston, 1987-90; ind. broadcast cons. and prodr. Houston, 1990—; subscriber svcs./pub. rels. rep. Theatre Under the Stars, Houston, 1992-99. Judge Roanoke (Va.) Art Festival, 1972; judge, lectr. S.W. Tex. State U., San Marcos, 1978. Narrator: (film) Pas de Deux: A Dance of Two Countries: China and America, 1980, Just a Closer Walk With Thee, 1989, The English Countryside, 1992 (Silver Telly award narration 1994), Hall of the Americas, 1998, Voyages of Discovery, 2000, Houston Mus. of Natural Sci., numerous travel and indsl. videos; interviewee: Inflatable Sculpture, CBS-TV, 1969, Views on Art, Sta. WNYC-FM, 1975, Curtain!, Sta. KUHT-TV, 1980-81; prodr./host: Conversations with People in Arts, Sta. KPFT-FM, 1977; exec. prodr. 30th Anniversary Sta. KUHT Sock Hop, 1983; writer mus. catalogues; organizer various exhbns. Mem. selection com. N.Y. Drawing Soc., 1970; reader Taping For the Blind, 1987—; adv. bd. Cultural Arts Council Houston, 1978. Recipient Silver award Assn. for Community TV, 1981, Gold award Assn. for Community TV, 1982. Fellow Royal Soc. Arts. Clubs: TLC Four Seasons. Home: 7839 Fondren Rd Houston TX 77074-4601 Office: Pastorini/Bosby Talent Agy 3013 Fountain View Dr Houston TX 77057-6124 E-mail: tejase@sbcglobal.net. *The learning and practice of good manners would alleviate most of the problems we face today . . . and tomorrow.*

ENGLING, EZRA SAMUEL, Spanish and literature educator, researcher; b. Kingston, Jamaica, June 3, 1957; 1 child, El Hassane Aghazzaf. BA in Spanish and English with honors, U. W.I. Mona, St. Andrew, Jamaica, 1980, MA in Spanish, 1983, PhD in Spanish, 1986. English tchr. Calabar H.S., St. Andrew, 1980-81; asst. lectr. Spanish U. W.I., Mona, 1981-82, grad. asst. Spanish, 1984-86; Spanish tchr. Campion Coll., St. Andrew, 1982-84; lectr. in English Coll. Arts, Scis. and Tech. (now U. Jamaica), St. Andrew, 1983-84; prof. Spanish and world lit. Lincoln (Pa.) U., 1987-2001, chair dept. langs., 1993-98; prof. Spanish, Tex. A&M Internat. U., Laredo, 2001—. Founding mem., adv. bd. Moroccan Cultural Studies Ctr., Fes, 1996—. Author: A Critical Edition of Calderon's "La Aurora en Copacabana," 1994; contbr. articles to profl. jours. Translator Oxford (Pa.) Dist. Ct., 1990—; contbr. Oxford Neighborhood Svcs. Scholar NEH, 1989, Spanish Ministry of Culture, Almagro, Spain, 1991; Summer Lang. Inst. grantee United Negro Coll. Fund, 1996; sr. rsch. fellow Fulbright Found., Morocco, 1996-97. Mem. MLA, AAUP (sec. local chpt. 1992-94), Coll. Lang. Assn. (mem. study abroad scholarship com.), Assn. Hispanic Classical Theater. Avocations: reading, travel, music, computers. Office: Tex A&M Internat U Dept Lang & Lit Laredo TX 78045 Fax: 435-518-0020. E-mail: engling@tamiu.edu.

ENGLISH, BRUCE VAUGHAN, environmental consultant; b. Richmond, Va., Aug. 6, 1921; s. Pollard and Lucy Kelly (Rice) E.; m. Virginia Tejas McCall Shaw, Feb. 6, 1949. BS in Physics and Math., Randolph-Macon Coll., 1942; MS in Physics and Math., Ind. U., 1943; PhD in Physics, U. Va., 1958. Grad. asst. instr. army specialized tng. program/rsch. asst. Manhattan Dist. Engrs. Project; physics instr. Ind. U., Bloomington; asst. prof. physics army specialized tng. program Randolph-Macon Coll., Ashland, Va., 1943-44, assoc. prof., acting chmn. dept. physics, 1948-58, prof., chmn. dept., 1958-64; physicist, head high pressure lab. U.S. Navy Underwater Sound Reference Lab., Orlando, Fla., 1946-48; physicist, cons. historic preservation, pollution control and environment Ashland, 1964—; dir. Poe Found., Inc., Richmond, 1968-97, pres., 1973-92, life hon. pres., 1998—; pres., dir. Edgar Allan Poe Mus., Richmond, 1973-92. Pres. Pollution Control Assocs., Richmond, 1967-70. Co-pub.: Poe's Richmond, 1978; columnist Herald-Progress, 1971—; contbr. articles to Poe Messenger mag. Founding mem. Richmond Symphony, 1956; mem. Patrick Henry Scotchtown Com., Hanover County, Va., 1958—; pres. Hist. Richmond Found., 1967-70; bd. dirs. Church Hill Model Neighborhood Bd., Richmond, 1968-73; chmn. Bicentennial Com. for Hanover County, 1974-92, Drainage Com., Ashland, 1980s, Courthouse Com. for Hanover County, 1985—; lay reader, mem. vestry St. John's Ch., Church Hill, Richmond, Va., 1969-70; hon. pres. Poe Found., Inc., 1998. With USN, 1944-45. Named Hon. Citizen State of Md., 1990; Ford Faculty fellow, 1951-52, Danforth fellow, 1956-57, du Pont fellow, 1957-58; recipient Smithey Math Gold medal, 1942. Mem. AAAS, Am. Phys. Soc., Va. Acad. Sci., Va. Hist. Soc., Nat. Trust for Hist. Preservation, Irish Georgian Soc., Cousteau Soc. (founding), Air and Waste Mgmt. Assn., Nat. Soc. for Clean Air Gt. Britain, Soc. Descs. of Peter Francisco (founder, advisor), Nat. D-Day Mus. WWII (charter), City Tavern Club, Commonwealth Club, Farmington Country Club, Downtown Club, Phi Beta Kappa, Sigma Xi, Omicron Delta Kappa, Chi Beta Phi, Pi Delta Epsilon. Episcopalian. Achievements include research in project developing atomic bomb, increasing awareness of hazards of pollution since 1955, of Edgar Allan Poe's cosmology, cryptography, and other scientific writings.

ENGLISH, CHRISTINE A. accountant, business development manager; b. Rutland, Vt., Mar. 13, 1969; d. Sherman Charles and Barbara (Tunison) Andres; m. Charles Hynes English III, June 5, 1999. BS in Mktg., Rutgers U., 1991; MBA, U. S.C., 1998. Acct. Advantica, Spartanburg, S.C., 1992-95, AIMCO, Greenville, S.C., 1995-97; account exec. Robert Half Internat., Greenville, 1997-98; v.p. recruiting MBI Fin. Staffing, Greenville, 1999—2000; bus. devel. mgr. Arrow Electronics, 2000—. Spkr. in field. Mem. Inst. Mgmt. Accts., Inst. Internal Auditors, Golden Key, Beta Gamma Sigma. Avocations: reading, exercise, cooking, travel.

ENGLISH, DALE LOWELL, circuit court judge; b. Madison, Wis., Nov. 12, 1956; s. Richard Dale and Grace Elaine (Piehler) E.; m. Patricia Kay Becker, Sept. 11, 1982; children: Kristopher Scott, Shane Patrick. BA cum laude, Luther Coll., 1979; JD, Marquette U., 1982. Bar: Wis. Supreme Ct. 1982, U.S. Dist. Ct. (ea. and we. dist.) Wis. 1982, U.S. Ct. Appeals (7th cir.) 1986, U.S. Supreme Ct. 1988. Ptnr. Colwin & English Svc. Corp., Fond du Lac, Wis., 1982-94; atty. Wausau Ins. Cos., Appleton, Wis., 1994-96; judge Br. I Fond du Lac County Circuit Ct., Wis., 1996—. Mem. Fond du Lac County teen ct. adv. task force, 1999-, Fond du Lac County juvenile facility com., 2001, judicial exchange program; bd. dirs. Brooke Industries, vice chmn., 1990. Contbr. case studies. Mem. Fond du Lac Planning Commn., 1986-95; mem. adv. com. Legal Sec. Assocs. Degree Program, Fond du Lac, 1986; bd. dirs. Fond du Lac YMCA, 1988-95, 97-2001, sec., 1989, v.p., 1990-91, pres.-elect, 1992, pres., 1993, past pres.coun., 2001—; bd. dirs. Drug Awareness Resistance Edn. of Fond du Lac, Inc., 1989-96; bd. dirs. Fond du Lac Festivals, Inc., 1996-99. Mem. ABA, Nat. Conf. of State Trial Judges, Am. Judges Assn. (mem. employee ethics adv. com., 1996-97), Wis. Bar Assn., Wis. Trial Judges Assn. (employee ethics advocacy com., 1996-97), Fond du Lac County Bar Assn. (pres. 2001, treas. 1984-85), Jaycees (legal counsel 1983-85, state dir. 1983-84, bd. dirs. 1983-85), Omicron Delta Epsilon. Avocations: weight lifting, sports. Office: 160 S Macy St Fond Du Lac WI 54935-4241

ENGLISH, DONALD MARVIN, loss control representative; b. Raleigh, N.C., July 31, 1951; s. Marvin Lee and Lois (Woodard) E.; m. Rebecca Pritchard, Sept. 3, 1970 (div. 1977); m. Kathryn A. Sumner, July 3, 1993 (div. 1998). Student, Miami U., Oxford, Ohio, 1969-70, 73-74, U. Cin., 1977-78, Calif. State U., Fresno, 1980—; AA, Fresno City Coll., 1991; BA in Social Sci., Wash. State U., 2002. Cert. safety profl. and health mgr. Bd. Cert. Safety Profls. Ins. inspector Comml. Services, Cin., 1974-78, Ohio Casualty Ins. Co., Fresno, 1978-93; owner Loss Control Systems, Renton, Wash., 1993; sr. loss control specialist Scott Wetzel Svcs., Inc., Federal Way, Wash., 1993-96; sr. loss control territory mgr. Safeco Ins. Co., Seattle, 1996—. Sen., treas. extended deg. program Wash. State U., 1999—2002. Served with U.S. Army, 1970-73. Mem. Am. Soc. Safety Engrs., Soc. CPCU (cert.), Ins. Inst. Am. (assoc. in loss control mgmt. 1990), East Fresno Exch. Club (pres. 1984-85). Avocation: travel. Home: 6520 146th St SW Edmonds WA 98026-3523 Office: 4514 154th Pl NE Redmond WA 98052 E-mail: DonEngCSP@yahoo.com.

ENGLISH, EDMOND, retail company executive; Grad., Northeastern U. With Filene's Basement; buyer T.J. Maxx, 1983, various sr. level merchandising positions, 1983-95; sr. v.p., group exec. TJX Cos., Inc., Framingham, Mass., 1998-99, pres., COO, bd. dirs., 1999—, pres., CEO. Office: TJX Cos Inc 770 Cochituate Rd Framingham MA 01701-4672

ENGLISH, FLOYD LEROY, telecommunications company executive; b. Nicholas, Calif., June 10, 1934; s. Elvan L. and Louise (Corliss) E.; children from previous marriage: children: Roxane, Darryl; m. Elaine Ewell, July 3, 1981; 1 child, Christine. AB in Physics, Calif. State U., Chico, 1959; MS in Physics, Ariz. State U., 1962, PhD in Physics, 1965. Divsn. supr. Sandia Labs., Albuquerque, 1965-73; gen. mgr. Rockwell Internat.-Collins, Newport Beach, Calif., 1973-75; pres. Darcom, Albuquerque, 1975-79; cons in energy mgmt. and acquisitions Albuquerque, 1980-81; v.p. U.S. ops. Andrew Corp., Orland Park, Ill., 1981-82, pres., 1981-82, COO, 1981-82, CEO, 1983-92, also bd. dirs., 1982—, chmn. bd. dirs., pres., CEO, 1992-2000, 2000—, chmn., bd. dirs., 1982—. Bd. dirs. Internat. Engring. Consortium. Contbr. articles to profl. jours. Bd. dirs. Ill. Math. and Sci. Acad. Fund for Advancement of Edn. 1st lt. U.S. Army, 1954-57; capt. Res., 1957-69. Mem. IEEE, Execs. Club of Chgo. (bd. dirs.). Republican. Presbyterian. Office: Andrew Corp 10500 W 153rd St Orland Park IL 60462-3071

ENGLISH, GREGORY BRUCE, lawyer; b. Lynchburg, Va., Nov. 8, 1946; s. Edgar George and Mavis Clark (Daniel) E.; m. Elaine Coleman Patton, Sept. 18, 1971; 1 child, Erik Todd. B.A., Lynchburg Coll., 1969; J.D., U. Va., 1973; LL.M., George Washington U., 1979. Bar: Pa. 1973, U.S. Supreme Ct. 1977, U.S. Dist. Ct. (no. dist.) Ohio 1981, U.S. Ct. Mil. Appeals 1976, U.S. Ct. Appeals (6th cir.) 1981, Va. 1986, D.C. 1986, U.S. Dist. Ct. (ea. dist.) Va. 1986, U.S. Ct. Appeals (4th cir.) 1986. Atty., Navy Gen. Counsel, 1977-78; sr. trial atty. U.S. Dept. Justice, narcotic and dangerous drug sect., criminal div., Washington, 1978-86; ptnr. English & Smith, 1988—; staff judge advocate, maj. JAGC D.C. Army Nat. Guard, Washington, 1977— . Contbr. articles to profl. jours. Bd. dirs. ACLU, Lynchburg, Va., 1969; dir. Democratic Central Com., Lynchburg, 1969. Served to capt. JAGC, U.S. Army, 1973-77. Recipient Atty. Gen.'s Spl. Commendation award, 1981; Commr.'s Meritorious Service award IRS, 1982, Meritorious award Justice Dept., 1982, Outstanding Contbns. award Drug Enforcement Adminstrn., 1983, Meritorious Contbns. award, 1984; Carey Brewer Alumni award Lynchburg Coll., 1983. Mem. ABA. Republican. Unitarian. Clubs: U. Va. Student Aid Found. (Washington) (dir. 1977—), Lee Dist. Basketball Assn. (Alexandria, Va.) (commr. 1984-86).

ENGLISH, HENRY L. not-for-profit association executive; b. West Point, Miss., May 27, 1942; s. Flozell and Julie Pearl (Smith) E.; m. Denise Tulloch, Sept. 11, 1989; children: Nkrumah, Kenya, Jumaane, Kalmilah. Student, Malcolm X Coll., 1966-69; BA, U. N.H., 1972; MPA, Cornell U., 1974. Asst. dir. devel. Kittrell (N.C.) Coll., 1974-75; asst. adminstr. Jackson Park Hosp., Chgo., 1975-77; dir. planning, mktg. South Chgo. Hosp., 1977-85; pres., CEO Black United Fund of Ill., Chgo., 1985—. Co-chmn. United Black Voters of Ill., 1077-79; mem. Coalition to Save S. Shore Country Club, 1980-84; bd. dirs. COMPRAND, Ill., 1981-86; commr. Calumet Dist. Boy Scouts Am., Chgo., 1982-84. Named fellow Woodrow Wilson Nat. Fellowship Found., 1972-74; recipient Leadership award Boy Scouts Am., Chgo., 1983, Appreciation award, Svc. award Clara's House Shelter, Chgo., 1995. Mem Nat. Health Care Execs., Blacks in Devel. (Appreciation award 1993). Office: Black United Fund Ill 1809 E 71st St Chicago IL 60649-2000

ENGLISH, J. KALANI, state senator; Cert., Nat. Chengchi U., Taiwan, 1988; BA in Pacific Islands Studies, Hawai'i Loa Coll., 1989; Cert., East-West Ctr., 1991; MA in Pacific Islands Studies, U. Hawaii, 1995; Cert. Paralegal, Maui C.C., 1996; grad. Leadership Acad., Asian Pacific Am. Inst. Congl. Studies, 2000. Adminstrv. aide Hawaiian Affairs/State of Hawaii, 1991-92; case mgr. Hui No Ke Ola Pono, 1992-94; lectr. Maui C.C., 1991-94, Visitor Industry Tng. and Edn. Ctr., 1993-94; UN corr. Samoa News, 1994; assoc. editor Na Po'e Hawai'i Mag., 1994-95; advisor Permanent Mission of Federated States Micronesia to UN, 1993-96; chief of staff Hawaii State Senator Avery B. Chumbley, 1995-96; advisor polit. and devel. affairs Nat. Tropical Bot. Gardens, 1995-97; councilmem. Maui County Coun., County of Maui, 1997-2000; Dem. senator dist. 5 Hawaii State Senate, 2000—. Advisor U.S. Permanent Mission to UN, 1999; mem. Internat. Pushkin Bicentennial Com., 1999; head del. to Rapa Nui, 1999; mem. local govt. adv. com. U.S. EPA, 2000—; dep. head del. State of Hawaii Del. to People's Rep. China, 2001-; mem. ways and means, commerce, consumer protection, housing, health and human services, edn., water, land, energy and environ. coms. Hawaii State Senate, vice chair tourism, intergovtl. affairs. Contbr. articles to mags. and profl. jours. Mem. bd. dirs. Maui Arts and Culture Ctr., 1993—, Maui Econ. Devel. Bd., 1997-99, Hawaii Cultural Found., N.Y.C., 1996—, Honolulu Media Coun.; mem. Maui County Cable TV Pub. Access Consortium, 1997; mem. Coun. on Aging-County of Maui, 1998-2000; mem. exec. com., bd. dirs. Maui Visitor's Bur., 1999-2000. Mem. Maui C. of C. (bd. dirs.). Office: Hawaii State Senate State Capitol Rm 205 415 S Beretania St Honolulu HI 96813 Fax: 808 587-7230. E-mail: senenglish@Capitol.hawaii.gov.*

ENGLISH, JAMES FAIRFIELD, JR., former college president; b. Putnam, Conn., Feb. 15, 1927; s. James Fairfield and Alice Bradford (Welles) English; m. Isabelle Spotswood Cox, July 9, 1955; children: Alice, James Fairfield, Margaret, William. Grad., Loomis Sch., 1944; BA, Yale U., 1949; MA, Cambridge (Eng.) U., 1951; JD, U. Conn., 1956; HLD, Northeastern U., 1982, Trinity Coll., 1989; LLD, U. Hartford, 1971, St. Joseph Coll., West Hartford, Conn., 1982. With Conn. Bank & Trust Co., Hartford, 1951—, sr. v.p., 1961-63, exec. v.p., 1963-66, pres., 1966-70, chmn. bd., 1970-80; v.p. fin. and planning Trinity Coll., Hartford, 1977-81, pres., 1981-89. Trustee emeritus Loomis Chaffee Sch., Mystic Seaport Mus.; bd. dirs. Duncaster Found., Inc. With AUS, 1944—46. Episcopalian. Home: 31 Potter St Groton CT 06340-5734 also: 777 Prospect Ave West Hartford CT 06105-4204

ENGLISH, JOHN DWIGHT, lawyer; b. Evanston, Ill., Mar. 28, 1949; s. John Francis English and Mary Faye (Taylor) Butler; m. Claranne Kay Lundeen, Apr. 22, 1972; children: Jennifer A., Katharine V., Margaret E. BA, Drake U., 1971; JD, Loyola U., 1976. Bar: Ill. 1976, U.S. Dist. Ct. (no. dist.) Ill. 1976, U.S. Tax Ct. 1977. Assoc. Bentley DuCanto Silvestri & Forkins, Chgo., 1976-79; ptnr. Silvestri Mahoney English & Zdeb, Chgo., 1979-81; assoc. Coffield Ungaretti Harris & Slavin, Chgo., 1981-83; ptnr. Ungaretti & Harris, Chgo., 1983—. Instr. estate planning Loyola U., Chgo., 1982-87; instr. Ill. Inst. Continuing Edn. Estate Planning Short Course, 1998, 2001. Bd. dirs. Prince of Peace Luth. Sch., Chgo., 1977-83, Bethesda Home for the Aged, Chgo., 1981-89, 2000-03, Luth. Family Mission, Chgo., 1985-91; alderman Park Ridge (Ill.) City Coun., 1991-95; pres. congregation coun. St. Luke's Luth. Ch., Park Ridge, 2000—. Mem.: Chgo. Bar Assn. (former chmn. divsn. II probate practice com.), Ill. State Bar Assn., Phi Beta Kappa. Lutheran. Home: 631 Wisner St Park Ridge IL 60068-3428 Office: Ungaretti & Harris 3500 Three 1st Nat Bank Plz Chicago IL 60602

ENGLISH, JOSEPH THOMAS, physician, medical administrator; b. Phila., May 21, 1933; m. Ann Carr Sanger, Dec. 20, 1969; 3 children. AB, St. Joseph's Coll., 1954; MD, Jefferson Med. Coll., 1958. Intern Jefferson Med. Coll. Hosp., Phila., 1958-59; resident in psychiatry Inst. of Pa. Hosp., Phila., 1959-61, NIMH, Bethesda, Md., 1961-62; practice psychiatry, 1962—; psychiatrist Office of Dir., NIMH, 1964-65, asst. chief policy and program coordination, 1965-66, dept. chief office interagy. liaison, 1966; chief psychiatrist med. program div. Peace Corps, Washington, 1962-66; dep. asst. dir. health affairs OEO, Washington, 1966, asst. dir., 1966-68; adminstr. Health Services and Mental Health Adminstrn., HEW, 1968-70; pres. N.Y.C. Health and Hosps. Corp., 1970-73; chmn. dept. psychiatry St. Vincent's Hosp. and Med. Ctr., N.Y.C., 1973—; prof. psychiatry, chmn. dept. psychiatry N.Y. Med. Coll., N.Y.C., 1979—, assoc. dean, 1979—. Adj. prof. psychiatry Cornell U.; lectr. psychiatry Harvard U., 1978-89; vis. fellow Woodrow Wilson Nat. Fellowship Found., 1979—; chmn. interagy. task force emergency food and med. program for U.S. OEO-HEW, U.S. Dept. Agrl., 1968-69; chmn. Alaska Subcom. Fed. Health Programs Pres.'s Rev. Commn. Alaska, 1969-71; chmn. adv. com. on accessible environments for disabled Bldg. Rsch. Adv. Bd., Washington, 1974-76; chmn. exec. coord. panels on mental health svcs. delivery Pres.'s Commn. on Mental Health, 1977; mem. Health Adv. Coun. Gov. State N.Y., 1981; mem. profl. and tech. adv. com. for hosps. and accreditation program Joint Commn. Accreditation Hosps., 1984-86, vice chmn., 1986-88, chmn., 1988-89, commr., 2002--; mem. adv. panel on financing of psychiat. care NIMH, 1985-87; mem. commr.'s adv. com. N.Y.C. Dept. Mental Health, Mental Retardation and Alcoholism Svc., 1980-92; bd. dirs., chmn. nat. clin. adv. bd. Healthcare Svcs. Am., Inc., 1985-87. Author spl. reports on Peace Corps, other govtl. programs; editorial bd. The Psychiatric Times, 1985—; contbr. articles to profl. jours. Bd. dirs. Kennedy Child Study Ctr., 1975-93; trustee Menninger Found., 1993—, Sarah Lawrence Coll., 1986-90. Served to capt. USAF Res., 1958-63; sr. surgeon USPHS, 1963-66. Named One of Outstanding Young Men of Year U.S. Jr. C. of C., 1964; recipient John XXIII medal Coll. New Rochelle, N.Y., 1966; Meritorious award for exemplary achievement pub. adminstrn. William A. Jump Meml. Found., 1966; Flemming award, also personal commendation Pres. of U.S., 1968 Fellow Am. Psychiat. Assn. (pres. 1992-93, chmn. coun. on econ. affairs 1983-85, chmn. task force on prospective payment 1983—, chmn. task force and strategic planning 1993—), N.Y. Acad. Medicine, Am. Coll. Psychiatrists, Inst. Medicine of Nat. Acad. Scis.; mem. AMA, N.Y. Psychiat. Soc., Hosp. Soc. N.Y., Assn. for Acad. Psychiatry, N.Y. State Med. Soc., Am. Assn. Gen. Hosp. Psychiatrists, Group Advancement Psychiatry, Am. Coll. Mental Health Adminstrs., Am. Hosp. Assn., Greater N.Y. Hosp. Assn. (chmn. mental health and substance abuse svcs. com. 1975—), Cath. Health Assn. (com. on govt. rels. 1984-87), World Psychiat. Soc. (chmn. sect. on religion and psychiatry 1994—), Alpha Omega Alpha, Kappa Beta Phi, Alpha Sigma Nu. Office: St Vincent's Hosp & Med Ctr 203 W 12th St New York NY 10011-7762

ENGLISH, MARK GREGORY, lawyer; b. Mpls., Oct. 14, 1951; s. Earl Mark and Georgia Corrine (Lastrange) E.; m. Renee Ann Thielen, Aug. 31, 1979; children— Janelle, Brandon. B.E.E. with high distinction, U. Minn., 1973, J.D. magna cum laude, 1976. Bar: Minn. 1976, Mo. 1981. Assoc. Arvesen, Donoho, Lundeen, Hoff, Svingen & English and predecessor Arvesen Donoho Lundeen, Hoff & Svingen, Fergus Falls, Minn., 1976-77, ptnr., 1978-80; atty. Kansas City Power & Light Co., Mo., 1981-82, staff atty., 1982-86, sr. atty., 1986-88, dep. gen. counsel, 1988—. Gen. counsel Minn. Jaycees, Mpls., 1978-79. Recipient Silver medal Royal Soc. Arts, London, 1973. Mem. Mo. Bar Assn., Mensa. Home: 11101 W 120th St Overland Park KS 66213-2045 Office: Kansas City Power & Light Co 1330 Baltimore Ave Kansas City MO 64105-1910

ENGLISH, MARLENE CABRAL, management consultant; b. Lawrence, Mass., Apr. 28, 1954; d. Amick John and Mary Rose (Vasconcelos) Cabral; m. Richard Gayle English, June 24, 1978. BBA, U. Mass., 1976; ind. study Victorian Studies, Vassar Coll. Acct. mgr. Revlon, Inc., N.Y.C., 1977-79; tech. rep. Rapidata, Inc., N.Y.C., 1979-80; mgr.acctg. systems group Pannell, Kerr, Forster, Dallas, 1980-83; mgmt. cons. Blythe/Nelson, Dallas, 1983-84, Prism Cons., Arlington, Tex., 1984—. Sec., treas. Highland-Avery Industries, Inc., Dallas, 1988-95. Author: And God Created Woman, 1995. Tech. systems procurement & installation Rep. Nat. Conv., Dallas, 1984; dir. Faith Harvest Ministries, Inc., Dallas, 1990-95; sys. cons. Van Cliburn Internat. Piano Competition, Ft. Worth, 1985. Roman Catholic. Avocations: antique linen restoration, gardening, writing, christian works for children, classical piano. Home and Office: Prism Cons 4320 Rambling Creek Dr Arlington TX 76016-3418 E-mail: engl@juno.com.

ENGLISH, NICHOLAS CONOVER, lawyer; b. Elizabeth, N.J., Apr. 12, 1912; s. Conover and Sara Elizabeth (Jones) E.; m. Agnes N. Perry, Mar. 18, 1939 (div. 1947); children— Henry H. P., Anne Whitall (Mrs. Edward J. Wardwell); m. Eleanor Morss, May 1, 1948; children— Priscilla English Vincent, Sara (dec.), Sherman, Eleanor English Folta. Grad., Pingry Sch., 1929; AB magna cum laude, Princeton, 1934; LL.B., Harvard, 1937. Bar: N.J. 1937. Since practiced in, Newark; partner firm McCarter & English, 1947-77, of counsel, 1978—. Bd. dirs. Summit (N.J.) YMCA, 1950-57, pres., 1953-55; bd. dirs. Newark YMWCA, also pres.; chmn. exec. com. Ctrl. Atlantic Area YMCA, 1957-63; mem. nat. coun. YMCA, 1954, 58-81, v.p., 1959-60, mem. nat. bd., 1960-71, 73-81, vice chmn., 1969-71, treas., 1977-81; trustee N.J. Nat. Land Trust, 1983-93, Kent Place Sch., 1959—, pres., 1961-72, Pingry Sch., 1954-73; bd. dirs. Nat. Legal Aid Assn., 1953-56. Lt. USNR, 1943—45. Mem. ABA (ho. of dels. 1957-58), N.J. Bar Assn., Essex County Bar Assn., Am. Bible Soc. (bd. trustees 1964-93, sr. trustee 1993—), Am. Law Inst. Congregationalist. Home: 46 Meadow Lks Apt 04L Hightstown NJ 08520-3332 Office: McCarter & English 4 Gateway Ctr 100 Mulberry St Newark NJ 07102-0652

ENGLISH, PHILIP SHERIDAN, congressman; b. Erie, Pa., June 20, 1956; s. John Sr. and Otilie English; m. Christiane Weschler. BA in Polit. Sci., U. Pa., 1978. Contr. City of Erie, Pa., 1986-90; chief of staff Senator Melissa Hart, Harrisburg, Pa., 1990-92; ex-dir. Pa. Senate Fin. Com., Harrisburg, 1992-94; mem. U.S. Congress from 3rd Pa. dist. (formerly 21st), 1995—; mem. ways and means com., joint econ. com. Republican. Roman Catholic. Avocations: hiking, history, archaeology. Office: US Ho of Reps 1410 Longworth Ho Office Bldg Washington DC 20515-0001*

ENGLISH, QUE, public relations executive; b. N.Y.C., Sept. 20, 1963; d. Ernest and Zenolia Phillips; m. Timothy English; 1 child, Sarah. Grad., Stuyvesant HS, N.Y., 1981. Event coord. T. D. Jakes Ministries, Dallas, 1997—99; spl. projects coord. T. D. Jakes Enterprises, Dallas, 1999—2001; pub. rels. comm. specialist The Potter's House/T. D. Jakes, Dallas, 2001—. Bd. dirs. SLE Enterprises, Dallas, 1996—; gen. mgr. cons. Mike Murdock Ministries, Argyle, 1995—96; instr. Christian Women Leadership Develop., Dallas, 1999—; keynote spkr. Women of Excellence Conf., London, 2000—; CEO Kerwin Phillips Found., Dallas, 2001—; CEO, exec. prodr. On Q Prodns., Dallas, 2001—; Motivational Speaker University Texas Arlington, Arlington, United States, 2002. Playwright : O Happy Day!, 1999; author: (book) Will the Real Me Please Stand Up, 2000; prodr.: (films) A Song for Momma, 2001. Adv. Hutchins Prison, Dallas, 2001. Mem.: Woman to Woman Ministries (liaison 1997—2001). Avocation: writing. Office: Kerwin Phillips Found PO Box 570795 Dallas TX 75357 E-mail: kphillipsfoundation@yahoo.com.

ENGLISH, RAY, library administrator; b. Brevard, N.C., Dec. 11, 1946; s. Daniel Leon and Lois (Dorsett) E.; m. Allison Scott Ricker, Oct. 19, 1985; children: John, Michael. AB with honors in German, Davidson Coll., 1969; MA in German Lit., U. N.C., 1971, MSLS, 1977, PhD, 1978. Teaching asst. German dept. U. N.C., Chapel Hill, 1970-73, 74-75, rsch. asst., 1976; reference libr. Alderman Libr. U.Va., Charlottesville, Va., 1977-79; head reference libr. Oberlin (Ohio) Coll. Libr., 1979-89, assoc. dir., 1986-90; dir. librs. Oberlin (Ohio) Coll., 1990—, acad. advisor, 1980—. Lectr. in German, 1986—2000; vis. lectr. Sch. Libr. Sci., U. N.C., Chapel Hill, 1981; spkr. in field; mem. steering com. Scholarly Pub. and Acad. Resources Coalition, 1999—. Mem. editl. bd. Portal: Libraries and the Academy; contbr. German Acad. Exchange Svc. fellow, 1973-74. Mem.: ALA, Acad. Libr. Assn. Ohio, Libr. Adminstrn. and Mgmt. Assn., Assn. Coll. and Rsch. Librs. (bd. dirs., exec. com. 1996—98, chair scholarly comm. com. 2002—). Home: 83 S Cedar St Oberlin OH 44074-1559 Office: Oberlin Coll Library 148 W College St Oberlin OH 44074-1575 E-mail: ray.english@oberlin.edu.

ENGLISH, RICHARD ALLYN, sociologist, social work educator; b. Winter Park, Fla., Aug. 29, 1936; s. Wentworth and Mary English; m. Ireita Geraldine Williams, June 29, 1978 AB, Talladega Coll., 1958; MA (Woodrow Wilson fellow), U. Mich., 1959, MSW., 1964, PhD, 1970. Cert. Oxford U., Internat. Summer Sch. Forced Migration Refugee Ctr., Queen Elizabeth Hse, Oxford, England, 2001. Dir. vocat. and youth services Flint Urban League, Mich., 1959-61, acting exec. dir., 1961-62; social group worker Neighborhood Service Orgn., Detroit, 1963-65; mem. faculty Sch. Social Work, Wayne State U., 1965-67; lectr. U. Mich., Ann Arbor, 1967-70, asst. prof. social work, 1970-72, assoc. prof., 1972-83, prof., 1983—, assoc. v.p. acad. affairs, 1974-81; dean Howard U. Sch. Social Work, 1985—2000, prof., 1985—; interim provost and chief acad. officer Howard U., 2003—. Vis. scholar Paul Baerwald Sch. Social Work, Hebrew U., Jerusalem, 1975; vis. prof. Howard U., fall 1981; Am. Psychol. Assn.-Nat. Inst. Edn. fellow, 1981; Robert L. Sutherland chair in mental health and social policy U. Tex.-Austin Sch. Social Work, 1983-84, 84-85; cons. to various schs., social work, public sch. dists. and pvt. founds., 1969— ; pres. Council on Social Work Edn., 1981-84; bd. dirs. Nat. Resource Ctr. for Spl. Needs Adoption, Spaulding Sch. for Children, Chelsea, Mich., 1986—, Nat. Coun. Aging. Author: (with others) Inheriting the Earth: Child Welfare Policies and Practices for Minority Children, 1990; co-editor: Human Service Organizations: A Book of Readings, 1974; The Challenge for Mental Health: Minorities and Their World Views, 1984, (with W. Allen and J. Hall) Black Families, 1960-84: A Classified, Selectively Annotated Bibliography, 1986; co-editor: (with C. Guzzetta and A.J.Katz) Education for Social Work Practice: Selected International Models; The Professional School Dean: The Roles of Leadership (co-editor with M.J. Austin and F.L. Ahearn), 1997; mem. editorial bd. Black Caucus: Jour. Nat. Assn. Black Social Workers; contbr. articles to profl. jours. Mem. adv. panel Refugee Policy Group, mem. adv. bd. Nat. Assembly; bd. visitors Sch. Social Work U. Pitts.; bd. dirs. Youth for Understanding Internat. Exch., 1991—, Coalition for the Homeless; bd. advisors Ill. Inst. Mil. and Occupational Studies; adv. bd. Enterprise Found.; mem. vestry St. Mary's Episcopal Ch. Recipient Outstanding Service award Nat. Assn. Black Social Workers, 1983; Nat. Assn. for Equal Opportunity in Higher Edn. Disting. Alumni award, 1985, Presdl. award for Excellence in Social Work Edn., 1997; Whitney Young, Jr. scholar, Western Mich. U., 1988. Mem. Nat. Assn. Social Workers, Nat. Coun. Family Rels., Am. Sociol. Assn., Internat. Council Social Welfare, Internat. Assn. Schs. Social Work (bd. dirs.), ACLU (bd. dirs. nat. capitol area 1986—), The Emeritus Found. (bd. dirs.), Dept. Human Svcs. Commn., D.C. Govt., Nat. Network for Social Work Mgrs. (adv. bd.), Internat. Coun. Social Welfare (U.S. com., internat. bd.), Coun. on Social Work Edn., Nat. Assn. Black Social Workers, Nat. Assn. Deans and Dirs. Schs. Social Work. Home: 2724 Abilene Dr Chevy Chase MD 20815-3051 Office: Howard U Washington DC 20059-0001

ENGLISH, RICHARD PAUL, music educator; b. Buffalo, June 16, 1960; s. Paul John and Marilyn Marie English; m. Kiva Marie VanZandt, June 9, 1984; children: Daniel, Michael, Eric. MusB, SUNY, Fredonia, 1981, MusM, 1986. Instrumental music dir. Weedsport (NY) Ctrl. Sch., Weedsport, 1982—, fine arts dept. chmn., 2001—. Mem. The Cayugans Big Band, Auburn, NY, 1986—, dir., 1998—; cons. NY State Dept. Edn., Albany, 1999—. Pres. Jordan-Elbridge Sch. Bd., Jordan, NY, 1993—95, mem., 1991—97; sec. Seymour Lofft Pk. Assn., Elbridge, NY, 1998—; coach Jordan-Elbridge Cmty. Coun., Elbridge, NY, 1993—2002; bd. dirs. No. Cayuga Little League, Weedsport, 2000—02. Mem.: Profl. Musicians Ctrl. NY, Music Educators Nat. Conf., NY State Sch. Music Assn., Cayuga County Music Educators Assn. (pres. 2000—03), Am. Fedn. Tchrs., NY State United Teachers, Am. Fedn. Musicians, Weedsport Teachers Assn. (v.p. 1989—91), Am. Mensa, Phi Mu Alpha Sinfonia. Home: 120 Sylvan St Elbridge NY 13060 Office: Weedsport Central School E Brutus St Weedsport NY 13166

ENGLISH, R(OBERT) BRADFORD, marshal; b. Jefferson City, Mo. BS in Criminal Justice, Lincoln U., 1982; MPA, U. Mo., 1984. Residential juvenile counselor Cole County Juvenile Ctr., Jefferson City, Mo., 1972-74; patrolman Jefferson City Police Dept., 1975-76, detective, 1976-78; comdr. Mo. Capitol Police, Jefferson City, 1978-79, police chief, 1979-94; marshal U.S. Marshal Svc., Kansas City, Mo., 1994—. Chmn. ct. security com. U.S. Dist. Ct. (we. dist.) Mo., Kansas City, 1995—; mem. dirs. adv. and leadership coun. U.S. Marshall Svc., 1996—. Chmn. bd. dirs. Capitol Area Cmty. Svc. Agy., Jefferson City, 1994. Named Statesman of Month, News Tribune Co., 1994. Mem. Internat. Assn. Chiefs of Police (life), Masons. Democrat. Avocations: golf, scuba diving, walking, weight lifting. Office: US Marshal Svc 400 E 9th St Ste 3740 Kansas City MO 64106-2635

ENGLISH, ROBERT JOSEPH, electronic corporation executive; b. Jersey City, Dec. 5, 1932; s. John Joseph and Mary (Budrawiz) E.; m. Robyn Adele Allan, Dec. 27, 1958; children: Robert Joseph, Mark Allan, John Frederick. BS, St. Peters Coll., 1954; LL.B., Georgetown U., 1958; MBA, NYU, 1963. Bar: D.C. 1958, N.J. 1959, N.Y. 1984. Subcontract adminstr. ITT Fed. Labs. div., Nutley, N.J., 1959-60; with Fed. Electric Corp., Paramus, N.J., 1960—, sec., gen. counsel, 1964-66, dir. legal contracts, 1967-70; gen. counsel ITT Govt. and Comml. Services Group, 1970-72; v.p., sec., gen. counsel ITT Def. Communications and ITT Avionics divs., Nutley, 1972—; sec., gen. counsel Internat. Electric Corp., 1972—. Dir. ITT Fed. Support Services Inc., ITT Tech. Services Inc., Intelex Systems Inc., Providence, Base Services Inc., Paramus, Internat. Standard Engring. Inc., Paramus. Author: Business Contract Forms, Federal Government Subcontract Forms; contbr. articles to profl. jours. Trustee Mahwah Hist. Soc., N.J., 1978— . Served to 1st lt., Chem. Corps, U.S. Army, 1954-56. Mem. Am., Bergen, N.J., D.C., N.Y. bar assns., Phi Delta Phi. Home: 36 Sunnyside Rd Mahwah NJ 07430-1418 Office: 492 River Rd Nutley NJ 07110-3609

ENGLISH, STEPHEN FRANCIS, lawyer; b. Portland, Oreg., Jan. 17, 1948; BA with honors, U. Oreg., 1970; JD, U. Calif., San Francisco, 1973. Bar: Oreg. 1973; U.S. Dist. Ct. Oreg. 1973; U.S. Ct. Appeals (9th cir.) Oreg. 1980; U.S. Supreme Ct. 1982. Ptnr. Bullivant Houser Bailey, Portland, Oreg., 1983—. Mem. faculty Hastings Coll. Trial Advocacy, 1998—. Mem. ABA (vice-chair products liability com., 1996—, chair self insurers and risk mgrs. com. 1994-95, editor Self Insurers Newsletter 1987-89, chair non-profit, charitable and religious orgns. com. 1990-92)), Multnomah County Bar Assn., Oreg. State Bar Assn. (chair litigation sect. 1990-91, exec. com. 1987-91), Am. Bd. of Trial Adv. (treas. Oreg. chpt. 1996-98, sec. Oreg. chpt. 1998—), Oreg. Assn. of Def. Counsel (chair products liability practice group 1997-98), Def. Rsch. Inst. Office: Bullivant Houser Bailey 300 Pioneer Tower 888 SW 5th Ave Portland OR 97204-2089

ENGLISH, STEPHEN RAYMOND, lawyer; b. Key West, Nov. 25, 1946; s. Jack Raymond and Jean Clyde (Peightal) E.; m. Molly Munger, Oct. 7, 1978; children: Nicholas, Alfred. BA, UCLA, 1975; JD, Harvard U., 1975. Bar: Calif. 1975, U.S. Dist. Ct. (cen. dist.) Calif. 1976, U.S. Dist. Ct. (so. dist.) Calif. 1978, U.S. Dist. Ct. (ea. dist.) Calif. 1988, U.S. Ct. Appeals (9th cir.) 1992. Assoc. Agnew, Miller & Carlson, L.A., 1975-78, Morgan, Lewis & Bockius, L.A., 1978-85, ptnr., 1985-98, English, Munger & Rice, L.A., 1998—; co-dir. advancement project, 2000—. Lawyer rep. Ninth Cir. Jud. Conf., 1996-97. Pres. bd. dirs. Pub. Counsel, L.A., 1988-89, Inner City Law Ctr., L.A., 1992-93; bd. dirs. L.A. Legal Aid Found., 1999—. Mem. L.A. County Bar Assn. (mem. barristers exec. com. 1980-82, trustee 1990-92, chair pro bono coun. 1990-92, chair legal svcs. for poor 1993-95, mem. exec. com. litigation sect. 1994—, chair litigation sect. 2003—), L.A. County Bar Found. (pres. 1998-99). Office: English Munger & Rice 1545 Wilshire Blvd Ste 800 Los Angeles CA 90017-4694

ENGLISH, WILLIAM DESHAY, lawyer, director; b. Piedmont, Calif., Dec. 25, 1924; s. Munro and Mabel (Michener) E.; m. Nancy Ames, Apr. 7, 1956; children: Catherine, Barbara, Susan, Stephen. AB in Econs., U. Calif., Berkeley, 1948, JD, 1951. Bar: Calif. 1952, D.C. 1972. Trial atty., spl. asst. to atty. gen. U.S. Dept. Justice, Washington, 1953-55; sr. atty. AEC, Washington, 1955-62; legal advisor U.S. Mission to European Communities, Brussels, 1962-64; asst. gen. counsel internat. matters COMSAT, Washington, 1965-73; counsel Internat. Telecomm. Satellite Orgn., 1965-73; v.p., gen. counsel, dir. COMSAT Gen. Corp., 1973-76; sr. v.p. legal and govtl. affairs Satellite Bus. Sys., McLean, Va., 1976-86; v.p., gen. counsel Satellite Transponder Leasing Corp. (IBM), McLean, Va., 1986-87; pvt. practice Washington, 1987—; counsel Am. Space Transp. Assn., 1987-93, Washington Space Bus. Roundtable; gen. counsel Iridium, LLC, 1992-96, spl. counsel, 1996-2000. With USAAF, 1943-45. Decorated Air medal. Fellow Coun. on Econ. Regulation, 1985-91; mem. ABA, AIAA (chmn. com. legal aspects aeronautics and astronautics,1993-2000, chmn. allocation space launch risks subcom. 1987, chmn. orbital debris legal subcom.), Am. Competitive Telecomm. Assn. (bd. dirs. 1976-84, pres. 1983), D.C. Bar Assn., Fed. Comm. Bar Assn., State Bar Calif., Fgn. Policy Discussion Group, Met. Club, Chevy Chase Club. Home: 7420 Exeter Rd Bethesda MD 20814-2352 E-mail: w.english2@verizon.net.

ENGLISH, WILLIAM JOSEPH, engineer; b. Oil City, Pa., Nov. 29, 1941; s. William Frederick and Arlene (Eisenman) E.; m. Cecelia Colette Bronder, July 29, 1978; children: William E., Cecelia R., Timothy S. BA in Math., St. Vincent Coll., 1963; BSEE, Carnegie-Mellon U., 1964, MSEE, 1965, PhD in Space Sci., 1969. Antenna engr. Comsat Labs., Clarksburg, Md., 1970-77; dept. mgr., spacecraft engr. Intelsat, Washington, 1977-91, dir. engring., 1991-96; prin. engr. Comsat, Bethesda, Md., 1997—2000; sr. v.p. Worldspace, Washington, 2001—. Contbr. articles to profl. jours.; patentee in field. Mem. IEEE (mem. stds. com., mem. editl. rev. bd. Transactions on Microwave Theory and Techniques), Internat. Sci. Radio Union, Trout Unltd. (life), Nat. Capitol Skeet and Trap Club. Roman Catholic. Avocations: hunting, fishing. Home: 7419 Needwood Rd Derwood MD 20855-1934 Office: Worldspace 2400 H St Washington DC 20031

ENGLISH-ANDERSON, SAN DEI, minister; b. Jacksboro, Tex., Aug. 27, 1945; d. Robert March English and Ressie English; m. Donald Loren Anderson, Dec. 19, 2001; children: Traci Dixon, Tiara Cunningham, Joshua English. AA, Jarvis Christian Coll., Hawkins, Texas, 1965. Minister, assoc. pastor New Creation Outreach, Anaheim, Calif., 2001—02; producer/host Sonic Cable TV, San Luis Obispo, Calif., 1982—86; CEO Tiara Prodns., Mission Viejo, Calif., 1987—2002. V.p. ways & means Laguna Niguel Rep. Women Federated, 2000—01. Served USAF, 1964—65. Named "Miss Lake Como", Lake Como Parks & Receation, 1962, "Model of the Yr.", Foxes and Hares Model Assn., 1967, Ms. Royal Ambassador 2002, Mrs. Orange County Am., 2003. Mem.: Ctr. Stage/ Performing Arts Guild, Phenomenal Women Orgn. (pres., CEO). Avocation: writing, sewing, reading, dancing, meditating. Business E-Mail: strongmeat@cox.net.

ENGLUND, GAGE BUSH, dancer, educator; b. Sept. 7, 1931; d. Morris William and Margaret Wallace (Gage) Bush; m. Richard Bernanrd Englund, Dec. 1, 1959; children: Alixandra Gage, Rachel Rutherford. Student, Sch. Am. Ballet, 1960. Founder Birmingham Civic Ballet, 1952; mem. Robert Joffrey Ballet, N.Y.C., 1957-60, soloist, 1959-60; mem. Am. Ballet Theatre, N.Y.C., 1960-63, Huntington Dance Ensemble, L.I., N.Y., 1968-69; soloist Dance Repertory Co., 1969-72; tchr. ballet, assoc. chmn. Friends of Am. Ballet Theatre, N.Y.C., 1972—. Dir. Ala. By-Products Corp., 1971—77; rehearsal coach Am. Ballet Theatre II, 1973—85; mem. scholarship com. Am. Ballet Theatre Sch., N.Y.C., 1974—; rehearsal coach Joffrey Ballet II, 1985—95, Am. Ballet Theatre Studio Co., 1995—. Trustee Ballet Theatre Found., 1974—87, v.p., 1980—81; trustee Chapin Sch., 1982—2003, Animal Med. Ctr., N.Y.C., 1982—, Cancer Rsch. Inst., 1984—, Episcpoal Sch. N.Y., 1979—83; bd. dirs. Children's Hosp. Clinic, Birmingham, 1955—57, Spoleto Festival, U.S.A., 1980—83, Ala. State Ballet, 1967—, Birmingham Civic Ballet, 1952—67. Named Queen, Birmingham Festival Arts, 1957; recipient Silver Bowl award, 1957, Lucia Chase award for svcs. to Am. Ballet Theatre, Soc. Fine Arts U. Ala., 2001, Patron of the Arts award, 2002; scholar Ford Found., 1960. Mem.: Am. Guild Mus. Artists, Jr. League N.Y.C., Colonial Dames Ala., Colony Club, Lakewood Country Club. Episcopalian. Home: PO Box 469 17367 Scenic Hwy 98 Point Clear AL 36564

ENGORON, ARTHUR FREDERICKS, judge; b. NYC, May 22, 1949; s. Malcolm Wilson and Edna June (Fredericks) E.; 1 child, Ian Abbie Intrator Engoron. BA, Columbia Coll., 1972; JD, NYU, 1979. Bar: N.Y., U.S. Dist. Ct. (so. and ea. dists.) N.Y. 1980, U.S. Supreme Ct. 1996. Assoc. Olwine, Connelly, Chase, O'Donnell & Weyher, N.Y.C., 1979-81, Pryor, Cashman, Sherman & Flynn, N.Y.C., 1981-83; prin. law clk. for Hon. Martin Schoenfeld N.Y. State Supreme Ct., N.Y.C., 1991—2002; judge N.Y.C. Civil Ct., 2003—. Author: Manual for Small Claims Arbitrators, 2001. Newsletter editor Park River Ind. Dems., N.Y.C., 1994-96. Mem. Assn. of the Bar of the City of N.Y. (chairperson civil ct. com.), Coun. Jud. Adminstrn., Assn. Small Claims Arbitrators (pres.). Democrat. Avocations: politics, computers, chess, art, physical fitness. Home: 255 W 84th St Apt 11E New York NY 10024-4325 Office: NYC Civil Ct Rm 527D 851 Grand Concourse Bronx NY 10451 E-mail: artengoron@aol.com., aengoron@courts.state.ny.us.

ENGORON, EDWARD DAVID, food service consultant, television and radio broadcaster; b. Los Angeles, Feb. 19, 1946; s. Leo and Claire (Gray) E.; m. Charlene Scott, Oct. 7, 1970 (div. July 1982). BArch., U. So. Calif., 1969, MBA, 1973, PhD, 1974; MA, Cordon Bleu, Paris, 1975. Art dir. ABC, L.A., 1964-67, Paramount Pictures, L.A., 1967-68, Warner Bros. Pictures, Burbank, Calif., 1968-69; mktg. dir. Lawry's Foods Inc., Burbank, 1969-74; v.p. Warehouse Restaurants, Marina del Rey, Calif., 1968-72; pres. Perspectives, San Francisco, 1974-82, Perspectives Comm. Syndicated Talk Shows, L.A., 1986—94, China Rose Inc., Dallas, 1982-86; exec. v.p. T.G.I. Fridays Inc., Dallas, 1986-87; pres., chief exec. officer, bd. dirs. Guilt Free Goodies, Ltd., Vancouver, B.C., Can., 1986-90, Sugarless Co., L.A., 1986-90. Cons. Southland Corp., Dallas, 1982-86, Pizza Hut Inc., Wichita, Kans., 1975-87, Frank L. Carney Enterprises, Wichita, 1982-87, Safeway Stores, Inc., Freemont, Calif., Romacorp, Dallas, Bel-Air Hotel Co., L.A., Capital Cities-ABC, Hollywood, Nestle Foods, White Plains, Screiber Foods, Green Bay, Rich's Food Products, Buffalo, Arby's Inc., Ft. Lauderdale, Fla., Sizzler Internat., L.A., ednl. found. Nat. Restaurant Assn., Taco Bell, Inc., Irvine, Calif., Basic Am., Inc., San Francisco, Nat. Super Markets, St. Louis, Wok Fast, Inc., L.A., The Vons Cons., L.A., 1989—; pres. Sweet Deceit, Inc., Guilt-Free Goodies, Ltd.; co-host nationally syndicated radio talk show The Super Foodies, ABC. Author: (cookbook) Stolen Secrets, 1980; patentee pasta cooking sta., 1981, micro-wave controller, 1982. Bd. govs. Los Angeles Parks, 1971-74; mem. Fine Arts Commn., Tiburon, Calif., 1974-76. Mem. Foodsvc. Cons. Soc. Internat., Soc. Motion Picture Art Dirs., Food, Wine and Travel Writers Assn., Internat. Assn. Culinary Profls., Masons. Republican. Office: 11030 Santa Monica Blvd Ste 301 Los Angeles CA 90025-7514

ENGROS, ELAINE, nurse, case manager; b. Bklyn., Feb. 22, 1956; d. John and Josephine (Parcarelli) Diaz; m. Jeffrey Jay Waage, Aug. 29, 1976 (div. Aug. 1984); 1 child, John; m. Michael Gerard Engros, June 3, 2000. BS in Nursing, Adelphi U., 1987. RN, N.Y.; cert. BLS, in peripherally inserted catheter. Staff nurse St. Joseph's Hosp.-Cath. Med. Ctr., Flushing, N.Y., 1987-88; vis. nurse staff Healthforce Inc., Hempstead, N.Y., 1988-90; staff nurse surg. onc. South Nassau Cmty. Hosp., Oceanside, N.Y., 1990-94; vis. nurse, Ch. T.P.N. Svcs. Inc., Jericho, N.Y., 1990-94; IV therapy instr. All Ct. Ronkonkoma, N.Y., 1994; med. care rep., case mgr. catastrophic ... N.Y. State Ins. Fund, Hempstead, 1994-98; med. case mgr. ... 1998-99; field case mgr. Kemper Nat. Svcs., 1999—2000, Liberty ... 2001—. Catechist tchr. St. Thomas the Apostle, West He... 1984-88, St. Anne's, Garden City, N.Y., 1988-89. Mem. AN... surg. nurse), ANA, Homehealth Care Nurses Assn., N.Y. Sta... Case Mgmt. Soc. Am. Democrat. Roman Catholic. Home: ... Wantagh NY 11793-3644

ENGSTROM, ERIK, private equity investor; b. Taby, Stock... Kjell and Alice (Klarstrom) E. BS in Econs. & Bus. Adminstr... Econs., 1986; MS in Engring., Royal Inst. Technology, 1986 ... Mgmt. Program, Ecole des Hautes Etudes Comml., Paris, 19... U., 1988. Cons. and engagement mgr. McKinsey & Co., ... corp. devel. Bantam Doubleday Dell Pub. Group, Inc., N.Y... CFO, 1992-93, exec. v.p., chief adminstrv. officer, 1993-9... 1994-96, pres., COO, 1996-98; pres., CEO BDD N.Am. ... Random House Inc., N.Y.C., 1998-2001; ptnr. Gen. Atlanti... Conn., 2001—. Bd. dirs. Telemedia Comm. Inc., Svensk... laget SCA, Bonnier Books, Infogrames Entertainment, SA... Windham Svcs. to Families and Children, 1999—; mem. ... of Art, 1998—. Sgt. Swedish Army, 1983-84. Scholar Fulb... Mem. Swedish-Am. C. of C. (bd. dirs. 1998—). Office: ... Pickwick Plz Greenwich CT 06830

ENGSTROM, MARLENE M. volunteer; b. McIntosh, S.D., June 4, 1932; d. Alfred Palmer Hustad and Cora Alberta Haugen; m. E. Duane Engstrom, July 24, 1954; children: Christine, Peter, Rolf. BA, St. Olaf Coll., 1954. Receptionist, sec. Luth. Ch. of the Good Shepherd, Mpls., 1954-55; acting dir. stewardship Am. Luth. Ch. Women, Mpls., 1979, interim dir. for edn., 1980-81, vol. nat. pres., 1984-87; receptionist, devel. Crossways Internat., Mpls., 1990-91. Tape transcriber Minn. State Svc. for the Blind, St. Paul, 1964-78; bd. dirs. Luth. Deaconess Hosp., Mpls., 1972-83, Luther Theol. Sem./Am. Luth. Ch., St. Paul, 1974-82, Luther N.W. Theol. Sem./Am. Luth. Ch./Luth. Ch. Am./Evangelical Luth. Ch. Am., 1982-88; chmn. bd. regents Luther Sem., 1981, Luther N.W. Theol. Sem., 1982-84; v.p. Mpls. Area Synod/Evang. Luth. Ch. Am., Mpls., 1988-92; trustee Luth. Sem. Found., St. Paul, 1991-99. Recipient Disting. Alumni award St. Olaf Coll., Northfield, Minn., 1981. Mem. AMA Alliance, Minn. Med. Assn. Alliance (treas., 2nd v.p., Disting. Svc. award 1996), Hennepin Med. Soc. Alliance (pres. 1991-93), Phi Beta Kappa. Avocations: aerobics, genealogy, memoir writing, reading, photography.

ENGSTROM, STEPHANIE CLOES, wildlife artist, small business owner; b. L.A., Nov. 1, 1943; d. John Augustus Cloes and Margaret Virginia Gerlach; m. Jean-Claude Louis Engstrom, Sept. 1, 1962 (div. 1967); children: Dominique Yvette Lubow, Denise Collette Engstrom. Student, UCLA, U. Md., USDA Grad. Sch. licensee MMDS. Adminstrv. mgr. Microband Corp. Am., Washington, 1972-74; sr. mgmt. cons. various, 1976—; licensee Microwave MMDS, various, 1983—. Tchr. Fairfax County Adult Edn., Vienna, Va., 1991-92, creativity workshop Guild Natural Sci. Illustrators Internat. Conf., Evora U., Portugal, 2000, Coll. of the Atlantic, Bar Harbor, Maine, 2001, Palos Verdes Art Ctr., Calif., 2002—, Univ. of Kans., Lawrence, 2002; cofacilitator Artist's Way Sems. Borders Books & Music, Torrance, Calif., 1998. Cover artist: (book) International Studbook, Cheetah, Acinonyx, Jubatus, 1988; artist, writer Endangered Species Note Cards, 1986-90, Internat. Wildlife Rancher, 1989; juried group show Palos Verdes Art Ctr., 2000, 01, 02 (People's Choice award 2000); solo show, The Distinctive Edge, 2001. Pres. PTA, Hermosa Beach, Calif., 1971-72; vol. Smithsonian, Washington, 1982-94; keeper aide Nat. Zool. Pk., Washington, 1985-90. Mem. Guild Nat. Sci. Illustrators (artist, writer newsletter 1988-89, 99—, pres. So. Calif. chpt. 2000-02), Artists Open Group Palos Verdes Art Ctr. Avocations: amateur naturalist, amateur animal behaviorist, writing poetry. Home and Office: 500 Avenue G Apt 25 Redondo Beach CA 90277-6002

ENHORNING, GORAN, obstetrician, gynecologist, educator; b. Birkdale, Eng, Mar. 18, 1924; came to US 1986; s. Emil Augustin and Maria Rosina (von Haartman) E.; m. Louise Christina Carlberg, Apr. 16, 1955; children: Ulf, Dag and Peder (twins), Marianne. MD, Karolinska Inst., Stockholm, 1952, PhD in Physiology, 1961. Asst. prof. ob/gyn. Karolinska Inst., Stockholm, 1952-61; Fulbright scholar U. Utah, Salt Lake City, 1961-63, UCLA, 1963-64; assoc. prof. ob/gyn. Karolinska Inst., 1964-71, U. Toronto, Canada, 1971-75, prof. ob/gyn., 1975-86; prof. ob/gyn. and physiology SUNY, Buffalo, 1986—2002. Contbr. articles to profl. jour. initiation of concept that symptoms of asthma and infectious bronchiolitis may be due to a surfactant dysfunction, caused by airway inflammation, an allergic reaction, an inhalation of cold air, or a hydrolysis of surfactant phospholipids, catalyzed by phospholipase A2 (PLA2) and by lysophospholipase (LPL) from eosinophils. The way the surfactant dysfunction causes airway blockage, and thus breathing difficulties is demonstrated with the Capillary Surfactometer, a new instrument developed to simulate surfactant function in terminal airways. Home: 21 Oakland Pl Buffalo NY 14222-2008 E-mail: gee1@acsu.buffalo.edu.

ENK, SCOTT, editor, researcher, activist; b. Milw., Apr. 9, 1958; s. Kenneth and Audrey (Szymanowski) E. BA in Mass Comm. and Econs. with distinction, U. Wis., Milw., 1981. Pers. asst. Fleet Mortgage Corp., Milw., 1982, foreclosure asst., 1983, publs. designer, editor, writer, 1983-87; documentation editor, writer, tester Aardvark/McGraw-Hill, Milw., 1987-88; rsch./quality assurance editor Gareth Stevens, Inc., Milw., 1988-91; sr. editor Southea. Wis. Regional Planning Commn., Waukesha, 1992—2001; claims examiner, rschr. U.S. Dept. Vets. Affairs, Milw., 2002; proofreader, editor The Relizon Co., New Berlin, Wis., 2003; copy editor and proofreader Aciman Publs., Greendale, Wis., 2003—. Guest lectr. silent film history and women's roles in silent film Alverno Coll., Milw., 1991-93, 96, 2000-01, in English style and grammar and mass comm. ethics and values, 2000—, guest lectr. Pewaukee Area (Wis.) Hist. Soc., 1997; spkr., presenter on radio, TV shows. Editor, writer, rschr. reports, newsletters, manuals, children's books; contbr. articles, essays and editls. to various publs. Founder, pres. Greater Milw. chpt. Hear My Voice/Protecting Our Nation's Children, 1993—; mem. Milwaukee County Hist. Soc., 1984—, ACLU, 1987—; former officer Wis. Phi Beta Kappa Found., Inc.; sec. West Suburban Milw. chpt. NOW, 1984-89, pres., 1987—, newsletter editor, 1989-, chair fundraising com., 1983-84. Recipient awards in recognition of children's rights work United Foster Parents Assn. Greater Milw., 1995, Hear My Voice/Protecting Our Nation's Children, 1998; journalism scholar Milw. profl. chpt. Soc. Profl. Journalists, 1979, Harry J. Grant Found., Milw., 1979-81. Mem. NOW (chpt. rep. to state coun.), U. Wis. Milw. Alumni Assn. (Coll. Letters and Sci. scholar 1979), Mensa, Milw. 9 to 5, Nat. Model R.R. Assn., Phi Beta Kappa (bd. dirs. Greater Milw. Assn. 1984—, sec. 1985-90, pres. 1990-2001, designated pres. emeritus 2001—, del. to nat. triennial coun. 1988, 91, 94, 97, 2000), Phi Kappa Phi, Phi Alpha Theta, Sigma Epsilon Sigma, Phi Eta Sigma. Avocations: computers/internet, silent films and other media, political and social history, chess, architecture. Home: 3163 S 10th St Milwaukee WI 53215-4729 E-mail: senk@execpc.com.

ENKHSAIKHAN, JARGALSAIKHAN, ambassador; b. Ulaanbaatar, Mongolia, Sept. 4, 1950; m.; 6 children. Lawyer, State Inst. Internat. Rels., Moscow, 1974, PhD in Law, 1979. Sec, legal dept. Mongolia, N.Y.C., USSR, 1974-79; sec. Mongolian Mission to UN, N.Y.C., 1979-86; acting head of legal and planning depts. MFA, 1986-88; minister-counsellor Mongolian Embassy, Moscow, 1988-92; adviser Pres. of Mongolia, Ulaanbaatar, 1992-93; exec. sec. Mongolian Nat. Security Coun., Ulaanbaatar, 1993-96; permanent rep. Mongolia UN, N.Y.C., 1996—. Mem. UN Gen. Assembly sessions, 1975, 79-86, 92, 96-2000, v.p., 1997, chmn., 1998; rapporteur Sixth (Legal) Com. UNGA, 1979, vice chmn., 1981, chmn., 1998; vice chmn. Spl. Com. on Non-use of Force in Internat. Rels, 1983; Mongolian rep. Law of the Sea Conf., 1976-82. Contbr. articles on internat. law and internat. rels. to Mongolian publs.; also to publs. in Russia and U.S. Office: Permanent Mission Mongolia to UN 6 E 77th St New York NY 10021-1704

ENLOW, DONALD HUGH, anatomist, educator, university dean; b. Mosquero, N.Mex., Jan. 22, 1927; s. Donald Carter and Martie Blairene (Albertson) E.; m. Martha Ruth McKnight, Sept. 3, 1945; 1 child, Sharon Lynn. BS, U. Houston, 1949, MS, 1951; PhD, Tex. A&M U., 1955. Instr. biology U. Houston, 1949-51; asst. prof. biology West Tex. State U., 1955-56, instr. anatomy Med. Coll. S.C., 1956-57; asst. prof. U. Mich. Med. Sch., Ann Arbor, 1957-62, assoc. prof., 1962-67, prof. anatomy, 1969-72; dir. phys. growth program Center for Human Growth and Devel., 1966-72; prof., chmn. dept. anatomy W.Va. U. Sch. Medicine, Morgantown, 1972-77; Thomas Hill disting. prof., chmn. dept. orthodontics Case Western Res. Sch. Dentistry, Cleve., 1977-89, prof. emeritus, 1989—, asst. dean for rsch. and grad. studies, 1977-85, acting dean, 1983-86. Adj. prof. U. N.C., 1992—; guest lectr. 29 fgn. countries, 1963—. Author: Principles of Bone Remodeling, 1963, The Human Face, 1968, Handbook of Facial Growth, 1975, 3d edit., 1990, Essentials of Facial Growth, 1996; contbr. chpts. to 30 books, numerous articles to profl. jours. Served with USCGR, 1945-46. Recipient Outstanding Research award Tex. Acad. Sci., 1952 Fellow Royal Soc. Medicine, Am. Assn. Anatomists, Internat. Assn. Dental Research; hon. mem. Am. Assn. Orthodontists (Mershon Meml. lectr. 1968, Spl. Merit award 1969, award for outstanding contbns. to orthodontia, 1984), Gt. Lakes Orthodontic Soc., Cleve. Dental Soc., Cleve. Orthodontic Soc., Omicron Kappa Upsilon. Republican. Methodist. Home: 5 Arbutus Ln Whispering Pines NC 28327-9465 E-mail: donnlo@pinehurst.net.

ENNELS, EDWARD CHARLES, mathematician, educator; b. Salisbury, Md., July 19, 1976; s. Nathaniel Ennels and Anita Louise Jones. BA in Psychology, Salisbury U., 2000, postgrad. in Math., 2002—. Geriatric nurse's asst. Salisbury Nursing Home, Md., 1994—97; live-in vol. Little Sisters of Jesus and Mary, Salisbury, Md., 1995—97; residential counselor Go Getters, Inc., Salisbury, Md., 1997—2000; chem. dependency technician Hudson Health Svcs., Salisbury, Md., 1998—2000; residential counselor Villa Maria, Balt., 2000; math. instr. Wor-Wic Cmty. Coll., Salisbury, Md., 2001—; mid. sch. tchr. math. Salisbury Sch., Md., 2001—. Student govt. pres. Wor-Wic Cmty. Coll., Salisbury, Md., 1997—98; student govt. advisor Salisbury Sch., Md., 2001—; deacon, cmty. outreach Unity Christian Fellowship, Salisbury, Md., 2001—. Recipient scholarship, Shore Distbr., Inc., 1998, Md. Sys. Alumni Assn., 1999, award for outstanding contbn. to dept. psychology, Salisbury U., 2000. Mem.: APA, Nat. Coun. Tchr. of Math. Republican. Office: Salisbury Sch 6279 Hobbs Rd Salisbury MD 21802

ENNEST, JOHN WILLIAM, bank executive; b. Bad Axe, Mich., Oct. 14, 1942; s. William J. and Margaret J. (Kritzman) E.; m. Mary Ellen Sweeney, Jan. 27, 1968 (dec. 1995); children: John W., James G., Anne M.; m. Cheryll Ann Pease, Dec. 1997. BS, U. Detroit, 1964; MBA, Mich. State U., 1965. Pres.'s exec. Exch. Program, Washington, 1979-80; v.p. Nat. Bank Detroit, 1973-81, NBD Bank Corp., Detroit, 1981-83; exec. v.p., chief fin. officer Citizens Bank, Flint, Mich., 1983-85; chief fin. officer, treas. Citizens Banking Corp., Flint, Mich., 1985-87; sr. exec. v.p., chief oper. officer Citizens Bank, Flint, Mich., 1985-87, pres., chief exec. officer, 1987-91; vice chmn., chief oper. officer Citizens Banking Corp., Flint, Mich., 1991—; chmn. bd., CEO Comml. Nat. Bank of Berwyn, Ill., 1992—; also bd. dirs. Citizens Bank, Citizens Banking Corp., Flint, Mich. Bd. dirs. Citizens Bank, 1987-91, Citizens Banking Corp., 1991, Second Nat. Bank, Saginaw, 1991, Comml. Nat. Bank, Berwyn, Ill., 1991. Author: (with others) Changing World of Banking, 1974. Chmn. bd. United Way, Flint, 1989, C. of C., Flint, 1991; dir. Baker Coll. Recipient cert. of merit USDA, 1980. Mem. Fin. Execs. Inst., Detroit Athletic Club, Warwick Hills Club. Republican. Roman Catholic.

ENNIS, ALANA, chief of police; b. Durham, N.C., June 17, 1950; d. Lee Warren and Ruby Faye (Hurt) Settle; m. T.W. Ennis, Jan. 16, 1979 (div. May 1991); 1 child, Taylor Kathleen. BA, Stratford Coll., Danville, Va., 1971; MPA, N.C. State U., 1991. Police officer Durham (N.C.) Police Dept., 1976-92; chief of police U. N.C., Chapel Hill, 1992-95, Duke U., Durham, N.C., 1995-98, Burlington (Vt.) Police Dept. Ex officio Queen City Police Found., 2001—; bd. dirs. Durham (NC) Art Guild, 1997—99, Flynn Theatre, Burlington, 1999—2002, Lund Home, 2003—. Recipient Susan B. Anthony Trailblazer award, YWCA, 2001. Mem.: Vt. Women's Forum (pres. 2000—), Vt. Chiefs, Internat. Assn. Chiefs of Police (Civil Rights award 2001), Police Exec. Rsch. Forum, Nat. Assn. for Women Law Enforcement Execs. (founder, pres. 1995—96), Rotary Internat. Office: 1 North Ave Burlington VT 05401-5220

ENNIS, BRUCE CLIFFORD, lawyer; b. Dover, Del., Mar. 22, 1941; s. Clifford Morgan and Mary Elizabeth (Jones) E.; m. Diane Wallace, July 19, 1969; 1 child, Heather Diane. BA, W.Va. Wesleyan Coll., 1963; JD, Dickinson Law Sch., 1966. Bar: Del. 1969, U.S. Dist. Ct. Del. 1971. Ptnr. Schmittinger & Rodriguez, P.A., Dover, 1969—2001. Instr. Wesley Coll., Dover, 1970-78, Del. Tech. and C.C., Dover, 1978-98. Active United Meth. Ch., Dover. With U.S. Army, 1966-68. Mem. Del. State Bar Assn., Kent County Bar Assn. Home: 444 Troon Rd Dover DE 19904-2343

ENNIS, EDGAR WILLIAM, JR., lawyer; b. Macon, Ga., May 20, 1945; s. Edgar W. and Nelle (Branan) E.; m. Judith Anne Godfrey, June 29, 1974; children: William, Branan. BS in Engring. Sci., USAF Acad., Colorado Springs, Colo., 1967; JD, U. Ga., 1971. Bar: Ga. 1971. Commd. 2d lt. USAF, 1967, advanced through ranks to capt., 1970, resigned, 1975; asst. U.S. atty. U.S. Atty.'s Office-Mid. Dist. of Ga., Macon, 1975-88; U.S. atty. U.S. Dept. Justice, Macon, 1988-93; of counsel Haynsworth, Baldwin, Johnson & Harper, Macon, 1993-97; ptnr. Haynsworth, Baldwin, Johnson & Greaves LLC, Macon, 1998-99, Constangy, Brooks & Smith LLC, Macon, 1999—. Office: Constangy Brooks & Smith LLC 577 Mulberry St Ste 710 Macon GA 31201-8588 E-mail: eennis@constangy.com.

ENNIS, MICHAEL E. government agency administrator; BA in French and Internat. Rels., Concordia Coll., Moorhead, Minn.; MA in Govt./Nat. Security Studies, Georgetown U. Commd. 2d lt. USMC, 1972, advanced through grades to brig. gen., 2001; rifle platoon comdr., bn. embarkation officer Okinawa; recruiting officer Milw.; fgn. area officer Monterey, Calif., U.S. Army's Russian Inst., Garmisch, Germany; dept. G-2 9th Marine Amphibious Brigade, Okinawa; S-2 9th Marine Regiment, Okinawa; translator Washington-Moscow Hotline; naval rep. to CINC Potsdam, East Germany; ops. officer 2d Surveillance, Reconnaissance and Intelligence Group; asst. naval attache Moscow; mil. rep. to Azerbaijan; dir. of intelligence divsn., hdqrs.; AC/S G-2 III Marine Expeditionary Force, Okinawa; comdr. Joint Intelligence Ctr. Pacific, Pearl Harbor, Hawaii. Decorated Legion of Merit, Navy and Marine Corps Commendation medal with 1 gold star, Army Commendation medal, Army Achievement medal. Office: CMC (PAC) HQUSMC Pentagon Rm 5E671 2 Navy Annex Washington DC 20380-1775

ENNIS, MICHAEL PATRICK, psychologist, educator; b. Peoria, Ill., July 22, 1970; s. Donald Lee Ennis, Joanne Agnes Timmer. MA Exptl. Psychology, U. North Tex., 1997; MA Psychology, U. Calif., Davis, 2002. Teaching asst. U. Calif., Davis, 1998—2001; adj. faculty psychology Cosumnes River Coll., Sacramento, 2001—. Psychol. rschr. U. Calif., 1998—. Contbr. articles to profl. jours. Grantee psychology grantee, U. Calif., Davis, 1999—2002. Mem.: APA, Am. Psychol. Soc. Avocations: songwriting, guitar. Home: 910 L St Davis CA 95616 Office: U Calif One Shields Ave Davis CA 95616 Office Fax: (530) 752-2087. Personal E-mail: miennis@yahoo.com. Business E-Mail: miennis@ucdavis.edu.

ENNIS, THOMAS MICHAEL, management consultant; b. Morgantown, W.Va., Mar. 7, 1931; s. Thomas Edson and Violet Ruth (Nugent) E.; m. Julia Marie Dorety, June 30, 1956; children: Thomas John, Robert Griswold (dec.). Student, W.Va. U., 1949-52; AB, George Washington U., 1954; JD, Georgetown U., 1960. With Gov. Employees Ins. Co., Washington, 1956, 59, Air Transport Assn. Am., Washington, 1959-60; dir. ann. support program George Washington U., 1960-63; nat. dir. devel. Project HOPE, People to People Health Found., Inc., Washington, 1963-66; nat. exec. dir. Epilepsy Found. Am., Washington, 1966-74; exec. dir. Clinton, Eaton, Ingham Community Mental Health Bd., Lansing, Mich., 1974-83; nat. exec. dir. Alzheimer's Disease and Related Disorders Assn., Inc., Chgo., 1983-86; exec. dir., pres. The John Douglas French Alzheimers Found., L.A., 1986-96, pres. emeritus, 1996—. Clin. instr. dept. cmty. medicine and internat. health Georgetown U., 1967-74; adj. assoc. prof. dept. psychiatry Mich. State U., 1975-84; lectr. Univ. Ctr. for Internat. Rehab., 1977; cons. health and med. founds., related orgns.; cons. Am. Health Found., 1967-69, Reston, Va.-Georgetown U. Health Planning Project, 1967-70. Editl. bd. Am. Jour. Alzheimer's Disease, 1997—. Mem. adv. bd. Nat. Center for the Law and the Handicapped, 1971-74; advisor Nat. Reye's Syndrome Found.; mem. Nat. Com. for Research in Neurol. Disorders, 1967-72; mem. nat. adv. bd. Developmental Disabilities/Tech. Assistance System, U. N.C., 1971-78; nat. trustee Nat. Kidney Found., 1970-74, mem. exec. com. and bd. Nat. Capitol Area chpt., pres., 1972-74; bd. dirs. Nat. Assn. Pvt. Residential Facilities for Mentally Retarded, 1970-74; bd. dirs., mem. exec. com. Epilepsy Found. Am., 1977-84, Epilepsy Center Mich., 1974-83; nat. bd. dirs. Western Inst. on Epilepsy, 1969-72; bd. dirs., pres. Mich. Mid-South Health Systems Agy., 1975-78; sec. gen. Internat. Fedn. Alzheimer's Disease and Related Disorders, 1984-86; mem. panel Alzheimer's Disease Edn. and Referral Ctr., 1990-93; mem. Calif. State Coun. on Developmental Disabilities, 1997—; med. adv. bd. EdenCare Sr. Living Svcs., advisor Ctr. Aging, Washington, 1998—. World Rehab. Fund fellow Norway, 1980. Mem. Nat. Epilepsy League (bd. dirs. 1977-78), Mich. Assn. Cmty. Mental Health (pres. 1977-79), Nat. Coalition Rsch. Neurol. Disorders (dir. at-large 1991—), Scan Health Plan (bd. govs.), Phi Alpha Theta, Phi Kappa Psi. Home and Office: 23740 Killion St Woodland Hills CA 91367-5822

ENNIS, WILLIAM LEE, physics educator; b. Houston, Aug. 10, 1949; s. Arthur Lee and Helen Ennis; m. Constance Elizabeth Livsey, July 20, 1991. BS, Auburn (Ala.) U., 1974, BA, 1978. Rsch. tech. Nat. Tillage Lab., Auburn, Ala., 1974-76; tchr. Stanford Jr. H.S., Hillsborough, N.C., 1979-81; physics tchr., chmn. sci. dept. East H.S., Anchorage, 1981—. Chmn. Anchorage Sch. Dist. Physics Tchrs.; curriculum devel. sci. cons. Copper River Schs., Anchorage, 1991. Recipient Nat. Tchr. award Milken Family Found., 1999; named Tandy Tech. Outstanding Tchr., 1989-90, Tchr. of Excellence Brit. Petroleum, 1996, Brit. Petroleum Tchr. of Yr., 1996, Disting. Tchr., White House Commn. on Presdl. Scholars; Fermi Lab. scholar U.S. Dept. Energy, 1991. Mem. AAAS, Am. Assn. Physics Tchrs., Am. Phys. Soc., Nat. Sci. Tchrs. Assn., Alaska Sci. Tchrs. (life), Am. Mountain Guides Assn., Am. Alpine Club. Avocations: mountaineering, outdoor activities, sailing, computers. Office: East HS 4025 E Northern Lights Blvd Anchorage AK 99508-3588

ENNS, JOHN BENJAMIN, polymer scientist; b. Chilliwack, B.C., Can., May 31, 1948; came to U.S., 1973; s. John and Louise (Toews) E.; m. Mary Louise Campbell, Apr. 27, 1975. BS in Chemistry, U. B.C., Vancouver, 1973; MS in Polymer Sci., Case Western Res. U., Cleve., 1975; MA in Chem. Engring., Princeton U., 1980, PhD in Chem. Engring., 1982. Rsch. assoc. Midland Macromolecular Inst., Midland, Mich., 1975-77; mem. tech. staff AT&T Bell Labs., Whippany, N.J., 1981-89; sr. scientist Vistakon, J&J Vision Care, Jacksonville, Fla., 1989-98, prin. scientist, 1998—. Cons. (N.J.) Princeton U., 1986-89, Plastics Analysis Instruments, Inc., Princeton, 1981-2002. Contbr. articles to profl. jours. including Jour. Applied Polymer Sci., Polymer Preprints, Jour. Macromolecular Sci.-Physics, chpts. to books; editor: N.Am. Thermal Analysis Soc. Conf. Proc., 1994, Thermochimica Acta, 1998-99. Fellow Soc. Plastics Engrs. (tech. program com. 1994-2000, bd. dirs. plastics analysis divsn. 2000—, treas. 2001—); mem. N.Am. Thermal Analysis Soc. (awards chmn. 1986-87, treas. 1989-93, pubs. chmn. 1994-95, 97, conf. treas. 1990-96, exec. coun. 1986-87, 89-95, 97), North Jersey Thermal Analysis Group (program chmn. 1988-89), Am. Chem. Soc. (program chmn. 1987-89), Soc. Rheology. Mennonite Brethren Ch. Achievements include development of concept of the liquid-liquid transition in polymers; concept of the TTT and CHT diagrams for thermosetting polymers; 7 patents. Home: 9251 Jaybird Cir E Jacksonville FL 32257-5276 Office: Vistakon J & J Vision Care Inc 5985 Richard St Jacksonville FL 32216-5998 E-mail: jenns@visus.jnj.com., jbenns@bellsouth.net.

ENO, AMOS STEWART, natural resource foundation administrator; b. Princeton, N.J., Jan. 26, 1950; s. Amos and Alice Pardee (Stewart) E.; m. Marjorie Theresa Belli, Sept. 18, 1982; children: Amos Pinchot L., Angus Connelly. BA, Princeton U., 1972; MA, Cornell U., 1977. Staff asst. to asst. sec. U.S. Dept. Interior, Washington, 1974-76, spl. asst. to chief, office of endangered species, 1978-81; asst. dir. wildlife affairs Nat. Audubon Soc., Washington, 1981-82, dir. wildlife programs, 1982-86; dir. conservation programs Nat. Fish and Wildlife Found., Washington, 1986-91, exec. dir., 1991-99; pres. Resources First Group, South Freeport, Maine, 2000—. Pres. Resources First Found.; exec. dir. New Eng. Forestry Found., 2002—; bd. dirs. Strategic Environ. Rsch. and Devel. Program, U.S. Dept. Def., LightStream Corp., Hydrophilix Corp.; mem. coun. N.Am. Wetlands Conservation Coun., U.S. Dept. Interior. Editor FY 1987-93 Federal Agency Needs Assessment; editor reports. Recipient Frederick Douglas award, Princeton, 1972, Profl. Conservationist award Chevron, 1992, Pres. Conservation Achievement Awd., 1993, Nature Conservancy. Mem. Ivy Club. Avocations: tennis, running, photography. E-mail: amoseno@aol.com.

ENO, PAUL FREDERICK, editor, writer; b. Hartford, Conn., Mar. 30, 1953; s. Earl Bryan and Bernice Sarah (Landers) E.; m. Jaclyn Ann Blackmon, June 7, 1981; children: Jonathan David, Benjamin Thomas. AA, St. Thomas Sem., Bloomfield, Conn., 1973; BA in Philosophy, Wadhams Hall Coll., Ogdensburg, N.Y., 1975; postgrad., Trinity Coll., Hartford, Conn., 1976-78. Book series editor Warbrooke Pub. Ltd., Montreal, Que., Can., 1974-76; staff writer Pawtuxet Valley Daily Times, West Warwick, R.I., 1979-80; mng. editor Observer Publs., Smithfield, R.I., 1980-83; copy editor Providence Jour., 1985-91; freelance editor, writer and publisher, 1976—. Owner New River Press, Woonsocket, R.I., 1990—; exec. dir. Pickering Inst. for New Eng. Studies, 1999—. Author: Best of Times, 1992, Rhode Island: A Genial History, 1994, Underhill Days, 1995, Faces at the Window, 1995, Footsteps in the Attic, 2001; editor: John Brown's Adirondack Empire, 1988, Flexography: Principles and Practices, 1990; contbr. articles to mags. Vice chmn. Cumberland Hist. Dist. Commn., 1987-92; bd. dirs. New Eng. Confedn., 1997—. With USCGR, 1983-89. With USCGR, 1983—89. Recipient medal R.I. Hist. Soc., 1987. Mem. R.I. Press. Assn. (bd. dirs., treas. 1982-89, Best Editorial of Yr. 1981, 82), Cumberland Beagle Club. Avocations: riding, boating, model railroading, shooting. Home: 645 Fairmount St Woonsocket RI 02895-4012

ENOCH, CRAIG TRIVELY, state supreme court justice; b. Wichita, Kans., Apr. 3, 1950; BA, So. Meth. U., 1972, JD, 1975; LLM, U. Va., 1992. Bar: Tex. 1975, U.S. Dist. Ct. (no. dist.) Tex. 1976, U.S. Ct. Appeals (5th cir.) 1979; cert. Civil Trial Law. Assoc. Burford, Ryburn & Ford, Dallas, 1975-77; ptnr. Moseley, Jones, Enoch & Martin, Dallas, 1977-81; judge 101st Dist. Ct., Dallas, 1981-87; chief justice Tex. Ct. Appeals (5th dist.), 1987-92; justice Tex. Supreme Ct., Austin, 1993—. Mem. exec. bd. Dedman Sch. Law So. Meth. U., 1990—. Capt. USAFR, 1973-81. Recipient Outstanding Young Lawyer in Dallas, 1985, Disting. Alumni award for judicial svc. So. Meth. U. Dedman Sch. Law, 1999, J. Edward Finch Law Day Speech award, 2001. Fellow: Dallas Bar Found., Tex. State Bar Found., Am. Bar Found.; mem.: ABA (past chair exec. bd. appellate judges conf. jud. divsn.), Tex. Supreme Ct. (liaison to State Bar of Tex. 1999—), Am. Law Inst. Episcopalian.

ENOCH, JAY MARTIN, optometrist, vision scientist; b. NYC, Apr. 20, 1929; s. Jerome Dee and Stella Sarah (Nathan) E.; m. Rebekah Ann Feiss, June 24, 1951; children: Harold Owen, Barbara Diane, Ann Allison. *Jay Enoch has pride in his grandchildren, Jordan Michael and Ryan Samuel Enoch, David Jacob Dryfoos, and Julia Rose and Maxwell Jay Perry. Enoch's career stems from inspiration received at the Bronx High School of Science. Ample stimuli were provided by mentors at Columbia U. by Isidore Finkelstein and George Smelser, at OSU by Glenn Fry, at NPL in Teddington, England, by Walter Stanley Stiles, at Washington U. in St. Louis by Bernard Becker, in Berne by Hans Goldmann, and at U. Florida by Herbert Kaufman. Throughout, he was encouraged by his parents, grandfather, and his wife.* BS in Optics and Optometry, Columbia U., 1950; post grad., Inst. Optics U. Rochester, 1953; PhD in Physiol. Optics, Ohio State U., 1956; DSc (hon.), SUNY, 1993, Poly. U. Catalonia, 2002. Asst. prof. physiol. optics Ohio State U., Columbus, 1956-58; assoc. supr. Ohio State U. (Mapping and Charting Rsch. Lab.), 1957-58; fellow Nat. Phys. Lab., Teddington, England, 1959-60; rsch. instr. dept. ophthalmology Washington U. Sch. Medicine, St. Louis, 1958-59, rsch. asst. prof., 1959-64, rsch. assoc. prof., 1965-70, rsch. prof., 1970-74; fellow Barnes Hosp., St. Louis, 1960-64, cons. ophthalmology, 1964-74; rsch. prof. dept. psychology Washington U., St. Louis, 1970-74; grad. rsch. prof. ophthalmology and psychology Coll. Medicine U. Fla., Gainesville, 1974-80, grad. rsch. prof. physics, 1979-80; dir. Ctr. for Sensory Studies, 1976-80; dean Sch. Optometry, chmn. Grad. Group in Vision Sci. U. Calif., Berkeley, Calif., 1980-92, prof. optometry and vision sci., 1980-94, prof. of Grad. Sch., 1994—; prof. physiol. optics in ophthalmology U. Calif., San Francisco, 1980—. Exec. sec. subcom. on vision and its disorders of nat. adv. Neurol. Diseases and Blindness Coun., NIH, 1963-66; chmn. subcom. contact lens stds. Am. Nat. Std. Inst., 1970-77; mem. nat. adv. eye coun. Nat. Eye Inst., NIH, 1975-77, 80-84; exec. com., com. on vision NAS-NRC, 1973-76; mem. US Nat. Com. Internat. Commn. Optics, 1976-79; health sci. com. Systemwide Adminstrn. U. Calif., 1989-93, co-chmn. subcom. on immigrant health in Calif., 1993-94; mem. sci. adv. bd. Fight-for-Sight, 1988-92, Allergan Corp., 1991-93; mem. Lighthouse Internat., NY, 1989-96, chair, 1995, Pisart award com., bd. dir. 2001—; mem. com. on Refractive Errors WHO, 2002—. *As Executive Secretary of the Subcommittee on Vision and its Disorders, Enoch had opportunity to draft the plan for the future National Eye Institute, NIH. With limited modifications, this proved to be a seminal document. Enoch served for decades as liaison between ophthalmology and optometry, helped develop the infrastructure of modern visual and ophthalmic science, and aided in organizing modern optometry in India. He derived satisfaction during years in neonatal vision-care practice, as well as from his research on retinal receptor optics, etc., during his service as Dean at Berkeley, and in development of low vision services in the U.S.A. and India.* Mem. editl. bd.: Investigative Ophthalmology, 1965—75, Vision Rsch., 1974—80, Sight-Saving Rev., 1974—84, Sensory Processes, 1974—80; contbr. ; mem. editl. bd.: Internat. Ophthalmology, 1977—93, mem. editl. bd. optical scis.: Springer-Verlag, 1978—87, : Investigative Ophthalmology, 1983—88, mem. editl. bd.: Binocular Vision, 1984—, Clin. Vision Sci., 1986—93, Biomed. Optics, 1988—90, mem. editl. bd. biomed. scis.: Springer-Verlag, 1988—95, mem. editl. bd.: Annals of Ophthalmology, 1997—, assoc. editor for vision: Handbook of Optics, Optical Soc. Am., 1997—2001, mem. internat. editl. bd.: Ophthalmic and Physiol. Optics, 2002—. Nat. sci. adv. bd. Retinitis Pigmentosa Found., 1977-95; US rep. Internat. Perimetric Soc., 1974-90, also exec. com., chmn. Rsch. Group Standards; bd. dirs. Friends of Eye Rsch., 1977-88; trustee

Illuminating Engring. Rsch. Inst., 1977-81; bd. dir. Lighting Rsch. Bd., 1988-95; mem. bd. counselors U.C. San Francisco Sch. Dentistry, 1995—. 2d lt. US Army, 1951-52. Recipient Career Devel. award, NIH, 1963—73, Everett Kinsey award, Contact Lens Soc. Ophthalmologists, 1991, Berkeley citation, Festschrift U. Calif. Berkeley, 1996, Pisart award, Lighthouse Internat., 2001, Gaspar de Portola awrd, U. Calif. and Govt. of Catalunya, 2001. Fellow AAAS, Am. Acad. Optometry (Glenn A. Fry award 1972, Charles F. Prentice medal award 1974), Optical Soc. Am. (chmn. vision tech. sect. 1974-76, mem. book pub. com. 1996-2000), Am. Acad. Ophthalmology (honor award 1985); mem. Assn. for Rsch. in Vision and Ophthalmology (trustee 1967-73, pres. 1972-73, Francis I. Proctor medal 1977), Assn. for Rsch. in Vision and Ophthalmology Found., Concilium Ophthalmologicum Universale (chmn. visual functions com. 1982-86), Am. Optometric Assn. (low vision sect., Vision Care award 1987), Internat. Perimetric Soc. (hon. mem.), Ocular Heritage Soc. (medal 1997), Cogan Ophthalmic History Soc., Cosmos Club (Washington), Sigma Xi. Home: 54 Shuey Dr Moraga CA 94556-2621 Office: U Calif Sch Optometry Berkeley CA 94720-2020 E-mail: jmenoch@socrates.berkeley.edu.

ENOCHS, M. REBECCA, science educator; d. Jerome and Mary LeCompte Lawrence; m. Stephen F. Enochs; 1 child, S. Mark. BA, Oklahoma City U., 1967; PhD, U. Okla., 1972. Postdoctoral fellow U. Tex. Med. Sch., Houston, 1972—76; rsch. assoc. U. Mo., Columbia, 1976—78; asst. prof. Columbia Coll., Mo., 1978—81, Keimber Mil. Sch., Bounville, Mo., 1981—85; prof. Ctrl. Meth. Coll., Fayette, Mo., 1985—. Contbr. chapters to books; author: (numerous abstracts) Mo. Acad. Sci., 1993—2002. Recipient Gov.'s award, State of Mo., 1997. Mem.: Am. Chem. Soc., Omicron Delta Kappa (Oak Gold Chalk award 1996), Alpha Epsilon Delta. Avocations: reading, gardening, swimming, tennis, racquetball. Office: Ctrl Meth Coll 411 CMC Sq Fayette MO 65248

ENOMOTO, JERRY JIRO, protective services official; b. San Francisco, Jan. 24, 1926; BA, U. Calif., Berkeley, 1949, MA, 1951. Counselor San Quentin Prison Calif. Dept. Corrections, 1952-54, parole officer, 1955-56, supr. San Quentin Prison, 1956-58, supr. Deuel Vocat. Inst., 1958-59, supr. counselor San Quinten Prison, 1959-60, assoc. warden Deuel Vocat Inst., 1960-65, chief classification svcs., 1965-70, deputy supt. Soledad Prison, 1970-71, warden Calif. Correctional Inst., 1971-74, acting supt. Calif. Inst. Women, 1971-75, dir., 1975-80; ind. cons., 1980-94; fed. ct. monitor, 1994; U.S. marshal Ea. Dist. Calif., 1994—. Pres. & chmn. Japanese Am. Citizens League, 1987—. Mem.: Am. Correctional Assn. Office: US Marshalls Office US Courthouse 501 I St Ste 5600 Sacramento CA 95814-7304

ENOS, PAUL, geologist, educator; b. Topeka, July 25, 1934; s. Allen Mason and Marjorie V. (Newell) E.; m. Carol Rae Curt, July 5, 1958; children: Curt Alan, Mischa Enos Martin, Kevin Christopher, Heather Enos Wohlert. BS, U. Kans., 1956; postgrad., U. Tübingen, W.Ger., 1956-57; MS, Stanford U., 1961; PhD, Yale U., 1965. Geologist Shell Devel. Co., Coral Gables, Fla., 1964-68, research geologist Houston, 1968-70; from assoc. prof. to prof. geology SUNY, Binghamton, 1970-82; Haas Disting. prof. geology U. Kans., Lawrence, 1982-2000, prof., 2001—03, Haas disting. prof. emeritus, 2003—. Cons. to industry; sedimentologist Ocean Drilling, 1975, 92; rsch. vis. Oxford U., 1989, U. Erlangen, Germany, 1995-96; fgn. scientist Ministry Geology, People's Republic China, 1988; with Global Sedimentary Geology Project, 1988—, co-convener Working Group 4, 1992-2000. Co-author: Quaternary Sedimentation of South Florida, 1977, Mid-Cretaceous, Mexico, 1983; editor: Field Trips: South-Central New York, 1981, Deep-Water Carbonates, 1977; contbr. articles to sci. jours. Served to 1st lt. C.E., U.S. Army, 1957-59 Recipient Pettijohn medal Sedimentology, 2001; U. Liverpool fellow, 1976-77; NSF fellow, 1959-62; Fulbright fellow, 1956-57; Summerfield scholar, 1954-56 Mem. Soc. Econ. Paleontologists and Mineralogists (assoc. editor 1976-80, 83-87, Best Paper award 1969), Internat. Assn. Sedimentologists (assoc. editor 1983-87), Am. Assn. Petroleum Geologists, AAAS, Sigma Xi, Omicron Delta Kappa. Avocations: photography, diving, cycling, history. Office: U Kans Dept Geology Lawrence KS 66045-2124 Home: 1825 Castle Pine Court Lawrence KS 66047-2017

ENOS, RANDALL, cartoonist, illustrator; b. New Bedford, Mass., Jan. 30, 1936; s. Eugene and Isabel (Da Costa) E.; m. Leann Walker, June 23, 1956. Student, Boston Mus. Sch. Fine Arts, 1954-55. Art tchr. Famous Artists Schs., Inc., Westport, Conn., 1956-64; film designer Pablo Ferro Films, Inc., N.Y.C., 1964-66; free-lance illustrator and film designer Westport, 1966—; part-time tchr. Parsons Sch. Design, N.Y.C., 1975-84; lectr., tchr. Syracuse U. Designed films for maj. Am. corps.; illustrator for maj. publs. including N.Y. Times, Time Mag., also children's books, posters; represented in numerous illustrators and art dirs. anns., other anthologies and mus. collections; created comic strips. Recipient Cannes TV award, 1964 Mem. Soc. of Illustrators. Democrat. Avocations: collecting antique harpoons and other whale craft, studying history of American whaling. Home: 402 N Park Ave Easton CT 06612-1248 E-mail: renos@optonline.net.

ENQUIST, LYNN WILLIAM, molecular biologist; b. Denver, Oct. 23, 1945; s. Clarence Andrew and Doris Alice (Hajenga) E.; m. Kathleen Marie Siverson, Aug. 10, 1968; 1 child, Brian Joseph. BS, S.D. State U., 1967; PhD, Va. Commonwealth U., 1971. Postdoctoral fellow Roche Inst. of Molecular Biology, Nutley, N.J., 1971-73; staff fellow NIH, Bethesda, Md., 1973-77, staff scientist, 1977-81; rsch. dir. Molecular Genetics Inc., Minnetonka, Minn., 1981-84; rsch. leader DuPont Cen. Rsch., Wilmington, Del., 1984-90; sr. rsch. fellow DuPont Merck Pharm. Co., Wilmington, 1991-93; prof. molecular biology Princeton (N.J.) U., 1993—, assoc. chair dept. molecular biology, 2003—. Editor Jour. Virology, 1994-2001, editor in chief, 2002--; mem. editorial bd. Jour. of Virology, 1979-81, 89-91, 91-94, Virology, 1992-94; contbr. numerous articles to profl. jours.; patentee in field; author: Experiments with Gene Fusions, 1984, Principles of Virology: Molecular Biology, Pathogenesis and Control, 2000. Named Disting. Alumnus, Va. Commonwealth U., 1983, S.D. State U., 1984; recipient Pres.'s award Disting. Tchg. Princeton U., 2001. Mem. AAAS, Am. Acad. Microbiology, Am. Soc. for Microbiology, Am. Soc. for Virology, Soc. for Neurosci. Avocations: fishing, skiing, reading, music, gardening. Office: Dept Molecular Biology Princeton University 314 Schultz Laboratory Princeton NJ 08544-0001 E-mail: enquist@molbio.princeton.edu.

ENQUIST, PHILIP, architectural firm executive; BS, U. of So. Calif., 1974, M in Arch., 1979. Assoc. Skidmore, Owings and Merrill, Chgo., 1983—90, assoc. ptnr., 1990—94, dir. planning, 1994—96, ptnr. in charge urban design and planning, 1996—. Ptnr.-in-charge Harvard U. N. Campus Master Plan, 2001, Tampa Cultural Arts Dist. Master Plan, 2001. Chair Am. Inst. of Archs., 1999; vice chair AIA Regional/Urban Design PIA, 1998, local fourm chair, 1997, nat. livable cmtys. com.; bd. mem. Friends of Downtown Chgo.; mem. U.S./China Bldg. Coun., 1999—2000. Fellow, Am. Inst. of Arch., 2003; grantee Welton Beckett Fellowship, 1976, Gamble House Fellowship, 1976. Mem.: Urban Land Inst., Chgo. Arch. Found., Am. Planning Assn., Lambda Alpha Internat. Office: 224 S Michigan Ave Ste 1000 Chicago IL 60604 Fax: 312-360-4545. E-mail: somchicago@som.com.*

ENRICO, EUGENE JOSEPH, music educator; b. Red Lodge, Mont., July 25, 1944; s. Joseph Eugene Enrico and Margaret Elizabeth Souders; m. Sherry Lee Enrico, Aug. 12, 1970. MusB, BA, MA in Musicology, U. Mont., 1966; PhD in Musicology, U. Mich., 1970. Asst. prof. Saginaw Valley State Coll., University Center, Mich., 1970—73; postdoctoral rsch. fellow Smithsonian Instn., Washington, 1973; asst. prof. U. Louisville, 1973—76; assoc. prof. U. Okla., Louisville, 1976—83, prof., 1983—95, Ruth Vern Davis Reaugh prof. music, 1995—. Dir. Early Baroque Performance Workshop, Lake Tahoe, NV, 1980—84; artistic dir. Accademia Filarmonica, Norman, Okla., 1983—; dir. Ctr. for Music TV, Norman, 1990—; lectr. nat. lecture tours Waverly Consort, 1989, 91, 92. Author: (book) The Orchestra at San Petronio, 1976; prodr.(dir.): (PBS TV program) 1492: A Portrait in Music, 1992, Isabella d'Este: First Lady of the Renaissance, 2002, (early music TV series) www.ou.edu.earlymusic. Recipient Gov.'s Art award, State of Okla., 1993, Outstanding Fine Arts Faculty award, Coll. Fine Arts, U. Okla., 1996. Mem.: Am. Musical Instrument Soc., Early Music Am., Am. Musicol. Soc. Office: Univ of Oklahoma Sch of Music Norman OK 73019 E-mail: ejenrico@ou.edu.

ENRICO, ROGER A. soft drink company executive; Former v.p. sales and mktg. Pepsi-Cola Metropol Bottling Co. Inc., Purchase, N.Y.; chmn., CEO Pepsico Worldwide Beverages, Purchase, 1987; CEO, chmn. bd. dirs. Pepsico, Inc., 1996—2001; vice-chmn, 2001. Office: Pepsico Inc 700 Anderson Hill Rd Purchase NY 10577-1444 E-mail: ceo@pepsi.com.

ENRIGHT, CYNTHIA LEE, illustrator; b. Denver, July 6, 1950; d. Darrel Lee and Iris Arlene (Flodquist) E. BA in Elem. Edn., U. No. Colo., 1972; student, Minn. Sch. Art and Design, Mpls., 1975-76. Tchr. 3d grade Littleton (Colo.) Sch. Dist., 1972-75; graphics artist Sta. KCNC TV, Denver, 1978-79; illustrator No Coast Graphics, Denver, 1979-87; editorial artist The Denver Post, 1987—. Illustrator (mag.) Sesame St., 1984, 85; illustrator, editor "Tiny Tales" The Denver Post, 1991-94. Recipient Print mag. Regional Design Ann. awards, 1984, 85, 87, Phoenix Art Mus. Biannual award, 1979. Mem. Mensa. Democrat. Home: 1210 Ivanhoe St Denver CO 80220-2640 Office: The Denver Post 1560 Broadway Denver CO 80202-5177 E-mail: leenright@aol.com.

ENRIGHT, GEORGANN MCGEE, healthcare educator; b. Chgo., Nov. 8, 1943; d. George Daniel and Marjorie (Altenburg) McGee; m. John Joseph Enright, 1967; children: Sean, Erin, Emily, Katherine. BSN cum laude, U. Mich, 1965; cert., Patricia Stevens Career Coll., 1966; postgrad., Edison State Community Coll.; MS, Wright State U., 1994. Staff nurse, med. surg. U. Hosp., Ann Arbor, Mich., 1965-66; float nurse, med. surg. ICU Christ Community Hosp., Oak Lawn, Ill., 1966; staff nurse, med. surg. Saratoga Gen. Hosp., Detroit, 1967; med.-surg. float nurse, staff nurse neurosurgery and neurology Ohio State U. Hosp., Columbus, 1967-68; clin. nurse, team leader Planned Parenthood Miami Valley, Dayton, Ohio, 1970-71; float nurse, med. surg. pediatrics Stouder Hosp., Troy, Ohio, 1974-75; staff nurse adolescent and adult mental health unit Upper Valley Med. Ctr., Troy, 1983—2001; from instr. to asst. prof. Sinclair C.C., Dayton, 1993—. Instr. Edison State C.C., Piqua, Ohio, 1990-95. Mem. Am. Psychiat. Nurses Assn., Nat. Alliance for Mentally Ill (pres. Miami City), Dayton Area Psychiatric Nurses Assn., Sigma Theta Tau, Phi Kappa Phi, Alpha Lambda Delta. Home: 103 S Monroe St Troy OH 45373-2932 E-mail: georgann.enright@sinclair.edu.

ENRIGHT, STEPHANIE VESELICH, investment company executive, financial consultant; b. L.A., Mar. 24, 1929; d. Stephen P. and Violet (Guthrie) Veselich; m. Robert James Enright (dec. Sept. 1982); children: Craig James, Brent Stephen, Erin Suzanne, Kyle Stephen. BA, U. So. Calif., 1952, MS, 1975. Fin. and engring. cons. Orange County, Santa Ana, Calif., 1976-79; fin. cons. The Sim-Ehrflo Group, Newport Beach, Calif., 1979-81; pres. Enright Fin. Cons., Torrance, Calif., 1981—; fin. columnist Copley/Daily Breeze Newspaper, Torrance, Calif., 1982—. Adj. faculty mem. UCLA, U. So. Calif.; pres. Pacific Home Builders. Author: Family Wealth Counseling: Getting to the Heart of the Matter, 1999, Strictly Business, 2001; contbr. Mem. Com. Assn. of the Peninsula, Palos Verdes, Calif., 1986; found. dir. Little Co. of Mary Hosp., Torrance; dir. endowment com. Pa. Art Assn.; adv. bd. Assistance League; bd. dirs. Pa. Symphony Soc., 1991, El Camino Coll. Found., Torrace Libr. Found.; adv. bd. Switzer Ctr. Bloombergs Top Wealth Mgnr., 2002-03. Mem. Fin. Planning Assn. (bd. dirs., officer 1982-84, Planner of Month award 1984), Nat. Assn. Women Owners, Nat. Assn. Fin. Edn., Registry Profl. Planners, Fin. Planning Assn., Torrance C. of C., Assistance League (bd. dirs. South Bay), Women in Constrn., Trojan Club and League (bd. dirs. 1978-79, 91—). Republican. Avocations: traveling, writing. Office: 21515 Hawthorne Blvd Ste 1050 Torrance CA 90503-6517 E-mail: senright@enrightfinancial.com.

ENRIQUEZ, MANUEL HIPOLITO, physician; b. Angeles City, Philippines, Aug. 19, 1953; came to U.S., 1982; s. Antonio S. and Milagros D. (Hipolito) E.; m. Mary Diane Maloney, June 22, 1985; children: Steven. Katie. BS, U. of the East, 1974, MD, 1979. Diplomate internal medicine, pulmonary disease and critical care medicine. Intern Philippine Gen. Hosp., Manila, 1980; resident Mercy Hosp., Buffalo, 1982-85; fellow Wayne State U. Sch. Medicine, Detroit, 1985-87; dir. respiratory therapy Humana Hosp. Clinch Valley, Richlands, Va., 1987-88; staff pulmonologist VA Med. Ctr., Asheville, N.C., 1989-99, also dir. med. ICU, 1990-99, med. dir. respiratory therapy, 1997-99; flight surgeon USAF Clinic, Charleston AFB, S.C., 1991-99; cons. assoc. Duke U. Med. ctr., Durham, NC, 1989-99; sr. physician TVA Nuclear, Chattanooga, 2000—; sr. flight surgeon 134th Med. Squadron McGhee Tyson Air NG Base, Tenn. Cons. in field. Med. officer CAP, Asheville, 1990-99, sr. programs officer, 1993-99. Fellow: ACP, Am. Coll. Chest Physicians; mem.: Soc. USAF Flight Surgeons, Res. Officers Assn., Aerospace Med. Assn., Am. Coll. Occupl. and Environ. Medicine. Roman Catholic. Avocations: flying, jogging, reading, computers. Office: TVA EB 10B-C 1101 Market St Chattanooga TN 37402

ENROTH-CUGELL, CHRISTINA ALMA ELISABETH, neurophysiologist, educator; b. Helsingfors, Finland, Aug. 27, 1919; came to US, 1956, naturalized, 1962; d. Emil and Maja (Syren) E.; m. David W. Cugell, Sept. 5, 1955. MD, Karolinska Inst., 1948, PhD, 1952; Hon. Doctors Degree, U. Helsinki, Finland, 1994. Resident Karolinska Sjukhuset, 1949-52; intern Passavant Meml. Hosp., 1956-57; with Northwestern U., Evanston, Ill., 1959-91, prof. emeritus, 1991—, prof. dept. neurobiology and physiology and dept. biomedical engring., 1974—; mem. vision rsch. program com. Nat. Eye Inst., 1974-78, mem. nat. adv. eye coun., 1980-84. Contbr. articles to profl. jour. Recipient Ludwig von Sallman award Internat. Assn. Rsch. in Vision and Ophthalmology, 1982. Fellow Am. Inst. Med. and Biol. Engring., Am. Acad. Arts and Sci.; mem. Am. Assn. Rsch. in Vision and Ophthalmology (co-recipient Friedenwald award 1983, recipient W.H. Helmerich III award 1992), Soc. Neurosis., Am. Physiol. Soc., Physiol. Soc. (U.K.) Office: Northwestern U McCormick Sch Engring Technl Inst 2145 Sheridan Rd Evanston IL 60208-0834 E-mail: enroth@northwestern.edu.

ENSENAT, DONALD BURNHAM, ambassador, lawyer; b. New Orleans, Feb. 4, 1946; s. A.G. and Genevieve (Burnham) E.; m. Taylor Harding, June 5, 1976; children: Farish, Will. BA, Yale U., 1968; JD, Tulane U., 1973. Bar: La. 1973, U.S. Ct. Appeals (5th cir.) 1974, U.S. Supreme Ct. 1975, U.S. Ct. Appeals (11th cir.) 1982, Tex. 1991. Legis. asst. Congressman Hale Boggs, U.S. Ho. of Reps., Washington, 1969-70, legis asst. Congresswoman Lindy Boggs, 1973-74; personal aide Hon. George Bush, Houston, 1970; asst. atty gen. State of La., New Orleans, 1975-80; assoc., dir., mng. dir. Carmouche, Gray, & Hoffman, A.P.L.C., New Orleans, 1981-89; mng. dir. Hoffman Sutterfield Ensenat, A.P.L.C., New Orleans, 1989-92, sr. dir., 1994-97; of counsel Locke Liddell & Sapp, PC, New Orleans, 1997-2001; U.S. Chief of Protocol Washington, 2001—. U.S. amb. to Brunei, 1992-93. Bd. dirs. World Trade Ctr., New Orleans, chmn. fin. com., 1990-92, exec. com., 1993-2001, pres.-elect, 1995, pres., 1996, chmn. bd. dirs., 1997. With USAR, 1968-74. Mem. State Bar Tex., La. State Bar Assn., Maritime Law Assn. U.S., Yale Alumni Assn. La. (bd. dirs. 1976-92, 94—, pres. 1980-82), Assn. Yale Alumni (rep. 1976-79). Republican. Roman Catholic. Avocation: sports. Home: 5527 Hurst St New Orleans LA 70115 Office: US State Dept S/CPR 2201 C St NW Washington DC 20520

ENSENAT, LOUIS ALBERT, surgeon; b. Merida, Mexico, Oct. 24, 1915; s. Frank and Guadalupe F. (Ensenat) E.; m. Ruth Ogden, July 9, 1943; children: Gloria Louise, Tinita Ruth, Louis Albert, Rita Joan, Barbara Jean, Michael Monroe. BS, Tulane U., 1938, MD, 1941; MSc in Medicine, U. Pa., 1953. Diplomate Am. Bd. Surgery, Am. Bd. Abdominal Surgery. Intern Charity Hosp., New Orleans, 1941-42, resident surgery Monroe, La., 1942, Lakeshore Hosp., New Orleans, La., VA Hosp., New Orleans, La., Batavia, N.Y.; fellow in surg. pathology Tulane U. Sch. Med.; preceptorship in surgery Biloxi (Miss.) VA Hosp.; staff surg. VA Hosp., Montgomery, 1946-52; pvt. practice surgery Pasadena, Tex., 1952-62, New Orleans, 1962—. Founder, adminstr. Mercy Hosp. Pasadena, 1954-62, chief surgery, 1954-62; founder, dir. Gulf Coast Home Builders, Inc.; trustee Angiology Research Found., 1986—. Author articles in field. Trustee, Big State Factors Corp. Served from lt. (j.g.) to lt. comdr. USN, 1942-46. Decorated Purple Heart, Bronze Star. Fellow: Am. Coll. Angiology (pres.), French Soc. Phlebology; mem.: AMA, Am. Med. Writers Assn., N.Y. Acad. Scis., Am. Soc. Abdominal Surgeons, Hawthorne Surg. Soc., Tulane U. Emeritus Club (bd. govs.). Home and Office: 1224 St Charles Ave Apt 210 New Orleans LA 70130-4334

ENSIGN, GREGORY MOORE, lawyer; b. Cleve., June 3, 1949; s. Gerald Edward and Patricia Mae (Komlos) E.; m. Nancy Beth Udelson, Jan. 9, 1977 (div.); children: Julie Ann, Jennifer Brooke; m. Cathryn Rae Halas, Oct. 24, 1987. BA, Ohio Wesleyan U., 1971; JD, Capital U., 1975. Bar: Ohio 1975, U.S. Dist. Ct. (so. dist.) Ohio 1975, U.S. Dist. Ct. (no. dist.) Ohio 1978, U.S. Ct. Appeals (6th cir.) 1984. Mgr. legal sect. Dept. Mental Health and Mental Retardation, Columbus, Ohio, 1972-77, chief counsel, 1977-78; assoc. Weltman, Strachan and Green Co., L.P.A., Cleve., 1978-79; ptnr. Sindell, Sindell & Rubenstein, Cleve., 1979-86; v.p. adminstrn., gen. counsel, sec. Kirkwood Industries, Inc., Cleve., 1986—. Contbr. articles to profl. jours. Mem. University Heights Communications and Devel. Commn., Ohio, 1981-84. Mem. ABA, Ohio State Bar Assn., Cleve. Bar Assn., Rotary. Republican. Office: Kirkwood Industries Inc 4855 W 130th St Cleveland OH 44135-5182

ENSIGN, JOHN D. retired military officer; b. New Britain, Conn., Aug. 20, 1956; s. Donald Lester and Gloria June (Ragna) Ensign; m. Rayna F. Goldberg, 1980 (div. 1985); children: Katrina, Natalie; m. Sandra Gray-Harris, 1987 (div. 1989); 1 child, Brandon. AS in Gen. Studies, Manchester (Conn.) C.C., 1986; BA in Sociology and Comm., U. Ariz., 1996; MA in Interdisciplinary Studies, U. Tex., 1997; postgrad. in Sociology, S.D. State U., 2001—02. Commd. 2d lt. USMC, 1974, inf. unit leader, marine security guard, recruiter, 1974—96, spl. ops., 1983, 1983—84, 1991, ret., 1996; instr. sociology Sanford-Brown Coll., Hazelwood, Mo., 2000, S.D. State U., Brookings, 2001—02. Crisis intervention vol. Hotline for Help, Brattleboro, Vt., 1994—95; recreation vol. Avery Heights Nursing Home, Conn., 2000—01; mem. budget adv. com. City of Tucson, Tucson. Mem.: VFW (life), Conn. Traumatic Brain Injury Assn., Golden Key. Avocations: sports, reading, art. Home: 6201 E Pima St Apt 1 Tucson AZ 85712-3022

ENSIGN, JOHN E. senator, former congressman; b. Roseville, Calif., Mar. 25, 1958; s. Mike and Sharon E.; m. Darlene Sciarretta Ensign; 1 child, Trevor. Student, UNLV; B in Gen. Sci., Oreg. State U., 1981; D of Veterinary Medicine, Colo. State U., 1985. Owner animal hosp., Las Vegas; gen. mgr. Gold Strike Hotel & Casino, 1991, Nev. Landing Hotel & Casino, 1992; mem. U.S. Congress from 1st Nev. dist., Washington, 1994-98; mem. ways and means com., subcom. health, subcom. human resources; mem. com. on resources, 1995-98; U.S. senator from Nev., 2000—. Candidate for U.S. Sen., 1998-99. Republican. Office: 9808 Moon Valley Pl Las Vegas NV 89134-6738*

ENSIGN, RICHARD PAPWORTH, transportation executive; b. Salt Lake City, Jan. 20, 1919; s. Louis Osborne and Florence May (Papworth) E.; m. Margaret Anne Hinckley, Sept. 5, 1942; children: Judith Ensign Lantz, Mary Jane Ensign Hofmeister, Richard L., James R., Margaret. BS, U. Utah, 1941. With Western Air Lines, 1941-70, v.p. in-flight service, 1963-70, v.p. passenger service, 1970, Pan Am. World Airways, 1971, sr. v.p. field mgmt., 1972-74, sr. v.p. mktg., 1974-75; exec. v.p. Western Airlines, 1975-82; pres. R.P. Ensign & Assocs., 1982—; spl. asst. to pres. Marriott-Host, Marriott Corp., 1990-91; spl. asst. to chmn. Caterair Internat. Corp., 1991-96. Chmn. Utah Nat. Adv. Coun., 1984-86; bd. dirs. Western Airlines, 1980-81, Pacific Area Travel Assocs., 1976-81, Marriott Airport Svc. Co., Osaka, Japan, 1986-92; resident dir. Marriott Internat. Corp., Seoul, People's Republic of Korea. Patentee in field. Nat. fund raising chmn. U. Utah, 1982-83, 83-84. Recipient Disting. Service award Fla. Internat. U., 1973; named Disting. Alumnus U. Utah, 1976, 86, recipient merit award of honor, 1985. Mem. Nat. Aeros. Assn. Clubs: Lochinvar. Republican. Mem. Lds Ch. Home: 3848 Malibu Country Dr Malibu CA 90265-4717

ENSIGN, WILLIAM LLOYD, architect; b. Trinidad, W.I., Dec. 14, 1928; s. Lloyd Gordon and Evelyn Barbara (Hobson) E.; m. June G. Pollinger, July 10, 1954; children: David Gordon, Evan Alexander. BSA.E., BSC.E., U. Colo., 1950; M. Arch., Columbia U., 1952. Mem. firm McLeod & Ferrara (Architects), Washington, 1955-65; ptnr. McLeod Ferrara & Ensign, 1965-72; pres. McLeod Ferrara Ensign, 1972-80; asst. architect of the Capitol Washington, 1980-95; acting architect of the Capitol Washington, 1995-97; ind. cons. Md., 1997—. Trustee Tax-Free Trust Ariz., Tax-Free Fund Utah; mem. D.C. Zoning commn., U.S. Capitol Police Bd., Nat. Capital Meml. Commn.; bd. dirs. Pa. Ave. Devel. Corp. Mem. Adv. Coun. Hist. Preservation, U.S. Capitol Guide Bd.; acting dir. U.S. Bot. Garden; trustee Nat. Bldg. Mus. With C.E.C., USNR, 1952-55. Fellow AIA (dir., past pres. Washington chpt., chmn. various coms.); mem. Nat. Trust Hist. Preservation, Nat. Capitol. Hist. Soc., Lambda Alpha Internat. (v.p.). Episcopalian.

ENSLEN, PAMELA CHAPMAN, lawyer; b. Detroit, Dec. 29, 1953; d. Ralph Nicholas Chapman and Roberta Margaret Clarke McLaughlin; m. Richard Alan Enslen, Nov. 20, 1985; 1 child, Alan Gennady Robert. BMus, U. Mich., 1976, MMus, 1977; JD, Wayne State U., 1981. Bar: Mich. 1981, Calif. 1996, U.S. Dist. Ct. (ea. and we. dists.) Mich. 1981, U.S. Ct. Appeals (6th cir.) 1983, U.S. Supreme Ct. 1983. Pre-hearing atty. Mich. Ct. Appeals, Detroit, 1981-83; fed. law clk. U.S. Dist. Ct., We. Dist. Mich., Kalamazoo, 1983-85; sr. ptnr. Miller, Canfield, Paddock & Stone, Kalamazoo, 1985-2001; fed. pub. defender We. Dist. Mich., 2001—03; sr. counsel Miller, Canfield, Paddock & Stone, Kalamazoo, 2003—. Lectr., cons., arbitrator, author and mediator in field. Co-founder, bd. dirs. Cmty. Dispute Resolution Ctr. Kalamazoo County, 1988—; bd. dirs. Am. Cancer Soc., Kalamazoo, 1991—. Named Mich. Lawyer of the Yr., Mich. Lawyers Weekly, 1998. Master: Am. Inns of Ct.; fellow: Am. Bar Found.; mem.: ATLA, ABA (standing com. on dispute resolution 1990—93, governing coun. dispute resolution sect. 1994—97, chair dispute resolution sect. 1997—98, sect. del. Ho. of Dels. 1999—, standing com. on fed. jud. improvements 2001—03), Fed. Bar Assn. We. Mich. (mem. governing bd. 2003—, bd. dirs.), Nat. Order of Barristers (mem. John Marshall award com. 2003), Women Lawyers of Mich. (regional rep. 1989—90), Kalamazoo Trial Lawyers Assn., Kalamazoo County Bar Assn. (chair law day com. 1989, bd. dirs. 1996—99), Mich. Bar Assn. (counsel sect. on arbitration and alternative dispute resolution 1985—98), Am. Mensa, Pi Kappa Lambda. Democrat. Avocations: reading, music. Office: Miller Canfield 444 W Michigan Kalamazoo MI 49007

ENSLEN, RICHARD ALAN, federal judge; b. Kalamazoo, May 28, 1931; s. Ehrman Thrasher and Pauline Mabel (Dragoo) E.; m. Pamela Gayle Chapman, Nov. 2, 1985; children— David, Susan, Sandra, Thomas, Janet, Joseph, Gennady. Student, Kalamazoo Coll., 1949-51, Western Mich. U., 1955; LL.B., Wayne State U., 1958; LL.M., U. Va., 1986. Bar: Mich. 1958, U.S. Dist. Ct. (we. dist.) Mich. 1960, U.S. Ct. Appeals (6th cir.) 1971, U.S. Ct. Appeals (4th cir.) 1975, U.S. Supreme Ct 1975. Mem. firm Stratton, Wise, Early & Starbuck, Kalamazoo, 1958-60, Bauckham & Enslen, Kalamazoo, 1960-64, Howard & Howard, Kalamazoo, 1970-76, Enslen & Schma, Kalamazoo, 1977-79; dir. Peace Corps, Costa Rica, 1965-67; judge Mich. Dist. Ct., 1968-70; U.S. dist. judge Kalamazoo, 1979—; chief judge, 1995-2001. Mem. faculty Western Mich. U., 1961-62, Nazareth Coll., 1974-75; adj. prof. polit. sci. Western Mich. U., 1982—. Co-author: The Constitutional Law Dictionary: Volume One, Individual Rights, 1985; Volume Two, Governmental Powers, 1987, Constitutional Deskbook: Individual Rights, 1987, (with Mary Bedikian and Pamela Enslen) Michigan Practice, Alternative Dispute Resolution, 1998. Served with USAF, 1951-54. Named Person of the Century-Law and Courts, The Kalamazoo Gazette, 1999; named to Great Am. Judges, ABC-Clio, 2003; recipient Disting. Alumni award, Wayne State Law Sch., 1980, Western Mich. U., 1982, Outstanding Practical Achievement award, Ctr. Pub. Resources, 1984, award for Excellence and Innovation in Alternative Dispute Resolution and Dispute Mgmt., Legal Program; scholar, Jewel Corp., 1956—57, Lampson McElhone, 1957. Mem. ABA (standing com. on dispute resolution 1983-90), Mich. Bar Assn., Am. Judicature Soc. (bd. dirs. 1983-85), Sixth Cir. Jud. Coun. Office: US Dist Ct 410 W Michigan Ave Kalamazoo MI 49007-3757

ENSLIN, THEODORE VERNON, poet; b. Chester, Pa., Mar. 25, 1925; s. Morton Scott and Ruth May (Tuttle); m. Mildred Marie Stout, Aug. 1, 1945 (div.); children— Deirdre, Jonathan Morton; m. Alison Jane Jose, Sept. 14, 1969; 1 son, Jacob Hezekiah. Studied mus. composition with Nadia Boulanger, Cambridge, Mass., 1943-44. Author: New Sharon's Prospect, 1965, To Come To Have Become, 1966, Forms (5 vols.), 1970-74, The Country of Our Consciousness, 1971, The Median Flow, 1975, Synthesis, 1975, Carmina, 1976, Ranger, 2 vols., 1978-80, Music for Several Occasions, 1985, Small Suite for Solo Flute, 1985, The Weather Within, 1986, Case Book, 1987, From Near the Great Pine, 1988, Love and Science, 1990, Little Wandering Flake of Snow, 1991, Gamma-UT, 1992, The House of the Golden Windows, 1993, Music in the Key of C, 1995, Communitas, 1996, Propositions for John Taggart, 1996, Thumbprint on Landscape, 1997, Skeins, 1998, Then and Now Selected Poems, 1999, Sequentiae, 1999; readings and seminars various colls. and univs.

Recipient Niemann award for weekly newspaper column The Cape Codder, 1955, Hart Crane Meml. award, 1969; Disting. Vis. Prof. Bowling Green State U., 1989. Mem. Am. Found. for Homoeopathy. Address: RFD Box 289 Kansas Rd Milbridge ME 04658

ENSMINGER, DALE, mechanical engineer, electrical engineer; b. Mt. Perry, Ohio, Sept. 26, 1923; s. Charles Henry and Mary Elpha (Koehler) Ensminger; m. Lois Elizabeth Hamilton, Mar. 25, 1948; children: Martha Jean, Laura Lee, Charles Robert, Jonathan Dale, Mary Ann, Daniel Joseph; m. Patricia Ann Evans, June 7, 2002. BSME, BSEE, Ohio State U., 1950, postgrad., 1950-53. Registered profl. engr., Ohio. Rschr. Battelle Meml. Inst., Columbus, Ohio, 1950, prin. rschr.; sr. rschr. Battelle Columbus Labs., mgr. ultrasonics, sr. rsch. scientist, 1984-88. Cons. in field. Author: Ultrasonics, 1973, 2d edit. 1988; contbr. articles to profl. jours., chpts. to books; patentee in field; contbr., reviewer Am. Soc. Non-Destructive Testing Handbook, 1989—. Sec. Columbus Prison Assn., 1950—; dean, dir. Columbus Bible Inst., 1952—97; mem. bd. Fundamental Bapt. Mission of Trinidad and Tobago; mem. session (governing body) Calvary Bible Ch., 1953—89, clk.of session, 1953—84. Recipient Cert. of Recognition, NASA, 1975. Mem.: ASM, Ultrasonic Industry Assn., Soc. for Non-Destructive Testing, Acoustical Soc. Am. Home: 198 E Longview Ave Columbus OH 43202-1236

ENSMINGER, JOHN J. publishing executive, lawyer; b. Colfax, Wash., July 11, 1946; s. M. Eugene and Audrey H. Ensminger; m. Joan Teresa Kay, Sept. 12, 1993. BA, U. Calif., Berkeley, 1968; JD, Hastings Coll. Law, San Francisco, 1974; LLM, NYU, 1985. Bar: NY. Sr. editor Warren, Gorham & Lamont, NYC, 1987—88, exec. editor, 1988—94, sr. mng. editor, 1994—95; dir. periodicals and svcs. Rsch. Inst. Am., NYU, 1995—2000; pres. Delta Hedge Publs., Bklyn., 2000—. Mem.: ABA (mem. com. banking and savings instns. tax sect. 2003—), Indian Inst. Fin. (editl. bd. 1999—), Internat. Assn. Fin. Engrs. Avocation: ballroom dancing. Office: Delta Hedge Publs PO Box 25664 Brooklyn NY 11202-5644

ENSMINGER, JOHN JAY, writer, poet, minister, counselor; b. June 25, 1945; m. Cynthia Re Fugate, Feb. 18, 1983. BTh, Southwest Bible Sem., Springfield, Mo., 1967; PhD, Univ. Metaphysics, Studio City, Calif., 1997. Caseworker State of Mo., 1974—2002, ret., 2002; jewelry designer and gem collector Ageless Wonders, Trenton, Mo., 1984—2003; metaphysical min. Univ. Metaphysics, Studio City, Calif., 1996—2003; freelance author, poet Trenton, Mo., 1984—. Mem. bd. Comprehensive N.W. Mental Health, Trenton, Mo., 1986—87. Author: On Earth as it is in Heaven, 2003. Recipient Citizenship award, DAR, 1959, Editors Choice award, Nat. Poetry Libr., 1991. Avocations: antiques, gardening, rock and gem collector, rare books. Office: Ageless Wonders 603 Rural St Trenton MO 64683-2737

ENSMINGER, LUTHER GLENN, chemist, consultant; b. Mt. Perry, Ohio, Oct. 17, 1919; s. Charles Henry and Mary Elfa (Koehler) E.; m. Emma Jean Couch, May 12, 1951 (dic. Apr. 1973); children: Luther, Douglas, Phillip, Deborah; m. How Leng Cheng, Nov. 11, 1983 (div. Dec. 1988); m. Lee Rose Olson, Oct. 19, 1992. B.Sc., Ohio State U., 1942, B.Sc., 1948. Chemist FDA, Cin., 1948-56, chemist, lab. supr. Los Angeles, 1956-59, sci. adminstr. Washington, 1959-79; sci. cons. Arlington, Va., 1979—. Vol., tutor for immigrant high sch. and coll. students (YMCA awards for outstanding tutoring work 1992, 93). Contbr. articles to profl. jours. Sec. Lee-Ballston Citizens Assn., 1965-75. Served with U.S. Army, 1942-45. Recipient Seven Who Care award, 1990, Outstanding Svc. to Cmty. award YMCA Met. Washington, 1996. Fellow Assn. Ofcl. Analytical Chemists (exec. sec. 1967-79, mem. exec. com. 1960-79), Beta Gamma Sigma; mem. Am. Shoppers Panel, Nat. Family Opinion World Group. Republican. Presbyterian. Address: 631 N Edison St Arlington VA 22203-1430

ENSSLIN, ROBERT FRANK, JR., retired association executive and military officer; b. Jacksonville, Fla., Feb. 22, 1928; s. Robert Frank Sr. and Pauline (Harper) E.; m. Fae Finter, Sept. 29, 1951; children: Robert III, Clyde, Paul, John. BA in Art, U. N.C., 1950; grad., F.A. Officer Candidate Sch., Ft. Sill, Okla., 1952, U.S. Army Command Staff Coll., 1969, U.S. Army War Coll., 1978. Commd. U.S. Army, 1952, advanced through grades to maj. gen., 1992; sales and adv. mgr. Sears, Roebuck & Co., Durham N.C. and Tampa, Fla., 1953-60; v.p. Louis Benito Advt., Tampa, 1960-67; pres. Ensslin & Hall Advt., Tampa, 1967-81; adj. gen. Fla. Nat. Guard, St. Augustine, Fla., 1982-92; exec. dir. Nat. Guard Assn. U.S., Washington, 1992-95. Chair mil. adv. com. Office of Gov., Tallahassee, Fla., 1982-92. Pub. Nat. Guard mag., 1990-95; contbr. articles to profl. jours. Pres. Guidance Ctr. of Hillsborough, Tampa, 1964, Am. Cancer Soc., Tampa, 1968; gov. Fla. Advt. Fedn., 1964-65; mem. res. forces policy bd. Dept. Def., Washington, 1987-90; pres. Mcht.'s Assn. Fla., 1963-64; mem. VA Vets. Cemetery Bd., 1999—. Decorated D.S.M., P.U.C., Legion of Merit, M.S.M., ARCOM. Mem. Am. Assn. Advt. Agys. (bd. dirs. 1978-81), Assn. of U.S. Army (trustee 1985-91, dir. Sunshine chpt.), N.G. Assn. U.S. (sec. 1986-88, v.p. 1988-90, pres. 1990-92, exec. dir.), Army and Navy Club. Home: 5903 Mt Eagle Dr Apt 414 Alexandria VA 22303-2527 E-mail: rensslinjr@aol.com.

ENSTICE, WAYNE, art educator, writer; s. John Franklin and Eleanor Frances Enstice; m. Marie Frances Geditz, Aug. 28, 1967; children: Timothy Jon, Kirsten Anne Inquilla, Nicolas Brett. BFA, Pratt Inst., 1965; MA, U. N.Mex, 1969. From instr. to assoc. prof. U. of Ariz., Tucson, 1970—90; prof., chmn. dept. Ind. State U., Terre Haute, 1990—95; prof., dir. U. of Cin. Sch. or Art, 1995—2000, prof., 2000—. Co-author: (textbook) Drawing/Space, Form, & Expression, 1990, 3rd edit., 2003, Jazz Spoken Here, 1992, paperback edit., 1994; contbr. chapters to books; exhibitions include Alternative Mus., NYC, Drawing Ctr., Diverse Works Gallery, Houston, Kiosk Mus., Mex., Getler/Pall/Saper Gallery, N.Y.C., 313 Gallery, NYC, SPACE Gallery, LA, Represented in permanent collections U. N.Mex., U. Ark., U. NC, Chapel Hill, U. Ariz. Mus. Art, Roswell Museum and Art Ctr., Ariz. Commn. on Arts, Yuma Art Mus, Libr. of Congress. Vol. Peace Corps, Freetown, Sierra Leone, 1965—67; chmn. Vis. Arts Alliance, Cin., 1998—99; bd. dirs. Tucson Mus. Art, 1977—78, Arts ILLIANA, Terre Haute, Ind., 1993—95. Individual Artist's grantee, SummerFair, Inc, Cin., 2001, Artist-in-Residence grantee, Roswell Mus. and Art Ctr., Roswell, N.Mex, 1984—85. Office: U Cin Sch of Art Cincinnati OH

ENSTROM, JAMES EUGENE, epidemiologist; b. Alhambra, Calif., June 20, 1943; s. Elmer Melvin, Jr. and Klea Elizabeth (Bissell) E.; m. Marta Eugenia Villanea, Sept. 3, 1978. BS, Harvey Mudd Coll., Claremont, Calif., 1965; MS, Stanford U., 1967; PhD in Physics, 1970; M.P.H., UCLA, 1976. Research assoc. Stanford Linear Accelerator Center, 1970-71; research physicist, cons. Lawrence Berkeley Lab. U. Calif., 1971-75; Celeste Durand Rogers cancer research fellow Sch. Pub. Health, UCLA, 1973-75; Nat. Cancer Inst. postdoctoral trainee, 1975-76; cancer epidemiology researcher, 1976-81; assoc. research prof., 1981—. Program dir. for cancer control epidemiology Jonsson Comprehensive Cancer Center, 1978-88, research epidemiologist, 1988—, sci. dir. tumor registry, 1984-87, mem. dean's council, 1976—; cons. epidemiologist Linus Pauling Inst. Sci. and Medicine, 1976-94; cons. physicist Rand Corp., 1969-73, R&D Assos., 1971-75; mem. sci. bd. Am. Council on Sci. and Health, 1984—. Author papers in field. NSF predoctoral trainee, 1965-66; grantee Am. Cancer Soc., 1973—, Nat. Cancer Inst., 1979—; Preventive Oncology Acad. award, 1981-87. Fellow Am. Coll. Epidemiology; mem. Soc. Epidemiologic Research, Am. Heart Assn., Am. Pub. Health Assn., Am. Phys. Soc., AAAS, N.Y. Acad. Scis., Galileo Soc. Office: U Calif Sch Pub Health Los Angeles CA 90024

ENSTROM, WALTER GORDON A. minister; b. Chgo., Oct. 15, 1931; s. Walter A. and Edla Viola (Carlson) E.; m. Helen Marie Fahning, June 29, 1957; children: Karen Lynn, Mark Alan, Jon Erick. BS, U. Ill.; MS, U. Minn.; MDiv, North Park Seminary. Lic. minister. Pastor Evangelical Covanent Ch., Savonburg, Kans., 1957-59; assoc. pastor Albany Park Luth. Ch., Chgo., 1959-60, Immanuel Evangelical Covenant Ch., Chgo., 1960-61; pastor Vista Evangelical Covenant Ch., New Richland, Minn., 1961-66, Evangelical Covenant Ch., Lanyon, Iowa, 1966-67, United Meth. Ch., Danbury, Iowa, 1968-78, United Ch. of Christ and German City Evangelical Ch., Oto and Hornick, Iowa, 1978-94. Interim pastor Evangelical Covenant Ch., Sloan, Iowa, 1985. Vol. Mercy Med. Ctr., Sioux City, Iowa, 1995—. With U.S. Army, 1953-55. Mem. Northwest Iowa Scandinavian Soc., Sioux city Genealogy Soc., Am. Legion, German Am. club, Stroke Club. Republican. Avocations: genealogy, coin and stamp collecting, gardening, swimming. Home: 2240 Old Hwy 141 Hornick IA 51026

ENTCHEV, PAVLIN BORISSOV, aerospace and mechanical engineer; m. Natalya Verkhusha, Dec. 19, 1998; 1 child, Bogdan. MS, Belarussian State Poly. Acad., Minsk, Belarus, 1994; PhD, Tex. A&M U., 2002. Postdoctoral rsch. assoc. Tex. A&M U., College Station, Tex., 2002—. Mem.: AIAA, ASME. Office: Aerospace Engring Dept Texas A&M U College Station TX 77843-3141

ENTE, GERALD, pediatrician; b. N.Y.C., July 18, 1930; s. Louis M. and Minnie (Lackfish) E.; m. Phyllis Warch, Aug. 27, 1995; children: Peter, William. BS, Union Coll., 1951; MD, NYU, 1955. Diplomate Am. Acad. Pediatrics. Intern Kings County Hosp., Bklyn., 1955-56, resident in pediat., 1958-59, Bronx Mcpl. Hosp., 1959-60; pvt. practice Westbury, N.Y., 1960—; clin. instr. pediat. Einstein Med. Sch., 1960-64, Meadowbrook, 1960-65, asst. attending pediat., 1965-68, clin. assoc. dir. of newborn svcs., 1968-70; clin. dir neonatology Nassau County Med. Ctr., 1970-88, attending physician pediat., 1974—; assoc. clin. prof. pediat. emeritus SUNY Med. Coll., Stony Brook, N.Y., 1985-99; attending pediatrician Winthrop U. Hosp., 1997—. Schneider Children's Hosp., 1997—. Med. dir. Trya Hostel, 1974-77, Fellowship Med. Labs, 1974-80; pediatric cons. Project Headstart, 1972, Westbury med. dir., 1966-76; cons. staff physician SUNY Coll. at Old Westbury, 1971-82, physician in-charge, 1972-79; cons. Westinghouse Electric Co., 1971-72, GenTel Electric Co., 1972, mem. Westbury Health Coun., 1974-78; dir. neonatology Ctrl. Gen. Hosp., 1980-90, chmn. pediats., 1990-94; profl. adv. bd. L.I. Inst. for Tng. in the Psychotherapies, 1979-81; mem. rsch. panel Med. World News, 1979-81. Author: (with others) Handbook of Neonatology, 1974, Pediatricians Manual Vol. I & II, 1977, Management of Prader Willi Syndrome, 1988; contbr. numerous articles to profl. jours.; assoc. editor Nassau County Med. Ctr. Proceedings, Nassau County Med. Soc. Bull., Schneider Children's Hosp. Bull. Bd. dirs. Offspring Dance Group, 1976-92; chmn. L.I. physicians United Way, 1983-84. Capt. U.S. Army Res., 1956-58. Recipient Samaritan award N.Y. Assn. Brain Injured Children, 1968, Man of Yr.; Resident's Teaching award Nassau County Medical Soc., 1972, Outstanding Attending of the Yr. Winthrop Univ. Hosp., 1998. Fellow Am. Acad. Pediatrics (PREP fellowship award 1979-85, PREP awards 1980-86, 93, 96, 98, 2000, 02, exec. bd. chpt. 2), Royal Soc. of Pediatrics, Royal Soc. of Health, Internat. Coll. Pediatrics, Nassau Acad. of Medicine; mem. AMA (Physicians Recognition award 1980-84, 86, 87, 89, 91, 93, 96, 98, 2000, 02), N.Y. State Med. Soc., Nassau County Med. Soc. (exec. com.), World Med. Assn., Nassau Acad. Medicine (sect. on pediatrics), Pan Am. Med. Assn. (diplomate), World Med. Soc., Assn. Am. Soc. Photobiology, Internat. Transactional Analysis Assn., Am. Holistic Med. Assn., Nassau Acad. Medicine (pres., 2001-), N.Y. State Fraternal Order of Police Surgeons' Lodge (pres. 1998—, Assoc. Mem. of Yr. 2003). Office: 530 Old Country Rd Westbury NY 11590-4500 E-mail: entedoc@aol.com.

ENTEMAN, WILLARD FINLEY, philosophy educator; b. Glen Ridge, N.J., Oct. 21, 1936; s. Verling Clair and Elizabeth Vance Rutherford (Dailey) E.; m. Kathleen Ffolliott, June 18, 1960; children: Sally Holyoke, David Finley. BA, Williams Coll., 1959, LL.D (hon.), 1978; MBA, Harvard U., 1961; MA, Boston U., 1962, PhD, 1965; LL.D. (hon.), Colby Coll., 1980. Instr. in philosophy Wheaton Coll., 1963-65, asst. prof., 1965-69, assoc. prof., 1969-70; assoc. prof., chmn. dept. philosophy Union Coll., Schenectady, 1970-72, provost and assoc. prof., 1972-78; pres., prof. Bowdoin Coll., 1978-81; provost, v.p. acad. affairs R.I. Coll., Providence, 1982-90, prof. philosophy, 1982—; exec. v.p., dir. Bibliotech, Inc., 1984-96. Mem. New Eng. Bd. Higher Edn., 1978-81 ; 2d v.p., trustee Colby-Bates-Bowdoin Ednl. Telecasting Corp., 1978-81. Author: Managerialsim: The Emergence of a New Ideology, Retirement 101: How TIAA-CREF Members Should Deal with the Dramatic Changes in Their Pensions; editor: The Problem of Free Will, 1967; contbr. articles to profl. publs. Trustee Regional Meml. Hosp., Brunswick, Maine, 1978-81, Hotchkiss Sch., 1980-90, Eckerd Coll., 1987—; mem. long-range planning com. Portland (Maine) Sch. Art, 1979-81; vice chmn. bd. trustees R.I. Coun. on Econ. Edn. Named One of 100 Top Young Leaders in Higher Edn., Change mag., 1978. Mem. Nat. Assn. Ind. Colls. and Univs. (dir.), Brunswick C. of C. (trustee 1978-81) Office: RI Coll 600 Mt Pleasant Ave Providence RI 02908-1924

ENTENMAN, JOHN ALFRED, lawyer; b. White Plains, NY, Apr. 14, 1948; s. Alfred Morris and Mae Muriel (Hamilton) Entenman. BA, U. Mich., 1970; JD, Harvard U., 1973. Bar: Mich. 1973, US Dist. Ct. (ea. dist.)/Mich. 1973, US Ct. Appeals (6th cir.) 1974, US Supreme Ct. 1974. Assoc. Dykema Gossett et al., Detroit, 1973—80, ptnr., 1980; adj. prof. labor law U. Detroit Sch. Law, Detroit, 1975—78. Mem.: Indsl. Rels. Rsch. Assn., ABA, State Bar Assn. Mich., Renaissance (Detroit), Theta Delta Chi (sr. exec. 1969—70). Home: 638 Westchester Rd Grosse Pointe MI 48230-1824 Office: Dykema Gossett 400 Renaissance Ctr Ste 35 Detroit MI 48243-1501

ENTERKIN, JAMES EDWARD, JR., lawyer; b. Newton, Mass., July 23, 1952; s. James Edward and Mary Isabelle (MacKinnon) E.; m. Susan Ivy Enterkin, July 3, 1977; children: James Andrew, Elizabeth Ivy. BA with distinction cum laude, Cornell U., 1974; JD, Boston U., 1977; postgrad., Harvard U., 1983, Emory U., 1987. Bar: Mass. 1977, U.S. Dist. Ct. Mass. 1978, U.S. Ct. Appeals (1st cir.) 1981. Atty. New England Electric System, Westborough, Mass., 1977-81; atty., from asst. counsel to sr. counsel John Hancock Life Ins. Co., Boston, 1981—. Mem. bd. advisors Cognistar, Inc., Southborough, Mass., 2000—. Co-author: Model Form Note Purchase Agreement, 1994, Financial Covenants Reference Manual, 1996. Mem. Gov.'s Task Force Coastal Zone Mgmt., Commonwealth of Mass., 1980-81; spkr. Am. Coll. of Investment Counsel, N.Y.C., 1995; amb. Cornell Alumni Admissions Amb. Network, 1987—; mem. St. Matthew Parish Religious Edn. Bd., Southborough, 1989-2002. Fellow Am. Coll. of Investment Counsel; mem. Am. Corp. Counsel Assn. Roman Catholic. Avocations: golfing, skiing, painting, music. Office: John Hancock Life Ins Co PO Box 111 Boston MA 02117-0111

ENTESSAR, TAHMINEH, political scientist, educator; b. Tehran, June 22, 1953; arrived in U.S., 1972; d. Fatollah and Azar Entessar; m. Robert Beller Weisenfeld, Aug. 18, 1984; 1 child, Aryan Entessar Weisenfeld. BA cum laude, Webster U., 1975; MA, So. Ill. U., Edwardsville, 1977; PhD, St. Louis U., 1983. Tchr. secondary sch. Springboard to Learning, St. Louis, 1978—83; adj. prof. Webster U., St. Louis, 1983—2001, lectr., grad. adviser, 2001—. Guest commentator Sta. KTVI-TV, St. Louis, 1991, World News Report, St. Louis, 1984—97; guest analyst St. Louis Post Dispatch, 1990. Mem.: AAUP, Pi Sigma Alpha. Avocations: classical music, jogging, piano. Office: Webster U 470 E Lockwood Ave Saint Louis MO 63119 Fax: 314-968-7403. E-mail: entessar@webster.edu.

ENTEZARI-TAHER, MOHAMMAD, neurologist, researcher; b. Tehran, Iran, Feb. 13, 1962; arrived in U.S., 1996; s. Yadollah Entezari-Taher and Monireh Mihanparast; m. Zohreh Taher, May 13, 1995. MD, Tehran U., 1987. Diplomate Am. Bd. Electrodiagnostic Medicine, Am. Bd. Psychiatry and Neurology. Asst. prof. neurology Tehran U. Med. Schs., 1991—93; intern in internal medicine U. Utah, Salt Lake City, 1996—97, resident in neurology, 1997—2000; neurologist Neurol. Assocs., American Fork, Utah, 2000—. Vis. prof. U. B.C., Vancouver, Canada, 1995—96; adj. prof. U. Utah, Salt Lake City, 2000—; co-investigator Eccles Inst. Human Genetics, Salt Lake City, 1999—. Contbr. articles to profl. jours. Recipient Specialist award, Iranian Ministry Health, 1992, Jasper prize, Can. Congress Neurol. Sci., 1995. Fellow: Am. Assn. Electrodiagnostic Medicine; mem.: AMA, Utah Med. Assn., Am. Acad. Neurology. Office: Neruol Assocs 52 N 1100 E American Fork UT 84003 Business E-Mail: metaher@msn.com.

ENTHOVEN, ALAIN CHARLES, economist, educator; b. Seattle, Sept. 10, 1930; s. Richard Frederick and Jacqueline E.; m. Rosemary Fenech, July 28, 1956; children: Eleanor, Richard, Andrew, Martha, Nicholas, Daniel. BA in Econs., Stanford U., 1952; M.Phil. (Rhodes scholar), Oxford (Eng.) U., 1954; PhD in Econs, MIT, 1956. Instr. econs. MIT, Cambridge, 1955-56; economist The RAND Corp., Santa Monica, Calif., 1956-60; ops. research asst. Office of Dir. Def. Research and Engring., Dept. Def., Washington, 1960; dep. comptroller, dep. asst. sec. U.S. Dept. Def., Washington, 1961-65, asst. sec. for systems analysis, 1965-69; v.p. for econ. planning Litton Industries, Beverly Hills, Calif., 1969-71; pres. Litton Med. Products, Beverly Hills, 1971-73; Marriner S. Eccles prof. pub. and pvt. mgmt. Grad. Sch. Bus. Stanford (Calif.) U., 1973-2000, prof. health care econs. Sch. Medicine, 1973-2000; sr. fellow Ctr. for Health Policy, Stanford U., 2000—. Cons. The Brookings Instn., 1956-60; vis. assoc. prof. econs. U. Wash., 1958; mem. Stanford Computer Sci. Adv. Com., 1968-73; cons. The RAND Corp., 1969— ; mem. vis. com. in econs. MIT, 1971-78; mem. vis. com. on environ. quality lab. Calif. Inst. Tech., 1972-77; mem. Inst. Medicine, Nat. Acad. Scis., 1972— ; mem. vis. com. Harvard U. Sch. Pub. Health, 1974-80; cons. Kaiser Found. Health Plan, Inc., 1973— ; vis. prof. U. Paris, 1985, London Sch. Hygiene and Tropical Medicine, 1998-99; vis. fellow St. Catherine's Coll., Oxford U., Eng., 1985, New Coll., 1998-99; dir. Hotel Investors Trust, 1986-87, PCS Inc., 1987-90, Caresoft, 1996-2002, Rx Intelligence, 2000—, eBenX Inc, 2001-03. Contbr. numerous articles on def. spending and on econs. and pub. policy in health care to profl. jours.; author: (with K. Wayne Smith) How Much is Enough? Shaping the Defense Program 1961-69, 1971, Health Plan: The Only Practical Solution to the Soaring Cost of Medical Care, 1980; editor (with A. Myrick Freeman III) Pollution, Resources and the Environment, 1973, Theory and Practice of Managed Competition in Health Care Finance, 1988, In Pursuit of an Improving National Health Service, 1999. Bd. dirs. Georgetown U., Washington, 1968-73, Jackson Hole Group, 1993-96; bd. regents St. John's Hosp., Santa Monica, 1971-73; chmn. Gov's Taskforce Managed Health Care Improvement, 1997-98, vis. com. Harvard U. Kennedy Sch. Govt., 1998-2003. Recipient President's award for disting. fed. civilian svc., 1963, Disting. Pub. Svc. medal Dept. Def., 1968, Baxter prize for health svcs. rsch., 1994, Bd. Dirs.' award Healthcare Fin. Mgmt. Assn., 1995, Ellwood award Found. for Accountability, 1998, Rock Carling fellow, Nuffield Trust, 1999 Mem. Am. Assn. Rhodes Scholars, Am. Acad. Arts and Scis., Integrated Healthcare Assn. (bd. dirs. 1999—), Phi Beta Kappa. Home: 1 McCormick Ln Atherton CA 94027-3033 Office: Stanford Univ Grad Sch Business Stanford CA 94305-5015 E-mail: enthoven@stanford.edu.

ENTMAN, ROBERT MATHEW, communications educator, consultant; b. Bklyn., Nov. 7, 1949; s. Bernard and Rose (Jacobson) E.; m. Francie Seymour, June 1, 1979; children: Max, Emily. AB, Duke U., 1971; PhD, Yale U., 1977; M in Pub. Policy, U. Calif., Berkeley, 1980. Asst. prof. Dickinson Coll., Carlisle, Pa., 1975-77, Duke U., Durham, N.C., 1980-89; postdoctoral fellow U. Calif., 1978-80; assoc. prof. comm. Northwestern U., Evanston, Ill., 1989-94; prof. comm. N.C. State U., Raleigh, 1994—, dir. Ctr. for Info. Tech. and Policy, 1999—. Adj. prof. U. N.C., Chapel Hill, 1995-98; Lombard vis. prof. Harvard U., 1997; cons. subcom. on telecom. U.S. Ho. of Reps., Washington, 1982, Nat. Telecom. and Info. Adminstrn., Washington, 1984-85, Aspen Inst., Washington and Aspen, Colo., 1986—; mem. working group Commn. on TV Policy, 1990-96; guest scholar Woodrow Wilson Ctr., Washington, 1989. Author: Democracy without Citizens, 1989, (monograph) Blacks in the News, 1991, Diversifying Broadcast Media, 1998, The Black Image in the White Mind, 2000; co-author: Media Power Politics, 1981; co-editor Mediated Politics: Communication in the Future of Democracy, 2000, (book series) Communication, Society and Politics, 1998—; also articles. Recipient McGannon award for comm. policy rsch., 1993, Mott award, 2000, Lane award, 2000, Goldsmith Book prize, 2002; rsch. grantee Markle Found., 1984, 86, 88, 95, Chgo. Cmty. Trust, 1989-92, 95-97; rsch. fellow Ameritech., 1989-90. Mem. Am. Polit. Sci. Assn. (coun. polit. comm. sec. 1990-91, mem. editl. bd. Polit. Comm. 1992—, mem. editl. bd. Jour. Comm. 1994-98, mem. editl. bd. Comm. Law and Policy 1994-2002, sec.-treas. polit. comm. sec. 1996-99, vice chair 1999-2000, chair 2000-01), Social Sci. Rsch. Coun. (mem. working group on media and fgn. policy 1990-93). Avocations: wine collecting and tasting, tennis. Office: NC State U Dept Comm PO Box 8104 Raleigh NC 27695-8104

ENTORF, RICHARD CARL, retired management consultant; b. Gettysburg, S.D., Feb. 11, 1929; s. Carl Luke and Violet (Carr) E.; m. Dorothy Ann Alexander, Nov. 23, 1951; children: Mark, Kimberly. BS, U. Calif. at Berkeley, 1952. Methods engr. Boeing Aircraft Corp., 1957; successively prodn. mgr., dir. mfg., v.p. ops., v.p., gen. mgr., pres. Riverside Cement Co. div. Amcord, Inc., Los Angeles, 1957-75; successively v.p., gen. mgr. Fla. div., sr. v.p. Gen. Portland Inc., Dallas, 1975-81; sr. v.p. Fla. Crushed Stone Co., Leesburg, Fla., 1982-84, pres., 1984-89; pvt. practice mgmt. cons. Leesburg, 1989-99; retired, 1999. Served with USAF, 1953-57. Home: 17 Juniper Knoll Ln Kennebunkport ME 04046-6323 E-mail: dentorf1@aol.com.

ENTREMONT, PHILIPPE, conductor, pianist; b. Rheims, France, June 7, 1934; came to U.S., 1953; s. Jean and Renée (Monchamps) E.; m. Andree Ragot, Dec. 21, 1955; children: Félicia, Alexandre. Student, Conservatoire National Superieur de Musique, Paris, Jean Doyen. Founder, artistic dir. Santo Domingo Music Festival, 1997—. Profl. debut at 17, Barcelona, Am. debut at 19, Nat. Gallery, Washington, 1953, pianist-condr. debut Mostly Mozart Festival, N.Y.C, 1971; rec. artist CBS, Teldec, EMI, Schwann and ProArte records; guest condr. Pitts. Symphony, Royal Philharm. Orch. Nat. de France, Montreal Symphony, San Francisco Symphony, Phila. Orch., Detroit Symphony, numerous others; prin. condr. Netherlands Chamber Orch., 1993—; prin.-guest condr. Israel Chamber Orch., 1994-96, condr. laureate, 1996—; lifetime mus. dir. Vienna Chamber Orch., 1975-91, chief laureate, 1991—; mus. dir. New Orleans Symphony Orch., 1981-85, Denver Symphony, 1986-89, others; prin. guest condr. Shanghai Broadcasting Symphony Orch., 2002—. Decorated Officer of the Legion of Honor, Legion of Honor, Officer de l'Order National du Merite: Austrian First Class Cross of Honor for the Arts and Scis., Comdr. in Order of Arts and Letters, 1998; A finalist Queen Elizabeth of Belgium Internat. Concours, 1952; Grand Prix Marguerite Long-Jacques Thibaud Competition, 1953; Harriet Cohen Piano medal, 1953; 1st prize Jeunesses Musicales; Grand Prix du Disque, 1967, 68, 69, 70; Edison award, 1968; Nominee Grammy award, 1972. Former mem. Academie Internationale de Musique Maurice Ravel (pres. 1975-80) Office: care Audrey Michaels 122 E 76th St New York NY 10021-2833 E-mail: ampubrel@aol.com.

ENTRUP, MICHAEL HARRY, anesthesiologist; b. Jersey City, N.J., Aug. 12, 1957; BS, Boston Coll., 1979; MD, U. Medicine and Dentistry N.J., 1984. Diplomate Am. Bd. Anesthesiology, Nat. Bd. Med. Examiners. Staff anesthesiologist Lahey Clinic, Burlington, Mass., 1988—, dir., cardiac anesthesiology, 1990—2001, vice-chairman, dept. of anesthesiology, 2000—01, med. dir., oper. rm., 2001—, chmn., dept. anesthesiology, 2001—. Mem., hosp. bd. Lahey Clinic, Burlington, Mass., 2001—; asst. clin. prof. of anesthesiology Tufts U. Sch. Medicine, Boston, 1997—; physician bd. mem. Commonwealth of Mass. Bd. of Registration of Perfusion, Mass., 2001—; bd. dirs. Nat. Youth Leadership Forum in Medicine, 2000—; mem., critical care com. Lahey Clinic, Burlington, Mass., 1993—, chmn., blood utilization com., 1994—2001, vice chair, oper. rm. com., 2001—, mem., fin. and ops. com., 2000—, mem., grad. med. edn. com., 2001—. Contbr. articles to profl. jours. Mem./officer Palisades Pk. Vol. Ambulance Corps, Palisades Park, NJ, 1973—83; Eagle Scout Boy Scouts Am.; mem. Wayland Pub. Schools Found., Wayland, Mass., 1996—97; bd. dirs. Am. Heart Assn. (Mass. affiliate), 1995—97. Mem.: Mass. Med. Soc., N.J. Med. Sch. Alumni Assn., Mass. Anesthesia Coun. on Edn. (bd. dirs. 1991—2002, pres. 1995—97, v.p. 1994—95), Mass. Soc. Anesthesiologists (immediate past-pres. 2002—03, pres. 2001—02, pres.-elect 2000—01, v.p. 1999—2000, sec. 1997—99, dir. med. edn. 1996—2001), Am. Soc. Anesthesiologists (ho. of dels. 1999—2002). Office: Lahey Clinic 41 Mall Rd Burlington MA 01805 Office Fax: 781-744-2273. E-mail: michael.h.entrup@lahey.org.

ENTWISLE, DORIS ROBERTS, sociology educator; b. Wilbraham, Mass., Sept. 28, 1924; d. Charles Edwin and Helen (McMenigall) Roberts; m. George Entwisle, Aug. 31, 1946; children: Barbara, Beverly, George H.; m. 2d Donald Roberts, Nov. 12, 1993. BS, U. Mass., 1945; MS, Brown U., 1946; PhD, Johns Hopkins U., 1960. Postdoctoral fellow Social Sci. Research Council Johns Hopkins U., Balt., 1960-61, research assoc. edn. and elec. engring., 1961-64, part-time asst. prof., 1964-67, assoc. prof., 1967-71, prof. sociology and engring. sci., 1971-98, prof. emerita, 1998—2003, rsch. prof., 2003—. Mem. com. on child devel. and pub. policy NRC, 1982-87. Harvard vis. com. for sociology dept., 1986-91. Author: (with S.G. Doering) The First Birth, 1981, (with L.A. Hayduk) Early Schooling, 1982, (with K.L. Alexander and Susan Dauber) The Success of Failure, 1984, 2d edit., 2002, (with K.L. Alexander, L.S. Olson) Children, Schools and Inequality, 1997; editor: Sociology of Education, 1975-78; assoc. editor Am. Sociol. Rev., 1972-75, 95-98; co-editor Jour. Rsch. in Adolescence, 1990-94. Guggenheim fellow, 1976-77 Fellow

APA, Am. Sociol. Assn. (chair sect. children); mem. Am. Ednl. Rsch. Assn., Soc. Rsch. in Child Devel. (pub. com. 1987-93, chair 1989-91, governing coun. 1993-99). Office: Johns Hopkins U 530 Mergenthaler Baltimore MD 21218 E-mail: entwisle@jhu.edu.

ENTWISTLE, ANDREW JOHN, lawyer, consultant; b. Rockville Centre, N.Y., Apr. 13, 1959; s. Michael Joseph and Frances (Deluca) E. BA in Govt. and Internat. Relations, U. Notre Dame, 1981; JD, Syracuse U., 1984. Bar: N.Y. 1985, N.J. 1986, U.S. Dist. Ct. (ea. and so. dists.) N.Y. 1986, U.S. Ct. Appeals (2d cir.) 1986, U.S. Dist. Ct. N.J. 1987, U.S. Ct. Appeals (3d cir.) 1989, U.S. Dist. Ct. (no. dist.) N.Y. 1993, U.S. Supreme Ct. 1993, Ill. 2001, D.C. 2002. Assoc. D'Amato & Lynch, N.Y.C., 1984—86, Wilson, Elser, Moskowitz, Edelman & Dicker, N.Y.C., 1986—89, Mudge Rose Guthrie Alexander & Ferdon, N.Y.C., 1989—91; ptnr., chmn. litigation dept. Wohl & Entwistle, LLP, N.Y.C., 1992—98. Mng. ptnr. Entwistle & Cappucci LLP, N.Y.C., 1998—; dir. PetroChemNet, Inc., 1997-98, Globalnet Venture Ptnrs., LLC, 1999, CheMatch, Inc., 1998; chmn. Network Buddy, Inc., 2000—; spl. mediator U.S. Bankruptcy Ct. for So. Dist. N.Y.; N.E. regional editor (jour.) The Bus. Suit, Def. Rsch. Inst., 1997-2001. Exec. com. Bd. Cath. Big Bros. of N.Y., 1995-98, dir., 1998-; mem. Housing Bd. Town of North Salem, N.Y., 1996-2000; chmn. Sports Buddies, Inc., 1998—; dir. Linden Hill Sch., 2001—. Mem. ABA, N.Y. Bar Assn., N.J. Bar Assn., Ill. State Bar Assn., D.C. Bar Assn., Assn. Trial Lawyers Am., Nat. Assn. Pension Plan Attys., Coun. Instnl. Investors (edn. sustainer), Nassau County Bar Assn., N.Y. Trial Lawyers Assn., Westchester County Bar Assn., Assn. Bar City N.Y., Fed. Bar Coun., Def. Rsch. Inst. Avocations: golf, whitewater kayaking, skiing, fly fishing, mountaineering. Office: 299 Park Ave New York NY 10171 Home: 1 Old Katonah Dr Katonah NY E-mail: aentwistle@entwistle-law.com.

ENTY, RICHARD MCDOUGALD, rail transportation administrator; b. Pittsburgh, Pa., May 20, 1953; s. Dorothy (McDougald) and Frank Edward Enty; m. Deborah Cooper, Aug. 8, 1987; children: Lauren Artha, Richard Douglass McDougald, Terricha Marie Bradley. BA, U. of Pa., 1975; MPA, Cleve. State U., 1996. Light rail operator Greater Cleve. Regional Transit Authority, 1978—83, transp. planner, 1978—83, rail adminstr., 1983—89, long range planner, 1989—2001, planning team leader, 2001—. Mem. & sec. of bd. of trustees Cuyahoga Valley Scenic RR, Penninsula, Ohio, 1996—; mem., environ. justice task force Transp. Rsch. Bd., Washington, 2002—. Pres. North Coast Chpt., Tuskegee Airmen, Inc., Cleve., 1996—2003; mem., bd. of directors & chair, devel. com. Tuskegee Airmen, Inc., Arlington, Va., 2003—. Mem.: Regional Sci. Assn. (assoc.), Smithsonian Nat. Air & Space Mus. (assoc.), Aircraft Owners & Pilots Assn. (assoc.). D-Conservative. Catholic. Avocations: bicycling, travel, flying, public transit, passenger railroads. Home: 1915 East 89th St Cleveland OH 44106-2007 Office: Greater Cleveland Regional Transit Auth 1240 West 6th St Cleveland OH 44113 Office Fax: 216-771-4424. Personal E-mail: rmenty@mail.multiverse.com. E-mail: renty@gcrta.org.

ENTZI, JOHN A. music educator; b. Drexel, N.C., July 17, 1952; s. Edward Paul and Claudia (Setzer) Entzi; m. Karen Russell, Jan. 4, 1989. BME, U. N.C.-Greensboro, 1974; MA, Appalachian State U., 1978; D of Musical Arts, U. S.C.-Columbia, 1999. Dir. Concert Bands and Jazz Ensembles N.C. State U., Raleigh. Mem.: N.C. Bandmasters Assn., Music Educators N.C., Nat. Band Assn., Internat. Trumpet Guild, Internat. Assn. Jazz Educators. Home: 455 St Jiles Dr Clayton NC 27540 Office: NC State Univ Bands Campus Box 7311 Raleigh NC 27695*

ENTZMINGER, JOHN NELSON, JR., federal agency administrator, electronic engineer, researcher; b. Memphis, Dec. 17, 1936; s. John Nelson and Josephine Chambers (Marshall) Entzminger; m. Nancy May Burg, Sept. 9, 1961; children: David Marshall, Rebecca Louise. BSEE magna cum laude, U. S.C., 1959; MSEE, Syracuse U., 1968. Elec. engr. Bell Telephone Labs., Winston-Salem, N.C., 1959; project engr. Rome Air Devel. Ctr., Griffiss AFB, N.Y., 1960-66, sect. chief, communications, 1966-73, br. chief, communications and control, 1973-81, tech. dir. intelligence and reconnaissance, 1981-83; dir. tactical tech. Def. Advance Rsch. Project Agy., Washington, 1983-91, chief advanced tech., 1991-95; sr. staff mem. Inst. for Def. Analyses, Alexandria, Va., 1996-98; dep. for technology Def. Airborne Reconnaissance Office, Washington, 1996-98; pres. Entzminger Assocs. Consulting Firm, 1998—. Contbr. articles to profl jours. Elder Christian Assembly, Vienna, Va., 1985—. Fellow: IEEE, AIAA (assoc.); mem.: Phi Beta Kappa, Tau Beta Pi. Republican. Achievements include patents in field. Avocations: flying, carpentry, mechanics, skiing. Home: 3203 Dominy Ct Oakton VA 22124-2008 E-mail: jentzminger@ieee.org.

ENYEART, JAMES L. museum director; b. Auburn, Wash., Jan. 13, 1943; s. Lyle F. and Emma A. (Ham) E.; m. Roxanne Enyeart Malone, Sept. 7, 1964; children: Mara, Sascha, Megan. BFA, Kansas City Art Inst., 1965; MFA, U. Kans., 1972. Dir. Albrecht Gallery Art, St. Joseph, Mo., 1967-68; curator photography, assoc. prof. Spencer Mus. Art, U. Kans., 1968-76; exec. dir. Friends of Photography, Carmel, Calif., 1976-77; dir., adj. prof. art Ctr. for Creative Photography, U. Ariz., 1977-89; dir. Internat. Mus. Photography at George Eastman House, Rochester, N.Y., 1989-95; Anne and John Marion prof., dir. Marion Ctr. Photo. Art Coll. Santa Fe, 1995—. Mem. numerous panels, adv. bds. and commns. in field, including peer panel Nat. Endowment for Arts, Mus. Challenge Grants, 1993; adv. bd. Am. Photography Inst., NYU, 1991—; others; cons. in field. Author: Creative Camera, 1976, Francis Bruguiere, 1977, Jerry Uelsmann: Twenty-Five Years, A Retrospective, 1982, Edward Weston's California Landscapes, 1984 (Am. Inst. Graphic Arts award), Land, Sky, and All That Is Within: Visionary Photographers of the Southwest, 1998, The Nature of Photographs, 1998, Harmony of Reflected Light: The Photographs of Arthur Wesley Dow, 2001, Photographer, Writer, and the American Scene, 2002, others; (with R.D. Monroe, Philip Stokes) Three Classic American Photographs: Texts and Contexts, 1982; contbr. Edward Weston Omnibus, 1984, Contemporary Photographers, 1983, 2d rev. edit., 1986-87; editor: Decade by Decade: A Survey of Twentieth Century American Photography, 1989; co-editor: Henry Holmes Smith: Collected Writings 1935-1985, 1986; contbr. introductions to Andreas Feininger: A Retrospective, 1986, Aaron Siskind: Terrors and Pleasures, 1931-1980, 1982, W. Eugene Smith: Master of the Photographic Essay, 1981, Landscapes 1975-1979, 1981, Photography of the Fifties: An American Perspective, 1980, George Fiske, Yosemite Photographer, 1980, Peekamoose, 1973; editor Kans. Album, 1977, Heinecken, 1980, The Archive, 1988, Image, 1989—; designer print study rm. Spencer Mus. Art, U. Kans., 1976, Ctr. Creative Photography, U. Ariz., 1989; author, curator exhbn. Judy Dater: Twenty Years; represented in collections Albrecht Gallery, St. Joseph, Mo., Mus. Art, U. Kans., Bibliotheque Nationale, Paris, Internat. Mus. Photography at George Eastman House, Rochester, Sheldon Meml. Gallery, Lincoln, Nebr., Nat. Mus. Am. Art; numerous other publs. Commr. Kans. Arts Commn., 1973-74; selection com. Ariz. Gov.'s Arts Awards, 1984; creative arts award com. Brandeis U., Waltham, Mass., 1990—; adv. bd. Aaron Siskind Found., 1981—, W. Eugene Smith Meml. Fund, Inc., 1983—; nom. com. MacArthur Found., 1982; rev. panel Bush Found. Fellowships, St. Paul, 1980. Recipient Josef Sudek medal Ministry Culture, Union Visual Arts, Czechoslovakia, 1989, Photokina Obelisk award, Fed. Republic Germany, 1982, Internat. Achievement award Photographic Soc. Japan, 1994, others; grantee NEA, 1973, 74, 75; Hon. Rsch. fellow U. Exeter, 1974, OAS fellow, 1966-67, John Simon Guggenheim Meml. fellow, 1987; fellow John S. and James L. Knight Found. Nat. Millennium Survey, 1998; named 100 Most Important People in Photography Am. Photo, 1998; grantee Nat. Endowment for the Arts, 1973—; other awards in field. Mem. Am. Assn. Art Mus. Dirs., Am. Assn. Art Mus., Am. Photography Inst. (adv. bd. 1991—), Am. Photog. Hist. Soc. (hon. life), Oracle (co-founder), Deutschen Gesellschaft fur Photographie (hon. mem.), others. Office: Coll Santa Fe Marion Ctr Photographic Art 1600 Saint Michaels Dr Santa Fe NM 87505-7615

ENYEDY, GUSTAV, JR., chemical engineer; b. Cleve., Aug. 23, 1924; s. Gustav and Mary (Silay) E.; m. Zoe Agnes Zachlin, Aug. 25, 1956 (div.); children: Louise Elaine, Roseann Marie, Arthur Gustav, Lillian Alice, Edward Anthony; m. Barbara Martha Ludwig Holley, May 9, 1987. BS in Chem. Engring., Case Inst. Tech., 1950, MS, 1955. Registered profl. engr., Ohio. Engr., Rayon Tech. div. E.I. duPont, Richmond, Va., 1950-51; project engr. Grasselli Chem. Div., Cleve., 1951-54; devel. engr. Diamond Alkali (Soda Products), Painesville, Ohio, 1954-60; process engr. Central Engring., Cleve., 1960-61, staff engr. research dept. Painesville, 1961-65, supr. computer services, 1965-68; mgr. Diamond Shamrock Corp., Painesville, 1968-73; engring. cons., 1973-85; pres. PDQS, Inc., 1975—. Lectr. chem. engring. Fenn Coll., Cleve., 1957-61, Cleve. State U., 1975-76 Contbr. articles to tech. jours., textbooks. Treas., cubmaster, chmn. Gates Mills Cub Scout Pack, 1970-71, 75-78. Served with AUS, 1943-46. Decorated Bronze Star medal, Combat Inf. badge. Fellow Am. Inst. Chem. Engrs., Am. Assn. Cost Engrs. (tech. v.p. 1966-68, pres. 1969-70, speakers' bur. program 1971-89, O.T. Zimmerman Founder's award and hon. life mem., 1992); mem. Hungarian Geneal. Soc. of Greater Cleve. (founder 1996), Tau Beta Pi, Pi Delta Epsilon. Home and Office: 7830 Sugarbush Ln Gates Mills OH 44040-9317 *Do each job with complete integrity. Do not gain favor by giving in to outside pressure to slant results.*

ENZEL, DAVID HOWARD, lawyer; b. Pitts., Jan. 21, 1955; s. Abram and Dora Enzel. BA, U. Pitts., 1976, JD, 1979. Bar: Pa. 1979, D.C. 1981. Chief atty. for fair housing enforcement HUD, Washington, 1979-91; spl. counsel Office of Thrift Supervision, Washington, 1991-2000; dep. asst. sec. for enforcement and programs HUD, Washington, 2000—. Mem. Phi Beta Kappa. Avocations: running, photography. Office: HUD Dep Asst Sec for Enforcement and Programs 451 7th St SW Washington DC 20410

ENZI, MICHAEL BRADLEY, senator, accountant; b. Bremerton, Wash., Feb. 1, 1944; s. Elmer Jacob and Dorothy (Bradley) E.; m. Diana Buckley, June 7, 1969; children: Amy, Bradley, Emily. BBA, George Wash. U., 1966; MBA, Denver U., 1968. Cert. profl. human resources, 1994. Pres. NZ Shoes, Inc., Gillette, Wyo., 1969-95, NZ Shoes of Sheridan, Inc., Wyo., 1983-96; acctg. mgr. Dunbar Well Svc., Inc., Gillette, 1985-97; mem. Wyo. Ho. of Reps., Cheyenne, 1987-91, Wyo. State Senate, Cheyenne, 1991-96; senator from Wyo. U.S. Senate, 1997—. Chmn. bd. dirs. 1st Wyo. Bank, Gillette, 1978-88; chmn. Senate Revenue Com., 1992-96. Mayor City of Gillette, 1975-82; pres. Wyo. Assn. Mcpls., Cheyenne, 1980-82. Sgt. Wyo. Air NG, 1967-73. Mem. Wyo. Order of DeMolay (state master councilor 1963-64), Wyo. Jaycees (state pres. 1973-74), Masons (Sheridan and Gillette lodges), Scottish Rite, Shriners, Lions, Sigma Chi. Republican. Presbyterian. Avocations: fishing, bicycling, soccer. Home: 431 Circle Dr Gillette WY 82716-4903 Office: US Senate 290 Russell Senate Bldg Washington DC 20510-0001 E-mail: senator@enzi.senate.gov.*

EODICE, MICHAEL THOMAS, aerospace engineer, biomedical engineer; b. Detroit, Sept. 28, 1954; s. Patrick Joseph and Joan Anna Eodice; m. Shamssi Shekarforoosh, Aug. 3, 1992. BA in Math., San Jose (Calif.) State U., 1990; MS in Engring. Mgmt., Stanford U., 1997, PhD in Mech. Engring., 2000. Space systems engr. GE, Moffett Field, Calif., 1984-86; control systems engr. Micro Craft Inc., Moffett Field, 1986-89; aircraft elec. systems engr. Sverdrup Tech., Inc., Moffett Field, 1989-92; STS-47 experiment mgr. NASA, Moffett Field, 1992-94, STS-90 experiment mgr., 1995-98, EMCS project mgr., 2000—. Contbr. articles to profl. jours., confs. Intertial navigation systems specialist Calif. Air N.G., Moffett Field, 1986-90; vol. for sci. U.S. Geol. Survey, Menlo Park, Calif., 1992-93; mem. Rep. Presdl. Task Force, Yuba City, Calif., 1982-83. With USAF, 1972-81. Decorated Air medal with 4 oak leaf clusters, USAF Commendation medal; recipient medal of merit Rep. Presdl. Task Force, 1982, Vol. Svc. award U.S. Geol. Survey, 1993, Bronze award Lincoln Design Competition, James F. Lincoln Arc Welding Co., 1999. Episcopalian. Avocations: travel, radio, flying, ice hockey. Office: NASA Ames Rsch Ctr Moffett Field CA 94035 Fax: (650) 604-0399. E-mail: meodice@mail.arc.nasa.gov.

EOM, SEAN BOCK, education educator, researcher; b. Korea (South), Jan. 9, 1949; s. Mahn Kyu Eom and Jong Ye Won; m. Soon Young Koh; children: Caroline Young, Alexander Sean. MBA, Seoul Nat. U., 1974—87; MS, U. of SC., 1978—80; PhD, U. of Nebr.- Lincoln, 1981—85. Asst. prof. Auburn U., 1985—89; assoc. prof. Mid. Tenn. State U., 1989—92; vis. prof. So. Ill. U., 2001; prof. SE Mo. State U., 1992—. Sr. editor, ency. of info. systems Academic Press, San Diego, 1998—. Mem. editl. bd. Jour. of Global Info. Tech. Mgmt., 1997—, Jour. of the Korea Indsl. Info. Systems Soc.; author: Decision Support Systems Research, 1999, Decision Support Systems Research and Its Reference Disciplines: A Research Guide to the Literature and an Unobtrusive Bibliography with Citation Frequency, 2003, Author Cocitation Analysis using Custom Bibliographical Databases - An Introduction to the SAS Systems, 2003; co-editor: Encyclopedia of Information Systems, 2002. Copper Dome Faculty fellow in rsch., Coll. of Bus., SE Mo. State U., 1998—2000, 1994—96. Mem.: Assn. for Info. Systems, The Inst. For Ops. Rsch. and Mgmt. Sciences, Decision Sci. Inst. Home: 3308 Lakewood Dr Cape Girardeau MO 63701 Office: Southeast Missouri State University 1 University Plaza Cape Girardeau MO 63701 Home Fax: 573-651-2992; Office Fax: 573-651-2992. Personal E-mail: sbeom@semovm.semo.edu. E-mail: sbeom@semovm.semo.edu.

EPCAR, RICHARD MICHAEL, actor, writer, director; b. Denver, Apr. 29, 1955; s. George Buck and Shirley (Learner) E.; m. Ellyn Jane Stern, Aug. 15, 1982; children: Jonathan Alexander, Jacqueline Elizabeth. BFA in Performing Arts, U. Ariz., 1978; postgrad., U. So. Calif., L.A., 1980, U. Calif., 1981, Am. Film Inst., 1982. Pres. Epcar Entertainment, LA, 1986—. Actor (films) including Memoirs of an Invisible Man, DC Collins, Incident of War, Street Hawk, Escape to Love, Not of This World, (TV series) Diagnosis Murder Columbo, Beverly Hills 90210, Cheers, General Hospital, Guns of Paradise, Matlock, Who's the Boss?, Sonny Spoons, Moonlighting, Highway to Heaven, Amazing Stories, Fast Times, Crazy Like a Fox, Hell Town, Stir Crazy, Santa Barbara, Days of our Lives, (animated series) Teknoman 2 Lead Voices; author 7 episodes, co-dir. Ghost in the Shell (film & lead voice- series), Transformers (co-author and lead voice), Digimon (dir. first season), Lupin the Third (dir. and lead voice), Robotech, Honey Bee Hutch, X-Men; dir. of Crimes of Father Amaro (acad. award nomination); dir and author, Widow of St. Pierre (acad. award nomination) Mostly Martha, Emperor and Assassin, Iron Monkey, Mission Kashmir, Shiri, Double Vision, and Omhyosi; co-dir., co-author, lead voice Eagle Riders, 2 lead voices Digimon, lead voice Flint; co-dir., co-author, lead voices Samurai X; (on stage) Why a Hero, Dracula, An Evening with Lincoln, Real Inspector Hound, Richard II; actor, writer (play) (on stage) The Vow, Take My Wife...Please!, 1980; wrote and directed English adaptation of Acad. award winning Cinema Paradisco, Belle Epoque (Acad. Award winner), Women on the Verge of a Nervous Breakdown (Acad. Award nomination), Eat Drink Man Woman (Acad. Award nominated), Fencing Master (Acad. Award nominated); dir. (for TV) A Cowboy Christmas. Mem. LA Zoo Assn., 1983-90, 91, 94, Natural History Mus., LA, 1989-91, Earth Save, LA, 1990, LA Mus. Art, 1991; host fall festival Sta. KCET-Pub. TV, LA, 1980; active Am. Cancer Soc. Recipient Haldeman Found. scholarship, U. Ariz., 1973-78; named Nat. Best Actor of Yr., Nat. Players, 1977, CPC Repertory Group, 1980; recipient Irene Ryan Soloist award, 1978. Avocations: weight lifting, tennis, music, art. E-mail: tallactor@aol.com.

EPEL, DAVID, biologist, educator; b. Detroit, Mar. 26, 1937; s. Jacob A. and Anna K. E.; m. Lois S. Ambush, Dec. 18, 1960; children: Andrea, Sharon, Elissa. AB, Wayne State U., 1958; PhD, U. Calif.-Berkeley, 1963. Postdoctoral fellow Johnson Research Found., U. Pa., 1963-65; asst. prof. Hopkins Marine Sta., 1965-70; assoc. prof., then prof. Scripps Instn. Oceanography, 1970-77; Jane and Marshall Steel Jr. prof. marine scis. Hopkins Marine Sta., Stanford U., Pacific Grove, Calif., 1977—; acting dir. Hopkins Marine Sta., Pacific Grove, 1984—88. Co-dir. embryology course Marine Biol. Lab, Woods Hole, 1974—77. Mem. editl. bd. Acta Histochemica, Biol. Bull, Zygote. Bd. dirs. Rsch. Inst., Monterey Bay Aquarium, 1987-89, trustee, 1985-88. Guggenheim fellow, 1976-77, Overseas fellow Churchill Coll., Cambridge, Eng., 1976-77; recipient Allen Cox medal for fostering excellence in undergrad. rsch. Stanford U., 1995. Fellow AAAS (mem.-at-large, sect. G 1979-84, chmn. sect. on biol. scis. 1998—), Calif. Acad. Scis.; mem. Am. Soc. Cell Biology (mem. council 1978-80), Soc. Devel. Biology, Internat. Soc. Devel. Biology, Soc. Integrative and Comparative Biology (chairperson devel. and cell biology sect. 1990-92). Home: 25847 Carmel Knolls Dr Carmel CA 93923-8845 E-mail: depel@stanford.edu.

EPHRON, NORA, writer, director; b. N.Y.C., May 19, 1941; d. Henry and Phoebe (Wolkind) E.; m. Dan Greenburg (div.); m. Carl Bernstein (div.); children: Jacob, Max; m. Nicholas Pileggi. BA, Wellesley Coll., 1962. Reporter N.Y. Post, 1963-68; free-lance writer, 1968—; contbg. editor, columnist Esquire mag., 1972-73, sr. editor, columnist, 1974-78; contbg. editor N.Y. mag., 1973-74. Author: Wallflower at the Orgy, 1970, Crazy Salad, 1975, Scribble Scribble, 1978, Heartburn, 1983, Nora Ephron Collected, 1991; screenwriter: (with Alice Arlen) Silkwood (nominated Acad. award for best original screenplay), 1983, Heartburn, 1986, Cookie, 1989, When Harry Met Sally (nominated Acad. award, BAFTA award for best screenplay), 1989, My Blue Heaven, 1990; dir., screenwriter (with Delia Ephron) This Is My Life, 1992, Mixed Nuts, 1994, Michael, 1996, You've Got Mail, 1998; co-screenwriter, dir. Sleepless in Seattle (nominated Acad. award for best original screenplay), 1993; prodr., dir. Lucky Numbers, 2000; screenwriter, prodr. Hanging Up, 2000; playwright Imaginary Friends, 2002. Mem. Writers Guild Am., Authors Guild, Dirs. Guild of Am., Acad. Motion Picture Arts and Scis.*

EPHROSS, PAUL HULLMAN, social work educator; b. Boston, Oct. 22, 1935; s. Israel Wolfson and Bessie (Hullman) E.; m. Joan Ettinger, 1959; children: Sara Anne, Peter Joseph, David Benjamin; m. Joan Weiss, Dec. 30, 1990. AB, Harvard Coll., 1955; M in Social Work, Boston U., 1957; PhD, U. Chgo., 1969. Lic. cert./clin. social worker, Md.; qualified expert witness. Social worker Jewish Community Ctr., Boston, 1957-59; social worker, social work adminstr. Jewish Community Ctrs., Chgo., 1959-66; lectr. Chgo. City Coll., 1966-68; instr. Loyola U., Chgo., 1967-68; from asst. prof. to assoc. prof. U. Md., Balt., 1968-74, prof. social work, 1974—, clin. prof. psychiatry, 1989-94, dir. PhD program, 1976-81; psychotherapist, cons. Md. Sexuality Resource Ctr., Balt., 1987-93; adj. prof. Balt. Hebrew U., 1998—2001. Cons. Md. State Dept. Edn., Balt. city and various other Md. counties, 1970-94, Juvenile Svcs. Agy. State of Md., Balt., 1972-82, Associated Cath. Charities, Inc., Balt., 1975-76, Nat. Assn. Social Workers, Silver Spring, Md., 1985-87, Md. State Dept. Health and Mental Hygiene, 1989—. Co-author: Working Effectively with Administrative Groups, 1987, Groups that Work, 1988, 2d edit., 2004, Human Behavior Theory and Social Work Practice, 1991, Group Work With Populations at Risk, 1997, 2d edit., 2003, Ethnicity and Social Work Practice. 1998; co-editor: Group Work: Expanding Horizons, 1993; contbr. articles to profl. jours. Bd. dirs. Balt. Hebrew Congregation, 1969-71, Associated Jewish Charities, Inc., Balt., 1980-84, Balt. Jewish Cmty. Rels. Coun., 1984-98; mem. Amateur Chamber Music Players, 1965-94. Named Alumnus of Yr., Sch. of Social Work, Boston U., 1984; rsch. and tng. grantee fed. & State of Md. agencies, 1977-92. Mem. Nat. Assn. Social Workers, Coun. on Social Work Edn., Assn. for the Advancement of Social Work with Groups (bd. dirs. 1987-93, sec. 1989-93), Soc. for the Scientific Study of Sex, Am. and Eastern Sociol. Assns., U. Club (bd. dirs. Balt. 1987-93), Democrat. Jewish. Avocations: chamber music (flute, piano), jewish & european history, boston red sox. Office: 525 W Redwood St Baltimore MD 21201-1705 E-mail: PEPHROSS@SSW.UMARYLAND.EDU.

EPLEE, ROBERT EUGENE, geophysicist; b. Morehead, Ky., Nov. 20, 1958; s. Robert Eugene and Mary Mullins Eplee. BS in Physics, U. N.C., 1981; PhD in Planetary Scis., U. Ariz., 1987. Postdoctoral rsch. fellow U. Ariz., Tucson, 1987—88; assoc. scientist Applied Rsch. Corp., Landover, Md., 1988—89, Gen. Scis. Corp., Laurel, Md., 1989—92; rsch. scientist Sci. Applications Internat. Corp., Beltsville, Md., 1992—. Asst. dist. commr. Nat. Capital Area Coun., Boy Scouts Am., Bethesda, Md., 1992—2002, dist. commr., 2002—; elder Laurel (Md.) Presbyn. Ch., 1990. Recipient Group Achievement award, NASA, 1990, 1993, 1999, Pub. Svc. Group Achievement award, 2001, Silver Beaver award, Nat. Capital Area coun. Boy Scouts Am., 2002, Eagle Scout award, Boy Scouts Am., 1976; Grad. Student Rschrs. fellow, NASA, 1985—87. Mem.: Am. Geophys. Union. Democrat. Presbyterian. Achievements include research in Calibration Scientist for the SeaWiFS Project at NASA Goddard Space Flight Center. Home: 407 Carroll Ave Laurel MD 20707-4220 Office: SAIC Code 970-2 NASA Goddard Space Flight Ctr Greenbelt MD 20771

EPLER, GARY ROBERT, physician, author, educator; b. Chico, Calif., Apr. 5, 1944; s. Deane Chandler and Kathryn Louise (McNeil) E.; m. Joan Susan Weidman, Sept. 10, 1983; children: Gregory C., Brett H. MD, Tulane U., 1971; MPH, Harvard U., 1978. Diplomate in internal medicine and pulmonary medicine Am. Bd. Internal Medicine. Intern Harlem Hosp., Columbia U., 1971-72; resident U. Hosp., Boston, 1974-76, pulmonary medicine fellowship, 1975-78; asst. prof. medicine Sch. Medicine Boston U., 1978-85, assoc. clin. prof. medicine, 1985-96, Harvard U., Boston, 1995—; med. dir. respiratory therapy, chmn. dept. medicine New England Bapt. Hosp., Boston, 1983-98, med. dir. rehab. unit, 1983-98. Parasitology rsch. fellow Tulane U., Cali, Colombia, 1969-70, USPHS, Ctrs. Disease Control, 1972-74; tuberculosis cons. CDC Vietnamese Refugee Camps, Eglin AFB, Fla. and Indiantown Gap, Pa., 1975, Cuban Refugee Camp, Indiantown Gap, 1980; med. cons. CDC, Vietnamese Refugee Programs in Hong Kong, Thailand, Philippines, Malaysia, Indonesia; vis. attending physician U. Hosp., Boston City Hosps. and Boston VA Hosp., 1978-98, Brigham and Women's Hosp., Boston, 1999—; med. dir. Occupational Health Ctr., Wilmington, Mass; vis. prof. Kyoto (Japan) U., 1990; many others. Author book on diseases of bronchioles, 1994; editor book on occupational lung diseases; editl. reviewer New England Jour. Medicine, Annals of Internal Medicine, Jour. AMA, Am. Rev. Respiratory Diseases, Chest, Jour. Respiratory Medicine, Jour. Western Medicine, Jour. Rheumatology, European Respiratory Jour.; contbr. chpts. to books, more than 85 articles to sci. jours. Lt. comdr. USPHS, 1972-74. Recipient cert. of appreciation Am. Lung Assn. Mass.; named one of Outstanding Med. Specialists in U.S., Town and Country Mag., 1989. Fellow ACP, Am. Coll. Chest Physicians (chmn. com. on occupational and environ. health 1987-88, v.p. New England States chpt. 1989-91, pres. chpt. 1991-93); mem. AMA (alt. del. 1987-93), Am. Soc. Law and Medicine (treas. 1983-85, Disting. Svc. award 1985), Am. Coll. Physician Execs., Mass. Thoracic Soc. (mem. coun. 1980-84, sec.-treas. 1984-85, pres. 1986-88), Mass. Med. Soc. Office: Brigham and Women's Hosp Pulmonary/Critical Care Med 75 Francis St Boston MA 02115-6106

EPLEY, LEWIS EVERETT, JR., lawyer; b. Ft. Smith, Ark., Apr. 28, 1936; s. Lewis Everett and Evelyn (Wood) E.; m. Donna Louise Swopes, Feb. 24, 1962. BS, JD, U. Ark., 1961. Bar: Ark. 1961. Formerly practiced in Eureka Springs, Ark.; city atty., 1969-71; chmn. bd. Bank of Eureka Springs, Ark., 1990-93, vice-chmn., 1993—, also bd. dirs. Del. Ark. Constl. Conv., 1969-70; apptd. spl. assoc. justice Ark. Supreme Ct., 1984. Mem. Ark. Bldg. Svcs. Coun., 1975-80, chmn., 1976-78; mem. Carroll County Cen. Dem. Com., 1964-68; bd. dirs. Eureka Springs Ozark Folk Festival, 1964-69, Ark. Cancer Rsch. Ctr., N.W. Ark. Radiation Therapy Inst., 1984-91, pres. bd. dirs., 1989; chmn. adv. bd. Eureka Springs Mcpl. Hosp., 1963-71; mem. Beaver Lake Adv. Com., 1982-89; trustee U. Ark., 1989-99, chmn. bd. trustees, 1996-98; bd. dirs. U. Ark. Found., 1994—, Mashburn Scholarship Found., 1993-2002; past dir. Washington Regional Med. Found.; mem. Carroll County Com. for Study of Long-Term Health Care Needs, 1990-93; mem. devel. coun. Eureka Springs Hosp., 1997-2001. Fellow Ark. Bar Assn. (del. 1975-78), Am. Inns of Ct. (mem. emeritus W. B. Putnam chpt. 1990-97), Carroll County Bar Assn. (past pres.), Eureka Springs C. of C. (dir., past pres.), Fayetteville Rotary Club, Phi Alpha Delta, Kappa Kappa Psi. Baptist. Home: 2805 Brandon Cir Fayetteville AR 72703

EPLING, RICHARD LOUIS, lawyer; b. Waukegan, Ill., Aug. 16, 1951; s. Carrol Franklin and Mary Teresa Epling; m. Suzanne Braley, Aug. 4, 1973. BA in English and History magna cum laude, Duke U., 1973; JD, U. Mich., 1976. Bar: Ill. 1977, U.S. Dist. Ct. (no. dist.) Ill. 1977, U.S. Ct. Appeals (7th cir.) 1979, Ariz. 1981, U.S. Dist. Ct. Ariz. 1981, U.S. Ct. Appeals (9th cir.) 1982, N.Y. 1988, U.S. Ct. Appeals (2d cir.) 1988, U.S. Dist. Ct. (ea. and so. dists.) N.Y. 1989. Law clk. to presiding justice Mich. Supreme Ct., Southfield, 1976-77; assoc. Katten, Muchin & Zavis, Chgo., 1977-81; ptnr. Brown & Bain, P.A., Phoenix, 1981-88, Sidley & Austin, N.Y.C., 1988-92, Pillsbury Winthrop LLP and predecessor firm, N.Y.C., 1992—. Assoc. conferee Nat. Bankruptcy Conf., Washington, 1985-93. Contbr. articles to profl. jours. Mem. Am. Bankruptcy Inst., Phi Beta Kappa. Office: Pillsbury Winthrop LLP One Battery Park Plz New York NY 10004

EPP, DIANNE NAOMI, secondary educator; b. Yankton, S.D., Oct. 1, 1939; d. Willard H. and Florence A. (Leigh) Waltner; m. Anthony R. Epp, Aug. 18, 1964; children: Alain-René Epp Weaver, Rachel Epp Buller. BA in Chemistry, Bethel Coll., 1961; MA, U. Mo., 1963; cert. etudes, L'Ecole d'Administration, Brussels, 1965. Chemistry instr. Bethel Coll., North Newton, Kans., 1963-64; sci. tchr. Ecole Secondaire, Sundi-Lutete, Zaire, 1965-67; rsch. chemist FMC Glass Lab., Golden, Colo., 1967-70; vis. instr. Nebr. Wesleyan U., Lincoln, 1973-74, 77-79, 1980-81; chemistry tchr. East High Sch., Lincoln, 1982-93, 94—; vis. scholar Miami U., Oxford, Ohio, 1993-94. Cons. NSF Doing Chemistry Videodisc, 1988; cons. small scale CD ROM Synapse Corp., Lincoln, 1993. Author: Chemical Manfacturing: The Process of Mixing, 2000,

Experimental Design: The Chemistry of Adhesives, 1998, Product Testing: The Chemistry of Ice Cream, 1998; cons. editor: Starting at Ground Zero, 1989; author: (monograph series) A Palette of Color, 1995; contbr. articles to profl. jours. Recipient Excellence in Teaching award Cooper Found., 1990, Excellence in High Sch. Chemistry Teaching award Am. Chem. Soc., 1990, 91, Presdl. award for Excellence in Sci. and Math. Teaching NSF, 1994, Kiewit Found. Tchg. award, 1997, 01. Mem. Nat. Sci. Tchrs. Assn. Office: East High Sch 1000 S 70th St Lincoln NE 68510-4297

EPP, DONALD JAMES, economist, educator; b. Hastings, Nebr., June 23, 1939; s. Abram W. and Edith Elizabeth (Harrison) E.; m. Cathryn Jean Cronn, Dec. 10, 1961; children: Eric Alan, Amy Elizabeth. BS, U. Nebr., 1961; MS, Mich. State U., 1964, PhD, 1967. Instr. Mich. State U., East Lansing, 1965-67; asst. prof. agrl. econs. Pa. State U., University Park, 1967-71, assoc. prof., 1971-81, prof., 1981—2002, prof. emeritus, 2003—; asst. dir. Environ. Resources Rsch. Inst., 1981—2002. Cons. to environ. firms, state and fed. agys. Author: (with John W. Malone, Jr.) Introduction to Agricultural Economics, 1981; contbr. articles to profl. jours. and tech. pubs. Served with F.A., U.S. Army, 1961-62. Mem. NE Agrl. and Resource Econs. Assn. (pres. 1995-96), Sigma Xi, Gamma Sigma Delta. Home: 550 Brittany Dr State College PA 16803-1423 Office: Pa State U 105 Armsby Bldg University Park PA 16802-5600

EPP, ELDON JAY, religion educator; b. Mountain Lake, Minn., Nov. 1, 1930; s. Jacob Jay and Louise (Kintzi) E.; m. ElDoris Balzer, June 13, 1951; children: Gregory Thomas, Jennifer Elizabeth. AB magna cum laude, Wheaton Coll., 1952; BD magna cum laude, Fuller Theol Sem., 1955; STM, Harvard U., 1956, PhD, 1961. Spl. rsch. asst. Princeton Theol. Sem., 1961-62; vis. instr. Drew U. Theol. Sch., 1962; asst. prof. religion U. So. Calif. Grad. Sch. Religion, 1962-65, assoc. prof., 1965-67, assoc. prof. classics, 1966-68; assoc. prof. religion Case Western Res. U., Cleve., 1968-71, prof. religion, Harkness prof. bibl. lit., 1971-98, prof. emeritus, 1998—, dean humanities and social scis., 1977-85, dean emeritus, 1998—; acting dean Western Res. Coll., Cleve., 1984; chmn. dept. religion Case Western Res. U., Cleve., 1982-98. Lectr. Harvard Divinity Sch., 2001-02, vis. prof., 2002-03; Am. exec. com. Internat. Greek New Testament Project, 1968-88; mem. N.Am. Com., 1989—; mem. accreditation rev. coun. North Ctrl. Assn. Commn. on Insts. Higher Edn., 1986-90, mem. appeals panel, 1992-95, cons. evaluator corps, 1983-98; panelist NEH, 1978, 80, 90, 2000; reader John Simon Guggenheim Meml. Found., 1991-94; Kenneth W. Clark lectr. Duke U., 1986; Ratner lectr. Case Western Res. U., 1998; bd. dirs. New Testament Lang. Project, 1999—. Author: The Theological Tendency of Codex Bezae Cantabrigiensis in Acts, 1966; co-author: Studies in the Theory and Method of New Testament Textual Criticism, 1993; co-editor: New Testament Textual Criticism: Its Significance for Exegesis, 1981, The New Testament and Its Modern Interpreters, 1989; assoc. editor Jour. Bibl. Lit., 1971-90; editor Critical Rev. of Books in Religion, 1991-94, Studies and Documents, 1991-2001; mem. editl. bd. Soc. Bibl. Lit. Monograph Series, 1969-72, Soc. Bibl. Lit. Centennial Publs., 1975-86, Studies and Documents, 1971-2001, Critical Rev. of Books in Religion, 1987-94; exec. sec. Hermeneia: A Critical and Historical Commentary on the Bible, 1962—, mem. editl. bd., 1966—; contbr. more than 40 scholarly articles to profl. jours. Active Boy Scouts Am., 1975-78; Bd. mgrs. St. Paul's Episcopal Cathedral, L.A., 1964-68, clk., 1967-68. Harvard Faculty Arts and Scis. fellow, 1958-59, Rockefeller doctoral fellow in religion, 1959-60; postdoctoral fellow Claremont Grad. Sch., 1966-68; Guggenheim fellow, 1974-75; NEH grant, 1988. Mem. AAUP 1963-98(mem. chpt. exec. com. 1970 72), Am. Acad. Religion 1961-98(sect. pres. 1965-66), Soc. Bibl. Lit. (chmn. textual criticism seminar 1966, 71-84, mem. permanent Centennial com. 1975-80, mem. coun. 1980-82, 85-87, 2002-, del. Coun. on Study of Religion 1980-82, chair nominating com. 1985-87, mem. fin. com. 1997—, v.p. 2002, pres. 2003, chmn. com. on programs and initiatives 2003—), Studiorum Novi Testamenti Societas, Cath. Bibl. Assn., Am. Soc. Papyrologists, New Testament Colloquium (chmn. 1974), Soc. Mithraic Studies, Egypt Exploration Soc., Phi Beta Kappa. *Personal philosophy: Two essentials for life and livelihood are integrity and maturity. Integrity, in the abstract, is soundness, but in practical terms means incorruptibility, while maturity is basically the capacity to tolerate ambiguity. As individuals and as a society, we cannot afford to abandon integrity or to stifle maturity.*

EPP, GARRETT WAYNE, music educator; b. Reedley, Calif., July 4, 1944; s. William "Howard" and Verna Myrtle (Janzen) E. BA in Music Edn., Bethel Coll., 1967; MusM, M Sacred Music, So. Meth. U., 1975; Mus D, U. Mo., Kansas City, 1993. Cert. elem., secondary tchr., Ind., Kans. Choral dir. grades 4-12 Stockton (Kans.) Unified Sch. Dist., 1967-70; edn. coord./counselor/tchr. Mpls. City Workhouse, 1970-73; supr. music/choral dir. grades 7-12 South Adams Schs., Berne, Ind., 1975-88; pvt. voice tchr. part-time Shawnee Mission South H.S., Overland Park, Kans., 1990-91; artist-in-residence/pvt. voice instr. Paseo Acad. Fine & Performing Arts, Kansas City, Mo., 1991-93; adj. faculty, pvt. voice instr. Kansas City (Kans.) C.C., 1993; secondary choral coord., choral dir. Olathe (Kans.) North H.S., Olathe, 1993—. Profl. singer Kansas City (Mo.) Chorale, 1998—; profl. singer/sect. leader St. Michael's & All Angels Episcopal Ch., Overland Park, 2000—; dir. music Trinity United Meth. Ch., Kansas City (Kans.), 1989-93; founder, music dir. Kansas City Singers, 1991; guest conductor Kansas City Symphony Chorus, 1991. Ch. choir director various Kans., Ind. chs., 1966-93; founder, music dir. Stockton (Kans.) Cmty. Chorus, 1967-70; dir., conductor other singing groups, 1970-93; soloist with several major choruses; mem. chorus other groups. Recipient U. Mo. Kansas City Chancellor's Non-Resident award, 1988-90, Perkins Sch. Theology Tuition award, 1974-75, Bethel Coll. Music Theory assistantship, 1965-67. Mem. Internat. Fedn. Choral Music, Am. Choral Dirs. Assn., Music Educators Nat. Conf., Nat. Assn. Tchrs. of Singing, Nat. Educators Assn., Coll. Music Soc., Phi Kappa Phi, Pi Kappa Lambda. Mennonite. Achievements: one of 160 singers selected by audition from throughout the world to perform in Carnegie Hall with the Robert Shaw/Carnegie Hall Festival Chorus, 1990, 92, 94, 99. Office: Olathe North H S 600 E Prairie St Olathe KS 66061-3355 Business E-Mail: geppon@mail.olathe.k12.ks.us.

EPP, MARY ELIZABETH, technologies consultant; b. Buffalo, Aug. 7, 1941; d. John Conrad and Gertrude Marie (Murphy) Winkelman; m. Harry Francis Epp, Aug. 31, 1963. BA in Math., D'Youville Coll., 1963; MS in Math., Xavier U., 1970, MBA in Fin., 1981, MBA in Mktg., 1987. Registered provisional auditor, Ohio, 65. Systems analyst GE, Evendale, Ohio, 1965-71, Palm Beach Co., Cin., 1972-73; hardware systems engr. Procter & Gamble, Cin., 1973-76; systems engr. CalComp Inc., Anaheim, Calif., 1980-84; software engr. SDRC Inc., Cin., 1984-86; advanced systems project mgr. SAMI/Burke Mktg., Cin., 1986-89; ptnr., dir. strategic planning Info. Advantage, Inc., Cin., 1989-91; internat. product control specialist Cincom Systems Inc., Cin., 1991-94; corp. profl. svcs., mgr. methods & tools, prin. cons. Sybase, Inc., Cin., 1995—2002. Cons. Shelley & Sands, Zanesville, Ohio, 1983-85. Contbr. articles to profl. jours. Active Fairfield Charter Rev. Commn., 1981-83. Mem. AAUW (br. treas. 1975-79, state women's chair 1979 80, state treas. 1980-82), NAFE, IEEE, Assn. Computing Machinery (treas. Cin. chpt. 1987-88, pres. 1988-89, program co-chair 1989-90), Nat. Computer Graphics Assn., Nat. Fedn. Music (Ohio fedn. music parade chair 1979-81.), Mercy Hosp. Aux. Club (treas. 1978-79), Musical Arts Club. Republican. Roman Catholic. Avocations: bridge, skiing, music, fishing, travel, dog training and showing. Home: 4242 Stahlheber Rd Hamilton OH 45013-8941

EPPELE, DAVID LOUIS, columnist, author; b. Jersey City, Apr. 4, 1939; s. Joseph Anton and Lena Marie (Tadlock) E.; m. Gladys Emily Padilla (div. 1975); children: David D., Joseph E.; m. Geneva Mae Kirsch, July 7, 1977. Student, N.Mex. State U., 1958, U. N.Mex., 1966, U. Portland, 1972. Field botanist, SW Deserts and Mex., 1947—2003, N.Mex. Cactus Rsch., Belen, 1953-62; dir. Ariz. Cactus and Succulent Rsch., Bisbee, 1984—; editor Ariz. Cactus News, 1984—; columnist Western Newspapers, 1987—. Author (newspaper column) On the Desert, 1986—; author: On the Desert, 1991, On The Desert, vol. 2, 2000; editor: Index of Cactus Illustrations, 1990, Desert in Bloom, 1989. Mem. Mule Mountain Dem. Party, Bisbee, 1978—. With USN, 1958-59. Mem. AAAS, Cactus and Succulent Soc. Am., N.Mex. Acad. Sci., Bisbee C. of C. Avocations: photography, music. Home and Office: Ariz Cactus 8 S Cactus Ln Bisbee AZ 85603-6356

EPPELHEIMER, LINDA LOUISE, software educator; b. Ames, Iowa, Dec. 10, 1949; d. Allyn Francis and Ada Geraldine (Hough) Van Dyke; m. Donald Mark Eppelheimer, Mar. 10, 1973; children: Matthew Allyn, Carrie Louise. BS, Mich. State U., 1972; AD, We. Wis. Tech. Inst., La Crosse, Wis., 1984. Tchr. jr. high sch., Onalaska, Wis., 1973-74, LaCrescent (Minn.) High Sch., 1974-75; instr. adult edn. WWTI, 1974-84; from programmer mgr. tng. Winnebago Software Co., Caledonia, Minn., 1984—2000, mgr. tng., 2000—; ISO 9001 mgmt. rep., 1994—97. Contbr. chpt. to book and articles to profl. jours. Mem. Sch. Bd., LaCrescent, 1991-98, pres., 1994-97; leader 4-H Clubs, Houston County, Minn., 1985-95. Mem. ALA, Am. Soc. for Quality. Avocations: hiking, camping, gardening, birdwatching. Home: 1230 County Rd # 6 La Crescent MN 55947 Office: Sagebrush Corp 131 Bissen Street Caledonia MN 55921-1356

EPPEN, GARY DEAN, business educator; b. Austin, Minn., Apr. 28, 1936; s. Marldene Fredrick and Elsie Alma (Wendorf) E.; m. Ann Marie Sathre, June 14, 1958; children: Gregory, Peter, Paul, Amy. AA, Austin Jr. Coll., 1956; BS, U. Minn., 1958, MSIE, 1960; PhD, Cornell U., 1964; Hon. Doctorate, Stockholm Sch. Econs., 1998. Prof. mgmt. European Inst. Advanced Studies, Brussels, 1972-73; assoc. dean Grad. Sch. Bus., U. Chgo., 1969-75, prof. indsl. adminstrn., 1970—, assoc. dean Ph.D. studies, 1978-85, dir. internat. bus. exchange program, 1977-92, dir. Life Officers Investment Seminar, 1975-88, dir. Fin. Analysts Seminar, 1982-88, Robert Law prof., 1989-97, dir. exec. program, 1989-94, Keller Disting. Svc. prof., 1997-2001, dep. dean part-time programs, 1998-2001, dean emeritus, 2001—, Keller Disting. Svc. prof. emeritus, 2001—. Francqui prof. Cath. U. Leuven, Belgium, 1979; Urwitz vis. prof. Stockholm Sch. Econs., 1994; external examiner U. W.I., 1979-82; dir. Landauer, Inc., Hub Group, Inc., Hornet Capital, LLC. Author: (with F.J. Gould) Quantitative Concepts for Management, 1979, (with Metcalfe and Walters) The MBA Degree, 1979, (with F.J. Gould and C.P. Schmidt) Introductory Management Science, 1984; editor: Energy the Policy Issues, 1975; contbr. articles to profl. jours. FMC Faculty Rsch. scholar, 1986-89. Home: 3107 N Snead Dr Goodyear AZ 85338 E-mail: gary.eppen@gsb.uchicago.edu.

EPPERSON, ERIC ROBERT, company executive, film producer; b. Oregon City, Oreg., Dec. 10, 1949; s. Robert Max and Margaret Joan (Crawford) E.; m. Lyla Gene Harris, Aug. 21, 1969; 1 child, Marcie. BS, Brigham Young U., 1973, M of Acctg., 1974; MBA, Golden Gate U., 1977, JD, 1981. Instr. acctg. Brigham Young U., Provo, Utah, 1973-74; supr. domestic taxation Bechtel Corp., San Francisco, 1974-78; supr. internat. taxation Bechtel Power Corp., San Francisco, 1978-80; mgr. internat. tax planning Del Monte Corp., San Francisco, 1980-82, mgr. internat. taxes, 1982-85; internat. tax specialist Touche Ross & Co., San Francisco, 1985-87; dir. internat. tax Coopers & Lybrand, Portland, 1987-89; exec. v.p., chief fin. officer Epperson Dayton Sorenson Prodns., Inc., Salt Lake City, 1989-90, Epperson Prodns., 1990-92; exec. dir. The Oreg. Trail Found., Inc., Oregon City, 1992-93; pres., chmn. bd. MFD Ltd., Portland, Oreg., 1993—; pres. Oreg. Trail Films, Ltd., 1998—, Morgan's Ferry Prodns., LLC, 1998—, Lakeboat Prodns., L.L.C., 1999—, Oregon Trail Television, Ltd., 1999, Oregon Trail Promotions, Ltd., 1999. Author: (with T. Gilbert) Interfacing of the Securities and Exchange Commission with the Accounting Profession: 1968 to 1973, 1974; producer (film) Without Evidence, 1995, Morgan's Ferry, 1999, Lakeboat, 2000, exec. producer (film) Dream Machine, 1989, Live & Learn, 2001, (TV series) Live & Learn, 2000, Dixie Chick "Fly Tour", 2000. Scoutmaster Boy Scouts Am., Provo, 1971-73, troop committeeman, 1973-74, 83—, vice-chmn. ranch devel. com., Butte Creek; mem. IRS Vol. Income Tax Assistance Program, 1972-75; pres. Youth First Found. Inc., 2000--, Mut. Improvement Assn., Ch. Jesus Christ of Latter-day Saints, 1972-74, pres. Sunday sch., 1977-79, tchr., 1974-80, ward clk., 1980-83, bishopric, 1983-87; bd. dirs. Oreg. Art Inst. Film Ctr., Oreg. Trail Coordinating Coun., Hist. Preservation League of Oreg. Mem. World Affairs Coun., Japan/Am. Soc., Internat. Tax Planning Assn., Internat. Fiscal Assn., Oreg. Trail Coordinating Coun. (exec. bd.), Oreg. Hist. Soc., U.S. Rowing Assn., Oreg. Calif. Trail Assn., Royal Photographic Soc., Commonwealth Club, Multnomah Athletic Club. Republican. Office: PMB 180 25 NW 23d Pl Ste 6 Portland OR 97210-5599

EPPERSON, KRAETTLI QUYNTON, lawyer, educator; b. Ft. Eustis, Va., May 2, 1949; s. Dimpster Eugene Sr. and Helen Walter (Davidson) E.; m. Kay Lawrence, Aug. 22, 1970; children: Kraettli L., Kristin J., Kevin Q., Keith W. BA in Polit. Sci., U. Okla., 1971; MS in Urban and Policy Scis., SUNY, Stony Brook, 1974; JD, Oklahoma City U., 1978. Bar: Okla. 1979, U.S. Dist. Ct. (we. dist.) Okla. 1984, Fed. Claims Ct. 1997. Urban planner Gov.'s Office of Community Affairs and Planning, Oklahoma City, 1974-75; adminstr. of pub. transp. planning Okla. Dept. of Transp., Oklahoma City, 1975-79; title examiner Lawyers Title of Oklahoma City, Inc., 1979-80; gen. counsel, v.p. Am. First Land Title Ins. Co., Oklahoma City, 1980-82; assoc. Ferguson & Litchfield, Oklahoma City, 1982-85; of counsel Ames & Ashabranner, Oklahoma City, 1986-88, ptnr., 1989-93, Cook & Epperson, Oklahoma City, 1994-97, Oklahoma City, 1997—2002, Rolston, Hamill, Epperson, Myles & Nelson, 2002—. Adj. prof. law Okla. land titles Oklahoma City U., 1982—; instr. real property Okla. Bar Rev., 1998—; instr. real property titles Grad. Realtors Inst., 1998-99. Author: Basye Clearing Land Titles, 1998-2000, contbr., 2001-; contbg. author, editor: Vernon's Oklahoma Forms 2d-Real Estate, 2000—; contbr. articles to profl. jours. Asst. scoutmaster Boy Scouts Am., Oklahoma City, 1984-88, 1993-2000, asst. cubmaster, 1989-90, cubmaster, 1990-91, webelos leader, 1991-95, dist. vice-chair, 2000-01, dist. chair, 2001—. 2d lt. USAR, 1971. Recipient Dist. Svc. award, Boy Scouts Am., 2001. Mem. ABA (vice-chmn. conveyancing com. 1987-88, 93-94, chmn. 1991-93, chmn. state customs and practice subcom. 1987-88, project chmn. title exam. standards nat. survey 1988—), Am. Land Title Assn. (legis. com. 1981-82, jud. com. 1981-82), Okla. Bar Assn. (real property sect. 1979—, dir. 1982-88, 94-95, chmn. 1985-86, project chmn. Okla. Title Exam. Standards Handbook project 1982-85, mem. title exam. standards com. 1980—, chmn. 1992—, legis. liaison com. 1986-92, co-chmn. abstracting standards com. 1982-84), Oklahoma City Real Property Lawyers Assn. (dir. 1985-91, pres. 1990-91), Oklahoma City Comml. Law Attys. Assn. Republican. Episcopalian. Avocations: skeet, storytelling, camping. Home: 3029 Rock Ridge Ct Oklahoma City OK 73120-5731 Office: 4334 NW Expressway St Ste 174 Oklahoma City OK 73116-1574 E-mail: kqelaw@aol.com.

EPPERSON, MARGARET FARRAR, civic worker; b. Hickman, Ky., Feb. 9, 1922; d. John Henry and Helen Margaret (Thompson) White; m. Liberty Weir Birmingham III, June 14, 1947 (dec. Feb. 1965); children: Margaret W., Elizabeth J., Richard L. (dec. Feb. 1997); m. Ralph Cameron Epperson, Sept. 18, 1971 (dec. Dec. 2000). Student, Washington Sch. Art, 1940; BA magna cum laude, Judson Coll., Marion, Ala., 1945; postgrad., Lambuth Coll., Jackson, Tenn., 1964. Cert. secondary tchr., Ky. Tchr. biology and typing Robert L. Osborne High Sch., Marietta, Ga., 1945-46; tchr. typing Hickman High Sch., 1946-47; tchr. day care ctr. Southside Bapt. Ch., Jacksonville, Fla., 1972-73; sec. to min. of Edn. Jacksonville, Fla., 1973; file clk. Epperson Appraisers, Pensacola, Fla., 1986-87. Formerly substitute tchr. various high schs. and jr. high schs., staff mem. Ridgecrest Bapt. Assembly, summer 1946, 1971. Exhibited in art shows, Jackson, Tenn., 1957, 58, West Tenn. Exec. Club, 1958-59. Pres. Alexander Sch. PTA, Jackson, 1959—60, devotional chmn., 1956—57, chmn. rm. mothers, 1957—58, 1st v.p., 1958—59; sec. Reelfoot Lake coun. Girl Scouts U.S.A., 1969—71, troop mother, cookie chmn., 1958—65, PTA sec. Jackson, Tenn. H.S., 1967—68, 1970—71; PTA 1st v.p. Jackson, Tenn. Ctrl. Coun., 1960—61; vol. ARC, Jackson, 1955, Meml. Med. Hosp. Aux., Jacksonville, 1978—86, Am. Heart Assn., 1987—90, Sacred Heart Hosp. Aux., Pensacola, 1986—; life mem., Jacksonville Children's Hosp. Aux., 1974—; hostess designer show house Jacksonville Symphony Guild, 1979—80; show house com. Pensacola Symphony Guild, 1996, 1997, 1999, 2003; active Newcomers Club Greater Pensacola Area, 1988—, Bon Appetit Luncheon Group, 1986—87, sunshine chmn., 1987—88, sec., 1988—89, nominating com., 1993—94, scholarship com., 1993—94, newcomer's book club group program chmn., 1995—96; publicity chmn. MacDowell Music Club, Jackson, 1954—55, program chmn., 1957—58, social chmn., 1959—60, parliamentarian, 1961; com. mem. Jackson Cmty. Concert Assn., 1958—64; mem. women's bd. Bapt. Health Care Found., 1993—; chmn. invitations and tickets com. for Style Show Friends of Libr., 1993—94, 2002, life mem., 1996—, Bapt. Health Care Found., 1996—; active Friday Musicale of Jacksonville, Fla., 1979—86, Escambia County Coun. on Aging, 1996—; assoc. mem. Nat. Mus. Women in Arts, 1998; vol. Campfire Boys and Girls, 1999; mem. libr. staff First Bapt. Ch., 2001—; mem. Pensacola Little Theatre, 2002—03, Music Study Club, 2002—03; dir. Women's Missionary Union Bapt. Ch., 1976—78, mission support chmn., 1992—94, sec., 1995; mem. aux. assn. Jackson Madison County Bar, 1960—65. Mem. AAUW (sec. 1988-90, 2d v.p. 1990-92, tel. com. 1993—, br. area rep. cmty. problems Tenn. 1970-71, chmn. Tenn. divsn. cultural interests 1969-70, Fla. chmn. interest groups 1977-78), DAR (treas. 1981-82, chmn. Am. Heritage 1989-91, chmn. mag. 1991-93, chmn. vol. cmty. svcs. 1998-99), UDC (sec. Jacksonville chpt. 1979-81, historian Jacksonville chpt. 1981-83, sec. Pensacola chpt. 1989-90, corr. sec. Pensacola chpt. 1992-94, mem. com. chmn. 1993-94, chmn. patriotic activities 1998-99, com. for children of confederacy 1998-2000, telephone com. 2000-01), Christian Women's Club (prayer chmn. 1991—, book chmn. 1987, 88, 92-94, hostesses asst. chmn. 1994—), Pensacola Fedn. Garden Clubs (pres. Poinciana Circle 1989-91, pres. Bells of Ireland Circle 1978-80, civic chmn., 1991, sec. Alderman Park Cir., Jacksonville 1980-82), Judson Coll. Alumnae Assn. of Pensacola (pres. 1993—, exec. bd. 1993—), Tenn. Fedn. Garden Clubs (pres. Jackson Jr. 1958-60, 60-70, chmn. exec. bd. 1970-71, chmn. flower show 1968). Avocations: giving book reviews, coal mining industry, volunteering.

EPPERSON, ROBERT DALE, farmer; b. Santa Maria, Calif., Jan. 12, 1947; s. Joseph Cary and Lina Marcille Epperson; m. Loretta Jolan Lambrecht, July 20, 1968; children: Andrea, David, Sara, Mary. BS, Calif. State U., Fresno, 1968, MS, 1970. Farmer, Kerman, Calif., 1974—; v.p. Epperson's Market, Inc., Kerman, 1974-79; dir. grants and contracts Calif. State U., Fresno, 1984-89; sr. environ. planner Calif. Dept. Transp., Fresno, 1989-2000; resource mgr. U.S. Bur. Reclamation, Fresno, 2000—. Mem. Nat. Agrl. Stats. Adv. Com., Washington, 1999—, mem. mktg. and strategic planning com. Sun-Maid Growers Bd. Dirs., Kingsburg, Calif., 1987—, mem. fin. com., 1987—, mem. pers. com., 1990—, chair fin. com., 1996—, chair ethics com., 1997—, chair mktg. and strategic planning com., 1990-96; dir. Sun-Diamond Growers, Pleasanton, Calif., 1988-97, mem. audit com., 1995-97, mem. ethics com., 1996-97: mem. Raisin Adminstrv. Com., Fresno, 1985—; mem. audit com. Raisin Adminstrv. Com., Fresno, 1995, vice-chair grades and stds. com., 1992-96. Chair safety and environ. protection subcom. Joint Army, Navy, NASA and Air Force Com. on Rocket Propulsion, L.A., 1979-83; admissions liaison officer USAF Acad., Colorado Springs, 1993-99; pres. Bethel Luth. Congregation, Fresno, 1977-79, youth group leader, 1974-79; youth group leader St. Olaf Luth. Ch., Garden Grove, Calif., 1980-83, Hope Luth. Ch., Fresno, 1984-88; Explorer Scout liasion Air Force Armament Lab., Eglin AFB, Fla., 1972-74. Capt USAF, 1979-83. Mem. Am. Chem. Soc. Republican. Avocations: genealogy, history, plant physiology, travel, reading. Home: 6685 N Feland Ave Fresno CA 93711 Office: US Bur Reclamation 1243 N St Fresno CA 93721-1813 E-mail: bobepperson@worldnet.att.net., repperson@mp.usbr.gov.

EPPERSON, STELLA MARIE, artist; b. Oakland, Calif., Nov. 6, 1920; d. Walter Peter and Martha Josephine (Schmitt) Ross; m. John Cray Epperson, May 10, 1941; children: Therese, John, Peter. Student, Calif. Coll. Arts & Crafts, 1939, 40-41, 56; postgrad., Art Inst., San Miguel d'Allende, Mex., 1972. Portrait artist Oakland Art Assn., 1956—, San Francisco Women Artists, 1962—, Marin Soc. Artists, Ross, Calif., 1971—. Art docent Oakland Mus., 1969-71, mem. women's bd., 1971—, art chmn. fund raiser, 1971-89, art guild chmn., 1965-69, chmn. exhbt. Japanese artists in Brazil, Kaiser Ctr., Oakland, for honoring artist Xavier Martinez, event honoring Neil Armstrong, Calif. Coll. Arts and Crafts. One-woman shows include Oakland Mus. Auction, 1993, Univ. Club, San Francisco, 1994; exhbns. include Women's Art Gallery, San Francisco, Kaiser Ctr., St. Mary's Coll. Hearst Gallery, numerous others; commd. portrait Mrs. Evangelina Macapagal, Malacalang Palace. Recipient San Francisco Women Artists, 1989, Oakland Art Assn., 1991, 1997, 2000, Marin Soc. Artists, 1992, Figurative Subject First award, Oakland Art Assn. Mem. Oakland Art Assn. (1st award in small format show 1998, 1999 Artistic award in Kaiser Ctr. Gallery Exhibit, Merit award 2000, Artistic award 2001), San Francisco Women Artists, Marin Art Assn., U. Calif. Berkeley Faculty Club, Orinda Country Club. Republican. Roman Catholic. Avocations: dress design, gourmet cooking, tennis. Home: 31 Valley View Rd Orinda CA 94563-1432

EPPERSON, WALLACE W., JR., investment banker; b. Richmond, Va., Feb. 16, 1948; s. Wallace W. and Dorothy Sue (Kelley) E.; m. Kathryn J. Nelson, Dec. 28, 1969; children: Kelley Seay, Wallace W. III. BS in Fin., U. Va., 1970; MBA, Coll. William and Mary, 1971. CFA. Furniture analyst, v.p. Scott & Strongfellow, Richmond, 1971-76; furniture analyst, sr. v.p. Wheat First Securities, Richmond, 1976-91; furniture analyst, mng. dir. Mann, Armistead & Epperson, Richmond, 1991—. Mem. Richmond Soc. Fin. Analysts. Office: Mann Armistead & Epperson 119 Shockoe Slip Richmond VA 23219-4121

EPPES, THOMAS EVANS, advertising executive, public relations executive; b. N.Y.C., Aug. 10, 1952; s. Benjamin F. and Eileen (Evans) E.; m. Jennie Spradling, Aug. 2, 1980; children: Benjamin, Jared, Michael. BS, U. So. Miss., 1974. Reporter Jackson (Miss.) Daily News, 1974-75, 76-77, Clearwater (Fla.) Sun, 1975-76; pub. info. coord. Miss. Rsch. and Devel. Ctr., Jackson, 1976-78; press sec. Gov. Bill Waller for U.S. Senate, Jackson, 1978, Maurice Dantin for U.S. Senate, Jackson, 1978; dir. pub. rels. Days Inns Am., Atlanta, 1978-82, Mgmt. Sci. Am., Atlanta, 1982-85; pres., pub. rels. Price-McNabb, Asheville, N.C., 1985-91, pres., 1992—. Spkr. nat. confs. on comms. and mktg. Bd. dirs., communications chmn. United Way of Asheville and Buncombe, 1986-87; campaign dir. Jacksonians for Mayor, Jackson, 1976; bd. advisors U. of Colo., Boulder Inc. Sch. Fellow Pub. Rels. Soc. Am. (counselor's acad., exec. bd. counselor's acad. 1998-2000, Coll. of Fellows 2000, Silver Anvil award 1993), Internat. Assn. Bus. Communicators (Gold Quill award 1980, 81), Internat. Comms. Agy. Network (v.p.2002), Charlotte C. of C. (bd. dirs. 1997). Avocation: golf. Office: Price-McNabb 2800 Bank America Corp Ctr Charlotte NC 28202

EPPES, WILLIAM DAVID, arts/humanities supporter; s. Talmadge DeWitt and Annie Lou (McCord) E. AB, Coll. of William and Mary, 1939; BS in LS, Vanderbilt U., 1940; student, U. Miami, U. Manchester (Eng.), 1950, Columbia U., 1950; MA, NYU, 1959; student, U. Durham, Eng., 1987. Reference asst. George Washington U., 1944—48, Calif. State U., San Francisco, 1948—49; head, stack personnel Butler Libr. Columbia U., N.Y.C., 1954-58; assoc. prof. Kean State Coll., N.J., 1958-61; asst. libr. Cooper Union, N.Y.C., 1961-70. Founder Film Classics League, St. Petersburg, Fla., 1950; co-founder Backstage Gallery, St. Petersburg Jr. Coll., 1950, Littlebury Eppes Meml. Libr., Westover Ch., Va.; adv. bd. Coral Gables (Fla.) Hist. Preservation Bd. Rev., 1979-81; trustee Greenwich Village Trust for Hist. Preservation, Inc., 1980, pres., 1980-84, 1984-90; cons. Hist. Buckingham (Va.) Inc., 1987—; hon. commr. Eleanor Roosevelt Monument Fund, Inc., N.Y.C. Author: The Empire Theatre (1893-1953), 1978, Gertrude Michael-A Star of the Golden Age of Hollywood, 1985, Montgomery (Ala.) Theatre 1822-1985, 1986; contbr. articles to mags. and hist. jours. Bd. dirs. St. Petersburg Symphony Orch., 1950-54; exec. bd. Assn. Village Homeowners, N.Y.C., 1969-82, Assocs. of Earl Gregg Swem Libr., Coll. of William and Mary, 1973-86; benefactor Jonathon Daniels Sch., Keene, N.H., 1998, Apple Hill Chamber Orch., Sullivan, N.H., 1998, Kean State Coll., 1999—; benefactor, hist. cons. Redfern Performing Arts Ctr. Keene (N.H.) State Coll., 2000—; pres. coun. Va. Hist. Soc., 1982; profl. advisor McLeod Plantation, Sea Island Hist. Soc., S.C. Mem. Theater Hist. Soc. (rsch. and reference com. 1977-81), Author's Guild, Inc., W&M Choir, Va. Hist. Soc. (pres.'s coun. 1993—, exec. coun. 1995), Sea Island Hist. Soc. (profl. adv. bd. 2000). Republican. Home: 14 Rivermead Rd Peterborough NH 03458-1701

EPPINGER, JAMES EDWARD, educational administrator; b. New Castle, Pa. s. James Fredrick and Gretchen Pauline Dover (Heasley) E.; divorced; children: David, Nicholas, Alicia, James. BA, Slippery Rock U., 1977; postgrad., Nova Southeastern U., 1987; JD, Stetson U., 1992. Bar: Fla. Tchr. math. Faith Christian Sch., Sarasota, Fla., 1981-89, adminstr., 1988-89; law clk. James Kennedy, St. Petersburg, Fla., 1990; tchr. mat. Tabernacle Christian Sch., Sarasota, 1991-95; atty. pvt. practice, Bradenton, Fla., 1992-98; headmaster, adminstr. Faith Christian Sch., 1995-98; cons. and substitute tchr., 1998—. Avocation: theology. Office: PMB 118 6094 14th St W Bradenton FL 34207-6007

EPPINK, JEFFREY FRANCIS, energy and environment consultant; b. Whittier, Calif., Jan. 31, 1955; s. Reno Paul and Bertine (Gilje) I.; m. Sheryl Ann Baumberger, Aug. 27, 1977; children: Christina Michelle, Michael Jeffrey. BS, Calif. State Poly. U., 1978; MS, U. So. Calif., 1981; MBA, Va. Poly. Inst.

and State U., 1996. Planetary scientist Jet Propulsion Lab., Pasadena, Calif., 1979-81; explorationist Chevron Overseas Petroleum Inc., San Ramon, Calif., 1981-91; project mgr. ICF Kaiser Internat., San Francisco, 1991-92; diplomacy fellow Asia Bur. U.S. Agy. Internat. Devel., Washington, 1992-93; project mgr. ICF Kaiser Internat., Fairfax, Va., 1993-98; v.p. Advanced Resources Internat., Inc., Arlington, Va., 1998—. Mem. AAAS, Am. Assn. Petroleum Geologists, Soc. Exploration Geophysicists, Internat. Assn. Energy Econs. Republican. Roman Catholic. Avocations: travel, long distance swimming, planetology, woodworking. Home: 13503 King Charles Dr Chantilly VA 20151-3325 Office: Advanced Resources Internat 1110 N Glebe Rd Arlington VA 22201-4795 E-mail: jeffeppink@aol.com.

EPPLEIN, LAWRENCE ELLIOTT, hospitality management educator; b. Balt., Apr. 10, 1943; s. Samuel Carroll and Bess Bittman Epplein; m. Dianne Ellen Davidson, Jan. 12, 1967 (div. June 1995); children: Rochelle, Meira; m. Jeanette Giesen Epplein, May 7, 1996. BS, U. Balt., 1965; MBA, George Washington U., 1968. Cert. hospitality educator Ednl. Inst. Am. Hotel and Lodging Assn. Instr. bus. Tidewater C.C., Chesapeake, Va., 1969—70; pres., owner Village Inn Pizza Parlors, Norfolk, Va., 1970—85, Cafe 21, Norfolk, Va., 1985—93; asst. prof. Norfolk State U., 1993—, acting chair dept. tourism and hospitality, 1997—, exec. dir. Hampton Roads Hospitality Edn. and Tng. Initiative, 1999—. Pres. Adventures, Inc., Norfolk, 1982—, Va. Espresso Sales Corp., Norfolk, 1995—. Treas. Va. Stage Co., Norfolk, 1979—85; trustees Tidewater Performing Arts Soc., Norfolk, 1988—92; co-pres. Norfolk Chamber Consort, 1997—2002. Named to Golden Fork Hall of Fame, Portfolio Mag., Norfolk, 1987; Workforce Devel. grantee, U.S. Dept. Labor, Norfolk, 1999. Mem.: AAUP, Congress Hotel, Restaurant and Instnl. Educators, Nat. Restaurant Assn. Avocations: classical music, cooking. Home: 620 Maury Ave Norfolk VA 23517

EPPLER, JEROME CANNON, private financial advisor; b. Englewood, N.J., Mar. 16, 1924; s. William E. and Aileen (Vaughan) E.; m. Debora Nye Eppler; children: Stephen Vaughan, William Durand, Margaret Nye, Elizabeth Scott, Edward Curtis. BSME, Tex. A&M U., 1946; MBA, U. Pa., 1949. With Gen. Electric Supply Corp., Newark, 1949-50; investment banker Equitable Securities Corp., Nashville, mgr. Houston, 1950-53; gen. ptnr. Cyrus J. Lawrence & Sons, N.Y.C., 1953-61; mem. N.Y. Stock Exch.; owner Eppler & Co., Denver, 1961; bd. dirs. Esmark, Inc., 1965—84; ltd. ptnr. Alex Brown & Sons, Balt., 1982-84; bd. dirs. Chgo. Milw. St. Paul & Pacific Ry., 1958-63, Chemex Pharms., 1984-88; prin. Olympic Capital Ptnrs., Seattle, 1995-2000. Dir. Advanced Rsch. Sys., Inc., Seattle, 1997-99, Pvt. Asset Mgmt., Inc., Bellevue, Wash.; chmn. bd. United Screen Arts, Inc., L.A., 1966-73; bd. dirs. VisionTek, Inc., Boulder, Colo., 1998-2001; chmn., bd. dirs. Life Ins. Co. Calif., 1967-77, I.S.I. Corp., 1967-77, Tessco Techs. Inc., Hunt Valley, Md., World Wide Life Assurance Co., London, 1972-77, Windsor Life Ins. Co., London, 1972-77; mem. indsl. adv. com. U. Calif., San Diego, 1978-93; dir. Telecredit, Inc., L.A., 1976-90, Brooktree Corp., San Diego, 1983-86, QTron, Inc., San Diego, 1995-97; chmn. Global Leadership Coun., Coll. Bus., Colo. State U., Ft. Collins, Colo. Trustee emeritus Scripps Clinic and Research Found., La Jolla; former trustee Drew U. (N.J.), 1966-67, Morris Mus. Arts & Scis. (N.J.), 1954-76, Met. Opera Assn., 1980-82, Wharton Grad. Sch. Bus. N.Y., 1972-86. Lt. (j.g.) USNR, 1942-46. Mem. Wharton Grad. Bus. Sch. Club, Castle Pines Golf Club, River Bend Country Club (Tequesta, Fla.). Presbyterian. Office: Eppler & Co 2800 S University Blvd #22 Denver CO 80210

EPPLER, RICHARD ANDREW, chemical engineer, educator, consultant; b. Lynn, Mass., Apr. 30, 1934; s. Walter T. and Faith E. (Marden) E.; m. Ruth Marilyn Coon, June 20, 1959; children: Katherine R., Rebecca E., Walter R., Douglas R., Bruce A. BS, Carnegie-Mellon U., 1956; MS, U. Ill., 1958, PhD, 1960. Registered profl. engr., N.Y. Research chemist Corning (N.Y.) Glass Works, 1959-65; research scientist Mobay Chem. Corp., Balt., 1965-84; supr. ceramics Olin Corp., New Haven, 1984-86; cons. Eppler Assocs., Cheshire, Conn., 1986—; assoc. prof. chem. engring. U. Lowell, Mass., 1986-89. Over 20 patents in field; contbr. articles to profl. jours. Served with USAR, 1960. Fellow Am. Ceramic Soc. (v.p. 1984-85, John Marquis award 1974), ASTM (chmn. com. 1980-85, 92-97, merit award 1984); mem. Am. Chem. Soc., Electrochem. Soc., Sigma Xi. Republican. Congregationalist. Home and Office: Eppler Assocs 400 Cedar Ln Cheshire CT 06410-2222

EPPLEY, FRANCES FIELDEN, retired secondary education educator, author; b. Knoxville, Tenn., July 18, 1921; d. Chester Earl and Beulah Magnolia (Wells) Fielden; m. Gordon Talmage Cougle, July 25, 1942; children: Russell Gordon Eppley, Carolyn Eppley Horseman; m. Fred Coan Eppley, Mar. 8, 1953; 1 child, Charlene Eppley Sellers. BA in English, Carson Newman Coll., 1942; MA, Winthrop U., 1963. Tchr. East Corinth (Maine) Acad., 1942-43, pub. schs., Charlotte, N.C., 1950-53, 59-83, Greenville, S.C., 1954-56, Spartanburg, S.C., 1957-58; Head Start tchr., summers 1964-68. Author: First Baptist Church: Its Heritage, 1982, Flint Hill Church, 1984, Religion and Astrology, 1991, Astrology and Prophecy, 1992, Sammy's Song, Jericho, Aunt Lillian's Sea Foam Candy, The First Astrologer, 1993, The Story of William Fielden, 1998, Search for an Ancestor, 1999, Christmas Magnus, Stella and the Sitting Stone, Messiah, An Immediate Family, 1999, The Signs of Your Life, 2000, Another Mary, 2000, The Winter Solstice, 2001, Of Course Your Child Can Read!, 2002, Columbus: The Race Home, 2003; : Canada Trilogy, 2003; : Canada Trilogy, 2003, Wacky Kings and Mystic Things, 2003, The Yellow River, 2003. Mem. hist. com. N.C. Bapt. Conv., 1985-88. Alpha Delta Kappa Grantee, 1970. Mem. NEA, N.C. Social Studies Conf., Writers Assn., Alpha Delta Kappa, Pi Kappa Delta, Alpha Psi Omega. Baptist. Home: 4119 Bannockburn Pl Apt B Charlotte NC 28211 E-mail: ffielden@bellsouth.net.

EPPLEY, ROLAND RAYMOND, JR., retired financial services executive; b. Balt., Apr. 1, 1932; s. Roland and Verna (Garrettson) E.; m. LeVerne Pittman, June 20, 1953; children: Kimberly, Kent, Todd. BA, Johns Hopkins U., 1952, MA, 1953; D.C.S. (hon.), St. John's U., 1984. Pres., chief exec. officr Comm. Credit Computer, Balt., 1962-68; pres., chief exec. officer CIPC, Balt., 1968-71; vice chmn. Eastern States Monetary, Lake Success, N.Y., 1982-88; pres., chief exec. officer, dir. Affiliated Financial, Wilmington, Del., 1983-85, Eastern States Bankcard, Lake Success, N.Y., 1971-88; ret., 1988; chmn. bd. Eppley-Tongue Assocs., Inc. Adj. prof. St. John's U., 1973-88; bd. dirs. Ea. States Monetary, Veritas Inc., Hanover Investment Funds, Janel Hydraulics, Vista Funds, J.P. Morgan Mut. Funds; chmn. bd. Hanover Funds, 1989-96, Eppley-Tongue Assocs., Inc., 1992-95. Chmn. bd. trustees Calgary Bapt. Ch., Balt., 1969-71; chmn. investment com. Community Ch., Manhasset, N.Y., 1983-88; bd. advisors St. John's U., 1973-88; active Trinity Meth. Ch., Palm Beach Gardens, Fla.; mem. Johns Hopkins U. Alumni Coun., 1996-99. Recipient Disting. Service award St. John's U., 1981, 84 Laucheimer grantee, 1952-53 Mem.: Cypress Links Country Club, Electronic Funds Transfer Assn., Am. Mgmt. Assn. Pres.'s Assn., Data Processing Mgmt. Assn., Am. Bankers Assn., Mensa, Tequesta Country Club, Cypress Yacht Club, City Club of Palm Beaches, Hillendale Country Club, Madison Sq. Garden Club, Meadowbrook Club, Plandome Country Club (dir. 1977—86), PGA Country Club, Ibis Country Club, Palm Beach Yacht Club, Shriners, Masons, Sigma Phi Epsilon (citation), Beta Gamma Sigma, Omicron Delta Epsilon, Phi Beta Kappa. Republican. Home: 24 Windward Isle West Palm Beach FL 33418-8001 also: 510 Greenwood Rd Towson MD 21204-3760 E-mail: rreppley@aol.com. *Throughout my life, most of what I had planned did not work out. However, by being prepared for opportunities, I was able to take advantage of the unexpected.*

EPPS, CHARLES HARRY, JR., retired orthopaedic surgery educator; b. Balt., July 24, 1930; BS magna cum laude, Howard U., 1951, MD, 1955. Intern Freedmen's Hosp., 1955-56, resident, 1956-57, mem. staff, 1961—2001; resident D.C. Gen. Hosp., Washington, 1958-60, vis. staff, 1961-98, orthopaedic med. officer for handicapped and crippled children's svc., 1961-98; instr. orthopaedic surgery Howard U., Washington, 1961-64, asst. prof., 1964-68, assoc. prof., 1968-73, prof., 1973-96, prof. emeritus, 1996—2001, chief divsn. orthopaedic surgery, 1968-88, dean Coll. Medicine, 1988-94, exec. dean Coll. Medicine, 1994-95; v.p. health affairs, acting exec. dir., CEO Howard U. Hosp., Washington, 1994-96; spl. asst. to pres. for health affairs Howard U., 1996-2001; ret., 2001. Assoc. prof. Johns Hopkins U., 1971; mem. staff VA Hosp., Washington, Cafritz Meml. Hosp., Providence Hosp.; cons. USN Med. Ctr., Bethesda, Md., Walter Reed Army Med. Ctr. Capt. M.C., U.S. Army, 1961-62. Fellow ACS; mem. AMA, Nat. Med. Assn., Ea. Orthop. Assn., Am. Orthop. Assn., Am. Acad. Orthop. Surgery.

EPPS, HARLAND WARREN, astronomy educator, optical design consultant; b. Hawthorne, Calif., July 29, 1936; s. Harland Garner and Nydia Dolly (Gall) E.; m. Louise Rodney Daniels, June 5, 1962 (div. Jan. 1970); m. Susan Lou Markowitz, Oct. 10, 1976 (div. Feb. 1983); children: Melody Amanda, Brenden Putty; m. Johanna Helen Archer, Nov. 23, 1991; children: Helena Dolly, Naomi Lauren. Student, U. Vienna, Austria, 1956-57; BA, Pomona Coll., 1959; MS, U. Wis., 1961, PhD, 1964. Asst. prof. astronomy San Diego State U., 1964-65, UCLA, 1965-70, assoc. prof., 1970-76, prof., 1976-89; astronomer, prof. astronomy Lick Obs., Santa Cruz, Calif., 1989—, U. Calif., Santa Cruz, 1989—. Cons. Steward Obs., Tucson, 1972—, Lick Obs., 1970—, Smithsonian Astrophys. Obs., Cambridge, Mass., 1984—, Los Alamos (N.Mex.) Nat. Lab., 1984—, Mount Wilson and Las Campanas Observatories, 1987—, Calif. Inst. Tech., 1988—. Assoc. editor for instrumentation: Publs. of Astron. Soc. of the Pacific, 2003—; contbr. articles to profl. jours. Mem. USAF Sci. Adv. Bd., 1989-93. Grantee NSF, Air Force Cambridge Rsch., U. Calif. Regents Opportunity Fund, NASA. Mem. Am. Astron. Soc., Internat. Astron. Union, Soc. Photooptical Instrumentation Engrs., Sigma Xi. Avocation: classical and flamenco guitar. Office: U Calif UCO/Lick Obs Natural Scis 2 Rm 191 Santa Cruz CA 95064 E-mail: epps@ucolick.org.

EPPS, JAMES HAWS, III, lawyer; b. Johnson City, Tenn., Sept. 15, 1936; s. James Haws and Anne Lafayette (Sessoms) E.; m. Jane Mahoney, Oct. 9, 1976; children from previous marriage--James Haws IV, Sara Stuart. BA, U.N.C., 1955-59; JD, Vanderbilt U., 1962. Bar: Tenn. 1962, U.S. Dist. Ct. Tenn. 1962, U.S. Ct. Appeals (6th cir.) 1971, Interstate Commerce Commn. Bar 1962, U.S. Supreme Ct. 1967. Prin. Epps & Epps, Johnson City, Tenn. City atty. Johnson City, 1967—, Johnson City Bd. Edn., 1967-86; spl. counsel State of Tenn., 1966-70; former gen. counsel Appalachian Flying Svc. Inc., ET&WNC Transp. Co., Inc. First bd. govs. Transp. Law Jour. Past bd. dirs. Washington County Mental Health Assn., East Tenn. and Western N.C. Transp. Co., East Tenn. and Western N.C. R.R., Tennolina Corp., Appalachian Air Lines, Inc., Appalachian Flying Svc., Inc., Farmers and Mchts. Bank, Limestone, Tenn., budget com. United Fund of Johnson City, 1964-68, Assault Crime Counsel Early Support Svcs. Inc., Safe Passage Inc., Johnson City Homeless Coalition, Home Base Adv. Coun., Johnson City/Washington County Health Coun. adv. com.; former legal adviser Appalachian coun. Girl Scouts U.S.A.; mem. Tenn. Law Revision Commn., 1970-71; legal counsel Salvation Army, mem. adv. bd. 1974—, exec. com. 1977—, 1st v.p. adv. bd. 1991, pres. adv. bd. 1993, 94, mem. property com.; chmn. Family Violence Coun.; legal counsel Washington County Humane Soc., Inc.; mem. Civil Def., 1967—; chmn. Washington County for Tenn. Leukemia Soc., 1991; mem. exec. com. Washington County Dem. Party, Tenn Bicentennial Commn., exec. and fin. coms.; past mem. bd. dirs. Tenn. Mental Health ASsn. Fellow Tenn. Bar Found.; mem. ABA, Fed. Bar Assn., Nat. Orgn. Legal Problems Edn., Am. Counsel Assn., Nat. Assn. R.R. Trial Counsel, Internat. Mcpl. Lawyers Assn. (bd. dirs. 1982—, state chmn. Tenn. 1988-89, ethics and environ. coms. 1989—, regional v.p. 1989-92, chmn. resolutions com. 1989-90, lectr., trustee, 1992—, chmn. dues and alternatives revenue 1996-97, budget and fin., federalism com. 1996—, state league counsel rev. com. 1997, awards com., 1999—, bd. mem. policy adv. com. 2000, 1st v.p. 2001, pres. 2002-03), Nat. Legal Aid Defender Assn., Tenn. Bar Assn., Am. Judicature Soc., Washington County Bar Assn. (past pres.), Tenn. Mcpl. Attys. Assn., Assn. ICC Practitioners (past com. profl. ethics and grievences), Transp. Lawyers Assn., Motor Carrier Lawyers Assn., Johnson City C. of C. (Disting. Service award 1968), Internat. Platform Assn., Lawyers Com. for Civil Rights Under Law, World Peace Through Law Ctr., Tenn. Lung Assn., Tenn. Correctional Assn., Tenn. Taxpayers Assn. (past bd. dirs.), Tennesseans for Better Transp., U.S. Supreme Ct. Hist. Soc., Def. Rsch. Inst., Tipton Haynes Hist. Assn. (past dir.), Hurstleigh Club, Unaka Rd. and Gun Club, Highland Stable Club, North Johnson City Bus. Club (dir., past pres. 1966-67), Nat. Lawyers Club, East Tenn. State U. Century Club, Boys'Club (charter, Johnson City/Washington County), Masons, Elks (legal counsel 1963-67), Phi Delta Phi, Phi Delta Theta. Episcopalian. Office: 115 E Unaka Ave Johnson City TN 37601-4623 also: PO Box 2288 Johnson City TN 37605-2288

EPPS, LEON ANTHONY, government official; b. Balt., Dec. 7, 1943; s. Leon and Lorraine (Brown) E.; m. Roberta Lee Redd, Nov. 4, 1967; 1 child, Leon Anthony Jr. BS in Chemistry and Edn., Morgan State U., 1966; MA in Inorganic Chemistry, PhD in Inorganic Chemistry, Johns Hopkins U., 1984. Rsch. technician dept. pharmacology Johns Hopkins U., Balt., 1966-67, chemistry technician, demonstrator dept. chemistry, 1969-79, head teaching asst., 1979-80, postdoctoral fellow divsn. radiation health scis., 1984-85, rsch. assoc. dept. environ. health scis., 1985-86; asst. prof. dept. chemistry Morgan State U., Balt., 1978-80; sr. rsch. scientist dept. radiopharm. rsch. and devel. Centocor, Inc., Malvern, Pa., 1986-90, sr. rsch. scientist dept. molecular biology, 1990-93; reviewer FDA, Rockville, Md., 1993-99, expert rev. chemist, 1999—. Contbr. articles to profl. jours. With USN, 1967-69. Recipient Letter of Commendation U.S. Naval Rsch. Inst., NIH Nat. Rsch. Svc. award, NIH postdoctoral fellowship. Mem. AAAS, Am. Chem. Soc., Drug Info. Assn., Alpha Chi Sigma. Roman Catholic. Avocations: chess, tennis, singing, walking, drawing. Home: 2808 Lindin Way Woodstock MD 21163 Office: FDA CBER 1401 Rockville Pike Ste 200 Rockville MD 20852-1448 E-mail: epps@cber.fda.gov.

EPPS, ROSELYN ELIZABETH PAYNE, pediatrician, educator; b. Little Rock, Dec. 11, 1930; d. William Kenneth and Mattie Elizabeth (Beverly) Payne; m. Charles Harry Epps, Jr., June 25, 1955; children: Charles Harry III (dec.), Kenneth Carter, Roselyn Elizabeth, Howard Robert. BS, Howard U., 1951, MD, 1955; MPH, Johns Hopkins U., 1973; MA, Am. U., 1981. Intern Freedmen's Hosp., Howard U., Washington, 1955-56, pediatric resident, 1956-59, chief resident, 1958-59; practice medicine specializing in pediatrics Washington, 1960; med. officer, pediatrics D.C. Dept. Pub. Health, Washington, 1961-64, dir. Clinic for Retarded Children, 1964-67, chief Infant and Pre-Sch. div., 1967-71, dir. children and youth project, 1970-71, dir. maternal and crippled children services, 1971-75; chief Bur. Clin. Services D.C. Dept. Human Services, Washington, 1975-80, acting commr. pub. health, 1980; instr., asst. research investigator Howard U. Coll. Medicine, Washington, 1960-61, prof. Dept. Pediatrics and Child Health, 1980-98, chief divsn. child devel., dir., 1985-89, dir. Child Devel. Ctr., 1985-89; rsch. assoc., vis. scientist smoking tobacco and cancer program, div. cancer prevention and control Nat. Cancer Inst. NIH, Washington, 1989-91; expert Nat. Cancer Inst. NIH, Pub. Health Applications Br., Bethesda, Md., 1991-97; scientific program adminstr. Nat. Cancer Inst. Pub. Health Applications Branch, Bethesda, Md., 1997-98; med. pub. hlth cons., 1998—; sr. program advisor for women's health programs Women's Health Inst., Howard U., Wash., 1999—. Chmn. task force to prepare comprehensive child care plan for D.C. Dept. Human Services, 1973-74; mem. nat. task force on pediatric hypertension Heart, Lung and Blood Inst., NIH, 1975; chmn. rsch. grants rev. com. maternal and child health and crippled children's svcs. HEW, Rockville, Md., 1978-80; sec. Commn. Licensure to Practice Healing Arts, Washington, 1980; trustee med. svc. D.C. Blue Shield Plan Nat. Capital Area, 1980; chmn. sec.'s adv. com. on rights and responsibilities of women HEW, Washington, 1981; dir. high-risk young people's project Howard U. Hosp., 1981-85; Washington coord. Know Your Body Program Am. Health Found., N.Y.C., 1982-91; mem. bd. advs. Coll. Home Econs. Ohio State U., Columbus, Ohio, 1983-87; adv. com. Nat. Ctr. for Edn. in Maternal and Child Health Georgetown U., Washington, 1983-89; nat. steering com., subcom. chmn. Healthy Mothers, Healthy Babies Coalition, Washington, 1983-90, mem. nominating com., 1991; cons. sickle cell disease NIH, 1984-88, Govt. Liberia and World Bank, 1984, UN Fund for Population Activities, N.Y. and Caribbean, 1984, filmstrip Miriam Berg Varian/Parents Mag. Films, 1978; bd. dirs. Vis. Nurse Assn., Inc., Washington, 1983-89; pres. bd. dirs. Hosp. for Sick Children, Washington, 1986-90, bd. dirs., 1984-94; frequent guest lectr. Weekly columnist Your Child's Health, Afro-Am. Newspaper, Washington, 1960-63; contbr. articles syndicated column Nat. Newspaper Pubs. Assn., 1982, Nat. Newspaper Assn., 1986-87; co-author audiocassettes; exhibitor sci. program; contbr. more than 90 articles to profl. jours. US trustee Children's Internat. Summer Villages, Casstown, Ohio, 1969—76, pres., 1974—75; trustee nat. bd. Palmer Meml. Inst., Sedalia, NC, 1969—71, Ford's Theater, Washington, 1973—79; bd. mgrs. YWCA of DC, 1970—83, vice chmn., 1975—76; v.p. Jack and Jill of Am., Inc., Washington, 1970—71; nat. bd. dir. Ctr. Population Options, Washington, 1980—86, Alexander Graham Bell Assn. for Deaf, Washington, 1974—78; bd. dir. Washington Performing Arts Soc., DC, 1971—81, v.p., 1979—81, hon. dir., 1981—. Recipient Leadership and Meritorious Service in Medicine award Palmer Meml. Inst., 1968, 14th Ann. Fed. Women's award CSC, Washington, 1974, Superior Performance award D.C. Govt., 1975, Meritorious Community Service award Howard U. Sch. Social Work Alumni Assns. and vis. com., 1980, Cert. Commendation Mayor of D.C., 1981, Roselyn Payne Epps M.D. Recognition Resolution of 1983 Council D.C., 1983, Disting. Vol. Leadership award March of Dimes Birth Defects Found., 1984, Community Svc. award D.C. Hosp. Assn., 1990, Physician of Yr. award Women's Med. Assn. N.Y.C., 1990, 91; named Outstanding Vol. in Leadership category YWCA Nat. Capital Area, 1983; inducted into D.C. Women's Hall of Fame D.C. Commn. for Women, 1990; grantee Robert Wood Johnson Found., Princeton, N.J., 1982, div. maternal and child health HHS, Rockville, Md., 1986; honored Tribute Resolution of 1981 declaring Feb. 14 Dr. Roselyn Payne Epps Day, Council of D.C., 1981; recipient Ophelia Settle Egypt award Planned Parenthood of Met. Washington, 1991, Advocacy award Soc. Advancement Women's Health, 1996, Horizon award Nat. Assn. Negro Bus. and Profl. Women's Clubs, 1999, Dorothy I Height award, Nat. Coun. of Negro Women, 2001, Lifetime Achievement award, Girls Inc., 2003. Fellow Am. Acad. Pediatrics (alt. state chmn. D.C. 1973-75, exec. com. D.C. chpt. 1983-94, pres. D.C. chpt. 1988-91, sec. cmty. pediatrics sect. 1973-75, cert. appreciation 1979, mem. coun. of child and adolescent health, cmty. and internat. health sect., charter mem., exec. com. 1992-94); mem. Acad. Medicine, AMA (alt. del. Nat. Med. Assn. 1983-85), Am. Med. Women's Assn. (chmn. pub. health com. 1973-75, pres. br. 1 1974-76, sec. 1988, v.p. 1989, pres-elect nat. 1990, pres. 1991, found. founding pres. 1992, bd. dirs. 1992-97, chmn. nominating com. 1993, Physician of Yr. award 1991, Cmty. Svc. award 1990, Elizabeth Blackwell award 1992), Women's Forum Washington, Med. Soc. D.C. (exec. bd. 1990, sec. 1990, pres.-elect 1991, pres. 1992, chair exec. bd. 1993, ann. Cmty. Svc. award 1982), Am. Pediatric Soc., D.C. Hosp. Assn. (Cmty. Svc. award 1990), Am. Pub. Health Assn. (action bd. 1977-79, joint policy com. 1978-79, gov. council 1978-81), Met. Washington Pub. Health Assn. (gov. council 1975-78, 81-83, ann. award 1981), Nat. Med. Assn. (chmn. pediatric sect. 1977-79, Ross Labs. award 1979, Outstanding Svcs. to Children during Internat. Yr. of Child award 1979, Meritorious Service Appreciation award 1979, W.M. Cobb co-lectr. 1985, mem. Coun. on Maternal and Child Health, 1974-92, chmn. 1979-89, ann. Roselyn Payne Epps Symposium 1994—, Grace Marilyn James award for Disting svc. Pediatric sect. 1991, Achievement award 1993, ann. Roselyn Payne Epps symposium 1994—), Am. Hosp. Assn. (maternal and child health sect. governing coun. 1989, 1992-94, maternal and child health nominating com. 1991), Soc. for the Advancement of Women's Health Rsch. (award for advocacy 1996), The Women's Forum of Washington, Alpha Omega Alpha, Delta Omega, Alpha Kappa Alpha. Mem. United Ch. of Christ. Clubs: Pearls (pres. 1984-86), Carrousels (corr. sec. 1978-80), Links (pres. Met. chpt. 1986-89) (Washington), Cosmos. Lodge: Zonta, Internat. Women's Forum. Home and Office: 1775 N Portal Dr NW Washington DC 20012-1014

EPPS, WILLIAM DAVID, priest; b. Jan. 15, 1951; s. William E. Epps Jr.; m. Cynthia Scott Douglas; children: Jason, John, James. B in Social Work, East Tenn. State U., 1975; ThM, Internat. Sem., 1981; DMin, Berean Christian Coll., 1981; MA, Assemblies of God Theol. Sem., 2000; postgrad., Trinity Episcopal Sch. Min., 2002—. Lic. to ministry Assemblies of God, 1978, ordained, 1980; ordained priest Evangelical Episcopal Ch., 1995, received into Charismatic Episcopal Ch., 1996; lic. to preach United Meth. Ch., 1974. Youth worker State St. United Meth. Ch., Bristol, Va., 1971-72; minister youth Wesley Meml. United Meth. Ch., Johnson City, Tenn., 1973-74; pastor Taylor Meml. United Meth. Ch., Johnson City, 1974-75, Chuckey United Meth. Cir., Greene County, Tenn., 1975-77, Orebank Assembly of God, Kingsport, Tenn., 1978-79; minister edn. Trinity Assembly of God, Johnson City, 1979-80; minister outreach 1st Assembly of God, Grand Junction, Colo., 1980-83; sr. pastor Trinity Fellowship, Peachtree City, Ga., 1983-96; rector Christ the King CEC, Peachtree City, Ga., 1996—; mem. bishop's coun. Ga. Diocese, 1997—; canon to the ordinary Archdiocese of Armed Forces CEC, Diocese of Ga. Presbyter South Atlanta sect. Ga. Dist. Assemblies of God; chaplain Peachtree City Police Dept., Fayette County Sheriff's Dept., Atlanta divsn. FBI, Fulton County Police Acad., Senoia Police Dept.; chmn. 1990 N. Ga. Intercessory Prayer Gathering, Atlanta; mem. Ga. Dist. Evangelism Com., area evangelism rep.; mem. Coll. of Fellows of The Acad. Parish Clergy. Contbg. editor, Strategies for the 90's: A Pastoral Evangelism Handbook, Sursum Corda; columnist Citizen Newspapers, 1996—; contbr. articles to profl. jours. With USMC; U.S. Army N.G. Recipient Ga. Press Assn. Editorial award 1986, Cert. of Appreciation, Ga. Dist. Women's Ministries, 1989, many others. Mem. Fellowship Christian Athletes, Evang. Tchr. Tng. Assn. (honor mem.), Internat. Conf. Police Chaplains (Ga. post cert. police officer, Ga. post cert. chaplain, cert. master chaplain), Fayette County Ministerial Assn. (past pres.).

EPRIGHT, CHARLES JOHN, retired aerospace engineer; b. Bklyn., Jan. 11, 1932; s. Charles and Margaret Mary (Tripoli) E.; m. Mary Lucy Bono, May 29, 1954; children: Daniel John, Michael James, Marisa Epright Becker, Victoria Epright Carmona, Maria Carmela. BS in Math., U. Nev., 1965; MS in Engring. Mgmt., Northeastern U., 1971. Sr. engr. Raytheon, Andover, Mass., 1970-78, Delmo-Victor, Belmont, Calif., 1978-79; advanced systems engring. specialist Lockheed Missile and Space Co., Austin and Sunnyvale, Tex. and Calif., 1979-87; engring. scientist Tracor Aerospace, Austin, 1987-89; staff engr. Lockheed Engring. and Sci. Co., Houston, 1989-99. Civic adv. Salem-in-Action, NH, 1977-79; dir. Reachout, Salem, NH, 1976-79; cmty. action com. mem. N.H. Com. for Adopted and Foster Children, Manchester, NH, 1978-79, Runaway Hotline, Austin, 1984-88, 99—, Restorative Justice, Travis County, Tex., 2001—, Middle Earth Spectrum Shelter, Austin, 1987-89; mem. pub. responsibility com. Mental Health/Mental Retardation, Austin, 1988-89; bd. dirs., v.p. Assn. Retarded Citizens, Webster, Tex., 1989-93; mem. outreach Covenant House Tex., Houston, 1990-99. With USAF, 1950-70. Decorated Legion of Merit; recipient Family of Yr. award Sons of Italy, 1968, 69. Mem. Air Force Assn. (life), DAV, Am. Legion. Lodges: KC (grand knight 1968-69). Roman Catholic. Avocations: stamp collecting, photography, collecting old books. Home: 7500 Bender Dr Austin TX 78749-3105

EPSTEIN, ALAN BRUCE, lawyer; b. Passaic, N.J., Sept. 20, 1944; s. Jerome P. and Stella M. (Goldfinger) E.; m. Eve Teichholz, June 21, 1966; children: Jason, Dylan. BA, Temple U., 1967, JD, 1969. Bar: Pa. 1970, U.S. Dist. Ct. (ea. dist.) Pa. 1970, U.S. Ct. Appeals (3d cir.) 1972, U.S. Ct. Appeals (5th cir.) 1977, U.S. Dist. Ct. (cen. and we. dists.) Pa. 1987, U.S. Supreme Ct. 1988, U.S. Ct. Appeals (9th cir.) 2000. Assoc. firm Freedman, Borowsky & Lorry, Phila., 1969-77; ptnr. firm Jablon, Epstein, Wolf & Drucker, Phila., 1977-99; shareholder Spector, Gadon & Rosen, Phila., 1999—. Pres. Judicate Nat. Pvt. Ct. System, Phila., 1983-88. Fellow Pa. Bar Found., Coll. Labor and Employement Lawyers; mem. ABA, ATLA, Pa. Trial Lawyers Assn. (bd. govs. 1984-86), Phila. Trial Lawyers Assn., Pa. Bar Assn., Phila. Bar Assn., Temple Am. Inn Ct. (bd. dirs. 1994—, pres. 2001—, nat. edn. chair 2000—). Jewish. Home: 404 S Camac St Philadelphia PA 19147-1112 Office: Spector Gadon & Rosen PC Seven Penn Ctr 1635 Market St Fl 7 Philadelphia PA 19103-2217 E-mail: aepstein@lawsgr.com.

EPSTEIN, ALVIN, actor, director, singer, mime; b. Bronx, N.Y., May 14, 1925; s. Harry and Goldie (Rudnick) E. Student, Queens Coll., 1941-43, Ecole de Mime Etienne Decroux, Paris, 1947-51, Sanford Meisner Profl. Class, N.Y.C., 1951-52. Tchr. Chamber Theatre, Israel, Neighborhood Playhouse, N.Y.C., Circle in Sq. Theatre Sch., N.Y.C., Yale Drama Sch., 1968-77, Am. Repertory Theatre Inst.; acting artistic dir. Yale Repertory Theatre, 1972-73, assoc. artistic dir., 1973-77; artistic dir. Guthrie Theatre, Mpls., 1978-79. Mem. faculty Salzburg Am. Seminar, 1972, Aspen Music Festival, 1980-82. Actor Theatre de Mime Etienne Decroux, Paris, 1947-51, Habima Theatre, Israel, 1952-55; made Am. profl. debut with Marcel Marceau, Phoenix Theatre, N.Y.C., 1955; has appeared in many Broadway, off-Broadway touring and regional prodns., including The Fool in Orson Welles' King Lear, N.Y.C., 1956, Lucky in original Broadway prodn. Waiting for Godot, 1956, Puck in A Midsummer Night's Dream, Empire State Music Festival, N.Y., 1956, O'Killigain in Purple Dust, N.Y.C., Clov in Endgame, N.Y.C., Luc Delbert in No Strings, N.Y.C., title role in Enrico IV, Milw., Chgo., Beranger in The Pedestrian in the Air, Chgo., Theseus and Oberon in A Midsummer's Night Dream, N.Y.C., Octave in Clerambard, N.Y.C., various roles in Postmark Zero, N.Y.C., Landau in The Latent Heterosexual, Los Angeles, Sgt. in Dynamite Tonite, N.Y.C.; appeared in Whores, Wars and Tin Pan Alley, Chgo., New Haven, N.Y.C., Easthampton, A Place Without Doors, Long Wharf Theatre, New Haven, Staircase Theatre, N.Y.C., Goodman Theatre, Chgo., on U.S. tour, Los Angeles, Washington, 3 Plays by Samuel Beckett, Harold Clurman Theater, N.Y.C., 1983-84, Mark Taper Forum Los Angeles, Library of Congress, Washington, 1984, Jerusalem Festival, 1985; directed and acted Hamm in

Endgame, Samuel Beckett Theatre, Cherry Ln. Theater, N.Y.C., New Mayfair Theater, Los Angeles, Jerusalem Festival, 1985; mem. Yale Repertory Theatre, New Haven, 1968-77; playing leading parts Dynamite Tonite, God Bless, Story Theatre, The Bacchae, Greatshot, Crimes and Crimes, Olympian Games, Gimpel the Fool, Woyzeck, Don Juan, Macbett (Ionesco), The Tempest, Happy End, The Possessed, Bingo, Ivanov, Crossing Niagara, N.Y.C. Manhattan Theatre Club, Ghosts, Three Sisters, School for Scandal, Good Woman of Setzuan, 6 Characters in Search of an Author, Right You Are (If You Think You Are), Uncle Vanya, King Stag (Gozzi), Platanov, Mastergate, In Twilight (Chekhov Short Stories), The Miser (Moliere), Once In A Lifetime (Kaufman and Hart), When We Dead Awaken (Ibsen), Gloucester in King Lear, Polonius in Hamlet, Lord Summerhays in Misalliance (Shaw), Media Amok (C. Durang), Judge Brack in Hedda Gabler, Dr. Lombardi in The Servant of Two Masters (Goldoni), Dream of the Red Spider (Ribman), Iva Vasilyevich in Black Snow (Bulgakov-Dewhurst), Silence, Cunning, Exile (S. Greenman), directed and played Duncan and Scottish Doctor in Macbeth, King Henry in Henry IV Parts 1 & 2 (Shakespeare), Dr. Rance in What the Butler Saw (Orton), Firs in the Cherry Orchard (Chekhov), Patty O'Dowd in "A Touch of the Poet (O'Neill), Krapp's Last Tape, Ohio Impromptu, Agamemnon, Waiting for Godot, Henry V, Threepenny Opera, Beckett Trio: Eh Joe, Ghost Sonata, Nacht Und Träume, The Tempest, Tartuffe, Slaughter City, Am. Repertory Theatre, Cambridge, Mass., Value of Names, Androcles and the Lion, Hartford Stage Co., Waltz of the Toreadors, Roundabout Theatre, N.Y.C., Peachum in Three Penny Opera, Lunt-Fontanne Theatre, 1989; dir. The Rivals, Caligula, Seven Deadly Sins, Bourgeois Gentleman, Rise and Fall of the City of Mahagonny, The Tempest, A Midsummer Night's Dream, Troilus and Cressida, Julius Caesar, Old Times, Marriage of Figaro, Boys From Syracuse, Endgame, Importance of Being Earnest, Heartbreak House, others at Yale Repertory Theatre, Am. Repertory Theatre, Williamstown Theatre Festival, Richard III, Becket Trio; narrator Oedipus Rex, Cantata Singers; appeared in many TV shows on all networks, including The Doctors on NBC-TV, 1981-82, Doing Life NBC-TV film, 1986; dir. The Pretenders, Beggars Opera; appeared in Marriage, A Kurt Weill Cabaret for Guthrie Theatre, with Martha Schlamme in A Kurt Weill Cabaret for Bijou Theater, N.Y.C., on tour throughout U.S., Argentina, Brazil, Israel, 1979-85; co-founder, actor Berkshire Theatre Festival, Stockbridge, Mass., 1966, playing Antrobus in Skin of Our Teeth, Shylock in Merchant of Venice; dir. Colette, Berkshire Theatre Festival, Stockbridge, Mass., 1974; appeared in Schlamme and Epstein Sing Bernstein and Blitzstein, Aspen Music Festival, HB Studio N.Y.C., Am. Repertory Theatre, Cambridge, Mass., 1981, When the World Was Green, Olympic Arts Festival, The Cabinet of Dr. Caligari, Man and Superman; (film) Never Met Picasso, Thomas Edison in The Wizard of Menlo Park with Boston Pops, The Devil in Stravinsky's Soldier's Tale, Jordan Hall, Boston, Alice Tully Hall, N.Y.C., GBS in Dear Liar, on U.S. tour, Cadmus in The Bacchae, Shlink in In The Jungle of Cities, Lee Strasberg in Nobody Dies on Friday, Old Man in When The World was Green, Internat. Festival, Moscow Art Theatre, Russia, 1997-98, voice overs for documentary Africans in America, Old Gobbo and Tubal in Merchant of Venice, Am. Repertory Theatre, Cambridge Mass., narrator Philosopher's Stone by Mozart et al, Boston Baroque, Jordan Hall, Boston, Old Man in Charlie in The House of Rue, American Repertory Theatre, Cambridge, Leonard in film The Living Room Waltz, 1998-99; various roles in series of Samuel Beckett Radio Plays for Nat. Pub. Radio, 1987-88, Voice of the Bookseller in Walt Disney's Beauty and the Beast, 1991, The Gentleman from Boston (film), Passionada (film), Count Shabelsky in Ivanov (Indep. Reviewers New England award: Best Supporting Actor 1999), McLeavy in Loot, Honecker in Full Circle, Camillo in The Winters Tale, Tiresias in Sophocles' Antigone, The General in Chekhov's The Wedding, Dr. Blenkinsop in Shaw's The Doctor's Dilemma, John of Gaunt in Richard II, American Repertory Theatre, 1999-2001, Kurt Weill Songs Dengenerate and Otherwise Market Theatre, Cambridge, Mass, 2001, Ragpicker in The Madwoman of Chaillot, Neighborhood Playhouse, N.Y.C.; Dr. Gianonni in Enrico IV; Herald in Marat/Sade; Old Man in Lysistrata, Am. Repertory Theatre; Mr. Zurmer in Psychoanalysis Changed My Life (film); Morrie in Tuesdays with Morrie, N.Y. Stage and Film Co., Vassar Coll., 2001-2002, Minetta Lane Theatre, N.Y.C., 2002-03. Bd. dirs. Theatre Communications Group, N.Y.C., 1975-77. Served with AUS, 1943-46, ETO. Recipient Brandeis Creative Arts award, 1966, Obie award for Dynamite Tonite, 1968, Torch of Hope award, 1994, Elliot Norton prize Boston Theatre Critics, 1996, Jason Robards award for dedication to the theater, 2001, Best Cabaret award Ind. Reviewers of New Eng., 2002, Spencer Cherashore Lifetime Dedication to Not-for-profit Theatre award, 2003; Ford Found. grantee, 1959-60; Trumbull Coll. fellow, Yale U.; named Most promising Actor, Variety poll, 1956. Address: 82 Highland Rd Brookline MA 02445-7041

EPSTEIN, ARTHUR BARRY, optometrist; b. NYC, May 28, 1951; s. Morris Leo and Sadelle Jeanette (Posner) E.; m. Marilyn Sue Golomb, May 25, 1974; children: Rebecca Meryl, Emily Louise. BS in Psychology, CUNY, 1973; OD, SUNY, N.Y.C., 1977. Clin. instr. optometry SUNY, N.Y.C., 1977-78; pvt. practice L.I., 1978-82; pvt. practice limited to contact lenses North Shore Contact Lens & Vision Cons., P.C., Roslyn, N.Y., 1982—, Ophthalmic Cons. L.I., Rockville Centre, N.Y., 1990-99. Ophthalmic industry cons., 1992—; attending staff North Shore U. Hosp., Manhasset, N.Y., 1990—, dir. contact lens svc., 1992—; clin. adj. asst. prof. Northeastern State U., Talequah, Okla.; mem. adv. com. Rigid Gas Permeable Lens Inst.; med. adv. bd. Nat. Keratoconus Found.; dir. med. adv. bd. Surgicaleyes Found., 1998-2001,v.p. ctr. for Keratoconus. Contbg. editor Contact Lens Forum, 1989-91; clin. editor Optometric Mgmt., 1995; directing editor Optometric Mgmt., 1995-2001; mem. editl. bd. Eye & Contact Lens; contbg. author Specialty Contact Lenses: The Fitter's Guide, 1995, Clinical Contact Lens Practice, 1997, Clinical Ocular Pharmacology, 2001, LASIK: Clinical Comanagement, 2001; chief optometric editor: Optometric Management, 1998-2001; rev., dir. Optometric Programs, 2001—; exec. editor Rev. of Contact Lenses, 2001—; chief med. editor Optometric Physician, 2001—; contbr. over 180 articles to profl. jours. Fellow: Am. Acad. Optometry; mem.: Am. Optometric Assn. (vice-chair contact lens and cornea sect.). Avocations: cycling, amateur radio. Office: North Shore Contact Lens 1025 Northern Blvd Ste 94 Roslyn NY 11576-1506

EPSTEIN, ARTHUR WILLIAM, physician, educator; b. N.Y.C., May 15, 1923; s. Jacob E. and Anne (Bass) E.; m. Leona Cruce, Mar. 2, 1955; children: David Byron, Nona Kathryn, Emily Vera, James Jacob. AB, Columbia U., 1944, MD, 1947. Intern Mt. Sinai Hosp., N.Y.C., 1947-48, resident, 1949-50; clin. asst. Norristown (Pa.) State Hosp., 1948-49; faculty Tulane U., New Orleans, 1954—, asso. prof. psychiatry and neurology, 1959-64, prof., 1964—; pvt. practice medicine, specializing in neuropsychiatry New Orleans, 1964—; prof. emeritus Tulane U., 1993—. Vis. physician Charity Hosp., New Orleans, 1951-99; cons. U.S. Army Hosp., New Orleans, 1958-64; mem. med. staff Tulane Med. Center Hosp., 1976— Author: An Anatomist's Dream of Love, 1966, The Dissecting Room, 1978, The Lady and the Serpent, 1981, A Contemporary Religious Svc., 1987, Bridge Cross, 1989, Dreaming and Other Involuntary Mentation: An Essay in Neuropsychiatry, 1996, Poems of Later Life, 1999; contbr. articles to profl. jours. Med. adviser Social Security Adminstrn., 1968-93; bd. dirs. Ednl. Rsch. and Treatment Ctr., New Orleans. Served with M.C. USNR, 1956-58. Named Psychiatrist of Yr. La. Psychiatric Assn., 1992. Fellow AAAS, Am. Psychiat. Assn. (life, leisure time and its uses com.), Am. Acad. Psychoanalysis (pres. 1987-88, Silverberg award 1985), Am. Acad. Neurology; mem. Soc. Biol. Psychiatry (v.p. 1979-80, pres.-elect 1980-81, pres. 1981-82), Am. Epilepsy Soc., Alpha Omega Alpha. Home: 1664 Robert St New Orleans LA 70115-4975 Office: DePaul-Tulane 1040 Calhoun St New Orleans LA 70118-5914 *Amid the hurly-burly, keep awe and wonder. Pursue the ideal.*

EPSTEIN, BARBARA, editor; b. Boston, Aug. 30, 1929; d. Harry W. and Helen (Diamond) Zimmerman; children: Jacob, Helen. BA, Radcliffe Coll., 1949. Editor N.Y. Rev. Books, N.Y.C., 1963—. Office: NY Rev of Books 1755 Broadway Fl 5 New York NY 10019-3743 E-mail: bepstein@nybooks.com.

EPSTEIN, BEN IRVING, management consultant; b. Chgo., Aug. 20, 1917; s. Joseph and Clara (Raskin) Epstein; m. Phyllis Shapiro Epstein, May 16, 1942 (dec.); children: Robert, Joseph(dec.). Grad. H.S., Chgo. Salesman Lidnel Sanger Rep., Kansas City, Mo., 1935—38; terr. sales mgr. Corp. Corp., Chgo., 1939—51; ctrl. divsn. sales mgr. Thor Corp., Cicero, Ill., 1952—56; nat. sales mgr. Regal Ware Corp., Kewaskum, Wis., 1956—57; v.p. sales Textile Mills, Chgo., 1959—66; asst. to the pres. Miracle White, Chgo., 1966—72; v.p. nat. accounts Associated Mills/Pollenex, Chgo., 1975—84. Founding family Temple Shalom, Milw., 1944; bd. mem. Burt Children's Ctr., San Francisco, 1985. Achievements include design of laurel table lamps; ladies blouses. Avocations: literature, music, antiques, birdwatching. Home: 6925 N Kolmar Ave Lincolnwood IL 60712

EPSTEIN, BRUCE HOWARD, lawyer; b. Dallas, Jan. 30, 1952; s. Raymond Howard and Thelma (Romotsky) Epstein; m. Toni Rosas, Aug. 28, 1988; children: Marianne Corinne, Peter Louis. Student, U. Calif., San Diego, 1970-71; AB in Polit. Sci. with honors, U. Calif., Riverside, 1974; JD, U. Calif., San Francisco, 1977. Bar: Calif. 1977, U.S. Dist. Ct. (no. dist.) Calif. 1977, U.S. Dist. Ct. (ctrl., ea., and so. dists.) Calif. 1990, U.S. Ct. Appeals (9th cir.) 1990, U.S. Supreme Ct. 1990. Dep. dist. atty. San Bernardino County Dist. Atty.'s Office, San Bernardino, Calif., 1977-83; sr. assoc. Atwood, Hurst, Knox & Anderson, San Jose, Calif., 1983-85; dep. city atty. San Jose City Atty.'s Office, 1985-86; pvt. practice Campbell, Calif., 1985-87; asst. v.p., counsel Lawyers Title Ins. Corp., Pasadena, Calif., 1987—, Lawyers Title Co., Pasadena, 1987—, Transnation Title Ins. Co., Pasadena, 1998—, Commonwealth Land Title Ins. Co., Pasadena, 1998—. Asst. v.p., counsel Land Am. Fin. Group, Pasadena, 1998—; real estate broker, Burbank, Calif., 1983—2000; lectr. Evergreen Coll., San Jose, Calif., 1986—87; instr. Minimum Continuing Legal Edn., 1997—, Escrow Agt. Profl. Devel., 1997—; mem. claims awareness com. Calif. Land Title Assn., 1997—; pres. Robert Louis Stevenson Sch. Site Coun., 1997— 2001. Active R. L. Stevenson PTA; site coun. Robert Louis Stevenson Sch., 2001—02; active Am. Cancer Soc., Am. Lung Soc., Santa Barbara Zoological Gardens, David Starr Jordan PTA, Am. Diabetes Assn., 1977—, Smithsonian Instn., 1990—, Jewish Found. for the Righteous, 1990—, Am. Air Mus. in Britain. Mem.: Calif. State Sheriffs' Assn., Alzheimer's Assn., Am. Heart Assn., Nat. Air and Space Soc., Los Angeles County Bar Assn., Calif. Bar Assn., Planetary Soc., Nat. Space Soc., Simon Wiesenthal Ctr., Zool. Soc. San Diego, Calif. Sci. Ctr., Natural History Mus. Los Angeles County, Descanso Gardens Guild, Greater L.A. Zool. Assn., Anti Defamtion League, Am. Mus. Natural History. Democrat. Jewish. Avocations: writing, sports, painting. Office: Land Am 55 S Lake Ave Ste 600 Pasadena CA 91101-2688

EPSTEIN, CHARLES JOSEPH, physician, medical geneticist, pediatrics and biochemistry educator; b. Phila., Sept. 3, 1933; s. Jacob C. and Frieda (Savransky) E.; m. Lois Barth, June 10, 1956; children: David Alexander, Jonathan Akiba, Paul Michael, Joanna Marguerite. AB, Harvard U., 1955, MD, 1959; DS, Northeastern Ohio U., 1997. Diplomate: Am. Bd. Medical Genetics. Intern in medicine Peter Bent Brigham Hosp., Boston, 1959-60, asst. resident in medicine, 1960-61; research assoc., med. officer and sect. chief Nat. Heart Inst. and Nat. Inst. Arthritis and Metabolic Diseases, NIH, Bethesda, Md., 1961-67; research fellow in med. genetics U. Wash., 1963-64; assoc. prof. pediatrics and biochemistry U. Calif., San Francisco, 1967-72, prof., 1972—, chief divsn. med. genetics. dept. pediatrics, 1967—, co-dir. program in human genetics, 1997—. Investigator Howard Hughes Med. Inst., 1976-81; mem. human embryology and devel. study sect. NIH, 1971-75; mem. mental retardation rsch. com. Nat. Inst. Child Health and Devel., 1979-83, chmn., 1981-83; mem. com. for study inborn errors of metabolism NRC, 1972-75; mem. sci. adv. bd. Nat. Down Syndrome Soc., 1981-99, chmn., 1984-99, mem. nat. adv. bd., 1999—, also bd. dirs.; mem. recombinant DNA adv. com. NIH, 1985-90, mem. human gene therapy subcom., 1987-91, chmn. residency review com. med. genetics, 1993-99; mem. sci. adv. bd. Buck Inst., 2002—; Stanley Wright Meml. lectr. Western Soc. Pediatric Rsch., 1986; William Potter lectr. Thomas Jefferson U., 1987; George H. Fetterman lectr. U Pitts., 1989; faculty rsch. lectr. U. Calif., San Francisco, 1994; Mary Hulings Edens lectr. U. Tex. Med. Br., Galveston, 1996; Ida Cordelia Beam lectr. U. Iowa, 1998; Donald L. Thurston meml. lectr. Washington U., St. Louis, 1999, others. Author: The Consequences of Chromosome Imbalance: Principles, Mechanisms and Models, 1986; editor: Human Genetics, 1984-95, The Neurobiology of Down Syndrome, 1986, Oncology and Immunology of Down Syndrome, 1987, Am. Jour. Human Genetics, 1987-93, Molecular and Cytogenetic Studies of Non-disjunction, 1989, Molecular Genetics of Chromosome 21 and Down Syndrome, 1990, Morphogenesis of Down Syndrome, 1991, Down Syndrome and Alzheimer Disease, 1992, Phenotypic Mapping of Down Syndrome and other Aneuploid Conditions, 1993, Etiology and Pathogenesis of Down Syndrome, 1995; assoc. editor Rudolph's Textbook of Pediatrics, 18th edit., 1986, 20th edit., 1996; mem. editl. bd. Biology Reprodn., 1974-78, Cytogenetics and Cell Genetics, 1975-80; mem. editl. bd. Am. Jour. Med. Genetics, 1977—, sr. editor, 1995-99, adv. editor, 2000—; mem. editl. bd. Devel. Genetics, 1983-85, Jour. Embryology and Exptl. Morphology, 1983-85, Human Gene Therapy, 1990-98, Human Mutation, 1992-99, Human Genetics, 1995-99, Down Syndrome Quar., 1996—, Trends in Genetics, 1997—, Cmty. Genetics, 1998—, Annual Review of Human Genetics and Genomics, 1999—, Mechanisms of Aging and Development, 2000—. Served with USPHS, 1961-63. Named to Hall of Fame, Central High Sch. of Phila., 2001; recipient Henry A. Christian award, Harvard Med. Sch., 1959, Rsch. Career Devel. award, NIH, 1967—72, Nancy and Daniel Weisman Charitable Found. award, 1990, Lifetime Achievement award in genetic scis., March of Dimes Birth Defects Found., Col. Harland Sanders, 1995, 6th World Congress on Down Syndrome award, 1997, Disting. Rsch. award, The Arc of the U.S., 1998, Premio Internat. Phoenix-Anni Verdi Perle Rsch. Geneticke, Italian Soc. Human Genetics, 1999, Allan award, Am. Soc. Human Genetics, 2001. Fellow AAAS; mem. AMA, Am. Bd. Med. Genetics (bd. dirs. 1988-93, v.p. 1989, pres. 1990-91), Genetics Soc. Am., Am. Fedn. Clin. Rsch., Am. Soc. Human Genetics (bd. dirs. 1972-75, 87-93, 97-98, pres.-elect 1995, pres. 1996), Am. Soc. Biochemistry and Molecular Biology, Soc. Pediatric Rsch. (coun. 1972-75), Am. Coll. Med. Genetics (pres. elect 2001-02, pres. 2003--), Western Soc. Clin. Investigation, Western Soc. Pediatric Rsch., Am. Soc. Clin. Investigation, Am. Soc. Cell Biology, Soc. Devel. Biology, Am. Pediatric Soc., Western Assn. Physicians (coun. 1993-95), Assn. Am. Physicians, Soc. Inherited Metabolic Disorders, Inst. Medicine (Nat. Acad. Scis.), Calif. Acad. Medicine, Phi Beta Kappa, Alpha Omega Alpha. Jewish. Achievements include research numerous publs. on human and med. genetics, devel. genetics and biochemistry. Office: U Calif Dept Pediatrics U585L San Francisco CA 94143-0001

EPSTEIN, DANIEL MARK, poet, dramatist, biographer; b. Washington, Oct. 25, 1948; s. Donald David and Louise Marietta (Tillman) E.; m. Wendy Roberts, May 29, 1976 (div. 1994); children: Johanna Ruth, Benjamin Robert; m. Jennifer Bishop, 1994; children: Theodore John, Nathaniel David. AB magna cum laude with highest honors in English, Kenyon Coll., 1970; postgrad., U. Va., 1970-71; M.F.A. h.c., Norwich U. Asst. mgr. Automatic Enterprises, Washington, 1967-70; disting. scholar-in-residence Randolph-Macon Woman's Coll., 1982; writer-in-residence Towson State U., 1983-90. Cons. lit. div. Nat. Endowment for Arts, Washington, 1973; lectr. USIS tour German univs., 1977, tour, Africa, 1978; asst. prof. Johns Hopkins U.; bd. dirs. Balt. Theatre Project; co-founder Balt. Poet's Theatre. Poet-in-residence, NDEA grantee, Garrett County, Md., 1972; master poet Md. Arts Coun. Artists-in-the Schs. program, 1974-77; appeared in numerous poetry readings; books of poetry include Appearances, 1969, No Vacancies in Hell, 1973, The Follies, 1977, Young Men's Gold, 1978, The Book of Fortune, 1982, Spirits, 1987, The Boy In The Well, 1995, The Traveler's Calendar, 2002, stories and essays include Star of Wonder, 1986, Love's Compass, 1990; biographies include Sister Aimee, 1993, Nat King Cole, 1999, Edna St. Vincent Millay, 2001; plays include Jenny and the Phoenix, 1977, The Midnight Visitor, 1981, The Leading Lady 1999, others; translator Euripides' The Bacchae, 1998. Recipient Robert Frost prize, 1969; Prix de Rome AAAL, 1977; Danforth Found. grantee, 1971; Nat. Endowment for Arts fellow, 1974; Guggenheim fellow, 1983 Fellow Am. Acad. in Rome; mem. Phi Beta Kappa. Address: 843 W University Pkwy Baltimore MD 21210-2911

EPSTEIN, DAVID GUSTAV, lawyer; b. Alexandria, La., Dec. 7, 1943; s. Isaac and Alice (Fried) Epstein; m. Diane Floca, Feb. 16, 1969; children: Daniel Stewart, Charles Abraham. LLB, U. Tex., 1966; LLM, Harvard U., 1969. Bar: Tex. 1966, Ariz. 1967, Ark. 1979, Ga. 1989. Asst. prof. N.C. Sch. Law, 1970-74; prof. law U. Tex., 1974-79, Fulbright and Jaworski prof. law, 1982-85; dean Sch. Law U. Ark., 1979-82; dean and prof. bankruptcy law Southeastern Bankruptcy Law Inst., Emory U., Atlanta, 1985-89; ptnr. King & Spalding, 1989-97, of counsel, 1998—. Charles E. Tweedy Jr. chair in law Law Sch. U. Ala., 1998—; Bruce W. Nichols vis. prof. law Harvard U., 2002. Author: (book) Bankruptcy (3 vols.), 1992, Business Structures, 2002, Making and Doing Deals, 2002, Bankruptcy in a Nutshell, 6th edit., 2002. Mem.: Am. Coll. Bankruptcy, Am. Law Inst., Nat. Bankruptcy Conf., Order of Coif. Democrat. Jewish. Office: King & Spalding 191 Peachtree St NE Ste 40 Atlanta GA 30303-1740

EPSTEIN, DAVID L. ophthalmologist, educator; b. Chgo., June 23, 1944; BA, Johns Hopkins U., 1965, MD, 1968; M of Med. Mgmt., Tulane U., 2001. Diplomate Am. Bd. Ophthalmology; cert. Med. Mgmt., Am. Coll. Physician Execs. Med. intern King County Hosp. and Univ. Hosp./U. Wash., Seattle, 1968-69; rsch. fellow Howe Lab. Ophthalmology Mass. Eye and Ear Infirmary/Harvard Med. Sch., Boston, 1969-70, 72, resident in ophthalmology, 1973-75, glaucoma clin. rsch. fellow, 1975-76; from instr. to assoc. prof. ophthalmology Harvard U. Med. Sch., 1976-91; prof. ophthalmology U. Calif., San Francisco, 1991-92; prof., chmn. dept. ophthalmology Duke U. Med. Sch., Durham, N.C., 1992—; chief of ophthalmology Duke U. Hosp., 1992—, Joseph A.C. Wadsworth clin. prof. ophthalmology, 1996—. Vis. scientist Nat. Eye Inst., 1988; mem. Nat. Eye Health Edn. Program; lectr. in field. Mem. editorial bd. Archives of Ophthalmology, 1985-94; contbr. numerous articles to profl. jours.; patentee in field. Recipient numerous awards and honors; grantee Nat. Eye Inst., Am. Health Assistance Found., Rsch. to Prevent Blindness, others. Mem. AAAS, AMA, Am. Coll. Physician Execs., Assn. for Ocular Pharmacology and Therapeutics, Assn. VA Ophthalmologists, N.C. Soc. Ophthalmology (ARVD advocacy com., sci. policy subcom.), N.C. Med. Soc., Durham-Orange County Med. Soc., Assn. Univ. Profs. in Ophthalmology, Glaucoma Soc. Internat. Congress Ophthalmology, Am. Glaucoma Soc., Internat. Soc. for Eye Rsch., Assn. for Rsch. in Vision and Ophthalmology, Am. Acad. Ophthalmology. Phi Beta Kappa, Sigma Xi, Alpha Omega Alpha. Home: 9123 S Lowell Rd Bahama NC 27503-8757 Office: Duke U Med Ctr Dept Oph Box 3802 Wadsworth Bldg Durham NC 27710

EPSTEIN, DAVID M. publishing executive; b. Chgo., Feb. 20, 1946; s. Bernard G. and Marjorie P. (McCormack) E.; m. Ryba L. Tregilgas, Apr. 11, 1968; children: Daniel, Miriam. AB, UCLA, 1968; MA, U. Ill., 1971. Assoc. editor Scott, Foresman and Co., Glenview, Ill., 1971-80, courseware splst., 1980-81; editor Richard D. Irwin Inc., Homewood, Ill., 1981-83, mgr. composition, 1983-89; assoc. pub. Am. Libr. Assn., Chgo., 1989-98; mgr. Creative Svcs. PricewaterhouseCoopers LLP, Chgo., 1998—2001, Mellon HR Svcs., 2002—. Author: Electronic Text Management, 1984; editor: U.S. in Literature, 1978, Books of the Fairs, 1991, Feeling Overworked: When Work Becomes Too Much, 2001; mng. editor: World Encyclopedia Libr. and Info. Sci., 1996, Frontiers of World Class Learning, 1998. Bd. dirs. Chgo. Concerned Jamaicans. Jewish. Avocations: aviation history, writing, jazz history. Office: Mellon HR/Buck Cons 1 North Dearborn Chicago IL 60602

EPSTEIN, EDWARD LOUIS, lawyer; b. Walla Walla, Wash., Jan. 10, 1936; s. Louis and Marie (Barger) E.; m. Marilyn K. Young, Dec. 29, 1962; children: Lisa Marie, Rachel Ann. BA with great distinction, Stanford U., 1958; LLB magna cum laude, Harvard U., 1961. Bar: Oreg. 1962, U.S. Dist. Ct. Oreg. 1962, U.S. Ct. Appeals (9th cir.) 1963. Assoc. Stoel Rives LLP, Portland, Oreg., 1962-67, ptnr., 1967—. Past sec., bd. dirs. Portland Hosp. Facilities Authority; trustee Good Samaritan Hosp. and Med. Ctr., Portland, 1972-78, pres., 1978; past trustee Morrison Ctr. for Youth and Family Svcs., Oreg. Assn. Hosps. Found. Mem. ABA, Am. Bar Found., Am. Health Lawyers Assn., Oreg. Bar Assn., Multnomah County Bar Assn., Multnomah Athletic Club, Univ. Club, Harvard Law Rev., Phi Beta Kappa. Office: Stoel Rives LLP 900 SW 5th Ave Ste 2600 Portland OR 97204-1268 E-mail: elepstein@stoel.com.

EPSTEIN, ELAINE MAY, lawyer; b. Phila., May 29, 1947; d. Sidney and Helen (Brill) Epstein; m. James A. Krachey, July 25, 1987; stepchildren: Ross Krachey, Anna Krachey. BA, U. Pa., 1968; MA, Yale U., 1971; JD, Northeastern U., 1976. Assoc. Law Offices of P.J. Piscitelli, Brockton, Mass., 1975-78; ptnr. LoDolce & Epstein, Brockton, 1978-94, Todd & Weld, Boston, 1994—. Mem. Bd. Bar Overseers, Boston, 1984-88; trustee Mass. Continuing Legal Edn., Boston, 1991-93. Mem. editl. bd. Mass. Lawyers Weekly, 1993-98. Fellow Mass. Bar Found. (trustee 1993-98); mem. ABA, Mass. Bar Assn. (pres. 1992-93), Women's Bar Assn. (pres. 1979-80). Democrat. Jewish. Home: 4 Manns Hill Cres Sharon MA 02067-2267 Office: Todd & Weld 28 State St Fl 31 Boston MA 02109-1775

EPSTEIN, EMANUEL, plant physiologist; b. Duisburg, Germany, Nov. 5, 1916; came to U.S., 1938, naturalized, 1946; s. Harry and Bertha (Lowe) E.; m. Hazel L. Leask, Nov. 26, 1943; children: Jared H. (dec.), Jonathan H. BS, U. Calif., Davis, 1940, MS, 1941; PhD, U. Calif., Berkeley, 1950. Plant physiologist Dept. Agr., Beltsville, Md., 1950-58; lectr., assoc. plant physiologist U. Calif.-Davis, 1958-65, prof. plant nutrition, plant physiologist, 1965-87, faculty rsch. lectr., 1980, prof. botany, 1974-87, prof. and plant physiologist emeritus (active), 1987—. Cons. to govt. and pvt. agys. Author: Mineral Nutrition of Plants: Principles and Perspectives, 1972; mem. editl. bd. Plant Physiology, 1962-71, 76-92, CRC Handbook Series in Nutrition and Food, 1975-84, The Biosaline Concept: An Approach to the Utilization of Underexploited Resources, 1978, Saline Agriculture: Salt-Tolerant Plants for Developing Countries, 1990, Plant Sci., 1981-89, Advances in Plant Nutrition, 1981-94, Soil Science and Plant Nutrition, 1998—; contbr. articles to profl. jours. With U.S. Army, 1943-46. Recipient Gold medal Pisa (Italy) U., 1962; Guggenheim fellow, 1958; Fulbright sr. research scholar, 1965-66, 74-75, award of honor, Am. Soc. Agronomy Calif. Chapter, 2002. Fellow AAAS (pres. Pacific divsn. 1990, Fifty-Yr. Life mem. award 1999); mem. Nat. Acad. Scis., Am. Soc. Plant Biologists (Charles Reid Barnes Hon. Life Membership award 1986), Japanese Soc. Plant Physiologists, Scandinavian Soc. Plant Physiology, Am. Inst. Biol. Scis., Am. Soc. Agronomy Calif. (award of honor, 2002), Common Cause, Save-the-Redwoods League, U. Calif. Davis Club, Calif. Aggie Alumni Assn. (Alumni citation for Excellence, 1999), Nature Conservancy, Sigma Xi. Achievements include rsch., publs. on ion transport in plants, mineral nutrition and salt rels. of plants, salt tolerant crops, and silicon in plant biology. Office: UC Soils & Biogeochemistry Land Air & Water Resources 1 Shields Ave Davis CA 95616-8627 E-mail: eqepstein@ucdavis.edu.

EPSTEIN, ERVIN HAROLD, JR., dermatologist, educator, researcher; b. Oakland, Calif, Mar. 6, 1941; s. Ervin Harold Sr. and Selma E.; m. Sally Ann Fain, Aug. 11, 1963; children: Adam, Stephanie, Emily. AB, Harvard Coll., 1962; MD, U. Calif., San Francisco, 1966. Diplomate Am. Bd. Dermatology. Intern Barnes Hosp., Washington U., St. Louis, 1966-67; resident in dermatology Harvard U., Boston, 1967-68; clin. assoc. dermatol. br. NIH, Bethesda, Md., 1968-70, resident fellow in biochemistry, 1970-71; resident in dermatology NYU Med. Sch., 1971-72; asst. to clin. prof. dept. dermatology U. Calif. Med. Sch., San Francisco, 1972—, asst. to rsch. dermatologist, 1972—. Prin. investigator various rsch. grants NIH Bethesda, 1972—; mem. gen. medicine study sect. 1987-91, mem. adv. coun. Nat. Inst. Arthritis, Musculoskeletal and Skin Diseases, 1993-96. Co-editor: Skin Surgery, 1977, 3rd edit., 1988; editor: Progress in Dermatology, 1982-87; assoc. editor: (audio tape) Dialogues in Dermatology, 1977-84, author numerous rsch. papers, 1966—. Lt. USPHS, 1968-70. Mem. Soc. Investigative Dermatology (sec.-treas. 1984-89, pres.-elect 1990 91, pres. 1991-92), Dermatology Found. (trustee 1981-83, 84-91), Am. Dermatol. Assn. (treas. 1992-96), Harvard Club San Francisco (v.p.). Jewish. Office: San Francisco Gen Hosp 1001 Potrero Ave Rm 269 San Francisco CA 94110-3594

EPSTEIN, FRANKLIN HAROLD, physician, educator; b. Bklyn., May 5, 1924; s. Max and Fannie (Geduld) E.; m. Sherrie Spivack, Aug. 12, 1951; children: Mark, Ann, Sara, Jonathan. BA, Bklyn. Coll., 1944; MD, Yale U., 1947; Doctor Honoris Causa, Med. Acad., Gdansk, 1992. Diplomate: Am. Bd. Internal Medicine (chmn. subsplty. bd. in nephrology 1969-72). Asst. prof. medicine Yale U., 1954-59, assoc. prof., 1959-66, prof. medicine, 1966-72, chief, divsn. metabolism, 1965-72; prof. medicine Harvard U., 1972—, H.L. Blumgart prof. medicine, W. Applebaum prof. medicine; dir. Thorndike Meml. Lab., Boston City Hosp., 1972; physician-in-chief Beth Israel Hosp., 1973-80, dir. renal divsn., 1980-93; Macy Found. fellow and vis. scientist Oxford (Eng.) U., 1980-81. Cons. to surgeon gen. U.S. Army, 1964-80; mem. metabolism study sect. USPHS, 1962-66; pres. Mt. Desert Island Biol.Lab., 1986-95. Editor: Yearbook of Medicine, 1967-96; assoc. editor: Jour. Clin. Investigation, 1957-62, New Eng. Jour. Medicine, 1982-2001, Quar. Jour. Medicine, 1984-93; contbr. papers, book chpts. on renal physiology, disease of kidneys. Capt. M.C., U.S. Army, 1950-53. Recipient Rsch. Career award, USPHS, 1964, John P.

Peters award, Am. Soc. Nephrology, 1985, Bywaters award, Internat. Soc. Nephrology, 1999, David Hume award, Nat. Kidney Found., 2003. Fellow AAAS, Assn. Physicians Gt. Britain and Ireland, Royal Coll. Physicians; mem. Am. Soc. Clin. Investigation (v.p. 1970), Assn. Am. Physicians, Interurban Clin. Club, Sigma Xi, Alpha Omega Alpha. Jewish. Home: 294 Buckminster Rd Brookline MA 02445-5801 Office: 330 Brookline Ave Boston MA 02215-5400 E-mail: fepstein@caregroup.harvard.edu.

EPSTEIN, GARY MARVIN, lawyer; b. Bklyn., Nov. 28, 1946; s. Arthur and Juliett (Winick) E.; m. Jeralyn Needel, June 29, 1969; children: Daniel, Deborah. BSEE, Lehigh U., 1968; JD, Harvard U., 1971. Bar: D.C. 1971, U.S. Ct. Appeals (3d cir.) 1973, U.S. Supreme Ct. 1975, U.S. Ct. Appeals (9th cir.) 1988. Engr. Gordon Engring. Co., Wakefield, Mass., 1967-70; assoc. Arent, Fox, Kinter, Plotkin & Kahn, Washington, 1971-79, ptnr., 1979-81; chief Common Carrier Bur. FCC, Washington, 1981-83; ptnr., head telecom. group Latham & Watkins, Washington, 1983—. Pub. mem. Adminstrv. Conf. U.S., 1983-86; chmn. adv. com. reduced orbital spacing FCC, 1983-86; chmn. adv. Com. World Radiocomms. Conf., FCC, 1994-96; dir. D.C. Appleseed Ctr., 2001—, vice chmn., 2002—, vice chair, 2003-, Appleseed Found., 2002—, v.p., 2002-. Bd. dirs. Appleseed Found., 2002—. Mem. ABA, D.C. Bar Assn., Eta Kappa Nu, Tau Beta Pi. Home: 1111 23d St NW Apt PH1F Washington DC 20037-2809 Office: Latham & Watkins 555 11th St NW Washington DC 20004-2585 E-mail: Gary.Epstein@lw.com.

EPSTEIN, IRVING ROBERT, chemistry educator; b. Bklyn., Aug. 9, 1945; s. Milton and Marion (Hillsberg) E.; m. Ellen Bea Fisher, Oct. 31, 1971; children: David, Peter. AB, Harvard U., 1966, MA, 1968, PhD, 1971; diploma, Oxford U., 1967. NATO postdoctoral fellow Cambridge U., 1971; asst. prof. dept. chemistry Brandeis U., Waltham, Mass., 1971-75, assoc. prof., 1975-81, prof., 1981—, Helena Rubinstein prof., 1989—94, chmn., 1983-87, dean arts & scis., 1992-94, provost, sr. v.p. for acad. affairs, 1994-2001. NSF faculty profl. devel. fellow Max Planck Inst., Göttingen, Germany, 1977-78. Editl. adv. bd. Jour. Phys. Chemistry, 1982-89; assoc. editor Chaos, 1990—; editl. bd. Interjour. Complex Sys., 1995—; contbr. articles to profl. jours. Recipient tchr.-scholar award Dreyfus Found., 1973; Nat. Merit scholar, 1962-66, Marshall scholar, 1966-67, Woodrow Wilson fellow, 1968, Guggenheim fellow, 1977, 87, Humboldt fellow, 1977, NSF fellow, 1977-78. Mem. Am. Chem. Soc. (Liebmann award), Phi Beta Kappa. Home: 28 Otis St Newton MA 02460-1803 Office: Brandeis U MS 015 Waltham MA 02454-9110 E-mail: epstein@brandeis.edu .

EPSTEIN, JASON, publishing company executive; b. Cambridge, Mass., Aug. 25, 1928; s. Robert and Gladys (Shapiro) E.; children: Jacob, Helen. BA, Columbia U., 1949, MA, 1950. Editor Doubleday & Co., 1951-58; v.p., editorial dir. Random House, Inc., N.Y.C., 1958-97. Co-founder N.Y. Rev. Books; founder Libr. of Am.; founder Reader's Catalog. Author: The Great Conspiracy Trial, 1970; co-author: Easthampton, a history and guide, 1975, Book Business, 2001; contbr. articles to various publs. Recipient John Jay award Columbia Coll., 1988, Lifetime Achievement award Nat. Book Award, 1988, Curtis Benjamin award Assn. Am. Pubs., 1993, Lifetime Achievement award Guld Hall, 2001, Lifetime Achievement award Nat. Book Critics Cir., 2002. Mem. Council Fgn. Relations, Phi Beta Kappa. Home: PO Box 1143 Sag Harbor NY 11963-0039 E-mail: Jasepstei@aol.com.

EPSTEIN, JAY STUART, federal regulator; married; 2 children. BA cum laude, Harvard U., 1969; MD, Downstate Med. Coll., 1976. Resident internal medicine George Washington U. Hosp., Washington, 1976-79, clin. fellow infectious diseases, 1979-81; sr. staff fellow rsch. divsn. virology office biologics rsch. & review FDA, Rockville, Md., 1981-85, chief immunochemistry lab., 1984-86, chief retrovirology lab. divsn. transfusion sci., 1986-92, acting dept. dir., 1990-92, dir. divsn. transfusion transmitted diseases, 1993-95, acting. dir. Office Blood Rsch. and Rev., 1993-95, dir., 1995—. Rsch. asst. Moffit Hosp., San Francisco, 1971-73; part time physician Potomac (Md.) Village Med. Ctr., 1981-83; part time house physician Capitol Hill Hosp., Washington, 1981-83. With USPHS, 1985-88. Nat. Merit scholar, 1965, Harvard Coll. scholar, 1965, N.Y. State Regents Medicine scholar, 1969. Mem. AAAS, Infectious Diseases Soc. Am., Greater Washington Area Infectious Diseaes Soc., Alpha Omega Alpha. Home: 1922 Foxhall Rd Mc Lean VA 22101-5535 Office: Office Blood Rsch & Review FDA CBER HFM-300 1401 Rockville Pike Rockville MD 20852-1448 E-mail: epsteinj@cber.fda.gov.

EPSTEIN, JEFFREY MARK, neurosurgeon; b. Newark, Apr. 7, 1951; s. Herbert Joseph and Roberta Laura (Sank) E.; m. Ronit Adler. BA, Johns Hopkins U., 1973; MD, Autonomous U. Guadalajara, Mex., 1979. Diplomate Am. Bd. Neurol. and Orthopedic Surgery, Am. Bd. Pain Mgmt. 5th channel clerkship Newark Beth-Israel Med. Ctr., 1979-80; intern in surgery Muhlenberg Hosp., Plainfield, N.J., 1980-81; resident in neurosurgery SUNY-Downstate and Kings County Hosp. Ctr., Bklyn., 1981-85, chief resident neurosurgery, 1985-86; instr. neurosurgery SUNY-Downstate Med. Ctr., 1986-87, asst. prof. neurosurgery, 1987-88; pvt. practice, Babylon, N.Y., 1988—. Contbr. articles to Anesthesia Jour., to Pain Physician. Mem.: Am. Bonanza Soc., Suffolk County Med. Soc., Med. Soc. State N.Y., N.Y. State Neurosurgery Soc., Lloyd Harbor Yacht Club, Alpha Epsilon Delta (v.p. 1973). Jewish. Avocations: skiing, sailing, flying. Office: 51 John St Ste 4 Babylon NY 11702-2928

EPSTEIN, JEREMIAH FAIN, anthropologist, educator; b. N.Y.C., Feb. 14, 1924; s. Joseph and Carol (Fain) E.; divorced; children— Anne, Louise, Suzanne. BS in Agr, U. Ill., 1949, MA in Anthropology, 1951; PhD, U. Pa., 1957. Lectr. Hunter Coll., N.Y.C., 1954-58; research scientist anthropology U. Tex., Austin, 1958-60, mem. faculty, 1958—, prof. anthropology, 1970-97; prof. emeritus, 1997—. Fieldwork in, Mex., Belize, Honduras, France, U.S. Contbr. articles to profl. jours. Served with AUS, 1942-45. Decorated Purple Heart; grantee NSF, 1963, 64; grantee Wenner Gren Found., 1961; grantee U. Tex. Inst. Latin Am. Studies, 1963, 75; grantee U. Tex., 1988; Fulbright-Hays fellow, 1964; Mellon Found. fellow in Latin Am. studies, 1988; U. Tex. faculty rsch. assignment, 1988. Mem. Am. Anthrop. Assn., Soc. Am. Archaeology, AAAS, Soc. Mexicana Anthropologia. Office: U Tex Dept Anthropology Austin TX 78712 E-mail: jepstein@mail.utexas.edu.

EPSTEIN, JEREMY G. lawyer; b. Chgo., Sept. 28, 1946; s. Joseph and Gayola (Goldman) E.; m. Amy Kallman, Sept. 15, 1968; children: Joshua, Abigail. BA summa cum laude, Columbia U., 1967; BA, Cambridge U., Eng., 1969, MA, 1973; JD, Yale U., 1972. Bar: N.Y. 1973. Law clk. to judge Arnold Bauman U.S. Dist. Ct. (so. dist.) N.Y., 1972-74; asst. U.S. atty. So. Dist. N.Y., 1974-78; ptnr. Shearman & Sterling, N.Y.C., 1982—. Vol. Lawyers for the Arts; bd. dirs. Fund for Modern Cts. Fellow Am. Coll. Trial Lawyers, Phi Beta Kappa. Office: 599 Lexington Ave Fl C2 New York NY 10022-6030

EPSTEIN, JOEL DONALD, lawyer; b. N.Y.C., July 3, 1947; s. Samuel B. and Estelle (LeBas) E.; m. Janet Chall, Sept. 27, 1981; children: Joshua Lee, Jenny Leigh. BA, CCNY, 1970; JD, Syracuse U., 1973. Assoc. Viscardi & Steinman, P.C., N.Y.C., 1973-79, Samuel A. Almon, N.Y.C., 1979-92, Law Offices John Guglielmo, 1992-97, Law Offices Anne D. Pope, N.Y.C., 1997-2001. Bar: N.Y. 1974. Small claims arbitrator N.Y.C. Civil Ct., 1982—; arbitrator Am. Arbitration Assn., N.Y.C., 1979—. Mem. N.Y. State Bar Assn. Home: 6 Hillside Ave Great Neck NY 11021-3236 Office: McDonnell Adels & Goodstein 5 Dakota Dr Lake Sucess NY 11042 E-mail: mreppy105@aol.com.

EPSTEIN, JOHN HOWARD, dermatologist; b. San Francisco, Dec. 29, 1926; s. Norman Neman and Gertrude (Hirsch) E.; m. Alice Thompson, Nov. 1953; children: Norman H., Janice A., Beverly A. BA, U. Calif., Berkeley, 1949, MD, 1952; MS, U. Minn., 1956. Diplomate Am. Bd. Dermatology (dir. 1974-84, pres. 1981-82). Intern Stanford U. Med. Ctr., 1952-53; resident in dermatology Mayo Clinic, Rochester, Minn., 1953-56; practice medicine specializing in dermatology San Francisco, 1956—; chief dermatology Mt. Zion Hosp., 1970-80. Clin. prof. U. Calif. Med. Sch., San Francisco, 1972— ; cons. Letterman Army Med. Center, U.S. Naval Hosp., San Diego. Chief editor Archives of Dermatology, 1973-78; asst. editor Jour. Am. Acad. Dermatology, 1978-88; contbr. over 275 articles to profl. jours. With USNR, 1944-46. Fellow ACP; mem. Am. Acad. Dermatology (pres. 1981-82, Silver award for exhibit 1962, Gold award 1969), Soc. Investigative Dermatology (v.p. 1979-80), Am. Dermatol. Assn. (bd. dirs. 1983-88, pres. 1990-91), N.Am. Dermatology Soc., Pacific Dermatol. Assn. (pres. 1985-86), Brit. Dermatol. Soc., Danish Dermatol. Soc., Polish Dermatol. Soc., San Francisco Dermatol. Soc. (pres. 1963-64), Am. Soc. Photobiology (councilor 1983-86), Academia Mexicana and Dermatologia (hon.), European Acad. Dermatology and Venerology (hon.), La Societe Francaise de Dermatologie & de Syphiligraphie, Spanish Dermatol. Soc. Office: 450 Sutter St Rm 1306 San Francisco CA 94108-4002

EPSTEIN, JONATHAN STONE, mechanical engineer, lawyer; b. White Plains, NY, May 11, 1957; s. Gerald Samual Epstein and Mary Holt Griffin; m. Jennifer Clair Wolfram, Aug. 7, 1997. BSME, Colo. State U., 1980; PhD, Va. Polytech. Inst., 1983; JD, U. Idaho, 2000. Bar: Idaho 2000; LL.M. Securities and Fin. Reg. Georgetown Univ. Law Ctr., 2003. Fellow Oxford U., England, 1984; sr. engring. spl. INEEL, Idaho Falls, 1984-88, cons. engr., 1990-97; asst. prof. Ga. Tech., Atlanta, 1988-90; sci. fellow Stanford U., Palo Alto, Calif., 1994-95; sci. adv. US Dept. Def., Washington, 1995-97; policy analyst US Dept. Commerce, Washington, 1999-2000; AAAS sci. fellow Office Senator Bingaman, N.Mex., 2000—. Cons. Rockwell Internat., Atlanta, 1988-90, INEEL, Idaho Falls, 1997-00. Editor Optics and Lasers in Engring., 1990-97, Soc. Experimental Mechanics., 1993-97. Recipient Disting. Lectr. award Associated Western U., 1994. Mem. Soc. Experimental Mechanics (chmn. com. 1990-94, 94-97, 95-96, Brewer award 1996), Office: INEEL MS 2218 PO Box 1625 Idaho Falls ID 83415-0001 E-mail: jonathan_epstein@bingaman.senate.gov.

EPSTEIN, JOSEPH MARC, lawyer; b. Phila., Oct. 31, 1944; s. Arthur and Shirley (Rubenstone) E.; m. Susan Nancy Landerson, June 25, 1967; children: Daniel, Samara. BA, SUNY, Buffalo, 1966; JD, NYU, 1969. Bar: N.J. 1969, U.S. Dist. Ct. N.J. 1969, U.S. Ct. Appeals (3d cir.) 1971, U.S. Dist. Ct. Colo. 1973, U.S. Ct. Appeals (10th cir.) 1980, U.S. Supreme Ct. 1973, Nebr. 1993, Wyo. 1993. Assoc. Neville & Pendleton, Denville, N.J., 1970-71; asst. U.S. Atty. Newark, 1971-73; assoc. Kripke, Carrigan & Bragg, Denver, 1973-75; ptnr. Epstein & Gilbert, Denver, 1975-78; pvt. practice Denver, 1978-80; ptnr. Kripke, Epstein & Lawrence, P.C., Denver, 1980-95; ADR specialist JAMS/Endispute n/k/a JAMS, Denver, 1995-2000, Conflict Resolution Svcs., Inc., Denver, 2000—. Lectr. in field. Contbr. articles to profl. jours. Bd. dirs. Colo. Assn. Retarded Citizens, 1976-80, Theodore Herzl Day Sch., 1981-84. Recipient Leadership award Denver C. of C., 1978-79. Fellow Internat. Acad. Mediators (founder 1997); mem. ATLA (bd. govs. 1990-92), Colo. Bar Assn., Denver Bar Assn., Colo. Trial Lawyers Assn. (past v.p., pres.-elect, pres.), Trial Lawyers for Public Justice (bd. dirs.). Republican. Jewish. Office: Kripke Epstein & Lawrence PC 4710 El Camino Dr Englewood CO 80111-1152

EPSTEIN, JUDITH ANN, judge; b. L.A., Dec. 23, 1942; d. Gerald Elliot and Harriet (Hirsh) Rubens; m. Joseph I. Epstein, Oct. 4, 1964; children: Mark Douglas, Laura Ann. AB, U. Calif., Berkeley, 1964; MA, U. San Francisco, 1974, JD, 1977. Bar: Calif. 1978, U.S. Dist. Ct. (no. dist.) Calif 1978, U.S. Supreme Ct. 1983, U.S. Ct. Appeals (9th cir.) 1984. With social svcs. dept. Sutter County, Yuba City, Calif., 1964-66; bus. devel. assoc. Yuba County C. of C., Marysville, Calif., 1968-70; rsch. clk. Calif. Supreme Ct., San Fransisco, 1977; ptnr. Crosby, Heafey, Roach & May, Oakland, Calif., 1978-91; gen. counsel and sec. Valent USA Corp., 1991-98; fellow The Commonwealth Club of Calif., 1999—2001; appellate judge Calif. State Bar Ct., 2002—. Lectr. U. Calif. Grad. Sch. Journalism in Media Law, Berkeley, 1987-91; bd. dirs. Sierra Pacific Steel, Hayward, Calif.; adj. prof. U. San Francisco, 1999—. Bd. dirs., v.p. Oakland Ballet, 1980-92; mem. bd. counselors U. San Francisco Sch. Law, 1994; trustee U. San Francisco, 1996—; bd. dirs. San Francisco Bay area Girl Scouts U.S., 1998—, East Bay Cmty. Found. Recipient Pres.'s award Oakland Ballet, James Madison Freedom of Info. award Soc. Profl. Journalists, 1992; award for Disting. Achievement, Girl Scouts U.S., 1995. Fellow Am. Bar Found.; mem. Calif. Women Lawyers Assn., Alameda Bar Assn., Berkeley Tennis Club.

EPSTEIN, LEE JOAN, political science educator; b. N.Y.C., Mar. 17, 1958; d. Kenneth Maurice and Ann (Buxbaum) Spole BA magna cum laude, Emory U., 1980, MA, 1982, PhD, 1983. Mallinckrodt Disting. Univ. prof. polit. sci. Washington U., St. Louis, 1998—, prof. law, 2000—. Author: Conservatives in Court, 1985; co-author: Supreme Court and Legal Change, 1992, The Choices Justices Make, 1998, Courts, Judges, and Politics, 2002, Constitutional Law for a Changing America, 2002, The Supreme Court Compendium, 2003; contbr. articles to profl. jours., chpts. in books. Mem. Am. Polit. Sci. Assn., Midwest Polit. Sci. Assn., Law and Soc. Assn., Pi Sigma Alpha, Alpha Epsilon Phi. Jewish. Avocations: skiing, tennis. Office: Washington U Dept Polit Sci PO Box 1063 Saint Louis MO 63188-1063 E-mail: epstein@artsci.wustl.edu.

EPSTEIN, LIONEL CHARLES, lawyer; b. N.Y.C., Apr. 7, 1924; s. David and Carrie (Roth) E.; m. Sarah Louise Gamble, June 10, 1951 (div. Apr. 12, 1983); children: David Bradley, James Roth, Richard Aldis, Miles Owen, Sarah Carianne; m. Elizabeth Pendelton Streicher, Nov. 10, 1990. BA, NYU, 1947; LL.B., Harvard U., 1950. Bar: N.Y. 1950, D.C. 1953, U.S. Supreme Ct. 1955. With office gen. counsel U.S. Navy Dept., 1950-52; tax div. U.S. Justice Dept., 1952-57; mem. firms Ginsburg & Leventhal, 1957-67, Epstein, Friedman, Duncan & Medalie, Washington, 1967-74; mem. firm Jones, Day, Reavis & Pogue, Washington, 1975-84, of counsel, 1984-86; chmn. EFO Capital Mgmt. Inc., Washington, 1984—. Spl. asst. to R. Sargent Shriver Peace Corps, 1962; Bd. dirs. Expt. in Internat. Living, Mus. Modern Art, N.Y.C., Com. on Illustrated Books and Prints, Washington Print Club. Author art exhbn. catalogs. Served with inf. AUS, 1942-45. Decorated Purple Heart, Knight's Cross 1st class Order St. Olav (Norway). Mem. ABA, Harvard Club (N.Y.). Clubs: Lawyers (founding mem.), Harvard. Home: 700 New Hampshire Ave NW Washington DC 20037-2406 Office: 21 Dupont Cir NW Ste 330 Washington DC 20036-1549 E-mail: lepstein@efocapitalmgmt.com.

EPSTEIN, MARK ROBERT, electronics manufacturing executive; b. N.Y.C., Feb. 7, 1943; s. Albert David and Edith (Prager) Epstein; children: Paul, Jeff. BS, MIT, 1963, MS, 1964; PhD, Stanford U., 1968. Rsch. assoc. Stanford Electronic Labs., 1967-68; mgr. R&D Northrop Page Engrs. Inc., Vienna, Va., 1968-74; program dir. Computer Sci. Corp., Falls Church, Va., 1974-76; staff asst. Theater C3 Office of Sec. of Def., Washington, 1976-80; dep. for C3 and intelligence Office of Sec. of Army, Washington, 1980-86; sr. v.p. Qualcomm Inc., San Diego, 1986—. Vice-chair Circles bd. Kennedy Ctr. for the Performing Arts, Washington, 1998—; mem. Wilson coun. Woodrow Wilson Internat. Ctr. for Scholars, 2002—; mem. MIT Corp. Mem. IEEE (sr.), MIT Club Washington (bd. dirs. 1998—, pres. 2002-03), Sigma Xi. Avocations: swimming, piano, dancing, golf. Home: 9209 Fox Meadow Ln Potomac MD 20854 Office: Qualcomm Inc 9209 Fox Meadow Ln Potomac MD 20854 E-mail: mepstein@qualcomm.com.

EPSTEIN, MARSHA ANN, public health administrator, physician; b. Chgo., Feb. 4, 1945; 1 child, Lee Rashad Mahmood. BA, Reed Coll., 1965; MD, U. Calif., San Francisco, 1969; MPH, U. Calif., Berkeley, 1971. Diplomate Am. Bd. Preventive Medicine. Intern French Hosp., San Francisco, 1969-70; resident in preventive medicine Sch. Pub. Health, U. Calif., Berkeley, 1971-73; fellow in family planning dept. ob-gyn. UCLA, 1973-74; med. dir. Herself Health Clinic, L.A., 1974-79; pvt. adult gen. practitioner L.A., 1978-82; dist. health officer L.A. County Pub. Health, L.A., 1982—2001, area med. dir., 2001—. Part-time physician U. Calif. Student Health, Berkeley, 1970-73; co-med. dir. Monsenior Oscar Romero Free Clinic, L.A., 1992-93. Mem.: APHA, Calif. Acad. Preventive Medicine, So. Calif. Pub. Health Assn., L.A.-Am. Med. Women's Assn., Am. Med. Women's Assn., Am. Coll. Physician Execs. Democrat. Jewish. Avocations: dancing, native plants, meditating. Office: Tucker Health Ctr 123 W Manchester Blvd Inglewood CA 90301 E-mail: mepstein@dhs.co.la.ca.us.

EPSTEIN, MARVIN MORRIS, retired construction company executive; b. Cleve., June 2, 1928; s. Isadore Elchanan and Rose (Gevelber) E.; m. Lois M. DeSure, June 10, 1957; children: Deborah L. Epstein Merkin, David A. BA with highest honors, U. Mich., 1951; attended, Western Res. U., 1947-49, Ohio State U., 1953, Cleve. State U., 1995-98. Reporter Cleve. Plain Dealer, 1951-52; editor AP, Columbus, Ohio, 1953-55; asst. mng. editor Times-Star, Cin., 1956-57; cons. Eden & Assocs., Cleve., 1959-60; sr. exec. The Austin Co., Cleve., 1961-93, sr. v.p., 1990—93, ret., 1993. Editor Internat. News Milw. Jour., 1958-59; contbr. articles to profl. jours. Active Greater Cleve. Growth Assn., 1975-90; mem. bd. overseers, visiting com. Case Western Res. U., Case Inst. Tech., Cleve., 1981-85; bd. dirs. The Stearns Collection, Ann Arbor, Mich., 1990-93, World Affairs Coun. of Desert; trustee Cleve. Music Sch. Settlement, 1989-90; mem. Presdl. Societies, Univ. Mich., 1980—, Vis. Com. Coll. Lit., Sci. and the Arts, U. Mich., 1989-92; trustee Cleveland Heights-University Heights Pub. Libr., 1997-99. With U.S. Army, 1946-47. Recipient McNaught Gold medal U. Mich., 1951, Disting. Svc. award, 1998. Mem. Soc. Profl. Journalists (life), U. Mich. Alumni Assn. (pres. Cleve. chpt. 1975-76), Heights Regional C. of C. (pres. 1992). Democrat. Home: 36598 Fan Palm Way Palm Desert CA 92211-2383 Fax: (760) 360-2942.

EPSTEIN, MELVIN, lawyer; b. Passaic, N.J., Jan. 4, 1938; s. Hyman and Lillian (Rozenblum) E.; m. Rachel Judith Stein, Dec. 20, 1964; children: Jonathan Andrew, Emily E. Landau. AB, Harvard U., 1959, LLB, 1962. Bar: N.Y. 1963. Assoc. Stroock & Stroock & Lavan, L.L.P., N.Y.C., 1962-71, ptnr., 1972—. Bd. dirs. Hillel of N.Y.C.; mem. schs. com. Harvard U., 1984—. Mem. N.Y. State Bar Assn., Assn. of Bar of City of N.Y. Democrat. Jewish. Office: Stroock & Stroock & Lavan LLP 180 Maiden Ln New York NY 10038-4925 E-mail: mepstein@stroock.com.

EPSTEIN, MICHAEL ALAN, lawyer; b. N.Y.C., June 26, 1954; s. Herman and Lillian (King) E. BA, Lehigh U., 1975; JD, NYU, 1979. Bar: N.Y., 1980, US. Dist. Ct. (so., ea. dists.) N.Y., 1980. Ptnr. Weil, Gotshal & Manges, N.Y.C., 1979—. Lectr. in field. Author: Modern Intellectual Property, 1984, 3d edit., 1994, International Intellectual Property, 1992, Epstein on Intellectual Property, 4th edit., 2001; editor: Corporate Counsellors Deskbook, 1982, 3d edit., 1990, Biotechnology Law, 1988, The Trademark Law Revision Act, 1989, Trade Secrets, Restrictive Covenants and Other Safeguards, 1986, Online-Internet Law, 1997; co-editor, mem. editl. bd. Jour. Proprietary Rights, The Computer Lawyer, The Intellectual Property Strategist, The Cyberspace Lawyer; contbr. articles to profl. jours. Trustee Jonas Salk Found., Am. Health Found. Donald L. Brown fellow in trade regulation NYU Sch. Law, 1978-79. Mem. ABA, N.Y. State Bar Assn. Home: 1020 Park Ave New York NY 10028-0913 Office: Weil Gotshal & Manges 767 5th Ave Fl Conc1 New York NY 10153-0119

EPSTEIN, RANDY J. physician, ophthalmologist; b. Chicago, Ill., Jan. 8, 1955; s. Benita M. LoGiudice; m. Kayla G. Schieber, June 17, 1979; children: Rachel H., Sarah A, Joshua N. MD, Rush Med. Coll., Chgo., 1976—80; BS, U of Ill., Urbana, IL, 1972—76. Diplomate Am. Bd. of Ophthalmology, 1986. Ceo Chgo. Cornea Consultants, Ltd., Highland Pk., Ill., 1986—; assoc. prof. Dept. of Ophthalmology, Rush Med. Coll., Chgo., 1986—. Mem. Lions Club, Highland Pk., Ill. Recipient One of Chicago's Top Doctors, Chgo. Mag., 2001. Achievements include Honor Award, AMerican Academy of Ophthalmology. Office: Chicago Cornea Cons 806 Central Highland Park IL 60035 Office Fax: 847-432-8241. E-mail: corneas@aol.com.

EPSTEIN, RAYMOND, engineering and architectural executive; b. Chgo., Jan. 12, 1918; s. Abraham and Janet (Rabinowitz) E.; m. Betty Jadwin, Apr. 7, 1940; children: Gail, David, Norman, Harriet. Student, MIT, 1934-36; BS, U. Ill., 1938. Registered architect registered profl. engr. With A. Epstein & Sons Internat., Inc., Chgo., 1938—, chmn. bd., 1961-83, chmn. exec. com., 1983—. Bd. dirs., life trustee United Israel Appeal; past sec., hon. dir. Am. Jewish Joint Distbn. Com.; mem. exec. com. Nat. Jewish Cmty. Rels. Adv. Coun.; v.p. nat. bd. Jewish Telegraphic Agy.; mem. citizens bd. Loyola U.; past pres. Coun. Jewish Fedns., Welfare Funds, Inc., Jewish Welfare Fund Met. Chgo., Jewish United Fund, Young Men's Jewish Coun.; past sec. Jewish Fed. Met. Chgo.; past chmn. budget com., bd. govs. Jewish Agy.; past trustee Chgo. Med. Sch; past bd. dirs. United Jewish Appeal; past exec. com. Meml. Found. Jewish Culture; past chmn. pub. affairs com., past chmn. campaign Jewish United Fund Met. Chgo.; past. sec. Welfare Coun. Met. Chgo.; past bd. dirs. Chgo. Bldg. Congress; life dir. Mt. Sinai Med. Rsch. Found.; trustee, past dir. Ampal-Am. Israel Corp. Decorated comdr. Legion of Honor Ivory Coast, 1982; recipient Disting. Alumnus award U. Ill., 1974, Julius Rosenwald Meml. award Jewish Fedn. Chgo., 1974, Citation Brandeis U., 1992; named to City of Chgo. Sr. Citizens Hall of Fame, 1991. Fellow Soc. Civil Engr. France, Soc. Am. Registered Architects; mem. NSPE, ASCE, Am. Concrete Inst., Western Soc. Engrs., Assn. Engrs. and Architects in Israel, French Engrs. in the U.S., Inc., Pi Lambda Phi. Clubs: Standard (past trustee), Illini, MIT, Caxton (Chgo.). Home: 4950 S Chicago Beach Dr Chicago IL 60615-3207 Office: 600 W Fulton St Chicago IL 60661-1100 E-mail: raye@thepowhatan.com.

EPSTEIN, ROBERT MARVIN, anesthesiologist, educator; b. NYC, Mar. 10, 1928; s. Nathan B. and Rebecca Epstein; m. Lillian Ray Cohen, Dec. 31, 1950; children: Judith Susan, Neal Myron, Charles Benjamin. BS with distinction, U. Mich., 1947, MD cum laude, 1951. Diplomate Am. Bd. Anesthesiology (dir. 1972-84, pres. 1979-80). Intern U. Mich. Hosp., 1951—52; resident in anesthesiology Presbyn. Hosp., NYC, 1952—53, 1955—56; instr. in anesthesiology and fellow in medicine Columbia U., 1956—57, assoc., 1957—59, asst. prof., anesthesiology, 1959—65, assoc. prof., 1965—70, prof., 1970—72, U. Va., Charlottesville, 1972—74, Alumni prof., 1974—87, Disting. prof., 1987—92, Harold Carron prof., 1992—2002, dept. chmn., 1972—96, Harold Carron prof. emeritus, 2002—. Mem. anesthesiology tng. com. Nat. Inst. Gen. Med. Scis., NIH, 1966—69; mem. com. on anesthesia NRC, 1970—71; mem. Nat. Bd. Med. Examiners, 1982—90, Am. Bd. Med. Specialities, 1974—95. Editor: Anesthesiology, 1974—79; contbr. Bd. dirs., sec. U. Va. Health Svcs. Found., 1980—90, pres., 1990—93; trustee Ednl. Commn. for Fgn. Med. Grads., 1991—95, vice chmn., 1993—95; bd. dirs. QualChoice of Va., 1997—2000. With U.S. Army, 1953—55. Fellow Guggenheim fellow, Oxford U., England, 1966—67, N.Y. Heart Assn., 1956—57; scholar in-residence, Inst. Medicine NAS, 1997, sr. scholar, Va. Health Policy Ctr., 1997—. Fellow: Royal Coll. Anaesthetists (Eng.); mem.: W.T.G. Morton Soc., Assn. Univ. Anesthesiologists (pres. 1973—74), Anaesthetic Rsch. Soc. (U.K.), Am. Soc. Pharmacology and Exptl. Therapeutics, Soc. Acad. Anesthesia Chmn. (rep. to Coun. Acad. Soc. Assn. Am. Med. Coll. 1984—91, mem. coun.), Am. Soc. Anesthesiologists, Am. Physiol. Soc., Inst. Medicine NAS, AAAS, Alpha Omega Alpha, Sigma Xi, Phi Beta Kappa. Office: Dept Anesthesiology PO Box 800710 Charlottesville VA 22908-0710 E-mail: rme@virginia.edu.

EPSTEIN, RONALD M. family medicine physician, educator; b. N.Y.C., Jan. 29, 1955; s. Jules Irwin and Joan Gray Epstein; m. Deborah Fox, Aug. 25, 1984; children: Eli, Malka. BA in Music, Wesleyan U., 1976; postgrad., Columbia U., 1980; MD, Harvard U., 1984. Diplomate Am. Bd. Family Practice; lic. MD, N.Y. Instr. medicine U. Rochester (N.Y.) Sch. Medicine and Dentistry, 1988-89, instr. family medicine, 1989-90, asst. prof. family medicine and psychiatry, 1990-96, assoc. prof., 1996—2002, prof. family medicine and psychiatry, 2002—; practice medicine Jacob W. Holler Family Medicine Ctr., Rochester. Mem. editl. bd. Dimension Humana, Jour. Family Practice, Atencion Primaria; article reviewer Family Medicine, Jour. Gen. Internal Medicine, Jour. AMA, Archives of Family Medicine, Jour. Family Practice; contbr. articles to profl. jours. Scholar Robert Wood Johnson Found., Princeton, 1994-98; Fulbright Sr. lectr. Inst. d'Etudis de la Salut, Spain, 1997-98. Mem. Am. Acad. Family Physicians, Am. Acad. Physicians and Patients (membership com. 1992-94), Internat. Ctr. for Family Medicine, Assn. for Behavioral Sci. in Med. Edn., Soc. of Tchrs. of Family Medicine. Avocations: playing harpsichord, cycling, skiing. Office: Jacob W Holler Family Medicine Ctr 885 South Ave Rochester NY 14620-2318 E-mail: Ronald_Epstein@urmc.rochester.edu.

EPSTEIN, SETH PAUL, immunologist, infectious disease researcher; b. N.Y.C., Sept. 11, 1958; s. Donald and Eileen (Schulman) Epstein; m. Ivy Chatanow, June 23, 2002. BA in Chemistry with high honors, Brandeis U., 1980; MD, Autonomous U. Guadalajara, Mex., 1984. Med. extern Pontiac (Mich.) Gen. Hosp., 1984; postdoctoral rsch. fellow Mich. Cancer Found., Detroit, 1985-86, NYU Med. Ctr., N.Y.C., 1987-91, asst. rsch. scientist, 1991; rsch. asst. Mt. Sinai Med. Ctr., N.Y.C., 1991-96, instr., asst. prof., 1997—. Contbr. articles to profl. jours. Tng. fellow NIH, 1987; grantee Dermatology Found., Inc., 1990. Mem. Assn. Rsch. in Vision and Ophthalmology, Phi Beta Kappa. Achievements include rsch. on cyclosporine A rapamycin transforming growth factor interferon-gamma relating to cytokine-induced upregulation of Langerhans cells, cell chemotaxis into the cornea and skin and treatment of herpetic keratitis; sunscreen prevention of Ultraviolet-activated herpes simplex; novel treatments for herpes simplex and adenovirus ocular infections. Office: Mount Sinai Med Ctr Dept Ophthalmology 1 Gustave L Levy Pl New York NY 10029-6500

EPSTEIN, SHERRY STEIN, lawyer; b. Idaho Falls, Idaho, Jan. 15, 1960; d. Seymour S. and Lucille R. (Richman) S. AB, Vassar Coll., 1981; JD, U. Pitts., 1985; MBA, Cleveland State U., 1994. Bar: Pa. 1985, U.S. Dist. Ct. (we. dist.) Pa. 1985, D.C. 1986, Ohio 1986, Fla. 1986, U.S. Dist. Ct. (no. dist.) Ohio 1986, U.S. Ct. Appeals (3d cir.) 1986, U.S. Ct. Appeals (6th cir.) 1987, U.S. Dist. Ct. D.C. 1988, U.S. Ct. Appeals (D.C. cir.) 1989, U.S. Supreme Ct. 1990. Account rep. West Svcs., Inc., Pitts., 1985-86; law clk. to judge Superior Ct. Pitts., 1986; assoc. Wickens, Hazen & Panza, Lorain, Ohio, 1986-88; legal counsel Advanced Med. Systems, Inc., Geneva, Ohio, 1988-95; sr. atty. Reminger & Reminger Co., L.P.A., Cleve., 1995; gen. counsel ATC Lighting & Plastics, Inc., 1996—. Bd. dirs. Lorain County Legal Aid Soc., Elyria, Ohio, 1988-89, Ash/Craft Industries; interviewer Cleve. and Cuyahoga Counties Joint Com. on Applications for Cuyahoga County for admission to Supreme Ct. of Ohio, Cleve., 1987-94; instr. Am. Inst. Paralegal Studies, Cleve., 1988-90; v.p., bd. dirs. Tree of Knowledge Learning Ctr. Inc., 1999—. Bd. dirs. Case Western Res. U. Friends of Eldred Theater, 1995—, Starting Point, 1996—2002, Mt. Sinai Cmty. Ptnrs., 1995—2000. Mem. ABA, Fla. Bar Assn., D.C. Bar Assn., Ohio Bar Assn., Cleve. Bar Assn., Ashtabula County Bar Assn. Avocation: teaching. Office: ATC Lighting & Plastics Inc 107 N Eagle St Geneva OH 44041-1161

EPSTEIN, SIDNEY, architect, engineer; b. Chgo., 1923; m. Sondra Berman, Sept. 4, 1987; children from previous marriage: Donna Epstein Barrows, Laurie Epstein Lawton. BS in Civil Engring. with high honors, U. Ill., 1943. Various positions A. Epstein & Sons Internat.; chmn. bd. dirs. A. Epstein & Sons Internat., Inc., Chgo. Dir. Amal. Trust & Savs. Bank, Polk Bros. Found., Michael Reese Found.; trustee emeritus Northwestern Mut. Life Ins. Co. Founder, bd. dirs., past chmn. Chgo. Youth Ctrs.; past chmn. bd. trustees Michael Reese Hosp. and Med. Ctr.; bd. govs., life mem. U. Chgo. Hosps. and Clinics; life trustee Orchestral Assn. Chgo. Mem.: Standard Club (life; past pres.), Chi Epsilon, Phi Eta Sigma, Phi Kappa Phi, Sigma Tau, Tau Beta Pi, Sigma Xi. Home: 1430 N Lake Shore Dr Chicago IL 60610-6682 Office: A Epstein & Sons Internat Inc 600 W Fulton St Chicago IL 60661-1100 E-mail: sidneyepstein@epstein-isi.com.

EPSTEIN, SIDNEY, retired editor; b. Wilmington, Del., Oct. 11, 1920; s. Abraham and Ida (Kelrick) E.; m. Eleni Sakes, Mar. 30, 1957; 1 dau., Diane. Student, George Washington U., 1937-41. With Washington Herald, 1937-54; city editor Washington Times-Herald, 1952-54, Washington Star, 1958-68, asst. mng. editor, 1968-74, mng. editor, 1974-78, exec. editor, 1978-81, assoc. pub. and editor, 1981, also dir. Served to capt. USMCR, 1942-46. Mem. Sigma Delta Chi (hall of fame 1981). Home: 5901 MacArthur Blvd NW Washington DC 20016

EPSTEIN, STEPHEN ROGER, financial executive; b. Chgo., Nov. 25, 1947; s. Maurice and Gertrude (Ades) E.; m. Christine Marie Kudrys, June 10, 1979; 1 child, Jorie Anne. Student, U. Ill., 1965-69; BSBA, Roosevelt U., 1977. Mgr. collection and billing Field Enterprises Ednl. Corp., Chgo., 1971-73; asst. mgr. cost acctg. dept. Sun Electric Corp., Crystal Lake, Ill., 1973-77; fin. analyst Wilson Sporting Goods Co., River Grove, Ill., 1978-79; mgr. cost acctg. dept. Salerno-Megowen Biscuit Co., Niles, Ill., 1980-81; mgr. fin. planning dept. Nachman Corp., Des Plaines, Ill., 1981-82, controller, 1982-83; controller ops. div. Helene Curtis, Inc., Chgo., 1983-88, dir. cost mgmt., 1988-90; dir. cost and performance mgmt. svcs. Checkers, Simon & Rosner, Chgo., 1990-93; sr. mgr., practice leader advanced cost mgmt. Grant Thornton, Chgo., 1993-95; CFO Aquion Ptnrs., L.P., Elk Grove Village, Ill., 1995-97, CIO, 1998; dir. mfg. cons. FERS Bus. Svcs., Inc., Chgo., 1998-99; v.p., CFO Perfection Spring and Stamping Co., Mt. Prospect, Ill., 1999—. Speaker in field. Assoc. mem. Leukemia Rsch. Found., Chgo., 1974—. Staff sgt. Ill. N.G., 1970-77. Mem. Inst. Mgmt. Accts., Am. Prodn. and Inventory Control Soc., Inst. Mgmt. Cons., Am. Mgmt. Assn., Am. Radio Relay League. Avocations: electronics, photography, physical fitness. Office: 1449 E Algonquin Rd Mount Prospect IL 60056 E-mail: stephene@pss-corp.com.

EPSTEIN, SUSAN BAERG, librarian, consultant; b. Chgo., Feb. 28, 1938; d. Philip William and Alice (Mackenzie) Ruppert; m. William Baerg, 1960 (div. 1971); children: Elisabeth, William Philip, Sara Margaret; m. A. H. Epstein, 1977 (div. 1981). BA in Econs., Wellesley Coll., 1960; MLS, Immaculate Heart Coll., 1972. Systems analyst IBM, San Jose, Calif., 1960-63, Control Data Corp., Palo Alto, Calif., 1963-64; dir. tech. and automation svcs. Huntington Beach (Calif.) Pub. Libr., 1972-74, asst. city libr., 1974-78; spl. asst. to county libr. L.A. County Pub. Libr., L.A., 1978-81, chief tech. svcs., 1979-81; pres. Susan Baerg Epstein, Ltd., Costa Mesa, Calif., 1981—. Columnist Libr. Jour., 1984—. Mem. ALA (chair com.), Calif. Libr. Assn. (councilor 1973-80). Office: 1992 Lemnos Dr Costa Mesa CA 92626-3534

EPSTEIN, WILLIAM LOUIS, dermatologist, educator; b. Cleve., Sept. 6, 1925; s. Norman N. and Gertrude (Hirsch) E.; m. Joan Goldman, Jan. 29, 1954; children: Wendy, Steven. AB, U. Calif., Berkeley, 1949, MD, 1952. Mem. faculty U. Calif., San Francisco, 1957—, assoc. prof. div. dermatology, 1963-69, prof. div. dermatology, 1969—, dir. dermatol. rsch., 1957-70, acting chmn. div. dermatology, 1966-69, chmn. dept. dermatology, 1970-85. Cons. dermatology Outpatient Dept.; cons. various hosps. Calif. Dept. Public Health; cons. Food and Drug Adminstrn., Washington, 1972—, Dept. Agriculture, 1979; dir. div. research Nat. Program Dermatology, 1970-73; Dohi lectr., Tokyo, 1982; Beecham lectr., 1988-89; Nippon Boehringer Ingelheim lectr. 18th Hakone Symposium on Respiration, Japan, 1990. Decorated medal of honor Order of the Rising Sun, gold rays with neck ribbon (Japan). Mem. AAAS, AMA, Am. Soc. Cell Biology, Am. Acad. Dermatology and Syphilology (nominating com. 1984), Am. Contact Dermatology Soc. (hon.), Pacific Dermatologic Assn., Am. Fedn. Clin. Rsch., Am. Contact Dermatitis Soc. (hon.), Soc. Investigative Dermatology (bd. dirs., pres. 1985), Am. Dermatol. Assn., Assn. Profs. Dermatology (sr. mem.), Dermatology Found. (pres. 1986-87), Phi Beta Kappa, Sigma Xi. Home: 267 Golden Hinde Psge Corte Madera CA 94925-1953 Fax: 415-681-9165. E-mail: wle@itsa.ucsf.edu.

EPSTEIN, WILLIAM MAURICE, social work educator; b. Bklyn., Feb. 5, 1944; s. Harry and Lillian Epstein. BA, Bklyn. Coll., 1967; MSW, U. Pitts., 1968; DSW, Columbia U., 1977. Spl. asst. U.S. Dept. HEW, Washington, 1968-71; exec. cons. Office of Legal Counsel U.S. Dept. Justice, Washington, 1973-74; mem. staff NAS, Washington, 1975-77; asst. prof. SUNY, Buffalo, 1978-85; prof. social work U. Nev., Las Vegas, 1992—. Cons. USPHS, Washington, 1977-78, Integrated Mental Health, Rochester, N.Y., 1985-86, Office of Gov., State of Miss., Jackson, 1987. Author: Dilemma of American Social Welfare, 1993, Illusion of Psychotherapy, 1995, Welfare in America, 1997, Children Who Could Have Been, 1999, American Policy Making, 2002. Mem. Am. Sociol. Assn. Democrat. Jewish. Home: PO Box 70715 Las Vegas NV 89170 Office: U Nev Las Vegas 4505 Maryland Pkwy Las Vegas NV 89154 E-mail: wepstein@ccmail.nevada.edu.

EPSTEIN, YAKOV M, education educator, psychologist; s. Elchanan Ephrayim and Malka Epstein; m. Helane S. Rosenberg, Feb. 14, 1989; children: Deborah Joy Jackel, Jennifer. PhD, Columbia U., 1963—68. Clinical Psychology License NJ Bd. of Psychol. Examiners, 1981. Assoc. dir. Ctr. for Math., Sci., and Computer Edn., Rutgers U., 1988, dir., 1998—. Prof. Dept. of Psychology, Rutgers U., 1980—. Associate editor Journal of Applied Social Psychology (Heather Bruce Thierman Online Angel award, 1997). Lead religious services Cong. Ansche Chesed, New York, 1989—2002. Recipient Educator of the Yr., Electronic Learning Mag.; NSF, 1999—2003. Fellow: APA. Office: Rutgers University - CMSCE 118 Frelinghuysen Rd Piscataway NJ 08854 8019 Home Fax: 732-445-3477; Office Fax: 732-445-3477. Personal E-mail: yepstein@rci.rutgers.edu.

EPSTIEN, JAY ALAN, lawyer; b. Newark, May 23, 1951; s. Leonard and Lorraine (Pedd) E.; children: Jessica, Shira; m. Nancy Elizabeth Kirsch, June 1, 1996. BS, Case Western Res. U., 1973; JD, Cornell U., 1976. Bar: D.C. 1976, N.J. 1976, U.S. Supreme Ct. 1977. Indsl. engr. Ortho Pharm., Somerset, N.J., 1973, Shaw, Pittman, Potts & Trowbridge, Washington, 1976—2000, ptnr., 1984—2000, chmn. bus. dept., 1994-95; mng. ptnr. Rudnick, Wolfe, Epstien & Zeidman, Washington, 1996-99; D.C. co-mng. ptnr. Piper Rudnick LLP, Washington, 1999—, co-chmn. real estate dept., 2003—. Mem.: Anglo-Am. Real Property Inst., Am. Coll. Real Estate Lawyers (bd. govs. 2001—), Internat. Coun. Shopping Ctrs. (chmn. D.C. govt. affairs 1989—96). Avocations: tennis, golf. Home: 3617 Shepherd St Chevy Chase MD 20815-4131 Office: Piper Rudnick LLP 1200 19th St NW Fl 7 Washington DC 20036-2430

ERASMUS, CHARLES JOHN, anthropologist, educator; b. Pitts., Sept. 23, 1921; s. Percy Thomas and Alice E.; m. Helen Marjorie O'Brien, Feb. 18, 1943; children: Thomas Glen, Gwendolyn. BA, UCLA, 1942; MA, U. Calif., Berkeley, 1950, PhD, 1955. Field ethnologist Smithsonian Instn., Colombia, 1950-52; applied anthropologist AID, Western S.Am., 1952-54; research assoc. culture exchange project U. Ill., Champaign-Urbana, 1955-59; vis. prof. anthropology Yale U., New Haven, 1959-60; assoc. prof. U. N.C., Chapel Hill, 1960-62, U. Calif., Santa Barbara, 1962-64, prof., 1964-87, prof. emeritus, 1987—, chmn. dept. anthropology, 1964-68. Author: Man Takes Control: Cultural Development and American Aid, 1961, In Search of the Common Good: Utopian Experiments Past and Future, 1977, Contemporary Change in Traditional Communities of Mexico and Peru, 1978. Served with USN, 1942-45. Home: 6190 Barrington Dr Santa Barbara CA 93117-1758 Office: U Calif Dept Anthropology Santa Barbara CA 93106

ERB, BLAIR DILLARD, SR., internist; b. Bristol, Va., Nov. 23, 1930; s. Harley Ellsworth and Louise (Dillard) E.; m. Sally Erb, June 20, 1953 (dec. Aug. 1998); children: Blair Dillard Jr., Mary Louise Erb Layton, Roy Ellsworth; m. Charlotte Carr Sanders, June 14, 2003. BS, U. Tenn., 1952, MD, 1953. Diplomate Am. Bd. Internal Medicine. Intern City of Memphis Hosps.-U. Tenn., 1953-54; resident in internal medicine U. Tenn., Memphis, 1955, 57-59, fellow in cardiology, 1959-60; mini-resident in occupl. medicine U. Cin., Ohio, 1981-83; pvt. practice Jackson, Tenn., 1960—; mem. staff dept. cardiology Jackson Clin., 1960-93; active staff Jackson-Madison County Gen. Hosp., Jackson, 1960-92, chief of staff, 1981-82, sr. staff, 1992—. Contbr. numerous articles to med. jours., including Am. Heart Jour., Jour. Occupl. Health and Safety, Tenn. Jour. Medicine, others. Flight surgeon USAF, 1955-57, maj. M.C., USAFR, 1955-65. Nat. rsch. fellow in electrophysiology Am. Heart Assn.; grantee Jackson C. of C., 1969, Memphis Regional Med. Program, 1971. Fellow ACP (gov. Tenn. region 1977-81, Laureate award 1996), Am. Coll. Cardiology, Am. Coll. Chest Physicians, Am. Coll. Sports Medicine (bd. trustees 1977-80), Am. Heart Assn. (bd. dirs. 1971-72), Am. Coll. Occupl. and Environ. Medicine, Wilderness Med. Soc. (bd. dirs. 1987-91, pres. 1989-91), Tenn. Heart Assn. (pres. 1971-72). Presbyterian. Avocations: travel, fly fishing, mountaineering. Home: 1729 N Highland Ave Jackson TN 38301

ERB, DONALD, composer; b. Youngstown, Ohio, Jan. 17, 1927; s. Tod and Janet (Griffith) E.; m. Lucille Hyman, June 10, 1950; children: Christine, Matthew, Stephanie, Janet. BS, Kent State U., 1950; MusM, Cleve. Inst. Music, 1953, MusD (hon.), 1984; MusD, Ind. U., 1964. Tchr. Cleve. Inst. Music, 1953-61, composer-in-residence, 1966-81, disting. prof. of composition, 1987-96; Meadows prof. composition So. Meth. U., 1981-84; composer-in-residence St. Louis Symphony, 1988-91; resident composer Am. Acad., Rome, 1991. Vis. asst. prof. rsch. electronic music Case Inst. Tech., 1965-67; composer-in-residence Dallas Symphony, 1968-69, Aspen Music Festival, 1993, Schweitzer Inst., 1994, 95; vis. prof. Ind. U., 1975-76, Calif. State U., L.A., 1977; prof. composition Ind. U., 1984-87; staff composer Bennington Composers Conf., 1969-73; resident composer June in Buffalo, 1984-96, composer-librettist panelist Nat. Endowment for Arts, 1973-79, chmn., 1977-79; performed at Warsaw Autumn Festival, 1971, 73, 94—; artist-in-residence Atlantic Ctr. for Arts, 1995. Composer: Dialogue for Violin and Piano, 1958, Correlations for Piano, 1959, Music for Violin and Piano, 1959, String Quartet No. 1, 1960, Sonata for Harpsichord and String Quartet, 1962, Chamber Concerto, 1961, Sonneries for Brass Choir, 1961, Four for Percussion, 1962, Bakersfield Pieces, 1962, Cumming's Cycle, 1963, Concertant for Harpsichord and Strings, 1963, Symphony of Overtures, 1964, VII Misc, 1964, Fallout?, 1964, Reticulation, 1965, Phantasma, 1965, Concert Piece 1, 1966, Diversion for Two, 1966, Stargazing, 1966, Concerto for Solo Percussion and Orchestra, 1966, Andante for Piccolo, Flute and Alto Flute, 1966, String Trio, 1966, Summermusic, 1966, Kyrie, 1967, Reconnaissance, 1967, In No Strange Land, 1968, the Seventh Trumpet, 1969, Basspiece, 1969, Klangfarbenfunk I, 1970, God Love You Now, 1971, Fanfare, 1971, The Purple-Roofed Ethical Suicide Parlor, 1972, Harold's Trip to the Sky, 1972, Concerto for Trombone and Orchestra, 1976, Quintet, 1976, Music for a Festive Occasion, 1976, Concerto for Violoncello and Orchestra, 1976, The Hawk, 1979, Cenotaph, 1979, Sonata for clarinet and percussino, 1980, Concerto for trumpet and orch., 1980, The Devil's Quickstep, 1982, Prismatic Variations, 1983, Concerto for clarinet and orch., 1984, The Rainbow Snake, 1985, The Dreamtime, 1985, Concerto for orch., 1985, Concerto for brass and orch., 1986, Three Poems for violin and piano, 1987, Solstice, 1988, Woody, 1988, Symphony for winds, 1989, String Quartet # 2, 1989, Five Red Hot Duets, 1989, Ritual Observances, 1991, Drawing down the Moon, 1991, Concerto for violin and orch., 1992, Evensong, 1993, Sonata for solo violin, 1994, Remembrances, 1994, Changes, 1994, Sonata for harp, 1995, Sunlit Peaks and Dark Valleys, 1995, String Quartet # 3, 1995, Suddenly It's Evening, 1997, others. Served with USNR, 1945-46. Recipient Disting. Alumni award Ind. U. Sch. Music, Naumberg Rec. award, 1974, Disting. Alumnus award Kent Sate U., 1982, Ohioana citation, 1978, award Am. Acad. Inst. Arts and Letters, 1985, Libr. of Congress Commn., 1987, Grammy nominee, 1994, Koussevitzky Commn., 1994, Fromm Found. Commn., 1994, Meet the Composer Commn., 1994, Ohioana Libr. Career award 1998, letter of distinction Am. Music Ctr., 2001; Ford Found. composer-in-residence Bakersfield, Calif., 1962-63; Rockefeller Found. grantee for performance Symphony of Overtures, 1965, grantee Nat. Coun. on Art, 1967-68, Nat. Endowment for Arts, 1980, 84, 91; Guggenheim fellow, 1965-66, fellow Bellagio Study and Conf. Ctr., 1979, 89, USA-Can. fellow NEA, 1995. Mem. Am. Music Center (pres. 1982-85), Broadcast Music, Cleve. Composers Guild, League ISCM (nat. adv. bd.). Home: 4073 Bluestone Rd Cleveland OH 44121-2465 E-mail: donalderb@aol.com.

ERB, DORETTA LOUISE BARKER, polymer scientist; b. Upper Darby, Pa., June 21, 1932; d. Ralph Merton and Pauline Kaufman (Isenberg) B.; m. Robert Allan Erb, June 27, 1953; children: Sylvia Ann, Susan Doretta, Carolyn Joy. BS in Pharmacy, Phila. Coll. Pharmacy and Sci., 1954. Registered pharmacist, Pa. Pharmacist Borland's Pharmacy, Upland, Pa., 1954—65; rsch. scientist Franklin Rsch. Ctr., ATC div. Calspan Corp., Norristown, Pa., 1974—93; owner, pres. SiliClone Studio, Valley Forge, Pa., 1982—. Mem. Sigma Xi (chpt. sec. 1990-93). Presbyterian. Achievements include co-invention of intrinsic coloration techniques for highly realistic external prostheses including production of Human Coloration System for silicone prosthetics and special effects; inventor Feclone/simulated fecal material for product testing. Home and Office: PO Box 86 Jug Hollow Rd Valley Forge PA 19481-0086

ERB, HELEN K. musician, educator; b. New Orleans, Sept. 29, 1942; d. Gerald Clifford Kerr and Doris Edna Toennies; m. Richard H. Erb, June 1, 1972; 1 child, Peter Michael Graham; m. Herbert H. Taylor, June 1964 (div. Feb. 1968). BA in German Lit., Swarthmore Coll., 1963. English hornist New Orleans Symphony, 1964—90, Santa Fe Opera, 1965—70, Houston Symphony, 1965—67; instr. oboe Loyola U. Coll. Music, New Orleans, 1970—85, 1995—; English hornist La. Philharm. Orch., New Orleans, 1990—. Mem. faculty Nat. Youth Orch. Can., Toronto, 1980, Toronto, 90; chair, vice chmn. pers. com. La. Philharm. Orch., 1990—96. Mem.: Am. Fedn. Musicians. Democrat. Avocations: tennis, hiking, gardening. Home: 7739 Cohn St New Orleans LA 70118

ERB, RICHARD LOUIS LUNDIN, resort and hotel executive; b. Chgo., Dec. 23, 1929; s. Louis Henry and Miriam (Lundin) E.; m. Jean Elizabeth Easton, Mar. 14, 1959; children: John Richard, Elizabeth Anne, James Easton, Richard Louis II. BA, U. Calif., Berkeley, 1951, postgrad., 1952; student, San Francisco Art Inst., 1956. Cert. hotel adminstr. Asst. gen. mgr. Grand Teton Lodge Co., Jackson Hole, Wyo., 1954-62; mgr. Mauna Kea Beach Hotel, Hawaii, 1964-66; v.p., gen. mgr. Caneel Bay Plantation, Inc., St. John, V.I., 1966-75; gen. mgr. Williamsburg (Va.) Inn, 1975-78; exec. v.p., gen. mgr. Seabrook Island Co., Johns Island, S.C., 1978-80; v.p., dir. hotels Sands Hotel and Casino, Inc., Atlantic City, 1980-81; v.p., gen. mgr. Disneyland Hotel, Anaheim, Calif., 1981—82; COO Grand Traverse Resort, Grand Traverse Village, Mich., 1982—93; gen. mgr. Stein Eriksen Lodge, Deer Valley, Utah, 1993-96; pres. The Erb Group, 1996—. Pres. Spruce-Park Mgmt. Co., 1989; mem. adv. bd. travel and tourism Mich. State U., 1992-96; vice-chmn. Charleston (S.C.) Tourism Coun., 1979-81; bd. dirs. Anaheim Visitors and Conv. Bur., 1981-82, Grand Traverse Conv. and Visitors Bur., 1985-90, U.S. 131 Area Devel. Assn., 1983-93; sr. cons. Cayuga Hosp. Advisors, 1996—. Contbr. articles to trade jours. Vice-pres. V.I. Montessori Sch., 1969-71, bd. dirs., 1968-76; bd. dirs. Coll. of V.I., 1976-79; adv. bd. U. S.C., 1978-82, Calif. State Poly. Inst., 1981-82, Orange Coast C.C., 1981-82, Northwestern Mich. Coll., 1983-93; adv. bd. hospitality mgmt. program Ea. Mich. U., 1989-93; trustee Munson Med. Ctr., Traverse City, 1985-93; bd. dirs. Traverse Symphony Orch., 1984-88, N.A. Vasa, 1987-89; adv. panel Mich. Communities of Econ. Excellence Program, 1984-88; mem. hospitality adv. bd. Utah Valley State Coll., 1994-98. Lt. arty. U.S. Army, 1952-54. Named hon. prof. Mich. State U. Hotel Sch., 1992—. Fellow Edn. Inst.; mem. Am. Hotel and Motel Assn. (dir. 1975-77, 90-94, exec. bd. 1991-94, Service Merit award 1976, Lawson Odde award 1993, Gold Medalist Membership award 1993, trustee Ednl. Inst. 1977-83, mktg. com., exec. com. 1978-83, chmn. projects and programs com. 1982-98, AH&MA resort com. 1986-96, AH&MA condominium com. 1985-96, chmn. ratings com. 1988-96, Ambassador award 1986, Blue Ribbon task force 1988-89, Resort Exec. of Yr. 1988), Caribbean Hotel Assn. (1st v.p. 1972-74, dir. 1970-76, hon. life mem., Extraordinary Service Merit award 1974), V.I. Hotel Assn. (pres. chmn. bd. 1971-76, Merit award 1973), Calif. Hotel Assn. (dir. 1981-82), Caribbean Travel Assn. (dir. 1972-74), Internat. Hotel Assn. (dir. 1971-73), S.C. Hotel Assn. (dir. 1978-82), Am. Hotel Assn. Edn. Inst., (Lamp of Knowledge award 1988), Va. Hotel Assn., Williamsburg Hotel Assn. (bd. dirs. 1975-78), Atlantic City Hotel Assn. (v.p. 1981-82), Atlantic City Casino Assn. (dir. 1981-82), Cornell Soc. Hotelmen, Mich. Travel and Tourist Assn. (bd. dirs. 1983-94, treas. 1986, sec. 1987, v.p. 1988, mktg. com. 1986-93, govtl. affairs com. 1986-93, chmn. edn. com. 1983-84, chmn. bd. 1989-90, Mich. Hotelier of Yr. 1991), Mich. Restaurant Assn. (bd. dirs. 1989-91, chmn. adminstrv. com. 1989-90), Mich. Gov.'s Task Force on Tourism, 1986-87, Grand Island Adv. Commn., Grand Traverse C. of C. (bd. dirs. 1984-89), Nat. Restaurant Assn., Utah Hotel and Motel Assn. (bd. dirs. 1994-96, treas. 1996), Leadership Grand Traverse (exec. com. 1984-92, fellow 1992), Park City Lodging Assn. (bd. dirs. 1993-96), Park City C. of C. (bd. dirs. 1994-97), Tavern Club, Rotary (Paul Harris fellow 1990), Beta Theta Pi. Congregationalist. E-mail: RichardErb@aol.com.

ERB, ROBERT ALLAN, physical scientist; b. Ridley Park, Pa., Jan. 30, 1932; s. John Walter and Roma (Chapman) E.; m. Doretta Louise Barker, June 27, 1953; children— Sylvia Ann, Susan Doretta, Carolyn Joy. BS in Chemistry, U. Pa., 1953; MS, Drexel Inst. Tech., 1959; PhD, Temple U., 1965. Chemist Gates Engring. Co., Wilmington, Del., 1953-54; with Franklin Research Center, div. Franklin Inst. (later div. Arvin/Calspan), Phila., 1954-93, sr. staff chemist, 1965-68, prin. scientist, 1968-81, Inst. fellow, 1981-84, staff scientist, 1985-93; tech. dir. SiliClone Studio, Valley Forge, Pa., 1993—. Mem. AAAS, Am. Anaplastology Assn. (pres. 1996-97), Am. Chem. Soc., Soc. Plastics Engrs., The Franklin Inst., Sigma Xi. Presbyterian. Inventor human simulators, medical and prosthetic devices, solar collectors, permanent systems for dropwise condensation, contraceptive systems, composites using waste plastics. Home and Office: PO Box 86 Valley Forge PA 19481-0086 *Success is to know God's will for your life and to do it.*

ERBE, GARY THOMAS, artist; b. Union City, N.J., Sept. 2, 1944; s. Herman Charles and Florence (Bertone) Erbe; m. Zeny Erbe; children: Kim, Chantell. Student pub. schs., Union City. One man shows Pace Gallery, Houston, 1970, Veldman Gallery, Milw., 1971, New Britain Mus. Am. Art, 1976, 95, Summit (N.J.) Art Ctr., 1976, Bergen Cmty. Mus., Paramus, N.J., 1979, Alexander Gallery, N.Y.C., 1982, 85, N.J. State Mus., Trenton, 1983, Butler Inst. Am. Art, Youngstown, Ohio, 1985, 94, 95, Sordon: Art Gallery, Wilkes Barre, Pa., 1985, Montclair Art Mus., N.J., 1988, Westmoreland (Pa.) Mus. Art, 1988, Canton (Ohio) Art Inst., 1988, Woodmere Art Mus., Phila., 1988, James A. Michener Art Mus., Doylestown, Pa., 1995, Boca Raton (Fla.) Mus. Art, 1995, ACA Gallery, N.Y.C., 1998, Springfield (Mo.) Art Mus., 1999, The Nat. Arts Club, N.Y.C., 2000; exhibited in group shows Newark Mus., 1971, Rutgers U., 1971, Heritage Gallery, N.Y.C., 1972, N.J. State Mus., 1972, 75, The Baseball Hall of Fame, Cooperstown, N.Y., 1991, Morris Mus., N.J., 1994, ACA Gallery, N.Y.C., 1998, Springfield Art Mus., Mo., 1999, Albuquerque Mus., 1999, Meridian Internat. Ctr., Washington, 1999, Mus. Fine Arts, Hanoi, Vietnam, 1999, Mus. Fine Arts, Ho Chi Minh, Vietnam, 1999, Painting Inst., Shanghai, China, 1999, Singapore Mus. Art, 1999, CIPTA Gallery, Jakarta (Indonesia) Arts Ctr., 1999—, Met. Mus. of Manila, Iran, Albuquerque Mus., 1999, Met. Mus. Manila, The Philippines, 2000, ACA Gallery, N.Y.C., 2000, Bradford Brinton Meml. Mus. Wyo., 2002, Meridian Internat. Ctr., Washington, 2002, Topkapi Mus., Turkey, 2002, Ankara Mus. Turkey, 2002, Hanager Arts Ctr., Cairo, Egypt, 2003, Alexandria, Egypt, 2003, Rabat, Morocco, 2003, Casablanca, Morocco, 2003, Allied Mus., Berlin, Germany, 2003, Trompe L'Oeil Internat., Eleanor Ettinger Gallery, N.Y.C., 2003, Harmon-Meek Gallery, Naples, Fla., 2003; represented in permanent collections Butler Inst. Am. Art, N.J. State Mus., New Britain Mus. Am. Art, Montclair Art Mus., Woodmere Art Mus., Archives Am. Art, Nat. Arts Club, N.Y.C., Springfield (Mo.) Art Mus. Recipient Julius Hallgarten award NAD, 1975, 1st award Salmagundi Club, 1975, Noyes Mus., N.J., 1992, The Gilmore Romans Meml. award Allied Artists Am., 1993; nat. mid-yr. 1st pl. award Butler Inst. Am. Art, 2002, Silver medal Audubon Artists, N.Y.C., 2002. Mem. Allied Artists Am. (Gold medal of honor 1975, 84, 91, John Young-Hunter Meml. award 1982, 85, Emily Lowe award 1989), Conn. Acad. Fine Arts, Assoc. Artists N.J., Audubon Artists (Emily Lowe award 1991, Beatrice Jackson Humphreys Meml. award 1992, Stephan Hirsch Meml. award 1994, gold medal of honor 1998, silver medal 2002), Allied Artists Am. (pres. 1994—), Nat. Arts Club (N.Y.C., 1st award 99th Ann. Members Exhbn., Salzman award 100th Ann. Members Exhbn. 1998, Nat. Midyear 1st pl. award Butler Inst. Am. Art 2002, Art Medal for Life Achievement in the Arts, 2003), Artists Fellowship, Inc. (N.Y.C., trustee 1997—), Trompe L'Oeil Soc. Artists. Achievements include development of contemporary approach to Am. Trompe l'oeil called Levitational Realism, extention of school to 3 dimensional compositions, oil on bronze. Office: 539 42nd St Union City NJ 07087-2606

ERBE, JANET SUE, medical surgical, orthopedics and pediatrics nurse; b. Hamilton, Ohio, Aug. 25, 1952; d. Robert A. and Evon R. (Walls) Schlotterbeck; m. Gene Erbe. ADN, Miami U., Hamilton, 1972; BS summa cum laude, Coll. Mt. St. Joseph, 1989. Cert. managed care nurse; cer. in neonatal resuscitation, basic life support. Asst. nurse mgr. Ft. Hamilton-Hughes Hosp., Hamilton, 1972-97; med. analyst Anthem Blue Cross-Blue Shield, Mason, Ohio, 1997—. Mem. ANA, ONA (legiis. liason). Home: 549 Beeler Blvd Hamilton OH 45013-6075 Office: 4361 Irwin Simpson Rd Mason OH 45040-9479

ERBE, YVONNE MARY, music educator, marketing specialist, guidance counselor; b. Wausau, Wis., Nov. 18, 1947; d. Rudolph Anton and Lucille Virginia Karlen; children: Daniel, Heather. BMus Edn., U. Wis., Madison, 1969, postgrad.; MA in Guidance/Counseling Edn Psychology, Eastern Ky. U., Richmond. Lic. music educator, Wis. Music-vocal tchr. Bayport H.S., Greenbay, Wis., 1969-70; tchr. bassoon, oboe U. Wis., Greenbay, 1969-70; jr. high choral dir. Kenosha Unified Schs., Wis., 1970-76; adjudicator, clinician, 1969—. Univ. supr.-edn. U. Wis.-Parkside, Kenosha, 1976-78; mem. parent adv. com. Northern Hills Sch. and Onalaska Mid. Sch., 1987-88; mktg. specialist Metro Prodns., La Crosse, Wis., 1984-85; tchr. music elem., jr. high sch., sr. high, LaCrosse, Wis.; secondary high sch. choral dir., Lexington, Ky., 1988-99, guidance counselor, 1999—. Parent vol. coord. Fauver Hill Sch., 1983-84; sec. exec. bd. Great River Festival of Arts, La Crosse, 1982-83, 1st v.p. exec. bd., chmn. adult choral workshop and performance, chmn. swing choir workshop, 1983-84, pres. bd. dirs., 1984-85; pres. La Crosse Area Newcomers Club, 1982-83; tchr. Confraternity of Christian Doctrine, 1985-88, bd. dirs. La Crosse Boy Choir, 1985-88; condr. Lexington Children's Choir, 1995-96; upward bound instr. Eastern Ky. U., 1994-95; conductor Ctrl. Ky. Youth Choruses, 1995-98. Mem. NEA, Ky. Edn. Assn., Ky. Counseling Assn., Ky. Adminstrs. Assn., Sigma Alpha Iota. Roman Catholic. Avocations: tennis, cross-country skiing, aerobic exercises, needlecrafts, gourmet cooking.

ERBELE, ROBERT S. state legislator; m. Susan Erbele; 4 children. Student, U. Sioux Falls, North Dakota State U. Rancher Bison; EMT-B; choral music dir., 1999—2000; mem. N.D. Senate from 28th dist., Bismark, 2001—; vice chair Senate AG Committee; senate Human Svcs. Com. Dir. Logan County Hist. Soc. Mem. N.D. Buffalo Assn. (v.p.). Republican. Office: 6512 51st St Ave SE Lehr ND 58460 E-mail: rerbele@state.nd.us.

ERBER, THOMAS, physics educator; b. Vienna, Dec. 6, 1930; m. Audrey Burns. BSc, MIT, 1951; MS, U. Chgo., 1953, PhD in Physics, 1957. Asst. prof. physics Ill. Inst. Tech., Chgo., 1957-62, assoc. prof., 1962-69, prof., 1969—, prof. math., 1986—, disting. prof., 1999—. Vis. scientist Stanford Linear Accelerator Ctr., 1970; prof. physics U. Graz, 1971, 82, hon prof., 1971—; prof. physics UCLA, 1978-79, 84-85, 87—, U. Grenoble, 1982; prof. physics U. Chgo., 1998-99; adv. bd. rsch. corp. Mem. editl. bd. Acta Physica Austriaca. Rsch. fellow, Brussels, Belgium, 1963-64. Fellow: Inst. Physics (U.K.), Am. Math. Soc., Am. Phys. Soc.; mem.: IEEE (life sr.), Nuclear, Plasma & Magnetics Soc., Am. Acad. Mechanics, Am. Radio Relay League, Magnetics Soc., Oesterreichische Physikalische Gesellschaft, European Phys. Soc. Office: Ill Inst Tech Dept Physics Chicago IL 60616

ERBER, WILLIAM FRANKLIN, gastroenterologist; b. N.Y.C., June 1, 1941; s. Sigmund and Marcia (Picard) E.; m. Ingrid Amelia Friedler, Dec. 25, 1967; children: Gregory, Karina, Jonathan, Joanna, Jeremy. BS, Muhlenberg Coll., 1963; MD, U. Health Sci., Chgo., 1967. Diplomate Am. Bd. Internal Medicine and Gastroenterology. Intern Maimonides Hosp., 1967-68, resident, 1968-69, 71-72; fellowship in gastroenterology Albert Einstein Coll. of Medicine, 1973-75; rsch. fellow Hadassah Hosp., Jerusalem, 1971-72; clin. asst. prof. Health Sci. Ctr., Bklyn., 1975—. Cons. Crohn's Colitis Found., N.Y.C., 1975—, H.I.P., N.Y.C., 1975—; attending gastroenterologist Maimonides Med. Ctr., Bklyn., 1975—. Author: Internal Medicine Review, 1979; contbr. articles to profl. jours. Maj. USAF, 1969-71. Fellow: ACP, Am. Coll. Gastroenterology; mem.: Am. Gastroenterol. Assn. Avocations: music, piano, skiing. Office: 591 Ocean Pkwy Brooklyn NY 11218-5913 Home: 159 Beach 147th St Neponsit NY 11694

ERBES, JOHN ROBERT, engineering executive; b. LaSalle County, Ill., Sept. 13, 1946; s. Robert William and Jeanette Marie (Brey) E. Cert. of Indsl. Engring. Tech., Allied Inst. Tech., 1966; BS in Gen. Engring., Kennedy Western U., Utah, 1993. Engring. project mgr. Methode Electronics, Inc., Carthage, Ill., 1977 , Vol. Reading is Fundamental, Bus. Ptnrs. Com., Boy Scouts Am. Recipient Award of Merit, Silver Beaver award, 1989. Mem.: Soc. Plastics Engrs., Soc. Automotive Engrs., Six Sigma Green Belt Apprentace. Roman Catholic. Avocations: gardening, storytelling, woodworking. Home: 1260 E County Road 1200 Warsaw IL 62379-3409 Office: Methode Electronics Inc PO Box 130 Carthage IL 62321-0130

ERBS, THOMAS J. lawyer, arbitrator; b. St. Louis, Aug. 31, 1936; s. Harry G. and Jeanne (Tinsley) E.; m. Mary Anne Gansmann, Aug. 23, 1958; children: Scott, Michelle, Todd, Jeanne. BS in Acctg., U. Notre Dame, 1958, JD, 1960. Bar: Mo. 1960, Ill. 1963. Ptnr. Erbs & Erbs P.C., St. Louis, 1960—, pres., 1973—. Arbitrator Fed. Mediation Service, 1974— ; adv. dir. U.S. Bank, St. Louis. Mem. Nat. Acad. Arbitrators, ABA, St. Louis Bar Assn., Am. Arbitration Assn. Office: Erbs & Erbs PC 1650 Des Peres Rd Ste 135 Saint Louis MO 63131-1899

ERBSEN, CLAUDE ERNEST, journalist; b. Trieste, Italy, Mar. 10, 1938; came to U.S., 1951, naturalized, 1956; s. Henry M. and Laura Elena (Treves) E.; m. Jill J. Prosky, July 16, 1959; 1 dau., Diana Lisa; m. Hedy Miriam Cohn, Apr. 7, 1970; children— Allan Henry, Michael David. BA cum laude, Amherst Coll., 1959; Inter-Am. Press Assn. scholar, U. Andes, Bogota, Colombia, 1960. Reporter-printer Amherst Jour.-Record, 1955-57; staff reporter El Tiempo, Bogota, 1960; with AP, 1960-1965, newsman in, Miami, Fla., Washington; to chief of bur. Brazil, 1965—69; exec. rep. for Latin Am., 1969—70; bus. mgr., adminstrv. dir. AP-Dow Jones Econ. Report, London, 1970-75; dep. dir. world services AP, N.Y.C., 1975-80; v.p., dir. AP-Dow Jones News Svcs., London, 1980—87; v.p., dir. world services AP, N.Y.C., 1987—. Bd. dirs. World Press Inst., St. Paul Served to lt. USNR, 1961-65. Recipient San Giusto D'Oro award City of Trieste, 1995. Mem. Internat. Press Inst., Coun. Fgn. Rels., World Assn. of Newspapers. Home: 27 Stratton Rd Scarsdale NY 10583-7556 Office: AP 50 Rockefeller Plz New York NY 10020-1605

ERBSKORN, AMY GORDON, healthcare executive; b. Cleve., Mar. 31, 1957; d. William Livingston and Thelma Jean (Crea) Gordon; m. Eugene Alan Erbskorn, Aug. 16, 1980; children: Jason William, Lea Christine. Student, Ohio State U., 1975-76; BA, Ohio U., 1979; MBA, Case Western Res. U., 1980. Mktg. product specialist Avery Internat. Corp., Painesville, Ohio, 1980-82; biomed. sales rep. Allegiance divsn. Cardinal Health, Chgo., 1982-83, product mgr., 1983-87; advt. account exec. Abelson-Taylor, Chgo., 1987-88; product mgr. oral contraceptives Bristol-Myers Squibb, Princeton, N.J., 1988-91, sr. product mgr. women's healthcare, 1991-94, dir. women's healthcare, 1994-95, dir. cardiovascular mktg., 1996; dir. diabetes care product mktg. Roche Diagnostics, Indpls., 1996-97, v.p. diabetes care mktg., 1997-2000; advt. sr. v.p. Gerbig, Snell/Weisheimer & Assocs., Westerville, Ohio, 2000—02; v.p. mktg. Integrity Pharm. Corp., Indpls., 2002—03; v.p. N.Am. sales and mktg. and internat. mktg. LifeScan, Inc., a Johnson & Johnson Co., Milpitas, Calif., 2003—. Children's ch. dir. Bible Fellowship Evang. Free Ch., Yardley, Pa., 1994-96. Mem. Healthcare Businesswommen's Assn. Republican. Home: 2281 Doccia Ct Pleasanton CA 94566

ERCANBRACK, GENE, food products executive; b. Provo, Utah, Nov. 27, 1941; s. Weldon Monroe and Lillian Hannah Ercanbrack; m. Aloma Richins, July 1, 1988; children: Gaylon Richins, Charles, Richard, Glenn, Christie Ercanbrack Johnsonstepchildren: Devine Taylor, Brett Richins. Student, Weber State U., 1960—62. Sgt. Utah Hwy. Patrol, Salt Lake City, 1967—98; gen ptnr. Ercanbrack Enterprises, Morgan, Utah, 1979—; sheriff Morgan County Sheriffs Office, 1999—. Mem. com. bd. Utah Law Enforcement Planning, Salt Lake City, 1999—; bd. dirs. Utah Behavioral Task Force, UTah Safe Sch. Consortium. Del. Morgan County State Reps., 1999—; bd. dirs. Morgan County Fair Bd., 2000—. Morgan County Farm Bur., 2000—. Mem.: Utah Sheriff's Assn., Western States Sheriff's Assn., Nat. Sheriff's Assn., Chiefs Police Assn. Mem. Lds Ch. Avocations: travel, hunting, sports, cultural events. Office: Morgan County Sheriffs Office PO Box 1047 48 W Young St Morgan UT 84050 Office Fax: 801-829-0605. Business E-Mail: gercanbrack@morgan.state.ut.us.

ERCKLENTZ, ALEXANDER TONIO, investment executive; b. N.Y.C., July 13, 1936; s. Enno Wilhelm and Hildegard (Schlubach) E.; children: Alexander Tonio Jr., Christina Titaua, Nicholas Ley BA, Yale U.; postgrad, NYU. Various positions Brown Brothers Harriman & Co., N.Y.C., 1959-77, ptnr., 1978—. Bd. dirs. AXA Art Ins. Corp., Stinnes Corp. Pres. Am. Berlin Opera Found.; trustee Am. U. Beirut; pres. Friends of Inst. U.S. Studies Univ. of London. Mem.: Field Club, Stanwich Club, Down Town Assn., The Links. Republican. Roman Catholic. Office: Brown Brothers Harriman & Co 140 Broadway New York NY 10005-1101

ERCKLENTZ, ENNO WILHELM, JR., lawyer; b. N.Y.C., Jan. 27, 1931; s. Enno Wilhelm and Hildegard (Schlubach) E.; m. Mai A. Vilms, Sept. 20, 1969; children: Cornelia, Stephanie. AB, Columbia U., 1954; JD, Harvard U., 1957. Bar: N.Y. 1958. Assoc. Curtis, Mallet-Prevost, Colt & Mosle, N.Y.C., 1957-60; sec., gen. counsel Channing Fin. Corp., N.Y.C., 1960-69; v.p., sec., gen. counsel Inverness Mgmt. Corp., N.Y.C., 1969-75; pvt. practice N.Y.C., 1975-78; ptnr. Whitman & Ransom, N.Y.C., 1978-87, Greeven & Ercklentz, N.Y.C., 1987-98; pvt. practice N.Y.C., 1998—. Author: Modern German Corporation Law, 1979. Mem. ABA, N.Y. State Bar Assn., Assn. of Bar City of N.Y., Am. Fgn. Law Assn. Republican. Roman Catholic. Office: Enno W Ercklentz Jr PC 630 5th Ave Ste 1905 New York NY 10111-0100 E-mail: ennoerck@aol.com.

ERDEL, SALLY ELIZABETH, nurse; b. Peoria, Ill., Mar. 28, 1952; d. Robert William and Mary Maxine (Vick) Birky; m. Timothy Paul Erdel, Aug. 28, 1977; children: Sarah Beth, Rachel Elaine, Matthew Robert. AA summa cum laude, Ft. Wayne Bible Coll., 1972; grad. with highest honor, West Suburban Hosp., Oak Park, Ill., 1975; BSN with high honor, U. Ill. Med. Ctr., Chgo., 1977, MS, 1980. Staff nurse West Suburban Hosp., 1975-77; tchg. asst. U. Ill. Med. Ctr., 1980; staff nurse Highland Park (Ill.) Hosp., 1981-82, Carle Found. Hosp., Urbana, Ill., 1982-87; asst. prof. Bethel Coll., Mishawaka, Ind., 1994—. Acting program dir. divsn. of nursing, Bethel Coll., Mishawaka, Ind., 1995-97, program dir., 1997-2002; staff nurse St. Joseph's Hosp., Mishawaka, Ind., 1994-97; seminar/workshop spkr., 1982—; clin. nurse specialist, 1985—87; campus nurse, Jamaica Theol. Sem., Kingston, Jamaica, 1988-93, lectr. abnormal psychology, 1992-93; thesis sec. Caribbean Grad. Sch. Theology, Kingston, Jamaica, 1988-93; nursing cons. Devel. and Behavioral Evaluation Svcs., South Bend, Ind., 1994; team mem. Med. Group Mission, Liberia, 1975; vol. clinic nurse St. Andrew's Settlement, Kingston, 1991-93; co-leader Bethel Coll. Task Force Team Jamaica, 2001; missionary World Ptnrs., 1987-94; mem. instnl. animal care and use com. U. Notre Dame, 1996-98; program evaluator Nat. League for Nursing Accrediting Commn., 1997—, mem. evaluation rev. panel ADN programs, 2003—; nursing instr. Kaplan programs, 2003—. Bd. dirs., sec. Renewed Ministries, Inc. Mem. ANA, Missionary Ch. Hist. Soc., Ill. Mennonite Hist. and Geneal. Soc., Mich. Anabapt. Historians, Ind. Nurses Assn., Sigma Theta Tau. Home: 56111 Francis Ave Mishawaka IN 46545-7507 Office: Bethel Coll Divsn Nursing 1001 W Mckinley Ave Mishawaka IN 46545-5509

ERDELJAC, DANIEL JOSEPH, retired manufacturing company executive; b. Farmington, W.Va., Aug. 27, 1932; s. Phillip John, Mary M. (Hudak) E.; m. Constance June Sabatino, June 25, 1955; children— Daniel J. II, James M., Mary L., Laurie A. Grad. high sch., Farmington, W.Va. Materials mgr. South Union Coal Co., Edna, W.Va., 1952-60; plant mgr. Interpace Corp., various locations, 1960-70; pres., exec. v.p. Hydro Conduit Corp., Houston, 1970-92, pres., 1980-82, ret., 1992; divsn. mgr. Brooks Products, Houston, 1995-96, ret., 1996. Past chmn. Am. Concrete Pipe Assn. Roman Catholic. Avocations: grandchildren, investments.

ERDELY, STEPHEN LAJOS, music educator; b. Szeged, Hungary, May 6, 1921; came to U.S., 1949, naturalized, 1954; s. Jeno and Vilma (Lengyel) Erdelyi; m. Beatrice Eppinelle, Sept. 28, 1952. Absolutorium, Nat. Franz Liszt Music Acad., 1939-44, Franz Josef U., 1944; PhD, Case Western Res. U., 1962. Faculty Ohio State U., Toledo, 1966-73; prof. music M.I.T., Cambridge, Mass., 1973—, dir. music, 1976—; mem. faculty Divsn. Continuing Edn. Harvard U. Rsch. assoc. Milman Perry Collection, Harvard U., faculty mem. divsn. continuing edn. Soloist, Munich (Ger.) Chamber Music Dept., 1946-49, Cleve. Orch., 1951-66, concert artist with, The Erdely Duo, 1951—; Author: Methods and Principles of Hungarian Ethnomusicology, 1965, Music of South Slavic Epics From The Bihac Region of Bosnia, 1995; contbr. articles to profl. jours. Am. Philos. Soc. grantee, 1962; Am. Council Learned Socs. grantee, 1964; Nat. Endowment for Arts grantee, 1974-77, 83-85 Mem. Am. Musicol. Soc. Soc. for Ethnomusicology (councilor 1970-73), Internat. Folk Music Council, Ohio Folklore Soc. (pres. 1967-69), Internat. Musicology Soc., Coll. Music Soc. Office: MIT Dept Humanities Cambridge MA 02139 Fax: 978-371-7046.

ERDELYI, EILEEN EDITH, financial planner and advisor; b. Glendale, Calif., Aug. 12, 1951; m. Alex Erdelyi, Jr., Dec. 11, 1971; children: Stephen Alex, Diana Lynn. Cert. real estate salesperson, Lumbleau Real Estate Sch., L.A., 1985; stock market investment cert., Pacific Sch. Fin., Pasadena, Calif., 1985; cert. fin. planning program, U. So. Calif., 1987; cert. fin. planner, Coll. Fin. Planning, Denver, 1988; AAS, Palomar Coll., San Marcos, Calif. Lic. real estate salesperson, Calif.; CFP; lic. series 63 and 7 Nat. Assn. Securities Dealers; lic. in health and disability ins., life agt. Calif. Supervising clk. dept. pub. social svcs. and dept. probation Los Angeles County, L.A., 1969-75; broker assoc. Red Carpet Real Estate, Tujunga, Calif., 1986-88; assoc. fin. advisor prudent planning-alliance adv. group NBC Employees Fed. Credit Union, Burbank, Calif., 1988-89; fin. advisor, affiliate Alliance Adv. Group, Inc., Chatsworth, Calif., 1989-94; real estate sales assoc. Key Real Estate, Escondido, Calif., 1989-94; fin. advisor Capital Planning Concepts, San Diego, 1994-95; sr. fin. advisor Alliance Adv. & Securities, Inc., Escondido, 1995—. Former press chmn., treas., v.p., pres. Sunland Woman's Club Jrs. of Calif. Fedn. Woman's Clubs, 1978-88, also former bd. dirs. Verdugo Met. dist. Named Jr. of Yr., Woman's Club Jrs., 1981. Avocations: gardening, water sports, creative writing. Address: PO Box 300822 Escondido CA 92030-0822 Office: 3390 Auto Mall Dr Ste 200 Westlake Village CA 91362

ERDEN, SYBIL ISOLDE, artist; b. N.Y.C., Nov. 30, 1950; d. Mark and Annelise (Stautner) E.; m. Philip M. Freund, July 7, 1970 (div. 1978); m. Jerry Buley, June 15, 1991 (div. 1998). Student, Acad. of Art, San Francisco, 1970-71, San Francisco Art Inst., 1971-73, Ariz. State U., 1992-93. Lectr. Calif. Coll. Arts and Crafts, 1978, Tempe Fine Art Ctr., 1985, Collins Gallery, San Francisco, 1986, Collage Art Appreciation Group, Colorado Springs, Colo., 1987, South Park Sch. Dist., Fairplay, Colo., 1987, Al Collins Sch. Graphic Design, 1989-90, Cerro Coso C.C., Calif., 1991, Chico State U., 1991; tchr. workshops City of Phoenix, 1991, Cerro Coso C.C., Calif., 1991, Chico State U., 1991, Phoenix Coll., 1992-94, Cochise Coll., 1993; guest spkr. Tempe Art Ctr. Seminar for Artists, 1993, Mesa C.C., 1994-96. Exhibited in group shows including San Francisco Art Inst., 1973, The Bush Street Gallery, San Francisco, 1977, The Top Floor Gallery, San Francisco, 1979, I-Beam, San Francisco, 1980, Diablo Valley Coll., Walnut Creek, Calif., 1980, The Stable, San Francisco, 1982, Tempe Fine Arts Ctr., 1985, Collins Gallery, San Francisco, 1986, 89—, Berkeley (Calif.) Art Ctr., 1986, The Cave, San Francisco, 1981, Alwun House, Phoenix, 1985, 87-93 (award 1989), Grand Canyon Coll., Phoenix, 1988, N.Mex. Jr. Coll., 1988, 90 (award 1990), San Francisco State U., 1988, Pa. State U., 1989, Ohio State U., 1989, Mendocino Art Ctr., 1990, Jewish Cmty. Ctr., Denver, 1990, Cerro Coso C.C., Kern County, Calif., 1990-91, Chico State U., 1991, Sierra Arts Found., 1991, Ea. N.Mex. U., 1992, Shemer Art Ctr., Phoenix, 1991, Chico (Calif.) State U., 1992, Sierra Arts Found., Reno, 1992, Movemiento Artistico del Rio Salado Artspace, 1993-98, IOA Artspace, Oklahoma City, 1995, Ariz. State U., 1996, Tempe Pub. Libr., 1996, La Bandera Vieja nat. traveling exhibit Ariz. Commn. on Arts; executed mural office of Dr. Peter Eckman, San Francisco, 1977, HandBall Express, San Francisco, 1981; archived by Smithsonian Mus. Archive Am. Art, Washington; columnist Cages Bird Hobbyist, 1996—; contbr. articles to popular mags. Founder, pres., dir. Oasis Sanctuary Found., to 1998. Mem. Am. Surrealist Initiative, Ariz. Visionary Alternative (founder, dir. 1984-85, 87-95), Movemiento Artistico del Rio Salado Artspace (artist mem.), LIC Rehabber For The Birds Rehab. Found., Am. Fedn. Aviculturists. Democrat. Jewish. Avocations: motorcycles, wildlife rescue and rehabilitation, aviculturist.

ERDMAN, JEAN, dancer, choreographer; b. Honolulu, Feb. 20, 1916; d. John Pinney and Marion (Dillingham) Erdman; m. Joseph Campbell, May 5, 1938 (dec. Oct. 1987). Diploma, Sarah Lawrence Coll., 1936; DArts (hon.), Bard Coll., 1992. Prin. dancer Martha Graham Dance Co., 1938; organized Jean Erdman Dance Group, 1944, performer, choreographer, 1944-54; dir. dance dept. Bard Coll., Annandale-on-Hudson, N.Y., 1954-57; creator, producer, performer Jean Erdman Theater of Dance, 1957-72; co-founder Theater of the Open Eye, 1972. Creator, head Dance Theater program NYU Sch. Arts, 1966-71; artist-in-residence arts festivals in Vancouver, Honolulu, Tokyo, L.A., San Francisco, Boulder; pres. Joseph Campbell Found., Honolulu; choreographer The Transformations of Medusa, 1942, Ophelia, 1946, The Perilous Chapel, 1949, The Coach with the Six Insides, 1960, Gauguin in Tahiti, 1972, Moon Mysteries, 1965, The Dream of Kitamura, 1978, The Minotaur Among Us, 1985. Jean Erdman Scholarship endowment, U. Hawaii. Recipient Obie award, 1963, Vernon Rice award Drama Desk, 1963, Drama Desk award, 1972, Heritage award Nat. Dance Assn., 1993, Manhattan award Manhattan Mag., 1994, Tony nomination. Mem. Century Club, Outrigger Canoe Club, Am. Dance Guild, Sacred Dance Guild (hon.). Office: 136 Waverly Pl Apt 14D New York NY 10014-6823

ERDMAN, JOSEPH, lawyer; b. Havana, Cuba, Dec. 14, 1935; s. Jonas and Miriam (Rimsky) E.; children: Harley, Andrew; m. Rosemary Hill, Apr. 20, 1992. BA, U. Va., 1956; postgrad., U. Mich., 1956-57; LLB, Fordham U., 1960. Bar: N.Y. 1960, Fla. 1975. Assoc. Wormser Koch Kiely-Alessandroni, N.Y.C., 1960-62; ptnr. Greenbaum, Wolff & Ernst, N.Y.C., 1962-82, Proskauer Rose LLP, Fla. and N.Y.C., 1982—, chmn. personal planning dept., 1991—. Lectr. radio, panels, NYU Inst. Taxation, 1978, U. Va. Law Sch., 1999—. Author: Complete Guide to Marital Deduction in Estate Planning, 1978, Effective Drafting Under the Revised Uniform Principal and Income Act, 1991; contbr. articles to profl. jours. Co-chmn. Westchester for Carter Campaign, 1976; pres. Scarsdale Synogogue, 1978-79; mem. Planned Giving Coun. U. Va., 1992—, Arts Coun., 1999—; bd. trustees U. Va. Coll. Arts & Scis., 1997—; adv. coun. Bayly Mus. With U.S. Army, 1957-58. Fellow Am. Coll. Trust and Estate Coun.; mem. N.Y. State Bar Assn., Fla. Bar Assn., Jefferson Soc. Va., Phi Beta Kappa, Boca Raton Resort and Club, Boca West Club, Farmington Country Club (Va.). Home: 19539 Island Court Dr Boca Raton FL 33434-5153 also: 4 Farmington Dr Charlottesville VA 22901-3241 Office: Proskauer Rose LLP One Boca Pl 2255 Glades Rd Ste 340 Boca Raton FL 33431-7382 also: 1585 Broadway New York NY 10036-8200

ERDMAN, PAUL EMIL, author; b. Stratford, Ont., Can., May 19, 1932; (parents Am. citizens); s. Horace Herman and Helen E.; m. Helly Elizabeth Boeglin, Sept. 11, 1954; children: Constance Anne Catherine, Jennifer Michele. Student, Concordia Coll., Ft. Wayne, Ind., 1950-51, Concordia Sem., St. Louis, 1952-53; BA, Concordia Coll., St. Louis, 1954; BS, Georgetown U., 1956; MA, PhD, U. Basel, Switzerland, 1958. Econ. cons. European Coal and Steel Community, Luxembourg, Luxembourg, 1958; internat. economist Stanford Research Inst., Menlo Park, Calif., 1958-61; exec. v.p. Electronics Internat. Capital Ltd., Hamilton, Bermuda, 1962-64; vice chmn. United California Bank in Basel A.G., 1965-70. Cons. RAI Corp., TV corp., Italy.; host Moneytalk Sta. KGO, ABC, San Francisco, 1983-86, commentator, 1987—. Author: Swiss-American Economic Relations, 1959, Die Europaeische Wirtschaftsgemeinschaft und die Drittlaender, 1960, The Billion Dollar Sure Thing, 1973, The Silver Bears, 1974, The Crash of '79, 1976, The Last Days of America, 1981, Paul Erdman's Money Book: An Investor's Guide to Economics and Finance, 1984, The Panic of '89, 1987, The Palace, 1988, What Next? 1988, The Swiss Account, 1991, Warning to the Yen, 1992, Zero Coupon, 1993, Tug of War, 1996, The Set-Up, 1997; contbg. editor, columnist M Inc. mag., 1987-92; columnist The Nikon Keizai Shimbun, 1987-88, The Japan Post, 1989—, CBS Market Watch, 1998—; contbr. articles, revs. to popular mags. Mem. bd. advisors program in internat. bus. diplomacy Sch. fgn. Service, Georgetown U., Washington, 1980—, faculty mem. Georgetown leadership seminar, 1982—. Recipient Champion Media award for econ. understanding Amos Tuck Sch. Bus. Administrn., Dartmouth Coll., 1984 Mem. Authors Guild, Mysters Writers Am. (Edgar award 1974), PEN Am. Ctr. Lutheran. Address: 1817 Lytton Springs Rd Healdsburg CA 95448-9145 E-mail: erdman@sonic.net.

ERDMAN, PHILIP, state legislator, farmer; b. Scottsbluff, Nebr., Apr. 7, 1977; BS in Agrl. Scis., U. Nebr., 2000. Mem. Nebr. Legis. from 47th dist., Lincoln, 2001—. Cons. strategic planning Farmland Industries, Inc.; football recruiter U. Nebr., Lincoln. Mem. adv. bd., mem. curriculum com. Coll. Agrl. Scis. and Natural Resources, 1999-2000; del. Nebr. State Rep. Conv., 2000, Morrill County Rep. Conv., 2000. Mem. Fellowship Christian Athletes, Nat. FFA Alumni, Nebr. FFA Alumni (state pres. 1996-97), Rock Jaycees, Bayard FFA Alumni, Cheyenne County C. of C., Alpha Zeta, Gamma Sigma Delta. Home: Rural Rt 1, Box 314 Bayard NE 69334 Office: Rm 1101 State Capitol Lincoln NE 68509

ERDMAN, SOL, non-profit organization administrator; b. N.Y.C., July 10, 1944; s. Joseph Barch and Therese (Mioduscewski) E. AB, Cornell U., 1965; MBA, Harvard U., 1971. Co-mgr. options arbitrage Oppenheimer & Co., N.Y.C., 1972-76, mgr., 1977-84, sr. v.p., 1979-84; prin. Sol Erdman, Venture Fin., N.Y.C., 1984-94; pres. Democracy 2000, N.Y.C., 1995—2001, Ctr. for Collaborative Democracy, N.Y.C., 2002—. Co-author: Reinventing Congress for the 21st Century, 1995. Bd. dirs. Nat. Taxpayers Union, Washington, 1986—. 1st lt. U.S. Army, 1966-69, Korea. Office: Ctr for Collaborative Democracy 200 E End Ave Apt 11D New York NY 10128-7800

ERDMANN, JAMES BERNARD, educational psychologist; b. Oct. 27, 1937; s. George C. and Emma (Hiltebrand) E.; m. Rebecca Susan Lindsay; children: Theodore Michael, Carolyn Louise, Christopher Joseph, Timothy James. Grad. cum laude, Pontifical Coll., Josephinum, 1959; MA, Loyola U., Chgo., 1964, PhD, 1966. Rsch. asst. Psychometric Lab. Loyola U., 1960-63, rsch. assoc., project dir., 1963-65, acting dir., 1965-66, assoc. dir., 1967-69, instr. dept. psychology, 1964-66, asst. prof. measurement program, 1967-69; assoc. prof. Sch. Edn. and Sch. Human Medicine, eval. coord. Office Med. Edn., R & D, Mich. State U., 1969-70; dir. divsn. ednl. measurement and rsch. Assn. Am. Med. Colls., Washington, 1970-87; clin. assoc. prof. psychiatry and behavioral scis. George Washington U. Sch. Medicine and Health Scis., 1973-87; assoc. dean adminstrn. and spl. projects Jefferson Med. Coll., Thomas Jefferson U., Phila., 1987-89, assoc. dean adminstrn. and univ. registrar, 1990-2001, prof. medicine (edn.) dept. medicine, 1993—, sr. assoc. dean faculty affairs, 2001—; dean Jefferson Coll. Health Professions Thomas Jefferson U., Phila., 2002—. Contbr. articles to profl. jours. Mem. Am. Ednl. Rsch. Assn., Nat. Coun. Measurement in Edn., Assn. Am. Med. Coll. Roman Catholic. Home: 408 Bickmore Dr Media PA 19086-6909 Office: 130 S 9th St Philadelphia PA 19107-5233 E-mail: james.erdmann@jefferson.edu.

ERDMANN, JOACHIM CHRISTIAN, physicist; b. Danzig, June 5, 1928; s. Franz Werner and Maria Magdalena (Schreiber) E.; m. Ursula Maria Wedemeyer, Aug. 24, 1957; children: Michael Andreas, Thomas Christian, Maria Martha Dorothea. Doctorate, Tech. U. Braunschweig, Germany, 1958. Physicist Osram Labs., Augsburg, Germany, 1954-60; sr. rsch. scientist Boeing Sci. Rsch. Labs., Seattle, 1960-72, Boeing Aerospace Co., Seattle, 1972-73; prin. engr. Boeing Comml. Airplane Co., Seattle, 1973-81, sr. prin. engr., 1981-84, Boeing Aerospace (Boeing Def. and Space Group), Seattle, 1984—90; tech. cons., 1990—. Vis. prof. Max Planck Inst. for Metals Rsch., Stuttgart, Germany, 1968-69; lectr. Tech. U. Stuttgart, 1968-69; pres. Optologics Inc., Seattle, 1973-94. Author: Heat Conduction in Crystals, 1969; contbr. articles to profl. jours. Mem. Am. Phys. Soc., Optical Soc. Am., Soc. Photo Optical Instrumentation Engrs. Achievements include research in cryogenics, statistical physics and opto electronics. Home: 14300 Trillium Blvd SE Apt 8 Bothell WA 98012-1300 Office: Boeing Def & Space Group PO Box 3999 Seattle WA 98124-2499 E-mail: joachime@juerdmann.com.

ERDNER, JON W. small business owner, securities trader; b. Pitts., Nov. 4, 1942; s. William John and Marie Dorothy (Filipietz) E.; m. Joyce Ann Girouard, Dec. 1, 1990; children: Niki Lee, Kassandra Marie. Student, U. Pitts., 1961-64; BA in Psychology, Kent (Ohio) State U., 1967. Pres. Erdner Enterprises, Inc., Pitts., 1967—; exec. v.p. Investment Timing Svcs., Inc., Washington, Pa., 1978-88, pres., owner, 1988-95, also bd. dirs.; owner Stormy Acres Farm & Stable, Washington, 1984—, ITS AssetMgmt., 1995—; pres., owner Erdner Enterprises, Inc., Washington, Pa., 1995—; owner Atlas Brokerage Co., Washington, Pa., 1998—. Mem. Internat. Assn. Fin. Planners, U.S. Trotting Assn., Pa. Harness Horse Assn., Meadows Standardbred Owners Assn., Kent State U. Alumni Assn., Masons, Shriner. Republican. Avocations: radio, classical music, bridge. Home: 52 Hatfield Ln Canonsburg PA 15317-4918 Office: ITS Asset Mgmt LP & Erdner Enterprises Inc 1720 Washington Rd Washington PA 15301-8919

ERDÖS, ERVIN GEORGE, pharmacology and biochemistry educator; b. Budapest, Hungary; came to U.S., 1954; naturalized, 1959; s. Andor and Aranka (Breuer) E; m. Sara F. Rabito, May 30, 1986; children from previous marriage: Martin, Peter, Philip. Grad., U. Budapest Sch. Medicine, 1950; MD, U. Munich, 1950. With hosp., Munich, 1951; rsch. assoc. in biochem. rsch. lab. U. Munich, 1952-54; rsch. assoc. Mercy Hosp., Pitts., 1955-58; fellow in biochemistry, ind. rsch. Mellon Inst., Pitts., 1958-63; asst. prof. pharmacology U. Pitts., 1958-61, assoc. prof., 1961-63; prof. pharmacology U. Okla. Sch. Medicine, Oklahoma City, 1963-73, George Lynn Cross rsch. prof., 1970-73; prof. pharmacology, internal medicine U. Tex., Southwestern Med. Sch., Dallas, 1973-85; prof. pharmacology and anesthesiology, dir. Peptide Rsch. Lab. U. Ill. Coll. Medicine, Chgo., 1985—. Vis. prof. Tulane U., 1963; Disting. Fulbright prof., 1975; vis. scientist U.S.-Japan Coop. Sci. Program, NSF, 1966; vis. prof. dept. pharmacology Rush Med. Coll., Chgo., 1993—; cons. in field; mem. coms. Nat. Heart and Lung Inst. Editor books; mem. editorial bd. jours. Recipient gold medal Frey-Werle Found., Munich, 1988, Disting. Faculty award U. Ill. Coll. Medicine, 1992; Deutsche Forschungsgemeinschaft fellow, 1954; Wellcome Rsch. travel grantee, 1964; Univ. scholar U. Ill., 1990. Fellow: Am. Heart Assn. (mem. adv. bd. Coun. for High Blood Pressure Rsch. 1972—, Ciba award for hypertension rsch. 1994, Rsch. Achievement award 1995); mem.: Am. Soc. Biochemistry and Molecular Biology, Hungarian Acad. Sci. (fgn.) (hon.), Am. Soc. Pharmacology and Exptl. Therapeutics. Office: U Ill Coll Medicine Dept Pharmacology MC 868 835 S Wolcott Ave Chicago IL 60612-7340 E-mail: egerdos@uic.edu.

ERDRICH, LOUISE (KAREN ERDRICH), fiction writer, poet; b. Little Falls, Minn., June 7, 1954; d. Ralph Louis and Rita Joanne (Gourneau) E.; m. Michael Anthony Dorris, Oct. 10, 1981 (dec. Apr. 1997); children: Abel (dec.), Sava, Madeline, Persia, Pallas, Aza. BA, Dartmouth Coll., 1976; MA, Johns Hopkins U., 1979. Vis. poet, tchr. N.D. State Arts Council, 1977-78; tchr. writing Johns Hopkins U., Balt., 1978-79; communications dir., editor Circle-Boston Indian Council, 1979-80; textbook writer Charles Merrill Co., 1980. Author: (textbook) Imagination, 1981; (poetry) Jacklight, 1984, Baptism of

Desire, 1989; (novels) Love Medicine, 1984 (Nat. Book Critics Circle award for fiction 1984, Virgina McCormick Scully prize 1984, L.A. Times award for best novel 1985, Sue Kaufman prize for first fiction Am Acad. and Inst. of Arts and Letters 1985), The Beet Queen, 1986, Tracks, 1988, (with Michael Dorris) The Crown of Columbus, 1991, (with Dorris) Route 2, 1991, The Bingo Palace, 1994, The Blue Jay's Dance: A Writer's Year with Baby, 1995, Tales of Burning Love, 1996, The Antelope Wife, 1998; (children's) Grandmother's Pigeon, 1997, The Birchbark House, 1999; contbr. short stories, essays and poems to popular mags., other publs. Johns Hopkins U. teaching fellow, 1979; Macdowell Colony fellow, 1980; Yaddo Colony fellow, 1981; vis. fellow Dartmouth Coll., 1981; Guggenheim fellow, 1985-86; recipient numerous awards for profl. excellence including Nelson Algren award, 1982, Pushcart prize, 1983, Nat. Mag. Fiction award, 1983, 87, First prize O. Henry awards, 1987. Mem. PEN (exec. bd. 1985-90),, Am. Acad. Arts and Letters, Authors Guild, Western Lit. Assn. Address: c/o Andrew Wylie Agy 250 W 57th St Ste 2114 New York NY 10107-2199 Office: PO Box 476 Cornish Flat NH 03746*

ERENBERGER, TIMOTHY, writer; b. Iowa City, Iowa, Feb. 1, 1971; s. Douglas V. and Judith A. Erenberger; m. Angela Rachelle Ross. Author: (book) Fangs of the Serpent, 2000, Grandfather's Tale, 2001, Abacar the Wizard, 2001. Avocations: martial arts, target shooting, hunting, paintball. Personal E-mail: timerenberger@hotmail.com.

ERENBURG, STEVEN ALAN, communications executive; b. Bklyn., Sept. 8, 1937; s. Harry and Sophie (Karp) E.; m. Mary Kabasakalian, Nov. 10, 1970; children: Aram Lee, Mariam Jennifer. BEE, Pratt Inst., 1957; MS in Systems Sci., Bklyn. Poly. Inst., 1970. Project engr. Kearfott Co., Wayne, N.J., 1957-66; program mgr. Kollsman Instrument Corp., Syosset, N.Y., 1966-70; editor Electronic Design mag., N.Y.C., 1970-71; mng. editor EDN mag., Boston, 1971-73; mgr. pub. relations AT&T Bell Labs., Murray Hill, N.J., 1973-77; v.p., dir. corp. rels. ITT Corp., N.Y.C., 1977-98, ret., 1998; cons. Hill and Knowlton Pub. Rels., N.Y.C., 2000—. Bd. dirs. Hybrid Data Systems, Inc., Rahway, N.J. Patentee Gyrocompass, 1965. Mem. IEEE (sr. mem., dir. external affairs com. 1974-79), Belgian Am. C. of C. (bd. dirs.). Democrat. Avocation: photography. Home: 35 S Mountain Rd Millburn NJ 07041-1505

ERENGIL, MEHMET ERDAL, aeronautical engineer, researcher; b. Yalova, Cyprus, Sept. 10, 1964; arrived in U.S.A., 1982; s. Kadir and Sevim Erengil; m. Miriam Jacqueline Balduff, Dec. 28, 1990; children: Haven Kennedy, Justice Remington. BS with hons. in Engring., Case We. Res. U., 1986; MS in Engring., U. Tex., Austin, Tex., 1989, PhD, 1993. From post-doctoral fellow to rsch. assoc. Inst. Advanced Tech. U. Tex., Austin, 1994—2000, rsch. assoc. Inst. Advanced Tech., 2000—. Cons. in field. Contbr. articles to profl. jours. Scholar, Cyprus-Am. Scholarship Program, 1982—86. Mem.: AIAA (sr.), Nat. Def. Indsl. Assn. Achievements include development of guidance, navigation and control concept for precision strike. Avocations: camping, photography, soccer, scuba diving, swimming. Home: 8420 Asmara Drive Austin TX 78750 Office: Inst for Advanced Technology 3925 W Braker Lane Ste 400 Austin TX 78759 E-mail: erengil@iat.utexas.edu.

ERENS, JAY ALLAN, lawyer; b. Chgo., Oct. 18, 1935; s. Miller S. and Annette (Goodman) R.; m. Patricia F. Brett, Aug. 21, 1960 (div. May 1985); children: Pamela B., Bradley B.; m. Patrice K. Franklin, June 15, 1985; 1 child, Cameron Jay. BA, Yale U., 1956; LLB, Harvard U., 1959. Bar: Ill. 1960. Law clk. to Justice John M. Harlan U.S. Supreme Ct., Washington, 1959-60; pvt. practice Chgo., 1960-64; founding and sr. ptnr. Levy and Erens (name changed to Erens and Miller 1985), Chgo., 1964-86; sr. ptnr. Hopkins & Sutter, Chgo., 1986-2001; with Foley & Lardner, Chgo., 2001—. Lectr. law Northwestern U., Chgo., 1961-63; spl. asst. atty. gen. State Ill., Chgo., 1964-70. Trustee Latin Sch. Chgo., 1975-80. Mem. ABA, Chgo. Bar Assn. Office: Foley & Lardner 321 N Clark St Chicago IL 60610 E-mail: jerens@foleylaw.com.

ERENSTEIN, ALAN, emergency room nurse, medical education consultant; Grad., Aliquippa Hosp Sch. Radiology, Pa., 1974; student, Aliquippa Hosp. Sch. Radiology, New Wilmington, Pa., 1974; AA in Gen. Studies, LPN, Beaver County C.C., Monaca, Pa., 1977, AS in Nursing, RN, 1979. RN, Fla.; registered radiologic technologist. LPN Hamot Med. Ctr., Erie, Pa., 1977-78; team leader Trauma-Neuro ICU and Stepdown Unit Allegheny Gen. Hosp., Pitts., 1979-81, staff nurse Emergency Room, 1981; flight nurse LifeWATCH HCA Wesley Med. Ctr., Wichita, Kans., 1981-91, contigency and float pool, 1991-92, hyperbaric nurse, 1991-92; ER nurse, relief charge nurse, clin. coord., team leader JFK Med. Ctr., Atlantis, Fla., 1992-95; aeromed. specialist Bizjet Air Ambulance, West Palm Beach, Fla., 1994-95; med. edn. cons. Med. Edn. Cons. Am., Tampa, 1994-97; with disaster team Cutler Ridge (Fla.) Field Hosp., 1992; response team Kans. Tornado Wesley Med. Ctr., Wichita, 1991; emergency rm./trauma nurse DelRay Med. Ctr., 1996—. Paramedic clin. coord. Hutchinson (Kans.) C.C., 1989; skills lab coord. Advanced Trauma Life Support Course, HCA Wesley Med. Ctr., Wichita, 1989-92; lectr. various med. ctrs., univs. and confs. Author: Trauma in Pregnancy, 1990; co-author: LifeWATCH Transport Manual, 1988; contbr. Society Trauma Nurses: Instructor's Resource Manual for Trauma Nursing, The Pregnant Trauma Patient Module, 1998. Mem. Soc. Trauma Nurses, Nat. Flight Nurses Assn. Office: Delray Med Ctr 5352 Linton Blvd Delray Beach FL 33484-6514 Home: PO Box 1109 Lake Worth FL 33460 E-mail: aerenstein@aol.com.

ERESHEFSKY, LARRY, psychopharmacologist educator, consultant; b. Bklyn., Mar. 10, 1952; s. Sam and Claire (Geller) E.; m. Elke S. Weisburd, Sept. 1, 1974; children: Benjamin Jacob, Sabrina Hope. Pharm.D., U. So. Calif., 1976. Cert. in psychiat. pharmacy. Resident in psychiat. pharm. practice, Calif.; rsch. asst. UCLA, 1970-73; clin. instr. U. So. Calif., 1976-77; asst. prof. U. Tex., Austin, 1977-82; assoc. prof., 1982-88; Regents chair in psychopharmacology, 1985—; prof. pharmacology and psychiatry Health Sci. Ctr., San Antonio, 1982—; program dir., 1983—; prof. clin. pharmacy, 1988-96; chmn. postdoct. tng., 1990—. Cons. in field; adv. com. Novartis, Inc., 1988—, Janssen Pharmaceutica Inc., 1995—, Wyeth-Ayerst Labs., 1995—, Hoechst Marion Roussel, 1997—; mem. adv. com. on psychopharmacologic drugs FDA, 1992-95; co-dir. clin. rsch. unit San Antonio State Hosp., 1995—; prin. investigator pivotal trials developing psychotropic medications, evaluating drug-drug interactions; mem. neurology and psychiatry panel U.S. Pharmacopeial Conv., 1985—; co-founder, past chmn., Coll. Psychiat. and Neurologic Pharmcacists, pres. elect, 2003—. Editor: Psychopharmacy Newsletter, 1990-94, Coll. on Psychiat. and Neurologic Pharmacists Newsletter, 1994-98; mem. editl. bd. Am. Jour. Hosp. Pharmacy, 1988-98, Drug Therapy Perspectives, 1990—, Primary Psychiatry, 1994-2000; contbr. articles to profl. jours. Recipient award Wilford Hall USAF Med. Ctr. Fellow Am. Coll. Clin. Pharmacy (chmn. clin. practice affairs 1987-88, bd. regents 1989-94); mem. Am. Soc. Hosp. Pharmacists (SIG officer 1980-82, mem. coun. edn. affairs 1982-83, chmn. psychopharmacology 1982), AAAS, Am. Assn. Colls. Pharmacy, Am. Soc. Health Sys. Pharmacists (chair-elect clin. pharmacy splsts. coun. 1997-98, chair sect. clin. splsts. 1999—), N.Y. Acad. Sci., Phi Kappa Phi, Rho Chi. Avocations: sailing, snorkeling, hiking, reading. Office: U Tex Health Sci Ctr 7703 Floyd Curl Dr San Antonio TX 78284-6200

ERFANI, SHERVIN, academic administrator, engineering educator; b. Tehran, Iran, Mar. 28, 1948; came to U.S. 1982; s. Ibrahim and Rashedeh (Naraghi) Erfani; m. Janet E. Kovar, Dec. 30, 1982. MSEE, U. Tehran, Iran, 1971; MS, So. Meth. U., 1974, PhD in EE, 1976. Asst. prof. Nat. U. Iran, Eveen, 1978-82; rsch. assoc. So. Meth. U., Dallas, 1982-83; asst. prof. U. Mich., Dearborn, 1983-85; mem. tech. staff Lucent Techs. Bell Labs., Holmdel, NJ, 1985—2002; prof., chmn. dept. elec. and computer engring. U. Windsor, Canada, 2002—. Vis. prof. U. P.R., 1992-93; adj. prof. dept. elec. engring. and computer sci. Stevens Inst. Tech., Hoboken, N.J., 1996-2000; mem. rsch. staff Racal-Datacom, Ft. Lauderdale, Fla., 1997-98. Translator: Elec. Engring. textbook, Circuit Design & Synthesis, 1985; assoc. editor Computers and Elec. Engring.: An Internat. Jour.; sr. editor Jour. of Network and Systems Mgmt.; contbr. articles to profl. jours. 2d lt. Signal Corps. Iranian Army, 1972—73. Mem. IEEE (sr., v.p. S.E. Mich. chpt. 1985), Inst. Elec. Engrs. U.K. (chartered engr.), N.Y. Acad. Scis., Tau Beta Pi, Eta Kappa Nu. Moslem. Avocations: flying, numismatics, antiques, philately. E-mail: erfani@uwindsor.ca.

ERGEN, CHARLES, communications professional; BS in Bus. and Acctg., U. Tenn.; MBA, Wake Forest U. Founder, chmn., CEO Echostar Comms., Littleton, Colo., 1980—. Office: Echostar Comms 5701 S Santa Fe Littleton CO 80120

ERHART, JOHN JOSEPH, lawyer; b. Rush City, Minn., May 20, 1952; m. Debra Elaine Borris, Oct. 22, 1988; children: Laura Frances, Jenna Rae. BA, St. John's U., 1974; JD, Georgetown U., 1977. Bar: Minn. 1977, U.S. Dist. Ct. Minn. 1977, U.S. Ct. Appeals (8th cir.) 1978. Law clk. Judge Gerald W. Heaney U.S. Ct. Appeals (8th cir.), Duluth, Minn., 1977-79; shareholder Fredrikson & Byron, Mpls., 1979—. Office: Fredrikson & Byron 4000 Pillsbury Ctr 200 S 6th St Minneapolis MN 55402-1425 E-mail: jerhart@fredlaw.com.

ERIBO, FESTUS, mass communication educator, journalist; b. Benin City, Edo, Nigeria, June 16, 1950; arrived in U.S., 1985; s. Wilfred Omovbe and Grace Iroguehi Eribo; m. Luba N. Eribo, Aug. 24, 1978; children: Brenda, Hilda. MA, Leningrad (Russia) State U., 1979; PhD, U. Wis., 1989. Tchr. Edo Coll., Benin City, 1971; pub. rels. mgr. Ribway Group Cos., Benin City, 1971-73; prin. info. officer Dept. Info., Benin City, 1980-89; asst. prof. East Carolina U., Greenville, 1990—95, assoc. prof., 1995—2002, prof., 2002—. Co-author: Window on Africa: Democratization and Media Exposure, 1993, Press Freedom and Communication in Africa, 1997, Journalism and Mass Communication in Africa: Cameroon, 2002; author: In Search of Greatness: Russia's Communications with Africa and the World, 2001. Mem. Assn. for Edn. in Journalism and Mass Comm. Home: 402 Lancelot Dr Greenville NC 27858-8647 Office: East Carolina U Sch Com Greenville NC 27858

ERICHSEN, PETER CHRISTIAN, foundation administrator; b. Kentfield, Calif., Aug. 4, 1956; s. Hans Skabo and Ruth Elsie (Henderson) E. AB magna cum laude, Harvard U., 1978, JD cum laude, 1981. Bar: Mass., Pa. Assoc. Ropes & Gray, Boston, 1981-90, ptnr., 1990-93; dep. asst. atty. gen. U.S. Dept. Justice, Washington, 1993-96; assoc. counsel to Pres. The White House, 1996-97; v.p., gen. counsel U. Pa., U. Pa. Health Sys., 1997—2001; v.p., gen. counsel, sec. J. Paul Getty Trust, 2001—. Bd. govs. Phila. Stock Exch., 1999—. Vestryman Trinity Ch., Boston, 1987-91, 92-93, mem. bd. gov., also mem. search com., 1992-93; founding dir. Trinity Hospice, Boston, 1988-93. Mem. Groton Sch. Alumni Assn. (v.p. 1985-89). Office: 1200 Getty Ctr Dr Los Angeles CA 90049-1681 E-mail: perichsen@getty.edu.

ERICHSEN-HUBBARD, ISABEL JANICE, music educator; b. LaCrosse, Wis., June 18, 1935; d. Frank Peter August and Janice May (Grutzmacher) Erichsen; m. Allan Paterson, Apr. 4, 1959; children: Janel Isabel, John Allan. BS in K-8 Edn. with honors, U. Wis., Madison, 1957, MS in Edni. Adminstrn., 1979, postgrad., 1980. Tchr. Kenosha (Wis.) Bd. Edn., 1957-60; tchr. supr. Madison (Wis.) Bd. Edn., 1968—. Coop. tchr. sr. program U. Wis. master tchr. seminars, 1978—; pvt. piano and vocal coach, 1950—; choir dir. St. Mary's Luth. Ch., Kenosha, 1959-61; mem., soloist Madison Meth. Ch., 1960—, Cath. Diocesan Choir, 1981-83, U. Wis. Choral Union Choir, New Horizons Jazz and Concert Bands (horn and trumpet); v.p. Wis. Health Initiative, 1994—. Author: Reading Techniques Using the Newspapers, Magazines, 1975, Spell It Again Sam, 1978, Hidden Curriculum, 1979; contbr. to Kenosha Kindergarten Teacher's Handbook, 1958. Program chair YWCA, 1961-65, bd. dirs., membership svcs., 1991—; chmn. UNICEF, 1960, Meth. Coop. Nursery Sch., 1960; info. chmn. Am. Cancer Soc., Dane County, 1960-68; bd. dirs., sec. Friends of Meth. Hosp., 1986—, also vol. escort, info. desk, gift shop, chapel musician, patient rep., coffee shop, info. svcs. McConnell Hall; bd. dirs., trustee Meriter Hosp., patient rep., R.S.V.P. Sch. Liaison Dane County, 1977-88, ret. vol., 2001; vocal and piano adjudicator Wis. Assn. Music Schs., 1984—; vol. campaign solicitor Am. Players Theatre, 1987-90; chmn. Ptnrs. Campaign West Madison, YMCA, bd. dirs. YMCA Dane County, 1996—; active Meth. Women's Soc., United Ch. Women, Madison Symphony League Assn., U. Wis. Coop. Mentor Program, 1987-91, Opera Buffs, Wis. Exec. Mansion Guides; mem. Bosom Buddies, 1998—; vol. Komen Race for the Cure, Madison chpt., 1998—, Relays for Life, Am. Cancer Soc., Middleton, Cross Plains, Madison relays, 1998—, Breast Cancer Recovery Found., Inc., 1998—, Sunnyhill Nursing Home, 1990-2000; life mem. and Oral History participant Middleton Hist. Soc.; docent Ten Chimmeys Found., Lunt-Fontane Home, Genesse Depot, Wis.; adjudicator cultural arts 4-H Fair, 2000—, Dane, Rock, Sauk counties; bd. dirs. TEAM Survivor, 2003—. Recipient Carol award Madison Jaycette Club, 1966, 3d grand prize Wis. State Jour. Cookbook, 1971, Golden Apple award Madison Met. Sch. Dist., 1988, Mature Lifestyles winner, 1993-95, Firstar Recipe winner Capital Times Recipe Contest, 1995, Vol. Yr. award MAREA, 1999, YMCA Key Leader award, Wis., 2002. Mem. NEA, Wis. Edn. Assn., Madison Tchrs. Inc. (grievance com. 1987-89), Lafollette Area Lang. Arts Cadre, Madison Met. Sch. Dist. Human Rels. Cadre, Social Studies K-12 Cadre, U. Wis. Alumni Assn. (life, co-hostess chmn., mentor program-edn. adminstrn. cadre, 25th and 40th class reunion com., chmn. Day on Campus 2001-2003, Attic Angels intern 2003), Middleton Area Hist. Soc. (lie), Madison Metro Women's Club (hostess chmn.), Metro Gourmet Couples Club, Madison Civics Club (hostess chair, pub. affairs spkr., pres. 1999-2000, mem. 90th anniversary com. publ. 2002—), Cherokee Country Club, Jr. Golf Club (dir. 1974-75), Euterpe Music Club (v.p. 1997-98, mem. com. 2002—), Sigma Alpha Iota (Music Sword of Honor, past alumni pres., sec. Patroness com. 1991—, v.p. membership, editor 2002-2003), Chi Omega (alumni sec. 1970-87, ho. bd. corp.), Phi Delta Kappa (life). Home: 6708 Clovernook Rd Stonefield Village Middleton WI 53562-3871

ERICK, MIRIAM ANNA, dietitian, medical writer; b. Norwich, Conn., Apr. 1, 1958; d. Eugene A. and Toini (Lampi) E. BS, U. R.I., 1978; MS, U. Bridgeport, 1992. Cert. diabetes educator. Morning sickness cons. Brigham and Women's Hosp., Boston, perinatal dietitian; sr. staff dir. The Morning Sickness Nutrition Clinic; mem. faculty Harvard Med. Sch., 1994—; part-time practice morning sickness mgmt. Author: No More Morning Sickness: A Survival Guide for Pregnant Women, 1993, Morning Sickness: All Night and All Day, 1994, Take Two Crackers and Call Me in the Morning!, A Real Life Guide for Surviving Morning Sickness, 1995; contbr. articles to profl. jours. Recipient Ross award for women's health, ADA Found., 1996. Mem. Am. Dietetic Assn., Am. Bot. Coun., Am. Coll. Ob-Gyn., Authors Guild. Avocations: horseback riding, culinary experimentation, hiking, horse statue photography, theater, medical, short story, and poetry.. Home: 1980 Commonwealth Ave # 23 Brighton MA 02135 Office: Brigham and Women's Hosp 75 Francis St Brookline MA 02446-6638

ERICKSEN, JERALD LAVERNE, retired engineering scientist, educator; b. Portland, Oreg., Dec. 20, 1924; s. Adolph and Ethel Rebecca (Correy) E.; m. Marion Ella Pook, Feb. 24, 1946; children: Lynn Christine, Randolph Peder. BS, U. Wash., 1947; MA, Oreg. State Coll., 1949; PhD, Ind. U., 1951; DSc (hon.), Nat. U. Ireland, 1984, Heriot-Watt U., 1988. Mathematician, solid state physicist U.S. Naval Research Lab., 1951-57; faculty Johns Hopkins U., 1957-83, prof. theoretical mechanics, 1960-83; prof. mechanics and math. U. Minn., Mpls., 1983-90; cons. Florence, Oreg., 1990—. Served with USNR, 1943-46. Recipient Bingham medal, 1968, Timoshenko medal, 1979, Engring. Sci. medal, 1987. Mem. Internat. Liquid Crystal Soc. (hon.), Nat. Acad. Engring., Soc. Rheology, Soc. Natural Philosophy, Soc. Interaction Mechanics and Math., Soc. Engring. Sci., Royal Irish Acad. (hon.). Home and Office: 5378 Buckskin Bob Dr Florence OR 97439-8320

ERICKSON, ALAN ERIC, librarian; b. Boston, Feb. 6, 1928; s. Elmer Eric and Ethel M (Winch) Erickson; m. June Andersen, July 14, 1951; children: Kim, John, Martha, William. AB, Middlebury Coll., 1949; MA, Boston U., 1955, PhD, 1960; MSL.S., Simmons Sch. Library Sci., 1969. Cert. teacher Mass. Instr. Boston U., 1954-60; staff scientist Worcester Found. for Exptl. Biology, Shrewsbury, Mass., 1960-66; sci. specialist library Harvard U., Cambridge, Mass., 1966-91; librarian Cabot Sci. Library, 1973-91; assoc. librarian for adminstrn. Harvard Coll., Cambridge, Mass., 1970-72; assoc. librarian Harvard Coll. Sci., 1984-91; ret., 1991. Consult Marine Biol Labs, Wood Hole, Mass., 1981—82; trustee BIOSIS Info Serv, 1988—93, chmn bd dirs, 1993. Contbr. articles to profl jours. Trustee David Turner Scholarship Fund, Needham, Mass., 1970—; bd. govs. Greater Boston 32 degree Masonic Learning Ctr. for Children, Inc.; trustee Carter Mem Meth Ch, Needham, Mass., 1964—66. Lt col USAFR, 1951—73, ret USAFR. Recipient Woolsey Bible Prize, Middlebury Col, Vt, 1949. Mem.: Harvard Univ Retirees Asn (pres. 1995—97), Needham Ret Men's Club (pres. 1999, 2000), Sigma Xi. Avocations: gardening, woodworking, bicycling.

ERICKSON, ARTHUR CHARLES, architect; b. Vancouver, B.C., Can., June 14, 1924; s. Oscar and Myrtle (Chatterson) E. Student, U. B.C., Vancouver, 1942-44; BArch., McGill U., Montreal, Que., Can., 1950; LLD (hon.), Simon Fraser U., Vancouver, 1973, U. Man., Winnipeg, Can., 1978, Lethbridge U., 1981; D.Eng. (hon.), Novia Scotia Tech. Coll., McGill U., 1971; LittD (hon.), U. B.C., 1985, Frank Lloyd Wright Sch. Arch., 2001, MArch (hon.), 2001. Asst. prof. U. Oreg., Eugene, 1955-56; assoc. prof. U. B.C., 1956-63; ptnr. Erickson-Massey Architects, Vancouver, 1963-72; prin. Arthur Erickson Architects, Vancouver, 1972-91, Toronto, Ont., Can., 1981-91, Los Angeles, 1981-91, Arthur Erickson Archtl. Corp., Vancouver, 1991—. Prin. works include Can. Pavilion at Expo '70, Osaka (recipient first prize in nat. competition, Archtl. Inst. of Japan award for best pavilion), Robson Square/The Law Courts (honor award), Mus. of Anthropology (honor award), Eppich Residence (honor award), Habitat Pavilion (honor award), Sikh Temple (award of merit), Champlain Heights Cmty. Sch. (award of merit), San Diego Conv. Ctr., Calif. Plz., L.A., Fresno City Hall, Can. Embassy, Washington, MacMillan Bloedel Bldg., Roy Thompson Hall, Bank of Can., Koerner Libr., U.B. C. Liu Internat. Conf. Ctr., U. B.C. Scotibank Dance Ctr., Vancouver Internat. Glass Mus., Tacoma, Wash. Mem. com. on urban devel. Coun. of Can., 1971; bd. dirs. Can. Conf. of Arts, 1972; mem. design adv. coun. Portland Devel. Commn., Can. Coun. Urban Rsch.; trustee Inst. Rsch. on Pub. Policy. Capt. Can. Intelligence Corps., 1945-46. Recipient Molson prize Can. Coun. Arts, 1967, Triangle award Nat. Soc. Interior Design, Royal Bank Can. award, 1971, Gold medal Tau Sigma Delta, 1973, residential design award Can. Housing Coun., 1975, August Perret award Internat. Union Archiects Congress, 1975, Chgo. Architecture award, 1984, Gold medals Royal Archtl. Inst. Can., 1984, French Acad. Architecture, 1984, Pres. award excellence Am. Soc. Landscape Architects, 1979; named Officer, Order of Can., 1973, Companion Order of Can., 1981. Fellow AIA (hon., Pan Pacific citation Hawaiian chpt. 1963, Gold medal 1986), Royal Archtl. Inst. Can. (award 1980), Royal Inst. Brit. Archs. (hon.), Royal Inst. Scottish Archs. (hon.), Frank Lloyd Wright Found. (hon., 2000); mem. Archtl. Inst. B.C., ARCAB Wash. State Archtl. Assn., Coll. d'arquitectos de España (hon.), Coll. d'architectos de Mex. (hon.), Royal Can. Acad. Arts (academician), Heritage Can., S.F.U. Faculty Club. Office: Arthur Erickson Archtl Corp 1672 W 1st Ave Vancouver BC Canada V6J 1G1

ERICKSON, BARBARA MARTHA, historian, writer, florist; b. Knoxville, Tenn., July 17, 1932; d. William Vivian and Elza Cleo (Nichols) Slatery; m. Eugene William Erickson, Aug. 21, 1954; children: Randall William, Jacqueline Barbara. BA, U. Tenn., 1954. Asst. bridal cons. LeGrands Jewelers, Chattanooga, Tenn., 1952-54; organizer patient file room Erlanger Hosp., Chattanooga, 1934; floral arranger Stevens Florists, Spring Valley, N.Y., 1956-58; sec. treas. Erickson Olds, Inc., Monsey, N.Y., 1968-92, Toyota of Rockland, Monsey, 1992. Floral arranger Schweizers Florist, Pearl River, N.Y., Dykstras Florists, Spring Valley, N.Y. Author: (children's hist. drama) Lure of the Kakiat, 1956, 200 Years of Brick Church History, 1974, What in the World is a Rotary Ann?, 1983, Diary of the West New Hempstead Dutch Reformed Church, 2000; editor Rockland Rep. Reporter Rockland County Young Rep. Club, 1950's, 60's, The Tempo of Brick Church West New Hempstead Reformed Ch., Spring Valley, N.Y., 1958-98; contbr. articles to mags., jours., chpt. to book. Historian West New Hempstead Reformed Ch., 1961-2002; co-chmn. bi-centennial Town of Ramapo, N.Y., 1976; sponsor, participant Canine Companions for Independence, 1990—, Ramapo Children of Chernobyl project, 1998-2000. Recipient Gov.'s Newsletter award Dist. Gov. Rotary Internat., 1984, Town Svc., Humanitarian awards Town of Ramapo, 1991; named First Families of Tenn. East Tenn. Hist. Soc., 1995; Paul Harris fellow, 1982. Mem. Valley Garden Club (hon., pres. 1962-65), Valley Star Order of the Ea. Star (matron, pres. 1960), Suffern Woman's Club (mem. exec. bd. 1996-2002), Sons of Norway (Tubfrim chmn. Norrone chpt. 2001—, exec. bd., 1996-2002), Atlantic Coast Old Timers Racing Assn., Rockland County German-Am. Club (sec. 2002—), DAR (chpt. scrapbook chmn. 2003, Shatemuc, N.Y., assoc. mem. Mary Blount Chptr., Tenn.), Pearl River Rotary Club (hon.), Norrona Lodge, German-Am. Club, Phi Mu. Mem. Reformed Ch. in Am. Avocations: writing, golf, scuba diving, camping, travel. Home: 179 W Maple Ave Monsey NY 10952-1733

ERICKSON, DENNIS, professional football coach; b. Everett, Wash., Mar. 24, 1947; m. Marilyn, children: Bryce, Ryan. BS Phys. Educ., Montana State U. Grad. asst. coach Montana State U., 1969, Washington State U., 1970; head football coach Billings Central H.S., Billings, Mont., 1970; backfield coach Montana State U., 1971-73; offensive coordinator, head coach U. Idaho, 1974-75, 1982-85; offensive coordinator Fresno State U., 1976-78, San Jose State U., 1979-81; head coach U. Wyoming, 1986, Washington State U., 1987-88, U. Miami Hurricanes, 1989-95, Seattle Seahawks, 1995-98, Oregon State U., 1999—2003, S.F. 49ers, 2003—. All-Big Sky quarterback, 1966-68, honorable All-American; head coach NCAA Divsn. 1A football champions, 1989, co-champions (with U. Wash.), 1991; fishing, golf. Office: SF 49ers 4949 Centennial Blvd Santa Clara CA 95054-1229

ERICKSON, DIANE QUINN, lawyer, artist, small business owner; b. La Grange, Ill., Oct. 8, 1959; d. Stanley Brittian Sr. and Marilyn Agnes (Miller) Quinn; m. Russell Lee Erickson, Mar. 9, 1985. BS in Psychology, U. Ill., 1981; JD, Valparaiso U., 1984. Bar: Ill. 1985. Assoc. Dreyer, Foote, et al, Aurora, Ill., 1984-87; trust officer, atty. 1st Nat. Bank Des Plaines, Ill., 1987-89; owner Erickson Art & Frame, Naperville, Ill., 1988—. Mem. Brain Rsch. Found. Mem. NAFE, Ill. Bar Assn., DuPage County Bar Assn., N.W. Suburban Bar Assn., Chgo. Bar Assn. Lutheran. Avocations: tennis, travel, dance, skiing. Home: 6413 Greene Rd Woodridge IL 60517-1485 Office: 6804 Hobson Valley Rd Ste 118 Woodridge IL 60517

ERICKSON, DIANE SUE, singer, artist, educator, moderator, music kinesiologist; b. Chgo., Dec. 31, 1955; d. Robert Donald and Iatser Cathline (Ortiz-Mortz) E. Student, Art Inst. Chgo., 1973-74; BMus, Roosevelt U., 1978; MMus with honors, Ind. U., 1991; postgrad., Schola Cantorum Basiliensis, Basel, Switzerland, 1991-95, Royal Coll. Art, London, 1993. Dress designing asst. Caron Inc., Chgo., 1973; floral asst. Betty Ries, Chgo., 1973; secretarial work Dean's Office U. Chgo. Law Sch., 1973-74; sales exec. Chgo., 1974-78; tchr. U. Chgo. Lab. Sch., 1978-88; tchr. dept. music theory Ind. U. Sch. Music, Bloomington, 1989-91; tchr., head art dept. Internat. Sch. Basel, 1991-95; dir. music St. George's Eng. Sch., Cologne, 1995-96. Soprano recitals and concerts in Austria, Brazil, Can., Eng., Germany, The Netherlands, Switzerland, U.S.; host for Melody Time, Deutsche Welle Internat. Radio, Cologne, 1996—. European debut and tour with Sequentia, Germany and Utrecht Early Music Festival, The Netherlands, 1990; live broadcasts on Am., Dutch, German and Swiss radio programs, CD recs. Recipient award in music theory Theodore Presser Mus. Pub., 1976. Mem. Phi Kappa Lambda. Avocations: fine arts, nature, reading, sports. Home: Kalscheurer Weg, Weg U3 D-50969 Cologne Germany

ERICKSON, EDWARD LEONARD, biotechnology company executive, administrator; b. Chgo., Dec. 7, 1946; s. Leonard Gerald and Eleanore Antoinette (Picek) E.; m. Helen Leonora Masten, Dec. 29, 1979. BS in Math., Ill. Inst. Tech., 1968, MS in Math., 1970; MBA in Gen. Mgmt., Harvard U., 1980. Mktg. rep. IBM, Miami, Fla., 1975-76; sr. systems engr. Advanced Tech., Inc., McLean, Va., 1976-78; cons. Bain & Co., Boston, 1979-80; sr. assoc. Resource Planning Assocs., Washington, 1980-82; dir. RPA Mgmt. Cons., London, 1982-83; dir. corp. devel. Amersham Internat. plc., Little Chalfont, Eng., 1983-86, gen. mgr. internat. ops., 1986-88; v.p. fin. ops. The Ares-Serono Group, Boston, 1988-90; pres. Serono-Baker Diagnostics (The Ares-Serono Group), Allentown, Pa., 1990-91; pres., CEO, dir. Cholestech Corp., Hayward, Calif., 1991-93, DepoTech Corp., La Jolla, Calif., 1993-98; pres., CEO, chmn. Immunicon Corp., 1998—. Bd. dirs. NaPro Biotherapeutics. Contbr. articles to profl. jours. Trustee Invention Factory. Lt. USN, 1970—75. John L. Loeb fellow Harvard U., 1980, George F. Baker scholar, 1980, NASA fellow, 1968-70. Mem. Am. Soc. Clin. Oncology (affiliate), Am. Assn. Pharm. Scientists. Republican. Avocations: tennis, skiing. Home: 6887 Tohickon Hill Rd Pipersville PA 18947-1415 E-mail: EErickson@direcway.com.

ERICKSON, ELAINE MAE, composer, poet; b. Des Moines, Iowa, Apr. 22, 1941; d. Iver Carl and Ruth Eloise (Johnson) E. MusB, Wheaton Coll., 1964; MusM, Drake U., 1967. Pvt. piano tchr., Des Moines, 1964—; music libr. Main Pub. Library, Des Moines, 1965-67; composer-in-residence Ford Found. Fellowship, Ft. Lauderdale, Fla., 1967-68; tchr. piano music theory Drake U., Des Moines, 1969-72; pianist Ctr. for New Music State U. Iowa, Iowa City,

1974-76; piano tchr. Waxter Ctr., Balt., 1988-89, Church Lane Elem. Sch., Balt., 1989-90; tchr. music composition Ctrl. Coll., Pella, Iowa, 1993-96; composer-in-residence Charles Ives Ctr. Am. Music, New Milford, Conn., 1981—83, 1993. Guest composer Meet the Composer, Saranac Lake, NY, 1987; touring artist Very Spl. Arts Iowa, 1994—. Author (poetry) Separate Trains, 1988, A Visit Home, 1990, Solo Drive, 1992, Portraits and Selected Poems, 1994, The Cottage, 2001; writer 5 operas, 3 performed at Peabody Conservatory, Balt., 1986-91; contbr. poetry to numerous jours. Pianist various retirement homes, Balt., Des Moines, 1978—, music appreciation tchr., Balt., 1991-93, Des Moines, 1993—; organist Divinity Luth. Ch., Towson, Md., 1987-88. Recipient Pyle Commn. award Iowa Composers Forum, Des Moines, 1997, composition award Nat. League Am. Pen Women, 1992; touring grantee Iowa Arts Coun., 1974-75, 81-82. Democrat. Avocation: photography. Home and Office: 3700 Hillsdale Dr Des Moines IA 50322-3947

ERICKSON, ERIC HERMAN, JR., entomologist, scientist; b. Denver, Apr. 26, 1940; s. Eric Herman Sr. and Emma Rocelia E.; m. Ruth C. Ashford, Aug. 29, 1962 (div. 1983); 2 children: Eric H. III, Jeffrey Paul; m. Lucille Erickson, Feb. 15, 1992; 1 child, Bill Schad. BS, Colo. State U., 1963, MS, 1965; PhD, U. Ariz., 1970. Rsch. entomologist North Ctrl. States Bee Rsch. unit USDA, Madison, Wis., 1970-78, rsch. leader, 1978-86, Carl Hayden Bee Rsch. Ctr., Tucson, 1986—2002; ret., 2002. Author: A Scanning Electron Microscope Atlas of the Honey Bee, 1986. 1st. lt. U.S. Army, 1966-68. Recipient J.I. Hambleton award Ea. Apicultural Soc., 1986, Outstanding Svc. Western Apicultural Soc., 1995, Outstanding Scientist of Yr. USDA Agrl. Rsch. Svc., 1997. Avocations: woodworking, gardening, fishing. Office: Carl Hayden Bee Rsch Ctr 2000 E Allen Rd Tucson AZ 83719 E-mail: e.h.Erickson@worldnet.att.net.

ERICKSON, FREDERICK DAVID, education and anthropology educator; b. Rhinelander, Wis., Nov. 12, 1941; s. Lennart and Marie (Holdren) E.; m. Jane Wright, Sept. 5, 1968 (div. 1987); children: Lennart, David; m. Joanne Straceski, Jan. 8, 1994. BMus, Northwestern U., 1963, MMus, 1964, PhD, 1969; MS, U. Pa., Phila., 1986. Ordained permanent deacon (nonstipendiary) Episcopal Ch., Boston, 1975. Asst. prof. edn. U. Ill., Chgo., 1968-71; asst. to assoc. prof. edn. Harvard U., Cambridge, Mass., 1971-78; prof. edn. and medicine Mich. State U., East Lansing, 1978-85; prof. edn. U. Pa., Phila., 1985-98; George Kneller prof. anthropology of edn. UCLA, 1998—; dir. urban edn. studies ctr. Corinne A. Seeds Univ. Elem. Sch., UCLA, 2000—. Dir. Ctr. Urban Ethnography, U. Pa., 1985-98. Sr. co-author: The Counselor as Gatekeeper, 1982, Sights and Sounds of Life in Schools, 1983; editor Anthropology and Edn. Quar. Deacon asst., Ch. St. John the Evangelist, Boston, 1975-78, Ch. St. Mary in Palms, L.A., 2000--; asst. chaplain, Episcopal Ministry at Mich. State U., 1978-85; deacon asst. Ch. St. Martin in the Fields, Chestnut Hill, Phila., 1989-96; instr. liturgics and homiletics, Sch. of the Diaconate, Episcopal Diocese of Pa., 1996-98. Grantee NIMH, 1970-73; Berkowitz prof., U. Pa., 1995-98; fellow Ctr. Advanced Study in Behavioral Scis., Stanford, 1998-99. Fellow Nat. Acad. Edn., Soc. Applied Anthropology; mem. Am. Anthropol. Assn. (Spindler award 1990), Am. Ednl. Rsch. Assn. (v.p. divsn. G 1987-88, Disting. Rsch. award 1984), Coun. on Anthropology and Edn. (pres. 1977-78). Episcopalian. Avocations: music, cooking, hunting, sailing. Office: UCLA Grad Sch Edn and Info Stud Moore Hall Box 951521 Los Angeles CA 90095-1521 E-mail: ferickson@gseis.ucla.edu.

ERICKSON, GARWOOD ELLIOTT, computer consulting company executive, entrepreneur; b. Little Silver, N.J., Jan. 8, 1946; s. Gustaf Walter and Martha Lake (Adams) Erickson; m. Carol Wyborski, July 21, 1973; children: Christopher Lake, Jason Edward. AB, Dartmouth Coll., 1967; BE, Thayer Computer Sci., 1968, ME, 1969; MBA, U. Mich., 1974. Sys. analyst Ford Motor Co., Dearborn, Mich., 1969-72, sect. supr., 1972-82, mgr., 1982-83; corp. dir. mgmt. info. svcs. Hoover Universal, Ann Arbor, Mich., 1983-86, Vickers, Inc., Troy, Mich., 1986-89, dir. sales, 1989-90, dir. quality mgmt., 1990-93; chief info. officer R.L. Polk & Co., Taylor, Mich., 1993-96; owner, COO Great Lakes Technols. Group, Southfield, Mich., 1996—2002; owner, mng. ptnr. Erickson Ptnrs., L.L.C., Farmington, Mich., 2002—. Bd. dirs. Digital Detroit, Automation Alley. Sec. Trayer Lakes Cmty. Assn., Ann Arbor, 1977; mem. Oakland County Econ. Devel. Commn.; mem. adv. com. Oakland U. Fellow Advanced Rsch. Projects Agy., 1967—69. Mem.: Detroit Soc. Info. Mgrs. (pres. 2001—), Dartmouth Club (pres. Ann Arbor 1982—86). E-mail: gerickson@ericksonpartners.com.

ERICKSON, GEORGANNE MORRIS, nursing administrator, nursing educator, psychiatric-mental health consultant; b. Dayton, Ohio, Dec. 23, 1939; d. Arthur McKinley and Fannie Thelma (Shroyer) Morris; children: Heather Lee Smith Peacock, Kimberly Reneé Smith Knobbe; m. Miles Alden Erickson. BSN, Ohio State U., 1963; postgrad., Wright State U., 1983-85; MS in Nursing Svc. Adminstrn., U. So. Miss., 1989. Cert. psychiat.-mental health nurse ANA. Several med. positions, 1960-75; asst. dir. insvc. edn. Grandview Hosp., Dayton, Ohio, 1975-79; asst. dir. nursing svc. Kettering (Ohio) Convalescent Ctr., 1979; PSRO nurse reviewer long-term care Region II Med. Rev. Corp., Dayton, 1979-81; psychiat. nurse VA Med. Ctr., Dayton, 1981-85; chem. dependency nurse Gulf Oak Hosp., Biloxi, Miss., 1987-88; psychiat.-mental health nurse cons., contract home health nurse Quality Home Health Care, Biloxi, 1988-90; clin. instr. Miss. Gulf Coast Community Coll., Gulfport, 1989-90; contract home health nurse Coastal Plains Pub. Health Dist. IX, Miss. State Dept Health, Gulfport, 1989-90; dir. quality assurance/edn. Profl. Home Health Agy., Biloxi, 1990; dir. nursing Sand Hill Hosp., Gulfport, 1990. Adj. clin. faculty William Carey Coll., Gulfport, 1990, night shift charge nurse med.-surg. and psychiatry Biloxi Regional Med. Ctr., 1992-95; vol. regional liaison officer peer assistance program Ohio Nurses Assn., 1983-85, La. Nurses' Network Impaired Profls. La. State Nurses Assn., 1990. Vol. divsn. probation Harrison County Family Ct., 1990-92, ARC Disaster Health Svcs., 1994—, Keesler AFB Health Promotion Program, 1995-96, ARC Blood Svc., 1996—; mem. Miss. Gulf Coast C. of C. Maturity Health Resource Coun., 1998-99, Miss. Gulf Coast Helpline, 1999—. Mem. ANA, Miss. Nurses Assn., Ohio Nurses Assn., Ohio State U. Sch. Nursing Alumni Assn., Sigma Theta Tau, Gamma Beta Phi. Home: 2434 W Shore Dr Biloxi MS 39532-3022

ERICKSON, GERALD MEYER, classical studies educator; b. Amery, Wis., Sept. 23, 1927; s. Oscar Meyer and Ellen Claire (Hanson) E.; m. Loretta Irene Eder, Feb. 11, 1951; children: Rachel, Viki, Kari BS, U. Minn., 1954, MA, 1956, PhD, 1968. Cert. secondary sch. tchr., Minn. Tchr. Edina-Morningside Pub. Sch., Minn., 1956-65, 66-67; vis. lectr. U. Minn., Mpls., 1965-66, asst. prof., 1968-71, assoc. prof., 1971-83, prof. classical studies, 1983-95, prof. emeritus, 1995—. Exchange prof. Moscow State U., 1980, 86; vis. prof. U. Ill., 1967, 68, Coll. of William and Mary, 1984; bd. regents La. Univ. System, 1981, chmn. evaluation team for classics programs; reader Coll. Bds. Advanced Placement Program, 1975-77, chief reader, 1978-81; cons., lectr. in field Assoc. editor, mem. editorial staff Nature, Society and Thought, 1987—; author, lectr. various TV and radio courses Served with U.S. Mcht. Marine, 1945-46, U.S. Army, 1946-47, PTO; served to capt. USAF, 1951-53 NEH grantee, 1977-79; recipient award Horace T. Morse Amoco Found., 1984 Mem. Minn. Classical Conf. (pres. 1971-74), Minn. Humanities Conf. (pres. 1974-75), Classical Assn. Midwest/South (Ovatio award 1971). Avocations: short-wave radio listening; bicycling. Home: 121 E 51st St Minneapolis MN 55419-2605 Office: 305 Folwell Hall 9 Pleasant St SE Minneapolis MN 55455-0194

ERICKSON, HOWARD HUGH, veterinarian, physiology educator; b. Wahoo, Nebr., Mar. 16, 1936; s. Conrad and Laurene (Swanson) E.; m. Ann E. Nicolay, June 6, 1959; children: James, David. BS, DVM, Kans. State U., 1959; PhD, Iowa State U., 1966. Commd. 1st lt. U.S. Air Force, 1959, advanced through grades to col., 1979; veterinarian U.K., 1960-63; vet. scientist Sch. Aerospace Medicine, Brooks AFB, Tex., 1966-75; dir. rsch. and devel. aerospace med. divsn. Brooks AFB, 1975-81; prof. physiology Kans. State U., Manhattan, 1981—, acting head dept. anatomy and physiology, 1989—90, Roy W. Upham prof. vet. medicine, 2001—. Sci. adv. bd. Morris Animal Found., Englewood, Colo., 1990-93; cons. Tex. Higher Edn. Coordination Bd., Austin, 1990-91; clin. asst. prof. U. Tex. Health Sci. Ctr., San Antonio, 1972-81; vis. mem. grad. faculty Tex. A&M U., College Station, 1967-81; affiliate prof. Colo. State U., Fort Collins, 1970-75. Editor: Animal Pain, 1983; contbr. articles to profl. jours. Trustee Kans. State U. Golf Course Rsch. and Mgmt. Found., Meadowlark Cmty. Found. Recipient Alumni Achievement award Midland Luth. Coll., Fremont, Nebr., 1977, Merck award for Creativity, 1993, Bayer Excellence in Equine Rsch. award Am. Vet. Med. Assn. Coun. on Rsch., 2000. Fellow AAAS, Royal Soc. Health, Aerospace Med. Assn. (assoc.); mem. Am. Vet. Med. Assn. (chmn. coun. on rsch. 1984), Am. Physiol. Soc. (exec. bd.), Optimists Club (trustee). Republican. Lutheran. Home: 1700 Kings Rd Manhattan KS 66503-7550 Office: Kans State U Coll Vet Medicine Dept Anatomy and Physiology Manhattan KS 66506 E-mail: erickson@vet.ksu.edu.

ERICKSON, JAMES CLIFFORD, III, anesthesiologist, educator; b. Phila., Oct. 7, 1927; MD, Temple U., 1953, MS in Anesthesiology, 1958. Diplomate Am. Bd. Anesthesiology, Pain Mgmt. Intern, resident anesthesiology Temple U. Hosp., Phila., 1953-57; from instr. to asst. prof. Temple U., Phila., 1957-67; prof., chief anesthesist Woman's Med. Coll. Pa., 1967-69; prof. anesthesiology Jefferson Med. Coll., 1969-80, Northwestern U. Med. Sch., Chgo., 1980-98, prof. emeritus, 1998—. Anesthesiologist Northwestern Meml. Hosp., Chgo., 1980—98. Vol. cons. Wood Libr.-Mus. Anesthesiology, 1998—. Fellow: Soc. Clin. and Exptl. Hypnosis, Am. Coll. Pain Medicine, Am. Coll. Anesthesiology; mem.: AMA, Soc. Clin. and Exptl. Hypnosis, Am. Soc. Regional Anesthesia, Am. Soc. Clin. Hypnosis, Internat. Assn. Study Pain, Internat. Soc. Hypnosis, Internat. Soc. Hypnosis, Am. Acad. Pain Medicine, Am. Soc. Anesthesiologists, Northwestern Emeriti Orgn. (pres. 2002—03). Office: 2425 Cardinal Ln Wilmette IL 60091-2334 E-mail: jceric@northwestern.edu.

ERICKSON, JAMES GARDNER, retired artist, cartoonist; b. International Falls, Minn., Apr. 11, 1925; s. Albin Edwin and Edna Lucille (Thomas) E. Student, Hundredmark Art Sch., Mpls., 1946-47. Comml. artist Pillsbury Co., Mpls., 1947-50; sign painter Tri-State Display Ctr., Mpls., 1950-64, Displaymasters, Inc., Mpls., 1964-80, Signdesign, Inc., St. Paul, 1980-90; ret., 1990. Contbr. cartoons to publs. including Daily Worker, 1949-67, E.H.J. Am. Freeman. With U.S. Army, 1943-46, MTO. Decorated Inf. Combat Badge. Mem. ACLU, 36th Divsn. Assn. (life). Avocations: oil painting, cartoons, reading. Home: PO Box 336 Hot Springs MT 59845-0336

ERICKSON, JAMES PAUL, retired financial service company executive; b. Williston, N.D., Dec. 19, 1929; s. Carl Henry and Alice Ione (Borden) E.; m. Shirley Patricia Julian, Oct. 16, 1954; children— Christopher, Lisa Kasl BS in Humanities and Social Sci., N.D. State U., 1991. Underwriter Mut. of Omaha, 1957-62, staff asst., 1962-68; asst. treas. Mut. of Omaha Fund Mgmt. Co., 1968-72, v.p., 1972-76, exec. v.p., 1976-81, exec. v.p., chief operating officer, 1981-87, pres., 1987-93; pres., CEO Mut. of Omaha Investors Svcs., 1993-96. Bd. dirs. Am. Bapt. Homes of Midwest. Life trustee N.D. State U. Devel Found.; bd. dirs. Millard Town Ctr. Cmty. Found. Served USAF, 1952—56. Mem. Happy Hollow Country Club. Republican. Home: 6220 S 118th Plz Omaha NE 68137-4403

ERICKSON, LARRY RAY, dermatologist; b. Rapid City, S.D., July 17, 1937; s. Lawrence Ervin and Doris Geraldine (Nelson) E.; m. Valerie Jeanne Hiatt, Aug. 23, 1980; children: Melanie, Timothy, Jonathan, Lisa, Sarah, Daniel. BA, St. Olaf Coll., 1959; MD, U. Minn., 1963. Diplomate Am. Bd. Dermatology. Commd. capt. USAF, 1964, advanced through grade to lt. col., 1971; resident in dermatology U. Colo. Med. Ctr., Denver, Colo., 1966-69; pvt. practice Lakewood, Colo., 1973-95; dermatologist Med. West Assoc., Springfield, Mass., 1995-98, Fla. Health Care Plans, Daytona Beach, 1998—. Contbr. articles to profl. jours. Fellow Am. Acad. Dermatology. Lutheran. Avocations: running, racquetball, skiing, scuba diving, reading. Home: 5488 Red Tail Dr Port Orange FL 32128-4502 Office: Fla Health Care Plans 350 N Clyde Morris Blvd Daytona Beach FL 32114-2733

ERICKSON, LINDA RAE, educator; b. Huron, S.D., Aug. 17, 1948; d. Robert Emil and Esther (Schorzman) E. BS, U. Nebr., 1966; MA, U. No. Colo., Greeley, 1970; cert., U. Denver, 1990. Cert. elem. tchr., adminstr., prin. Spl. edn. resource tchr., Ignacio, Colo., 1983-85; elem. tchr. Woodland Park, Colo., 1985-86; tutor spl. edn. Am. Sch. London, 1987; elem. tchr. Borough of Brent, London, 1987, Internat. Sch. Hampstead, London, 1987-88; tchr. spl. edn. Carronhill Sch. for Handicapped, Stonehaven, Scotland, 1988-89; elem. tchr. Littleton (Colo.) Pub. Schs., 1970-83, 89-01; staff developer Pub. Edn. Bus. Coalition, 2001—; affiliate faculty Regis U., 2001—. Enrichment program coord. Sandburg Sch., 1991; co-chair Alternative Authentic Assessment Com., 1991—2001, Sandburg Parent Adv. Com., 1993—96; facilitator Littleton Pub. Schs., 1977—83, 1990—2001; workshop presenter Nat. Coun. Tchrs. English, Nat. Coun. Social Studies, WNET-TV Sta.; mem. Littleton Dist. Assessment Com., 1997—2001; chair Mother/Daughter Book Club, 1997—; affiliate faculty, supr. student tchrs. Regis U., 2001—; presenter in field. Active Fawcett Soc., London, 1987-89, NEA-Colo. Edn. Assn. Women's Caucus, 1979-01; mem. Sandburg Sch. mother/daughter book club, 1996—; founder mother/son book club, 1999-2000. Woman of Yr. nominee Littleton Jaycees, 1982; fed. grantee Use of Group Paperbacks in the Elem. Classroom, 1978. Mem. ASCD, NEA (women's leadership tng. cadre 1978-85), NOW, Colo. Edn. Assn., Littleton Edn. Assn. (bd. dirs., chair unit-bargaining team 1976-85), Internat. Reading Assn. (chair Pikes Peak 1986, Colo. coun. children's books award com. 1993-97, workshop presenter, reader meets writer com. co-coun. 1996—, tutor comitis crisis ctr. for homeless 1995-97, conf. presenter), Nat. Coun. Tchrs. English (co-lang. arts soc. exec. bd. dirs. 1995-97, co-chair storytelling contest 1997-98, mem. editl. bd. 1997-2001, presenter state conf. 1997), Planned Parenthood, Sierra Club, Alpha Delta Kappa, Phi Delta Kappa. Democrat. Lutheran. Avocations: skiing, water skiing, scuba diving, mountain biking, gardening. Home: 439 Saddlewood Cir Highlands Ranch CO 80126-2284

ERICKSON, MARY (MOLLY) LOUISE, speech pathology/audiology services professional, educator; b. Sacramento; d. Norvin Elwood and Cecilia Mabel Erickson. MusB, Calif. State U., 1981; MusM, U. So. Calif., 1984, PhD in Speech Sci. and Tech., 1989; MA in Comm. Processes and Disorders, U. Fla., 1996. V.p. Ximicon Corp., Manhattan Beach, Calif., 1986—90; pres. Erickson Consulting, Gainesville, Fla., 1986—90; tech. cons. Tucker-Davis Techs., Gainesville, Fla., 1994—95; clin. fellow Vanderbilt Voice Ctr., Nashville, 1996—97; asst. prof. U. Tenn., Knoxville, 1997—. Consulting editor Acustica, Am. Jour. Speech Language Pathology, Jour. Acoustical Soc. Am., Logopedics, Phoniatrics, and Vocology. Fellow, Kappa Kappa Gamma, 1982—83, U. So. Calif., 1988—89; grantee, U. Tenn., Knoxville, 1998, Thord-Gray Meml. Fund, The Am.-Scandinavian Found., 2000; scholar, Sacramento Opera Assn., 1979, Fla. Assn. Speech-Lang. Pathologist and Audiologists, 1996; Voice scholar, Sacramento Saturday Club, 1980, Sr. Rsch. scholar, Fulbright-Hays Found., 2000. Mem.: Voice Found., Am. Speech-Lang. and Hearing Assn. (cert. clin. competence 1997), Acoustical Soc. Am. Office: U Tenn Knoxville 578 S Stadium Hall Knoxville TN 37996

ERICKSON, MARY EVELYN, artist, writer; d. Henry Austin Chaney and Gulli Ingeborg Johnson; m. Alexander Erickson, Mar. 5, 1988; m. Clyde Fahler Bush, Feb. 12, 1955 (div. Sept. 8, 1977); children: Catherine Anne Bush, Timothy Alan Bush, Donald Edward Bush, Laura Ellen Kalitta. Paralegal, Wichita State U., 1977, BA in Gen. Studies, 1984. Author: (novels) Ten Times Have the Lilies Blown, 2002; exhibitions include visual; two-dimentional. Vol. Hospice of the Grand Valley, Grand Junction, Colo., 2002—03. Recipient Best of Show for pastel painting, Palisade Art Lovers, 1994, Apples, Aspen and Art Show Com., 1998, 1st Pl. award in poetry, AAUW and Mesa State Coll. Found., 2001, 1st Pl. Award in creative nonfiction, 2001. Mem.: Inside- Out Writers Group (corr.), Pastel Soc. of Colo. (corr.), Pastel Soc. of Am. (assoc.), Phi Kappa Phi (corr.). Home: 1870 S Deer Park Cir Grand Junction CO 81503

ERICKSON, PETER BROWN, librarian, scholar, writer; b. Worcester, Mass., Aug. 11, 1945; s. Irving Peter and Elinor (Brown) E.; m. Tay Gavin, June 30, 1968 (dec. Oct. 1998); children: Andrew Sven, Ingrid Adriana, Benjamin Peter. BA, Amherst Coll., 1967; postgrad., U. Birmingham, Birmingham, Eng., 1967-68; PhD, U. Calif., 1975; MSLS, Simmons Coll., 1984. Asst. prof. Williams Coll., Williamstown, Mass., 1976-81; fellow Wesleyan U., Middletown, Conn., 1981-82, vis. asst. prof., 1982-83; rsch. lib. Clark Art Inst., Williamstown, Mass., 1985—. Author: Patriarchal Structures in Shakespeare's Drama, 1985, Rewriting Shakespeare Rewriting Ourselves, 1991 (paperback edition, 1994); contbr. essays and book and theater reviews to profl. jours; editor: Festschrift: Shakespeare's Rough Magic, Renaissance Essays in Honor of C.L. Barber, 1985, Making Trifles of Terrors: Redistributing Complicities in Shakespeare, 1997, Early Modern Visual Culture: Representation, Race, and Empire in Renaissance England, 2000. Recipient Amherst Meml. Fellowship, Amherst Coll., 1967-68, Worldwide Books Pub. award, 2001, 03; Kent fellow Soc. for Values in Higher Edn., 1981-82. Mem. Shakespeare Assn. of Am., Renaissance Soc. of Am., Modern Language Assn., Appalachian Mt. Club, Phi Beta Kappa. Avocations: running, hiking, canoeing. Home: 81 Buxton Hill Rd Williamstown MA 01267-2773 Office: Clark Art Inst 225 South St # 8 Williamstown MA 01267-2891 E-mail: peter.erickson@clarkart.edu.

ERICKSON, PHILLIP ARTHUR, lawyer, corporate executive; b. Duluth, Minn., June 27, 1941; s. Carl Edward and Velma Cecilia (Pera) Erickson; children: Michael Phillip, Amy Diane. BA, U. Minn., 1967, JD, 1970. Bar: Minn. 1970, U.S. Supreme Ct. 1981, U.S. Ct. Appeals (fed. cir.) 1989. Gen. counsel, sec. North Ctrl. Cos., Inc., St. Paul, 1970—73; gen. counsel JFP Enterprises, Duluth, 1973—74; corp. counsel, sr. v.p. law and corp. sec. The Cornelius Co., Anoka, Minn., 1974—86; sr. v.p., corp. sec. IMI Cornelius Inc., 1986—88; sr. v.p. legal and regulatory affairs IMI Group Inc., Mpls., 1988—. Mem. adv. com. legal assistance for people with devel. disabilities Christian Edn. Com. Social Ministry, mem. facilities com., mem. singles fellowship com.; coach Plymouth Athletic Assn.; mem. parents adv. com., acad. com. Wayzata W Jr. High Sch.; mem. program evaluation and rev. com. Bklyn. Park Elem. Sch.; bd. dirs., past pres. Homeward Bound, Inc., 1981—83; past. dir. Mpls. Assn. Retarded Citizens; deacon St. Philip Lut. Ch., usher social ministry com.; mem. stewardship com. Prince of Peace Lut. Ch. Mem.: ABA, HHennepin County Bar Assn., Minn. State Bar Assn., Rotary (Mpls., City Lakes chpt.). Home: 14605 34th Ave N Minneapolis MN 55447-5229 Office: IMI Group Inc 1 Cornelius Pl Anoka MN 55303-1583

ERICKSON, RALPH D. retired physical education educator, small business owner, consultant; b. Beresford, S.D., June 25, 1922; s. John Henning and Ester Christina (Lofgren) E.; m. Nancy Erickson, Sept. 1949 (div. 1961); m. Patricia Erickson, Apr. 1973 (div. 1975); m. Karen Ann Erickson, June 1, 1989; 1 child, Karina Ann. BS in Phys. Edn., Northwestern U., 1949, MA in Edn., 1953. Swim instr., coach Chgo. Park Dist., 1946-54; social studies tchr., swim coach Elmwood Park (Ill.) High Sch., 1954-65; swimming, water polo coach Loyola Univ., Chgo., 1965-87, assoc. prof. phys. edn., 1971-87; salesman Alexander Hamilton Inst., Chgo., 1966-69; tchr. Chgo. Bd. Edn., 1969-70. Bd. dirs. Capital Investments & Ventures Corp., Santa Ana, Calif., 1983-93, Cosmopolitan Comm., Santa Ana, 1991-93; vice chmn. Internat. Profl. Assn. Diving Inst., Santa Ana, 1966-93. Author: Under Pressure, 1961, Discover the Under Water World, 1971, V/W Navigation, 1972, Search and Recovery, 1973. Sgt US Army, 1942-45 Recipient Reach Out award Diving Equipment Mfg. Assn.; named to Ill. H.S. Swimming Coaches Hall of Fame, 1982, Athletic Hall of Fame Loyola U. Chgo., 1986. Mem. Profl. Assn. Diving Instrs. (co founder) Home and Office: 17307 Whippoorwill Trl Leander TX 78645-9734

ERICKSON, RALPH O. botany educator; b. Duluth, Minn., Oct. 27, 1914; s. Charles W. and Stella (Sjostrom) E.; m. Elinor M. Borgstedt, June 17, 1945; children: Diane Erickson Field, Elizabeth Erickson. BA, Gustavus Adolphus Coll., 1935; MS, Washington U., St. Louis, 1941; PhD, Washington U., 1944. Instr. Gustavus Adolphus Coll., 1935-39; asst. chemist Western Cartridge Co., East Alton, Ill., 1942-44; instr., then asst. prof. botany U. Rochester, N.Y., 1944-47; mem. faculty U. Pa., Phila., 1947—, prof. botany, 1954-85, prof. emeritus, 1985—, chmn. grad. group botany, 1957-68, acting dir. div. biology, 1961-63, chmn. grad. group biology, 1968-76, acting chmn. dept. biology, 1977-78. Contbr. articles to profl. jours. Guggenheim fellow Calif. Inst. Tech., 1954-55 Mem. AAAS, Bot. Soc. Am., Soc. Devel. Biology (pres. 1959), Am. Inst. Biol. Scis., Sigma Xi. Home: 3300 Darby Rd Apt 3319 Haverford PA 19041-1071 E-mail: erickson@snip.net.

ERICKSON, RAY CHARLES, retired wildlife biologist; b. St. Peter, Minn., Jan. 30, 1918; s. Isaac and Martha Ernestina (Ziebarth) Erickson; m. Patricia Katherine Miles, Jan. 8, 1950 (div. Nov. 8, 1951); 1 child, Susan Eileen; m. Helen Josephine Haworth, Sept. 10, 1953 (dec. Nov. 16, 1996); children: Joanne Louise, David Wayne, Thomas Alan; m. Grace Margarie Hayes, May 2, 2001. Student, George Washington U., 1939—40; AB, Gustavus Adolphus Coll., 1941; MS, Iowa State U., 1942, PhD, 1948. Wildlife biologist U.S. Fish and Wildlife Svc., Burns, Oreg., 1948—57, rsch. staff specialist divsn. wildlife rsch. Washington, 1957—65, supr. biology wildlife rsch. program Laurel, Md., 1965—80; ret., 1980. Mem., scientist Oreg. Natural Heritage Adv. Coun., Salem, 1990—. Contbr. articles to profl. publs. Lt. (j.g.) USNR, 1943—46, PTO. Named Disting. Alumnus, Gustavus Adolphus Coll., 1991; recipient Disting. Svc. award, U.S. Dept. of Interior, 1968, Spl. Conservation award, Nat. Wildlife Fedn., 1975, Wildlife Conservation award, Zool. Soc. San Diego, 1979. Mem.: Whooping Crane Conservation Assn. (life), Washington Biologists' Field Club (pres. 1967—70). Lutheran. Achievements include organizer endangered wildlife research program to study wildlife species in the wild and in captivity. Avocations: nature watching, fishing, photography, travel. Home: 3010 Twin Oak Pl NW Salem OR 97304

ERICKSON, RAYMOND, music historian, musician; b. Mpls., Aug. 2, 1941; s. Ray F. and Irene E. (Banko) E.; m. Carole A. DeSaram, May 15, 1982. BA with high honors, Whittier (Calif) Coll., 1963; PhD, Yale U., 1970. Acting instr. history music Yale U., New Haven, 1968-70; rsch. fellow IBM Sys. Rsch. Inst., N.Y.C., 1970-71; asst. prof. music Queens Coll., CUNY, Flushing, 1971-75, elected mem. Doctoral Programs in Music, 1976—, prof., 1981, chair dept. music, dir. Aaron Copland Sch. Music, 1978-81. Author: "Musica enchiriadis" and "Scolica enchiriadis", 1995, DARMS: A Reference Manual, 1976; editor: Schubert's Vienna, 1997; artist (CD) From rosey Bow'rs: Music of Henry Purcell, 1994; contbr. articles to profl. jours. Acad. dir. Aston Magna Found. for Music and Humanities, Inc., Great Barrington, Mass., 1978—; bd. dirs. ex officio Godwin-Ternbach Mus., Flushing, 1993-2000, Aston Magna Found. Decorated officer's cross Order of Merit (Germany; rsch. fellowship Alexander von Humboldt Assn. of Am., Stiftung, Freiburg, Munich and Saxony, Germany. 1977-78, 84-85, 99. Mem. Alexander von Humboldt Assn. Am. (pres.), Am. Musicology Soc., Early Music Am., Phi Beta Kappa (hon.), Pi Delta Phi (hon.), Omicron Delta Kappa. Avocations: wine, travel, languages. Office: Queens Coll CUNY Flushing NY 11367-1597

ERICKSON, RICHARD AMES, physicist, emeritus educator; b. Bryant, S.D., Sept. 12, 1923; s. Ray and Mabel Gabriella (Arneson) E.; m. Frances Irene Boyd, June 13, 1943; children: Donna Mae, Jeanne Marie (Mrs. Paul Mahoney), David Ray, Kristine Ann (Mrs. Scott Stewart). B.Sc., S.D. Sch. Mines and Tech., 1944; PhD, Tex. A. and M. U., 1952. Predoctoral fellow Oak Ridge Inst. Nuclear Studies, 1949-51; asst. prof. physics U. Tenn., 1951-54; asst. prof. Ohio State U., 1954-61, assoc. prof., 1961-74, prof., 1974-79, prof. emeritus, 1979—; prof. of physics Ind. U. (ITM/MUCIA), Shah Alam, Malaysia, 1987-89; sec. faculty Ohio State U., 1975-77. Cons. Lockheed Research Lab., Palo Alto, Calif., 1964, AID, India, 1965; Mem. Univ. Area Commn., Columbus, Ohio, 1973-74 Contbg. author: Methods of Experimental Physics, vol. 3, 1961; Contbr. articles to profl. jours. Served with USNR, 1944-46. Home: 325 W Grant St Spearfish SD 57783-2334

ERICKSON, ROBERT PORTER, genetics researcher, educator, clinician; b. Portland, Oreg., June 27, 1939; s. Harold M. and Marjorie S. (Porter) E.; m. Sandra De'Ath, June 20, 1964; children: Andrew Ian, Colin De'Ath, Tanya Nadene, Tracy Lynn, Michelle Lee, Christof Phillipe. BA, Reed Coll., 1960; MD, Stanford U., 1965. Diplomate Am. Bd. Pediat., Am. Coll. Med. Genetics. Asst. prof. pediatrics U. Calif.-San Francisco Med. Sch., 1970-75; vis. scientist Institut Pasteur, Paris, 1975-76; assoc. prof. human genetics and pediat. U. Mich., Ann Arbor, 1976-80, prof., 1980-90, dir. divsn. pediat. genetics, 1985-90. Vis. scientist Imperial Cancer Rsch. Fund, London, 1983-84; Holsclaw Family prof. human genetics and inherited diseases dept. pediat. U. Ariz., 1990—; vis fellow Hughes Hall, U. Cambridge, 1996-97. Mem. editl. bd. Jour. Reproductive Immunology, 1978-89, Dictionary of Lab. Tech., 1983, Molecular Reprodn. and Devel., 1989-99, Antisense R&D, 1992—, Jour. Rare Diseases, 1995-98, Jour. Applied Genetics, 2000—, Reviews in Mutation Rsch., 2001—; contbr. over 300 articles to sci. jours. and books. With USPHS, 1967-69. Guggenheim fellow, Paris, 1975, Eleanor Roosevelt fellow, London, 1983; Fogarty Sr. Internat. fellow, 1996, Burroughs Wellcome travel fellow, 1996; Fulbright grantee, London, 1983, NIH grantee, 1971—. Mem. Am. Soc. Human Genetics, Soc. Pediat. Rsch., Am. Pediat. Soc. Avocations: skiing, backpacking. Home: 5200 N Camino Real Tucson AZ 85718-5029 E-mail: erickson@peds.arizona.edu.

ERICKSON, ROBERT STANLEY, lawyer; b. Kemmerer, Wyo., Apr. 17, 1944; s. Stanley W. and Dorothy Marie (Johnson) E.; m. Alice Norman, Dec. 27, 1972; children: Robert Badger, Erin Elizabeth, Andrew Carl, Scott Stanley, Courtney Ellen, Brennan Marie. BS in Bus., U. Idaho, 1966; JD, U. Utah, 1969; LLM in Taxation, George Washington U., 1973. Bar: U.S. Supreme Ct. 1973, U.S. Ct. Appeals (9th cir.) 1980, U.S. Dist. Ct. Idaho 1973, U.S. Tax Ct. 1969, Idaho 1973, Utah 1969. Assoc. atty. Office of Chief Counsel, Dept. Treasury, Washington, 1969-73; assoc. Elam, Burke, Jeppesen, Evans & Boyd, Boise, Idaho, 1973-77; ptnr. Elam, Burke, Evans, Boyd & Koontz, Boise, 1977-81; spl. counsel Holme Roberts & Owen, Salt Lake City, 1981-83; ptnr. Hansen & Erickson, Boise, 1983-85, Hawley Troxell Ennis & Hawley, Boise, 1985—. Contbr. articles to profl. jours. Named Citizen of Yr., Boise Exch. Club, 1980. Fellow Am. Coll. of Trust and Estate Counsel (past Idaho chmn. 1993—); mem. ABA (sect. on taxation, com. state and local taxes), IRS/Western Region Bar Assn. (mem., past chmn. liaison com. Idaho co-chair local task force IRS non-filer program 1993), Idaho State Bar (founding chmn. taxation, probate and trust law sect.), Utah State Bar (tax and estate planning sect.), Boise Estate Planning Council, Idaho State Tax Inst. (exec. com., numerous other local and nat. coms.). Mem. Lds Ch. Office: Hawley Troxell Ennis & Hawley First Interstate Ctr 877 Main St Ste 1000 Boise ID 83702-5884

ERICKSON, RODNEY ALLEN, university executive, provost; b. Frederic, Wis., Oct. 3, 1946; s. Reuben Alexander and Elva Imogene (Bergman) E.; m. Sharon Lea Young, May 3, 1969; children: Craig, Jeffrey. BA, U. Minn., 1968, MA, 1970; PhD, U. Wash., 1973. Asst. prof. U. Wis., Madison, 1973-77, Pa. State U., University Park, 1977-79, assoc. prof., 1979-84, prof., 1984—, dean grad. sch., 1995-99, v.p. for rsch., 1997-99, exec. v.p., provost, 1999—. Staff sgt. USAR, 1966-72. Simon Sr. rsch. fellow U. Manchester (England), 1982, Census rsch. fellow NSF, Washington, 1989; sr. rsch. scholar Fulbright Commn., Washington, 1982. Mem. Am. Geographical Soc. (councilor 1984-96). Avocations: grain farming, windsurfing, skiing. Office: Pa State U 201 Old Main University Park PA 16802-1503 Fax: (814) 863-8583. E-mail: rae@psu.edu.

ERICKSON, RONALD A. retail executive; JD, U. Minn. CEO Holiday Cos., Mpls. Office: Holiday Companies PO Box 1224 Minneapolis MN 55440-1224*

ERICKSON, SALLY ALICE, social welfare administrator; d. Vincent N. and Marcia C. Erickson; m. John Edward O'Shea, Apr. 2, 2000. BA in Sociology and Anthropology, Occidental Coll., 1982; MSW, U. Hawaii, 1997. Dir. pub. rels. and pub. svcs. Burke Mus., Seattle, 1987—93; project dir. Safe Haven Mental Health Kokua, Honolulu, 1995—99; exec. dir. Coun. for the Homeless, Vancouver, Wash., 1999—. Contbr. articles to profl. jours. Democrat. Office: Coun for the Homeless 2500 Main St Vancouver WA 98660

ERICKSON, STACY LYNN, literature educator; b. Oshkosh, Wis., Aug. 25, 1977; d. Rand Edward and Vicki Lynn Erickson. BA in English and Spanish, Ripon Coll., 2000; postgrad., U. Iowa, 2000—. Instr. rhetoric U. Iowa, Iowa City, 2001—03, instr. lit., 2003—, co-leader profl. devel. program rhetoric dept., 2002. Mem.: MLA. Democrat. Presbyterian. Avocation: tennis. E-mail: st_erickson@yahoo.com.

ERICKSON, VIRGINIA BEMMELS, chemical engineer; b. Sleepy Eye, Minn., June 19, 1948; d. Gordon Boothe and Marion Mae (Rieke) Bemmels; m. Larry Douglas Erickson, Sept. 6, 1969; children: Kirsten Danielle, Dean Michael. Diploma in nursing, Swedish Hosp. Sch. Nursing, 1969; BSChemE, U. Wash., 1983, MChemE, 1985, MEd, 1999. RN. Asst. head nurse N. Meml. Hosp., Mpls., 1970-73; intensive care RN Swedish Med. Ctr., Seattle, 1973-83; research asst. U. Wash., Seattle, 1983-85; instrumentation and control engr. CH2M Hill, Bellevue, Wash., 1985—, mgr. dept., 1988-93, mgr. info. mgmt., 1994—, v.p., 1995-99; calculus tchr. Shoreline Sch. Dist., Seattle, 1999—. Cons. instrumentation and control engr. Mem. editl. adv. bd. Control. Leader Girl Scouts U.S., Seattle, 1985; rep. United Way, 1986—; supt. Seattle Ch. Sch., 1983. Recipient cert. Achievement, Soc. Women Engrs., 1983, Teenfeed, 1990. Mem.: AAUW, Instrument Soc. Am., Tau Beta Pi. Democrat. Methodist. Avocations: running, soccer, music, cooking. Home: 6026 24th Ave NE Seattle WA 98115-7009 Office: Shoreline Sch Dist 15343 25th Ave NE Seattle WA 98155-7321 E-mail: virginia.erickson@shorelineschools.com.

ERICKSON, W(ALTER) BRUCE, business and economics educator, entrepreneur; b. Chgo., Mar. 4, 1938; s. Clifford Eric and Mildred B. (Brinkmeier) E. BA, Mich. State U., 1959, MA, 1960, PhD in Econs., 1965. Rsch. assoc. subcom. on antitrust and monopoly U.S. Senate, 1960-61; asst. prof. econs. Bowling Green (Ohio) U., 1964-66; asst. prof. bus. and govt. Coll. Bus. Adminstrn., U. Minn., Mpls., 1966-70, assoc. prof., 1971-75, prof. dept. mgmt., 1975—, prof., chmn. dept. mgmt., 1977-80, co-chmn., then chmn., 1988-92. Bd. dirs. various bus., non-profit and venture capital orgns.; cons. rock salt antitrust cases for atty. gens. Mich., cons. rock salt antitrust cases for atty. gens. Calif., Ill., Wis., Minn.; cons. U.S. Justice Dept. Author: An Introduction to Contemporary Business, 4th edit., 1985, Government and Business, 1980, 2d edit., 1984, International Business, 1998; co-author: International Business, 1998; bd. editors Antitrust Law and Econs. Rev., Jour. Indsl. Orgn.; contbr. articles to profl. jours. Bd. dirs. Found. for Constl. Edn. and the Citizens League, 1991-92; mem. ethics com. Ebenezer System, Minn. Mem. Am. Econ. Assn., Royal Econ. Soc. Office: Carlson Sch Mgmt 321 19th Ave S Minneapolis MN 55455-0438

ERICKSON, WILLIAM HURT, retired state supreme court justice; b. Denver, May 11, 1924; s. Arthur Xavier and Virginia (Hurt) E.; m. Doris Rogers, Dec. 24, 1953; children: Barbara Ann, Virginia Lee, Stephen Arthur, William Taylor. Degree in petroleum engring., Colo. Sch. Mines, 1947; student, U. Mich., 1949; LLB, U. Va., 1950; PhD in Engring. (hon.), Colo. Sch. of Mines, 2002. Bar: Colo. 1951. Pvt. practice, Denver; state supreme ct. justice Colo. Supreme Ct., 1971-96, state supreme ct. chief justice, 1983-86; faculty NYU Appellate Judges Sch., 1972-85. Mem. exec. Commn. on Accreditation of Law Enforcement Agys., 1980-83; chmn. Pres.'s Nat. Commn. for Rev. of Fed. and State Laws Relating to Wiretapping and Electronic Surveillance, 1976. Chmn. Erickson Commn., 1997, Owens Columbine Rev. Commn., 2000-01; chmn. gov.'s Columbine Rev. Commn., 1999-2001. With USAAF, 1943. Recipient Disting. Achievement medal Colo. Sch. Mines, 1990. Fellow Internat. Acad. Trial Lawyers (former sec.), Am. Coll. Trial Lawyers, Am. Bar Found. (chmn. 1985), Internat. Soc. Barristers (pres. 1971); mem. ABA, (bd. govs. 1975-79, former chmn. com. on standards criminal justice, former chmn. coun. criminal law sect., former chmn. com. to implement standards criminal justice, mem. long-range planning com., action com. to reduce ct. cost and delay), Colo. Bar Assn. (award of merit 1989), Denver Bar Assn. (past pres., trustee), Am. Law Inst. (coun. 1973—), Practising Law Inst. (nat. adv. coun., bd. govs. Colo.), Freedoms Found. at Valley Forge (nat. coun. trustees, 1986—), Order of Coif, Scribes (pres. 1978). Home: 10 Martin Ln Englewood CO 80110-4821

ERICSON, ALVIN CHARLES, marketing professional, consultant; b. Pittsfield, Mass., June 25, 1955; s. Alvin Justin and Bernice Martha (Bence) E. BS, MIT, 1977; MBA, Northeastern U., 1985. Draftsman Unistress Corp., Pittsfield, Mass., 1977-79; sales rep. San-Vel Concrete Corp., Littleton, Mass., 1979-82; mktg. dir. New Eng. region Precast/Prestressed Concrete Inst., Chgo., 1982-88; ind. cons. tech. mktg., 1988—. Mem. Mass. Soc. Profl. Engrs. (treas. Met. chpt. 1984-87, pres. 1988-89), Boston Soc. Civil Engrs. (chmn. structural group 1990-91), Am. Concrete Inst. (bd. dirs. 1983-91, pres. New Eng. chpt. 1989-90, mem. 550 com. on precast structures), Soc. Am. Mil. Engrs., Precast/Prestressed Concrete Inst. (mktg. com. 1987-1999, bridge producers com. 1989-2000, seismic com. 1991—, erectors com. 1990-2000, chmn. student edn. com. 1997-2003, bd. dirs 2000-03), Mensa. Republican. Lutheran. Avocations: swimming, scuba diving, skiing, travel, flute. Home and Office: PO Box 367897 Bonita Springs FL 34136-7897

ERICSON, DAVID FRANK, political scientist, educator; b. Chgo., June 18, 1950; s. Arthur Edward Ericson and Ruth Irene Kessel. BA in Polit. Sci., Wayne State U., 1972; MA in Polit. Sci., U. Mich., 1973, MA in Journalism, 1976; PhD in Polit. Sci., U. Chgo., 1987. Journalist Jackson (Mich.) Citizen-Patriot, 1977, Detroit News, 1978-80; instr. Oberlin (Ohio) Coll., 1986-87; prof. Wichita (Kans.) State U., 1992—. Vis. prof. Washington U., St. Louis, 1987—89, U. Chgo., 1990—91. Author: (book) The Shaping of American Liberalism: The Debates Over Ratification, Nullification, and Slavery, 1993, The Debate Over Slavery: Antislavery and Proslavery Liberalism in Antebellum America, 2001; editor: The Liberal Tradition in American Politics: Reassessing the Legacy of Amercian Liberalism, 1999; contbr. articles to profl. jours. Postdoctoral fellow, John M. Olin Ctr. Study History Polit. Culture, U. Chgo., 1989—90, Summer Rsch. grantee, NEH, 1994. Mem.: So. Polit. Sci. Assn., Western Polit. Sci. Assn., Midwest Polit. Sci. Assn., Am. Polit. Sci. Assn., Phi Beta Kappa, Pi Sigma Alpha. Avocations: tennis, basketball. Home: 402 N Bluff St Wichita KS 67208-3729 E-mail: david.ericson@wichita.edu.

ERICSON, JAMES DONALD, lawyer, insurance executive; b. Hawarden, Iowa, Oct. 12, 1935; s. Elmer H. and Martha (Sydness) E.; children: Linda Jean, James Robert. BA in History, State U. Iowa, 1958, JD, 1962. Bar: Wis. 1965. Assoc. Fitzgerald, Brown, Leahy, McGill & Strom, Omaha, 1962-65; with Northwestern Mut. Life Ins. Co., Milw., 1965—, asst. to pres., 1972-75, dir. policy benefits, 1975-76, v.p., gen. counsel, sec., 1976-80, sr. v.p., 1980, exec. v.p., 1987, pres., 1990, chief operating officer, 1991-93, pres., CEO, 1993-2000, chmn., CEO, 2000-2001. Dir. MGIC Investment Corp., Green Bay Packaging Inc., Kohl's Corp., Marcus Corp., Northwestern Mut. Investment Svcs., Frank Russell Co.; immediate past chmn. Am. Coun. Life Ins. Bd. dirs. Wis. Taxpayers Alliance, Competitive Wis., Inc., Greater Milw. Com., Milw. Redevel. Com., United Way, Met. Milw. Assn. Commerce, Med. Coll. Wis., Milw. Sch. Engring.; trustee Lawrence U., Com. for Econ. Devel., Boys and Girls Club Greater Milw., Lyric Opera Chgo. Mem. ABA, Assn. Life Ins. Counsel (hon.), Wis. Bar Assn., Milw. Club (bd. dirs.), Phi Beta Kappa. Republican. Presbyterian. Office: Northwestern Mut 777 E Wisconsin Ave Ste 3010 Milwaukee WI 53202-4703

ERICSON, JON MEYER, academic administrator, rhetoric theory educator; b. Three Forks, Mont., Aug. 1, 1928; s. George Edward and Olga Young (Meyer) E.; m. Amy Knutson, Aug. 19, 1951; children: Jon, Beth, Joel, Ingrid. BA, Pacific Luth. Coll., 1952; MA, Stanford U., 1953, PhD, 1961. Instr. argumentation, pub. speaking, rhetorical theory and criticism Tex. Luth. Coll., Seguin, 1953-54; asst. prof. Pacific Luth. Coll., Tacoma, 1954-57; instr., dir. forensics Stanford (Calif.) U., 1959-61, asst. prof., 1961-64; from assoc. prof. to prof., dept. head Cen. Wash. State U., Ellensburg, 1964-70, prof. dept. speech communication, 1988-95; dean sch. liberal arts Calif. Poly. State U., San Luis Obispo, 1970-88, dept. dir. London Study Program, 1984-96. Co-author: The Debater's Guide, 1961; contbg. author: Demosthenes on the Crown, 1967, Public Speaking as Dialogue, 1970; contbr. articles to profl. jours. and books Pres. Pacific Forensic League, 1961-62, No. Calif. Forensic Assn., 1962-63; mem., trustee Pacific Luth. Theol. Sem., Berkeley, 1961-64. Served with USN, 1946-48. Danforth tchr., 1957; Univ. Honors scholarship Stanford U., 1957-61. Lutheran. Avocations: tennis, gardening. Home: 741 Pasatiempo Dr San Luis Obispo CA 93405-1033 E-mail: joneric741@aol.com.

ERICSON, RICHARD VICTOR, sociologist, educator, law educator, academic administrator; b. Montreal, Que., Can., Sept. 20, 1948; s. John William and Elizabeth Mary (Hinkley) Ericson; m. Diana Lea McMillan, May 31, 1969; 1 child, Matthew Simon. BA, U. Guelph, Ont., 1969; MA, U. Toronto, Can., 1971; PhD, Cambridge U., Eng., 1974, LittD, 1991. From asst. prof. to assoc. prof. U. Toronto, 1974—82, prof. sociology, prof. criminology, 1982-93, dir. Ctr. Criminology, 1992-93; prof. sociology, prof. law U. B.C., Vancouver, Canada, 1993—, prin. Green Coll., 1993—. Vis. rsch. prof. Coll. Pub. Programs Ariz. State U., Tempe, 1991; vis. fellow Inst. Criminology Cambridge U., 1979, 1984—85, Churchill Coll. Cambridge U., 1979, 1984—85, All Souls Coll., Oxford, 1998—99; vis. prof. U Paris X-Nanterre, 1999; assoc. mem. Ctr. Urban and Cmty. Rsch., Goldsmiths Coll., U. London, 2000—. Co-author: (book) Negotiating Control, 1989, Representing Order, 1991, Policing the Risk Society, 1997, Insurance as Governance, 2003; author: Making Crime, 2d edit., 1993. Hon. vis. fellow, Green Coll., Oxford, 1993—, Sr. fellow, Massey Coll., Toronto. Fellow: Royal Soc. Can. Home: Principals Residence Green College at U BC Vancouver BC Canada V6T 1Z1 Office: Green College at U BC 6201 Cecil Green Park Rd Vancouver BC Canada V6T 1Z1

ERICSON, ROBERT WALTER, lawyer; b. Highland Park, Ill., June 24, 1948; BA, Johns Hopkins U., 1970, MA, 1971; JD, U. Va., 1976. Bar: Ill. 1976, N.Y. 1992. Ptnr. Winston & Strawn, N.Y.C. Mem.: N.Y. State Bar Assn. Office: Winston & Strawn 200 Park Ave Fl 41 New York NY 10166-4401 E-mail: rericson@winston.com.

ERICSON, ROGER DELWIN, lawyer, forest resource company executive; b. Moline, Ill, Dec. 21, 1934; s. Carl D. and Linnea E. (Challman) E.; m. Norma F. Brown, Aug. 1, 1957; children: Catherine Lynn, David. AB, JD, Stetson U., DeLand, Fla., 1958; MBA, U. Chgo., 1971. Bar: Fla. 1958, Ill. 1959, Ind. 1974. Atty. Brunswick Corp., Skokie, Ill., 1959-62; asst. sec., asst. gen. counsel Chemetron Corp., Chgo., 1962-73; asst. v.p. Inland Container Corp., Indpls., 1973-75, v.p., gen. counsel, sec., 1975-83, Temple-Inland, Inc., 1983-94, of counsel, 1994—. V.p., sec. bd. dirs. Inland Container Corp.; dir., pres., co-CEO Kraft Land Svcs., Inc., Atlanta, 1978-88; bd. dirs., v.p. Guaranty Holdings Inc., Dallas; v.p. Temple-Inland Fin. Svcs., Inc., Austin, 1990-94; bd. dirs. Temple-Inland Forest Products, Temple-Inland Real Estate Investment, Inc., Temple-Inland Realty Inc. Trustee Chgo. Homes for Children, 1971-74; mem. alumni coun. U. Chgo., 1972-76; mem. Palatine Twp. Youth Commn., 1969-72; sect. chmn. Chgo. Heart Assn., 1972, 73; alumni bd. dirs. Stetson U.; bd. dirs. Temple-Inland Found; mem. Safe and Drug-Free Comm. Collier County Sch. Bd., 1996—. Mem. ABA, Am. Arbitration Assn. (nat. panel comml. arbitrators), Am. Soc. Corp. Secs., Am. Forest Products Assn. (past mem. govt. affairs com. and legal com.), Am. Corp. Counsel Assn., Ind. Bar Assn., Fla. Bar Assn., Chgo. Bar Assn., Indpls. Bar Assn. (chmn. corp. counsel sect., mem. profl. responsibility com. 1982), Collier County Bar Assn., Indpls. C. of C. (govt. affairs com.), Plum Grove Club (pres. 1967), The Club at Olde Cypress, Omicron Delta Kappa, Phi Delta Phi. Office: PO Box 110218 Naples FL 34108-0104 *Concentrate on the desired final result of any activity. Never forget your family, co-workers, friends.*

ERICSON, RUTH ANN, retired psychiatrist; b. Assaria, Kans., May 15; d. William Albert and Anna Mathilda (Almquist) E. Student, So. Meth. U., 1945-47; BS, Bethany Coll.; MD, U. Tex., 1951. Intern Calif. Hosp., L.A., 1951-52; resident in psychiatry U. Tex. Med. Br., Galveston, 1952-55; psychiatrist Child Guidance Clinic, Dallas, 1955-63; clin. instr. Southwestern Med. Sch., Dallas, 1955-72; practice medicine specializing in psychiatry Dallas, 1955-2000; ret., 2002. Cons. Dallas Intertribal Coun. Clinic, 1974-81, Dallas Ind. Sch. Dist., U.S. Army, Welfare Dept., Tribal Concerns, Alcoholism, Adv. Bd. Intertribal Coun. Recipient Disting. Svc. award, Am. Med. Women's Assn., 1999, Alumni award of merit, Bethany Coll., Lindsborg, Kans., 2000, Recognition award 5 State Regional Sci. Fair, Dallas Morning News, 2001. Fellow Am. Geriatrics Assn., Royal Soc. Medicine; mem. So. Med. Assn. (life), Tex. Med. Assn. (life), Dallas Med. Assns. (life), Am. Psychiat. Assn. (life), Tex. Psychiat. Assn., North Tex. Psychiat. Assn., Am. Med. Women's Assn. (Disting. Svc. award 1999), Dallas Area Women Psychiatrists, Alumni Assn. U. Tex. (Med. Br.), Navy League (life), Air Force Assn., Tex. Archaeol. Soc. (life, 45 Yr. Recognition award 2002), Dallas Archaeol. Soc. (hon. life, pres. 1972-73, 82-84, 89-91, 97-99, archival rschr., pres. 1997-99, historian 1997—), South Tex. Archaeol. Soc., Tarrant County Archeol. Soc., El Paso Archeol. Soc., N.Mex. Archaeol. Soc., Paleopathology Soc., Internat. Psychogeriatric Assn. (Famous Women of the 20th Century), VASA Lodge, Alpha Omega Alpha, Delta Psi Omega, Alpha Psi Omega, Pi Gamma Mu, Lambda Sigma, Alpha Epsilon Iota, Mu Delta. Lutheran. Home: 4007 Shady Hill Dr Dallas TX 75229-2844

ERICSON, WILLIAM B. orthopedic hand surgeon; MD, Harvard U., 1983. Diplomate Am. Bd. Orthopedics and Hand Surgery. Orthop. hand surgeon Winchester (Mass.) Hand Surgery, 1990—. Fellow: ACS, Am. Acad. Orthop. Surgeons; mem.: MOA (pres. 1997—98), ASSH. Achievements include discovery of anatomic basis of repetitive strain injuries. Office: Winchester Hand Surgery 611 Main St Winchester MA 01890

ERICSSON, KARL ANDERS, cognitive psychologist, educator, researcher; b. Bromma, Sweden, Oct. 23, 1947; came to U.S., 1977; s. Karl Olov and Ingrid Linnea Ericsson; m. Anna-Lena Ericsson, Oct. 25, 1970 (dec. Apr. 1980); children: Jens, Lina; m. Natalie Jean Sachs, Dec. 20, 1985. BA, U. Stockholm, 1970, PhD in Cognitive Psychology, 1976. Asst. prof. dept. psychology U. Colo., Boulder, 1980-86, assoc. prof., 1986-92, prof., 1992-93; Conradi eminent scholar, prof. psychology Fla. State U., Tallahassee, 1992—. Disting. scholar lectr. dept. psychology U. Alta., Edmonton, Can., 2001; fellow Ctr. for Advanced Study in Behavoiral Scis., Stanford, Calif., 2002-03. Author: Protocol Analysis, 1984, Toward a General Theory of Expertise, 1991, The Road to Excellence, 1996, Expert Performance in Sport: Recent Advances in the Study of Sport Expertise, 2003. Fellow APA (Stanley Hall lectr. 2000). Office: Dept Psychology Fla State Univ Tallahassee FL 32306-1270 E-mail: ericsson@psy.fsu.edu.

ERICSSON, NEIL R. economist, consultant; b. Chgo., Sept. 25, 1954; BA in Econs., Yale U., 1976; MSc in Econometrics and Math. Econs., London Sch. Econs., 1978, PhD in Econs., 1982. Economist Fed. Res. Bd., Washington, 1983—; rsch. officer Nuffield Coll., Oxford, England, 1983. Cons. IMF, Washington, 1995—, World Bank, Washington, 1999; rsch. prof. George Washington U., Washington, 1996—; vis. cons. Res. Bank Australia, Sydney, 1993—94, Sydney, 1998, Bank of Norway, Oslo, 1995—97. Editor: (book) Testing Exogeneity, Understanding Economic Forecasts; contbr. articles to profl. jours. Erskine fellow, U. Canterbury, 1998. Mem.: Sigma Xi, Royal Statis. Soc., Royal Econ. Soc., Econometric Soc., Am. Statis. Assn. (program chair, bus. and econ. sect. 1998—98), Am. Econ. Assn., Am. Friends of the London Sch. Econs. (chmn. of the scholarship com. 1999—2001). Avocations: choral singing, scuba diving, cross country skiing, hiking. Office: Fed Reserve Board Stop 20 2000 C St NW Washington DC 20551 E-mail: ericsson@frb.gov.

ERICSSON, RONALD JAMES, applied biology executive; b. Belle Fourche, S.D., July 17, 1935; s. Arnold L. and Virginia Y. (Clarkson) E.; m. Jean Marie Hodge, Aug. 19, 1956; children: Julie Ann, Scott Alan. BS, Colo. State U., 1957; MS, U. Ky., 1961, PhD, 1964. Postdoctoral fellow U. Wis., Madison, 1963-64; sr. rsch. scientist Upjohn Co., Kalamazoo, Mich., 1964-71; adj. assoc. prof. Western Mich. U., Kalamazoo, 1964-71; spl. cons. Schering AG, Berlin, 1971-73; investigator Inst. Rsch. in Human Reprodn., Tehran, Iran, 1973-74; pres. Gametrics Ltd., Sausalito, Calif., 1974-85, Alzada, Mont., 1985—, Androscore Corp., Alzada, Mont., 1987—. Pres. Lonesome Country Ltd. Ranch, Alzada, 1969—, Bull Pine Properties Ltd. Ranch, Aladdin, Wyo., 2002—. Co-author: Getting Pregnant in the 1980's, 1982; contbr. over 75 articles to profl. publs. With U.S. Army, 1958, capt. Res., 1958-68. Mem. AAAS, Am. Assn. Tissue Banks, Am. Soc. Reproductive Medicine, Am. Soc. Andrology, Assn. for Study of Animal Behavior, Endocrine Soc., Soc. for Advancement of Contraception, Soc. for Explt. Biology and Medicine, Soc. for Study of Fertility, Soc. of Study of Reproduction, Sigma Xi. Achievements include patents in methods for preventing impregnation, rodent sterilant process, determination of capacitation of sperm employing fluorescent form of tetracycline, controlling fertility, fractionation of sperm, sperm fractionation and storage, method of increasing incidence of female offspring, method of increasing economic value of breeding stock semen, method used in testing human males for fertility, kit for testing human males for fertility. Office: Gametrics Ltd HC 69 Box 50 PO Box 68 Alzada MT 59311-9501 Fax: 307-878-4499. E-mail: gametrics@childselect.com.

ERICSSON, SALLY CLAIRE, not-for-profit organization administrator; b. Madison, Wis., Jan. 16, 1953; d. William H. and JoAnn (Finnell) E.; m. Thomas A. Garwin, Oct. 7, 1979; children: Rachel, Benjamin. B in Urban and Regional Planning, U. Ill., 1976; M in Pub. Policy, Harvard U., 1981. Legis. analyst Dem. Steering and Policy Com, Washington, 1982-87; adminstr. asst. Rep. Sam Geidenson U.S. Ho. Reps., Washington, 1987-89; legis. asst. to Sen. John F. Kerry U.S. Senate, Washington, 1989-90; asst. to pres. for policy and rsch. Svc. Employees Internat. Union, Washington, 1990-93; assoc. under sec. for econ. affairs U.S. Dept. Commerce, Washington, 1993-96, dep. chief of staff, 1996-97; assoc. dir. for natural resources Coun. on Environtl. Quality, Exec. Office of the Pres., 1997-99; dir. outreach Pew Ctr. on Global Climate Change, Arlington, Va., 1999—. Home: 1805 Monroe St NW Washington DC 20010-1014 Office: Pew Ctr on Global Climate Change 2101 Wilson Blvd Ste 550 Arlington VA 22201-3038

ERIKSEN, CHARLES WALTER, psychologist, educator; b. Omaha, Feb. 4, 1923; s. Charles Hans and Luella (Carlson) E.; m. Garnita Tharp, July 22, 1945 (div. Jan. 1971); children: Michael John, Kathy Ann; m. Barbara Becker, Apr. 1971. BA summa cum laude, U. Omaha, 1943; PhD, Stanford, 1950. Asst. prof. Johns Hopkins U., Balt., 1949-53, research scientist, 1954-55; lectr. Harvard U., Cambridge, Mass., 1953-54; mem. faculty U. Ill., Urbana, 1956—, prof., 1959-93, prof. emeritus, 1993—. Rsch. cons. VA, 1960-80; mem. psychobiology panel NSF, 1963; mem. exptl. psychology study sect. NIH, 1958-62, 66-70; Pillsbury Meml. lectr. Cornell U., 1966; keynote address 1st Internat. Congress on Visual Search, U. Durham, U.K., 1988, European Congress for Cognitive Psychology, Elsinore, Denmark, 1993; invited lectr. Max Planck Inst., Munich, 1993, Universidad Autonoma de Madrid, 1993, U. of Salamanca, Spain, 1993. Author: Behavior and Awareness, 1962; editor Am. Jour. Psychology, 1968; prin. editor Perception and Psychophysics, 1971-93; cons. editor Jour. Exptl. Psychology, 1965-71, Jour. Gerontology, 1980—; contbr. articles to profl. jours. Recipient Stratton award Am. Psychopath. Assn., 1964, NIMH Research Career award, 1964 Fellow AAAS; mem. Am. Psychol. Soc., Psychonomic Soc., Soc. Exptl. Psychologists, Midwestern Psychol. Assn., Sigma Xi. Home: 22485 State Highway 133 Oakland IL 61943-6822 Office: U Ill Psychol Bldg 603 E Daniel St Champaign IL 61820-6232 E-mail: eriksen@Gulftel.com., erikbarb@consolidated.net.

ERIKSEN, DAN OLUF, film director; b. Seattle, Sept. 24, 1925; s. Oluf and Esther K. (Andersen) E.; m. Delphina I. Brownlee, Apr. 20, 1954 (div. 1960); 1 child, Lynn Michele. Student, U. Wash., 1946-47. Film dir. numerous feature films and commls.; asst. dir. including The Pawnbroker, 1965, A Thousand Clowns, 1965, Truman Capote's Christmas Memory, 1966, The Group, 1966; dir. A Midsummer Night's Dream, 1966. USMC, 1943-45. Mem. Dirs. Guild Am. Lutheran. Avocations: reading, listening to classical music, walking. Home and Office: 129 Old Hwy Wilton CT 06897-3110

ERIKSEN, ERIK FINK, endocrinologist, osteoporosis researcher; b. O. Jerstal, Denmark, Feb. 8, 1953; s. Christian Frede and Signe (Fink) Eriksen; children: Morten Fink, Mads Fink. MD, Aarhus U., Denmark, 1980; D of Med. Sci., Aarhus U., 1989. Diplomate Endocrinology and Internal Medicine. Cons. Aarhus (Denmark) U. Hosp., 1980-82; rsch. fellow Aarhus Amtssygehus, 1982-85; postdoctoral fellow Mayo Clinic, Rochester, Minn., 1985-87; clin. fellow Aarhus U. Hosp., 1987-89, asst. prof. internal medicine, 1989-96, assoc. prof. internal medicine, 1996—2002, cons. endocrinology and internal medicine, 1994—2001, chmn. dept. endocrinology, 1995—2002; med. dir. Eli Lilly & Co., Indpls., 2002—. Author: Osteoporosis, 1992, 2002, Histomorphometry, 1993; mem. editl. bd. Osteoporosis Int., 1989, Bone, 1988, Bone Mineral Rsch., 1988-98, Scandinavian Jour. Musculoskeletal Rsch., 1992; sci. editor European Jour. Clin. Investigation; contbr. articles to profl. jours. Mem. European Calcified Soc., Danish Soc. Internal Medicine, Danish Endocrine Soc. (bd. dirs.), Am. Soc. Bone and Mineral Rsch. (Young Investigator award 1987), Danish Bone and Tooth Soc. (chmn.), Internat. Osteoporosis Found. (mem. scientific adv. com.). Office: Eli Lilly & Co Lilly Corp Ctr Indianapolis IN 46285

ERIKSON, G(EORGE) E(MIL) (ERIK ERIKSON), anatomist, archivist, historian, educator, information specialist; b. Palmer, Mass., May 3, 1920; s. Emil and Sofia (Gustafson) Erikson; m. Suzanne J. Henderson, Apr. 23, 1950; children: Ann, David, John, Thomas. BS, Mass. State Coll. (now U. Mass.), 1941; MA in Biology, Harvard U., 1946, PhD in Biology, 1948. Reader in history of sci. and learning Harvard U., 1943—45, asst. prof. gen. edn. in biology, 1949—52, lectr. anthropology, 1965; instr. anatomy Harvard Med. Sch., 1947—49, rsch. fellow anatomy, 1949—52, assoc. in anatomy, 1952—55, asst. prof. anatomy, 1955—65, assoc. curator Warren Anat. Mus., 1961—65; prof. med. sci. Brown U., Providence, 1965—90, prof. emeritus, 1990—, chmn. sect. morphology, 1968—85, co-chmn. sect. population biology, morphology & genetics and chmn. for anatomy, 1985—90; vis. prof., Dept. Anatomy and Cellular Biology Harvard U. Med. Sch., 1990—91; vis. lectr. in surgery Med. Sch. Harvard U., 1991—; anatomist dept. surgery Mass. Gen. Hosp., Boston, 1990—; pres. Erikson Biog. Inst., Inc., Providence, 1990—. Adv. bd. Reed Elsevier, 1990; anatomist various Boston Hosps., 1952—82, Mass. Gen. Hosp. Sch. Med. Illus., 1947—60, Mass. Gen. Hosp., 1990—, Lahey Clinic, Boston, 1947—60; anatomist depts. surgery, orthopedics, rehab. and neurosurgery R.I.

Hosp., 1967—; cons. anatomist Surg. Techniques Illus., 1976—80; cons. Dorlands Illus. Med. Dictionary, Rockefeller Found. med. and pub. health, S. Am., 1949; specialist State Dept., Brazil, 1962; adj. mem. faculty R.I. Sch. Design, 1970—; Kate Hurd Mead lectr. Coll. Physicians Phila., 1977; Raymond C. Truex lectr. Hahnemann U. Sch. Med., 1985. Fellow Sheldon traveling, Ctrl. Am., 1946, Guggenheim, S. Am., 1949, Fulbright, Brazil, 1962. Mem.: Assn. of Anatomy Chairmen (emeritus), Oral History Medicine, Am. Assn. History Medicine (coun. 1972—74), Am. Assn. Anatomists (historian and archivist 1972—86, archivist 1986—90, historian and archivist 1990—), Am. Assn. Phys. Anthropologists (archivist and co-historian 1981—), History Sci. Soc. (life), Alpha Omega Alpha Honor Med. Soc. (faculty election 1957). Achievements include research in new world primates and gen. intellectual history, especially biology and medicine; development of of database on over 420,000 careers without limits of time, place, or field with extensive institutional, subject, geographical analyses. also: Erikson Biog Inst 242B Meeting St Providence RI 02906-2221 E-mail: gee@biographical.org.*

ERIKSON, KAI, sociologist, educator; b. Vienna, Feb. 12, 1931; came to U.S., 1933, naturalized, 1937; s. Erik H. and Joan (Serson) E.; m. Joanna M. Slivka, Jan. 27, 1961; children: Keith S., Christopher J. BA, Reed Coll., 1953; MA, U. Chgo., 1955, PhD, 1963. Instr. psychiatry U. Pitts., 1959-63; assoc. prof. Emory U., Atlanta, 1963-66; prof. sociology Yale U., New Haven, 1966—, master Trumbull Coll., 1969-73; editor Yale Rev., 1979-89. Author: Wayward Puritans, 1966, Everything in Its Path, 1976, A New Species of Trouble, 1994. With AUS, 1955-57. Fellow Am. Sociol. Assn. (MacIver award 1967, Sorokin award 1977, pres. 1984-85); mem. Soc. Study Social Problems (pres. 1970-71), Eastern Sociol. Soc. (pres. 1980-81) Home: 53 Quarry Dock Rd Branford CT 06405-4655 Office: Yale U Dept Sociology PO Box 208265 New Haven CT 06520-8265

ERISMAN, JAMES A. lawyer; b. Wilmington, Del., Jan. 29, 1940; s. Hudson H. and Madeleine (Poinsett) E.; m. Jane Sarius, June 12, 1965; children: James B., Samantha S. BS, U. Del., 1963; JD, Dickinson Sch. Law, Carlisle, pa., 1966. Bar: Del. 1966, U.S. Dist. Ct. Del. 1967, U.S. Supreme Ct. 1972; diplomate Nat. Bd. Trial Advocacy. Military judge USMC, 1969-70; dep. atty. gen. State of Del., Wilmington, 1970-72; spl. rate counsel Del. Pub. Svc. Commn., Dover, 1972-73; ptnr. Erisman & VanOgtrop, Wilmington and Newark, 1972—. Contbr. articles to profl. jurs. With USMC, 1967-70. Fellow The Roscoe Pound Found., Trial Lawyers for Pub. Justice; mem. Am. Bd. Trial Advocates (pres. Del. chpt. 1996), Assn. Trial Lawyers Am. (bd. govs. 1985-94, trustee 1988-91, 93-95, 97-99), Million Dollar Advocates Forum, Del. Trial Lawyers Assn. (pres. 1982-83, 85-86), Am. Coll. Barristers (sr. counsel), Am. Jury Found. (trustee), Richard S. Rodney Inn of Ct. (bencher). Home: 1502 Pennsylvania Ave Wilmington DE 19806-4318 Office: Erisman and van OgTrop 1224 King St Wilmington DE 19801-3289 E-mail: jerisman@devolaw.com.

ERK, FRANK CHRIS, biologist, educator; b. Evansville, Ind., Dec. 17, 1924; s. Carl Benjamin and Matilda (Schumacher) E.; m. Ruth Parker Hobgood, June 12, 1948; children: Susan Patrick Erk Tierney, Elisabeth Carlene Erk Smith, Stephanie Diane Erk Lutostanski. AB magna cum laude, U. Evansville, 1948; PhD in Genetics, Johns Hopkins U., 1952. Jr. instr. Johns Hopkins U., Balt., 1948-51, Adam T. Bruce fellow, 1951-52, Lalor faculty fellow, 1956; assoc. prof. biology, chmn. dept. Washington Coll., Chestertown, Md., 1952-57, dir. coll. choir, 1952-57; prof. biology SUNY, L.I. Ctr., Oyster Bay, 1957-61, chmn. divsn. sci. and math., 1957—60, chmn. dept. biology, 1958-61, dir. univ. choir, 1957-61; prof. biol. scis. SUNY, Stony Brook, 1962-81, prof. biochemistry and cell biology, 1981-90, prof. emeritus, 1990—, chmn. dept. biology, 1962-67, 76-78. Vis. assoc. prof. biology, Carnegie intern in gen. edn. U. Chgo., 1954-55; rsch. collaborator Masonic Med. Rsch. Lab., Utica, N.Y., 1968-71; vis. investigator Poultry Rsch. Ctr., Agrl. Rsch. Coun., U. Edinburgh, Scotland, 1964-65, Genetics Inst., U. Milan, Italy, 1965, U. Sussex, Eng., 1971-72, 85-86, Galton Lab., U. Coll. London, Eng., 1978-79, U. Edinburgh, 1979; vis. prof. U. Essex, Eng., 1978-79; asst. examiner Internat. Baccalaureate Program, Geneva, 1977-82, cons., 1976-84; cons., writer Biol. Scis. Curriculum Study, Boulder, Colo., 1960-70, 85-90; senator statewide SUNY Faculty Senate, 1967-69, pres., 1969-71; chair Emeritus Faculty Assn. SUNY, Stony Brook, 1990-00, acting master honors coll., 1991-92; dir. Madrigal Singers, Stony Brook, 1963-71; mem. examining com. Advanced Placement Biology Coll. Entrance Exam. Bd., 1967-71, chmn., 1973-77; genealogy chair Three Village Hist. Soc., East Setauket, N.Y., 1996-00. Author: (with others) Biological Science: Molecules to Man, 1963, 68, (with others) Biological Sciences: Interaction of Experiments and Ideas, 1965, 70, Biological Science: An Ecological Approach, 1987, William Sidney Mount: Family, Friends, and Ideas, 1999; editor: (with others) Evolution, Mammals and Southern Continents, 1972; exec. editor Quar. Rev. Biology, 1966-69, editor, 1969-99; mem. editl. bd. Jour. Biol. Edn., London, 1976-90. 1st lt. USAAF, 1943-46, PTO. Mem. AAAS, AAUP, Am. Genetics Assn. (coun. 1978-81), Genetics Soc. Am., Soc. Genetics Can., Nat. Assn. Biology Tchrs., Am. Soc. Zoologists, Soc. for Study Evolution, Human Biology Coun., SUNY Emeritus Faculty Assn. (chmn. 1990-00), Sigma Xi, Phi Beta Chi, Omicron Delta Kappa. Home: 3118 Gracefield Rd Apt 310 Silver Spring MD 20904-7849

ERKKILA-RICKER, BARBARA HOWELL, writer, photographer; b. Boston, July 11, 1918; d. John William and Adelia Parsons (Jones) Howell; m. Onni R. Erkkila, Apr. 27, 1941 (dec. 1981); children: John W., Kathleen L., Marjorie A.; m. G. Ashton Ricker, FEb. 5, 2000. Student, Boston U. Evening Coll., 1959-62. Corr. Gloucester (Mas.) Daily Times, 1936-53, feature writer, 1953—, women's editor, 1967-72, cmty. news editor, 1972-74; freelance article writer for mags., 1953—. Editor weekly mag. Essex County Newspapers, Gloucester, 1973, editl. asst., 1974-85, writer, photographer, 1970—; tchr. Russian, Ipswich (Mass.) Pub. Schs., evenings, 1962-63; jewelry designer; quarry historian. Author: Hammers on Stone, 1981, Village at Lane's Cove, 1989; editor Lane's Cove Cook Book, 1954. Mem. price panel OPA, 1944-46; mem. ARC nurse's aide class Addison Gilbert Hosp., 1942-43; mem. Gloucester Hist. Commn., 1967-69, 93-2000; formerly active Girl Scouts U.S.A.; sec. Lanesville C.C., 1957-94; apptd. granite industry cons. Cape Ann (Mass.) Hist. Assn. Mus., 1997. Recipient 2d prize for feature writing UPI, 1970, historian award Town of Rockport, 1978, First Walker Hancock award City of Gloucester, 1999. Mem. Sandy Bay Hist. Soc., Ohio Geneal. Soc., Cape Ann Hist. Assn., North Shore Rock and Mineral (charter), North Shore Button Club. Congregationalist. Home and Office: 7 School St North Chelmsford MA 01863-2109 E-mail: BarickGran@aol.com.

ERKONEN, WILLIAM E. radiologist, medical educator; BS, U. Iowa, 1955, MD, 1958. Diplomate Am. Bd. Radiology. Intern U. Oreg., Portland, 1959; pvt. practice; resident in radiology U. Iowa Coll. Medicine, Iowa City, 1968-71; pvt. practice, 1971-87; faculty U. Iowa Coll. Medicine, 1988-94, asst. prof. radiology, 1994-98, assoc. prof., 1995-98, co-dir. Electric Differential Multimedia Lab., 1993—, assoc. prof. emeritus, 1998—. Rschr. in med. informatics and med. student instrn. and edn.; mem. anatomy and interdisciplinary com. Nat. Bd. Med. Licensure Exam., 1999—2001. Editor: (textbook) Radiology 101; contbr. articles to profl. jours.; developer electronic med. textbooks. Recipient numerous certs. of merit Radiology Soc. N.Am.; named Tchr. of Yr., U. Iowa Coll. Med., 1990, 93, 96; recipient Disting. Tchr. award for jr. faculty in clin. scis. Alpha Omega Alpha. Fellow Am. Coll. Radiology. Office: Univ Iowa Coll Medicine Dept Radiology Iowa City IA 52240

ERLA, KAREN, artist, painter, collagist, printmaker; b. Pitts., Nov. 17, 1942; d. Jack and Lenore (Kamons) Franklin; children: Stephanie, Joan. BFA, George Washington U., 1965; postgrad., Parsons Sch. Design, 1979-81, Carnegie Inst., 1958-59, Boston U., 1960-62, Pratt Inst., 1980-82, NYU, 1982. Solo exhbns. include Phoenix Gallery, N.Y.C., 1985, E.L. Stark Gallery, N.Y.C., 1988, Bertha Urdang Gallery, N.Y.C., 1986, Bennett and Siegel Gallery, 1989, 90, U. of South, Sewanee, Tenn., Manhattanville Coll., Purchase, N.Y., 1982, Printmaking Council of N.J., 1982, Bennet Siegel Gallery, N.Y.C., 1990, Bryant Gallery, N.Y.C., 1990, Queens Coll., N.Y.C., 1991; group shows include Herbert Johnson Mus. Art, Atlanta Coll. Art, Van Straaten Gallery, Chgo., Greene Gallery, Guilford, Conn., Nat. Mus. of Am. Art, Washington, D.C., Fine Arts Museum of L.I., N.Y., Zimmerli Mus., New Brunswick, N.J., Printmaking Council of N.J., Somerstown Studios and Gallery, Somers, N.Y., Cork Exhbn. in Lincoln Ctr., Fay Gold Gallery, Atlanta, 1984, Boston Printmakers 37th Nat. Exhbn., 1985, The Print Club's 61st Internat. Juried Exhbn., Phila., Schering-Plough Corp. Gallery, Madison, N.J., New Brunswick, N.J., Australian Nat. Gallery, 1989, E.L. Stark Exhbn., 1990, Am. Embassy, 1990, others; represented in permanent collections at Balt. Mus. of Art, Herbert F. Johnson Mus., Cornell U., Bklyn. Mus. Art, Huntsville Mus. Art, Ala., L.A. County Mus. Art, Met. Mus. Art, N.Y., Nat. Museum Am. Art, Australian Nat. Gallery, Smithsonian Inst., New Orleans Mus. Art, Phila. Mus. Art, Tampa Mus., Fla.; featured in Monograph of Karen Erla (text by Ronnie Cohen) 1988, Monoprints Karen Erla (text by Dr. Mary Lee Thompson), Paintings: Karen Erla (text by Bertha Urdang and E.L. Stark); featured in Newsday as New Yorker mag.; solo exhibitions E.L. Stark Gallery, Bertha Urdang Gallery, N.Y.C. Harrison Library, Harrison, N.Y. Manhattanville Coll., Purchase, N.Y., Sound Shore Gallery, N.Y.C., The Print Club 62d Internat., Phila. Recipient Nat. Art award, Pa., 1959, Herbert F. Johnson Mus., Cornell U.; Mamroneck Artists Guild award, 1983. Mem. World Print Council, Printmaking Council N.J., Artists Equity, Pratt Graphic Ctr., L.A. Printmaking Soc. Avocations: music, reading, traveling. Address: PO Box 202 White Plains NY 10603-0202

ERLAND, SHIRLEY MAY, nurse; b. N.Y.C., Sept. 24, 1947; Diploma, Meth. Hosp. Sch. Nursing, Bklyn., 1968; BSN, Molloy Coll., 1981; MSN, Adelphi U., 1987; postgrad., N.Y. Coll. Wholistic Health, 1998-2000. RN, N.Y.; cert. AMMA therapeutic message therapy traditional Chinese medicine, 2000. Surg. nurse Meth. Hosp., Bklyn., 1968-70; staff nurse J.B. Thomas Hosp., Peabody, Mass., 1971-73, Mercy Med. Ctr., Rockville Ctr., NY, 1973—88, critical care nurse, 1975—87, staff nurse CCU, 1978-86, asst. head nurse, 1986-87, instr. staff edn., 1988—97, ednl. mgr., 1998—, Holistic Nursing,: therapeutic message, imagery, stress mgmt., nutrition Rockville Centre, NY. Contbr. articles to profl. jours. Mem. Nurses Assn. of the Counties of L.I., Transcultural Nursing Soc., Am. Holistic Nurses Assn., Assn. Critical Care Nurses, Internat. Assn. Interactive Imagery, Sierra Club, Sons of Norway, Sigma Theta Tau, Phi Sigma Tau. Home: 2120 Wantagh Ave Wantagh NY 11793-3916 Office: Mercy Med Ctr 1000 N Village Ave Rockville Centre NY 11570-1000 E-mail: sme924@aol.com.

ERLANDSON, DAVID ALAN, education administration educator; b. Chgo., Jan. 10, 1936; s. Gerald Kenneth and Anna Marie Schlichting E.; m. Gwyneth Ellen Jones, Sept. 21, 1957; children: Paul William, Linda Ann, Daniel Lindsay, Charles David. AB Wheaton (Ill.) Coll., 1956; MS, No. Ill. U., 1962; EdD, U. Ill., 1969. Cert. supr. all grades, Ill. Tchr. jr. high sch. Geneva (Ill.) Pub. Schs., 1959-62, Unit 4 Schs., Champaign, Ill., 1962-63, dir. gifted program, 1965-68, asst. prin., 1969-71; tchr. Univ. High Sch., Urbana, Ill., 1963-64; asst. prof. SUNY, Buffalo, 1964-65; dir. Ctr. for Upgrading Ednl. Services, Champaign, 1968-69; asst. prof. Queens Coll. CUNY, Flushing, 1971—77; prof. ednl. adminstrn. Tex. A&M U., College Station, 1977—, head dept. ednl. adminstrn., 1984-92. Dir. Prins.' Ctr., Tex. A&M U., 1983-85, 93-01. Author: Strengthening School Leadership, 1976, Doing Naturalistic Inquiry, 1993, Organizational Oversight, 1996; co-author: School Special Services, 1979, Measurement and Evaluation, 1999, The Emerging Principalship; co-editor School Leadership Library; contbr. 127 articles to books and profl. jours. Served to 1st lt. USMC, 1956-59. Mem. Nat. Assn. Secondary Sch. Prins. (commn. on standards for principalship 1985-88), Am. Ednl. Rsch. Assn., Phi Delta Kappa, Phi Kappa Phi. Democrat. Home: 1107 Glade St College Station TX 77840-4434 Office: Tex A&M U Dept Ednl Adminstrn College Station TX 77843-4226

ERLANDSON, PATRICK J. medical association administrator; Corp. controller, chief acctg. officer UnitedHealth Group, Minnetonka, Minn., 1997-2000, CFO, 2000—. Office: UnitedHealth Group 9900 Bren Rd E Minnetonka MN 55343 also: UnitedHealth Group PO Box 1459 Minneapolis MN 55440-1459

ERLANGER, BERNARD FERDINAND, biochemist, educator; b. N.Y.C., July 13, 1923; s. Leo and Frieda (David) E.; m. Rachel Fenichel, June 23, 1946; children: Laura, Louis, Leon. BS with highest honors, CCNY, 1943; MA, NYU, 1949; PhD, Columbia U., 1951. Chemist U.S. Indsl. Chems. Co., Inc., Newark, 1943-44; tech. adviser Manhattan Project, U.S. Army, Los Alamos, 1944-46; prodn. mgr. Hexagon Labs., Inc., N.Y.C., 1946-48; faculty Columbia, 1951—, prof. microbiology, 1966—; vis. scientist Instituto Superiore di Sanita, Rome, 1961-62, Inst. Cell Biology, Shanghai, People's Republic of China, 1978. Mem. Fulbright-Hays Award Com., 1966-72; invited expert analyst biochem. and molecular biology edit. Chemtracts; mem. study sect. neurol. C, NIH, 1985-88. Recipient 600th Anniversary medal Copernican Med. Acad., Cracow, Poland, 1979,Sigma Alpha/Mu Gamma award N.Y. Heart Assn., Townsend Harris medal CUNY, 1995; Fulbright scholar U. Republic of Uruguay, 1967, Guggenheim fellow Inst. Phys.-Chem. Biology, Paris, 1969, Am. Cancer Soc. scholar Pasteur Inst., Paris, 1979. Recipient Physicians and Surgeons Disting. Svc. award Columbia U., 1996. Mem. Am. Chem. Soc., Am. Soc. Biol. Chemists, Biochem. Soc., N.Y. Acad. Scis. (mem. conf. com. 1978), Soc. Exptl. Biol. Medicine (assoc. editor proceedings 1981-88), Harvey Soc., Am. Soc. Immunologists, N.Y. Heart Assn., Am. Soc. Photobiology, Phi Beta Kappa, Sigma Alpha Mu (Gamma award). Achievements include research in mode of action of antibiotics and on cancer; investigation of mechanisms of enzyme catalysis; investigation of macromolecules concerned with genetics immunology of fullerenes, photoregulation, biological receptors; investigation of immunochemistry of buckminsterfullerenes, nanobiotechnology. Home: 16316 15th Dr Flushing NY 11357-2935 Office: Columbia U 701 W 168th St New York NY 10032-2704 E-mail: bfel@columbia.edu. *The scientist, like the artist, contributes most when he allows his work to be an extension of his individuality. The risks to his ego and security are great, but success brings with it the satisfaction of making a personal imprint on the future of society.*

ERLANGER, RICHARD ALAN, investment executive; b. Waterbury, Conn, July 21, 1941; s. Meyer B. and Freda F. (Freilich) E.; m. Catherine Ann Porter, July 1, 1963. AB, Hamilton Coll., 1963; MBA, Columbia U., 1969. Fin. trainee GE Co., 1963—66; cons. Arthur D. Little Inc., Cambridge, Mass., 1969-74, McKinsey & Co. Inc., NYC, 1974-80; mgr. Alexander & Alexander Inc., NYC, 1980-87; pres. Erlanger Holdings, Inc., Greenwich, Conn., 1987—. Treas. Green-Links, New Canaan, Conn.; trustee New Canaan Nature Ctr. Lt. (j.g.) USN, 1966-68, Vietnam. Avocations: ice hockey, aerobics, weight lifting, reading. Home: 103 Seminary St New Canaan CT 06840-4504 Office: Erlanger Holdings Inc 2 Sound View Dr Greenwich CT 06830-6471 E-mail: richarderlanger@go.com.

ERLANSON, DEBORAH MCFARLIN, state program administrator; b. Watertown, N.Y., Oct. 17, 1943; d. Raymond Thomas and Alberta Antoinette (Schultz) McF.; m. David Norman Erlanson, Sept. 10, 1966 (dec. Aug. 1998); 1 child, Joshua David. AA in Liberal Arts, Dutchess C.C., 1964; BA in Psychology, Am. Internat. Coll., 1966; MS in Edn., So. Ill. U., 1972. Coord. occupancy tng. Decatur (Ill.) Housing Authority, 1975-76, coord. target projects program, 1976-77, coord. spl. svcs., 1977-78, asst. dir. planning, 1978-82, dir. program devel., 1982—. Spkr. in field; cons. Piatt County Housing Authority, Monticello, Ill., 1985-89, Woodford Homes, Inc., Decatur, 1985-86. Steering com. Near West Restoration and Preservation Soc., Decatur, 1985-86, bd. dirs., 1986—, v.p., 1992—; mem. steering com. Cmtys. in Partnership, 1991—, bd. dirs., 1993—; mem. Decatur Advantage 20/20, 1993, Macon County Literacy Coun., 1992-95; parent group counselor Macon County Parents Anonymous, Decatur, 1976-80; mem. health divsn. Decatur Coun. Cmty. Svcs., 1978-84; bd. dirs. YWCA, Decatur, 1992-95; adv. bd. Ill. Housing Devel. Authority, 1993—. Mem. Nat. Assn. Housing/Redevel. Ofcls. (mem. state exec. bd. 1983-93, mem. profl. devel. com. 1983-93, state exec. bd. 1983-93, state pres. 1984-87, regional pres. 1993-95, profl. devel. faculty 1986—, nat. bd. govs. 1987—, vice chair 1987-89, v.p. profl. devel. 1987-89, task force on product devel. 1987, mem. task force on elderly housing issues 1990-91, mem. Award of Excellence jury 1991-98, regional pres. 1993-95, sr. v.p. 1995-97, chair futures working group 1996-97, pres. 1997—, Charles A. Thompson award 1991, William R. Hammond award 1993), Decatur Women's Network, Internat. City Mgmt. Assn. Avocations: historic preservation, swimming. Home: 465 W Macon St Decatur IL 62522-3122 Office: Decatur Housing Authority 1808 E Locust St Decatur IL 62521-1565

ERLEBACHER, ALBERT, history educator; b. Ulm, Württemburg, Fed. Republic of Germany, Sept. 28, 1932; came to U.S., 1937; s. Alfred Samuel and Rosa (Wertheimer) E.; m. Dolores Adler, Aug. 20, 1961; children: Seth Allen, Steven John, Ross Maier. BA, Marquette U., 1954, MA, 1956; PhD, U. Wis., 1965. Cert. prin., Wis. Tchr. Independence (Wis.) H.S., 1954-55, Cen. H.S., Sheboygan, Wis., 1956-59; prin. Lone Rock (Wis.) H.S., 1960-62; asst. prof. U. Wis., Oshkosh, 1962-65; prof. DePaul U., Chgo., 1965—, chmn. history dept., 1982-88. Dist. 69 Sch. Bd., Skokie, Ill., 1978-81; faculty adv. com. State Bd. Higher Edn., Champaign, Ill., 1974-80, 92-97. Mem. Temple Judea-Mizpah. Mem. AAUP, Am. Hist. Assn., State His. Soc. Wis. Home: 8232 Kilbourn Ave Skokie IL 60076-2614 Office: DePaul U 2320 N Kenmore Ave Chicago IL 60614-3210 E-mail: aerlebac@condor.depaul.edu.

ERLEBACHER, ARLENE CERNIK, retired lawyer; b. Chgo., Oct. 3, 1946; d. Laddie J. and Gertrude V. (Kurdys) Cernik; m. Albert Erlebacher, June 14, 1968; children: Annette Doherty, Jacqueline. BA, Northwestern U., 1967, JD, 1973. Bar: Ill. 1974, U.S. Dist. Ct. (no. dist.) Ill. 1974, U.S. Ct. Appeals (7th cir.) 1974, Fed. Trial Bar 1983, U.S. Supreme Ct. 1985. Assoc. Sidley & Austin, Chgo., 1974-80, ptnr., 1980-95, ret., 1996. Fellow Am. Bar Found.; mem. Order of Coif. E-mail: Erlebacher@comcast.net.

ERLEBACHER, MARTHA MAYER, artist, educator; b. Jersey City, Nov. 21, 1937; d. Desiderius and Mary Mayer; m. Walter Erlebacher, June 26, 1961 (dec. Aug. 1991); children: Adrian Immanuel, Jonah Daedalus. Student, Gettysburg (Pa.) Coll., 1955-56; B of Indsl. Design, Pratt Inst., 1960, MFA, 1963. Indsl. designer, illustrator Arthur Wagner Assocs., N.Y.C., 1956-61; tchr. anatomy and figure drawing U. of Arts, Phila., 1978-94. Tchr. Phila. Coll. Art, 1966-68, 78-94; tchr. anatomical drawing and painting Grad. Sch. Figurative Art, N.Y. Acad. Art, N.Y.C., 1992—, others; guest lectr. Grad. Sch. Art Yale U., 1974, Vassar Coll., Poughkeepsie, N.Y., 1975, Phila. Coll. Art, 1976, U. Conn., Storrs, 1977, Tyler Sch. Art Temple U., 1978, Med. Coll. Pa., Phila., 1987, N.Y. Acad. Art, 1990, others; vis. artist colls. and univs. including U. Wis., Oshkosh, 1979, Syracuse U., 1986-87, U. Mich., 1988, Calif. State U., 1989, 91, Tulane U., New Orleans, 1992, Kalamazoo Inst. Arts, 1989; panelist arts shows, 1978—; juror U. Del., 1979, N.Y. Statewide Bi-Annual, Trenton, 1984, Moss Rehab. Hosp., Phila., 1985, Tex. Nat. '98, Nacogdoches. Exhibited in one-person shows at Robert Schoelkopf Gallery, N.Y.C., 1973, 75, 78, 80, 82, 85, Dart Gallery, Chgo., 1976, 78, 83, Koplin Gallery, L.A., 1989, 91, Kalamazoo Inst. Arts, 1989, Fischbach Gallery, N.Y.C., 1993, 95, The More Gallery, Phila., 1993, 97, 2000, Hackett-Freedman Gallery, San Francisco, 1999, 2002, Arnot Mus., Elmira, NY, 2001, Forum Gallery, N.Y.C., 2003, others; exhibited in group shows Bklyn. Mus., 1960, Phila. Art Alliance, 1967, Suffolk Mus., Stony Brook, N.Y., 1971, Pratt Manhattan Ctr., 1971, Am. Acad. Arts & Letters, N.Y.C., 1973, 76, 87, Yale U. Art Gallery, 1973, Phila. Civic Ctr., 1974, Mus. Art, Penn. State U., 1974, 76, N.Y. Cultural Ctr., 1975, Libr. Congress, 1975, U. Notre Dame, 1976, Ringling Mus. Art, Sarasota, Fla., 1976, Fogg Art Mus. Harvard U., Cambridge, Mass., 1976, Art Gallery Boston U., 1977, Penn. Acad. Fine Arts, 1978, 81, 82, Phila. Mus. Art, 1979, Centro Colombo Americano, Bogota, Colombia, 1979, Fendrick Gallery, Washington, 1980, Print Club, Phila., 1980, 88, Albright-Knox Gallery, Buffalo, 1981, Woodmere Art Gallery, Phila., 1982, Univ. Art Mus., Santa Barbara, Calif., 1983, N.J. State Mus., Trenton, 1984, Hudson River Mus., Yonkers, N.Y., 1986, Sch. Fine Arts Gallery Ind. U., 1987, Sherry French Gallery, N.Y.C., 1988, 91, 92, Jack Wright Gallery, Palm Beach, Fla., 1992, Contemporary Realist Gallery, San Francisco, 1993, 94, Gerald Peters Gallery, Sante Fe, 1993, Fletcher Gallery, Sante Fe, 1994, Arnot Mus., Elmira, 2000, many others; represented in pvt. and pub. collections including Cleve. Mus. Art, Ball State U., Muncie, Ind., AT&T Co., Inc., Chgo., U. Notre Dame, Art Inst. Chgo., Fogg Mus. of Art, Fed. Reserve Bank, N.Y.C., Penn. Acad. Fine Arts, Phila., Valparaiso U., Phila. Mus. Art, Libr. Congress, Flint Inst. Arts, N.J. State Mus., others. Recipient Bertha Shay award Cheltenham Art Ctr., 1967, Netsky-Sernaker Meml. prize, 1973, Vivian and Meyer P. Potamkin prize, 1974; Yaddo fellow, 1966, 73, sr. fellow Nat. Endowment for Arts, 1982, fellow Pa. Coun. on Arts, 1988; grantee Ingram Merrill Found., 1978, Mellon Venture Fund, 1987; also other grants and awards. Home: 7733 Mill Rd Elkins Park PA 19027-2708 E-mail: mmayererlebacher@aol.com.

ERLENBORN, JOHN NEAL, lawyer, educator, former congressman; b. Chgo., Feb. 8, 1927; s. John H. and Veronica M. (Moran) E.; m. Dorothy C. Fisher, May 10, 1952; children: Debra Lynn, Paul Nelson, David John. Student, U. Notre Dame, 1944, U. Ill., 1945-46; JD, Loyola U., Chgo., 1949. Bar: Ill. 1949. With law office Joseph S. Perry, Wheaton, 1949-50; partner firm Erlenborn & Bauer, Elmhurst, 1952-63, Erlenborn, Bauer and Hotte, 1963-71; mem. 89-97th congresses from 14th Dist., Ill., 1965-83, 98th congress from 13th dist., Ill., 1983-85; asst. states atty. DuPage County, Ill., 1950-52; mem. Ill. Ho. of Reps. from DuPage County, 1956-64; ptnr. Seyfarth, Shaw, Fairweather & Geraldson, Washington, 1985-92, of counsel, 1993-94. Bd. dirs. Custodial Trust Co., Princeton, N.J.; mem. U.S. Dept. Labor Employee Retirement Income Security Act Adv. Coun., 1985-89, chmn., 1985-86; adj. prof. Georgetown U. Law Ctr., 1994-2002; mem., vice chair Legal Svcs. Corp., 1989-90, 1996—, pres. 2001-03. Trustee The Aerospace Corp., 1990-99, chair audit and fin. com., 1999; advisor U.S. Delegation to ILO 78th and 79th Session, Geneva. With USNR, 1944-46. Mem.: Former Mems. of Congress (bd. dirs. 1993—, sec. 1995—96, treas. 1996—97, v.p. 1998—2000, pres. 2000—02). E-mail: JErlenborn@aol.com.

ERLENMEYER-KIMLING, L. psychiatrist, researcher; b. Princeton, N.J. d. Floyd M. and Dorothy F. (Dirst) Erlenmeyer; m. Carl F. E. Kimling. BS magna cum laude, Columbia U., 1957, PhD, 1961; DSc (hon.), SUNY, Purchase, 1997. Sr. rsch. scientist N.Y. State Psychiat. Inst., N.Y.C., 1960-69, assoc. rsch. scientist, 1969-75, prin. rsch. scientist, 1975-78, dir. div. devel. behavioral studies, 1978—, chief med. genetics, 1991—; asst. in psychiatry Columbia U., 1962-66, rsch. assoc., 1966-70, from asst. prof. to assoc. prof. psychiatry and genetics, 1970—78, prof., 1978—. Vis. prof. psychology New Sch. Social Rsch., 1971—97; mem. peer rev. group NIH, 1976—80; mem. work group guidance and counseling Congl. Commn. Hungtinton's Disease, 1976—77; mem. task force intervention Pres.'s Commn. Mental Health, 1977—78; mem. initial rev. group NIMH, 1981—85; mem. adv. bd. Croatian Inst. Brain Rsch., 1991—93. Editor: (book) Life-Span Research in Psychopathology, 1986; issue editor: Differential Reproduction, Social Biology, 1971, Genetics and Mental Disorders, Internat. Jour. Mental Health, 1972, Genetics and Gene Expression in Mental Illness, Jour. Psychiat. Rsch., 1992, Measuring Liability to Schizophrenia: Progress Report, 1994; mem. editl. bd. Schizophrenia Bull., 1978—; issue editor: Schizophrenia Bull., 1994; mem. editl. bd. Social Biology, 1970—79, Jour. Preventive Psychiatry, 1980—84, Croatian Med. Jour., 1991—, Neurology/Psychiatry/Brain Rsch., 1991—, Neuropsychiat. Genetics, —, Am. Jour. Med. Genetics, 1992—. Recipient Disting. Investigator award, Merit award, NIMH, 1989—96, William K. Warren Schizophrenia Rsch. award, Internat. Congress Schizophrenia Rsch., 1995, Lifetime Achievement award, Internat. Soc. of Psychiatric Genetics, 2002; grantee, NIMH, 1966—69, 1971—, Scottish Rite Com. Schizophrenia, 1970—74, 1984—87, 1989—94, W. T. Grant Found., 1978—86, MacArthur Found., 1981, Stnaley Found., 1995—, NARSAD, 1996—2000. Fellow: APA, Am. Psychol. Soc., Am. Psychopath. Assn.; mem.: AAAS, Soc. Study Social Biology (bd. dirs. 1969—84, 1992—96, sec. 1972—75, pres. 1975—78), N.Y. Acad. Scis., Internat. Soc. Psychiat. Genetics (Lifetime Achievement award 2002), Behavior Genetics Assn. (mem.-at-large 1972—74, Theodosius Dobzhansky award 1985), Am. Soc. Human Genetics, Sigma Xi, Phi Beta Kappa. Office: NY State Psychiat Inst Dept Med Genetics 1051 Riverside Dr Mail Unit 6 New York NY 10032-2603 E-mail: le4@columbia.edu.

ERLICH, JACOB NATHAN, lawyer; b. Milford, Mass., Mar. 27, 1940; s. Jack and Sara (Londner) E.; m. Laura Yessin, Sept. 17, 1967; children— Adam and Shari. B.S. in Mech. Engring., Worcester Poly. Inst., 1962; J.D., Georgetown U., 1966. Bar: D.C. 1967, U.S. Ct. Appeals (D.C. cir.) 1967, Mass. 1972, U.S. Supreme Ct. 1972, U.S. Patent and Trademark Office, Canadian Patent Office.Patent examiner U.S. Patent Office, Washington, 1962-67. chief patent adviser USAF, Waltham, Mass., 1967-95, ptnr. Perkins, Smith & Cohen, Boston, 1995—; Bd. dirs. Citizens Scholar. Found., Bedford, Mass., 1979—, v.p., 1984-85, pres., 1985-86; mem. Bd. Standards, Bedford, 1978-88, exec. working group Fed. Tech. Transfer, 1987-95. Contbr. articles to profl. jours. Recipient Spl. Achievement award Dept. Air Force, 1969-72, 73-79, 80-83, Superior Performance award Dept. Air Force, 1981-84, Sci. Achievement award, 1983, Merit Pay award superior svc., 1984-95; Disting. Service award Worcester Poly. Inst., 1982, 83, 87. Mem. Worcester Poly. Inst. Alumni Coun.,Boston Patent Law Assn. (sec. 1981, v.p. 1982, pres.-elect. 1983, pres. 1984, bd. govs. 1979, 81-85, chmn. LES, 1987-91, chmn. AIPLA, 1983-90, bd. dirs. NE chpt. tech. transfer soc. 1990-95), ASME (pres. 1961-62), Intellectual Property Law Assn. (rep. nat. coun. 1984-92, faculty nat. intellectual property

law inst. 1994, intellectual property inst. for corp. counsel 1994). Club: Georgetown Patent Law (treas. 1965-66). Home: 19 Fox Run Rd Bedford MA 01730-1141 Office: Perkins Smith & Cohen One Beacon St Boston MA 02108-3106

ERLICH, VICTOR, Slavic languages educator; b. Petrograd, Russia, Nov. 22, 1914; came to U.S., 1942, naturalized, 1943; s. Henryk and Sophie (Dubnov) E.; m. Iza Sznejerson, Feb. 27, 1940; children: Henry Anthony, Mark Leo. MA, Free Polish U., Warsaw, 1937; PhD, Columbia U., 1951; MA (hon.), Yale U., 1963. Asst. lit. editor New Life mag., Warsaw, 1937-39; research writer Yiddish Ency., 1942-43; from asst. prof. to prof. Slavic lit. and langs. U. Wash., 1949-63; Bensinger prof. Russian lit. Yale U., 1963-85, chmn. dept. Slavic langs., 1963-68, 78-81, prof. emeritus, 1985—; Del. congress Fedn. Modern Lang. and Lit., 1957, Internat. Congress Slavists, Sofia, 1963, Warsaw, 1973, Congress Internat. Comparative Lit. Assn., Belgrade, 1967. Author: Russian Formalism: History, Doctrine, 1955, The Double Image: Concepts of The Poet in Slavic Literatures, 1964, Gogol, 1969, Modernism and Revolution: Russian Literature in Transition, 1994; editor: Twentieth Century Russian Criticism, 1975, Pasternak: Twentieth-Century Views, 1977. Served with AUS, 1943-45, ETO. Decorated Purple Heart.; Ford Fellow, 1953-54; Fulbright lectr. U. Leyden, 1957-58; Guggenheim fellow, 1958, 64, 76-77; Nat. Endowment for Humanities fellow, 1968-69 Mem. Am. Assn. Advancement Slavic Studies (v.p.), MLA (exec. council), Internat. Assn. Slavic Langs. and Lits. (exec. council 1957-62), AAUP, Am. Comparative Lit. Assn., Am. Soc. Aesthetics. Home: 25 Glen Pkwy Hamden CT 06517-1402 Office: Yale Univ Dept of Slavic Languages New Haven CT 06520

ERLICH PENCHUK, SARA, social worker, psychotherapist; b. N.Y.C., Aug. 1, 1948; d. Henry and Raye (Marsa) Erlich; children: Andrew Henry, Matthew David. BA, U. New Haven, 1969; cert. in social work, Fordham U., 1975, MSW, 1977; PsyD, So. Calif. U. Profl. Studies, 2000. Cert. sch. social work specialist; cert. social worker, N.Y.; diplomate in clin. social work; lic. clin. social worker. With Assn. Retarded Citizens, Bergen-Passaic Counties, 1973—88, social worker, 1978-88, Bd. Edn., Leonia, N.J., 1979-82, Englewood, N.J., 1978-80; pvt. practice Teaneck, N.J., 1982—. Dir. PsychoTherapeutics, Inc., Teaneck; adj. faculty Fairleigh Dickinson U., 1981-86; cons. and lectr. in field. Mem. NASW, Acad. Cert. Social Workers, Am. Anorexia/Bulemia Assn. Avocations: travel, reading. Office: 154 Bennett Rd Teaneck NJ 07666-5652

ERLICHSON, MIRIAM, fundraiser; b. Bronx, NY, July 26, 1948; d. Jack and Bess (Hyatt) E.; m. Walter Forman, Sept. 26, 1970 (div. 1975); m. Victor Petrusewicz, July 17, 1980. BA in English, CCNY, 1969, MA in English, 1976; postgrad., Hunter Coll., 1970-71; JD, Pace U., 1993. Cert. secondary tchr., N.Y. Tchr. English Intermediate Sch. 84, Bronx, 1972-78; coord. ann. and planned giving N.Y. Hosp.-Cornell Med. Ctr., N.Y.C., 1979-90; sr. devel. assoc. I.H. Found., Inc., N.Y.C., 1996-98, assoc. dir. N.E. region, 1998—2002; devel. comms. mgr. G.H. Ednl. Found., Inc., N.Y.C., 2002—03. Bd. dirs. 77 Settler Corp. Mem. N.Y. County Lawyers Assn., Jane Austen Soc. (Eng.), N.Y.S. Bar, Phi Beta Kappa.

ERLICHT, LEWIS HOWARD, broadcasting company executive; b. N.Y.C., Aug. 6, 1939; s. Harry and Estelle (Silk) E.; m. Wilma Binder, June 10, 1961; children: Paul Jon, Jamie Blake. BA in Psychology, L.I. U., 1962. With ABC-TV, 1962—, account exec., 1965-70; sales mgr. Sta. WABC-TV, 1970-73, gen. sales mgr., 1973-74; gen. mgr. Sta. WLS-TV, Chgo., 1974-77, v.p. programming N.Y.C., 1977-79; v.p., asst. to pres. ABC Entertainment, Los Angeles, 1979-80, sr. v.p., asst. to pres., 1980-81, sr. v.p. prime time programming, 1981-83, pres., 1983-85, ABC Circle Films, Los Angeles, 1985-86; pres., chief operating officer New World Broadcasting, Los Angeles, 1986-87; pres. LHE, Inc., 1986—. Cons. Scandinavian Broadcasting Systems, 1989-91. Served with USAF, 1956-60.

ERLICK, JUNE CAROLYN, director; b. Boston; d. Gerald Jerome and Miriam Erlick. BA, Barnard Coll., 1969; MS in Journalism, Columbia U., 1970. Fellow Inter-Am. Press Assn., Bogota, Colombia, 1977; corr. Nat. Cath. Reporter, Bogota, 1977—84, Miami Herald, Time Mag., Bogota, Managua, 1984—88, Fairchild News Svc., Berlin, 1988—92; editor, Casa Internacional ABC/Capital Cities, N.Y.C., 1993—97; publs. dir., David Rockefeller Ctr. L.Am. Studies Harvard U., Cambridge, Mass., 1997—. Alumni bd. Columbia Grad. Sch. Journalism, 1993—; editor ReVista mag., 1997—. Vol. interpreter PAIR Project, Boston, 1997—. Fulbright fellow, Guatemala, 2000. Mem.: Nat. Assn. Hispanic Journalists. Avocations: Scrabble, reading, photography, cooking. Office: David Rockefeller Ctr L Am Studies Harvard U 61 Kirkland St Cambridge MA 02138 E-mail: jerlick@fas.harvard.edu.

ERLINGER, JAMES H., III, lawyer; b. St. Charles, N.J., Sept. 30, 1958; s. James H. II and Nancy (Willbrand) E.. BSBA, U. Mo., 1981, MBA, 1983; JD, 1985. CPA; bar: Mo. 1985. Ptnr., mem. exec. com. Bryan Cave LLP, St. Louis, 1985—. Office: Bryan Cave LLP 211 N Broadway Ste 3600 Saint Louis MO 63102-2733

ERMAN, ANDREW DAVID, civil engineer; b. L.A., Sept. 28, 1963; s. Paul and Rachelle (Monté) E. BSCE, U. Calif., Berkeley, 1985; MBA, U. S.C., 1998. Registered profl. engr., Calif. Civil engring. asst. I L.A. Dept. Pub. Works, 1986, civil engring. asst. II, 1986-88, civil engring. asst. III, 1988-90, civil engring. assoc. I, 1990, acting civil engr., 1990-91; civil engring. assoc. L.A. Dept. Water & Power, 1991—2001; staff engr. L.A. Bur. St. Svcs., 2001—. Pres. Berkeley chpt. Circle K Internat., 1984-85; v.p. Barrington-Tarryhill Homeowners Assn., L.A., 1987—; cantor Jewish temple. Recipient cert. of excellence L.A. Bur. Engring. Quality Circle, 1988, citation L.A. Bd. Pub. Works, 1988, cert. of appreciation L.A. councilwoman, 1990; Alumni scholar Calif. Alumni Assn., 1981, H.J. Hjul scholar, 1981. Mem. ASCE. Home: 612 S Barrington Ave Apt 412 Los Angeles CA 90049-4423 Office: LA Bur St Svcs 600 S Spring St Fl 12 Los Angeles CA 90014

ERMOLAEV, HERMAN SERGEI, Slavic languages educator; b. Tomsk, Russia, Nov. 14, 1924; came to U.S., 1949, naturalized, 1956; s. Sergei and Vera (Kozminykh) E.; m. Tatiana Kuzubova, June 8, 1975; children: Michael, Natalia, Katherine. Student, U. Graz, Austria, 1949; BA, Stanford U., 1951; MA, U. Calif.-Berkeley, 1954, PhD, 1959. Mem. faculty Princeton U., 1959—, prof. Slavic langs. and lits., 1970—. Author: Soviet Literary Theories, 1917-1934, The Genesis of Socialist Realism, 1963, 77, Mikhail Sholokhov and His Art, 1982, Censorship in Soviet Literature, 1917-1991, 1997, Mikhail Sholokhov and His Art (in Russian), 2000; co-author: Sholokhov's Tikhii Don, A Commentary, 1997; also articles; translator: Untimely Thoughts (Gorky), 1968, 95. McCosh fellow, 1967-68 Mem. Am. Assn. Advancement Slavic Studies, Am. Assn. Tchrs. Slavic and East European Langs. (pres. 1971-72) Home: 206 Moore St Princeton NJ 08540-3404 E-mail: ermolaev@princeton.edu.

ERMOLAEVA, MARIA D. bioinformatician, researcher; Diploma in Bio-physics(hon.), Moscow State U., 1995, PhD in Physics and Math., 1997. Postdoctoral rschr. Pa. State U., University Park, Pa., 1997—99; staff scientist Inst. for Genomic Rsch., Rockville, Md., 1999—; lectr. Johns Hopkins U., Rockville, Md., 2002—. Contbr. articles to profl. jours. Office: Inst Genomic Rsch 9712 Medical Ctr Dr Rockville MD 20850 E-mail: mariae@tigr.org.

ERNEST, DOUGLAS JEROME, librarian; b. Billings, Mont., Mar. 31, 1947; s. Clarence Henry and Ruth (Imhof) E. BA in History, U. Colo., 1969, MA in History, 1975; MA in Libr. Sci., U. Denver, 1970. Reference libr. Florence (S.C.) County Libr., 1970-73, Mo. Western State Coll., St. Joseph, 1975-81; social scis., humanities libr. Colo. State U., Ft. Collins., 1981—. Author: (book) Agricultural Frontier to Electronic Frontier, 1996; also articles. Chair High Plains Regional Libr. Svc. Sys. Bd., 2000-01. Recipient Lit. award Colo. Libr. Assn., 1996. Mem. Wilderness Soc., Nature Conservancy, Phi Beta Kappa, Beta Phi Mu. Democrat. Unitarian Universalist. Avocations: hiking, nature study. Home: 1625 W Elizabeth St Apt J-1 Fort Collins CO 80521-4465 Office: Colo State U Morgan Libr Fort Collins CO 80523-0001 E-mail: Doug.Ernest@colostate.edu.

ERNEST, J. TERRY, ocular physiologist, educator; b. Sycamore, Ill., June 26, 1935; married, 1965; 2 children. BA, Northwestern U., 1957; MD, U. Chgo., 1961, PhD in Visual Sci., 1967. Prof. ophthalmology U. Wis., 1977-79; prof., chmn. ophthalmology Ind. U., 1980-81; prof. ophthalmology U. Ill., 1981-85; prof., chmn. ophthalmology U. Chgo., 1985—, Cynthia Chow prof., 2002—. Mem visual sci. A study sect., NIH, 1975-78, chmn. 1978-79, chmn. visual disorders study sect., 1979-80; rsch. prof. Rsch. to Prevent Blindness, Ind., 1981-84; mem. Vision Rsch. Program Com., 1982-84. Founding editor, Key, 1986-88; editor, Year Book of Ophthamology, 1982-88, Investigative Ophthalmology and Visual Sci., 1988-92. Recipient Rsch. Career Devel. award NIH, 1972. Mem. AAAS, Am. Ophthalmol. Soc., Am. Acad. Ophthalmology (Honor award 1982), Assn. Rsch. Vision and Ophthalmology. Achievements include research in ocular circulation with special emphasis on glaucoma and diabetic retinopathy using various methods of in vivo blood flow measurements. Office: U Chgo Visual Sciences Ctr 5841 S Maryland Ave MC2114 Chicago IL 60637-1454

ERNEST, MICHAEL VANCE, SR., research chemist; b. Balt., July 27, 1941; s. Charles Vernon and Pauline Maurette (McHenry) E.; m. Barbara Lee Hipp, July 22, 1961; children: Deborah, Sheryl, Michael Jr. AA, Balt. Jr. Coll., 1965; BS in Physics, Loyola Coll., 1970, BA in Math., 1974, MBA, 1979. Asst. to chief chemist Hynson, Wescott, Dunning, Balt., 1960-62; lab. technician A.W.R. Grace & Co., Columbia, Md., 1962-70, jr. rsch. chemist, 1970-75, assoc. rsch. chemist, 1975-76, rsch. chemist, 1976-79, sr. rsch. chemist, 1979-90, rsch. assoc., 1990—2002, sr. prin. scientist, 2002—. Contbr. articles to profl. jours.; 25 patents in field. Avocations: woodworking, furniture making, fitness training. Office: WR Grace and Co 7500 Grace Dr Columbia MD 21044-4098 E-mail: Michael.V.Ernest.Sr@grace.com.

ERNO, MARGARET JEAN, social worker, consultant; b. Barre, Vt., Feb. 24, 1950; d. Gilbert Higley and Florence Erno; 1 adopted child, Roy Anthony. BA, Trinity Coll., Burlington, Vt., 1974; postgrad., Long Ridge Writers Group, 2002—. First aid instr. ARC, Burlington, 1971—86; EMT U. Vt., Burlington, 1973—76. Floor specialist IBM, Essex Junction, Vt., 1981—93. Bd. mem. Vocat. Rehab., Burlington, 1973—75; ceramic artist Vt. Ceramic League, Burlington, 1990—; active Young Vt. Reps., Burlington, 1972. Mem.: Internat. Women's Writing Guild. Independent. Episcopalian. Home and Studio: 30 Hayward St Burlington VT 05401

ERNST, CHESTER NELSON, manufacturing company executive; b. Harrisburg, Pa., Apr. 6, 1948; s. H. Nelson and Blanche E. (Stillwell) E.; m. Norma Marie DeGhetto, Feb. 21, 1971; children: Patrick, Terrence, Douglas, Katherine. BS, U.S. Mil. Acad., 1970; MBA, U. Chgo., 1984. Commd. 2d lt. U.S. Army, 1970, advanced through grades to capt., 1973, resigned, 1975; prodn. planner Masonite Corp., Towanda, Pa., 1975-76, mgr. prodn., inventory control Chgo., 1976-79; mgr. prodn., inventory control indsl. sealing div. EG&G Sealol, Elmhurst, Ill., 1979-82, materials mgr. indsl. sealing div., 1982-83, ops. mgr. indsl sealing div., 1983-88; materials mgr. ITT McDonnell and Miller, Chgo., 1988-92; mfg. ops. mgr. ITT McDonnell & Miller, Chgo., 1992-2000; value based six sigma champion ITT Fluid Handling Divsn., Morton Grove, Ill., 2000—02, lean mfg. master, 2003—. Fellow Am. Prodn. and Inventory Control Soc. Republican. Roman Catholic. Home: 516 Irvington Ct Bartlett IL 60103-4653 Office: ITT Bell & Gossett Fluid Handling Divsn 8200 N Austin Ave Morton Grove IL 60053 E-mail: chernst@attbi.com.

ERNST, CHRISTOPHER MARK, lawyer; b. Cleve., Dec. 1, 1966; s. Chalmer Mark and Helen Elizabeth (Gibson) E. BA, Tufts U., 1988; JD, Case Western Res. U., 1991. Bar: Ohio 1991, U.S. Dist. Ct. Ohio 1992, U.S. Ct. Appeals (6th cir.) 1995, U.S. Supreme Ct. 2001. Law clk. Cuyahoga County Ct. of Common Pleas, Cleve., 1992; ptnr. Ernst & Dowling, 1992-96; prin. Ernst & Co., LPA, 1996-97; assoc. Weston Hurd Fallon Paisley & Howley, 1997—99, ptnr., 2000—. Vol. in-house counsel Call For Action, WJW TV-8, 1993-96; vol. counsel Legal Aid Soc. Mem. Playhouse Sq. Ptnrs., Cleve., 1992—2000; trustee, 1995—2000, mem. exec. com., 1995—98, chair activities com., 1995—96, chair fiduciary com., 1996—97, chair leadership devel., 1997—98; trustee Cuyahoga County Corrections Planning Bd., 1996—; pres. Cuyahoga County Young Dems., 1999—2000. Mem.: ABA (cyberspace law com.), Cuyahoga County Bar Assn. (trustee 1996—2001, jud. selection com. 1997—98, co-chair jud. selection com. 1998—99, cert. grievance com. 1997—2001), Ohio State Bar Assn., Mensa. Avocation: jazz trombone. Office: 50 Public Sq Cleveland OH 44113-2201

ERNST, DANIEL PEARSON, lawyer; b. Des Moines, Sept. 30, 1931; s. Daniel Ward and Thea Elaine (Pearson) E.; m. Ann Robinson, April 14, 1956; children: Ellen, Daniel R., Ruth Ann. BA, Dartmouth Coll., 1953; JD, U. Mich., 1956. Bar: Iowa 1956, Ill. 1964, Mich. 1980. Assoc. Clewell Cooney & Fuerste, 1960-64; ptnr. Nelson Stapleton & Ernst, Stapleton & Ernst, Stapleton Ernst & Sprengelmeyer, East Dubuque, Ill., Nelson Stapleton & Ernst & Sprengelmeyer, Dubuque, Iowa, 1964-79; pvt. practice Dubuque, 1979-80; ptnr. Ernst & Cody, Dubuque, 1981-84, Daniel P. Ernst, P.C., Dubuque, 1984-90, Vincent Roth & Ernst, P.C., Galena, Ill., 1991; pub. defender State of Iowa, Dubuque, 1991-96; pvt. practice Dubuque, 1997—. U.S. trustee 1979-91. Capt. USAF, 1957-60, U.S. Coast Guard Aux. Mem. ABA, Iowa State Bar Assn. (bd. govs. 1985-89), Dubuque County Bar Assn. (2d v.p. 1979-80, 1st v.p. 1980-81, pres. 1981-82), Ill. State Bar Assn., Jo Daviess County Bar Assn., State Bar Assn. Mich., Grand Traverse-Leelanau-Antrim Bar Assn. Democrat. Avocations: swimming, boating. Office: Attorney-at-Law 899 Mount Carmel Rd Dubuque IA 52003-7946 Fax: 563-582-0324. E-mail: ernstdan@mchsi.com.

ERNST, EDWARD WILLIS, retired electrical engineering educator; b. Great Falls, Mont., Aug. 28, 1924; s. Paul Wilson and Grace Vio (Woodmore) E.; m. Helen Kitty Todd, Jan. 29, 1950 (dec. Mar. 1975); children: Deborah Kitty, Thomas Edward (dec.); m. Margaret Frances Patton, Sept. 13, 1975 (dec. Feb. 2002); children: Alan Harmon, Ruth Margaret, Betty Carol; m. Barbara Allen Moye, Apr. 26, 2003. BS, U. Ill., 1949, MS, 1950, PhD, 1955. Rsch. engr. GE, Syracuse, N.Y., 1955, Stewart-Warner, Chgo., 1955-58; assoc. prof. U. Ill., Urbana, 1958-68, prof., 1968-89, assoc. head elec. engring., 1970-85, assoc. dean engring., 1985-89; Allied-Signal prof. engring. U. S.C., Columbia, 1990-2000, ret., 2000. Program dir. NSF, Washington, 1987-90; chmn. Engring. Accreditation Commn., Accreditation Bd. for Engring. Tech., N.Y.C., 1985-86, pres., 1989-90. Pres. Mckinley Found., Champaign, Ill. 1968-72. Recipient Linton Grinter award Accreditation Bd. Engring. and Tech., 1992. Fellow IEEE (v.p. 1981-82, Centennial medal 1984, EAB Meritorious Achievement award in accreditation activities 1985), AAAS, ABET, Internat. Engring. Consortium (bd. dirs.), Am. Soc. for Engring. Edn. (editor Jour. Engring. Edn. 1992-96). Presbyterian. Avocations: photography, hiking, reading. E-mail: ernst@engr.sc.edu.

ERNST, JOHN ALLAN, clinical neuropsychologist; b. Seattle, June 27, 1955; s. Gene Allan and Maxine Joan (Weedon) Ernst. BA magna cum laude, U. Calif., San Diego, 1977; MS, San Diego State U., 1979; PhD, U. Mont., 1983. Diplomate Am. Bd. Clin. Neuropsychology, Am. Bd. Profl. Psychology, lic. psychologist Wash. Postdoctoral fellow U. Wash., Seattle, 1983-84; psychologist Western State Hosp., Lakewood, Wash., 1984-85; postdoctoral rsch. fellow U. Queensland, Brisbane, Australia, 1985-87; neuropsychologist St. Joseph Med. Ctr., Tacoma, 1987—. Mem. Wash. State Exam. Bd. Psychology, 1995—2000. Contbr. articles to profl. jours.; mem. editl. bd. Rehab. Psychology and Aging, SCI Psychosocial Process, 1994—98. Mem.: others, Pacific N.W. Neuropsychological Soc. (pres. 2001—02), Nat. Acad. Neuropsychology, Internat. Neuropsychological Soc., Am. Acad. Clin. Neuropsychology. Avocations: music appreciation, art appreciation. Office: Saint Joseph Med Ctr Dept Psychology PO Box 2197 Tacoma WA 98401-2197 E-mail: johnaernst@chiwest.com.

ERNST, JOHN LOUIS, management consultant; b. Pine Bluff, Ark., Dec. 24, 1932; s. Albert C. and Christine (Vinent) E.; m. Lois R. Geraci, June 12, 1971; children: Ann Marie, Catherine Teresa, Laura Elizabeth, Christine Margaret. BS, Spring Hill Coll., Mobile, Ala., 1954; postgrad., Georgetown U. Law Sch., 1956-57. Stockbroker Washington Planning Co., 1957-58; pub. rels.-sales exec. Am. Airlines, Washington, Phila. and N.Y.C., 1958-62; account exec. Ted Bates Advt. Agy., N.Y.C., 1962-65; sr. v.p., mgmt. dir. Marschalk Advt. Agy., N.Y.C., 1965-68; dir. Interpub. Svc. Corp., 1967-69; sr. v.p., mng. dir. McCann-Erickson Advt. Agy., N.Y.C., 1969-70; pres. Ernst-Van Praag, N.Y.C., 1970-75; chmn. bd. A.V.E. Corp., N.Y.C., 1974-75, Advt. to Women, Inc., N.Y.C., 1975-86; pres. Bellvinent Communications, Inc., N.Y.C., 1986—, Art Vault Internat., N.Y.C., 1996—. Capt. USMC, 1954-57. Mem. Amyotrophic Lateral Sclerosis (Lou Gehrig's Disease) Assn. (chmn. bd. dirs., CEO Greater N.Y.C. chpt. 1997—), Players Club. Address: 20 Monroe Ave Spring Lake NJ 07762-1717

ERNST, KATHRYN FITZGERALD, management, marketing consulting firm executive, author; b. N.Y.C., Nov. 12, 1942; d. Joseph Michael and Helen Ann (Dougherty) Fitzgerald; m. John Lyman Ernst, Dec. 7, 1971 (div. Apr. 1977). BA in Econs., Wells Coll., Aurora, N.Y., 1963; postgrad N.Y. U., 1964. Portfolio analyst Donaldson, Lufkin & Jenrette, N.Y.C., 1966-68; asst. v.p. Prentice-Hall, Englewood Cliffs, N.J., 1968-74; v.p. Franklin Watts/Grolier, N.Y.C., 1975-77; mktg. mgr. ITT, N.Y.C., 1977-80; mng. dir. Warburg, Paribas Becker, N.Y.C., 1980-82; pres., owner Ernst Assocs., Inc., N.Y.C., 1982—. Author: Danny and His Thumb, 1972, Mr. Tamerin's Trees, 1978 (Nat. Sci. Tchrs. award 1979), Owl's New Cards, 1979 (ALA-Children's Choice award 1980), Charlie's Pets, 1980, Indians: The First Americans, 1981, ESP McGee & The Mysterious Magician, 1984, The Complete Calorie and Carbohydrate Counters for Dining Out, 1987. Bd. dirs. Cmty. Svc. Coun. Greater Harlem. Recipient Outstanding Achievement award Fed. Govt., 1966, Pub. Achievement award Christopher Soc., 1973, Acad. Women Achievers YWCA, 1979. Mem. Direct Mktg. Assn. (Echo award 1985). Avocations: bridge, chess, golf, modern art, jazz. Home: 333 E 53rd St New York NY 10022-4911

ERNST, MARK A. diversified financial services company executive; m. Annette Ernst; two children. Degree in Acctg. & Fin. summa cum laude, Drake U.; MBA, U. Chgo. With tax, investment and corp. adv. svcs. dept. Coopers & Lybrand; v.p., gen. mgr. tax and bus. svcs. divsn. Am. Express Co., Mpls., sr. v.p. workplace fin. svcs., sr. v.p.; exec. v.p., COO H&R Block, Inc., 1998-99, pres., COO, 1999—, also bd. dirs. Office: H&R Block 4400 Main St Kansas City MO 64111-1812

ERNST, RALPH AMBROSE, poultry specialist; b. Saline, Mich., July 5, 1938; s. Ambrose William and Catherine (Prosser) E.; m. Patricia F. Ernst, Feb. 20, 1988. BS in Agrl. Edn., Mich. State U., 1959, MS in Poultry Sci., 1963, PhD in Poultry Sci., 1966. Rschr., tchg. asst. Mich. State U., East Lansing, 1961-66; poultry specialist U. Calif., Davis, 1966—. Mem. Calif. Assn. Farm Advisors and Specialists, Poultry Sci. Assn. (bd. dirs. 1985-86, newsletter editor 1986-91, Extension award 1978), World Poultry Sci. Assn., Coun. Agrl. Sci. & Tech., Alpha Zeta Office: Univ Calif Dept Animal Sci Davis CA 95616 E-mail: raernst@ucdavis.edu.

ERNST, RICHARD ROBERT, chemist, educator; b. Winterthur, Zurich, Switzerland, Aug. 14, 1933; s. Robert and Irma (Brunner) E.; m. Magdalena Kielholz, Oct. 9, 1963; children: Anna Magdalena, Katharina Elisabeth, Hans-Martin Walter. Diploma Chemistry, ETH Zurich, 1956, DSc in Tech., 1962; PhD (hon.), ETH-Lausanne, Switzerland, 1986, Technische Hochschule, Munich, 1989, U. Zurich, 1994, U. Antwerp, 1997, U. Cluj-Napoca, 1998, U. Montpellier, 1999; PhD (hon.), Charles U., Prague, 2002. Scientist ETH-Zurich, 1962-63, privatdozent, 1968-70, asst. prof., 1970-72, assoc. prof., 1973-76, prof., 1976—; scientist Varian Assocs., Palo Alto, Calif., 1963-68. Cons. Spectrospin AG, Fällanden, Switzerland, 1978—, v.p. bd. dirs. Numerous inventions, patents in field. 1st lt. ACS-Dienst, 1953-88, Swiss mil. Recipient Silver medal ETH-Zurich, 1962, Ruzicka prize, 1968, Gold medal Soc. Magnetic Resonance in Medicine, San Francisco, 1983, Benoist prize Swiss Fedn. Confedn., Berne, 1986, Kirkwood award Yale U., 1989, Ampere prize, 1990, Wolf prize in chemistry, 1991, Louisa Gross Horwitz prize Columbia U., 1991, Nobel prize in chemistry, 1991, award for Achievements in Magnetic Resonance EAS, 1992. Mem. NAS (India), Deutsche Akademie Leopoldina, Acad. Europaea, Schweizerische Chemische Gesellschaft, Royal Soc. London, Österreichische Gesellschaft für Analytische Chemie, Am. Phys. Soc., U.S. Nat. Acad. Sci., Am. Acad. Arts and Scis., Schweizerische Akademie d. Tech. Wiss., Russian Acad. Scis. Avocations: tibetan art, music. Office: Lab F Phys Chem ETH-Hongerberg 8093 Zurich Switzerland

ERNST, ROGER, international studies educator, consultant; b. N.Y.C., June 2, 1924; s. Morris L. and Marguerite (Samuels) E.; m. Jean O'Mara, Mar. 15, 1952; children: Deborah, David. BA cum laude, Williams Coll., 1948; german fgn. area and lang. study, U. Md., 1944; grad., Nat. War Coll., 1956. Austria desk officer Marshall Plan State Dept., 1948-50; asst. dir NATO, Dept. Def., 1950-55; asst. dir. planning Dept. Def., 1956-59; mem. staff President's Com. Study Fgn. Aid Program, 1958-59; joined U.S. Fgn. Svc., 1959; asst. dir. AID mission to India, 1959-62; rep. Peace Corps in India, 1961-62; dep. dir. AID mission to China, 1962-64, AID mission to Korea, 1964-68; dir., econ. minister AID mission to Ethiopia, 1968-73; dir.-minister AID mission to Thailand, Bangkok, 1973-76; spl. cons. to adminstr. tech. applications Tech. Assistance Bur., AID, Washington, 1976-77; coord. So. African devel. analysis Bur. for Africa, 1977-78, U. Hawaii Coll. Tropical Agr., Honolulu, 1978-80, Small Island States in So. Pacific; cons. on devel., 1980—; pres. Devel. Consultancy Internat., Inc., 1982-86; vis. fellow, lectr. on Asian affairs East-West Ctr., Hawaii, 1985-98. Lectr. cruise ships, 1989-96; mem. sr. adv. com. Vector Borne Disease and Control Project AID, 1990—; adj. prof. Internat. Studies Program, U. South Fla., Tampa, 1994-2001. Asst. sec. U.S. Group Control Coun., Berlin, 1946-47; vol. Jr. Achievement instr. Tampa Bay area elem., middle and high schs., lectr. Elder Hostels, 2000-, Capt. AUS, 1943-47. Decorated Bronze Star; Civic Merit medal Republic of Korea; recipient William A. Jump award for exemplary pub. service. Mem. Nantucket Hist. Assn. Lodges: Rotary. Home: 9176 Highland Ridge Way Tampa FL 33647-2277 *Success comes from: good preparation; "no indecision, no regret" when taking action; "catching the tide"; Having "fun" while doing; Being experimental and able to correlate the unrelated elements in a situation. Management succeeds when managers focus on directing people's energies, not money nor physical resources which are finite.*

ERNST, WALLACE GARY, geology educator; b. St. Louis, Mo., Dec. 14, 1931; BA, Carleton Coll., 1953; MS, U. Minn., 1955; PhD, Johns Hopkins U., 1959. Geologist U.S. Geol. Survey, Washington, 1955-56; fellow (Geophys. Lab.), Washington, 1956-59; mem. faculty UCLA, 1960-89, prof. geology and geophysics, 1968-89, chmn. geology dept. (now earth and space scis. dept.), 1970-74, 78-82, dir. Inst. Geophysics and Planetary Physics, 1987-89; dean Stanford Sch. of Earth Scis., 1989-94; prof. geol. and environ. scis. Stanford (Calif.) U., 1989—, Benjamin M. Page prof., 1999—, dean Sch. of Earth Scis., 1989-94. Author: Amphiboles, 1968, Earth Materials, 1969, Metamorphism and Plate Tectonic Regimes, 1975, Subduction Zone Metamorphism, 1975, Petrologic Phase Equilibria, 1976, The Geotectonic Development of California, 1981, The Environment of the Deep Sea, 1982, Energy for Ourselves and Our Posterity, 1985, Cenozoic Basin Development of Coastal California, 1987, Metamorphic and Crustal Evolution of the Western Cordillera, 1988, The Dynamic Planet, 1990, Integrated Earth and Environmental Evolution of the Southwestern United States, 1998, Planetary Petrology and Geochemistry, 1999; editor: Earth Systems: Processes and Issues, 2000, (with R.G. Coleman) Tectonic Studies of Asia and the Pacific Rim--A Tribute to Benjamin M. Page, 2000, (with J.G. Liou) Ultrahigh-Pressure Metamorphism and Geodynamics in Collision-Type Orogenic Belts, 2000. Trustee Carnegie Instn. of Washington, 1990—. Recipient Miyashiro medal Geol. Soc. Japan, 1998. Mem. NAS (chmn. geology sect. 1979-82, chair class I 2000—), AAAS, Am. Philos. Soc., Am. Geophys. Union, Am. Geol. Inst., Geol. Soc. Am. (pres. 1985-86), Am. Acad. Arts and Sci., Geochem. Soc., Mineral Soc. Am. (recipient award 1969, pres. 1979-80). Office: Stanford U Dept Earth & Environ Scis Green Earth Sci #209 Palo Alto CA 94303-1823

ERNSTEIN, JULIE H. archaeologist, educator, researcher; b. Washington, D.C., July 3, 1962; d. Edith Ellis and Dennis N. Hevener; m. Alan D. Ernstein, July 10, 1982. BA in Anthropoloy, U. Md., 1984; MA in Archaeology, Boston U., 1987. Lectr. anthropology, faculty rschr. U. Md., College Park, 1987—, project/staff archaeologist, 1987—90; prin. investigator, project archaeologist, and project oral historian Rsch. Project Administered through Coop. Agreement between U. of Md. and City of Bowie Museums, College Park, 1999—2002. Archaeologist, historian Balt. Ctr. Urban Archaeology/Balt. City Life Mus., 1991—93; program asst, outreach coord. Martin Marietta Grad. Fellows Program, Balt., 1992—95; mem. gov.'s cons. com. nat. register hist. places Md. Hist. Trust, Crownsville, 1998—; archaeology/preservation cons Ctr. for

History Now, Haddonfield, NJ, 1998—2000; mem. landscape adv. panel Corp. for Jefferson's Poplar Forest, Forest, Va., 1999—; archaeology/preservation cons. Ea. Shore Heritage, Inc., Chestertown, Md., 2003—; lectr. sociology-anthropology Washington Coll., Chestertown, 2003—. Contbr. chapters to books, articles and reviews. Fellow, Boston U., 1984—85, Assn. Field Archaeology, 1985—87. Mem.: Soc. Indsl. Archeology, Soc. Hist. Archaeology, Recent Past Preservation Network (sec., bd. mem. 2002—), Preservation Md., Nat. Trust Hist. Preservation, Md. Heritage Alliance (sec. 2002—), Coun. NE Hist. Archaeology, Coun. Md. Archeology (v.p., pres. 1998—2002), Archeol. Soc. Md., Lambda Alpha, Omicron Delta Kappa, Phi Beta Kappa, Alpha Phi Omega. Home: 4115 Rainier Ave Mount Rainier MD 20712-1740 Office: Dept Anthropology Univ Md College Park MD 20742 Office Fax: 301-314-8305. E-mail: jernst@anth.umd.edu.

ERNZEN, MARY ANNE, women's health nurse, clinical nurse specialist; m. Phillip Ernzen; children: Becky, Ted. BSN magna cum laude, Wichita State U., 1986, MSN, 1991. Cert. childbirth educator; cert. in ambulatory women's health. Clin. nurse specialist, dir. patient edn./patient educator for assocs. in women's health, Wichita; mgr. post-partum home visit program birth ctr. planning com. Wesley Med. Ctr., Wichita. Lectr. in transcultural nursing; rschr. post partum adaptation; adj. faculty Wichita State U. Dept. Nursing, Braille Transcription Svcs., Am. Red Cross; breast feeding educator Birth Enhancement, Inc. Contbr. articles to profl. jours. Trustee Kans. Found. Vision Awareness; braille transcriber ARC; reader Wichita Radio Svc. for the Blind. Mem. AWHONN, ASPO, ICEA, Transcultural Nursing Soc., Assistance League Wichita, Sigma Theta Tau, Phi Kappa Phi.

ERON, LEONARD DAVID, psychology educator; b. Newark, Apr. 22, 1920; s. Joseph I. and Sarah (Hilfman) E.; m. Madeline Marcus, Mar. 21, 1950; children: Joan Hobson, Don, Barbara Christensen. BS, CCNY, 1941; MA, Columbia U., 1946; PhD, U. Wis., 1949. Diplomate Am. Bd. Profl. Psychology. Asst. prof. psychology and psychiatry Yale U., New Haven, 1948-55; dir. research Rip Van Winkle Found., 1955-62; prof. psychology U. Iowa, Iowa City, 1962-69; research prof. U. Ill.-Chgo., 1969-89; emeritus rsch. prof. of the social sci. in psychology, 1989—; rsch. scientist prof. psychology Inst. for Social Rsch., U. Mich., Ann Arbor, 1992—. Author 8 books, editor Jour. Abnormal Psychology, 1973-80; assoc. editor Am. Psychologist, 1986-90; contbr. numerous articles to profl. jours. Served to 1st lt. AUS, 1942-45 Fulbright lectr., Free U. Amsterdam, 1967-68; recipient Fulbright Sr. Scholar award, Queensland U., Australia, 1976-77, James McKeen Cattell Sabbatical award, U. Rome, 1984-85. Fellow AAAS, Am. Psychol. Assn. (chair commn. violence and youth 1991-93, Disting. Contbns. to Knowledge award 1980, Gold medal award for Life Contbn. to Psychology in the Pub. Interest 1995), Am. Orthopsychiat. Assn.; mem. Midwestern Psychol. Assn. (pres. 1985-86), Internat. Soc. for Rsch. in Aggression (pres. 1989-90). Office: U Mich Inst for Social Rsch 426 Thompson St Ann Arbor MI 48104-2321 E-mail: lderon@umich.edu.

EROSH, WILLIAM DANIEL, advertising executive; b. N.Y.C., Feb. 8, 1956; s. Walter William and Dorothy Irene (Ricci) E.; m. Violet A. Payton; children: Pamela, Justin. BS in Econs., Wagner Coll., 1978. CPA, N.Y. Staff acct. Henry F. Malarkey and Co., CPA's, N.Y.C., 1977-79; sr. acct. Perel Smolin and Co., CPA's, N.Y.C., 1979-81; tax supr. Deloitte Haskins and Sells, CPAs, N.Y.C., 1981-84; asst. v.p., dir. tax compliance 1st Boston Corp., N.Y.C., 1984-87; 1st v.p., contr., dir. taxes Security Capital Corp., N.Y.C., 1987-90; prin. Ernst & Young, N.Y.C., 1990-95; v.p. corp. fin. E.D.&F. Man, Inc., N.Y.C., 1995-98; sr. v.p. E.D.&F. Man Global Markets, N.Y.C., 1998-99; sr. v.p. dir. acctg. Saatchi & Saatchi, N.Y.C., 1999-2000; CFO Healthcare Resources Group, Inc., N.Y.C., 2000—. Mem. AICPA Republican. Roman Catholic. Avocations: golf, scuba diving. Home: 74 Main St Holmdel NJ 07733-2344 Office: Healthcare Resources Group Inc 375 Hudson St New York NY 10014 E-mail: werosh@bellatlantic.net.

ERRAMPALLI, DEENA, molecular plant pathologist, researcher; b. Machilipatnam, India, Mar. 7, 1958; arrived in Can., 1992; d. Stephen Devadatham and Mary Bharathi (Kondaveti) E.; m. Andrew Robert Piggott, June 19, 1993. BS, Andhra U., India, 1976; MS, Banaras Hindu U., India, 1979; PhD, Okla. State U., 1990. Rsch. assoc. Internat. Crops Rsch. Inst. for the Semi Arid Tropics, Andhra Pradesh, India, 1980-84; rsch. asst. Okla. State U., Stillwater, 1985-89, tchg. asst., 1985, postdoctoral rsch. assoc., 1989-92; postdoctoral rsch. fellow U. Toronto, 1992-95; rsch. molecular biologist U. Guelph, Ont., Can., 1995-97; rsch. scientist So. Crop Protection and Food Rsch. Ctr., Agr. and Agri-Food Can., Vineland Station, Ont., 1998—. Mem. editl. bd. for dictionary Can. Soc. Soil Sci., 1998-2000; contbr. more than 82 articles to profl. jours., books, popular agrl. mags., confs. and workshops. Mem. Social Svc. League, Vijayawada, India, 1973-76. Electron Microscopy grantee Okla. State U., 1986-89. Mem. Am. Phytopath. Soc. (co-moderator 1986), Can. Phytopath. Soc., Okla. Acad. Sci., Sigma Xi. Mem. United Ch. of Can. Avocations: water color painting, cooking. Office: Agr & Agri-Food Can POB 6000, 4902 Victoria Ave Vineland Station ON Canada L0R 2E0

ERRINGTON, NORMAN, television producer, photographer; b. Middlesbrough, Yorkshire, England, Nov. 13, 1936; s. Nathan Errington and Ruth Havercroft; 1 child, Mark. Leading aircraftsman RAF/ Fighter Command, Leeming, England, 1951—54; mng. dir. Mark Printing Co., Middlesbrough, England, 1954—60; pres. Vistavision TV Prodn., Tampa Bay, Fla., 1961—78; photo journalist New Port Richey Press, New Port Richey, Fla., 1978—84; tv prodr. Telemart Programming & Prodn., Bayonet Point, Fla., 1993—. Publisher: TV Today, 1986; prodr.: (TV series) What's New, 1989; (TV films) In Search of.The Fountain of Youth, 1984; author: One Life Less Ordinary, A Memoir, 2002. Founder, pres. Brit. Am. Assn., Tampa Bay, Fla., 1986—90. With Fighter Command Royal Air Force, 1954—57, England. Master: Freemasons (25 yr. pin 1998). Avocations: world war 2 historian, travel. Office: Norman Errington TV Productions Box 34669 Bayonet Point FL 34669 Home Fax: 727-863-2871. Personal E-mail: NormanErrington@aol.com. Business E-Mail: NormanErrington@aol.com.

ERSEK, GREGORY JOSEPH MARK, lawyer, business administrator; b. Cleve., Aug. 30, 1956; s. Joseph Francis and Mary H. (Hurchanik) E. AB, Columbia U., 1977; MBA, U. Pa., 1979; JD, U. Fla., 1984; cert. cir. civil mediator, Fla. Internat. U., 1998. Bar: Fla. 1986, U.S. Dist. Ct. (so. dist.) Fla. 1987. Cons. fin. valuation Am. Appraisal Co., Princeton, N.J., 1979-80; mgr. import-export Marie L. Veslie Co., Coral Gables, Fla., 1980-85; assoc. Lunny, Tucker, Karns & Brescher, Ft. Lauderdale, Fla., 1986; dir. legal dept. Horizons Rsch. Labs. Inc., Ft. Lauderdale, 1986-89, sr. corp. planner, 1988-89; gen. counsel Unisco Corp., Ft. Lauderdale, 1989-93, TRICORD Corp., Ft. Lauderdale, 1990-93, Irish Times, Inc., Ft. Lauderdale, 1993-97; dir. corp. fin. dept. & sr. corp. counsel Canton Fin. Svcs. Corp., subs. Cyber Am. Corp., Salt Lake City, 1995-96; gen. counsel Greenstreet Capital Corp., Investment Bankers, Las Vegas, 1996-99, Gaelic Pub. Devel., Inc., Ft. Lauderdale, 1998—, Premier Fin. Corp., Jacksonville, 1998—. Sec.-treas. Sorkar Group, Inc., Ft. Lauderdale, 1987-89; CEO Am. CompuShopper, Inc., 1989-98; with legal dept. Pfizer Inc., NYC, 1983; co-founder, mgr. Poland/US Trade and Mktg. Consortium, 1989—; pres. Corp. Exec. with Spinal Cord Injury, 2002—; sec. Dir. Pub. Co. with Spinal Cord Injury, 2002—; mem. Philip C. Jessup Internat. Moot Ct. team, 1983; gen. counsel Biltmore Vacation Resorts, Inc., f/k/a Cyber Info., Inc., Las Vegas, 1997-99, Avalon Group, Inc., Cedar Rapids, Iowa, 1997-99. Editor Medscanner, med. industry newsletter, 1987-89. Mem. venture coun. forum; alumnus Internat. House, N.Y.C., 1984. Mem. Fla. Bar Assn., Nat. Assn. Securities Dealers (nat. arbitration com. 1991-98), Assn. Attys. with Disabilities (exec. dir. 2002—), Coun. on Fgn. Rels. (local com.), Corp. Execs. with Spinal Cord Injury (pres. 2002—), Dirs. Pub. Co. with Spinal Cord Injury (sec. 2002—), Wharton Club South Fla. Avocations: travel, books. Home and Office: 17820 NW 18th Ave Miami Gardens FL 33056-4949

ERSEK, ROBERT ALLEN, plastic surgeon, inventor; b. Ridley Twp., Pa., June 19, 1938; s. Joseph Martin and Theda Louise (Kromes) E.; m. Gerry Avenelle Mullins, Mar. 28, 1958; children: Stephanie Louise, Cynthia Leigh. BS, Morris Harvey Coll., 1961; MD, Hahnemann Med. Coll., 1966. Diplomate Nat. Bd. Med. Examiners; cert. Am. Bd. Plastic Surgery. Intern surgery U. Minn. Hosps., Mpls., 1966-67; research fellow U. Pa., 1962, Hahnemann Med. Coll., Phila., 1963-65; med. fellow dept. surgery U. Minn., 1967-73; resident dept. plastic and reconstructive surgery Tulane U., New Orleans, 1975-77; fellow in plastic surgery U. Miss., Jackson, 1978; clin. instr. plastic surgery U. Tex. Health Sci. Center, San Antonio, 1979. Chmn. bd., dir. Med. Gen. Inc., 1969— ; dir., med. dir. Genetic Labs., 1970—, Emerald Airlines, Inc.; chmn. bd. Remedco, 1980— ; bd. dirs., med. dir. Genetic Labs Wound Care; chmn. Personique Inc., 1996; bd. dirs. Plastic Surgery Co.; dean Lipoplasy Univ. Author: Pain Control, 1981; Co-editor: Organ Perfusion and Preservation, 1969; contbr. articles to med. jours.; patentee numerous surg. devices. Bd. dirs. Austin Civic Ballet. Served to maj. USAF, 1973-75. Recipient Alan Edelsohn prize Hahnemann Med. Coll., 1966; Grand award for exhibit Student Am. Med. Assn. Squibb Nat. Contest, 1967; award of excellence in med. writing Minn. Medicine, 1970 Fellow ACS; mem. AMA, AAUP, NAS, Am. Coll. Emergency Physicians, La. Med. Soc., Soc. for Cryosurgery, Am. Soc. Plastic and Reconstructive Surgeons, Am. Soc. Artificial Internal Organs, Am. Med. Writers Assn., Smithsonian Inst., Nat. Assn., Flying Physicians, Am. Trauma Soc., Tex. Med. Assn., Travis County Med. Soc., Am. Burn Assn., Lipoplasty Soc. N.Am. (bd. dirs.), Serpent Soc., Aesculpulation Soc., Austin Knights of Symphony (chmn. Personique Inc. 1996), Phi Kappa Delta. Office: 630 W 34th St Austin TX 78705-1229 E-mail: ersek@ensek.com.

ERSGAARD, OLE KRISTIAN, marketing and management consultant, business developer; b. Copenhagen, Sept. 9, 1948; s. Poul V. and Aase K. (Agenskov) E.; m. Liselotte Larsen; June 21, 1993; 1 child, Joachim. Diploma in pub. relations, NKI, Stockholm, 1971; Diploma in Mktg., Danish Comml. Colls., Cph., (now Niels Brock Copenhagen Bus. Coll.), 1975; postgrad., Danish Coll. Commerce, London, 1979, London Sch. Fgn. Trade, 1981, London Poly., 1982, DMC/INSEAD France, 1988-89; cert. in Art History, U. Copenhagen, 1998; cert. in Adult Tchrs. Edn., Ctr. for Higher Edn., Denmark, 2003. Erhvervsoekonom MDM Danish profl. bus. qualification, 1980; cert. bus. economist, 1986. Comml. trainee, advt. and mktg. trainee, advt. coord. and mktg. adv. various comml. enterprises and advt. agencies, Denmark, 1966-76; advt. mgr. (worldwide) Ostermann Petersen Bros. Ltd., Denmark, 1977-79; group advt. mgr. IN-WEAR A/S, Denmark, 1979-82; group mktg. dir. Carli Gry Internat. A/S, Denmark, 1983-84; mgmt. cons. Denmark, 1984—. Dep. gov. Am. Biog. Inst. (life), mem. editl. adv. bd., 1992—; dep. dir. gen. (life) Internat. Biog. Ctr., Cambridge, Eng., 1994—. Contbr. articles to profl. jours. Mem. Think-Tank Centre Democrates, 1990-92; adviser Coun. Danish Merc. Assn., 1991-96. Recipient Internat. Cultural diploma. Fellow Australian Inst. Coordinated Rsch. (life); mem. Inst. des Hautes Etudes Economiques et Sociales Belgium (hon.), Inst. Dirs., Danish Merc. Assn (chmn. bd. region south br. 1989-91), Soc. of Futurology, Assn. of Book Workmanship-The Graphic Arts Inst. Denmark, Danish European Movement (chmn. bd. West Zealand br. 2001—, bd. dirs. 2001—). Home: Vedelsgade 9 DK-4180 Soro Denmark

ERSHLER, WILLIAM BALDWIN, biogerontologist, educator; b. Syracuse, N.Y., Jan. 13, 1949; s. Irving Leonard and Eunice (Baldwin) E.; m. Joan Lipstein, Nov. 6, 1971; children: Rachel Eve, Leah Rose. BA, Case Western Res. U., 1970; MD, SUNY Upstate Ctr., Syracuse, 1974. Diplomate Am. Bd. Internal Medicine, Am. Bd. Med. Oncology, Am. Bd. Hematology. Asst. prof. U. Vt., Burlington, 1980-85; assoc. prof. U. Wis., Madison, 1985-89, prof. medicine, 1989-96, dir. U. Wis. Inst. on Aging, 1989-96, head geriatrics, 1989-96; dir. geriatric rsch. Edn. and Clin. Ctr. William Middleton VA Hosp., Madison, 1991-96; prof. medicine, dir. Glennan Ctr. Geriatrics & gerontolog Eastern Va. Medical Sch., Norfolk, 1996-97; dir. Inst. Advanced Studies in Aging and Geriatric Medicine, Washington, 1998—, Nat. Geriatrics Rsch. Consortium, 1998—; rsch. edn. dir. Extended Care Info. Network, 1999—. Dir. Geriatric Oncology Consortium, 2001—. Editor Jour. Gerontology, 1996-2000; contbr. articles to profl. jours. Recipient Geriatric Leadership award NIH, 1990-96; NIH grantee, 1989—. Fellow Gerontologic Soc. Am.; mem. Am. Geriatrics Soc., Am. Assn. Cancer Rsch., Am. Soc. Clin. Oncology, Am. Soc. Hematology, Assn. Dirs. Acad. Geriatrics (councilor). Jewish. Avocations: running, photography, travel. Office: 1700 Wisconsin Ave NW Washington DC 20007 E-mail: wershler@iasia.org.

ERSKINE, JAMES LORENZO, physics educator; b. Seattle, Oct. 25, 1942; s. Lawrence A. and Elizabeth (Woodbury) E.; m. Julie Ann Grant; children: Michael Grant, John Lawrence. BSEE, U. Wash., 1964, MSEE, 1966, PhD in Physics, 1973. Sr. engr. and cons. Boeing Co., Seattle, 1967-74; rsch. asst. prof. dept. physics U. Ill., Urbana, 1974-77; asst. prof. dept. physics U. Tex., Austin, 1977-82, assoc. prof., 1982-86, prof., 1986—. Trull Centennial prof. Trull Found. U. Tex., 1986. Contbr. numerous articles in fields of solid state physics, magnetism and magnetic materials, surface physics, surface chemistry, and instrumentation. Grantee NSF, R.A. Welch Found., other fed. and pvt. agys. Fellow Am. Phys. Soc.; mem. Am. Vacuum Soc. Office: U Tex Grad Sch Dept Of Physics Austin TX 78712

ERSKINE, JOHN MORSE, surgeon; b. San Francisco, Sept. 10, 1920; s. Morse and Dorothy (Ward) E. BS, Harvard U., 1942, MD, 1945. Diplomate Am. Bd. Surgery. Surg. intern U. Calif. Hosp., San Francisco, 1945-46; surg. researcher Mass. Gen. Hosp., Boston, 1948; resident in surgery Peter Bent Brigham Hosp., Boston, 1948-53; George Gorham Peters fellow St. Mary's Hosp., London, 1952; pvt. practice in medicine specializing in surgery San Francisco, 1954-98; asst. clin. prof. Stanford Med. Sch., San Francisco, 1956-59; asst., assoc. clin. prof. U. Calif. Med. Sch., San Francisco, 1959—. Surg. cons. San Francisco Vets. Hosp., 1959-73. Contbr. articles to profl. jours., chpts. to books. Founder No. Calif. Artery Bank, 1954-58, Irwin Meml. Blood Bank, San Francisco, commr., pres., 1969-74; bd. dirs. People for Open Space-Greenbelt Alliance, 1984-98, adv. coun., 1998—; chmn. adv. coun. Dorothy Erskine Open Space Fund. Capt. with U.S. Army, 1946-48. Fellow ACS; mem. San Francisco Med. Soc. (bd. dirs. 1968-72), San Francisco Surg. Soc. (v.p. 1984), Pacific Coast Surg. Assn., Am. Cancer Soc. (bd. dirs. San Francisco br. 1965-75), Calif. Med. Assn., Olympic Club, Sierra Club. Democrat. Unitarian Universalist. Avocations: mountaineering, tree farming, garden work, walking, reading. Home and Office: 233 Chestnut St San Francisco CA 94133-2452 E-mail: johnmerskine@aol.com.

ERSKINE, KALI (WENDY COLMAN), psychoanalyst; b. Flushing, N.Y., July 6, 1950; d. Leo M. and Ray (Fine) Colman BS, Tufts U., 1972; MA, NYU, 1977, PhD in Occupational Therapy, 1984; postgrad., Phila. Sch. of Psychoanalysis, 1988-92. Cert. psychoanalyst. Occupational therapist Extended Family Ctr., San Francisco, 1973-74; cons. child abuse San Francisco, 1974-75; sr. occupational therapist Roosevelt Hosp., N.Y.C., 1975-77; adj. instr. occupational therapy dept. NYU, N.Y.C., 1977-80; asst. prof. occupational therapy dept. Boston U., 1980-83; dir. grad. edn. occupational therapy, dept. assoc. prof. Temple U., Phila., 1984-87; cons. curriculum design Kean Coll. N.J., Union, 1985-88; cons. spl. projects, vice provost for rsch.- grad. studies Temple U., Phila., 1987-88; evaluation rsch. coord. Nat. Inst. Adolescent Pregnancy, Phila., 1986-90; pvt. practice psychotherapy and psychoanalysis, 1988—. Tng. and supervising analyst Phila. Sch. of Psychoanalysis. Editor VAPS Aviso newsletter, 1998-2000; contbr. articles to profl. jours. and texts in occupl. therapy and psychoanalysis (under names Wendy Colman and Kali Erskine). Fellow Am. Occupl. Therapy Assn.; mem. APA (Divsn. psychoanalysis), Nat. Assn. Advancement Psychoanalysis, Vt. Assn. for Psychoanalytic Studies, Soc. Phila. Sch. Psychoanalysis. Achievements include being first person to earn doctorate in occupational therapy. Office: Montpelier Psychoanalytic Group 201 Kildrummy Way Montpelier VT 05602 E-mail: ccpsygal.ke@verizon.net.

ERSKINE, WILLIAM CRAWFORD, academic administrator, accountant, health facility administrator; b. Seattle, Feb. 29, 1924; s. Alwin Crawford and Emilie Hildred (Davies) E.; m. Mary Jean Hopkins, Feb. 28, 1946; children: Scott Crawford, Nancy Page. BA in Bus. Adminstrn., U. Wash., 1950. CPA, Wash. Auditor Arthur Andersen & Co., 1950-54; sr. auditor Ansell Johnson & Co., CPAs, Seattle, 1956-59; contr. Food Giant Stores, Seattle, 1959-64; comptr. U. Wash., Seattle, 1964-70; v.p. bus. U. Colo., Boulder, 1970-74; exec. v.p. U. Nebr. system, Lincoln, 1974-80; v.p. bus. affairs U. Tex., El Paso, 1980-88; ret., 1988. Dir. West Tex. Higher Edn. Authority, El Paso, 1982-88, Sunwest Bank El Paso, 1986-96, Providence Hosp. P.H.A., Inc., 1994-96; cons. Educator Cons. Panel GAO, 1978-86. Treas. St. Francis on the Hill Episcopal Ch., 1996-99. With U.S. Air Corps, WWII. Mem.: Coronado Country Club (treas. 1990—93). Home: 6136 Los Robles Dr El Paso TX 79912-1933 E-mail: werskine@elp.rr.com.

ERSPAMER, PETER ROY, humanities educator, writer; b. Duluth, Minn., Sept. 28, 1959; s. Ernest Gordon and Jean Alice (McDonell) E. Student, U. Freiburg, 1980—84; BA, Grinnell Coll., 1982; MA, U. Wis., 1986, PhD cum laude, 1992; postgrad., U. Bonn, 1989—91. Vis. asst. prof. German Winona (Minn.) State U., 1992-93, U. Mo., Columbia, 1993-94, Ft. Hays State U., Hays, Kans., 1994-96, organizer holocaust symposium, 1996. Vis. scholar Boston U., summer 1997; lectr. German Ind. U./Purdue U., Indpls., 1997-98; vis. asst. prof. German Marquette U., Milw., Fall 1999; vis. lectr. German Carroll Coll., Waukesha, Wis., 2000; adj. prof. history and English, Mt. Senario Coll., West Allis, Wis., 2000-02. Author: The Elusiveness of Tolerance: The Jewish Question from Lessing to the Napoleonic Wars, 1997 (Choice mag. Outstanding Acad. Book of 1997); contbg. author: The Yale Companion to Jewish Writing and Thought in German Culture, 1997, Literature and Ethnic Discrimination, 1997, Reader's Guide to Judaism, 2000, Literature and Music, 2002; contbg. author: Reference Guide to Holocaust Literature, 2002, History in Dispute: The Holocaust, 2003. Vol. tutor NAACP, Madison, 1985. Rsch. grantee Fulbright Commn., Bonn, Germany, 1989-91, pub. grantee Lucius N. Littauer Found., 1996, summer seminar grantee NEH, 1997. Mem. MLA, Lessing Soc., Goethe Soc., Western Jewish Studies Assn., Am. Hist. Assn. Democrat. Unitarian Universalist. Avocations: writing, swimming, bookworming. Home: 313 NW 4th Avenue Rochester MN 55901 E-mail: perspamer@yahoo.com.

ERSTAD, LEON ROBERT, lawyer; b. Tyler, Minn., Aug. 3, 1947; s. Clifford and Josie (Dellberg) E.; m. Nancy Youel, July 19, 1969; children: Eric, Andrew, Jonathan. BSBA, U. Minn., 1969; JD cum laude, Temple U., 1976. Bar: Minn. 1976, U.S. Dist. Ct. Minn. 1976, U.S. Ct. Appeals (8th cir.) 1992, U.S. Supreme Ct. 1994; cert. ct. mediator. Ptnr. Chadwick, Johnson & Condon, P.A., Mpls., 1976-90, Erstad & Riemer P.A., 1990—. Adj. instr. law William Mitchell Coll., St. Paul, 1985-94; Fulbright lectr. Moldova State U., Chisinau, 2002-03; spkr. at profl. seminars. Contbr. articles to profl. jours. Bd. dirs. Loring Nicollet Cmty. Ctr., Mpls., 1981-91, Minn. Returned Peace Corps Vols., Mpls., 1980-86, pres., 1980-81; trustee Lynnhurst Congrl. Ch., 1997—, deacon, 1994-97. Named alumni of notable achievement U. Minn. Mem. ABA, Minn. State Bar Assn., Minn. Def. Lawyers Assn. (bd. dirs. 1999-2000, sec. 2000-01, treas. 2001-02, v.p. 2002-03, pres. 2003—), Def. Rsch. Inst., Def. Lawyers Assn. Home: 4700 Dupont Ave S Minneapolis MN 55409-2324 Office: Erstad & Riemer PA 200 Riverview Office Tower 8006 34th Ave S Minneapolis MN 55425 E-mail: lerstad@erstad.com.

ERTAN, ATILLA, medical educator, physician, researcher, health facility administrator; b. Eskisehir, Turkey, June 21, 1940; arrived in US, 1969; s. Rasim and Veliye E.; m. Inci E. Ertan, June 2, 1973; children: Basak, Baris R. MD, Ankara (Turkey) U. Med. Sch., 1963, Internal Medicine, 1967. Intern Ankara U. Med. Sch., 1963—64, resident in internal medicine, 1964—67; instr, medicine U. Pa., Phila., 1969—71, fellow in gastroenterology, 1971; assoc. prof. Ankara U. Med. Sch., 1972—76, prof., 1976—82, Tulane U. Med. Sch., New Orleans, 1982—90, chief GI, 1985—90, interim chair, 1989—90; prof., chief GI BCM/TMH, Houston, 1990—2000; prof., med. dir. dept. digestive diseases Meth. Hosp., Houston, 1990—. Founder Turkish GI Rsch. Fund, Ankara, 1996. Editor: Best Practice of Med. Gastroent., 1998; mem. editl. bd.: Digestive Disease Sci., 1994—, Ann. Med. Sci., 1999—, Med. Sci., 2002—; contbr. over 140 articles to profl. jours., chapters to books. Named Hon. Citizen, City of New Orleans, 1989, Best Physician, CCFA, 1996; named one of Top Drs. in Am., 1997—2003; recipient Med. Sci. award, TUBITAK, 1992. Master: Am. Coll. Gastroenterology; mem.: ASGE, AAAS, Am. Gastroenterol. Assn. (Disting. Clinician award 2003), Turkish GI Soc. (hon. pres. 1996), L'Union Med. Balkanique (hon. Best Rschr. award 1973), So. Soc. Clin. Investigation, Am. Fedn. Med. Rsch. Achievements include research in biliary and pancreatic disorders, Barrett's esophagus and inflammatory bowel diseases. Avocations: travel, reading, exercise. Home: 6337 Mercer St Houston TX 77005 Office: 6560 Fannin St Ste 2208 Houston TX 77030

ERTEKIN, TURGAY, petroleum engineer educator, researcher, consultant; b. Ayvalik, Turkey, July 9, 1947; s. Mehmet and Guzin Ertekin; m. Ayse Filiz Unal, Nov. 14, 1975; children: Elif, Emre. Ph.D., Penn State U., University Park, Pennsylvania, 1975—78; M.Sc., Mid. East Tech. U., Ankara, Turkey, 1969—71, B.Sc., 1964—69. Prof. and chair of petroleum and natural gas engring. Penn State U., University Park, Pa., 2002—; rsch. and tchg. asst. of petroleum engring. Mid. East Tech. U., Ankara, Turkey, 1970—74; prof. of petroleum and natural gas engring. and george e. trimble chair in earth and mineral sciences Penn State U., University Park, Pa., 2001—, assoc. head of energy and geo-environmental engring., 1998—2001, chmn. and prof. of petroleum and natural gas engring., 1987—98, chmn. and assoc. prof. of petroleum and natural gas engring., 1984—87, assoc. prof. of petroleum and natural gas engring., 1983—84, asst. prof. of petroleum and natural gas engring., 1978—83, rsch. and tchg. asst. of petroleum and natural gas engring., 1975—78; instr. of petroleum engring. Mid. East Tech. U., Ankara, Turkey, 1974—75. Petroleum and natural gas engring. cons. Turgay Ertekin Engring. Cons., State College, Pa., 1978—; exec. editor Soc. of Petroleum Engineers, Formation Evaluation Jour., Richardson, Tex., 1992—94. Author: (book writing) Gas Well Testing: Theory, Practice and Regulations (Pub. by IHRDC, 1982), Technical Editor Workshop (Pub. by SPE, 1992), Reservoir Simulation (pub. by IHRDC, 1995), Basic Applied Reservoir Simulation (Pub. by SPE, 2001). Program com. memberships Soc. of Petroleum Engineers, Richardson, Tex., 1974—2003. Recipient Matthew J. and Anne C. Wilson Outstanding Tchg. Award, Penn State U. Coll. of Earth and Mineral Sciences, 1982, Quentin E. and Louise L. Wood Fellow in Petroleum and Natural Gas Engring., Penn State U. Bd. of Trustees, 1990-2001, Penn State U. Grad. Faculty Tchg. Award, Penn State U. Grad. Sch., 1995, Soc. of Engineers Disting. Achievement Award for Petroleum Engring. Faculty, Bd. of Directors of Soc. of Petroleum Engineers, 1998, Matthew J. and Anne C. Wilson Outstanding Svc. Award, Penn State U., Coll. of Earth and Mineral Sciences, 1999, Faculty Svc. Award, Penn State U., 2000, George E. Trimble Chair in Earth and Mineral Sciences, Bd. of Trustees of Penn State U., 2001, Soc. of Petroleum Engineers Lester C. Uren Award, Bd. of Directors of Soc. of Petroleum Engineers, 2001, Soc. of Petroleum Engineers Disting. Mem. Award, Bd. of Directors of Soc. and Petroleum Engineers, 2001. Mem.: Chamber of Petroleum Engineers of Turkey, Petroleum Soc. of Can. Inst. of Mining, Am. Soc. of Engring. Edn., Soc. of Indsl. and Applied Math., Soc. of Petroleum Engineers (various com. memberships, com. chair positions 1974—2003). Achievements include Authored and co-authored more than 150 technical articles published in petroleum engineering journals and conference proceedings; Presented more than 20 workshops and shortcourses on various topics in petroleum and natural gas engineering; Gave More Than 120 Invited Lectures And Seminars In More Than 30 Different Countries; supervised the M.S research programs of more than 45 students; Supervised The Research Programs Of More than 25 Doctoral Students. Office: Pennsylvania State University 115 Hosler Building University Park PA 16802 Office Fax: 814-863-1875. E-mail: turgay@pnge.psu.edu., eur@psu.edu.

ERTEL, ALLEN EDWARD, lawyer, former congressman; b. Williamsport, Pa., Nov. 7, 1936; s. Clarence and Helen (Froehner) E.; m. Catharine Bieber Klepper, June 20, 1959; children: Taylor John (dec.), Edward Barnhardt, Amy Sara. BA, Dartmouth Coll., 1958, MSBA, MS, 1959; LL.B., Yale U., 1965. Bar: Pa., Del., U.S. Supreme Ct. Law clk. U.S. Dist. Ct. of Del., 1965-66; ptnr. Candor, Youngman, Gibson & Gault, Williamsport, 1967-72, Ertel & Kieser, Williamsport, 1972-76; dist. atty. Lycoming County, Pa., 1967-76; mem. 95th-97th Congresses from 17th Pa. Dist.; ptnr. Reed Smith Shaw & McClay, Williamsport, 1985-88; pvt. practice Williamsport, 1988—. Del. Democratic. Nat. Conv., 1972; Dem. nominee for gov. of Pa., 1982, for atty. gen. of Pa., 1984. Served with USN, 1959-62. Mem. Pa. Bar Assn., Del. Bar Assn., Dartmouth Soc. Engrs., Lions. Lutheran. Home: 2245 Heim Hill Rd Montoursville PA 17754-9699 Office: 800 W 4th St Williamsport PA 17701-5901

ERTEL, GARY ARTHUR, accountant; b. Racine, Wis., Feb. 16, 1954; s. Arthur and Jean Ann (Potterville) E.; m. Judith Marie Vasy, Aug. 9, 1975; children: James Arthur, Emily Marie. BSBA in Acctg. cum laude, Drake U., 1975; MBA cum laude, Marquette U., 1984. CPA, Wis.; cert. cash mgr. Mem. staff Arthur Andersen & Co., Milw., 1975-77; mgr. Jezzo, Deppisch & Co., Cedarburg, Wis., 1978; gen. actg. mgr. to asst. sec.-treas. and contr. Grede Foundries, Inc., Milw., 1978—. Mem. Amateur Radio Emergency Svc., Milw., 1984—; bd. dirs. Grace Evang. Luth. Ch., Milw., 1984-87, stewardship com., 1980-89. Mem. AICPAs, Wis. Inst. CPAs (chmn. acctg. careers com. 1979-87, bd. dirs. southeastern chpt. 1988, chmn. long-range planning com. 1987-90, sec.-treas. 1989-90, pres. 1991-93, fin. com. 1993-95, Svc. award 1989-94), Nat. Cash Mgmt. Assn. (edn. com. 1989-93), Am. Foundrymens Soc. (treas. Wis. chpt. 1994-96), Wis. Cash Mgmt. Assn. (program com. 1985-87, v.p. 1987,

pres. 1988, bd. dirs. 1989-98), Risk and Ins. Mgmt. Assn., Fin. Execs. Inst., Milw. Civil War Roundtable, Sons of Union Vets. of the Civil War, Western Raquet Club (fin. com. 1993—, bd. dirs. 1993-98, v.p. 1995, pres. 1996). Avocations: skiing, tennis, amateur radio, golf, flying. Home: 765 Talon Trl Brookfield WI 53045-6648 Office: Grede Foundries Inc 9898 W Bluemound Rd Milwaukee WI 53226-4365 E-mail: gertel@gredce.com., gertel@execpc.com.

ERTEL, RUTH ROBINSON, lawyer, government official; b. Feb. 9, 1943; BA, George Mason U., Fairfax, Va., 1974; JD, George Washington U., 1983. Bar: D.C. Program analyst/writer U.S. Women's Bur., Washington, 1975-84; atty. U.S. Dept. Labor, Washington, 1984-87, OSC, Washington, 1987-96; assoc. spl. counsel for investigation Office of Spl. Counsel, Washington, 1996—. Mem. D.C. Bar Assn. Office: Office of Spl Counsel 1730 M St NW Ste 300 Washington DC 20036-4531

ERTL, RITA MAE, elementary education educator; b. Appleton, Wis., Dec. 22, 1939; d. Irving John and Bertha Helen (Van Ryte) Petrie; m. Andrew Philip Ertl, June 12, 1971; children: Kristyn Marie, Jessica Lynn. Student, Silver Lake Coll., 1961-71. Religious instr. for mentally handicapped Holy Name Parish, Sheboygan, Wis., 1965-69; tchr. grade 3 Holy Name Sch. (name now Holy Family Sch.), Sheboygan, 1969-72, learning ctr. coord., 1984—2001; tchr. aide Holy Family Sch., 2001—. Tchr. grade 2 St. Mary's Sch., Sheboygan Falls, 1961-69; mem. CCD bd. Holy Name Sch. Co-founder Human Rights Assn., Sheboygan, 1960-69. Avocations: sewing, reading, good music, volunteer work, gardening.

ERTL, WOLFGANG, German language and literature educator; b. Sangerhausen, Germany, May 27, 1946; came to U.S., 1969; m. Mary R. Clough, Aug. 30, 1969. BA equivalent in German and English, Philipps U., Marburg, Germany, 1969; MA in German, U. N.H., 1970; PhD in Germanic Langs. and Lits., U. Pa., 1975. Lectr. German U. Pa., Phila., 1974-76; asst. prof. German Swarthmore (Pa.) Coll., 1976-77, U. Iowa, 1977-82, assoc. prof., 1982-88, prof., 1988—, chmn. dept. German, 1988-96. Author: Stephan Hermlin and Tradition, 1977, Nature and Landscape in the Poetry of the GDR: Walter Werner, Wulf Kirsten, and Uwe Gressmann, 1982, (with Christine Cosentino) On Volker Braun's Lyric Poetry, 1984; co-editor: GDR Poetry in Context, 1988; co-editor Glossen: An Internat. Bi-Lingual Scholarly Jour. on Lit., Film, and Art in the German Speaking Countries After 1945; co-editor (with C. Cosentino and W. Muller) Taking Stock German Literature after Unification: Contributions to the 1st Carlisle Symposium on Modern German Literature, glossen: 10, 2000, Crosscurrents--German Literature(s) and the Search for Identity: Selected Papers from the 2nd Carisle Symposium on Modern German Literature, glossen 15, 2002; co-editor At the Milennium: Focus on German Literature, 2003, contbr. chpts. to books, revs. and articles to profl. jours. Resident dir., Academic Year In Freiburg, Germany, 2000-01. May Brodbeck Humanities fellow, 1987. Mem. MLA, N.E. MLA, Am. Assn. Tchrs. German, German Studies Assn. Office: U Iowa Dept German 526 Phillips Hall Iowa City IA 52242-1323

ERTWINE, DEAN R. retired military officer; b. Danville, Pa., Sept. 15, 1950; m. Linda Zeplin; 2 children. BS, U.S. Mil. Acad., 1972; MS in Phys. Chemistry, D in Chemistry, Lehigh U.; grad., Army Command Gen. Staff Coll., Indsl. Coll. Armed Forces. Commd. 2d lt. U.S. Army, advanced through grades to brig. gen.; early assignments include forward observer, asst. exec. officer, then exec. officer Battery B; liaison officer 33d field arty. 1st infantry divsn. U.S. Army Europe, 7th Army, Germany; gunnery instr., combat devels. staff officer, comdr. Battery A, 2d bn., 37th field arty., Ft. Sill, Okla., 1976-80; from instr. to asst. prof. chemistry U.S. Mil. Acad., West Point, N.Y., 1982-85; dep. divsn. chem. officer 9th chem. co., 9th inf. divsn., Ft. Lewis, Wash., 1985-87; dep. G-3, then sec. of Gen. Staff 9th inf. divsn., Ft. Lewis, Wash., 1987—88; chief arty. and hazards br., then exec. officer, then dir. material testing U.S. Army Dugway Proving Ground, Utah, 1989—91; comdr. U.S. Army Cold Regions Test Ctr., Ft. Greely, Alaska, 1991-93; comdr. fire support armaments ctr. U.S. Army Armaments Rsch., Devel. and Engrng. Ctr., Picatinny Arsenal, N.J., 1994-96; exec. officer to asst. sec. Army Rsch., Devel. & Acquisition U.S. Army, Washington, Md., 1996-97; dep. sys. acquisition U.S. Army Comm. and Electronics Command, Ft. Monmouth, N.J., 1997-99; comdg. gen. U.S. Army Devel. Test Command, Aberdeen Proving Ground, Md., 1999—2003; ret. U.S. Army, 2003. Decorated Legion of Merit with 1 oak leaf cluster, Meritorious Svc. medal with 4 oak leaf clusters, Army Commendation medal with 1 oak leaf cluster, others. E-mail: cg@dtc.army.mil.

ERVIN, ANTHONY, Olympic athlete; b. Burbank, Calif., May 26, 1981; s. Jack and Sherry Ervin. Recipient Gold medal 50-meter freestyle Sydney Olympics, 2000, gold medal 50m free, silver medal 400m free relay at Olympic Games, won gold medal 50m free, 100m free, World Championships, 2001, won silver medal 50m free, 400m fee, Pan Pacific Championships, 2002; All Star Team Member, 2002, Am. record holder in 50y, 100y free and 100m free, world record holder in 50m free, US Open record holder in 100m free; ranked 2nd in world for 50m free, 1st in 100m free, 2001 Office: USA Swimming 1 Olympic Plz Colorado Springs CO 80909-5746

ERVIN, BILLY MAXWELL, management consultant; b. Dante, Va., July 29, 1933; s. Willie Beldon and Ollie Lowel (Biggs) Ervin; m. Barbara Frances Walsh, June 27, 1971; 1 child, Honore McDonough 1 stepchild, Kerry Thompson;1 child from previous marriage, Michael. BS, U.S. Naval Acad., 1955; grad., Navy Nuclear Power Training, 1961; M in Marine Affairs, U. R.I., 1971; postgrad., U. Mass., 1989. Commd. ensign USN, 1955, advanced through grades to capt., 1975, chief engr. aircraft carrier, 1969-70, destroyer capt., 1971-73, project mgr., 1973-78, head logistics br., 1978-80, head rsch. and devel. br., 1980-82, insp. gen. Europe London, 1982-85, ret., 1985; adminstr. Baystate Eye Care, P.C., Springfield, Mass., 1986-88; mgr. engring. adminstrn. and planning Kaman Aerospace Corp., Bloomfield, Conn., 1990-92; chief oper. officer Conn. Orthopaedic and Sports Medicine Ctr., Vernon, CT, 1992-97; bus. mgr. engring. Kaman Aerospace Corp., Bloomfield, 1997-2000; mgmt. cons. Bloomfield, 2000—. Decorated Bronze Star; recipient Meritorious Svc. Medal award Pres. of the U.S., 1985. Mem. Naval War Coll. Found., Navy League, St. Andrew's Soc., Clan Irwin Assn. Avocations: antique cars, genealogy. Home: 20 Magnolia Ter Springfield MA 01108-2512 E-mail: max.ervin@1955.usna.com.

ERVIN, CHARLES PHIFER, JR., retired military officer, education educator; b. Morganton, N.C., Nov. 30, 1942; s. Charles P. Ervin Jr. and Eunice (Cuthbertson) Ervin; m. Margie Berry Ervin, Sept. 10, 1962 (div. Aug. 1989); children: Eunice Anita, Charles III, Todd. BS in Sociology, N.C. A&T State U., 1965; MA in Mgmt., Ctrl. Mich. U., 1978; PhD in Social Found. of Edn., Ga. State U., 2001. Commd. 2d lt. U.S. Army, 1965, advanced through grades to lt. col., chief pers. svcs. officer, 1980—81, insp. gen., adjutant Camp Casey, Republic of Korea, 1983—84, manpower staffing officer, Pentagon, 1984—87, dep. cmty. comdr., resource mgr., 1987—89; prof. mil. sci. SROTC Ft. Valley State Coll., Ft. Valley, 1989—93; ret. U.S. Army, 1993; sr. army ROTC instr. Northeast H.S., Macon, Ga., 1993—96; state coord. edn. homeless children and youth program Fla. Dept. Edn., Fla. A&M U., Tallahassee, 1996—; asst. prof. Fla. A&M U., Tallahassee, 2001—. Bd. dirs. Tallahassee Coalition for Homeless, 1997—, Fla. Coalition for Homeless, Orlando, 1998—. Named one of 100 Black Men of Mid. Ga., CME Ch., Warner Robins, Ga., 1991. Mem.: NAACP, Ret. Officers Assn., Nat. Assn. for Edn. Homeless Children & Youths, Urban League, Mason, Alpha Phi Alpha. Democrat. Methodist. Avocation: running. Home: 8691 Alexandrite Ct Tallahassee FL 32309 Office: Fla A&M Univ Dept Secondary Edn Coll Edn Tallahassee FL 32301 Fax: 850-599-8485. E-mail: cervin42@aol.com.

ERVIN, CLARK KENT, federal agency administrator; grad., JD, Harvard Coll. With Office of Nat. Svce., Tex., 1989—91; asst. sec. of state State of Tex., 1995—99; dep. atty. gen., gen. counsel Tex. Atty. Gen.'s Office; insp. gen. U.S. Dept. of State, Washington, 2001—. Scholar Rhodes scholar. Office: US Dept of State Inspector Gen 2201 C St NW Washington DC 20520 Office Fax: 202-647-7660.

ERVIN, PATRICK FRANKLIN, nuclear engineer; b. Kansas City, Kans., Aug. 4, 1946; s. James Franklin and Irma Lee (Arnett) E.; m. Rita Jeanne Kimsey, Aug. 12, 1967; children: James, Kevin, Amber. BS in Nuclear Engring., Kans. State U., 1969, MS in Nuclear Engring., 1971; postgrad., Northeastern U., 1988. Registered profl. engr., Ill., Colo., Calif., Idaho, Wash.; cert. paleontology paraprofl., Colo. Reactor health physicist Dept. Nuclear Engring. Kans. State U., Manhattan, 1968-69, rsch. asst. Dept. Nuclear Engring., 1969-72, sr. reactor operator, temp. facility dir. Dept. Nuclear Engring., 1970-72; system test engr. Commonwealth Edison Co., Zion, Ill., 1972—74, shift foreman, 1973, shift foreman with sr. reactor operator lic., 1974-76, prin. engr., 1976-77, acting operating engr., 1977, tech. staff supr. Byron, Ill., 1977-81; lead test engr. Stone & Webster Engring. Corp., Denver, 1982-83, project mgr., 1982-95, ops. svcs. supr., 1982-86, asst. engring. mgr., 1986-89, cons. engr., 1989-94; sr. cons., 1994—96; decommisioning program mgr. Rocky Flats Closure project Kaiser-Hill Co., Denver, 1996—2001; prin. project mgr. CH2M Hill Constructors, Inc., Denver, 2001—. Contbr. articles to profl. jours. Served with U.S. Army N.G., 1971-77. Mem. Am. Nuclear Soc. (Nat. and Colo. chpts.), Am. Nat. Standards Inst. (working group on containment leakage testing). Independent. Roman Catholic. Avocations: paleontology, hunting, fishing, camping, stamp collecting. Home: 2978 S Bahama St Aurora CO 80013-2340 Office: 9189 S Jamaica St Englewood CO 80112 E-mail: pevin@ch2m.com.

ERVIN, ROBERT MARVIN, lawyer; b. near Ocala, Fla., Jan. 19, 1917; s. Richard William and Carrie (Phillips) E.; m. Frances Anne Cushing, Dec. 25, 1941; children: Anne Cushing (Mrs. Henry Lamar Rowe), Robert Marvin. BSBA, U. Fla., 1941, LLB, 1947. Bar: Fla. 1947. Of counsel Ervin, Chapman & Ervin, Tallahassee, 1947—; U.S. referee in bankruptcy No. Dist. Fla., part time, 1952-72. Mem. Fla. Constn. Revision Commn., 1966-68; Trustee U. Fla. Law Center Assn.; mem. founders com., mem. bd. visitors Fla. State U. Coll. Law. Served with USMC, 1941-45, PAO; col. ret. Recipient Disting. Svc. award for legal edn. John B. Stetson U., 1966, Disting. Svc. award Armed Forces League, 1966, Medal of Hon. award Fla. Bar Found., 2003; named to Fla. Housing Hall of Fame, 1993. Fellow Am. Bar Found. (chmn. 1989-90); mem. ABA (ho. of dels. 1966-91, bd. govs., 1979-82, chmn. sect. criminal justice 1975-76, mem. resource devel. coun., audit com., vice chmn. sr. lawyers div., chmn. special com. on fiscal policy 1984-85), Am. Coll. Trial Lawyers (bd. regents 1983-84), Am. Law Inst., Am. Judicature Soc., Fla. Bar (pres. 1965-66, Disting. Svc. award 1966), Fla. Supreme Ct. Hist. Soc. (pres. 1986 87, chmn. trustees 1987-98), Am. Bar Retirement Assn. (pres. 1980-82), Nat. Conf. Referees in Bankruptcy (pres. 1963-64), Ret. Officers Assn., Elks, Fla. Blue Key, Phi Alpha Delta, Alpha Kappa Psi. Baptist. Home: 530 N Ride Tallahassee FL 32303-5127 Office: PO Box 1170 223 S Gadsden St Tallahassee FL 32301-1811

ERVIN, SPENCER, lawyer; b. Bala, Pa., Nov. 25, 1932; s. Spencer and Miriam Williams (Roberts) E.; m. Florence Wetherill Schroeder, Sept. 12, 1964; children: Margaret, Mary, Miriam, Helen. AB, Harvard U., 1954, JD, 1959. Bar: Pa. 1960, Maine 1995, U.S. Supreme Ct. 1963. Staff counsel Philco Corp., Phila., 1959-62; assoc. Ringe & Dewey, Phila., 1962-64; ptnr. Ringe, Tate & Ervin, Phila., 1964-72, Gratz, Tate, Spiegel, Ervin & Ruthrauff, Phila., 1972-92, Hepburn, Willcox, Hamilton & Putnam, Phila., 1992-96, Largay Law Offices, Bangor, Maine, 1996-97; pvt. practice, Bass Harbor, Maine, 1998—. Bd. dirs. Mt. Desert Island Biol. Lab. Bd. dirs., officer Neighborhood Club, Bala Cynwyd, Pa., 1969-89. Lt. USNR, 1954-56. Republican. Episcopal. Home and Office: PO Box 383 Bass Harbor ME 04653-0383 E-mail: law@spencerervin.com.

ERVIN, SUSAN CHADWICK, lawyer; b. Aberdeen, Md., May 16, 1951; d. A.R. and Ellyn (Wiegert) E. BA, Mt. Holyoke Coll., 1973; JD, Rutgers U., 1976. Bar: N.Y. 1977, D.C. 1985. Assoc. Kronish, Lieb, Shainswit, Weiner & Hellman, N.Y.C., 1976-78, Kramer, Levin, Nessen, Kamin & Frankel, N.Y.C., 1978-83; asst. gen. counsel Commodity Futures Trading Commn., Washington, 1983-86, assoc. dir. div. of trading and markets, 1986-87, dep. dir., chief counsel div. of trading and markets, 1987-97; counsel Dechert, Price & Rhoads, Washington, 1998-2000; ptnr. Dechert LLP, Washington, 2001—. Mem. ABA, Assn. Bar City N.Y. Office: Dechert 1775 Eye St NW Washington DC 20006 E-mail: susan.ervin@dechert.com.

ERVINE, TIMOTHY DUWAYNE, utilities executive; b. Covington, Va., Feb. 15, 1963; s. Randolph DuWayne and Mary Evelyn (McCutcheon) E.; m. Teresa Lee Gadd, Feb. 25, 1984; children: Alison Lee, Casey Beth. Student, Jackson River Vocat., 1981, Tri-County Tech. Coll., 1988-90; BS in Safety Engring, Kennedy-Western U., 1996. Cert. utility safety adminstr. Nat. Safety Coun.; cert. provl. environ. auditor; cert. hazard control mgr. From attendant to asst. mgr. Stonewall Svc. Sta., Covington, 1976-81; safety and loss prevention insp. Va. Power, Warm Springs, Va., 1981-86; with BE & K Constrn. Co., 1985-86, project safety dir., 1986, Georgetown, S.C., 1986; safety specialist Duke Power Co., Salem, S.C., 1986-90, safety and security supr., 1990-91, Great Falls, S.C., 1991-94, safety and indsl. hygiene cons. Charlotte, NC, 1994-98, health and safety mgr., 1998—2001, mgr. environ. health and safety, 2001—. Mem., del. Va. Assn. Vol. Rescue Squads, 1978-83; del. Va. Firemen's Assn., 1978-83. Named Fireman of the Yr. Dunlap Fire and Rescue Squad, 1979, 81. Mem. Am. Soc. Safety Engrs., Am. Indsl. Hygiene Assn. Methodist. Avocations: auto racing, hunting, fishing, carpentry. Home: 419 Woodland Rd Covington VA 24426-6321 Office: Duke Power Co 526 S Church St Charlotte NC 28202-1802 E-mail: tdervine@duke-energy.com.

ERVING, CLAUDE MOORE, JR., career officer, pilot; b. St. John's, N.F., Can., Sept. 10, 1952; s. Claude Moore Sr. and Ingeborg (Mauss) E.; m. Donna Lee Mathis, June 17, 1978; children: Zachary C., Allyson B., Michael J. M. BS in Geography, USAF Acad., 1975. Commd. 2d lt. USAF, 1975, advanced through grades to lt. col., 1979; check pilot, instr. 85th Flying Tng. Squadron, Laughlin AFB, Tex., 1976-80; flight examiner, instr. pilot, flight comdr. 460th Fighter Interceptor Tng. Squadron, Peterson AFB, Colo., 1980-82; flight comdr. 49th Fighter Interceptor Squadron, Griffiss AFB, N.Y., 1982-85; chief of tng. 18th Tactical Fighter Squadron, Eielson AFB, Alaska, 1985-86; chief of flight safety, asst. chief of safety 343d Tactical Fighter Wing, Eielson AFB, Alasaka, 1986-88; chief ops. plans div. and exec. officer to dep. comdr. ops. for 11th Air Force and Alaskan NORAD region Hdqrs. Alaskan Air Command, Elmendorf AFB, 1988-92; comdr. 94th airmanship tng. squadron USAF Acad., Colo., 1992-94, dep. dir. pub. affairs, 1994-96; ret., 1996. Aircraft accident investigator USAF, worldwide, 1986-96; pilot Fed. Express Corp. Mem.: Internat. Soc. of Aviation Safety Investigators, CAP ((flight comdr.) 1990—93). Republican. Avocations: hunting, fishing, camping, traithalons, flying. Home: 3811 Gunwale Ct Anchorage AK 99516-7601

ERWAY, LAWRENCE CLIFTON, JR., biologist, educator; b. Lawrenceville, Pa., Apr. 27, 1938; s. Lawrence Clifton and Mary (Gearhart) Erway; m. Louise Vieth, June 25, 1960; children: Lauri, Leslie, Lisa, Lawrence C., III. BA, Barrington Coll., R.I., 1960; MA, Brown U., Providence, 1963; PhD, U. Calif., Davis, 1967. Prof. U. Cin., 1967—2002, prof. biol. scis. emeritus, 2003—. Contbr. Mem.: Assn. Rsch. Otolaryngology. Baptist. Achievements include research in deafness in mic; susceptibility to noise induced hearing loss; vestibular behavioral defects in mice and preventing them by manganese suplementation. Home: 422 Grove Ave Cincinnati OH 45215 Office: Univ of Cincinnati PO Box 210006 Cincinnati OH 45221-0001

ERWIN, BETTY, bank executive; b. Charlotte, N.C., Nov. 11, 1945; d. John and Lula Bell Erwin; children: Wanda E. Dae, Johnny Maurice. BTh, Teamers Sch. of religion, 1989; BD, Teamers Sch. of Religion, 1991; BA, Shaw U., 1996; M in Christian Edn., Pheiffer U., 1998; Doctorate of Min., New Life Theol. Sem., 2000. Asst. buyer First Union, Charlotte, NC, 1986—97; courier specialist First Union Nat. Bank, Charlotte, 1997—2001. Mem.: Alpha Chi. Home: 3045 La Salle St Charlotte NC 28216

ERWIN, DONALD CARROLL, plant pathology educator; b. Concord, Nebr., Nov. 24, 1920; s. Robert James and Carol (Sexson) E.; m. Veora Marie Endres, Aug. 15, 1948; children: Daniel Erwin, Myriam Erwin Casey. Student, Wayne State (Nebr.) Tchrs.Coll, 1938-39; BSc, U. Nebr., 1949, MA, 1950; PhD, U. Calif.-Davis, 1953. Jr. plant pathologist U. Calif., Riverside, 1953-54, asst. plant pathologist, 1954-60, assoc. plant pathologist, 1960-66, prof. plant pathology, 1966—, emeritus prof., 1991. Sr. author: Phytophthora Diseases Worldwide, 1996; editor: Phytophthora: Its Biology, Taxonomy, Ecology and Pathology, 1983; contbr. articles to profl. jours. With U.S. Army, 1942-46; ETO. Nathan Gold fellow, 1949, Guggenheim fellow, 1959. Mem.: Am. Phytopathol. Soc. (fellow), Sigma Xi. Democrat. Roman Catholic. Office: U Calif Dept Plant Pathology Riverside CA 92521-0001

ERWIN, DOUGLAS HAMILTON, museum director, paleobiologist; b. L.A., Mar. 27, 1958; s. John Daniel and Ann E. AB, Colgate U., 1980; PhD, U. Calif., Santa Barbara, 1985. Asst. prof. dept. geol. sci. Mich. State U., East Lansing, 1985-90; assoc. curator dept. paelobiology U.S. Nat. Mus. Natural History, Washington, 1990-93, curator dept. paelobiology, 1993—; interim dir. Natural Mus. of Natural History, 2002—03. Mem. Paleontol. Soc., AAAS, Geol. Soc. Am. Office: Smithsonian Instn 10th St Constitution Ave NW Washington DC 20560

ERWIN, ELMER LOUIS, vintager, cement consultant; b. Visalia, Calif., Oct. 6, 1926; s. Louis Nelson and Myra Erla (Hector) E.; m. Jeanne Prothero, Feb. 27, 1954; children: Catherine Lynn, Christopher Lawrence. BS, U. Calif.-Berkeley, 1950. Registered profl. engr., Calif. With Kaiser Cement Corp., Oakland, Calif., 1957-80, v.p. mfg. and distbn., 1980-87; freelance vintager. Cons. internat. cement plant projects.

ERWIN, FRANCES SUZANNE, artist; b. Stockton, Calif. d. Frederick Bedford and Clara Jackquiline (Seale) Davis; widow; 9 children. Student, Thomas Leighton Sch. Fine Arts, San Francisco, 1964-70, Sergie Bongart Sch., Rexburg, Idaho, 1972-73, various master artists, various cities, 1972—. Represented by The Main Street Gallery, Pleasanton, Calif., The Phantom Gallery, Hayward, Calif. Portrait painting instr. Roy Johnson Sch., Castro Valley, Calif., 1993—, San Lorenzo (Calif.) Sch., 1995—; lectr. on visual arts, various San Francisco Bay area locations, 1987—. One-woman shows include Hayward Art Coun. Gallery, Hayward, Calif., 2002; group exhbns. include The Triton Mus., San Jose, Calif., 2002; portrait painter numerous pvt. commns include Alameda County Ct. House, 1990, recreation facilities in Castro Valley and Hayward, 1991-92, Moreau H.S., Hayward, 1993, San Francisco World Trade Club, 1994, Eden Hosp., Castro Valley, 1994, Sakura Corp. Mus., Osaka, Japan, 1996; designed image for Sakura Corp. Judge various county fairs and open art shows, Alameda County, Contra Costa County, and Santa Clara County (all in Calif.), 1988—. Recipient Best of Show award Alameda County Fair, Pleasanton, Calif., 1989, Best of Class, 1990; recipient Purchase and Founders awards Pastel Soc. Fla., 1996, Silver Medal awards (3) Alameda County Fair, 1999, 2 Silver Medal awards, 2002. Mem. Pastel Soc. of Am. (signature mem.), Am. Soc. Portrait Artists, Pastel Soc. of the West Coast (signature mem., co-founder, bd. dirs., events chair 1985-87, v.p. 1987-88, pres. 1988-89, adv. bd. mem. 1989—, Plaques 1988, 89, Art of the West award 1994), Knickerbocker Artists USA (signature mem.), Nat. League Am. Pen Women. Republican. Roman Catholic. Avocations: photography, sculpting, gardening. Home: The Painted Portrait 22125 Orange Ave Castro Valley CA 94546-6937 E-mail: franportraits@aol.com.

ERWIN, FRANK WILLIAM, personnel research and publishing executive; b. Elizabeth, N.J., Nov. 22, 1931; s. Frank J. and Jessie (Rugero) E.; m. Bridget E. Taddeo, June 26, 1965. BA cum laude, NYU, 1957. With MBS, 1957-62, asst. to pres., asst. sec. to bd. dirs., 1960-62; dep. dir. div. selection, dir. recruiting ops. Peace Corps, 1962-65; exec. asst. to sec. labor, 1965-68; pres., chmn. Richardson, Bellows, Henry & Co., Inc., 1968-99; advisor FBI, 1995—, ePredix, Inc., 1999—, Nat. Skills Stds. Bd., 2001—. Chmn. fin. com. Our Lady of Lourdes Ch.; pres. Ridge House Condominium, 2002—; v.p. Ridge House Condominium, 2001—. Served with AUS, 1949-52. Mem. Am. Psychol. Assn., Internat. Assn. for Advancement Pschology, Soc. for Indsl. and Organizational Psychology, Personnel Testing Coun. of Metro. Washington. Home: 2310 S Rolfe St Arlington VA 22202-1545 Office: 1400 S Joyce St # 115 Arlington VA 22202

ERWIN, GOODLOE Y. physician, land company executive; b. Athens, Ga., June 14, 1919; s. Howell Cobb and Llucy Gratten (Yancey) E.; m. Patricia Graham, Sept. 27, 1947; children: Alexander Wales, Charles Graham, Leslie Erwin Moose, Catharine. BS in Chemistry, U. Ga., 1940; MD, Emory U., 1943. Diplomate Am. Bd. Internal Medicine. Intern Grady Meml. Hosp., Atlanta, 1944; resident in medicine VA Hosp., Salt Lake City, 1947-48; pvt. practice internal medicine St. Marys Hosp., Athens Ctrl. Hosp., 1948-87; pres. Erwin Land Co., Athens, 1987—. Dir. respiratory therapy dept. Athens Gen. Hosp., 1963-75, dir. CCU, 1965-70. Pres. Athens Hist. Soc., 1992-94; bd. dirs. Athens Cmty. Chest, 1950-60. 1st lt. M.C., U.S. Army, 1944-46, ETO. Fellow Am. Coll. Chest Physicians, Am. Coll. Cardiology; mem. Ga. Heart Assn. (pres. 1957-58, Disting. Svc. award 1964), Ga. Lung Assn. (pres. 1973-74), Ga. Soc. Internal Medicine (pres.), Phi Beta Kappa, Alpha Omega Alpha. Baptist. Avocations: genealogy, golf, swimming. Home: 354 Milledge Cir Athens GA 30606-4334

ERWIN, JAMES WALTER, lawyer; b. Carthage, Mo., Nov. 18, 1946; s. Charles Max and Juanita Carmen (Adams) E.; m. Vicki Berger, Dec. 30, 1972; children: Elizabeth Susan, James Bryan. B.A., Southwest Mo. State U., 1968; M.A., U. Mo., 1972, J.D., 1976. Bar: Mo. 1976, Ill. 1977, U.S. Dist. Ct. (ea. and we. dists.) Mo. 1976, U.S. Ct. Appeals (8th cir.) 1976, U.S. Supreme Ct. 1979, U.S. Dist. Ct. (so. dist.) Ill. 1984, U.S . Ct. Appeals (7th, 10th and fed. cirs.) 1990. Assoc. firm Thompson Coburn, St. Louis, 1976-83, ptnr., 1984—; adj. lectr. Washington U., St. Louis, 1980-84. Lead articles editor Mo. Law Rev., 1976. Pres. Nursery Found. St. Louis, 1989-92; treas. Educare Learning Ctr., 2002—. Served to 1st lt. U.S. Army, 1968-70. Mem. ABA, Bar Assn. Met. St. Louis, Ill. State Bar Assn., Order of Coif. Democrat. Roman Catholic. Home: 532 W Jewel Ave Saint Louis MO 63122-2515 Office: Thompson Coburn One US Bank Plz Saint Louis MO 63101-1643 E-mail: jerwin@thompsoncoburn.com.

ERWIN, JOAN LENORE, artist, educator; b. Berkeley, Calif., Feb. 12, 1932; d. Ralph Albert and Dorothy Christine (Wuhrman) Potter; m. Byron W. Crider, Jan. 28, 1956 (div. May 1975); children: Susan Lynne Crider Adams, Gayle Leann Crider; m. Joseph G. Erwin Jr., May 28, 1976; children: Terry, Ray, Steve, Tim. BS, U. So. Calif., 1954; MS in Sch. Adminstrn., Pepperdine U., 1975. Cert. tchr., Calif.; registered occupational therapist, Calif. Occupational therapist Calif. State Hosp., Camarillo, 1955-56, Harlan Shoemaker Sch., San Pedro, Calif., 1956-57; tchr. Norwalk (Calif.) Sch. Dist., 1957-59, Tustin (Calif.) Sch. Dist., 1966-68, Garden Grove (Calif.) Sch. Dist., 1968-92; freelance artist Phelan, Calif., 1976—; comml. artist Morningstar Creations, Fullerton, Calif., 1982-92; substitute tchr. Snowline Sch. Dist., Phelan, Calif., 1994—; owner, artist Plumfrog Creations, Phelan, 2000—03. Artist Y.U.G.O., Los Alamitos, 1977-87; organizer 34th Annual Open Internat. Exbhn. Art, San Bernardino County Mus., 1999; resident artist High Desert Ctr. for the Arts, Victorville, 2000—. Pet portrait artist, U.S. and Eng., 1978—85, author, artist Biblical coloring books, 1985—90; Exhibited in group shows at San Bernardino County Mus., Redlands, Calif., Riverside Art Mus., Wildlife Artist Assn. Bd. dirs. San Bernardino County Mus., Fine Arts Inst. Calif. Elks scholar, 1952-53; grantee Ford Found., 1957-58, Mentor Tchr. Program, 1986. Republican. Baptist. Avocations: gardening, travel. Home: 10080 Monte Vista Rd Phelan CA 92371-8371 E-mail: jaybird92371@yahoo.com.

ERWIN, JOSEPH ARNOLD, political organization worker, advertising executive, creative director; b. Florence, S.C., Oct. 23, 1956; s. Henry Brooks Erwin and Isabel (Williams) Kelly; m. Gretchen Elaine Getchell, June 16, 1984; 1 child, Douglas Getchell. BA in Polit. Sci., Clemson U., 1979; postgrad., Sch. of Visual Arts, 1985. Media buyer Leslie Advt., Greenville, S.C., 1980-81, asst. account exec., 1981-82, account exec., 1982, Benton & Bowles, Spartanburg, S.C., 1982-83, Benton & Bowles (merged with DMB&B), N.Y.C., 1983-86; pres., founder Erwin-Penland, Inc., Greenville, 1986—; chmn. S.C. Dem. Party, 2003—. Cons. Walter Johnson Vol. Com., Greenville, 1986—; cons., vol. communications div. Greenville C. of C., 1987-88; bd. dirs. Freedom Weekend Aloft, Inc. Mem. Palmetto (S.C.) Project, 1989—; mem. staff Palmetto Boys State, Charleston, 1977—; vol. Greenville Little Theatre Bd., 1987—; mem. advt. rev. com. Better Bus. Bur. Mem. Am. Advt. Fedn. (5 Addy's 1984, 7 Addy's 1989, 14 Addy's 1990, 10 Addy's 1991), Am. Assn. Advt. Agys. Democrat. Episcopalian. Avocations: tennis, automobile racing, politics. Home: 208 Idonia Dr Taylors SC 29687-3813 also: 125 E Broad St Greenville SC 29601*

ERWIN, JUDITH ANN (JUDITH ANN PEACOCK), writer, photographer, lawyer; b. Decatur, Ga., Jan. 4, 1939; d. Milo Eugene and Lucy Isabelle (Simpson) Peacock; m. William Wofford Erwin, Sept. 5, 1959 (div. Mar. 1982); children: William Wofford Jr., Allison Sheridan (Norton). AA, Fla. C.C., 1987; BA summa cum laude, Jacksonville U., 1989; JD, U. Fla., 1993. Cert. mediator, custody evaluator. Photography instr., freelance writer, Jacksonville, Fla., 1986-91; freelance dance photographer, 1984-91; theater and dance critic Folio Weekly, Jacksonville, Fla., 1987-89; writer dance VUE mag.; founder On Our Own, 1991; pvt. practice lawyer. Pres. Ballet Guild, Jacksonville, 1973—75, Ballet Repertory Jacksonville, 1979—80; freelance costume designer, Jacksonville, 1981—86; mem. grand rev. dance panel Fla. Dept. Cultural Affairs, 1996—97, 2002; seminar spkr. in field; child custody evaluator. Mem. editorial staff Kalliope, Jour. Women's Art, 1989-91; editor-in-chief U. Fla. Jour. of Law and Pub. Policy, fall 1993; editor Jacksonville Trial Lawyers Newsletter. Mem. del.'s council Art's Assembly Jacksonville, 1979-80. Mem. AAUW, ATLA, Nat. Soc. Arts and Letters, Nat. League Am. Pen Women, Fla. Bar Assn., Phi Kappa Phi, Phi Theta Kappa. Republican. Episcopalian.

ERWIN, LINDA MCINTOSH, librarian, consultant; b. Austin, Tex., June 22, 1939; d. William Erwin and Martha (Ferguson) McIntosh; m. Kenneth James Erwin, June 7, 1962 (div. Feb. 1986); 1 child, Jason Emerson. BA magna cum laude, U. Tex., 1961, MLS, 1968. Tchr. Spanish, Victoria (Tex.) H.S., 1961-62, El Campo (Tex.) H.S., 1962-63, Del Valle (Tex.) H.S., 1963-66; libr. U. Tex., Austin, 1968-69, Corpus Christi Pub. Librs., 1981-89; cons. South Tex. Libr. Sys., Corpus Christi, 1989-99, asst. coord., 1999—. Ford Found. scholar, 1966-67. Mem. ALA, Tex. Libr. Assn., Pub. Libr. Assn., Phi Beta Kappa, Alpha Phi Sigma Delta Pi. Office: South Tex Libr Sys 805 Comanche St Corpus Christi TX 78401-2715

ERXLEBEN, WILLIAM CHARLES, lawyer, consultant; b. Chgo., Dec. 18, 1942; s. Walter Oscar and Sarah Louise (Githens) E.; m. Gayle Amelia Reichmuth, Aaug. 28, 1965; children: David William, Jennifer Renée. BS in Bus., Miami U., Oxford, Ohio, 1963; JD, Stanford U., 1966. Bar: Wash. 1969. Asst. state atty. gen. Wash. State Atty. Gen.'s Office, Olympia, 1968-70; exec. asst. U.S. atty. Dept. Justice, Seattle, 1970-72; regional dir. FTC, Seattle, 1972-79; lectr. Grad. Sch. Bus., U. Wash., Seattle, 1979-85; ptnr. Foster, Pepper & Shefelman, Bellevue, Wash., 1985-91, Lane Powell Spears Lubersky, Olympia, 1991-93; pres., CEO, Data I/O Corp., Redmond, Wash., 1993-98, bd. dirs., 1979-98, cons., 1998—. Chmn., dir. Advanced Digital Tech., Bellevue, 1983-85. Contbr. articles to law revs. Counsel Wash. Assn. for Children and Adults with Learning Disabilities, Seattle, 1985-93; chmn. Portwatch, Seattle, 1985; mem. advt. rev. com. BBB, Seattle, 1982; bd. dirs. Wash. Citizens for Recycling, Seattle, 1980-84; Dem. nominee for Wash. State Atty. Gen., 1988, Wash.Ho. of Reps., 1982; mem., chmn. Newcastle City Planning Commn., 2002—; mem. Newcastle City Coun., 2002—. Recipient Excellence in Supervision award FTC, 1975, Disting. Svc. award, 1979; Sloan exec. fellow Stanford U. Grad. Sch. Bus., 1975-76. Mem. ABA, Wash. State Bar Assn. (sec.-treas. antitrust subcom 1981-83). Home: 7625 120th Pl SE Newcastle WA 98056-1791

ERZINGER, DENNIS EUGENE, SR., factory automation executive; b. Elkins, W.Va., Feb. 21, 1951; s. Vincent Joseph and Jacqueline (James) E.; m. Kathy Parneace McClam, June 22, 1974; children: Amberlyn Marie, Dennis E. Jr. AA, Charles County C.C., La Plata, Md., 1971; BS in Acctg., Carson-Newman Coll., 1973. Sales rep. Skil Corp., Miami, Fla. and Atlanta, 1973-75, Black & Decker Corp., Atlanta, 1975-78, internat. mktg. mgr. Towson, Md., 1978-80, mktg. mgr. research and devel., 1980-83; product mgr. robotic and vision systems dept. Gen. Electric Corp., Orlando, Fla., 1983-86; mktg. mgr. Vistronic, Honeywell Inc., Denver, 1986-87, Advanced Indsl. Sensors Microswitch div. of Honeywell, Denver, 1988-89; dir. mktg. Perton Controls div. Square D Co., Chatsworth, Calif., 1989-91; pres. David Vincent Group, Thousand Oaks, Calif., 1991-2000, Heathsville, Va., 2000—. Cons. Johns Hopkins Univ., Balt., 1981; instr. Goucher Coll., Towson, 1982-84; guest lectr. U. of Bus. and Econs., Almata, Kazakstan, 1991. Named hon. citizen Kazakstan Republic, 1991. Mem. Am. Mktg. Assn., Licensing Exec. Soc., Soc. Mfg. Engrs., AAAS. Republican. Baptist. Avocations: coaching high school and junior hockey, Russian history and terrorism, astronomy, astrophysics.

ESAHAK, GEORGE MICHAEL, lawyer; b. Tucson, July 27, 1958; s. James and Bernice (Lindquist) E. BA, Yale U., 1980; JD, Northwestern U., 1983. Bar: Ariz. 1983, U.S. Ct. Appeals (9th cir.) 1983, U.S. Dist. Ct. Ariz. 1983. Assoc. Jennings Strouss & Salmon, Phoenix, 1983-88, ptnr., 1988—. Campaign vol. John McCain for Senator, Phoenix, 1984, Jon Kyl for Congressman, 1986. Mem. ABA, Ariz. Bar Assn., Maricopa County Bar Assn., Maricopa County Bar Found., Am. Judicature Soc., Phoenix C. of C., Captain's Club, IBM Ring 55 Club, Phi Beta Kappa. Republican. Avocations: triathlete, magic. Office: Jennings Strouss & Salmon Ste 1100 201 E Washington St Phoenix AZ 85004-2385 E-mail: esahakgage@jsslaw.com.

ESAKI, HOWARD YUJI, economist; b. Monterey, Calif., Oct. 20, 1953; s. George T. and Jean M. (Oishi) E. AB, Princeton U., 1975; MA, Yale U., 1977, PhD, 1981. Economist Fed. Res. Bank N.Y., N.Y.C., 1980-87; v.p. Shearson/Lehman/Hutton, N.Y.C., 1987-88; assoc. dir. Moody's Investors Svc., N.Y.C., 1988-93; exec. dir. Morgan Stanley & Co., N.Y.C., 1993—. Office: Morgan Stanley & Co 1585 Broadway New York NY 10036

ESAKI, LEO, physicist, foundation executive, university president; b. Osaka, Japan, Mar. 12, 1925; arrived in U.S., 1960; s. Soichiro and Niyoko (Ito) Esaki; m. Masako Kondo, May 31, 1986; children from previous marriage: Nina Yvonne, Anna Eileen, Eugene Leo. BS, U. Tokyo, 1947, PhD, 1959. With Sony Corp., Japan, 1956—60; with Thomas J. Watson Research Center, IBM, Yorktown Heights, NY, 1960—92, IBM fellow, 1967—92, mgr. device research, 1965—92; dir. IBM-Japan, 1975—92; pres. U. Tsukuba, Ibaraki, Japan, 1992—98; chmn. Sci. and Tech. Found. of Ibaraki, 1998—; pres. Shibaura Inst. of Tech., Tokyo, 2000—. Decorated Order of Culture Govt. of Japan, Grand Cordon Order of Rising Sun; recipient Stuart Ballantine medal, Franklin Inst., 1961, Japan Acad. award, 1965, Nobel prize in Physics, 1973. Fellow: IEEE (Morris N. Liebman Meml. prize 1961, medal of Honor 1991), Am. Vacuum Soc. (bd. dirs. 1973—74), Japan Phys. Soc., Am. Phys. Soc. (councillor-at-large 1971—74); mem.: NAE (fgn. assoc.), NAS (fgn. assoc.), Japan Acad., Russian Acad. Scis. (fgn.), Academia Nacional de Ingenieria Mex. (corr.), Max-Planck Gesellschaft, Am. Philos. Soc., Am. Philos. Soc., Am. Acad. Arts and Scis. Achievements include discovery of Esaki tunnel diode, 1957; pioneering research in semiconductor superlattices and quantum wells. Office: Shibaura Inst of Tech Minato-ku Tokyo 108-8548 Japan also: Tsukuba Internat Congress 2-20-3 Takezono Tsukuba Ibaraki 305-0032 Japan also: PO Box 851 Katonah NY 10536-0851 E-mail: leoesaki@sic.shibaura-it.ac.jp.*

ESBER, EDWARD MICHAEL, JR., software company executive; b. Cleve., June 22, 1952; s. Edward Michael and Joanne Helen (Saah) E.; m. Margaret Renfrow, July 19, 1980; children: Dianne Michelle, Paul Andrew, Alexander Joseph. BS in Computer Engring., Case Western Res. U., Cleve., 1974; MSEE, Syracuse U., N.Y., 1976; MBA, Harvard U., Cambridge, 1978. Assoc. engr. IBM, Poughkeepsie, N.Y., 1974-76; mktg. mgr. Tex. Instruments, Lubbock, Tex., 1978-79; v.p. mktg. Visi Corp., San Jose, Calif., 1979-83; exec. v.p. mktg. and sales Ashton-Tate, Torrance, Calif., 1984, pres., COO, 1984—, pres., chief exec. officer, 1984—, chmn., chief exec. officer, 1986-90; pres., COO Creative Labs, Milpitas, Calif., 1993-94; chmn., CEO Creative Insights, Sunnyvale, Calif., 1994-95; CEO, pres. Solo Point, Los Gatos, Calif., 1995—98, chmn., 1995—98; CEO The Esber Group, Los Gatos, 1990; chmn. Esber Group, Los Altos Hills, Calif., 1990—. Bd. dirs. Quantum Inc. Trustee Case Western Res. U. Mem. Am. Electronic Assn. Republican. Office: The Esber Group 13430 Country Way Los Altos CA 94022-2434

ESBERGER, KAREN ANN, school nurse; b. Waxahachie, Tex., Jan. 17, 1948; d. James Tolivar Kay Jr. and Phama Duke; m. Michael Esberger, May 19, 1973; children: Edward James, Michael Douglas. BSN, Baylor U., 1970; MSN, U. Tex., 1973; PhD, U. North Tex., 1977. RN. Instr. Kilgore (Tex.) Coll., 1970-71, 72-73; instr., assoc. prof. Baylor U., Dallas, 1973-80; assoc. prof. U. Tex., Arlington, 1980-82, Dallas Bapt. U., 1982-83; sch. nurse Midlothian (Tex.) Ind. Sch. Dist., 1983—. Rsch. cons. Harris Hosp., Fort Worth, Tex., 1980-82; instr. first aid for little people 1st graders ARC, 1986-88, instr. basic aid tng. for 5th graders, 1998— Author: The Dukes of Grenada, 1988; co-editor: Nursing Care of the Aged, 1989; accompanist: The Master's Quartet; contbr. articles to profl. jours., chpts. to books. Sec. A.H. Meadows Libr. Bd., Midlothian, 1984—; mem. Hist. Adv. Bd., Midlothian, 1998—, Ellis County AIDS Edn. Task Force, 1988-93, First Bapt. Ch., Midlothian, 1954—; v.p. Kay Family Assn. Mem. DAR, Tex. Assn. Sch. Nurses, Baylor Alumni Assn., Assn. Tex. Profl. Educators, Sigma Theta Tau. Avocations: genealogy, piano, reading, gathering data on local history. Home: PO Box 116 Midlothian TX 76065-0116 Office: Midlothian Ind Sch Dist 100 Walter Stephenson Rd Midlothian TX 76065-3418

ESCALANTE, JUAN, performing company executive; children: Juan, Eduardo. Devel. mgr., human resources dir. Miami City Ballet; asst. dir. fin. N.Y.C. Ballet; mng. dir. Ballet of Fla., Fla., 2002—. Mem. bd. trustees Chaminade-Madonna Coll. Prep., Hollywood, Fla. Office: 500 Fern St West Palm Beach FL 33401 Business E-Mail: Jescalante@balletflorida.com.

ESCALANTE, JUDSON ROBERT, business consultant; b. Schenectady, N.Y., Jan. 31, 1930; s. James S. and Katherine H. (Judson) E.; m. Charlotte D. Carpenter, June 7, 1958; children: David J., Katherine Anne. BA, Union Coll., 1953. Asst. estate planning officer Nat. Comml. Bank, Albany, N.Y., 1955-65; founder, v.p., sec., dir. Fidelity Bank of Colonie, Latham, N.Y., 1966-69; area dir. Gen. Bus. Svcs., Latham, 1969-81, Micro Bus. Svcs., 1981—2003. V.p. fin. Gad Cruise Lines, Inc., 1987-88; instr. in field. Bd. dirs., treas. Capital Artists Opera Co., 1970-74, 79; mem. fund dr. com. Union Coll., 1979-80; vestryman, treas. Episcopal Ch.; treas., chief fin. officer Chatham Vis. Nurse Assn., 1983-89; trustee Chatham Vis. Nurse Assn. Profit Trust, 1985-96; auditor Chatham Conservation Found., 1985-95. With U.S. Army, 1953-55. Mem. Colonie C. of C. (treas., bd. dirs. 1972-76), Union Coll. Alumni Soc. (pres. 1971-73, Alumni Gold medal 1978), Dutch Settlers Soc. Albany. Home: 400 Old Comers Rd Chatham MA 02633-1315 E-mail: judcape@capecod.net.

ESCALERA, KAREN WEINER, marketing professional; b. Phila., Dec. 7, 1944; d. George Joseph Weiner and Gladys Lieberman; m. Alfonso G. Escalera, Sept. 8, 1978. BA cum laude, U. Pa., 1966. Prof. Nat. U., Bogota, Columbia, 1966-67; assoc. editor United Bus. Publs., N.Y.C., 1967-68; account exec. Jacobson/Wallace/Westphal, N.Y.C., 1968-69; dir. pub. rels. for western hemisphere Hilton Internat., N.Y.C., 1969-79; chmn., CEO, owner KWE Assocs., Inc., N.Y.C., 1979—2002; pres., CEO KWE Group, Inc., 2002—. Contbg. author: Hospitality Management; also articles. Bd. dirs. Children's Home Soc., Miami, Fla., 1997—. Recipient Winthrop Grice award Hotel Sales and Mktg. Assn., 1993; named All Star in Travel, Inside PR mag., 1990. Mem.: Soc. Am. Travel Writers, Pub. Rels. Soc. Am. (Silver Anvil award). Avocations: travel, gardening, tennis. Office: 4425 Ponce de Leon Blvd Miami FL 33146

ESCALET, FRANK DIAZ, art gallery owner, artist, educator; b. Ponce, P.R., Mar. 16, 1930; s. Frank Thillet and Concepcion Rodriquez (Diaz) E.; m.Shirley Leslie Fanner, Sept. 29, 1953 (div. Aug., 1955); children: Judith Alicia, Sudan Edith Escalet Barry; m. Marjorie Janet Gaydash-Huebner, July 19, 1964; 1 child, Frank Daniel (dec.). Owner, operator Talent Shop, N.Y.C., 1955-58, House of Escalet, N.Y.C., 1958-71, Pandora's Box, Eastport, Maine, 1971-73, Cobbler's Bench Art Gallery, Pembroke, Maine, 1973-82, House of Escalet Gallery, Kennebunkport, Maine, 1982-84, House of Escalet Studios, Kennebunkport, 1984—. Tchr. leathercraft Pasamaquoddy Reservation, Perry, Maine, 1971-72, Vocat. Sch. for Retarded Children, Calais, Maine, 1972-73. One-man traveling show Czechoslovakia, Russia, Poland, Yugoslavia, Hungary, Ukraine, 1991—; represented in permanent collections at Naprstkovo Mus., Prague, Union of Artists, Moscow, Bratslavia Primitive Mus., Slovakia, Frydek-Mistek Mus. No. Moravia, Museo Chicano, Phoenix, S.E. Tex. Art Mus., Beaumont, Arch. M. Huntington Gallery, Austin, Tex., Housatonic Mus., Bridgeport, Conn., Orgn. of Am. States Art Mus., Washington, Maryknoll (N.Y.) Sisters Ctr., Mus. City N.Y., 1998; featured on pub. TV, 1978, 82, 89; works in permanent collections Mus. City of N.Y., Ellen Noel Mus. Art of Permian Basin, Odessa, Tex., Dowd Fine Arts Mus., Cortland, N.Y., New Britain Mus. Am. Art; artist: Song and Dance Man acrylic, 1996. With US Air Force, 1947-54. Recipient numerous internat. and U.S. awards. Avocations: photography, antiques, gardening, travel, reading. Home and Office: House of Escalet Studios 24 Fletcher St Kennebunk ME 04043-6707 E-mail: escalet@gwi.net.

ESCARRAZ, ENRIQUE, III, lawyer; b. Evergreen Park, Ill., Aug. 30, 1944; s. Enrique Jr. and Mary Ellen (Bandy) E.; children from previous marriage; Erin Christine, Martina Mary; m. Patricia Jane Escarraz; children: Sarah Ellen, James Lee, Jason F. BA, U. Fla., 1966, JD, 1968. Bar: Fla. 1969, U.S. Dist. Ct. (so. and mid. dists.) Fla. 1969, U.S. Ct. Appeals (5th cir.) 1971, U.S. Ct. Appeals (11th cir.) 1981. VISTA atty. Community Legal Counsel, Chgo., 1968-69; mng. atty. Fla. Rural Legal Services, Ft. Myers, 1969-71; pvt. practice law St. Petersburg, Fla., 1971-82, 85-87, 88—; ptnr. Anderson & Escarraz, St. Petersburg, 1982-85; asst. gen. counsel U. South Fla., 1987-88; assoc. James L. Eskald Law Office, Largo, Fla., 1988. Part-time atty. Pub. Defender's Office Fla. 6th Cir., St. Petersburg, 1973-74; bd. dirs. Gulf Coast Legal Svcs., Inc., 1989—, pres., 1994-96. Vol. Cmty. Law Prog., Inc.; coord. James B. Sanderlin for Judge, Pinellas County, Fla., 1972-76; mem. ACLU Legal Panel, St. Petersburg, 1972—; cooperating atty. NAACP Legal Def. Edn. Funds, Inc., N.Y.C., 1973—; pres. Creative Care, Inc., Clearwater, Fla., 1974-80; mem. allocations com. United Way, Pinellas County, 1976, 1978-81; pres., treas. Cmty. Youth Svcs., Inc., St. Petersburg, 1977-82; co-chmn. Blue Ribbon Com. Pinellas County Dem. Exec. Com., 1977-82; mem. Fla. HRS Dist. V Adv. Coun., Pinellas County, 1982, St. Petersburg Human Rels. Rev. Bd., 1984, 90—, St. Petersburg Adult Cmty. Band, 1989-2003, Greater St. Petersburg Second Time Around Marching Band, 1990-92; mem. adv. bd. Jacquelyn Elvera Hodges Johnson Fund, 1990—. Mem.: FBA, ATLA, ABA, St. Petersburg Bar Assn. (pro bono com. 1988, 1995—2001, diversity com. 2000—), Nat. Assn. Social Security Claimant Reps., Show Me the Money Investment Club Pinellas (founding mem., 1st pres. 2002), Greater Pinellas County Dem. Club (sec.-treas. 1989—97, bd. dirs. 1997—2001). Office: 2121 5th Ave N Saint Petersburg FL 33713-8013 also: PO Box 847 Saint Petersburg FL 33731-0847

ESCHBACH, JOSEPH WETHERILL, nephrology educator; b. Detroit, Jan. 21, 1933; s. Joseph William and Marguerite (Wetherill) E.; m. Mary Ann Charles, June 16, 1956; children: Cheryl Louise, Ann Elizabeth, Joseph Charles. BA, BS, Otterbein Coll., 1955; MD, Jefferson Med. Coll., 1959. Practitioner nephrology and internal medicine Minor and James Med., Seattle, 1965—; dir. home dialysis U. Wash., Seattle, 1965-72, clin. asst. prof. div. nephrology, 1967-70, clin. assoc. prof. div. nephrology, 1970-75, clin. prof. div. nephrology, 1975-85, clin. prof. divs. nephrology and hematology, 1985—. Cons. Ortho Pharm., Raritan, N.J., 1987-88, Amgen, Thousand Oaks, Calif., 1985-91. Co-editor: Erythropoietin: Molecular, Cellular and Clinical Biology, 1991; contbr. articles to jours. in field, chpts. to textbooks. Trustee First Ave. Svc. Ctr., 1976-86; pres. bd. trustees Northwest Kidney Ctr., Seattle, 1985-87 (Haviland award 1991). Recipient Disting. Svc. award Seattle Jaycees, 1979, Alumni Achievement award Otterbein Coll., 1991. Fellow: ACP; mem.: AMA, Washington Assn. Biomed. Rsch. (pres. 1999—2001), King County Med. Soc. (pres. 1987), Internat. Soc. Nephrology, Am. Soc. Nephrology, Inst. Medicine of NAS. Presbyterian. Avocations: squash, woodworking, singing. Home: 770 96th Ave SE Bellevue WA 98004-6502 Office: Minor & James Medical 515 Minor Ave Ste 300 Seattle WA 98104-2187

ESCHENBACH, CHRISTOPH, conductor, pianist; b. Breslau, Silesia, Germany, Feb. 20, 1940; Attended, Hamburg (Germany) Conservatory, State Conservatory Music, Cologne, Germany; D, U. Houston. Performed with leading orchs. including Concertgebouw, Amsterdam, The Netherlands, Paris Orch., London Symphony, Berlin Philharm., Carnegie Hall debut with Cleve. Orch., 1969, toured Europe, N.Am. and S.Am., Israel, Japan, appeared at festivals including, Salzburg, Austria, Lucerne, Switzerland, Bonn, Germany, Aix-en-Provence, France, Pacific Music Festival, 1990—94, chief condr. Staatsphilharmonie Rheinland-Pfalz, Germany, 1979, first prin. guest condr. Tonhalle Orch., Switzerland, 1981, chief condr., 1982, rec. artist Deutsche Gammophon, Polydor, EMI, Virgin Classics, London, 1989, artistic dir. Schleswig-Holstein Music Festival, Germany, music dir. Hamburg NDR Symphony Orch., Orch. de Paris, 2000, Houston Symphony, 1988—99, Phila. Orch., 2003—. Decorated officers cross German Order Merit, comdrs. cross; named artistic dir., Ravinia Music Festival, 1995, award, Munich Internat.; recipient Leonard Bernstein award, Pacific Music Festival, 1993. Office: care Columbia Artists Mgmt Inc 165 W 57th St New York NY 10019-2201 Mailing: Houston Symphony Orch 615 Louisiana St Ste 102 Houston TX 77002*

ESCHENMOSER, ALBERT, chemist; b. Erstfeld, Aug. 5, 1925; s. Alfons and Johanna (Oesch) E.; m. Elizabeth Baschnonga, 1954; 3 children. Dr. Nat. Sci., Swiss Fed. Inst. Tech., 1951; student Collegium Altdorf, Kantonsschule St. Gallen, ETH Zurich; Dr.rer.nat. (hon.), U. Fribourg, 1966; DSc (hon.), U. Chgo., 1970, U. Edinburgh, 1979, U. Bologna, 1989, U. Frankfurt, 1990, U. Strasbourg, 1991, Harvard U., 1993, Scripps Rsch. Inst., La Jolla, Calif., 2000. Privatdozent organic chemistry Swiss Fed. Inst. Tech., 1956, assoc. prof., 1960, prof. organic chemistry, 1965; prof. Skaggs Inst. Chem. Biology Scripps Rsch. Inst., La Jolla, Calif., 1996. Contbr. articles to profl. jour. Recipient Kern award, Swiss Fed. Inst. Tech., 1949, Werner award, Swiss Chem. Soc., 1956, Ruzicka award, Swiss Fed. Inst. Tech., 1958, Fritzsche award, Am. Chem. Soc., 1966, Marcel Benoist prize, Swiss Govt., 1973, R.A. Welch award in Chemistry, Houston, 1974, Kirkwood medal, Yale, 1976, A.W.V. Hofmann-Denkmünze, GDCh., 1976, Dannie Heinemann prize, Akademie der Wissenschaften Göttingen, 1977, Davy medal, Royal Soc. London, 1978, Tetrahedron prize, Pergamon Press, 1981, G. Kenner award, U. Liverpool, 1982, Arthur C. Cope award, Am. Chem. Soc., 1984, Wolf prize for chemistry, Wolf Found., Israel, 1986, Cothenius medal, Leopoldina Halle, 1991, Orden Pour le mérite für Wissenschaften und Künste, 1992, Oesterreichisches Ehrenzeichen für Wissenschaft und Kunst, 1993, Nakanishi prize, Chem. Soc. Japan, 1998, Paracelsus prize, Swiss Chem. Soc., 1999, Grande Medaille d'Or, Acad. de Sci., Paris, 2001, A.I. Oparin medal, Internat. Soc. Study Origin of Life, 2002, Roger Adams award, Am. Chem. Soc., 2003. Mem. Am. Acad. Arts and Sci. (fgn.), Nat. Acad. Sci. US (fgn. assoc.), Akademie der Wissenschaften (corr. mem. Göttingen), Deutsche Akademie der Naturforscher Leopoldina (Halle), Royal Soc. (fgn. London), Pontificial Acad. (Vatican), Acad. Europe (London), Croatian Acad. Sci. Arts (corr. mem. Zagreb). Home: Bergstrasse 9 8700 Kuesnacht Switzerland Office: ETH Hönggerberg HCI H309 CH-8093 Zurich Switzerland E-mail: eschenmoser@org.chem.ethz.ch.

ESCHETE, MARY LOUISE, internist; b. Houma, La., Feb. 8, 1949; d. Marshall John and Louise Esther (Davis) E.; m. Lorphy Joseph Bourque, July 7, 1979. BS, La. State U., 1970; MD, La. State U. Med. Ctr., Shreveport, 1974. Diplomate, Am. Bd. Internal Medicine. Resident in internal medicine La. State U. Med. Ctr., Shreveport, 1974-77, staff instr., 1979, fellow in infectious disease, 1979; pvt. practice Houma, 1980-83; staff, dept. internal medicine South La. Med. Assocs., Houma, 1983—. Chmn. infection control Terrebonne Gen. Hosp., 1981—2000, 2002—, mem. performance improvement, 2000—; chmn. infection control S. La. Med. Ctr., 1983—; pub. health dir. Region III, 1993—98, pub. health infectious disease cons., 1998—. Contbr. articles to med. jours. Bd. dirs. Houma Battered Women's Shelter, 1983-87, Houma YWCA, 1987-94; mem. Roche Nat. AIDS Adv. Bd., 1993; Triparish vol. activist, 1994. Named Citizen of Yr. Regional and State Social Workers, 1992, Outstanding Dr. in South East. Mem. ACP, AAAS, AMA, Infectious Disease Soc., Am. Soc. Microbiology, So. Med. Assn. (grantee 1978), N.Y. Acad. Sci., La. State Med. Soc., Terrebonne Parish Med. Soc. (sec. 1982-83, treas. 1988-89, 98—, v.p. 1993-94, pres. 1994-95), Krewe of Hyachinthians (pres. 1989-90, 94-95, bd. dirs. 1990-96), Houma Jr. Women's Club (reporter 1988-89, rec. sec. 1989—, pres.-elect 1991-93, pres. 1993-95, chaplain 1998—2002), Alpha Epsilon Delta. Democrat. Roman Catholic. Avocation: gardening. Home: 3984 Highway 311 Houma LA 70360-8115 Office: Chabert Med Ctr 1978 Industrial Blvd Houma LA 70363-7055

ESCHWEILER, PETER QUINTUS, planning consultant; b. Milw., Nov. 2, 1932; s. Alexander Chadbourne Jr. and Dorothy Quincy (Adams) E m. Mickie Pauline Symonds, Aug. 13, 1955; children Susan Marie, Steven Adams. BA, Cornell U., 1955, M of Regional Planning, 1957. Assoc. planner Frederick P. Clark & Assocs., Rye, N.Y., 1960-66; chief planner Westchester County, White Plains, N.Y., 1967, dep. commr. of planning, 1968-69, commr. of planning, 1969-91; advisor Hudson River Valley (N.Y.) Greenway Cmtys. Coun., 1991—2000, Nassau County (N.Y.) Planning Commn., 1997-98. Chmn. Westchester County Drought Mgmt. Task Force, 1991-2002, Westchester County Geographic Info. Sys. Task Force, 1998—; pres. Pleasantville (N.Y.) Housing Devel. Fund Co., Inc., 1997-2002; mem. mission planning task force Presbytery of Hudson River, 1994, 1997, 2002, chmn., 1997; mem. Mt. Pleasant Pub. Libr. Men's Group, 1991—, chmn., 2002—; dir. Westchester County Hist. Soc., 2001—; pres. Pleasantville Cmty. Housing Devel. Orgn., Inc., 2002—. 1st lt. USAF, 1957-60. Mem. Am. Inst. Cert. Planners, Nat. Assn. County Planning Dirs. (pres. 1984-85), N.Y. State Assn. Counties (pres. 1980-81, Recognition award 1991), N.Y. Assn. County Planning Dirs. (pres. 1970, bd. dirs. 1969-91), Nat. Assn. Counties (bd. dirs. 1987-89), Nat. Assn. Regional Couns. (bd. dirs. 1988-89), Am. Soc. for Photogrammetry and Remote Sensing (bd. dirs. North Atlantic region 1987-97, 99—, sec.-treas. 1988-97, Bausch and Lomb Photogrammetric award 1957, Meritorious Svc. award 1997), Cornell Club (N.Y.C.), Rotary (pres. White Plains 1985-86), Sigma Chi. Presbyterian. Avocations: skiing, photography, computers. Home and Office: 36 Wilton Rd Pleasantville NY 10570-2022

ESCOBAR, ELAINE OFELIA, television producer, writer; b. Santa Barbara, CA, Nov. 9, 1946; d. Catarino Hilly and Ofelia (Valdez) Escobar. HS dip., Sacred Heart Acad., Tampa, Fl, 1963—65. Spkr. Sch. Enrichment Resource, Tampa, Fla., 1980—2002; prodr. Publ. Access TV, Tampa, Fla., 1990—94, host, 1990—94, writer, 1990—94. Author: (novels) Love Wizard for You, 1989, (comic book) Children Save Planet Earth, 1994, (plays), 1995. Mem. Bd. of Dir. Easter Seals, West Coast Tampa, Fla., 1978—99. Recipient Svc. to Mankind, Firefighters Sertoma /Fla., 1981—83, Gallantry, Easter Seals/ Fla., 1989, Vol. of the yr., Mayor Dick Greco/ Fla., 1990, Golden Cassett award for outstanding TV host., 1992. Achievements include pres. of my own non-profit Co."Wizard Prodn.". The comic book and play features the character "Love Wizard" after myself. Avocations: gardening, art, theater.

ESCOBAR, ISABEL CRISTINA, education educator; b. Curitiba, Parana, Brazil, May 10, 1973; d. Elias Antonio Silva and Vera Maria Pietruza; m. Alan Edward Kurtzweg, Dec. 4, 1999. BS, U. of Ctrl. Fla., 1993—96, MS, 1996—96, PhD in Civil Engring., 1997—2000. Cert. Fla. State Bd. Profl. Engineers, 1995. Asst. prof. U. of Toledo - ChEE Dept., 2000—. Grantee Sci. to Achieve Results Fellowship, EPA, 1997-2000. Mem.: Soc. of Women Engineers, Am. Chem. Soc., Water Environment Fedn., Am. Water Works Assn., Assn. of Environ. Engrng. and Sci. Professors. Office: University of Toledo - ChEE Department 2801 West Bancroft St MS 305 Toledo OH 43606-3390 Office Fax: 419-530-8086. E-mail: isabel.escobar@utoledo.edu.

ESCOTO, LUZ, language educator; arrived in U.S., 1984; d. Victor Manuel Becerra and Luz Maria Escoto; m. James Cameron, Jan. 4, 1984 (div. 1984); 1 child, Ivan Becerra. BA in Edn., St. Mary's U., San Antonio, 1993; MA in Spanish and Portuguese, Rice U., 1997; postgrad., U. Tex. Spanish instr. U. Tex., Austin, 1997—. Spkr. in field. Vol. San Antonio Mus. Art, 1994; vol., ESL organizer Pilgrim Luth. Ch., Houston, 1995. Hon. scholar, St. Mary's U., San Antonio, 1990—93, Presdl. scholar, Rice U., Houston, 1994—96. Mem.: Alfa Sigma Lambda. Avocations: writing, travel, cooking, movies. Office: Univ Tex Austin Spanish and Portuguese Dept University Station B3700 Austin TX 78712-1155

ESCUTIA, MARTHA, state senator; b. East Los Angeles, Calif. m. Leo Briones; 2 children. BA in Pub. Adminstrn. with honors, U. So. Calif; JD, GEorgetown U.; postgrad., Nat. Autonomous U., Mexico City. Sr. rsch. atty. Los Angeles County Superior Ct.; pvt. practice with law firm specializing in civil litigation, L.A.; mem. Calif. State Assembly, 1992-98, Calif. State Senate, 1998—, chmn. health and human svcs. com. V.p. govt. affairs and pub. policy United Way of L.A. Recipient numerous awards for pub. svc. Democrat. Office: Calif State Senate State Capitol Rm 5080 Sacramento CA 95814 also: Ste 125 12440 E Imperial Hwy Norwalk CA 90650*

ESER, SEMIH, science educator, consultant, researcher; PhS, Penn State U., 1981—86. Dir. (research in coking) Coke Deposition and Carbonization, Needle Coke; contbr. publications in jours. Carbon, Fuel, Energy & Fuels, IEC Rsc. Office: Penn State U 101 Hosler Bldg University Park PA 16802 Office Fax: 814-865-3248. E-mail: seser@psu.edu.

ESFANDIARY, DARA SADIGH, information technology executive; b. Tehran, Iran, July 7, 1964; s. Mohsen Sadigh and Mary (Nieradka) Esfandiary; 1 child, Lily Veronica. BS, George Washington U., 1990. Asst. dir. budget Sch. Gov. and Bus. Adminstrn. George Washington U., Washington, 1986-87

software programming, systems analysis cons. Davison Assocs., Washington, 1987-89; sr. computer specialist Orkand Corp., Washington, 1989-91; dir. devel. Elm Svcs. Corp., Rockville, Md., 1991-92; v.p., chief info. officer Software Engring. Solutions Corp., Washington, 1992-94; ADP sect. leader U.S. Dept. of Interior/Fish Wildlife Svc., Washington, 1994-2000; sr. data mgmt. officer Internat. Monetary Fund, Washington, 2000—. Info. sys. and bus. tech. cons. SES Corp., Washington, 1985—2000, leadership tng., 1996—2000, knowledge discovery and data visualization cons., 1997—; parliamentary procedure trainer, pres. Free & Wild Club Toastmasters Internat., Washington, 1995. Contbr. articles to profl. jours. Participant Re-enactment of Laying U.S. Capital/Cornerstone, Washington, 1995. Mem.: IEEE, Am. Mgmt. Assn., Toastmaster Internat. (chpt. pres. 1995, head fraternal orgn. 1996—97), Mensa. Avocations: scuba diving, tennis, Tae Kwon Do, skiing, opera. Home: 4401 Sedgwick St NW Washington DC 20016-2713

ESFANDIARY, MARY S. physical scientist, operations consultant; b. Passaic, N.J., June 27, 1929; d. Peter J. and Veronica R. (Kida) Nieradka; m. Mohsen S. Esfandiary; children: Homayoun Austin, Dara S. BS in Chemistry, St. John's U., 1951; postgrad., Polytechnic Inst. N.Y., 1955-56. Research chemist Picatinny Arsenal, Dover, N.J., 1951-56; supr. phys. sci. Bur. Mines, Washington, 1956-61; asst. to dir. research Nat. Iranian Oil Co., Tehran, 1961-64; lectr. U. Tehran and Aryamehr Inst. Tech., Tehran, 1961-64, 69-73; dir. internat. affairs Acad. of Scis., Tehran, 1977-79; chief geog. names br. Def. Mapping Agy., Washington, 1981-86, chief prodn. mgmt. office, 1986-87, chief support div., chief inventory mgmt. div., 1987-90, chief product mgmt. dept., 1990-92, dep. dir. distbn. mgmt. ops. Combat Support Ctr., 1993, chief, co-prodn. mgmt. divsn., 1993-94, chief divsn. internat. ops. coprodn. mgmt., 1993-96; ops. mgmt., 1996; dir. MS svcs., 1997—. Contbr. papers and articles to tech. jours., 1952-78. Pres. UN Delegations Women's Club, N.Y.C., 1967-69, v.p., program dir., 1964-67; pres. Diplomatic Corps. Com. for Red Cross, Bangkok, Thailand, 1974-76; v.p., bd. dirs. Found. for Blind of Thailand, Bangkok, 1973-77. Recipient Badge of Honor for Social Service, Thailand, 1975, 1st Class medal Red Cross, Thailand, 1976. Home and Office: 4401 Sedgewick St NW Washington DC 20016-2713

ESHAGIAN, JOSEPH, ophthalmologist; b. Iran, Mar. 15, 1951; s. Ebrahim and Touran (Monasebian) E. BS with honors, U. Mich., 1971; MD, SUNY, Syracuse, 1975. Diplomate Am. Bd. Ophthalmology. Intern U. Mich. Hosp., Ann Arbor, 1975-76; resident in ophthalmology U. Iowa Hosp., Iowa City, 1976-79, assoc. dept. ophthalmology, 1979; practice medicine specializing in ophthalmology, L.A., 1980—. Contbr. articles to med. jours. Mem. AMA, Am. Acad. Neurology, Assn. Rsch. in Vision and Ophthalmology, Am. Assn. Ophthalmology, Contact Lens Assn. Ophthalmologists, Med. Eye Svcs. Calif., Am. Acad. Ophthalmology, Calif. Med. Assn., Los Angeles County Med. Assn., Am. Soc. Contemporary Ophthalmology, Internat. Glaucoma Congress. Office: 1211 N Vermont Ave Ste 200 Los Angeles CA 90029-1748

ES-HAQ, FEREIDOUN, minister, marriage and family therapist; b. Hamadan, Iran, June 7, 1956; arrived in U.S., 1979; s. Samuel Es-Haq and Alice Yeganeh. BA, Azusa Pacific U., 1980, MA, 1987; DMin, Carolina U. Theology, 1997; M in Pastoral Counseling, Andersonville Bapt. Sem., 1999, ThD, 2003. Cert. Internat. Assn. Christian Counselors. Pastor Assyrian Evang. Ch., Turlock, Calif., 1980—85, organizing pastor San Jose, Calif., 1981—92; asst. pastor Santa Teresa Hills Presbyn. Ch., San Jose, 1985—86; organizing pastor Iranian Christian Ch., San Jose, 1987—94, Bet-Eil Assyrian Ch., San Jose, 1992—, S. Bay Iranian Ch., San Jose, 1994—2000. Bd. dirs. Conservative Bapt. Assn. No. Calif. and Nev., Saratoga, Calif.; adj. prof. San Jose Christian Coll., 1987—94. Translator: Disciple, 1982, 1997, Be Mature, 1998, How to Handle Adversity, 1999, other books from English to Farsi. Cmty. adv. Assyrian cmty., San Jose, 1987—; welfare adv. Bet-Eil Assyrian Ch., San Jose, 1992—. Avocations: choir directing, composing music. Office: Bet-Eil Assyrian Ch PO Box 24278 San Jose CA 95154

ESHBAUGH, W(ILLIAM) HARDY, botanist, educator; b. Glen Ridge, N.J., May 1, 1936; s. William Hardy Eshbaugh Jr. and Elizabeth (Stephen) Henderson; m. Barbara Keller, Sept. 6, 1958; children: David Charles, Stephen Hardy, Elizabeth Wendy Brown, Jeffrey Raymond. BA, Cornell U., 1959; MA, Ind. U., 1961, PhD, 1964. Lectr. in botany Ind. U., Bloomington, 1962; spl. asst. to chief ecology and epidemiology br. Dugway (Utah) Proving Ground, 1964-65; asst. prof., curator herbarium So. Ill. U., Carbondale, 1965—66; from asst. prof. to prof. botany Miami U., Oxford, Ohio, 1967—98, chmn. dept. botany, 1983-88, prof. emeritus, 1998. Cur., Willard Sherman Turrell Herbarium, Miami U., 1967-82; assoc. program dir. NSF, Washington, 1982-83; co-chmn. steering com. Systematics Agenda 2000-Charting the Biosphere; adv. bd. Am. Bot. Coun., 1996—; instr. Internat. Rainforest Workshops, 1991-99. Co-author: (Book) The Vascular Flora of Andros Island, Bahamas, 1988; contbr. articles to profl. jours. Bd. dirs. Childrens Environ. Trust Found., 1992-94; pres. Elizabeth Wakeman Henderson Charitable Found., 1997—. Capt. U.S. Army, 1964-65. Named Citizen of Yr., Oxford, Ohio, 2002. Fellow: AAAS, Inst. Environ. Scis., Ohio Acad. Sci.; mem.: Internat. Field Studies (trustee 1989—95), Internat. Orgn. Plant Biosystematists (coun. 1987—89, ad hoc com. 1989—92, N. Am. treas. 1992—95), Assn. Systemic Collections (bd. dirs. 1981—84, rep.-at-large), Nature Conservancy (vice chmn. Ohio chpt. 1970—75, trustee 1970—77), Atlantic Salmon Fedn. (bd. dirs. 2002—05), Bot. Soc. Am. (pres. 1988—89, Merit award 1992), Soc. Econ. Botany (v.p. 1982—83, pres. 1983—84), Am. Soc. Plant Taxonomists (pres. 1991—92), Am. Inst. Biol. Scis. (pres. 1995), Nat. Audubon Soc. (bd. dirs. 1993—, vice-chmn.). Methodist. Avocations: camping, fly fishing, photography, sailing, swimming. Home: 209 Mckee Ave Oxford OH 45056-9059 Office: Miami U Dept Botany Oxford OH 45056 E-mail: eshbauwh@muohio.edu.

ESHELMAN, RALPH ELLSWORTH, maritime historian, vertebrate paleontologist, cultural resource consultant; b. Mt. Holly, N.J., Mar. 20, 1947; s. Ralph Mengel and Grace Elizha (Bozarth) E.; m. Evelyne Margaret Herman, June 3, 1974; 1 child, Erich Ellsworth. AA, Prince George's C.C., 1967; BS, SUNY, Stony Brook, 1969; MS, U. Iowa, 1971; PhD, U. Mich., 1974. Phys. sci. aide U.S. Geol. Survey, Washington, 1965-69; dir. Calvert Marine Mus., Solomons, Md., 1974-90; rsch. assoc. Smithsonian Inst., Washington, 1976—. Owner Eshelman & Assocs., 1994—; cons. Nat. Maritime Initiative, Nat. Park Svc., 1993-2000, USCG, 1995-98; project dir. Md. War of 1812 Initiative, 1998—; cons. Am. Battlefield Protection program Nat. Park Svc., 1999-2002, cons. Star-Spangled Nat. Historic Trail study, 2002—; lectr. on expedition cruise ship Explorer, 1991—; study leader for nat. and internat. trips Smithsonian Instn., 1998—; dir. paleontological field camp Mus. of Middle Appalachians, 2000—. Contbr. articles to profl. jours. Grantee Sigma Xi, 1972, Nat. Geog. Soc., 1981, 86. Mem. Nat. Maritime Preservation Task Force (vice chmn. 1983-84), Md. Soc. Underwater Archeology (trustee 1984-86), Historical Trust, Md. Humanities Coun. (trustee 1984-89, 2d v.p. 1987-89), Coun. Am. Maritime Mus. (exec. com. 1983-89, v.p. 1988-89, pres. 1990), Solomons Environ. and Archeol. Rsch. Consortium (founding chmn. 1987), Nat. Maritime Alliance (co-chair 1994-95), Nat. Lighthouse Mus. (pres. steering com., trustee 1998—, 2nd v.p.), The Nature Conservancy (Md. chpt. v.p. sci. and stewardship 1996-2001). Avocations: spelunking, snorkeling, canoeing, hiking, swimming. Home and Office: 12178 Preston Dr Lusby MD 20657-2905 E-mail: ree47@comcast.com.

ESHELMAN, WILLIAM ROBERT, librarian, editor; b. Oklahoma City, Aug. 23, 1921; s. Cyrus Lenhert and Fern (Reed) E.; m. Mimi Blau, July 3, 1952 (div. Aug. 1956); m. Eve Kendall, June 21, 1957 (div. Apr. 1975); children: Ann, Benjamin, Zachary; m. Pat Rom, Dec. 29, 1977. BA, Chapman Coll., L.A., 1943; MA, UCLA, 1950; BLS, U. Calif. at Berkeley, 1951. Conscripted in civilian pub. service, Waldport, Oreg., 1943-46; ptnr. Untide Press, Pasadena, Calif., 1946-65; teaching asst. UCLA, 1949-50, library asst., 1950; faculty Los Angeles State Coll., 1951-65, asst. librarian, 1954-59, coll. librarian, 1959-65; librarian, prof. bibliography Bucknell U., 1965-68; editor Wilson Library Bull., 1968-78; pres. Scarecrow Press, Metuchen, N.J., 1979-86; proprietor The Press at the Camperdown Elm, Wooster, Ohio, 1987-93. Editor: Take Hold Upon the Future: Letters on Writers and Writing by William Everson and Lawrence Clark Powell, 1938-1946, 1994; author: No Silence! A Library Life, 1997; contbg. author: Perspectives on William Everson, 1992; mem. editl. bd. Choice, 1966-71. Bd. dirs. Grolier Edn. Corp., 1979-86; mem. adv. council edn. for librarianship U. Calif., 1961-64; mem. acad. senate Calif. State Colls., 1964-65. Mem. AAUP (v.p. L.A. State Coll. 1958-59, pres. 1964-65). ALA (winner Libr. Periodicals award 1960, editorial com. 1964-66, mem. coun. 1972-76, com. accreditation 1977-79), Calif. Libr. Assn. (chmn. intellectual freedom com., pres. so. dist. 1965, editor Calif. Libr. jour. 1960-63), Assn. Coll. and Rsch. Librs. (publs. com.), Assn. Calif. State Coll. Profs., ACLU, Friends Com. Legis., N.J. Libr. Assn. (hon.), Rounce and Coffin Club (L.A.; sec.-treas. 1953-56), Typophiles Club (N.Y.C.). Home and Office: 3645 SW 52nd Pl Portland OR 97221-2113 E-mail: eshrom@aol.com.

ESHER, BRIAN RICHARD, chief executive officer; b. N.Y.C., Sept. 1, 1948; s. John Conrad and Elizabeth (Carley) E.; children: Justin John, Christopher Ryan. BS in Bus. Mgmt. magna cum laude, Fairleigh Dickinson U., Madison, N.J., 1971, MBA summa cum laude, 1975. Mgr. Litton Industries, Morristown, 1972-75; industry mgr. AT&T Long Lines, Somerset, N.J., 1975-77; v.p. Transaction Mgmt., Inc., Montgomeryville, Pa., 1977-79; dir. mktg. Burroughs Corp., Detroit, 1980-82, exec. office Detoit, 1982-84, v.p. Rochester, N.Y., 1984-85; sr. v.p., gen. mgr. ITEK Graphic Systems Divsn., 1985-88; exec. v.p. A.B. Dick Co., Chgo., 1988-89; chmn., pres., CEO Environ. Control Group, Inc., Maple Shade, N.J., 1989, pres., CEO, chmn., 1990-96; dir., chmn, CEO MLX Corp., 1990-96, also bd. dirs.; chmn, pres., CEO Pameco Corp., Norcross, Ga., 1992-96; prin. SE. Tech. Opportunities Fund LLC., 1998—; chmn., CEO Storm Consulting LLC, 2000—; chmn., pres & CEO, Coe Mfg., Co., 2002—03, pres., chmn., 2003—; CEO Coe Newnes/McGehee, 2002—03, pres., chmn., 2003—. With U.S. Army, 1967-69, Vietnam. Decorated D.S.C., Silver Star, Bronze Star, Purple Heart (3). Mem. Assn. of MBA Execs., Phi Omega Epsilon (Membership award 1971). Republican. Avocation: tennis. Home: 300 Morton Manor Ct Alpharetta GA 30022-6253 Office Fax: 678-291-9138. E-mail: brian@stormconsultingllc.com.

ESHER, JACOB AARON, lawyer, mediator; b. Boston, Oct. 25, 1950; s. Eli Abraham and Irma (Hoffman) Etscovitz; m. Susan Riedle Foucault, June 1975 (div. Sept. 1979); m. Linda Ann Robinson, May 9, 1984; children: Joel Harry Robinson, Samantha Blihn Robinson. BA, Brandeis U., 1972; JD magna cum laude, U. San Francisco, 1977. Bar: Calif. 1977, Mass. 1985, U.S. Dist. Ct. (no. dist.) Calif. 1977, U.S. Dist. Ct. (ea. dist.) Calif. 1979, U.S. Dist. Ct. Mass. 1985. Assoc., Murphy, Weir & Butler, San Francisco, 1977-79; assoc. counsel, legal dept. Bank of Am., San Francisco, 1979-82; pvt. practice Law and Mediation Offices of Jacob Aaron Esher, Petaluma, Calif., 1982-84; ptnr. Riemer & Braunstein, Boston, 1984-90, Rubin and Rudman, Boston, 1990-99; sr. mediator JAMS, Boston, 1996—; ptnr. Riley & Esher, Cambridge, 1999—. Author: Mediation Manual, ABI, 1996, (songs) Blindspot, 1998; contbr. chpts. to books. Mem. Am. Bankruptcy Inst. (chair ADR subcom. 1994—), Boston Bar Assn. (chair ADR subcom. 1995-98). Office: Riley & Esher LLP 69 Thorndike St Cambridge MA 02141 E-mail: jesher@rileyesher.com.

ESHERICK, JOSEPH WHARTON, history educator; b. Ross, Calif., Aug. 14, 1942; s. Joseph Esherick and Rebecca (Wood) Watkin; m. Judy Teng, June 7, 1965 (div. 1978); children: Joseph Scott, Christopher Michael; m. Ye Wa, June 17, 1984; 1 child, Lisl Ye. BA, Harvard U., 1964; MA, U. Calif., Berkeley, 1966, PhD, 1971. Rsch. assoc. U. Mich., Ann Arbor, 1970-71; from asst. prof. to full prof. U. Oreg., Eugene, 1971-90; Hsiu prof. Chinese Studies U. Calif., San Diego, 1990—. Author: Reform & Revolution in China, 1976, Origins of Boxer Uprising, 1987; editor: Lost Chance in China, 1974; co-editor, contbr.: Chinese Local Elites & Patterns of Dominance, 1990; co-author: Chinese Archives: An Introductory Aride, 1996; editor, contbr.: Remaking the Chinese City, 1900-1950, 2001. Frank Knox fellow Harvard U., 1964-65; Am. Coun. Learned Studies grantee, 1977-78, Nat. Acad. Sci. grantee, 1979-80, 88-89. Mem. Assn. for Asian Studies (chair China and Inner Asia coun. 1990-91), Am. Hist. Assn. Democrat. Avocations: skiing, tennis, camping. Home: 4679 Robbins St San Diego CA 92122-3034 Office: U Calif Dept of History La Jolla CA 92093

ESHLEMAN, SILAS KENDRICK, III, retired psychiatrist; b. Gainesville, Fla, June 28, 1928; s. Silas Kendrick Jr. and Aileen Hope (McClamroch) E.; m. Judith Cooper, July 3, 1954; 1 child, Diane Eshleman Djordjevic. BS, U. Fla., 1949; MD, U. Pa., 1953. Diplomate Nat. Bd. Med. Examiners, Am. Bd. Psychiatry and Neurology, Am. Bd. Med. Psychotherapists, Am. Bd. Forensic Examiners. Mem. med. staff St. Joseph Hosp. (now Lancaster Regional Med. Ctr), Lancaster, Pa., 1959—, chmn. dept. psychiatry, 1968-88; mem. med. staff Lancaster Gen. Hosp., 1959-98; pvt. practice Lancaster, 1959-97; ret., 1997. Cons. in psychiatry VA Med. Ctr., Lebanon, Pa., 1961-92, NIH Project, 1978—; mem. various med. staff coms. Assoc. editor Jour. Lancaster County Hist. Soc., 1998—; contbr. articles to profl. jour. Trustee Lancaster County (Pa.) Hist. Soc., 1997—98; bd. dirs. Quest for Learning, Lancaster, Pa., 1998—, pres., 2002—. Capt. M.C. U.S. Army, 1955—57. Fellow: Coll. Physicians of Phila., Am. Psychiat. Assn. (life; disting., Disting. life); mem.: AAAS, AMA, Pa. Soc. Sons of Revolution, Lancaster Cliosophic Soc. (program chmn. 1983—84), Internat. Assn. Torch Clubs (pres. Lancaster chpt. 1981—82, 2001—02). Episcopalian. Avocations: natural history, gardening, woodland management. Home: PO Box 306 Paradise PA 17562-0306

ESHLEMAN, VON RUSSEL, electrical engineering educator; b. Darke County, Ohio, Sept. 17, 1924; married; 4 children. BEE, George Washington U., 1949; MS, Stanford U., 1950, PhD in Elec. Engring., 1952. Rsch. assoc. Radio Propagation Lab. Stanford (Calif.) U., 1952-56, from instr. to prof. elec. engring., 1956-61, prof. elec. engring., co-dir. Ctr. Radar Astronomy, 1961-82, dir. Radioscience Lab., 1974-83. Cons. NAS, Nat. Bur. Stds., SRI Internat., Jet Propulsion Lab.; mem. Internat. Astronaut Congress, Internat. Astron. Union, Internat. Sci. Radion Union; dir. emeritus Watkins-Johnson Co.; mem. radio sci. teams for Pioneer, Mariner, Voyager, Galileo spacecraft studies of the planets. Fellow AAAS, IEEE, Am. Geophys. Union, Royal Astronomy Soc.; mem. NAE. Achievements include rsch. in radar astronomy, planetary exploration, ionospheric and plasma physics, radio wave propagation, astronautics. Office: Stanford U Radar Astronomy Ctr Packard EE Bldg 309 Stanford CA 94305-9515 E-mail: eshleman@nova.stanford.edu.

ESHOM-OVIATT, CORINA MAY, air transportation executive; b. Moab, Utah, Aug. 25, 1967; d. Marvin Edward Eshom and Sandra Irene Peterson. BS in Anthropology, U. Utah, 1990. Cert. EMT Utah. Dir. environ. safety and health AgriDyne Techs., Salt Lake City, 1988-94; environ. engr. Dugway (Utah) Proving Ground Lockheed Martin, 1995-99, supr. agt. test support sect., 1999—. Vol. firefighter/EMT Terra (Utah) Fire Dept., 1999—2001; instr., instrn. trainer ARC, Salt Lake City, 1984—2003, dir. 1st aid sta. team, mem. health and safety com., 1992—94; leader Utah Girl Scouts, Dugway, 2000—01. Mem. Am. Chem. Soc., Am. Legion Aux. (Secondary Edn. scholar 1985), Am. Philatelic Soc., Utah Firefighters Assn., Tooele County Backcounty Horsemans Club Mem. Lds Ch. Avocations: stamp collecting, hiking, climbing, quilting, carpentry. Home: 261 W Utah Ave Tooele UT 84074 Office: Lockheed Martin Bldg 4239 Dugway Proving Ground Dugway UT 84022 E-mail: oviatt@dpg.army.mil.

ESHOO, ANNA GEORGES, congresswoman; b. New Britain, Conn., Dec. 13, 1942; d. Fred and Alice Alexandre Georges; children: Karen Elizabeth, Paul Frederick. AA with honors, Canada Coll., 1975. Chmn. San Mateo County Dem. Ctrl. Com., Calif., 1978-82; chair Human Rels. Com., 1979-82; mem. U.S. Congress from 14th Calif. dist., 1993—; at-large minority whip; mem. energy and commerce com., intelligence com. Chief of staff Calif. Assembly Spkr. Leo McCarthy, 1981; regional majority whip No. Calif., 1993-94. Co-founder Women's Hall of Fame; chair San Mateo County (Calif.) Dem. Party, 1980; active San Mateo County Bd. Suprs., 1982-92, pres., 1986; pres. Bay Area Air Quality Mgmt. Dist., 1982-92; mem. San Francisco Bay Conservation Devel. Commn., 1982-92; chair San Mateo County Gen. Hosp. Bd. Dirs. Democrat. Roman Catholic. Office: US Ho Reps 205 Cannon Ho Office Bldg Washington DC 20515-0001*

ESHOO, BARBARA ANNE RUDOLPH, academic official; b. Worcester, Mass., Sept. 27, 1946; d. Charles Leighton and Irene Isabella (Wheeler) Rudolph; divorced; 1 child, Melissa Clinton; m. Robert Pius Eshoo, July 11, 1981. Student, Morehead State U., 1964-66, U. N.H., 1974, 75; BA, New England Coll., 1976. Asst. to dir. Currier Gallery Art, Manchester, N.H., 1976-78, coord. pub. rels., 1979-82; dir. pub. rels. Daniel Webster Coll., Nashua, N.H., 1982-87, chief advancement officer, 1988-95; v.p. instnl. advancement Ea. Conn. State U., Willimantic, 1995—. Mem. faculty Currier Art Ctr., Manchester, 1977-79; bd. advisers New Eng. Coll. Art Gallery, Henniker, N.H., 1989-91. Advisor on planned giving United Way, Nashua, 1989-90; com. mem. Manchester Mayor's Task force on Youth Affairs, 1986-88, Manchester Bd. of Sch. Commn., 1986-90; del. N.H. Sch. Bds. Assn., 1988-90; trustee, bd. sec. Manchester Hist. Assn., 1989-95; mem. Mayor's Com. on Leadership, Manchester, 1988-91; bd. dirs. Swiftwater coun. Girl Scouts U.S., 1990-95; chairperson parents com. Bennington Coll. Mem.: Assn. Fundraising Profls., Coun. for Advancement and Support of Edn., Assn. Governing Bds. of Univs. and Colls. (planning com., facilitator), Conn. Com. on Planned Giving, Nat. Com. on Planned Giving, Am. Coun. on Edn. (state of Conn. rep. Office Women in Higher Edn.), Conn. Women in Higher Edn., Nat. Soc. Fundraising Execs. (bd. dirs., v.p. pub. affairs N.H./Vt. chpt. to 1995), Newcomen Soc. Conn. (treas. 1997—99), Rotary (Nashua West chpt. 1990—95), Advt. Club N.H. (bd. dirs., v.p. 1980—82). Office: Ea Conn State U 83 Windham St Willimantic CT 06226-2211 E-mail: eschoob@easternct.edu.

ESKANDARIAN, EDWARD, advertising agency executive; b. Telford, Pa., Nov. 20, 1936; s. Michael and Katherine (Arslanian) E.; m. Nancy Rose Boujicanian, June 20, 1965; children: Wendy, Christopher, Jill. BS, Villanova U., 1958; MBA, Harvard, 1965. Engr. Pitman Dunn Labs., Phila., 1958-60; project engr. GE, Phila., 1961-63; v.p., account supr. Compton Advt., Inc., N.Y.C., 1965-71; chmn., chief exec. officer HBM/Creamer Inc., Boston, 1971-88; chmn. Della Femina McNamee, Boston, 1988-89; chmn., CEO Arnold Comm., Boston, 1989-2000, Arnold Worldwide Ptnrs., Boston, 2000—. Overseer Boston Symphony, 1987—, Boston Mus. Sci., 1987—; trustee U. Richmond. With USAF, 1959-60. Mem. Am. Assn. Advt. Agys. (sec.-treas. 1988-89, ea. region gov.-at-large 1989-91), New Eng. Broadcasters Assn. (pres. 1982-83), Advt. Club Boston (pres. 1977-78, trustee 1980—), Harvard Bus. Sch. Assn. Boston (pres. 1984-85), Harvard Club, Algonquin Club, Weston Golf Club, Jupiter Hills Club, Oyster Harbors Club, Willowbend Club, Caves Valley Club. Home: 300 Boylston St Boston MA 02116-3923 Office: Arnold Worldwide Ptnrs 101 Huntington Ave Boston MA 02199-7606

ESKELIN, JOHN THURSTON, city planner; b. Santa Monica, Calif., June 2, 1946; s. Arthur Frederick and Catherine Marshall (Mason) E.; m. Stephanie Elizebeth Pearson, June 27, 1980; 1 child, Jack. BS in City Planning, Calif. Polytechnic U., 1972; M in Urban Planning, cert. in urban design, U. Wash., 1989. Asst. planner San Luis Obispo (Calif.) County, 1972-74; assoc. planner City of El Cerrito, Calif., 1974-78; planning mgr. Woldemar & Assocs., Richmond, Calif., 1978-82; planning dir. Park City (Utah) Mcpl. Corp., 1982-85; planning cons. Land Planning and Devel. Assocs., Seattle, 1985-87; neighborhood devel. mgr. City of Seattle, 1987—. Coll. lectr. series coord. U. Wash. Coll. Arch., 1985-87. Editor: Park City Developer's Guide, 1984 (Am. Planning Assn. award 1985); editor: (video) San Juan Futures, 1987 (Am. Planning Assn. award 1987); contbr. articles to profl. jours. Mem. housing adv. com. City of El Cerrito, 1977-78; bd. dirs. Epiphany Parish Vestry, Seattle, 1989-91. Recipient Valle scholarship U. Wash., 1987. Mem. Am. Assn. Cert. Planners (cert.), Am. Planning Assn., Wash. Athletic Club, Seattle Tennis Club. Avocation: urban design and planning. Office: Seattle Dept Neighborhoods 700 3rd Ave Ste 400 Seattle WA 98104-1872

ESKEW, JAMES ROBERT, otolaryngologist; b. Abilene, Tex., Nov. 3, 1949; MD, U. Tex., San Antonio, 1977. Diplomate Am. Bd. Otolaryngology. Intern Meth. Hosp., Dallas, 1977-79; resident in otolaryngology U. Tex. Med. Br., Galveston, 1979-82; hosp. staff mem. So. Austin Hosp., Tex.; pvt. practice Austin, 1982—. Mem. ACS, AMA, Am. Acad. of Otolaryngology, Travis County Med. Soc. (pres. 2003). Office: Austin ENT Clinic 4207 James Casey St Ste 301 Austin TX 78745-1193

ESKEW, MICHAEL L. package distribution company executive; BS in Indsl. Engring., Purdue U., 1972; postgrad., Butler U., U. Pa. Various positions UPS, Inc., Germany, 1972-82, indsl. engring. mgr. northwest region, 1982-91, dist. mgr. Cen. Jersey dist., 1991-93, corp. indsl. engring. mgr., 1993, corp. v.p. indsl. engring, 1994—96, group v.p. engring., 1996—99, exec. v.p., 1999—2002, vice chmn., 2000—02, chmn., CEO, 2002—. Office: UPS Inc 55 Glenlake Pkwy NE Atlanta GA 30328-3474

ESKEW, R. ALLEN, architect, director; MA architecture, UC/Berkeley; BS, LSU. Founder/dir. Eskew Architects, 1989—2001. Mr. Eskew is a highly sought after individual for boards and civic activites. Architectural design, Aquarium of the Americas, New Orleans Mus. of Art, New Orleans Fair Grounds Grandstand, South Carolina Aquarium. Fellow: Am. Inst. of Arch. (fellow 2003). He has also established his expertise as a talented facilitator of design processes and strategic planning. He brings particular focus to the early stages of project devel. To achieve objectives, he concentrates on design and programming criteria, implementation strategies and budget modeling. Office: Eskew, Dumez, Ripple 1 Canal Pl, 365 Canal St, Ste 3150 New Orleans LA 70130*

ESKEW, RHEA TALIAFERRO, newspaper publisher; b. Lebanon, Tenn., Nov. 16, 1923; s. Robert Edward and Sammie (Taylor) E.; m. Nancy Portlock Hall, June 13, 1953; children: Rhea Taliaferro, Elizabeth Vaughan Overman, Tucker Alexander, Hall Edward. Student, U. Tenn., 1941-42; BA, Emory U., 1948. With UPI, 1948-55, bus. rep., 1951-55; dept. pub. relations So. Bell Telephone Co., 1955-56; with UPI, 1956-73, gen. mgr. communications, 1963-64, So. div. mgr. Atlanta, 1964-73; v.p., gen. mgr. Greenville (S.C.) News-Piedmont, 1973-77, pub., 1978-84; pres. Multimedia Newspaper Co., 1978-85, sr. exec., 1984-88. Bd. dirs. Order of the Palmetto. Pres. Greenville Cmty. Planning Coun., 1989, hon. bd. dirs., 1997—; hon. bd. dirs. United Way, 1997—; vice-chmn. Greenville Symphony Endowment, 1998-2003. With AUS, 1942-45, ETO. Mem. S.C. Press Assn. (pres. 1981), So. Newspaper Pubs. Assn. (pres. 1982-83), Greenville Country Club, Poinsett Club. Methodist. Home: 400 Huntington Rd Greenville SC 29615-4210 E-mail: mrrheat@aol.com.

ESKIN, BARRY SANFORD, court investigator; b. Pitts., Mar. 6, 1943; s. Saul and Dorothy (Zaron) E.; m. M. Joyce Rosalind, Sept. 12, 1965; 1 child, David. AA, L.A. City Coll., 1963; BA, Calif. State U., L.A., 1965; JD, Citrus Belt Law Sch., 1976. Bar: Calif. 1976. Social service worker San Bernardino (Calif.) Dept. Pub. Social Services, 1965-77; assoc. Law Office of Lawrence Novack, San Bernardino, 1978; ct. investigator San Bernardino Superior Ct., 1978, supervising investigator, 1978—2003. Pro bono atty. Mex. Am. Commn., 1977-78. Mem. ARC Svc. Ctr. Advising Bd., San Bernardino, 1980-82; bd. dirs. Golden Valley Civ. Assn., San Bernardino, 1978-81, Congregation Emanuel, San Bernardino, 1984-87, bd. dirs. 1994-96. Mem. ABA, Calif. Assn. of Superior Ct. Investigators (pres. 1980-81, treas. 1984-85, bd. dirs., chmn. guardianship legis. com.), San Bernardino County Bar Assn., B'nai B'rith (pres. Paradise Lodge 1988), Alpha Phi Omega. Democrat. Jewish. Avocations: reading, photography, baseball. Office: San Bernardino Superior Ct 351 N Arrowhead Ave Rm 200 San Bernardino CA 92415-0240

ESKIN, BERNARD ABRAHAM, obstetrics and gynecology educator, medical researcher; b. Atlantic City, Feb. 12, 1928; s. Joseph H. and Goldie Celia (Schwartz) E.; m. Debra Lynn Kimelblot, June 11, 1955; children: Gregg Carl, JoAnne Hillary, Catherine Ruth. BS in Chemistry and Biology, Princeton U., Rutgers U., 1947; MS in Endocrinology, Rutgers U., 1949; MD, Albany Med. Coll., 1955. Diplomate Nat. Bd. Medicine, Am. Bd. Ob./Gyn; MD, Pa., N.J., N.Y. Teaching and rsch. fellow Rutgers U., New Brunswick, N.J., 1948-49, Woods Hole (Mass.) Marine Biology, 1950, Brown U., Providence, 1950-51, Woman's Med. Coll., Phila., 1960-67, asst. prof. ob./gyn. and reproductive endocrinology, 1965-70, assoc. prof., 1971-79; chief sect. reproductive endocrinology, ob./gyn. Med. Coll. of Pa. and Albert Einstein Med. Ctr., Phila., 1967-82; prof. ob./gyn., reproductive endocrinology Drexel U. Coll. Medicine, Phila., 1979—; assoc. prof. psychiatry Med. Coll. Pa./Drexel U. Coll. Medicine, Phila., 1976—, prof. pharmacology, 1993—; dir. Ctr. for Menopause and Geripause/Drexel U. Coll. of Medicine. Clin. prof. ob./gyn. Robert Wood Johnson Med. Sch., New Brunswick, 1967—. Author: Midlife Can Wait, 1995, Breast Disease for Primary Care Physicians, 1999; author, editor: Menopause, 4th rev. edit., 2000, others, The Geripause: Medical Management During the Late Menopause, 2003; numerous patents in field. Bd. dirs. Main Line Symphony Orch., Wayne, Pa., 1982—. Lt. USNR, 1943-46. Recipient Fogarty Internat. Rsch. award, 1998; grantee NIH, ACS, others, 1965—; Hartford Found. fellow, 1960-65; Nat. Found. for Infantile Paralysis fellow, 1951. Fellow Am. Coll. Ob./gyn. (life), Soc. Senologie (bd. dirs. 1984-88), Phila. Coll. Physicians; mem. Am. Thyroid Assn., Am. Assn. Cancer Rsch., Endocrine Soc.,

Am. Soc. Reproductive Medicine (life), Pa. Med. Soc. (state rep. 1987—), Phila. County Med. Soc. (bd. dirs. 1991—), Rutgers Univ. Fedn. (bd. dirs. 1993—), Rutgers U. Regional Alumni Clubs (chmn. 1994—), N.Am. Menopause Soc. Jewish. Avocations: classical viola, jazz alto saxophones, clarinet. Office: Rsch Lab Drexel U Coll of Med 3300 Henry Ave Philadelphia PA 19129 also: 4190 City Ave Ste 418/Rowland Hall Philadelphia PA 19131 Fax: 215-477-6107. E-mail: bae22@drexel.edu.

ESKIN, DAVID J. cardiologist; b. Phila., May 2, 1942; MD, U. Pa., 1967. Diplomate Am. Bd. Internal Medicine, Am. Bd. Cardiology. Intern Bronx Mcpl. Hosp. - Einstein, N.Y.C., 1967-68; resident in medicine Hosp. U., Pa., 1970-72, fellow in cardiology, 1972-74; chief of staff, v.p. med. Abington Meml. Hosp., Pa.; assoc. clin. prof. medicine U. Pa. Sch. Medicine. Trustee Abington Meml. Hosp. Fellow: ACP, Am. Heart Assn., Am. Coll. Cardiology; mem.: AMA, U. Pa. Sch. Medicine Alumni Soc. (exec. com.), Alpha Omega Alpha. Office: Abington Med Specs 1235 Old York Rd Ste 222 Abington PA 19001-3800

ESLER, ANTHONY JAMES, historian, novelist, educator; b. New London, Conn., Feb. 20, 1934; s. Jamie Arthur and Helen Wilhelmina (Kreamer) E.; m. Carol Eaton Clemeau, June 17, 1961 (div. 1988); children: Kenneth Campbell, David Douglas; m. Helen Campbell Walker, July 24, 1992. BA, U. Ariz., 1956; MA, Duke U., 1958, PhD, 1961. Mem. faculty Coll. William and Mary, 1962-99, prof. history, 1972-99. Vis. prof. Northwestern U., 1968-69. Author: The Aspiring Mind of the Elizabethan Younger Generation, 1966, Bombs, Beards and Barricades: 150 Years of Youth in Revolt, 1971, The Youth Revolution: The Conflict of Generations in Modern History, 1974, Castlemayne, 1974, Hellbane, 1975, Lord Libertine, 1976, Forbidden City, 1977, The Freebooters, 1979, Babylon, 1980, Bastion, 1980, Generations in History: An Introduction to the Concept, 1982, The Generation Gap in Society and History: A Select Bibliography, 1984, The Human Venture, 5th edit., 2003, The Western World: A Narrative History, 2d edit., 1997; co-author: A Survey of Western Civilization, 1987, World History: Connections to Today, 1997, 2d edit., 2001, 3rd edit., 2003. Fulbright fellow U. London, 1961-62; research fellow Am. Council Learned Socs., 1969-70; Fulbright travel grantee Ivory Coast and Tanzania, 1983 Mem. World Hist. Assn., Am. Hist. Assn., Authors Guild, Amnesty Internat. Home: 416 Harriet Tubman Dr Williamsburg VA 23185 Office: Coll William and Mary Dept History Williamsburg VA 23187-8795 E-mail: anthonyesler@aol.com.

ESLINGER, KENNETH N. social sciences educator; s. Kenneth N. and Pearl May E.; m. Denise Marie Juba, July 22, 1979. BA, Ind. State U., Terre Haute, Ind., 1963; MA, The Ohio State U., Columbus, 1968, PhD, 1971. Asst. prof. of sociology Ohio State U., Columbus, 1972—73, The Cleve. State U., 1973—80; asst. prof. sociology John Carroll U., University Heights, Ohio, 1980—85, assoc. prof. sociology, 1985—, acting chair dept. sociology, 1995—96, chair dept. sociology, 1997—. Contbr. articles. Mem. Dem. Nat. Com., 1993—2003; adv. com., congressman Cleve., 1983—84; organizer higher edn. field gubernatorial campaign, Cleve., 1982; organizer Higher Edn. Organizer, Cleve. Mem.: Am. Sociol. Assn., North Ctrl. Sociol. Assn. (v.p. 1997—99), Soc. Study Social Problems, Nat. Coun. Family Rels. Democrat. Avocations: bass fishing, fly fishing. Office: John Carroll U 20700 North Park Blvd University Heights OH 44118

ESLINGER-BROWN, VANESSA PAULINE, humanities educator; b. Murfreesboro, Tenn., Dec. 28, 1951; d. Walter Clarence and Clare Marie Eslinger; m. Wilbur Edwin Brown Jr., Nov. 28, 1987; children: Celeste Gabrielle Brown, Cameron Yates Brown, Savannah Clare Brown. B Speech and Comm., U. Mont., 1973; MEd, U. Va., 1983, EdD, 1986. Cert. secondary tchr. Va. Substitute tchr. Eugene (Oreg.) Pub. Schs., 1976—78; coach, drama dir., English tchr. MatoacaH.S., Ettrick, Va., 1978—82; rsch. asst. U. Va., Charlottesville, 1986—87; adj. lectr. Germanna C.C., Locust Grove, Va., 1987—89; adj./asst. prof. No. Va. C.C., Woodbridge, 1987—89; adj./sr. lectr. Mary Washington Coll., Fredericksburg, Va., 1990—94, sr. lectr., 1994—95; prof. gen. studies Stayer U., Fredericksburg, 1996—, chmn. dept. gen. studies, 1999—. Piano tchr., Fredericksburg, 1997—. Vol. magic cir. Women's Shelter for Help and Emergency, Charlottesville, 1982—87; Bible sch. tchr. Shiloh New Site Bapt. Ch., Fredericksburg, 1989—99. Recipient Outstanding Vol. award, Women's Shelter for Help and Emergency, 1985. Mem.: Nat. Assn. Tchrs. English, Va. Assn. Tchrs. English, Nat. Forensics League, Thespians Soc. Democrat. Methodist. Avocations: swimming, piano, reading, cooking. Home: 10415 Edinburgh Dr Spotsylvania VA 22553 Office: Strayer U 4500 Plank Rd Fredericksburg VA 22407 E-mail: veb@strayer.edu.

ESMAELI, BITA, ophthalmologist; b. Tehran, Iran, Mar. 6, 1963; came to U.S., 1978; d. Mohammed T. Esmaeli and Nahid Hidaji; m. Howard Gutstein (div.); 1 child, Brett Ferdosi Gutstein. BS in Biology, Rhodes Coll., 1984; MA in Cell Physiology, U. Calif., Santa Barbara, 1984; MD, Chgo. Med. Sch., 1990. Bd. cert. Am. Bd. Ophthalmology; lic. physician, Calif., Mich., Tex. Intern Ill. Masonic Med. Ctr., Chgo., 1990-91; resident in ophthalmology U. Mich., Ann Arbor, 1991-94; fellow in ophthalmic plastic and reconstructive surgery U. Toronto, Ont., Can., 1995-96; staff ophthalmologist St. Joseph Mercy Hosp., Ann Arbor, 1994-98; asst. prof., chief ophthalmology sect. M.D. Anderson Cancer Ctr., Houston, 1998—. Adj. asst. prof. ophthalmology Baylor Coll. Medicine, 1998—. Contbr. numerous articles to profl. jours. Recipient Janet M. Glasgow Meml. citation Am. Med. Women's Assn., 1990, Muscular Dystrophy Assn. Med. Student Rsch. award, 1987; Rhodes Coll. Sci. scholar, 1980-84. Fellow Am. Acad. Ophthalmology; mem. AMA, Am. Soc. Ophthalmic Plastic and Reconstructive Surgery (Merril Reeh Pathology award 1997), Assn. for Rsch. in Vision and Ophthalmology, Assn. for Women in Ophthalmology, Am. Acad. Ophthalmology, Alpha Omega Alpha. Avocations: live classical concerts, persian rugs (history and collection), wine tasting, international ophthalmology. Home: 2324 Bolsover St Houston TX 77005-2612 Office: MD Anderson Cancer Ctr Box 62 1515 Holcombe Blvd Houston TX 77030-4009

ESMAILZADEH, EBRAHIM, mechanical engineering educator, consultant; b. Mashhad Khorasan, Iran, Apr. 6, 1944; s. Mohammad and Fakhrolsharieh (Riaz) E.;m. Rouhangiz Daei Sadeghi, July 15, 1977; children: Reza, Ali. BSc with honours, U. London, 1967, MPhil, 1969, PhD, 1971. Chartered engr., U.K. Lab. instr. U. London, 1967-71; asst. prof. Arya-Mehr U. Tech., Tehran, 1971-75; vis. assoc. prof. MIT, Cambridge, Mass., 1976-77; prof. Sharif U. Tech., Tehran, 1980-89, univ. disting. prof., 1992-97, v.p., 1979-80; prof. dir. mfg. engring. program U. Ontario, Oshawa, Canada. Vis. prof. U. Victoria, Can., 1990-91, 97—; rsch. advisor Ministry of Heavy Industry, Iran, 1982-84; tech. cons. in field. Author textbooks and jour. articles on mech. engring.; mem. editl. bd. nat. and internat. jours.; spkr. in field. Named Excellent Prof., Iranian Soc. Mech. Engrs., 1994, Exemplar Prof. of Iranian Univs., 1993. Fellow Instn. Mech. Engrs. Eng., ASME; mem. Soc. Automotive Engrs., Iranian Acad. Scis. Tehran (chair mech. engring. dept. 1995-97), Iranian Soc. Control and Instrumentation Engrs. (dir. 1994). Avocations: chess, photography, music, ball games, skiing. Office: U Ontario Inst Tech 2000 Simcoe St N Oshawa ON Canada L1H 7K4

ESMOND, CHERI SUE, secondary school educator; b. Oak Park, Ill., Oct. 16, 1943; d. Fred W. and Shirley C. (Reiser) Wassmundt; m. Jack B. Esmond, Aug. 22, 1964; children: Jill Esmond Letbetter, Heather Esmond Camden. BS in Maths., U. Ill., 1965, MEd in Secondary Edn., 1966. Cert. secondary edn. tchr., Tex., Ill., N.Y., Mich.; lic. real estate broker, Ill. Tchr. Mahomet (Ill.) Seymour H.S., 1965-67, Ottawa (Ill.) H.S., 1972-73, Klein (Tex.) H.S., 1977—2000, Tomball Coll., 2000—02, Montgomery Coll., 2002—. Yearbook judge Nat. Scholastic Press Assn., Mpls., 1967-73. Treas. Jr. Guild Adv. Bd., Houston, 1989-90, provisional coord., 1990-92. Mem. Nat. Coun. Tchrs. of Maths., Tex. Assn. Gifted and Talented, Tex. Math. and Sci. Coachess Assn. (Number Sense Coach of Yr. 1997, 99, 2000, Sweepstakes Coach of Yr. 1997-2000), Raveneaux Country Club, U. Ill. Alumni Assn., Cypress Creek Investment Club (treas. 2002—), Chi Omega Alums (pres. 1995-97), Kappa Delta Pi. Avocations: travel, scuba diving, golf. Home: 10835 Clubhouse Cir Magnolia TX 77354-6915 E-mail: esmond@hal-pc.org.

ESP, BARBARA ANN LORRAINE, educational researcher, educator; b. Bklyn., Nov. 10, 1947; d. Lawrence Joseph and Evelyn (Webber) Barbeire; m. Edward J. Esp, Aug. 31, 1968; children: Jacqueline, Michelle. BA, Adelphi U., 1969; PhD, Hofstra U., 1978. Counselor, tchr. U.S. Army Dept. Def., Wildflecken, Fed. Republic of Germany, 1970-73; adj. asst. prof. Hofstra U., Hempstead, N.Y., 1974-81; cons., rsch. program evaluator various sch. dists. N.Y., 1982-86; program rsch. analyst N.Y. State Div. Parole, N.Y.C., 1986-88; dir. pupil pers. svcs. Cleary Sch. for Deaf, Nesconset, NY, 1989—. Adj. prof. St. Joseph's Coll., Patchogue, NY, 2000—. Contbr. articles to profl. jours. Leader Girl Scouts U.S., Farmingville, N.Y., 1976-78; bd. dirs. Nassau-Suffolk Counties Alzheimers Assn., Patchogue, N.Y., 1984-86. Hofstra U. fellow, 1975-76. Republican. Roman Catholic. Home: 2 Jacqueline Dr Manorville NY 11949-2615

ESPALDON, ERNESTO MERCADER, plastic surgeon, former senator; b. Sulu, Philippines, Nov. 11, 1926; arrived in Guam, 1963; s. Cipriano Acuna Espaldon and Claudia (Cadag) Mercader); m. Leticia Legaspi Virata, May 31, 1952; children: Arlene Espaldon Ramos, Vivian Espaldon Wolff, James, Diane, Karl, Ernesto Jr. AA, U. Philippines, Manila, 1949; MD, U. Santo tomas, Manila, 1954; postgrad., U. Okla., 1959, Washington U., St. Louis, 1961. Diplomate Am. Bd. Plastic Surgery. Plastic surgeon Guam Meml. Hosp., Agana, 1963—, chief surgery, 1965-69; pres., plastic surgeon Espaldon Clinic, Agana, 1969—; senator Guam Legislature, Agana, 1974-80, 86-92, chmn. Com. on Health, Welfare and Ecology and Com. on Ethics and Standards, 1974-80. Vis. prof. Bicol Med. and Edn. Ctr., Legaspi City, The Philippines, 1980—; cons. plastic surgery U.S. Naval Hosp., Guam, 1972-76; chmn. com. on advance health care Assn. Pacific Islands Legislators, 1988-92, Coll. Assurance Plan Pre-Need Ednl. Plan, Guam, 1979—; bd. dirs. Coll. Assurance Plan Pension, Philippines, Coll. Assurance Plan, Philippines. Author: With The Bravest, 1996. Pres., founder Guam Balikbayan Med. Mission, Agana, 1974—; organizer, co-founder Aloha Med., Mission, Honolulu, 1982—. Guerrilla comdr. Sulu (Philippines) Area Command, 1943-46, 2d lt. Philippine Army, 1946-47. Recipient Thomas Jefferson award for pub. svc. Am. Inst. Pub. Svc., Washington, and Honolulu Advertiser, 1983, Raja Baguinda award for humanitarian svc. 6th Centennial Celebration of Islam in The Philippines, 1980; named Most Outstanding Filipino Overseas Philippine Govt. and Philippine Jaycees for Pub. Svc., 1982, Most Outstanding Cmty. Filipino Leader of Guam Philippine-Am. Cmty., 1979, Man of Yr. and Disting. Svc. award Inst. Philippine Am. Affairs, Hawaii, 1983; named Most Outstanding Alumni Achiever for Humanitarian Svc., U. Santo Tomas, 1981, Ernesto M. Espaldon profl. chairship in plastic and reconstructive surgery U. Santo Tomas, 1995. Fellow ACS, Philippine Coll. Surgeons; mem. AMA, Pan Pacific Surg. Assn., Guam Med. Soc. (pres. 1970-72, chief del. to AMA 1973-76), KC. Republican. Roman Catholic. Home: PO Box CE Agana GU 96932-8982

ESPARZA, MONICA, nursing administrator; b. El Paso, Tex., Jan. 1, 1965; d. Gilbert Esparza, Edna Esparza. BSN, U. Tex., 1989. RN 1990. Staff nurse neonatal ICU Thomason Gen. Hosp., El Paso, Tex., 1990—95; flight nurse transporter Medflight, 1993—96; acute dialysis coord. Fresenius Med. Care Acutes, 1997—98; dir. nursing Fresenius Med. Care, 1999—. Preceptor neonatal ICU Thomason Gen. Hosp., El Paso, 1991—92. Mem.: Am. Nephrology Nurses Assn., Sigma Theta Tau. Avocation: travel. Office Fax: 915-599-2896. Personal E-mail: RNTexas@aol.com. Business E-mail: Monica.Esparza@fmc-na.com.

ESPAT, N. JOSEPH, surgeon; b. Guatemala, Guatemala, Jan. 8, 1964; came to U.S., 1971; s. Nocif and Elba Marina (Godoy) E.; m. Jacqueline A. Ellis, Apr. 5, 1997; children: Riley Bridget, Zackary Joseph. BS in Biology, U. South Fla., 1985, BA in Philosophy, 1986; MD, U. Fla., 1990; MS, U. Ill., 2002. Diplomate Am. Bd. Surgery. Intern U. Fla. Shands Hosp., Gainesville, Fla., 1990-91, resident, 1991-92; rsch. fellow U. Fla. Labs., Gainesville, Fla., 1992-94; sr. resident U. Fla. Shands Hosp., Gainesville, Fla., 1994-96, chief resident, 1996-97; fellow surg. oncology Meml. Sloan Kettering Hosp., N.Y.C., 1997-99; assox. prof. hepatobiliary surgery U. Ill., Chgo., 1999—. Mem. Shands Institutional com. grad. medical edn., 1996-97, code com. Shands Hosp., 1995-96; med. team NASA Space Shuttle Univ. Fla., 1992-95, lectr. Project Smoke Free 2000, 1992-94. Contbr. numerous articles to profl. jours. Recipient Harry M. Vars Rsch. award, 1993, James Euwing travel award, 1993, Jonathan Rhoads Career Devel. award 1999, Stanley Dudrick Rsch. Scholar award 2002. Mem. ACS, AMA, Assn. Acad. Surgery, Soc. Leukocyte Biology, Soc. Surg. Oncology, So. Med. Assn., Southeastern Surg. Congress, Alpha Omega Alpha. Home: 474 N Lakeshore Dr Chicago IL 60611-3400

ESPE, MATTHEW J. manufacturing executive; With GE, 1980—2002; pres. GE Plastics Netherlands, 1994—99, GE Plastics Europe, 1999—2000; pres., CEO GE Lighting, 2000—02, IKON Office Solutions, Inc., 2002—, chmn., 2003—. Office: 70 Valley Stream Pkwy Malvern PA 19355*

ESPEGARD, DUAINE C. state legislator; m. Phyllis Espegard; 3 children. BBA, Aakers Bus. Coll. Pres., CEO Bremer Bank; mem. N.D. Senate from 43d dist., Bismark, 2001—. Mem. NDAK Commn. Econ. Devel. Republican. Office: 3649 Lynwood Cir Grand Forks ND 58201 E-mail: despegar@state.nd.us.

ESPENLAUB, MARGO LINN, women's studies educator, writer, artist; b. Decorah, Iowa, May 1, 1944; d. Lloyd Wilson and Margaret Mary (Seegmiller) Ruid; children: Arn R. Johnson, Cara C. Johnson. BA in Philosophy, U. Colo., 1983, M in Humanities, 1985; PhD in Women's Studies, The Union Inst. Grad. Sch., 1995. Assoc. dir. student devel., mem. faculty U. Denver, The Women's Coll. Mem. women's studies faculty Inst. for Ethics, U. Denver; colloqium coord. Front Range Feminist Scholars, Denver, 1991-98; faculty coord. TWC Student Writer's Club. Co-author: Women's Studies: Thinking Women, 1993; gen. editor Voices of the Women's Coll. Mem. biomed. ethics com. Kaiser Permanente, Denver, 1986-96. Mem. Nat. Women's Studies Assn., Colo. Women's Agenda, Nat. Mus. Women in the Arts. E-mail: mespenla@du.edu.

ESPERO, WILLIAM (WILLIE C.), state senator; BA in bus. mgmt., Seattle U., 1982. Exec. sec. City and County of Honolulu Neighborhood Commn., 1987—94; ops. coord. Coalition for a Drug Free Hawaii, 1995; property mgr. Chaney, Brooks and Co., 1995—96; gen. mgr. Ewa by Gentry Cmty. Assn., 1996—2000; rep. Hawaii State House, 1999—2002; senator Hawaii State Senate, 2002—. Pres. Ewa Beach Cmty. Assn.; past pres. Ewa Beach Cmty. Trust Fund. Recipient Kapolei Outstanding Achievements award, 1998, 1999. Democrat. Office: State Capitol Rm 228 415 S Beretania St Honolulu HI 96813 Fax: 808-586-6361. E-mail: senespero@Capitol.hawaii.gov.*

ESPESETH, ROBERT D. park and recreation planning educator; b. Cameron, Wis., July 11, 1930; s. Robert I. and Mary (Willemssen) E.; m. Mary Ann Krepps, Dec. 30, 1952; children: Robert D. Jr., Steven R., Michael W., Karen S. BS in Landscape Architecture, U. Wis., 1952, MS in Landscape Arch./Regional Planning, 1956. Registered landscape architect, Ill., Neb. Park planner div. state forest and parks Wis. Conservation Dept., Madison, 1955-56; chief park planning bureau state parks and recreation Wis. Dept. Natural Resources, Madison, 1956-67; with Genessee County Park and Recreation Commn., Flint, Mich., 1967-73; asst. prof. dept. leisure studies U. Ill., Champaign, 1973-79, assoc. prof., 1979-95; ret., 1995. Expert witness, Champaign, Ill., 1974—. Author monographs, Site Planning of Park Areas, 1987, Developing a Bed and Breakfast Business Plan, 1988, Use of Conservation Easements, 1990, Community Park and Recreation Planning, 1994. Commr. Champaign County Forest Preserve Dist., Mahomet, Ill., 1974-86; bd. dirs. Green Meadows coun. Girl Scouts USA, 1975-83. With USN, 1952-54, capt. USNR, ret. Recipient Disting. Svc. award Am. Inst. Park Execs., 1965, Scroll Honor award Navy League U.S., 1973. Fellow Ill. Park and Recreation Assn. (bd. dirs. 1977); mem. Nat. Soc. Park Resources (Meritorious Svc. award 1985), Nat. Recreation and Park Assn. (trustee 1989-95, Park Profl. of Yr. award 1992), Univ. Club (past pres. U. Ill.). Avocations: golf, gardening, fishing, biking. Office: U Ill 1206 S 4th St Ste 104 Champaign IL 61820-6920 E-mail: respeset@uiuc.edu.

ESPINA-RUIZ, OSKAR, clarinet, educator; b. Bilbap, Spain, Aug. 15, 1971; s. Carlos Espina-Carrion and Delia Ruiz-Auinaco; m. Noriko Nagasawa, Aug. 1, 1998. Prof. degree, Leioa Conservatory of Music, Leioa, Spain, 1983—91; MFA, SUNY, Purchase, N.Y., 1993—95; DMA, SUNY, Stony Brook, N.Y., 1996—2003. Assoc. clarinetist Bilbao Symphony Orch., Bilbao, Spain, 1987; tchg. asst. of Charles Neidich Purchase Conservatory, Stony Brook, NY, 1991; clarinet master classes Conservatories, Spain, 1994; tchg. asst. of Charles Neidich SUNY, Stony Brook, 1991; clarinet faculty Bloomindale Sch. of Music, N.Y.C., 2002. Mem. European Mozart Found., 1995; soloist clarinetist Bilbao Symphony, Spain, 1994—; conducting Purchase Conservatory, Stony Brook, 1991—; guest prof. 9 Conservatories in China including Shanghai, and Central in Beijing., China, 1999; music dir. and founding mem. Musika Bizia Summer Festival, Gernika, Spain, 1994—99, Huesca Chamber Music Festival, Heusca, Spain, 2000—01. Musician (with Ernach Tria): (songs) toured Spain, 1994—, (CD) Prion, —; musician: (songs) Basque Heart, 2001—; composer (Conducted several works) (Chamber Music) Purchase Conservatory, 1991—; rsch. Julian Menendez great works:. Recipient Dow Music Award, Bilboa Conservatory, 1987, Top Clarinetist Award Winner, Olga Koussevitzky Competition for Woodwinds, 1999, Winner, Artists Internat. Annual N.Y. Debut Award, 1999, Award of the County, County Council of Bizkaia, Pres. Award, Purchase Conservatory, Finalist Diploma, Buffet Crampon Internat. Clarinet Competition, 1995; grantee 3 Grants for rsch. on Basque composers, Basque Govt., 2000. Office: Kobaltone PO Box 615 New York NY 10025

ESPINO, DAVID V. geriatrician, family practice physician; b. San Antonio, Sept. 2, 1956; s. Virgil and Estelle Espino; m. Denise Renee, Dec. 7, 1985; children: Raquel, Silas. AS, San Antonio Coll., 1977; BS, U. Tex., San Antonio, 1979; MD, U. Tex., Galveston, 1983. Asst. prof. U. Tex. Health Sci. Ctr., San Antonio, 1987-92, assoc. prof., 1992-99, prof., 1999—, chief div. geriatrics, vice chair for rsch., 1987. Dir. Geriatric Clinic, Univ. Health Sys., San Antonio, 1994, dir. Cognitive Disorders Clinic, San Antonio, 1996—; mem. Internat. Congress on Rural Aging, 1998; prin. investigator Hartford Geriatrics Ctr. Excellence, N.Y.C., 1998; mem. adv. coun. Nat. Inst. Aging, San Antonio, 1998— Editor: Ethnogeriatrics Clinics of Geriatric Medicine, 1995; contbg. editor: Family Medicine Review II Sattinger Group, 1999; contbr. 23 chpts. to books. Bd. dirs. Morningside Ministries Nursing Home, San Antonio, 1989—; mem. Target 90 Task Force, San Antonio, 1989-90; bd. dirs. Vis. Nurses, San Antonio, 1990-92, San Antonio Food Bank, 1997. Named Outstanding Faculty, Hispanic Faculty Assn., San Antonio, 1998, Paredes Disting. Internat. Lectureship U. Guadalajara, Mexico, 1998. Methodist. Avocation: photography. Home: 1420 Wiltshire Ave San Antonio TX 78209-6051 Office: U Tex Health Sci Ctr 7703 Floyd Curl Dr San Antonio TX 78229-3901 E-mail: espino@uthscsa.edu.

ESPINOSA, CARLOS, golfer; b. Reynosa, Mexico, Nov. 4, 1961; m. Annette Marie Espinosa, 1 child, Karla Marie. Degree in fin., U. Houston. Profl. golfer Canadian Profl. Golf Tour, 1988—. Avocations: music, reading, sports. Office: c/o Canadian Tour 212 King St W Ste 203 Toronto ON Canada M5H 1K5

ESPINOSA, HORACIO DANTE, mechanical engineering educator, consultant; b. Resistencia, Chaco, Argentina; s. Horacio Dante Espinosa and Maria Azucena Batocchio; m. Dora Graciela Rodriguez, Nov. 17, 1957; children: Leandro, Juan. B in Civil Engring., Northeastern U., Resistencia, 1982; MSc in Structural Engring., Poly. Milan, 1987; MS, Brown U., 1989, PhD, 1992. Asst. prof. Northeastern U., Resistencia, 1982-85; rsch. asst. Poly. Milan, 1985-87, Brown U., Providence, 1987-92; asst. prof. Purdue U., West Lafayette, Ind., 1992-97, assoc. prof., 1997-99, Northwestern U., Evanston, Ill., 2000—. Cons. Planta Tamet, Resistencia, 1982-83, State House Planning, Resistencia, 1983-85, Raytheon Sys. Co., Dallas, 1998—, Argonne (Ill.) Nat. Lab., 2001—, U. Ill., Chgo., 2000—; rev. panelist NSF, Washington, 1994—. Contbr. chpt. to book and articles to profl. jours. Recipient Rsch. awards NSF, Civil and Mech. Systems Divsn., 1992, 94, 97, 2000, 01, Rsch. awards Army Rsch. Office, 1995, 96, FAA, 2001, Rsch. awards Air Force Office Sci. Rsch., 1996, 97, 2000, Young Investigator award NSF, 1996-2001, Young Investigator award Office Naval Rsch., 1997-2001. Fellow Am. Acad. Mechanics (editor Mechanics mag. 1998--); mem. IEEE, AAAS, ASME (Svc. Appreciation award 1996), Am. Ceramic Soc., Materials Rsch. Soc.

ESPINOSA, RESURRECCION, playwright, theater director, writer; b. Tijola, Almeria, Spain, Dec. 19, 1956; arrived in U.S., 1978; d. Juan Espinosa Mesas and Carolina Rodriguez Jimenez; m. Charles William Frink, Sept. 12, 1988. Licentiate in philosophy and letters, U. Granada, Spain, 1982. Bilingual tchr. New London (Conn.) Pub. Schs., 1983—84; instr. hispanic studies Conn. Coll., New London, 1985—93; part-time instr. U. R.I., Kingston, 1993—98, dir., founder Teatro Latino Estudiantil, 1998—; dir., founder Teatro Latino de New London, 2000—; master tchg. artist Conn. Commn. on Arts, Hartford, 2001—; theater dir. New London Pub. Schs., 2002—. Pub. spkr. R.I. Com. for Humanities, Providence, 2000—; lectr., evaluator Conn. Humanities Coun., Middletown, 1991, Middletown, 92. Author: (book of plays) El Gaucho Vegeteriano and Other Plays, 1995, Don Quijote in America, Plays in English and Spanish, 2002, (book of poems) Waking Dream, 1998, (comic strip) Amanda y Rocinante, 1995—. Active New London Main St., 2000—, Trinity Encore, Providence, 2000—. Recipient Cmty. Svc. award, Centro de la Comunidad, New London, 1991, Pioneers Project award, 1999, Lambda Upsilon Lambda, 2002; grantee, United Way, New London, 2001—02, Palmer and Bodenwein Funds, Hartford, 2001—02, RISCA, 1998, RICH, 2000, Conn. Com. Arts, 2002. Mem.: Am. Assn. Tchrs. Spanish and Portuguese. Avocations: photography, walking, playing with cat, plants, music. Home: 265 Gardner Ave New London CT 06320-3026 E-mail: teatrol@etal.uri.edu.

ESPINOSA, RUBEN, education educator, consultant; b. Riverside, Calif., June 27, 1948; s. Robert William and Delfina Martinez Espinosa; m. Joanne Espinosa. BA in Sociology, U. Calif., Riverside, 1971; M in Sociology, Stanford U., 1973, PhD in Sociology, 1975. Dir. Calif. Sch. Fin. Project, San Diego, 1975—80, Multifunctional Resource Ctr., San Diego, 1988—92; asst. prof. San Diego State U.-Coll. Edn., 1975—99, assoc. prof., 1980—82, full prof., 1983—. Conducted over 1000 tng. workshops, advisor over 25 doctoral coms. Contbr. over 34 pubs. and books. Office: Dept Edn Polit Studies 5551 Maryland Ave La Mesa CA 91942-1519 Business E-mail: espinosa@mail.sosuiadu.

ESPIRICUETA, SYLVIA, counseling administrator; b. Chgo., June 17, 1960; d. Zeferino Sáenz and Maria Delua; m. Valentine Espiricueta, July 26, 1986; 1 child, Valentine IV. BS in Edn. magna cum laude, Pan Am. U., Edinburg, Tex., 1983; MS in Edn., Counseling, Guidance, U. North Tex., 1990. Cert. counselor Tex., tchr. Tex. Bilingual tchr. Mission Sch. Dist., Tex., Austin Ind. Sch. Dist., Tex., Irving Ind. Sch. Dist., Tex.; tchr. Spanish Mesquite Ind. Sch. Dist., Tex.; binlingual psychotherapist MHMR, Dallas, Galaxy Ctr., Garland, Tex.; elem. sch. counselor Grand Prairie Ind. Sch. Dist., Tex., Arlington Ind. Sch. Dist., Tex. Whole brain tutor, Dallas, Ft. Worth, 1998—; lectr. in field; bilingual storyteller Arlington Pub. Libr., 2002. Singer (songwriter): (CD) After the Rain Comes the Sun, 2003; author: Positive Choices, 1996, Teach to Reach, 2002, Choosing to Learn to Climb, 2002. Internat. singer, songwriter. Finalist Festival Cancion Latin Am., Calif., 2003. Mem.: ASCAP, San Diego Songwriters Guild, Ft. Worth Songwriters Assn. E-mail: espiricuetasylvia@hotmail.com.

ESPOSITO, BONNIE LOU, marketing professional; b. Chgo., July 20, 1947; d. Ralph Edgar and Dorothy Mae (Groh) Myers; m. Frank Merle Esposito, Aug. 15, 1969 (div. Sept. 1985); children: Mario Henry, Elizabeth Ann. BA, George Williams Coll., 1969. Caseworker Little Bros. of the Poor, Chgo., 1969-72; dir. Little Bros.-Friends of the Elderly, Mpls., 1972-78; organizer Community Crime Prevention, Mpls., 1978-81; owner Espo Inc./Mario's Ristorante, Mpls., 1978-85; mktg. mgr. City of Mpls. Energy Office, 1981—; dir. mktg. and tng. The Energy Collaborative, 1987-93; dir. mktg. Ctr. for Energy and Environment, Mpls., 1989-95; dir. WINGS program Employment Action Ctr., Mpls., 1995-97; dir. Minn. Office Citizenship and Vol. Svcs., Mpls., 1997—2002; exec. dir. Account Ability Minn., 2002—. V.p., bd. dirs. Resource Alternatives, Inc.; sec. bd. dirs. Golden Girl Homes, 2002—. Bd. dirs. Vital Aging Network, 2002; bd. dir. Golden Girls Homes, 2002—. Recipient Disting. Leadership award, Minn. Assn. Vol. Adminstrn., 2002. Mem. NAFE (bd. dirs. Monday Night Network 1988), Midwest Direct Mktg. Assn., Minn. Multi-Housing Assn., Nat. Apt. Assn., Profl. Assn. for Consumer Energy Edn. (bd. dirs. 1993—, chmn. fin. com.). Office: Office Accountability Minn 2314 Univ Ave Ste 12 Saint Paul MN 55114

ESPOSITO, JOSEPH ANTHONY, lawyer; b. Spokane, Wash., Oct. 4, 1941; s. Charles Esposito and Angela (Migliuri) E.; m. Joyce A. Chastek, July 7, 1966; children: Kate, Molly, Jill, Sara, Amy. BBA, Gonzaga U., 1963, JD, 1969. Bar Wash., U.S. Dist. Ct. Wash., U.S. Ct. Appeals (9th cir.). Law clk. to presiding justice Wash. State Ct. Appeals, Spokane, 1969-70; lawyer in prin. Dellwo Rudolph and Grant, Spokane, 1970-73; ptnr. Trezona Lorenz and Esposito Spokane, 1973-85; prin. Esposito, Tombari and George, Spokane, 1985—. Trustee St. Joseph's Children's Home, Spokane, 1970-85, Gonzaga Preparatory

Sch., 1982-88; legal counsel, bd. dirs. Spokane Jr. C. of C., 1969-75; bd. dirs. Spokane Legal Svcs. Bd., 1970-75. Recipient svc. award Spokane Jr. C. of C., 1973. Mem.: Wash. Bar Assn., Rotary, Manito Golf and Country Club. Roman Catholic. Avocations: golf, fly fishing, hunting. Office: Esposito Tombari and George 960 Paulsen Bldg Spokane WA 99201

ESPOSITO, JOSEPH LOUIS, lawyer; b. New Haven, Conn., Nov. 2, 1941; s. Joseph Henry and Camille (Carrano) E.; m. Nancy Giller, June 17, 1967 (div. 1973); m. Maddalena Fiorillo, Dec. 17, 1977 (div. 1986); 1 child, Giulio; m. Katherine Valenzuela, Oct. 26, 1996. BS, Fairfield U., 1964; MA, NYU, 1968, PhD, 1970; JD, U. Ariz., 1986. Bar: Ariz. 1987, U.S. Dist. Ct. (9th cir.) Ariz. 1987, U.S. Supreme Ct. 1991, U.S. Ct. Appeals (fed. cir.) 1998. Assoc. prof. philosophy Bradley U., Peoria, Ill., 1968-70, prof. philosophy, 1970-76; editor, 1974-80; with various bus. ventures, 1981-88; assoc. Smitherman and Sacks, Tucson, 1987-88; ptnr. Smitherman, Sacks and Esposito, Tucson, 1988-89, Smitherman & Esposito, Tucson, 1989-91; pvt. practice Tucson, 1992—. Rsch. prof. Inst. for Studies in Pragmatism, Tex. Tech. U., Lubbock, 1975-84; vis. scholar U. Ariz., 2001-03. Author five philosophy books; contbr. articles to profl. jours. Mem. Am. Philos. Assn. Avocation: travel. Office: 630 N Craycroft Rd Ste 250 Tucson AZ 85711-1456 E-mail: jespo@earthlink.net.

ESPOSITO, MARK MARIO, lawyer; b. Petersburg, Va., Nov. 27, 1958; s. Marion Francis and Mary Josephine (Straccioni) E.; m. Suzanne Marie Daley, Apr. 1988; children: Mark Francis, David Anthony. BS, James Madison U., 1980; JD, U. Richmond, 1984. Bar: Va. 1984, U.S. Dist. Ct. (ea. dist.) Va. 1984, U.S. Ct. Appeals (4th cir.) 1984, U.S. Supreme Ct. 1994. Assoc. Eliades & Eliades, Hopewell, Va., 1984-87; ptnr., dir. Hundley & Johnson, Richmond, Va., 1987—.

ESQUEDA, OCTAVIO JAVIER, religious studies educator; b. Guadalajara, Mex., Nov. 19, 1972; s. Javier and Leticia Esqueda; m. M. Angelica Angelica de la Torre, July 18, 1998. Licenciatura in Lit., U. Guadalajara, 1997; MA in Christian Edn., Dallas Theol. Sem., 2000; PhD in Higher Edn., U. North Tex., 2003. Prof., Cuba. Bd. mem. Howard Ctr. Christian Studies, Dallas, 2002—. Recipient Anna L. Agre award Ctr. Bibl. Studies Tchg., Dallas Theol. Sem., 2000. Achievements include research in Theological Seminaries in Cuba. Home: 3719 Mockingbird Lane Dallas TX 75205 Personal E-mail: oesqueda@hotmail.com.

ESQUER, DEBORAH ANNE, elementary school educator; b. Omaha, Oct. 28, 1950; d. Thomas Ross and Carolyn Mae (Wright) Woods; m. Mario H. Esquer, Aug. 21, 1971 (div. Apr. 1991); children: Mario, Michael. BA, Ariz. State U., 1972, MA in Edn., 1972, 78; postgrad., Ottawa U., Phoenix, 1990-92. Cert. elem. tchr., spl. edn. Tchr. Paradise Valley Sch. Dist., Phoenix, 1972—. Precinct commmitteewoman Scottsdale Dem. Com.; committeewoman Ariz. Dem. Com.; mem. Valley Leadership Class, 1999-2000; bd. dirs. Wesley Cmty. Ctr., 2000—, bd. pres.; mission team co-chair Paradise Valley United Meth. Ch.; bd. dirs. ASU Coll. Edn. Alumni. Tchr. venture grantee, Phoenix, 1988. Mem. NEA, Ariz. Edn. Assn., Ariz. Reading Coun., Paradise Valley Edn. Assn., Paradise Valley Reading Coun., Phoenix Art Mus., Ariz. Hist. Soc., Paradise Valley Jr. Women's Club (corr. sec. 1991-92), Alpha Delta Kappa (pres. 1986 88, ctrl. dist. treas. 1986-88, corr. sec. 1992-94, treas. 1994—, state com.), Alpha Phi. Democrat. Methodist. Office: Desert Springs 6010 E Acoma Dr Scottsdale AZ 85254-2599

ESQUIBEL, EDWARD V. psychiatrist, clinical medical program developer; b. Denver, May 28, 1928; s. Delfino C. and Beatrice (Solis) E.; m. Elaine F. Telk (div. 1961); children: Roxanne, Cyndi, Allen, James; m. Lillian D. Robb, 1961; children: Amanda, Ramona. MD, U. Colo., 1958. Diplomate Am. Bd. Psychiatry and Neurology. Assoc. chief svc. Ill. State Psychiat. Inst., Chgo., 1964-66; dir. undergrad. program psychiatry, asst. prof. psychiatry Chgo Med. Sch., 1966-68; cons. and supr. group therapy Lake County Mental Health Clinic, Gary, Ind., 1968-72; pvt practice Daytona Beach, Jacksonville, Fla., 1972-82; chief forensic svcs., dir. div. maximum security and inst. rsch. Colo. State Hosp., Pueblo, 1981; assoc. clin. prof. psychiatry Quillen-Dishner Coll. Medicine, Johnson City, Tenn., 1982-84; clin. psychiatrist VA Outpatient Clinic, Riviera Beach, Fla., 1984-86; mental health coord., supr. VA, Pensacola, Fla., 1986-88; assoc. chief staff, ambulatory care VA Med. Ctr., Ft. Lyon, Colo., 1988-90, Carl Vinson VA Med. Ctr., Dublin, Ga., 1990-91; staff physician VA Med. Ctr., Sheridan, Wyo., 1993—, chief psychiat. svcs. Lake City, Fla., 1993-94; contract physician, 1995—. Contbr. articles to profl. jours. Sgt. U.S. Army, 1948-52. Recipient Plaque Recognition award Southeastern Psychiat. Inst., 1964, Internat. Pers. Creative award, 1972, Key to City Daytona Beach, 1975, Hosp. Dirs. commendation VA, 1991. Avocations: gardening, arts and crafts, reading. Home and Office: 801 Gospel Island Rd Inverness FL 34450-3592

ESQUIVEL, AGERICO LIWAG, retired research physicist; b. Manila, June 5, 1932; came to U.S., 1957, naturalized, 1971; s. Enrique Frias and P. R. (Liwag) E. AB, Berchmans Coll., Manila, 1955; MA, Berchmans Coll., 1956; PhD, St. Louis U., 1963. Rsch. assoc. St. Louis U., 1961-63; rsch. scientist Research Inst. Advanced Studies, Balt., 1963, Materials Research Lab., Martin Co., Orlando, Fla., 1964-65; sr. rsch. engr. Materials Tech. Labs. Boeing Co., Seattle, 1965-71; postdoctoral fellow Advanced Research Projects Agy., U. So. Calif., L.A., 1971-73; mem. tech. staff Hughes Aircraft Co., Culver City, Calif., 1973-76; mem. tech. staff Semicondr. Process and Device Ctr., Tex. Instuments Inc., Dallas, 1976-98. Presenter internat. symposia, U.S., Japan, Europe. Contbr. articles to sci. jours. NSF postdoctoral fellow, 1963. Mem. IEEE Elec. Devices Soc. (sr. mem.), Am. Phys. Soc., Electrochem. Soc., Sigma Xi, Pi Mu Epsilon. Achievements include 16 U.S. patents issued on submicron CMOS process integration, development, device characterization, process/device computer simulation, trench isolation, buried multilevel interconnect systems, nonvolatile memory devices; contbr. papers to jours. and procs. on X-ray, electron diffaction, radiation hardening, cathodoluminescence in GaAs, deep level transient spectroscopy, x-ray lithography, high density nonvolatile memories, trench isolated electronically programmable read-only memories (EPROMs), sub-0.25 micron Complementary Metal Oxide Semiconductor (CMOS) transistors and fabrication process, 0.18 micron CMOS logic transistor technology, Ultra Large Scale Integrated (ULSI) CMOS device process integration and characterization.

ESREY, ELIZABETH GOVE GOODIER, chemist, biologist; b. West Chester, Pa., Mar. 25, 1964; d. Robert Egan and Mary Ellen (Winslow) Goodier; m. James David Esrey, Nov. 28, 1987; children: Briana, Steven. BA in Biology, Maryville Coll., 1986. Lab. tech. Franklin Co., Wilmington, Del., 1987, Stine Haskell Rsch. Labs., DuPont, Newark, Del., 1987-91, chemist, 1991-93, biochemist, 1993—, biochemist herbicide biomechanisms Agrl. Product Discovery, 1993-94, biologist plant and fungal biochemistry, 1994-97, biologist high throughput screening/assay devel. biol. leads, 1998-99, lead generation screening, lead characterization, 1999-2000, site of action assay devel., 2000—, mem. safety resource team, 1996-98. Owner Beth's Homemade Breads & Pies Middletown, Del., 1987—. Active Chesapeake Bay Girl Scouts, 1998—. Recipient DuPont Agr. Products Global Tech Divsn. Achievement award, 1997; named to Outstanding Young Women of Am., 1987, 97. Republican. Episcopalian. Office: Stine Haskell Rsch Labs PO Box 30 Newark DE 19714-0030 E-mail: elizabeth.g.esrey@usa.dupont.com.

ESREY, WILLIAM TODD, telecommunications company executive; b. Phila., Jan. 17, 1940; s. Alexander J. and Dorothy (B.) E.; m. Julie L. Campbell, June 13, 1964; children: William Todd, John Campbell. BA, Denison U., Granville, Ohio, 1961; MBA, Harvard U., 1964. With Am. Tel & Tel. Co., also N.Y. Tel. Co., 1964-69; pres. Empire City Subway Ltd., N.Y.C., 1969-70; mng. dir. Dillon, Read & Co. Inc., N.Y.C., 1970-80; exec. v.p. corp. planning United Telecommunications, Inc. (now Sprint), Westwood, Kans., 1980-81, exec. v.p., CFO, 1981-82, 84-85, CEO, 1985—90; chmn., CEO Sprint Corp., Westwood, Kans., 1990—. Bd. dirs. Exxon Mobil Corp., Duke Energy Corp., Gen. Mills, Inc. Bd. dirs. Midwest Rsch. Com. for Econ. Devel. Mem. Mission Hills Country Club, River Club, Links Club, Kans. City Country Club, Phi Beta Kappa. Office: Sprint 2330 Shawnee Mission Pkwy Shawnee Mission KS 66205-2090

ESRICK, JERALD PAUL, lawyer; b. Moline, Ill., Oct. 1, 1941; s. Reuben and Nancy (Parson) E.; m. Ellen Feinstein, June 18, 1966; children: Sara Elizabeth, Daniel Michael. BA, Northwestern U., 1963; JD, Harvard U., 1966. Bar: Ill. 1966, U.S. Dist. Ct. (no. dist.) Ill. 1967, U.S. Supreme Ct. 1974, U.S. Ct. Appeals (9th cir.) 1985, U.S. Ct. Appeals (7th cir.) 1967. Law clk. U.S. Dist. Ct. (no. dist.) Ill., 1966-68; assoc. Wildman, Harrold, Allen & Dixon, Chgo., 1968-73, ptnr., 1973—, also chmn. firm mgmt. com., 1987-90. Lectr. Northwestern U., 1984-93, Coll. Arts and Scis. bd. visitors, 1993—, Nat. Panel Comml. Arbitrators, Am. Arbitration Assn. Pres. bd. trustees Nat. Lekotek Ctr., Evanston, Ill., 1989-93, U.S. Toy Libr. Assn., 1987-88; bd. dirs. Evanston Mental Health Assn., 1984-86, Fund for Justice, 1969-95, Lawyers' Com. for Civil Rights, 1974-84. Fellow Am. Coll. Trial Lawyers; mem. ABA, Ill. State Bar Assn., Chgo. Coun. Lawyers (bd. dirs., sec., founding mem.), Chgo. Bar Assn., Lawyers Club Chgo. Avocations: running, skiing, sailing, windsurfing, classical music. Home: 1326 Judson Ave Evanston IL 60201-4720 Office: Wildman Harrold Allen & Dixon 225 W Wacker Dr Ste 3000 Chicago IL 60606-1229 E-mail: esrick@wildmanharrold.com.

ESSA, LISA BETH, elementary school educator; b. Nov. 19, 1955; d. Mark Newyla and Elizabeth (Warda) Essa. BA, U. Pacific-Stockton, 1977, MA in Curriculum and Instrn. Reading, 1980. Cert. tchr. elem., multiple subject and reading specialist Calif. Libr. media specialist Delhi (Calif.) Elem. Sch. Dist., 1978-80; reading clinic tutor San Joaquin Delta C.C., Stockton, Calif., 1980; libr. media specialist Hayward (Calif.) Unified Sch. Dist., 1980—. Chair curriculum coun. Hayward Unified Sch. Dist., 2000—01; support provider Beginning Tchr. Support Assessment, 2000—01. Supr. San Francisco host com. Dem. Nat. Conv., 1984. Named Master Tchr., Intel Teach to the Future; recipient Hon. Svc. award, 1999. Mem.: Hayward Unified Tchrs. Assn., Calif. Tchrs. Assn., Jr. League San Francisco. Episcopalian. E-mail: chalktalk1@aol.com.

ESSANDOH, HILDA BRATHWAITE, kindergarten educator; b. N.Y.C., Feb. 19, 1925; d. Charles Christopher and Millicent Marian (Boxill) Brathwaite; m. Samuel O. Essandoh, June 11, 1959; children: Millicent Efua, Yvonne Araba, Dorothy Esi. BA, Hunter Coll., 1959; MS, Bank Street Coll. Edn., 1976, profl. diploma in supervision-adminstrn., 1980. Cert. nursery, kindergarten, 1st-6th grades, sch. adminstrn. and supervision. Tchr. kindergarten N.Y.C. Bd. Edn., 1962-91. Recipient Ely Trachtenberg award. Home: 548 W 165th St New York NY 10032-4942

ESSANDOH, LOUIS KOFI, cardiologist; b. Ghana, 1954; MD, Yale U., 1981. Diplomate Am. Bd. Internal Medicine, Am. Bd. Cardiology. Intern Mayo Clinic, Rochester, Minn., 1982-83, resident in internal medicine, 1983-85, fellow in cardiology, 1985-88; pvt. practice Annapolis, Md. Asst. prof. medicine Johns Hopkins U., Balt. Office: 2002 Medical Pa Annapolis MD 21401

ESSARY, ANDREW CHARLES, philosophy educator, financial analyst; b. Dallas, Oct. 6, 1950; s. Charles Eugene and Dorothy (Miller) E.; m. Carol Anne Kuhn, Aug. 15, 1969; 1 child, Kerry Alise Berry. Student, Richland Coll., Dallas, 1974-80; BBA, So. Meth. U., 1984; MA, U. Tex. at Dallas, Richardson, 1994. Fin. analyst Tex. Instruments, Dallas, 1972-93; auditor Trinity Industries, Dallas, 1993-95; dir. Lovers Lane Animal Hosp., Dallas, 1995-98; assoc. prof. philosophy Collin County C.C., Plano, Tex., 1995—; sr. fin. analyst U. Tex. Southwestern Med. Sch., Dallas, 1998—. Freelance writer, newspaper columnist on ethics, 1998.d Named Outstanding Alumni, U. Tex. at Dallas, 1997; scholar Endowed Essary Family's Single Parent scholarship, Collin County C.C. Found., 1998—. Mem. Mensa, Profl. Assn. Dive Instructors (cert. dive master). Avocations: scuba diving, photography, gardening, motorcycling, tai chi. Office: U Tex Southwestern Med Sch Ste NB7 208A 5323 Harry Hines Blvd Dallas TX 75390-9072 Fax: 214-648-4080. E-mail: andy.essary@utsouthwestern.edu.

ESSEGAIER, SKANDER, education educator, researcher; b. Binzart, Tunisia, Jan. 6, 1969; s. Bechir Sghaier and Leila Bahri; m. Hanan Askalan. BS in Stats. and Econs., ENSAE, 1993; MS in Math., London Sch. of Econs., 1993; PhD, Columbia U., 1999. Fin. analyst Banque Nationale de Paris, N.Y.C., 1991—92; jr. ptnr. Maghreb Fin. Group, Tunis, Tunisia, 1994—95; sr. mgr. Tuninvest Fin. Group, 1999—2000; asst. prof. NYU, N.Y.C., 2000—03, Wharton Sch., U. of Pa., 2003—. Recipient Mktg. Doctoral Consortium, Columbia U., 1998; fellow, 1995—99; grantee, NATO, 1999; scholar Merit scholar, Govt. of Tunisia, 1986—89, Mary Trevelyan scholar, Internat. Students Ho., London, 1992—93. Mem.: INFORMS, Am. Mktg. Assn., Beta Gamma Sigma. Office Fax: 212-995-4006.

ESSER, ARISTIDE HENRI, psychiatrist; b. Padalarang, Java, Indonesia, May 11, 1930; came to U.S., 1961; s. Samuel Jonathan and Anganita (Tawalujan) E.; m. Ada Reif; children: Jonathan Hendrik, Jessica. MD, U. Amsterdam, The Netherlands, 1955. Diplomate Am. Bd. Psychiatry and Neurology. Med. dir. N.S. Kline Rsch. Inst., Orangeburg, N.Y., 1962-69; dir. rsch. Letchworth Village, Thiells, N.Y., 1969-71; dir. Ctrl. Bergen Cmty. Mental Health Ctr., Paramus, N.J., 1971-77; med. dir. Mission for Immaculate Virgin, S.I., N.Y., 1977-80; dir. quality assurance Bronx (N.Y.) Psychiat. Ctr., 1980-85; unit chief for supportive rehab. Rockland Psychiat. Ctr., Orangeburg, 1985-88, chief geriat. divsn., 1988-90; pvt. practice, 1989; cons. psychiatrist St. Dominic's Home, Blauvelt, 1990—2001; attending psychiatrist Good Samaritan Hosp., Suffern, NY, 1990—2002, Rye (N.Y.) Hosp. Ctr., 1990—. Rsch. prof. NYU Med. Ctr., N.Y.C., 1985-94; pres. Psychiatry P.C., 1989—, Palisades Practice Mgmt., Inc., 1998—, Psychiatry Evaluation Treatment and Rehab. Assocs., PLLC, 1999—. Co-author: Mental Illness: A Homecare Guide, 1989, Chi Gong: The Ancient Chinese Way to Health, 1990; co-editor: Behavior and Environment, 1971, Design for Communality and Privacy; editor Jour. Man-Environment Sys., 1969— (Internat. Design award 1973). Recipient travel grant City of Leyden, The Netherlands, 1960; Lederle Labs. fellow Yale U., 1961. Fellow AAAS (life), Am. Psychiat. Assn. (life); mem. Soc. for Biol. Psychiatry, Soc. for Gen. Systems Rsch., Am. Acad. Acupuncture (founding), Assn. for Study Man-Environment Rels. (founding). Home: 435 S Mountain Rd New City NY 10956-5731 Office: 337 N Main St Ste 2 New City NY 10956-4310 Office Fax: (845) 639-3031. E-mail: pbhppmc@att.net.

ESSER, CARL ERIC, lawyer; b. Montclair, N.J., Feb. 12, 1942; s. Josef and Elly (Graber) E.; m. Barbara A. B. Stelzer, Oct. 12, 1968; children: Jennifer, Eric, Brian. AB, Princeton U., 1964; JD, U. Mich., 1967. Bar: Pa. 1967. Assoc. Reed Smith LLP, Phila., 1967-72, ptnr., 1973—2002; pvt. practice Phila., 2003—. With USMCR, 1960-66. Mem. ABA, Pa. Bar Assn., Pa. Lawyers Fund for Client Security (bd. dirs., chmn.), Octavia Hill Assn. (chmn. bd. dirs.), German Am. C. of C. (bd. dirs.); Racquet Club, Penllyn Club, Mfrs. Golf and Country Club. Republican. Office: 2500 One Liberty Pl Philadelphia PA 19103 E-mail: cesser@reedsmith.com.

ESSER, JAMES MARK, cardiovascular and interventional radiologist; b. Madison, Wis., Aug. 1, 1960; s. John Michael Esser and Helen Josephine (Brown) Butterworth. MD, SUNY, Buffalo, 1985. Diplomate Am. Bd. Radiology, Nat. Bd. Med. Examiners. Transitional resident John Burns Sch. Medicine-U. Hawaii, Honolulu, 1985-86, asst. clin. instr. surgery, 1985-86; resident in diagnostic radiology Beth Israel Med. Ctr.-Mt. Sinai Sch. Medicine, N.Y.C., 1986-90; fellow in vascular and interventional radiology St. Luke's-Roosevelt Hosp., N.Y.C., 1990-91; clinical fell. Cardiovasc. and Interv. Rad., Columbia Coll. of Physicians and Surgs., 1990-91; attending staff emergency dept. Bellevue Hosp., N.Y.C., 1988-91; attending radiologist Elmhurst Hosp., N.Y.C., 1990-91, St. Mary's Hosp., West Palm Beach, Fla., 1991-92, Med. Ctr. Hosp., Punta Gorda, Fla., 1992-93, Welborn Hosps. & Clins., Evansville, Ind., 1993-94, St. Mary's Med. Ctr., Evansville, 1993—, Cmty. Meth. Hosp., Henderson, Ky., 1994—98, Perry County Meml. Hosp., Tell City, Ind., 1994—99, St. Mary's Ctr. for Her, Evansville, 1995—, Vencor Hosp., Louisville, 1998—2001, Jasper Meml. Hosp., Jasper, Ind., 1998—2000, Wellington Regional Med. Ctr., West Palm Beach, Fla., 2000—, Regional Med. Ctr., Madisonville, Ky., 2000—. Pres., v.p. N.Y.C. Soc. Physicians for Social Responsibility, 1987-90. Clin. fellow Columbia Coll. Physicians and Surgeons, 1990-91. Mem. AAAS, Am. Coll. Radiology, Radiol. Soc. N.Am., Soc. Cardiovasc. and Interventional Radiology, Am. Roentgen Ray Soc., Ky. Med. Assn., Henderson County Med. Soc., N.Y. Roentgen Soc., Nat. Trust Historic Preservation. Roman Catholic. Avocations: jogging, surfing, rock climbing. Home and Office: 612 N Main St Henderson KY 42420

ESSER, JOSEPH ALLEN, editor; b. Arnold, Pa., Jan. 9, 1939; s. Joseph Frank and Helen Elizabeth Esser. BS in Social Sci., John Carroll U., 1961. From staff writer to assoc. editor Broadcasting Publs. Inc., Washington, 1965-91; assoc. editor Reed Elsevier, New Providence, N.J., 1991—. Mem. Soc. Profl. Journalists, Washington Ind. Writers, Deadline Club. Avocations: shortwave radio, tennis, jazz. Office: Broadcasting & Cable Yearbook 630 Central Ave New Providence NJ 07974-1541 E-mail: joe.esser@bowker.com.

ESSEX, MYRON ELMER, microbiology and virology educator; b. Coventry, R.I., Aug. 17, 1939; s. Myron Elmer Essex and Ruth Hazel (Knight) Esses; m. Elizabeth Katherine Jordan, June 19, 1966; children: Holly Anne, Carrie Lisa. BS, U. R.I., Kingston, 1962; DVM, Mich. State U., East Lansing, 1967; MS, Mich. State U., 1967, DSc (hon.), 1988; PhD, U. Calif., Davis, 1970; MA (hon.), Harvard U., 1979; DSc (hon.), U. R.I., 1987; DSc (hon.), U. Madrid, 1989, U. Md., 1992; DSc (hon.), U. Kinshasa, Zaire, 1995. Research fellow Karolinska Inst., Stockholm, 1970—72; asst. prof. Harvard U., Cambridge, Mass., 1972—76, assoc. prof., 1976—78, prof., chmn. dept. microbiology, 1978—81, chmn. dept. cancer biology, 1981—97, chmn. dept. immunology and infectious diseases, 1997—, Mary Woodard Lasker prof. health scis., 1989—, chmn. AIDS Inst., 1988—. Mem. sci. adv. bd. Cambridge Biosci. Corp., 1982—93, Virus Rsch. Inst., 1993—; cons. Diacrin, Cin. Co-editor: Viruses in Cancer, 1980, AIDS:Etiology, Diagnosis, Treatment and Prevention, 1992, 1997, Human T-cell Leukemia Viruses, 1984, AIDS in Africa, 1994; contbr. articles; patentee test for human T leukemia virus infection and AIDS blood tests and vaccines. Bd. sci. counselors Nat. Cancer Inst., 1982—93; sci. adv. bd. ARC, 1985—89; v.p. sci. affairs Internat. Retrovirol. Assn. HTLV and Related Viruses, 1995—; sec. gen. Internat. Assn. Rsch. on Leukemia, 1995—97, pres., 1997; mem.Lasker award jury Albert & Mary Lasker Found., 1982—84, 1987—92; bd. dirs. Pierre Dick/Virbac Found.; mem. adv. bd. AIDS Assn., 1990—; mem. sci. adv. bd. Until There's A Cure, 1995—, Internat. AIDS Vaccine Initiative, Rockefeller Found., 1996—, Sabin Found., 1996—, Inst. for Internat. Vaccine Devel., 1997—, Virus Rsch. Inst., 1992—; bd. dirs. Hong Kong Cancer Ctr., 1994—. Recipient Bronze medal, Am. Cancer Soc., 1978, Ralston-Purina Rsch. award, 1985, Outstanding Investigator award, Nat Cancer Inst., 1985, Lifetime Rsch. award, 1995, Disting. Alumnus award, Mich. State U., Lasker award, 1986, Carnation Rsch. award, 1987, Disting. Alumnus award, U. Calif., Davis, 1987, Presdl. medal of honor, Govt. of Senegal, 1991, Ann. award, Am. Assn. Vet. Epidemiologists, 1992, Gold-Headed Cane award, 1995, Alumni Excellence award, U. R.I., 1994; scholar Leukemia Soc. Am., 1972, Am. Cancer Soc. Nat Cancer Inst., 1973—. Fellow: Infectious Disease Soc. Am., Am. Assn. Microbiology, AAAS; mem.: Internat. Retrovirology Assn. (v.p.), Leukemia Soc. Am. (adv. bd. 1978—83, 1985—), Am. Cancer Soc. (mem. rsch. com. Mass. br. 1975—86), Soc. Gen. Microbiology, Reticuloendothelial Soc., Nat. Acad. Practitioners, Am. Soc. Virology, Internat. Assn. Rsch. in Leukemia (pres.), Am. Assn. Immunologists, Am. Assn. Cancer Rsch., AVMA, Inst. Medicine of NAS. Office: Harvard Sch Pub Health Immunology & Infectious Dis 651 Huntington Ave Boston MA 02115-6009

ESSIG, ALVIN, physiology educator; b. Canton, Ohio, Feb. 16, 1923; s. Samuel Essig and Yetta Hershlekevitch; m. Caroline Eileen Wechsler, Sept. 11, 1960; children: Steven, Rina. BS, Harvard U., 1944; MD, Ohio State U., 1948. Instr. to assoc. in medicine Harvard Med. Sch., Boston, 1961-65; asst. prof. medicine Tufts Univ. Sch. of Medicine, Boston, 1966-68, assoc. prof. of medicine, 1968-73, assoc. prof. physiology, 1971-73; lectr. in biophysics Harvard Med. Sch., Boston, 1970-75; prof. physiology and rsch. prof. medicine Boston U., 1973-91, prof. emeritus physiology and medicine, 1991—. Vis. scientist MIT, 1975-88; study sect. mem. NIH, Bethesda, Md., 1976-79, 79-80. Co-author: (book) Bioenergetics and Linear Nonequilibrium Thermodynamics, 1983. Mem. Salt and Water Club, Am. Physiol. Soc., Biophys. Soc., Soc. Gen. Physiologists. Avocations: music, reading. Office: Boston U Sch of Medicine 80 E Concord St Boston MA 02118

ESSIG, ERHARDT HERBERT, English educator; b. Sawyer, Mich., May 24, 1913; s. William Gustav and Wilhelmina Augusta (Kirchner) E.; m. Viola Katherine Waldschmidt, Aug. 24, 1946. MA, U. Tex., 1939; DPhil, Northwestern U., 1951. Instr., dean students Concordia Coll., Austin, Tex., 1936-40; instr. Concordia High Sch., Ft. Wayne, Ind., 1940-46; asst. prof. Valparaiso (Ind.) U., 1946-51, assoc. prof., 1951-56; prof., chmn. humanities Concordia Sr. Coll., Ft. Wayne, 1956-77; assoc.faculty Ind. U.-Purdue U., Ft. Wayne, 1976-83. Vis. prof. St. Francis Coll., Ft. Wayne, 1964-77; cons., spkr. in field. Author: History of Holy Cross Lutheran Church, 1995; contbr. articles to profl. jours. Grad. scholar Northwestern U., 1949-50. Mem. Modern Lang. Assn., Colonial Park Assn. (bd. dirs. 1972-74, pres. bd. dirs. 1972-73). Independent. Lutheran. Avocations: sports, travel, reading. Home: 1905 Colony Dr Fort Wayne IN 46825-5009

ESSIG, KATHLEEN SUSAN, university official, management consultant; b. Denver, July 5, 1956; d. Robert and Ethel Essig. BS in BA, Colo. State U., 1979, MS, 1987. CPA, Colo. Personal fin. planner, v.p. fin. Successful Money Mgmt., Ft. Collins, Colo., 1987-88; accts. payable technician Colo. State U., Ft. Collins, 1980-81, supr. comml. accts. receivable, 1981-83, gen. acct. II, 1983-85, supr. student loans, 1985-87, supr. accts. receivable, acct. II, 1988-89, cost acct. III, 1989-94, univ. ofcl., contr., 1994; univ. mgmt. cons. KPMG Peat Marwick, Denver, 1994-97, 1995-97; mgr. prin. cons. Oracle Corp., Redwood Shores, Calif., 1998—. Mem. Am. Bus. Women's Assn. (v.p. 1985, Woman of Yr. 1985), Nat. Assn. Accts. Avocations: photography, golf, skiing, scuba diving.

ESSIN, EMMETT MOHAMMED, JR., obstetrician, gynecologist; b. Sherman, Tex., Jan. 2, 1920; s. Emmett Mohammed Sr. and Lela Priscilla (Tallent) E.; m. Margaret Cummings, Dec. 31, 1939 (dec.); children: Emmett III, William Robert, Ellen Priscilla, Warren Namon; m. Norma J. Shytles, Jan. 28, 2001. BA, Austin Coll., 1940; MD, U. Tex., Galveston, 1943. Intern U. Tex., John Sealy Hosps., Galveston, 1943-44, resident in ob./gyn., 1944-45; mem. med. staff Wilson N. Jones Meml. Hosp., Sherman, Tex., 1946—, chief med. affairs, 2000—. Chief staff Wilson N. Jones Meml. Hosp., Sherman, 1976-77, chief ob-gyn., 1987-88; bd. dirs. Devel. Bd. Wilson N. Jones Meml. Hosp., Am. Bank, Sherman; ; founder, pres., ptnr. Essin Clinic, Sherman, 1946-89. Charter bd. dirs. Texoma Blood Bank, Sherman, 1975. Lt. USNR, 1945-46. Recipient Disting. Alumnus award Austin Coll., 1987, Sherman H.S., 1993; Paul Harris fellow Rotary Internat.; laureate Texoma Bus. Hall of Fame, 2001. Mem. ACOG (founding), Grayson County Med. Soc. (past pres.), Tex. Med. Assn., Willard R. Cooke Ob-Gyn. Soc. (past pres.), So. Med. Soc., Am. Coll. Abdominal Surgery, Am. Soc. Fertility, Tex. Ob-Gyn. Soc. (life), Rotary Internat. (Sherman rotary vocational svc. award medicine and health, 1999). Presbyterian. Avocations: fishing, people. Home: 1016 Crestview Dr Sherman TX 75092-5239 Office: Essin Med Bldg 600 N Highland Ave Sherman TX 75092-5601

ESSLINGER, JOHN THOMAS, lawyer; b. Ephrata, Pa., Aug. 11, 1943; s. Doster Alvin and Lucy Mildred (Ream) E.; m. Patricia Lynn Smith, Aug. 15, 1970; 1 child, John David. BA, Yale U., 1965; JD, Georgetown U., 1973. Bar: D.C. 1973, U.S. Dist. Ct. D.C. 1974, U.S. Supreme Ct. 1974, U.S. Ct. Appeals (D.C. cir.) 1974. Assoc. Morgan, Lewis & Bockius, Washington, 1973-76; ptnr. Schmeltzer, Aptaker & Shepard, P.C., Washington, 1976—. Capt. USMC, 1966-70, Vietnam. Decorated Purple Heart, Bronze Star, Gold Star. Mem. ABA, Bar Assn. D.C., D.C. Bar Assn., Maritime Adminstrv. Bar Assn. Episcopalian. Avocations: golf, wine, baseball. Home: 9102 Brierly Rd Chevy Chase MD 20815-5655 Office: Schmeltzer Aptaker & Shepard PC 2600 Virginia Ave NW Ste 1000 Washington DC 20037-1922

ESSMAN, ALYN V. photographic studios company executive; b. St. Louis, May 3, 1932; BBA, Washington U., St. Louis, 1953. Chmn. & CEO CPI Corp., St. Louis. Office: CPI Corp 1706 Washington Ave Fl 8 Saint Louis MO 63103-1717

ESSMAN, ROBERT NORVEL, artist, graphic designer; b. St. Louis, Feb. 6, 1937; s. Paul M. and Rose (Solinsky) E. BFA, State U. of Iowa, 1959. Artist Simplicity Pattern Co., N.Y.C., 1961-62, Life Mag., N.Y.C., 1962-68, art dir., 1969, Show Mag., N.Y.C., 1969-70, Bus. Week Mag., N.Y.C., 1970-74; logo designer, creative dir. N.Y.C. Bicentennial Commn., N.Y.C., 1974-76; art dir. People Weekly Mag., N.Y.C., 1974-82; art dir., pres. Bob Essman: Design, The Cricket Press, N.Y.C., 1982—. Pubr./design dir.: Revival: Theatrical History

Revisited, 1992-94. Bd. dirs. League for the Hard of Hearing, 1977-99, recording sec. 1987-95, hon. bd., 1999—; bd. dirs. Hampton-Booth Theatre Libr., 1993-94, sec., 1994. Recipient Vol. of Yr. award League for the Hard of Hearing, 1990, Excellence of Design award, Advt. Club of N.Y., 1977, Art Dirs. Club of N.Y., 1978, Gen. Excellence Nat. Mag. award Am. Soc. Mag. Editors, 1973. Mem.: Overseas Press Club (Designer Dateline 1991—92, New Club Logo 1994), Soc. Pub. Designers (bd. dirs. 1972—79, pres. 1976—79, Excellence of Design award 1972, 1973, 1975, 1976, 1978), Am. Inst. Graphic Arts (Excellence of Design award 1980), Dutch Treat Club (book designer 1989—, compiled membership history The Whole Who 1995, Gold medal 2003), The Players Club (bd. dirs. 1979—85). Address: Bob Essman Design 20 W Canal St Apt 113 Winooski VT 05404-2132 Home and Office: Apt 113 20 W Canal St Winooski VT 05404-2132 E-mail: bobessman@adelphia.net.

ESSMYER, MICHAEL MARTIN, lawyer; b. Abilene, Tex., Dec. 6, 1949; s. Lytle Martin Essmyer and Roberta N. Essmyer Nicholson; m. Cynthia Rose Piccolo, Dec. 27, 1970; children: Deanna, Mike, Brent Austin. BS in Geology, Tex. A&M U., 1972; postgrad., Tex. Christian U., 1976; JD summa cum laude, South Tex. Coll. Law, 1980. Bar: Tex. 1980, U.S. Dist. Ct. (no., so., ea. we. dists) Tex. 1982, U.S. Ct. Appeals (5th cir.) 1981, U.S. Ct. Appeals (9th cir.) 1990, U.S. Ct. Appeals (1st cir.) 1993, U.S. Ct. Appeals (7th cir.) 1995, U.S. Ct. Appeals (fed. cir.) 1985, U.S. Ct. Claims, 1981, U.S. Supreme Ct. 1991. Briefing atty. Supreme Ct. Tex., Austin, 1980-81, Haynes & Fullenweider, Houston, 1981-89, Essmyer & Hanby, Houston, 1989-92; atty. Essmyer & Assocs., Houston, 1992-94; pres. Essmyer & Tritco, LLP, Houston, 1994-95, Essmyer, Tritco & Clary, LLP, Houston, 1995-99, Essmyer & Tritco, LLP, Houston, 1999—. Lead article editor South Tex. Law Jour., 1979. Dem. candidate for state rep., Bryan, Tex., 1972; del. Dem. Party, Houston, 1982, 84; precinct chmn. Harris County Dem. Exec. Com., Houston, 1983-86. Capt. USAF, 1972-78. Nat. Merit Scholar, 1968-72. Mem. ABA, Houston Bar Assn., Tex. Trial Lawyers Assn. (dir. 1996—), Harris County Trial Lawyers Assn. (dir. 1997—), Assn. Trial Lawyers Am., Tex. Criminal Def. Lawyers Assn., Tex. Bar Found., Harris County Criminal Lawyers Assn. (dir. 1986-87), Fed. Bar Assn., Houstonian Club, The Petroleum Club of Houston, The Co. Onstage. Roman Catholic. Home: 1122 Glourie Dr Houston TX 77055-7506 Office: Essmyer & Tritico LLP 4300 Scotland St Houston TX 77007-7328 E-mail: essmyer@flash.net.

ESSNER, ROBERT ALAN, pharmaceutical executive; b. N.Y.C., Oct. 26, 1947; s. Arthur and Charlotte (Levy) E.; m. Rosalind Esser, July 24, 1969 (div. June 1986); children: Elizabeth, Emily; m. Anne Essner, May 23, 1987; children: Elizabeth, Emily, Benjamin. Various positions Sandoz Pharms. Corp., East Hanover, N.J., 1978-86, v.p., 1986-87, corp. v.p., COO bus. mgmt., 1987; pres. Sandoz Consumer HealthCare Group, Parsippany, N.J., 1987, Wyeth-Ayerst Labs., Phila., 1987-97; exec. v.p. Am. Home Products, Madison, N.J., 1997-2000, pres., 2000—; CEO Am. Home Products (now Wyeth), Madison, NJ, 2001—. Mem. Pharm. Mfs. Assn. Avocation: antique photography. Office: Wyeth 5 Giralda Farms Madison NJ 07940-0874

ESTABROOK, BROOKE KENDELL, instructional technologist; b. San Francisco, Oct. 24, 1965; d. Milton James Zibel; m. Brent Fishinghawk; children: Austin, Madison. BA in Psychology, UCLA, 1987; MS in Kinesiology/Sport Psychology, U. N. Tex., 1990; MS in Tchg. Computer Sci., U. Ill., 1997. Asst. to coach UCLA Mens Swimming Team, 1987—88; tchg. fellow U. N. Tex., Denton, 1988—90; sport psychology cons. So. Meth. U. Mens Swimming and Diving, Dallas, 1989; tchr., site dir. Princeton Rev., Anaheim, Calif., 1990—97; coach, instr. Long Beach (Calif.) C.C., 1990—91; instr. Rancho Santiago C.C., Santa Ana, Calif., 1990—91, Parkland C.C., Champaign, Ill., 1993—2001, Mesa (Ariz.) C.C., 1997—. Cons. Amateur Athletic Found., L.A. Author: Gym Access, 1994, Sports Psychology Online, 1998. Recipient Presdl. Sports award, 1996, 97; named Outstanding Young Am., 1998. Avocations: sports, reading, computers. Office: Mesa CC 1833 W Southern Ave Mesa AZ 85202-4822

ESTABROOK, REED, artist, educator; b. Boston, May 31, 1944; s. F. Reed and Nancy (Vogel) E.; 1 son, August. B.F.A., R.I. Sch. Design, Providence, 1969; M.F.A., Art Inst. Chgo., 1971. Instr. U. Ill., 1971-74; asst. prof. U. No. Iowa, Cedar Falls, 1974-78, assoc. prof., 1978-83, head dept. photog. program, 1974-83; advisor visual arts Iowa Arts Council, Des Moines, 1977-78, mem. art purchase com., 1977-78; chmn. photog. dept. Kansas City Art Inst., Mo., 1983-84; prof., coordinator Photo Dept. San Jose State U., 1984-89, 92-95. Bd. dirs. San Francisco Camera Work, 1987-90; Fulbright exch. tchr. Sheffield Poly., Eng., 1990-91. Exhibited one-man shows, Sioux City Art Ctr., Iowa, 1981, Klein Gallery, Chgo., 1982, James Madison U., Harrisonburg, Va., 1983, Orange Coast Coll., Costa Mesa, Calif., 1983, Portland State U., Oreg., 1983, others, group shows, Isetan Mus. of Art, Tokyo, 1993, U. Colo., Boulder, 1977, 82, Mus. Modern Art, N.Y.C., 1978, 82, 84, Santa Barbara Mus. Art, Calif., 1979, San Francisco Mus. Modern Art, 1982, 90, Hokkaido Obihito Mus. of Art, Tokyo, 1993, Royal Coll. Art, London, 1994, Mus. Fine Art, Santa Fe, N.Mex., 1994, 96, San Jose Inst. Contemporary Art, 1996, San Francisco Mus. Modern Art, 1996, Sheppard Gallery U. Nev., Reno, others; represented permanent collections, Mus. Modern Art, N.Y.C., Mpls. Inst. Arts, Hallmark Collection, Kansas City, Mo., Boise Gallery Art, Idaho, Walker Art Ctr., Mpls., R.I. Sch. Design, U. Colo., Fogg Mus. Art, Harvard U., Spencer Mus. Art, U. Kans., Lawrence, Internat. Mus. Photography, Rochester, N.Y., Art Inst. Chgo., Humbolt State U., Arcata, Calif., Smithsonian Instn., Washington, San Francisco Mus. Modern Art, J. Paul Getty Mus., Santa Monica, Calif., Honolulu Acad. Arts. W.R. French fellow Art Inst. Chgo., 1971; Nat. Endowment for Arts fellow, 1976 Fellow Soc. Contemporary Photo; mem. Soc. for Photog. Edn. Home: 482 Chetwood St Oakland CA 94610-2649 Office: San Jose State U Sch Art & Design San Jose CA 95192-0089 E-mail: reed@reedestabrook.net.

ESTABROOK, ROBERT HARLEY, journalist; b. Dayton, Ohio, Oct. 16, 1918; s. Charles and Christianne M. (Harley) E.; m. Mary Lou Stewart, Dec. 22, 1942; children: John Stewart, James Ross, David Morse, Margaret Harley. AB, Northwestern U., 1939; postgrad., Am. Press Inst., Columbia, 1947; LHD (hon.), Colby Coll., 1972. City editor Emmet County Graphic, Harbor Springs, Mich., 1936; editor Daily Northwestern, Northwestern U., 1938-39; reporter Cedar Rapids (Iowa) Gazette, 1939-40, editorial writer, 1940-42, Washington Post, 1946-53, editor editorial page, 1953-61, corr., 1961-62, chief fgn. corr., 1962-65, UN and Can. corr., 1966-71; editor, pub. Lakeville (Conn.) Jour., 1971-86, pub. emeritus, cons., 1987—. Lectr. journalism U. Md., 1948-49; India Editor Exchange Program, 1987. Served from pvt. to capt. AUS, 1942-46; in charge Army newspaper and radio sta. 1945, Brazil. Recipient John Peter Zenger award U. Ariz., 1979, Eugene Cervi award, 1980, Horace Greeley award, 1980, Yankee Quill award Acad. New Eng. Journalists, 1983; named to New Eng. Cmty. Newspaper Hall of Fame, 2000. Mem. Nat. Conf. Editorial Writers (founder, life mem. pres. 1951), Council Fgn. Relations, Conn. Council on Freedom of Info. (chmn. 1981-82, Stephen Collins award, 1989), New Eng. Press Assn. (pres. 1983), Rotary Club, Phi Beta Kappa, Sigma Delta Chi (award for best editorial 1954), Deadline Club (Pulitzer Prize juror 1988, 89, award for UN corr. 1969, Golden Quill award for best editorial 1973, 78, Herbert Brucker award 1977), Delta Tau Delta. Unitarian Universalist. Office: Lakeville Jour 33 Bissell St Lakeville CT 06039-1688 Personal E-mail: restabrook01@snet.net.

ESTABROOK, RONALD WINFIELD, chemistry educator; b. Albany, NY, Jan. 3, 1926; s. George Arthur and Lillian Florence (Childs) E.; m. June Elizabeth Templeton, Aug. 23, 1947; children: Linda Estabrook Gilbert, Laura Estabrook Verinder, Jill Estabrook Wisehart, David. BS, Rensselaer Poly. Inst., 1950; PhD, U. Rochester, 1954, D.Sc. (hon.), 1980; MD (hon.), Karolinska Inst., Stockholm, 1981. Johnson Research Found. fellow U. Pa. Sch. Medicine, 1955-58; research assoc., 1958-59; asst. prof. phys. biochemistry, 1959-62; assoc. prof., 1961-65; prof., 1965-68; Virginia Lazenby O'Hara prof. biochemistry, 1968—; chmn. biochemistry U. Tex. Southwestern Med. Ctr., Dallas, 1968-82; dean U. Tex. Health Sci. Center (Grad. Sch. Biomed. Scis.), 1973-76; Cecil and Ida Green Chair of Biomedical Scis., 1990—; acting dir. Green Ctr. for Reproductive Biology Scis. U. Tex. Southwestern Med. Ctr., Dallas, 1997-99; chmn. basic sci. rev. com. VA, 1972-74. Cons. in field; bd. sci. advisors St. Judes Hosp., Memphis, 1978-81; chmn. bd. toxicology and environ. health NAS, 1980-85; governing bd. NRC, NAS, 1986-89; mem. Atlantic Richfield Sci. Adv. Coun., 1981-87; mem. coun. Inst. Medicine, NAS, 1984-89, report rev. com.; chmn. bd. sci. overseers Med. Rsch. Inst. San Francisco; mem. Robert Wood Johnson Found. Commn. on Med. Edn., bd. sci. advisors ILSI Found.; treas. Fedn. Am. Socs. Exptl. Biology, 1992-94; treas. 17th Internat. Congress of Biochemistry and Molecular Biology; chmn. Philip Morris USA SAB, 2002—; mem. SAB Kansas City Life Sci. Inst., 2002—. Exec. editor Archives of Biochemistry and Biophysics, 1966-73, 77-92, chmn. editorial bd., 1984-90; exec. editor Cancer Research, 1980-84; editor Jour. Pharmacology and Exptl. Therapeutics, 1969-74, Xenobiotica, 1970—, Life Scis., 1973-84; contbr. articles to profl. jours. Served with USNR, 1943-46. Recipient Patton Prize British Toxicology Soc., 2002, Disting. Scientist award Fedn. Am. Socs. Exptl. Biology, 1977, Claude Bernard medal U. Montreal, 1969. Mem. NAS, Inst. Medicine, Pan Am. Assn., Biochem. Socs. (sec.-gen. 1972-75), Am. Assn. Med. Schs. (adminstrv. bd. council acad. socs.; task force cost med. edn. 1971-72, liaison com. med. edn. 1975-80), Am. Soc. Biol. Chemists (treas. 1985-91), Internat. Soc. for Study Xenobiotics (pres. 1988-90), Am. Soc. Pharmacology and Exptl. Therapeutics, OXYgene (founder 1989), Sigma Xi. Home: 5208 Preston Haven Dr Dallas TX 75229-3040 Office: U Tex Southwestern Med Ctr 5323 Harry Hines Blvd Dallas TX 75390-9038 E-mail: estabroo@utsw.swmed.edu., REstab6741@aol.com.

ESTAVER, PAUL EDWARD, writer, poet; b. Springfield, Mass., Mar. 7, 1924; s. Edward Andrew and Lillian Marguerite (Moore) E.; m. Marina Brodie, Feb. 15, 1964 (div. Feb. 1973); 1 child, Donna Estaver Hall; m. Lynn Inez Lala Tabb, May 24, 1975; children: Emile R. Tabb, Tari Tabb Clem, Todd Tabb. AB, Boston U., 1948, MA, 1949. Dept. dir. Office of Law Enforcement Programs Law Enforcement Assistance Adminstrn., Washington, 1968-69, dir. civil disorders divsn., 1969-71; dep. dir. Nat. Ctr. for Dispute Settlement, Washington, 1973-75; dir. reference and dissemination divsn. Nat. Inst. Justice, Washington, 1976-95. Author: (poetry) Salisbury Beach-1954, 1984, (novels) His Third, Her Second, 1989, (novel in verse) Snake, 2003. Cpl. U.S. Army, 1943-46, ETO. Recipient Va. prize for fiction Va. Commn. for Arts, 1984, fellowship in poetry Nat. Endowment for Arts, 1987, Asst. Atty. Gen.'s award U.S. Dept. Justice, 1987, Heroes of Reinvention award V.P. of U.S., 1995. Mem. Internat. Soc. for Panetics. Avocations: jazz musician, antique clock restoration, horse farming, breeding standard poodles. Home: 6309 Pilgrims Rest Rd E Warrenton VA 20187-2854

ESTEBAN, MANUEL ANTONIO, academic administrator, language educator; b. Barcelona, June 20, 1940; arrived in U.S., 1970; s. Manuel and Julia Esteban; m. Gloria Ribas, July 7, 1962; 1 child, Jacqueline. BA in French with 1st class honors, U. Calgary, Can., 1969, MA in Romance Studies, 1970; PhD in French, U. Calif., Santa Barbara, 1976. From asst. prof. to prof. French and Spanish langs. and lit. U. Mich., Dearborn, 1973-87, assoc. dean, 1984-86, acting dean Coll. Arts, Scis., and Letters, 1986-87; dean arts and scis. Calif. State U., Bakersfield, 1987-90; provost, v.p. acad. affairs Humboldt State U., Arcata, Calif., 1990-93; pres., prof. French and Spanish Calif. State U., Chico, 1993—2003, pres. emeritus, prof. emeritus, 2003—. Bd. dirs. Calif. Joint Policy Coun. Agr. and Edn., 1995—. Author: (book) Georges Feydeau, 1983; contbr. to book revs. and articles to profl. publs. Trustee Enloe Hosp. Fellow, U. Mich., 1982—83; Woodrow Wilson fellow, 1969, Doctoral fellow, U. Calif., Santa Barbara, 1970—73, Can. Coun. Doctoral fellow, Govt. of Can., 1970—73, Rackham grantee, U. Mich., 1979. Mem.: Am. Assn. State Colls. and Univs., Am. Coun. Edn., Sierra Health Found. (bd. dirs. 1998—), Greater Chico C. of C. Avocations: golf, woodworking, glass blowing. Office: Calif State Univ O'Connell 407 Chico CA 95929-0003

ESTEFAN, NABIL, finance and business executive; b. Beirut, July 30, 1956; came to U.S., 1980; s. Joseph George and Marie (Zahr) E.; m. Fadia Elia, July 26, 1980; children: Kareem, Dana. BA in Bus. Adminstrn. summa cum laude, New Eng. Coll., Sussex, Eng., 1980; MBA Fin. and Investments summa cum laude, George Washington U., 1982. CPA, Md. Bank analyst Standard & Chartered Bank, Beirut, 1973-75; fin. analyst Internat. Fin. Svcs., Washington, 1985-86; contr. Online Computer Sys., Inc., Germantown, Md., 1986-91, v.p. fin., 1991-93; CFO Reed Tech. and Info. Svcs., Ft. Washington, Pa., 1993-96; v.p. fin. Pepsi-Cola Internat., Somers, N.Y., 1996-97, dir. planning, 1997; pres., owner Optimum Capital Mgmt., 1998—. Mem. AICPA, Am. Mgmt. Assn. Avocations: skiing, tennis, reading, classical music, opera. Home: 1114 Hillcrest Rd Narberth PA 19072-1224

ESTELL, DAVID B. psychologist, educator; b. San Diego, Calif., June 28, 1973; s. Robert Gordon and Helen Marie (Husby) Estell. BS in Psychology, U. Calif.-Davis, 1995; MA in Devel. Psychology, U. N.C., 1999, PhD of Devel. Psychology, 2001. Postdoctoral fellow Ctr. Devel. Sci. U. N.C., Chapel Hill, 2001—02; asst. prof. Ind. U., Bloomington, 2002—. Contbr. Mem.: AAAS, APA, Soc. for Rsch. on Child Devel. Office: Ind Univ Sch Edn Rm 4010 201 N Rose Ave Bloomington IN 47405-1006*

ESTELL, DORA LUCILE, retired educational administrator; b. Ft. Worth, Mar. 3, 1930; d. Hugh and Hattie Lucile (Poole) E. BA, East Tex. Bapt. U., 1951; MA, U. North Tex., 1959; EdD, East Tex. State U., 1988. Tchr. Mission (Tex.) Ind. Sch. Dist., 1951-53; tchr., adminstr. Marshall (Tex.) Ind. Sch. Dist., 1953-68; dep. dir. Region VII Edn. Svc. Ctr., Kilgore, Tex., 1968-94, ret., 1994. Contbr. articles to profl. jours. Bd. dir. South Milan County United Way, Richards Meml. Hosp. Named Rockdale Citizen of Yr., 2001. Mem. Rockdale C. of C. (bd. dirs.), Phi Delta Kappa. Baptist. Avocations: photography, gardening. Home: 611 W Bell Ave Rockdale TX 76567-2809

ESTEP, ARTHUR LEE, lawyer; b. Forsyth, Mo., Dec. 4, 1932; s. Raymond B. and Nancy Mabel (Melton) E.; m. Joan Marie Hayes, June 16, 1956; 1 child, Sallie Ann Estep Warren. BS, U. Mo., 1954; JD, U. Ariz., 1959, honors grad., 1989. Bar: Ariz. 1959, Calif. 1959. Trust officer 1st Nat. Bank, San Diego, 1959-60; dep. city atty. City of San Diego, 1960-61; pvt. practice San Diego, 1961—. Bd. visitors U. Ariz., Tucson, 1986-96. 1st lt. USMC, 1950-56, Korea. Recipient Outstanding Svc. to Legal Profession award San Diego Bar Assn., 1986. Diplomate Am. Bd. Trial Advs. (pres. San Diego chpt. 1991, mem. nat. bd. dirs. 1990-96). Office: Hughes & Nunn 450 B St Ste 2000 San Diego CA 92101

ESTEP, JOHN HAYES, religious organization administrator, clergyman; b. Bellwood, Pa., June 30, 1930; s. Kenneth and Anna Emily Estep; m. Dorothy L. Nash, Aug. 21, 1951; children: Heidi Ann, John H. Jr. BA, Wheaton (Ill.) Coll., 1953; MDiv, Denver Sem., 1956, DD (hon.), 1980. Ordained to ministry Bapt. Ch., 1956. Asst. pastor Forest City Bapt. Ch., Rockford, Ill., 1956-62; pastor, sr. min. Calvary Bapt. Ch., Longmont, Colo., 1962-69; dir. ch. rels. Mission to the Americas, Wheaton, 1969-80, CEO, 1980-95. Bd. dirs. Colo. Christian U., Denver, 1964-71, Denver Sem., 1968-70. Mem. Nat. Assn. Evangelicals (officer 1988-96), Nat. Black Evang. Assn. (bd. dirs. 1992—). Baptist. Avocations: golf, travel, reading, music. Office: CB Ministries 1501 W Mineral Ave Littleton CO 80120-5612 E-mail: jacke@cbamerica.org.

ESTEP, MYRNA LYNNE, systems analyst, philosophy educator; b. Whitesville, W.Va., Jan. 7, 1944; d. Modest Schaeffer and Mary Magdalene E.; m. Richard Keith Schoenig, June 5, 1971; 1 child, Debora Lynne. BA, Ind. U., 1970, MS, 1971, PhD, 1975; postgrad., U. Tex., 1993. Assoc. instr. Ind. U., Bloomington, 1972-75; asst. prof. U. Tex., San Antonio, 1975-78; rsch. edn. specialist Acad. Health Scis., San Antonio, Tex., 1979-84; program systems analyst, field researcher USMC, U.S. Navy, Quantico, Va., 1984-87; grad. faculty, advisor U. Zimbabwe, 1987-89; rsch. systems analyst San Antonio, 1990—; adj. faculty in philosophy U. of Incarnate Word, San Antonio, 1996-99, Our Lady of the Lake U., San Antonio, 1996-98. Grad. faculty U. Zimbabwe, Harare; advisor to ministries of higher edn. and labour, manpower planning and social welfare, Zimbabwe, 1987-89. Author: The Relation Between Theoretical and Procedural Knowing, 1975, A Theory of Immediate Awareness: Self-Organization and Adaptation in Natural Intelligence, 2003; co-editor (with E.S. Maccia and others): Women and Education, 1975; reviewer (for jours.); contbr. articles. Recipient Best Paper award U. Vienna, Austria, 1992. Mem. AAAS, Internat. Soc. Gen. Systems Rsch., Austrian Soc. Cybernetics, Math. Assn. Am., N.Y. Acad. Sci., Phi Kappa Phi. Home: 16022 Oak Grove Dr San Antonio TX 78255-1128 E-mail: emathematica@aol.com.

ESTEP, ROBERT LLOYD, lawyer; b. Marion, Va., Dec. 20, 1939; s. Lanson Eugene and Clara Nell (White) E.; m. Elizabeth Grayson Werth, July 10, 1971; 1 child, Laura White. BA with Honors, U. Va., 1962, JD, 1973. Bar: Ill. 1973, U.S. Dist. Ct. (no. dist.) Ill. 1973, Tex. 1984. From assoc. to ptnr. Isham, Lincoln & Beale, Chgo., 1973-83; ptnr. Jones, Day, Reavis & Pogue, Dallas, 1983—. Served to capt. U.S. Army, 1966-70, Vietnam.. Woodrow Wilson fellow, U. Va., 1962. Mem. Tex. Bar Assn., Law Club Chgo., Spl. Forces Assn., Phi Beta Kappa. Republican. Lutheran. Home: 6331 Park Ln Dallas TX 75225-2108 Office: Jones Day Reavis & Pogue 2727 N Harwood St Dallas TX 75201-1515

ESTERHAI, JOHN LOUIS, JR., surgeon, medical educator; b. Phila., Oct. 23, 1946; s. John Louis and Louise K. (Moyer) E.; m. Carol Jean Keely, Apr. 12, 1969; children: Staci June, Gregory Wayne. BA, Gettysburg Coll., 1968; MD, Temple U., 1972. Intern in surgery Temple U. Health Sci. Ctr., Phila., 1973; flight surgeon USAF, Kadena AFB, Okinawa, Japan, 1973-76; resident in orthop. surgery U. Pa. Sch. Medicine, 1977-80; asst. prof. orthopedic surgery Hosp. U. Pa., Phila., 1980-87, assoc. prof. orthopedic surgery, 1987-2000, prof. orthopedic surgery, 2000—. Editor: Musculoskeletal Infection, 1992. Maj. USAF, 1973-76. Recipient award Am. Orthopedic Assn., 1989, Assn. Bone and Joint Surgeons, 1994. Fellow Am. Acad. Orthopedic Surgeons, ACS; mem. Internat. Soc. Fracture Repair, Orthopaedic Rsch. Soc., Musculoskeletal Infection Soc. (pres. 1997-98). Office: Hosp U Pa Dept Orthopaedic Surgery 3400 Spruce St Philadelphia PA 19104-4206

ESTERHAMMER, ANGELA, literary theorist, educator; d. Hermann and Marianne E.; married, Feb. 20, 1989. BA, U. Toronto, 1983; postgrad., U. Tübingen, Germany, 1983-84; PhD, Princeton U., 1990. Asst. prof. dept. modern langs. U. Western Ont., London, Canada, 1989—94, assoc. prof., 1994—99, prof., 2000—, chair dept., 2000—. Vis. prof. Free U. Berlin, 1996—98. Author: Creating States: Studies in the Performative Language of John Milton and William Blake, 1994, The Romantic Performative: Language and Action in British and German Romanticism, 2000; editor Romantic Poetry, 2002, translator (and introduction): Two Stories of Prague by R.M. Rilke, 1994; contbr. articles to profl. jours. Recipient Protégé award, Toronto Arts Award Found., 1988, John Charles Polanyi prize, Govt. of Ont., 1990, Hellmuth Prize for Achievement in Rsch., 2002; Whiting fellow in Humanities, Princeton U., 1988, Alexander von Humboldt Found. rsch. fellow, Free U. Berlin, 1996—97. Mem. MLA, N.Am. Soc. for Study of Romanticism (founding mem.), Can. Comparative Lit. Assn. (pres. 2003—), Internat. Comparative Lit. Assn. Mem. United Ch. of Can. E-mail: angelae@uwo.ca.

ESTERLY, KATHERINE LOUISE, pediatrician; b. Norristown, Pa., Oct. 11, 1925; d. Harold Davis and Inez (Morgan) E. BS, Ursinus Coll., 1947; MD, Temple U., 1951. Diplomate Am. Bd. Pediat., Am. Bd. Neonatology. Intern Del. Hosp., Wilmington, 1951-52, pediatric resident, 1952-54; pvt. practice Wilmington, 1954-84; dir. neonatology Christiana Care Health Sys., Newark, 1984-94, chmn. pediatrics, 1994—. Med. dir. Children and Families First, Wilmington, 1955— (J. Thompson Brown award 1993); mem. med. adv. bd. March of Dimes, Del., 1975—. Recipient Trailblazer award Del. Women's Agenda, 1989, medal of honor Del. Pub. Health Assn., 1995, Medal of Distinction, U. Del., 1997; named to Women's Hall of Fame, Del. Commn. on Women, 1991. Home: PO Box 3658 Wilmington DE 19807-0658 Office: Christiana Care Health Sys PO Box 6001 Newark DE 19718-0001

ESTERLY, NANCY BURTON, physician; b. N.Y.C., Apr. 14, 1935; d. Paul R. and Tanya (Pasahow) Burton; m. John R. Esterly, June 16, 1957; children: Sarah Burton, Anne Beidler, John Snyder, II, Henry Clark, II. AB, Smith Coll., 1956; MD, Johns Hopkins U., 1960. Intern, then resident in pediatrics Johns Hopkins Hosp., 1960-63, resident in dermatology, 1964-67; instr. pediatrics Johns Hopkins U. Med. Sch., 1967-68; instr., trainee La Rabida U. Chgo. Inst.; also dept. pediatrics U. Chgo. Med. Sch., 1968-69; asst. prof. Pritzker Sch. Medicine, U. Chgo., 1969-70, assoc. prof., 1973-78; asst. prof. dermatology Abraham Lincoln Sch. Medicine, U. Ill., 1970-72, assoc. prof. dermatology and pediatrics, 1972-73; dir. div. dermatology, dept. pediatrics Michael Reese Hosp. and Med. Ctr., Chgo., 1973-78; prof. pediatrics and dermatology Northwestern U. Med. Sch., 1978; head div. dermatology, dept. pediatrics Children's Meml. Hosp., Chgo., 1978-87; prof. pediatrics and dermatology Med. Coll. Wis., Milw., 1987—; head div. dermatology, dept. pediatrics Children's Hosp. Wis., Milw., 1987—. Editor: Pediatric Dermatology, 1983—; contbr. numerous articles to profl. jours. Recipient David Martic Carter award, Am. Skin Assn., 2002, Lifetime Career Educator award, Dermatology Found., 2002. Mem.: Wis. Pediat. Soc., Women's Dermatol. Soc., Soc. Pediat. Dermatology (1st Lifetime Achievement award 1998), Soc. Pediat. Rsch., Am. Acad. Pediatrics, Soc. Investigative Dermatology, Wis. Dermatol. Soc., Am. Dermatol. Assn., Am. Acad. Dermatology, Internat. Soc. Pediat. Dermatology, Sigma Xi. Office: 9200 W Wisconsin Ave Milwaukee WI 53226-3522

ESTEROW, MILTON, magazine editor, publisher; b. Bklyn., July 28, 1928; s. Bernard and Yetta (Barash) E.; m. Jacqueline Levine, Jan. 6, 1951; children: Judith, Deborah. Student, Bklyn. Coll., 1946-49. Reporter N.Y. Times, N.Y.C., 1948-63, asst. to cultural news dir., 1963-68; assoc. dir. Kennedy Galleries, N.Y.C., 1968-72; editor, pub. ARTnews, N.Y.C., 1972—; chmn. ARTnewsletter, 1975—, Esterow Communications Corp., 1981, Annellen Publs., 1982. Lectr. numerous colls., univs., museums. Author: The Art Stealers, 1966. Office: ARTnews LLC 48 W 38th St Fl 9 New York NY 10018-6238

ESTES, ANDREW HARPER, lawyer; b. Pecos, Tex., Dec. 16, 1956; s. Bobby Frank and Gayle (Harper) E.; m. Deidre Dement, Mar. 19, 1976; children: Andrew Kimble, Jada Catherine. BA, Tex. Tech U., 1977; JD, Baylor Sch. Law, 1979. Bar: Tex. 1980, U.S. Dist. Ct. (no. dist.) Tex. 1980, U.S. Dist. Ct. (we. dist.) Tex. 1981, U.S. Ct. Appeals (5th cir.) 1982, U.S. Supreme Ct. 1983, U.S. Tax Ct., U.S. Ct. Appeals (10th cir.) 1987. Ptnr. Lynch, Chappell & Alsup P.C., Midland, Tex., 1980—. Mem. admissions com. Dist. 16, State Bar Tex., 1982-85, bd. dirs., 1999-2002. Mem. Tex. Tech. U. Coll. Edn. Devel. Coun., Lubbock, 1986-87; vol. Big Bros., Midland, 1983—, bd. dirs., 1985-89; bd. dirs. Hearthstone Temporary Children's Shelter, 1988-92; mem. bd. dirs. Tex. Book Festival, 2001-. Named Big Brother of Yr., Big Bros./Big Sisters of Midland, 1985; recipient Trimble Vol. Svc. award, Leadership Midland Alumni, 1986, Pro Bono Atty. award West Tex. Legal Svcs., 1991. Mem. ABA, Midland County Young Lawyers Assn. (sec., treas. 1987-88, Outstanding Young Lawyer of Midland County 1992), Midland County Bar Assn. (sec., treas. 1987-88, v.p. 1992-93, pres. elect. 1993-94, pres. 1995-96), State Bar Tex. (Dist. 16 grievance com. 1990-93, chmn. 1992-93, bd. dirs. 1999-2002), Tex. Young Lawyers Assn. (bd. dirs. 1987-89), Tex. Bd. Legal Specialization (cert.), Phi Delta Phi. Presbyterian. Home: 1505 Princeton Ave Midland TX 79701-5760 Office: Lynch Chappell & Alsup PC The Summit Bldg 300 N Marienfeld St Fl 7 Midland TX 79701-4345

ESTES, CARL LEWIS, II, lawyer; b. Ft. Worth, Feb. 9, 1936; s. Joe E. and Carroll E.; m. Gay Gooch, Aug. 29, 1959; children: Adrienne Virginia, Margaret Ellen. BS, U. Tex., 1957, LL.B., 1960. Bar: Tex. 1960. Law clk. U.S. Supreme Ct., 1960-61; assoc. firm Vinson & Elkins, Houston, 1961-69, ptnr. 1970—2002. Bd. dirs. Houston Grand Opera Assn., Houston Arboretum. Fellow Am. Bar Found., Tex. Bar Found.; mem. ABA, Internat. Bar Assn., Am. Law Inst., Am. Coll. Probate Counsel, Tex. Bar Assn., Internat. Fiscal Assn., Internat. Acad. Estate and Trust Law. Fellow Am. Bar Found., Tex. Bar Found.; mem. ABA, Internat. Bar Assn., Am. Law Inst., Am. Coll. Probate Counsel, Tex. Bar Assn., Internat. Fiscal Assn., Internat. Acad. Estate and Trust Law, Asia Soc. (bd. dirs.).

ESTES, CAROLYN ANN HULL, retired elementary school educator; b. Memphis, June 11, 1933; d. Elmer Franklin and Annie Vernon (Jeter) Hull; m. Robert Marion Estes, June 4, 1955; children: Robert Franklin, David Carlton. BS, Memphis State U., 1955; postgrad., U. Tenn., 1958, Nat. Coll. Edn., 1968, N. Tex. State U., 1970, Tex. Christian U., 1984, U. Tex., Arlington, 1985. Cert. elem. and secondary tchr., Tex. 4th grade tchr. Memphis City Schs., 1955-56, 63-66; 6th grade tchr. Knoxville (Tenn.) City Schs., 1957-58; 3d grade tchr. Elk Grove Village (Ill.) Schs., 1968-69; sci. tchr. Stripling Middle Sch., Ft. Worth Ind. Sch. Dist., 1970-76; 5th grade tchr. Eastern Hills Sch., Ft. Worth Ind. Sch. Dist., 1976-78; 5th grade honors tchr. Westcreek Elem. Sch., Ft. Worth Ind. Sch. Dist., 1978-91, computer instr., technol. coord., 1991-96; ret., 1996. Author: Hull's Heritage, 1986; contbg. author: Hardeman County History, 1979, also curriculum materials. Life mem. Tex. Coun. PTA, program chairperson, 1984-86; mem., bd. dirs. Ft. Worth Geneal. Assn. Named Walt Disney Salutes the Am. Tchr. Alternate, 1994, 2000 Most Memorable Tchrs., Baylor U. Mem. Nat. Edn. Assn., DAR (Outstanding Am. History Tchr. award 1988), Te

State Tchrs. Assn., Ft. Worth Classroom Tchrs. (faculty liaison 1983-86, chmn. Tchr. Ethics and Profl. Standards 1989, Tchr. of Yr. 1985), Sigma Kappa (alumnae chpt., Significant Sigma award 1990). Home: 141 Club House Dr Weatherford TX 76087-4001

ESTES, CARROLL LYNN, sociologist, educator; b. Fort Worth, May 30, 1938; d. Joe Ewing and Carroll (Cox) E.; 1 child, Duskie Lynn Gelfand Estes. AB, STanford U., 1959; MA, So. Meth. U., 1961; PhD, U. Calif., San Diego, 1972; DHL (hon.), Russell Sage Coll., 1986. Rsch. asst., asst. study dir. Brandeis U. Social Welfare Rsch. Ctr., 1962-63, rsch. assoc., 1964-65, project dir., 1965-67; vis. lectr. Florence Heller Grad. Sch., 1964-65; rsch. dir. Simmons Coll., 1963-64; asst. prof. social work San Diego State Coll., 1967-72; asst. prof. in residence dept. psychiatry U. Calif., San Francisco, 1972-75, assoc. prof. dept. social and behavioral scis., 1975-79, prof., 1979-92, chair dept. social and behavioral scis., 1981-93, coord. human devel. tng. program, 1974-75; dir. Aging Health Policy Rsch. Ctr., 1979-85, Inst. for Health and Aging, 1985-99. Faculty rsch. lectr. U. Calif., 1993. Author: The Decision-Makers: The Power Structure of Dallas, 1963; co-author: Protective Services for Older People, 1972, U.S. Senate Special Committee on Aging Report, Paperwork and the Older Americans Act, 1978, The Aging Enterprise, 1979 Fiscal Austerity and Aging, 1983, Long Term Care of the Elderly, 1985, Political Economy, Health and Aging, 1984, The Long Term Care Crisis, 1993, The Nation's Health, 2001, 7th edit., 2003, Critical Gerontology, 1999, Social Policy and Aging, 2001, Social Theory, Social Policy and Aging, 2003; contbr. articles to profl. jours. Mem. Calif. Commn. on Aging, 1974-77; cons. U.S. Senate Spl. Com. on Aging from 1976, Notch Commn. U.S. Commn. Social Security, 1993-94; bd. dirs. Nat. Com. to Preserve Social Security and Medicare, 2002—. Recipient Matrix award Theta Sigma Phi, 1964, award for contbns. to lives of older Californians, Calif. Commn. on Aging, 1977, Helen Nahm Rsch. award U. Calif., San Francisco, 1986, Woman Who Would Be Pres. League of Women Voters, 1998. Mem. Inst. Medicine of NAS, ACLU, Am. Sociol. Assn. (Disting. Scholar award Aging and Life Course 2000), Assn. Gerontology in Higher Edn. (pres. 1980-81, recipient Beverly award 1993, Tibbitts award 2000), Am. Soc. on Aging (pres. 1982-84, Leadership award 1986), Geronotol. Soc. Am. (Kent award 1992, pres. 1995-96), Older Women's League (v.p. 1994-97), Soc. Study Social Problems, Alpha Kappa Delta, Pi Beta Phi. Democrat. Office: U Calif San Francisco Inst Health & Aging 3333 California St Ste 340 San Francisco CA 94118-1944

ESTES, EDWARD RICHARD, JR., engineering consultant, engineer, retired educator; b. Richmond, Va., Mar. 2, 1925; s. Edward Richard Sr. and Mamie Cleveland (Bugg) E.; m. Elizabeth Hood Lee, Oct. 28, 1950; children: Virginia Lee Zimmerman, Susan Page, Edward Richard III, Elizabeth Anne, William Thomas. B in Engring., Tulane U., 1945; MS, Va. Polytech. Inst., 1948. Structural engr. Baskerville & Son, Richmond, 1947-48; asst. prof. Sch. Engring. U. Va., Charlottesville, 1948-55; rsch. engr. Am. Inst. Steel Constrn., N.Y.C., 1955-60; dir. engring. Fla. Steel Corp., Tampa, 1960-66; dir. engring. dept. Montague-Betts Co., Lynchburg, Va., 1966-68; chief rsch. engr. Am. Iron & Steel Inst., N.Y.C., 1968-69; engring. mgr. Rep. Steel Corp., Youngstown, Ohio, 1969-72; cons. engr. Estes & Assocs., Youngstown, 1972-78, Norfolk, Va., 1978—; prof. Old Dominion U., Norfolk, 1978-94, prof. emeritus, 1994, chmn. civil engring. tech. dept., 1978-84, assoc. dean coll. engring. and tech., 1984-88. Cons. in field. Contbr. articles to profl. jours. With USNR, 1943-46. Fellow ASTM (award of merit 2000), ASCE (pres. Norfolk chpt. 1983-84); mem. Am. Welding Soc. (disting., sect. chmn. 1986-87, A.F. Davis Silver medal 1964), Am. Iron and Steel Inst. (specification com.), Rsch. Coun. on Structural Connections (chmn. 1974-79), Norfolk Yacht and Country Club, Rotary. Republican. Methodist. Avocations: golf, tennis. Home and Office: 7611 Nancy Dr Norfolk VA 23518-4635

ESTES, ELAINE ROSE GRAHAM, retired librarian; b. Springfield, Mo., Nov. 24, 1931; d. James McKinley and Zelma Mae (Smith) Graham; m. John Melvin Estes, Dec. 29, 1953. BSBA, Drake U., 1953, tchg. cert., 1956; MSLS, U. Ill., 1960. With Pub. Libr. Des Moines, 1956-95, coord. extension svcs., 1977-78, dir., 1978-95, ret., 1995. Lectr. antiques, hist. architecture, libraries; mem. conservation planning com. for disaster preparedness for libraries. Author bibliographies of books on antiques; contbr. articles to profl. jours. Mem. State of Iowa Cultural Affairs Adv. Coun., 1986—94, Nat. Commn. on Future of Drake U., 1987—88; chmn. Des Moines Mayor's Hist. Dist. Commn.; mem. nominations review com. Iowa State Nat. Hist. Register, 1983—89; chmn. hist. subcom. Des Moines Sesquecentennial Com., 1993, Iowa Sister State Commn., 1993—95; mem. com. 40th Anniversary Drake U. Alumni Weekend, 50 Yr. Drake Alumni Weekend, 2003; mem. July 4 com. Iowa Sesquecentennial; nat. exch. dir. Friendship Force, 1997; mem. nat. adv. bd. Cowles Libr., 1998—; mem. Gov.'s Iowa Centennial Meml. Found., 1998—; mem. acquisition com. Salisbury House; mem. cultural ctr. task force African Am. Hist. Mus., 1999; mem. Iowa author com. Pub. Libr. Des Moines Found., 2001—03; mem. Terrace Hill Commn., 2001—; bd. dirs. Des Moines Art Ctr., 1972—83, hon. mem., 1983—; bd. dirs. Friends of Libr. USA, 1986—92, Henry Wallace House Found., Iowa Libr. Centennial Com., 1990—91. Recipient Recognition award Greater Des Moines, YWCA, 1975, Disting. Alumni award Drake U., 1979, Woman of Achievement award YWCA, 1989, Excellence in Hist. Preservation award City of Des Moines, 1994, Contribution to Cmty. award Connect Found., 1995; named Textbook Project in her honor, Forest Libr., 2002; named to Wall of Fame, YWCA, 2003. Mem.: ALA (30th Anniversary Honor Roll for Intellectual Freedom 1999), Iowa Soc. Preservation Hist. Landmarks (bd. dirs. 1969—97), Libr. Assn. Greater Des Moines Metro Area (chmn. 1992, pres.), Iowa Urban Pub. Libr. Assn., Iowa Libr. Assn. (life; pres. 1978—79), Iowa Antique Assn., Terrace Hill (Gov.'s Mansion) Soc. (bd. dirs. 1972—, v.p. 1991—93, pres. 1993—96), Links Inc. (40th ann. com. 1997), Drake U. 50 Yr. Club, Questers Inc. Club (pres. 1982, state 2d v.p. 1984—86, 1st v.p. 1990—2000, pres. 1997, state pres. 2000—03, pres. 2001—03), Rotary (history com. 2001), Proteus (pres. 2003—04).

ESTES, JAMES PAUL, financial services company executive; b. Fullerton, Calif., Oct. 28, 1946; s. Paul Herbert and Dorothy Jane E.; m. Denise Suzanne, June 7, 1968; 1 child, Jill Nicole. BA, Calif. State U., Fullerton, 1968, MBA, 1973; PhD, Calif. Coast U., 1998. CFP, CPCU, CLU, ChFC. Divsn. supr. All State Ins. Co., Santa Ana, Calif., 1971-74; dept. mgr. Nat. Auto and Casualty Ins. Co., L.A., 1974-76; mktg. specialist Met. Property and Casualty Ins. Co., Orange, Calif., 1976-77; v.p. Caroon & Black, Orange, 1978-81; pres. Oxford Fin. Corp., Orange, 1981-84; v.p. Metmor Ins. Agy., Orange, 1984-87; divsn. mgr. Cuna Mut. Inst. Corp., Pomona, Calif., 1987-96; regional sales mgr. Auto Club So. Calif., L.A., 1996-97; pres., CEO Arrowhead Fin. Group, San Bernardino, Calif., 1997—. Mem. adv. bd. Calif. State U., San Bernardino, 1998—. Lt. USN, 1968-71. Mem. Internat. Assn. Fin. Planning, Chartered Property & Casualty Underwriters Soc., Fin. Planning Assn., Phi Kappa Tau. Avocations: tennis, golf, reading, writing. Office: Arrowhead Fin Group 303 E Vanderbilt Way Ste 150 San Bernardino CA 92408-3574 E-mail: Jim_Estes@arrowheadcu.org.

ESTES, MARK ERNEST, law librarian; b. Topeka, July 18, 1950; s. Jack E. and Bonnita A. (Hatfield) E.; m. Elizabeth M. Stever Wrenn, Jan. 16, 1978. BA, magna cum laude, Ottawa U., Kans., 1972; JD, MLL, U. Denver, 1977. Law librarian, asst. prof. law U. LaVerne, Calif., 1978-80; librarian Holme Roberts & Owen LLP, Denver, 1980—; cons. Calif. Inst. for Women, Frontera, 1979-80. Bd. dirs. U.S. Cycling Fedn., 1981-83; exec. dir., legis. lobbyist Bicycles Now, Denver, 1973-74; bd. chair Colo. Lir. Resource Sharing and Info. Access, 1994-95, active, 1995—; pres. Bicycle Racing Assn. Colo., 1976-77. Mem. Am. Assn. Law Libraries (constn. and membership com. 1980—, pres. 1992-93, fin. long range planning com. 1993-94, chair govt. rels. com., task force on value of law librs. 1995-96, ann. meeting program selection com. 1997—), Pvt. Law Libraries (exec. bd. 1982-83), Colo. Bar Assn. (law and tech. com. 1981-82), Colo. Consortium Law Libraries (v.p. 1980-81, sec.-treas. 1976-77), Southwestern Assn. Law Libraries (pvt. libraries com. 1981-82). Home: 2374 Glencoe St Denver CO 80207-3248 Office: Holme Roberts & Owen LLP 1700 Lincoln St Ste 4100 Denver CO 80203-4541

ESTES, RICHARD, artist; b. Kewanee, Ill., 1932; Student, Chgo. Art Inst., 1951-55. Exhbns. include Whitney Mus. Am. Art, Mus. Modern Art, Guggenheim Mus., all N.Y.C., Rockhill Nelson Mus., Kansas City, Mo., Toledo Mus., Chgo. Art Inst., Des Moines Art Ctr., Mus. Contemporary Art, Chgo., High Mus. Art, Atlanta, Hirshorne Mus., Washinton, Richmond, Va. Mus. Art, Mus. Contemporary Art, Vienna, Austria, Ludwig Collection, Cologne, Fed. Republic Germany; numerous exhbns. including Documenta V, Kassel, Fed. Republic Germany, 1972, Venice Biennale, 1972, Whitney Mus. Ann., 1972, Va. Mus. Fine Arts, 1974, Boston Mus. Fine Arts, 1975, 78, Allan Stone Gallery, 1983, Adams-Middleton Gallery, Dallas, 1984, Greenville (S.C.) County Mus. Art, 1984, Whitney Mus. Am. Art, N.Y., 1982, Martha White Gallery, Louisville, 1984, Heckscher Mus., Huntington, N.Y., 1984, Walter Moos Gallery, Toronto, Ont., Can., 1984, Byer Mus. Arts, Evanston, 1984, Daimaru Mus., Osaka, Japan, 1985, Mus. Art, Ft. Lauderdale, 1986. Contemporary Art Ctr., New Orleans, 1986, San Francisco Mus. Modern Art, 1986-87, 90, Carpenter Ctr., Harvard U., 1990, Portland (Maine) Mus. Art, 1991, Whitney Mus., Stamford, Conn., 1991-92; traveling retrospective exhibit in Japan, Tokyo, Osaka and Hiroshima, Am. Fedn. of Arts; traveling print show various mus., 1993-95; one-man show at Marlborough Gallery, 1995, 97, 98, Centro Cultural Recoleta, Buenos Aires, 1999, Fine Art (London) Ltd., 2000. Address: 300 Central Park W New York NY 10024-1513

ESTES, ROBERT LEWIS, ophthalmologist; b. Nashville, Mar. 17, 1950; s. Moreau Pinckney and Bertha (Lewis) E.; m. Cassandra Lee Dillon, Aug. 18, 1973; children: Daniel Joseph, Jonathan Lewis. BS, Stanford U., 1972; MD, UCLA, 1976. Diplomate Am. Bd. Ophthalmology, Nat. Bd. Med. Examiners. Intern Santa Clara Valley Med. Ctr., San Jose, 1976-77; resident in ophthalmology U. Mich., Ann Arbor, 1978-81; fellow in pediatric ophthalmology Ind. U., Indpls., 1981-82; pvt. practice Nashville, 1982—. Chief divsn. ophthalmology Bapt. Hosp., Nashville, 1987-89, active staff, 1982—; active staff Centennial Med. Ctr., Nashville, 1982—, Vanderbilt Med. Ctr., Nashville, 1995—. Fellow Am. Acad. Ophthalmology; mem. AMA, Am. Assn. for Pediatric Ophthalmology, Tenn. Acad. Ophthalmology, Davidson County Pediatric Assn. Roman Catholic. Avocations: golf, computer programming, weight training, running. Office: 2011 Murphy Ave Ste 308 Nashville TN 37203-2023 E-mail: rlestesm@bellsouth.net.

ESTES, SCOTT ELLIOTT, music educator; b. Hopkinsville, Ky., Sept. 7, 1971; s. Gary Dale Estes, Patricia Ann Estes. B in Music Edn., U. Ky., 1994. Cert. State Bd. Cert. Tchr. Ky. Asst. dir. bands Lexington HS, Lexington, Tenn., 1994—95; dir. bands College View Mid. Sch., Owensboro, Ky., 1995—97, Beechwood H.S., Ft. Mitchell, Ky., 1997—98, Christian County HS, Hopkinsville, Ky., 1998—. Instr. saxophone North Hardin H.S., Radcliff, Ky., 1999—; adjudicator solo and ensemble Ky. Music Educators Assn., Louisville, 1999—. Recipient Outstanding Young Band Dir. Ky., Phi Beta Mu, 1998. Democrat. Avocations: tennis, movies, saxophone, conducting. Home: 190 Petsch Ln Hopkinsville KY 42240 Office: Christian County HS 220 Glass Ave Hopkinsville KY 42240

ESTES, STEPHEN ARTHUR, dermatologist; b. Rochester, N.Y., July 7, 1947; s. Cameron and Ruth (Madden) E.; m. Barbara Jane Carbary, May 29, 1977; children: Cameron, Jessica. BS, Purdue U., 1969; MD, U. Rochester, 1973. Diplomate Am. Bd. Dermatology. Intern Tucson Hosp., 1973-74; resident Johns Hopkins Hosp., Balt., 1974-77; instr. dermatology U. Ariz. Med. Ctr., Tucson, 1977-78; assoc. prof. U. Cin., 1978-85; pvt. practice Cin., 1985—. Contbr. more than 50 articles to profl. jours. Mem. Cin. Dermatol. Assn. (sec.-treas. 1994-96, pres. 1997-98), Ohio Dermatology Assn. (trustee 1993-96). Home: 1227 Ridgecliff Dr Cincinnati OH 45215-2031 Office: 800 Compton Rd Unit 28 Cincinnati OH 45231-3850

ESTES, WILLIAM KAYE, psychologist, educator; b. Mpls., June 17, 1919; s. George D. and Mona Estes; m. Katherine Walker, Sept. 26, 1942; children: George E., Gregory W. Mem. faculty Ind. U., 1946—62, prof. psychology, 1955—60, research prof. psychology, 1960—62; faculty research fellow Social Sci. Research Council, 1952—55; lectr. psychology U. Wis., 1949; vis. prof. Northwestern U., 1959; fellow Center Advanced Study Behavioral Scis., 1955—56; spl. univ. lectr. U. London, 1961; prof. psychology, mem. Inst. Math. Studies Social Scis., Stanford, 1962—68; prof. Rockefeller U., 1968—79, Harvard U., 1978—89, prof. emeritus, 1989—; prof. Ind. U., 1999—. Chmn. Office Sci. and Engring. Personnel NRC, 1982—85, chmn. com. on prevention of nuclear war, 1984—89. Author: An Experimental Study of Punishment, 1944, Learning Theory and Mental Development, 1970, Models of Learning, Memory and Choice, 1982, Statistical Models in Behavioral Research, 1991, Classification and Cognition, 1994; co-author: Modern Learning Theory, 1954; contbr. articles to profl. jours.; editor: Handbook of Learning and Cognitive Processes, 1962—68, Psychol. Rev., 1977—82, Psychol. Sci., 1990—94; Jour. Exptl. Psychology, 1958—62. With AUS, 1944—46. Recipient U.S. Nat. medal of Sci., 1997. Fellow: AAAS, APA (pres. divsn. exptl. psychology 1958—59, Disting. Sci. Contbn. award 1962, gold medal for lifetime achievement in psychol. sci. 1992), Am. Acad. Arts and Scis.; mem.: NAS, Fedn. Behavioral Psychol. and Cognitive Scis. (v.p. 1988—91), Midwestern Psychol. Assn., N.Y. Acad. Scis. (life), N.Y. Acad. Scis. (hon.), Soc. Exptl. Psychologists (Warren medal 1963). Home: 2714 E Pine Ln Bloomington IN 47401-4423 Office: Ind U Psychology Bldg Bloomington IN 47405 E-mail: wkestes@indiana.edu.

ESTEVA, FRANCISCO JAVIER, physician, researcher; b. Bueu, Galicia, Spain, Jan. 16, 1964; came to U.S., 1990; s. Carlos Esteva and Anunciacion Lorenzo; m. Maria J. Pastoriza-Regueira, June 2, 1991; 1 child, Eduardo. MD, U. Zaragoza, Spain, 1988. Diplomate Am. Bd. Internal Medicine, Am. Bd. Med. Oncology. Resident in internal medicine Cooper Hosp./U. Med. Ctr., Camden, N.J., 1991-94; fellow in med. oncology Georgetown U., Washington, 1994-97, instr. medicine, 1997; asst. prof. medicine U. Tex. M.D. Anderson Cancer Ctr., Houston, 1997—. Mem. spkrs. bur. Genentech, Inc., San Francisco, 1998—, Astro-Zeneca, Wilmington, Del., 1998—. Author: Hormones and Growth Factors in Development and Neoplasia, 1998, Monoclonal Antibody-Based Therapy of Cancer, 1998, Hematology-Oncology Clinics in North America, 1999; contbr. articles to profl. jours. Recipient rsch. award Nat. Cancer Inst., 1999—. Mem. ACP, Am. Soc. Clin. Oncology, Am. Assn. for Cancer Rsch., Assn. for Patient-Oriented Rsch., Am. Soc. Breast Disease, European Soc. for Med. Oncology. Avocations: travel, reading. Office: MD Anderson Cancer Ctr 1515 Holcombe Blvd Box 424 Houston TX 77030-4009

ESTEVE, EDWARD V. lawyer; b. N.Y.C., May 29, 1937; m. Mildred Briand, June 10, 1961; children: Greg, Christopher, Kimberly. Grad., NYU, 1959; LLB, JD, N.Y. Law Sch., 1962. Ptnr. Taitz, Bernard & Esteve, Patchogue, N.Y., to 1997, Pelletreau & Pelletreau, Patchogue, 1997—98, Roe Wallace Esteve Taroff & Taitz, 1999—. Adj. prof. Touro Coll. Law, Huntington, N.Y., 1995—; mem. com. on character and fitness, 2d dept. N.Y. Appellate Divsn., 1991—. Bd. dirs. Red Cross (Suffolk chpt.), Adelante of Suffolk, La Union Hispanica, Three Village Youth Coun., 1972-90, Brookhaven Meml. Hosp., Patchogue, 1995—; v.p., officer Suffolk Acad. Law, 1977-89. Mem. N.Y. State Bar Assn. (gen. practice sect. 10th and 11th jud. dist. v.p. 1981-82, pres. com. access justice 1990-96), Suffolk County Bar Assn. (pres. 1989-90, bd. dirs. and exzc. com. 1977-93). Avocation: aviation. Office: Roe Wallace Esteve Taroff & Taitz LLP 31 Oak St PO Box 352 Patchogue NY 11772 Fax: 631-475-9882.

ESTHER, QUEEN, playwright, scriptwriter, actor; d. James Monroe and Ivory Boone Pooser. BA, The New Sch., 1994. Performer: (plays) Whoa, Jack!, Harlem Song (Audelco Award nomination for best supporting actress, 2002), RENT, Stagedoor Canteen (Drama Desk Award to Tribeca Playhouse, 2002, NY Drama Desk Award for Tribeca Playhouse, 2002), The Moxie Show; singer (songwriter): (recording) Mighty (as blues duo Hoosegow); performer: (one person show) Queen Esther: Unemployed Superstar, (TV series) The It Factor. Recipient Governor's Honor's Program, State of Ga., 1982, Arts Recognition and Talent Search (Merit award), Nat. Found. for the Arts, 1983; Scholarships in Acting, The U. of Tex. at Austin, 1983. Born Again Christian. Avocations: apologetics, travel, writing, reading. Personal E-mail: info@queen-esther.com.

ESTIN, HANS HOWARD, investment executive; b. Prague, Czechoslovakia, Sept. 8, 1928; came to U.S., 1941, naturalized, 1946; m. Martha McCormick, Oct. 1990; children from previous marriage: Hilary Parker, Alexandra Howard; stepchildren: Sargent L. Goodchild, Jr., Abigail Goodchild, McKay Goodchild. AB, Harvard U., 1949; LL.D., Merrimac Coll., 1972, Boston U., 1977. Vice chmn., pres., chmn. bd. Harbor Nat. Bank, Boston, 1964-67; vice chmn. N.Am. Mgmt. Corp., Boston, 1974—. Trustee Putnam Group Mut. Funds, 1972-2001. Former trustee New Eng. Aquarium; chmn. bd. trustees Boston U., 1969-76; mem. Schepens Eye Rsch. Inst.; former bd. overseers Boys and Girls Clubs Boston, Inc. 1st lt. USAF, 1951-55. Decorated Knight, Order of Crown, Belgium, 1983, Order of Leopold, Belgium, 1990; named Hon. Consul of Belgium at Boston, 1970-90. Mem. Somerset Club (Boston), Essex County Club (Manchester, Mass.). Home: 600 Summer St Manchester MA 01944-1626 Office: NAm Mgmt Corp Ten Post Office Sq Boston MA 02109

ESTLER, SUZANNE E. education educator; b. Paterson, N.J., Sept. 16, 1944; d. Louis Calder and Beatrice VanderVoort Estler; life ptnr. Paula D. Johnson. BA, Rutgers U., New Brunswick, N.J., 1966; MA, Ohio U., Athens, OH, 1969; PhD, Stanford U., Calif., 1978. Grad. asst. Stanford U., 1973—76; resident dir. Ohio U., Athens, 1967—69; asst. dir. of residences SUNY Binghamton, Vestal, NY, 1969—70, dir. of residences, 1970—71, coord. of student svcs. coll. in the woods, 1971—73; vis. instr. of higher edn. Claremont Grad. Sch., Claremont, Calif., 1976—77; asst. prof. of higher edn. U. of Wash., Seattle, 1979—84; assoc. prof. of higher ednl. leadership U. of Maine, Orono, 1984—, dir. of equal opportunity, 1986—97. Cons. Nat. Ctr. for Higher Edn. Mgmt. Systems, Boulder, Colo., 1978—80. Contbr. articles to profl. jours, chpts. to books. Pres. Audubon Expdn. Inst., Belfast, Maine, 1988—2003. Recipient Janet Badger Vol. award, Rape Response Svcs., 1998, M Club, U. of Maine, 1999; Thomas James Jr. fellowship, Stanford U., 1975—76. Mem.: Assn. for the Study of Higher Edn., Am. Ednl. Rsch. Assn. Avocations: lobstering, boating, travel, reading, gardening. Office: University of Maine Merrill Hall Orono ME 04469-5749 Office Fax: 207-581-3120. E-mail: estler@umit.maine.edu.

ESTREN, MARK JAMES, business and media consultant, TV producer, author; b. N.Y.C., July 12, 1948; s. Solomon and Elaine Estren; m. S. Amber Gordon, July 4, 1986; children: Meredith, Nicholas. BA in Classics and English cum laude, Wesleyan U., 1968; MS in Journalism, Columbia U., 1970; MA in English and Psychology, U. Buffalo, 1973, PhD in English and Psychology, 1978. Producer, reporter, anchor Stas. WBEN & WBEN-TV, Buffalo, 1971-75; exec. producer Stas. WCBS-Radio and TV, N.Y.C., 1975-76, Sta. WCAU-TV, Phila., 1976-79; sr. producer ABC News, N.Y.C. and Washington, 1979-80; editor Phila. Inquirer, 1980-81, Miami (Fla.) Herald, 1980-81; exec. producer The Nightly Bus. Report, Miami, Fla., 1981-84; sr. v.p., gen. mgr. Fin. News Network, N.Y.C. and L.A., 1984-87; editor-in-chief High Tech. Bus. mag., Boston and N.Y.C., 1987-89; exec. v.p. Infotechnology, Inc., N.Y.C. and Washington, 1987-90, UPI, Washington, 1988-90; founder, pres. UPI TV, Fairfax, Va., 1989-90; pres., chief exec. officer TransCentury Comm., Inc., Easton, Conn. and McLean, Va., 1984—. Adj. prof. Columbia U., 1987-89; webmaster www.infodad.com, 1999—. Author: A History of Underground Comics, 1974, rev. edit., 1987, 89, 93; co-author: In a Word, 1992; contbg. editor Miami Herald, Bottom Line/Personal, Bottom Line/Tomorrow, Boardroom Reports, Bottom Line/Business, Bottom Line/Health, Washington Office Mag., Moneysworth, Parent Weekly, Va. Parent News. Trustee Boston Cath. TV Ctr., 1987-89; vice chmn. Arthritis Found., Washington, 1992-94, chmn. commn. com., 1990-92. Pulitzer Found. fellow, 1970. Avocations: classical music, herpetology. Office: 1163 Old Gate Ct Mc Lean VA 22102-2532 E-mail: infodad@juno.com.

ESTRIN, DEBORAH PERRY, human resources executive; b. Waynesboro, Va., Dec. 28, 1948; d. James William and Annie Lee (Miller) Perry; m. Abbott Simon Estrin, Feb. 6, 1982. BS in Humanities, U. Tenn., 1982; MBA, Fairleigh Dickerson U., 1988. Dir. human resources Ciba Geigy Pharms., Summit, N.J., 1983-89; v.p. human resources Geneva Pharms. divsn. Ciba Geigy Pharms., Broomfield, Colo., 1989-91, USPCI subs. Union Pacific, Houston, 1994-96, N.Y. Power Authority, White Plains, 1994-96; sr. v.p. human resources Phila. Gas Works, 1996-98; v.p. human resources Maersk-Sealand, Inc., Madison, N.J., 1999-2000; mng. ptnr. Fitzgerald Addison Group LLC, 2001—. Adj. prof. Audrey Cohen Coll., 1994-96; dir. ENS Charon Found. for Global Mgmt. Studies; dir. Found. Global Mgmt. Studies, Paris, S.C. Ctr. for Dispute Resolution; bd. dir. Beaufort County Transportation Authority. Mem. Beaufort County Transp. Authority. Office: 86 Helmsman Way Hilton Head Island SC 29928 E-mail: fitzaddison@aol.com.

ESTRIN, GERALD, computer scientist, engineering educator, academic administrator; b. N.Y.C., Sept. 9, 1921; married; 3 children BS, U. Wis., 1948, MS, 1949, PhD in Elec. Engring., 1951. Rsch. engr. electronic computer project Inst. Advanced Study, Princeton, 1950-53, 55-56; dir. electronic computing project Weizmann Inst. Sci., Israel, 1953-55; assoc. prof. engring. UCLA, 1956-58, prof., 1958-91, prof. emeritus, 1991—, chmn. dept. computer sci., 1979-82, 85-88. Mem. adv. bd. applied math. div. Argonne Nat. Lab., 1966-68, mem. assoc. univs. rev. com. for chmn., 1976-77, mem. adv. bd. applied math. div., 1974-80, adv. com. NASA Space Applications, 1983-86; dir. Computer Communications, Inc., 1966-67, Systems Engring. Labs., 1977-80; mem. internat. program com. Internat. Fedn. Info. Processing Congress, 1968; internat. program chmn. Jerusalem Conf. Info. Tech., 1971; mem. math. and computer sci. research adv. com. AEC; mem. sci. com., operating bd. Gould, Inc., Rolling Meadows, Ill., 1981-86; bd. govs. Weizmann Inst. Sci., 1971-96, gov. emeritus, 1996—. Lipsky fellow, 1954, Guggenheim fellow, 1963, 67; recipient Disting. Svc. award U. Wis., 1975, Jerusalem Conf. on Info. Tech. Spl. Recognition award, 1978, NASA Commendation, 1986, Computer Pioneer award IEEE Computer Soc., 1995. Fellow AAAS, IEEE (disting. spkr. 1980), Assn. Computing Machinery (nat. lectr. 1966-67). Office: UCLA BH4731 Dept Computer Sci Los Angeles CA 90095-0001 E-mail: gestrin@cs.ucla.edu.

ESTRIN, HERBERT ALVIN, financial consultant, entertainment company executive; b. Jamaica, N.Y., May 4, 1925; s. Joseph and Minnie (Haskell) E.; m. Phyllis Glassman, Jan. 28, 1951; children— Myrna Hope, Richard Lawrence. BS in Acctg, N.Y. U., 1949. With Columbia Pictures Industries, Inc., N.Y.C., 1953-73, v.p., 1971-73; v.p., treas., chief fin. officer Prudential Bldg. Maintenance Corp., N.Y.C., 1973-79; v.p., treas. Bolt Corp., South Laguna, Calif., 1979; sr. v.p. fin. and adminstrn. Warner Home Video Inc. subs. Warner Communications, 1981-83; dir. ops. adminstrn. United Satellite Communications Inc., 1983-85; v.p. fin. and adminstrn. Rainbow Home Video div. Rainbow Program Enterprises Co., 1986-88; fin. cons., 1986—. Served with U.S. Army, 1943-46.

ESTRIN, KARI (KAREN RUTH ESTRIN), artist and tour manager, agent, consultant; b. Plainfield, N.J., Nov. 5, 1954; d. Herman Albert and Pearl (Simon) E. BA with honors, Ramapo Coll. of N.J., 1976. Founder, exec. dir. Black Sheep Concerts and Publs., Inc., Cambridge, Mass., 1980-86; editor The Black Sheep Rev., 1982-85; co-producer (album) Great Acoustics, 1985; artist mgr., agt. Tony Rice/Rounder Records, 1981-85; tour mgr. Suzanne Vega/A&M Records, 1985, Peter Murphy Tour/Island Records, 1987, Kevin Brown Ryko Disc/Chrysalis, 1991; founder, cons. Palomine Mgmt., 1984—92; asst. producer Newport Folk Festival Festival Prodns., Inc., N.Y.C., 1987; artist and tour mgr. 3 Mustaphas 3/Ryko Disc, 1988-91, artist asst. Suzy Bogguss/Capitol Records, 1989; mgr. Kanda Bongo Man, 1991, 93; tour mgr. Irma Thomas/Rounder Records, 1993, Papa Wemba/Real World Records, 1995; booking & spl. events dir. Caffe Milano, 1998; owner, prin. Kari Estrin, Mgt., Cons., Nashville, 1995—. Nat. promoter Rounder Records, Cambridge, Mass., 1979; asst. to dir. Berkshire Mt. Bluegrass Festival, Hillsdale, NY, 1980—81, assoc. producer Gt. N.E. Prodns., Townsend, Mass., 1986; chairperson events ECO, Nashville, 1990; bd. dirs., vol. Sta. WPLN, 1991—92, pres. vol bd. dirs., 1993—94; cons. Marie Watson Meml. Festival, Wilkesboro, NC, 1992—93, asst. festival dir., 1993; co-founder Chris Austin Songwriting Contest, Naahville/Wilkesboro, 1992—93; assoc prodr. Pickin' for Merle series N.C. Pub. TV, Rsch. Triangle Park, 1992; artist mgr. Wayland Pattom, 1993—94; talent coord. Pro Events Summer Lights, 1997; nat. advt. mgr. Sing Out ! mag., 1995—96; co-prodr. Americana Music Assn. Conv., Nashville, 2000; club booking agt. Radio Cage, Nashville, 2000—01, 3rd and Lindsley, Nashville, 2002; host and prodr. The Acoustic Beat Radio Show, 2002. Editor: How to be Your Own Booking Agent and Save Thousands of Dollars, 1997. Bd. dirs. Hey, Rube Folk Music Orgn., 1983-86, Folk Arts Network, Cambridge, 1983-85, Folk Arts Ctr. of New Eng., Cambridge, 1982-84; sec., newsletter editor Eastwood Neighbors Bd., 1995-97. Avocations: catering and cooking, traveling, performing arts. Home and Office: 1415 Sumner Ave Nashville TN 37206-2533

ESTRIN, MELVYN J. computer products company executive; Co-chmn., co-CEO Nat. Intergroup, Inc., Carrollton, Tex., 1997—; co-chmn., co-CEO McKesson Health Corp., Carrollton, Tex., 1996; also bd. dirs.; chmn. U. Rsch. Corp., Bethesda, Md. Mng. ptnr. Centaur Ptnrs., L.P.; chmn., pres., CEO Am. Health Svcs.; v.p., dir. Spectro Industries; founder First Women's Bank of Md.; pres. FWB Bancorporation, Rockville, Md.; chmn. FWB Bancorporation.;

chmn. Estrin Internat., Inc.; with Estrin Realty and Devel. Corp.; bd. dirs. Washington Gas Light Co. Trustee U. Pa.; active Endowment Bd. of the Kennedy Ctr., The Econ. Club of Washington, The Washington Opera; nat. vice chmn. State of Israel Bonds; apptd. by Pres. Bush commr.Nat. Capital Planning Commn.; apptd. Nat. Coun. for the Performing Arts, John F. Kennedy Ctr. Recipient Eleanor Roosevelt Humanities award for Community Svc., 1986. Office: Univ Rsch Corp 7200 Wisconsin Ave Ste 600 Bethesda MD 20814-4811 also: Foxmeyer Health Corp 5910 N Central Expy Ste 1780 Dallas TX 75206-5174

ESTRIN, RICHARD WILLIAM, real estate broker, retired newspaper editor; b. NYC, Apr. 16, 1932; s. Max and Ruth (Lillienthal) E.; m. Alison Kiendl Stewart, Mar. 13, 1971. BA, CCNY, 1953; grad., Realtor Inst., 2000. Reporter Pk. Row News Svc., NYC, 1953-55; with Newsday, Inc., Long Island, NY, 1955-85, sucessl. Sunday news editor, Part II editor, sr. editor news, until 1983, exec. news editor N.Y.C. Newsday, 1983-85; weekend editor Herald-Tribune, Sarasota, Fla., 1985-86, news editor, 1986-90, asst. mng. editor, 1990-97; v.p. Longview Realty, Longboat Key, Fla., 1999-2001, pres., 2001—. Recipient First Place Lifestyle Journalism awards J.C. Penney-U. M., 1974, 75 Mem. Kiwanis, Phi Beta Kappa. E-mail: longviewrealty@att.net.

ESTRIN, THELMA AUSTERN, retired electrical engineer; b. N.Y.C., Feb. 21, 1924; d. I. Billy and Mary (Ginsburg) Austern; m. Gerald Estrin, Dec. 21, 1941; children: Margo, Judith, Deborah. BSEE, U. Wis., Madison, 1947, MSEE, 1948, PhD, 1951; DSc. (hon.), U. Wis., 1990. Cert. clin. engr. Research engr. UCLA Brain Research Inst., 1960-70, dir. data processing, 1970-80; prof. computer sci. UCLA, 1980—; dir. div. electronics, computer and systems engring. NSF, Washington, 1982-84; dir. extension dept. engring. and sci., asst. dean Sch. Engring. and Applied Sci., UCLA, 1984-89; ret. Trustee Aerospace Corp., 1979-82; mem. biomed. tech. resources com. NIH, 1981-86; mem. U.S. Army Sci. Bd., 1982-84; mem. energy engring. bd. NRC, 1985-88. Contbr. articles to tech. jours. Mem. Los Angeles Women in Bus. Recipient Disting. Contbn. to Engring. Edn. award NSPE, 1985, Achievement award Soc. Women Engrs. 1981, Disting. Svc. citation U. Wis., 1976. Fellow Soc. Women Engrs., AAAS (fellow, chair engring. sect. 1989), IEEE (fellow, bd. dirs. 1979-80, exec. v.p. 1982, recipient Centennial medal 1984, pres. Engring. in Medicine and Biology Soc. 1977, Haraden Pratt Svc. award 1991). Jewish.

ESTY, JOHN CUSHING, JR., writer, teacher, advisor to non-profit boards; b. White Plains, N.Y., Aug. 9, 1928; s. John Cushing and Virginia (Place) E.; m. Katharine Woolsey Cole, Dec. 21, 1955; children: Daniel Cushing, Paul Cameron, Benjamin Cole, Joshua Dwight. BA, Amherst Coll., 1950, LHD (hon.), 1970; MA, Yale U., 1951; postgrad., U. Calif., Berkeley, 1959-60. Asst. dean, asst. dir. admissions Amherst Coll., 1953-58, asso. dean, 1958-63, lectr. math., 1958-63; headmaster Taft Sch., Watertown, Conn., 1963-72; research asso. in edn. Harvard U., 1972-73; scholar-in-residence U. Mass. Sch. Edn., 1972-73; sr. staff asso. Edn. Devel. Center, Newton, Mass., 1973-74; staff asso. Rockefeller Bros. Fund, N.Y.C., 1973-78; pres. Nat. Assn. Ind. Schs., 1978-91; adj. lectr. U. Mass., 1978—. Pres. bd. Coun. for Am. Pvt. Edn., 1987-89. Author: Choosing Private School, 1974. Trustee Amherst Coll., 1970-76; trustee, bd. chmn. Greeley Found., Mass., 1991-2000; dir., founder Recruiting New Tchrs., Inc., 1988—; assoc. for bd. devel. Nat. Ctr. Nonprofit Bds., 1993—. 1st lt. USAF, 1951-53. Mem. Phi Beta Kappa, Sigma Xi. Clubs: Univ. (N.Y.C.), Century Assn. (N.Y.C.).

ESWEIN, BRUCE JAMES, II, human resources executive; b. San Mateo, Calif., Oct. 26, 1951; s. Bruce James and Janet Gordon (Copeland) E.; m. Sarah Anne Shames, Feb. 7, 1981 (div.); children: Thomas Jonathan, Elizabeth Anne. Student, U. Wash., 1969-71; AB, U. Calif.-Berkeley, 1973, MBA, 1977. Brand asst. Clorox Co., Oakland, Calif., 1977-79, coll. rels. mgr., 1979-83; mgr. exec. recruitment and devel. BBDO Worldwide, N.Y.C., 1983-84, v.p., 1984-87, v.p. personnel adminstrn., 1987-88, v.p. human resources, mgr. worldwide tng. and devel., 1988-89, v.p. human resources internat., 1989-90, v.p., dir. human resources internat., 1990-95, sr. v.p., dir. human resources internat., 1995-97; cons. The Newman Group, N.Y.C., 1997—. Mem. Soc. for Human Resources Mgmt., U. Calif. at Berkeley Bus. Sch. Alumni Assn. (bd. dirs. 1980-83), Phi Beta Kappa, Chi Psi (v.p. 1972-73, bd. dirs. 1979-82, trustee ednl. trust 1983-84, trustee emeritus 1984—). Episcopalian. Home: 27 Scenic Dr Apt H Croton On Hudson NY 10520-1822 E-mail: esweinb@bestweb.net.

ETCHESON, WARREN WADE, business administration educator; b. Bainbridge, Ind., May 15, 1920; s. Raymond W. and Rosetta (Evans) E.; m. Marianne Newgent, May 30, 1947; children: Denise Elene, Crayton Wade. BS, Ind. U., 1943; MA, U. Iowa, 1951, PhD, 1956. Adminstrv. sec., exec. sec., nat. sec. Delta Chi Nat. Fraternity, 1946-56; lectr. Santo Tomas U., Manila, 1946, U. Iowa, 1951-54; asst. prof. U. Wash., 1954-56, assoc. prof., 1956-60, prof. Sch. Bus. Adminstrn., 1960-90, assoc. dean Bus. Adminstrn., 1974-87, prof. emeritus, 1990—. Fulbright prof. Istanbul, Turkey, 1963-64. Author: Pazarlama, 1964, Consumerism, 1972. Served to lt. U.S. Army, 1942-46. Mem. Alpha Kappa Psi, Phi Eta Sigma, Beta Gamma Sigma, Delta Chi. Home: 6625 NE 132nd St Kirkland WA 98034-1614

ETEFIA, FLORENCE VICTORIA, school psychologist; b. Alton, Ill., Feb. 13, 1946; d. Esau and Pearl (Taylor) Anthony. BA, Mich. State U., 1968; MAT, Oakland U., Rochester, Mich., 1972; EdS, Wayne State U., 1977, MA, 1987, postgrad. Cert. tchr. mentally impaired, Mich.; spl. edn. supr., Mich.; cert. tchr. mentally impaired, learning disabled, K-8 gen. edn., psychology, Mich. Special edn. tchr. Sch. Dist. of Pontiac, Mich. Mem. NEA, Mich. Edn. Assn., Pontiac Edn. Assn., Delta Sigma Theta. Home: 3035 Debra Ct Auburn Hills MI 48326-2044

ETEROVICH MAGUIRE, KAREN ANN, actress, writer; b. Cleve., Feb. 24, 1961; d. Anthony William and Alice (Troyan) Eterovich; m. John Gordon Maguire. BA, U. Akron, Ohio, 1983; MFA, U. S.C., Columbia, 1989. Actress ArtReach Touring Theatre, Cin., 1983—85; actress, office mgr. Indpls. Shakespeare Co., 1984—86; grad. tchg. asst. U. S.C., Columbia, 1986—89; acting intern Shakespeare Theatre, Washington, 1987—88; resident profl. tchg. assoc. Cornell U., Ithaca, NY, 1991—92; actress Ind. Repertory Theater, Indpls., 1993; actress, producer, dir. Love Arm'd Productions, N.Y.C., 1993—. Producer Cosmic Leopard Productions, N.Y.C., 1994—2002; publicity cons. Fertile Ground Inc., N.Y.C., 1995—97. Actor: (Multi-Media Play) Love Arm'd, Aphra Behn & Her Pen, 1997 (Listed in Grants & Awards). Recipient Juliet Hardtner Endowment for Women in the Arts, McNeese State U., 2000, NEH Endowment for Faculty Devel., Albertson Coll.of Idaho, 2000, N.Y. State Coun. on the Arts Decentralization Program, Keuka Coll., 2001. Avocations: skiing, swimming, tennis. Office: Love Arm'd Productions P O Box 2668 Times Sq Station New York NY 10108-2668 Personal E-mail: karen_eterovich@hotmail.com. Business E-Mail: karen_eterovich@hotmail.com.

ETGEN, ANN, ballet educator, artistic director, choreographer; b. Dallas; d. Eddy R. Etgen and Myrtle (Applegate) Etgen; life ptnr. Bill Atkinson, Aug. 16, 1961. Dance, active Arts Magnet Sch., 1980, 81, 82, 83. Dancer Met. Opera Ballet, N.Y.C., 1958—60. Artistic dir. Etgen-Atkinson Sch. of Ballet, Dallas, 1962—; Dallas Met. Ballet, 1964—; dance panel Tex. Fine Arts Com., 1978—79. Dancer (Broadway musicals) Brigadoon, Carousel; guest dancer Omnibus History of Dance for Agnes De Mille, 1957, host S.W. Regional Ballet Festival, 1973, Creator (ballets) Dallas Met. Ballet. Recipient choreography plan award, Nat. Assn. Regional Ballet, 1983; grantee NEA choreography grantee, 1976, Tex. Fine Arts Commn., 1973, 1976—77, Mobile Oil, 1979, 500 Inc., 1978—79. Mem.: S.W. Regional Ballet Assn. (membership chmn. 1986—87), Nat. Assn. Regional Ballet. Presbyterian. Office: Etgen Atkinson Ballet School 6815 Hillcrest Ave Dallas TX 75205-1308

ETGES, FRANK JOSEPH, parasitology educator; b. Chgo., June 18, 1924; s. Joseph Peter and Anna Marie (Foss) E.; m. Ruth Camille Storkan, Sept. 20, 1948 (div. June 1984); children: Robert J., William J., Anne C., David J., Thomas J.; m. Lesta Judith Cooper-Freytag, July 6, 1985. AB, U. Ill., 1948, MS, 1949; PhD, NYU, 1953. Asst. prof. U. Ark., Fayetteville, 1953-54, U. Cin., 1954-59, assoc. prof., 1959-66, prof. parasitology, 1966-95; prof. emeritus, 1995—. Rsch. assoc. U.S. Army Tropical Rsch. Med. Lab., San Juan, P.R., 1961-62; guest investigator London Sch. Tropical Medicine and Hygiene, 1971-72. Sgt. U.S. Army, 1943-46, ETO, PTO. NSF rsch. grantee, 1959-65; La. State U. Med. Sch. rsch. fellow, Santo Domingo, P.R., 1961-62, 64, 65, 67, 69; postdoctoral fellow NIH, London, 1971-72, WHO, Egypt, Sudan, Rhodesia, 1975. Mem. Am. Soc. Parasitologists (editorial com.), Am. Soc. Tropical Medicine and Hygiene, Am. Microscopical Soc. (v.p. 1970), Royal Soc. Tropical Medicine and Hygiene, Australian Soc. Parasitology, Soc. Protozoologists, Midwestern Parastiologists (pres. 1969), Helminthol. Soc. Washington, Sigma Xi. Avocations: travel, golf. Home: 8284 Sunfish Ln Maineville OH 45039-8978 Office: U Cin Dept Biol Scis Cincinnati OH 45221-0006 E-mail: cooperlj@ucfwcu.rwc.uc.edu.

ETHAN, CAROL BAEHR, psychotherapist; b. N.Y.C., May 30, 1920; d. Irving and Sadie (Goldman) Baehr; m. Sy Ethan, Mar. 18, 1955; children: Willa Capraro, Barbara. Trained, Greenwich Inst. Psychoanalytic Studies, 1965-70; BA in Psychology with honors, NYU, 1978; MA in Psychology, New Sch. Social Rsch., 1981. Tchr. Queens Coll., 1956-57; consumer psychology rschr., cons., 1950-70; staff psychotherapist Fifth Ave. Ctr. Counseling & Psychotherapy, 1965-70; psychotherapist pvt. practice, N.Y.C., 1967—. Vol. social rehab. program Queens County Mental Health Soc., 1965—66; Dem. committeewoman Queens County, 1960. Recipient Founders Day award, NYU, 1978; Internat. Coun. Sex Edn. and Parenthood fellow, Am. U. Fellow: Am. Orthopsychiat. Assn.; mem.: APA, Am. Psychotherapy Assn. (cert. diplomate), N.Am. Assn. Masters in Psychology (cert.), Internat. Acad. Behavioral Medicine, Counseling and Psychotherapy (clin. mem.), Family and Divorce Mediation Coun. N.Y., Am. Mental Health Counselors Assn., N.Y. State Assn. Practising Psychotherapists (cert.). Address: 235 W 76th St New York NY 10023-8210 E-mail: cethan@nyc.rr.com.

ETHEREDGE, FOREST DEROYCE, former state senator, former university administrator; b. Dallas, Oct. 21, 1929; s. Gilbert Wybert and Theta Erlene (Tate) E.; m. Joan Mary Horan, Apr. 30, 1955; children: Forest William, John Bede, Mary Faith, Brian Thomas, Regina Ann. BS, Va. Poly. Inst. and State U., 1951; MS, U. Ill., 1953; postgrad., Northwestern U., 1953-55; PhD, Loyola U., Chgo., 1968. Mem. faculty City Colls. Chgo., 1955-65, chmn. phys. sci. dept., 1963-65; dean instrn. Rock Valley Coll., 1965-67, v.p., 1966-67; pres. McHenry County Coll., 1967-70, Waubonsee Community Coll., 1970-81; Ill. state senator Ill. State Senate, 1981-93, higher edn. com., 1981-91, mem. intergovtl. coop. commn., 1982-91, co-chmn. legis. info. system, 1983-93, minority spokesman appropriations I com., 1986-93; prof. pub. adminstrn. Aurora (Ill.) U., 1991-2001, dean Sch. of Bus. and Profl. Studies, 1994-99, dean emeritus, 1999—. Author: School Boards and the Ballot Box, 1989. Bd. dirs. Ill. Math. and Sci. Acad. Mem.: Rotary (pres. Aurora chpt. 1978-79). Republican. Roman Catholic. Home: 843 Hardin Ave Aurora IL 60506-4936 E-mail: fethered@aurora.edu., fethered@prodigy.net.

ETHERIDGE, BOB, congressman; b. Lilington, N.C., Aug. 7, 1941; BS Campbell U., 1965. Commr. Harnett County, 1972—76; mem. NC Ho. Reps., 1978—88; supt. Pub. Inst. Dept., Raleigh, NC, 1989—96; mem. U.S. Congress from 2d N.C. dist., Washington, 1997—; mem. agr. com., sci. com.; mem. Select Com. on Homeland Security. Democrat. Office: US House of Reps 1533 Longworth Ho Office Bldg Washington DC 20515-3302*

ETHERIDGE, DIANA CAROL, internet business executive; b. Alliance, Nebr., Mar. 18, 1940; d. Elvon Lynn and Enola Nadene Howe; m. Brian Newman Etheridge, May 30, 1940; children: Melissa Ann, Juliana Lynn. Student, U. Geneva, Switzerland, 1960-61; BA, U. Denver., 1962; MA, Simmons Coll., 1981. Cert. tchr., Colo., Fla.; real estate lic., Fla., Va., Md., D.C., 2000; cert. internatl property specialist, Nat. Assn. of Realtors, 1994-00. Tchr. French, science, English Denver Pub. Schs., 1962-63, 64-68; tchr. 7th grade and French PreK-7th grade St. Anne's Episcopal Sch., Denver, 1974-76; tchr. 6th grade and French Collegiate Sch., Denver, 1976-80; real estate agt. Merrill Lynch, Prudential, Long & Foster, Treder Realty, Potomac, Md. and Titusville, Fla., 1982—; pres., founder e-dea. inc., Merritt Island, Fla., 1997—, Cybernastics, Inc., Merritt Island, 1999—, Flexystems/Flexhome, 2000—. Mem. No. Va. Coun. Comml. Realtors, Fairfax, Va., 1993—95, Govtl. Internat. and Info. Svcs. Coms., Fairfax, Internat. Real Estate Inst., Alexandria, Minn., 1996—2001, World Trade Ctr. Inst., Balt., 1995; cert. internat. property specialist Nat. Assn. Realtors, 1994—2000, judge Who is Today's Realtor, 1995. House bill proofreader Colo. State Legislature, Denver, 1970; campaign staff mem. U.S. Congressman Dave Weldon, Melbourne, Fla., 1996, 1998, 2000; hon. chmn. Fla. bus. adv. coun. Nat. Rep. Congl. Com., 2003. Recipient Lifetime award Prudential Preferred Properties, 1990. Mem.: Fla. Bus. Adv. Coun. Nat. Rep. Congl. Com. (hon. chmn. 2003), Montgomery Assn. Realtors (Lifetime award), Nat. Assn. Realtors, Nat. Assn. Home Builders, Nat. Assn. Women in Constrn., Hospitality and Info. Svcs. Internat. Club, Welcome to Washington Internat. Club, Long and Foster Pres.'s Club (life), Brevard County Newcomer's Club, Million Dollar Club, Optimists Club (past pres. Capital City), Phi Beta Kappa, Pi Beta Phi. Achievements include patents for building construction. Avocations: skiing, swimming, scuba diving, hiking, aerobics. Business E-Mail: info@e-dea.com.

ETHERIDGE, JOHN GREEN, retired pathologist; b. Macon, Ga., May 4, 1932; s. Hubert Calvin and Mary Lee (Aultman) E.; m. Anita Dawn Bruce, June 8, 1955; children: Debra Lynn, Bonnie Gay, John Bruce, Brian Dale. AB, Mercer U., 1954; MD, Med. Coll. Ga., 1958. Pathologist Med. Ctr. Ctrl. Ga., Macon, 1965—2000. Chief of staff Med. Ctr. Ctrl. Ga., Macon, 1981; chmn. bd. Medcen Found., Macon, 1991-92. Capt. USN, 1959-61. Fellow Am. Soc. Clin. Pathologists (state counselor), Coll. Am. Pathologists; mem. So. Med. Assn., Gen. Assn. Pathologists (sec.), Med. Assn. Ga. (del.), Ocmulgee Med. Pathology Assn. (chmn. bd. 1982-97). Methodist. Avocations: tennis, fishing, travel, reading. Home: 6848 Colaparchee Rd Macon GA 31210-7221

ETHERIDGE, MARGARET DWYER, medical center director; b. Atlanta, Jan. 5, 1938; d. Philip Fitzgerald and Mary Catharine (Dwyer) E.; m. Roy Charles McCracken, May 5, 1975; m. William Bertram Smitheram, Aug. 17, 1985. BA, Emory U., 1960; M in Health Adminstrn., Washington U., St. Louis, 1973. Registered record administr., 1960-71; spl. asst. to dir. VA Med. Ctr., Roseburg, Oreg., 1973-74; hosp. administrn, specialist VA Central Office, Washington, 1974-75; asst. dir. trainee VA Med. Ctr., Phila., 1976, assoc. dir. Hampton, Va., 1976--80, Buffalo, N.Y., 1980-81; presdl. exchange exec. Kimberly Clark Corp., Neenah, Wis., 1981-82, Roswell, Ga., 1981-82; dir. VA Med. Ctr., Grand Island, Nebr., 1982-94; interim dir. Grand Island-Hall County Health Dept., 1996-97; instr. Cerritos Coll., 1969-70. Bd. dirs. Project 2M Coordinating Coun., Inc., Grand Island, 1985-87, Hall County Leadership Unlimited, Inc., 1990. Bd. dirs. Grand Island Area United Way, 1987-90 (pres. 1989), Grand Island Concert Assn, 1987-92, Ctrl. Nebr. Goodwill Industries, Inc., 1987-93 (pres. 1991-92). Fellow Am. Coll. Healthcare Execs. (life); mem. rev. bd. State of Nebr. Foster Care, Am. Hosp. Assn., Fed. Exec. Assn. (pres. Grand Island chpt. 1987), Nebr. Hosp. Assn., Grand Island C. of C. (bd. dirs. 1988-92, legis. affairs com 1984-85, priorities com. 1984-85, govtl. affairs com. 1984-88, nominating com. 1991-92, 94-95, audit com. 1992-93, pres. club 1993-94), Rotary Internat. Club #1485 (v.p. 1998-2000, pres. 2000-2001, District 5630 Group Study Exchange Team Leader to South Korea District 3710, 1999, Paul Harris fellow), Riverside Golf Club. Roman Catholic. Home: 1429 Stagecoach Rd Grand Island NE 68801-7374 E-mail: montuma@juno.com.

ETHINGTON, RAYMOND LINDSAY, geology educator, researcher; b. State Center, Iowa, Aug. 28, 1929; s. Lindsay E. and Hilda Ruby (Weuve) E.; m. Leslie Ann Nielsen, June 15, 1955; children: Elaine Marie, Mary Frances. BS, Iowa State U., 1951, MS, 1955; PhD, U. Iowa, 1958. Asst. prof. geology Ariz. State U., Tempe, 1958-62; asst. prof. U. Mo., Columbia, 1962-65, assoc. prof., 1965-68, prof., 1968-2000, prof. emeritus, 2000—. With U.S. Army, 1951-53. NSF grantee, 1966, 87. Fellow Geol. Soc. Am.; mem. Soc. Econ. Paleontologists and Mineralogists (editor Jour. Paleontology 1969-74, spl. pubs. editor 1980-83, chmn. publs. com. 1974-76, pres. 1989-90, pres. SEPM Found., Inc., 1993-98), Pander Soc. (chief panderer 1990-98), Am. Assn. Petroleum Geologists, Palaeontol. Assn. G.B., Paleontol. Soc. Mem. Lds Ch. Home: 1012 Pheasant Run Columbia MO 65201-6252 Office: U Mo Dept Geol Sci Columbia MO 65211-0001 E-mail: EthingtonR@missouri.edu.

ETHRIDGE, JOSEPH ALFRED, manufacturing executive (heavy); BBA in Acctg., U. N. Tex., 1963, MBA in Fin., 1967. Comptr. currency Asst. Nat. Bank Examiner, Dallas, 1968-69; staff acct. to mng. ptnr. Coopers & Lybrand, 1970-90; sr. v.p. fin., treas. Sammons Enterprises Inc., Dallas, 1990—. Office: Sammons Enterprises Inc 5949 Sherry Ln Ste 1900 Dallas TX 75225

ETHRIDGE, LARRY CLAYTON, lawyer; b. Houston, Feb. 27, 1946; s. Robert Pike and Gladys Jeannette (Grant) E.; m. Edith Kirkbride Gilbert, May 21, 1977; children: Elizabeth Kirkbride, Grant Harbin. BA, Duke U., 1968; JD cum laude, U. Louisville, 1975. Bar: Ky. 1975, U.S. Dist. Ct. (we. dist.) Ky. 1980, U.S. Ct. Appeals (6th cir.) 1981, U.S. Dist. Ct. (ea. dist.) Ky. 2003. Intern Adv. Commn. on Intergovtl. Rels., Washington, 1975-76; asst. dir. model procurement code project ABA, Washington, 1976-80; ptnr. Mosley, Clare & Townes, Louisville, 1980-97, Ackerson Mosley & Yann, 1998—2003, Ackerson & Yann, Louisville, 2003—. Cons. ABA model procurement code project, Washington, 1980-82; panel mem. N.Y. State Procurement Rev., 1984—. Co-author: Supplement to Annotations on the Model Procurement Code, 1991, Annotations, 3d edit., 1996. Elder Highland Presbyn. Ch., Louisville, clk. of session, 1989-90, 96-2001; vol. Am. Cancer Soc.; gen. counsel Mobile Riverine Force Assn., 1995—. Lt. USNR, 1969, Vietnam, Cambodia, and Japan. Recipient Disting. Svc. award Nat. Inst. Govtl. Purchasing, 1987. Fellow Am. Bar Found. (life); mem. ABA (chmn. coord. com. on a model procurement code 1985-96, co-chmn. model procurement code revision project steering com. 1997—, coun. mem., state and local govt. law sect. 1988—, sect. publs. dir. 1990-93, comms. dir. 1993-95, sec. 1995-96, vice-chmn. 1996-97, chmn. elect 1997-98, chmn. 1998-99, Donald M. Davidson award), AAA Ky. (bd. dirs. 1990-96, sec., gen. counsel 1996—), Ky. Bar Assn., Louisville Bar Assn., Jefferson Fordham Soc., U. Louisville Law Alumni Assn. (pres. 1990-92), U. Louisville Alumni Assn. (exec. com., pres.-elect, pres. 2003—, Alumni Svc. award), Duke Club Ky. (pres. 1992-94), Waggener H.S. Alumni Assn. (pres. 1996-97), Univ. of Louisville Club (bd. dirs. 1997—, treas. 2000—, v.p. 2002—). Republican. Presbyterian. Avocations: gardening, travel, golf, bicycling, reading. Home: 2402 Longest Ave Louisville KY 40204-2125 Office: Ackerson & Yann 401 W Main St Ste 1200 Louisville KY 40202-2806 E-mail: lethridge@amy-law.com.

ETHRIDGE, MARK FOSTER, III, writer, publisher, media consultant; b. Winston-Salem, N.C., May 28, 1949; s. Mark F. Jr. and Margaret Burns (Furbee) E.; m. Kay Stover, Aug. 12, 1972; children: Emily Vigland, Mark Furbee. Grad., Phillips Exeter Acad., 1967; AB cum laude, Princeton U., 1971. Reporter AP, Boston, 1971-72, The Charlotte (N.C.) Observer, 1972-88, dep. metro editor, 1978-79, mng. editor, 1979-88; pub. The Bus. Jour. of Charlotte, 1989-98; pres. Carolina Parenting, Inc., 1991—, Cotter Group, Harrisburg, N.C., 1998-2001. Bd. dirs. Bioethics Resource Group Ltd. Mem. editl. bd. PBS Frontline. Mem. exec. com. Princeton Alumni Coun., 2001—. Nieman fellow Harvard U., 1986. Presbyterian. Home: 5516 Gorham Dr Charlotte NC 28226-6414 Office: Carolina Parenting Inc 1100 S Mint St Charlotte NC 28203 E-mail: methridge@charlotteparent.com.

ETIENNE, MICHELE, financial consultant; b. Cap Haitien, Haiti, Oct. 16, 1946; d. Raymond and Claudia (Prophete) Kersaint; m. Ernst Etienne, Mar. 2, 1967; children: Patrick, Bernard. BBA, Baruch Coll., 1976. Dir. fin. Martha Graham Ctr., N.Y., 1973-98; fin. adv. Lee Strasberg Theatrical Inst., N.Y., 1999—. Pres. Primevere Club; mem. Casegha. Home: 84-15 168th St Jamaica NY 11432 Office: Lee Strasberg Theatrical Inst 115 E 15th St New York NY 10003-2188 E-mail: metienne16@aol.com.

ETIM, TERRIS, geriatrics nurse; b. Roxboro, NC, June 12, 1955; d. Ambrose and Odell Vinnie Harris; m. Albert Etim (div. June 1, 1996); 5 children. Grad., Atlantic County Vo-Tech, 1986. LPN Nurse Works, Langhorne, Pa., Ocean Side Nurse Home, Atlantic City; skilled home LPN Divsn. of Disabilities, Hamman, NJ; LPN Caring Inc., Pleasantville, NJ; CSR-technician Atlantic City Hosp.; LPN Our Ladies Residence, Pleasantville, NJ, Ea. Pines Nursing Home, Atlantic City. Author: In the Valley of Dry Bones, 2001. Trustee Full Gospel Ch., 1975—90. Recipient bronze star, African Am. Women's Network, achievement in field of health, Camden County Bd. of Freeholders. Mem.: Hostes Club, Mt. Pleasant Bapt. Ch. Home: 111 N 2nd St Pleasantville NJ 08232-2425

ETKIN, LAURENCE D. geneticist, educator; b. Phila., Mar. 7, 1945; s. Harry and Mollie Etkin; m. Lorraine Farkas Etkin, Mar. 26, 1967; children: Marc, Scott, Craig. BS, Temple U., 1966; PhD, Ind. U., 1977. Vis. instr. Ind. U., 1977; postdoctoral fellow U. Calif., Berkeley, 1977—79; asst. prof. U. Tenn., Knoxville, 1979—83, U. Tex. M.D. Anderson Cancer Ctr., Houston, 1984—86, assoc. prof., 1986—92, prof., 1992—, Abell-Hanger Found. prof. genetics, 1997—. Adv. panel for devel. mechanisms NSF, 1995—97; ad hoc mem. sci. adv. com. in nucleic acids and proteins Am. Cancer Soc., 1991; NICHD spl. emphasis study sect. NIH, 2002—, devel. biology study sect., 2003—. Mem. editl. adv. bd.: Internat. Rev. Cytology: A Survey of Cell Biology, 1998—, editor-in-chief: Differentiation, 2000—. With USN, 1968—70. Grantee, NIH, NSF, March of Dimes; NDEA Title IV fellow, Georgetown U., 1971—72, postdoctoral fellow, Am. Cancer Soc., U. Calif., Berkeley, 1977—79. Fellow: AAAS; mem.: Internat. Soc. Differentiation (bd. dirs. 1993—), Am. Soc. for Cell Biology (mem. congl. liaison com. 1995—), Soc. for Developmental Biology. Avocation: photography. Office: Univ Tex MD Anderson Cancer Ctr 1515 Holcombe Blvd Houston TX 77030

ETLING, TERRY DOUGLAS, state agency administrator; b. Akron, Ohio, Jan. 24, 1943; s. Harold A. and Betty Jean (Newton) E.; m. Rosalind Joyce Gallogly, Dec. 26, 1966 (div. Mar. 1983); children: Allison Irene, Bret Newton. BS, Ohio State U., 1966; MEd, Kent (Ohio) State U., 1968. Vocat. rehab. counselor Apple Creek (Ohio) State Hosp., 1966-67, rehab. unit supr., 1967-69; coord. facility and program devel. Ohio Bur. Vocat. Rehab., Columbus, 1969-71; supr. rsch., planning and devel. div. Ohio Rehab. Svcs. Commn., Columbus, 1971-73, chief rsch., planning and devel. div., 1973-77, dep. adminstr., 1977-80, dir. bur. program support, 1980-91, retired, 1991; cons. pvt. practice, 1991—; mgr. program devel. MEDVOC Mgmt., Inc., Columbus, 1992-93, dir. program devel., 1993—. Mem. nat. adv. com. The Therapeutic Community of Upper Valley Med. Ctrs., J.M. Found. Search for Excellence in Vocat. Programs; mem. exec. com. chmn. standards com., trustee Commn. on Accreditation Rehab. Facilities, Tucson, 1985-89; chmn. Nat. State Facility Specialists Conf., Chgo., 1989; regional adv. coun. Rehab. Inst. Chgo. Rsch. and Tng. Ctr. in Prevention and Treatment of Spinal Cord Injury; dir. program devel. project boss Community Bankers Assn. Ohio, 1993-94; cons. Fla. Divsn. Vocat. Rehab., 1994—, Fla. Rehab. Adv. Coun., 1997—; adv. bd. dirs. Nat. Results Coun., St. Paul. Contbr. articles to profl. jours.; commentator for profl. papers Jour. of Rehab. Adminstrn., 1991—. Past pres. Assn. for Developmentally Disabled, Columbus, bd. dirs., 1977-88; ins. adv. coun. Good Samaritan Med. Ctr., Zanesville, Ohio, State Com. Purchase Products and Svcs. Severly Handicapped, 1977-88; chmn. Nat. Results Coun., Mpls., 1995—, apptd. CEO, 1996, 97. Recipient Spl. Recognition award Commn. on Accreditation Rehab. Facilities, 1976, Meritorious Svc. award Ohio Industries for Handicapped 1984, Disting. Svc. award Ohio Rehab. Counselors Assn., 1988, Mary Thiel award Fla. Assn. Rehab. Facilities, 1997. Mem. Vocat. Rehab. (mem. facility com.), Ohio Assn. Rehab. Facilities (former agy. liaison to bd. dirs.), Nat Rehab. Assn., Assn. for Developmentally Disabled (bd. dirs. 1987-88), SAR Ohio State U. Alumni Assn., Union League Club, Delta Sigma Phi. Home: The Four Seasons # 403 333 Sunset Dr Fort Lauderdale FL 33301-2641 E-mail termar733@aol.com.

ETO, HAJIME, information scientist, educator; b. Tokyo, June 16, 1935; s Yoshio and Kikuko (Tamari) E. BA, U. Tokyo, 1959, MA, 1962; MS, U. Calif Berkely, 1967; PhD, Tokyo Inst. Tech., 1979. Rschr. Hitachi Ltd., Tokyo 1962-76; prof. U. Tsukuba, Japan, 1976-99, Chiba Keizai U., Japan, 1999— prof. emeritus U. Tsukuba, 1999—. *He approaches to technology innovations i relation with organizational and policy innovations and is applying manage ment scientific approaches to administrative and judicial services including th behaviors of the tax complaint tribunal as well as the supreme court, both which take innovations into little consideration.* Author, editor: R & Management Systems in Japanese Industry, 1984, R & D Strategies in Japa 1993; mem. editl. bd. Scientometrics Jour., 1979—, Human Sys. Mgm 1980-84, Internat. Jour. of the Sci. of Scis., 1994—, Internat. Jour. Svc. Tec & Mgmt., 1998—; contbr. sci. articles to profl. jours. Recipient Fulbrig scholarship U.S.-Japan Edn. Com., 1966. Mem. AAAS, Internat. Soc. Scient

metrics and Informetrics (mem. coun. 1993—, mem. editl. bd. 1995—), Japan Assn. for Philosophy Sci. (mem. coun. 1970-92), Japan Soc. for Sci. Policy (bd. dirs. 1994-96, coun. 1997—), Assn. of France on Cybernetics, Econs. and Tech. (mem. editl. bd. 1985—), N.Y. Acad. Sci. Home: Nakano 3-43-17-305 Nakano-ku Tokyo 164-0001 Japan Personal E-mail: etohajime@mac.com. Business E-Mail: eto@cku.ac.jp.

ETRA, DONALD, lawyer; b. N.Y.C., July 23, 1947; s. Harry and Blanche (Goldman) E.; m. Paula Renee Wiener, Dec. 28, 1985; children: Harry, Dorothy, Anna, Jonathan. BA, Yale U., 1968; MBA, JD, Columbia U., 1971. Atty. to Ralph Nader, Washington, 1971-73; trial atty. U.S. Dept. Justice, Washington, 1973-77, asst. U.S. atty. L.A., 1978-81; ptnr. Sidley & Austin, L.A., 1983-95, Law Offices of Donald Etra, L.A., 1995—. Co-author: Citibank, 1973. Office: Law Offices of Donald Etra 2029 Century Park East Ste 1020 Los Angeles CA 90067 E-mail: etralaw@aol.com.

ETRA, LIONEL, lawyer; b. N.Y.C., July 22, 1942; s. Max Jacob and Reba (Zuckerbraun) E. AB, Columbia Coll., 1964; JD, Harvard U., 1967; LLM in Taxation, NYU, 1978. Atty. Karelsen Karelsen Lawrence & Nathan, N.Y.C., 1969-77, Roberts & Holland, N.Y.C., 1977—. Avocations: photography, flute playing, running. E-mail: letra@rhtax.com.

ETRIS, SAMUEL FRANKLIN, trade association research consultant; b. Port Huron, Mich., Dec. 3, 1922; s. Samuel and Mildred Susan (Davis) E.; m. Mary Jane Lytle, June 29, 1957; children: Andrew Brooke, Edward Lytle. AB, Temple U., 1947; MS, Rutgers U., 1951. With Foote Mineral Rsch. Labs., Phila., 1947-49, spl. asst. to mng. dir. for nat. affairs, editor, 1967-80; editor ASTM, Phila., 1967-76. Sr. cons. Klein of Saks, Inc., Washington; mgrs. Silver Inst., Gold Inst.; mem. numerical data adv. bd. NRC. Contbr. articles and editorials to profl. publs. Tchr. measurement course Phila. Pkwy. Sch.; Scoutmaster Boy Scouts Am., 1954-57, troop com. chmn., 1957-61; convenor 1st Internat. Conf. on Gold and Silver in Medicine, Bethesda, Md., 1987. Served to 1st lt. USAAF, 1944-46, CBI; Served to 1st lt. USAF, 1951-52. Recipient Scoutmaster's Key award, 1957 Mem. Am. Ceramic Soc. (emeritus). Home and Office: 115 Runnymede Ave Wayne PA 19087-4014 E-mail: sfetris@erols.com.

ETTEL, ZITA MOAK, nursing administrator, food services executive; b. Blythewood, S.C., Feb. 11, 1922; d. George Washington and Johhnie Louise (Halstead) Moak; m. James Hughlon Lylos, Oct. 24, 1949 (dec. June 1960); 6 children; m. James Phillip Ettel, Dec. 25, 1995. RN, Elizabeth Buxton Sch. Nursing, 1941. Carpenter Blythewood Shop, S.C., 1938; RN Elizabeth Buxton, Va., 1942; armament electrician, welder Columbia, SC, 1943; aircraft mechanic Army Air Base, Columbia, 1944; charge nurse Providence Hosp., Columbia, 1945; decorator Macy Dept. Store, N.Y.C., 1947; auto mechanic, 1948; food svc. supr. Columbia Hosp., 1959; psychoanalyst Hall Inst., Columbia, 1964; RN Valley Meml. Hosp., Grand Forks, N.D., 1965; beautician Columbia, 1970—76; orthop. nurse Vet. Hosp., Columbia, 1973, 1980-85. Author: My Abused Childhood, Tommy Turtle, 1955, (poems) Farewell, The Christmas Promise, Too Many; inventor. Nurse Am. Red. Cross, Ft. Monroe, Va., 1942, Ft. Jackson, 1943; driver Blind Assn., Columbia, S.C., 1970; former ch. organist, Sunday Sch. tchr., sec. Luther League. With U.S. Air Force, 1943. Recipient Editor's Choice award Nat. Libr. Poetry, 1996, Golden Poet award World of Poetry, 1989, 91 Mem. N.Y. Acad. Scis. Home: 1001 Confederate Ave Columbia SC 29201

ETTENGER, ROBERT BRUCE, physician, nephrologist; b. Phila., Sept. 17, 1942; s.Ervin Earl and Sylvia (Goodstein) W.; m. Angela Joan Castellano Ettenger; children: Allison, Jessica. BA, U. Pa., 1964; MD, 1968. Maj. U.S. Army, El Paso, 1971-73; asst. prof. pediat. Children's Hosp. of L.A., 1976-80, Sch. Medicine UCLA, 1980-84, asst. prof., 1984-89, prof., 1989—, head divsn. pediat. nephrology dept. pediat., 1990—, vice chmn. clin. affairs, 1990—; med. dir. pediat. renal transplant program UCLA Med. Ctr., 1983—, dir. historcom patibility lab., 1987—2001, vice chief staff, 2002—. Mem., chairperson sub bd. nephrology Am. Bd. Pediat., Chapel Hill, N.C., 1986-91; cons. Immunosuppressive Adv. Com. Food and Drug Adminstrn., Bethesda, Md., 1994—, Biologics and Immune Response Modifiers, Food and Drug Adminstrn., Bethesda, 1994—; mem. biol. sci. adv. com. U.S. Renal Data Sys., Ann Arbor, Mich., 1993-2000. Mem. editl. bd, Transplantation, Pediat. Nephrology, Pediat. Transplantation; contbr. articles to profl. jours. Coach, mem. exec. bd. AYSO Soccer, Santa Monica, Calif., 1994-2001, Bobby Sox Softball, 1995-97, YWCA Basketball, 1995-2000; mem. med. adv. bd. Nat. Kidney Found., L.A., 1993—; mem. sports and phys. edn. adv. com. Santa Monica Sch. Dist. Recipient Ortho Biotech Lectureship Urologic Soc. for Transplantation, 1990, Continuing Svc. award Nat. Kidney Found., L.A., 1991, 92, 94. Fellow Internat. Soc. of Nephrology, Internat. Pediat. Nephrology Assn., Am. Acad. Pediat., Am. Soc. Transplant Physicians (pres. 1984-85), Am. Pediat. Soc., Am. Soc. of Nephrology, Am. Soc. of Pediat. Nephrology, Soc. for Pediat. Rsch., Transplantation Soc (Best Drs. in Am. 1992-2002), United Network For Organ Sharing (regional councillor at region 5, bd. dirs. 2000-02). Jewish. Avocations: distance running, youth sports. Office: UCLA Med Ctr A2-383 Dept Pediatrics 10833 Le Conte Ave Los Angeles CA 90095-3075

ETTENSOHN, FRANK ROBERT, geologist, educator; b. Cin., Feb. 6, 1947; s. Robert Frank and Aileen Frances (Keman) E.; m. Beth Mosher, June 3, 1978; children: Clare Marie, Marc Francis. BS, U. Cin., 1969, MS, 1970; PhD, U. Ill., 1975. Lic. profl. geologist, Ky. Tchr. math. Greenhills (Ohio)-Forest Park City Sch. Dist., 1971; from asst. prof. to prof. geology U. Ky., Lexington, 1975—2003, tech. editor Jour. of Paleontology, 1994-97, bd. dir. Inst. Mining and Minerals Rsch., 1992-93, acting chmn., 1985-86, chmn. dept. geol. sci., 1997—; instr. Kiis Inst., Salzburg, Austria, 2004—; tubist Lexington Brass Band, 2003—04. Geology adv. com. Coun. for Internat. Exch. Scholars, 1993-96, chmn., 1994-96; bd. dir., v.p. Ky. Mus. Natural History, 1991-; tech. adv. com. Ea. Oil Shale Symposium, 1992-94; dir. U.K. Geology Field Camp, 1977-81, 84-85, 92-93, 95, 97-98, 2001; adv. com. Ky. Water Resources Rsch. Inst., 1998-2001; faculty math. and sci. edn. program U. Ky. Coll. Edn., 1999-; adv. bd. Appalachian Math. Sci. Partnership, 2003-; cons. in field; expert witness. Contbr. articles to profl. jour. Capt. C.E., AUS, 1970. Fenneman fellow, 1969-70; U. Ill. fellow, 1971-74; grantee U.S. Dept. Energy, 1976-81, NSF, 1987-90, US Bur. Mines, 1990-91, Ky. Coun. on Higher Edn., 1998-2002, NSF/EPSCOR, 2002-, Geol. Soc. Am.; Fulbright lectr. US Govt., Soviet Union, 1989. Fellow Geol. Soc. Am. (jt. chmn., field trip chmn. ann. mtg. southeastern sect. 2001-02); mem. AAAS, Paleontol. Soc., Paleontol. Assn., Paleontol. Rsch. Inst., Internat. Paleontol. Assn., Ky. Acad. Sci., Am. Geophys. Union, Nat. Assn. Geosci. Tchr., Nat. Earth Sci. Tchr. Assn., Fulbright Assn., Phi Beta Kappa, Sigma Xi, Phi Kappa Phi, Sigma Gamma Epsilon. Roman Catholic. Avocations: phlately, numismatics, scouting, soccer. Home: 1631 Duntreath Dr Lexington KY 40504-2352 Office: U Ky Dept Geol Scis Lexington KY 40506-0053

ETTER, ALAN YANCY, legal administration executive; b. Fayette, Mo., May 25, 1949; s. Kern W. and Nina B. Etter; m. Linda L. Glisan, Dec. 28, 1971; children: Christy L., Katie A. BS in Edn., S.E. Mo. State U., 1971; M Equivalent, Indsl. Coll. Armed Forces, 1991; MPA, Troy State U., 1996. Comms. ens. USN, 1971, advanced through grades to capt., 1993; commanding officer USS Lawrence, Norfolk, Va., 1989-90, USS Pharris, Norfolk, 1991-92; dep. sr. mem. Propulsion Examining Bd., Norfolk, 1992-95; commanding officer Atlantic Bd. Inspection and Survey, Norfolk, 1995-98; ret. USN, 1998; exec. dir. Jackson Kelly PLLC, Charleston, W.Va., 1998—. Surface warfare officer Navy Mil. Pers. Command, Washington, 1988. Referee U.S. Soccer Fedn., Va., 1987-98; girls coord. Beach FC youth soccer orgn., Virginia Beach, Va., 1992-93. Decorated Legion of Merit. Mem. Assn. Legal Adminstrs., Ret. Officers Assn., Indsl. Coll. Armed Forces Alumni, Ducks Unltd. Avocation: decoy carving. Home: 9 Beacon Hl Charleston WV 25311-9718 Office: Jackson Kelly PLLC 1600 Laidley Tower Charleston WV 25301-2189 E-mail: aetter@jacksonkelly.com.

ETTER, DAVID PEARSON, poet, editor; b. Huntington Park, Calif., Mar. 18, 1928; s. Harold Pearson and Judith (Goodenow) E.; m. Margaret Ann Cochran, Aug. 8, 1959; children: Emily Louise, George Goodenow. BA, U. Iowa, 1953. Editor Northwestern U. Press, Evanston, Ill., 1961-63; asst. editor Ency. Brit., Chgo., 1964-66, staff writer, 1966-69; staff editor Compton's Ency., Chgo., 1969-73; manuscript editor No. Ill. U. Press, DeKalb, 1974-80; free-lance writer, editor, 1980-87; textbook order checker, packer McDougal, Littell and Co., St. Charles, Ill., 1988-94; instr. creative writing Elgin (Ill.) C.C., 1995—97. Author: (poetry) Go Read the River, 1966, The Last Train to Prophetstown, 1968, Strawberries, 1970, Voyages to the Inland Sea, 1971, Crabtree's Woman, 1972, Bright Mississippi, 1975, Well You Needn't, 1975, Central Standard Time: New and Selected Poems, 1978, Alliance, Illinois, 1978, Open to the Wind, 1978, Riding the Rock Island Through Kansas, 1979, Cornfields, 1980, West of Chicago, 1981, Boondocks, 1982, Alliance, Illinois Complete Edition, 1983, Home State, 1985, Live at the Silver Dollar, 1986, Selected Poems, 1987, Midlanders, 1988, Electric Avenue, 1988, Carnival, 1990, Sunflower County, 1994, I Want to Talk About You, 1995, How High the Moon, 1996, Next Time You See Me, 1997, The Essential Dave Etter, 2001, Greatest Hits, 2002; contbr. poems to lit. mags., anthologies, textbooks. With AUS, 1953-55. Home: 628 E Locust St Lanark IL 61046-1130

ETTER, GREGG WAYNE, SR., police officer, educator; b. Hutchison, Kans., Oct. 17, 1952; s. Lendell Wayne and Imojean (Swearingen) E.; m. Pamela Lynn Scoggins, June 30, 1979 (div. Oct. 1989); children: Gregg Jr., Alexander P., Nicholas V., Benjamin J.; m. Bonnie Lou Arnold, Dec. 10, 1991. B of Gen. Studies in Polit. Sci., Wichita State U., 1976, M in Adminstrn. Justice, 1981; diploma, USAF Air Command & Staff Coll., 1978; EdD, Okla. State U., 2000. Lt. Sedgwick County Sheriff's Dept., Wichita, Kans., 1977—; instr. Butler County C.C., El Dorado, Kans., 1991—97, Newman U., Wichita, 1997—. Contbr. articles to profl. jours. Unit comdr. Civil Air Patrol, Wichita, 1974-94 Recipient Fredrick Milton Thrasher award, Nat. Gang Crime Rsch. Ctr., 1995, 1998. Mem. Am. Soc. Law Enforcement Tnrs., Kans. Peace Officers Assn., Kans. Sheriff's Assn., North Okla./South Kans. Peace Officers Assn., Am. Correctional Assn., Am. Soc. Criminology, Brit. Soc. Criminology, Acad. Criminal Justice Scis., Am. Jail Assn. Republican. Episcopalian. Office: Sedgwick County Sheriff'sDept 525 N Main St Wichita KS 67203-3702

ETTER, ORVAL, b. Appleton, Colo., July 30, 1915; s. Wayne and Laura (Carpenter) E.; m. Mary Field, Aug. 11, 1939; children: John, Kristina, Hanya, Ted. BS, U. Oreg., 1937, JD with honors, 1939. Rsch. asst. Bur. Mcpl. Rsch., U. Oreg., Eugene, 1939-45, rsch. atty., 1960-65, assoc. prof. pub. affairs and adminstrn., 1968-80; ret., 1980. Sec. Far West, Fellowship of Reconciliation, Berkeley, Calif., 1946-57; pub. adminstrn. analyst bur. pub. adminstrn., U. Calif., Berkeley, 1957-60; legal adviser numerous county charter coms., Oreg., 1962-78; gen. counsel Portland Area Met. Study Commn., 1965-71; of counsel Harrang, Long, Watkinson and Arnold, Eugene, 1971-81. Author: Municipal Home Rule On and Off: Unconstitutional Law in Oregan Now and Then, 1991, Municipal Home Rule in Oregon: Unfulfilled Revolution, 1993; Oreg. corr., Nat. Civic Rev., 1968-81; contbr. articles Oreg. Law Rev., 1940-82, Fellowship (monthly jour.), 1947-55, Nat. Civic Rev. (monthly of Nat. Mcpl. League), 1970-80, We. City (monthly of We. Leagues of Mcpltys.), 1942-45, (monthly jour.) Human Quest, 2001-03. Pres., Eugene Symphony Assn., 1965-72. Mem. Phi Beta Kappa. Democrat. Home: 3080 Potter St Eugene OR 97405-4277

ETTER, PETER ERICH, retired school district administrator; b. Lauenstein, German, Sept. 11, 1941; came to U.S., 1950; s. Friedrich Wilhelm and Luise Emma Bertha (Etter) Schnoek; m. Sharon Emily Sperle, Aug. 1, 1964; children: Michael Erich, Kristina Elaina, Marcus Edward. Student, U. Wis. Milw., 1960-62; BS, U. Wis. Whitewater, 1965, MS, 1969. Cert. elem. tchr., jr. high tchr., German tchr., elem. prin., sch. dist. adminstr. Tchr. Germantown (Wis.) Schs., 1964-66; tchr., prin., adminstr. Darien (Wis.) Consol. Sch., 1966-79; sch. dist. adminstr. New Glarus (Wis.) Pub. Sch., 1979-2001; German tchr. Oregon (Wis.) Pub. Sch., 2001—. Bd. dirs. Amcore Bank, New Glarus; bilingual tour guide Swiss Air, New Glarus, 1988, 90—; tchr. German Madison (Wis.) Area Tech. Coll., 1983—. Pres. Wilhelm Tell Guild, New Glarus, 1986—; mem. Green County Libr. Bd., Monroe, Wis., 1989—; mem. New Glarus com. for Swiss Ctr. of N.Am., New Glarus Hist. Soc. Mem. Wis. Dept. Pub. Instrn. (Leadership Acad.), Wis. Assn. Sch. Dist. Adminstrs. Lutheran. Home: N9111 Old Madison Rd New Glarus WI 53574-9739 E-mail: pete_etter@yahoo.com.

ETTER, ZANA CLAIRE, media library director; b. Camden, N.J., June 6, 1950; d. Clair V. and Zana Irene Cathers; m. Markus Ernst Etter, May 28, 1988; 1 child, Erich. Student, U. Lausanne, Switzerland, 1970; BA in French, Rutgers U., 1972, MEd, 1979, MLS, 1986. Cert. French, German and ESL tchr., N.J. Cataloguer Princeton (N.J.) U., 1973-79; info. specialist Edn. Improvement Ctr., Princeton, 1979-82; supr., libr. assoc. Rutgers U. Tech. Svcs., New Brunswick, N.J., 1982-87; dir. media libr. univ. medicine and dentistry Robert Wood Johnson Med. Sch., Piscataway, N.J., 1987—. Tchr. ESL West Windsor-Plainsboro (N.J.) Schs., 1978, YMCA, Princeton, 1981; tchr. French East Windsor Adult Sch., Hightstown, N.J., 1981; pvt. practice tutoring English, Plainsboro, N.J., 1981-84. Contbr. articles to profl. jours. Mem. Med. Libr. Assn., Acad. Health Info. Profls. of Med. Libr. Assn. (sr. mem.), Health Scis. Libr. Assn. N.J. Avocations: skiing, tennis, writing. Office: Robert Wood Johnson Med Sch 675 Hoes Ln Piscataway NJ 08854-5627

ETTERER, SEPP, industrial relations specialist, consultant, application developer; b. Munich, Aug. 31, 1944; arrived in U.S., 1955, naturalized, 1962; s. Josef and Ingeborg Anna (Fierlings) Etterer; m. Judith Annette Shell, Feb. 25, 1978; children: Jonathan Sepp, Julia Anne, Joseph William;children from previous marriage: Victoria Marie, Christina Diane, Kurt. BSEE, Mich. State U., 1966. Lic. comml. pilot. Assoc. ele. engr. Boeing Co., 1966-67; pulp mill supr., plant safety engr. Procter & Gamble Co., 1970-76; sr. safety rep. Bechtel Power Co., 1976-77; plant safety supt. Hooker Chems. & Plastics Corp., 1977-78; indsl. relations dir. Interstate Lead Co. Inc., Leeds, Ala., 1978-85; regional personnel and safety dir. Structl. Steel Fabrication div. Trinity Industries, Inc., Birmingham, Ala., 1985-89; safety mgr. freight car div. Trinity Industries, Bessemer, Ala., 1989-94; pres. SMOsys, Birmingham, 1994—. Indsl. rels. software developer, cons.; v.p. Le Marche aux Fleurs, Inc., 1986—97. Author: (book) Take It-It's Yours, 1975, Sky Pig, 1976, Equity 5, 1980, (software) SMOsys M7 Indsl. Rels. Mgmt., 2003. Capt. USAF, 1967—70. Mem.: Soc. Human Resource Mgmt., Air and Water Mgmt. Assn., Am. Indsl. Hygiene Assn., Am. Soc. Safety Engrs. (past pres.). Home: 1315 Wickford Rd Birmingham AL 35216-2903 Office: PO Box 661333 Birmingham AL 35266-1333

ETTINGER, DAVID SEYMOUR, medical oncologist; b. Bklyn., Mar. 16, 1942; s. Harry and Frieda (Rose) E.; m. Phyllis Evellen Katz, June 4, 1964; children: Laura, Daniel, Kathryn. BA, Yeshiva Coll., 1963; MD, U. Louisville, 1967. Intern Albany (N.Y.) Med. Coll., 1967-68; fellow in medicine Mayo Clinic, Rochester, N.Y., 1968-71; fellow in med. oncology Johns Hopkins U. Sch. Medicine, Balt., 1973-75, instr. oncology, 1975-76, instr. medicine, 1975-77, asst. prof. oncology, 1976-81, asst. prof. medicine, 1977-81, assoc. prof. oncology, 1981-82, assoc. prof. medicine, 1981-93, prof. oncology, 1992—, prof. medicine, 1993—; assoc. dir. for clin. rsch. Johns Hopkins Oncology Ctr., Balt., 1992—. Mem. editorial bd. Oncology: Internat. Jour. of Cancer Rsch. and Treatment, Jour. Cancer Rsch. and Clin. Oncology, The Oncologist, Expert Rev. of Anticancer Therapy; editor-in-chief: Current Treatment Options in Oncology; contbr. chpts. to books, numerous articles to profl. jours. Pres. Md. divsn. Am. Cancer Soc., 1994-96. Maj. U.S. Army, 1971-73. Fellow ACP; mem. Eastern Coop. Oncology Group, Am. Soc. Clin. Oncology, Am. Assn. for Cancer Rsch., Internat. Assn. for Study of Lung Cancer, Am. Soc. Therapeutic Radiology and Oncology, Connective Tissue Oncology Soc. Office: Bunting Blanstein CRB 1650 Orleans St Baltimore MD 21231

ETTINGER, HARRY JOSEPH, industrial hygiene engineer, project manager; b. N.Y.C., July 20, 1934; s. Morris and Pauline (Waxman) E.; m. June Kopf, June 14, 1958; children: Linda E., Steven E., Robert A. BCE, CCNY, 1956; MCE, NYU, 1958. Registered profl. engr., N.Mex.; cert. indsl. hygienist. Sanitary engr. USPHS, Bethesda, Md., 1958-61; staff mem. Los Alamos (N.Mex.) Nat. Lab., 1961-71, alt. group leader, 1971-74, group leader, 1974-80, program mgr., 1981-87; project dir. Occupational Safety and Health Adminstrn., Washington, 1987-89; tech. rsch. coord. Los Alamos (N.Mex.) Nat. Lab., 1989-91, program mgr., 1991-93, chief scientist environ., safety and health divsn., 1993-97, acting dep. divsn. dir., 1995-96, lab. assoc., 1997-99, cons., 1999—. Cons. divsn. reactor licensing USAEC, 1970-71, cons. EPA, 1972-74, various industries, 1970—; cons. to adv. com. on nuclear facility safety DOE, 1990-91; mem. adj. faculty U. Ark., Little Rock, 1969-90, San Diego State U., 1981-86; vis. faculty Tex. A&M U., College Station, 1981-99; faculty affiliate Colo. State U., Ft. Collins, 1983—; mem. exec. com. toxic substances rsch. and tchg. program U. Calif., 1984-90; mem. stds. steering group DOE Lab. Dirs. Environ. and Occupational Health, 1990-96; mem. liaison com. NIOSH/NORA. Contbr. jour. articles and tech. reports on indsl. hygiene, aerosol physics, respiratory protection. Active Los Alamos County Utility Bd., 1968-70, 78-82, chmn., 1970; vice chmn. Los Alamos County Planning and Zoning Commn., 1974-76, mem., 1972-76, 97-01. Fellow: Am. Indsl. Hygiene Assn. (chmn. aerosol tech. com. 1968—70, mem. aerosol tech. com. 1968—78, editl. rev. bd. 1979—87, aerosol tech. com. 1980—84, bd. dirs. 1987—90, editl. rev. bd. 1990—91, v.p. 1991—92, pres.-elect 1992—93, pres. 1993—94, respirator com. 1995—, editl. rev. bd. 1995—, Edward Baier award 1990, Donald Cummings award 2003); mem.: Internat. Occupl. Hygiene Assn. (bd. dirs. 1994—97), Internat. Soc. Respiratory Protection (bd. dirs. 1985—88, 1995—97, mem. editl. bd. NSC J safety rsch. 2001—), Am. Conf. Govtl. Indsl. Hygiene (Meritorious Achievement award 1985), Am. Bd. Indsl. Hygiene (bd. dirs. 1979—85, chmn. 1983—85), Am. Assn. Aerosol Rsch., Am. Acad. Indsl. Hygiene (editor newsletter 1997—2001). Democrat. Jewish. E-mail: Junee@rt66.com.

ETTINGER, JAYNE GOLD, physical education educator; b. N.Y.C., Oct. 18, 1954; d. Benjamin and Joan Louise (Hyman) Gold; m. Brian K. Ettinger, July 10, 1988; 1 child, Bradley Joseph. AA, Green Mountain Coll., Poultney, Vt., 1973; BS, Cortland State Coll., 1975; MS, Western Conn. State Coll., 1981. Lic. phys. edn. tchr., N.Y. Phys. edn. tchr. Lakeland Cen. Schs., Shrub Oak, N.Y., 1975— . Volleyball ofcl. Hudson Valley Bd. of Ofcls., 1984-88, pres., 1987-89. Coord. Jump Rope for Heart, Mohegan Lake, N.Y., 1988—, Basketball Shoot Contest, Easter Seal Soc., 1989—, Hopping-Disability Awareness, 1992-99. Mem. AAHPERD, N.Y. State Assn. Health, Phys. Edn., Recreation and Dance, Lakeland Fedn. Tchrs. (sec. 1985-97), Kappa Delta Pi. Office: George Washington Elem Sch 3634 Lexington Ave Mohegan Lake NY 10547-1244

ETTINGER, JOSEPH ALAN, lawyer; b. N.Y.C., July 21, 1931; s. Max and Frances E.; children: Amy Beth, Ellen Jane. BA, Tulane U., 1954, JD with honors, 1956. Bar: La. 1956, Ill. 1959. Asst. corp. counsel City of Chgo., 1959-62; pvt. practice, Chgo., 1962-73, 76-80; sr. ptnr. Ettinger & Schoenfield, Chgo., 1980-92; pvt. practice, Chgo., 1993—. Assoc. prof. law Chgo.-Kent Coll., 1973-76; chmn. Village of Olympia Fields (Ill.) Zoning Bd. Appeals, 1969-76; chmn. panel on corrections Welfare Coun. Met. Chgo., 1969-76; spl. state appellate defender State of Ill., 1997-98. Contbr. articles to profl. publs. Capt. JAGC, U.S.Army, 1956-59. Recipient svc. award Village of Olympia Fields, 1976. Mem. Chgo. Bar Assn., Assn. Criminal Def. Lawyers (gov. 1970-72). E-mail: joeett@aol.com.

ETTINGER, LAWRENCE JAY, pediatric hematologist and oncologist, educator; b. Bklyn., Dec. 17, 1947; s. Joseph and Blanche (Mittman) E.; m. Alice G. Renick. BA, Case Western Res. U., 1969, MD, 1973. Intern in pediatrics U. Md. Hosp., Balt., 1973-74, resident in pediatrics, 1974-75, Children's Hosp. Buffalo, 1975-76; fellow in pediatric hematology-oncology Roswell Park Meml. Inst. and Children's Hosp. Buffalo, 1976-78; asst. prof. pediatrics U. Rochester (N.Y.) Sch. Med. and Dentistry, 1978-81, U. So. Calif., L.A., 1981-84; assoc. prof. U Medicine and Dentistry N.J., Robert Wood Johnson Med. Sch., New Brunswick, chief div. pediatric hematology-oncology, 1984-98; lectr. in pediats. Coll. Physicians and Surgeons Columbia U., 1998-2000; chief divsn. pediat. hematology/oncology St. Peter's Univ. Hosp., 1998—; assoc. clin. prof. pediatrics Coll. Physicians and Surgeons Columbia U., 2000 . Sickle cell adv. com. N.J. State Dept. Health, 1998—. Contbr. articles to profl. jours.; manuscript reviewer Cancer, Mayo Clinic Proceedings, Jour. Pediat. Hematology-Oncology, Brit. Jour. Cancer, Med. Pediat. Oncology, Am. Jour. Perinatology. Mem. adv. com. Pediatric Oncology Adv. Group, N.J. Commn. Cancer Rsch., 1986—; mem. med. adv. bd. Inst. for Children with Cancer and Blood Disorders, 1991-98; field reader Office of Orphan Products Devel. FDA, 1988—; mem. spl. rev. com. NIH, 1992, 95; mem. cancer ad hoc com. Ocean County (N.J.) Health Dept., 1996-98. Recipient Univ. Excellence award for patient care U. Medicine and Dentistry, N.J., 1991, Pride of N.J. award and Clara Barton Med. Svc. award Gov. of N.J., 1992, N.J. Pride award in health, 1993; grantee N.J. Commn. on Cancer Rsch., Trenton, 1987-89, Valerie Fund, Maplewood, N.J., 1985-90, The Upjohn Co., Kalamazoo, 1984-86, Wyeth-Ayerst Rsch., Phila., 1992-94, Enzon Inc., Piscataway, N.J., 1992-94, Amgen, Inc., Thousand Oaks, Calif., 1992-94, Inst. for Children with Cancer and Blood Disorders, 1991-98, Sanofi Winthrop, 1996; Jr. Faculty Clin. . Fellow Am. Cancer Soc., 1980-83. Fellow Am. Acad. Pediatrics (exec. com. sect. on hematology-oncology 1997-2000); mem. AMA, Acad. Medicine N.J., Ea. Soc. Pediatric Rsch., Am. Assn. Cancer Rsch., Am. Soc. Clin. Oncology, Am. Soc. Hematology, Am. Soc. Pediatric Hematology-Oncology, Am. Cancer Soc. (svc. and rehab. com. N.J. divsn. 1985-96, vice chmn. 1988-89, 92-94, chmn. 1994-96, bd. trustees, exec. com. 1994-96), Oncology Soc. N.J., Children's Cancer Group (prin. investigator 1997-98), Internat. Soc. of Pediatric Oncology, Children's Oncology Group, Phi Beta Kappa. Avocations: photography, travel. Office: St Peter's U Hosp 254 Easton Ave PO Box 591 New Brunswick NJ 08903-0591 E-mail: lettinger@saintpetersuh.com.

ETTINGHAUSEN, THOMAS ANDREW DAVID, investment banker, writer; b. Washington, D.C., Feb. 26, 1959; s. Richard and Elizabeth (Sgalitzer) E. AB, Princeton U., 1983; MBA, UCLA, 1989. Analyst The First Boston Corp., L.A., N.Y.C., 1983-88; v.p. Paribas Properties, Inc., L.A., N.Y.C., 1988-90, The Yarmouth Group, N.Y., 1990-92, Jones Lang Wootton, N.Y., 1992-93; v.p., sr. credit officer Moody's Investors Svc., N.Y., 1993-98; v.p. Merrill Lynch Internat., Inc., Hong Kong, Tokyo, and London, 1998—. Trustee N.Y. Inst. Spl. Edn., Bronx. Mem. The Ivy Club, The Princeton Club of N.Y., The Rockaway Hunting Club, Phi Gamma Delta. Avocations: flying, tennis, fishing, antiquing. Home: 24 Armour Rd Princeton NJ 08540-3004 Office: Merrill Lynch Internat Merrill Lynch Fin Ctr 2 King Edward St London EC1A 1HQ England E-mail: thomas_ettinghausen@ml.com.

ETTLICH, WILLIAM F. electrical engineer; b. Spokane, Wash., Jan. 7, 1936; s. Fred Ernest Ettlich and Dorothy Sue (Olney) Nicholls; m. Alice Dianne Lawton, Aug. 24, 1958; children: Pamela, Daniel. BS, Oreg. State U.; PMD-25, Harvard U. Registered profl. engr., Oreg., Calif., Nev., Colo., Ohio. Project engr. CH2M-Hill Corp., Corvallis, Oreg., 1959-65; pres. Neptune Microfloc, Corvallis, 1965-74; v.p. Culp Wesner Culp, Cameron Park, Calif., 1974-86; exec. v.p. CWC-HDR, Inc., Cameron Park, 1986-88, HDR Engring., Inc., El Dorado Hills, 1988—. Pres. Cameron Estates CSD, Cameron Park, 1977-80. Contbr. tech. articles to jours.; patentee in field. Bd. dirs. Marshall Hosp.; trustee emeritus Marshall Hosp. Found. and Hosp. Bd. Mem. IEEE (sr.), Instrument Soc. Am., Rotary (pres. Cameron Park club 1987-88). Republican. Presbyterian. Avocations: skiing, woodworking. Home: 3417 Strolling Hills Rd Cameron Park CA 95682-9632 Office: HDR Engring 271 Turn Pike Dr Folsom CA 95630-8098 E-mail: bettlich@hdrinc.com.

ETTORE, JOSEPH R. discount department store chain executive; Pres., CEO, Jamesway Corp., until 1994; pres., CEO Ames Dept. Stores Inc., Rocky Hill, Conn., 1994—, chmn., 1999—. Recipient numerous industry awards and honors, including Humanitarian of Yr. award Housewares Charity Found., Retail Exec. of Yr. award Discount Merchandiser mag., Discounters in Svc. to Cmty. award Discount Store News, Bus. Leadership award U. Hartford, Corp. Leadership award Nat. Coun. on Aging, 1st award for edn. excellence Sch. and Home Office Products Assn. Found., 1999. Mem. Internat. Mass Retail Assn. (chmn.). Office: Ames Dept Stores Inc 2418 Main St Rocky Hill CT 06067-2598

ETTRE, LESLIE STEPHEN, chemist; b. Szombathely, Hungary, Sept. 16, 1922; came to U.S., 1958, naturalized, 1965; s. Stephen and Mary Therese (Dunay) E.; m. Kitty Polonyi, May 16, 1953; 1 child, Julie Suzanne. Diploma Chem. Engring, U. Tech. Scis., Hungary, 1945, D.Tech. Scis. Chemist G. Richter Pharm. Works, Budapest, Hungary, 1946-49; rsch. chemist Rsch. Inst. for Heavy Chem. Industries, Veszprem, Hungary, 1949-51, head tech. office, 1951-53; sr. lectr. chemistry U. Veszprem, 1951-53; head indsl. dept. Research Inst. for Plastics Industry, Budapest, 1953-56; chemist Lurgi Cos., Frankfurt, Fed. Republic Germany, 1957-58; applications chemist Perkin-Elmer Corp., Norwalk, Conn., 1958-60, product specialist, 1960-62, chief applications chemist, 1962-68, sr. staff scientist, 1972-87, sr. scientist, 1987-90. Exec. editor Ency. Indsl. Chem. Analysis John Wiley & Sons, N.Y.C., 1968-72; rsch. assoc. dept. engring. and applied scis. Yale U., New Haven, 1977-78, adj. prof., 1989-95, rsch. affiliate, 1995—; adj. prof. U. Houston, 1978-88; chmn. various symposia on chromatography, intermittantly, 1972-93; co-chmn. Summer

Symposium on Analytical Chemistry Miami U., Oxford, Ohio, 1973; lectr. in U.S., Can., Europe, Asia, Africa, Australia; participant lecture tours of Chromatography Coun. of Acad. Scis., USSR, 1976, 78, 79, 80, 81, 86, 88, Estonian Acad. Scis., 1979-81, Chinese Acad. Scis., 1980, 85, 87, Georgian Acad. Sci., 1981. Recipient Commemorative Chromatography medal Acad. Scis., USSR, 1978, M.S. Tswett award, 1978, L.S. Palmer award Minn. Chromatography Forum, 1980, A.J.P. Martin award Brit. Chromatography Discussion Group, 1982, Outstanding Svc. award Western Carolinas Chromatography Discussion Group, 1987, M.J.E. Golay award Internat. Symposium on Capillary Chromatography, 1992, Jubilee award, 1998, Golden Diploma U. Tech. Scis., Budapest, 1995, Dimick award Pitts. Conf. on Analytical Chemistry and Applied Spectroscopy, 1998, Cs Horvath award Conn. Separations Sci. Coun., 2001. Fellow Am. Inst. Chemists; mem. ASTM (chmn. subcom. rsch. com. E-19, 1966-70, subcom. on nomenclature of com. E-19, 1970-73), Am. Chem. Soc. (award in chromatography 1985), Chromatography Soc. (exec. com. 1982-89), N.Y. Acad. Scis., Internat. Union Pure and Applied Chemistry (nomenclature com. 1981-91), Hungarian Chem. Soc. (hon.; Heureka award 2001). Office: Beardsley Station PO Box 6274 Bridgeport CT 06606-0274 Fax: 203-371-5765. E-mail: lsettre@snet.net.

ETULAIN, RICHARD WAYNE, historian, educator; b. Wapato, Wash., Aug. 26, 1938; s. Sebastian and Mary Lou (Gillard) E.; m. Joyce Oldenkamp, Aug. 18, 1961; 1 child, Jacqueline Joyce Etulain Partch. BA in History, BA in English, N.W. Nazarene Coll., Nampa, Idaho, 1960; MA in Am. Lit., U. Oreg., 1962, PhD in Am. History and Lit., 1966; DHL, Northwest Nazarene U., 2000. Grad. asst. U. Oreg., Eugene, 1963—66; asst. prof. N.W. Nazarene Coll., 1966—68; assoc. prof. Eastern Nazarene Coll., Quincy, Mass., 1968—69; postdoctoral grantee Dartmouth Coll., Hanover, 1969—70; from assoc. prof. to prof. history Idaho State U., Pocatello, 1970—79; prof. history U. N.Mex., Albuquerque, 1979—2001, prof. emeritus, 2001—. Postdoctoral fellow U. Nev., Reno, 1973-74; bd. trustees N.W. Nazarene U., 2003—. Author: Owen Wister, 1973, Ernest Haycox, 1988, The American West: A Twentieth-Century History, 1989, Re-imagining the Modern American West: A Century of Fiction, History, Art, 1996, Telling Western Stories: From Buffalo Bill to Larry McMurtry, 1999; editor/co-editor: Basque Americans, 1981, Conversations: Wallace Stegner on History and Literature, rev. edit., 1990, The Twentieth-Century West: Historical Interpretations, 1989, Basques of the Pacific Northwest, 1991, Religion in Modern New Mexico, 1997, By Grit and Grace: Eleven Women Who Shaped the American West, 1997, Myths and the American West, 1998, Portraits of Basques in the New World, 1999, Does the Frontier Experience Make America Exceptional?, 1999, With Badges and Bullets: Lawmen and Outlaws in the Old West, 1999, The Hollywood West: Lives of Film Legends Who Shaped It, 2001, New Mexican Lives, 2002, César Chávez: A Brief Biography, 2002, Wild Women of the Old West, 2003, The American West in 2000, 2003; contbr. over 400 articles and rev. to profl. jours. Sunday sch. tchr., mem. ch. bd., Pocatello, Portland and Albuquerque, 1970—. Recipient Wrangler/Western Heritage award Nat. Cowboy Hall of Fame, 1997, Excellence in Humanities award N.Mex. Endowment for Humanities, 1998, Gaspar Perez de Villagra award N.Mex. Hist. Soc., 2001; NEH Minority fellow, 1973-74; NHPC Hist. Editing fellow, 1969-70, postdoctoral fellow U. Nev., Reno, 1973-74. Mem. Western Lit. Assn. (pres. 1979-80), Western History Assn. (pres. 1998-99, Best Book in Western History award 1997), Orgn. Am. Historians. Democrat. Mem. Ch. of the Nazarene. Avocations: book collecting, travel, writing. Home: 14559 SE Megan Way Clackamas OR 97015 E-mail: baldbasq@unm.edu.

ETZ, JANE (HELEN JANE ETZ), hospital review analyst; b. Riverside, Calif., Feb. 21, 1938; d. James Wycoff Van Derpool and Mildred Thelma Carr; m. William Arthur Ward, Aug. 9, 1958 (div. 1978); children: Arthur Scott Ward, Wendolyn Zee (Ward) Warwick; m. Charles Frederick Etz, Jan. 26, 1980. BSN, Calif. State U., Dominguez Hills, 1996. RN Calif; cert. Pub. Health Nurse, Calif.; cert. case mgr. Clinic nurse Gridley (Calif.) Farm Labor Camp, 1965-67; staff nurse Chico (Calif.) Cmty. Hosp., 1972-75, patient care coord., 1975-80; head nurse King Abdulaziz Air Base Hosp., Dhahran, Saudi Arabia, 1980-81; utilization mgr. Chico Cmty. Hosp., 1981-91, dir. quality mgmt., 1991-94; dir. utilization mgmt. discharge planning and social svcs. Chico Cmty. Hosp., Inc., 1994-98; utilization mgr. Enloe Med. Ctr., Chico, 1998-2001, clin. regulatory analyst, 2001&. V.p., bd. dirs. Peg Taylor Adult Day Health, Chico, 1996—, sec. and bd. mem., 1993-96; pres. elect Butte/Glenn/Tehema County (Calif.) chpt. Am. Diabetic Assn., 1996-99, pres. 1999-2000. Mem. North Sierra Quality/Utilization Assn. (pres. 1981-82), Chico Book Club, Caribou Investment Club. Episcopalian. Avocations: books, investing, bicycle touring, birding, gardening. Office: Enloe Med Ctr 1351 Esplanade Chico CA 95926-3330 E-mail: jcetz@aol.com.

ETZEL, JAMES EDWARD, environmental engineering educator; b. Reading, Pa., Nov. 9, 1929; s. Edward John and Ruth Anna (Getrost) E.; m. Barbara Dawn Shoup, Sept. 3, 1950; children: Pamela Dawn, Gregory John, Mark Raymond, Scott Edward, Christopher James. BS in Sanitation Engring., Pa. State U., 1951; MSCE, Purdue U., 1955, PhD, 1957. Registered profl. engr., Ind. Engr. Capitol Engring. Co., Dillsburg, Pa., 1951, du Pont Co., Wilmington, Del., 1957-58; engr., dir. research Roy F. Weston, engrs., Newtown Sq., Pa., 1958-59; mem. faculty Purdue U., 1959-90, prof. environ. engring., 1964-90, Water Refining Co. prof., 1978-83, head environ. engring. area Sch. Civil Engring., 1971-90, prof. emeritus environ. engring., 1990—; v.p. Heritage Environ. Svcs., Inc., 1990—. Chmn. Tippecanoe County (Ind.) Solid Wastes Com., 1971-86; mem. W. Lafayette Environ. Commn., 1968-76; cons. to industry, 1960—. Patentee in field. Served with C.E., 1951-53, AUS. Named Outstanding Prof. in Civil Engring. Purdue U., 1979 Mem. Water Pollution Control Fedn. Ind. Water Pollution Control Assn. (past pres.) Lutheran. Home and Office: 710 Cardinal Dr Lafayette IN 47909-9036

ETZEL, RUTH ANN, pediatrician, epidemiologist, educator; b. Milw., Apr. 6, 1954; d. Raymond Arthur and Marian Dorothy Etzel. Student, St. Olaf Coll., 1972-73; BA in Biology summa cum laude, U. Minn., 1976; MD, U. Wis., 1980; PhD, U. N.C., 1985. Resident in pediat. N.C. Meml. Hosp., Chapel Hill, 1980-83; adj. asst. prof. pediat. Emory U. Sch. Medicine, Atlanta, 1985-87; epidemic intelligence svc. officer Ctr. Environ. Health Ctrs. Disease Control, Atlanta, 1985-87, med. epidemiologist Ctr. Environ. Health and Injury Control, 1987-90, chief air pollution and respiratory health br., 1991-96, asst. dir. preventive medicine residency program, 1992-97; dir. divsn. epidemiology and risk assessment Office Pub. Health and Sci., Food Safety and Inspection Svc., USDA, Washington, 1998—2001; adj. prof. environ. and occupl. health George Washington U., Washington, 2000—. Mem. preventive medicine and pub. health test com. Nat. Bd. Med. Examiners, 1992—94; mem. U.S. Med. Licensing Exam. Step 2 Preventive Medicine and Pub. Health Test Material Devel. Com., 1992—94. Contbr. articles to profl. pubs.; editor: book Handbook of Pediatric Environmental Health, 1999—. Recipient Arthur S. Flemming award, DC Jaycees, 1991; Robert Wood Johnson Clin. scholar, U. N.C., 1983—85, MacPherson scholar, 1972. Fellow: Am. Acad. Pediats. (mem. com. environ. hazards, Ctrs. Disease Control and Prevention liaison 1986—92, chmn. sect. epidemiology 1988—92, ex-officio 1993—94, chmn. com. environ. health 1995—99, editor Handbook Pediatric Environmental Health 1999—2003); mem.: APHA, Internat. Soc. Environ. Epidemiology, Soc. Pediatric Epidemiol. Rsch., Ambulatory Pediatric Assn. (mem. rsch. com. 1987—, comms. dir. 2002—), Delta Omega, Phi Beta Kappa. E-mail: retzel@earthlink.net.

ETZIONI, AMITAI, sociologist, educator; b. Cologne, Germany, Jan. 4, 1929; s. Willi Falk and Gertrude Hannauer (Falk) E.; m. Minerva Morales, Sept. 14, 1965 (dec. Dec. 20, 1985); children: Ethan, Oren, Michael, David, Benjamin; m. Patricia Kellogg, Nov. 6, 1992. BA, Hebrew U., Jerusalem, 1954, MA, 1956; PhD in Sociology, U. Calif., Berkeley, 1958; LittD (hon.), Rider Coll., 1980, Gov.'s State U., 1987; LLD (hon.), U. Utah, 1991; LHD (hon.), Colo. Coll., 1994, Conn. Coll., 1994. Mem. faculty Columbia U., 1958-80; rsch. assoc. Inst. War and Peace Studies, 1961, prof. sociology, 1967, chmn. dept., 1969-78; dir. Ctr. for Policy Rsch., 1968—; guest scholar Brookings Instn., 1978-79; sr. advisor White House, 1979-80; univ. prof. George Washington U., Washington, 1980—, dir. Inst. for Communitarian Policy Studies, 1995—; Thomas Henry Carroll Ford Found. vis. prof., grad. sch. bus. Harvard U., Cambridge, Mass., 1987-89. Bd. dirs. Ctr. for Policy Rsch., Washington; mem. Econ. Forum The Conf. Bd., 1983-85; founder Ctr. for Comm. Policy Studies, George Washington U., 1995—; dir., founder Inst. Communitarian Policy Studies, 1995; developed organizational analysis, a typology based on means used to control participants in orgns., how orgns. change, survive and are integrated into larger social units. Author: A Comparative Analysis of Complex Organizations, 1961, Modern Organizations, 1964, Political Unification, A Comparative Study of Leaders and Forces, 1965, Studies in Social Change, 1966, the Active Society, 1968, Genetic Fix, 1973, Social Problems, 1975, An Immodest Agenda, 1982, Capital Corruption, 1984, The Moral Dimension, 1988, The Spirit of Community, 1993, The New Golden Rule, 1996, The Limits of Privacy, 1999, The Road to the Good Society, 2001, The Monochrome Society, 2001; editor: The Responsive Community, 1990—; editorial bd. Sci. Mag., 1969-71; contbr. numerous articles to profl. jours. With Israeli Army. Social Sci. Rsch. Coun. faculty fellow, 1960-61, 67-68; fellow Ctr. for Advanced Study in Behavioral Scis., 1965-66; Guggenheim fellow, 1968. Fellow AAAS; mem. Am. Sociol. Assn. (pres. 1995), Soc. for the Advancement Socio-Econs. (founder 1989), The Communitarian Network (founder 1993), Inst. Medicine. Office: George Washington U Rm 703 2130 Gelman Libr St NW Washington DC 20052-0001

ETZKOWITZ, HENRY, educator, consultant; b. N.Y.C., July 9, 1940; s. Benjamin and Mary E.; m. Michelle Baker; 1 child, Alexander. BA, U. Chgo., 1962; PhD, New Sch. U., 1969. Assoc. prof. SUNY, Purchase, N.Y., 1972—. Dir. Sci. Policy Inst. Author: MIT and the Rise of Entrepreneurial Science, 2002, The Triple Helix, 2003; co-author: Public Venture Capital, 2001, Athena Unbound: the Advancement of Women in Science and Technology, 2000; co-editor: Capitalizing Knowledge, 1998, Universities in the Global Knowledge Economy, 1997. Home: 325 Riverside Dr New York NY 10025-4162 E-mail: henryetzkowitz@earthlink.net.

ETZOLD, HERMAN ALBERT, clergyman, theology educator; b. Farrar, Mo., Mar. 10, 1915; s. Martin Gottlieb and Selma Bertha (Stueve) E.; m. Mabel Marie Traugott, Aug. 31, 1942; children: Thomas, Mary Vanagas, Elisabeth Schroeder, Rhoda Finck, Bonnie Johnson, Rachel Eaton, Peter. MS in Edn., Ind. U., 1970; MST, Luth. Sch. Theology, Chgo., 1972; DMin, Concordia Theol. Sem., Ft. Wayne, Ind., 1985. Ordained to ministry Lutheran Ch., 1942. Pastor Signal Hill Luth. Ch., Belleville, Ill., 1942-48, St. Stephen Luth. Ch., St. Louis, 1948-53, Trinity Luth. Ch., Bloomington, Ill., 1953-60, Our Savior Luth. Ch., St. Charles, Mo., 1960-62; prof., dean of students Concordia Coll., Ft. Wayne, 1962-77; prof. St. Paul's Coll., Concordia, Mo., 1977-78; prof. theology Concordia U., Seward, Nebr., 1978—. Sr. mentor Calif. Luth. U., Thousand Oaks, Calif., 1983; vis. prof. Christ Coll., Irvine, Calif., 1983-84; v.p. Ctrl. Ill. dist. Luth. Ch.-Mo. Synod, Springfield, 1957-60; mem. Bd. Luth. World Relief, St. Louis, 1957-68. Author sermons in 10 vols. of Concordia Pulpit, devotions in Portals of Prayer, articles on Luth. confessions in The Lutheran Witness, 1971. Mem. 4th of July Planning Com., Seward, 1980-83. Aid Assn. for Luths. study grantee, 1964-85. Mem. Kiwanis Club. Democrat. Avocations: gardening, travel, computer. Home: 445 N Columbia Ave Seward NE 68434-1601

EU, MARCH FONG, ambassador, former state official; b. Oakdale, Calif., Mar. 29, 1929; d. Yuen and Shiu (Shee) Kong; children by previous marriage: Matthew Kipling Fong, Marchesa Suyin Fong; m. Henry Eu, Aug. 31, 1973; stepchildren: Henry, Adeline, Yvonne, Conroy, Alaric. Student, Salinas Jr. Coll.; BS, U. Calif.-Berkeley, 1943; MEd, Mills Coll., 1947; EdD, Stanford U., 1956; postgrad., Columbia U., Calif. State Coll.-Hayward; LLD, Lincoln U., 1984; LLB (hon.), Western U., 1985; DHL (hon.), Northrup Coll., 1991; LLB (hon.), Pepperdine U., 1993. Chmn. divsn. dental hygiene U. Calif. Med. Center, San Francisco, 1948-56; dental hygienist Oakland (Calif.) Pub. Schs., 1948-56; supr. dental health edn. Alameda County (Calif.) Schs.; lectr. health edn. Mills Coll., Oakland; mem. Calif. Legislature, 1966-74, chmn. select com. on agr., foods and nutrition, 1973-74; mem. com. natural resources and conservation, com. commerce and pub. utilities, select com. med. malpractice; chief of protocol State of Calif., 1975-83, sec. of state, 1975-94; amb. to Federated States of Micronesia, Am. Embassy, Pohnpei, 1994—. Chmn. Calif. State World Trade Commn., 1983-87; ex-officio mem. Calif. State World Trade Commn., 1987—; spl. cons. Bur. Intergroup Relations, Calif. Dept. Edn.; ednl., legis. cons. Sausalito (Calif.) Pub. Schs., Santa Clara County Office Edn., Jefferson Elementary Union Sch. Dist., Santa Clara H.S. Dist., Santa Clara Elementary Sch. Dist., Live Oak Union H.S. Dist.; mem. Alameda County Bd. Edn., 1956-66, pres., 1961-62, legis. adv., 1963, Assembly Retirment Com., Assembly Com. on Govtl. Quality Com., Assembly Com. on Pub. Health; pres. Alameda County Sch. Bds. Assn., others; U.S. advisor Shenzhen Internat. Ent. Co., Ltd., Shenzhen, Guangzhou, China, 1997; internat. hon. advisor 4th World Chinese Entrepreneurs Conv., Vancouver, B.C., 1997; hon. chmn. Sino-Am. Inst. Human Resources, L.A., 1997; U.S. advisor Internat. Hort Exposition for 1999, Kunming, Yunnan, 1997; exec. adv. bd. Asian Am. Policy Rev. Bd., Washington, 1998, others; adj. prof. on regional and continuing edn. Calif. State U., Sacramento, 2000; S.E. Asia advisor Startec Global Telecomm., Inc.; bd. dirs. East L.A. Coll. Found.; adv. bd. for canonization of Blessed Junipero Serra, Santa Barbara, Calif., 2000-01; hon. advisor Internat. Leadership Found., Sacramento, Calif., 2000; adj. prof., sr. adv. Calif. State U. Coll. Continuing & Regional Edn., Sacramento, 2000; sr. advisor S.E. Asia, Startec Global Oper. Co., Bethesda, Md., 2000; bd. regents presdl. adv. com. So. Calif. U. Health Scis., Whittier, Calif., 2002. Mem. adv. bd. for canonization of Father Junipero Sierra, Franciscan Fathers, Santa Barbara, Calif., Internat. Leadership Found. Recipient Citizen of Yr. award Chinese-Am. United for Self Employment, 1996, Govt. Svc. award friends of Mus. of Chinese Am. History, L.A., 1997, Cmty. Svc. award Coll. of San Mateo, Ann. Humanitarian award Women's Ctr., Coll. of Law, San Diego, Asian Am. on the Move award for politics L.A. City Employees Asian Am. Assn., Outstanding Svc. to Cmty. award Irish-Israeli Italian Soc.. San Francisco, Disting. C.C. Alumni award Calif. C.C. and Jr. Coll. Assn., Outstanding Woman award Nat. Women's Polit. Caucus, Daisy award Calif. Landscape Contrs. Assn., 1980, Milton Shoong Hall of Fame Humanitarian award, 1981, Citizen of the Yr. award Coun. for Civic Unity of San Francisco Bay Area, 1982, Woman of the Yr., Dems. United, San Bernardino, 1986, Woman of Achievement Award of Distinction, San Gabriel Valley YWCA, 1987, Disting. svc. award Rep. of Honduras, 1987, Woman of the Yr. award Santa Barbara County Girls Club Coalition, 1987, Polit. Achievement award Calif. Dem. Party, Black Caucus, 1988, 1989, JFK Am. Leadership award Santa Ana Dem. Club, 1989, Cmty. Leadership award Torat-Haijun Hebrew Acad., 1990, Mother of the Yr. award No. Am. TV Corp., 1999, Lifetime Achievement award Orgn. Chinese Ams. Inc., 1999, Outstanding Overseas Chinese award San Francisco Chinese Benevolent Assn. and Chinese Consol. Women's Assn. San Francisco, 2001, Outstanding Citizen award Chinese Am. Citizens Alliance, 2002, Spirit of Am. award Chinese Am. Citizen's Alliance, 2003, numerous others; March Fong Eu ann. achievement award named in her honor Nat. Notary Pub. Assn. Fellow Internat. Coll. Dentists; mem. Navy League (life), Am. Dental Hygienists Assn. (pres. 1956-57), No. Calif. Dental Hygienists Assn., Oakland LWV, AAUW (area rep. in edn. Oakland br.), Calif. Tchrs. Assn., Calif. Agrl. Aircraft Assn. (hon.), Calif. Sch. Bd. Assn., Alameda County Sch. Bd. Assn. (pres. 1965), Alameda County Mental Health Assn., Calif. Pub. Health Assn. Northern Divsn. (hon.), So. Calif. Dental Assn. (hon.), Bus. and Profl. Women's Club, Soroptimist (hon.), Hadassah (life), Ebell Club (L.A.), Chinese Retail Food Markets Assn. (hon.), Chinese Women's Assn. Singapore, Am. Assn. Singapore, Pilot Club Internat., Clara Barton Soc. Am. Red Cross (L.A. chpt.), Delta Kappa Gamma, Phi Alpha Delta (hon.), Phi Delta Gamma (hon.), others. Democrat. Avocation: painting.

EUBANK, DAVID LYNN, lawyer, consultant; b. Lexington, Ky., May 3, 1950; s. Elbert H. and Thelma C. Eubank; m. Lenora A. Eubank, Apr. 12, 1980; 1 child, Mitchell. B of Cmty. Planning, U. Cin., 1974; MPA, JD, U. Dayton, 1989. Bar: Ohio 1989, U.S. Supreme Ct. 1996, U.S. Ct. Appeals (6th cir.) 1991, U.S. Dist. Ct. (so. dist.) Ohio 1990. Exec. dir. Longmont (Colo.) Downtown Devel. Authority, 1980-85; city atty. City of Beavercreek, Ohio, 1991-97; law dir. City of Kettering, Ohio, 1997—. Prin. SFDG Cons., Cin., 1975-80. Mem. Montgomery County, Ohio Cmty. Human Svcs. Levy Rev. Bd., Dayton, 1990-96. Mem. Am. Inst. Cert. Planners. Office: City of Kettering Law Dept 3600 Shroyer Rd Kettering OH 45429

EUBANK, EDWARD J. music educator; b. Des Moines, Iowa, Feb. 12, 1961; s. Harold F. and Jeannine T. Eubank; m. Christina R. Kowalczyk, May 12, 1984; children: Brandon J., Amanda L. MusB, Am. Conservatory Music, Chgo., 1983; MA in Ednl. Adminstrn., Govs. State U., 1996. Type 75 Administrative Certificate, General Administrative E Ill., 1996, Special K 12, Type 10 Teaching Certificate Music Ill., 1991. Orch./choral dir. Mother Guerin H.s., River Grove, Ill., 1991—93; dir. orch. Cmty. Unit Dist. #300, Algonquin, Ill., 1993—94, Maine Twp. H.S. East, Park Ridge, Ill., 1994—2000, chmn. dept. fine arts, 2000—. Mem. Park Ridge Cultural Arts Coun., 2001—; founder Maine East String Acad. Violinist, cantor music ministry St. Elizabeth Seton Cath. Ch., Orland Hills, Ill., 1990—2002. Mem.: ASCD, Nat. Assn. Music Edn., Tri-M Music Honor Soc. (hon.). Avocations: travel, reading, hiking, golf. Office: Maine Township High School East 2601 W Dempster St Park Ridge IL 60068

EUBANK, J. THOMAS, lawyer; b. Port Arthur, Tex., Mar. 17, 1930; s. J.T. and Ada (White) E.; m. Nancy Moore, Feb.10, 1956; children: John, Marshall, Stephen, Laura. BA, Rice U., 1951; JD, U. Tex., 1954. Bar: Tex. 1954, U.S. Supreme Ct. 1960. With Baker Botts L.L.P., Houston, 1954-90, sr. ptnr., 1979-90, sr. counsel, 1999—; dir. Sentinel Trust Co., L.B.A., 1997—. Mem. joint editl. bd. Uniform Probate code, 1972-86. Bd. govs. Rice U., 1985-91. Mem. ABA (chmn. sect. real property, probate and trust law 1978-79), Am. Coll. Trust and Estate Counsel (pres. 1984-85, pres. Found. 1986-89, Trachtman lectr. 1986), State Bar Tex. (chmn. sect. real estate, probate and trust law 1972-73, Lifetime Achievement award 2003), Am. Bar Found., Tex. Bar Found., Houston Philos. Soc., Rice U. Alumni Assn. (pres. 1979-80, Rice Gold medal 1992), Am. Law Inst., Internat. Acad. Estate and Trust Law, Houston Country, Coronado, Allegro, Thalia, Chevaliers du Tastevin. Home: 26 Liberty Bell Cir Houston TX 77024-6303 Office: 910 Louisiana St Houston TX 77002-4995 E-mail: tom.eubank@bakerbotts.com.

EUBANKS, EUGENE EMERSON, education educator, consultant; b. Meadville, Pa., June 6, 1939; s. Nelson Eubanks and Emily (Princes) Jackson; m. Audrey Hunter, Aug. 4, 1962; children: Brian, Regina. BS, Edinboro (Pa.) State U., 1963; PhD, Mich. State U., 1972. Tchr. Cleve. Pub. Schs., 1963-68, unit prin., 1968-70; asst. prof. U. Del., Newark, 1972-74; asst. dean U. Mo., Kansas City, 1974-79, dean, 1979-88, prof. edn. and urban affairs, 1988—; dept. supt. Kansas City Pub. Schs., 1984-85. Contbr. articles to profl. jours. Cons. Urban League, 1978—, legal def. fund NAACP, 1978, Cleve. Found., 1978, U. Wis., 1988; bd. dirs. Operation PUSH, 1982-87, Mid-Continent Girl Scouts, Kansas City, 1983—, Genesis Sch., 1984—; chair Desegration Monitoring Com., 1985—. Mem. Am. Assn. Coll. Tchr. Edn. (pres. 1988-89), Nat. Alliance Found. (chmn. 1984-85), Black Sch. Educators (edn. commn.). Home: 12737 Oakmont Dr Kansas City MO 64145-1140 Office: U Mo Sch Edn 5100 Rockhill Rd Kansas City MO 64110-2481 E-mail: EubanksE@UMKC.edu.

EUBANKS, JESSICA LYNN, protective services official; b. Helena, Mont., Dec. 7, 1965; d. Houston Caldwell and Gloria Jane Eubanks; 1 child, David Fulton III. BA in Criminal Justice, U. Ark., Little Rock, 1989, BA in Psychology, 1990; M in pub. admin., Helena, 2003. Probation officer Mcpl. Probation Svcs., Little Rock, 1986—88; DWI specialist Family Svc. Agy., North Little Rock, Ark., 1988—92; patrolman Little Rock Police Dept., Little Rock, 1992—. Instr. emergency med. tech.; instr. law enforcement officers. Mem.: Little Rock Police Spl. Response Unit, Little Rock Black Police Assn., Little Rock Fraternal Order of Police. Democrat. Baptist. Avocations: reading, travel, cooking, crafts.

EUBANKS, OMER LAFAYETTE, data communications consultant, systems engineer; b. Atlanta, Nov. 28, 1956; s. Omer LaFayette and Frances (Dix) EuB.; m. Joy Kay Gantt, Nov. 15, 1979; children: Matthew Christopher, Timothy Mark. BS, Vanderbuilt U., 1979; D of Computer Sci., Crown Ch. U., 2001. Cert. computer profl., Ga. Sys. programmer U. Tenn., Nashville, 1978-79, Equifax, Inc., Atlanta, 1979-85; sr. sys. programmer Advanced Techs., Inc., Norcross, Ga., 1985-86; sr. comm. sys. programmer Atlanta Jour. Constitution, 1987-89; sys. programmer Suntrust Banks, Atlanta, 1989-90; sr. comm. analyst Life Ins. Co. of Ga., Atlanta, 1990-91; cons. Sys. Ctr., Inc., Reston, Va., 1991-93; integration cons. Candle Corp., Atlanta, 1999—. Cons. Corinthian Software, Marietta, Ga., 1987, North Fulton Healthcare Assn., Roswell, Ga., 1990-99, ISSC-Windward Tech. Ctr., 1994, AT&T Universal Card Svcs., 1994, WORLDSPAN, 1994-96, Advantis, 1996, IBM, 1997, GE Capital, 1997, Candle Corp., 1997—. Bd. dirs. Wills Park Youth Baseball Assn., 1995-96—; deacon Roswell First Bapt., 1989—, vice chair deacon bd., 1994, chmn. student minister search com., 1996, mem. future devel. com., 1991-94, chair, 1994, mem pers. com., 1995-98, vice chair, 1998. NSF grantee, 1974. Mem. NRA (patron), N.Am. Hunting Club (life), Pi Kappa Alpha. Baptist. Avocations: hunting, fishing, baseball. Home: 355 Hickory Flat Rd Alpharetta GA 30004-2612 Office: Candle Corp Ste 1730 Bldg One 2727 Paces Ferry Rd Atlanta GA 30339 E-mail: oeubanks@aol.com.

EUBANKS, RACHEL AMELIA, music educator; b. San Jose, Calif. d. Joseph Sylvester and Elizabeth Amelia (Gant) E. BA, U. Calif., Berkeley, 1945; MA, Columbia U., 1947; DMA, Pacific Western U., 1980. Chmn. music dept. Wilberforce (Ohio) U., 1949-50; founder, pres. Eubanks Conservatory of Music and Arts, L.A., 1951—. Author: Musicianship, 1961; composer: Cantata, 1947, Trio, 1977, Symphonic Requiem, 1980, Sonata for Piano, 1992, 5 Interludes for Piano, 1996, Easter Suite for Organ, 1995, also chamber music, songs, piano solos; publ.: Musicianship, Vol. I, II plus tapes, "Five Interludes" for piano, Vivace Press, "Vietnamese Love Song" for violin and piano, Hildegard Publ. Rosenthal fellow Columbia U., 1946; recipient Cmty. awards City of L.A., 1982, Crenshaw Chamber of Congress, 1986, Calif. Legis. Assembly, 1991, County of L.A., 1991, Phelan award, 1948. Mem. Internat. Alliance of Women in Music, Alpha Mu Honor Soc. Avocation: travel. Office: Eubanks Conservatory of Music and Arts Box 191 6709 La Tijera Blvd Los Angeles CA 90045 Office Fax: 323-293-9182.

EUBANKS-POPE, SHARON G. real estate company executive, entrepreneur; b. Chgo., Aug. 26, 1943; d. Walter Franklyn and Thelma Octavia (Watkins) Gibson; m. Larry Hudson Eubanks, Dec. 20, 1970 (dec. Jan. 1976); children: Rebekah, Aimée; m. Otis Eliot Pope, June 7, 1977; children: O. Eliot Jr., Adrienne. BS in Edn., Chgo. Tchrs. Coll., 1965; postgrad., Ill. Inst. Tech., 1967, John Marshall Law Sch., 1970, Governor's State U., 1975-76. Educator, parent coord. Chgo. Bd. Edn., 1965-77; owner, ptnr. Redel Rentals, Chgo., 1977—. Bd. dirs. Jack and Jill of Am. Found. Adminstrv. bd. St. Mark United Meth. Ch., Chgo., 1967, bd. trustees, 1988; com. chair Englewood Urban Progress Ctr., Chgo., 1973; coord., educator LWV, 1975-76; chair comms. Marian Cath. H.S., 1999—, adv. bd.. Named Outstanding Sch. Parent Vol., Chgo. Bd. Edn., 1977; recipient Outstanding Cmty. Law Class award LWV, 1975-76, Christian Leadership award United Meth. Women, Chgo., 1985. Mem.: NAACP, NAFE, Nat. Assn. Realtors, Am. Soc. Profl. and Exec. Women, St. Mark Cmty. Devel. Corp., Jack and Jill Am., Inc. (Chgo. chpt. journalist 1989—91, Midwestern region sec./treas. 1993—95, nat. treas. 1998—2000, founder Parents for Parity in Edn. 1992, pres. Eubanks-Pope Devel. Co., Inc. 1993, parliamentarian of Parity 1991), Jack & Jill of Am. Found. (bd. dirs. 1995—2000), Links, Inc., Alpha Beta Gamma (female exec. del. to China People to People Amb. program 1998). Office: Redel Rentals 4338 S Drexel Blvd Chicago IL 60653-3536

EUDALY, NATHAN H. insurance company executive; b. El Paso, Tex., Sept. 10, 1955; s. Nathan H. and Marie (Saddler) E.; m. A. Jean Eudaly, Nov. 27, 1982; 1 child, Daniel. BA with honors, Baylor U., 1976; Postgrad., U. Tex./Southwestern Theol., Seminary; Exec. Edn., U. Pa., Duke U. Cert. managed healthcare profl. V.p., sec. and treas. Med Con, Inc., Ft. Worth, Tex., 1980-84; sr. v.p., chief fin. officer NYLCare Health Plan, Irving, Tex., 1984-99; chmn., pres., CEO, 1999—. Bd. dirs. NYLCare Health Plans of the Southwest, Inc., Irving, NYLCare Health Plans of the Gulf Coast, Inc.; exec. officer; adj. to com. that reviewed the HMO solvency regulations for the Tex. Dept. of Ins. Bd. dirs., past pres. Ft. Worth Civic Orchestra; bd. dirs. The Family Place - Dallas County, exec. com., treas. bd. dirs., chair fin. com. Mem. Am. Acad. Med. Adminstrs., Am. Mgmt. Assn., Baylor U. Fin. Officers Assn., DFW Health Industry Coun., Healthcare Fin. Mgmt. Assn. Mem. Vineyard Fellowship. Avocation: performing and visual arts. Office: Nylcare Health Plans 4500 Fuller Dr Irving TX 75038-6529

EUGENE, JOHN, lawyer; b. Glen Cove, N.Y., Aug. 18, 1940; s. Edward and Asimina (Stergionis) E. BS, St. Peter's Coll., Jersey City, 1961; JD, Rutgers U. Newark, 1964. Bar: N.J. 1966, D.C. 1968, U.S. Dist. Ct. N.J. 1966, U.S. Supreme Ct. 1970, N.Y. 1972, Fla. 1977, U.S. Dist. Ct. (so. and ea. dists.) N.Y. 1984. Spl. agt. U.S. Treasury Dept., Washington, 1965-67; pvt. practice Metuchen, N.J., 1967—. Mem. Nat. Coll. Criminal Def. Lawyers (grad. charter class 1972). Office: 475 Main St PO Box 449 Metuchen NJ 08840-0449

EUGENIDES, JEFFREY, writer; b. Detroit, Mich., Mar. 8, 1960; married; 1 child. BA in English magna cum laude, Brown U., 1983; MA in English and Creative Writing, Stanford U., 1986. Fellow Berliner Kunstlerprogramm of DAAD, Am. Acad. Berlin. Author: (book) The Virgin Suicides, 1993, Middlesex, 2002 (Pulitzer prize for fiction, 2003); contbr. fiction to popular mags. and anthologies. Recipient Whiting Writer's award, Henry D. Vursell Meml. award, Am. Acad. Arts and Letters, Pulitzer prize for fiction, 2003; fellow, Guggenheim Found., NEA. Office: Farrar Straus & Giroux 19 Union Sq W New York NY 10003

EUGSTER, ALBRECHT KONRAD, veterinarian, laboratory director, emeritus; b. Langenegg, Austria, Dec. 10, 1938; came to US, 1964; s. Anton Ferdinand and Joseffina (Laesser) E.; m. Kathe Ella Dittrich, Feb. 12, 1965; children— Cristopher, Susan D.V.M., Vet. Coll., Vienna, Austria, 1963; PhD, Colo. State U., 1970. Diplomate Am. Coll. Vet. Microbiologists. Practice vet. medicine, Austria, 1963-64; rsch. assoc. S.W. Found. Rsch. and Edn., San Antonio, 1964-67; head diagnostic microbiology Tex. Vet. Med. Diagnostic Lab., Coll. Sta., 1970-80, exec. dir., 1980- 2002, vet. med. cons., 2002—. Columnist jour. The Cattleman Mem. Am. Assn. Vet. Lab. Diagnosticians (pres. 1987), AVMA, Tex. Veterinary Med. Assn. (Disting. Achievement award 1984), World Assn. Vet Lab Diognosticians (pres. 1999-2001), Am. Veterinarian Epidemiology Soc. (hon. diploma) Lodges: Kiwanis (pres. 1984-85). Roman Catholic. Avocation: skiing. E-mail: keugster@tamu.edu.

EULE, NORMAN LOUIS, lawyer; b. Bklyn., Jan. 5, 1947; m. Ellen D. Luks, June 21, 1971; 1 child, Alex. BA in Polit. Sci. cum laude, Bklyn. Coll., 1968; JD with highest honors, George Washington U., 1974; postgrad., Columbia U., 1968-71. Bar: D.C. 1974. Assoc. Pierson, Ball & Dowd, Washington, 1974-81, ptnr., 1981-89, Reed, Smith, Shaw & McClay, 1989-94, Ridberg, Press & Sherbill LLP, Bethesda, Md., 1995—; adj. prof. Am. U./Washington Coll. of Law. Speaker and author tax, bus. and employee benefits matters. Mem. editl. bd. Tax Strategies; contbr. articles to profl. jours. Past pres. Congregation Beth El, Montgomery County, Md. Mem. ABA, Fed. Comm. Bar Assn., Bar Assn. of D.C., Bar Assn. of Md., Order of Coif. Office: Ste 650 Three Bethesda Metro Ctr Bethesda MD 20814 E-mail: neule@rpslaw.com.

EULERT, CORNEUAX H, drama therapist, educator; b. Bucharest, Romania, Dec. 11, 1942; arrived in US, 1974; d. Nicolae and Elisabeth Hancu; m. Donald Eulert, Aug. 10, 1974 (div. Aug. 1984); 1 child, Alexander. MFA, U. San Diego, 1974—79, Dramatic Arts Conservatory of Drama, 1961—66. Registered drama therapist Nat. Assn. of Drama Therapy. Actress Nat. Theatre, Romania, 1966—74; adj. prof., 1977—2000, drama therapist Kaiser Pomerante, Positive Choice Clinic, San Diego, 1993—. Author: Magic Chest, 1998. Recipient Best Debut award, Old Globe Theatre, San Diego, 1980; fellowship, Assn. of Teachers of Preventive Medicine, 1991—2001. Democrat. Greek Orthodox. Avocations: music, travel, art, theater. Office: Kaiser Pomerante 7035 Convoy Ct San Diego CA 92111

EURICH, NELL P. educator, author; b. Norwood, Ohio, July 28, 1919; d. Clayton W. and Adah (Palmer) Plopper; m. Alvin C. Eurich, Mar. 15, 1953 (dec. 1987); children: Juliet Ann, Donald Alan; m. Maurice Lazarus, 1988. AA, Stephens Coll., 1939; BA, Stanford U., 1941, MA, 1943; PhD, Columbia U., 1959. Dir. student union U. Tex., 1942-43; resident counselor Barnard Coll., 1944-46; asst. to pres. Woman's Found., 1947-49; officer charge pub. relations State U. N.Y., 1949- 52; acting pres. Stephens Coll., 1953-54; asst. prof. English NYU, 1959-64; academic dean New Coll., Sarasota, Fla., 1965; dir. project to reorganize curriculum Aspen (Colo.) Pub. High Sch., 1966; dean faculty, prof. English Vassar Coll., 1967-70; provost, dean faculty, prof. English, v.p. acad. affairs Manhattanville Coll., N.Y., 1971-75; sr. cons. Internat. Council for Ednl. Devel., 1975-82, Acad. for Ednl. Devel., 1982-88. Mem. nat. selection com., chmn. Rocky Mountain regional com. Nat. Endowment Humanities, 1966-67, cons., 1970-71; mem. Middle States commn. Marshall Scholarships, 1967-68; chmn. Northeastern region, 1969-71; mem. U.S. Commn. on Ednl. Tech., HEW, 1968-69; mem. overseer's vis. com. on summer sch. and univ. extension Harvard, 1969-75; mem. panel of judge's Fed. Woman's award, 1969; cons. Acad. for Ednl. Devel., 1970-71; mem. career minister rev. bd. U.S. Dept. State, 1972; participant Ditchley Conf. V, 1973; mem Rhodes Scholarship Selection Com., 1976; moderator exec. seminar Aspen Inst. for Humanistic Studies, 1977, 79, 80; dir. Adult Learning Project Carnegie Found. for Advancement Teaching, 1985-90; advisor Nat. Acad. of Engring., 1987-88; vis. com. Neuro Scis., Mass. Gen. Hosp. Author: Science in Utopia, 1967, Higher Education in Twelve Countries: A Comparative View, 1981, (with B. Schwenkmeyer) Great Britain's Open University, 1971, Corporate Classrooms, 1985, The Learning Industry, 1991; contbg. author: (Alvin Toffler) Learning for Tomorrow, 1974, From Parnassus: Essays for Jacques Barzun, 1976; contbr. articles to profl. jours. Past trustee Bank Street Coll., Salisbury Sch., Hudson Guild Neighborhood House, Colo. Rocky Mountain Sch., Bennington Coll.; trustee Carnegie Coun. on Policy Studies in Higher Edn., 1977—80, Carnegie Found. for Advancement of Teaching, 1978—84; trustee emeritus New Coll. Found., 1964—2001. Mem. MLA, Am. Assn. Colls. (spl. com. on liberal studies 1966-70), World Soc. Ekistics, Nat. Coun. Women (hon.), Century Assn. N.Y.C. Home: 144 Brattle St Cambridge MA 02138-2202

EURICH, RICHARD REX, lawyer; b. Lancaster, Pa., Apr. 12, 1947; s. Richard Roy and Mary Elizabeth (Kiehl) E.; m. JoAnn Samsa, June 27, 1970; 1 child, Richard. BA cum laude, Am. U., 1969; JD cum laude, Harvard U., 1972. Bar: Mass. 1972, U.S. Dist. Ct. Mass. 1973, U.S. Ct. Appeals (1st cir.) 1975. Assoc. Morrison, Mahoney and Miller, Boston, 1972-76, ptnr., 1976—. Elected Town Meeting Mem., Town of Lexington, 1996-99; mem. exec. bd. Lexington Town Meeting Mems. Assn., 1998-99, Lexington Appropriation Com., 2000— Fellow Mass. Bar Found.; mem. ABA, Mass. Bar Assn. (chmn. ins. com.), Def. Rsch. Inst., Mass. Def. Lawyers Assn., Internat. Assn. Def. Counsel. Roman Catholic. Home: 7 Pitcairn Pl Lexington MA 02421-7108 Office: Morrison Mahoney and Miller 250 Summer St Fl 1 Boston MA 02210-1181 E-mail: reurich@mail.mm-m.com.

EUSDEN, JOHN DYKSTRA, theology educator, minister; b. Holland, Mich., July 20, 1922; s. Ray Anderson and Marie (Dykstra) E.; m. Joanne Reiman, June 14, 1950; children: Andrea Bonner, Alan Tolles, John Dykstra Jr., Sarah Jewell. AB, Harvard U., 1943; postgrad., Harvard Law Sch., 1946; BD cum laude, Yale U., 1949, PhD in Religion, 1954. Ordained to ministry United Ch. of Christ, 1949. Instr. in religion Yale U., 1953-55, asst. prof., 1955-60; assoc. prof. religion, chaplain Williams Coll., Williamstown, Mass., 1960-70, Nathan Jackson prof. Christian theology, 1970-90, vis. prof. environ. studies, 1990-92; vis. prof. religion and asian studies Mt. Holyoke Coll., Mass., 1992-93; min. 1st Congl. Ch., Bennington, Vt., 1991—; cons. Asian programs and environ. studies Williams Coll., Williamstown, Mass., 1992—. Lectr., research fellow Kyoto U., 1963-64, 76, 81-82; theologian-in-residence Am. Ch. in Paris, 1972; lectr. Doshisha U., Kyoto, Japan, 1976, 82; bd. dir. Associated Kyoto Program, Japan. Author: Puritans, Lawyers and Politics in Early 17th Century England, 1958, 68, Zen and Christian: The Journey Between, 1981, The Spiritual Life: Learning East and West, 1982, (with John H. Westerhoff III) Sensing Beauty: Aesthetics, the Human Spirit, and the Church, 1998, Thirsting for Healing and Wholeness, 2003; contbr. articles to profl. jours.; translator, editor, author introduction: The Marrow of Theology (William Ames), 1975, 86; author introduction: Zen Buddhism and Christianity in Y. Takeuchi Festschrift (Japanese edition), 1993, Christology: The Dialogue of East and West in Christology in Dialogue, 1993, Chinese Healing: A Practical Mysticism in John Sahadat Festschrift, 2002. Mem. adv. coun., campus ministry program Danforth Found., 1966-70; bd. dirs. Wellesley Coll. Parents Assn., 1972-75, pres., 1974-75; rsch. fellow Ctr. for Study of Japanese Religion, Kyoto, 1976-94; trustee Lingnan Found., N.Y.C., 1964—, Buxton Sch., Williamstown, Mass., 1970-83, Chewonki Found., Wiscasset, Maine, 2002—; leader trips, People's Republic of China, 1978, 81, 86, 88, 90, 94. 1st lt. USMCR, 1943-45. Scholar Harvard U.; faculty fellow Am. Assn. Theol. Schs., 1958-59, Sterling fellow Yale U., 1950-53, fellow Folger Shakespeare Libr., 1958-59, 71-72; Lilly postdoctoral grantee, 1963-64, Danforth campus ministry grantee, 1963-64; fellow Am. Council Learned Socs., 1967-68; Fulbright rsch. travel grantee, 1967-68; research fellow U. Utrecht, Netherlands, 1968; rsch. grantee Williams Coll., 1976. Mem. AAUP, Am. Acad. Religion, Am. Soc. Ch. History, Am. Soc. Christian Ethics, Nat. Assn. Coll. and Univ. Chaplains, Soc. Values in Higher Edn., Appalachian Mountain Club, Randolph Mountain Club (pres. 1973-75). Home: 75 Forest Rd Williamstown MA 01267-2028 Office: Williams Coll Stetson Hall Williamstown MA 01267

EUSKIRCHEN, GEORGE JOHN, business administration and economics educator; b. Cin., Sept. 25, 1941; s. George August and Roselle Margaret (Werner) E.; m. Carol Marie Iannitto, Sept. 7, 1965; children: Ghia Marie, Susanne Eugenie, George Werner. BA, U. Cin., 1963, PhD, 1974. Lectr., instr. U. Cin., 1967-73; asst. prof. bus. adminstrn. and econs. Thomas More Coll., Ft. Mitchell, Ky., 1973-75, assoc. prof., 1975—, chmn. dept., 1975-82, 89—. Pres. Cin. Foundry Co., 1970-81. Referee Jour. Econs., 1984—. Mem. Am. Econ. Assn., Miami Valley Bus. Economists, Omicron Delta Epsilon, Delta Tau Delta. Avocations: bicycling, tennis, golf. Office: Thomas More Coll Fort Mitchell KY 41017

EUSTACE, DUDLEY GRAHAM, diversified financial services company executive; b. July 3, 1936; m. Carol Diane Zakrajsek; 2 children. BA in Econs., U. Bristol. Chartered acct. With John Barrit & Son, Hamilton, Bermuda, 1962, Internat. Resort Facilities, Ont., 1963, Alcan Aluminium, Ltd., Montreal, Vancouver, Buenos Aires, Rio de Janeiro, Madrid & U.K., 1964-87, Brit. Aerospace plc, 1987, fin. dir., 1988-92; mem. group mgmt. com. Philips, 1992—, exec. v.p. fin., 1993-97, vice chmn., 1997—; now chmn. Smith & Nephew plc, London. Mem. coun. dept. exports, credits guarantee Resigweb, 1992; mem. supervisory bd. Aegon N.V.; mem. adv. coun. Bayerische Landes-Bank; chmn. supervisory bd. Origin N.V. Mem. Assn. Monetary Union Europe. Avocations: philately, gardening, reading. Office: Smith & Nephew plc Heron House 15 Adam St London WC2N 6LA England

EUSTER, JOANNE REED, retired librarian; b. Grants Pass, Oreg., Apr. 7, 1936; d. Robert Lewis and Mabel Louise (Jones) Reed; m. Stephen L. Gerhardt, May 14, 1977; children: Sharon L., Carol L., Lisa J. Student, Lewis and Clark Coll., 1953-56; BA, Portland State Coll., 1965; MLibrarianship, U. Wash., 1968, MBA, 1977; PhD, U. Calif., Berkeley, 1986. Asst. libr. Edmonds C.C., Lynnwood, Wash., 1968-73, dir. libr.-media ctr., 1973-77; libr. Loyola U., New Orleans, 1977-80; libr. dir. J. Paul Leonard Libr., San Francisco State U., 1980-86, Rutgers State U. N.J., New Brunswick, 1986-89, v.p. info. svcs., 1989-91, v.p. univ. librs., 1991-92; libr. dir. U. Calif., Irvine, 1992-97; ret., 1997. Cons. Coll. S.I., Union Ejidal, La Penita, Nayarit, Mexico, 1973, Univ. D.C., 1988; co-cons. Office of Mgmt. Svcs. Assn. of Rsch. Librs., 1979—; bd. regents, Kansas; mem. adv. coun. Hong Kong U. Sci. and Tech. Librs., 1988—, Princeton U. Libr., 1988-92, U. B.C., Can., 1991—. Author: Changing Patterns of Internal Communication in Large Academic Libraries, 1981, The Academic Library Director, Management Activities and Effectiveness, 1987; columnist Wilson Libr. Bull., 1993-95; contbr. articles to profl. jours. Pres. Seattle Repertory Orgn.; trustee Seattle Repertory Theatre. Mem. ALA, Calif. Libr. Assn., Assn. Coll. and Rsch. Librs. (pres. 1987-88), Rsch. Librs. Group (chair bd. dirs. 1991-92).

EUSTICE, FRANCIS JOSEPH, lawyer; b. LaCrosse, Wis., Feb. 2, 1951; s. Frank R. and Cecelia T. (Babler) E.; m. Mary J. McCormick, July 28, 1971; children: Cristen L., Tara L. BS in Chemistry, Kansas Newman Coll., 1976; JD, U. Wis., 1980. Bar: Wis. 1980, U.S Dist. Ct. (ea. and we. dists.) Wis. 1980, U.S. Tax Ct. 1981, U.S. Ct. Appeals (7th cir.) 1990, U.S. Dist. Ct. (no. dist.) Ill. 1993. With Eustice, Laffey & Sebranek, S.C. and predecessor firms, Sun Prairie, Wis., 1980—. Bd. dirs., pres. Sun Prairie Devel. Corp., 1989—. Bd. dirs. Exch. Ctr. for Prevention of Child Abuse, Inc., Dane County, Wis., 1984-95. Sgt. USAF, 1973-77. Mem. Wis. Bar Assn., Dane County Bar Assn., Sun Prairie C. of C. (bd. dirs., pres., amb. 1987—), Sun Prairie Exch. Club (sec., pres., bd. dirs. 1980—). Office: PO Box 590 100 Wilburn Rd Ste 202 Sun Prairie WI 53590-0590 E-mail: f.eustice@els-law.com.

EUSTICE, JAMES SAMUEL, legal educator, lawyer; b. Chgo., June 9, 1932; s. Burt C. and Julia (Bohon) E.; m. LaVaun Schild, Jan. 29, 1956 (dec. 1994); m. Carol Fonda, Nov. 1995; children: Cynthia, James M. BS, U. Ill., 1954, LLB, 1956; LLM in Taxation, NYU, 1958. Bar: Ill. 1956, N.Y. 1958. Assoc. White & Case, N.Y.C., 1958-60; prof. law NYU, 1960—; counsel Kronish Lieb, N.Y.C., 1970—. Author: (with Kuntz) Federal Income Taxation of Subchapter S Corporations, 2001, (with Bittker) Federal Income Taxation of Corporations and Shareholders, 2000. Mem. ABA, N.Y. State Bar Assn., Am. Coll. Tax Counsel, Order of Coif. Club: University (N.Y.C.). Republican. Presbyterian. Office: NYU Sch Law 40 Washington Sq S New York NY 10012-1005

EUSTICE, RUSSELL CLIFFORD, consulting company executive, academic director; b. Hackensack, N.J., July 11, 1919; s. Russell C. and Ethel (Hutchison) E.; m. Veronica B. Dabrowski, Mar. 14, 1946; children: Russell Clifford, David A., Paul M. BA, Colgate U., 1941; MBA, Am. U., 1973. With Vick Chem. Corp., N.Y.C., 1941-42, 46-47, Johnson & Johnson, N.Y.C., 1947-61, divsn. sales mgr., 1954-61; nat. sales mgr. Park & Tilford divsn. Schenley Affiliates, N.Y.C., 1961-62; pres. Mid-Atlantic Assos., Inc., Prospect Harbor, Maine, 1962—. Dir. Small Bus. Inst., Husson Coll., Bangor, Maine, 1979-88, alt. regional rep. New England Region - Svc. Corps. Ret. Execs., SBA, 1991—; asst. prof. bus. adminstrn., 1979-88; part-time instr. mktg. The Am. U., Washington, 1970-74; active VISTA; bus. develop. specialist Washington-Hancock Community Agy., 1989. Capt. AUS, 1942-46. Mem. Assn. Mil. Surgeons, Res. Officers Assn., Assn. Mktg. Educators, SBA, Alpha Tau Omega. Republican. Methodist. Home: 1732 Spring Lilly Ln Hillsborough NC 27278-8492 also: 211 S Gouldsboro Rd Gouldsboro ME 04607

EUSTIS, ALBERT ANTHONY, lawyer, diversified industry corporate executive; b. Mahanoy City, Pa., Nov. 8, 1921; m. Mary Hampton Stewart, Apr. 25, 1959; children: Thomas Stewart, David Anthony. BS, Columbia U., 1948; LL.B., Harvard U., 1951. Bar: N.Y. 1952, U.S. Dist. Ct. (So. dist.) N.Y 1955. Atty. firm Kelley, Drye & Warren, N.Y.C., 1951-61; atty. W.R. Grace & Co., N.Y.C., 1961-66, asst. gen. counsel, 1966-76, v.p., gen. counsel, sec., 1976-78, sr. v.p., gen. counsel, sec., 1978-82, exec. v.p., gen. counsel, sec., 1982-87; of counsel Holland & Knight, Washington, 1987—. Chmn. bd. trustees, spl. counsel Found. for President's Pvt. Sector Survey on Cost Control; adj. prof. law Fordham Law Sch. Served with AUS, 1942-46. Mem. ABA, Am. Arbitration Assn. (bd. dirs., comml. arbitration panel)

EUSTIS, LYNN ELEANOR, music educator, vocalist; b. Bklyn., N.Y. d. Richard James and Carole Anne Eustis. MusB, Bucknell U., 1987; MusM, Curtis Inst. Music, 1990; MusD, Fla. State U., 1998. Opera soloist Nat. Opera Co., Raleigh, NC, 1991—93; asst. prof. voice/opera Howard Payne U., Brownwood, Tex., 1998—99; chair voice dept. Belvoir Ter. Fine Arts Program, Lenox, Mass., 1998—2001; asst. prof. voice U. North Tex. Coll. Music, Denton, 1999—. Chair dr. musical arts com. U. North Tex. Coll. Music, Denton, 2002—; master class clinician Des Moines Metro Opera, Indianola, Iowa, 2002. Singer: (soloist) Mahler Festival, 2002, 2003, (baroque opera soloist) Les arts florissants, Concert Royal; singer/historian (lecture recital) Vocal Music in Theresienstadt 1941-45; singer/historian: Concert Royal, 2002; singer: (oratoro soloist) Mozart Great Mass in C Minor, (soloist) Various Repertoire, (concert soloist) Carmina burana (Orff). Recipient First Pl. Opera Competition, Suncoast Opera Guild, 1998; scholar, Tallahassee Opera Guild, 1997; Grad. Tchg. Assistantship, Fla. State U., 1995—98, Dissertation Rsch. Travel grantee, 1997—98. Mem.: Coll. Music Soc., Nat. Assn. Tchrs. Singing (bd. mem. Dallas-Ft. Worth chpt.), Phi Beta Kappa (Mu chpt.). Home: 2411 Interstate 35E South #1722 Denton TX 76210 Office: Univ North Texas Coll Music PO Box 311367 Denton TX 76203-1367 Office Fax: 940-565-2002. E-mail: leustis@music.unt.edu.

EUSTIS, RICHMOND MINOR, lawyer; b. New Orleans, Nov. 24, 1945; s. David and Molly Cox (Minor) E.; m. Catherine Luise Baños, Apr. 15, 1971; children: Richmond Minor Jr., Julie Bransford, Joshua Leeds, Molly Minor. BA in Econs., U. Va., 1967; JD, Tulane U., 1970. Bar: La. 1970. Assoc. Phelps Dunbar, New Orleans, 1970-75; ptnr. Monroe and Lemann, New Orleans, 1975-96; founder, ptnr. Eustis, O'Keefe & Gleason LLC, New Orleans, 1996—. Bd. dirs. New Orleans Bd. of Trade. Bd. dirs. Children's Bur., 1976-88, treas., 1984. Mem. La. Bar Assn., New Orleans Bar Assn. (chmn. torts and ins. com. 1992-95), Maritime Law Assn., S.E. Admiralty Law Inst., Am. Inns of Ct., Boston Club, La. Club. Republican. Episcopalian. Avocation: fishing. Home: 289 Audubon St New Orleans LA 70118-4841 Office: Eustis & O'Keefe 228 Saint Charles Ave Ste 1010 New Orleans LA 70130-2686

EUSTIS, ROBERT HENRY, mechanical engineer; b. Mpls., Apr. 18, 1920; s. Ralph Warren and Florence Louise E.; m. Katherine Vik Johnson, Mar. 20, 1943; children— Jeffrey Nelson, Karen V. B.M.E., U. Minn., 1942, MS, 1944; Sc.D., M.I.T., 1953. Instr. U. Minn., 1942-44; research scientist NASA, 1944-47; asst. prof. M.I.T., 1947-51; chief engr. Thermal Research and Engring. Corp., 1951-53; mgr. heat and mech. sect. S.R.I. Internat., 1953-55; mem. faculty dept. mech. engring. Stanford U., 1955-90, prof., 1962, dir. high temperature gasdynamics lab, 1961-80, assoc. dean engring., 1984-88. Chmn. tech. adv. coun. Emerson Electric Corp.; prin Eustis Designs, 1990—. Contbr. articles to profl. jours. Recipient medal Soviet Sci. Acad., 1973 Fellow: AAAS, ASME, AIAA. Home: 862 Lathrop Dr Palo Alto CA 94305-1053 Office: Stanford Univ Dept Mech Engring Stanford CA 94305 E-mail: rheustis@stanford.edu.

EUTSEY, DWAYNE EUGENE, writer, editor; b. Havre de Grace, Md, Oct. 10, 1964; s. Sara Laverne and David Arnold Rhoades(Stepfather); m. Amy Louise Jordan, Jan. 12, 1967; children: Jordan, Gina, Martin. B, U. Md., 1988; cert. in theol. studies, Georgetown U., 1993, M in Liberal Studies, 1997. Web editor, asst. newsletter editor Phillips Internat., Inc., Potomac, Md., 2000—01; sr. comm. expert Delmarva Found., Easton, Md., 2001—. Adj. instr. U. Md., Coll. Pk., United States, 1999; instr. Georgetown U. Sch. Summer and Continuing Edn., Washington, 1999. Editor: (book) Palliative Care Patient & Family Counseling Manual, 1997; contbr. articles to profl. jour. Literacy tutor Montgomery County Literacy Coun., Rockville, Md., 1991—92; grief counselor, peace activist Hospice Frederick (Md.) County. Scholar Mark Twain scholar. Mem.: Unitarian Universalist (v.p., Easton). Unitarian Universalist. Avocations: guitar, poetry, community activism. Home: 9 Wrightson Ave Easton MD 21601 Personal E-mail: deutsey@hotmail.com.

EVAN, BRYAN J. electronics executive; b. Great Falls, Va. m. Sarah Evan; 2 children. BA, St. Anselm Coll., 1983. With engring. and prodn. support segment Raytheon Co.; pres. Raytheon Tech. Svcs. Co., 2001—; v.p. Raytheon Co., Reston, Va., 2002—. Office: Raytheon Co Ste 500 12160 Sunrise Valley Dr Reston VA 20191*

EVAN, WILLIAM MARTIN, sociologist, educator; b. Ostrow, Poland, Dec. 17, 1922; BA, U. Pa., 1946; PhD, Cornell U., 1954. Instr. sociology Princeton U., 1954-56; asst. prof. Columbia U., 1956-59; research sociologist Bell Telephone Labs., Murray Hill, N.J., 1959-62; assoc. prof. sociology and mgmt. MIT, 1962-66; prof. U. Pa., Phila., 1966—. Cons. to govt. agys. and pvt. industry, 1960—; Ford vis. prof. sociology Grad. Sch. Bus., U. Chgo., 1971-72; vis. fellow Wolfson Coll., U. Oxford, 1978-79. Author: (with others) Preventing World War III, 1962, Law and Sociology, 1962, Organizational Experiments, 1971, Interorganizational Relations, 1976, Organization Theory, 1976, Frontiers in Organization and Management, 1980, The Sociology of Law, 1980, Knowledge and Power in a Global Society, 1981, The Arms Race and Nuclear War, 1987, Social Structure and Law, 1990, Organization Theory. Research and Design, 1993, (with Ved P. Nanda) Nuclear Proliferation and the Legality of Nuclear Weapons, 1995, (with Mark Manion) Minding the Machines: Preventing Technological Disasters, 2002. Social Sci. Rsch. Coun. tng. fellow, 1951-52, Fulbright fellow, 1952-53; Russell Sage Found. resident, 1956-58. Fellow AAAS; mem. Am. Sociol. Assn., Internat. Sociol. Assn., Internat. Inst. Mgmt. Scis., Law and Soc. Assn., Internat. Studies Assn. Clubs: U. Pa. Faculty, Phila. Art Alliance. Home: 311 S Smedley St Philadelphia PA 19103-6717 Office: Dept Sociology and Dept Mgmt Univ Pa Philadelphia PA 19104 E-mail: evanw@wharton.upenn.edu.

EVANGELATOS, GREGORY GERASIMOS, city planner; b. Torrance, Calif., July 27, 1949; s. Gerasimos and Sophie E.; m. Jeanine Marie VanDeVort, Mar. 24, 1978; 1 child, Gregory Michael. BA, UCLA, 1971; M of Regional and City Planning, U. Okla., 1974. Cert. planner AICP. Asst. planner City of Manhattan Beach, Calif., 1975-77; cmty. planner Washoe Coun. of Govt., Reno, 1977-78; zoning enforcement City of Sparks, Nev., 1978-80, sr. planner, 1980-84, prin. planner, 1984-87, planning dir., 1987-95; v.p., prin. planner FPE Engring. and Planning, Reno, 1995—2003; devel. mgr. Landmark Homes and Devel., Inc., Carson City, Nev., 2003—. Chmn. ad-hoc zoning comm. City of Reno, 1997-99, regional transp., 1991; mem. comm., tech. adv. chmn. Gov.'s CDBG State of Nev., Carson City, 1987. Bd. dirs. YMCA, Reno-Sparks, 1992-94; mem. We. Inds. Nev., Reno, 1998—, Am. Hellenic Edn. Progressive Assn., Reno, 1986—. Recipient Mayor's commendation City of Sparks, 1983, Gov.'s Energy award, State of nev., Carson City, 1987, Outstanding Planning Accomplishment award Am. Planning Assn., Las Vegas, 1992. Mem. Exec. Assn., Econ. Devel. Authority, Urban Land Inst., No. Nev. Network, Nev. Am. Planning Assn. (pres. 1978—, Planner of Yr. 1990). Democrat. Home: 1365 Hilltop Rd Reno NV 89509-3973 Office: Landmark Homes & Devel Inc PO Box 21670 3086 Silversage Dr Ste 101 Carson City NV 89701

EVANGELIOU, CHRISTOS C. researcher, educator; b. Kyrtoni, Lokris, Greece, Dec. 23, 1946; s. Constantinos I. Evangeliou and Maria I. Soteriou; m. Karen M. Weidenheim, Sept. 2, 1979. BA, U. Athens, Greece; MA, Emory U., PhD, 1979. From asst. to prof. Towson U., Md., 1996—. Vis. prof. Miss. State U., Stakrville, 1980—81, Appalachian State U., Boone, NC, 1984—85. Author: The Hellenic Philosophy; assoc. editor: journal Skepsis; co-editor: Jour. Neoplatonic Studies; contbr. articles to profl. jours. V.p. Internat. Soc. for Neoplatonic Studies, Norfolk, Va., 1997—2002. With Greek Army, 1970—72. Scholar Othon-Athena Stathatos, Athens Acad. Arts and Sciences, 1974—76. Mem.: Am. Philos. Assn. Achievements include research in Aristotle's Categories and Porphyry. Office: Towson University Philosophy Department 800 York Road Towson, MD Office Fax: 410-704-4398. Personal E-mail: cevang@aol.com. E-mail: cevangeliou@towson.edu.

EVANGELISTA, ALLAN, podiatrist, medical researcher; b. Quezon City, Manila, The Philippines, June 23, 1970; came to U.S., 1990; s. Go Guan and Ana Evangelista. BA in Biology, U. La Verne, Calif., 1991; MDiv in Family, Pastoral Care and Counseling, Fuller Theol. Sem., Calif., 1996; MPH in Epidemiology, Loma Linda U., Calif., 1998; D of Podiatric Medicine, Temple U., Phila., 2002. Ordained and lic. Evangel. min. Supr., administrv. asst. D.G. Engring. Works, Butuan City, The Philippines, 1988-90; host, server, cashier Coco's Bakery & Family Restaurant, Pomona, Calif., 1991-92; tchg. asst. U. La Verne, Calif., 1991; project supr., computer graphic designer Interior Corner, Monterey Park, Calif., 1992-93; inter libr. loan processor Fuller Sem. Libr., Pasadena, Calif., 1995-96; assoc. pastor New Life Christian Ctr., El Monte, Calif., 1992—; rsch. assoc. U. So. Calif. Cardiovasc. Lab., L.A., 1993—. Fin. investment analyst, San Gabriel, Calif., 1993—; fin. trustee New Life Christian Ctr., El Monte, Calif., 1994—, pastoral care/marriage counselor First Assembly of God Ch., El Monte, Calif., 1994—. Contbr. articles to med. jours. Vol. San Gabriel Valley Med. Ctr., 1992; med. outreach coord. First Assembly of God Ch., El Monte, 1994—; youth pastoring/Bible tchr. Christian Reform Ch., West Covina, Calif., 1995—; chaplain UCLA Med. Ctr., Westwood, 1996. Recipient Ednl. Excellence award Alpha Kappa Alpha, Chgo., 1995; Harding Found. scholar, 1995-96, Fuller Theol. Sem. scholar, 1995-96. Mem. AAAS, ACA, APHA, Am. Fedn. Med. Rsch. (trainee investigator award 1994), Internat. Assn. Marriage and Family Counselors, Am. Podiatric Med. Assn., Am. Heart Assn. (rsch. coun. 1999), Am. Diabetes Assn. Avocations: basketball, swimming, drawing, traveling, cooking. Home: 10231 Timberland Point Dr Tampa FL 33647-2836 E-mail: allevan@hotmail.com.

EVANGELISTA, ANITA LORETTA, freelance writer, psychologist, nurse, publishing executive; b. L.A., Nov. 9, 1952; d. Carl A. and Etta L. (Erickson) Anderson; m. Nick F. Evangelista, 1979; children: Jamie, Justin. Student, Pepperdine U., 1970-71, U. So. Calif., 1972; BSN, S.W. Mo. State U., Springfield, 2001, grad. nursing and psychology, 2001—. RN; cert. clin. hypnotherapist. Asst. to dir. internat. fin. Max Factor, L.A., 1972-73; asst. to 2d mgr. steel dept. Sumitomo Shoji, L.A., 1973-75; freelance writer, 1975—; columnist Mo. Farm Mag., Clark, 1984-87; adminstr. West Plains (Mo.) Coun. on Arts, 1986-91; editor Ranch Dog Trainer mag., West Plains, 1990-92; mng. editor Fencers Quar., 1999—. Spkr., lectr. Mid West Hypnosis Conv., Chgo., 1983; cons. film dir. R. Wise, Hollywood, Calif., 1977; reader Llewellyn Pub., 1997—. Author: Hypnosis-A Journey into the Mind, 1980, Dictionary of

Hypnotism, 1991, How to Develop a Low-Cost Family Food Storage System, 1995, How To Live Without Electricity and Like It, 1997, Backyard Meat Production, 1997, (with N. Evangelista) Blood Lust Chickens and Renegade Sheep: A First Timer's Guide to Country Living, 1999, (with N. Evangelista) Country Living is Risky Business, 2000, (with N. Evangelista) The Women Fencer, 2001; indexer: Tikkum Olam, 1996; contbr. articles to mags., periodicals including Mother Earth News, Sci. Digest, Reason, Chronicles, Backwoods Home, Small Farmers Jour., Practical Farmer of Iowa, Fate, Maine Organic Gardner, Dairy Goat Jour., numerous others. Vol. Ozark Med. Ctr., West Plains, 1995-98, ARC, 1999. Recipient TZ 1st prize Twilight Zone Mag., 1989, 1st place Fine Arts Heart of the Ozarks Fair, 1989. Mem.: Advanced Practice Nurses of the Ozarks, Parapsychology Assn., Mo. Psychol. Assn., Cath. Med. Assn., Ozark Area Psychol. Assn., Am. Psychology Soc., Internat. Assn. Clin. Hypnotherapists, Calif. Profl. Hypnotist Assn. (chpt. pres. L.A. 1976—82), Am. Soc. Clin. Hypnosis, Am. Holistic Nurses Assn., Am. Soc. Psychical Rsch., Sigma Theta Tau, Psi Chi, Alpha Sigma Lambda, Phi Theta Kappa. Roman Catholic. Achievements include research in apolipoprotein E4 in Alzheimer's linguistic expression; Parkinson's disease and visual scanning; Alzheimer's disease and divorce; assessing single-question screening tool for problem drinking; learning hypnotizability. E-mail: evangel@atlascomm.net.

EVANGELISTA, NICK FORREST, fencing master, writer, publisher; b. Glendale, Calif., Jan. 25, 1949; s. Joseph Norman and Marianne (Williamson) E.; m. Anita Loretta Evangelista, Aug. 5, 1979; children: Jamie Alexandre, Justin Alyn. Student, S.W. Mo. State U., 2001—. Fencing master Faulkner Sch. Fencing, L.A., 1973-81, Evangelista Sch. Fencing, L.A., 1981-85, Peace Valley, Mo., 1985—2000, Springfield, Mo., 2001—, St. Louis Classical Fencing Soc., 1998—, S.W. Mo. State U. Fencing Soc., 2001—; farmer Peace Valley, 1985—; historian, 1989—. Author: The Encyclopedia of the Sword, 1995, The Art and Science of Fencing, 1996, Fighting with Sticks, 1998, Blood-Lust Chickens and Renegade Sheep, 1999, The Inner Game of Fencing, 2000, Country Living Is Risky Business, 2000, The Woman Fencer, 2001; editor-in-chief Vet. Fencers Quar. aka Fencers Quarterly Mag., 1999—; fencing editor Ency. Brit., 2000—; contbr. articles to profl. jours. Fundraiser West Plains (Mo.) Coun. on Art, 1987-91. Recipient 1st Ann. Fiction awards Crosscurrents Mag., 1981. Mem. U.S. Fencing Assn., Nat. Soc. Collegiate Scholars, Phi Alpha Theta, Alpha Sigma Lambda. Roman Catholic. Avocations: paleontology, book collecting, cartooning, Latin. E-mail: evangel@atlascomm.net.

EVANOFF, GEORGE C. b. W. Deer, Pa., June 5, 1931; s. Christ and Luba (Georgieff) E.; m. Mary E. Yelavich, Nov. 21, 1964; 1 son, Michael. BS cum laude, U. Detroit, 1952, MBA, 1956. Engr. Gen. Motors Corp., Detroit, 1953-57; supervisory, mgmt. and exec. positions in sales, marketing, and product devel. Ford Motor Co., Dearborn, Mich., 1957-68; staff v.p. mktg., v.p. corporate planning, v.p. corporate devel. RCA Corp., N.Y.C., 1968-76; with Norton Simon, Inc., Los Angeles and New York, 1977-82; v.p. corp. planning, interim pres. Max Factor & Co., 1977-78; pres. Max Factor Internat., 1979-82; pres., chief exec. officer Cordura Publs., Inc., San Diego, 1984-86; mgmt. cons., 1987-88; pres., chief exec. officer Tago, Inc., Burlingame, Calif., 1989-92; ret. Ind. cons., pvt. investor, 1993-96. Commd. officer USAF, 1952—53, capt. Res. USAF. Roman Catholic.

EVANOFSKI, BERNARD PETER, Roman Catholic priest; b. Wilkes-Barre, Pa., June 18, 1948; s. Peter Thomas and Margaret Ann (Wilk) E. BA, Wilkes U., 1970; MA, Temple U., 1972; MDiv, Pope John XXIII Sem., Weston, Mass., 1986. Cert. sch. psychologist, Pa.; ordained priest, 1986. Psychologist Elwyn (Pa.) Inst., 1971-72, White Haven (Pa.) Ctr., 1972-75, Luzerne Intermediate Unit, Kingston, Pa., 1976-82; asst. pastor St. Mary's Ch., Dickson City, Pa., 1986-92; pastor St. Patrick's Ch., Nicholson, Pa., 1992-96, St. Anthony's Ch., Larksville, Pa., 1996-2001; parochial vicar St. Bernard Ch., Holmes, Fla., 2001—. Auditor Scranton (Pa.) Diocesan Tribunal, 1987-2001. Pres. Jr. Kosciuszko Assn., Wilkes-Barre, 1976-82. Mem.: Polish Am. Congress (rec. sec. 1976—82), KC (3d degree 2001). Democrat. Roman Catholic. Avocations: travel, swimming, fitness. Home: 4255 Gulf Dr Unit 111 Holmes Beach FL 34217 Office: St Bernard Church 248 South Harbor Dr Holmes Beach FL 34217

EVANS, ALBERT, dancer; b. Atlanta, Ga. Student, Patsy Bromleys Terpsichore Expressions, Sch. Am. Ballet, 1986. Mem. corps de ballet N.Y.C. Ballet, 1988—91, soloist, 1991—95, prin., 1995—. Dancer (ballets) Agon, Danses Concertantes, A Midsummer Nights Dream, The Nutcracker, Stravinsky Violin Concerto, Symphony in Three Movements, Gershwin Concerto, Ash, The Beethoven Seventh, Jeu de Cartes, Swan Lake, The Beethoven Seventh, The Sleeping Beauty, Appalachia Waltz, Steel and Rain, Open Strings, Swerve Poems, Duke!. Office: NYC Ballet NY State Theatre 20 Lincoln Ctr Plz New York NY 10023-6913

EVANS, ALFRED LEE, JR., advertising executive; b. Kansas City, Mo., Sept. 16, 1940; s. Alfred Lee and Laura Edith (Redman) E.; m. Jean Perpetua Corcoran, Aug. 29, 1970 (div. Mar. 1994); children: Amanda Corcoran, Cynthia Redman, Cassandra Lee, Nicholas Carpenter; m. Georgiana Coyle Mundy, July 9, 1994. BA, Princeton U., 1962. Account exec. Ted Bates & Co., N.Y.C., 1963-66, Papert Koenig Lois Inc., N.Y.C., 1967-68; v.p. account supr. Lois Holland Callaway, Inc., N.Y.C., 1969-74, v.p. mgmt. supr., 1975, sr. v.p. mgmt. supr., 1976, Norman Craig & Kummel, N.Y.C., 1977-80, Laurence, Charles, Free & Lawson, N.Y.C., 1981-84, 85—, exec. v.p., mem. ops., 1988-95, mem. bd. dirs.; sr. v.p. Wolf Group, N.Y.C., 1995-2000, Bates USA, NYC, 2000—. Recipient summer travel award Carnegie Found., 1960; scholar Princeton U., 1958-62. Episcopalian. Home: 1530 Palisade Ave Fort Lee NJ 07024-5470 Office: Bates USA 498 Seventh Ave New York NY 10018

EVANS, ARTHUR HAINES, JR., educational consultant, researcher; b. Mount Holly, N.J., Apr. 25, 1940; s. Arthur Haines and Betty Ogden (Dougherty) E.; m. Gay Dell Goodwin, Aug. 13, 1967; children: Kristna Jan, Ross Neil. AB cum laude, Princeton U., 1962; MBA, Stanford U., 1964; PhD in Higher Edn., U. Calif., Berkeley, 1970. Cert. cmty. supt., adminstr. and tchr., Calif. Bus. instr. City Coll. San Francisco, 1964-70; assoc. dean instrn. West Hills Coll., Coalinga, Calif., 1970-74; assoc. project dir. Pima C.C., Tucson, 1974-75, asst. to dean, 1975-79, asst. to pres., 1979-91; field faculty No. Ariz. U., Tucson, 1991—99; pres. Evans and Assocs., Tucson, 1991—. Rsch. cons. Pima County Interfaith Coun., Tucson, 1991-97; rsch. and evaluation coord. Ariz. Interfaith Network, 1998—. Bd. mem. Soc. for Coll. and Univ. Planning, 1977-79, United Way Greater Tucson, 1987-90; pres. Tucson Trade Bur., 1987-90, Tucson Almaty Sister Cities, 1990-92; founding pres. United Way of Ariz., 1989-90; mem. Common Govt. Rels. Coun. for Advancement of Edn., 1990-92. Kellogg fellow U. Calif., Berkeley, 1969. Methodist. Avocations: swimming, bicycling, hiking, traveling. Office: Evans and Assocs PO Box 43693 Tucson AZ 85733-3693

EVANS, BARTON, JR., analytical instrument company executive; b. Washington, Dec. 11, 1947; s. Barton and Viola (Gompf) E.; m. Harriet Andrea Neves, Nov. 20, 1983. BA in Econs., Claremont McKenna Coll., 1970; BS in Engring., MS in Engring., Stanford U., 1972. Sr. engr. Lockheed Missiles and Space Co., Sunnyvale, Calif., 1976-77, Dionex Corp., Sunnyvale, 1977-79, engring. mgr., 1979-81, dir. engring., 1981-83, v.p. engring., 1983-84, v.p. ops., 1984-93, sr. v.p. ops., 1993-2001, exec. v.p., COO, 2001—03; pvt. practice, 2003—. 1st lt. U.S. Army, 1972-75; col. USAR, 1976-2002, ret. 2002—. Mem.: ASME, Res. Officers Assn., Assn. U.S. Army, Psychol. Ops. Assn., Civil Affairs Assn. (dir.). Achievements include co-inventor conductivity detector. Office: Dionex Corp 541 Lakeside Dr Sunnyvale CA 94085-4003

EVANS, BERNARD WILLIAM, geologist, educator; b. London, July 16, 1934; came to U.S., 1961, naturalized, 1977; s. Albert Edward and Marjorie (Jordan) E.; m. Sheila Campbell Nolan, Nov. 19, 1962. BSc, U. London, 1955; PhD, Oxford U., Eng., 1959. Asst. U. Glasgow, Scotland, 1958-59; departmental demonstrator U. Oxford, 1959-61; asst. research prof. U. Calif., Berkeley, 1961-65, asst. prof., 1965-66, assoc. prof., 1966-69; prof. geology U. Wash., Seattle, 1969—2001, chmn. dept. geol. scis., 1974-79; emeritus prof. U. Washington, 2001—. Contbr. articles to profl. jours. Recipient U.S. Sr. Scientist award Humboldt Found., Fed. Republic Germany, 1988-89; Fulbright travel award, France, 1995-96. Fellow Geol. Soc. Am., Mineral Soc. Am. (pres. 1993-94, award 1970), Geochem. Soc., Geol. Soc. London, Mineral. Soc. Gt. Britain, Swiss Mineral. Soc. Home: 8001 Sand Point Way NE Apt C55 Seattle WA 98115-6399 Office: U Wash Dept Earth and Space Scis PO Box 351310 Seattle WA 98195-1310 E-mail: bwevans@u.washington.edu.

EVANS, BILL (JAMES WILLIAM EVANS), dancer, choreographer, educator, arts administrator; b. Lehi, Utah, Apr. 11, 1940; s. William Ferdinand and Lila (Snape) E.; married, Aug. 27, 1962 (div. 1965); 1 child, Thaïs. BA in English, U. Utah, 1963, MFA in Modern Dance, 1970; dance student various pvt. dance schs. and studios; cert. in laban and bartenieff, U. Utah, 1997. Apprentice Harkness Ballet Co., N.Y.C., 1966; mem. Chgo. Ballet and Lyric Opera Ballet, 1966-67; teaching asst. dept. ballet and modern dance U. Utah, 1967-68, faculty Virginia Tanner Creative Dance Program, 1968-73, asst. prof. modern dance, 1974-76, dancer, tchr., choreographer, artistic coordinator, mem. Repertory Dance Theatre, 1967-74; artistic dir. Dance Theatre Seattle, 1976-83; artistic dir., resident tchr., choreographer Winnipeg's Contemporary Dancers, Man., Can., 1983-84; assoc. prof., coord. dance program dept. kinesiology Ind. U., Bloomington, 1986-87, 87-88, artistic dir. Ind. Dance Theatre, 1986-88; head dance program dept. theatre and dance U. N.Mex., Albuquerque, 1988-93; prof. dance, 1993—; artistic dir. univ. Contemporary Dance Ensemble U. N.Mex., Albuquerque, 1989-93, dir., founder Univ. Youth Dance Camp, 1990, dir., founder Magnificio Youth Dance Groups, 1991-96. Artistic dir. Bill Evans Dance Co., toured U.S., Europe, Mex. 1975-99; Bill Evans Summer Insts. of Dance and Summer Festivals of Dance, Bill Evans Solo Dance Repertory, 1976—, Bill Evans Dance Co. Sch., Seattle; vis. prof. dance div. U. Wash., 1976-81; artistic advisor Fairmount Dance Theatre, Cleve., 1974-75; guest artist in residence Dance Dept., U. Utah; artist in resident Ill. U., Harvard U. Summer Sch., choreographer in residence Repertory Dance Theater; dir., choreographer N.Mex. Repertory Theatre, Santa Fe and Albuquerque; mem. Artists in Edn. Bank, Utah arts council; dance/movement specialist Artist-in-Schs. program Nat. Endowment for Arts; founder, dir. Celebrate Youth Summer Dance Inst., 1993-98; artistic coord. SW Am. Coll. Dance Festival, 1994; guest artist Kala Chhaya Cultural Ctr., India, 1993—; toured Karnataka, Maharastra, India. Free-lance dancer, 1969—, including Berlin Ballet, 1969, Jacob's Pillow Dance Festival, Lee, Mass., 1973, Harvard U., 1973, 74, 90; choreographer over 170 works for various ballet and modern dance cos., 1967—; mem. editl. bd. Dance Connections, 1997. Am. Arts Alliance rep. before House and Senate appropriations coms., 1979. Served as officer U.S. Army, 1963-65. Recipient various choreographic awards, grants and fellowships from Nat. Endowment for Arts, 1972-75, 77-83, Utah Bicentennial Com., 1976, Art Found., Western States Arts Fedn., Wash. Arts Commn., King County Arts Commn., Seattle Arts Commn., Man. Arts Council, Ind. Arts Commn., N.Mex. Arts Div., U. N.Mex. Found., U. N.Mex. Coll. Fine Arts, Ind. U., Multidisciplinary Ventures Fund, U. N.Mex. Rsch. Allocations Com., City of Albuquerque, BRAVO award Albuquerque Arts Alliance, 1997, 2003, N.Mex. Gov.'s award for excellence and achievement in the arts, 2001; Guggenheim fellow, 1976-77, Am. Coll. Dance Fest., regional awards, 1986,87, 89-90, nat., 1986, 90; recipient Teaching Plaudit award nat. Dance Assn., 1981, scholar artist, 1997; named adjudicator and guest artist 1st Nat. Ballet Festival Regional Dance Am., 1997-99. Mem. Dancers, Inc. (adv. bd.), Nat. Dance Assn. (chair performance divsn. 1993—), Am. Coll. Dance Festival Assn. (bd. dirs. 1992—, U.S. rep. 1st internat. coll. dance festival Japan 1993). Office: U NM Dance Program Ctr for the Arts Dance Program Fine Art Ctr Albuquerque NM 87131-0001 E-mail: beran@unm.edu.

EVANS, BOB OVERTON, electronics executive, director; b. Grand Island, Nebr., Aug. 19, 1927; s. Walter Bernard and Lillian (Overton) Evans; m. Maria Bowman, Nov. 19, 1949; children: Cathleen L., Robert W., David D., Douglas B. BEE, Iowa State U., 1949. Electric operating engr. No. Ind. Pub. Svc. Co., Hammond, 1949—51; with IBM, 1951—62, from v.p. devel. data systems divsn. to v.p. engring., programming and tech., 1962—84; ptnr. Hambrecht and Quist, 1984—88; mng. ptnr. Tech. Strategies and Alliances, Menlo Park, Calif., 1988—2001; pres., CEO Interactive Voice Systems, Monrovia, Calif., 1997—99; ptnr. Rocket Ventures, Menlo, 2002—. Mem. Rep. of China Sci. and Tech. Adv. Com., 1981—95; strategic adv. bd. Rep. of China, 1984—95; elec. engring. vis. com. MIT, Cambridge, 1971—85; chmn. Foothill Rsch. Inc., 1984—85, Cambridge Tech. Group, McLean, Va., 1999—, VCommand.com, 1999—; pres. Vanguard Internat. Semi-conductor Corp., 1995—96; pres., CEO Ridge Computers Inc., 1986—88; mem. Def. Sci. Bd., 1970—74, Stark Draper Labs., Inc., 1972—2001; bd. dirs. Md. Nat. Bank, Santa Barbara Labs., Integrated CMOS Sys., Inc., V Mark Software, Cullinet Software, Micrognosis, Inc., Athena Sys., Planning Rsch. Corp., Cambridge Rsch. Assocs. Excellence in Comms. Corp., Dotcast, Equator Techs.; bd. overseers Superconductivity Super Collider, 1991—93. Exec. bd. Nat. Capital Area coun. Boy Scouts Am., 1967—69; trustee Rensselaer Poly. Inst., 1972—84, N.Y. Pub. Libr., 1980—84; elder Presbyterian Ch. Lt. (j.g.) USNR, 1945—46. Named to Datamation Hall of Fame, 1987; recipient Disting. Pub. Svc. award, NASA, Disting. Alumni citation, Iowa State U., Disting. Achievement citation, 1991, Nat. medal of tech., 1985, Very Large-Scale Interpretation Outstanding Contbn. award, Republic of China, 2001. Fellow: IEEE (chmn. computer group conf. 1970, Armstrong award 1984), Assn. Computing Machines; mem.: Aerospace Industries Assn. (exec. bd.), Nat. Security Indsl. Assn., Profl. Group Electronic Computers, Nat. Acad. Engring. (trustee), Armed Forces Comm. and Electronics Assn. (trustee). Presbyterian. Achievements include design of large digital electric computers. Home: 170 Robin Rd Hillsborough CA 94010-6632 Office: Rocket Ventures #B-1S170 3000 Sand Hill Rd Menlo Park CA 94025-7113 E-mail: bevans6@attglobal.net.

EVANS, BONITA DIANNE, adult education educator; b. N.Y.C., Jan. 14, 1940; d. Roy Simon and Verna (Ashton) Evans; m. Robert John Watts, Aug. 1981 (div. 1996); 1 child, Helena Watts. BA, U. Canberra, Australia, 1990; MDS, Monash U., Melbourne, Australia, 1992; PhD, Walden U., Minn., 1996. With Dept. of Prime Minister and Cabinet, Australian Dept. Fgn. Affairs, Canberra, 1986—88; devel. rsch. officer Aboriginal Hostels, Canberra, 1986—88; cultural affairs asst. U.S. Embassy, Canberra, 1988—90; mem. Diplomatic Corps UN Mission to Nambia, S.W. Africa, 1978; field officer Israeli/Egyptian border UN Peacekeeping Forces, 1979—80; adj. prof. English Montclair State U., NJ, 1996—2000; vis. prof. Rutgers U., Newark, 1999—2000; mem. internat. adv. bd., literacy/ESL instr. New Cmty. Corp./Hispanic Devel. Corp, Newark, 2000—03; faculty African and African-Am. studies and Women's Studies depts. William Paterson U.; tchr. bilingual dept. Essex County Coll., 2003—. Author: Youth in Foster Care, 1997, Kijani, 2002, New Hope Rising, 2002.

EVANS, BRUCE DWIGHT, lawyer; b. Mt. Hope, W.Va., May 27, 1934; s. M. Albert and Eleanor E. (Fowler) E.; m. Sallie Lee Hazen, Aug. 24, 1957 (div. Jan. 1974); children: Scott C., Leigh F., Randolph D.; m. Doris M. Stritzinger Webster, Sept. 2, 1978. AB, Princeton U., 1956; LL.B., Harvard U., 1959. Bar: N.Y. 1960, Pa. 1970. Assoc. Debevoise, Plimpton, Lyons & Gates, N.Y.C., 1959-68; ptnr. Reed Smith Shaw & McClay, Pitts., 1969-96. Trustee Ellis Sch., Pitts., 1972-78. Mem. ABA, Pa. Bar Assn., Allegheny County Bar Assn., Rivers Club, Phi Beta Kappa Republican. Episcopalian. Office: 625 Liberty Ave Ste 2800 Pittsburgh PA 15222-3110

EVANS, CAROL ROCKWELL, nursing administrator; b. New Orleans, Jan. 8, 1953; d. Daniel Raymond Sr. and Helen (Fischer) Rockwell; divorced; children: Nikki Elizabeth, Mimi Michelle. ADN, La. State Med. Ctr., 1990. RN, La.; cert. ACLS, BLS, cert. case mgr.; lic. life and health ins. agent. Life and health ins. agt. La. Ins. Agts. Assn., New Orleans, 1975-95; dir. case mgmt. and utilization rev. Associated Med. Rev. Svcs., Metairie, La., 1986-95; charge nurse med-surg. telemetry unit Elmwood Med. Ctr., Jefferson, La., 1990—; RN specialist III ICU dept. St. Charles Gen. Hosp., New Orleans, 1993—; dir. med. mgmt. Nat. Health Resources, Inc., Metairie, La., 1995-99, Med. Care Solutions, Inc., 1999—2002; owner Case Mgmt. Svcs., Metairie, 2002—. Lobby La. Health Care, Baton Rouge, 1991. Mem. ANA, NAFE, Case Mgmt. Soc. Am., Individual Case Mgmt. Assn., Assn. Respiratory Care, New Orleans Continuity Care, La. Managed Healthcare Assn. (Great Nurses award 1997). Republican. Roman Catholic. Avocations: sports, dancing, swimming, traveling, theater. Home: 6316 York St Metairie LA 70003-3557 Office: Case Mgmt Svcs PO Box 74137 Metairie LA 70033-4132 E-mail: CRocky108@aol.com.

EVANS, C(AROLINE) SUE, educator; b. Bethel, Ohio, July 14, 1948; d. Raymond George Brown and Relva Olive Spears-Brown; m. Gary W. Evans, June 18, 1966; children: Rhonda Fannin, Gary Lee, Daniel Ray, Rebekah Sue, David Jonathan. Assoc. of Applied Bus., So. State C.C., Hillsboro, Ohio, 1989; BS, Wilberforce U., 1999. Leader, lectr. Weight Watchers, Inc., West Union, Ohio, 1974-80; lab. asst. So. State C.C., Sardinia, Ohio, 1989-92, 93-99, coord., instr., 1999—; project sec. Ford Motor Co., Batavia, Ohio, 1992-93, coord./instr., 1999—. Adv. bd. mem. Your Place Bd., Sardinia, Family/Cons. Sci., Seaman, Ohio. Author: Broken Wings Fly, 2003. Bd. dirs. United Ch. of God, South Portsmouth, Ohio, Adam Brown Counties Econ. Opportunities Inc., 2001—. Mem.: Take Off Pounds Sensibly (leader). Home: 1525 Moores Rd Seaman OH 45679 Office: So State CC 12681 US 62 Sardinia OH 45171 E-mail: sevans@sscc.edu.

EVANS, CHARLES ALBERT, microbiology educator; b. Mpls., Feb. 18, 1912; s. Albert Grant and Susan Briery (Thompson) E.; m. Allie Ann Christman, Dec. 22, 1939; children: Nicholas J. (dec.), Susan Ethel, Thomas Charles, Carol Ann. BS, U. Minn., 1935, MD, 1937, PhD, 1943. Diplomate Am. B. Med. Microbiology. NRC fellow U. Rochester, 1941-42; rsch. supr. Minn. State Dept. Conservation, Mpls., 1942-43; asst. prof. dept. bacteriology U. Minn., Mpls., 1942-44, assoc. prof. dept. bacteriology, 1944-46; assoc. dir. Fred Hutchinson Cancer Rsch. Ctr., Seattle, 1971-75; prof. dept. microbiology U. Wash., Seattle, 1946-82, chmn., 1946-70, prof. emeritus, 1982—. Mem. nat. cancer coun. USPHS, Bethesda, Md., 1958-59,64-67; chmn. rsch. adv. coun. Am. Cancer Soc., 1967-70. Contbr. over 100 articles to profl. jours. Recipient numerous rsch. grants from NIH and Am. Cancer Soc. Mem. Am. Soc. for Microbiology (hon., pres. 1959-60), Soc. for Infectious Diseases (emeritus), Am. Assn. for Cancer Rsch. (emeritus), Am. Acad. Microbiology (mem. bd. govs. 1959-65, chmn. 1960-61). Avocations: birding, photography. Home: 7739 29th Ave NE Seattle WA 98115-4616 Office: U Wash Sch Medicine Dept Microbiology Seattle WA 98195-0001 E-mail: evansmic@u.washington.edu.

EVANS, CHARLES H. federal judge; b. 1922; BA, U. Ill., 1947, JD, 1948. Asst. atty. gen. State of Ill., 1949—56, 1962—76; pvt. law practice, 1957—62; magistrate judge Ill. Ctrl., Springfield, 1977—. Served with USAAF, 1942—45. Office: 110 US Courthouse 600 E Monroe St Springfield IL 62701-1626

EVANS, CHARLES HAWES, JR., immunologist, health science educator; b. Orange, N.J., Apr. 16, 1940; s. Charles Hawes and Jean Marie (Robinson) E.; m. Nancy Margaret Engel, Aug. 21, 1965; 1 child, Heather Leigh. BS, Union Coll., Schenectady, N.Y., 1962; MD, PhD, U. Va., 1969. Diplomate Nat. Bd. Med. Examiners. Intern in pediatrics U. Va., Charlottesville, 1969-70, resident in pediat., 1970-71; rsch. assoc. Nat. Cancer Inst., Bethesda, Md., 1971-75, chief tumor biology sect., 1975-98; commd. capt. USPHS, Bethesda, 1971-98; sr. advisor for biomed. and clin. rsch. Nat. Acad. Scis., Washington, 1998—2002; prof. health studies Georgetown U., Washington, 2002—. Mem. arts and scis. coun. U. Va., 1987-97, v.p., 1993-97; trustee Suburban Hosp., Bethesda, 1988-97. Contbr., co-contbr. over 125 med. and sci. articles to profl. jours. Recipient John Horsley prize for med. rsch. U. Va., 1982, officers citation USPHS, 1980, commendation medal, 1985, unit commendation, 1992, Outstanding Svc. medal 1996; Sir Henry Wellcome medal and prize Assn. Mil. Surgeons U.S., 1990. Fellow AAAS, Am Inst. Chemists, Am. Acad. Med. Adminstrs.; mem. Am. Assn. for Cancer Rsch., Am. Assn. Immunologists, Am. Coll. Physician Execs., Clin. Immunology Soc. (charter), Azalea Soc. Am. (gov. 1983-89, editor The Azalean Jour. 1983-88, Frederic P. Lee commendation 1984, Disting. Svc. award 1989), Sigma Xi, Alpha Omega Alpha. Democrat. Presbyterian. Avocations: horticulture, piano, philately. Home: 9233 Farnsworth Dr Potomac MD 20854-4504 Office: Georgetown U Sch Nursing and Health Studies 3700 Reservoir Rd NW Washington DC 20057 E-mail: che3@georgetown.edu.

EVANS, CHARLES WAYNE, II, biologist, researcher; b. Athens, Ohio, Aug. 9, 1929; s. Charles Wayne nd Florence Louise (Sheets) Evans Claypool; m. Jo F. Burt, 1978 (div. 1959); children: Charles Wayne III, James Friedrich (dec.), John Burns, Elizabeth Burt; m. Patricia Anne Baker, 1971; children: Debbie Jo, Caralyn Michele. Student, Tex. A&M U., 1947-51, BA, 1957, postgrad., 1963-65, U. Houston, 1969-70. Seismologist Universal Seismic Expt., Beaumont, Tex., 1958-65; marine biologist CRI/VIERS, St. Thomas, U.S. Virgin Islands, 1965-71; geologist Dr. C. B. Claypool, Beaumont, Tex., 1971-76; research biologist Panthera-Marine-Internat., Ltd., Belize, C.A., Beaumont, pres., chief exec. officer, 1976—; research biologist Synetics Inc. Las Vegas, 1979-82, bd. dirs., treas., 1979; research biologist SAC Research Ctr., 1982-88; pres. Jordhammer, Inc., Las Vegas, 1980—; bd. dirs. Ant Fire, Inc., Beaumont, 1985-89, Caribbean World enterprises, Ltd., New Orleans & Belize, 1987—; pres., dir. rsch. Invicta Corp., 1988. Cons. I.Q. Tech., Houston, 1994—96, Eradicator Corp., Houston, 1994—98, Aire-Mate Inc., Westfield, Ind., Terminator Techs., Inc., San Jose, Calif., 1999. Co-inventor Jordhammer, 1982, Earthfire Injection System, 1988. Sus. mem. Rep. Nat. Com., Washington, 1982; charter mem. Ellis Island Found., N.Y.C., 1983—; founder, pres. Caribbean Inst. Natural Sci., St. Thomas, 1967-70; with N.G., 1945-47. SAC Research Ctr. grantee, 1983, Dr. C.B. Claypool grantee, 1963, 78. Mem. AAAS, Smithsonian Assocs., Am. Mus. Natural History (assoc.)., N.Y. Acad. Sci., Internat. Oceanographic Found., Entomol. Soc. Am., World Wildlife Fund, Aggie Club, Century Club, Lions. Avocations: music, chess, big game fishing.

EVANS, CHARLIE ANDERSON, chemist; b. Columbus, Ga., Dec. 29, 1945; s. James William and Mollie Ree (Carter) E.; m. Phyllis Angela Roberts, Dec. 16, 1967 (div. 1992); children: Timothy Anderson, Laurin Stephen, Paul Thomas. BS, Ga. Inst. Tech., 1968; PhD, U. Ga., 1974. Postdoctoral fellow Centre d'Etudes Nucleaire, Grenoble, France, 1973-74, U. Western Ont., London, 1974-76; applications chemist Varian Assocs., Florham Park, N.J., 1976-80, JEOL, Cranford, N.J., 1980-81, mgr. applications lab., 1981-84; scientist Berlex Labs., Cedar Knolls, N.J., 1984-87; sr. prin. scientist Schering-Plough Corp., Bloomfield, N.J., 1987-90, devel. fellow, 1990—. Part-time insr. Ga. Inst. Tech., Atlanta, 1967-68; adj. asst. prof. Drew U., Madison, N.J., 1978; adj. prof. Fairleigh Dickinson U., 1988—. Contbr. articles to profl. jours. With U.S. Army, 1969-71. Muscogee Found. scholar, 1964-68; NSF summer fellow, 1967; NDEA Title IV fellow, 1971-73; Fulbright-Hays fellow, 1973-74. Mem. AAAS, Am. Chem. Soc. (chmn. NMR discussion group 1988, 94), N.Y. Acad. Sci., Internat. Soc. Magnetic Resonance. Democrat. Presbyterian. Office: Schering Plough Rsch Inst K15-0450 2015 Galloping Hill Rd Kenilworth NJ 07033-1300 E-mail: charlie.evans@spcorp.com., andy.evans@verizon.net.

EVANS, CHARLOTTE MORTIMER, communications consultant, writer; b. Newton, NJ, Nov. 26, 1933; d. Karl Otto and Wilhelmina (Otterbach) Pfau; m. John Atterbury Mortimer, Nov. 20, 1964; children: Meredith Elizabeth, Mandy Leigh; m. G. Robert Evans, Sept. 4, 1982. Student, Douglass Coll., 1952—54; BS, RN, Columbia U. Presby. Hosp., 1957; postgrad., Columbia U. Presbyn. Hosp., 1957—59, NYU, 1959—60; MPA, Coll. of Notre Dame, 1979. Spl. assignment nurse Columbia-Presbyn. Med. Center, N.Y.C., 1957—59; med. advt. copywriter Paul Klemtner & Co., N.Y.C., 1959—61, William Douglas McAdams Agy., N.Y.C., 1961—62; account exec. Arndt, Preston, Chapin, Lamb & Keen, N.Y.C., 1962—63; Rocky Mountain corr. Med. World News, Denver, 1963—64; owner Publicite, Denver; gen. mgr. Center Mktg. Assn., Palo Alto, Calif., 1964—66; freelance writer, pub. rels. and mgmt. cons. Woodside, Calif., 1966—85; pres. Communications for Youth, 1979—. Mem. Palo Alto-Stanford Hosp. Aux., 1968—72; pub. rels. assistance Peninsula Children's Ctr., Palo Alto, 1968—73, Triton Mus. Art, San Jose, Calif., 1966—70; health component Early Childhood Com. Woodside Elem. Sch. Dist.; past chair, mem., bd. dirs. ct.-apptd. spl. advocate program CASA-Kane County, 1989—96; mem. San Mateo County Mental Health Adv. Bd., Friends of Woodside Libr. Bd., 1983—85, Nat. CASA advocate program, 1989; vol. Nat. Com. for Prevention Child Abuse and Neglect, 1987—96; acting chair founder Chicagoland Media & Children Com., 1993—96; adv. com Our Children's Place, Kane County, 1995—98; mem. Rep. Senatorial Inner Cir. 1982—86; chmn. citizens adv. com. San Mateo County Juvenile Social Svcs. mem. adv. com. South County Youth and Family Svcs. Program; mem Statewide Citizens Adv. Com. on Child Abuse and Neglect, Ill. Dept. Children and Family Svcs., 1987-1999, 1987—99; chair adv. com. to Congressman Dennis Hastert on Family and Child Legis., 1990—92; bd. dirs. N.J. Jr. C. of C./UNICEF/African Project, 1960—61, Natividad Ranch, first-time offender program, 2001—, Friends of the Monterey Symphony, 2000—. Home and Office: PO Box 223380 Carmel CA 93922-3380

EVANS, CHERYL LYNN, elementary school principal; b. Dec. 22, 1956; BS, Okla. State U., 1988, MS, 1998. Tchr. Olive (Okla.) Elem. Sch., 1988-90, Sunnyside Elem. Sch., Cushing, Okla., 1990-98, prin., 1998—. Home: PO Box 723 Stillwater OK 74076

EVANS, DANIEL FRALEY, JR., lawyer; b. Indpls., Apr. 19, 1949; s. Daniel Fraley and Julie (Sloan) E.; m. Marilyn Schultz, Aug. 11, 1973; children: Meredith, Benjamin, Suzannah, Theodore. BA, Ind. U., 1971, JD, 1976. Bar: Ind. 1976, U.S. Dist. Ct. (so. dist.) Ind. 1976, U.S. Ct. Appeals (7th cir.) 1983, U.S. Supreme Ct. 1983. Assoc. Sparrenberger, Duvall, Tabbert, Lalley & Newton, Indpls., 1976-77; ptnr. Duvall, Tabbert, Lalley & Newton, Indpls., 1977-81, Bayh, Tabbert & Capehart, Indpls., 1981-85, Baker & Daniels, Indpls., 1985—. Chmn. Ind. Bd. Correction, Indpls., 1976-88, Qyaule for Senate Com., 1980, 86, Quayle for v.p. com.; mem. Fed. Jud. Merit Sel. Com., Indpls., 1981-88, Adminstrv. Conf. U.S., 1983-88; chmn. Indpls. Dist. Fed. Home Loan Bank Bd., 1987-90, Fed. Housing Fin. Bd., 1990-93; vice chmn. Methodist Health Group, Inc., 1996—, Cir. Investors, Inc., 1997—; vice chmn. Hudson Inst., Inc., 1996—, Cir. Investors, Inc., 1994-99; chancellor South Ind. Conf. United Meth. Ch., 1998—; gen. coun. Citizens Gas Utility, 1999—; bd. dirs. Clarian Health Ptnrs., Inc., Indpls., Downtown, Inc., 1992-96, Meth. Hosp. Ind. Mem. Ind. Bar Assn., Indpls. Bar Assn., Woodstock Club, Indpls. Club. Republican. Methodist. Office: Baker & Daniels 300 N Meridian St Ste 2700 Indianapolis IN 46204-1782

EVANS, DARRELL J. higher education educator; b. Pocatello, Idaho, Dec. 3, 1937; s. Cedric Coffin and Elsie Christine (Jensen) E.; m. Laurel Bradley, June 13, 1955 (div. Apr. 1962); children: Mark Bradley, Athena Denice; m. Penny L. Deay, Aug. 1963 (div. June 1980); 1 child, Dana Jacqueline; m. Judith Claire Peterson, Feb. 10, 1984 (div. Apr. 1993); m. Leiola Irene Reeder, Aug. 4, 1995 (div. July 1996). AA, San Diego Jr. Coll., 1967; BA, San Diego State Coll., 1969; MA, UCLA, 1970; PhD, U. Idaho, 1997. Cert. tchr. art advanced secondary, Idaho, advanced secondary vocat. specialist, Idaho, C.C. cert., Calif. Asst. art instr. Chula Vista (Calif.) Sch. Dist., summer 1968; dir. arts and crafts Camp Roosevelt, Mountain Center, Calif., summer 1970; art tchr., intern Blackfoot (Idaho) High Sch., 1971-72; chief illustrator-draftsman USN, 1972-84; tch. and art tchr. McCall (Idaho)-Donnelly High Sch., 1984-97; asst. prof. art edn. U. Tex., El Paso, 1997-98; assoc. prof. art edn. Ala. A&M U., Huntsville, 2000—. Art tchr. Fairfield (Calif.) Suisun Evening Sch., 1973-74; art instr. U. Md.-Naples, Italy, 1975-76; mem. panel Idaho Commn. on Arts, Boise, 1990, 91, 94; owner Evans Design Inc., McCall, Idaho, 1989-2000, Huntsville, 2000—; mem. fine arts framework writing com. Schs. 2000, Idaho State Dept. Edn., 1994; co-chair art 5-12 curriculum writing com. Idaho State Dept. Edn. With USN, 1954-84, ret. 1984. Art Coun. scholar UCLA Art Coun., 1969-70. Mem. Nat. Art Edn. Assn. (chair tech. com. dels. assembly 1995). Avocation: residential archtl. design. Home: 2319 Gallatin St SW Huntsville AL 35801-3825

EVANS, DAVID A(LBERT), chemistry educator; b. Washington, D.C., Jan. 11, 1941; s. Albert Edward and Iris (Hill) Evans Yohe; m. Selena Anne Welliver, Dec. 27, 1962; 1 child, Bethan Hill AB, Oberlin Coll., 1963; PhD, Calif. Inst. Tech., Pasadena, 1967; MA (hon.), Harvard U., Cambridge, 1983. Asst. prof. chemistry UCLA, 1967-72, assoc. prof., 1972-73, prof., 1974; prof. chemistry Calif. Inst. Tech., Pasadena, 1974-83, Harvard U., Cambridge, 1983—, Abbott and James Lawrence prof. chemistry. Mem. com. on chem. scis. NRC; cons. to pharm. industry; lectr. in field Contbr. more than 125 articles of profl. jours.; hon. editor Tetrahedron and Tetrahedron Letters, 1981—; mem. editorial adv. bd. Jour. Am. Chem. Soc., 1983—88. Recipient Camille and Henry Dreyfus Tchr.-Scholar award Dreyfus Found., 1971-76; Alfred P. Sloan Found. fellow, 1972-74; Disting. Teaching award UCLA Alumni Assn., 1973; Tetra Hedron award, 1998; Prelog Medal, 1999.; Caltech. Disting. Alumni award, 2002. Mem. Am. Chem. Soc. (award for creative work in synthetic organic chemistry 1984, Arthur C. Cope Award, 2000), Nat. Acad. Scis. (award 1984) Home: 39 Pine Hill Ln Concord MA 01742-4414 Office: Harvard U Dept of Chemistry Chemical Biology Dept of Chemistry 12 Oxford St Cambridge MA 02138-2902

EVANS, DAVID ALLAN, English educator; b. Sioux City, Iowa, Apr. 11, 1940; s. Arthur Clarence and Ruth (Lyle) E.; m. Janice Kay Johnson, July 4, 1958; children: Shelly Evans Moreau, David Allan Jr., Karlin Evans Bauer. BA, Morningside Coll., 1962; MA, U. Iowa, 1964; MFA, U. Ark., 1973. Asst. U. Iowa, Iowa City, 1965, U. Ark., Fayetteville, 1971-72; asst. prof. English, Adams State Coll., Alamosa, Colo., 1966-68, S.D. State U., Brookings, 1968-78, prof., 1978—, writer-in-residence, 1997—; poet laureate SD, 2002. Faculty exch. prof. Yunnan Normal U., Kunming, China, 1988—89; poet laureate, SD, 2002—. Author: (poetry chapbook) Among Athletes, 1970, (poetry) Train Windows, 1976, Real and False Alarms, 1980, Hanging Out with the Crows, 1990, Decent Dangers, 2001, (essays) Remembering the Soos, 1982; (with Jan Evans) Double Happinesss: Two Lives in China, 1995; co-editor: From Language to Idea, 1970, Statement and Craft, 1972, The Sport of Poetry/The Poetry of Sport, 1979; editor: New Voices in American Poetry, 1973; gen. editor, writer What the Tall Grass Says, 1982. Writing mentor S.D. State Prison, Sioux Falls, 2001—; mem. steering com. Brookings Arts Coun., 2001—; active participant artist in schs. SD Arts Coun. Named S.D. Centennial Poet, 1989; recipient Exemplary Tchr. award Guangdong U. Fgn. Studies, 1999; athletic scholar Augustana Coll., 1958-60, Breadloaf scholar, Vt., 1973, Fulbright scholar, China, 1992-93, 98-99; writing grantee Nat. Endowment for Arts, 1975, 80, grantee S.D. Arts Coun., 1981, artist grantee Bush Found., 1990. Mem. Poetry Soc. Am. Democrat. Avocations: racquetball and other exercise, reading, travel. Home: 1432 2nd St Brookings SD 57006 Office: SD State U Scobey Hall 008 Box 504 Brookings SD 57007 E-mail: evanspl@brookings.net.

EVANS, DAVID ALUN, otolaryngologist; b. Midland, Mich., Mar. 11, 1960; BS with distinction, U. Mich., 1981, MD with distinction, 1984. Diplomate Am. Bd. Otolaryngology. Intern St. Joseph Mercy Hosp., Ann Arbor, Mich., 1984-85; resident in otolaryngology-head and neck surgery U. Mich., Ann Arbor, 1985-89; pvt. practice Sacramento ENT; sr. mem. staff Sutter Hosps., Sacramento; mem. staff Mercy Gen. Hosp., Sacramento. Fellow ACS; mem. AMA, Am. Acad. Otolaryngology-Head and Neck Surgery, Phi Beta Kappa, Alpha Omega Alpha. Office: Sacramento ENT 3810 J St Sacramento CA 95816-5521 E-mail: devans@sacent.com.

EVANS, DAVID CHARLES, retired elementary school educator; b. Cleve., Sept. 23, 1945; s. Howard Robert and Verna Eileen (Stark) E.; m. Nancy Ellen Smith, Aug. 10, 1968; children: Charles Ray, James Neal. BS in Edn., Otterbein Coll., Westerville, Ohio, 1967; MEd, Kent State U., 1970. Cert. tchr., elem. prin., Ohio. Tchr. 6th grade Columbus (Ohio) City Schs., 1967; tchr. grades 4-6, team leader Parma (Ohio) City Schs., 1967-77; tchr. 6th grade Southwestern City Schs., Grove City, Ohio, 1978; tchr. grades 5-8 Upper Arlington (Ohio) City Schs., 1978—2002, also team leader, summer sch. tchr.; supr. student tchrs., interns and field experience students Ashland U., Ohio, 2002—. Coord. Dist. Washington trip Recipient Golden Apple Achiever award Ashland Oil, Inc., 1995, 96, others, Golden Apple award Upper Arlington Civic Assn., 1989, 91; named to Outstanding Young Men in Am., 1974, Over-All Tchr. of Yr. in Upper Arlington Schs., State of Ohio Ho. Representatives, 1995; Jennings scholar, 1972. Mem. NEA, Ohio Edn. Assn., Upper Arlington Edn. Assn. (pres. 1982-83), Nat. Mid. Sch. Assn., Nat. Coun. Tchrs. English. Home: 4323 Stratton Rd Columbus OH 43220-4371

EVANS, DAVID LYNN, management consultant; b. Red Oak, Iowa, June 26, 1941; s. John Louis and Margaret Alice (Young) E.; m. Mary Susan Ricke, Aug. 4, 1963; children: John Louis, Mary Lynn, Sarah Leigh, Michael Ricke. BS, Iowa State U., 1964; MBA, U. Pa., 1966. Mem. staff Deere & Co., Moline, Ill., 1964-92; mgr. John Deere Info Systems, Moline, 1983-87; dir. fin. Deere & Co., Moline, 1987-92; exec. v.p. Rocky Mountain Internet, Denver, 1997-98; v.p. Netbeam. Inc., 1999-2000; pres. Evanwood Corp., Evergreen, Colo., 1992—; CEO Rose Creek Ridge Corp., 2003—. Bd. dirs. Conen Internat., Inc.; v.p. John Deere Leasing Co., bd. dirs. John Deere Receivables, Inc.; bd. dirs., chmn. audit com. Pearl Mut. Funds, 1977—; chmn. audit com. Data Transmission Network Corp., 1986-95; mng. dir. Evans Farms, 1972—; dir. World Federalists Assn., 1980-90, v.p. midwest region 1977-82; dir. Campaign for UN Reform, 1979-82, 1980-81, treas, 1982-88; trustee John Deere Dealer Group Ins. Trust, 1981-85; chmn. fin. rels. com. Am Fin. Svcs. Assn., 1991-92; chmn. Nat. Assn. Corp. Dirs., 1991—; cons. corp. fin. N.Am., India and China. Elder Presbyn. Ch. Mem.: Iowa Mfrs. Assn. (chmn. econ. edn. com. 1979—81), Denver World Affairs Coun. (program chair 2002—), Denver Coun. Fgn. Rels., UN Assn., am. Econ. Assn., Quad Cities World Affairs Coun. (pres. 1984, 1992). Republican. Home and Office: Evanwood Corp 32500 El Diente Ct Evergreen CO 80439-9773 E-mail: Dave@Evanwood.com.

EVANS, DENNIS HYDE, chemist, educator; b. Grinnell, Iowa, Mar. 28, 1939; s. Leonard Hyde and Clara Ethel (Parmley) E.; m. Ruth Elizabeth Turnbull, June 28, 1958 (div. July 1986); children: Susan Katherine, John Hyde, Andrew Turnbull; m. Mary Jean Wirth, Aug.2, 1986. BS, Ottawa U., 1960; A.M., Harvard U., 1961, PhD, 1964. Instr. chemistry Harvard U., Cambridge, 1964-66; asst. prof. chemistry U. Wis., Madison, 1966-70, asso. prof., 1970-75, prof., 1975-84, Meloche-Bascom prof. chemistry, 1984-86, chmn. dept., 1977-80, assoc. dean Coll. of Letters and Sci., 1983-86; prof. chemistry U. Del., Newark, 1986—. Contbr. articles to profl. jours. Named Danforth fellow, 1960 64, NIH fellow, 1961-64; recipient C.N. Reilley award Soc. for Electroanalytical Chemistry, 1993. Fellow Electrochem. Soc. (M.M. Baizer award Organic and Biol. Electrochemistry Divsn. 2004); mem. Am. Chem. Soc., Internat. Soc. Electrochemistry, Soc. for Electroanalytical Chemistry (pres. 1993-95). Baptist. Home: 26 E Parkway Pky Elkton MD 21921-2042 Office: U Del Dept Chemistry Newark DE 19716 E-mail: dhevans@udel.edu.

EVANS, DONALD FOSTER, quality engineer, computer consultant; b. Atlanta, Sept. 27, 1949; s. Marlin Donald Evans and Winnefred Irene (Pelton) Yow; divorced; 1 child, Randi Leigh. Grad., USAF Sch. Electronics, Biloxi, Miss., 1969; student, Evergreen Community Coll., San Jose, Calif., 1980, San Jose City Coll., 1986. Cert. quality mgr. Am. Soc. Quality, quality engr. Am. Soc. Quality, calibration technician Am. Soc. Quality. Enlisted USAF, 1968, advanced to staff sgt., 1973, resigned, 1979; tng. instr. Sylvania Tech. Systems, Sunnyvale, Calif., 1979-80, Ampex Inc., Redwood City, Calif., 1980-82; master technician Convergent Techs., San Jose, 1983-84; sr. electronics technician Atari, Sunnyvale, 1982-83, Forté Data Systems, San Jose, 1984-86, Alps Electric Inc., San Jose, 1986-98; quality engr. KLA-Tencor, San Jose, 1999; quality engr., mgmt. rep. Mitsubishi Electric & Electronics U.S.A., Inc., Sunnyvale, Calif., 1999—2003; sr. quality engr. ISIS Surface Mounting, San Jose, 2003—. Mem. Silicon Valley Gay Men's Chorus, San Jose, 1989-95; bd. dirs. Necisities & More, 1989, Project Disseminate Info. on AIDS by Phone Lines, San Francisco, 1990, St. Raphael Orthodox Ch. Mem. Assn. Computing Machinery, Math. Assn. Am., Am. Soc. for Quality. Avocations: reading, music, computers, fishing. Home: 1213 N San Pedro St San Jose CA 95110-1436

EVANS, DONALD CHARLES, JR., lawyer; b. New London, Conn., Nov. 1, 1938; s. Donald Charles and Henrietta Agnes (Perkins) E.; m. Magda Anna Wehr, Apr. 30, 1966; children: Donald Charles III, Sean Thomas. BA, U. Miami, 1961; JD, U. Fla., Gainesville, 1967; LLM, NYU, 1968. Bar: Fla. 1967, D.C. 1974, U.S. Tax Ct. 1974. Legis.-adminstrv. asst. Fla. State Senate, 1967; atty.-adviser legis. and regulations divsn. Office Chief Csl., IRS, 1968-71; legis. latty. U.S. Congress Joint Com. on Internal Revenue Taxation, Washington, 1971-74; mem. Williams & Jensen PC, Washington, 1974-83, Evans & Assocs., Washington, 1983—. 1st lt. AUS, 1963-65. Mem. ABA, Fla. Bar Assn. (gov. 1979-83), D.C. Bar Assn., U. Fla. Alumni Assn. (pres. D.C. chpt. 1974-75), Fla. State Soc. (dir. 1972-77). Home: 9315 Winbourne Rd Burke VA 22015-1755 Office: Evans & Assocs Ste 300 1201 Pennsylvania Ave NW Washington DC 20004

EVANS, DONALD L. secretary of commerce; b. Houston, 1946; m. Susan Marinis; three children: Lisa Moon, Jennifer, Donald L. BS in Mech. Engring., U. Tex. Austin, 1969, MBA, 1973; LHD (hon.), U. S.C., 2001. Mgmt. to chmn. bd. dirs. and CEO Tom Brown, Inc., Denver, 1975-2001; sec. U.S. Dept. Commerce, Washington, 2001—. Bd. dirs. TMBR/Sharp Drilling, Inc., bd. regents U. Tex., 1995, chmn. bd., 1997—. Bd. Trustees Meml. Hosp. & Med. Ctr., 1990-94; bd. dirs. The Gladney Fund, 1992-96, Scleroderma Rsch. Found., 1992-00; campaign chair United Way of Midland, 1981, pres., 1989; bd. regents U. Tex., 1995-96, chmn., 1997 98; bd. dirs. Scleroderma Rsch. Found; active United Way, campaign chair, 1981, pres., 1989; mem. Gov. Bush gubernatorial campaign, 1994, 98; chmn. Bush/Cheney Presdl. campaign, 2000. Named to U. Tex. Red McCombs Sch. Bus. Hall of Fame, 2002; recipient Disting. Alumnus award, U Tex., 2002. Mem. Independent Petroleum Assn. Am., Young Presidents Orgn., Rocky Mtn. Oil & Gas Assn., Permian Basin Petroleum Assn., All-Am. Wildcatters, Nat. Petroleum Council. Republican. Methodist. Office: Sec of Commerce Rm 5516 14th & Constitution Ave NW Washington DC 20230

EVANS, DORINDA, art history educator; b. Wakefield, Mass., Mar. 5, 1944; d. George Jelly and Priscilla (White) E.; 1 adopted child, Antonia Tamsen. BA, Wheaton Coll., Norton, Mass., 1965; MA, U. Pa., 1967; PhD, U. London, 1972. Mus. curator Nat. Gallery Art, Washington, 1967-69; asst. prof. U. Ill., Chgo., 1972-74; vis. curator Phila. Mus. Art, 1974-75; guest curator Nat. Portrait Gallery, Washington, 1975-78; asst. prof. art history Emory U., Atlanta, 1978-84, assoc. prof., 1984—2002, prof., 2002—. Author: Benjamin West and His American Students, 1980, Mather Brown, 1982, The Genius of Gilbert Stuart, 1999; contbr. articles to profl. jours. Paul Hamlyn grantee Courtauld Inst. Art, U. London, 1970-71; fellow Samuel H. Kress Found., 1971-72, sr. postdoctoral fellow Smithsonian Instn., 1986-87, Joshua C. Taylor rsch. fellow Nat. Mus. Am. Art, 1991. Office: Emory U Art History Dept Atlanta GA 30322-0001 E-mail: devan03@emory.edu.

EVANS, DOUGLAS HAYWARD, lawyer; b. Providence, July 21, 1950; s. Jerrold Merton and Gladys Jean (Snelgrove) E.; m. Sarah Edwards Cogan, May 28, 1983; children: Anne Morrill, Thomas Taylor Seelye, Elizabeth Hayward. AB, Franklin and Marshall Coll., 1972; JD, Cornell U., 1975. Bar: N.J. 1975, U.S. Dist. Ct. N.J. 1975, N.Y. 1976, U.S. Dist Ct. (so. dist.) N.Y. 1991. Assoc. Windels, Marx, Davies & Ives, N.Y.C., 1975-85, Sullivan & Cromwell, N.Y.C., 1985-90, spl. counsel, 1990—. Faculty NYU Inst. Fed. Taxation, N.Y.C., 1984; counsel, treas., pres. St. David's Soc. State of N.Y., N.Y.C., 1985—; bd. dirs. Friends of Washington Sq. Park, 1989—, Washington Sq. Assn., 1992—, 1st Presbyn. Ch. Nursery Sch., 1999—. Co-Author: Estate Accounting, 1980, Probate and Estate Administration, 1982, Administration of Estates, 1985, Settling An Estate, 1989; editor-in-chief, co-author: Probate and Administration of New York Estates, 1995, 2d edit., 2001; also articles. Trustee Franklin and Marshall Coll., 1994—, Grace Ch. Sch., N.Y.C., 1997—, vice chmn., 2000-01, chmn., 2001—; mem. Ch. Club of N.Y., Salmagundi Club, N.Y.C. Fellow: Am. Coll. of Trust and Estate Coun.; mem.: ABA, Assn. of the Bar of the City of N.Y. (com. on estate and gift taxation), N.Y. County Lawyers Assn. (not-for-profit com.), N.Y. State Bar Assn. (estate litig. and adminstrn. of trusts and estates com., com. on CLE, chmn. 1991—94), N.J. Bar Assn., Pi Gamma Mu, Phi Alpha Theta, Phi Delta Phi, Phi Beta Kappa. Episcopalian. Home: 43 Fifth Ave New York NY 10003-4368 Office: Sullivan & Cromwell 125 Broad St Fl 28 New York NY 10004-2489

EVANS, DOUGLAS MCCULLOUGH, surgeon, educator; b. Vandergrift, Pa., July 31, 1925; s. Archibald Davis and Helen Irene (McCullough) E.; m. Thelmajean Volkers, Aug. 1, 1959; children: Matthew Kirk, Daniel Scott. MD, Western Res. U., 1952; postgrad., U. Mich., 1956-58. Diplomate Am. Bd. Surgery. Resident in surgery Henry Ford Hosp., 1952-57, chief resident in surgery, 1957-58, mem. surgery staff, 1959-60, Akron (Ohio) Gen. Hosp., 1960-70; chmn. dept. surgery Akron Gen. Med. Ctr., 1971-90, rsch. cons.; prof. and chmn. surgery emeritus Northeastern Ohio U. Coll. Medicine. Served with AUS, 1943-46. Fellow: ACS; mem.: AAAS, AMA, N.Y. Acad. Scis., Ohio Med. Assn., Midwest Surg. Soc., Soc. Critical Care Medicine, Metastasis Rsch. Soc., Am. Assn. Cancer Rsch. Republican. Presbyterian. Office: 400 Wabash Ave Akron OH 44307-2433

EVANS, DVORAH A. organization executive, professional organizer; b. Dallas, Aug. 14; d. Theresa Evans. Student, Prairie View A&M U., 1987-91. Cert. meeting profl. Leasing agt. B-G Personnel, Dallas, 1991; paralegal Law Office Robinson, West & Gooden P.C., Dallas, 1991-92; asst. spl. projects mgr. Dallas Black C. of C., 1992-93, dir. convs. and tourism, 1993—. Mem. Meeting Profls. Internat. (bd. dirs. Dallas/Ft. Worth chpt. 2001—, mem. internat. mktg. com. 2000—, Star of the Month 2000), Nat. Coalition Black Meeting Planners (mem. com.), Religious Confs. Mgmt. Assn., Tex. Travel Industry Assn., Alpha Kappa Alpha. Baptist. Avocations: travel, reading, dancing, cooking. Office: Dallas Black C of C 2838 Martin Luther King Jr Dallas TX 75215 Fax: 214-421-5200. E-mail: dae@dbcc.org.

EVANS, EDWARD SPENCER, JR., entomologist; b. Woodbury, N.J., Aug. 7, 1943; s. Edward Spencer and Hazel Louise (Flagg) E.; m. Marilyn Dale Kernohan, Aug. 13, 1966 (div. 1981); children: Tracey Lynn, Edward Spencer III; m. Sandra Ruth Ehrhardt, June 9, 1984. BS, Rutgers U., 1965, MS, 1967, PhD, 1975. Cert. entomologist. Asst. wildlife biologist N.J. Div. Fish and Game, Tuckahoe, 1964; grad. asst. dept. entomology Rutgers U., New Brunswick, N.J., 1965-67, 69-73; entomologist U.S. Army Environ. Hygiene Agy., Aberdeen Proving Ground, Md., 1973 76, pesticide coord., 1976-83, supervisory entomologist, 1983—. Chmn. Armed Forces Pest Mgmt. Bd., Washington, 1988-92; adj. asst. prof. Uniformed Svcs. U. Health Scis., Bethesda, Md., 1986—. Co-author: Pesticides, 1991; contbr. articles and tech. reports to profl. jours. Chmn. long range planning com. Bel Air (Md.) United Meth. Ch., 1988, mem. bldg. com., 1990—; coach youth baseball Recreation Coun., Joppatowne, Md., 1980-85. Capt. U.S. Army, 1967-69, Korea. Mem. ASTM (chmn. com. F-35, 1983-89), Am. Mosquito Control Assn., Entomol. Soc. Am., Sigma Xi, Alpha Zeta. Home: 1309 Beckett Ct Bel Air MD 21014-2736 Office: US Army Ctr Health Promotion & Preventive Med Aberdeen Proving Ground MD 21010-5403 E-mail: esevans@comcast.net.

EVANS, ELIZABETH ANN WEST, retired realtor; b. Xenia, Ohio, Mar. 28, 1933; d. Millard Stanley and Elizabeth Denver (Johns) West. BA, Ohio U., 1966, MA, 1968, Cert. GRI, 1993. Sec. various orgns., Ohio, 1952-61; tchr. Ohio U., Athens, 1966-67, Zanesville, 1968-72, Collier County Pub. Schs., Naples, Fla., 1972-77; sales Helen's Hang Ups, Naples, 1978-79; mgr. pvt. practice Wilmington, Ohio, 1979-87; adminstrv. asst. Powell Assocs., Cambridge, Mass., 1987-90; real estate agt. Bill Evans Realty, Inc., Naples, 1989-90, Howard Hanna Real Estate Svcs., Naples, 1991-93, Downing-Frye Realty, Inc., Naples, Fla., 1993-97, Downing-Frye Referral Network Realty Inc., Naples, 1997—2002, ret., 2002. Fellow: Phi Beta Kappa; mem.: DAR (chaplain 1988—90, chmn. Motion, Picture, Radio and TV 1992—94, asst. chaplain 1994—96, chaplain 2000—01, chmn. pub. rels. 2003—), Kappa Alpha Theta (50-yr. mem.), Phi Kappa Phi, Phi Sigma Iota. Republican. Presbyterian. Avocation: leading group discussions. Home: 182 Cape May Dr Wilmington OH 45177

EVANS, ELIZABETH E. physical therapist, educator; d. Richard John and Adele Cameron Evans. BS, Springfield Coll., 1962, MEd, 1970; phys. therapy cert., U. Pa., 1971; PHD, U. Conn., 1983. Vol. Peace Corps, 1963—65; tchr., coach Longmeadow (Mass.) H.S., 1965—69; prof. Springfield (Mass.) Coll., 1971—. Vol. programmer for swim/gym for handicapped children and recreation programs for blind children U.S. Sport and Wellness Ctr. for Persons with Disabilities, Springfield, 1998—. Mem.: Am. Assn. for Mental Retardation, Am. Alliance for Health Phys. Edn., Recreation and Dance. Office: Springfield Coll Judd Gym Alden St Springfield MA 01109

EVANS, ELLEN FRASCA, pharmaceutical company executive; b. Morristown, N.J., Feb. 23, 1959; d. Louis Anthony and Mary Eileen Frasca; m. Peter Alan Evans, Aug. 13, 1983; children: Paul Alexander, Kyle Stokes, James Morris. BA summa cum laude, Yale U., 1981; MBA, U. Pa., 1985. Compensation rsch. analyst Hay Assocs., Phila., 1981-83; cons. Deloitte & Touche, Phila., 1985-91; sr. fin. planning U.S. Biosci. Inc., West Conshohocken, Pa., 1991-92, dir. bus. devel., 1992-94, dir. health econs., 1994-95, dir. bus. devel. strategic alliances, 1995-98, sr. dir. bus. devel. and new product planning, 1998-99; dir. project mgmt. and bus. devel. MedImmune Oncology, West Conshohocken, 1999-2000; v.p., sr. licensing exec. BTG Internat. Inc., Gulph Mills, Pa., 1993—. Grants com. mem. Snave Found., Phila., 1993—. Mem. Licensing Execs. Soc., Am. Assn. Cancer Rsch., Merion Cricket Club, Bryn Mawr Running Club, Yale Club Phila. (past pres. 1994-96), Brant Beach Yacht Club, Phila. Skating Club, Phi Beta Kappa, Sigma Xi, Beta Gamma Sigma. Avocations: running marathons, fitness. Office: BTG Internat Inc Five Tower Bridge 300 Barr Harbor Dr 7th Fl West Conshohocken PA 19428-2998

EVANS, ERIC ALAN, lawyer; b. Bend, Oreg., Mar. 17, 1949; s. Byron Fletcher and Margaret Jeanette Evans; m. Anne Van Vechten Myers Evans, July 26, 1975; children: Ryan, Katharine, Andrew. BA, U. of Pa., 1971; JD, Albany Law Sch. of Union U., N.Y., 1976. Bar: N.Y. 1977, Fed. 1977. Banking & comml. lawyer Harter, Secrest & Emery LLP, Rochester, NY, 1976—78, mgmt. labor lawyer, 1978—, chair, labor dept., 1992—95, unit mgr., bus., 1998—2000, mng. ptnr., 2000—. Bd. mem. Kirkhaven, Rochester, NY, 1994—2000; nominating com. United Way of Greater Rochester, NY, 2002; bd. mem. Rochester Bus. Alliance, NY, 2003. Mem.: Mgmt. Attorneys Conf., Genesee Valley Club. Office: Harter Secrest & Emery LLP 1600 Bausch & Lomb Pl Rochester NY 14604-2711 E-mail: eevans@hselaw.com.

EVANS, ERSEL ARTHUR, consulting engineer executive; b. Trenton, Nebr., July 17, 1922; s. Arthur E. and Mattie Agnes (Perkins) E.; m. Patricia A. Powers, Oct. 11, 1945 (div.); children: Debra Lynn (dec.), Paul Arthur. BA, Reed Coll., Portland, Oreg., 1947; PhD, Oreg. State U., 1950. Registered profl. engr., Calif. With Gen. Electric Co., 1951-67, supr. ceramics research and devel., 1961-64; mgr. plutonium devel. Vallecitos Lab., Pleasanton, Calif., 1964-67; mgr. fuels and materials dept. Battelle Meml. Inst., Richland, Wash., 1967-70; with Westinghouse Electric Corp., 1970-87; v.p. Westinghouse Hanford Co., Richland, 1972-87, v.p., lab. tech. dir., 1985-87, ret., 1987, cons., 1987—. Mem. Tech. Assistance Adv. Group for Three Mile Island Recovery, 1981-86; mem. rev. Com. EBR-II, U. Chgo., 1989-91, 94—; mem. Japan Tech. Panel for Nuclear Power, NSF, 1989-90; mem. alt. applications of laser isotope separations tech. com. NRC, 1991-92, separations and tech. study, 1991-95, 96; del. Atlantic Coun. U.S.-Japan Conf. on Global Energy Issues, Maui, 1994, 96. Mem. vis. com. U. Wash. Served with USNR, 1943-45. Recipient Westinghouse Order of Merit; DuPont fellow, 1950-51; recipient Mishima award Am. Nuclear Soc., 1995. Fellow Am. Nuclear Soc. (Spl. Merit award 1964, Spl. Performance award 1980 Fed. Design Achievement award 1991, Walker Cisler medal 2001), Am. Inst. Chemists, Am. Soc. Metals, Am. Ceramic Soc.; mem. NAE, Phi Kappa Phi, Sigma Xi. Achievements include patents in field. Home and Office: Park Row # 45 701 Kettner Blvd San Diego CA 92101-5908 E-mail: ersel3@cox.net. *Inspiration and guidance for my career have often been provided by Justice Oliver Wendell Holmes, "certainty generally is illusion, and repose is not the destiny of man." (Harvard Law Review 1897)*

EVANS, ESSI H. research scientist; b. Bad-Schwalbach, Germany, Jan. 12, 1950; came to U.S., 1951, naturalized, 1957; d. John H. (b. Horst H. Jahn) and Jean E. (von Schwerin); m. Everett M. Turner Jr., Aug. 16, 1974. BS in Agr., U. Md., 1972; MS in Animal Sci., U. Guelph, 1974, PhD in Animal Sci., 1976. Polymer chemist Monarch Rubber Co., Balt., 1972; rsch. asst., tchg. asst. U. Guelph, Ont., 1972-76; project dir. animal nutrition Can. Packers Inc., Toronto, Ont., 1976-85, tech. mgr. animal nutrition and animal health, 1986-89, rsch. mgr., 1989-90, gen. rsch. and nutrition mgr. shur-gain divsn., 1990-93, mgmt. dir., 1993-2000, v.p. Shur Gain, 2000—02; CEO Tech. Adv. Svcs. Inc., 2002—. Farm cons.; guest lectr. Hubbard Farms fellow, 1975-76; NRC Indsl. postdoctoral fellow, 1976-79. Contbr. articles to sci. jours. and profl. at sci. confs. James Harris scholar, U. Md., 1972; recipient Hamilton Milk Prodrs. award, 1973, 74; Ont. Ministry of Agr. and Foods Provincial Lottery grantee, 1980-83. Mem. AAAS, Am. Soc. Animal Sci., Am. Dairy Sci. Assn., Am. Assn. Vet. Nutritionists, Coun. for Agrl. Sci. and Tech., Nat. Feed Industry Assn., Can. Feed Industry Assn. Republican. Home and Office: 64 Scugog St Bowmanville ON Canada L1C 3J1 E-mail: essievans@sympatico.ca.

EVANS, EVAN, petroleum executive; b. N.Y.C., May 19, 1925; s. John William Jr. and Therese Rosemary (Guilfoyle) E.; m. Natalie Coe Holbrook, Feb. 20, 1968; children: Megan, Meredith, Rhys, Valerie, Cynthia, David. Student, St. Lawrence U., 1942-43, 46, BS, 1949, MIT, 1951. Engr. Calif. Tex. Oil Corp., N.Y.C., 1951-55, 1955-57, refinery ops. asst., 1957-60, Rotterdam, 1960-62, refinery plant mgr., 1963, refinery specialist, 1963-65; refinery project mgr. King Wilkinson, Antwerp, Belgium, 1966-68; v.p. United Refining Co., Warren, Pa., 1972-81, dir., 1974-81, 96—. Pres. Kiantone Pipeline, 1970-81; v.p. Western Crude Oil Inc., 1981-83; pres. Wesco Internat. Inc., 1981-83, Holvan Properties Inc., Madison, Conn., 1985—; dir. U.S. Energy Sys., Belgian

Refining Corp., 1993-96, Alexander-Allen Inc., 1994-2002. Chmn. Am. Sch. Rotterdam, 1961-62. With USN, 1943-46. Mem. N.Y. Athletic Club. Address: 331 Old Toll Rd Madison CT 06443-1710

EVANS, FRANKLIN BACHELDER, marketing educator emeritus; b. Chgo., Feb. 9, 1922; s. Franklin B. and Arline (Brown) E.; m. Barbara V. Both, Sept. 16, 1943; children: Mary A., Amy B., Geoffrey B., Christopher G. AA, U. Chgo., 1941, AB, 1943, MBA, 1954, PhD, 1959. Asst. prof. mktg. U. Chgo., 1957-64; prof. mktg. U. Hawaii, 1964-69; prof. advt. Northwestern U., 1969-80, prof. emeritus, 1981—. Cons. to bus. and industry; researcher on consumer motivation. Contbr. articles to profl. jours. Served with U.S. Army, 1943-45. Decorated Bronze Star. Home: 4215 Harding Pike Apt 708 Nashville TN 37205 *Education should develop intellectual power. The ideal education is not specialized or pre-professional; it is not utilitarian. The intellectual tools for developing the mind start with the three R's and the liberal arts. Specialization can follow later.*

EVANS, GARY LEE, communications educator and consultant; b. Davison, Mich., June 26, 1938; s. Joe Howard and Annie Annette (Colden) E.; m. Katherine Strand; children: Gary James, Aimee Lynn; stepchildren: John E. Holkeboer, Maja K. Holkeboer. BA, Wayne State U., 1962; MA, U. Mich., 1965, PhD, 1977. Prof. organizational and intercultural communication Eastern Mich. U., Ypsilanti, 1964—. Pres. Comm. Rsch. and Tng. Assocs.; cons. Volvo Corp., GM Corp., Ford Motor Car Co., Mich. Pub. Schs. and other ednl. instns.; speaker in field; instr., Davos, Switzerland, 1989; internat. program instr., Australia, New Zealand, Switzerland. Mem. Peace Corps Tng. and Teaching. Named Outstanding Continuing Educator of the Yr., Ea. Mich. U., 1994, Disting. Sr. Tchg. Award, 1998, Disting. Faculty Mem., 1998, Disting. Tchg. award Ea. Mich. U. Alumni, 2001. Mem. Internat. Communication Assn., Speech Communication assn., Mich. Acad. Sci., Arts and Letters (communication chmn. 1982), Mich. Speech Communication Assn. (communication chmn. 1978—), Golden Key Nat. Honorary Soc., Phi Kappa Phi (pres. 1998—), Delta Sigma Rho, Pi Kappa Delta. Home: 11350 Pleasant Shore Dr Manchester MI 48158-9739 Office: Ea Mich U 121 Quirk Hall Ypsilanti MI 48197-2220

EVANS, GAY GOODWIN, nurse; b. Wink, Tex., Aug. 3, 1938; d. Lloyd Otis and Lila Muriel (States) Goodwin; m. Arthur Haynes Evans Jr., Aug. 13, 1967; children: Kristna Jan, Ross Neil. BS, Okla. Bapt. U., 1959; MS, U. Minn., 1966; cert. family nurse practitioner, U. Ariz., 1975. RN, Ariz. Pub. health nurse San Mateo (Calif.) County Health Dept., 1964-66; instr. City Coll. San Francisco, 1967-68; asst. prof. U. San Francisco, 1968-70, Calif. State U., Fresno, 1972-73; instr. W. Hills C.C., Coalinga, Calif., 1972; family nurse practitioner El Rio Health Ctr., Tucson, 1974—2002. Dir. The Health Edn. Project for At-Risk Populations, Tucson, 1990—. Mem. ANA, Ariz. State Nurses Assn. (program chair 1977-78, pres. chpt. II 1979-80), Ariz. Pub. Health Assn., Sigma Theta Tau. Methodist. Avocations: hiking, reading, travel. Office: El Rio Health Ctr 839 W Congress St Tucson AZ 85745-2819

EVANS, GEORGE WILLIAM, economics educator; b. NYC, Apr. 3, 1949; s. George William II and Marjorie Woodard Evans; m. Pauline Andrews; children: David George, Marc Paul. BA, Oxford (Eng.) U., 1972, U. Calif., Berkeley, 1973, MA, 1976; PhD, U. Calif., 1980. Lectr. Stirling U., Scotland, 1978-81; asst. prof. econ. Stanford U., Calif., 1981-87; lectr., sr. lectr., reader London Sch. Econ., 1987-92; George Watson's and Daniel Stewart's Chair Polit. Economy Edinburgh U., Scotland, 1993-94; John B. Hamacher Chair Econ. U. Oreg., Eugene, 1993—. Author: Learning and Expectations in Macroeconomics, 2001; contbr. over 40 articles to profl. jour., including Am. Econ. Rev., Rev. Econ. Studies, Econometrica, Quar. Jour. Econ., others. Rsch. grantee NSF,others. Mem. Phi Beta Kappa. Office: Dept Econs 1285 U Oreg Eugene OR 97403-1285

EVANS, GERALDINE ANN, academic administrator; b. Zumbrota, Minn., Feb. 24, 1939; d. Wallace William and Elda Ida (Tiedemann) Whipple; m. John Lyle Evans, June 21, 1963; children: John David, Paul William. AA, Rochester Community Coll., 1958; BS, U. Minn., 1960, MA, 1963, PhD, 1968. Cert. tchr., counselor, prin. and supt., Minn. Tchr. Hopkins (Minn.) Pub. Schs., 1960-63; counselor Anoka (Minn.) Pub. Schs., 1963-66; cons. in edn. Mpls., 1966-78; policy analyst Minn. Dept. Edn., St. Paul, 1978-79; dir. personnel Minn. Community Coll. System, St. Paul, 1979-82; pres. Rochester (Minn.) Community Coll., 1982-92; chancellor Minn. C.C. System, St. Paul, 1992-94; exec. dir. Ill. C.C. Bd., Springfield, 1994-96; chancellor San Jose (Calif.) Evergreen C.C. Dist., 1996—. Mem. San Jose Workforce Investment Bd., 2000—; mem. legis. and adv. com. Calif. C.C. League, 1998-2002. Mem. Gov.'s Job Tng. Coun., St. Paul, 1983—94, chair, 1992—94; mem. Silicon Valley Pvt. Industry Coun., 1997—2000, Workforce Silicon Valley, 1998—2002; trustee Golden Gate U., 1997—; moderator Mizpah United Ch. Christ, Hopkins, 1982; mem. complete count com. U.S. Census, Santa Clara County, 2000; vice chair, bd. dirs. Wayzata (Minn.) Sch. Bd., 1980—83; bd. dirs. Minn. Tech. Ctr., Rochester, 1991—92; sec.-treas. Coun. North Ctrl. Cmty. and Jr. Colls., 1990—92; mem. ACE Commn. on Edn. Credit and Credentials, 1992—96. Winner Rochester C. of C. Athena award, 1990, San Jose YWCA Exec. award, 1998; Inst. Ednl. Leadership fellow, Washington, 1978-79. Mem. Nat. League Nursing (bd. assoc. degree accreditation rev. 1990-93, exec. com. 1993-96), Am. Assn. Cmty. Colls. (workforce commn. 2000-03), Am. Assn. Cmty. Jr. Colls. (bd. dirs. 1984-87), North Ctrl. Assn. Cmty. and Jr. Colls. (evaluator 1985-96), Silicon Valley C. of C., La Raza Roundtable, Rotary. Congregationalist. Avocations: travel, gardening. E-mail: geraldine.evans@sjeccd.cc.ca.us.

EVANS, GREGORY RANDOLPH DEAN, plastic surgeon, educator; b. Lynwood, Calif., Sept. 4, 1958; s. Richard Dean and Lavon Ilene Evans; m. Ruth Ellen Anderson, Mar. 15, 1986; children: Brandon, Brogan. BS in Psychobiology, U. So. Calif., L.A., 1980, MD, 1985. Resident in gen. surgery L.A. County/U. So. Calif. Med. Ctr., 1985—90; resident in craniofacial microvascular surgery Md. Inst. Emergency Med. Svcs. Sys., 1992-93; resident in plastic and reconstrv. surgery Johns Hopkins Hosp./U. Md., 1993; clin. assoc. prof. divsn. plastic surgery Baylor Coll. Medicine, Houston, 1993-2000; adj. assoc. prof. U. Tex., Houston, 1993-2000; assoc. prof. dept. plastic surgery U. Tex. M.D. Anderson Cancer Ctr., Houston, 1993-2000; prof. surgery, chief divsn. plastic surgery U. Calif., Irvine, 2000—. Adj. prof. bioengring. Rice U., Houston, 1993-2000; study sect. reviewer for neurosci. NIH, 1999; lectr. in field. Contbr. articles to profl. jours. Johns Hopkins Hosp./U. Md. Combined Programs Jr. Clin. Rsch. awardee, 1992, Chmn. Rsch. Grants Com./Plastic Surgery Ednl. Found. grantee, 1998-2000; U. Tex. M.D. Anderson Cancer Ctr. Faculty scholar, 1999—; Godina lectr. ASRM, 2000. Fellow ACS; mem. Am. Soc. Plastic and Reconstrv. Surgeons, Soc. of Surg. Oncology, Tissue Engring. Soc., Plastic Surgery Rsch. Coun. Avocations: golf, skiing. Office: Univ Calif-Irvine Med Ctr 200 S Manchester Ave Orange CA 92868-3201 E-mail: gevans@uci.edu.

EVANS, HAROLD EDWARD, banker; b. Detroit, Apr. 23, 1927; s. Harold J. and Mary Esther (Keenoy) E.; m. Patricia Mae Persons Willy, Mar. 28, 1982; children by previous marriage: D'lorah Ann, M'liss Lorraine, David Keenoy, Craig Edward. BBA, U. Mich., 1950; cert., Bank Adminstrn. Inst., U. Wis., 1968, Stonier Grad. Sch. Banking, Rutgers U., 1975. Auditor Second Nat. Bank Saginaw, Mich., 1952-61, controller, 1961-73, sr. v.p., cashier, sec., chief fin. officer, 1973-92; founder, chmn. art collection, 1976-92; mem. selection com., 1992-2001; v.p. loan rev. officer Citizens Banking Corp., Flint, Mich., 1986-92. Sec.-treas. 2d Nat. Corp., 1973-88, Century Life Ins. Co., Mich., 1973-93; lectr. Robert Perry Sch. Banking, Ctrl. Mich. U. Mem. Saginaw Citizens Coun. for Ctrl. Bus. Dist., 1970-89; mem. adv. bd. Urban Renewal, chmn. econ. base study com., 1954-55; chmn. Downtown Saginaw Beautification Commn., 1968-83, Greater Saginaw Beautification Residential Com., 1965-68, 1988-97; chmn. Saginaw Valley State U. Humanities Series Com., 1990—; sec., trustee Saginaw Osteo. Hosp., 1960-84; treas., trustee Saginaw Symphony Orch., 1965-72; past trustee Saginaw His. Mus.; treas., dir. United Rehab. Svcs., 1954-65, Temple Theater Arts Assn., 1980-87; fin. officer Saginaw CAP, 1978-84; trustee, treas. Saginaw Valley Dancers, 1977-93; trustee Hartley Nature Ctr. Found., 1987—, Saginaw Hall of Fame, 1989—; mem. adv. bd. Health Source Saginaw, Inc., 1991—, sec. adv. bd., 1993, 96, vice chmn., 1997, chmn., 1998; mem. steering com. Cathedral Dist. Renewal, 1990—; mem. com. for advancement Saginaw Valley State U., 1992—, mem. com. Stuart and Vernice Gross History Lit. award, 1996-2000; mem. com. for advancement Saginaw Area Enrichment Commn., 1992-2002, Saginaw Twp. Art in Pub. Place Commn., 1991—, Delta Coll. Pub. Radio Fund Raiser Com., 1990-97, Temple Theater Film Selection com., 1998-2003; mem. awards panel Theatre Guild Midland Ctr. for the Arts. With USNR, 1945—46. Recipient Saginaw Arts award Community Enrichment Commn., 1992; nominee Gov's. Art award, 1996. Mem. Saginaw C. of C., Bank Adminstrn. Inst. (life; pres. Ea. Mich. conf. 1955-56, v.p. Mich. chpt. 1958-59), Valley Film Soc. (bd. dirs. 1991—), Tri-County Econ. Club, Econ. Club Detroit, Internat. Torch Club (Saginaw Valley chpt. 1993—), U. Mich. Alumni Club (Saginaw chpt.), Optimists (bd. dirs. Breakfast Club 1960-80, treas. 1961-63, pres. 1970-72), Mich. Women's Hall of Fame (elector 1992-93), Friends Theodore Roethke, U.S. Navy League. Home: 17 Riverside Blvd Saginaw MI 48602-1077 also: 1710 N Charles St Saginaw MI 48602-4848

EVANS, HARRY LAUNIUS, pathology educator; b. Mobile, Ala., June 11, 1948; s. Aurelius A. and Anne (Hathaway) E.; m. Cheryl J. Winfrey, June 6, 1970 (div. Dec. 1990); children: Thomas H., Sarah S. BS, Stetson U., 1970; MD, U. Fla., 1974. Diplomate Am. Bd. Pathology. Resident in pathology Vanderbilt U. Med. Ctr., Nashville, 1974-75; fellow in dermatopathology Mayo Clinic, Rochester, Minn., 1977-78; fellow in pathology U.Tex.-M.D. Anderson Cancer Ctr., Houston, 1975-77, asst. prof. pathology, 1978-82, assoc. prof., 1982-90, prof., 1990—. Contbr. articles to med. jours. Mem. U.S.-Can. Acad. Pathology, Arthur Purdy Stout Soc. Surg. Pathologists. Avocations: mountain climbing, music, crossword puzzles. Office: U Tex-MD Anderson Cancer Ctr Dept Pathology 1515 Holcombe Blvd Houston TX 77030-4009

EVANS, HOWARD MORGAN, acupuncturist, zero balancer; b. Phila., Dec. 4, 1943; s. Nathaniel Hathaway and Marjory Ada (Morgan) E.; m. Jennie Boyd Bull, Sept. 13, 1969 (div. June 1972); m. Vicki Cohn Pollard, Oct. 25, 1982; children: Tanya Louise, Justin Benjamin. BSCE, Swarthmore (Pa.) Coll., 1965; MS in Environ. Engring. Sci., Johns Hopkins U., 1967; Lic. in Acupuntcure, Coll. Traditional Acupuncture, 1989; M in Acupuncture, Acad. for Five Element Acupuncture, 2001. Cert. in Zero Balancing. Rsch. asst. NAS, Washington, 1966; h.s. dir. Am. Friends Svc., Balt., 1968-71; dir. People's Cmty. Clinic, Balt., 1971-73, Balt. Exptl. H.S., 1972-77, Haystack Mountain Sch. of Crafts, Deer Isle, Maine, 1977-88; pres. Merlin Design, Blue Hill, Maine, 1988—, Chair adv. bd. Worsley Inst. for Classical Acupuncture, Miami Lakes, Fla., 1995-97; mem. Maine Arts Commn., Augusta, 1980-87; acuuncturist, 1988—; mem. faculty Zero Balancing, 1996—, Acad. for Five Element Acupuncture, Hallandale, Fla., 1997—. Bd. dirs. Blue Hill Co-op, Inc., 1997—, Morgan Bay Zendo, Surry, Maine, 1998—. Mem. Maine Assn. Acupuncture and Oriental Medicine (pres. 1990-93, 94-96). Mem. Soc. of Friends, Buddhist. Avocations: sailing, crafts. Office: Traditional Acupuncture PO Box 838 Blue Hill ME 04614-0838 E-mail: howard7@downeast.net.

EVANS, HUGH E. pediatrician, educator; b. N.Y.C., July 6, 1934; s. David and Geraldine (Krebs) E.; m. Ruth L. Orloff, June 5, 1960 (dec. Mar. 1999); children: Margo Lynn, Marc Douglas. AB cum laude, Columbia U., 1954; MD, SUNY Downstate Med. Center, 1958. Intern Johns Hopkins Hosp., Balt., 1958-59, asst. resident, 1959-60; sr. asst. resident NIH, Bethesda, Md., 1960-62, chief resident outpatient dept., 1962-63; pvt. practice Bellaire, Ohio, 1963-66; assoc. dir. pediatrics Harlem Hosp. Center, N.Y.C., 1966-73; dir. dept. pediatrics Jewish Hosp. and Med. Center, Bklyn., 1973-85; prof. pediatrics U. Medicine and Dentistry of N.J., Newark, 1985—, prof. preventive medicine and community health, 1991—, chmn. dept. pediatrics, 1985-90; dir. dept. pediatrics U. Hosp., Newark, 1985-90, mem. attending staff, 1985—. Assoc. clin. prof. pediatrics Columbia U., 1968-73; prof. pediatrics SUNY Downstate Med. Center, Bklyn., 1973-85; cons. Englewood (N.J.) Hosp., Hackensack (N.J.) Hosp.; trustee Bergen-Passaic County Lung Assn., 1973-85. bd. of gov. coun., Am. Assn. U. Prof., U. Medicine and Dentistry, 2001-. Author: (with Leonard Glass) Perinatal Medicine, 1976, Lung Diseases of Children, 1979, 2d edit., 1985, The Hidden Campaign: The Medical History of President Franklin D. Roosevelt and the 1944 Election, 2002; editor: Hospital Care of Children and Youth, 1986, Jour. Perinatology, 1985—; contbr. articles to profl. jours., chpts. to textbooks. Served to sr. asst. surgeon USPHS, 1960-62. Mem. Soc. Pediat. Rsch., Harvey Soc., Am. Soc. Microbiology, Am. Acad. Pediat. (com. on hosp. care 1982-85, chmn. 1985-88, task force on pediat. AIDS 1987-92), Am. Thoracic Soc., Am. Pediat. Soc., Soc. Exptl. Biology and Medicine, N.Y. Pediat. Soc. (pres. 1982-83), Am. Polit. Sci. Assn., Bklyn. Acad. Pediat. (v.p. 1976, pres. 1977), Infectious Diseases Soc., Med. Soc. N.J. (mem. spl. com. AIDS 1993-95), Alpha Omega Alpha. Home: 165 Serpentine Rd Tenafly NJ 07670-2739 Office: U Medicine and Dentistry NJ MSB-F586 185 S Orange Ave Newark NJ 07103-2757 E-mail: evanshe@umdnj.edu.

EVANS, JACK, city official; b. Oct. 31, 1953; Student, U. Pa., U. Pitts. Past atty. divs. enforcement SEC, Washington; past co-founder ward 2 Dem. Com., Washington, past chmn. rules and procedures com.; pres. Washington D.C. Dem. Party, 1988; city councilman, chmn. ward 2 Washington D.C. City Coun., 1991—; assoc. Baker & Hostetler Law Firm. Chmn. pro tempore Washington (D.C.) City Coun., 2000—. Mem. Dupont Cir. Adv. Neighborhood Commn., 1988—.*

EVANS, JACK R. (J. GLENN EVANS), writer, poet; b. Wewoka, Okla., Dec. 21, 1930; s. John and Jimmie Devonia (Gordon) Glenn; m. Lucille Wallace, May 28, 1957 (div. 1967); m. Barbara Ann (Lubic) Conroy, Oct. 26, 1968; 1 stepchild, Barbara Ann Conroy. BS, East Ctrl. U., Ada, Okla., 1956. Stockbroker Hinton Jones Co., Seattle, 1966-68; stockbroker, v.p. Fox Roff Co., Seattle, 1968-70, John R. Lewis Co., Seattle, 1970-73; stockbroker, pres. Securities Exch., Seattle, 1973-76; pres., stockbroker, investment banker Securities Corp. of Wash., Seattle, 1976-84; pub. SCW Publs., Seattle, 1984—; poetry editor, pub. PoetsWest Online, Seattle, 1998—; freelance poet, writer, historian Seattle, 1986—; poetry curator Seattle City Coun. "Words' Worth", 2001. Bd. dirs. Seattle Freelances, 1995-2002; mem. adv. bd. U. Wash. Writers Program. Author: Little History of Pike Place Market, 1991, Swedes From Whence They Came, 1993, Seattle Poems, 1996, Window in the Sky, 1996, Levant F. Thompson: Hop King, Banker, Senator, 1992, Little History of Bothell Washington, 1988, Little History of Gig Harbor Washington, 1988, Little History of North Bend-Snoqualmie, 1990, Little History of Renton Washington, 1987, (CD) Window in the Sky, 1999; editor: Klondike Gold Rush Centennial Anthology, 1997, Chasing His Dreams: Life of Entrepreneur, 2002, Broker Jim, 2002, Buffalo Tracks, 2003. Contest dir., bd. dirs. Klondike Gold Rush Centennial Celebration, Wash. State, 1997. Cpl. USAF, 1954. Recipient Faith Beamer Cooke award Wash. Poets Assn., 1999, Seattle FreeLances Outstanding Writer award, 2003, Nat. winner Rock Rover Poetry Contect, 2003, 2d pl. winner William STafford award, 2002. Mem. Assn. King County Hist. Orgn. (past pres.), Pacific N.W. Hist. Guild (past v.p.), Wash. Poets Assn. (bd. dirs. 1997—), PoetsTable. Avocations: hiking, history, reading. Office: SCW Publs 1011 Boren Ave # 155 Seattle WA 98104-1325

EVANS, JAMES, engineer; b. Stamford, Conn., Mar. 6, 1927; m. Charlotte Evans, June 11, 1949 (dec. 1974); children: Donald, Richard, Kenneth; m. Miriam Evans, July 5, 1984. BSEE, Cooper U., 1949; MA in Physics, Columbia U., 1950; PhD in Physics, Bklyn. Polytech. Inst., 1953. Engr. IBM, Yorktown Heights, N.Y., 1960-65; engr., cons. Ridgefield, Conn., 1965-73; engr. Schlumberger, Ridgefield, 1973-76, Diag. Ret. Systems, Oakland, N.J., 1977-80, Trans-Lux, Norwalk, Conn., 1980-85; engr., cons. Stamford, 1985—. With USN, 1944-45. Home: 65 Glenbrook Rd Stamford CT 06902-2970

EVANS, JAMES BRIAN, geophysics educator; b. Baker City, Oreg., June 25, 1946; s. James Richard and Ruth Mary (Hue) E.; m. Marcia Louise Killam, Aug. 25, 1974; children: Megan Hue, Rebecca Brower, Tristan Isaac. BS cum laude, U. Idaho, 1968; MS in Geophysics, U. Minn., 1975; PhD, MIT, 1978. Postdoctoral assoc. dept. earth, atmos., planetary sci. MIT, Cambridge, 1978-79; asst. prof. dept. geology and geophysics Princeton (N.J.) U., 1980-83; asst. prof. dept. earth, atmos., planetary sci. MIT, Cambridge, 1983-88, assoc. prof. dept. earth, atmos., planetary sci., 1988-93, prof. dept. earth, atmos., planetary sci., 1993—. Cons. various indsl. orgns. and govt. panels. Editor: (book; with T.F. Wong) Fault Mechanics and Transport Properties of Rock, 1992; contbr. articles to sci. jours. Lt. USN, 1969-72, Vietnam. Recipient von Humboldt Soc. award for sr. scientists, 1996, U. Minn. Alumni Outstanding Achievement award, 2001. Mem. Am. Ceramic Soc., Am. Geophys. Union, Phi Beta Kappa, Sigma Xi. Democrat. Office: MIT 54-718 Cambridge MA 02139-4307 E-mail: brievans@mit.edu.

EVANS, JAMES E. lawyer; b. 1946; BA, Mich. State U., 1968; JD, Ohio State U., 1970. Bar: Ohio 1971. Assoc. Keating, Muething & Klekamp, 1971-76; v.p., gen. counsel Am. Fin. Corp., Cin., 1976—, now sr. v.p., dir. Office: Am Fin Corp 1 E 4th St Cincinnati OH 45202-3717

EVANS, JAMES HANDEL, university administrator, architect, educator; b. Bolton, Eng., June 14, 1938; came to U.S., 1965. s. Arthur Handel and Ellen Bowen (Ramsden) E.; m. Carol L. Mulligan, Sept. 10, 1966; children: Jonathan, Sarah. Diploma of Architecture, U. Manchester, Eng., 1965; MArch., U. Oreg., 1967; postgrad., Cambridge (Eng.) U., 1969-70. Registered architect, Calif., U.K.; cert. NCARB. Assoc. dean. prof. architecture Calif. Poly. State U., San Luis Obispo, 1967-78; prof. art and design San Jose (Calif.) State U., 1979—, assoc. exec. v.p., 1978-81, interim exec. v.p., 1981-82, exec. v.p., 1982-91, interim pres., 1991-92, pres., 1992-95; vice chancellor Calif. State U System, Long Beach, CA, 1995-96; planning pres. Calif. State U. Channel Islands, Ventura, 1996-2001; pres. HE Cons. Inc., 2001—. Cons. Ibiza Nueva, Ibiza, Spain, 1977-80; vis. prof. Ciudad Universitaria, Madrid, 1977; vis. lectr. Herriott Watt U., Edinburgh, 1970; mem. adv. com. Army Command Staff Coll., Ft. Leavenworth, Kans., 1988. Trustee Good Samaritan Hosp., San Jose, 1987-90; bd. dirs. San Jose Shelter, 1988-90; dir. San Jose C. of C., 1991-94, Ventura County Mus. History and Art. Sci. Rsch. Coun. fellow Cambridge U., 1969-70. Fellow AIA; mem. Royal Inst. Brit. Architects, Assn. Univ. Architects. Avocation: golf. E-mail: jhevans@adelphia.net.

EVANS, JAMES HURLBURT, retired transportation and natural resources executive; b. Lansing, Mich., June 26, 1920; s. James L. and Marie (Hurlburt) E.; m. Mary Johnston Head, 1984; children by previous marriage: Eric B. (dec. 1996), Carol E. Jepperson, Joan E. Madsen. AB, Centre Coll., 1943, DHL (hon.), 1987; JD, U. Chgo., 1948; LLD (hon.), Millikin U., 1978. Bar: Ill. 1949. Atty., loan officer Harris Trust & Savs. Bank, Chgo., 1948-56; sec.-treas. Reuben H. Donnelley Corp., Chgo., 1956-57; v.p., dir. Reuben H. Donnelley Corp. (merged with Dun & Bradstreet 1961), N.Y.C., 1957-62; v.p. fin. Dun & Bradstreet, 1962-65, also bd. dirs.; pres. Seamen's Bank for Savs., N.Y.C., 1965-68, chmn. bd., 1968, trustee, 1965-78; pres. Union Pacific Corp., N.Y.C., 1969-77, chmn., CEO, 1977-85. Ret. dir. AT&T, GM Corp., Citicorp/Citibank, Met. Life Ins. Co., Bristol-Myers, Dun & Bradstreet, Anaconda Corp. Bd. govs. ARC, 1970-76, nat. fund chmn. 1974-78; hon. trustee, former vice chmn. John F. Kennedy Ctr. for Performing Arts; life trustee Nat. Recreation Found., pres. 1971-75, U. Chgo., Ctr. Coll. Ky., Ctrl. Park Conservancy; founding mem. Citizens Adv. Com. on Environ. Quality, 1966-70. Served to lt. USNR, 1943-46; life gov. N.Y. Presbyn. Hosp. Mem. ABA, Bus. Council, Phi Beta Kappa, Omicron Delta Kappa, Delta Kappa Epsilon. Clubs: Racquet and Tennis, Links, Knickerbocker (N.Y.C.); Metropolitan, Alfalfa (Washington); Maidstone (East Hampton); Bohemian (San Francisco). Presbyterian. Office: 375 Park Ave Ste 2005 New York NY 10152-2099

EVANS, JAMES MIGNON, architect; b. Memphis, May 9, 1938; s. Mignon Kemper and Elizabeth Louise (Fulcher) E.; m. Gayle Jean Dupont, Aug. 21, 1965; children: Matthew Moseby, Benjamin Dupont, Bolin Briscoe. BA, Rice U., 1960; MFA in Architecture, Princeton U., 1962. Registered architect, Tenn., Va., Calif., Ariz., N.Y. Intern architect Perkins & Will Ptnrship., Washington, 1965-66; architect Doxiadis Assocs., Washington, 1966-68, Gassner Nathan & Browne, Memphis, 1969-70, prin., 1970-87, Nathan/Evans/Taylor, Memphis, 1987-95, Nathan/Evans/Taylor/Coleman/Foster, Memphis, 1995—. Mem. bldg. code rev. and adv. bd. Memphis and Shelby Counties, 1980-83; mem. Memphis Heritage Adv. Com., 1980-84. Bd. dirs. Dismas Ho., Memphis, 1989—94, pres., 1992, 1993; bd. dirs. Theatre Memphis; trustee Grace-St. Luke's Episcopal Sch., Memphis, 1980—86, pres., 1984—85; mem. vestry Grace-St. Luke's Episcopal Ch., 1983—86, 1990—93, 2001—, jr. warden, 1992, 1993. Served with U.S. Army, 1963—65. Lowell M. Palmer fellow, 1961-62; recipient Sylvan award Lumberman's Club of Memphis, 1983, 85, Excellence award Masonry Inst. Tenn., 1980, 89, 91, Energy Design Honor award TVA, 1988. Mem. AIA (treas. 1978, peer reviewer 1987—, Honor award 1978, 94, mem. exec. com. Memphis chpt., mem. past pres. coun. 2001-03, chmn. awards com. 2001-03), Tenn. Soc. Architects (bd. dirs. 1977-80, Excellence award 1978, 81, 96,, 97, Honor award 1981, 89, 91), Memphis Inst. Architects (v.p. 1980, pres. 1981), Memphis Rotary (chmn. ambassadorial scholarship com. 2003—). Clubs: Univ. of Memphis. Avocations: jogging, gardening, reading. Office: Nathan Evans Taylor Coleman Foster 17 W Pontotoc Ave Ste 101 Memphis TN 38103

EVANS, JANET, former Olympic swimmer; b. Placentia, Calif., Aug. 28, 1971; Degree in comms., U. So. Calif., 1994. Competed Atlanta Olympic Games, 1996; swimming coach U. So. Calif., host Janet Evans Invitational. Named U.S. Swimmer of Yr., 1987, USOC Sportswoman of the Yr.; recipient 4 Gold medals, 400m Freestyle, 800m Individual Medley, Seoul Olympic Games, 1988, 3 Gold medals, 800m Freestyle, 400m Freestyle, 400m Individual Medley, Barcelona Olympic Games, 1992, Silver medal, 400m Freestyle, 1992, Wubber 40th Nat. Title-400m Freestyle, Phillips 66 Nat. Swimming Championships, Indpls., 1994. Office: US Swimming Inc One Olympic Plaza Colorado Springs CO 80909-5724

EVANS, JO BURT, communications executive, rancher; b. Kimble County, Tex., Dec. 18, 1928; d. John Fred and Sadie (Oliver) Burt; m. Charles Wayne Evans II, Apr. 17, 1949; children: Charles Wayne III, John Burt, Elizabeth Wisart. BA, Mary Hardin-Baylor Coll., 1948; MA, Trinity U., 1967. Owner, mgr. Sta. KMBL, Junction, Tex., 1959-61; real estate broker Junction, 1965-74; staff economist, adv. on 21st Congl. Dist., polit. campaign Nelson Wolff, 1974-75; asst. mgr., bookkepper family owned ranches/rental property Junction, 1948—; gen. mgr. TV Translator Corp., Junction, 1968—, sec.-treas., 1980—. Treas., asst. to coord. Citizens for Tex., 1972; historian Kimble Hist. Soc.; mem. Com. of Conservation Soc. to Save the Edwards Aquifer, San Antonio, 1973; homecoming chmn. Sesquicentennial Yr., Junction; treas., asst. coord. New Consitution, San Antonio, 1974; legis. chair Hill Country Women, Kimble County, 1990—; cashier Texan Theatre; campaign chmn. for Challenge U. Mary Hardin, Baylor, 2000. Named an outstanding Texan, Tex. Senate, 1973. Mem. AAUW (scholarship named in honor 1973), Nat. Translator Assn., Daus. Republic Tex., Tex. Sheriffs Assn., Nat. Cattlewomens Assn., Internat. Platform Assn., Bus. and Profl. Women (pres. 1981-82). Republican. Mem. Unity Ch. Home: PO Box 283 Junction TX 76849-0283 Office: 618 Main St Junction TX 76849-4635

EVANS, JOEL RAYMOND, marketing educator; b. N.Y.C., Sept. 17, 1948; s. Joseph and Betty Evans; m. Linda Ruth, Dec. 19, 1970; children: Jennifer Faith, Stacey Beth. BA, Queens Coll., 1970; MBA, Bernard M. Baruch Coll., 1974; PhD, CUNY, 1975. MBA dir. Hofstra U., Hempstead, N.Y., 1975-77, asst. prof., 1975-79, assoc. prof., 1979-84, prof. mktg., 1984—, assoc. dean, 1981-82, chmn. dept. mktg. and internat. bus., 1978-85, RMI disting. prof. bus., 1989—, co-dir. retail mgmt. inst., 1989-96, co-dir. bus. rsch. inst., 1992-96. Cons. NCR, Pepsico, ARA/Slater Food Svcs., McCrory, Fortunoff, also other orgns. Co-author: Readings in Marketing Management, 1984, Principles of Marketing, 3d edit., 1995, Retail Management, 9th edit., 2004, Marketing, 8th edit., 2002, Can. edit., 2000. Recipient Disting. Service award, Hofstra U., 1982, Hofstra U. Sch. Bus. Dean's award, 1979, 81, 98; named One of Outstanding Young Men of Am., 1979. Mem. Am. Mktg. Assn., Acad. Mktg. Sci., Mktg. Educators Assn., Am. Collegiate Retailing Assn., Southwestern Mktg. Assn., Soc. for Mktg. Advances, Beta Gamma Sigma. Avocations: jogging, tennis. Home: 14 Melrose Ln Commack NY 11725-1615 Office: 134 Hofstra U Dept Mktg & Internat Bus 222 Weller Hall Hempstead NY 11549

EVANS, JOHN CLIFFORD, statistician; b. Boggabri, NSW, Australia, Oct. 28, 1948; arrived in U.S., 2001; s. Gordon Clifford and Olive Mary Evans; m. Patricia Marie Breau, Dec. 14, 1957; children: Julian, Cara, Gabrielle, Daniel. BScAgr. in Biometry, U. Sydney, 1971, MScAgr. in Biometry, 1978; PhD in Stats. and Biometry, Cornell U., 1983. Biometrician Australian Dept. Agr., Sydney, 1971—89; mgr. math., stats. and databases Australian Water Techs., Sydney, 1989—96; clin. stats. mgr. Polartechnics, Sydney, 1996—2001; mgr. data mgmt. and biostats. Boston Scientific, Natick, Mass., 2001—. Contbr. articles to profl. jours. Ofcl., meet dir. USA Swimming, Gardner, Mass., 2001—. Mem.: Am. Assn. Pharm. Scientists, Internat. Biometrics Soc. Office: Boston Scientific 1 Boston Scientific Pl Natick MA 01760-1537 E-mail: evansj1@bsci.com.

EVANS, JOHN DAVID DANIEL, judge; b. Feb. 5, 1944; children: Reagan, Quentin Cory, Jonathan. BA, U. Western Ont., 1967; LLB, Windsor Law Sch., 1972. Bar: Ont. 1974. Assoc. W.L.S. trivett, Q.C., Orillia, Ont., 1974, Robert J. Carter, Q.C., Toronto, Ont., 1975-76; ptnr. Evans, Kukurin, Timmins, Ont., 1976-77, Perras, Evans, Kukurin & Huot, Timmins, Ont., 1977-80, Riopelle, Evans, Chornyj and Carr, Timmins, 1980-84; apptd. judge Criminal divsn. Provincial Ct., Ont., 1984-90, apptd. regional sr. judge ctrl. east region, 1990-98, sr. judge. Faculty law St. Clair C.C., No. C.C., Laurentian U. Mem. Criminal Lawyers Assn., Can. Bar Assn., Am. Judges Assn. (bd. govs.). Roman Catholic. Avocations: sports, hockey playing. Office: Ont Ct Justice 3 Dominion St Bracebridge ON Canada P1L 2E6 E-mail: John.D.Evans@jus.gov.on.ca.

EVANS, JOHN DERBY, telecommunications company executive; b. Detroit, June 3, 1944; s. Edward Steptoe and Florence (Allington) E.; m. Susan Blair Allan, Apr. 7, 1973 (div. Nov. 1986); children: John Derby, Courtenay Boyd. AB, U. Mich., 1966. Pres. Evans Comm. Sys. Inc., Charlottesville, Va., 1970-72; v.p., gen. mgr. Capitol Cablevision Corp., Charleston, W.Va., 1972-76; regional mgr. Am. TV and Comm. Corp., Denver, 1974-76; exec. v.p., COO Arlington (Va.) TeleCom. Corp., 1976-83; pres. Arlington Cable Ptnrs. Ltd., 1983-94, Suburban Cable Ptnrs., Brooklyn Pk., Minn., 1985-89, Hauser Comm., N.Y.C., 1985-94, Evans Telecomm. Co., 1983—; chmn., CEO Waterford Marine Inc., Middleburg, Va., 1996—. Staff asst. sec. planning and devel. Dept. HEW, Washington, 1976; bd. dirs. Eisenhower World Affairs Inst., 1990-2003, chmn. strategic planning com., 1997-2003, vice chmn. 1999-2003; vice chmn. bd. dirs. Signature Theater, Inc., Arlington, Va.; co-founder, bd. dirs. Cable Satelliter Pub. Affairs Network (C-SPAN), 1979—, exec. com., 1982-93, 98—, chmn., 1991-93, chmn. fin. com., 1997—; pres. Montgomery Cablevision (LP), Rockville, Md., 1986-94, Washington Metro Cable Club, 1981—; bd. dirs. Falcon Comm. Co., L.A., Falcon Cable TV, 1998-2000; GBR Scientific, Balt., 1999-2000; v.p. North Ctrl. Cable Comm. Co., Roseville, Minn., 1986-92; mng. gen. ptnr. Waterford Farm Partnership, Middleburg, Va., 1993—; Siciliano forum lectr. U. Utah, 1998; future makers lectr. Emory U., 1999; bd. dirs., Nelson Cable Co., Lovingston, Va.; spkr. in field. Trustee C Span Ednl. Found., 1994—. Signature Theater, Arlington; chmn. bd. trustees Evans Found., 1994—; chmn. Cancer/AIDS Rsch. Network, Balt.; mem. steering com. Inst. Human Virology U. Md., Balt., 1996—; bd. dirs. Internat. Cancer and AIDS Rsch. Found., 1996-2000, Internat. AIDS Vaccine Initiative, N.Y.C., 2002—, treas., 2003—, chmn. fin. and audit com., 2003—; bd. dirs., Hollings Cancer Ctr., Charleston, S.C.; adv. com. AIDS Rsch. Inst. U. Calif., San Francisco; mem. vis. com. Coll. LS and A, U. Mich., 1994—, mem. pres.'s adv. bd., 1998—, mem. commn. on info. tech., 2000—; chmn. Waterford Project Inc., 2000—; lectr. Inst. of the Humanities, U. Mich., 2000; keynote spkr. Exec. Summit on Internat. Health Philanthropy Royal Coll. Physicians, London, 2001; inaugural lectr. Mich. State U. Quello Ctr. for Telecom. Law and Regulation, 2001. Mem. Nat. Cable TV Assn. (nat. chmn. awards com. 1981, bd. dirs. 1982—, chmn. govt. rels. com. 1985-86, chmn. elections, bylaws com. 1991-97, mem. regulatory policy com. 1991-95, mem. conv. com. 1999-00, Pres. award 1979, Vanguard award 1984, convention com. 1998—), Va. Cable Assn. (bd. dirs. 1979—, v.p. 1982, pres. 1983, 84, Hall of Fame, 2001), Asia-Pacific Conf. Sci. and Tech. Leaders (U.S. del. 1996), Caribbean Acad. of Sci. (U.S. del. 10th ann. meeting 1998), Farmington Country Club, Boars Head Sports Club (Charlottesville), Washington Golf and Country Club (Arlington), Key West Yacht Club, Cable TV Adminstrn., Mktg. Soc. (bd. dirs. 1985). Republican. Episcopalian. Home and Office: Evans Telecoms 1617 White St Key West FL 33040 E-mail: jdevans@msn.com.

EVANS, JOHN JOSEPH, management consultant, executive, educator, writer; b. St. Louis, Mar. 1, 1940; s. Roy Joseph and Henrietta Frances (Schweizer) E.; children: Todd, Karlyn, Jane, Mark. BA, Centenary Coll., 1962; postgrad., Syracuse U., 1969, U. Wis., 1971, Harvard Bus. Sch., 1970—73; MBA, Pepperdine U., 1972, DSc (hon.), 1974. Pres., CEO Evans Distbg. Cos., La., 1962-72, Evans & Co., La., 1966—; v.p., corp. sec. Lee Nat. Life Ins. Co., La., 1973; pres., CEO La. REIT; v.p. mktg. UMB, 1974; divsn. gen. mgr. AgMet, La., 1974-76; gen. mgr. Exxon Ofc Products, L.A., 1976-78; pres., CEO Universal Mfg. Corp., L.A., 1982; corp. dir. tng. & devel. Mitchell Internat., San Diego, 1983-87, Sun Electric Corp., Crystal Lake, Ill., 1988-90; corp. dir. tng. Chilton Publs., Radnor, Pa., 1990-92. Adj. prof. Centenary Coll., Golf Acad. San Diego. Bd. dirs. ARC; trustee Grad. Sch. Sales Mgmt. and Mktg.; chmn. bd. dirs. N. La. Mental Health Hosp.; co-chair United Way, 1965-69. Recipient awards United Way, 1965-69, ITVA awards, 1987-88. Mem. Nat. Beer Wholesalers Assn. (adv. dir.), Sales and Mktg. Execs. of Shreveport (pres.), S.W. Sales and Mktg. Execs. Coun. (pres.), Young Pres. Orgn., Pres.'s Assn., Conf. Bd., Aspen Inst., Sales and Mktg. Execs. Internat., Am. Soc. Tng. and Devel., Am. Soc. Pers. Adminstrn., Syracuse U. Grad. Sch. Sales Mgmt. and Mktg. Alumni Assn. (past pres., past trustee), Westlake Village C. of C. (past v.p., bd. dirs.), Shreveport C. of C. Pers. and Indsl. Rels. Assn. (vice chmn., bd. dirs.), Harvard Club San Diego. Home and Office: 11305 Affinity Ct 131 San Diego CA 92131-2758

EVANS, JOHN ROBERT, former university president, physician; b. Toronto, Oct. 1, 1929; s. William Watson and Mary Evelyn Lucille (Thompson) E.; m. Jean Gay Glassco, 1954; children: Derek, Mark and Michael (twins), Gillian, Timothy, Willa. MD, U. Toronto, 1952; DPhil (Rhodes scholar), Oxford U., 1955; LLD (hon.), Dalhousie U., McMaster U., McGill U., 1972, Queen's U., 1974, Wilfred Laurier U., 1975, York U., 1977, U. Toronto, 1980, U. Western Ont., 1982, Yale U., 1978; DSc (hon.), Meml. U., 1973, U. Montreal, 1977, Royal Mil. Coll., 1989; DHL (hon.), Johns Hopkins U., 1978; D Univ. (hon.), U. Ottawa, 1978, U. Limbourg, The Netherlands, 1980. Intern Toronto Gen. Hosp., 1952—53, chief resident physician, 1958—59; practice medicine specializing in cardiology Toronto, 1961—72; assoc. dept. medicine U. Toronto Med. Sch., 1961—65, prof., 1972—, pres. univ., 1972—78, pres. emeritus, 1995—; dir. population, health and nutrition dept. World Bank, Washington, 1979—83; chmn. Allelix Inc., Mississauga, 1983—99; physician Toronto Gen. Hosp., 1961—65; dean Faculty Medicine McMaster U., Hamilton, 1965—72, v.p. health scis., 1967—72; chmn. Torstar Corp., Toronto, 1993—, Alcan Aluminium Ltd., Montreal, 1995—2002; vice chmn. NPS-Allelix Inc., 1999—. Bd. dirs. Torstar Ltd., Toronto, MDS Health Group, Toronto; hon. fellow London Sch. Hygiene and Tropical Medicine, Univ. Coll., Oxford, Eng.; chmn. Can. Found. Innovation, 1997—. Trustee Rockefeller Found., N.Y.C., 1982—95, chmn., 1988—95, African Med. Rsch. Found., Canada, 1986—90; trustee Walter and Duncan Gordon Charitable Found., Toronto, 1991—2000, chair, 1998—2000. Decorated Companion Order of Can., Order of Ont.; named, Can. Med. Hall of Fame, 2000; recipient Gairdner Found. Wightman award, Gairdner Found., 1992, FNG Starr medal, Can. Med. Assn., 2002; scholar Markle scholar, 1960—65. Master: ACP; fellow: Inst. Corp. Dirs., Royal Coll. Physicians (London), Royal Coll. Physicians and Surgeons Can., Royal Soc. Can. Home: 58 Highland Ave Toronto ON Canada M4W 2A3 Office: Torstar Ltd 1 Yonge St Toronto ON Canada M5E 1P9

EVANS, JOHN T. finance educator, consultant, social sciences educator, researcher; b. Albany, NY, Mar. 31, 1941; s. Horace S. and Maurine F. (Sassé) Evans; m. Barbara E. Ferman, Nov. 28, 1982 (dec. June 1993). BA, Columbia U., 1965; MA, New Sch. U., 1969, PhD, 1989. V.p. Syntony Sound, Inc., NYC, 1979—81; pres. Econ. Sys. Corp., NYC, 1981—; instr. Baruch Coll., NYC, 1986—88; prof. Manhattan Inst. Mgmt., NYC, 1988—91; asst. prof. LI U., Bklyn., 1991—98, assoc. prof., 1998—, chmn. bus. dept., 2001—. Author: From Trade Surplus to Deficit, 1995; co-author: Childrens TV Commercials, 1974, Globalization in the 21st Century, 1999, Globalization and Labor Force Composition, 2001. Campaign mgr. Congrl. race, Albany, NY, 1968. Mem.: Am. Econ. Assn., Internat. Trade & Fin. Assn., Columbia Club. Avocations: travel, history, reading. Office: LI Univ 1 University Plz Brooklyn NY 11201 Fax: 212-533-3277.

EVANS, JOHNNIE P. retired elementary school educator; b. Mobile, Ala., Sept. 6, 1924; s. Johnnie Price Evans Sr. and Josie Lee Evans; m. Carol J. Cannon, June 19, 1972 (dec. Mar. 1993); children: Katrina Holt, Pablo, Phillip. BA, Lincoln U., 1950; MS, So. Ill. U., 1966, PhD, 1975. Elem. tchr. Dept. of Edn., Jeffersoncity, Mo., secondary tchr., supt. of sch. Reading specialist,math asst. St. Louis (Mo.) Pub. Sch., 1979—91; adv. bd. Dist. Supt. of Sch., St. Louis. Mem. YMCA, St. Louis, 1994—, NAACP, St. Louis, 2003. Steward USN, 1943—46. Recipient Honors award, Harris Stowe Coll., 1964 Mem.: Cathedral Choir, Kappa Delta Pi (hon.), Phi Delta Kappa, Kapppa Alpha Psi. Meth. Avocations: travel, writing, swimming, reading, creative writing. Home: 3505 Oakdale Ave Saint Louis MO 63121

EVANS, JOY, foundation administrator; b. Waterbury, Conn., Feb. 15, 1940; 4 children. Student, Hartford Coll. for Women, 1959. Weekly radio personality Young Stars on Parade Sta. WBRY, Waterbury, 1951-58; exec. sec. dir.'s office Discover Am. Travel Orgns., Washington, 1962-71; exec. sec. adminstr.'s office Nat. Ctr. for Housing Mgmt., Washington, 1971-72; exec. sec. mgr.'s office Nat. Visitor's Ctr. Nat. Park Svc. Dept. Interior, 1972-73; staff asst. divsn. pub. programs Nat. Endowment for Humanities, Washington, 1973-81, pub. info. officer, office of the chair, 1981—. Founding chair fed. woman's com. Nat. Endowment for Humanities, 1980-82, liaison White House task force on the humanities and arts 1981-82. Staff newsletter editor Not Hardcopy Newsletter, 1996-98. Mem. Annandale Homeowner's Assn. (pres. Terrace Townhouses 1989-92, TTA newsletter editor 1988-92), Soc. Govt. Meeting Planners (D.C. chpt. 1991-92). Commencement Addr., Nat. Coll. of Business and Tech., Charlottesville, Va., 2002. Roman Catholic. Avocations: music, art, dance, photography, theater, feng shui. Office: Nat Endowment for Humanities Rm 402 1100 Pennsylvania Ave NW Washington DC 20506-0001

EVANS, JUDITH ANN FUTRAL, artist; b. Ft. Smith, Ark., Feb. 18, 1939; d. Charles Thomas and Wilma Hazel (Matthews) Futral; m. Jeptha Armstrong Evans, June 16, 1963 (div. 1976); children: Clara Hartley, Jeptha Armstrong III. BA, U. Ark., 1961; MFA, U. Iowa, 1964. Founder Blue Mountain Gallery, N.Y.C., 1980; theatrical scenic artist United Scenic Artists, N.Y.C., 1984—. Exhbns. include Butler Inst. Am. Art, Youngstown, Ohio, 1985, 88, 92, Sherry Franch Gallery, N.Y.C., 1997-2003, Ethel Sergeant Smith Gallery, Wayne, Pa., 1997, Sotheby's N.Y.C., 1996, Park Ave Atrium, N.Y.C., 1996, Lincoln Ctr. Gallery, N.Y.C., 1995, Metlife Windows, N.Y.C., 1994, Blue Mountain Gallery, N.Y.C., 1990, 92, 94, 96, Elaine Benson Gallery, Bridgehampton, N.Y., 1988, 92, Heckscher Mus. Art, Huntington, N.Y., 1996, Chesapeake Gallery, Centreville, Md., 2002, Doran Gallery, Tulsa, 2002, 03; represented in permanent collections Avon Corp., N.Y.C., U.S. Air, Phila., Tafapolsky & Smith LLP, San Francisco, Towers Perrin, Stamford, Conn., Giro Credit Bank, Vienna, Austria and N.Y.C., Shearson Lehman Hutton, Frankfort, Germany, N.Y.C., Dewey, Ballantine, N.Y.C., Maimonides Med. Ctr., N.Y.C., Hunter Coll., N.Y.C., Cedar Crest Coll., Allentown, Pa., Mincron Corp., N.Y.C., Castrol Corp., Inc., N.J., So. Ark. U., Magnolia, N.Y. Presbyn. Hosp., N.Y.C., Cary Ellis Co., Houston, Broadacre Mgmt. Co., Chgo.; included in The Best of Acrylic Painting, 1996, The Best of Oil Painting, 1996, Landscape Inspirations, 1997. Mem. United Scenic Artists, Am. Women in Radio and TV. Democrat.

EVANS, LANCE, psychology educator; b. Midland, Tex., Oct. 21, 1963; s. Graham Evans Frank and Field Allen Frances; m. Bea Bright, Mar. 15, 1997. BS, Auburn U., 1982; MA, U. Ala., 1998; PhD, Ind. State U., 2002. Postdoc. fellow U. Okla. Health Scis. Ctr., Oklahoma City, 2002—. Vol. coach YMCA, Birmingham, Ala., 1992-98. Recipient William Van Til award for scholarly writing, 2000, E.G. Roeber award; rsch. grantee Ind. Stat U., 1998-2000, Midwest Ctr. for Rural Health, 2000. Mem. APA, ACA, Kappa Delta Pi, Chi Sigma Iota, Phi Kappa Phi. E-mail: lancer6322@hotpop.com.

EVANS, LANCE MICHAEL, real estate board executive; b. Rochester, N.Y., Nov. 18, 1961; s. Charles Lee and Marlain Roan (Wahlberg) E.; m. Cheryl Ann Cummings, June 30, 1984. BA, SUNY, Potsdam, 1983; M Bus. and Policy Studies, SUNY, Saratoga Springs, 1995. Tchr. math. So. Cayuga Ctrl. Sch. Dist., Poplar Ridge, N.Y., 1983-84, Parishville (N.Y.) Ctrl.Sch., 1984-85; salesman Electrolux, Potsdam, N.Y., 1985; circulation office mgr. Watertown (N.Y.) Daily Times, 1985-91; dir. Salvation Army Thrift, Watertown, 1991-93; exec. dir. Sci-Tech Ctr. No. N.Y., Watertown, 1993-97; swim coach YMCA Blue Sharks, Watertown, 1997-99; dislocated worker assistance rep. N.Y. State Dept. Labor, Watertown, 1998; crew leader U.S. Bur. of the Census, 1998; exec. officer Jefferson-Lewis Bd. Realtors, Inc., 1998—. Bd. dirs. Downtown Bus. Assn., Watertown, 1994-98, v.p. 1996-97; mem. alumni bd. SUNY, Potsdam, 1984—; pres. adminstrv. bd. 1st United Meth. Ch., Watertown, 1994-96, pres. Watertown Assn. of Chs., 1996-97; mem. First Night Watertown Com., 1997-98; event coord. YMCA Cmty. Cup, 1994—; exec. officer St. Lawrence County Bd. Realtors, 2001-. Masters swimmer, YMCA Cmty. Cup, 1993—. Mem. Rotary of Watertown (bd. dirs. 2001-2004). Republican. Avocations: reading, swimming. Office: 215 Washington St Ste B9 Watertown NY 13601-3332 E-mail: levans@nnymls.com.

EVANS, LANE, congressman; b. Rock Island, Ill., Aug. 4, 1951; s. Lee Herbert and Joycelene (Saylor) E. BA, Augustana Coll., 1974; JD, Georgetown U., 1978. Bar: Ill. 1978. Mng. atty. Western Ill. Legal Assistance Found., Rock Island, 1978-79; mem. nat. staff Kennedy for Pres., Washington, 1978-80; atty., ptnr. Community Legal Clinic, Rock Island, Ill., 1981-82; mem. 98th-108th Congresses from 17th Ill. Dist., 1983—; mem. nat. security com., ranking mem. vets. affairs com., armed svcs. com. Served with USMC, 1969-71. Mem. AmVets, Am. Legion, Marine Corps League, Vietnam Vets Ill. Democrat. Roman Catholic. Office: US Ho of Reps 2211 Rayburn HOB Washington DC 20515-1317*

EVANS, LAWRENCE E. lawyer, educator; b. Houston, Mar. 30, 1950; s. Lawrence Edgar and Edith (Kinzy) E.; m. Nancy Campbell, Aug. 20, 1977; children: Christopher, Laura. BA, Washington & Lee U., 1973; JD, South Tex. Coll., 1977. Bar: Tex. 1977, Mo. 1989; registered patent atty. Lawyer Gunn, Lee & Miller, Houston, 1977-88, Herzog, Crebs & McGhee, St. Louis, 1988-2000, Blackwell, Sanders, Peper, Martin LLP, St. Louis, 2000—. Adj. prof. Washington Univ. Sch. of Law, St. Louis. Mem. Metro. Bar Assn. St. Louis (chmn. Patent, Trademark and Copyright sect. 1994), Internat. Trademark Assn., Am. Intellectual Property Law Assn. Office: Blackwell Sanders Peper Martin LLP 720 Olive St Ste 2400 Saint Louis MO 63101 E-mail: levans@blackwellsanders.com.

EVANS, LINDA KAY, publishing company executive; b. Tipton, Ind., June 16, 1945; d. Walter K. and Helen S. (Fakes) E. BA in English, Purdue U., 1968. Asst. to mng. editor Random House Pubs., N.Y.C., 1969-71; asst. to dir. editorial svcs. Sch. div. McGraw-Hill Book Co., N.Y.C., 1971-75, mgr. state contracts and inventory dept., 1975-88; bookstore owner, pres. The Literary Bookshop, N.Y.C., 1988-93; prodn. mgr. trade div. Simon & Schuster, N.Y.C., 1994—. Pub. cons. for sch. textbooks Prentice Hall Book Co., Englewood Cliffs, N.J., 1992-93. Recipient Holiday Window Display award to Lit. Bookshop, Greenwich Village C. of C., 1990. Avocations: reading, antique collecting, furniture making, travel. Office: Simon & Schuster Trade Div 1230 Ave of the Americas New York NY 10020-1586

EVANS, LOUISE, investor; b. San Antonio; d. Henry Daniel and Adela (Pariser) E.; m. Thomas Ross Gambrell, Feb. 23, 1960. BS, Northwestern U., 1949; MS in Clin. Psychology, Purdue U., 1952, PhD in Clin. Psychology, 1955. Lic. marriage, family and child counselor Calif.; Nat. Register of Health Svc. Providers in Psychology; lic. psychologist, Calif., N.Y. (inactive); diplomate Clin. Psychology, Am. Bd. Profl. Psychology. Intern clin. psychology Menninger Found. Topeka (Kans.) State Hosp., 1952-53; postdoctoral fellow clin. child psychology Menninger Clinic, Topeka, 1955-56; staff psychologist Kankakee (Ill.) State Hosp., 1954-55; head staff psychologist child guidance clinic Kings County Hosp., Bklyn., 1957-58; dir. psychology clinic Barnes-Renard Hosp.; instr. med. psychology Sch. Medicine Washington U., 1959-60; clin. rsch. cons. Episc. City Diocese, St. Louis, 1959-60; pvt. practice Fullerton, Calif., 1960—93; fellow Internat. Coun. Sex Edn. and Parenthood, 1984, Am. U., Washington. Psychol. cons. Fullerton Cmty. Hosp., 1961-81; staff cons. clin. psychology Martin Luther Hosp., Anaheim, Calif., 1963-70; chair, participant psychol. symposiums, 1956—; spkr., lectr. in field. Contbr. articles on clin. psychology to profl. publs. Elected to Hall of Fame Ctrl. H.S., Evansville, Ind., 1966; recipient Svc. award Yuma County (Ariz.) Head Start Program, 1972, Statue of Victory Personality of Yr. award Centro Studi E. Ricerche Delle Nazioni, Italy, 1985, Alumni Merit award Northwestern U. Coll. Arts and Scis., 1997; named Miss Heritage, Heritage Publs., 1965. Fellow AAAS (emeritus), APA (clin. divsn. psychology of women divsn., divsn. psychotherapy, cons. divsn., dir. exec. bd. 1976-79, Recognition award Internat. divsn. 2002), Acad. Clin. Psychology, Am. Assn. Applied and Preventive Psychology (charter), Royal Soc. Health Eng. (emeritus), Internat. Coun. Psychologists (dir. 1977-79, sec. 1962-64, 73-76, 2 awards 2003), Am. Orthopsychiat. Assn. (life), World Wide Acad. Scholars of N.Z. (life), Am. Psychol. Soc. (charter), L.A. Soc. Clin. Psychologists (exec. bd. 1966-67); mem. AAUP (emeritus), Calif. Psychol. Assn. (life, ins. com. 1961-65), L.A. County Psychol. Assn. (emeritus), Orange County Psychol. Assn. (charter founder, exec. bd. 1961-62), Am. Pub. Health Assn. (emeritus), Internat. Platform Assn., N.Y. Acad. Scis. (emeritus), Purdue U. Alumni Assn. (life, past pres. coun., mem. dean's club, Citizenship award 1975, Disting. Alumni award 1993, Old Master 1993), Northwestern U. 1851 Soc. (Coll. Arts and Scis. Merit award 1997), Ctr. Study Presidency, Soc. Jewelry Historians USA (charter), Alumni Assn. Menninger Sch. Psychiatry, Sigma Xi (emeritus). Achievements include development of innovative theories and techniques of clinical practice; acknowledged pioneer in development of psychology as science and profession both nationally and internationally, and in marital and family therapy, and in consulting to hospitals and clinics. Office: PO Box 6067 Beverly Hills CA 90212-1067 Fax: 310-474-1361.

EVANS, MARGARET A. volunteer; b. N.Y.C., Jan. 20, 1924; d. Bernard J. and Katherine (Walsh) Markey; m. John Cullen Evans, Jr., Nov. 24, 1951. BA, Coll. Mt. St. Vincent, 1944; postgrad., Columbia U. Rep. N.Y. Telephone Co., 1944; pers. office Sak's 34th, N.Y.C., 1944-45, tng. supr. selling and non-selling depts., 1945-49, spl. assignment for store mgr., 1949-50; non-selling tng. supr. Gimbel Bros. and Saks 5th Inc., 1950-51; rep. Gimbels and Sak's 34th at NCCJ Retail Group meeting, 1949-50; instr. textile painting for ARC Chelsea Navy Hosp., 1952-54. ARC vol., 1980-92. Bd. dirs. Marblehead Hosp. Aid Assn., 1954, pres. 1955-58; sec. Mass. Hosp. Assn. Coun. of Hosp. Auxilliaries, 1957-59, chmn. North Shore region, 1959-61, chmn.-elect 1961-62, state chmn., 1962-64; exofficio trustee Salem Hosp.; trustee Mary A. Alley Hosp., 1956-79, chmn. bd. 1974-79; mem. Welcome Wagon of Fairfield/Easton (Conn.), 1979-83; chmn. Fairfield/Easton Theatre Group, Fifth Wheel Club of Fairfield, 1983-85. Mem. Alumnae Assn. Coll. Mt. Saint Vincent, Arrangers of Marblehead (chmn. garden therapy 1967-79), Marblehead Women's Newcomers (pres. 1953). Home: 108 Cedarwood Ln Fairfield CT 06825-1308

EVANS, MARGARET ANN, human resources administrator, business owner; b. Great Bend, Kans., Dec. 26, 1947; d. Freddy Florence and Peggy (Hawkins) Green; m. Carl Evans, Aug. 13, 1972 (dir.); children: Carl André, Christopher Dion. B in Psychology, U. Mo., 1971, MPA, 1972. Pers. specialist Met. Jr. Coll., Kansas City, Mo., 1972-73; employee rels. specialist Amoco Oil Co., Kansas City, 1973-74; classification specialist Richards-Gebaur AFB, Mo., 1974-75; employee rels. officer Govt. Employee Hosp. Assn., Kansas City, 1977-84, mgr. pers., 1984-87, dir. human resources, 1987—. Mem. pers. com. Sta. KKFI, Kansas City, 1989—; mem. cert. bd. Human Resource Inst., exam devel. dir., 1994-95, sec.-treas., 1995-96. Sec. and v.p. Booster Club, Hickman Mills High Sch., Kansas City, 1989—; bd. dirs. Saturday Scholars, 2000-02. Ford Found. fellow U. Mo., 1971; recipient Contbr. of Yr. award Human Resource Mgmt. Assn., 1992, Pres. award 1993, 1995; named One of Kansas City's 100 Most Influential Kansas Citians KC Globe Most Influential African Ams. of Kansas City, 1993, 95, 96, 97. Mem. NAFE, Soc. Human Resources Mgmt. (pers. rsch. com. Kansas City chpt. 1989—, nat. com. 1990—, sec.-treas. Mo. state coun. 1992-93, bd. dirs., v.p. at large 1999-2000, v.p. Area IV 2000, 02, 03), Pers. Mgmt. Assn. (co-chmn. coll. rels. 1981), Urban League, NAACP, Links, Inc., ASTD, Alpha Kappa Alpha (chair midwestern regional conf., 1996, Outstanding Grad. Soror). Home: 10216 E 96th St Kansas City MO 64134-2309 Office: Govt Employee Hosp Assn 17306 E Us Highway 24 Independence MO 64056-1808

EVANS, MARGARET UTZ, secondary school educator; b. Gladwyne, Pa. d. Joseph H. and Marion Irwin (Laughead) Utz; m. James Irvin Evans. BA, King's Coll., Briarcliff Manor, N.Y.; MA, Ea. Bapt. Theol. Sem., Wynneword, Pa. Tchr. Menaul High Sch., Albuquerque, Haverford Sch. Dist., Havertown, Pa., Penn-Delco Sch. Dist., Aston, Pa. Recipient Wilbor T. Elmore prize in history, James A. Barkley award in history. Mem. NEA. Home: 820 Montico Rd Wilmington DE 19803-4007

EVANS, MARK IRA, obstetrician, geneticist; b. Bklyn., May 14, 1952; s. Robert Bernard and Sonia Beatrice Evans. BS in Psychology, Tufts U., 1973; MD, SUNY, Bklyn., 1978. Diplomate Am. Bd. Ob-Gyn, Am. Bd. Med. Genetics. Resident in ob-gyn U. Chgo., 1979—82; med. genetics fellow NIH, Bethesda, Md., 1982—84; dir. reproductive genetics Hutzel Hosp. Wayne State U., Detroit, 1984—2001, Charlotte B. Failing prof. ob-gyn. and human genetics Ctr. Molecular Med./Path., 1991—2001, disting. prof., 2000, dir. Ctr. for Fetal Diagnosis and Therapy, 1985—2001, dir. human genetics program, 1996—2001, chmn., chief, 1998—2001; prof., chmn. ob-gyn, prof. human genetics, dir. fetal therap Hahnemann Hosp., Phila., 2000—02; dir. fetal therapy program MCP Hahnemann U., 2000—02; dir. Inst. Genetics and Fetal Medicine, prof. ob-gyn. St. Lukes Roosevelt Hosp. Ctr./Columbia U., N.Y.C., 2002—. Mem. adv. bd. Ehlrs Danlos Found., L.A., 1986—, Corning Metpath, Quest Diagnostics, 1988-2000, Lab. Corp., 2003—, Nat. Adv. Bd. on Ethics in Reprodn., Washington; mem. ethics com. Am. Coll. Ob-Gyn., 1987-90, Molecular Medicine and Genetics, Wayne State U. Author: (textbooks) Pretest: Obsterics and Gynecology, 6th rev. edit., 1991, 9th edit., 2000, (with C.C. Lin) Intrauterine Growth Retardation, 1984, (with others) Fetal Diagnosis Therapy: Science, Ethics and the Law, 1989, Reproductive Risks and Prenatal Diagnosis, 1992, The New Reproductive Genetics, 1993, Maternal Genetic Disease, 1996, Invasive Outpatient Procedures in Reproductive Medicine, 1997, Principles and Practice of Medical Therapy in Pregnancy, 1998, Study Guide, 1998, The Unborn Patient, 2001, Contemporary Therapy for Obstetrics & Gynecology, 2002; (with Evans and Rodeck) Ultrasound and Fetal Therapy, 2000; (with Evans, Platt and De La Cruz) Fetal Therapy, 2000; editor: (with others) The Genetic Revolution and Obstetrics and Gynecology, 2002, New Genetics for the Clinician, 2002; contbr. articles to profl. jours. Fellow Am. Coll. Ob-Gyn. (course coordination com. 1996-99), Am. Coll. Med. Genetics (founder); mem. AMA (nat. ultrasound task force 1990-91), Internat. Fetal Medicine Surgery Soc. (pres. 1986-87, 96-97), Am. Soc. Human Genetics, Soc. Gynecol. Investigation, Ctrl. Assn. Ob-Gyn. (bd. dirs. 1998-2000), Soc. Perinatal Obstetricians, Am. Gynecol. and Obstetrics Soc. Jewish. Office: Inst for Genetics and Fetal Medicine St Lukes Roosevelt Hosp Ctr 1000 10th Ave Ste 11A-11 New York NY 10019 E-mail: IGFM@chpnet.org.

EVANS, MARSHA JO ANNE, nursing administrator; b. Watseka, Ill., Aug. 18, 1951; d. Robert Lewis and Jane Eleanor (Orr) Niles; m. Larry E. Evans, Sept. 16, 1973 (div. Aug. 1997); 1 child, Melinda Joy. BSN, So. Ill. U., 1973. Staff nurse Sevier County Hosp., Sevierville, Tenn., 1973-75; asst. DON Fair Oaks Nursing Home, Edward A. Utlaut Meml. Hosp., Greenville, Ill., 1975-76; insvc. coord., infection control nurse, nursing supr. Fayette County Hosp., Vandalia, Ill., 1976-83, quality assurance coord., 1983-88; infection control coord. St. Anthony's Meml. Hosp., Effingham, Ill., 1988-94, outpatient svcs. rep., 1994-96, home care mgr., 1996-98; utilization mgmt. case mgr. St. John's Hosp., Springfield, Ill., 1998—2002; infection control facilitator St. John's Hosp, Springfield, Ill., 2002—03; chief clin. officer Pana Cmty. Hosp., Pana, Ill., 2003—. Office: Pana Cmty Hosp 101 E Ninth St Pana IL 62557

EVANS, MARSHA JOHNSON, non-profit association administrator, former career officer; b. Springfield, Ill., Aug. 12, 1947; d. Walter Edward Johnson and Alice Anne Field; m. Gerard Riendeau Evans, June 30, 1979. AB, Occidental Coll., 1968; MA, MA in Law & Diplomacy, Fletcher Sch., 1977; postgrad., Nat. War Coll., 1988-89. Commd. ensign USN, 1968, advanced through grades to rear admiral, 1993; mideast policy officer Commander-in-Chief, U.S. Naval Forces, Europe, London, 1977-79; spl. asst. to sec. treasury U.S. Treasury Dept., Washington, 1979-80; staff analyst Office of Chief Naval Ops., Washington, 1980-81; dep. dir. Pres. Commn. on White House Fellowships, Washington, 1981-82; exec. officer Recruit Tng. Command, San Diego, 1982-84; commanding officer Naval Tech. Tng. Ctr., San Francisco, 1984-86; battalion officer, sr. lectr. polit. sci. U.S. Naval Acad., Annapolis, Md., 1986-88; chief of staff San Francisco Naval Base, 1989-91, Naval Acad., Annapolis, Md., 1991-92; exec. dir. of the standing com. on mil. and civilian women Dept. of the Navy, 1992-93; comdr. Navy Recruiting Command, Washington, 1993-95; supt. Naval Postgrad. Sch., Monterey, Calif., 1995-97; CEO, nat. exec. dir. Girl Scouts U.S.A., N.Y.C., 1998—2002; president American Red Cross, 2002—. Interim dir. George C. Marshall European Ctr. Security Studies, Garmisch Partenkirchen, Germany, 1996-97; nat. exec. dir. Girl Scouts. Am., 1998—. White House fellow, 1979; Chief Naval Ops. scholar, 1976. Mem. Mortar Bd., Phi Beta Kappa. Office: Am Red Cross 430 17th St NW Washington DC 20006-5307

EVANS, MARTIN FREDERIC, lawyer; b. Nashville, June 12, 1947; s. Robert Clements and Adelaide Hawkins (Roberts) E.; m. Margaret Carroll Kidder, Apr. 17, 1982. BA, U. Va., 1969; JD, Yale U., 1972. Bar: N.Y. 1973, U.S. Dist. Ct. (so. dist.) N.Y. 1973, U.S. Ct. Appeals (2d cir.) 1974, U.S. Ct. Appeals (D.C. cir.) 1981, U.S. Supreme Ct. 1981, D.C. 1982. Assoc. Debevoise & Plimpton, N.Y.C., 1972-80, ptnr., 1981—. Researcher Nat. Commn. for Rev. of Antitrust Laws and Procedure, Washington, 1978. Mem. ABA (sect. for antitrust law), Assn. of Bar of City of N.Y., Phi Beta Kappa. Office: Debevoise & Plimpton 919 Third Ave New York NY 10022-6225

EVANS, MARTIN G. management educator; b. Cardiff, Wales, Nov. 28, 1939; s. Griffith Thomas and Dorothea F.N. (Bradley) E.; m. Nancy Remage, Aug. 3, 1968; children: Lisa, Katherine. Frim prof. to prof. emeritus U. Toronto Rotman Sch. Mgmt., 1966—. Contbg. author: Variations in Organizational Science: A Conference in Honor of Donald T. Campbell, Thousand Oaks, California, 1999; contbr. articles to prof. jours., including Can. Jour. Adminstrv. Scis., Am. Psychologist, Orgnl. Behavior and Human Performance. Fellow: APA, Am. Psychol. Soc.; mem.: Acad. Mgmt. (co-webmaster rsch. methods divsn., disting. edn. award 2001). Home: 48 Grisword St Cambridge MA 02138 Office: U Toronto Rotman Sch Mgmt Toronto ON Canada M5S 3E6 E-mail: evans@mgmt.utoronto.ca.

EVANS, MARY JOHNSTON, corporate director; b. Shawnee, Okla., Feb. 28, 1930; d. Paul Xenophon and Helen Elizabeth (Alford) Johnston; children by previous marriage: Marcy Head Benson, Paul Johnston Head, Eric Talbott Head; m. James H. Evans, 1984. Student, Wellesley Coll., 1947-48, U. Okla., 1949. Dir. Amtrak, 1974-80, vice-chmn., 1975-79. Bd. dirs. Household Internat., Inc., Saint-Gobain Corp., Sunoco, Inc., Delta Air Lines, Inc., Moody's Corp. Pres. Jr. League Oklahoma City, 1968-69; trustee Nat. Coun. Crime and Delinquency, 1971-75, Presbyn. Med. Ctr., Oklahoma City, 1969-75; trustee Brick Presbyn. Ch., 1985-89; bd. dirs. St. Anthony Hosp., 1973-75; bd. visitors U. Pitts. Grad. Sch. Bus., 1978-85; trustee Mary Baldwin Coll., Staunton, Va., 1976-83, Carnegie Hall, 1985-92. Recipient Law Day award-Liberty Bell award Okla. Bar Assn., 1971, Disting. Svc. award U. Okla., 1981; named one of Top 100 Corp. Women Bus. Week mag., 1976; named to Okla. Hall of Fame, 1978 Mem. Conf. Bd. (Sr.), Colony Club, River Club, Maidstone Club (East Hampton, N.Y.), Pi Beta Phi. Presbyterian (elder). Address: 920 5th Ave New York NY 10021-4160 also: 32 Windmill Ln East Hampton NY 11937-3605

EVANS, MIKE, professional basketball coach; m. Kim Evans; children: Michael, Rachelle, D'Ambra. Postgrad, Kansas State U., 1978. Guard San Antonio Spurs, Milw. Bucks, Cleve. Cavaliers, Denver Nuggets, dir. player personnel, tv analyst, asst. coach, head coach, 2002—. Named Big Eight Player of the Year, Kansas State U., 1977, 1978. Office: Denver Nuggets 1000 Chopper Cir Denver CO 80204 E-mail: nuggetsmail@pepsicenter.com.

EVANS, MYRON WYN, physicist, researcher; b. Craigcefnparc, Wales, May 26, 1950; came to US, 1986; s. Edward Ivor and Mary (Jones) E.; m. Laura Jean Joseph, Feb. 18, 1988. BSc, Aberystwyth U., Wales, 1971, PhD, 1974, DSc, 1977. Jr. rsch. fellow Wolfson Coll., Oxford, 1975; advanced fellow Sci. and Engring. Rsch. Coun., Aberystwyth, 1978-83; vis. scientist Cornell U., 1989-92, U. Zurich, 1989-90; prof. Alpha Found., Budapest, Hungary, 1995—; dir., chmn. bd. Alpha Found. Inst. for Advanced Study, 1998—. Chmn. bd. dirs. Alpha Inst. for Advanced Study; nat. com. British Sci. and Engring. Rsch. Coun.; rsch. assoc. Pa. State U., 1992; 1st sci. coord. European Molecular Liquids Group, 1980; sr. assoc. Pa. State U., 1990; sci.-tech. advisor Plaid Cymru, 1991; vis. prof. Trinity Coll., Dublin, 1985, IBM, Kingston, N.Y., 1986, York U., Toronto, 1995, Indian Statis. Inst., Calcutta, 1995; vis. scientist U. Pisa and Scuala Normale Superiore, 1980, U. Zurich, 1990, Cornell U., 1989, 91. Editor Modern Nonlinear Optics, 1997, The Enigmatic Photon, 1994-99; author: The Enigmatic Photon, 5 vols. 1994-99, Molecular Dynamics, 1982, Molecular Diffusion, 1984, Memory Function Approaches to Stochastic Problems in Condensed Matter, 1985, Dynamical Processes in Condensed Matter, 1985, Simulaton and Symmetry in Moledular Diffusion and Spectroscopy, 1992, The Photon's Magnetic Field, 1992, The Photomagneton in Quantum Field Theory, 1994, Water in Biology, Chemistry and Physics, 1996, Classical and Quantum Electrodynamics and the B Field, 1999, Contemporary Optics and Electrodynamics, 2001, (with David Clements) Higher Symmetry Electrodynamics in Special and General Relativity, (with Lawrence B. Crowell) Lecture Notes in Nigher Symmetry Electrodynamics; contbr. over 650 articles to profl. jours. Leverhulme fellow, Humboldt fellow, Brit. Imperial Chem. Industries fellow, 1974, NRC Can. fellow, 1974, Jr. Rsch. fellow Wolfson Coll., Oxford, 1975, Brit. Ramsay Meml. fellow, 1976, IBM fellow; recipient Harrison Meml. prize Royal Soc. Chemistry, London, 1978, Meldola medal, 1979, Disting. Am. Scientist award Assn. Disting. Am. Scientists, 2000. Mem. Optical Soc. Am., Am. Inst. Physics, NY Acad. Sci., Sigma Pi Sigma. Republican Nationalist. Avocations: poetry, landscape photography, athletics. also: 50 Rhyddwen Rd Craigcefnparc Swansea SA6 5RA Wales England Office: Alpha Found Inst Physics 11 Rutafa St Budapest Hungary Home: PO Box 6828 Ithaca NY 14851-6828

EVANS, NOLLY SEYMOUR, lawyer; b. Augusta, Ga., Sept. 16, 1927; s. Nolly Seymour and Laura (Taylor) E.; m. Judith Anne Leach, Feb. 18, 1965; children: Samantha, Meredydd, Clelia, Nolly. BFA in Music, U. Ga., 1948, MA in English Lit., 1950; LLB, Yale U., 1956; LLD, Yale Law Sch., 1971. Bar: N.Y. 1956. Assoc. firm Milbank, Tweed, Hadley & McCloy, N.Y.C., 1956-64; fin. counsel Amax, Inc., N.Y.C., 1964-70; gen. counsel Gilman Paper Co., N.Y.C., 1970-74; gen. counsel, sec. Crouse-Hinds Co., Syracuse, N.Y., 1976-82; counsel Hancock & Estabrook, Syracuse, N.Y., 1982-83; prin. Nolly S. Evans Law Offices, Syracuse, 1983-93. Docent Homewood House Mus., Balt. With U.S. Army, 1947—48. Mem. Confrerie des Chevaliers du Tastevin, Grand Officier of Sous Commanderie de Etats-Unis, N.Y., Commanderie de Bordeaux, Le Grand Conseil de Bordeaux, Jurade de St. Emilion, Connetable de Guyenne, Royal Over-Seas Club (London), and others. Home: 647 W University Pkwy Baltimore MD 21210-2907

EVANS, NORMAN ALLEN, retired civil engineering educator; b. Spearfish, S.D., Dec. 3, 1922; s. Allen C. and Claire (Doscher) E.; m. Jean Cole, Dec. 26, 1943; children— Douglas Robert, Elizabeth Ann, Garth William, Mathew. BS, S.D. State U., 1944; MS, Utah State U., 1947; PhD, Colo. State U., 1963. Registered profl. engr., Colo. Asst. prof. N.D. State U., Fargo, 1947-51; from asst. prof. to prof. civil engring. Colo. State U., Ft. Collins, 1951-59, prof., head dept. agrl. engring., 1956-69, dir. Environ. Resources Ctr., 1966-78, assoc. dir. Expt. Sta., 1970-71, dir. Office Gen. Univ. Research, 1970-72. Dir. Water Resources Research Inst., 1966-88; cons. in field; dir. Engrs. Council for Profl. Devel., 1970-76; mem. Colo. Water Pollution Control Commn., 1966-80, vice chmn., 1970-72; mem. Fort Collins City Water Bd., 1963-88, chmn., 1966-68, 81-88, vice chmn., 1963-66, 68-81; dir. Poudre Landmarks Found., 1996—, pres., 2000, 01. Served to 1st lt. AUS, 1944-46. Fellow AAAS, Am. Soc. Agrl. Engrs. (v.p. 1968-70); mem. ASCE, Sigma Xi, Phi Kappa Phi, Chi Epsilon, Alpha Epsilon, Gamma Sigma Delta. Home: 1847 Michael Ln Fort Collins CO 80526-1535

EVANS, OWEN BEVERLY, neurologist; b. Little Rock, Oct. 23, 1946; s. Owen Beverly and Patricia Claire (Weny) E.; m. Lynn Murray, June 5, 1971; children: Kathryn Boone, Owen William. BA, Vanderbilt U., 1969, MD, 1973. Diplomate Am. Bd. Pediatrics, Am. Bd. Psychiatry & Neurology. Intern Children's Orthopedic Hosp. & Med. Ctr., Seattle, 1973-74; lt. USNMC, 1974-76; resident pediatrics Vanderbilt U. Sch. Medicine, Nashville, 1976-77, resident neurology, 1977-80, asst. prof., 1980-83; assoc. prof. neurology, pediatrics U. Miss., Jackson, 1983-88, prof., chmn. dept. pediatrics, 1989—. Author: Manual of Child Neurology, 1987. Mem. AMA, Am. Acad. Pediatrics, Am. Acad. Neurology, Assn. Med. Sch. Pediat. Dep. Chmn., So. Child Neurology Soc., So. Soc. Pediat. Rsch., Ctrl. Miss. Pediat. Soc., Child Neurology Soc. Office: U Miss Med Ctr Dept Pediatrics 2500 N State St Jackson MS 39216-4500

EVANS, PAMELA R. sales and marketing executive; b. Hoisington, Kans., Aug. 25, 1957; d. John Roy and Sarah Mace (Alder) E. BS in Bus., U. Kans., 1980. Sales rep. Home & Automotive Products div. Union Carbide Corp., Seattle, 1981, dist. sales mgr. Syracuse, N.Y., 1981-82, mktg. assoc. Danbury, Conn., 1982-84, assoc. product mgr., 1984; asst. product mgr. Grocery Products div. Ralston Purina, St. Louis, 1984-85, product mgr., 1985-86, Eveready Battery Co. subs. Ralston Purina, St. Louis, 1986-88, group dir. mktg., 1988-90; dir. mktg. Consumer Products div. Esselte Pendaflex, 1990-91; dir. new bus. devel. Olympus Am., Inc., Woodbury, NY, 1991—94; v.p. mktg. consumer products group Olympus Am., Woodbury, NY, 1994—2001; pres. blueprints, inc., New Hope, Pa., 1994—2000, The SJI Cos., St. Louis, 1998-2000; sr. v.p. sales and mktg. The Sentry Group, Rochester, NY, 2000—03. Bd. advisors Electri-Cord Mfg. Co.; bd. dirs. Humane Soc., Rochester, NY. Avocations: music, sports, reading, photography. Office: 900 Linden Ave Rochester NY 14625 E-mail: pamalert@aol.com.

EVANS, PAT TERRELL, financial consultant; b. New Orleans, June 5, 1931; d. Paul W. and Catherine Rappold Terrell; m. Harry L. Evans, Aug. 5, 1950 (dec. Apr. 20, 1979); children: Debra, Matthew, Erin. BA, Southeastern La. U., 1953; postgrad., Harvard U., 1981. Documentary film prodr. WBRZ-TV, Baton Rouge, 1962—73; dir. Gov.'s Office of Women's Svcs., Baton Rouge, 1974—82; cons. KPMG-Peat Marwick, New Orleans, 1988—90; pres. Pat Evans and Assocs., New Orleans, 1990. Mgr. polit. campaigns, New Orleans, 1983—96; European coord. U.S. Baltic Found., Lithuania, Latvia and Estonia, 1997—99; cons. U.S. AID, Sarajevo, 2000. Sponsor Narcotics Anonymous, Women's Prison, St. Gabriel, La., 1973—83; founder La. Polit. Caucus, Baton Rouge, 1972, Ctr. for Women and Govt., 1992. Named to Women's Hall of Fame, Ctr. for Women and Govt., 1994; recipient Disting Svc. award, Welfare Rights, 1974, Outstanding Svc. award, La. Mental Health Assn., 1975. Democrat. Roman Catholic. Home: 2301 Magazine St New Orleans LA 70130 Office: Internat Project for Nonprofit Leadership 3330 N Causeway Blvd Metairie LA 70002

EVANS, PATRICIA MCCORMICK, clinical therapist; b. Cheraw, S.C. d. Foris Linsley and Mary Lucille Jackson; children: Robert, Antonio, Ronnie Jr. BA in Sociology, Coker Coll., 1996; MA in Counseling, Webster U., 1999; postgrad., Walden U., 2000—. Cashier Wal-Mart, Cheraw, SC, 1996—97; instr. South Piedmont C.C., Polkton, SC, 1997—2001; social worker Richmond County Dept. Social Svcs., Rockingham, SC, 2000—01; facilitator grief counseling group Richmond County Hospice. Founder, dir. Edn. Mentoring/Tutoring Program, Chesterfield, S.C., 2000—; founde,r pres. Maknadifrens, Inc. Author of poems. Vol. Richmond County Hospice. Mem.: Am. Correctional Assn., Am. Counseling Assn. Democrat. Baptist. Home: PO Box 882 Cheraw SC 29520 Office: Carolina Behavioral Svcs LLC Divsn Mentor Network 1219 Rockingham Rd Ste 12 Rockingham NC 28379 E-mail: cateyes@peedeeworld.net.

EVANS, PAUL DALE, economist, educator; b. Pocatello, Idaho, May 26, 1946; s. Paul Rex and Helen Mary Evans; m. Lin Jiang Evans; 1 child, Helen Victoria. SB, MIT, 1969; MS, U. Chgo., 1971, PhD, 1976. Asst. prof. Stanford (Calif.) U., 1976—84; assoc. prof. U. Houston, Houston, 1984—87, Ohio State U., Columbus, 1987—90, prof., 1990—. Contbr. articles to profl. jours.; editor: Jour. of Money, Credit and Banking, 1992—. Achievements include research in elucidated effects of government policies on the economy; elucidated the dynamics of how economies grow. Office: Ohio State U Dept Econs 1945 N High St Columbus OH 43210 E-mail: evans.21@osu.edu.

EVANS, PAUL F. protective services official; m. Karen O'Connor; 1 child, Paul III. JD cum laude, Suffolk U., 1978. Police commr. Boston Police Dept., 1994—. Bd. dirs. Police Athletic League, YMCA, City Year. Mem. VFW, Semper Fidelis Soc., Internat. Assn. Chiefs of Police, Police Exec. Rsch. Forum. Office: Office of Police Commr 1 Schroeder Plaza Boston MA 02120-2014

EVANS, PAUL VERNON, lawyer; b. Colorado Springs, Colo., June 19, 1926; s. Fred Harrison and Emma Hooper (Austin) Evans; m. Patricia Gwyn Davis, July 27, 1964 (dec. Dec. 2001); children: Paula Jean, Bruce, Mike, Mark, Paul; m. Betty J. Haynes, 2002; m. Frances Irene Pool, Sept. 7, 1947 (div. 1963). BA cum laude, Colo. Coll., 1953; JD, Duke U., 1956. Bar: Colo. 1956, U.S. Dist. Ct. Colo. 1956, U.S. Supreme Ct. 1971, U.S. Ct. Appeals (10th cir.) 1974. Field mgr. Keystone Readers Service, Dallas, 1946-50; sole practice Colorado Springs, 1956-60; ptnr. Goodbar, Evans & Goodbar, 1960-63; sr. ptnr. Evans & Briggs Attys., Colorado Springs, 1963-95; ret., 2001. City atty. City of Fountain, Colo., 1958—62, City of Woodland Park, Colo., 1962—78; atty. Rock Creek Mesa Water Dist., Colorado Springs, 1963—2002. Author instruction materials. Precinct com. man Republican Com., Colorado Springs, 1956-72. Served with USNR, 1944-46, PTO. Recipient Jr. C. of C. Outstanding Achievement award, 1957. Mem. Colo. Mining Assn., Am. Jud. Soc., ABA, Colo. Bar Assn. (com. chmn. 1966-67, 84), El Paso County Bar Assn. (com. chmn. 1956—0, Assn. Trial Lawyers Am., Colo. and Local Trial Lawyers, Tau Kappa Alpha (pres.), Phi Beta Kappa. Clubs: Optimist (pres. 1966-67). Republican. Home: 244 Cobblestone Dr Colorado Springs CO 80906-7624 E-mail: paulvevans@msn.com.

EVANS, PETER KENNETH, advertising executive; b. Brighton, Eng., Apr. 18, 1935; s. Percy Edward and Doris (McCoy) E.; m. Juana Santana Ramirez, Mar. 31, 1956; children: Luis Miguel, Linda Rosa Del Rocio, Pilar De Los Angeles. Student, Varndean Sch., Brighton, 1946-50. Asst. art dir. Grant Advt., Toronto, Ont., Can., 1958-61; creative group head Goodis, Goldberg, Soren, Toronto, 1961-63; v.p., creative dir. Baker/BBDO, Toronto, 1963-65; creative dir. Kenyon & Eckhardt, Toronto, 1965-67, Mexico City, 1967-68; exec. v.p., creative dir. Vladimir & Evans Inc., Miami, Fla., 1968-71; pres., creative dir. Evans & Ciccarone Inc., Miami, 1971-91; mktg. cons., 1991—; proprietor Peter Evans Pipes, 1994—2001, Peter Evans Woodcrafting Solutions, 1998—; cartoonist The Islander News, Key Biscayne, Fla., 1996—; pres. Peter Evans Response Mktg. & Advt., 1996—, Peter Evans Creative Svcs., 1997—. Instr. advt. Fla. Internat. U., Miami, 1974. Author: Jumpstart Marketing for the New Business Owner, 1993, Treasure Your Teeth, 1998; broadcaster radio reading svc. Sta. WLRN-FM (NPR affiliate), Miami, 1990—; playwright: Ruiz, 1982, Unconscious, 1996, Lost, 1997, Bang, 1998; actor: Scrooge, Social Security, 2000; inventor bed elevator, blind dog head protector, perfect wood carvers bench, sander-expander. Leader Jr. Achievement, Miami, 1968; asst. leader Boy Scouts Am., Miami, 1970; bd. dirs. Key Biscayne Music & Drama Club, Miami Bach Soc. Armament technician RAF, Fassberg, Germany, 1953-55, ETO. Recipient awards Can. TV Commercials Festival, N.Y. Art Directors Show, Clio awards, Andy awards, 100 Best U.S. TV Commercials, Printing Industry Am. awards, 24 Top U.S. New Product Introductions, Miami Big Mike awards, Miami Addy awards, Fla. State Addy awards, Fla. Press Assn. awards; named 100 Top U.S. Creative Men Ad Day/USA, Art Dir. of Yr. Greater Miami Ad Fedn. Mem. NAUI, PADI, Dramatists Guild, Nat. Wood Carvers Assn., Am. Birding Assn., Nat. Audubon Soc., Key Biscayne Beach Club, South Fla. Woodcarvers Club. Anglican. Home and Office: 285 W Mashta Dr Key Biscayne FL 33149-2419 E-mail: kpeterevans@yahoo.com.

EVANS, PETER YOSHIO, ophthalmologist, educator; b. Tokyo, Dec. 19, 1925; came to the U.S., 1957; s. Paul Yuzuru Kawai and Vicki Wichgraf Evans; m. Helga Kemp, Sept. 19, 1953; children: Johannes, Marina, Michael, André, Thomas, Ursula, Christiane. MD, Innsbruck U., 1951. Resident Innsbruck (Austria) and Frankfurt (Germany) Univs., 1951-55; intern Sisters Charity Hosp., Buffalo, N.Y., 1957-58; chief dept. ophthalmology D.C. Gen. Hosp., 1958-63; fellow Georgetown U., Washington, 1958-59, program dir. div. ophthalmology, 1963-69, chmn., 1969-83, prof., 1973-92, prof. emeritus, 1992—. Cons. D.C. Columbia Lighthouse for the Blind, 1959-63; sr. cons. D.C. Child and Maternal Welfare Dept., 1961-74; exec. v.p. Joint Commn. Allied Health Pers. in Ophthalmology, St. Paul, 1981-96; bd. dirs. Internat. Eye Found., 1999—. Author, producer scientific films; contbr. articles to profl. jours.; editor numerous jours. Recipient Man of Decade award, Joint Commn. on Allied Health Pers. in Ophthalmology, 1997, Promotion of Peace and Vision award, Internat. Eye Found., 2002. Fellow Am. Acad. Ophthalmology (Disting. Svc. award 1982), Austrian Ophthalm. Soc. (First Fuchs Meml. Lectr. 1975), German Ophthalm. Soc., Am.-Austrian Soc. (pres. 1989-91), Cosmos Club D.C. Lutheran. Avocations: skiing, violin, philately, photography, bridge. Home and office: 3113 Lewis Pl Falls Church VA 22042-2511 E-mail: pye19@cs.com.

EVANS, RICHARD JAMES, mechanical engineer; b. Wabash, Ind., Nov. 26, 1960; s. Tommy Lewis E. and Joyce Anne (Leckrone) Wert; children: Matthew Thomas, Kari Lynn, Jenna Marie. BSME, Rose-Hulman Inst. Tech., 1983; MBA with honors, Ind. U., 1993. Registered profl. engr., Ky., Ind.; cert. lighting efficiency profl. Sales engr. Johnson Controls, Inc., Indpls., 1983-90, sales team leader in healthcare mktg., 1990-93, br. mgr. Evansville, Ind., 1993-95, area installation mgr., 1995-98, area svc. mgr., 1998-2000, area sales mgr., 2000—. Active Sons of Am. Legion, Wabash, 1989—. Energy award U.S. Dept. Energy, 1995. Mem. ASHRAE (pres. ctrl. Ind. chpt. 1991-92, bd. dirs. 1992-93, Presdl. award of Excellence 1992), NSPE, Assn. Energy Engrs. (cert. energy mgr.), Ind. Soc. Profl. Engrs. (v.p. ctrl. Ind. chpt. 1997-98, pres. 1998-99, bd. dirs. 1999-2000 Mathcounts co-chair 1999-2002), Ind. Soc. Hosp. Engrs., Beta Gamma Sigma, Lambda Chi Alpha (housing corp. bd. 1996-2000, sec. 1999-2000). Home: 10478 Magenta Dr Noblesville IN 46060-8398 Office: Johnson Controls Inc 1255 N Senate Ave Indianapolis IN 46202-2200

EVANS, RICHARD LLOYD, financial services company executive; b. Seattle, Oct. 16, 1935; s. Lloyd Herman and Dorleska L. (Rotta) E.; m. Judith Anne Sahlberg, Dec. 20, 1958; children: Dallas J., Douglas L., Daniel A., Marjorie A., Rebecca M. BA in Bus. Adminstrn., U. Wash., 1957. CLU; chartered fin. cons. Agt. Phoenix Mut. Life Ins. Co., Seattle, 1960-69; chmn. R.L. Evans Co. Inc., Seattle, 1969—; mng. prin. Evans Capital Mgmt. Assocs., Seattle. Spkr. on ins. and fin. planning to numerous orgns., 1975—; adv. Orcas Island Found., 1996-99. adv. bd. Wash. U. Business Sch., adv. bd. Prostate Cancer, Wash U. Medical Sch. Mem. exec. bd. Chief Seattle coun. Boy Scouts Am., 1976-2003; chmn. N.W. Theol. Union, Seattle, 1984-88; mem. San Juan County Pk. Bd., 1996—, chmn., 2000-02; co-chmn. San Juan County Hotel-Motel Tax Adv. Bd., 1995—; pres. Orcas Island Garden Club, 1999-2000. Lt. USN, 1957-59. Recipient award of merit Chief Seattle coun. Boy Scouts Am., 1984. Mem. Am. Soc. CLU, Am. Soc. Chartered Fin. Cons., Nat. Assn. Life Underwriters, Wash. State Assn. Life Underwriters (bd. dirs. 1973-79, pres. 1977-78), Seattle Assn. Life Underwriters (v.p. 1972-73), Assn. Advanced Underwriting, Million Dollar Round Table, Estate Planning Coun. Seattle, Rainier Club, Rotary (dir.). Republican. Presbyterian. Home: 871 Deer Point Rd Olga WA 98279-9518 Office: 600 Stewart St Ste 1210 Seattle WA 98101-1255 E-mail: evans@interisland.net.

EVANS, RICHARD TAYLOR, aerospace engineer, consultant; b. Denver, July 2, 1940; s. Lawrence T. Evans and Geraldine E. (Shoemaker) Dorsey; m. Mary W. Kalmar, Apr. 10, 1965; children: Christine M., Richard G. AB Pre-Engring., Columbia U., N.Y.C., 1962; BS in Elec. Engring., Colo. U., Boulder, 1964; MS in Aerospace Engring., Air Force Inst. of Tech., Dayton, Ohio, 1969; PhD in Aerospace Engring., U. Tex., Austin, Tex., 1980. Launch crew commdr., instr. Minuteman Missile Wing, Malmstrom AFB, Mont., 1965-69; minuteman, guidance project officer Space and Missile Sys. Orgn., Norton AFB, Calif., 1969-74; tech. rep. Charles Stark Draper Lab, Cambridge, Mass., 1974-76; grad. student Aerospace & Engring. Mechanics, Austin, Tex., 1976-79; dep. dir. Aerospace-Mechs. Scis. F.J. Seiler Rsch. Lab. USAF Acad., USAF Acad., Colo., 1979-83; site activation commdr. Joint Cruise Missile Program Office Sicily, 1983-84; dir. Sys. Deployment Cruise Missile Program Office, Crystal City, Va., 1984-87; deputy dir. Advanced Strategic Missile Sys. USAF, Norton AFB, Calif., 1987-90, Minuteman program mgr., 1990-92; tech. cons. SDIO TASC, Arlington, Va., 1992-94; tech. cons. Iridium Satellite Comms. TASC, Inc., Chandler, Ariz., 1994-95, tech. cons. to Nat. Imaging and Mapping Agy., other agys. Reston, Va., 1995-96, tech. cons. intelligence agys. Chantilly, Va., 1996—. Contbr. articles to profl. jours. Col. USAF, 1965-92. Mem. AIAA (sr., chpt. chair), Armed Forces Commn. & Electronics Assn., Air Force Assn., Internat. Coun. Sys. Engring. Republican. Avocations: backpacking, tennis, skiing, chess, photography. Home: 2181 Wolftrap Ct Vienna VA 22182-5190 Office: Northrop Grumman-TASC 4801 Stonecroft Blvd Chantilly VA 20151-3822 E-mail: rtevans@tasc.com., rtevans@erols.com.

EVANS, ROBERT, JR., economics educator; b. Sterling, Colo., Mar. 20, 1932; s. Robert and Mary Louise (Paradise) E.; m. Lois Ellen Herr, Nov. 6, 1955 (dec. 1994); children: Karen E., Robert, Janet K., Thomas W., L. Midori, Laura E., Katherine Joan; m. Marian Elizabeth Grotheer, Dec. 26, 1996. SB, MIT, 1954; PhD (Hillman fellow), U. Chgo., 1959. Asst. prof. indsl. relations MIT, 1959-65; assoc. prof. Brandeis U., Waltham, Mass., 1965-71, prof., 1971—. Atran prof. labor econs., 1975-98, chmn. dept. econs., 1970-72, 73-75, 84-87, dean Coll. Arts and Scis., 1975-81; retired, 1998. Vis. prof. Keio U., Tokyo, 1966-67, 72-73, 82-83, 88-89, 94-95; rsch. dir. study on prison industries Can. Corrections Assn., 1968-69. Author: Public Policy Toward Labor, 1965, The Labor Economics of Japan and the United States, 1971, Developing Policies for Public Security and Criminal Justice, 1973. Mem. Acton (Mass.) and Acton Boxborough Regional Sch. Com., 1971-72, 74-82, 84-88, regional chmn., 1972, 79-80, 85-86, town chmn., 1975-77; mem. Acton Fin. Com., 1997—, chair, 2000-2003. With U.S. Army, 1955-57. Fulbright Rsch. scholar, Japan, 1982-83, 88-89; Abe fellow, Japan, 1994-95. Mem. Am. Econ. Assn., Indsl. Relations Assn., Assn. Asian Studies. Home: 4 Old Meadow Ln Acton MA 01720 E-mail: revans@world.std.com.

EVANS, ROBERT DAVID, legal association executive; b. Vergennes, Vt., Mar. 1, 1945; BA, Yale U., 1966; JD, U. Mich., 1969. Bar: Ill. 1969. Assoc. Sachnoff Schrager Jones & Weaver, Chgo., 1969-72; asst. dir. divsn. pub. svc. activities ABA, Chgo., 1972-73, asst. dir. govtl. rels. office Washington, 1973-78, assoc. dir. govtl. rels. office, 1978-82, dir. govtl. affairs office, 1982—, assoc. dir., dir. Washington Office, 1988—. Mem. Washington Grove (Md.) Town Coun., 1977-81, 98—, Washington Grove Town Planning Commn., 1977-81, 98—; mayor Washington Grove, 1981-83; vice chmn. assns. divsn. Nat. Capital Area United Way, 1986, chmn., 1987. Recipient Spl. Achievement award Nat. Legal Aid and Defender Assn., 1990. Fellow ABA (life), Am. Bar Found.; mem. Am. Law Inst. Home: PO Box 332 Washington Grove MD 20880-0332 Office: ABA 740 15th St NW Fl 8 Washington DC 20005-1019

EVANS, ROBERT JAMES, architect; b. Alameda, Calif., Apr. 15, 1914; s. Edwin Florence and Idella Mary (Cranna) E.; m. Carol Ann Benton, Sept. 11, 1937; children: Joan Carlson, Ann Blakeman, Marcia Mothorn. AB, U. Calif., Berkeley, 1935. Registered architect, Calif. Draftsman Wm. C. Hays Architect, San Francisco, 1935-37, U. Calif., 1937-41, architect, 1941-45, univ. architect, 1945-72, asst. v.p., 1971-72; cons. architect Marshall, Calif., 1973—; asst. to chancellor U. Mich.-Flint, 1972-73; supervising architect U. Calif., Davis, 1942-45, Berkeley, 1948-55; cons. architect campus plan U. Ryukus, Okinawa, 1969; cons. architect campus paln U. N.C., Greensboro, 1979-82. Cons. architect campus plan Kabul U., Afghanistan, 1955, U. Hawaii, 1960-62, Salk Inst., San Diego, 1983-84. Founder Tomales Bay Assn., Marshall Calif., 1964. Fellow AIA (emeritus), Assn. Univ. Architects (emeritus, pres. 1955-57), Richmond Yacht Club (treas. 1961) Address: 18545 Hwy 1 Marshall CA 94940

EVANS, ROBERT VINCENT, sales and marketing executive; b. Mobile, Ala., Sept. 21, 1958; s. William Alexander Evans and Katherine Barbara (Doerr) Davidson; children: James Vernon, Chelsea Marie, Layla Annelise. BS in Computer Info. Systems, BS in Tech. Mgmt., Regis U., Denver, 1987; postgrad. in Mgmt., U. Wash., 1995. Electrician Climax (Colo.) Molybdenum Co., 1978—82; applications engr. Honeywell, Inc., Englewood, Colo., 1982—83, sales engr., 1983—87; sys. engr. Apple Computer, Inc., Seattle, 1987—88, mgr. regional sys. engring. Portland, Oreg., 1988—96, dist. sales mgr. Seattle, 1997—2002; v.p. Bulldog Beach Interactive, Seattle, 2002—. Author: Anthology of American Poets, 1981. Dir. Operation Lookout, Seattle, 1989; mem. Rep. Nat. Com.; commr. dist. chmn. Boy Scouts Am. Recipient USMC Blues award, Marine Corps Assn. Leatherneck award, 1977, Denver Post Outstanding Svc. award, 1983, N.Y. Zool. Soc. Hon. medal, James West fellowship award, Paul Harris fellowship award, Silver Beaver award Boy Scouts Am., 1998. Mem. Am. Mgmt. Assn., Am. Platform Assn., Mensa, Rotary, Kiwanis. Republican. Mem. Northwest Cmty. Ch. Avocations: reading, church ministry, family activities. Office: Bulldog Beach Interactive 4302 SW Alaska St #2000 Seattle WA 98116-

EVANS, ROD L. philosophy educator; b. Norfolk, Va., Mar. 23, 1956; s. Irving Furman and Evelyn (Werth) Evans. BA, Old Dominion U., Norfolk, Va., 1978; MA in Philosophy, U. Va., 1981, PhD in Philosophy, 1987. Prof. dept. philosophy and religious studies Old Dominion U., Norfolk, 1989—. Lectr. in field. Co-author (with Irwin M. Berent): (book) Drug Legalization: For and Against, 1992, Weird Words, 1995, The ABC of Cat Trivia, 1996, The Quotable Conservative: The Giants of Conservatism on Liberty, Freedom, Individual Responsibility and Traditional Virtues, 1996, The Right Words: The 350 Best Things to Say to Get Along with People, 1992, Getting Your Words' Worth: Discovering and Enjoying Phantonyms, Gramograms, Anagrams, and Other Fascinating Word Phenomena, 1993, The Dictionary of Highly Unusual Words,

1997, Fundamentalism: Hazards and Heartbreaks, 1988, Legalized Gambling: For and Against, 1997, Sexicon: The Ultimate X-Rated Dictionary, 2002; co-author: (with John Carpenter) Matching Wits with the Million Dollar Mind: The World's Hardest Trivia Quizzes From Americas First Quiz Show Millionaire, 2002. Recipient Outstanding Tchr. of the Yr. for Students with Disabilities award, Old Dominion U., 2001, Armada Hoffler Weekend Coll. Teaching award, 2003. Avocations: reading, exercising. Home: 8582 Chesapeake Blvd Unit 303 Norfolk VA 23503-5450 Office: Old Dominion University Dept Philosophy/Religious Studies Norfolk VA 23529

EVANS, ROGER, lawyer; b. Syracuse, Apr. 18, 1951; s. David Longfellow and Louise Maude (Crawford) Evans; children: Jonathan Longfellow, Gillian Crawford, Catherine Leigh, Skylar Elizabeth, Valerie Lynn, Joel Brian. AB, Cornell U., 1974; postgrad., Columbia U., 1976-77; JD, Harvard U., 1977. Bar: Ohio 1977, U.S. Dist. Ct. (no. dist.) Ohio 1978, Tex. 1981, U.S. Dist. Ct. (no. dist.) Tex. 1981, U.S. Dist. Ct. (so. dist.) Tex. 1997, U.S. Ct. Appeals (5th, 6th and 11th cirs.) 1981, U.S. Ct. Appeals (10th cir.) 1982, U.S. Tax Ct. 1989, U.S. Dist. Ct. (we. and ea. dists.) Tex. 1998. Assoc. Jones, Day, Reavis & Pogue, Cleve., 1977-81, Dallas, 1981-84; ptnr. Shank, Irwin & Conant, Dallas, 1985, Gardner, Carton & Douglas, Dallas, 1986-88, Vinson & Elkins, Dallas, 1988-91; pvt. practice Dallas, 1991-2001; ptnr. Mathis & Donheiser, Dallas, 2001—. Bd. dirs., gen. counsel Equest, Inc., Dallas, 1986—88; instr. trial advocacy, instr. law and econs. So. Meth. U. Sch. Law; instr. labor law Baylor U.; mem. faculty Nat. Inst. Trial Advocacy. Gen. counsel, bd. dirs. Freedom Ride Found., Dallas, 1985-86; cmty. svcs. bd. mgmt. YMCA, 1990-92; bd. dirs. Legal Svcs. Corp. North Tex., 1991-92; adv. bd. dirs. Providence Christian Sch. Tex., Inc., 1995-2000. Recipient Advocacy award, Dallas Epilepsy Assn., 1995. Mem. Tex. Bar Assn., Dallas Bar Assn., Cornell U. Alumni Assn. (class pres. 1984-89), Harvard U. Law Sch. Alumni Assn. No. Ohio (sec. 1978-81), Harvard Club. Office: 2001 Ross Ave Ste 4600 Dallas TX 75201 E-mail: revans@mathisdonheiser.com.

EVANS, ROSEMARY HALL, civic worker; b. Lenox, Mass., Mar. 25, 1925; d. Alfred A. and Rosamond (Morse) Hall; m. Richard Morse Colgate, Jan. 1, 1949; children: Jessie Morse, Margaret Auchincloss, Pamela Morse; m. James H. Evans, July 1, 1972 (div. 1984). Trustee Menninger Found., Topeka, Princeton (N.J.) Theol. Sem.; founding mem., life trustee Nat. Recreation and Park Assn., Washington; past dir. Nat. Audubon Soc., N.Y.C.; former collaborator Nat. Park Svc. Mem. Colony Club (N.Y.C.), Lenox (Mass.) Club, Profile Club (Sugar Hill, N.H.). Avocations: walking, gardening, reading, farming, bird watching.

EVANS, TERENCE THOMAS, federal judge; b. Milwaukee, Wisc., Mar. 25, 1940; s. Robert Hansen and Jeanette (Walters) Evans; m. Joan Marie Witte, July 24, 1965; children: Kelly Elizabeth, Christine Marie, David Rourke. BA, Marquette U., 1962, JD, 1967. Bar: Wis. 1967. Law clk. to justice Wis. Supreme Ct., 1967—68; asst. dist. atty. Milw. County, 1968—70; pvt. practice law Milw., 1970—74; cir. judge State of Wis., 1978—80; judge, then chief judge U.S. Dist. Ct. (ea. dist) Wis., Milw., 1979—95; judge U.S. Ct. Appeals (7th cir.), 1995—. Mem.: ABA, Milw. Bar Assn., State Bar Wis. Roman Catholic. Office: US Courthouse & Federal Bldg 517 E Wisconsin Ave Rm 721 Milwaukee WI 53202-4504*

EVANS, TERESA RINALDI, music educator, vocalist; d. Joseph Rinaldi and Josephine Ann Bakane; m. Marion Baker Evans, Nov. 5, 1990; m. Thomas Edward Hildebrand, May 5, 1976 (div. Sept. 10, 1990); 1 child, Thomas Edward Hildebrand Jr. M in Vocal Performance, NYU, 1995. Prof. voice Warren Wilson Coll., Swannanoa, NC, 1976—80, U. N.C., Asheville, 1978—85. Mem. New Canaan Woman's Rep. Scholar, Exch. Club, 1957. Mem.: NATS. Avocations: directing, piano, languages, travel, senior citizens.

EVANS, THELMA JEAN MATHIS, internist; b. East St. Louis, Ill., Jan. 29, 1944; d. Clemmie and Catherine (Rose) Mathis; m. Timothy Charles Evans, June 29, 1968; children: Cynthia Marie, Catherine Elizabeth (twins). BS in Zoology with honors, U. Ill., 1967; MD, U. Ill., Chgo., 1969. Intern, then resident U. Ill. Hosp., Chgo., 1969-71, fellow in pulmonary medicine, 1971-73; med. dir., acute care unit Presbyn.-St. Luke's Hosp., Chgo., 1973-75, asst. to dir. emergency svcs., 1975-77; staff physician Health Specialists, S.C., Chgo., 1977-80, AT&T (Western Electric), Cicero, Ill., 1980-85, Health First, Inc., Chgo., 1985-89, Michael Reese Health Plan, Chgo., 1989-98; mem. adv. bd. Advocate Profl. Group, Chgo., 1998—; bd. dirs. Advocate Health Care Network, Chgo., 2000—. Instr., Rush Med. Coll., Chgo., 1973-84; tuberculosis control officer, infectious disease sect. Chgo. Dept. Health, 1976-77. V.p., Com. to Elect Timothy C. Evans, Chgo., 1989. Grantee, Chgo. Lung Assn., 1972-73. Fellow ACP; mem. Am. Soc. Internal Medicine, NAACP, AMA. Democrat. African Methodist Episcopal. Avocations: photography, gardening, collecting thimbles, bells and music boxes. Office: Advocate Health Ctrs 9831 S Western Ave Chicago IL 60643-1791

EVANS, THOMAS EDGAR, JR., title insurance agency executive; b. Toronto, Ohio, Apr. 17, 1940; s. Thomas Edgar and Sarah Ellen (Bauer) E.; m. Cynthia Lee Johnson, Feb. 23; children: Thomas Edgar, Douglas, Melinda, Jennifer. BA, Mt. Union Coll., 1963. Tchr., Lodi, Ohio, 1963-64; salesman Simpson-Evans Realty, Steubenville, Ohio, 1964-65, Shadron Realty, Tucson, 1965-67; real estate broker, co-owner Double E Realty, Tucson, 1967-69; escrow officer, br. mgr., asst. county mgr., v.p. Ariz. Title Ins., Tucson, 1969-80; pres. Commonwealth Land Title Agy., Tucson, 1980-82, also dir.; pres. Fidelity Nat. Title Agy., 1982-90; bd. govs. Calif. Land Title Assn., 1990—; exec. v.p. Fidelity Nat. Title Ins. Co., 1990-92; v.p. Inland Empire Divsn. Fidelity Nat. Title, 1991-93, pres. Orange County divsn., 1993-2000, exec. v.p., regional mgr., 2000—. Bd. dirs. Western Fin. Trust Co., Fidelity Nat. Fin. Inc., Fidelity Nat. Title Ins. Co., Fidelity Nat. Title Agy. Pinal, The Griffin Co., Computer Market Place, Inc., e Market Place, Chgo. Title Ins. Co.; bd. dirs., chmn. bd. Cochise Title Agy., TIPCO; v.p., dir. A.P.C. Corp. Named Boss of Yr., El Chaparral chpt. Am. Bus. Women's Assn., 1977. Mem. Calif. Land Title Assn. (pres. 1995-96), So. Ariz. Escrow Assn., So. Ariz. Mortgage Bankers Assn. (bd. dirs. 1982-85), Ariz. Mktg. Bankers Assn., Old Pueblo Businessmen's Assn. Tucson, Tucson Bd. Realtors, Ariz. Assn. Real Estate Exchangors (bd. dirs. 1968-69), Land Title Assn. Ariz. (pres. 1984), So. Ariz. Homebuilders Assn., Tucson Real Estate Exchangors (pres. 1968), Pacific Club, Ctr. Club, Old Pueblo Courthouse Club, La Paloma Club, Ventana Country Club, Centre Ct. Club, Coto de Casa Country Club, Montecito Country Club, Elks Club, Pima Jaycees (dir. 1966), Sertoma (charter pres., chmn. bd. Midtown sect. 1968-70), Sunrise Rotary, Old Pueblo Club, South Coast Repertory (trustee 1996-2000), Blue Key, Sigma Nu. Home: 3260 Braemar Dr Santa Barbara CA 93109 Office: 4050 Calle Real Ste 210 Santa Barbara CA 93110-3413

EVANS, THOMAS PASSMORE, business and product licensing consultant; b. West Grove, Pa., Aug. 19, 1921; s. John and Linda (Zeuner) E.; m. Lenore Jane Knuth, June 21, 1947; children: Paula S., Christina L., Bruce A., Carol L. BS in Elec. Engring., Swarthmore Coll., 1942; M in Engring., Yale U., 1948. Registered profl. engr., Pa. Engr. atomic power divsn. Westinghouse Electric Corp., Pitts., 1948-51; dir. R&D AMF, Inc., N.Y.C., 1951-60; dir. rsch. O.M. Scott & Sons Co., Marysville, Ohio, 1960-62; v.p. R&D W. A. Sheaffer Pen Co., Fort Madison, Iowa, 1962-67; dir. rsch. Mich. Tech. U., Houghton, 1967-80; dir. rsch., mem. faculty Berry Coll., Mt. Berry, Ga., 1980 88, prof. bus. adminstrn., 1980-86. Lt. USN, 1943-46. Mem. IEEE, AAAS. VFW, Am. Forestry Assn., Nat. Defense Industl. Assn., Am. Phys. Soc., Soc. Plastics Engrs., Yale Sci. and Engring. Assn., Nat. Coun. Univ. Rsch. Adminstrs., Air Force Assn., Am. Legion, Hunter Mus. Art, Nat. Trust Hist. Preservation, Yale Club of Ga., Sigma Xi, Tau Beta Pi. Achievements include patents in field. Home: 1220 Broadrick Dr Apt 1222 Dalton GA 30720-2809

EVANS, THOMAS WILLIAM, lawyer; b. N.Y.C., Dec. 9, 1930; s. William J. and R. Helen (Stenvall) E.; m. Lois deBaun Logan, Dec. 22, 1956; children: Heather, Logan, Paige. BA, Williams Coll., 1952; JD, Columbia U., 1958; EdD, Piedmont Coll., 1993. Bar: N.Y. 1958, U.S. Supreme Ct. 1961. Assoc. Simpson, Thacher & Bartlett, N.Y.C., 1958-64; asst. coun. to spl. state commn. of investigation, spl. dep. asst. N.Y. Atty. Gen., 1964-65; assoc. Mudge Rose Guthrie Alexander & Ferdon, N.Y.C., 1965-66, ptnr., 1967-93, of counsel, 1993-94. Founder MENTOR, nat. law-related edn. program for pub. sch. students, 1983; mem. Pres.'s Pvt. Sector Initiatives Adv. Coun. Author: The School in the Home, 1973, Admissions Practices (Center for Public Resources), 1986, Mentors, 1992. Chmn. Nat. Symposium on Partnerships in Edn., 1983-90; chmn. bd. trustees Columbia U. Tchrs. Coll., 1991-98, trustee, 1985—, adj. prof. of ednl. adminstrn., 1992-95; co-chmn. N.Y. Korean Vets. Meml. Commn.; chmn. The Mentor Ctr., L.C., 1998-2003. With USMC, 1952-54. Mem. Fed. Bar Coun. (pres. 1989-90, trustee 1981—), Century Assn. Republican. Episcopalian. Home: 9660 W Bay Harbor Dr Apt PHE Miami FL 33154 E-mail: thoswevans@aol.com.

EVANS, TOMMY NICHOLAS, obstetrician/gynecologist, educator; b. Batesville, Ark., Apr. 12, 1922; s. James Rufus and Carrye Mae (Goatcher) E.; m. Jessica Ray Osment, June 12, 1945; 1 child, Laura Kathreen AA, Mars Hill Jr. Coll., 1940; student, Duke U., 1940-41; AB, Baylor U., 1942; MD, Vanderbilt U., 1945. Intern U. Mich. Hosp., Ann Arbor, 1945-46, asst. resident ob-gyn, 1948, resident, 1948-49, jr. clin. instr., 1949-50, sr. clin. instr., 1950-51, instr., 1951-54, asst. prof., 1954-56, assoc. prof., 1956-60, prof., 1960-65; prof. ob-gyn Wayne State U., Detroit, 1965-83, dean Sch. Medicine, 1970-72, dir. C.S. Mott Ctr. Human Growth and Devel., 1973-83; sr. attending physician Hutzel Hosp., 1966-83, chief ob-gyn, 1966-82, vice chief of staff, 1967-70, chief of staff, 1970-74, trustee, 1975-78; mem. teaching, surgeon Harper-Grace Hosps., 1965-83, chief gynecology Harper div., 1970-83, chief ob-gyn, 1975-83; chief gynecology, sr. attending physician Detroit Receiving Hosp., 1965-83; chief gynecology U. Colo., Denver, 1983-89, vice chmn. ob-gyn., 1983-89, prof. emeritus ob-gyn., 1989—. Cons. pediatric surgery Children's Hosp.; cons. Sinai Hosp. William Beaumont Hosp., Wayne County Gen. Hosp.; past mem. med. adv. com. Detroit Med. Ctr. Corp. Bd. dirs. Alan Guttmacher Inst. Fellow Am. Assn. Ob-Gyn.; mem. Am. Coll. Obstetricians and Gynecologists (past exec. bd., past pres.), ACS (adv. council ob-gyn credentials com. 1983-85, bd. govs. 1982-86), Am. Fedn. Clin. Research, Am. Fertility Soc., Am. Gynecol. Club (past pres.), Am. Gynecol. Soc. (past pres.), Am. Gynecol. and Obstetrical Soc. (council), AMA, Am. Med. Soc. Vienna, Am. Pub. Health Assn., Am. Soc. Andrology (exec. council), Am. Soc. Study Sterility, Anthony Wayne Soc., Assn. Profs. Ob-Gyn (past chmn. nominating com.), Central Assn. Ob-Gyn (past pres.), Charlie Flowers Ob-Gyn Soc., Chgo. Gynecol. Soc., Continental Gynecol. Soc., Detroit Acad. Medicine, Detroit Cancer Club (past mem. program com.), Engring. Soc. Detroit, Greater Detroit Area Hosp. Council Inc., Internat. Fedn. Ob-Gyn (exec. bd.), Internat. Soc. Advancement Humanistic Studies in Gynecology, Miami Obstet. and Gynecol. Soc., Mich. Assn. Retarded Children, Mich. Cancer Found. (trustee), Mich. Council Study of Abortion, Mich. Soc. Ob-Gyn (past pres.), Mich. State Med. Soc. (past exec. council), Mich. United Cerebral Palsy Assn., Norman Miller Gynecol. Soc. (past pres.), Ob-Gyn Soc. N.Y., Planned Parenthood League, Pan Am. Med. Assn., Royal Soc. Medicine, Soc. Study of Reprodn., Soc. Ob-Gyn of Can., S. Atlantic Assn. Ob-Gyn, numerous others. Republican. Presbyterian. Office: 7501 E Thompson Peak Pkwy Apt 233 Scottsdale AZ 85255-4533

EVANS, VICTOR MILES, retired funeral home, cemetery company executive; b. Hines, Minn., Dec. 8, 1939; s. Miles Byron and Millicent (Owen) E.; m. Joyce M. Dexter, Dec. 17, 1960; children: Terri, Ross, Jana, Stephanie, Anthony. BBA, U. Minn., 1962. CPA, Ill. Staff acct. McGladrey, Hansen, Dunn, Rock Island, Ill., 1962-64; chief fin. officer Roy & E. Roth Co., Rock Island, 1964-69; sr. v.p. Svc. Corp. Internat., Houston, 1969-92, ret., 1993. Republican. Baptist. Avocations: racquetball, skiing. E-mail: vicevans@aol.com.

EVANS, WALTER REED, retired engineering executive, consultant; b. El Paso, Tex., Oct. 25, 1921; s. Charles Reed and Ruby Estelle (Simpson-Rountree) E.; m. Frances Adelaide Lounsbury, Jan. 15, 1942 (dec. 1975); children: Sandra Frances, Roger Reed, Sharon Adelaide; m. Dorothy May Cuthbertson, 1975; stepchildren: Jack W., William D., Charles T. Rogers. BS in Mech. Engring., U. Tex. Registered profl. engr. La., Tex. Engring. and mech. supr. Celanese and Exxon Corps., Tex. and Venezuela, 1948-57; plant mgr., pres. Falcon Chem. Corp., Lake Charles, La., 1957-59; cons. SIP, Inc., Houston, 1960-62; instrument engr. Exxon, Aruba, 1963, mech. mgr., 1964-65, chief engr., 1966-71, divsn. head, 1972; project mgr. S & B, Inc., Houston, 1973-79; mech. mgr. Arabian Am. Oil Co., Ras Tanura, Saudi Arabia, 1979-81; pvt. practice mech. engring. cons., 1982-88; Tex. state coord., lobbyist ASME, Austin, 1988-94; prof., competency monitor Tex. State Bd. Engring. Registration, 1995-99. Founder, v.p. Structural Metals, Inc. divsn. Comml. Metals, Inc., Seguin, Tex., 1947-48; trustee Teal Petroleum Co. divsn. W.R. Grace Co., 1975-79; apprentice mechanic, aircraft engine, Kelly Field, Tex., 1939; owner's rep. Himont, Inc. divsn. Dupont, 1984-85. Author: Aircraft Engine Overhaul, 1942. Enlisted Tex. N.G., 1938; lt. USAAF, 1942-44, ETO. Fellow ASME (life); mem. NSPE (life), NRA, Squires Bus. Men's Orgn., Austin Amateur Radio, Men's Garden Club, Austin Rifle Club. Republican. Episcopalian. Avocations: hunting, fishing, stamp/coin collecting, gardening, reading. Home and Office: 11279 Taylor Draper Ln Apt 329 Austin TX 78759-3965

EVANS, WAYNE LEWIS, lawyer; b. Bluefield, W.Va., Mar. 30, 1954; s. Douglas Evan and Wanda (Shrewsberry) E.; m. Cheryl Jane Richardson, June 28, 1980; children: Lisa Marie, Jason Lloyd. BA summa cum laude, U. N.C., Greensboro, 1976; MS, Radford U., 1978; diploma, Roanoke Police Acad., 1980; JD, Wake Forest U., 1984. Bar: W.Va. 1984, U.S. Dist. Ct. (so. dist.) W.Va. 1984, U.S. Ct. Appeals (4th cir. 1989); cert. Va. Cert. Bds. Zoning Appeals Programs. Probation/parole officer Va. Dept. Corrections, Tazewell, Va., 1976-77; dep. sheriff Roanoke County Sheriff Dept., Salem, Va., 1979-81; summer assoc. Katz Kantor & Perkins, Bluefield, W.Va., 1982; ptnr. Katz, Kantor & Perkins, Bluefield, 1985—; summer assoc. Gardner, Moss, Brown & Rocovich, Roanoke, 1983; assoc. Law Office of John H. Shott, Bluefield, 1984-85; sec. Bandy Minerals Corp., 2001—. V.p., sec. WELD Enterprises, 1989-95; mem. Campaigning With Lee-Civil War Roundtable, Va. Tech., 1994, 95, 96, 97; mem. mentoring program W.Va. State Bar, 2002—; speaker at seminars. Mem. Bd. Zoning Appeals, Bluefield, 1991—, chmn., 2000—; participant Career Awareness, Mercer County (W.Va.) Schs., 1989, 92; coach Odyssey of the Mind, Tazewell County (Va.) Schs., 1994, 95, 96, 97, judge, 1999; vol. United Way, Mercer and Tazewell Counties, 1989; chmn. com. PTA, Dudley Primary Sch; leader Boy Scouts Am., Bluefield, Va., 1996-99, 2000—; pres. Graham Middle Sch. PTA, Bluefield, 1997-98; pres. Graham H.S. Band Boosters, 1999-00. Mem. ATLA, W.Va. Trial Lawyers Assn., Fincastle Country Club, Phi Beta Kappa, Psi Chi, Phi Kappa Phi. Avocations: golf, tennis, civil war history. Home: 45 College Dr Bluefield VA 24605-1736 Office: Katz Kantor and Perkins 307 Federal St Bluefield WV 24701-3005

EVANS, WILLIAM DAVIDSON, JR., lawyer; b. Memphis, Jan. 20, 1943; s. William D. and Maxey (Carter) Evans; m. Eileen McKenna, June 19, 1971; children: William D., Carter M., Alexander B. BA, Vanderbilt U., 1965; JD, U. Tenn., 1968; LLM, Georgetown U., 1985. Bar: Tenn. 1968, D.C. 1988, Md. 1996. Spl. agt. FBI, N.Y.C., 1968-72; ptnr. Glankler, Brown, Gilliland, Chase, Robinson & Raines, Memphis, 1972-82; trial atty. environ. enforcement sect. U.S. Dept. of Justice, Washington, 1982-86; of counsel Washington, Perito & Dubuc, Washington, 1986-91, Graham & James, Washington, 1991-93; ptnr. Rich and Henderson, P.C., Annapolis, Md., 1993-98; sr. asst. county atty. Anne Arundel County Office of Law, Annapolis, 1998—. Editor: Digest Environ. Law of Real Property, 1986—90, Environ. Hazards, 1989—90; contbr. Mem. environ. issues group George Bush for Pres. Campaign, Washington, 1987—88, Robert Dole for Pres. Campaign, Washington, 1995—96. Mem.: ABA, Environ. Law Inst., Md. Bar Assn., D.C. Bar Assn. Republican. Roman Catholic. Home: Apt 111A 3900 Cathedral Ave NW Washington DC 20016 Office: Anne Arundel County Office Law 2660 Riva Rd Annapolis MD 21401-7305 E-mail: billevansjr@hotmail.com.

EVANS, WILLIAM LEE, biologist, educator; b. Calvert, Tex., Aug. 28, 1924; s. James Herman and Lilly Australia (O'Neal) E.; m. Lillian Mary Madden, July 30, 1948; children: Kathy A., David C., Susan D. BA with honors, U. Tex., Austin, 1949, MA, 1950, PhD, 1955. Mem. faculty U. Ark., Fayetteville, 1955-89, prof. zoology, 1968-89, prof. emeritus, 1989, chmn. gen. biology, 1967-70. Mem. pre-med. com. Fulbright Coll. Arts & Scis., 1982-89, chmn. 1987-89. Author articles, lab. manuals. Capt. AUS, 1942-46, USAF, 1951-52. Decorated Air medal with Oak Leaf cluster USAF; recipient Classrm. Tchg. award, Omicron Delta Kappa, 1959; grantee, NSF, 1959—62, U. Ark. Found., 1979, Fullbright Coll. Arts and Sci., 1982. Mem. Ark. Acad. Sci. (treas. 1972-82, pres. 1984-85), Orthopterists Soc., Am. Philatelic Soc., Phi Beta Kappa, Sigma Xi, Phi Eta Sigma, Phi Sigma. Home and Office: # 201 2410 Chestnut Terrace Ct Odenton MD 21113-0746

EVANS, WILLIAM MCKEE, historian, educator; b. St. Pauls, N.C., Sept. 17, 1923; s. John Browne and Alfreda Pittard Evans; children: Owen Thomas, Katherine Ann Smith, Daniel George, Laura Ellen. PhD in History, U. N.C., 1965. Asst. prof. to prof. history Calif. State Poly. U., Pomona, 1968—88, prof. emeritus, 1988—. Author: Ballots & Fence Rails, 1968, 1995, To Die Game, 1972, 2nd edit., 1996. With U.S. Army, 1943—46. Mem.: So. Hist. Assn. (membership/program com.), Orgn. Am. Historians, Am. Hist. Assn. Home: 390 W La Verne Ave Pomona CA 91767-2335

EVANS, WINTHROP SHATTUCK, retired lawyer; b. Santa Monica, Calif., June 21, 1939; s. Clifford E. and Luella (Wyble) E.; m. Carlene D. Buschena, June 26, 1965; children: Theresa, Shalene, Shanna, Michelle. AA, Fullerton Coll., 1969; BA, Calif. State U., Fullerton, 1973; JD, Western State U., Fullerton, 1980. Bar: Calif. 1980. Enlisted U.S. Navy, 1957, commd. ensign, 1961, advanced through grades to lt. comdr., 1969; served with U.S. Naval Res., 1965-76, ret. lt. comdr., 1976; airline capt. Am. Airlines, L.A., 1965-97; pvt. practice law Placentia, Calif., 1980—2001; ret., 2001. Mem. Calif. Bar Assn., Orange County Bar Assn., Aircraft Owners and Pilots Assn. Republican. Roman Catholic. Office: PO Box 532 Placentia CA 92871-0532 E-mail: winevans@juno.com.

EVANS, YONYNAH SCHUB (NINA EVANS), child psychiatrist; b. Phila., Apr. 10, 1933; d. Pincus and Rosa (Brind) Schub; m. Richard C. Evans, Dec. 4, 1959; children: Risa, Seth. BS, U. Pa., 1954, postgrad., 1954-56; MD, Columbia U., 1958. Diplomate Am. Bd. Child Psychiatry, Am. Bd. Psychiatry and Neurology. Intern Columbia U. Presbyn. Hsop., N.Y.C., 1958-59, resident, 1959-61, Jacobi Hosp., Bronx, 1968-73; liaison child psychiatry pediat. Montefiore Hosp., Bronx, N.Y., 1973-78; asst. prof. Albert Einstein Coll. Medicine, Bronx, 1974-79; coord. child psychiatry Westchester Jewish Cmty. Svcs., Hartsdale, N.Y., 1978-83, med. dir., 1983—2001. Lectr., workshop leader Albert Einstein Coll. Med., 1978—80, Columbia U., N.Y.C., 1980—95, Cape Cod Summer Seminars, Wilfleet, Mass., 1984—92, Rockland Children's Hosp., NY, 1995—96; lectr., supr. family therapy Columbia U., N.Y.C., 1987—93. Child Psychiatry fellow Jacobi Hosp. Bronx, 1971-73. Mem. Phi Beta Kappa. Avocations: watercolor painting, down-river canoeing, gardening. Home and Office: 54 N Broadway Tarrytown NY 10591 E-mail: docevans@earthlink.net.

EVANS-O'CONNOR, NORMA LEE, secondary education educator, consultant; b. Vanceburg, Ky., Sept. 4, 1952; d. Herbert Martin and Nellie Irene (Parker) E.; 1 child, Karen. AB, Morehead State U., 1975; MEd, Xavier U., 1982; EdS, Nova Southeastern U., 2001. Cert. tchr. Fla., Ky., Tenn., Ohio. Tchr. Forest Hills Sch. Dist., Cin., 1977-83, Osceola County Schs., Kissimmee, Fla., 1983—. Dean of students, curriculum resource tchr., chair sch. adv. coun. Osceola High Sch., activities dir., 1997—, head social studies dept.; mem. student coun. bd. Nat. Assn. Secondary Sch. Prins., Va., 1990—91; staff mem. Horatio Alger Assn.; cons. Walt Disney World, Lake Buena Vista, Fla., 1991—; retail theft operative Walt Disney World Co., Lake Buena Vista, 1988—; movie checker Theatrical Entertainment Svcs., L.A., 1990—2000. Nominated for Nat. Tchrs. Hall of Fame, 1997-98. Mem. NEA, Nat. Assn. Workshop Dirs., Osceola County Tchrs. Orgn., Phi Delta Kappa. Democrat. Roman Catholic. Avocations: basketball, softball, cheerleading. Office: Osceola County Schs 420 S Thacker Ave Kissimmee FL 34741-5963 E-mail: nleoc@cfl.rr.com.

EVANSON, BARBARA JEAN, middle school education educator; b. Grand Forks, N.D., Aug. 15, 1944; d. Robert John and Jean Elizabeth (Lommen) Gibbons; m. Bruce Carlyle Evanson, Dec. 27, 1965; children: Tracey, John, Kelly. AA, Bismarck State Coll., 1964; BS in Spl. and Elem. Edn., U. N.D., 1966. Tchr. spl. edn. Winship Sch., Grand Forks, 1966-67, Simle Jr. High, Bismarck, 1967-70; tchr. Northridge Elem. Sch., Bismarck, 1980-86, Wachter Middle Sch., Bismarck, 1986—. Cons. Dept. Pub. Instrn., Bismarck, 1988—, Chpt. I, Bismark, 1989—, McRel for Drug Free Schs., Denver, 1990-95. Co-founder The Big People, Bismarck, 1978-95; mem. task force Children's Trust Fund, N.D., 1984; senator N.D. Legislature, Bismarck, 1989-94; mem. N.D. Bridges Adv. Bd., 1991-97, DPI English Adv. Com., 1993—; co-facilitator Lead Mid. Sch. for Carnegie, 1994-97, N.D. Health Adv. Com., 1993-94, N.D. Tchr.'s Fund for Retirement, State Investment Bd. 1996—; co-founder, bd. dirs. Neighbors Network, 1983—. Recipient Gold Award Bismarck Norwest Bank, 1985; named Tchr. of Yr., N.D. Dept. Pub. Instrn., 1989, Legislator of Yr., Children's Caucus, 1991, Outstanding Alumnae, Bismarck State Coll., 1991, Milken Nat. Tchr. of Yr., 1995-96, KX Golden Apple award, 1999. Mem. N.D. Reading Assn., N.D. Coun. of Tchrs. of English., NEA, N.D. Edn. Assn., Bismarck Edn. Assn. Avocations: clown, walking, reading, travel, remodeling. Office: Wachter Middle Sch 1107 S 7th St Bismarck ND 58504-6533

EVANSON, PAUL JOHN, utilities executive; b. N.Y.C., June 16, 1941; s. Edwin F. and Barbara (Marconi) E.; m. Carol Louise Cordaro, Aug. 21, 1965; 1 child, Lisa J. BBA, St. John's U., N.Y., 1963; JD, Columbia U., 1966; LLM, NYU, 1970. CPA, N.Y.; Bar: N.Y. 1966. Mgr. Arthur Andersen & Co., N.Y.C., 1966-73; exec. v.p. Moore McCormack Resources, Inc., Stamford, Conn., 1973-88; pres., chief oper. officer Lynch Corp., Greenwich, Conn., 1988-92; sr. v.p., CFO FPL Group, Inc., Juno Beach, Fla., 1992-95; pres. FPL Co., Juno Beach, 1995—2003; pres., CEO, chmn. Allegheny Energy, Inc., Hagertown, Md., 2003—. Bd. dirs. Lynch Corp. (AMEX), So. Energy Homes, Inc. (NASDAQ). Chmn., pres. YMCA, Stamford, 1982-88. Mem. Country Club of Darien. Avocations: tennis, reading. Office: Allegheny Energy, Inc 10435 Downsville Pike Hagerstown MD 21740-1766*

EVANSON, ROBERT VERNE, pharmacy educator; b. Hammond, Ind., Nov. 3, 1920; s. Evan and Dorothy (Gordon) E.; m. Helen Louise Wolber, June 29, 1947; children: Yvonne Louise Evanson Nash, Karen Denice Evanson Ivanson. BS in Pharmacy, Purdue U., 1947, MS in Indsl. Pharmacy, 1949, PhD in Pharmacy Adminstrn., 1953. Apprentice pharmacist Physician's Supply Co., Hammond, 1946; grad. asst. pharmacy Sch. Pharmacy, Purdue U., 1947-48, mem. faculty, 1948—, prof. pharm. adminstrn., 1963-86, head dept., 1966-72; assoc. head dept. pharmacy practice, 1982-86; prof. emeritus, 1986—. Cons. in field. Contbr. articles to profl. jours.; contbg. author: Central Pharm. Jour., 1964-72. Served with AUS, 1943-46. Recipient Lederle Faculty award, 1964; award for faculty excellence in pharmacy adminstrn. Nat. Assn. Retail Druggists, 1985; Robert V. Evanson Walgreen scholarship, 1986—. Fellow Am. Found. Pharm. Edn., Am. Pharm. Assn.; mem. Ind. Pharm. Assn., Am. Assn. Coll. Pharmacy (dir., Disting. Educator award 1982), Am. Assn. Coll. Pharmacy Council Faculties (chmn. 1985-86), Acad. Pharm. Scis., Acad. Pharmacy Practice, Soc. Preservation and Encouragement Barbershop Quartet Singing in Am., Sigma Xi. Mem. Fed. Ch. W. Lafayette. Home: 400 Lindberg Ave West Lafayette IN 47906-2032

EVARTS, WILLIAM MAXWELL, JR., lawyer; b. N.Y.C., June 3, 1925; m. Helen Rulison Coleman, Aug. 28, 1948; children: Holly Evarts Bartow, Kate, Alice. AB, Harvard U., 1949, LL.B., 1952. Bar: N.Y. 1953, U.S. Ct. Appeals (2d cir.) 1961, U.S. Dist. Ct. (so. and ea. dists.) N.Y. 1974. Assoc. Winthrop, Stimson, Putnam & Roberts, N.Y.C., 1952-62, ptnr., 1962-97, sr. counsel, 1997—. Bd. dirs. Trust for Pub. Land, San Francisco, United Hosp. Fund, N.Y.C., Scenic Hudson, Poughkeepsie, The Clark Found., N.Y.C.; chmn., 1996-2000, cons. mem., 2001– ; chmn. distbn. com. N.Y. Cmty. Trust. Sgt. U.S. Army, 1943-46, ETO. Mem. Assn. of Bar of City of N.Y. Office: Pillsbury Winthrop LLP 1 Battery Park Plz New York NY 10004-1490

EVATT, PARKER, former state commissioner, former state legislator; b. Greenville, S.C., Aug. 27, 1935; s. H.D. and Ruby (Parker) E.; m. Jane Mangum, Sept. 2, 1960; children: Katherine, Alan. BS, U. S.C., 1958, M.Criminal Justice, 1978; LLD, Presbyn. Coll., 1977. Exec. dir. Alston Wilkes Soc., Columbia, S.C., 1965-87; mem. S.C. Ho. of Reps., 1975-87; commr. S.C. Dept. Corrections, 1987-95; sr. v.p. Just Care, Inc., 1996—. Mem. adminstrv. bd. Virginia Wingard Meml., United Meth. Ch., del. to gen. conf., 1972, del. to jurisdiction confs., 1972, 76, 80, 84; past lay leader Columbia Meth. Dist. Served with USN, 1958-60. Recipient numerous awards and citations from civic, religious and profl. orgns. Mem. S.C. Youth Workers Assn. (past pres.), Christian Action Coun. (bd. govs. 1968-71), S.C. Andrews Jaycees (Ifie), Nat. Assn. Social Workers (named Citizen of Yr. S.C. chpt. 1978), Internat. Halfway Assn. (v.p. 1973-76), Res. Officers Assn. (v.p. Columbia chpt.), Naval Rsch. Assn. (past pres. Carolina chpt.), Rotary, Pi Kappa Alpha. E-mail: PElake156@aol.com.

EVDOKIMOFF, MERRILY WEBER, nursing administrator, community health nurse; b. Pontiac, Mich., July 16, 1945; d. Earl H. and Lillian (Simpson) Weber; m. Victor Evdokimoff, Oct. 14, 1972; children: Justin, Amy. BSN, U. Mich., 1967; MS in Nursing, Boston U., 1984. RN, Mass. Nursing supr. East Seal Home Health Care, Boston, 1985-88; COO Vis. Nurse & Community Health, Inc., Lexington, Mass., 1988-95; home care cons., 1995-99; adminstr. Acton (Mass.) Nursing Svc., 1999—. Named Shirley Titus scholar, U. Mich., 1983. Mem. Mass. Home and Health Assn. (co-chair data com.), Sigma Theta Tau. Home: 246A Burroughs Rd Boxboro MA 01719-1320 E-mail: mevdokimoff@town.acton.ma.us .

EVDOKIMOVA, EVA, prima ballerina assoluta, choreographer, director, producer, actress; b. Geneva, Dec. 1, 1948; parents Am. citizens; m. Michael Gregori, 1982. Student, Munich State Opera Ballet Sch., Royal Ballet Sch., London; studied privately with Maria Fay (London), Vera Volkova (Copenhagen), Natalia Dudinskaya (Leningrad), 1964-66; student in Music Studies, Guild Hall Sch. Music, London, 1964—66, Juilliard Sch., 1998—2000; student in Drama Studies, H.B. Studio, N.Y.C., 1997—2000. Pres. of jury Rudolf Nureyev Internat. Ballet Competition, Budapest, 1994, 96, 98; chm. Jury Varna Internat. Ballet Competition, Bulgaria, 1996; ballet mistress Boston Ballet, 2002-03; drama performances 5 off off Broadway drama prodns., 1997-2002; contemporary dance performances created for her by Igal Perry, Henning Rubsam, Angela Jones; simultaneous translation and interpretation between English, French, German, Russian, Italian, Danish. Latin Studies. Debut Royal Danish Ballet, Copenhagen, 1966; Prima Ballerina Assoluta, Deutsche Oper Berlin, 1969-90; frequent guest artist with numerous major ballet cos. worldwide including London Festival Ballet, English Nat. Ballet, Am. Ballet Theatre, Paris Opera Ballet, La Scala, Kirov Ballet, Tokyo Ballet, Teatro Colon, Nat. Ballet of Can., and all other major nat. ballet cos.; premiered roles in all Rudolf Nureyev's classical ballet prodns. (ptnr. over 15 years); appeared in over 16 classical and modern ballets with Rudolf Nureyev across the world; repertoire of more than 130 roles includes Swan Lake, Giselle, La Sylphide, Sleeping Beauty, Romeo and Juliet, Don Quixote, La Bayadere, Onegin, Raymonda; created roles in many contemporary ballets for stage, film and TV; film appearances include The Nutcracker, La Sylphide, Cinderella, A Family Portrait, The Romantic Era, Invitation to the Dance, Portrait of Eva Evdokimova, and others. Recipient Diploma, Internat. Ballet Competition, Moscow, 1969; winner Gold medal Varna Internat. Ballet competition, 1970; awarded title Prima Ballerina Assoluta, Berlin Senate, 1973, Berlin Critic's Prize, 1974; first fgn. mem. Royal Danish Ballet, first Am. and Westerner to win any internat. ballet competition, first Am. to perform with Kirov Ballet, 1976, first Am. to perform in Peking after the Cultural Revolution, 1978, first and only Am. dancer with portrait in permanent collection, Mus. Drama and Dance, Leningrad, St. Petersburg, Russia, only Am. performer ever to be honored in a German opera house, Grand Défilé ceremony, 1990 Deutsche Oper Berlin; recipient letter for meritorious svc. from Pres. Bush, 1990, numerous other awards; holder world record for 67 curtain calls with 40 minute standing ovation, Berlin, 1990.

EVELETH, JANET STIDMAN, law association administrator; b. Balt., Sept. 6, 1950; d. John Charles and Edith Janet (Scales) Stidman; m. Donald P. Eveleth, May 11, 1974. BA, Washington Coll., 1972; MS, Johns Hopkins U., 1973. Counselor Office of Mayor, Balt., 1973-75; asst. dir. Gov. Commn. on Children, Balt., 1975-78; lobbyist Balt., 1978-80; comm. specialist Med. Soc., Balt., 1980-81; dir. pub. affairs Mid-Atlantic Food Dealers, Balt., 1981-84; dir. comm. Home Builders Assn., Balt., 1984-87, Md. Bar Assn., Balt., 1987—. Contbr. articles to profl. jours. Recipient Gov. citation State of Md., 1993, Citizen citation City of Balt., 1993. Mem.: NAFE, Nat. Assn. Bar Execs. (chmn. pub. rels. sect. 1994—95, Achievement award 1995, E.A. Wally Richter award 1997, Luminary award 1999, 2001), Md. Soc. Assn. Execs. (pres. 1992—93), Am. Soc. Profl. Women, Pi Lambda Theta, Alpha Chi Omega. Office: Md Bar Assn 520 W Fayette St Baltimore MD 21201-1781 E-mail: jeveleth@msba.org.

EVELYN, DOUGLAS EVERETT, museum director; b. Ossining, N.Y., Sept. 19, 1941; s. Everett Edward and Marie Georgette (Davis) Evelyn; m. Martha Ellen Hutchins MacCornack, Aug. 14, 1965; children: Sarah Ellen Bordac, Elizabeth Jane. BA cum laude, Wesleyan U., Middletown, Conn., 1963; PhD, George Washington U., 1997. Staff asst., then adminstrv. asst. to dir. Am. Assn. Mus., 1963—67; adminstrv. asst. Dem. Nat. Com., 1968; assoc. cons. Monroe Bush & Assocs. (mgmt. cons.), Washington, 1969; various positions to dep. dir. Nat. Portrait Gallery, Smithsonian Instn., Washington, 1969-79; dep. dir. Nat. Mus. Am. History, Smithsonian Instn., Washington, 1979-92, Nat. Mus. Am. Indian, Smithsonian Instn., Washington, 1992—. Co-author: (book) On This Spot: Pinpointing the History of Washington D.C., 1992. Mem.: Internat. Coun. Mus. (U.S. com. bd. dirs. 2000—), Am. Assn. State and Local History (coun. 1987—96, v.p. 1990, pres. 1992—94), Am. Assn. Mus. (treas. 1979—82), Cultural Alliance Greater Washington (coun. 1977—84, treas. 1983—84). Home: 23 King Pl NW Washington DC 20007-1029 Office: Smithsonian Inst Nat Mus Am Indian Washington DC 20560-0001

EVEN, FRANCIS ALPHONSE, lawyer; b. Chgo., Sept. 8, 1920; s. George Martin and Cecilia (Neuman) E.; m. Margaret Hope Herrick, Oct. 16, 1945; children: Janet Beth, Dorothy Elizabeth. BS in Mech. Engring, U. Ill., 1942; JD, George Washington U., 1949. Bar: D.C. bar 1949, Ill. bar 1950. Engr. GE, 1945-49; ptnr. Fitch, Even, Tabin & Flannery (patent and trademark law), Chgo., 1952—. Mem. bd. edn., River Forest, Ill., 1963-69; trustee West Suburban Hosp., Oak Park, Ill., 1974-77; mem. bd. Ill. State Hist. Soc., 2000-03. With combat engrs., U.S. 3d inf. divsn., 1942-45. Fellow Am. Coll. Trial Lawyers (emeritus); mem. ABA, Am. Intellectual Property Law Assn. (bd. mgrs. 1963-66), Ill. Bar Assn., Chgo. Bar Assn., Intellectual Property Law Assn. Chgo. (bd. mgrs. 1972-73, pres. 1984), No. Ill. Ct. Hist. Assn. (pres.), Union League Club (Chgo.), Oak Park (Ill.) Country Club, Chgo. Literary Club. Republican. Home: 1018 Park Ave River Forest IL 60305-1308 Office: 120 S La Salle St Chicago IL 60603-3403

EVEN, RANDOLPH M. lawyer; b. 1943; BS, U. Calif.; JD, Calif. Western Sch. Law. Bar: Calif. 1969. Atty. Even, Crandall, Wade, & Lowe and predecessor firm Genson, Even, Crandall & Wade, P.C., Woodland Hills, Calif. Mem. Am. Bd. Trial Advocates, Assn. So. Calif. Def. Counsel (bd. dirs. 1978-80, 93-98). Office: Even Crandall Wade & Lowe 21031 Ventura Blvd Ste 801 Woodland Hills CA 91364-2240

EVENBECK, SCOTT EDWARD, university official, psychologist; b. Findlay, Ohio, Aug. 14, 1946; s. Benjamin F. and Norma H. (Kelley) E.; m. Elizabeth Ann Jones, Aug. 14, 1970 (div. July 1995); 1 child, Benjamin F. III. AB, Ind. U., 1968; MA, U. N.C., 1971, PhD, 1972. Asst. prof. psychology Ind. U.-Purdue U., Indpls., 1972-76; asst. dean Purdue U. Sch. Sci., 1977-79, assoc. dean, 1979-80, assoc. dir. adminstrv. affairs, assoc. prof. psychology, 1976—, assoc. dir. adminstrv. affairs, 1980-85, dir. continuing studies, 1985—; assoc. dean Ind. U. Sch. Continuing Studies, 1985-88, assoc. dean of faculties, 1988-90, assoc. vice chancellor, 1990—, dean univ. coll., 1997. Bd. dirs. Parent Info. Resource Ctr., 1977-85; exec. v.p. Assn. for Continuing Higher Edn., 1990-93, bd. dirs., 1993-2000, v.p., 1996—, pres.-elect, 1997, pres.98-99. Contbr. articles in field to profl. jours., books. Mem. exec. com., asst. treas., v.p., pres. Am. Lung Assn. Ctrl. Ind., bd. dirs., 1985—, v.p., 1986; pres. Am. Lung Assn. Ind., 1988; mem. nat. coun. Am. Lung Assn., 1991-94; bd. dirs. Christamore House, 1985-94; sec. Indpls.-Searborough Peace Games, 1977-80; mem. bd. Consortium Endowed Episcopal Parishes, 1992—, v.p., 1994-96, pres., 1996-99; dep. gen. Episcopal Ch. Conv., 1988, 91, 94, 97, 2000, 03, standing commn. on human affairs, 1995-98, standing commn. on domestic mission and evangelism, 1997—, chair edn., 2000-03; sec. Diocese Indpls., 1995—; mem. program com. Indpls. Urban League, 2002—; bd. dirs. Campus Ministries, 2002—. USPHS trainee, 1968-72. Arthur R. Metz scholar Ind. U., 1964-68. Mem. APA, Nat. Coun. Univ. Rsch. Adminstrs. (mem. exec. com. 1979-80), Indpls. C. of C. (mem. exec. com. spkrs. bur.), Ind. Soc. Chgo. (v.p. 2000—), Masons. Republican. Episcopalian. Home: 5115 E 74th Pl Indianapolis IN 46250-2529 Office: 815 W Michigan St Indianapolis IN 46202-5199

EVENHUIS, HENK J. research company exxecutive; b. Ontario, Calif., Apr. 10, 1943; s. Kornelus and Harmina (Vermeer) E.; m. Cynthia Wheelus, Jan. 31, 1964; children: John, Karen. BS in Acctg., Calif. State Poly. U., Pomona, 1967; MBA in Fin., U. Santa Clara, 1976. V.p., CFO, Ferix Corp., Fremont, Calif., 1983-85, Trimedia Corp., Fremont, 1985-86, Corvus Systems Corp., San Jose, Calif., 1986-87; sr. v.p., CFO, Lam Rsch. Corp., Fremont, 1987—. Bd. dirs. Credence Corp., Fremont. Mem. Fin. Execs. Inst. (bd. dirs. Santa Clara, Calif. 1988-90). Avocations: skiing, golf. Office: Fair Isaac & Co Inc 120 N Redwood Dr San Rafael CA 94903

EVENS, MARTHA WALTON, computer science educator; b. Boston, Jan. 1, 1935; d. Clarence Russell and Virgene (Dupka) Walton; m. Leonard Evens, Sept. 13, 1958; children: Sarah Helen, Samuel Robert, Anne Chaia. AB in Math., Bryn Mawr Coll., 1955; postgrad., U. Paris, 1955-56; AM in Math., Radcliffe Coll., 1957; PhD in Computer Sci., Northwestern U., Evanston, Ill., 1975. Staff mem. MIT Lincoln Lab., Bedford, Mass., 1957-60; asst. prof. computer sci. Ill. Inst. Tech., Chgo., 1975-81, assoc. prof. computer sci., 1981-86, prof. computer sci., 1986—. Author: Lexical Semantic Relations, 1980; editor: Relational Models of the Lexicon, 1988; assoc. editor Am. Math. Monthly, 1976-81, Computational Linguistics, 1984-86; editorial bd. Cambridge Univ. Press Series in Natural Language Processing, 1986-90. Precinct capt. Dem. party of Evanston, 1972-75. Recipient fellowship, Fulbright, U. Paris, 1955-56. Mem. Assn. for Computational Linguistics (pres. 1984). Episcopalian. Home: 2026 Orrington Ave Evanston IL 60201-2912 Office: Computer Sci Dept Ill Inst Technology 10 W 31st St Chicago IL 60616-3729 E-mail: evens@iit.edu.

EVENS, RONALD GENE, radiologist, medical center administrator; b. St. Louis, Sept. 24, 1939; s. Robert and Dorothy (Lupkey) E.; m. Hanna Blunk, Sept. 3, 1960; children: Ronald Jr., Christine, Amanda. BA, Washington U., 1960, MD, 1964, postgrad. in bus. and edn., 1970-71. Intern Barnes Hosp., St. Louis, 1964-65; resident Mallinckrodt Inst. Radiology, St. Louis, 1965-66, 68-70; rsch. assoc. Nat. Heart Inst., 1966-68; asst. prof. radiology, v.p. Washington U. Med. Sch., 1970-71, prof., head dept. radiology, dir., 1971-72, Elizabeth Mallinckrodt prof., head radiology dept., 1972-99, prof. med. econs., 1988—; pres., sr. exec. ofcr. Barnes-Jewish Hosp., St. Louis, 1999—. Radiologist-in-chief Barnes Hosp., St. Louis, 1971-99; radiologist-in-chief Children's Hosp., 1971-99, pres., chief exec. officer, 1985-88; vice chancellor fin. Washington U., St. Louis, 1988-91; mem. adv. com. on splty. and geog. distbn. of physicians Inst. Medicine, Nat. Acad. Scis., 1974-76, Hickey lectr., 1976, Carmen lectr. Calif. U., 1985, Kiewit lectr. Eisenhower Med. Ctr., 1986; Hornick lectr. U. Pitts., 1986; ann. orator Can. Radiol. Soc., 1984; Hodes lectr. Jefferson U., 1991—; Smith lectr. Royal Coll. Physicians, Edinburgh, 1992; Seaman lectr. Columbia Presbyn., 1992; dir. Boatmens Bank Inc., Mallinckrodt Group Inc., Right Choice Inc., Blue Choice, Inc.; chmn. bd. Med. Care Group St. Louis, 1980-86. Contbr. over 210 articles to profl. jours. Active Boy Scouts Am., 1975—; elder Glendale Presbyn. Ch., 1971-74, Kirkwood Presbyn. Ch., 1983-86. Served with USPHS, 1966-68. Advance Acad. fellow James Picker Found, 1970; recipient Disting. Svc. award. St. Louis C. of C., 1972; named Disting. Eagle Scout Nat. Coun., 1983. Fellow Am. Coll. Radiology (chair elect 1995, chair bd. chancellors 1996—); mem. AMA (editl. bd. JAMA), Mo. Radiol. Soc. (pres. 1977-78), Soc. Nuclear Medicine (trustee 1971-75), St. Louis Med. Soc., Mo. State Med. Assn., Soc. Chmn. Acad. Radiology Depts. (pres. 1979), Radiol. Soc. N.Am., Assn. Univ. Radiologists (pres. 1988), Am. Roentgen Ray Soc. (pres. 1989), Phi Beta Kappa, Alpha Omega Alpha (Sheard-Sanford award). Office: Barnes Jewish Hosp Mallinckrodt Inst Radiology Barnes Jewish Plz Saint Louis MO 63110-1016 Address: Barnes-Jewish Hosp One Barnes-Jewish Hospital Plz Saint Louis MO 63110

EVENSEN, EDWARD ARTHUR, elementary school educator; b. Claremont, N.H., Aug. 18, 1949; s. Edwin Arthur and Doris Mae (Stockwell) E.; m. Anne Stella Rogers, July 14, 1973; children: Erik Andrew, Keira Lindsay. BMus in Edn., Boston U., 1971; MS, U. N.H., 1972. Cert. music edn. grades K-12, N.H. Instrumental music tchr. Oyster River Schs., Durham, N.H., 1971-72; dir. music grades K-12 Alton Ctrl. Schs., N.H., 1972-74; music tchr. Claremont Jr. High, N.H., 1974-86; instrumental music tchr. grades 7-12 Woodstock Union High, Vt., 1986-88; dir. music grades 4-12 Whitcomb High, Bethel Elem., Bethel, Vt., 1989-92; dir. music grades K-8 Plainfield Elem., Meriden, NH, 1992—2001; instrumental music tchr. grades 5-12 Sunapee Schs., NH, 1993—95; music tchr. grades K-6 Albert Bridge Sch., Brownsville, Vt., 1995—96, 1999—2000; music tchr. grades 5-8 Cornish (N.H.) Elem., 1999-2001; coord. music fest. N.H. Mid. Sch., 2000—02; music tchr. 1-8 Alstead, N.H., 2001—. Adjudicator woodwinds New England Music Festival, 1976-92; adjudicator woodwinds/vocal Vt. All-State/Dists., 1973—; dir. Claremont Am. Band, N.H., 1969—; musical dir. Off Broad St. Players, Claremont, N.H., 1992-98, 2000, 02; music festival coord., Vt., 1992, N.H., 2000, host, 1981, 84, 95. Mem. NEA, ASCD, Music Educators Nat. Conf., New England Band Dirs. Assn., Assn. Concert Bands. Avocations: clarinet, saxophone and flute jazz performance, mgb cars, numismatics, woodworking. Home: 216 Broad St Claremont NH 03743-2685

EVENSON, MERLE ARMIN, chemist, educator; b. LaCrosse, Wis., July 27, 1934; s. Ansel Bernard and Gladys Mabel (Nelson) E.; m. Peggy L. Kovats, Oct. 5, 1957; children— David A., Donna L. BS in Chem. Physics and Math., U. Wis., LaCrosse, 1956; MS in Guidance, MS in Sci. Edn., Madison, 1960, PhD in Analytical Chemistry, 1966. Diplomate Am. Bd. Clin. Chemists, v.p., 1978-81. Tchr. math. and physics St. Croix Falls (Wis.) High Sch., 1956-57; tchr. chemistry Central High Sch., LaCrosse, 1957-59; instr. dept. medicine U. Wis., Madison, 1965-66, asst. prof., 1966-69, assoc. prof., 1971-75, prof., 1975—, prof. dept. pathology, 1979—; asst. dir. clin. lab. Univ. Hosps., 1965-66, dir. clin. chemistry lab., 1966-69, dir. toxicology lab., 1971-87. Chmn. Gordon Rsch. Conf. on Analytical Chemistry, 1978; vis. lectr. Harvard Med. Sch., 1969-71; mem. staff Peter Bent Brigham Hosp., Boston, 1969-71; cons. on analytical and clin. chemistry to AEC, 1968-93, Am. Chem. Soc., Nat. Bur. Standards, FDA, NIH, study sect. mem. 1968-72, ad hoc memberships, 1973-87. Bd. editors: Chemical Instrumentation, 1973-87, Analytical Chemistry, 1974-77, Jour. Analytical Toxicology, 1976-79, Selected Methods in Clin. Chemistry, 1977-81; editor: Contemporary Topics in Analytical and Clincal Chemistry, 1974-83; contbr. numerous chpts. to books, articles to profl. jours.; patentee continuous oil hemoperfusion unit. NIH fellow, 1970-71, NSF, 1959-62; recipient Maurice O. Graff Disting. Alumni award U. Wis., LaCrosse, 1981 Mem. AAAS, Acad. Clin. Lab. Physicians and Scientists, Am. Assn. Clin. Chemists (bd. editors Clin. Chemistry 1970-80, nat. chair pub. rels. com. 1973-78, diplomat 1974, v.p. 1978-81), Am. Chem. Soc. (com. on clin. chemistry 1973-93), Sigma Xi, Kappa Delta Pi. Office: U Wis 1300 University Ave Madison WI 53706-1510 *As a teacher, the fostering of the development of creativity in people who then make contributions to our society is an exciting process. The most significant professional reward I receive is the observation of the successes of others with whom I have interacted and taught.*

EVENSON, ROBERT EUGENE, economist, educator; b. Elmore, Minn., July 25, 1934; s. Edven Herbert and Annie Cecilia (O'Toole) Evenson; m. Bonnie Lee Leak, Dec. 7, 1952 (div. 1959); children: Nancy Lynn, Patsy Ann; m. Judi Joan Ungrodt, June 11, 1967; children: Joseph Robert, Sarah Judith. BA in Bus. Adminstrn., U. Minn., 1961, MS, 1964; PhD, U. Chgo., 1968. Farmer E.H. Evenson & Son, Minnesota Lake, Minn., 1952—60; asst. prof. U. Minn., Mpls. and St. Paul, 1966—68; vis. asst. prof. So. Meth. U., Dallas, 1968—69; assoc. prof. econs. Yale U., New Haven, 1969—74; assoc. vis. prof. Agrl. Devel. Coun., N.Y.C., 1974—77; prof. Yale U., New Haven, 1977—. Cons. World Bank, Washington, 1970—, U.S. AID, 1970—. Author: Agricultural Research and Productivity, 1975, Technology and Income, 1990; editor: Science and Technology: Lessons for Development, 1990. Fellow, NSF, 1964. Fellow: AAAS, Am. Agrl. Econs. Assn.; mem.: Econometric Soc., Am. Econ. Assn. Home: 322 Audubon Ct New Haven CT 06510

EVERARD, ERIC, company administrator; b. Brussels, July 10, 1964; s. Patrick and Elschen (Schäfer) E.; m. Muriel Morettini; children: Emilie, Juliette, Fanny, Arthur. Grad. in applied econs., Econonique Appliquee, Belgium, 1986. Founder, mng. dir. student mags. Univers-Cite, Brussels, 1985-87, Kampus/Knack, Brussels, 1987-88, European Student Fair, Brussels, 1988-91; adminstr. Associated Comm. Industries/Nat. Info. and Distbn., Brussels, 1989-91; gen. mgr. Reed Exhbns., Brussels, 1991-95; mng. dir. Ki Ptnrs. Group, Brussels, 1997-99, ARTEXIS, S.A., Brussels, 1998—, Best of Group SA, 2001—. Mng. dir. Co-Case, Brussels, 1990—, Reed Roularta, Brussels, 1994—, MIP-TV/MIPCOM, 1995-96, Chateau de Beggen S.A., Luxembourg; v.p. Euresco, Brussels, 1993—. Avocations: plane flying, motorcycling, skiing, antiques and modern art. Office: ARTEXIS SA Blvd Louis Schmidt 97 B-1040 Brussels Belgium

EVERARD, GERALD WILFRED, lawyer, trust company executive; b. Green Bay, Wis., Sept. 25, 1952; s. Wilfred A. and Regina P. (Arendt) E.; m. Paula M. Devroy, Sept. 17, 1977. BA, St. Norbert Coll., 1974; JD, U. Wis., 1977. Bar: Wis. 1977. Assoc. Boaroman, Suhr, Curry & Field, Madison, Wis., 1977-81; trust officer 1st Wis. Nat. Bank, Madison, 1981—. Law instr. U. Wis., Madison, 1985. Bd. dirs. Cen. YMCA, Madison, 1983-86. Mem. Wis. Bar Assn., Dane County Bar Assn., ABA. Office: US Bank PO Box 7900 Madison WI 53707-7900 E-mail: jay.everard@usbank.com.

EVERARD, NOEL J. structural engineer, educator; b. New Orleans, La., Dec. 24, 1923; s. James J. and Lydia (Rehm) Everard; m. Courtney LeBlanc, Sept. 9, 1950; children: Ann Everard Fielder, Michael Scott. BS in Civil Engring., La. State U., Baton Rouge, 1948, MS in Civil Engring., 1957; PhD in Civil Engring., Tex. A&M U., College Station, 1962. Registered profl. engr., La., 1948, Tex., 1960. Instr. civil engring. La. State U., Baton Rouge, 1948—49; assoc. ptnr. David W. Godat & Assocs., New Orleans, 1949—56; asst. prof. civil engring. La. State U., Baton Rouge, 1956—60; assoc. prof. civil engring. U. Tex., Arlington, 1960—62, prof. civil engring., 1962—89, chmn. civil engring. dept., 1973—83, prof. emeritus, 1991—. Cons. engr. Dr. Noel J. Everard & Assocs., Arlington, Tex., 1964—; internat. lectr. structural engring. Author: (text book) Reinforced Concrete Design, 1966, 3d edit., 1993; contbr. articles to profl. jours. Capt. U.S. Army, 1942—46, PTO. Fellow: ASCE (life); mem.: Structural Engrs. Assn. Tex., Am. Concrete Inst. (hon. Delmar Bloem Disting. Svc. award 1971, Joe W. Kelly award for outstanding educators 1984), Phi Kappa Phi, Pi Mu Epsilon, Chi Epsilon, Tau Beta Pi, Sigma Xi. Roman Catholic. Home: 4310 Downsview Ct Arlington TX 76016 Office: Dr Noel J Everard & Assocs 4310 Downsview Ct Arlington TX 76016 E-mail: neverard@netscape.net.

EVERBACH, OTTO GEORGE, lawyer; b. New Albany, Ind., Aug. 27, 1938; s. Otto G. and Zelda Marie (Hilt) E.; m. Nancy Lee Stern, June 3, 1961; children: Tracy Ellen, Stephen George. BS, U.S. Mil. Acad., 1960; LLB, U. Va., 1966. Bar: Va. 1967, Ind. 1967, Calif. 1975, Mass. 1978. Counsel CIA, Langley, Va., 1966-67; corp. counsel Bristol-Meyers Co., Evansville, Ind., 1967-74, Alza Corp., Palo Alto, Calif., 1974-75; sec., gen. counsel Am. Optical Corp., Southbridge, Mass., 1976-81; assoc. gen. counsel Warner-Lambert Co., Morris Plains, N.J., 1981-83; v.p. Kimberly-Clark Corp., Neenah, Wis., 1984-86, sr. v.p., gen. counsel, 1986—, sr. v.p. law & govt. affairs, 1988—. Served with U.S. Army, 1960-63. Mem. Am. Bar Assn., Mass. Bar Assn., Ind. Bar Assn., Calif. Bar Assn. Office: Kimberly-Clark Corp DFW Airport Sta PO Box 619100 Dallas TX 75261-9100

EVERDELL, WILLIAM, retired lawyer; b. N.Y.C., May 29, 1915; s. William and Rosalind (Romeyn) E.; m. Eleanore Darling, July 2, 1940; children: William Romeyn, Coburn Darling, Preston. BA, Williams Coll., 1937; LLB, Yale U., 1940. Bar: N.Y. 1941. Assoc. Debevoise & Plimpton, N.Y.C., 1940-49, ptnr., 1949-85, of counsel, 1986-88. Contbr. articles to profl. jours. Trustee Woods Hole Oceanographic Instn., Mass., 1978-86; mem. exec. com., 1981-86, hon. trustee, 1987—; trustee, mem. exec. com. Cold Spring Harbor Lab., N.Y., 1987-93. Served to lt. comdr. USNR, 1942-45, PTO, ATO. Fellow Am. Bar Found.; mem. ABA, Assn. of Bar of City of N.Y. (mem. exec. com. 1960-64), N.Y. State Bar Assn. (chmn. com. corp. law 1971-73). Clubs: The Links (gov. 1959-62) (N.Y.C.). Episcopalian. Avocations: sailing; golf.

EVERDELL, WILLIAM ROMEYN, humanities educator, educator; b. NYC, June 25, 1941; s. William and Eleanore (Darling) E.; m. Barbara Scott, Dec. 21, 1966; children: Joshua William, Christian Romeyn. AB, Princeton U., 1964; MA, Harvard U., 1965; PhD, NYU, 1971. Asst. English Lycee Arago, Paris, 1963-64; chmn. dept. history St. Ann's Sch., Bklyn., 1972-73, head upper shc., 1973-75, co-chmn. dept. history, 1975-84, dean humanities, 1984—. Adj. instr. NYU, N.Y.C., 1984-85, 86, 87, 89; steering com. U.S. history assessment Nat. Assessment Ednl. Progress, 1991-92; rev. panel NEH Tchr. Fellowships, U.S. Dept. Edn. Blue Ribbon Schs., 1992; ednl. testing svc. World History AP Exam. Devel. Com., 1999-2000. Author: The End of Kings, 1983, 2d edit., 2000, Christian Apologetics in France, 1987, The First Moderns, 1997; co-author: Rowboats to Rapid Transit, 1974; contbr. articles and poems to profl. jours. and newspapers. With USMC, 1966-68. Recipient Poetry prize Acad. Am. Poets, 1963; Fullbright travel grantee, Paris, 1963; Woodrow Wilson fellow, 1964, 70, NEH fellow, 1985, 90; NEH/Wallace Found. tchr./scholar, 1990-91. Mem. Internat. Soc. Intellectual History, Nat. Coun. History Edn., Am. Hist. Assn., N.Y. Acad. Sci., Orgn. History Tchrs. (pres. 2002—), East Ctrl. Am. Soc. 18th Century Studies (pres. 1997), Bklyn. Hist. Soc., New Eng. Soc. Bklyn., Rembrandt Club. Democrat. Episcopalian. Avocation: bicycling. Office: St Ann's Sch 129 Pierrepont St Brooklyn NY 11201-2793 E-mail: Everdell@aol.com.

EVERED, CHARLES B. writer, educator; b. Passaic, Nj, Nov. 12, 1964; s. Charles Joseph and Marie Theresa Evered; m. Wendy Rolfe Evered, Nov. 28, 1998; children: Margaret Adele, John O'Hara. MA, Yale U., New Haven, Connecticut, 1991; BA, Rutgers U., Newark, New Jersey, 1987. Educator Emerson Coll., Boston, Mass., 2002—; writer Whitman Coll., Walla Walla, Wash., 2001—02; educator Rider U., Lawrenceville, NJ, 1999—2000, Carnegie Mellon U., Pittsburgh, Pa., 1997—98; screenwriter Dreamworks Studio, Universal City, Calif., 1993—96; writer Amblin Productions, Universal City, Calif., 1991—92. Bd. mem. Dahlia Theatre, Los Angeles, Calif., 2000—; libr. bd. mem. Madison Libr., Madison, NJ, 2000—01; writer NJ Shakespeare Festival, Madison, NJ, 1994—98. Author: (book) Shoreham amd Other Plays, Size of the World and Other Plays (Berrilla Kerr, 1998). Lt. (j.g.) USN, 2000—, New York. Recipient Albee Award, Albee Found., 1991, Audrey Wood Award, Yale U., 1991, Eugene O'Neill Award, 1990. Mem.: Writers Guild of Am. (event com. 1993—2002), Navy Res. Assn. (ops. officer 1999), Yale Club of NYC. Unitarian Universalist. Avocations: baseball, tennis, skiing, fishing, hiking. Home: 35 Keep St Madison NJ 07940 Office: Emerson College 120 Boylston Street Boston MA 02116 E-mail: cbevered@aol.com.

EVERETT, AUBREY LEIGH, musician; b. Houston, Tex., Dec. 14, 1979; d. Richard and Arlene Lafosse; m. Gavin William Everett, Dec. 22, 2001. MusB Performance, Tex. Tech U., Lubbock, 1998—2001, MusM Performance, 2001—03. Guest asst. Galveston Symphony, Tex., 1997—97, Midland-Odessa (Tex.) Symphony, 2001—01, Abilene (Tex.) Philharm., 2001—01; adminstrv. internship Lubbock (Tex.) Symphony Orch., 2002, guest prin., 2002; guest asst. Big Spring (Tex.) Symphony Orch., 2002. Recipient Outstanding Music Scholar, Tex. Tech U., 2001, Excellence in Performance, Phi Kappa Lambda, 2002, Concerto Competition Winner, Symphonic Wind Ensemble, 2002. Mem.: Mu Phi Epsilon (pres. 2001—03). Personal E-mail: raineighbow@hotmail.com.

EVERETT, CARL BELL, lawyer; b. Plainfield, N.J., Mar. 23, 1947; s. Edward F. and Catherine (Bell) E.; m. Julie Elizabeth Lund, June 25, 1971; children: Andrew, Martha. BS Chem. Engring., MIT, 1969; JD, U. Houston, 1973. Bar: Tex. 1974, Del. 1974, Pa. 1987, U.S. Dist. Ct. Del. 1977, U.S. Dist. Ct. (ea. dist.) Pa. 1987, U.S. Ct. Appeals (6th cir.) 1977, U.S. Ct. Appeals (5th cir.) 1978, U.S. Ct. Appeals (1st cir.) 1979, U.S. Ct. Appeals (D.C. cir.) 1979. Sr. counsel E.I. du Pont de Nemours & Co. Inc., Wilmington, Del., 1974-86, Liebert, Short, FitzPatrick & Hirshland, Phila., 1986-87; with Saul Ewing, LLP, Phila., 1987—. Home: 813 Valley Rd Havertown PA 19083 Office: Saul Ewing LLP 1500 Market St Philadelphia PA 19102-2186

EVERETT, C(HARLES) CURTIS, retired lawyer; b. Omaha, Aug. 9, 1930; s. Charles Edgar and Rosalie (Cook) E.; m. Joan Rose Bader, Sept. 7, 1951; children: Jeffrey, Ellen, Amy, Jennifer. BA cum laude, Beloit Coll., 1952; JD, U. Chgo., 1957. Bar: Ill. 1957. Pvt. practice, Chgo., 1957-91; ptnr. Bell, Boyd, Lloyd, Haddad & Burns, 1965-81, successor firm Bell, Boyd & Lloyd, 1981-91; v.p. law, sec., gen. counsel AMRE, Inc., Dallas, 1991-96; v.p. law, sec., gen. counsel, bd. dirs. Am. Remodeling, Inc., Dallas, 1992-96; v.p. Canre Remodelling, Inc., Dallas, 1992-94. V.p., sec. Hans Bader, Cons., Inc., Clearwater, Fla., 1954-99, also bd. dirs.; vis. com. U. Chgo. Law Sch., 1986-89; lectr. Ill. Inst. CLE. Mem. editl. bd. U. Chgo. Law Rev., 1956-57; contbr. articles to profl. jours. Chmn. So. Suburban area Beloit Coll. Ford Found. challange program, 1964-65; pres. The Players, Flossmoor, 1970-71; bd. govs. Lake Shore Dr. Condominium Assn., 1986-91. With AUS, 1952-54. Mem. ABA, Ill. Bar Assn., Chgo. Bar Assn. (mem. securities law com. 1960-91), U. Chgo. Law Sch. Alumni Assn. (dir. 1973-76, pres. Chgo. chpt. 1979-80), Legal Club, Law Club,

Monroe Club (bd. govs. 1976-97), Univ. Club Chgo., Order of DeMolay (past master counselor Rock River chpt.), Order of Coif, Sigma Chi, Phi Alpha Delta. Mem. Cmty. Ch. (deacon). Home: 532 Long Reach Dr Salem SC 29676-4214

EVERETT, CHARLES ROOSEVELT, JR., airport executive; BA in Urban Studies, U. Pa., 1984. Transp. planning engr. Gannett Fleming, Inc., Harrisburg, Pa., 1986-88; transp. systems planner II Schimpeler Corradino Assoc., Louisville, 1988-89; project mgr. transp. planning Woolpert Cons., Dayton, Ohio, 1989-91; dir. Syracuse (N.Y.) Met. Transp. Coun., 1991-94; commr. dept. aviation City of Syracuse, 1994—2003, dir. city ops., 2003—. Bd. dirs. Hancock Field Devel. Corp., Aviation/Aerospace Edn. Found.; presenter in field. Contbr. articles to profl. jours. Maj. N.Y. ANG.; with N.Y. Air NG. Mem.: Transp. Rsch. Bd., Inst. Transp. Engrs. (trans. planners coun. N.Y. Upstate sect. pres. 1993—94, 1996—97, sec. 1995, tech. com., high speed inter-city rail svc. planning 1988—92), N.Y. Aviation Mgmt. Assn. (v.p. 1997, pres. 1998—99), Am. Assn. Airport Execs. Office: City of Syracuse 233 E Washington St Syracuse NY 13202 E-mail: ceverettc@ci.syracuse.ny.us.

EVERETT, CHERYL ANN, music educator, pianist; b. Crawfordsville, Ind., July 7, 1945; d. Howard Dennis and Thelma Louise (Rutledge) P. Student, DePauw U., 1975. Church organist Christian Sci. Ch., Methodist Ch., Presbyn. Ch., Crawfordsvill, Ind., 1958—; celeste player Indpls. Philharmonic Orch., 1994—; accompanist Wabash Coll. Glee Club, Crawfordsville, 1997—; adj. instr. piano Wabash Coll., 2003—. Adj. instr. piano Wabash Coll., 2003; chmn. Ind. Jr. Festival Nat. Fedn. Music Clubs, 1984-94, Indpls Jr. Festival Nat. Fedn. Music Clubs, 1984-94, Indpls. West Festival, 2000—; chmn. Indpls. West Festival, 2000—; performed in recitals and master classes of Internat. Workshops in Italy, Eng., France, Can., Switzerland, 1986-89, with Internat. String Orch. in workshops in Eisenstadt, Austria, 1989; adjudicator Tippecanoe Piano Tchrs. Lafayette, Ind, 1993-97, Logansport (Ind.) Piano Tchrs., 1993-97, Stickley Meml. Competition, South Bend, Ind., 1989, Ind. State Fair Young Hoosier Pianists Competition. Founder, dir. Presbyn. Artists Concert Series, Crawfordsville, 1991; founder, organizer Montgomery County Multi-keyboard Extravaganza featuring 170 players, Crawfordsville, 1995-97. Chosen 15 times Ideal Lady, Sunshine Soc. Girls, 1977-97. Mem. Indiana Music Tchrs. Assn. (chair monster concert 1998, Tchr. of Yr. 1999), Nat. Music Tchrs., Indpls. Piano Tchrs. (pres. 1986-88), Nat. Guild of Piano Tchrs., Crawfordsville Music Club (pres. 1989), Ind. Fedn. Music Clubs, Nat. Fedn. Music Clubs. Avocations: sewing, needlework, quilting. Home: 207 S Water St Crawfordsville IN 47933-2536 E-mail: ceverett@link2000.net.

EVERETT, CLAUDIA KELLAM, retired special education educator; b. Mobile, Ala., Dec. 28, 1933; d. Claude M. and Minnie L. Kellam; m. Thomas Sherwood Everett Sr., June 18, 1953; children: Thomas Sherwood Jr., Sherilisa Ann. BA magna cum laude, Roberts Wesleyan Coll., 1958; MS summa cum laude, Barry U., 1988. Cert. English, spl. edn. tchr. Fla., N.Y. Tchr. Dade County Pub. Schs., Miami, Fla., 1959-67, Carol City Elem. Sch., Miami, 1967-77; pers. mgr., payroll supr. Harrington Cos., Miami, 1977-81; honors English tchr. Citrus Grove Jr. HS, Miami, 1981-87, spl. edn. tchr. Citrus Grove Mid. Sch., Miami, 1987-90; tchr. severely emotionally disturbed children Hilton (N.Y.) HS, 1990-91; tchr. emotionally disturbed and mentally retarded, learning disabled Hill Elem. Sch., Brockport, NY, 1991-92; tchr. emotionally/learning disabled, mentally retarded Oliver Mid. Sch., Brockport, 1991—2001; ret., 2001. Cons. cmty. benevolent agys., Miami, 1969—83; pvt. tutor, 2001—. Author: numerous poems. Youth dir. Ctrl. Alliance Youth, Miami, 1960—80; cmty. advisor youth affairs Carol City, Miami, 1970—87; founder, pres. Tchr.-Parent Study Group, Miami, 1970—80; 1st v.p., sec., treas. PTA Carol City, 1967—77; pres. Teens to S.Am. Christian Missionary Alliance, Miami, 1978—80, cons. tech. action, 1980—90. Recipient Svc. award, Christian Missionary Alliance Cmty., 1980, Youth in Action award, S.Am. Missions, 1978. Mem.: S.E. Edn. Opportunities Handicapped, Coun. Exceptional Children (mem. divsn. learning disabilities 1989—, mem. divsn. mentally retarded 1989—, mem. divsn. emotionally handicapped 1989—). Republican. Avocations: reading, photography, tutoring, writing for children, visiting elderly in nursing homes. Home: 2355 Westside Dr Rochester NY 14624-1933

EVERETT, ELBERT KYLE, marketing executive, consultant; b. Knoxville, Tenn., June 17, 1946; s. David Abraham and Lois (Hill) E.; m. Jane Harville, June 13, 1967; 1 child, Evelyn Anne. Student, E. Tenn. U., 1965-67. Sales rep. Met. Life Ins. Co., Knoxville, 1968-70, Creative Displays, Knoxville, 1970-73; market mgr. ctrl. and No. Calif. Nat. Advt. divsn. 3M Co., Stockton, from 1973, dist. mgr. western dist. Fresno, 1984; owner Jane Everett's Country Wholesale Furniture Mfg.; sr. cons. Profl. Practice Systems, Inc., Eastern U.S., 1990—2001; ptnr. Everett Mgmt. Group, 1990—2001; CFO, KDI Facility Svcs., 2001—. Advt. cons. athletic dept. U. Pacific, Fresno State U.; lectr. outdoor advt. and mktg. San Joaquin Delta Coll., Fresno City Coll., Fresno State U., W.Va. Optometric Conv., Ind. Optometric Conv.; mgmt. cons. in med. field; lectr. in field. Mayor City of Indian Hills, Ky.; mem. steering com. Jefferson County Governance; mem. subcom. on tourism State of Nev.; ons. Stockton Civic Theater; bd. dirs. Jefferson County League of Cities. Served with AUS, 1964. Recipient cert. of recognition U.S. Treasury Dept., 1977-78, 82-83, recognition award for best design Advt. Age, 1974, 83, Ky. col., 1995, 2 recognition awards outdoor Advt. Assn. Am., 1973, Cert. of Appreciation United Way, 1978, 81, 82, 83. Mem. U. Pacific Athletic Found., Fresno State Found., Stockton C. of C., Fresno C. of C., Advt. Club Sacramento, Advt. Club Fresno, Internat. Platform Assn., Fresno State Athletic Found., Phi Sigma Kappa. Baptist. E-mail: kjeverett@aol.com.

EVERETT, G. STEVEN, music educator; b. Rome, Ga., Aug. 3, 1953; s. James R. and Charline H. Everett; m. Yayoi Uno Everett, Mar. 10, 1953 (div. Aug. 1993); 1 child, Charlsa Taul. MusB in History, Fla. State U., 1975, MusM in Theory, 1976, MusM in Performance, 1977; DMA in Composition, U. Ill., 1988. Lectr. music Ohio No. U., Ada, 1977—78; assoc. prof. music Kennesaw State U., Marietta, Ga., 1978—91; chair, assoc. prof. music Emory U., Atlanta, 1991—. Vis. prof. Princeton U., NJ, 1999; artistic dir. Thamyris New Music Ensemble, Atlanta, 1995—. Composer: over 35 works; performer: computer music compositions in 15 countries in N.Am., Europe, Asia. Recipient Rockefeller Residency award, Rockefellar Found., 1998, First Prize Composition award, Internat. Trumpet Guild, Manchester, Eng., 2001. Mem.: Internat. Computer Music Assn. Office: Emory Univ Dept Music 1804 N Decatur Rd Atlanta GA 30322

EVERETT, HOBART RAY, JR., engineer, naval officer, consultant, researcher; b. Charleston, S.C., Nov. 29, 1949; s. Hobart Ray and Ruth (Humphreys) E.; m. Rachael Patricia Lewis, Dec. 30, 1971 (div. Dec. 1995); children: Todd Ashley, Rebecca Nicole. BEE, Ga. Inst. Tech., 1973; MSME, Naval Postgrad. Sch., 1982. Commd. ensign USN, 1973, advanced through grades to comdr., 1988, asst. engr. USS Nitro, 1975-77, engring. recruiter for officer programs, 1977-80, robotics coord. Naval Sea Sys. Washington, 1983-84, dir. Office of Robotics and Autonomous Sys., 1984-86, autonomous sys. project office Naval Ocean Sys. Ctr. San Diego, 1986-88, chief engr. USMC teleoperated vehicle program, 1988-89, assoc. head advanced sys. divsn., 1988-93. Cons. to Computer Scis. Corp., Falls Church, Va., 1993-94; assoc. divsn. head robotics Space and Naval Warfare Sys. Ctr., San Diego, 1994—; founder DoD Robotics and Artificial Intelligence Database, 1983; Navy rep. to tri-svc. Joint Tech. Panel for Robotics, 1984-86; guest lectr. in robotics U. Md., U. PA., 1983-86, U. Calif., San Diego, 1988; robotics rschr. Naval Ocean Sys. Ctr.; prin. tech. cons. U.S. Army Mobile Detection Assessment and Response Sys. interior program, 1990-93; tech. dir. Joint Army-Navy Mobile Detection Assessment and Response Sys. interior and exterior program, 1993—. Author: Sensors for Mobile Robots, 1995, (with Borenstein and Feng) Sensors and Techniques for Mobile Robot Positioning, 1996; contbg. author Robotics Age mag., 1982-86, Sensors mag., 1987—; mem. editl. bd., contbg. author Robotics and Autonomous Sys. mag.; contbr. 90 tech. publs.; inventor 1st autonomous sentry robot; patentee in field. Decorated Navy Commendation, 1981, 86; recipient Naval Sea Sys. Command award for Acad. Excellence, 1982, Woelful award for Acad. Excellence, Naval Sea Sys. Command, 1983, Gen. Dynamics award for Acad. and Mil. Accomplishment, 1973, Spl. Act award Dept. Def., 1999, Navy Meritorious Civilian Svc. award, 2000, SSC San Diego Lauritsen-Bennet award for excellence in engring., 2001. Mem. IEEE, Soc. Mfg. Engrs. (sr.), Robotics Inst. Am., Nat. Svc. Robot Assn. (bd. dirs. 1991-93), Assn. Unmanned Vehicle Sys. Internat., Sigma Xi. Office: Space & Naval Warfare Sys Ctr Code D3701 53406 Woodward Rd San Diego CA 92152-7383 E-mail: everett@spawar.navy.mil.

EVERETT, JAMES, JR., lawyer; b. Buffalo, Oct. 26, 1957; s. James William and Esther (Kratzer) Everett. BA in Polit. Sci., Coll. Wooster (Ohio), 1979; JD, SUNY, Buffalo, 1984; LLM in Banking Law with honor, Boston U., 1985. Bar: N.Y. 1985, U.S. Dist. Ct. (we. dist.) N.Y. 1989, U.S. Dist. Ct. (no. dist.) N.Y. 1990, U.S. Supreme Ct. 1991. Officer Emil A. Kratzer Co., Inc., Buffalo, 1980—2001; assoc. John C. Peters, P.C., Hartford, Conn., 1986-87; assoc. counsel for banks, corps., ins. and sml. bus. N.Y. State Assembly, Albany, N.Y., 1987-88; asst. counsel for banks, commerce, real property, fin. N.Y. State Senate Majority, 1988-94; v.p., counsel for state proceedings and taxation Securities Industry Assn., 1995-98; gen. ptnr. Everett Law, 1998—; capital markets counsel NY State Ins. Dept., 2001—. Speechwriter for chair policy com. for nat. adv. counsel on women's edn. programs. Observer, Nat. Conf. Commr. on Uniformed State Laws Trust Code Drafting Com.; spkr fin. svcs. Nat. Com. State Legislators, Exec. Enterprises. Author N.Y. Law Revision Commn. Review on Leasing Remedies, Forward to Bowne Securities Regulation Compilations; contbg. editor Barnert Reports; contbr. to Buffalo News, Bus. Ins., Corp. Fin. Week, The Bank Letter, The Bond Buyer, Compliance Reporter. Mem. judicial nominating com. Erie County (N.Y.) Rep. Com., 1979-2001; deacon N. Presbyn. Ch., Amherst, N.Y. Recipient Cummings-Rumbaugh prize Coll. of Wooster, Harmony Heights Sch. Pub. Svc. award. Mem. ABA (com. on state regulation of securities), Am. Corp. Counsel Assn., N.Y. State Bar Assn. (banking law com.), Assn. Bar City N.Y., Nat. Assn. Life Cos., Nat. Assn. for Variable Annuities. Republican. Avocations: hiking, cycling, travel. Home: 602 Baxter Ct Delmar NY 12054 E-mail: everettlaw@msn.com.

EVERETT, JAMES JOSEPH, lawyer; b. San Antonio, May 7, 1955; BA, St. Mary's U., San Antonio, 1976; JD, Tex. So. U., 1980. Bar: U.S. Dist. Ct. Ariz. 1987, U.S. Tax Ct. 1980, U.S. Ct. Appeals (9th cir.) 1988. Sr. trial atty. IRS, Phoenix, 1980-87; ptnr. Brnilovich & Everett, Phoenix, 1987-89; owner Law Offices of James J. Everett, Phoenix, 1989—; of counsel Broadbent, Walker & Wales, 1991-95. Mem. ATLA, ABA (bus. and tax sects.), Fed. Bar Assn., Tex. Bar Assn., Ariz. Bar Assn., State Bar Ariz. (cert. tax specialist), Maricopa County Bar Assn., Ariz. Tax Controversy Group, Valley Estate Planners (Phoenix), Ctrl. Ariz. Estate Planners, Ariz. Soc. Boutiques, St. Thomas Moore Soc. Office: Ste 225 2999 N 44th St Phoenix AZ 85018 E-mail: james.everett@azbar.org.

EVERETT, KAREN JOAN, retired librarian, genealogy educator; b. Cin., Dec. 12, 1926; d. Leonard Kelly and Kletis V. (Wade) Wheatley; m. Wilbur Mason Everett, Sept. 25, 1950; children: Karen, Jan, Jeffrey, Jon, Kathleen, Kerry, Kelly, Shannon. BS in Edn. magna cum laude, U. Cin., 1976, postgrad., 1982-85, Coll. Mt. St. Joseph, 1981-86, Xavier U., Cin., 1985-87, U. Cin., 1982-85, Miami U., 1987. Libr. S.W. Local Schs., Harrison, Ohio, 1967-97, dist. media coord., 1980-97, dist. vol. dir., 1980-97, ret., 1997; instr. genealogy U. Cin., 1998—. Tchr. genealogy U. Cin., 1997—; cons. in field; bd. dirs. U. Cin. ILR; lectr. in field. Contbr. articles to profl. jours. Pres. Citizens Adv. Coun., Harrison, Ohio, 1981-84, 88—, Citizens Adv. Coun., 1989; state chmn. supervisory div. Ohio Ednl. Libr./Media Assn.; mem. Ohio Ambulance Licensing Bd., 1991—. Named Woman of the Yr., Cin. Enquirer, 1978, Xi Eta Iota, 1979, named PTA Educator of the Yr., 1981, others. Mem. NEA, Ohio Ednl. Libr./Media Assn. (chair supervisory div. 1990—, bd. dirs. 1993-94), Ohio Edn. Assn., S.W. Local Classroom Tchrs. Assn., Hamilton County Geneal. Soc. (bd. dirs. 1992—). Avocations: flying, travel, genealogy. Office: U Cin PO Box 210146 Cincinnati OH 45221-0146

EVERETT, MARK ALLEN, dermatologist, educator; b. Oklahoma City, May 30, 1928; s. Mark Ruben and Alice (Allen) E.; 1 son, Howard Dean. BA in Polit. Sci., U. Okla., 1947, MD, 1951; USAF intern in pub. health. Intern in pediatrics U. Mich. Med. Sch., 1951, resident in dermatology, 1954-57, instr. dermatology, 1956-57; intern in pub. health Tulane Med. Sch., 1951; mem. faculty U. Okla. Med. Sch., 1959-98, chmn. dept. dermatology, 1964-96, prof. dermatology, head dept., 1967-96, adj. prof. pathology and anatomy, 1975-98, prof., interim head dept. pathology, 1979-84, Regents prof., 1982-98, Regents prof. emeritus, 1998—, chmn. faculty bd., 1974-90; chief staff Okla. Meml. Hosp., 1980-85. Vice chmn. bd. Bone and Joint Hosp., Oklahoma City, 1976-85; chmn. Internat. Com. for Dermatopathology, 1980-86; bd. dirs. Am. Bd. Dermatology, 1985-96, pres. elect, 1994, pres., 1995. Author 200 articles in field, chpts. in books. Pres. Okla. Ballet Soc., 1973, 77-80, Oklahoma City Chamber Orch., 1979-81, Chamber Music Okla., 1989-2001; pres. bd. trustees Everett Found., 1961—; adv. bd. World Lit. Today, 1970-85, Bizzell Libr. Soc., 1982—; bd. visitors Coll. of Fine Arts, U. Okla., 1990-2002, Coll. of Arts and Scis., 1996-99; bd. dirs. Red Earth Inc., 1997-, trustee, 2000, v.p., 2001—; chair Mus. Com., 1997-2001, Art Com., 2001-03; bd. dirs. Jacobson House, 2002—. With USAF, 1952-54. Recipient Bronze medal U. Okla. Fedn., Mayor's award for Lifetime Contbn. to Arts, Oklahoma City, 1989, Gov.'s Arts award, 1993; grantee Am. Cancer Soc., NIH. Mem. AMA, Am. Acad. Dermatology (chmn. long-range planning coun. 1975-80, dir. 1978-82, chmn. coun. on sci. assembly 1985), Assn. Profs. Dermatology (pres. 1976-78), Am. Soc. Dermatopathology (pres. 1980), Am. Assn. Cancer Rsch., Internat. Acad. Pathology, Am. Dermatol. Assn. (bd. dirs. 1990-95, pres. 1995-96), Am. Soc. Clin. Investigation, Soc. Investigative Dermatology, Radiation Rsch. Soc., Okla. Med. Soc., Coll. Physicians Phila., N.Y. Acad. Scis., N.Mex. Dermatol. Soc., Pacific Dermatol. Assn., South Ctrl. Dermatol. Soc., Austrian Dermatology Soc. (hon.), Polish Dermatology Soc. (hon.), Brit. Assn. Dermatology (hon.), RRC Dermatology RRC Dermapathology, Gourgerot Soc., Societè Française de Dermatologie (hon.), Lotos Club (N.Y.C.), Equestrian Order of the Holy Sepulchre, Phi Beta Kappa. Democrat. Roman Catholic. Home and Office: 1211 N Shartel Ave Ste 202 Oklahoma City OK 73103-2425 Fax: 405-235-8000.

EVERETT, MICHAEL DAVID, economist, educator; b. Cin., Jan. 30, 1938; s. Rollin H. and Eleanor (Sutermeister) Everett; m. Caryl Ann Reed, May 24, 1964 (div. 1991); children: Fric Reed, Alexander Myer; m. Linda M. Jewell, 1993. AB, Wash. U., St. Louis, 1960; PhD in Econs., Wash. U., 1967. Instr. El Colegio de Mex., 1967—68; asst. prof. Fla. State U., Tallahassee, 1968—73; assoc. prof. U. So. Miss., Hattiesburg, 1973—77; prof. East Tenn. State U., Johnson City, 1977—. Past mem. Transp. Rsch. Bd., Washington, 1973—84; cons. on bicycle transp. for physical fitness; mem. numerous other conservation com.; analyst, cons. econ. impact of mil. build-up. Author: (book) Understanding Profit Oriented Marketing: A Guide for Students and Managers, 1986; contbr. articles to profl. jours. Served with U.S. Army, 1956. Recipient winner age group, Warriors Path Triathlon, Tenn., 1983, 1984, award for outstanding paper on edn., 1982, winner age group, State of Tenn. Bicycle Road Races, 1980; fellow, NDEA, 1962—67, Wash. U. Mem.: Am. Soc. Traffic and Transp. (cert. examination com. 1978—84), Am. Econ. Assn., Tenn. Back Country Horse Men (rancher). Democrat. Achievements include Active civil rights movement, early 1960s; set up workshops studying peasant economics central Mex., late 1960s, early 1970s. Home: 1322 Centenary Rd Kingsport TN 37663-3953

EVERETT, MIKE, lawyer; b. McCrory, Ark., Mar. 12, 1948; s. John Grant and Mary Lucille (Pohnka) E.; m. Betsy Ann Milwre, Jan. 19, 1968 (div. July 1975); m. Laurel Casey, Dec. 27, 1977; children: Michael Wayne, Casey Toye. BA, Ark. State U., 1970; JD, U. Ark., 1973. Pvt. practice, Marked Tree, Ark., 1973—; mem. Ark Senate from 23rd dist., Little Rock, 1971—2002. Maj. U.S. Army res. Fellow Ark. Bar Found.; mem. Ark. Bar Assn. Democrat. Avocations: cooking, reading. Address: 412 Broadway St Marked Tree AR 72365-1406*

EVERETT, PAUL MARVIN, physicist; b. Toledo, Ohio, Mar. 15, 1940; s. Arthur Marvin and Elizabeth Bernice Everett; m. Sandra Lee McClelland; children: David, Christopher. BS Physics, Case Inst. Tech., Cleve., 1962; PhD, Case Western Res. U., 1968. Rsch. assoc. La. State U., Baton Rouge, 1968—71, adminstrv. asst., 1971—72; asst. prof. physics U. Ky., Lexington, 1972—79; mem. tech. staff Tex. Instruments Ctrl. Rsch. Labs., Dallas, 1979—83; unit mgr., sect. mgr., br. mgr. McDonnell Douglas Microelectronics Ctr., St. Louis, 1983—89; br. mgr. McDonnell Douglas Electronic Sys. Co., St. Louis, 1989—90; chief scientist, product mgr. Magnavox New Eng. Rsch. Ctr., Sudbury, Mass., 1990—91; bus. devel. mgr., program mgr. Litton Electron Devices, Tempe, Ariz., 1992—96; pres., owner Everett Cos. LLC, Phoenix, 1996—. Apptd. Ahwatukee Foothills Village Planning Com. - City of Phoenix, 1998—. Fellow, NASA, 1965—67; grantee, The Rsch. Corp., 1974—76. Mem.: IEEE, IEEE Phoenix Area Consultants Network (pres. 2002—), Sigma Xi. Office: Everett Companies LLC 3825 E Mtn Vista Dr Phoenix AZ 85048-7374 Office Fax: 480-706-4753. Business E-Mail: peverett@everettinfrared.com.

EVERETT, RALPH BERNARD, lawyer; b. Orangeburg, S.C., June 23, 1951; s. Francis G.S. and Alethia (Hilton) E.; m. Gwendolyn Harris, June 22, 1974. BA, Morehouse Coll., 1973; JD, Duke U., 1976. Bar: N.C. 1977, D.C. 1979. Adminstrv. asst. N.C. Dept. Labor, 1976-77; legis. asst. Office of Sen. Ernest F. Hollings, Washington, 1977-82; minority chief counsel, staff dir. U.S. Senate Com. on Commerce, Sci., Transp., Washington, 1983-87, chief counsel, staff dir., 1987-89; ptnr. Paul, Hastings, Janofsky and Walker, LLP, Washington, 1989—. Bd. dirs. Shenandoah Life Ins. Co., Cumulus Media Inc.; mem. adv. bd. Norfolk So. Corp., Washington, 1991—; life mem. bd. visitors Duke U. Sch. Law; former mem. Pres.'s Bd. Advisors on Historically Black Colls. and Univs.; head U.S. Del. to World Telecomm. Conf., 1998; U.S. amb. to 1998 Internat. Telecomm. Union Plenipotentiary Conf. Former trustee Nat. Urban League, N.Y.C., 1990, 92; senate liaison Clinton/Gore Presdl. Campaign, Washington, 1992; former mem. Congl. Award Found., McLean, Va., 1993—; former mem. Fed. City Coun. Mem.: Econ. Club Washington, Phi Beta Kappa, Alpha Phi Alpha. Office: Paul Hastings Janofsky & Walker LLP 10th Fl 1299 Pennsylvania Ave NW Washington DC 20004-2400 E-mail: ralpheverett@paulhastings.com.

EVERETT, RICHARD G. newspaper editor; b. New Brunswick, N.J., Sept. 20, 1950; s. Richard D. and Patricia L. Everett; m. Mary Worth, Aug. 26, 1972; children: Laura Worth, Kathryn Worth. BA in English Lit., Colgate U., 1972. Reporter Daily Advance, Dover, NJ, 1974—77; headline writer The Star-Ledger, Newark, 1977—80, asst. night city editor, 1980—84, asst. city editor, 1984—92, metro editor, 1992—95, asst. mng. editor, 1995—96, mng. editor, 1996—. Office: The Star-Ledger One Star Ledger Plaza Newark NJ 07102-1200

EVERETT, ROBERT RIVERS, electrical engineer; b. Yonkers, N.Y., June 26, 1921; s. Chester Mckenzie and Ruth (Melius) Everett; m. Helen Louis Burns, Oct. 21, 1966 (div. Oct. 1972); children: Robert, Bruce, Douglas, Theodore, Michael; m. Ann Theresa Russell, Mar. 26, 1982; 1 child, David; m. Jean McGrath, Nov. 4, 1972 (dec. Nov. 1980). BSEE, Duke U., 1942; MSEE, MIT, 1943; DEE (hon.), Northeastern U., Boston, 1985. Tech. staff Servo-mechanisims Lab MIT, 1943—51, assoc. dir. Digital Computer Lab., 1951—56, assoc. div. head. Lincoln Lab., 1951—56, div. head Lincoln Lab., 1956—58; tech. dir. MITRE Corp., Bedford, Mass., 1958—59, v.p. tech. ops., 1959—69, exec. v.p., 1969, pres., 1969—86, trustee, 1969—. Bd. dirs. Digital Equipment Corp.; mem. Mass. Gen. Hosp. Corp., Boston; mem. sci. adv. bd. USAF; mem. def. sci. bd. Pentagon, 1986—, chmn., 1988—89; adv. bd. Strategic Def. Initiative. Contbr. numerous articles to profl. jours. Recipient Disting. Engring. Alumnus award, Duke U., 1978, Disting. Pub. Svc. medal, Dept. of Def., 1983, Gold medal, Armed Forces Comm. and Electronics Assn., 1985, Nat. medal of tech. Fellow: IEEE; mem.: AAAS, NAE, Assn. Computing Machinery, Cosmos Club. Republican. Achievements include patents for magnetic drum memories, display devices.

EVERETT, TERRY, congressman; b. Dothan, Ala., Feb. 15, 1937; m. Barbara Pitts. Owner, pres. The Union Springs Herald; mem. U.S. Congress from 2nd Ala. Dist., Washington, 1992—; nat. security com., agriculture com., veterans' affairs com., and select com. on intelligence. Served in USAF, 1955—59. Republican. Office: US Ho of Reps 2312 Rayburn Bldg Washington DC 20515-3603*

EVERETT, TOM, actor; b. Oreg. MFA, NYU Sch of Arts, London Acad. Music/Drama Arts. Actor: (films) The Alamo, XXX, Pearl Harbor, Air Force One, My Fellow Americans, Dances With Wolves, Thirteen Days, Crazy as Hell, Mi Amigo, Vaya Con Dios (aka Hard Time Romance), Best of the Best, The Goodbye Girl, Beverly Hills Cops, Prison, Messenger of Death, Die Hard 2, Earth and the American Dream, Leatherface, Hollywood Vice Squad, others; (Broadway plays) Elizabeth I, Habeas Corpus, Emminent Domain, A Midsummer Night's Dream; numerous Off-Broadway and regional theatre plays; (TV movies) Last Rites, Crash Landing: The Rescue of Flight 232, To Heal A Nation, Gore Vidal's Billy the Kid, Lady Mobster, Double Jeopardy, The Return of Mike Hammer, Thirteen Days to Glory, others; (TV shows) C.S.I. Miami, For the People, Alias, The Beast, The District, C-16, Pretender, JAG, E.R., Profiler, Picket Fences, Space Above and Beyond, Murder She Wrote, Cheers, LA Law, Hill Street Blues, Cagney and Lacy, Birdland, Newhart, Secret Agent Man, others; songwriter/singer (RCA album): Porchlight On In Oregon; (ind. album) Still Waters (A Collection of Years). Scholar Jacobs Pillow Dance Festival, Perry Mansfield Dance and Drama Sch.; fellow NYU Sch. of Arts, ITT Internat. Fellowship/Fulbright Competition, London Acad. of Music and Dramatic Arts. Mem. The Actors Studio. Roman Catholic. Avocations: cello, guitar, country-western music.

EVERETT, WENDY ANN, toy designer; b. East Lansing, Mich., May 6, 1950; d. Donald Franklin and Mary Margaret (Marshall) E. BA in Edn., Fine Arts, Mich. State U., 1972; M in Early Childhood Devel., Fairfield (Conn.) U., 1989. Elem. sch. tchr. Fraser (Mich.) Pub. Schs., 1973-77; creative dir. WFR Ribbon Corp., N.Y.C., 1977-79; pres. Wendy Everett Creations, Westport, Conn., 1979—. Author: The Gift Book, 1986, Active Bulletin Boards, 1979; composer (children's musical) The Vegetable Garden, 1973 (children's TV show) The Dream Makers, 1990; regular guest (TV show) Our Home; contbr. articles to mags.; designer Barbie Doll Fashions, 1983—, Care Bears, Strawberry Shortcake, Cabbage Patch Doll Clothes, Americana Crafts, ET Quilt, ET Wallhanging, 1983, Stenciling Hunt Mfg. Co. Kits, 1979—, Pastime Industries Crafts, 1990, Bath Buddies toy line, 1989—, ednl. toys for Princess Fabrics, N.Y.C., 1992—; painter large acrylic and gold leaf polo paintings; featured artist in Polo Players Mag. and Equine Image Mag. Nat. spokeperson for Smithsonian's 150 Birthday TV tour. Mem. Cooper Hewitt Mus. Received Artist of Yr. award Greenwich (Conn.) Polo Club, 1998. Mem. Nat. Arts Club (N.Y.C.), Black Rock Yacht Club, N.Y. Yacht Club, Phi Beta Kappa. Congregationalist. Avocations: painting, dancing, golf, classical piano, polo. Home: 1123 Sasco Hill Rd Fairfield CT 06430-6346

EVERETT, WOODROW WILSON, electrical engineer, educator; b. Newton, Miss., Oct. 11, 1937; s. Woodrow Wilson and Katherine (Thrash) E.; m. Cherry Donna Sarff, Aug. 23, 1958; children: Woodrow W., Leanne Everett Traver. B.E.E., George Washington U., 1959; MS, Cornell U., 1965, PhD, 1968. Project engr. Scott Paper Co., 1959, Ithaca (N.Y.) Rsch. Labs., Atlantic Rsch. Corp., 1962-64; postdoctoral program dir. Rome (N.Y.) Air Devel. Ctr., 1964-75; chmn. bd. N.E. Consortium for Engring. Edn., St. Cloud, Fla., 1975—. Bd. dirs. Device Assos. Corp. N.Y., Masonwood, Inc., Sunoric Corp., ITG, Inc., Thrash Homestead Corp., The Cherwood Corp., SCEEE Svc. Corp. Author works in field. Democratic committeeman, Madison County, N.Y., 1976-79; pres. Village of Groton (N.Y.) Appeals Bd., 1966-69; chmn. Groton Planning Bd., 1968-69. Served with USAF, 1959-62. Fellow IEEE (life); mem. Air Force Assn. (life), Res. Officers Assn. (life), Am. Soc. Engring. Edn. Clubs: Rotary. Home: Cherwood-Alligator Lake 1161 Walnut Grove Rd Bridgeport NY 13030 Office: 1101 Massachusetts Ave Saint Cloud FL 34769-3733

EVERETT NOLLKAMPER, PAMELA IRENE, legal management company executive, educator; b. L.A., Dec. 31, 1947; d. Richard Weldon and Alta Irene (Tuttle) Bunnell; m. James E. Everett, Sept. 2, 1967 (div. 1973); 1 child, Richard Earl; m. Milton Nollkamper, Dec. 20, 2000. Cert. Paralegal, Rancho Santago Coll., Santa Ana, Calif., 1977; BA, Calif. State U.-Long Beach, 1985; MA, U. Redlands, 1988. Owner, mgr. Orange County Paralegal Svc., Santa Ana, 1979—; pres. Gem Legal Mgmt. Inc., Fullerton, Calif., 1986—; co-owner Bunnell Publs., Fullerton, Calif., 1992-96. Instr. Rancho Santiago Coll., 1979-96, chmn. adv. bd., 1980-85; instr. Fullerton Coll., 1989-2002, Rio Hondo Coll., Whittier, Calif., 1992-94; advisor Saddleback Coll., 1985—, North Orange County Regional Occupational Program, Fullerton, 1986-99, Fullerton Coll. So. Calif. Coll. Bus. and Law; bd. dirs. Nat. Profl. Legal Assts. Inc., editor PLA News. Author: Legal Secretary Federal Litigation, 1986, Bankruptcy Courts and Procedure, 1987, Going Independent--Business Planning Guide, Fundamentals of Law Office Management, 1994. Republican. Avocation: reading. Office: 940 Manor Way Corona CA 92882 E-mail: 2Pan@attbi.com.

EVERHART, JAMES GRAY, retired manufacturing executive; b. Pitts., Aug. 29, 1915; s. Samuel Dunlap Everhart, Frances Pillow Gray; m. Levada Marie Hamilton, Mar. 9, 1940; children: Rodney Lee, Gary Eugene, Barbara Eileen Phillips. BSEE, Pa. State U., 1938; grad. mgmt. course, Am. Mgmt. Assn., 1960. Registered profl. engr., Ohio, 1938. From engring. inspector to mgr. engring. Transformer divsn. Line Material Industries, Zanesville, Ohio, 1938—55; mgr. plant Tex. Fibre Products McGraw-Edison Co., Sherman, Tex., 1955—57, v.p., gen. mgr., pres. Ill. Edison Porcelain divsn. Line Material Industries Macomb, Ill., 1957—66, gen. mgr. Line Material Industries Zanesville, 1966—70; v.p. mfg., gen. mgr. Utility Sys. divsn. A.B. Chance Co., Centralia, Mo., 1970—80, exec. v.p., 1970—80; pres. Pitman divsn. Emerson Electric Co., Kansas City, Mo., 1976—80; ret., 1980. Author: Strategic Business Planning, 1974, 1991, Business Insights for the Advancing Supervisor, 1975, Comprehensive Plan for the City of Centralia, Mo., 1987. Fellow: IEEE (life); mem.: Am. Mgmt. Assn. (lectr., seminar leader 1969—75, v.p. mfg. coun. 1973—75, pres.'s coun. 1977—80, Disting. Svc. award 1975), Nat. Elec. Mfrs. Assn. (distbn. transformer sect. 1948—55, chmn. high voltage insulator sect. 1964—65, bd. dirs. power equipment divsn. 1973—77, chmn. high voltage insulator sect. 1974—76), Boone County Hist. Soc. (bd. dirs., exec. com., Long Range Planning Program author 2001), Centralia Hist. Soc. (bd. dirs.), Rotary Internat., Toastmasters Internat., Eta Kappa Nu, Sigma Tau, Tau Beta Pi. Republican. Methodist. Achievements include patents for electric transformers. Avocation: music. Home: 902 Eastmont Dr Centralia MO 65240

EVERHART, LEON EUGENE, retired career officer; b. Abilene, Kans., Jan. 14, 1928; s. Charles Francis and Florence Etta (Amess) E. BS with distinction, Ariz. State U., 1957; postgrad., U. Tenn., 1965. Commd. 2d lt. USAF, 1952, advanced through grades to col., 1970, ops. officer Berlin Air Safety Ctr., 1961-63, project officer Missile Devel. Ctr., 1963-65, chief spl. projects div. Missile Devel. Ctr., 1965-66, tactical fighter pilot, flight commander, 1967-68, system program dir. Aero. Systems Div., 1968-72, dir. test engring. Devel. and Test Ctr. Eglin AFB, Fla., 1973-78, comdr. Air Force Western Test Range Vandenberg AFB, Calif., 1978-82, ret., 1982. Cons. in field. Speaker on big-game hunting in Africa and wildlife conservation for various civic and ednl. orgns. Mem. Amateur Trapshooting Assn. Ohio, NRA. Avocations: golf, trapshooting, big-game hunting, deep-sea fishing. Home: 1285 Oak Knolls Rd Santa Maria CA 93455-4302

EVERHART, ROBERT PHILLIP (BOBBY WILLIAMS), entertainer, songwriter, recording artist; b. St. Edward, Nebr., June 16, 1936; s. Phillip McClelland and Martha Matilda (Meyer) E.; m. Sheila Dawn Armstrong, Feb. 14, 1992; 1 child, Bobbie Lhea. Student, U. Nebr., 1959-62; Assoc. in Radio-TV, Iowa Western Coll., 1971, Assoc. in Graphic Arts, 1974; diploma in Journalism, London Sch. Journalism, 1983; spl. studies Mex. Indian culture, U. Okla., 1990—. Disc jockey various stas., Omaha and Juneau, Alaska, 1959-63; songwriter Royal Flair Music, BMI Pub., Walnut, Iowa, 1964—. Prodr. Bus Stop radio program, 2000—. Host prodr. (TV series) Old Time Country Music, (radio show) Old-Time Music Hour; prodr. The Great Plains and Prairie music Tour, World Music Events, American Traditional Music and Dance Festival, 1998, 2000--; rec. artist Folkway Records, N.Y.C., 1970—, Smithsonian Inst., Westwood Records, Wales, 1981, Folk Variety Records, Europe, 1980—, Allied Records, The Philippines, OGA Records, Austria, Otro Records, Poland, Prairie Music Records, Unltd. Prodns., internat. concert artist performing traditional Am. country and folk music; curator, owner Pioneer Music Instrument Mus., Am. Country Music Hall of Fame, Am. Old Time Fiddlers Hall of Fame, Capt.'s Quarters Bed & Breakfast, all located in Walnut, Iowa, and Vera Cruz, Mex., Oaktree Opry, Anita, Iowa; festival promoter Nat. Old-Time Country Music Contest and Pioneer Exposition, 1976—, Am. Traditional Music and Dance Festival, Nat. Traditional Music Performer Awards, 1991—; pres. Nat. Traditional Country Music Assn., Inc., 1982—; regular performer La. Hayride, 1985—; editor: Tradition Country Music Mag., 1980—; author: Clara Bell, 1976, Hart's Bluff, 1977, Listen to the Mockingbird, 1995; (poetry) Silver Bullets, 1979, Savage Trumpet, 1980, Prairie Sunrise, 1982, Snoopy Goes to Mexico, 1983; prodr. (TV shows) Bus Stop, Tradition, Country Life, Country Style; (TV scripts) The Life of Jimmie Rodgers, 1984, Matecombe Treasure, 1984, The Ghost of Carl Herrmann, 1993, Listen to the Mockingbird, 1998; recs. include: Let's Go, Dream Angel, She Sings Sad Songs, Love to Make Love, Bad Woman Blues, Fishpole John, Time After Time, Street Sleepers, No One Comes Near, Berlin Folksinger My Sweet Love Aint Around Compact Disc release on Otro Records, Dear Grand Ole Opry, 2001; host (TV) Old Time Country Music, 1990-97. With USN, 1954-59. Named to Profl. Musicians and Entertainers Club Iowa Hall of Fame, 1994, Country Music Showcase Internat. Hall of Fame, 1995, Am.'s Old Time Country Music Hall of Fame; Ky. col., 1995; recipient Lifetime Achievement award World Music Events, Vienna, 1998, Kitty Wells/Johnny Wright Country Music Leadership award, 2000; honored as Tenn. Amb. of Goodwill by Gov. Don Sundquist, 2000; honored by Iowa State Legis., 2001, 03. Mem. Internat. Coun. Festivals Fedn., Great Plains Old Time Music Assn., Acad. Country Music, Nat. Bluegrass Assn., Ill. Traditional Country Music Assn., Tri-State Bluegrass Assn., Ky. Cols., Internat. Bluegrass Music Assn., Soc. for Preservation of Bluegrass Music of Am., Profl. Musicians Club of Iowa, Midwest Prodrs. Assn. (chmn.), Internat. Assn. Fairs and Expositions, Carribean Club. Independent. Lutheran. Avocations: scuba diving, traveling. Office: Country Opera House PO Box 492 Anita IA 50020-0492 also: Nat Traditional Country Music Assn PO Box 492 Anita IA 50020-0492 E-mail: bobeverhart@yahoo.com.

EVERHART, THOMAS EUGENE, retired university president, engineering educator; b. Kansas City, Mo., Feb. 15, 1932; s. William Elliott and Elizabeth Ann (West) E.; m. Doris Arleen Wentz, June 21, 1953; children: Janet Sue, Nancy Jean, David William, John Thomas. AB in Physics magna cum laude, Harvard, 1953; MSc, UCLA, 1955; PhD in Engring., Cambridge U., Eng., 1958. Mem. tech. staff Hughes Research Labs., Culver City, Calif., 1953—55; mem. faculty U. Calif., Berkeley, 1958—78, prof. elec. engring. and computer scis., 1967—78, Miller research prof., 1969—70, chmn. dept., 1972—77; prof. elec. engring., Joseph Silbert dean engring. Cornell U., Ithaca, 1979—84; prof. elec. and computer engring., chancellor U. Ill., Urbana-Champaign, 1984—87; prof. elec. engring. and applied physics, pres. Calif. Inst. Tech., Pasadena, 1987—97, pres. emeritus, 1997—. Fellow scientist Westinghouse Rsch. Labs., Pitts., 1962-63; guest prof. Inst. Applied Physics, U. Tuebingen, Germany, 1966-67, Waseda U., Tokyo, Osaka U., 1974; vis. fellow Clare Hall, Cambridge, U., 1975; chmn. Electron, Ion and Photon Beam Symposium, 1977; cons. in field; mem. sci. and ednl. adv. com. Lawrence Berkeley Lab., 1978-85, chmn., 1980-85; mem. sci. adv. com. GM, 1980-89, chmn., 1984-89; bd. dirs. Saint-Gobain Corp., Raytheon Co.; tech. adv. com. R.R. Donnelly & Sons, 1981-89; sr. sci. advisor W.M. Keck Found., 1997—; pro-vice chancellor Cambridge U., 1998. Chmn. Sec. of Energy Adv. Bd., 1990-93; bd. dirs. KCET, 1989-97, Corp. for Nat. Rsch. Initiatives; trustee Calif. Inst. Tech., 1998—; mem. bd. overseers Harvard U., 1999—. Marshall scholar Cambridge U., 1955-58, NSF sr. fellow, 1966-67, Guggenheim fellow, 1974-75. Fellow IEEE, AAAS, ASEE, Royal Acad. Engring.; mem. NAE (ednl. adv. bd. 1984-88, mem. com. 1984-89, chmn. 1988, coun. 1988-94, 96-2002), Microbeam Analysis Soc. Am., Electron Microscopy Soc. Am. (coun. 1970-72, pres. 1977), Coun. on Competitiveness (vice-chmn. 1990-96), Assn. Marshall Scholars and Alumni (pres. 1965-68), Athenaeum Club, California Club, Sigma Xi, Eta Kappa Nu. Home: PO Box 1639 Santa Barbara CA 93116-1639 Office: Calif Inst Tech Office Pres Emeritus/202-31 1200 E California Blvd Pasadena CA 91125-0001

EVERINGHAM, JAMES THEODORE, lawyer; b. Buchanan, Mich., May 22, 1939; s. James H. and Ruth L. (French) Everingham; m. Marcia J. Devenney, Aug. 19, 1961; children: Scott J., Linda B., Bradford A. AB, Albion Coll., 1961; JD, U. Mich., 1964. Bar: Mich. 1965, U.S. Dist. Ct. (ea. dist.) Mich. 1965. Assoc. Cross, Wrock, Miller, Vieson & Kelly, Detroit, 1964—67, Dykema, Gossett, Spencer, Goodnow, Trigg, 1967—75, ptnr., 1975—. Treas. Clair Crawford Meml. Handicapped Assn., 1981—84, v.p., 1984—. Mem.: ABA, Detroit Bar Assn., Mich. Bar Assn., Detroit Yacht Club (dir. 1978—, sec. 1980—81, rear comdr. 1981—82, comdr. 1983—84). Office: Dykema Gossett 400 Renaissance Ctr Ste 3800 Detroit MI 48243-1603

EVERITT, ALICE LUBIN, labor arbitrator; b. Dec. 13, 1936; d. Isador and Alice (Berliner) Lubin. BA, Columbia U., 1968, JD, 1971. Assoc. Amen, Weisman & Butler, N.Y.C., 1971-78; spl. asst. to dir. Fed. Mediation and Conciliation Svc., Washington, 1978-81; pvt. practice labor arbitration Washington, N.Y.C., 1981-87, Petersburg, Va., 1987—. Mem. various nat. mediation and arbitration panels including Fed. Mediation and Conciliation Svc., U.S. Steel and United Steelworkers, Am. Arbitration Assn. Editor Dept. Labor publ., 1979. Mem. Am. Arbitration Assn., Soc. Profls. Dispute Resolution, Indsl. Rels. Rsch. Assn., Civil War Roundtable of Richmond, Petersburg Planning Commn. Office: 541 High St Petersburg VA 23803-3859

EVERITT-NEWTON, KATHERINE EVELYN, international management consultant; b. Cleve., Sept. 2, 1957; BS, Bowling Green State U., 1979, MBA, 1981. Sci. systems analyst Eli Lilly & Co., Indpls., 1981-83, systems tng. cons., 1983-84; customer liaison mgr. Ind. U., Bloomington, 1985, prodn. ops. mgr. Indpls., 1985-86; prin. systems cons. Wang Labs., Inc., Carmel, Ind., 1986-93; mgmt. cons. AMT-Sybex (I) Ltd., Dublin, 1994-99; sr. cons. mgr. AMT-Sybex, Ltd., U.K., Letchworth, 1999—. Cons. Ind. Univ., Bloomington, 1984-85, Allied Irish Bank, Dublin, Ireland, 1990-91. Contbr. (book) Introduction to Business, 1980, Introduction to Accounting, 1981, Computers and Data Processing, 1981. Republican. Presbyterian. Avocations: scuba diving, photography, biking, crafts, horseback riding. Office: AMT-Sybex Ltd Spirella Bldg Bridge Rd Letchworth SG6 4ET England Home: 2 Beaulieu Close Bracknell, Berkshire RG12 9QL England E-mail: Katherine_everitt-newton@amt-sybex.com.

EVERLY, GEORGE STOTELMYER, JR., psychologist, psychophysiologist, educator, mathematician; b. Balt., May 31, 1950; s. George Stotelmyer and Kathleen Webster E.; children: Marideth, George III, Andrea. BS, U. Md., 1972, MA, 1974, PhD, 1978; postdoctoral tng., U. Miami, 1983-85, Harvard U., 1985-86. Lectr. U. Md., College Park, 1975-80; assoc. prof. psychology, dir. psychophysiology lab. Loyola Coll., Balt., 1980-85, prof. psychology, 1985—; dir. psychol. svcs. div. Homewood Hosp. Ctr. Johns Hopkins Health System, Balt., 1990-92; CEO, chmn. bd. dirs. Internat. Critical Incident Stress Found., Balt., 1989-95; chmn. emeritus, 1995—; CEO, Inst. Advanced Studies Crisis and Disaster Mgmt., Balt., 1995—2000. Vis. scholar Harvard U., 1985-87, vis. lectr. medicine Harvard Med. Sch., 1987-88; NGO rep. to UN, 1997—; mem. adj. faculty Johns Hopkins U. Sch. Hygiene and Pub. Health, 1998— Author: Occupational Health Promotion, 1985; The Nature and Treatment of the Stress Response, 1981, Psychotraumatology, 1995, Innovations in Disaster and Trauma Psychology, 1995; The Stress Mess Solution, 1980, Critical Incident Stress Management, 1999, Critical Incident Stress Debriefing, 2001, Personality Guided Treatment of PTSD, 2003; co-author: Controlling Stress and Tension, 6th edit., 2000; Experiencing Health, 1985; Personality and Its Disorders, 1985, The Assessment of Human Stress, 1987, Clinical Guide to Treatment of the Human Stress Response, 1989, 2d edit., 2001; founding and exec. editor Internat. Jour. Emergency Mental Health, 1999—; rschr., developer The Everly Behavioral Survey, 1982. Recipient cert. of honor Balt. City Police Dept., 1981, Prof.'s medal Weiner U., Lima, Peru, 1997. Fellow Acad. Psychosomatic Medicine, Am. Inst. Stress (trustee); mem. APA, Soc. Behavioral Medicine, Am. Acad. Behavioral Medicine.

EVERLY, JACK, conductor; b. Richmond, VA; Grad., Ind. U. Prin. condr. Am. Ballet Theatre, N.Y.C., 1984—98; mus. dir. & condr. Ameritech's Yuletide Celebration, Indianapolis Symphony Orchestra, 1994—; music advisor Symphonic Pops Consortium, 1998—; principle pops condr. Indianapolis Symphony Orchestra, 2002—. Conducted shows including Hello, Dolly!, 1978, A Chorus Line, They're Playing Our Song, Showboat, Kismet, Carousel, The Mikado, Hazel Kirk, others; conductor Vancouver Symphony, San Diego Symphony, Lake George Opera Festival, Pacific Symphony, Ravinia Festival; music dir., orchestrator In Performance at the White House; conductor world premiers at Am. Ballet Theatre include Sir Kenneth MacMillan's Requiem, Agnes de Mille's The Informer, Mikhail Baryshnikov's Giselle and Swan Lake. Office: Indianapolis Symphony Orchestra 32 E Washington St Ste 600 Indianapolis IN 46204*

EVERNHAM, RAY, race team owner; Team owner, founder Evernham Motorsports, Statesville, NC, 2001—; founder Evernham Performance Parts, Evernham Mktg. Svcs., Evernham Engine Techs. Broadcaster ABC, ESPN; spkr. maj. corps. including NASA, STIHL, GE, Valvoline; keynote spkr. Fast Co., Performance Racing Industry. Recipient three-time champion crew chief, NASCAR Winston Cup. Office: Evernham Motorsports 160 Munday Rd Statesville NC 28677-9665

EVERS, GENE, writer; b. N.Y.C., Mar. 26, 1951; s. Lee Evers and Pauline (Leviton) Stein. AA in Liberal Arts, Nassau C.C., Garden City, N.Y., 1973; BA in Humanities, SUNY, Old Westbury, 1982. Writer L.I. Bus. Rev., Plainview, N.Y., 1978-82; staff Quaker Homecraft, Plainview, 1983-84; ind. writer Bethpage, NY, 1992—. Staff Nassau Ctr. for the Developmentally Disabled, Woodbury, N.Y., 1978-84. Author: (movie script) The Ancient Star of Christmas, 1997, (poem) I Long for the Love of Thee, (poem) My Beloved, (song) The Falling Rain; songwriter A Christmas Song, 1997, Candles of Love, The Northern Wind, We're Flying, Ohio, The Very Last Time; author of poetry, short stories. Named Disting. Poet of the Yr., Internat. Soc. Poets, Owings Mills, Md., 1997; inductee Hall of Fame, Internat. Soc. Poets, 1996. Mem. Writers Guild, Internat. Platform Assn. Avocations: model trains, weight lifting, studying history, philosophy and literature. Home: 2296 Lincoln St Bellmore NY 11710-

EVERS, WILLIAM DOHRMANN, lawyer; b. San Francisco, May 6, 1927; s. Albert John and Sepha (Pischel) E.; m. Edwina Bigelow Benington, Aug. 26, 1950 (div. May 1978); children: Elliot B., Anne B., Albert John II, William Dohrmann Jr.; m. Britte-Marie Emblad, May 27, 1978. BA, Yale U., 1949; LLB, JD, U. Calif., Berkeley, 1952. Bar: Calif. 1952. Assoc. Chickering & Gregory, San Francisco, 1953-56; legal asst. to commr. SEC, 1956-57; assoc. atty. Allen, Miller, Groezinger, Keesling & Martin, San Francisco, 1957-60; ptnr. Pettit, Evers & Martin, San Francisco, 1960-78; chmn. On-Line Bus. Sys., Inc., 1980-82; chmn., CEO Precision Techs., 1982-87; ptnr. Chickering & Gregory, San Francisco, 1986-89, Sullivan, Roche & Johnson, San Francisco, 1989-95, Miller, Mailliad & Culver LLP, San Francisco, 1995-96, Evers & Andelin LLP, San Francisco, 1996-97, Evers & Hendrickson LLP, 1997-2000, Foley & Lardner, 2000—. Pres. Econ. Devel. Council City and County of San Francisco, 1978-80; chmn. San Francisco Bay Conservation and Devel. Commn., 1972-75; pres. Calif. Roadside Council, 1959-60; chmn. SPUR, San Francisco, 1975-78; chmn. assistance and adv. council Calif. Gov.'s Office Planning and Research, 1977-78; founder, pres. Planning and Conservation League, 1965-68; mem. air quality adv. bd. EPA, 1970-73; vice chmn. San Francisco Republican County Central Com., 1959-63; trustee Marin County Day Sch., 1967-70, 79-82, Katherine Branson Sch., 1976-78; bd. dirs. Yosemite Nat. Inst., 1981—, chmn. 1988-90; mem. governing council Wilderness Soc., Washington, 1984-96; chmn. Calif. Capital Access Forum, 1996—; vice chmn. TechVentures Network, 2002—. With USN, 1944-45. Mem. ABA, San Francisco Bar Assn., State Bar Calif., Bohemian Club (San Francisco). Home: 2019 Lyon St San Francisco CA 94115-1609 E-mail: wevers@foleylaw.com. *Intelligence, industry, integrity and humor are the essential elements for business or professional success and, of these, integrity is the most important.*

EVERS, WILLIAMSON MOORE, education policy analyst, political scientist; b. San Francisco, Oct. 18, 1948; s. Henry Kaspar and Emily Stout Evers; m. Leslie Carver Johnson, Apr. 30, 1994; m. Mary Therese Gingell (div.); children: Daniel Kenneth, Pamela Ruth. BA in Polit. Sci., Stanford U., 1972, MA in Polit. Sci., 1978, PhD in Polit. Sci., 1987. Editor-in-chief Inquiry Mag., San Francisco, 1976—80; vis. asst. prof. Emory U., Atlanta, 1987—88; nat. and vis. fellow Hoover Instn., Stanford (Calif.) U., 1988—94, rsch. fellow, 1995—. Adj. assoc. prof. Santa Clara (Calif.) U., 1995—98; commr. State Calif. Commn. for the Establishment Academic Content and Performance Stds., Sacramento, 1996—98; mem. math. content rev. panel State Calif. Standardized Testing and Reporting Program, Sacramento, 1998—, mem. history-social sci. content rev. panel, 1999—; mem. adv. bd. Calif. History-Social Sci. Project, L.A., 1999—; mem. Koret Task Force on K-12 Edn., Hoover Instn., Stanford, 1999—, Nat. Ednl. Rsch. Policy and Priorities Bd., Washington, 2001—02; commr. White Ho. Commn. on Presdl. Scholars, Washington, 2001—. Author: (public policy research) Victims' Rights, 1996; editor, contbr.: public policy research National Service: Pro & Con, 1990, What's Gone Wrong in America's Classrooms, 1998; co-editor: School Reform: The Critical Issues, 2001, School Accountability, 2002, Teacher Quality, 2002. Mem. edn. adv. com. Bush-Cheney Transition, 2000—01; edn. policy advisor Richard Riordan Gubernatorial Campaign, 2001—02, William Simon Gubernatorial Campaign, 2002; bd. dirs. East Palo Alto (Calif.) Charter Sch., 1997—. Episcopalian. Office: Hoover Instn Stanford Univ Stanford CA 94305-6010

EVERSE, JOHANNES, biochemist, researcher; b. Yerseke, The Netherlands, Dec. 2, 1931; came to U.S., 1960; s. Marinus Everse and Cornelia Geertruida Mulder; m. Kathleen Eleanor Dervin (dec. Mar. 1988); children: Magdalena Cornelia, Stephen Jay, Linda Ann; m. Melissa Lea Gunn, July 30, 1993. MA, Brandeis U., 1971; PhD, U. Calif., San Diego, 1973. Lab. asst. Philips-Duphar, N.V., Weesp, The Netherlands, 1952-60; rsch. assoc. Brandeis U., Waltham, Mass., 1960-69; assoc. specialist U. Calif., San Diego, 1969-73, asst. rsch. chemist, 1973-76; assoc. prof. Tex. Tech U. Health Sci. Ctr., Lubbock, 1976-80, prof., 1980—. NATO sr. vis. prof. U. Milan, Italy, 1980-81; vis. prof. U. Utrecht, The Netherlands, 1989; vis. rsch. scientist Letterman Army Inst. of Rsch., San Francisco, 1989-91. Contbr. over 60 articles to profl. jours.; co-editor 5 books; patents immobilization of streptokinase. Grantee NIH, 1975—, Am. Cancer Soc., 1980-81, Robert A. Welch Found., 1977-83, US Dept. Edn., 1996-2000. Mem. Am. Cancer Soc., Am. Soc. Biol. Chemists, Am. Assn. Cancer Rsch., Tex. Faculty Assn. (exec. com. 1999—). Avocation: restoration of 1953-1955 Kaiser automobiles. Home: 2613 Newcomb St Lubbock TX 79415-1707 Office: Tex Tech U Health Scis Ctr 3601 4th St Lubbock TX 79430-0001 E-mail: johannes.everse@ttmc.ttuhsc.edu.

EVERSLEY, FREDERICK JOHN, sculptor, engineer; b. Bklyn., Aug. 28, 1941; s. Frederick William and Beatrice Agnes (Syphax) E. BSE.E., Carnegie-Mellon U., 1963. One-man shows include Whitney Mus. Am. Art, N.Y.C., 1970, Nat. Acad. Sci., Washington, 1976, 81, L.A. Inst. Contemporary Art, 1976, Santa Barbara Mus., 1976, Newport Harbor Art Mus., 1976, Oakland Mus. Art, 1977, Palm Springs (Calif.) Desert Mus., 1978, AIA, 1981, Va. Mus., 1981, Bacardi Art Gallery, Miami, 1984, Laband Art Gallery, 1985, Loyola Marymount U., L.A., Hokin Gallery, Palm Beach, Fla., 1988, Juda Gallery, London, 1988, Eva Cohen Gallery, Chgo., 1991, Lorenzelli Arte, Milan, 1992, Pavilion of Saudi Arabia, Expo 92, Seville, Spain, 1992; represented in permanent collections Smithsonian Instn., Washington, IRS Nat. Hdqtrs., New Carrollton, Md., Calif. State Coll., L.A., Oakland (Calif.) Art Mus., Milw. Art Center, Whitney Mus. Am. Art, N.Y.C., John Marin Meml. Collection, N.Y.C., U., Kans. Art Gallery, Lawrence, Long Beach (Calif.) Mus. Art, Currier Gallery Art, Manchester, N.H., Taft Mus. Art, Cin., Cranbrook Art Gallery, Bloomfield Hills, Mich., Nat. Acad. Sci., Washington, Nat. Collection Fine Arts, Washington, MIT, Cambridge, Neuberger Mus. Art, Purchase, N.Y., Newport Harbor Art Mus., Newport Beach, Calif., Guggenheim Mus., N.Y.C., Smith Coll. Mus. Art, Northhampton, Mass., Nat. Air and Space Mus., Mus. Contemporary Art, L.A., Palm Springs Desert Mus., Rose Mus. of Art, Brandis U., Boston, Sammlung Goetz, Munich Germany, IRS hdqs., New Carrollton, Md., 1996, Rossini Sculpture Park, Briosco, Italy, 1999; artist in residence Nat. Air and Space Mus., Washington, 1977-80. Nat. Endowment Arts grantee, 1972 Mem. L.A. Inst. Contemporary Art, Artworkers Coalition. Address: 1110 Abbot Kinney Blvd Venice CA 90291-3314

EVERSOLE, KELLYE ANNE, government relations and public affairs consultant; b. Wichita Falls, Tex, Apr. 28, 1958; d. John Lewis and Frankye Louise (Atchley) E. BA (hons.), George Washington Univ., 1983. Staff asst. US Senator David Boren, Washington, 1979-81, legis. asst., 1981-88; profl. staff mem. US Senate Com. on Agri., Nutrition and Forestry, Washington, 1988-89; exec. dir. Fed. Crop Ins. Commn, Washington, 1989-90; pres. Eversole Assoc., Washington, 1991—. Cons. Nat. Corn Growners Assn., St. Louis, 1995-2002, Am. Seed Trade Assn., Washington, 1998-2002, Am. Phytopathol. Soc., 2001—, Alliance Animal Genome Rsch., 2001—, Battelle Meml. Inst., 2001--, Minn.Corn Growers Assn., 2000--, Kans. State Univ., 2003-, Iowa Corn Growers Assn., 2002-, Va. Bioinformatics Inst., 2002-. Appt. mem. USTR/USDA Agricultral Policy Adv. Com., Washington, 1994-98. Recipient Outstanding Performance award Nat. Corn Growers Assn., 1999. Mem. AAAS, Soc. Women Environmental Profl. (founding, bd. dir.), ABA Agrl. Mgmt. Task Force Adv. Com., Am. Phytopathol. Soc., Alliance for Animal Genomics. Office: Eversole Assoc 5207 Wyoming Rd Bethesda MD 20816 E-mail: eversole@eversole.biz.

EVERSOLE, SANDRA JOY, operating room nurse; b. Leesville, La., Nov. 15, 1955; d. Marvin Henry and Joy Marie (Caraway) Miller; m. Robert Dean Eversole, July 6, 1974; children: Brandi, Jennifer, Brian. ADN, Brazosport-Galveston Coll., 1977. Cert. oper. rm. nurse. Staff nurse med.-surg. Sweeny (Tex.) Community Hosp., 1977-78; staff nurse oper. rm. Sweeny (Tex.) Cmty. Hosp., 1978-82, Polly Ryon Hosp., Richmond, Tex., 1982-91, asst. mgr. oper. rm., 1991—97; asst. dir. Surg. Svcs., 1997—99, mgr. perioperative svcs., 1999—. Designer intraoperative record, 1990, 99. Active PTA, Band Boosters Club. Mem.: Brazos Bend Assn. Oper. Rm. Nurses (pres.-elect 1998, pres. 1999, newsletter editor 2000—03, pres.-elect 2001, pres. 2002, pres.-elect 2003), Assn. Oper. Rm. Nurses (cert.). Mem. United Ch. Of Christ. Avocations: crossword puzzles, cross-stitching. Home: 15426 John Miller Rd Guy TX 77444-9516 Office: Polly Ryon Hosp 1705 Jackson St Richmond TX 77469-3246

EVERSON, JEAN WATKINS DOLORES, librarian media technical assistant, educator; b. Forest City, N.C., Feb. 14, 1938; d. J.D. Watkins and Hermie Roberta (Dizard) Watkins; children: Curtis Bryon, Vincent Keith. BS Elem. Edn., U. Cin., 1971, M Secondary Edn., 1973. Cert. X-ray technician. Educator Cin. Pub. Schs., Cin., 1965—2002, classroom tchr., parent/school coord., 1965—2002; work study coord. Butler County Edn. Ctr., Fairfield, Ohio, 1997—98; long term sub. Brown County -Georgetown Sch. Sys., Gerogetown, Ohio, 1993; sr. staff asst., cpc/alcohol substance abuse, inc. Cin. Pub. Schs., Cin., 1992—93; libr. tech. media; libr. media tech. asst. langsam libr. University of Cin.cinnati-Langsam Library, Cincinnati. Dir. and coord. tutoring program So. Baptist Ch., Cincinnati, 1990—91. Author: (booklet) Gospel Music: Copywrite Laws, 1987 (1987). Prodr./dir./coord. city music festival in music hall Cin. Pub. Schs., 1972—77. Mem.: Ohio Assn. Suprs. and Work Study Coords., Music Educator Nat. Conf. Baptist. Avocations: travel, walking. Home: PO Box 8337 West Chester OH 45069 Office: Cin City Pub Schs-Woodward 7001 Reading Rd Cincinnati OH 45237 Home Fax: 513-858-6880; Office Fax: 513-758-1279. Personal E-mail: jeanwatkinseverson@msn.com. Business E-Mail: eversoj@cpsboe.k12.oh.us.

EVERSON, MARK W. federal agency administrator; b. NY, Sept. 10, 1954; BA, Yale U., 1976; MS, NYU, 1977. With Arthur Andersen & Co., N.Y.C., Reagan Adminstrn., 1982—88, with USIA, 1982—85, spl. asst. to Atty. Gen. Edwin Meese, Dept. Justice, 1985, exec. assoc. commr., dep. commr. Immigration and Naturalization Svc.; exec. Pechiney Group, 1988—98; group v.p. fin. SC Internat. Svcs., Inc., 1998—2001; contr. fed. fin. mgmt. Off. of Mgt. and Budget, Washington, 2001—03, dep. dir. for mgmt., 2002—03; commr. IRS, Washington, 2003—. Office: IRS 1111 Constitution Ave NW Washington DC 20224-0002*

EVERSON, MARTIN JOSEPH, lawyer; b. San Francisco, Feb. 8, 1948; s. Joseph Martin and Virginia (Smith) E.; m. Lucille Jacobsen, Apr. 10, 1981; children: Diana, Andrew, Cynthia. BA, Georgetown U., 1970; JD, U. Calif., San Francisco, 1977. Bar: Calif. 1977, U.S. Dist. Ct. (no. dist.) Calif. 1977, bd. cert. trial adv.: Nat. Bd. Trial Advocacy. Dep. dist. atty. San Mateo County Dist. Atty.'s Office, Redwood City, Calif., 1977-78; assoc. Anderson, Galloway & Lucchese, Walnut Creek, Calif., 1978-85, ptnr., 1985—2001, Galloway, Lucchese & Everson, Walnut Creek, Calif., 2001—. Capt. USMC, 1971-74. Mem. ABA, Assn. Def. Counsel, Dep. Dist. Atty. Assn., Am. Bd. Trial Advocates, Alameda County Bar Assn., Contra Costa County Bar Assn. Roman Catholic. Avocations: golf, fishing. Office: Galloway Lucchese & Everson 1676 N California Blvd Ste 500 Walnut Creek CA 94596-4183 Business E-Mail: meverson@glattys.com. E-mail: mjeverson@msn.com.

EVERSON, STEVEN LEE, lawyer, real estate executive; b. Philippi, W.Va., June 16, 1950; s. Billie Lee and Mildred Ann (Hill) E.; m. Donna Janine Chmielarz, May 29, 1976; 1 child, Michael. BA in Math. magna cum laude, W. Va. U., 1972; JD, Northwestern U., 1979. Bar: Colo. 1979. Tax sr. acct. Deloitte, Haskins & Sells, Colorado Springs, Colo., 1979-82; v.p., sec., treas. The Schuck Corp., Colorado Springs, 1982—. Instr. real estate U. Colo. Project bus. instr. Jr. Achievement, 1985—87; treas. Steve Schuck for Gov. Com., 1988—98; bd. dirs. Silver Key Sr. Svcs., Inc., 2000—, Boys and Girls Club of Pikes Peak

Region, Colorado Springs, 1987—90, UCCS Exec. Club, Colorado Springs, 1988—90; bd. dirs., past chmn. Pikes Peak Found. Mental Health, Colorado Springs, 1986—2001, treas., 2001—; past chmn. Pikes Peak Mental Health Ctr. Sys., Inc., treas., 2001—. Capt. USAF, 1972—76. Named Vol. of Yr., Pikes Peak Mental Health Ctr., 1999, 2002. Mem. Phi Beta Kappa. Republican. Mem. Ch. of Christ. Avocations: racquetball, skiing, softball, golf, tennis, vol. coaching youth sports teams. Home: 1690 Colgate Dr Colorado Springs CO 80918-8106 Office: The Schuck Corp 2 N Cascade Ave Ste 1280 Colorado Springs CO 80903-1601

EVERS-WILLIAMS, MYRLIE, cultural organization administrator; b. Vicksburg, Miss., Mar. 17, 1933; m. Medgar Evers (dec. June 1963); 3 children; m. Walter Edward Williams (dec. 1995). Student, Alcorn State U.; BA in Sociology, Pomona Coll., 1968, honorary degree; cert., Simmons Coll.; honorary degree, Medgar Evers Coll., Spelman Coll., Columbia Coll., Chgo., Bennett Coll., Tougaloo Coll., Pomona Coll. Mem. staff, sec. NAACP; dir. planning Claremont (Calif.) Colls., 1968-70; v.p. advt. & publicity Seligman & Latz, N.Y.C., 1973-75; dir. consumer affairs Atlantic Richfield Co.; commr. Pub. Works Bd., L.A., 1987-95; chmn. NAACP, 1995-98. Civil rights leader, lectr. Author: For Us the Living, 1967, Watch Me Fly, 1999; contbg. editor Ladies Home Jour. Candidate for Congress in Calif., 1970; candidate for L.A. City Coun., 1987; head So. Calif. Dem. Women's Divsn.; convener Nat. Women's Polit. Caucus; founder, chmn. Medgar Evers Inst. Named Woman of Yr., Glamour Mag., 1995, Ms. Mag., 1995, one of Women of Yr., Ladies Home Jour., 1996; recipient Mary Church Terrell award Delta Sigma Theta, 1996, Althea T.L. Simmons Social Action award, 1998; recipient Spingarn award, NAACP, Atlanta, 1998; recipient Trumpeter's award, Nat. Consumers League, New Orleans, 1998; named one of 200 most influential women, Vanity Fair mag., Jan. 1999. Office: MEW Assocs Inc 15 SW Colorado Ave Bend OR 97702-1150

EVERT, CHRIS (CHRISTINE MARIE EVERT), retired professional tennis player; b. Ft. Lauderdale, Fla., Dec. 21, 1954; d. James and Colette Evert; m. John Lloyd, Apr. 17, 1979 (div.); m. Andy Mill, July 30, 1988; children: Alexander James, Nicholas Joseph, Colton Jack. Amateur tennis player, until Dec. 1972; profl. tennis player, 1972-89; ret. from tennis, 1989; owner Evert Enterprises/IMG, Boca Raton, Fla., 1989—; Olympics commentator CBS Sports, 1992. Commentator NBC Sports tennis events; winner numerous tournaments including U.S. Jr. Championship, 1970, 71, U.S. Open, 1975, 76, 77, 78, 80, 82, Wimbledon Singles, 1974, 76, 81, doubles, 1976, Australian Open, 1982, 84, French Open Singles, 1974, 75, 79, 80, 83, 85, 86, Virginia Slims, 1972, 73, 75, 77, 87, European Women's Open, Geneva, 1987, Eckerd Open, 1987; spl. advisor to U.S. Nat. Tennis Team by U.S. Tennis Assn.; bd. dirs. Internat. Tennis Hall of Fame; trustee Womens Sports Found. Star 3 vols. VCR instrnl. tennis tapes, 1991—; corp. spokesperson and rep., appearing in TV commls. and print advertisements; host and organizer Chris Evert Pro-Celebrity Tennis Classic, 1989, 90, 92, 93, 94, 95, 96, 97, 98, 99. Founder Chris Evert Charities, Inc., Healthy Start. Recipient Lebair Sportsmanship trophy, 1971; named Female Athlete of Yr. AP, 1974, 75, 77, 80, Athlete of Yr. Sports Illustrated, 1976, Greatest Woman Athlete of Last 25 Years Women's Sports Found., 1985, Flo Hyman award Women's Sports Found., 1990, Providencia award Palm Beach County Conv. and Visitors Bur., 1991; named one of Top 10 Romantic People of 1989, Korbel; Inducted Madison Sq. Garden Walk of Fame, 1993, inductee, Internat. Tennis Hall of Fame, 1995. Mem. U.S. Lawn Tennis Assn. (Top Women's Singles Player award 1974), Nat. Honor Soc., Fla. Sports Found. (bd. dirs.), Women's Tennis Assn. (pres. 1982 91, exec. com., Sportsmanship award 1979, Player Svc. awards 1981, 86, 87).

EVERT, SANDRA FLORENCE (SANDRA WHEELER), medical/surgical nurse; b. Saginaw, Mich., Sept. 18, 1949; d. Charles William and Florence Arlene (Babcock) Wheeler; m. Raymond Clyde Evert, Jan. 20, 1968; children: Christine Michelle, Raymond Clyde II. AD cum laude, Lansing C.C., 1986. Med./surg. staff nurse E.W. Sparrow Hosp., Lansing, Mich., 1986—. Mem. First United Pentecostal Ch. of Grand Ledge, Mich. Mem. Apostolic Ch. Avocations: camping, bible reading, christian music, family, church functions. Home: 10 Willard Ct Grand Ledge MI 48837-1356

EVERT, THOMAS L., III, music educator; b. Phila. AA, Bucks County C.C., 1988; BA, Trenton State Coll., 1990; MA in Edn., Beaver Coll., 1991, MEd, 2001. Cert. music tchr. K-12, supr. curriculum and instrn., elem. prin., secondary prin. Pa., music tchr. K-12, supr., prin./supr., sch. bus. adminstr., sch. adminstr. N.J. Tchr. Music Trenton Sch. Dist., NJ, 1992—99, disciplinarian, 1999—. Coord., supr. summer sch. Trenton Sch. Dist., 2000—; adj. prof. Music Beaver Coll./Arcadia U., Glenside, Pa., 1993—, acting chairperson Music Dept., 2002—. Mem.: Musician Union Phila. #77, Trenton Educators Assn., N.J. Educators Assn. Office: Arcadia Univ Music Dept 450 S Easton Rd Glenside PA 19038-3215*

EVERTON, MARTA VE, retired ophthalmologist; b. Luling, Tex., Nov. 12, 1926; d. T.W. and Nora E. (Eckols) O'Leavy; B.A., Hardin-Simmons U., 1945; M.A., Stanford U., 1947; M.D., Baylor U., 1955; postgrad. N.Y.U.-Bellevue Hosp., 1956-57; m. Robert K. Graham, Oct. 15, 1960; children: Marcia, Christie, Leslie Fox. Intern, Meth. Hosp., Houston, 1955-56; resident in ophthalmology Baylor Affiliated Hosps., Houston, 1956-59; clin. instr. ophthalmology Baylor U., 1959-60; asst. clin. prof. ophthalmology Loma Linda U., 1962-73; practice medicine specializing in ophthalmology, Houston, 1959-60, Pasadena, Calif., 1961-74, Escondido, Calif., 1974-98. Mem. Am. Acad. Ophthalmology, Alpha Omega Alpha. Home: 3024 Sycamore Ln Escondido CA 92025-7433

EVERTS, CONNOR, artist; b. Bellingham, Wash., Jan. 24, 1926; s. William Edward and Sophia (Mehan) E.; children: Anon Connor, Meigan Mariko, Geoffrey, Tamura; m. Judith Asa Colman, Dec. 12, 1994. AA, El Camino Coll., 1950; BA, U. Wash., 1952. Mem. faculty dept. art Calif. State U., Northridge, 1960-62; mem. faculty dept. art Calif. Inst. Arts, 1962-65, Calif. State U., Long Beach, 1965, San Francisco Art Inst., 1966, U. So. Calif., 1967-69, U. Calif., Riverside, 1972-76; graphics chmn. Cranbrook Acad. Art, Bloomfield Hills, Mich., 1976-81. Exchange prof. Prahran Coll. Advanced Studies, Melbourne, Australia; artist in residence Calif. Inst. Tech., 1970-71 One man shows include Pasadena Art Mus., 1960, Michael Walls Gallery, San Francisco, 1967-69, Los Angeles Mcpl. Gallery, 1971, Meckler Gallery, Los Angeles, 1979, World Print Council, 1982, retrospective exhibit, Los Angeles Mus., 1983, Orange County Ctr. for Contemporary Art, 1986, Whatcom Mus. Art, 1987, Print Works Gallery, Chgo., 1988, 90, Ruth Bachofner, L.A., 1986, 89, Dominguez Hills State U., 1989, Joy Emery Gallery, Detroit, 1990, Claremont Gallery, L.A., 1995, Flowers Gallery, London, 1999, Oceanside Mus., 2001; Retrospective 1948-2002 at Union Ctr. for the Arts, L.A.; exhibited in group shows at Tokyo Biann. Painting Exhbn, 1967, Homage to Lithography, Mus. Modern Art, N.Y.C., 1969, Printmaking, Oskokunst Forening, Oslo, Norway, 1974, Mint Mus., 1987, Kunstsamm-Luggen Der Veste Coburg, 1988; represented in permanent collections, Chgo. Art Inst., Long Beach Mus. Art, Los Angeles County Mus. Art, Milw. Art Mus., Mus. Modern Art, N.Y.C., Pasadena Art Mus., San Francisco Mus. Modern Art, Washington Gallery Modern Art, others. Pres. adv. bd. Los Angeles Mcpl. Gallery, 1968. With USCG, 1946. Mem. AAUP, L.A. Printmaking Soc., Mich. Assn. Printmakers, Artists Equity. Studio. 2351 Sonoma St Torrance CA 90501-3130 *Circumstances, time and place of birth, sex, race, religion, economic status, and the resultant formulative years, determine the rough shape of our lives. But we, above all, are the largest factors in determining the kinds of persons we become. Let it be by conscious choice. If we will be shaped, let it be by ideas and challenge.*

EVERY, MICHAEL A. state legislator; m. Laura Every; 4 children. Student, Milton Coll., 1981. Sales mgr. Double Z Broadcasting; mayor City of Minnewauken, N.D.; mem. N.D. Senate from 12th dist., Bismark, 2001—. Coun. pres. City of Minnewauken. Democrat. Office: PO Box 56 Minnewaukan ND 58351-0056 E-mail: mevery@state.nd.us.

EVETT, RUSSELL DOUGHERTY, internist, educator; b. Norfolk, Va., Feb. 1, 1932; s. Edward Hall and Elizabeth (Dougherty) E.; m. Mary Gail Kirby, Aug. 18, 1956; children: Stephen, Anne, Gail, John. BS, Randolph-Macon Coll., 1953; MD, Med. Coll. Va., 1957; MS in Medicine, Mayo Clinic and U. Minn., 1963. Diplomate Am. Bd. Internal Medicine. Intern DePaul Hosp., Norfolk, 1957-58; fellow in internal medicine Mayo Clinic, Rochester, Minn., 1960-63; pvt. practice internal medicine Norfolk, 1964—. Pres. med. staff Leigh Meml. Hosp., Norfolk, 1970-72; chmn. dept. internal medicine Norfolk Gen. Hosp., 1972-74; assoc. prof. medicine Eastern Va. Med. Sch., 1974— ; mem. staff Med. Center Hosps., DePaul Hosp., to 1998; mem. Va. Health Info. Bd., 1997—; bd. dirs. Med. Coll. Va. Found., 1998—. Served with USNR, 1958-60. Mem. Va. Health Info. Bd., 1997—, Norfolk Cmty. Svcs. Bd., 2000—. Served with USNR, 1958-60. Fellow ACP (Laureate award 1997); mem. Va. Gastroenterol. Soc. (pres. 1975-77), Norfolk Acad. Medicine (pres. 1976-77), Med. Soc. Va. (pres. 1994-95), AMA (alt. del. 1985-95, del. 1995-99), Norfolk Cmty. Svcs. Bd., So. Med. Assn., Norfolk Yacht and Country Club, Harbor Club, Phi Beta Kappa, Omicron Delta Kappa, Alpha Omega Alpha. Methodist. Home: 6147 Studeley Ave Norfolk VA 23508-1044 E-mail: rdemd@att.net.

EVEY, MERLE KENTON, lawyer; b. Altoona, Pa., Oct. 9, 1930; s. Merle Houser and Dorothy Ellen (Miller) E.; m. Veronica Nuala Moran, Sept. 1, 1962; children: Eileen Veronica, Kathleen Marie. BA, Pa. State U., 1952; JD, Dickinson Sch. of Law, 1955. Bar: Pa. 1956, U.S. Dist. Ct. (we. dist.) Pa. 1959, U.S. Supreme Ct. 1959. Ptnr. Evey, Routch, Black, Dorezas, Magee & Levine, Hollidaysburg, Pa., 1957—. Bd. dirs. Hollidaysburg Trust Co., Omega Fin. Corp., State College, Pa. Chmn. adv. bd. Pa. State U., Altoona; bd. dirs., solicitor Home Nursing Affiliates, Altoona, Pa., 1978—; solicitor County of Blair, Pa., 1978—, Blair County Hosp. Authority, Hollidaysburg, 1978—. Served with U.S. Army, 1955—57. Mem. ABA, Blair County Bar Assn. (bd. govs. 1964-67, pres. 1982-83), Pa. Bar Assn. (ho. of dels. 1980-83, bd. govs. 1983-86). Clubs: Spruce Creek (Pa.) Rod & Gun. Lodges: Masons. Republican. Methodist. Avocation: golf. Home: PO Box 16 Elm St Sylvan Hills Hollidaysburg PA 16648 Office: Evey Routch Black et al 401 Allegheny St Hollidaysburg PA 16648-2011 E-mail: mevey@eveyroutch.com .

EVGENOV, OLEG V. medical scientist; b. Arkhangelsk, Russia, July 24, 1970; arrived in U.S., 2002; s. Victor E. and Kapitalina A. Evgenov; m. Natalia V. Ermakova, Aug. 20, 1999; children: Daniel O., Dennis O. MD with distinction, No. State Med. U., Arkhangelsk, 1993; PhD, U. of Tromsø, Norway, 2001. Lectr. No. State Med. U., Arkhangelsk, 1993—95; rsch. and tchg. asst. U. of Tromsø, Tromsø, 1995—97, rsch. assoc., 1997—2001; scientist Inotek Pharms. Corp., Beverly, Mass., 2002, Mass. Gen. Hosp., Boston, 2002—. Contbr. articles to profl. jours. Finalist Resident Rsch. Contest, N.Y. State Soc. of Anesthesiologists, 2000; recipient Fellowship award, Internat. Sepsis Forum, 2000, Silver Medal of Distinction, Russian Ministry of Gen. Edn., 1987; fellow, Norwegian Rsch. Coun., 1997—2001. Mem.: Am. Physiol. Soc. (corr.), Am. Thoracic Soc. (corr.). Office: Mass Gen Hosp Dept Anesthesia CLN 309 55 Fruit St Boston MA 02114 Office Fax: 617-724-7768. E-mail: evgenov@etherdome.mgh.harvard.edu.

EVIATAR, LYDIA, pediatric neurologist; b. Bucharest, Romania, Apr. 7, 1936; came to U.S., 1966; d. Joseph and Ghitea (Scheinberg) Tamir; m. Abraham Eviatar, Oct. 9, 1956; children: Joseph, Daphne. BSc, Faculte des Scis., Strasbourg, 1954; MD, Hadassah Hebrew U., Jerusalem, 1961. Diplomate Am. Bd. Pediatrics. Intern and resident Tel Hashoner Hosp., Tel Aviv, 1961-65; U.C.P. fellow UCLA, 1966-67, fellow in pediatric neurology, 1967-69; pediatric neurologist Bronx (N.Y.) Lebanon Hosp., 1970-79; resident in neurology Montefiore Hosp. Med. Ctr., Bronx, 1973-75; pediatric neurologist L.I. Jewish Med. Ctr., 1979-86; chief pediatric neurology Schneider Children's Hosp., New Hyde Park, N.Y., 1986-99; from assoc. prof. to prof. pediatrics and neurology Albert Einstein Coll. Medicine, Bronx, N.Y., 1989-99, chief emeritus, 1999. Co-author: (with others) Pediatric Neurology, 1988. Grantee Nat. Inst. Neurol. Disease and Blindness, 1970-77, Acad. Cerebral Palsy, 1980-81, Richmond award, 1981; recipient teaching award Am. Acad. Otolaryngology, 1983. Fellow Am. Acad. Pediatrics, Am. Acad. Neurology (cert. neurologist, child neurologist). E-mail: eviatar@lij.edu.

EVNIN, ANTHONY BASIL, venture capital investor; b. N.Y.C., Mar. 10, 1941; s. Oscar B. Evnin and Nina (Fradkin) Schick; m. Judith P. Ward, June 9, 1962; children: Luke B., Timothy W. BA, Princeton U., 1962; PhD, MIT, 1966. With Union Carbide Corp., 1966-71, Story Chem., 1971-74; gen. ptnr. Venrock Assocs., N.Y.C., 1974—. Bd. dirs. Caliper Techs. Corp., Mountain View, Calif., Sonic Innovations, Inc., Salt Lake City. Trustee Princeton U., 1997—, Rockefeller U., 1999—. Office: Venrock Assocs 30 Rockefeller Plz Fl 56 New York NY 10112-0256

EVRIGENIS, JOHN BASIL, obstetrician/gynecologist; b. Athens, Greece, Feb. 23, 1929; came to U.S., 1951; s. Basil I. and Maria (Soteriou) E.; m. Sophia M. Goritsan, June 22, 1952; children: Maryellen, E. Debbie, W. Gregory, John Jr. BA, U. Athens, 1947, MD, 1951. Diplomate Am. Bd. Ob-Gyn. Intern Providence Hosp., Portland, Oreg., 1951-52, resident in gen. practice medicine, 1952-53; resident in ob-gyn Emanuel Hosp. and U. Oreg. Med. Sch., Portland, 1953-56; pvt. practice specializing in ob-gyn Sacramento, 1956—. Assoc. clin. prof. ob-gyn Med. Sch., U. Calif., Davis, 1975—; chief ob-gyn dept. Mercy Hosp., Sacramento, 1972-73. Mem. AMA, Am. Fertility Soc., Pan-Am. Med. Soc., Royal Soc. Medicine, Royal Soc. Health, Sacramento County Med. Soc., Calif. Med. Assn., So. Calif. Ob-Gyn. Assembly, Am. Soc. Gynecol. Laproscopists, Am. Soc. Abdominal Surgeons, No. Calif. Ob-Gyn. Soc. (pres. 1975-76), Dynamis Club, Ahepa, Del Paso Country Club, Northridge Country Club, Sutter Club, Sacramento Club, Lions, Elks, Masons, Rotary Club. Eastern Orthodox. Avocations: reading, travel, golf, history, statistics. Home and Office: 2845 Calle Vista Way Sacramento CA 95821 E-mail: evrig@aol.com.

EWALD, LAURA ANNE, school librarian; b. Bryn Mawr, Pa., May 20, 1961; d. Thomas M. and Sharon C. Ewald. BA in Classical Studies, U. of Wash., 1985; BA in Drama, Ctrl. Wash. U., 1990; MLS, Ind. U., 1998; MA in Orgnl. Comm., Murray (Ky.) State U., 2003. Reference libr. Ind. U., Bloomington, Ind., 1998; reference instrn. libr. Murray (Ky.) State U., 1998—. Mem.: ALA, Theatre Libr. Assn., Ky. Libr. Assn., Beta Phi Mu. Avocations: community and educational theatre, puppet theatre.

EWALD, ROBERT FREDERICK, insurance association executive; b. Newark, May 5, 1924; s. Frederick J. and Florence M. (Reiley) E.; m. Jeanine Martinez, Jan. 3, 1976; children: Robert, Steven; children by a previous marriage: William F., John C., George E. BS in Bus. Adminstrn. with spl. honors in Econs., Rutgers U., 1948. Asst. corp. auditor Prudential Ins. Co., Newark, Houston, Chgo., 1948-61; audit mgr. N.Y. Life Ins. Co., N.Y.C., 1962-64; treas. Mass. Gen. Life Ins. Co., Boston, 1965-68; adminstrv. v.p., controller Res. Life Ins. Co., Dallas, 1969-70; pres. Nat. Ben Franklin Life, Chgo., 1971-77; trustee, pres. Rockford (Ill.) Blue Cross Plan, North Cmties. Health Plan, Inc., 1979-82; dir., chmn. audit com. Guaranty Reasurance Corp., 1993-95; exec. dir. Guaranty Sys. Cons. LTD, Guaranty Assn., Chgo. Served with U.S. Army, 1943-46. Fellow Life Mgmt. Inst.; mem. Fin. Execs. Inst., Am. Arbitration Assn., Adminstrv. Mgmt. Soc., Mensa, Nat. Orgn. Life and Health Ins. Guaranty Assn. (emeritus dir., chmn. mems. coun. 1992-95, chmn. exec. com.), VFW. Home: 12 Wisner St Park Ridge IL 60068-3546 E-mail: bobewald@attbi.com.

EWALD, WILLIAM BRAGG, JR., author, consultant; b. Chgo., Dec. 8, 1925; s. William Bragg and Mary Ann (Niccolls) E.; m. Mary Cecilia Thedieck, Dec. 6, 1947 (dec. Feb. 1997); children: William Bragg, Charles Ross, Thomas Hart Benton. AB, Washington U., 1946; MA, Harvard U., 1947, PhD, 1951. Instr. English, humanities Harvard U., Cambridge, 1951-54; spl. asst. on White House staff, asst. to Sec. Interior Washington, 1954-61; with IBM, Armonk, 1961-88. Author: The Masks of Jonathan Swift, 1954, The Newsmen of Queen Anne, 1956, Eisenhower the President, 1981, Who Killed Joe McCarthy?, 1984; McCarthyism and Consensus, 1987; asst. to former Pres. Eisenhower in preparation of 2-vol. memoirs, White House Years, 1961-64. Pres. Bruce Mus. Assocs., Greenwich, 1972-73; vestry mem. Christ Ch., Greenwich, 1986-89; bd. dirs. Eisenhower World Affairs Inst., 1984-91. Grantee Am. Philos. Soc., 1952, Harvard Found. Advanced Study and Research, 1952-53; Eisenhower Exchange fellow, 1960. Mem. Judson Welliver Soc., Phi Beta Kappa. Clubs: Cosmos (Washington); Round Hill (Greenwich). Republican. Episcopalian. Home and Office: 3 Dewart Rd Greenwich CT 06830-3418

EWALD, WILLIAM BRAGG, III, law educator, philosopher, educator; b. Washington, Sept. 30, 1954; s. William Bragg Ewald Jr. and Mary Thedieck. BA, AM, Harvard U., 1976, JD, 1981; PhD, Oxford (England) U., 1978. Jr. rsch. fellow Queen's Coll., Oxford, 1982—88; mem. Inst. for Advanced Study, Princeton, NJ, 1988—89; Jean Monnet fellow European U. Inst., Florence, Italy, 1989—91; asst. prof. law and philosphy U. Pa., Phila., 1991—96, prof. law and philosophy, 1996—. Editor: From Kant to Hilbert, 1996. Trustee St. Mark's Sch., Southborough, Mass., 1999—. Grantee, Alexander von Humboldt Stiftung, Göttingen, Germany, 1984—86. Home: 1520 Flat Rock Rd Narberth PA 19072 Office: U Pa Law Sch 3400 Chestnut St Philadelphia PA 19104 E-mail: wewald@law.upenn.edu.

EWALT, JACQUELYN MARIE, biologist; b. Pitts., May 20, 1968; d. Thomas A. and Veronica Ewalt. BS, La Roche Coll., Pitts., 1991; student, Duquesne U., 1993. Biology lab. asst. La Roche Coll., 1990-91; environ. chemistry Allegheny County Health Dept., Pitts., 1992; gen. biology lab. instr., faculty liasion Duquesne U., Pitts., 1992-93; molecular biology rsch. asst. MaGee Womens Rsch. Inst., Pitts., 1993-95; with client collections dept. Quest Diagnostics Inc. (formerly Corning Clin. Labs.), Pitts., 1995-97, biologist microbiology lab., 1997-99, virology lab., 1999-00; quality control specialist ARC, Phila., 2000—. Sci. teaching asst. La Roche Pre-Coll. Program, Pitts., 1991; judge Pitts. Regional Sci. and Engring. Fair. Vol. histology lab. Ohio Valley Gen. Hosp., McKees Rocks, Pa., 1991; judge Pjas local competition Holy Trinity Sch., 1993, 1994, 1995, Pitts. Regional Sci. and Engring. Fair; vol. Carnegie Sci. Ctr., Pitts.; lab. tech. Am. Red Cross Nat. Testing Lab., Nucliecic Acid Testing Lab., Phila., 2000—. Named faculty scholar Duquesne U., 1992-93; recipient Best Composition award Nat. Aviary Photo Contest. Mem. AAAS, Am. Inst. Biol. Scis., Nat. Audubon Soc., Pitts. Zool. Soc. Avocations: art, music, theater, photography. Home: Apt B2 542 Knightsbridge Ct Andalusia PA 19020

EWAN, DAVID E. lawyer; b. Camden, N.J., June 23, 1959; s. Eugene H. and Catherine T. (Stannard) E.; m. Lisa J. Draves, Sept. 12, 1998. BA, Dickinson Coll., 1981; JD, Rutgers U., 1991. Bar: N.J. 1991, Pa. 1991, Fla. 1992, Colo. 1994, U.S. Dist. Ct. N.J. 1991, U.S. Ct. Appeals (3d cir.) 1992. Legal intern Camden County Prosecutor, 1989; law clk. U.S. Ct. Appeals (3d cir.), Phila., 1990-91; assoc. Begley, McCloskey & Gaskill, Moorestown, NJ, 1991—2001; pres. Computer Network SOS, Inc., 2002—. Cons. N.J. Land Title Assn., 2000—; sr. adj. prof. paralegal program Burlington County Coll., Pemberton, N.J., 1996—. Mem.: Assn. for Info and Image Mgmt. Internat., Property Records Industry Assn. (bd. dirs. 2003—, co-chair real property law com. 2003—), Am. Ednl. Rsch. Assn. Home: 400 N Haddon Ave Unit 50 Haddonfield NJ 08033-1731 Office: PO Box 102 Haddonfield NJ 08033

EWAN, GEORGE THOMSON, physicist, educator; b. Edinburgh, Scotland, May 6, 1927; arrived in Can., 1952; s. Alexander Farmer and Jeannie Young (Taylor) E.; m. Maureen Louise Howard, Aug. 7, 1952; children: Elizabeth Louise, Robert Alexander. BS with 1st class honors, Edinburgh U., 1948, PhD, 1952; DSc (hon.), Guelph U., 2001, Laurentian U., 2002. Asst. lectr. Edinburgh U., 1950-52; rsch. assoc. McGill U., Montreal, Que., Can., 1952-55; asst. to sr. rsch. officer Atomic Energy of Can., Ltd., Chalk River, 1955-70; prof. physics Queen's U., Kingston, Ont., Can., 1970-94; prof. emeritus, 1994—; head dept. Queen's U., Kingston, Ont., Can., 1974-77. Vis. scientist Lawrence Berkeley (Calif.) Lab., 1966. Ford Found. fellow Niels Bohr Inst., Copenhagen, Denmark, 1961-62; Japan Soc. Promotion of Sci. fellow, Tokyo, 1986; recipient Radiation Industry award Am. Nuclear Soc., 1967. Fellow Royal Soc. Can., Royal Soc. Edinburgh, Am. Phys. Soc.; mem. Can. Assn. Physicists (Gold medal Achievement in Physics 1987). Mem. United Ch. Can. Avocations: golf, walking, reading. Office: Queen's U Physics Dept Kingston ON Canada K7L 3N6

EWAN, WILLIAM KENNETH, lawyer; b. Riverdale, Md., May 15, 1943; s. Richard Kenneth and Dorothy Alice (Spencer) E.; m. Naomi Ruth Browne, July 31, 1971; 1 child, Andrea Sue. BS, Ind. U., 1964, JD, 1967. Bar: Ind. 1967, U.S. Dist. Ct. (so. dist.) Ind. 1967, U.S. Ct. Mil. Appeals 1976. Pvt. practice law, Lawrenceburg, Ind., 1974—. Unit sec. Salvation Army, chmn. kettle drive. Capt. USNR, 1967-99, ret. Decorated Meritorious Svc. Medal USN. Mem. Ind. State Bar Assn., Dearborn-Ohio County Bar Assn. (pres. 1976-78), Ind. U. Alumni Assn., Ind. U. Alumni Club Dearborn County (pres. 1976), Am. Legion. Methodist. Avocations: photography, hiking Appalachian Trail, sailing, golf. Home: 9636 Old State Road 350 Aurora IN 47001-9343 Office: 210 W High St Lawrenceburg IN 47025-1910 E-mail: bewan@one.net.

EWANCHUK, MICHAEL, retired school system administrator; b. Gimli, Man., Can., Mar. 14, 1908; s. Wasyl and Paraskeva Ewanchuk; m. J. Muriel Smith, Aug. 2, 1941 (dec. 1997). Student, Detroit City Coll., 1928—30; BA, U. Man., 1939, BEd, 1941, MEd, 1950; LLD (hon.), U. Winnipeg, 1979; D in Canon Law (hon.), St. John's Coll., U. Man., 1989. H.s. prin.; apptd. sch. inspector, 1946—73; ret., 1973. Chmn. Ukrainian Curriculum com. U. Man., lectr. stats. and testing; statistician Man. H.S. exams. and std. tests; chmn. editl. com. Secondary Edn. in Can. Author: Pioneer Settlers: Ukrainians in the Dauphin Area 1896-1926 (Shevchenko meda., Ukrainian Can. Congress), Sisler and His Times, Vita: A Ukrainian Community, Spruce, Swamp and Stone, Pioneer Profiles: Ukrainian Settlers in Manitoba, Hawaiian Ordeal: Ukrainian Contract Workers 1897-1910, Reflections and Reminiscences: Ukrainians in Canada, Young Cossack, a novella, Pioneer Ukrainian Settlers, William Kurelek: The Suffering Genius, East of the Red: Early Ukrainian Settlements, East of the Red: Early Ukrainian Settlements North of the Dawson Trail, Vertical Development: A New Generation of Ukrainian Canadians; contbr. articles to profl. jours. Flight lt., navigation and pers. counseling RCAF, World War II. Recipient Queen's Jubilee medal, Lt. Gov. Hon. Peter Liba, 2002. Fellow: Can. Coll. Tchrs.; mem.: Ukrainian Acad. Arts and Sci., Can. Assn. Sch. Supts. (pres.), Man. Inspectors' Assn. (pres.), U. Man. Alumni Assn. (pres.).

EWBANK, THOMAS PETERS, lawyer, retired banker; b. Indpls., Dec. 29, 1943; s. William Curtis and Maxine Stuart (Peters) E.; m. Alice Ann Shelton, June 8, 1968; children: William Curtis, Ann Shelton. Student, Stanford U., 1961-62; AB, Ind. U., 1965, JD, 1969. Bar: Ind. 1969, U.S. Tax Ct. 1969, U.S. Dist. Ct. (so. dist.) Ind. 1969, U.S. Supreme Ct. 1974; cert. trust & fin. advisor. Legis. asst. Ind. Legis. Coun., 1966-67; estate and inheritance tax adminstr. Mchts. Nat. Bank, Indpls., 1967-69; assoc. Hilgedag, Johnson, Secrest and Murphy, Indpls., 1969-71; asst. gen. counsel Everett I. Brown Co., Indpls., 1971-72; with Mchts. Nat. Bank & Trust Co. (now Nat. City Bank), Indpls., 1972-95; from probate adminstr. to sr. v.p. & sr. trust officer, pres. Mechants Capital Mgmt., Inc., Ind., 1990-93; ptnr. Krieg DeVault LLP, Indpls., 1995—. Contbr. articles to profl. jours. Asst. treas. Ruckelshaus for US Senator Com., 1968; candidate for Ind. Legislature, 1970, 74; bd. dir. Noble Found. Ind., 1997-99, Indpls. Art Ctr., 1997-2002, Ruth Lilly Found., 1997-2002, Ctr. Philanthropy, Ind. U., Indpls., 1998-2002, Benjamin Harrison Home Found., 1994—, v.p., 1996-98, pres., 1998-2000; Arthur Jordan Found., 2002-, sec., 2003-; chmn. adv. com. ARC, 1987—. Fellow: Ind. Bar Found (life); mem.: ABA, Indpls. Bar Found. (treas. 1976-81), Ind. Bar. Assn., Indpls. Bar Assn., Estate Planning Coun. Indpls. (pres. 1982—83), English Speaking Union Indpls., Kiwanis (Circle K Internat. trustee 1963 64, pres. 1964-65, chmn. internat. com. 1988-90, George Hixson Diamond fellow, past treas. Indpls. club) (Career Achievement award 2001), Meridian Hills Country Club, Blue Key. Republican. Baptist. Office: One Indiana Sq Ste 2800 Indianapolis IN 46204-2017 E-mail: tewbank@kdlegal.com.

EWELL, A. BEN, JR., lawyer, businessman; b. Elyria, Ohio, Sept. 10, 1941; s. Austin Bert and Mary Rebecca (Thompson) E.; m. Suzanne E.; children: Austin Bert III, Brice Ballantyne, Harrison Dale, Jonathan Eli, Tucker Benjamin. BA, Miami U., Oxford, Ohio, 1963; JD, Hasting Coll. Law, U. Calif., San Francisco, 1966. Bar: Calif. 1966, U.S. Dist. Ct. (ea. dist.) Calif. 1967, U.S. Supreme Ct. 1982, U.S. Ct. Appeals (9th cir.) 1967. Pres. A.B. Ewell, Jr., A. Profl. Corp., Fresno, 1984-98, The Clarksfield Co., Inc., Fresno, 1989—; formerly gen. counsel to various water dists. and assn.; gen. counsel, chmn. San Joaquin River Flood Control Assn., 1984-88; CEO Millerton New Town Devel. Co., 1988-94, chmn., 1994-96; pres. Millerton Open Space and Natural Resource Plan, 1999—; regional v.p. Western Water Co., Fresno, 2001—; pres. Lake Millerton Marinas, LLC. Mem. task force on prosecution, cts. and law reform Calif. Coun. Criminal Justice, 1971-74; columnist, The Willington Enterprise; mem. Fresno Bulldog Found., Calif. State U.; mem. San Joaquin

Valley Agrl. Water commn., 1979-88; co-chmn. nat. adv. coun. SBA, 1981, 82, mem. 1981-87; bd. dirs. Fresno East Cmty. Ctr., 1971-73; mem. Fresno County Water Adv. Com., 1989; chmn. various area polit. campaigns and orgns., including Reagan/Bush, 1984, Deukmejian for Gov., 1986; mem. adv. com. St. Agnes Med. Ctr. Found., 1983-89; trustee U. Calif. Med. Edn. Found., 1989-90, Fresno Met. Mus. Art, History and Sci., active, 1989—, mem. adv. com., 1993-94; bd. dirs. Citizens for Cmty. Enrichment, Fresno, 1990-93; mem. Police Activities League, 1995—; pres. Fresno Conv. and Visitors Bur., 2003—. Bd. dirs. Fresno Conv. and Visitors Bur., 1997—, pres. 2003—; co-chmn., ministry resources First Congl. Ch., 2003—. Mem. Millerton Lake C. of C., Brighton Crest Country Club (pres. 1989-96), Copper River Country Club, Phi Alpha Delta, Brighton Crest Golf and Country Club, Sigma Nu Office: 410 W Fallbrook Ave Ste 102 Fresno CA 93711-5830

EWELL, DENA LYNETTE, administrative management executive; b. Washington, May 27, 1966; d. Deo and Connie (Hoskinson) Clure; m. Charles Raymond Ewell, Jr., Feb. 2, 1993. Computer Sci., George Mason U., 1987. Security officer CIA, Washington, 1984-88; customer svc. rep. Sprint, Reston, Va., 1988-89; exec. asst. Summer Cons., Inc., McLean, Va., 1989-91; adminstr. Waterfall Trucking, Centreville, Va., 1991-95; bookkeeper Greg Sound & Comm., Chantilly, Va., 1994-96; fin. cons. Genesis Tech. Group, Sterling, Va., 1996; sr. fin. analyst, fin. adminstr. Gestalt Sys., Inc., Vienna, Va., 1996-99; exec. asst., strategic alliances specialist Motient Corp., Reston, Va., 1999-2000; mgr., bus. devel. eStara, Inc., 2000—03; adminstrv. mgr. Lansdowne (Va.) Cmty. Devel., LLC, Va., 2001—03; adminstr. Convergys Corp., Reston, 2003—. Recipient Presdl. Acad. Achievement award Dept. Edn., 1984. Mem.: NAFE, Nat. Assn. for Search and Rescue, The Wolf Edn. and Rsch. Ctr. Avocations: reading, hiking, auto racing, contemporary dancing. Office: Convergys Corp 11800 Sunrise Valley Dr #800 Reston VA 20191 E-mail: dena.ewell@convergys.com.

EWELL, JOHN ALBERT, III, mathematician, educator; b. Newellton, La., Feb. 28, 1928; s. John Albert Ewell II and Carolyn E. (Fay) Ewell; m. Perdy Viola Lavik, Oct. 15, 1960; children: Ginger Astri, Lars Albert, Philip Adrian. BS, Morehouse Coll., 1948; postgrad., U. Colo., 1949—51; MA, UCLA, 1955, PhD, 1966. Tchr. Sci. Lincoln H.S., Camden, Ark., 1948—49; asst. prof. Math. So. U., Baton Rouge, 1955—57, Calif. State U. Long Beach, 1961—66; postdoctoral fellow U. Manitoba, Winnipeg, Canada, 1966—67; asst. prof. Math. York U., Toronto, Canada, 1967—70; assoc. prof. Math. Calif. State U., Rohnert Park, 1970—73, No. Ill. U., DeKalb, 1973—98, prof. emeritus, 1998—. Contbr. Avocations: opera, music, walking. Office: Northern Ill Univ DeKalb IL 60115

EWEN, H.I. physicist; b. Chicopee, Mass., Mar. 5, 1922; s. Arthur and Ruth Frances (Fay) E.; m. Mary Ann Whitney, Feb. 11, 1956; children: Donald, Jim, Bruce, Mark, David, Deborah, Daniel, Rebecca. BA, Amherst Coll., 1943; MA, Harvard U., 1948, PhD, 1951. Mem. faculty Amherst Coll., 1943; co-dir. Harvard Radio Astronomy Program, 1952-58, rsch. assoc. astronomy dept., 1958—80; v.p. Millitech Corp., South Deerfield, Mass., 1989-2000; rsch. prof. Sch. Engring. U. Mass., 2000—. Pres. Ewen Knight Corp., Weston, Mass., 1952-88, Ewen Dae Corp., 1958-88, E.K. Assocs., 1993—; sci. advisor to Cin. Electronics Corp. for USAF Air Weather Svc.; mem. Global Solar Radio Telescope Network, 1977-86. Contbg. author: Advances in Microwaves, vol. 5, 1970, Electromagnetic Sensing of the Earth from Satellites, 1967, Geoscience Instrumentation, 1974, also articles; co-discoverer 21 cm interstellar hydrogen line, 1951; remote sensing of atmospheric ozone distribution (resonant line at 102 GHz), 1966. Served to lt. USNR, 1943-46. NRC fellow, 1946-49; recipient svc. award Harvard Coll., 1977. Fellow AAAS (life), IEEE (Morris E. Leeds award 1970), Am. Acad. Arts and Scis.; mem. Am. Astron. Soc. (Tinsley prize 1988), Phi Beta Kappa, Sigma Xi.

EWERS, JAMES BENJAMIN, JR., director; b. Winston-Salem, N.C., Sept. 29, 1948; s. James Benjamin and Mildred (Holland) E.; m. Deborah Leufroy, Aug. 3, 1989; children: Courtney, Christopher, Aaron. BA, Johnson C. Smith U., 1970; MA, Cath. U. Am., 1971; EdD, U. Mass., 1981. Tchr. D.C. Pub. Schs., 1971-75; asst. dir. admissions Stockton State Coll., Pomona, N.J., 1976-78; dir. admissions and registration U. Md., Princess Anne, Md., 1978-83; v.p. student affairs Livingstone Coll., Salisbury, N.C., 1983-87, Dillard U., New Orleans, 1987-90, Savannah (Ga.) State U., 1990-94, assoc. exec. dir. for student affairs; active Middletown Red Cross, 1996—2000. Trustee Middletown Regional Hosp. Active Middletown Civil Svc. Commn., 1998—; bd. dirs., pres. YMCA, Middletown, 1996—; bd. dirs. Malachi, 1999—. Recipient Image award NAACP, 1998, Image award Applause Mag., 1999; named Hometown Hero Cin. Enquirer Newspaper, 1999. Mem. Nat. Assn. Student Personnel, Am. Assn. Higher Edn., Middletown Rotary (bd. dirs. 1998—), Alpha Phi Alpha, Phi Kappa Phi. Office: Miami U 4200 E University Blvd Middletown OH 45042

EWERS, PAUL JOSEPH, priest; b. Cin., Feb. 14, 1937; s. Paul Joseph Ewers, Sr. and Marie Margarete Rodenberg. Student, Verona Fathers' Coll., Monroe, Mich., 1957—61. Ordained priest Roman Cath. Ch., Milan, 1965. Assoc. and vocation dir. Comboni Mission Ctr., Yorkville, Ill., 1965—66; assoc. pastor Santa Ysabel (Calif.) Indian Mission, 1966—68, Comboni Missionaries, Esmeraldas, Ecuador, 1968—78, vocation and mission promotor Montclair, NJ, 1978—82, Monroe, Mich., 1982—88, assoc. pastor Quinindé, Ecuador, 1988—97, mission promotor Montclair, 1997—. Fundraiser Rocafuerte (Ecuador) Jr. H.S., 1970—73, English and religion tchr., 1971—73. Avocations: history, steam engines, solar energy, camping, computers. Home: PO Box 138 88 High St Montclair NJ 07042-0138 Office: Comboni Mission Ctr PO Box 138 88 High St Montclair NJ 07042-0138

EWICK, RAY (CHARLES RAY EWICK), librarian; b. Shelbyville, Ind., Sept. 13, 1937; s. Laurel R. and Loraine Pearl (Tufts) E.; m. Joann Hotchkiss, June 14, 1958; children— David Lee, Jeffrey Allen. BA, Wabash Coll., 1962; MA, Ind. U., 1966. Cons. Ind. State Library, Indpls., 1966-68, asst. dir., 1968-72, dir., 1978—. Dir. Rolling Prairie Libraries, Decatur, Ill., 1972-78 Mem. ALA, Ind. Library Assn., Phi Beta Mu. Office: Ind State Library 140 N Senate Ave Indianapolis IN 46204-2296

EWIN, DABNEY MINOR, surgeon; b. New Orleans, Dec. 7, 1925; s. James Perkins and Lucille Havard (Scott) E.; m. Ethelyn Alexander Sherrouse, June 6, 1951 (div. 1968); children: Dabney Jr., Constance, Walton, Christopher, Leila; m. Marilyn Allison Abernathy, June 29, 1968. MD, Tulane U., 1951. Intern Jefferson-Hillman Hosp. U. Ala., Birmingham, 1951, resident, 1951-54, Ochsner Found. Hosp., New Orleans, 1954-56; chief resident Huey P. Long Charity Hosp., Pineville, La., 1956-57; pvt. practice, 1957—. Staff surgeon Touro Infirmary, New Orleans, East Jefferson Gen. Hosp., Metairie, La., Charity Hosp. La.; clin. prof. surgery and psychiatry Tulane Med. Sch.; clin. prof. psychiatry La. State U. Contbr. articles to profl. jours. Bd. dirs. Christ Sch., 1979-85; sr. class Sunday sch. tchr. Trinity Episc. Ch., 1960-66. Fellow ACS; mem. AMA, Am. Trauma Soc. (dir. 1975-79), Am. Burn Assn., Am. Coll. Occup. and Environ. Medicine (spkr. Ho. of Dels., 1973-75), Am. Bd. Med. Hypnosis (past pres.), Am. Soc. Clin. Hypnosis (past pres.), La. State Med. Soc., Orleans Parish Med. Soc., Surg. Assn. La., New Orleans Surg. Soc., Alton Ochsner Surg. Soc. (past sec.), So. Med. Assn. (chmn. sect. on indsl. medicine and surgery 1966-67), Soc. for Clin. and Exptl. Hypnosis, La. Psychiat. Med. Assn. Republican. Avocations: fishing, tennis. Office: 318 Baronne St New Orleans LA 70112-1606

EWIN, GORDON OVERTON, retired lawyer, farmer; b. New Orleans, June 1, 1923; s. James Perkins and Lucille Havard (Scott) E.; m. Katharine Elise Keller, Sept. 6, 1947; 1 dau., Katharine Adair. BA, Tulane U., 1943, JD, 1948; postgrad. Faculté de Droit, U. Paris, 1948-49. Bar: La. 1948, U.S. Dist. Ct. (ea. dist.) La. 1949, U.S. Ct. Appeals (5th cir.) 1949. Assoc. Milling, Saal, Saunders, Benson & Woodward, New Orleans, 1949-52; ptnr. Ewin & Robertson, New Orleans, 1952-55; staff atty. Humble Oil & Refining Co., New Orleans, 1955-59; ptnr. Chaffe, McCall, Phillips, Toler & Sarpy, New Orleans, 1959-93; pres. Greenwood Planting Co., 1979-89; ptnr. Green Field Farms, 1984-91; bd. dirs. Prodrs. Mut. Gin, Greenwood Plantation LLC. Active Young Life Adv. Coun., 1972; vestryman Trinity Ch. 1976-80; bd. dirs. New Orleans Philharm. Orch., 1961, Garden Dist. Assn., 1967-74, pres., 1973-74; bd. dirs. Friends of the Cabildo, 1976-82, pres., 1981-82. Lt. (j.g.) USNR, 1943-46; PTO. Mem. New Orleans Bar Assn. (treas.), La. Bar Assn., La. Club, Boston Club, Soc. Colonial Wars (past La. gov.). Episcopalian. Home: Greenwood Plantation PO Box 403 Cheneyville LA 71325-0403

EWING, BENJAMIN BAUGH, environmental engineering educator, consultant; b. Donna, Tex., Apr. 4, 1924; s. Joshua Fulkerson and Bula Betty (Baugh) E.; m. Elizabeth Malone, Apr. 3, 1947; children: Melissa, Douglas Malone, Frederick Joshua. BS, U. Tex., Austin, 1944, MS, 1949; PhD, U. Calif. at Berkeley, 1959. Diplomate: Am. Acad. Environ. Engrs. Instr., asst. prof. U. Tex., Austin, 1947-55; assoc. in civil engring., asst. research engr. U. Calif. at Berkeley, 1955-58; assoc. prof., prof. U. Ill., Urbana, 1958-85, prof. emeritus, 1985—, dir. Water Resource Center, 1966-73, dir. Inst. for Environ. Studies, 1972-85, dir. emeritus, 1985—. Cons. engr., 1959— Research and publs. in water quality mgmt. and pollution control, water treatment, wastewater treatment, water resources mgmt. Trustee Urbana and Champaign San. Dist., 1974-80; public mem. Ill. Water Resources Commn., 1975-84. Served to lt. (j.g.) CEC. USNR, 1943-46. Recipient Epstein award dept. civil engring. U. Ill., 1961, Harrison Prescott Eddy award for noteworthy research, 1968 Fellow ASCE; mem. Am. Water Works Assn. (life), Water Environment Fedn. (life), Assn. Environ. Engring. Profs. Emeritus. Home: 4374 Cedar Pl Lummi Island WA 98262-8672

EWING, BLAIR GORDON, federal official; b. Kansas City, Mo., Dec. 3, 1933; s. Lynn Moore and Margaret (Blair) E.; m. Barbara F. Thompson, Jan. 3, 1959 (div. Nov. 1991); children: Blair Gordon, Chatham Boyd; m. Martha L. Brockway, Apr. 30, 1994. AB, U. Mo., 1954; postgrad., U. Bonn, Germany, 1957-58; AM, U. Chgo., 1960. Reporter Chgo. City News Bur., 1958-59, UPI, 1959-60, Traffic World Mag., 1960-61; instr. polit. sci. Chgo. City Jr. Coll., 1961-62, SUNY, Binghamton, 1962-67; planning and mgmt. cons. Harold Wise and Assocs., Washington, 1967-69; program analyst Office of Asst. Sec. HEW, Washington, 1969-70; dir. criminal justice planning D.C. Govt., 1970-72; dir. dept. pub. safety Met. Washington Coun. Govts., 1972-74; dir. planning and evaluation divsn. U.S. Dept. Justice, Washington, 1974-78; dep. dir. Nat. Inst. Law Enforcement and Criminal Justice Dept. Justice, 1976—. Acting dir., 1977-79; asst. dir. U.S. Office Pers. Mgmt., Washington, 1979-81, dep. dir., 1981-83; sr. exec. U.S. Office Mgmt. and Budget, 1983-86; dir. Mgmt. Improvement, Dept. Def., 1986-98; adj. prof. Law Ctr., Georgetown U., 1971-74. Author: Peace Through Negotiation: The Austrian State Treaty, 1966; contbr. articles to profl. jours. Mem. Montgomery County (Md.) Human Rels. Commn., 1975-76; mem. Montgomery County Bd. Edn., 1976-98, pres., 1982-83, 90-91; elected mem. coun. Montgomery County, 1998-2002 pres., 2000-01. With U.S. Army, 1954-56. Recipient Disting. Svc. award Office Pers. Mgmt., 1981, U.S. Dept. Def. Disting. Civil Svc. award, 1990, Presdl. Rank award Meritorious Sr. Exec., 1990; Rotary Found. fellow U. Bonn, 1957-58; Woodrow Wilson fellow, 1956-57. Mem. Phi Beta Kappa. Democrat. Home: 3 Park Valley Rd Silver Spring MD 20910-5424 Office: Montgomery County Coun 100 Maryland Ave Rockville MD 20850-2322

EWING, DAVID CHARLES, automobile dealership executive; b. Canton, Ohio, Sept. 27, 1942; s. Stanley Clement; m. Penni Lynn West, Sept. 10, 1966; 1 child, Amy Lynn. BSBA, Bowling Green State U., 1964; MBA, Western Res. U., 1966. 1st lt. USAR, 1966-72; mgr. truck sales Ewing Chevrolet, Canton, 1966-72, mgr. lease sales, 1972-75, mgr. new car sales, 1975-81, gen. mgr., 1981-88; owner, pres. Ewing Chevrolet, Inc., Canton, Ohio, 1988—. Trustee Malone Coll., Canton, 1979-90; chmn. adminstrv. bd. Ch. of Savior, United Meth. Ch., 1989-92, chmn. found., 1992-97; trustee Ohio and Erie Canal Corridor Coalition. Mem. Greater Canton C. of C., Nat. Automobile Dealers Assn., Ohio Automobile Dealers Assn. (trustee), Stark County Automobile Dealers Assn. (past pres.), Antique Automobile Club Am. (life), Brookside Country Club, Rotary (pres. Canton 1989-90, dist. 6650 gov. 1996-97), Glenmoor Country Club, Elks, Vintage Chevrolet Club of Am. (life), Alpha Tau Omega. Republican. Home: 2545 Glenmont Rd NW Canton OH 44708-1341 Office: Ewing Chevrolet Inc 929 Cleveland Ave NW Canton OH 44702-1895 E-mail: dce1914@aol.com.

EWING, EDGAR LOUIS, artist, educator; b. Hartington, Nebr., Jan. 17, 1913; s. David E. and Laura (Buckendorf) E.; m. Suzanna Peter Giovan, Feb. 12, 1941. Grad., Art Inst. Chgo., 1935; studied in France, Eng., Italy, 1935-37. Mem. faculty Art Inst. Chgo., 1937-43, U. Mich., Ann Arbor, 1946; asst. prof. fine arts U. So. Calif., 1946-54, assoc. prof., 1954-59, prof., 1959-78, Disting. prof. emeritus, 1978—; Mellon prof. Carnegie-Mellon U., Pitts., 1968-69. One-man shows M.H. DeYoung Meml. Mus. Art, San Francisco, 1948, Santa Barbara Mus. of Art, 1952, Long Beach Mus. Art, 1955, Dalzell Hatfield Galleries, Los Angeles, 1954, 56, 58, 61, 63, 65, Hewlett Gallery-Carnegie Mellon U., Pitts., 1969, Nat. Gallery, Athens, Greece, 1973, Los Angeles Mcpl. Art Gallery, 1974, Palm Springs (Calif.) Desert Mus., 1976-77, Fisher Gallery U. So. Calif., 1978, Fisher Gallery, U. So. Calif., 1993-94; group exhbns. Cin Art Mus., Corcoran Gallery Art, Washington, Denver Art Mus., Dallas Mus. Fine Arts, Fort Worth Art Ctr., Met. Mus., N.Y.C.; represented: San Francisco Mus. Art, Dallas Mus. Fine Arts, Ft. Worth Art Ctr., Met. Mus., N.Y.C., Sao Paulo (Brazil) Mus. Art, Wichita Art Mus., Fisher Gallery, U. So. Calif., 1994. Served with C.E., U.S. Army, 1943-46, PTO. Recipient Aberle Florscheim Meml. prize for Oil Painting, Art Inst. Chgo., 1943, Purchase award for oil painting Los Angeles County Mus. Art, 1952, Samuel Goldwyn award, 1957, Ahmanson Purchase award City of Los Angeles Exhbn., 1962, Disting. Prof. Emeritus award U. So. Calif., 1987; Edward L. Ryerson fellow, 1935; Louis Comfort Tiffany grantee, 1948-49, Jose Drudis Fund grantee, Greece, 1967; named one of 100 Artists-100 Yrs., Art Inst. Chgo., 1980. Mem. AAUP, Nat. Watercolor Soc. (v.p. 1952, pres. 1953) Democrat.

EWING, ELISABETH ANNE ROONEY, priest; b. San Bernardino, Calif. m. James E. Ewing. Student, Mt. San Antonio Coll., 1978. Ordained priest Communion Evang. Episcopal Ch., 1998, ordained to ministry Meth. Ch. Pastor, gen. overseers, CEO St. Matthew's Nationwide Chs., N.Y.C. Mem. Rand Rsch. Corp.; mem. diplomat cir. L.A. World Affairs Coun. Co-editor: (book) Church History, 1996—98, The Church Visible, 1996—98, Life After Death, 1996—98, Bible Lessons, 1996—98; head pub. rels., assoc. editor Pinnacle Today Internat. Mag.; assoc. editor: St. Matthew Tribune. Recipient St. Augustine cross, Archbishop of Canterbury. Mem.: Knights of Malta (dame).

EWING, FRANK MARION, lumber company executive, industrial land developer; b. Albany, Ga., Apr. 24, 1915; s. Frank Marion and Alpharetta (Tucker) E.; m. Hanna Anderson, June 15, 1935; children: Grace Marit (Mrs. Paul Atherton), Linda Tucker (Mrs. Richard R. Mace), Frances Marion (Mrs. Brian Tennery); m. Jo Anne Bacon Hilley, Mar. 12, 1964; children: (adopted) Kathleen Melinda, Wayne Edgar, Andrew L.; m. Marilyn Hassett Petrie, Mar. 2, 1973; m. Judith H. Viets, July 24, 1999. BA (Sereno Gaylord scholar), Yale U., 1936. Pres., chmn. bd. Frank M. Ewing Co., Inc., Washington, 1937—, Lumber Distbn. Co., Petersburg, Va., 1942-57; Pres., chmn. bd. Ewing Lumber & Millwork Corp., Beltsville, Md., 1958-71; chmn. bd. Kettler Bros. Inc., Gaithersburg, Md., 1965-88; developer Beltsville Indsl. Center, 1950-89. Bd. dirs. Washington Mut. Investors Fund.; mem. industry adv. com. WPB, 1942-46; industry adv. com. to sec. commerce, 1947-50, dep. and later acting asst. sec. def., 1955-56; mem. bd. Met. Washington Bd. Trade, 1957-61 Gen. campaign chmn. Prince Georges Community Chest, 1955; bd. dirs. Childrens Hosp., Washington. Mem. Prince Georges C. of C. (pres. 1956-57) Clubs: Kiwanian (bd. dirs. Prince Georges 1948-52), Mason., Chevy Chase, Metropolitan, Burning Tree (Washington); St. Andrew's Royal and Ancient Golf (Scotland), Tryall Club (Jamaica). Home: 5610 Wisconsin Ave PH 20C Chevy Chase MD 20815-4415 Office: 5610 Wisconsin Ave PH20C Chevy Chase MD 20815-4415

EWING, GUIN PORTER, historian, art collector; b. Albuquerque, Sept. 20, 1921; s. G. Porter and Rose Betty (Ellersdorfer) Ewing. BA, UCLA, 1943, MEd, 1950, MA, 1954, CPhil, 1963. Tchr. Inglewood (Calif.) H.S., 1947-50; prof. L.A. City Coll., 1955-2001; instr. UCLA Extension, 1958-70, Calif. State U., Dominguez Hills, 1968-69. Fulbright lectr., Denmark, 1960—61. With1946 U.S. Army, 1942. Mem.: Am. Fedn. Tchrs. Home: 7510 Amestoy Ave Van Nuys CA 91406

EWING, JACK, communications executive; b. Chgo., Jan. 21, 1945; s. John Cullen and Irene Leone (Roeder) E.; m. Sharon Jean Tomlinson, Oct. 13, 1973. BA in English, Parsons Coll., 1966; MA in English, SUNY, Oswego, 1970. Cert. tchr., N.Y., Mont. Copy chief, pub. svc. dir. Wolf Radio, Syracuse, N.Y., 1970-73; copywriter Silverman and Mower Advt., Syracuse, 1973-74; pres. Mr. E Enterprises, Syracuse, 1974-77; copy chief PJ&L Advt., Syracuse, 1977-80; creative dir. BBW Advt., Boise, Idaho, 1980-82, WRC Advt., Boise, 1986, 92-95; pres. Ewing Concepts and Copy, Boise, 1982-92, 95—. Author: A Freshman's Confessions, 1962, Soft More, College Stud, 1963, Freak-out, 1998, Kissing Asphalt, 2000; editor: Lite 'N Up, 1996; author numerous poems, short stories, articles. Recipient Essay Contest award Syracuse Newspapers, 1973, others. Mem. Log Cabin Lit. Ctr. Avocations: reading, stamp and coin collecting, music, archaeology, cross-country skiing. Office: Ewing Concepts and Copy PO Box 571 Boise ID 83701-0571 E-mail: citizenew@aol.com.

EWING, JACK ROBERT, accountant; b. San Francisco, Feb. 14, 1947; s. Robert Maxwell and Blanche Julia (Diak) E.; m. Joan Marie Coughlin Ewing, Nov. 25, 1967; children: Theresa Marie Ewing, Christina Ann Ewing. BS, U. Mo., 1969. CPA. Staff acct. Fox & Co., St. Louis, 1969-70; radio station opr. USAF, Mountain Home, Idaho, 1970-72; internal auditor Air Force Audit Agy., Warren, Wyo., 1972-74; supr. auditor Fox & Co., St. Louis, 1974-79; audit mgr. Erickson, Hunt & Spillman, P.C., Ft. Collins, Colo., 1979-82; stockholder, owner Hunt, Spillman & Ewing, P.C., Ft. Collins, Colo., 1982-93; owner Jack R. Ewing, CPA, 1993—. Mem., pres. Parent Adv. Bd., Beattie Elem. Sch., 1982-83, 86-87; mem. Entrepreneur of Yr. Selection Com., Ft. Collins, Colo., 1989-92, Suicide Resource Ctr. of Larimer County, Ft. Collins, Colo., 1992—, pres., 1998—, bd. dirs.; mem. Leadership Ft. Collins-Class of 1992, State of Colo. Mental Health Planning Coun., 1993—; dir. treas. One West Contemporary Art Ctr., 1989-97—, Ctr. for Diversity in Work Place, 1991—; pres., adv. bd. Larimer County Bd. Mental Health, 1992-99; v.p. Colo. Behavioral Healthcare Coun., 1995-97; mem. mental health pro bono project, 1996-97; mem. gov.'s citizen panel on suicide prevention, 1998—; indicators and outcomes com. Mental Health Performance; planning steering com. Mental Health and Substance Abuse. Mem. Am. Inst. CPAs, Colo. Soc. CPAs. Avocations: writing, hiking. Office: 3112 Meadowlark Ave Fort Collins CO 80526-2843

EWING, JAMES E. priest; m. Elisabeth Anne Rooney. DD, ThD. Ordained priest Communion Evang. Episcopal Chs., 1951. Sr. pastor, gen. overseer, pres. bd. govs. and counselors St. Matthew's Nationwide Chs., N.Y.C., 1951—. Mem. Rand Rsch. Corp.; mem. diplomat cir. L.A. World Affairs Coun. Co-author, editor: book Church History, The Church Visible, Life After Death, Bible Lessons, pub., editor, author: Pinnacle Today. With USAF, 1953—57. Recipient St. Augustine cross, Archbishop of Canterbury. Mem.: Sovereign Order St. John of Jerusalem, Knights of Malta.

EWING, JOHN HARWOOD, mathematics educator; b. Bronxville, N.Y., Nov. 25, 1944; s. Robert Edward and Virginia (Harwood) E.; m. Janice Rusche, May 22, 1965; children: Scott Andrew, Jennifer Beth, Amy Sarah. BS, St. Lawrence U., Canton, N.Y., 1966; MS, PhD, Brown U., 1971; DS (hon.), St. Lawrence U., 1996. Instr. Dartmouth Coll., Hanover, N.H., 1971-73; asst. prof., assoc. prof. math. Ind. U., Bloomington, 1973, prof., chmn. dept., 1986-89, 92-95; exec. dir. Am. Math. Soc., Providence, 1995—. Sci. and Engring. rsch. Coun. fellow U. Newcastle, Eng., 1980-81; Sonderforschungsbereicht fellow U. Goettingen, Germany, 1985-86; series editor Springer-Verlag, N.Y.C., 1987-95. Author: Puzzle It Out, 1981; editor: Numbers, 1990, Celebrating 50 Years of Mathematics, 1991, A Century of Mathematics, 1994, Towards Excellence, 1999; editor-in-chief Math. Intelligencer, 1980-86, Am. Math. Monthly, 1992-96; also over 40 articles. Mem. AAAS, Am. Math. Soc., Math. Assn. Am. (Lester R. Ford award 1976, George Polya lectr. 1991-92, Polya award 1996). Episcopalian. Office: Am Math Soc 201 Charles St Providence RI 02904 E-mail: jhe@ams.org.

EWING, JOSEPH GRAHAM, family practice physician; b. Grand Junction, Colo., Mar. 29, 1942; s. Eugene Graham and Elizabeth (Brown) E.; m. Dena Louise, June 26, 1992; three children. BS, U. Nebr., 1965; MD, U. Nebr. Coll. Medicine, 1973. Intern U.S. Navy, Oakland, Calif., 1973-74, med. officer Alameda, Calif., 1974-75; pvt. practice Coronado, Calif., 1975-92; faculty U. Wyo., Cheyenne, 1992-95; residency program dir. U. Tex. Med. Br., Conroe, Tex., 1995—; pres. Conroe Med. Edn. Found., 2001—. Office: Conroe FP Residency 704 Old Montgomery Rd Conroe TX 77301 Office Fax: 936-539-3635. Business E-Mail: jgewing@lonestarfamily.org. E-mail: josephgewing@cs.com.

EWING, JOSEPH NEFF, JR., retired lawyer; b. Bryn Mawr, Pa., Nov. 10, 1925; s. Joseph Neff and Anne (Ashton) E.; m. Margaret Converse Howe, Dec. 22, 1951; children: Margaret E. Lloyd, Anne A., Elizabeth M. Peifer AB, Princeton U., 1947; JD, U. Pa., 1953. Bar: Pa. 1954, U.S. Tax Ct. 1992, U.S. Supreme Ct. 1978. Assoc. Saul, Ewing, Remick & Saul, Phila., 1953-63, ptnr., 1963-95, of counsel, 1996—. Bd. govs. Main Line Health, Inc., 1988-95; trustee The Bryn Mawr Hosp., 1969-96, Bryn Mawr Hosp. Found., 1981-98, Hist. Sugartown, Inc., Malvern, Pa., 1990-98; trustee Dunwoody Village, Inc., 1997--, 2d vice chmn. 1999-2003, 1st vice chmn., 2003--; chancellor Clan Ewing in Am., 1998—. Chmn. Willistown Twp. Planning Commn., Malvern, 1960-69, chmn. bd. suprs., 1970-82, chmn. zoning hearing bd., 1985-95, East Goshen Twp., chmn. Zoning Hearing Bd., 1996—; pres. bd. trustees Embreeville (Pa.) State Hosp., 1965-72, chmn. spl. contacts divsn. Phila. United Fund, 1965-66; mem. hosp. coun. Mental Health Assn., Southeastern Pa., Phila., 1967-68; elder Paoli (Pa.) Presbyn. Ch., 1970-72. Mem. ABA, Phila. Bar Assn. (med.-legal com. 1962-76, chmn. 1971), Phila. Assn. Def. Counsel (pres. 1973), Nat. Assn. R.R. Trial Counsel, Pa. Soc. Healthcare Attys. (pres. 1975-77), Waynesborough Country Club (v.p. 1965-69), Hershey's Mill Golf Club. Avocations: sailing, photography, gardening, genealogy. Home: 1109 Lincoln Dr West Chester PA 19380-5721

EWING, KY PEPPER, JR., lawyer; b. Victoria, Tex., Jan. 7, 1935; s. Ky Pepper and Sallie (Dixon) E.; m. Almuth Rott, Apr. 6, 1963; children: Kenneth Patrick, Kevin Andrew, Kathryn Diana. BA cum laude, Baylor U., 1956; LLB cum laude, Harvard U., 1959. Bar: D.C. 1959, U.S. Supreme Ct 1963. Assoc. firm Covington & Burling, Washington, 1959-64; partner firm Prather, Seeger, Doolittle, Farmer & Ewing, Washington, 1964-77; dep. asst. atty. gen. antitrust div. Dept. Justice, Washington, 1978-80; ptnr. Vinson & Elkins, Washington, 1980—2001, of counsel, 2002—. Mem. Washington Inst. Fgn. Affairs. Author: Competition Rules for the 21st Century: Principles from America's Experience, 2003; co-editor-in-chief: State Antitrust Practice and Statutes, 3 Vols., 1990; mem. antitrust adv. bd. Antitrust and Trade Regulation Report Bur. Nat. Affairs, 1990—; mem. edit. bd. Antitrust Report Matthew Bender & Co., 1993—. Pres. Potomac Valley League, 1977, Carderock Springs Citizens Assn., 1975-78. Fellow: Am. Bar Found. (life); mem.: ABA (chmn. legis. com. antitrust sect. 1987—91, coun. antitrust sect. 1991—94, fin. officer antitrust sect. 1994—96, chmn. FTC/Dept. Justice working group 1994—97, mem. Ho. of Dels. 1996—98, vice chair antitrust sect. 1998—99, chair-elect antitrust sect. 1999—2000, chair antitrust sect. 2000—01, chmn. nominating com. antitrust sect. 2002—03), D.C. Bar Assn., Inter-Am. Bar Assn., Internat. Bar Assn. (editl. bd. Bus. Law Internat.), Am. Soc. Internat. Law, Met. Club. Democrat. Episcopalian. Home: 8317 Comanche Ct Bethesda MD 20817-4561 Office: Vinson & Elkins 1455 Pennsylvania Ave NW Washington DC 20004-1013 E-mail: kewing@velaw.com.

EWING, MARILYN, English educator; b. Rochester, N.H., Oct. 19, 1940; d. Thomas Kirby and Ida Maryann (Scala) McKee; m. Richard Edwin Ewing, June 29, 1963 (div. Nov. 1974); 1 child, Julie E. BA cum laude, U. N.H., 1962; MA, U. No. Colo., 1974; PhD, U. Colo., 1982. Tchr. Portsmouth (N.H.) H.S., 1962-63, Green Springs (Ohio) Local Sch., 1964-66; tchg. asst. U. No. Colo., Greeley, 1973-77; tchg. asst., part-time instr. U. Colo., Boulder, 1977-82; from asst. prof. to assoc. prof. English, Eastern Oreg. U., La Grande, 1982—. Translator poems by Pablo Neruda, Colo.-North Rev., 1976; columnist The Longmont (Colo.) Ledger, 1971; author essays and article. Recipient Svc. award Oreg. Women in Higher Edn., 1999. Mem. NOW, MLA, Nat. Coun. Tchrs. English, Oreg. Writing Project (mem. steering com. 1994—), Lambda Pi. Office: Eastern Oreg U 1 University Blvd La Grande OR 97850-2807

EWING, MARTIN S. astronomer, electrical engineer; b. Albany, N.Y., May 4, 1945; s. Galen Wood and Alice (Sipple) E.; m. Eva Reissner, June 11, 1966; children: Margaret, Robert, Eric. BA, Swarthmore Coll., 1966; PhD, MIT, 1971. Mem. prof. staff Calif. Inst. Tech., Pasadena, 1971-89; vis. assoc. CSIRO Div. Radiophysics, Sydney, Australia, 1985-86; dir. sci. and engring. computing facility Yale U., New Haven, 1989-98, dir. info. tech., faculty engring., 1998—2002. Author: Forth Manuel D'Application, 1984; contbr. articles to profl. jours. Mem. AAAS, Am. Astron. Soc., Am. Soc. Engring. Edn., Internat. Union Radio Sci. Avocations: writing, amateur radio. E-mail: ewing@alum.mit.edu.

EWING, MARY, lawyer; b. Shreveport, La., Feb. 21, 1948; d. George and Christine (Cocek) Hengy; m. Robert Craig Ewing, Aug. 30, 1981; 1 child, Kyle Ross. BA, U. Colo., 1972; JD, U. Denver, 1975. Bar: Colo. 1975, U.S. Supreme Ct. 1979. Assoc. Johnson & Mahoney, Denver, 1975-80; ptnr. Branney, Hillyard, Ewing & Barnes, Englewood, Colo., 1980-85, Bucholtz, Bull & Ewing, Denver, 1985-96, Ewing & Ewing PC, Englewood, Colo., 1996—. Asst. prof. law U. Denver, 1977-78, part time prof. 1978—; mem. faculty Nat. Inst. Trial Advocacy, 1984-89; instr. nat. session 1984, 85, 87, Nat. Bd. Trial Advocacy, regional session, 1984-89; bd. trustees Lowell Whiteman Sch., Steamboat Springs, Colo., 2001—. Chmn. Denver County Task Force, 1976—77, mem., 1990; treas. Cen. Com. 1st Congl. Dist., 1976—77; v.p. Young Rep. League Denver, 1975, pres., 1976; mem. govt. rels. com. Jr. Symphony Guild, 1978—; mem. legal com. County Horse Assn., 1990—; mem. bd. trustee The Lowell Whiteman Sch., Steamboat Springs, Colo., 2000—; mem. capital campaign com. Denver Dumb Friends League; bd. dirs. Steamboat Springs Arts Coun., Emerald City Opera Guild, 2003. Mem. ABA, Colo. Bar Assn. (ethics com.), Denver Bar Assn. (vice chmn. new lawyers assistance com. 1977), Colo. Women's Bar Assn., Rocky Mountain Dressage Soc. (sec. High Plains chpt. 1979-80, chmn. constn. and by-laws com. 1988—), Assn. Trial Lawyers Am., Colo. Trial Lawyers Assn. (bd. govs., chmn. interprofl. com. 1980—, bd. dirs. polit. action com. 1989—, exec. bd. 2000—), Douglas County Bar Assn., Am. Arbitration Assn., Nat. Bd. Trial Advocacy (cert. 1983), Yellowstone Assn. (bd. dirs. 2003—), Am. Trakehner Assn., Rocky Mountain Trakehner Assn. (v.p. 1987), Arapahoe Hunt Club, Greenwood Athletic Club, Kappa Beta Pi (pres. 1977-78). Home: Nonesuch Farm 4256 S Perry Park Rd Sedalia CO 80135-8207 Address: 3601 S Pennsylvania St Englewood CO 80110-3753 E-mail: MaryEwingEsq@aol.com.

EWING, MARY EILEEN, radiologic technologist; b. Morning Sun, Iowa, Aug. 26, 1926; d. Frank Leeman and Myrtle Marguerite (Mehaffy) Steele; m. Dean Willard Ewing, Mar. 29, 1952; children: John, Eileen, Diane, Denise. BS in Radiologic Tech., St. Louis U., 1948. Registered technologist. Staff technologist Mo. Pacific Hosp., St. Louis, 1948-52, Blanchard Valley Hosp., Findlay, Ohio, 1968-69, asst. chief technologist, 1969-80, asst. dir. dept., 1980-90. Clin. instr. Lima (Ohio) Tech. Coll., 1978-90; sec. N.W. Libr. Dist. Exec. Bd., 1988-97. Trustee McComb (Ohio) Pub. Libr., 1957-2002; pres. Libr. Bd., McComb, 1967-2002; elder ck. of session, 1994—. Mem.: Nat. Soc. DAR (Ft. Findlay chpt. sec. 1993—94, regent 1995—2001), Mansfield China Painters, Internat. Porcelain Artists and Tchrs. (treas. 2002—), Mansfield World Orgn. China Painters (pres. 2000—01), Philomath Club (pres. 1958, 1995—98). Democrat. Presbyterian. Avocations: porcelain painting, reading, genealogy, bridge, pinochle clubs. Home: 103 W South St Mc Comb OH 45858 E-mail: dwewing@bright.net.

EWING, MICHAEL SNYDER, producer, film company executive; b. Kalamazoo, Mich., Mar. 29, 1960; s. Robert Earl and Juan Marie Snyder. Student, We. Mich. U., 1979, Am. Acad. Dramatic Arts, N.Y.C., 1980, Stella Adler Conservatory, 1979-81, Actors Studio, 1981, Stella Adler Conservatory, 1980-84. Theater dir., co-prodr., L.A., 1985, N.Y.C., 1986-87; asst. to prodr. Paramount Pictures, L.A., 1988, asst. prodr., 1989-90, assoc. prodr., 1991-95; co-prodr. Warner Bros., 1995-96; pres. Greenhaven Films, L.A., 1995—2001; pres. Greenhaven Films Sony Pictures Corp., Culver City, Calif., 2001—. Dir., co-prodr. (plays) World Premiere, Tigers Wild, L.A., 1985, N.Y.C., 1986-87; asst. to prodr. (film) The Naked Gun: From the Files of Police Squad, 1988; asst. prodr.: (film) Nothing But Trouble, 1990, Crazy People; assoc. prodr.: Naked Gun 2-1/2: The Smell of Fear, 1991, Naked Gun 33 1/3: The Final Insult, 1993, Tommy Boy, 1994; co-prodr.: (film) My Fellow Americans, 1996, Nutty Professor 2, 1999, Anger Management, 2003; exec. prodr. 50 First Kisses, 2003. Office: Callahan Filmworks/Sony Pictures Corp Hedy Lamarr Bldg 10202 W Washington Blvd Culver City CA 90232

EWING, PATRICK ALOYSIUS, professional basketball coach; b. Kingston, Jamaica, Aug. 5, 1962; m. Rita Ewing; children: Patrick Aloysius, Randi. BFA, Georgetown U., 1985. Basketball player N.Y. Knickerbockers, N.Y.C., 1985—2000, Seattle SuperSonics, 2000—01, Orlando Magic, Fla., 2001—02; asst. coach Washington Wizards, 2002—. Mem. U.S. Olympic Basketball Teams, 1984, 92. Named Divsn. I Most Outstanding Player, NCAA, 1984, Coll. Player of Yr., Sporting News, 1985, 1985, Rookie of Yr., NBA, 1986; named to All-Am. 1st team, Sporting News, 1985, All-Star team, 1986, 1988—93, All-Am. 2d team, 1983—84, NBA All-Star team, 1986—95, All-NBA 2d team, 1988, All-Defensive 2d team, 1988, 1989, All-NBA 2d team, 1989, All-NBA 1st team, 1990, All-NBA 2d team, 1991, All-Defensive 2d team, 1992, All-NBA 2d team, 1992; recipient Naismith award, 1985, Gold medal, U.S. Olympic Basketball Team. Achievements include being a player in NCAA divsn. I championship team, 1984; being a holder of NBA Finals series record for most blocked shots (30), 1994; being co-holder of NBA finals single-game record most block shots (8), 1994. Office: Washington Wizards 601 F St NW Washington DC 20004

EWING, RAYMOND CHARLES, retired ambassador; b. Cleve., Sept. 7, 1936; s. Thomas Davis and Marion (Andrews) E.; m. Jerelyn Patten, Jan. 19, 1962; children: Gregory, Thomas, Joyce, Lillian Patten. BA, Occidental Coll., 1957; MPA, Harvard U., 1970. Joined Fgn. Svc., Dept. State, 1957; various assignments in Washington, Bern, Switzerland, Rome, Lahore, Pakistan, Vienna, Tokyo, 1957-1977; dir. Office So. European Affairs, Dept. State, Washington, 1977-79; mem. Sr. Seminar, Washington, 1979-80; dep. asst. sec. of state for European affairs, 1980-81; amb. to Cyprus, 1981-84; dean Sch. Lang. Studies Fgn. Svc. Inst., Washington, 1985-87; dir. Office Career Devel. and Assignments, Dept. State, 1987-89; amb. to Ghana, 1989-92; chargé d'affaires, a.i. to Tanzania, 1992; ret., 1993; mng. editor Mediterranean Quarterly, Washington, 1994—. Mem. Am. Fgn. Svc. Assn., Diplomatic and Consular Officers (ret.), Cyprus Am. Archaeol. Rsch. Inst. (bd. mem. 2000). Presbyterian. Avocations: tennis, golf, travel, reading.

EWING, RAYMOND PEYTON, educator, author, management consultant; b. Hannibal, Mo., July 31, 1925; s. Larama Angelo and Winona Fern (Adams) E.; m. Audrey Jane Schulze, May 7, 1949; 1 child, Jane Ann. AA, Hannibal La-Grange Coll., 1948; BA, William Jewell Coll., 1949; MA in Humanities, U. Chgo., 1950. Sr. editor Commerce Clearing House, Chgo., 1952-60; dir. corp. communications Allstate Ins. Cos. & Allstate Enterprises, Northbrook, Ill., 1960-85, dir. issues mgmt., 1979-85; pres. Issues Mgmt. Cons. Group, 1985—; assoc. prof., founding dir. grad. corp. pub. rels. program Medill Sch. Journalism Northwestern U., Evanston, Ill., 1986-89, prof., 1989-90; vis. prof., 1990-91. Pub. rels. dir. Chicago Mag., 1966-67, book columnist, 1968-70; staff Book News Commentator, Sta. WRSV, Skokie, Ill., 1962-70. Author: Mark Twain's Steamboat Years, 1981, Managing the New Bottom Line, 1987, Handbook of Communications in Corporate Restructuring and Takeovers, 1992; contbr. articles to mags. Mem. Winnetka (Ill.) Libr. Bd., 1969-70; pres. Skokie Valley United Crusade, 1964-65; bd. dirs. Suburban Community Chest Coun., Onward Neighborhood House, Chgo.; mem. House Commerce Com., Pvt. Sector Foresight Task Force, 1982-83. Served with AUS, 1943-46, ETO. Mem. Pub. Rels. Soc. of Am. (accredited; Silver Anvil awards for pub. affairs, 1970, 72, for fin. rels. 1970, for bus. spl. events 1976, chmn. nat. pub. affairs sect. 1984), Publicity Club of Chgo. (v.p. 1967, bd. dirs. 1966-68; Golden Trumpet award for pub. affairs, 1969, 70, 72, 79, for fin. rels. 1970), Insurers Pub. Rels. Coun. (pres. 1980-81), Issues Mgmt. Assn. (founder, pres. 1981-83, chmn. 1983-84, Disting. Profl. Contbns. award 1994), Internat. Sculpture Ctr., Mensa, World Future Soc., U.S. C. of C. (trends and perspective coun.), Chgo. Poets and Writers Found. (pub. rels. dir. 1966-67), Union League (Chgo.), Internat. Sculpture Ctr. Home: 316 Richmond Rd Kenilworth IL 60043-1139

EWING, RICHARD EDWARD, mathematics, chemical and petroleum engineering educator; b. Kingsville, Tex., Nov. 24, 1946; s. Floyd Ford and Olivia Clara (Henrichson) E.; m. Rita Louise Williams, Aug. 8, 1970; children: John Edward, Lawrence Alan, Bradley William. BA, U. Tex., 1969, MA, 1972, PhD, 1974; doctorate (hon.), U. Bergen, Norway, 1996, Shadong U., China. Asst. prof. Oakland U., Rochester, Mich., 1974-77, Ohio State U., Columbus, 1977-80, assoc. prof., 1980-81; sr. rsch. mathematician Mobil R & D Corp., Dallas, 1980-82, assoc. mathematician, 1982-83; prof. math., petroleum and chem. engring. U. Wyo., Laramie, 1983-92, J.E. Warren dist. prof. energy and environ., 1984-92, dir. Enhanced Oil Recovery Inst., 1984-92, dir. Inst. for Sci. Computation, 1986-92, dir. Ctr. for Math. Modeling, 1986-92, Wold Centennial chair in energy, 1991-92; dean Coll. Sci. Tex. A&M U., College Station, 1992-2000, prof. math. and engring., 1992—, dir. Inst. for Sci. Computation, 1992—, disting. rsch. chair TEES, 1992, dir. Acad. Advanced Telecom. and Learning Techs., 1996-2000, Dist. prof. math. and engring., 1998—, v.p. for rsch., 2000—; chair in sci. computing Mobil Tech. Co., 1999—, Harrison Endowed chair in Sci., 1999—. Adj. prof. Rice U., Houston, 1980—84, U. Tex., 1998—; adv. res. Inst. Petroleum, Beijing, 1987—; adv. Rsch. Inst. Petroleum, 1987—; steering com. Ctr. for Fluid Dynamics and Geoscis., Columbia, SC, 1987—; hon. prof. Shandong U., China, 1987; adv. bd. Ctr. Sci. Computing, Jyväskylä, Finland, 1990—, Improved Oil Recovery Ctr., Bergen, Norway, 1990—, Interdisciplinary Ctr. Computational Sci., Heidelberg, Germany, 1992—, Inst. Biosci. Tech., Houston, 1992—; acad. adv. bd. Dow Chem., 1994—; exec. com. Patnership Computational Scis., Oak Ridge Nat. Lab., 1991—98; pres. Environ. Modelling and Analysis Corp., 1991—; sci. adv. bd. Inst. for Math. Scis., Alta, Canada, 1996—; bd. dirs. Nat. space Biomed. Rsch. Inst., Houston Tech. Ctr., Associated Western U., Southeastern U. Rsch. Assocs., Oak Ridge Assocs. U., Tex. Healthcare and Biosci. Inst., Tex. Soc. Biomed. Rsch.; adv. coun. NASA, 2001—, Tex. Coun. on Environ. Tech., 2001—; hon. guest rschr. Wuhan U., China, 1997—; adj. prof. U. Tex., Houston, 1998—; sci. bd. Indsl. Math. Inst., U. S.C., 1999—; cons. in field; coun. mem. Harte Rsch. Inst., 2001—. Author: The Mathematics of Reservoir Simulation, 1983, Mathematical Modeling in Energy and Environmental Sciences, 1988; contbr. articles to sci. jours., chpts. to books. Cubmaster Boy Scouts Am., Dallas, 1981, Webelos leader, 1982, asst. scoutleader, Laramie, 1984, asst. scoutmaster, College Station, 1995—. Recipient numerous rsch. grants NSF, Dept. Energy, NRC, DOD, oil cos., others, 1978—. Fellow AAAS; mem. Soc. Petroleum Engrs., Soc. Indsl. and Applied Math. (trustee 1986-93), Am. Math. Soc., Math. Assn. Am., Internat. Assn. for Math. and Computers in Simulation, Internat. Assn. Computer Mech. (trustee 1991—), Inst. for Advancement Sci. Computing (trustee 1987-93), Geoscis. Inst. (bd. dirs. 1988-92), N.Y. Acad. Scis., Internat. Computer Club (sci. coun. 1989—). Democrat. Avocations: skiing, tennis, stamp and coin collecting. Home: 2004 Indian Trl College Station TX 77845-5600 E-mail: richard-ewing@tamu.edu.

EWING, ROBERT CLARK, lawyer; b. Lower Merion, Pa., Nov. 26, 1957; m. Cheralynn Kennedy, Mar. 22, 1986; children: Edward, Jaesun; stepchildren: Kristin, Shannon. BS in Fin., Pa. State U., 1980; JD, Villanova U., 1983. Bar: Pa. 1983, U.S. Dist. Ct. (ea. dist.) Pa. 1985, U.S. Ct. Appeals (3rd cir.) 1987, U.S. Supreme Ct. 1987. Ranger Pa. State Park Svc., 1976-78, Valley Forge Nat. Park, 1979; police officer Ocean City (Md.) Police Dept., 1980-81, Springfield Twp. Delaware County, 1992-99; assoc. Lagoy & Lyons, West Chester, Pa., 1983-86, Ronald H. Silverman, P.C., King of Prussia, Pa., 1986-88, Anthony J. McNulty & Assocs., Media, Pa., 1988-91; pvt. practice Media, Pa., 1991—. Contbr. articles to profl. jours. Mem. Lima (Pa.) Fire Co., 1973—, bd. dirs., 1981-88; mem. Media (Pa.) Fire Co., 1988—; bd. dirs. Hank Nacrelli Scholarship Fund, 1988-97, Delaware County Emergency Health Svcs. Coun., 1986-93; active Delaware County Critical Incident Stress Mgmt. Program, Media, 1987—. Mem. ATLA, Delaware County Bar Assn., Pa. Trial Lawyers Assn. Office: 115 N Monroe St PO Box 728 Media PA 19063

EWING, ROBERT CRAIG, lawyer, educator; b. Glen Ridge, N.J., May 9, 1953; s. Donald Graham and Barbara (Hansen) E.; m. Mary Arnold Hengy, Aug. 30, 1981; 1 child, Kyle Ross. BA, Middlebury Coll., 1976; JD, Denver U., 1980. Bar: Colo. 1980, Mass. 1981, U.S. Dist. Ct. Colo. 1980, U.S. Ct. Appeals (10th cir.) 1984, Maine 1997. Assoc. Hall & Evans, Denver, 1981-84; part-time prof. Metro. State Coll., Denver, 1983-88; ptnr. Holme, Roberts & Owen, Denver, 1984-95; CEO, founder skifreestyle.com; shareholder EWing & Ewing, PC; bd. dirs. State Adv. Council on Emergency Med. Services, Denver, 1981-83; emergency med technician Am. Coll. Surgeons, Colo. Dept. Health, Denver, 1979— ; bd. dirs. McArthur Ranch Homeowners Assn., 1981-85; mem. Am. Trakehner Assn., Columbus, Ohio, 1983— . Author: Emergency Medical Personnel and the Law, 1982, Electromagnetic Fields at the Millenium-Should We Tresspass Against Us, 1991; editor Legal Information Rev., 1983; Trends in Law Report newsletter, 1983-84. Named Charles A. Dana Scholar Middlebury Coll., Vt., 1975. Mem. Colo. Bar Assn., Denver Bar Assn., Am. Trial Lawyers Assn., Colo. Trial Lawyers Assn. Republican. Presbyterian. Clubs: Araphaoe Hunt (Littleton); Greenwood Athletic. Home: 4256 S Perry Park Rd Sedalia CO 80135-8207

EWING, RUSSELL CHARLES, II, physician; b. Tucson, Aug. 16, 1941; s. Russell Charles and Sue M. (Sawyer) E.; children: John Charles, Susan Lenore. BS, U. Arizona, 1963; MD, George Washington U., 1967. Diplomate Am. Bd. Family Practice. Intern L.A. County-U. So. Calif. Med. Ctr., L.A., 1967-68; gen. practice in medicine and surgery Yorba Linda and Placentia, Calif., 1990-96; correctional psychiatrist, 1998—; gen. practice in medicine and surgery Brea, Calif., 1996-97; mem. staff St. Jude's Hosp., Fullerton, Calif., 1970-98, Placentia Linda Cmty. Hosp., 1972-98; vice chief staff, 1977-78; chief staff, 1978-80; bd. dirs., 1974-81; sec., dir. Yorba Linda Med. Group, Inc., 1974-90. Bd. dirs. We. Empire Savs. & Loan Assn., Calif., Ewing Enterprises. Bd. dirs. Yorba Linda YMCA, 1973-88, pres., 1973-74, 81. With USN, 1968-70. Fellow Am. Acad. Family Practice; mem. AMA, Am. Coll. Physician Execs., Calif. Med. Assn. (ho. of dels. 1978-90, 92-99, trustee 1990-92), Orange County Med. Assn. (bd. dirs. 1983-90, pres. 1988-89). Republican. Episcopalian. Home and Office: 2300 Iron Pt Rd #1113 Folsom CA 95630-8489

EWING, SIDNEY ALTON, veterinary medical educator, parasitologist; b. Emory University, Ga, Dec. 1, 1934; s. Aubrey Coleman and Grace Eliza (Prickett) E.; m. Margaret Jane Steffens, Aug. 16, 1963; children— Holly Annette, Ann Krull, Leah Grace. BSA, DVM, U. Ga., 1958; MS, U. Wis., 1960; PhD, Okla. State U., 1964. Instr. U. Wis., 1960; mem. faculty Okla. State U., Stillwater, 1960—65, 1968—72, prof., head dept. vet. parasitology, microbiology and public health, 1968—72, 1979—84, prof., 1984—91, interim assoc. dean for acad. affairs, 1991—92, 2001—03, Wendell H./Nellie G. Krull endowed prof. vet. parasitology, 1992—; assoc. prof. Kans. State U., 1965—67; prof., head dept. Miss. State U., 1967—68; prof., dean Coll. Vet. Medicine, U. Minn., St. Paul, 1972—78. Mem. adv. bd. Morris Animal Found., Denver, 1967-69, cons., 1969-78; mem. animal health com. NRC, 1971-75; mem. adv. panel U.S. Pharmacopeial Conv., 1980-95. Recipient Outstanding Tchr. of Yr. award Okla. State U. Coll. Vet. Medicine, 1970, SmithKline Beecham award for rsch. excellence Okla. State U., 1991, A.M. Mills award for outstanding contbns. to vet. medicine, 1993, Good Neighbor award Radio Sta. WCCO, Mpls.-St. Paul, 1978; commendation Gov. Minn., 1978; named Veterinarian of Yr., State of Okla., 1997; named to Okla. Higher Edn. Hall of Fame, 2000, Disting. Vet. Parasitologist Am. Assn. Vet. Parasitologists, 2002. Mem. AAUP, AVMA, Am. Assn. Vet. Parasitologists, Am. Soc. Parasitologists, Am. Vet. Med. History Soc., Am. Soc. Rickettsiology, World Assn. Advancement Vet. Parasitology, Conf. Rsch. Workers in Animal Diseases (coun. 1980-85, v.p. 1983-84, pres. 1984-85), Soc. Vector Ecology, Soc. Tropical Vet. Medicine, Minn. Vet. Med. Assn., Okla. Vet. Med. Assn., NY Acad. Sci., Southwestern Assn. of Parasitologists (program officer, pres. elect 2001-02, pres. 2002-2003), Sigma Xi, Phi Kappa Phi, Phi Zeta, Alpha Zeta, Alpha Psi (past nat. pres.), Gamma Sigma Delta, Aghon, Omicron Delta Kappa. Office: Okla State U Dept Vet Pathobiology Stillwater OK 74078-2005 E-mail: saewing@cvm.okstate.edu.

EWING, THOMAS WILLIAM, former congressman, lawyer; b. Atlanta, Ill., Sept. 19, 1935; m. Connie Lupo, 1981; children: Jane, Kathryn, Sam, Christine Lupo, John Lupo, Stephanie Lupo. BS, Millikin U., 1957; JD, John Marshall Law Sch., Chgo., 1968. Asst. state atty. Livingston County, 1968-73; ptnr. Satter Ewing Beyer & Spires, Pontiac, Ill., 1969-91; mem. Ill. Ho. of Reps., 1974-91, U.S. Congress from 15th Ill. Dist., 1991-2001; mem. sci. com., agr. subcom., transp. and infrastructure coms., house adminstrn. com. Mem. agr. com. Ill. Ho. Reps., chmn. subcom. on risk mgmt. and specialty crops, subcom. on dept. ops., nutrition and fgn. agr., transp. and infrastructure com., aviation subcom., water resources and environment subcom., joint econ. com., former dep. minority leader, chmn. policy com., house revenue com., 1980, co-chmn. Ill. Econ. and Fiscal Commn., co-chmn. Legis. Space Needs Commn. Rep. precinct committeeman; del. Rep. Nat. Conv., 1980, 84, 88, 96, 2000; committeeman 15th Congl. Dist., 1986-93. With U.S. Army, 1958, USAR, 1957-63. Recipient Best Legislator award Nat. Rep. Legislator of the Yr. award, 1982, Ill. Small Businessmen Assn., 1983, 85, 87, Friend of Agr. award Ill. Agrl. Assn., 1985, 87, 89, 91, Legislator of Yr. award Ill. Assn. Homes for the Aging, 1986. Mem. Livingston County Bar Assn., Pontiac C. of C. (past exec. dir., past pres.), Livingston County Farm Bur., Elks, Moose, Masons. Republican. Methodist. E-mail: TWewing@yahoo.com.

EWING, WAYNE HILLEY, film producer, director, writer; b. Washington (D.C.), Oct. 25, 1948; s. Frank Marion and Joanne (Bacon) E. BA, Yale Coll., 1970; MA in Communications, U. Tex., 1971. Prin. Wayne Ewing Films, Aspen, Colo., 1972—. Producer, dir.: Breakfast with Hunter, 2003, If Elected, 1972, Cowboys, 1974, Copland at 75, 1975, Six Great Ideas with Bill Moyers, 1982, A Journey to Russia, 1983, The Bloods of 'Nam, 1987, Gangs, Cops and Drugs, 1989, The New Hollywood, 1990, Breakfast with Hurtez, 2003; dir. TV spl.: Women Behind Bars, 1988; dir., dir. photography Homicide: Life on the Street, 1993. Office: Wayne Ewing Films PO Box 1751 Aspen CO 81612-1751

EWING, WAYNE TURNER, coal company executive; b. Beech Creek, Ky., Dec. 1, 1933; s. O.E. and Elizabeth E.; m. Jane Gray, June 3, 1960; children—Allyson, Sally. BA, Georgetown Coll.; MA, Western Ky. U. With Peabody Coal Co., 1963-85, pres., 1983-85, Peabody Devel. Co., St. Louis, 1985-90; cons. Peabody Holding Co., St. Louis, 1992-93; sr. v.p. Kerr McGee Corp., Oklahoma City, 1993-96; owner The Ewing Co., Bonita Springs, Fla., 1996—. With U.S. Army, 1955-57. Mem. Nat. Mining Assn., Ill. Coal Assn., Pelican Nest Country Club. Fax: 239-948-0719. E-mail: wewing@mindspring.com.

EWOH, ANDREW IKEH EMMANUEL, political science educator; b. Enugu, Nigeria, Nov. 20, 1959; came to U.S., 1981; s. Lazarus Ngene and Virginia Nnenna (Ani) E.; married; children: Tyrone, Emmanuel, Andy, Chelsey. BS in Bus. Adminstrn., U. La., Lafayette, 1984; MPA in Pub. Adminstrn., So. U., Baton Rouge, 1986; MA in Polit. Economy, U. Tex., Dallas, 1991, PhD in Polit. Economy, 1993. Grad. intern Office Housing and Tech. Assistance La. Dept. Urban and Community Affairs, Baton Rouge, 1985-86; teaching asst. So. U., Baton Rouge, 1985-86, Sch. Social Scis., U. Tex.-Dallas, Richardson, 1990-92, rsch. asst., 1991, instr., 1993; instr. bus. divsn. Richland Coll., Dallas, 1993; adj. prof. dept. pub. affairs Tex. So. U., Houston, 1986-89, 93; adj. prof. Sch. Bus. and Pub. Adminstrn. U. Houston-Clear Lake, 1994; assoc. prof. polit. sci. Prairie View (Tex.) A&M U., 1993—, polit. sci. program coord., 1993—. Vis. scholar Iowa Social Sci. Inst., U. Iowa, Iowa City, 1997. Editor in Chief: African Soc. Sci. Review; acting editor Issues in Polit. Economy, 1991-92; contbr. articles to profl. jours. Grad. rsch. fellow Tex. Higher Edn. Coord. Bd., Rsch. Programs Divsn., Austin, Tex., 1990, grad. fellow Minnie K. Patton Scholarship Found., 1991-92, 92-93. Fellow Acad. Polit. Sci.; mem. Am. Soc. Pub. Adminstrn. (mem. Pub. Com.), Assn. for Budgeting and Fin. Mgmt., Am. Acad. Polit. and Social Sci., Am. Polit. Sci. Assn., Ctr. for Study of Presidency, Southwestern Social Sci. Assn., Southwestern Polit. Sci. Assn. Home: PO Box 691824 Houston TX 77269-1824 E-mail: Andrew_Ewoh@pvamu.edu., AEwoh@aol.com.

EWY, GORDON ALLEN, cardiologist, clinician, researcher, educator; b. Brenham, Kans., Aug. 5, 1933; s. Marvin John and Hazel Miller (Allen) E.; m. Priscilla Ruth Weldon; children: Kim Elizabeth, Gordon Stuart, Mark Allen. BA, U. Kans., 1955, MD, 1961. Resident, house officer Georgetown U. Hosp., Washington, 1961-64, cardiology fellow, 1964-65; instr. medicine Georgetown U., Washington, 1965-68, asst. prof., 1968-69, U. Ariz., Tucson, 1969-70, assoc. prof., 1970-75, prof. medicine, 1975—, chief cardiology, dir. cardiology fellowship program, 1982—, assoc. head dept. medicine, 1986-94, dir. Sarver Heart Ctr., 1991—. The Gordon A. Ewy MD Endowed chair cardiovasc. medicine, 2002—. Editor: Cardiovascular Drugs and Management of Heart Disease, 1982, 93, Current Cardiovascular Drug Therapy, 1984, Manual of Cardiovascular Diagnosis and Therapy, 5th edit., 2002; author numerous sci. publs.; contbr. numerous revs. to profl. jours., chpts. to books. Lt. (j.g.) USNR, 1955-57. Fellow ACP, Am. Heart Assn. (mem. clin. coun., nat. faculty advanced cardiac life support 1982-84, chmn. nat. programs subcom. 1982, bd. dirs. Ariz. chpt. 1975-82, 84-89, tchg. fellow 1970-75), Am. Coll. Cardiology (chmn. learning ctr. com. 1988-91, trustee 1992-97), Alpha Omega Alpha. Republican. Avocation: travel. Office: Ariz Health Scis Ctr 1501 N Campbell Ave Tucson AZ 85724-0001 E-mail: gaewy@aol.com.

EXARHOS, GREGORY JAMES, physical chemist, research scientist; b. Milw., Oct. 27, 1948; s. James Nick and Helen Ann Exarhos; m. Catherine Ann Scarborough, Jan. 13, 1979; children: Annemarie Louise, Alexander James, Stephen Anthony, Caroline Elizabeth. Ph.D., Brown U., Providence, RI, 1970—74; A.B. (Magna cum laude), Lawrence U., Appleton, WI, 1966—70. Lab. fellow Pacific NW Nat. Lab., Richland, Wash., 2002—; sr. staff scientist Pacific NW Nat. lab., Richland, Wash., 1994—2002; staff scientist Pacific NW Nat. Lab., Richland, Wash., 1986—94, sr. rsch. scientist, 1980—86; asst. prof. (chemistry) Harvard U., Cambridge, Mass., 1974—80. Adj. prof. of physics Wash. State U., Pullman, Wash., 1973—; mem., bd. dirs. Internat. Tech. Corp., Research Triangle Park, NC, 2002—; gen. chair, internat. conf. on metall. coatings and thin films AVS, San Diego, 2002, chair, long range planning com., New York, NY, 1997—2000; cons. NJDI, Phila., 1979—80; mem., bd. visitors Wash. State U., Pullman, Wash., 1997—2001; co-chair for ann. symposium on optical materials for high power lasers SPIE, Bellingham, Wash., 1997—; sec. vacuum metallurgy divsn. IUVSTA, Brussels, 1998—2001, chmn. vmd, 2001—; mem., bd. dirs. AVS, New York, 1998—2000. Author: (185 peer-reviewed jour. publs.) Thin Solid Films, JVST, JPC, (Best Paper Award, 2003). Recipient FLC (Fed. Lab. Consortium) Tech. Transfer Award: Prodn. of Ceramic Powders Using the Glycine/Nitrate Process, Fed. Govt. (DOE), 1993, R&D 100 Award: Glycine-Nitrate Process for Synthesizing Ceramic Powders ;, DOE, 1992. Fellow: Am. Ceramic Soc. (hon.). R-Conservative. Achievements include patents for Preparation of Thin Ceramic Films via an Aqueous Solution Route; Metal Oxide Ceramic Powders and Thin Films and Methods of Making Same; Polymer-Ceramic Molecular Composites and Methods of Making; Electrochemical Process for Making Thin Inorganic-Organic Composite Pol; Apparatus for Photocatalytic Destruction of Internal Combustion Engine Emissions During Cold Start; Electrochemically Induced Conductivity in Transparent Transition Metal Oxide Films. Avocations: horseback riding, music (clarinet), bicycling, reading, swimming. Office: Pacific NW Nat Lab PO Box 999 MS K2-44 Richland WA 99352 Office Fax: 509-375-2186. E-mail: greg.exarhos@pnl.gov.

EXE, DAVID ALLEN, electrical engineer; b. Jan. 29, 1942; s. Oscar Melvin and Irene Marie (Mattis) E.; m. Lynn Rae Roberts (dec.); m. Mary Ann Savilla; children: Doreen Lea, Raena Lynn. BSEE, S.D. State U., 1968; MBA, U. S.D., 1980; postgrad., Iowa State U., 1969-70, U. Idaho, 1978-80. Registered prof. engr., Idaho, Oreg., Minn., S.D., Wash., Wyo., Utah, N.Y., Ind. Wis. Applications engr. Collins Radio, Cedar Rapids, Iowa, 1969-70; dist. engr. Bonneville Power Adminstrn., Idaho Falls, Idaho, 1970-77; instr. math. U. S.D., Vermillion, 1977-78; CEO EXE Engring., Idaho Falls, 1978-83, Greenfield, Minn., 1985—. Safety mgr. CPT Corp., Eden Prairie, Minn., 1983-85; owner, CEO Exe Inc., Eden Prairie, 1983—; chmn. bd. Applied Techs. Idaho, Idaho Falls, 1979—; chmn., CEO Azimuth Cons., Idaho Falls, 1979-81; v.p. D & B Constrn. Co., Idaho Falls, 1980-83; bd. dirs., v.p., COO Nat. Multi-Housing Corp., 1989. Tech. advisor Nat. Earth Day, 1991; apptd. Minn. State Bd. Profl. Engrs., 1991. With USN, 1960—64. Mem. IEEE, NSPEA (exec. com), Nat. Contracts Mgrs. Assn., Mensa, Am. Legion, VFW, Masons, Elks, Lions (sec.). Office: Indsl Engring Inc 11451 Valley Creek Rd Woodbury MN 55129 Fax: 651-436-1947.

EXEROWA, DOTCHI RUSSEVA, chemist, researcher; b. Varna, Bulgaria, May 20, 1935; d. Russi Mitev and Alexandra Nikolova (Karagyozova) E.; m. Dimo Nikolov Platikanov, April 22, 1962; 1 child, Iva. MSc, U. Sofia, Bulgaria, 1958; PhD, Bulgarian Acad. Sci., Sofia, 1969; DSc, Bulgarian Acad. Sci., 1987. Cert. physical chemistry. Resercher Inst. Physical Chemistry, Bulgarian Acad. Sci., Sofia, 1958-72, sr. researcher, 1972-88, head dept. colloids and surfaces, prof., 1983—. Assoc. prof. U. Sofia, 1972-88; chmn. Specialized Sci. Coun. Physical Chemistry, 1992—; sci. achievements in liquid thin films and surfaces;

co-chair 9th Internat. Conf. on Surface and Colloid Sci., Sofia, Bulgaria; lectr. in field. Mem. editl. bd. Adv. Colloid Interface Sci., 1990-95, Colloid Jour., 1993--, Colloids & Surfaces, 1999--, Colloid and Polymer Sci., 2001--; contbr. over 2170 articles to profl. jours. Recipient Kliment Ohridsky medal, Bulgaria, 1983, first prize Union Bulgarian Scientists, Bulgaria, 1987, Acad. prize, Bulgaria, 1995. Mem. Gen. Assembly of Bulgarian Acad. Sci., Internat. Assn. Colloid and Interface Scientists (coun. mem. 1990-94), Internat. Assn. Lung Surfactant Sys., N.Y. Acad. Scis. Anticommunist. Eastern Orthodox. Avocation: art. Home: 24 Gen Parensov 1000 Sofia Bulgaria Office: Inst Physical Chemistry Bulgarian Acad Sci 1113 Sofia Bulgaria

EXLER, SAMUEL, retired advertising executive, writer; b. Bklyn., July 7, 1922; s. Harry and Regina Exler; m. Florence Schoenbaum, June 20, 1948 (div. 1976); children: Judith Nora, Harriet Elizabeth. BA, Bklyn. Coll., 1943. With advt. agencies, N.Y.C., NY. Author: (children's book) Growing and Changing, 1957, (poetry book) Ambition, Fertility, Loneliness, 1982; contbr. poems to lit. mags. and anthologies. Pvt. 1st class infantry U.S. Army, 1942—45, ETO. Decorated Bronze Star U.S. Army, ETO Ribbon with 3 battle stars. Home: 307 E Roumfort Rd Philadelphia PA 19119-1031

EXON, J(OHN) JAMES, former senator; b. Lake Andes, S.D., Aug. 9, 1921; s. John James and Luella (Johns) E.; m. Patricia Ann Pros, Sept. 18, 1943; children: Stephen, Pamela, Candace. Student, U. Omaha, 1939-41; LLD (hon.), Creighton U., 1991, Doane Coll., 1995; LittD (hon.), U. Nebr., 1997. Mgr. Universal Finance Corp., Nebr., 1946-53; pres. Exon's, Inc., Lincoln, Nebr., 1954-71; gov. State of Nebr., 1971-79; mem. U.S. Senate, Nebr., 1979-96. Mem. Armed Svcs. Com., ranking Min. mem. of budget com., ranking Min. mem. commerce, sci. and transp. subcom. of consumer affairs, fgn. commerce and tourism. Active state, local, nat. Democratic coms., 1952— ; del. Dem. Nat. Conv., 1964, 72, 74, 76, 88, 92; former Dem. nat. committeeman. Served with Signal Corps AUS, 1942-45. Mem. Am. Legion, VFW, Masons (33rd degree), Shriners, Elks, Eagles, Optimist Internat. Home: 1615 Brent Blvd Lincoln NE 68506-1867

EXPOSITO, DAISY, advertising executive; b. Cuba; arrived in U.S., 1964; Creative dir. Bravo Group, N.Y.C., 1981—85, sr. v.p., gen. mgr., 1985—90, CEO, chmn., 1990—. Named one of N.Y.'s Top 100 Top Minority Execs., Crain's N.Y. Bus., 100 Outstanding Hispanic Women in Comm., Hispanic Mag.; recipient Corp. Achiever of the Yr. award, Nat. Hispanic Acad. Media Arts & Scis., Salute to Model award, Am. Advt. Fedn. Dist. 2. Mem.: Assn. Hispanic Advt. Agys. (pres.), Internat. Arts Rels., Am. Assn. Advt. Agys. Found., Inc. (bd. dirs.), Nat. Coun. La Raza, Hispanic Fedn., New Am.'s Alliance. Office: Bravo Group 20 Cooper Sq New York NY 10003*

EXUZIDES, ALEX, statistician, researcher; b. Bönn, Germany, Dec. 30, 1964; arrived in U.S., 1986; s. Haralambos and Photini Exuzides. BA, U. Patras, Greece, 1986; PhD, U. Calif., Davis, Calif., 1996. Sr. scientist Exponent, Menlo Pk., Calif., 1996—. Contbr. articles to profl. jours. Mem.: Am. Statis. Assn., Am. Pub. Health Assn. Office: 149 Commonwealth Dr Menlo Park CA 94103

EYBERG, DONALD THEODORE, JR., architect; b. Mpls., July 8, 1944; s. Donald Theodore and Helen Irene (Young) E.; m. Sally Jo Birch, Dec. 30, 1967; children: Jon, Erin. Student, Mankato State U., 1962-64; BArch, U. Minn., 1968. Registered architect, Minn., Fla., Tex. Planner Midwest Planning and Rsch., Mpls., 1966-67; designer Matson-Wegleitner, Mpls., 1967-68; architect Ellerbe Assocs., Mpls., 1968-76, exec. architect, 1977-82, v.p., 1983-2000; prin. Devine, deFlon, Yaeger, Inc., Mpls., 2000—. Prin. works include Providence Civic Ctr., 1971, Dahlgren Hall U.S. Naval Acad., Annapolis, Md., 1973 (numerous awards), Rupp Arena/Hyatt Regency Hotel, Lexington, Ky., 1975 (numerous awards), Huntington (W.Va.) Civic Ctr., 1977, Charleston (W.Va.) Civic Ctr., 1980 (Merit award Athletic Bus. 1981), Hartford (Conn.) Coliseum, 1981 (numerous awards), Mpls. Coll. Art and Design, 1982, Children's Theater Co., Mpls., 1983, Mpls. Inst. Arts, 1984, Ocean Ctr., Daytona Beach, Fla., 1985, Manatee Ctr., Bradenton, Fla., 1985, Thirteen Hundred Biscayne Bldg. Study, Miami, 1985 (Minn. Paper Architect award AIA), Santa Clara (Calif.) Conv. Ctr., 1986, expansion, 1995, Mayo Civic Ctr., Rochester, Minn., 1986, Santa Clara Golf and Tennis Ctr., 1986 (Merit award Athletic Bus. 1988), Nat. Hockey Ctr., St. Cloud, Minn., Lawrence Joel Vet. Meml. Coliseum, Winston-Salem, N.C. (Merit award Athletic Bd. 1991), Hubert H. Humphrey Metrodome Expansion, Mpls., Austin (Tex.) Conv. Ctr., Reino Aventura Arena, Mexico City, Minn. Twins Baseball Club Office Expansion, Mpls., Summit Arena Expansion, Houston, 1993, Santa Clara (Calif.) Conv. Ctr. Expansion, Commonwealth Conv. Ctr. Expansion. Louisville, Miami Arena Expansion, Von Braun Conv. Ctr. Expansion, Aquatics Ctr. and Gymnasium U. Chgo., Payne Whitney Gym Planning Study and Renovation/Expansion, Yale U., Univ. Hall rebuild U. Va., Charlottesville, Springfield (Mass.) Civic Ctr. expansion and plaza, Walter A. Haas Jr. Pavilion, U. Calif., Berkeley, track/football stadium Claremont (Calif.) Coll., Target Ctr. Upgrades, Mpls. Track/Football stadium, fieldhouse St. Johns U., Collegeville Mn., Taylor Ctr. Arena, Minn. State U., Makato, Grand Ctr., Grand Rapids, Mich., Austin (Tex.) Conv. Ctr. expansion, Whittier Coll. track/football stadium, Calif., Atlantis Hotel & Casino Showroom, Paradise Island, Bahamas, St. Cloud State Univ. football stadium, Minn., Fargo Dome Arena, N.D., Gibson-Nagurski U. Minn. Football Complex addition, Mpls., Ameristar Casino Conf. Ctr., Kansas City, Mo., U. Minn. Baseball Stadium, Mpls. Mem. AIA, Urban Land Inst., Minn. Soc. Architects (Merit award 1977), Nat. Coun. Archtl. Registration Bd., Mpls. Soc. Fine Arts. Home: 6600 Dakota Trail Minneapolis MN 55439-1119 Office: Berger Devine Yaeger Inc 201 SE Main St Ste 221 Minneapolis MN 55414 Fax: (623) 623-7810. E-mail: deyberg@ddyinc.com.

EYERMAN, DAVID JOHN, software engineer; b. Oak Park, Ill., June 14, 1966; s. Thomas Jude and Mary Kathryn E.; m. Regan Veasey, Aug. 5, 1995. BS in Computer Sci., Am. U., Washington, 1988, MS in Computer Sci., 1989. Microcomputer project mgr. U.S. Dept. Treasury, Washington, 1987-89; assoc. programmer IBM, Milford, Conn., 1989-90, adv. software engr. Dallas, 1990-97, sr. software engr. Santa Teresa Lab. San Jose, Calif., 1997—. Dir. Thomas J. and Mary Kay Eyerman Found., Chgo., 1992—. Mem. The 500, Inc., Dallas, 1991-97, Voce Forte, The Dallas Opera, 1993-97, Shakespeare Festival of Dallas, 1994-97. Mem. IEEE, Assn. Computing Machinery. Roman Catholic. Avocations: private pilot, cooking, wine. E-mail: dreyerman@earthlink.net.

EYES-PENN, Chief PIERCING See TURNBULL, DAVID JOHN

EYKAMP, PAUL W. academic administrator; b. Evansville, Ind., Oct. 1964; s. G. Richard and Rita Eykamp. AB cum laude, Washington U., 1987; MA, PhD, U. Calif., San Diego, 1995. Dir. coun. student fees U. Calif., San Diego, 1994-96, sr. policy analyst Oakland, 1996-98, coord. long range enrollment analysis and database devel., 1998—. Web designer Eykamp Consulting, Alamo, Calif., 1994—; presenter in field. Author: Political Control of State Universities: The Effect of Political Control of State Research University on Quality and Funding, 1995; dir. (TV) The Grove Unplugged, 1996. Mem. Am. Polit. Sci. Assn., Assn. Instl. Rsch., Calif. Assn. Instl. Rsch., U. Calif. San Diego Bay Area Alumni Assn. (pres. 1999—), Washington U. Bay Area Alumni Club (pres. 1997—), Alpha Kappa Psi (dir. rsch. 1991-95), Omnicron Delta Epsilon, Nu Xi. Office: U Calif Oakland 1111 Franklin St Oakland CA 94607 Fax: 510-987-9447. E-mail: paul@eykamp.net.

EYKMAN, CHRISTOPH W. language educator; b. Frankfurt, Germany, Dec. 6, 1937; arrived in U.S., 1964; s. Alfred and Irmgard Eykman; m. Ecke E. Schmidt, Sept. 23, 1945; children: Alexander, Mathias. PhD, U. Bonn, 1964. Asst. prof. Antioch Coll., Yellow Springs, Ohio, 1964—68; from asst. prof. to prof. Boston (Mass.) Coll., 1968—84, prof., 1984—. Author: Die Funktion des Hasslichen, 1965, 2d edit., 1969, Geschichts pessimismus, 1970, Denk und Stilformen des Expressionismus, 1974, Phanomenologie der Interpretation, 1977, Der Intellekfuelle, 1992, Ästhetishe Erfahrung, 1997, Die geringen Dinge, 1999, Über Bilder Schreiben, 2003. Home: 10 Alfred Rd Framingham MA 01701 Office: Boston College 140 Commonwealth Ave Framingham MA 01701

EYLER, BONNIE, lawyer; b. Cumberland, Md. d. George Raphael and Elizabeth (Binnix) E. BS in Nursing, Widener U., 1969; MS, Boston U., 1974; JD, Nova U., 1983. Bar: Fla. 1984, U.S. Dist. Ct. (so. dist.) Fla. 1984. Registered nurse at several hosps. in the Boston and Phila. areas, 1974-84; assoc. Conrad, Scherer & James, Ft. Lauderdale, Fla., 1984-90; ptnr. Santone, Eyler & Lury, P.A., Ft. Lauderdale, 1990-95, Sonneborn Rutter Cooney Klingensmith & Eyler P.A., West Palm Beach, Fla., 1995-2000; of counsel Glick & Retamar, Boca Raton, Fla., 2001; ptnr. Adams, Coogler, Watson, Merkel, Barry & Kellner, PA, W. Palm Beach, Fla., 2002—. Mem. ATLA, ABA, Fla. Bar Assn., Palm Beach County Bar Assn., The Am. Assn. Nurse Attys. Office: Adams Coogler Watson Merkel Barry & Kellner PA 1555 Palm Beach Lakes Blvd Ste 1600 West Palm Beach FL 33402

EYLER, DAVID PAUL, music educator; s. Thomas Eyler and Ruth Bergeron; m. Barbara Johnson, Aug. 12, 1978. BS, Frostburg (Md.) State U., 1977; MusM, The Ohio State U., 1979; DMA, La. State U., 1985. Music dir.: Frostburg State U. percussion ensemble Frostburg State U., Frostburg, Md., 1973—77; grad. tchg. assoc. Sch. Music Ohio State U., Columbus, Ohio, 1977—79; grad. tchg. asst. Sch. Music La. State U., Baton Rouge, 1979—84; dir. of bands/dept. chairperson Redemptorist Jr. and Sr. HS, Baton Rouge, 1984—85; asst. prof. of music Ind. U. of PA, Ind., Pa., 1986—86; dir. of bands St. Jude Sch., Baton Rouge, 1986—87; assoc. prof. of music Concordia Coll., Moorhead, Minn., 1987—. Prin. Percussionist Susquehanna Festival Theater Orch., Harford, Md., 1971—73; prin. timpanist Potomac Symphony Orch., Potomac, Md., 1976—77; percussionist Columbus (Ohio) Symphony Orch., 1977—79; prin. percussionist Baton Rouge (La.) Symphony New Hyperion Ragtime Orch., 1979—84, Baton Rouge (La.) Symphony Orch., 1979—87; trap set drummer La. Soundstage Orch., Baton Rouge, 1981—85; prin. percussionist Baton Rouge (La.) Opera Orch., 1982—87; percussionist Rapides (La.) Symphony Orch., Alexandria, 1986—86, Lake Charles (La.) Symphony Orch., 1986—86; prin. timpanist Fargo-Moorhead Symphony Orch., Fargo, ND, 1987—. Author: Twenty-Two Progressive Studies, Etudes and Duets for Snare Drum, Music For Percussion, Inc.; composer: (music compositions) Triple Threat, Perpetual Motion, Fanfare and Dance for Solo Timpani, 7/8 Stomp, Watching The Time Go By, Latino: Trio for Latin Instruments, Tricastourine: A Multiple Percussion Solo, March Time for Percussion Trio, Changing Times for Solo Snare Drum, Bajo Los Pinos, Arrangements of Silent Night, Somewhere Over the Rainbow; contbr. articles to profl. jours. Chmn. orch. com. Baton Rouge (La.) Symphony Orch., 1986—87; chair, orch. com. Fargo-Moorhead (N.Dak.) Symphony Orch., 2000—; v.p. Minn. Percussive Arts Soc. Chpt., 1995—, bd. of trustees Fargo-Morhead (N.Dak.) Symphony Assn., 1995—2001; bd. trustees Percussive Arts Soc., 1998—. Fellow Danforth Grad. fellowship, 1977; grantee NEXUS grant, Lake Region Arts Coun., 1998, N.Dak. State U., 1999, Lake Region Arts Coun., 2001, Hendrickson Study grant, Concordia Coll., 2002, Lake Region Arts Coun., 2002; scholar Charles E. Lutton Meml. Merit-scholarship, 1976. Mem.: Music Educators Nat. Conf. (corr.), Coll. Music Soc. (corr.), Percussive Arts Soc. (assoc.; bd. of dir. 1998—2002, grants 1990—99), Pi Kappa Lambda Nat. Music Honor Soc. (hon.), Phi Mu Alpha Sinfonia Frat. (corr.; pres. 1976—77). Conservative. Pentecostal. Home: 2545 S 14th Street Fargo ND 58103 Office: Concordia College 901 S 8th Street Moorhead MN 56562

EYLER, JOHN H., JR., retail toy and game company executive; b. 1948; m. Dolores Eyler; 3 children. Grad., U. Wash.; MBA, Harvard U. With May Dep. Stores Co.; pres., CEO, May D&F, Denver, from 1980; chmn., CEO MainStreet divsn. Fed. Dept. Stoers, Inc.; CEO retail subs. Hartmarx, Chgo.; chmn., CEO FAO Schwarz, 1992-2000; pres., CEO Toys 'R' Us, Inc., Paramus, N.J., 2000—, also bd. dirs. Bd. dirs. Dona Karan Internat. Inc. Office: Toys 'R' Us Inc 461 From Rd Ste 2 Paramus NJ 07652-3524

EYMAN, ROGER ALLEN, minister; b. Canton, Ill., Mar. 16, 1942; s. Silbert Lionel and Ruth Maxine (Noland) E.; m. Priscilla Ann Baker, Dec. 24, 1979; 1 child, Hans Roger. AA, Orange Coast Coll., Costa Mesa, Calif., 1969; BA in Psychology, Calif. State U., L.A., 1971; MMin, Bethany Theol. Sem., 1975, DMin summa cum laude, 1991. Ordained to ministry Am. Evang. Christian Ch./Gen. Conf., 1983. Missionary Gospel Mission Ch., Liberia, Costa Rica, 1974-76, 1976-79; founder, pastor Ch. of Calvary Grace of Ariz., Tucson, 1984-89, Ch. of Calvary Grace of Alaska, Anchorage, 1989—. Ins. claims cons., Anchorage, 1989—. Fellow Internat. Ministerial Fellowship, AECC Gen. Conf., Internat. Chaplains Assn., Alaska Club. Republican. Office: Ch of Calvary Grace Alaska 3107 W Colorado Ave # 241 Colorado Springs CO 80904-2040

EYMANN, RICHARD CHARLES, lawyer; b. Hanover, N.H., June 6, 1945; BS, U. Oreg., 1968; JD, Gonzaga U., 1976. Bar: Wash. 1976, U.S. Dist. Ct. (ea. dist.) Wash. 1978, U.S. Ct. Appeals (9th cir.) 1987, U.S. Dist. Ct. (we. dist.) Wash. 1989, U.S. Supreme Ct. 1995. Ptnr. Eymann, Allison, Fennessy, Hunter Jones, P.S., Spokane, Wash. Mem. ABA (founder, chmn. nat. appellate advocacy competition 1975-84, bd. advs. 1985-93), ATLA, Wash. State Bar Assn. (bd. govs. 1997-98, pres. elect 1998-99, pres. 1999-2000), Wash. State Trial Lawyers Assn. (bd. govs. 1984-86, 88-95, legis. steering com. 1990-96, membership chair 1984-85, v.p. East 1991-92, fin. com. 1994-95, Trial Lawyer of Yr. 1995, pres. 1996-97), Wash. Trial Lawyers for Pub. Justice (bd. dirs. 1994-98), Am. Bd. Trial Advocates, Spokane County Bar Assn., Am. Inns of Ct. (barrister 1986, master of the bench 1990, Charles L. Powell & Inn pres. 1991-93), Damage Attys. Round Table. Office: Eymann Allison Fennessy Hunter & Jones PS 601 W Main Ave Ste 801 Spokane WA 99201 E-mail: eymann@eahjlaw.com.

EYNON, STEVEN SCOTT, minister; b. Jacksonville, Fla., July 4, 1961; s. John Jerry and Sally Ann Eynon; m. Lori Hunter, June 25, 1983; children: Christopher, Steven. BA summa cum laude, Fla. Christian Coll., Kissimmee, 1984; MMin, Ky. Christian Coll., 1992. Ordained to ministry Christian Ch., 1984. Min. youth Winter Haven (Fla.) Christian Ch., 1982-84, 1st Christian Ch., Clearwater, Fla., 1985-94; sr. min. Cmty. Christian Ch., Ft. Lauderdale, Fla., 1994—. Adj. instr. Fla. Christian Coll., 1988, 90, sec. of trustee, 1996-98; v.p. Fla. Christian Youth Conv., Orlando, 1986; bd. dirs. Christianville Mission, Haiti, 1991-96, chmn. bd. dirs., 1993-94; v.p. Fla. Christian Conv., 1998, pres. 1999; active Fla. Ch. Planters Leadership Team, 2003. Author: (with others) Ideas, vol. 42, 1987, Good Stuff, vol. 4, 1988, Directions for Your Journey, 2002. Mem. Nat. Right to Life, Washington, 1983-93; vol. Spl. Olympics, Clearwater, 1985-94; scouting coord. Boy Scouts Am., Clearwater, 1986-94; pres. Fla. Christian Coll. Alumni Assn., Kissimmee, 1987-88, v.p., 1985-87; bd. trustees Fla. Christian Coll., 1995-2000; pres. South Fla. Minister's Assn., 1997-98; with mgmt. team LifePoint Christian Ch., 2001-. Named Outstanding Young Min., N.Am. Christian Conv., 1989. Mem. Christ in Youth Planning Coun. (advisor 1986-88), Christian Edn. Conf. (dir. 1988), Nat. Eagle Scout Assn. Home: 9590 NW 31st Pl Sunrise FL 33351-7157 Office: Community Christian Ch 155 NW 112th Ave Fort Lauderdale FL 33325-2526

EYRE, IVAN, artist, educator; b. Tullymet, Sask., Can., Apr. 15, 1935; s. Thomas and Kay E.; m. Brenda Fenske, June 14, 1957; children: Keven, Tyrone. Mem. faculty U. N.D., 1958-59; mem. faculty U. Man., Winnipeg, Can., 1959-92, prof. drawing and painting, 1975-92, head drawing dept. 1974-78, prof. emeritus, 1994—; founding mem. Winnipeg Art Gallery, 1996. One-man shows include: Montreal Mus. Fine Arts, 1964, Winnipeg Art Gallery, 1964, 66, 74, 82, 88, 92, Fleet Galleries, Winnipeg, 1965, 69, 71, Albert White Galleries, Toronto, 1965, Atelier Vincitore Gallery, Brighton, Eng., 1967, Yellow Door Gallery, Winnipeg, 1966, Mount Allison U., 1968, Mendel Art Gallery, Saskatoon, 1968, Jerrold Morris Gallery, Toronto, 1969, 71, 73, Frankfurter Kunst Kabinett, Frankfurt, Ger., 1973, Burnaby Art Gallery, 1973, McIntosh Gallery, U. W. Ont., 1973, Siemens Werk, Erlangen, Germany, 1974, N.B. Mus., St. John, 1976, Gallery I.I.I., U. Manitoba, 1977, 94, Nat. Gallery Can., Ottawa, 1978, Equinox Gallery, Vancouver, 1978, 81, 82, Robert McLaughlin Gallery, Oshawa, 1980, Mira Godard Gallery, Toronto, 1978, 79, 80, 90, 92, 94, 96, 99, 2002, Rodman Hall Arts Centre, St. Catherines, Ont., 1980, Art Gallery Windsor, Ont., 1981, Beaverbrook Art Gallery, Fredericton, N.B., 1981, London (Ont.) Regional Art Gallery, 1981, Sir George Williams Galleries, Montreal, 1981, MacDonald Stewart Art Centre, Guelph, Ont., 1981, Brian Melnychenko Gallery, Winnipeg, 1981, 87, The Ctr. for Inter-Am. Rels. N.Y., 1982, Burlington (Ont.) Art Ctr., 1982, Winnipeg Art Gallery, 1982, Can. Cultural Centre, Paris, 1982, Can. House Gallery, London, Eng., 1982, Talbot Rice Gallery, Edinburgh, Scotland, 1982, The Art Gallery of Greater Victoria, Can., 1973, 82, 99, Evelyn Aimis Fine Art Gallery, Toronto, 1985, 87, The Nat. Gallery of Can., Ottawa, 1988, Ivan Eyre: Personal Mythologies: Images of the Milieu: Figurative Paintings 1957 to 1988 touring Can., Winnipeg Art Gallery, 1989, Nickle Arts Mus., Calgary, 1989, Edmonton Art Gallery, 1989, London (Can.) Regional Art Gallery, 1989; 49th Parallel Gallery, NYC, 1988, Edmonton Art Gallery, 1995, Mackenzie Art Gallery, 1996, Assiniboine Park Pavilion Gallery, Winnipeg, 1998, 99, 2000, 01, 02, Art Gallery of Hamilton, 1999, Loch & Mayberry Fine Art, Winnipeg, 2000; group shows include: London Regional Art Gallery, 1964, Agnes Lefort Gallery, Montreal, 1964, Nat. Gallery, Ottawa, 1965, 67, 74, Yellow Door Gallery, Winnipeg, 1965, Art Gallery of Ont., Toronto, 1968, Montreal Mus. Fine Arts, 1964, 70, 76, Primera Biennial Americana De Artes Graficas, Cali, Columbia, 1971, Art Gallery Ont., 1970, 76, Winnipeg Art Gallery, 1967, 76, 90, 92, 95, 2002, Glenbow-Alta. Inst., Calgary, 1976, Vancouver Art Gallery, 1977, Mendel Art Gallery, Saskatoon, 1977, 82, 2002, Harbourfront Art Gallery, Toronto, 1977, Edmonton (Alta., Can.) Art Gallery, 1981, 99, 2000, Printworld, US, 1982, Barcelona, Spain, 1982, Seattle Art Fair, 1987, LA Art Fair, 1986, 87, Chgo. Art Fair, 1989, Maison de la Culture Cotes-des-Neiges, Montreal, 1992, Galerie de la Ville Dollard-des-Ormeaux, Que., Can. Coun. Art Bank, 1993, Drabinsky Gallery, Toronto, 1993, Hong Kong Art Fair, 1993, Expo '93, Taejon, South Korea, 1993, Loch and Mayberry Fine Art, Winnipeg, 1997, Mira Godard Gallery, Toronto, 1998, 2001, Royal Can. Acad. Arts Prairie Region Exhbn., Winnipeg, 1997, travelling to Regina, 1998, Calgary, 1998, Victoria, 1999, Markham, Ont., 1999, Mackenzie Art Gallery, Regina, 2001; represented in permanent collections, Assiniboine Pk. Pavilion Gallery Art Collection, Winnipeg, Winnipeg Art Gallery, Nat. Gallery, Ottawa, Vancouver Art Gallery, Edmonton Art Gallery, Montreal Mus. Fine Arts, Art Gallery Ont., Toronto. Decorated Queen's Silver Jubilee medal, Queen's Golden Jubilee medal; nominee Molson prize, 1996; named sr. grantee, Can. Coun., 1966, 1977; recipient Gold medal, Acad. of Italy, 1980, Jubilee award, U. Man. Alumni, 1982, Outstanding Achievement medal, Internat. Biograph.Ctr., 1998. Mem. Royal Can. Acad. Arts Achievements include being subject of book Ivan Eyre (Woodcock), 1981; subject of various documentary films. Home: 1098 Des Trappistes St Winnipeg MB Canada R3V 1B8

EYRE, PAUL P. lawyer; b. Dublin, Mar. 13, 1947; BA, U. Wis., 1971, JD, 1975. Bar: Wis. 1975, Ohio 1982. Asst. regional dir. FTC, Washington, 1977-79, regional dir., 1979-82; ptnr. Baker & Hostetler, Cleve. With USN, 1967-69. Mem. Ohio Bar Assn. Office: Baker & Hostetler 3200 Nat City Ctr 1900 E 9th St Ste 3200 Cleveland OH 44114-3475

EYRE, PETER, dean; B of Vet. Medicine and Surgery, U. Edinburgh Scotland, 1960, BS in Biomed. Sci., Pharmacology, 1962, Phd in Pharmacoloy/Toxicology, 1965. Postgrad. fellow U. Edinburgh, 1960—63, lectr. pharmacology, 1963—68; assoc. prof. pharmacology U. Guelph, Canada, 1972—85, prof. pharmacology/toxicology, 1972—85, chmn. dept. biomed. scis., 1979—85; assoc. dir. Can. Ctr. for Toxicology U. Guelph and U. Toronto, Canada, 1982—85; prof. pharmacology Va.-Md. Regional Coll. Vet. Medicine, Va. Tech., 1985—; dean Va.-Md. Regional Coll. Vet. Medicine, Va. Tech and U. Md., 1985—. Mem.: Assn. Am. Vet. Med. Colls. (pres. 2003—04), Am. Acad. Vet. Pharmacology and Therapeutics, Md. Vet. Med. Assn., Va. Vet. Med. Assn., Am. Vet. Med. Assn., Royal Coll. Vet. Surgeons London. Office: Va Tech Duckpond Dr Phase II Blacksburg VA 24061*

EYRING, HENRY BENNION, bishop; b. Princeton, N.J., May 31, 1933; s. Henry and Mildred (Bennion) E.; m. Kathleen Johnson, July 27, 1962; children: Henry J., Stuart J., Matthew J., John B., Elizabeth, Mary Kathleen. BS, U. Utah, 1955; MBA, Harvard U., 1959, PhD, 1963; D of Humanities (hon.), Brigham Young U., 1985. Asst., then assoc. prof. Stanford U., Palo Alto, Calif., 1962—71; pres. Ricks Coll., Rexburg, Idaho, 1972—77; dep. commr. edn., then commr. LDS Ch., Salt Lake City, 1977—85, presiding bishopric, 1985—92, mem. 1st Quorum of the Seventy, 1992—95, mem. Quorum of the Twelve, 1995—. Author: To Draw Closer to God, 1997; co-author: The Organizational World, 1973. With USAF, 1955—57. Recipient Sloan faculty fellowship, MIT, 1963—64. Avocations: swimming, painting, woodcarving. Office: LDS Ch Quorum of the Twelve 47 E South Temple Salt Lake City UT 84150-9701*

EYRING, MAXINE LOUISE, small business owner, esthetician; b. Baltimore, MD, Sept. 17, 1946; d. William Charles Whippo and Catherine Marie Bennett; m. William John Eyring (div.). Student, Catonsville C.C., Baltimore, 1964. Lic. estetician Md., 1979. Owner Maxime's Skin and Nail Care, Annapolis, Md., 1980—88; with Salon West, Annapolis, 1988—89, Lord's and Lady's Salon, Annapolis, 1989—91; esthetician Robert Andrew Day Spa, Gambills, Md., 1991—97, Vincent's Masterpiece Internat. Day Spa, Annapolis, 1997—2000, Rumors of Annapolis, 2000—02; mgr. Esthencian Vincent's Masterpiece Internat. Day Spa, 2002—. Democrat. Lutheran.

EYSTER, CHARLES RICHARD, lawyer, oil and gas exploration executive; b. Ballinger, Tex., Dec. 2, 1930; s. Charles Francis and Mildred Maurine (Butler) E.; m. Agnes Christian Welsh, Feb. 11, 1961; children: Richard, Maury, John. BBA, Tex. A&M U., 1953; LLB, U. Tex., 1958. Bar: Tex. 1957, U.S. Supreme Ct. 1967. Lawyer Coastal States, Corpus Christi, Tex., 1959-61; head land and legal svcs. Alamo Gas, San Antonio, 1961-64; lawyer Forest Oil, San Antonio, 1964—68; pvt. practice law San Antonio, 1968—. Mgr. Corcel, LC, Waco, Tex., 1992-2000, Agarita Trading Co., LLC, San Antonio, 1996-99. Capt. USMC, 1953-61, Korea. Episcopalian. Avocations: family, oil and gas exploration. Home: 240 E Huisache Ave San Antonio TX 78212-3029 Office: PO Box 12372 San Antonio TX 78212-0372

EYSTER, MARY ELAINE, hematologist, educator; m. Robert E. Dye, Jan. 2, 1965; children: Robert E. Dye, Charles Dye. AB, Duke U., 1956, MD, 1960. Intern. N.Y. Hosp.-Cornell Med. Coll., N.Y.C., 1960-61, resident in medicine, 1961-63, fellow in hematology, 1963-66, instr. medicine, 1966-67, asst. prof. medicine, 1967-70; asst. prof. medicine Milton S. Hershey Med. Ctr. Pa. State U., Hershey, 1970-73, assoc. prof. Milton S. Hershey Med. Ctr., 1973-82, prof. Milton S. Hershey Med. Ctr., 1982—, chief hematology divsn., dept. medicine Coll. Medicine, 1973-96. Bd. dirs. Hemophilia Ctr. Cen. Pa., 1973—, AIDS Clin. Trials Unit Pa. State U., 1987—; faculty rsch. assoc. Am. Cancer Soc., 1966-71; mem. State Hemophilia Adv. Com, 1973—, chmn., 1977-79, 1988-90; mem. policy bd. Coop. F VII inhibitor study Nat. Heart, Lung and Blood Inst., 1975-79; mem. med. and sci. adv. counc. Nat. Hemophilia Found., 1976-77, 83-89, chmn. med. adv. com. Del. Valley chpt., 1979-82; co-investigator, mem. multi-agy. task force on AIDS HHS, 1982-83; mem. blood products adv. com. FDA, 1985-89; exec. com. NIH-NIAID Clin. Trials, 1988-90; mem. forum on blood safety and availability Inst. of Med., 1993-95. USPHS grantee, 1976-95. Fellow ACP; mem. Am. Fedn. Clin. Rsch., World Fedn. Hemophilia, Am. Soc. Hematology, Internat. Soc. Thrombosis and Haemostasis, Insternat. Soc. Hematology, Pa. Soc. Hematology and Oncology (bd. dirs. 1982-85), Am. Assn. for Study of Liver Diseases, Phi Beta Kappa, Alpha Omega Alpha. Office: Milton S Hershey Med Ctr PO Box 850 Hershey PA 17033-0850

EYTON, JOHN TREVOR, senator, business executive; b. Quebec, Que., Can., July 12, 1934; s. John and Dorothy Isabel (dec.) E.; m. Barbara Jane Montgomery, Feb. 13, 1955; children: Adam Tudor, Christopher Montgomery, Deborah Jane Findlay, Susannah Margaret Belton, Sarah Elizabeth Eyton Gould. BA, U. Toronto, Can., 1957, JD, 1960; LLD, U. Waterloo, 1992; D Civil Law (hon.), U. Kings Coll., 2002. Bar: Ont. 1962, created Queen's Counsel. Read law Tory, Tory, DesLauriers & Binnington, Toronto, Ont., 1960-62, assoc., 1962-67, ptnr., 1967-79; pres., CEO Brascan Ltd., Toronto, 1979-90, chmn., 1990-98; chancellor U. King's Coll., Halifax, 1996—2001; senator Senate of Can., Ottawa, Ont., Can., 1990—. Bd. dirs. Brascan Corp., Toronto, Coretec Inc., Gen. Motors of Can. Ltd., Noranda Inc., Coca Cola Enterprises Inc., IMAX Corp.; bd. dirs., chmn. Ivernia West Inc.; bd. govs. Can. Sports Hall of Fame; adv. bd. Nestle. Gov. Can. Olympic Found. Decorated Order of Can., 1986; recipient Mexican Aguila Azteca award, 2000. Mem. Upper Can. Law Soc., Can. Bar Assn., Toronto Club, York Club, Caledon Mountain Trout Club, Devil's Pulpit Golf Club (Caledon), The Rideau Club (Ottawa), Royal Palm Yacht and Country Club (Boca Raton). Progressive Conservative. Anglican. Avocations: ski, golf. Office: 44 Victoria St Ste 400 Toronto ON Canada M5C 1Y2 also: Senate of Can Parliament Bldgs Rm 561-S Ottawa ON Canada K1A 0A4 Home: 44 Adelarde St 400 Toronto ON Canada

EZAKI-YAMAGUCHI, JOYCE YAYOI, dietitian; b. Kingsburg, Calif., Mar. 18, 1947; d. Toshikatsu and Aiko (Ogata) Ezaki; m. Kent Takao Yamaguchi, Oct. 28, 1972; children: Kent Takao, Jr., Toshia Ann. AA, Reedley Coll., 1967; BS in Foods and Nutrition, U. Calif., Davis, 1969. Dietetic intern Henry Ford Hosp., Detroit, 1969-70, staff dietitian, 1970-71; renal dietitian Sutter Meml.

Hosp., Sacramento, 1971-72; therapeutic dietitian Mt. Sinai Hosp., Beverly Hills, Calif., 1972-73; clin. dietitian Pacific Hosp., Long Beach, Calif., 1973-77; consulting dietitian Doctor's Hosp., Lakewood, Calif., 1976-77; clin. dietitian Mass. Gen. Hosp., Boston, 1977-78, Winona Meml. Hosp., Indpls., 1978-80; renal dietitian Fresno (Calif.) Community Hosp., Calif., 1980—. Author: (computer program) Dialysis Tracker, 1987; author: (with others) Cultural Foods and Renal Diets for the Dietitian, 1988, Standards of Practice Guidlines for the Practice of Clinical Dietetics, 1991. Religious chair Fresno Dharma Sch. Fresno Betsuin Buddhist Temple, 1994—; sec. Japanese Lang. Sch., 1997-01. Mem. Nat. Kidney Found. (exec. com. coun. renal nutrition 1991-98, region V rep., nutrition editor, chair patient and pub. edn. com. 1992-93, chair elect comms. chair 1994-95, chair 1995-96, past chair 1997-98, chair nominations com., chair rsch. grant com., Disting. Svc. award 1996, Nat. Kidney Found./Coun. on Renal Nutrition Recognized Renal Dietitian award 1999), Am. Dietetic Assn. (bd. cert. renal nutrition specialist, renal practice group 1993-98, renal practice group nominating com. chair 1999), No. Calif/No. Nev. chpt. Nat. Kidney Found. (disting. achievement award coun. on renal nutrition 1993, co-chair-elect 1993-94, co-chair 1994-95, co-past chair 1995-96, treas., corr. sec.). Buddhist. Avocations: computers, cross stitch. Office: Cmty Med Ctrs CAPD Fresno & R Sts Fresno CA 93715-2094

EZASHI, TOSHIHIKO, molecular biologist; b. Takefu, Fukui, Japan, July 24, 1962; came to U.S., 1995; s. Shunei and Kazuko Ezashi; m. Mine Ezashi, Mar. 12, 1995. BS, Azabu U., Sagamihara, Japan, 1986, MS, 1988; PhD, Gumma U., Maebashi, Japan, 1993. Rsch. assoc. Osaka Biosci. Inst., Suita, Japan, 1992-95; postdoctoral fellow U. Mo., Columbia, 1995-99, rsch. asst. prof., 1999—. Author: Yeast Hybrid Technologies, 2000; contbr. articles to profl. jours.; inventor in field. Recipient Encouragement award Osaka Biosci. Inst,. 1994, travel award Internat. Soc. for Interferon and Cytokine Rsch., 1997, Poster Contest and Presentation award Molecular Biology Week 98, U. Mo., 1998. Mem. Soka Gakkai Internat. (dist. leader Kansas City N.E. chpt. 1999—, group leader 1996-99). Buddhist. Avocations: hiking, biking, reading books. Home: 3415 Madrid Ln Columbia MO 65203 Office: U Mo 920 E Campus Dr 158 ASRC Columbia MO 65211 E-mail: etoshihiko@socket.net.

EZEKWE, MICHAEL OBI, animal science educator; b. Abatete, Anambra, Nigeria, Nov. 16, 1944; came to U.S., 1972; s. Okudo Ebudike and Ogaobaka (Anyaralu) E.; m. Edith Ifeyinwa Uzodinma, May 18, 1974; children: Obi, Kenechi, Ifemefuna, Chijioke, Nneamaka. BS with honors, U. Nigeria, 1971; MS, Pa. State U., 1974, PhD, 1977. Rsch. scientist Va. State U., Petersburg, 1978—, coord. program, 1993-97; assoc. prof., dir. Swine Devel. Ctr. Alcorn State U., Lorman, Miss., 1997—. Cons. in field. Contbr. articles to Jour. Animal Sci., Growth, Devel. and Aging, Va. Jour. Sci., Nutrition Report Internat., Hormone and Metabolic Rsch., Jour. Am. Oil Chemists Soc., Plant Foods Human Nutrition, Ann. Reciprocal Meats Conf. Eucharistic min. St. Joseph's Ch., Port Gibson, Miss., 1999—. USDA-CSRS grantee, 1986—. Mem. Am. Soc. Animal Sci., Am. Soc. Nutritional Scis., KC, Sigma Xi, Gamma Sigma Delta. Roman Catholic. Achievements include discovery of usefulness of maternal diabetes in developing fetal pigs; patent in demonstrating the beneficial effects of purslane plant in lowering plasma cholesterol and triglycerides. Office: Alcorn State U Box 1374 1000 Alcorn State U Dr Lorman MS 39096-9400 E-mail: ezekwe@lorman.alcorn.edu.

EZELL, WAYLAND L. biologist, educator; b. Stockton, Calif., Dec. 31, 1937; s. Doyle Landreth Ezell and Elaine Mildred Cromer; m. Sue Ellen Schlegel, June 10, 1961 (dec. Dec. 1990); children: Charles, David, Elizabeth; m. Yvette Victoria Villeneuve-Ezell, May 24, 1992. BA, U. of the Pacific, 1959, MA, 1962; PhD, Oreg. State U., 1970. Instr. biology Ventura (Calif.) Coll., 1962—66; prof. biology St. Cloud (Minn.) State Coll., 1970—99; ret. Environ. cons., Copperopolis, Calif., 1999—. Contbr. articles to profl. jours. Commr. Calaveras County Fish and Game Commn., 2000—; active Copperopolis Cmty.Plan Commn., 2000—. Grantee, NSF, 1971—73. Mem.: Calif. Native Plant Soc., Calif. Bot. Soc., Am. Soc. Plant Taxonomists. Avocations: poetry, writing, wildflower photography. Home: 2403 Pamo Ct Copperopolis CA 95228

EZELLE, ROBERT EUGENE, diplomat; b. Mattoon, Ill., Dec. 5, 1927; s. Zonner Robert and Nina Leora (Smith) E.; m. Lesly Marion Hopkins, Apr. 30, 1955; children: Robert, Lesley, John, Paul. Student, U. So. Calif., 1947-49, U. Bonn, 1954-56, U. Munich, 1956-57; PhD, U. Vienna, 1960; MS (Sloan fellow), Stanford Grad. Sch. Bus., 1977; Dr.h.c., Nat. U., 1981. Instr. Bonn, Munich and Vienna, 1954-60; dir. lang. sch., San Mateo, Calif., 1960-61; joined U.S. Fgn. Svc., 1961; internat. rels. officer State Dept., Washington, 1961-62, staff asst. Nat. Interdeptl. Seminar, 1962-63; assigned Hong Kong, 1963-65, Bern, Switzerland, 1965-69, Naples, Italy, 1969-72; chief consular affairs sect. Am. Embassy, Bonn, 1972-75; internat. rels. officer State Dept., Washington, 1975-76; dep. consul gen. Am. Embassy, London, 1977-80; consul gen. Am. Consulate Gen., Tijuana, Mex., 1980-84, Am. Embassy, Paris, 1984-88, 1988—90; cons., internat. trade, 1990—. Served with USAF, 1949-53. Recipient Gold medal City of Paris, 1988, Superior Honor award Dept. State, 1988. Address: 27606 N Regal Rd Chattaroy WA 99003

EZENWA, JOSEPHINE NWABUOKU, social worker; b. Oct. 20, 1959; d. Igwe Silas O. and H.R.H. Veronica A. Ezenwa. BA psychology and human Svc.(hon.), Fontbonne Coll., St. Louis, 1980; MSW, Washington Univ., St. Louis, 1981; post grad., St. Louis U., 1991-93. Rsch. dir. Nat. Benevolent Assn., St. Louis, 1981-89; tchr. U. City Sch. Dist., St. Louis, 1989-94; therapist Presbyn. Children's Home, St. Louis, 1994-95; social worker St. Louis Regional Med. Ctr., 1995-97; founder, chair St. Louis Regional Med. Ctr. Dialysis Support Group, 1995-97; social worker St. Louis U. Hosp., 1997; CEO and pres. BBS Care U.S.A., Inc., St. Louis, 1997-2000; pres. BBS Charities, Inc., St. Louis, 2000—; chair Bus. Adv. Coun. Nat Rep. Congl. Com., St. Louis, 2002—. Founder and chair St. Louis Regional Med. Ctr. Dialysis Support Group, 1995-97; chair long range planning com. Washington U.; co-chair Bus. Adv. Coun., 2002; presenter in field. Chair bus. adv. coun. Nat. Rep. Congl. Com., 2002—. Recipient Nat. Leadership award, St. Louis Regional Med. Ctr. Dialysis Support Group, 2002. Mem. NASW, NAFE, Coun. Nephrology Social Workers; Nat. Assn. Forensic Counselors; Nat. Assn. Cognitive Behavioral Therapists, Washington U. Sch. Social Work Alumni Assn. (bd. dir.); Creve Coeur-Olive C. of C.; Lions Club. Avocations: choreography, fashion cons., event coord., design, travel. Office: St Louis U Hosp 3536 Vista Grand Saint Louis MO 63110 also: BBS Care USA Inc 8420 Delmar Blvd Ste 505 Saint Louis MO 63124-2180

EZHARATH, JOSEPH, pastor; b. Punnathura, Kerala, India, May 6, 1936; arrived in U.S., 1994; s. Punnoose Ezharath, Elizabeth Ezharath. BS in Philosophy, S.H. Sem., Poonamallee, India, 1962, MDiv, 1966. Ordained minister 1966. Parish min. Diocese of Vijayawada, Andhra Pradeth, India, 1966—94, Mater Dolorosa Ch., Paden City, W.Va., 1994—. Home and Office: 302 E Main St Paden City WV 26159

EZRATI, MILTON JOSEPH, investment manager, economist, writer; b. N.Y.C., May 22, 1947; s. Al and Edythe Ezrati; m. Lynda Lamare, July 1970 (div.); m. Susan Arlene Graham, June 19, 1976; 1 child, Isabel Diana. BA in Econs., SUNY, Buffalo, 1969; M Social Sci. in Math. Econs., Birmingham (Eng.) U., 1973. Econ. specialist Citibank, N.Y.C., 1971-73; economist Chase Manhattan Bank, N.Y.C., 1973-77, Lionel Edie & Co., N.Y.C., 1977-78, chief economist, 1978-81, Mfrs. Hanover Investment Corp., N.Y.C., 1981-83, chief economist and strategist, 1983-85, sr. v.p., dir. rsch., 1985-87; chief investment officer Nomura Asset Mgmt., N.Y.C., 1987-99; sr. economist and strategist Lord, Abbett & Co., Jersey City, N.J., 2000—. Author: Kawari: How Japan's Economic and Cultural Transformation Will Alter the Balance of Power Among Nations, 1999; contbr. articles to profl. and popular jours. Mem. Am. Econs. Assn., Nat. Assn. Scholars, Old Westbury Horseman's Assn. Methodist. Avocations: riding and training horses, skiing. Office: Lord Abbett & Co 90 Hudson St Jersey City NJ 07302

EZZEDINE, SOUHEIL M. physicist, researcher; PhD, Ecole des Mines de Paris, 1989—94. Scientist U. Calif., Berkeley, 1994—99; scientist, engr. Lawrence Livermore Nat. Lab., Calif., 1999—. Scientist Ecole des Mines de Paris, 1989—94; cons. Weiss Associates, Emeryville, Calif., 1999. Contbr. articles to profl. jours. Mem.: NGWA, SIAM, ISBA, IAMG, AGU. Office: Lawrence Livermore Natl Lab 7000 East Ave Livermore CA 94550 Office Fax: 925-424-3155. E-mail: ezzedine1@llnl.gov.

EZZELL, CATHERINE, librarian; b. Canadian, Tex., Apr. 2, 1950; d. Ben Roach and Nancy Catherine E. BA in English, Sam Houston State U., 1972; MLS, Tex. Womans U., 1977. Asst. childrens libr. Bryan Pub. Libr., 1972-76; tech. svc. student clerk Tex. Womans U., Denton, 1976-77; tech. svc. libr. Bryan Pub. Libr., 1977—. Mem.: Tex. Libr. Assn., Brazos Heritage Soc., Tex. Women's U. Alumni Assn. Avocations: writing poetry, reading. Office: Bryan Pub Libr 201 E 26th St Bryan TX 77803-5389

FAALEVAO, AVIATA FANO, attorney general, political organization worker; b. Fagalele, Leone, Am. Samoa, Mar. 3, 1946; s. Faalevao Amitoelau Fano and Safua Akulu Pepe; m. Lia Sausau Faamausili, June 29, 1970; children: Aviata Jr., Sualua, Lora-Tufanua, Lia-Chalene, SauSau, Tafamoa. Student, Warren Wilson Coll.; BS, U. Tenn., 1969; JD, Valparaiso U., 1974. Bar: Pa. 1974, Am. Samoa 1975. Asst. atty. gen. Am. Samoa, 1975-78, dep. atty. gen., 1978-80, atty. gen., 1980—93; pvt. practice, 1993—; state chmn. Rep. Party, Pago Pago, 1996—. Mem. com. on resolutions Rep. Nat. Conv., 1992. V.p. PTA Pago Pago Sch., 1978—. Mem. Nat. Assn. Attys. Gen., Pa. Bar Assn., Am. Samoa Bar Assn. (v.p.). Mem. Congregational Christian Ch. Am. Samoa. Office: Republican Party American Samoa PO Box 6171 Pago Pago AS 96799*

FAATZ, JEANNE RYAN, councilperson; b. Cumberland, Md., July 30, 1941; d. Charles Keith and Myrtle Elizabeth (McIntyre) Ryan; children: Kristin, Susan. BS, U. Ill., 1962; postgrad., Harvard U., 1984; MA, U. Colo., Denver, 1985. Instr. speech dept. Met. State Coll., Denver, 1985-98; sec. to majority leader Colo. Senate, 1976-78; mem. Colo. Ho. Reps. from Dist. 1, 1979-98; dir. Colo. Sch.-to-Career, 1999—2001; councilwoman City of Denver, 2003—. Former ho. asst. majority leader. Past pres. S.W. Denver YWCA Adult Edn. Club; former mem. bd. mgrs. S.W. Denver YMCA; past pres. Harvey Park (Colo.) Homeowners Assn. Gates fellow, Harvard U., 1984. Home: 2903 S Quitman St Denver CO 80236-2208

FABBRI, ANNE R. art critic, curator; b. Norristown, Pa. d. Remo and Anna Wild (Butterworth) F.; m. Joseph Henry Butera (div.); children: Virginia, Remo, Joseph F. (Jay). AB cum laude, Radcliffe Coll.; MA in Art History, Bryn Mawr Coll., 1971. Art lectr. Villanova U., Pa., 1971-73, Drexel U., Phila., 1974-76; art critic, art editor The Drummer, Phila., 1976-79; art critic The Bulletin, Phila., 1978-80; dir. Alfred O. Deshong Mus., Widener U., Chester, Pa., 1980-82, The Noyes Mus., Oceanville, N.J., 1982-91; dir. Paley Design Ctr. Phila. U., 1991-2001; art critic Phila. Daily News, Art in Am., Art Matters, The Art Newspaper, Am. Artist, 1998—; lectr. arts adminstrn. Rosemont Coll., 2000—, lectr. humanities, 2001—. Bd. dirs. Phila. Vol. Lawyers for the arts, 2001—; mem. adv. com. Main Line Art Ctr.; chair adv. com. Art in City Hall, Phila., 1999-2003; chair New Visions, Phila. Furniture Exhbn., 1998—. Chair, mem. adv. com. Art in City Hall, 1999—. Vis. NEH fellow U. Calif.-Berkeley, 1980, Princeton U., 1981; recipient John Cotton Dana award Mus. N.J. Assn. Mus., 1991. Mem. Am. Assn. Museums, Coll. Art Assn., Internat. Assn. Art Critics, Amici Ctr. for Italian Studies (bd. advisors 1987—91). Home and Office: 642 Valley View Ln Wayne PA 19087-2024 E-mail: arfabbri@aol.com.

FABE, DANA ANDERSON, state supreme court chief justice; b. Cin., Mar. 29, 1951; d. George and Mary Lawrence (Van Antwerp) F.; m. Randall Gene Simpson, Jan. 1, 1983; 1 child, Amelia Fabe Simpson. BA, Cornell U., 1973; JD, Northeastern U., 1976. Bar: Alaska 1977, U.S. Supreme Ct. 1981. Law clk. to justice Alaska Supreme Ct., 1976-77; staff atty. pub. defenders State Alaska, 1977-81; dir. Alaska Pub. Defender Agy., Anchorage, 1981—. Judge Superior Ct., Anchorage; justice Alaska Supreme Ct., Anchorage, 1996—, chief justice, 2000—. Named alumna of yr. Northeastern Sch. Law, 1983, alumni pub. svc. award, 1991. Office: Alaska Supreme Ct 303 K St Fl 5 Anchorage AK 99501-2013

FABENS, ANDREW LAWRIE, III, lawyer; b. Washington, Apr. 8, 1942; s. Andrew Lawrie Jr. and Alicia Gordon (Hail) F.; m. Martha Leigh Leingang, June 24, 1966; children: Andrew Lawrie IV, Jennie Leigh. AB, Yale U., 1964; JD, U. Chgo., 1967. Bar: Ohio 1967. Assoc. Thompson, Hine and Flory, Cleve., 1967-74; ptnr. Thompson Hine LLP (formerly Thompson, Hine and Flory), Cleve., 1974—, chmn. estate planning and probate area, 1988-94. Contbr. articles on estate planning and related topics to profl. publs. Pres. Family Health Assn., Cleve., 1978-80, 83-84; trustee A.M. McGregor Home, East Cleveland, Ohio, 1991—, chmn., 2001—; trustee Bascom Little Fund, Cleve., 1985—, Great Lakes Basin Conservancy, 1999—; vestryman Christ Episcopal Ch., Shaker Heights, Ohio, 1972-77. Fellow Am. Coll. Trust and Estate Counsel; mem. Ohio State Bar Assn. (bd. govs. estate planning, trust and probate law sect. 1983—, treas. 1997-99, sec. 1999-2001, vice-chmn. 2001-03, chmn. 2003—), Probate Law Jour. Ohio (adv. bd.), Cleve. Bar Assn. (speaker, com. mem. 1976—), Cleve. Skating Club, Rowfant Club (fellow 2000-03), The Novel Club (sec. 1986-88, pres. 1995-97), The Union Club. Home: 2280 Woodmere Dr Cleveland OH 44106-3604 Office: Thompson Hine LLP 3900 Key Ctr 127 Public Square Cleveland OH 44114-1216

FABER, JOHN M. state representative; b. Colby, Kans., Oct. 22, 1952; m. Renee Faber; 3 children. Ptnr. Faber & Faber Farms, Triumph Seed Co.; mem. Kans. Ho. of Reps., 1997—. Mem. sch. bd., 1993—97; pres. sch. bd., 1995—97; leadership coun. Colby Coll.; area wide bd. control Northwest Kans. Vocat. Tech.; mem. N.W. Kans. Libr. Svc. Ctr.; coun. Our Savior's Luth Ch.; mem. Luth. Parish Western Kans.; pres. bd. dirs. N.W. Kans. Heritage; bd. dirs. Goodland Coop., Brewster Coop. With U.S. Army, 1971—72. Mem.: Compassionate Friends. Republican. Lutheran. Office: 181-W State Capitol 300 SW 10th Ave Topeka KS 66612 Address: HC 2 Box 130 Brewster KS 67732-9302*

FABER, MICHAEL WARREN, lawyer; b. N.Y.C., June 7, 1943; s. Carl Faber and Harriet Ruth Cohen; m. Adele Zolot, Apr. 16, 1975; children: Evan, Jenna. AB, Hunter Coll., 1964; JD, Fordham U., 1967. Bar: N.Y. 1967, D.C. 1972, U.S. Ct. Claims, 1972, U.S. Supreme Ct. 1972, Colo. 1993. Gen. atty. FCC, Washington, 1967-69, trial atty., 1969-71, atty. advisor to Commr. T.J. Houser, 1971; assoc. Peabody, Rivlin, Lambert & Meyers, Washington, 1971-73; ptnr. Peabody, Lambert & Meyers, Washington, 1973-84, Reid and Priest, Washington, 1984-93, mem. exec. com., 1986-92; prin. The Faber Group, Cascade, Colo., 1993-94; pres. USA Volleyball Ctrs. LLC, Colorado Springs, Colo., 1995-96; owner The Pantry Restaurant, Green Mountain Falls, Colo., 1996—2001; prin. Crossroads Cons., LLC, Cascade, Colo., 2001—; dir. Workforce Partnership study Pikes Peak Workforce Investment Bd., Colorado Springs, Colo., 2003—. Cons. White House Office Telecomm. Policy, 1976; chmn. organizing com. Nat. Volleyball League. Bd. dirs. Washington Very Spl. Arts, 1986-93; mem. Telecom. Policy Adv. Com., Colo. Springs, 2002-, SAFE Com., Colo. Springs, 2002-; pres. Manitou Springs Edn. Assn., Manitou Springs, 2002-; dir. Workforce Partnership Project, Pikes Peak, Workforce Investment Bd., Colorado Springs, Colo. Mem. N.Y. Bar Assn., D.C. Bar Assn., Fed. Communications Bar Assn., Colo. Bar Assn. E-mail: mwfaber@aol.com.

FABER, NEIL, advertising executive; b. N.Y.C., May 21, 1938; m. Susan Somer, Jan. 28, 1962; children: Cynthia Farber-Wolf, Amy Farber, Gary Faber. BS, MBA, NYU, 1960. Rsch. analyst Alfred Politz, N.Y.C., 1958-60; eastern sales svc. mgr. ABC, N.Y.C., 1960-63, media supr. Batten, Barton, Durstein & Osborn, N.Y.C., 1964-67; sr. account exec. Wells, Rich, Greene, N.Y.C., 1967-73; v.p., dir. media Della Femina Advt., N.Y.C., 1973-79; founder, pres. Neil Faber Media Inc. Mktg. Media Planning/Buying Co., N.Y.C., 1979—; pres. NexGen Media Worldwide Inc. Assoc. prof. mktg. NYU, 1982-2000; lectr. in field. One of the first to develop and introduce new media interactive course at NYU and to utilize web for course exams.; contbr. articles to profl. jours., consumer mags. Recipient Master Communicator award Advt. Agy., Workshop award, Seminar award Mktg. Media. Avocations: music, sports. Office: NexGen Media Worldwide Inc 108 W 57th St New York NY 10019-2210 E-mail: nfaber@nexgenmedia.com.

FABER, PETER LEWIS, lawyer; b. N.Y.C., Apr. 29, 1938; s. Alexander W. and Anne L. Faber; m. Joan Schuster, June 14, 1959; children: Michael, Julia, Thomas. AB, Swarthmore Coll., 1960; LLB, Harvard U., 1963. Bar: N.Y. 1964. Assoc. Wiser, Shaw, Freeman, Ickes & Williams, Rochester, N.Y., 1963-65, Parker, Chapin & Flattau, N.Y.C., 1965-66; ptnr. Harter, Secrest & Emery, Rochester, N.Y., 1966-82, Winthrop, Stimson, Putnam & Roberts, N.Y.C., 1982-84, Kaye, Scholer, Fierman, Hays & Handler, N.Y.C., 1984-95, McDermott, Will & Emery, N.Y.C., 1995—. Mem. adv. com. NYU Ann. Inst. on State & Local Taxation; mem. N.Y. State Coun. on Fiscal and Econ. Priorities, 1991-95. Contbr. articles to profl. jours. Chmn. Rochester Econ. Devel. Com., 1979-82; pres. Rochester Philharm. Orch., Inc., 1980-82; bd. dirs. Met. Rochester Devel. Coun., Harley Sch., 1978-81; mem. fin. com. Monroe County Dem. Party, 1979-82; active N.Y.C. Partnership. Fellow Am. Bar Found., Am. Coll. Tax Counsel; mem. ABA (chmn. tax sect. 1991-92, vice chmn. 1986-88, chmn.-elect 1990-91, chmn. com. corp. stockholder relationships tax sect. 1980-82, liaison to IRS for North Atlantic region, vice chmn. spl. com. on integration 1979-81, sec. tax sect. 1984-86), N.Y. State Bar Assn. (chmn. sect. taxation 1976-77, exec. com. sect. taxation 1969—), N.Y. C. of C. (chmn. tax com. 1988—, trustee 1989—, exec. com. 1990—), Monroe County Bar Assn., Am. Law Inst. (tax project adv. group), Rochester Area C. of C. (trustee 1980-82). Home: 300 Central Park W New York NY 10024-1513 Office: McDermott Will & Emery 50 Rockefeller Plz Fl 12 New York NY 10020-1600

FABER, ROBERT CHARLES, lawyer; b. N.Y.C., June 26, 1941; s. Sidney G. and Beatrice (Siebert) F.; m. Carol Z. Zimmerman, Aug. 15, 1965; 1 child, Susan Faber. BA, Cornell U., 1962; JD, Harvard Law Sch., 1965. Bar: N.Y. 1966; U.S. Dist. Ct. (so. dist.) N.Y. 1967; U.S. Ct. Appeals (2nd cir.), U.S. Ct. Appeals (fed. cir.) 1982; U.S. Supreme Ct. 1971; U.S. Patent and trademark Office 1967. Atty., ptnr. Ostrolenk, Faber, Gerb & Soffen, LLP, N.Y.C., 1965—. Lectr. Practicing Law Inst., N.Y.C., 1974—. Author: Landis on Mechanics of Patent Claim Drafting, 3d edit. 1990, 4th edit. 1996. Mem. Am. Intellectual Property Law Assn., N.Y. Intellectual Property Law Assn., Harvard Club of N.Y. Office: Ostrolenk Faber Gerb & Soffen LLP 1180 Ave of Americas New York NY 10036-8401

FABER, SANDRA MOORE, astronomer, educator; b. Boston, Dec. 28, 1944; d. Donald Edwin and Elizabeth Mackenzie (Borwick) Moore; m. Andrew L. Faber, June 9, 1967; children: Robin, Holly. BA, Swarthmore Coll., 1966, DSc (hon.), 1986; PhD, Harvard U., 1972; DSc (hon.), Williams Coll., 1996. Asst. prof., astronomer Lick Obs., U. Calif., Santa Cruz, 1972-77, assoc. prof., astronomer, 1977-79, prof., astronomer, 1979—; Univ. Prof. U. Calif., Santa Cruz, 1996—. Mem. astronomy adv. panel NSF, 1975-77; vis. prof. Princeton U., 1978, U. Hawaii, 1983, Ariz. State U., 1985; Phillips visitor Haverford Coll., 1982; Feshbach lectr. MIT, Cambridge, Mass., 1990; Darwin lectr. Royal Astron. Soc., 1991; Marker lectr. Pa. State U., 1992; Bunyan lectr. Stanford U., 1992; Tomkins lectr. U. Calif., San Francisco, 1992; Mohler lectr. U. Mich., 1994; mem. Nat. Acad. Astronomy Survey Panel, 1979-81Nfat. Acad. Com. on Astronomy and Astrophysics 1993-1995; chmn. vis. com. Space Telescope Sci. Inst., 1983-84; co-chmn. sci. steering com. Keck Obs., 1987-92, leader DEIMOS spectrograph team, 1993—; mem. Wide Field Camera team Hubble Space Telescope, 1985-97, user's com., 1990-92, mem. advanced radial camera selection team, 1995,co-chmn. TAC review comm., 2002; mem. treas. pgm. advis. comm. 2002-; mem. Calif. Coun. on Sci. and Tech., 1989-94,; Com. on Future Smithsonian Instn., 1994-95; mem. White House Space Sci. Workshop, 1996, Waterman Awards Com., NSF, 1997-99, Nat. Medal of Sci. selection com., 1999-2001; mem. Plumian Prof. selection com. Cambridge U., 1998—. Assoc. editor: Astrophys. Jour. Letters, 1982-87; editorial bd.: Ann. Revs. Astronomy and Astrophysics, 1982-87; contbr. articles to profl. jours. Trustee Carnegie Instn., Washington, 1985—; bd. dirs. Ann. Revs., 1989—, SETI Inst., 1997—; editl. affairs com. Ann. Revs., 1996—; exec. com. Ann. Revs., 1998—; Scripps Instn. Oceanography Coun., 2000--; bd. overseers Fermilab, 2002--. Recipient Bart J. Bok prize Harvard U., 1978, Director's Distinguished Lectr. award Livermore Nat. Lab., 1986; NASA Group Achievement award, 1993, DeVaucouleurs medal U. Tex., 1997; Carnegie Lectr. Carnegie Inst. Washington, 1988, 99; NSF fellow, 1966-71; Woodrow Wilson fellow, 1966-71; Alfred P. Sloan fellow, 1977-81; listed among 100 best Am. scientists under 40, Sci. Digest, 1984, listed among 50 best Am. Women scientists, Discover Mag., 2002; Tetelman fellow, Yale U., 1987. Fellow Calif. Coun. on Sci. and Tech.; mem. NAS (vice chair adv. panel on cosmology 1993, rsch. in astronomy commn. on orgn. and mgmt. astrophysics 2001, co-chmn. TAC rev. commn. 2002, mem. treas. program adv. commn. 2002--), Am. Philos. Soc. Am. Acad. Arts and Scis., Calif. Acad. Scis., 1998—, Am. Astron. Soc. (councilor 1982-84, Dannie Heineman prize 1986), Internat. Astron. Union, Am. Philos. Soc., Phi Beta Kappa, Sigma Xi. Office: U Calif Lick Obs Santa Cruz CA 95064 E-mail: faber@ucolick.org.

FABER, TRUDY, music educator; b. Clifton, N.J., Dec. 10, 1938; d. Jacob Gerard and Olive Kievit; m. J. Arthur Faber, Aug. 5, 1960; children: James Stephan, Jonathan Leigh. BA in Music, Calvin Coll., 1960; postgrad., Amsterdam Conservatory, 1960—61, U. Toronto, Can., 1962—63; MA in Music, Smith Coll., 1966. Cert. ch. musician Presbyn. Ch. Am. Asst. instr. organ Calvin Coll., Grand Rapids, Mich., 1961—62; elem. music tchr. Sylvan Christian Schs., Grand Rapids, Mich., 1961—62; H.S. English tchr. Northampton (Mass.) H.S., 1963—64; prof. music Wittenberg U., Springfield, Ohio, 1966—, chair dept. music, 1995—. Organ, harpsichord recitalist Covenant Presbyn. Ch., Springfield, 1972—, organist, 1973—; clinician Am. Guild Organists, 1986—; pre-concert lectr. Springfield Symphony Orch., 1988—; lectr. in field. Fulbright scholar, 1960. Avocations: reading, bicycling, boating, hiking, travel. Home: 2910 Nauset St Springfield OH 45503 Office: Wittenberg Univ Box 720 Springfield OH 45501

FABIAN, D'ARLINE D. music educator; b. Detroit, Aug. 27, 1940; d. Edwin and Alva Orr DeJongh; m. Robert Henry Fabian, Aug. 14, 1964; 1 child, Douglas Stuart. BA in Psychology, U. Mich., 1963, MSW, 1964; MusB, Millikin U., 1986. Social worker Family Counseling Ctr., Hackensack, NJ, 1967, DeKalb-Rockdale Tng. Ctr., Atlanta, 1971; casework trainer Choctaw Child Advocacy Program, Philadelphia, Miss., 1977; freelance piano tchr. Springfield, Ill., 1980—85, Easton, Pa., 1990—92, Greenville, SC, 1986—90, Charlotte, NC, 1992—. Adjudicator state auditions S.C. Music Tchrs. Assn., 2002. Vol. usher N.C. Blumenthal Performing Arts Ctr., Charlotte, 2002, 2003. Mem.: Charlotte Piano Tchrs. Forum (asst. treas. 1997—99), N.C. Music Tchrs. Assn. (Charlotte dist. piano contest chair 1997—99, western divsn. state piano contest chair 2001, 2002), Music Tchrs. Nat. Assn. (cert.). E-mail: fabianpiano@webtv.net.

FABIAN, HANS J. education educator; b. Elbing, Germany, Aug. 1, 1926; arrived in U.S., 1941; s. Morris F. and Johanna E. Fabian; m. Myra Lou Williamson, Aug. 19, 1951. BA, Syracuse U., Syracuse, N.Y., 1950, MA, 1952, MS, 1954; PhD, Ohio State U., 1963. Libr. dir., asst. prof Wilmington Coll., Wilmington, Ohio, 1954—61; asst. prof., German Ohio U., Athens, Ohio, 1962—63; libr. Ohio State U., Columbus, Ohio, 1963—64; asst. prof., German U. Mich., Ann Arbor, Mich., 1964. Resident dir. Study Abroad U. Mich., Ann Arbor, Mich., 1968—69, Ann Arbor, 1975—76, asst. dean, 1970—73, dir. German House, 1975. Contbr. articles to profl. jours. Cpl. intelligence U.S. Army, 1944—46, Germany. Grantee Rsch. Grant, NEH, Washington, 1979, U. Mich., 1980. Mem.: Modern Lang. Assn. (life). Avocations: sailing, skiing, swimming, travel. Home: 2320 Walter Dr Ann Arbor MI 48103-3453 Home Fax: 734-665-1769. E-mail: hjf@umich.edu.

FABIAN, JANE, former ballet company executive, Mng. dir. Nashville Ballet. Office: Nashville Ballet 3630 Redmon Dr Nashville TN 37209-4827

FABIAN, JEANNE, entrepreneur, executive recruiter; b. Wilkes Barre, Pa., June 25, 1946; d. Joseph A. and Dorothy (Cannon) F.; m. Christopher Sykes, Sept. 7, 1968 (div. Mar. 1979). BBA, Baruch Coll., N.Y.C., 1969; MBA, Hofstra U., Hempstead, N.Y., 1979; postgrad., N.Y. Coll. Osteo. Medicine, 1998—. CPA, N.Y. Auditor Arthur Andersen & Co., N.Y.C., 1969-73; planning analyst Avon Products, Inc., N.Y.C., 1973-75; fin. analyst Revlon, Inc., N.Y.C., 1975-77; acctg. mgr. Am. Standard, Inc., N.Y.C., 1977-78; sr. fin. analyst Texaco, Inc., Harrison, N.Y., 1979-82; asst. dir. Harper & Row Pubs., Inc., N.Y.C., 1983-86, exec. recruiter, 1986-89; owner Fabian Assocs., Inc., N.Y.C., 1989—. Contbr. articles to profl. jours., including Archives of Biochemistry and Biophysics, Synlett. Treas., bd. dirs. Stanwix Apts. Corp., Forest Hills, N.Y., 1983—. Mem. AICPA, N.Y. State Soc. CPAs., Golden Key Nat. Hon. Soc. Avocations: real estate investments, international travel, science studies, photography. Office: Fabian Assocs Inc 521 5th Ave Fl 17 New York NY 10175-1799

FABIAN, KAREN, publishing executive, small business owner; b. Chgo., June 30, 1958; d. Arthur H. and Gerda Themer; m. Edward G. Fabian, May 17, 2002; children: Kirsten K. Welch, Erika E. Welch, Thomas M. McGowan. Owner and

mgr. The McGowan News Svc., Morris, Ill., 1997—, Ratava Publs., Morris, 1999—, Fabian's Fashions, Morris, 2002—. Pres. KET Corp., Morris, 1999—. Author: Vox Nihilo, 1999, Suffer My Children No More, 2001. Avocation: drag racing. Home: 407 W Jackson St Morris IL 60450-1728 E-mail: McGowanNews@aol.com., RatavaPubl@aol.com., FabiansFashions@aol.com.

FABIAN, LARRY LOUIS, university administrator; b. Aurora, Ill., May 25, 1940; s. Louis and Emma (Mayer) F.; m. Terese Sulikowski, Dec. 1, 1978; children: Christopher, Laura. BA, Cath. U. Am., 1961, MA, 1963; PhD, Columbia U., 1971. Staff mem. Bur. Intelligence and Research, Dept. State, Washington, 1962; staff mem. Carnegie Endowment for Internat. Peace, N.Y.C., 1964; research staff fgn. policy studies program Brookings Instn., Washington, 1965-71, research asso., co-dir. program on tech. and Am. fgn. policy, 1971-73; sr. assoc., dir. Middle East program Carnegie Endowment for Internat. Peace, Washington, 1974-77, sec., 1977-94; sr. v.p., COO, Coun. on Fgn. Rels., N.Y.C., 1994-95; v.p. Shorebank Corp., Chgo., 1996-98; deputy commr. Chgo. Dept. Housing, 1998; v.p., exec. sec. bd. trustees, exec. dir. N.Y. office Am. U. in Cairo, 1998—. Cons. Hudson Inst., N.Y.C., Rockefeller Found. Author: Soldiers without Enemies, 1971, (with others) Regimes for the Ocean, Outer Space and Weather, 1973, Andrew Carnegie's Peace Endowment, 1985; co-editor: Israelis Speak: About Themselves and the Palestinians, 1976. Mem. Coun. on Fgn. Rels., Century Assn. Roman Catholic. Office: Am U in Cairo NY Office 420 5th Ave Fl 3D New York NY 10018-2729

FABIAN, SUSAN JEAN, language educator; d. Charles Vincent and Helen Rosalie F.. MA in English Lang. and Lit., U. Chgo., Chgo., Ill., 1981. Cert. English and lang. arts tchr. Instr. English, lectr. Moraine Valley C.C., Palos Hills, Ill., 1981—86; instr. English Maria H.S., Chgo., 1987—90, Acad. of Our Lady H.S., Chgo., 1990—93; instr. English, lectr. Richard J. Daley Coll., Chgo., 1987—, St. Xavier U., Chgo., 1999—. Mem.: AAUP, MLA, Nat. Coun. Tchrs. English. Office: St Xavier U 3700 W 103rd St Chicago IL 60655

FABREGA, HORACIO, JR., psychiatry and anthropology educator; b. Phila., Jan. 6, 1934; s. Horacio and Maria (Stewart) F.; m. Joan Sporkin, June 7, 1957; children: Andrea Melanie, Michele Marie. BA, U. Pa., 1952-56; MD, Columbia U., 1956-60. Resident Yale U., New Haven, 1961-64; rsch. assoc. Walter Reed Army Inst. Rsch., Washington, 1964-66; asst. prof. psychiatry Baylor Coll. Medicine, Houston, 1966-69; assoc. to full prof. psychiatry Mich. State U., East Lansing, 1969-77; prof. psychiatry and anthropology U. Pitts., Pa., 1977—. Postdoctoral fellow in cultural psychiatry U. Tex., Austin, 1966-67; cons. NIMH, Washington, 1970—; pres. Soc. for Med. Anthropology, Am. Anthropol. Assn., Washington, 1972. Editorial bd.: Culture Medicine and Psychiatry, 1976-85, Psychiatry, 1992—, Psychosomatic Medicine, 1993—; author: Illness and Shamanistic Curing in Zinacantan, 1973, Disease and Social Behavior, 1974, Evaluation of Sickness and Healing, 1997, Origins of Psychopathology, 2002; contbr. articles to profl. jours. Capt. U.S. Army, 1964-66. Fellow Coll. Am. Psychiatrists, Am. Psychiat. Assn. Avocations: squash racquets, social history, literature, rock climbing. Home: 257 Kenforest Dr Pittsburgh PA 15216-1133 Office: Univ Pitts 3811 Ohara St Pittsburgh PA 15213-2593

FABRI, PETER J. surgeon, educator; b. Dec. 9, 1947; m. Sharon E. Schur. BA, Northwestern U., 1969; MD, Loyola U., Maywood, Ill., 1973. Assoc. prof. surgery Ohio State U., Columbus, 1984-86; prof. surgery U. South Fla. Coll. Medicine, Tampa, 1986—, program dir. gen. surgery residency, 1988-94, prof. dept. pharmacology and therapeutics, 1990—, dir. divsn. general surgery, 1992-94, assoc. dean grad. med. ed., 1993—; chief surgery James A. Haley Vets. Hosp., Tampa, 1986—2002, interim chief of staff, 1991-92; assoc. dean for VA affairs, 2002; acad. affiliations officer VISN8, 2002. Pres. Am. Soc. for Parenteral and Enteral Nutrition, 1995. Author Nutrition in Inflammatory Bowel Disease, 1992, Replacement of Central Vascular Catheters, 1993, The Remedial Year in Surgical Training: An Institutional Experience, 1997, The Endocrine Surgeon and Endocrine Neopolasms, 1997. Chmn. field adv. com. in surgery Dept. Vets. Affairs, Washington, 1996; mem. spl. task force in surgery Undersec. Dept. Vets. Affairs, Washington, 1998. Mem. AMA, Am. Coll. Surgeons, Am. Cancer Soc., Am. Surg. Assn., Endocrine Surgeons (program dir. 1992), Phi Sigma Kappa. Avocations: sailing, skiing, reading. Office: James A Haley Vets Hosp (111) 13000 Bruce B Downs Blvd Tampa FL 33612-4745 Fax: (813) 910-3029. E-mail: pfabri@hsc.usf.edu.

FABRICAND, BURTON PAUL, physicist, educator; b. N.Y.C., Nov. 22, 1923; s. Irving Kermit and Frances (Sobler) F.; m. Heather C. North, Dec. 15, 1972; children by previous marriage: Nicole Diane, Lorraine Stewart. AB, Columbia U., 1947, A.M., 1949, PhD, 1953. Project engr. Philco Corp., Phila., 1952-54; lectr., research asso. U. Pa., 1954-56; sr. research scientist Columbia Hudson Labs., Dobbs Ferry, N.Y., 1957-69; prof. physics Pratt Inst., Bklyn., 1969-92, prof. emeritus, 1992—; mng. ptnr. Fabricand Assocs., 1970—. Cons. Moore Sch. Elec. Engring., U. Pa., 1954-60, Indsl. Electronic Hardware Corp., N.Y.C., 1960-64; investment mgr. Beating the Street Fund, 1996—; bd. dirs. Murphey, Marseilles, Smith & Nammack, N.Y.C. Author: Horse Sense: A New and Rigorous Application of Mathematical Methods to Successful Betting at the Track, 1965, Beating the Street, 1969, Horse Sense: Updated and Expanded Edition, 1976, The Science of Winning: A Random Walk on the Road to Riches, 1979, Abolish the Income Tax: A New and Rigorous Inquiry into the Wealth of Nations, 1986, Symmetry in Free Markets in Symmetry—Unifying Human Understanding, 1989, The Science of Winning: A Random Walk Along the Road to Investment Riches, 1996; contbr. numerous articles on atomic and nuclear physics and oceanography. Served U.S. Army, 1942-46. Mem. Am. Phys. Soc., Sigma Xi. Home: PO Box 1107 New Milford CT 06776 Office: PO Box 1107 New Milford CT 06776-1107

FABRICANT, ARTHUR E. lawyer, corporate executive; b. N.Y.C., Aug. 8, 1935; s. Henry and Rita (Wilson) F.; children: Jill, Mary, John, James, Ann. AB, U. St. Andrews, Scotland, 1954, Union Coll., 1956; JD, Harvard U., 1959. Bar: N.Y. 1960. Atty. spl. group organized crime Office U.S. Atty. Gen., 1959-60; mem. firm Abeles & Clark, N.Y.C., 1960-61; v.p. Seligman & Latz Inc., N.Y.C., 1962-67, pres. internat. divsn. London, 1967-84, COO, pres., 1984-85; chmn. Essanelle Holdings, Ltd., Bermuda, 1985-96, Elizabeth Arden, Inc., 1992-2000. Bd. dirs. Elizabeth Arden Holdings Inc. Fellow Inst. Dirs.; mem. Royal Wimbledon Golf Club; Lyford Cay Club. Home: Old Warren Farm Wimbledon Common England Office: AE Fabricant & Co 39 Camp Rd London SW19 4UR England E-mail: arthurfab@aol.com.

FABRICANT, JILL DIANE, technology company executive; b. L.A. d. I. Robert and Lillian (Solid) F. BA, Mills Coll., 1971; MA, Occidental Coll., 1971; PhD, McGill U., 1976. Postdoctoral fellow Pasteur Inst., Paris, 1976-78; scientist NASA-Johnson Space Ctr., Houston, 1978-79; asst. prof. U. Tex. Med. Br., Galveston, 1979-82; pres. Biosyne Corp., Houston, 1982-88; v.p. bioscis. KVM Techs., Inc., Houston, 1989-90; pres. OvTex Corp., Houston, 1991—96; dir. The Enterprise NASA, Johnson Space Ctr., Houston, 1993—96; pres., CEO FlowGenix Corp., Webster, Tex., 1996—99; CEO Medicine for Humanity, San Juan Capistrano, Calif., 2000—01; dir. emerging technologies O'Melveny Consulting, LLC, L.A., 2002; pres. JFabricant and Assocs., Dana Point, Calif., 2002—. Mem. adv. bd. Houston Tech. Ctr., 1999—; trustee Mills Coll., 2000—, ATSC, Newport Beach, 2002—; bd. dirs. SGCC. Contbr. articles to sci. jours. Mem.: Am. Soc. Cell Biologists, Sigma Xi. Achievements include patents in field of sperm sexing and early-embry sexing, ovulation detection and FlowRad cell surface modification. Home: 34363 Dana Strand Dana Point CA 92629-2706 E-mail: jfabricant@aol.com.

FABRICANT, ROBERT E. federal agency administrator; b. N.Y., N.Y., 1963; BA, Drew U., 1985; JD, Cath. U., 1990. Chief counsel Gov. Christine Todd Whitman, 2000—01; gen. counsel EPA, Washington, 2001—. Office: EPA 1200 Pennsylvania Ave NW MC 2310A Washington DC 20460

FABRIKANT, CRAIG STEVEN, psychologist; b. Buffalo, Jan. 8, 1952; s. Benjamin and Laurine Miriam (Zucker) F.; m. Carol Diane Golub, Nov. 6, 1977; children: Chad Adam, Carly. BA, Fairleigh Dickinson U., 1974, MA, 1977; PhD, Fla. Inst. Tech., 1983. Intern in psychology N.J. Dept. Human Svcs., Trenton, 1977-78; clin. psychologist North Jersey Devel. Ctr., Totowa, 1978-85, Cedar Grove Residential Ctr.; chief psychologist Hackensack (N.J.) Med. Ctr., 1985-96; pvt. practice, 1984—. Adj. instr. Montclair State Coll., 1980-82; part-time instr. Fairleigh Dickinson U.; cons. psychology N.J. Dept. Labor and Industry, Newark, 1980—. Author profl. papers. Mem. APA, Assn. Advancement Behavior Therapy, N.J. Psychol. Assn. Home: 750 Martin Ave Oradell NJ 07649-2300 Office: 106 Old Hook Rd Westwood NJ 07675-2421 E-mail: shring106@aol.com.

FABRIS, JAMES A. journalist; b. Cleve., Aug. 6, 1938; s. Andrew and Geraldine (Foretic) F.; m. Donna Wilker, Dec. 26, 1960; children— Julia, John, James F., Gerald, Andrew, Fredric Student, Case Western Res. U., Cleve., 1956-58. Reporter Bklyn.-Parma News, Parma, Ohio, 1954-58; editorial staff Lake County News-Herald, Willoughby, Ohio, 1958-67, Chgo. Daily News, 1967-77, Chgo. Sun-Times, 1977-84, dep. mng. editor, 1984-86; mng. editor N.Y. Post, N.Y.C., 1986-89; editorial staff New York Daily News, 1990-92; deputy mng. editor Cleve. Plain Dealer, 1992—. Recipient Marshall Field award Field Enterprises, 1974; Soc. of Publ. Designers award, 1978 Roman Catholic. Home: 20791 Lake Rd Rocky River OH 44116-1335 Office: Cleve Plain Dealer 1801 Superior Ave Cleveland OH 44114-2107

FABRIZIO, LOUIS MICHAEL, educator; b. N.Y.C., Feb. 3, 1952; s. Fiore and Concetta (Del Bove) F.; m. Betsy Jo Jackson, Apr. 9, 1977 (div. Aug. 1984); 1 child, Erin; m. Katherine Kilburn, Nov. 21, 1987; children: Clair, Maria. BS in Physics, Georgetown U., 1974; MS in Edn. Adminstrn., N.C. State U., 1979. Tchr. math. and sci. Kalorama Children's Program, Washington, 1974; Head Start edn. dir. Wake County Opportunities, Inc., Raleigh, N.C., 1975, dir. head start, 1975-77; edn. cons. N.C. Dept. of Pub. Instruction, Raleigh, 1978, evaluation cons., 1979-81, CTB McGraw-Hill, Monterey, Calif., 1982-88, sr. evaluation cons., 1990-92; nat. evaluation cons., instr. software cons. CTB Macmillan/McGraw-Hill, Monterey, 1993; nat. assessment cons. CTB/McGraw-Hill, Monterey, Calif., 1994-96; dir. divsn. accountability svcs. N.C. Dept. Pub. Instrn., Raleigh, 1996—. Fellow Edn. Policy Fellowship Program, Washington, 1979. Active Dem. Nat. Com., N.C., 1988—, N.C. Dem. Com., 1990—. Mem. ASCD, Coun. for Basic Edn., Am. Ednl. Rsch. Assn., N.C. Assn. for Rsch. Edn. (sec. 1984-87, pres. 1988), Georgetown U. Alumni Assn. (chmn. admissions com. ea. N.C. 1985-89), Phi Delta Kappa (bd. dirs. 1985-89, historian 1999-01, Svc. Key 1990). Avocations: music, reading, sports, travel. Home: 1719 Park Dr Raleigh NC 27605-1610 Office: 301 N Wilmington St Raleigh NC 27601-2825 E-mail: Lfabrizi@dpi.state.nc.us., Lfabrizio@aol.com.

FABRYCKY, WOLTER JOSEPH, engineering educator, author, industrial and systems engineer; b. Springfield, N.Y., Dec. 6, 1932; s. Louis Ludwig and Stephanie (Wadis) F.; m. Luba Swerbilow, 1954; children: David Jon, Kathryn Marie. BS, Wichita State U., 1957; MS, U. Ark., 1958; PhD, Okla. State U., 1962. Instr. indsl. engring. U. Ark., 1957-60; from asst. to assoc. prof. indsl. engring. and mgmt. Okla. State U., 1962-65; from assoc. prof. to prof. indsl. and sys. engring. Va. Poly. Inst. and State U., Blacksburg, 1965-88, John L. Lawrence prof., 1988-95, founding chmn. systems engring., 1969-76, assoc. dean engring., 1970-76, dean rsch. divsn., 1976-81, Lawrence prof. emeritus, sr. rsch. scientist, 1995-99, Lawrence prof. emeritus, 1999—. Chmn. Acad. Applications Internat., Inc., 1998—. Author: (with G.J. Thuesen) Engineering Economy, 1950, 9th edit., 2001, (with G.J. Thuesen and D. Verma) Economic Decision Analysis, 1974, 3d edit., 1998, (with B.S. Blanchard) Systems Engineering and Analysis, 1981, 3d edit., 1998, (with P.M. Ghare and P.E. Torgersen) Applied Operations Research and Management Science, 1984, (with J. Banks) Procurement and Inventory Systems Analysis, 1987, (with B.S. Blanchard) Life-Cycle Cost and Economic Analysis, 1991; editor: (with J.H. Mize) Prentice-Hall International Series in Industrial and Systems Engineering, 1972—. Recipient Lohmann medal Okla. State U., 1992; Ethyl Corp. doctoral fellow Okla. State U., 1960-62. Fellow AAAS, Inst. Indsl. Engrs. (exec. v.p. 1982-84, trustee, Book of Yr. award 1973, Outstanding Educator award 1990), Internat. Coun. on Sys. Engring. (charter, nat. bd. dirs. 1995-97, Pioneer award 2000); mem. Am. Soc. Engrng. Edn. (v.p. 1977-78, bd. dirs., Grant award 1995), Ops. Rsch. Soc. Am., Sigma Xi, Alpha Pi Mu (v.p., bd. dirs. 1992—), Tau Beta Pi. Home: 1200 Lakewood Dr Blacksburg VA 24060-2005 Office: Va Poly Inst and State U Blacksburg VA 24061 E-mail: fab@vt.edu.

FABUNAN, RUBEN G, research scientist; b. San Marcelino, Zambales, Philippines, Mar. 15, 1945; arrived in U.S., 1979; s. Roman Battad Fabunan, Sr. and Feliza Pescador Garcia; m. Annie Pilapil Fabunan, Dec. 1973; children: Maritess, Farahnaz, Eileen. BS pre-med, Univ. Philippines, Diliman, Quezon City, 1966; MD, Southwestern Univ. Matias H. Aznar Meml. Coll. of Medicine, Philippines, 1973. Contract med. worker Gov. of Iran, 1976—79; founder Fabunan Med. Clin., San Marcelino, Philippines, 1975; independent med. rschr. Gen. Medicine, 1975—; chmn. Fil-Am Tech Inc, 2001—. Recipient First Place award in Biotechnology "Poison Antidote", Invention Convention, Calif., 1997. Mem.: Am. Soc. of Patent Holders (life), Philippine Med. Assn. (life). Achievements include patents for Fabunan injection Viral Treatment for HIV/AIDS, Influenza & Dengue Fever; Envenomation antidote: snakebite, Catfish sting and other poisons; Monitor Diaper; invention of Dr Shoe Boy Driving footguard. Home: 329 N Vendome St Los Angeles CA 90026

FACCINTO, VICTOR PAUL, artist, gallery administrator; b. Albany, Calif., Oct. 30, 1945; s. Victor A. and Betty Jean (Smith) Pearson; 1 dau., Denise Michelle. BA in Psychology, Calif. State U.-Sacramento, 1969, MA in Art, 1972. Instr. art Calif. State U., 1972-74; asst. to dir. Nancy Hoffman Gallery, N.Y.C., 1974-78; dir. art gallery Wake Forest U., Winston Salem, 1978—, art faculty, 1983—. Founding mem. multi-media performance group Three People, 1990. One-person shows include Millennium, 1996, 2003, Mus. Modern Art, N.Y.C., 1975, Collective for Living Cinema, N.Y.C., 1976, Phyllis Kind Gallery, N.Y.C., 1980, 82, 87, N.C. Mus. Art, 1986, Helander Gallery, N.Y.C., 1991, Millennium Film Workshop, N.Y.C., 1996, 2003, Cleve. Performance Art Festival, 1998, Southeastern Ctr. for Contemporary Art, N.C., 1999, Madison (Wis.) Art Ctr., 2000; group shows include Am. Visionary Art Mus., Md., 2002, Whitney Mus. Am. Art, 1972, 73, 74, Mus. Modern Art, N.Y.C., 1978, Barbara Gladstone Gallery, N.Y.C., 1983, Monique Knowlton Gallery, N.Y.C., 1983, Helander Gallery, Palm Beach, Fla., 1988, 90; represented in permanent collections Mus. Modern Art, N.Y.C., Philip Morris, Inc.; animated film maker: Shameless, 1974. N.Y. CAPS fellow, 1977; N.C. Arts Council fellow, 1982, 86, 2000; recipient 1st prize NYU Small Works Competition, 1983 Baptist. Home: 1950 Cliffside Dr Pfafftown NC 27040-9507 Office: Wake Forest U PO Box 7232 Winston Salem NC 27109-7232 E-mail: faccinto@wfu.edu.

FACE, WAYNE BRUCE, small business owner; b. Everett, Mass., June 20, 1942; s. Ward Jr. and Margaret Irene (Keil) F.; m. Sharon Lucille Blythe, Mar. 25, 1967; children: Jonathan Jacob, Joseph Matthew. ASA, Bentley Coll., 1962, BSA, 1967; MBA, Pepperdine U., 1975; EdD, Vanderbilt U., 1986. Div. analyst Varian Assocs., Palo Alto, Calif., 1969-71, sr. fin. analyst, 1972-75; acctg. mgr. Veeco Instruments, Sunnyvale, Calif., 1971-72; product line controller Nat. Semiconductor, Santa Clara, Calif., 1975-76; assoc. prof. Hawthorne Coll. of Bus., Antrim, N.H., 1976-86, dept. chmn., 1983-86; owner Learn to Live, Warner, N.H., 1986-88; acctg. mgr. N.H. Correctional Industries, Concord, 1988-91; owner Sharway Gifts, Warner, 1991-93; part-time transp. aide NFI North, Concord, N.H., 1993—. Contbr. to Mensa Rsch. Jour. Advisor Jr. Achievement, Palo Alto, 1971-73; den leader Cub Scouts, Warner, 1990-91; coach Kearsarge Youth Basketball, New London, N.H., 1991-93; bd. dirs. Kearsarge Children's Ctr., Warner, 1987-88. With U.S. Army, 1964-67, Korea. Democrat. Avocations: sports, golf, chess, reading. Home and Office: 45 W Main St Warner NH 03278-4213

FACEY, JOHN ABBOTT, III, lawyer; b. Springfield, Mass., June 14, 1950; s. John Abbott Jr. and Mary Agnes (Murphy) F.; m. Patricia Marie Otto, Sept. 27, 1975; children: Justin Abbott, Christopher John, Michael Edward. BA, Coll. of the Holy Cross, 1972; JD, Suffolk U., 1975. Bar: Mass. 1975, Vt. 1976, U.S. Dist. Ct. Vt. 1977. Assoc. Bishop & Crowley, Rutland, Vt., 1975-81; ptnr. Keyser, Crowley, Banse & Facey, Rutland, 1981-90, Reiber Kenlan Schwiebert & Facey, P.C., Rutland, 1990—. Corporator Rutland Regional Med. Ctr.; trustee Rutland Free Libr., 1988-94, pres., 1989-90; bd. dirs. Downtown Devel. Corp., 1990-94; mem. Rutland City Planning Commn., 1994—, chair, 1996—. Mem. ABA, Mass. Bar Assn., Vt. Bar Assn. (title stds. subcom.), Rutland County Bar Assn., New Eng. Land Title Assn., Rotary (bd. dirs. 1989-95, pres. 1991-92). Republican. Roman Catholic. Avocations: skiing, tennis, travel. Home: 82 Davis St Rutland VT 05701-3308 Office: Reiber Kenlan Schwiebert & Facey 71 Allen St Rutland VT 05701-4570 E-mail: jfacey@reiberlaw.com.

FACHNIE, H(UGH) DOUGLAS, film manufacturing company official; b. Windsor, Ont., Can., Sept. 8, 1952; arrived in U.S., 1958; s. Harold Lennox Fachnie and Mary Jane (Schultz) MacKenzie. B Gen. Studies, U. Mich., 1973. Salesman Quarry, Inc., Ann Arbor, Mich., 1974, store mgr. Ann Arbor and Saginaw, Mich., 1974-77; dist. mgr. Fotomat Corp., San Diego, 1977-80, dir. ops. Wilton, Conn., 1980-81, dir. merchandising, 1981-83; mgr. optical products Fuji Photo Film U.S.A., Inc., N.Y.C., 1983-84, product mgr. consumer film Elmsford, N.Y., 1984-89, sr. product/packaging mgr. film and one-time use cameras, 1989-94, mktg. mgr. consumer photo, 1995-97, 98-00; comml. planning and logistics mgr. profl. and photofinishing Fuji Phot Film USA, Inc., Elmsford, N.Y., 1998-2000, dir. mktg., color paper and chems., comml. imaging divsn., 2000—. Mem. AAAS, Photog. Mktg. Assn., Digital Imaging Mktg. Assn., Am. Prodn. and Inventory Control Soc., Profl. Photographers Assn. Republican. Avocations: home maintenance, flying, photography, audiophile, curling. Home: 30 Fleetwood Dr Danbury CT 06810-7010 Office: Fuji Photo Film USA Inc 555 Taxter Rd Elmsford NY 10523-2394 E-mail: d.fachnie@att.net.

FACKLAM, ROGER LEE, engineer, physicist; b. Abilene, Kans., May 22, 1955; s. Kenneth L. and Elaine Facklam; m. Sue Ann Dudzik, Mar. 11, 1989; children: Ryan, Jason. BS in Physics, Kans. State U., 1976; postgrad., U. Mo., Kansas City, 1977; MS in Engring. Physics, Air Force Inst. Tech., 1983; postgrad., U. N.Mex., 1983-86. Rsch. asst. Kans. State U., Manhattan, 1973-76; lab. instr. U. Mo., Kansas City, 1976-77; analyst Kittpeak Nat. Obs., Tucson, 1978-79; engr. Rockwell Internat., Albuquerque, 1986-90; sr. engr. Nichols Rsch. Corp., Arlington, Va., 1990-93, E-Sys., Falls Church, Va., 1993-94; patent rschr. Matt Kasap, Inc., Arlington, Va., 1994-96; sr. engr. SPARTA, Inc., Arlington, 1996—. Pvt. practice patent cons., Burke, Va., 1994-96; sci. engring. and tech. asst. Missile Def. Agy., Missile Def. Nat. team, Ballistic Missile Def. Orgn. Airborne Laser (ABL) program and sys. engring. office. Editor, conf. chair: OE LASE'93; co-author: ABL Report to Congress, 2001; author 17 other publs. Capt. USAF, 1979—86. Recipient Best Paper award AIAA, 1982, Air Force Commendation medal Meritorious Svc., Outstanding Tech. Achievement USAF Avionics Lab. AAA divsn. Mem. Mercedes Benz Club, Sigma Pi Sigma. Achievements include 3 patents: laser clock, laser dispersion controller and laser self-injection locking. Office: SPARTA Inc 1911 N Fort Myer Dr Ste 800 Arlington VA 22209-1604

FACKLER, JOHN PAUL, JR., chemistry educator; b. Toledo, July 31, 1934; s. John P. and Ruth (Moehring) F.; m. Naomi Paula Steege, Sept. 2, 1956; children: Katherine G., Cheryl R., Karla S., John M., Dorothy L. Student, MIT, 1952; BA, Valpraiso U., 1956, D.Sc. (hon.), 1987; PhD, MIT, 1960. Jr. chemist Sun Oil Co., 1953-56; teaching asst. MIT, 1956-59, research assoc., 1960; asst. prof. U. Calif., 1960-62, Case Inst. Tech., 1962-64; assoc. prof. chemistry Case Western Res. U., 1964-69, prof., 1970-82, chmn. dept., 1972-77; dean Coll. Sci., Tex. A&M U., 1983-91, Disting. prof. chemistry, 1987—; Wilhelm Manchot Forschung prof. Tech. U., Munich, 1992. Vis. prof. U. Calif. at Santa Barbara, 1969; Fulbright lectr. Colombia, 1969; cons. in chemistry Central State U., 1967-69; chmn. Inorganic Synthesis Corp., 1987-90. Author: Symmetry in Coordination Chemistry, 1971; editor: Symmetry in Chemical Theory, 1973, Inorganic Syntheses, Vol. 21, 1982, Modern Inorganic Chemistry Series, Plenum; contbr. articles to profl. jours. Bd. dirs. Luth. Met. Ministry, 1969-72; bd. dirs. Luth. High Sch. Assn., 1974-80, chmn., 1979. NSF summer fellow, 1959; J.S. Guggenheim fellow, 1976; Bye fellow Robinson Coll., U. Cambridge, 1992; recipient Tech. Achievement award Cleve. Tech. Soc., 1971 Fellow AAAS, Am. Inst. Chemists; mem. Am. Chem. Soc. (councilor 1972-73, chmn. elect 1974, chmn. Cleve. sect. 1975, chmn. elect 1978, chmn. inorganic divsn. 1979, Morley medal Cleve. sect. 1987, Southwest regional award 1990, Disting. Achievement award 2001, chair, Chemistry Sect.), Gordon Rsch. Conf. (council 1979-82, trustee 1982-89, chmn. 1989), Tex. Acad. Sci. (bd. dirs. 1987-90), Chem. Soc. London, Am. Crystal. Assn., N.Y. Acad. Scis., Sigma Xi, Phi Lambda Upsilon, Phi Delta Theta. Lutheran. Home: 4770 Enchanted Oaks Dr College Station TX 77845-7649 Office: Tex A&M U Chem Dept College Station TX 77842-3012

FACOS, JAMES FRANCIS, English language educator, author; b. Lawrence, Mass., July 28, 1924; s. Chris and Theresa (McAdam) F.; m. Cleo John Chigos, Dec. 1, 1956; children: Theresa-Katina, Elizabeth Joy, Anthony John. AB in English, Bates Coll., Lewiston, Maine, 1949; MA in English, Fla. State U., 1958; DHL, Norwich U., Northfield, Vt., 1989. Instr. Vt. Coll., Montpelier, 1959-72; asst. prof. Norwich U., Northfield, Vt., 1972-73, assoc. prof., 1973-83, prof., 1983-89, prof. emeritus, 1989—. Author: (novel) The Silver Lady, 1972, 95, (poems) Morning's Come Singing, 1981, (plays) The Piper O' The May, 1962, A Day of Genesis, 1969, One Daring Fling, 1978, (novella) Fugitives' Fair, 1985, (novella) Jezzy, 2002; represented in permanent collection 20th Century Archives Mugar Meml. Libr., Boston U. Staff sgt. USAF, 1943-45, ETO. Decorated DFC, Air medal; recipient The Alden award Dramatists' Alliance, Palo Alto, Calif., 1956, Walter Peach award Poetry Soc. Vt., Burlington, 1962, Corinne Davis award Poetry Soc. Vt., Burlington, 1970, Norwich U. Found. award for disting. svc., 1992. Home: 333 Elm St Montpelier VT 05602-2213

FACTOR, ALFRED, lawyer; b. Providence, June 27, 1931; s. Benjamin Factor and Jennie Singer; m. Marilyn Presel, July 22, 1956; children: Jeffrey, Robyn. BS, U. R.I., 1956; JD, Boston U., 1956. Bar: R.I. 1956, U.S. Ct. Appeals (1st cir.) 1958. Assoc. Kirshenbaum & Kirshenbaum, Cranston, R.I., 1956-77, v.p., 1973-77, pres., 1977—. Bar examiner, R.I., 1987-97, chmn. bd., 1995-96. Office: Kirshenbaum & Kirshenbaum 888 Reservoir Ave Cranston RI 02910-4414

FADDEN, DELMAR MCLEAN, retired electrical engineer; b. Seattle, Nov. 10, 1941; s. Gene Scott and Alice Elizabeth (McLean) F.; m. Sandra Myrene Callahan, June 22, 1963; children: Donna McLean, Lawrence Gene. BSEE, U. Wash., 1963, MSEE, 1975. Lic. comml. pilot, Wash. With Boeing Comml. Airplane Co., Seattle, 1969-99, chief engr. flight deck, 1988-90, chief engr. 737/757 avonics/flight sys., 1990-96, integration mgr. cabin sys., 1996-98, integration mgr. airplane svcs., 1999; ret.; product cons. Sandel Avionics Co., San Diego, 1999—, ARNAV Systems Inc., Payallup, Wash., 2001—, Boeing Connexion, Seattle, 2002—03. Contbr. articles to profl. jours. Capt. USAF, 1963-69. Mem. AIAA, IEEE, Human Factors Soc., Soc. Automotive Engrs. (vice chmn. G-10 com. 1981-91, chmn. systems integration task group 1990-96), Mountaineers Found. (pres. 1998-2001), Am. Alpine Club, Mountaineers Club (pres. 1984-86). Achievements include 2 patents in field. Home: 5011 298th Ave SE Preston WA 98050 E-mail: delfadden@cs.com.

FADE, RICHARD, information technology executive; BS in Fin., Fla. State U. From mgr. to sr. v.p. Microsoft, Redmond, Wash., 1984, sr. v.p., 1986—. Office: One Microsoft Way Redmond WA 98052-6399

FADELEY, ELEANOR ADELINE, secondary education educator; b. Phila., Aug. 30, 1924; d. Nicholas William and Eleonora (Miceli) Battafarano; m. Herbert John Fadeley, Jr., Feb. 8, 1947; children: Herbert John, Brett Duane, Theresa Jane, Scott Lewis. BS, Drexel U., 1946; postgrad. Sch. Law, Temple U., 1949-51. Exec. trainee Lit Bros., Phila., 1946-47; sec. Hyde-Rakestraw, cotton yarn brokers, Phila., 1947-48; lab. asst. pub. rels. rep. Indsl. By Products & Rsch. Corp., Phila., 1948-51; tchr. Atlantic City Friends Sch., 1957-58; subs. tchr. Troy (N.Y.) Pub. Schs., 1970-71, 78-86; curriculum chmn. Friends of W. Kenneth Doyle Mid. Sch., Troy, 1977-78; English and sci. asst. Troy Pub. Schs., 1976-77. Legis. chmn. Samaritan Hosp. Aux., 1975-78, v.p., 1978-79; bd. dirs. Rensselaer County Am. Cancer Soc., 1980-83; chmn. Town of Brunswick Residential Crusade, 1982; vol. Bellevue Maternity Hosp., Niskayuna, N.Y. Mem. AAUW (mem. chmn., sec.-treas. Ea. area interbr. coun. 1981-82, vice-chmn. 1982-83, pres. Troy br. 1979), Home Econs. Legis. Monitors, Drexel Alumnae Assn., St. Johns Altar Guild, N.Y. State Gen. Fedn. Women's Clubs (Rensselaer County chmn. 1980-82, internat. chmn. 3d dist., scholarship chmn. 3rd dist. 1994-2002, 3rd dist. nominating com.), Embroiders' Guild Am. Inc. (N.Y. capital dist. chpt.), Panhellenic Alumnae Assn. Schenectady, Panhellenic Garden Club (pres. 1983-84, sec.-treas. 1990-91, v.p. 1994-95), Troy Woman's Club (pres. 1976-78, v.p. 1982-83, 96-98, bd. dirs. 1993-95, 99-2001, 2003—, vol. Stories Offer Activity Read 1993-95, mem. permanent funds bd. 1995-98, chmn. ann. luncheon 1998-2002), Alpha Sigma Alpha (life). Republican. Episcopalian. Home: 150 Tallmadge Pl Albany NY 12208-1086

FADELY, JAMES PHILIP, educator, writer; b. New Castle, Ind., Jan. 10, 1953; s. Harry Ellison and Viola (Clapp) F.; m. Sally Jane Fehsenfeld, Aug. 16, 1975; children: James Philip Jr., Adele Langsdale. BA, Hanover Coll., 1975; MA, Ind. U., 1977, PhD, 1990. Tchr. Brookstone Sch., Columbus, Ga., 1975-76, Savannah (Ga.) Country Day Sch., 1979-83; lectr. Ind. U., Indpls., 1984—; tchr., asst. headmaster St. Richard's Sch., Indpls., 1988-90, tchr., 1990-91, dir. admission and fin. aid, tchr., 1991-2000; dir. mktg./pub. rels., history tchr., dir. coll. counseling Univ. H.S., 2000—. Nat. bd. dirs. English-Speaking Union, exec. com., 1998-2001, pres. Indpls. br., 2002—; v.p. Ind. Libr. and Hist. Bd., 1997—; lectr. Butler U., 1985, U. Indpls., 1995. Author: A Brief History of St. Richard's School, 1960-1995, 1995, Thomas Taggart: Public Servant, Political Boss, 1856-1929, 1997, The Origins of Woodstock Club, 1997; contbr. articles to profl. jours. Dem. nominee 6th Dist. of Ind. for Congress, 1990; friend Woodrow Wilson House. Mem.: Hist. Deerfield, Hist. Madison, Nat. Assn. Coll. Admission Counseling, Ind. Hist. Soc. (grant 1991—94), Ind. Assn. Historians, Hist. Landmarks Found. Ind., Nat. Coun. for History Edn., Am. Hist. Assn., Lanier Mansion Found., Soc. Ind. Pioneers (bd. govs. 2001—), Hanover Coll. Alumni Assn. (bd. dirs. 1985—88), Marion County Hist. Soc., Nat. Trust for Hist. Preservation, Leelanau Hist. Soc., Woodstock Club, Hanover Club Indpls. (bd. dirs. 1988—96), Indpls. Lit. Club, Leland (Mich.) Yacht Club, Phi Delta Theta. Democrat. Roman Catholic. Avocation: travel. Home: 9146 N Kenwood Dr Indianapolis IN 46260-1400 Office: Univ HS 2825 W 116th St Carmel IN 46032 E-mail: fadely@worldnet.att.net.

FADEN, LEE JEFFREY, technical consultant and expert referral company executive; b. Phila., Dec. 18, 1953; s. Myer I. and Thelma A. (Lehrich) F.; m. Susan D. Rosen, Aug. 19, 1978; 3 children. BS in Acctg., Pa. State U., 1976; MBA, Temple U., 1979. Purchasing, advt. and sales exec. Royal Distbrs., Colmar, Pa., 1974-79; co-CEO The TASA Group, Inc., Blue Bell, Pa., 1979—. Fin. advisor Unami One Lodge, The Order of the Arrow, Boy Scouts Am., 2001—. Chmn. troop com. Boy Scouts Am., Dresher, Pa., 1963-99, asst. scoutmaster troop 3, Hatboro, 2001—; mgr. Horsham (Pa.) Little League, 1991-2000; coach, mgr. Horsham Soccer Assn., 1994—; coach Hatboro YMCA Roller Hockey, 1999—. Inducted to Chapel of Four Chaplains Phila., 1980; recipient Vigil Honor, Boy Scouts Am., 2003. Mem. Assn. Records Mgrs. and Adminstrs. Internat., Am. Fin. Assn., Am. Mgmt. Assn., Greater Phila. C. of C., Unami One Lodge (fin. adv. 2000—), Order of the Arrow (Vigil Honor 2003). Avocations: scouts, camping, clay modelling, bicycling, computers. Office: The TASA Group Inc 1166 Dekalb Pike Blue Bell PA 19422-1853

FADEN, RUTH R. medical educator, ethicist, researcher; BA, U. Pa., 1970; MA, U. Chgo., 1971; MPH, U. Calif., Berkeley, 1973, PhD, 1976. Sr. rsch. scholar Kennedy Inst. Ethics, Georgetown U., 1978—; prof. health policy and mgmt. Johns Hopkins U., Balt., 1986—, joint appointment in medicine, Sch. of Medicine, 1992—, prof., Philip Franklin Wagley chair in biomed. ethics, 1995—, exec. dir. Phoebe R. Berman Bioethics Inst., 1995. Chair pres.'s adv. com. on human radiation expts., 1994—95; chmn. adv. panel on reproductive hazards in workplace Office Tech. Assessment, 1984—85; mem. com. on risk perception and comm. NAS, 1987—88; mem. panel on confidentiality and data access om. on Nat. Stats. and Social Sci. Rsch. Coun., 1989—91; mem. Alcohol, Drug Abuse, and Mental Health Adminstrn., AIDS Adv. Com., 1990—92; mem. Workshop on Biomed. Ethics in U.S. Pub. Policy Office Tech. Assessment, 1992; mem. adv. bd. Finding Common Ground Project: The Reproductive Rights and Needs of Women and the Emerging Conflict in Maternal and Child Health, 1992—93; mem. Adv. Panel on Prospects for Health Tech. Assessment Office Tech. Assessment, 1992—93; co-chair com. on legal and ethical issues relating to inclusion of women in clin. studies Inst. Medicine, 1992—93, mem. com. on clin. rsch. in pub. interest, 1996—97, mem. bd. on health scis. policy, 1995—, mem. com. on battlefield radiation exposure criteria, Med. Follow-Up Agy., 1996—98, mem. adv. com. on strategies to protect health of deployed U.S. forces, 1998—99; chmn. acv. com. on human radiation expts. Human Radiation Expts., 1996; mem. nat. adv. coun. for human genome rsch. NIH, 1996—97; mem. adv. bd. to nat. info. resource on ethics and human genetics Kennedy Inst. Ethics, 1996—99; mem. privacy law adv. com. Ctrs. for Disease Control and Prevention, Coun. State and Territorial Epidemiologists, Assn. State and Territorial Epidemiologists, and Nat. Coun. State Legislators, 1998—; mem. genetics adv. com. Genetics Legis. Project, 1999—2001. Author (with T.L. Beauchamp, J. Wallace and L. Walters): Ethical Issues in Social Science Research, 1982; author: (with T.L. Beauchamp) A History and Theory of Informed Consent, 1986; author: (with G. Geller, M. Powers) AIDS, Women and the Next Generation, 1991; author: (with A.C. Mastroianni, D. Federman) Women and Health Research: Ethical and Legal Issues of Including Women in Clinical Studies, vol. I, 1994, vol. II, 1994; author: (with N. Kass) HIV, AIDS and Childbearing: Public Policy, Private Lives; mem. editl. bd.: The Millbank Quarterly, 2000—. Fellow: APA, Hastings Ctr. (fellow's coun.); mem.: APHA, Am. Soc. for Bioethics and Humanities, Forum on Bioethics (co-founder, former chmn.), Am. Assn. Bioethics (organizing com.), Inst. Medicine. Office: Phoebe R Berman Bioethics Inst Hampton House 352 624 N Broadway Baltimore MD 21205-1996 E-mail: rfaden@jhsph.edu.

FADER, DANIEL NELSON, English language educator; b. Balt., Jan. 4, 1930; s. Maurice Abraham and Ida Eunice (Browne) F.; m. Martha Alice Agnew, Oct. 8, 1955 (div. 1982); children: Paul Frederick, Lisa Jeanine; m. Christine Verzar, Oct. 15, 1988. BA, Cornell U., 1952, MA, 1954; PhD, Stanford U., 1963. Research scholar Christ's Coll., Cambridge (Eng.) U., 1955-57; acting instr. Stanford (Calif.) U., 1957-61; instr. U. Mich., Ann Arbor, 1961-63, from asst. prof. to assoc. prof., 1963-73, prof. English lang. and lit., 1973-76, prof. English, chmn. English composition bd., 1976-83, prof. English, 1983-98, prof. emeritus, from 1998. Lectr., cons. in field. Author: books including Hooked on Books, 1966, The Naked Children, 1971, 96, Paul and I Discover America, 1975, (with others) New Hooked on Books, 1976; contbr. articles to profl. jours. Served with U.S. Army, 1954-55. Mem. ACLU. Home: Truro, Mass. Died June 23, 2003.

FADER, HENRY CONRAD, lawyer; b. Bronx, Dec. 2, 1946; s. Michael and Ruth (Filler) F.; m. Linda L. Koch, Nov. 23, 1969; children: Melanie, Danielle. AB, U. Rochester, N.Y., 1968; MEd, Temple U., 1970; JD, Syracuse (N.Y.) U., 1973. Bar: Pa. 1973, U.S. Dist. Ct. (ea. dist.) Pa. 1973, N.J. 1988. Ptnr. Fox, Rothschild, O'Brien & Frankel, Phila., 1973-92, Schnader, Harrison, Segal & Lewis, Phila., 1992—2003, chmn. health law dept., 1993—2003; ptnr. Pepper Hamilton LLP, Phila., 2003—. Chmn. Fox Rothchild Health Law Group, 1985-92. Bd. dirs., solicitor Eagleville (Pa.) Hosp., 1987—; bd. dirs. Beth Am Synagogue, Abington, Pa., 1988—; first vice chmn. bd. dirs. Pa. Chamber Bus. and Industry, 1994—; past pres. e-Pennsylvania Alliance; chmn. bd. dirs. Intercultural Family Svcs., Inc., 1998—. Mem. ABA, Pa. Bar Assn., Phila. Bar Assn., Nat. Assn. Bond Lawyers, Am. Health Lawyers Assn. Avocations: tennis, reading, gardening, home improvements. Office: Pepper Hamilton LLP 3000 Two Logan Sq 18th and Arch Sts Philadelphia PA 19103 E-mail: faderh@pepperlaw.com.

FADER, SEYMOUR JEREMIAH, management and engineering consulting company executive; b. N.Y.C., Feb. 9, 1923; s. Louis and Bertha (Stachel) F.; m. Shirley Ruth Sloan, June 26, 1951; children: Susan Deborah, Steven Micah Student, CCNY, 1938-42; BSEE, U. Pa., 1949, MBA in Indsl. Mgmt., 1950. Mgr. prodn. Bogue Elec. Mfg. Co., Paterson, N.J., 1950-56; mgr. planning and control Rowe Mfg. Co., Whippany, N.J., 1956-58; cons., engr. Koor Crafts & Industries, Ltd., Tel Aviv, 1958-59; dir. mfg. ops. ESC Electronics Corp., Palisades Park, N.J., 1959-62; mgr. mfg. Artistic Mfg., Sun Chem. Corp., Carlstadt, N.J., 1962-66; mgr. ops. Fairchild Instrumentation Fairchild Camera & Instrument Corp., Clifton, N.J., 1966-67; v.p. Graphic Products, Inc., Hackensack, N.J., 1967-69; gen. mgr., v.p. Berkey Tech., Berkey Photo, Inc., Woodside, N.Y., 1969-72; pres. Suste Assocs., Paramus, N.J., 1972—. Asst. prof. mgmt. Ramapo Coll., Mahwah, N.J., 1972-75, assoc. prof., 1975-80, prof. mgmt. and indsl. rels., 1980-83, prof. emerigus, 1993—, bd. dirs., creator Ramapo Coll. USA-Eng. Study Abroad programs, 1983-93; program coord., exec. dir. Overseas Program, Southside Va. C.C., 1994-95; adj. prof. mgmt. Grad. Sch. Bus., Fordham U., 1982—; arbitration panelist Better Bus. Bur. of Bergen, Passaic and Rockland Counties, 1983—; creator, exec. program dir. overseas program Coll. Consortium for Study Abroad, 1995—. Author: Fundamentals of Management for First0Line Supervisors, 1974, The Manufacturing Manager, 1975; co-author: Jobmanship, 1979; contbr. articles to profl. jours.; patentee coreless reeler, desk-tip copier, photo-copier. Mem. pub. health study N.J. State Assembly Commn. on Conservation, Natural Resources, Air and Water Pollution, 1972-73; commr. Paramus Environ. Commn., 1973-78, vice chmn., 1977-78, chmn. inventory and land use com., 974-78. With U.S. Army, 1942-45. Mem. Am. Mgmt. Assn. (cert. of achievement 1974), Am. Arbitration Assn. (panelist), Am. Inst. Indsl. Engrs., Soc. Advancement of Mgmt., Nat. Panel Consumer Arbitrators, Am. Prodn. and Inventory Control Soc., Delta Mu Delta. Home and Office: 377 Mckinley Blvd Paramus NJ 07652-4725

FADER, SHIRLEY SLOAN, writer; b. Paterson, N.J. d. Samuel Louis and Miriam (Marcus) Sloan; m. Seymour J. Fader; children: Susan Deborah, Steven Micah Kimchi. BS, MS, U. Pa. Writer, journalist, author, Paramus, N.J. Chmn., coord. ann. writers seminar Bergen C.C., 1973-76. Author: (books) The Princess Who Grew Down, 1968, From Kitchen to Career, 1977, Jobmanship, 1978, Successfully Ever After, 1982 (Brit. edit. 1985), Wait a Minute: You Can Have It All, 1993, paperback edit., 1994; (columns) Jobmanship, People and You, Family Weekly mag., 1971-82, How to Get More From Your Job, Glamour mag., 1978-81, Start Here, Working Woman mag., 1980-88, Work Strategies, Working Mother mag., 1987-88, Women Getting Ahead, Ladies Home Jour., 1980-90, How Would You Handle It, New Idea mag., 1984—, Moving Up, Woman mag., 1989-90, Career Expert "Ask the Experts", Woman's World mag., 1992-95; contbg. editor Family Weekly, 1971-82, Glamour mag., 1978-81, Working Woman mag., 1980-88, Working Mother mag., 1987-88, Ladies Home Jour., 1980-90, Woman mag., 1989-90; contbr.: (book) Foundations of English, 2002; contbr. articles on career, relationships and travel to mags. worldwide.. Mem. Authors Guild, Am. Soc. Journalists and Authors (moderator ann. writer's conf. 1971-2000, nat. v.p. 1976-77, mem.-at-large nat. exec. coun. 1976-78, 83-86, nat. sec., mem. exec. coun. 1995-96), Nat. Press Club, Newswomen of N.Y. Address: 377 Mckinley Blvd Paramus NJ 07652-4725

FAER, A.M. magazine publishing consultant, poet; b. N.Y.C., Oct. 25, 1944; s. Meyer and Violet (Shecter) F.; m. 1967 (div. 1996); children: Daniel, Stacy; m. Fran Brennan, June 1999. Prodn. mgr. McGraw Hill Publ., N.Y.C., 1969-72; customer svc. mgr., scheduling mgr. Rumford Nat. Graphics, Concord, N.H., 1972-77; v.p. mfg. LFP, Inc., L.A., 1978-82, v.p. ops., sr. v.p., 1983-84; founder, pres. The Jared Co., Scottsdale, Ariz., 1981—. Instr. UCLA; spkr. in field. Contbr. to books and mags. Mem. Western Publ. Assn. (bd. dirs. 1996—). Avocations: writing, art, travel. Office: The Jared Co 7119 E Shea Blvd Ste 264 Scottsdale AZ 85254-6107

FAERBER, ABIGAIL HOBBS, physician, farm manager; b. Columbus, Ohio, Aug. 30, 1943; d. Theodore Caleb and Olliffe Elizabeth (Litchfield) Hobbs; m. George Oswald Faerber, Feb. 19, 1966; children: Rachel, Peter, George. BA, Ohio Wesleyan U., 1964; MS, U. Ill., 1966; DO, Ohio U., 1985. Bd. cert. in family practice, 1992. Physician, mgr. Dist. Physicians Inc., Columbus, Ohio, 1986-97; physician Asian Am. Health Initiative Clinic, 2000—02. Adj. clin. faculty Ohio U. Coll. Medicine, Athens, Ohio, 1986-96; physician DH Family Practice VIII, Columbus, Ohio, 1995-96; mgr. Scioto Cliff Farms, Delaware, Ohio, 1995-97; bd. dirs. Nat. Alumni Ohio U., Athens, 1989-92; medicine adv. bd. Ohio U. Coll. Osteo., 1994—. Bd. dirs. Columbus Chamber Music Soc., 1977-83; mem. Beaux Art Columbus Mus. Art, 1971-82. Recipient Cmty. Svc. award Ciba Geigy, 1986. Mem. Am. Osteo. Assn., Ohio Osteo. Assn., Ohio State Med. Assn., Franklin County Med. Soc., (chair of credentials com., 1991-93), Republican. Lutheran. Avocations: sailing, hiking, reading, travel. Home: 7547 Dublin Rd Delaware OH 43015-9237 Office: Dist Physicians Inc 7547 Dublin Rd Delaware OH 43015-9237

FAERBER, GARY J. surgeon, educator; s. John and JoAnn Faerber; m. Kathleen A. Cooney; children: Meg, Tim. BS in Biology, Washington U., 1980; MD, Temple U., 1984. Resident urol. surgery U. Mich., Ann Arbor, 1989—92; asst. prof. U. Mich. Med. Sch., Ann Arbor, 1992—98, assoc. prof., 1998—. Cons. Olympus Inc. Mem.: Mich. Urologic Soc. (pres.-elect 2002—03). Office: Univ Mich Med Ctr 1500 E Medical Center Dr Ann Arbor MI 48109

FAERBER, KENT WILLIAM, foundation administrator, consultant; b. St. Louis, May 28, 1941; s. Otto and Elsie (Buchmueller) F.; m. Lorena Brigham, June 12, 1965. AB, Amherst Coll., 1963; LLB, Harvard U., 1966. Bar: Mo. 1966, Mass. 1990. Atty. Husch Eppenberger, St. Louis, 1968-74; terminals mgr. Marine Petroleum Co., St. Louis, 1974-77; alumni sec. Amherst (Mass.) Coll., 1977-86, sec. for alumni rels. and devel., 1986-94, sr. advisor to pres., 1994; cons. Amherst, 1995—; devel. officer Cmty. Found. of Western Mass., Springfield, 1996-99, pres., 1999—. Pres. Amherst Inn Co., 1981-86, dir., 1978—; dir., chair Case, Dist. I, 1990-93. Bd. dirs. Wildwood Cemetery Assn., Amherst, 1986—; founder, bd. dirs., pres. Amherst Club, 1984; trustee Jones Libr., Amherst, 1996-99; vestry Grace Episcopal Ch., 1997, treas., 1998, sr. warden, 1999; trustee Martha Dickinson Bianchi Trust (Evergreens), Amherst, 2000-03; bd. govs. Emily Dickinson Mus., 2003—. Mem. Mo. Bar Assn., Mass. Bar, Amherst Club. Home: 11 Mcintosh Dr Amherst MA 01002-3345 Office: Cmty Found Western Mass 1500 Main St Springfield MA 01115-0001

FAETH, GERARD MICHAEL, aerospace and mechanical engineering educator, researcher; b. N.Y.C., July 5, 1936; s. Joseph and Helen (Wagner) F.; m. Mary Ann Kordich, Dec. 27, 1959; children: Christine Louise, Lorraine Vera, Elinor Jean. BME, Union Coll., 1958; MS, Pa. State U., 1961, PhD, 1964. Instr. mech. engrng. Pa. State U., University Park, 1958-59, research asst., 1959-64, asst. prof., 1964-68, assoc. prof., 1968-74, prof., 1974-85, prof. emeritus, 1985—; Modine prof., head gas dynamics labs. U. Mich., Ann Arbor, 1985—. Vis. prof. Air Force Office Sci. Rsch., Washington, 1983-84; cons. GM, Warren, Mich., 1977-1992, Applied Rsch. Lab., Pa. State U., 1964-85; prof.-in-residence GM Inst., Detroit, 1983. Mem. editorial bd. Combustion Sci. and Tech., 1979-99, Ann. Rev. Numerical Fluid M echanics and Heat Transfer, 1985—, Atomization and Sprays, 1989—, Progress in Energy and Combustion Sci., 1991—, Internat. Jour. Multiphase Flow, 1997—; contbr. numerous articles to profl. jours. Rep. Precinct Chmn. Centre County, Pa., 1977-84; bd. dirs. Eagles Mere (Pa.) Assn., 1982-88, Eagles Mere Park Assn., 1978-85. Recipient Outstanding Engr. Alumnus award, Pa. State Univ. Alumni Assn., 1990, Pub. Svc. medal, NASA, 1999, Highly-Cited Rschr. cert., Inst. Sci. Info., 2000, Appreciation award, Helwan U., Cairo, 2002. Fellow: AAAS, AIAA (editor-in-chief 1997—2002, editl. adv. bd. 2003—, Propellants and Combustion award 1993), ASME (tech. editor 1981—84, sr. tech. editor 1985—90, Meml. award heat transfer divsn. 1988); mem.: NAE, Phi Kappa Phi, Am. Phys. Soc., Combustion Inst. (dep. editor 1984—90, tech. editor 1990—96, bd. dirs. 1990—96), Sigma Xi, Pi Tau Sigma. Episcopalian. Office: U Mich 3000 FXB Bldg Ann Arbor MI 48109-2140 Home: PO Box 1468 Ann Arbor MI 48106-1468 E-mail: gmfaeth@umich.edu.

FAFIAN, JOSEPH, JR., management consultant; b. N.Y.C., Apr., 1939; s. Joseph M. and Mary (Alonso) F.; m. Nathalie Coluccio, Oct. 5, 1963; children: John Joseph, Michael Francis. BA, Bklyn. Coll., 1959. Assoc. actuary U.S. Life Ins. Co., N.Y.C., 1959-67; 2d v.p. USLIFE Corp., 1967-69, v.p., 1969-72, sr. v.p. ops., 1972-76, exec. v.p. life ins., 1976-77, sr. exec. v.p. life ins., 1977-78; pres., chief exec. officer, dir. U.S. Life, 1978-80; pres., dir. Beneficial Nat. Life Ins. Co., N.Y.C., 1980-82, chmn. bd., CEO, 1982-84; founder, pres., CEO, Fafian and Assocs., Inc., S.I., N.Y., 1984—. Dir. Assoc. Madison pres., COO, 1982-84; acting pres. Maine & Fidelity Life Ins. Co., 1985-86; bd. dirs. Columbian Mut., Columbian Family, Columbia Life. Served with N.G., 1962-67. Fellow Soc. Actuaries; mem. Acad. Actuaries. Home: 74 Mason St Staten Island NY 10304-3106 Office: 1 Edgewater Plz Ste 204A Staten Island NY 10305-4900 E-mail: josephfafian@cs.com. *Guide my actions by three principles: Always be proud of what I am doing; Always seek to improve what I am doing; Always learn more about what I am doing.*

FAGA, ANTHONY, JR., sales operations professional; b. N.Y.C., Mar. 9, 1949; s. Anthony and Susie (Strivelli) F.; m. Helen Theresa Behrens, July 24, 1971; children: Cheryl Ann, Michael Anthony, Dennis John. BS in Biology, St. Francis Coll., Bklyn., 1970; MBA, Fordham U., 1973. Various field positions IBM, N.Y., 1970-85, program mgr. Corp. I/S, 1985-87, mgr. mktg. ops. Higher Edn. Milford, Conn., 1987-92, program mgr. Networking Somers, N.Y., 1992-95, sr. program mgr. Software Group, 1996-97, sales performance cons. Software Group, 1998-99, program dir. Software Group, 2000—. Troop com. chmn. Boy Scouts Am. Troop 76, Ridgefield, Conn., 1987-92, Eagle scout, advisor, 1992-2000. Roman Catholic. Avocations: traveling, reading, computing, music. Home: 21 Whitlock Ln Ridgefield CT 06877-1524 Office: IBM Software Group Rt 100 Somers NY 10589 E-mail: faga@us.ibm.com.

FAGALY, WILLIAM ARTHUR, curator; b. Lawrenceburg, Ind., Mar. 1, 1938; s. William James and Dorothy Rae (Wheeler) F. BA, Ind. U., 1962, MA, 1967. Asst. registrar Art Mus., Ind. U., Bloomington, 1965-66; registrar New Orleans Mus. Art, 1966—67, curator collections, 1967-73, chief curator, 1973-80, asst. dir for art, 1980-2001, Francoise Billion Richardson curator African art, 1997—; curator art U. Art Mus. U. La. Lafayette, 2002—. Guest curator La. Folk Painting exhibit, Mus. Am. Folk Art, 1973, Exhbn. of Contemporary Painting, Corcoran Gallery of Art, Washington, 1989, Arthur Roger Gallery, New Orleans, 1990, Geography of the Body: The Art of Mignon Faget, Contemporary Arts Ctr., 1995, Preacher Art, Phyllis Kind Gallery, N.Y.C., 1997, Watercolor U.S.A. 1999, Springfield (Mo.) Art Mus., 1999, Nat. Works on Paper, McNeese State U., Lake Charles, La., It's a Wonderful World, Contemporary Arts Ctr., New Orleans, 2003, Aristides Logothetis, Cue Art Found., N.Y.C., 2003; adv. panel visual arts and crafts divsn. arts La. Arts Coun., 1978—81, 1992; panelist Nat. Endowment Arts GSA Art in Architecture Commn., 1974, 76, 78; guest lectr. S.S. Rotterdam, 1983, H.M.S. Queen Elizabeth II, 1986, Sotheby's, NY, 1996; cons. Liberian Pavilion La. World Expn., 1984, Shapes of Power, Belief and Celebration: African Art from New Orleans Collections, 1989, Fritz Bultman: A Retrospective, 1993, Wyo. Art Mus., Laramie, 1995, Oreg. Biennial, Portland Art Mus., 1995, Roots of Am. Jazz: African Mus. Instruments from New Orleans Collections, 1995, He's the Prettiest: A Tribute to Big Chief Allison "Tootie," Mont.'s 50 Yrs. of Mardi Gras Indian Suiting; selection panelist McKnight Found. Fellowship Program, Minn. Coll. Arts and Design, Mpls., 1986, So. Arts Fedn., NEA Arts Regional Artists Fellowships, 1990; selecton panelist 1984 Visual Arts Fellowships, Wyo. Arts Coun., 1993; selection panelist Adolph and Esther Gottlieb Found. Artist Fellowships, N.Y.C., 1995, Western States Art Fedn./NEA, 1996; bd. dirs. Ctr. for African and African-Am. Studies, So. U., New Orleans, Sac-O-Lait-The Keith Sonnier Found., 2002—; bd. advisors Wilkinson County Mus., Woodville, Miss.; adj. curator Univ. Art Mus., U. La., Lafayette, 2002—; founder art activities bus. FUN (Fagaly Unltd.), 2001—. Contbr. articles to profl. jours. NEA fellow, 1985; Visual Arts and Media fellow Miss. Arts Commn., 1994, Visual Arts fellow Wyo. Art Coun., 1994; recipient Mayor's Arts award City of New Orleans, 1997, Gov.'s Arts award La. State Arts Coun., 1997, Charles E. Dunbar Jr. Career Svc. award La. Civil Svc. League, 1999, Isaac Delgado Meml. award Fellows of New Orleans Mus. of Art, 2001. Mem. Am. Assn. Mus. (mem. vis. com. for Tampa Mus. Art accreditation program 1999). Episcopalian. Home: 915 Saint Philip St New Orleans LA 70116-2407 Office: PO Box 19123 New Orleans LA 70179-0123 Office Fax: 504-484-6662. Personal E-mail: bfagaly@hotmail.com. Business E-Mail: bfagaly@noma.org.

FAGAN, FREDERIC, neurosurgeon; b. Bklyn., Oct. 18, 1935; s. Jack and Sophie (Altschuler) F.;m. Donna Fagan, Mar. 1, 1969; children: Gabrielle, Samantha. BA, Ohio State U., 1958. Intern Santa Monica (Calif.) Hosp., N.Y.C., 1959; resident N.Y. Hosp., N.Y.C., Calif., 1960. Cons. AMA, L.A., 1980—. Dir. Smithsonian Assocs., Washington, 1995, U.S. Holocaust Meml. Mus., Washington, 1995. Named Surgeon of Yr. MacMillan Industries, Santa Clara, Calif., 1989. Mem. N.Y. Acad. Scis., NRA (dir. 1995). Home: 11102 Excelsior Dr Apt 9E Norwalk CA 90650-5646 Office: Woodruff Hosp 3800 Woodruff Ave Long Beach CA 90808-2125

FAGAN, GEORGE DAVIDSON, lawyer; b. New Orleans, Mar. 16, 1959; s. William Ranson and Suzanne (Duvall) F.; m. Andrea Derks, Aug. 20, 1988; children: Connor, Kathryn. BA cum laude, Washington & Lee U., 1981; JD, La. State U., 1984. Bar: La. 1984. Assoc. Hammett, Leake & Hammett, New Orleans, 1984-87; ptnr. Leake & Andersson, New Orleans, 1987—, mng. ptnr., 1999—. Mem. alumni bd. La. State U. Law Sch., Baton Rouge, 1994-99. Named to Best Lawyers in Am., 2001—. Mem. Fed. Ins. and Def. Counsel. Office: Leake & Andersson LLP 1700 Energy Ctr 1100 Poydras St New Orleans LA 70163-1701

FAGAN, WILLIAM F. ecologist; b. 1970; m. Meredith L. Brittain. BA in Biology (hons.), U. of Del., 1992; PhD in Zoology, U. of Wash., 1996. Postdoctoral fellow Nat. Ctr. for Ecol. Analysis and Synthesis, Santa Barbara, Calif., 1996—97; asst. prof. Ariz. State U., Tempe, 1997—2002; assoc. prof. U. of Md., Coll. Pk., 2002—. Author: (jour. articles) Am. Naturalist, Ecology, Procs. of the Nat. Acad. of Scis. of the U.S. of Am. Guggenheim Fellow, John Simon Guggenheim Meml. Found., 2001. Mem.: Phi Beta Kappa (Herbert Ellis Newman award (Alpha of Del. Chpt.) 1991). Avocations: shell collecting, hiking. Office: Univ of Md Dept of Biology College Park MD 20742

FAGAN, WILLIAM THOMAS, JR., urologist; b. Rutland, Vt, Sept. 21, 1923; s. William T. Sr. and Irene (Hevey) F.; m. Joy A. Lipman; children from previous marriage: Susan A. Barry, William T. III. BS, U. Vt., 1945, MD, 1948. Diplomate Am. Bd. Urology. Intern Mary Fletcher Hosp., 1948-49; resident Med. Ctr. Hosp. Vt., Burlington, 1949-52, attending physician urology, 1952-86, emeritus attending, 1986—; assoc. prof. U. Vt., Burlington, 1954; chief urology dept. Fanny Allen Hosp., Winooski, Vt., 1956-86. Cons. in urology Littleton Hosp., NH, 1961-92, Cottage Hosp., Woodsville, NH, 1981-92. Contbr. articles to profl. jour. Decorated Legion of Merit. Fellow ACS; mem. NY Acad. Sci., Am. Urol. Assn., Am. Geriatric Soc., AMA, Royal Soc. Medicine, Assn. Mil. Surgeons US Avocations: reading, raising and marketing Maine wild blueberries and forest products. Home and Office: PO Box 1508 Stowe VT 05672-1508

FAGEN, LESLIE GORDON, lawyer; b. N.Y.C., Apr. 12, 1950; s. Herman and Estelle (Garber) F. BA, Yale U., 1971; JD, Columbia U., 1974. Bar: N.Y. 1975, D.C. 1985, U.S. Dist. Ct. (so. and ea. dists.) N.Y. 1975, U.S. Ct. Appeals (2d cir.) 1975, U.S. Ct. Appeals (3d cir.) 1991, U.S. Ct. Appeals (7th and fed. cirs.) 1993; U.S. Supreme Ct. 1978. Law clk to judge U.S. Dist. Ct. (ea. dist.) N.Y., Bklyn., 1975; assoc. Milbank, Tweed, Hadley & McCloy, N.Y.C., 1975-76; from assoc. to ptnr. Paul, Weiss, Rifkind, Wharton & Garrison, N.Y.C., 1976—. Former adj. faculty Cardozo Law Sch., CCNY. Vice-chmn., pres. and trustee The Ednl. Alliance, Inc., 1993—. Mem. N.Y. State Bar Assn., Assn. Bar City N.Y. Office: Paul Weiss Rifkind Wharton & Garrison Ste 2330 1285 Avenue Of The Americas Fl 21 New York NY 10019-6028

FAGG, GEORGE GARDNER, federal judge; b. Eldora, Iowa, Apr. 30, 1934; s. Ned and Arleene (Gardner) Fagg; m. Jane E. Wood, Aug. 19, 1956; children: Martha, Thomas, Ned, Susan, George, Sarah. BSBA, Drake U., 1965, JD, 1958. Bar: Iowa 1958. Ptnr. Cartwright, Druker, Ryden & Fagg, Marshalltown, Iowa, 1958—72; judge Iowa Dist. Ct., 1972—82, U.S. Ct. Appeals (8th cir.), 1982—99, sr. judge, 1999—. Faculty Nat. Jud. Coll., 1979. Mem.: Iowa Bar Assn., Order of Coif. Office: US Ct Appeals US Courthouse Annex 110 E Court Ave Ste 455 Des Moines IA 50309-2044

FAGG, RUSSELL, judge, lawyer; b. Billings, Mont., June 26, 1960; s. Harrison Grover and Darlene (Bohling) F.; m. Karen Barclay, Feb. 13, 1992. BA, Whitman Coll., 1983; JD, U. Mont., 1986; MJS, U. Nev., 1999. Law clerk Mont. Supreme Ct., Helena, Mont., 1986-87; atty. Sandall Law Firm, Billings, Mont., 1987-89; city prosecutor City of Billings, Mont., 1989-91; dep. atty. Yellowstone County, Billings, Mont., 1991-94; mem. Montana State Legislator, Helena, 1991-94; judge State Dist. Ct. (13th dist.) Mont., Billings, 1995—. Dir. Midland Empire Pachyderm Club, 1988-94, pres. 1990-91; chmn. judiciary com. House of Reps., 1993-94. Named Outstanding Young Montanan, Mont. Jaycees, 1994; Young Life Spirit award, 2002. Avocations: hiking, fishing, skiing, reading. Home: 3031 Rimview Dr Billings MT 59102-0955 Office: PO Box 35027 Billings MT 59107-5027

FAGGIN, FEDERICO, electronics executive; b. Vicenza, Italy, Dec. 1, 1941; came to U.S., 1968, naturalized, 1978; s. Giuseppe and Emma (Munari) F.; m. Elvia Sardei, Sept. 2, 1967; children: Marzia, Marc, Eric. Grad., Perito Industriale Instituto A. Rossi, Vicenza, 1960; D.Physics, U. Padua, Italy, 1965. Sect. head Fairchild Camera & Instrument Co., Palo Alto, Calif., 1968-70; dept. mgr. Intel Corp., Santa Clara, Calif., 1970-74; founder, pres. Zilog Inc., Cupertino, Calif., 1974-80; v.p. computer systems group Exxon Enterprises, N.Y.C., 1981; co-founder, pres. Cygnet Technologies, Inc., Sunnyvale, Calif., 1982-86; co-founder, CEO Synaptics, Inc., San Jose, Calif., 1986-99, chmn.,

1999—. Recipient Marconi Fellowship award, 1988, W. Wallace McDowell award IEEE Computer Soc., 1994, Kyoto prize, 1997; inducted Nat. Inventor's Hall of Fame, 1996. Achievements include developing silicon gate tech. for MOS fabrication, first microprocessor. Office: Synaptics Inc 2381 Bering Dr San Jose CA 95131-1125

FAGIN, BARRY STEVEN, computer science educator, writer; b. Boston, Sept. 2, 1960; s. Arnold D. Fagin and Lois R. Roisman; m. Michele Berdinis Fagin, Aug. 11, 1985; children: Max, Erica. AB magna cum laude, Brown U., 1982; PhD, U. Calif., Berkeley, 1987. Asst. prof. engring. sci. Thayer Sch. of Engring., Dartmouth Coll., Hanover, N.H., 1987-94; prof. computer sci. USAF Acad., Colorado Springs, Colo., 1994—. Contbr. articles to profl. jours. Co-founder Families Against Internet Censorship, Colorado Springs, 1996—; info. dir. ACM SIGCAS, N.Y.; mem. Rocky Mountain Skeptics, Colorado Springs. Recipient Civil Liberties award ACLU, 1996; sr. fellow Independence Inst.; Fulbright scholar St. Petersburg (Russia) Tech. State U., 2001. Jewish. Avocations: snowboarding, mountain climbing, scuba, freestyle frisbee. Office: USAF Acad Dept Computer Sci 2354 Fairchild Dr Colorado Springs CO 80840 Fax: 719-333-3338. E-mail: barry.fagin@usafa.af.mil.

FAGIN, CLAIRE MINTZER, nursing educator, administrator; b. NYC; d. Harry and Mae (Slatin) Mintzer; m. Samuel Fagin, Feb. 17, 1952; children: Joshua, Charles. BS, Wagner Coll., 1948; MA, Tchrs. Coll. Columbia, 1951; PhD, NYU, 1964; DSc (hon.), Lycoming Coll., 1983, Cedar Crest Coll., 1987, U. Rochester, 1987, Med. Coll. Pa., 1989, U. Md., 1993, Wagner Coll., 1993, Loyola U., 1996; DSc (hon.), Case Western Res. U., 2002; LLD (hon.), U. Pa., 1994; DHL (hon.), Hunter Coll., 1993, Rush U., 1996, Johns Hopkins U., 2003. Staff nurse, clin. instr. Sea View Hosp., S.I., N.Y.; clin. instr. Bellevue Hosp., N.Y.C.; psychiat. nurse cons. Nat. League for Nursing, N.Y.C.; asst. chief psychiat. nursing svc. clin. ctr. NIH; rsch. project coord. dept. psychiatry Children's Hosp., Washington; instr., assoc. prof. psychiat.-mental health nursing NYU, N.Y.C., dir. grad. programs in psychiat. mental health nursing, 1965—69; chmn. nursing dept., prof. Herbert H. Lehman Coll., CUNY, N.Y.C., 1969—77; dir. Health Professions Inst., Montefiore Hosp. and Med. Ctr., 1975—77; Margaret Bond Simon dean sch. of nursing U. Pa., Phila., 1977—92, Leadership chair prof., 1992—96, interim pres., 1993—94, dean emeritus, prof. emeritus, 1996—. Project leader Millbank Found.; dir. program bldg. acad. geriatric nursing John A. Hartford Found.; bd. dirs. Provident Mut. Ins. Co., chmn. audit com., 1985—96, exec. com., 1986—97, adv. com., 1996—2003, audit com., 1978—96, Salomon, Inc., 1994—97; bd. dirs., comp. com. Radian Inc.; bd. dirs. Vis. Nurse Soc. N.Y., 1998—; bd. dirs., chair audit com. N.Y. Acad. Medicine, 1998—; spkr., cons. in field. Contbr. articles. Named Disting. Dau. Pa., 1994; recipient Achievement award, Wagner Coll., 1956, Tchrs. Coll., 1975, Disting. Alumna award, NYU, 1979, Founders award, Sigma Theta Tau, 1981, Hon. Recognition award, ANA, 1988, Woman of Courage award, Women's Way, 1990, Alumni Merit award, U. Pa., 1991, Leadership award, Trustee Coun. Pa. Women First, 1991, Caring award, Phila. Vis. Nurses Assn., 1994, Lillian Wald award, N.Y. Vis. Nurses Assn., 1994, Hildegard Peplau award outstanding contbn. psych-nursing, 1994, Living Legend award, Am. Acad. Nursing, 1998, Pres. medal, NYU, 1998, Nightingale Lamp award, Am. Nurses Found., 2002; disting. scholar, 1984, hon. fellow, Royd Coll. Nursing, 2002. Fellow: Royal Coll. Nursing (hon.); mem.: Nat. League for Nursing (pres. 1991—93), Am. Orthopsychiat. Assn. (bd. dirs. 1972—75, exec. com. bd. dirs. 1973—75, pres. 1985—86), Am. Acad. Nursing (governing coun. 1976—78), Inst. Medicine of NAS (governing coun. 1981—83, chmn. bd. health promotion and disease prevention 1991—94). Address: 200 Central Park S Apt 12E New York NY 10019-1415 Office: U Pa Sch Nursing 354 Neb Bldg Philadelphia PA 19104-6096

FAGIN, DAVID KYLE, natural resources executive; b. Dallas, Apr. 9, 1938; s. Kyle Marshall and Frances Margaret (Gaston) F.; m. Margaret Anne Hazlett, Jan. 24, 1959 (dec. July 1999); children: David Kyle, Scott Edward; m. Terry Lee Craig, Dec. 6, 2002. BS in Petroleum Engring., U. Okla., 1960; postgrad., Am. Inst. Banking, So. Meth. U. Grad. Sch. Bus. Adminstrn. Registered profl. engr., La., Okla., Tex. Trainee Exxon-Mobil (formerly Magnolia Petroleum Co.), 1955—56; jr. engr., engr., then ptnr. W.C. Bednar Petroleum Cons., Dallas, 1958—65; petroleum engr. Bank of Am. N.A. (formerly First Nat. Bank Dallas), Dallas, 1965—68; v.p. Rosario Resources Corp. (merged 1980 with AMAX Inc.), N.Y.C., 1968—75; pres. Alamo Petroleum Corp., 1968—82; exec. v.p. Rosario Resources Corp. (now Alcoa/Phelps Dodge), N.Y.C., 1975—77, dir., 1975—80, pres., COO, 1977—82; chmn., dir., pres., CEO Fagin Exploration Co., Denver, 1982—86; pres., COO, bd. dirs. Barrick Gold Ltd. (formerly Homestake Mining Co.), Toronto, Canada, 1986—91; CEO & chmn. Golden Star Resources Ltd., Denver, 1992—96, dir., 1992—; chmn., CEO Western Exploration and Devel. Ltd., Denver, 1997—2000, dir., 1997—2001. Bd. dirs. all T. Rowe Price Pub. Mut. Funds, Balt., Pacific Rim Mining Corp. (formerly Dayton Mining Co.), Vancouver, B.C., Mineral Info. Inst., Canyon Resources Corp. Bd. dirs. Denver Area coun. Boy Scouts Am., 1993—; bd. visitors U. Okla. Sch. Engring., 1995-98, 99—, chmn., 2002—; Nat. Mining Hall of Fame and Mus., 1997—; dir. Teen Challenge of Colo., 2002—. Mem. AIME (chmn. Dallas sect. of Soc. Petroleum Engrs. 1975, chmn. investment fund 1979-82), Soc. Mining, Metallurgy and Exploration (dir. 1996-97), Soc. Petroleum Engrs., Mining and Metall. Soc. Am., Internat. Mining Profls. Soc. (dir., exec. com., v.p. 1999, pres. 2001-2002).

FAHERTY, DAVID MILES, musical instrument repairman; b. Ft. Worth, Tex., July 8, 1954; s. Frank Patrick and Laura Gene Faherty. Grad., Tarrant County Jr. Coll., 1977. Owner, pres. D.M. Faherty Music Co., Ft. Worth, 1978—. Mem. U.S. Jaycees, Ft. Worth, 1985-94, Ft. Worth City Band, 1978—; pres. Tarrant County Jaycees, 1988-89. Mem. Ft. Worth City Band (v.p. 1984-85), Nat. Assn. of Profl. Band Instrument Repair Technicians (clinician tchr.). Roman Catholic. Avocations: hunting, fishing, musical performance. Office: D M Faherty Music Co PO Box 11102 Fort Worth TX 76110-0102 E-mail: milessax@napbirt.org.

FAHERTY, JOHN KEVIN, insurance broker, consultant; b. San Benito, Tex., Nov. 1, 1952; s. Frank Patrick and Laura Lewis (Kelly) F.; m. Marion Cumming Kilpatrick, Nov. 29, 1980; children: Sean, Colin. BA with honors in behavioral scis., St. Edward's U., Austin, Tex., 1975; MS in counseling psychology, North Tex. State U., 1979; spl. edn. cert., U. Tex., Tyler, 1981. Lic. psychol. assoc., assoc. sch. psychologist, Tex. Tchg. fellow, rschr. North Tex. State U., Denton, 1977-80; sch. psychologist Windham Sch. Sys., Tennessee Colony, Tex., 1980-87, Ft. Worth Ind. Schs., 1988-91, edn1. cons., 1991—; ins. broker Faherty Ins. Svcs., Ft. Worth, 1991—. Mem. pub. rels. com. Palestine (Tex.) Ind. Schs., 1986-87; rep. area adv. coun. Tex. Youth Commn., 1989-91; ex-officio mem. Tex. Commn. on Alcohol and Drug Abuse, 1991-93; mem. broker adv. panel Harris Meth. Health Sys., Arlington, Tex., 1996-99. Author: (coll. workbook) Statistical Measurement in Psychology, 1980; co-author 12 tech. reports; contbr. articles to profl. jours. Chpt. pres. Palestine Jr. Chamber, 1985-86, state program mgr., 1986-87, state v.p., 1987-88; den leader and treas. Cub Scout pack 499, Ft. Worth, 1991-97. Named one of Outstanding Young Men Am., 1988, 91; recipient Seiji Horiuchi award U.S. Jaycees, 1987, Career Achievement award Gen. Agts. and Mgrs. Assn. Ft. Worth chpt., 1991; Jaycees Internat. senator, 1988. Mem. Ft. Worth Life Underwriters Assn. (exec. com., sec.-treas. 1995, v.p. 1997-98, pres.-elect 1998-99, pres. 1999-2000, dir. region II Tex. Assn. Ins. and Fin. Advisors 2000—01, Cmty. Vol. Svc. award 1997), Tex. Jr. Chamber Senate (exec. com., pres. 1996-97, Thomas E. Humphrey Meml. award as Outstanding State Senate Pres. 1997, Career Svc. award 2003), Tex. Jaycees Found., Inc. (bd. dirs., rep. 1990-92), John Ben Shepperd Leadership Forum (governing bd., rep. 1990-91), Tex. Leaders Round Table (life, Lone Star leader 1994-), Leading Producers Round Table (pres.'s coun. 1993-2001), Eagles Club (life 2003). Republican. Roman Catholic. Avocations: rsch., writing, motorcycle rallies, swimming, charitable work in cmty. Home: 7200 Francisco Dr Fort Worth TX 76133-6708 Office: Faherty Ins Svcs 3701 S University Dr Fort Worth TX 76109-3719 E-mail: kfaherty@hotmail.com.

FAHERTY, ROBERT LOUIS, publishing executive; b. St. Louis, Sept. 26, 1939; s. Justin Louis and Elizabeth Veronica (Quigley) F.; m. Claudia C. Hutchison, Jan. 10, 1969; children: Kathleen Marie, Timothy Robert, Mark Robert, Megan Elizabeth, Bridget Justine. BA magna cum laude, Cath. U. Am., 1961, MA, 1962; STL cum laude, Pontifical Gregorian U., Rome, 1966. Editor St. Louis Rev., 1967-69, Ency. Britannica, Chgo., 1969-72; mng. editor sci./Benefic Press Harcourt Brace Jovanovich, Chgo., 1972-73; mng. editor Scholarly Press, Detroit, 1973-75; co-founder, editor-in-chief Reference Publs., Algonac, Mich., 1975-77; editor-in-chief Congl. Budget Office, Washington, 1977-84; dir. Brookings Instn. Press, Washington, 1984—. Lectr. Howard U. Grad. Pub. Inst., 1985-89; mem. adv. com. on pub. and comm. programs U. Va., 1994—, instr., 1995—. Contbr. articles to profl. jours. Trustee, treas. Ela Area Pub. Libr. Dist., Lake County, Ill., 1973-74; bd. dirs. United Cmty. Ministries, Fairfax County, Va., 1992-99, pres., 1995-99; chmn. Algonac Recreation Commn., 1976-77; mem. bioethics com. for Mid-Atlantic region Kaiser Permanente HMO, 1989-99; mem. Fairfax County, Va., Human Svcs. Coun., 1999—. Curators' scholar U. Mo., 1957, Basselin Found. scholar Cath. U. Am., 1959. Mem. Assn. Am. Univ. Presses (bd. dirs. 1991-94, 97-2000, pres. 1998-99), Assn. Am. Pubs. (bd. dirs. 2001—). Home: 4303 Mission Ct Alexandria VA 22310-3353 Office: Brookings Instn 1775 Massachusetts Ave NW Washington DC 20036-2103 E-mail: rfaherty@brookings.edu.

FAHEY, BARBARA STEWART DOE, public agency administrator; b. Chgo., Aug. 9, 1950; d. William Bethel and Doris (Charn) Doe. BA, U. Colo., 1972; MA, Sangamon State U., 1975. Dir. Wilderness Study Project, Springfield, Ill., 1973-75, Environ. Ctr., Boulder, Colo., 1976-79; natural resource specialist U.S. Bur. Reclamation, Denver, 1977-78; rsch. assoc. Nat. Conf. State Legislatures, Denver, 1979-80; asst. to transp. dir. City of Boulder, 1980-81, project mgr., 1981-85, parking coord., 1985-90, open space planner, 1991-92; interpretive park naturalist Jefferson County, Golden, Colo., 1992, adminstr. Nature Ctr., 1993-95; county dir. Colo. State U. Coop. Extension in Jefferson County, 1995—. Vice chmn. Boulder County Energy Adv. Com., Boulder, 1987; bd. mem. County Bd. Rev., Boulder, 1984-86, Historic Boulder, 1991-92. Bd. mem. Colo. Open Space Coun., Denver, 1979-80; mem. Leadership Boulder C. of C., 1986. Named Young Career Woman Colo. Bus. and Profl. Women's Fedn., Denver, 1981; recipient Innovation award Denver Coun. Govts., 1985, State Dir.'s Merit award, 1997, Nat. Program Leadership award Assn. Natural Resources Ext. Profls., 2002. Mem. Nat. Assn. Interpretation, Denver Botanic Gardens, Denver Mus. Sci. and Nature, Colo. Native Plant Soc., Boulder Bus. and Profl. Women (treas. 1983-84, v.p. 1987-88, pres. 1989-90, winner speech contest 1985), Sierra Club (bd. mem. Sangamon Valley Group 1973-75). Avocations: cross-country skiing, backpacking, hiking, classical and folk music. Office: 15200 W 6th Ave Ste C Golden CO 80401-6588

FAHEY, HALLIE JOAN MILLER, lawyer; b. McHenry, Ill., July 2, 1965; d. Charles Peter and Joan Kathryn (Bauer) Miller; m. Brian Joseph Fahey, Nov. 18, 1995; 1 child, Cameron Miller Fahey. BS, Butler U., 1987; postgrad., Boston Coll., 1987-88; JD, U. Ill., 1990. Bar: Ill. 1990. Assoc. Schiff Hardin & White, Chgo., 1990-95, Blatt Hammesfahr & Eaton, Chgo., 1995-97; from assoc. to ptnr. Meckler Bulger & Tilson, Chgo., 1997—2001; ptnr. Ross Dixon & Bell, Chgo., 2001—. Republican. Roman Catholic. Avocations: photography, architecture. Office: Ross Dixon & Bell Three First Na Plz 70 W Madison Ste 525 Chicago IL 60602

FAHEY, JAMES EDWARD, brokerage house executive; b. N.Y.C. s. John Michael and Kathleen Rose Fahey; 2 children. BBA, MBA, Iona Coll. Registered investment advisor. Territory asst. European Am. Bank, N.Y.C., 1978-80; internat. analyst Texaco, Inc., White Plains, N.Y., 1981-83; mgr. internat. treasury Am. Standard Inc., N.Y.C., 1984-88; asst. treas. Perkin Elmer Internat., Inc., 1988-91; sr. mgr. internat. treasury Perkin Elmer Corp., Norwalk, Conn., 1988-91; sr. v.p. investments, corp. client group dir. Smith Barney, N.Y.C., 1991—. Active Friends of Am. Cancer Soc., N.Y.C., 1986—; mem. leadership com. Tristate Cure Autism Now, 2002—. Mem. Friendly Sons of St. Patrick (N.Y.C.), Rep. Senatorial Inner Circle. Office: Smith Barney 250 Park Ave New York NY 10177-0001

FAHEY, JOHN M., JR., book publishing executive; Pres., CEO, chmn. Time Life Inc., Alexandria, Va., 1996; exec. v.p., chair ops. office Nat. Geog. Soc., Washington, 1997—, pres., CEO, 1998—, Explorers Hall, Washington. Office: Nat Geographic Soc 1145 17th St NW Washington DC 20036-4701

FAHEY, MIKE, mayor; b. Kansas City, Kansas ; 4 children. Postgrad, Creighton Univ., 1973. Mayor City of Omaha, 2001—; ret. CEO Am. Land Title Co., former owner. Bd. Holy Name Housing, Am. Red Cross Heartland Chpt., Creighton Prep H.S.; chmn. Omaha Planning Bd., 1981. Office: 1819 Farnam St Ste 300 Omaha NE 68183

FAHEY, PATRICIA ANNE, editor; b. Methuen, Mass., Aug. 6, 1957; d. Edward James and Evelyn Fay (Benedix) Howard; m. Thomas Francis Fahey, Jr., Mar. 5, 1982; children: Ryan Thomas, Caitlin Elizabeth (dec.), Emily Catherine. AA in Liberal Arts with highest honors, No. Essex Community Coll., Haverhill, Mass., 1977; BA in English magna cum laude, Notre Dame Coll., Manchester, N.H., 1987; MEd in Elem. Edn., Notre Dame Coll., 1995. News reporter Salem (N.H.) Observer, 1975-77, news editor, 1977-78; news corr. Union Leader Corp., Manchester, N.H., 1978-80, lifestyle reporter, 1980-82, news reporter, 1982-86, copy editor, 1986—; elem. tchr. Concord (N.H.) Sch. Dist., 1994—. Mem. Future Planning Commn., Town of Auburn, N.H., 1983-84; mem. adv. bd. Manchester Assn. Retarded Citizens, 1984-85. Recipient Community Service award Am. Cancer Soc., 1985. Mem. Internat. Reading Assn., Nat. Coun. Tchrs. of Math., Granite State Reading Coun., Concord Edn. Assn., The Newspaper Guild. Congregationalist. Avocations: skiing, travel, photography, interior decorating. Home: 8 Chestnut Pasture Rd Concord NH 03301-7900 Office: 40 Sewalls Falls Rd Concord NH 03301-4649

FAHEY, RICHARD PAUL, lawyer; b. Oakland, Calif., Nov. 2, 1944; s. John Joseph and Helene Goldie (Whetstone) F.; m. Suzanne Dawson, June 8, 1968; children: Eamon, Aaron Chad. AA, Meritt Coll., 1964; BA, San Francisco State Univ., 1966; JD, Northwestern U., 1971. Bar: N. Mex., 1971, U.S. Dist. Ct., N. Mex., 1972, U.S. Ct. Appeals (10th cir.) 1972, Ohio 1973, U.S. Dist. Ct. (no. and so. dists.), U.S. Supreme Ct. 1975. Atty. in charge Dinebeiina Nahiilna Be Agaditahe, Shiprock, New Mexico, 1971-73; asst. atty. genl. State of Ohio, Columbus, OH, 1973-76; ptnr. Fahey & Schraff, 1976-80; atty. Sanford, Fisher, Fahey, Boyland & Schwarzwalder, 1980-84; of counsel Knepper, White, Arter & Hadden, 1984-85; ptnr. Arter & Hadden, 1985-99; of counsel Vorys Sater Seymour and Pease LLP, 2000—02, ptnr., 2003—; adj. prof. law Capital U., 1976-86, Ohio State Univ., 1986-87; chmn. Ohio Oil and Gas Regulatory Rev. Commn., 1986-87. Author: Underground Storage Tanks A Primer of the Federal Regulatory Program, 2d edit., 1995; contbr. articles to profl. jours. Vol. Peace Corps., Liberia, 1966—68; active Columbus Pub. Schs. Bd. Edn., 1986—93, pres., 1989; trustee Godman Guild Settlement House, 1976—82, Ohio Environ. Coun., 1981—83; adv. bd. WCBE Pub. Radio; Charter rev. com. Columbus City, 1998—99; exec. com. Dem. Party, Ohio, 1996—2002; trustee Downtown Columbus, Inc., 1989, Pilot Dogs, Inc., 1993—, pres., 2001, 1999—2003, Cmty. in Sch., 2000—. Grantee, Russell Sage Found., 1969. Mem. ABA (vice chair Sonreel water quality com. 1993-97), Ohio Bar Assn., N. Mex. Bar Assn., Columbus Bar Assn., Columbus Bar Found. Democrat. Unitarian Universalist. Avocations: travel, fishing, reading, jogging, skiing. Home: 449 E Dominion Blvd Columbus OH 43214-2216 Address: 58 Camino Nevoso Santa Fe NM 87505 Office: Vorys Sater Seymour and Pease LLP 52 E Gay St Columbus OH 43215

FAHEY-CAMERON, ROBIN, artist, photographer, writer; b. Bangor, Maine, Mar. 7, 1943; d. Oswald R. and Georgina Marie (Barbin) Fahey; m. Gordon W. Vogel, June 27, 1966 (dec. 1993); 1 child, Darren Taggert. BA in Studio Art, U. Minn., 1968; grad., LaJolla Acad. Advt. Arts, Calif., 1984. Tech. dir. The Peppermint Tent, Mpls., 1968; costume designer St. Joseph (Minn.) Coll., 1968-69; copywriter, graphic artist Western Word and Picture Co., Sausalito, Calif., 1984-86; creative dir. 20/20 Catalogue, San Francisco, 1986-89; mng. ptnr. Felisous Films, Emeryville, Calif., 2003—. Owner-dir. William Lester Gallery, Point Reyes Station, Calif. Author: Games of Deception, 1989, The Inner Door, 1996, Gate Between the Worlds, 1998; art dir. Wakeup-a Felisous film, 2002. Mem. En Couleur (signature), Am. Impressionist Soc. Avocation: gardening.

FAHIEN, LEONARD AUGUST, physician, educator; b. St. Louis, July 26, 1934; s. John Henry and Alice Katherine (Schubkegel) F.; m. Rose Marian Burmeister, June 21, 1958; children: Catherine Fahien Reuter, Lisa Fahien Uldrich, James. AB, Washington U., St Louis, 1956; MD, Washington U., 1960. Intern U. Wis., Madison, 1960-61; surgeon NIH, Bethesda, Md., 1964-66; asst. prof. dept. pharmacology U. Wis. Med. Sch., Madison, 1966-69, asso. prof., 1969-74, prof., 1974—, asso. dean, 1979-83; vis. prof. Inst. Protein Rsch. Osaka U., Japan, 1991; prof. El Julios U. Barcelona (Spain), 1997. Contbr. chpts. to books; contbr. articles to profl. jours. Served with USPHS, 1964-66. Numerous NIH grants, 1966— Mem. Phi Beta Kappa, Sigma Xi. Lutheran. Home: 3212 Topping Rd Madison WI 53705-1435 Office: 426 S Charter St Madison WI 53715-1626 E-mail: lafahien@facstaff.wisc.edu.

FAHLBECK, DOUGLAS ALAN, corporate development executive; b. Worcester, Mass., Dec. 27, 1945; s. Robert L. and Evelyn (Drury) F.; m. Jean A. Reardon, Aug. 22, 1970; children: Susan, Lauren. BS in Bus. Adminstrn., Boston U., 1967. Audit mgr. Arthur Andersen & Co., Boston, 1967-76; contr., treas. BTR, Inc., Providence, 1977-81; CFO Textron Fin. Corp., Providence, 1982-95; v.p. mergers and acquisitions Textron Inc., Providence, 1995—. Served as sgt. USMC, 1967-73. Mem. Am. Inst. CPA's., Mass. Soc. CPA's. Avocations: skiing, water skiing.

FAHLE, MANFRED, ophthalmology researcher; b. Duesseldorf, Germany, Dec. 10, 1950; s. Fritz and Helma (Westerfeld) F.; m. Sigrid Henke, Aug. 3, 1979; children: Nora Katharina, Till Patrick Jakob; m. Karoline Spang, Aug. 4, 2001. Degree in Biology, U. Goettingen, Fed. Republic Germany, 1972; degree in medicine, U. Giessen, Fed. Republic Germany, 1973; MA in biology, U. Mainz, Fed. Republic Germany, 1975; MD, U. Tuebingen, Fed. Republic Germany, 1977. Fellow Max-Planck Inst. for Biol. Cybernetics, Tuebingen, 1977-81; head electrophysiol. lab. Univ. Eye Clinic, Tuebingen, 1981-88; vis. scientist U. Calif., Berkeley, 1984, MIT, Cambridge, Mass., 1989-90; fellow German Rsch. Coun., Tuebingen, 1990-93; prof. ophthalmology, head sect. visual sci. Univ. Eye Hosp., Tuebingen, 1994-98; head Inst. Brain Rsch. IV human-neurobiology U. Bremen, Germany, 2000—. Wiersma vis. prof. Calif. Inst. Tech., Pasadena, 1996; prof., head dept. optometry and visual sci. City U., London, 1998-99; prof. human neurobiology U. Bremen, Germany, 1999—; vis. prof. Univ. Coll., London, 1999-2002, vis. prof. Applied Vision Rsch. Ctr., City Univ., 2000—; mem. acad. senate, U. Bremen, 2003—. Mem. editl. bd. German Jour. Ophthalmology, 1991-97, Neuroophthalmology, 1993-2003, Vision Rsch., 1994—. Bd. dirs. Grad. Program Neurobiology, Tuebingen, 1986-91, Drug Rsch. Program, Tuebingen, 1996-99; mem. acad. senate Bremen Univ., 2003—. Recipient Heisenberg award German Rsch. Coun., 1989, prize von Humboldt/Max-Planck Soc., 1992. Avocations: music, literature, sailing, windsurfing. Home: Graf-Moltkestr 56 D28211 Bremen Germany Office: Inst Human Neurobiology Argonnenstr 3 D28211 Bremen Germany E-mail: mfahle@uni-bremen.de.

FAHLGREN, H(ERBERT) SMOOT, advertising executive; b. Parkerburg, W.Va., Aug. 17, 1930; s. C. Herbert and Julia (Smoot) Fahlgren; m. Judith Anne Henniger, Dec. 7, 1952; children: Steven, Becky, John. Student, U. Va., 1949-52; BSBA, Marietta Coll., 1952. Chmn. bd. dirs. Fahlgren, Parkersburg, W.Va., 1962—. Bd. dirs. United Nat. Bank. Elder 1st Presbyn. Ch., Parkersburg; bd. dirs. W.Va. U. Found. Recipient Spirit of Live award, 1998. Mem.: W.Va. Round Table, Am. Assn. Advt. Agys. (treas. 1978—79, dir. 1981—). Home: 199 Thoroughbred Ln Parkersburg WV 26104 Office: PO Box 1628 418 Grand Park Dr Ste 321 Parkersburg WV 26102-1628 E-mail: hsfahlgren@fahlgren.com.

FAHMY, IBRAHIM MOUNIR, hotel executive; b. Alexandria, Egypt, July 4, 1943; came to U.S., 1986; s. Ambassador Mounir Ibrahim and Aziza (Kelada) F.; m. Brenda Lee Chenier, Sept. 18, 1970 (div. Jan. 1991); children: Susan Lee, Christine Lynn; m. Ann Marie Jones, Oct. 15, 1995; 1 child, Laila Ann. Certs., St. Mark's Coll., Alexandria, 1949-63; student, U. Alexandria, 1962-63. V.p., gen. mgr. King Edward Hotel, Toronto, Canada, 1982—86; sr. v.p. Can. Forte Hotels Inc., N.Y.C., 1986—95; exec. v.p. Forte Hotels Inc., San Diego, 1986—95; mng. dir. The Carlton, Washington, 1995—99, The Essex House, NY, NY, 1999—2002, Egypt-Starwood Hotels and Resorts Worldwide, Cairo, 2002—. Former dir. Hotel Assn. Met. Toronto, Ont. Hostelry Inst.; mem. adv. com. Humber Coll. Vol. Kidney Found., Muscular Dystrophy, The Can. Children's Found. Mem. Internat. Wine and Food Soc., St. Botolph Club. Avocations: skiing, english riding, squash, theatre, skeet and sporting clay shooting. Home and Office: Sheraton Cairo Hotel Towers and Casino PO Box 11 Cairo 11511 Egypt

FAHN, JAY, commercial bank executive, consultant, art dealer; b. Dallas, Aug. 19, 1949; s. Eli and Marion Fahn. BA, Williams Coll., 1971; PhB, MPhil. in Internat. Relations, Oxford (Eng.) U., 1975. Assoc. Citibank, N.A., N.Y.C. and Nairobi, Kenya, 1976, asst. v.p. Seoul, Republic of Korea, 1981-83; mgr. Citibank, N.A., Ltd., Johannesburg, Republic of South Africa, 1977-79; resident v.p. Citibank Zambia, Ltd., Lusaka, 1979-81; v.p. Citicorp U.S.A., Chgo., 1983-85, First Nat. Bank of Chgo., 1989-91, LaSalle St. Securities, Chgo., 1989-90, Citicorp Investment Bank, Chgo., 1985—; sr. v.p. Hyde Park Bank, Chgo., 1991—. Chmn. corp. contbns. com. Citicorp, Chgo., 1985—; prin., pres. Fahn & Assocs., Ltd., Chgo., 1986—; prin., owner Orca Aart Gallery, Chgo., 1987—; vis. lectr. geopolitics DePaul U., Chgo., 1990—. Author: Chimbuko, 1986; contbr., editorial assoc.: Government by the People, 1971, Edward Kennedy and the Camelot Legacy, 1975. Nat. youth coord. Nat. Humphrey for Pres. Com., Washington, 1971-72; mem. com. on fgn. affairs Chgo. Coun. Fgn. Rels., 1989. Recipient Oxford U. scholarship, 1973, 74. Mem. Williams Club, Adventurers, Chgo. Zool. Soc. (governing mem. 1993—), North Michigan Ave. Assn. (bd. exec. com. 2000—). Avocations: flying, camping, wildlife, history, scuba. Home: 131 S Scoville Ave Oak Park IL 60302 Office: Hyde Park Bank & Trust 1525 E 53rd St Ste 502 Chicago IL 60615-4584

FAHN, STANLEY, neurologist, educator; b. Sacramento, Nov. 6, 1933; s. Ernest and Sylvia F.; m. Charlotte, June 21, 1958; children: Paul N., James D. BA, U. Calif.-Berkeley, 1955, MD, 1958. Diplomate Am. Bd. Neurology. Resident in neurology Neurol. Inst., N.Y., 1959-62; rsch. assoc. NIH, 1962-65; mem. faculty Columbia U., N.Y.C., 1965-68, prof. neurology, 1973-78, H. Houston Merritt prof., 1978—, dir. Morris K. Udall Parkinson Disease Rsch. Ctr., 1999—2003; mem. faculty U. Pa., Phila., 1968-73. Dir. Dystonia Rsch. Ctr., 1981-97; sci. dir. Parkinson's Disease Found., 1979—; chmn. adv. com. peripheral and ctrl. nervous sys. drugs FDA, 1987-89, 91-96. Editor Movement Disorders, 1985-95; assoc. editor Neurology, 1977-87. With USPHS, 1962-65 Grantee NIH, 1974—77, 1980—82, 1984—91, 1994—. Mem.: Inst. of Medicine, Dystonia Med. Rsch. Found. (hon. life, bd. dirs. 1998—), Movement Disorder Soc. (pres. 1988—91), Am. Neurol. Assn. (v.p. 1987—88, chair jour. oversight com. 1994—96), Am. Acad. Neurology (chair edn. com. 1986—93, v.p. 1993—97, pres.-elect 1999—2001, pres. 2001—03). Home: 155 Edgars Ln Hastings On Hudson NY 10706-1107 Office: 710 W 168th St New York NY 10032-2603

FAHNER, HAROLD THOMAS, marketing executive; b. Detroit, Sept. 4, 1940; s. Harold L. and Beatrice H. (Craig) F.; m. Patricia A. (Churchvara), Aug. 25, 1962; children: Michael, Janet, Peter. BS in Econ., U. Detroit, 1962. Sales dept. Dun and Bradstreet, Inc., N.Y.C., 1963-67; mgr. sales tng. Blue Cross Blue Shield, Detroit, 1967-70; mgr. sales, mgmt. tng. A.O. Smith Harvestore Products, Inc., Arlington Heights, Ill., 1970-76, dist. sales mgr., 1976-77, ea. regional mgr., 1977-79, mktg. cons., 1980-82; v.p. mktg. Neuero Corp., West Chgo., Ill., 1982-85; v.p. sales and mktg. Atwater Group, Inc., Mpls., 1985-87; v.p. corp. mktg. Blue Cross Blue Shield of Fla., Inc., Jacksonville, Fla., 1988—2003; prin. Sales and Mktg. Assocs., Jacksonville, Fla., 2003—. Instr. Internat. Sales Mgmt. Inst.; lectr. in mktg., sales field. Author: The Problem Solving Approach to Selling, 1975; The Sales Manager's Model Letter Book, 1976, 2d edit., 1987; Successful Sales Management, 1983. Bd. trustees, Grad. Sch. Sales Mgmt. and Mktg., Syracuse Univ. Mem. Sales and Mktg. Exec. Assn. Internat. (sr. v.p., bd. dir. Jacksonville chpt.) Home: 1601 Ocean Dr S Jacksonville FL 32250-6362 E-mail: halsmktg@att.net.

FAHNESTOCK, JEAN HOWE, retired civil engineer; b. Pitts., May 22, 1930; d. James Murray and Hazel Margaret (Alberts) F. AA, Stephens, 1950; BS in Civil Engring., Carnegie-Mellon, 1955. Registered profl. engr., Ill., Mich., Iowa. Sr. project mgr. De Leuw, Cather & Co., Chgo., 1955-92. Design mgr. De Leuw, Cather & Co., Kuwait, 1978-81, Abu Dhabi, 1981-85, Kennedy Expy. and Elgin-O'Hare Expy., Chgo., 1985-92. Fellow ASCE (life); mem. NSPE, Ill. Soc. Profl. Engrs. (life). Republican. Presbyterian. Avocations: bridge, travel, politics. Home: 4606 W Bryn Mawr Ave Chicago IL 60646-6632 E-mail: jhf4606@aol.com.

FAHRBACH, RUTH C. state legislator; b. N.Y.C. Grad. high sch., East Meadow, N.Y. Mem. Dist. 61 Conn. Ho. of Reps., 1981—, minority whip. Appropriations com., pub. health com., legis. mgmt. com. Active Windsor Rep. Town Com., Order Women Legislators; mem. Windsor Bd. Edn., 1977-81, v.p., 1979-80; bd. dirs. Celebrate Windsor!, Inc., 2001--. Mem. First Dist. Rep. Womens Club, Fedn. Rep. Women, Civitan Club Windsor (past pres), Nat. Order of Women Legislators, Conn. Order of Women Legislators (sec.), Conn. Fedn. of Rep. Women, Nat. Fedn. of Republican Women, St. Casimir's Lithuanian Club Women's Aux. Home: 592 Poquonock Ave Windsor CT 06095-2204 Office: Legis Office Bldg Rm 4200 Hartford CT 06106-1591 E-mail: ruth.fahrbach@housegop.po.state.ct.us.

FAHRENKOPF, FRANK JOSEPH, JR., lawyer; b. Bklyn., Aug. 28, 1939; s. Frank J. and Rose (Freeman) F.; m. Mary Ethel Bandoni, Aug. 25, 1962; children: Allison Marie, Leslie Ann, Amy Michelle. BA, U. Nev., 1962; JD, U. Calif., Berkeley, 1965. Bar: Nev. 1965, D.C. 1983. Assoc. atty. Breen & Young, Reno, 1965-67; ptnr., atty. Sanford, Sanford, Fahrenkopf & Mousel, Reno, 1967-75, Fahrenkopf, Mortimer, Sourwine, Mousel & Sloane, Reno, 1976-85, Hogan & Hartson, Washington, 1985—; pres., CEO Am. Gaming Assn., 1995—. Instr. criminal law U. Nev., 1967-82; panelist reporter Citizens Conf. on Nev. Cts., 1968; mem. Nev. Bd. Bar Examiners, 1971-85; judge pro tem Reno Municipal Ct., 1972-85; mem. faculty Nat. Jud. Coll., Reno, 1974-83; chmn. Coun. for the Future, Nat. Jud. Coll., 1990-94, bd. trustees, 1995-2000. Chmn. lawyers divsn. United Fund, 1969-70, chmn. Rep. Nat. Com., 1983-89; chmn. Nev. Rep. Com., 1975-83, gen. counsel, 1972-75; No. Nev. co-chmn. Com. for Re-election of Pres., 1972; mem. exec. bd. Nev. Rep. Cen. Com., 1969; nat. committeeman Nev. Young Reps., 1969-73; mem. Rep. Nat. Com., 1975-89; del. Rep. Nat. Conv., 1972, 76, 80, 84, 88; chmn. Western States Rep. Chmn.'s Assn., 1978-83; nat. chmn. Rep. State Chmn.'s Assn., 1981-83; bd. dirs. Nev. Cancer Soc., chmn., 1978-87; bd. dirs. Washoe County Legal Aid Soc., Babe Ruth Baseball League, Nev. Opera Guild, Reno YWCA, Sierra Sage coun. Camp Fire Girls, 1974-76, Nat. Endowment Democracy, 1938-93, Am. Coun. Young Polit. Leaders, 1983-89; co-chmn. Nat. Commn. on Presdl. Debates, 1987—, Commn. on Nat. Polit. Conv., 1989-93; vice chmn. Ctr. Democracy, 1995-98; dep. chmn. Internat. Dem. Union, 1983-98; chmn. Pacific Dem. Union, 1983. With AUS, 1957. Recipient Disting. Service award U.S. Jaycees, 1973, Humanitarian award NCCJ, 1981 Mem. Am. Judicature Soc., Comml. Law League Am., ABA (mem. gov. coun. gen. practice sect., internat. law com., chmn. Coalition for Justice 1993-95), Am. Trial Lawyers Assn., No. Nev. Trial Lawyers Assn. (v.p. 1969), State Bar Nev., Washoe County Bar Assn. (pres. 1973-74), Execs. Assn. Reno (dir. 1973-74), Nat. Assn. Gaming Attys. (v.p. 1981, pres. 1982-83), Barristers Club Nev. (v.p. 1969-73), Alpha Tau Omega. Office: 555 13th St NW Ste 1010E Washington DC 20004-1147 E-mail: agafjf@aol.com. *I believe each of us as a citizen of this country has an obligation to serve the community, state and nation. The rights of citizens and benefits of citizenship must be balanced by a duty to serve others.*

FAHRER, FRANKLIN JAMES, music educator; b. New Rockford, N.D., Sept. 6, 1949; s. Arnold Franklin and Lois Jeanette Fahrer; m. Karen Sue Harrold; children: Nicole, Amanda. BA in Vocal/Music Edn., Northeastern Ill. U., 1971; MusM, Northwestern U., Evanston, Ill., 1974. Vocal tchr. Sunset Ridge Sch., Northfield, Ill., 1971—73, Sidney (Ohio) City Schs., 1974—. Mem.: Sons Am. Legion (dir. Legion Post 217 Singing Soldiers 1974—, 2d Dist. Educator of the Yr. 1998), Lions. Avocations: hunting, fishing, dog training. Office: Sidney HS 1215 Campbell Rd Sidney OH 45365

FAHRINGER, CATHERINE HEWSON, retired savings and loan association executive; b. Phila., Aug. 1, 1922; d. George Francis and Catherine Gertrude (Magee) Hewson; m. Edward F. Fahringer, July 8, 1961 (dec.); 1 child, Francis George Beckett. Grad. diploma, Inst. Fin. Edn., 1965. With Centrust Bank (formerly Dade Savs. and Loan Assn.), Miami, 1958-85, v.p., 1967-74, sr. v.p., 1974-82, sec., 1975-79, head savs. personnel and mktg. divsn., 1979-83, exec. v.p. office of chmn., 1984, dir., 1984-90, co-chmn. audit com. of bd. dirs., 1990; referral assoc. Referral Network Inc. subs. Coldwell Banker, 1990—. Pub. arbitrator NASD, 1999—. Contbr. articles to profl. jours. Trustee United Way of Dade County (Fla.), 1980-87, chmn. audit com. 1982-84, trustee, Pub. Health Trust, Dade County, 1974-84, sec. 1976, vice chmn., 1977-78, chmn. bd., 1978-81; mem. adv. coun. Women's Bus. Devel. Ctr., Fla. Internat. U., 1993-95; mem. spl. steering com. Breast Cancer Task Force, Jackson Meml. Hosp., 1991; hon. bd. govs. U. Miami, Soc. for Rsch. in Med. Edn.; trustee South Fla. Blood Svc., Miami, 1979-84, vice chmn., 1980, chmn., 1981-84; trustee Dade County Vocat. Found., 1977-81; trustee Fla. Internat. U. Found., 1976-90; trustee emeritus, 1990, v.p. bd., 1978-81, pres. 1982-84; bd. dirs. Sta. WPBT-TV, 1984-2002, founding lifetime dir., 1995, chmn. budget and fin. com., 1986, mem. exec. com. 1985-92, sec. 1987, investment com., 1988-90, vice chmn. 1988-92, mem. fin. com., 1992, chmn. audit and control com., 1994, 2000, 2001, mem., 1997-98; bd. dirs., mem. nominating com. Girl Scout Coun., Tropical Fla., 1985-89, chmn. 1988-89, mem. long range planning com., 1986-88; citizens oversight com. Dade County Pub. Sch. System, 1986-90, chmn. 1988-90; bd. dirs. New World Sch. of Arts, 1987-90, chmn. devel. com., 1987-90, chair New World Sch. of Arts Gala, 1990; mem. Disaster Relief Com., chair Hurricane Disaster Relief Distbn. Ctr., 1992; mem. fin. commn., chmn. capital improvement fund com. Coral Gables Congrl. Ch., summer concert series com., chmn. refreshement sub-com.; commd. Stephen min., 1995—; mem. grievance com. 11th Jud. Cir. Fla. Bar, 1988-92; bd. trustees United Protestant Appeal, 1994-96; mem. parking adv. bd. City of Coral Gables, 1997-98, bd. of adjustments, 1998—, vice chmn., 2001—2003, chmn.2003—; mem., 3rd v.p. Bush chpt. Women's Cancer Assn. U. Miami, 1997-99, 2nd v.p., treas. and parliamentarian, 1999-2001, chmn. meml. fund, 1998-2003, 3rd v.p., 2002-03. Named Women of Yr. in fin., Zonta Internat., 1975, amb., Air Def. Arty., 1970, U.S. Army Air Def. Command, 1970, Woman of Yr. in Sports, Links Club, 1986, First Lady of Athletics, Fla. Internat. U., 2003; recipient Trail Blazer award, Women's Coun. of 100, 1977, Cmty. Headliner award, Women in Comm., 1983, Outstanding Citizen of Dade County award, 1984, Honors and Recognition award, Golden Panthers Club of Fla. Internat. U., 1989, Disting. Svc. and Leadership award, Fla. Internat. U., 1991, apprecation, New World Sch. of the Arts, 1990, Meritorious Pub. Svc. award, Fla. Bar, 1991, Outstanding Svc. award, Country Club Coral Gables, 2001, hon. BA, U. Hard Knocks Alderson-Broaddus Coll., 1987, Key to City of Coral Gables for Cmty. Svc., 2000, Dedicated Svc. award, Women's Cancer Assn. of U. Miami, 2001, Outstanding Svc. Award, 2001. Mem.: LWV, Women's Union of Russia, Fla. Women's Alliance (bd. dirs. 1983—91, pres. 1987—89), Internat. Women's Alliance, Savs. and Loan Pers. Soc. South Fla., Savs. and Loan Mktg. Soc. South Fla. (past pres.), Inst. Fin. Edn. (life; nat. dir., past pres. Local Greater Miami chpt.), Greater Miami Women's Golf Assn. (social dir. 1999—2001), Greenway Women's Golf Assn. (treas. 1988—89), Biltmore Women's Golf Assn., Fla. Internat. U. Athletics Club, Golden Panther Club (bd. dirs. 1988—, v.p. 1991, pres. 1992—94), Links Fla. Internat. U. Club (v.p. 1992, bd. dirs., sec.), Country Club of Coral Gables (treas. women's golf assn 1988—89, sec., bd. dirs., found. trustee 1993, v.p. bd. dirs. 1994, pres. 1995, chmn. bldg. restoration, capital improvement and maintenance com. 1995—99, bd. advisor 1996—99, liaison City of Coral Gables 1997—99, rear commodore The Fleet, vice-commodore 1998, commodore 1999, publicity chmn. woman's bd. 2000—01, pres. women's golf assn. 2001—02, mem. adv. bd. govs. 2003), Dade Bus. and Profl. Women's Club (past pres.). Democrat. *Success is putting forth your full effort and loving what you do. Dreams take time, but you can make them happen if you believe in yourself and in your dreams.*

FAHRLANDER, HENRY WILLIAM, JR., management consultant; b. Hamilton, Ohio, June 24, 1931; s. Henry William and Frances L. (Mitchel) F.; m. Shirley Fontenot, July 16, 1955; children: Henry W. III, Pauline Ann. BSEE, McNeese State U., 1956; cert. indsl. mgmt., So. Meth. U., 1965. Registered profl. engr., Calif.; registered lead auditor; cert. profl. cons. Design engr. Gen. Electric Co., Evendale, Ohio, 1956-60, quality mgr. St. Petersburg, Fla., 1960-65; quality system evaluation mgr. Tex. Instruments Co., Dallas, 1965-68; quality assurance dir. Recognition Equipment Corp., Dallas, 1968-72; dir. engring. Gen. Computer Systems, Addison, Tex., 1972-75; prin. H.W. Fahrlander & Assocs., Richardson, Tex., 1976—. Instr. Dallas County Community Coll., Mesquite, Tex., 1972-78. Contbr. articles to profl. jours. Dir. adv. com. Dallas County Community Coll. Dist. at Richland Coll., 1965-68. Served with USAF, 1952-56, including Korea. Sr. mem. Am. Soc. Quality (chmn. Dallas sect. 1971-72, chmn. adminstrv. applications div. Milw. 1976-77, cert. quality engr., reliability engr.). Republican. Roman Catholic. Office: HW Fahrlander & Assocs 640 Downing Dr Richardson TX 75080-6117

FAHRNBRUCH, DALE E. retired state supreme court justice; b. Lincoln, Nebr., Sept. 13, 1924; s. Henry and Bessie M. (Osborne) F.; m. Margaret L. Hunt, July 4, 1952; children: Rebecca Kay Fahrnbruch Braymen, Daniel D. (dec.). AD in Journalism, U. Nebr., 1948, BS in Law, 1950; JD, Creighton U., 1951; LLM, U. Va., 1986. Bar: Nebr. 1951, U.S. Ct. Appeals (8th cir.) 1969. City editor Jour. Newspaper, Lincoln, 1951-52; asst., then dep. county atty. Lancaster County, Lincoln, Nebr., 1952-55, chief dep. county atty., 1955-59; ptnr. Beynon, Hecht & Fahrnbruch, Lincoln, 1959-73; dist. judge Nebr. Lincoln, 1973-87; justice Nebr. Supreme Ct., Lincoln, 1987-97.

FAHY, JOSEPH THOMAS, lawyer; b. Uxbridge, Mass., July 9, 1919; s. John Francis and Josephine Mary (Rooney) F.; m. Marie C. McOsker, May 7, 1955; children: Margaret Ellen, Joseph Thomas Jr., John Fergus, Mary Celine. AB, Coll. of Holy Cross, 1941; LLB, Harvard U., 1948. Bar: Mass. 1948, U.S. Dist. Ct. Mass. 1954, U.S. Ct. Appeals (1st cir.) 1971, U.S. Supreme Ct. 1971. Assoc. Peabody, Brown, Rowley & Storey, Boston, 1948-56, ptnr., 1957-80; prin. Joseph T. Fahy, P.C., Boston, 1981-92; ptnr. Peabody & Brown, Boston, 1981-92, counsel, 1992-99, Nixon Peabody LLP, Boston, 1999—. Mem. ABA, Boston Bar Assn., Harvard U. Law Sch. Assn., Alpha Sigma Nu, Delta Epsilon Sigma, Holy Cross Club (past bd. dirs.), Harvard Club, K.C. Avocation: american history. Office: Nixon Peabody LLP 101 Federal St Fl 11 Boston MA 02110-1800

FAHY, MICHAEL P. civil and environmental engineer; b. St. Louis, Nov. 15, 1950; s. William P. and Constance V. (Stark) F.; m. Anna Louise Hyder, Feb. 23 1985; stepchildren: David Groseclose, Lisa Lingnau, Steven Groseclose, Michael Groseclose, Scott Groseclose. BS in Geol. Engring., U. Mo., Rolla, 1973; MS in Civil and Environ. Engring., U. Colo., 1977. Registered profl. engr., N.Mex., Kans., Tex.; registered profl. geologist, Mo. Geologist Willard Owens Assocs., Denver, 1973-75; rsch. specialist U.S. Geol. Survey, Denver, 1975; lab. rschr. U.S. Bur. of Mines, Boulder, Colo., 1975-77; staff engr. W.A. Wahler & Assocs., Palo Alto, Calif., 1977-78; water and fuel engr. Pub. Svc. of N.M., Albuquerque, 1978-88; asst. water engr. Topeka Water Divsn., 1989-94; water rights engr. El Paso (Tex.) Water Utilities, 1994-98, planning and devel. mgr., 1998—. Contbr. articles to profl. jours. Tech. presenter Optimists Club, Topeka, 1992; developer water rights presentation for cmty. orgns. in El Paso, 1996. Recipient 1st Place presentation in groundwater sect. Ann. Conf. Assn. Engring. Geologists, 1995. Mem. NSPE (grader mathcounts 1994, 96, 98, mathcounts chpt. coord. 2001-02), Am. Water Works Assn. (recipient rsch. proposal award 1994, safety com. 1996-99), Assn. Engring. Geologists (GIS com. 1997). Democrat. Roman Catholic. Avocations: photography, gardening, fishing, reading, museums. Home: PO Box 26883 El Paso TX 79926-6883 Office: El Paso Water Utilities PO Box 511 1154 Hawkins Blvd El Paso TX 79961-0001 E-mail: mpfahy@epwu.org.

FAHY, NANCY LEE, food products marketing executive; b. Schenectady, N.Y., Aug. 15, 1946; d. Christopher Mark and Frances (Lee) F.; m. Steven Neil Wohl, June 8, 1968 (div. Apr. 1978). BS cum laude, Miami (Ohio) U., 1968. Educator Palatine (Ill.) Pub. Schs., 1968-70, Glencoe (Ill.) Pub. Schs., 1970-78; sales rep. Keebler Co., Elmhurst, Ill., 1978-80, dist. mgr., 1980-82, account mgr., 1982-83, zone mgr., 1983-85, account mgr., 1985-89, regional mktg. mgr. Coll. Pk., Ga., 1989—. Vol. Lincoln Park Zool. Soc., Chgo., 1975-78. Mem. Food Products Club, Merchandising Execs. Club (bd. dirs. 1984-85), Grocery Mfgs. Sales Execs. Club (bd. dirs. 1984-85, asst. sec. 1987, treas. 1988, 1st v.p. 1989), Phi Beta Kappa. Avocations: gardening, literature, skiing, antiques. Office: Keebler Co 4751 Best Rd Ste 140 College Park GA 30337-5616 E-mail: Nancy_Fahy@keebler.com.

FAI, GHULAM NABI, cultural organization administrator; b. Badgam, Srinigar, Kashmir, Apr. 16, 1949; came to U.S., 1980; s. Habib Ullah and Habba Bano Syed; m. Ning-Yang Chang, Mar. 12, 1961; children: Muzzammil Sayyid, Zahra Sayyid. MA, Aligarh U., India, 1979; PhD in Mass Comm., Temple U., 1989. Exec. dir. Kashmiri Am. Coun., Washington; founding chmn. Internat. Inst. Kashmir Studies, London, 1983—. Mem. Supreme Coun., Kashmir Fedn.; presenter confs. Editor-in-chief Kashmir Report, 1989—; contbr. articles to newspapers and profl. jours., including Chgo. Tribune, Wall St. Jour., Fin. Times, others. Office: 733 15th St NW Ste 1100 Washington DC 20005-2112 Fax: 202-393-0062. E-mail: uchang9999@aol.com.

FAIG, KENNETH WALTER, actuary, publisher; b. Cin., Aug. 24, 1948; s. Kenneth Walter and Edith Frances (Kennedy) F.; m. Carol Ann Gaber, May 19, 1979; children: Edith Mary, Walter Gerard. BA, Northwestern U., 1970. Asst. v.p. N.Am. Co. for Life and Health Ins., Chgo., 1973-87; assoc. actuary Allstate Life Ins. Co., Northbrook, Ill., 1987-89; mgr. Polysystems Inc., Chgo., 1989—. Pub. books for Moshassuck Press, 1987—. Recipient Spencer L. Kimball award Nat.. Assn. Ins. Commrs., 1997. Fellow Soc. Actuaries; mem. Am. Acad. Actuaries, Latin Litury Assn., R.I. Geneal. Soc., Foster Preservation Soc., Nat. Amateur Press Assn., The Fossils. Roman Catholic. Avocations: history of actuarial science, genealogy. Home: 2311 Swainwood Dr Glenview IL 60025-2741

FAIGEN, ANNE GUSSIN, secondary school educator, writer; d. Carl and Yetta Smilovitz Gussin; m. Mark R. Faigen, June 15, 1952; children: Susan L., Lynne E. Faigen (Deceased), Janet Faigen Schultz, David S. BA, U. of Pitts., 1948—52, MA, 1958—62. Cert. tchr. Pa. Bd. Edn., 1970. Tchr. Penn Hills Sch. Dist., Pitts., Pa., 1989—; novelist Royal Fireworks Press, Unionville, NY, 1997—. Advt. copywriter. Author: (young adult novel) Finding Her Way. Vol. reader of novels Radio Info. Svc. (for blind and print-impaired), Pitts., 1977—2003; bd. mem. Friends of Carnegie Libr., Pa.; spkr. H.S. classes, mother/daughter book groups; allegheny county com. woman Dem. Party, Pitts., 1996—99; bd. of trustees Temple Sinai, Pitts., 1999—2003; spkr. to educators/parents of gifted adolescents Pa. Assn. for Gifted Edn., Pitts., 1998. Avocations: travel, hiking, reading, theater. Home: 5561 Woodmont St Pittsburgh PA 15217 Personal E-mail: marknann@telerama.com.

FAIGNANT, JOHN PAUL, lawyer, educator; b. Proctor, Vt., Mar. 24, 1953; s. Joseph Paul and Ann (DeBlasio) F.; children: Janelle, Melissa. BA, U. New Haven, 1974; JD, George Mason U., 1978. Bar: Va. 1978, Vt. 1979, U.S. Dist. Ct. Vt. 1979, U.S. Ct. Appeals (4th cir.) 1979, U.S. Supreme Ct. 1992. Assoc. Griffin & Griffin, Rutland, Vt., 1978-79, Miller, Norton & Cleary, Rutland, 1979-84, ptnr., 1984-87, Miller, Cleary and Faignant PC, Rutland, 1988-91, Miller & Faignant, Ltd., Rutland, 1991-97, Miller Faignant & Whelton PC (now Miller Faignant & Behrens), Rutland, 1997—. Adj. prof. Coll. St. Joseph, Rutland, 1982-90. Mem. Rutland Town Fire Dept., 1989—; mem., pres. No. New England Def. Counsel, 1995-96. Mem. Va. Bar Assn., Vt. Bar Assn., Assn. Trial Lawyers Am., Def. Rsch. Inst., Am. Bd. Trial Advocates. Roman Catholic. Avocation: antique trucks. Home: RR 1 Box 3762 Rutland VT 05701-9214 Office: Miller Faignant & Behrens PC 36 Merchants Row PO Box 6688 Rutland VT 05702-6688

FAILING, GEORGE EDGAR, editor, clergyman, educator; b. Kingston, Ont., Can., Nov. 25, 1912; s. Roy Augustus and Nellie (Richardson) F.; m. Phyllis Ogden, Apr. 12, 1939; children: Bunnie Jean, Alice Joy, Lynn Odgen. BA magna cum laude, Houghton Coll., 1940, Litt.D., 1960; MA, Duke U., 1947; D.D., So. Wesleyan U., 1996. Ordained to ministry Wesleyan Meth. Ch., 1938. Pastor in, Fillmore, N.Y., 1935-41, Louisville, 1941-44, Marion, Ind., 1953-56; prof. Cen. S.C. Wesleyan Coll., 1944-47; prof. theology Houghton (N.Y.) Coll., 1947-53, dir. pub. rels., 1947-53; editor Sunday sch. lit., pastor Wesleyan Meth. Ch., Marion, Ind., 1956—59; editor Wesleyan Meth., 1959-68; chancellor Satellite Christian Inst., San Diego, 1968-73; prof. Greek and N.T. United Wesleyan Coll., Allentown, Pa., 1973; gen. editor Wesleyan Advocate, Marion, 1973-84. Author: 1 Corinthians, 1963, The Way of Holiness, 1970, Presence, 1977, Secure and Rejoicing, 1980, Did Christ Die for All?, 1980; contbg. author: Ency. World Methodism, 1974; contbg. author, editor: And They Shall Prophesy, 1978, With Open Face, 1983, Way of Wonder, 1983, History of the Wesleyan Ch., 1991, Death Has No Dominion, 1991. Mem. gen. bd. trustees Wesleyan Meth. Ch. Am., 1959-68, 74-84; pres. Presence, Inc., 1979—. Recipient Spl. Alumnus award United Wesleyan Coll., 1969, Houghton Coll., 1983. Mem. Soc. Bibl. Lit. and Exegesis, Evang. Press Assn. (pres. 1965-67), Am. Schs. Oriental Rsch. Avocations: photography, travel. Home: PO Box 1867 Easley SC 29641-1867 Office: 102 Fernwood Dr Easley SC 29640-8831

FAILINGER, MARIE ANITA, law educator, editor; b. Battle Creek, Mich., June 29, 1952; d. Conard Frederick and Joan Anita (Lang) F.; children: Joanna, Kristina. BA, Valparaiso U., 1973, JD, 1976; LLM, Yale U., 1983; postgrad., U. Chgo., 1990. Bar: Ind. 1976, U.S. Dist. Ct. (no. dist.) Ind. 1976, U.S. Dist. Ct. (so. dist.) Ind. 1977, U.S. Ct. Appeals (7th cir.) 1979, Minn. 1984, U.S. Supreme Ct. 1980. Prof. of law Hamline U., St. Paul, 1983 , assoc. dean, 1990-93. Editor: Jour. of Law and Religion, 1988—; contbr. articles, book revs. to profl. publs. Treas. Am. Indian Policy Ctr., 1993—; sec. Church Innovations Inst.; treas. Luth. Innovations. Mem. Minn. Women Lawyers (bd. dirs. 1989-90), Am. Assn. Law Schs. (chair poverty sect. 1984-88, exec. com. law and religion sect.), Ctrl. Minn. Legal Svcs. Bd., Nat. Equal Justice Libr. (bd. dirs. 1989—). Democrat. Mem. Evang. Luth. Ch. Am. Office: Hamline U Sch Law 1536 Hewitt Ave Saint Paul MN 55104-1284

FAILLACE, WALTER JOSEPH, medical educator; b. Piazza Armerina, Italy, May 3, 1952; came to U.S., 1954; s. Joseph Frank and Caterina (Amato) F.; m. Robin Lisa Wind, Dec. 10, 1978. BS in Biology cum laude, Bklyn. Coll., 1974; MD, U. Rome, 1980. Diplomate Am. Bd. Neurol. Surgery. Asst. prof. neurosurgery and pediat. U. Fla., Jacksonville, 1988-94, assoc. prof. neurosurgery and pediat., 1994—2002; with The Dean Clnic, Madison, Wis., 2002—. Contbr. articles to profl. jours. Founding mem. Duval county chpt. Think First, Jacksonville, 1993—; participant Children's Miracle Network, Jacksonville, 1988. Rsch. grantee SAnofi-Winthrop, Ciba Geigy. Fellow ACS; mem. Am. Brain Injury Consortium. Democrat. Roman Catholic. Avocations: hiking, birding, museums, music, gardening. Office: The Dean Clnic Dept Neurosurgery 1313 Fish Hatchery Rd Madison WI 53715

FAILS, THOMAS GLENN, geologist; b. Unity Twp., Ohio, Feb. 28, 1928; s. T. Glenn and Mary C. (Adams) F.; m. Mary Ivy Schmid, Mar. 1, 1959; children— Glenn Michael, Nora Anne. Geol. Engr., Colo. Sch. Mines, 1954; M.A. in Geology, Columbia U., 1955. Cert. petroleum geologist, profl. geologist. Geologist, Shell Oil Co., New Orleans, 1956-66; dist. geologist Trend Exploration Ltd., New Orleans, 1967-69, v.p., London, 1970-75; geologist, petroleum prodr., Denver, 1975; ind. geologist, petroleum prodr., Denver, 1975—; pres., owner Raven Exploration Corp., Denver, 1977—; v.p., dir. Pannonian Energy, Inc., Denver, 1998-2000; pres., dir. Pannonian Internat., Ltd., Denver, 2000-, dir. Galaxy Energy Corp., Denver, 2003-; trustee Bridge Trust, Denver, 1990-93; mem. Colo. Geol. Survey Adv. Com., 1991-94. Author book diapiric structures, Gulf Coast, U.S.; contbr. 11 peer-reviewed sci. papers. Served with USMC, 1946-48, 50-51. Disting. Pub. Svc. to earth sci. RMAG, 1993. Fellow Geol. Soc. London; mem. Am. Assn. Petroleum Geologists, Am. Inst. Profl. Geologists (v.p. 1995, pres. 1999, Martin van Couvering Meml. award 2001), Petroleum Exploration Soc. Gt. Britain (dir. 1974-75), Rocky Mountain Assn. Geologists. Republican. Lutheran. Home: 965 S Monroe St Denver CO 80209-4939 Office: 4101 E Louisiana Ave Ste 412 Denver CO 80246-3431 E-mail: thomgeol@aol.com.

FAIN, CHERYL ANN, translator, editor; b. Providence, May 16, 1953; d. Harry and Pearl (Friedman) F. Student, U. Salzburg, Austria, 1973-74; BA with high distinction, U. R.I., 1975; MA, postgrad. cert. Eng.-German Transl., Monterey Inst. Internat. Studies, 1978. Freelance German and French transl. various govt. agys., transl. burs., record co., pvt. clients, Washington, Balt. and Monterey, Calif., 1976—; in-house German and French med. translator Social Security Adminstrn., Balt., 1984-94; German/French trans., sci. and tech. specialist Embassy of Switzerland, Washington, 1994—. Mem. Swiss delegation to the European Space Agy. Internat. Space Sta. Working Group, Washington, D.C. Translator: Perspectives on Mozart, 1978, also various articles and liner notes, program notes, U.S., Switzerland. Mem. Am. Translators Assn. (accredited for translation from German-English, French-English), Sci. Diplomats' Club of Washington, Phi Kappa Phi. Avocations: international travel, performance in operas, choral concerts and plays. Home: 2401 Calvert St NW Apt 421 Washington DC 20008-2667 Office: Embassy of Switzerland 2900 Cathedral Ave NW Washington DC 20008-3499

FAIN, JOEL MAURICE, lawyer; b. Miami Beach, Fla., Dec. 11, 1953; s. William Maurice and Carolyn Genievive (Baggett) F.; m. Moira Joan Slocum, June 15, 1974; children: Hannah Ruth, Dylan Michael, Rachel Joan. BA, Yale U., 1975; JD, U. Conn., 1978. Bar: Conn. 1978, U.S. Dist. Ct. Conn. 1978, U.S. Ct. Appeals (2d cir.) 1989, U.S. Supreme Ct. 1999. Assoc. Kahan, Kerensky, Capossela, Levine & Breslau, Vernon, Conn., 1978-83, ptnr., 1984-90, mng. ptnr., 1990-91; ptnr. Morrison, Mahoney & Miller, Hartford, Conn., 1992—. Chmn. Youth Adv. Bd., Tolland, Conn., 1983-92; chmn. Tolland Town Coun., 1995-97. Mem. ABA, Conn. Bar Assn., Tolland County Bar Assn. (pres. 1991-92), Assn. Trial Lawyers Am., Conn. Trial Lawyers Assn., Lions (pres. 1987-88). Democrat. Congregationalist. Home: 140 Huyshope Ave Hartford CT 06106-2857 Office: Morrison Mahoney & Miller 1 Constitution Plaza Hartford CT 06103-4506

FAIN, JOHN NICHOLAS, biochemistry educator; b. Jefferson City, Tenn., Aug. 18, 1934; s. Samuel Clark and Virginia Manson (Hunt) F.; m. Ann Duff, June 7, 1958; children: Margaret Ann, John Nicholas Jr., James Clark. BS magna cum laude, Carson-Newman Coll., 1956; PhD in Biochemistry, Emory U., 1960. Rsch. assoc. Emory U., Atlanta, 1960-61; NSF fellow NIH, Bethesda, Md., 1961-62, postdoctoral fellow USPHS, 1962-63; biochemist NIH and Nat. Inst. Arthritis and Metabolic Diseases, Bethesda, 1963-65; asst. prof. Brown U., Providence, 1965-68, assoc. prof., 1968-71, prof., 1971-85, chmn. biochemistry, 1975-85; Van Vleet prof., dept. chmn. U. Tenn., Memphis, 1985-2000, Van Vleet prof. of molecular scis., 2000—. Contbr. numerous articles to sci. jours. Del. gen. assembly United Presbyn. Ch., Providence, 1972. Recipient Disting. Alumnus award Carson-Newman Coll., 1986; fellow Cambridge U., 1977-78; NIH Fogarty fellow, 1984-85; Macy Faculty scholar, 1977-78. Mem. Am. Soc. Biol. Chemists. Democrat. Office: U Tenn Health Scis Ctr Coll Medicine Dept Mol Scis 858 Madison Ste GO1 Memphis TN 38163 Fax: 901-448-7360. E-mail: jfain@utmem.edu.

FAINGOLD, EDUARDO DANIEL, language and linguistics educator, researcher; b. La Plata, Argentina, Sept. 6, 1958; arrived in US, 1990; s. Enrique and Annie (Turkenich) Faingold; m. Sonia D Hocherman, 1 child, Noam. BA in English and French, Hebrew U., Jerusalem, Israel, 1984, MA in English, 1987; PhD in Linguistics, Tel-Aviv U., 1992. Vis. scholar Tech. U. Berlin, 1988-89, UCLA, 1990-92, SUNY, Stony Brook, 1992-95; asst. prof. U. Tulsa, 1995—2002, assoc. prof., 2003—. Advisor UNESCO, 1998; guest prof. Hebrew U., Jerusalem, 1984; vis. prof. U. Calif., Santa Barbara, 2001; vis. scientist Max Planck Inst., Leipzig, 2002. Author: The Case for Fusion: Ladino in Balkans and the Eastern Turkish Empire, 1989, Child Language, Creolization and Historical Change, 1996, Composition Codex, 2002, The Development of Grammar in Spanish and the Romance Languages, 2003, Multilingualism from Infancy to Adolescence, 2003, mem. editl. bd.: S.W. Jour. Linguistics, 1997, book rev. editor:, 1999—; contbr. articles to profl. jours. Recipient Fozis Research Prize, 1989, Tel-Aviv Univ Cult Doctoral Prize, 1991, Teaching Award, Univ Tulsa, 1997; grantee, NEH, 2000—02; Book Publ. grantee, German Sci. Found., 1996, Faculty rsch. grantee, U. Tulsa, 1996—2003, DAAD fellow, 2002. Mem.: MLA, Internat. Phonetic Assn., Internat. Acad. Linguistic Law, Salzburg Seminal Alumni Assn., Internat. Linguistic Assn., Linguistic Soc. Am., Linguistic Assn. S.W., Internat. Clin. and Linguistics Assn. Office: U Tulsa 600 S College Ave Tulsa OK 74104-3126

FAINSTEIN, NORMAN, college president; m. Susan Fainstein; 2 children. BS with highest honors, MIT, 1966, PhD with highest distinction, 1971. Prof., dep. chair undergrad. programs in gen. studies, dir. summer session dept. sociology Columbia U., N.Y.C., 1971—76; prof., assoc. dean acad. affairs Grad. Sch. Mgmt. and Urban Professions New Sch. for Social Rsch., N.Y.C., 1983—87; prof., dean Sch. Liberal Arts and Scis. Baruch Coll. CUNY, 1987—95; prof., dean of faculty Vassar Coll., Poughkeepsie, NY, 1996—2001; pres. Conn. Coll., New London, 2001—. Author: 4 books; contbr. numerous articles to profl. jours. Active Poughkeepsie Inst., Andrew W. Mellon Found. Fellow Woodrow Wilson, NSF, Stouffer, Harvard-MIT Joint Ctr. for Urban Studies. Office: Conn Coll 270 Mohegan Ave New London CT 06320*

FAIR, EVERETT NEIL, public administrator; b. Humboldt, Tenn., Nov. 27, 1964; s. Lydia Frances and Travis Neal Fair. BBA, U. of Memphis, Memphis, Tennessee, 1983—92. Exec. dir. Beacons & Bridges, Inc., Jonesboro, Ark., 2002—; pub. adminstrn. specialist No. Ky. Area Devel. Dist., Florence, Ky.,

2000—02; cmty. devel. specialist Pennyrile Area Devel. Dist., Hopkinsville, Ky., 1998—2000. Bd. mem. Greater Paducah Chamber of Commerce, Paducah, Ky., 1994—95, Purchase Area Devel. Dist., Mayfield, Ky., 1995—96, the Minority Econ. Devel. Initiative, Hopkinsville, Ky., 1998—99. Mem.: Ky. City/County Mgmt. Assn., Nat. Forum for Black Pub. Administrators, Am. Soc. of Pub. Administrators, Govt. Fin. Officers Assn. Home: 607 Gladiolus Drive A-3 Jonesboro AR 72404 Personal E-mail: efair2460@msn.com.

FAIR, HUDSON RANDOLPH, recording company executive; b. Evanston, Ill., Aug. 15, 1953; s. Harry Joel Jr. Fair and Virginia (Gauntlett) Kowcz. BS in Speech, Northwestern U., 1976, MA in Speech, 1979. Mktg. rep. Calumet Refining Co., Chgo., 1975-78, Calumet Petro-Chems., Inc., Houston, 1977-78, Stellavox, S.A., Schaumburg, Ill., 1986-87, Nagra Magnetic Recorders, Inc., N.Y.C., 1987-91; pres. Ealing Mobile Recording, Ltd., Chgo., 1981—. Music prodr. WFMT Radio, Chgo., 1992—, Ravinia Festival, 1997—; cons. in field. Prodr. more than 125 classical albums, 1981—. Speech writer Rep. George Bush Presdl. Campaign, Chgo., 1979-80. Recipient Chorus award for best choral rec., 1989, Deutsche Schallplatten-preis for best chamber music record Juilliard String Quartet, 1998; grantee Ill. Arts Coun., 1982-86, Nat. Endowment for Arts, 1986. Mem. NARAS (bd. govs. 1991-95, 96-2000, nat. trustee 1993-95), Audio Engring. Soc., Engring. and Rec. Soc. (bd. dirs. 1987—, chmn. 1991-92). Republican. Episcopalian. Avocations: travel, motorcycles, skiing. Office: Ealing Mobile Rec Ltd 6538 N Sayre Ave Chicago IL 60631 E-mail: ffur1@sbcglobal.com.

FAIR, JAMES RUTHERFORD, JR., chemical engineering educator, consultant; b. Charleston, Mo., Oct. 14, 1920; s. James Rutherford and Georgia Irene (Case) F.; m. Merle Innis, Jan. 14, 1950; children: James Rutherford III, Elizabeth, Richard Innis. Student, The Citadel, 1938-40; BS, Ga. Inst. Tech., 1942; MS, U. Mich., 1949; PhD, U. Tex., 1955; DSc (hon.), Wash. U., 1977; HHD (hon.), Clemson U., 1987. Rsch. engr. Shell Devel. Co., Emeryville, Calif., 1954-56; with Monsanto Co., 1942-52, 56-79; engring. dir. corp. engring. dept. Monsanto Co. (World hdqrs.), St. Louis, 1969-79; McKetta chair chem. engring. U. Tex., Austin, 1979—. Dir., v.p. Fractionation Research, Inc., Bartlesville, Okla., 1969-79; pres. James R. Fair Inc., 1981—. Author: North Arkansas Line, 1969, Distillation, 1971, Louisiana and Arkansas, 1997, Distillation, 1998; contbr. numerous articles to profl. publs. Recipient profl. achievement award Chemical Engineering mag., 1968, King award U. Tex., 1987. Fellow AIChE (bd. dirs. 1965-67, Walker award 1973, Practice award 1975, Founders award 1977, Inst. lectr. 1979, Separation Tech. award 1994); mem. NSPE, NAE, Am. Chem. Soc. (Separation Sci. and Tech. award 1993), Am. Soc. Engring. Edn., Faculty Club U. Tex., Headliners Club (Austin), Sigma Nu. Republican. Presbyterian. Home: 2804 Northwood Rd Austin TX 78703-1603 Office: U Tex Dept Chem Engring Separations Rsch Progr Austin TX 78712 E-mail: fair@che.utexas.edu.

FAIR, JEAN EVERHARD, retired education educator; b. Evanston, Ill., July 21, 1917; d. Drury Hampton and Bess Marion (Everhard) F. BA, U. Ill., 1938; MA, U. Chgo., 1939, PhD, 1953. Tchr. Evanston (Ill.) Twp. High Sch., 1940-48, 1954-58; tchr. U. Minn. High Sch., 1948-49, U. Ill. High Sch., 1951-53; prof. edn. Wayne State U., Detroit, 1958-82, now prof. emeritus. Cons. in edn.; cons. Mich. Ednl. Goals, Objectives and Assessment in Social Studies; reviewer of position statements for teaching and learning, standards, assessment and other manuscripts for Nat. Coun. Social Studies. Contbr. articles to profl. jours. Mem. AAUW, Nat. Council for Social Studies (pres. 1972, dir. 1958-61, 73-75), Assn. for Supervision and Curriculum Devel., Social Sci. Edn. Consortium, LWV, Phi Beta Kappa. Mem. United Ch. Christ. Home: Apt 281 16351 Rotunda Dr Dearborn MI 48120-1158

FAIR, MARCIA JEANNE HIXSON, retired educational administrator; b. Scobey, Mont. d. Edward Goodell and Olga Marie (Frederickson) Hixson; m. Donald Harry Mahaffey (div. Aug. 1976); 1 child, Marcia Anne (dec.); m. George Justin Fair, Mar. 26, 1997. BA in English, U. Wash.; MA in Secondary Edn., U. Hawaii, 1967. Cert. secondary and elem. tchr. and adminstr. Tchr. San Lorenzo (Calif.) Sch. Dist., 1958-59, Castro Valley (Calif.) Sch. Dist., 1959-63, vice prin., 1963-67, Sequoia Union High Sch. Dist., Redwood City, Calif., 1967-77, asst. prin., 1977-91, ret., 1991. Tchr. trainer Project Impact Sequoia Union Sch. Dist., Redwood City, 1986-91; mem. supr.'s task force for dropout prevention, 1987-91, Sequoia Dist. Goals Commn. (chair subcom. staff devel. 1988); mentor tchr. selection com., 1987-91; mem. Stanford Program Devel. Ctr. Com., 1987-91; chairperson gifted and talented Castro Valley Sch. Dist.; mem. family svcs. bd., San Leandro, Calif. Vol. Am. Cancer Soc., San Mateo, Calif., 1967, Castro Valley, 1965; chair Carlmont H.S. Site Coun., Belmont, Calif., 1977—91; active Nat. Trust for Hist. Preservation; Neighborhood Beautification project dir. Bridle Trails Cmty. Club, 1999—2001; mem. Golden Grads. scholarship com. Roosevelt H.S., Seattle, 2000—; Sunday sch. tchr. Hope Luth. Ch., San Mateo, 1970—76. Recipient Life Mem. award Parent, Tchr., Student Assn., Belmont, 1984, Svc. award, 1989, Exemplary Svc award Carlmont High Sch., 1989, 92; named Woman of the Week, Castro Valley, 1967, Outstanding Task Force Chair Adopt A Sch. Program San Mateo (Calif.) County, 1990. Mem. ASCD, AAUW, DAR, Assn. Calif. Sch. Adminstrs. (Project Leadership plaque 1985), Sequoia Dist. Mgmt.Assn. (pres. 1975, treas. 1984-85), Met. Mus. Art, Smithsonian Instn., Libr. of Congress Assocs. (charter), Am. Heritage - The Soc. of Am. Historians, Internat. Platform Assn., Animal Welfare Advocacy, Woodrow Wilson Internat. Ctr. Scholars, Nat. Geographic Soc., The Nat. Mus. Women in the Arts, Am. Mus. Natural History (charter mem.), Delta Kappa Gamma, Alpha Xi Delta (Order of Rose award 1997). Avocations: oil painting, travel, tap dancing, redecorating, writing poetry. *Personal philosophy: Life is short, so make haste to be kind to one another.*

FAIRBAIRN, JOYCE, Canadian government official; b. Lethbridge, Alta., Can., Nov. 6, 1939; m. Michael Gillan (dec.). BA in English, U. Alta., 1960; B Journalism, Carleton U., 1961. Mem. news staff Ottawa (Ont., Can.) Jour., 1961; mem. staff parliamentary press gallery UPI, Ottawa, 1962-64; mem. staff parliamentary bur. F.P. Publs., 1964-70; legis. asst., sr. legis. advisor Prime Minister of Can. Pierre Elliott Trudeau, 1970-84, comms. coord., 1981-83; mem. Senate for Province of Alta., 1984—, appt. to privy coun., leader govt., 1993-97, minister with spl. responsibility for literacy, 1993-97, spl. advisor for literacy, 1997. Mem. Spl. Senate Com. on Youth, Senate Standing Coms. on Transp. and Comm., Legal and Constl. Affairs, Fgn. Affairs, Agr. and Forestry, mem. senate social affairs com.; founding mem. standing com. on Aboriginal peoples; chair spl. com. on Anti-Terrorism, 2001, Friends of the Can. Paralympics; vice chair Nat. Liberal Caucus and Western and No. Liberal Caucus, 1984-91; co-chair nat. campaign com. Liberal Party of Can., 1991. Past mem. senate U. Lethbridge. Inducted into Kainai Chieftainship, Blood Nation; hon. col. 18th Air Def. Regt., Royal Can. Army. Office: Can Senate 571-S Centre Block Ottawa ON Canada K1A 0A4

FAIRBAIRN, SYDNEY ELISE, lawyer; b. Fullerton, Calif., Feb. 20, 1963; d. Robin H. and Yvonne A. Fairbairn. BA in Rhetoric, BA in Anthropology, U. Calif., Berkeley, 1982; JD, Golden Gate U., 1985. Bar: Calif. 1986. Pvt. practice, San Rafael, Calif., 1986—. Atty. YWCA, San Anselmo, Calif., 1995—. Mem. Marin County Bar Assn. (chair ins. sect. 1999—), Marin County Women's Bar Assn. (pres. 2002-03), Mission San Rafael, Rotary. Democrat. Office: Ste A-110 Seven Mt Lassen Dr San Rafael CA 94903 E-mail: s.e.fairbairn@att.net.

FAIRBAIRN, URSULA FARRELL, human resources executive; b. Newark, Feb. 5, 1943; d. Henry C. and Clara J. (Ziefle) Otte; m. William Todd Fairbairn III, May 14, 1978; children: W. Todd, Mary. BA, Upsala Coll., 1965; MAT in Math., Harvard U., 1966. Instr., numerous mktg. positions IBM, N.Y.C., 1966-78; exec. asst. to sec., White House fellow U.S. Treasury Dept., Washington, 1973-74; exec. asst. to chmn. bd., group dir. IBM, Armonk, N.Y., 1978-79, v.p. mgmt. svcs., then v.p. mktg. ops. west, 1980-84, dir. pers. resources, 1984-87, dir. bus. and mgmt. edn., 1987, dir. edn., 1987-89, dir. edn. and mgmt. devel., 1989-90; sr. v.p. human resources Union Pacific Corp., Bethlehem, Pa., 1990-96; exec. v.p. human resources and quality Am. Express Co., N.Y.C., 1996—. Bd. dirs. VF Corp., Greensboro, N.C., Air Products Corp., Allentown, Pa., Sunoco Corp., Phila. Contbg. author: Managing Human Resources in the Information Age, 1991. Mem. Com. of 200, Catalyst, N.Y.C.; vice-chair Nat. Acad.-HR; chair Pers. Round Table. Mem. Bus. Roundtable, Employee Rels. Com., Labor Policy Assn. (bd. dirs., mem. exec. com.). Avocations: gardening, art, reading, walking, travel. Office: Am Express Co 35 N Moore St New York NY 10013

FAIRBANK, RICHARD D. diversified financial services company executive; Chmn., CEO Capital One Fin. Corp., McLean, Va. Office: Capital One Fin Corp 1680 Capital One Dr Mc Lean VA 22102-3491

FAIRBANK, ROBERT HAROLD, lawyer; b. Northampton, Mass., Mar. 4, 1948; s. William Martin and Jane (Davenport) F.;children: Sarah Julia, David Kivy. AB in Polit. Sci., Stanford U., 1972; MLS, U. Calif.-Berkeley, 1973; JD, NYU, 1977. Bar: Calif. 1977, U.S. Dist. Ct. (cen. and no. dists.) Calif. 1978, U.S. Dist. Ct. (so. dist.) Calif. 1993. Assoc. Gibson, Dunn & Crutcher, L.A., 1977-84, ptnr., 1985-96; co-founding ptnr. Fairbank & Vincent, 1996—. Lawyer rep., co-chair 9th cir. Jud. Conf. Ctrl. Dist., 2000—02; bd. dirs. 9th Jud. Cir. Hist. Soc., 2003—. Author: Effective Pretrial and Trial Motions, 1983, California Practice Guide: Civil Trials and Evidence (The Rutter Group 1993, with yearly updates); mem. editl. bd. NYU Law Rev., 1975-76. Named One of Top 100 Bus. Lawyers in L.A., L.A. Bus. Jour., 1995. Mem. Assn. Bus. Trial Lawyers (co-founder San Francisco and Orange County chpts., bd. govs. 1984-85, treas. 1986-87, sec. 1987-88, v.p. 1988-89, pres. 1989-90), L.A. County Bar Assn. (fed. cts. com. 1983-85), Jud. Coun. Calif. Adv. Com. on Local Rules (subcom. chair on civil trial rules). Office: Fairbank & Vincent 11755 Wilshire Blvd Ste 2320 Los Angeles CA 90025-1501 E-mail: rfairbank@fairbankvincent.com.

FAIRBANKS, DAVID NATHANIEL FOX, physician, surgeon, educator; b. Ann Arbor, Mich., Mar. 31, 1936; s. Avard Tennyson and Beatrice Maude (Fox) F.; m. Sylvia West, June 17, 1959; children: David W., Lisa Marie, E. Jefferson, Galen J. BS, U. Utah, 1959, MD, 1963. Diplomate Am. Bd. Otolaryngology. Resident in otolaryngology surgery Johns Hopkins Hosp., Balt., 1963-69; grands adminstr. NIH, Bethesda, Md., 1969-71; mem. rotating staff Project HOPE, Kingston, Jamaica, 1971; clin. prof. otolaryngology George Washington U., Washington, 1970—, dir. divsn. otolaryngology, 1976-84. Med. bd. Project HOPE, Millwood, Va., 1971—; cons. NIH, Bethesda, Md., 1971—; co-dir. Sleep Disorders Ctr., Sibley Meml. Hosp. Washington D.C., 1994—. Author: Antimicrobial Therapy in Otolaryngology, 1981, 11th edit., 2003, Snoring and Obstructive Sleep Apnea, 1987, 3d edit., 2002; contbr. articles to profl. jours., chpts. to books. Missionary Ch. of Jesus Christ of Latter-day Saints, Calif., 1956-58. With USPHS, 1969-71. Johns Hopkins U. fellow, 1968-69. Fellow ACS, Am. Acad. Otolaryngology (dir. 1983-85, Disting. Svc. award 1999), Am. Rhinological Soc., Triol. Soc.; mem AMA, Am. Sleep Disorders Assn., Med. Soc. D.C. (bd. dirs. 1984-86), Met. Ear, Nose and Throat Soc. (pres. 1976), Phi Beta Kappa, Sons of the Am. Revolution, Sons of the Utah Pioneers. Republican. Mem. Lds Ch. Avocations: banjo, folk music, farming, family band. Office: Ear Nose and Throat Med Group 2021 K St NW Ste 210 Washington DC 20006-1003

FAIRBANKS, JONATHAN LEO, museum curator; b. Ann Arbor, Mich., Feb. 19, 1933; s. Avard T. and Beatrice Maude (Fox) F.; m. Louise Ann Eckenbrecht, Feb. 12, 1954; children: Theresa Louise Fairbanks Harris, Hilary-Ann. BFA, U. Utah, 1953; student, Pa. Acad. Fine Arts, 1956-57; MFA, U. Pa., 1957; MA, U. Del., 1961. From curatorial asst. to assoc. curator Winterthur Museum, Del., 1961-71; co-founder Am. Prints Confs., 1970—; founder dept. Am. decorative arts and sculpture Mus. of Fine Arts Boston, 1971—99, Katharine Lane Weems curator Am. decorative arts/sculpture; v.p. Antiques Am., Inc., Boston, 1991—. Adj. lectr. U. Del.; instr. U. Utah Ext., Brigham Young U. Ext., W.Va. U. Ext.; adj. prof. Am. New Eng. studies program Boston U.; trustee Tex. Pioneer Arts Found.; trustee, incorporator Dublin Seminar for Early New Eng. Folklife; rsch. assoc. Dept. Art History, Boston U. Curator exhbns. and catalogues Paul Revere's Boston--1735-1818, New England Begins, The Seventeenth Century, Glass Today, U.S. Dept. State, 2003; exhibited paintings at Haley & Steele, Boston, 2001, 02; author: American Furniture 1620 to the Present, 1981; mural executed Hall of Earth History, Acad. Natural Scis., Phila., 1957. Bd. dirs. Revere House, Boston, Fairbanks House, Dedham, The Connick Found.; former mem. Com. for Preservation White House; pres. Decorative Arts trust; former trustee Forest Hills Cemetery, Longfellow's Wayside Inn, Shirley-Eustis House. Winterthur fellow, 1959-61; recipient Disting. Service award Antiques Monthly, 1983, Robert H. Lord award for excellence in hist. studies. Emmanuel Coll., 1983, medal Excellence Craft, Soc. Arts & Crafts, Boston, 1997, Ellen Banning Ayer award for Contbns. to the Cultural Life of Boston, 1999, award of distinction The Furniture Soc., 2003. Fellow Pilgrim Soc., Am. Inst. Conservation, Am. crafts Coun. (hon.); mem. Victorian Soc. Am. (past v.p., Lifetime Achievement award Am., New Eng. chpt. 2000), Internat. Inst. Conservation, Am. Assn. Mus., Soc. Archtl. Historians, Nat. Trust for Hist. Preservation, Colonial Soc. Mass., Decorative Arts Soc. (v.p. 1978-79, C.F. Montgomery award 1983), Westwood Hist. Soc. (pres. 1978-81), Am. Soc. Interior Designers (hon.), Mass. Hist. Soc., Am. Antiquarian Soc., Colonial Soc., Walpole Soc., St. Botolph Club. Office: Editor At Large Catalogue of Antiques & Fine Arts 125 Walnut St Watertown MA 02472

FAIRBANKS, MARY KATHLEEN, computer scientist, researcher; b. Manhattan, Kans., June 4, 1948; d. Everitt Edsel and Mary Catherine (Moran) Fairbanks. BS, St. Norbert Coll., 1970; postgrad., Calif. Family Study Ctr., 1981-82. Neuropsychology rschr. U.S. VA Hosp., Sepulveda, Calif., 1970-76; mgr. print shop Charisma In Missions, City of Industry, Calif., 1976-77; neuropsychology rschr. L.A. County Women's Hosp., 1977-79; mem. tech. staff Computer Scis. Corp., Ridgecrest, Calif., 1979-81; systems programmer Calif. State U., Northridge, 1982-84; bus. systems analyst World Vision, Monrovia, Calif., 1984-86; configuration analyst Teledyne System Co., Northridge, 1986-87; applications sys. analyst Internat. Telephone and Telegraph/Fed. Electric Corp., Altadena, Calif., 1987-88; supr. data analysts OAO Corp., Altadena, 1988—2001; computer scientist Computer Scis. Corp., Altadena, 2001—. Co-author, contbr.: Serotonin and Behavior, 1973, Advances in Sleep Research, vol. 1, 1974. Mem. St. Mary's Cath. Cmty. Theatre. Mem.: Digital Equipment Computer Users Soc., So. Calif. Application Sys. Users Group, OAO Mgmt. Assn. Roman Catholic. Avocations: photography, reading, music, hiking, camping. Home: 37607 Lasker Ave Palmdale CA 93550-7721 Office: Computer Scis Corp 540 W Woodbury Rd Altadena CA 91001-5388 Business E-Mail: mfairbanks@csc.com. E-mail: fairbanks376@earthlink.net.

FAIRBANKS, RICHARD MONROE, III, lawyer, former ambassador at large; b. Indpls., Feb. 10, 1941; s. Richard Monroe, Jr. and Mary Evans (Caperton) F.; m. Anne Shannon O'Connor, June 13, 1962; children: Woods Alexander, Jonathan Barcroft. AB, Yale U., 1962; JD magna cum laude, Columbia U., 1969. Bar: D.C. Assoc. Arnold & Porter, 1969-71; spl. asst. to adminstr. EPA, 1971; staff asst. Domestic Council, Exec. Office of Pres., White House, 1971-72, assoc. dir. energy, environ. and natural resources, 1972-74; founding ptnr. firm Ruckelshaus, Beveridge & Fairbanks, Washington, 1974-81; asst. sec. congressional relations Dept. State, 1981-82, ambassador, spl. negotiator for Middle East peace process, 1982-83, ambassador-at-large, 1984-85; ptnr. Paul, Hastings, Janofsky & Walker, 1986-89, mng. ptnr., 1990-92, sr. counsel, 1992-94, Ctr. for Strategic and Internat. Studies, Washington, 1992-94, mng. dir. for domestic and internat. issues, 1994-99, pres., CEO, 1999-2000, counselor, 2000—. Adj. prof. law Georgetown U., Washington, 1971-72; dir. Fairbanks Broadcasting Co., 1974-81; bd. dirs. SEACOR SMIT Inc., GATX Corp., SPACEHAB, Inc.; sr. counselor Am. Enterprise Inst., 1985-90; pres. U.S. nat. com. for Pacific Econ. Coop., 1986-92; internat. chair Pacific Econ. Coop. Coun., 1991-92, U.S. vice chair 1992—; mem. Pres.'s Task Force on U.S. Internat. Broadcasting, 1991. Founder, 1st pres. Washington chpt. Am. Refugee Com., 1978, mem. nat. bd. dirs., 1977-93; trustee Meridian House Internat., 1978-93; mem. com. natural resources Rep. Nat. Com., 1977-80; mem. Pres.'s Citizens Adv. Com. Environ. Quality, 1974-77; bd. visitors Columbia U. Sch. Law. Officer USN, 1962-66. Mem.: Ctr. for Strategic and Internat. Studies (adv. bd. 1989, bd. trustees 2000), Coun. Am. Ambassadors, Coun. Fgn. Rels., D.C. Bar Assn., ABA, Indian Creek Club, Roaring Fork Club, Chevy Chase Club, Yale Club (N.Y.C.), Metropolitan Club Washington, Ocean Reef Club, Burning Tree Club, Anglers Club. Office: Ctr Strategic & Internat Studies 1800 K St NW Washington DC 20006-2202 E-mail: rfairban@csis.org.

FAIRBANKS II, WILLIAM LOUIS, anthropologist, educator; b. San Francisco, Calif., Mar. 26, 1937; s. William Louis and Drusilla Talbot Fairbanks; m. Carole Anne Fairbanks, Jan. 24, 1959; children: William Louis Fairbanks III, Christine Genevieve Holdstock, Judy Diane Irons. AA, Santa Rosa Jr. Coll., Santa Rosa, CA, 1957; BA, San Jose State Coll., San Jose, CA, 1961, MA, 1962; PhD, U. Calif. Santa Barbara, Santa Barbara, CA, 1975. Social sci. educator Yuba City Union H.S., Yuba City, Calif., 1962—66; anthropology educator Cuesta Coll., San Luis Obispo, Calif., 1966—. Mem.: Am. Anthrop. Assn., Calif. Mission Studies Assn. (exec. bd. mem. 2001—02), Southwestern Anthrop. Assn. (pres. 2000—00). United Methodist. Achievements include Organized program for community college students to travel across the U.S. and interview people in their fields. Avocations: basketball, bridge, wine, walking, rose gardening. Office: Cuesta College PO Box 8106 San Luis Obispo CA 93403

FAIRCHILD, DORCAS SEXTON, English educator; b. Persia, Tenn., June 21, 1938; d. Philip Riley Sr. and Eula Kate (Robinette) Sexton; m. Joe Elmer Fairchild, Apr. 2, 1969. BS, East Tenn. State U., 1960. Cert. secondary English and social studies tchr., Tenn. English tchr. Rogersville (Tenn.) H.S., 1960-80, Cherokee Comprehensive H.S., Rogersville, 1980—, chmn. English dept., 1993—. Sponsor Beta Club, Rogersville, 1984—, Stock Market Game, Rogersville, 1989—. Sunday sch. tchr. Marion Robinette Meml. Ch., Rogersville, 1975—. Mem. NEA, Tenn. Edn. Assn., East Tenn. Edn. Assn., Hawkins County Edn. Assn., Nat. Coun. Tchrs. of English, Tenn. Coun. Tchrs. of English, Delta Kappa Gamma (pres. 1972-74). Republican. Avocations: reading, walking, crocheting. Home: 110 Par 3 Cir Rogersville TN 37857-3916 Office: Cherokee Comprehensive HS 2927 Highway 66 S Rogersville TN 37857-5169

FAIRCHILD, EDWARD HAROLD, chemist, researcher; b. Wadsworth, Ohio, Oct. 31, 1943; s. Dennsion and Marietta Smith Fairchild; m. Linda Maria Lutz, July 29, 1967; children: Joseph Edward, Daniel Ian. BS in Chemistry, Wright State U., 1970; MS in Natural Products Chemistry, The Ohio State U., 1972, PhD in Natural Products Chemistry, 1976. Group leader analytical chemistry Sherex Chem. Co., Dublin, Ohio, 1979—87; mgr. analytical svcs. Henkel Corp. (formerly Quantum Chem.), Cin., 1987—90; dir. sci. support Lonza Inc., Annandale, NJ, 1990—97; v.p. R&D Mona Industries, Paterson, NJ, 1997—99; v.p. R&D americas Uniqema, New Castle, Del., 1999—. Contbr. articles to profl. jours. Sgt. USAF, 1964—68. Mem.: Soc. for Cosmetic Chemists, Am. Oil Chemists Soc. (bd. soap & detergents divsn. 2000—03), Chem. Splty. Manufacturers Assn. (bd. antimicrobial divsn. 1995—97), Consumer Splty. Products Assn. (bd. detergent products 1999—2002), Am. Chem. Soc. Home: 101 Berwyck Ct Newark DE 19702 Office: Uniqema 1000 Uniqema Blvd New Castle DE 19720 Office Fax: 302-574-1790. Personal E-mail: edfairchild@comcast.net. E-mail: ed.fairchild@uniqema.com.

FAIRCHILD, JOHN BURR, publishing executive; b. Newark, Mar. 6, 1927; s. Louis W. and Margaret (Day) F.; m. Jill Lipsky, June 8, 1950; children: John Longin, James Burr, Jill and Stephen L. (twins). BA, Princeton, 1950. Mem. rsch. dept. J.L. Hudson Co., Detroit, 1950-51; with Fairchild Publs., Inc., N.Y.C., 1951—; pub. Women's Wear Daily, Daily News Record, 1960—, editor in chief corp. publs., 1964-65, pub. dir., 1965-66, pres., 1966-70, chmn. bd., chief exec. officer corp. publs., 1970-97, ret., 1997. Exec. v.p., dir. Capital Cities/ABC, Inc., exec. v.p. Author: The Moonflower Couple, The Fashionable Savages, Chic Savages; editor-at-large W Mag., Women's Wear Daily, 1997. Served with AUS, 1947-48. Decorated chevalier de L'Ordre National de Merite, France; grade de chevalier de la Légion d'Honneur, France, officier des Arts et Lettres, France. Mem.: Travellers (Paris, France), Tir aux Pigeons (Paris, France); Century (N.Y.C.). Office: Fairchild Publs 7 W 34th St New York NY 10001-8100

FAIRCHILD, JOSEPH VIRGIL, JR., accounting educator; b. New Orleans, Nov. 26, 1933; s. Joseph Virgil and Georgiana Malone (Bourgeois) F.; m. Judith Champagne, Aug. 12, 1961; children: Georgianna, Joseph, Benjamin. BS in Geology, La. State U., 1956, MBA, 1963, PhD, 1975. CPA, La. Geologist United Core, Inc., Houston, 1956-57; assoc. acct. Humble Oil & Refining Co., New Orleans, 1963-64; ptnr. L.A. Champagne & Co., Baton Rouge, 1964-69; pvt. practice acctg. Thibodaux, La., 1969-2000; ret., 2000; asst. prof. acctg. Nicholls State U., Thibodaux, 1969-75, assoc. prof., 1975-76, prof., 1976-84, disting. prof. acctg., 1984—2000, asst. dean Coll. Bus., 1985-86, dir. grad. bus. studies, 1982-85, disting. prof. emeritus, 2002—; prof. acctg. Henderson State U., Arkadelphia, Ark., 2000—. Rsch. reviewer USAF Bus. Rsch. Mgmt. Ctr., Wright-Patterson AFB, Ohio, 1974-84; cons. Def. Sys. Mgmt. Coll., Ft. Belvoir, Va., 1980-81; faculty senate v.p. govt. com., chmn. dean's search com. Author: (with others) The Acquisition and Distribution of Commercial Products, 1980, 1985-86, 1986-87, 1987-88 and 1988-89 Income Tax Guides for State Legislators; contbr. articles to profl. jours.; actor: (TV, movies) The Kingfish-TNT, Orleans-CBS, Deadman Walking; (plays) South Pacific, Arsenic and Old Lace, Brigadoon, Damn Yankees. Mem. St. Genevieve Sch. Bd., Thibodaux, 1979-83, E.D. White Cath. H.S. Bd., 1985-87, chmn. fin. com., 1985-87; lector St. Genevieve Ch., 1975—, choir, 1989—. 1st lt. USAF, 1957-60, lt. col. USAFR ret. Recipient Acad. Excellence award Henderson State U., 2003; Trueblood Prof. Touche-Ross Found., N.Y.C., 1987. Mem. AICPA, Soc. La. CPA's (lectr. seminars, La.'s Outstanding Acctg. Educator 1994), Am. Acctg. Assn., Nat. Assn. Accts., Nicholls State U. Alumni Assn. (Hon. Alumnus award 1991, Case Educator of Yr. 1994). Roman Catholic. Avocations: flying, skiing, photography, fishing. Home: 412 Plater Dr Thibodaux LA 70301-5616 Office: Nicholls State U Dept Acctg Thibodaux LA 70310-0001

FAIRCHILD, MARK ROBIN, theology studies educator; b. Corry, Pa., July 23, 1954; s. Donald Gerald and Ethel Mae Fairchild; m. Darlene Annette Marsh, July 22, 1978; children: Peter Nathanael, Hannah Elizabeth, Ennea Alene, Malina Mae. BS in Biology (Genetics), Pa. State U., 1976; BA in Bible and Theology, Toccoa Falls (Ga.) Coll., 1980; MDiv in Specialized Curriculum, Asbury Theol. Sem., Wilmore, Ky., 1982; MPhil in Bibl. Studies, Drew U., 1984, PhD in Bibl. Studies, 1989. Adj. prof. Drew U., Madison, NJ, 1986; prof. bible and religion Huntington Coll., Huntington, Ind., 1986—. Author: Eleven Articles in Eerdmans Dictionary of the Bible; contbr. articles and revs. to profl. jours. Grantee NEH, 1992, 2002. Mem.: Evang. Theol. Soc., Cath. Bibl. Assn., Inst. for Bibl. Rsch., Soc. of Bibl. Lit. Home: 5917 N Clear Creek Rd Huntington IN 46750 Office: Huntington Coll Huntington IN 46750 Personal E-mail: mfairchild@huntington.edu. E-mail: mfairchild@huntington.edu.

FAIRCHILD, PHYLLIS ELAINE, school counselor; b. Franklin, La., Feb. 23, 1927; d. Joseph Virgil and Georgiana (Bourgeois) F. BS in Chemistry and Biology, U. Southwestern La., 1946; postgrad., La. State U., 1949-50, MEd in Guidance, 1966. Cert. chemistry, biology, gen. sci., Spanish and social studies tchr., counselor, La. Tchr. sci. St. Mary Parish Sch. Bd., Franklin, 1952-58, counselor, 1977-82; tchr. sci. Am. Dependent Schs., Yokohama, Japan, 1958-60, London, Lakenheath, Eng., 1960-61, Ramey AFB, PR, 1961-62, Norfolk (Va.) City Schs., 1962-63, Iberville Parish Sch. Bd., Plaquemine, La., 1963-66; tchr. sci., counselor East Baton Rouge Parish Sch. Bd., Baton Rouge, 1966-77; counselor Hanson Sch. Bd., Franklin, 1982-94, 96-98; ret., 1998. Mem. adv. com. La. Dept. Edn., Baton Rouge, 1976, 78. Mem. DAR (regent Attakapas chpt. 2003—), La. Landmarks Soc., Cath. Daugs. Am. (co-chmn. religious litergy 1992-94), Fortnightly Lit. Club (pres. 1982-83), Sigma Delta Pi, Pi Gamma Mu, Kappa Kappa Gamma, Delta Kappa Gamma (chmn. membership, scholarship, profl. affairs 1971-77, parliamentarian 1996-98). Avocations: reading, walking, piano, writing. Home: 214 Morris St Franklin LA 70538-6127

FAIRCHILD, ROBERT CHARLES, pediatrician; b. Kansas City, Mo., Dec. 22, 1921; s. Charles Clement and Ada Mae (Baker) F.; m. Patricia Louise Russell, May 28, 1964; children—Robert, Nancy, Rex Hartman, Dan Hartman Student, Kansas City Jr. Coll., 1938-40; BA, U. Kans., 1942, MD, 1950. Diplomate Am. Bd. Pediatrics. Intern Kansas City Gen. Hosp., 1950-51; resident in pediatrics U. Kans. Med. Ctr., 1951-53; practice medicine specializing in pediatrics Mission, Kans., 1953-70; dir. area clinics Children's Mercy Hosp., Kansas City, Mo., 1970-74, dir. outpatient services, 1974-88, ret., 1991. Prof. pediatrics emeritus U. Mo.-Kansas City Sch. Medicine; mem. adv. com. Assoc. Degree nursing program Johnson County Community Coll. Contbr. articles to med. jours. Served to maj. U.S. Army, 1942-46 Decorated Bronze Star; recipient Physician's Recognition award AMA, 1990; Porter scholar U. Kans. Sch. Medicine, 1950. Mem. AMA, Am. Acad. Pediatrics, Mo. State Med.

Assn., Met. Med. Soc. of Kansas City, Greater Kansas City Pediatric Soc., Kansas City S.W. Clin. Soc., Alpha Omega Alpha, Nu Sigma Nu, Sigma Nu. Presbyterian. Home: 8425 Reinhardt Ln Shawnee Mission KS 66206-1316

FAIRCHILD, SAMUEL WILSON, professional services company executive, former federal agency administrator; b. Ft. Eustis, Va., July 16, 1954; s. Henry Howell and Ruby Mae (Love) F.; m. Linda Elizabeth Doremus, May 17, 1986; children: Elizabeth Christine, Samuel Bruce. BS, BA, Coll. of William and Mary, 1977. Cons. ITT, Inc., Smithfield, Va., 1977; v.p., gen. mgr. P.A., Inc., Hampton, Va., 1977-83; sr. policy advisor Exec. Office of the Pres., Washington, 1983-89; dep. asst. sec. U.S. Dept. Transp., Washington, 1989-91; v.p., sr. fellow Ctr. for Tech. and Pub. Policy Rsch. BDM Internat., Inc., McLean, Va., 1991-94; ptnr. Galland, Kharasch, Morse & Garfinkle, p.c., Washington, 1993-99; v.p. PA Cons. Corp., Arlington, Va., 1999—. Chmn. bd. dirs. Schiphol N.Am.Holdings; bd. dirs., founder, pres. GKMG Cons. Svcs., Washington. Author, editor: Moving America, 1989. Active Boy Scouts Am., Irving, Tex., 1972—, mem. World Scout Bur., Geneva, 1972-80, Coun. for Excellence in Govt.; mem. exec. bd. Nat. Capital Area Coun. Boy Scouts Am., 1990—, Patriots Path coun., 1999—, Scouting Century Found., 1999—; co chmn. ARC, Alexandria, Va., 1988-90. Recipient Disting. Alumni award Christopher Newport Coll., 1990; Usry Garland scholar Coll. William and Mary/Christopher Newport Coll., 1975. Mem. Nat. Aviation Assn., Coun. for Excellence in Govt., Aero Club. Presbyterian. Avocations: photography, music. Home: PO Box 341 Brookside NJ 07926-0341

FAIRCHILD, THOMAS E. federal judge; b. Milw., Dec. 25, 1912; s. Edward Thomas and Helen (Edwards) Fairchild; m. Eleanor E. Dahl, July 24, 1937; children: Edward, Susan, Jennifer, Andrew. Student, Princeton, 1931—33; AB, Cornell U., 1934; LLB, U. Wis., 1938. Bar: Wis. 1938. Practiced, Portage, Wis., 1938—41, Milw., 1945—48, 1953—57; atty. OPA, Chgo., Milw., 1941—45; hearing commr. Chgo. Region, 1945; atty. gen. Wis., 1948—51; consultant Office of Price Stabilization, 1951; U.S. atty. for Western Dist. Wis., 1951—52; justice Supreme Ct. Wis., 1957—66, U.S. Ct. Appeals for 7th Circuit, 1966—75; chief judge, 1975—81; sr. judge, 1981—. Dem. candidate Senator from Wis., 1950, 1952. Mem.: KP, FBA, ABA, Am. Law Inst., Am. Judicature Soc., Dane County Bar Assn., 7th Cir. Bar Assn., Milw. Bar Assn., Wis. Bar Assn., Phi Delta Phi. Democrat. Mem. United Church Of Christ. Office: US Courthouse Rm 2764 219 S Dearborn St Chicago IL 60604-1702

FAIRCLOTH, DUNCAN MCLAUCHLIN (LAUCH FAIRCLOTH), former senator, businessman, farmer; b. Sampson County, N.C., Jan. 14, 1928; s. James McLaughlin and Mary (Holt) F.; m. Nancy Ann Bryan, May 26, 1967 (div.); 1 child, Anne. Various positions Faircloth Construction, car dealerships, land-clearing, milling, banking, concrete, comml. real estate; farmer Coharie and Faircloth farms; chmn. N.C. Hwy. Commn., 1969-73; sec. N.C. Commerce, 1977-83; U.S. senator from N.C., 1993-99. Mem. Banking Housing & Urban Affairs Com., chmn. subcom. HUD Oversight and Structure; chmn. Environ. & Pub. Works subcom. of Clean Air Wetlands Pvt. Property and Nuclear Safety; appropriations com., sm. bus. com. Republican. Presbyterian. Office: PO Box 496 Clinton NC 28329-0496

FAIRES, ROSS NORBERT, manufacturing company executive; b. Indpls., July 20, 1934; s. Herbert C. and Thelma (Wood) F.; m. Glady Ann Caley, Dec. 20, 1954; children: Kurt J., Eric S., Jay A. BA, Wabash Coll., 1958; MBA, Ind. U., 1959. Advt. mgr. Cummins Engine Co., Columbus, Ind., 1959-62; pres. Arvin Industries div. Housewares, Columbus, 1962-75, Tibbals Flooring Co., Oneida, Tenn., 1976-91; chmn. Faires Group, Chattanooga, 1991—. Bd. dirs. AmSouth Bank, Knoxville, Tenn. Bd. dirs. Knoxville Zoo, Knoxville Mus. Art, Nat. Symphony Orch., Washington, Webb Sch., Knoxville, St. Mary's Hosp. Found., Am. Symphony Orch. League, East Tenn. Comm. Found., Helen Ross McNabb Found.; bd. regents State of Tenn., 1984-91; mem. bd. advisors McCallie Sch. for Boys, Chattanooga; trustee Wabash (Ind.) Coll., Maryville Coll. Mem. Tenn. Bus. Assn. (bd. dirs.), Tenn. BAnd Assn., Leadership Knoxville, Cherokee Country Club, Sea Pines Country Club. Presbyterian. Home and Office: 904 Cherokee Blvd Knoxville TN 37919-7847

FAIRFIELD-SONN, JAMES WILLED, management educator and consultant; b. Nashua, N.H., Aug. 21, 1948; s. David Alexander and Christine Mary (Fairfield) Sonn; m. Lynn Groark, July 3, 1982; children: Anne Madeline, James Willed, Jr., John Thomas. MS, Cornell U., 1979; MA, Yale U., 1980, MPhil, 1982, PhD, 1985. Mgr. office adminstrn. Hartford Ins. Group, Indpls., 1972-76; asst. prof. mgmt. U. Hartford, West Hartford, Conn., 1982-88, assoc. prof., 1988—2002, prof., 2002—, chmn. mgmt. dept., 1987-90, dir. exec. MBA, 1993-95. Pres. Fairfield-Sonn Assocs., Centerbrook, Conn., 1981—; v.p. bd. dirs. ENCOMPASS Software. Author: Corporate Culture and the Quality Organization, 2001; contbr. articles and revs. to profl. jours. Named Outstanding Tchr. of Yr., Barney Sch., 1999; Cornell U. indsl. and labor rels. fellow, 1977-78, Yale U. fellow, 1978-82, Olin fellow, 1981. Mem.: Assn. Yale Alumni (chmn. grad. and profl. schs. com. 1982—83), Ea. Acad. Mgmt., Acad. Mgmt. Republican. Congregationalist. Avocations: tennis, travel, gardening. Home and Office: PO Box 1047 Old Lyme CT 06371-0998 E-mail: jimfs@fairfield-sonn.net.

FAIRHURST, CHARLES, civil and mining engineering educator; b. Widnes, Lancashire, Eng, Aug. 5, 1929; came to US, 1956, naturalized, 1967; s. Richard Lowe and Josephine (Starkey) F.; m. Margaret Ann Lloyd, Sept. 7, 1957; children: Anne Elizabeth Charlet, David Lloyd, Charles Edward, Catherine Mary Kotz, Hugh Richard, John Peter, Margaret Mary Evans. BEng with honors, U. Sheffield, Eng., 1952, PhD, 1955; DSc, U. Sheffield, 1998; D in Engring. (hon.), St. Petersburg Mining Inst., Russia, 1995, Inst. Nat. Poly de Lorraine, France, 1996; DSc (hon.), U. Minn., 2000. Mining engr. trainee Nat. Coal Bd., St. Helens, England, 1949-56; research assoc. prof. U. Minn., Mpls., 1956-67, head Sch. Mineral and Metall. Engring., 1967-70, prof. dept. civil and mineral engring., 1970-94, prof. dept. civil engring., 1994-97, head dept., 1972-87, T.W. Bennett Prof. mining engring. and rock mechanics, 1983-97, prof. emeritus, 1997—. Sr. cons. Itasca Group Inc., Mpls.; cons. Petrobras, Brazil, Spie. Batignolles, France, Charbonnages de France; Geodesio, France, chmn. US Com. Rock Mechanics, 1971-74, Waste Isolation Pilot Plant Panel NAS/NRC, Carlsbad, N.Mex., 1989-96; chmn. study underground nuclear testing in French Polynesia, Internat. Geomechanics Commn., 1995-98; mem. bd. radioactive waste mgmt. NAS/NRC, 1987-94, vice chmn., 1989-94; adv. prof. Tongji U., Shanghai, 1994. Mem. Conseil Sci. ANDRA (France), 1994—, Mon. Geol. Rep. Consulting Bd., Yucca Mountain, 1999-2001; mem. sci. and tech. panel Office of Civilian Radioactive Waste Mgmt., US Dept. Energy, 2002-. Mem. AIME, ASCE (chmn. rock mechanics com. 1978-80), Internat. Soc. Rock Mechanics (pres. 1991-95), Am. Rock Mechanics Assn. (pres. 1995-97), Am. Underground Constrn. Assn. (pres. 1976-77), Royal Swedish Acad. Engring. Sci. (fgn.), US Nat. Acad. Engring., Sigma Xi. Roman Catholic. Home: 417 5th Ave N South Saint Paul MN 55075-2035 Office: 417 Fifth Ave N South Saint Paul MN 55075-2035 E-mail: fairh001@tc.umn.edu.

FAIRLEIGH, JAMES PARKINSON, music educator; b. St. Joseph, Mo., Aug. 24, 1938; s. William Macdonald and Mable Emily (Parkinson) F.; m. Marlane Alberta Paxson, June 25, 1960; children: William Paxson, Karen Evelyn. MusB, U. Mich., 1960; MusM, U. So. Calif., 1965; PhD, U. Mich., 1973. Instr., asst. prof. Hanover (Ind.) Coll., 1965-75; assoc. prof. R.I. Coll., Providence, 1975-80; prof., head music dept. Jacksonville (Ala.) State U., 1980—2001, prof. emeritus music, 2001—. Dir. of music First Presbyn. Ch., Anniston, Ala., 1981-2001; presenter, lectr. at meetings of profl. orgns., 1974-. Contbr. articles to profl. jours., mags., 1966—. Served to 1st lt. U.S. Army, 1960-62. Mem. Am. Musicol. Soc., Ala. Music Tchrs. Assn. (cert., treas. 1982-86, 1st v.p. 1986-88, pres. 1988-90), Coll. Music Soc. (southern chpt. exec. bd. 1996-98), Music Tchrs. Nat. Assn. (cert.), Assn. Ala. Coll. Music Adminstrs. (sec., treas. 1985-89, pres. 1989-91), Phi Beta Kappa, Phi Kappa Phi, Pi Kappa Lambda, Phi Eta Sigma, Phi Mu Alpha Sinfonia. Republican. Avocations: water-skiing, swimming, backpacking.

FAIRLEIGH, MARLANE PAXSON, retired management educator; b. Three Rivers, Mich., Feb. 28, 1939; d. Ronald Edward and Evelyn May (Roth) Paxson; m. James Parkinson Fairleigh, June 25, 1960; children: William Paxson, Karen Evelyn. MusB, U. Mich., 1960; MBA, Jacksonville State U., 1986. Cert. econ. devel. fin. profl. Nat. Devel. Coun., 1989. Mem. adj. faculty Providence Coll., 1976-80, R.I. Coll., Providence, 1978-80; grad. asst. news bur. and info. ctr. Jacksonville (Ala.) State U., 1983-84, grad. asst. Coll. Commerce, 1984-85; bus. cons. Jacksonville State U. Small Bus. Devel. Ctr., 1985-96. Presenter in field. Contbr. articles to profl. jours.; soprano soloist (songs) Coll. Music Soc. Internat. Conf., Berlin, Germany, 1995, Vienna, Austria, 1997, (chamber music recitals) Auburn U., Jacksonville State U., 1998, Gadsden, Ala., 2001, lectr.-recitalist (songs) U. Ala., Tuscaloosa, 1997, U. Ctrl. Fla., Orlando, 1999, Jacksonville State U., 1999, State U. West Ga., 1998, Valdosta State U., 2001, U. South Fla., Tampa, 2003, recitalist (chamber music) Colonial Dames Am., Gadsden, Ala., 2001, Gadsden Music Club, 2001. Chair Jacksonville State U. campus United Way Calhoun County, 1986-87. Mem. Coll. Music Soc., Sigma Beta Delta. Avocations: vocal performing, water skiing, swimming, hiking. Home: 13116 Janda Rd Seneca SC 29672

FAIRMAN, JARRETT SYLVESTER, retail company executive; b. Anderson, Ind., Feb. 22, 1939; s. Charles Lawton and Ruth (Rich) F.; m. Delores Rae Anderson, Nov. 13, 1960; children: Adele Suzanne, Jarrett Scott, Angela Christine. BS, Purdue U., 1961. Exec. trainee, div. mgr. Sears, Marion, Ind., 1963-67, mdse. mgr., asst. store mgr., Bloomington, Ind., 1967-69, asst. retail sales mgr. sporting goods, Chgo., 1969-71, territorial mdse. mgr. sporting goods, toys and bus. equipment, Dallas, 1971-78; regional v.p. retail ops. White's Home and Auto Stores, 1978-81; pres. Banner, Hendrik & Grant Co., Inc., Dallas, 1981-86; pres. Rapid Distbg. Co. (subs. Otasco), Tulsa, 1986-88; v.p. devel. Coast-to-Coast Home and Auto, Denver, 1988-89; pres. Fairman and Assocs., Inc., 1989-94; pres., CEO Fairman Properties, Inc., 1994—. Served with U.S. Army, 1961-63. Republican. Lutheran. Home and Office: 2006 Hillcrest Ct Mc Kinney TX 75070-4010

FAIRMAN, JOEL MARTIN, broadcasting executive; b. N.Y.C., Mar. 12, 1929; s. Philip A. and Isabelle (Glackman) Feinberg; m. Claire Martin, Oct. 1, 1959; children: Elizabeth, David, Helen. BA, Amherst Coll., 1952; JD, Yale U., 1955. Assoc. Patterson Belknap & Webb, N.Y.C., 1956-61; asst. to pres., v.p. Gianis & Co., Inc., N.Y.C., 1961-65; sr. v.p. and mng. dir. corp. fin. communications group Prudential-Bache Securities and predecessor firms, N.Y.C., 1965-83; chmn. Faircom Inc., 1984-98; vice chmn. Regent Comm., Inc., 1998—2001, also bd. dirs.; chmn. North Shore Strategies Inc., 2001—. Home: Bayville Rd Locust Valley NY 11560-2003 Office: North Shore Strategies 333 Glen Head Rd Glen Head NY 11545-1947

FAIROBENT, DOUGLAS KEVIN, computer programmer; b. Detroit, Jan. 10, 1951; s. Jack Edward and Doris Kathleen (Kennedy) F.; m. Paulette Marie Gillig, June 13, 1981. BS in Physics, U. Mich., 1972, MS in Physics, 1975, PhD in Theoretical Condensed Matter Physics, 1978. Engr. Ford Motor Co., Allen Park, Mich., 1978-80, lectr. physics Ohio State U., Columbus, 1980-82; sr. systems programmer Rockwell Internat., Columbus, 1982-85, Cin. Milacron, 1985-90, Quantum Chem. Co., Cin., 1990-96; sys. adminstr. Cath. Healthcare Ptnrs., Cin., 1996—. Contbr. articles to Phys. Rev., other publs. Mem. Am. Phys. Soc. (life). Avocations: ice hockey, classical piano. Office: Catholic Healthcare Partners 615 Elsinore Pl Cincinnati OH 45202-1459 E-mail: dkfairobent@health-partners.org.

FAIRWEATHER, ROBERT GORDON LEE, lawyer; b. Rothesay, N.B., Can., Mar. 27, 1923; s. Jack H.A.L. and Agnes Charlotte (Mackeen) F.; m. Nancy E. Broughall, June 1, 1946; children— Michael, Wendy, Hugh. B.C.L., U. N.B., 1949, LL.D. (hon.), 1973, St. Thomas U., 1977, Queens U., 1978, St. Francis Xavier U., 1980, York U., 1993. Called to bar N.B 1949, created Queen's Counsel 1958. Partner firm McKelvey, MacAulay, Machum & Fairweather, St. John, 1957-77; atty. gen. N.B., 1958 60; chief Can. Human Rights Commn., Ottawa, Ont., 1977-87; chmn. Immigration and Refugee Bd., Ottawa, 1987-92. Mem. Legis. Assembly N.B., 1952-62, M.P., 1962-77. Served with Royal Can. Navy, 1941-45. Decorated officer Order of Can.; recipient Outstanding Achievement award of pub. svc. Govt. Can., 1990, Humanitarian of the Yr. award Can. Red Cross, 1999, New Brunswick Pioneer of Human Rights award, 2002; Ryerson Poly. U. fellow, 1993. Home: 2865 Rothesay Rd Apt 43 Rothesay NB Canada E2E 5V1

FAISON, SETH SHEPARD, retired insurance broker; b. N.Y.C., Jan. 18, 1924; s. John Williams and Caroline Goree (Shepard) F.; m. Susan Tyler, Apr. 14, 1956 (dec. 1978); children: Katharine Faison Spencer, Seth Shepard, Sarah, Ann Badger; m. Sara Williams Rose Chew, Mar. 29, 1980; stepchildren: Sara Holten Chew, Katherine Rose Chew, Arthur Duncan Chew. BA with honors and distinction, Wesleyan U., 1947. Personnel mgr. NBC, N.Y.C., 1948-53; divsn. mgr. Am. Mgmt. Assn., N.Y.C., 1953-58; asst. v.p. Johnson & Higgins, N.Y.C., 1958-68, v.p., 1968-89; ret., 1989. Chmn. Bklyn. Acad. Music, 1966-72, hon. chmn., 1979—; trustee Bklyn. Inst. Arts and Scis., 1963-81, v.p., 1965-71, exec. v.p., 1971-74, vice-chmn., 1974-79, chmn., 1979-81; trustee/gov. Bklyn. Mus. Art, 1972-91, vice-chmn. 1976-91, trustee 1993—; trustee Bklyn. Hosp., 1963—, v.p. 1968-82, vice-chmn., 1982-93, chmn., 1993-02; bd. govs. Hosp. Trustees of N.Y. State, 1992-97, chmn., 1995-97; trustee Poly Prep., 1962-77, N.Y. Presbyn. Healthcare Sys., 1998-03; bd. dirs. Police Athletic League N.Y., 1957-73, Chelsea Theater Center, 1969-77; regent St. Francis Coll., Bklyn., 1961-70; mem. N.Y.C. Commn. for Cultural Affairs, 1981-91. Lt. (j.g.) USNR, 1943-46. Recipient N.Y. State award for Bklyn. Acad. Music (rehab. of 1 of state's most venerable theaters), 1969. Mem. Citizens Union, Huguenot Soc. Am., The Heights Casino Club, Rembrandt Club, Ihpetonga Club (Bklyn.), Bellport Bay Yacht Club (N.Y.). Unitarian (sr. deacon). Home: 1 Pierrepont St Apt 10B Brooklyn NY 11201-3302 E-mail: maisonfaison@earthlink.net.

FAISON, W. MACK, lawyer; b. Roanoke Rapids, N.C., Oct. 25, 1945; BA, N.C. Ctrl. U., 1966; JD, Harvard U., 1969. Bar: N.Y. 1970, Mich. 1972. Mem. Miller, Canfield, Paddock and Stone, Detroit. Mem. local rules adv. com. Ea. Dist. Mich., U.S. Dist. Ct., civil justice reform act adv. com. Mem. ABA, State Bar Mich., Nat. Bar Assn., Detroit Bar Assn., Wolverine Bar Assn., Am. Coll. of Trial Lawyers. Office: Miller Canfield Paddock & Stone 150 W Jefferson Ave Ste 2500 Detroit MI 48226-4416

FAISS, ROBERT DEAN, lawyer; b. Centralia, Ill., Sept. 19, 1934; s. Wilbur and Theresa Ella (Watts) F.; m. Linda Louise Chambers, Mar. 30, 1991; children: Michael Dean Faiss, Marcy Faiss Ayres, Robert Mitchell Faiss, Philip Grant Faiss, Justin Cooper. BA in Journalism, Am. U., 1969, JD, 1972. Bar: Nev. 1972, D.C. 1972, U.S. Dist. Ct. Nev. 1973, U.S. Supreme Ct. 1977, U.S. Ct. Appeals (9th cir.) 1978. City editor Las Vegas (Nev.) Sun, 1957-59; pub. info. officer Nev. Dept. Employment Security, 1959-61; asst. exec. sec. Nev. Gaming Commn., Carson City, 1961-63; exec. asst. to gov. State of Nev., Carson City, 1963-67; staff asst. U.S. Pres. Lyndon B. Johnson, White House, Washington, 1968-69; asst. to exec. dir. U.S. Travel Adminstrn., Washington, 1969-72; ptnr., chmn. adminstrv. law dept. Lionel, Sawyer & Collins, Las Vegas, 1973—. Mem. bank secrecy Act Adv. Group U.S. Treasury. Co-author: Legalized Gaming in Nevada, 1961, Nevada Gaming License Guide, 1988, Nevada Gaming Law, 1991, 95, 98. Recipient Bronze medal Dept. Commerce, 1972, Chris Schaller award We Can, Las Vegas, 1995, Lifetime Achievement award Nev. Gaming Attys. Assn., 1997; named One of 100 Most Influential Lawyers in Am. and premier U.S. gaming atty., Nat. Law Jour., 1997. Mem. ABA (chmn. gaming law com. 1985-86), Internat. Assn. Gaming Attys. (founding, pres. 1980), Nev. Gaming Attys. Office: Lionel Sawyer & Collins 300 S 4th St Ste 1700 Las Vegas NV 89101-6053

FAITH, JAMES ALBERT, JR., minister; b. Dalton, Ga., Aug. 24, 1972; s. James Albert Faith Sr. and Ida Frances Faith. B in Ch. Music, Shorter Coll., 1996; MusM, S.W. Baptist Theol. Seminary, 1999. Ordained minister 2000. Minister music & worship First United Meth. Ch., Granbury, Tex., 1997—. Asst. dir. Granbury Civic Chorus, Granbury, 2001—. Mem.: Am. Guild Eng. Handbell Ringers, Hymn Soc. U.S. & Can., Am. Guild of Organists. Methodist. Avocations: golf, tennis. Home: 3703 Mission Ct Granbury TX 76049 Office: First United Methodist Church 205 East Pearl St Granbury TX 76048 Fax: 817-573-7196. E-mail: jfaith@fumcgranbury.org.

FAITH, MARSHALL E. grain company executive; Chmn. The Scoular Co., Omaha. Office: The Scoular Co Scoular Bldg 2027 Dodge St Ste 300 Omaha NE 68102-1229

FAITH, TRISTAN, counselor; b. Indiana, Pa., July 12, 1953; children: Shawn Hill, Joshua Hill. BA Transpersonal Psychology, Burlington Coll., Burlington, VT, 1997; Master's Counseling, Southwestern Coll., Santa Fe, 2000. Owner Ford Gallery (Art), Fairfax, Va., 2002—02; newspaper column writer Old Town Crier, Fairfax, Va.; spokesperson No. Va. Mental Health Alliance, Va.; regression therapist and lectr. Recipient Best in Show Art award, Prince William County, VA, 1986. Home: 7203 Park Shores Center Madison WI 53703

FAITHFULL, TIMOTHY WILLIAM, petroleum industry executive, b. Winchester, Hampshire, Eng., June 10, 1944; arrived in Can., 1999; s. Horace William and Mary Elizabeth Faithfull; m. Prudence Eyre String, July 7, 1973; children: Kaisi, William, Joseph. BA, Keble Coll., Oxford, Eng., 1967; MA, U. Oxford, 1972. Gen. mgr. Kenya Shell, Nairobi, 1989; area coord. Shell Internat., 1989-93; v.p. crude oil trading SITCO, Eng., 1993-96; chmn., CEO, Shell Ea. Petroleum Ltd., Singapore, 1996-99; pres., CEO, Shell Can. Ltd., Calgary, Alta., Can., 1999—, also bd. dirs. Bd. trustees Starehe Boys Ctr., Kenya, 1995—. Mem. Calgary Petroleum Club, Calgary Golf and Country Club, United Oxford and Cambridge Univs. Club. Anglican. Avocations: sailing, golf. Office: Shell Can Ltd PO Box 100 400 4th Ave SW Calgary AB Canada T2P 2H5

FAJANS, JACK, physics educator; b. N.Y., Nov. 17, 1922; s. Harry and Fanny Fajans; m. Eleanor Belfert, Mar. 5, 1944; children— Anita, Joel. B.Chem.Engring., CCNY, 1944; PhD, M.I.T., 1950. Engr. Western Electric Co., Kearny, N.J., 1944; group mgr. Sylvania Electric Co., Bayside, N.Y., 1950-53; mem. faculty Stevens Inst. Tech., Hoboken, N.J., 1953—, prof. physics, 1953-88, prof. emeritus, 1988—, dean grad. sch., 1974-84. Exchange prof. Kabul U., Afghanistan, 1963-65, 67-69; cons. in field, 1956— Author; patentee in field Served with AUS, 1944-46. Mem. Am. Phys. Soc., M.I.T. Alumni Assn., CCNY Alumni Assn., Sigma Xi. Home: 1133 Magnolia Rd Teaneck NJ 07666-2745

FAJANS, STEFAN STANISLAUS, retired internist; b. Munich, Mar. 15, 1918; arrived in U.S., 1936, naturalized, 1942; s. Kasimir M. and Salomea (Kaplan) Fajans; m. Ruth Stine, Sept. 6, 1947; children: Peter S., John S. BS, U. Mich., Ann Arbor, 1938, MD, 1942. Intern Mount Sinai Hosp., N.Y.C., 1942—43; research fellow U. Mich., 1946—47, rsch. fellow, 1949—51, resident, 1947—49; mem. faculty U. Mich. Med. Sch., 1950—, prof., 1961—88, prof. emeritus, 1988—. Mem. endocrinology study sect. NIH, 1958—62, mem. diabetes and metabolism tng. grants com., 1966—70, mem. nat. diabetes adv. bd., 1987—91; chief divsn. endocrinology and metabolism Mich. Diabetes Rsch. and Tng. Ctr., 1973—87, dir., 1977—86; chmn. Am. zone internat. sci. adv. com. Congresses Internat. Diabetes Fedn., 1977—79; Banting meml. lectr., 1978. Contbr. articles med. publs. Mem. career devel. com. VA Med. Rsch. Svcs., 1987—91. Officer M.C. U.S. Army, 1943—46. Fellow rsch. fellow in medicine, ACP, 1949—50, Life Ins. Med. Inst., 1950—51. Master: ACP; mem.: NAS (sr. mem. inst. med.), Ctrl. Soc. Clin. Rsch., Assn. Am. Physicians, Am. Soc. Clin. Investigation, Am. Fedn. Clin. Rsch., Endocrine Soc. (v.p. 1970—71, coun. 1967—71, 1978—81), Am. Diabetes Assn. (pres. 1971—72, Banting medal 1972, Banting Meml. award 1978), Alpha Omega Alpha, Sigma Xi. Home: 827 Asa Gray Dr # 360 Ann Arbor MI 48105-2566 Office: PO Box 0354 Ann Arbor MI 48109-0354 E-mail: sfajans@umich.edu.

FAJARDO, SARAH ELIZABETH JOHNSON, financial consultant; b. Montgomery, Ala., July 27, 1956; d. Robert Kellogg and Mary Loretta (Franks) Johnson; m. Thomas Ronald Fajardo, Sept. 5, 1987; children: Emilia Katherine, Roberto Thomas. BA in Anthropology, U. Ariz., 1979; postgrad., Inst. Fin. Edn., Tucson, 1985-87. Resident advisor Tucson Job Corps, 1980-81; felony release specialist Pretrial Release of Pima County, Tucson, 1981-82; dir. retention counseling Tucson Coll. Bus., 1982-84; teller, new account rep. Western Savs., Tucson, 1984-86; stockbroker Western Savs./Invest, Tucson, 1986-87; fin. planner Boucher, Oehmke & Quinn, Tucson, 1987-89, Consolidated Investment Svcs., 1989-92; registered rep. Plan Am., 1992—93; designed and developed investment dept. Nat. Bank Ariz., 1993—95; fin. cons. pvt. client svcs. Wells Fargo Investment (formerly Norwest), 1995—. Mgr. telemarketing dept. Ariz. Theatre Co., Tucson, 1988-89. Contbr. articles to profl. jours. Mem. com. Tucson Tomorrow, 1988; founding mem. Brewster Ctr. for Victims of Family Violence, Tucson, 1982-86; vol. Peace Corps, Senegal, Africa, 1979; chair ann. awards banquet events YWCA Women on the Move, 1991, grad. leadership tng. program, 1990; mem. investment adv. and fin. com. So. Ariz. Ctr. Against Sexual Assault, 2002-03; bd. dirs. Ariz. Children's Assn.; chair fin. com. Planned Parenthood So. Ariz., 1993, bd. dirs. Mem. Resources for Women (group leader of money talks 1987), NAFE, Successful Bus. Referral Club, Indsl. Recreation Coun. (treas. 1986-87), Greater Tucson Econ. Coun. (small bus. task force 1992—). Democrat. Avocations: gourmet cooking, bicycling, weight training, running, gardening. Office: Wells Fargo Investments Wells Fargo Pvt Client Svcs 2195 E River Rd Ste 105 Tucson AZ 85718

FAJORS, NIQUE, policy advisor; b. Boston, Nov. 2, 1967; s. Herb and Blanche Christine Fajors; m. Faiza Abdallah Zarroug. BSBA, Suffolk U., 1989; MBA, Harvard U., 1993. Brand mgmt. Procter & Gamble, Cin., 1993-95; exec. v.p. Digital Telemedia, Inc., N.Y.C., 1995-97; mgr. bus. devel. Schlumberger, Paris, 1997-98; pres. Valuecreation.com LLC, N.Y.C., 1998—99; pres. consumer mktg. svcs. Bounty SCA Worldwide, Chgo., 1999—2001; sr. policy advisor Office of the Sec. Dept. Commerce, 2002—. Bd. dirs. ProMonde, Inc. Prodr. (ednl. video) The Invisible Men, 1995; author: Cultural & Economic Revitalization, 1999. Mem.: Coun. Fgn. Rels. Avocations: travel, photography. Home: 4443 13th St NE Washington DC 20017 Office: Office of the Sec Dept Commerce 1401 Constitution Ave NW Washington DC 20230 E-mail: nfajors@earthlink.net.

FAKHARZADEH, FREDERICK F. surgeon; b. N.Y.C., July 2, 1955; s. Mehdi and Sigrun Kristin (Fridriksdottir) F.; m. Patricia Fleming, Sept. 3, 1983; children: Kristine, Stephanie, Daniel, Eric. BA magna cum laude, Cornell U., 1976; MD, Columbia U., 1980. Diplomate Am. Bd. Orthop. Surgery. Intern Roosevelt Hosp., N.Y.C., 1980-81, resident in surgery, 1981-82; resident in orthop. surgery Columbia-Presbyn. Med. Ctr., N.Y.C., 1982-85; hand surgery fellow Thomas Jefferson U., Phila., 1985-86; pvt. practice Paramus, N.J., 1986—. Attending surgeon, Hackensack Med. Ctr., N.J., 1986—; asst. attending surgeon Holy Name Hosp., Teaneck, N.J., 1986—; active med. staff Pascack Valley Hosp., Westwood, N.J., 1986—; active med. staff, The Valley Hosp., Ridgewood, N.J., 1987—; clin. asst. prof. U. Medicine and Dentistry of N.J., Newark, 1990-2001. Contbr. articles to profl. jours. Coord. girl's basketball, Recreation League, Oradell, N.J., 1995-2002, coach, 1993-2001; coach girl's softball, Oradell Little League, 1993-2000. Fellow Am. Acad. Orthopaedic Surgeon; mem. Am. Soc. Surgery of the Hand, N.Y. Soc. for Surgery of the Hand, AMA, Med. Soc. of N.J., Bergen County Med. Soc. Avocations: photography, fishing, basketball, golf. Office: 22 Madison Ave Paramus NJ 07652-2721 E-mail: fredfak@aol.com.

FAKLER, MARY EDITH, English educator; b. Mt. Vernon, N.Y. d. Charles A. and Kathleen Deierlein; m. Helmut K. Fakler; children: Marè, Wayne, Kate, Marissa, Heidi. BA in English, SUNY, New Paltz, 1991, MA in English, 1994. Instr. English SUNY, New Paltz, 1992—, Mt. St. Mary Coll., Newburgh, NY, 1994—2001; instr. Acad. and Artistic Adventures Gifted Program Bishop Dunn Sch., Newburgh, 1996—. Home: 150 Plains Rd Walden NY 12586-2443 Office: SUNY JFT 706 Manheim Blvd New Paltz NY 12561 E-mail: faklerm@newpaltz.edu.

FAKUNDINY, LYDIA, English language educator; b. Pezinok, Slovakia, June 20, 1941; came to U.S., 1951; d. Albert and Elisabeth Fakundiny. BA in English with honors, Smith Coll., 1963; BPhil, St. Anne's Coll., Oxford, Eng., 1965, BLitt, 1967. From instr. to asst. prof. English, Ea. Ky. U., Richmond, 1966-69; from asst. to assoc. prof. English, Fed. City Coll. (now U. D.C.), Washington, 1969-74; from lectr. to sr. lectr. English, Cornell U., Ithaca, N.Y., 1981—. Editor: (anthology) Art of the Essay, 1991; co-author: (with Joyce Elbrecht) The Restorationist, 1993. Marshall scholar Oxford U., 1963-65, hon. Woodrow Wilson scholar, 1963—. Mem. Phi Beta Kappa. Democrat. Office: Cornell U Dept English Ithaca NY 14850 E-mail: lef5@cornell.edu.

FAKUNDINY, ROBERT HARRY, geologist, educator, consultant; b. Manitowoc, Wis., Feb. 11, 1940; s. Walter P. and Ann (Kakes) F.; m. Anne J. Finch, Jan. 28, 1978. BA in Geology, U. Calif., Riverside, 1962; MA in Geology, U. Tex., 1967, PhD in Geology, 1970. Vol. U.S. Peace Corps, Ghana, 1963-65; assoc. seicntist and sr. scientist N.Y. State Geol. Survey, Albany, 1970-78, state geologist and chief, 1978—. Adj. asst. prof. SUNY, Albany, 1975-87; cons. to

profl. groups, industries and govt. agys. Contbr. articles to profl. jours. Trustee Esquatak Town Hist. Soc., 1983-86; bd. dirs. N.E. Sci. Found., 1988-91; advisor New Eng. River Basins Commn., 1973-75; mem. site selection com. CoCorp, 1978-93; mem. com. on energy resources IOCC, 1978-79; mem. com. on oil and gas info. and data base mgmt., 1989—; chmn. Ian Campbell award com. Am. Geol. Inst., 1995-96; chmn. N.Am. Com. on Stratigraphic Nomenclature, 1988. Hogg fellow U. Tex., 1969; numerous scholarships and grants. Fellow AAAS, Geol. Soc. Am. (mgmt. bd. engring. geology divsn. 1987, chmn. N.E. sect. geology and pub. policy com. 1991-97), Geol. Assn. Can., Chartered Geologists Geol. Soc. London, N.Y. Acad. Scis.; mem. Am. Assn. Petroleum Geologists (George V. Cohee Pub. Svc. award 1997), Am. Geophys. Union, Assn. Am. State Geologists (v.p. 1989-90, pres.-elect 1990-91, pres. 1991-92, chmn. low-level radioactive waste com. 1980-86, chmn. radon com. 1990-91, chmn. earth sci. edn. com. 1993-99), Am. Inst. Profl. Geologists (cert., nat. selection com. 1991-95, chmn. nat. selection com. 1993-94, del. to USSR, 1990, nat. sec. 1996-97, pres.-elect 2000, pres. 2001), John T. Galey Sr. Meml. Pub. Svc. award 1993, Presdl. cert. of merit, 1994), Nat. Assn. Geology Tchrs., Assn. Earth Sci. Editors, Soc. Exploration Paleontologists and Mineralogists, Assn. Engring. Geologists, Assn. Women Geoscientists, Assn. Geoscientists for Internat. Devel., Multi Agy. Group for Neotechnics in Ea. Can., Buffalo Assn. Profl. Geologists, Ctrl. N.Y. Assn. Profl. Geologists, Nat. Assn. Black Geologists, Geophysics Hudson-Mohawk Profl. Geologists Assn. (bd. dirs. 1995-97), N.Y. State Coun. Profl. Geologists, Sigma Xi, Sigma Gamma Epsilon. Achievements include research in seismic hazard determination, application of glacial studies to environmental issues, geology of low-level radioactive waste disposal, geologic structure of Adirondack Mountains, landslides. Home: 3288 River Rd # 9J Rensselaer NY 12144-5121 Office: NY State Geol Survey CEC 3140 Albany NY 12230-0001 E-mail: rfakundi@mail.nysed.gov.

FALA, HERMAN C. lawyer; b. Phila., Oct. 15, 1949; s. Herman Anthony and Rose Maria (Iannetti) F.; m. Helen E. Perry, June 26, 1971; 1 child, Danielle. BS summa cum laude, U. Notre Dame, 1971; JD cum laude, Harvard U., 1974. Bar: Pa. 1974, U.S. Dist. Ct. (ea. dist.) Pa. 1974. Assoc. Wolf, Block, Schorr & Solis-Cohen, Phila., 1974-82, ptnr., 1982—. Chair real estate dept. Wolf, Block, Schorr & Solis-Cohen. Editor: The Philadelphia Lawyer, 1977—. Bd. dirs. The Wilma Theatre, Phila., 1986—, chmn., 1995-97. Mem. ABA, Pa. Bar Assn., Phila. Bar Assn. (v.p. 1997, chair exec. com. real property sect. 1998) Phi Beta Kappa. Avocations: photography, amateur astronomy, travel, cooking, writing. Office: Wolf Block Schorr & Solis-Cohen 22d Fl 1650 Arch St Fl 22D Philadelphia PA 19103-2029

FALB, PETER LAWRENCE, mathematician, educator, investment company executive; b. N.Y.C., July 26, 1936; s. Harry and Bertha (Kirschner) F.; m. Karen Forslund, Oct. 9, 1971; children— Hilary, Alison AB, Harvard U., 1956, MA, 1957, PhD, 1961. Mem. staff Mass. Inst. Tech. Lincoln Lab., Cambridge, 1960-66; asso. prof. applied math. U. Mich., Ann Arbor, 1966; prof. Brown U., Providence, 1967—; prin., treas. Dane, Falb, Stone & Co., Inc., Boston, 1977—. Chmn. Barberry Corp., 1968-85; also bd. dirs.; bd. dirs. FES Computing Co., LTCQ, Inc., Toreador Royalty, Infolenz, LTC Media; mng. dir. F-Co. Holdings Co.; vis. prof. Lund (Sweden) Inst. Tech., summers 1971, 72, 74, 76, 78; cons. NASA, Bolt, Beranek & Newman Co. Author: (with M. Athans) Optimal Control: An Introduction to the Theory and its Applications, 1966, (with R. Kalman and M. Arbib) Topics in Mathematical System Theory, 1969, (with J. deJong) Some Successive Approximation Methods in Control and Oscillation Theory, 1969; Methods of Algebraic Geometry in Control Theory, Part I: Scalar Linear Systems and Affine Algebraic Geometry, 1989, Methods of Algebraic Geometry in Control Theory, Part II: Multivariable Linear systems and Projective Algebraic Geometry, 1999. Home: 245 Brattle St Cambridge MA 02138-4614 Office: Dane Falb Stone & Co Inc 15 Broad St Ste 406 Boston MA 02109-3803 also: Brown U Box F Providence RI 02912 E-mail: plf245@aol.com.

FALBAUM, BERTRAM SEYMOUR, law educator, investigator; b. N.Y.C., July 28, 1934; s. Abraham and Shari (Greenfield) Falbaum; m. Roberta Jessie Oberstone, Sept. 1, 1957; children: Vance Leonard, Stacy Lynn. AA, L.A. City Coll., 1961; BS with honors, Calif. State U., L.A., 1962; postgrad., George Washington U., 1966—68; MPA, Syracuse U., 1972. Lic. pvt. investigator Va., Washington, Ariz. Agt. U.S. Customs Svc., L.A. and Nogales, Ariz., 1961—66, spl. agt. Washington, 1969—73; instr. Treasury Law Enforcement Sch., Washington, 1966—69; dep. chief law enforcement U.S. Fish & Wildlife Svc., Washington, 1973—78, spl. projects officer, 1978—79; sr. criminal investigator U.S. Dept. Justice (office spl. investigations), Washington, 1979—86; v.p. The Investigative Group, Inc., Washington, 1986—92; pres. Investigative Dynamics, Inc., Tucson, 1992—. Adj. prof. Am. U., 1977—78, 1990—91; bd. dirs. Forensic Scis. Corp.; adv. bd. Found. Genetic Medicine, Inc. Chmn. troop com. Nat. Capital Area coun. Boy Scouts Am., Centreville, Va., 1974—77; bd. dirs. 88-CRIME, 1998, pres., 2002. Served with USAF, 1953—57. Recipient commendations, U.S. Customs Svc., U.S. Dept. Justice. Fellow: Am. Bd. Forensic Examiners; mem.: INTELNET (adv. bd. 1997—), Vidocq Soc., Customs Spl. Agt. Assn. (pres. 1994—), Internat. Assn. Law Enforcement Intelligence Analysts, Global Investigators Network, World Investigators Network, Calif. Assn. Licensed Investigators, Pvt. Investigators Assn. of Va., Pvt. Investigators and Security Assn., Nat. Assn. Chief of Police, Fraternal Order of Police, Fraternal Order of Border Agts., Fed. Law Enforcement Officers Assn., Ariz. Assn. Lic. Pvt. Investigators (bd. dirs. 1994—96, pres. 1997, 2000), Nat. Coun. Investigation and Security Svcs. (bd. dirs. 1998), Assn. of Former Intelligence Officers, So. Ariz. Counter Intelligence Corps Assn., Am. Criminal Justice Assn. (life; chpt. pres. 1959—61), Internat. Assn. Chiefs of Police (life), Am. Coll. Forensic Examiners (life; cert.), Internat. Narcotic Enforcement Officers Assn., Nat. Assn. Legal Investigators, World Assn. Detectives, Coun. Internat. Investigators (treas. 2002—, cert.), Nat. Dist. Attys. Assn., Am. Soc. Indsl. Security (cert. protection profl.), Assn. Cert. Fraud Examiners (cert.), Am. Law Enforcement Officers Assn., Am. Fedn. Police, Fed. Criminal Investigators Assn., Am. Judicature Soc., Assn. Fed. Investigators (bd. dirs. 1979—86, cert. profl. investigator), 88-CRIME (bd. dirs. 1998—, pres. 2002—), La Paloma Country Club (golf com. and handicap chmn. 1994—95, vice chmn. 1996—98, chmn. 1999—2000, vice chmn. 2002, bd. dirs. 2003), Chantilly Country Club (v.p. for golf 1978, 1980, 1981, 1983, bd. dirs. 1984, chmn. bd. 1985—89), Lambda Alpha Epsilon (life). Home: 4921 N Fort Verde Trl Tucson AZ 85750-5903 E-mail: bertfalbaum@compuserve.com.

FALCI, DENNIS MICHAEL, sales executive, pharmaceutical executive; b. Astoria, N.Y., May 16, 1968; s. Robert P. and Elaine A. F.; m. Caroline Mueller, Aug. 14, 1994; children: Derek Michael, Devin Walter. BS Mktg., Seton Hall U., 1990; MBA in Pharm. Mktg., Fairleigh Dickinson U., 1996. Sales mgr. Macy's, Morristown, N.J., 1990-91; area sales mgr. Aventis Pharms., 1991-99, regional account mgr., 1999—. Mem. planning bd. Hanover Twp., Whippany, N.J., 1996, 97, 98. Home: 6 Forest Way Morris Plains NJ 07950-3263 Office: Aventis Pharms 6 Forest Way Morris Plains NJ 07950-3263

FALCO, EDIE, actress; b. Northport, NY, July 5, 1963; BFA, SUNY, Purchase, NY, 1986. Appeared in films Sweet Lorraine, 1987, The Unbelievable Truth, 1990, Trust, 1990, Time Expired, 1992, Laws of Gravity, 1992, I Was on Mars, 1992, Bullets Over Broadway, 1994, Backfire!, 1995, The Addiction, 1995, Layin' Low, 1996, The Funeral, 1996, Breathing Room, 1996, Firehouse, 1997, Cost of Living, 1997, Cop Land, 1997, Trouble on the Corner, 1997, A Price Above Rubies, 1998, Hurrican Streets, 1998, Judy Berlin, 1999, Random Hearts, 1999, Overnight Sensation, 2000, Death of a Dog, 2000, Sunshine State, 2002 (Best Supporting Acress award LA Film Critics Assn. 2002, Golden Satellite award best supporting actress 2003); appeared in TV movies The Sunshine Boys, 1995, Jenifer, 2001; appeared in TV series Oz, 1997-99, The Sopranos, 1999- (Golden Globe award best actress in a drama 2000, 03, Emmy for best actress 1999, 2001, 2003, Actor of Yr., Am. Film Inst. 2001, Golden Satellite award 2002, SAG award 2003); TV guest appearances include Homicide: Life on the Street, 1993-94, 97, Law & Order, 1993-94, 97, New York Undercover, 1995; film dir. Rift, 1993; TV prodr. Stringer, 1999; theater appearances include Side Man, 2000, The Vagina Monologues, 2001, Frankie and Johnny in the Clair de Lune, 2002. Office: c/o Sandra Marsh Mgmt 9150 Wilshire Blvd Ste 220 Beverly Hills CA 90212-3429*

FALCO, MARIA JOSEPHINE, political scientist, academic administrator; b. Wildwood, N.J., July 7, 1932; d. John J. and Mafalda M. (Barbieri) F. AB, Immaculata (Pa.) Coll., 1954; student, U. Florence, Italy, 1954-55; MA, Fordham U., 1958; PhD, Bryn Mawr (Pa.) Coll., 1963; postdoctoral rsch. fellow, Yale, 1965-66; quantitative data analysis, U. Mich., 1968; mgmt. program, Carnegie-Mellon U., 1983. Instr., then asst. prof. history and polit. sci. Immaculata Coll., Pa., 1957-63; asst. prof. polit. sci. Washington Coll., Chestertown, Md., 1963-64; rsch. asst. Genevieve Blatt; candidate for U.S. Senator from Pa., 1964-65; asst. prof., then assoc. prof. polit. sci. Le Moyne Coll., Syracuse, N.Y., 1966-73, chmn. polit. sci. dept., 1967-73; prof. polit. sci. Stockton State Coll., Pomona, N.J., 1973-76; chmn. social and behavioral scis. faculty U. Tulsa, 1976-79; dean Coll. Arts and Scis., Loyola U., New Orleans, 1979-85; prof. polit. sci. Loyola U., New Orleans, 1985-86; v.p. acad. affairs DePauw U., Greencastle, Ind., 1986-88, prof. polit. sci., 1988-93, prof. emerita, 1993—. Speaker in field; adj. prof. polit. sci. Tulane U., New Orleans, 1996-97. Author: Truth and Meaning in Political Science: An Introduction to Political Inquiry, 1973, Bigotry: Ethnic, Machine and Sexual Politics in a Senatorial Election, 1980; editor: Through the Looking Glass: Epistemology and the Conduct of Political Inquiry: An Anthology, 1979, Feminism and Epistemology: Approaches to Research in Women and Politics, 1987, Feminist Interpretations of Mary Wollstonecraft, 1996; cons. editor Political Parties and the Civic Action Groups:; contbr. articles and book revs. to profl. jours. Mem. Mayor's Task Force on Future of New Orleans, 1983-85, Women's Equity Action League, 1979-81, LWV, 1960-63, 82-84; bd. dirs. Inst. for Human Rels., Loyola U., Inst. Human Understanding, New Orleans, 1985-86; pres. Syracuse chpt. New Dem. Coalition, 1970-71; mem. pres.'s coun. Loyola U., New Orleans, 1997-2000. Fulbright scholar U. Florence, Italy, 1954-55; faculty fellow in state and local politics Nat. Ctr. for Edn. in Politics, 1964. Mem. AAUP (v.p. LeMoyne chpt. 1971-72), Womens Caucus Polit. Sci. (pres. 1976, named Mentor of Distinction 1989), Am. Polit. Sci. Assn. (Benjamin Evans Lippincott award com. 1976, chmn. sect. program com. 1975, com. acad. freedom and profl. ethics, chair com. for outstanding conv. paper award women and politics rsch. sect. 1990-91), Midwestern Polit. Sci. Assn. (com. status of women), Northeastern Polit. Sci. Assn., S.W. Polit. Sci. Assn. (outstanding conv. paper com.), Founds. Polit. Theory Group, Common Cause, Great Lakes Coll. Assn. (dean's coun. 1986-88), Assn. Jesuit Colls. and Univs. (dean's coun. 1979-85), Assn. Am. Colls. (coun. for liberal learning 1985-87), Western Polit. Sci. Assn., Ind. Polit. Sci. Assn. (pres., chair 1992-93), Ind. Social Sci. Assn., So. Polit. Sci. Assn., Jefferson Parish LWV (bd. dirs. 1999—, pres. 2001-02), Jefferson Parish Bus. and Profl. Women (1st v.p. 2002-). Roman Catholic. Home: 4817 Belle Dr Metairie LA 70006-2274 E-mail: falco@loyno.edu. *Despite the fact that it's difficult being a woman in a man's world, I'm glad I'm a woman.*

FALCON, CHUCK TILTON, psychologist, writer; b. Akron, Ohio, Oct. 10, 1954; s. Jack Zack and Virgie Helen Falcon. BA, Kent State U., Kent, OH, 1976; MS, U. Fla., Gainesville, FL, 1980—85. Geriatric deaf caretaker Benjamin Schowe, Akron, Ohio, 1972—73; drug crisis staff Akron's Ho. Extending Aid on Drugs, Akron, Ohio, 1973—75; teacher's aide Weaver Sch., Akron, Ohio, 1975—76; mental health worker St. Elizabeth's Hosp., Washington, 1976—76; substitute educator Weaver Sch., Akron, Ohio, 1978—78; therapeutic program staff Sagamore Hills Children's Psychiat. Hosp. (name changed to Western Res. Psychiat. Hosp.), Northfield, Ohio, 1978—79; asst. educator psychology U. Fla., Gainesville, Fla., 1980—81; psychology practicum VA Med. Ctr., Gainesville, Fla., 1983—84; psychology practicum Corner Drugstore, Gainesville, Fla., 1984—84; pub. Sensible Psychology Press, Lafayette, La., 1985—; disabilities services coord. Deaf Action Ctr., Lafayette, La., 1990—92, sign lang. interpreter, 1990—. Adj. comm. disorders educator Delgado CC, New Orleans, 1997—; spkr. in field. Author: Happiness and Personal Problems: Psychology Made Easy, Psychology Made Easy, Family Desk Reference to Psychology. Avocations: gardening, stained glass craft, cooking, dancing, artwork. Office: Sensible Psychology Press PO Box 2687 Lafayette LA 70502 Office Fax: 337-667-7950.

FALCONE, ANTHONY, mechanical engineer; b. Pottstown, Pa., Nov. 13, 1952; s. Anthony and Rose (Savelloni) F.; m. Suzanne Marie diSilvestro, July 14, 1991; children: Mark Anthony, Ann Marie. BS in Mech. Engring., Drexel U., 1975. Registered profl. engr., Pa. Coop. engr. Goodyear Tire & Rubber Co., Inc., Akron, Ohio, 1973-74; engr. Am. Air Filter Co., Inc., Louisville, 1975-76, sales engr. King of Prussia, Pa., 1976-82; sr. facility engr. Merck & Co., Inc., West Point, Pa., 1982-94; mfr. rep. AB&G Assocs., Inc., Bala Cynwyd, Pa., 1994-96; dist. sales rep. Spirax Sarco, Inc., Allentown, Pa., 1996—. Mem. The Entrepreneurial Inst., Phila., 1991—. Advisor, Jr. Achievement, Norristown, Pa., 1984; adminstr. MATHCOUNTS, Warminster Twp., Pa., 1986—. Mem.: NSPE. Avocations: piano, music, physical fitness, collecting, outdoors activities. Home: 12 Old Dutch Rd Harleysville PA 19438-3079 Office: Spirax Sarco Inc 1150 Northpoint Blvd Blythewood SC 29016

FALCONE, PATRICIA JEANNE LALIM, investor, foundation administrator; b. Montevideo, Minn., Oct. 12; d. Clarence I. and Eva (Corneliusen) Lalim; m. Alfonso Benjamin Falcone, Oct. 22; children: Christopher Lalim Falcone, Steven Lalim Falcone. BS, U. Minn.; MS, PhD, U. Wis. Former libr. asst. U. Minn., St. Paul; former singer/performer Mpls.; former asst. prog. dir. U. Wis. Meml. Union, Madison; former instr. U. Wis., Madison; medical executive A.B. Falcone, M.D., Ph.D., Fresno, Calif.; pres. Dr. A.B. Falcone Meml. Found., U. Calif., Berkeley Coll. of Chemistry. Pvt. investor lectr. in field Patricia Lalim Falcone; contbr., presenter various confs. and seminars. Contbr. articles to profl. jours.;, author various ednl. and profl. pamphlets; former artist/craftsman (textile designs) U. Wis. Traveling exhibit. Bd. dirs. Fresno/Madera Med. Polit. Action Com., Medical Soc., 1985-89, 1990, treas. 1997-2001, Philip Lorenz Meml. Keyboard Concert, (bd. dirs. 1988—); mem. Supts. Roundtable, Fresno Unified Sch. Dist., 1989; chmn. U. Calif., Fresno com. to bring UC campus to Fresno area, 1987—; chmn. Parent Adv. Com. for Gifted and Talented, Fresno Unified Sch. Dist., 1985, mem. 1984—; citizens adv. coun. U. Calif., San Joaquin, 1991—. Fellow U. Wis.; scholar. Mem. AAUW, Med. Alliance of Fresno/Madera County Med. Soc. (exec. bd. 1989—), Assn. for Acad. Excellence (chmn. 1988-91), Edison Computech Assn., Am. Scandinavian Found., U.S. English, Kappa Omicron Nu, Pi Lambda Theta, Phi Delta Gamma, pres. Alpha Beta chpt., Pacific Legal Found., Fresno/Verona, Italy Sister City (com. mem. 2001-), St. George Greek Orthodox Church Community, Lutheran Brotherhood. Avocations: genealogy, swimming, travel, cross country skiing. Office: PO Box 14030 Pinedale CA 93650-4030 also: Riverview Tower # 1707 1920 First St South Minneapolis MN 55454-1055 Fax: 612-659-1359; Office Fax: 559-439-0549.

FALCONE, ROBERT EDWARD, surgeon; b. Sulmona, Italy, Apr. 12, 1950; s. Joseph and Sophie (Kosier) F.; 1 child, Melissa. Student, Cleve. State U., 1968-71; BA in Chemistry magna cum laude, Kent (Ohio) State U., 1973; MD cum laude, Ohio State U., 1976, postgrad., 1987-90. Mem. staff and teaching faculty Grant Med. Ctr., Columbus, Ohio, 1981—, dir. trauma svcs., 1985-98, dir. surg. ICU, med. dir. life flight, 1988-95, chmn. dept. surgery, 1989-90, med. co-dir. med flight; v.p. trauma and critical care svcs. Grant/Riverside Med. Ctr. Hosps., 1998-99, sr. v.p. trauma, 1999-2000, sr. ops. officer, 2001—, COO, 2002. Chmn. Ohio Com. on Trauma, 1994—2000; chmn. nutritional support com. Riverside Meth. Hosp., Columbus, Ohio, 1983—84; med. dir. Franklin County Paramedic Sch., Columbus, 1992—95; pres. Ctrl. Ohio Trauma Sys., 1997—2000, chmn. med. bd., 2001—; clin. assoc. prof. Ohio State U. Coll. Medicine, Columbus, 1985—2000, clin. prof. surgery, 2001—; surg. product adv. Ethican, Inc., 1984—85, Bd. Cardiosurgery, Inc., 1986—87; lectr. in contg. medicine edn. Merck Sharp & Dohne, Inc., 1986—90, Squibb & Sons, Inc., 1989—90, Roerig Divsn. Pfizer, Inc., 1994—99. Contbr. numerous articles to profl. jours. Fellow ACS, Soc. Critical Care Medicine; mem. Am. Assn. Surgery for Trauma, Pan-Am. Trauma Soc., Soc. Internat. de Chirurgie, Ea. Assn. Surgery for Trauma, Ctrl. Surg. Assn., Alpha Omega Alpha, Sigma Psi. Avocations: music, art, martial arts. Office: Grant Med Ctr 111 S Grant Ave Columbus OH 43215-4701 Fax: 614-566-8043. E-mail: rfalcone@ohiohealth.com.

FALCONE, TOMMASO, reproductive endocrinologist; b. Montreal, Que., Can., Nov. 28, 1953; came to U.S., 1995; s. Michele and Domenica Falcone. Med. degree, McGill U., Montreal, 1981. Bd. cert. in reproductive endocrinology and laparoscopic surgery. Reproductive endocrinologist McGill U., Montreal, 1984-94, Cleve. Clinic Found., 1995—. Editor: Congenital Malformations of Female Genital Tract, 1999; co-author: Atlas of Endoscopic Techniques in Gynecology, 2000. Mem. Am. Soc. Reproductive Medicine. Office: Cleve Clinic Found Dept Gyn-A-81 9500 Euclid Ave Dept Gyn-a81 Cleveland OH 44195-0001 E-mail: falcont@ccf.org.

FALCONER, ETTA ZUBER, mahtematics educator; b. Tupelo, Miss., Nov. 21, 1933; d. Walter Alexander and Zadie Montgomery Zuber; m. Dolan P. Falconer, Sept. 1, 1955 (dec. Feb. 9, 1994); children: Dolan P. II, Alice Falconer Wilson, Walter Z. BA, Fisk U., 1953; MS, U. Wis., 1954; PhD, Emory U., 1969; MS, Atlanta U., 1982; DSc (hon.), U. Wis., 1996. Instr. Okolona (Miss.) Coll., 1954—63; from asst. prof. to assoc. prof. Spelman Coll., Atlanta, 1965—71; assoc. prof. Norfolk (Va.) State Coll., 1971—72; chair dept. math. Spelman Coll., Atlanta, 1972—82, chair divsn. natural scis., 1975—91, assoc. provost for sci. programs, 1991—98, Callaway prof. math., 1982—. Author: (book chpts.) A Century of Mathematics Meetings, 1996, DIMACS, Series in Discrete Mathematics and Theoretical Computer Science, Vol. 34, 1997; contbr. articles to profl. jours. Recipient Louise Hay award, Assn. Women in Math., 1995, Giants in Sci. award, Quality Edn. for Minorities, 1995. Fellow: AAAS (Mentor award for lifetime achievement 2002); mem.: Am. Math. Soc., Nat. Assn. for Mathematicians (sec. 1970—72). Home: 3415 Spreading Oak Dr SW Atlanta GA 30311

FALCONER, MARGUERITE ELIZABETH, artist; b. Boston, July 5, 1919; d. Edward Henry and Marguerite Marie (McCarthy) Walsh; m. Charles Bowman Falconer, July 7, 1942 (dec. Apr. 1975); children: Charles Edward, Susan Jane Falconer; m. Frederick Cyrille Cuthbertson, Jan. 12, 1991 (dec. Mar. 1999). Student, Mus. Fine Arts, Boston, De Cordova Mus., Lincoln, Mass. Artist, proprietess McElwain-Falconer Gallery, Chatham, Mass., 1969—, sole propr., 1987-92, Falconer's, Chatham, 1992—. Co-founder Chatham Creative Arts Ctr. Represented in permanent collections at Cape Mus. Fine Arts. Mem. Archtl. Rev. Bd., Chatham, 1979-87; bd. dirs. Lower Cape Arts Lottery Coun.; mem. vestry St. Christopher's Episcopal Ch., Chatham, Mass. Mem. Am. Artists Profl. League, Nat. Mus. Women in Arts Archives, Women Painter's West, Copley Soc. Boston, Cape Mus. Fine Arts, Cape Cod Conservatory Music and Arts, Nat. Gallery Am. Art Smithsonian Inst. Archives, L.a. Contemporary Art Assn., Lower Cape Arts and Humanities, Copley Soc., Salmagundi Club. Episcopalian. Avocations: swimming, writing, music, travel, reading.

FALDO, NICK (NICHOLAS ALEXANDER FALDO), professional golfer; b. Hertfordshire, Eng., July 18, 1957; m. Gill Faldo; children: Natalie, Matthew, Georgia. Profl. golfer PGA, 1976—; mem. European Ryder Cup Team, 1977, 79, 81, 83, 85, 87, 89, 91, 93, 95, 97, World Cup Team, 1977, 91, 98, Dunhill Cup Team, 1985, 86, 87, 88, 91, 93, Nissan Cup Team, 1986, Kirin Cup Team, 1987, Four Tours Championship Team, 1990. Winner Brit. Open, 1987, 90, 92, Brit. Youths Amateur Championship, 1975, English Amateur Championship, 1975, Colgate PGA Championship, 1978, Brit. PGA Championship, 1978, 80, 81, Car Care Plan Internat., 1984, Spanish Open, 1987, French Open, 1988, Volvo Masters, 1988, Volvo PGA Championship, 1989, Dunhill Brit. Masters, 1989, Peugeot French Open, 1989, Suntory World Match Play, 1989, The Masters, 1989, 90, Irish Open, 1991, Carroll's Irish Open, 1992, 93, Brit. Open, 1992, Scandinavian Masters, 1992, GA European Open, 1992, Toyota World Matchplay, 1992, Johnnie Walker Classic, 1993, Doral/Ryder Open, 1995; named European Rookie of Yr., 1977; recipient MBE award, 1987; leading money winner European Tour, 1983, 92, winner Master Tourn., 1996, Nissan Open, 1997, elected World Golf Hall of Fame, 1997. Office: care IMG 1 Erieview Plz Ste 1300 Cleveland OH 44114-1715

FALENDER-ZOHN, CAROL ANN, psychologist; b. Indpls., Aug. 22, 1946; d. Allison E. and Dorothy R. Falender; m. Martin S. Zohn, June 8, 1980; children: David, Daniel. BA, Vassar Coll., 1968; MA, U. Wis., 1969, PhD, 1973. Asst. dir. tng. San Fernando Valley Child Guidance Clinic, Northridge, Calif., 1978-92; dir. rsch. & tng. St. John's Child & Family Devel. Ctr., Health Ctr., Santa Monica, Calif., 1992-2000; lectr., cons., clin. prof. dept. psychology UCLA, 2000—. Presenter in field. Mem.: APA, Calif. Psychol. Assn. (chair divsn. II edn. and tng. 1997—99, sec. divsn. 37 2002—). Avocations: biking, running. Office: 1158 26th St # 189 Santa Monica CA 90403 E-mail: cfalende@ucla.edu.

FALEOMAVAEGA, ENI FA'AUAA HUNKIN, congressman; b. Vailoatai Village, Am. Samoa, Aug. 15, 1943; m. Hinanui Bambridge Cave; children: Temanuata Tuilua'ai, Taualai, Nifae, Vaimoana, Leonne. BA in Polit. Sci. and History, Brigham Young U., 1966; JD, U. Houston, 1972; LLM, U. Calif., Berkeley, 1973. Bar: Am. Samoa, U.S. Supreme Ct. Adminstrv. asst. Am. Samoa del. to Washington, 1973-75; staff counsel to house com. on interior and insular affairs U.S. House of Reps., Washington, 1975-81; dep. atty. gen. Am. Samoa, 1981-84, lt. gov., 1984-89; territorial del. from Am. Samoa U.S. Ho. Reps., 1988; rep. U.S. Congress from Samoa, 1989—; mem. internat. rels. com., resources com. Chmn. Gov.'s Task Force for Reorgn. of the Adminstrn., Am. Samoa Adv. Fisheries Council, 1985—, Gov.'s Adv. Com. on Grants Programs, 1985—; mem. nat. lt. gov.'s mission to Egypt, Jordan and Saudi Arabia, South Pacific Leaders Orientation Mission to Paris, 1987; leader Am. Samoa's del. to South Pacific Conf., Noumea New Caledonia, 1987; keynote speaker and leader Am. Samoa's del. to Pacific Trade/Investment Conf., 1986. With U.S. Army, 1966-69, including Vietnam, USAR, 1985—. Recipient Alumni Svc. award Brigham Young U., 1979; named Chieftain Faleomavaega, leone Village. Mem. Nat. Conf. of Lt. Govs., Nat. Assn. Secs. of State, Navy League of U.S., VFW, Nat. Am. Indian Prayer Breakfast Group, Lions (charter mem. Pago Pago chpt.), Go for Broke Assn. (life; pres. Samoa chpt.). Democrat. Office: US Ho Reps 2422 Rayburn HOB Washington DC 20515

FALES, HALIBURTON, II, lawyer; b. N.Y.C., Aug. 7, 1919; s. DeCoursey and Dorothy Mildred (Mitchell) F.; m. Katharine Ladd, Dec. 27, 1941; children: Nancy, Haliburton, Priscilla, Lucy, William E. Ladd. Student, Harvard U., 1938-41; LLB, Columbia U., 1947. Bar: N.Y. 1948, U.S. Supreme Ct. 1957. Assoc. firm White & Case, N.Y.C., 1947-58, ptnr. firm, 1959-88, of counsel, 1988-90, ret. ptnr., 1991—. Spl. master Appellate div. 1st dept. N.Y. State Supreme Ct., 1983—, chmn. departmental discipline com., 1991—96, special counsel, 1997—; nat. ctr. for state courts Warren Burger Assoc., 2002. Author: Trying Cases A Life in the Law, 1997; contbr. articles to profl. jours. Trustee, pres. emeritus Pierpont Morgan Libr.; trustee St. Barnabas Hosp., 1949-96, trustee emeritus, 1996—; sr. warden St. Luke's Ch., 1967-93; bd. dirs. Union Theol. Sem., 1986-94; bd. visitors Columbia Law Sch., 1993-98, emeritus, 1998—. Lt. comdr. USNR, 1941-45. Recipient Columbia U. medal, 1994. Fellow Am. Bar Found., N.Y. Bar Found., Inst. Judicial Adminstrn., Am. Coll. Trial Lawyers; mem. ABA, Albert Gallatin Assocs., Am. Judicature Soc., Am. Law Inst. (life), Assn. of Bar of City of N.Y., N.Y. County Lawyers Assn. (William Nelson Cromwell award 1998), N.Y. State Bar Assn. (pres. 1983-84, chair task force on the prof., 1994-96), Columbia Law Sch. Assn., Inc. (pres. 1991-92), St. Paul's Sch. Alumni Assn. (v.p. 1988-92), Alumni Fedn. Columbia U. Home: 560 Pottersville Rd Gladstone NJ 07934-2046 Office: c/o White & Case 1155 Ave of Americas New York NY 10036-2711

FALES, HENRY MARSHALL, chemist; b. N.Y.C., Feb. 12, 1927; s. Henry Marshall and Cecile Marie (Vatet) F.; m. Caroline Eleanor McCullagh, Dec. 20, 1947; children: Marsha Kent Fales Mazz, Suzanne Kent Fales Palmer, Henry Richard. BSc in Chemistry, Rutgers U., 1948, PhD in Organic Chemistry, 1953. Instr. Rutgers U., New Brunswick, N.J., 1953; rsch. chemist, lab. chief Nat. Heart, Lung and Blood Inst., NIH, Bethesda, Md., 1953—2003; adj. prof. anatomy, physiology and genetics USEHS. With USN, 1944-46. Recipient Superior Svc. award U.S. Govt., 1973, 86, Profl. Svc. award Wash. Chpt. of Alpha Chi Sigma, 50 Yr. Svc. award, NIH, NHLBI. Mem. Am. Chem. Soc., Am. Soc. Mass Spectrometry (mem.-at-large, sec., v.p. programs, pres., past pres.). Avocations: fishing, stained glass. Home: 3114 Gracefield Rd Apt # 315 Silver Spring MD 20904-7854 Office: NIH NHLBI Bldg 50 Rm 3305 50 South Dr MSC 8014 Bethesda MD 20842-8014 E-mail: hmfales@helix.nih.gov.

FALETRA, ROBERT, technology company executive; Pres. Tech. Solutions Group, CMP Media, LLC, Waltham, Mass. E-mail: rfaletra@cmp.com.

FALEY, R(ICHARD) SCOTT, lawyer; b. Trenton, N.J., Aug. 18, 1947; s. Henry and Winifred (Goeke) F.; m. Josepha Ann Bartlett, Aug. 29, 1970; children: Scott Joseph, Zachary Lorin, Katherine Winifred. BA, Georgetown U., 1969, JD, 1972; LLM, George Washington U., 1975. Bar: D.C. 1973, U.S. Tax Ct. 1973, U.S. Dist. Ct. D.C. 1973, Mont. 1996. Assoc., ptnr. Danzansky, Dickey, Tydings, Quint & Gordon, Washington, 1972-78; prin. R. Scott Faley, P.C., Washington, 1978—. Bd. dir. Fed. Employees News Digest, Inc., Fairfax, Va., 1980—; bd. dir., pres. NCC Trout Unltd., 1985—; del. Mid Atlantic Coun. Trout Unltd., 1985—, v.p., 1992—; bd. dirs. Falling Springs Greenway, Inc.,

Chambersburg, Pa. Inst. for Safety Analysis, Inc., Rockville, Md., 1980-89. Contbr. articles to profl. jours. Mem. instnl. rev. com. Sibley Meml. Hosp., Washington, 1980—. Capt. USAF, 1974. Mem. ABA, FBA, Univ. Club, Boca Bay Pass Club, The Williams Club, Alpha Phi Omega, Phi Alpha Delta. Roman Catholic. Home: 25 Primrose St Chevy Chase MD 20815-4228 Office: Ste 401 5100 Wisconsin Ave NW Washington DC 20016-4119 Fax: 202-363-7355. E-mail: faleyfish@aol.com.

FALEY, ROBERT LAWRENCE, retired instruments company executive; b. Bklyn., Oct. 13, 1927; s. Eric Lawrence and Anna (Makahon) F.; m. Mary Virginia Mumme, May 12, 1950; children: Robert Wayne, Nancy Diane. BS in Chemistry cum laude, St. Mary's U., San Antonio, 1956; postgrad., U. Del., 1958-59. Chemist E.I. Dupont de Nemours & Co., Inc., Wilmington, Del., 1956-60; sales mgr. F&M Sci., Houston, 1960-62; pres. Faley Assocs., Houston, 1962-65; sales mgr. Tech. Inc., Dayton, Ohio, 1965-70; biomed. mktg. mgr. Perkin-Elmer Co., Norwalk, Conn., 1967-69; mktg. dir. Cahn Instruments, L.A., 1970-72; pres. Faley Internat., El Toro, Calif., 1972-93, Status Internat., Las Vegas, Nev., 1993-97. Internat. spkr. in field; dir. Whatman Lab. Products Inc., 1981-82, Status Instrument Corp., 1985-87; tech. mktg. cons. Whatman Ltd., Abbott Labs., OCG Tech., Inc., Pacific Biochem., Baker Commodities, Bausch & Lomb Co., Motorola Inc., Whatman Inc., Filtration Scis. Corp., PMC Industries, UVP, Inc., Ericomp, Inc., Data I/O. Contbr. articles on technique of gas chromatography to profl. jours. Mem. adv. com. on sci., tech., energy and water U.S. 48th Congl. Dist., 1985-87. With USMS, 1944-47, 1st lt. USAF, 1948-53. Named Charter mem. Aviation Hall of Fame. Fellow AAAS, Am. Inst. Chemists (life); mem. ASTM, Am. Chem. Soc. (life), Instrument Soc. Am. (life), Inst. Environ. Scis., Aircraft Owners and Pilots Assn., U.S. Power Squadrons, VFW (life), Ret. Officers Assn., Silver Wings Fraternity (life, Golden mem.), Masons, Delta Epsilon Sigma (life). Home: 27850 Espinoza Mission Viejo CA 92692-2156

FALK, BARBARA MARIE, psychologist; b. Nov. 16, 1940; PhD, U. Ill., 1972. Asst. prof. U. Ill., Champaign-Urbana, 1972-73; staff psychologist St. Louis Juvenile Ct., 1973-74, supr. psychologist, 1974-80; pvt. practice Chesterfield, Mo., 1977—. Pres. Cmty. H.S. Dist. 218 Tchrs. Assn., Blue Island, Ill., 1969. Office: St Johns Health Ctr 1585 Woodlake Dr Ste 115 Chesterfield MO 63017-5740 E-mail: barbarafalk@earthlink.net.

FALK, BERNARD HENRY, trade association executive; b. N.Y.C., Sept. 10, 1926; s. Max and Sadie (Orwin) F.; m. Iris G. Tannenbaum, June 13, 1954; children: Cindy, Amy, David. BEE, CCNY, 1950; postgrad., Columbia Sch. Bus., 1954. Field engr. RCA, 1950-52; sales engr. Gen. Precision Corp., 1953-56; exec. sec. Nat. Elec. Mfrs. Assn., 1956-65, v.p. govt. rels., 1966-71, pres., 1972-91, vice chmn., 1991-92; chmn. adv. com. elec. goods Dept. Commerce; pres. elect Internat. Electrotech. Commn., 1994-95, pres., 1995—2000. Mem. exec. adv. com. nat. power survey FPC; mem. Bus. Adv. Coun. on Fed. Reports; chmn. liaison com. White House Trade Assn.; bd. dirs. Underwriters Labs., trustee, 1992-2001; co-chmn. EC 92 com. Dept. Commerce, 1991—. Served with USNR, 1944-46. Mem. Am. Nat. Standards Inst. (dir.), Am. Soc. Assn. Execs. (v.p. 1978, dir., chmn. Key industries assn. Council 1985-86), N.Y. State Soc. Assn. Execs. (pres. 1975), U.S. C. of C. (bd. dirs.). Home: 14 Bermuda Lake Dr Palm Beach Gardens FL 33418-4583

FALK, CHARLES H. (HARRY FALK), brokerage house executive; With Czarnikow-Rionda, 1958—82; Richco Sugar, 1982—84; chmn. Coffee, Sugar & Cocoa Clearing Assn., 1983—91; with Louis Dreyfus Corp., 1984—; bd. mgrs. Coffee, Sugar & Cocoa Exch., Inc., 1989—90, vice chmn., 1990, chmn., 1991—95; vice chmn. N.Y. Bd. Trade, LI, 2000, chmn., 2000—, acting pres. & CEO, 2002—03, pres., CEO, 2003—. Office: NY Bd Trade 23-10 43rd Ave Long Island City NY 11101*

FALK, DIANE M. research director, librarian, editor, writer; b. N.Y.C. d. Leon H.E. Falk and J. Constance Moorehead (Lilienthal) Stephenson. BA in English and World Lit., Columbia U., 1973, MLS, 1979. Test bibliog. enhancement N.Y. Times Info. Svc., Inc., N.Y.C., 1980—; rsch. libr., documents analyst Atlantis Energy and Minerals, N.Y.C., 1980-81; project coord. legal dept. GAF Corp., N.Y.C., 1981-82; cataloger Exxon Edn. Found., N.Y.C., 1982; indexer, fact-checker H. W. Wilson & Co., Bronx, N.Y., 1982; bibliog. orgn. The Rockefeller Found., N.Y.C., 1983; rsch. info. specialist Harkavy Info. Svc., N.Y.C., 1983-84, Newsworld Comm., N.Y.C., 1985, features writer, 1977—78, rsch. (clippings) libr., 1985; dir. rsch., head libr., editl. rsch. specialist The World & I mag.: The Mag. for Lifelong Learners, Washington, 1986—. Copy editor, rsch. mgr. HSA-UWC, N.Y.C. and Washington, 1974-75, 86; reference asst. Lehman Libr., Columbia U., N.Y.C., 1978; rsch. libr., documents analyst UN Ctr. for Transnational Corps., 1979; coord., conf. participant Ambs. for Peace, 2001–, Svc. for Peace. Editor-in-chief FOCUS, 1979-80; contbr. articles to profl. jours. English and comms. prof., vol. United to Serve Am., Washington Saturday Coll., Howard U., Washington, 1992-94; ofcl. tour guide Washington Times Found. and Corp.; conf. coord. Internat. Acad. Arts, Literary, Bus., Legal and Polit. Groups and Issues, 1991—; instr., conf. demonstrator for internet and other knowledge mgmt. tech. rsch. resources; vol. Ambs. for Peace Seminars, 2001-03; sponsor, participant Svc. for Peace, 2002. Recipient Corp. award Washington Times Corp., 1997. Mem. ALA, Spl. Librs. Assn., D.C. Libr. Assn., Intellectual Freedom Interest Group (chairperson 1996-97, com. chair 2002-03), Rsch. and Reference Interest Group, Women's Fedn. for World Peace (sec. D.C. chpt. 1993—), Internat. Leadership Seminars (staff vol. 1991—), Internat. Fedn. for World Peace (signature campaign staff 1990-91, vol. 1990—, acting sec. 1993—), The Prosperity Coun. (editor newsletter 1991), Inst. Mus. and Libr. Svcs. Avocations: photography, arts, travel, writing. Home: 508 Columbia Rd NW Washington DC 20001-2904 Office: The World & I: The Mag for Lifelong Learners Libr and Rsch Dept 3600 New York Ave NE Washington DC 20002-1947 E-mail: dmfalk@worldandimag.com., research@worldandimag.com., library@worldandimag.com.

FALK, EDGAR ALAN, public relations consulting executive, writer; b. Bklyn., Nov. 4, 1932; s. Ralph P. and Lillian (Freud) F. AB, NYU, 1954, postgrad., 1957-59. Pub. rels. asst. Western Electric Co., N.Y.C., 1957-59; dir. pub. rels. Ritter, Sanford, Price & Chalek, N.Y.C., 1959-60; account supr. pub. rels. Batten, Barton, Durstine & Osborn, N.Y.C., 1960-67; group dir. pub. rels. N.W. Ayer & Son, N.Y.C., 1967-73; v.p., dir. pub. rels. div. Cunningham & Walsh, Inc., N.Y.C., 1973-79; dir. communications NBA, 1979-81; pres. Ed Falk Communications, N.Y.C., 1981—. Spkr. nat. convs. retailing orgns. Author: 1,001 Ideas To Create Retail Excitement, 1994; rev.edit. 2003, contbg. editor, writer for several retail publs. Mem. Kings County Rep. County Com., 1958-61. 1st lt. U.S. Army, 1954-56; lt. col. Res. ret. Recipient Freedoms Found. award, 1971 Mem. Pub. Rels. Soc. Am. (recipient Silver Anvil award 1970, 71, 73), The Author's Guild, Res. Officers Assn., Retired Officers Assn. Home: 301 E 78th St New York NY 10021-1322 Office: Ed Falk Communications 509 Madison Ave Ste 1400 New York NY 10022-5501

FALK, HEINRICH RICHARD, theater and humanities educator; b. Frankfurt, Germany, May 3, 1939; came to U.S., 1947; s. Heinrich Wilhelm Karl and Janet Elizabeth (Prentice) F.; m. Joyce Duncan, Aug. 14, 1965. BA, Wittenberg U., 1960; PhD, U. So. Calif., 1970. Instr. mgmt. tng. div. Union Bank, L.A., 1963-64; lectr. U. So. Calif., L.A., 1964-67; instr. Chapman Coll., Orange, Calif., 1966-67; prof. Calif. State U., Northridge, 1967—. Resident dir. Calif. State U., Madrid, 1986-87; vis. prof. Shanghai Theatre Acad., China, 1993, coord. Internat. Programs, 2000-2002. Editor: Theatre Jour. (book review sect.), 1981-83. Spl. cons. and project writer, Fine Arts and Humanities Framework com., State of Calif., 1967-72. Recipient post-doctoral scholar U. Calif., 1970-72; Younger Humanist fellow, Nat. Endowment Humanities, Madrid, Barcelona, 1972-73, Del Amo Found., Madrid, 1977-78, Asian Cultural Coun., China, 1993, Aston Magna Acad. Nat. Endowment for the Humanities, 1995; grantee Nat. Endowment for the Humanities, 1982. Mem. Internat. Soc. for Eighteenth-Century Studies, Internat. Fed.for Theatre Rsch., Am. Soc. for Theatre Rsch., Am. Soc. Eighteenth-Century Studies, Instituto Feijoo de Estudios del Siglo XVIII, Sociedad Espanola de Estudios del Siglo XVIII. Home: 2726 Cuesta Rd Santa Barbara CA 93105-3708 Office: Calif State U Dept Theatre Northridge CA 91330-8320 E-mail: heinrich.falk@csun.edu.

FALK, JAMES NATHAN, not-for-profit organization administrator, consultant; s. Leo J and Eugenia (Etheridge) Falk; m. Terrell E. Held, June 2, 1979; children: Todd Nathan, Ashleigh Elizabeth. BA, Wash. and Lee U., Lexington, Va., 1977; MA, U. of Va., Charlottesville, 1982. Dir. of edn. Mid. East Inst., Washington, 1978—80; dep. dir. Egypt Today, Washington, 1980—81; v.p. First City Nat. Bank of Houston, Houston, 1982—92; regional dir. Inst. Internat. Edn., Houston, 1992—99; v.p. - devel. Nat. Ctr. for Policy Analysis, Dallas, 1999—2001; pres. World Affairs Coun. Greater Dallas, Tex., 2001- . Adv. dir. U. of North Tex./Internat. Affairs Com., Denton, Tex., 2001; mem. Houston Com. on Fgn. Rels., Houston, 1982—99, Dallas Com. on Fgn. Rels., Dallas, 1999; mem., internat. rels. adv. commn. City of Plano, Plano, Tex., 2002; bd. dirs. Nat. Coun. for Internat. Visitors, Washington, 1994—99, World Affairs Couns. of Am., Washington, 2002, The Tower Club, Dallas, 2002, Dallas Internat. Sch., Dallas, 2001. Mem.: Assn. of Profl. Fundraisers (cert. 2001). Avocations: tennis, running, dog training, travel. Office: World Affairs Coun Greater Dallas 325 N St Paul Street #550 Dallas TX 75201

FALK, JOAN FRANCES, public relations executive; b. Flushing, N.Y., Jan. 15, 1936; d. Leo Carl Hjalmar and Frances Louise (Masin) F. Cert., Parsons Sch. Design, N.Y.C., 1955; BS, NYU, 1956, MBA, 1958. Assoc. editor Fairchild's Fin. Manual, N.Y.C., 1956-58; editor, costs mgr. Western Printing & Lithographing, N.Y.C., 1958-61; dir. rsch. and costs Grolier, Inc., N.Y.C., 1961-64; budget supr. Ted Bates & Co., N.Y.C., 1965-82; bus. mgr. N.W. Ayer Pub. Rels. (Div. of N.W. Ayer, Inc.), N.Y.C., 1982-95, Diamond Info. Ctr. (Div. of N.W. Ayer, Inc.), N.Y.C., 1992-95, Diamond Info. Ctr. (disvn. of J. Walter Thompson, Inc.), N.Y.C., 1995-99; bus. cons. Contbr. photographs to Grolier Internat., 1964, Encyclopedia Brittanica, 1970. Active Broadway Flushing Homeowners; vol. fundraiser pub. broadcast TV, WNET, N.Y.C., WLIW, L.I. Mem. Daus. of Nile (Queen of al Kahbay Temple # 22 1970, supreme temple officer 1980; mem. Pyremus Temple 1994), Order Ea. Star (matron of Pleiades #206 1962, dist. dep. grand matron 1987, mem. advance #588, Grand Historian of N.Y. 2003), Orgn. Triangles (past queen of Rising Star #69), Nat. Leadership Coun. (Capital award 1991), Bayside H.S. Alumni Assn. (past rec. sec.). Republican. Lutheran. Avocations: photography, gardening. Home: 164-16 32nd Ave Flushing NY 11358-1418 E-mail: jffklaf@yahoo.com.

FALK, JULIA S. linguist, educator; b. Englewood, N.J., Sept. 21, 1941; d. Charles Joseph and Stella Sableski; m. Thomas Heinrich, Jan. 20, 1967; 1 child, Tatiana Prentice. BS, Georgetown U., 1963; MA, U. Wash., 1964, PhD, 1968. Instr. linguistics Mich. State U., East Lansing, 1966-68, asst. prof., 1968-71, assoc. prof., 1971-78, prof., 1978-2001, asst. dean Coll. of Arts and Letters, 1979-81, assoc. dean Coll. Arts and Letters, 1981-86, prof. emerita, 2001—. Vis. scholar U. Calif., San Diego, 2000—; cons. on lang. and law, lang. and gender, bias-free communication. Author: Linguistics and Language, 1973, 2d revised edit., 1978, Women, Language and Linguistics, 1999; contbr. articles on history of linguistics to profl. jours. Fellow Woodrow Wilson Found., 1963, NDEA Title IV, 1963-66, NSF, 1965; recipient Paul Varg Alumni award for Teaching, 1993, Faculty Profl. Women's Assn. Outstanding U. Woman Faculty award, 1999. Mem.: N.Am. Assn. History of Lang. Scis. (pres. 2000), Linguistic Soc. Am. Home: 8939 Caminito Verano La Jolla CA 92037-1606

FALK, LLOYD LEOPOLD, water pollution control consultant; b. Ocean Grove, N.J., Nov. 6, 1919; s. Leroy and Della (Blum) F.; m. Eleanor Ruth McCoy, Sept. 9, 1945; children: David Lawrence, Laurie Ann, Gary Lee. BS in Chemistry, Rutgers U., 1941, PhD in Sanitation, 1949. Rsch. assoc. Rutgers U., New Brunswick, N.J., 1945-49; cns. E.I. duPont de Nemours & Co., Wilmington, Del., 1949-76, prin. cons., 1977-81; cons. Wilmington, Del., 1982—. Scientific and tech. adv. com., Del. Estuary Program, 1990-96; sea grant adv. coun. U. Del., 1995-97. Contbr. articles to profl. jours. Water resources adv. com. Water Resources Agy. for New Castle County, Del., 1974-91. 1st lt. USAF, 1943-45, ETO. Fellow Delmarva Ornithol. Soc. (pres. 1969-71); mem. Am. Chem. Soc. (life), Water Environment Fedn. (life), Am. Birding Assn., Md. Ornithol. Soc., Am. Recorder Soc., Phi Beta Kappa, Phi Lambda Upsilon, Sigma Xi. Home: 123 Bette Rd Wilmington DE 19803-3430

FALK, MARSHALL ALLEN, retired university dean, physician; b. Chgo., May 23, 1929; s. Ben and Frances (Kamins) F.; m. Marilyn Joyce Levoff, June 15, 1952; children: Gayle Debra, Ben Scott. BS, Bradley U., 1950; MS, U. Ill., 1952; MD, Chgo. Med. Sch., 1956. Diplomate Am. Bd. Psychiatry. Intern Cook County Hosp., Chgo., 1956-57; resident Mt. Sinai Hosp., Chgo., 1964-67; gen. practice medicine Chgo., 1959-64; resident in psychiatry, faculty dept. psychiatry Chgo. Med. Sch., 1964-67, prof., acting chmn. dept. psychiatry, 1973-74, dean, 1974-92, v.p. med. affairs, 1981-82, exec. v.p., 1982-91, dean emeritus, emeritus prof. psychiatry, 1991—. Med. dir. London Meml. Hosp., 1971-74; mem. cons. com. to commr. health City of Chgo., 1972-82; mem. Ill. Gov.'s Commn. to Revise Mental Health Code, 1973-77, Chgo. Northside Commn. on Health Planning, 1970-74, Ill. Hosp. Licensing Bd., 1981-91. Contbr. articles to profl. jours. Trustee John F. Kennedy Hosp., Antlantis, Fla., 1993-95, cons., 1991-92; trustee Quantum Found. for Health, Palm Beach, Fla., 1995—; vice chmn. grants com. Quantum Found., 1997—; trustee Finch U./Chgo. Med. Sch., 1998—, chmn. bd. trustees, 1998—. Capt. AUS, 1957-59. Recipient Bd. Trustees award for rsch. Chgo. Med. Sch., 1963, Disting. Alumni award Chgo. Med. Sch., 1976, Alumnus of Yr. award Bradley U., 1990. Fellow Am. Psychiat. Assn., Am. Coll. Psychiatrists; mem. Ill. Coun. Deans (pres. 1981-83), Coun. Free Standing Med. Sch. Deans (bd. dirs. 1984-92, pres. 1989-91), Sigma Xi, Alpha Omega Alpha. E-mail: maf/mjf@aol.com. *Consistent effort, with an attempt to make decisions based on situations as they occur— with as little prejudgment as possible.*

FALK, MARVIN WILLIAM, historian, bibliographer; b. Wichita, Kans., Jan. 29, 1943; s. Melvin Leroy and Martha Louise (Crew) F.; m. Helen Amanda Widman, June 7, 1969 (div. May 1985); children: Karl, Adelia, Stuart; m. Sylvie Denise Savage, June 21, 1998. BA, U. Minn., 1965; MA, U. Mass., 1966; PhD, U. Iowa, 1976. Arctic bibliographer U. Alaska, Fairbanks, 1975-81, curator rare books, 1981—. Author: Alaska, 1995, (series) Rasmuson Translation Series, 13 vols., 1985—; compiler: Alaskan Maps, 1983. Pres. Fairbanks Sch. Bd., 1985-86. Mem. Alaska Hist. Soc. (pres. 1978-80). Avocation: photography. Home: 865 Gold Pan Rd Fairbanks AK 99712-2041 Office: U Alaska Fairbanks PO Box 756808 Fairbanks AK 99775-6808 E-mail: ffmwf@uaf.edu.

FALK, PETER HASTINGS, publishing company executive, author, art dealer; b. New Haven, Oct. 27, 1950; s. Wilbur Nelson and Patricia (Hastings) F.; m. Laurie Rosenfield, 2001; children from previous marriage: Kristen, Kerrin, Kendall. AB, Brown U., 1973; BFA, R.I. Sch. Design, 1975. Pres. Falk Art Mgmt., LLC, Madison, Conn., 1977—. Editor Artnet, N.Y.C., 1995—96, Artprice.com, France, 2000—03. Author: The Photographic Art Market, 1981, Who Was Who in American Art, 1985, Dictionary of Signatures and Monograms of American Artists: Colonial Period to Mid 20th Century, 1988, The Annual Exhibition Record of the National Academy of Design: 1901-1950, 1989, The Annual Exhibition Record of the Art Institute of Chicago: 1888-1950, 1991, The Biennial Exhibition Record of the Corcoran Gallery: 1907-1967, 1991, Art Price Index International, others; author exhbn. monographs. Mem. Art Librs. Soc. (Wittenborn award 1985), Brown Rowing Assn. (steward). Avocations: tennis, rowing, skiing. Office: Sound View Press PO Box 833 Madison CT 06443-2165

FALK, ROBERT HARDY, lawyer; b. Houston, Dec. 27, 1948; s. Arnold Charles and Sara Holmes (Pierce) Falk; m. Donna Kay Watts, Aug. 18, 1973 (div. Apr. 27, 1980); children: Dorian Danielle, Dillon Holmes; m. Patricia K. Stampley, Nov. 5, 1994. BS summa cum laude, U. Tex., 1971; BA cum laude, Austin Coll., 1972; JD, U. Tex., 1975. Bar: Tex. 1975, D.C. 1977, U.S. Dist. Ct. (so. dist. Tex.) 1975, U.S. Patent Office, U.S. Ct. Appeals (5th cir.) 1976, Ct. Customs and Patent Appeals 1976, N.C. 1979, U.S. Dist. Ct. (we. dist. N.C.) 1982, U.S. Dist Ct. (no. dist. Tex.) 1984, U.S. Ct. Appeals (fed. cir.) 1982, U.S. Ct. Appeals (5th cir.) 1983, U.S. Ct. Internat. Trade 1985, U.S. Dist. Ct. (no. dist.) Tex. 1987. Process engr. Exxon Co., USA, Baytown, Tex., 1971-72; atty. Pravel, Wilson & Gambrell, Houston, 1975-77; patent and trademark counsel Organon Inc. div. Akzona, Inc., Asheville, N.C., 1977-84; ptnr. Hubbard, Thurman, Tucker & Harris, Dallas, 1984-91; dir. Geary, Glast & Middleton, P.C., Dallas, 1992; mng. ptnr. Falk, Vestal & Fish, LLP, Dallas, 1992—2003, Falk & Fish, LLP, Dallas, 2003—; pres. Robert Hardy Falk, P.C., 1983—. Pres. Haw Creek Vol. Fire Dept., Asheville, 1980-84; deacon Cen. Christian Ch., Dallas, 1985-89. Recipient Bar Register of Preeminent Lawyers 2003 for Intellectual Property Law and Patent Lawyers, Am. Intellectual Property Law Assn., 2003; fellow, U. Tex., 1972. Mem. ABA, ATLA, Am. Patent Law Assn., Am. Intellectual Property Law Assn., Tex. Bar Assn., NC Bar Assn., DC Bar Assn., Dallas Bar Assn., Dallas Patent Law Assn., Licensing Execs., Univ. Club (Dallas), Gleneagles Country Club (Plano), Plaza of the Ams. Club (Dallas). Republican. Avocations: golf, fishing. Mailing: PO Box 794748 Dallas TX 75379 E-mail: falk@patent.net., robertfalk@sbcglobal.net.

FALK, STANLEY LAWRENCE, historian, consultant; b. N.Y.C., Mar. 11, 1927; s. Nathan Isaac and Katherine (Sagal) Falk; m. Evelyn Rhea Lightman, Mar. 25, 1956; children: Lisa, Karen. BA, Columbia U., 1945; postgrad., U. Mich., 1945; MA, Georgetown U., 1952, PhD, 1959. Historian U.S. Army, Washington, 1949—54, Am. U., Washington, 1954—56, Joint Chiefs of Staff, Washington, 1956—59; sr. historian Chief Mil. History U.S. Army, Washington, 1959—62; prof. nat. security affairs, prof. internat. rels. Indsl. Coll. Armed Forces, Washington, 1962—74; chief historian USAF, Washington, 1974—80; dep. chief historian SE Asia U.S. Army, Washington, 1980—82; ret., 1982. Hist. cons., Alexandria, Va., 1983—; lectr. Nat. Def. U., Smithsonian Instn., Air War Coll., Army War Coll., Nat. Inst. Def. Studies, Tokyo, China Armed Forces U., Taipei, Georgetown U., Washington, Howard U., Fairfax County Libr. Sys. Author: Bataan: The March of Death, 1962; author: (textbook) The International Arena, 1964; author: Decision at Leyte, 1966; author: (textbook) Human Resources for National Strength, 1966, The National Security Structure, 1967, The Environment of National Security, 1967, The Environment of National Security, rev. edit., 1973, Defense Military Manpower, 1969; editor: The World in Ferment, 1970, The World in Ferment, 2d edit., 1974; author: Liberation of the Philippines, 1971, Bloodiest Victory: Palaus, 1974, Seventy Days to Singapore, 1975; author: (with Harry Yoshpe) Organization for National Security, 1963; editor (with Warren Tsuneishi): MIS in the War Against Japan, 1995; contbr. With U.S. Army, 1945—48, col. USAR, 1948—77. Recipient Disting. Svc. award, Indsl. Coll. of Armed Forces, 1962—74, Outstanding Performance award, Dept. Air Force, 1975—76, Meritorious Svc. medal, Dept. of Army, 1977, Ofcl. Commendation, 1980, 1981, Civilian Svc. award, 1982. Mem.: Assn. U.S. Army, Nat. Assn. Ret. Fed. Employees, Soc. for History in Fed. Govt., Orgn. Am. Historians, Am. Hist. Assn., Soc. Historians of Am. Fgn. Rels., Soc. Mil. History, WWII Studies Assn., Phi Alpha Theta. Home: 2310 Kimbro St Alexandria VA 22307-1822

FALK, STEVEN B. newspaper publishing executive; Worked for Gannett Newspapers, 1983—87; various positions San Francisco (Calif.) Newspaper Agy., 1987—98, pres., CEO, 1998—2000; pres., COO San Francisco (Calif.) Chronicle, 2000—, assoc. pub., 2000—03, pub., 2003—. Office: San Francisco Chronicle 901 Mission St San Francisco CA 94103-2905*

FALK, THOMAS J. paper company executive; Chmn., CEO Kimberly-Clark Corp., Irving, Tex., 2002—, also bd. dirs. Office: Kimberly-Clark Corp 351 Phelps Dr Irving TX 75038-6507*

FALK, WILLIAM JAMES, lawyer; b. Kew Gardens, N.Y., Aug. 15, 1952; s. Sam and Bertha (Schwartzwald) F.; m. Laurie Jean Dombrowski, June 24, 1973; children: Douglas Charles, Andrew Stephen, Edward Allaire. BS, Ill. Inst. Tech., 1973, JD cum laude, Suffolk U., 1977; LLM in Taxation, Washington U., St. Louis, 1982. Bar: Mass. 1977, Mo. 1981. Trial atty. IRS Office of Dist. Counsel, St. Louis, 1977—81; assoc. Thompson & Mitchell, St. Louis, 1982—83, ptnr., 1984—96, Thompson Coburn LLP, St. Louis, 1996—99; mem. Lewis, Rice & Fingersh, L.C., St. Louis, 1999—. Contbg. author: Missouri Taxation Law and Practice, 1987, 96; contbr. articles to legal jours. Mem. ABA, Mo. Bar Assn., Bar Assn. Met. St. Louis (chmn. taxation sect. 1992-93, mem. exec. com. 1992-93). Avocations: camping, music. Office: Lewis Rice & Fingersh LC 500 N Broadway Ste 2000 Saint Louis MO 63102-2147

FALKENSTEIN, KARIN EDITH, elementary school principal; b. Michigan City, Ind., Feb. 12, 1950; d. Martin Victor and Helen Marion (Hedberg) Sandstrom; m. Chrles William Falkenstein Jr., July 13, 1985; 1 stepchild, Amanda Ann. BA in Elem. Edn., Spl. Edn., Mich. State U., 1972, MA in Reading Instrn., 1975. Spl. edn. tchr. Hesperia (Mich.) Pub. Schs., 1972-73, Buchanan (Mich.) Community Schs., 1973-79, elem. prin. Moccasin Sch., sch. farm coord., 1979-80; elem. prin. Ottawa Sch., Buchanan (Mich.) Community Schs., 1980—; dist. spl. edn. supr., 1980—; gifted and talented coord. Ottawa Sch., Buchanan (Mich.) Community Schs., 1980—, elem. coord., k-12 testing coord. and k-5 curriculum dir., 1993—. Instr. Ind. U., South Bend, 1981—; presenter spl. edn. workshops. Active Big Bros./Big Sisters of Berrien & Cass Inc., 1982—97, 1999—2003, v.p., 1985, 2002, pres., 1988, big sister, 2000—; active Buchanan Fine Arts Coun., 1987—, treas., 1988—93, sec., 1996—99, pres., 1999—; active Redbud Area Ministries LOVE, Inc., 1985—89, pres., 1988—89; active Hospice Bereavement Care, 1987—, PTA, 1988—; pres. Coll. Edn. Alumni Assn. Bd., 1988—89; Sun. sch. tchr. First United Meth. Ch., 1982—, trustee, 1986—91, Christian Edn. chairperson, 1988—90; bd. dirs. Berrien Coun. for Children, 1987—91, mem. edn. com., 1984—91; bd. dirs. Four Flags Samaritan Ctr., 1985—, Mich. Gateway Cmty. Found., Buchanan, 1997—. Recipient Nat. Disting. Prin.'s award, 1989, Mich. Legis. recognition, 1989, Pres.'s award Mich. State U. Coll. Edn. Alumni Assn., 1987, Mich. State U. Nat. Alumni Assn. Svc. award 1995, Golden Nugget award for spl. edn., 1983, Milken Found. Family Educator award, 1993; named Mich. Outstanding Practicing Prin., 1988, Region 5 Prin. award, 1989. Mem. Mich. Elem. and Mid. Sch. Prins. Assn. (membership chair 1984-86, profl. devel. chair 1983-84, pres. 1987-88), ASCD, CEC, Tri-County Coun. of Women in Ednl. Adminstrn. (profl. devel. chair 1983-84, pres. 1985-87, historian 1987-92), Spl. Edn. Dirs. and Coords. for Berrien County, Internat. Reading Assn., Mich. Reading Assn., Mich. State U. Alumni Assn. (nat. bd. v.p. 1992-93, treas. 1991-92, pres. 1993-94, Svc. award 1995), Phi Delta Kappa. Office: Buchanan Community Schs 109 Ottawa St Buchanan MI 49107-1136 E-mail: kfalkens@remc11.k12.mi.us.

FALKENSTEIN, RALPH JAY, ophthalmologist; b. N.Y.C., June 1, 1943; s. Henry and Hedy (Reinemann) F.; m. Jean Ellen Rosenberg, June 4, 1965; children: Andrew, Eric, Kendra. BA, Columbia U., 1965; MD, Yale U., 1969. Pvt. practice, Danbury, Conn., 1974—, Danbury Eye Physicians and Surgeons, Danbury, 1990—. Mem. Am. Acad. Ophthalmology. Office: Danbury Eye Physicians and Surgeons 69 Sand Pit Rd Ste 101 Danbury CT 06810-4005 Fax: (203) 778-6238.

FALKIE, THOMAS VICTOR, mining engineer, mining executive; b. Mount Carmel, Pa., Sept. 5, 1934; s. Victor J. and Aldona H. Falkie; m. Jean C. Broscius, Nov. 27, 1957 (dec. Apr. 2001); children: Ann, Thomas, Lawrence, Michael, Christine. BS in Mining Engring., Pa. State U., 1956, MS in Mining Engring., 1958, PhD in Mining Engring., 1961. Fellow, research asst. Pa. State U., University Park, 1956-61, prof., head mineral engring. dept., 1969-73; various staff and managerial positions Internat. Minerals and Chem. Corp., Skokie, Ill., 1961-69, Bartow, Fla., 1961-69; dir. U.S. Bur. Mines Dept. of Interior, Washington, 1974-77; chmn. Berwind Natural Resources Corp., Phila., 1977, bd. dirs. Adj. prof. indsl. engring. U. Fla./U. So. Fla., 1966; cons. UN, 1971—73; nat. arbitrator joint industry health and safety com. United Mine Workers and Bituminous Coal Operators Assn., 1973; chmn. coal task force project ind. study U.S. Govt., 1974; chmn. interagy. task force Fed. Coun. Sci. and Tech., 1975—76; mem. bd. mineral and energy resources NRC, 1982—88; mem. adv. com. mining and mineral resources rsch. Dept. of Interior, 1988—94. Contbr. articles to profl. jours. Recipient Disting. Alumnus award, Pa. State U. Mineral Engring. Dept., 1995. Mem.: AIME (hon.), Am. Coal Found. (chmn. 1993—), Mining and Metall. Soc. Am., Nat. Acad. Engring. (councillor 1994—2000), Nat. Mining Assn. (bd. dirs. 1979—2002, exec. dir. 2002—), Pa. Coal Assn. (bd. dirs. 1980—90), Soc. Mining Engrs. of AIME (bd. dirs. 1971—75, v.p. 1977—79, chmn. Phila. sect. 1980—81, bd. dirs. 1984—87, pres. 1988, disting. mem., Erskine Ramsay medal 1991, Disting. Svc. award 2001), Union League Club (Phila.), Tau Beta Pi, Sigma Gamma Epsilon. Republican. Roman Catholic. Home: 347 Echo Valley Ln Newtown Square PA 19073-1619 Office: Berwind Natural Resources Corp 3000 Centre Sq W 1500 Market St Philadelphia PA 19102-2100

FALKINGHAM, DONALD HERBERT, oil company executive; b. Lexington, Ill., Dec. 13, 1918; s. William Bishop and Violet (Ashabran) F.; m. Mary Margaret Chalmers, Aug. 23, 1947 (dec. Nov. 1993); children: Deanna Beth Falkingham Worst, Janis Kay Falkingham Fenwick; m. Joella Hall, May 23, 1998. BS, Mo. Sch. Mines, 1941; Profl. Engr., U. Mo., Rolla, 1973. Registered profl. engr., land surveyor, Wyo. Field engr. Amoco, Rangely, Colo., 1951-53; dist. engr. Amoco Producing Co., Cody, Wyo., 1953-59, div. engr. Casper, Wyo.,

1959-61, dist. supt. New Orleans, 1961-68; pres. Amoco UK Exploration Co., London, 1968-70, Amoco Iran Oil Co., Tehran, 1970-71; co-chmn. bd. dirs. Pan Am. Iran Oil Co., Teheran, 1970-71; gen. mgr. producing dept. Amoco Internat. Oil Co., Chgo., 1972-77; pres. Amoco Drilling Svcs., Chgo., 1975-77, Ocean-wide Constrn. Co., St. Helier, Isle of Jersey, 1977-78; chmn. bd. World Maritime, Bermuda, 1977-78; ptnr., co-owner Falcar Energy Co., Houston, 1978—; mng. dir. hydrocarbon devel. McDermott Inc., Bucharest, Romania, 1994-95; mng. dir. EuroMAC, Sofia, Bulgaria, 1994-95. Dist. chmn. Am. Petroleum Inst., 1961; com. mem. Am Bur. Shipping, Bldg. and Classing Offshore Drilling Units, N.Y.C., 1966-68; chmn. exploration and production forum, Oil Industry Internat., London, 1974-77. Pres. bd. trustees, Presbyterian Ch., Cody. Pilot U.S. Army, 1942-45, ETO, maj. ret. Decorated D.F.C., Air medal with oak leaf cluster. Mem. Soc. Petroleum Engrs. (dist. chmn. 1967), Petroleum Club (pres. Casper chpt.), Cody Country Club (pres.), Masons, Shriners. Republican. Avocation: travel. Home (Summer): 11515 Barnett Valley Rd Sebastopol CA 95472-9554 Office: Falcar Energy Co PO Box 1323 Montgomery TX 77356-1323 Home (Winter): Sun Island Dr Pres 307 Saint Petersburg FL 33707 E-mail: donfalky@aol.com.

FALKNER, FRANK TARDREW, physician, educator; b. Hale, Eng., Oct. 27, 1918; arrived in U.S., 1956, naturalized, 1963; s. Ernest and Ethel (Letten) Falkner; m. June Dixon, Jan. 1948; 2 children. MD, Cambridge U., 1945. Diplomate Am. Bd. Clin. Nutrition. Intern London Hosp., 1945; resident Guys Hosp., London, 1947—48, Children's Hosp., Cin., 1948—50; practice medicine specializing in pediat. England, 1948—56, 1948—56, Louisville, 1956—70, Yellow Springs, Ohio, 1971—79; chmn. dept. pediat. U. Louisville, 1963—70; dir. Fels Rsch. Inst., Yellow Springs, 1971—79; Fels prof. pediat., prof. obstetrics and gynecology U. Cin. Coll. Medicine, 1979—79; prof. child and family health U. Mich., 1979—81; prof. and chmn. maternal and child health U. Calif., Berkeley, 1981—89, prof. pediat. San Francisco, 1981—89, prof. emeritus Berkeley, 1989—. Editor-in-chief International Child Health, syndicated columnist on children's and young people's health; contbr. articles to profl. jours. Recipient Fellowship to Am. Meml. Hosp. created in his name, 2000. Fellow: Royal Coll. Pediat. and Child Health, Am. Acad. Pediat.; mem.: French Pediatric Soc., Inst. Medicine NAS (sr.), Am. Pediatric Soc. Home: 145 Forest Ln Berkeley CA 94708-1519 Office: U Calif Sch Pub Health Maternal And Child Health Berkeley CA 94720-0001 E-mail: ffalknermd@aol.com.*

FALKNER, JAMES GEORGE, SR., foundation executive; b. Spokane, Wash., Dec. 24, 1952; s. Albert Andrew and Amanda Rosalia (Reisinger) F.; m. Joleen Rae Ann Brown, June 22, 1974; children: James Jr., Jayson, Jerin, Jarret. BS in Acctg., U. Wash., 1975. CPA, Wash. CPA LeMaster & Daniels, Spokane, 1975-80; treas. Dominican Sisters Spokane, 1980-95; pres. Dominican Outreach Found., Spokane, 1995—. Bd. dirs. Providence Svcs. Ea. Wash., chmn. fin. com., exec. com., 2002—; mem. bishop's fin. coun. Diocese of Spokane, 1990-96; mem. investment adv. com. Gonzaga Prep. H.S., 1995-99, Sinsinawa Dominican Sisters, 1995—; mem. investment adv. com. Spokane Cath. Investment Trust, 1997—, chmn. investment com.; bd. dirs. Transitions, treas. exec. com., 2003—. Bd. dirs. sch. bd. St. Mary's Ch., Veradale, Wash., 1986-89, 90, sch. found., 1987-2000; mem. acctg. dept. adv. com. Spokane Falls C.C., 1989—. Mem.: Nat. Notary Assn., Wash. State Soc. CPAs (Spokane Wash. bd. dirs., pres. 1998—2002, strategic planning com. 2001—03), AICPA, Healthcare Fin. Mgmt. Assn. (bd. dirs. 1982—85). Avocations: coaching baseball, golf, soccer, carpentry. Office: Dominican Outreach Found 3102 W Fort George Wright Dr Spokane WA 99224-5203

FALKNER, WILLIAM CARROLL, lawyer; b. Baird, Tex., Mar. 26, 1954; s. Vernon Lee and Eunice Vera (Fore) F.; m. Linda May (Tilley), May 23, 1987; children: Heather Lynn, Holly Ann. BA in Govt., Tarleton State U., Stephenville, Tex., 1976; JD, Stetson U., Gulfport, Fla., 1984. Bar: Fla. 1984, U.S. Dist. Ct. (mid. dist.) Fla. 1985, U.S. Ct. Appeals (11th cir.) 1985. Asst. co. atty., sr. asst. co. atty. Pinellas County Atty.'s Office, Clearwater, Fla., 1985—. Editor Res Ipsa, Clearwater, Fla., 1992-93; contbr. articles to profl. jours. Col. U.S. Army Res., 1976—. Mem. ABA, Fla. Bar Assoc., Clearwater Bar Assoc. Baptist. Avocations: reading, writing, sports, biblical studies. Office: Pinellas County Atty's Office 315 Court St Clearwater FL 33756-5165 E-mail: bfalkner@co.pinellas.fl.us.

FALKOF, MELVIN MILTON, retired food products company executive; b. Boston, June 2, 1919; s. Philip and Esther (Lavine) F.; m. Lucille Beatrice Weintraub, Feb. 6, 1944; children: Ellen Beth Feinberg, Bonnie Dee Blodgett, Moshe Richard, Bradley Benjamin. BS, MIT, 1939; MS, U. Minn., 1941. V.p. Darling Distbg. Corp., N.Y.C., 1946-58; mgr. mdse. Cortland Furniture Mfg. Co., Inc., N.Y.C., 1958-59; dir. Topco Assocs., Inc., Skokie, Ill., 1959-85; vol. exec. Internat. Exec. Svc. Corps, Stamford, Conn., 1987, 88, 95, dir. regional Cairo, Egypt, 1989, 90; counselor Svc. Corps Ret. Execs., Chgo., 1990—. Chmn. Svc. Corps Ret. Execs., Chgo., 1993-95. Maj. U.S. Army, 1941-46. Mem. MIT Alumni Assn., Boston Latin Sch. Alumni Assn., Phi Lambda Upsilon, Gamma Alpha. Jewish. Avocations: tennis, travel. Home: 2500 Indigo Lane 333 Glenview IL 60025-8306 Office: Svc Corps Retired Execs 500 W Madison St Chicago IL 60661-2511 E-mail: meluf@earthlink.net.

FALKOWSKI, EDWARD J. executive consultant, business coach; b. Manchester, Conn. s. John E. and Carmella M. Falkowski; m. Brenda L. Falkowski, July 2, 1943; children: B. June Ashway, Richard S., Lance E. BS in Chem. Engring., Worcester Poly. Inst., 1965; MBA, We. New Eng. U., 1968. Various positions E.I. duPont, Wilmington, Del., 1966—79; regional dir. DuPont Japan Ltd., Tokyo, 1979—85; bus. dir. E.I. duPont, Wilmington, 1985—95; v.p., gen. mgr. Ceco Environ., Conshohocken, Pa., 1996—99; pres. Brenlan Assoc. Inc., Mt. Pleasant, SC, 1999; bd. dir. Touch of Glass, 2000—01; ad. bd. Media Services, Mr. Pleasant, SC, 2000—01. Com. mem., Nat. Recycling Coalition, Washington, 1993-95; mem. Environ. Export Coun., Washington, 1996-99; com. chmn., Am. Polyester Film Mfrs., 1994-95. Mem. Nat. Assn. Bus. Coaches (dir. adv. bd. 2000-01), Charleston Metro C. of C. Avocation: golf. Office: Brenlan Assocs Inc Suite C-171 1150 Hungry Neck Blvd Mount Pleasant SC 29466 E-mail: brenlan@onebox.com.

FALKOWSKI, THERESA GAE, chemistry educator; b. El Paso, Tex., Mar. 19, 1958; d. Chester Doan and Patricia Ann Harman; m. Henry Steven Falkowski, May 16, 1981. AA, Potomac State Coll., 1978; BA, W.Va. U., 1980. Lab. asst. Potomac State Coll., Keyser, W.Va., 1977-78, gen. chem. prep rm. mgr., 1986—, chem. lab. instr., 1995-99; chem. lab. tchg. asst. W.Va. U., Morgantown, 1981-83, chem. lab. tech., 1981-85, adj. instr. chemistry, 1999—. Cons. USS N.C. Battleship Meml., Wilmington, 1981—; mem. haz-mat response team Potomac State Coll., 1993—. Author: Clark Hall of Chemistry: A Pictorial History, 1996, Laboratory Manual for Chemistry 112, 1996; illustrator: Laboratory Manual for Chemistry 115/116, 1991. Mem. Am. Chem. Soc., W.Va. Acad. Sci., Carnegie Mus. Natural History and Sci. Ctr., The Nat. Maritime Ctr., The N.C. Aquarium Soc., The Mote Marine Lab. Avocations: model building, world war ii history, aircraft identification, science fiction. Office: Potomac State Coll Fort Ave Keyser WV 26726

FALKSON, CARLA ISADORA, medical oncologist; b. Pretoria, South Africa, Apr. 6, 1959; d. Geoffrey and Hendrika Cornelia (Van Dyk) F.; m. Ben Bothma, Feb. 20, 1990; children: Sarah, Alexandra. MB, ChB, U. Pretoria, South Africa, 1982, MMed, 1989, MD, 1994. Registered specialist physician, subsplty. med. oncology, med. practitioner; cert. European Soc. Med. Oncology. Intern 1 Mil. Hosp., Pretoria, 1982-83; med. officer, lectr. dept. cancer chemotherapy U. Pretoria, 1983-84, registrar, lectr. dept. internal medicine, 1984-86, 87-89; specialist, sr. lectr. dept. med. oncology Pretoria Acad. Hosp., U. Pretoria, 1989-91; clin. fellow med. oncology U. Tex. Sys. Cancer Ctr., M.D. Anderson Hosp. & Tumor Inst., Houston, 1986-87; prin. specialist, sr. lectr. dept. med. oncology U. Pretoria, 1992-94, assoc. prof., prin. specialist, sr. lectr., 1994-98, prof., head dept. med. oncology, 1998-2001; prof. medicine divsn. hematology and oncology U. Ala., Birmingham, 2001—. Med. dir. breast health ctr. U. Ala., 2001—, Comprehensive Cancer Ctr, chair breast cancer working group; chmn. metastatic malignant melanoma study Eastern Coop. Oncology Group, 1990-94, co-chmn., 1999, mem. melanoma-sarcoma disease oriented com. and subcom., 1990—, mem. toxicity monitoring com., 1994, task force for cost effectiveness analysis, 1994, mem. outcomes com., 1994—, mem. gynecology-oncology com., 1995-98, prin. investigator, 1995-2001; chmn. ECOG Audit com., 1998-99; clin. expert European Med. Cmty, 1994; cons. in the field. Contbr. articles to profl. jours., chpts. to books. Co-chair Study for Advanced Esophagus Cancer. Avon scholar U. Ala., 2001. Mem. Am. Soc. Clin. Oncology, European Soc. Med. Oncology, South African Soc. Med. Oncology, South African Lymphoma Study Group, U. Tex. M.D. Anderson Assocs., Gastrointestinal Malignancies Com., Breast Cancer Com., ECOG Publication Com., Med. Rsch. Coun. So. Africa Ehtics Com., U. Pretoria Rsch. Protocol and Ethics Com., Am. Assn. Cancer Rsch., Third World Orgn. Women in Sci., European Orgn. Rsch. and Treatment of Cancer, Australian/New Zealand Lymphoma Study Group, ECOG Publcations Com. Avocations: literature, music, art, computers, gardening. Office: WTI 275 1530 3rd Ave South Birmingham AL 35296-3300 E-mail: carla.falkson@ccc.uab.edu., cfalkson@uab.edu.

FALL, ATLEY See BALL, WILLIAM LEE

FALL, DOROTHY ELEANOR, librarian; b. Havre de Grace, Md., Feb. 4, 1945; d. James Huey Jr. and Blanche Cecelia (JOhnson) Fall. BA, Lake Erie Coll., 1967; MEd, Westfield State Coll., 1976; EdD, Nova U., 1995. Cert. tchr. Mass, Va. Tchr. Big Spring (Tex.) Sch. System, 1968; substitute tchr. Dept. Defense Schs., Clark AFB, Philippines, 1969-70; tchr. Fayetteville (N.C.) Sch. System, 1971-72, Granby (Mass.) Pub. Schs., 1973-78; eligibility tech. State of Conn., Danbury, 1980-85; libr. Loudoun Country Day Sch., Leesburg, Va., 1990—. Ednl. liaison Granby Pub. Schs., Granby Pub. Libr., 1973-78; libr. trustee Loudoun County Libr. System, 1990-94; lectr. Shenandoah U., Winchester, Va., 1994—; adj. prof. edn. Mary Baldwin Coll. Contbr. articles to newspapers and jours. Vol. ARC, Ala, Ohio, Philippines, 1960-69, United Way, Conn., Va., 1984-86, Am. Cancer Soc., Va., 1988; pres. P.E.O. sisterhood, 1988-90; bd. dirs. Vol. Svcs., Loudoun County, 2002—; mem. Cmty. of Caring. Named Hidden Heroine Girl Scouts Am., 1976. Mem. ALA, ASCD, Va. Libr. Assn., Va. Edn. Media Assn., P.E.O. Presbyterian. Avocations: herb gardening, catering, decorating, calligraphy, sewing. Office: Loudoun Country Day Sch 237 Fairview St NW Leesburg VA 20176-2009

FALL, GORDON FREDERICK FRANCIS, family physician; b. Seattle, Nov. 12, 1937; s. James Davis and Freda Phyllis (Hardwick) F.; m. Sylvia Carole Burnham, Mar. 20, 1971; chlidren: Andrea Christine, Laurie Kathleen, James Gordon. BS, U. Wash., 1959, MD, 1963. Diplomate Am. Bd. Family Practice. Resident in family practice U. Kans., Kansas City, 1963-65, pvt. practice Hickman Mills (Mo.) Clinic, 1966, Olympic Med. Ctr., Seattle, 1966—. Maj. U.S. Army N.G., 1964-71. Mem. Am. Acad. Family Practice, Wash. State/King County Acad. Family Practice, Wash. State Med. Assn., King County Med. Soc., Christian Med. Soc. (pres. local chpt. 1969-72), Phi Beta Kappa. Republican. Presbyterian. Avocation: tennis. Home: 1922 NW Blue Ridge Dr Seattle WA 98177-5426 Office: Olympic Med Ctr 7715 24th Ave NW Seattle WA 98117-4412 E-mail: gfall@hotmail.com.

FALL, JOHN ROBERT, management and information technology consultant; b. Rockford, Ill., Sept. 21, 1943; s. Robert Duane and Ruth (Hart) F.; m. Maria Pilar McClintock, Sept. 22, 1990; children: Brian Alexander, Amado Magtoto, Roehl Magtoto. BA, San Diego State U., 1965. Systems engr. IBM, San Diego, 1965-70; v.p. Computer Intelligence Corp., San Diego, 1970-71; dir. corp. devel. Userware Internat., Escondido, Calif., 1972-73; pres. Fall Cons Internat., Inc., L.A., 1974—. Author: Living With a Fast Idiot, 1980. Office: 3016 Waverly Dr # 104 Los Angeles CA 90039- also: 101-A Landmark Villa I Kaimito St Valle Verde II Metro Manila Philippines E-mail: jrfall@fallconsulting.com.

FALL, MARIJANE EATON, counselor educator; b. Sanford, Maine, Oct. 4, 1940; d. Harold Vincent and Estella Anne (Prescott) Eaton; m. David William Fall (div. 1985); children: David Gregory, Gretchen, Amy. BA, Nasson Coll., 1963; MS, U. So. Maine, 1986; EdD, U. Maine, 1991. Lic. profl. counselor, Maine; lic. mental health counselor, Iowa; nat. cert. counselor. Counselor Wiscasset and Damariscotta (Maine) Pub. Schs., 1986—89; pvt. practice Westport Island, Maine, 1987—92, Iowa City, 1993—95, Gorham, Maine, 1995—; lectr. II counseling U. So. Maine, Gorham, 1991—92, assoc. prof., 1995—2002, prof., 2002—; asst. prof. U. Iowa, Iowa City, 1992—95. Mem. adj. faculty U. Maine, Orono, 1990; cons. Big Bros. and Big. Sisters, Damarcocotta, Maine, 1989-92, Iowa Test of Basic Skills, Iowa City, 1993—; supr. play therapists, Maine, then Iowa, 1992—. Mem. editl. bd. Sch. Counselor, 1993—; contbr. articles to profl. publs., chpts. to books. Troop leader, cons. Girl Scouts U.S., Sanford, Maine, 1978-84; pres. bd. dirs. Sanford Young Men's Christian Assn., 1981—, hon. life mem., 1983. George Nasson scholar Nasson Coll., Springvale, Maine, 1963. Mem. ACA (cert.), North Cen. Assn. Counselor Edn. Suprs., Play Therapy Assn., N. Atlantic Regoin Assn. Counselor Edn. (pres. 1999-2000), Assn. Counselor Edn. (exec. bd. 1999-2000), Maine Assn. Play Therapy (founder 1999, bd. dirs. 1999—). Mem. Soc. Of Friends. Avocations: walking, writing, reading, friends. Office: U So Maine 400 Bailey Hall Gorham ME 04038 E-mail: mjfall@usm.maine.edu.

FALLAT, MARY ELIZABETH, pediatric surgeon; b. Auburn, N.Y., May 1, 1953; d. George and Elizabeth (Sluty) F.; m. Ch. Thomas Walker, Jr., Dec. 16, 1989; children: Krista Penland Walker, Alexander Michael Walker, Andrew Colin Walker. BA, Northwestern U., 1975; MD, SUNY, Syracuse, 1979. Attending surgeon Kosair Children's Hosp., Louisville, 1987—, dir. trauma svcs., 1988—; asst. prof. surgery U. Louisville, 1987-93, assoc. prof. surgery, 1993—2001, prof. surgery, 2001—; mem. active staff U. Louisville Hosp. (formerly Humana Hosp.-U. Louisville), 1988—. Mem. prof. cons. staff Frazier Rehab. Ctr., Louisville, 1990—; bd. dirs. Ky. Organ Donor Affiliates, Louisville, 1989—; chmn. trauma com. Kosair Children's Hosp., 1988—. Contbr. articles to profl. jours. Crusade for Children grantee WHAS-TV, Louisville, 1989, Alliant Cmty. Trust Fund grantee Alliant Health Sys., Louisville, 1990-93, 96, Emergency Svcs. Children Fed. Grantee, 1992, 96, 99, 2000; trauma/EMS Sys. grantee Dept. Health and Human Svcs., Maternal Child Health Bur., 2000, 01; named Outstanding Vol. Prof., Kosair Children's Hosp. and U. Louisville, 1990. Fellow ACS, Am. Acad. Pediats.; mem. AMA, Soc. U. Surgeons, Am. Trauma Soc., Assn. Acad. Surgery,Am. Assn. Surgery Trauma, Ea. Assn. Surgery Trauma, Brit. Assn. Pediat. Surgeons, Am. Pediat. Surg. Assn., Southeastern Surg. Congress, So. Med. Assn., Ky. Med. Assn., North Am. Soc. Pediat. and Adolescent Gynecology, Am. Soc. Andrology. Roman Catholic. Office: 233 E Gray St Ste 708 Louisville KY 40202

FALLDING, HAROLD JOSEPH, sociology educator; b. Cessnock, New South Wales, Australia, May 3, 1923; s. Frederick and Alice Bessie (Chopping) F.; m. Margaret Hurlstone Hardy, Dec. 18, 1954; children: Marion, Ruth, Helen. Cert. Libr. Sch., Pub. Libr. New South Wales, 1941; BSc, U. Sydney, Australia, 1950, BA, 1951, diploma of edn., 1952, MA with honors, 1955; PhD, Australian Nat. U., 1957. Tchr. h.s. English and history New South Wales Dept. Edn., 1952-53; sr. rsch. fellow in sociology, dept. agrl. econs. U. Sydney, 1956-58; sr. lectr. sociology U. New South Wales, 1959-62; vis. assoc. prof. Grad. Sch., Rutgers U., N.J., 1963-65; prof. U. Waterloo, Ont., Can., 1965-88, disting. prof. emeritus, 1989—. Author: The Sociological Task, 1968, The Sociology of Religion: An Explanation of the Unity and Diversity in Religion, 1974, Drinking, Community and Civilization. The Account of a New Jersey Interview Study, 1974, The Social Process Revisited, 1990; poems Word of the Tangling Fire, 1969, Collected Poetry, 1997. Mem. Clare Hall, U. Cambridge. Fellow Royal Soc. Can.; mem. Am. Sociol. Assn., Can. Inst. Internat. Affairs, Can. Soc. Sociology and Anthropology, Internat. Soeiol. Assn., Soc. Sci. Study of Religion, Assn. Sociology of Religion, Social Sci. Fedn. Can. (dir.) Mem. United Ch. Can. Home: 40 Arbordale Walk Guelph ON Canada N1G 4X7 Office: Sociology Dept U Waterloo Waterloo ON Canada N2L 3G1 *My life has seemed like a series of arrivals at the same crossroads, compelling me to confirm a decision on priorities made very early, that loyalty to truth comes before achievement. Any achievements have consequently seemed surprises—like spin-offs from giving effect to that loyalty.*

FALLEK, ANDREW MICHAEL, lawyer; b. Bklyn., Aug. 15, 1956; m. Elaine Friedman, June 4, 1984. BA, U. Pa., 1978; JD, Vanderbilt U., 1981. Bar: N.Y. 1982, U.S. Dist. Ct. (so. and ea. dists.) N.Y. 1985, U.S. Ct. Appeals (2d cir.) 1991, U.S. Ct. Appeals (D.C. cir.) 1993. Assoc. Belson, Connolly & Belson, N.Y.C., 1981-84; pvt. practice Bklyn., 1984—. Dir. Bklyn. Bar Found. Editor in-chief Bklyn. Barrister. Mem. N.Y. State Bar Assn., Bklyn. Bar Assn. (judiciary com., continuing legal edn. com., trustee), Def. Rsch. Inst. Office: One Whitehall St 16th Flr New York NY 10004

FALLER, DONALD E. marketing and operations executive; b. Jersey City, Mar. 1, 1927; s. Louis John and Gertrude Louise (Hupfield) F.; m. Dolores Adeline Smith, Aug. 28, 1948; children: Mark William, Kyle Lindsay Fernandez, Kimberly Willard, Donald Mark, Krystn Judith, Kelly Bridget Christina Weir. BS, Mich. State U., 1948. Prodn. mgr. Sealtest Foods Kraft, Detroit, 1958-60, dist. mgr., 1960-67, div. mktg. mgr. Cleve., 1967-70; v.p. mktg. Citrus Cen. Inc., Orlando, Fla., 1970-78, exec. v.p. mktg. and adminstrn., 1978-83, chief exec. officer, 1980-83; gen. sales mgr. Sunkist Growers Inc., Ontario, Calif., 1984-88, dir. sales, fin. and ops., 1988-90; pres., CEO Trinity Mktg. Cons., Longwood, Fla., 1990—. Bd. dirs. Combank Apopka Freedom Savs. & Loan Assn., Winter Park, Fla., Calif.-Ariz. Citrus League. Bd. dirs. Pace Sch., Alamonte Springs, Fla., 1976-82. Mem. Nat. Juice Products Assn. (pres.), Blue Key, Alpha Zeta (pres. 1947-48) Clubs: Sweetwater Country (Longwood, Fla.). Republican. Office: Trinity Mktg Cons 732 Riverbend Blvd Longwood FL 32779-2349

FALLER, DOROTHY ANDERSON, international agency administrator; b. Chgo., July 6, 1939; d. Albert T. and Lillian G. (Chalbeck) Anderson. Student, Ill. Wesleyan U., 1956-59; AB, U. Ill., 1959-60; MSSA, Case Western Res. U., 1975. lic. social worker; m. Adolph Faller, Sept. 5, 1959; children: Carl, Kurt. Child welfare worker Klamath County Pub. Welfare Commn., Klamath Falls, Oreg., 1960-67; social svc. cons. Ind. State Dept. Pub. Welfare, 1968-72; adminstrv. asst. Berea (Ohio) Children's Home, Berea, 1974; rsch. asst. Case Western Res. U., Sch. Applied Social Scis., 1975, Mandel Sch. Applied Social Scis.; social svcs. supr. Ohio Dept. Pub. Welfare, Cleve., 1975-81; exec. dir. Cleve. Internat. Program, 1981-99, 1981-99; sec. gen., CEO Coun. Internat. Programs USA, 1999—2002; pres. Faller Internat. Tng., 2002—. Cons. to Cleve. Found., Am. Sickle Cell Anemia Found., John A. Yankey & Assocs.; field instr. Case Western Res. U., 1976-77, lectr., 1981; dir. African Internship Project Substance Abuse Prevention, 1992-95; dir. Ghana Conf., 1995, Cmty. Criminal Justice Adminstrn. grant, Romania, 1999-2001; reestablishing Sch. of Social Work, Addis Abba U., Ethiopia, 2002--; instr. conflict resolution and fundraising, Addis Ababa; mem. adv. coun. Mandel Ctr. Non-Profit Orgns., 1995-96, Case Western Res. U. Editor, contbr. Ohio Children's Budget Project: A Public Policy Study, 1975. Bd. dirs. West Shore Unitarian Ch., 1978-81, 2000-03, Volgograd Free Speech Forum, 1995-2001. Hon. by Fulbright Assn., 1999. Mem. Acad. Cert. Social Workers (cert.), Nat. Assn. Social Workers (unit chair state bd., exec. com. nat. bd. dirs. 1985-88, chmn. Internat. Activities Com. of Nat. Bd. 1986-89, program com. 1989-91, del. Internat. Fedn. Social Workers, Sweden, 1988, Cleve. unit Social Worker of Yr. 1986, del. from Ohio to del. assembly 1990, conf. chair ann. mtg. profession 1993), Nat. Fulbright Assn. (life), Case Western Res. U. Sch. Applied Social Scis. Alumni Assn., Sigma Kappa (pres. 1959), Alpha Lambda Delta (pres. 1956). Home: 6889 Columbia Rd Olmsted Falls OH 44138-1523 Office: 1700 E 13th St Ste 4ME Cleveland OH 44114-3213 E-mail: dorothyfaller@cs.com.

FALLER, JASON, physician; b. Rochester, Pa., Jan. 21, 1953; m. Karen; children: Avery, Morley, Ellery. BA, U. Pa., 1973, MD, 1977. Sr. attending physician St. Luke's Roosevelt Hosp., N.Y.C., 1982—, chief, Arthritis Clinic, 1990—. Fellow ACP, Am. Coll. Rheumatology.

FALLER, RHODA, lawyer; b. N.Y.C., Dec. 21, 1946; d. Benjamin and Marion (Mediasky) Sragg; m. Stanley Grossberg, Apr. 12, 1973 (div. Oct. 1983); children: Joseph Seth, Daniel Benjamin; m. Bernard Martin Faller, May 31, 1987. BS, SUNY, Stony Brook, 1967; MS, Pace U., 1973; JD, N.Y. Law Sch., 1978. Bar: N.Y. 1979, N.J. 1979, U.S. Dist. Ct. N.J. 1979, Fla. 1980, U.S. Dist. Ct. (ea. and so. dists.) N.Y. 1982, Ky. 1996, U.S. Dist. Ct. (ea. dist.) Ky. 1997. Assoc. Fuchsberg & Fuchsberg, N.Y.C., 1982-91, DeBlasio & Alton, P.C., N.Y.C., 1991-95, Rhoda Grossberg Faller, Esq., Teaneck, 1995-96, Becker Law Office, Louisville, Ky., 1997-2000; pvt. practice Louisville, 2000—. Mem.: Women Lawyers Assn., Louisville Bar Assn., Fla. Bar Assn., N.Y. State Bar Assn., Ky. Bar Assn., Ky. Acad. Trial Attys., Nat. Assn. Women Bus. Owners, Assn. Trial Lawyers Am., Million Dollar Advocates Forum. Democrat. Jewish. Home: 213 Mockingbird Gardens Dr Louisville KY 40207-5718 Office: Law Office of Rhoda Faller PLLC 455 S 4th St Ste 310 Louisville KY 40202

FALLER, SUSAN GROGAN, lawyer; b. Cin., Mar. 1, 1950; d. William M. and Jane (Eagen) Grogan; m. Kenneth R. Faller, June 8, 1973; children: Susan Elisabeth, Maura Christine, Julie Kathleen. BA, U. Cin., 1972; JD, U. Mich., 1975. Bar: Ohio 1975, Ky. 1989, U.S. Dist. Ct. (so. dist.) Ohio 1975, U.S. Ct. Claims 1982, U.S. Ct. Appeals (6th cir.) 1982, U.S. Supreme Ct. 1982, U.S. Tax Ct. 1984, U.S. Dist. Ct. (ea. dist.) Ky., 1991. Assoc. Frost & Jacobs, Cin., 1975-82; ptnr. Frost & Jacobs LLP, Cin., 1982-2000; mem. Frost Brown Todd LLC, Cin., 2000—. Assoc. editor Mich. Law Rev., 1974-75; contbg. author: MLRC 50-State Survey of Media Libel and Privacy Law, 1982-93, MLRC 50-State Survey of Media Libel Law, 1999-, MLRC State Survey of Employment Libel and Privacy Law, 1999-. Bd. dirs. Summit Alumni Coun., Cin., 1983-85; trustee Newman Found., Cin., 1980-86, Cath. Social Svc., Cin., 1984-93, nominating com., 1985-88, sec., 1990; mem. Class XVII Leadership Cin., 1993-94; mem. exec. com., def. counsel sect. Media Law Resource Ctr., 1998-2002, chmn. membership com., 2003; pres., def. counsel sect. Libel Def. Resource Ctr., 2001; mem. parish coun. St. Monica-St. George Ch., 1996-2000. Recipient Career Women of Achievement award YWCA, 1990. Mem. ABA (co-editor newsletter media litig. 1993-97), FBA, Ky. Bar Assn., No. Ky. Bar Assn., No. Ky. Women's Bar Assn., Ohio Bar Assn. (chair media law com.), Cin. Bar Assn. (com. mem.), Potter Stewart Inn of Ct., U. Cin. Alumni Assn., Arts & Scis. Alumni Assn. (bd. govs. U. Cin. Coll. 1988-2000), U. Mich. Alumni Assn., Mortar Bd., Leland Yacht Club, Coll. Club, Clifton Meadows Club, Phi Beta Kappa, Theta Phi Alpha. Roman Catholic. Home: 5 Belsaw Pl Cincinnati OH 45220-1104 Office: Frost Brown Todd LLC 2200 PNC Ctr 201 E 5th St Cincinnati OH 45202-4182

FALLER, THOMPSON MASON, philosophy educator; b. Louisville, Apr. 26, 1938; s. Louis Joseph and Katherine Thompson Faller; m. Madeleine O'Brien, Aug. 22, 1969; 1 child, Thompson Mason II. BA, St. Mary's Coll., 1962; MA, Xavier U., 1964; PhD, U. Salzburg, Austria, 1969. From instr. to prof. U. Portland, Oreg., 1964—. Instnl. rev. bd. mem. Providence Health Sys., Portland, 1990—; vis. prof./animal rsch. rev. com. mem. Oreg. Health Scis. U., Portland, 1991—. Authro: Axiology: F. Brentano, 1983; contbr. chpts. to books. Chair com. for scholars Reagan/Bush Election Com., Washington, 1984, 88; pres. Portland-Sapporo Sister City Assn., 1997-99, bd. dir. 1987—; com. mem. Portland Sister City Coun., 1998—; v.p. Cascade Coun. Boy Scouts, Portland, 2000—; bd. dir. Nat. Cath. Ednl. Assn., 1994-. Recipient Pilgrim shell, Patriach of Jerusalem, Jerusalem, 1996, named Danforth Assoc., Danforth Found., St. Louis, 1976, J.F. Kennedy Man of Yr., KC, Portland, 1993, Fulbright fellow, Washington, 1968—69, Silver Beaver, Boy Scouts Am., 2003. Mem. AAUP, Nat. Assn. Bds. Edn. (chair exec. com. 1991-2001, exec. com. 1991—), Nat. Cath. Edn. Assn. (bd. dirs. 1994—), Nat. Assn. Fgn. Student Affairs, Internat. Ho. of Japan, Knights of Malta (knight), Knights of the Holy Sepulchre (knight), Delta Epsilon Sigma. Roman Catholic. Avocations: raquetball, classical music, football, traveling. Home: 4684 NW Brassie Pl Portland OR 97229-0901 Office: Univ Portland 5000 N Willamette Blvd Portland OR 97203-5798 E-mail: faller@up.edu.

FALLET, GEORGE, civil engineer; b. Berlin, Pa., May 18, 1920; s. John and Anna (Hrobak) F.; m. Sybil Lorene DeLoach, Apr. 30, 1949; children: George Michael, Carol Ann, Mary Jane. BCE, Poly. Inst. Bklyn., 1957, MSCE, 1963. Registered profl. engr., N.H., N.Y.; registered land surveyor, N.Y. Asst. engr. Balt. & Ohio R.R., S.I. Rapid Transit Rwy., Staten Island, N.Y., 1946-53; structural designer H.K. Ferguson Co., N.Y.C., 1953-58; civil engr. U.S. Corps Engrs., N.Y.C., 1958-60; structural engr. U.S. Naval Facilities Command, N.Y.C., 1960-68, Fed. GSA, N.Y.C., 1968-85; dep. dir. bldg. dept. City of Nashua, N.H., 1986-89; cons. engr. Nashua, 1989—. Mem. subcom. U.S. Com. on Seismic Safety, Washington, 1978-85. Active Community Planning Bd., Staten Island, 1975-81. Recognized for Outstanding Citizenship Borough of Staten Island, 1980. Fellow ASCE (Robert Ridgway award 1957), NSPE (GSA Nat. Engr. of the Yr. 1981), Soc. Am. Mil. Engrs., Chi Epsilon, Tau Beta Pi. Republican. Home: 32 Watersedge Dr Nashua NH 03063-1120 Office: PO Box 3233 Nashua NH 03061-3233 E-mail: gfallet@aol.com.

FALLETTA, JO ANN, musician; b. N.Y.C., Feb. 27, 1954; d. John Edward and Mary Lucy (Racioppo) F.; m. Robert Alemany, Aug. 24, 1986. BA in Music, Mannes Coll. Music, N.Y.C., 1976; MA in Music, Juilliard Sch., N.Y.C., 1983;

PhD in Musical Arts, 1989; doctorate (hon.), Marian Coll., Wis., 1988, Old Dominion U., 1996, Canisius Coll., 2000. Music dir. Queens Philharmonic, N.Y.C., 1978-91, Den. Chamber Orch., Colo., 1983-92; assoc. condr. Milw. Symphony, Wis., 1985-88; music dir. Women's Philharmonic, San Francisco, 1986-96; music dir., condr. Long Beach Symphony, Calif., 1989-00; music dir. Va. Symphony, Norfolk, 1991—, Buffalo Philharm., 1999—. Stokowski Conducting Competition, Toscanini Conducting award. Office: ICM Artists LTD 40 W 57th St Fl 16 New York NY 10019-4098

FALLETTA, JOHN MATTHEW, pediatrician, educator; b. Arma, Kans., Sept. 3, 1940; s. Matthew John and Norma (Luke) F.; m. Carolyn Ontjes, June 22, 1963; children: Elizabeth, Matthew. AB, U. Kans., 1962, MD, 1966. Diplomate Am. Bd. Pediat., Am. Bd. Hematology-Oncology. Intern in mixed medicine Kans. U. Med. Ctr., Kansas City, 1966-67; surgeon Epidemic Intelligence Svc., Tex. Children's Hosp. USPHS, Houston, 1967-69; asst. instr. pediat. Baylor Coll. Medicine, Houston, 1967-69, resident, 1969-71, chief resident Tex. Children's Hosp., 1971, postdoctoral fellow hematology-oncology, 1971-73, asst. prof. pediat., 1973-76; assoc. prof. Duke U., Durham, N.C., 1976-83, prof., 1984—, chief divsn. hematology-oncology, 1976-94, dir. Clin. Pediat. Lab., 1976-95. Chmn. transfusion com. Duke U. Med. Ctr., 1978—, mem. exec. com. med. staff, 1978—, instl. rev. bd. human rsch., 1979—, chmn., 1994—; mem. instl. rev. bd. human rsch. Baylor Coll. Medicine, 1974-76; mem. acad. coun. Duke U., 1982 86, 87-96, 98-2000, exec. com., 1988, faculty compensation com., 1988—, faculty com. on univ. governance, 1988, trustee-faculty com. to rev. pres., 1989, search com. for pres., 1992; cons. pediat. hematologist-oncologist Charlotte (N.C.) Meml. Hosp., 1978-, mem. Copernicus Independent Review Bd., 2002-; mem. med. adv. bd. Children's Cancer Rsch. Fund, 2001-. Contbr. more than 120 articles to Nature, Am. Jour. Ophthalmology, Pediat., New England Jour. Medicine, Clin. Pediat. Oncology, others. Cons. pediat. hematologist-oncologist Project Hope, Pediatric Inst., Krakow, Poland, 1979—; prin. investigator Pediat. Oncology Group, 1981-95, chmn. epidemiology com., mem. prin. investigator's exec. com., new agts. and pharmacology com.; chmn. prophylactic penicillin study I Nat. Heart, Lung and Blood Inst., NIH, 1982-86, chmn. study II, 1987-95; active Cancer Ctr. Support Rev. Com. Nat. Cancer Inst. NIH, 1986-90, NIH Reviewers Res., 1990—, Cancer Clin. Investigation Rev. Com., 1991-96, chmn., 1995-96; trustee Ronald McDonald House Charities, 1986—; mem. med. adv. bd. Children's Cancer Rsch. Fund, 2001—. Mem. Am. Assn. Cancer Rsch., Am. Acad. Pediat., Am. Pediat. Soc., Am. Soc. Clin. Oncology, So. Soc. Pediat. Rsch. (pres. 1981-82), Soc. Pediat. Rsch., N.C. Pediat. Soc., N.C. Med. Soc., Phi Beta Kappa, Alpha Omega Alpha, Children's Rsch. Fund, Nat. Med. Advisory Bd. Office: Duke U Med Ctr PO Box 2991 Durham NC 27710-2991

FALLIN, MARY COPELAND, lieutenant governor; b. Warrensburg, Mo., Dec. 9, 1954; d. Jospeh Newton and Mary (Duggan) Copeland; children: Christina, Price. BS, Okla. State U., 1977. Bus. mgr. Okla. Dept. Securities, Oklahoma City, 1979-81; state travel coord. Okla. Dept. of Tourism, Oklahoma City, 1981-82; sales rep. Associated Petroleum, Oklahoma City, 1982-83; mktg. dir. Brian Head (Utah) Hotel & Ski Resort, 1983-84; dir. sales Residence Inn Hotel, Oklahoma City, 1984-87; dist. mgr. Lexington Hotel Suites, Oklahoma City, 1988-90; real estate assoc. Pippin Properties, Inc., Oklahoma City, 1990-94; state rep. Okla. Ho. of Reps., Oklahoma City, 1990-94; lt. gov. State of Okla., Oklahoma City, 1995—. Chmn. Nat. Conf. Lt. Govs. Mem., del. Okla. Fedn. Rep. Women; mem. Am. Legis. Exch. Coun., Nat. Conf. State Legislatures. Named Nat. Legislator of the Yr., Okla. Ladies in the News, Guardian of Small Bus. award; named Woman of Yr. Ladies in Comm., 1998, Girl Scouts Am., 1998, Bi-liner award, 1997. Republican. Presbyterian. Office: State Capitol Rm 211 Office of Lt Governor Oklahoma City OK 73105*

FALLIS, ALBERT MURRAY, microbiology educator; b. Minto Twp., Ont., Can., Jan. 2, 1907; s. William Robert and Martha Melissa (Millen) F.; m. Ada Ruth Bostock, Sept. 21, 1938; children— Alexander Graham, Hugh Murray, Bruce William BA, U. Toronto, Ont., 1932, PhD, 1937. Research fellow Ont. Research Found., Toronto, 1932-47, dir. parasitology, 1947-66; prof. parasitology U. Toronto, 1952-75, head dept., 1952-72, prof. emeritus, 1975—, assoc. dean Sch. Grad. Studies, 1967-71, mem. governing council, 1972-73. Cons. Ont. Rsch. Found., Toronto, 1966-68, WHO, Geneva, 1966, 71; vis. prof. Meml. U. Nfld., 1975-76. Author: Parasites, People and Progress, Historical Recollections, 1993; contbr. articles to profl. jours. Erskine fellow Canterbury U., N.Z., 1975 Fellow Royal Soc. Can.; mem. Am. Soc. Parasitologists (v.p., pres. 1979, emeritus), Can. Soc. Zoologists (hon. mem.), Am. Soc. Tropical Medicine and Hygiene (emeritus), Can. Assn. Adv. Vet. Parasitology (hon. mem.), Wildlife Disease Assn. (emeritus mem.), Royal Can. Inst. (pres. 1955-56, hon. editor 1951-52), Soc. Protozoologists (hon., emeritus), Masons. Avocations: woodworking; photography; gardening; historical research. Home: # 149 43 Aylmer Ave Ottawa ON Canada K1S 4R5

FALLON, FRANCIS E(DWARD), lawyer, corporation executive; b. N.Y.C., Jan. 19, 1926; s. Francis Patrick and Mary Nora (Curry) F.; m. Adelaide Monica Haley, Dec. 26, 1953; children: Joseph F., Stephen F., Francis P., Donna Marie, Louise C., James C.. BA, St. John's U., 1950; LLB, Columbia U., 1953. Bar: N.Y. 1953. Atty. New Haven and Hartford R.R., N.Y.C., 1954-56, GAF Corp., N.Y.C., 1956-58, Curtiss-Wright Corp., Lyndhurst, N.J., 1958-61, corp. sec., 1961—. Mem. Planning Bd. Clarkstown, New City, N.Y., 1976-83. Served with USN, 1944-46, PTO. Mem. Am. Soc. Corp. Secs., Assn. Corp. Counsel N.J. (sec. 1983-84). Democrat. Roman Catholic. Avocation: golf. Home: 26 Concord Dr New City NY 10956-4037 Office: Curtiss-Wright Corp 1200 Wall St W Lyndhurst NJ 07071-3680

FALLON, HAROLD JOSEPH, physician, pharmacology and biochemistry educator; b. N.Y.C., Aug. 13, 1931; s. Harold Joseph and Martha A. (Hansen) Fallon; m. Jo Ann Brouse; children: Thomas, Michael, Elisabeth, John. BA, Yale U., 1953, MD, 1957. Diplomate Am. Bd. Internal Medicine. Intern in medicine N.C. Meml. Hosp., Chapel Hill, 1957—58, asst. resident in medicine, 1958—59, chief resident in medicine, 1961—62; clin. assoc. NIH, 1959—61; postdoctoral fellow dept. biochemistry Duke U. Sch. Medicine, 1963—64; asst. prof. medicine U. N.C. Sch. Medicine, Chapel Hill, 1963—71, asst. prof. biochemistry, 1966—71, assoc. prof. medicine, 1967—70, chief divsn. clin. pharmacology, toxicology, environ. health, 1968—74, vice chmn. dept. medicine, 1968—71, assoc. prof. pharmacology, 1969—70, prof. medicine and pharmacology, 1970—74, assoc. prof. biochemistry, 1971—74, acting chmn. dept medicine, 1971—72; William Branch Porter prof. medicine, chmn. dept. medicine Va. Commonwealth U.-Med. Coll. Va., Richmond, 1974—93; dean, Sch. of Med. U. Ala., Birmingham, 1993—97, assoc. dean grad. med. edn. Sch. Medicine, 1997—99; home sec. Inst. Medicine, Washington, 1999—. Vis. scientist U. Utrecht, The Netherlands, 1972—73; vis. scholar U. Munich Med. Faculty, 1988—89; mem. numerous med. coms. and couns.; rsch. fellow Yale U. Sch. Medicine, 1962—63. Editl. bd. Gastroenterology, Clin. Research, Hepatology, mem. adv. editl. bd. Jour. Lipid Rsch., mem. editl. com. Jour. Clin. Investigation, 1971—76, contbr. numerous articles to med. jours. Exec. com. YMCA, Richmond, 1984—. Served with USPHS, 1959—62. Named Outstanding Affiliate appointee, Sch. Basic Scis., 1984; recipient Sinsheimer award, 0975—1970, Rsch. Career Devel. award, 1968, Burroughs Wellcome award, 1974, Med. Coll. Va. Deans award, 1981, Founders medal, So. Soc. for Clin. Investigation, 1997. Master: ACP (regent, chair bd. regents 1991—98); mem.: AMA, AAAS, Internat. Assn. for Study Liver Disease (councillor 1982—84), also numerous others, Am. Soc. Pharmacology Exptl. Therapeutics, Gastroenterology Rsch. Group (mem. steering com. 1970—74, sec.-treas. 1973—74), Am. Assn. for Study Liver Disease (pres. 1979, mem. publ. com. 1983—), Am. Liver Found. (bd. dirs. 1981), Am. Gastroenterol. Assn. (mem. governing bd. 1978—82), Am. Fedn. Clin. Rsch., Am. Clin. Climatol. Assn., So. Soc. for Clin. Investigation (councillor 1971—74, presl. 1976—77), Am. Soc. for Clin. Investigation (councillor 1975—76, v.p. 1975—76), Assn. Profs. Medicine (councillor, pres. 1987—88), Assn. Am. Physicians (pres. 1991), Commonwealth Kiawah Island Club. Presbyterian. Home: 40 Marsh Edge Ln Kiawah Island SC 29455-5731 Office: Inst Medicine NAS Bldg 2101 Constitution Ave NW Washington DC 20418-0007

FALLON, PAT, artist, educator; b. Cartagena, Colombia, Nov. 2, 1939; (parents Am. citizens); d. Carlos Fallon and Maureen (Bryne) Fallon Laird; m. Ronald Patrick Conner, Dec. 26, 1960 (div. June 1976); children: Haldey Kathryn Conner, Kenneth Fallon Conner. BA, Antioch Coll., 1962; BFA, Cleve. Inst. Art, 1980; MFA, Kent State U., 1982. Prof. Ursuline Coll., Cleve., 2001—. Exhibitions include nat. and internat., U.S., Ireland, Germany. Vol., advisor art com. N.E. Ohio Coalition Homeless, Cleve., 1996—97. Fellow, Ohio Humanities Coun., 1986—94. Mem.: Founds. Art Theory and Edn., Coll. Arts Assn., Amnesty Internat. Democrat. Roman Catholic. Home: 3300 Kenmore Rd Shaker Heights OH 44122-3462 Office: Ursuline Coll 2550 Lander Rd Cleveland OH 44124-4318

FALLON, RAE MARY, psychology educator, early childhood consultant; b. N.Y.C., Apr. 13, 1947; d. Frank J. and Santa A. T.; m. John J. Fallon, 1972; children: Sean, Christopher. BA, CUNY, 1968, MA, 1971; PhD, Fordham U., 2001. Cert. N-6 tchr., spl. edn. tchr., N.Y. Elem. tchr. Pub. Sch. 1, Bronx, NY, 1968—72; pre-sch. tchr. Valley Nursery Sch., Walden, NY, 1972—73; tchr. spl. edn. Orange-Ulster Bd. Coop. Edn. Svcs., Goshen, NY, 1973—75, early childhood specialist, 1982—89; instr. edn. Mt. St. Mary Coll., Newburgh, NY, 1989—93, asst. prof., 1993—2001, assoc. prof. psychology, 2001—. Early childhood cons., Montgomery, N.Y., 1989—; mem. early childhood com. Valley Ctrl. Sch. Sys., Montgomery, 1994. Mem. West Street Sch. Cmty. Sch. Bd., Newburgh, 1990—; mem. early intervention com. Orange County Health Dept., Goshen, 1993—; chmn. program com. Montgomery Rep. Club, 1990-94. Mem. ASCD, Coun. for Exceptional Children, Assn. for Edn. Young Children (regional coord. 1991-92), Kiwanis, Delta Kappa Gamma (pres. Alpha chpt. 2002-04), Phi Delta Kappa. Roman Catholic. Office: Mt St Mary Coll 330 Powell Ave Newburgh NY 12550-3412

FALLON, ROBERT THOMAS, English language educator; b. N.Y.C., June 6, 1927; s. John Edward and Winifred (Hanigan) F.; m. Mary Snyder, May 18, 1953 (div. May 1971); children: Frances Fallon Schuster, Robert Thomas Jr. BS, U.S. Mil. Acad., 1949; MA in History, Canisius Coll., 1960; MA in English, Columbia U., 1962, PhD in English, 1965. Commd. 2nd lt. U.S. Army, 1949, advanced through grades to lt. col., 1965, ret., 1970; assoc. prof. English LaSalle U., Phila., 1970-78, prof. English, 1978-95; prof. emeritus, 1995—. Author: Captain or Colonel: The Soldier in Milton's Life and Art, 1984, Milton in Government, 1993, Divided Empire: Milton's Political Imagery, 1995, A Theatergoer's Guide to Shakespeare, 2001, A Theatergoer's Guide to Shakespear's Themes, 2002, The Christian Soldier, 2003; contbr. articles to profl. publs. NEH fellow, 1990-91; Am. Coun. Learned Socs. grantee-in-aid, 1980. Mem. MLA, Cromwell Assn., Milton Soc. Am. (treas. 1977-86, v.p. 1987, pres. 1988), John Donne Soc. (mem. exec. com. 1991-93). Avocation: tennis. Home: River Rd Lumberville PA 18933

FALLON, STEPHEN MICHAEL, humanities educator; b. Washington, Sept. 18, 1954; s. William Francis and Margaret Mary (Barry) F.; m. Nancy Anne Hungarland, May 30, 1981 (dec. Feb. 2000); children: Samuel, Claire, Daniel. AB in English, Princeton U., 1976; MA in English, McGill U., 1978; PhD in English, U. Va., 1985. Asst. prof. liberal studies U. Notre Dame, 1985-90, assoc. prof. liberal studies, English, 1990—. Author: Milton among the Philosophers, 1991; co-founder great books course for homeless; contbr. essays in books and articles to profl. jours. Fellow Nat. Endowment Humanities, 1988-89, 95-96, Am. Coun. Learned Socs.; recipient Outstanding Tchr. award, Notre Dame Arts and Letters Coll., 2001. Mem. Modern Lang. Assn., Milton Soc. Am. (James Holly Hanford award 1991, exec. com. 1990-92), Phi Beta Kappa. Avocations: soccer, bicycling, opera. Office: U Notre Dame 368 Decio Hall Notre Dame IN 46556-5644

FALLON, WILLIAM J. career officer; b. East Orange, NJ, Dec. 30, 1944; m. Mary Elizabeth Trapp; children: Susan, Barbara, William, Christina. BA, Villanova U., 1967; MA in Internat. Studies, Old Dominion. Advanced through grade to adm. USN; pilot USS Ranger, 1969; comdr. attack squadron 65 USS Dwight D. Eisenhower, 1984-85; dep. comdr. carrier air wing 8 USS Nimitz; comdr. attack wing 1 Naval Air Sta. Occana, Va., 1989-90, USS Theodore Roosevelt, 1991, comdr. carrier group 8, 1995; comdr. Theodore Roosevelt battle group, comdr. Battle Force 6th Fleet; dep. comdr. in chief, chief staff U.S. Atlantic Fleet, Norfolk, Va., 1996-98, commdr. 2d Fleet, Striking Fleet Atlantic, 1997—2000; vice chief naval ops. U.S. Navy, Washington, 2000—.*

FALLS, KATHLEENE JOYCE, photographer; b. Detroit, July 3, 1949; d. Edgar John and Acelia Olive (Young) Haley; m. Donald David Falls, June 15, 1974; children: Daniel John, David James. Student, Oakland Community Coll., 1969-73, Winona Sch. Profl. Photography, 1973-80, postgrad., 1988, 90. Lic. ham radio-technician class. Printer Guardian Photo, Novi, Mich., 1967-69; printer, supr. quality control N.Am. Photo, Livonia, Mich., 1969-76; free lance photographer Livonia, 1969-76; owner, pres. Kathy Falls, Inc., Carleton, Mich., 1976—2001; instr. digital imaging Monroe County (Mich.) C.C., 1994-95. Instr. continuing edn. Monroe County C.C., 1981-83; nat. artisan judge Congl. H.S. Art Competition, 1985-2000; owner Picture Perfect, Carleton, 1987; co-owner Haleys Gift Shoppe, Dundee, Mich., 1989; pub. info. officer Am. Radio Relay League, 1998-2000. Author: (booklet) Emergency Photo-Retouching for Photographers, 1988; editor The Hertzian herald, 1998; contbr. articles to profl. jours.; represented in spl. categories in the Nat. Loan Collection, Profl. Photographers Am., 1980, 81, 83, 87, 2002; represented in permanent Collections Monroe County Hist. Mus., Archives Notre Dame; newsletter editor Hertzian Herald. Active Big Bros. and Big Sisters, Monroe, 1986—87; corr. sec. Monroe Women's Ctr., 1986—88; mem. Amateur Radio Emergency Svc.; pres. Our Lady of Knock divsn. Laoh Adrian, Laoh State Bd., 2001—; Catechist St. Parick's Ch., Carleton, 1984—87, mem. parish coun., 1998—2000; bd. dirs. Ladies Ancient Order of Hibernians. Recipient Photographic Craftsman degree, 1989, numerous awards granted by profl. photographic orgns.; editor: Hertzian Herald. Mem.: NAFE, Nat. Orgn. Women Bus. Owners, Monroe C. of C. (chmn. council women bus. owners), Monroe County Fine Arts Coun. (pres. 1998—2000), Am. Photog. Artisans Guild (bd. dirs. 1987—, Photog. Artisan degree 1989, Artisan Laurel degree 1991, pres. 1992, exec. sec. 2001—, editor Palette Page 2001—, exec. dir. 2002, coun. mem.), Profl. Photographers Am. (photographic specialist degree 1988, cert. profl. photog. specialist, Photog. Craftsman degree 1990, cert. electronic imager), Profl. Photographers Mich. (artisan chair 1982—83, bd. dirs. 2000—, dir. 2001—, Best of Show award 1976, 1981, 2001, Artist of Yr. 1980, 1991), Detroit Profl. Photographers Assn. (artisan chmn. 1981—82, bd. dirs. 1987—, Best of Show award 1981, 1983), Am. Soc. Photographers, Hillsdale Art Guild, Toastmasters, Monroe County Radio Comms. Assn., Ladies Ancient Order of Hibernians (bd. dirs. 1998—99), Monroe Camera, Hillsdale County Amateur Radio Club, Scarab Club Detroit, Internat. Club. Republican. Roman Catholic. Avocations: guitar, piano, drawing, travel, camping. Home and Office: 14940 Carpenter Rd Camden MI 49232 E-mail: katfalls@tdi.net.

FALLS, ROBERT ARTHUR, artistic director; b. Springfield, Ill., Mar. 2, 1954; s. Arthur Joseph and Nancy (Stribling) F. BFA, U. Ill., 1976. Artistic dir. Wisdom Bridge Theatre, Chgo., 1977-86, Goodman Theatre, Chgo., 1987—; dir. Pravda (Howard Brenton and David Hare), Guthrie Theater, Mpls., 1989, The Speed Of Darkness (Steve Tesich), Belasco Theatre, N.Y.C., 1991, The Iceman Cometh (Eugene O'Neill), Goodman Theatre, 1990, Abbey Theatre, 1992, Dublin, The Night of the Iguana (Tennessee Williams), Goodman Theatre, 1994, Death of a Salesman, Goodman Theatre, 1998; additional directing credits: Griller, The Young Man from Atlanta, A Touch of the Poet, The Night of the Iguana, The Rose Tatoo, On the Open Road, The Tempest, Three Sisters, Galileo, Landscape of the Body, Book of the Night, Pal Joey. Revivals include: Getting Out, In the Belly of the Beast: Letters from Prison, Of Mice and Men, Wings, Mother Courage and Her Children, Hamlet; directed Am. premieres: Pravda, The Misanthrope, Standing on My Knees, The Food Chain, subUrbia, The Consul and Susannah; Won Tony award for Best Revival, 1999, Death of a Salesman. Office: Goodman Theatre 170 N Dearborn St Chicago IL 60601-3205

FALOCCO, JOE, theater educator, actor; s. John and Minnie Francis Falocco; m. Melissa Anne Barnes, May 15, 2001. BA, De Paul U., 1997; MFA, Roosevelt U., 2000. Acting tchr. Trollwood Sch., Fargo, ND, 2000; asst. prof. Ark. State U., Jonesboro, 2000—. Actor Tex. Shakespeare Festival, Kilgoe, 1998—99, Okla. Shakespeare Festival, Durant, 2001; dir. Shakespeare Festival of Ark., Little Rock, 2002. Mem.: SAG, Soc. Am. Fight Dirs., Actors Equity Assn. Home: 141 E Corriher Ave Salisbury NC 28144

FALOON, WILLIAM WASSELL, physician, educator; b. Pitts., July 6, 1920; s. Joseph Coulter and Martha Louise (Wassell) F.; m. Roberta Jane Emery, Sept. 11, 1948; children: Karen F. Durham, Nancy F. Dodd, William W. BA, Allegheny Coll., 1941; MD, Harvard U., 1944. Diplomate Am. Bd. Internal Medicine; cert. registered arbitrator; ordained as deacon Presbyterian, 1958, elder, 1963. Intern Pa. Hosp., Phila., 1944-45; asst. resident in medicine Albany (N.Y.) Hosp., 1945-46, resident in medicine, 1946-47; rsch. fellow in medicine Harvard Med. Sch., Thorndike Meml. Lab., Boston City Hosp., 1947-48; asst. prof. oncology, instr. medicine Albany Med. Coll., 1948-50; instr. medicine SUNY Coll. Medicine, Syracuse, 1950-51, asst. prof., 1951-56, assoc. prof., 1956-64, prof. medicine, 1964-68; program dir. Adult Clin. Rsch. Ctr., Syracuse, 1965-68; physician-in-chief, dir. clin. rsch. and edn. Santa Barbara (Calif.) Gen.-Cottage Hosps., 1968-69; prof. medicine U. Rochester (N.Y.) Sch. Medicine, 1969-92, emeritus prof. medicine, 1992—; mem. Univ. Senate, 1971-74; mem. staff Strong Meml. Hosp., Rochester, Highland Hosp., 1969-90, chief medicine, 1970-80, dir. gastroenterology and nutrition, 1970-86; sr. attending physician The Genesee Hosp., 1990-91. Mem. editl. bd. Am. Jour. Clin. Nutrition, 1970-76; contbr. articles to profl. jours. Bd. mgrs. Camp Dudley YMCA, 1962-67, 69-74, chmn. bd., 1966-67, 71-73; bd. dirs. Onondaga County Met. Health Coun., Syracuse, 1959-61; mem. adv. com. Onondaga County Health Dept., 1966-68; bd. dirs. Am. Liver Found., 1982-92, pres. we. N.Y. chpt., 1982-83. Fellow ACP, Rochester Acad. Medicine (dir. 1979-82); mem. Am. Fedn. Clin. Rsch. (councillor 1956-59), AAAS, Onondaga County Med. Soc. (exec. com. 1964 66), Am. Assn. for Study Liver Disease, Am. Inst. Nutrition, Am. Soc. Clin. Nutrition, Endocrine Soc., Am. Gastroent. Assn., Western Soc. for Clin. Rsch., Med. Soc. Monroe County, Internat. Assn. for Study Liver, Assn. Program Dirs. Internal Medicine (councillor 1978-80), N.Y. State Dept. Health (bd. profl. med. conduct N.Y. State 1986-97), Island Profl. Rev. Orgn. (cons. 1991-94), Nat. Health Lawyers Assn. (dispute resolver), Gt. Lakes Interurban (sec. 1977-84), Ea. Gut, Oak Hill Country Club (Rochester). Presbyterian. Home: 4 Whitecliff Dr Pittsford NY 14534-2926 E-mail: remfaloon@aol.com.

FALSGRAF, WILLIAM WENDELL, lawyer; b. Cleve., Nov. 10, 1933; s. Wendell A. and Catherine J. F.; children: Carl Douglas, Jeffrey Price, Catherine Louise. AB cum laude, Amherst Coll., 1955, LLD (hon.), 1986; JD, Case Western Res. U., 1958. Bar: Ohio 1958, U.S. Supreme Ct. 1972. Ptnr. Baker & Hostetler, Cleve., 1971—2002; ret., 2002. Chmn. vis. com. Case Western Res. U. Law Sch., 1973-76; trustee Case Western Reserve U., 1978-90, chmn. bd. overseers, 1977-78; trustee Cleve. Health Mus., 1975-90, Hiram Coll., 1989—; chmn. bd. trustees Hiram Coll., 1990-99. Recipient Disting. Service award; named Outstanding Young Man of Year Cleve. Jr. C. of C., 1962. Fellow Am. Bar Found., Ohio Bar Found.; mem. ABA (chmn. young lawyers sect. 1966-67, mem. ho. of dels. 1967-68, 70—, bd. govs. 1971-75, pres. 1985-86, bd. dirs. Am. Bar Endowment 1974-84, 87-97), Am. Bar Ins. Plans Cons. (pres. 1991—), Ohio Bar Assn. (mem. coun. of dels. 1968-70), Cleve. Bar Assn. (trustee 1979-82), Amherst Alumni Assn. (pres. N.E. Ohio 1964), The Country Club, LaPaloma Country Club. Home: 616 North St Chagrin Falls OH 44022-2514 Office: Baker & Hostetler LLP 3200 National City Ctr Cleveland OH 44114-3485 E-mail: wfalsgraf@bakerlaw.com.

FALTER, ROBERT GARY, nursing home administrator, educator; b. N.Y.C., Sept. 14, 1943; s. Lawrence Zane and Helen (Smith) F.; m. Kathleen Ann Burrill, July 9, 1982; children: John William Wright III, Jason Michael Wright. AA, St. John's U., Jamaica, N.Y., 1965, BA, 1967; MA, Kean Coll. of N.J., 1973; MBA, Cornell U., 1976; PhD, Walden U., 1993. Lic. nursing home adminstr., notary public. Adminstrv. resident N.Y. Hosp./Cornell Med. Ctr., N.Y.C., summer 1975; mgr. ophthalmology Hahnemann Med. Coll. & Hosp., Phila., 1976-77; dir. out-patient clinic USPHS Ctr. for Disease Control, Atlanta, 1977—78; project officer ambulatory care data systems USPHS Div. Hosps. and Clinics, West Hyattsville, Md., 1978-80; assoc. dir. ambulatory care USPHS Hosp., Boston, 1980-81; adminstr. family medicine Sch. of Medicine U. Tenn., Memphis, 1981-82; asst. v.p. customer svc./instnl. benefits Blue Cross/Blue Shield of N.Y., N.Y.C., 1982-86; assoc. v.p. ops. S.I. Hosp., 1986-87; assoc. dir. adminstrv. svcs. divsn. fed. employee occupational health USPHS Region II, N.Y.C., 1988-89; health/resources and svcs. adminstr. Rockville, Md., 1989; materiel mgmt. officer, dep. br. chief, 1989, health care adminstr. individual ready res. USPHS, Rockville, 1989-90, chief program liaison unit, 1990-91, chief budget officer BOP/HSD, 1991-93, chief br. budget and mgmt. support, 1993-99; chief health svcs. officer Office of the Surgeon Gen./Pub. Health Svc., 1995-99; adminstrv. officer Fed. Med. Ctr., Fed. Bur. Prisons, Devens, Ayer, Mass., 1999-2000, quality risk mgr., 2000, health care adminstr. correctional med. svcs. MCI-Shirley-Medium, Mass., 2000—02; adminstr.-in-tng. Clark Manor Healthcare Ctr., 2002; asst. adminstr. Tower Hill Ctr. for Health and Rehab., 2002—03, Harborlights Nursing and Rehab. Ctr., 2002; interim adminstr. Avery Manor Rehab. and Nursing Ctr., Needham, Mass., 2003; adminstr. Linda Manor Extended Care Facility, Leeds, Mass., 2003—. Chmn. hosp. and med. care adminstrs. Health Svcs. Profl. Adv. Com., 1989-91; co-chmn. centennial symposium planning com. Health Svcs. Officers, 1989; lectr. fiscal mgmt. Christian Bros. U., Memphis, 1982; lectr. health econs. grad. program in health svcs. adminstrn. Salve Regina Coll., Newport, R.I., 1984; mem. assoc. grad. faculty, acad. advisor Ctrl. Mich. U. Coll. of Extended Learning Health Svcs. Adminstrn., 1995—; adj. asst. prof. divsn. nursing rsch. Uniformed Svcs. U. Health Scis. Grad. Sch. Nursing, Bethesda, 1996-2001; adj. instr. Vanderbilt U., Sch. Nursing, Nashville, 1999—; sr. lectr. Western New Eng. Coll., Springfield, Mass., 2000-; bd. dirs. Nat. Commn. on Correctional Health Care, 1991-94, mem. program com., 1991-92, mem. publs. com., 1991-94, mem. exec. com., 1992-94, mng. editor Jour., 1994-97; adj. asst. prof. preventive medicine and biometrics, Health Svcs. Adminstrn., Uniformed Svcs. U. of Health Scis., Bethesda, 1999-2001. Bd. dirs. Vis. Nurse Assn. Memphis, Inc., 1982; mem. cmty. adv. bd. Primary Health Care for Srs., Allston-Brighton Med. Care Coalition, Boston, 1981; usher coord. St. Michael's Cath. Ch., Poplar Springs, 1989-91. Served with U.S. Army, 1968-71; capt. USPHS, 1977-81, 88-2001. Recipient Capt. Stanley J. Kissel, Jr. award USPHS/Health Svcs. Officer, 1994, Surgeon Gen.'s Exemplary Svc. medal USPHS, 1996, 99. Fellow: Mil. Offices Assn. Am. (pres. Worcester County chpt. 2002—), D.C.-Md.-Va. Hosp. Assn. (chmn. liaison com. 51st ann. conv. 1991), Am. Acad. Med. Adminstrs. (hon.), Am. Coll. Healthcare Execs. (editl. bd. Healthcare Execs. 1986—88, book reviewer Hosp. and Health Svcs. Adminstrn.); mem.: Commd. Officers Assn. USPHS (sec. Atlanta chpt. 1978), Assn. Mil. Surgeons U.S. (reviewer Mil. Medicine 1989—, cons.), Healthcare Mgmt. Assn. Mass., Assn. Health Care Adminstrs. Nat. Capital Area, Anchor and Caduceus Soc. (charter), Reserve Officers Assn. U.S. (newsletter editor Montgomery County chpt. 1989), KC (warden St. Michael's of Poplar Springs coun. 1990—91, chancelor 1991—92). Avocations: teaching, travel, writing, consulting. Home: 50 Deerfield Rd Shrewsbury MA 01545-1571 E-mail: rgf4@cornell.edu.

FALTER, VINCENT EUGENE, retired army officer, consultant; b. Akron, Ohio, Dec. 20, 1932; s Alois S. and Prunella (Scharf) F.; m Anna Marta Stephen, Sept. 6, 1958; children: Vincent Eugene, Laura Diane B.E., U. Nebr.-Omaha, 1963; grad., Command and Gen. Staff Coll., 1968, U.S. War Coll., 1973; M.P.A., Shippensburg State Coll., 1972. Enlisted U.S. Army, 1953, commd. 2d lt., 1954, advanced through grades to maj. gen., 1981, served with 750th F.A. Bn., 1954-57, served with Mortar Battery 2d BG 60th Inf., 1958-59, served with hdqrs. 1st Cav. Div., 1959-60, instr. F.A. Sch., 1960-63, battery comdg. officer B battery 17th F.A. Bn., 1963-64, asst. G-1, 7th Army, 1964-66, exec. officer 2d Bn., 13th F.A. Bn., 1966-67; staff officer Dept. Army Office Dept. Chief of Staff for Ops., Washington, 1968-70; comdg. officer 2d Bn. 19th F.A. U.S. Army, Vietnam, 1970-71, exec. officer F.A. Br. Washington, 1971-72, sec. F.A. Sch., 1973-74, comdg. officer 75th F.A Group, 1974-76; dir. nuclear and chem. ops. Dept. Army, Office Dep. Chief of Staff for Ops., Washington, 1977-79; comdg. gen. VII Corps Arty. U.S. Army, Germany, 1979-81, dep. insp. gen., 1981-82, with Office Chief of Staff, 1982-83; comdg. gen. Mil Personnel Ctr., 1983-85; dep. dir. ops. Def. Nuclear Agy., Washington, 1985-86, dep. asst. to sec. def. for atomic energy, 1986-88; ret., 1988; founder The Copley Group, nat. security cons., 1988—. Mem. NRC/NAS. Decorated Def. D.S.M. with oak leaf cluster, Army D.S.M., Legion of Merit with 2 oak leaf clusters, Bronze Star with 3 oak leaf clusters, Air Medal with 15 oak leaf clusters Mem. F.A. Assn., Rotary. Roman Catholic. Home: 7914 Colorado Springs Dr Springfield VA 22153-2719 Office: Dir Ops MPRI Alexandria VA 22314

FALVEY, MARY C. management consultant; b. Detroit, Oct. 28, 1941; d. Lawrence C. and Mathilde G. Falvey. BA in Econs. with honors, Cornell U., 1963; MBA, Harvard U., 1967. Systems engr. IBM Corp., N.Y.C., 1963-65; mgmt. cons. McKinsey & Co., Inc., N.Y.C., 1967-75; v.p. Citibank, N.Y.C., 1975-78, head asset servicing divsn., 1977-78; sr. v.p., dir., head adminstrn.

divsn., mem. exec. com. Blyth Eastman Dillon & Co., Inc., N.Y.C., 1978-80; pres. Falvey Autos, Inc., Troy, Mich., 1979—93, also chmn. bd. dirs.; pres. M.C. Falvey Assocs., Inc., N.Y.C., 1980-81, 1982—; v.p. fin. Shaklee Corp., San Francisco, 1981—82. Bd. dirs. Golden Gate Bank, San Francisco Classical Voice, World Affairs Coun. Calif.; mem. Band of Angels. Mem. Com. N.Y. Philharm., 1975—77, Adv. Coun. Social Security, 1979—80, Pres. Reagan's Transition Task Force Social Security, 1979—80, Nat. Commn. Social Security Reform, 1982—83; chmn. St. Francis Hosp. Found., 1998—99; trustee San Francisco Performances, 1981—93, chmn. bd. trustees, 1984—91; mem. composite com. Med. Licensing Exam., 1995—2000; mem. Internat. Women's Forum; bd. dirs. St. Francis Hosp. Found., 1992—2000, San Francisco Symphony, Philharmonia Baroque Orch. Havard Bus. Sch. grantee, 1965-67. Mem. Harvard Bus. Sch. Assn. No. Calif. (dir.), Commonwealth Club Calif., Univ. Club (dir. 1993-96 San Francisco). Republican. Presbyterian. Home and Office: 2100 Pacific Ave Apt 4A San Francisco CA 94115-1546 E-mail: falveyassoc@earthlink.net.

FALVEY, PATRICK JOSEPH, lawyer; b. Yonkers, N.Y., June 29, 1927; s. Patrick J. Falvey and Nora Rowley Falvey; m. Eileen Ryan, June 29, 1963; 1 child, Patrick James. Student, Iona Coll., 1944-47; JD cum laude, St. John's U., Jamaica, N.Y., 1950. Bar: N.Y. 1951, U.S. Supreme Ct. 1972. Law asst. Port Authority of N.Y. and N.J., 1951, atty., 1951-65, chief condemnation and litigation, 1965-67, asst. gen. counsel, 1967-72, gen. counsel, 1972-91, gen. counsel, asst. exec. dir., 1979-87, dep. exec. dir., 1987-91, spl. counsel, 1991—. Advisor U.S. del. to UN Com. on Internat. Trade Law, U.S. State Dept. Pvt. Trade Law; advisor to U.S. del. UN diplomatic confs. on treaty on liability of ops. of transport terminals, N.Y. County Lawyers Assn., 1992—. With USN, 1945-46. Recipient Howard S. Cullman Disting. Svc. medal Port Authority of N.Y. and N.J., 1982, 91; Loftus award and Trustee's Honoree Iona Coll., 1982. Fellow Am. Bar Found.; mem. ABA (chmn. urban state and local govt. law sect. 1983-84, vice-chmn. model procurement code project 1979—, sect. del. 1987-90, Award for Lifetime Achievement in Local Law 2000), Assn. Bar City N.Y., N.Y. County Lawyers Assn., Internat. Assn. Ports and Harbors (hon., legal counsellors com., arbitrator, mediator trade and comml. matters, cons. transp. and trade studies). Address: PMB 81 Pondfield Rd Ste 338 Bronxville NY 10708-3818 E-mail: woodlawnfalvey@aol.com.

FALVO, CATHEY E. medical educator, director, pediatrician; d. Benjamin Eisner and Rita Teumin; m. Kenneth Anthony Falvo, Dec. 17, 1966; 1 child, Jessica Aimee. AB, U. Rochester, 1963; MD, SUNY, 1968; MPH, Columbia U., 1977. Diplomate Am. Bd. Pediats., 1975, Am. Bd. Preventive Medicine, 1975, lic. N.Y., 1969. Attending physician in pediats. Roosevelt Hosp., N.Y.C., 1973—78; pediatrician Open Door Health Ctrs., Ossining, NY, 1978—92; dir. epidemiology Sch. Pub. Health N.Y. Med. Coll., Valhalla, NY, 1981—92, dir. internat. and pub. health, 1992—. Cons. Westchester County Dept. Health, White Plains, NY, 1979—81; mem. adv. com. EPA, Washington, 1998—2001; cons. UNICEF, N.Y.C., 1996—97. Med. cons. Project Hearts and Minds Vietnam, Greenwich, Conn., 1994—2000; co-chmn. women and environ. UN Commn. Status Women, N.Y.C., 1994—2000; mem. nat. bd. Physicians for Social Responsibility, Washington, 1993—. Fellow: Am. Coll. Preventive Medicine, Am. Acad. Pediats.; mem.: APHA (section coun. epidemiology 1975—, grantee 1990—97). Avocations: theater, opera, swimming, cooking, travel. Office: School of Public Health New York Medical College Valhalla NY 10595 E-mail: falvo@nymc.edu.

FALWELL, JERRY L. minister; b. Lynchburg, Va., Aug. 11, 1933; s. Carey H. and Helen V. (Beasley) Falwell; m. Macel Pate, Apr. 12, 1958; children: Jerry L., Jeannie, Jonathan. BA, Bapt. Bible Coll., Springfield, Mo., 1956; DD (hon.), Tenn. Temple U.; LLD (hon.), Calif. Grad. Sch. Theology, Cen. U., Seoul, Korea. Founder, pastor Thomas Rd. Bapt. Ch., Lynchburg, Va., 1956—; founder Liberty U., 1971, Moral Majority Inc., 1979—89; chancellor Liberty U. Host TV show Old Time Gospel Hour; lectr in field. Author: Listen, America!, 1980, The Fundamentalist Phenomenon, 1981, Finding Inner Peace and Strength, 1982, When It Hurts Too Much to Cry, 1984, Wisdom for Living, 1984, Stepping Out on Faith, 1984, Champions for God, 1985, IF I Should Die Before I Wake, 1986, Strength For the Journey, 1987, New American Family, 1992, Falwell: A Autobiography, 1997, Fasting Can Change Your Life, 1998; co-author: Church Afflame, 1971, Capturing a Town for Christ, 1973. Named Christian Humanitarian of Yr., Food for the Hungry Internat., Number One Most Admired Conservative Man Not in Congress, Conservative Digest, 1983, Most Influential Ctrl. Virginian of 20th Century, News and Advance, Lynchburg, Va., 1999; named one of Most Influential People in Am., U.S. News & World Report, 1983, 10 Most Admired Men, Good Housekeeping, 1982, 1984, 1986; named to Hall of Fame, Nat. Religious Broadcasters, 1985; recipient Clergyman of Yr. award, Religious Heritage Am., 1979, Jabotinsky Centennial medal, 1980, Two Hungers award, Food for the Hungry Internat., 1981. Mem.: Nat. Assn. Religious Broadcasters (bd. dirs.). Baptist. Address: Liberty U 1971 University Blvd Lynchburg VA 24502-2269

FAM, AMIR Z. engineering educator, researcher; b. Alexandria, Egypt, Aug. 5, 1969; arrived in U.S., 2000; s. Zakaria Y. Fam and Marcelle S. Basaly; m. Hala H. Doch, Mar. 2, 1976. BS in Civil Engring., Alexandria U., 1991; MS in Structural Engring., U. Man., Winnipeg, Man., Can., 1996, PhD in Structural Engring., 2000. Rsch. asst. Geo-tech. Lab. Alexandria U., 1990—91, instr. 1st yr. engring., 1991—92; structural engr. Consultants Engring. Firm, Alexandria, 1991—93; grad. tchg. and rsch. asst. U. Man., Winnipeg, 1993—2000; vis. grad. student U. Calgary, Canada, 1997—97; post-doctoral rsch. assoc. and lectr. N.C. State U., Raleigh, 2000—02; asst. prof. and Can. Rsch. Chair in Innovative and Retrofitted Structures Queen's U., Kingston, Canada, 2002—. Cons. and rschr. in field; presenter in field. Contbr. articles to profl. jours. Vol. tutor Alexandria U., 1991—93; tutor aboriginal engring. students U. Man., Winnipeg, 1994—98; bd. mem.. St. Mark Coptic Orthodox Ch., Winnipeg, Canada, 1995—96, youth leader, 1993—2000; bd. mem.. St. Mina Coptic Orthodox Ch., Kingston, Canada, 2002; mem. engring. coun. St. Mary Coptic Orthodox Ch., Raleigh, 2001—02. Soldier Egyptian Navy, 1992—93. Recipient Best Paper award, Can. Network of Centers of Excellence on Intelligent Sensing for Innovative Structures, ISIS Can., 2000, Travel award, Office Rsch. Svcs., Queen's U., 2002; fellow, U. Man., 1997; scholar, Natural Scis. and Engring. Rsch. Coun. Can., NSERC, 1997—99. Mem.: Syndicate Engrs. Egypt, Am. Soc. Composites, Am. Concrete Inst. (mem. fiber reinforced polymer reinforcement com.). Achievements include research in Modeling of the First Concrete Bridge in the World Fully Prestressed and Reinforced for Shear Using Carbon Fiber Reinforced Polymers, Taylor Bridge, Manitoba, Canada; Comprehensive Studies on Structural Performance of an Innovative Concrete-Filled Fiber Reinforced Polymer (FRP) Tubes; development of Confinement Model for Fiber Reinforced Polymer - Confined Concrete. Avocations: reading, swimming, travel, tennis. Home: 802 Woodside Dr Kingston ON Canada K7P 1T2 Office: Dept Civil Eng Queens Univ Ellis Hall 58 University Ave Kingston ON Canada K7L 3N6 Office Fax: 613-533-2128. E-mail: fam@civil.queensu.ca.

FAMIGLIETTI, NANCY ZIMA, computer executive; b. Hartford, Conn., Nov. 10, 1956; d. Joseph and Angeline (Morello) Zima; m. Arthur R. Famiglietti Jr., May 23, 1981. BA in Math., Computer Sci. cum laude, Eastern Conn. State Coll., Willimantic, 1978. Sr. programmer analyst Hamilton Standard, Windsor Locks, Conn., 1978-82; system analyst Cigna Corp., Hartford, 1982-83, system designer, 1983-86, lead system designer, 1986-89; system advisor Aetna Life & Casualty Co., Hartford, 1989-93, system adminstr., 1993-94, sr. sys. adminstr., 1994-95, bus. sys. mgr., 1995-98; with Hartford Life, Windsor, Conn., 1998, bus. cons., 1998-2000, team leader, 2000-2001, mgr., 2001—. Active Windsor (Conn.) Hist. Soc. Mem. Kappa Mu Epsilon. Avocations: reading, walking, crafts, swimming, bicycling. Home: 81 Mcgrath Rd South Windsor CT 06074-1123

FAMMERÉE, RICHARD ARTHUR NOEL, poet, composer, performing artist; BA in Creative Writing and Internat. Lit., Beloit Coll. Former chmn. art. dept. The Found., Chgo.; former pres. Artists Coalition; former dir. Chgo. Arts Emerging, BHF Atelier, Chgo.; dir. Poetry in Process, 1996-2000, Nomadica, 1996—, First Words, 2001—; founder, artistic dir. Full Body Poetry, 2001—. Mem. adv. bd. The Poetry Ctr. of Chgo., 2001. Author: Lessons of Water and Thirst, 2000, Innocent, 2003, poems and songs; editor: Lap of Poetical Literary Jour., 1997—98; dir.: Poetry and Its Music International, 1999—, Sacred Site, 1999—, Voice Palace, 2000—, First Words, 2001—, Full Body Poetry, 2001—; dir., prodr.: Live From Mars, 2002, Live From Beyond Mars, 2003, A Spiritual Banquet of Poetry and Music, 2003; dir.: Art Spoken, Art Sung, 2003; co-dir.: Linnaeus & Fammerée, 1996—. Avocations: world travel, french studies. Home and Office: PO Box 223 Beverly Shores IN 46301-0223 E-mail: fammeree@att.net.

FAN, CHIEN, aerospace engineer, researcher; b. Haimen, China, Apr. 1, 1930; s. Chin Meng Fan and Shi Mei Shih; m. Ning Sun Chang, May 3, 1958; children: Albert W., May S., Marie S. BSME, Nat. Taiwan U., 1954; MSME, U. Ill., 1958, PhD, 1964. Asst. prof. Fla. State U., Tallahassee, 1961—65; rsch. specialist Lockheed Missiles and Space Co., Huntsville, Ala., 1965—74, staff engr. Sunnyvale, Calif., 1974—79, project engr., 1980—84, supr., 1985—91, sr. staff engr., 1989—94; ret., 1994. Vis. scientist to Republic of China NSF, Washington, 1970; lecturing scientist China Sci. and Tech. U., Hei-Fe, 1995. Contbr. articles to profl. publs. Chmn. bd. dirs. Fan Chin-Meng/Fan Heng Father/Son Scholarship Fund Found., Haimen, China, 1994—. Recipient Hdqrs. award, NASA, 1986, Hdqrs. award (2), 1994, The LMSC Pres. award, 1984. Mem.: AIAA, ASME, N.Y. Acad. Scis., Am. Soc. Engring. Edn., Sigma Xi, Pi Mu Epsilon. Achievements include development of Monte Carlo computer simulation techniques for molecular flow problems. Avocations: bridge, travel. Home: 10989 Ronald Way Cupertino CA 95014

FAN, CONG, music educator; d. Shi-Huang Fan and Feng-Li Guo. Mus D Arts, Temple U., Phila., 2000—03, MusM Arts, 1998—2000; MusB Arts, Ctrl. Conservatory of Music, Beijing, China, 1993—97. Opera coach Nat. Opera Ho. of China, Beijing, 1997—98; piano tchr. Ctrl. Conservatory of Music, Beijing, 1997—98; opera coach Temple U., Phila., 1998—2000, piano tchr., 2000—, recital accompanist, 2000—, part-time faculty, 2003—. Ch. organist United Meth. Ch., Phila., 1998—; concert pianist Rotary Clubs, Phila., 2000—, Music Teachers Nat. Assn., Phila., 2000—, Piano Teachers Congress of NY, New York, NY, 2002—. Recipient William A. Singer Meml. Award, Temple U., 1999; fellow Martha Ellen Fisher Tye Fellowship, Am. Inst. of Musical Studies, 2002; scholar Kennedy Music Scholarship, Am. Embassy, 2001, Ann. Full-tuition Scholarship, Temple U., 1998-2003, Ann. Tchg. Assistantship, 1998-2003. Mem.: Music Teachers Nat. Assn. (licentiate; cin. 2000—03), Pi Kappa Lambda Music Soc. (hon.; phila. 1999—2003, first prize 1999), Nat. Music Honor Soc. (hon.; phila. 1999—2003, first prize 1999). Achievements include Winning of Frinna Awerbuch International Piano Competition; Winning of Pennsylvania Piano Competition; Winning of Pi Kappa Lambda Competition; Winning of Young Artist's Competition; Winning of Competition's of Chinese Piano Compositions. Avocations: travel, aerobics, walking.

FAN, GUANGWEI, seismologist; b. Tianjin, China; arrived in U.S., 1986; s. Jingtao and Jingli (Wang) F.; m. Lin Guo; 1 child, Diana Ying. PhD, U. Ariz., 1992. Tchg./rsch. asst. N.Mex. State U., Las Cruces, 1986-89; rsch. assoc. U. Ariz., Tucson, 1990-92, rsch. scientist, 1992-96; postgrad. rschr. U. Calif., Santa Cruz, 1996—. Editl. bd. Seismol. Abstract, Beijing, 1979-86; contbr. articles to profl. jours. Recipient Amoco prize Amoco Corp., 1992. Mem. Am. Geophys. Union, Seismol. Soc. Am., Sigma Pi Sigma. Avocations: music, reading. Office: IGPP Dept of Earth Sci U Calif Santa Cruz 1156 High St Santa Cruz CA 95064

FAN, HUNG Y. virology educator, consultant; b. Beijing, Oct. 30, 1947; s. Hsu Yun and Li Nien (Bien) Fan. BS, Purdue U., 1967; PhD, MIT, 1971. Asst. research prof. Salk Inst., San Diego, 1973-81; asst. prof. U. Calif., Irvine, 1981-83, assoc. prof., 1984-88, prof., 1988—, dir. Cancer Rsch. Inst., 1985—, acting dean Sch. Biol. Scis., 1990-91. Editor: Jour. Virology, 1998—; contbr. NIH grantee, 1973—, grant review coms., 1973—; Woodrow Wilson Found. grad. fellow, 1967, Helen Hay Whitney Found. postdoctorate fellow, 1971. Fellow AAAS, Am. Acad. Microbiology; mem. Am. Soc. Microbiology, Am. Soc. Virology, Am. Assn. Cancer Rsch. Avocation: chamber music. E-mail: hyfan@uci.edu.

FAN, LELAND LANE, pediatrician, educator, medical researcher; b. Houston, Oct. 5, 1948; s. Paul H. and Joyce Wang Fan; m. Anne Leslie Manning; children: Tamara Young, Jacqueline Knox, Timothy, Elizabeth. BS, Baylor U., 1970, MD, 1973. Pediat. intern and resident U. Calif., San Francisco, 1973—75; pediat. resident U. Colo., Denver, 1975, pediat. pulmonary and critical care fellow, 1976—78; asst. prof. pediat. U. N.Mex., Albuquerque, 1978—82; asst. prof., assoc. prof., prof. pediat. U. Colo. Health Scis. Ctr., Denver, 1982—95; prof. pediat. Baylor Coll. Medicine, Houston, 1995—. Dir. pediat. ICU U. N.Mex., Albuquerque, 1978—82; chief pulmonary svcs. Children's Hosp., Denver, 1982—89; chief clin. pulmonary svcs. Nat. Jewish Med. and Rsch. Ctr., Denver, 1989—95, dir. pediat. spl. care unit, 1989—95; assoc. and sr. faculty Nat. Jewish Med. and Rsch. Ctr., Denver, 1989—95; dir. pediat. pulmonary fellow Baylor Coll. Medicine, Houston, 1995—2000; dir. pediat. bronchoscopy lab. Tex. Children's Hosp., Houston, 1995—. Editor: (pediat. sect.) UpToDate in Pulmonary and Critical Care Medicine, 2002; contbr. chapters to books, articles to profl. jours. Recipient Outstanding Tchg. award, Nat. Jewish Fellows, 1993, 1995; fellow, Am. Lung Assn., 1977. Fellow: Am. Acad. Pediat.; mem.: Am. Thoracic Soc. Office: Baylor Coll Medicine One Baylor Plaza Houston TX 77030

FAN, QI, mechanical engineer; b. Wuhan, China, Aug. 5, 1963; PhD, U. Ill., Chgo., 2001. Assoc. prof. Wuhan Transp. U., 1987—98; rsch. asst. prof. U. Ill., Chgo., 2001—02; bevel gear theoretician Gleason Work, 2002—. Author: Computer Methods in Applied Mechanics and Engineering, 2001. Recipient Chinese Scholarship award, Chinese Scholarship Coun., 1997, Thomas Bernard Hall prize, Inst. Mech. Engring., London, 2001. Mem.: ASME, AIAA.

FAN, TAI-SHEN LIU, dietitian; b. Taichung, Taiwan, Nov. 15, 1950; came to the U.S., 1976; d. Chi-Pei and Ching-Lien Liu; m. Chien-Chung Fan, Feb. 22, 1975; 1 child, Caroline. BA in Social Edn., Nat. Taiwan Normal U., Taipei, 1972; AS in Med. Lab. Tech., Miami (Fla.)-Dade Cmty. Coll., 1980; BS in Nutrition and Med. Dietetics, U. Ill., Chgo., 1986. Lic. dietitian State of Ill. Dept. Profl. Regulation. Counselor, tchr. Ta-Li Girls' Jr. H.S., Taipei, 1972-73, chief counselor, tchr., 1973-76; clin. dietitian Suburban Hosp. and Sanitariam, Hinsdale, Ill., 1986-87, St. Francis Hosp., Evanston, Ill., 1987—. Dean of acads. Chinese Cultural and Ednl. Assn. (CCEA)-Chinese Lang. Sch., Skokie, Ill., 1993-95, rec. sec., 1995-96, asst. prin., dean acads., 1996-97; trustee Chinese Cultural and Ednl. Assn., 2000-02. Cheng-Fu Hsieh Meml. scholar, Taipei, 1971, Yun-Wu Wang scholar, Taipei, 1971. Mem. Am. Dietetic Assn. (registered dietitian), Ill. Dietetic Assn., U. Ill. Alumni Assn., Chinese Cultural and Ednl. Assn. (trustee 2000—), Phi Tau Phi, Phi Theta Kappa. Avocations: reading, cooking. Office: 7701 N Lincoln PO Box 4572 Skokie IL 60076-4572 E-mail: taishen.fan@mindspring.com.

FAN, XIJUN, education educator; b. Yuncheng, China, Oct. 8, 1947; s. Hanting and Errui (Liu) F.; m. Shufen Tian, May 31, 1971; children: Yalin, Binghui. BSc, Beijing Normal U., 1970, MSc, Shandong Normal U., 1981. Lectr. Liaocheng (China) Edn. Coll., 1972-75, Shandong Normal U., Jinan, Cina, 1983-88, assoc. prof., 1988-93, prof., 1993—. Vis. scholar Beijing U., 1986-87; sr. vis. scholar Ariz. State U., Tempe, 1993-97. Contbr. articles to profl. jours. Recipient Sci. and Tech. Progress award Edn. Com. of Shandong Province, 1990, 92, Sci. and Tech. Progress award of Shandong Province, 1999. Mem. Chinese Optical Soc., Chinese Phys. Soc., Optical Soc. Am.adr Office: Shandong Normal U East Wenhua Rd Jinan Shandong China 250014 E-mail: fanxj108@beelink.com.

FAN, Z. HUGH, chemist, biomedical engineer; b. Qidong, Jiangsu, China, Jan. 23, 1966; came to U.S., 1994; BS, Yangzhou Tchr.'s Coll., 1985; PhD, U. Alta., Edmonton, Can., 1993. Lectr. Yangzhou Tchr.'s Coll., 1985-89; postdoctoral fellow Iowa State U., Ames, 1994-95; mem. tech. staff Sarnoff Corp., Princeton, NJ, 1995-2000; prin. scientist Aclara BioSci. Inc., Mountain View, Calif., 2000—02; assoc. prof. U. Fla., Gainesville, 2003—. Contbr. articles to profl. jours, chapters to books. Mem. AAAS, Am. Chem. Soc., Electrochem. Soc. Achievements include patents for miniaturized analyzer, biochip, microfluids from Sarnoff Corp., Princeton, NJ, 1996-1998. Office: U Fla Dept Mech and Aerospace Engring PO Box 116250 Gainesville FL 32611-6250

FANCHER, EDWIN CRAWFORD, psychologist, educator; b. Middletown, N.Y., Aug. 29, 1923; s. Frank Dane and Elizabeth (McGarr) F.; m. Vivian Kramer, Nov. 8, 1969; children: Bruce Daniel, Emily Jill. BA, The New Sch. U., 1949, MA, 1951. Psychologist Linden (N.J.) Mental Hygiene Clinic, 1955-58; therapist Cmty. Guidance Svc., N.Y.C., 1958-88; pvt. practice psychology, counseling N.Y.C., 1958—; co-founder, dir. Washington Sq. Inst. Psychotherapy and Mental Health, N.Y.C., 1960-70. Co-founder, pub. Village Voice, N.Y.C., 1955-74; dir. Orange County Telephone Co., Middletown, N.Y., 1946-60; cons. Plumsock Fund, Indpls., 1974-96, pres. 1985-96; founding pres. N.Y. Sch. for Psychoanalytic Psychotherapy and Psychoanalysis, 1978—. Founder, past chmn. N.Y. Neighborhoods Coun. on Narcotics Addiction. Served with U.S. Army, 1943-46. Decorated two Bronze stars. Mem. APA, Internat. Psychoanalytical Assn., Am. Inst. Psychotherapy and Psychoanalysis, Am. Orthopsychiat. Assn., N.Y. State Psychol. Assn., N.Y. Sch. for Psychoanalytic Psychotherapy and Psychoanlysis (pres. 1978—), N.Y. Freudian Soc. (mem. faculty tng. analyst 1985—), Gipsy Trail. Democrat. Home: 40 5th Ave New York NY 10011-8843 Office: 33 Greenwich Ave New York NY 10014-2701 E-mail: edwinfancher@earthlink.net.

FANCHER, MICHAEL REILLY, newspaper editor, newspaper publishing executive; b. Long Beach, Calif., July 13, 1946; s. Eugene Arthur and Ruth Leone (Dickson) F.; m. Nancy Helen Edens, Nov. 3, 1967 (div. 1982); children: Jason Michael, Patrick Reilly; m. 2d Carolyn Elaine Bowers, Mar. 25, 1983; Katherine Claire, Elizabeth Lynn. BA, U. Oreg., 1968; MS, Kans. State U., 1971; MBA, U. Wash., 1986. Reporter, asst. city editor Kansas City Star, Mo., 1970-76, city editor, 1976-78; reporter Seattle Times, 1978-79, night city editor, 1979-80, asst. mng. editor, 1980-81, mng. editor, 1981-86, exec. editor, 1986—, v.p., exec. editor, 1989-95; sr. v.p., 1995—. Bd. dirs. Blethen Maine Newspapers, Walla Walla Union-Bulletin, Yakima Herald Rep. Ruhl fellow Hall of Achievement, U. Oreg., 1983 Mem. Am. Soc. Newspaper Editors, Soc. Profl. Journalists, Nat. Press Photographers Assn. (Editor of Yr. 1986). Office: Seattle Times PO Box 70 1120 John St Seattle WA 98111-0070 E-mail: mfancher@seattletimes.com.

FANCHER, PAUL STRIMPLE, research scientist; b. San Antonio, Jan. 5, 1932; s. Paul and Katherine Althea (Johnson) F.; m. Mary Kuhns, June 26, 1954; children; Katherine, Janet, Louise, Rebecca. BS in Engring., U. Mich., 1953, MS in Engring., 1959, Profl. Degree, 1961. Rsch. asst. U. Mich., Ann Arbor, 1957-59, rsch. assoc., 1959-61, assoc. rsch. scientist, 1961-70, rsch. scientist, 1970-98, sr. rsch. scientist, 1998—2000, sr. rsch. scientist emeritus, 2000—. Mem. sci. com. Vehicle Sys. Dynamics, Cranfield, Eng., 1991-95; mem. exec. com., dir. rsch. Gt. Lakes Ctr. for Truck and Transit Rsch., Ann Arbor, 1994-99. Contbr. articles to profl. jours. With U.S. Army, 1953-56. Fellow Soc. Automotive Engrs. (chmn. vehicle dynamics com. 1992-2002); mem. Internat. Assn. Vehicle Sys. Dynamics. Avocations: gardening, traveling, fishing. Office: Univ Mich Transp Rsch Inst 2901 Baxter Rd Ann Arbor MI 48109-2150 E-mail: fancher@umich.edu.

FANCHER, RICK, lawyer; b. Tucson, July 27, 1953; s. James Richard and Margaret Mae (Gum) F.; m. Cecelia Francis Baney, July 12, 1975; children: Jeffery Reed, Ashley Kristin. BA, Trinity U., 1975; JD, U. Tex., 1978. Bar: Tex. 1979, U.S. Dist. Ct. (we. and so. dists.) Tex. 1981, U.S. Ct. Appeals (5th cir.) 1981. Law clk. U.S. Dist. Ct., Corpus Christi, Tex., 1978-80; asst. atty. City of Corpus Christi, 1980; assoc. Gibbins, Burrow & Bratton, Austin, Tex., 1981, John L. Johnson, Corpus Christi, 1982-85; ptnr. Thornton, Summers, Biechlin, Dunham & Brown, Corpus Christi, 1985-99, Barker, Leon, Fancher & Matthys, Corpus Christi, 2000—. Mem. Tex. Bar Assn., Tex. Bd. Legal Specialization (cert. personal injury trial law). Democrat. Avocations: jogging, bicycling, hunting, golf. Home: 4502 Lake Bistineau Dr Corpus Christi TX 78413-5261 Office: Barker Leon Fancher & Matthys 1200 First City Tower II 555 N Carancahua St Corpus Christi TX 78478-0002 E-mail: rfancher@blfmlaw.com.

FANCHI, JOHN RICHARD, physicist, educator, industrial technologist; b. Pontiac, Ill., Nov. 17, 1952; s. John Anton and Shirley Mae (Andersen) F.; m. Katherine Frances Goedecke, Aug. 22, 1976; children: Anthony Clifford, Christopher John. BS in Physics, U. Denver, 1974; MS in Physics, U. Miss., 1975; PhD in Physics, U. Houston, 1977. Rsch. asst. Denver Rsch. Inst., 1970-74; rsch. engr. Getty Oil Co., Houston, 1978-79, Cities Svc. Co., Tulsa, 1979-81; sr. engr. Keplinger & Assocs., Tulsa, 1981-84; advanced sr. engr. Marathon Oil Co., Littleton, Colo., 1984-95, Houston, 1995-98; pres. Access Pubs., Denver, 1990-93; prof. Colo. Sch. Mines, Golden, 1998—; co-owner Fanchi Enterprises Cons., 1998—. Adj. prof. physics U. Tulsa, 1980-81; vis. scientist Colo. Alliance for Sci., Denver, 1989-95; lectr. Arapahoe C.C., 1992; instr. engring. and math. U. Houston, 1996-97 Author: Parametrized Relativistic Quantum Theory, 1993, Principles of Applied Reservoir Simulation, 2nd edit., 2001, Math Refresher for Scientists and Engineers, 2nd edit., 2000, Integrated Flow Modeling, 2000, Shared Earth Modeling, 2002; referee: Soc. of Petroleum Engrs., 1981—, Founds. of Physics Jour., 1988—; contbr. Ctrl. com. Colo. Reps., Denver, 1974; coord. coun. Littleton Pub. Schs., 1989-91, v.p., sch. bd., 1993-95; coach YMCA, Littleton, 1987-92; chmn. accountability com. Runyon Elem. Sch., Littleton, 1990-91. U. Miss. fellow, 1974-75, U. Houston, 1975-77; Colo.-Wyo. Acad. Sci. grantee, 1972. Mem. Am. Phys. Soc., Soc. Petroleum Engrs. (disting.), Internat. Assn. Relativistic Dynamics (co-founder, pres. 1998—). Lutheran. Achievements include development of software models of fluid flow in porous media; pioneered devel. of parametrized relativistic quantum theory; application of high technology to model performance and manage devel. of world-class size oil and gas fields; research on the effect of laser radiation on chemical reactions. Home: 180 Eagle Dr Golden CO 80403-7775 E-mail: jfanchi@mines.edu.

FANELLI, JOSEPH JAMES, retired public affairs executive, consultant; b. Hartford, Conn., Mar. 22, 1924; s. George A.M. and Nicoletta (Lamarra) F.; m. Pirkko Annikki Saarinen, Aug. 30, 1958; children: George Tauno, John Timo, Christina Colette. BS in Fin., Syracuse U., 1949; cert. mgmt., Mich. State U., 1969; MA in Internat. Affairs, Cath. U. Am., 1995. Stockbroker G.H. Walker & Co., N.Y.C. and Hartford, Conn., 1949-51; broker, br. mgr. Schibo Corp., Jersey City and Boston, 1952-55; asst. dir. devel. U. Hartford, 1955-56; spl. asst. U.S. Rep. Edwin H. May Jr., Washington, 1957-58, U.S. Senator Prescott Bush, Washington, 1959-62; asst. mgr., then mgr. pub. affairs dept. U.S. C. of C., Washington, 1963-75; pres. Bus.-Industry Polit. Action Com., Washington, 1975-93. Editor: Enhancing the Image of Business, 1972. Mem. U.S. Jaycees, Hartford, 1950-58; internat. dir. Conn. Jaycees, 1956; mem. Md. Rep. State Ctrl. Com., Montgomery County, 1970; vol. Cmty. Chest, ARC, Conn. and Md.; active numerous polit. campaigns at local, regional, and state levels, 1956—. Staff Sgt. USAF, 1943-46, PTO. Recipient Legion of Hon. award Chapel of the Four Chaplains, 1980, Scholastic Hon. award Alpha Kappa Psi, 1949. Mem. U.S. C. of C., Nat. Assn. Mfrs. (pub. affairs steering com. 1976—), World Affairs Coun. Washington, Greater Washington Sigma Chi Alumni Assn. (cmty. amb. to France, designee Experiment in Internat. Living 1954, Significant Sig award 1991), D.C. Lions Club (pres. 1984-85, Lion of Yr. 1987, 92), Internat. Club, Univ. Club. Republican. Roman Catholic. Avocations: travel, politics, sports, music, international relations. Home: 11602 Monticello Ave Silver Spring MD 20902-1710

FANELLI, MICHAEL PAUL, music educator; b. Evanston, Ill., Feb. 12, 1943; s. George and Gloria (Del Carlo) F.; m. Carla Jean Saiger, May 28, 1978. BMus, U. Ill., 1968, EdD in Music Edn., 2000; MA in Music History, U. Mo., 1981. Cert. tchr. K-12, Mo., Iowa. Instr. of double bass U. Mo., Columbia, 1968-74; double bass artist-in-residence Stephens Coll., Columbia, 1968-75; profl. double bassist St. Louis Philharmonic, 1975-83; instr. instrumental music Sch. Dist. of the City of Ladue, Mo., 1983-87; instr. of music U. No. Iowa, Cedar Falls, 1987—; instr. of double bass Grinnell (Iowa) Coll., 1996—. Founder, music dir. No. Iowa Jr. Orchestra, Cedar Falls, 1990-92; music dir. No. Iowa Youth Orchestra, 1994—; distance learning instr. music iowa Comms. Network, U. No. Iowa, 1995—; adv. bd. Iowa Alliance for Arts Edn., Des Moines, 1994—. Contbr. articles to profl. jours.; contbg. author: American String Teacher, 1997. Double bassist U. Ill., U.S. State Dept. tour of S.Am., 1964. Microcomputer grantee U. No. Iowa, Cedar Falls, 1989, 92, 95-98. Mem. Iowa String Tchrs. Assn. (pres. 1996-98, Disting. Svc. award 1992, Cert. for Outstanding Contbn. 1996), Iowa Sch. Orchestra Assn. (pres. 1992-96), Am. String Tchrs. Assn. (editl. com. 1997—, Outstanding Contbr. 1995-97), Suzuki Assn. of the Americas (column editor 1992—), Mo. String Tchrs. Assn. (sec.-treas. 1983-87), Kappa Delta Pi. Avocations: Am. art history, photography, fly fishing. Home: 203 Parkgate Rd Cedar Falls IA 50613-1953 Office: Univ No Iowa Price Lab Sch Cedar Falls IA 50613

FANELLI, ROBERT D. surgeon; BS magna cum laude, U. Richmond, 1982; MD, Med. Coll. of Pa., 1986. Diplomate Am. Bd. Surgery, Nat. Bd. Med. Examiners; cert. BLS, ACLS, Advanced Trauma Life Support; cert. DEA; controlled substance permit, Mass. Residency in surgery The Stamford (Conn.) Hosp., 1986-88; integrated residency in gen. surgery Mich. State U., East Lansing, 1988-91; fellow dept. surgery Mt. Sinai Med. Ctr. Cleve., 1991-92; gen. and laparoendoscopic surgeon Surg. Specialists of Western New Eng., P.C., Pittsfield, Mass., 1992—; pres., 1992—; surg. dir. New Eng. Pain Diagnosis and Treatment Ctr., Pittsfield, 1996-99; vice chmn. dept. surgery Berkshire Med. Ctr., 2000—03, dir. surg. endoscopy, 2002—. Surgeon Berkshire Med. Ctr., Pittsfield, 1992—; dir. endoscopic svcs. Hillcrest Hosp., Pittsfield, 1993-2001; dir. edn. in laparoendoscopic surgery Berkshire Med. Ctr. Residency Program in Surgery, 1996-99; asst. prof. surgery U. Mass. Med. Sch.; tchg. assoc. premed. program Williams Coll.; conf. presenter in field. Contbr. articles to profl. publs. Recipient U. Richmond Acad. Honors award, 1980, Va. Inst. for Sci. Rsch. Undergrad. award in Biology, U. Richmond, 1981, John Neasmith Dickinson Meml. Rsch. award in Biology, U. Richmond, 1981, Brownell Found. Resident Rsch. award in Gen. Surgery, McLaren Regional Med. Ctr., 1989, Flint Acad. of Surgery Resident Rsch. award, 1990, Mich. State U. Dept. of Surgery Resident Rsch. award, 1992; named Outstanding Resident Instr. of Yr. in Gen. Surgery, Mich. State U., 1990-91. Fellow ACS (membership selection com. dist. #1 Mass. chpt.); mem. Am. Soc. Gastrointestinal Endoscopy, Soc. Am. Gastrointestinal Endoscopic Surgeons (co-chair of Guideline Com. (new name for Std.), rep. to Am. Soc. Gastrointestinal Endoscopy stds. of practice com. mem. flexible endoscopy and rural surgery task force coms. (ends effective Oct. 2003), Am. Neuromodulation Soc., Soc. for Surgery of Alimentary Tract, Soc. Am. Gastrointestinal and Endoscopic Surgeons (co-chair stds. and practice com. 2002--), Mass. Med. Soc., Berkshire Dist. Med. Soc., Phi Beta Kappa, Sigma Xi, Gamma Sigma Epsilon, Phi Eta Sigma. Achievements include development of surgical instrumentation and technology. Avocations: snow skiing, boating, tennis. Office: Surg Specialists Western New Eng 510 North St Ste 202 Pittsfield MA 01201-4111

FANG, CHENG-SHEN, chemical engineering educator; b. Taipei, Taiwan, Mar. 29, 1936; came to U.S., 1962; s. Hou-Chin and Roumouy Fang; m. Fei-Ying Fang, Oct. 5, 1972. BSChemE, Nat. Taiwan U., Taipei, 1958; MSChemE, U. Houston, 1965, PhD in Chem. Engring., 1968. Registered profl. engr., La. Postdoctoral fellow U. Houston, 1968-69; prof. chem. engring. U. La., Lafayette, 1969—. Presenter in field. Co-author: Oceanography-Contemporary Reading, 1996; creater (computer software) ChemCalc 2, ChemCalc 3, 1985; contbr. articles to profl. jours. Mem. AIChE, Soc. Petroleum Engrs. Office: U La Dept Chem Engring Madison Hall Rex St Lafayette LA 70504-0001 E-mail: fangcs@louisiana.edu.

FANG, JOONG, philosopher, mathematician, educator; b. Piongyang, Korea, Mar. 30, 1923; arrived in U.S., 1948, naturalized, 1962; s. Gabiong and Igab (Kim) Fang; children: Eva Maria, Guido Andreas. Student, Chuo U., Tokyo, 1939-41; BS, Coll. Tech. Seoul, Korea, 1944; MA, Yale U., 1950; PhD, U. Mainz, Germany, 1957. Asst. prof. math. Jinhae Coll., also U. Pusan, Republic of Korea, 1945-48, Valparaiso (Ind.) U., 1958-59, St. John's U., 1959-61, U. Alaska, 1961-62; assoc. prof. No. Ill. U., 1963-67; prof. math. and philosophy Memphis State U., 1967-73; prof. philosophy Old Dominion U., Norfolk, Va., 1974-90, prof. emeritus, 1990—. Vis. prof. U. Münster, Germany, 1971. Author: (book) Das Antinomienproblem, 1957, Abstract Algebra, 1963, Kant-Interpretation, I, 1967, Numbers Racket: The Aftermath of the "New Math", 1968, Towards a Philosophy of Modern Mathematics, I, Bourbaki, 1970, II, Hilbert, 1970, Mathematicians from Antiquity to Today, I, 1972, Sociology of Mathematics and Mathematicians, 1975, The Illusory Infinite: A Theology of Mathematics, 1976, Logic Today, Basics and Beyond, 1979, Linguistic Sense of the Japanese (in Japanese), 1984, Kant and Mathematics Today, 1997, Learning, East and West, 2002, Docta Ignorantia, 2003; editor: Philosophia Mathematica, 1964—92. Mem.: Am. Philos. Assn., Am. Math. Soc. Address: 9745 Oakview Dr North VA 23128-9041

FANG, MARK (YANCHU FANG), geneticist; b. Yue Yang, Hunan, China; came to U.S., 1987; s. X. Fang and Y. Qu. BS, DVM, Hunan Agrl. U., Changsha, China, 1981; MS, Western Ky. U., 1990; PhD, U. Wis., 1996. From instr. to asst. prof. Hunan Agrl. U., Changsha, 1982-84; editor Hunan Sci. and Tech. Pub. Ho., Changsha, 1985-88; rsch. asst. Western Ky U., Bowling Green, 1989-90; rsch. specialist state lab. U. Wis., Madison, 1991-92, rsch. asst., 1993-96; postdoctoral fellow U. Calif., Berkeley, 1997-98, Yale U., New Haven, 1998-99; chief sci. officer Regene Bio Sci. Internat. Inc., Berkeley, 1999—2001; CEO, U.S. BioTech. Sources, 2001—. Vis. scholar PIC, Franklin, Ky., 1987-88. Editor: Dairy Production in China, 1986, Practice Manual in Food Microbiology, 1988; co-author: Swine Production in China, 1987, Sanitary Control in Canned Food Processing, 1987. Mem. Am. Endocrinology Soc., Plant and Animal Genome Soc., Internat. Embryo Transfer Soc., Mouse Genetics. Avocations: basketball, ping pong, fishing.

FANGANELLO, JOSEPH MICHAEL, lawyer; b. Denver, Nov. 16, 1941; s. Anthony and Imogene (Baskett) F.; m. JoAnne Craig, Aug. 13, 1966; children: Joseph Duffy, Anne, Joan. BA, Regis Coll., 1963; JD, U. Colo., 1968. Bar: Colo. 1968. Law clk. Denver Dist. Ct., 1968-69; sole practice Denver, 1968-82; ptnr. Joseph M. Fanganello, P.C., Denver, 1982—. Officer, dir. numerous Colo. cos., 1968—. Bd. dirs., counsel Denver Opera Co., 1977-80. Mem. Denver Bar Assn., Colo. Bar Assn. Office: Joseph M Fanganello PC 1650 Washington St Denver CO 80203-1407

FANGER, MARK, psychologist, psychotherapist, consultant; b. Boston, Dec. 6, 1943; AB in Polit. Sci., Syracuse U., 1965; EdM in Psychology, Boston State Coll., 1972; EdD in Counseling Psychology, Boston U., 1977; grad. Clin. Consultation Program, Boston Inst. for Psychotherapy, 1984. Lic. psychologist, Mass., Nat. Register in Psychology. Clin. dir. Milford Assistance Program Community Mental Health Ctr., Milford, Mass., 1971-74; clin. cons. drug treatment program Boston City Hosp., 1975-77; staff psychologist Bay Area Psychiat. Assocs., Burlington, Mass., 1977-80, Suburban Counseling Assocs., Weston, Mass., 1977-80; clin. supr. Whiteman House, Survival, Inc., Quincy, Mass., 1982-84; pvt. practice psychotherapy, Newton Highlands, Mass., 1978—. Mem. adj. faculty dept. counseling psychology Boston U., 1976-77, dept. psychology Boston State Coll., 1977-79; mem. adj. faculty Antioch's Inst. Open Edn., Cambridge, Mass., 1979-80; mem. adj. faculty, supr. family therapy Mass. Sch. Profl. Psychology, Newton, 1982-83; group psychotherapy cons. People for People, Inc., Framingham, Mass., 1990-92; mem. faculty group psychotherapy tng. program Northeastern Soc. for Group Psychotherapy, 1991-98; bd. dirs. Youth Enrichment Svcs., Inc., Boston; presenter in field; condr. workshops. Recipient Svc. of Self award Rotary Club, Franklin, Mass., 1974; grantee Mass. Gen. Hosp., 1975. Fellow: Mass. Psychol. Assn.; mem.: APA, Consortium for Psychotherapy, Northeastern Soc. Group Psychotherapy (membership com. 1986—88, program com. 1988—94, faculty tng. program group psychotherapy 1991—99, bd. dir. 1994—97, inst. com. 1995—2001, chair inst. com. 1996—2001, bd. dir. 1999—2001), Soc. for Family Therapy and Rsch. (edn. com. 1984—87), Psychologists for Social Responsibility, Am. Mental Health Alliance New Eng. (charter), Phi Delta Kappa, Pi Lambda Theta. Office: 4 Hartford St Newton Highlands MA 02461-1553

FANGEROW, KAY ELIZABETH, nurse; b. Thomas, Okla., June 27, 1952; d. Byron Frederick and Wilma Jean (Bickford) Mayfield; children: David Andrew, Sarah Elizabeth. Student, Oral Roberts U., 1970-71; BS in Nursing magna cum laude, Calif. State U., Long Beach, 1975; MS in Health Care Adminstrn., U. LaVerne, 1991. RN, Calif.; cert. pub. health nurse. Staff nurse pediatrics service Long Beach Meml. Hosp., 1974-75, Riverside (Calif.) Community Hosp., 1975-76, Parkview Community Hosp., Riverside, 1982-84; supervising pub. health nurse County Health Dept., San Bernardino, Calif., 1976—, coord. sch. based and sch. linked health care svcs., 1994—, grant writer, 1994—. Cons. Am. Home Health, Santa Ana, Calif., 1986—. Instr. Inland Counties chpt. Am. Cancer Soc., Riverside, 1977—; mem. cmty. action coun. San Bernardino Cty. Youth Justice Ctr., 1999—. Mem. Am. Pub. Health Assn. (co-author abstract 1986, 87, 89, coordinator hypertension worksite project, diabetes control project, pub. health nursing homeless project, presenter ann. meeting 1986, 87, 89), Pub. Health Nurse Group (chmn. 1977-78, vice chmn. profl. performance com. 1978, sec. peer rev. com. 1978), San Bernardino County Asthma Coalition, Sigma Theta Tau (Gamma Alpha chpt., honoree for child abuse prevention supervising pub. health nurse of yr. 2002). Democrat. Home: PO Box 3308 Running Springs CA 92382-3308 E-mail: kfangerow@dph.sbcounty.gov.

FANGMANN, HEATHER ANN, secondary educator, English; b. Wichita, Kans., Sept. 22, 1973; d. Ronald George and Joice Mary Fangmann. BSE in English, Emporia State U., 1996, MA in English, 2003. Cert. English educator, 5-12. Substitute tchr. USD 394/260, Rose Hill/Derby, Kans., 1996-97; tchr. English USD 490, El Dorado, Kans., 1997—. Tchr. Sylvan Learning Ctr., Wichita, 1997-98. Author: (poem) Quivira, 1995. Mem. Assistance League of Wichita, 1995—. English scholar Emporia State U., 1993-96. Mem. Nat. Coun. Tchrs. English. Republican. Avocations: soccer, poetry, running, reading. Home: 1275 S Topeka St El Dorado KS 67042-3791 Business E-Mail: hfangmann@eldoradoschools.org.

FANIZZA, MICHAEL ANTHONY, art educator; b. Killeen, Tex., July 18, 1954; s. Michael and Arleen Fanizza; m. Sanja Softic; 1 child, Olivia Virginia. BA, U. Ill., Chgo., 1981; MFA, Va. Commonwealth U., 1984. Asst. prof. Ohio U., Athens, 1984—86, Chico (Calif.) State U., 1986—88; chair, assoc. prof. Old Dominion U., Norfolk, Va., 1988—99; prof. Mich. State U., East Lansing, 1999—. Prin. Michael Fanizza Designs, Haslett, Mich., 1999—. Artist (graphic design) MF Designs Poster (1st pl. am. Assn. Museums, 1999), Fifteenth Ann. Rosen Sculpture Catalog (Am. Graphic Design award, 2002). Mem.: AIGA, Coll. Art Assn. Home: 1051 Wild Ginger Trl Haslett MI 48840 Office: Mich State U 313 Kresge Art Ctr East Lansing MI 48824 Office Fax: 517-432-3938. E-mail: fanizza@msu.edu.

FANN, MARGARET ANN, counselor; b. Pasco, Wash., July 16, 1942; d. Joseph Albert David and Clarice Mable (Deaver) Rivard; m. Jerry Lee Fann, June 13, 1986; children: Brenda Heupel, Scott Sherman, Kristin Johnson, Robert Lack III. AA, Big Bend C.C., Moses Lake, Wash., 1976; BA in Applied Psychology magna cum laude, Ea. Wash. U., 1977, MS in Psychology, 1978. Cert. mental health counselor, Wash.; cert. chem. dependency counselor II, nat. cert. addictions counselor II, cert. in chronic psychiat. disability. Intern counselor Linker House Drug Rehab., Spokane, Wash., 1976-78; drug counselor The House drug program, Tacoma, Wash., 1978-80; exec. dir. Walla Walla (Wash.) Commn. Alcohol, 1980-82; dir. Cmty. Alcohol Svcs. Assn., Kennewick, Wash., 1982-86; primary care coord. Carondelet Psychiat. Care Ctr., Richland, Wash., 1986-90; part-time instr. Ea. Wash. U., Cheney, 1981-88; instr. Columbia Basin Coll., Pasco, 1990-93; adminstr. Action Chem. Dependency Ctr., Kennewick, 1993—. Bd. dirs. Benton-Franklin County Substance Abuse Coalition, Pasco, Kennewick, Richland, 1990—. Vol. Pat Hale for Senator, Kennewick, 1994. Mem. Am. Counselors Assn., Nat. Mental Health Counselors Assn., Wash. State Mental Health Counselors Assn., Tri-Cities Counselors Assn., Phi Theta Kappa. Avocations: Triathlons (swim, bike, run), Native Am. culture and artifacts. Office: Action Chem Dependency Ctr 552 N Colorado St Ste 5525 Kennewick WA 99336-7779 also: Benton-Franklin County MICA Detoxification Ctr 1020 E 7th Ave Kennewick WA 99336-5936

FANNIN, CAROLINE MATHER, library administrator; b. N.Y.C., July 22, 1959; d. Alfred Bruce and Marjorie Evelyn (Burns) Brown; m. John Paul Fannin, Jan. 12, 1991; stepchildren: Scott A., Brian W. BA, Wheaton Coll., 1982; MLS, Rutgers U., 1984. Profl. libr., N.J. Info. analyst Montclair (N.J.) Pub. Libr., 1979-85, br. supr., 1985-90; dir. Louis Bay 2d Libr., Hawthorne, N.J., 1990-92; exec. dir. Bergen-Passaic Regional Libr. Coop., Hawthorne, 1992-93; writer, 1993—; dir. Ridgefield Park (N.J) Pub. Libr., 2000—02; expansion coord. Montclair Pub. Libr., 1995-99, pub. svc. chief, 2003—. Co-author: (book chpts.) Abortion: Library in a Book, 1991, Capital Punishment: Library in a Book, 1991, Distinguished African Americans in Aviation and Space Sciences, 2001; author articles. Mem. Hawthorne Aux Police, 1994—; bd. dirs. Bergen-Passaic Regional Libr. Coop., Hawthorne, 1991—92, Highlands Regional Libr. Coop., Denville, NJ, 2000—02. Mem.: ALA, N.J. Libr. Assn. Office: Montclair Pub Libr 50 S Fullerton Ave Montclair NJ 07042 E-mail: fannin@montlib.org.

FANNIN, PAUL ROBERT, political party official; BA, Stanford U., 1957; JD, U. Ariz., 1963. Bar: Ariz. Former gov. State of Ariz.; U.S. Senator from Ariz., 1964—76; chmn. Ariz. Rep. Party, 2001—. State bar lectr. govt. rels. Bd. dirs., past chmn. Barrow Neurol. Inst. Found.; mem. Alexis de Tocqueville Soc., United Way; mem., state govt. liaison Phoenix Thunderbirds. Mem.: Maricopa County Bar Assn., Phi Alpah Delta. Office: Collier Ctr 201 E Washington St Ste 1600 Phoenix AZ 85004-2382 Office Fax: 602-257-5299.*

FANNIN, TOM, architectural firm executive; BArch with honors, U. Tex., 1970; MArch, Tex. A&M U., 1972. Dir. health planning FKP Arch., 1998—. Lectr. in field. Mem.: AIA (mem. com. on architecture for health), Acad. Architecture for Health (mem. Houston chpt.), Nat. Coun. Archtl. Registration Bd. Cert., Am. Coll. Healthcare Archs. (founding mem.), Am. Coll. Healthcare Execs., Am. Soc. Hosp. Engring. Avocations: travel, art. Office: 8 Greenway Plz Ste 300 Houston TX 77046-0899*

FANNING, BARRY HEDGES, lawyer; b. Olney, Tex., Dec. 5, 1950; s. Robert Allen and Carolyn (Parker) F.; m. Rebecca Sue Cobbs, May 24, 1975 (dec. Mar. 1997); m. Sherri Winn Perry, Mar. 6, 1999. BBA, Baylor U., 1972, LL.B., 1973. Bar: Tex. 1973, Fla. 1974, U.S. Dist. Ct. (no., ea. we. and so. dists.) Tex. 1974, U.S. Ct. Appeals (5th and 11th cirs.) 1974. Mem. firm Fanning, Harper & Martinson, Dallas, 1974—. Social v.p. Dallas Symphony Orch. Guild, 1975-77; mem. Dallas Regional Young Life Bd., 1977—, fund raising chmn., 1982-84, 86-88, 97—; bd. dirs., membership/mktg. com., Downtown YMCA, 1997—, chmn. cmty. svcs. fund dr., 2003; mem. Russell Perry Free Enterprise Banquet Com., Dallas Bapt. U.; mem. Miss Tex. Pageant Bd., 2003—. Mem. ABA (vice chmn. young lawyers com. 1980, pub. rels. com. torts sect.), Baylor U. Student Found. (steering com. 1971-72), Baylor Alumni Assn. (bd. dirs. 1978-82, 95), Tryon Coterie (pres. 1971), Highland Park Forensics Found. (pres. 1993-95), Preston Ctr. Legal Assn. (sec. 1993-94, bd. dirs. 1994-95), Dervish Club, Calyx Club, Dallas Baylor Club (bd. dirs. 1976-84, pres. 1981-82), Christian Men's Club, Phi Eta Sigma, Omicron Kappa Delta, Phi Delta Theta. Baptist. Home: 4400 Lorraine Dallas TX 75205 Office: Fanning Harper & Martinson 4849 Greenville Ave Ste 1300 Dallas TX 75206

FANNING, DELVIN SEYMOUR, soil science educator; b. Copenhagen, N.Y., July 13, 1931; s. Clarence Roscoe and Faye Theodora (Hays) F.; m. Mary Christine Balluff, Nov. 22, 1958 (dec. Aug. 1994); children: Michael Christopher, Maurine Faye, Christine Kay; m. Emily Louise Wenzel Manning, Nov. 15, 1997. BS, Cornell U., 1954, MS, 1959; PhD, U. Wis., 1964. Cert. profl. soil scientist. Soil scientist Soil Conservation Svc., USDA, 1954, 59-62; grad. rsch. asst. dept. of soils U. Wis., Madison, 1960-64; from asst. prof. to prof. dept. natural resource scis. and landscape arch. U. Md., College Park, 1964-99, emeritus prof., 1999—. Vis. prof. Tech. U. of Munich, Germany, 1971-72, USDA Soil Conservation Svc., Washington, 1986; rsch. assoc. Tex. A&M U., College Station, 1979. Co-author: (with M.C.B. Fanning) Soil: Morphology, Genesis, and Classification, 1989, co-editor Acid Sulfate Weathering, 1982; contbr. entries in Encys., chpts. in books, articles to profl. jours.. Bass singer Holy Redeemer Ch. Choir, College Park, Md., 1968—. With U.S. Army, 1954-56. Fellow Am Soc. Agronomy, Soil Sci. Soc. Am. Democrat. Roman Catholic. Achievements include definition, description and naming of processes for sulfide mineral accumulation in soils sulfidization and sulfide mineral oxidation to form sulfuric acid, and reaction of sulfuric acid with soils to form new minerals sulfuricization. Home: 4809 Ravenswood Rd Riverdale Park MD 20737-1115 Office: U Md Dept Nat Resource Scis and Landscape Arch College Park MD 20742-4452 E-mail: delvindel@aol.com., df3@umail.umd.edu. *Know the earth and live in harmony.*

FANNING, GARY LEE, anesthesiologist; b. Rochester, N.Y., July 19, 1940; MD, SUNY, Syracuse, 1966. Diplomate Am. Bd. Anesthesiology. Intern Strong Meml. Hosp., Rochester, N.Y., 1966-67, resident in anesthesiology, 1967-70; staff Mary Greeley Med. Ctr., Ames, Iowa, 1972-91, Hauser-Ross Surg. Ctr. Inc., Sycamore, Ill., 1991—. Mem. AMA, Am. Soc. Anesthesiologists, Alpha Omega Alpha. Office: Hauser Ross Eye Inst 2240 Gateway Dr Sycamore IL 60178-3155 Fax: 815-756-1226. E-mail: glfanning@aol.com.

FANNING, RONALD HEATH, architect, engineer; b. Evanston, Ill., Oct. 5, 1935; s. Ralph Richard and Leone Agatha (Heath) F.; m. Jenine Vivian Schnelle, Jan. 9, 1960; children: Anthony Lee, Traycee Anne. BArch, Miami U., Oxford, Ohio, 1959. Registered architect in 24 states; registered profl. engr. in 13 states Nat. Coun. of Archtl. Registration Bds., Nat. Coun. of Engring. Examiners, Chmn. bd. Fanning/Howey Assocs., Inc., Celina, Ohio, 1959—. Mng. ptnr. Manning Partnership, Celina 1978—, F/H Bldg. Partnership, 1986-2003; trustee Fanning Family Charitable Remainder Trust, 2003—. Chmn. Mercer County Young Reps., Celina, 1962-65. Recipient Fred B. Joyner Profl. Achievement award Delta Gamma chpt. Pi Kappa Alpha, 1997. Mem. NSPE, Am. Inst. Architects, Coun. Ednl. Facility Planners Internat. (Great Lakes Midwest regional membership chmn. 1992-97, pres. Great Lakes Midwest region coun. ednl. facility planners internat. 1997-98), Ohio Soc. Profl. Engrs., Ohio Soc. Architects, Soc. Mktg. Profl. Svcs., Fla. Ednl. Facilities Planners Assn., Buckeye Assn. Sch. Adminstrs., Coun. Ednl. Facility Planners Internat. (membership chmn. 1994-96, dir. 1997-2002, pres.-elect 2002-2003, pres. 2003—, cert.). Methodist. Avocations: tennis, bowling, golf. Home: 422 Magnolia St Celina OH 45822-1254 Office: Fanning Howey Assoc Inc PO Box 71 Celina OH 45822-0071 E-mail: rfanning@fhai.com.

FANNING, WILLIAM HENRY, JR., computer specialist; b. N.Y.C., Feb. 12, 1917; s. William Henry and Terese Genevieve (Moloney) F.; m. Mary Major Winter, Sept. 5, 1940; children: Hugh M. (dec.), Helen A. Smith, Mary M., Gerard, William Henry III. BA, Fordham U., 1940; postgrad., Cath. U., 1940-41, Jersey City State Coll., 1977, Pace U., 1989-91. Exch. clerk N.Y. Times, 1938-40; Greek and German instr. Gonzaga High Sch., Washington, 1940-41; reporter, copy editor Nat. Cath. News Svc., Washington, 1941-48, news editor, 1948-55; dir. Rome News Bur., Radio Free Europe, 1955-57, dir. news and info. svcs., 1957-59, dir. Paris News Bur., 1959-60; editor The Cath. News, N.Y.C., 1960-66; freelance writer CBS-TV, N.Y.C., 1966-68, Harcourt Brace Jovanovich, N.Y.C., 1967-72; v.p. promotion and advt., pop music producer/agt. Diamond Prodns., Ltd., N.Y.C., 1967-69; analyst CGA Computer Assocs., Holmdel, N.J., 1969-73; programmer/analyst to sr. systems specialist Equitable Life Assurance Soc. U.S., N.Y.C., 1973-87; computer and network mgr. Mayor's Office of Midtown Enforcement, N.Y.C., 1988-94. Cons. Bill Fanning Productivity Systems, Westport Point, Mass., 1966—; lectr. journalism Good Counsel Coll., White Plains, N.Y., 1967-69; head U.S. Cath. Bishops Press Rels. Office, Rome-2d Vatican, 1962; mem. pres.'s com. Employment of the Handicapped, 1947-66. Bd. dirs. Westchester Cath. Edn. Coun., N.Y.C., 1963-69; mem. Archdiocese Edn. Coun., N.Y.C., 1961-66. Lt. USNR, 1942-45. Mem. N.Y. Acad. Scis., Writers Guild Am., Phi Kappa Theta (hon.). Roman Catholic. Home and Office: Box 234 Westport Point MA 02791-0234

FANNING, WILLIAM JAMES, professional baseball team executive, radio and television broadcaster; b. Chgo., Sept. 14, 1927; s. Frank and Gladys Leona (Lighter) F. BA in phys. edn., Buena Vista Coll, 1951; M in Phys. Edn., U. Ill., 1961. Profl. baseball player Chgo. Cubs, 1954, 56, 57; player, mgr. Tulsa Oilers, Tex. League, 1958, Dallas Rangers, Am. Assn., 1959-60, Venezuela, Eau Claire Braves, Wis., 1961-62; spl. assignment scout Milw. Braves, 1963-64, asst. gen. mgr., 1964-66; asst. gen. mgr., farm and scouting dir. Atlanta Braves, 1966-67; 1st dir. Major League Scouting Bur., 1968; gen. mgr. Montreal Expos., 1968-73, v.p., gen. mgr., 1973-77, v.p. player devel., 1977-81, field mgr., 1981-84, v.p. player devel. and scouting, 1982-86, spl. cons. baseball ops., 1989—; radio and TV broadcaster, 1987-88. Spl. cons. baseball ops., 1989-92; major league scout Colo. Rockies, 1993-99; radio baseball show CJAD, Montreal, 1993-2000; spl. asst. to gen. mgr. Toronto Blue Jays, 2001, amb. to amateur baseball Toronto Blue Jays 2002, 2003. Served with U.S. Army, 1945-47. Inducted into Can. Baseball Hall of Fame, 2000, Montreal Expos Hall of Fame, 2000. Methodist. Home and Office: 154 Tiner Ave Dorchester ON Canada N0L 1G2 Address: One Blue Jays Way Ste 3200 Toronto ON Canada M5V 1J1 E-mail: wordsarepoetry@rogers.com.

FANNJIANG, ALBERT, mathematician, educator; arrived in U.S., 1987; s. W.-C. and W.-Y. Fannjiang; m. Jean Fannjiang, Mar. 19, 1988; children: Clara, Dominic. PhD, NYU, 1992. Asst. prof. computational and applied math. UCLA, 1992—95; asst. prof. U. Calif., Davis, 1995—99, assoc. prof., 1999—2003, prof. math., 2003—. Contbr. rsch. articles to profl. jours. Recipient U. Calif.-Davis Chancellor fellowship, U. of Calif., 2001—06; grantee, NSF, 1996—2003. Mem.: Am. Math. Soc. (Centennial fellow 2002). Achievements include research in mathematical theory of random media. Office: U Calif Dept Math One Shields Ave Davis CA 95616-8633 Office Fax: 530-752-6635.

FANONE, JOSEPH ANTHONY, lawyer; b. Sharon, Pa., Apr. 14, 1949; s. Anthony and Nancy Fanone; children: Michael, Kathleen, Peter. AB, Georgetown U., 1971, JD, 1974. Bar: Pa. 1974, D.C. 1980. Asst. atty. gen. Pa. Dept. of Justice, 1974-77; assoc. Squire, Sanders & Dempsey, Washington, 1977-81, Ballard, Spahr, Andrews & Ingersoll, Washington, 1981-83, ptnr., 1983-94, Piper & Marbury, Washington, 1994-95, Ballard, Spahr, Andrews & Ingersoll, Washington, 1996—. Mem. ABA. Office: Ballard Spahr Andrews & Ingersoll 601 13th St NW Ste 1000 Washington DC 20005-3807

FANOS, KATHLEEN HILAIRE, osteopathic physician, podiatrist; b. Bremerhaven, Germany, Aug. 18, 1956; came to U.S., 1957; d. Homer Dantangelo and Ilse Helmar (Ochs) F. AAS in Music, Nassau C.C., Garden City, N.Y., 1976; BS in Music Edn., Hofstra U., 1978, postgrad., 1978-79; D Podiatric Medicine, Coll. Podiatric Med. and Surg., Des Moines, 1987; DO, Coll. Osteo. Med. and Surg., Des Moines, 1994. Diplomate Am. Bd. Internal Medicine. Tchr. music McKenna Jr. H.S. and Eastlake Elem. Sch., Massapequa, N.Y., 1978-79; musician numerous profl. orgns., N.Y., Iowa, 1979—; preceptorship in podiatry Bayshore, N.Y., 1987-88; pvt. practice podiatry Hyde Park, West Roxbury and Brookline, Mass., 1988-91; resident in internal medicine Winthrop U. Hosp., Mineola, N.Y., 1994-97; internist Cmty. Med. Assocs., Jackson, NJ, 1997-2000, Ocean County Family Care, Jackson, 2000—03, Hinds Internaal Medicine, Jackson. Ins. med. examiner Portamedic, Burlington, Mass., 1988-91. Mem. AMA, ACP, Am. Bd. Internal Medicine, Am. Soc. Internal. Medicine, Am. Osteo. Assn., Am. Coll. Osteo. Family Physicians, N.Y. State Internal Medicine Soc., Phi Theta Kappa, Pi Kappa Lambda, Sigma Sigma Phi, Phi Delta Epsilon. Avocations: music, tennis, bowling, skiing, travel. E-mail: kmozartf@aol.com.

FANOUS, NIKKI HOBERT, lawyer; b. Lubbock, Tex., July 2, 1967; d. Tony R. Hobert and Ann A. (Moorhouse) Gibbs; m. David Elias Fanous, Apr. 27, 1996; 1 child, Ashley Jordan. BA, So. Meth. U., 1987; JD, La. State U., 1993. Bar: Tex. 1993. Assoc. Page & Addison, P.C., Dallas, 1994-96; ptnr. Jackson Walker, L.L.P., Ft. Worth, 1996—. Mem. ABA, State Bar Tex., Tarrant County Bar Assn., Greater Ft. Worth Comml. Real Estate Women, Comml. Real Estate Women Network. Republican. Presbyterian. Avocations: travel, reading, scuba diving. Office: Jackson Walker LLP 301 Commerce St Ste 2400 Fort Worth TX 76102-4124

FANSELOW, JULIE RUTH, writer; b. Springfield, Ill., July 26, 1961; d. Byron and Ruth Leona (Neumann) F.; m. Bruce Edward Whiting, Apr. 25, 1992; 1 child, Natalie. BS in Journalism, Ohio U., 1982. Reporter Salem (Ohio) News, 1982-85; editor Vindicator, Youngstown, Ohio, 1985-89; reporter Times-News, Twin Falls, Ohio, 1989-91; pvt. practice writer Twin Falls, 1991—. Co-founder Guidebookwriters.com. Author: Traveling the Oregon Trail, 1993, new edit., 2001, Traveling the Lewis and Clark Trail, 1994, 3d edit., 2003, Idaho Off The Beaten Path, 1998, new edit., 2002, Texas (Lonely Planet), 1999, 2d edit., 2002, British Columbia (Lonely Planet), 2001; contbr. articles to nat. publs. Recipient 1st place for mag. writing Idaho Press Club, 1992, 1st place for guidebook Nat. Assn. for Interpretation, 1993. Mem. Am. Soc. Journalists and Authors, Soc. Am. Travel Writers, Lewis and Clark Trail Heritage Found., Oreg.-Calif. Trail Assn. Unitarian Universalist. Avocations: kayaking, travel, reading, arts, hiking. Home and Office: Fanselow Comm 1511 9th Ave E Twin Falls ID 83301-6611

FANT, CLYDE EDWARD, JR., religion educator; b. Marshall, Tex., Nov. 14, 1934; s. Clyde Edward and Margaret (Moos) F.; (div.); children: Brian H., Carol E., Julie A.; m. Cheryl Hammock, Nov. 9, 1984. BA, Baylor U., 1956; BD, Southwestern Bapt. Seminary, Ft. Worth, 1960, ThD, 1964. Ordained to ministry Bapt. Ch., 1956. Pastor First Bapt. Ch., Belcher, La., 1958-62, Ruston, La., 1962-66; prof. of preaching Southwestern Bapt. Seminary, Ft. Worth, 1966-75; pastor First Bapt. Ch., Richardson, Tex., 1975-82; pres. Internat. Bapt. Sem., Ruschlikon/Zurich, Switzerland, 1982-83; dean of chapel, prof. religious

studies Stetson Univ., Deland, Fla., 1985-2000, O.L. Walker Prof. Christian Studies emeritus, 2000—; dir. Fla. Winter Pastor's Sch., 1985—. Vis. prof. of preaching Divinity Sch., Duke U., Durham, NC, Southea. Bapt. Sem., Wake Forest, NC, 1983—85. Author, editor 20 Centuries of Great Preaching (13 vols.), 1971; author: Preaching for Today, 1977, Bonhoeffer: Worldly Preaching, 1991, The Misunderstood Jesus: Ten Lost Keys to Life, 1996; co-author: An Introduction to the Bible, 1991, rev. edit., 2001, A Guide to Biblical Sites in Greece and Turkey, 2003. Recipient Fulbright scholarship, Tubingen, Fed. Republic of Germany, 1956, Venting award/Outstanding Sr., Southwestern Bapt. Sem., 1960. Mem.: Soc. Bibl. Lit. Democrat. E-mail: cfant@stetson.edu.

FANT, GENE CLINTON, JR., English language educator; b. Laurel, Miss., June 30, 1963; s. Gene C. and Ramona Faith (Hankins) F.; m. Lisa Anne Williams, Mar. 25, 1989. BA, James Madison U., 1984; MA, Old Dominion U., 1987; MDiv, New Orleans Bapt. Theol. Sem., 1991; MEd, PhD, U. So. Miss., 1995. Instr. Hampton (Va.) City Schs., 1985-87; instr. of English Gloucester (Va.) County Schs., 1987-89, Phillips Coll., Metairie, La., 1989-90, William Carey Coll., Hattiesburg, Miss., 1991-92; teaching asst. in English U. So. Miss., Hattiesburg, 1992-94, asst. dir. dept. edn., 1994-95, aide to univ. pres., 1995; asst. prof. Miss. Coll., Clinton, 1995—2002; assoc. prof., chair English dept. Union U., Jackson, Tenn., 2002—. Cons. Miss. River Ministry, Jackson, 1992. Author: Petrarchan Hagiography in Wroth, 1995, Expectant Moments, 1999; contbr. articles to profl. jours. Crisis counselor, New Orleans, 1990-92. Linwood Orange fellow U. So. Miss., 1993. Mem. MLA, Conf. on Christianity and Lit. (Daub-Maher prize 1994), Philological Assn. La., Gamma Beta Phi. Avocations: film studies, sports, travel. Office: Union U Box 3142 1050 Union University Dr Jackson TN 38305

FANTA, GEORGE FREDERICK, chemist, researcher; b. Chgo., Aug. 30, 1934; s. George and Hermina Fanta; m. Carmen Viola Amado, Sept. 7, 1957; children: Steven George, Linda Carmen Troemel, Julie Anita Carson. PhD, U. Ill., 1960. Rsch. chemist Ethyl Corp., Ferndale, Mich., 1960—63, USDA, Peoria, Ill., 1963—. Contbr. articles to profl. jours. Mem.: Am. Chem. Soc. Achievements include patents in field. Home: 33 Diamond Point Morton IL 61550-1186 Office: USDA 1815 N University St Peoria IL 61604 Office Fax: 309-681-6691. E-mail: fantagf@ncaur.usda.gov.

FANTA, PAUL EDWARD, chemist, educator; b. Chgo., July 24, 1921; s. Joseph and Marie (Zitnik) F.; m. LaVergne Danek, Sept. 3, 1949; children—David, John. BS, U. Ill., 1942; PhD, U. Rochester, 1946. Postdoctoral research fellow U. Rochester, 1946-47; instr. Harvard, 1947-48; mem. faculty Ill. Inst. Tech., 1948—, prof. chemistry, 1961-84, prof. emeritus, 1984—. Exchange scholar Czechoslovak Acad. Sci., Prague, 1963-64, Soviet Acad. Sci., Moscow, 1970-71 Contbr. articles to profl. jours. NSF fellow Imperial Coll., London, Eng., 1956-57 Mem. Am. Chem. Soc., Sigma Xi, Phi Lambda Upsilon. Home: 947 Clinton Ave Oak Park IL 60304-1821

FANTAUZZI, ANTHONY JOSEPH, III, lawyer; b. Saratoga Springs, NY, May 11, 1974; s. Anthony Joseph and Elizabeth Fantauzzi; m. Michelle Elizabeth Woodward, Jan. 20, 2001. BA, Union Coll., 1996; JD, U. Miami, Fla., 1999. Bar: Fla. Assoc. Bavol Bush & Sisco, PA, Tampa, Fla., 2000—. Mem.: ABA, Hillsborough County Bar Assn., Fla. Bar Assn. Roman Catholic. Office: Bavol Bush & Sisco PA PO Box 3423 100 S Ashley Dr Ste 2100 Tampa FL 33601 E-mail: afant@bbs-law.net.

FANTE, RONALD LOUIS, engineering scientist; b. Phila., Oct. 27, 1936; s. Frank Louis and Jeanne Gloria (Bossone) F.; m. Clara Connie Patalano, Apr. 23, 1961; children: Robert, Richard, Karen. BS, U. Pa., 1958; MS, MIT, 1960; PhD, Princeton U., 1964. Sr. scientist AVCO Corp., Wilmington, Mass., 1964-71, Air Force Cambridge Rsch. Labs., Bedford, Mass., 1971-80; asst. v.p. Textron Def. Systems, Wilmington, 1980-87; corp. fellow The MITRE Corp., Bedford, 1988—. Author: Signal Analysis and Estimation, 1988; contbr. numerous articles to jours. in field; mem. editl. bd. Waves in Random Media. Recipient Atwater Kent prize U. Pa., 1958, Dept. Labs. Achievement award USAF, 1974, Marcus O'Day prize USAF, 1975, I Migliori award Pirandello Lyceum, 1989, MITRE Corp. Best Paper prize, 1992, 2002, IEEE Disting. Lectr., 1995, 96. Fellow IEEE (editor in chief Transactions 1983-86, Third Millennium medal 2000, Scheklunoff prize 2002), Optical Soc. Am., Inst. Physics; mem. Electromagnetics Acad., Internat. Union Radio Sci. Roman Catholic. Home: 26 Sherwood Rd Reading MA 01867-3743 Office: MITRE Corp Burlington Rd Bedford MA 01730-1306 E-mail: rfante@mitre.org.

FANTINI, ALVINO E. language educator, humanities educator, consultant; b. Phila., June 11, 1936; s. Alvino and Maria Domenica Fantini; m. Beatriz Céspedes de Fantini, Jan. 22, 1966; children: A. Mario, Carla Alina. BA, U. Pa., 1958; MA, U. Tex., 1962, PhD, 1974; postgrad., U. N.Mex., 1977. Interpreter, translator U.S. Army; lang. coord. U.S. Peace Corps, Afghanistan; prof. U. Católica, La Paz, Bolivia; sr. faculty, dir. bilingual-multicultural edn. Sch. for Internat. Tng., Brattleboro, Vt. Dir. Lang.-Culture Ctr. Sch. for Internat. Tng., dir. The Experiment Press; ednl. cons. Fedn. of The Experiment, Putney, Vt., CISV Internat., Newcastle, England; mem. nat. fgn. lang. com. Am. Coun. on Tchg. of Fgn. Langs., Tarrytown, NY. Editor: The SIETAR Internat. Jour.; author: Language Acquisition of a Bilingual Child, 1972, rev. edit., 1974; mem. editl. bd.: Internat. Jour. Intercultural Rsch. Bd. dirs. Esperantic Studies Found., Vancouver, Canada; pres. Internat. Soc. Intercultural Edn., Tng. and Rsch., 1988—94. With intelligence units U.S. Army, 1960—63. Recipient Primus Inter Pares, Soc. for Intercultural Edn., Tng. and Rsch., 2000, citation, Fedn. of The Experiment, New Zealand, 2001. Mem.: Nat. Assn. Bilingual Educators (presenter), Nat. Fgn. Lang. Stds. Com. (bd. dirs. 1994—97), Acad. Intercultural Rsch. (bd. dirs.). Office: Sch for Internat Tng Kipling Rd Brattleboro VT 05302 Fax: 802-258-3316. E-mail: alvino.fantini@sit.edu.

FANTINO, EDMUND, psychology educator; b. N.Y.C., June 30, 1939; s. Claudio Fantino and Mary Lentini; m. Stephanie Stolarz, Sept. 22, 1977; children: Ramona Emily, Marin Antonia. BA, Cornell U., 1961; PhD, Harvard U., 1964. Asst. prof. psychology Yale U., New Haven, 1964—67; prof. psychology and neurosci. group U. Calif., San Diego, 1967—. Pres. Soc. for Exptl. Analysis of Behavior, 1985—87. Author: Introduction to Contemporary Psychology, 1975, The Experimental Analysis of Behavior: A Biological Perspective, 1979; contbr. over 100 articles to profl. jours.; editor: Jour. Exptl. Analysis of Behavior, 1987—91. Grantee, NIMH, 2001—. Office: U Calif San Diego Dept Psychology La Jolla CA 92093-0109 Office Fax: 858-534-7190. E-mail: efantino@ucsd.edu.

FANTOZZI, DONALD ROBERT, music educator; b. Torrington, Conn., Mar. 27, 1957; s. Donald Robert Fantozzi, Sr and Martha Fantozzi; m. Janet Rosen, Aug. 9, 1986; children: Danielle Rose, Donald Robert Fantozzi, III. MusB, Hartt Sch. of Music, Hartford, CT, 1979; M in Mus. Edn., Western Conn. State U., Danbury, 1989; postgrad., Ctrl. Conn. State U., New Britain, 1992. Cert. tchr. Conn. Dept. of Edn. Gen. music/orch. tchr. Cloonan Mid. Sch., Stamford, Conn., 1979—80; instrumental music tchr. Fairfield Pub. Schs., Conn., 1980—86, New Canaan H.S., Conn., 1986—88, Avon Mid. Sch., Conn., 1988—. Band cochairperson No. Regional Mid. Sch. Music Festival, Conn.; state band chmn. CMEA; instrumental tchr. New Horizens Band; cons./tester Functional Forms Reeds; presenter Conn. Music Educators Conv. Author: (journal articles) CMEA Journal, musician performances in numerous ensembles; composer/arranger (arrangements for concert band). Den leader Cub Scouts; deacon Ctrl. Congl. Ch.; bd. mem. Concert Soc. of Westchester County, NY. Mem.: Conn. Music Educators Assn., Phi Beta Mu, Modern Music Masters (life). Achievements include development of Committee member on the development of State Music Assessment Guidelines. Avocations: travel, fly fishing, hiking, reading. Home: 107 Woodlawn Drive Torrington CT 06790 Office: Avon Middle School 375 West Avon Road Avon CT 06001

FANTOZZI, PEGGY RYONE, geologist, environmental planner; b. Providence, Feb. 2, 1948; d. Eugene Baker and Cynthia (Bragg) Ryone; m. Thomas Allen Collins, Jan. 4, 1969 (div. 1985); children: Christin, Cindi; m. Thomas Edward Fantozzi, Mar. 22, 1985 (div. 1989); 1 child, Amy. BA in Earth Scis., Bridgewater State Coll., 1969; MS in Geology, Franklin and Marshall Coll., 1971. Registered sanitarian, Mass.; cert. wastewater treatment operator grade 4-M; cert. soil evaluator. Project mgr. Coastal Zone Mgmt. Grant, Eastham, Mass., 1980-81; geologist, project mgr. BSC Group/Cape Cod, Barnstable Village, Mass., 1982-88; sr. environ. scientist A.M. Wilson Assocs., Osterville, 1988-94, Daylor Consulting Group, Braintree, Mass., 1994-97. Instr. earth scis. and geology Bridgewater (Mass.) State Coll., 1972-74, Cape Cod C.C., West Barnstable, Mass., 1979-82; cons. conservation and health bds. Town of Bourne, Mass., 1984-85; mem., chair State Comm. for the Conservation of Soil, Water and Related Resources, 1996—; mem. Nat. Resources Conservation and Devel. Coun., 1998. Bd. dirs., v.p. Assn. for Preservation of Cape Cod, Orleans, Mass., 1979-85; bd. trustees Cape Cod Mus. Natural History, Brewster, 1982-85; advisor Barnstable County Marine Resources program, 1980-82; chmn. Eastham Conservation Commn., 1978-82, Selectmen's Task Force on Local Pollution, Bourne, 1985-87; del. Barnstable County Water Resources Adv. Coun., 1979-89, Bourne Shore and Harbor Com., 1989-92; rep. Tri-Town Septage treatment Facilities Planning Commn., Eastham, Orleans, citizen's adv. com. groundwater discharge program Mass. Dept. EPA, 1987-88, Surface Water Quality, 1990, 93, Mass. Bays Program Citizen Adv. Steering Com., 1992—; pres. Mass. Assn. Conservation Dists., 1995-98; chair Mass. State Commn. for the Conservation of Soil, Water and Related Resources, 1998—. Grantee USDA-Natural Resources Conservation Svc., 1997-98. Mem. Nat. Assn. Conservation Dists. (dir.), Mass. Health Officers Assn., Mass. Water Works Assn., Monument Beach Civic Assn. Home: 25 Shore Rd Buzzards Bay MA 02532-5425 Office: Land Use Permitting 25 Shore Rd Bourne MA 02532-5425

FANUELE, FRANK JOHN, engineering executive; b. N.Y.C., June 19, 1938; BSEE, Rensselaer Poly. Inst., 1960. Elec. engr. GE, 1960-64; project engr. Fairchild Electrometrics Corp., 1964-69; sys. engring. mgr. Mech. Tech. Inc., 1969-84; tech. sales mgr. Brown & Sharpe Mfg. Co., 1984-86; tech. mktg. mgr. Robotic Vision Sys., 1989; pres. Fanuele Enterprises, Albany, N.Y., 1986—. Achievements include transforming state of the art research and development activities into practical implementation in military, aerospace, automotive sectors and general factory automation. Office: Fanuele Enterprises 256 Partridge St Albany NY 12208-2624 E-mail: afanuele@nycap.rr.com.

FANUELE, MICHAEL ANTHONY, retired electronics engineer, research engineer; b. Bronx, N.Y., Feb. 24, 1938; s. Joseph A. and R. Fanny (Rubino) F.; m. Joyce L. Cassidy, May 23, 1964; children: Gina M., Peter A. BEE, NYU, 1959; MSEE, Rutgers U., 1968. Electronics engr. U.S. Army Combat Surveillance & Target Acquisition Lab., Fort Monmouth, N.J., 1960-72, sr. electronics engr. 1972-80, project officer, 1980-81, dir. ISTA systems div., 1981-85; chief systems and signals analysis div. U.S. Army Electronic Warfare, Reconnaissance Surveillance and Target Acquisition Ctr., Fort Monmouth, N.J., 1985-88; sr. rsch. engr. Ga. Tech. Rsch. Inst., Ga. Inst. Tech., 1988-2001; ret., 2001. Cons. in field; chmn. dept. electomagnetic engring. U.S. Army Internal Tng. Program, Ft. Monmouth, 1968-78, advisor, 1978-88; Army chmn. Tri-Svc. Radar Symposium Steering Group, Ft. Monmouth, 1973-88; Army mem. Internat. Tech. group, 1977-81, Internat. Radar Panel, 1984-88; coord., instr. radar short course Ga. Tech. Patentee in field; contbr. articles to profl. jours. 2d lt. U.S. Army, 1959-60. Mem. IEEE (sr.), Assn. Old Crows. Lodges: KC (treas. Brickton, N.J. 1968-70). Roman Catholic. Avocations: boating, photography, woodworking, collecting records, model railroading. Home: 440 Colleen Ct Toms River NJ 08755-7376 E-mail: mfanuele@verizon.net.

FANUS, PAULINE RIFE, librarian; b. New Oxford, Pa., Feb. 14, 1925; d. Maurice Diehl and Bernice Edna (Gable) Rife; m. William Edward Fanus, June 20, 1944; children: Irene Weaver, Larry William, Daniel Diehl. BS, Pa. State U., 1945; MLS, Villanova U., 1961; postgrad., Temple U., 1986—. Periodical libr. Tex. Coll. Arts Industries, Kingville, 1945; tchr. nursery sch. Studio Sch., Wayne, Pa., 1953-55; libr. circulation, reference Franklin Inst., Phila., 1963-66; asst. libr. Ursinus Coll., Collegeville, Pa., 1966; catalog libr., instr. Eastern Coll., St. Davids, Pa., 1967-71; head libr. Agnes Irwin Sch., Rosemont, Pa., 1971-93, head libr. emeritus, 1993—. Book reviewer The Book Report. Mem. AAUP (chpt. sec. Eastern Coll. 1970-71). Home: 78 Holly Dr New Holland PA 17557-9476

FANWICK, ERNEST, lawyer; b. N.Y.C., Feb. 28, 1926; s. Jacob and Jeanette (Lossof) F.; m. Lee Nathan, Sept. 1, 1951; children: Lewis, Leslie, Eric. BS in Elec. Engring., Pa. State U., 1948; JD, Columbia U., 1951. Bar: N.Y. 1952, Conn. 1988, U.S. Patent Office 1952, U.S. Ct. Appeals (2d cir.) 1952, U.S. Supreme Ct. 1958, U.S. Ct. Appeals (fed. cir.) 1982. Sr. patent atty. ITT Fed. Telecom. Labs., Nutley, 1951-55; div. counsel Avion div. ACF, Paramus, N.J., 1955-57; patent counsel Burndy Corp., Norwalk, Conn., 1957-65, dir. legal dept., 1965-75, gen. counsel, 1975-82, v.p., gen. counsel, sec., 1982-89. Mem. faculty Practising Law Inst., N.Y.C., 1964-97; lectr. Conf. Legal Execs., Pa., 1970, 72. Bd. dirs. Aid to Retarded, Stamford, Conn., 1982-87, mem. exec. com., 1997—; bd.dirs. Assn. Jewish Family and Children's Agys., 1992-2000, Jewish Family Svcs., Stamford, 1989-2000; alternate mem. Zoning Bd. Appeals, Stamford, 1990-96; active Am. ARbitration Assn.; mem. Arbitration panel N.Y. Stock Exch., Am. Stock Exch., Nat. Assn. Security Dealers. Lt. U.S. Army, 1943-47. Mem. ABA, Conn. Bar Assn., Conn. Patent Law Assn. (pres. 1966), N.Y. Intellectual Property Law Assn., The Corp. Bar Assn., Am. Intellectual Property Assn., Am. Arbitration Assn., Masons. Fax: 203-322-4764. E-mail: ernest@fanwick.com.

FAPPIANO, TARA C. lawyer; b. New Haven, Mar. 9, 1973; d. Anthony Bernard and Christine (Shrude) Fappiano; m. Charles Turner Zegers, Oct. 3, 1998. BA, Fordham U., 1995; JD, St. John's Sch. Law, Jamaica, N.Y., 1998. Bar: N.J. 1998, N.Y. 1999, Conn. 1999; notary pub., N.Y. Paralegal Law Offices of Kevin J. Quaranta, Bronx, N.Y., 1993-95; law clk. Law Offices of Anthony D. Perri, N.Y.C., 1996-97; assoc. Verner Simon, LLP, N.Y.C., 1997-00, Ohrenstein & Brown, LLP, N.Y.C., 2000—. Articles editor St. John's Jour. Legal Commentary, 1997-98. Mem. N.Y. State Bar Assn., N.Y. County Lawyers Assn. Roman Catholic. Avocations: travel, cooking, wine, reading. E-mail: tara.fappiano@oandb.com.

FARABELLI, STEPHEN J. accountant, finance educator; b. Phila., Nov. 16, 1950; s. James and Anne Farabelli; m. Elizabeth A. Wilson, Sept. 22, 1973; children: Jill Patricia, James Stephen, Leah Rachel, Suzanne Michelle. BTh, Bethany Bible Coll. and Seminary, 1994; Assocs. in Acctg., McGraw Hill Inst., 1995; MBA, Cambridge State U., 1999. Ordained Bapt. min. Pa., 1985. Asst. pastor youth Calvary Bapt. Ch., Pottstown, Pa., 1983—85; pastor New Testament Bapt. Ch., Royersford, Pa., 1985—90; sales rep. Abeka Books, Pensacola, Fla., 1990—92; tchr. Riverside (Calif.) Chrsitian High Sch., 1993—2001; contr. Fourth St. Rock Crusher Inc., San Bernardino, Calif., 2001—02, City Electric Inc., Riverside, 2002—03; dir. ops. Raincross Med. Group Inc., Riverside, 2003—. Adv. bd. mem. Grace Ind. Bapt. Missions, Doylestown, Pa., 1985—90; adj. prof. U. Redlands (Calif.) Sch. Bus., 2000—, Devry U. Sch. Bus., Pomona, Calif., 2000—02. Author: (newsletter) The How to Study Newsletter, 1996—. Coach H.S. football. Cpl. USMC, 1969—72, Vietnam. Named to, Outstanding Young Men of Am., 1985—. Republican. Home: 11215 Arlington Ave Riverside CA 92505

FARABI-NANCE, KHADIJAH, writer; b. Junction City, Kans., Apr. 30, 1938; d. Signey Charles Rucker and Maxine Lillian Barnes; m. Lawrence Lorenzo Hammond, May 10, 1952 (div. Oct. 1, 1966); children: Lawrence Hammond, Jeffrey Hammond, Charisse Hammond, Crystal Hammond, Roger Hammond, Leann Hammond, Syadia Hammond. BA in English, African-Am. Studies, Met. State Coll., Denver, 1977. Founder, pres. Syadia Creations; founder Nudijah Prodns. Mem. adv. bd. Operation Push, Denver, 1975, Cleo Parker Dance Co., Denver, 1976—82; cons. Compton Welfare Rights, Calif., 1991—97. Author: Wish Words Story Poet, Chocolate Thief. Mem.: Internat. Black Writer and Artist (Poetry prize 1999). Avocations: refinishing furniture, renewing throw away items, reading. Home: 1051 Pioneer Ave Wilmington CA 90744

FARABOW, FORD FRANKLIN, JR., lawyer; b. Charlotte, N.C., Jan. 6, 1938; s. Ford Franklin and Louise (Botts) F.; children— Ford Franklin, III, Amy Kathryn, Andrew Leighton. BS in Chem. Engring., Clemson U., 1959; JD with honors, George Washington U., 1963. Bar: D.C. bar 1965, S.C. bar 1963. With law dept. Swift & Co., Washington, 1959-62; assoc. Nexsen & Pruet, Columbia, S.C., 1962-64; with patent dept. Hercules, Inc., Wilmington, Del., 1964-65; ptnr. Finnegan, Henderson, Farabow, Garrett & Dunner, Washington, 1965—. Lectr. to ABA, Am. Patent Law Assn., also others. Contbr. articles to profl. publs. Mem. ABA, S.C. Bar Assn., Am. Judicature Soc., Bar Assn. D.C., Am. Patent Law Assn., U.S. Trademark Assn. (chmn. internat. adv. group), Am. Chem. Soc., Clemson U. Alumni Assn., Giles S. Rich Am. Inns of Ct., Tiger Brotherhood, Order of Coif, Phi Eta Sigma, Delta Theta Phi, Bethesda (Md.) Club (bd. dirs. 1987), TPC Club at Avenel, Franklin Sq. Club, Clemson IPTAY. Home: 9107 Belmart Rd Potomac MD 20854-1620 Office: Finnegan Henderson Farabow Garrett & Dunner 1300 I St NW Washington DC 20005-3315

FARACI, JOHN VINCENT, JR., paper company executive; b. Summit, N.J., Feb. 16, 1950; s. John V. and Joan (Abbot) F.; m. Heath Holland. BA, Denison U., 1972; MBA, U. Mich., 1974. With Internat. Paper Co., 1974-88; fin. analyst N.Y.C., 1974-75; bus. analyst Statesville, N.C., 1975-76; plant contr. Kalamazoo, 1976-77; staff analyst N.Y.C., 1977-78; mgr. mktg. Mobile, Ala., 1978-80; dir. planning N.Y.C., 1980-83; gen. mgr. western ops. Gardiner, Oreg., 1983-85; gen. mgr. wood products group Dallas, 1985-88; v.p., gen. mgr. Masonite div., Chgo., 1988-91; CFO International Paper, Purchase, NY, 1991—. Republican. Avocations: mountain and rock climbing, flying, collecting Am. antique furniture, tennis, water skiing. Office: Internat Paper 2 Mahanttanville Rd Purchase NY 10577-2196

FARAGE, MICHAEL N. career officer; BSBA, Ctrl. Mich. U., 1970; grad., Squadron Officer Sch., 1974; MBA, U. No. Colo., 1979; grad., Air Command and Staff Coll., 1984, Air War Coll., 1988. Commd. 2d lt. USAF, 1971, advanced through grades to maj. gen., 2000; helicopter pilot 48th Aerospace Rescue Recovery Squadron, Fairchild AFB, Wash., 1972-75, 40th Rescue and Recovery Squadron, Nakhon Phanom Royal AFB, Thailand, 1975; T-37 instr. pilot and flight examiner 35th Flying Tng. Squadron and 64th Flying Tng. Wing, Reese AFB, Tex., 1976-81; plans officer 23d Air Force, Scott AFB, Ill., 1981-83; comdr. detachment 4 40th Aerospace Rescue and Recovery Squadron, Hill AFB, Utah, 1984-86, ops. officer, 1986-87; comdr. detachment 370 Air Force Res. Officer Tng. Corps U. Mass., Amherst, 1988-90; dir. ops. Hdqs. Air Force Res. Officer Tng. Corps, Maxwell AFB, Ala., 1990-92; comdr. 81st Tech. Tng. Group, Keesler AFB, Miss., 1992-94, 58th Spl. Ops. Wing, Kirtland AFB, N.Mex., 1994-97; dep. comdg. gen. Joint Spl. Ops. Command, Ft. Bragg, N.C., 1997-99; comdr. 37th Tng. Wing, Au Edn. and Tng. Command, Lackland AFB, Tex., 1999—. Office: Au Edn and Tng Command 37th Tng Wing Ste 242 Lackland A F B TX 78236

FARAGHAN, GEORGE TELFORD, photographer; b. Phila., July 8, 1926; s. Joseph Telford and Sarah (Earnest) F.; m. Ida Jane Hanley, Dec. 8, 1948; children: Karen, Kurt, Kim, Kyle, Ken. Student, Pa. State U., 1947; grad. comml. photography magna cum laude, Yawn Sch. Photography, Phila., 1949. Printer Thomas Melvin Studio, Phila., 1949-50, printer, asst. Willard Steward Studio, Wilmington, Del., 1950-51; freelance photographer Phila., 1951-52; owner George Faraghan Studio, Phila., 1953—. Inventor spl. camera unit to photograph U.V. photo damage caused by exposure to the sun used in pharm. rsch. With USN, 1944-46, PTO. Recipient 3 George Berry awards, Profl. Photographers Assn. Del. Valley, Phila. Art Dirs. Shows awards, N.Y Art Dirs. Show Neographics award; photograher 50 Best of Ads of Yr., 1960. Mem. Phila. Art Dir.'s Club (over 100 awards). Republican. Office: 940 N Delaware Ave Philadelphia PA 19123-3111

FARAGO, JOHN MICHAEL, law educator, hearing officer, consultant; b. N.Y.C., Mar. 8, 1951; s. Ladislas and Liesel (Mroz) F.; m. Sharon Cramer, Nov. 11, 1972 (div.); m. Jeanne Elaine Martin, Dec. 5, 1985; 1 child, Max Farago; stepchildren: Belle Iskowitz, Sarah Iskowitz. BA, MAT, Harvard U., 1972; JD, NYU, 1978, postgrad., 1975-78. Assoc. dean, prof. Valparaiso (Ind.) U. Sch. Law, 1978-82; assoc. prof., assoc. dean for acad. planning CUNY Law Sch., N.Y.C., 1982—86, assoc. prof., dir. systems, 1986—90; assoc. dean for acad. affairs N.Y. Law Sch., N.Y.C., 1990—92; assoc. prof. CUNY Law Sch., N.Y.C., 1992—. Spl. edn. hearing officer Ind. Edn. Dept., 1979-82, N.Y.C. Bd. Edn., 1982—; hearing officer N.Y. State vocat. Edn., N.Y.C., 1993-98; adj. prof. Tchrs. Coll., 1998; cons. in field Co-author: Junk Food, 1978, Current & Emerging Issues in Special Education, 2002, Special Education Primer; editor: The Family, 1975; editl. bd. Ctr. for Computer-Assisted Legal Instrn., 1997—; contbr. articles to profl. jours. Search coord., chancellor search N.Y.C. Bd. Edn., 1995. Home: 1225 Park Ave New York NY 10128-1758 Office: CUNY Law Sch 65-21 Main St Flushing NY 11367 E-mail: Farago@mail.law.cuny.edu.

FARAH, BADIE NAIEM, computer information systems educator, consultant; b. Nazareth, Palestine, Jan. 15, 1946; came to U.S., 1970; naturalized, 1983. s. Naim R. and Afifi F. BS, Damascus U., 1967, MA, 1968; MS, Wayne State U., 1973; MSIE, Ohio State U., 1976, PhD, 1977. Teaching asst. Wayne State U., Detroit, 1971-73; research assoc. Ohio State U., Columbus, 1973-77; sr. systems analyst Gen. Motors Co., Detroit, 1977-78; asst. prof. Oakland U., Rochester, Mich., 1978-82; asst. prof. computer systems Eastern Mich. U., Ypsilanti, 1982-86, assoc. prof., 1986-90, prof., 1990—. Advisor to bd. dirs. S & G Grocer Co., Detroit, 1979-81, vis. gen. mgr., 1980-81. Author: Business Information Systems: Development and Implementation, 1990, 2nd edition, 1995; co-author: Integrated Case Studies in Accounting Information Systems, 1987; contbr. articles to profl. jours. Mem. Am. Inst. Indsl. Engrs., Assn. for Computing Machinery (exec. council Met. Detroit chpt.), Ops. Research Soc. Am., Inst. Mgmt. Scis. (sec. SE Mich. chpt.), Mich. Acad. Sci., Arts and Letters, AAUP, Alpha Pi Mu, Beta Gamma Sigma, Phi Kappa Phi. Syrian Orthodox (pres. local ch. bd.). Research on data communications and networks of computers, e-commerce, management information. Home: 37 Foxboro Dr Rochester Hills MI 48309 Office: Ea Mich U Computer Info Sys Ypsilanti MI 48197 E-mail: badie.farah@emich.edu.

FARAH, CAESAR ELIE, Middle Eastern and Islamic studies educator; b. Portland, Oreg., Mar. 13, 1929; s. Sam Khalil and Lawrice Farah; m. Irmgard Tenkamp, Dec. 13, 1987; 1 child, Elizabeth;children from previous marriage: Ronald, Christopher, Ramsey, Laurence, Raymond, Alexandra. Student, Internat. Coll. Am. U. Beirut, 1941-46; BA, Stanford U., 1952; MA, Princeton U., 1955, PhD, 1957. Pub. affairs asst., cultural affairs officer ednl. exchanges USIS, New Delhi, 1957-58, Karachi, Pakistan, 1958; asst. to chief Bur. Cultural Affairs, Washington, 1959; asst. prof. history and semitic langs. Portland State U., 1959-63; asst. prof. history Calif. State U.-Los Angeles, 1963-64; assoc. prof. Near Eastern studies Ind. U., Bloomington, 1964-69; prof. Middle Eastern and Islamic history U. Minn., Mpls., 1969—, chmn. South Asian and Middle Eastern studies, 1988-91. Guest lectr. Fgn. Ministry, Spain, Iraq, Iran, Ministry Higher Edn., Saudi Arabia, Yemen, Turkey, Kuwait, Qatar, Tunisia, Morocco, Syrian Acad. Scis., Acad. Scis., Beijing; vis. scholar Cambridge U., 1974; resource person on Middle East media and svc. group, Minn., 1977—; bd. dirs., chmn. Upper Midwest Consortium for Middle East Outreach, 1980—; vis. prof. Harvard U., 1964, 65, Sanaa U., Yemen, 1984, Karl-Franzens U. Austria, 1990, 91, 1997—98, Ludwig-Maximilian U., Munich, 1992—93; vis. Fulbright-Hays scholar U. Damascus, 1994; vis. lectr. Am. U. Beirut, 2001; exec. sec., editor Am. inst. Yemeni Studies, 1982—86; sec.-gen., exec. bd. dirs. Internat. Com. for Pre-Ottoman & Ottoman Studies, 1988—2000, v.p., 2000—; fellow Rsch. Ctr. Islamic History, Istanbul, 1993, Ctr. Lebanese Studies & St. Anthony Coll., Oxford, England, 1994; vis. cons. Sultan Qaboos U., Oman, 2000. Author: The Addendum in Medieval Arabic Historiography, 1968, Islam: Beliefs and Observances, 7th edit., 2003, Eternal Message of Muhammad, 1964, 3d edit., 1981, Tarikh Baghdad li-Ibn-al-Najjar, 3 vols., 1980—83, 2d edit., 1986, al-Ghazali on Abstinence in Islam, 1992, Decision Making in the Ottoman Empire, 1992, The Road to Intervention: Fiscal Policies in Ottoman Mount Lebanon, 1992, The Politics of Interventionism in Ottoman Lebanon, 2000, The Sultan's Yemen, 2002, Ottomans & Arabs, 2002, First Arab Traveler to Latin America, 2003; contbr. articles to profl. jours.; mem. editl. bd.: Digest of Middle East Studies. Mem. Oreg. Rep. Committeeman, 1960—64. Named Fulbright-Hayes lectr., 1993—94; recipient cert. of merit, Syrian Ministry Higher Edn.; fellow, Am. Coun. Learned Socs., 1953, Am. Rsch. Ctr. Egypt, 1966—67, Fulbright Tgn. and Rsch., Germany, 1992—93, Ford Found., 1966, Am. Philos. Soc., 1970—71; grantee Participants Program, Dept. State Am., 1981, 1984, 1993, Minn. Humanities Comm., 1981, 1985, 1989, 1995, 1998, 2001, Am. Inst. Yemeni Studies, 1999, Coun. Am. Overseas Rsch. Ctrs., 2000, Travel to Collection, NEH, 1989, others; scholar Fulbright Rsch., 1966—67, 1985—86, 1992—93. Mem.: Turkish Studies Assn., Am. Assn. Tchrs. Arabic (exec. bd.), Mid. East Studies Assn. N.Am., Am. Hist. Assn., Royal Asiatic Soc. Gt. Britain, Am. Oriental Soc., Stanford U. Alumni Assn. (Leadership Recognition award), Princeton Club, Stanford Club Minn. (dir., pres. 1979), Phi Alpha Theta, Pi Sigma Alpha. Greek Orthodox. Home: 5125 Blake Rd S Edina MN 55436-1125 Office: Univ Minn 839 Soc Sci Towers Minneapolis MN 55455 Fax: 612-624-9383. Business E-Mail: farah001@umn.edu.

FARAH, KIMBERLY SUE, chemistry educator, researcher; b. Morristown, N.J., Apr. 6, 1962; d. Basil Said and Barbara (Donald) F. BS, Va. Tech. U., 1984; MSE, U. Lowell, 1989; PhD, U. Mass., 1993. Asst. prof. Lasell Coll., Newton, Mass., 1993-98, assoc. prof., dept. head, 1998—. Faculty cons. Kennedy-Western U., Thousand Oaks, Calif., 1994—; mem. adv. bd. exercise physiology Lasell Coll., Newton, 1995—. Author: (book chpt.) Advances in Applied Spectroscopy, 1997; contbr. articles to profl. jours.; mem. editl. bd. Micro-chemical Jour., Lake Charles, La., 1997-99. Mem. scholarship com. Girl Scouts Am., Manchester, N.H., 1996—. 1st lt. U.S. Army, 1984-88, Korea, Ala. Grantee State St. Found., Boston, 1995-97. Mem. Am. Chem. Soc., Soc. for Applied Spectroscopy. Avocations: horseback riding, flute, biking. E-mail: kfarah@lasell.edu.

FARAH, ROGER, retail company executive; Former chmn., chief exec. officer Rich's, Atlanta, Federated/Allied Merchandising Svcs., N.Y.C.; chmn., CEO, Woolworth Corp. (name changed to Venator Group), N.Y.C., 1994-00, also bd. dirs.; pres. & COO Polo Ralph Lauren Corp., N.Y.C., 2000—. Office: Polo Ralph Lauren Corp 650 Madison Ave New York NY 10022-1029

FARAHANI, MAHNAZ, chemist, scientist; b. Tehran, Iran, June 27, 1952; came to U.S., 1975; d. Mohamad and Ghodsieh Farahani; m. Mohamad Alsheikhly, Apr. 19, 1990; 1 child, Melody Alsheikhly. MS, U. Bridgeport, 1978; PhD, Am. U., Washington, 1985. With Am. U., Washington, 1985-88; rsch. scientist Am. Dental Assn., Gaithersburg, Md., 1988-98; scientist FDA, 1998—. Contbr. articles to profl. jours.; patentee for Color-matched, Ambient-light Visual Comparator; inventor Std. Reference Material SRM 4500. Mem. ASTM. Avocations: swimming, reading, music, photography. Home: 9225 Cambridge Manor Ct Potomac MD 20854 Office: FDA HFD-645 7500 Standish Pl Rockville MD 20855-2764 Business E-Mail: farahanim@cder.fda.gov.

FARAIDY, ABDULAZIZ ABDULLAH, national public security officer; b. Taif, Saudi Arabia, May 15, 1945; m. Nora I. Zaki; children: Faris, Waleed, Yasir, Najah, Nayef, Bander, Nouf. BS, Calif. State U., L.A., 1970; MPA, U. So. Calif., L.A., 1978, PhD in Pub. Adminstrn., 1982. Comdr. of shooting range Pub. Security, Riyadh, 1970-72, chief armament dept., 1972-73, chief instr. officers inst., 1973-75, chief instr. non-commd. officer inst., 1975, hosp. adminstr., 1975-76, Security Forces Hosp., Riyadh, 1982-84; gen. dir. asst., med. svcs. dept. Ministry of Interior, Riyadh, 1984-86; dir. officers dept. Civil Def., Riyadh, 1986-87, dir. warning and monitoring dept., 1987-90; dir. region Civil Def. for Baha, 1990-92; vice comdr. Civil Def. for Riyadh Region 1992-97, gen. dir., 1997—. Mem. Am. Soc. for Pub. Adminstrn., Am. Soc. Safety Engrs., Fire Engring. Soc. Avocations: swimming, tennis. Home: PO Box 26894 Riyadh 11496 Saudi Arabia

FARAONE, TERI, public relations executive; b. N.Y.C., July 6, 1953; d. Seymour and Marilyn (Lutsky) Dickstein; m. Ted Faraone, June 1, 1988 (div. 2003). BA, Kean Coll. of N.J., Elizabeth, 1979; MA, CUNY, 1996; MA, postgrad., Columbia U., 1999—. Asst. mgr. Citicorp, N.Y.C., 1982-88; mgr. Faraone Comms., N.Y.C., 1988-92, dir. acct. svcs., 1990-92, v.p., 1992-94, pres., 1994—. Mem. NATAS. Office: Faraone Communications Inc 75 W End Ave New York NY 10023-7853

FARARA, JOSEPH MONTGOMERY, library director; b. Boston, Mar. 19, 1958; s. Joseph Clinging and Elizabeth Mary (Mulcahy) F.; m. Nancy Ruth Blood, Nov. 24, 1984; 1 child, Keegan James. BA in English, Bates Coll., 1980; MS in Info. Sci., Simmons Coll., 1984. Cataloging asst. Mus. Fine Arts, Boston, 1984; reference libr. RISD, Providence, R.I., 1984-85; rsch. libr. F.W. Faxon Co., Westwood, Mass., 1985-87; reserves and circulation libr. Hilles Libr., Harvard U., Cambridge, 1987-90; libr. dir. Johnson (Vt.) State Coll., 1990—, assoc. dean tech., 1995—2002, chief tech. officer, 2002—; dir. libr. planning Vt. State Colls., 2003—. Host: (radio show) Fancy Eatin' Table, 1990—. Recipient Faculty Rsch. grant Johnson (Vt.) State Coll., 1992, Learning Communities grant Vt. State Colls., Waterbury, 1993. Mem. Lamoille County Librs. Assn. (pres. 1993—), Vt. State Colls. Libr. Coun. (chmn. 2002—). Sandinista Track Club, B.A.B. Office Club at West Main. Republican. Episcopalian. Office: John Dewey Libr Johnson State Coll Johnson VT 05656

FARARO, THOMAS JOHN, sociologist, educator; b. N.Y.C., Feb. 11, 1933; s. Joseph and Anna (Marcello) F.; m. Irene Johanna Fannasch, Dec. 30, 1955; children: Ramona, Raymond. BA, CCNY, 1959; PhD, Syracuse U., 1963. Asst. prof. sociology Syracuse (N.Y.) U., 1963-64; vis. scholar Stanford (Calif.) U., 1964-67; prof. U. Pitts., 1967-99, chmn. dept. sociology, 1980-85, Disting. Svc. prof., 1999—. Author: Mathematical Sociology, 1973, Mathematical Sociology, Japanese translation, 1980, The Meaning of General Theoretical Sociology, 1989 (transl. into Japanese 1996), Social Action Systems, 2001; co-author: Generating Images of Stratification, 2003; editor: Mathematical Ideas and Sociological Theory, 1984; co-editor Rational Choice Theory, 1992, The Problem of Solidarity, 1998; assoc. editor Jour. Math. Sociology, 1978— ; mem. editl. bd. Am. Jour. Sociology, 1977-79, Am. Sociol. Rev., 1980-82, Social Networks, 1978-82, Sociol. Theory, 1988-90, Sociol. Forum, 1989-92. With USAF, 1952-56. Grantee, Social Sci. Rsch. Coun., 1968, NSF, 1969-72. Mem. Am. Sociol. Assn. (chair math. sociol. sect. 1998-99), Internat. Network for Social Network Analysis, Sociol. Rsch. Assn. Office: U Pitts Dept Sociology 230 S Bouquet St Pittsburgh PA 15213-4015 E-mail: tjf2@pitt.edu. *I have devoted my intellectual life to the advancement of theoretical sociology by the use of mathematical methods in presenting theories, clarifying and formalizing concepts, representing social processes and social structures, and explaining social phenomena.*

FARB, THOMAS FOREST, financial executive; b. N.Y.C., Oct. 28, 1956; s. Peter and Oriole (Horch) F.; m. Stacy Siana Valhouli, Apr. 29, 1961; children: Peter Forest Valhouli-Farb, Siana Louisa Valhouli-Farb, Andreas John Valhouli-Farb. AB, Harvard U., 1980. Rsch. assoc. Mass. House Ways and Means Com., Boston, 1976-78; asst v.p. Bank of Boston, 1980-83; v.p., CFO and gen. mgr. ea. ops. Symbolics, Inc., Burlington, Mass., 1983-89; sr. v.p., CFO & controller Airfund Corp., Lexington, Mass., 1989-92; v.p. corp. devel., chief fin. officer and treas. Cytyc Corp., Marborough, Mass., 1992-94; exec. v.p., CFO, treas. Interneuron Pharms., Inc., Lexington, Mass., 1994-98; gen. ptnr., CFO Summit Ptnrs., Boston, 1998—. Bd. dirs. Fair, Issac and Co., San Rafael, Calif., Redwood Trust, Inc., Mill Valley, Calif., Saf-T-Med. Inc., Barrington, Ill., Symon Comms., Dallas. Mem. Fin. Execs. Inst., Bus. Assocs. Club, Treas. Club Boston, Newcomen Soc. Home: 1228 Lowell Rd Concord MA 01742-5527 Office: Summit Partners 222 Berkeley St 18th Fl Boston MA 02116

FARBANISH, THOMAS, sculptor; b. Endicott, N.Y., Mar. 21, 1963; BFA, Rochester Inst. Tech., 1986. Asst. Artpark, Lewiston, N.Y., 1986, Wheaton Village, Millville, N.J., 1989; instr. Golden Glass Sch., Cin., 1990, Corning Bus. Devel. Ctr., 1991; faculty Tyler Sch. Art, Pa., 1991, Urban Glass, N.Y., 1992, Pilchuck Glass Sch., Stanwood, Wash., 1993-94, 97, gaffer, 1996-97; faculty Haystack Sch. Crafts, Maine, 1993, Penland Sch., N.C., 1993, Rochester (N.Y.) Inst. Tech., 1994, 97. Tchg. asst. Pilchuck Glass Sch., Stanwood, 1986, 87, 90, Saxe emerging artist in residence, 1988; lectr. in field. One-man and two-man shows include Snyderman Gallery, Phila., 1987, Sarah Squeri Gallery, Cin., 1990, AVA Gallery, Lebanon, N.H., 1992, Artspace, Kohler Art Ctr., Sheboygan, Wis., 1993, Robert L. Kidd Gallery, Birmingham, Mich., 1994, William Traver Gallery, Seattle, 1991, 94, 95, Heller Gallery, N.Y.C., 1995; group shows include Glass Gallery, Bethesda, Md., 1984, 85, Germanow Gallery, Rochester, 1984, Morris Mus., Morristown, N.J., 1985, Upton Hall Galleries, Buffalo, 1985, Courtyard Galleries, Balt., 1986, Huntington (W.Va.) Mus. Art, 1986, Heller Gallery, N.Y.C., 1986, 87, 91, 92, 94, 95, 97, Ward Gallery, 1987, Somerstown Gallery, Somers, N.Y., 1987, Snyderman Gallery, Pa., 1987, Am. Craft Mus., N.Y.C., 1988, So. Alleghenies Mus. Art, Loretto, Pa., 1988, Grohe Gallery, Boston, 1989, Robert L. Kidd Gallery, Birmingham, 1989, 96, William Traver Gallery, Seattle, 1990, 92, 93, Sotheby's, N.Y.C., 1990, Gallery Nakama, Tokyo, 1991, Lehman Gallery, N.Y.C., 1993, Christies, N.Y.C., 1993, Bellevue (Wash.) Art Mus., 1994, Habitat Galleries, Birmingham, 1994, Leedy Voulkos Gallery, Kansas City, Mo., 1995, Philabaum Gallery, Tucson, 1995, Huntsville (Ala.) Mus. Art, 1996; represented in permanent collections Huntsville Mus. Art, Am. Craft Mus., Prescott Collection, Wash., Huntington Mus. Art, Davis Wright and Jones, Wash., Wheaton (N.J.) Mus. Am. Glass, Pilchuck Glass Sch., Wash., Rochester Inst. Tech. Creative Glass Ctr. Am. fellow Wheaton Village, 1985, 90, Visual Artist fellow Nat. Endowment Arts, 1988, 94; Pilchuck Galss Sch. scholar, 1987; Mid Atlantic Arts Found. grantee, 1990. Office: c/o William Traver Gallery 110 Union St Ste 200 Seattle WA 98101-2028

FARBER, BERNARD JOHN, lawyer; b. London, Feb. 27, 1948; came to U.S., 1949; s. Solomon and Regina (Wachter) F.; m. Mary Lee Mueller, Feb. 14, 1987; children: Zachary, Anne. BS, U. of State of N.Y., Albany, 1978; JD, Ill. Inst. Tech., 1983. Bar: Ill. 1983, U.S. Dist. Ct. (no. dist.) Ill. 1983, U.S. Ct. Appeals (7th cir.) 1985, U.S. Tax Ct. 1986, U.S. Ct. Mil. Appeals 1986, U.S. Supreme Ct. 1987, U.S. Ct. Appeals (6th cir.) 1988, U.S. Ct. Appeals (4th cir.) 1989, U.S. Ct. Appeals (11th cir.) 1990. Instr. legal writing Chgo.-Kent Law Sch. Ill. Inst. Tech., 1983-85, computer rsch. atty., 1985-86, adj. prof. law, 1987—; legal editor Longman Fin. Svcs., Chgo., 1986-87; rsch. counsel publs. Ams. for Effective Law Enforcement, Chgo., 1987—. Instr. Law Scholastic Aptitude Test; preparation course BAR/BRI, Chgo., 1984-88; v.p. Brickton Montessori Sch., Chgo., 1992-93; sec. bd. dirs., 1993-95. Mng. editor: Chgo.-Kent Law Rev., 1981-82, editor-in-chief, 1982-83; co-author: Protective Security Law, 1996; editor: (with others) Dow Jones-Irwin Handbook of Micro Computer Applications in Law, 1987, Illinois Law of Criminal Investigation, 1986; contbr. articles to profl. jours. Elected mem. Local Sch. Coun., Agassiz Elem. Sch., Chgo., 1996—, chmn., 1999-2004, vice-chmn. 2002-2003. Mem. ABA, Ill. State Bar Assn., Chgo. Bar Assn., Sci. Fiction Rsch. Assn., Mensa. Avocations: history, computers, science fiction. Home and Office: 1126 W Wolfram St Rear Chicago IL 60657-4330 E-mail: bernfarber@aol.com., bernardjfarber@voyager.net.

FARBER, DONALD CLIFFORD, lawyer, educator; b. Columbus, Nebr., Oct. 19, 1923; s. Charles and Sarah (Epstein) F.; m. Ann Eis, Dec. 28, 1947; children: Seth, Patricia. BS in Law, U. Nebr., 1948, JD, 1950. Bar: N.Y. 1950. Assoc. Newman, Hauser & Teitler, N.Y.C., 1950-58; pvt. practice, N.Y.C., 1958-80; of counsel Conboy, Hewitt, O'Brien & Boardman, N.Y.C., 1980-84; ptnr. Tanner Propp Fersko & Sterner, N.Y.C., 1984-95, Farber & Rich LLP, N.Y.C., 1995-98; of counsel Hartman & Craven LLP, N.Y.C., 1998—2000, Jacob Medinger & Finnegan LLP, N.Y.C., 2000—. Prof. law York U., Toronto, Ont., Can., 1970, 72-73; prof. theatre law Hofstra Law Sch., Hempstead, N.Y., 1974-75; prof. New Sch. for Social Rsch., N.Y.C., 1972—, Hunter Coll., 1978. Author: From Option to Opening, 1968, 4th edit., 1st Limelight edit., 1988, Producing on Broadway, 1969, Actor's Guide: What You Should Know About the Contracts You Sign, 1971, Producing, Financing and Distributing Film, 1973, 2d edit., 1991, The Amazing Story of the Fantasticks: America's Longest Running Play, 1991, Producing Theatre, A Comprehensive Legal and Business Guide, 1981, 3d Limelight edit., 1997, Common Sense Negotiation-The Art of Winning Gracefully, 1996; gen. editor (10 vol. series, author theatre vol.) Entertainment Industry Contracts-Negotiating and Drafting Guide. With AUS, 1941-44, ETO. Mem. Order of Coif. Home: 14 E 75th St New York NY 10021-2657 Office: Jacob Medinger & Finnegan LLP 1270 Ave of Americas New York NY 10020 E-mail: donaldc14@aol.com., dcfarber@jmfnylaw.com.

FARBER, DONNA SYLVIE, marketing professional; b. Johannesburg, Mar. 24, 1973; d. Darryl Michael and Ruth Inri Farber. BA with honors, McGill U., 1995; MBA, George Washington U., Washington, D.C., 1997. Mktg. specialist Ernst & Young, Toronto, Canada, 1996—98; mktg. dir. Washington office Hale and Dorr LLP, 1998—2001, Latham & Watkins, 2001—. Master: Legal Mktg. Assn. (bd. dirs. Mid-Atlantic chpt. 1999). Office: Latham & Watkins 555 11th St Ste 1000 Washington DC 20004 Office Fax: 202-637-2201. Personal E-mail: donna.farber@lw.com. Business E-Mail: donna.farber@lw.com.

FARBER, EMMANUEL, pathology and biochemistry educator; b. Toronto, Ont., Can., Oct. 19, 1918; s. Morris and Mary (Madorsky) Farber; m. Ruth Diamond, Apr. 21, 1942 (dec. Apr. 22, 1993); 1 child, Noami Beth; m. Henrietta K., Apr. 28, 2000. MD, U. Toronto, 1942; PhD in Biochemistry, U. Calif., 1949; D Medicine and Surgery (hon.), U. Turin, Italy, 1985. Diplomate Am. Bd. Pathology. Intern, then resident in pathology Hamilton (Ont.) Gen. Hosp., 1942-43; fellow in cancer rsch. Am. Cancer Soc. U. Calif., 1947-49, Hektoen Inst. Med. Rsch., Cook County Hosp., Chgo., 1949-50; from instr. to assoc. prof. pathology and biochemistry Tulane U., New Orleans, 1950-59, Am. Cancer Soc. Rsch. prof., 1959-61; prof., chmn. pathology dept. U. Pitts., 1961-70; Am. Cancer Soc. Rsch. prof., sr. investigator Fels Rsch. Inst., Temple U. Sch. Medicine, Phila., 1970-74, prof., dir., 1974-75; prof., chmn. pathology dept. U. Toronto, 1975-85, prof. dept. pathology, dept. biochemistry, 1985, prof. emeritus, 1985—; mem. staff, pathologist-in-chief Toronto Gen. Hosp., 1975-85; chmn. dept. pathology Toronto Western Hosp., 1975-85; prof. dept. pathology and cell biology Jefferson Med. Coll., Phila., 1994—; prof. dept. pathology S.C. Cancer Ctr.-U. S.C. Sch. Medicine, Columbia, 1999—, rsch. prof./cons., 1999—. Vis. scientist Toxicology Rsch. Unit Med. Rsch. Coun. Lab., Carshalton, Eng., 1959; vis. prof. Courtauld Inst. Biochemistry. Middlesex Hosp. Med. Sch., London, Eng.,1968-69; vis. prof., lectr. Krakower U. Ill., Chgo., 1989; mem. Surgeon Gen.'s adv. com. on smoking and health, 1962-64; mem. pathology B study sect. NIH, 1962-66, chmn. 1963-66, chem. pathology study sect, 1980-82, metabolic pathology study sect., 1987-89; mem. pathology com. NAS Nat. Rsch. Coun., 1965-66; mem. adv. panel 5 on med. scis. U.S.-Japan coop. sci. program, 1965, panel D Nat. Cancer Inst. Can., 1977-79, panel I com. on food safely and food safety policy NAS, 1978-79; mem. rev. bd. Alachlor Can., 1985-87; mem. sci. adv. bd. Armed Forces Inst. Pathology, 1966-70, Nat. Ctr. Toxicology Rsch., 1973-74; mem. nat. adv. cancer coun. USPHS, 1966-70; mem. com. Cancer Rsch. Tng. Grants Nat. Cancer Inst., 1971-72; mem. bd. sci. overseers Jackson Lab., 1972-81; trustee 1972-74; cons. HEW, 1964-67, St. Michael's Hosp., Toronto, 1976-85, Sunnybrook Med. Centre, Toronto, 1976-85, Wellesley Hosp., 1976-85, Mt. Sinai Hosp., 1976-85, N.Y. Gen. Hosp., 1977-85. Editor: Biochemical Pathology, 1966, The Biochemistry of Disease Series Vols. 1-12, 1971-87, Toxic Liver Injury, 1979, Toxic Injury of the Liver, 1980, Pathogenesis of Liver Diseases, 1987; mem. editorial bd., assoc. editor Cancer Rsch., Teratogenisis Carcinogenesis and Mutagenesis; mem. editorial bd. Oncology News, Internat. Jour. Cancer, Chem. Biological Interactions, Carcinogenesis, Liver, Hepatology, Lab. Investigation; assoc. editor Toxicologic Pathology; contbr. numerous articles to profl. jours. Capt. Med. Corp. Royal Can. Army, 1942-46. Recipient Parke-Davis award Am. Soc. Exptl. Pathology, 1958, Bertha Goldblatt Teplitz Meml. award, 1961, Samuel R. Noble Found. award, 1976, fellow Royal Soc. Can., Eastman Kodak award Nat. Acad. Clin. Biochem., 1986, Founders' award Chem. Industry Inst. Toxicology, 1987, Disting. Pathologist award U.S. and Can. Acad. Pathologists, 1992; named Schofield Meml. lectr. U. Guelph, 1984, Alexander Breslow Meml. lectr. George Washington U., 1986, Robert E. Greenfield lectr. U. Nebr., 1987, Disting. lectr. Roswell Pk. Meml. Inst., 1988; NIH fellow Nat. Cancer Inst., 1969-70. Mem. AAAS, Am. Assn. Cancer Rsch. (GHA Clowes Meml. award 1984, hon. mem. 1995), Am. Assn. Pathologists (Rous-Whipple award 1982), Am. Chem. Soc., Am. Soc. Biochemistry Molecular Biology, Am. Soc. Investigative Pathology (Gold Headed Cane award 1995), Am. Gastroenterol. Assn., Am. Assn. Study Liver Disease, Biochem. Soc., Can. Assn. Pathologists (William Boyd lectr. 1986), Can. Biochem. Soc., Histochem. Soc., U.S.-Can. Acad. Pathology (Maude E. Abbott lectr. 1987, Disting. Pathologist award 1992), Jap. Cancer Assn. (hon.), N.Y. Acad. Scis., Ont. Assn. Pathologists, Ont. Med. Assn., Pathol. Soc. Gt. Britain Ireland (hon.), Soc. Exptl. Biology and Medicine, Soc. Toxicology (U.S. chpt.), Soc. Toxicology Can., Soc. Toxicologic Pathologists (hon.). Office: U SC Sch Medicine Dept Pathology & Cancer Ctr Columbia SC 29209 E-mail: twoakinlov@aol.com.

FARBER, EVAN IRA, librarian; b. N.Y.C., June 30, 1922; s. Meyer M. and Estelle H. (Shapiro) F.; m. Hope Wells Nagle, June 13, 1966; children: Cynthia, Amy, Jo Anna, May Beth; stepchildren: David Nagle, Jeffrey Nagle, Lisa Nagle. AB, U. N.C., 1944, MA, BLS, U. N.C., 1953; DHL (hon.), St. Lawrence U., 1980, Susquehanna U., 1989, Ind. U., 1996. Instr. polit. sci. U. Mass., Amherst, 1948-49; librarian State Tchrs. Coll., Livingston, Ala., 1953-55; chief serials and binding div. Emory U. Library, Ga., 1955-62; head librarian Earlham Coll., Richmond, Ind., 1962-94, coll. libr. emeritus, 1994—. Cons. Bates Coll., Eckerd Coll., Colo. Coll., Hartwick Coll., Macalester Coll., Maryville Coll., Knox Coll., Ill. Coll., Messiah Coll., Hiram Coll., Centenary Coll., Colby Coll., Ga. State U., Ripon Coll., Hampshire Coll., Reed Coll., Williams Coll., NEH, Lilly Endowment, North Ctrl. Assn., Assn. Am. Colls., Pew Meml. Trust. Author: (with Andreano and Reynolds) Student Economists Handbook, 1967, Classified List of Periodicals for the College Library, 5th edit., 1972; assoc. editor: Southeastern Librarian, 1959-62; asst. editor: Explorations in Entrepreneurial History, 1964-66; co-editor: Earlham Rev., 1965-72; editor: Combined Retrospective Index to Book Revs. in Scholarly Jours., 1886-1974, 1979-83, Combined Retrospective Index to Revs. in Humanities Jours., 1802-1974, 1983-85, (with Ruth Walling) Essays in Honor of Guy R. Lyle; columnist: Choice Mag., 1974-80, Library Issues, 1982-88; mem. editl. bd. Coll. and Undergrad Librs., Internet and Higher Edn. Recipient Acad./Rsch. Libr. of the Yr., 1980, B.I. Libr. of Yr. award, 1987. Mem. Assn. Coll. and Rsch. Librs. (pres. 1978-79, bd. dirs. 1989-93), ALA (council 1969-71, 79-83). Home: 304 SW H St Richmond IN 47374-5243 Office: Earlham Coll Lilly Libr Richmond IN 47374 E-mail: evanf@earlham.edu.

FARBER, HARRISON W. critical care physician, medical educator; b. Ware, Mass., May 5, 1947; s. Seymour J. and Harriet W. (Wirtschafter) F. BS, Duke U., 1969; MD, George Washington U., 1977. Diplomate Am. Bd. Internal Medicine, Am. Bd. Pulmonary Diseases, Am. Bd. Critical Care Medicine. Intern Med. Coll. Va., Richmond, 1977-78, resident, 1978-80, chief resident, 1980-81; fellow in pulmonary/critical care Boston U. Sch. Medicine, 1981-84, asst. prof., 1984-89, assoc. prof., 1989-94, prof., 1994—; staff physician Boston City Hosp., 1984—, med. dir. respiratory therapy, 1986 , dir. med. intensive care unit, 1985—; staff physician Univ. Hosp., Boston, 1984—; med. dir. respiratory therapy Mattapan Hosp., Boston, 1986—; dir. pulmonary hypertension ctr. Boston Med. Ctr., 2001—. Mem. spl. care unit adv. com. Boston City Hosp., chmn., 1992—, mem. code com., respiratory therapy com., diversion task force, com. on house officer performance, physicians comm. task force, clin. and edn. com., residency tchg. skills; spkr. numerous confs. in field. Contbr. over 100 articles and abstracts to profl. jours., chpts. to books; reviewer Am. Jour. Respiratory Cell and Molecular Biology, Am. Jour. Physiology, Jour. Cellular Physiology, Jour. Clin. Investigation, Circulation Rsch., Annals Internal Medicine, Chest, Endothelium, Am. Jour. Respiratory and Critical Care Medicine, Exptl. Eye Rsch. Active Nat. Youth Leadership Forum. Recipient Am. Lung Assn. Rsch. award, 1983-84, Career Investigator award, 1992—, Mass. Thoracic Soc. Rsch. award, 1984-85, NIH-NHLBI New Investigator award, 1985-88; biomed. rsch. grantee Univ. Hosp., 1984-85; rsch. grantee Am. Lung Assn.; 1986-88; program project grantee NIH-NHLBI, 1986-91; grantee Am. Heart Assn. Mass. Affiliate, 1989-91, NIH-NHLBI, 1992-96. Mem. AAAS, Am. Coll. Chest Physicians, Am. Thoracic Soc., Am. Heart Assn. (cardiopulmonary coun.), Am. Fedn. Clin. Rsch., Am. Physiologic Soc., Am. Soc. Cell Biology (congl. liaison com.), Am. Soc. Clin. Investigation. Avocations: travel, running, cycling, endurance sports. Office: Boston U Sch Medicine Pulmonary Ctr 715 Albany St R304 Boston MA 02118-2307 E-mail: hfarber@lung.bumc.bu.edu.

FARBER, ISADORE E. psychologist, educator; b. St. Joseph, Mo., May 21, 1917; s. Jacob and Rose (Malkin) F.; m. Billie Frances Gulko, May 5, 1942; children: Ronna Ellen (dec.), Deborah. Student, St. Joseph Jr. Coll., 1934-36; BA, U. Mo., 1939, MA, 1940; PhD, U. Iowa, 1946. Instr. psychology U. Rochester, 1946-47; asst. prof. to prof. psychology U. Iowa, 1947-64; vis. prof. U. Wis., 1955, Stanford, 1960; research cons. Med. Sch., U. of Okla., 1956-57; prof. psychology U. Ill., Chgo., 1964-84, prof. emeritus, 1984—, head dept. psychology, 1964-68, 76-81. Vis. prof., sr. Fulbright fellow Hebrew U., Jerusalem, 1971-72. Founding editor Jour. Exptl. Research in Personality, 1965-71; editor Psychology series, Dodd, Mead & Co., 1965-73; cons. editor Jour. Abnormal and Social Psychology, 1955-61, Jour. of Personality, 1955-61, Jour. Abnormal Psychology, 1973-79; contbr. articles to profl. jours. Served with Q.M.C. AUS, 1941-42; to 2d lt. USAAF, 1942-45. Fellow APA, Am. Psychol. Soc.; mem. Midwestern Psychol. Assn. (past pres.), Psychonomic Soc., Midwest Com. for Rational Inquiry, Phi Beta Kappa, Sigma Xi. Jewish. Home: 7912 Church St Morton Grove IL 60053-1628

FARBER, JOHN J. chemical company executive; b. Timisoara, Rumania, Aug. 23, 1925; s. Eugene and Magda (Reiter) F.; m. Maya Kleyman, June 28, 1953; children: Sandra, Deborah, Michael, Claudia. MS, U. Cluj, Timisoara, 1948; PhD, Poly. Inst. Bklyn., 1956. Rsch. chemist Sun Chem. Co., N.Y.C., 1951-52; cons. Soc. des Peintures et Vernis Bouvet, Tournus, France, Verneba A.G. Neuallschwill, Basel, Switzerland, Foster Grant Co., Inc., Leominster, Mass., Chemische Fabrik Kalk GmbH, Koln, Kalk, Germany, Asahi Chem. Industry Co., Ltd., Tokyo, 1953-56; chmn. bd., chief exec. officer ICC Industries, Ind., N.Y.C.; chmn. Primex Plastics Corp., Oakland, N.J.; pres. Dover Chem. Corp., Ohio. Dir., chmn. Electrochem. Industries (Frutarom) Ltd., Haifa, Israel. Mem. Am. Chem. Soc., Soc. Plastics Industry, Soc. Plastics Engrs., Nat. Petroleum Refiners Assn., Chem. Mfrs. Assn. Office: ICC Industries Inc 460 Park Ave New York NY 10022-1906

FARBER, KENNETH LAWRENCE MEYERS, management consultant; s. Lawrence Jerome and Barbara Holland Meyers; m. Courtney Meyers Farber, Sept. 21, 1996; children: Benjamin Peter Meyers, Ruby Meyers. SM in Nuc. Engring., MIT, 1987, SM in Tech. and Policy, 1989. CEO Mirada Solutions, Inc., Burlington, Mass., 1997—98, Organic Software, Inc., Concord, Mass., 1998—. Libertarian. Office: Organic Software Inc 30 Monument Sq Concord MA 01742 Personal E-mail: kenlmf@rcn.com.

FARBER, LILLIAN, retired photography equipment company executive; b. N.Y.C., Aug. 4, 1920; d. Louis and Fannie (Disraeli) Bachrach; m. Leonard L. Farber, Nov. 3, 1940 (div. 1975); children: Lindy Linder, Robert D. (dec.), Peggy, Felicia Gervais. BA, NYU, 1940; MA, Sarah Lawrence Coll., 1966. Co-dir. Upward Bound Sarah Lawrence Coll., Bronxville, N.Y., 1966-70, dean student svcs., 1973-76; v.p., owner Zone VI Studios, Inc., Newfane, Vt., 1976-90, ret., 1990. One-woman photography shows include, Vt., N.Y. V.p. Greenburgh LWV, Hartsdale, NY, 1955—63; family adv. Westchester Coun. Social Agys., White Plains, NY, 1970—73; pres. bd. trustees Free Libr., Newfane, 1977—97; trustee Marlboro (Vt.) Coll., 1982—, chmn. bd. trustees, 1982—97; trustee Vt. Coun. on the Arts, 1992—96; mem. Vt. Bicentennial Commn., 1990—91; state committeewoman N.Y. State Dem. Com., 1968—70. Mem. ACLU. Avocation: photography. Home: 10 Wiswall Hill PO Box 265 Newfane VT 05345-0265

FARBER, MARTIN STUART, rheumatologist; b. N.Y.C., May 26, 1950; MD, PhD, Albert Einstein Coll. Medicine, 1979. Intern in internal medicine Boston City Hosp., 1979-80, resident in internal medicine, 1980-82; fellow in rheumatology Boston U., 1982-84; chief rheumatology Ellis Hosp., Schenectady, N.Y., 1987—, St. Clare's Hosp., Schenectady, 1990—. Mem.: ACP, Arthritis Found. (bd. dirs. 1990—, chmn. 1994—95, 2003), Am. Coll. Rheumatology. Office: 124 Rosa Rd Ste 381 Schenectady NY 12308-2104

FARBER, PATRICIA ANN, secondary education educator; b. Balt., June 15, 1945; d. George Earle and Joy Lucille (Hankins) Reynolds; m. Stuart L. Farber. BA in English and Music, Calif. State U., Long Beach, 1967, MA in Ednl. Adminstrn. summa cum laude, 1983, postgrad., 1987. Cert. tchr. math., English and music, cert. in adminstr. svcs., Calif. Instr. kindergarten-6th grade Garden Grove (Calif.) Unified Sch. Dist., 1968-72, math. and English curriculum specialist, 1976-78; field curriculum cons. Allied Edn. Coun., Chgo., 1973 75; tchr. math./computers Palm Desert (Calif.) Mid. Sch., 1983-85; mentor math. tchr. Bellflower (Calif.) H.S., 1985-98, chair dept. math., 1993-98; math. tchr. La Quinta H.S., 1998—. Author curricula, math. placement and proficiency exams. Chair jr. aux. Children's Meml. Hosp., Long Beach, 1978-83; v.p. Long Beach Civic Light Opera Guild, 1978-83. Recipient Jaime Escalante award L.A. Ednl. Partnership/ARCO, 1992, Outstanding Educator award Johns Hopkins U., 1994, Congl. Dist. citation 1996, NBC TV Crystal Apple award, 1997, Golden Apple award KESQ (ABC) TV, 2001; Mark Taper fellow, 1994; Tandy Tech. scholar, 1994, 95. Mem. ASCD, NEA, Calif. Tchrs. Assn., Assn. for Elem. Edn., Calif. State U. Alumni Assn., Phi Delta Kappa. Avocations: boating, travel, tennis. Home: 350 Monrovia Ave Long Beach CA 90803-1933 Office: La Quinta HS 79-225 Westward Ho Dr La Quinta CA 92253 E-mail: patriciaf@surf.dsusd.k12.ca.us.

FARBER, ROSANN ALEXANDER, geneticist, educator; b. Charlotte, N.C., Nov. 21, 1944; d. J. Wilson Jr. and June Adell (Childs) Alexander; m. Gerald Lee Farber, July 28, 1966 (div. Jan. 1969); m. Thomas Douglas Petes, July 20, 1973; children: Laura Elizabeth Petes, Diana Christine Petes. AB in Biology, Oberlin Coll., 1966; postgrad., U. Pitts., 1967-68, Albert Einstein Coll. Medicine, 1969; PhD in Genetics, U. Wash., 1973. Diplomate in clin. cytogenetics and clin. molecular genetics Am. Bd. Med. Genetics. Postdoctoral fellow Nat. Inst. for Med. Rsch., London, 1973-75; rsch. assoc. Children's Hosp. Med. Ctr., Boston, 1975-77; from asst. prof. to assoc. prof. U. Chgo.,

1977-88; assoc. prof. dept. pathology and lab. medicine, program molecular biology and biotechnology, curriculum genetics and molecular biology U. N.C., Chapel Hill, 1988-97, prof., 1997—, prof. dept. genetics, 2001—. Mem. U. N.C. Lineberger Comprehensive Cancer Ctr., 1996—. Contbr. articles to profl. jours. NIH grantee, 1978—. Mem. AAAS, Am. Soc. Human Genetics. Achievements include research in human molecular genetics, somatic cell genetics, cancer genetics. Home: 612 Morgan Creek Rd Chapel Hill NC 27517-4928 Office: U NC CB 7525 Brinkhous-Bullitt Bldg Chapel Hill NC 27599

FARBER, SAUL JOSEPH, physician, educator; b. N.Y.C. s. Isodor and Mary (Bunim) Farber; m. Doris Marcia Balmuth; children: Joshua M., Beth Mina Farber Loewentheil. AB, NYU, 1938, MD, 1942; PhD (hon.), Tel Aviv U., 1983. Diplomate Am. Bd. Internal Medicine. Intern Sinai Hosp., Balt., 1942—43; rsch. resident Goldwater Meml. Hosp., N.Y.C, 1946—47; resident Bellevue Hosp., N.Y.C, 1947—48; fellow NYU, 1948—49, instr., asst. prof. medicine, 1953—62, assoc. prof., 1962—66, prof., chmn. dept. medicine, 1966—, Frederick H. King prof. medicine, 1978—, dean for acad. affairs Sch. Medicine, 1978—98, acting dean Sch. of Medicine, 1963—66, 1979—81, 1982—, provost, dean sch. medicine, 1987—98, chmn., 1998—99. Co-chmn. N.Y. State Health Adv. Coun., 1975—80; chmn. Com. on Resource Requirements of VA Health Care Systems NRC, 1974—77; mem. adv. com. on long term care chronic illness Robert Wood Johnson Found., 1979—, co-chmn. clin. nurse scholars adv. com., 1982—; mem. med. adv. bd. Hadassah; mem. adv. com. Harold C. Simmons Arthritis Rsch. Ctr., U. Tex. Health Sci. Ctr., Dallas, 1983—86; organizing chmn. Fedn. Coun. Internal Medicine, 1975; splty. advisor Naval Med. Command, Washington, 1985—86. Contbr. articles to profl. jours. Recipient Career Scientist award, Health Rsch. Coun., N.Y.C., 1960—65, Med. Alumni Achievement award, NYU Sch. Medicine Alumni Assn., 1966, Gt. Tchr. award, NYU Alumni Fedn., 1973, Alumni Assn. Achievement award, Washington Sq. Coll. Arts and Sci., NYU, 1978, Alumni Meritorious Svc. award, NYU Alumni Fedn., 1984, Wise medal, Tel Aviv U., 1990, The Albert Gallatin medal, NYU, 1993, The Abraham Flexner award for Disting. Svc. to Med. Edn., 1995. Master: ACP (pres. 1984—85, regent 1978—86, Disting. Tchr. award 1986, Alfred Stengal Meml. award 1992); mem.: Acad. Health Ctrs. (adv. com. 1981—), Am. Physiol. Assn., Am. Clin. and Climatol. Assn., Inst. Medicine NAS, Interurban Clin. Club, Assn. Am. Physicians, Am. Soc. Clin. Investigation (sec.-treas. 1951—60, councillor 1960—63), Am. Soc. Internal Medicine (Disting. Internist of Yr. award 1976), Sigma Theta Tau (hon.). Office: NYU Sch Medicine 550 1st Ave New York NY 10016-6402

FARBER, STEVEN GLENN, lawyer; b. Phila., July 20, 1946; s. Isadore Irving and Sylvia (Galperin) F.; children: Jamie, Daniel, Zoey, Avi. BBA, Temple U., 1968, JD, 1972. Bar: Pa. 1972, U.S. Dist. Ct. (ea. dist.) Pa. 1972, U.S. Dist. Ct. Appeals (3d cir.) 1972, N.Mex. 1975, U.S. Dist. Ct. N.Mex. 1975, U.S. Ct. Appeals (10th cir.) 1979, U.S. Supreme Ct. 1980. Asst. defender Pub. Defender Assn. Phila., 1972-74; acting dist. pub. defender State of N.Mex., Santa Fe, 1975-76, asst. atty. gen., 1976-78; pvt. practice Santa Fe, 1978—. Mem. N.Mex. Bd. Legal Specialization, 1986-90, chmn., 1991-93. Mem. Santa Fe Mcpl. Home Rule Charter Commn., 1997; bd. dirs. Ptnrs. in Edn., 1997—2002, Santa Fe County United Way, 1998—2002; elected city councilor City of Santa Fe, 1992—96; bd. dirs. Temple Beth Shalom, 1997—, v.p., 2000—01, pres., 2002—03. Mem. Nat. Assn. Criminal Def. Lawyers (vice-chmn. continuing legal edn. com. 1990-91), N.Mex. Lawyers Guild (pres. 1980-81), N.Mex. State Bar Assn. (bd. dirs. criminal law sect. 1980-83, chmn. 1981-82), N.Mex. Criminal Def. Lawyers Assn. (bd. dirs. 1991, treas. 1996), First Jud. Dist. Criminal Def. Lawyers Assn. (sec. 1999). Democrat. Jewish. Office: PO Box 2473 306 Catron St Santa Fe NM 87504-2473 E-mail: sgfsaf@aol.com.

FARBER, WALTER T. assyriologist, educator; b. Stuttgart, Germany, Oct. 3, 1947; m. Gertrud Flügge. PhD, Eberhard-Karls-Universität, Tübingen, Germany, 1973; habilitation, Ludwig-Maximilians-Universität, Munich, 1980. Asst. prof. Ludwig-Maximilians-Universität, Munich; assoc. prof. U. Chgo., 1980—90, prof. Assyriology, 1990—. Tablet collection curator Oriental Inst., Chgo., 2002—. Author: (scholarly monograph) Beschwörungsrituale an Ischtar und Dumuzi, 1977, Schlaf, Kindchen, schlaf!, 1989, (philatelic handbook) Rejected Mail Germany, 1945-49, 1994. Fellow NEH, 1995. Mem.: Brit. Sch. Archaeology in Iraq, Am. Oriental Soc., Germany Philatelic Soc. Avocations: playing classical music, philately, travel. Office: Univ Chgo 1155 E 58th St Chicago IL 60637 Office Fax: 773-702-9853. E-mail: w-farber@uchicago. edu.

FARBERMAN, HAROLD, conductor, composer; b. N.Y.C., Nov. 2, 1930; s. Louis and Lena (Kramer) F.; m. Corinne Curry, June 22, 1958; children: Thea, Lewis. Diploma, Juilliard Sch. Music, 1951; BS, New England Conservatory Music, 1956, MS, 1957. Prin. guest condr. Bournemouth Sinfonietta; founder, dir. Conductors Inst., 1980—. Dir. Stokowski Conducting Competition, 1994; prof. conducting Hartt Sch. Author: The Art of Conducting Technique; percussionist, Boston Symphony Orch., 1951-63, condr., New Arts Orch., Boston, 1955-63, guest condr., Royal Philharm. Orch., London, Denver Symphony Orch., BBC Symphony, Victoria (Can.) Philharm., Miami (Fla.) Philharm., N.Y. Philharm., New Philharmonia Orch., London, Orchestre de Lille, France, Stockholm Philharm., Swedish Radio Orch., Danish Radio Orch., Malmö (Sweden) Symphony Orch., Sydney (Australia) Symphony, Melbourne (Australia) Symphony, Perth (Australia) Symphony, Brisbane (Australia) Symphony, London Smyphony Orch., English Chamber Orch., condr., Colorado Springs (Colo.) Philharm., 1967-68, music dir., condr., Oakland Symphony Orch., 1971-79, rec. artist (condr. or composer) for, Columbia, Capitol, Mercury, Vanguard, Cambridge, Serenus, Boston records, rep. U.S. in, Paris Internat. Composition Competition, 1959; Composer symphonies, string quartet, chamber music, operas, jazz.; pioneered recorded works of Charles E. Ives., Michael Haydn. Scholar Juilliard Sch. Music, 1947-51. Mem. Condrs. Guild (founder, bd. dirs. summer inst.), Nat. Assn. Composers and Condrs. Address: PO Box 543 Germantown NY 12526

FARBISH, ALFRED B. waterproofing materials executive; b. Phila., Sept. 18, 1923; s. Sidney Almeyer and Rachel Bucks Farbish; m. Rita Fayer, Oct. 11, 1951 (dec. July 1995); children: Michael Bucks, Peter Bertram. Student, Oxford (Eng.) U., 1945; BA, U. Pa., 1948. Civil engr. Corps of Engrs., Phila., 1956-59; quality control Barrett divsn. Allied Chem., N.Y.C., 1959-65; sales mgr. Am. Cyanamid, Wakefield, Mass., 1965-71; v.p. Rubber & Plastics Corp., Long Island City, NY, 1972-89; pres., owner Nervastral, Inc., Greenwich, Conn., 1989—. Patentee in field. 1st lt. arty. U.S. Army, 1948-53; lt. col. USAR ret., 1983. Republican. Avocations: rowing, fencing. Home: 351 Pemberwick Rd Apt 916 Greenwich CT 06831 Office: Nervastral Inc 100 Melrose Ave Ste 206 Greenwich CT 06830

FARCI, PATRIZIA, medical educator, researcher; b. Villasimius, Italy, Feb. 2, 1954; came to U.S., 1989; d. Miniato and Eleonora (Scuda) F.; m. Paolo Lusso; 1 child, Emanuele. MD, U. Cagliari, Italy, 1979, cert. infectious diseases, 1983, cert. gastroenterology, 1987. Intern in internal medicine U. Cagliari, 1979-83, asst. prof., 1984-92, head hepatology sect., 1985—, assoc. prof. medicine, 1992—2000, prof. medicine, 2000—. Vis. scientist Free Hosp., London, 1983-85, Lab. of Infectious Diseases/NIAID/NIH, Bethesda, Md., 1989-96; adj. investigator LID/NIAID/NIH, Bethesda, 1997—. Contbr. more than 140 articles to profl. jours. Mem. Am. Assn. for the Study of Liver Diseases. Roman Catholic. Avocations: music, reading, travel. Office: LID NIAID/NIH Bldg 50 Rm 6531 9000 Rockville Pike Bethesda MD 20892-0001 also: Dept Med Scis U Cagliari via S Giorgio 12 09124 Cagliari Italy Fax: 39-070-510064. E-mail: farcip@pacs.unica.it.

FARCUS, JOSEPH JAY, architect, interior designer; b. McKeesport, Pa., June 17, 1944; s. Howard E. and Fannie (Meyers) F.; m. Jeanne Cohen, Dec. 31, 1983; children: David Evensky, Daniel, Elizabeth. BArch, U. Fla., 1967. Registered architect, Fla.; cert. Nat. Coun. Archtl. Registration Bds. Designer Morris Lapidus Assocs., Miami Beach, Fla., 1967-77; prin. Joseph Farcus Architect, Miami, Fla., 1977—. Featured speaker: Modern Ship Architecture, intl. conf., Natl. Maritime Museum, London, 1996, Pres.' Invitatio Lectr. Royal Instn. Naval Architects, London, 1997; spkr. in field. Published in newspapers and mags. including Hotel and Restaurant Design, Fabrics & Architecture, Travel Weekly, World Cruise Industry Rev., Internat. Cruise & Ferry, Seatrade Rev., Archtl. Record; mem. editl. adv. bd. Internat. Cruise and Ferry Rev., London, 1994; archtl. and interior designer for largest cruise ship ever built, 1996; patentee ship funnel design; design work on ships subject of show Design Mus., London, 1999-2000. Bd. dirs. Am. Jewish Com., Miami, 1991—, Bass Mus. of Art, Miami Beach, 1999; mem. nat. bd. govs. Am. Jewish Com., 2002-. Featured interior architect largest passenger ship ever built Guiness World Book Records, 1998. Mem. Constrn. Specifications Inst. Home and Office: 5285 Pine Tree Dr Miami FL 33140-2109

FARE, ELIZABETH CAROL, music educator; d. Jay John Potter and Mary Elizabeth Jund; m. Jason Anthony Fare, Oct. 19, 1996; 1 child, Nicholas Joseph. B in Sociology, St. Norbert Coll., DePere, Wis., 1993; MSW, U. Wis, Milw., 2001—01. Probation officer asst. US Cts., Milw., 1995—99; probation officer US Courts, Milwaukee, Wis., 1999—2000; piano instr. Oconomowoc, Wis., 2000—. Mem.: Nat. Fedn. Music Clubs (assoc.), Milw. Music Tchrs. Assn. (assoc.), Wis. Music Tchrs. Assn. (assoc.; treas. 2003—). Avocations: reading, walking, gardening, travel.

FARELL CUBILLAS, ARSENIO, former Mexican government official; Sec. of patronage, Independent Nat. U. of Mexico, 1952—66; prof., tech. advisor Independent Nat. U. of Mexico, 1956—73; prof. Latin Amer. U., 1967—68; chief Federal Commission of Electricity, 1973—76, Mexican Inst. of Soc. Insurance, 1976—82; sec. Work and Social Forecast, 1982—94; chief Nat. Coord. of Public Security, 1994; comptroller gen. Govt. of Mex., Mexico City, 1996—2000; now official Partido Revolucionario Institutional. Office: Partido Rev Institutional Insurgentes Norte No 59 Edif 2 Col Buenavista 06359 Mexico

FARENTHOLD, FRANCES TARLTON, lawyer; b. Corpus Christi, Tex., Oct. 2, 1926; d. Benjamin Dudley and Catherine (Bluntzer) Tarlton; children: Dudley Tarlton, George Edward, Emilie, James Doughterty, Vincent Bluntzer (dec.). AB, Vassar Coll., 1946; JD, U. Tex., 1949; LLD, Hood Coll., 1973, Boston U., 1973, Regis Coll., 1976, Lake Erie Coll., 1979, Elmira Coll., 1981, Coll. Santa Fe, 1985. Bar: Tex. 1949. Pvt. practice, 1949-65, 67-76, 80—; mem. Tex. Ho. of Reps., 1968-72; dir. legal aid Nueces County, 1965-67; pres. Wells Coll., Aurora, N.Y., 1976-80; asst. prof. law Tex. So. U., Houston, Thurgood Marshall disting. vis. prof., 1994-95. Lawyer; b. Corpus Christi, Tex., Oct. 2, 1926; d. Benjamin Dudley and Catherine (Bluntzer) Tarlton; children: Dudley Tarlton, George Edward, Emilie, James Doughterty, Vincent Bluntzer (dec.). AB, Vassar Coll., 1946; JD, U. Tex., 1949; LLD, Hood Coll., 1973, Boston U., 1973, Regis Coll., 1976, Lake Erie Coll., 1979, Elmira Coll., 1981, Coll. of Santa Fe, 1985. Bar: Tex. 1949. Pvt. practice, 1949-65, 67-76, 80—; mem. Tex. Ho. of Reps., 1968-72; dir. legal aide Nueces County, 1965-67; asst. prof. law Tex. So. U., Houston; pres. Wells Coll., Aurora, N.Y., 1976-80; disting. vis. prof. Thurgood Marshall Tex. So. U., Houston, 1994-95. Mem. Human Relations Com., Corpus Christi, 1963-68, Corpus Christi Citizen's Com. Community Improvement, 1966-68; mem. Tex. adv. com. to U.S. Commn. on Civil Rights, 1968-76; mem. nat. adv. council ACLU; mem. Orgn. for Preservation Unblemished Shoreline, 1964—; Dem. candidate for Gov. of Tex., 1972; del. Dem. Nat. Conv., 1972, 1st woman nominated to be candidate v.p. U.S., 1972; nat. co-chmn. Citizens to Elect McGovern-Shriver, 1972; chmn. Nat. Women's Polit. Caucus, 1973-75; mem. Dem. platform com., 1988; trustee Vassar Coll., 1975-83; bd. dirs. Fund for Constl. Govt., Ctr. for Devel. Policy, 1983—, Mexican Am. Legal Def. and Ednl. Fund, 1980-83; chmn. Inst. for Policy Studies, 1986-91; mem. bd. dirs. Rothko Chapel, 1997—. Recipient Lyndon B. Johnson Woman of Year award, 1973. Mem. State Bar Tex. Mem. Human Rels. Com., Corpus Christi, 1963-68, Corpus Christi Citizens Com. Cmty. Improvement, 1966-68; mem. Tex. adv. com. to U.S. Commn. on Civil Rights, 1968-76; mem. nat. adv. coun. ACLU; mem. Orgn. for Preservation Unblemished Shoreline, 1964—; Dem. candidate for Gov. of Tex., 1972; del. Dem. Nat. Conv., 1972, 1st woman nominated to be candidate v.p. U.S., 1972; nat. co-chair Citizens to elect McGovern-Shriver, 1972; chmn. Nat. Women's Polit. Caucus, 1973-75; mem. Dem. Platform Com., 1988; trustee Vassar Coll., 1975-83; bd. dirs. Fund for Constl. Govt., Ctr. for Devel. Policy, 1983—, Mexican Am. Legal Def. and Ednl. Fund, 198--83; chmn. Inst. for Policy Studies, 1986-91; bd. dirs. Rothko Chapel, 1997—, chmn., 2001—. Recipient Lyndon B. Johnson Woman of Yr. award, 1973, Lifetime Svc. award Dem. Party of Tex., 1998. Mem. State Bar Tex. Office: 2929 Buffalo Speedway Apt 1813 Houston TX 77098-1710

FARES, MICHAEL ISSAM, bank executive, investor, philanthropist; s. Issam Michael Fares and Oumayma Farah; m. Lara Rizk. Mng. dir., CEO Wedge Bancorp B.V., 1988—97; dir. Wedge Bank M.E., 1985—97, chmn., 1991—97; dir. Wedge Bank (Switzerland), 1985—94, chmn., 1991—94; dir. Wedge Group Internat., Tex., 1987—; chmn. Wedge Real Estate S.A.L., 1985—97; co-founder, dir. Lebanon Holdings, Luxembourg, 1997—. Co-founder, pres. Fares Found., 1984—. Bd. visitors Fletcher Sch. Law and Diplomacy, Mass., 1992-2003; internat. adv. coun. Am. U. Beirut, N.Y., 1992-96; trustee Balamand U., Lebanon, 1994—, Am. U. Beirut, 1996—.

FARGEY, MICHAEL ANDREW, special education educator; b. Morristown, N.J., Jan. 31, 1955; s. Thomas Archibald and Bertha Elizabeth Fargey; m. Barbara Majeski Fargey, June 23, 1990. AA in Fine Arts, Bergen C.C., Paramus, N.J., 1991; BA in Spl. Edn., William Paterson U., Wayne, N.J., 1998. Cert. tchr. of handicapped, elem. edn. N.J. Spl. edn. tchr. Elizabeth (N.J.) Bd. Edn., 1999—2002, Bridgewater-Raritan Bd. Edn., Bridgewater, 2002—. Tutor Home Ednl. Svcs., Somerville, NJ, 2001—. Mem.: Coun. for Exceptional Children. Avocations: painting, running, weight lifting. Mailing: 64 S 23d St Kenilworth NJ 07033

FARGIS, PAUL MCKENNA, publishing consultant, book developer, editor; b. NYC, Mar. 19, 1939; s. George Bertrand and Elizabeth Harlin (McKenna) F.; m. Elizabeth Hackett, Aug. 22, 1964; children: John Hackett, Alison Katherine; m. Dawn Sangrey, Apr. 23, 1977; 1 child, Christopher Sangrey. Student, Cath. U. Am., 1958; B in Social Sci., Fairfield U., 1961; MA (Publ. Tuition scholar), NYU, 1962. Editorial asst. Prentice-Hall, Inc., Englewood Cliffs, NJ, 1961-62; editor Hawthorn Books, Inc., NYC, 1963-67, v.p., editorial dir., 1967-71; v.p., editor-in-chief Thomas Y. Crowell Co. and Funk & Wagnalls divs. Dun-Donnelley Pub. Corp., NYC, 1971-77; editor-in-chief Apollo Books, NYC, 1972-77; mng. dir. Thomas Y. Crowell div. Harper and Row, NYC, 1977-78; founder, pres. and pub. The Stonesong Press, Inc., 1978—2003. Dir., sec. Round Stone Press, Inc., 1990-2001; pub. Grand Ctrl. Press, 2001-2003; mem. adv. bd. Grad. Sch. Corp. and Polit. Comm., Fairfield U., 1969-81; pub. arbitrator Am. Arbitration Assn., 1982-2002. Author: The Consumer's Handbook, 1966, rev. edit., 1974, Company's Coming, 1965; Am. editor: Twentieth Century Ency. Catholicism, 1963-67; editor-in-chief: The New York Public Library Desk Reference, 1989; co-author: Perks and Parachutes, 1997; co-editor: The Big Book of Life's Instructions, 1995; contbr. articles to profl. jour.; patentee in field. Exec. dir. Harrison (NY) Town Recreation Commn., 1970-72; dir. Harrison Town Forum, 1969-73; former bd. dir. US Cath. Hist. Soc.; trustee Unitarian Universalist Fellowship of No. Westchester. Mem. Am. Book Coun. (bd. dir. 1987-88), Am. Book Producers Assn. (pres. 1986-87, bd. dir. Charitable Book program 1987-89), Book Industry Study Group. Unitarian Universalist. Avocations: carpentry, stonework, travel, hiking, sculpture. Office: 11 E 47th St New York NY 10017-1919

FARGO, HEATHER, mayor; Mayor City of Sacramento, Calif. Office: City Hall 915 I St Sacramento CA 95814 E-mail: hfargo@cityofsacramento.org.

FARGO, THOMAS BOULTON, career officer; b. San Diego, Calif., 1948; Grad., U.S. Naval Acad., 1970. Commd. ensign USN, 1970, advanced through ranks to adm.; various assignments to comd. U.S. Naval Forces, Cen. Command/Comdr., U.S. Fifth Fleet; dep. chief of naval opers., comdr. U.S. Pacific Fleet; comdr. U.S. Pacific Command, Honolulu, 2002—. Decorated Disting. Svc. medal (4 times), Def. Superior Svc. medal, Legion of Merit (3 times), others; recipient James Bond Stockdale award for Inspirational Leadership, 1989.

FARHADI, ASHKAN, physician, researcher; b. Shiraz, Iran, Mar. 5, 1965; arrived in U.S., 2000; s. Gholam Ali Farhadi and Sadat Eyni; m. Ziba Ranjbaran, June 20, 1990; children: Arghavan, Nilgoun. Med. Diploma, Shiraz U., Iran, 1989; Internal Medicine Splty., Shiraz U., 1992; Gastroenterology subspeciality, Beheshti (Nat.) U., Tehran, Iran, 1994; M in clin. rsch., Rush U., 2001—03; Internal Medicine Splty., Rush U., Ill., 2003. Lic. MD Ill. Regulation dept., 2002, Iran Med. Assn., 1989. Rsch. fellow Rush U., Chgo., 2000—; chmn., dept. of medicine Mazandaran U., Sari, Iran, 1998—99, asst. prof. of medicine, 1994—99, Beheshti (Nat.) U., Tehran, 1992—94. Author: (book) Irritable Bowel Syndrome, Peptic Ulcer. Recipient Presdl. award, Am. Coll. of Gastroenterology, 2002, Sr. Fellow award, 2002, Third Pl. in the Bd. of Gastroenterology, Mister of Health and Sciences, Iran, 1994, First Pl. in the Bd. of Internal Medicine, 1992, Best Young Investigator, The Iranian Med. Assn., 1990; Award for Rsch., Am. Coll. of Gastroenterology, 2001. Achievements include invention of creeping colonoscope; automated hot biopsy needle and device. Office: Rush Medical Coll 1725 W Harrison St Ste 206 Chicago IL 60612 Office Fax: 312-563-3883. Personal E-mail: ashkan_farhadi@rush.edu. E-mail: ashkan_farhadi@rush.edu.

FARHAT, CAROL SUE, motion picture company executive; b. Santa Monica, Calif. d. Annis Farhat; 1 child, Michael. Assoc. degree, Inst. Audio Rsch., 1976-78; student, Otis Parsons Art Inst., 1980—84, UCLA, 1984-90; BA in Bus., Music, Antioch U., 1992. Co-founder, recording studio mgr. The Village Recorder, L.A., 1972-78; audio engr. The Village Recorder Studio, L.A., 1978-79; music adminstr. 20th Century Fox Film Corp., Beverly Hills, Calif., 1980-82, music supr., 1983-86, music dir., 1986-92, supr. internat. music Tokyo, 1993; music prodr. Scopus Films, England, 1987-89; songwriter Music Experts Ltd., Santa Monica, Calif., 1989-90; v.p. music 20th Century Fox Film Corp., 1994—2002; v.p. TV music and feature Am. Fedn. Musicians advisor 20th Century Fox Music, 1995-99. Author: China Diary, 1992; composer (music book) Children's Songbook, 1991; songwriter (for film) Rockin' Reindeer, 1990; prodr. (soundtrack) Ally McBeal Show (double platinum record award 1998).. Recipient Emmy award contbn. recognition for Simpsons TV-show music, 1990, 96, 97, 98, King of the Hill, 1999, Grammy award contbn. recognition for Malcolm in the Middle TV-show music, 2002. Mem. BMI, NATAS, NARAS, Women in Film, Am. Film Inst., Pacific Composers Forum, Entertainment Industry Counsel. Avocations: classical ballet, botany, ethnomusicology, photography. Office: 20th Century Fox Film Corp Bldg 19 Rm 130 PO Box 900 Beverly Hills CA 90213-0900

FARHAT, GEORGES ANTOUN, anesthesiologist; b. Lebanon, Feb. 17, 1966; MD, St. Joseph U., 1989. Intern Staten Island U. Hosp., 1989-90; resident in surgery St. Elizabeth Hosp. Med. Ctr., Youngstown, Ohio, 1990-91; resident in internal medicine St. Lukes Roosevelt Hosp., N.Y.C., 1991-92; resident in anesthesia Baylor Coll. of Medicine, Houston, 1992-95; fellow in pain mgmt. Cleve. Clinic Found., 1995-96; staff Tex. Inst. Pain Medicine, Fort Worth, 1996—. Mem. Am. Soc. Anesthesiology, Am. Soc. Regional Anesthesia, Internat. Anesthesia Rsch. Soc., Am. Acad. Pain Medicine, Am. Acad. Pain Mgmt., Tex. Soc. Anesthesiologist. Office: Ste 202 1305 Airport Fwy Bedford TX 76021

FARHI, DIANE C. pathologist and researcher; b. Cleve., Nov. 27, 1951; d. Victor and Betty D. (Brown) F.; children: Joseph, Ariela, Michael. BA, U. Mich., 1973, MD, 1977. Intern and resident U. Colo. Health Scs. Ctr., Denver, 1977-81; asst. prof. pathology U. Colo. Health Sci. Ctr., Denver, 1981-84, Case Western Res. U., Cleve., 1984-90, assoc. prof., 1990; assoc. prof. pathology U. Tex.-Southwestern Med. Ctr., Dallas, 1990-91, Emory U., Atlanta, 1991-96, prof. pathology, 1996-99; with GLM, Atlanta, 1999—2000, Quest Diagnostics, Inc., Tucker, Ga., 2000—. Editl. bd. Am. Jour. Clin. Pathology. Fellow Coll. Am. Pathology; mem. European Assn. for Hematopathology, Soc. for Hematopathology, Am. Soc. Clin. Pathology. Office: Quest Diagnostics Inc 1777 Montreal Cir Atlanta GA 30084 E-mail: diane.c.farhi@questdiagnostics.com.

FARHO, JAMES HENRY, JR., mechanical engineer, consultant; b. Omaha, June 28, 1924; s. James Henry and Mary (Mena) F.; m. Dummer Ree Mitchem, Nov. 12, 1946; children: Sandra, Joann, Wayne. BSME, U. Nebr., 1965. Enlisted USN, 1942, advanced through grades to sr. aviation chief machinist, 1942-62, ret., 1962; engr. Exxon Rsch. & Engring. Co., Florham Park, N.J., 1965-66, project engr., 1966-68, sr. project engr., 1968-70, engring. group head, 1970-71, engring. sect. head, 1971-78, sr. staff advisor Clinton, N.J., 1978-85; cons. engr. Lighthouse Point, Fla., 1985—. Cons. Exxon Prodn. Rsch., Houston, 1985, Swiki Anderson & Assocs., Bryan, Tex., 1986-87, Glaxo Pharms., Research Triangle, N.C., 1988-91. Mem. VFW, Fleet Res. Assn., Am. Legion, Elks, Sigma Xi. Republican. Roman Catholic. Home and Office: 2401 NE 33rd St Lighthouse Point FL 33064

FARHY, RODOLFO DAVID, internist, cardiologist; b. Las Varillas, Argentina, May 4, 1963; m. Iris Farhy, Sept. 2, 1989; children: Eli, Sara, Dina, Hadassah. MD, Nat. U. Cordoba, 1985. Diplomate Am. Bd. Internal Medicine, Cardiovascular Diseases. Resident in internal medicine Henry Ford Hosp., Detroit, 1993-95, fellow in hyper vascular rsch., 1990-93; fellow cardiology Cleve. Clin. Found., 1995-98; cardiologist Detroit, 1998—. Office: 31500 Telegraph Rd Ste 010 Bingham Farms MI 48025

FARIAS, JOSEPH G. priest, consultant; b. Passaic, N.J., June 3, 1949; s. Joseph J. and Anita M. Farias. BA, St. Mary's Sem. Coll., Catonsville, Md., 1971; STM, St. Mary's Sem. & U., Balt., 1975; MA, Notre Dame U., 1984. Diocesan youth dir. Diocese of Paterson, Clifton, NJ, 1976—79, dir. worship and spirituality, 1988—97; assoc. pastor St. Philip the Apostle Ch., Clifton, 1979—82; cath. chaplain Drew & Fairleigh Dickinson Univs., Madison, NJ, 1982—89, Drew & Fairleigh Dickinson Universities, Madison, NJ, 1997—; pastor St. Bernard Ch., Rockaway Twp., NJ, 1992—2002; aux. chaplain Archdiocese for the Mil. Svcs. USA, Washington, 1994—. Liturgical cons. In-Spire Worship Resources, Convent Station, NJ, 1988—; bd. dirs. Pallotti Ctr., Paterson; chaplain Phi Sigma Kappa Internat. Frat., Inpls., 1999—. Contributing editor: worship book Catholic Liturgy Book. Advisor Phi Sigma Kappa Frat., Madison, 1982—; police chaplain Police Dept., Rockaway Twp., 1998—2002; mem. N.J. Commn. on Children & Youth, Trenton, 1977—79; grand coun. dir. Phi Sigma Kappa Internat. Frat., Indpls., 1995—; trustee Morris Rugby Corp., Morristown, 2000—02. Mem.: N.Am. Acad. Liturgy. Roman Catholic. Avocation: technology. Office: Catholic Campus Ministry-Drew University 36 Madison Ave Madison NJ 07940 Personal E-mail: jfarias@drew.edu.

FARIAS BOUVIER, NESTOR, consulting company executive; b. Santa Fe, Argentina, July 23, 1941; s. Americo Farlas and Nelly Bouvier Samyn; m. Marina Lopez Anadon (div.); m. Maria Elena Daro, Jan. 5, 1988; children: Gaston, Martina. Degree in chem. engring., U. Nat. Litoral, Santa Fe, 1964; MBA, Iese. Navarra U., Barcelona, Spain, 1968. Pres., CEO Sapin Ltd., Brazil, 1973-78; pres. Sapin S.A. Bus. Cons., Buenos Aires, 1975—. Petroquimica Bahia Blanca, Buenos Aires, 1984-87; pres., CEO Austral Airlines, Buenos Aires, 1987-89; CEO, bd. dirs. Met. Railway SA, Argentina, 1992-94; CEO DGT Electronics S.A., Argentina, 1977-99; pres. Nucleo Electrca S.A., 2000—01. Contbr. papers on bus. policy/mgmt. to profl. jours. Industry sec. of state Argentine Govt., 1985. Roman Catholic. Avocations: tennis, skiing, horseback-riding. Office: Sapin SA Bus Cons Cordoba 669 8 1054 Buenos Aires Argentina

FARICY, JOHN HARTNETT, JR., lawyer; b. Augsburg, Germany, Nov. 5, 1955; came to U.S., 1956; s. John Hartnett and Mary Helen Sarah (Bowe) F. BA, Tulane U., 1977; JD, William Mitchell Coll. Law, St. Paul, 1982. Bar: Minn. 1982, U.S. Dist. Ct. Minn. 1983, U.S. Ct. Appeals (2d cir.) 1987, U.S. Supreme Ct. 1988. Ptnr. Faricy & Roen, P.A., Mpls., 1996—. Mem. Univ. Club of St. Paul. Office: Faricy & Roen PA 333 S 7th St Minneapolis MN 55402-4200

FARICY, RICHARD THOMAS, architect; b. St. Paul, June 1, 1928; s. Roland J. and Clare (Sullivan) F.; m. Carole Murphy, June 24, 1961; children: Althea, Bridget. Registered architect, Minn. V.p. The Cerny Assocs., Mpls., 1961-71; exec. v.p. Winsor/Faricy Architects, Inc., St. Paul, 1971-96; founding prin. Symmes Maini McKee Assoc./Winsor Faricy, St. Paul, 1996—2001; cons. arch. Collaborative Design Group, 2001—. Pres. Minn. Archtl. Found., 1986; trustee Am. Mus. Asmat Art, 1995—. Prin. works include: Raughurst Libr., Jamestown, N.D., Warren E. Burger Libr. at William Mitchell Coll. Law, St. Paul, Collier County Courthouse, Naples, Fla., Bandana Sq., St. Paul, Como Park Conservatory Restoration, St. Paul, Earl Brown Heritage Ctr., Brooklyn Center, Minn. Pres. Merrick Community Ctr., St. Paul, 1969; pres. Ramsey County Hist. Soc., 1981-82; chmn. Blue Cross Blue Shield Minn., 1974-77, HMO Minn., 1974-76; bd. dirs. Minn. State Arts Bd., 1988-94, HealthEast

Found., 1987-99, James J. Hill Reference Libr., 1996-99; bd. dirs. Friends St. Paul Pub. Libr., 19862000, pres., 1992-95; trustee Minn. Mus. Art, 1980-86; commr. St. Paul Heritage Preservation Commn., 1986-87, 2002—; bd. zoning appeals, St. Paul, 2001-; vice chmn. Mounds Midway Found., 1987-91; bd. dirs. sponsor bd. Bapt. Hosp. Fund, 1991—. 1st lt. USAR, 1952-57. Fellow AIA (nat. housing com. 1984-92, trustee AIA Benefit Ins. Trust 1986-89); mem. Minn. Soc. Architects (dir. 1973-77, chair Ins. Trust 1984-86), St. Paul AIA (pres. 1974), St. Paul Athletic Club (pres. 1980). Home: 2211 St Clair Ave Saint Paul MN 55105-1136 Office: Collaborative Design Group Inc Ste 300 1501 Washington Ave South Minneapolis MN 55454 E-mail: rfaricy@collaborativedesigngroup.com.

FARID, FARID O. mathematics educator; MS, U. of London, U.K., 1982; PhD in Math., U. of Calgary, Can., 1988. Vis. math prof. U. of Cin., 1999—2000, Pacific Luth. U., Tacoma, 2000—01; math prof., rschr., supr. U. of Minn., Morris, 2002—. Author: (author of a research paper in math) Linear and Multilinear Algebra, (math. rsch. papers) Linear Algebra and Its Applications, Procs. of the Am. Math. Soc., Procs. Indian Acad. Sci; co-author: Can. Jour. of Math. Fellow Post Doctoral Fellowship, U. of Toronto, 1989, U. of Guelph, 1992; scholar Rsch. and Tchg. Scholarships, U. of Calgary, 1984—88.

FARINA, MARIO G. lawyer; b. Newark, Nov. 1, 1927; s. Gerardo and Marianna F.; m. Lois R. Wachman, Apr. 11, 1955; children: Jay E., Wendy D., F. William. BS in Edn., Montclair State U., 1949; MA in Adminstrn., Seton Hall U., 1955, JD, 1960. Bar: N.J. 1963, N.Y. 1982, U.S. Dist. Ct. N.J. 1963, U.S. Supreme Ct. 1977. Atty. N.J. Pub. Defenders Office, Elizabeth, 1968-86; pvt. practice Clark, N.J., 1963—. Sgt. U.S. Army, 1950-52. Mem. Union County Bar Assn. Democrat. Roman Catholic. Avocation: writing. Office: 990 Raritan Rd Clark NJ 07066-1740 E-mail: mariogfarina@aol.com.

FARINELLA, PAUL JAMES, retired arts institution executive; b. Trenton, N.J., Sept. 28, 1926; s. Nicholas F. and Grace (Cubberly) F.; m. Margaret Pippitt, May 29, 1948; children: Dianne, Deborah. BS in Commerce and Bus. Adminstrn., Rider Coll., 1953. C.P.A., N.J. Pub. acct. Peat, Marwick, Mitchell & Co., Newark, 1953-61; assoc. comptroller U. Rochester, N.Y., 1961-67; v.p. bus. and fin., sec., treas. Ithaca Coll., 1967-76; pres., trustee Munson-Williams-Proctor Inst., Utica, N.Y., 1977-90, sr. advisor to bd., 1990-91. Served with USAAF, 1945-47.

FARINELLI, JEAN L. public relations executive; b. Phila., July 26, 1946; d. Albert J. and Edith M. (Falini) F. BA, Am. U., Washington, 1968; MA, Ohio State U., Columbus, 1969. Asst. pub. relations dir. Dow Jones & Co., Inc., N.Y.C., 1969-71; account exec. Carl Byoir & Assocs., Inc., N.Y.C., 1972-74, v.p., 1974-80, sr. v.p., 1980-82; pres. Tracy-Locke/BBDO Pub. Relations, Dallas, 1982-87, Creamer Dickson Basford, Inc., N.Y.C., 1987-88, chmn., chief exec. officer, 1988-98; pres., chief exec. officer Eurocom Corp. & PR (U.S.), 1991, Corp. Graphics, Inc., 1992; pres. Farinelli Cons. Group, LLC, 1999—. Dir. The Cologne Life Reinsurance Co., 1997-99. Recipient PR CaseBook, PR Reporter, N.H., 1984, Silver Spur, Tex. Pub. Rels. Assn., Dallas, 1985, Matrix award Women in Comms., 1993. Mem.: Nat. Found. for Infectious Diseases (former trustee), Arthur W. Page Soc. (treas., v.p. adminstrn. and fin.), Internat. Pub. Rels. Assn. (pub. rels. seminar), Nat. Investor Rels. Inst., The Women's Forum (bd. dirs.), Women in Comms. (chmn. 1995, dir. 1999—, Matrix award 1993), Pub. Rels. Soc. Am. (Silver Anvil award chmn. 1987, acad. exec. bd. 1990—91, trustee found., Silver Anvil award 1980—81, 1985, Excalibur award Houston chpt. 1985, Best of Show Silver Anvil award 1998). Office: 20 Sutton Pl S New York NY 10022-4165

FARIS, CHARLES OREN, civil engineer; b. Plymouth, Idaho, Sept. 8, 1924; s. Brady V. and Ellen (Alta) F.; m. Dorothy Phillips, Dec. 21, 1979; children from a previous marriage: Ellen Eileen, Nancy Claire. BSCE, Oregon State U., 1949. Registered profl. engr., Idaho, Oreg., Wash., Calif., Ariz., Colo., Kans., S.C., Va., Mont., Mo., Ark. Engr. Consol. Builders Inc., Mill City, Oreg., 1949-52; asst. supr. plant design State of Punjab, Nangal, India, 1952-54; office engr. dam divsn. Morrison-Knudsen Inc., Ione, Wash., 1954-55, chief plant engr. Strawberry, Calif., 1955, plant engr. divsn. constrn. Boise, Idaho, 1955-57, plant mgr. divsn. constrn., 1957-64; plant mgr. Western divsn. constrn. Dravo Corp., Bellevue, Wash., 1964-66, asst. mgr. Western divsn. constrn., 1966-67, dist. mgr. Seattle, 1967-71; ptnr. Hamlin-Faris Co., Bellevue, 1971-73; pres. Hamlin-Faris Internat. Inc., Bellevue, 1973-91, Faris Assocs. Inc., Bellevue, 1973—. Cons. in field to Am. and fgn. contractors and govtl. orgns. With U.S. Army, 1943-46, PTO. Fellow ASCE; mem. NSPE, Am. Concrete Inst., U.S. Com. Large Dams, Wash. Athletic Club. Republican. Mem. First Ch. Christ. Avocations: power boating, running, cycling, trail biking. Home: 9949 Lake Washington Blvd NE Bellevue WA 98004-6068 Office: Faris Assocs Ste B218 1750 112th Ave NE Bellevue WA 98004-3770

FARIS, JAMES VANNOY, interventional cardiologist, cardiology educator, hospital executive; b. July 18, 1943; s. Vannoy and Maudeline (Freeman) F.; m. Jacqueline Claire Bexell, July 1, 1978; children: Nathan James, Jamie Lynn, Jenna Claire, Brittany Jean, James Vannoy III, Janessa Marie. AB, Ind. U., 1965, MD, 1968. Diplomate Am. Bd. Internal Medicine, Am. Bd. Cardiology, Am. Bd. Interventional Cardiology. Intern, resident Ind. U. Med. Ctr., Indpls., 1968-71, asst. prof. medicine, 1976-80, assoc. prof. medicine, radiology, 1980-99; chief of staff Richard L. Roudebush VA Med. Ctr., Indpls., 1983-95, chief sect. cardiology, 1995-99; clin. assoc. prof. medicine, med. scis. program Ind. U., Bloomington, 1999—. Asst. dean sch. medicine Ind. U., 1983-95. Maj. U.S. Army, 1971-73, Vietnam. Grantee Ind. Heart Assn., VA Cooperative Study, 1999-2000. Fellow Am. Coll. Cardiology; mem. AMA, Ind. State Med. Assn., Indpls. Med. Soc. (pres. 1998-99), Monroe Owen County Med. Soc. (pres. 2003), Alpha Omega Alpha, Alpha Epsilon Delta. Republican. Methodist. Avocations: snow skiing, tennis, water skiing. E-mail: jfaris@ima-md.com.

FARISH, WILLIAM S. U.S. ambassador to United Kingdom; m. Sarah Farish. Student, U. Va. Stockbroker Underwood, Neuhaus and Co., Houston; pres. Navarro Exploration Co.; founding dir. Eurus, Inc., Capital Nat. Bank, Houston; pres. W.S. Farish and Co., Houston; owner Lane's End Farm, Versailles, Ky., 1980—; amb. to U.K. London, 2001—. Former chmn. Churchill Downs Inc. Past organizing mem. Houston chpt. Nat. Urban League; chmn. Houston Parks Bd. Office: The American Embassy 24 Grosvenor Sq London W1A 1AE England*

FARISON, JAMES BLAIR, electrical biomedical engineer, educator; b. McClure, Ohio, May 26, 1938; s. Blair Albert and Marie Lucille (Ballard) F.; m. Gail Donahue, Mar. 30, 1961; children: Jeffrey James, Mark Donahue. BS summa cum laude in Elec. Engring, U. Toledo, 1960; MS, Stanford U., 1961, PhD, 1964. Registered profl. engr., Tex., Oh. Asst. prof. elec. engring. U. Toledo, 1964-67, asso. prof., 1967-74, prof., 1974-95; asst. dean engring., 1969-71; dean engring. U. Toledo, 1971-80, prof. elec. engring. and computer sci., 1995-98; prof. bioengring., 1996-98; prof., chmn. dept. engring. Baylor U., Waco, Tex., 1998—. Adj. prof. Med. Coll. Ohio, 1987-98. Contbr. articles on control sys. design and image processing to profl. jours. Recipient Outstanding Young Man of 1971 award Toledo Jr. C. of C., 1972, Boss of Year award Limestone chpt. Am. Bus. Women's Assn., 1973, Toledo's Engr. Yr. award, 1984, Outstanding Tchr. award U. Toledo, 1986; named Disting. Alumnus, U. Toledo, 1983. Fellow Ohio Acad. Sci. (Centennial honoree 1991); mem. IEEE (sr. mem., Toledo Elec. Engr. of Yr. 1972, 74, 76), NSPE, Ohio Soc. Profl. Engrs. (Young Engr. of Yr. 1973, Citation 1983, Outstanding Engring. Educator 1984), Toledo Soc. Profl. Engrs. (Young Engr. of Yr. 1973), ASME, Biomed. Engring. Soc., Am. Soc. Engring. Edn. (Outstanding Campus Rep. 2003), Machine Vision Assn., Soc. Mfg. Engrs. (sr. mem.), Internat. Soc. Optical Engring., Instrumentation, Sys. and Automation Soc. (sr. mem.), Tex. Soc. Profl. Engrs., Soc. Woman Engrs. (sr. mem.), Blue Key, Sigma Xi, Tau Beta Pi, Pi Mu Epsilon, Phi Kappa Phi, Eta Kappa Nu (Outstanding Young Elec. Engr. 1971). Home: 9613 Old Farm Rd Waco TX 76712-6402 Office: Baylor U PO Box 97356 Waco TX 76798-7356 E-mail: Jim_Farison@baylor.edu.

FARISS, BRUCE LINDSAY, endocrinologist, educator; b. Allisonia, Va., July 22, 1934; s. Alven Pierce and Hetty Jo (Lindsay) F.; m. Cheryl Louise Tomasie, Jan. 18, 1975; children: Bruce LIndsay, Melissa, Margaret, Susan, Henry, Sarah Jane, Caroline, Adam. BS, Roanoke Coll., 1957; MD, U. Va., 1961. Diplomate in internal medicine and endocrinology Am. Bd. Internal Medicine. Med. intern U. Va. Hosp., Charlottesville, 1961-62; commd. capt. M.C. U.S. Army, 1962, advanced through grades to col., 1976; gen. med. officer Ft. Monroe, Va., 1962-63; resident in internal medicine Brooke Gen. Hosp., Ft. Sam Houston, Tex., 1963-66; fellow in endocrinology U. Calif., San Francisco, 1966-68; chief endocrine service Madigan Gen. Hosp., Tacoma, 1968-71, chief clin. rsch. svc., 1968-76, asst. chief dept. medicine, 1972-73, dir. endocrine fellowship program, 1971-76, chief dept. clin. investigation, 1979-85, dir. endocrine-metabolism fellowship tng. program, 1979-85; cons. internal medicine MEDCOM Europe, 1976-79; cons. endocrinology to surgeon gen. U.S. Army, 1979-85; with dept. biology Va. Poly. Inst., Blacksburg, 1987-99; sec., treas. Radford Cmty. Hosp., 1998—2000, vice chmn., 2000—02, chmn., 2002—. Contbr. articles to profl. jours. Mem. Bd. Suprs., Pulaski County, Va., 1988—, vice chmn., 2000-; mem. Pulaski County Planning Commn., 1992—; mem. Pulaski County Recreation Com., 1989-93. Decorated Legion of Merit with oak leaf cluster; recipient Meritorious Svc. aard Office of Surgeon Gen. of Army, 1977, Roanoke Coll. medal, 1982. Fellow: ACP; mem.: AACE, Am. Assn. Clin. Endocrinologists, N.Y. Acad. Sci., So. Med. Assn., Am. Diabetes Assn. (trustee 1986—89), Endocrine Soc. (ednl. com. 1980—83), Am. Fedn. Clin. Rsch., S.W. Va. Med. Soc., Alpha Omega Alpha.

FARKAS, ANDREW, library director emeritus, educator, writer; b. Budapest, Hungary, Apr. 7, 1936; came to U.S., 1956; s. Miklos and Renee (Schwartz) F. Student, Eotvos Loránd U. Law, Budapest, 1954-56; BA, Occidental Coll., Los Angeles, 1959; MLS, U. Calif., Berkeley, 1962. Asst. bibliographer U. Calif., Davis, 1962-63, gift and exchange librarian, 1962-65, asst. head acquisitions dept., 1965-67, chief bibliographer, 1966-67; asst. mgr. Walter J. Johnson, Inc., N.Y.C., 1967-70; dir. libraries, prof. library sci. U. North Fla., Jacksonville, 1970—2003. Dir. Emeritus U. Library, U. North Fla., program com. mem. Fla. Gov.'s Conf. on Librs., Tallahassee, 1978; expert witness IRS, Atlanta, 1981, cons., Washington, 1982; Sharp & Gay, 1995. Author, editor: Titta Ruffo: An Anthology, 1984, (with Enrico Caruso Jr.) Enrico Caruso: My Father & My Family, 1990, (with Anna-Lisa Björling) Jussi, 1996; author: (annotated bibliography), Opera and Concert Singers, 1985; editor: (ann. handbook) Librarians Calendar, 1984—, Opera Biographies Series, Great Voices Series, Lawrence Tibbett, Singing Actor, 1989; contbr. editor: The Opera Quarterly, 1993—. Mem. Coun. Interinstnl. Planning, Jacksonville, 1983-85. With U.S. Army, 1959-61. Mem. ALA. Avocations: research, creative writing, travel, photography, book and record collecting. Office: U North Fla 4567 Saint Johns Bluff Rd S Jacksonville FL 32224-2646 E-mail: afarkas@unf.edu.

FARKAS, CAROL GARNER, nurse, administrator; b. N.Y.C., Apr. 26, 1936; d. Charles Harry and Phyllis (Levine) Schotland; m. Theodore Arthur Garner, 1956 (dec. 1971); children: Charles Hugh Farkas Garner, Judi Beth Garner Farkas, Andrea Lee Garner Farkas Krupen; m. Robin Lewis Farkas, Oct. 17, 1972; adopted children: Bradford Lewis Farkas, Andrew Lawrence Farkas. BSN with distinction, Cornell U., 1976; MPH, Columbia U., 1980. Nursing dir. Am. Inst. Life Threatening Illness and Loss Columbia Presbyn. Med. Ctr., N.Y.C., 1980—. Del. white House Conf. Aging, N.Y. State Gov.'s Conf. Aging; mem. N.Y. State Hospice Adv. Group, 1979-81; mem. adv. com. office health mgmt, N.Y. State Dept. Health, 1979-81; mem. select com. financing and licensure, com. legis. cdn. Nat. Hospice Orgn., 1980—; vol. adminstr., practitioner in sympton control psychiatry dept. Meml. Sloan-Kettering Cancer Ctr., N.Y.C., 1981-96; mem. Choice in Dying, 1991-92, Nat. Coun. Death and Dying, 1990-91, Soc. Right to Die, 1982-90; co-chair med. student conf. nursing com. Columbia Presbyn., N.Y.C., 1992. Co-editor: Nursing and Thanatology, 1982; contbr. articles to profl. publs., chpts. to books. Bd. mem. N.Y. State Task Force on Life and the Law, 1994-97. Mem. Sigma Theta Tau. Home: PO Box 9223 485 Indian Springs Dr Jackson Hole WY 83002 Fax: 307-734-8006. E-mail: rfarkas@inventfund.com.

FARKAS, DANIEL FREDERICK, food science and technology educator; b. Boston, June 20, 1933; m. Alice Bridgetta Brady, Jan. 25, 1959; children: Brian Emerson, Douglas Frederick. BS, MIT, 1954, MS, 1955, PhD, 1960. Lic. chem. engr., Calif. Commd. U.S. Army, 1954, advanced through grades to major, 1968, ret., 1974; staff scientist Arthur D. Little, Cambridge, Mass., 1960-62; asst. prof. Cornell U. Agrl Expt. Sta., Geneva, N.Y., 1962-66; rsch. leader We. regional rsch. ctr. USDA, Albany, Calif., 1967-80; prin. Daniel F. Farkas Assocs., 1976—; prof., chair dept. food sci. U. Del., Newark, 1980-87; v.p. process R & D Campbell Soup Co., Camden, N.J., 1987-90; Jacobs-Root prof., head dept. food sci. and tech. Oreg. State U., Corvalis, 1990-2000, prof. emeritus, 2000—. Contbr. more than 50 articles to peer-reviewed sci. and tech. jours. Fellow Inst. Food Technologists (Nicholas Appert medal 2002); mem. AICE, Am. Chem. Soc. (profl.), Sigma Xi. Achievements include 5 U.S. patents for centrifugal fluidized bed food drying system, application of ultra-high hydrostatic pressure to food preservation.

FARKAS, LESLIE GABRIEL, plastic surgeon; b. Ruzomberok, Hungary, Apr. 18, 1915; s. Charles Samuel and Olga (Kustra) F.; m. Susanna Gál, Oct. 23, 1971; 1 child, Julia. MD, U. Istropolitana, Bratislava, 1941; PhD, Charles U., Prague, 1959; DSc, Charles U., 1968. Resident surgeon Mil. Hosp. and Field Svc., Czechoslovakia, 1941-45; resident in plastic surgery Charles U., Prague, 1945-48, asst. prof., 1948-65, assoc. prof., 1965-68; dep. dir. plastic surgery rsch. lab. Czechoslovak Acad. Scis., 1963-68, dir. divsn. cong. anomalies, 1963-68; clin. fellow divsn. plastic surgery Hosp. Sick Children, Toronto, Ont., Can., 1968-69, rsch. fellow divsn. exptl. surgery, 1969-70, asst. scientist Rsch. Inst., 1970-77, sr. scientist, 1977-81, dir. plastic surgery lab. Rsch. Inst., 1970-81, asst. prof., 1970-78; assoc. prof. U. Toronto, 1978-81, spl. rsch. lectr., 1981-82, assoc. rsch. prof., 1982—; cons. dept. nephrology Children Hosp. Dalhausie U., Halifax. Cons. dept. surgery and Rsch. Inst., Hosp. for Sick Children, Toronto, 1981—, dir. craniofacial measur. lab., 1986—; cons. cleft palate program U. Iowa, 1975-78, dept. neurology Shriver Ctr., Waltham, Mass., 1984-95; cons. Gulian U. Med. Scis., Rasht, Iran, 1999—, Ctr. for Neuropsychiat. Outcome and Rehab. Rsch., Hillside Hosp./Glen Oaks, Albert Einstein Coll. Medicine, N.Y., 2000—; divsn. plastic surgery Royal Victoria Hosp., Montreal, Que.; mem. panel 5th Internat. Congl. Plastic Reconstructive Surgery, Melbourne, Australia, 1971; mem. panel cleft-lip nose Am. Cleft Palate-Craniofacial Assn., Hilton Head, S.C., 1991; invited vis. expert med. anthropometry Min. Health Govt. of Singapore, 1987; invited tchr. course med. anthropometry orthodontics Orthodontic and Human Scis. Congress U. Med. Sch., Szeged, Hungary, 1996; session chmn. 8th Internat. Congress on Cleft Palate and Related Craniofacial Abnormalities, Documentation, Anthropolmetry, Database, Singapore, 1997. Author: Hypospadias, 1967, Constructive, Reconstructive and Esthetic Surgery of the Male Urogenital Tract, 1973, Anthropometry of the Head and Face in Medicine, 1981, Anthropometric Facial Proportions in Medicine, 1987, Anthropometry of the Head and Face, 2d edit., 1994; contbr. numerous articles to sci. jours. Recipient Cert. Excellence for rsch. in attractive face Am. Soc. Aesthetic Plastic Surgery, Boston, 1985, Aleš Hrdlička Commemorative medal Czechoslovakia Acad. Scis., Prague, 1992, Vis. Scholar award dept. pediats. faculty medicine U. Calgary, Can., 1992, Salamon Frigyes Commemorative medal Orthodontic Soc. Hungary, 1996, Best Paper of the Yr. award for Surface Anatomy of the Face in Down's Syndrome: Anthropometric Proportion Indices in the Craniofacial Regions in Jour. Craniofacial Surgery, 2002; Med. Rsch. Coun. grantee, 1970-72, Atkinson Charitable Found. grantee, 1973-76, Smythe Found. Can. grantee, 1976-81, Physicians Svcs., Inc. grantee, 1991-99. Fellow Royal Coll. Surgeons, mem. Acad. Medicine Toronto, Am. Soc. Plastic and Reconstructive Surgeons (mem. faculty symposium reconstructive auricle 1972), Can. Soc. Plastic Surgeons, Plastic Surgery Rsch. Coun., Can. Assn. Anatomists, Biomat. Soc. Can., Can. Craniofacial Soc., Internat. Soc. Craniomaxillofacial Surgery, Japanese Soc. Aesthetic Plastic Surgery (hon.), Roman Catholic. Home: 59 Claywood Rd Willowdale ON Canada M2N 2R3 Office: Hosp for Sick Chldn/Pl Surg 555 University Blvd Toronto ON Canada M5G 1X8 E-mail: lfarkas@interlog.com.

FARKAS, PAUL STEPHEN, gastroenterologist; b. N.Y.C., 1952; s. Benjamin J. and Ellen (Tanner) F.; m. Esta Miriam Cantor, June 24, 1973; children: Melanie Sharon, Joshua David. AB magna cum laude with distinction in psychology, Brandeis U., 1972; MD, Tufts U., 1976. Diplomate Am. Bd. Internal Medicine, Am. Bd. Gastroenterology. Intern Baystate Med. Ctr., Sprinfield, Mass., 1976-77, resident in internal medicine, 1977-79; fellow in gastroenterology Albert Einstein Coll. Medicine, Bronx, N.Y., 1979-81; asst. clin. prof. medicine Tufts U., Boston, 1985—; med. advisor Med. Assist Program Springfield Tech. C.C., 1989—. Co-dir. med. edn. Mercy Hosp., Springfield, 1990-95, chmn. dept. gastroenterology, 1995—, dir. libr., 1988-97, mem. exec. com., 1995—, treas. med. staff, 1999—; mem. adv. bd. VNA, Springfield, 1984-88; adj. asst. prof. clin. pharmacology Mass. Coll. Pharmacy, Boston, 1982—. Author: Diagnostic Diagrams Gastroenterology, 1985; contbr. book chpts., articles and revs. in field. Bd. dirs. B'nai Jacob Synagogue, Springfield, 1987-88, Com. for Longmeadow, Mass., 1989, Yeshiva, Longmeadow, 1994-99; trustee Mercy Hosp., 1997-98. Fellow ACP (cmty. based excellence in tchg. award 2000); mem. AMA, Am. Coll. Gastroenterology, Am. Gastroent. Assn., Am. Soc. Gastrointestinal Endoscopy, New Eng. Soc. Gastrointestinal Endoscopy. Office: 299 Carew St Springfield MA 01104-2301

FARLEY, ANDREW NEWELL, lawyer, consultant; b. Brownsville, Pa., Oct. 31, 1934; s. Andrew Polycarp and Sarah Theresa (Landymore) F.; m. Marta Olha Pisetska, May 5, 1963; children— Andrew Daniel, Mark Landymore. AB, Washington and Jefferson Coll., 1956; MPA, U. Pitts., 1962, JD, 1961; diploma, U.S. Army Command and Gen. Staff Coll., 1972, Indsl. Coll. Armed Forces, 1967; grad., U.S. Army War Coll., 1976. Bar: Pa. 1962, U.S. Supreme Ct. 1965. Assoc. Reed Smith Shaw & McClay, Pitts., 1961-65, ptnr., 1966-91; cons. Pitts., 1992—. Bd. dirs. Corp Devel. USAM Mid-Atlantic and Ohio; mng. dir. USAM-Nat., 1992-95; Am. Arbitration Assn. Nat. Panel Comml. Disputes, 1995—; mediator JAMS-Endispute, 1996—; sec.-treas. Internat. Acad. Mediators, 1996-2000; lectr. in fed. jurisprudence and adminstrv. law U. Pitts.; adminstrv. asst. Pa. Atty. Gen., 1959; counsel to Pa. Constl. Conv., 1968; mem. Pa. Atty. Gen.'s Task Force on Adminstrn., 1970. Assoc. editor Pitts Legal Jour., 1963— (mem. exec. com.); contbr. articles to profl. jours. Bd. dirs. Ind. Sch. Chmn. Assn., World Affairs Coun., Pitts., Pitts. Opera, 1986-95; sec., bd. dirs. Found. for Calif. U. Pa.,; mem. adv. bd. Western Pa. Advanced Tech. Ctr., Internat. Resuscitation Rsch. Ctr., U. Pitts. Med. Sch., Mon Valley Renaissance; mem. bd. visitors U. Pitts. Grad. Sch. Pub. and Internat. Affairs; trustee Thiel Coll., 1989-95. Brig. gen. U.S. Army. Decorated Meritorious Svc. medals, Dept. Def. and U.S. Army, Army Commendation medals; recipient Gubernatorial citation Commonwealth of Pa., 1978, Omicron Delta Kappa award, 1960; Nat. Def. Transp. Assn. fellow, 1956; named Mon Valley Renaissance MVP, 1987. Mem. Internat. Acad. Mediators, Pa. Bar Assn. (chmn. sect. internat. law, bd. editors, jud. adminstrn. com., statewide computer com. for the cts., alternative dispute resolution com.), Allegheny County Bar Assn. (fee determination com.), Am. Law Inst., Nat. Health Lawyers Assn., Am. Arbitration Assn., Soc. for Profls. in Dispute Resolution, Assn. U.S. Army (pres. Ft. Pitt chpt., pres. Pa.), Sr. Army Res. Comdrs. Assn. (exec. com.), Pitts. Athletic Assn., Duquesne Club, Pa. State Grange, Masons. Home: 54 N Manorcliff Pl The Woodlands Spring TX 77382

FARLEY, BARBARA L. lawyer; b. Abington, Pa., Nov. 13, 1949; d. Vincent Lanza Jr. and Noreen Marie Cathcart; m. David Allen Farley, July 8, 1972. BS in Fin. and Acctg., Drexel U., 1970; JD, Rutgers U., 1973; LLM in Taxation, Villanova U., 1988. Bar: N.J. 1974, Pa. 1974, U.S. Tax Ct. 1975. Pres. Barbara Lanza Farley, A Profl. Corp., Phila., Haddonfield, N.J., 1975—. Office: 325 Chestnut St Ste 915 Philadelphia PA 19106-2609 Also: 13 Wilkins Avenue Haddonfield NJ 08033

FARLEY, BARBARA SUZANNE, lawyer; b. Salt Lake City, Dec. 13, 1949; d. Ross Edward Farley and Barbara Ann (Edwards) Farley Swanson; m. Arthur Hoffman Ferris, Apr. 9, 1982 (div. 1995); children: Barbara Whitney, Taylor Edwards; m. Michael L. Levine, Aug. 7, 1999. BA with honors, Mills Coll., 1972; JD, U. Calif.-Hastings, San Francisco, 1976. Bar: Calif. 1976. Extern law clk. to justice Calif. Supreme Ct., San Francisco, 1975; assoc. Pillsbury, Madison & Sutro, San Francisco, 1976-78, Bronson, Bronson & McKinnon, San Francisco, 1978-80, Goldstein & Phillips, San Francisco, 1980-84; ptnr., head litigation Rosen, Wachtell & Gilbert, San Francisco, 1984-89; of counsel Lempres & Wulfsberg, Oakland, Calif., 1989—99; pvt. practice, 2000—. Founder, pres. and CEO Fiducety Tech. Inc.; arbitrator U.S. Dist. Ct. (no. dist.) Calif., San Francisco, 1981—, Calif. Superior Ct., San Francisco, 1984—89; judge pro tem San Francisco Mcpl. Ct., 1983—; probation monitor Calif. State Bar, 1990—2002; del. to the Calif. Bar San Francisco Bar Assn., 2003; spkr., author Nat. Bus. Inst. Estate Adminstrn., 2000; spkr. Lorman Edn. Svcs. Tax Exempt Orgns. Contbg. author Calif. Continuing Edn. of the Bar, Nat. Bus. Inst., Lorman Edn. Svcs.; mng. editor Hastings Coll. of Law-U. Calif.-San Francisco Constl. Law Quar., 1975-76; civil litigation reporter. Mills Coll. scholar, 1970-72, U. Calif.-Hastings, San Francisco scholar, 1973-76. Mem. ATLA, San Francisco Bar Assn., Calif. Trial Lawyers Assn., San Francisco Bar Assn. (del. Calif. State Bar 2003), Alameda Bar Assn.

FARLEY, BENJAMIN WIRT, religious studies educator, writer; b. Manila, Aug. 6, 1935; s. Wirt Pamplin and Bessie (Campbell) White F.; m. Alice Anne Gamble; children: John David, Bryan Kirk. AB, Davidson Coll., 1958; BD, Union Theol. Sem., Richmond, Va., 1963, ThM, 1964, PhD, 1976. Ordained to ministry Presbyn. Ch., 1963. Instr. Lees-MacRae Coll., Banner-Elk, N.C., 1973-74; asst. prof. bible, religion, philosophy Erskine Coll., Due West, S.C., 1974-78, assoc. prof., 1978-84, Younts prof., 1985—, chair bible, religion, philosophy dept., 1978-91. Author: The Hero of St. Lo, 1986, Mercy Road, 1986, The Providence of God, 1988, Corbin's Rubi-Yacht, 1992, In Praise of Virtue, 1994, Son of the Morning Sky, 1999; translator, editor: Calvins Sermons on the Ten Commandments, 1980, Calvin's Treatises Against the Anabaptists and Against the Libertines, 1982, Calvin's Sermons on the Book of Micah, 2003; co-translator: Calvin's Ecclesiastical Advice, 1991; contbr. articles to profl. jours. Chair Bi-Racial Com., Franklin, Va., 1967-68, pres. of the Calvin Studies Soc. in America, 1997—. Named Writer of the Season, Nostalgia mag., 1990; Fund for Theol. Edn. fellow, 1970; Thomas Carey Johnson scholar Union Theol. Sem., 1963. Mem. Am. Philos. Assn., Calvin Studies Soc. (pres. 1997-99), Coloquium on Calvin Studies, Internat. Calvin Congress, Omicron Delta Kappa. Republican. Avocations: golf, sailing, hunting, fishing, hiking.

FARLEY, CAROLE, soprano; b. Le Mars, Iowa, Nov. 29, 1946; d. Melvin and Irene (Reid) F.; m. Jose Serebrier, Mar. 29, 1969; 1 dau., Lara Adriana Francesca. MusB, Ind. U., 1968. Fulbright scholar Hochschule für Musik, Munich, 1968-69. (Musician of Month, Musical Am./Hi Fidelity 1977), Am. debut at Town Hall, N.Y.C., 1969, Paris debut, Nat. Orch., 1975, London debut, Royal Philharmonic Soc., 1975, S.Am. debut, Teatro Colon, Philharmonic Orch., Buenos Aires, 1975; soloist with, major Am. and European symphony orchs., 1970—, soloist, Welsh Nat. Opera, 1971, 72, Cologne Opera, 1972-75, Phila. Lyric Opera, 1974, Brussels Opera, 1972, Lyon Opera, 1976, 77, Strasbourg Opera, 1975, Linz Opera, 1969, N.Y.C. Opera, 1976, New Orleans Opera, 1977, Cin. Opera, 1977, Met. Opera Co., N.Y.C., 1977—, Zurich Opera, 1979, Chgo. Lyric Opera, 1981, Can. Opera Co., 1980, Düsseldorf Opera, 1980, 81, 84, Palm Beach Opera, 1982, Theatre Mcpl. Paris, 1983, Theatre Royale dela Monnaie Brussels, 1983, Teatro Regio, Turin, Italy, 1983, Nice Opera (France), 1984, 86, 87, 88, Cologne Opera, 1985, Teatro Comunale, Florence, Italy, 1985, BBC Opera, 1987, TeatroColon, Buenos Aires, 1987, 88, 89, Opera de Montpellier (France), 1988, 94, Theatre des Champs Elysees, Paris, 1988, Helsinki Festival, 1989, Tchaikovsky Opera Arias Pickwick/IMP Records, 1993, Met. Opera Premiere Shostakovich Opera Lady Macbeth of Mtzensk, 1994, Theatre Capitole de Toulouse Wozzeck, 1994, internat. tour with Nat. Chamber Orchestra of Toolouse, 2003; on New Zealand Broadcasting Commn. Orchestral Tour, 1986; TV film for ABC Australia La Voix Humaine, also co-producer compact disc and video for BBC, London, 1990; co-producer compact disc and video The Telephone, 1990; recorded compact disc Weill, 1992, Metro. Opera Shostakovich: "Lady Macbeth", 1994, Strausslieder with Czech Philharmonic, 1995, Les Soldats Morts, 1995 (Grand Prix du Disque); recorded for Deutsche Gramophone (Diapason d'or prize 1997), Chandos, CBS, BBC, ASV, RCA, Ricercar and Varese-Sarabande records, London/Decca Records, IMP Masters, Pickwick; new CD Naxos: Selected Songs Ned Rorem, 2001, The Songs of Ernesto Lecuona For Bis Records, 2003; Argentine premier Bomarzo by Alberto Finastera, Teatro Colón Buenos Aires, 2003. Recipient Abiati prize for her role as Lulu, Italy, 1984, Deutsche Schallplatten award for recording Carole Farley Sings French Songs, 1988; named Alumni of Year, U. Ind., 1976. Mem. Am. Guild Mus. Artists. Home: 270 Riverside Dr New York NY 10025-5209 E-mail: caspi123@aol.com. *A young opera singer today has a much greater responsibility than his predecessors 50 years ago. The age of the 200-pound soprano expiring of consumption at the end of La Traviata is a thing of the past. Now we must "look" the part, and be able to act as well as sing.*

FARLEY, EDWARD RAYMOND, JR., mining and manufacturing company executive; b. S.I., N.Y., Sept. 30, 1918; s. Edward Raymond and Ruth Veronica (Joyce) F.; m. Irene Daly, Feb. 19, 1948; children— Thomas Joyce, Nancy

Seaver, Jane Campbell, Edward Raymond III. AB, Princeton, 1940; JD, Harvard, 1943. Bar: N.Y. bar 1944. With firm Simpson, Thacher & Bartlett, N.Y.C., 1944-55; v.p. Atlas Corp., N.Y.C., 1956-64, chmn. bd. dirs., 1964-87, pres., 1966-87, also chmn. exec. com. Trustee, chmn. exec. com. Lincoln Savs. Bank, Bklyn., 1973-84; dir. Am. Nuclear Energy Council, 1979-89. Active local United Fund; trustee, pres. bd. Lawrenceville Sch., 1970-85; trustee, chmn. bd. Princeton Med. Center, 1976— ; assoc. trustee U. Pa., 1988—. Decorated Knight of Malta Mem. Nat. Football Hall of Fame (pres. Delaware Valley chpt.), Atomic Indsl. Forum, U. Pa. Grad. Sch. Edn. (bd. gov.'s 1988—), Dial Lodge (trustee) Beden's Brook Club (Princeton), Pretty Brook Tennis Club (Princeton), Nassau Club (Princeton), Springdale Golf Club (Princeton). Home: 188 Parkside Dr Princeton NJ 08540-4815 Office: 353 Nassau St Princeton NJ 08540-4623

FARLEY, GAIL CONLEY, retired librarian; b. Mead, Okla., July 9, 1936; s. William Conley and Marguerite Gaines (Austin) F. BS in History, Sul Ross State U., 1957; MS in Libr. Sci., East Tex. State U., 1970. Tchr. San Felipe Ind. Sch. Dist., Del Rio, Tex., 1963-64, Natalia (Tex.) Ind. Sch. Dist., 1964-65; libr. Medina Valley Ind. Sch. Dist., Castroville, Tex., 1965-77, La Pryor (Tex.) ind. Sch. Dist., 1977-78, McCamey (Tex.) Ind. Sch. Dist., 1978-92; reporter Medina County Sheriff's Res., 1973-75, pres., 1975-77. With U.S. Army, 1957-60. Mem. Tex. Libr. Assn., Tex. Assn. Sch. Librs., NRA (life), Tex. Rifle Assn. (life). Home: PO Box 965 Mc Camey TX 79752-0965

FARLEY, JAMES NEWTON, manufacturing executive, engineer; b. Hutchinson, Kans., Nov. 8, 1928; s. James N. Farley and Elizabeth (Martin) Sanders; m. Nancy J. Hollabaugh, Apr. 30, 1956; children: Sarah Huskey, Timothy, Barbara Carré, James, Stuart. BSEE, Northwestern U., 1950. Registered profl. engr., Ill. Test engr. GE, Schenectady, N.Y., 1950-51; sales engr. Allen Bradley Co., Milw., 1953-54, Chgo., 1954-60; sales mgr. SpeedFam Corp., Skokie, Ill., 1960-64, pres. Des Plaines, Ill., 1964-87, chmn. bd. dirs., 1987-97; pres., CEO Speedfam-IPEC, Inc., Chandler, Ariz., 1987-92, CEO, chmn. bd. dirs., 1992-97, chmn. bd. dirs., 1997-2001, chmn. emeritus, 2001—02. Bd. dirs. Lovejoy, Inc., Downers Grove, Ill., Extrude Hone Corp., Irwin, Pa., imortgage.com, Scottsdale, Ariz. With U.S. Army, 1951-53. Recipient Alumni Merit award Northwestern U., 1996. Mem. Assn. for Mfg. Tech., Oriental Order of Groundhogs. Democrat. Episcopalian. Office: Novellus Sys Inc 300 N 56th St Chandler AZ 85226-2405

FARLEY, JAMES PARKER, retired advertising agency executive; b. Newark, Sept. 16, 1924; s. James Joseph and Margaret (Parker) F.; m. Irene Florence Reinert, July 1, 1950; children: James Bernard, Catherine Elizabeth, Robert Craig, Margaret Patricia. BA in Bus. Adminstrn, Rutgers U., 1949. Asst. to advt. mgr. Gen. Electric Co., Syracuse, N.Y., 1949-51, merchandising mgr. Bridgeport, Conn., 1951-56; account dir. McCann-Erickson, Inc., N.Y.C., 1956-62; pres., chief exec. officer McCann Erickson-Hakuhodo, Tokyo, 1963-78, chmn., chief exec. officer, 1978-79, chmn., 1979-82; exec. v.p., regional mgr. Pacific, McCann-Erickson Internat., N.Y.C., 1972-82. Dir. McCann-Erickson Internat., N.Y.C., 1974-82, Hakuhodo, Inc., Tokyo, 1963-82. Served with USNR, 1943-46. Mem. Internat. Advt. Assn., Am. C. of C. Japan, Am.-Japan Soc., Fgn. Corr. Club Japan, Fgn. Corr. Club Hong Kong, Japan Soc. N.Y.C., Young Pres. Orgn., Zeta Psi. Clubs: Tokyo Am. (past pres.); Patterson (Fairfield, Conn.), Royal Hong Kong Yacht; Met. (N.Y.C.); N.Y. Athletic. Home: 62 Rivergate Dr Wilton CT 06897-4137

FARLEY, JAN EDWIN, lawyer; b. Bartlesville, Okla., Dec. 4, 1948; s. Earl Franklin Farley and Martha Lynn Crisp; m. Sybil Anne Bova, Aug. 3, 1974; children: Elizabeth Anne, Christopher George. BA magna cum laude, Midwestern U., Wichita Falls, Tex., 1971; cert. Inst. Advanced Internat. Studies, U. Paris, 1973; JD with honors, U. Tex., 1975. Bar: Tex. 1975. Assoc. Baker & Botts, Houston, 1975-81; asst. sec., asst. gen. counsel Weatherford Internat. Inc., Houston, 1981-85 ; asst. gen. counsel ARA Services, Inc., Houston, 1986-87, v.p., gen. counsel health and edn. svcs. sector, 1987—; lectr. in internat. comml. trans. U. Houston Law Sch., 1976. Sec. Houston-Nice Sister City Assn., 1977-78. Rotary Found. fellow U. Paris, 1972-73. Mem. ABA, Tex. Bar Assn., Houston Bar Assn. (treas. internat. law sect. 1981, exec. council 1982-85, chmn.-elect 1985-86, chmn. 1986-87), Petroleum Equipment Suppliers Assn. (corp. counsel com., steering com. 1983-85), U. Tex. Internat. Law Jour. Alumni Assn. (pres. 1980-81), Houston Athletic Club. Presbyterian. Home: 2927 Deer Creek Dr Sugar Land TX 77478-4267 Office: ARA Services Inc 10205 Westheimer Rd # 1142 Houston TX 77042-3115

FARLEY, JOHN JOSEPH, III, federal judge; b. Hackensack, N.J., July 30, 1942; s. John Joseph and Patricia (Earle) F.; m. Kathleen Mary Wells, June 27, 1970; children: Maura, Brendan, Thomas, Caitlin. AB in Econs., Holy Cross Coll., 1964; MBA, Columbia, 1966; JD cum laude, Hofstra U., 1973. Bar: N.Y. 1974, D.C. 1975, U.S. Supreme Ct. 1977. Trial atty. torts sect. civil div. U.S. Dept. Justice, Washington, 1973-78, asst. dir. torts br. civil div., 1978-80, dir. torts br. civil div., 1980-89; judge U.S. Ct. of Appeals for Vets. Claims, Washington, 1989—. Mem. faculty OPM Exec. Seminar Ctrs., Denver, 1980—, Columbus Sch. Law Catholic U. Am., 2003; lectr. Atty. Gen's. Advocacy Inst., Washington, 1976-89, FBI Acad., Quantico, Va., 1978-88; lectr. Columbus Sch. Law, Cath. U. Am., 2003. Editor-in-chief Hofstra Law Rev., 1971-73; contbr. articles to profl. jours. Vice-chmn. bd. dirs. Amputee Coalition of Am., 1997—. Served to capt. U.S. Army, 1966-70, Vietnam. Decorated Bronze Star with V device and 3 oak leaf clusters, Purple Heart with oak leaf cluster; recipient Sr. Exec. Service Spl. Achievement award U.S. Dept. Justice, 1984, Civil Div. Spl award U.S. Dept. Justice, 1980; Samuel Bronfman fellow, 1964-65, Dean's award for Disting. Hofstra Law Sch. Alumni, 1995, Disting. Alumni medal Hofstra U. Sch. of Law, 1986; inducted into Massapequa H.S. Hall of Fame, 1999. Mem. Fed. Bar Assn. (1st chmn. vets. law sec. 1990-91). Roman Catholic. Avocations: skiing, tennis, bicycling, reading. Office: US Court Of Appeals for Vets Claims 625 Indiana Ave NW Ste 900 Washington DC 20004-2917

FARLEY, JOHN JOSEPH, library science educator emeritus; b. N.Y.C., Mar. 19, 1920; s. John Anthony and Margaret (Green) F.; m. Rita Johnston, Feb. 26, 1944; children— Janet, Eugene, Marian, Joseph, Veronica. BA, Cath. U., 1940; MA, Columbia U., 1950, MS, 1953; PhD, NYU, 1964. Tchr., N.Y.C. schs., 1940-50; high sch. librarian, 1952-53, W. Hempstead, N.Y., 1953-58; curriculum dir. Sewanhaka Central High Sch. Dist., N.Y., 1958-60; successively asst. prof., asso. prof., chmn. dept. library scis. Queens Coll. of CUNY, 1960-67; vis. prof. library sci. San Jose State Coll., Calif., 1967; prof. library sci. SUNY-Albany, 1967-85, prof. emeritus, 1985—, dean Sch. Library and Info. Sci., 1967-77. Cons. in field, 1958—. Author: Introduction to Library Science, 1969, also articles. Served with USAAF, 1943- 46. Recipient Founders Day award N.Y. U., 1964, Pius X medal for disting. service to confraternity Christian doctrine, 1966 Mem. ALA, AAUP, Nat. Council Tchrs. English Democrat. Roman Catholic. Home: 100 Saratoga Blvd Saratoga Springs NY 12866-9194

FARLEY, JOSEPH MCCONNELL, lawyer; b. Birmingham, Ala., Oct. 6, 1927; s. John G. and Lynne (McConnell) F.; m. Sheila Shirley, Oct. 1, 1958 (dec. July 1978); children: Joseph McConnell, Thomas Gager, Mary Lynne. Student, Birmingham-So. Coll., 1944-45; BSME, Princeton U., 1948; student, U. Ala., 1948—49; LLB, Harvard U., 1952; LHD (hon.), Judson Coll., 1974; LLD (hon.), U. Ala. at Birmingham, 1983. Bar: Ala. 1952. Assoc. Martin, Turner, Blakey & Bouldin, Birmingham, 1952-57; ptnr. successor firm Martin, Balch, Bingham & Hawthorne, 1957-65; exec. v.p., dir. Ala. Power Co., 1965-69, pres., dir., 1969-89; v.p. So. Electric Generating Co., 1970-74, pres., dir., 1974-89; exec. v.p. nuclear, bd. dirs. The So. Co., Birmingham, 1989-90; pres., CEO So. Nuclear Oper. Co., Birmingham, 1990-91, chmn., CEO, 1991-92, also bd. dirs.; exec. v.p., corp. counsel So. Co., 1991-92; of counsel Balch & Bingham, LLP, Birmingham, 1993—. Bd. dirs. N.A., Torchmark Corp., SVI Corp.; mem. exec. bd. Southeastern Electric Reliability Coun., chmn., 1974-76; bd. dirs. Edison Electric Inst.; bd. dirs. Southeastern Electric Exch., pres., 1984; adv. dir. So. Co., 1992-97; bd. dir. emeritus Am. South Bancorp. Mem. Jefferson County Republican Exec. Com., 1953-65; counsel, mem. Ala. Rep. Com., 1962-65; permanent chmn. Ala. Rep. Conv., 1962; alternate del. Rep. Nat. Conv., 1956; bd. dirs. Ala. Bus. Hall of Fame, Birmingham Area YMCA (hon. dir.); chmn. bd. trustees So. Rsch. Inst., 1970-99; trustee Tuskegee U., 1981-2002; trustee Children's Hosp. Birmingham, pres. bd. trustees 1983-85; mem. Pres.'s Cabinet U. Ala.-Tuscaloosa; bd. visitors U. Ala. Sch. Commerce, chmn., 1991-93. Served with USNR, 1948; now lt. ret. Mem. ABA, NAM (bd. dirs. 1987-92), Ala. Bar Assn., Birmingham Bar Assn., Inst. Nuclear Power Ops. (bd. dirs. 1982-89, chmn. 1987-89), U.S. Coun. for Energy Awareness (bd. dirs. 1985-92), Am. Nuclear Energy Coun. (chmn. bd. dirs. 1987-92), Newcomen Soc. N.Am., Birmingham Country Club, Shoal Creek Club, The Club, Mountain Brook Club, Summit Club, Rotary, Phi Beta Kappa, Kappa Alpha, Tau Beta Pi, Beta Gamma Sigma (hon.). Episcopalian. Home: 3333 Dell Rd Birmingham AL 35223-1319 Office: Balch & Bingham LLP PO Box 306 Birmingham AL 35201-0306

FARLEY, JOSEPH MICHAEL, human relations executive, editor, publisher; b. Phila., Dec. 28, 1961; s. Francis William Farley and Joanne Hafer; m. Juan Xu, Aug. 25, 1988; children: Sean David, Alexander Dmitri Xiahou Farley. BA, St. Joseph's U., 1983; MA, Temple U., 1988. Social worker trainee dept. human svcs. City of Phila., 1985, clk. II revenue dept., 1986; mngt. trainee Phila. Commn. on Human Rels., 1987-88, pub. rels. splst., 1989-94, human rels. rep., 1994—99, human rels. supr. compliance div., 1999—; editor, pub. Cynic Press, Phila., 1995—. Author: January, 1986, Souvenir or Evolution, 1996, Wolf Poems, 2000, For the Birds, 2001; editor Axe Factory Rev., 1986—. Shop steward dist. coun. 47 AFSCME, 2000—, del., 1994-96. Avocation: martial arts. Home: 2653 Sperry St Philadelphia PA 19152 Office: Phila Commn Human Rels 34 S 11th St 6th Fl Philadelphia PA 19107

FARLEY, MARGARET WILHELMINA, librarian; b. Hallam, Nebr., June 29, 1919; d. Benjamin Wilhelm Buhrmann and Wilhelmina Talena Asseln-Buhrmann; m. Cecil Morgan McClouston, July 9, 1945 (dec. Jan. 1951); m. Robert Laverne Farley, Apr. 29, 1954 (dec. Sept. 9, 1992). Student, U. Nebr., 1936—39; diploma, Pepin Acad. Fashion, 1940; student, Mt. San Antonis Coll., 1986, Calif. State U., 1986—90. Spl. diets State Mental Hosp., Lincoln, Nebr., 1939—40; sewing, alterations Dayton Dept. Store, Mpls., 1940—41; inspector (WWII) New Brighton Cartridge, 1941—43; art dir. Internat. Inst., St. Paul, 1943—45; libr. L.A. County Libr., Downey, 1959—80; children's libr. in charge cataloging La Crecenta (Calif.) Pub. Libr. Mem.: Antelope Valley Allied Arts Assn., Rep. Women, Palmdale Women's Club, Newcomers Club. Republican. Avocations: art, gardening, sewing. Home: 4326 Avoca Ave Palmdale CA 93552

FARLEY, PEGGY ANN, finance company executive; b. Phila., Mar. 12, 1947, d. Harry E. and Ruth (Lloyd) F.; m. Reid McIntyre, Dec. 31, 1985 (div.); 1 child, Margaret Ruth Farley. AB, Barnard Coll., 1970; MA with honors, Columbia U., 1972. Admissions officer Barnard Coll., N.Y.C., 1973-76; adminstr. Citibank NA, Athens, Greece, 1976-77; cons. Orgn. Resources Counselors, N.Y.C., 1977-78; sr. assoc. Morgan Stanley and Co. Inc., N.Y.C., 1978-84; mng. dir., CEO AMAS Securities Inc., N.Y.C., 1984-98; also bd. dirs. AMAS Securities, Inc., N.Y.C.; pres., CEO Ascent Asset Mgmt. Adv. Svc., Inc., N.Y.C., 1998-99. Pres., CEO, bd. dirs. Ascent/Meredith Asset Mgmt. Inc., N.Y.C., 1999—, Ascent/Meredith Portfolio Mgmt. Inc., N.Y.C., 1999—; bd. dirs. Robert R. Meredith & Co. Inc., N.Y.C.; partner Ascent Med. Tech. Fund, 1999-; mng. dir. Ascent Pvt. Equity, 1999-, Ascent Capital Adv., 2001-. Author: The Place Of The Yankee And Euro Bond Markets In A Financing Program For The People's Republic of China, 1982, Ascent Quar. Rev. Mem. Columbia U. Seminar on China-U.S. Bus. Mem. China Inst., Fgn. Policy Assn., Met. Club, Econ. Club of N.Y. Republican. Presbyterian. Avocations: gardening, film, swimming. Home: 908 Owassa Rd Newton NJ 07860-4015 Office: Ascent/Meredith Asset Mgmt Inc 712 5th Ave New York NY 10019-4108 E-mail: pfarley@amam.net.

FARLEY, ROSEMARY CARROLL, mathematics and computer science educator; b. N.Y.C., Apr. 7, 1952; d. Joseph William and Nancy (Flaherty) C.; m. Dennis Michael Farley, Oct. 10, 1976; children: Christopher, Mary Ann, Brian, Nancy. BS, Coll. Mt. St. Vincent, 1974; MS, NYU, 1976, PhD, 1991. Instr. Fordham U., Bronx, N.Y., 1976-79, Manhattan Coll., Bronx, N.Y., 1979-82, assoc. prof., 1989—; assoc. prof. Coll. Mt. St. Vincent, Bronx, 1982-88. Mem. Math. Assn. Am., Am. Math. Soc., Am. Statis. Assn. Democrat. Roman Catholic. Home: 120 Bennett Ave Yonkers NY 10701-6310 Office: Manhattan Coll Manhattan Coll Pky Bronx NY 10471

FARLEY, ROY CARL, counselor educator; b. Dierks, Ark., Feb. 21, 1942; s. Embra and Mildred (Efird) F.; m. Omagene Cowan, May 29, 1969; children: Susanne, Justin. BA, Henderson State U., 1964; MS, Ctrl. Ark. U., 1972; EdD, U. Ark., 1978. Rehab. counselor, adminstr. Ark. Rehab. Svcs., Little Rock, 1967-74; dir., prof. rehab. edn. Ark. Rsch. & Tng. Ctr., Hot Springs, 1974-99; prof., counselor edn. U. Ark., Fayetteville, 1999—. Contbr. over 200 workshops & seminars for rehab. and mental health profls. Author, co-author 15 comprehensive tng. packages for rehab. and mental health profls. including The Advanced Facilitative Case Management Series, Relationship Skills for Career Enhancement, Rational Behavior Problem-Solving, Employability Assessment and Planning, Know Thyself: A Strategy for Empowering and Involving Consumers in the Vocational Assessment Process; contbr. over 50 articles to profl. jours., also book chpts., monographs, conf. procs.; presenter 53 papers at confs. & meetings. Home: 2670 E Tulip Ct Fayetteville AR 72701-2889 Office: U Ark 134 Grad Edn Bldg Fayetteville AR 72701 E-mail: rfarley@uark.edu.

FARLEY, TERRENCE MICHAEL, banker; b. N.Y.C., Mar. 6, 1930; s. Terrence M. and Mary A. (Dundon) F.; m. Audrey E. Churchill, June 8, 1952; children: Elizabeth C., Peter, Matthew. BBA, CCNY, 1955. With Brown Bros. Harriman & Co., N.Y.C., 1951—, ptnr., 1972—, mng. ptnr., 1983-95. Trustee Children's Specialized Hosp., Mountainside, NJ. Mem. Univ. Club, Links Club, Echo Lake Country Club (Westfield, N.J.), Wianno Club (Osterville, Mass.). Home: 309 Hillside Ave Westfield NJ 07090-2902 Office: Brown Bros Harriman & Co 140 Broadway New York NY 10005-1101

FARLEY, THOMAS T. lawyer; b. Pueblo, Colo., Nov. 10, 1934; s. John Baron and Mary (Tancred) F.; m. Kathleen Maybelle Murphy, May 14, 1960; children: John, Michael, Kelly, Anne. BS, U. Santa Clara, 1956; LLB, U. Colo., 1959. Bar: Colo. 1959, U.S. Dist. Ct. Colo. 1959, U.S. Ct. Appeals (10th cir.) 1988. Dep. dist. atty. County of Pueblo, 1960-62; pvt. practice Pueblo, 1963-69; ptnr. Phelps, Fonda & Hays, Pueblo, 1970-75, Petersen & Fonda, P.C., Pueblo, 1975—. Bd. dirs. Pub. Svc. Co. Colo., Wells Fargo Pueblo, Wells Fargo Sunset, Health Net, Inc., Colo. Pub. Radio. Minority leader Colo. Ho. of Reps., 1967-75; chmn. Colo. Wildlife Commn., 1975-79, Colo. Bd. Agr., 1979-87; bd. regents Santa Clara U., 1987—; commr. Colo. State Fair; trustee Cath. Found. Diocese of Pueblo, Great Outdoors Colo. Trust Fund. Recipient Disting. Svc. award U. So. Colo., 1987, 93, Bd. of Regents, U. Colo., 1993. Mem. ABA, Colo. Bar Assn., Pueblo C. of C. (bd. dirs. 1991-93), Rotary. Democrat. Roman Catholic. Office: Petersen & Fonda PC 215 W 2d St Pueblo CO 81003-3251

FARMAKIDES, JOHN BASIL, lawyer; b. Symi Island (Dodecanese), Italy; s. Basil John and Anna Maria (Zouroudis) F.; m. Maria T. Kambanis, July 12, 1964; children: Basil J., George S. BS, Case Western Res. U., 1950; JD with honors, George Washington U., 1956; LL.M., Georgetown U., 1958. Bar: D.C. 1957, U.S. Supreme Ct. 1958, Va. 1986. Patent examiner U.S. Patent Office, 1955-59; atty. U.S. Air Force, 1960-61, NASA, 1961-70, mem. bd. contract appeals, 1968-70; asst. gen. counsel NSF, 1970-72; mem. NRC appeals bd. AEC (NRC), 1972-75; chmn. bd. Dept. Energy, Washington, 1975-84; ptnr. Whitney & Dempsey, Washington, 1985-88; arbitrator, 1988—. Adj. prof. in law Am. U. Law Sch., 1964-72; U.S. del. Internat. Conf. on Govt. Computer Experts, Geneva, 1972; chmn. FCST Subcom. on Legal Aspects of Info Sys., 1969-72; cons. HEW, NSF; chmn. Nat. Conf. on Legal Aspects of Computerized Info. Sys.-FCST, 1969-72; comdg. officer, dir. Joint Army, Navy, Air Force Spl. Analyn Divsn., USAR, 1971-74; mem. U.S. Chinese Workshop on Computerized Info. Sys., NAS, 1972. Contbr. articles to profl. jours. Pres. Cosmos Club Hist. Preservation Found. Recipient letters of appreciation U.S. Army, HEW, NASA, NSF; Exceptional Service medal Dept. Energy. Mem. ABA, Fed. Bar Assn., IEEE, Am. Arbitration Assn., Am. Soc. Pub. Adminstrn., Am. Hellenic Ednl. Progressive Assn., Phi Delta Phi. Clubs: Cosmos, Washington Golf, Nat. Lawyers.

FARMAKIS, GEORGE LEONARD, education educator; b. Clarksburg, W.Va., June 30, 1925; s. Michael and Pipitsa (Roussopoulos) F. BA, Wayne State U., 1949, MEd, 1950, MA, 1966, PhD, 1971; MA, U. Mich., 1978; postgrad., Columbia U., Yale U., Queens Coll. Tchr. audio-visual aids dir. Roseville (Mich.) Pub. Schs., 1951-57; tchr. Birmingham (Mich.) Pub. Schs., 1957-61, Highland Park (Mich.) Pub. Schs., 1961-90; substitute tchr. Grosse Pointe Pub. Schs., 1990—2003. Lectr. Oakland County C.C., 1990-92, Lawrence U., 1990-98, Oakland U., 2000—; instr. Highland Park C.C., 1966-68, Wayne County C.C., 1969-70; assoc. mem. grad. faculty Coll. Edn. Wayne State U., 1988-89; founder Ford Sch. Math. High Intensity Tutoring Program, 1971; chairperson Highland Park Sch. Dist. Curriculum Coun. and Profl. Staff Devel. Governing Bd., 1979-82; pres. Mich. Coun. Social Studies, 1985-86; founder, dir. Mich. Social Studies Olympiad, 1987; founder, editor Mich. Social Studies Jour., 1986; participant ESEA Title I/Nat. Diffusion Network. Author, translator: Letters of Nicholas Gysis, 1842-1901; co-author: Michigan School Finance Curriculum Guide; contbr. poems to books of poetry, articles to Focus jour. Cpl. USNG, 1948-51. Recipient spl. commendation Office of Edn., 1978, Outstanding Svc. award Nat. Coun. Social Studies, 1987, Presdl. award Mich. Coun. Social Studies, 1988, 96. Mem. ASCD (bd. dirs. Mich. chpt. 1983-86), Internat. Reading Assn., Am. History Assn., Nat. Coun. Social Studies (pres. SIG-CASE 1987-88, pres. JESIG 1988-89), Am. Philol. Assn., U. Mich. Alumni Assn., Wayne State U. Coll. Edn. Alumni Assn. (bd. dirs. 1985-86), Mich. Reading Assn., Masons (32 degree), Shriners, Ancient Accepted Scottish Rite, Phi Delta Kappa (Outstanding Educators award 1988). Greek Orthodox. Home: 15215 Windmill Dr Macomb MI 48044-4929

FARMAN, ALLAN GEORGE, radiologist, oral pathologist, educator; b. Birmingham, Eng., July 26, 1949; came to the U.S., 1980; s. George (dec.) and Lily (Hewitt) F.; m. Taeko Takemori, May 21, 1996. B Dental Surgery, U. Birmingham, 1971; PhD, U. Stellenbosch, Cape Town, South Africa, 1977, DSc (hon.), 1996; EdS, U. Louisville, 1983, MBA with distinction, 1987. Diplomate Am. Bd. Oral and Maxillofacial Radiology, Japanese Bd. Oral and Maxillofacial Radiology; specialist registration in oral pathology South African Med. and Dental Coun.; lic. Ky. Bd. Dentistry. Sr. lectr. oral pathology U. Stellenbosch, Cape Town, 1974-77; head dept. oral biology U. Riyadh, Saudi Arabia, 1978-79; prof., head divsn. radiology and imaging scis. Dental Sch., U. Louisville, 1980—; clin. prof. dept. diagnostic radiology Med. Sch., U. Louisville, 1990—. Cons. Joint Commn. for Dental Bd. Examination, Chgo., 1984—92, NIH, Bethesda, Md., 1990—; rep. to internat. DICOM com. Am. Dental Assn., 2001—. Author: Oral and Maxillofacial Diagnostic Imaging, 1993; editor: Advances in Maxillofacial Imaging, 1997, (oral and maxillofacial radiology sect.) Oral Surgery, Oral Medicine, Oral Pathology, Oral Radiology and Endodontics, 1988-95; co-editor CARS Proceedings, 1998—, Computer-Assisted Radiology and Surgery, 1998-; mem. editl. bd. Cranio, Oral Radiology, Acta Stomatologica Croatia, Sarundl, contbr. 250 articles to profl. jours. Mem. Am. Dental Assn., Internat. Assn. Dental Rsch., Japanese Soc. Oral and Maxillofacial Radiology, Internat. Assn. Dento Maxillofacial Radiology (pres. 1994-97, trust fund chmn. 1997-), Internat. Congress and Exposition on Computed Maxillofacial Imaging (initiator, founder, organizer 1995—), Am. Acad. Oral and Maxillofacial Radiology (editor 1988-95), Am. Assn. Dental Schs. (chmn. oral radiology sect. 1988-89). Office: U Louisville Sch Dentistry 501 S Preston St Louisville KY 40292-1701

FARMAN, RICHARD DONALD, energy company executive; b. San Francisco, Aug. 20, 1935; s. Carl Edward Jr. and Doris May (Muntz) Farman; m. Suzanne Hotchkiss, Sept. 12, 1956; children: Michael H., Charles S. BA in Econs. cum laude, Stanford U., 1957, LLB, 1963. Cert. Calif. Bar, 1964. Pvt. practice law, Palo Alto, Calif., 1963—69; with Unionamerica, Inc., 1969—78, exec. v.p., sec., gen. counsel, 1969—75, exec. v.p. Unionamerica Ins. Group, 1976—78; v.p. Pacific Enterprises, 1978—82, pres. Pacific Lighting Energy Systems and Cen. Plants, Inc., 1982—86, vice chmn. So. Calif. Gas Co., L.A., 1987—88, chmn. bd., CEO, 1989—93, pres., COO, 1993—98, CEO, 1998; chmn., CEO Sempra Energy, San Diego, 1998—2001; lead ind. dir. Catellus Dev. Corp, 1997—. Bd. dirs. Union Bank, Sentinel Group Funds, Inc., Nat. Bus. Higher Edn. Forum. Lt. USN, 1957—60. Mem.: LA Area C. of C. (bd. dirs., exec. com.), Natural Petroleum Coun., Interstate Nat. Gas Assn. Am., Pacific Coast Gas Assn., Am. Gas Assn. (past chmn., bd. dirs., exec com. 1988—), City Club on Bunker Hill, LA Country Club, Calif. Club. Republican. Avocations: golf, fishing, racquetball, music. Office: Catellus Dev Corp 201 Mission St 2nd Fl Van Nuys CA 91405

FARMAN-FARMAIAN, GHAFFAR, investment company executive; b. Tehran, Iran, Jan. 14, 1930; s. Abdol Hossein Mirza and Massoumeh (Tafreshi) F-F.;m. Jahan Aalam, Aug. 5, 1956; children: Massoumeh, Amir Hossein, Ali Reza, Afsar. D.L.C. with honors, Loughborough (Eng.) Coll., 1951; MS, U. Ill., 1953; PhD, U. Calif., Berkeley, 1958. Head power div. Karadj Water & Power Orgn., Tehran, 1961-64; mem. Iranian Nat. Com. on Electro-Tech. Standards, Tehran, 1966-79; pres. Armed Forces Communication & Electronic, Tehran, 1970-71; chmn. IEEE, Tehran, 1972-73; mem. Iranian Nat. Com. on Energy Ministry of Water and Power, Tehran, 1972-79; co-founder, chmn. ASEA Iran Co., Tehran, 1973-79; vice chmn. Bank of Tehran, 1973-79; co-founder, bd. dirs. Tehran Ins. Co., 1975-79; pres. Univest Corp., N.Y.C., 1982—, Astle Properties Inc., Houston, 1989—. Author tech. papers. Chmn. bd. trustees Cmty. Sch., Tehran, 1975—79. Recipient 1st prize Inst. Elec. Engrs., 1956, 57, Alfred Noble prize Am. Inst. Civil Engrs., 1958. Mem. IEEE (life), Armed Forces Communication & Electronic Assn. (life). Avocations: financial planning, tennis, hiking. Office: PO Box 3221 CH-1211 Geneva 3 - Rive Switzerland

FARMEN, RAGNE KRISTIN BENTSEN, molecular biologist, researcher; b. Ringerike, Norway, July 27, 1966; d. Torgeir and Oddveig (Oppen) Bentsen; m. Peder Espen Farmen, Aug. 23, 1997; children: Paal Christian, Thomas Aleksander. BS in Molecular Biology with honors, U. East Anglia, Norwich, Eng., 1989; MS in Forensic Sci., Strathclyde U., Glasgow, U.K., 1991; PhD in Toxicology, U. Oslo, Norway, 2000. Sr. engr. DNA lab. Nat. Inst. Forensic Sci., Oslo, 1989-90; rsch. student No. Ireland Forensic Sci. Lab., Belfast, 1991; product specialist cellular immunology Dynal A.S., Oslo, 1992-93; toxicologist, rschr. Nat. Inst. Occupl. Health, Oslo, 1993-2000; molecular biologist, rschr. dept. oncology Regional Hosp., 2001—. Contbr. articles to profl. jours. Rep., Assn. for Norwegian Students Abroad, U. East Anglia, 1987-89. Recipient grant Confederation of Norwegian Bus. and Industry, 1993-96, 98. Mem. Forensic Sci. Soc. Avocations: golf, tennis. Home: Johns Johnsensgt 12 4021 Stavanger Norway Office: Rogaland Ctrl Hosp PO Box 8100 4068 Stavanger Norway E-mail: rkfarmen@start.no.

FARMER, CORNELIA GRIFFIN, lawyer, consultant, hearings official; b. NYC, Mar. 3, 1945; d. John Bastin and Elizabeth McCue (Sussman) Griffin; m. William Paul Farmer, Jan. 8, 1972; children: Suzanne Elizabeth, John Paul. BA, Mt. Holyoke Coll., 1967; M in Regional Planning, Cornell U., 1970; JD, Marquette U., 1978. Bar: Wis. 1978, Pa. 1981, Minn. 1996, Oreg. 1999, Ill. 2001. Planner Frederick P. Clark Assoc., Rye, N.Y., 1970-71, Tri State Regional Planning Com., N.Y.C., 1971-72, State of Wis. and City of Milw., 1973-75; assoc. Friebert & Finerty, Milw., 1978-80, Baskin & Sears, Pitts., 1981-82; cons. County of Allegheny, Pitts., 1983; adj. faculty U. Pitts., 1986-94; jud. law clk. Commonwealth Ct. of Pa., Pitts., 1992-95; pvt. practice Mpls., 1996—99; staff atty., hearings ofcl. Lane Coun. Govts., Eugene, Oreg., 1999—2001. Vic-chmn. loan monitoring com. Pitts. Countywide Corp., 1981—87; child adv. Allegheny County Pro Bono Program, Pitts., 1986—92; mediator Dispute Resolution Ctr., St. Paul, 1998—99; adj. faculty U. Wis., Milw., 1978—79. Book rev., referee books, articles. Vol. polit. campaigns Milw., Pitts. and Eugene, 1972-2000; bd. trustees Falk Sch. Fund; v.p. PTA Falk Lab. Sch. U. Pitts., 1985-89; ct. monitor abuse cases WATCH, Mpls., 1996-99; pres. Class of 1967 Mt. Holyoke Coll., 1992-97, reunion co-chair, 1987, 2000-02, head class agt., 2002—; vol., WITS tutoring and mentoring program, 2002-, SMART, Eugene, Oreg., WITS, Chgo. Mem. ABA, APA, Chgo. Bar Assn., Silver Bay Assn. Coun., Mt. Holyoke Coll. Alumnae Assn. (alumnae vol.). Mt. Holyoke Club Pitts. (pres., treas.).

FARMER, DEBRA, academic administrator, educator; d. Alvin and Annette Alberts; children: Dan, Krista. BA in Psychobiology, U. of Colo., 1977; BE, Metro State Coll., 1983; MA in Spl. Edn., U. of Colo., 1992. Dir. disability services Colo. Mountain Coll., Steamboat Springs, 1993—. Mem.: CEC, LDA, Phi Theta Kappa (assoc.; advisor). Office: Colo Mountain Coll 1330 Bob Adams Dr Steamboat Springs CO 80477 E-mail: dfarmer@coloradomtn.edu.

FARMER, DEWAYNE MARK, director, photographer; b. Morristown, Tenn., Mar. 16, 1960; s. Ernest Jr. and Doris Ann Farmer; m. Daphney Cheri Pilkey, Nov. 16, 1956; children: April Pilkey Akins, Heather Pilkey Barnes, Clinton Pilkey. BS in Music Edn., Tenn. Tech. U., 1983; M in Music Edn., U. So. Miss.,

1989, postgrad., 1997—. Profl. tchg. cert. Tenn., tchg. cert. Miss., cert. tchr. evaluator Miss., profl. tchr. Ga. Dir. bands Sweetwater (Tenn.) H.S., 1983—84, Bledsoe County H.S., Pikeville, Tenn., 1985—89, Dougherty Comprehensive H.S., Albany, Ga., 1989—92, Brantly County Mid. Sch., Nahunta, Ga., 1992—93, Jefferson Mid. Sch., Jefferson City, Tenn., 1996—2002, Metter H.S., Ga., 2002—; pvt. practice photographer Jefferson City, 1983—. Supr. music student tchrs. U. So. Miss., Hattiesburg, 2001—02. Recipient Grad. Tchg. assistantship, U. So. Miss., 2001-2002. Mem.: NEA, Ga. Music Educators Assn., Tenn. Edn. Assn., Tenn. Secondary Sch. Band Dirs. Assn., E. Tenn. Sch. Band and Orch. Assn., Music Educators Nat. Conf. Avocation: photography. Home: 475 N Kennedy St Metter GA 30439 Office: Metter High School RR3 Box 1500 Metter GA 30439 Personal E-mail: mfarmer@pineland.net.

FARMER, EVAN R. academic administrator, dermatologist, researcher; b. Richmond, Va. BS in Biology, Va. Mil. Inst.; MD, M in History Ideas, John Hopkins U. Diplomate Am. Bd. Dermatology, cert. in dermatopathology. Past Kampen-Norins prof., past chmn. dept dermatology Sch. Medicine Ind. U.; formerly with Armed Forces Inst. Pathology, Washington; past resident in dermatology John Hopkins U., past dep. dir. dept. dermatology, dir. depts. dermatopathology, oral pathology, 1977, past rschr. in graft-versus-host disease; dean, provost Ea. Va. Med. Sch., Norfolk. Past vol. All Africa Leprosy Rehab. and Tng. Ctr., Addis Ababa, Ethiopia. Office: Ea Va Med Sch Office Dean Lewis Hall PO Box 1980 Norfolk VA 23501

FARMER, GUY OTTO, II, lawyer; b. Washington, Jan. 7, 1941; s. Guy Otto and Rose Marie (Smith) F.; m. Drema Houchins, Jan. 27, 1963; children: Caroline E., Guy Otto III. BA in Polit. Sci., W.Va. U., 1963; JD, U. Va., 1966. Bar: Fla. 1966, U.S. Dist. Ct. (mid. dist.) Fla. 1966, U.S. Ct. Appeals (5th cir.) 1967, U.S. Ct. Appeals (11th cir.) 1970, U.S. Supreme Ct. 1970, U.S. Ct. Appeals (6th cir.) 1991, U.S. Ct. Appeals (2d cir.) 1997, cert.: Fla. Bar (specialist in labor and employment law). Assoc. to ptnr. Mahoney, Hadlow & Adams, Jacksonville, Fla., 1966-82; ptnr. Smith & Hulsey, Jacksonville, 1982-88, Foley & Lardner, Jacksonville, 1988—2003, Holland & Knight, Jacksonville, 2003—. Contbr. articles to profl. jours. Bd. dirs. N.E. Fla. Hospice, Jacksonville, 1987-93, Children's Home Soc., Jacksonville, 1988-91, N.E. Fla. Safety Coun., Jacksonville, 1988—. Fellow: Am. Bar Found.; mem.: ABA (com. on EEO law and Nat. Labor Rels. Act), Acad. Fla. Mgmt. Attys. (bd. dirs. 2000—), Def. Rsch. Inst., Jacksonville Bar Assn., Fla. Bar Assn., Epping Forest Yacht Club, Ponte Verda Club, The River Club. Democrat. Methodist. Avocations: reading, gardening, boating, sports. Home: 4244 San Jose Blvd Jacksonville FL 32207-6343 Office: Holland & Knight 50 N laura St Ste 3900 Jacksonville FL 32202 E-mail: gfarmer@hk.com.

FARMER, HELEN SWEENEY, psychology educator; b. Ottawa, Can., Dec. 23, 1929; d. Henry Bertrum and Mabel Sarah (Switzer) Sweeney; m. James A. Farmer Jr., Jan. 25, 1955; children: James Sweeney, David Sargent, Paul Alexander. BA, Queens U., Can., 1952; BD, Union Theol. Sem., 1955; MA, Columbia U., 1969; PhD, UCLA, 1972. Lic. psychologist, Ill. Dir. evaluation svcs. INSGROUP, Long Beach, Calif., 1971-74; asst. prof. counseling psychology U. Ill., Urbana, 1974-81, assoc. prof., 1981-87, prof., 1987—98, sr. scholar, 1995—, prof. emerita, 1998—. Author: (with Tom Backer) New Career Options for Women: Counselor's Sourcebook, 1977, New Career Options for Women: A Woman's Guide, 1977, Diversity and Women's Career Development: Adolescence to Adulthood, 1997; contbr. articles to profl. jours. Queens U. scholar, 1949, Can. govt., 1949-52; grantee Nat. Inst. Edn., 1974, 76, 78, NSF, 1991; recipient Mentoring Grad. Students award U. Ill., 1997. Fellow APA (divsn. sec., Disting. Sr. Contbr. to counseling psychology 1995, Divsn. Counseling, Woman of Yr. 1999), Am. Psychol. Soc.; mem. ACA, Am. Ednl. and Rsch. Assn. (divsn. v.p. 1984-86). Avocations: collecting sea shells, snorkeling. Home: 2204 S Staley Rd Champaign IL 61822-9763 Office: U Ill Sch Edn Dept Ednl Psychology Champaign IL 61820 Fax: 217-244-0726. E-mail: hfarmer@uiuc.edu.

FARMER, JAMES A., II, lawyer; b. N.Y.C., May 23, 1956; BA, Rutgers U., New Brunswick, 1978; JD, Rutgers U., Camden, 1981. Bar: N.J. 1982, Pa. 1981. Sr. trial attorney Office of Pub. Defender, Camden, N.J., 1983—. Vol. Phila. Com. for Homeless, 1989; vol. Big Bros./Big Sisters Assn., Phila., 1983-95; mem. Chapel of 4 Chaplains Legion Honor, 1986; mem. bd. dirs. Onwards, Inc. Prison Pre-Release Ctr., 1994-2000. Recipient Cert. of Appreciation for Outstanding Efforts Big Brother/Big Sister Assn., 1988. Mem. Rutgers Alumni Assn., Rutgers Camden Sch. Law Alumni Assn., Phi Beta Kappa, Phi Sigma Iota. Democrat. Home: 4633 Spruce St Philadelphia PA 19139-4542 Office: Office of Pub Defender 101 Haddon Ave Ste 8 Camden NJ 08103-1468 Fax: 856-614-3503.

FARMER, JAMES ALEXANDER, JR., retired education educator; b. N.Y.C., Mar. 12, 1931; s. James A. and Margaret (Belknap) F.; m. Helen Sweeney, Jan. 25, 1955; children: James S., Paul A. BA, Hamilton Coll., 1953; MDiv, Union Theol. Sem., 1956; MA, Columbia U., 1968, EdD, 1969. ordained by United Ch. of Christ, 1956. Pastor Oxford (Conn.) Congl. Ch., 1956-59; founding pastor United Ch. of Hayward, Calif., 1959-63; minister of adult edn. Riverside Ch., N.Y.C., 1963-69; asst. prof. UCLA, 1969-74; assoc. prof. U. Ill., Urbana/Champaign, 1974-93, prof. continuing edn., 1993-98, prof. emer., 1998—. Cons. Am. Acad. Orthopaedic Surgeons, 1970—, Am. Orthopaedic Soc. for Sports Medicine, 1985—. Co-author: Psychomotor Skills in Orthopaedic Surgery, 1981, Instructional Design: Implications From Cognitive Science, 1991. Recipient George D. Rovere Edn. award Am. Orthopaedic Soc. for Sports Medicine, 1994, Career Achievement award U. Ill. Coll. Edn. Mem.: Adult Edn. Assn. of USA (pres. 1975), Am. Osteo. Acad. Orthopedics (hon.). Avocations: fishing, snorkeling, diving. Home: 2204 S Staley Rd Champaign IL 61822-9763 E-mail: jfarmer@uiuc.edu.

FARMER, JANENE ELIZABETH, artist, educator; b. Albuquerque, Oct. 16, 1946; d. Charles John Watt and Regina Mortimere (Brown) Kruger; m. Michael Hugh Bolton, Apr. 1965 (div.); m. Frank Urban Farmer, May 1972 (div.). BA in Art, San Diego State U., 1969; postgrad., U. San Diego, San Diego State U., U. Calif., San Diego, 1983—85. Owner, operator Iron Walrus Pottery, 1972-79. Tchr. Cath. schs., San Diego, 1983—86, Ramona Unified Sch. Dist., 1986—, mentor tchr., 1994—98; tchr. environ. art San Diego Natural History Mus., 1996—97, San Diego Wild Animal Park, 1996; cons. tchr. Ramona Unified Sch. Dist., 2002—03; instr. Extension Dept. U. Calif., San Diego, 2003. Exhibited in group shows at San Diego Mus. Art, San Diego City Adminstrn. Bldg., University City Libr., San Diego, Art Scene Gallery, San Diego, Kauai, Hawaii, Am. Soc. Interior Designers, San Diego, Sierra Club Bookstore, San Diego, Quail Bot. Gardens, Encinitas, Calif. Mem. Coronado Arts and Humanities Coun., 1979-81; edn. adv. com. La Jolla (Calif.) Playhouse, 1996; edn. com. Calif. Wolf Ctr., 1999-2001, U. Calif. San Diego Extension, 2003. Grantee Calif. Arts Coun., 1980-81, resident artist, instr. U. Calif., San Diego; U. San Diego grad. fellow Dept. Edn., 1984. Roman Catholic. Home: # 35 4435 Nobel Dr San Diego CA 92122-1559 E-mail: farmerj4@mac.com.

FARMER, JOHN J. state commissioner, former state attorney general; b. June 24, 1957; m. Beth Gates. BA, Georgetown U., 1979, JD, 1986. Law clk. hon. Alan B. Handler N.J. Supreme Ct. Justice; assoc. Riker, Danzig, Scherer, Hyland and Perretti, Morristown, 1988—90; asst. U.S. atty. Dist. N.J., 1990—94; dep. chief counsel, sr. assoc. counsel to the Gov., 1994—97; chief counsel to the Gov., chief law enforcement officer State of N.J., Trenton, 1997—99, atty. gen., 1999—2002; Commr. State of N.J. Comm. on Investigation, Trenton, 2002—. Adj. prof. law Seton Hall U. Law Sch., 1993—97; chmn. Juvenile Justice Commn. Mem.: Nat. Assn. Attys. Gen. (co-chair health care fraud, abuse and adv. com.). Republican. Office: 28 W State St 10th Fl Trenton NJ 08625-0045*

FARMER, KENNETH, JR., military officer; b. Leeds, Ala. BS, Auburn U.; MD, U. Ala.; grad., Army Command Gen. Staff Coll., Army War Coll. Diplomate Am. Bd. Family Practice. Commd. 2d lt. U.S. Army, advanced through grades to maj. gen.; early assignments include Eisenhower Army Med. Ctr., Ft. Gordon, Ga., 9th Med. Detachment and Health Clinic, Heilbronn, Germany, 1976-79; other early assignments include Keller Army Hosp., West Pt., N.Y.; divsn. surgeon 101st Airborne divsn. Ft. Campbell, Ky.; dep. comdr. clin. svcs. Ft. Campbell Hosp.; chief family practice residency tng. program Eisenhower Army Med. Ctr.; comdr. 85th Evacuation Hosp. Dhahran, Saudi Arabia, 1990-91; comdr. Bayne-Jones Army Cmty. Hosp., Fort Polk, L.A.; command surgeon U.S. European Command, Stuttgart, Germany, 1994-97; comdr. Darnall Army Cmty. Hosp. and U.S. Army Med. Dept. Activity, Ft. Hood, Tex.; comdg. gen. 44th Med. Brigade, Ft. Bragg, NC, 1999-2000, Western Regional Med. Command, Tacoma, 2000—, lead agt. TRICARE NW/Reg., commanding gen., 2000—02. Decorated Legion of Merit with 3 oak leaf clusters, Bronze Star, Meritorious Svc. medal with 3 oak leaf clusters, Army Commendation medal, others. Fellow Am. Acad. Family Physicians (Robert Graham Physician Exec. award 2001).

FARMER, LINDA L. philosophy educator; d. Denis Joseph Farmer and Yvonne Marie Proulx; m. Michael D. Khatib, Aug. 12, 1989. PhD in Philosophy, U. Ottawa, 1997. Asst. prof. philosophy U. St. Thomas, St. Paul, 1997—99; assoc. prof. philosophy Wright State U., Dayton, Ohio, 1999—. Contbr. articles to profl. jours. Grantee, Fonds pour la formation de chercheurs et aide a la recherche, Govt. Que., 1993—95. Mem.: Am. Cath. Philos. Assn., Am. Philos. Assn. Office: Wright State U 3640 Colonel Glenn Hwy Dayton OH 45435-0001 Office Fax: 937-775-2892. E-mail: linda.farmer@wright.edu.

FARMER, MARILYN, volunteer; b. Watseka, Ill., Jan. 23, 1943; d. Melvin Charles Perzee and Marjorie Elaine Korte; m. David H Farmer, Apr. 19, 1969; children: David H, Deborah J Carsten, John C(dec.), Theresa A Murphy. AA, Joliet Jr. Coll., 1994. Clk. CNA Ins., Chgo.; clk./receptionist Boy Scouts of Am., Munster, Ind.; program dir. Southlakey YMCA, Brownpoint, Ind., 1978—86, Hobart YMCA, Hobart, Ind., 1986—88; adminstrv. asst. Will Grundy Home Builders, Joliet, Ill., 1988—95; cmty. dir. Mar. of Dimes, Joliet, Ill., 1995—96; exec. dir. New Lenox Chamber, New Lenox, Ill., 1996—98. Com. mem. Joliet Will County Continuim of Care, Ill., 1998—; sec./treas. Midwest dist. Assn. Gospel Rescue Mission, Kans. City, Kans., 2001—03. Mem.: Council Working Women, Cmty. Services Coun., Joliet Ecumenical Clergy Assn. Avocations: travel, reading. Office: Morningstar Mission Ministries 350 E Washington Joliet IL 60433 Office Fax: 815-726-9450. E-mail: morningstar@iols.net.

FARMER, MARY BAUDER, artist; b. San Diego, Nov. 30, 1953; d. Chester Robert and Dixie (Cook) Bauder; m. L. Michael Dowling, July 1990. BS, Auburn U., 1986; postgrad., Ga. State U., 1992—; ind. study with Joan Snyder; BFA in Studio Arts, Atlanta Coll. Art, 2003. Exec. dir. Birmingham Woman's Med. Clinic, Ala., 1975-80; pres. Beacon Clinic, Montgomery, Ala., 1980-83; ptnr. Hill, Rose and Farmer, Atlanta, 1988-90; owner, mgr. Studio M. Farmer, Atlanta, 1990—; creative dir., pres. Twin Studios, Inc., Atlanta, 1995-97. V.p. Global Interests Inc., 1990—. Author, pub.: The Landlord's Primer for Georgia: A Self-Help Guide for Inexperienced Landlords. Mem. pub. rels. com. Project Open Hand, Ga. Citizens for Arts; mem. Bus. Com. for Arts. Mem. LWV, Ga. Women's Agenda (founder), Omicron Delta Kappa. Democrat. Studio: 535 Means St Atlanta GA 30318

FARMER, RICHARD GILBERT, physician, foundation administrator, medical advisor, healthcare consultant; b. Kokomo, Ind., Sept. 29, 1931; s. Oscar Irvin and Elizabeth Jane (Gilbert) Farmer; m. Janice Mae Schrank, Nov. 29, 1958; children: Amy Lynn, David Richard. Student, Ind. U., 1949—52; MD, U. Md., 1956; MS in Medicine, U. Minn., 1960. Diplomate Am. Bd. Internal Medicine, Gastroenterology. Fellow in internal medicine Mayo Clinic, Rochester, Minn., 1957—60; mem. staff Cleve. Clinic Found., 1962—91, chmn. dept. gastroenterology, 1972—82, chmn. div. medicine, 1975—91, mem. med. exec. com., 1975—91, bd. govs., 1974—79, mem. exec. com. bd. trustees, 1975—77; sr. med. advisor Bur. for Europe Agy. for Internat. Devel. U.S. Dept. State, Washington, 1992—94; cons. health care Eastern Europe and former Soviet Union, 1994—96; med. dir. Quality Health Internat., Boston, 1997—98; cons. Scandinavian Care, 1998—. Clin. prof. medicine (gastroenterology) Georgetown U. Med. Ctr., Washington, 1992—; mem. nat. adv. bd. Nat. Commn. Digestive Diseases, 1977—79; mem. nat. sci. adv. bd. Nat. Found. Ileitis and Colitis, 1973—91, chmn. grants rev. com., 1981—85; mem. Coun. Subsplty. Socs. in Internal Medicine, 1978—85; mem. com. to assess quality care in Medicare program, GAO and ways and means com. U.S. Ho. of Reps., 1986—89; cons. Am. Medico-Legal Found., Phila., 1996—, Inst. for Health Policy Analysis, Washington, 1996—; med. dir. Eurasian Med. Edn. Program (Russian Fedn.), 1998—. Editor 6 books; contbr. over 275 articles to sci. jours., in books. Lt. comdr. USNR, 1960—62. Recipient Jubilee medal, Charles U. Prague, 1998. Master: ACP (gov. Ohio 1980—84, health and pub. policy com. 1982—91, chmn. med. tech. assessment com. 1985—86, regent 1985—91, chmn. 1986—88, chmn. clin. practice subcom. 1988—91, del. to AMA 1989—94, Spl. Presdl. citation 1984), Am. Coll. Gastroenterology (trustee, exec. com. 1975—80, pres. 1978—79); mem.: Internat. Orgn. for Study Inflammatory Bowel Disease (dep. chmn. 1982—86), Interstate Postgrad. Med. Assn. (pres. 1983—84), Inst. Medicine of NAS (life), Am. Gastroent. Assn. (commn. on future 1973—74, tng. and edn. com. 1975—78, chmn. subcom. grad. edn. 1975—78), Assn. Program Dirs. in Internal Medicine (founding pres. 1977—79, Founder's award 1993). Democrat. Mem. Soc. Of Friends. Home and Office: 9126 Town Gate Ln Bethesda MD 20817-4111 Fax: 301-365-6202. E-mail: RG.JM.FARMER@worldnet.att.net.

FARMER, ROBERT LINDSAY, lawyer; b. Portland, Oreg., Sept. 29, 1922; s. Paul C. and Irma (Lindsay) F.; m. Carmen E. Engebretson, Sept. 8, 1943; children: Cort W., Scott L., Eric C. BS, UCLA, 1946; LLB, U. So. Calif., 1949. Bar: Calif. 1949. Since practiced in L.A.; mem. Farmer & Ridley, L.A., 1949—. Trustee Edward James Found., West Dean Estate, Chichester, Eng. Served with AUS, 1943-46. Mem. ABA, Los Angeles County Bar Assn., Order of Coif, Beta Gamma Sigma, Kappa Sigma, Phi Delta Phi, Annandale Golf Club (Pasadena, Calif.). Home: 251 S Orange Grove Blvd Apt 1 Pasadena CA 91105-1766 Office: 444 S Flower St Los Angeles CA 90071-2901

FARMER, SUSAN LAWSON, broadcasting executive, former secretary of state; b. Boston, May 29, 1942; d. Ralph and Margaret (Tyng) Lawson; m. Malcolm Farmer, III, Apr. 6, 1968; children: Heidi Benson, Stephanie Lawson. Student, Garland Jr. Coll., 1960-61, Brown U., 1961-62. Mem. Providence Home Rule Charter Commn., 1979-80; sec. of state State of R.I., Providence, 1983-87; pres., CEO Sta. WSBE-TV R.I. PBS, Providence, 1987—. Spl. adv. R.I. Family Ct., 1978-83; mem. nat. voting stds. panel Fed. Election Commn. co-chmn. Nat. Voter Edn. Project; mem. electoral coll., 1984; chmn. Gov.'s Com. on Ethics in Govt., 1985-86; mem. teaching facility and adv. panel Internat. Ctr. on Election Law and Adminstrn.; mem. nat. edn. adv. com. Pub. Broadcasting System, 1987-89; trustee Eastern Ednl. TV Network, 1987-95; mem. R.I. Task Force on Tech., 1995—, R.I. Info. Mgmt. Commn., 1997; bd. dirs., mem. exec. com. Program Resources Group, 1993-2001; mem. Gov.'s Telecom. Task Force, 2000—; mem. nat. media adv. com. WomenFuture, 2002—. Bd. dirs. Justice Resources Corp., Marathon House, Inc., R.I. Council Alcoholism, R.I. Hist. Soc., Planned Parenthood (R.I. chpt.), R.I. Rape Crisis Ctr., The Newport Inst.; mem. Mayor's Task Force on Child Abuse, R.I. Film Commn.; v.p. Miriam Hosp. Found.; mem. adv. com. Women in Polit. and Govtl. Careers Program, U. R.I., 1985—; mem. adv. bd. Com. for Study of Am. Electorate-Ford Found. Project-Efficacy in State Voting Laws, 1986; mem. Commn. to Study Length of Election Process, 1985-87; steering com. Nat. Fund for America's Future, Project Vote R.I.; bd. dirs. Dawn for Children Tng. Thru Placement; pres. Channel 36 Found.; bd. dirs. R.I. Anti-Drug Coalition Exec. Com., Nat. Forum for Pub. TV Execs., 1998—, chmn., 1999. Named Woman of Yr., Nat. Women's Polit. Caucus, 1980. Mem. LWV, NATAS (bd. govs. New Eng. chpt. 1995—), N.E. Assn. Schs. and Colls. (com. on tech. and course instns.), So. Ednl. Comms. Assn. (bd. dirs. 1993-96), R.I. Women's Polit. Caucus (Woman of Yr. 1980), Bus. and Profl. Women (Woman of Yr. 1984), Common Cause, Save the Bay, Providence Preservation Soc., Orgn. State Broadcasting Execs, Agawam Hunt Club, Mill Reef Club (Antigua, West Indies), Nat. Assn. of Ams. Pub. TV Stas. (trustee 1996—), Nat. Acad. TV Arts and Scis. (bd. govs. N.E. chpt. 1995—), Nat. Ednl. Telecomms. Assn. (bd. dirs. 1997—, Nat. Forum Pub. TV Execs. (bd. dirs. 1998—, chmn. 1999). Home: 147 Lloyd Ave Providence RI 02906-1552 Office: RI PBS 50 Park Ln Providence RI 02907-3124 E-mail: sfarmer@RIpbs.org.

FARMER, TERRY D(WAYNE), lawyer; b. Oklahoma City, May 1, 1949; s. Gayle V. and Allene (Edsall) F.; m. Nicole M. Charlebois; children: Grant L., Tyler M. BA, U. Okla., 1971, JD, 1974. Bar: Okla. 1974, N.Mex. 1975, U.S. Dist. Ct. N.Mex. 1976, U.S. Ct. Claims 1975, U.S. Ct. Appeals (10th cir.) 1977, U.S. Supreme Ct. 1980. Asst. trust officer First Nat. Bank of Albuquerque, 1974-75; assoc. Nordhaus, Moses & Dunn, Albuquerque, 1975-78, ptnr., 1978-80; dir. Moses, Dunn, Farmer & Tuthill, P.C., Albuquerque, 1980—. Pres. Albuquerque Lawyers Club, N. Mex., 1982-83. Fellow N.Mex. Bar Found.; mem. N.Mex. Bar Assn. (pres. Young Lawyers div., 1978-79), Okla. Bar Assn., N.Mex. Trial Lawyers. Office: Moses Dunn Farmer & Tuthill PC PO Box 27047 Albuquerque NM 87125-7047

FARMER, THOMAS WOHLSEN, neurologist, educator; b. Lancaster, Pa., Sept. 18, 1914; s. Clarence R. and Laura (Wohlsen) F.; m. Phyllis McCormick, July 19, 1941; children: Pamela Farmer Henderson, Thomas Wohlsen. AB, Harvard U., 1935, MD, 1941; MA, Duke U., 1937; postgrad., U. Copenhagen, 1957-58, U. Calif., San Diego, 1971-72. Diplomate: Am. Bd. Psychiatry and Neurology (dir. 1969—, pres. 1977). Intern Pa. Hosp., Phila., 1941-42; resident Boston City Hosp., 1942-43, Johns Hopkins Hosp., 1943-44, 46-47; mem. staff N.C. Meml. Hosp., Chapel Hill, 1952—; instr. medicine Johns Hopkins U., 1947-48; asst. prof. neurology Southwestern Med. Sch., U. Tex., Dallas, 1948-49, asso. prof., 1949-50, prof., 1950-52, prof. medicine, acting chmn. dept. medicine, 1951-52; prof. neurol. medicine, head div. neurology U. N.C., Chapel Hill, 1952—, Sarah Graham Kenan prof. medicine, 1975—. Author: Pediatric Neurology, 1964, 3d edit., 1983, Neurologia Pediatrica, 1972. Served with USNR, 1944-46. Mem. Am. Acad. Neurology (nat. sec. 1955-57), Am. Neurol. Assn., Am. Acad. Neurology, ACP, AMA, Assn. Research Nervous and Mental Diseases, Child Neurology Soc. Home: 1304 Mason Farm Rd Chapel Hill NC 27514-4604 Office: U NC Sch Medicine Clin Scis Bldg Chapel Hill NC 27514

FARMER, WESLEY STEVEN, police officer; b. Albuquerque, Dec. 1, 1950; s. Dewey B. Farmer and Bernice (Willie) Maloch. BA, Calif. Bapt. U., 1972; MPA, Calif. State U., San Bernardino, 1989; grad., FBI Nat. Acad., 1991. Police officer San Bernardino (Calif.) Police, 1973-79, police detective, 1979-84, police sgt., 1984-89, police lt., 1989-2001, capt., 2001—. Adj. faculty Riverside (Calif.) C.C., 1989, 92. Contbr. articles to profl. jours. Mem. Rotary, San Bernardino, 1983-84; bd. dirs. Alliance for Children and Families, Milw., 1995—. Mem. ASPA (bd. dirs. 1992-96), Family Svc. Agy. (bd. chair 1993-96, Svc. award 1995). Republican. Avocations: community service, fishing, camping, hiking. Office: San Bernardino Police PO Box 1559 San Bernardino CA 92402-1559 E-mail: Farmer_We@sbcity.org.

FARMER, WILLIAM H. political organization worker, lawyer; b. Nashville, Nov. 10, 1947; BA, Austin Peay State U., 1971; JD, U. Tenn., 1974. Bar: Tenn. 1974. Asst. U.S. atty. U.S. Dist. Ct. (mid. dist.) Tenn., 1978-84; adv. gen. State of Tenn., 1984-86; mem. Waller Lansden Dortch & Davis, Nashville, 1986—2002, Farmer & Luna, PLLC, Nashville, 2002—. Instr. Southeast Paralegal Inst., 1981-87, Vanderbilt U., 1987—; nat. chmn. Fed. Defender Adv. Com., 1983-84; hearing officer Bd. Profl. Responsibility, 1985—; lands commr. U.S. Dist. Ct. (mid. dist.) Tenn. 1987—; bd. dirs. Capital Case Resource Ctr. Tenn. Mem. Fed. Bar Assn. (pres. 1981-82), Am. Judicature Soc., Tenn. Bar Assn., Tenn. Assn. Criminal Def. Lawyers, Tenn. Trial Lawyers Assn., Nashville Bar Assn., Phi Delta Phi. Office: Farmer & Luna 333 Union St Ste 300 Nashville TN 37201

FARNAM, JAFAR, allergist, immunologist, pediatrician; b. Tabriz, Iran, Dec. 18, 1945; MD, Faculty Medicine Tabriz, 1972. Diplomate Am. Bd. Pediatrics, Am. Bd. Allergy and Immunology. Intern U. Ill. Hosp., Chgo., 1977-78; resident in pediatrics Christ Hosp.- Rush U., Oaklawn, 1978-80; fellow in allergy & immunology U. Tex. Med. Br., Galveston, 1980-82, clin. assoc. prof. internal medicine; with Clear Lake Regional Hosp. Mem. Am. Acad. Pediat., Am. Acad. Allergy, Asthma, and Immunology, Am. Coll. Allergy, Asthma, and Immunology, Tex. Med. Assn., Tex. Allergy Soc. Office: Allergy Asthma Ctr 450 Medical Center Blvd Ste 204 Webster TX 77598-4229 E-mail: farnammd@aol.com.

FARNATH, DOROTHY WHITMYER, recruitment company executive; b. Hammonton, N.J., Mar. 3, 1942; d. Theodore George and Dorothy Priest Whitmyer; children: Melissa Scott Ciliberti, Theodore George. BS in Med. Tech., U. Pa., 1964. Med. tech. Thomas Jefferson U. Medicine, Phila., 1966-69; supr. South Jersey Urology Assocs., Cherry Hill, N.J., 1977-84; supr., mgr. 227 Labs., Phila., 1984-88; pres. Dorothy Whitmyer Farnath & Assocs., Inc., Marlton, N.J., 1988—. Pres. Championship Family Restaurant, Trenton, N.J., 1995—; gen. mgr. GDV Enterprises, Trenton, 1995—; owner Hair Sta., Haddon Heights, N.J., 1994—; co-owner Hardshell Cafe, Marlton, N.J., 2000—. Mem. Rep. Nat. Com., Washington, 1994—. Mem. U.S. C. of C. Avocations: reading, genealogy. Office: 104 Centre Blvd Ste B Marlton NJ 08053-4130

FARNEN, RUSSELL FRANCIS, political scientist, educator; b. New Haven, Apr. 18, 1933; s. Russell and Anna (Ryan) F.; m. Christa Sigrid, Sept. 21, 1979; children: Edward Reid, Monika K. Germaine.8 BS, Ctrl. Conn. State U., 1957; MA, Syracuse U., 1960, PhD, 1963. Instr. Syracuse (N.Y.) U., 1957-60; asst. prof. U. Fla., Gainesville, 1960-64; assoc. examiner Ednl. Testing Svc., Princeton, N.J., 1964-67; assoc. prof. polit. sci. Vanderbilt U., Nashville, 1967-72; prof. polit. sci. James Madison U., Harrisonburg, Va., 1972-77, SUNY, Saratoga Springs, 1977-81, U. Conn., Storrs, 1981—. Cons. U.S. Dept. Edn., Washington, 1994—; vis. scholar Harvard Sch. Pub. Health, Boston, 1989—. Author: Integrating Political Science, Education and Public Policy, 1990; co-editor, contbr. Politics, Sociology and Economics of Education, 1998, Political Participation, Socialization and Education, 2003; co-author: Democracy, Authoritarianism and Education, 2000, Tolerance in Transition, 2001, Democracies in Transition, 2001; mng. editor Politics, Groups and the Individual, 1997—, editl. contbr. Nationalism, Identity and Ethnicity, 1994, Democracy, Socialization and Conflicting Loyalties in East and West, 1997. Cpl. U.S. Army, 1950-51. Mem. Internat. Polit. Sci. Assn., AAUP, APA. Independent. Avocations: golf, tennis, swimming, jogging. Office: U Conn 85 Lawler Rd West Hartford CT 06117-2620 E-mail: htfdadm2@uconnvm.uconn.edu.

FARNHAM, ANTHONY EDWARD, English language educator; b. Oakland, Calif., July 2, 1930; s. Willard Edward and Frances Fern (Hicks) F.; m. Frances Anne Larkey, Dec. 28, 1957; children: Allen Nicholas, Timothy John. AB, U. Calif.-Berkeley, 1951; MA, Harvard U., 1957, PhD, 1964. Instr. English Mt. Holyoke Coll., South Hadley, Mass., 1961-64, asst. prof., 1964-69, assoc. prof., 1969-72, prof., 1972-99, dept. chmn., 1979-85, prof. emeritus, 1999—. Editor: A Sourcebook in the History of English, 1969; author: Statement and Search in the Confessio Amantis, Mediaevalia 16, 1993. Served with M.I. U.S. Army, 1953-56. Mem. MLA, Am. Cath. Hist. Assn., Medieval Acad. Am., Assn. Literary Scholars and Critics, Dante Soc., New Chaucer Soc., Phi Beta Kappa. Roman Catholic. Home: 23 Atwood Rd South Hadley MA 01075-1601 Office: Mt Holyoke Coll Dept English 50 Coll St South Hadley MA 01075-6421

FARNHAM, CLAYTON HENSON, lawyer; b. New Brunswick, N.J., Aug. 18, 1938; s. Richard Bayles and Naomi Shropshire (Henson) F.; m. Katharine Gross, Sept. 16, 1967; children: Julia Kernan, Richard Bayles II. BA, U. of the South, 1961; LLB, U. Ga., 1967. Bar: Ga. 1968, U.S. Dist. Ct. (no., so. and mid. dists.) Ga. 1968, U.S. Supreme Ct. 1978, U.S. Dist. Ct. (no. dist.) Miss. 1978, U.S. Ct. Appeals (5th cir., 11th cir.) 1968, (4th cir.) 1980, U.S. Ct. Appeals (8th cir.) 1992. Law clk. to judge U.S. Dist. Ct., Atlanta, 1967-69; from assoc., to ptnr. Swift, Currie, McGhee & Hiers, Atlanta, 1969-82; ptnr. Drew, Eckl & Farnham, Atlanta, 1983—. Contbr. articles to profl. jours. Lt. (j.g.) USNR, 1961-64. Mem. ABA (coun. TIPS sect. 1989-92), Internat. Assn. Def. Counsel (com. chmn. 1987-89), Ansley Golf Club, Lawyer's Club Atlanta, Old War Horse Lawyer's Club. Home: 30 Inman Cir NE Atlanta GA 30309 Office: Drew Eckl & Farnham 800 W Peachtree St NW PO Box 7600 Atlanta GA 30357 E-mail: cfarnham@deflaw.com.

FARNHAM, DAVID ALEXANDER, lawyer, banker; b. Washington, Sept. 7, 1946; s. Waller and Leslie (Thompson) F. BA, Yale U., 1969; JD, Columbia U., 1975. Bar: Md. 1977, Va. 1981, U.S. Dist. Ct. Md. 1979, U.S. Dist. Ct. (we. dist.) Va. 1981, U.S. Ct. Appeals (4th cir.) 1981. Asst. counsel Bankers Trust Co., N.Y.C., 1975-76; assoc. Weinberg & Green, Balt., 1976-80; legal compliance officer Dominion Bankshares Corp., Roanoke, Va., 1980-82, v.p., corp. counsel, 1983-89, sr. v.p. corp. counsel, 1989—. Author: (with Earl E. McGuire, Jr.) A Banker's Guide to IRAs, 1982. With U.S. Army, 1969-72. Mem. ABA,

Md. Bar Assn., Va. State Bar, Roanoke City Bar Assn. Episcopalian. Club: Yale (N.Y.C.); Jefferson (Roanoke). Home: PO Box 8682 Roanoke VA 24014-0682 Office: Dominion Bankshares Corp 10 S Jefferson St Roanoke VA 24011-1331

FARNHAM, SHERMAN BRETT, retired electrical engineer; b. New Haven, June 23, 1912; s. Charles Sherman and Antoinette (Brett) F.; children: Anne Valerie, John Brett. BS, Yale U., 1933, MEE, 1935. Registered profl. elec. engr., N.Y., Mass., N.J. Lab. asst. Yale U., New Haven, 1933-35; test engr. GE, Schenectady, N.Y., 1935-36, design engr. Phila., 1936-37, application engr. Schenectady, 1937-55, engring. mgr. Boston, 1955-66; chief elec. engring. Chas T. Main, Inc., Boston, 1966-80, ret., 1980. Contbr. articles and tech. papers to profl. jours.; patentee in field. Fellow IEEE (chmn. Boston sect. 1962-63, Centennial medal 1984). Republican. Congregationalist. Avocation: gardening. Home: 10 Rivermead Rd Peterborough NH 03458-1701

FARNHAM, TIMOTHY, training and education administrator; b. Arlington, Calif., Mar. 1, 1947; s. Jack Pershing and Joyce Maureen (Evans) F.; m. Sue Ann Newton Frantz, Oct. 25, 1969 (div. Jan. 1975); children: Kevin, Kara; m. Paula Eleen Kerner, Nov. 25, 1978; children: Melinda, Elyse. BBA summa cum laude, Nat. U., 1990. Equipment engr. Pacific Bell, San Diego, 1980-86, design engr., 1986-87; mgr. instrn. and devel. Bellcore, Lisle, Ill., 1987-89, mgr. tng. and edn., 1991-95; tech. engr. Pacific Bell, San Ramon, Calif., 1989-91, 95-96; regional mgr. new tech. and applied R & D Teleport Comm. Group, Walnut Creek, Calif., 1996-99; dir. tng. and edn. Telecordia Techs. Inc., 1999—. Lead presenter wireless comm. curriculum Bellcore; presenter tech. confs., orgns. including UN APEC Agy., Bangkok, USTA Showcases, Western Comm. Forum, Network '90s Conf., San Francisco, Expo Comm, Mex., Mexico City, Inst. for Internat. Rsch., Beverly Hills, Calif. Contbr. articles to profl. conf. procs. Sgt. USAF, 1965-68. Mem. IEEE, N.Y. Acad. Scis. Avocations: reading, playing guitar, genealogy research. Office: 863 Dover Cir Benicia CA 94510-3651 E-mail: farnham4@pacbell.net.

FARNSWORTH, E(DWARD) ALLAN, lawyer, educator; b. Providence, June 30, 1928; s. Harrison Edward and Gertrude (Romig) F.; m. Patricia Ann Nordstrom, May 30, 1952; children: Jeanne Scott, Karen Ladd, Edward Allan (dec.), Pamela Ann. BS, U. Mich., 1948; MA, Yale U., 1949; JD (Ordronaux prize 1952), Columbia U., 1952; LLD (hon.), Dickinson Law Sch., Pa. State U., 1988; Docteur en Droit (hon.), U. Paris, 1988, U. Louvain, 1989. Bar: D.C 1952, N.Y. 1956. Mem. faculty Columbia U., N.Y.C., 1954—, prof. law, 1959—, Alfred McCormack prof. law, 1970—. Vis. prof. U. Istanbul, U. Dakar, 1964, U. Paris, 1974-75, 90, 93, Harvard Law S ch., 1970-71, Stetson Coll. Law, 1991, 94, U. Mich., 1994; mem. faculty Salzburg Seminar Am. Law, 1963, Columbia-Leyden-Amsterdam program on Am. law, 1964, 69, 73, 85, San Diego Inst. Internat. and Comparative Law, Paris, 1982, 94, Tulane Summer Inst., Paris, 1995, 98, 99, 00, Rhodes, 1996, China Ctr. for Am. Law Study, Beijing, 1986; dir. orientation program on Am. law Assn. Am. Law Schs., 1965-68; U.S. rep. UN Commn. on Internat. Trade Law, 1970-81; reporter Restatement of Contracts 2nd, 1971-80; cons. N.Y. State Law Revision Commn., 1956, 58, 59, 61, P.R. comml. code revision, 1988-91; mem. coms. validity and agy. internat. sales contracts Internat. Inst. Unification Pvt. Law, Rome, 1966-72, mem. governing coun., 1978-98; mem. adv. com. on pvt. internat. law Sec. of State, 1985-89; spl. counsel city reorgn. N.Y.C. Coun., 1966-68; U.S. del. Vienna Conf. on Internat. Sales Law, 1980, Bucharest and Geneva Conf. on Internat. Agy., 1979, 83. Author: Changing Your Mind: The Law of Regretted Decisions, 1998, An Introduction to the Legal System of the United States, 3d edit., 1993; (with J. Honnold, S. Harris, C. Mooney, and C. Reitz) Cases and Materials on Commercial Law, 5th edit., 1993; (with W.F. Young and C. Sanger) Cases and Materials on Contracts, 6th edit., 2001, Cases and Materials on Negotiable Instruments, 4th edit., 1993, Treatise on Contracts, 1982, 3d edit., 1999; (with V. Mozolin) Contract Law in the USSR and the United States, 1987, Farnsworth on Contracts, 3 vols., 1990, 2nd edit., 1998, United States Contract Law, 1992, 2d revised edit, 1999. Capt. USAAF, 1952-54. Fellow British Acad.; mem. ABA (Theberge award for pvt. internat. law 1996), Am. Philos. Soc., Am. Law Inst., Assn. of Bar of City of N.Y. (chmn. com. on fgn. and comparative law 1967-70, chmn. spl. com. on products liability 1979-82), Phi Beta Kappa, Phi Delta Phi. Unitarian Universalist. Home: 201 Lincoln St Englewood NJ 07631-3158 Office: Columbia U 435 W 116th St New York NY 10027-7201 E-mail: allan@law.columbia.edu.

FARNSWORTH, ELIZABETH, broadcast journalist; b. Mpls., Dec. 23, 1943; d. H. Bernerd and Jane (Mills) Fink; m. Charles E. Farnsworth, June 20, 1966; children: Jennifer Farnsworth Fellows, Samuel. BA, Middlebury Coll., 1965; MA in History, Stanford U., 1966; LLD (hon.), Colby Coll., 2002. Reporter, panelist PBS World Press, KQED, San Francisco, 1975-77; reporter InterNews, Berkeley, Calif., 1977-80; freelance TV and print reporter, San Francisco, 1980-91; fgn. corr. MacNeil/Lehrer News Hour, San Francisco, 1991-95; chief corr., prin. substitute anchor News Hour with Jim Lehrer, Arlington, Va., 1995-97, San Francisco, 1997-99, sr. corr., 1999—. Co-author: El Bloqueo Invisible, 1974; prodr., dir. documentary Thanh's War, 1991 (Cine Golden Eagle award); contbr. articles to various publs. Mem. adv. bd. Berkeley Edn. Found., 1990-95, U. Calif. Sch. Journalism, Berkeley; mem. nat. adv. bd. Ctr. Investigative Reporting, 2001-; bd. dirs. Data Ctr., Oakland, Calif., 1993-95. Recipient Golden Gate award San Francisco Film Festival, 1984, Best Investigative Reporting award No. Calif. Radio, TV News Dirs.' Assn., 1986, Blue Ribbon, Am. Film and Video Festival, 1991, Silver World medal N.Y. Film Festivals, 2001; nominee Emmy award, 2002. Mem. AFTRA, NATAS, World Affairs Coun. No. Calif. (bd. dirs. 1998—), Nat. Adv. Writers Corps, Phi Beta Kappa. Presbyterian. Avocations: gardening, hiking, writing poetry.

FARNSWORTH, FRANK ALBERT, retired economics educator; s. Frank Adelbert and Lancing Claudine (Miller) F.; m. Ruth Coburn, June 26 1943 (dec. Dec. 1970); children: Frank A., Ruth Farnsworth Eldridge, John C.; m. Elizabeth Hoyt Martire, Dec. 26, 1971 (dec. June 1988); children: Elizabeth M. Cutter-Hickman, Amy Martire, John Martire. AB in Econs. with honors, Colgate U., 1939; AM, Harvard U., 1946, PhD, 1952. With dept. econ. Colgate U., 1941-87, prof., 1957-87, ret., 1987. Dept. chmn., vis. rsch. assoc. Grad. Bus. Sch., Harvard U., 1947-48; Fulbright prof. Norwegian Sch. Econ., Bergen, 1954-55; vis. prof. small bus. Wake Forest U., 1975; vis. fellow Massey Coll.-U. Toronto, Ont., Can., 1968; ex-officio mem. Madison County Indsl. Devel. Agy.; bd. dir. Otter Valley Press, Inc., Am. Tree Farmer, Svc. Corp. of Ret. Execs.; cons. in field. Mem. AAUP, Am. Mgmt. Assn., N.Y. State Econ. Devel. Coun., Masons, Alpha Chi Epsilon, Alpha Delta Phi. Republican. Baptist. Home: 17 E Kendrick Ave Hamilton NY 13346-1311 Office: 1119 Wheeler Rd Brandon VT 05733-8922 E-mail: vtotter@together.net., farnsworth@Mail.Colgate.Edu.

FARNSWORTH, STEPHEN JAMES, political science educator, writer; b. Burlington, Vt., Apr. 25, 1961; s. Willis H. and Margaret L. Farnsworth. BA in Govt., Dartmouth Coll., 1983; BA in History, U. Mo., Kansas City, 1990; MA in Govt., Georgetown U., 1993, PhD in Govt., 1997. Staff reporter Kansas City Star & Times, 1985-90; nat. econs. corr. Fairchild News Svc., Washington, 1990-93; rschr. Ctr. for Study of Responsive Law, Washington, 1993-94; lectr. Georgetown U., Washington, 1994-95; sr. lectr. polit. sci. Mary Washington Coll., Fredericksburg, Va., 1995, instr. polit. sci., 1996-97, asst. prof. polit. sci., 1997—2002, assoc. prof., 2002—. Author: Political Support in a Frustrated America; co-author: (with S. Robert Lichter) The Nightly News Nightmare: Network Television's Coverage of U.S. Presidential Elections, 1988-2000; contbr. articles to profl. jours. Mem. Am. Polit. Sci. Assn., Midwest Polit. Sci. Assn., So. Polit. Sci. Assn. Office: Mary Washington Coll 1301 College Ave Fredericksburg VA 22401-5300 E-mail: sfarnswo@mwc.edu.

FARNSWORTH, T. BROOKE, lawyer; b. Grand Rapids, Mich., Mar. 16, 1945; s. George Llelwyn and Gladys Fern (Kennedy) Farnsworth; m. Connie D. Hedblom, June 15, 1996; children: Leslie Erin, T. Brooke. BS in Bus., Ind. U., 1967; JD, Ind. U., Indpls., 1971. Bar: Tex. 1971, U.S. Dist. Ct. (so. dist.) Tex. 1972, U.S. Tax Ct. 1972, U.S. Ct. Appeals (5th cir.) 1977, U.S. Ct. Appeals (D.C. Cir.) 1977, U.S. Supreme Ct. 1978, U.S. Ct. Appeals (11th cir.) 1982, U.S. Dist. Ct. (we. dist.) Tex. 1988, U.S. Dist. Ct. (no. dist.) Tex. 1994, U.S. Ct. Appeals (10th cir.) 2003. Adminstrv. asst. to treas. of State of Ind., Indpls., 1968-71; assoc. Butler, Binion, Rice, Cook & Knapp, Houston, 1971-74; counsel Damson Oil Corp., Houston, 1974-78; prin. Farnsworth & Assocs., Houston, 1978-90, Farnsworth & von Berg, Houston, 1990—. Contbr. articles on law to profl. jours. Mem.: ATLA, ABA, Tex. Trial Lawyers Assn., Fed. Energy Bar Assn., Houston Bar Assn., State Bar Tex., Fed. Bar Assn., Champions Golf Club, Loch Lomond Golf Club, Olympic Club. Republican. Home: 6038 Pebble Beach Dr Houston TX 77069 Office: Farnsworth and von Berg 333 N Sam Houston Pkwy E Ste 300 Houston TX 77060-2414

FARON, FAY CHERYL, private investigator, writer; b. Kansas City, Mo. d. Albert David and Geraldine Fay (Morgan) F. Student, Glendale (Ariz.) C.C., 1967-68, Ariz. State U., 1968-71, U. Ariz., 1971-72. Lic. pvt. investigator, Calif. Owner Monogramation, San Francisco, 1976-80; assoc. prodr. Sta. KGO-TV, San Francisco, 1980-81, Power/Rector, San Francisco, 1982-83; owner Office in the City, San Francisco, 1982-83, The Rat Dog Dick Detective Agy., San Francisco, 1983—. Lectr., spkr. San Francisco U., 1984—, San Francisco Assn. Legal Assts., 1984—, Commonwealth Club San Francisco, 1987, Calif. Collectors Coun., San Francisco, 1992—, Book Passage Mystery Writers Conf., 1997-99. Author: A Private Eye's Guide to Collecting a Bad Debt, 1991, Missing Persons, 1997; author/editor: The Instant National Locator Guide, 1991, 2nd edit., 1993, 3rd edit, 1996, Rip-Off, 1998; columnist Ask Rat Dog, 1993—; host, writer: (Court TV Crime Story Spl.) Rip-Offs and Scams, 2000. Co-founder, pres. bd. ElderAngels, San Francisco. Subject of Jack Olsen's book, Hastened to the Grave, 1998. Mem. Nat. Assn. Investigative Specialists, Nat. Assn. Bunco Investigators (asst.), Profls. Against Confidence Crimes (asst.), Sisters in Crime. Avocations: biking, camping, horseback riding, river rafting, travel.

FARON, ROBERT STEVEN, lawyer; b. N.Y.C., Jan. 10, 1947; s. Jack and Ceil Faron; m. Linda A. Baumann, May 18, 1975; children: Gregory Andrew, Douglas James, Daniel Scott. BS in Engring., Princeton U., 1968; JD, Columbia U., 1975. Bar: D.C. 1975, U.S. Ct. Appeals (D.C. cir.) 1978, U.S. Ct. Appeals (4th cir.) 1986, U.S. Ct. Claims 1986. Systems engr. IBM Corp., Holmdel, N.J., 1968-69; atty. U.S. Dept. of Commerce, Washington, 1975-76; fgn. svc. officer U.S. Dept. of State, Washington, 1976-77; assoc. LeBoef, Lamb, Leiby & MacRae, Washington, 1977-82; of counsel Lane & Mittendorf, Washington, 1982-84, Brown, Roady, Bonvillian & Gold, Washington, 1984-85; ptnr. Alagia, Day, Marshall, Mintmire & Chauvin, Washington, 1986-90; dep. asst. gen. counsel for environ. Dept. of Energy, Washington, 1990-93; asst. gen. counsel Amerada Hess Corp., 1993-97; sr. advisor PHB Hagler Bailly, Inc., Washington, 1997-2000; pvt. practice, 2001— Chair energy com. D.C. Bar sect. environ. energy and nat. resources. Contbr. articles to profl. jours. Capt. USAF, 1969—72. Mem. ABA (chmn. TIPS energy resources law com. 1988-89, 91-97, mem. TIPS profl. issues com. 1989-92, coordinating group energy law 1989-94), Assoc. Internat. de Droit des Assurances (chmn. U.S. pollution law working party 1986-89). Office: Law Offices Ste 708 1330 New Hampshire Ave NW Washington DC 20036 E-mail: rsfaron@verizon.net.

FARQUHAR, JOHN WILLIAM, physician, educator; b. Winnipeg, Man., Can., June 13, 1927; arrived in U.S., 1934; s. John Giles and Marjorie Victoria (Roberts) Farquhar; m. Christine Louise Johnson, July 14, 1968; children: Margaret F., John C.M.;children from previous marriage: Bruce E., Douglas G. AB, U. Calif., Berkeley, 1949; MD, U. Calif., San Francisco, 1952. Intern U. Calif. Hosp., San Francisco, 1952—53, resident, 1953—54, 1957—58, post-doctoral fellow, 1955—57; resident U. Minn., Mpls., 1954—55; rsch. assoc. Rockefeller U., N.Y.C., 1958—62; asst. prof. medicine Stanford (Calif.) U., 1962—66, assoc. prof., 1966—73, prof., 1978—, C.F. Rehnborg prof. in disease prevention, 1989—2000; dir. Stanford Ctr. Rsch. in Disease Prevention, 1973—98; dir. collaborating ctr. for chronic disease prevention WHO, 1985—99; prof. health rsch. and policy, 1988—. Mem. staff Stanford U. Hosp.; chair Victoria Declaration Implementation com. Author: The American Way of Life Need Not Be Hazardous to Your Health, 1978, 1987; author: (with Gene Spiller) The Last Puff, 1990; author: The Victoria Declaration for Heart Health, 1992, How to Reduce Your Risk of Heart Disease, 1994, The Catalonia Declaration: Investing in Heart Health, 1996, Worldwide Efforts to Improve Heart Disease, 1997; author: (with Spiller) Diagnosis Heart Disease: Answers to Your Questions about Recovery and Lasting Health, 2001; contbr. articles to profl. jours. Served with U.S. Army, 1944—46. Recipient James D. Bruce award, ACP, 1983, Myrdal prize, 1986, Dana award for Pioneering Achievement in Health, Dana Found., 1990, Nat. Cholesterol award for Pub. Edn., Nat. Cholesterol Edn. Program of NIH, 1991, Rsch. Achievement award, Am. Heart Assn., 1992, Order of St. George for Svc. to Autonomous Govt. of Catalonia, 1996, Joseph Stokes Preventive Cardiology award, Am. Soc. Preventive Cardiology, 1999, Ancel Keys Meml. lectureship, Am. Heart Assn., 2000. Mem.: Internat. Heart Health Soc., Soc. Behavioral Medicine (pres. 1991—92), Am. Heart Assn. (coun. epidemiology and prevention), Am. Soc. Clin. Investigation, Inst. Medicine NAS, Gold Headed Cane Soc., Alpha Omega Alpha, Sigma Xi. Episcopalian. Office: Stanford U Sch of Medicine Ctr Rsch in Disease Prevention 730 Welch Rd Palo Alto CA 94304-1583 Fax: 650-723-7018. E-mail: JFarquhar@stanford.edu.

FARQUHAR, MARILYN GIST, cell biology and pathology educator; b. Tulare, Calif., July 11, 1928; d. Brooks DeWitt and Alta (Green) Gist; m. John W. Farquhar, June 4, 1952; children: Bruce, Douglas (div. 1968); m. George Palade, June 7, 1970. AB, U. Calif., Berkeley, 1949, MA, 1952, PhD, 1955. Asst. rsch. pathologist Sch. Medicine U. Calif., San Francisco, 1956-58, assoc. rsch. pathologist, 1962-64, assoc. prof., 1964-68, prof. pathology, 1968-70; rsch. assoc. Rockefeller U., N.Y.C., 1958-62, prof. cell biology, 1970-73, Sch. Medicine Yale U., New Haven, 1973-87, Sterling prof. cell biology and pathology, 1987-90; prof. pathology cell molecular medicine U. Calif., San Diego, 1990—, chair divsn. cellular and molecular medicine, 1991-99, prof. cellular & molecular medicine, chair dept. cellular & molecular medicine, 1999—. Mem. editorial bd. numerous sci. jours.; contbr. articles to profl. jours. Recipient Career Devel. award NIH, 1968-73, Disting. Sci. medal Electron Microscope Soc., 1987, Gomori medal Histochem. Soc., 1999, A.N. Richards award Internat. Soc. Nephrology, 2003. Mem.: NAS, Internat. Soc. Nephrology (A.N. Richards award 2003), Am. Soc. Nephrology (Homer Smith award 1988, Gottschalk award 2002), Am. Assn. Investigative Pathology (Rous Whipple award 2001), Am. Soc. Cell Biology (pres. 1981—82, E.B. Wilson medal 1987), Am. Acad. Arts and Scis. Home and Office: U Calif San Diego Sch Med 12894 Via Latina Del Mar CA 92014-3730

FARQUHAR, ROBERT NICHOLS, lawyer; b. Dayton, Ohio, Apr. 23, 1936; s. Robert Lawrence and Mary Frances (Nichols) F.; m. Elizabeth Lynn Bryan, Aug. 29, 1959 (div. 1971); children: Robert Nichols, Laura Ann; m. Carol A. Smith, Dec. 27, 1975. AB, Kenyon Coll., 1958; JD, Cornell U., 1961. Bar: Ohio 1961, Mich. 1993, U.S. Dist. Ct. (so. dist.) Ohio 1962, U.S. Ct. Appeals (6th cir.) 1966, U.S. Supreme Ct. 1978. Assoc. Altick & McDaniel, Dayton, 1961-69; ptnr. Gould, Bailey & Farquhar and predecessor firms, Dayton, 1969-78, Brumbaugh, Corwin & Gould, Dayton, 1978-80, Altick & Corwin, Dayton, 1981—, pres., 1996—. Bd. dirs. Ohio Law Abstract Pub., Columbus; city atty., Centerville, Ohio, 1969—, Oakwood, Ohio, 1997—2003; sec., gen. counsel Miami Conservancy Dist., 1990—; bd. commrs. character and fitness Ohio Supreme Ct., 1988-94, 97-2003, chair, 2000-02. Mem. Montgomery County Rep. Ctrl. Com, 1965-69, exec. com., 1968-69; bd. dirs. Centerville Hist. Soc., 1971-75, pres. 1973-74; trustee Montgomery County Legal Aid Soc., 1972-76; trustee Dayton Law Libr. Assn., 1972—, pres., 1980-86; mem. governing bd.äv. bdä Carillon Hist. Park, Dayton, chair, 1999-2001; mem. congressional screening com. U.S. Naval Acad., 1979-83. Mem. ABA (ho. of dels. 2001—), Ohio State Bar Assn. (chmn. legal ethics and profl. conduct com. 1982-86, exec. com. 1988-91, coun. of dels. 1988—), Dayton Bar Assn. Found. (pres. 1984-90), Dayton Bicycle Club, Dayton Lawyers Club, Delta Phi, Phi Delta Phi. Episcopalian. Home: 1731 Ladera Trl Dayton OH 45459-1403 Office: Altick & Corwin 1700 One Dayton Ctr 1 S Main St Dayton OH 45402-2024 E-mail: nikfar@aol.com., farquhar@altickcorwin.com.

FARQUHAR, ROBIN HUGH, former university president; b. Victoria, B.C., Can., Dec. 1, 1938; s. Hugh Ernest and Jean (MacIntosh) F.; m. Frances Harriet Caswell, July 6, 1963; children: Francine Jean, Katherine Lynn, Susan Ann. BA with honors, U. B.C., 1960, MA, 1964; PhD, U. Chgo., 1967; Hon. Diploma in Adult Edn., Red River C.C., 1989. Tchr., counsellor, coach Edward Milne Secondary Sch., Sooke, B.C., 1962-64; assoc. dir., then dep. dir. Univ. Council Ednl. Adminstrn., Columbus, Ohio, 1966-71; chmn. ednl. adminstrn. dept., asst. dir. Ont. Inst. Studies in Edn., Toronto, 1971-76; prof. U. Toronto, 1974-76; prof., dean Coll. Edn., U. Sask., Saskatoon, 1976-81; prof., pres. U. Winnipeg, 1981-89, Carleton U., Ottawa, Ont., 1989-96, prof. policy pub. and adminstrn., 1996—; spl. advisor to pres. of Salzburg Seminar, 2002. Author: The Humanities in Preparing Educational Administrators, 1970, Preparing Educational Leaders: A Review of Recent Literature, 1972; editor: Social Science Content for Preparing Educational Leaders, 1973, Educational Administration in Australia and Abroad: Analyses and Challenges, 1975, Canadian and Comparative Educational Administration, 1980, The Canadian School Superintendent, 1989, Advancing Education: School Leadership in Action, 1991, Advancing the Canadian Agenda for International Education, 2001; mem. editl. bd. Jour. Edn. Adminstrn., 1973-86. Served with Can. Navy Res., 1956-64. Recipient Edward L. Bernays Found. prize, 1968, Commemorative medal for 125th Anniversary of Confedn. of Can., 1993, Ottawa-Carleton Partnership award of excellence for leadership, 1996, Can. Bur. Internat. Edn. award of Merit, 1998; named Hon. Citizen, City of Winnipeg, 1989; hon. mem. Scouts Can., 1992. Fellow Commonwealth Coun. Ednl. Adminstrn. (former pres.); mem. Can. Bur. Internat. Edn. (former chmn.), Can. Soc. Study Edn. (former pres.), Can. Edn. Assn. (former dir.), InterAm. Soc. for Ednl. Adminstrn. (former dir.), Ottawa-Carleton Econ. Devel. Corp. (former dir.), Ottawa-Carleton Rsch. Inst. (former dir.), Corp. Higher Edn. Forum (former dir.), Nat. Acad. of Sch. Execs. (former dir.). E-mail: rfarquha@ccs.carleton.ca.

FARQUHARSON, GORDON MACKAY, lawyer, director; b. Charlottetown, P.E.I., Can., July 12, 1928; s. Percy Alfred and Rachel Lillian (MacKay) F.; m. Judy Lynne Bridges, Oct. 10, 1980; children: Trevor, Jordan; children by previous marriage: Douglas, Tanyss, Rob, Caryn. BA, U. Toronto, 1950; LL.B., Osgoode Hall Law Sch., 1954. Bar: Called to Ont. bar 1954; Queen's Counsel 1965. Pvt. practice, Toronto, 1954—; ptnr. Lang Michener, 1964—. Dir. Valleydene Corp. Ltd., Doverhold Investments Ltd. Mem. University Club (Toronto), Craigleigh Ski Club, Phi Gamma Delta (pres. 1950). Home: 419 Brunswick Ave Toronto ON Canada Office: BCE Pl 181 Bay St Ste 2500 Toronto ON Canada M5J 2T7

FARQUHARSON, PATRICE ELLEN, primary school educator; b. West Haven, Conn., Feb. 10, 1956; d. Robert Douglas and Margaret Ellen (Dietle) Farquharson; children: Julia, Elena. BS in Edn., U. Conn., 1978; MS in Edn., So. Conn. State U., 1984; EdD, Nova Southeastern U., 1995. Cert. tchr., adminstr., Conn. Asst. dir. West Haven (Conn.) Child Devel. Ctr., 1978-82, exec. dir., 1982-96, 97—; edn. cons. dept. pediatrics div. child and family studies U. Conn., 1993-95; mgmt. cons. West Haven Child Devel. Ctr., Inc., 1996—; asst. prof. early childhood, dir. early childhood programs Teikyo-Post U., Waterbury, Conn., 1996—. Adj. prof. U. Conn. Inst. Pub. Policy, 1996; cons. early childhood edn., workshop presenter, Internat. and New Eng., 1987—; profl. cheerleader The New Eng. Patriots football team, 1980; dir., ptnr. New Eng. Cheerleading Camp, West Haven, 1982-84; cheerleading coach U. New Haven, 1982-90; textbook webguide developer Thomson Pub., 2001; online course developer Teikyo Post U. Conn. Early Childhood Edn. Coun. scholar, 1993-96. Mem. AAUW, Nat. Assn. Edn. Young Children, Conn. Assn. Edn. Young Children, Coalition for Children (Jimmy Fund Cmty. Svc. award 2001), Dirs. Forum, Gov. Adv. Coun. Early Childhood Edn., South Ctrl. Conn. Agy. on Aging (adv. coun.), West Haven Rotary Club. Avocations: ballet, jazz dancing, horseback riding, reading, traveling. Home: 5 Sunflower Cir West Haven CT 06516-6229 Office: West Haven Child Devel Ctr 201 Noble St West Haven CT 06516-6047

FARR, CHARLES SIMS, lawyer; b. Hewlett, N.Y., June 29, 1920; s. John Farr and Hazel (Zealy) Sims; m. Mary Randolph Rue, Dec. 21, 1946 (dec. Dec. 1980); children: Charles Sims, Virginia Farr Ramsey, Randolph Rue, John II; m. Muriel Tobin Byrnes, Oct. 13, 1990. Student, Princeton U., 1938-40; LLB, Columbia U., 1948. Bar: N.Y. 1949, Fla. 1984. Assoc. White & Case, N.Y.C., 1948-58, ptnr., 1959-88, of counsel, 1989-92, ret. Contbr. articles to profl. publs. Chmn. Commonwealth Fund, N.Y.C., 1976-93; trustee St. Luke's-Roosevelt Hosp. Ctr., 1968-92, Gen. Theol. Sem., 1968-77, N.Y. Zool. Soc., Kent Sch.; mem. bd. fgn. parishes Protestant Episcopal Ch., 1954-78, pres. 1977; chancellor to pres. bishop Protestant Episcopal Ch. in U.S.A., 1977-85; vestryman St. James Ch., N.Y.C., 1966-76; sr. warden, 1973-76, jr. warden, 1984-86; mem. coun. Rockefeller U., 1980-92; former mem. bd. visitors Columbia U. Sch. Law. Lt. comdr. USN, 1941—45, ETO, MTO, PTO. Recipient medal Columbia U. Alumni Assn., 1977. Fellow Am. Coll. Probate Counsel (regent 1960-75), Am. Bar Found.; mem. ABA (chmn. tax aspects decendent's estates 1974-76, div. dirs. real property, probate and trust law sect. 1976-78, chmn. com. application securities laws to fiduciaries 1974-76), N.Y. State Bar Assn. (chmn. trusts and estates com. 1966-68), Assn. of Bar of City of N.Y. (com. profl. responsibility 1972-74), Century Club (trustee 1992-95), Links Club, River Club, Pilgrims Club, Yeamans Hall (S.C.). Independent. Home: PO Box 9455 900 Yeamans Hall Rd Charleston SC 29410 also: 200 E 66th St Apt E802 New York NY 10021-9192

FARR, DAVID C.M. non-profit organizational business development, consultant; s. Charles E. and Jean C. Farr; m. Diana J. Keech, Aug. 10, 1991; children: Peter I.D., Rachel H.G. BFA, Colo. State U., 1982—86; M in Urban Regional Planning, U. Colo., Denver, 1986—88; MDiv, Denver Sem., 1993—96. Advancement officer Denver Sem., 1993—96; maj. gifts dir. Promise Keepers, Denver, 1996—2000; sr. cons. TouchPoint Solutions, Colorado Springs, 2000—02, The Elevation Group, Colorado Springs, 2002—. Key man Promise Keepers, Denver, 1993—2000. Recipient Order of Omega, Internat. Pan Hellenic Coun., 1985, 1986. R-Consevative. Christian. Avocations: running, tennis, writing. Office: The Elevation Group 5145 Centennial Blvd Ste 220 Colorado Springs CO 80919

FARR, DAVID N. electronics executive; BS in Chemistry, Wake Forest U.; MBA, Vanderbilt U. With Emerson, 1981—, exec. v.p., 1997—99, sr. exec. v.p., COO, 1999—2000, CEO, 2000—. Office: Emerson 8000 W Florissant Ave PO Box 4100 Saint Louis MO 63136

FARR, DONALD EUGENE, engineering scientist; b. Clinton, Iowa, July 1, 1933; s. Kenneth Elroy and Nellie Irene (Bailey) F.; m. Sally Joyce Brauer, Mar. 8, 1954; children: Erika Lyn Farr Leventis, Jolene Karyn Farr Walters. BA in Engring. Psychology, San Diego State U., 1961; MT with honors, Nat. U., 1974; postgrad., Calif. Pacific U., 1976-80. Human factors specialist Bunker Ramo Corp., Canoga Park, Calif., Germany, 1964-69; sr. design specialist Gen. Dynamics, San Diego, 1955-63, 69-76; tech. staff Sandia Nat. Labs., Albuquerque, 1977-80; group supr., sr. tech. advisor The Babcock and Wilcox Co., Lynchburg, Va., 1980-82; dir. human factors sys. Sci. Applications, Inc., Lynchburg, 1982-83; human engring. scientist Lockheed Calif. Co., Burbank, 1983-91; MANPRINT mgr. Teledyne Electronic Sys., Northridge, Calif., 1991-94; human engring. scientist, program mgr. Symvionics, Inc., Pasadena, Calif., 1994—. Ergonomics safety cons. govt., industry and academia, 1977—; instr. human factors/design psychology Art Ctr. Coll. of Design, Pasadena, Calif., 2000—. Contbr. articles to profl. jours. Precinct capt., voter registration vol. Rep. Party, 1963—; lectr., support group Am. Diabetes Assn., L.A., 1993—. With USN, 1952-53. Scholarship USN, 1953; recipient Admiral's award NSIA, 1963. Mem. Human Factors and Ergonomics Soc. (pres. San Diego, L.A. chpt.), Internat. Numismatic Soc. (pres. 1973-75), Am. Nuclear Soc. (human factors chair 1980-82), Am. Legion, NRA Golden Eagles (honor role). Lutheran. Avocations: bridge, numismatics, genealogy, computer graphics, travel. Home: 20054 Avenue Of The Oaks Newhall CA 91321-1361 Office: Symvionics Inc 3280 E Foothill Blvd Ste 200 Pasadena CA 91107-3187 E-mail: dfarr@earthlink.net.

FARR, G(ARDNER) NEIL, retired lawyer; b. L.A., Jan. 9, 1932; s. Gardner and Elsie M. (Schuster) F.; m. Lorna Jean, Oct. 26, 1957; children: Marshall Clay, Jennifer T., Thomas M. BA, U. Calif., Berkeley, 1957; JD, U. Calif., San Francisco, 1960. Bar: Calif. 1961, U.S. Supreme Ct. 1977; cert. specialist family law Calif. Bd. Specialization. Dep. dist. atty. Solano County, 1961-66; recreation commr. City of Fairfield, 1964-66; dep. dist. atty. Kern County, 1966-69; ptnr. Law Offices Young Wooldridge, Bakersfield, Calif., 1969—, Judge protem Kern County Superior Ct. Chmn. Kern County Juvenile Justice Commn. With USNR, 1949-53. Mem. ABA, Calif. Bar Assn., Kern County Bar Assn. (pres. 1984, past pres. family law sect.). Office: Young Wooldridge 1800 30th St Fl 4 Bakersfield CA 93301-1919 Fax: 661-327-1087.

FARR, IVANNE ESTELLE, small business owner, consultant, artist, sculptor; b. Texarkana, Ark., Feb. 7, 1940; d. Franklin Lynnwood and Leone Faye (Seedig) F.; m. William D. Alsup, Aug. 27, 1960 (div. Aug. 1975); children: Joe Farr, Mark De Witt, Lara LeAnne. Student, S.W. Tex.U.; cert. diamond,

Gemological Inst. Am., 1979. Founder, owner Ivanne et Cie, Inc., Corpus Christi, Tex., 1976—; v.p. Internat. Agri-Ventures, Inc., Corpus Christi, 1985—89; owner Bosque River Valley Breeders, Ltd., Emu prodn. facilities, Meridian, Tex., 1990—97. Cons. C.I.C.C., Inc., Montreal, Can., 1985, Mexican Jewelers Assn., Mexico City, 1988, Jireh Resources, Inc., Paris, 1988; co-founder, charter pres. Bosque County Tourism Coun., Inc., 1992; co-founder Farr Rsch. Internat.; cons. Bibl. Archaeology Mus., Springfield, Mo., 1997; co-founder, chmn., chair Odyssey of Flight, 1991-94; chmn. John A. Lomax Gathering Trading Post Silent Auction, 1991-94; bd. dirs. Econ. Opportunities Advancement Corp., Region XI, 2002—. Mem. Mus. Oriental Culture; bd. dirs. Chem. Dependency Unit South Tex., Coastal Bend Youth City, Palmer Drug Abuse Program; bd. of govs., chmn. membership com. Art Mus. South Tex.; chmn. bd. govs., co-founder Alliance for Justice Found., Inc., 1988—; docent Fossil Rim Wildlife Ctr., Glenrose, Tex.; pres. Bosque County Tourism Coun., 1999-2003; co-founder Bosque County Chisholm Trail Cowboy Gathering Trail Ride and Rendezvous, 2000-01, Tex. Chisholm Trail Cowboy Heritage Celebration, 2002-03, co-chmn., 2002, founding pres. Tex. Chisholm Trail Assn. Mem. Gemological Inst. Am., Coast Conservation Assn., Inst. Tex. Cultures (amb.), Jewelers Assn. Am., Marine Mil. Acad. Parents Assn., Navy League (bd. dirs.), Norwegian Soc. Tex., PTA, Scandinavian Soc. South Tex. (co-founder), Tex. Jewelers Assn., Internat. Group (co-founder), Corpus Christi C. of C. (bd. dirs.), Corpus Christi Area Econ. Devel. Corp. (internat. com.), Am. Emu Assn., Tex. Emu Assn., Emu Coop., Am. Assn. Museums, Ducks Unltd., Mid-Morning Group (co-founder), Daus. of the King Internat., SWT Alumni Assn.. Republican. Episcopalian. Avocations: water skiing, snow skiing, travelling, sailing, opera. E-mail: farrlands@hotmail.com., ifarr@pardners.org.

FARR, JESSE F. federal agency administrator; b. Scranton, Pennsylvania, Feb. 5, 1915; s. Edward Farr Jr. and Leah Frisby Farr; m. Mary Elizabeth Davison; children: Lee Anne Geiger, Jesse Edward. Student, Powell Bus. Coll., Scranton, 1934—35; BS, Lafayette Coll., 1938. Chief indsl. rate analysis Phila. Electric Co., 1941—42; asst. legal attaché Am. Embassy, Paris, 1965—68; spl. agent unit chief FBI, Washington, staff supr. Balt. Author: (short stories) Nuke Sub Sold. Former pres. Beach Lake Vol. Fire Dept.; 1st reader Christian Sci. Ch., Towson, Md. Mem.: Beach Lake Hunting Club (former pres.).

FARR, LONA MAE, non-profit executive, business owner; b. Phila., June 4, 1941; d. Alonzo Schroeder and Lillyan (Nickels) F.; m. Malcolm J. Gross, Aug. 24, 1963 (div. Mar. 1976); children: Andrea Lillyan, Stacey Jane, John Farr; m. David V. Voellinger, Sept. 27, 1981. AB in History and English, Muhlenberg Coll., 1962; MS in Edn., Temple U., 1968; PhD in Philanthropy, Union Inst., 1995. Advanced cert. in fund raising. Master tchr. Swain Sch., Allentown, Pa., 1962-63; tchr. St. Monica's Sch., Berwyn, Pa., 1963-65, Hebrew Day Sch., Scranton, Pa., 1965-66; pub. rels. assoc. Muhlenberg Coll., Allentown, 1973-75, dir. alumni affairs, 1975-77; dir. devel. and pub. rels. De Sales U., Allentown, 1977-81; dir. pub. rels. Good Shepherd Home, Allentown, 1981-84, dir. devel., 1984-87, group exec., v.p. instnl. devel., 1987-92; v.p. instl. devel. Luth. Home at Topton, Pa., 1992-96, spl. adv. to pres., 1996—; prin. Farr Healey Cons. LLC, 1996—. Author: A Story of Two Cultures: The Germans and the Puerto Ricans, 2000; prodr. (films) More Than a Name, 1983 (Golden Eagle award 1984), Venture of Faith, 1984 (silver medal N.Y. Film Festival 1985), Spirit of Good Shepherd Day, 1987, Aspects of Topton, 1993 (1st place PANPHA), Topton New Century, 1993 (1st place PANPHA), They Came to Topton, 1994, A Gift of Love, 1995, (video) The Best You Can Be, 1988; contbr. articles to profl. jours. Bd. dirs. Muhlenberg Coll.; past bd. dirs. Kids Peace, Allentown Symphony, Baum Sch. Art, Allentown, United Way Lehigh Valley; past adviser Lehigh County Human Svcs., Allentown, 1986-91; mem. exec. bd. Harris York Condo Assn., 2000—. Recipient Disting. Sales award Sales and Mktg. Execs. Lehigh Valley, 1984, 1st place award in mktg. and pub. rels. Pa. Assn. Nonprofit Homes for Aging, 1994. Mem.: Appalachian Health Care Pub. Rels./Mktg. Assn. (pres. 1987), Nat. Soc. Fund Raising Execs. (founding pres. Ea. Pa. chpt. 1986—88, vice chair profl. enhancement bd. dirs. 1987—, past chair cert. bd., vice chair profl. advancement com., Girl Scout Disting Alumni award, Outstanding Exec. award 1988, Fund Raising Exec. of Yr. 1988), Nat. Soc. Hosp. Devel., Pub. Rels. Soc. Am., Muhlenberg Coll. Alumni Assn. (pres. 1981—85), Ea. Pa. BBB (bd. dirs.), Quota Club (pres. Allentown 1986—88), Liberty Bell Rotary (Allentown, pres. 1993—94, asst. dist. gov. rotary dist. 7430 2000—02). Avocations: reading, walking, travel, gourmet cooking. Home and Office: 2485 Houghton Ln Macungie PA 18062 *To live life to its fullest, endeavor each day to reach out to others in love; open your mind to learn something new, and lead others to do the same. This is living by what I call the Four "L's".*

FARR, MARCIA ELIZABETH, English and linguistics educator; b. Berkeley, Calif., Mar. 25, 1944; d. Richard Arthur and Mary Margaret (Bollinger) F.; m. David Lee Whiteman, July 30, 1966 (div. July 1981); 1 child, Julianna Downing; m. Michael David Maltz, Dec. 2, 1984; stepchildren: David Selby, Robert Reeves. BA in English, Ohio Wesleyan U., 1965; MA in Linguistics, Am. U., 1970; PhD in Linguistics, Georgetown U., 1976. Sr. rsch. assoc. Nat. Inst. of Edn., Washington, 1976-82; assoc. to full prof. English and linguistics U. Ill., Chgo., 1982—2002; prof. of edn. and English Ohio State U., 2002—. Adv. bd. Ctr. for the Study of Writing, U. Calif., Berkeley, 1986-96. Co-author: Language Diversity and Writing Instruction, 1986; editor: Variation in Writing, 1981, Ethnolinguistic Chicago: Language and Literacy in the City's Neighborhoods, 2003; author: (with others) Cultural Performances, 1994, Literacy Across Communities, 1994, Mexico en Fiesta, 1998; editl. bds. jours.; gen. editor rsch. series Hampton Press, Cresskill, N.J., 1992-2000, Ablex Publs., Norwood, N.J., 1982-92. Rsch. fellow in Mex., Fulbright Found., 1995-96; rsch. grant Spencer Found., 1990-93, 95-98, 99-00, NSF, 1988-90; recipient Mentor Network award Spencer Found., 1995-97. Fellow Am. Anthropol. Assn.; mem. Am. Assn. for Applied Linguistics (exec. com., program chair 1981), Internat. Assessment of Literacy (U.S. nat. com.), Nat. Coun. of Tchrs. of English (commn. on English lang.). Avocations: dance, mystery novels and films. Office: Ohio State U Coll Edn 29 W Woodruff Ave Columbus OH 43210 E-mail: farr.18@osu.edu.

FARR, MICHAEL KEOGH, investment company executive; b. Washington, Apr. 24, 1961; s. Harry Hull and Joyce Keogh Farr; m. Laurie Fishburn, Apr. 1, 1989; children: Robert, Margaret. BA, U. of the South, 1984. Sch. master Pomfret (Conn.) Sch., 1984-87; stock broker, v.p. Wheat First Securities, Washington, 1987-90; stock broker, prin. Alex Brown & Sons, Washington, 1990-96; pres. Farr, Miller & Washington, LLC, 1996—; chmn. FMW Trust Co., Sioux Falls, S.D., 1999—. Expert commentator CNN TV, 1998—, WJLA Channel 7 TV. Chmn. Paul Berry Acad. Scholarship Found., Washington, 1995—, Nation's Capital Progress Found., Washington, 1997—; bd. dirs. The Salvation Army, Washington, 1999—; trustee The Heights Sch., Potomac, Md., 1995—. Recipient Outstanding Young Alumnus Achievement award U. of the South, 1999; named Top 10 Outstanding Brokers of Yr. Registered Rep. mag., 1994. Mem. Washington Assn. of Money Mgrs., Nat. Econs. Club, Met. Club of Washington, Chevy Chase Club, Rehoboth Beach County Club. Republican. Roman Catholic. Avocations: hunting, fishing, golf, sailing. Office: Farr Miller & Washington LLC 1020 19th St NW Ste 200 Washington DC 20036-6101

FARR, REETA RAE, special education administrator; b. Edhube, Tex., Jan. 15, 1926; d. Paul Ray and Verna (Biggerstaff) Wright; m. Gerald Edward Self, June 1, 1946 (dec. Dec. 1977); children: Eddie, Lee; m. Barnie B. Farr Jr., Dec. 28, 1978 (wid. Mar. 1997). BS, Southeastern Okla. State U., 1959, MS, 1963. 1st grade tchr. Sherman (Tex.) Pub. Schs., 1959-61, Denison (Tex.) Pub. Schs., 1961-64, spl. edn. tchr., 1964-72, spl. edn. counselor, 1972-76, spl. edn. diagnostician, 1976-85, dir. spl. edn., 1985-94. Named Educator of Yr. Denison Edn. Assn., 1991. Mem. NEA, AAUW (pres. 1981-83), Tex. State Tchrs. Assn. (local pres. 1971), Tex. Ednl. Diagnostician Assn., Tex. Assn. Counseling and Devel., Phi Delta Kappa (sec.-treas. 1983, del. 1978-99), Delta Kappa Gamma. Mem. Ch. Of Christ. Avocation: reading. Home: 23000 2d Fork Rd Ola ID 83657-5015 E-mail: rfarr@bigskytel.com.

FARR, SAM, congressman; b. Calif., July 4, 1941; m. Shary Baldwin; 1 child, Jessica. BSc Biology, Willamette U., 1963; student, Monterey Inst. Internat. Studies, U. Santa Clara. Vol. Peace Corps, 1963-65; budget analyst, cons. Assembly com. Constl. Amendments; bd. suprs. Monterey (Calif.) County; rep. Calif. State Assembly, 1980-93; mem. U.S. Congress from 17th Calif. dist., 1993—; mem. appropriations com., agr. and military constrn. subcoms. Named Legislator of Yr. Calif. 9 times. Democrat. Avocations: photography, skiing, fly fishing, spanish. Office: Ho of Reps 1221 Longworth Bldg Washington DC 20515-0517*

FARR, WALTER EVANS, chemist, chemical engineer; b. Houston, Miss., June 19, 1938; s. Walter Evans Farr Sr. and Evelyn Foster Farr; m. Sue Beasley Farr, Dec. 20, 1964; children: Ralph, Cynthia, Kimberly. BS in chemistry, Miss. State U. Chemist, engr. Wesson Oil, Memphis, 1960—64; refinery mgr. Wesson Oil., 1964—68; refineries mgr. ADM, Decautr, Ill., 1968—80; corp. tech. dir. Anderson Clayton & Co., Houston, 1980—87, Kraft Foods, Memphis, 1987—93; v.p., refined oils Owensboro Grain Co., Owensboro, Ky., 1993—98; dir. refined oils Desmet Process and Tech., Marietta, Ga., 1998—2003; prin. Farr Rsch. Internat., Olive Branch, Miss., 2003—. Co-author: (book) Introduction to Fats and Oils, 2001. Fellow: Am. Inst. of Chemists; mem.: Am. Oil Chemists Soc. Democrat. Meth. Achievements include co-inventor of novel oil refining process (patented). Avocations: hunting, fishing, travel. Home and Office: Farr Rsch Internat 4863 Stone Park Blvd Olive Branch MS 38654

FARRAGHER, CLARE M. state legislator; b. Richmond Hill, N.Y., Dec. 11, 1941; m. Liam; children: Irene, Anne Marie, Kathleen, Mary Clare. Student, St. John's U. Mem. N.J. Assembly, Trenton, 1987—. Asst. minority whip, 1990-91, dep. spkr., 1989-90, 96—, mem. Legis. Svcs. Commn., 1990-95, vice-chair ins. com., mem. trans. and comm. com.; mem. Am. Legis. Exch. Coun., 1987—, N.J. chmn., 1990-2003, chmn., Telecom and Info. Tech. Task Force, 2003-; mem. Nat. Conf. Ins. Legislators, 1992—, v.p., 1998, pres.-elect, 1999, pres. 2000—; mem. Joint Commn. on Auto Ins. Reform, 1998-99, Appropriations Commn., 2000—, Banking & Ins. Commn., 2000-, Assembly Budget Com. (current). Past sr. citizen liaison Freehold Twp., committeewoman, 1982-91, police commr., 1984; dep. mayor, 1984, 88, mayor, 1985; mem. Monmouth County Rep. Com., 1978—; treas. Freehold Twp. Rep. Club; exec. com. Rep. Women of 90's. Named Ins. Legislator of Yr., Am. Legis. Exch. Coun., 1995. Mem. Nat. Order Women Legislators, Nat. Coun. Ins. Legislators (v.p.), N.J. Assn. Elected Women Ofcls. (bd. dirs.). Home: 40 Enright Ave Freehold NJ 07728-2062 Office: 3rd Fl 400 W Main St Freehold NJ 07728-2539

FARRALL, GEORGE WILLIAM, marketing executive; b. Beverly, Mass., Feb. 16, 1959; s. Robert Arthur and Nancy Mary (Georgi) F.; m. JoAnn Steigler. BS in Mgmt, Fairfield U., 1981. Ops. mgr. Interstate Yacht Maintenance, Rye, N.Y., 1978-81; div. mgr. Amerco, Phoenix, 1981-82, ops. mgr., 1982-83; product mktg. mgr., specialist Clairex Electronics, Mt. Vernon, N.Y., 1983-88, mgr. product mktg., 1988-90; sales mgr. Tyco Backplanes, Stafford Springs, Conn., 1990-91; pres. LDC Communications, Stamford, Conn., 1991-95; dir. sales Blue Chip Mktg., Stamford, 1995-97; nat. account dir. The Sr. Network, Stamford, 1997-98; COO LLS/Group Four Imaging, Mamaroneck, N.Y., 1998-2001; exec. v.p. bus. devel. Allegra Sys., Inc., Ridgefield, Conn., 2001—. Cons. Lowall Distbg. Corp., Rye, 1988—, also bd. dirs. Active Rye Pub. Sch. System, N.Y., 1980. Mem. Nat. Desktop Pub. Assn., Am. Mgmt. Assn., Am. Mktg. Assn., N.Y. Direct Mktg. Assn., Am. Yacht Club, Mystic Seaport. Democrat. Home: 24 Standish Dr Ridgefield CT 06877-4721 Office: Allegra Sys Inc PO Box 1402 Ridgefield CT 06877

FARRALL, HAROLD JOHN, retired accountant; b. Harvard, Nebr., Mar. 25, 1918; s. John William and Olive Almira (Frazell) F. BSBA, Nebr. U., 1940. Clerk teletype ctr. Bur. Aeronautics, Washington, 1946-47; cost acct. Bur. Reclamation Br. Office Region 7, Grand Island, Nebr., 1948-53, fin. officer Ainsworth, Nebr., 1953-54; payroll acct. to supervisory operating acct. Bur. Reclamation Hdqs. Region 7, Denver, Colo., 1955-72; accts. payable supr. Dutton-Lainson Co., Hastings, Nebr., 1974-85; ret., 1985. Author: The Rise and Fall of the United States, 1990, 2d edit., 1998. With U.S. Army, 1941-45. Regents scholarship U. Nebr., 1936. Mem. DAV, VFW, Am. Legion, Ind. order of Odd Fellows, Fed. Govt. Accts. Assn., Mensa. Avocation: big band music.

FARRAND, GEORGE NIXON, JR., marketing professional; b. N.Y.C., Apr. 1, 1936; s. George Nixon and Pauline (Merchant) F.; m. Elyn Marie Hallberg, Aug. 26, 1961; 1 child, Kathryn Elyn (dec. 1985). BSBA, Lehigh U., 1958; postgrad. in bus. adminstrn., NYU, 1962. Advt. and promotions writer Union Carbide Corp., N.Y.C., 1959-62; account exec. McCann-Erickson, Inc., N.Y.C., 1962-63, Vick Chem. Co., N.Y.C., 1963-64; sr. account exec., supr. Grey Advt., Inc., N.Y.C., 1964-65; products mktg. mgr. Hoffmann-LaRoche, Inc., Clifton, N.J., 1965-67; dir. new markets Inmont Corp., N.Y.C., 1967-69; sr. v.p. Bliss/Grunewald, Inc., N.Y.C., 1969-73; pres., CEO, Farrand Mktg. Assoc., Inc., Vernon, N.J., 1973—, Farrand Enterprises, Vernon, N.J., 1983—. Sgt. U.S. Army, 1959. Mem. Sales Execs. Club N.Y.C., Lehigh U. Alumni Club (past treas. and pres.). Republican. Avocations: sports, interior decorating, travel, music. Home: 13 Bucky Ln Vernon NJ 07462 Fax: 973-764-0826.

FARRAND, WILLIAM RICHARD, geology educator; b. Columbus, Ohio, Apr. 27, 1931; s. Harvey Ashley and Esther Evelyn (Bowman) F.; m. Claudine Brickmann, Aug. 17, 1962 (div. 1983); children: Frederic Hervé, Anne Marie; m. Carola Hill Stearns, Dec. 6, 1988; 1 child, Michelle Diane. BS in Geology, Ohio State U., 1955, MS in Geology, 1956; PhD, U. Mich., 1960. Rsch. assoc. Lamont Geol. Obs. Columbia U., N.Y., 1960-61, asst. prof., 1961-64; rsch. assoc. in geology U. Mich., Ann Arbor, 1962; postdoctoral rsch. fellow NAS/NRC, Strasbourg, France, 1963-64; asst. prof. geol. scis. U. Mich., Ann Arbor, 1965-67, assoc. prof. geol scis., 1967-74, prof., 1974-2000, prof. emeritus, 2000—, curator analytical collections Mus. Anthropology, 1975-2000, dir. Exhibit Mus., 1993-2000. Vis. prof. U. Strasbourg, France, 1964-65, Hebrew U., Jerusalem, 1971-72, U. Colo., Boulder, 1983, U. Tex., Austin, 1986; fellow Inst. for Advanced Study, Ind. U., 1985; mem. archaeometry panel NSF, 1989-91; apptd. mem. U.S. Nat. com. Internat. Quaternary Assn., 1989-99, chair, 1995-99; sr. fellow Inst. for Study Earth and Man, So. Meth. U., Dallas, 1991—. Mem. editorial bd. Quaternary Sci. Review, Paleorient, Jour. Archaeological Sci., Review Archaeology, Stratigraphica Archaeologica; contbr. articles and maps to profl jours. With U.S. Army, 1951-53. Fellow AAAS, Geol. Soc. Am. (mem. panel quaternary geology and geomorphology divsn. 1978, vice chmn. archaeological geology divsn, 1979, chmn, 1980, Archaeological Geology award 1986), Ohio Acad. Sci., 1994-96; mem. Am. Quaternary Assn. (sec. 1978-90, program chmn. biennial meeting 1980, pres. 1994-96), Mich. Acad. Sci., Arts and Letters, Internat. Union for Quaternary Rsch. (chmn. working group on Southwest Asia commn. paleoecology early man 1975-83), L'Assn. Francaise pour l'Etude de Quaternaire, Sigma Xi, Phi Beta Kappa. Office: U Mich Mus Anthropology 4009 Ruthven Mus Ann Arbor MI 48109-1079 E-mail: wfarrand@umich.edu.

FARRAR, ANDREW LOCKETT, agricultural education educator; b. Clarksville, Va., Apr. 5, 1937; s. Albert Adolphus and Elizabeth (Merritt) F.; m. Mavis Ann Wray, June 18, 1960; 1 child, Angela LaVonia. BS, Va. State U., 1960, MS, 1972. Post-profl. tchg. cert. in agr. Sci. tchr. Mecklenburg Sch. Bd., Boydton, Va., 1960-61; agrl. tchr. Pittsylvania County Sch. Bd., Chatham, Va., 1961-84; supr. agr. Va. Dept. Edn., Richmond, 1984-91. Chmn. dept. Northside, Gretna Jr. Hi, Gretna, Va., 1967-84; mem. state adv. bd. Future Farmers of Am., Richmond, 1984; chmn. Pittsylvania County Agr. Tchrs., Gretna, 1976; team mem. So. Assn. Accreditation, Richmond, 1984-91; adv. bd. Young Farmers of Va., 1985; chmn. J.R. Thomas New Farmer and New Homemakers of Am. Scholarship Found., Petersburg, Va., 1968—; mem. exec. bd. Va. State Agr. Alumni, Petersburg, 1984—. Contbr. articles to profl. jours. Mem. Councilman Town of Gretna, 1978-84, planning commn., 1978-84; bd. dirs. Pittsylvania County Med. Svc. Ctr., Chatham, Va., 1976-84; deacon Second Bapt. Ch., 1984; trustee John Tyler Cmty. Coll., Chester, Va., 1988-96; charter mem. Prince George Econ. Alliance, 1997. Recipient Sound Off for Agr. award Nat. Vocat. Ag. Tchrs., New Orleans, 1980, Disting. Svc. award 1991; inducted into Sports Hall of Fame, Va. State U., 1989 Mem. Ret. Tchrs. Assn. Old Dominion Ag. Tchrs. (state pres. Va. 1969), Dist. D Retired Tchrs. (chmn. 1991-97), Va. Ret. Tchrs. Assn. Ipar liamentarian 2003), Va. State U. Agr. (awards com. 1985-97, plaque 1994), Petersburg-Prince George (chmn. 1994), NAACP. Democrat. Avocations: growing and exhibiting plants and vegetables, golf. Home: 4329 Prince George Dr Prince George VA 23875-2610 E-mail: mafar@aol.com.

FARRAR, CONSTANCE MOSHER, marketing executive; b. Cambridge, Mass., Aug. 24, 1925; d. Curtis Howard and Jeannette (Shaw) Mosher; m. Robert Stewart Perkins, Sept. 21, 1946 (div. Oct. 1954); m. Franklin Ernest Farrar, Feb. 4, 1961; 1 child, Bruce Stewart. CLU degree, Am. Coll. Fin. Svc. Profls., 1961; BLS in Interdisciplinary Studies, Boston U., 1981. Chartist Liberty Mut., N.Y.C., 1945-46; asst. cashier, bookkeeper Columbian Nat., Boston, 1946-51; v.p. Baystate Fin. Svcs., Boston, 1951- . Lay Eucharistic min., lay reader, mem. vestry Episcopalian Ch. Recipient Nat. Quality award, 1970-2000, named Businessman of Yr., Nat. Rep. Congl. Com. Bus. Adv. Coun., 2003. Mem. NAACP (life), New Eng. Leaders Assn. (life), Nat. Assn. Ins. and Fin. Adv. (past bd. dirs., Nat. Quality award for 30 years), Soc. Fin. Svc. Profls., Boston Estate Planning Coun., Golden Key Soc., Zonta (chair status of women com.), Order Ea. Star (past Worthy Matron), Zonta Club of Newton (treas., past pres.). Republican. Avocations: camping, hiking. Home: 1508 Great Plain Ave Needham MA 02492-1237 Office: Baystate Fin Svcs 1 Exeter Plz Ste 1400 Boston MA 02116-2848

FARRAR, DONALD KEITH, retired financial executive; b. Indio, Calif., May 18, 1938; s. Keith and Sarah S. (Turner) F.; m. Jo Ann Puttler, Dec. 16, 1961; children: Daniel K., Donald S., Douglas S., Kimberly. BSBA, U. So. Calif., 1960; MBA, Harvard U., 1965. With planning div. Paul Revere Life Ins. Co., Worcester, Mass., 1965, budget supr., 1966, asst. to pres., 1967, asst. sec., 1968-73, v.p. investment, 1969-73; v.p. planning Avco Corp., Greenwich, Conn., 1973-74, sr. v.p., chief acct. officer, 1975-77, exec. v.p., 1978-81, pres., 1981-85, also bd. dirs.; sr. exec. v.p., pres. Avco Ops. Textron Inc., Providence, R.I., 1985-89, sr. exec. v.p. ops., 1985-89, also bd. dirs.; pres., CEO IMO Industries, Lawrenceville, N.J., 1993-94, chmn., CEO, 1994-97. Pvt. investor 1990-93, 98—, retired. With USNR, 1960-63. Home: 5 Prairie Grass Irvine CA 92603

FARRAR, DONNA BEATRICE, hospital official; b. Ayer, Mass., Feb. 4, 1950; d. Raymond H. and Shirley E. (Perham) F. B Music Edn., U. Mass., Lowell, 1971; MDiv, Bangor Theol. Sem., 1979; D Ministry, Christian Theol. Sem., 1987; M Family Studies, U. Ky., 1997. Tchr. music Billerica (Mass.) Pub. Schs., 1971-76; chaplain intern various hosps., Bangor, Maine, 1979; assoc. pastor Emanuel United Ch., Hales Corners, Wis., 1980-82; chaplain resident Ind. U & Meth. Hosp., Indpls., 1982-85; assoc. chaplain Ohio State U. Hosp., Columbus, 1985-87; assoc. dir., dir. Ind. U. Med. Ctr., Indpls., 1987-92; dept. dir. U. Ky. Hosps., Lexington, 1992—. Mem.: Am. Assn. Marriage and Family Therapists (lic. marriage family therapist). Democrat. Mem. Christian Ch. Avocations: reading, felines, dancing, travel, art. Office: U Ky 800 Rose St # H-118 Lexington KY 40536-0293

FARRAR, ELAINE WILLARDSON, artist; b. L.A. d. Eldon and Gladys Elsie (Larsen) Willardson; children: Steve, Mark, Gregory, JanLeslie, Monty, Susan. BA, Ariz. State U., 1967, MA, 1969, PhD, 1990. Tchr. Camelback Desert Sch., Paradise Valley, Ariz., 1966-69; mem. faculty Yavapai Coll., Prescott, Ariz., 1970-92, chmn. dept. art, 1973-78, instr. art in watercolor, oil, acrylic painting, intaglio, 1971-92, instr. art relief intaglio and monoprints, 1971-92; grad. advisor Prescott Coll. Master of Arts Program, 1993-97. (one-woman shows) R.P. Moffat's, Scottsdale, Ariz., 1969, Art Ctr., Battlecreek, Mich., 1969, The Woodpeddler, Costa Mesa, Calif., 1979, (group shows) Prescott (Ariz.) Fine Arts Assn., 1982, 1984, 1986, 1989, 1990—95, 1996, 1997, (invitational group shows) The Elements, 2001, Collage & Works on Paper, 2002, (group shows) N.Y. Nat. Am. Watercolorists, 1982, Ariz. State U. Women Images Now, 1986, 1987, 1989, 1990—92, Prescott Fine Arts Assn., 1999, 2001; Exhibited in group shows at Prescott Fine Arts Assn., 1999, 2001; (group shows) Prescott Fine Arts Assn., 2002. Mem., curator Prescott Fine Arts Visual Arts com., 1992-97, Works on Paper, 2002; mem. exec. com., 1996-98; bd. dirs. Prescott Fine Arts Assn., 1995-98, Friends Y.C. Art Gallery Bd., 1992-97. Mem. Northern Ariz. Watercolor Assn., Mountain Artists Guild (past pres.), Women's Nat. Mus. (charter Washington chpt.), mus. of North Ariz. and Phoenix Art Mus., Kappa Delta Pi. *Through the visual arts many ideas and feelings are expressed that would otherwise be lost to the communication of these thoughts to others—a vital link to understanding...and vital to helping release ideas through art therapy when one has been unable to verbalize thoughts and ideas and whether analyzed or not the path is cleared away...universal as is music and dance!.*

FARRAR, FRANK LEROY, lawyer, former governor; b. Britton, S.D., Apr. 2, 1929; s. Virgil William and Venetia Soule (Taylor) F.; m. Patricia Jean Henley, June 5, 1953; children— Jeanne Marie, Sally Ann, Robert John, Mary Susan, Ann M. BS, U. S.D., 1951, LL.B., 1953; LL.D., Huron Coll. Bar: S.D. 1953. Practiced law, Britton, 1957-63; agt. IRS, 1955-57; judge Marshall County, S.D., 1958, state's atty., 1959-62; atty. gen. State of S.D., 1963-69, gov., 1969-70; ptnr. Farrar & Spiry, Britton, S.D., 1970—. Chmn. Cardinal and Gold Ins. Co., Frank L. Farrar & Assocs., Performance Bankers, Inc., Capital, Fulda, Beresford, Wanbay, Sidney, Uptown, Versailles, Glenrock, Wolf Point Bancorps., Inc., NW Investment Inc., Carlton Agy., Inc., 1st Agy. Hasting, Cairo, First, Inc., Peoples Holding Co.; adv. bd. dirs. Citicorp, Correspondent Resources Inc. Past pres. Pheasant council Boy Scouts Am.; past chmn. S.D. March of Dimes; past fund raising chmn. S.D. Mental Health Assn.; bd. dirs. Rural Coalition Am.; chmn. Marshall County Republican Party, 1959; asst. sgt.-at-arms Rep. Nat. Conv., 1960. Served to capt. U.S. Army Recipient Alumnus Achievement award U. S.D., 1981, named Alumnus of Yr. Sch. Bus., 1979; named Sr. Olympics Athlete of the Yr. for S.D., 4th All Am. for Triathlon, 1999; named to Hall of Fame Sr. Olympics, S.D. Mem. S.D. Bar Assn., Ind. Bar Assn., Wash. Bar Assn., S.D. States Attys. Assn. (asst. pres.), Nat. Dist. Attys. Assn., Alpha Tau Omega, Phi Delta Phi. Lodges: Masons, Shriners, Jesters, Lions, Elks, Odd Fellows, Sportsmen. Address: PO Box 936 Britton SD 57430-0936

FARRAR, JAMES MARTIN, chemistry educator; b. Pitts., June 15, 1948; s. Martin W. and Lorraine H. (Williams) F.; m. Kathy June Meyer, Mar. 20, 1971; children: Stacey Elizabeth, Andrew Martin. AB, Washington U., 1970; MS, U. Chgo., 1972, PhD, 1974. Postdoctoral rschr. Lawrence Berkeley (Calif.) Lab., 1974-76; asst. prof. U. Rochester, N.Y., 1976-82, assoc. prof., 1982-86, prof., 1986—, chair dept. chemistry, 1997-2000. Vis. fellow Joint Inst. Lab. Astrophysics, Boulder, Colo., 1987-88. Mem. editl. bd. J.W. Wiley Pubs., 1992—. Recipient fellowship Alfred P. Sloan, 1981-85. Fellow Am. Phys. Soc.; mem. Am. Chem. Soc. Office: Univ Rochester Dept Chemistry Rochester NY 14627

FARRAR, JOHN THRUSTON, health facility administrator; b. St. Louis, June 26, 1920; s. Benedict and Ruth Elizabeth (Gregg) F.; m. Joan Hayward Niedringhaus, May 20, 1947 (div. Feb. 1964); children: John Hayward, Leslie Tweedy; m. Pamela Sedgwick Gibson, May 15, 1966 (div. Mar. 1994); children: Elizabeth Gregg, Anne Dandridge; m. Rowena Kay Bryan, Oct. 28, 1995. AB, Princeton U., 1942; MD, Washington U., St. Louis, 1945. Diplomate Am. Bd. Internal Medicine, Am. Bd. Gastroenterology. Intern St. Louis County Hosp., Clayton, Mo., 1945-46; asst. resident in pathology Boston City Hosp., 1948-49; intern in medicine Mass. Meml. Hosps., Boston, 1949-50, asst. resident in medicine, 1950-51, rsch. assoc. divsn. gastroenterology, 1951-54; instr. medicine Boston U. Sch. Medicine, 1954-55; asst. prof. clin. medicine Cornell U. Coll. Medicine, N.Y.C., 1956-63; assoc. prof. medicine Med. Coll. Va., Richmond, 1963-65, chmn. divsn. gastroenterology, 1963-78, prof. medicine, 1965-92, assoc. dean vets. affairs, 1979-90, prof. emeritus, 1992—. Chief gastroenterology sect. med. svc. Vets. Hosp., N.Y.C., 1955-63; assoc. chief of staff rsch. devel. Vets. Affairs Med. Ctr., N.Y.C., 1956-63; cons. gastroenterology McGuire Vets. Affairs Med. Ctr., Richmond, 1963-78, chief of staff, 1979-90; nat. adv. panel nat. program rev. com. VA, 1965-69; adv. com. gastrointestinal drugs FDA, Washington, 1971-74, 77-82, cons., 1976-77; grants rev. com. Nat. Found. Ileitis Colitis, Inc., 1975-79, nat. scientific adv. com. 1975-79; chmn. long range planning com. Nat. digestive Diseases Edn. Info. Clearinghouse, 1983-85, chmn. scientific Evaluation subcom. 1983-85, chmn. exec. com. advisors, 1983-90; mem. steering com. Internat. Conf. Gastrointestinal Motility, 1975-81, chmn. steering com., 1977-79; chmn. Am. Bd. Gastroenterology, 1979-83; mem. bd. govs. Am. Bd. Internal Medicine, 1979-85; first vice-chmn. Coalition Digestive Desease Orgns., 1983-85; pres. Digestive Disease Nat. Coalition (formerly Coalition Digestive Disease Orgns.), 1986-91; rsch. com. Am. Fedn. Aging Rsch., 1983-89; assoc. dep. chief med. dir. Dept. Vets. Affairs, Vets. Affairs Ctrl. Office, Washington, 1990-91, dep. chief med. dir., 1991-93, acting under sec. health, 1993-94, dep. under sec. health, 1994-95; assoc. chief of staff extended care Vets. Affairs med. Ctr., Martinsburg, W.Va., 1995—. Author: (chpts.) Miniaturization, 1961, Modern Trends in Gastroenterology, 1961, Medicine, Essentials of Clinical Practice, 1970, Medical Engineering, 1974, Gastrointestinal Motility, 1971, Scientific

Foundations of Gastroenterology, 1980, Tratado De Gastroenterologia Y Hepatologia, 1982, Clinics in Gastroenterology, 1982, Clinical Medicine, 1983, Social Security Practice Guide, 1986, Surgical Management of the Elderly Patient, 1992; editor: Practice of Medicine, Vol. Gastroenterology, 1973-78; mem. editl. bd. Am. Jour. Digestive Diseases, 1959-64, 88—, editor, 1968-76, Gastroenterology, 1964-68, Am. Jour. Med. Electronics, 1962-82; mem. editl. coun. Rendiconti Romani di Gastro-enterologia, 1969-89; contbr. over 55 articles to profl. jours. Bd. trustees Elk Hill Farm for Boys, 1974-80; pres. Goochland Family Svc. Soc., 1975-76, 79-81. Capt. U.S. Army Med. Corps., 1946-48. Mem.: ACP (coun.subspecialty socs. 1985—88, chmn. gastroenterology com. 1985—88, chair Washington 1986, chair San Francisco 1987), Am. Liver Found. (bd. dirs. 1986—, chmn. 1990—94), Am. Clin. Climatol. Assn., Am. Gastroent. Assn. (rssch. com. 1968—71, nat. liaison com. 1971—73, 1977—80, treas. 1972—77, chmn. publs. com. 1977—80, gov. bd. 1972—77, 1980—89, v.p 1980—81, pres.-elect 1981—82, pres. 1982—83, chmn. com. pub. policy and govt. rels. 1986—89, historian, archivist 1989—98), Am. Fedn. Clin. Rsch. Home: 113 Falling Creek Cir Williamsburg VA 23185-1482

FARRAR, RICHARD BARTLETT, JR., school system administrator; b. Penn Yan, N.Y., Apr. 25, 1939; s. Richard B. and Margaret M. (Stevenson) F. BS, Houghton Coll., 1960; MEd, Frostburg (Md.) State U., 1990. Cert. wildlife biologist. Sci. tchr. Hinckley (Maine) Sch., 1960-61, Concord (Mass.) High Sch., 1962-64; program dir. Mass. Audubon Soc., Lincoln, 1964-65; instr. U. Ill., Chgo., 1966-68; chair sci. dept. Woodstock Country Sch., 1968-73; exec. dir. Vt. Inst. Natural Sci., Woodstock, 1971-73, N.J. Audubon Soc., Franklin Lakes, 1974-78; field exec. Nat. Wildlife Fedn., Washington, 1979-81; wildlife biology cons. Washington, 1982-86; lead sci. tchr. Garrett County Bd. Edn., Oakland, Md., 1987-97; dir. PPEPTEC High Schs., Tucson, 1997—. Rsch. advisor Coastal Facilities Rev. Act, State of N.J., Trenton, 1977-78; mem. State of N.J. Natural Resources Coun., 1978-79; advisor Savage River State Forest Coun., 1991-92; NASA sci. tchr. amb., 1994—; mem. legisl. subcom. on edn. State of Ariz., 2000—. Author: Birds of East-Central Vermont, 1971, The Hungry Snowbird, 1975, The Birds' Woodland, 1976; editor Vt. Natural History mag., 1970-73, N.J. Audubon mag., 1974-78; contbr. articles to popular and sci. publs. Treas. League for Conservation Legis., N.J., 1978; dir. Mid.-Atlantic Naturalist Soc., Md., 1981-82. Recipient Outstanding Biology Tchr. award Nat. Assn. Biology Tchrs., 1971, Conservation award Connecticut River Watershed Coun., 1971, Children's Sci. Book award Children's Libr. Coun., 1975, NSTA, 1976. Mem. Assn. for Supervision and Curriculum Devel., Nat. Coun. for Tchrs. Math., Internat. Reading Assn., Nat. Sci. Tchrs. Assn., Nat. Coun. for Social Studies, Rotary (treas. Friendsville, Md. 1988). E-mail: rfarrar2@earthlink.net.

FARRAR, STANLEY F. lawyer; b. Santa Ana, Calif., 1943; BS, U. Calif., Berkeley, 1964, JD, 1967. Bar: Calif. 1968, N.Y. 1969. Mem. Sullivan & Cromwell LLP, L.A. Mem. ABA (chmn. subcom. on bank holding cos. and nonbank activities banking law com. 1980-85, chmn. letters credit subcom. uniform comml. code com. 1982-88, sect. bus. law), State Bar Calif. (chmn. fin. instns. com. 1981-82). Office: Sullivan & Cromwell LLP 1888 Century Park E Los Angeles CA 90067-1725 E-mail: farrars@sullcrom.com.

FARRAR, STEPHEN PRESCOTT, glass products manufacturing executive; b. Concord, N.H., Jan. 27, 1944; s. Prescott Samuel and Katherine (Hitchcock) F.; m. Kathleen D. Clark, Dec. 28, 1968 (dec.); children: Sheila E. Bermudez, Stephen Prescott Jr.; m. Rose Marie Bucar, July 4, 1998. BA, Bowdoin Coll., 1965; MSFS, Georgetown U., 1967. Internat. economist U.S. Dept. Commerce, Washington, 1966-72, Office of Mngt. and Budget, Washington, 1972-80, chief econ. affairs br. IAD, 1980-86; dir. internat. econ. affairs NSC, Washington, 1986-88, spl. asst. to Pres. and sr. dir. internat. econ. affairs, 1988-89; dep. exec. sec. Econ. Policy Coun., The White House, Washington, 1989-92; spl. asst. to Pres. for Policy Devel. Office of Policy Devel., the White House, Washington, 1989-92; chief of staff Office of the U.S. Trade Rep., Washington, 1992-93; dir. internat. bus. Guardian Industries Corp., Auburn Hills, Mich., 1993—. Mem. Coun. on Fgn. Rels. Republican. Avocations: tennis, running. Office: Guardian Industries Corp 2300 Harmon Rd Auburn Hills MI 48326-1714 E-mail: sfarrar@guardian.com.

FARRAR, SUSAN CLEMENT, choreographer, performing company executive, writer; b. Billerica, Mass., Nov. 10, 1917; d. Joseph Anthony Clement and Emily Potsus; children: Michelle, Douglas, Lisa, Paul. BA in Theater and Sci., U. Maine, 1999; student, Kings Coll., London, 1999. Dir., choreographer Spring St. Dance Theater, Bethel, Maine, 1957—2001. Author: Samantha on Stage, 1980, Emily and Her Cavalier, 1984, Broken Promises, 2002, short stories. Recipient Children's Book Coun. award, 1984, Internat. Young Readers award, 1984, West Australian Young Readers award, 1984, Maine Book Mark award, 1984. Home: 16 Spring St Bethel ME 04217 E-mail: missue@megalink.net.

FARRAR, THOMAS C. chemist, educator; b. Independence, Kans., Jan. 14, 1933; s. Otis C. and Agnes K. F.; m. Friedemarie L. Farrar, June 22, 1963; children: Michael, Christian, Gisela. BS in Math., Chemistry, Wichita State U., 1954; PhD in Chemistry, U. Ill., 1959. NSF fellow Cambridge U., Eng., 1959-61; prof. chemistry U. Oregon, Eugene, 1961-63; chief, magnetism sect. Nat. Bur. Standards, Washington, 1963-71; dir. R & D Japan Electron Optics Lab., Cranford, N.J., 1971-75; dir. instr. NSF, Washington, 1975-79; prof. chemistry U. Wis., Madison, 1979—. Chmn. adv. com. MIT Nat. Magnetics Lab., Cambridge, Mass., 1979-84. Author: Introduction to Pulse NMR Spectros, 1989, Density Matrix Theory, 1995; contbr. over 120 articles to profl. jours. Recipient Silver medal Dept. Commerce, Washington, 1971, Silver medal Nat. Science Found., Washington, 1979. Fellow Wash. Acad. Science; mem. Am. Chem. Soc. (sec.-treas. Wis. sect. 1986-89), Am. Physical Soc. Office: Univ Wis Dept Chemistry 1101 University Ave Madison WI 53706-1322 E-mail: tfarrar@chem.wisc.edu.

FARRAR-MYERS, VICTORIA ANNE, political scientist; b. Albany, Dec. 26, 1968; d. John Cecil and Sally Anne F.; m. Jason Bryan Myers, Aug. 27, 1966. BS, Russell Sage Coll., 1990; MA, U. Ill., 1992; PhD, U. Albany SUNY, 1997. Assoc. prof. U. Tex., Arlington, 1998—, assoc. dean, 2003—. Co-author: Legislative Labyrinth: Congress and Campaign Finance Reform, 2001, American Political Parties, 2001, The Presidency and the Law After Clinton, 2002, Anticipating Madame President, 2003; contbr. articles to profl. jours. Rsch. grantee Dirksen Congrl. Ctr., 2000, U. Tex., Arlington, 2000. Mem.: So. Polit. Sci. Assn., Western Polit. Sci. Assn. (exec. bd. 2002—), Am. Polit. Sci. Assn. (pres. rsch. group exec. bd. 1998—, Congrl. fellow 1997—98), Phi Kappa Phi. Avocations: coin collecting, travel, the arts, pets. Office: U Tex Arlington Dept Polit Sci Arlington TX 76019 Fax: 817-272-2525. E-mail: victoria@uta.edu.

FARREHI, CYRUS, cardiologist, educator; b. Malayer, Iran, Jan. 26, 1935; s. Mansoor and Nikzad (Agah) F.; m. Z. Jane Christensen, June 6, 1964; children: Peter M., Paul C., Lisa N., Mary M. MD, U. Tehran, 1958. Diplomate: Am. Bd. Internal Medicine, Am. Bd. Cardiovascular Diseases, added qualifications in interventional cardiology. Intern Wayne County Gen. Hosp., Eloise, Mich., 1959-60, resident, 1960-62; fellow in cardiology U. Oreg. Med. Sch., 1962-64; teaching fellow dept. medicine U. Alta., 1964-66; asst. prof. medicine U. Oreg.; also dir. cardiac catheterization lab. VA Hosp., Portland, Oreg., 1966-69; chmn. dept. medicine McLaren Regional Med. Ctr., Flint, Mich., 1971-73; founding dir. cardiovascular diagnostic service McLaren Gen. Hosp., 1973-85; clin. assoc. prof. medicine Mich. State U., 1973-78, clin. prof., 1978—; chief of staff McLaren Regional Med. Ctr., 2001—. Cons. cardiovascular diseases, Flint, 1969— ; bd. dirs. Ind. Practice Assocs., 1979-86, sec., 1979-83; adj. prof. health care, Sch. Health Scis., U. Mich., Flint, 1981-84 Contbr. articles med. jours. Fellow A.C.P., Royal Coll. Physicians and Surgeons of Can., Am. Coll. Cardiology, Clin. Council Am. Heart Assn., Genesee County Med. Soc. (dir. 1980—, pres. 1999-2000); mem. Detroit Heart Club. Roman Catholic. Home: 8398 Old Plank Rd Grand Blanc MI 48439-2041 Office: 1116 S Linden # 14 Flint MI 48532

FARRELL, ANNE VAN NESS, foundation executive; b. Peking, China, July 17, 1935; came to U.S. 1935; d. C. Peter and Virginia (Cheatham) Van Ness; m. E. Robert Farell, June 17, 1955; children: Virginia Farrell Day and Susan Farrell Johnson. BA, U. Wash., 1960. Dir. devel. Seattle Children's Home, 1978-80; exec. v.p. The Seattle Found., 1980-84, pres., CEO, 1984—, dir. WM funds, 1993—. Bd. dirs. Wash. Mut. Bank, Blue Cross of Wash. and Alaska, REI Corp. Author: Puget Soundings, 1989. Regent Seattle U., 1986—, trustee, 2001—; pres. bd. trustees Lakeside Sch., 1992-94; bd. dirs. Nature Conservancy, 1990-95, Ind. Sector, Wash., 1990-95, Girl Scouts U.S., N.Y.C., 1974-83. Recipient Cmty. Svc. award YWCA, Seattle, 1984, Girl Scout of Yr. award, Seattle, 1986, A.K. Guy award for Outstanding Cmty. Svc. Mem. Pacific N.W. Grantmakers Forum (pres. 1984-85), N.W. Devel. Officers Assn. (pres. 1983-84), Wash. Women's Forum, Seattle, Jr. League, Greater Seattle C. of C., Rotary (pres. Seattle chpt. 1997-98). Republican. Episcopalian. Home: 1620 43rd Ave E # 15C Seattle WA 98112-3222 Office: The Seattle Found 425 Pike St Ste 510 Seattle WA 98101-4026

FARRELL, CLIFFORD MICHAEL, lawyer; b. Gallup, N.Mex., Jan. 17, 1956; s. Francis and Carolyn Louise (Evans) F.; m. Mary E. Moore, Oct. 22, 1994. BA, Moravian Coll., 1978; JD, Capital U., 1982. Bar: Ohio 1982, Pa. 1983, U.S. Dist. Ct. (we. dist.) Pa. 1983, U.S. Ct. Appeals (3d cir.) 1983, U.S. Dist. Ct. (so. dist.) Ohio 1984, U.S. Ct. Appeals (6th cir.) 1984, U.S. Ct. Appeals (4th and 11th cirs.) 1985, U.S. Supreme Ct. 2002. Staff atty. HHS, Columbus, Ohio, 1982-83; mem. firm Robert N. Peirce, Jr., P.C., Pitts., 1983-84, Barkan & Neff Co., L.P.A., Columbus, 1984-88; ptnr. Farrell & Golian, Columbus, 1988-91, Manring & Farrell, Columbus, 1991—. Mem. Ohio Mock Trial Program, N.W. Civic Assn. Mem. ABA, ATLA, Ohio Bar Assn., Ohio Acad. Trial Lawyers (chair social security sect. 2000-02), Franklin County Trial Lawyers Assn., Pa. Bar Assn., Allegheny County Bar Assn., Columbus Bar Assn. Home: 3199 Martin Rd Dublin OH 43017-1451

FARRELL, CRAIG, hotel executive; married; 4 children. AD in Transp. and Travel., Coll. of DuPage; BA, DePaul U., Chgo. Dir. travel mktg. Choice Hotels Internat., 1984-85; v.p. travel industry mktg. Days Inns, 1985-90; sr. v.p. worldwide sales Hospitality Franchise Sys., 1990-94; pres., CEO Choice Hotels Can., Inc., Misissauga, Ont., Can., 1994—; bd. dirs. Can. Tourism Commn., 1998—; planning com. SATH World Congress for Travellers with Disabilities, 1998—. Mem. Tourism Industry Assn. Can. (bd. dirs.), Travel Tourism Rsch. Assn. (pres. S.E. chpt. 1988-90), Can. Profl. Sales Assn., Can. Franchise Assn., Hotel Assn. Can. (bd. dirs.). Office: Choice Hotels Can Inc 5090 Explorer Dr 5th Fl Mississauga ON Canada L4W 4T9 Fax: (905) 624-7796. E-mail: craig_farrell@choicehotels.ca.

FARRELL, EDGAR HENRY, building components manufacturing executive, lawyer; b. Aug. 31, 1924; s. Edgar Henry and Lillian Sarah (Lancaster) Farrell; m. Mary Louise Whelan, May 3, 1952; children: Brooke Larkin Cragan, Elizabeth Lancaster, Kimberley Hopkins. Student, Tex. A&M U., 1943, Stanford U., 1943—45, George Washington U., 1948—49; JD, U. Md., 1950; postgrad., Harvard U., 1965. Exec. sales asst. A.C. Gilbert Co., N.Y.C., 1950; asst. legal counsel U.S. Senate Crime Com., 1951; zone mgr. Life Mag., N.Y.C., 1951—52; account exec. Time Mag., N.Y.C., 1952—55, Phila., 1955—59, Detroit, 1959—62; nat. automotive sales mgr. Worldwide Automotive Products, Detroit, 1962—64, divsn. sales mgr., 1964—68, sales mgr., 1968; regional mgr. Comms./Rsch. Machines, Inc., Mich., Ohio, 1968; ctrl. advt. dir. Petersen Pub. Co., Detroit, 1969; CEO Internat. Concrete Bldg. Group, London, 1972—79; asst. to pres. Dillon Co., Akron, Ohio, 1979—80; pres., CEO Component Bldgs. Group, Woodbury, Conn., 1980—96; v.p. Mktg. Contrs. Mkt. Pl., Cornwall Bridge, Conn., 1993—96; assoc. pub. Bus. Digest Housatonic Valley Pub. Co., New Milford, Conn., 1996—97; mem. constrn. panel Am. Arbitration Assn., 1992; pres. Motorhome Holidays Internat., Camp Can. Inc., BEK Press, Camp Am., Inc. Housing cons. Saudi Arabia, Nigeria, Sri Lanka. Author: Computer Center Construction, 1984, Walls on Wheels, 1993. Trustee Baldwin Libr., Birmingham, Mich., 1962—65; publicity chmn. Youth for Eisenhower Com., N.Y.C., 1952. Lt. U.S. Army, 1945—46, PTO. Recipient Low Cost Housing award, Ministry of Housing, Sri Lanka, 1979. Mem.: Nat. Assn. Home Bldrs., Am. Mktg. Assn., Gen. Soc. Mayflower Descendants, Phi Alpha Sigma, Gamma Eta Gamma, Phi Delta Theta. Republican. Episcopalian. Home: 1 Woodbury Hl Woodbury CT 06798-2958 Office: Bee Publ Co 5 Church Hill Rd Newtown CT 06470-1605

FARRELL, EDMUND JAMES, retired English language educator, author; b. Butte, Mont., May 17, 1927; s. Bartholomew J. and Lavinia H. (Collins) F.; m. Jo Ann Hayes, Dec. 19, 1964; children: David, Kevin, Sean. AB, Stanford U., 1950, MA, 1951; PhD, U. Calif., Berkeley, 1969. Chmn. English dept. James Lick H.S., San Jose, Calif., 1954-59; supr. secondary English, U. Calif., Berkeley, 1959-70; adj. prof. English, U. Ill., Urbana, 1973-78; prof. English edn. U. Tex., Austin, 1978-92, prof. emeritus, 1992—; pres. Farrell Ednl. Svcs., Inc., Austin, 1981-97; ret., 1997. Participant revision lit. objectives Nat. Assessment of Ednl. Progress, Denver, 1972-73, 78; mem. adv. com. Ctr. for the Book, Libr. of Congress, 1980-86; chmn. adv. com. on English, Coll. Bd., N.Y.C., 1974-79, mem. council acad. affairs, 1978-79; guest lectr. local, state and nat. confs. of English tchrs., 1954—; reader compositions for advanced placement program Rider Coll., Princeton, N.J., 1969, 72-77; pres. Calif. Assn. Tchrs. English, 1962-63; sr. cons. EMC Masterpiece Series, 1999—. Author: (with others) Exploring Life Through Literature, 1964, Counterpoint in Literature, 1967, Projection in Literature, 1973, Outlooks Through Literature, 1973, Fantasy: Forms of Things Unknown, 1974, Science Fact/Fiction, 1974, Comment, 1976, Myth, Mind and Moment, 1976, I/You, We/They, 1976, Traits and Topics, 1976, Reality in Conflict, 1976, To Be, 1976, Arrangement in Literature, 1979, Purpose in Literature, 1979, Album U.S.A., 1983, Discoveries in Literature, 1985, classic edit., 1989, Patterns in Literature, 1985, classic edit., 1989, Transactions with Literature, 1990, The Perceptive I, 1997. With USN, 1945-46. Fellow Nat. Conf. Rsch. on Lang. and Literacy; mem. Nat. Coun. Tchrs. English (field rep. 1970-71, asst. exec. sec. 1971-73, assoc. exec. dir. 1973-78, chmn. commn. lit. 1979-83; trustees rsch. found. 1983-85; fund for tchg. of English 1993-96, Disting. Svc. award 1982, James R. Squire award 1999), Tex. Joint Coun. Tchrs. of English (pres. 1986-87, Disting. English Educator award 1989-90, Disting. Lifetime Svc. award 1999). Unitarian Universalist. Home: 6500 Sumac Dr Austin TX 78731-4117 Office: U Tex Dept Curriculum and Instrn Austin TX 78712

FARRELL, EDWARD WAGNER, retired dentist, educator; b. Jan. 12, 1921; Dentist VA Ohio, 1948—50; pvt. practice dentistry Youngstown, Ohio, 1952—62; dental dir. Ariz. Dept. Health, Phoenix, 1965—69, Fla. Dept. Health, Jacksonville, 1969—75; dir. dental aux. edn. Ind. U. Shc. Dentistry, N.W. Campus, Gary, 1975—86, ret. Served with U.S. Army, 1943—45, served with USN, 1946—48. Republican.

FARRELL, EILEEN MARIE, nurse, administrator; b. N.Y.C., Oct. 8, 1950; d. William James and Ann Marie (Hogan) F.; m. Steven Agronick, 1993. BSN, Columbia U., 1972, MPH, 1986; master's cert. in Info. Sys., Pace U., 1991. Cert. BCLS, nursing informatics. Staff nurse Vanderbilt Clinic Columbia Presbyn. Med. Ctr., N.Y.C., 1972-74, sr. supr. evenings emergency svcs. Vanderbilt Clinic, 1974-77, sr. supr. days Vanderbilt Clinic, 1978-80, adminstrv. nurse clinician emergency svcs., 1980-86, tng. coord. info. sys. divsn. nursing, 1986-93, nursing liaison ambulatory care, 1982, nurse practice adv., 1989-93; mgr. nursing informatics Meml. Sloan Ketterig Cancer Ctr., N.Y.C., 1993-97; nursing informatics specialist N.Y. Hosp., N.Y.C., 1997-98; edn. mgr. Mt. Sinai Hosp. Home Health Agy., N.Y.C., 1998-2000, mgr. clin. info. sys., 2000—01; project ops. adminstr. Mt. Sinai Hosp., 2001—. Preceptor, cons. Edna McConnell Clark and Columbia U. Sch. Nursing, 1978-86; preceptor ambulatory care Columbia U. Sch. Pub. Health, 1980-82; preceptor information systems N.Y.U. Grad. Sch. Nursing, 1992-93; tchr. seminars in field. Mem. NAFE, Women in Health Mgmt., N.Y. State Nurses Assn., Columbia U. Presbyn. Hosp. Alumnae Assn. Office: Mt Sinai Hosp NSG Adminstrn MC1 Level 1425 Madison Ave E Bldg Box 1168 New York NY 10029 E-mail: farrelle@msn.com.

FARRELL, FRANCINE ANNETTE, psychotherapist, educator, author; b. Long Beach, Calif., Mar. 26, 1948; d. Thomas and Evelyn Marie (Lucente) F.; m. James Thomas Hanley, Dec. 5, 1968 (div. Dec. 1988); children: Melinda Lee Hanley Flynn, James Thomas Hanley Jr.; m. Robert Erich Haesche, June 3, 1995. BA in Psychology with honors, Calif. State U., Sacramento, 1985, MS in Counseling, 1986. Lic. marriage and family therapist, Calif.; nat. cert. addiction counselor. Marriage, family and child counselor intern Fulton Ct. Counseling, Sacramento, 1987-88; pvt. practice psychotherapy, Sacramento, 1988—. Instr. chem. dependency studies program, Calif. State U., Sacramento, 1985-94, acad. coord. chem. dependency studies program, 1988-90; instr. cert. program in alcohol and drug studies U. Calif.-Davis Extension Programs, 1997-98; trainee Sobriety Brings a Change, Sacramento, 1986-87; assoc. investigator, curriculum coord. Project S.A.F.E., Sacramento, 1990-91; presenter Sacramento Conf., ACA, 1986, 88, 89, 91, 92, Ann. Symposium on Chem. Dependency, 1993. Presenter (cable TV series) Trouble in River City: Charting a Course for Change, 1991, H.O.W. Seminar Series, 1988-2000. Mem. AAUW, Calif. Assn. Marriage and Family Therapists, Calif. Assn. Alcoholism and Drug Abuse Counselors (bd. dirs. region 5, 1988-90), Phi Kappa Phi. Roman Catholic. Avocations: photography, writing, boating. Office: 2740 Fulton Ave Ste 100 Sacramento CA 95821-5184 Fax: 916-971-0388. E-mail: ffarrell@sbcglobal.net.

FARRELL, GREGORY ALAN, biomedical engineer; b. Bklyn., May 12, 1942; s. Edmond William and Edna Florence (Williams) F.; m. Mary Louise Lupiani, Sept. 3, 1966; children: Juliana Eden, Cristina Elizabeth. BSME, Cooper Union, 1964; MS in Biomed. Engring., Columbia U., 1972, postgrad., 1972—. Mech. engr. Gen. Dynamics, San Diego, 1964-65, Rochester, N.Y., 1965-67; rsch. asst. Columbia U. Med. Sch., N.Y.C., 1968-69; instr. pathology N.Y. Med. Coll., 1969-72; rsch. engr. Technicon Instruments Corp., Tarrytown, N.Y., 1972-82; mgr. mech. engring. Baker Instruments Corp., Allentown, Pa., 1982-84, prin. mech. engr., 1984-86; prin. engr. Nat. Patent Devel. Corp., N.Y.C., 1986-87; project engr. Bayer Diagnostics (formerly Miles Diagnostics) (formerly Technicon Instruments), Tarrytown, 1987-90, new product devel. mgr., 1990—; prin. staff engr. Tarrytown, 2000—; mgr. mech. engring., 2001—. Patentee in field; contbr. articles to profl. jours. Winner med. design excellence award, Indsl. Designers Soc. Am., 1998. Democrat. Roman Catholic. Achievements include development of of several automated clinical hematology, chemistry and immunology instruments. Home: 447 Hillcrest Rd Ridgewood NJ 07450-1520 Office: Bayer Diagnostics 511 Benedict Ave Tarrytown NY 10591-5005 E-mail: gregory.farrell.b@bayer.com.

FARRELL, HAROLD MARON, JR., chemist; b. Pottsville, Pa., Sept. 5, 1940; s. Harold M. and Marie G. (Daley) F.; m. Susan Gares, June 15, 1963; children: Judith A., Jonathan K. BS in Chemistry, Mt. St. Mary's Coll., 1962; MS in Biochemistry, Pa. State U., 1965, PhD, 1968. Postdoctoral fellow USDA Eastern Regional Rsch. Ctr., Phila., 1967-69, rsch. chemist, 1969-75, supervisory rsch. chemist, 1975—. Contbr. articles to profl. jours. and chpts. to books. Pres. Old York Rd. Community Concerts, Abington, Pa., 1991-2000, Glenside (Pa.) United Ch. of Christ, 1987-91; active troop 354 Boy Scouts Am., Willow Grove, Pa., 1980-90, cubmaster pack 336, 1978-80; trustee Upper Moreland Libr., Willow Grove, Pa., 2001-. Fellow Sigma Xi; mem. Am. Chem. Soc., Am. Dairy Sci. Assn. (com. chair 1976-00, bd. dirs. 1995-98, Borden award 1985), Am. Soc. for Biochemistry and Molecular Biology, Fed. Animal Sci. Soc. (bd. dirs. 1999—2002), Phila. Biochemists Club (treas.-sec. 1978-80). Avocations: choir singing, music. Home: 500 Inman Ter Willow Grove PA 19090-3614 Office: USDA 600 W Mermaid Ln Wyndmoor PA 19038 E-mail: hfarrell@arserrc.gov.

FARRELL, HERMAN DENNY, JR., state legislator, political organization worker; married; children: Monique, Herman D. III. Mem. N.Y. State Assembly, 1974—. Mem. rules com., dem. nat. com., 1988—, Black and Puerto Rican Caucus; chmn. N.Y. dem. party, assembly banks com., 1979-94; dem. dist. leader, 1973—. Del. Dem. Nat. Conv.; chmn. N.Y. County Dem. Com., 1981—, now also vice chmn. exec. com. Named Man of Yr., N.Y. State Supreme Ct. Officer's Assn. Address: 2541-55 A Clayton Powell Jr Blvd New York NY 10039*

FARRELL, JOHN BRENDAN, lawyer; b. Gary, Ind., Jan. 26, 1946; s. Edward Lawrence and Margaret (Byrnes) F.; m. Sue Ann Schulte, June 8, 1974; children: Sean Edward, Brian Patrick, Joseph Brendan. BA Marquette U., 1968; JD Thomas F. Cooley Law Sch., Lansing, Mich., 1977. Bar: Mich. 1977, U.S. Dist. Ct. (we. dist.) Mich. 1977. Midwest div. claims supt. Foremost Ins. Co., Grand Rapids, 1974-77 (sr. litigation counsel 1986—), claims atty., 1978-81, claims counsel, 1981-84, asst. v.p. claims, 1984—, assoc. Seth Barsky, Southfield, 1977-78; ptnr. Hibbs, Welch & MacApine P.C., Grand Rapids. Sec., Kentwood Zoning Bd. Appeals, 1982—; mem. Kentwood Citizens Safety Commn., 1983; adviser Jr. Achievement, Grand Rapids, 1980. Mem. Def. Research Inst., Mich. Def. Trial lawyers Assn., Assn. Trial Lawyers Am., ABA, Fedn. Ins. Defense Counsel (assoc.), Macomb County Bar Assn. Republican. Roman Catholic. Club: Charlevoix. Home: 660 Ten Point Dr Rochester Hills MI 48309-2549 Office: Hibbs Welch & MacAlpine PC 71 North Ave Mount Clemens MI 48043-5543

FARRELL, JOHN L., JR., lawyer, business executive; b. N.Y.C., Jan. 24, 1929; s. John Lawrence and Edna (Ziegler) F.; m. Beverly H. Farrell; children: John Lawrence III, Maureen, Jayne, Dianne, Michael. BA, St. Peters Coll., N.J., 1950; LL.B., St. John's U., 1955; MBA, NYU, 1960. Bar: N.Y. 1956. Asst. counsel ACF Industries, Inc., N.Y.C., 1955-61; counsel, sec., asst. to chmn. Knox Glass, Inc., N.Y.C., 1961-68; adminstrv. liaison Williams Cos., Tulsa, 1968-69; cons. on mergers and acquisitions, 1969-71; sr. v.p. law and adminstrn., sec. U.S. Filter Corp., N.Y.C., 1971-82; pres., chief operating officer FRACORP, Tulsa, 1983-84; cons. on mergers, acquisitions and fin. Frates Enterprises, Tulsa, 1984-87; prin. The Morgan Investment Group, Tulsa, 1988—; chmn. exec. com. Diagnetics, Inc., Tulsa, 1989-96. Mem. Ardsley (N.Y.) Sch. Bd., 1965-68. Served to 1st lt. U.S. Army, 1951-53. Republican. Roman Catholic. Home: 2128 E 60th Pl Tulsa OK 74105-7021

FARRELL, JOSEPH, movie market analyst, producer, entertainment research company executive, writer, sculptor, designer; b. N.Y.C., Sept. 11, 1935; s. John Joseph and Mildred Veronica (Dwyer) F. AB summa cum laude, St. John's Coll., 1958; A.M., U. Notre Dame, 1959; JD, Harvard U., 1965. Bar: N.Y. 1965. With firm Milbank, Tweed, Hadley & McCloy, N.Y.C., 1964-65; exec. assoc. Carnegie Corp. N.Y., 1965-66; exec. v.p., chief oper. officer Am. Council of Arts, 1966-71; cons. Rockefeller Bros. Fund, Spl. Projects, 1966-74, exec. v.p., 1974-77; vice chmn. Louis Harris & Assocs. (Harris Poll), N.Y.C., 1978; chmn., CEO, Nat. Rsch. Group, Inc., subs, VNU, L.A., London and Tokyo, 1978—. Movie market analyst and cons., 1978—; movie exec. producer, 1986—; sculptor, 1958—; designer Farbino Furniture, 1982—. Author, editor: Americans and the Arts, 1973, 75, Museums: USA, 1973, The Cultural Consumer, 1973, The U.S. Arts and Cultural Trend Data System, 1977; author: (novel) Birds of Prey, 1998; screenwriter The Foundation, Second Son, 1990—. Mem. Gov. N.Y. Task Force on Arts, 1975; founder, bd. dirs. Vol. Lawyers for Arts, 1968-76; bd. dirs. Arts and Bus. Coun. N.Y., 1973-76; bd. advisors Actors Studio, 1983-90. Woodrow Wilson fellow, 1958; named among Top 100 Influential People in Hollywood, Premiere mag., 1998, 99. Office: NRG 5900 Wilshire Blvd 29th Fl Los Angeles CA 90036-5013

FARRELL, JOSEPH CHRISTOPHER, retired mining executive, services executive; b. Boston, Sept. 27, 1935; s. Joseph C. and Ellen G. (Luttrell) F.; children: Christopher, Michael, John. BSEE, Northeastern U., 1958; MBA, Harvard U., 1963. Lic. pvt. pilot. Ensign USN, 1958, advanced through grades to lt. comdr., resigned, 1968; asst. treas. Freeport Indonesia, N.Y.C., 1968-72; treas. Queensland Nickel, Townsville, Australia, 1972-75; v.p. Freeport Minerals, N.Y.C., 1975-78; pres. Freeport Gold, Elko, Nev., 1978-84; exec. v.p., dir. Pittston Co., Greenwich, Conn., 1984-89, pres., COO, 1989-91, chmn., CEO, Stamford, Conn., 1991-98; ret., 1998. Bd. dirs. Aeroquip-Vickers, Inc., Maumee, Ohio, Universal Corp., Richmond, Va., ASA Corp., Johannesburg; mem. Northeastern U. Corp., Nev. Commn. Mining and Natural Resources; trustee Va. Commonwealth U. Sch. Engring.; bd. visitors James Madison U. Mem. AIME, World Coal Inst. (hon. mem.), Harvard Club, The Commonwealth Club Richmond, Sky Club (N.Y.C.), Blind Brook Club, Country Club of Va., Rotary. Office: 15 Avenue De La Mer Apt 2602 Palm Coast FL 32137-2290

FARRELL, JOSEPH MICHAEL, steamship company executive; b. Yonkers, N.Y., June 7, 1922; s. Joseph Michael and Mary Elizabeth (Powers) F.; m. Cloatta Grace Pennington, Dec. 6, 1946; children: Cloatta M., Anthony J., Christopher J., Janice E. BS in Marine Transp., U.S. Mcht. Marine Acad., 1943; postgrad., Columbia U., 1948-50, Fordham U., 1947-48. Commd. ensign USNR, 1943, advanced through grades to capt., 1960; ret., 1968; mgr. Great Lakes Svc., States Marine LInes, 1960-62; European mgr. States Marine Lines, Bremerhaven, Germany, 1962-65; exec. v.p. Waterman S.S. Corp., Washington, 1965-95. V.p. Hammond Leasing Corp., Mobile, Ala., 1967-89, Waterman S.S. Co. of Del., 1967-89; pres. Waterman Oceanic Corp., 1974-89; sr. v.p. Ctrl. Gulf Lines, 1993-95; v.p. Internat. Shipholding Corp., 1993-95. Recipient Outstanding Profl. Achievement U.S. Merchant Marine ACad., 1968-88; invested Knight of Malta, 1988. Mem. Propeller Club U.S. (v.p., bd. govs. 1967-68, U.S. Exec.

com. 1984-95), Nat. Def. Transp. Ass.n, Navy League, Congressional Country Club, Univ. Club, George Town Club (Washington), Siwanoy Country Club (Bronxville, N.Y.). Home: 4701 Willard Ave Apt 1214 Chevy Chase MD 20815-4625

FARRELL, KENNETH ROYDEN, economist; b. Ont., Can., Jan. 17, 1927; naturalized, 1958; s. William R. and Velma V. (Wood) F.; m. Mary Souter, Sept. 7, 1951; children: Janet, Betty, Deborah, Robert, Patricia, Lisa. BS, U. Toronto, Ont., 1950; MS, Iowa State U., 1955, PhD, 1958. Economist U. Calif., Berkeley, 1957-71; dep. adminstr. USDA, Washington, 1971-77, adminstr., 1977-81; dir. Nat. Ctr., Resources for the Future, Washington, 1981-87; v.p. U. Calif., Oakland, 1987-95, v.p. emeritus, 1995—. Economist Nat. Food Commn., Washington, 1965-66, Nat. Productivity Commn., Washington, 1972-73; mem. Presdl. Task Force, Washington, 1982; cons. Robert Nathan Assocs., 1983-84. Contbr. articles to profl. jours.; author (with others) books. Lt. Royal Can. Navy Reserve, 1946-48. Fulbright scholar U. Naples (Italy), 1963-64. Fellow AAAS, Am. Agrl. Econs. Assn. (bd. dirs. 1973-76, pres. 1976-77, named for Disting. Pub. Policy Contbn. 1980, 92); mem. Internat. Assn. Agrl. Econs., Commonwealth Club Calif., Phi Kappa Phi, Gamma Sigma Delta. Avocations: golf, gardening, literature. Office: Univ Calif 300 Lakeside Dr Ste 604 Oakland CA 94612-3534 E-mail: fkcnmar2001@aol.com., Kenneth.farrell@ucop.edu.

FARRELL, MARGARET, magazine publisher; BA, Fordham U. With Time Inc., 1975—90; assoc. pub. Reader's Digest, 1990—92; pub. Marie Claire, 1994-97; v.p., pub. Country Living Gardens, N.Y.C., 1997– 2000, sr. v.p. Family Cir. G+J USA, 2000 –, pub. Family Cir., 2000—. Office: G+J USA Publishing 375 Lexington Ave New York NY 10017-5514*

FARRELL, MARGARET DAWSON, lawyer; b. Bellingham, Wash., July 23, 1949; d. Sterling Jacob and Irene Hegg; m. David S. Farrell, June 10, 1972; children: Lindsay S., Charles D. BA cum laude, Smith Coll., 1971; postgrad., Georgetown U., 1971-72; JD, U. Cin., 1974. Bar: Ohio 1974, U.S. Dist. Ct. (so. dist.) Ohio 1974, R.I. 1976, U.S. Dist. Ct. R.I. 1976. Assoc. Frost & Jacobs, Cin., 1974-76; from assoc. to ptnr. Tillinghast, Collins & Graham, Providence, 1976—81; ptnr. Hinckley, Allen & Snyder LLP, Providence, 1981—. Lectr. Bryant Coll., 1979-80; dir., sec. Bank R.I., 1996—, Bancorp R.I., Inc., 2000—. Trustee Women and Infants Hosp., Providence, 1981—, sec., 1982-96, vice chair, 1996– ; bd. dirs. Women and Infants Corp., Providence, 1989—, sec., 1989-96, vice chair, 1996—; trustee, sec. Providence Preservation Soc. Revolving Fund, 1982-88; trustee Butler Hosp., 1995—, Care New England Health Sys., 1996—, R.I. Hist. Soc., 1980-85, Gordon Sch., East Providence, R.I., 1990-95; trustee Hosp. Assn. R.I., 1989-2003, mem. exec. coun., 1998-2003; trustee, sec., pres. Found. for Repertory Theatre, R.I., 1978-84; R.I. del. Am. Hosp. Assn. Congress Hosp. Trustees, 1993-98; mem. R.I. Bd. Regents for Elem. and Secondary Edn., 1987-90. Mem. ABA, R.I. Bar Assn. Avocations: golf, sailing, skiing, horseback riding. Office: Hinckley Allen & Snyder LLP 1500 Fleet Ctr Providence RI 02903-2319

FARRELL, MARIAN LOUISE, nursing educator; b. Carbondale, Pa. m. James Farrell; children: Jess, Dan, Sara, Rebecca. BSN, Coll. Miseracordia, Dallas, Pa., 1976, MSN, 1985; MS, Syracuse U., 1992; PhD, Adelphi U., 1992. Cert. CRNP, CNS. Nurse instr. Lach Co. Tech., Scranton, Pa., 1978—81, Commonwealth Med. Ctr., Scranton, 1981—87; asst. prof. nursing Marywood U., Dunmore, Pa., 1987—90; prof. nursing U. Scranton, 1990—. Author: Private Practices; contbr. articles to profl. jours. Chmn. March of Dimes. Mem.: Susan G. Komen NE Affiliate, Mar. of Dimes, Am. Cancer Soc. Office: U Scranton 800 Linden St Scranton PA 18510-2429

FARRELL, PATRICIA ANN, psychologist, educator, writer; b. N.Y.C. d. Joseph Alexander and Pauline Farrell. BA, Queens Coll.; MA, PhD, NYU. Lic. psychologist, N.J., Fla.; cert. online computer instr. Assoc. editor Pubs. Weekly Mag., N.Y.C.; editor Bestsellers Mag., N.Y.C.; assoc. editor King Features Syndicate, N.Y.C.; staff psychologist, intake coord. Mid-Bergen Cmty. Mental Health Ctr., Paramus, NJ; instr. Bergen C.C., Paramus, 1978-94; prof. clin. psychology Walden U., 1995—2001. Resident clin. psychology Am. Inst. for Counseling, N.J., 1990-91; cons. Family Counseling Svc. of Ridgewood, N.J., 1984; clin. psychology intern Marlboro (N.J.) Psychiat. Hosp., 1984-85, staff psychologist, 1985-87; rsch. analyst Mt. Sinai Sch. Medicine, 1987-88; account exec., sr. med. writer Manning, Selvage and Lee, N.Y.C., 1988-90; sr. clin. psychologist, mem. med. staff Greystone Pk (N.J.) Psychiat. Hosp., 1990-96; pvt. practice psychology, Englewood, N.J.; health sci. editor Time Warner Cable, Channel 10 News, 1995-2000; med. specialist N.J. Divsn. Disability Determination, 1997—; police surgeon Boro Ft. Lee, N.J., 1998—; psychiatry preceptor U. Medicine and Dentistry N.J. Med. Sch.; cons. pharm. clin. protocols; psychologist, expert moderator on anxiety and panic WebMD, 2000—. Guest radio and TV shows including The View, The O'Reilly Factor, ABC Sports Spl., ABC World News Tonight, Court TV, CNN Radio, Newsweek-on-Air, Voice of Am., Family Talk, Up Front Tonight, Pros and Cons, Local Live, USA Radio Network, Ken Hamblin Show, KNU Radio, Fox Beyond the News, Real Talk, Jay Thomas Radio Show, Sally Jessy Raphael, Montel Williams, Gordon Elliott Show, Inside Edit., Am. Jour., Joan Rivers Show, Fox Cable News, Good Day N.Y., Mark Walberg, Am. After Hours, Dini, The Shirley Show, Camilla Scott, USA Live, Alive and Wellness with Carol Martin, News Talk, Maury Povich, Caucus N.J., It's Your Call, One-on-One, The Carnie Wilson Show, AP Newswire, Judge for Yourself TV Show, N.Y.C. 10 O'Clock News, Cosmo, Redbook, Self, Fitness, Latina Maxim, Washington Post, Fox & Friends, Eyewitness News, Reuters TV, Timeout N.Y., Detroit News, Chgo. Tribune, Home Office Computing, Working Woman, N.Y. Post, Boston Globe, NY Daily News, New Woman, Phila. Enquirer, WPIX-TV, N.Y., UPN 9 News, WWOR-TV News, WNRR-TV, In Your Interest, LTV, Channel 10 News, On Campus, Sta WTTM, WSNJ, WHSI-TV, Bloomberg News, UPI News, KGAB, WSAR, Don Weeks Show, Common Concerns, WHSE-TV, Alan Nathan's Battle Lines, Dirk Van NBC radio, Ruth Koscielak Show, Voice of Am., WTOP, Redbook, Ramp, Fox & Friends, Eyewitness News, Cork Talks Back, TalkSport, The Week, Reuters TV, Bev Smith Show, Fitness, The Oregonian, Arnie Arneson Show, Talk Am., Real Simple, Marie Claire, Seventeen, Parents, Shape, PHysical, Christian Single, Mental Health Law Report; author: (manual) Alzheimer's Disease Assessment Scale test, How To Be Your Own Therapist, 2002; contbr. book chpt. to Innovations in Clin. Practice: A Source Book, 15th edit., 2000; contbr. articles to Writer's Digest, Real World, Postgrad. Medicine, newspapers. Bd. dirs., chmn. med. liaison com. liaison to dept. psychiatry Bergen Pines County Hosp., Paramus, 1994-95. McDonald's rsch. grantee, 1994-95; recipient Sci. award Rotary Club. Avocations: fitness, racquetball, kite-flying. Office: PO Box 1525 Englewood Cliffs NJ 07632-0283 E-mail: pfarrell@ix.netcom.com.

FARRELL, PHILIP M. dean, physician, educator, researcher; b. St. Louis, Nov. 26, 1943; m. Alice Yeakle; children: Michael Henry, David Sean, Bridget Mary AB, St. Louis U., 1964, MD, PhD, St. Louis U., 1970. Diplomate Am. Bd. Pediatrics. Asst. prof. dept. child health Washington U., Washington, 1975; asst. prof. dept. pediatrics U. Wis., Madison, 1977-78, assoc. prof. pediatrics, 1978-82, prof. pediatrics, 1982—, chmn. dept. pediatrics, 1985-95, affiliate scientist Wis. Regional Primate Research Ctr., 1978, affiliate faculty dept. nutrition scis., 1978, dir. Pediatric Pulmonary Specialized Ctr. of Research, 1981-85, co-dir. Cystic Fibrosis Ctr., 1983-85, dean Med. Sch., 1995—. Sr. investigator pediatric metabolism br. Nat. Inst. Arthritis, Metabolism and Digestive Diseases NIH, Bethesda, Md., 1974-75, chief sect. on devel. biology and clin. nutrition Neonatal and Pediatric Medicine br. Nat. Inst. Child Health and Human Devel., 1975, chief Neonatal and Pediatric Medicine br., 1975 Editor: Lung Development: Biological and Clinical Perspectives, 1982 Avalon Found. scholar, 1965-67, Thurston Meml. scholar, 1966-70; Fogarty Internat. fellow, 1985 Mem. Am. Chem. Soc., Am. Acad. Pediatrics, Soc. Pediatric Research, Am. Thoracic Soc., Soc. Exptl. Biology and Medicine, Am. Inst. Nutrition, Am. Soc. Clin. Nutrition, Wis. Assn. Perinatal Care, Sigma XI, Phi Beta Kappa, Alpha Omega Alpha. Office: Univ Wis Office of Dean 1300 University Ave Rm 1217 Madison WI 53706-1510

FARRELL, SHARON ELAINE, retired real estate broker; b. Boston, Nov. 8, 1941; d. Winston Cushman and Evelyn (Murphy) Lawson; m. James E. Waldron, Oct. 15, 1961 (div. Apr. 1987); children: Peter M., Kathleen M.; m. Richard J. Farrell, May, 1994. Grad., Realtors Inst., 1987; BS, Stonehill Coll., 1998. Cert. residential specialist. Den mother Cub Scouts Boy Scouts Am., East Bridgewater, 1972-76, den leader, coach, 1976-78; mem. com., 1978-79. Mem. Am. Soc. Notaries (life), Green Key Soc., Beta Xi, Theta Alpha Kappa. Roman Catholic. Avocations: reading, travel. Home: 10 Colewood Rd East Bridgewater MA 02333-1687

FARRELL, TERESA JOANNING, lawyer; b. L.A., Sept. 17, 1958; d. Harold T. and Helen Dolores Joanning; m. Michael P. Farrell, Oct. 18, 1986. BA, U. Calif., San Diego, 1980; JD, U. Calif., 1986. Bar: Calif. 1986, U.S. Dist. Ct. (ctrl. dist.) Calif. 1987. Assoc., spl. counsel Gibson, Dunn & Crutcher LLP, Irvine, Calif., 1986-98, ptnr., 1999—. Bd. dirs. Second Harvest Food Bank, Orange, Calif., 1993—, The Harvesters, Newport Beach, Calif., 1993—, Pretend City--The Children's Mus. of Orange County, Newport Beach, Calif., 2001—. Mem. Calif. State Bar Assn. (real property sect.), Internat. Coun. Shopping Ctrs. Office: Gibson Dunn & Crutcher LLP 4 Park Plz Ste 1400 Irvine CA 92614-8557

FARRELL, W. JAMES, metal products manufacturing company executive; b. N.Y.C., 1942; BA, U. Detroit, 1965. Salesman Ill. Tool Wks., Inc., Glenview, Ill., exec. v.p., pres., chmn. bd., chmn. bd., CEO, 1996—. Office: Illinois Tool Wks Inc 3600 W Lake Ave Glenview IL 60025-5811

FARRELL, WARREN THOMAS, author; b. N.Y.C., June 26, 1943; s. Thomas Edward and Muriel (Levy) F.; m. Ursie Otte Fairbairn, June 19, 1966 (div. 1977); m. Liz Dowling, Aug. 4, 2002. BA in Social Sci., Montclair State U., 1965; MA in Political Sci., U. Calif., L.A., 1966; PhD in Political Sci., NYU, 1974; D. of Humane Letters, Profl. Sch. Psychology, San Diego, 1985. Diplomate Am. Bd. Sexology; cert. tchr. NJ. Adj. asst. prof. Sch. of Medicine U. Calif., San Diego, 1986—88; candidate for Gov. Calif. 2003 Recall Election, First Candidate in US History on ballot as "Fathers' Issues" Candidate; cons. & spkr. Young Presidents' Orgn., 2003; cons. in field. Author: The Liberated Man, 1975, Why Men Are The Way They Are, 1986, 87, 88, The Myth of Male Power, 1993, 94, Women Can't Hear What Men Don't Say, 1999 (Book-of-the-Month Club 1999), Father and Child Reunion, 2001; contbr. articles to profl. jours; TV appearances include Oprah, Donahue, The Today Show, Larry King Live, ABC World News with Peter Jennings, Crossfire, CBC's Newsworld, CNN Special on Candidacy, 2003; TV spls. ABC's 20/20, ABC (Australia), BBC (Britian), CBC (Can.), People Mag., Parade Mag., Japan Times, N.Y. Times, Wall St. Jour., Time, Forbes, Der Spiegel, Mac Leans, London Times, So. China Morning Post, others. Recipient Outstanding Contribution award Calif. Assn. Marriage Family Therapists, 1988, Pioneer in the Psychology of Fatherhood award Onstep Inst. Mental Rsch., 2000; named Top 100 Thought Leaders worldwide Fin. Times, 2000. Mem. Nat. Coalition Free Men (adv. bd. 1996—2002, best book 1986), Nat. Congress Fathers & Children (bd. dirs. 1992—, best book 1993), Nat. Org. Women (N.Y.C Chpt. bd. dirs. 1970-73), Children's Rights Council (adv. bd. 1985—), Am. Coalition of Fathers and Children (bd. dirs. 96-98). Unitarian Universalist. Achievements include books published in more than 50 countries and more than 10 languages. Home and Office: 2982 Las Olas Ct Carlsbad CA 92009 E-mail: warren@warrenfarrell.com.

FARRELL, WILLIAM CHRISTOPHER, lobbyist; b. Amsterdam, N.Y., Dec. 30, 1951; s. Francis M. and Margaret (Holmes) F.; m. Mary E. Crowley-Farrell, Sept. 1, 1979; children: Eliza Carolyn, Luke Jeremiah. AB in Polit. Sci., Providence (R.I.) Coll., 1974; MA in Polit. Sci., Rutgers U., New Brunswick, N.J., 1979; student post-grad studies, George Washington U., 1983-87. Social worker Dublin (Ireland) Com., 1980-81; legis. analyst State and Fed. Assocs., Washington, 1981-82; computer mgr. Rep. Gerry Sikorski, 1982; legis. asst. Rep. Bill Richardson, 1982-84; legis. dir. Rep. Tommy Robinson, 1984-89; lobbyist, organizer Nat. Assn. Retired Fed. Employees, 1989—. Bd. mem. Action in Montgomery, Montgomery County, 1994—. Mem. Kemp Mill Civic Assn., Silver Spring, Md., 1987—, Montgomery Democrats, Rockville, Md., 1993—, Capital Area Polit. Sci. Assn., Washington, 1993—; coach Montgomery Soccer, Inc.; leader Boy Scouts Am., Silver Spring, Md., 2002. Fellow Eagleton Inst. of Politics, Rutgers U., New Brunswick, N.J., 1977. Mem. St. Andrew Apostle Parish, Pi Sigma Alpha. Avocations: hiking, biking, rafting, theater, soccer. Office: National Assn Retired Fed Employees 606 N Washington St Alexandria VA 22314-1914 E-mail: cfarrell@narfe.org.

FARRELL, WILLIAM EDGAR, sales executive, infosystems specialist, management consultant; b. Jeanette, Pa., Mar. 13, 1937; s. Arthur Richard and Lelia (Ryder) F.; m. Sara Lynnette Swing, Aug. 20, 1960; children: Wendy J., Tracy L., Rebecca J. BS in Edn., Pa. State U., 1959. Location mgr. IBM Corp., Dover, Del., 1969-72, corp. lobbyist Washington, 1972-74, planning cons., 1974-78, nat. mktg. mgr., 1978-80, exec. asst., 1980-81, account exec. Denver, 1981-87, policy exec., 1987-91; pres., CEO Weatherall Co., Inc., Englewood, Colo., 1993-97; chief info. officer, v.p. info. tech. & purchasing Wild West, Inc., Kearney, Nebr., 1998—2001; v.p. sales Skydex Tech., Inc., Englewood, Colo., 2001—. CFO, Wide Horizon, Inc., Denver, 1987-92, chmn. bd. trustees, 1989-92; pres. Exec. Mgmt. Cons., 1987—; sec.-treas. Electronic Shoe Enterprises Inc., 1991-94; mem. Colo. Info. Mgmt. Commn., 1992-95; bd. dirs. Energaire Corp. Founding mem. River Falls Community Assn., Potomac, Md., 1975; first reader First Ch. of Christ Scientist, Chevy Chase, Md., 1976-80; chmn. Amigo's De Ser; bd. dirs. Rocky Mountain Ser, 1991-92. Recipient Outstanding Contbn. award IBM Corp., 1968. Republican. Avocation: flying instrument S.E.L. airplanes.

FARRELL LOGAN, VIVIAN, actress; b. N.Y.C. m. Harvey Lewis, Aug. 5, 1979 (dec. Aug. 1980); m. Tracy Harrison Logan, June 3, 1984 (dec. Sept. 1996). BS in Edn., Syracuse U.; MA in Theatre, NYU. Tchr. elem. sch. Levittown (N.Y.) Schs., 1965-75. Tchr. workshops Coll. of Cape Breton, N.S., Can., 1977-79. Appearances include (stage) Gateway Playhouse, Bellport, N.Y., Playhouse 3200, Richmond, Va., Bartke's Dinner Theatre, Tampa, Fla., (film) Impulse; narrator for Nutcracker, Eglevsky Ballet Co. with L.I. Symphony Orch., Nassau Coliseum, Uniondale, N.Y., 1978-79; appeared as The Musical Storyteller and as Amelia Earhart in her one-woman play, Queen's Theatre in the Park Flushing Meadows, 1998, Lincoln Ctr., N.Y.C., Carnegie Recital Hall, N.Y.C., 1978-80, also in various libraries and schs., N.Y. area; performer, 1978—, writer, performer (album) The Musical Storyteller, 1978; author: (children's book) Robert's Tall Friend: A Story of the Fire Island Lighthouse 10th anniv. ed. 1997, 2d printing 1999, appearing numerous schs., librs. in Author Narrates Her Book Robert's Tall Friend, 1989—, 3rd printing, 2002 (named Ofcl. Children's Book of Town of Babylon 2002, also Ofcl. Book of Suffolk County), 1989—; appearing N.Y.C schs. and on tour in one-woman play Amelia, My Courageous Sister, 1993—. Nassau County (N.Y.) Office Cultural Devel grantee, 1986—, N.Y. State Coun. on the Arts grantee, 1986—. Mem. Actors Equity Assn., SAG, AFTRA, Twelfth Night Club, Ninety-Nines, Alpha Psi Omega, Zeta Phi Eta. Avocations: flying, tennis. Office: PO Box 734 Lindenhurst NY 11757-0734

FARRELLY, BOBBY (ROBERT LEO RARRELLY JR.), writer, producer, director; b. Cumberland, R.I., 1958; m. Nancy Farrelly; 2 children. Student, Rensselaer Poly. Inst. Writer, prodr. Outside Providence, 1999; writer, co-prodr. Dumb and Dumber, 1994; exec. prodr., writer, dir. There's Something About Mary, 1998; writer, prodr., dir. Me, Myself and Irene, 2000, Shallow Hall, 2001; writer Bushwacked, 1995; dir. Kingpin, 1996; dir., prodr. Osmosis Jones, 2001; prodr. Say It Isn't So, 2001. Recipient Screenwriter of Yr. ShoWest Conv., 1999. Office: Creative Artists Agy c/o Adam Kantor 9830 Wilshire Blvd Beverly Hills CA 90212-1825

FARRELLY, MARK JOHN, retired theologian, priest; b. St. Louis, Oct. 20, 1927; s. John Joseph Farrelly and Cordelia Mary Gross. STD, Cath. U. Am., 1962. Ordained Benedictine Priest St. Anselm's Abbey, Washington, D.C., 1955. Prof. theology De Sales Sch. Theology, Washington, 1967—97. Author: (books) Predestination, Grace and Free Will, 1964, God's Work in a Changing World, 1985, Belief in God in Our Time, 1992, Faith in God through Jesus Christ, 1997; contbr. articles over 100 articles and reviews to prof. jours. Mem.: Cath. Theol. Soc. Am. (lectures given at conventions). Roman Catholic. Avocation: conducting spirituality workshops. Home: 4501 S Dakota Ave NE Washington DC 20017 Office: St Anselm's Abbey 4501 S Dakota Ave NE Washington DC 20017 Fax: 202-269-2312. E-mail: Mjfarrelly@aol.com.

FARRELLY, PETER JOHN, screenwriter; b. Phoenixville, Pa., Dec. 17, 1956; s. Robert Leo and Mariann (Neary) F. BA, Providence Coll., 1979; MFA, Columbia U., 1987. Salesman U.S. Lines, Inc., Boston, 1979-81; bartender various libationary locales, Boston, 1981-85; screenwriter Paramount Columbia and Disney Studios, Los Angeles, 1985—. Author Outside Providence, 1988; co-writer (TV spls.) Our Planet Tonight, 1987, Paul Reiser: Out on a Whim, 1987; writer (film) Dumb & Dumber, 1994, Bushwhacked, 1995, There's Something About Mary, 1998; dir. (film) Dumb & Dumber, 1994, Kingpin, 1996, There's Something About Mary, 1998; prodr. There's Something About Mary, 1998, Outside Providence, 1999; writer, co-dir, prodr.: Me, Myself & Irene, 2000, Shallow Hal, 2002. Mem. Writers Guild Am. West. Roman Catholic.

FARREN, ANN LOUISE, chemist, information scientist, educator; b. Portage, Pa., Dec. 5, 1926; dJ. Edward and Ann (Conrad) F. AB, U. Pa., 1948. Biochemist Jefferson Med. Coll./Valley Forge Hosp., Phila./Phoenixville, Pa., 1948-52; organic chemist Smith, Kline & French Labs., Phila., 1952-53; chemist Rohm & Haas Co., Phila., 1953-56; head info. office Am. Chem. Soc. News Svc., N.Y.C., 1956-59; with BIOSIS, Phila., 1959—, profl. rels. officer, 1962-74, mgr. edn. bur., 1974-78, sr. edn. specialist, 1978-95, lead database specialist, 1996-98, ret., 1998, ednl cons., 1998—. Bd. dirs. Delaware Valley Sci. Coun., 1972—. Fellow AAAS; mem. Am. Chem. Soc. (bd. dirs. Phila. sect., Ullyot award 1993), Am. Inst. Biol. Scis., Nat. Assn. Sci. Writers. Home: 5720 Wissahickon Ave Apt D19 Philadelphia PA 19144-5610 E-mail: alf12@aol.com.

FARREN, CAROL ELESE, facility management consultant; b. Glen Ridge, N.J., Dec. 10, 1944; d. Merritt Freeman and Katherine Elizabeth Farren; m. Steven Charles Bagdan, May 17, 1969 (div. Sept. 1975); m. Dennis DeBenedetto, Oct. 26, 1991 (div. Feb. 1996). BS, Cornell U., 1966; postgrad., Parsons Sch. Design, 1967; MBA, NYU, 1979. Cert. facility mgr. 1993, mgmt. cons. Inst. Mgmt. Cons., 2002. Adminstrv. coord. Maria Bergson Assocs., N.Y.C., 1967-69; adminstrv. mgr. J. Gordon Carr & Assocs., N.Y.C., 1969-70; adminstrv. dir. interiors dept. Carson Lundin & Thorson Architects, N.Y.C., 1970-73; purchasing agt., corp. designer AOL Time Warner Inc., N.Y.C., 1973-76, dir. facilities dept., 1979-88; pres., founder CD/3 Design, N.Y.C., 1976-79, Facility Mgmt. World Wide Ltd., N.Y.C., 1988—; chmn., COO, founder Sharon Springs Heights Devel. Inc., East Durham, N.Y., 1990—. Mem. adv. bd. design and environ. analysis dept. Cornell U., Ithaca, N.Y., 1988-97; mem. curriculum com. Real Estate Inst. NYU, N.Y.C., 1988-90; mem. adv. bd. Profl. Office Design mag., N.Y.C., 1989-90; assoc. prof. facility mgmt. masters degree program Pratt Inst., Bklyn., 1992-96; facility mgmt. panelist USN, 2002-03. Author (ref. textbook) Planning and Managing Interior Projects, 1988, 2d edit., 1999 (IFMA-GNY Author of Yr. 1999); contbr. articles to mags. and jours. Fellow Internat. Facility Mgmt. Assn. (pres. 1987-88, v.p. Greater N.Y. chpt. 1985-86, bd. dirs. 1985-2003, spkr. 1989-91, named Profl. Mem. of Yr. 1994), NRCC (N.Y. Businessman of Yr., 2001, mem. bus. adv. coun.); mem. Profl. Women in Constrn., Inst. of Mgmt. Cons. (ethics com.), Facility Mgmt. Cons. Coun. (pres.-elect 2002—). Republican. Episcopalian. Avocations: skiing, rock climbing, white water inflatable kyaking, wind surfing, gardening. Office: Facility Mgmt World Wide Ltd 7080 Route 81 East Durham NY 12423-1159 Fax: 518-239-4462. E-mail: fmww@earthlink.net

FARRINGTON, BERTHA LOUISE, retired nursing administrator; b. Poteet, Tex., Jan. 20, 1937; d. Leonard Gilbert and Janie (Hernandez) Lozano; m. James Charles Farrington, Jan. 30, 1965; children: Mark Hiram, Robert Lee. BSN, Tex. Women's U., 1960; NP, U. Tex., 1984. RN, Tex. Charge nurse emergency rm. Parkland Meml. Hosp., Dallas; head nurse emergency rm./day surgery Bapt. Meml. Hosp., Pensacola, Fla.; asst. dir. health svcs. U. Tex. Southwestern Med. Ctr., Dallas, dir. student health svcs., ret., 2002. Cons. Student Health Com. E-mail: j.bfarrington@sbcglobal.net.

FARRINGTON, BUFORD LEE, lawyer; b. Kansas City, Mo., July 30, 1947; s. James Spencer and Beverly Jeanne F.; m. Diane M., Aug. 17, 1968; children: Whitney B., Jay D. BS in Pub. Administrn., U. Mo., 1969, JD, 1975. Bar: Mo. 1975. Atty., shareholder Humphrey, Farrington, & McClain, P.C., Independence, 1981—. Co-author: Independent Administration. Chmn. election bd. Jackson Co., Independence, 1986-91, mem., chmn. Rep. Com., Kansas City, 1994—; chmn. Charter Amendment Com., Independence, 1984. Fellow Am. Coll. Trust and Estate Counsel. Republican. Methodist. Office: Humphrey Farrington & McClain PC 221 W Lexington Ave Ste 400 Independence MO 64050-3722

FARRINGTON, GREGORY C. university administrator; b. Bronxville, N.Y. B in Chemistry, Clarkson U., 1968; AM in Chemistry, Harvard U., 1970, PhD in Chemistry, 1972; degree (hon.), U. Uppsala, Sweden, 1984. Staff sci. GE, Schenectady, N.Y., 1972-79; assoc. prof. materials sci. and engring. U. Pa., 1979-84, prof., 1984, chair dept. materials sci. and engring., 1984-87, dir. Lab. for Rsch. on Structure of Matter, 1987-90, dean Sch. Engring. and Applied Sci., 1990-98; pres. Lehigh U., 1998—. Office: Lehigh U Office of the Pres 27 Memorial Dr West, Alumni Memorial Bld Bethlehem PA 18015 E-mail: gcf2@lehigh.edu.

FARRINGTON, HELEN AGNES, personnel director; b. Queens, N.Y., Dec. 1, 1945; d. Joseph Christopher and Therese Marie (Breazzano) F. AS, Interboro Inst., N.Y.C., 1965; AA, Ohio State U., 1983, BS in Human Resource Mgmt., 1987; Mgmt. cert., U. Mich., 1980. Pers. adminstr. Am. Electric Power Co., N.Y.C., 1974-79; supr. human resources Ohio Power divsn. Am. Electric Power Co., Newark, 1979-87; dir. human resources Citizens Utilities Co., Stamford, Conn., 1987-88; mgr., exec. search firm Arthur Lyle Assocs., Norwalk, Conn., 1988-89; dir. human resources CaroLee Designs, Inc., Greenwich, Conn., 1990-92, ind. HR cons., 1992-95; dir. human resources The Gartner Group, Stamford, 1993-95; prin., chief people officer HFA Resources LLC, Niwot, Colo., 1996—. Bd. dirs.-at-large MARC, non-profit, Lakewood, Colo., bd. dirs. Boulder Cmty. Hosp. Aux. Bd., 2003. Mem.: NAFE, Consultants Forum, Boulder Area Human Resources Assn., Colo. Human Resources Assn., Soc. Human Resources Mgmt., Am. Soc. Profl. Female Execs., Am. Mgmt. Assn. Office: PO Box 438 Niwot CO 80544-0438

FARRINGTON, HUGH G. wholesale food and retail drug company executive; b. 1945; married BA, Dartmouth Coll., 1968. With Hannaford Bros., Scarborough, Maine, 1968—, exec. v.p., 1981-84, pres., chief operating officer, 1984-92, pres., CEO, 1992—, dir. Office: Hannaford Bros Co PO Box 1000 Portland ME 04104-5005

FARRINGTON, JERRY S. utility holding company executive; b. Burkburnett, Tex., 1934; BBA, North Tex. State U., 1955, MBA, 1958. With Tex. Electric Service Co., 1957-60; v.p. Tex. Utilities Co. (parent co.), Dallas, 1970-76, pres., 1983-87, chmn., CEO, 1987-95, chmn., 1995-98; pres. Dallas Power & Light Co., 1976-83; chmn., CEO Tex. Utilities Fuel Co., Tex. Utilities Mining Co., Dallas, 1987-95, chmn. emeritus, 1998—. Office: Tex Utilities Co Energy Plz 1601 Bryan St Fl 41 Dallas TX 75201-3401

FARRINGTON, JOHN WILLIAM, academic administrator, dean, research scientist; b. New Bedford, Mass., Sept. 25, 1944; s. John James Grace and Hazel Evelyn F.; m. Shirley Gale Hutchinson, May 28, 1966; children: Karen Lee Sabetta, Jeffrey William. BS in chemistry, U. Mass. Dartmouth, 1966, MS in chemistry, 1968; PhD in oceanography, Univ. R.I., 1972. Grad. tchg. asst. U. Mass. Dartmouth, New Bedford, Mass., 1966-68; summer rsch. fellow Biochemical Rsch. Labs. Dow Chemical Co., Midland, Mich., 1968; grad. rsch. asst. Graduate Sch. of Oceanography, URI, Kingston, R.I., 1968-69, fed. water quality adminstrn. fellow, 1969-71; postdoctoral investigator, asst., assoc., sr. scientist Woods Hole (Mass.) Oceanographic Inst. Chemistry Dept., 1971-88; dir. coastal rsch. ctr. Woods Hole Oceanographic Inst., 1982-87; Michael P. Walsh prof., dir. Environmental Scis. Program, U. Mass., Boston, 1988-90; assoc. dir. edn., dean, sr. scientist Woods Hole Oceanographic Inst., 1990—2002, v.p. for acad. programs, dean, 2002—. Cons. several companies, adv. nat., internat. organizations with respect to oceanography. Contbr. over 120 sci. jour. articles and book chpts. Trustee Bermuda Biological Station for Rsch, Bermuda, N.Y., 1990—, New Bedford Aquarium, 1998—, Big Brother/Big Sisters, Cape Cod and the Islands, Mass., 1998-2002; asst. cub master, Weblos leader Falmouth Pack, St. Barnabas Ch., Falmouth, Mass., 1978-79. Recipient

Best Paper award Organic Geochemistry Divsn./Geochemical Soc., Marine Educator award Mass. Marine Educators Assn., 1996, Excellence in Rsch. award URI Alumni/ae Assn., Kingston, 1998, USGS Amb. of Sci. award, 2001, David B. Stone award N.E. Aquarium, 2001. Mem. Am. Chem. Soc., Am. Geophysical Union, Am. Assn. for the Advancement of Sci., Oceanography Soc., Estuarine Rsch. Fedn., N.Y. Acad. Sci., Sigma Xi/Woods Hole Chpt. (pres. 1995-96). Protestant. Office: Woods Hole Oceanographic Inst MS #31 360 Woods Hole Rd Woods Hole MA 02543-1536

FARRINGTON, ROBERT MARTIN, language educator; b. Bay City, Mich., Aug. 3, 1939; s. Donald Charles and Mary Ellen (Jeuderine) Farrington; m. Merrel L. Amins, July 4, 1965; 1 child, Jessica Deborah Farrington Ruthkopf. BA, Mich. State U., 1961, MA, 1965; PhD, NYU, 1980. Cert. tchr. English, French, Spanish N.Y. Faculty Mich. State U., East Lansing, 1961—63; tchr. Lycée Vauvenargues, Aix-en-Provence, France, 1963—65, Mount Vernon H.S., NY, 1966—67, Byran Hills H.S., Armonk, NY, 1967—78, Scarsdale Schs., NY, 1978—95; instr. Westchester C.C., Valhalla, NY, 1991—2002, Columbus State C.C., Ohio, 2002—. Writer/editor/cons. The Coll. Digest, Larchmont, NY, 1983—87. Author: (monograph) European Lyric Folkdrama, 2001, (novels) Mockwasaka: Red-haired Woman, 2003; contbr. Grantee Fulbright Travel grantee, Inst. Internat. Edn., 1963; French Govt. fellow, 1963. Mem.: Phi Beta Kappa. Avocation: swimming. Office: Columbus State Univ Spring St Columbus OH

FARRINGTON-HOPF, SUSAN KAY, plumbing and heating contractor; b. Seattle, Dec. 17, 1940; d. Donald Robert and Dorothy May (Graf) Little; m. Edwin Terry Farrington, Sept. 4, 1959 (div. Apr. 1972); children: Cathe T., Jacqueline M.; m. William Desmond Hopf, Nov. 20, 1983. BA cum laude, U.S. Internat. U., 1975, MA, 1976. Program spkr. AMR Internat., N.Y.C., 1977-82; pres. Dawson Plumbing & Heating Co., Seattle, 1979—. Tng. cons. Fred Sherman, Inc., San Marcos, Calif., 1982—; cons. Pacific S.W. Airlines, San Diego, 1977, Dept. Labor Job Corps, Moses Lake, Wash., 1978. Developer assertive mgmt. workshop, 1976. Mem. Seattle Execs. Assn. (bd. dirs., treas., v.p., pres. 1993—), Nat. Bath and Kitchen Assn., Nat. Assn. Plumbing Heating Cooling Contractors, Master Builders Assn. Avocations: skiing, sailing, gardening. Home: 16419 261st Ave SE Issaquah WA 98027-8214 Office: Dawson Plumbing & Heating Co 1522 12th Ave Seattle WA 98122-3908

FARRIOR, EVAN BELL, special education educator, writer; b. Jersey City, June 2, 1952; BA, N.J. City U., 1977. Cert. tchr. of the handicapped. Supr. Occupl. Ctr. Hudson County, Jersey City, 1978—83; tchr. spl. edn. Jersey City Pub. Sch., 1983—. Advocate for spl. needs Farrior Advocacy Svc., Jersey City, 1983—. Author: (book) Enoch: A Faith Tale, 1995, Love Is a Strange Thing, 2003. Notary pub. Farrior Notary Svcs., Jersey City, 1995—; pres., owner Farrior Enterprise, Jersey City, 2002—; pres. Evan B. Farrior Ministries Inc., Jersey City, 1995—. Named Golden Poet, World of Poetry, 1986, 1987, 1988, 1989, 1990, 1991, 1992; recipient citation, County of Hudson, 1991, Svc. award, Afro Am. Indsl. Women's Club, 1988, citation, County of Hudson, 1999. Mem.: NEA, CEC, Flagship Interval Assn. Inc., Interval Internat., Spl. Olympics, N.J. State Coun. on Arts, Hudson County Coun. on Arts, Nat. Notary Assn., Famous Poet Soc. (Famous poet 1998, 1999, 2000, Famous Poet 2001, 2002, 2003), Internat. Soc. Poets (Poet of Yr. 1999, 2000, Editor's Choice 2000, Poet of Yr. 2001, Editor's Choice 2001, Poet of Yr. 2002, Editor's Choice 2002, Poet of Yr. 2003), Authors League of Am., Inc., Author's Guild, Am. Christian Writers, Feed the Children, N.J. Performing Arts Ctr., Learning Resource Ctr.-N/NS, N.J. Edn. Assn., Hudson County Edn. Assn., Jersey City Edn. Assn. Assembly Of God. Avocations: traveling, writing, cooking, singing, listening to music. Home: 348 5th St Jersey City NJ 07302-2345 Home Fax: 201-656-0619. Personal E-mail: Enoch348@aol.com.

FARRIS, CHARLES, JR., obstetrician, gynecologist; b. Greenville, Miss., Oct. 2, 1925; MD, U. Tenn., Memphis, 1951. Diplomate Am. Bd. Ob-Gyn.; cert. menopause clinician. Intern Charity Hosp., New Orleans, 1951-52, resident ob-gyn., 1952-55; mem. staff Bapt. campus Meml. Med., New Orleans; assoc. prof. Ochsner Clinic Tulane U., New Orleans; pvt. practice New Orleans. Fellow AMA, ACS, ACOG, New Orleans Ob-Gyn. Soc.; mem. Internat. Menopause Soc., N.Am. Menopause Soc. Office: Womens Pavilion Ochsner Clinic 4429 Clara St Ste 640 New Orleans LA 70115-8243

FARRIS, FRANK A. mathematician, educator, editor; s. Ragene A. and Marjorie Farris; life ptnr. William O. Beeman. BA, Pomona Coll., 1977; PhD, MIT, 1981. Asst. prof. math. Santa Clara (Calif.) U., 1984—88, assoc. prof. math. and computer sci., 1988—. Editor Math. Mag. Math. Assn. Am., Washington, 2001—. Recipient Trevor Evans award, 2001. Mem.: Phi Beta Kappa. Unitarian-Universalist. Avocation: singing. Office: Santa Clara Univ 500 El Camino Real Santa Clara CA 95053 E-mail: ffarris@scu.edu.

FARRIS, JEFFERSON DAVIS, university administrator; b. Springdale, Ark., Sept. 30, 1927; s. Jeff D. and Loretta J. (Grunder) F.; m. Patricia Ann Camp, July 31, 1948; children— Rebecca, Elizabeth, Jefferson Davis III. BS in Engring, U. Central Ark., 1949; MA, Peabody Coll., 1950; M.P.H. (USPHS fellow), U. Mich., 1957; Ed.D., U. Ark., 1963; DHL, Sch. of Ozarks, 1981. Tchr. public high sch., Pine Bluff, Ark., 1950-57; dir. public health edn. Ark. Dept. Health, Little Rock, 1957-61; prof. health edn. U. Central Ark., Conway, 1961-86, chmn. dept. health and phys. edn., 1961-68, dean, 1968-75, univ. pres., 1975-86; nat. exec. dir. Nat. Assn. Intercollegiate Athletics, Kansas City, Mo., 1986-91. Mem. adv. com. Nat. Endowment Humanities; chair U.S. Collegiate Sports Coun., 1988-91. Editor: A Guide for School Health Education, 1956, Handbook for Elementary Physical Education, 1964. Mem. Ark. Gov.'s Council on Youth Fitness; bd. dirs. Conway (Ark.) Meml. Hosp., 1971-86, civilian aide for Ark. to sec. of army, 1979-81. Served with USN, 1946-48. Named Layman of Yr. Ark. Assn. Dentistry for Children, 1970 Mem. Ark. Assn. Deans (pres. 1968-75), Nat. Assn. Intercollegiate Athletics. Clubs: Rotary (pres. local, Paul Harris fellow 1986). Methodist. Home: 2 Delavaga Cir Hot Springs National Park AR 71909-6009 E-mail: jeffpat@cswnet.com.

FARRIS, JEROME, federal judge; b. Birmingham, Ala., Mar. 4, 1930; s. William J. and Elizabeth (White) Farris; 2 children. BS, Morehouse Coll., 1951, LLD, 1978; MSW, Atlanta U., 1955; JD, U. Wash., 1958. Bar: Wash. 1958. Mem. Weyer, Roderick, Schroeter and Sterne, Seattle, 1958—59; ptnr. Weyer, Schroeter, Sterne & Farris and successor firms, Seattle, 1959—61, Schroeter & Farris, Seattle, 1961—63, Schroeter, Farris, Bangs & Horowitz, Seattle, 1963—65, Farris, Bangs & Horowitz, Seattle, 1965—69; judge Wash. State Ct. of Appeals, Seattle, 1969—79, U.S. Ct. of Appeals (9th cir.), Seattle, 1979—95, sr. judge, 1995—. Lectr. U. Wash. Law Sch. and Sch. Social Work, 1976—; mem. faculty Nat. Coll. State Judiciary, U. Nev., 1973; adv. bd. Nat. Ctr. for State Cts. Appellate Justice Project, 1978—81; founder First Union Nat. Bank, Seattle, 1965, dir., 1965—69; mem. U.S. Supreme Ct. Jud. Fellows Commn., 1997—; mem. Jud. Conf. Com. on Internat. Jud. Rels., 1997—2000. Del. The White House Conf. on Children and Youth, 1970; mem. King County (Wash.) Youth Commn., 1969—70; vis. com. U. Wash. Sch. Social Work, 1977—90; mem. King County Mental Health-Mental Retardation Bd., 1967—69; past bd. dirs. Seattle United Way; mem. Tyee Bd. Advisers, U. Wash., 1984—88, bd. regents, 1985—97, pres., 1990—91; trustee U. Law Sch. Found., 1978—84, Morehouse Coll., 1999—; mem. vis. com. Harvard Law Sch., 1996—. With Signal Corps U.S. Army, 1952—53. Recipient Disting. Svc. award, Seattle Jaycees, 1965, Clayton Frost award, 1966. Fellow: Am. Bar Found. (chair of fellows 2000, bd. dirs. 1987, exec. com. 1989—97); mem.: ABA (exec. com. appellate judges conf. 1978—84, chmn. conf. 1982—83, exec. com. appellate judges conf. 1987—88, del. jud. adminstrn. coun. 1987—88, sr. lawyers divsn. coun. 1998—), State-Fed. Jud. Coun. State Wash. (vice-chmn. 1977—78, chmn. 1983—87), Wash. Coun. on Crime and Delinquency (chmn. 1970—72), U. Wash. Law Sch., Order of Coif (mem. law rev.). Office: US Ct Appeals 9th Cir 1030 US Courthouse 1010 5th Ave Seattle WA 98104-1181

FARRIS, PAUL LEONARD, agricultural economist; b. Vincennes, Ind., Nov. 10, 1919; s. James David and Fairy Julia (Kahre) F.; m. Rachel Joyce Rutherford, Aug. 16, 1953; children: Nancy, Paul, John, Carl. BS, Purdue U., 1949; MS, U. Ill., 1950; PhD, Harvard U., 1954. Asst. prof. agrl. econs. Purdue U., West Lafayette, Ind., 1952-56, assoc. prof., 1956-59, prof., 1959-90, prof. emeritus, 1990—, head dept. agrl. econs., 1973-82; agrl. economist Dept. Agr., Washington, 1962; project leader for meat and poultry Nat. Commn. Food Mktg., Washington, 1965-66. Editor: Market Structure Research, 1964, Future Frontiers in Agricultural Marketing Research, 1983; contbr. articles to profl. jours. Served with AUS and USAAF, 1941-46. Fellow Am. Agrl. Econs. Assn.; mem. Am. Econ. Assn. Home: 1510 Woodland Ave West Lafayette IN 47906-2376 Office: Purdue U Dept Agrl Econs West Lafayette IN 47907

FARRIS, R. WESLEY, II, neurologist; b. Waynesboro, Va., Oct. 2, 1969; s. Roger Wesley and Evelyn (Crane) Farris; m. Joan Beatrice Stalzer, Sept. 2, 2000. BS in Biology, Coll. William and Mary, 1991; MD, U. Va., Charlottesville, 1996. Diplomate Am. Bd. Psychiatry and Neurology 2001. Intern Mass. Gen. Hosp., Boston, 1996—97; neurology resident Mass. Gen. and Brigham and Women's Hosp., Boston, 1997—2000, chief resident neurology, 1999—2000; behavioral neurology fellow Brigham and Women's Hosp., Boston, 2000—02; instr. Harvard Med. Sch., Boston, 2000—. Neurology cons. Winchester (Mass.) Hosp., Lawrence Meml. Hosp., Medford, Mass., 2000—. Contbr. articles to profl. med. jours. Fellow, Howard Hughes Med. Inst., 1994—96. Mem.: Am. Acad. Neurology, Soc. Neurosci. Achievements include research in interaction between diabetes, Alzheimer's disease, and an enzyme named "insulin degrading enzyme". Avocations: reading, travel. Home: 332 Broadway Unit # 4 Cambridge MA 02139 Office: Ctr Neurologic Diseases 77 Ave Louis Pasteur Boston MA 02115

FARRIS, ROBERT GENE, transportation company executive; b. Bartlesville, Okla., June 21, 1930; s. Carlton Kittrell and Ruby Lee (Richeson) F.; m. Betty C. Raimond, Dec. 28, 1951; children: Robert Raimond, William Carlton, Jonathan Bradley. BBA, U. Tex., 1952. Safety dir. Valley Transit Co., Inc., Harlingen, Tex., 1955-56, pers. dir., 1956-57, v.p., 1957-62, pres., 1963-99, chmn. bd., also bd. dirs., 1963—. Bd. dirs. Tex. State Bank, Harlingen, Tex. Regional Bancshares, McAllen, Tex., Millennium Fuels Corp., Dallas. Pres. Harlingen Indsl. Found., 1968-69; v.p. Rio Grande coun. Boy Scouts Am., 1971-72; trustee Marine Mil. Acad., Harlingen, 1977—; bd. dirs. Tex. Tourist Coun., Austin, 1980-84; past crusade chmn. Am. Cancer Soc.; past mem. bd. 1st United Meth. Ch., Harlingen. lst lt. U.S. Army, 1952-54, Korea. Named Friend of Tex. Transit, Tex. Dept. Hwys. and Pub. Transp., 1978. Mem. Nat. Bus Traffic Assn. (bd. dirs. 1980-85), Tex. Motor Transp. Assn. (bd. dirs. 1976-80), Harlingen C. of C. (pres. 1967-68), Rio Grande Valley C. of C. (pres. 1975-76), Algodon Club (past pres.), Phi Gamma Delta. Methodist. Office: Valley Transit Co Inc 219 N A St Harlingen TX 78550-3410 E-mail: bbrfarris@aol.com.

FARRIS, TRUEMAN EARL, JR., retired newspaper editor; b. Sedalia, Mo., June 2, 1926; PhB in Journalism, Marquette U., Milw., 1948; MA in Polit. Sci., U. Wis.-Milw., 1989. Reporter Milw. Sentinel, 1945-62, asst. city editor, 1962-75, city editor, 1975-77, mng. editor, 1977-89. Juror Pulitzer Prizes, 1985-86; mem. dean's coun. Student Publs. Bd., Coll. of Comm., Journalism and Performing Arts, Marquette U., 1987-92; mem. bd. visitors U. Wis., Milw., 1991-2000; mem. commitment adv. panel, U. Wis., Milw., 2000; bd. dirs. Wis. Masonic Jour., Newspaper of State Grand Lodge, 1993—. Author series of stories: Japan, 1980. Served with U.S. Army, 1955 Recipient By-Line award Marquette U., 1987; named to Milw. Press Club Media Hall of Fame, 1989. Mem. AP Mng. Editors Assn. (dir. 1980-87, editor ann. reports 1979-85), Milw. Soc. Profl. Journalists (pres. 1982-83), Milw. Press Club (pres. 1968, several reporting awards, editorial writing award 1957, included Media Hall of Fame 1989), Civil War Round Table (sec.), Mil. Order Loyal Legion of U.S. (recorder). Methodist. Avocations: reading, genealogy, civil war history. Home: 3192 S 80th St Milwaukee WI 53219-3501 Office: Milwaukee Sentinel PO Box 371 Milwaukee WI 53201-0371

FARRON, ROBERT, physician, family practice; b. N.Y.C., May 17, 1947; s. Irving and Anne (Zavoznick) F.; m. Lorraine Herzberg, May 27, 1972; children: Cory, Eric, Jeffrey. BS, CCNY, 1968; DO, Kansas City Coll. Osteo. Med., 1972. Diplomate Am. Bd. Family Practice, Am. Osteo. Bd. Family Practice. Intern Interboro Gen. Hosp., Bklyn., 1972-73; practice medicine specializing in family practice Far Rockaway, N.Y., 1973—, Valley Stream, N.Y., 1978—; attending physician Peninsula Hosp. Ctr., Far Rockaway, N.Y., 1985—. Asst. prof. family practice N.Y. Coll. Osteopathic Medicine. Recipient Physicians Recognition award AMA, 1983, 86, 89, 92, 95, 98. Fellow Am. Acad. Family Physicians; mem. Am. Osteo. Assn., N.Y. Osteo. Soc., Am. Osteo. Coll. Family Practice, Mensa, N.Y. State Med. Soc., Nassau County Med. Soc. Avocation: boating. Office: 2240 Mott Ave Far Rockaway NY 11691-3070 also: 201 E Merrick Rd Valley Stream NY 11580-5952 E-mail: BOBFMX@netscape.net.

FARROW, MARGARET ANN, former state official; b. Kenosha, Wis., Nov. 28, 1934; d. William Charles and Margaret Ann (Horan) Nemitz; m. John Harvey Farrow, Dec. 29, 1956; children: John, William, Peter, Paul, Mark. Student, Rosary Coll., 1952-53; BS in Polit. Sci. and Edn., Marquette U., 1956, postgrad., 1975-77. Tchr. Archdiocese of Milw., 1956-57; trustee Elm Grove Village, Wis., 1976-81, pres., 1981-86; mem. Wis. Assembly, Madison, 1986-89, Wis. Senate from 33rd dist., Madison, 1989—2001; lt. gov. State of Wis., 2001—03. Chair govt. effectiveness, 1998-2001, asst. majority leader, 1998; mem. joint com. on audit, 1993-97, mem. joint survey com. on tax exemptions, 1993-97, chair Wis. women's coun., 1991—, Rep. caucus chair, 1996, 99, mem. coun. on workforce excellence, 1995—, mem. Wis. glass ceiling commn., 1993—; mem. Senate Com. on edn., 1999, Senate com. on labor, 1999. Republican. Home: W 262 # 2402 Deer Haven Dr Pewaukee WI 53072-4572*

FARROW, ROBERT SCOTT, economist, educator; b. LA, Dec. 5, 1952; s. Robert Bruce and Eleanor (Dietrich) Farrow; m. Elaine A. Farrow, July 3, 1988. BA, Whitman Coll., Walla Walla, Wash., 1974; MA, Wash. State U., 1980, PhD, 1983. Rschr. Frank LeRoux Inc., Walla Walla, Wash., 1975—77; economist Coun. on Wage and Price Stability, Exec. Office of the Pres., Washington, 1979, Minerals Mgmt. Svc., U.S. Dept. Interior, Washington, 1985—86; ptnr. West Ten Organic Farm, Walla Walla, 1975—90; asst. prof. Carnegie Mellon U., Pitts., 1982—89, assoc. prof., 1989—93, dir. ctr. study improvement regulation, prin. rsch. economist, 1998—; sr. economist, assoc. dir. Coun. on Environ. Quality, Exec. Office of Pres., 1990—92; assoc. Dames and Moore, 1994—98; chief economist U.S. GAO, 2002—. Vis. assoc. prof. Pa. State U., 1997—98; cons. Office Tech. Assessment, Coun. Wage and Price Stability, Harvard Inst. Internat. Devel., Orgn. Econ. Coop. and Devel.; cons., sprk. on offshore oil and gas devel., econ. instruments for environ. policy; mem. sci. com. outer continental shelf adv. bd. U.S. Dept. Interior, 1990—93; mem. effluent task force EPA, 1994—96; mem. man and biosphere directorate U.S. Dept. State, 1992—95. Author: (book) Managing the Outer Continental Shelf Lands, 1990; contbg. author, rschr.: book The Myth of U.S. Agricultural Prosperity, 1976; co-editor: Improving Regulation, 2001; environ. editor: Hist. Statistics of the U.S. Rev. com. for the aged and disadvantaged United Way, Pitts., 1988—89; trustee Miami Valley Bus. Economists, 1994—95. Fellow Marine Policy, Woods Hole Oceanog. Inst., 1988—89, Sr., 1998; grantee, Charles A. Lindbergh Fund, 1984. Mem.: Assn. Environ. and Resource Econs. (editl. coun., nominating com. 1989—92), Am. Econs. Assn., Pitts. Athletic Assn., Phi Kappa Phi. Avocation: collecting first edition books. Office: US GAO 441 G St NW Washington DC 20548

FARRUG, EUGENE JOSEPH, SR., retired lawyer; b. Detroit, May 22, 1928; s. Michael and Bridget Mary (Foley) F.; m. Dolores Marie Augustine, Apr. 14, 1951; children: Elizabeth Marie Streit, Eugene Joseph Jr., Matthew Augustine, Pamela Ann, Bridget Louise, Donna Michele. BBA, U. Mich., 1950, JD, 1958. Bar: Ill. 1958, U.S. Dist. Ct. (no. dist.) Ill. 1958; U.S. Supreme Ct. 1980. With Lincoln-Mercury divsn. Ford Motor Co., Dearborn, Mich., 1950, with Aircraft Engine divsn., 1951; assoc. McKenna, Storer, Rowe White & Farrug, Dearborn, 1958-62, ptnr., 1962-92, of counsel, 1992—. Mem. Citizens of Greater Chgo., 1970-80, pres., 1976-79. Served with USN, 1951-55. McGreggor Fund scholar, 1946; Mich. Bd. Realtors scholar, 1949. Mem. Ill. Bar Assn., Chgo. Bar Assn., DuPage County Bar Assn., Am. Judicature Soc., Cath. Lawyers Guild, Phi Alpha Delta. Lodges: Kiwanis (pres. 1964). Home: 708 W Hinsdale Hinsdale IL 60521 Fax: 630-323-1162.

FARSHIDI, ARDESHIR B. cardiologist, educator; b. Kerman, Iran, June 13, 1945; arrived in U.S., 1972, naturalized, 1977; s. Jamshid and Farangis Farshidi; m. Katayoon Kavoussi, Jan. 2, 1982. MD, Tehran U., 1969. Diplomate Am. Bd. Internal Medicine, Am. Bd. Cardiovasc. Disease, Am. Bd. Cardiac Electrophysiology. Intern, Washington, 1972—73; resident U. Pa., Phila., 1973—75, resident in cardiology, 1975—77, electrophysiologist, 1977—78; asst. prof., assoc. prof. medicine U. Conn., Farmington, 1978—84; dir. electrophysiology LA Heart Inst., 1984—90; dir. arrhythmia ctr. Los Robles Regional Med. Ctr., 1990—. Dir. electrophysiologist U. Conn., Farmington, 1982—84, attending cardiologist, 1982—84; co-dir. electrophysiology, asst. prof. medicine Yale U., 1979—82; attending cardiologist Yale U. Hosp., 1979—82; chief cardiology sect. VA Hosp., Newington, Conn., 1982—84. Rschr. Am. Heart Assn., 1981. Lt. Iranian Army, 1969—72. Fellow: ACP, Am. Heart Assn., Am. Coll. Cardiology; mem.: Am. Electrophysiologic Soc., Am. Fedn. Clin. Rsch. Achievements include research in clin. cardiac electrophysiology and arrhythmia. Home: 3011 Grandoaks Dr Westlake Village CA 91361-5563 Office: 2100 Lynn Rd Ste 220 Thousand Oaks CA 91360-8036

FARSON, DAVE FOREST, engineering educator; b. Marietta, Ohio, Sept. 10, 1958; s. Robert F. and Martha Clark F.; m. Paula M. Mourant, Aug. 31, 1991; children: Forrest, Ellis. PhD, Ohio State U., 1987. Rsch. assoc. Pa. State U., State College, 1988-95; assoc. prof. Ohio State U., Columbus, 1995—. Fellow Laser Inst. Am. (pres. 1997, dir. 1993—); mem. Am. Welding Soc. (Adams Meml. membership award 1998). Office: Ohio State U 1971 Neil Ave Columbus OH 43210

FARSON, RICHARD EVANS, psychologist; b. Chgo., Nov. 16, 1926; s. Duke Mendenhall and Mary Gladys (Clark) F.; m. Elizabeth Lee Grimes, May 21, 1954 (div. 1962); children: Lisa Page, Clark Douglas; m. 2d Dawn Jackson Cooper, Jan. 4, 1964 (div. 1990); children: Joel Andrew, Ashley Dawn, Jeremy Richard. BA, Occidental Coll., 1947, MA, 1951; postgrad., UCLA, 1948-50; PhD, U. Chgo., 1955. Dean Sch. Design Calif. Inst. Arts, Valencia, 1969-73; pres. Esalen Inst., Big Sur and San Francisco, 1973-75; faculty Saybrook Inst., San Francisco, 1975-79; pres. Western Behavioral Scis. Inst., La Jolla, Calif., 1958-68; chmn. bd. Western Behavior Scis. Inst., La Jolla, Calif., 1968-79, pres., 1979—. Dir. Internat. Design Conf. in Aspen, Colo., 1971-2001, pres. 1976-80, 94-97; nat. bd. dirs., pub. dir. AIA, 1999-2001. Editor: Science and Human Affairs, 1967; author: Birthrights, 1974, Management of the Absurd: Paradoxes in Leadership, 1996, (with others) The Future of the Family, 1969, (with Ralph Keyes) Whoever Makes the Most Mistakes Wins: The Paradox of Innovation, 2002. Served to lt. j.g. USNR, 1955-57. Ford Found. fellow, Harvard U. Bus. Sch., 1953-54. Mem. Am. Psychol. Assn., Sigma Xi, Psi Chi Home: 252 Prospect St La Jolla CA 92037-4225 E-mail: rfarson@wbsi.org.

FARUKI, CHARLES JOSEPH, lawyer; b. Bay Shore, N.Y., July 3, 1949; s. Mahmud Taji and Rita (Trownsell) F.; m. Nancy Louise Glock, June 5, 1971 (div. Oct. 1995); children: Brian Andrew, Jason Allen, Charles Joseph Jr.; m. Michelle F. Zalar, June 15, 1996. BA summa cum laude, U. Cin., 1971; JD cum laude, Ohio State U., 1973. Bar: Ohio 1974, U.S. Dist. Ct. (no. and so. dists.) Ohio 1975, U.S. Ct. Appeals (9th cir.) 1977, U.S. Tax Ct. 1977, U.S. Supreme Ct. 1977, U.S. Ct. Appeals (6th cir.) 1978, U.S. Dist. Ct. (no. dist.) Tex. 1979, U.S. Dist. Ct. (ea. dist.) Ky. 1982, U.S. Ct. Appeals (D.C. cir.) 1982, U.S. Ct. Customs and Patent Appeals 1982, U.S. Ct. Appeals (4th cir.) 1986, U.S. Ct. Appeals (2d cir.) 1989, U.S. Ct. Appeals (fed. cir.), 1991, U.S. Ct. Appeals (8th cir.) 1997. Assoc. Smith & Schnacke, Dayton, Ohio, 1974—78, ptnr., 1979—89; founder, mng. ptnr. Faruki Ireland & Cox PLL, Dayton, 1989—. Lectr. in field. Contbr. articles in field. Trustee Dayton Bar Assn. Found., 1997-2003, pres., 2002-03. Served to capt. U.S. Army Res., 1971-79. Fellow Am. Bar Found., Am. Coll. Trial Lawyers (complex litigation com. 1993-98, Ohio state com. 1998—, chair 2004—); mem. ABA, Fed. Bar Assn. (officer and exec. com. Dayton chpt. 1988-93, pres. 1991-92), Ohio State Bar Assn. (bd. govs. Antitrust sect. 1992—), Dayton Bar Assn. (officer 1992-94, pres. 1994-95, 2002-03, trustee 1997—), Def. Rsch. Inst., Human Factors and Ergonomics Soc. (affiliate mem.), Fed. Cir. Bar Assn. Avocation: numismatics. Home: 300 Fairforest Cir Dayton OH 45419-1308 Office: Faruki Ireland & Cox PLL 500 Courthouse Plz SW Dayton OH 45402 E-mail: cfaruki@fgilaw.com.

FARWELL, ALBERT EDMOND, retired government official, consultant; b. Providence, June 7, 1915; s. Albert Potter and Elizabeth (Shelmerdine) F.; m. Elizabeth Fuller Thurlow, May 18, 1940 (dec. Apr. 21, 1975); children: Bruce Albert, Christopher James; m. Gertrude Cochran Ridgely, Sept. 9, 1978. AB, Brown U., 1935; MA, U. Ariz., 1937. Various non govtl. positions, 1939-45; exec. dir. Fgn. Trade Found., 1945-46; sr. editor Bur. Nat. Affairs, Washington, 1946-48; chief procedures and publ. br. Dept. Commerce, 1948-49; econ. analyst ECA, Greece, 1949-51; dep. dir. strategic controls div. Dept. Commerce, 1951-52; program analyst MSA, FOA, 1952-54; chief Near East div. FOA, ICA, 1955; chief Program Office Nr. East and So. Asia ICA, 1956-59; spl. asst. to undersec. mut. security Dept. State, 1959-60; dep. dir. AID, Nepal, 1960-65; dir. Costa Rica, 1965—67; dep. dir. Laos, 1967, dir., 1968; assoc. dir. Vietnam, 1968-73; dir. labor rels. Washington, 1973-74; cons. vector-borne disease control, econ. devel. planning and adminstrn., 1974—; pres. Alphi Assos., 1979—. Recipient Meritorious Service award ICA, 1953, 55, Meritorious Service award Dept. State, 1960; Pub. Safety award Govt. of Costa Rica, 1967; Vietnam Service award AID, 1970; Superior Honor award, 1974; Presdl. Order of Merit; Def. Honor medal; numerous others. Mem. Am. Acad. Polit. and Social Sci., Soc. Labor Relations Profls., Am. Fgn. Service Assn. Address: 2831 Oakton Manor Ct Oakton VA 22124-3016 E-mail: gealfar@aol.com.

FARWELL, DOUG GEORGE, music educator; b. Madison, Wis., Mar. 22, 1964; s. Harold Fredrick Farwell, Jr. and Wanda Joyce Farwell; m. Donna Marie Gwozdz, May 28, 1988; children: Donica Beth, Darcy Lee. Student, U. Tex., Arlington, 1984; MusB, N.C. Sch. of the Arts, 1986; MusM, SUNY, Stony Brook, 1987; D in Musical Arts, U. Ill., 1994. Grad. asst. SUNY, Stony Brook, 1986—87, U. Ill., Champaign-Urbana, 1990—93; asst. prof. music Ea. Ill. U., Charleston, 1991—91, U. Mo., Kansas City, 1994—95; assoc. prof. music Valdosta (Ga.) State U., 1995—, asst. to the dean Coll. of the Arts, 2002—. Chair music tech. com. Valdosta State U., 1995—, chair brass area, 1995—, dir. computer assisted music instrn. lab., 1997—, dir./advisor and campus min., 2000—, tenured and grad. faculty; presenter in field. Composer electroacoustic music for trombone & tape. Mem. Valdosta Symphony Orch., 1995—2003, Albany (Ga.) Symphony Orch.; campus min. Cath. Newman Ctr. Valdosta State U., 2000—03; mem. Parish Coun., Valdosta, 2000—03, Internat. Trombone Assn., Valdosta, 1984—2003. Named to All-State Band, Tex. Music Educators Assn., 1981; fellow, U. Ill., 1990; scholar, U. Tex., Arlington, 1982—84, N.C. Sch. of the Arts, 1984—86. Mem.: Ga. Music Educators Assn. (presenter 1995—2003), Music Tchrs. Nat. Assn., Internat. Trombone Assn. Democrat. Roman Catholic. Achievements include design of Computer Assisted Music Instruction Lab. Avocations: computer music design, racquetball. Office: Valdosta State Univ Music Dept 1500 N Patterson St Valdosta GA 31698 Personal E-mail: dfarwell@valdosta.edu. E-mail: dfarwell@valdosta.edu.

FARWELL, ELWIN D. minister, educational consultant; b. Branch County, Mich., May 1, 1919; s. Don J. and Dessa (Clingan) F.; m. Helen Irene Hill, Aug. 23, 1942; children: Don Lucian, Helen Kay, James Lyman, Judith Anne. BS, Mich. State U, 1943, MS, 1947; EdD, U. Calif. at Berkeley, 1959; BD, Pacific Lutheran Theol. Sem., Berkeley, 1959; LLD (hon.), Loras Coll., 1969, Valparaiso U., 1980, Luther Coll., 1986, Dana Coll., 1992, Calif. Luth. U., 1994; LHD (hon.), St. John's U., 1981; St. Olaf Coll., 1982. Instr. animal husbandry Mich. State U., 1947-49, asst. prof., 1949-55; cons. point 4 program State Dept. U. Nacional, Colombia, 1952; adminstrv. asst. to chmn. Center Study Higher Edn., U. Calif. at Berkeley, 1956-59; ordained to ministry Luth. Ch., 1958; pastor in Andrew, Iowa, 1959-61; academic dean Calif. Luth. Coll., Thousand Oaks, Calif., 1961-63; pres. Luther Coll., Decorah, Iowa, 1963-82; vis. scholar U. Calif.-Berkeley, 1982; profl. cons., 1983—; pres. Dana Coll., Blair, Nebr., 1985-86; dir. study theol. edn. Luth. Ch. U.S.A., 1984-86; adminstrv. cons. Pacific Luth. Theol. Sem., 1987-88; interim bishop Nebr. Synod Evan. Luth. Ch. in Am., 1990; interim pastor St. Paul Luth. Ch., Monona, Iowa, 1990-91, 97; interim bishop Rocky Mountain Synod Evangel. Luth. Ch. in Am., 1993-94. Author: Livestock Development and Selection, 1951, (with others) Stability of Change, 1964; contbr. articles to profl. jours., encys. Mem. Iowa Gov.'s Com. Conservation Natural Resources, 1964-68, Iowa Gov.'s Commn. Coop. State and Local Govt., 1964-66; mem. Iowa Coordinating Coun. Higher Edn., 1967-70, pres., 1968-69; chmn. Com. Intergovtl. Coop. and Comm., 1964-65, Gov.'s Com. on Govt. Reorgn., 1966, State Adv. Com. on Cmty. and Jr. Coll., 1965-69; mem. exec. com. Iowa Assn. Pvt. Colls. and Univs., 1964-73, 76-78, chmn., 1971-72; chmn. Coun. Coll. Pres.'s Am. Luth. Ch., 1976-77; mem. exec. com. Norwegian-Am. Mus. Assn., 1965-71; chmn. World Brotherhood Found., 1962-77; chmn. Iowa Coll. Found., 1968-69; mem. Iowa Campaign Fin. Disclosure Commn., 1977-91, chmn., 1980-81, 87-89; mem. Iowa Mental Health Adv. Coun., 1978-81, Am. Scandinavian Found.; bd. govs. Calif. Luth. Ednl. Found., 1957-59; bd. dirs. Inst. European Studies,

1977-81; bd. Nat. Luth. Campus Ministry, 1966-69; pres. Luth. Ednl. Conf. N.Am., 1973-74, mem. legis. policy com., 1978-81; counselor Luth. Coun. U.S.A., 1975-79; bd. dirs. Gundersen Med. Found., La Crosse, Wis., 1976-81; bd. regents Dana Coll., 1986-95; trustee Iowa Natural Heritage Found., 1983-92, Iowa Humanities Found., 1992-2002; bd. dirs. Luth. Social Svc. of Iowa, 1992-95, Winneshiek County Hosp. Found., 1992-97. Capt. U.S. Army, 1943-46, PTO. Decorated Knight's Cross 1st class Order St. Olav, 1975, Knight's Cross 1st class Order No. Star, 1977 (Sweden); recipient Disting. Patriarchs award Mich. State U., 1993. Mem. Ctrl. State Coll. Assn. (dir. 1964-76, chmn. 1967), Nat. Assn. Ind. Colls. and Univs. (bd. dirs. 1977-78), Oneota Golf and Country Club (pres. 1987-89), Rotary, Phi Beta Kappa, Phi Delta Kappa, Alpha Gamma Rho, Alpha Zeta. Lutheran. Home: 504 Locust Rd # 3 Decorah IA 52101-1002 E-mail: farwelle@martin.luther.edu.

FARWELL, GEORGE WELLS, retired physicist; s. Raymond Forrest Farwell and Mary Gust (Ashley) Farwell; m. Ruth Margaret Kircher, Mar. 24, 1945 (div. 1976); children: Jacqueline, Lawrence, Bruce, Barbara Alexander. SB magna cum laude, Harvard U., 1941; PhD Physics, U. Chgo., 1948. Asst. in physics Manhattan Dist., Radiation Lab., U. Calif., Berkeley, 1941—43; physicist Manhattan Dist., Los Alamos Sci. Lab., N.Mex., 1943—46; fellow Inst. for Nuc. Studies, U. of Chgo., 1946—48; asst. prof. of physics U. of Wash., Seattle, 1948—55, assoc. prof. of physics, 1955—59, prof. of physics, 1959—87, assoc. dean of grad. sch., 1959—65, asst. v.p., 1965—67, acting dir., divsn. of marine resources, 1967—68, v.p. for rsch., 1967—76; prof. emeritus of physics and v.p. for rsch. emeritus Universtiy of Wash., Seattle, 1987—; vis. scientist Inst. Theoretical Physics, U. Copenhagen, 1960—61. Dir. KING Broadcasting Co., Seattle, 1967—82; trustee Universities Space Rsch. Assn., Washington, 1969—76; mem. organizing com. 11th Internat. Radiocarbon Conf., Seattle, 1982. Contbr. articles to numerous sci. jours. Mem. Oceanog. Commn. Wash., Olympia, 1969—71, Project SEA USE Coun., Seattle, 1970—71; trustee Pacific Sci. Ctr., Seattle, 1975—79, found. assoc., 1980—. Fellow, NSF, 1960—61; grantee, US AEC, the M.J. Murdoch Charitable Trust, and NSF. Fellow: Am. Phys. Soc.; mem.: The Mountaineers, Swiss Alpine Club, Sigma Xi (chpt. pres.), Phi Beta Kappa. Achievements include research in experimental nuclear physics and environmental earth and marine sciences; spontaneous fission process; nuclear structure physics; time reversal invariance in nuclear reactions; radiocarbon in the environment; paleoclimatology through radiocarbon dating of pollen in sediments using ultrasensitive mass spectrometry with accelerators; co-discovery of plutonium-240. Office: U Wash Ctr Exptl Nuclear Physics & Astrophysics Box 354290 Seattle WA 98195 Business E-Mail: farwell@npl.washington.edu.

FARWELL, HAROLD FREDERICK, JR., English language educator; b. Oak Park, Ill., Apr. 9, 1934; s. Harold Frederick and Dorothy Delma (Cobb) F.; m. Joyce G. Farwell, Feb. 10, 1961; children: Douglas G., Beth Elene, Amy Kathleen, Ellen Claudia. BA, U. Chgo., 1960, MA, 1961; PhD, U. Wis., Madison, 1970. Instr. English Drake U., Des Moines, 1960-61; asst. prof. U. Cin., 1966-70; assoc. prof., prof. Western Carolina U., Cullowhee, N.C., 1970—, dir. English grad. program, 1980-90, 97-00. Ranger U.S. Park Svcs., Great Smokies Nat. Park, 1983. Author: The Metamorphoses of Madam Butterfly, 2003; editor: Smoky Mountain Voices, 1993; reporter Opera News, 1982—; editor, reporter The Arts Jour. With USN, 1956-58. Fulbright sr. lectr., The Phillipines, 1986-87, Indonesia, 1991; rsch. grantee Western Carolina U., 1974, 93, 94, 97; SDIP grantee U. Tex., 1981; China Field Study grantee, 1995, 96; Ctr. for Tchg. Excellence fellow Western Carolina U., 1992-94; fellow East-West Ctr., Honolulu, 1997, 99. Mem.: Dictionary Soc. N.Am., Melville Soc. Avocations: nature study, gardening. Home: PO Box 838 Cullowhee NC 28723-0838 E-mail: hal_farwell@aol.com., farwell@wcu.edu.

FARWELL, HERMON WALDO, JR., parliamentarian, educator, former speech communication educator; b. Englewood, NJ, Oct. 24, 1918; s. Hermon Waldo and Elizabeth (Whitcomb) Farwell; m. Martha Carey Matthews, Jan. 3, 1942. AB, Columbia U., 1940; MA, Pa. State U., 1964. Commd. USAF, 1940, advanced through grades to maj., various positions, 1940—66, ret., 1966; instr. aerial photography Escola Tecnica de Aviaçao, Brazil, 1946—48; mem. faculty U. So. Colo., Pueblo, 1966—84, prof. emeritus speech comm., 1984—; cons., tchr. parliamentary procedure. Author: Point of Opinion: The Majority Rules - A Manual of Procedure for Most Groups: Parliamentary Motions: Majority Motions, Point of Opinion - An Anthology of Parliamentary Simplicity; editor: The Parliamentary Jour., 1981—87; contbr. articles to profl. jours. Mem.: VFW, Nat. Assn. Parliamentarians, Ret. Officers Assn., Commn. on Am. Parliamentary Practice (chmn. 1976), Am. Inst. Parliamentarians (nat. dir. 1977—87), Air Force Assn., Am. Legion. Home and Office: 65 MacAlester Rd Pueblo CO 81001-2052

FARWELL, NANCY LARRAINE, public relations executive; b. Sellersville, Pa., May 2, 1944; d. Warren Gregory and Mary Rita (Zaniboni) F. BA, Pa. State U., 1966. Asst. TV rep. H.R. TV Reps., Phila., 1966-68; various positions Hawthorne Advt. Inc., Phila., 1968-73; dir. employee rels. Colonial Penn Group, Inc., Phila., 1973-75, mgr. press rels., 1976-78, mgr. pub. rels., 1978-82; dir. communications Provident Mutual Life Ins. Co., Phila., 1982-83, asst. v.p., communications, 1983-87; pres. Nancy Farwell Assocs., Phila., 1987-90; v.p. Anne Klein & Assocs., Inc., Mt. Laurel, N.J., 1990-92, sr. v.p., 1992-97, sr. v.p., COO, 1998-2001, sr. v.p. strategic planning, 2001—. Adv. bd. City of Phila. Century IV Tall Ships, 1982. Author: (photo essay) Philadelphia, 1976; contbr. chpt. to home health care marketing book. Founder, co-chair Portico Row Neighborhood Assn., Phila., 1989-92; bd. dirs. Washington Square West Project Area Com., Phila., 1990-92, Boys and Girls Clubs of Metro Phila. Adv. Coun., 1991—; adv. com. Phila. 6th Police Dist., 1990-92. Mem. Pub. Rels. Soc. Am. (9 Pepperpot awards, Award of Excellence, Silver Anvil award of Excellence), Phila. Pub. Rels. Assn. Office: Anne Klein & Assocs Inc Three Greentree Ctr Ste 200 Marlton NJ 08053

FARWELL, WALTER MAURICE, vocalist, educator; b. Sidney, Iowa, Mar. 29, 1928; s. Clyde Ross and Erma Leona (Liggett) F. B.Mus.Edn., U. Mo., Kansas City, 1950; MA, U. Iowa, 1953. Vocal music tchr. pub. schs., Fayette, Iowa, 1953-59; head voice tchr. Wartburg Coll., Waverly, Iowa, 1960-61; vocal music tchr. pub. schs., Tipton, Iowa, 1961-67, music educator Davenport, Iowa, 1967-90. Choir dir. Meth. Ch., Fayette, Tipton, 1953—; vocal soloist, 1953—; organist Replacement Tng. Ctr., Ft. Bragg, N.C., 1951-52. Author: (4 vols.) History of Fremont County, Iowa, 1968-91; contbr.: Bells of Stony Creek, 1994; editor: Court Records Atchison County, Mo. (pamphlet), 1985; cons. (county history) Thumbprints in time, 1996; contbr. historical articles to profl. pubs. Cpl. U.S. Army, 1950-52. Recipient Am. Legion award, 1941. Mem. NEA, Davenport Area Ret. Tchrs. Assn., Fremont County Hist. Soc. (charter). Methodist. Avocation: historical and genealogical research. Home: 549 E 4th St Tipton IA 52772-1933 E-mail: farwellwalter@hotmail.com.

FASEL, IDA, English language educator, writer; b. Portland, Maine, May 9, 1909; d. I.E. Drapkin and Lilian Rose Harwich; m. Oscar A. Fasel, Dec. 24, 1946 (dec. Apr. 1973). BA summa cum laude, Boston U., 1931, MA, 1945; PhD, U. Denver, 1963. Mem. faculty English U. Conn., New London, Midwestern U., Wichita Falls, Tex., Colo. Woman's Coll., Denver; prof. English U. Colo., Denver, 1962-77, prof. emerita of English, 1977. Presenter in field; contest judge. Translator from French and Italian, editl. cons.: Baroque and Renaissance Lyrics, 1962; author (poetry): On the Meanings of Cleave, 1979 (Nortex Publ. award); author: The Study of Writing Poetry, 1983; author: (poetry) Where Is the Center of the World?: Selections From Seven Chapbooks, 1981-1991, 1999 (U. Fla. and Before the Rapture Press prize chapbooks), All Real Living Is Meeting, 1999, The Difficult Inch, 2000, Journey of a Hundred Years, 2002, Air, Angels and Us, 2002, Waking to Light, 2002 (Best Chapbook Angels Without Wings Found. 2003), Aureoles, 2002; translator: Renaissance and Baroque Lyrics, 1962; contbg. author: The Study and Writing of Poetry, 1983; contbr. articles to profl. jours., chpts. to books, poetry to anthologies and jours. Faculty Rsch. fellow U. Colo., 1979; recipient Disting. Alumni honor Boston U., 1979, Alumni Poetry prize, 1983, 85, Before the Rapture Chapbook prize, 1985, Colo. Poet Honor, Friends of Denver Pub. Libr., 1991, Panhandler Chapbook prize, U. West Fla., 1991, Prize Poems award Colo. Authors League, 1993-94. Mem. Milton Soc. Am. (life), Friends of Milton's Cottage (charter), Assn. Literary Scholars and Critics, Conf. on Christianity and Lit., Poetry Soc. Tex., Colo. Ctr. for the Book, Denver Woman's Press Club, Phi Beta Kappa. Avocations: ballet, Star Trek, collecting angels, piano, translating French poetry. Home: 165 Ivy St Denver CO 80220-5846

FASH, MICHAEL WILLIAM, cinematographer, director; b. London, Apr. 29, 1940; came to U.S., 1983; s. Alfred Norris and Katharine (Bell) F.; divorced; children: Alexandra, Nicholas, Katharine. Attended, Richmond Art Sch., London, 1959. Dir. of photography BBC, London, 1959-69, Thames TV, London, 1969-80. Cinematographer: (TV movies) Naked Civil Servant, 1975 (British Acad. award 1976), The Sun is God, 1975 (British Acad. nomination 1976), The One and Only Phyliss Dixie, 1978 (British Acad. nomination 1978), Bill, 1979 (Emmy for Best Picture 1980), Movie Stars Daughter, 1978 (Emmy for Best Photography 1979), Sara Plain and Tall, 1993, Christy, 1993, Grace and Glory, 1998, Love Letters, 1998, Double Platinum, 1998, Nero Wolfe Golden Spiders, 1999, The John Denver Story, 1999, Strong Medicine, 2001; (features) Britannia Hosp., 1981, Betrayal, 1982, The Whales of August, 1986, Entertaining Angels: The Dorothy Day Story, 1996, The Confession, 1997; dir. TV series Christy, 1993, Second Noah, Strong Medicine, 2000, 01, 02, Dinotopia, 2002; dir. numerous TV commls. Recipient award British Soc. of Cinematographers, London, 1977. Mem. IATSE, Dirs'. Guild Am. Avocations: tennis, skiing, sailing, fly fishing, painting. Home and Office: 4314 Marina City Dr Apt 618 Marina Del Rey CA 90292 also: Lenhoff and Lenhoff 830 Palm Ave West Hollywood CA 90069 E-mail: mwfast@aol.com.

FASH, VICTORIA R. healthcare company executive; Sr. v.p. bus. strategy Dun & Bradstreet Corp., 1995-96; exec. v.p., CFO Cognizant, 1996—; exec. v.p., chmn., CEO IMS Internat., Westport, Conn., 1999—. Bd. dirs. Orion Capital Corp. Office: IMS Health Inc 1499 Post Rd Fairfield CT 06430-5940

FASHING, EDWARD MICHAEL, ranch owner, physical sciences educator; b. Chgo., Jan. 27, 1936; s. Michael George and Leontine (LeClercq) F.; m. Annette Louise Lubker, Jan. 29, 1959; children: Anita Fashing Kiska, Mary Fashing Schillig, Edward Jr., James, John. BS in Chemistry, Loyola U., Chgo., 1960; MS in Chemistry, DePaul U., 1968; postgrad., U. Mo., 1982-84. Cert. jr. coll. chemistry tchr., Ill. Instr. geology, phys. sci., chemistry of hazardous materials Triton Coll., River Grove, Ill., 1969-81; Simmental cattle and sheep rancher Cedar Ln. Farm, Sturgeon, Mo., 1973—; asst. prof. N.E. Mo. State U. (Truman State), Kirksville, 1981-82; chemistry asst. U. Mo., Columbia, 1982-84; instr. physics Columbia (Mo.) Coll., 1986; summerreading tchr. Centralia Elem. Sch., 1998—2002. Writer, news commentator, show moderator, producer Farm Forum Sta. KOPN-Radio, 1985-89; freelance reporter, columnist, proofreader, editor Am. Agr. Reporter and Mo. Am. Agr. Newsletter, 1990—; mem. editl bd., writer religious and cultural cyber jour. Just Good Company, 2002—. Leader 4H, Sturgeon, 1974—84, 1988; creator posters Mo. Rural Crisis Ctr., Columbia, 1986—93, bd. dirs., 1989—92; publicity dir. Am. Agrl. Movement Grassroots, 1985, demonstrator, 1985, spokesman Chgo. demonstrations, 1984, 1985, 1986; mem. Nat. Farm Org.; v.p. coms. Am. Agr. Movement Inc. of Mo., 1991—; bd. dirs. Farm Alliance of Rural Mo., 1986—89, 1995—, pres., 1997—99, v.p., 1999—2001; mem. N.Am. Farm Alliance, Orgn. for Competitive Markets; lobbyist Nat. Farmers Union, 1990; Dem. rep. Mo. State Conv., 1988; Roman Cath. ch. cantor, lector, extraordinary min. NSF grantee, 1966, 76; 2d place winner steer carcass judging contest Mo. State Fair, 1995; breeder of 10 winning steer carcasses, 1973-99, Boone County, Mo. and Mo. State Fair, 1995, 2000. Mem.: AAAS, Phi Delta Kappa, Am. Corn Growers Assocs., Mo. Stockmans Assn., Mo. Simmental Assn., Am. Simmental Assn., Am. Chem. Soc. Democrat. Avocations: rockhounding, gardening, writing, entomology. Address: Cedar Ln Farm 2898 Audrain Road 114 Sturgeon MO 65284-2023 E-mail: emfashing@socket.net.

FASI, FRANK FRANCIS, state legislator; b. East Hartford, Conn., Aug. 27, 1920; BS, Trinity Coll., Hartford, 1942. Mem. Hawaii Senate, 1959—; Dem. mayor City and County of Honolulu, 1969-81, Rep. mayor, 1985-94; resigned, 1994; owner Property & Bus., Honolulu, 1995. Mem. Dem. Nat. Com. for Hawaii, 1952-56; del. 2d Constl. Conv., 1968; mem.-at-large Honolulu City Coun., 1965-69; non-partisan candidate for Mayor of Honolulu, 2000. Served to capt. USMCR. Mem. Pacific-Asian Congress Municipalities (founder, past pres., exec. dir.), VFW (former comdr. Hawaii dept.), AFTRA (past v.p.). Office: 401 Waiakamilo Rd Ste 201 Honolulu HI 96817-4955 *Personal philosophy: Moderate/Conservative. I believe in a free enterprise system as the foundation of our economy and in state's rights. I believe that the less government from Washington D.C. the better. I also have a strong belief in Christ Jesus.*

FASICK, ADELE MONGAN, information services consultant; b. N.Y.C., Mar. 18, 1930; d. Stephen Leo and Florence (Geary) Mongan; m. Frank Fasick, Aug. 14, 1955 (div. 1986); children: Pamela, Laura, Julia. BA, Cornell U., 1951; MA, Columbia U., 1954, MSLS, 1956; PhD, Case Western Reserve U., 1970. Libr. N.Y. Pub. Libr., 1955-56, L.I.U., Bklyn., 1956-58; asst. prof. Rosary Coll., River Forest, Ill., 1970-71; prof. U. Toronto, 1971-96, dean Faculty of Libr. and Info. Sci., 1990-95. Adj. prof. San Jose State U., 1999—, U. .C., 2002—. Author: Managing Children Services in Public Libraries, 1991, 2d edit., 1998, Beauty Who Would Not Spin, 1987; co-author: ChildView, 1987; editor: Lands of Pleasure, 1990; editor International Research Abstracts: Youth Library Services, 1993—. Mem. ALA (com. on accreditation 1990-92), Assn. Libr. Svc. to Children (exec. bd. 1980-84), Assn. Librs. and Info. Sci. Edn. (pres. 1992), Internat. Fedn. Libr. Assn. (sec./treas. sect. on reading 1997—). E-mail: amfasick@earthlink.net.

FASKE, DONNA See KARAN, DONNA

FASKIANOS, IRINA A. organization executive; b. Dover, N.H., Apr. 20, 1968; d. James Charles and Maria Liadis Faskianos; m. Thomas T. DePatie, June 25, 1994. BA, Yale U., 1989, MusM, 1990. Profl. flutist, N.Y.C., 1990-95; spl. asst. Bette Bao Lord and Winston Lord, N.Y.C., 1991-95; assoc. prodr. America and the World on NPR Coun. on Fgn. Rels., N.Y.C., 1995-97, asst. dir. media projects, 1997-99, dep. nat. dir. nat. program, 1999—2000, nat. dir., nat. program, 2001—02, v.p. nat. and outreach programs, 2002—. Mem. Campaign 2000 adv com. Coun. Fgn. Rels., N.Y.C., 1999-2000. Mem. Coun. Fgn. Rels. Office: Coun on Fgn Rels 58 E 68th St New York NY 10021

FASMAN, ZACHARY DEAN, lawyer; b. Chgo., Oct. 27, 1948; s. Irving D. and Lillian V. (Vilatzer) F.; children: Jonathan, Benjamin, Rebecca. BA, Northwestern U., 1969; JD, U. Mich., 1972. Bar: Ill. 1972, D.C. 1977, N.Y. 2001, U.S. Supreme Ct. 1977. Assoc., then ptnr. Seyfarth, Shaw et al, Chgo. and Washington, 1972-81; ptnr. Wald, Harkrader et al, Washington, 1981-83, Crowell & Moring, Washington, 1983-88, Paul, Hastings, Janofsky & Walker, Washington, 1988—2000, NYC, 2000—. Author: Equal Employment Audit Handbook, 1983, Employment Law Compliance Manual, 1988, What Business Must Know About The ADA, 1992. Mem. ABA (labor law sect., litig. sect.), Coll. Labor and Employment Lawyers, Order of Coif. Home: 201 E 79th St Apt 15B New York NY 10021 Office: Paul Hastings Janofsky & Walker 75 E 55th St New York NY 10022 Office Fax: 212-318-6837. E-mail: zacharyfasman@paulhastings.com.

FASON, RITA MILLER, lawyer; b. Fargo, ND, July 12, 1935; d. John Maurice Miller and Mary Dullea; divorced; children: Catherine, John, William, Richard. BA in History, Rice Inst., 1957; JD, U. Houston, 1979. Bar: Tex. 1979. Pvt. practice John Graml & Assocs., Houston, 1979—; ptnr. Brady & Fason, Houston, 1981-82; pvt. practice Houston, 1982—. Eucharistic min. St. Anne's Cath. Ch., Houston, 1988—; pres. bd. dirs. Wellsprings, Houston, 1989-95. Mem. Assn. Women Attys. (com. 1979—). Avocations: gardening, traveling. Home: 2121 Peckham St Houston TX 77019-6431 Office: 3212 Smith St Ste 202 Houston TX 77006-6622

FASS, PETER MICHAEL, lawyer, educator; b. Bklyn., Apr. 11, 1937; s. Irving and Bess (Fordin) F.; m. Deborah K. Orshan, May 6, 1989; 1 child, Olivia Jae; children from previous marriage: Brian Samuel, Lyle Williams. BS in Econs. with honors, U. Pa., 1958; JD cum laude, Harvard U., 1961; LLM, NYU, 1964. Bar: N.Y. 1965; CPA. From assoc. to ptnr. Carro, Spanbock, Fass, Geller, Kaster & Cuiffo, N.Y.C., 1968-86; ptnr. Kaye, Scholer, Fierman, Hayes & Handler, N.Y.C., 1988-95, Battle Fowler LLP, N.Y.C., 1995-2000, Proskauer Rose LLP, N.Y.C., 2000—. Adj. asst. prof. real estate NYU; lectr. Practising Law Inst., N.Y. Law Jour., Instl. mag., Ill. Inst. Continuing Legal Edn.; spl. cons. Calif. Commr. of Corps Real Estate Adv. Com.; mem. ad hoc com. Real Estate Securities and Syndication Inst., chmn. regulatory legis and taxation com., 1975-76; mem., dir. participant/real estate com. NASD, 1991-94. Co-author: Tax Advantaged Securities, 1977—, Real Estate Syndication Handbook, 1985-87, Tax Aspects of Real Estate Investments, 1988—, Blue Sky Practice Handbook, 1987—, Real Estate Investment Trusts Handbook, 1987—, S Corporation Handbook, 1985—, Tax Advantaged Securities Handbook, 1979—; contbr. articles to profl. jours. Recipient Haskins award for outstanding achievement in N.Y. State C.P.A.s exam., 1964 Mem. ABA (chmn. real estate investment com., real property, probate and trust sect.), N.Y. State Bar Assn., Am. Inst. CPA's, N.Y. State Soc. CPA's, Pi Lambda Phi, Beta Gamma Sigma, Beta Alpha Psi. Home: 115 Central Park W New York NY 10023-4153 Office: Proskauer Rose LLP 1585 Broadway New York NY 10036-8299 E-mail: pfass@proskauer.com., reitman411@aol.com.

FASS, RONNIE, gastroenterologist, director; b. Rehovot, Israel, Nov. 14, 1958; s. Mordechai and Sali Sarah Fass; m. Shira Sarah Fass; children: Hagar, Ofer, Sharon. BMS, Ben Gurion Univ. of Negev, Beer-Sheva, Israel, 1984, MD, 1987. Cert. internal medicine bd. cert., 1992, gastroenterology bd. cert., 1997. Asst. prof. medicine U. Ariz., Tucson, 1996—2001, assoc. prof., 2001—; staff gastroenterologist So. Ariz. VA Health Care Sys., 1996—. Dir. GI mobility Lab. So. Ariz. VA Health Care Sys., Tucson, 1996—; dir. of GI Fellowship Rsch. U. Ariz. Health Svc. Ctr., 1997—2000, dir. motility lab., 2001—. Lt. Israeli Defense Forces, 1977—81. Recipient Clin. Rsch. award, Am. Coll. Gastroenterology, 1999, 2001, Glaxo Inst. Digestioc Health, 1999. Office: Southern Ariz VA Health Care System 3601 S North Ave 1-111G-1 Tucson AZ 85723

FASSEL, JIM, professional football coach; b. Anaheim, Calif., Aug. 31, 1949; m. Kitty Fassel; children: John, Brian, Jana, Mike. Collegiate coach various, including Fullerton C.C., Weber State U., Stanford, 1973-83; asst. head coach/offensive coord. Denver Broncos, 1993, 94; quarterback coach Oakland Raiders, 1995; offensive coord., quarterback coach Ariz. Cardinals, 1996; asst. coach N.Y. Giants, 1991-92, head coach, 1997—. Drafted by Chgo. in seventh round of 1972 NFL Draft. Office: NY Giants Giants Stadium East Rutherford NJ 07073

FASSETT, JOHN D. retired utility executive, consultant; b. East Hampton, N.Y., Jan. 30, 1926; s. Howard J. and Irene (Darby) F.; m. Betty Jean Conrad, Aug. 4, 1947; children— Ellen Joy Fassett Mermin, John D., Lora Jean Fassett Mason. BA cum laude, U. Rochester, 1948; JD cum laude, Yale U., 1953; LLD (hon.), Ky. Wesleyan Coll., 1999. Law clk. to assoc. justice Stanley F. Reed U.S. Supreme Ct., Washington, 1953-54; assoc. Wiggin & Dana, New Haven, 1954-58, ptnr., 1958-73; v.p., gen. counsel United Illuminating Co., New Haven, 1973, pres., 1974-75, chief exec. officer, 1976-84, chmn. bd., 1985-87. Author: UI—History of an Electric Company, 1991, New Deal Justice: The Life of Stanley Reed of Kentucky, 1994, The Shaping Years: A Memoir of My Youth and Education, 2000. Served with U.S. Army, 1943-46, 1st lt., 1950-51 Republican. Avocations: tennis, reading, writing. Home: 2600 Croasdaile Farm Pkwy Durham NC 27705-1331

FASSETT, STEPHANIE A. lawyer; b. Monte Vista, Colo., Feb. 28, 1968; d. Robert Charles Fassett and Karen Fassett Herbold. BS, U. Idaho, 1990, JD, 1994. Law clk. Twin Falls County, Twin Falls, Idaho, 1994-96; assoc. Benoit, Alexander, Sinclair, Harwood & High, Twin Falls, 1996—. Cons. to various orgns. on employment law issues, 1996—. Editor Idaho Law Rev., 1994; contbr. articles to profl. jours. Bd. dirs. United Way, Twin Falls, 1996-97. Mem. PEO, Order of DeMolay (adv. staff 1984—, Cross of Honor for Adult Leadership 1999). Office: Benoit Alexander et al 126 2d Ave N Twin Falls ID 83301

FASSIHI, MOHAMMAD REZA, engineering executive; s. Reza and Fassihi; m. Terry C Fassihi; children: Samad children: Mansoor. PhD, Stanford U., Calif., 1981. Acting asst. prof. Stanford Univ., Stanford, Calif., 1980—81; rsch. engr. ARCO O&G Co, Plano, Tex., 1981—84; staff rsch. engr. Amoco O&G Co, Tulsa, 1984—93; staff reservoir engr. Amoco Eurasia, Houston, 1994—99; reservoir engr. leader BP Amoco, Sunbury, England, 1999—2000; pre-project mgr. BP, Sunbury, England, 2001—02, learning and devel. mgr. Houston, 2002—. Tech. editor SPE, Richardson, Tex., 1981—94. Contbr. scientific papers (Best paper Award, Can. SPE, 1990, Best Paper, SPE Calif. Regional Meeting, 1980). Industry rep United Way, Houston, Tex., 1985—94. Mem.: SPE (Disting. spkr. 2003—). Office: BP Am 501 Westlake Pk Blvd Houston TX 77079 Office Fax: 281-366-7820. E-mail: fassihr@bp.com.

FASSLER, CRYSTAL G. marketing consultant; b. Marion, Ohio, Mar. 15, 1942; d. Lloyd C. and Iola M. (Runkle) Mahaffey; student public schs., Prospect, Ohio; m. Donald D. Fassler, May 6, 1960; 1 son, Curtis A. Media buyer H. Swink Advt., Marion, 1968-73; media buyer and planner Tracey Locke Advt., Columbus, Ohio, 1973-74, Lord, Sullivan & Yoder Advt., Marion, 1974-82; youth conselor State of Ohio Employment Services, Marion, 1982-83; nat. mktg. consultant WMRN-AM and FM, Marion, 1983-84, gen. mgr., 1985; gen. sales mgr. WRFD Radio, Columbus, 1986-90; gen. sales mgr. Stas. WMAN-AM and WYHT-FM, Mansfield, Ohio, 1990-92, media cons., Dimension Media Svcs., Marion, Ohio, 1992-93, cons., Credit Bur. Co., Marion, 1993-94, ptnr. Media Mktg. Strategies, 1994-1998, Vizual Express, Marion, 2001—. Home and Office: Visual Express Ptnr Ctr St Marion OH 43302-7352 E-mail: fishal1@aol.com.

FASSOULIS, SATIRIS GALAHAD, communications company executive; b. Syracuse, N.Y., Aug. 19, 1922; s. Peter George and Anastasia P. (Limpert) F. BA, Syracuse U., 1945. V.p. Commerce Internat. Corp., 1949-75; chmn. Global Comm. Co., N.Y.C., 1976—, Global Def. Products Inc., N.Y.C., 1976—; pres. CIC Internat. Ltd., 2000—, Columbia Defence Corp., 2000—; chmn. CIC Aerospace Corp. Dir Comml. Exports (Overseas) Ltd., U.K., CIC Internat. Ltd., N.Y.C., Colombia Technology Corp., Colombia Energy Corp., Africa One Ltd. Mem. U.S. Congl. Adv. Bd.; bd. dirs. Better Life Enterprises for the Blind, Inc.; chmn. Internat. Cultural Exch. 1st lt. USAAF, 1941-45. Decorated Purple Heart, Air medal with 3 oak leaf clusters, Prisoner of War medal. Mem. N.Y. C. of C., Am. Def. Preparedness Assn., Navy League U.S., Armed Forces Comm. and Electronics Assn., U.S. Naval Inst., Air Force Assn., Assn. of U.S. Army, Internat. Platform Assn., N.Y. Athletic Club, Order of Ahepa. Republican. Episcopalian. Home: 20 Waterside Plz New York NY 10010-2612 Office: 5 Marine View Plz Apt 310 Hoboken NJ 07030

FAST, JULIUS, author, editor; b. N.Y.C., Apr. 17, 1919; s. Barnett Arthur and Ida (Miller) F.; m. Barbara Hewitt Sher, June 8, 1946; children: Jennifer, Melissa, Timothy Hewitt. BA, NYU, 1941. Sr. writer Smith, Kline & French Pharms., Phila., 1955-57; chief dept. med. communications Purdue Fredericks, N.Y.C., 1957-62; feature editor Med. News, 1962-63; sr. editor Med. World News, 1963-64; editor Ob-Gyn Observer, N.Y.C., 1965-75. Author: (mystery novels) Watchful at Night, 1945, Bright Face of Danger, 1946, Walk in Shadow, 1948, Model for Murder, 1956, Street of Fear, 1959, (fiction) What Should We Do About Davey?, 1987, (sci. fiction) League of Grey-Eyed Women, 1970, (nonfiction) Blueprint for Life, 1963, Beatles, 1968, What You Should Know About Sexual Response, 1966, Body Language, 1970, Incompatibility of Men and Women, 1971, You and Your Feet, 1971, The New Sexual Fulfillment, 1972, Bisexual Living, 1974, The Pleasure Book, 1975, Creative Coping, 1976, The Body Language of Sex Power and Aggression, 1977, Psyching Up, 1978, Weather Language, 1979, Talking Between the Lines, 1979, Body Politics, 1980, The Body Book, 1981, Sexual Chemistry, 1983, Ladies Man, 1983, The Omega-3 Breakthrough, 1987, Subtext, 1990, Legal Atlas of the United States, 1996, Courtroom Communication Skills, 1994, Trunk Full of Trouble, 2002. Served with AUS, 1942-46. Recipient Mystery Writers Am. award, 1944 Home: 720 West End Ave Apt 1608 New York NY 10025-6299

FAST, KENNETH H. lawyer; b. Newark, Apr. 1929; s. Moe M. and Eva H. Fast; m. Judith Nicholson, Nov. 23, 1969; children: Jonathan Nicholson, Madelaine M. BA, Lafayette Coll., 1951; LLB, Yale U., 1954. Bar: N.J. 1954, D.C. 1954, U.S. Ct. Appeals (3d cir.) 1958, U.S. Supreme Ct. 1960. Ptnr. Fast & Fast, East Orange, N.J., 1957-86, Fox & Fox, Livingston, N.J., 1987—. Trustee Weisberger Fund for Age, Poor and Needy, Raritan, N.J., 1969—. 1st lt. USAF, 1955-57. Mem. N.J. State Bar Assn., Essex County Bar Assn. Home: 91 Fairfield Dr Short Hills NJ 07078-1718

FAST, LINDA LEE, music educator; b. Lewiston, Idaho, Aug. 28, 1943; d. Lawrence Russel and Lissa LaVerne Kuykendall; children: Michelle Denise Collins, Mark David. BA, Warner Pacific Coll., Portland, Oreg., 1966. Tel. operator Pacific NW Bell, Lewiston, Idaho, 1960—65; youth dir. Capitola

Cmty. Ch. of God, Capitola, Calif., 1966—68; pvt. piano and voice tchr. Olympia, Clarkston, WallaWalla and Centralia, Wash., 1968—2003; preschool tchr. Happy Day Child Care Ctr., Centralia, Wash., 1985—91; sch. tchr. Centralia Christian Sch., Centralia, Wash., 1995. Jr. high youth dir. Richmond Ch. of God, Portland, Oreg., 1964—66; children's choir dir. Centralia (Wash.) Cmty. Ch. of God, 1982—85, youth choir dir., 1985—88, coll. and young adult leader and tchr., 1986—99, English handbell dir., 1988—2003; ch. pianist and vocalist Ch. of God, Lacey, Clarkston, Walla Walla & Centralia, Wash., 1968—70; youth dir. First Ch. of God, Clarkston, Wash., 1970—73, children's choir dir., Walla Walla, Wash., 1977—82; family camp program dir. Pacific NW Assn. Chs. of God, Centralia, 1995—97; youth choir dir. Olympia-Lacey Ch. of God, Lacey, Wash., 1973—77; dir. of summer jr. camp We. Wash. Assn. of the Churches of God, Olympia, 1975. Sec. Salvation Army Harbor Light, Portland, 1963—64; worship leader for womens retreat Ch. of God, Nevada City, Nev., 1994—94, worship leader for women's retreats Olympia and Easton, Wash., 1994—99, women's retreat spkr. Edmonds, Walla Walla, Spokane, Clarkston and Centralia, Wash., 1998—2003. Mem.: Lewis County Music Tchrs. Assn. (assoc.; chmn. of auditions Young Artists Master Series 1978—2003, chmn. of auditions Ribbon festival 1978—2003, pres., v.p., sec. 1978—2003, affil. with Wash. State Music Tchrs. Assn. and Music Tchrs. Nat. Assn., Music Tchr. of Yr. 2000). Republican. Avocations: grandparenting, entertaining, reading, gardening, travel. Home: 814 Eshom Rd Centralia WA 98531

FASTENAU, PHILIP S. neuropsychologist, educator; s. Emmett H. and Doris P. Fastenau; m. Dana R. Atkinson. BA in Sociology, Concordia Coll., 1984; MS in Exptl. Psychology, Appalachian State U., 1988; PhD in Clin. Psychology, Mich. State U., 1994. Lic. health svc. provider in psychology Ind. Lectr. Appalachian State U., Boone, NC, 1989; instr. Mich. State U., East Lansing, 1991—93; postdoctoral fellow U. of Mich. Med. Ctr., Ann Arbor, 1994—96; asst. prof. Ind. U. Purdue U. Indpls., 1996—2002, assoc. prof., 2002—; mem. exec. bd. Ctr. for Therapeutic Behavioral Neurosci., Indpls., 2002—. Instr. Appalachian State U., Boone, NC, 1989; assessment coord., supr. Mich. State U. Psychol. Clinic, East Lansing, 1991—93; instr. Mich. State U., East Lansing, 1991—93; mem. grad. faculty Purdue U., West Lafayette, Ind., 1996—, assoc. mem. grad. faculty, 1997—; affiliated scientist Ind. U. Ctr. for Aging Rsch., Indpls., 1999; cons. neuropsychologist Riley Hosp. for Children, Indpls., 1999—; team neuropsychologist Indpls. Colts, 1999—; adj. asst. prof. clin. psychology Ind. U. Sch. Medicine, Indpls., 2001—; presenter in field. Contbr. articles to profl. jours. Recipient Jr. Investigator Travel award, Nat. Inst. of Neurol. Disorders and Stroke and The Epilepsy Found., 2000, Jr. Investigator Rsch. award, Epilepsy Found. of Am., 1996; grantee, NIH/Nat. Inst. of Neurol. Disorders and Stroke, 2000—07, NIH/Nat. Inst. of Nursing Rsch., 2002—04, Cyberonics, Inc., 1998—99, Epilepsy Found., 1999—2000, Eli Lilly & Co., 2000, U.S. Dept of Edn. and Rehab. Svcs. Adminstrn., 1997—2000, NIH/Nat. Inst. of Nursing Rsch., 1997—2002, Clarian Health Ptnrs., 1999—2001. Mem.: AAUP, APA (Dissertation award 1992), Ind. Psychol. Assn., Midwestern Neuropsychological Group, Epilepsy Found. Am. (grantee 1997—98), Am. Epilepsy Soc., Nat. Acad. of Neuropsychology, Internat. Neuropsychol. Soc., Alpha Kappa Delta (life), Psi Chi (life). Achievements include invention of created and published Extended Complex Figure Test, a psychometric test of visual-spatial memory used in diagnosing neurological disorders. Office: Ind U Purdue U Indpls Psych (LD 124) 402 N Blackford St Indianapolis IN 46202-3275

FASTHUBER-GRANDE, TRAUDY, financial services company executive; b. Wels, Austria, July 26, 1950; came to U.S., 1974; d. Franz X. and Friederike (Enzlmuller) Fasthuber; m. John J. Grande, Mar. 27, 1987. Student, U. Vienna, 1973-74; BA, Rutgers U., 1976. CFP; registered investment advisor. Program dir. Alt's Gymnastics, inc., Shrewsbury, N.J., 1974-80; v.p. Tangible Resource Group, Inc., Red Bank, N.J., 1980-81, Grande Fin. Svcs., Inc., Oakhurst, N.J., 1987—; sr. fin. planner Raymond James & Assocs., Inc., Naples, Fla., 1982-85; registered prin. Raymond James Fin. Svcs., Inc., Oakhurst, 1985—. Hostess TV program Wall St.-Main St., Naples, 1983-84; guest speaker Am. Heart Assn., Fla., 1984-85; lectr. various women's investment seminars, N.J., 1986—; adminstr. Am. Psychiat. Assn. Mem. Retirement Program, 1990—; lectr. Johns Hopkins U., 1992—. Mem. Inst. Cert. Fin. Planners. Avocations: skiing, music, running, travel, swimming. Office: Grande Fin Svcs Inc Ste 7 257 Monmouth Rd Bldg B Oakhurst NJ 07755-1500 E-mail: traudy.grande@raymondjames.com.

FASTIFF, WESLEY J. lawyer; b. Fall River, Mass., July 19, 1932; s. Jacob Fastiff and Ida Bertman; m. Bonnie Barmon, Dec. 29, 1963; children: Pamela Fastiff Ellman, Eric Barmon Fastiff. LLB, Harvard U., 1959. Bar: Calif., D.C., U.S. Dist. Ct. (no., ea., ctrl. dist.) Calif., U.S. Ct. Appeals (2nd, 9th cir.), U.S. Supreme Ct. Lawyer, chmn. bd. Littler Mendelson, San Francisco, 1963—. With USN, 1954-56. Office: Littler Mendelson 650 California St Fl 20 San Francisco CA 94108-2702

FASTIGGI, ROBERT L. religious studies educator; b. Montclair, N.J., Feb. 20, 1953; s. Caesar and Mary Fastiggi; m. Kathleen Marie Kobus; children: Mary, Anthony, Clare. AB, Dartmouth Coll., 1974; MA, Fordham U., 1976, PhD, 1987. Religion and English tchr. Archbishop Stepinac H.S., White Plains, NY, 1978—79; staff worker Office of Spiritual Devel., Larchmont, NY, 1978—80; religion tchr. Immaculate Conception H.S., Montclair, 1980—81; religion and English tchr. St. Joseph-By-The-Sea H.S., S.I., NY, 1981—84; religion tchr. Cardinal Gibbons H.S., Ft. Lauderdale, Fla., 1984—85; asst./assoc. prof. St. Edward's U., Austin, Tex., 1985—99; assoc. prof. Sacred Heart Maj. Seminary, Detroit, 1999—. Com. chair MDiv Degree Com., Detroit, 1999—; mem., advisor Am. Bioethics Adv. Commn., Stafford, Va., 2002—. Author: Natural Theology of Yves de Paris, 1991; contbr. articles to profl. jours. Mem.: Soc. Cath. Social Scientists, Fellowship Cath. Scholars, Am. Acad. Religion. Roman Catholic. Avocations: walking, bicycling. Home: 3991 Dudley St Dearborn Heights MI 48125 Office: Sacred Heart Maj Seminary 2701 Chicago Blvd Detroit MI 48206

FATEMI, RAY S. mechanical engineer, consultant; b. Tehran, Iran, July 18, 1959; arrived in U.S., 1978; s. Mohamed and Zahra Fatemi; m. Marjaneh Nemati, June 16, 1982; children: Nikoo, Laudan. BS in Biomed. Engring., U. Iowa, 1983, MS in Mech. Engring., 1985, PhD in Mech. Engring., 1989. Rsch. asst. U. Iowa, Iowa City, 1983—89; tchg. faculty Kirkwood C.C., Iowa City, 1986—89; rsch. asst. prof. U. Akron, Ohio, 1990—93; prin., cons. ACUU-TEK of Ohio, Akron, 1993—; sales cons. GM Indsl., Bedford Heights, Ohio, 1995—96; v.p. engring. Ruger Equip., Inc., Uhrichsville, Ohio, 1995—2000; project engr. mgr. JRB Co., Inc., Akron, 2000—. Adj. faculty U. Akron, 1993—. Contbr. articles. Treas. Ft. Island Swim Club, Fairlawn, Ohio, 1999—2002. Grantee, NRC, 1990—91, U. Akron, 1991—93. Mem.: ASME, Ohio Acad. Sci., Biomed. Engring. Soc. Achievements include patents in field. Home: 462 Gresham Dr Akron OH 44333 Office: JRB Co Inc 820 Glaser Pky Akron OH 44306

FATEMI, SAEID, language educator, writer, researcher; b. Yazd, Iran; s. Mohammad Ali and Saltanat Fatemi; m. Minoo Varzegar; children: Delaram, Arezou. BA in French Lang. Lit., BA in Law, U. Tehran, 1947, PhD in Persian Lit., 1950; PhD in Comparative Lit., U. Paris, 1953. Assoc. prof. U. Tehran, 1953-65, prof., 1965—. Translator of French into Persian UNESCO; vis. prof. Princeton U., Kent State U.; over 70 presentations at nat. and intern. confs. Author: Greek and Roman Mythology, A Collection of Poems; author, translator: Formation of the Rural Education; translator: Human Rights, Human Against Ignorance; chief editor Bakhtare-Emruz Daily Newspaper, Tehran; translator Courier, Payam; editor PAYAM; contbr. over 500 articles to profl. jours. Leader Iran-e-Emruz Polit. Party, 1978-80; elected mem. supreme coun. Nat. Front Iran, 1960—; del. Internat. Ct. of Justice; polit. prisoner in Iran, 1953-62. Mem. Internat. Coun. Philosophy and Human Scis., Assn. Writers and Poets. Avocations: reading, writing. Home: 290 Anderson Ave # 6K Hackensack NJ 07601 E-mail: varzegar@aol.com.

FATHAUER, THEODORE FREDERICK, meteorologist; b. Oak Park, Ill., June 5, 1946; s. Arthur Theodore and Helen Ann (Mashek) F.; m. Mary Ann Neesan, Aug. 8, 1981. BA, U. Chgo., 1968. Cert. cons. meteorologist. Rsch. aide USDA No. Dev. Labs., Peoria, Ill., 1966, Cloud Physics Lab., Chgo., 1967; meteorologist Sta. WLW Radio/TV, Cin., 1967-68, Nat. Meteorol. Ctr., Washington, 1968-70, Nat. Weather Svc., Anchorage, 1970-80, meteorologist-in-charge Fairbanks, Alaska, 1980-98, lead forecaster, 1998—. Instr. U. Alaska, Fairbanks, 1975-76, USCG Aux., Fairbanks and Anchorage, 1974—; specialist in Alaska meteorology. Contbr. chpt to book Denali's West Buttress, 1997, Living With the Coast of Alaska, 1997; contbr. articles to weather mags. and jours. Bd. dirs. Fairbanks Concert Assn., 1988—; bd. dirs. No. Alaska Combined Fed. Campaign, 1996—, campaign chmn., 1996-97; bd. dirs. Friends U. Alaska Mus., 1993—, pres., 1993-95, sec. 1997-98; bd. visitors U. Alaska Fairbanks, 1995—; bd. dirs. Fairbanks Symphony Assn., 1994—, sec., 1994-2001, treas., 2001-; bd. trustees U. Alaska Found., 1997—, mem. coll. fellows, 1993—, exec. com., 1997—, vice chair, 1998-99, chair, 2000-01; mem. adv. bd. Salvation Army Fairbanks Corps, 1997—. Recipient Outstanding Performance award Nat. Weather Service, 1972, 76, 83, 85, 86, 89, Fed. Employee of Yr. award, Fed. Exec. Assn., Anchorage, 1978. Fellow Am. Meteorol. Soc. (scientific and tech. adv. com. for coastal environments, 1998-, TV and radio seals of approval, co-chmn. Conference on Coastal Env. 2003), Royal Meteorol. Soc.; mem. AAAS, Am. Geophys. Union, Western Snow Conf., Arctic Inst. N.Am. (exec. sec. U.S. Corp. 1998—), Oceanography Soc., Can. Meteorol. and Oceanographic Soc., Greater Fairbanks C. of C., Am. Sailing Assn. Republican. Lutheran. Avocations: reading, music, skiing, canoeing. Home: PO Box 80210 Fairbanks AK 99708-0210 Office: Nat Weather Svc Forecast Office Internat Arctic Rsch Ctr U Alaska PO Box 757345 Fairbanks AK 99775-7345 E-mail: theodore.fathauer@noaa.gov.

FATO, GILDO E. lawyer, chemical engineer; b. Chgo., Mar. 27, 1928; s. Frank and Mary Louise (Phillipi) F.; m. Marie A. Matz, Sept. 18, 1954; children: Barbara Ann, Debra R., Karen M. BS in Chem. Engring., Ill. Inst. Tech., 1950; JD, DePaul U., 1960; postgrad., John Marshall Law Sch., 1960-63. Sr. chemist, patent asst. Ditto, Inc., Chgo., 1950-61; patent counsel Fansteel Metall. Corp., North Chicago, Ill., 1961-64; divsn. patent counsel Abbott Labs., North Chicago, Ill., 1964-83; asst. patent counsel Am. Hosp. Supply Corp., Evanston, Ill., 1983-86; sr. counsel E.I. duPont de Nemours & Co., Evanston, Ill., 1986-89; pvt. practice Libertyville, Ill., 1989—. Co-inventor transfer sheet. Served with U.S. Army, 1946-47, PTO. Mem. ABA, Ill. Bar Assn., Patent Law Assn.. Chgo., Toastmasters Bicycle Club (v.p., sec. 1977-80, Lake County, Ill.). Home and Office: 515 Ash St Libertyville IL 60048-2706

FATT, WILLIAM R. hospitality company executive; b. Toronto, Ont., Can., Mar. 11, 1951; BA in Econs., York U., Toronto. Auditor Thorne Riddell, Toronto, 1973-75; asst. contr. Revenue Properties Co. Ltd., Toronto, 1975-77; acctg. analyst The Consumers Gas Co., Toronto, 1977-78; asst. treas. Hiram Walker Resources, Toronto, 1978-82, treas., 1982-84, v.p., treas., 1984-86; v.p. Morgan Bank of Can., Toronto, 1986-88; treas. Can. Pacific Ltd., Toronto, 1988, v.p., treas., 1988-90, v.p. fin. and acctg., CFO, 1990-94, exec. v.p. and CFO Toronto and Calgary, 1994; CEO Fairmont Hotels & Resorts (formerly Can. Pacific Hotels Corp.), Toronto, 1998—; also bd. dirs. Vice chmn., trustee Legacy Hotels Real Estate Investment Trust; bd. dirs. Jim Pattison Group Inc., Toronto Gen. Western Hosp. Found., Embridge Inc., Sun Life Fin. Inc., EnCana Corp. Office: Fairmont Hotels & Resorts 100 Wellington St W # 1600 Toronto ON Canada M5K 1B7

FATTAH, CHAKA, congressman, former state legislator; b. Phila., Nov. 21, 1956; m. Renée Chenault; 3 children. Student, Phila. C.C., 1976; M. in Govt., U. Pa., 1986; student, Harvard U. Mem. Pa. Ho. of Reps., 1982-88, Pa. State Senate, 1988-94; congressman, Pa. 2nd Dist. U.S. House Reps., Washington, D.C., 1995—. Mem. house adminstr. com., com. on appropriations, VA-HUD subcom. Founder Am. Cities Conf. and Found.; leader task force Child Devel. Initiative, Phila.; founder, convenor Grad. Opportunities Conf., Pa.; chmn. exec. com. Pa. Higher Edn. Assistance Agy.; creator Jobs Project. Recognized nationally for outstanding leadership Time Mag.'s roster of Amer.'s most promising leaders, 1994, Ebony Mag.'s one of 50 Future Leaders, 1984; recipient Pa. Pub. Interest Coalition's State Legislator of Yr. award. Democrat. Baptist. Office: US House Reps 2301 Rayburn Hob Washington DC 20515-0001 : 4104 Walnut Street Philadelphia PA 19104*

FATUM, DELORES RUTH, school counselor; b. Kingston, NY, Aug. 1, 1945; d. Robert and Dorothy Beatrice (Van Demark) F. BS, Winthrop U., 1968; MEd, Ga. Coll., Milledgeville, 1973; EdS, Ga. So. U. Cert. couselor, Ga.; practice tchr. supr. Sch. couselor Laurens County Bd. of Edn., Dublin, Ga.; EdS counseling educator Ga. So. U. Regional coordinator Outdoor Edn., Ga. Dept. of Natural Resources, Atlanta. Author: (manuals) Georgia Outdoor Education, Student Services for Lauren County. Mem. Am. Counseling Assn., Am. Sch. Counselors Assn., Nat. Mid. Sch. Assn., Profl. Assn. Ga. Educators. (v.p. Laurens county chpt.), Ga. Sch. Counselors Assn. (chair U.S. Congl. Dist. 8). Home: 573 Coleman Ln Dublin GA 31021-4439 Office: W Laurens Mid Sch 332 W Laurens School Rd Dublin GA 31021-1570

FATZINGER, JAMES A. S. construction educator, estimator; b. Bethlehem, Pa., Jan. 27, 1926; s. James Andrew and Cora Ellen (Steigerwalt) F.; m. Mary Lois Beckman, June 10, 1972. Student, Pa. State Coll., 1943-44, Moravian Coll., 1957-58, Fullerton Jr. Coll., 1972-73. Journeyman various cos., 1951-72; supr. 3M Co., Montpelier, Ohio, 1966-67; journeyman Endicott Brass Co., Montpelier, 1967; substation operator Pub. Svc. Elec. and Gas Co., Newark, 1959-65; constrn. estimator various cos., 1972—; contractor Calif. and Ariz., 1980-85; constrn. instr. Mesa (Ariz.) C.C., Rio Salado C.C., Mesa, 1974-78, C.C. of So. Nev., Las Vegas, 1978-97, U. Nev., Las Vegas, 1992-97. Pres., owner Basic Estimating Ltd., Las Vegas, 1978-99. Author: Basic Estimating for Construction, 1996, Blueprint Reading for Construction, 1997. Trustee Tech. Sch., Fullerton Jr. Coll., 1986-92; scoutmaster Boy Scouts Am., Bethlehem, 1950-60, commr., Huntington Beach, Calif., 1976-77. 1st sgt. U.S. Army, 1944-46, ETO. Mem. Am. Soc. Profl. Estimators (cert.; emeritus). Republican. Avocations: motor home travel, music.

FAUCETTE, GLORIA MARIE, accountant, educator; b. Burlington, N.C., Aug. 29, 1948; d. Jesse Graham and Mildred Kathryn Faucette. BA in Social Scis., Elon Coll., 1982; BS in Acctg., N.C. A&T State U., 1991; MBA, Elon Coll., 1993. Social worker Alamance County Dept. Social Svcs., Burlington, NC, 1974-89; instr. acctg. and bus. N.C. A&T State U., Greensboro, NC, 1991-99, N.C. AT&T State, Greensboro, NC, 2000—01; acct. Cobb Ezekiel Brown and Co., Graham, NC, 1999—2000; bus. tchr. Hawfields Mid. Sch., 2001—. Mem. acad. rels. com. Inst. Internal Auditors, Greensboro, 1996-97; cons. bus. ednl. career decisions mid/secondary sch. students. Contbr. articles to profl. jours. Mem. AICPA, N.C. Assn. CPA (mem. acctg. edn. com. 1995-97; chair careers in acctg. com. 1999), Beta Alpha Psi, Beta Gamma Sigma Democrat. Methodist. Avocations: child abuse/neglect issues, higher education for underpriveleged, small business consulting.

FAUCETTE, MERILON COOPER, retired elementary educator; b. Washington, Ark., Oct. 17, 1931; d. Andrew and Narciss (Tyus) Cooper; m. Clarence William Faucette, Jr., May 17, 1958 (dec. 1982); children: Billie Reneé, Gwenevere Yvetta. BS, Ark. Bapt. Coll., Little Rock, 1953; MEd, Henderson State U., Arkadelphi, Ark., 1975. Tchr. Searcy (Ark.) Sch. Dist., 1953-61, Pulaski County Spl. Sch. Dist., Searcy, 1961-86; ret., 1986. Mem.: Telephone Pioneers Am. (assoc.).

FAUCHIER, DAN R(AY), mediator, arbitrator, educator, construction management consultant; b. Blackwell, Okla., Sept. 27, 1946; s. Wallace Monroe and Betty Lou F.; m. Sylvia Stephanie Chan Fauchier, Mar. 15, 1969; 1 child, Angele Calista Fauchier; m. Jonah Keri, 1997. BA cum laude, Southwestern Coll., 1964-68; student, Sch. Theology, Claremont, Calif., 1968-69, Claremont Grad. Sch., 1969-70. Lic. bldg. contractor, Calif.; cert. arbitrator and mediator. Min. of youth First United Meth. Ch., Winfield, Kans., 1964-68, First Congl. Ch., Riverside, Calif., 1968-69; adminstr. Calif. Youth Authority, Chino and Paso Robles, Calif., 1969-76; tchr. Chaffey Coll., Rancho Cucamonga, Calif., 1971-74; dir. Pacific Fin. Svcs., Beverly Hills, Calif., 1977-81; pres. Littlefields Corp., Santa Maria and Corona del Mar, Calif., 1978-81; cons. Hughes Helicopters, Oasis Oil, Jakarta, Indonesia, 1981; systems designer Teltrans Corp., L.A., 1982-85; project mgr. Pacific Sunset Builders, L.A., 1985-87, DW Devel., Fontana, Calif., 1987-90; owner Fauchier Group Builders, San Diego, 1988—; pres. Empire Bay Devel. Corp., San Bernardino, Calif., 1991-92; project mgr. White Sys. L.A. Ctrl. Libr., 1993; dir. project mgmt. White Sys. divsn. Pinnacle Automation, Inc., San Diego, 1993-95; dir. project mgmt.; dir. design logistics White Systems divsn. Pinnacle Automation, Inc., San Diego, 1995-97; v.p. SDC & Assocs., San Diego and Washington, 1997-2000; tchr. Power Summit, 2000—, dir., bd. advisors, 2001—. Founding dir. Neighborhood Restoration Project, San Bernardino, Calif., 1991-92; cons. project mgr. White Sys., Inc., Cin. Pub. Libr., 1997, FCC Document Mechanization Project, 1998; instr. U. Calif. San Diego, 1998-2001; Inst. Constrn. Mgmt., arbitrator and mediator Arbitration Works, 1999—, Saddle Island Inst., 1999—; instr. San Diego State U., 2001—, mediator panelist La Jolla Ctr. Dipsute Resolution, 2003-. Contbr. cons.: President's Commission on Criminal Justice, 1972; co-author: Consumer Credit, 1984. Deputy Registrar Voters San Bernardino, Calif., 1975; mem. Skid Row Mental Health Adv. Bd., L.A., 1986, Chaffey Coll. Adv. Bd. Rancho Cucamonga, Calif., 1991-95, chmn. Bus. Security Alliance, San Bernardino, Calif., 1992. Named Nat. fellow Woodrow Wilson Fellowship, Princeton, N.J., 1968-69; Grad. scholar State of Calif., Claremont, 1969. Mem. Associated Gen. Contractors (chmn. edn. com. 1999-2001), Am. Subcontractor Assn. (chmn. mktg. com. 1999-2000), Associated Builders and Contractors, Nat. Elec. Contractors Assn., Forensics Cons. Assn., Nat. Found. for Dispute Rev. Bds., Engring. Gen. Contractors Assn. (pub. works advocate), ABA Constrn. Industry Forum, Self-Realization Fellowship, Christmas in April (bd. dirs., v.p. 1999-2000), Habitat for Humanity, Internat. Platform Assn., Inst. for Cmty. Econ., Homeless Coalition, People for Ethical Treatment of Animals, Rainforest Alliance. Avocations: painting, photography, writing. Home: PMB249 9921 Carmel Mountain Rd San Diego CA 92129-2813 E-mail: dan@danzpage.com.

FAUCI, ANTHONY STEPHEN, health facility administrator, physician; b. Bklyn., Dec. 24, 1940; s. Stephen A. and Eugenia A. Fauci. AB, Coll. of Holy Cross, 1962; MD, Cornell U., 1966; DSc (hon.), Coll. Holy Cross, 1987, Georgetown U., 1990, Hahnemann U., 1990, Mt. Sinai Sch. Medicine, 1990, Universita di Roma, 1990, St. John's U., 1991, Long Island U., 1992, Med. Coll. Wis., 1993, Bard Coll., 1993, Bates Coll., 1993, SUNY, Farmingdale, 1994, U. Conn. Health Ctr, 1994, Duke U., 1995. Diplomate Am. Bd. Internal Medicine, Am. Bd. Allergy and Immunology (bd. dirs. 1984 to date), Am. Bd. Infectious Diseases. Intern N.Y. Hosp.-Cornell Med. Ctr., 1966—67, asst. resident in medicine, 1967—68, chief resident dept. medicine, 1971—72; clin. assoc. Nat. Inst. Allergy and Infectious Diseases-NIH, Bethesda, Md., 1968—70, sr. staff fellow, 1970—71, sr. investigator, 1972—74, head, clin. physiology sect., 1974—80, dep. clin. dir., 1977—80, chief Lab. Immunoregulation, 1980—, dir., 1984—; dir. Office of AIDS Rsch., NIH, assoc. dir. NIH for AIDS Rsch., 1988—94. Cons. Naval Med. Ctr., Bethesda, 1972—. Contbr. With USPHS, 1968—96. Recipient meritorious svcs. award, USPHS, 1979, Arthur S. Fleming award, 1983, Squibb award, Infectious Diseases Soc., 1983, Commrs. Spl. Citation, FDA, 1984, Clemons von Pirquet award, Georgetown U. Med. Ctr., 1986, Disting Clin. Educator award, NIH Clin. Ctr., 1988, Leadership award, Columbus Citizens Found., Inc., 1988, spl. award for rsch. in AIDS, Nat. Hemophilia Fedn., 1989, Lee P. Brown Nat. Pub. Svc. award, Nat. Acad. Pub. Adminstrn. and Nat. Soc. for Pub. Adminstrn., 1989, numerous awards, Duke U., AMA, Children's Hosp., Nat. Med. Ctr., Surgeon Gen., Am. Assn. Physicians for Human Rights, Nat. Health Coun., Nat. Found. Infectious Disease, Helen Hayes award for med. rsch., 1989, Excellence in Pub. Svc. award, Com. for Support of Pub. Svc., 1990, Lifetime Sci. award, Inst. Advanced Studies in Immunology and Aging, 1990, Internat. Chiron prize, 1990, Pres. award, N.Y. Acad. Sci., 1990, Thomas H. Ham-Louis R. Wasserman award, Am. Soc. Hematology, 1992, Dr. Nathan Davis award, AMA, 1992, Outstanding Achievement award, Howard U., 1992, Humanitarian award, Tiro a Segno Fedn., 1993, Cartwright prize, Columbia U. Coll. Physicians and Surgeons, 1993, Commr. of Honor award, SUNY-Farmingdale, 1994, Theobald Smith award, Albany Med. Coll., 1995, Coord. Com. award, ABA, 1996, David Rumbough Sci. award, Juvenile Diabetes Fedn. Internat., 1996, award, Nat. Coun. Internat. Health, 1996, March of Dimes Fedn., 1996, Ellen Browning Scripps medal, Scripps Fedn. Medicine and Rsch., 1996, Md. Gov.'s Citation, 1997, Thomas J. D'Alesandro Jr. award, Assoc. Italian Am. Charities, 1997, San Marino prize for medicine, 1997, John P. McGovern award, Am. Med. Writers Assn., 1997, many others. Master: AAAS (Westinghouse award 1988); fellow: Am. Acad. Microbiology, Am. Acad. Arts and Scis., ACP (Richard and Hinda Rosenthal award 1995, John Phillips Meml. award 1997), Am. Acad. Allergy, Am. Acad. Allergy and Immunology (hon.), Am. Med. Writers Assn. (hon.), N.Y. Acad. Medicine (hon.); mem.: Royal Acad. Medicine (Spain), Royal Danish Acad. Sci. and Letters (fgn.), Inst. Medicine of NAS, Assn. of Am. Physicians (recorder 1988—93, councillor 1993—), Am. Soc. for Clin. Investigation, Infectious Diseases Soc. Am., Commd. Officers Assn. USPHS (Pub. Health Leader of Yr. award), Internat. AIDS Soc., Am. Fedn. Clin. Rsch. (pres. 1980—81), Am. Soc. Cell Biology, Am. Soc. Virology, Am. Assn. Immunologists (program chmn. 1982—85, Kober lectr. 1988). Roman Catholic. Avocations: running, tennis. Office: Nat Inst Allergy & Infectious Diseases 31 Ctr Dr Msc 2520 Bethesda MD 20892-0001

FAUDE, WILSON HINSDALE, museum director, consultant; b. Hartford, Conn., Feb. 20, 1946; s. John Paul and Helen (Hinsdale) Faude; m. Janet Bailey, 1985; children: Sarah Hinsdale, Paul Bailey. BA, Hobart Coll., 1969; MA, Trinity Coll., 1975. Curator Mark Twain Meml., Hartford, 1971—78; exec. assoc. to v.p. for devel. U. Hartford, West Hartford, Conn., 1981—85; exec. dir. Old State House, Hartford, 1978—81, 1985—2001, exec. dir. emeritus, 2002—. Commr. Conn. Arts Commn., 1975—83, hon. mem. 350th commn., 1984—86; commr. Conn. Hist. Commn., 1980, chmn., 1984—96. Author: (book) Renaissance of Mark Twain's House, 1977, The Great Hartford Picture Book, 1985, The Old Photograph Series: Hartford, 1994, The Old Photograph Series: Hartford, vol. II, 1995, The Old Photograph Series: Hartford, vol. III, 1997, Lost Hartford, 2000; author: (with others) Connecticut Firsts, 1978, 1985, 1996, 2000, Birthplace of Democracy, 1979; contbr. articles to profl. jours. Reader Talking Books for the Blind and Handicapped Conn. Vols. Svcs., 1986—; mem. faculty Cooperstown Seminars, NY, 1979—80, 1984—88; corporator Hartford Art Sch., West Hartford, 1980—98; mem. Conn. Heritage Task Force, 1980—82; corporator Hartford Hosp., 1992—; bd. dirs. Conn. Equestrian Ctr., 1996, Stowe Ctr., 1996—97, Conn. Women's Hall of Fame, 1996—; trustee Renbrook Sch., West Hartford, 1984—85; hon. trustee Mark Twain Ho., 1997—. With U.S. Army, 1969—71. Named Capt., 1st Co. Gov. Foot Guard, 1979—, Civitan Man of the Yr., 1997; recipient 1st prize needlepoint, Ea. State Expn., 1997, Disting. Adv. for the Arts award, State of Conn., 1998, Thomas Hooker award for disting. cmty. svc., Ancient Burying Ground Assn., 1999. Mem.: Pub. Rels. Soc. Am. (Pub. Svc. Merit award 2001), Mark Twain Meml., Century Assn., Nat. Arts Club, Druid Soc. Episcopalian. Home and Office: 42 Fulton Pl West Hartford CT 06107-1128 E-mail: wilsonfaude@attbi.com.

FAUDREE, RALPH J. academic administrator, mathematician, educator; b. Durant, Okla., Aug. 23, 1939; s. Ralph J. Faudree Sr. and Vinita Faudree; m. Patricia Lee Newsom; children: Paja, Jill. BS in Math. and Physics, Okla. Bapt. U., Shawnee, 1961; MS in Math., Purdue U., 1962, PhD in Math., 1964. Instr. math. U. Calif., Berkeley, 1964—66; asst. prof. math. U. Ill., Urbana, 1966—71; assoc. prof. math. Memphis State U., 1971—76, prof. math., 1976—, chmn. dept. math., 1983—94, dean Coll. Arts and Scis., 1995—2000, interim pres., 2000—01, provost, 2001—. Recipient Emminent Faculty award, Bd. Visitors - U. Memphis, 1994. Mem.: Am. Math. Soc. Home: 5370 Normandy Rd Memphis TN 38120 Office: University of Memphis Southern Ave Memphis TN 38152 Office Fax: 901-678-3643. Personal E-mail: rfaudree@memphis.edu. Business E-Mail: rfaudree@memphis.edu.

FAUL, JOHN LAURENCE, medical educator; s. Peter James Faul and Noreen Moloney. MA, MB, BCh, BAOI, Trinity Coll. Dublin, 1991, MD, 1998. Cert. specialist in respiratory and gen. medicine Irish Med. Coun., 2001. Asst. prof. medicine divsn. pulmonary and critical care medicine Stanford (Calif.) U., 2000—. Assoc. med. dir. Lung and Heart/Lung Transplantation Program Stanford U. Recipient Cecil Lehman Mayer Rsch. award, Am. Coll. Chest Physicians, 1995. Fellow: Am. Bd. Sleep Medicine; mem.: Royal Coll. Physicians. Achievements include research in airway inflammation in asthma and pulmonary vascular disease. Office: Divsn Pulmonary Med Rm H3149 300 Pasteur Dr Stanford CA 94305-5236 E-mail: jfaul@stanford.edu.

FAUL, JUNE PATRICIA, education specialist; b. Detroit; d. John William and Shirley Olive (Block) Lynch; m. George Johnson Faul, EdD, Dec. 22, 1949; children: Robert M., Alison. BA, U. Calif., Berkeley, 1952. Cert. elem. tchr., Calif. Tchr. Tulare County (Calif.) Schs., 1945-46, Tulare City Schs., 1946-48, Visalia (Calif.) City Schs., 1948-49, Richmond (Calif.) City Schs., 1951-52, Pacific Grove (Calif.) Sch. Dist., 1965-85; designated English tchg. specialist State of Calif., 1969—; edn. cons. Leo A. Meyer Assocs., Inc., Hayward, Calif., 1993—. Prin. Group Four Assocs.; lectr. Calif. State U., Fresno, 1969, U. Calif.,

Santa Cruz, 1970. Co-author: The New Older Woman, 1996. Apprd. mem. first human rels. commn. City of Richmond, 1962-64; mem. adv. bd. Family Resource Ctr.; founding mem., 1st pres. Monterey (Calif.) Peninsula Child Abuse Prevention Coun., 1974; hon. life mem. Calif. PTA; bd. dirs. Carmel Cultural Commn., 1964-67, Harrison Meml. Libr. Bd., Carmel, Calif., 1978-84; bd. dirs. Monterey Peninsula Airport Dist., 1980—; co-founder 100 Women Supporting Women, Monterey Peninsula Coll., 1997. Mem. Am. Assn. Airport Execs., Friends of Hopkins Marine Sta. (founer, bd. dirs.), Carmel Heritage (founder, bd. dirs.), Monterey NAACP (life), Monterey Mus. Art (life), Monterey Symphony Guild (life). Democrat. Avocation: writing. Home: PO Box 4365 Carmel CA 93921-4365 E-mail: patfaul@aol.com.

FAULCON, CLARENCE AUGUSTUS, musician; b. Phila., Aug. 8, 1928; s. Leroy Cortez and Addie Theresa Faulcon; m. Jacqueline Beach; 1 child, David. BS in Music Edn. and Supervision, U. Pa., 1950, MS in Music Edn., 1952; MusD in Musicology, Phila. Conservatory of Music, 1962. Instrumental music tchr. Sulzberger Jr. H.S., Phila., 1951—63; chair music dept. Cazenovia Coll., Cazenovia, NY, 1963—68; chair, full prof. music dept. Morgan State U., Balt., 1968—93, First MSU Jazz Festival, 1969, First MSU Black Symphony Orch. Symposium with Balt. Symphony Orch., 1973; accompanist, 1982—; piano and vocal team with wife, 2000—. Chair Wholistic Ministry Chs. Take a Corner, Wilmington, Del., 1994—; cons. world culture and bus. Faulcon, Inc., Hockessin, 1994—; lectr., performer various arts and humanities congresses six countries and the U.S. Libr., NASA and student libr. exch. program advisor Afganistan Del. Cmty. Together Com., Wilmington, 2002. Grantee Gates Grant, Del. Libr. Sys., 1970—2002; Found. Digital Divide Tech. Access grantee, 2001, NSF grantee, 1991—92, Gates grantee. Mem.: Internat. Biog. Ctr. (del. 2002), Pa. Hist. Soc., Sigma Pi Phi. Baptist. Avocations: Bible study, music history. Home and Office: PO Box 670 Hockessin DE 19707

FAULCONER, JAMES E. humanities educator; b. Warrensburg, Mo., Sept. 27, 1947; m. Janice K. Allen, Dec. 19, 1970; children: Christian James, Matthew Allen, Rebecca Elyse, Elisabeth Anne Malmgren. PhD, Pa. State U., 1977. Prof. Brigham Young U., Provo, Utah, 1975—. Dean gen. edn. and honors Brigham Young U., Provo, 1997—2000, assoc. dean gen. edn. and honors, 1994—97, dept. chair philosophy, 1989—94; vis. prof. Cath. U., Belgium, 1995—96. Author: Romans 1: Notes and Reflections; co-author: Introduction to Logic; editor: Transcendence in Philosophy and Religion; co-editor: Appropriating Heidegger; founding editor Epoche: A Jour. for History of Philosophy, board of editors. Dist. chairperson Dem. Party, Provo, 1993—95. Fellow Alcuin Gen. Edn. fellow, Brigham Young U., 1988—91; scholar, 1991—94. Mem.: Heidegger Conf. (sec.-convenor 1994), Soc. Phenomenology and Existential Philosophy. Democrat. Mem. Lds Ch. Avocations: cooking, travel. Office: Brigham Young U Provo UT 84602 Personal E-mail: james_faulconer@byu.edu. E-mail: james_faulconer@byu.edu.

FAULCONER, ROBERT JAMIESON, pathologist, educator; b. Sedlescombe, Sussex, Eng., July 11, 1923; came to U.S., 1925, naturalized, 1932; s. Robert Hoffman and Gladys Alice (Jamieson) F.; m. Virginia Myrl Davis, Aug. 11, 1945; children: Anne Faulconer Hurley, Elisabeth Myrl, Mary Waite, John Edmund. BS, Coll. William and Mary, 1943; MD, Johns Hopkins U., 1947; DSc (hon.), Ea. Va. Med. Sch., 1998. Diplomate Am. Bd. Pathology. Intern Johns Hopkins Hosp., 1948, fellow, 1948-49; resident Presbyn.-U. Pa. Med. Ctr., Phila., 1949-52; pathologist DePaul Hosp., Norfolk, Va., 1954-78, pathologist, dir. labs., 1965-78; clin. prof. pathology Med. Coll. Va., 1972-79; prof. pathology Ea. Va. Med. Sch., 1974-94, chmn., 1978-93, prof. emeritus, 1994—. Cons. pathologist U.S. Naval Hosp., Portsmouth, Va., VA Hosp., Hampton, Va., Children;s Hosp., Norfolk, Va. Beach Gen. Hosp.; chmn. Health Svcs. Adv. Bd., Norfolk; mem. adv. com. Va. Cancer Registry. Med. editorial bd. Histology and Histopathology Jour.; contbr. articles on pathology to profl. publs. Pres. Va. div. Am. Cancer Soc., 1963-66, mem. nat. bd. dirs., exec. and sci. rev. coms.; bd. visitors Coll. William and Mary, 1972-76, 79-87, chmn. William and Mary Olde Guarde, 1997-98. With USNR, 1943-46, M.C., U.S. Army, 1952-54. Recipient J. Shelton Horsley award merit Va. div. Am. Cancer Soc., 1966, Alumni medallion Coll. William and Mary, 1985 Fellow AAAS; mem. AMA, Internat. Acad. Pathology, Am. Soc. Clin. Pathologists, Coll. Am. Pathologists, Am. Assn. Anatomists, Am. Soc. Clin. Oncology, Am. Assn. Phys. Anthropologists, Va. Soc. Pathology (pres. 1958-59), Norfolk Acad. Medicine (pres. 1964-65), Am. Assn. History of Medicine, Am. Assn. Pathologists, Assn. Pathology Chmn., Cypher Soc. (Coll. William and Mary), Norfolk Yacht and Country Club, Town Point Club (bd. govs.), Commonwealth Club (Richmond), Sigma Xi. Episcopalian. Home: 1507 Buckingham Ave Norfolk VA 23508-1354 Office: Ea Va Med Sch Med Coll of Hampton Roads PO Box 1980 Norfolk VA 23501-1980

FAULES, BARBARA RUTH, elementary education educator, retired; b. Austin, Texas, Mar. 10, 1940; d. Milton Friedrich Hausmann and Ruth Elizabeth Hornbuckle; m. John Wilson Faules, May 30, 1967. BA cum laude, Harding U., 1962; MA in Curriculum and Instrn., U. Mo., Kansas City, 1995. Cert. elem. tchr., Mo. Tchr. 4th grade Searcy Grammar Sch., Ark., 1962-64, Pulaski County Spl. Sch., Little Rock AFB Elem., Jacksonville, Ark., 1964-67; tchr. grades 3, 4, and 6 Butcher Greene Elem. Consol. Sch. Dist. #4, Grandview, Mo., 1967-98, ret., 1998. Contbr. (poetry) Sunrise and Soft Mist, 1999 (Editor's Choice 1999). Mem. Nat. Congress Parents and Tchr. (hon. life mem.). Mem. Ch. of Christ. Avocations: freelance photography, writing, gardening, reading, traveling. Home: 305 Valley Ct Smyrna TN 37167-5509 E-mail: Tchow1101@aol.com.

FAULK, MARSHALL WILLIAM, professional football player; b. New Orleans, Feb. 26, 1973; Student, San Diego State U. Running back Indpls. Colts., 1994-99, St. Louis Rams, 1999—. Named to Sporting News Coll. All-Am. 1st Team, 1991-93, NFL Rookie of Year 1994; selected to Pro Bowl, 1994, named outstanding player, 1994. Office: c/o St Louis Rams One Rams Way Bridgeton MO 63045

FAULKNER, JULIA ELLEN, opera singer; b. St. Louis, Nov. 1, 1957; d. Seldon and Dona Leah (Clark) F. MusB cum laude, Ind. U., 1980, MusM, 1983. Instr. voice No. Ariz. U., Flagstaff, 1984, Iowa State U., 1984-85; solo artist San Francisco Opera Ctr., 1985-86, Wolftrap Opera Co., Vienna, Va., 1986, Bavarian State Opera, Munich, 1987-91, Vienna (Austria) State Opera, 1991-97, Metropolitan Opera, N.Y.C., 1997—; studio voice tchr., 1998—2002; mem. faculty U. Wis. Sch. Music, 2003—. Solo performances with opera cos. and theaters at La Scala, Carnegie Hall, N.Y.C., Met. Opera, N.Y.C., L.A. Philharm., San Francisco Philharm., also in Miami Fla., Berlin, Hamburg, Germany, Lyon, Jerusalem, Bordeau, Stockholm, Amsterdam and Genoa; dir. Oklahoma and Old Maid and the Thief, Flagstaff, 1984; rec. artist Elektra, 1990, Der Rosenkavalier, 1991, Rossini, Semiramide, Schumann, Genoveva; recorded Pergolese Stabat Mater Deutsche Grammophone Das Paradis und die Peri, Verdi's Falstaff. Recipient award Met. Opera, N.Y.C., 1985, 3d prize Whitaker Internat. Voice Competition, 1985, Festspiel prize Bavarian State Opera, 1988. Democrat. Office: Sch of Music Univ Wis Madison WI 53703

FAULKNER, KARL MAX, photography director; b. Lubbock, Tex., June 1, 1961; s. William Paul Jr. and Fredericka Rahm F.; m. Helena Catherine Foret, Aug. 13, 1988; 1 child, Katherine Alexandra. Student, Tex. Tech. U., 1979-81. Staff photographer Odessa (Tex.) Am., 1981-83, chief photographer, 1984; staff photographer Ft. Worth Star-Telegram, 1984-85, photo editor, 1985-94, dir. photography, 1994—. Mem. adv. bd. Tex. Tech. U. Mass Comm., Lubbock, 1992—. Photo editor: Shattered: The Tarrant Tornadoes, 2000. Mem.: Nat. Press Photographer's Assn., Soc. Profl. Journalists (v.p. 2000—01, pres. 2001—02), Ridotto Club. Home: 2205 Windsor Pl Fort Worth TX 76110 Office: Ft Worth Star-Telegram 400 W 7th St Fort Worth TX 76102 Fax: 817-390-7206. E-mail: mfaulkner@star-telegram.com.

FAULKNER, LARRY R. dean, educator, researcher, writer; MD, U. Wash., 1974. Diplomate Am. Bd. Psychiatry and Neurology. Resident U. Ark.; dean, prof. U. S.C. Sch. Medicine, 2002—. Rschr., writer in field. Contbr. articles to profl. jours. Fellow NIH. Office: 6311 Garner's Ferry Rd Columbia SC 29208

FAULKNER, LARRY RAY, university official, chemistry educator; b. Shreveport, La., Nov. 26, 1944; s. James Clifford and Doris Louise (Koch) Faulkner; m. Mary Ann Jordan, Aug. 14, 1965; children: Brian Jordan, Susan Louise. BS, So. Meth. U., 1966; PhD, U. Tex., Austin, 1969; DSc (hon.), So. Meth. U., 2000. Asst. prof. chemistry Harvard U., Cambridge, Mass., 1969—73; prof. chemistry U. Tex., Austin, 1983—84, pres., 1998—; asst. prof. U. Ill., Urbana-Champaign, 1973—75, assoc. prof., 1975—79, prof., 1979—83, prof. chemistry, dept. head, 1984—89, dean Coll. Liberal Arts and Sci., 1989—94, provost and vice chancellor acad. affairs, 1994—98. Mem. Materials Rsch. Lab, 1978—90. Author (with A.J. Bard): Electrochemical Methods, 1980, 2d edit., 2001; editor: Jour. Electroanalytical Chemistry, 1980—85; mem. edit. bd.: Jour. Electrochem. Soc., 1975—80. Recipient U.S. Dept. Energy award, 1986. Fellow: Electrochem. Soc. (v.p. 1988—91, pres. 1991—92, Edward Weston fellow 1969, Young Author's prize 1976, Edward Goodrich Acheson medal 2000), Am. Acad. Arts and Scis.; mem.: Soc. Electroanalytical Chemistry (Charles N. Reilly award 1998), Am. Chem. Soc. (award in analytical chemistry 1992), Phi Kappa Phi, Phi Beta Kappa (Grad. Rsch. award Tex. Gamma chpt. 1969—70). Home: 5310 Western Hills Dr Austin TX 78731-4822 Office: Office of Pres U Tex at Austin PO Box T Austin TX 78713-8920 E-mail: president@po.utexas.edu.

FAULKNER, LEWIS L. architect; b. Memphis, Aug. 31, 1937; s. Lewis L., Sr. and Vera J. Faulkner; m. Sherry A. Vaughn, July 20, 1984; children: Keli Lynn, Craig Randall, Heather Ann. BArch, Tex. A&M U., 1960. Registered architect, Colo., Va., Md., D.C., Nat. Coun. Archtl. Registration Bds. Designer draftsman Harrell & Hamilton, Dallas, 1963-65; project architect Hallum & Wrightsman, Dallas, 1966-69; project dir. Neuhaus & Taylor, Dallas, 1970-74; prin. Faulkner Cos., Dallas, 1975-79; project dir./v.p. Woodward & Taylor, Dallas, 1980-82; prin., CEO Faulkner Assocs., Dallas, 1983-86; resident architect RTKL, McLean, Va., 1987—. Sr. architect Harry Weese Assocs., Washington, 1987-91; dir. of architecture/v.p. HTB, Inc., Washington, 1991-93, chief architect FBI, FBI Acad., 1993-2001. Project dir.: The Plaza Hotel, Ft. Worth (AIA Dallas Design award 1982), Knights of Pythias, Ft. Worth (Tex. Soc. of Architecture Design award 1983), Block 42 West, Ft. Worth (AIA Dallas Design award 1983), Northpark Ctr., Dallas (AIA Dallas 25-Yr. Design award 1990). 2d lt. artillery U.S. Army, 1960-63, Korea. Mem. AIA, Dallas AIA, Tex. Soc. Architects Republican. Baptist. Avocations: carpentry, woodworking, home building.

FAULKNER, LYNN LEROY, research scientist; b. Fort Wayne, Ind., June 24, 1941; s. Robert LeRoy and Joy Elizabeth Faulkner; m. Carole Ann Hearold; children: Michael L., Michele A. BSc, Purdue U, 1965, MSc, 1966, PhD, 1969. Post doctorial fellow Purdue U, 1970; prof. The Ohio State U, Columbus, 1970—78; program mgr. Bettelle Meml. Inst., Columbus, 1979—. Bd. mem. Dept. of Mech. Engrng., Columbus, 1978—, Ctr. for Automotive Rsch., Columbus, 1988—; indsl. bd. Ohio State U, Columbus. Editor (in chief): Handbook of Indsl. Noise Control, 1976; editor: Marcel Dekker. Mech. Engrng., 1984; editor: (Sr.) Handbook of Machinery Dynamics, 2000. Achievements include patents in field of Acoustic Degasification of Pressurized Liquids; Method and Appaaratus for Automated Fiber Optic Assembly. Avocations: hunting, fishing, gardening. Office: Battelle Memorial Institute 505 King Ave Columbus OH 43201

FAULKNER, ROBERT LLOYD, advertising executive, graphic designer; b. Chgo., Nov. 8, 1934; s. L. Lester and Agnes Elizabeth (Irons) F.; m. Elizabeth Alice Thomas, June 14, 1958; children: Anne Elizabeth, Lynn Marie, Thomas Robert. BFA in Advt. Design, U. Ill., 1958. Account exec. Brad Sebstad Advt., Chgo., 1966—67; sr. account exec. D'Arcy Advt. Co., Chgo., 1967—70; v.p. Wm. A. Robinson Inc., Northbrook, Ill., 1970—71; nat. mdse. and promotion mgr. James B. Beam Distilling Co., Chgo., 1971—73; v.p. Coord. Advt., Chgo., 1973—77, Grant/Jacoby Inc., Chgo., 1977—79, Kennedy Advt., Chgo., 1979—86; exec. v.p. Kamen/Faulkner Inc., Chgo., 1986—89; pres., owner Bob Faulkner Corp., Westchester, Ill., 1989—. Course coord., advt. lectr. grad. level advt. courses Northwestern U. and Roosevelt U., Chgo., 1980-85. Author: Learn to Cross Country Ski, 1976; co-author: Cross-Country Skiing for Everybody, 1975. Dir. Western Springs Hist. Soc., 1992-95; mem. Illegitimate Theatre of Western Springs. Recipient numerous advt. awards. Mem. Bus. Mktg. Assn. (Cert. Bus. Communicator), Nat. Ski Patrol (life), Model T Ford Owners Assn., Sports Car Club Am., Portage Lake Yacht Club. Episcopalian. Avocation: fine art painting. Home and Office: 11523 Burton Court Westchester IL 60154

FAULKNER, WALTER THOMAS, lawyer, director; b. New Haven, Sept. 17, 1928; s. Walter Thomas and Alice Marion (McGushin) F.; m. Joan Lee Hills, Mar. 17, 1956; children: John, Andrew, George, Susan. AB, Providence Coll., 1952; LL.B., Columbia U., 1955. Bar: N.Y. State 1956. Since practiced in, N.Y.C.; assoc. firm Rogers, Hoge & Hills, 1959-65, ptnr., 1965-86, Kelley Drye & Warren, 1987—. Sec. Sterling Drug Inc., 1973-78, Bacardi Corp., 1975-96. Bd. govs. Sound Shore Med. Ctr. Westchester. Served with AUS, 1946-48. Mem. Assn. of Bar of City of N.Y., ABA, N.Y. State Bar Assn., Am. Soc. Corp. Secs. Home: 64 Woodbine Ave Larchmont NY 10538-3525 Office: Kelley Drye & Warren 101 Park Ave New York NY 10178-0062

FAULMANN, ROGER R. music educator; b. Mt. Clemens, Mich., Jan. 27, 1938; m. Jo D. Dunbar, Dec. 27, 1964; 1 child, Bryan A. BME, Baldwin-Wallace Coll., 1960; MusM, U. of Mich., 1967. Cert. tchr. Fla., 1985. Instrumental gen. music dir. Fraser (Mich.) Pub. Schs., 1960—63; instrument/gen. music tchr. Port Huron (Mich.) Pub. Schs., 1963—64; dir. of bands Lake Orion (Mich.) Cmty. Schs., 1963—67; percussion prof. and band dir. Ill. State U., Normal, Ill., 1967—80; dir. of bands and percussion S.Dak. State U., Brookings, SD, 1980—83; dir. of bands Miami-Dade (Fla.) County Schs., 1985—2000. Mem. faculty Interlochen (Mich.) Arts Ctr., 1963—76; prof. and band dir. Ill. State U., 1967—80; cons. Fleisher-Hinton Music, Denver, 1983—85; guest condr. in field. Contbr. articles to profl. jours.; percussionist: numerous internat. venues. Mem.: Kiwanis Internat., Benevolent and Protective Order of Elks. Moderate. Episcopalian. Avocations: model trains, holocaust research. Home: 10386 West Marion Dr Traverse City MI 49686 Personal E-mail: rfaulmann@aol.com.

FAUNCE, SARAH CUSHING, former museum curator; b. Tulsa, Aug. 19, 1929; d. George Jr. and Helen Pauline (Colwell) F. BA, Wellesley Coll., 1951; MA, Washington U., St. Louis, 1959; postgrad., Columbia U., 1960-63. Tchr. history Hartridge Sch., Plainfield, N.J., 1954-56; tchr. art Mary C. Wheeler Sch., Providence, 1958-59; instr. art history Barnard Coll., N.Y.C., 1962-64; sec. adv. council art history Columbia U., 1963-70, registrar, curator, 1965-70; exhbn. cons. Jewish Mus., N.Y.C., 1968-70; curator paintings and sculpture Bklyn. Mus. Art, 1970-98, curator emeritus, project dir. Courbet Catalogue Raisonné project, 1998—. Author: Courbet, 1993; exhbn. catalog author: Anne Ryan Collages, 1974, Carl Larsson, 1982; author, editor: Belgian Art 1880-1914, 1980, Courbet Reconsidered, 1988, In the Light of Italy: Corot and Early Plein Air Painting, 1996; editor: Northern Light: Realism and Symbolism in Scandinavian Painting 1880-1910, 1982. Travel grantee Columbia U., 1963 Mem. AAM-ICOM, Coll. Art Assn., Phi Beta Kappa. Democrat. Home: 28 E 92nd St New York NY 10128-0616 Office: Courbet Catalogue Raisonne Project 432 E 75th St New York NY 10021-3403

FAUNCE, WILLIAM DALE, clinical psychologist, researcher, consultant; b. Lansing, Mich., Dec. 4, 1947; s. Lucius Dale and Wilhelmina (Hall) F.; m. Leigh Brown, Dec. 17, 1995. BA, Mich. State U., 1972; MA, Calif. State U., L.A., 1978; PhD in Clin. Psychology, U. So. Calif., 1983. Lic. psychologist, N.C., Md. Psychology intern Brentwood (Calif.) VA, 1981-82; clin. psychologist UCLA Neuropsychiat. Inst., Westwood, Calif., 1983, Coldwater Canyon Hosp., North Hollywood, Calif., 1983-84, So. Peninsula Community Mental Health Ctr., Homer, Alaska, 1984-86; pvt. practice Homer, Alaska, 1986-87; cons. Santa Cruz, Calif., 1987-90; clin. psychologist, program dir. Broughton State Hosp., Morganton, N.C., 1990-92; mem. faculty Appalachian State U., Boone, N.C., 1992-97; pvt. practice cons., 1997—. Co-author: (chpt.) Imagery, 1984; contbr. articles to profl. jours. Fellow NIMH; mem. APA, Union Concerned Scientists. Avocations: creative writing, guitar, travel, foreign languages. Home and Office: 1026 Ellicott Dr Bel Air MD 21015-3440

FAUNTLEROY, CARMA CECIL, arts administration executive; b. Lynchburg, Va., July 7, 1954; BA in History, Coll. of William & Mary, 1976; MA in Art History, George Washington U., 1985; MBA in Internat. Bus., Rutgers U., 1992. Fin. officer The Textile Mus., Washington, 1985—86; dir. coll. galleries and arts mgmt. program Sweet Briar (Va.) Coll., 1986—89; assoc. dir. Jane Voorhees Zimmerli Art Mus., New Brunswick, NJ, 1989—93; exec. dir. Queens (N.Y.) Mus. Art, 1993—98, 2001—02; dir. found. and corp. philanthropy Nat. Trust for Hist. Preservation, Washington, 1998—2001. Trustee N.J. Assn. Ms., Trenton, 1990-93; project evaluator N.J. Com. for Humanities, New Brunswick, 1990-93; GOS field reviewer Inst. Mus. Svcs., 1989-90, 93, 99, 2002. Author: (catalogue) Japanese Woodblock Prints from the Sweet Briar Collection, 1989; contbr. to mags. and newsletters. Mem. Internat. Coun. Mus., Am. Assn. Mus., Assn. Fund Raising Profls., ArtTable (bd. dirs. 1995-98), Mus. Trustee Assn. (adv. coun. of dirs. 1996-97). Office: PO Box 11402 Washington DC 20008 E-mail: carmafauntleroy@aol.com.

FAURE, GUNTER, geology educator; b. Tallinn, Estonia, May 11, 1934; s. Arnulf and Stella (von Harpe) F.; m. Barbara L.L. Goodell, Sept. 5, 1959 (div. Feb. 1985); children: Mary Jennifer, John Eric, Pamela Anne, David Christopher; m. Teresa M. Mensing, June 4, 1988. B.Sc., U. Western Ont., 1957; PhD, MIT, 1961; fellow, Sch. Advanced Studies, 1961-62. Asst. prof. geology Ohio State U., 1962-65, assoc. prof., 1965-68, prof., 1968—2002, prof. emeritus, 2002—; field work Antarctica. Author: (with J.L. Powell) Strontium Isotope Geology, 1972, Principles of Isotope Geology, 1977, 2d edit., 1986, 3rd edit., 2004, Principles and Applications of Geochemistry, 1991, 2d edit., 1998, Origin of Igneous Rocks, 2001; editor-in-chief Jour. Isotope Geoscience, 1983-88; exec. editor Geochimica et Cosmochimica Acta, 1989-97; assoc. editor Geochimica et Cosmochimica Acta, 1989-99; contbr. articles to profl. jours. Recipient univ. gold medal in honors geology, U. Western Ont., 1957, disting. tchg. award, Ohio State U., 1970, 1983, 1999, Antarctic Svc. medal, 1976. Fellow Geol. Soc. Am., Geochem. Soc., European Assn. Geochemistry; mem. Planetary Soc., Meteoritical Soc., Internat. Assn. Geochemistry and Cosmochemistry (v.p. 1992-96, pres. 1996-2000, newsletter editor 1999-2002). Office: 125 S Oval Mall Columbus OH 43210-1308 E-mail: faure.1@osu.edu.

FAURI, ERIC JOSEPH, lawyer; b. Lansing, Mich., Feb. 16, 1942; s. Fedele Fauri and Iris M. Petersen; m. Sherrill Lynn Nurenberg, July 15, 1969; children— Lauren, Nadia, Kirk. B.A., U. Del., 1963; J.D. with distinction, U. Mich., 1966. Bar: Mich. 1967, U.S. Dist. Ct. (ea. dist.) Mich. 1967, U.S. Dist. Ct. (we. dist.) Mich. 1972, U.S. Ct. Appeals (6th cir.) 1974. Assoc. Dykema, Gossett, Spencer, Goodnow & Trigg, Detroit, 1966-71; Parmenter Forsythe, Rude et al, Muskegon, Mich., 1971-73; ptnr. Parmenter, Forsythe, Rude et al, Muskegon, 1973—; Parmenter O'Toole, 1992—. Served to capt. U.S. Army, 1967-68. Mem. ABA, State Bar Mich. Office: Parmenter O'Toole 175 W Apple Ave PO Box 786 Muskegon MI 49443-0786

FAUROT, ELLEN F. librarian; b. Cullman, Ala., Mar. 19, 1947; d. Edward J. and Demaris (Childers) Fortenberry; m. William Lorin Faurot, Jr., Sept. 14, 1968; children: Susan Diane, John Mark. BS, Auburn U., 1980; MLS, U. Ala., 1988. A cert. sch. libr. Bus. tchr. Demopolis (Ala.) Acad., 1982-86, Demopolis High Sch., 1985-87; pub. svcs. libr. Livingston (Ala.) U. Libr., 1988-91; dir. libr. svcs. Bowling Libr. Judson Coll., Marion, Ala., 1991—. Mem. Friends of the Libr., Demopolis, 1989—, Marengo County Hist. soc., Demopolis, 1992—, Demopolis Arts Com., 1991—. Recipient William Stanley Hoolie award U. Ala., Tuscaloosa, 1988. Mem. ALA, Ala. Libr. Assn. (moderator), Ala. Assn. Women In Edn., U. Ala. Alumni Assn. Baptist. Avocations: reading, gardening. Home: 835 Amberwood Dr Tuscaloosa AL 35405 9615 Office: Judson Coll Bowling Libr Marion AL 36756

FAUST, ANNE SONIA, lawyer; b. Aug. 27, 1936; d. Alfred and Geneva Dora (Barnett) F. BA, U. Hawaii, 1960; cert. in Pub. Affairs, Coro Found. Internship, 1961; JD, Harvard U., 1964. Bar: Hawaii, 1964. Dept. corp. counsel City and County of Honolulu, 1964-66; asst. rschr. Legis. Ref. Bur., Honolulu, 1966-69; assoc. counsel Legal Aid Soc., Honolulu, 1969-70; dep. atty. gen. State of Hawaii, Honolulu, 1970-72; atty., exec. officer Hawaii Pub. Employment Rels. Bd., Honolulu, 1972-80; 1st dep. corp. counsel County of Maui, Wailuku, Hawaii, 1980-81; chief antitrust div. Dep. Atty. Gen. State of Hawaii, Honolulu, 1981-86; chief Regulatory Hawaiin Homelands Hawaii Housing Authority Div. Dept., Hawaii, 1986-95. Supervising dep. atty. gen., land and transp. divsn. Dept. Atty. Gn. State of Hawaii; ex-officio mem. Gov.'s Com. Status of Women, Hawaii, 1971-72; mem. Hawaii Bd. Bar Examiners, 1975-79. Mem. ABA (membership chmn. Hawaii 1965), Phi Beta Kappa, Phi Kappa Phi. Mem. Ch. of Christ. Club: Obedience Tng. of Hawaii (Honolulu) (treas. 1982-87). Home: 47-415 A Kapehe St Kaneohe HI 96744-4845 Office: Dept Atty Gen 465 S King St Honolulu HI 96813-2911

FAUST, DONNY D. music educator; b. Durango, Colo., May 24, 1953; s. Melvin E. and Eloise L. Faust; 1 child, Jennifer Jo. BA, Ft. Lewis Coll., Durango, Colo., 1976; MPA, U. Colo., Colorado Springs, 1979; grad. in MAED Adminstrn., U. Phoenix, 2002. Cert. K-12 prin., K-12 music tchr. Ariz., 1992, Community College; Music, History, ESL, Ed Admin. State of Ariz. Coll. Bd., 1992. Tchr. band/music Willcox Pub. Sch., Ariz., 1994—95; asst. prin. Marana Sch. Dist., Ariz., 1995—96; tchr. music/band and history Superior Sch. Dist., Ariz., 1996—97; tchr. band 5-12 San Carlos Sch. Dist.; tchr. K-8 music and 5-8 band Roosevelt Sch. Dist., Phoenix, 1997—. Adj. instr. Cochise C.C., Willcox, Ariz., 1996; ballet folklorico Roosevelt Sch. Dist., Phoenix, 1997—; adj. instr. music Chandler-Gilbert C.C., Ariz., 1998—; adj. instr. ESL Mesa C.C., Ariz., 2000—; trombone musican Fiesta Bowl parade, Phoenix, 2001—. Contbr. H.S. NCAA accreditation team. Water cmty. of bond issues City of Chandler, Ariz. Recipient Outstanding Band award, Rodeo Parade Com., 1994, Best Band in Class, Colo. State Fair, 1988, Outstanding Student Dance performance, Nat. Assn. for Bilingual Edn., 2001. Mem.: NEA (assoc.), Music Educators Nat. Conf. (corr.), Nat. Assication for Bilingual Edn. (assoc.), Phi Delta Kappa (corr.). Achievements include research in Color-coding of Musical Notes to Music Instruction; San Carlos Apache Study, National Endowment Fellowship Study 1994. Home: PO Box 7648 2119 West Tulsa St Chandler AZ 85246 Personal E-mail: dondfaust@earthlink.net.

FAUST, NAOMI FLOWE, education educator, poet; b. Salisbury, N.C. d. Christopher Leroy and Ada Luella (Graham) Flowe; m. Roy Malcolm Faust, Aug. 16, 1948. AB, Bennett Coll; MA, U. Mich., 1945; PhD, NYU, 1963. Elem. tchr. Pub. Schs. Gaffney (S.C.); tchr. English, French, phys. edn. Atkins H.S., Winston-Salem; instr. English Bennett Coll. and So. U., Scotlandville, La., 1944-46; prof. English Morgan State Coll., Balt., 1946-48; tchr. English Greensboro (N.C.) Pub. Schs., 1948-51, N.Y.C. Pub. Schs., 1954-63; prof. edn. Queens Coll. of CUNY, Flushing, 1964-82; writer, lectr., poetry readings, 1982—. Lectr. in field. Author: Discipline and the Classroom Teacher, 1977; (poetry) Speaking in Verse, 1974, All Beautiful Things, 1983, And I Travel by Rhythms and Words, 1990; contbr. poetry to jours. Named Tchr.-Author of 1979, Tchr.-Writer; recipient Cert. of Merit for Poem Cooper Hill Writers Conf., 1970, Achievement award L.I. br. AAUW, 1985, Poet of the Millennium award Internat. Poets Acad., Excellence in World Poetry award Internat. Poets Acad., 2002; named Internat. Eminent Poet, Internat. Poets Acad. Mem. AAUP, AAUW, Acad. Am. Poets, Nat. Coun. Tchrs. English, Nat. Women's Book Assn., Nat. Assn. Univ. Women (L.I. br.), World Poetry Soc. Intercontinental, N.Y. Poetry Forum, NAACP, United Negro Coll. Fund, Alpha Kappa Alpha, Alpha Kappa Mu., Alpha Epsilon. Home: 11201 175th St Jamaica NY 11433-4135

FAUST, WILLIAM ROSCOE, physicist; b. Shawnee, Okla., Mar. 9, 1918; s. Hugh Graham and Bertha Adele (Weinmann) F.; m. Mary Cone Dees, Jan. 23, 1942; children: Hugh H., Margaret Adele, Mary Elizabeth. BSEE, Okla. State U., 1939; MSEE, Ill. Inst. Tech., Chgo., 1941; PhD in Physics, U. Md., 1949. Physicist Naval Rsch. Lab., Washington, 1941-55, assoc. supt. Radiation Divsn., 1956-64, supt. Application Rsch. Divsn., 1964-69, assoc. dir. rsch., 1969-72, ret., 1972; chief nuclear rsch. Convair, Ft. Worth, 1955-56. Contbr. articles to profl. jours.; patentee in field. Mem. Sons Am. Revolution, Prince Georges County, Md., 1980—. Fellow Am. Phys. Soc., Wash. Acad. Sci., Philos. Soc. Washington; mem. AAAS. Home: 1665 Heather Ln Huntingtown MD 20639-4108 E-mail: wrfaust@chesapeak.net.

FAUTH, JOHN J. venture capitalist; Chmn., dir., pres., CEO Churchill Capital, Inc., Mpls. Office: Churchill Capital Inc 333 S 7th St Ste 2400 Minneapolis MN 55402-2435

FAUVER, JOHN WILLIAM, mayor, retired business executive; b. Detroit, Dec. 11, 1921; s. John Newton and Margaret Burns (Schofield) F.; children: John, Johanna, Jeffrey; m. Irene Byerlein. BSM.E., U. Mich., 1943. With J.N.

Fauver Co., Madison Heights, Mich., from 1946, now ret. chmn., chief exec. officer. Dir. Beaumont Hosp. Found. Mayor City of Bloomfield Hills, Mich., 1976-77, 81—, city commr., 1972—; trustee Cranbrook Schs., 1970-80; pres. Boys and Girls Clubs of S.E. Mich., 1972, bd. dirs. Capt. AUS, 1942-46. Mem. Nat. Indsl. Distbrs. Assn. (pres. 1979-80), Fluid Power Ednl. Found. (trustee), Johns Island Country Club, Bloomfield Hills Country Club, Orchard Lake Country Club, Rotary (past pres. Detroit chpt.). Republican. Presbyterian. Home: 3475 Bloomfield Club Dr Bloomfield Hills MI 48301-2102 Home (Summer): 341 Llwyd's Ln Vero Beach FL 32963

FAUX, JEFF (GEOFFREY PETER FAUX), economist, writer; b. N.Y.C., June 18, 1936; s. George Frederick and Caroline Pauline (Goyanovic) Faux; m. Mary Ruth Robbins, June 11, 1957 (div. Dec. 1986); children: Thomas Geoffrey, George Frederick. AB, Queens Coll., 1959; postgrad., George Wash. U., 1963—65, Harvard U., 1971—72; HHD (hon.), U. New Eng., 1983. Economist Dept. Commerce, Washington, 1962, Dept. Labor, 1963—65, Dept. State, 1965—67; dir. econ. devel. divsn. Office Econ. Opportunity, 1967—70; fellow Inst. Politics Harvard U., Cambridge, Mass., 1970—71, dir. Ctr. for Cmty. Econ. Devel., 1972; co-dir. Nat. Ctr. for Econ. Alternatives, Washington, 1973—84; dir. Project on Indsl. Policy, 1984—85; pres. Econ. Policy Inst., 1985—. Contbg. editor The Am. Prospect, Boston, 1990—; mem. adv. bd. Ctr. for Pub. Integrity, Washington, 1991—98; mem. U.S. Nat. Adv. Council Econ. Opportunity, 1977—81; chair New Eng. Housing Devel. Corp., Boston, 1972—75. Author: New Hope for Inner City, 1971, The Party's Not Over, 1996; co-author: Star Spangled Hustle, 1972, Rebuilding America, 1984; co-editor: Reckoning Prosperity, 1996; mem. editl. bd.: Dissent, 1989—. Bd. dirs. Rural Am., Washington, 1974—78; mem. Planning Bd., Whitefield, Maine, 1977—79; chair Com. for Utility Rate Return, Augusta, 1977—81, Cmty on Maine Evonomy, 1976—80. Recipient Weinberg award, Wayne State U., 1991; fellow, Harvard U., 1970—71. Democrat. Office: Econ Policy Inst 1660 L St NW Ste 1200 Washington DC 20036-5632

FAVA, MAURIZIO, hospital administrator, researcher; b. Valdagno, Italy, May 8, 1956; came to U.S., 1985; s. Ezio Fava and Olga Danieli; m. Stefania Lamon, May 18, 1985; 1 child, Giovanni. Med. degree, U. Padua, Italy, 1982. Dir. depression rsch. program Mass. Gen. Hosp., Boston, 1990-94, dir. depression clin. and rsch. program, 1994—, assoc. chief psychiatry for clin. rsch., 2000—. Prof. psychiatry Harvard Med. Sch., Boston, 2002— Co-editor: Research Designs and Methods in Psychiatry, 1992. DuPont-Warren fellow Mass. Gen. Hosp., 1988. Mem. Am. Psychiat. Assn., Am. Coll. Neuropsychopharmacology. Office: Mass Gen Hosp ACC 812 15 Parkman St Boston MA 02114-3117 E-mail: mfava@partners.org.

FAVALORA, JOHN CLEMENT, bishop; b. New Orleans, Dec. 5, 1935; s. Felix J. and Leona M. (Stevens) F.. BA in Philosophy and History, Notre Dame Sem., New Orleans, 1958; STL, Pontifical Gregorian U., Rome, 1962; MEd, Tulane U., 1969. Ordained priest Roman Cath. Ch., 1962. Asst. pastor St. Theresa of the Child Jesus Ch., New Orleans, 1962—70; sec. to archbishop Archdiocese of New Orleans, 1963—65, vice chancellor, 1963—65; vice rector St. John Prep., New Orleans, 1964—67, 1968—71; dir. Office of Permanent Diaconate, New Orleans, 1971—74; adminstrv. asst. Notre Dame Sem., New Orleans, 1971—73, rector-pres., 1981—86; pastor St. Angela Merici Ch., Metairie, La., 1973—79; dir. Office of Vocations, New Orleans, 1979—81; bishop Diocese of Alexandria, La., 1986—89, Diocese of St. Petersburg, Fla., 1989—94; archbishop Diocese of Miami, 1994—. Ecclesiastical notary Archdiocese of New Orleans, 1962—64, pro-synodal judge, 1973—79; dean East Jefferson Deanery, New Orleans, 1974—77; vicar Pastoral Planning, New Orleans, 1976—81; chmn. Permanent Diaconate Adv. Com., New Orleans, 1984; consultor Archdiocese of New Orleans, 1984—86. Office: Archdiocese of Miami Pastoral Ctr 9401 Biscayne Blvd Miami Shores FL 33138*

FAVARO, MARY KAYE ASPERHEIM (MRS. BIAGINO PHILIP FAVARO), pediatrician, writer; b. Edgerton, Wis., Sept. 30, 1934; d. Harold Wilbur and Genevieve Catherine (Hyland) Asperheim; m. Biagino Philip Favaro, May 31, 1969; children: Justin Peter, Gina Sue. BS, U. Wis., 1956; MS, St. Louis Coll. Pharmacy, 1965; MD, U. Wis., 1969. Instr. pharmacology St. Louis U. and St. Mary's Hosp. Sch. Practical Nurses, 1959-64; staff pharmacist U. Hosps., Madison, Wis., 1964-65; intern Albany (N.Y.) Med. Center, 1969-70; resident, 1970-71; resident in pediatrics U. S.C., Charleston, 1971-72, asst. prof. pediatrics, 1973-75; pvt. practice pediatrics, 1974-99; ret. Author: Pharmacology, an Introductory Text, 2001; The Pharmacologic Basis of Patient Care, 1985. Mem. AMA. Roman Catholic. Home: 1407 Southwood Dr Surfside Beach SC 29575

FAVELUKES, HANNE ELSE, psychiatrist; b. The Netherlands, 1941; came to U.S., 1972; married; 2 children. Diploma in Psychol. Medicine, Royal Coll. Physicians and Surgeons, London, 1972. Diplomate Am. Bd. Psychiatry and Neurology; added qualifications in Geriatric Psychiatry. Resident in psychiatry Albert Einstein Coll. Medicine, 1972-75, instr. psychiatry, 1975-76; asst. in clin. psychiatry Columbia U. Sch. Medicine, 1976-82, instr. clin. psychiatry, 1982—; assoc. attending psychiatrist St. Luke's Hosp., 1976—; psychiat. dir. Greenwich House Sr. Citizens Consultation Ctr., N.Y.C., 1983—; psychiatrist Fedn. Employment Guidance Svcs. Manhattan Mental Health Ctr. Clinic, N.Y.C., 1992-93; psychiatrist Health Ins. Plan of N.Y. Manhattan Mental Health Svc., N.Y.C., 1994—. Mem. Am. Psychiat. Assn., Am. Assn. Geriatric Psychiatry, Internat. Soc. for Trauma and Stress. Office: Ctrl Park West Med 2 W 86th St New York NY 10024-3666

FAVOR, LESLI JOANNA, writer, researcher; b. Dallas, Apr. 29, 1970; d. John Lewis and Linda June Frost; m. Stephen L. Favor, July 21, 1990. BA in English, U. Tex., Arlington, 1992; MA in English, U. North Tex., 1993, PhD in English, 1995. Writing tutor U. Tex., Arlington, 1991-92; grad. tchg. fellow U. North Tex., Denton, 1992-95, adj. prof. English, 1996; asst. prof. English Sul Ross State U.-Rio Grande Coll., Eagle Pass, Tex., 1996-98; coord. liberal arts Higher Rsch. Orgn., Austin, Tex., 1998—2001; freelance writer, editor, rschr. Dallas, 1998—. Author: Sex, Drugs, and Rock & Roll: Women as Casualties of Culture, 1998, Beneath the Candy Coating: The Foreign and the Female in Arthur Conan Doyle, 1999, Everything You Need to Know About Growth Spurts and Delayed Growth, 2002, Francisco Vázquez de Coronado: Famous Journeys to the American Southwest, 2003, The Iroquois Constitution, 2003, Italy: A Primary Source Cultural Guide, 2003, Martin Van Buren, 2003; book reviewer: (by Christine Froula) Modernism's Body: Sex, Culture, and Joyce, 1998, others; contbr. articles to profl. jours. Recipient Mary Patchell Grad. award U. North Tex., 1995, Craig B. Raupe scholarship U. North Tex., 1997, Faculty Rsch. Enhancement grant Sul Ross State U., 1998. Mem. Nat. Coun. Tchrs. English, Soc. Children's Book Writers and Illustrators, Tex. Libr. Assn. Avocations: reading fiction, creative writing, e-mailing friends, horseback riding, yoga, walking. Home: 18484 Preston Rd Ste 102 PMB 166 Dallas TX 75252-5474 E-mail: lfavor@DrFavor.com.

FAVORITE, MALAIKA, artist; b. Geismar, La., Feb. 7, 1949; d. Amos Joseph and Rosemary Favorite; m. Lewen Anthony Kellman, Dec. 10, 1988. BFA, La. State U., 1971, MFA, 1973. Instr. art Grambling (La.) State U., 1973-75, 76-78; artist in residence Assumption Parish (La.) Schs., 1975-76, Episcopal H.S., Baton Rouge, 1978-84; instr. of art La. State U., Baton Rouge, 1987-89, Augusta (Ga.) Coll., 1989-93; artist in residence Baton Rouge Arts Coun., 1993-95. (one-woman shows) Baton Rouge Gallery, 1988, South Shore Bank, Chgo., 1989, Posselt Baker Gallery, New Orleans, 1984, 1985, 1986, 1989, Paine Coll., Augusta, 1993, Stephens Coll.-Davis Art Gallery, Columbia, Mo., 1993, Camille Love Gallery, Atlanta, 1996, Columbia Theol. Sem., Decatur, Ga., 2000, Gertrude Herbert Inst. Art, Augusta, Ga., 2001, Auburn Avenue Rsch. Libr. African Am. Culture and History, Atlanta, 2001, Associate Gallery, Banners, McNeese Arts and Humanities Series, Lake Charles, La., 2001, (group shows) Stella Jones Gallery, New Orleans, 1997, 1999, JAZZ...a Montage of a Dream, Kansas City, Mo., 1999, (three person show) Stella Jones Gallery, New Orleans, La., 1999, designer (mural) West End Mall, Atlanta, 1999, painter, 1999, (commd. works) Absolut Vodka, 1997, Fulton County Arts Coun., 1998; contbr. poetry to anthologies. Asst. to chmn., program dir. Youth for Real, Geisman, 1994—. Grantee African-Am. Inst., 1975, Fulbright-Hays Found., 1998, Ga. Coun. for Arts, 1992, Delta Sigma Theta, 1987. Mem. Black Artist Network (v.p. 1996—), Women Caucus for Art (past officer). Democrat. Baptist. Avocations: reading, children's workshops, poetry.

FAVORS, ADOLPHUS C., JR., internist; b. Kansas City, Kans., Jan. 22, 1944; MD, U. Wash., 1973. Diplomate Am. Bd. Internal Medicine, Am. Bd. Med. Oncology. Intern Grady Meml., Atlanta, 1973-74; resident in internal medicine Emory-Grady Affil. Hosps., Atlanta, 1974-76; fellow in hematology/oncology U. Colo., Denver, 1977-78; fellow in med. oncology MD Anderson Tumor Inst., Houston, 1978-79. Mem. AMA, Am. Acad. Ins. Medicine, Nat. Med. Soc., Mo. State Med. Soc., St. Louis Metro Med. Soc., Mound City Med. Soc. Office: Gen Am Life Ins Co 13045 Tesson Ferry Rd Saint Louis MO 63128-3407

FAVORS, STEVE ALEXANDER, academic administrator; b. Texarkana, Tex., Dec. 30, 1948; s. Clarence L. and Erma (Newton) F.; m. Charlotte A. Edwards, Feb. 12, 1977; children: Steve A., Jonathan A. BS, Tex. A&M U., 1971, MS, 1973, EdD, 1978. Lic. in clin. counseling, Tex. Adminstrv. asst. to dean students Tex. A&M U., Commerce, 1975-77; v.p. student affairs Wiley Coll., Marshall, Tex., 1977-81, Dillard U., New Orleans, 1981-85; vice chancellor for student affairs U. New Orleans, 1985-90; v.p. student affairs Howard U., Washington, 1990-98; pres. Grambling (La.) State U., 1998—. Mem. Mid-Eastern Athletics Conf. Exec. Coun., 1990—; voting del. NCAA, 1990. Bd. dirs. New Orleans Found., 1985-90, Dollars for Scholars Found., 1983-90; mem. Urban League, New orleans, 1985-90. Recipient Appreciation award U. New Orleans Black Caucus, 1990, Man of the Yr. award Mt. Zion United Meth. Ch., New Orleans, 1988-89, Appreciation award Am. Counseling Assn. (Tex. So. Univ. chpt.), 1987, Svc. award Am. Coll. Pers. Assn., 1986. Mem. Nat. Assn. Student Pers. Adminstrs. (Disting. Svc. award 1988-89), Nat. Assn. for Student Affairs Pers., NAACP, Alpha Phi Omega, Phi Delta Kappa, Omega Psi Phi. Avocations: basketball, graphic designs, collecting sports cards. Office: Grambling State U Office Pres Grambling LA 71245-3091

FAVORULE, DENISE, publishing executive; Advt. dir. Stagebill Mag., 1993—96; advt. mgr. Prevention Mag., 1996—98, nat. advt. dir., 1998—99, assoc. pub., 1999—2000, v.p., pub., 2000—. Office: Rondale Press Inc 33 E Minor St Emmaus PA 18098-0099

FAVRE, BRETT LORENZO, professional football player; b. Pass Christian (Gulfport), Miss., Oct. 10, 1969; m. Deanna Tynes, July 1996; children: Brittany, Breleigh. Student, So. Miss. U., 1991. Quarterback Atlanta Falcons, 1991—92, Green Bay Packers, 1992—; first team all-pro Assoc. Press, 1995. Named MVP East-West Shrine Game, All Am. Bowl, NFL, 1995; named to Pro Bowl team, 1992, 1993, 1995, 1996. Office: Green Bay Packers PO Box 10628 Green Bay WI 54307-0628

FAVRE, GREGORY, publishing executive; b. New Orleans, Apr. 19, 1935; m. Beatrice Favre; children: Monica Kauppinen, Jeff. Asst. sports editor Atlanta Jour.; mng. editor Dayton Daily News; editor Palm Beach (Fla.) Post; news dir. Sta. WPLG-TV, Miami; editor Corpus Christi Caller-Times; mng. editor Chgo. Daily News, Chgo. Sun-Times; exec. editor Sacramento Bee, 1984—98; v.p. news The McClatchy Co., Sacramento, 1989—2001; disting. fellow The Poynter Inst. for Media Studies, St. Petersburg, Fla., 2001—. Bd. dirs. Found. for Am. Comms., Inter Am. Press Assn. Chmn. bd. advisors The Luth. Mag.; bd. visitors Medill Sch. Journalism, Northwestern U., Sch. Journalism, U. Calif.-Davis Med. Sch.; bd. mem. Knight Ctr. Specialized Journalism, U. Calif.-Davis Found. Named News Exec. of Yr., Calif. Press Assn., 1992; recipient Silver Em award, U. Miss., 1996, Catalyst award, Nat. Assn. Minority Media Execs., 1997. Mem.: Calif. Soc. Newspaper Editors (past pres.), Am. Soc. Newspaper Editors (past pres., past chmn. program com., readership com., journalism edn. com., future of newspapers com.). Office: The Poynter Inst for Media Studies 801 3rd St Saint Petersburg FL 33701-4920 E-mail: gfavre@poynter.org.

FAVRE, JACQUES, neurosurgeon; b. Neuchâtel, Switzerland, Apr. 7, 1964; s. Pierre and Michéle (Cottini) F.; m. Nicole Sanceau, Oct. 24, 1991; children: Léa, Brendan, Nolwenn. Cert. in parasitology, U. Neuchâtel, 1986; MD, U. Lausanne, Switzerland, 1988. Neurosurgery resident Ctr. Hospitalier Universitaire Vaudois, Lausanne, 1989-90, 91-94; surgery resident Neuchâtel, 1990-91; fellow in functional neurosurgery Oreg. Health Sci. U., Portland, 1995-96, clin. assoc. prof., 1999—. Author: (computer software) Pharmacology of Diuretics, 1988, NeuroStereo, Interspike, Grat-Q, 1990-96; contbr. articles to profl. jours. and books. Mem. European Soc. Stereotactic and Functional Neurosurgery, Am. Soc. Stereotactic and Functional Neurosurgery, World Soc. Stereotactic and Functional Neurosurgery, Swiss Neurosurgery Soc. Avocations: snowboarding, mountains, computers. Home: Chemin de la Duchesne 7 1806 St-Légier Switzerland Office: Forum Center Grand' Rue 3 1820 Montreux Switzerland E-mail: jfavre@neurochir.ch, jfavre@neurosurgery.ch.

FAVROT, HENRI MORTIMER, JR., architect, real estate developer; b. New Orleans, Apr. 23, 1930; s. Henri Mortimer and Helen Rebecca (Parkhurst) F.; m. Kathleen Loker Gibbons, Sept. 16, 1956; children: James P., Kathleen Favrot VanHorn, T. Semmes, Caroline. BArch, Tulane U., 1953; MArch, Harvard U., 1957. Lic. architect, La., Miss. Architect Favrot, Reed, Mathes & Bergman, New Orleans, 1955-56, Curtis & Davis, New Orleans, 1957-58; ptnr. Favrot & Grimball, New Orleans, 1958-62; pvt. practice architecture New Orleans, 1962-64; ptnr. Mathes, Bergman, Favrot & Assocs., New Orleans, 1964-69, Favrot & Shane, Metairie, La., 1969—. Chmn. La. Architects Selection Bd., Baton Rouge, 1976, 97. Prin. works include: Parktowne Townhouses, 1971 (Design Honor award La. Architects Assn.), Favrot & Shane Office Bldg., 1982 (Design Honor award New Orleans chpt. AIA). Mem. City Planning Commn., New Orleans, 1970-84, chmn., 1976, 77; commr. La. Housing Commn., Baton Rouge, 1985-86; bd. dirs. Met. Area Com., New Orleans, 1985-98, New Orleans Mus. Art, 1985-91, v.p., 1986-87; bd. dirs. Preservation Resource Ctr. of New Orleans, 1988-96, pres., 1994-96; bd. dirs. La. Landmarks Soc., 2001-; mem. bd. adminstrn. Tulane U., 1986-2000, emeritus, 2000—. Named Outstanding Alumnus award Tulane U. Sch. Architecture, 1985, Tulane U. Alumni Vol. of Yr., 1997, one of 10 Outstanding Persons Greater New Orleans, Family Svc. Soc., 2001; named Role Model for 2002 by Young Leadership Coun. of New Orleans. Mem. AIA (pres. New Orleans chpt. 1982), AIA La. (pres. 1984, Medal of Honor 2001), Archtl. Found. (bd. regents 1996—, chmn. 2000), New Orleans Apt. Assn. (pres. 1980), So. Yacht Club, New Orleans Lawn Tennis Club, New Orleans Country Club, Boston Club, La. Club, Stratford Club. Republican. Roman Catholic. Avocations: tennis, sailing, fishing, hunting. Home: 1400 State St New Orleans LA 70118-6047

FAW, MELVIN LEE, retired physician; b. Kansas City, Mo., Dec. 4, 1925; s. Floyd Butler and Ivalee Muriel (Harvey) F.; m. Anna Margaret Rose, July 17, 1948 (dec. Jan. 1997); children: Linda, Gary, David, Nancy; m. Rosemary Amelia Schoppert, Aug. 17, 2001 (dec. Aug. 2003). Student, U. Kans., 1943-44, Baylor U., 1945; BS magna cum laude, Washburn U., 1948; MD, Washington U., St. Louis, 1951. Diplomate Am. Bd. Internal Medicine. Intern Washington U. Service St. Louis City Hosp., 1951-52; asst. in medicine Washington U. Sch. Medicine, St. Louis, 1951-54; resident in internal medicine Washington U. Service St. Louis City Hosp., 1952-54, U. Kans. Hosp., Kansas City, 1954-55; practice medicine specializing in internal medicine and cardiology Welborn Clinic, Evansville, Ind., 1955-87, mng. ptnr., 1965-78. Pres. med. staff Welborn Hosp., 1980, chief medicine, 1958-64, dir. cardiovascular services, 1981-87; mem. So. Ind. Health Service Agy., 1976-80. Served with Inf. AUS, 1944-45 Decorated Bronze Star medal with V device oak leaf cluster, Purple Heart, Combat Infantryman Badge; recipient Disting. Service award U. Evansville, 1980 Fellow Am. Coll. Chest Physicians; mem. ACP, Am. Soc. Internal Medicine, AMA, Ind. Med. Assn., Vanderburgh County Med. Soc., Phi Kappa Phi Methodist. Home: 2400 E Chandler Ave Evansville IN 47714-2421 Office: Welborn Clinic 421 Chestnut St Evansville IN 47713-1297 E-mail: melfaw@sigecom.net.

FAWCETT, BERNADINE L. marriage and family counselor; b. Madison, Wis., Oct. 16, 1933; d. Alfred H. and Martha L. Engel; m. Robert D. Silverman, Dec. 2, 1951 (div. Oct. 1959); children: Lawrence D. Silverman, Anna L. Silverman; m. Lyman W. Fawcett, Dec. 25, 1959; 1 child, Lyman W. Jr. AA, Suffolk C.C., N.Y.; BA, SUNY, Stony Brook; cert. social worker, Fordham U. Counselor Marriage and Family Counseling of Patchogue, N.Y. Author: Hear My Cry, 1989; appearances on numerous TV and radio stations; presenter and speaker. Home: 86 Log Rd Patchogue NY 11772-1524

FAWCETT, CHRISTOPHER BABCOCK, civil engineer, construction and water resources company executive; b. N.Y.C., Dec. 17, 1951; s. George Gifford Fawcett Jr. and Andi Adams Emerson; m. Nina Beth Williamson, June 20, 1986 (div. Aug. 1993); 1 child, Kyle Christopher Adams. Student. U. Okla., 1969-72, Concordia U., Montreal, Que., Can., 1979-81; BS, Clarkson U., 1984. Lic. civil engr.; registered civil engr., N.Y. Owner C.B.F. Handyman Co., N.Y.C., 1974-77; v.p., gen. mgr. Fawcett & Fawcett, Inc., N.Y.C., 1977-84; project mgr. U.S. Army Corps Engrs., N.Y.C., 1985-86; asst. project mgr. N. Kruger Constrn., Inc., Locust Valley, N.Y., 1986-87; project mgr., engr. Finch, Pruyn & Co., Inc., Glens Falls, N.Y., 1987-98; propr. Caton Hill Enterprises, 1992—; project mgr., engr. Clough Harbour & Assocs., LLP, Albany, NY, 2000; project mgr. MLB Industries, Inc., Latham, NY, 2001; sr. project mgr. Santa Fe Constrn., Inc., N.Y.C., 2002—; judge h.s. competition N.Y. Acad. Scis., 2003—. Judge, N.Y. Acad. Scis., HS Sci. and Engring. Event, N.Y.C., 2003; founder, past chmn. Tri-County Nat. Engrs. Week and Nat. Jr. H.S. Mathcounts Competition programs, Glens Falls, 1987-98; founding sponsor Challenger Ctr. for Space Sci. Edn. Mem. NSPE, ASCE, N.Y. Acad. Scis., Nat. Space Soc. (charter), Engrs. for Edn., Order of Engr., Cousteau Soc. Avocation: scuba diving. Office: Caton Hill Enterprises 16 E 96th St Ste 2A New York NY 10128-

FAWCETT, COLLEEN, economist, educator; b. Akron, Ohio, Nov. 8, 1953; d. Gordon Dale and Doris Christine Williams; m. Brett William Frizzell (div. Jan. 1990); 1 child, Brett William Frizzell; m. Keith Richard Fawcett, June 26, 1998. BSHEC, Ohio U., 1975; MS, Nova Southwestern U., Ft. Lauderdale, Fla., 1992; PhD, U. San Jose, 1998. Home econs. tchr. Souers Jr. H.S., North Canton, Ohio, 1975—82, Forest Hill H.S., West Palm Beach, Fla., 1986—90, Wellington H.S., West Palm Beach, 1990—97; headmistress St. Davids in the Pines Episcopal Sch., West Palm Beach, 1997—2001; asst. prof. Wright State U., Celina, Ohio, 2001—. Presenter confs. in field. Mentor H.O.S.T.S., Celina West Elem. Sch., 2001—. Mem.: Nat. Assn. for the Edn. of Young Children. Republican. Episcopalian. Avocations: tennis, equestriene, photography. Office: Wright State Univ 7600 S Rt 703 Celina OH 45822

FAWCETT, DON WAYNE, retired anatomist; b. Springdale, Iowa, Mar. 14, 1917; s. Carlos J. and Mabel (Kennedy) F.; m. Dorothy Marie Secrest, 1941; children: Robert S., Mary Elaine, Donna, Joseph. AB cum laude, Harvard, 1938, MD, 1942; DSc (hon.), U. Siena, Italy, 1974, N.Y. Med. Coll., 1975, U. Chgo., 1977, U. Cordoba, Argentina, 1978; MD (hon.), U. Heidelberg, Germany, 1977; DVM (hon.), Justus Liebig U., Giessen-Lahn, Germany, 1977; DSc (hon.), Georgetown U., 1987, U. Rome, 1997. Intern surgery Mass. Gen Hosp., Boston, 1942-43; instr. anatomy Harvard Med. Sch., 1946-48, asso. anatomy, 1948-51, asst. prof. anatomy, 1951-55, Hersey prof. anatomy, 1958-80, James Stillman prof. comparative anatomy, 1962-80, sr. asso. dean preclin. affairs, 1975-77; prof. anatomy Cornell Med. Coll., 1955-58; scientist Internat. Lab. Research on Animal Diseases, Nairobi, Kenya, 1980-85. Author: The Cell, 1966, 2d edit., 1981, Textbook of Histology, 1968, 10th edit., 1975, 11th edit., 1986, 12th edit., 1993. Served as capt. M.C. AUS, 1943-46; bn. surgeon A.A.A. John and Mary Markle scholar med. sci., 1949-54; recipient Lederle Med. Faculty award, 1954 Fellow Am. Acad. Arts and Sci., Nat. Acad. Sci. U.S., Royal Microscopical Soc. (hon.); mem. AAAS, N.Y. Acad. Sci., Am. Assn. Anatomists (pres. 1964- 65, Henry Gray award 1983, Centennial medal 1987), N.Y. Soc. Electron Microscopists (pres. 1957-58), Histochem. Soc., Tissue Culture Assn. (v.p. 1954-55), Soc. Exptl. Biology and Medicine, Assn. Anatomy Chairmen (pres. 1973-74), Am. Soc. Zoologists, Am. Soc. Mammalogists, Electron Microscope Soc. Am. (Disting. Scientist award in Life Scis. 1989), Soc. Study Devel. and Growth, Harvey Soc., Am. Soc. Cell Biology (pres. 1961-62), Argentine Nat. Acad. Sci., Anat. Soc. So. Africa (hon.), Japanese Anat. Soc. (hon.), Anat. Soc. Australia and N.Z. (hon.), Japanese Electron Microscope Soc., Internat. Fedn. Soc. Electron Microscopy (pres. 1976-78), Am. Soc. Andrology (pres. 1977-78), Soc. Study Reprodn. (Carl Hartman award 1985), Mexican (hon.), Canadian (hon.) Assn. Anatomists. Address: 1224 Lincoln Rd Missoula MT 59802-3041

FAWCETT, DWIGHT WINTER, lawyer; b. Springfield, Ohio, Sept. 24, 1927; s. Dwight Ansley and Hazel (Winter) F.; m. Anne N. Langfitt, Apr. 27, 1957; children: Dwight P., Jane F. Dearborn, Donald N. B.S., Ind. U., 1948; J.D., Harvard U., 1951. Bar: Ill. 1951, U.S. Supreme Ct. 1975. Assoc. Mayer, Brown & Platt, Chgo., 1951-61, ptnr., 1961-91. Served with USN, 1945-46. Republican. Episcopalian. Clubs: Law; Indian Hill (Winnetka, Ill.); Lost Tree (North Palm Beach, Fla.). Home: 711 Locust St Winnetka IL 60093-2013

FAWCETT, JOHN SCOTT, real estate developer; b. Pitts., Nov. 5, 1937; s. William Hagen and Mary Jane (Wise) F.; m. Anne Elizabeth Mitchell, Dec. 30, 161; children: Holly Anne, John Scott II (dec.). BS, Ohio State U., 1959. Dist. dealer rep. Shell Oil Co., San Diego, 1962-66; dist. real estate rep. Shell Oil, Phoenix, 1967-69, region real estate rep. San Francisco, 1970-71, head office land investments rep. Houston, 1972-75; pres., CEO Marinita Devel. Co., Newport Beach, Calif., 1976—. Lectr. in land devel. related fields. With U.S. Army, 1960-61. Named Ky. Col., Gov. Ky., 1996. Mem. Internat. Platform Assn., Internat. Coun. Shopping Ctrs., Internat. Right of Way Assn., Internat. Inst. Valuers, Inst. Bus. Appraisers, Nat. Assn. Rev. Appraisers and Mortgage Underwriters, Am. Assn. Cert. Appraisers, Urban Land Inst., Nat. Assn. Real Estate Execs. (pres. L.A. chpt. 1975), Calif. Lic. Contractors Assn., Bldg. Industry Assn., U.S. C. of C., Town Hall of Calif., Ohio State U. Alumni Assn., Toastmasters (pres. Scottsdale Ariz. club 1968, pres. Hospitality T club 1964), U. Athletic Club, Phi Kappa Tau. Republican. Roman Catholic. Avocations: antiques, tennis, skiing. Home: 8739 Hudson River Cir Fountain Valley CA 92708-5503 Office: Marinita Devel Co 3835 Birch St Newport Beach CA 92660-2600

FAWCETT, JOHN THOMAS, archivist; b. West Branch, Iowa, Nov. 27, 1943; s. Floyd Thomas and Mary Helen (Miller) F.; m. Sharon Atchison, July 25, 1971 (div. 1993); children: Allen, Katherine. BA, U. Iowa, 1966; MA, U. Tex., 1978. Archivist, mus. tech. Herbert Hoover Libr., West Branch, Iowa, 1962-67; asst. acting dir., exec. dir. Herbert Hoover Libr. and Assn., West Branch, Iowa, 1983-87; archivist Office Presdl. Librs., Washington, 1967-68, supervisory and acting dir., 1978-83, asst. archivist, 1987-95; mil. aide to President of U.S. Exec. Office, Austin, Tex., 1968-70; supervisory archivist Lyndon B. Johnson Libr., Austin, 1970-78; pres. John T. Fawcett and Assocs., Inc., Washington, 1995—. Mem. exec. bd. Boy Scouts Am., 1984-87. Mem. Masons, Kiwanis (pres. 1985).

FAWCETT, JOY LYNN, soccer player; b. Inglewood, Calif., Feb. 8, 1968; m. Walter Fawcett; children: Katelyn Rose, Carli. Degree in phys. edn., U. Calif., Berkeley, 1990. Women's soccer coach UCLA, 1993-97, 1993—97. Named 3-time All-Am., 1987—89, Most Valuable Player, So. Calif., L.A. Times, 1987; named to, U. Calif. Berkeley Hall of Fame, 1997. Achievements include mem. U.S. Nat. Women's Soccer Team, 1987—; including 1991 World Cup, China; 1995 FIFA World Cup, Sweden; 1994 CONCACAF Qualifying Championship, Montreal; U.S. Olympic Festival, Denver, 1995; FIFA Women's World Cup, Sweden, 1995; gold medal U.S. Olympic Team, 1996; mem. Ajax of Manhattan Beach Club Soccer Team (champions U.S. Women's Amateur Nat. Cup, 1992, 93). Office: US Soccer Fedn 1801-1811 S Prairie Ave Chicago IL 60616

FAWCETT, LEE C. retired dean; b. Omaha, Nebr., May 15, 1941; s. Paul Wayne and Helen Rivola F.; m. Rita Margaret West, June 20, 1964; children: David, Daniel, Michael. BA in Polit. Sci., U. Chgo., 1963; MA in Ancient History, Wayne State U., 1970. Intern Detroit Country Day Sch., Birmingham, Mich., 1963—65; dir. fin. aid Kendall Coll., Evanston, Ill., 1965—68; assoc. dir., dir. fin. aid Wayne State U., Detroit, 1968—70; assoc. dean admissions and fin. aid Ea. Mich. U., Ypsilanti, Mich., 1970—75, dir. fin. aid, 1975—80, asst. to v.p. student svcs., 1980—81; asst. dean student svcs. Clackamas C.C., Oregon City, Oreg., 1981—91, assoc. dean rsch. and planning, 1991—97; ret., 1997. Pres. Mich. Student Fin. Aid Assn., Detroit, 1969—71; chair C.C. Rsch. and Planning Coun., Salem, Oreg., 1991—93. Treas. ACLU, Ann Arbor, Mich., 1972—76; cubmaster Boy Scouts Am., Ann Arbor, 1973—75; city councilor City of Lake Oswego (Oreg.), 1985—90; treas. Unitarian Ch., 1999—2001. Recipient Disting. Svc. award, Mich. Student Fin. Aid Assn., 1981. Democrat. Mem. Unitarian Ch. Avocations: reading, distributing library books to local shelters. Home: Apt 105 416 NW 13th Ave Portland OR 97209-2932 E-mail: lee_ritafawcett@attbi.com.

FAWCETT, MARIE ANN FORMANEK (MRS. ROSCOE KENT FAWCETT), civic leader; b. Mpls., Mar. 6, 1914; d. Peter Paul and Mary (Stepanek) Formanek; m. Roscoe Kent Fawcett, Mar. 16, 1935; children: Roscoe Kent, Peter Formanek, Roger Knowlton II, Stephen Hart. Cert., Harvard U., 1976-83. Chmn. of vols. Merry Go Round Club House and Mews, Greenwich, Conn., 1949-92, trustee, 1948-90, v.p., bd. dirs., 1949—, corr. sec., 1992—, chmn. entertainment, 1970-90; bd. dirs., vol. chmn., corr. sec. Nathaniel Witherell Hosp., Greenwich, 1952—, chmn. vols., 1956-89, corr. sec. aux. bd., 1956-94; bd. dirs., corr. sec. Nathaniel Witherell Auxiliary Hosp., 1952—. Chmn. vols. Greenwich Hosp., 1953-54; dist. chmn. ARC, Community Chest, Mental Health, 1946-50; vol. mentally retarded children Milbank Sch., Greenwich, 1958-92. Bd. dirs. Cerebral Palsy, Greenwich Symphony, 1956—, Greenwich Symphony Guild, 1956—, Putnam Indianfield Sch.; bd. dirs., corr. sec. Merry Go Round Mews, 1949—; bd. dirs. Multiple Sclerosis Soc., 1948—, v.p., 1970, corr. sec., 1958—; active drives for ARC, Community Chest, Leukemia, Muscular Dystrophy, Mental Health, Mentally Retarded Children Milbank Sch.; bd. dirs. Merry-Go-Round News for the Elderly, 1948—, Nathaniel Whitherell Hosp. for Elderly, 1952—, Greenwich Symphony Guild, 1956—, Travel Club Greenwich, 1982—; participating mem. Huxley Inst. Biosocial Rsch.; mem. polo com. Susan Cancer Fund, Pegasus Therapeutic Riding and Rusk Inst. Rehab. Medicine; trustee Menninger Found., Topeka. Named Woman of Year, Soroptimist Club, 1967; recipient Community Svc. award United Cerebral Palsy Assn. Fairfield County, 1972, Fund Drive award Cerebral Palsy, 1970, citations for 36 yrs. outstanding vol. svcs. Nathaniel Witherell Hosp. Aux., Conn. Dept. Health, 1977. Mem. Internat. Platform Assn., Smithsonian Inst., The Woman's Club of Greenwich, Travel Club of Greenwich (corr. sec., bd. dirs. 1982—), Charles F. Menninger Soc. (mem. Roll of Nonor 1998, Sustaining Excellence award). Home: 8141 12th Ave S Minneapolis MN 55425-1055

FAWCETT, SHERWOOD LUTHER, research laboratory executive; b. Youngstown, Ohio, Dec. 25, 1919; s. Luther T. and Clara (Sherwood) F.; m. Martha L. Simcox, Feb. 28, 1953; children: Paul, Judith, Tom. BS, Ohio State U., 1941; MS, Case Inst. Tech., 1948, PhD, 1950, Ohio State U., Gonzaga U., Whitman Coll., Otterbein Coll., Detroit Inst. Tech., Ohio Dominican Coll. Registered profl. engr., Ohio. Mem. staff Columbus Labs. Battelle Meml. Inst., 1950-64, mgr. physics dept., 1959-64; dir. Pacific Northwest Labs., Richland, Wash., 1964-67; trustee Battelle Meml. Inst., Columbus, Ohio, 1968-92, exec. v.p., 1967-68, CEO, 1968-84, pres., 1968-80, chmn., 1981-84, chmn. bd. trustees, 1985-87; assoc. trustee Columbus, Ohio, 1987-94. Chmn. bd. dirs. Transmet Corp. With USNR, 1941-46. Decorated Bronze Star; recipient Washington award Western Soc. Engrs., 1989. Mem. AIME, NSPE, Am. Phys. Soc., Am. Nuclear Soc., Am. Phys. Soc., Sigma Xi, Tau Beta Pi, Delta Chi, Sigma Pi Sigma. Home: 1852A Riverside Dr Columbus OH 43212-1875 Office: Transmet Corp 4290 Perimeter Dr Columbus OH 43228-1036

FAWELL, HARRIS W. lawyer, former congressman; b. West Chicago, Ill., Mar. 25, 1929; m. Ruth Johnson, 1954; children: Richard, Jane, John. Student, Naperville North Ctrl. Coll., 1949; LLD, Chgo. Kent Coll. Law, 1952. Ptnr. Fawell, James & Brooks, Naperville, Ill., 1954—84; mem. Ill. Senate, Springfield, 1963—77; gen. counsel Ill. Assn. Park Dists., 1977—84; mem. 99th-105th Congresses from 13th Ill. dist., 1985—98; of counsel James, Gustafson & Thompson, 1999—. Mem. Edn. and the Workforce Com., chmn. subcom. on employer-employee rels.; mem. House Sci. Com. Office: 1001 E Chicago Ave Ste 103 Naperville IL 60540-5500

FAWELL, REED MARQUETTE, III, lawyer; b. Miami Beach, Fla., Nov. 29, 1944; s. Reed Marquette Jr. and Betsy Page (McLean) F.; m. Anna Catherine Ikenberry, Dec. 27, 1969; children— Reed Marquette IV, Henry Pendleton. B.A., U. Va., 1967; J.D., U. Md., 1970. Bar: D.C. 1970, Md. 1970. Assoc. firm Glassie, Pewett, Dudley, Beebe & Shanks, P.C., Washington, 1970-75, ptnr., 1975-85, pres., 1982-85, of counsel, 1985-88; lawyer, real estate developer Rouse & Assocs., McLean, Va., 1985— ; of counsel McGuire, Woods, Battle & Boothe, McLean, Va., 1989—; pres. The Pendleton Adv. Group Ltd. Ptnrship., McLean, 1989—. Home: 4429 Garrison St NW Washington DC 20016-4055

FAWLEY, JOHN JONES, retired banker; b. Phila., Oct. 1, 1921; s. James L. and Edna (Jones) F.; m. Ann Kemp, Jan. 8, 1944; children: Jo Ann (Mrs. Richard High), Christine, James K. BS in Econs, U. Pa., 1948; grad., Rutgers U., 1957. With First Pa. Bank, Phila., 1948-69, sr. v.p., 1968-69; pres., dir. United Va. Bank/First & Citizens Nat. Bank, Alexandria, Va., 1969-72; exec. v.p. Indsl. Valley Bank, Phila., 1973-83, Dauphin Deposit Bank, Harrisburg, Pa., 1983-87. Lectr. Comml. Lending Sch., U. Okla., 1969 Former trustee Hahnemann U. With AUS, 1942-45. Mem. Robert Morris Assocs. (nat. pres. 1972-73), Masons. Home: Brittany Pointe Estates #2214 1001 Valley Ford Rd Lansdale PA 19446 also: Pinecrest Lake Pocono Pines PA 18350

FAX, CHARLES SAMUEL, lawyer; b. Balt., Sept. 12, 1948; s. David Hirsch and Eleanor Shirley (Lobe) F.; m. Nancy Lee Gruenberg, 1980 (div. 1995); children: Joanna May, Benjamin Zachary; m. Michele Weil, 1996. BA, Johns Hopkins U., 1970; JD with honors, George Washington U., 1973. Bar: D.C. 1974, N.Y. 1974, Md. 1990. Office of dist. atty. N.Y.C. (Bronx county), 1973-74; assoc. Truitt & Fabrikant, Washington, 1974-75, Chapman, Duff & Paul, Washington, 1975-79, ptnr., 1979-84, Porter, Wright, Morris & Arthur, Washington, 1985-89; sr. ptnr., co-chmn. lit. dept. Shapiro Sher Guinot & Sandler (formerly Shapiro and Olander), Balt., 1989—; mem. exec. com. Shapiro Sher Guinot & Sandler, Balt., 1999—; gen. counsel Parents and Children Together, Inc., 1992-98; apptd. mediator Cir. Ct. for Balt. City, 1994-98; spl. outside litigation counsel Commonwealth P.R. Dept. Justice, 1998-2001, Balt. City Mayor, 1994—95. Mem. faculty Exec. Enterprises, Inc., N.Y.C., Chgo., 1985-86; lectr. fed. personnel litigation Adminstrv. Law Inst., Washington, Chgo., San Francisco, 1982-83; lectr. Md. Mcpl. League, 1990-98; book rev. Cleve. Plain Dealer. Contbr. articles to newspapers and mags. Mem. Washington com. Sch. Arts and Scis., Johns Hopkins U., 1987—89; class of '70 agt. Johns Hopkins U., 1995—; bd. dirs. Md. region Jewish Nat. Fund, 2002—, chmn. exec. com., 2002—03, chmn. Md. region ann. campaign, 2002, pres., 2003—; bd. dirs. Am. Friends of Haifa Music Festival, 2002—. Mem. Johns Hopkins U. Soc. for 2d Decade, Tudor and Stuart Club, Johns Hopkins Club, Johns Hopkins Class of 1970 (class agt. 1995—), Alpha Delta Phi. Democrat. Jewish. Home: 10720 Gloxinia Dr North Bethesda MD 20852-3404 Office: Shapiro Sher Guinot & Sandler 36 S Charles St Ste 2000 Baltimore MD 21201-3147 E-mail: csf@shapirosher.com., csfax@aol.com.

FAXON, ALICIA CRAIG, art educator, department chairman; b. N.Y.C., July 27, 1931; d. William Donald and Clara Alicia (Harnecker) Craig; m. Richard Bremer Faxon, Feb. 21, 1953; children: Richard Paul, Thomas Hardwick. AB, Vassar Coll., 1952; MA, Radcliffe Coll., 1953, Boston U., 1971, PhD, 1979; DHL (hon.), Simmons Coll., 1998. Lectr. New Eng. Sch. Art and Design, Boston, 1974-77; acting dir. Danforth Mus., Framingham, Mass., 1977; teaching assoc. Boston U. Sch. for Art, 1978-79; vis. lectr. Simmons Coll., Boston, 1979-80, asst. prof. art, 1980-86, assoc. prof., 1986-91, chmn. dept. art and music, 1987-93, prof. art, 1991-93, alumnae endowed chair, 1992-93. Lectr. Sch. for Lifelong Learning, Harvard U., Cambridge, Mass., 1978-80; program chmn. Women's Studies Adv. Bd., 1982-84; R.I. editor Art New Eng., 1994-99. Author: Catalog Raisonnè of Prints of J.-L. Forain, 1982, Pilgrims and Pioneers, 1987, Dante Gabriel Rossetti, 1989; co-author: (with Liana Cheney and Kathleen Russo) Self-Portraits of Woman Painters, 2000; co-editor (with Susan Casteras) Pre-Raphaelite Art in its European Context, 1995; mem. editl. bd. Woman's Art Jour., 1989—. Mem. acquisitions com. Danforth Mus., 1974-89, trustee, 1975-77. Recipient Nan award for art criticism Art New Eng., 1987; grantee Nat. Endowment for Arts, 1982, Simmons Coll., 1984, NEH, 1989, 92. Mem. Coll. Art Assn. (chmn. preRaphaelite session 1990), Women's Caucus for Art (program co-chmn. 1986-88), Victorian Soc., 19th Century Art Historians Group, Vassar Coll. Alumnae Assn. Democrat. Episcopalian. Avocations: travel, writing.

FAXON, BRAD, professional golfer; b. Oceanport, NJ, Aug. 1, 1961; m. Bonnie Faxon (div.); children: Melanie, Emily, Sophie Lee. B in Econs., Furman U., 1983. Member PGA, professional golfer, 1983-. Co-sponsor Billy Andrade/Brad Faxon Charities for Children, 1991—; co-host CVS Charity Classic, 1999. Winner Provident Classic, 1986, Buick Open, 1991, New England Classic, 1992, The International, 1992, Heineken Australian Open, 1993, Freeport-McDermott Classic, 1997, B.C. Open, 1999. Achievements include being ranked 7th on PGA tour, 1992; mem. (nat. teams) Walker Cup, 1983, Ryder Cup, 1995, 97, Dunhill Cup, 1997, (PGA tour charity team) JCPenney Classic, 1999. Address: PGA 100 PGA Tour Blvd Ponte Vedra Beach FL 32082

FAXON, THOMAS BAKER, retired lawyer; b. Des Moines, Oct. 15, 1924; s. Ralph Henry and Prue (Baker) Faxon; m. Virginia Webb Johnson, Sept. 8, 1949; 1 child, Thomas Baker;1 child, Rebecca Webb Osgood. BA, Princeton U., 1949; LLB, Harvard U., 1952. Bar: Colo. 1953. Asst. prof., asst. dir. Inst. Govt. U. N.C., Chapel Hill, 1952-53; assoc. Pershing, Bosworth, Dick & Dawson, Denver, 1953-57; ptnr. Dawson, Nagel, Sherman & Howard, Denver, 1957-84; of counsel Sherman & Howard, Denver, 1984-92. Bd. trustees Colo. Legal Aid Found., Denver, 1984-91. Bd. dirs. Urban League Colo., Denver, 1964-67, Colo. chpt. UN Assn. of U.S.A., 1980-81, Recording for the Blind Colo., 1988-94; pres. bd. trustees 1st Unitarian Ch., Denver, 1960; mem. Denver Equality of Edn. Com., 1969. USAAF, 1943-46. Mem. Harvard Law Sch. Assn. Colo. (pres. 1968), Cactus Club Denver. Democrat. Address: 830 Race St Denver CO 80206-3734

FAY, ABBOTT EASTMAN, history educator; b. Scottsbluff, Nebr., July 19, 1926; s. Abbott Eastman and Ethel (Lambert) F.; m. Joan D. Richardson, Nov. 26, 1953; children: Rand, Diana, Collin. Grad., Scottsbluff (Nebr.) Jr. Coll.; BA, Colo. State Coll., 1949, MA, 1953; postgrad., U. Denver, 1961-63; cert. advanced study, Western State U., 1963. Tchr. Leadville (Colo.) Pub. Schs., 1950-52, elem. prin., 1952-54; prin. Leadville Jr. H.S., 1954-55; pub. info. dir., instr. history Mesa Coll., Grand Junction, Colo., 1955-64; asst. prof. history Western State Coll., Gunnison, Colo., 1964-76, assoc. prof. history, 1976-82, assoc. prof. emeritus, 1982—. Adj. faculty Adams State Coll., Alamosa, Colo., Mesa State Coll., Grand Junction, Colo., 1989—; propr. Mountaintop Books, Paonia, Colo.; bd. dirs. Colo. Assoc. Univ. Press; dir. hist. tours; columnist Valley Chronicle, Paonia, Best Years Beacon, Grand Junction, Guide Lines, Denver, The Historian, Fruita, Colo., Grand Mesa Byway News, Delta, Colo., Agewave: Get Up & Go!, Mpls.; profl. speaker in field; cons. Colo. Welcome Ctr., 1997—. Author: Mountain Academia, 1968, Writing Good History Research Papers, 1980, Ski Tracks in the Rockies, 1984, Famous Coloradans, 1990, I Never Knew That About Colorado, 1993, Beyond The Great Divide, 1999, To Think That This Happened in Grand County!, 1999, A History of Skiing in Colorado, 2000, More That I Never Knew About Colorado, 2000, The Story of Colorado Wines, 2002; playwright: Thunder Mountain Lives Tonight!; contbr. articles to profl. jours.; freelance writer popular mags. Founder, coord. Nat. Energy Conservation Challenge; travel cons. Colo. State Welcome Ctr., 1997-99; project reviewer NEH, Colo. Hist. Soc.; steering com. West Elk Scenic & Historic Byway, Colo., 1994—; founder Leadville (Colo.) Assembly, pres., 1953-54; mem. Advs. of Lifelong Learning, 1994—. Named Top Prof. Western State Coll., 1969, 70, 71; fellow Hamline U. Inst. Asian Studies, 1975, 79; recipient Colo. Ind. Pubs. award, 1998. Mem. Western Writers Am., Rocky Mountain Social Sci. Assn. (sec. 1961-63), Am. Hist. Assn., Assn. Asian Studies, Western History Assn., Western State Coll. Alumni Assn. (pres. 1971-73), Internat. Platform Assn. Profl. Guides Assn. Am. (cert.), Rocky Mountain Guides Assn., Colo. Antiquarian Booksellers Assn., Am. Legion (Outstanding Historian award 1981), Phi Alpha Theta, Phi Kappa Delta, Delta Kappa Pi. Home: 679 Brentwood Dr 11A Palisade CO 81526

FAY, CONNER MARTINDALE, retired business executive; b. Chillicothe, Mo., May 9, 1929; s. Vernon Martindale and Corinne (Conner) F.; m. Evelyn Caffey Buford, Dec. 2, 1961; children: Leslie Conner Francesca, Buford Martindale Edoardo, David Curtis Anselmo. BA, Yale U., 1951; MBA cum laude, Harvard U., 1953. Brand mgr. Procter & Gamble Co., Cin., 1956-62; mktg. mgr. Procter & Gamble Co. Italia, Rome, 1962-69; sr. v.p. Clairol Inc., N.Y.C., 1970-89; mgmt. cons., 1989-93. Mem. bd. fgn. parishes Am. Episcopal Ch., N.Y., 1977—, pres., 1989—; bd. dirs. St. Paul's Ch., Rome, 1977—, pres., 1989-2001; bd. dirs. St. James Ch., Florence, Italy, 1977—, pres., 1989-2000; vice chmn. St. Stephen's Sch., Rome, 1980-94; trustee Samuel and Lois Silberman Fund of N.Y. Cmty. Trust, 1993—; sr. warden St. Mary the Virgin Episcopal Ch., Chappaqua, N.Y., 1982-83, 91-93; chmn. coun. of advisors Hunter Sch. Social Work, CUNY, 1985-97, founding bd. dirs. 'Neath the Elms Found.; mem. univ. coun. and com. on devel. and alumni affairs Yale U. Class of 1951, 1996-98; chmn. of agts. Yale Alumni Fund, 1982-86, 1951 40th reunion gift chmn., 1991, 50th reunion gift co-chmn. 2001, vice chmn., 1994-96, chmn., 1996-98; bd. dirs. Yale Alumni Chorus Found., 2001—; bd. dirs. Katonah Mus. Art, 1995—, treas., 2001-03. Recipient Yale medal, 2000. Mem. Am. Indsl. Health Coun. (bd. dirs. 1979-91, chmn. 1988-89), Yale Glee Club Assocs. (pres. 1979-81, treas. 1996-2001), Yale Club, Mem Neath Elms Found. (trustee), 2002 — Republican. Avocation: music.

FAY, DAVID B. sports association executive; b. N.Y.C., Oct. 12, 1950; s. Peter Donald and Sarah (McGrath) F.; m. Joan Margaret Mcananey, June 2, 1979; children: Katherine, Mary Elizabeth. BA, Colgate U., 1972. Communications dir. Met. Golf. Assn., N.Y.C., 1975-78; tournament rels. mgr. U.S. Golf Assn., Far Hills, N.J., 1978-81, dir. rules and program devel., 1981-87, asst. exec. dir., 1987-89, exec. dir., 1989—; joint sec. World Amateur Golf Coun., 1991—. Office: USGA Golf House PO Box 708 Far Hills NJ 07931-0708

FAY, FRANK ALLEN, lawyer; b. Lafayette, Ind., Jan. 30, 1949; s. Dale Allen and Merry Ann (Fleming) R.; m. Carol Ann Olmutz, Oct. 1, 1982; children: Erica Fleming, Robert Allen. BA, Ohio State U., 1970, JD, 1973. Bar: Ohio 1973, U.S. Dist. Ct. (so. dist.) Ohio 1975, U.S. Supreme Ct. 1976, U.S. Tax Ct. 1977, U.S. Ct. Appeals (6th cir.) 1977, U.S. Dist. Ct. (no. dist.) Ohio 1980, U.S. Dist. Ct. (ea. dist.) Mich. 1983, U.S. Ct. Appeals (1st cir.) 1986; cert. civil trial adv. Nat. Bd. Trial Advocacy. Asst. pros. atty. Franklin County, Ohio, 1973-75, chief civil counsel, 1976-78; dir. econ. crime project Nat. Dist. Attys. Assn., Washington, 1975-76; assoc. Brownfield, Kosydar, Bowen, Bally & Sturtz, Columbus, Ohio, 1978, Michael F. Colley Co., L.P.A., Columbus, 1979-83; pres. Frank A. Ray Co., L.P.A., Columbus, 1983-93, 2000—, Ray & Todaro Co., LPA, Columbus, 1993-94, Ray, Todaro & Alton Co., L.P.A., Columbus, 1994-96, Ray, Todaro, Alton & Kirstein Co., L.P.A., Columbus, 1996, Ray, Alton & Kirstein Co., L.P.A., Columbus, 1996—98; sr. ptnr. Ray & Alton, L.L.P., Columbus, 1998—2000; adj. prof. Moritz Coll. of Law, Ohio State U., 2003—. Mem. seminar faculty Nat. Coll. Dist. Attys., Houston, 1975-77; mem. nat. conf. faculty Fed. Jud. Ctr., Washington, 1976-77; bd. editors Man. for Complex Litigation, Fed. Jud. Ctr., 1999—; bd. mem. bar examiners Ohio Supreme Ct., 1992-95, Rules Adv. Com., 1995-99. Editor: Economic Crime Digest, 1975-76; co-author: Personal Injury Litigation Practice in Ohio, 1988, 91. Mem. fin. com. Franklin County Rep. Orgn., Columbus, 1979-84; trustee Ohio State U. Coll. Humanities Alumni Soc., 1991-93, Nat. Coun. Ohio State U. Coll. Law Alumni Assn., 1998—; mem. Legal Aid Soc. of Columbus Capital Campaign Fund Cabinet, 1998. Capt. inf. U.S. Army, 1976. Named to Ten Outstanding Young Citizens of Columbus, Columbus Jaycees, 1976; recipient Nat. award of Distinctive Svc., Nat. Dist. Attys. Assn., 1977. Fellow: Ohio Acad. Trial Lawyers (pres. 1989—90, Pres.'s award 1986), Ohio State Bar Found., Roscoe Pound Found., Am. Coll. Trial Lawyers, Internat. Soc. Barristers, Columbus Bar Found. (trustee 2003—); mem.: ATLA (state del. 1990—92), ABA, Franklin County Trial Lawyers Assn. (pres. 1987—88, mem. com. jury instrns. 2002—, Pres.'s award 1990), Ohio State Bar Assn. (com. negligence law 1990—97), Million Dollar Advs. Forum, Columbus Bar Assn. (pres. 2001—02, Profl. award 1987), Am. Bd. Trial Advs. (pres.-elect, Ohio Chpt. 2003—), Inns. of Ct. (pres. Judge Robert M. Duncan chpt. 1993—94). Presbyterian. Home: 2030 Tremont Rd Columbus OH 43221-4330 Office: 175 S 3rd St Ste 350 Columbus OH 43215-5188 E-mail: far@raylaw.com.

FAY, JAMES ALAN, mechanical engineering educator; b. Southold, N.Y., Nov. 1, 1923; s. William Joseph, Jr. and Margaret (Keenan) F.; m. Agatha Marie Kelly, Jan. 12, 1946; children: David Anthony, Mark Bernard, Colin Michael, Jamie Martin, Peter Robert, Michele Marie. BS, Webb Inst. Naval Architecture, 1944; MS, MIT, 1947; PhD, Cornell U., 1951. Research engr. Lima-Hamilton Corp., 1947-49; asst. prof. engring. mechanics Cornell U., 1951-55; mem. faculty MIT, 1955-89, prof. mech. engring., 1960-89, prof. emeritus, 1989—. Cons. to govt. and industry; mem. NRC Environ. Studies Bd., 1973-78, 80-83 Author: (Text books) Molecular Thermodynamics, 1965, Introduction to Fluid Mechanics, 1994, Energy and the Environment, 2002; contbr. articles to profl. jours. Chmn. Boston Air Pollution Commn., 1969-72, Mass. Port Authority, 1972-77; bd. dirs. Union Concerned Scientists, 1978—, Conservation Law Found., 1984-94. Served with USNR, 1942-46. Overseas fellow Churchill Coll., Cambridge U., 1980; Fulbright lectr., India, 1990. Fellow Am. Acad. Arts and Scis., Am. Phys. Soc. (exec. com. div. fluid dynamics 1964-67), AAAS, AIAA (chmn. plasmadynamics com. 1966-68); mem. NAE, ASME, Air and Waste Mgmt. Assn., Sigma Xi. Home: 36 Spruce Hill Rd Weston MA 02493-2134 Office: MIT Rm 3-258 Cambridge MA 02139-4307 E-mail: jfay@mit.edu.

FAY, JOSEPH BARTLETT, not-for-profit marketing executive; b. Noblesville, Ind., Nov. 17, 1954; s. Charles Bartlett and Marie Dorothy (Quan) Fay. BA magna cum laude, Boston Coll., 1977; MBA magna cum laude, Columbia U., 1984. Assoc. brand mgr. Procter & Gamble, Cin., 1984-87; product mgr. Heinz USA, Pitts., 1987-92; dep. dir. Am. Lung Assn., N.Y.C., 1992-96; sr. dir. ARC, Washington, 1996-2000; v.p. Reading is Fundamental, Washington, 2000—02, Am. Lung Assn., N.Y.C., 2002—. Adj. lectr. Georgetown U., Washington, 2002. Lt. USN, 1978—82. Decorated Achievment medal USN. Mem.: Mensa. Unitarian Universalist. Avocations: pottery, sailing, environmental causes. Home: 119 Prospect Park W Brooklyn NY 11215 Office: Am Lung Assn 61 Broadway New York NY 10006

FAY, PETER THORP, judge; b. Rochester, N.Y., Jan. 18, 1929; s. Lester Thorp and Jane (Baumler) Fay; m. Claudia Pat Zimmerman, Oct. 1, 1958; children: Michael Thorp, William, Darcy. BA, Rollins Coll., 1951, LLD, 1971; JD, U. Fla., 1956; LLD, Biscayne Coll., 1975. Bar: Fla. 1956, U.S. Supreme Ct. 1961. Ptnr. firm Nichols, Gaither Green, Frates & Beckham, Miami, Fla., 1956—61, Frates, Fay, Floyd & Pearson (and predecessors), Miami, 1961—70; prof. Fla. Jr. Bar Practical Legal Inst., 1959—65; judge U.S. Dist. Ct. for So. Fla., Miami, 1970—76, U.S. Ct. Appeals (5th cir.), 1976—81, U.S. Ct. Appeals (11th cir.), 1981—94, sr. judge, 1994—; lectr. Fla. Bar Legal Inst., 1959—; faculty Fed. Jud. Center, Washington, 1974—94. Mem. Jud. Conf. Com. for Implementation Criminal Justice Act, 1974—82, Adv. Com. on Codes of Conduct, 1980—87, Adv. Com. on Appellate Rules, 1987—90; co-chmn. Nat. Jud. Coun. for State and Fed. Cts., 1990—. Mem. Orange Bowl Com., 1974—; dist. collector United Fund, 1957—70; mem. adminstrv. bd. St. Thomas U., 1970—; trustee U. Miami, Fla., 1989—; mem., supr. Ind. Counsel, 1994—. Lieutenant USAF, 1951—53. Mem.: ABA, Medico Legal Inst., John Marshall Bar Assn. (past pres.), Dade County Bar Assn., Fla. Bar Assn., Fla. Acad. Trial Attys., Law Sci. Acad., Miami C. of C., U. Fla. Alumni Assn. (dir.), Fla. Coun. of 100, Miami Club, Coral Oaks Club (Miami), Wildcat Cliffs Club (N.C.), Snapper Creek Lakes Club (Miami), Phi Delta Theta (past sec.), Phi Kappa Phi, Pi Gamma Mu (past pres.), Omicron Delta Kappa (past pres.), Phi Delta Phi (past pres.), Order of Coif. Republican. Roman Catholic.*

FAY, REGAN JOSEPH, lawyer; b. Cleve., Sept. 19, 1948; s. Robert J. and Loretta Ann (Regan) F.; married; children: John, Mary, Matthew, Jessica, Samantha. BS in Chem. Engring., MIT, 1970; JD with honors, George Washington U., 1974. Bar: Ohio 1974, U.S. Dist. Ct. (no. dist.) Ohio 1974, U.S. Patent Office 1973, U.S. Ct. Appeals (fed. cir.) 1974, U.S. Ct. Appeals (9th cir.) 1975, U.S. Dist. Ct. (ea. dist.) Wis. 1976, U.S. Dist. Ct. (no. dist.) Tex. 1986, U.S. Supreme Ct. 1988. Patent examiner U.S. Patent and Trademark Office, Washington, 1970-72; law clk. to presiding justice U.S. Ct. Customs and Patent Appeals, Washington, 1973-75; assoc. Yount & Tarolli, Cleve., 1975-79; assoc., then ptnr. Jones, Day, Reavis & Pogue, Cleve., 1979—. Lectr. patent and trademark law Case Western Res. U., Cleve., 1976-86. Mem. Cleve. Intellectual Property Law Assn (pres. 1996-97). Republican. Roman Catholic. Avocation: skiing. Office: Jones Day Reavis & Pogue 901 Lakeside Ave E Cleveland OH 44114-1190 E-mail: rjfay@jonesday.com.

FAY, RICHARD JAMES, mechanical engineer, executive, educator; b. St. Joseph, Mo., Apr. 26, 1935; s. Frank James and Marie Jewell (Senger) F.; m. Marilyn Louise Kelsey, Dec. 22, 1962; BSME, U. Denver, 1959, MSME, 1970. Registered profl. engr., Colo., Nebr. Design engr. Denver Fire Clay Co., 1957-60; design, project engr. Silver Engring. Works, 1960-63; research engr., lectr. mech. engring. U. Denver, 1963-74, asst. prof. Colo. Sch. of Mines, 1974-75, founder, pres. Fay Engring. Corp., 1971—. Served with Colo. N.G., 1962. Mem. Soc. Automotive Engrs. (past chmn. Colo. sect.), ASME (past chmn. Colo. sect., past regional v.p.), La Societe des Ingenieurs de L'Automobile (France). Contbr. articles to profl. jours.; patentee in field. Office: 5201 E 48th Ave Denver CO 80216-5316

FAY, ROBERT CLINTON, chemist, educator; b. Kenosha, Wis., Mar. 14, 1936; s. Clinton Edward and Selma (Lenz) F.; m. Carol Lee Baker, Aug. 25, 1960. AB, Oberlin Coll., 1957; postgrad., Wheaton Coll., 1957-58; MS, U. Ill., 1960, PhD, 1962. Teaching fellow Wheaton (Ill.) Coll., 1957-58; teaching asst. U. Ill., Urbana, 1958-59; inorganic chemist Nat. Bur. Standards, Washington, summers 1957-60; asst. prof. chemistry Cornell U., Ithaca, N.Y., 1962-68, assoc. prof., 1968-75, prof., 1975—. Vis. prof. chemistry Harvard U., Cambridge, Mass., 1990-91, contract prof. U. Bologna, Italy, 1992. Co-author: (text) Chemistry, 1995, 3d edit., 2001; contbr. articles to profl. jours. NSF fellow, 1960-62; NSF faculty fellow U. East Anglia, U. Sussex, Eng., 1969-70; Sci. and Engring. Research Council vis. fellow and NATO/Heineman sr. fellow Oxford (Eng.) U., 1982-83; NSF grantee, 1964-80; recipient Clark Disting. Teaching award Cornell U., 1980 Mem. Am. Chem. Soc., Royal Soc. Chem. (London), Am. Crystallographic Assn., Am. Sci. Affiliation, Sigma Xi, Phi Kappa Phi, Phi Beta Kappa, Phi Lambda Upsilon, Pi Mu Epsilon. Home: 318 Eastwood Ave Ithaca NY 14850-6202 Office: Cornell Univ Dept Chemistry/Chem Biology Baker Lab Ithaca NY 14853 E-mail: rcf4@cornell.edu.

FAY, TERRENCE MICHAEL, lawyer; b. Cleve., Feb. 25, 1953; s. J. Francis and Alice Wilsona (Porter) F.; m. Beverly Ann Luciow, Feb. 25, 1983; children: Robert Michael, Katherine Elizabeth. BA cum laude, Baldwin Wallace Coll., 1974, BS cum laude, 1975; JD, Ohio State U., 1978. Bar: Ohio 1978, U.S. Dist. Ct. (no. dist.) Ohio 1983, U.S. Dist. Ct. (so. dist.) Ohio 1987, U.S. Ct. Appeals (6th cir.) 1987, U.S. Dist. Ct. (no. dist.) Ind. 1992, U.S. Dist. Ct. (ea. dist.) Mich. 1993. Law clk. for chief adminstrv. law judge Ohio Power Siting Commn., Columbus, 1977-78; asst. atty. gen. environ. sect. Ohio Atty. Gen.'s Office, Columbus, 1978-87, chief civil atty., 1987-88; sr. assoc. Smith & Schnacke, L.P.A., Columbus, 1988-89, Benesch, Friedlander, Coplan & Aronoff, Columbus, 1989-90, ptnr., 1992—2001, chair hiring com., 1995—97; of counsel Frost, Brown Todd LLC, Columbus, 2002—. Bd. dirs. Hucksters, Inc., Columbus, 1990. Abrahms scholar, 1975; recipient Book award Lawyers Coop., Inc., 1978, Ohio Gov.'s Spl. Recognition award, 1988. Mem. Phi Alpha Theta, Omicron Delta Kappa, Pi Kappa Delta, Psi Chi. Office: Frost Brown Todd LLC One Columbus Ste 1000 10 W Broad St Columbus OH 43215-3467 E-mail: tfay@ftblaw.com.

FAY, THOMAS A. philosopher, educator; b. Utica, N.Y., July 18, 1927; s. Thomas A. and Theresa A. (Miller) F.; m. Evelyn C. DaCorta, Apr. 6, 1984 BA, Cath. U. Am., 1952; MA, U. Laval, Quebec, 1963; PhD, Fordham U., 1970. Asst. prof. philosophy St. Bernard Coll., 1963-64; mem. faculty St. John's U., Jamaica, N.Y., 1967—, prof. philosophy, 1977—; chmn. dept. philosophy St John's U., Jamaica, N.Y., 1974-80. Vis. prof. Drew U., 1969 Author: Heidegger: The Critique of Logic, 1977, And Smoking Flax Shall He Not Quench: Reflections on New Testament Themes, 1979; mem. editorial bd. Guidebook for Publishing Philosophy, 1977, 2d edit., 1986; contbr. articles to profl. jours.. Served with U.S. Army, 1945-46. Mem. Am. Cath. Philos. Assn. (pres. Met. chpt. 1975-81, exec. council 1976-79), Internat. Thomistic Soc. (v.p.), Internat. Soc. Metaphysics, Am. Philos. Assn., Medieval Acad. Am. Home: 20 Melody Ln Kings Park NY 11754-5026 Office: St Johns U Philosophy Dept Jamaica NY 11439-0001 E-mail: tafay@aol.com.

FAY, TONI GEORGETTE, communications executive; b. N.Y.C., Apr. 25, 1947; d. George E. and Allie C. (Smith) Fay. BA, Duquesne U., Pitts., 1968; MSW, U. Pitts., 1972, MEd, 1973; cert., Yale U. Drug Dependence Unit, 1973. Caseworker N.Y.C. Dept. Welfare, 1968-70; regional commr. Gov. Pa. Coun. Drugs and Alcohol, 1973-76; dir. social svcs. Pitts. Drug Abuse Ctr., 1972-73; dir. planning and devel. Nat. Coun. Negro Women, 1977-79; exec. v.p. D. Parke Gibson Assocs., 1979-82; mgr. cmty. rels. Time Inc. (now AOL Time-Warner Inc.), N.Y.C., 1982-83; dir. corp. cmty. rels. and affirmative action Time Inc. (now Time-Warner Inc.), N.Y.C., 1983-93, v.p., corp. officer, 1993-2001; pres. TGF Assocs., Englewood, N.J., 2001—. Bd. dirs. UNICEF, Congl. Black Caucus Found., NAACP Legal Def. Fund Bd., Franklin and Eleanor Inst., Apollo Theatre Found.; apptd. bd. advs. Nat. Inst. Literacy, 1996—, Corp. for Nat. and Cmty. Svc., 2000. Named Woman of Yr., Pitts. YWCA, 1975, N.Y.

Women's Forum; recipient Twin award YWCA of USA, 1987; named one 100 Top Women in Bus., Dollars and Sense Mag., 1986. Office: TGF Assocs 233 W Hudson Ave Englewood NJ 07631 Fax: 201-568-5157. E-mail: tonigfay@aol.com.

FAY, WILLIAM PATRICK, church administrator; b. Boston, Mass., Apr. 1, 1949; s. Warren Gerard Fay and Katherine Rose Fay (Kiernan). PhD, Cath. U. of Am., Washington, D.C., 1977—87; MA, Pontifical Gregorian U., Rome, Italy, 1973—74, S.T.B., 1970—73; BA, St. John Sem., Brighton, Massachusetts, 1966—70. Gen. sec. U.S. Conf. of Cath. Bishops, Washington, 2001—, assoc. gen. sec., 1995—2001. Sec. of the bd. of directors Cath. Relief Services, Baltimore, Md., 2001—. Roman Catholic. Avocations: reading, travel, skiing, cooking. Office: US Conference of Catholic Bishops 3211 4th Street NE Washington DC 20017-1194

FAYAD, PIERRE B. neurologist; b. Rechmaya, Lebanon, Nov. 20, 1956; s. Mansour Youssef and Marguerite (Chalhoub) F. MD, U. Rome, 1983. Diplomate Am. Bd. Psychiatry & Neurology. Intern Millard Fillmore Hosp., Buffalo, 1985-86; resident in neurology SUNY/Dent Neurol. Inst., Buffalo, 1986-89; fellow in vascular neurology Yale U., New Haven, 1989-91, inst. neurology, 1991-92, asst. prof. neurology, 1992-97, assoc. prof. neurology, 1997-2001; co-dir. Yale Cerebrovascular Ctr., New Haven, 1993-2001; dir. Yale Vascular Neurology Program, 1993—2001; chmn. dept. neurol. scis. U. Nebr. Med. Ctr., 2001—; Reynolds Centennial prof. neurol. scis. U. Nebr. Coll. Medicine, 2001—. Fellow stroke coun. Am. Heart Assn., Houston, 1991—. Mem. AMA, Am. Acad. Neurology. Office: Univ Nebraska Med Ctr 982045 Nebraska Med Ctr Omaha NE 68198-2045 Office Fax: 402-559-3341. E-mail: pfayad@unmc.edu.

FAYBUSOVICH, LEONID, mathematician, educator; b. Leningrad, Russia, Sept. 2, 1954; arrived in U.S., 1989; MSc, Poly. Inst., Leningrad, 1977; PhD, Harvard U., 1991. Prof. Univ. Notre Dame, Ind., 1991—. Contbr. more than 60 scientific papers. Grantee, NSF, 1994—. Mem.: Soc. for Indsl. and Applied Math. (mem. of editl. boards 1996—2002), Am. Math. Soc. Office: Univ Notre Dame Dep Math 233 Hurley Building Notre Dame IN 46556

FAYER, MICHAEL DAVID, chemist, educator; b. L.A., Sept. 12, 1947; s. William and Frieda Fayer; m. Terry Wolfe, Dec. 21, 1968; children: Victoria, William. BS, U. Calif., Berkeley, 1969, PhD, 1974. Asst. prof. chemistry Stanford (Calif.) U., 1974—80, assoc. prof. chemistry, 1980—84, prof. chemistry, 1984—2000, David Mulvane Ehrsam and Edward Curtis Franklin prof. of chemistry, 2000—. Author: (book) Elements of Quantum Mechanics, 2001; contbr. articles to sci. jours. Fellow Am. Acad. of Arts and Scis. fellow, 1999—, Guggenheim Found., 1983, Camille & Henry Dreyfus Found. fellow, Dreyfus Found., 1977, Alfred P. Sloan fellow, Sloan Found., 1977. Fellow: Am. Phys. Soc. (Earl K. Pyler prize for molecular spectroscopy 2000). Office: Stanford U Dept Chemistry Stanford CA 94305-5080 Personal E-mail: fayer@stanford.edu. E-mail: fayer@stanford.edu.

FAYER, STEVE, writer; b. Bklyn., Mar. 11, 1935; s. Saul S. and Pearl Ruth (Perlman) Fayer. BA with honors in English Lit., U. Pa., 1956. Promotion dir. WSBA-TV, York, Pa., 1956—58, WTOL-TV, Toledo, 1958—65; first mate Schooner C'est la Vie, Denmark, 1966; dir. audience promotion Kaiser Broadcasting, Oakland, Calif. and Boston, 1967—70; exec. v.p. Blackside, Inc., Boston, 1972—77; TV writer Boston, 1977—. Co-author: (non-fiction book) Voices of Freedom (One of the Notable Books of the Yr., N.Y. Times Book Rev., 1990), George Wallace: Settin' the Woods on Fire, 2000 (Writers Guild of Am. award, 2000); author: (TV films) (documentary) Mississippi: Is This America?, 1987 (Emmy Award, 1987), After the Crash, 1991, Frederick Douglass -- When the Lion Wrote History, 1994; co-author Malcolm X: Make It Plain, 1994 (George Foster Peabody award, Emmy award, The New York Festival Grand award for best TV documentary, Gold award Worldfest, Houston); author Africans in America: America's Journey Through Slavery, 1998—99 (George Foster Peabody award, Emmy award, 2000), (TV series) Eyes on the Prize, Parts 1 and 2, 1987—90 (DuPont Columbia Gold baton, DuPont Columbia Silver baton, George Foster Peabody award, Edward R. Murrow Brotherhood award, Christopher award, 6 Emmy awards), The Great Depression, 1993 (Dupont-Columbia Silver Baton, Emmy award, 4 Gold awards Worldfest, Houston Internat. Film Festival, 4 CINE Golden Eagles); series cons. (documentary TV series) America's War on Poverty, 1995 (DuPont-Columbia Silver Baton, Erik Barnouw award Orgn. Am. Historians, Grand award Worldfest, Houston, Silver Plaque, Chgo. Internat. Film Festival, CINE Golden Eagle), Chicano! History of the Mexican-American Civil Rights Movement, 1996, sr. creative cons. (documentary TV films) Driving Passion, 1995; author: numerous short stories. With USNR, 1952—60. Recipient Emmy award for writing, Nat. Acad. TV Arts and Scis., 1987, Spl. Jury award for documentary, Sundance Film Festival, 2000. Fellow: MacDowell Colony; mem.: Writers Guild of Am. (Award for TV Documentary 2000). Jewish.

FAYEZ, MEHANNI SAMUEL, finance educator; b. Mansourah, Egypt, Jan. 6, 1940; m. Claire Ramzi Bassili; children: Nancy, Dahlia. LLB, Cairo U., 1967; MBA in Internat. Fin., St. John's U., N.Y., 1976. Sales staff, then atty. in legal dept. The Arab Drug Co., Cairo, 1968—69; customer svc. officer Bankers Trust Co., N.Y.C., 1970—86; adj. assoc. prof. econs. SUNY, Farmingdale, 1987—; adj. prof. econs. and fin. Dowling Coll., Oakdale, NY, 1990—. Recipient Pride award for excellence in performance, svc., problem solving, creativity, Dowling Coll., 1995, 1999, Cert. of Appreciation for dedicated svc., SUNY, 1991. Mem.: AAUP, United Univ. Profs. (chmn. contract negotiations team 1995, 1999), N.Y. State United Tchrs. (del. 1990), Am. Fedn. Tchrs. (del. 1990). Home: 4 Tanyard Ln Huntington NY 11743 Office: Dowling College Idle Hour Blvd Oakdale NY 11769

FAYO, ANTHONY THOMAS, research scientist; b. Cornwall, N.Y., Aug. 12, 1966; s. Thomas Louis and Margaret Joy (Perno) F.; m. Corinne Renee Luckfield, Apr. 6, 1991. AS in physics, Dutchess C.C., 1987; BS, U. Albany, 1989. Mass spectral interpretation specialist Hewlett Packard. Chemist Camo Labs., Inc., Poughkeepsie, N.Y., 1989-90; group leader chemist Pace, Inc., Wappingers Falls, N.Y., 1990-92; mass spectrometry supr. Northeast Analytical, Inc., Schenectady, N.Y., 1992-93; rsch. scientist N.Y. State Dept Health, Albany, 1993—. Recipient Citizenship award New Paltz Knights of Columbus, 1984. Roman Catholic. Avocations: softball, woodworking, hockey, music. Home: 91 Whitney Dr Valatie NY 12184-5245 Office: NY State Dept Health Empire State Plaza PO Box 509 Albany NY 12201-0509

FAY-SCHMIDT, PATRICIA ANN, paralegal; b. Waukegan, Ill., Dec. 25, 1941; d. John William and Agnes Alice (Semerad) Fay; m. Dennis A. Schmidt, Nov. 3, 1962 (div. Dec. 1987); children: Kristin Fay Schmidt, John Andrew Schmidt. Student, L.A. Pierce Coll., 1959-60, U. San Jose, 1960-62, Western State U. of Law, Fullerton, Calif., 1991-92. Cert. legal asst., Calif. Paralegal Rasner & Rasner, Costa Mesa, Calif., 1979-82; paralegal, adminstr. Law Offices of Manuel Ortega, Santa Ana, Calif., 1982-92; sabbatical, 1992-94. Mem. editorial adv. bd. James Pub. Co., Costa Mesa, 1984-88. Contbg. author: Journal of the Citizen Ambassador Paralegal Delegation to the Soviet Union, 1990. Treas., Republican Women, Tustin, Calif., 1990-91; past regent, 1st vice regent, 2d vice regent NSDAR, Tustin, 1967—; docent Richard M. Nixon Libr. and Birthplace, 1993—, bd. dirs. Docent Guild, 1994-99; docent Orange County Courthouse Mus., 1992-94; chmn. Am. History Essay, 1999—. Mem. Orange County Paralegal Assn. (hospitality chair 1985-87). Roman Catholic. Avocations: theater, dance. Home: 13571 Hewes Ave Santa Ana CA 92705-2215 E-mail: gabriellex@pacbel.net.

FAZAKAS, ART HERSCHEL, writer, educator, editor; b. N.Y.C., Aug. 29, 1952; s. Arpard Albert Fazakas and Sylvia Vivian Siegel; m. Ruth Ann Cunningham, Nov. 7, 1992 (div. Jan. 20, 2000). BA in Math., CUNY, 1977. Sec. East Asia Nat. Coun. Chs., N.Y.C., 1997; tech. writer Eli Lilly & Co., Indpls., 1998; lead writer web content MSN Gaming Zone, Redmond, Wash., 1999; tech. editor Boeing Chem. Equipment, Auburn, Wash., 2000, Microsoft Windows, Redmond, 2000; self-employed home organizer Edmonds, Wash., 2002—. Writing instr. Indpls. Writers Ctr., Discover U, Seattle. Author: Microsoft spl. project Kasparov vs. the World; contbr. articles to mags. and websites. Vol. KCTS-TV Channel 9, Seattle, 2002—; fund raiser Seattle (Wash.) Symphony, 2003, Seattle (Wash.) Chamber Music Festival. Recipient Hon. mention for feature writing, Writers Digest mag., 1996, 1999. Mem.: Soc. for Tech. Comm., The Mountaineers, Hostelling Internat., Sierra Club. Democrat. Avocations: classical piano, hiking, bicycle touring, travel. Home: 103 13th Ave E # 30 Seattle WA 98102 E-mail: northwestart@yahoo.com.

FAZAL, SHEIKH, photographer; b. N.Y.C., 1965; BA, Princeton U., 1987. Exhibitions include Photographic Resource Ctr., Boston, 1994, Opsis Gallery, N.Y.C., 1994, PaceWildenstein MacGill, 1995, 1998, Schneider Gallery, Chgo., 1996, Internat. Ctr. Photography, N.Y.C., 1996, Diggs Gallery, Winston-Salem State U., 1997, Schneider Gallery, Chgo., 1998, Sprengel Mus., Hannover, Germany, 1998, others, Represented in permanent collections. Recipient Infinity award, Internat. Ctr. Photography, 1995, Ferguson award, Friends of Photography, 1995, Ruttenberg award, 1995, Mother Jones Internat. Documentary award, 1995, Leica Medal of Excellence, 1995; fellow Fulbright fellow in the arts, Kenya, 1992, Photography fellow, N.J. State Coun. on Arts, 1994, NEA, 1994. Office: Art in Context Ctr for Comm PO Box 336 New York NY 10276-0336 Fax: 212-759-8964.

FAZIO, EVELYN M. publisher; b. Hackensack, N.J. BA in History, U. Bridgeport, 1975; MA in History, U. Conn., 1977. Cert. social studies tchr., N.J. Tchr. social studies Cedar Grove (N.J.) High Sch., 1977-79; prodn. editor Prentice-Hall, Inc., Englewood Cliffs, N.J., 1980-82, devel. editor, 1982-83, acquisitions editor, 1983-85; sr. acquisitions editor P-H/Simon & Schuster, Inc., Englewood Cliffs, 1985-88; mng. editor Random House, Inc., N.Y.C., 1988—; exec. editor polit. sci., internat. rels. and policy studies Paragon House Pubs., Inc., N.Y.C., 1989-91; editorial dir. Marshall Cavendish Pubs., N. Bellmore, N.Y., 1992-95; v.p., pub. M.E. Sharpe, Armonk, N.Y., 1995-00; v.p. e-content acquisition Baher & Taylor, Bridgewater, NJ, 2001—03. Mem.: ALA (panelist Charleston conf. 2000, Open e-Book forum 2001).

FAZIO, PETER VICTOR, JR., lawyer; b. Chgo., Jan. 22, 1940; s. Peter Victor and Marie Rose (LaMantia) F.; m. Patti Ann Campbell, Jan. 3, 1966; children: Patti-Marie, Catherine, Peter. AB, Coll. of Holy Cross, Worcester, Mass., 1961; JD, U. Mich., 1964. Bar: Ill. 1964, U.S. Dist. Ct. (no. dist.) Ill. 1965, U.S. Ct. Appeals (7th cir.) 1972, U.S. Supreme Ct. 1977, D.C. 1981, U.S. Ct. Appeals (D.C. cir.) 1988, Ind. 1993. Assoc. Schiff, Hardin & Waite, Chgo., 1964-70, ptnr., 1970-82, 84-95, mng. ptnr., 1995—2000, chmn., 2001—; exec. v.p. Internat. Capital Equipment, Chgo., 1982-83, also bd. dirs., 1982-85, sec., 1982-87; exec. v.p., gen. counsel NiSource Inc., 2000—. Bd. dirs. Planmetrics Inc., Chgo., 1984-92, Chgo. Lawyers Commn. for Civil Rights Under Law, 1976-82, co-chmn., 1978-80; bd. dirs. Seton Health Corp. No. Ill., Chgo 1987-90, vice chmn., 1989-90. Trustee Barat Coll., Lake Forest, Ill., 1977-82; bd. dirs. St. Joseph Hosp., Chgo., 1990-95, mem. exec. adv. bd., 1984-89, chmn., 1986-89; vice chmn. bd. dirs. Cath. Health Ptnrs., 1995-99, chmn., 1999—; dir. exec. com. Ill. Coalition, 1994—, N.W. Ind. Forum, 1994-98. Mem. ABA (coun. 1991-94, chmn. sect. pub. utility, transp. and comm. law 2000-01), FBA, Ill. Bar Assn., Chgo. Bar Assn., Fed. Energy Bar Assn., Edison Electric Inst. (chmn. legal com. 1999-2001), Am. Gas Assn. (legal com.), Am. Soc. Corp. Secs., Met. Club, Econ. Club Chgo., Comml. Club Chgo. Office: Schiff Hardin & Waite 6600 Sears Tower 233 S Wacker Dr Chicago IL 60606-6473

FAZIO, SERGIO, medical educator, researcher; MD in Medicine summa cum laude, U. Rome, 1983; PhD in Molecular Biology, U. Siena, Italy, 1989. Intern and resident in internal medicine U. Rome, 1983—86; resident svc. of emergency medicine Gen. Hosp. Udine, Italy, 1984—85; fellow in metabolism dept. medicine Univ. Hosp. U. Rome, 1986—88; postdoctoral fellow Gladstone Inst. Cardiovasc. Disease, San Francisco, 1988—91, staff rsch. investigator, 1991—93; rsch. fellow Cardiovasc. Rsch. Inst. U. Calif., San Francisco, 1988—93; asst. prof. medicine and pathology, dir. lipid lab. Vanderbilt U., Nashville, 1993—, assoc. prof. medicine and pathology, co-dir. atherosclerosis rsch. unit. Ad hoc reviewer: Jour. Biol. Chemistry, Biochimica Biophysica Acta, Lipids, Arteriosclerosis and Thrombosis, Jour. of Lipid Rsch., Diabetes; contbr. articles to profl. jours. Recipient Pilot Project and Young Investigator award, CNRU, Established Investigatorship award, Am. Heart Assn., 1996, grant-in-aid, 1995, Joe C. Davies Found. scholarship. Fellow: Am. Heart Assn. (mem. coun. on arteriosclerosis); mem.: Am. Fedn. for Clin. Rsch. Office: Vanderbilt U Sch Medicine Divsn Cardioly 315 Mrb II 2220 Pierce Ave Nashville TN 37232-0001

FAZIO, VIC, former congressman; b. Winchester, Mass., Oct. 11, 1942; m. Judy Kern; children: Dana Fazio, Anne Fazio (dec.), Kevin Kern, Kristie Kern. BA, Union Coll., Schenectady, 1965; postgrad., Calif. State U., Sacramento. Journalist, founder Calif. Jour.; congl. and legis. cons., 1966-75; mem. Calif. State Assembly, 1975-78; mem. 96th -103rd Congresses from Calif. 3rd Dist., 1979-98; former chmn. Dem. Congl. Campaign Com.; chmn. Dem. caucus, house steering policy com.; mem. legis. br. appropriations subcom.; ranking mem. appropriations subcom. energy and water; mem. Ho. budget com. 97th-100th Congress; majority whip-at-large 96th-105th Congress; also co-chmn. Fed. Govt. Svcs. Task Force 96th-101st Congresses, former chmn. bipartisan com. on ethics; mem. approriations com. 105th Congress; sr. ptnr. Clark & Weinstock, Washington, 1999—. Former mem. Sacramento County Charter and Planning Commns. Bd. dirs. Asthma Allergy Found., Jr. Statesman, Nat. Italian-Am. Found. Coro Found. fellow; named Solar Congressman of Yr. Mem. Air Force Assn. Office: Clark & Weinstock Inc 52 Vanderbilt Ave New York NY 10017-3808

FAZZI, CHARLES, accounting educator; b. Phila., Sept. 10, 1948; s. Benjamin Carl and Connie (DiFranco) F.; m. Millicent Yvonne Andrews, May 15, 1976; children: Matthew, Stephen. BS, Pa. State U., 1970, MBA, 1974, PhD, 1983. Asst. prof. acctg. Ariz. State U., Tempe, 1977-79; bus. adminstrn. lectr. U. North Tex., Denton, 1979-82; asst. prof. acctg. Tex. Christian U., Ft. Worth, 1982-83; assoc. prof. acctg. Bucknell U., Lewisburg, Pa., 1983-88; Edgar T. Bitting prof. acctg. Elizabethtown (Pa.) Coll., 1988-92; prof., acad. dept. head Robert Morris Coll., Pitts., 1992—2002; prof., dir. grad. programs in acctg. St. Vincent Coll., Latrobe, Pa., 2002—. Vis. prof. acctg. Old Dominion U., Norfolk, Va., 1988; cons. Nat. Steel Corp., Inc., Pitts., 1988-90, Hercules, Inc., Wilmington, Del., 1984-90, Nat. Tax Seminars, Portland, Oreg., 1984-88; mem. acctg. adv. bd. McGraw-Hill, Inc., N.Y.C., 1992-93. Author: Study Guide for Financial Reporting and Analysis, 2002, Instructor's Manual for Advanced Accounting, 2003; co-author: Study Guide for Advanced Financial Accounting, 1986; contbr. articles to profl. jours. Recipient Dedication to Edn. award Beta Alpha Psi, 1981, Outstanding Grad. Asst. Tchr. award Pa. State U. Alumni Assn., 1975; fellow Deloitte & Touche, 1974, Book Industry Study Group, 1987. Mem. Am. Acctg. Assn. (various coms.), Inst. Mgmt. Accountants (nat. v.p. 1994-95). Avocations: golf, reading. Home: 1600 Whitney Court Dr 40 Latrobe PA 15650 Office: St Vincent Coll 300 Fraser Purchase Rd Latrobe PA 15650 E-mail: charles.fazzi@email.stvincent.edu.

FEAGLES, GERALD FRANKLIN, marketing executive; b. Kansas City, Kans., Dec. 8, 1934; s. George Joseph and Florence Ada (Johnson) F.; m. Eleanor Jean Holder, Aug. 31, 1957; 1 child, Gerald Franklin II. Student, Kansas City Jr. Coll., 1953-55. Mktg. and sales rep. Sears Roebuck and Co., Kansas City, 1963-70; br. mgr. SunarHauserman, Overland Park, Kans., 1970-86; mgr. bus. devel. govt. svcs. group The Austin Co., Kansas City, 1986-91; mgr. mktg.-indsl. divsn. Black & Veatch Architects & Engrs., Kansas City, 1991-93; mgr. ctrl. region Va. Metal Industries Inc., Orange, Va., 1994-96; mgr. bus. devel.-ctrl. region The Austin Co. Engrs. and Constructors, Kansas City, 1996—. Com. chmn. Boy Scouts of Am. Kansas City, 1973. Mem. Kansas City C. of C., Constrn. Specifications Inst., Prodrs. Coun., Internat. Facility Mgmt. Assn., Assoc. Gen. Contractors, Soc. Am. Mil. Engrs.

FEAGLES, ROBERT WEST, retired insurance company executive; b. Ft. Wayne, Ind., July 23, 1920; s. Ralph L. and Mary Anna (West) F.; m. Anita Marie MacRae, Sept. 15, 1951; children: Wendy Lee, Cuyler MacRae, Priscilla Jane, Patrick Emerson. BS, Ga. Inst. Tech., 1943, Am. Grad. Sch. of Internat. Mgmt., 1951; cert. of banking, Rutgers U. Grad. Sch. Banking, 1958. Sr. v.p. Citibank, N.A., N.Y.C., 1951-76, Travelers Ins. Co., Hartford, Conn., 1976-86; chmn., chief exec. officer Travelers Asset Mgmt. Internat. Corp., N.Y.C., 1979-87; vice chmn., chief exec. offcier The Conn. Ins. Co., Farmington, 1988-90. Bd. fellows Am. Grad. Sch. Internat. Mgmt., Glendale, Ariz., 1973—86; mem. adv. council Internat. Exec. Service Corps. Council, N.Y.C., 1970—86; chmn. Hartford Area Manpower Planning Coun., 1978-79, Hartford Area Pvt. Industry Coun., 1979-83, State job Tng. Coordinating Coun., Hartford, 1983-88. Served to capt. U.S. Army, 1943-47. Recipient Jonas Mayer award Am. Grad. Sch. Internat. Mgmt., 1978 Mem. Pers. Round Table (emeritus), Univ. Club (N.Y.C.), Royal Automobile Club (London), Fishers Island Club, Bent Pine Golf Club. Republican. Presbyterian. Home: 635 Riomar Dr Vero Beach FL 32963-2012 E-mail: rfeagles@cs.com.

FEAGLEY, MICHAEL ROWE, lawyer; b. Exeter, N.H., Feb. 1, 1945; s. Walter Charles and Laura (Rowe) F. BA, Wesleyan U., 1967; JD, Harvard U., 1973. Bar: Mass., Ill., U.S. Dist. Ct. (no. dist.) Ill., U.S. Dist. Ct. (ctrl. dist.) Ill., U.S. Ct. Appeals (6th, 7th, 8th and 10th cirs.), U.S. Supreme Ct. Assoc. Mayer, Brown, & Platt, Chgo., 1973-79; ptnr. Mayer, Brown, Rowe & Maw, Chgo., 1980—. Instr. Nat. Inst. Trial Advocacy, Chgo., 1977--, John Marshall Law Sch., Chgo., 1980-85. Served to 1st lt. U.S. Army, 1968-71, Vietnam. Fellow Am. Coll. Trial Lawyers; mem. ABA, Chgo. Coun. Lawyers, Chgo. Bar Assn., Union League Club (Chgo.). Office: Mayer Brown Rowe & Maw 190 S La Salle St Ste 3100 Chicago IL 60603-3441

FEAR, JUDITH A. music educator, director; b. Wichita, Kans., Oct. 2, 1938; d. William O. and Rachel V. Bannon; m. Larry C. Fear, July 1, 1960; children: Amy Fear Bishop, John Todd. BME, Wichita State U., 1960, MM, 1967. Tchr. vocal music South Haven Schs., Kans., 1960—62; tchr. English and Social Studies Ark. City Schs., Kans., 1962—65; tchr. vocal music Wichita H.S. West, Kans., 1965—66; grad. tchg. asst. Wichita State U., 1966—68, instr. piano dept., 1968—; instr. Bethel Coll., North Newton, Kans., 1981—89; dir. Coll. Fine Arts Inst., Wichita State U., 2000—. Mem.: Wichita Area Piano Tchrs. League (various offices), Nat. Guild Comty. Schs. of the Arts, Music Tchrs. Nat. Assn., Kans. Music Tchrs. Assn. (bd. dirs. 1980—90, editor KMTA sect. 1980—90). Office: Wichita State Univ 1845 Fairmount Wichita KS 67260-0071 Office Fax: 316-978-3951. E-mail: judith.fear@wichita.edu.

FEARING, WILLIAM KELLY, art educator, artist; b. Fordyce, Ark., Oct. 18, 1918; s. George David and Frankie (Kelly) F. BA, La. Tech. U., 1941; MA, Columbia U., 1950. Classroom tchr. Windfield Pub. Schs., La., La., 1942-43; prodn. illustrator Consolidated Vultee Aircraft, Fort Worth, 1943-45; prof. art Tex. Wesleyan Coll., Fort Worth, 1945-47, U. Tex., Austin, 1947-87, Ashbel Smith prof., 1983—, Ashbel Smith prof. emeritus 1987—. Author: (with C.I. Martin and E. Beard) Our Expanding Vision, 1960, The Creative Eye, 1969, 2d edit., 1979, (with E. Beard, N. Krevitsky, C.I. Martin) Art and the Creative Teacher, 1971, (with E.L. Mayton, B. Francis, E. Beard) Helping Children See Art and Make Art, 1982, (with E.L. Mayton and R. Brooks) The Way or Art Inner Vision Outer Expression, 1986; guest editor Tex. Quar., Creativity and the Human Spirit, vol. XVI, 1978; one man shows include El Paso Mus. Art, Esther Bear Gallery, Santa Barbara, 1964, Gallery Visual Arts, La. Tech. U., Ruston, 1966, U. Tex. Art Mus., Austin, 1967, Ft. Worth Art Ctr., 1969, Witte Meml. Mus., San Antonio, 1969, U. Tex. Art Mus., Austin, 1974, Mary Moore Gallery, LaJolla, 1975, Mary Moffett Gallery, La. Tech. U., 1976, DuBose Gallery, Houston, 1977, L and L Gallery, Longview, 1975, 78, Retrospective Spencer Gallery, Fine Arts Ctr., U. Ark.-Monticello, 1981, Mary Moffett Gallery, Sch. Art and Arch., La. Tech. U., 1981, Old Jail Art Ctr., Albany, Tex., 1985, Marion Koogler McNay Art Mus., San Antonio, 1986, Valley House Gallery, Dallas, 1992, 96, Robinson Galleries, Houston, 1995, Flatbed Press and Gallery, Austin, 1995, 97, Pascal/Robinson Galleries, Houston, 1999, U. Tex., Austin, 2002, Creative Rsch. Labs., 2002, Flatbed Internat. Press Galleries, Austin, 2002; exhibited in group shows at Carnegie Inst., Pitts., 1955, 56, 57, Pa. Acad. Art, Phila., 1954-56, Mus. Fine Arts, Houston, 1956-57, Dallas Mus. Fine Art, 1956-57, Munson-Williams-Proctor Inst., Utica, 1956-57, Edwin Hewitt Gallery, N.Y.C., 1957, Dallas Mus. Fine Art, 1958, Am. Fedn. Art, 1958, Mus. Fine Art of Little Rock, 1961, Colorado Springs Art Ctr., 1961, 63, Philbrook Art Ctr., Tulsa, 1963, Fort Worth Art Ctr., 1963, U. Ill., Urbana, 1955, 59, 63, Denver Art Mus., 1963, U. Ariz. and Ark Art Ctr., 1964-65, N.Y. World's Fair, Tex. Pavillion, 1964, Tex. Pavillion Hemistair, San Antonio, 1968, Tex. Tech U. Mus. Art, Lubbock, 1978, U. Tex.-Austin, 1979, Art Gallery Sch. Art and Architecture, La. Tech. U. Ruston, 1984, Jack S. Blanton Mus. Art (formerly Archer M. Huntington Art Gallery), U. Tex.-Austin, 1963-82, 83-91, 92-98, 99, 2000, 2001, Longview Mus. and Arts Ctr., Tex., 1962, 63, 75, 85, 90, 91, Amarillo Art Ctr., Tex., 1988, Dallas Mus. Fine Arts, 1991, Robinson Gelleries, Houston, 1993, 94, 96, 97, 98, 99, Valley House gallery, Dallas, 1994-99, 2001, Flatbed Press and Gallery, Austin, 1996, 97, 98, 99, 2000, 2001, Ga. Art Mus., U. Ga., Athens, 1997, Marion Koogler McNay Art Mus., San Antonio, 1997, 98, 99, 2000, 2001, Mus. of Big Bend, Sul Ross State U., Alpine, Tex., 1998, Nancy Wilson Scanlon Gallery, Helms Fine Art Ctr., Austin, 1999, Austin Mus. Art, 2000, Pascal Robinson Galleries, 2000, 2001, McKinney Contemporary Art Ctr., Dallas, 2000, Tex. Roots: Arlington Mus. Art, 2000, Ctr. for Visual Arts, Denton, Tex., 2000, Old Jail Art Ctr., Albany, Tex., 2001, San Angelo Art Mus., Tex., 2002, San Angelo (Tex.) Mus. Fine Art, 2002. Mem. Nat. Soc. Lit., and Arts, Austin Mus. of Art, Tex. Fine Arts Assn., Tex. Art Edn. Assn., Phi Kappa Phi. Home: 914 Calithea Rd Austin TX 78746-2716

FEARN, HEIDI, physicist, educator; b. Sutton-in-Ashfield, Eng., Aug. 21, 1965; came to U.S., 1989; d. Lawrence Leonard and Erika Hanna Elfrede (Kröger) F. BS in Theol. Physics with honors, Essex U., Colchester, Eng., 1986, PhD in Theol. Quantum Optics, 1989. Grad. lab. demonstrator Essex U., 1986-89; postdoctoral rsch. asst. Max Planck Inst. Quantum Optics, Garching, Germany, 1989; rsch. assoc. U. N.Mex., Albuquerque, 1989-91; lectr. physics Calif. State U., Fullerton, 1991-92, asst. prof. physics, 1992-95, assoc. prof. physics, 1995-97, prof. physics, 1997—. Vis. scholar U. Ariz., Tucson, 1989-91; cons. Los Alamos (N.Mex.) Nat. Lab., 1994—. Kavli Inst. Theoretical Physics scholar, 2003—. Mem. AAAS, Am. Phys. Soc. Office: Calif State U Physics Dept 800 N State College Blvd Fullerton CA 92831-3547

FEARN, ROBERT MORCOM, economics and business educator, consultant; b. Paterson, N.J., Oct. 10, 1928; s. William and Violet Emily (Bray) Fearn; m. Priscilla Anne Southard, Sept. 15, 1951; children: Diane C. Fearn Derosiers, Deborah A. Sears, Priscilla L. Fearn Graham, Robert W. AA, Boston U., 1950; BS in Commerce, Ohio U., 1952; MA in Econs., Wash. State U., 1955; PhD in Econs., U. Chgo., 1968. Intelligence officer CIA, Washington, 1954—63; from asst. to prof. econs. and bus. N.C. State U., Raleigh, 1965—96, dir. grad. programs econs., 1993—96, prof. emeritus, 1996—. Mem. athletics coun. N.C. State U., 1986—89; vis. prof. Duke U., Durham, NC, 1982, Sch. Econs. and Bus., Athens, 1986—87, Liaoning U., 1991; expert witness NLRB, Winston-Salem, NC, 1981—83; cons. Rsch. Triangle Inst., Research Triangle Park, NC, 1968—75; mem. Pres.'s Commn. Income Maintenance, Washington, 1970; mem. techno-econ. rsch. Group on mideast labor problems1997, 96; sigma one Ghanaian labor code rev., 99; mem. econ. study and ad hoc wage bd. City of Raleigh, 1974; others; mem. edil. video team on Kyrgyzstan, 99. Contbr. articles to profl. jours. Pres., v.p., bd. dirs. West Raleigh Civic Assn., 1968—72; vice chmn. Free Alliance for Improvement of Raleigh, 1968—71; scoutmaster, asst. scoutmaster, committeeman Occoneechee coun. Boy Scouts Am., Raleigh, 1970—80. Served U.S. Army, 1946—48. Mem.: Assn. Comparative Econ. Studies, Indsl. Rels. Rsch. Assn., So. Econ. Assn. (mem. bd. editors 1975—77), Am. Econ. Assn., Acad. Outstanding Tchrs., N.C. Faculty Senate (chmn. 1984—85, vice chmn. 1983—84), Raleigh Area Masters Swimming, U. Chgo. Club of N.C. (sec. 1982—83, 1983—84, bd. dirs. 1981—84), Alpha Kappa Lambda, Beta Gamma Sigma, Phi Kappa Phi (pres. 1992—93). Democrat. Unitarian-Universalist. Avocations: swimming, long distance backpacking, camping, sailing, photography. Home: 1032 High Lake Ct Raleigh NC 27606-8064 Office: NC State U Dept Econs PO Box 8110 Raleigh NC 27695-0001 Personal E-mail: BOBFearn@aol.com. Business E-Mail: Bob_Fearn@ncsu.edu.

FEARON, LEE CHARLES, chemist; b. Tulsa, Nov. 22, 1938; s. Robert Earl and Ruth Belle (Strothers) F.; m. Wanda Sue Williams, Nov. 30, 1971 (div. June 1998); m. Shirlene Olsen, Dec. 9, 2000. Student, Rensselaer Polytech. Inst., 1957-59; BS in Physics, Okla. State U., Stillwater, 1961, BA in Chemistry, 1962, MS in Analytical Chemistry, 1969. Rsch. chemist Houston process lab. Shell Oil Co., Deer Park, Tex., 1968-70; chief chemist Pollution Engrng. Internat., Inc., Houston, 1970-76; rsch. chemist M-I Drilling Fluids Co., Houston, 1976-83; cons. chemist Profl. Engr. Assocs., Inc., Tulsa, 1983-84; chemist Anacon, Inc., Houston, 1984-85; scientist III Bionetics Corp., Rockville, Md., 1985-86; sr. chemist L.A. County Sanitation Dist., Whittier, Calif., 1986; chemist Severn Trent Labs., West Sacramento, Calif., 1986-87; cons. chemist Branham Industries, Inc., Conroe, Tex., 1987-89; chemist 4, Lab

Accreditation sect. EAP, Wash. State Dept. Ecology, Manchester, 1989—. Cons. chemist Terra-Kleen, Okmulgee, Okla., 1988—94, Excel Pacific, Inc. & Precision Works, Inc., Camarillo, Calif., 1993—96, 2002—, Precision Works, Inc., 2002—. Patentee for environ. soil remediation tech., 1994. With U.S. Army, 1962—65. Fellow: Am. Inst. Chemists; mem.: AAAS, Am. Chem. Soc. Avocations: photography, travel. Home: PO Box 514 Manchester WA 98353-0514 Office: PO Box 488 Manchester WA 98353-0488 E-mail: limafox@charter.net., lfea461@ecy.wa.gov.

FEARRINGTON, ANN PEYTON, writer, illustrator, newspaper reporter, portraitist; b. Winston-Salem, N.C., Aug. 25, 1945; d. James Cornelius Pass Fearrington and Florence Moore (McCanless-Fearrington) Blackwood; m. Hege Hill Russ, Sept. 1967 (div. 1984); children: James Pass Fearrington Russ, Joseph Peyton Fearrington Russ; m. Vance Edwin Cox, Jr., June 17, 1985; 1 stepson, Charles Jonathan Cox. BA in Secondary Edn. and English, U. N.C., 1967; MS in Life Scis., Botany & Horticulture, N.C. State U., 1972. Mid. sch. tchr. Wake County Sch. Sys., Raleigh, 1967-71; landscape designer pvt. practice N.Y.C., Winston-Salem, N.C., 1972-83; corr. Raleigh News & Observer, 1993—. Writer/artist-in-residence Raleigh-Wake County Pub. Schs., 1997-2000. Author, illustrator: Christmas Lights, 1996, Little Green Book-18 Keys to Your Child's Reading Success, 1998 (Southeastern Newspaper Assn. Literacy award 1999), Teacher and Librarian Guide for the Little Green Book, 2000, Pequeño Libro Verde, 2000, Who Sees the Lighthouse?, 2002. Sch. libr. vol. Wake County Sch. Sys., Raleigh, 1985—; Sunday Sch. tchr. Highland United Meth. Ch., Raleigh, 1986-90. Recipient Literacy award, Southeastern Newspaper Assn., 1999. Mem.: N.C. Reading Assn. (James B. Hunt Literacy award 2001), Internat. Reading Assn., Soc. Children's Book Writers and Illustrators, Beatrix Potter Soc., N.C. State Univ. Club. Avocations: gardening, reading, sketching.

FEARS, JESSE RUFUS, historian, educator, academic dean; b. Atlanta, Ga., Mar. 7, 1945; s. Emory Binford Fears; m. Charlene Louise Bauer, July 9, 1966; children: Laura Elizabeth, Jesse Rufus IV. BA summa cum laude, Emory U., 1966; MA, Harvard U., 1967, PhD, 1971. Asst. prof. classical langs. Tulane U., New Orleans, 1971-72; asst. prof. history Indiana U., Bloomington, 1972-75, assoc. prof. history, 1975-80, prof. history, 1980-86; prof., chair classical studies Boston U., 1986-90, assoc. dean Coll. Liberal Arts, 1987-89, dir. humanities found., 1988-90; dean Coll. Arts and Scis. U. Okla., Norman, 1990-92, prof. Classics, 1990—, G.T. and Libby Blankenship prof. history of liberty, 1992—, dir. Ctr. for History of Liberty, 1992—; adj. scholar Okla. Coun. Pub. Affairs, 1996—. Adj. scholar Okla. Coun. Pub. Affairs, 1996—. Author: Princeps A Diis Electus, 1977, (monographs) The Cult of Jupiter, 1981, The Theology of Victory, 1981, The Cult of Virtues, 1981; books on audio and video tape: A History of Freedom, 2001, Famous Greeks, 2001, Famous Romans, 2001, The Life and Times of Winston Churchill, 2001; editor: (3 vols.) Selected Writings/Lord Acton, 1985-88; contbr. chpts. to books, numerous articles to profl. jours. Bd. dirs. Okla. Sch. Sci./Math., Oklahoma City, 1990—; pres. Vergilian Soc., 2002—. Recipient Judah P. Benjamin award, Military Order of Stars and Bars, 1996; Danforth fellow Danforth Found., 1966-71; fellow Am. Acad. in Rome, 1969-71, Guggenheim Found., 1976-77, Howard Found., 1977-78, Alexander Von Humboldt, 1977-78, 80-81, Ctr. for History of Freedom, Wash. U., 1989-90; grantee Am. Philos. Soc., 1972, 79, NEH, 1974, Am. Coun. Learned Soc., 1979, Woodrow Wilson, 1983, Kerr Found., 1994, 99, 2003, Zarrow Found., 2000, 2001, 2002; Sigma Chi Scholar in Residence, Miami U., 2003. Mem. AAUP, Am. Philol. Assn., Classical Assn. Middle West and South, Archaeol. Inst. of Am., Phi Beta Kappa, Golden Key Nat. Honor Soc. Office: U Okla Dept Classics Ctr History of Liberty Kaufman Hall Norman OK 73019 E-mail: jrfears@ou.edu.

FEATHERMAN, BERNARD, steel company executive; b. May 3, 1929; m. Sandra Green; children: Andrew C., John James. BS, Temple U., 1951; postgrad., Grad. Bus. Sch., 1951-52, Law Sch., 1952-54, Wharton Sch., U. Pa., 1965-66. Chmn. bd. dirs. Western Metal Bed Co., Phila., 1978-86; with CIATEQ USA, Inc., 1995-98; dir. Pa. Steel and Aluminum Corp. (now Pa. Steel Corp.), Bensalem, Pa., 1972—, Wardwell Retirement Complex, Saco, Maine, 1998—, Counselling Svcs., Inc., Saco, 1998-2000, Newsletter Pub. Co., Phila. Contbr. articles to profl. jours.; inventor electronics locking locker. Mem. exec. bd. Southeast chpt. Nat. Found. March of Dimes, 1969-82, vice-chmn., 1978-80; pres. Phila. Assn. for Retarded Citizens, 1975-77, trustee, 1983-96; trustee Phila. Devel. Disabilities Corp., 1991-96, Equity 591 F8AM, 1990-92; chmn. Mayor's Adv. Com. on Mental Health-Mental Retardation, Phila., 1979-92, bd. dirs. 1993; mem. tax policy and budget rev. com. City of Phila., fiscal adv. com., 1990; bd. dirs. Costar, Inc., 1989-92; co-chmn. Mayor's Sml. Bus. Adv. Com., Phila., 1979-92, mem., 1979-95; del. White House Conf. on Sml. Bus., 1980, Pa. del., 1995, vice-chmn., 1986; chmn. sml. bus. coun. Dem. Nat. Com., 1982-84; fin. chmn. Pa. Dem. Orgn., 1985-86; mem. adv. bd. Coll. Liberal Arts and Scis., Temple U., 1982-91, chmn. incubator program, 1989-91, chmn. Entrepreneurial Inst., 1990; co-dir. Entrepreneurial Inst. U. New Eng., 1996-98; adv. bd. West Chester (Pa.) State U. Bus. Sch., 1986-87, Frankford Hosp., 1983—; steering com. entrepreneurial forum Drexel U. Bus. Sch., 1988-91; chmn. 3d Congl. Sml. Bus. Coun., Phila., 1984-88; bd. dirs. Phila. Citywide Devel. Corp., 1984-96; bd. dirs. Phila. Loan Fund, Inc., 1987-88, ARC, York County, Sanford, Maine. Recipient award of appreciation Sml. Bus. Coun., Dem. Nat. Com., 1983; Gold medal of Honor Adult Trainees Found., Phila., 1976; citation White House Conf. on Sml. Bus., 1980; named Entrepreneur of Yr. Mid Atlantic Region Supporter of Entrepreneurship, 1990, Ea. Pa. Sml. Bus. Adv. of Yr. SBA, 1991. Mem. Assn. of Steel Distbrs. (nat. pres. 1975-76, 86-87, named Steel Distbr. of Yr. 1976), Inst. Am. Entrepreneurs (life), Shelving Mfrs. Assn. (nat. chmn. 1977-78), Pa. Soc., Assn. Steel Distbrs. (nat. pres. 1975-76, 86-87, Hunting Park-Germantown Bus. Assn. (pres. 1986-96), Biddeford/Saco C. of C. (bd. dirs. 2002-), Rotary, Masons (trustee), B'nai Brith (pres. 1980-82, Nat. Youth Svcs. award Quaker City lodge 1985). Home: PO Box 428A Kennebunkport ME 04046-1728

FEATHERMAN, SANDRA, university president, political science educator; b. Phila., Apr. 14, 1934; d. Albert N. and Rebe (Burd) Green; m. Bernard Featherman, Mar. 29, 1958; children: Andrew Charles, John James. BA, U. Pa., 1955, MA, PhD, U. Pa., 1978. Asst. prof. dept. polit. sci. Temple U., Phila., 1978-84, assoc. prof., 1984-91, asst. to pres., 1986-89, pres. faculty senate, 1985-86, dir. Ctr. Pub. Policy, 1986-91; vice chancellor acad. adminstrn., prof. polit. sci. U. Minn., Duluth, 1991-95; pres. U. New Eng., Biddeford, Maine, 1995—. Commr. New Eng. Assn. Schs. and Coll. Higher Edn. Commn., 2002—. Author: Jews, Black and Ethnics, 1979, Race and Politics at the Millenium, 2000; contbr. articles to profl. jours. Pres. Pa. Fedn. C.C., Girls Inc., nat. bd., 1971—74; sec. Maine Women's Forum, 2002—03; active Maine Compact for Higher Edn., 2003—; bd. dirs. Citizens Com. Pub. Edn. Phila., 1977—89, pres., 1979—81; trustee C.C. Phila., 1970—92, chmn. bd. trustees, 1984—86; life trustee, v.p. Samuel Fels Found., 1978—; bd. dirs. United Way SE Pa., 1977—89, United Way Pa., 1981—84, U. New Eng., Gulf of Maine Aquarium; nat. bd. dirs. Women and Founds.-Corp. Philanthropy, 1986—91; bd. dirs. Kennebec Girl Scout Coun., Va. Gildeslove Internat. Fund., 2003—, Vis. Nurse Assn., 2002—. Recipient Brooks Graves award, Pa. Polit. Sci. Assn., 1982, Cmty. Svc. award, City of Phila., 1984, Women's Achievement award, YWCA, 1989, Adminstr. of Yr. award, Minn. Women in Higher Edn., 1994, Champion of Econ. Growth award, Maine Devel. Found., 2002. Mem.: Am. Coun. Edn. (commn. on minorities in higher edn. 2001), Maine Ind. Colls. Assn. (pres. 1998 1998—2000), Greater Portland Alliance Colls. and Univs. (pres. 1997—98), Nat. Assn. Ind. Colls & Univs. (com. policy analysis & pub. rels. 2001—), Am. Polit. Sci. Assn., Maine Ind. Colls. Assn., AAUW (bd. dirs. Phila. chpt. 1975-78 1975—78, bd. dirs. Phila. chpt. 1980—91, pres. 1984—86, nat. chair internat. fellowships panel 1987—91, nat bd. dirs. 1993—, Outstanding Woman award 1986). Office: U New Eng Hills Beach Rd Biddeford ME 04005-9526

FEATHERS, GAIL M. WRATNY, social worker; b. Gowanda, NY, Nov. 19, 1958; d. Frank John and Elinor Louise (Miller) Wratny; m. Donald James Feathers, May 24, 1980; children: Ryan James, David John, Rachel Marie. BA in English, SUNY, Geneseo, 1982; MSW, Syracuse U., 1992. Cert. social worker. Staff U. Rochester (N.Y.) Med. Ctr., 1992; social worker cmty. of caring program Cath. Family Ctr., Rochester, 1993-95, Cath. Charities of Livingston County, Mt. Morris, N.Y., 1995-97; dir. social work Nicholas H. Noyes Meml. Hosp., Dansville, N.Y., 1997—. Social svcs. adv. com. Livingston County Dept. Social Svcs., Mt. Morris, 1993—, chair, 2000—01; social worker early intervention program Livingston County Dept. Health, 1996—2000; mem. Livingston County Teen Pregnancy Prevention Task Force, Mt. Morris, 1993—99, Livingston County Cmty. Resource Network, Mt. Morris, 1993—, chair, 1994—98; family and consumer edn. com. Cornell Coop. Ext., 1999—2002, bd. dirs.; mem. Wayland Cmty. Chest, 1997—2003, sec., 2001—03. Mem. Livingston-Wyoming Assn. Retarded Citizens, 1986—96, bd. dirs., 1987—96, chairperson advocacy com., 1988—92, children's svcs. com., 1988—91; organizer, mem. parents panel on children who have disabilities SUNY Geneseo and Livingston-Wyoming-Steuben Bd. Coop. Ednl. Svcs., 1988—94; mem. adv. coun. N.Y. State Senate Select Com. for the Disabled, NY, 1990—92; mem. Rochester Sch. Deaf Task Force, 1996; mem. deaf awareness panel SUNY Geneseo and Nat. Tech. Inst. for the Deaf, 1998—99. Mem.: NASW. Avocations: golf, reading. E-mail: gfeathers@noyes-hospital.org., rdfthr3307@aol.com.

FEATHERSTONAUGH, HENRY GORDON, psychologist, health facility administrator; b. Nov. 11, 1917; s. Henry Stuart and Evelyn (Borrow) Featherstonaugh; m. Nancy Ellen Couper, July 28, 1946 (div.), children: Wendy, Rusby. BS, U. Calif., Berkeley, 1939; MS, Lehigh U., 1974; PhD, U. Mo., 1978. Diplomate Am. Bd. Sexology. Chemist H. J. Heinz Co., Berkeley, Calif., 1938—40; dist. mgr. Union Carbide Corp., N.Y.C., 1945—73; geriatric svcs. coord. Ctr. Mental Health, Anderson, Ind., 1979—82; co-founder, pres. Living Skills Inst., Inc., Indpls., 1982—. Health svc. provider Nat. Register Health Svc. Providers Psychology, Ind. State Bd. Examiners Psychology; lectr. in field. Contbr. articles to profl. jours. Exec. bd. Madison County Coun. on Aging, 1979—. Served with U.S. Army, 1941—43 USAAF, 1943—45, ATO, CBI. Decorated Air medal with oak leaf cluster D.F.C.; tchg. asst. and tuition grantee, Lehigh U., 1972—73, rsch. grantee, U. Mo., 1974—78. Mem.: APA, Ind. Counselors Assn. on Alcohol and Drug Abuse, Phi Kappa Phi, Psi Chi. Office: 8204 Westfield Blvd Indianapolis IN 46240-2366

FEATHERSTONE, ALLEN MERRIL, economics educator; b. Elkhorn, Wis., Feb. 4, 1960; s. Marshall Paul and Marie Elizabeth F.; m. Lila Helen Nilson, Oct. 9, 1961; children: Andrew, Sarah, Nathan, Rachel. BS, U. Wis., River Falls, 1982; MS, Purdue U., 1984, PhD, 1986. Prof. agrl. econs. Kans. State U., Manhattan, 1986—. Grad. program dir. Dept. Agrl. Econ., Manhattan, 1992—; external evaluation panel BASIS Collaborative Rsch. Support Program, 1999—. Assoc. editor Am. Jour. Agrl. Econ., 1995-97; mem. editl. bd. Choices, 1990-92. Mem. Am. Agrl. Econ. Assn. (Oustanding Grad. Tchg. award 2002), Am. Fin. Assn., Western Agrl. Econs. Assn., So. Agrl. Econs. Assn. Republican. Baptist. Home: 4402 Harbour View Rd Manhattan KS 66503-9021 Office: Dept Agrl Econs 313 Waters Hall Manhattan KS 66506 4011 Fax: 785-532-6925. E-mail: afeather@ksu.edu.

FEAVEARYEAR, JOHN EDGAR, aerospace systems engineer; b. London, Dec. 28, 1933; arrived in arrived in U.S., 1959; s. Albert Edgar and Ruby Louisa (Castleton) Feavearyear; m. Kate Elizabeth Pert, July 27, 1957 (div. Aug. 2000); children: Sara, Susan, Simon, David; m. K. Faye Rafferty, Sept. 15, 2001. MA, Trinity Coll., Cambridge, Eng., 1958; BA, 1956. Engr. IBM, 1965-72; project mgr., 1972-82; functional mgr., 1982-91; engring. dir., 1991-94; project dir., 1994-96; tech. dir. Lockheed Martin Fed. Sys., Owego, NY, 1996-2000; dir. advanced programs aerospace sys. Lockheed Martin Integration Sys., Owego, NY, 2000, ret., 2003. Mem. tech. bd. Soc. Brit. Aerospace Cos., London, 1995—99 Mem.: IEEE (sr.). Republican. Unitarian Universalist. Home: 12 King Point Cir S Owego NY 13827-1146 Office: Lockheed Martin Int Sys 1801 State Rte MC Owego NY 13827-0041

FEAVER, GEORGE ARTHUR, political science educator; b. Hamilton, Ont., Canada, May 12, 1937; came to U.S., July 4, 1967; s. Harold Lorne and Doris Davies (Senior) F.; m. Nancy Alice Poynter, June 12, 1963 (div. 1978); m. Ruth Helene Tubbesing, Mar. 8, 1986 (div. 1991); children: Catherine Fergusson, Noah George, Anthea Jane, Elysia Beatta. BA with Honors, U. B.C., 1959; PhD, London Sch. of Econs., 1962. Asst. prof. Mt. Holyoke Coll., South Hadley, Mass., 1962-65; lectr., research assoc. London Sch. Econs. and Univ. Coll., London, 1965-67; assoc. prof. Georgetown U., Washington, 1967-68, Emory U., Atlanta, 1968-71, U.B.C., Vancouver, B.C., Canada, 1971-74, prof., 1974—2002, prof. emeritus, 2002—. Vis. fellow Australian Nat. U., Canberra, 1987, London Sch. of Econ., 1991-92. Author: From Status to Contract, 1969; editor: Beatrice Webb's Our Partnership, 1975; editor: The Webbs in Asia: The 1911-12 Travel Diary, 1992; co-editor: Lives, Liberties and the Public Good, 1987; contbr. articles to profl. jours., books. Fellow Canada Council, 1970-71, 74-75, Am. Council Learned Socs., 1974-75, Social Scis. and Humanities Research Council of Canada, 1981-82, 86-91. Mem. Can. Polit. Sci. Assn., Am. Polit. Sci. Assn., Am. Soc. for Polit. and Legal Philosophy, Conf. for Study of Polit. Thought, Inst. Internat. de philosophie politique, Travellers Club (London). Avocations: rambling, wine appreciation. Home: 4776 W 7th Ave Vancouver BC Canada V6T 1C6 Office: Univ British Columbia Dept Polit Sci Vancouver BC Canada V6T 1Z1 E-mail: feaver@interchange.ubc.ca.

FEAVER, PETER DOUGLAS, political science educator, consultant, defense analyst; b. Fountain Hill, Pa., Dec. 17, 1961; s. Douglas David and Margaret Ruth (Seaman) F.; m. Karen Michelle Geers, Aug. 11, 1990. BA in Polit. Sci., Lehigh U., 1983; MA in Polit. Sci., Harvard U., 1986, PhD in Polit. Sci., 1990. Tchg. fellow Harvard U., Cambridge, Mass., 1985-90, pre post doctoral fellow, 1985-90; post doctoral rsch. fellow Mershon Ctr., Ohio State U., Columbus, 1990-91; asst. prof. polit. sci. Duke U., Durham, NC, 1991—98, assoc. prof., 1998—2003, prof., 2003—; cons. Inst. for Def. Analysis, Alexandria, Va., 1985—98; dir. for def., policy and arms control Nat. Security Coun. Staff, White House, Washington, 1993-94. Freelance writer L.A. Times, Washington Post, Wall St. Jour., Weekly Std., 1990—; spkr. in field. Author: Guarding the Guardians, 1992, Armed Servants, 2003; co-author: Assuring Control of Nuclear Weapons, 1987, Choosing Your Battles, 2003; co-editor: Battlefield Nuclear Weapons, 1988, Soldiers and Civilians, 2001; assoc. editor Armed Forces and Society, mem. editl. bd. Security Studies. Recipient Disting. Tchg. award, Trinity Coll., 1994—95, Disting. Undergrad. Tchg. award, Duke U. Alumni Assn., 2001. Mem.: Inter Univ. Seminar on Armed Forces and Soc., Internat. Studies Assn., Am. Polit. Sci. Assn., Phi Beta Kappa. Evangelical. Avocations: golf, squash, basketball, swimming, choral music. Office: Duke U Dept Polit Sci Durham NC 27708

FEAZELL, JOHNNY RAY, physicians assistant; b. Springfield, Mo., July 18, 1945; s. Raymond Maurice and Rosemary (Bunting) F.; m. Jeannie Feazell, July 30, 1966; children: Johnna, Jonathan. BS in Criminal Justice, Drury Coll., 1980. Police officer Springfield Mo. Police Dept., 1969-72; physician's asst. Bur. of Prison's, Springfield, 1972-99, ret., 1999; at risk sch. tchr. Hurley (Mo.) R-1 Sch. Dist., 1999—. Pres. Parkview Legion Baseball, Springfield, 1990-94, Springfield Cath. Baseball Assn., 1995-2000; coach varsity baseball, Hurley, Mo., 1997, jr. high sch. basketball, Hurley, 1998; alternative sch. coord., GED instr. Hurley Sch., 1999—, athletic dir., 2002—. Home: 1002 W Portland St Springfield MO 65807-1946 Office: Hurley R-1 Sch Dist PO Box 248 Hurley MO 65675-0248

FEAZELL, THOMAS LEE, lawyer, business executive; b. Mount Hope, W.Va., Feb. 25, 1937; s. Thomas Lee and Drema Lyal (Walker) F.; m. Virginia Scott, Feb. 3, 1961; children— Ann Lindsay, Thomas Lee, Robert Kent Student, W.Va. U., 1954-56; BBA, Marshall U., 1959; LLB, Washington and Lee U., 1962. Bar: W.Va. 1962, Ky. 1965. Atty. Ashland Oil, Inc., Ky., 1965-74, sr. atty., 1975-76, gen. atty., 1976-78, asst. gen. counsel, 1978-79, assoc. gen. counsel, 1979-80, v.p., 1980, v.p., gen. counsel, 1981—, adminstrv. v.p., 1988-92, sr. v.p., gen. counsel, sec., 1992-99; ret., 1999; legal cons., 1999—. Bd. dirs. Arch Coal, Inc., Nat. City Bank of Ashland. Bd. dirs. Marshall U. Found., Inc., Huntington, W. Va., 1984—, The Yegar Scholars Bd., Marshall U., 1999—, The Conf. Bd.-Coun. Chief Legal Officers. Mem. ABA, W.Va. Bar Assn., Ky. Bar Assn., Maritime Bar assn., Assn. Trial Lawyers Am., Am. Corp. Counsel Assn. (API gen. com. on law), U.S. C. of C. (legal affairs coun.), Am. Soc. of Corp. Secs., Bellefonte Country Club. Democrat. Presbyterian.

FEAZELL, VIC, lawyer; b. Monroe, La., June 8, 1951; 1 child, Gregory Victor. BA, Mary Hardin Baylor Coll., 1972; JD, Baylor U., 1979. Bar: Tex. 1979, U.S. Dist. Ct. (5th cir.) 1988, U.S. Dist. Ct. (no. dist) 1988, U.S. Dist. Ct. (so. dist), 1989. Dir. drug abuse treatment program Mental Health-Mental Retardation, Waco, Tex., 1975-79; pvt. practice Waco, 1979-82; dist. atty. McLennan County, Tex., 1983-88; pvt. practice Austin, Tex., 1989-94; of counsel Rosenthal and Watson, Austin, 1995-2000; ptnr. Feazell, Rosenthal and Watson, Austin, 2001—. Pres. McLennan County Peace Officers Assn., Waco, 1984-87; pro bono def. counsel Henry Lee Lucas, 1989-94; expert legal corr. O.J. Simpson Trial, KTBC TV. Primary character: Careless Whispers, 1986 (Edgar award 1986); exec. prodr. Rhinos the Movie, Natural Selection, Final Redemption, Blood Sweat and Teeth, Rage in the Cage; pres. One Horn Prodns.; contbr. articles to profl. jours. Del. State Dem. Conv., Houston, 1988. Named Outstanding Young Alumni, U. Mary Hardin Baylor, Belton, Tex., 1985, Peace Officer of Yr., Waco JC's, 1986. Fellow Tex. Bar Found. (life); mem. ATLA, Nat. Assn. Criminal Def. Lawyers (life), Tex. Trial Lawyers Assn., Tex. Criminal Def. Lawyers Assn., State Bar Tex., Bar of U.S. Fifth Cir. Avocation: flim making. Office: Feazell Rosenthal & Watson PC 6601 Vaught Ranch Rd Ste 200 Austin TX 78730 E-mail: vic@vicfeazell.com.

FECHER, VINCENT JOHN, priest; b. Wilmette, Ill., Feb. 10, 1924; s. Joseph Martin and Emilia Cecilia (Siemer) F. D. Ch. History, Gregoriana, Rome, 1954; MA in Philosophy, Cath. U. Am., 1960; PhD, Angelicum, Rome, 1974; MA in Gerontology, Trinity U., San Antonio, 1981. Ordained priest Roman Cath. Ch., 1950. Sem. prof. Divine Word Sem., Techny, Ill., 1954-59, Manila, Philippines, 1959-64; sec. gen. Soc. of Divine Word, Rome, 1968-74; parish priest San Antonio Archdiocese, 1974—; pastor Sacred Heart Cath. Ch., Uvalde, Tex., 1980-92, St. John the Evangelist Ch., Hondo, Tex., 1995-99. Dean Uvalde deanery Diocese of San Antonio, 1980-86; sec. Diocesan Presbyteral Coun., 1980-86. Author: German National Parishes, 1955, Error, Deception, Incomplete Truth, 1974, Religion and Aging, 1982, The Lord and I, 1990, Man, Woman, and God, 1993; contbr. articles to profl. publs. Mem. adv. coun. Tex. Dept. Human Svcs., Austin, 1984-88 Mem. Nat. Fedn. Priests' Coun. (Tex. rep. 1980s), KC, Knights of Holy Sepulcher. Home: 8520 Cross Mountain Trl San Antonio TX 78255-2038 E-mail: countpas@texas.net.

FECHT, DANIEL R. psychologist, actor; b. St. Louis, Mo., Mar. 7, 1948; s. Edward William and Emmy Lou F. BA in Psychology, Ctrl. Mo. State U., Warrensburg, 1970; MS in Psychology, Ctrl. Mo. State U., 1974; PhD in Counseling Psychology, U. Mo. Kansas City, 1988. Lic. psychologist, Mo. Psychologist Clay Co. Health Dept., Liberty, Mo., 1974-84, mental health supr., 1984-86; psychology intern Fulton State Hosp., Mo., 1986-87; psychologist Swope Pkwy Health Ctr., Kansas City, Mo., 1987-95, Madison Ave Psychol. Svcs., Kansas City, 1995—. Cons. Comprehensive Mental Health Svcs., Independence, Mo., 1997—99, Nat. Child Care Accreditation Project, Kansas City, Mo., Midwest Law Enforcement Trainers Assn.; guest lectr. Regional Law Enforcement Acad., 1999, Midwest Law Enforcement Tng. Assn., 2001; actor. Author: (screenplay) Sorority Babes Unchained vs. the Ninja Zombies, 1995, Basic Self-Protection, 2000. Res. dep. sheriff Clay County Sheriffs Office, 1994—96. Sp/5 U.S. Army, 1970—72. Recipient Army Commendation Medal, K.C., Mo., 1981. Mem. Independent Film Makers Coalition, Mensa, Internat. Brotherhood Magicians. Avocations: magic, film-making, travel, fitness, self-defense. Office: Madison Ave Psychol Svcs 3100 Broadway St Ste 1104 Kansas City MO 64111-2495

FECHT, LORENE, surgical nurse; b. Keokuk, Iowa, July 13, 1949; d. Alvin and Norma Ruth (Jenkins) Fink; m. Herb Fecht, June 29, 1969; children: Kristie, Tiffanie, Lindsay, Lacey. Diploma, Burlington (Iowa) Med. Ctr., 1970; student, Robert Morris Coll., Carthage, Ill., Carl Sandburg Coll., Carthage, Southeastern Community Coll. Cert. BCLS, ACLS, cert. nurse in operating rm. nurse, neonatal resuscitation and neonatal resuscitation preceptor; registered nurse 1st asst. Physician's asst., Carthage; supr. RR, Cen. Supply; surgery supr. Meml. Hosp., Carthage, staff nurse in med.-surg. CCU; head nurse ambulatory surgery recovery rm. Keokuk Area Hosp., dir. surg. svcs., 1992—2002, dir. Surgery Ctr. Quincy, 2002—. Mem. Am. Soc. Past Anesth. Nurses, Soc. Gastrointestinal Nurses Am., Assn. Oper. Rm. Nurses (chpt. pres., vice chmn.), Iowa Orgn. Nurse Leaders. Office: The Surgery Ctr of Quincy 1025 Main St Quincy IL 62301

FECHTEL, VINCENT JOHN, legal administrator; b. Leesburg, Fla., Aug. 10, 1936; s. Vincent John and Annie Jo (Hayman) F.; m. Dixie Davenport, Feb 1992; children: John, Katherine, Elizabeth D., MaryKathcrine. BSBA, U. Fla., 1959. Mem. Fla. Ho. of Reps., 1972-78, Fla. Senate, 1978-80; parole commr. U.S. Dept. Justice, Chevy Chase, Md., 1983-96. Served with USNR and Fla. Nat. Guard. Mem. Alpha Tau Omega. Republican. Methodist. Home: 609 Cascade Ave Leesburg FL 34748-6323

FECHTER, LAURENCE DAVID, toxicology educator, researcher; b. N.Y.C., Dec. 23, 1945; BA, Clark U., 1967; MA, Kent State U., 1969; PhD, U. Rochester, 1973. Asst. prof. Johns Hopkins U., Balt., 1976-84, assoc. prof., 1984-93, prof., 1993; Mosier prof. toxicology U. Okla. Health Scis. Ctr., Oklahoma City, 1993—2002; rsch. sci. Loma Linda Vets. Assn. Rsch. and Edn., Loma Linda, Calif., 2002—. Cons. World Health. Editor: Proc. 4th Internat. Conf. on Combined Exposures to Environ. Factors, 1990; assoc. editor Neurotoxicology and Teratology, 1996-99, mem. editl. bd., 1989—; mem. editl. bd. Toxicol. Scis., 1997—, Neurotoxicology, 1994—. Fellow Acad. Toxicol. Scis.; mem. Soc. Toxicology (pres. neurotoxicology splty. sect. 1994), Internat. Neurotoxicol. Assn. (pres. 2001-03). Office: Research Svc Pettis VAMC 11201 Benton Street Loma Linda CA 92357

FECHT-GRAMLEY, MARY E. trauma specialist, health facility educator; b. Newport News, Va. d. Wilbur C. and Clara B. (Williams) Jessee; m. Albert P. Fecht Sr. (dec. Feb. 1989); children: Thomas C. (dec. Dec. 1992), Albert P. Jr.; m. Leon F. Gramley. Diploma in nursing, Copley Meml. Hosp., Aurora, Ill., 1970; BSN, No. Ill. U., 1974, MSN, 1975; PhD, Columbia Pacific U., 1981. Cert. trauma nursing core faculty, CEN, emergency comm. nurse, trauma nurse specialist, CPR instr., trainer, PALS, BLS, ACLS regional faculty instr. Clinical specialist Spl. Care Units, Good Samaritan Hosp., Downers Grove, Ill.; supr. nursing, instr. critical care Delnor Hosp., St. Charles, Ill.; coord. emergency med. svcs., trauma systems St. Joseph Med. Ctr., Joliet, Ill.; staff nurse, emergency dept. Delnor Cmty. Hosp., Geneva, Ill., 1986—; regional nurse coord. trauma specialist program Ill. Dept. Pub. Health, 1988-95; EMS trauma coord. Elmhurst (Ill.) Meml. Hosp., 1995—. Coord. numerous workshops, seminars; surveyor trauma ctr. applicants Ill. Dept. Pub. Health, 1988, 92; instr. numerous degreed nursing programs including ADN, BSN; spkr. numerous edn. programs including Ill. Nurses Week, Morris (Ill.) Hosp., 1983; trauma edn. coord. Loyola U. Med. Ctr., Maywood, Ill., 1997—99; mem. internat. faculty TNCC/ENPC Emergency Nurses Assn., 1998—2000; asst. prof. Sch. Nursing Aurora (Ill.) U., 1999—; editor magnet nursing project Delnor Cmty. Hosp., Geneva, 2001—02. Abstractor: Nursing Scan in Emergency Care, 1990—94, reviewer: Am. Jour. Nursing, 1996 -, Jour. Emergency Nursing, 2001—; contbr. articles to profl. jours., chapters to books; sect. editor: TNCC Textbook, 2000. Chair, faculty mem. Trauma and Critical Care Symposium, Chgo., 1992; outreach dir. Level 1 Trauma Ctr. Good Samaritan Hosp., Downers Grove, Ill., 1999—2001; chair position statement rev. work group Emergency Nurses Assn., 2000—02. Capt. USAR, 1978—81. Mem. Emergency Nurses Assn. (cert., chair edn, spl. interest group for Ill. coun., planning com. 1986-90, chair trauma com. 1993-95, pres. Ill. coun. 1990), No. Ill. Emergency Med. Svcs. Coords. Assn. (pres. 1989, v.p. 1988, sec.treas. 1987, award for Contbn. to Emergency Nursing Edn. 1992), Emergency Nurses Assn., Sigma Theta Tau.

FECK, LUKE MATTHEW, retired utility executive; b. Cin., Aug. 15, 1935; s. John Franz and Mercedes Caroline (Rielag) F.; m. Gail Ann Schutte, Aug. 12, 1961; children: Lisa, Mara, Paul. BA, U. Cin., 1957. Copyboy Cin. Enquirer, 1956, reporter, TV editor, columnist, 1957-64, asst. features editor, 1969-70, mag. editor, 1970, news editor, 1971-73, mng. editor, 1974-75, exec. editor, 1975, editor, 1976-80, Columbus Dispatch, 1980-89; sr. v.p. corp. comms. Am. Electric Power, Columbus, 1990-2000; ret. Pres. Ackerman and Feck Press, Inc., 1964-69, Feicke Web, Inc., 1974-75 Bd. dirs. Thurber House, MPW Indsl. Svcs., Inc., Acad. for Governance and Leadership. 1st lt. AUS, 1957-59. Mem. Pub. Rels. Soc. Am., Edison Electric Inst., Lit. Club Cin., Capital Club, Lakes Golf and Country Club, Torch Club of Columbus, Sigma Delta Chi (pres. chpt.), Phi Kappa Theta. Home: 6880 Worthington Rd Westerville OH 43082-9491

FECTEAU, FRANCIS ROGER, judge; b. Worcester, Mass., July 8, 1947; BA, Holy Cross Coll., 1969; JD, Boston Coll., 1972. Bar: Mass. 1972, U.S. Dist. Ct. Mass. 1973, U.S. Ct. Appeals (1st cir.) 1973. Asst. dist. atty. Worcester County Dist. Attys. Office, Worcester, 1973-79; assoc. Lawrence H. Fisher, Worcester, 1979-82, Healy & Rocheleau, Worcester, 1982-84, ptnr., 1984—96;

judge, 1996—. Instr. Anna Maria Coll., 1976—; apptd. Mass. Superior Ct., 1996. Mem. Worcester County Bar Assn. (exec. com. 1981-83), Mass. Bar Assn., Mass. Def. Lawyers Assn., Mass. Acad. Trial Lawyers, Am. Arbitration Assn., Am. Soc. Law and Medicine.

FECTEAU, ROSEMARY LOUISE, educational administrator, educator, consultant; b. Niagara, Wis., Aug. 7, 1930; d. Andrew Raymond and Julianna Agnes (Wodenka) Waitrovich; m. Jack Richard Fecteau Sr. (dec. Dec. 1994), June 12, 1954; children: Michele, Julienne, Gervaise, Jack Jr., Andrew, Anne-Marie. BA with high distinction, U. R.I., 1974; MS in Edn., U. Maine, 1976; MS in Ednl. Adminstrn., U. So. Maine, 1979; PhD, Columbia Pacific U., 1999. Cert. supt. schs. K-12. Sec. A.O. Smith Corp., Milw., 1949-54; sec. to Judge Irving W. Smith, Niagara, 1954-55; asst. tchr. Regional Resource Rm., Yarmouth, Maine, 1974-75; prin. Breakwater Sch., Cape Elizabeth, Maine, 1975-78; tchr. grades 6-8 Wells (Maine) Jr. H.S., 1978-79; dir. spl. svcs. Maine Sch. Adminstrv. Dist. 75, Bowdoin, Bowdoinham, Harpswell, Topsham, Maine, 1979-84; ednl. cons. various states, 1984—. Owner Serendipity Acres Sheep Farm; secondary handicapped task force State Dept. Edn., Augusta, 1980-81; chairperson nat. insvc. network U. Ind., Topsham, Maine, 1981-84; mem. policy adv. group Gov. John Baldacci, Maine, 2002. Mem. Maine Spl. Edn. Rev. Team; founder Project Co-Step and Project S.E.A.R.C.H.; mem. focus group Casco Bay Estuary Project Maine; brownie leader, girl scout cons. Girl Scouts Am., Erie, Pa., 1965-66; dir. women's Cursillo Movement, Erie, 1967; co-chair publicity St. Vincent Hosp., Erie, 1966-67; chair conservation commn. Town of North Yarmouth, 1987; del. Maine Dem. Conv., 1986; mem. policy adv. group Maine Gov. John Baldacci, 2002 Mem.: AAUW, Columbia Pacific U. Alumni Assn., Maine Children's Alliance, Physicians for Social Responsibility, Union of Concerned Scientists, Consumers for Affordable Health Care, Maine Organic Farmer and Gardener Assn., North Yarmouth Hist. Soc., U. So. Maine Alumni Assn. Avocations: music, arts, nutrition, physical fitness. Home: Serendipity Acres 140 W Pownal Rd North Yarmouth ME 04097-6819 E-mail: romyphd99@aol.com.

FEDAK, BARBARA KINGRY, retired technical center administrator; b. Hazleton, Pa., Feb. 7, 1939; d. Marvin Frederick and Ruth Anna (Wheeler) Siebel; m. Raymond F. Fedak, Mar. 27, 1993; children: Sean M., James Goldey. BA, Trenton State Coll., 1961; MEd, Lesley Coll., Cambridge, Mass., 1986. Registered respiratory therapist. Dept. dir. North Platte (Nebr.) Community Hosp., 1974-75; newborn coord. Children's Hosp., Denver, 1975-79; edn. coord. Rose Med. Ctr., Denver, 1979-81; program dir. respiratory tech. program Pickens Tech., Aurora, Colo., 1981-86; mktg. rep. Foster Med. Corp., Denver, 1986-87; staff therapist Porter Meml. Hosp., Denver, 1987-88; dir., br. mgr. Pediatric Svcs. Am., Denver, 1988-90; dir. clin. edn. Pickens Tech., Aurora, Colo., 1991—2000, divsn. chair health occupations, 1991—2000; ret., 2000. Site evaluator Joint Rev. Com. for Respiratory Therapy Edn., Euless, Tex. Co-editor: Am. Assn. Respiratory Care Record, 1998-2000. Met. coun. mem. Am. Lung Assn., 1987-91. Mem.: Colo. Assn. Respiratory Educators (chair 1991—96), Colo. Soc. Respiratory Care (sec. 1980—81, program com. 1982—92, dir. at large 1983—86, 1990—92), Am. Assn. for Respiratory Care (edn. sect. program com. 1992—2000, abstract rev. com. 1993—96, alt. del. ho. dels. 1997—98, del. 1999—2000, treas. ho. dels. 2001, 2002), Lambda Beta (sec./treas. exec. bd. 2003). Methodist. Avocations: reading, mountain biking, golf, singing, piano playing. Home: 11478 S Marlborough Dr Parker CO 80138-7318 E-mail: bobbinkf@aol.com.

FEDDE, G(ABRIEL) BERNHARD, retired lawyer; b. Bklyn., Mar. 7, 1909; s. Bernhard Andreas and Anna Mathea (Heggelund) F.; m. Johanna Borrevik, Aug. 14, 1957; m. Elizabeth Amy Ralston, Oct. 9, 1938 (div. 1955). AB, Williams Coll., 1930; postgrad., U. Munich, 1930-31, Columbia U., 1933-35; JD, U. Oreg., 1936; AM, Oreg. State U., 1964. Bar: Oreg. 1936. Pvt. practice law, Eugene, Oreg., 1938-43, Portland, Oreg., 1955-90; with forest svc. Civil Pub. Svc., Cascade Locks, Oreg., 1943-46; head relief mission Am. Friends Svc. Com., Oberhausen, Germany, 1946-48; lawyer Luth. World Fedn., Palestine, 1949-50. Adj. prof. Portland State U., 1955-90. Author: Norwegian-Swedish Crisis of 1905, 1964, also monographs. Mem. Scandinavian Heritage Found. (pres. 1985-90, 2001-02, bd. dirs. 1990-), Oreg. UN Assn. (bd. dirs. 1954-00), Norsemen's Fedn. Oreg. (pres. 1982-91), Scandinavian Club of Portland (pres. 1977-82). Lutheran. Home: 1919 NW Ramsey Crest Portland OR 97229-4209

FEDDER, NORMAN J. retired theater educator, playwright; b. N.Y.C., Jan. 26, 1934; s. Abraham Herbert and Harriet Dorothy (Solomon) Fedder; m. Deborah Pincus, Nov. 24, 1955; children: Jordan Michael, Tamar Beth Fedder Katz. Student, Johns Hopkins U., 1950-52; BA, CUNY, Bklyn., 1955; MA, Columbia U., 1956; PhD, NYU, 1962. Registered drama therapist; bd. cert. trainer. Asst. prof. English Trenton (N.J.) State Coll., 1960-61; assoc. prof. Indiana U. Pa., 1961-64, Fla. Atlantic U., Boca Raton, 1964-67; assoc. prof. drama U. Ariz., Tucson, 1967-70; Disting. prof. theatre Kans. State U., Manhattan, 1970-99, Disting. prof. emeritus theatre, 1999—. Adj. prof. interdisciplinary arts Nova Southeastern U., Ft. Lauderdale, 2002—; founder, dir. Israel Theatre Program, Tel Aviv. Author: (teleplay) We Can Make Our Lives Sublime, 1970, (plays) The Betrayal, 1978, Out of the Depths, 1998; author: (with Richard Lippman) (musical) The Buck Stops Here!, 1983. Mem.: Assn. Jewish Theatre (founding mem.), Nat. Assn. Drama Therapy (bd. dirs. 1990—99). Democrat. Jewish. Avocations: swimming, walking. Office: 7966 Lexington Club Blvd B Delray Beach FL 33446 E-mail: fedder@ksu.edu.

FEDDERS, JOHN MICHAEL, lawyer; b. Covington, Ky., Oct. 21, 1941; s. Aloysius Henry and Mary Margaret (Schmidt) F.; m. Barbara E. Baxter; children: Luke D., Mark A., Matthew C., Andrew M., Peter J. BA in Journalism, Marquette U., 1963; LL.B., Cath. U. Am., 1966. Bar: N.Y. 1967, D.C. 1967. Assoc. Cadwalader, Wickersham & Taft, N.Y.C., 1966-71; exec. v.p. Gulf Life Holding Co., Dallas, 1971-73; with firm Arnold & Porter, Washington, 1973-81; ptnr., 1975-81; dir. Div. of Enforcement, SEC, 1981-85; ptnr. Miller, Cassidy, Larroca & Lewin, 1985-87; sole practice Washington, 1987—. Lectr. corp. securities and fin. Contbr. articles to legal jours. Recipient Service award Marquette U., 1977, Achievement award Cath. U. Am. Alumni Assn., 1982, Chmn.'s award for excellence SEC, 1982, Supervisory Excellence award, SEC, 1983 Mem. ABA, Assn. Bar City N.Y., Sigma Delta Chi, Phi Alpha Delta. Republican. Roman Catholic. Office: 1914 Sunderland Pl NW Washington DC 20036-1608 E-mail: jfedders@erols.com.

FEDE, ANDREW THOMAS, lawyer, educator; b. Jersey City, N.J., Jan. 20, 1956; s. Andrew Paul and Dorothy Marie Fede. BA, Montclair State U., 1978; JD, Rutgers U., 1982. Bar: N.J. 1982, U.S. Dist. Ct. N.J., 1982, U.S. Ct. Appeals (3d cir.) 1986, U.S. Supreme Ct. 1987. Assoc. Contant, Atkins and Fede, LLC, Hackensack, 1982-90; ptnr. Contant, Atkins, and Fede, LLC, Hackensack, 1991—. Atty. Borough of Bogota, 1992, 96—, Bogota Planning Bd., 1985-86, Borough of Maywood, 1993-94, 98-2000, 2002-, Hasbrouck Heights Planning Bd., 1991-94, Borough of Norwood, 1998, Borough of Ridgefield Planning Bd., 2000, Ridgefield Bd. of Adjustment, 2001; adj. prof. Montclair State U., 1985-99. Author: People Without Rights: An Interpretation of the Fundamentals of the Law of Slavery in the U.S. South, 1992; contbr. articles to profl. jours. Rep. County Committeeman, 1979-95, mcpl. chmn., Bogota, 2000—; pres. Bd. Health, Bogota, 1983-89. Mem. ABA, N.J. Bar Assn., Bergen County Bar Assn., Am. Soc. for Legal History. Avocation: legal history. Office: Contant Atkins et al 25 Main St Hackensack NJ 07601

FEDER, ADAM BARRY, software engineer; b. Warsaw, N.Y., Mar. 10, 1972; s. Eric Leigh and Sharon Esther Feder. BS, MS, MIT, 1995. Tech. staff Silicon Graphics, Inc., Mountain View, Calif., 1995-98; co-founder Electric Arc LLC, Mountain View, Calif., 1998—2002; mem. tech. staff TiVo, Inc., Sunnyvale, Calif., 1999—2002, prin. engr., 2002—. Mem. Tau Beta Pi (assoc.), Eta Kappa Nu. Avocations: biking, camping, hiking, reading, scuba diving.

FEDER, ARTHUR A. lawyer, business executive; b. N.Y.C., Mar. 23, 1927; s. Leo and Bertha (Franklin) F.; m. Ruth Musicant, Sept. 4, 1949; children: Gwen Lisabeth, Leslie Margaret, Andrew Michael. BA, Columbia Coll., 1949; LLB, Columbia U., 1951. Bar: N.Y. 1951. Assoc. Fulton Walter & Halley, 1951-53; rsch. asst. Am. Law Inst. Fed. Income, Estate and Gift Tax Project, 1953-54; assoc., ptnr. Roberts & Holland, N.Y.C., 1954-66; ptnr. Willkie, Farr & Gallagher, N.Y.C., 1966-69, Fried, Frank, Harris, Shriver & Jacobson, N.Y.C., 1970-94, of counsel, 1994—; sr. adv. to exec. com. Herzog, Heine, Geduld Inc., N.Y.C., 1996—2001; counsel Geduld & Co., LLC, N.Y.C., 2002—, Cougar Trading, 2002—. Lectr. in law Columbia U., 1961-63; lectr. Am. Law Inst., NYU Inst. on Fed. Taxation, Practicing Law Inst., various profl. groups. Editor Columbia Law Rev., 1949-51; contbr. articles to profl. jours. With USN, 1945-46. Fellow Am. Coll. Tax Counsel; mem. ABA (taxation sect., chmn. com. on real property tax problems 1964-66, com. on legis. drafting 1968-84), Assn. of Bar of City of N.Y. (various coms.), N.Y. State Bar Assn. (taxation sect., co-chmn. various coms. 1982-86, sec. 1987-88, 2d vice chmn. 1988-89, vice chmn. 1989-90, chmn. 1990-91), Internat. Fiscal Assn. (coun. U.S.A. br. 1984-91), Am. Law Inst. (tax adv. group fed. income tax project), Univ. Club, Phi Beta Kappa. Democrat. Home: 25 W 81st St New York NY 10024-6023 Office: Cougar Trading 535 Madison Ave New York NY 10022 Home Fax: 212-877-2489; Office Fax: 212-319-8066. E-mail: afeder@nyc.rr.com., afeder@geduldco.com.

FEDER, DAVID L. lawyer; b. Mar. 13, 1949; s. Aaron and Edith (Forman) Feder; m. Deborah Kuzman, Nov. 1, 1980. BA, SUNY, 1971; JD, Northeastern U., 1974; LLM in Labor Law, NYU, 1975. Bar: Pa. 1975, U.S. Supreme Ct. 1977. Atty., adv. Fed. Labor Rels. Coun., Washington, 1975—79; dep. asst. gen. counsel Fed. Labor Rels. Authority, Washington, 1979—81, asst. gen counsel field mgmt. and legal policy, 1981—94, dep. gen. counsel, 1994—2003, acting gen. counsel, 2001—03, assoc. commn., social security adminstr., labor mgmt. and employee rels., 2003—. Home: 29 Shadow Point Ct Edgewater MD 21037-1212 Office: Fed Labor Relations Authority 1400 K St NW Washington DC 20424

FEDER, DONALD ALBERT, syndicated columnist; b. Troy, N.Y., Nov. 25, 1946; s. Harold Samuel and Esther Ruth (Whitman) F.; m. Andrea Helen Mills, Aug. 5, 1973; children: Helena, Anna, Jonathan, Aaron. BA cum laude, Boston U., 1969, JD, 1972. Bar: N.Y. 1973, Mass. 1976. Assoc. Pozefsky, Tocci & Pozefsky, Gloversville, N.Y., 1973-76; exec. dir. Citizens for Ltd. Taxation, Boston, 1976-79, Second Amendment Found., Bellevue, Wash., 1979-81, WEEI-NewsRadio, Boston, 1983-84; editor, pub. On Principle, Longmeadow, Mass., 1981-83; columnist, editorial writer Boston Herald, 1984—. Author: A Jewish Conservative Looks at Pagan America, 1992, Who's Afraid of the Religious Right?, 1996. Recipient 1st prize writing award AMY Found., 1992, Internat. Comm. award, Republic of China, 1998. Mem. Internat. Churhill Soc., Theodore Roosevelt Assn., Calvin Coolidge Meml. Found. Jewish. Avocations: history, gardening, hiking. Office: Boston Herald PO Box 2096 Boston MA 02106-2096

FEDER, GARY HAROLD, lawyer; b. Cin., Dec. 12, 1948; s. Max Henry and Marian Alice (Blumenthal) F.; m. Robin Melman; Aug. 19, 1973; children: Jessica, Amy. AB, Washington U., 1970, JD, 1974, LLM in Taxation, 1980. Bar: Mo. 1974, U.S. Dist. Ct. (we. and ea. dists.) Mo., U.S. Tax Ct., U.S. Ct. Appeals (8th cir.), U.S. Supreme Ct. Assoc. Team Four, Inc., St. Louis, 1974-78, Shifrin & Treiman, St. Louis, 1978-84, ptnr., 1984-88, Ziercher & Hocker, P.C., St. Louis, 1988-2000; mem. Husch & Eppenberger, LLC, 2000—. Sec. Sta. KWMU, St. Louis, 1984-86. Co-author: Tax Abatement Alternatives, 1978; editor in chief Urban Law Ann. Washington U. Law Rev., 1974. Treas. Clayton (Mo.) Sch. Dist., 1986-90; with City of Clayton Plan Commn./Archtl. Rev. Bd., 2003—. Office: Husch & Eppenberger LLC 190 Carondelet Plz Ste 600 Saint Louis MO 63105-1925

FEDER, HARRY SIMON, bank executive; b. N.Y.C., Aug. 20, 1953; s. Morris Louis and Lucy (Kraus) F.; m. Gilli Bortman, Mar. 1, 1977; children: Jean Ella, Laura Ann. BA in Econs., NYU, 1974; MBA in Internat. Fin., Syracuse U., 1976. Credit analyst Israel Discount Bank of N.Y., N.Y.C., 1977-78, with domestic lending, 1978-79, with internat. lending, 1979-81, asst. v.p. corr. banking, 1981-85, v.p. treasury, 1986-94, 1st v.p. treasury, 1995-96, mgr. corr. banking and treasury, 1996-2000, sr. v.p. treasury and non-bank product devel., 2001—. Avocations: collecting stamps and coins, travel. Home: 66 Dora Ln New Rochelle NY 10804-1006 Office: Israel Discount Bank NY 511 5th Ave Rm 1003 New York NY 10017-4997

FEDER, HELENE TERRY, lawyer; BA in English, UCLA, 1980; JD, Southwestern U., 1991; LLM, George Washington U., 1993. Bar: Calif. 1991, D.C. 1994. Legal intern U.S. Internat. Trade Commn.; legis. asst. intern Congresswoman Ileana Ros-Lehtinen. Vol. Gore/Lieberman 2000. Home: 10490 Wilshire Blvd Apt 505 Los Angeles CA 90024-4657

FEDER, MARTIN ELLIOTT, biology researcher and educator; b. Newark, Mar. 14, 1951; s. S. and A. C. (Gerwin) F.; m. Juliana Helen Huta, Aug. 19, 1973; children: Jonathan R. L., Alison F. L. BA summa cum laude, Cornell U., 1973; PhD, U. Calif., Berkeley, 1977. Postdoctoral fellow U. Chgo., 1977-78, asst. prof., 1979-85, assoc. prof., 1985-89, master biol. scis. collegiate div., assoc. dean div. biol. scis., 1988-91, prof. dept. organismal biology and anatomy, 1989—. Dozor lectr., 2000. Author, editor: Predator-Prey Relationships, 1986, New Directions in Ecological Physiology, 1987, Environmental Physiology of the Amphibians, 1992; mem. editorial bd. jour. Physiol. Biochemistry Zoology; Ann. Rev. Physiol., Journal of Experimental Biology, Jour. Thermal Biology; contbr. over 100 articles to profl. jours. Undergrad. Edn. Initiative award Howard Hughes Med. Inst., 1989-94; NSF grantee, 1978—; Andrew Mellon Found. fellow. Fellow AAAS; mem. Am. Physiol. Soc., Soc. Integrative Comparative Biology (pres. 1999-00), Soc. for Exptl.Biology, NIH Biomedical Rsch. and Tng. Study Sec.. founder/chair, Gordon Rsch. Conf. on Evolutionary and Ecological Functional Genomics, Phi Beta Kappa. Achievements include research on heat-shock proteins, evolutionary physiology and regulation of cutaneous gas exchange. Office: Univ Chgo Dept Organismal Biology and Anatomy 1027 E 57th St Chicago IL 60637-1508

FEDER, ROBERT, lawyer; b. N.Y.C., Nov. 29, 1930; BA cum laude, CCNY, 1953; LLB, Columbia U., 1953. Bar: N.Y. 1953, U.S. Tax Ct. 1956, U.S. Dist. Ct. (so. dist.) N.Y. 1973. V.p., gen. counsel Presdl. Realty Corp., White Plains, N.Y., 1953-71; ptnr. Cuddy & Feder LLP, White Plains, 1971—. Bd. dirs. Westchester County (N.Y.) Legal Aid Soc., 1972—, pres., 1974—78; adj. prof. sch. bus. Columbia U., N.Y.C., 1988—89; bd. dirs. Presdl. Realty Corp. (Amex), Interplex Industries, Inc., Stellaris Health Network, Inc., vice chmn., 2001—; adj. prof. Pace U. Law Sch., 1985—87. Pres. White Plains Cmty. Action Program, 1967—69; bd.. dirs. White Plains Hosp. Ctr., 1978—, also sec., treas., chmn., 1992—97, 2002—; commr. White Plains Housing Authority, 1984—2002; chmn. White Plains Jud. Rev. Com., 2003; trustee SUNY-Purchase Coll. Found., 1988—, vice-chmn., 1995—. Mem. ABA, N.Y. State Bar Assn., White Plains Bar Assn., Westchester County Bar Assn., Am. Coll. Real Estate Lawyers. Home: 9 Oxford Rd White Plains NY 10605-3602 Office: Cuddy & Feder LLP 90 Maple Ave White Plains NY 10601-5105 E-mail: rfeder@pipeline.com., rfeder@cfwlaw.com.

FEDER, ROBERT, television and radio columnist; b. Chgo., May 17, 1956; s. Harold J. and Selma (Reisberg) F.; m. Janet Gail Elkins, June 16, 1985; 1 child, Emily Jacklyn. BS in Journalism, Northwestern U., 1978. Reporter, news editor Lerner Newspapers, Chgo., 1974-78, mng. editor, 1978-80; reporter Chgo. Sun-Times, 1980-83, TV/radio columnist, 1983—. Project cons. (TV documentary) Radio Faces, 1989; contbr. (spl. report) Ency. Brittanica, 1983, World Book Ency., 1996. Recipient Page One award Chgo. Newspaper Guild, 1976; named Best Daily Newspaper Columnist, New City, 1997. Mem. Soc. Profl. Journalists, Chgo. Headline Club, Chgo. Newspaper Guild, Northwestern Club of Chgo., Skokie Hist. Soc. Office: Chgo Sun-Times 401 N Wabash Ave Chicago IL 60611-5642

FEDER, ROBERT ELLIOT, psychiatrist; b. Detroit, July 8, 1951; s. Norman W. and Helen (Kadushin) F.; m. Marsha Susan Cooper; children: Daniel, Elana. BS with high honors, U. Mich., 1972; MD, U. Wash., 1977. Diplomate Am. Bd. Med. Examiners, Am. Bd. Psychiatry and Neurology. Resident in psychiatry Yale U., New Haven, 1981; assoc. psychiatrist Elmcrest Psychiat. Inst., Portland, Conn., 1980-81; med. dir. inpatient psychiatry Beverly (Mass.) Hosp., 1981-83; chief psychiatrist Matthew Thornton Health Plan, Nashua, N.H., 1983-86; courtesy staff Nashua Meml. Hosp., 1983—, St. Joseph's Hosp., Nashua, 1984—; attending staff Cath. Med. Ctr., Manchester, N.H., 1988—; med. dir. Psychiatric Inst. Cath. Med. Ctr., Manchester, N.H., 1995-2000; dir. outpatient svcs. Charter Brookside Hosp., Nashua, 1986-95; assoc. med. dir. Brookside Hosp., Nashua, 1993-95; pvt. practice psychiatry Manchester, 1995—; med. dir. Behavioral Health Network, Concord, N.H., 2000—. Chmn. dept. psychiatry Nashua Meml. Hosp., 1988—93, chmn. credentials com., 1991—93; mem. N.H. State Med. Bd., 2001—. Contbr. articles in psychiatry to profl. jours. Recipient Exemplary Psychiatrist award Nat. Alliance for Mentally Ill, 1992, 94. Fellow Am. Psychiat. Assn. (dist. mem.); mem. AMA, Am. Assn. Gen. Hosp. Psychiatrists, Physicians for Social Responsibility, N.H. Psychiat. Soc. (pres. 1995-96, chmn. pub. affairs 1985-95, mem. exec. com. 1985—, N.H. rep. to Am. Psychiat. Assn. assembly 1996—), Am. Psychiat. Assn. Arts Assn. (sec.-treas. 1985-87), Phi Beta Kappa, Phi Eta Sigma. Democrat. Avocations: hiking, skiing, computer art, stained glass, music. Office: Behavioral Health Network Ste 300 One Pillsbury St Concord NH 03301-3556 E-mail: bfeder@bhninc.com.

FEDER, SAUL E. lawyer; b. Bklyn., Oct. 8, 1943; s. Joseph Robert and Toby Feder; m. Marcia Carrie Weinblatt, Feb. 25, 1968; children: Howard Avram, Fayge Miriam, Tamar Miriam, Michael Elon, David Ben-Zion Aaron, Alexandra Rachel, Evan Daniel, Sarah Lily, Maya Malka. BS, NYU, 1965; JD, Bklyn. Law Sch., 1968. Bar: N.Y. 1969, U.S. Ct. Appeals (2d cir.) 1969, U.S. Ct. Claims 1970, U.S. Customs Ct. 1972, U.S. Supreme Ct. 1972, U.S. Ct. Customs and Patent Appeals 1974. Mng. lawyer Queens Legal Svcs., Jamaica, N.Y., 1970-71; ptnr. Previte-Glasser-Feder & Farber, Jackson Heights, N.Y., 1972-73, Hein-Waters-Klein & Feder, Far Rockaway, N.Y., 1973-78, Regosin-Edwards-Stone & Feder, N.Y.C., 1979—. Spl. investigator Bur. Election Frauds, Atty. Gen.'s Office, N.Y.C., 1976-77, spl. dep. atty. gen., 1969-70; arbitrator, consumer counsel small claims div. Civil Ct. City of N.Y., 1974—. Pres. Young Israel Briarwood, Queens, N.Y., 1978; chmn. polit. affairs com. Young Israel Staten Island, 1985—; rep. candidate State of N.Y. Assembly, Queens, 1976; chmn. Stat Pac Polit. Action Com. Mem. N.Y. Bar Assn., Queens County Bar Assn., Nassau County Bar Assn., Am. Judges Assn., N.Y. Trial Lawyers Assn., Richmond County Bar Assn., Com. on Law and Pub. Affairs, Internat. Acad. Law & Sci., Am. Jud. Soc., Soc. Med. Jurisprudence, Am. Arbitration Assn. Republican. Home: 259 Ardmore Ave Staten Island NY 10314-4349 Office: Regosin Edwards Stone & Feder 225 Broadway Ste 613 New York NY 10007-3059 E-mail: sfeder@resflaw.com.

FEDERICI, WILLIAM VITO, newspaper reporter; b. Bklyn., June 22, 1931; s. Theodore and Margaret (DeMaio) F.; m. Arlene Ann McAuliffe, Oct. 1, 1955 (dec.); children: William Theodore, Robert Gerard. Student, Hofstra Coll., 1949-50, St. John's U., 1954-56. With N.Y. Daily News, 1950—, nat. corr., until 1965, spl. reporter, 1965-72, asst. city editor in charge investigations, 1975-79, Bklyn. editor, 1979—, Dir. spl. projects Office Spl. State Prosecutor, N.Y.C., 1972-75; exec. dir. corp. affairs Bklyn. Union Gas Co., 1987—. Author series on child abuse which initiated N.Y. laws to protect children, 1969. Served with USN, 1950-54, Korea. Recipient several journalism awards, including George Polk award Long Island U., 1970, Sigma Delta Chi award for met. reporting, 1975

FEDERING, ERIC K. congressional communications director, motion picture preservationist, educator, public policy advisor; b. Bronx, N.Y., Feb. 10, 1960; s. Abraham M. and Eileen (Katz) F.; m. Daphne V. Clones, May 2000. BA with Distinction, George Washington U., 1982. Aide U.S. Dept. State, Washington, 1979-81; founder, dir. motion picture restoration effort MAD WORLD Campaign, Washington, 1982-91; press sec., speechwriter for mem. of congress Rep. Norman Y. Mineta, Washington, 1987-93; supr. press information ctr. Dem. Nat. Conv., N.Y.C., 1992, mgr. press info. ctr. ops. Chgo., 1996; dir. comm. Pub. Works and Transp. Com. U.S. Ho. of Reps., Washington, 1993-94, Dem. dir. comm. Transp. and Infrastructure Com., 1994-97; press sec. Senator Joseph I. Lieberman, Washington, 1997-99; dir. bus. pub. policy and govt. affairs KPMG LLP, 1999—; dir. press info. ctr. ops. Dem. Nat. Conv., L.A., 2000; mem. transition team Sec.-Designate Norman Y. Mineta U.S. Dept. Commerce, 2000. Freelance writer, 1982-87; contract writer Larsen-Pomada Lit. Agts., San Francisco, 1984-96, Farber Literacy Agy., N.Y., 1996—; lectr. U. Queensland, Australia, Bond U., Australia, Australian Ctr. Am. Studies, East-West Ctr. Hawaii, 1992, U. Western Australia, Edith Cowan U., Australia, Curtin U., Australia, U. Melbourne, Australia, La Trobe U., Australia, Victoria U., Australia, U.S. Consulate, Melbourne, 1993, U.S. Consulate, Sydney, U.S. Embassy, Canberra, Finders U. So. Australia, 1995; mem. Com. for Econ. Devel. of Australia U. Tasmania, Australian Inst. of Internat. Affairs, James Cook U., 1996, Monash U. Australia, U.S.-Australia Bus. and Trade Coun., Com. for Econ. Devel. of Australia, Flinders U. So. Australia, 1998; congl. liaison to Smithsonian Instn. Bd. Regents, 1995; U.S. dir. Washington internship program The Flinders U. Australia, 1999-2003, U. Queensland, U. Wollongong, U. Western Australia, U. Canberra, Macquarie U., Deakin U., 2003—; founder, dir. Uni-Capitol Washington Internship Programme, 2003—. Press sec. to nat. co-chair Dukakis-Bentsen Presdl. Campaign, Washington, 1988; prin. Coun. for Excellence in Govt., 2002—; bd. dirs. Nat. Japanese Am. Meml. Found., 2003—. Recipient Commendation for Outstanding Achievement by Sec. of State, 1981. Mem. Phi Beta Kappa. Democrat. Avocations: sound recordings, motion pictures, theater restoration, photography. E-mail: efedering@kpmg.com.

FEDERLE, MICHAEL, publishing executive; Assoc. pub. Fortune Mag., N.Y.C., 1997—99, pub., 1999—. Office: Time Inc Time Life Bldg Rockefeller Ctr New York NY 10020-1393*

FEDERMAN, DANIEL DAVID, medical educator, academic administrator, endocrinologist; b. N.Y.C., Apr. 16, 1928; m. Elizabeth Buckley; children: Lise, Carolyn. BA, Harvard U., 1949, MD, 1953. Diplomate Am. Bd. Internal Medicine. Instr. to prof. Harvard Med. Sch., Boston, 1961—72, prof. medicine and dean for students and alumni, 1977—92, Carl W. Walter prof. medicine and med. edn., dean med. edn., 1992—; chmn. medicine Stanford Med. Sch., Palo Alto, Calif., 1972—77. Author: (med. textbook) Abnormal Sexual Development, 1967; editor: Scientific American Medicine. Master: ACP (pres. Phila. 1982—83). Office: Harvard Med Sch Office of Dean Bldg A-101 25 Shattuck St Boston MA 02115-6027

FEDERSEL, HANS-JÜRGEN, pharmaceutical company executive; b. Säter, Dalecarlia, Sweden, Mar. 16, 1949; s. Hans and Ilse Marie (Schild) F.; m. Sophie Linnéa Lovisa Åkergård, June 13, 1981; children: Christopher, Alexander, Lovisa Antonia. MSc, Royal Inst. Tech., Stockholm, 1973, PhD, 1980. Devel. chemist Astra Pharm. Prodn., Södertälje, Sweden, 1974-89, prin. devel. chemist, 1989-92; mgr. Astra Prodn. Chems., Södertälje, 1992-96, sr. mgr., 1996-97, dir. projects coordination and liaison, process R & D, 1998-99; lead project mgr. AstraZeneca R & D, Södertälje, 1999-2001, head of projects, 2001—. Assoc. prof. Royal Inst. Tech., Stockholm, 1990—. Contbr. articles to profl. jours.; patentee in field. Mem. Swedish Chem. Soc., Drug Info. Assn., Internat. Soc. Heterocyclic Chemistry. Avocations: piano playing, music (instrumental and opera), wine-tasting, dogs. Home: Igelkottsvägen 60 16757 Stockholm-Bromma Sweden Office: AstraZeneca R & D 151 85 Södertälje Sweden E-mail: hans-jurgen.federsel@astrazeneca.com.

FEDERSPIEL, ULRIK, diplomat; b. Copenhagen, 1943; s. Per and Elin F.; m. Birgitte Hartnack. Degree in polit. sci. cum laude, U. Aarhus, Denmark, 1970; MA in Internat. Rels., U. Pa., 1971. With Danish Fgn. Svc., 1971-77, first sec., 1977-81, spl. asst. to permanent sec. state of fgn. affairs Copenhagen, 1981-84, min. Danish Embassy Washington, 1984-89, asst. to fgn. min. and fgn. svc. commn., 1989-91, head fgn. ministry and fgn. svc., permanent sec. state of fgn. affairs, 1991-93, permanent sec. state prime min. office, sec. cabinet, sec. to the Queen coun. mins., chmn. various govt. coms. including European Union-Summit Com., 1993-97, amb. to Ireland, 1997-2000, amb. to U.S., 2000—. Lectr., then sr. lectr. internat. rels. U. Copenhagen, 1971-77, censor, 1990, mem. governing bd., 1993-97; rschr. Danish Fgn. Policy Inst., 1975-76; vis. lectr. George Washington U., Washington, 1985-86. Author: Integration in Theory and Practice, 1985; co-editor yearbook Danish Fgn. Policy Inst., 1981-83, Danish Ct. and Danish Govt., 1993-96. Hon. trustee Crown Prince Frederik Fund; Danish adv. bd. Humanity in Action. With Royal Danish Navy. Decorated comdr. 1st degree Order of Dannebrog, Grand Cross of Belgium, Finland, Iceland, Italy, Lithuania, Norway, Portugal. Office: Royal Danish Embassy 3200 Whitehaven St NW Washington DC 20008-3616 E-mail: wasamb@um.dk.

FEDEWA, LAWRENCE JOHN, management consulting firm executive, entrepreneur; b. Lansing, Mich., Oct. 31, 1937; s. Norman Anthony and Agnes G. (Murphy) F.; m. Theresa Kathryn Goeser, Aug. 18, 1962; children: Kirsten

Ann, Eric Christian, Lawrence John Jr. BA, Sacred Heart Sem., Detroit, 1959; postgrad., Mich. State U., 1960-61; PhD, Marquette U., 1969. Cert. high sch. tchr., Colo. Mem. editorial staff Denver Cath. Register, 1962-63; columnist Hi-Time mag., 1963-64; assoc. prof. St. Norbert Coll., De Pere, Wis., 1966-71; prof. philosophy, v.p. Park Coll., Kansas City, Mo., 1971-76, dean of the coll., 1971-74; founder, provost Park Coll./Crown Ctr., Kansas City, Mo., 1974-76; dir. internat. projects Control Data Corp., Washington, 1976-79; pres. Fedewa and Assocs., Washington, 1979-81; co-founder Internat. Inst. for Advanced Tech., Manila, 1978; v.p., sec., bd. dirs. Cordatum Inc., McLean, Va., 1981-90, pres., CEO, bd. dirs., 1990; pres. CEO, chmn. bd. Washington Tech. Group, Springfield, Va., 1990—; chmn., CFO Washington Inst. Tech., 1990-2000; CFO, chmn. bd. dirs. Internat. Health Corp., 1991-94; mng. exec. K.W. Tunnell Co. Fed. Svcs. Group, Washington, 1994—. Chmn., CEO, bd. dirs. Plowshares Internat., Inc., 1992-95; chmn. bd. dirs., CFO Health Interventions, Inc., 1993-95, chmn. WTG Fin. Svcs. Corp., 1995-99; pres. Cedarwood Arabians, 1994—; exec. dir. NEA Ednl. Computer Svc., Washington, 1983-87. Pub. Yellow Book of Computer Products for Edn., 1983-86; author, pub. Guide to the Software Assessment Procedure, 1983-87; author: The Ethics of Ecumenism, 1969, Social Ethics with a Big Beat, 1970, The Design and Development of Computer Interactive Videodisc (CIV) Lessons, 1985; Education in the Information Age, 1986, Safety Training For Railroad Operating Employees: Introduction of Interactive Video Disc Training to the Railroad Industry (A Case Study), 1987, Do Computers Help Teachers Teach?, 1987. Mem. rsch. and devel. com. Met. Washington YMCA, 1986-90; trustee The Dupuy Inst., Washington, 1992. Roman Catholic. Avocations: horseman, racquetball, tennis, history, biography. Office: Washington Tech Group Inc #900 6564 Loisdale Ct Ste 900 Springfield VA 22150-1822 *I have come to believe that perseverance may be the ultimate virtue. Frequently, the ability to keep trying, to stay the course, can be more important to success than talent, luck, contacts, creativity, even purity of heart.*

FEDOR, ALLAN JOHN, lawyer; b. Erie, Pa., Jan. 2, 1947; s. Alexander Joseph and Janet Fedor; m. Franell Prhne, Mar. 18, 1977. BS cum laude, Gannon U., 1973; JD, U. Akron, 1976; MBA, Pepperdine U., 1979. Bar: Ohio 1976, Hawaii 1978, Calif. 1981, Fla., 1990. mfg. mgr. GE Co., Erie, 1965-73; gen. counsel, Trilogy Ltd., Cupertino, Calif., 1985-86; Big Bros. of Hawaii, Honolulu, 1977-80. Author: (with others) Drafting Agreements for the Sale of Businesses, 2nd edit., 1988, California Business Incorporations, 1988. Served with JAGC, Capt. U.S. Army, 1977-80. Mem. Pub. Investors Arbitration Bar Assn. (bd. dirs. 1998—), Blue Key Bracton's Inn (pres. 1975). Republican. Roman Catholic. Office: Fedor & Fedor 10225 Ulmerton Rd Ste 8A Largo FL 33771-3522

FEDORNAK, MARY, school counselor, educator; b. Bridgeport, Conn., Nov. 13, 1949; d. Leo William and Carmella Margaret Baker; m. Michael Richard Fedornak, Aug. 7, 1982. BA in Edn., So. Conn. State U., 1980; MA in Sch. Counseling, Fairfield U., 1990. Cert. educator, sch. counselor, Conn. Tchr. Nichols Elem. Sch., Stratford, Conn., 1984—; counselor Stratford Evening H.S., 1996—. Active area PTA. Mem. NEA, ACA, Nat. Bd. Cert. Counselors, Conn. Edn. Assn. Avocations: gardening, reading, walking. Home: 14 Rosewood Ln Shelton CT 06484-5771

FEDOROCHKO, WILLIAM, JR., retired army officer, defense policy analyst; b. Bayonne, N.J., Sept. 6, 1940; s. William and Helen (Dinis) F.; m. Sandra L. Clements, Dec. 10, 1966; 1 child, Sharon. BA in Econs., Washington and Jefferson Coll., 1962; MA in Econs., U. Pitts., 1971. Commd. 2d lt. U.S. Army, 1962, advanced through grades to brig. gen., 1989; platoon leader, staff officer 14th Armored Cav. Rgt., Fed. Republic Germany, 1962-64; staff officer Dept. Army, Washington, 1973-76; comdr. 1st Armored Div. Materiel Mgmt. Ctr., 501st Supply and Transport Bn., Fed. Republic Germany, 1976-80; student Def. Systems Mgmt. Coll., 1980, Indsl. Coll. Armed Forces, 1981; spl. asst. for joint activities Office of Comdr., Army Materiel Command, Alexandria, Va., 1981-83; chief acquisition and support program analysis div. Office Chief of Staff Army, Washington, 1983-84; comdr. 13th Support Command, Ft. Hood, Tex., 1984-87; spl. asst. Office Under Sec. Def. for Acquisition, Washington, 1987-88, dep. dir. program integration, 1988-90; dep. dir. force structure and resources Joint Staff, J-8, Washington, 1990-93; ret., 1993; sr. policy analyst RAND, Washington, 1993-94; sr. fellow Logistics Mgmt. Inst., McLean, Va., 1994-98; policy analyst strategy, forces and resources divsn. Inst. for Defense Analyses, Alexandria, Va., 1998—. Decorated Legion of Merit with 4 oak leaf clusters, Def. D.S.M. with oak leaf cluster. Mem. Assn. Quartermasters. Baptist. Avocations: golf, tennis. Home: 11404 Stonewall Jackson Dr Spotsylvania VA 22553-4607 Office: Inst for Def Analyses 4850 Mark Center Dr Alexandria VA 22311-1882 E-mail: wfedoroc@ida.org.

FEDOROFF, NINA VSEVOLOD, research scientist, consultant, educator; b. Cleve., Apr. 9, 1942; d. Vsevolod N. and Olga S. (Snegireff) Stacy; m. D. Pfaff, 2000; children: Natasha, Kyr, James. BS, Syracuse U., 1966; PhD, Rockefeller U., 1972. Asst. mgr. transl. bur. Biol. Abstracts, Phila., 1962-63; flutist Syracuse (N.Y.) Symphony Orch., 1964-66; acting asst. prof. UCLA, 1972-74; postdoctoral fellow UCLA and Carnegie Inst. Washington, Los Angeles and Balt., 1974-78; staff scientist Carnegie Inst. Washington, Balt., 1978-95; dir., biotechnol. inst. Pa. State U., 1995—, Willaman prof. of life scis., 1995—, Evan Pugh prof., 2002—. Dir. Life Scis. Consortium, Pa. State U., 1996—; prof. dept. biology John Hopkins U., 1979-95; mem. devel. biology panel NSF, Washington, 1979-80; sci. adv. panel Office of Tech. Assessment, Congress, Washington, 1979-80; recombinant DNA adv. com. NIH, Bethesda, Md., 1980-84; sci. adv. com. Japanese Human Frontier Sci., 1988; sci adv. com. Competitive Rsch. Grants Office, USDA; mem. commn. on life scis., basic biology bd. NRC, NAS, 1984-90; bd. dirs. Genetics Soc. Am.; mem. bd. overseers Harvard U., 1988-91; trustee BIOSIS, Phila., 1990-96; mem. NAS Coun., 1991-94; dir. Internat. Sci. Found., 1992-93; mem. adv. com. Directorate for Biol. Scis., 1994-97; chmn., bd. dirs. Sigma-Aldrich Corp., 1996. Editor: Gene, 1981—84, Perspectives in Biology and Medicine, 1991—2001, Procs. Nat. Acad. Sci., 1996—2000; editor, bd. rev. editors: Sci., 1985, mem. sci. adv. bd.: The Plant Jour., 1991—98, book editor: various publs.; contbr. chapters to books articles to profl. jours. Recipient merit award NIH, 1990, Howard Taylor Ricketts award U. Chgo., 1990, Arents Pioneer Medal, Syracuse U., 2003; grantee NSF and USDA, 1979-84, NIH, 1984—, NSF, 1992—, NASA, 1997—. Mem.: AAAS, NAS (editor procs. 1995—), AAAS (bd. dirs. 2000—), Am. Acad. Arts and Scis., Nat. Sci. Bd., Sigma Xi (McGovern Sci. and Soc. medal 1997, 1997), Phi Beta Kappa (vis. scholar 1984—85, vis. scholar 1984—85), Sigma Xi, Phi Beta Kappa. Avocations: chamber music, gardening, skiing, tennis, flying. Home: 2398 Shagbark Ct State College PA 16803-3367 Office: Biotechnol Inst Pa State U University Park PA 16802

FEDOROV, SERGEI, hockey player; b. Pskov, Russia, Dec. 13, 1969; Forward Detroit Red Wings, 1990—. Mem. Stanley Cub. Champions, Detroit Red Wings, 2002; founder Sergei Fedorov Found., 1998—. Recipient Hart Trophy, 1994, Selke Trophy, 1994, Lester B. Pearson award, 1994, Player of Yr. award, Hockey News, 1994, Sporting News, 1999, Hockey Digest, 1994, Silver medal, Olympic Games, Nagano, Japan, 1998. Avocations: golf, boating, travel. Office: Detroit Red Wings 600 Civic Center Dr Detroit MI 48226 4419

FEDOROWICZ, JANE, information systems educator; b. Derby, Conn, Mar. 5, 1955; m. Michael Golibersuch, Sept. 3, 1984; children: Andrew, William. BS in Health Systems, U. Conn., 1976; MS, Carnegie-Mellon U., 1978, PhD in Systems Sci., 1981. Instr., lectr. Carnegie-Mellon U., Pitts., 1978-80; asst. prof. Northwestern U., Evanston, Ill., 1980-85; assoc. prof. Boston U., 1985-93; vis. assoc. prof. U. Mass., Boston, 1993-94; assoc. prof. Bentley Coll., Waltham, Mass., 1994-2000, Rae D. Anderson Chair in Accountancy and Info. Sys., 1999—. Gen. chair DSS-92, Chgo., 1992; mem. editl. bd. Info. Sys. Rsch., Providence, 1987-2000, Mgmt. Info. Sys. Quar., 1989-94; co-gen. chair Am. Conf. Info. Systems, 2001; mem. exec. com. om pre-cert. edn. AICPA, 1999-2002. Contbr. articles to profl. jour. Named J.L. Kellogg Rsch. Prof., Northwestern U., 1984-85; recipient Notable Contbn. to Lit. award AAA/IS sect., 1997; named Bentley Coll. Scholar of the Year, 2000. Mem. ACM, Am. Acctg. Assn., Assn. Info. Systems (v.p. 1997-2004), Inst. Ops. Rsch. and Mgmt. Sci. (coll. chair 1986-88, mem. coun. 1993-96). Roman Catholic. Achievements include rsch. on the impact of info. tech. on individuals and orgn. E-mail: jfedorowicz@bentley.edu.

FEDUCCIA, J. ALAN, biologist, educator; b. Mobile, Ala., Apr. 25, 1943; m. Margarette Olivia Taylor, Sept. 5, 1947. BS, La. State U., 1960; MA, PhD, U. Mich., 1969. Rsch. assoc. Smithsonian Instn., Washington, 1978—87; S. K. Heninger prof. U. N.C., Chapel Hill, 1994—, chmn. div. natural scis., 1996—97, chmn. dept. biology, 1997—2002. Bd. govs. U. N.C. Press, Chapel Hill, 1999—; Watkins vis. prof. Wichita State U., 2002. Author: Structure and Evolution of Vertebrates, 1975, The Age of Birds, 1980, Catesby's Birds of Colonial America, 1985, Birds of Colonial Williamsburg, 1989, The Origin and Evolution of Birds, 1996 (Excellence in Biol. Sci., Assn. Am. Pubs., 1996); contbr. articles to profl. jours.; interview appearances include Nat. Pub. Radio, BBC, Voice of Am., CNN, McNeil/Lehrer Report. Recipient Smithsonian Disting. Lectr., Smithsonian Instn., 2002. Fellow: AAAS (life), Am. Ornithologists' Union (life). Avocations: farming, golf. Home: 704 Wellington Dr Chapel Hill NC 27514 Office: Dept Biology U NC Coker Hall CB # 3280 Chapel Hill NC 27599-3280 Home Fax: 919-962-3690; Office Fax: 919-962-3690. Personal E-mail: feduccia@bio.unc.edu. Business E-Mail: feduccia@bio.unc.edu.

FEDUNOK, SUZANNE, librarian; b. Pitts., Apr. 23, 1945; d. Yaroslav and Angela S. (Balcius) F. AB, Bryn Mawr (Pa.) Coll., 1967; AM, U. Mich., 1969, AMLS, 1974. Editl., reference libr. Math. Revs., Ann Arbor, Mich., 1969-74, head libr., 1974-77; math, physics libr. Columbia U., N.Y.C., 1977-83, head reference, collection devel. Sci. & Engring Dept., 1983-85, asst. dir., 1985-90, SUNY, Binghamton, 1990-96; head Coles Sci. Libr. NYU, 1996—. Mem. ALA, Spl. Librs. Assn., Internat. Fedn. Libr. Assns. Office: NYU Bobst Libr 70 Washington Sq S New York NY 10012-1091 E-mail: suzanne.fedunok@nyu.edu.

FEE, WILLARD EDWARD, JR., otolaryngologist; b. Portchester, N.Y., June 10, 1943; s. Willard E. and Jane Frances (Cromwell) F.; m. Caroline Fee, June 13, 1965; children: Heather, Adam. BS cum laude, U. San Francisco, 1965; MD magna cum laude, U. Colo., 1969. Intern Harbor Gen. Hosp., Torrance, Calif., 1969-70; resident in gen. surgery Wadsworth VA Hosp., L.A., 1970-71; resident in head and neck surgery UCLA Sch. Medicine, 1971-74; asst. prof. Stanford (Calif.) U. Med. Ctr., 1974-80, assoc. prof. otolaryngology, 1980-86, prof., 1986—, Edward C. & Amy H. Sewall prof., 1996—, chmn. dept., 1980-00. Dir. Am. Bd. of Otolaryngology, Houston, 1985—; chmn. med. sch. faculty senate Stanford U., 1992-94. Editl. bd. Archives in Otolaryngology, Chgo., 1984-95; contbr. numerous articles to profl. jours. Mem. Collegium ORLAS-US (chmn. 1995-2001), Paul H. Ward Soc., Inc. (pres. 1988-89), Am. Soc. Head and Neck Surgery (pres. 1989-90), Am. Acad. Otolaryngology and Head and Neck Surgery, Calif. Soc. Otolaryngology (pres. 1995-99), Alpha Omega Alpha. Home: 27299 Ursula Ln Los Altos CA 94022-3222 Office: Stanford U Med Ctr Divsn Otolaryngology Edwards R135 300 Pasteur Stanford CA 94305-5328

FEEGEL, JOHN RICHARD, pathologist; b. Middletown, Conn., Nov. 16, 1932; s. Fred Benjamin and Eva Lilian (Kane) Feegel; m. Elaine Antoinette Blanchet, Feb. 1968; children: John R., Mark, Catherine, Elizabeth, Thomas. BS, Holy Cross Coll., 1954; MD, U. Ottawa, Ont., Can., 1960; JD, U. Denver, 1964; MPH, U. So. Fla., 1991. Bar: Colo. 1964, Fla. 1967, U.S. Dist. Ct. (mid. dist.) Fla. 1983; diplomate Am. Bd. Pathology (AP, FP). Intern St. Mary's Hosp., West Palm Beach, Fla., 1960—61; resident in pathology and forensic pathology Denver Gen. Hosp., Denver Coroner's Office, 1961—65; chief med. examiner Tampa, Fla., 1973—76; assoc. chief med. examiner State of N.C., 1976—77, Fulton County, Atlanta, 1977—83; ptnr. Mitzel, Mitzel & Feegel, Tampa, 1983—86; adj. assoc. prof. pathology U. N.C., Chapel Hill, 1976—77; assoc. prof. pathology Emory U., Atlanta, 1977—81; pvt. practice Tampa. Author: (novels) Autopsy, 1976 (Edgar award, 1977), Dance Card, 1980. Served to comdr. USPHS, 1965—67. Fellow: Am. Coll. Legal Medicine, Am. Acad. Forensic Scis., Coll. Am. Pathologists; mem.: ATLA. Republican. Roman Catholic. Home: 3002 W Waverly Ave Tampa FL 33629-8912 Office: Law Office of John R FeegelPA 401 S Albany Ave Tampa FL 33606-2019

FEELEY, KAREN ADLER, training services executive, consultant; b. Toms River, NJ, Nov. 8, 1966; d. Herman Alfred and Ruth Adler; m. T. Jens Feeley. BA in Chinese Area Studies, The Am. U., Washington, 1989; MBA, George Washington U., 1996. Tng. & devel. intern Magnet Interactive Studios, Washington, 1995; prin. cons. PwC Consulting, Arlington, Va., 1996—. Tchr. Tianjin Inst. of Tech., 1989—90. Literacy vol. Jewish Coalition for Literacy/Chinatown Beacon Ctr., San Francisco, 2000; English lang. tutor Bd. of Jewish Family Welfare Services, N.Y.C., 1991. Mem.: ASTD, Nat. S.D. Assn., Pacific N.W. Writers Assn., Soc. for Childrens Book Writers & Illustrators, Experience Music Project. Avocations: travel, reading, writing, kayaking, skiing. Office: IBM 1616 N Ft Myer Dr Arlington VA 22209

FEELEY, MALCOLM MCCOLLUM, law educator, political scientist; b. North Conway, N.H., Nov. 28, 1942; s. John Aloysius and Mildred (McCollum) F.; divorced; children: Jacob, Miriam, Amin. BA, Austin Coll., 1964; MA, U. Minn., 1966, PhD, 1969. Asst. prof. NYU, N.Y.C., 1968-72; fellow, lectr. Yale U., New Haven, Conn., 1972-77; prof. U. Wis.-Madison, 1977-84; prof. law U. Calif.-Berkeley, 1984—. V.p. Silbert-Feeley Assn., New Haven, 1975-83; editorial advisor Longman Inc., N.Y.C., 1979—. Author: The Process is the Punishment, 1979, The Policy Dilemma, 1981, Court Reform on Trial, 1983, Judicial Policy-Making, 1998; Editor: American Constitutional Law, 1985. Recipient Silver Gavel award, ABA, 1980, cert. merit, 1984; fellow Ctr. for Advanced Study, Stanford U., 2001—02. Mem. Law and Soc. Assn. (trustee 1975-80), Am. Polit. Sci. Assn. Democrat. Jewish. Avocations: canoeing, hiking, reading. Office: U Calif Sch Law Boalt Hall Ctr Study Law Society Hl Berkeley CA 94720-0001

FEELEY, MICHAEL JOHN, investment counselor; b. Bklyn., Aug. 3, 1944; s. John Joseph and Eileen Emily Feeley; m. Mary Ellen Feeley, Dec. 27, 1967 (div. Dec. 1995); children: John, Pamela, Jamie, Michelle. AB, Georgetown U., 1966; JD, Fordham U., 1969; MBA, Harvard U., 1971. V.p. Mitchell Hutchins, N.Y.C., 1971-75; mngr. Brown Bros. Harriman, N.Y.C., 1975-86; account exec. Carret Securities, N.Y.C., 1997-99, Brill Securities, N.Y.C., 1999—; pres. Feeley Wilcox, N.Y.C., 1986—; chmn. Sino Am. Devel. Corp., N.Y.C., 1993—. Author: The Decade Ahead, 1989. Parish coun. St. Teresa's, Summit, N.J., 1975-85; coach Summit Jr. Baseball, Summit, 1976-85. Mem. Baltusrol Golf Club, Harvard Club. Republican. Roman Catholic. Avocations: golf, cinema, books. Home: 71A New England Ave Summit NJ 07901-1842 Office: Sino Am Devel Corp 380 Rector Pl New York NY 10280-1441

FEELEY, TIMOTHY E. state representative; b. Hackensack, NJ, Feb. 3, 1956; m. Dr. Sue Feeley; children: Kate, Mary, Peggy;1 child, Jack. JD, W. Va. Univ. Coll. of Law, 1985; BS, The Warton Sch., Univ. of Pa., 1978. State Rep. House of Rep., Dist. 59, 1998—; atty. Pvt. practice, 1996—; asst. US atty. US Dept. of Justice, 1989—96. Bd. mem. Sch. Bd. of Ed., Oldham County, 1994—98; vice chair Econ. Devel.; mem. Ed., State Gov. Capt., JAGC U.S. Army, 1978—96, Germany. Caucuses: Backacre Task Force, 2000-present; Ky. Rails to Trails Task Force, 1999-present. Republican. Catholic. Office: Capitol Capitol Annex, Rm 413C Frankfort KY 40601 also: Dist PO Box 64 Crestwood KY 40014*

FEELISCH, MARTIN, research scientist, consultant; b. Remscheid, Northrhine Westfalia, Germany, June 18, 1959; s. Guenter Max and Hildegard Feelisch; m. Lucia del Pilar Revelo Silva, Jan. 28, 1999; m. Dorothee Briese, Jan. 9, 1986 (div. Jan. 19, 1999); children: Lucia Gabriela Revelo, Nicolas Constantin, Nicole Martina, Marco Laurenz. Pharmacy Technician, Pharmazeutisch-Technische Lehranstalt, Solingen, Germany, 1979—81; BSc, Heinrich-Heine-U., Dusseldorf, Germany, 1985; PhD summa cum laude, Heinrich-Heine-University, Dusseldorf, Germany, 1988. Venia legendi for Pharmacology & Toxicology U. Cologne, Germany, 1997, lic. pharmacist Head Provincial Govt. Dusseldorf, Germany, 1986, cert. specialist for drug info. Apothekerkammer Nordrhein, Germany, 1992, Expert Degree in Pharmacology German Pharmacological Soc., 1992. Vis. rsch. scientist The Wellcome Rsch. Labs., Beckenham, England, 1989—90; head dept. pharmacology Schwarz Pharma AG, Monheim, Germany, 1990—97, dir. pharmacology and internat. project coord., 1991—97; sr. lectr., sci. coord. Wolfson Inst., U. Coll. London, 1997—99; prof. molecular and cellular physiology La. State U. Health Scis. Ctr., Shreveport, 1999—. Co-founder, dir. The Nitric Oxide Soc., 1996—; cons. Lacer S.A., Barcelona, 1997—99; vis. prof. pharmacology U. Florence, Italy, 1999—99; sci. adv. bd. mem. Vasopharm Biotech GmbH, Giessen, Hessen, Germany, 2000—, NitroMed Inc., Bedford, Mass., 2003—. Author, editor: reference book Method in Nitric Oxide Research, mem. editl. bd.: Nitric Oxide Chemistry & Biology, 1993—, Endothelium, 1993—; contbr. articles to profl. jours. Named Hon. Sr. Lectureship in Pharmacology, U. Coll. London, 1998—99; fellow, Smith Kline Dauelsberg, 1987—88; grantee, Nat. Heart, Blood and Lung Inst., 2002 . Mem.: Nitric Oxide Soc. (dir. 1996—2003), Soc. for Free Radical Biology and Medicine, German Pharm. Soc., German Soc. for Cardiology, Heart and Circulation Rsch., German Soc. for Exptl. and Clin. Pharmacology and Toxicology (Fritz-Kulz prize 1990), Am. Physiol. Soc., Am. Heart Assn., Am. Chem. Soc. Achievements include patents in field. Home: 2017 South Kirkwood Dr Shreveport LA 71118 Office: LSU Health Scis Ctr 1501 Kings Hwy Shreveport LA 71130-3932 E-mail: mfeeli@lsuhsc.edu.

FEENEY, DANIEL ARTHUR, veterinary radiologist; b. Butte, Mont., June 1, 1950; s. Daniel Henry and Phyllis May (Herrin) F.; m. Janet May Emrick, June 16, 1973; 1 child, Russell Dominic. BS, Colo. State U., 1972, DVM, 1974; MS, U. Ga., 1978. Intern in small animal medicine Purdue U., West Lafayette, Ind., 1974-75; resident in vet. radiology U. Ga., Athens, 1975-78; from asst. prof. to assoc. prof. U. Minn., St. Paul, 1978-89, prof., 1989—. Cons. in vet. radiology, Mpls., 1983—. Co-author: Correlative Imaging Anatomy, 1991, Small Animal Radiology and Ultrasound, 2003. Mem. Am. Coll. Vet. Radiology (diplomate), Phi Kappa Phi, Sigma Xi. Avocations: camping, snowmobiling, boating, motorcycling. Home: 2932 108th Ln NW Coon Rapids MN 55433-3813 Office: U Minn 1352 Boyd Ave Saint Paul MN 55108-6100 E-mail: feene001@umn.edu.

FEENEY, DAVID WESLEY, lawyer; b. Phila., Nov. 1, 1938; s. William James McKay and Mary Catherine (Watkins) Feeney; m. Elizabeth Butler Shamel, Aug. 15, 1959; children: Shawn, Shari, David, Darryl. BS, Cornell U., 1960, LLB with distinction, 1963. Bar: U.S. Tax Ct. 1966, U.S. Dist. Ct. (so. dist.) N.Y. 1976, U.S. Ct. Claims 1976, U.S. Ct. Appeals (2d cir.) 1976. Assoc. Cadwalader, Wickersham & Taft, N.Y.C., 1963-64, 66-71, ptnr., 1971—. Served to 1st lt. U.S. Army, 1964-66. Mem. N.Y. State Bar Assn. (tax sect.), Cornell Club of N.Y.C. Republican. Presbyterian. Home: 1 Black Point Horseshoe Rumson NJ 07760-1500 Office: Cadwalader Wickersham et al 100 Maiden Ln New York NY 10038-4818

FEENEY, DON JOSEPH, JR., psychologist; b. Greenville, N.C., Jan. 17, 1948; s. Don Joseph Sr. and Louise (Saieed) Feeney; 1 child, Kelly Lynn. BA, Colgate U., 1971; MA, Gov.'s State U., 1973; PhD, Loyola U., Chgo., 1979. Registered psychologist Ill., Ind., diplomate Am. Bd. Psychol. Specialties, Am. Bd. Psychology, cert. addictions counselor; profl. coach Grow Tng. Inst., Inc. Clin. dir. Champaign (Ill.) Coun. on Alcoholism, 1976-79; pvt. practice psychology, hypnotherapy, family svcs. Downers Grove, Ill., 1979—, Dangerous Drugs Com., Chgo., 1979-80; psychologist Tri-City Mental Health Ctr., East Chicago, Ind., 1980-82; psychologist alcohol treatment program Christ Hosp., Oak Lawn, Ill., 1982—; cons. Cons. Psychol. Svcs. PC, Downers Grove, 1985—, ceo, 1998—. Chmn. adv. coun. alcoholism Govs. State U., University Park, Ill., 1979—82; devel., presenter self-hypnosis and wellness programs on smoking, weight control and chem. abuse. Author: Entrancing Relationships: Exploring the Hypnotic Framework of Addictive Relationships, 1999, Motif: The Transformative Creation of Self, 2001, Creating Cultural Motifs in the War Against Terrorism, 2003; contbr. articles to profl. jours.; guest cons. (TV series) Oprah Winfrey, Jerry Springer, Jenny Jones, others. Loyola U. fellow, 1976. Mem.: APA, Chgo. Coun. Fgn. Rels., Ill. Psychol. Assn. Roman Catholic. Avocations: chess, tennis, weightlifting, jogging, reading. Office: Cons Psychol Svcs PC 6900 Main St Ste 58 Downers Grove IL 60516-3455 E-mail: drdonjfeeneyjr@mycidco.com.

FEENEY, FLOYD FULTON, legal educator; b. Franklin, Ind., Sept. 26, 1933; s. Burla L. and Ona Marie (McMillin) F.; m. Peggy Ann Ballard, June 15, 1956; children: Elizabeth, Linda. BS in History with honors, Davidson Coll., 1955; LL.B., NYU, 1960. Bar: N.C. 1960, D.C. 1961. Law clk. U.S. Supreme Ct., 1961-62; spl. asst. to solicitor Dept. Labor, 1962-63; dep. spl. counsel Pres.'s Com. on Equal Employment Opportunity, 1963; asst. dir. Pres.'s Crime Commn., 1966-67; spl. asst. to adminstr. AID, 1963-68; prof. law U. Calif.-Davis, 1968—; mem. Calif. Atty. Gen.'s Research Adv. Council, 1985-90. Cons. Nat. Ctr. for State Cts., Nat. Inst. Justice, Brit. Home Office. Author: The Police and Pretrial Release, 1982, (with Roger Baron) Juvenile Diversion Through Family Counseling, 1976, (with Dill and Weir) Arrests Without Conviction, 1983, (with Philip Dubois) Lawmaking by Initiative, 1998. Served to 1st lt. U.S. Army, 1956-58. Fulbright scholar, 1995-96; recipient Pepperdine award, 1978 Mem. ABA, Am. Assn. Law Schs., Am. Law Inst., D.C. Bar Assn., N.C. Bar Assn., Assn. for Criminal Justice Research Calif. Home: 1228 Colby Dr Davis CA 95616-1719 E-mail: fffeeney@ucdavis.edu.

FEENEY, KELLY LYNN, management consultant; b. Chicago Heights, Ill., July 25, 1976; d. Don Joseph Jr. and Diane Feeney. Student, U. Sheffield, Eng., DePaul U., 1998—. Computer scientist, supr. Butler U., Indpls., 1994; orgnl. cons. Psychol. Consulting, Downers Grove, Ill., 1994-98. Analyst, rschr., clk. on market Chgo. Bd. Trade, 1995-96. Strategic planner Rep. Party, Chgo., 1996-97. Scholar Butler U., Indpls., 1995-96, DePaul U., Chgo., 1996—. Mem. Gamma Delta Sorority (treas. 1995-96). Roman Catholic. Avocations: art, music, arts, computer sciences, reading, philosophy. Office: Psychol Consulting 20146 S Pine Hill Rd Frankfort IL 60423

FEENEY, KENDALL GREER, art director, music educator; b. Pomona, CA, Apr. 26, 1958; d. John Francis Feeney, Carol McEuen Feeney; m. Anthony Michael Flinn. Bachelor of Music, University of Southern California, Los Angeles, California, 1978—80, Masters of Music, 1981—84. Artistic dir. ZEPHYR, Spokane, Wash., 1991—; faculty assoc. Ea. Wash. U., Cheney, 1990—. Guest spkr. Wash. State Music Tchrs. Assn., 1987—; faculty mem. Taubman Inst. Piano, Williamstown, Mass., 1997—. Musician: (Concert performer) Bellingham Music Festival, 2000, Round Top Festival Inst., 1983—84, New Coll. Festival, 1981, author essay writer for Clavier magazine. Board Member Hanford Education and Action League, Spokane, WA, 1986—99. Recipient Artist of the Yr. award, Spokane, Wash., 1997. Mem.: Music Teachers National Association. Avocation: Reading, gardening, animals, equestrian work, outdoors. Home: 1230 East 14th Ave Spokane WA 99202 Office: Eastern Washington University Music Department Cheney WA 99004 Personal E-mail: kgfeeney@earthlink.net. Business E-Mail: kfeeney@ewu.edu.

FEENEY, MARY KATHERINE O'SHEA, retired public health nurse; b. Niagara Falls, N.Y., July 10, 1934; d. James T. and Mary Elizabeth (Woodside) O'Shea; m. Gerald E. Feeney, Apr. 27, 1957; children: Patricia, Elizabeth, Susan, Kathleen. BSN, Niagara U., 1956; MS in Mgmt., SUNY, Binghamton, 1981. RN, N.Y.; hypnotherapist; Assessment Modified Reflexology for Nurses. Pub. health nurse Herkimer County (N.Y.) Pub. Health Nursing Svc.; ret. Past coord. Herkimer County Long Term Health Care; bd. dirs. Oneida/Herkimer Coalition for Smoke Free Mohawk Valley. Home: 146 State Route 169 Little Falls NY 13365-5017

FEENEY, MICHAEL THOMAS, civil engineer; b. Greensboro, N.C., Sept. 14, 1956; s. William Thomas and Helen Rae (Davis) F.; m. Mary Ryan Phillips, Oct. 26, 1985; children: William Patrick, Michael Ryan, Mary Patricia. BCE, N.C. State U., 1978, MCE, 1981. Registered profl. engr., Ga., Ala., S.C., Kans., Ind., Tenn., N.C., Va. Engr. trainee U.S. Corps Engrs., Wilmington, N.C., 1977-78, civil engr., 1979-80; engr. Golder Assocs. Inc., Atlanta, 1981-84, project engr., 1984-86, sr. engr., 1986-87, assoc., 1987-92; mgr. geotechnology Jordan, Jones & Goulding Inc., Atlanta, 1993—. Scoutmaster Boy Scouts Am., Atlanta, 1981-85, 2002—, den leader, 1996-2002, troop com., 2001-02; active pub. sch. system strategic planning team, Atlanta, 1990; com. mem. Homeowners Assn., Atlanta, 1990-2002. Mem. ASCE, Solid Waste Assn. N.Am., N.Am. Geosynthetics Soc. Republican. Roman Catholic. Achievements include research in landfill performance, leakage, and alternative liners closure. Office: Jordan Jones & Goulding Inc 6801 Governors Lake Pky Norcross GA 30021

FEENEY, TOM, congresswoman; b. Abington, Pa., May 21, 1958; m. Ellen Stewart. BA in Polit. Sci., Pa. State U., 1980; JD, U. Pitts., 1983. Mem. Fla. Ho. of Reps., 1990—94, 1996—2002, speaker, 2000—02; majority coun. liaison; mem. procedural coun. chair reapportionment com.; mem. econ. impact, govt. responsibility, justice couns.; U.S. rep. Florida, 2003—. Rep. nominee lt. gov., 1994; legis. del. chmn. Orange County, 1993, Seminole County, 1996; ambas-

sador to Macedonian Govt., Internat. Rep. Inst., 1995; bd. dir. U. Activity Ctr. Transp. Authority, Mosley's High-Tech Tutoring, Cornerstone Inc. Distbn. Ctr., OIA Kidsway Inc., James Madison Inst., former dir.; mem. bus. leadership coun. City of Light; mem. rep. exec. com. Orange and Seminole County; former Fla. chmn. Empowerment Network; former chmn. edn. task force Am. Legis. Exchang Coun., 1992-94. Recipient Outstanding Legislator of Yr. award Ctrl. Fla. Young Rep., 1991, 92, Am. Legis. Exchange Coun., 1992, So. Coll. Cmty. Svc. award, 1992, Orlando Leadership award, 1993, 40 Under 40 award Orlando Bus. Jour., 1996. Mem. East Orange C. of C., S.W. Volusia, C. of C., Sandord C. of C., Oviedo C. of C. Presbyterian. Avocations: history, politics, philosophy, reading. also: PO Box 622109 Oviedo FL 32762-2109 Office: 323 Cannon House Off Bldg Washington DC 20515*

FEENSTRA, LAURENCE HENRY, physician; b. Grand Rapids, Mich., Aug. 27, 1927; s. Henry and Agnes (Hofstra) F. m. June Elaine Nykamp, Aug. 15, 1952; children: Richard D., Lori Beth, David Scott, Cheryl Sue. BS, Calvin Coll., Grand Rapids, 1949; MD, U. Mich., 1952. Diplomate Am. Bd. Internal Medicine, Am. Bd. Geriatrics. Mem. staff, cons. Buttwerworth Hosp. (now Spectrum Health), Grand Rapids, 1958—, chief internal medicine, 1971-75, program dir. internal medicine, 1971-90. Mem. staff Blodgett Meml. Hosp., Grand Rapids, 1958-70, mem. courtesy staff, 1970—; mem. staff St. Mary's Hosp., Grand Rapids, 1958-70; clin. prof. medicine Mich State u., 1984—. Lt. M.C., USN, 1953-55. Fellow ACP; mem. AMA, Mich. State Med. Soc., Kent County Med. Soc., Mich. Athletic Club, East Hills Athletic Club. Avocations: traveling, tennis, sailing, skiing. Home: 2137 N Cross Creek Dr SE Grand Rapids MI 49508-8775 Office: Spectrum Health-Butterworth Hosp 100 Michigan St NE Grand Rapids MI 49503-2551 E-mail: larry.feenstra@spectrum-health.org.

FEESER, LARRY JAMES, civil engineering educator, researcher; b. Hanover, Pa, Feb. 23, 1937; s. Cyrus Myers and Arelia Cecilia (Stonesifer) F.; m. Patricia Marianne Reinhold, Aug. 19, 1961; children— Anne Elizabeth, David John BS in Civil Engring., Lehigh U., 1958; MS, U. Colo., 1961; PhD, Carnegie-Mellon U., 1965. Registered profl. engr., Colo., 1963, N.Y., 1974. From instr. to prof. civil engring. U. Colo., Boulder, 1958-71; prof., chmn. dept. civil engring. Rensselaer Poly. Inst., Troy, NY, 1974-82, assoc. dean engring., 1982-85, vice provost for computing and info. tech., 1985-90, prof. civil engring., 1990—, dir. ctr. for infrastructure and transp. studies, 1993-95. Cons. Jorgensen & Hendrickson Engrs., Denver Contbr. articles to profl. jour. Named to Those Who Made Marks in 1981, Engring. News Record, 1982; Ford Found. fellow, 1961-63; NSF Sci. Faculty fellow, 1971-72 Fellow Am. Concrete Inst., ASCE (hon., nat. dir. 1979-82), fellow, Nat. Soc. Profl. Engrs. (nat. v.p. 1998-99); mem. Am. Soc. Engring. Edn. Office: Rensselaer Poly Inst Dept Civil and Environ Engring Troy NY 12181

FEFFER, GERALD ALAN, lawyer; b. Washington, Apr. 24, 1942; s. Louis Charles and Elsie (Glick) F.; children: Andrew, John, Keith. BA with honors, Lehigh U., 1964; JD, U. Va., 1967. Bar: N.Y. 1968, D.C. 1980. Assoc. Mudge, Rose, Guthrie & Alexander, N.Y.C., 1967-71; asst. U.S. atty. So. Dist. N.Y., 1971-76, asst. chief criminal div., 1975-76; ptnr. Kostelanetz & Ritholz, N.Y.C., 1976-79; dep. asst. atty. gen. tax div. Dept. Justice, Washington, 1979-81; ptnr. Steptoe & Johnson, Washington, 1981-86, Williams & Connolly, Washington, 1986—. Mem. editl. bd. Busniess Crimes Bulletin: Compliance and Litigation; contbr. articles to profl. jours. Fellow Am. Coll. Tax Counsel, Am. Coll. Trial Lawyers; mem. ABA (criminal justice litigation and taxation sects.), Nat. Assn. Criminal Def. Lawyers, Nat. Inst. on Criminal Tax Fraud (chmn.). Office: Williams & Connolly 725 12th St NW Washington DC 20005-5901 Home: 3000 Garrison St NW Washington DC 20008-1032 also: # 306 2512 Q St NW Washington DC 20007-4310

FEFFERMAN, HILBERT, government official, lawyer; b. N.Y.C., June 5, 1913; s. Jacob and Sarah F.; m. Helen Libby Relkin, June 16, 1940. BS magna cum laude in philosophy(hon.), NYU, 1934; JD, Harvard U., 1937. Bar: N.Y. 1938, U.S. Supreme Ct. 1953. Pvt. practice, N.Y.C., 1938-41; atty. U.S. Housing and Home Fin. Agy., Washington, 1941-59, asst. gen. counsel for legislation, 1960-62, assoc. gen. counsel for ops., 1962-67; chief legislative counsel HUD, Washington, 1967-72; cons. Housing and Devel. Legislation, Bethesda, Md., 1973—. Lectr., vis. prof. city planning MIT, Cambridge, Mass., 1973-76. Contbr. articles to profl. jours. Recipient Disting. Svc. award HUD, 1968. Mem.: Phi Beta Kappa. Home and Office: 5661 Bent Branch Rd Bethesda MD 20816-1049

FEGAN, JEFFREY P. airport executive; BS in Geography, Frostburg U.; M in City Planning, Ga. Inst. Tech.; advanced airport mgmt. course, Internat. Aviation Mgmt. Tng. Inst., Montreal. Aviation cons., 1978-83; noise abatement officer Westchester County Airport, N.Y., 1983-84; chief planner Dallas/Ft. Worth Internat. Airport Bd., 1984, asst. dir., dir. planning and engring., 1989-93, dep. exec. dir. fin. and adminstrn., 1993-94, exec. dir., chief adminstr., exec. officer, 1994—. Mem. Airports Coun. Internat.-NA Environ. Affairs Com., Internat. Civil Airports Assn.-Passenger Facilitation World Com., Am. Assn. Airport Execs., Am. Planning Assn., Am. Inst. Cert. Planners. Office: DFW Int'l Airport Adminstrn PO Box 619428 Dallas TX 75261-9428*

FEGELY, EUGENE LEROY, retired humanities educator; b. Allentown, Pa., Dec. 10, 1930; s. Leroy Tracy and Viola Eliza (Sterner) F.; m. Margaret Ann Maconaghy, Sept. 18, 1954; children: Barbara, Laura, Hugh. BS in Edn., Temple U., Phila., 1956, MS in Edn., 1960. Cert. prin., tchr., edn. specialist. Tchr. Bucks County C.C., Newtown, Pa., 1970-78; instr. Craven C. C., New Bern, N.C., 1988—. Stage mgr., actor Bucks County Playhouse, New Hope, Pa., 1984-86; asst. to prodr.-dir. Worthy is the Lamb, Swansboro, N.C., 1988; pres. Imagerz, Inc. Author: Best of the Least, 1973; editor: Temple PDK, 1960-70, Rebel Rouser, 1995-99, Internat. Assn. Bus. Leaders, 2002-03; N.C. editor SERA Jour., 1990-2000. Recipient Citation, Pa. Ho. of Reps., Harrisburg, 1987. Mem. NEA (life), Actors Equity, Pa. State Edn. Assn. (life, pres. 1967-68, Plaque 1968), Phi Delta Kappa (life, area coord. 1970-78, plaque 1978). Republican. Methodist. Avocation: photography. Home: 115 Randomwood Ln New Bern NC 28562-9556 Office: PO Box 15544 New Bern NC 28561-5544

FEHELEY, LAWRENCE FRANCIS, lawyer; b. Phila., Oct. 9, 1946; s. Francis Edward and Dorothy May (Greenhalgh) F.; divorced; 1 child, Matthew Francis; m. Janet Kay Douglass, Apr. 6, 1979; children: Brendan Patrick, Lawren Kaitlin, Tyne Brielle. BA, Cornell U., 1969, JD with distinction, 1973. Bar: Ohio 1973, U.S. Dist. Ct. (so. dist.) Ohio 1974, U.S. Ct. Appeals (6th cir.) 1980, U.S. Supreme Ct. 1993. Assoc. Emens, Kegler, Brown, Hill & Ritter, Columbus, Ohio, 1973-77; ptnr. Emens, Hurd, Kegler & Ritter, Columbus, Ohio, 1977—, mng. dir., 1986; Dir., exec. com. Kegler, Brown, Hill & Ritter (formerly Emens, Hurd, Kegler & Ritter, Columbus, Ohio, 2000—. Bd. dirs. Netcare Corp. Fellow, Coll. Labor and Employment Lawyers, 2001—. Mem. ABA, Ohio Bar Assn. (bd. govs. labor law sect.), Columbus Bar Assn., Ohio State Bar Assn. (cert. specialist in labor and employment law 2001-). Republican. Episcopalian. Avocations: art, soccer. Office: Kegler Brown Hill & Ritter 65 E State St Ste 1800 Columbus OH 43215-4213

FEHLBERG, ROBERT ERICK, architect; b. Kalispell, Mont., Apr. 28, 1926; s. Otto Albert Erick and Mary Grace (Nelson) F.; m. LaDonna Karen Rognlie, May 31, 1953; children: Kolby J., Kenje A., Kurt E., Klee J. BS in Architecture, Mont. State U., 1951. Architect in tng. with Gehres D. Weed Architect, Kalispell, 1952-55; partner Weed & Fehlberg Architects, Kalispell, 1955-57; pvt. practice Kalispell, 1957-58; with Cushing Terrell Assos., Billings, Mont., 1958-72, partner, 1960-72; v.p. CTA Architects Engrs., Inc., Billings, 1973-87; ptnr. Collaborative Design Architects, Oakland, Calif., 1987-91, Robert Fehlberg Architects, Pleasanton, Calif., 1991—. Bd. dirs. Yellowstone Art Center Found., 1965-84, 1st pres., 1965; bd. dirs. Mont. Inst. Arts Found., 1976-86, pres., 1976-80, treas., 1980-86. Served with AUS, 1944-46. Recipient (with wife) Gov.'s award for arts, 1983 Fellow AIA (pres. Mont. 1965, nat. dir. 1971-74), Mont. Inst. Arts (pres. 1963-64); mem. Prodn. Systems for Architects and Engrs. (dir. 1971-74, chmn. 1974), East Bay AIA. Home: 7566 Rosedale Ct Pleasanton CA 94588-3762 also: PO Box 2431 Sitka AK 99835-2431

FEHLER, POLLY DIANE, neonatal nurse, educator; b. Harvard, Ill., Jan. 6, 1946; d. Arthur William and Charlotte (Stewart) Eggert; m. Gene L. Fehler, Dec. 26, 1964; children: Timothy, Andrew. AS, summa cum laude, Kishwaukee Coll., 1974; BSN, magna cum laude, No. Ill. U., DeKalb, 1977, MSN, summa cum laude, 1980. Cert. BLS, neonatal resuscitation instr., 1989-00. Ob-gyn. staff nurse Kishwaukee Hosp., 1977; community health nurse DeKalb County Health Dept., 1977-79; grad. teaching asst. No. Ill. Univ., 1978-80; adj. maternity instr. Auburn Univ., Montgomery, Ala., 1980-81; maternal/newborn nurse USAF Regional Hosp. Maxwell, Montgomery, Ala., 1980-81, nurse internship coord., 1981-83; edn. coord. USAF Hosp., Bergstrom, Austin, Tex., 1983-87; neonatal ICU & transport RN St. Mary's Hosp., Athens, Ga., 1988-90; nursing instr. Tri-County Tech. Coll., Pendleton, S.C., 1990-97, dept. head nursing program, 1998—. EMT, course lectr. U. Tex., Austin, 1984-86; counselor, vol. Hospice, 1984-87; sec., v.p. Shared Resources for Nurses, Austin, 1984-87; high blood pressure instr.-trainer Am. Heart Assn., 1986-87, home health staff nurse Interim Health Care, Anderson, S.C., 1991-94; expert witness St. Mary's Hosp., Athens, 1991-92; coord. NCLEX rev. course Health Edn. Systems, Inc., 1993-96; lectr. on interculturalism in nursing, 1993-99; mem. adv. bd. Tri-County Student Competencies, 1990-99, mem. advising team, 1995-2002, mini grant sel. com., 1992-93, 95-97, com. chmn., 1996-97, Tri-County Instrnl. Affairs com., 1998-2000, Y2K Coll. Planning Group, 1999-2000. Nursing textbook reviewer Addison Wesley Pubs., 1993-99, Mosby Yearbook, 1995-99, Saunders Publisher, 1999-2000. Nurse, med. evaluator Mass Casualty Exercises, Austin, 1984-87; tchr., sec. United Meth. Chs., Ill., Ala., Ga., S.C., 1970—; mem. alumni bd. No. Ill. U., DeKalb, 1979-80; mem. Malta Dist. Bd. Edn., 1979-80; judge Austin Sch. Dist. Sci. and Math. Fair, Austin, 1983-84; S.C. Gov.'s Guardian ad Litem Vol., 1995-99; vol. Oconee County Healthy Visions Task Force, 1996-98, S.C. Good Health Appeal Coll. Campaign Mgr., 1996, Oconee County Humane Soc., 1996-2002; mem. adv. coun. Oconee Kid's Health, 1997-99, Planning Work Force, 1998-99; mem. SC Nurses Assn. Continuing Edn. Approval Com., 1998-2000, SC Maternal Child Health Counc., 1999-2001. Capt. USAF, 1980-88. Decorated USAF Commendation medal with oak leaf cluster; recipient Sr. Nursing Class of Tri-County Tech. Coll. Instr. of the Yr. award, 1992, Nat. Inst. for Staff and Orgnl. Devel. Excellence award, 1995; Duke Power grantee Alliance 2020, 1997-02; Amy Cockcroft Leadership fellow, U. S.C., 2002-03. Mem. ANA, Nat. League for Nursing, S.C. Nurses Assn., S.C. Assn. Perinatal Nurses, S.C. Tech. Edn. Assn. (Educator of Yr. 2000), Nursing Faculty Orgn. (v.p. 1991-94, pres. 1998-2003), United Meth. Women (pres. 1998-99), S.C. Nursing Deans and Dirs. Coun. (nom. com. 2000-01), S.C. League for Nursing (bd. dirs.), RN-BSN-MSN Co-0p. Initiative (pres. 2002—), Sigma Theta Tau, Lambda Chi Nu. Meth. Avocations: reading, swimming, writing, walking. Home: 106 Laurel Ln Seneca SC 29678-2705 Office: Tri-County Tech Coll PO Box 587 Pendleton SC 29670-0587 E-mail: pfehler@tctc.edu.

FEHR, GREGORY PARIS, marketing and distribution company executive; b. Urbana, Ill., Nov. 10, 1943; s. Orval Joachim and Cuba Lucile (Paris) F.; m. Sharon Louise Burba, Jan. 21, 1965 (div. Jan. 1975); children: Kristina K., Gregory Tyson Howard; m. Kathleen Lorretta Meyers, Aug. 10, 1990. BS in Indsl. Engring., Okla. U., 1967; MBA, Drake U., 1977. Registered profl. mech. engr. Iowa, Okla., Ala.; cert. corrosion technologist, cathodic protection specialist. From engr. to sr. project engr. Fisher Controls Co., Marshalltown, Iowa, 1967-77; fgn. liaison GE, Portland, Maine, 1977-79; gen. mgr. Arabian Am. Oil Co., Dhahran, Saudi Arabia, 1979-81; v.p. Oil Tech. Svcs., Houston, 1981-85; mgr. materials engring. Standard Oil Prodn. Co., Houston, 1985-86; mgr. nuclear products Wyle Labs., Huntsville, Ala., 1986-88; sr. materials engr. Sci. Applications Internat., Las Vegas, Nev., 1988-96; v.p. GPF Mktg. and Distbn., Las Vegas, 1988—; sr. project mgr. Converse Cons. S.W., Inc., Las Vegas, 1996—2002; with Terracon Cons. Engrs. and Scientists, 2002—. Cons. task groups Am. Petroleum Inst., 1983-86, Electric Power Rsch. Inst., San Mateo, Calif., 1986-89; chmn. employee adv. coun. Sci. Applications Internat., Las Vegas, 1992. Contbr. articles and tech. papers to profl. jours. Pres. Marshalltown Tennis Assn., 1972-73; head swim coach YMCA/YWCA, Marshalltown, 1973-74; mem. adv. bd. Marshalltown C.C., 1975. Mem. NSPE, ASME, Nat. Assn. Corrosion Engrs., Am. Petroleum Inst., Am. Soc. Nondestructive Testing. Avocations: skiing, scuba diving, sailing, photography.

FEHR, J. WILL, newspaper editor; b. Long Beach, Calif., Mar. 8, 1926; s. John and Evelyn (James) F.; m. Cynthia Moore, Sept. 4, 1951; children— Michael John, Martha Ann BA in English, U. Utah, 1951. City editor Salt Lake City Tribune, 1964-80, mng. editor, 1980-81, editor, 1981-91. Served to 1st lt. USAF. 1951-53 Mem. Am. Soc. Newspaper Editors, Sigma Chi Home: 468 13th Ave Salt Lake City UT 84103-3229

FEHR, KENNETH MANBECK, retired computer systems company executive; b. Schuylkill Haven, Pa., Feb. 21, 1928; s. Theodore E. and Eva (Manbeck) F.; m. Jean Alice Greenawalt, June 28, 1952; children: K. Craig, Karen Jean, K. Todd. BS, Pa. State U., 1951; MBA, U. Pitts., 1953. With U.S. Steel Corp., 1951-62, div. controller, 1962; controller Interlake Steel Corp., Chgo., 1962-68; v.p. fin. Hallicrafters Co., 1968-71, E.W. Bliss Co., Salem, Ohio, 1971-74; treas. Alliance Machine Co., Ohio, 1974-86; pres. I.M.S. Corp., Hudson, Ohio, 1986-90, Fehr & Greenawalt Investments, Salem, Ohio, 1990—, Salem Security Storage, LLB, Salem, 2002—. Bd. dirs. Fegreen Inc.; pres. Salem Security Storage LLP; night sch. tchr. U. Pitts., 1956—57. Trustee Save Our Salem, Inc.; treas. Salem Renaissance. With USNR, 1945—46. Mem.: Nat. Assn. Accts., Fin. Execs. Inst., Salem Hist. Soc., Salem Preservation Soc., Salem-Golf Club, Kiwanis (chpt. pres.), Masons. Home: 725 S Lincoln Ave Salem OH 44460-3709 Office: 1210 So Ellsworth Ave Salem OH 44460

FEHR, LOLA MAE, health organization administrator; b. Hastings, Nebr., Sept. 29, 1936; d. Leland R. and Edith (Wunderlich) Gaymon; m. Harry E. Fehr, Aug. 15, 1972; children: Dawn, Cheryl, Michael. RN, St. Luke's Hosp., Denver, 1958; BSN magna cum laude, U. Denver, 1959; MS, U. Colo., Boulder, 1975. Dir. staff devel. Weld County Gen. Hosp., Greeley, Colo., 1972-76, dir. nursing, 1976-80; exec. dir. Colo. Nurses Assn., Denver, 1980-89; dir. membership Assn. Oper. Rm. Nurses, Inc., Denver, 1989-90, exec. dir., 1990-99; pres. Fehr Cons. Resources, Frisco, Colo., 1999—; exec. dir. Am. Soc. Bariatric Physicians, 2000—01; program dir. Colo. Ctr. for Nursing Excellence, 2003—; exec. dir. N.Y. State Nurses Assn. Editor Colo. Nurse, 1980-89. Recipient U. Colo. Alumni award, Colo. Nurses Assn. Profl. Nurse of the Yr. award. Mem. Am. Acad. Nursing, Nat. Assn. Parliamentarians, Am. Soc. Assn. Execs., Colo. Nurses Assn., Sigma Theta Tau.

FEHRENBACH, MARGARET JEAN, dental hygienist, educator; d. Victor John and Barbara Ann Rudolph; m. Jon Paul Fehrenbach. BS in Dental Hygiene, Marquette U., 1977; MS in Oral Biology, U. Wash., 1981, cert. in clin. rsch. methods, 1998. Pvt. practice dental hygiene ednl. cons., Seattle, 1997—; adj. faculty mem. dental hygiene program Marquette U., Milw., 1998—; online profl. continuing edn. author ArcMesa Educators Online Continuing Edn. for Health Profls., 1999—. Author, primary and contributory: oral biology textbooks WB Saunders, Phila., 1997—. Editl. advisor, reviewer: Jour. Practical Hygiene, 2002—; contbr. articles to profl. jours. Com. appointee, spkr., exhibitor, tobacco cessation reform project contbr., mem. Tobacco Prevention and Control Program, Wash. State Dept. Health, Seattle, 1990—2003. Mem.: Am. Dental Hygienists' Assn. (mem. coda rep. 1999—2002, reader adv. bd. mem. Access Mag.), Am. Dental Edn. Assn. (mem.exhibit reviewer). E-mail: margaret@dhed.net.

FEHRENBACH, T(HEODORE) R(EED), author, businessman; b. San Benito, Tex., Jan. 12, 1925; s. T.R. and Rose Mardel (Wentz) F.; m. Lillian Breetz, Aug. 22, 1951. BA magna cum laude, Princeton U., 1947. Field supr. Travelers Ins. Co., San Antonio, 1954-56; owner ind. ins. agy. San Antonio, 1956-69; mng. trustee Fehrenbach Trusts, 1970—; pres. Royal Poinciana Corp., San Antonio, 1971-92. Author: This Kind of War, 1963, This Kind of Peace, 1966, Lone Star (PBS TV Series 1985-86), 1968, Fire and Blood, 1973, Comanches, 1974, Seven Keys to Texas, 1983, Texas: A Salute From Above, 1985, others; contbr. numerous articles, stories to mags., U.S. fgn. periodicals. Mem. Tex. 2000 Commn., 1981-82; chmn. Tex. Hist. Commn., 1987-91; mem. design adv. com. Tex. Quarter Dollar, 2001-03. 1st lt. AUS, 1943-46, lt. col., 1950-53, Korea. Recipient Disting. Civilian Svc. medal, Freedoms Found. award, 1965, Evelyn Oppenheimer award, 1968, citations Tex. Ho. of Reps., 1969, 73, Tex. Legislature, 1977, 2003; T.R. Fehrenbach Book awards created in his honor Tex. Hist. Commn., 1986; named Disting. Citizen, San Antonio, 1973, Knight of San Jacinto, Primicerius Order of St. Maurice. Fellow Am. Numismatic Soc., Tex. State Hist. Assn.; mem. Philos. Soc. Tex., Authors Guild, Sci. Fiction Writers Am., Conopus Club, Argyle Club, Torch Club, Princeton Club of N.Y.C., Garden of the Gods Club (Colo.). Republican. Episcopalian. Home: 131 Mary D Ave San Antonio TX 78209-5667 Office: 5108 Broadway St # San San Antonio TX 78209-5746

FEHRIBACH, RONALD STEVEN, investment executive; b. Huntingburg, Ind., Nov. 2, 1949; s. Edwin Joseph and Stella Ann (Edele) F. BS in Polit. Sci., Ind. State U., 1974; postgrad., Rose Hulman Inst. Tech., 1974, Ind. U., 1977; MA, Eastern Ky. U., Richmond, 1980. Crew supr. Ahrens and Son's Nursery, Huntingburg, Ind., 1966-70; constrn. worker Nailer Constrn. Co., Huntingburg, 1971; fin. and program analyst HEW, Chgo., Washington, 1972; investment exec. Moseley, Hallgarten, Estabrook & Weeden Inc., Chgo., 1980-87, LaSalle St. Securities, Inc., Chgo., 1987-93, F.J. Garber & Co., Mesa, Ariz., 1993-95; pres. Fehribach Investments Inc., Chgo., 1986—2003; owner Mama's Place - The Legend Continues, Mesa, 1991—; investment exec. First Fin. Planners, Inc., Chesterfield, Mo., 1996—2001, Jefferson Pilot Securities Corp., 2003—, Fehribach Fin. Svcs. Inc., Ariz., 2003. Corp. comdr. Res. Officer Tng. Program, Terre Haute, 1973-74. Capt. U.S. Army, 1975-77, Korea; with Ind. Nat. Guard, 1977-79. Named Rookie of Yr., Moseley Assocs., Boston, 1983; recipient Outstanding Sales award Am. Fin. Group, Boston, 1986. Avocation: travel.

FEHRING, MARY ANN, secondary education educator; Secondary tchr. Bishop Noll Inst., Hammond, Ind. Named Outstanding High Sch. tchr. Inland Steel Ryerson Found., 1992. Office: Bishop Noll Inst 1518 Hoffman St Hammond IN 46327-1769

FEHRMAN, KENNETH RAY, educator, interior designer, author, researcher; b. San Antonio, Oct. 24, 1941; s. Oscar Fehrman and Ruth (Peabody) McVey; m. Cherie Christina Allen, Apr. 7, 1967. AA, Solano Coll., 1963; BA, San Francisco State U., 1965, MA, 1969; EdD, U. San Francisco, 1987. Lic. secondary tchr., Calif. Chair art dept. The Hamlin Sch., San Francisco, 1970-77; pres. Fehrman Interior Design Ltd., San Francisco, 1976—; environ. design instr. Rudolph Schaeffer Sch., San Francisco, 1978-80; dir. edn. Western Design Inst., San Francisco, 1979-81; prof. interior design San Francisco State U., 1980—2002. Author: (with others) Postwar Interior Design: 1945-1960, 1986, SuperColor, 1988, Death by Design, 1988, Color: The Secret Influence, 2000, 02; contbr. articles on design and decorative arts to mags.; exhibitor textile work and design projects at galleries, including San Francisco Mus. Modern Art, 1969-82. Mem. Internat. Soc. Interior Designers (founding pres., No. Calif. chpt., 1980-82), Internat. Interior Design Assn., Interior Designers Edn. Council. Office: San Francisco State U Consumer and Family Studies Dept 1600 Holloway Ave San Francisco CA 94132-1722

FEI, JAMES ROBERT, engineering executive, consultant; b. Tucson, May 24, 1947; s. Robert Fleming and Barbara Jean (Dukes) F.; m. Patricia Christine Wilson, Aug. 24, 1968; children: Robert Fleming, Christina Kalani. BSME, U. So. Calif., 1969; MS in Ocean Engring., U. Hawaii, 1973. Registered profl. engr., S.C., La., Tex., Ga., Va., N.H., N.C. Design engr. USN, Mare Island, Calif., 1969-70; project mgr. Pearl Harbor (Hawaii) Shipyard, 1970-73; mech. systems engr. Submarine Maintenance Monitoring Systems Office Dept. of the Navy, Washington, 1973-76; chmn., chief exec. officer Life Cycle Engring., Inc., Charleston, S.C., 1977—. Bd. dirs., adv. bd. Nat. Bank of S.C., 1985-92; mem. adv. coun. St. Francis Hosp., 1992-95; mem. pres.'s adv. coun. Med. U. S.C., Charleston, 1995-96; mem. Cold War Submarine Meml. Found., exec. com., bd. Mem. SCSPE, NSPE, ASME, Navy League. Republican. Avocations: golf, boating. Office: Life Cycle Engring Inc 4360 Corporate Rd Ste 100 North Charleston SC 29405-7445 E-mail: jim@lce.com.

FEI, YIJIAN, ophthalmologist, biomedical researcher; b. Luzhou, Sichuan, China, June 12, 1962; came to the U.S., 1993; s. Kaili Fei and Zhizheng Fu; m. Yueyi Zhang, Aug. 7, 1987; children: Tianming, Benjamin. MD, Luzhou Med. Coll., 1983; M in Med. Sci., West China U. Med. Scis., Chengdu, China, 1986. Resident, instr. dept. ophthalmology West China U. Med. Scis., Chengdu, 1984-88, asst. prof. dept. ophthalmology, 1988-92; vis. rsch. scientist U. Eye Hosp., Tübingen, Germany, 1992-93; rsch. fellow dept. opthalmology Med. Coll. Ga., Augusta, 1993-98; rsch. assoc. dept. ophthalmology and visual sci. Yale U., New Haven, 1998—. Author: Degenerative Retinopathies: Advances in Clinical and Genetic Research, 1991 (award Assn. Sci. and Tech., Chengdu, 1992), Retinal Diseases: Clinical and Basic Research, 1995; contbr. articles to profl. jours. Recipient Outstanding Young Scholar Acad. award West China U. Med. Scis., Chengdu, 1988, Outstanding Rsch. award Assn. Sci. and Tech. Chengdu City, 1989, Advancement Sci. and Tech. award Govt. Sichuan Province, Chengdu, 1993; named Outstanding Rschr., U.S. Immigration and Naturalization Svc., Tex., 1996; rsch. fellow Acad. Exch. Svc. Germany, Bonn, 1992. Fellow Chinese Assn. Ophthalmic Genetics (Outstanding Rsch. award 1987); mem. AAAS, Chinese Assn. Retinal Diseases, Assn. for Rsch. in Vision and Ophthalmology, N.Y. Acad. Scis. Achievements include introduced the modern molecular genetic and recombinant DNA technologies into the scientific communities of eye research in China; applied genetic linkage analysis and candidate gene approach to find out the genetic causes or molecular defects of some blinding or debilitating retinal diseases; successfully generated mouse models for the study of human retinal function, development and diseases. Home: 95 Kaye Vue Dr Apt 2L Hamden CT 06514-2332 Office: Dept Ophthalmology/Visual Sci Yale Univ Sch of Medicine 330 Cedar St New Haven CT 06510-3218

FEIBEL, FREDERICK ARTHUR, financial consultant; b. Chgo., Oct. 27, 1942; s. Fred and Emma Feibel; m. Marlene Ruth Edwards, Aug. 7, 1965; 1 son, Frederick Curtis. BSEE, Purdue U., 1964; MBA, Northwestern U., 1970. Project engr. Johnson Controls Corp., Milw., 1964-69; sr. mgmt. cons. Arthur Andersen & Co., Chgo., 1970-76; rep. pension fund evaluation A.G. Becker Securities Co., Chgo., 1976-77; spl. agt. Northwestern Mut. Life Ins. Co., Milw., 1977-82; pres. F.A. Feibel Fin. Assocs., Northbrook, Ill., 1982—. Chmn. Village of Northbrook Bicentennial Commn., 1975-76, Boy Scouts Am. Troop 67, 1990—; v.p. Northbrook Civic Found., 1977, pres., 1978, also bd. dirs.; deacon Northfield Cmty. Ch., 1978-81, 95-98, asst. treas., 1986—; trustee Northfield Rural Fire Dist., 2000—. Recipient Disting. Svc. award State of Ill., 1976, Northbrook Civic Found., 1983, 89, Civic Svc. award Northbrook B'nai B'rith, 1981-82, Vol Initiative of Pvt. Sector Recognition award Northbrook C. of C. and Industry, 1985, Vol. Appreciation award Northbrook Park Dist, 1987; named Northbrook Rotary Man of Yr, 1978-79, Hall of Fame III Festival Assn., 1992. Mem. Greater North Shore Estate Planning Coun., Eta Kappa Nu, Tau Beta Pi. Home: 1841 Western Ave Northbrook IL 60062-5041 Office: FA Feibel Fin Assocs PO Box 355 Northbrook IL 60065-0355

FEIBLEMAN, GILBERT BRUCE, lawyer; b. Portland, Oreg., Jan. 29, 1951; s. Herbert Frank and Bernice Feibleman; m. Ellen M. McDowell, June 20, 1981; 1 child, Benjamin David. BS, U. Oreg., 1972; JD, U. Pacific, 1976. Bar: Oreg. 1976, U.S. Dist. Ct. Oreg. 1976, U.S. Ct. Appeals (9th cir.). Assoc. Goodenough & Pierson, Salem, Oreg., 1976-78; mng. ptnr. Ramsay, Stein, Feibleman & Myers P.C., Salem, 1978-89, Ramsay, Stein & Feibleman P.C., Salem, 1989-94, Feibleman & Assocs. P.C., 1995—. Adj. prof. trial law and negotiation skills Willamette U.; adj. prof. bus. law Chemeketa Community Coll., Marion County, Oreg., 1977; arbitrator Marion County Ct., Salem, 1985—; referee juvenile ct., 1985; judge pro tem Oreg. Dist. Cts., 1982—, Oreg. Cir. Cts., 1987—; reference judge Marion County, 1989—. Fellow Am. Acad. Matrimonial Lawyers; mem. Assn. Trial Lawyers Am., Oreg. Trial Lawyers Assn., Oreg. Bar Assn. (arbitrator), Oreg. State Bar Assn. (bar counsel 1989—, sec. joint chiropractic com. 1989—, chair family juvenile law sect). Democrat. Avocations: skiing, gourmet cooking. Home: 552 Stagecoach Way SE Salem OR 97302-3925 Office: 1815 Commercial St SE Salem OR 97302-5203 E-mail: gil@feibleman-law.com.

FEIDER, GARY JOSEPH, newspaper editor; b. Sheboygan, Wis., Apr. 24, 1953; s. Joseph Nicholas and Elaine Sylvina (Schueller) F. BA, U. Wis., 1975. Editor, gen. mgr. The Sounder, Random Lake, Wis., 1975—. Editor Dancers' Dateline, Random Lake, 1992—. Roman Catholic. Avocations: competitive ballroom dancing, local and Wisconsin history. Home: W3672 County Road K Cedar Grove WI 53013-1478 E-mail: sounder@execpc.com.

FEIERSTEIN, MARK BARRY, pollster; b. N.Y.C., June 19, 1963; s. Saul and Rita Carol (Goldberg) F.; m. Itzel del Carmen Sclopis, June 27, 1991; 1 child, Bianca Pilar. BA, Tufts U., 1987; MA, Fletcher Sch. Law & Diplomacy, Medford, Mass., 1987. Editor, reporter Trumbull (Conn.) Times, summers 1981-83; Lyndon Baines Johnson intern U.S. Rep. Stewart McKinney, Washington, 1984; copy editor Hartford (Conn.) Courant, 1985; reporter Mexico City News, 1985-86; dep. western fin. dir. Dukakis for President Campaign, Boston, 1987; dir. Latin Am. programs Nat. Dem. Inst. Internat. Affairs, Washington, 1987-93; spl. asst. to U.S. amb. OAS, State Dept., Washington, 1993-97; sr. adviser elections AID, Washington, 1997-99; sr. assoc. Greenberg Quinlan Rosner Rsch., Inc., Washington, 1999—2002, assoc. v.p., 2003—. Mem. Toastmasters Internat. (club pres. 1996-97, area gov. 1997-98, 1st pl. area humorous speech contest 1995). Democrat. Jewish. Avocations: playing with my daughter, reading history, tennis, baseball. Home: 8608 Battailles Ct Annandale VA 22003-3608 Office: Greenberg Quinlan Rsch Inc 10 G St NE Washington DC 20002-4213 E-mail: cecilfire@aol.com.

FEIERSTEIN, MARK ERROL, retired lawyer; b. N.Y.C., May 22, 1948; s. Lester and Rose (Feingersh) F. BA, Miami U., Oxford, Ohio, 1970; MS in Bus., L.I. U., 1975; JD, N.Y. Law Sch., 1979. Bar: N.Y. 1979, U.S. Tax Ct., 1988. Assoc. Olvaney, Eisner and Donnelly, N.Y.C., 1977-79, Oppenheim, Appel and Co., N.Y.C., 1981-82; law guardian Family Ct. of N.Y., Westchester; atty. Article 18-B Panel, Westchester; of counsel Thomas and Sykes, Yonkers, N.Y., 1985-86; ret., 1996. Adminstrv. law judge N.Y.C. Taxi and Limousine Commn., N.Y.C. Parking Violations Bur., 1984-93, N.Y.C. Environ. Control Bd., 1987-99; arbitrator Civil Ct. of N.Y.C., N.Y. Stock Exch., 1988, Nat. Assn. Securities Dealers, 1989; hearing officer N.Y.C. Transit Adjudication Bur., Bklyn., 1987-88; expert in credit card fraud Tech. Adv. Svc. for Attys., Blue Bell, Pa. Author: Emergency Guidelines to Assist Individuals and Businesses Counter Credit Card Fraud, 1992. Mem. Bronx Citizens Com., N.Y., 1986. Mem. ABA, N.Y. State Bar Assn., N.Y. Law Sch. Alumni Assn., Am. Arbitration Assn. Jewish. Avocations: movies, theater, reading.

FEIG, BARRY W. surgeon, oncologist; MD, SUNY Health Sci. Ctr., Syracuse, 1984. Lic. Nat. Bd. Med. Examiners, Tex., Am. Bd. of Surgery, Pa., critical care Am. Bd. of Surgery, Pa. Assoc. prof. of surgery U.Tex. M.D. Anderson Cancer Ctr., Houston, 1991—. Editor: (handbook) The M.D. Anderson Surgical Oncology Handbook. Fellow: ACS (liaison, commn. on cancer); mem.: Am. Assn. for Clin. Rsch., Am. Soc. of Clin. Oncology, Southwestern Surg. Soc., Assn. for Acad. Surgery, Soc. of U. Surgeons, Soc. of Surg. Oncology, Soc. of Critical Care Medicine, Connective Tissue Oncology Soc. Office: U Tex MD Anderson Cancer Ctr Box 444 1515 Holcombe Blvd Houston TX 77030

FEIG, STEPHEN ALBERT, radiologist; b. N.Y.C., Jan. 21, 1942; AB, Columbia U., 1963; MD, NYU, 1967. Diplomate Am. Bd. Radiology. Intern Beth Israel Hosp., N.Y.C., 1967-68; resident in radiology Bronx Mcpl. Hosp.-Einstein, N.Y.C., 1968-71; chief, radiology U.S. Army Med. Ctr., Okinawa, Japan, 1971—73; radiologist Jefferson U. Hosp., Phila., 1973—99; prof. radiology Jefferson Med. Coll., Phila., 1973—99; radiologist Mount Sinai Hosp., N.Y.C., 1999—; prof. radiology Mount Sinai Sch. Medicine, N.Y.C., 1999—. Mem. Am. Coll. Radiology, Radiol. Soc. N.Am., Am. Roentgen Ray Soc. Office: Mount Sinai Hosp Dept of Radiology New York NY 10029-6574 Home: 200 Locust St Apt 21A Philadelphia PA 19106-3919

FEIG, STEPHEN ARTHUR, pediatrics educator, hematologist, oncologist; b. N.Y.C., Dec. 24, 1937; s. Irving L. and Janet (Oppenheimer) F.; m. Judith Bergman, Aug. 28, 1960; children: Laura, Daniel, Andrew. AB in Biology, Princeton U., 1959; MD, Columbia U., 1963. Diplomate Am. Bd. Pediatrics, Am. Bd. Hematology-Oncology. Intern Mt. Sinai Hosp., N.Y.C., 1963-64, resident in pediatrics, 1964-66; hematology fellow Children's Hosp. Med. Ctr., Boston, 1968-71, assoc. in medicine, 1971-72; asst. prof. pediatrics UCLA, 1972-77, chief div. hematology and oncology, sch. medicine, 1977—, assoc. prof., 1977-82, prof., 1982—, exec. vice chmn. dept. pediatrics sch. medicine, 1994—. Cons. Olive View Med. Ctr., Van Nuys, Calif., 1973—, Sunrise Hosp. dept. pediatrics, Las Vegas, Nev., 1980—; trustee L.A. chpt. Leukemia Soc. Am., 1978—; bd. trustees, 1984—; exec. com. subsect. hemotology/oncology Am. Acad. Pediadrics; bd. dirs. Camp Ronald McDonald for Good Times; active numerous other pediatric hosp. and med. sch. coms. Reviewer Am. Jour. Pediatric Hematology/Oncology, Blood, Pediatrics, Pediatric Rsch., Jour. Pediatrics; contbr. articles to profl. jours.; editl. bd. Jour. Pediat. Hematology & Oncology, Stem Cells. Served with USNR, 1966-68. Mem. Am. Soc. Hematology, Soc. Pediatric Research, Am. Pediatric Soc., Internat. Soc. Exptl. Hematology, Am. Assn. Cancer Research. Jewish. Avocation: native arts. Office: UCLA Sch Medicine Dept Pediatrics 10833 Le Conte Ave Los Angeles CA 90095-3075

FEIGAL, DAVID W., JR., health science association administrator; BS, U. Minn.; MD, Stanford U. Resident U. Calif., Davis, fellow San Francisco, former assoc. prof.; head divsn. anti-viral drug products Ctr. Drug Evaluation & Rsch. FDA, 1992-97, med. dep. dir. Ctr. Biologics Evaluation & Rsch., 1997-99, dir. Ctr. Devices and Radiological Health, 1999—. Office: Ctr Devices & Radiol Health FDA 9200 Corporate Blvd # 100E Rockville MD 20850-3229

FEIGELSON, BORIS N. physical chemist, researcher, materials scientist; b. Chirchik, Russia, June 19, 1957; s. Nikolay Iosifovich and Albina Andreevna Feigelson; m. Tatyana Ivanovna Moraru, Aug. 24, 1990; 1 child, Mariya. BS in Phys. Chemistry, Steel and Alloys Inst., 1978, MS, 1981; PhD, Inst. Pulsar, Moscow, 1999. Cert. engr./rschr. Engr./rschr. Inst. of Monocrystals, Siberian br. Soviet Acad. Sci., Novosibirsk, 1981-89, head high pressure/high temp. dept., 1989-91; chief scientist Adamas Co., Minsk, 1991-93, Technocrystal Co., Moscow, Russia, 1993-96; dir. R&D Ctr. Basis, Moscow, Russia, 1996-2001; sr. scientist GEO Ctrs., Naval Rsch. Lab., Washington, 2001—. Achievements include development of new HP-HT technology for growth of single diamond crystals; produced first synthetic gem quality single diamond crystals in the former Soviet Union; design of (built and operated) Technocrystal Co. and research and development basis in Moscow for growth of single diamond crystals. Avocations: swimming, running. Office: Naval Rsch Lab Electronics Sci and Tech Div Code 6861 Washington DC 20375 Fax: 202-404-4071. E-mail: borisf@estd.nrl.navy.mil., basisfbn@hotmail.com.

FEIGELSON, EUGENE B. dean; Dean SUNY Downstate Med. Ctr. Coll. Medicine, Bklyn., 1996—; interim pres. SUNY-Health Sciences Ctr. Brooklyn Coll. Medicine, 1997—99. Office: SUNY Downstate Med Ctr 450 Clarkson Ave Box 97 Brooklyn NY 11203-2098

FEIGEN, BRENDA S. lawyer, film producer, author; b. Chgo., July 7, 1944; d. Arthur Paul Feigen and Shirley (Bierman) Feigen Kadison; children: Alexis Feigen Fasteau. BA in Math. cum laude, Vassar Coll., 1966; JD, Harvard U., 1969. Bar: Mass. 1970, N.Y. 1971, Calif. 2001. Chief analyst Boston Redevel. Authority, 1969; assoc. firm Rosenman, Colin, Kaye, Petschek, Freund & Emil, N.Y.C., 1970; pvt. practice N.Y.C., 1970—, L.A., 2001—. Founder, coordinating dir. Women's Action Alliance, N.Y.C., 1970—72; co-founder Ms. Mag., 1971; dir. Nat. Women's Rights project ACLU, N.Y.C., 1972—74; ptnr. Fasteau and Feigen, N.Y.C., 1974—80; assoc. Hess, Segall, Guterman, Pelz & Steiner, N.Y.C., 1980—81; atty., motion picture agt. William Morris Agy., N.Y.C., 1982—87; pres. Brenda Feigen Prodns., N.Y.C. and L.A., 1987—97; ptnr. Baxter/Feigen Prodns., 1991—92, Berton & Feigen, Beverly Hills, 1992—94; of counsel Berton & Donaldson, Beverly Hills, 1994—96; gen. counsel Feigen/Parrent Lit. Mgmt., Bel Air, Calif., 1995—; co-pres. and gen. counsel Reel Life Women Prodn. Co., Bel Air, 1996—; chair Nat. Breast Cancer Edn. and Legal Ctr., Bel Air, 2001—; prof. UCLA Ext., 1990; guest spkr., panelist numerous confs., seminars; panelist Harvard Law Sch. seminar, 1999, Yale Law Sch. seminar, 1999, Calif. Lawyers for Arts, 1999—, L.A. Times Book Festival, 2001, Vassar Coll., 2001; co-chair Practicing Law Inst. Seminars on Entertainment Law, 1987, 88, Harvard Law and Harvard Bus. Schs. Entertainement Law Conf., 1999, Vassar Coll. Symposium on Entertainment Industry, 1998; practicing Law Inst., 1987, 88; bd. dirs. Calif. Lawyers for the Arts, 1996—, Population Media Ctr., 2003—; emerita mem. bd. dirs. Women's Action Alliance; adv. com. Am. Friends of Israel Mus., 2002—; moderator panel on employment law Harvard Law Sch., Celebration 50, 2003. Prodr.: (films, Orion Pictures) NAVY SEALS, 1990; author: Not One of the Boys: Living Life as a Feminist, 2000; contbr. Mem. adv. bd. Working Women United, nat. adv. bd. Take Our Daughters to Work, 1993—; bd. dirs. Film Forum, 1986-90; mem. Pen Ctr. USA West, 1996—, Authors' Guild, 1996—, Harvard Com. Entertainment, Sports and Cyberspace Law, 1997—; candidate for N.Y. State Senate, 1978; panelist L.A. Times Book Festival, 2001; adv. com. Am. Friends of Israel Mus., 2002—. Hon. Pres.'s fellow Columbia U., 1977, 78; participant Exec. Seminar, Aspen Inst., 1979. Mem. ABA (panelist film divsn.), ATLA, NOW (nat. legis. v.p., bd. dirs. 1970-71), Show Coalition (bd. govs. 1990-92), Calif. State Bar Assn., Los Angeles County Bar Assn., Nat. Employment Law Assn., N.Y. Civil and Criminal Cts. Bar Assn., N.Y. Women in Film (bd. dirs. 1985-86), Women's Action Alliance (co-founder, dir.), Nat. Women's Polit. Caucus (co-founder, nat. adv. com.), Nat. Employment Law Assn. Democrat. Office: Law Office of Brenda S Feigen 11150 W Olympic Blvd Ste 860 Los Angeles CA 90064 E-mail: bfeigen@feigenlaw.com.

FEIGEN, RICHARD L. art dealer, collector, writer; b. Chgo., Aug. 8, 1930; s. Arthur P. and Shirley (Bierman) F.; m. Sandra Elizabeth Canning Walker, Feb. 23, 1966 (div. 1978); children: Philippa Canning, Richard Wood Bliss; m. Margaret Langan Culver, Sept. 12, 1998 (div. 2002). BA, Yale U., 1952; MBA, Harvard U., 1954. Asst. treas. Beneficial Standard Life Ins. Co., LA, 1955—56; mem. N.Y. Stock Exchange, 1956—57; pres., dir. Richard L. Feigen & Co., Inc., NYC, 1957—. Mem. com. works fine art N.Y. State Office Bldg., Harlem; lectr. in field. Author: Tales from the Art Crypt, 2000; contbr. articles to profl. jours. Candidate, del. Dem. Nat. Conv., 1972; trustee John Jay Homestead Assn., Katonah, N.Y., 1979-90, Lincoln U., Pa., 1988-92; mem. pres.'s coun. U. South Fla. Fellow Mpls. Soc. Fine Arts, Met. Mus. Art, Art Inst. Chgo.; mem. Art Dealers Assn. Am. (bd. dirs. 1972-76, 97-99, 2001—), Harvard Bus. Sch. Assn., Century Assn., Arts Club, Casino Club. Home: Cantitoe House Cantitoe Rd Katonah NY 10536-9718 also: 1 rue Allent 75007 Paris France also: 960 Fifth Ave New York NY 10021-1708 Office: 34 E 69th St New York NY 10021-5016

FEIGENBAUM, ABRAHAM SAMUEL, nutritional biochemist; b. N.Y.C., Mar. 11, 1929; s. Benjamin and Pearl Feigenbaum; m. Hannah Devries, Aug. 17, 1952; children: Benjamin, Josef, Miriam. BS, Rutgers U., 1951, MS, 1959, PhD, 1962. Chemist E.R. Squibb, New Brunswick, N.J., 1954-57; rsch. asst. Rutgers U., New Brunswick, N.J., 1957-61; rsch. scientist, chief neuroendocrinology N.J. Bur. Rsch. in Neurology and Psychiatry, Skillman, 1961-73; dir. clin. nutrition, dir. clin. coordination Warren-Teed Pharm./Adria Labs., Inc., Columbus, Ohio, 1973-81; clin. project dir., dir. rsch. Pharm. Rsch. Inst., sub. Akzo, Columbus, Ohio, 1981-94; dir. clin. devel. Organon, Inc., West Orange, N.J., 1981-94; ret., 1994. Guest lectr. in nutrition Hahnemann Med. Coll., Phila., 1977-80. Mem. Bd. Edn., Highland Park, N.J., 1969-73, pres., 1970-72, v.p., 1972-73. NSF fellow, 1961. Mem. Am. Inst. Nutrition, Am. Chem. Soc., Soc. Exptl. Biology and Medicine. Home: 209 N 4th Ave Highland Park NJ 08904-2723

FEIGENBAUM, ARMAND VALLIN, systems engineer, systems equipment executive; b. N.Y.C., Apr. 6, 1920; s. S. Frederick and Hilda (Vallin) F. BS, Union Coll., 1942, DSc (hon.), 1992; MS, MIT, 1948, PhD, 1951; LHD (hon.), U. Mass., 1996; DSc (hon.), Mass. Coll. Liberal Arts, 2003. Engr. test program GE, Schenectady, 1942-45, factory tng. course, 1945-47, sales engr., 1947-48, supr. tng. mfg. personnel, 1948-50, asst. to gen. mgr. aircraft gas turbine divsn. Cin., 1950-52, mgr. aircraft nuclear propulsion dept. N.Y.C., 1952, co. mgr. quality control, 1956, co.-wide mgr. mfg. ops. and quality control, 1958-68; pres., CEO Gen. Systems Co., Inc., Pittsfield, Mass., 1968—; Nat. Acad. Engring. U.S., 1992—. Mem. bd. overseers Malcolm Baldridge Nat. Quality Program, Washington, D.C., 1988-91; pres. Internat. Acad. for Quality, 1966-79, chmn. bd. dirs., 1979—; adv. group U.S. Army, 1966—; lectr. MIT, U. Cin., Union Coll., U. Pa. Author: Quality Control-Principles and Practice, 1951, Total Quality Control-Engineering and Management, 1961, Management Programming, 1980, The Organization Process, 1980, Total Quality Control, 3d edit., 1983, Total Quality Control, 40th Anniversary edit., 1991, The Power of Management Capital, 2003; contbr. articles to profl. jours.; articles and speeches included in: Global Leaders in Quality, 2002. Chmn. inst. adminstrn., mgmt. coun. Union Coll., 1963— . Recipient Founders medal, 1977, medaille Georges Borel, Republic of France, 1988, Disting. Svc. award Nat. Inst. for Engring., Mgmt. and Sys., 1991, Disting. Leadership award Quality and Productivity Mgmt. Assn., 1993, Ishikawa/Harrington medal Asia-Pacific Quality Orgn., 1996; Armand V. Feigenbaum Mass. Quality award established by Gov. Mass., 1992, Singapore's Ngee Ann Polytechnic inaugurated the ann. Dr. A.V. Feigenbaum Gold medal award for outstanding quality assurance engring. grad., 1994, Mass. Gov.'s proclamation on 50th anniversary of book, 2001; fellow World Acad. Productivity Sci., 1993; Armand V. and Donald S. Feigenbaum Hall named in his honor Union Coll., 1996, Armand and Donald Feigenbaum Disting. Professorship named in his honor U. Mass. Med. Sch., 1998; recognized with the Outstanding Engring. Alumnus award, 2003. Fellow Am. Soc. Quality Control (pres. 1961-63, chmn. bd. 1963-64, Edwards medal 1966, Lancaster medal 1982, hon. mem. 1986, Feigenbaum award established 1999), World Acad. Productivity Sci.; mem. IEEE (life), NSPE (Disting. Svc. award 1991), ASME (life), AAAS (hon.), Nat. Security Indsl. Assn. (nat. award merit 1965), Inst. Math. Stats., Acad. Polit. and Social Scis., Am. Econ. Assn., Soc. Advancement Mgmt., Indsl. Rels. Rsch. Soc., Coun. Internat. Progress in Mgmt. (chmn. bd. 1968-70), China Assn. Quality Control (hon. advisor), Argentine Inst. Quality (hon.), Philippines Soc. for Quality Control (hon.), NAE. Home: 123 Ann Dr Pittsfield MA 01201-8405 Office: Berkshire Common South St Pittsfield MA 01201-6123

FEIGENBAUM, EDWARD ALBERT, computer science educator; b. Weehawken, N.J., Jan. 20, 1936; s. Fred J. and Sara Rachman; m. H. Penny Nii, 1975. BEE, Carnegie Inst. Tech., 1956, PhD in Indsl. Adminstrn., 1960; DSc (hon.), Aston U., U.K., 1989. From asst. prof. to assoc. prof. bus. adminstrn. U. Calif., Berkeley, 1960—65; from assoc. prof. computer sci. to prof. Stanford U., 1965—95, prin. investigator heuristic programming project and knowledge sys. lab., 1965—2001, chmn. dept. computer sci., 1976-81, emeritus, 2001—, dir. Computation Ctr., 1965-68, Kumagai prof. computer sci., 1995—2001, emeritus, 2001—; pres. Intelli Genetics Inc., 1980—82, mem. tech. adv. bd., 1983-86; chmn., dir. Teknowledge, Inc., 1981-82; dir. IntelliCorp, 1984-90; chief scientist USAF, 1994-97; Kumagai prof. computer sci. Stanford (Calif.) U., 1995—2001, emeritus, 2001—. Cons. to industry, 1957—; mem. computer and biomath. scis. study sect. NIH, 1968-72, mem. adv. com. on artificial intelligence in medicine, 1974-92; mem. Math. Social Sci. Bd., 1975-78; computer sci. adv. com. NSF, 1977-80; mem. Internat. Joint Coun. on Artificial Intelligence, 1973-83; bd. dirs. Design Power Inc., 1990; chief scientist, USAF, 1994-97; mem. sci. adv. bd. USAF, 1997-2000; sci. advisor Air Force Office Sci. Rsch., 2000-. Author: (with others) Information Processing Language V Manual, 1961, (with P. McCorduck) The Fifth Generation, 1983; author: (with R. Lindsay, B. Buchanan, J. Lederberg) Applications of Artificial Intelligence to Organic Chemistry: the Dendral Project, 1980; Editor: (with J. Feldman) Computers and Thought, 1963, (with A. Barr and P. Cohen) Handbook of Artificial Intelligence, 1981, 82, 89, (with Pamela McCorduck and H. Penny Nii) The Rise of the Expert Company: How Visionary Companies are using Artificial Intelligence to Achieve Higher Productivity and Profits, 1988, The Japanese Entrepreneur: Making the Desert Bloom, 2002; mem. editorial bd.: Jour. Artificial Intelligence, 1970-88. Trustee Charles Babbage Found. for the History of Info. Processing, U. Minn., 2000—; pres. Feigenbaum Nii Found., 2000—. Recipient Exceptional Civilian Svc. award USAF, 1997, Meritorious Civilian Sci. award USAF, 2000; Fulbright scholar, 1959-60; Feigenbaum medal established in his honor World Congress on Expert Systems, 1991. Fellow AAAI, AAAS, Am. Coll. Med. Informatics, Am. Inst. Med. and Biol. Engring.; mem. NAE, Assn. Computing Machinery (nat. coun. 1966-68, chmn. spl. interest group on biol. applications 1973-76, A.M. Turing award 1994), Am. Assn. Artificial Intelligence (pres. 1980-81), Am. Acad. Arts and Scis., Cognitive Sci. Soc. (coun. 1979-82), Sigma Xi, Tau Beta Pi, Eta Kappa Nu, Pi Delta Epsilon. Home: 1017 Cathcart Way Palo Alto CA 94305-1048 Office: Stanford U Knowledge Systems Lab Gates Computer Sci Rm 220 Stanford CA 94305-9020

FEIGENHOLTZ, SARA, state legislator; b. Chgo., Dec. 11, 1956; d. Bernard and Florence (Buky) F. Student, Northeastern Ill. U. Ill. state rep. Dist. 12, 1995—. Chmn. human svcs. com. Ill. Ho. of Reps., co-chair tobacco settlement proceeds distribution, vice-chair health care availabity com., mem. state govt. adminstrn. and appropriations human svcs. coms.; exec. dir. Cen. Lakeview Merchants Assn., 1993-94; former cons., Chgo. Mem. NOW, Nat. Coun. Jewish Women, Am. Jewish Coun. (gov. coun. 1994-95), Conf. Women Legislators, Phi Theta Kappa. Office: 1051 W Belmont Ave Chicago IL 60657-3327*

FEIGERT, FRANK BROOK, retired political science educator, writer; b. N.Y.C., Nov. 10, 1937; s. Morris Samuel Feigert and Anna (Frank) Spelke; m. Frances Goodside, June 17, 1961; children: Benjamin, Daniel. BA, Allegheny Coll., 1959; MA, U. Md., 1965, PhD, 1968. Instr. to asst. prof. Knox Coll., Galesburg, Ill., 1966—70; asst. to prof. SUNY, Brockport, 1970—77; prof. then regents prof. polit. sci. U. North Tex., Denton, 1997—2002; ret., 2002. Author: Canada Votes, 1988, Parties and Politics in America, 1976, Politics and Process of American Government, 1982, American Political Parties, 1984, American Party System and The American People, 1985; author: (with others) Political Analysis, 1972, 1976. Precinct leader Monroe County Dem. Com., NY, 1972—77, registration chmn., 1972; campaign chmn. State Assembly Campaign, Monroe County, 1974; bd. dirs. Participation, 2000—03. Served to capt. USAF, 1959—64. Fulbright-Hays sr. fellow, 1977—78. Mem.: Midwestern Polit. Sci. Assn., So. Polit. Sci. Assn., Am. Polit. Sci. Assn., U.S. Sailing Club, Dallas Corinthian Yacht Club (Oak Point, Tex.) (treas. 1983—89). Jewish. Avocations: reading, photography, travel. Home: 500 Court Sq Apt 404 Charlottesville VA 22902

FEIGHT, THEODORE J. financial planner; b. Alma, Mich., Oct. 18, 1946; s. William T. Feight and Wilma (Richardson) Recker; m. Kathleen Lischkge, June 13, 1969; children: Jay David, Richard Thomas, James Daryl, Brian Lynn. BS, Western Mich. U., Kalamazoo, 1972. Dist. mgr. Clark Oil, Milw., 1972-73; fin. planner Mut. Benefit Life Ins. Co., Lansing, Mich., 1973-78, Creative Fin. Design, Lansing, 1978—. Mem. Inst. CFP Registry, Denver, 1991—; bd. dirs., treas. Commemorative Bucks of Mich., Inc.; bd. dirs. CDP of Mich.; webmaster Michigancdp.com., Buckfax.com. Ghost writer book on fin. planning, 1984. Bd. dirs. The Adoption Cradle, Battle Creek, Mich., 1993-98. With U.S. Army, 1967-68, Viet Nam. Decorated DSM, Air medal with 2 bronze stars; winner nat. championship USAPC Powerlifting, 2001, 02, Powerlifting Nat. Championship, AAPF, 2001, WABDC, 2001, 02, ALWPC, 2002, World Championships, 2002. Mem. Fin. Planning Assn. (bd. dirs.), Inst. CFPs, Mich. State Assn. Life Underwriters (Nat. Pub. Svc. award 1980), Lansing Assn. Life Underwriters (bd. dirs. 1978-79), Mich. Cert. Divorce Planners (pres.), Mich. Fin. Planning Assn. (pres.-elect), Rotary Internat. (bd. dirs. 1979-81). Avocations: hunting, golf, Karate, cars, power lifting. Home and Office: Creative Fin Design 2112 Tulane Dr Lansing MI 48912-3546

FEIGIN, NANCY J. guidance counselor; b. N.Y.C., Sept. 14, 1953; d. Herbert and Estelle B. Mittleman; m. William Feigin, Aug. 25, 1974; children: Michael, Kim. BS, Syracuse U., N.Y., 1974; MS in Edn., Bank St. Coll. Edn., N.Y.C., 1976. Dir. guidance Westchester Hebrew H.S., Mamaroneck, NY. Cons. Kaplan, N.Y.C., Ptnrs. for Coll. Solutions, Pleasantville, NY. Office: Westchester Hebrew High Sch 856 Orienta Ave Mamaroneck NY 10543

FEIGIN, RALPH DAVID, medical school administrator, pediatrician, educator; b. N.Y.C., Apr. 3, 1938; s. Jack Bernard and Dorothy Phyllis (Strauss) F.; m. Judith Sue Zobel, June 26, 1960; children: Susan M., Michael E., Debra F. AB, Columbia U., 1958; MD, Boston U., 1962, DHL (hon.), 1998. Diplomate Am. Bd. Pediatrics, sub bd. for infectious diseases. Pediatric intern Boston City Hosp., 1962-63; pediatric resident Boston City Hosp. and Mass. Gen. Hosp., 1963-65; tchg. fellow pediatrics Harvard U. Med. Sch., 1964-65; rschr. U.S. Army Rsch. Inst. Infectious Diseases, Frederick, Md., 1965-67; chief resident children's svc. Mass. Gen. Hosp., 1967-68; from instr. to prof. pediatrics Washington U. Med. Sch., St. Louis, 1968-77, dir. divsn. infectious diseases dept. pediatrics, 1973-77; prof. pediatrics, chmn. dept. Baylor Coll. Medicine, Houston, 1977—, disting. svc. prof., 1990—, sr. v.p., 1992—96, dean med. edn., 1994—96, pres. and CEO, 1996—2003; physician-in-chief Tex. Children's Hosp., 1977—, exec. v.p., 1987-89; chief pediatric svc. Harris County Hosp. Dist., 1977—90; pediatrician-in-chief Methodist Hosp., 1979—; chief pediat. svc. Ben Taub Gen. Hosp., 1990—. Mem. adv. ad hoc study group on spl. infectious disease problems U.S. Army Med. R & D Command, 1974-83; vis. prof., cons. in field; pres. Pediatric Rsch. Found., 1982—. Co-editor: Nutrition and the Developing Nervous System, 1975, Textbook of Pediatric Infectious Diseases, 1981, 4th edit., 1997, Roundsmanship, 1989-93, Practices and Principles of Pediatrics, 1989, 2nd edit., 1993; mem. editorial bd. Pediatrics, 1978-90, consulting editor, 1993-94, assoc. editor, 1994—; mem. editorial bd. Jour. Pediatric Infectious Diseases; assoc. editor Jour. Infectious Diseases, 1984-88; editor-in-chief Seminars in Pediatric Infectious Diseases, 1990—; contbr. articles to med. jours., chpts. to books. With M.C., USAR, 1965-67. Recipient Rsch. Career Devel. award USPHS, 1970, Founders Day award Washington U. Med. Sch., 1977, Sr. Class Outstanding Tchr. award Baylor Coll. Medicine, 1978, 80, 81, 82, 83, 84, 85, 86, Minnie Stevens Piper Professorial award, 1984, John McGovern Outstanding Clin. Faculty award Baylor Coll. Medicine, 1986, 94, Disting. Alumnus award Boston U. Sch. of Medicine, 1989, Joseph St. Geme Jr. Leadership award in Pediatrics, Fedn. Pediatric Orgns., 1995, Disting. Faculty award Alumni Assn., Baylor Coll. of Medicine, 1994; named to Baylor Coll. Medicine Outstanding Tchr. Hall of Fame, 1984; Alumni Tchg. scholar Washington U. Med. Sch., 1975, Amer. Acad. Pediatrics Med. Educ. Lifetime Ach. Award. Fellow AAAS, Am. Microbiology; mem. AMA, Am. Pediatric Soc. (pres. 1997-98, Lifetime Achievement award, 1997), Am. Acad. Pediat., Infectious Diseases Soc. Am., Pediatric Infectious Disease Soc. (Disting. Physician award 1996), Inst. Medicine of NAS, N.Y. Acad. Scis., Tex. Med. Assn., Tex. Pediatric Soc., Harris County Med. Soc., Houston Pediatric Soc., Soc. Pediatric Rsch. (pres. 1982-83), Assn. Med. Sch. Pediatric Dept. Chairpersons (pres. 1991-93). Office: Baylor Coll Medicine Dept Pediats One Baylor Plz Houston TX 77030-3411

FEIGON, JUDITH TOVA, ophthalmologist, surgeon, educator; b. Galveston, Tex., Dec. 2, 1947; d. Louis and Ethel Feigon; m. Nathan C. Goldman; children: Michael G., Miriam G. AB, Barnard Coll., Columbia U., 1970; postgrad., Rice U., U. Houston, 1970-71; MD, U. Tex., San Antonio, 1976. Diplomate Am. Bd. Ophthalmology. Intern Mt. Auburn Hosp., Cambridge, Mass.; intern, clin. tchg. fellow Harvard U. Med. Sch., 1976-77; resident in ophthalmology Baylor Coll. Medicine, Houston, 1977-80, fellow in retina, 1980-82, clin. faculty, 1982-95; asst. prof. ophthalmology U. Tex. Med. Br., Galveston, 1982-85, clin. asst. prof., 1985-91, clin. assoc. prof., 1992—; pvt. practice medicine specializing ophthalmology, vitreoretinal diseases, surgery, Houston, 1983—. Physician advisor to Houston br. Tex. Soc. to Prevent Blindness, 1987-89, also bd. dirs.; mem. staff Meth., St. Lukes, Tex. Children's, St. Joseph's Hosp., Park Plaza; clin. faculty Baylor Coll. Medicine, 1992-95. Contbr. articles to profl. publs. Mem. Assn. Am. Physicians and Surgeons, Am. Acad. Ophthalmology, Tex. Med. Assn. Houston Ophthal. Soc., Harris County Med. Soc., U. Tex. San Antonio Alumni Assn., Am. Soc. Retina Specialists, Tex. Ophthalmol. Assn. Office: 7515 Main St Ste 650 Houston TX 77030-4599

FEIKENS, JOHN, federal judge; b. Clifton, N.J., Dec. 3, 1917; s. Sipke and Corine (Wisse) F.; m. Henriette Dorothy Schulthouse, Nov. 4, 1939; children: Jon, Susan Corine, Barbara Edith, Julie Anne, Robert H. AB, Calvin Coll., Grand Rapids, Mich., 1938; JD, U. Mich., 1941; LLD (hon.), U. Detroit, 1979, Detroit Coll. Law, 1981. Bar: Mich. 1942. Gen. practice law, Detroit; dist. judge Ea. Dist. Mich., Detroit, 1960-61, 70-79, chief judge, 1979-86, sr. judge, 1986—. Past co-chmn. Mich. Civil Rights Commn.; past chmn. Rep. State Central Com.; past mem. Rep. Nat. Com.; mem. com. visitors U. Mich. Law Sch. Past bd. trustees Calvin Coll. Fellow Am. Coll. Trial Lawyers; mem. ABA, Detroit Bar Assn. (dir. 1962, past pres.), State Bar Mich. (commr. 1965-71), U. Mich. Club (com. visitors). Office: US Dist Ct 851 Theodore Levin US Ct 231 W Lafayette Blvd Detroit MI 48226-2700

FEIL, LINDA MAE, tax preparer; b. Dallas, Oreg., Apr. 9, 1948; d. Fred Henry and Ruth Irene (Hoffman) F. AA, West Valley Community Coll., 1975; student, Golden Gate U. Ctr. for Tax Studies, 1975, Menlo Coll. Sch. Bus. Adminstrn., 1978. Enrolled agt. IRS; cert. in fed. taxation. Income tax preparer, office mgr. H & R Block, Inc., Santa Clara, Calif., 1972-74, asst. area mgr., 1974-76; propr. L.M. Feil Tax Service, Santa Clara, 1976-80; ptnr. Tennyson Tax Service, Santa Clara, 1980-81; owner McKeany-Feil Tax Service, San Jose, Calif., 1981-83, Feil Tax Service, San Jose, 1983-90, Richmond, Calif., 1990-96, Vallejo, Calif., 1996—. Mem. Nat. Soc. Pub. Accts., Nat. Assn. Enrolled Agts. (chpt. sec. 1981-83, chpt. v.p. 1983-84), Mission Soc. Enrolled Agts. (pres. 1984-85, Enrolled Agt. of Yr. 1985), Calif. Soc. Enrolled Agts. (bd. dirs. 1985-86). Office: Feil Tax Svc 824 Foothill Dr Vallejo CA 94591-3697 E-mail: feiltax@hotmail.com.

FEILER, JO ALISON, artist; b. L.A., Apr. 16, 1951; d. Alfred Martin (dec.) and Leatrice Lucille Feiler. Student, UCLA, 1969, Art Ctr. Coll. Design, L.A., 1970-72; BFA, Calif. Inst. Arts, 1973, MFA, 1975. Asst. dir. Frank Perls Gallery, Beverly Hills, Calif., 1969-70; photography editor Coast Environ. mag., L.A., 1970-72; art dir. Log/An Inc., L.A., 1975-82. One-woman shows Inst. Contemporary Art, London, 1975, Calif. Inst. Arts, Valencia, 1975, NUAGE, L.A., 1978, Susan Harder Gallery, N.Y.C., 1984; exhibited in numerous group shows, 1975—; represented in permanent collections including Nat. Portrait Gallery, London, Victoria and Albert Mus., London, Met. Mus. Art, N.Y.C., Mus. Modern Art, N.Y.C., Los Angeles County Mus. Art, Internat. Mus. Photography, Rochester, N.Y., Santa Barbara Mus. Art, Oakland Mus., Mus. Fine Arts, Houston, Bibliotheque Nat., Paris, Musee D'Art Moderne De La Ville De Paris, Fondation Vincent Van Gogh, Arles, France, others. Recipient cert. art excellence Los Angeles County Mus. Art, 1968, award Laguna Beach Mus. Art, 1976; Calif. Inst. Arts scholar, 1974. Mem. Royal Photog. Soc. Gt. Britain, Friends of Photography. Democrat. Avocations: cross-country skiing, tennis, collecting art and books, music.

FEIMAN, RONALD MARK, lawyer; b. N.Y.C., Feb. 28, 1951; s. Richard and Patricia Feiman; m. Hilary J. Ronner, Jan. 7, 1984. BA, Yale U., 1972; JD, MBA, NYU, 1977. Bar: N.Y. 1978., CPA, N.Y. Assoc. Gordon Altman Butowsky Weitzen Shalov & Wein, N.Y.C., 1977-85, ptnr., 1985-99, Mayer, Brown, Rowe & Maw LLP, 1999—. Mem. ABA (intellectual property law com., bus. law com.), AICPA (appointed to fin. svcs. industry taxation com.), Assn. Bar City N.Y., Yale Club. Office: Mayer Brown Rowe & Maw LLP 1675 Broadway New York NY 10019-5889 E-mail: rfeiman@mayerbrownrowe.com., ronald.feiman.es.72@aya.yale.edu.

FEIMAN, THOMAS E. investment manager; b. Canton, Ohio, Dec. 21, 1940; s. Daniel Thaviu and Adrienne (Silver) F.; m. Marilyn Judith Miller, June 26, 1966; children: Sheri, Michael. BS in Econs., U. Pa., 1962; MBA, Northwestern U., 1963. CPA, Calif. Staff acct. Arthur Young & Co., L.A., 1963-66; field auditor IRS, L.A., 1966-68; pvt. practice acctg. Thomas Feiman, C.P.A., L.A., 1968-69; ptnr. Wideman & Feiman, C.P.A.s, L.A., 1969-74; pres. Wideman, Feiman, Levy, Sapin & Ko, L.A., 1974-93; investment mgr., v.p. Schroder Wertheim & Co., Inc., 1993-96; CFO Spinal Home Health Systems, Inc., L.A., 1983-85; fin. cons., v.p. Merrill Lynch, 1996—; pres., dir. Urol. Scis. Rsch. Found., 1993—. Sr. instr. UCLA Extension, 1967-84. Trustee Temple Israel of Hollywood, Calif., 1981-83, treas., 1983-84. Recipient cert. of award IRS, 1967. Mem. AICPA, Calif. Soc. CPAs, Northwestern Bus. So. Calif. Club (pres. 1977-80), Northwestern Alumni of So. Calif. Club (trustee 1977-92, treas. 1977-90 L.A.). Republican. Jewish. Office: Merrill Lynch Ste 290E 6320 Canoga Ave Woodland Hills CA 91367

FEIN, IRVING ASHLEY, television and motion picture executive; b. Bklyn., June 21, 1911; s. Harry and Fannie (Milstein) F.; m. Florence Kohn, Dec. 25, 1941 (dec.); children: Michael Anthony, Patricia Ann; m. Marion Shepard Schechter, June 21, 1969. Student, U. Balt., 1928-29, U. Wis., 1930-32; LL.B., St. Lawrence U., 1936. Publicity and advt. dept. Warner Bros., N.Y.C., 1933-36; dir. exploitation and radio West Coast studios, 1936; asst. publicity dir. Samuel Goldwyn, 1941; dir. exploitation and radio Columbia Pictures, Hollywood, 1942; publicity, advt. dir. Amusement Enterprises, Inc., 1947; with CBS, Inc., 1948-56, dir. exploitation, 1950; dir. publicity and exploitation CBS Radio, Hollywood, 1951-53, dir. pub. relations, 1953-55, v.p. sales promotion, advt. and press info., 1955-56; pres. J & M Prodns., Inc., Beverly Hills, Calif., 1956-65; exec. v.p. J.B. Prodns., 1965-75; producer Jack Benny Programs, 1958-74; pres. TV Prodn. Co. Producer: George Burns TV spls., 1975-96, (films) Just You and Me Kid, Oh God! You Devil, Eighteen Again; author: Jack Benny: An Intimate Biography, 1976. Recipient Emmy award, 1961. Home: 1100 Alta Loma Rd Los Angeles CA 90069-2455

FEIN, LEONA MOSS, artist; b. N.Y.C., Apr. 6, 1930; d. Leo and Pauline (Binnick) Moss; m. Harris Abraham Fein, May 25, 1952 (dec. Oct. 25, 1988); children: Ellen Beth Fein Shapiro, Scott Martin, Eric Bruce. BA in Studio Art, Queens Coll., 1980. Instr. The Craft Students League, N.Y.C., 1972-87; owner Leona M. Fein Ltd., Nassau County, N.Y., 1982—. Lectr. Met. Mus. of Art, N.Y.C., 1970-80; cons., tchr. N.Y. Coun. Arts, N.Y.C., Elder Craftsman, N.Y.C. One-woman show Queens Coll., N.Y.C., 1981; gallery show Nabisco Internat. and more, 1986; artist-in-residence Queens Mus., N.Y.C.; represented in collection of Pres. Bill Clinton. Mem. Nat. Assn. Women Artists, Nat. Guild Decoupeurs, Guild Judaic Artists. Avocation: travel. Home and Office: 125 Knickerbocker Rd Plainview NY 11803-2629 E-mail: LeonaMFein@aol.com.

FEIN, LINDA ANN, nurse anesthetist, consultant; b. Cin., Dec. 10, 1949; d. Joseph and Elizabeth P. (Kannady) Stofle; m. Thomas Paul Fein, Dec. 11, 1971. Nursing diploma, Miami Vly. Hosp. Sch. Nursing, Dayton, Ohio, 1971, Wright State U., 1969; postgrad., U. Cin. Med. Ctr., 1978. Nursing asst. Miami Vly. Hosp, 1969-71; staff nurse operating rm. Cin. Children's Hosp. & Med. Ctr., 1971, 73, Peninsula Hosp., Burlingame, Calif., 1972-73; staff nurse operating rm., emergency rm. Doctor's Hosp., San Diego, 1972; staff nurse emergency rm. Ohio State U. Hosps., Columbus, 1973-75, head nurse operating rm., 1975-76; staff nurse anesthetist Bethesda Hosps., Cin., 1978-86, Mercy Hosp. Fairfield, Cin., 1986-95; locum tenens anesthetist Fort Hamilton-Hughes Hosp., Hamilton, Ohio, 1994—95, staff anesthetist, 1995—, Butler County Surgery Ctr., Hamilton, 2000—. Childbirth educator psychoprophylactic method, 1975—; critical care nursing cons. Med. Communicators & Assocs., Salt Lake City, 1985-89; ind. nursing cons., 1989—; co-owner Exec. Shops, Cin., 1982-85; spkr. in field. Search com. Cin. Gen. Hosp. Sch. Anesthesia for Nurses, 1981-82; bd. dirs. YWCA, 1988-91, Children's Diagnostic Ctr., 1989-95, pres. bd. dirs., 1994, Planned Parenthood, 1992-95. Recipient recognition award for profl. excellence First Nurse Anesthesia Faculty Assocs., 1982, Florence Nightingale awards, 1995. Mem. Miami Vly. Hosp. Sch. Nursing Alumni Assn., Cin. Gen. Hosp. Sch. Anesthesia for Nurses Alumni Assn., Nurse Anesthetists Greater Cin., Ohio Assn. Nurse Anesthetists, Am. Assn. Nurse Anesthetists, Am. Assn. Critical Care Nurses, Nat. Registry Cert. Nurses in Advanced Practice (cert.), Ohio Coalition Nurses with Specialty Cert., Am. Soc. Critical Care Medicine, Am. Trauma Soc., NAFE, Altrusa Internat. (officer 1985-92), Order Eastern Star. Republican. Methodist. Avocations: antiques, gourmet cooking, african violets, roses, swimming. Home: 650 History Bridge Ln Hamilton OH 45013-3659

FEIN, MICHAEL R. historian, educator; b. New London, Conn., Apr. 4, 1973; s. Maier Ort and Sonya Esther Fein; m. Marjorie Nan Feld, Oct. 10, 1999. BA, Columbia U., 1995; MA, Brandeis U., 1998, PhD, 2003. Tchg. asst. Brandeis U., Waltham, Mass., 1996—98, rsch. asst., 1996—2000; rsch. assoc. Harvard Bus. Sch., Boston, 1998—2001; adj. prof. Lesley U., Cambridge, 2002—; lectr. history Brandeis U., 2003—. Co-coord. evening hours for working families Margaret Fuller Neighborhood House Food Pantry, Cambridge, 1998—. Fellow, Miller Ctr. for Pub. Affairs, 2001—02; Crown fellow, Brandeis U., 1995—99. Mem.: Am. Polit. Sci. Assn., Orgn. Am. Historians, Am. Hist. Assn. Democrat. Jewish. Home: 100 Walnut St Watertown MA 02472 Business E-Mail: fein@brandeis.edu.

FEIN, OLIVER T. physician, medical school dean; b. May 5, 1940; BA, Swarthmore Coll., 1962; MD, Western Res. U., 1967. Attending Lincoln Hosp., Bronx, N.Y., 1975-77; dir. gen. medicine outpatient svcs. Columbia Presbyn. Hosp., 1977-93; Robert Wood Johnson health policy fellow U.S. Senate Majority Office, 1993-94; assoc. dean affiliations, prof. Weill Med. Coll. of Cornell U., N.Y.C., 1995—. Mem. editl. bd. Med. Care, 1998—. Recipient Elnora Rhodes Svcs. award, Soc. Gen. Internal Medicine, 1999, Haven Emerson award, Pub. Health Assn. N.Y.C., 2001. Mem.: APHA (chair med. care sect. 1997—99, governing coun. 2000—02), Physicians for Nat. Health Program (chair N.Y.C. chpt. 1995—). Office: Weill Med Coll/Cornell U 445 East 69th St Rm 420 New York NY 10021-4805 E-mail: ofein@med.cornell.edu.

FEIN, RASHI, health sciences educator; b. N.Y.C., Feb. 6, 1926; s. Isaac M. and Clara(Wertheim) F.; m. Ruth Judith Breslau, June 19, 1949; children: Alan, Michael, Karen, Bena (dec.). Student, Bridgeport Jr. Coll., 1942-43; BA, Johns Hopkins U., 1948, PhD, 1956; LittD (hon.), SUNY, 1996. Mem. staff Pres.'s Commn. on Health Needs, 1952; from asst. to assoc. prof. U. N.C., 1952-61; statistician Bur. of Census, 1958-59; sr. staff Pres.'s Council Econ. Advisers, 1961-63; sr. fellow Brookings Inst., 1963-68; prof. Harvard U., 1968-99, prof. emeritus, 1999; Heath Clark lectr. London Sch. Hygiene and Tropical Medicine, 1980; chmn. med. assistance adv. council to sec. HEW, 1967-69; mem. adv. com. research and devel. Social Security Adminstrn., 1968-71; mem. Nat. Manpower Policy Task Force, 1967-79, Office Tech. Assessment, Health Adv. Panel., 1981-86. Mem. spl. med. adv. group VA, 1987-91; mem. nat. adv. rsch. resources coun. NIH, 1995-99; chair nat. adv. com. Robert Wood Johnson Found. Scholars in Health Policy Rsch. Program; bd. dirs. Ctr. for Child Health Rsch., Am. Acad. Pediat. Author: Economics of Mental Illness, 1958, The Doctor Shortage: An Economic Diagnosis, 1967, (with Gerald Weber) Financing Medical Education: An Analysis of Alternative Policies and Mechanisms, 1971, (with Charles Lewis and David Mechanic) A Right to Health: The Problem of Access to Primary Medical Care, 1976, Alcohol in America: The Price We Pay, 1984, Medical Care, Medical Costs: The Search for a Health Insurance Policy, 1986, 89. Mem. bd. overseers Beth Israel Deaconess Med. Ctr., Boston; trustee Hebrew Rehab. Home for Aged, Boston; mem. com. of visitors Goucher Coll.; bd. dirs. Harvard Cmty. Health Plan Found., 1980—87; mem. tech. bd. Millbank Meml. Fund, 1975—78, 1986—90, bd. dirs., 1987—90. Recipient John M. Russell award for advancement knowledge in medicine, 1971; Fellow Inst. History Medicine Johns Hopkins, 1951-52; traveling fellow WHO, 1971 Mem. APHA, AAUP, Inst. Medicine of NAS (Adam Yarmolinsky medal for contbns.), Nat. Acad. Social Ins., Am. Econ. Assn., Am. Adv. Coun. World Orgn. for Ednl. Resources and Tech. Tng. Union. Jewish. Office: Harvard U Sch Medicine Dept Social Medicine 641 Huntington Ave 2d Fl Boston MA 02115-6019 E-mail: rashi_fein@hms.harvard.edu.

FEIN, RONNIE, writer, journalist; b. N.Y.C., June 5, 1943; d. William and Lily (Hoffman) Vail; m. Edward Fein, Nov. 15, 1969; children: Meredith, Gillian. BA, Northwestern U., 1964; LLB, NYU, 1967. Atty. Chadbourne, Parke, Whiteside & Wolff, N.Y.C., 1967-70, Rosenman, Colin, N.Y.C., 1970-71; dir. Ronnie Fein Sch. Creative Cooking, Stamford, Conn., 1971—; freelance demonstrator cooking, dept. stores various locations, 1971—; journalist Stamford Trader, 1980-81, The Advertiser, New Canaan, 1981-98, Times-Mirror/Tribune newspapers, 1984—, Consumer's Digest Mag., 1989—, Darien Times, 1993-98, Newsday, 1995—, Hersam-Acorn newspapers, 1997-98, L.A. Times Syndicate, 1999—, Westport Mag., 1999—, Greenwich Mag., 1999—. Contbg. editor The New Cook's Catalogue, 2000, Tribune Newspapers, 2001—; talk show host The New WNLK, Norwalk, Conn., 1984. Author: The Complete Idiot's Guide to Cooking Basics, 1995, 3d edit., 2000, The Complete Idiot's Guide to American Cooking, 2002. Alumni admissions dir. Fairfield County, Northwestern U., Evanston, Ill., 1985-98. Fellow Conn. Women's Culinary Alliance (charter, newsletter co-chmn. 1988-89, pres. 1996-97). Home: 32 Heming Way Stamford CT 06903

FEIN, SCOTT NORRIS, lawyer; b. N.Y.C., Oct. 22, 1949; s. Sidney and Charlotte (Blaustein) F.; m. Patricia Martinelli, Oct. 16, 1983. BA, Am. U., 1971; JD, Georgetown U., 1975; LLM, NYU, 1979. Bar: N.Y. 1976, U.S. Dist. Ct. (ea. dist.) N.Y. 1978, U.S. Dist. Ct. (no. dist.) N.Y. 1982, U.S. Dist. Ct. (so. dist.) N.Y. 1978, U.S. Dist. Ct. (we. dist.) N.Y. 1985. Asst. dist. atty. Nassau County, Mineola, N.Y., 1975-79; asst. counsel to Gov. Hugh Carey of N.Y., Albany, 1979-82, Gov. Mario Cuomo, 1982-83; ptnr. Whiteman Osterman & Hanna, Albany, 1983—; litigation counsel N.Y. State Civil Liberties Union, 1984—. Co-author: The Defense of Environmental Offenses. Mem. Assn. Trial Lawyers Am., ABA, N.Y. State Bar Assn. (co-chmn. environ. sect. criminal litigation com.). Office: Whiteman Osterman & Hanna LLP One Commerce Plaza Albany NY 12260 E-mail: sfein@woh.com.

FEIN, SEYMOUR HOWARD, pharmaceutical executive; b. N.Y.C., Oct. 28, 1948; s. Abner and Beatrice (Wolkoff) F.; m. Mary Louise Orizzonto, Apr. 1, 1979; children: Jessica Ann, David Thomas, Renee Elizabeth, Jonathan Parker. BA, U. Pa., 1970; MD, N.Y. Med. Coll., 1974. Intern Dartmouth-Hitchcock Med. Ctr., Hanover, N.H., 1974-75, resident in internal medicine, 1975-77; fellow in hematology, oncology Beth Israel Hosp., Harvard Med. Sch., Boston, 1977-80; instr. medicine Harvard Med. Sch., Boston, 1979-80; sr. rsch. physician Hoffmann-LaRoche, Nutley, N.J., 1980-83; dir. med. rsch. Miles Pharmaceuticals, West Haven, Conn., 1983-86, Rorer Pharmaceuticals, Fort Washington, Pa., 1986-87; v.p. med. rsch. Greenwich Pharmaceuticals, Fort Washington, 1987-88; dir. clin. rsch. and devel. Anaquest, Murray Hill, N.J., 1988-92; v.p. clin. rsch. and biostats. Oxford Rsch. Internat. Corp., Clifton, N.J., 1992-94; pres. Fein Consulting and Rsch. Svcs., New Canaan, Conn., 1994—; mng. ptnr. CNF Pharma LLC, 2002—. Chmn. ChiRhoClin Inc., 1996—. Mem. Am. Soc. Clin. Oncology, N.Y. Acad. Scis., AAAS. Republican. Jewish. Avocations: reading, cooking, tennis, gardening, travel.

FEIN, SHERMAN EDWARD, lawyer, psychologist; b. June 17, 1928; s. Samuel L. and Mildred B. (Sherman) F.; m. Myra N. Becker, Nov. 13, 1955; children: Dina, Julia, Sara. BA, Bowdoin Coll., 1949; JD, Boston U., 1953; MS, Springfield Coll., 1962; EdD, U. Mass., 1969; Sc.MD, Sch. Medicine, Ross U., Portsmouth, Dominica, West Indies, 1983; PhD, Kensington U., 1993. Bar: Maine 1952, Mass. 1953, U.S. Dist. Ct. Mass., 1957, U.S. Supreme Ct. 1965; diplomate Am. Bd. Med. Psychotherapists. Ptnr. Fein, Pearson & Emond, P.C., Springfield, 1953—; pvt. practice psychology Springfield, 1962—; hon. consul Republic of Nicaragua, 1999—. Author: Selected Cases on Shoplifting, 1975; Divorce Handbook, 1978. Sgt. USAF, 1950-52; to lt. col. CAP, 1953-77. Mem. ABA, Hampden County Bar Assn., Mass. Bar Assn., Assn. Trial Lawyers Am., N.Y. Acad. Scis., Am. Psychology-Law Assn., Masons, Shriners. Republican. Jewish. Home: 224 Longmeadow St Longmeadow MA 01106 Office: Fein Pearson Emond & Fein 52 Mulberry St Springfield MA 01105-1410

FEIN, THOMAS PAUL, software support specialist; b. Cin., Jan. 13, 1946; s. Harold Robert and Virginia May (Gray) F.; m. Linda Ann Stofle, Dec. 11, 1971. Student, Ohio State U., 1964-67, BBA, 1976; MBA, U. Phoenix, 2000. Programmer The Ohio Casualty Group, Hamilton, 1976, Am. Laundry Machinery, Cin., 1976; programmer/analyst Automated Data Systems, Cin., 1976-78, Savs. and Loan Data Corp., Cin., 1978-81, Champion Internat. Corp., Hamilton, 1981-85, data security adminstr., 1985-89, pers. computer software analyst, 1990-2000; owner Fein Solutions, Hamilton, 2000—. Bd. dirs. St. Raphael Social Svc. Agy., Inc. Mem. Cin. Personal Computer Users Group, Ohio State U. Alumni Assn. (life). Lodges: Masons (local trustee 1982-97, sec.-treas. 1982-97, chmn. scholarship com. 1983-86), Order of Eastern Star. Republican. Methodist. Avocations: sports, electronics, antiques, gardening, volunteering. Home: 650 History Bridge Ln Hamilton OH 45013-3659 E-mail: tom@feinsolutions.com., feint@fuse.net.

FEIN, WILLIAM, ophthalmologist; b. N.Y.C., Nov. 27, 1933; s. Samuel and Beatrice (Lipschitz) F.; m. Bonnie Fern Aaronson, Dec. 15, 1963; children: Stephanie Paula, Adam Irving, Gregory Andrew. BS, CCNY, 1954; MD, U. Calif., Irvine, 1962. Diplomate Am. Bd. Ophthalmology. Intern L.A. County Gen. Hosp., 1962-63, resident in ophthalmology, 1963-66; instr. U. Calif. Med. Sch., Irvine, 1966-69; faculty U. So. Calif. Med. Sch., 1969—, assoc. clin. prof. ophthalmology, 1979—; attending physician Cedars-Sinai Med. Ctr., L.A., 1966—, chief ophthalmology clinic svc., 1979-81, chmn. divsn. ophthalmology, 1981-85; attending physician L.A. County-U. So. Calif. Med. Ctr., 1969—; chmn. dept. ophthalmology Midway Hosp., 1975-78; dir. Ellis Eye Ctr., L.A., 1984—. Mem. editorial bd. CATARACT, Internat. Jour. of Cataract and Ocular Surgery, 1992—; contbr. articles to profl. jours. Chmn. ophthalmology adv. com. Jewish Home for Aging of Greater L.A., 1993—. Fellow Internat. Coll. Surgeons, Am. Coll. Surgeons; mem. Am. Acad. Ophthalmology, Am. Soc. Ophthalmic Plastic and Reconstructive Surgery, Royal Soc. Medicine, AMA, Calif. Med. Assn., L.A. Med. Assn. Home: 718 N Camden Dr Beverly Hills CA 90210-3205 Office: 415 N Crescent Dr Beverly Hills CA 90210-4860

FEINBERG, CHERYL LACKMAN, lawyer, mediator; b. Long Beach, Calif., May 29, 1957; d. Lawrence H. and Etta D. Lackman; children: Craig, Adriana. BA, UCLA, 1980; JD, Western State U., Fullerton, Calif., 1985. Bar: Calif. 1986, U.S. Dist. Ct. (ctrl. dist.) Calif. 1987, U.S. Ct. Appeals (9th cir.) 1987; cert. tchr., Calif. Atty. Law Offices of Lawrence H. Lackman, Long Beach, 1986—. Mediator L.A. Superior Ct., The Mediation Ctr., Costa Mesa, Calif., 1994-2000; instr. legal aspects of real estate Long Beach City Coll., 1989—; arbitrator Long Beach Bar Assn., 1990—. Cmty. atty. advisor The Jr. League of Long Beach, 1991-95; mem. exec. task force, fund raising com. Legal Aid Found. Long Beach, 1990-97; legal vol. Stand Down, Long Beach, 1997, 98, 2000, 01; mem. adv. com. Long Beach Vols. in Parole, 2001-02; mem. bd. trustees St. Mary Med. Ctr., 1998—, sec., 2001-03, vice chair, 2003—. Mem. Long Beach Bar Assn. (bd. govs. 1991-92, 96-97, sec./treas. 1998, v.p. 1999, pres.-elect 2000, pres. 2001), Women Lawyers of Long Beach (pres. 1989-90, Outstanding Lawyer of Yr. award 1998, Pro Bono award 1999), Calif. Women Lawyers (bd. govs. 1990-91), So. Calif. Mediation Assn. (chair Mediation Week 1997), Long Beach Bar Found. (bd. govs. 1998-2002). Office: Law Offices Lawrence H Lackman 3740 Long Beach Blvd Long Beach CA 90807-3310

FEINBERG, DAVID ERWIN, publishing company executive; b. Mpls., 1922; Grad., U. Minn., 1948. Chmn., chief exec. officer EMC Corp., St. Paul. Sec. bd. dirs., v.p. Paradigm Pub., Inc. Home: 111 Kellogg Blvd E Saint Paul MN 55101-1237 Office: EMC Corp 875 Montreal Way Saint Paul MN 55102-4245

FEINBERG, DENNIS LOWELL, dermatologist; b. Bridgeport, Conn., June 10, 1951; AB, Cornell U., 1973; MD, SUNY, Syracuse, 1976. Diplomat Nat. Bd. Med. Examiners, Am. Bd. Internal Medicine, Am. Bd. Dermatology. Intern U. Miami (Fla.) Affiliated Hosps., 1976-77, resident, 1977-78, Johns Hopkins Med. Inst., Balt., 1978-80; dermatologist pvt. practice, Washington, 1981, Stratford, Conn., 1981—. Sr. attending Bridgeport Hosp., 1981—; attending St. Vincent's Med. Ctr., Bridgeport, 1981—, cons. Milford (Conn.) Hosp., 1982—; asst. clin. prof. Yale U. Sch. Medicine, New HAven, Conn., 1985—. Fellow Am. Acad. Dermatology; mem. AMA, ACP, Atlantic Dermatol. Soc., New Eng. Dermatological Soc., Conn. Dermatology and Dermatologic Surgery Soc., Conn. State Med. Soc., Fairfield County Med. Assn., Greater Bridgeport Med. Assn., Syracuse Med. Alumni Assn. Office: 2875 Main St Stratford CT 06614-4937

FEINBERG, ELEN AMY, artist, educator; b. N.Y.C., Jan. 22, 1955; d. S.J. Feinberg BFA, Cornell U., 1976; student, Tyler Sch. of Art, Rome, 1974-75; MFA, Ind. U., 1978. Regent's prof. of art U. N.Mex., Albuquerque, 1978—, assoc. dean. Coll. Art. One-woman shows include Eason Gallery, Santa Fe, 1981, Touchstone Gallery, N.Y.C., 1984, Roger Ramsay Gallery, Chgo., 1987, Mekler Gallery, L.A., 1988, Graham Gallery, Albuquerque, 1992, Locus Gallery, St. Louis, 1996, 98, Inpost Gallery, Albuquerque, 1997, Sarah Morthland Gallery, N.Y.C., 1999, Ruth Bachofner Gallery, L.A., 1999, Galerie Rauminhalt, Vienna, 1999, Dist. Fine Arts, Washington, 2000, Plains Art Mus., Fargo, N.D., 2000, Insap III, Palermo, Italy, 2000, St. James Ctr. for Creativity, Vallella, Malta, Dist. Fine Arts, Washington, 2003, others; exhibited in group shows at Okun Gallery, Santa Fe, 1994, Ruth Siegel Gallery, N.Y.C., 1987, Bill Bace Gallery, N.Y.C., 1990, Locus Gallery, 1997, 98, Works Gallery, Long Beach, Calif., 1991, Mus. Fine Arts, Santa Fe, 1992, Albuquerque Mus., 1992, Thomas Barry Fine Arts, Mpls., 1993, Gallery A, Chgo., 1995, Ruth Bachofner Gallery, Santa Monica, Calif., 1998, Dist. Fine Arts, Washington, 1998, South Bend (Ind.) Regional Mus. Art, 1998, Byron Cohen Gallery for Contemporary Art, Kansas City, Mo., 1998, U.S. Dept. State Art in Embassies Program, Lilonque, Malawi, 1998, Cedar Rapids Mus. Art, 1998, Dist. Fine Arts, Washington, 1998-99, Ruth Bachofner Gallery, L.A., 1999, Locus Gallery, St. Louis, 1999, Dowd Fine Arts Mus., SUNY, Cortland, N.Y., 2000, Common Ground, Albuquerque, N.Mex., 2000, Tenn. Repertory Theatre. Nashville, 2001, Lost City Arts, N.Y.C., 2001, Graphic Arts Coun., N.Y C., 2001, Harrison Gallery, Williamstown, Mass., 2001, Metaphor Contemporary Art, Bklyn., N.Y., 2002, Oxford U., Magdalen Coll., Eng., 2003, Albuquerque Mus., 2003, Johnson Gallery Fire Arts Mus., U. N.Mex., Albuquerque, Saks Fifth Ave., N.Y.C., 2003, others; represented in pub. collections Israel Mus., Jerusalem, Fed. Chancellery Bundeskanzleramt, Vienna, Morgan Guarantee Trust, N.Y.C., IBM, Atlanta, others; pub. in The Inspiration of Astronomical Phenomena: Edition Malta, 2002. N.Mex. state rep. Friends of Art & Preservation in the Embassies. Recipient Ingram Merrill Found. award in painting, 1989, Ruth Chenven Found. award in painting, 1991, Basil H. Alkazzi award in painting, 1997; Painting fellow NEA, 1987, MacDowell Colony fellow, Peterbough, N.H., 1987, Burlington rsch. fellow U. N.Mex., 1991, Va. Ctr. for the Creative Arts fellow, Sweet Briar, 1998, Painting fellow St. James Ctr. for Creativity, Vallella. Malta, 2001, Presdl. Tchg. fellow U. N.Mex., 2002; grantee Montalvo Ctr. for Arts, Saratoga, Calif., 1981, 84, Rsch. grantee U. N.Mex. Coll. Fine Arts, 1992-99, Fulbright scholar Germany, 2000; named Regents Prof., U. N.Mex., 1994-97; Presdl. Tchg. fellow U. N.Mex., 2002—. Office: U NMex Dept Arts and Art Hist 1 Univ Campus Albuquerque NM 87131-0001

FEINBERG, GARY H. lawyer, retail company executive; b. Buffalo, Oct. 19, 1942; s. Harold and Edna (Kaufman) F.; BA, U. Pa., 1964; JD, SUNY, Buffalo, 1968; m. Ellen Talles, Mar. 5, 1977; 1 child, Kevin M. Admitted to N.Y. State bar, 1968. Various positions with NLRB, Washington, Phila., Buffalo, 1968-73; atty. labor relations dept. Montgomery Ward, Balt., 1973-81, asst. labor relations dir., 1981-86, asst. dir. labor relations, Chgo., 1986—. Mem. ABA, U.S. Golf Assn. Home: 601 E Palo Verde Dr Apt 23 Phoenix AZ 85012-1344 Office: Montgomery Ward 1 Montgomery Ward Plz Chicago IL 60671-0001

FEINBERG, GLENDA JOYCE, restaurant chain executive; b. Louisville, Feb. 8, 1948; d. Harold and Winnie Esther (McIntosh) F.; divorced; 1 child, Anthony John. Student, Purdue U., 1967-68, Ind. U., 1977-79. Cert. in restaurant and personnel mgmt. Beverage mgr. Don Ce Sar Beach Hotel, St. Petersburg Beach, Fla., 1979-80; catering dir. Best Western-Skyway Inn, St. Petersburg, Fla., 1980-83; gen. mgr. Village, Inc., St. Petersburg Beach, 1983-86; banquet mgr. Tradewinds Resort Hotel, St. Petersburg Beach, 1986-87; exec. mgr. Ponderosa, Inc., Clearwater, Fla., 1987-90; food and beverage dir. Days Inn Island Beach Resort, St. Petersburg Beach, 1990-92; owner, mgmt. cons., pvt. caterer G.F. Sans Inc., 1992—. Bd. dirs. AIDS Coalitions Pinellas, 1990. Mem. NOW, World Wildlife Fedn., Nat. Geog. Soc., Greenpeace, Amnesty Internat., Environ. Def. Fund, Nat. Audubon Soc., Nat. Arbor Day Found. Democrat.

FEINBERG, HERBERT, apparel and beverage executive; b. N.Y.C., June 20, 1926; s. Harry Feinberg and Dorothy (Hurwitz) Goldstein; m. Audrey Frank, Sept. 15, 1948 (div. Mar. 1972); children: Michael(dec.), Mark, Harry; m. Barbara Mays Jones, May 25, 1972 (div. June 1989); 1 child, Candice; m. Sandi Ann Gold, June 1989; 1 child, Tara. BS, U. Ill., 1949. Owner, v.p. Monsieur Henri Wines Ltd., N.Y.C., 1949-72; owner, pres. Hudson Valley Wine Village, Highland, N.Y., 1972—, Regent Champagne Cellars, Highland, N.Y., 1988. With USAF, 1944-46. Republican. Jewish. Avocations: tennis, boating. Home: 472 Mariner Dr Jupiter FL 33477

FEINBERG, JEFFREY ENOCH, educator, author; b. Chgo., Mar. 10, 1951; s. Sidney Theodore and Sher Lee F.; m. Patricia Elaine Feinberg, June 15, 1979; children: Avraham David, Zechariah Daniel, Shoshannah Tirzah. BA, Univ. Calif., Berkeley, 1972; MBA, MA, U. Chgo., 1976; MDiv, Trinity Internat. Univ., 1985, PhD, 1988. Instr. Trinity Coll., Deerfield, Ill., 1978-79,82-85; chair of econ./mgmt. Trinity Coll. Sch. of Econ./Mgmt., Deerfield, 1985; educator Adat Hatikvah Congregation, Chgo., 1988-91, interim leader, 1991; Rosh-Kehilah/leader Etz Chaim Congregation, Buffalo Grove, Ill., 1994—; pres. Peniel Cmty. Ctr., Lake Forest, Ill., 1991—, Found. for Leadership and Messianic Edn., Lake Forest, 1988—. Steering com. Union Messianic Jewish Congregations, Albuquerque, 1994—. Recipient Internat. Writer of the Year, Internat. Biog. Ctr., Cambridge, England, 2003. Office: Flame Foundation 234 Surrey Ln Lake Forest IL 60045-3474 E-mail: enoch@flamefoundation.org.

FEINBERG, JOSEPH, plastic surgeon; b. N.Y.C., Mar. 9, 1948; s. Harold and Pauline (Heimer) F.; m. Andrea Leigh Siegel, June 17, 1950; children: Matthew, Gregory. BA, Cornell U., 1969, MD, 1973. Resident gen. surgery N.Y. Hosp., Cornell Med. Ctr., 1973-76, resident plastic surgery, 1976-78; fellow reconstructive surgery Meml. Sloan Kettering, 1978; clin. instr. N.Y. Hosp., Cornell Med. Ctr., 1979-81, asst. prof., 1981—. Trustee Friend's Acad., Locust Valley, N.Y., 1993—. Office: 1201 Northern Blvd Manhasset NY 11030-3001

FEINBERG, KENNETH ROY, lawyer, law educator; b. Brockton, Mass., Oct. 23, 1945; s. Martin B. and Dorothy (Rubenstein) F.; m. Diane Shaff, June 29, 1975; children: Michael, Leslie, Andrew. BA cum laude, U. Mass., 1967; JD, NYU, 1970. Bar: N.Y. 1971, D.C. 1977, Mass. 1980. Asst. U.S. atty. So. Dist. N.Y., 1972-75; gen. csl. subcom. on adminstrv. practice and procedure Com. on Judiciary, U.S. Senate, 1975-77, spl. counsel, 1979-80; adminstrv. asst. Senator Edward M. Kennedy, 1977-79; mng. ptnr. Kaye, Scholer, Fierman, Hays & Handler, Washington, 1980-92; ptnr., founder The Feinberg Group, Washington, 1993—. Adj. prof. law Georgetown U. Law Ctr., 1979—. Trustee Dalkon Shield Claimants Trust; active Presdl. Adv. Commn. Human Radiation

Experiments, Presdl. Commn. Catastrophic Nuclear Accidents, 1989-90, Carnegie Commn. Task Force Sci. and Tech. in Judicial and Regulatory Decision Making, 1989-93, Nat. Judicial Panel, Ctr. Pub. Resources, Marine Spill Response Corp. Named one of 27 Future Leaders of Am. Major Firms, The Am. Lawyer, 1986, one of 100 Most Influential Lawyers in Am., Nat. Law Jour. Mem. Am. Arbitration Assn., Bar Assn. City N.Y., Bar Assn. D.C., Mass. Bar Assn. Home: 5200 Edgemoor Ln Bethesda MD 20814-2342 Office: The Feinberg Group 1120 20th St NW Ste 740S Washington DC 20036-3441

FEINBERG, LAWRENCE BERNARD, university dean, psychologist; b. Bklyn., June 2, 1940; s. Robert Erwin and Geraldine F.; m. Lynn J. Feinberg; children: Ronald, Nancy, Jillian. BA, U. Buffalo, 1961; MS, SUNY, Buffalo, 1963, PhD, 1966. Lic. psychologist, Calif. cert. rehab. counselor. Lectr. dept. counselor edn. SUNY, Buffalo, 1965-66; prof. spl. edn. and rehab. Syracuse U., 1966-77, dir. rehab. edn., 1967-77; prof. counselor edn. San Diego State U., 1977—2002, adj. prof. public health, 1981-96, assoc. dean grad. div. and research, 1977-98, acting dean Coll. Edn., 1984-85, acting dean grad. div. and research, 1986-87, exec. dir internat. programs, 1988-98, assoc. v.p. for rsch. and tech., 1998—2002, prof. emeritus, 2002—. Cons. psychologist VA Hosp., Syracuse, 1970-77; cons. Rehab. Services Adminstrn., HEW, Washington, 1976-77, Nat. Inst. Handicapped Research, U.S. Dept. Edn., 1982; chmn. Nat. Commn. Accreditation of Rehab. Edn., 1974-76; bd. dirs. Nat. Commn. Rehab. Counselor Cert., 1973-77 Author: (with others) Rehabilitation and Poverty: Bridging the Gap, 1969, Rehabilitation in the Inner City, 1970, Education for the Rehabilitation Services, 1974; cons. editor 6 profl. jours.; contbr. articles to profl. jours. Recipient 20 fed. grants, 4 nat. profl. service awards Fellow Am. Psychol. Assn. (treas. div. rehab. psychology 1980-83, pres. div. rehab. psychology 1984-85), Am. Psychol. Soc.; mem. Am. Rehab. Counseling Assn. (pres. 1973, dir. 1980-83), Am. Personnel and Guidance Assn. (dir. 1974), N.Y. State Rehab. Counseling Assn. (pres. 1970), Council Rehab. Counselor Educators (regional dir. 1969-71), Phi Beta Delta (pres. Delta chpt. 1987-89). Home: 5021 Bluff Pl El Cajon CA 92020-8212 Office: San Diego State U Grad Div And Rsch San Diego CA 92182

FEINBERG, LAWRENCE EDWARD, language educator, researcher; b. N.Y., Nov. 13, 1941; s. Samuel and Nettie (Weissman) Feinberg; m. Nana Nikolaishvili, Nov. 24, 1994. BA cum laude, Middlebury Coll., 1962; MA, Harvard U., 1964, PhD, 1969. Asst. prof. U. Colo., Boulder, 1967—70; from asst. prof. to assoc. prof. U. N.C., Chapel Hill, 1970—. Contbr. articles to profl. jour. Mem.: Linguistic Soc. Am., Am. Assn. Tchrs. Slavic and East European Langs., Am. Assn. for Advancement of Slavic Studies. Home: 1506 Halifax Rd Chapel Hill NC 27514 Office: Univ NC Dey Hall 418 CB 3165 Chapel Hill NC 27599-3165

FEINBERG, LINDA SONES, social worker, artist, writer; b. Brookline, Mass., Mar. 8, 1949; d. Israel Herman and Ruth Ida (Kendall) Sones; m. Steven Lappen, June 1971 (div. May 1978); m. Alec A. Feinberg, June 18, 1978; children: Marissa, Jennifer. BA, Boston U., 1970; MSW, Boston Coll., 1975. Social worker Dept. Pub. Welfare, Boston, 1970-73, supr. social svcs., 1973-79; social worker Andover, Mass., 1983-91, Newton, Mass., 1991-95, Lynnfield, Mass., 1995—99; author New Horizon Press, Far Hills, N.J., 1994—; psychotherapist Andover, 1999—. Author: I'm Grieving As Fast As I Can, 1994, Teasing: Innocent Fun or Sadistic Malice?, 1996. Mem. NASW. Home and Office: 22 Avery Ln Andover MA 01810-6401

FEINBERG, NORMAN MAURICE, real estate company executive; b. Bklyn., Nov. 28, 1934; s. Harry and Beatrice (Soroca) F.; m. Arline S. Itzkoff, Nov. 26, 1960; children: Mitchell, David. BS, NYU, 1956. Exec. Columbia Pictures Corp., N.Y.C., 1956-62; pres. Gateside Corp., Rye, N.Y., 1965—. Owner, gen. ptnr. 27 companies, Rye; bd. dirs. St. Marys Rehab. Ctr. for Children. Arbitrator Am. Arbitration Assn., N.Y.C.; trustee, vice-chmn. Bklyn. Mus.; bd. dirs. Assn. for Mentally Ill Children, Scarborough, N.Y; chmn. bd. St. Mary's Health Sys.; mem. adv. bd. Steven L. Newman Real Estate Inst. of Baruch Coll., CUNY. Mem. World Pres. Orgn., Young Pres. Orgn. (chmn.), Chief Execs. Officers. Avocations: art collecting, skiing, tennis, travel, languages. Home: 15 E 69th St New York NY 10021-4905 Office: Gateside Corp 555 Theodore Fremd Ave Rye NY 10580-1451

FEINBERG, RICHARD, anthropologist, educator; b. Norfolk, Va., Nov 4, 1947; s. Isadore and Rose Selma (Hartmann) F.; m. Nancy Ellen Grim, Apr. 15, 1978; children: Joseph Grim einberg, Kate Grim-Feinberg. AB, U. Calif., Berkeley, 1969; MA, U. Chgo., 1971, PhD, 1974. Asst. prof. anthropology Kent (Ohio) State U., 1974-80, assoc. prof., 1980-86, prof., 1986—. Mem. editorial bd. Kent State U. Press, 1990-93; chair Kent State U. Faculty Senate, 1997-98; pres. Kent Rsch. Group, 1997-98. Author: Anuta: Social Structure of a Polynesian Island, 1981, Polynesian Seafaring and Navigation, 1988; editor: Politics of Culture in the Pacific Islands, 1995, Seafaring in the Contemporary Pacific Islands, 1995, Leadership and Change in the Western Pacific, 1996, Oral Traditions of Anuta, 1998, The Cultural Analysis of Kinship: The Legacy of David M. Schneider, 2001, (with others) Oceania: An Introduction to the Cultures and Identities of Pacific Islanders, 2002. Kent State Rsch. Coun. grantee, 1983, 88, 00; Wenner-Gren Found. grantee, 1991. Fellow: Assn. for Social Anthropology in Oceania (newsletter editor 1986—90, program coord. 2000—03), Am. Anthrop. Assn.; mem.: Ctrl. States Anthrop. Soc. (bull. editor 1994—98, 2d v.p. 2002—03), Am. Ethnological Soc., Polynesian Soc. Avocations: camping, white water kayaking, scuba diving, folk music. Office: Kent State U Dept Anthropology Kent OH 44242-0001

FEINBERG, RICHARD ALAN, clinical psychologist; b. Oakland, Calif., Aug. 12, 1947; s. Jack and Raechel Sacks (Hoff) F. BA, Calif. State U., Hayward, 1969; MA in Clin. Psychology, Mich. State U., 1972, PhD, 1979. Cert. Nat. Register Health Svc. Providers in Psychology. Instr. Merritt Coll., Oakland, 1975-76; clin. psychology Highland Gen. Hosp., Oakland, 1976-79; assoc. Lafayette Ctr. Counseling and Edn., 1978-79; clin. psychology Tri-City Mental Health Ctr., Fremont, Calif., 1979-81, dir., 1981-86; pvt. practice, Fremont, 1976—. Participant profl. conf. USPHS fellow, 1969-71. Mem. APA, Calif. Psychol. Assn. Office: 38950 Blacow Rd Ste D Fremont CA 94536-7379

FEINBERG, ROBERT S. plastics company executive, marketing professional; b. Newark, May 14, 1934; s. Clarence Jacob and Sabina (Zorn) Feinberg. BA in English, BS in Chemistry, Trinity Coll., Hartford, Conn., 1955; MBA in Mkg., Fairleigh Dickinson U., 1966; diploma in advt., Assn. Indsl. Advt., 1967, NY Inst. Advt., 1967. Pres. Trebor Assocs. and Trebor Plastics Co., Teaneck, NJ, 1961—; mktg. cons. computer software Zettler Softwear Co., Burroughs Corp.; sr. coun. Yankelovich, Skelly and White, Inc.; cons. Greenwich Assocs.; co-chmn., ptnr. Edgeroy Co., Inc., Ridgefield and Palisades Park, NJ, 1973—, LeMont Sales Co., Teaneck, NJ, 1973—. Cons. plastics formulations W. R. Grace, Endicott Johnson, Brown Shoe Co., U.S. Shoe Co., Ciba, Uniroyal. Author: Olympia Shoe Co. (Harvard Case Book Series); poet. Mem.: U.S. Profl. Tennis Assn., Sell Overseas Am., Sporting Goods Mfrs. Assn., Soc. Plastics Engrs. (sr.), Bergen County Tennis League (v.p.), Ahdeek Tennis Club. Achievements include patents in polymer and mechanical engineering fields; co-inventor Edgeroy Ball Press (Internat. Tennis Hall of Fame). Home: PO Box 273 Teaneck NJ 07666-0273

FEINBERG, SHELDON NORMAN, pediatrician, educator; b. N.Y.C., Mar. 16, 1930; m. MaryEllen Wisker, Jan. 2, 1988; children: Lynn Ann, Bette Joan, Barbara Ellen, Paul Howard, John Joseph. MD, N.Y. Med. Coll., 1955. Diplomate Am. Bd. Pediat. Intern Bronx Mcpl. Hosp. Ctr., N.Y.C., 1955-56; resident Met. Hosp., N.Y.C., 1956-57; fellow pediatrics N.Y. Med. Coll., 1959-60; pediat. staff Passack Valley Hosp., Westwood, N.J., 1960-82; emergency physician various hosps., 1982-85; pediat. staff Hackensack (N.J.) U. Med. Ctr., 1985—; clin. asst. prof. pediat. U. Med. & Dentistry N.J., Newark, 1985—. Inventor infant scale guard, simple stool stain. Maj. USAF med. corps., 1957-59. Honor award Bergen County Med. Soc., 1965. Fellow Am. Acad. Pediat.; mem. AMA, N.J. Pediat. Soc. (pres. 1989-91, Honor award 1991). Home: 125 N Country Rd Mount Sinai NY 11766-1503

FEINBERG, TODD ELIOT, physician; b. N.Y.C., Mar. 11, 1952; s. Mortimer and Gloria Feinberg; children: Rachel, Joshua. BA, U. Pa., 1974; MD, Mount Sinai Sch. Medicine, 1978. Chief Yarmon Neurobehavioral and Alzheimers Disease Ctr. Beth Israel Med. Ctr., N.Y.C., 1986—. Assoc. prof. neurology and psychiatry Albert Einstein Coll. Medicine, 1995—. Author: Altered Egos: How the Brain Creates the Self; editor: Behavioral Neurology and Neuropsychology, 1997. Office: Beth Israel Med Ctr Yarmon Neurobev & Alzheimer 1st Ave at 16th St New York NY 10003-3804 E-mail: tfeinberg@bethisraelny.org.

FEINBERG, WILFRED, judge; b. N.Y.C., June 22, 1920; s. Jac and Eva (Wolin) Feinberg; m. Shirley Marcus, June 23, 1946; children: Susan Stelk, Jack, Jessica Iwedt. BA, Columbia U., 1940, LLB, 1946, LLD (hon.), 1985, Syracuse U., 1985; LLD (hon.), Bklyn. Law Sch., 1998. Bar: N.Y. 1947. Law clk. Hon. James P. McGranery U.S. Dist. Ct. (ea. dist.) Pa., 1947—49; assoc. Kaye, Scholer, Fierman & Hays, N.Y.C., 1949—53; ptnr. McGoldrick, Dannett, Horowitz & Golub, N.Y.C., 1953—61; dep. supt. N.Y. State Banking Dept., N.Y.C., 1958; judge U.S. Dist Ct. (so. dist.), N.Y.C., NY, 1961—66, U.S. Ct. Appeals (2nd cir.), N.Y.C., NY, 1966—; chief judge, 1980—88, sr. judge, 1991—. Mem. U.S. Jud. Conf. U.S., 1980—88, chmn. exec. com., 1987—88, mem. Devitt award com., 1989, 90, mem. long-range planning com., 1991—96; Madison lectr. NYU Law Sch., 1983; Sonnett lectr. Fordham U. Law Sch., 1984; Inaugural Howard Kaplan Meml. lectr. Hofstra U. Law Sch., 1986; The Future of Justice lectr. Inst. of Comparative Law, Chuo U., Japan, 1991. Editor-in-chief: Columbia Law Rev., 1946; contbr. With U.S. Army, 1942—45. Recipient Learned Hand medal for excellence in fed. jurisprudence, 1982, Gold medal, award for disting. svc. in the law, N.Y. State Bar Assn., 1990, medal for excellence, Columbia Law Alumni Assn., 1990, Pursuit of Justice award, Internat. Assn. Jewish Lawyers and Jurists, 1993, Disting. Pub. Svc. award, N.Y. County Lawyers Assn., 1994, Edward Weinfeld award, 1995, Ann. Wilfred Feinberg prize named in his honor for best student work at Columbia Law Sch. related to fed. cts., 1998. Mem.: ABA, Am. Law Inst., Am. Judicature Soc., N.Y. County Lawyers Assn., Assn. of Bar of City of N.Y., Phi Beta Kappa. Office: US Ct Appeals 2nd Cir Room 2004 US Court House Foley Sq New York NY 10007-1501

FEINDEL, JANET MADELLE, performing arts educator; b. Montreal, Que., Can., 1952; d. William Howard and Faith (Roswell) Feindel; m. Robert Arthur Haley, Aug. 25, 1984. Diploma with honors, George Brown Coll., Toronto, 1978; BA in Drama, U. Toronto, 1984; MFA in Drama, Carnegie Mellon U., 2002. Vis. asst. prof. U. Alta., Edmonton, Canada, 1989—90; asst. prof. Kent State U., Kent, Ohio, 1990—94; adj. prof. Voice/Acting Concordia U., Montreal, 1994—95; assoc. prof. Carnegie Mellon U., Pitts., 1996—. Coach Voice, Dialect Stratford Festival, Stratford, Ont., 1994—95, Shaw Festival, Niagara, Ont., 1990, Pitts., 2001—02. Author: (plays) A Particular Class of Women, 1987; contbr. Mem.: Voice and Speech Trainers Assn., Alexander Technique Internat., Assn. Can. TV and Radio Artists, Playwrights Guild Can., Alexander Alliance, Actors Equity, Voice Found. Avocation: yoga. Office: Carnegie Mellon Univ Sch Drama 5000 Forbes Ave Pittsburgh PA 15213-3890

FEINDEL, WILLIAM HOWARD HOWARD, neurosurgeon, consultant; b. Bridgewater, NS, Can., July 12, 1918; s. Robert Ronald Feindel and Annie Swansburg; m. Dorothy Faith Roswell Lyman, July 28, 1945; children: Christopher, Alexander, Patricia, Janet, Michael, Anna. BA, Acadia U., Can., 1939, DSc (hon.), 1963; MSc, Dalhousie U., Can., 1942; MD, CM, McGill U., Can., 1945, DSc (hon.), 1984; DPhil in Neuroanatomy, Oxford U., Eng., 1949; LLD (hon.), Mt. Allison U., 1983, U. Sask., Can., 1986. Diplomate Am. Bd. Neurol. Surgery; licentiate Med. Coun. Can. Rsch. asst. Montreal (Can.) Neurol. Inst., 1942-44, fellow in neuropathology, 1944-45, dir. neuro-isotope lab., 1959-88, dir. inst., 1972-84; dir. gen., dir. profl. svcs. Montreal Neurol. Hosp., 1972-84; rsch. asst., demonstrator in anatomy Oxford U., Eng., 1946-49; demonstrator in neurosurgery McGill U., 1951-52, lectr. neurosurgery, 1952-55, William Cone prof. neurosurgery, 1959-88, chmn. dept. neurology and neurosurgery, 1972-77, dir. Cone lab. neurosurg. rsch., 1959-88; assoc. prof. surgery U. Sask., 1955-56, prof. surgery, 1956-59; coord. rsch. in positron emission tomography Montreal Neurol. Inst. and Hosp., 1975-84, dir. brain imaging ctr., 1984-87, dir. neuro history project, 1987—; chancellor Acadia U., 1991-96, chancellor emeritus, hon. gov., 1996—. Prin. investigator brain tumor project NIH, Bethesda, Md., 1986-89, co-investigator rsch., 1989—, mem.-reviewer neurol. disorders program project rev., 1983-88, external reviewer spl. programs, 1989-95; lectr. dept. history medicine and sci. U. B.C., 1976-78; neurol. cons. St. Paul's and City Hosps., Saskatoon, sask., 1955-59; cons. neurosurgeon Royal Victoria Hosp. and Catherine Booth Hos., Montreal, 1959-79, Sherbrooke (Que.) Gen. Hosp., 1964-85, Montreal Gen. Hosp., 1978—; cons. Champlain Valley Physicians Hosp., Plattsburgh, NY, 1973-85; neurosurgeon-in-chief Montreal Neurol. Hosp., 1961-72, sr. neurosurgeon, 1985—; neurologist and neurosurgeon-in-chief Royal Victoria Hosp., 1971-85, cons. neurosurgeon, 1985—; mem. sci. com. Found. for Study Ctrl. and Peripheral Nervous Sys., Geneva,1983—; mem. expert panel on neurology WHO and Pan-Am. Health Orgn., 1976-94, cons. in neuroscis., 1996—; med. advisor to bd. Internat. Children's Inst., 1999—. Author more than 500 articles on epilepsy, neurosurgery, brain imaging and history of medicine; editor: Memory, Learning and Language—The Physical Basis of Mind, 1960, The Anatomy of the Brain and Nerves by Doctor Thomas Willis, tercentenary edit., 1965; co-editor: Dynamics of Brain Edema, 1976, Brain Imaging and Metabolism, 1985. Mem. bd. curators Osler Libr., McGill U., 1963—, curator Penfield Archive, 1976—, hon. assoc. libr. Osler Libr., 1964-65, hon. libr., 1996—; chmn. Publications Com.(osler library),1977-. bd. gov. Acadia U., 1981-89, mem. exec. com., 1984-86. Decorated officer Order of Can., 1982; Grand Officer de l'Ordre National du Québec, 2002, nominated for Canadian Med. Hall of Fame, 2002, Rhodes scholar Merton Coll. Oxford U., 1939; recipient Neilson award Hannah Inst. History Medicine, 1997, Golden Jubilee medal Queen Elizabeth II, 2003, Laureate Can. Med. Hall of Fame, 2003; William Feindel lectureship named in his honor, Montreal Neurol. Inst., 1994, William Feindel chair neuro-oncology endowed at Montreal Neurol. Inst. and McGill U., 2001. Fellow ACS, Royal Coll. Physicians and Surgeons Can., Royal Soc. Can.; mem. Am. Assn. Neurol. Surgeons, Am. Acad. Neurol. Surgeons (pres. 1976), Am. Neurol. Assn. (v.p. 1976), Am. Epilepsy Soc. (J. Kiffin Penry award 1998), Am. Soc. Neurol. Surgeons (v.p. 1978), Can. Neurosurg. Soc. (pres. 1968), Montreal Medico-Chirurg. Soc. (pres. 1974), Osler Soc. McGill U. (pres. 1945, hon. pres. 1985-88, 90-97), James McGill Soc. (pres. 1997), Acad. Mexicana Cirugia (hon.), Am. Osler Soc., Osler Club London (hon.), Univ. Club Montreal, Faculty Club McGill U., Indoor Tennis Club, Alpha Omega Alpha. Anglican. Avocations: medical history, travel, music, book-binding, maya culture. Office: Montreal Neurol Inst 3801 University St # 110 Montreal QC Canada H3A 2B4 E-mail: william.feindel@mcgill.ca.

FEINER, AVA SOPHIA, public affairs and management consultant, economist; b. Bklyn., Feb. 13, 1950; d. Ignace and Lola (Pasternak) F.; m. Clifford Douglas Stromberg, June 25, 1972; children: Kimberly Greta, Eric George. BA summa cum laude, Yale U., 1971; MA, Harvard U., 1974, PhD in Govt., 1978. Legis. asst. to U.S. Senator Bill Bradley, Washington, 1979-82; dir. internat. trade policy U.S. C. of C., Washington, 1982-83, mgr. internat. policy dept., 1983-85; corp. program dir. IBM, Washington, 1985-87, corp. dir. pub. affairs, trade and investment, 1987; pres. Feiner Pub. Affairs Cons., Washington, 1988—; co-founder, dir. Washington Alive! Inc., 1989-90; pres. Washington Networks, 1990—; mem. campaign and transition team Ehrlich for Gov., 2002; mem. Maryland State Ethics Commn., 2003. Teaching fellow Harvard U., Cambridge, Mass., 1972-74; lectr. nat. and internat. politics and econs., 1978—; bd. dirs., World Trade Forum, Washington, 1987-89; mem. Md. State Ethics Commn., 2003—. Co-author: American Excellence in A World Economy, 1987; contbr. articles on econs., trade, fgn. policy to various publs. Del. to Atlantic Coun. Young Leadership Program, Wis. and Can., 1978, 80, Aspen Inst. Exec. Seminar, 1982, Germany-U.S. Young Leadership Conf., San Francisco, 1982, Harbor Sch. Bd., 1992-93; co-chair Holton-Arms Sch. Silent Auction, 1995-96; mem. adv. com. Homeowners, 1999—, chmn., 2001—; 1st v.p. Potomac Women's Rep. Club., 2002, Ehrlich for Gov. of Md. campaign and transition team, 2002. Fgn. Policy fellow Brookings Instn., 1975-76, guest scholar, 1976-77; Carnegie Endowment for Internat. Peace fellow, 1975-76. Mem.: Trade Policy Forum, Coun. Fgn. Rels. (task force on women 1988—91, term membership com. 1988—91, internat. affairs fellows com. 1991—95, Washington program adv. com. 1995—98), Phi Beta Kappa. Avocations: photography, Karate, swimming, bicycling, tennis.

FEINER, JOEL S. psychiatrist; b. N.Y.C., July 14, 1938; s. Sol and Helen (Minkow) F. BA, Yale U., 1960; MD, Albert Einstein Coll. Medicine, 1964. Diplomate Am. Bd. Psychiatry and Neurology. Dir. dept. psychiatry Bronx (N.Y.) Psychiat. Ctr., 1985-87, devel. dir., 1987-92, pres. med. staff orgn., 1989-92; co-dir. residency tng. dept. psychiatry Albert Einstein Coll. Medicine, Bronx, 1979-83, dir. residency tng. dept. psychiatry, 1983-86, prof. dept. psychiatry, 1989-92, vis. prof. dept. psychiatry, 1992—, dir. div. social and community psychiatry dept. psychiatry, 1986-92, also chmn. Med. Sch. Minority Affairs Com.; prof. dept. psychiatry U. Tex. Southwestern Med. Sch., Dallas, 1992—; clin. and tng. dir. Mental Health Connections, 1992—; assoc. dir. residency tng. dept. psychiatry U. Tex. Southwestern Med. Sch., Dallas, 1993—. Cons. in field; editl. adv. com. Family Sys. Medicine, 1983-92; vis. faculty Family Inst. Westchester, Mt. Vernon, N.Y., 1985-92. Recipient Profl. of Yr. award Dallas Alliance for Mentally Ill, 1993, Pamela Blumenthal award Dallas Mental Health Assn., 1994, Profl. of Yr. award Tex. Alliance for Mentally Ill, 1995, Exemplary Psychiatrist award Nat. Alliance Mentally Ill, 1996, Spl. Svc. award Tex. Soc. Psychiat. Physicians, 1997; Career Tchg. fellow Albert Einstein Coll. Medicine, 1972-74. Fellow Am. Psychiat. Assn. (cons. Commn. on Homelessness, Poverty and Psychiatry, Mead Johnson fellow in pub. psychiatry selection com. 1986-89, Significant Achievement award 1995), Am. Family Therapy Acad. (charter); mem. Am. Orthopsychiat. Assn. (sect. 1987-90, program faculty chair 1985-86). Office: Southwestern Med Sch Mental Health Connections 5909 Harry Hines Blvd Dallas TX 75235-6209 *"Beware of closed systems" and from E.M. Forster, "only connect.".*

FEINER, STEVEN KEITH, computer science educator, consultant, lecturer; b. N.Y.C., Aug. 5, 1952; s. Louis and Claire Bernice (Shulman) F.; m. Michele Page, July 2, 1997. AB, Brown U., 1973, PhD, 1987. Asst. prof. Columbia U., N.Y.C., 1985-90, assoc. prof., 1991-99, prof., 2000—. Mem. steering com. IEEE Symposium on Info. Visualization, 1997—, IEEE and Assn. Computing Machinery Internat. Symposium on Mixed and Augmented Reality, 2000—, Internat. Symposium on Wearable Computers, 2001—. Co-author: Computer Graphics: Principles and Practice, 1990, Introduction to Computer Graphics, 1994, German transl., 1995, French transl., 1995, Polish transl., 1995, Spanish transl., 1996, Computer Graphics: Principles and Practice in C., 1995; assoc. editor ACM Transactions on Info. Sys., 1990-95, ACM Transactions on Graphics, 1995—; mem. editl. bd. IEEE Transactions on Visualization and Computer Graphics, 1994—, IEEE Computer Soc. Tech. Com. on Computer Graphics, 1994—. Grad. fellow IBM, 1981; recipient Instrnl. Technology Rsch. award ASTD, 1990, Young Investigator award Office Naval Rsch., 1991. Mem. IEEE Computer Soc., Assn. Computing Machinery, Spl. Interest Group on Computer-Human Interaction, Spl. Interest Group on Graphics. Office: Columbia U Dept Computer Sci, 450 CS Bldg 500 W 120th St New York NY 10027-6623

FEINGLASS, NEIL GORDON, anesthesiologist; b. Miami, Florida, 1957; MD, Vanderbilt Univ., 1983. Resident in anesthesiology U. Fla. Coll. Medicine, Gainesville, Fla., 1983-86, fellow in critical care medicine, 1986-87; fellow in cardiac anesthesia Tex. Heart Inst., 1986; cons. anesthesiologist, critical care medicine Mayo Clinic, Rochester, Minn., 1990—, chief of cardiac anesthesia, head intra operative echo svc., 1995—, dir. anesthesia info. svc.; dir. hosp. automation St. Luke's Hosp., Jacksonville, Fla., 2002—. Asst. prof. Mayo Grad. Sch. Medicine; mem. task force for electronic anesthesia sys., Anesthesia Patent Safety Found., 2002; reviewer, Jour. Cardio-Thoracle Vascular Anesthesia. Fellow Am. Coll. Chest Physicians; mem. AMA; Am. Bd. Echocardiography; Am. Surg. Assn.; Minn. Med. Assn.; Minn. Surg. Assn.; Am. Lung Assn. (regional bd. dir. 1999—); ZVMS. Office: Mayo Clinic Jacksonville 4500 San Pablo Rd S Jacksonville FL 32224-1865

FEINGOLD, DAVID SIDNEY, microbiology educator; b. Chelsea, Mass., Nov. 15, 1922; s. Louis Edward and Miriam (Young) F.; m. Batia Babette Haber, Nov. 15, 1949; children: Oded, Anat, Michele. BS, MIT, 1944; PhD, Hebrew U., Jerusalem, Israel, 1956. Chemist Lucidol Corp., Buffalo, 1944; jr. research biochemist U. Calif. at Berkeley, 1957-60; asst. prof. biology U. Pitts., 1960-62, asso. prof., 1962-65, prof., 1965—; prof. microbiology Sch. Medicine, 1966-93, prof. emeritus molecular genetics and biochemistry, 1993—. Contbr. articles to profl. jours. Served with USNR, 1944-46. Recipient State of Israel prize in natural sci., 1957, Career Devel. award NIH, 1965-75 Fellow Infectious Disease Soc. Am.; mem. Internat. Endotoxin Soc., Am. Soc. for Biochemistry and Molecular Biology. Home: 6420 Bartlett St Pittsburgh PA 15217-1832 E-mail: udpglcdh@juno.com.

FEINGOLD, RUSSELL DANA, senator, lawyer; b. Janesville, Wis., Jan. 2, 1953; s. Leon and Sylvia (Binstock) Feingold; m. Susan Levine, Aug. 21, 1977; children: Jessica, Ellen; m. Mary Speerschneider, Jan. 20, 1991; stepchildren: Sam Speerschneider, Ted Speerschneider. BA with honors, U. Wis.-Madison, 1975; postgrad., Magdalen Coll., Oxford U., Eng., 1975—77; JD with honors, Harvard U., 1979. Bar: Wis. 1979. Assoc. Foley & Lardner, Madison, 1979—82, LaFollette, Sinykin, Anderson & Munson, Madison, 1983—85, Goldman & Feingold, 1985—88; mem. Wis. Senate, 1983—92; U.S. senator from Wis., 1993—; mem. aging com., budget com., fgn. rels. com., judiciary com., senate Dem. policy com. U.S. Senate. Scholar, Wis. Honors scholar, 1971, Rhodes scholar, 1975. Mem.: Phi Beta Kappa. Democrat. Jewish. Office: US Senate 506 Hart Senate Office Bldg Washington DC 20510-0001 also: US Senators Office 1600 Aspen Commons Rm 100 Middleton WI 53562-4626

FEINGOLD, S. NORMAN, psychologist; b. Worcester, Mass., Feb. 2, 1914; s. William and Aida (Salit) F.; m. Marie Goodman, Mar. 24, 1947; children: Elizabeth Anne, Margaret Ellen, Deborah Carol, Marilyn Nancy. AB, Ind. U., 1937; MA, Clark U., 1940; EdD, Boston U., 1948; LLD, Edward Waters Coll., Saints Coll. Dir. vocat. svc., ednl. and vocat. dir. Hecht. Neighborhood House, Boston, 1940-43; exec. dir. Boston Jewish Vocat. Svc. and Work Adjustment Ctr., 1946-58; nat. dir. B'nai B'rith Career and Counseling Svcs., Washington, 1958-80; pres. Nat. Career and Counseling Svcs., 1980—; pvt. practice, 1980—. Exec. adviser Rehab. Services, Boston, 1953-58; dir. ednl. and vocat. workshop United Cerebral Palsy of Greater Boston, Inc., 1957-58; cons. to Scholarships, Fellowships and Loans News Service, Social Security Administrn., 1962—; instr., spl. lectr. Boston U., 1951-58; profl. lectr. Am. U. Rehab. Counseling Adv. Panel, 1963-65; mem. Am. Bd. Counseling Services, 1962-65, 70—. Author: It Pays to Advertise, 1975, Occupations and Careers, 1969, The Vocational Expert in the Social Security Disability Program, 1969, A Counselor's Handbook, 1972, Counseling for Careers in the 80's, 1979, Whither Counseling, 1981, Making It on Your Own, rev., 1991, A Guide to Financial Success, 1981, rev., 1985, Emerging Careers: New Occupations for the Year Two Thousand and Beyond, 1983, The Professional and Trade Association Job Finder, 1983, Getting Ahead: A Woman's Guide to Career Sources, 1983, Scholarships, Fellowships and Loans, Vol. 8, 1987, New Emerging Careers: Today, Tomorrow, and in the 21st Century, 1988, Futuristic Exercises: A Work Book for Emerging Lifestyles and Careers in the 21st Century and Beyond, 1989, Where the Jobs Are: A Comprehensive Directory of 1200 Journals Listing Career Opportunities, 1989, The Complete Job and Career Handbook: 101 Ways to Get from Here to There, 1993; past editor Counselors Information Service. Chmn. Gov.'s Council on Aging, 1956-58, Washington Bus.-Industry Group, 1963-64; mem. Pres.'s Com. on Employment Handicapped, 1950—; adv. com. Nat. Health Council; pres. Greater Boston Persn. and Guidance Assn., 1952-53; mem. Nat. Home Study Accrediting Commn.; chmn. human relations com. Dept. Agr. Grad. Sch.; profl. adv. bd. Epilepsy Found. 1st lt. AUS, 1943-46, ETO and PTO. Recipient Cmty. Svc. award B'nai B'rith, 1957, Brotherhood and Americanization award, 1958, Eminent Career award Nat. Capital Personnel and Guidance Assn. Fellow Am. Psychol. Assn.; mem. Am. Personnel and Guidance Assn. (pres. 1974-75), Mass., Nat. Vocat. Guidance Assn. (pres. 1968-69), Internat. Coun. Psychologists, Nat. Press Club, Nat. Rehab. Assn., Torch Club, New Century Club (bd. dirs. 1954-58), Phi Delta Kappa. Home: 1801 E Jefferson St # 442 Rockville MD 20852-4057 *Any success I may have attained is because of conscientiousness, a love of life, a high energy level, a supportive family, close friends, and being an optimist by temperament and conviction. I believe in people and the tremendous potential of all people. To me, everyone is a Very Important Person, who can make a contribution. My premise is that our most precious resource is people, and everything we do individually or collectively now or in the future depends on that conviction and acting accordingly.*

FEININGER, THEODORE LUX, artist; b. Berlin, June 11, 1910; s. Charles Lyonel and Julia (Lilienfeld) F.; m. Patricia Randall, Dec. 17, 1954; children: Lucas, Conrad, Charles. Grad., Bauhaus, Dessau, Germany, 1929. Instr. Sarah Lawrence Coll., 1950-52; lectr. drawing and painting Harvard U., 1953-62; instr. drawing and painting Boston Fine Arts Mus. Sch., 1962-75. Author:

Lyonel Feininger: City at the Edge of the World, 1965, Photographs of the 20s and 30s (illustrated catalogue), 1980; exhbns. include Am. Realists and Magic Realists, Mus. Modern Art, N.Y.C., 1943, Revolution and Tradition in Modern Am. Art, Bklyn. Mus., 1951, Whitney Mus. Am. Art Ann., N.Y.C., 1951, Am. Painters, MIT, 1954, Retrospective, Busch-Reisinger Mus., 1962, Wheaton Coll., 1973, Wamsutta Club, New Bedford, Mass., 1974, Prakapas Gallery, N.Y.C., 1980, Sacramento St. Gallery, Cambridge, Mass., 1982, Gallery on the Green, Lexington, Mass., 1986, 88, 90, 92, Achim Moeller Fine Art, N.Y.C., 1954-94, Staatliche Galerie Moritzburg Halle, Saale, Germany, 1998, Städtisches Mus. Karlsruhe, Germany, 2001; represented in permanent collections Mus. Modern Art, N.Y.C., Busch-Reisinger Mus. and Fogg Art Mus., Harvard U., Altonaer Mus., Hamburg, Germany, Schleswig-Holstein Landes Mus., Mus. Folkwang, Essen, Germany, Bauhaus Mus., Weimar, Germany, Getty Mus., Calif., Met. Mus., N.Y., L.A. County Mus., Stedelijk Mus., Amsterdam, Guggenheim Mus., N.Y., Staatliche Galerie Moritzburg, Germany. With U.S. Army, 1942-45. Mem. Westport Art Group. Democrat. Address: 22 Arlington St Cambridge MA 02140-2713 *The practice and teaching of art has shown me that I must seek progress on the basis of understanding and assimilating tradition; that every individual incorporates both revolutionary and conservative tendencies; and that the task of the individual lies in assessing and acting upon his findings, his own proportionate share of these two conflicting trends. I am Society, and Society cannot do without me.*

FEINLEIB, SIDNEY, technology company business executive; b. N.Y.C., Dec. 31, 1938; m. Hisako Azumi; 1 child, David. BA, Columbia U., 1960, MA, 1961; PhD, U. Minn., 1965. Cons. Arthur D. Little Inc., Cambridge, Mass., 1968-72; pres. Cons. Internat. Inc., Arlington, Mass., 1972—; prof. venture capital devel. Rikkyo U., Tokyo, 2002—. Author: Action for Productive Aging, 1997. Fin. com. Town of Arlington, 1996—. Mem. IEEE, Am. Chem. Soc. Achievements include development of UV circular dischroism spectrophotmeter, non-copyable paper, hand-held copier. Home: 30 Hamilton Rd Apt 401 Arlington MA 02474-8271 E-mail: consultint@aol.com.

FEINMAN, ALVIN, retired literature educator, poet; b. Bklyn., Nov. 21, 1929; s. Morris Feinman and Kaplan Frieda; m. Deborah Dorfman, Jan. 20, 1992. BA, Bklyn. Coll., 1951; MA, Yale U., 1953. Prof. lit. Bennington (Vt.) Coll., 1969—94; ret., 1994. Author: (poetry) Preambles, 1964, Poems, 1990. Fellow Fulbright Found., Heidelberg, 1954—55. Home: PO Box 655 North Bennington VT 05257

FEINMAN, STEPHEN ERWIN, art dealer, consultant, appraiser; b. N.Y.C., Sept. 29, 1932; s. Mark C. and Mildred (Rinzler) F.; m. Elizabeth Petrillo (div.); children: Gary, Stephanie Elena, Lily M., Ester Buchholtz Wolf. AB, Inst. Applied Arts, 1952; postgrad., CCNY, 1953-54. Pres. Breton Fabrics, Inc., N.Y.C., 1962-64, Gary Arts Ltd., N.Y.C., 1964-72, Multiple Impressions Ltd., N.Y.C., 1972-94, S.E. Feinman Fine Arts Ltd., N.Y.C., 1994—. Mem. Fine Art Trade System (exec. com.), Panther Orgn. Home: 60 E 8th St Apt 27D New York NY 10003-6522

FEINMARK, PHYLLIS S. KAPLAN, lawyer; b. Washington, Jan. 31, 1954; BA, Johns Hopkins U., 1975; JD, George Washington U., 1978. Bar: Md. 1978, D.C. 1991, U.S. Dist. Ct. Md. 1979, U.S. Ct. Appeals (4th cir.) 1979. Atty. advisor USDA, Washington, 1978-80; environ. cons. Royal Swedish Acad. Sci., Swedish Dept. Agr., Stockholm, 1980-83; asst. dist. counsel U.S. Army C.E., N.Y.C., 1985-90; sr. asst. regional counsel EPA, N.Y.C., 1990—. Lectr. on environ. law. Office: US EPA 290 Broadway New York NY 10007-1866

FEINOUR, JOHN STEPHEN, lawyer; b. Kingston, Pa., July 30, 1951; s. John Gouger and Ethel Cooke (Peterson) Feinour; m. Bernadette Barattini, Apr. 16, 1977; children: J. Stephen, Kathleen M. BA, Dickinson Coll., 1973; JD, Temple U., 1976. Bar: Pa. 1976, U.S. Dist. Ct. (mid. and ea. dists.): Pa. 1979, U.S. Supreme Ct.: 1983, bar: U.S. Ct. Appeals (3d cir.) 1988. Law clk. to presiding justice Dauphin County Ct. Common Pleas, Harrisburg, Pa., 1976—77; assoc. Nauman, Smith, Shissler & Hall LLP, Harrisburg, Pa., 1977—82, ptnr., 1982—93, mng. ptnr., 1993—2001. Arbitrator Dauphin County Ct. Common Pleas, 1982—84, chmn. arbitration bd., 1984—86. Dir. Art Assn. Harrisburg, Pa., 1988—97; moderator, bd. deacons, ruling elder Paxton Presbyterian Ch., Pa., 1982—83; bd. dirs. Camp Shikellimy br. Harrisburg Area YMCA, 1979—84; bd. dirs. Harrisburg Area, 1985—91. Mem.: ABA, Dauphin County Bar Assn. (ct. relations, alt. dispute resolution com.), Pa. Bar Assn. (alt. dispute resolution com., judicial adminstrn. com., Pa. jud. evaluation com., mem. investigative panel), ATLA (cert. mediator), Kappa Sigma (alumnus advisor 1982). Republican. Home: 333 Willow Ave Camp Hill PA 17011-3655 Office: 200 N 3rd St Harrisburg PA 17101-1585

FEINSILVER, DONALD LEE, psychiatry educator; b. Bklyn., July 24, 1947; s. Albert and Mildred (Weissman) Feinsilver. BA, Alfred U., 1968; MD, Autonomous U., Guadalajara, Mexico, 1974. Diplomate Am. Bd. Psychiatry and Neurology, Am. Bd. Forensic Psychiatry. Intern in medicine L.I. Coll. Hosp., Bklyn., 1975—76; resident in psychiatry SUNY-Bklyn., 1977—78, chief resident, 1979; asst. prof. psychiatry and surgery Med. Coll. Wis., Milw., 1980—85, assoc. prof., 1985—; dir. psychiat. emergency svc. Milw. County Mental Health and Med. Complexes, 1980—88; dir. med.-psychiat. unit Milw. Psychiat. Hosp./West Allis Meml. Hosp., 1988—. Contbr. articles to profl. jours.; editor: Crisis Psychiatry: Pros and Cons, 1982; mem. editl. bd.: Psychiat. Medicine Jour., 1983—. Mem.: AAAS, AMA, Acad. Psychosomatic Medicine, Am. Acad. Psychiatry and the Law, Am. Psychiat. Assn. Office: West Allis Psychiat Assocs 2424 S 90th St Milwaukee WI 53227-2455 E-mail: DFeinsilver@prodigy.net.

FEINSMITH, NORMAN, cardiovascular disease physician; b. Bklyn., Oct. 27, 1952; MD, Mt. Sinai Sch. Medicine, 1978. Diplomate Am. Bd. Internal Medicine, Am. Bd. Cardiovascular Disease. Intern Rutgers Affiliated Hosps., Piscataway, N.J., 1978-79, resident in internal medicine, 1979-81; fellow in cardiovascular disease Presbyn.-U. Pa. Med. Ctr., Phila., 1981-83; mem. staff Presbyn. Med. Ctr., Phila.; pres. med. staff Presbyn. U. Pa. Med. Ctr., Phila., 1998—2000. Assoc. prof. medicine U. Pa. Med. Sch. Fellow Am. Coll. Cardiology; mem. AMA. Office: Presbyn U Pa Med Ctr Phila Heart Inst 2C 39th and Market St Philadelphia PA 19104

FEINSMITH, PAUL LOWELL, lawyer; b. N.Y.C., July 30, 1941; s. Sydney William and Esther (Gell) Feinsmith; m. Sherry Raphael Feinsmith, May 28, 1967 (div. 1972); children: Jeremiah R., Deborah Gardner; m. Alicia Goldstein, Nov. 18, 1979; 1 child, Sylvie G. BA, U. Pa., 1962; JD, NYU, 1965. Bar: N.J. 1965, Ill. 1969, Fla. 1981. Assoc. Platoff Heftler Harker & Nashel, Esqs., Union City, NJ, 1965—69; v.p., gen. counsel Elgin & Waltham Watch Cos., Chgo., 1969—79, N.Y.C., 1972—76, Miami, Fla., 1979—82; ptnr. Hoffman Larin & Feinsmith, North Miami Beach, Fla., 1982—88; sole practice Miami, 1990—. Mem. Broward County Dem. Exec. Com., Fla., 1994—2000; pres. Nat. Kidney Found. Fla., 1981—85; mem. exec. com. Renal Network, 1982—; pres. NAPHT, 1984—86; co-founder, former chmn. Nat. Renal Coalition, Fla. Renal Coalition. Mem.: ABA, Fla. Bar Assn., B'nai B'rith. Democrat. Jewish. Home: 1730 N 55th Ave Hollywood FL 33021-3934 Office: 1111 Lincoln Rd Miami FL 33139-2452 also: 19098 W Dixie Hwy Aventura FL 33180

FEINSOD, ARTHUR BENNETT, theatre arts educator; b. N.Y.C., June 4, 1951; s. Robert Lewis and Kalma Jewel (Shapiro) F.; m. Mary Elizabeth Kramer, 1996; children: Lincoln Peterson, Simon Peterson. BA magna cum laude, Harvard U., 1973; MA, U. Calif., Berkeley, 1978; PhD, NYU, 1986. Artistic dir. Berkeley Lights Theater Ensemble, 1976—80; tchr. drama The Branson Sch., Ross, Calif., 1976—80; asst. prof. Trinity Coll., Hartford, Conn., 1985—92, assoc. prof., 1992—2001, chmn. theater and dance dept., 1986—89, 1993—2001; resident Dramaturg Hartford Stage Co., 1995—98; prof., chmn. theater dept. Ind. State U., Terre Haute, 2001—. Artistic dir. SummerStage, Terre Haute, 2001—. Author: (book) The Simple Stage, 1992; playwright (with Maurice Schneider) Play for Keeps, 1983, Malcolm's Call, 1996, playwright (with Mohammad Ghaffari) Dreams and Fires, 1997, playwright (adaptation of William Butler Yeats' Cuchulain plays) Sword Against the Sea, 1999, Table 17, 1999, The Curse of Sleepy Hollow, 2000, The Certainty of Glass, 2002; stage dir. True West, 1985; stage dir. Waiting for Godot, 1997, Comedy of Errors, 1998, Purgatory, 1998, Krapp's Last Tape, 1999, Rockaby, 1999, The Effect of Gamma Rays on Man-in-the-Moon Marigolds, 2000, The School for Wives, 2002. Pearl Hickman fellow U. Calif., 1973-75, NEH fellow, 1987, 95; recipient Arthur Hughes award Trinity Coll., 1991, Leaders in Diversity award, Pres.'s Commn., Ind. State U., 2003. Mem.: Phi Beta Kappa. Office: Ind State U Theater Dept 540 N 7th St Terre Haute IN 47809 Office Fax: 812-237-3954.

FEINSTEIN, ALLEN LEWIS, lawyer; b. N.Y.C., Apr. 18, 1929; s. Jacob and Kate (Goldberg) F.; m. Charlesa Joan Wolfe, Dec. 14, 1957. AB, CCNY, 1949; LLB, Columbia U., 1952. Bar: N.Y. 1952, U.S. Supreme Ct. 1958, Ariz. 1960, U.S. Dist. Ct. Ariz. 1960, U.S. Ct. Appeals (9th cir.) 1960. Assoc. Proskauer Rose Goetz & Mendelsohn, N.Y.C., 1955-59; law clk. to justice Supreme Ct. Ariz., Phoenix, 1959-61, 1st adminstrv. dir., 1961-64; pvt. practice law Phoenix, 1964-72, 1995—; ptnr. Daughton Feinstein & Wilson, Phoenix, 1972-86; sr. ptnr. Rawlins, Burrus, Lewkowitz & Feinstein, P.C., Phoenix, 1986-95. Mem. Phoenix Housing Code Com., 1968; vice-chmn. adv. com. State Legislative com. on Medicaid; mem. Phoenix Charter Review Com., 1969; mem. exec. com. Phoenix Sister City Commn., 1973-75 Author: First, Second and Third Reports of Courts of Arizona, 1962, 63, 64. Bd. dirs. Meml. Hosp. Phoenix, chmn., 1973-76, Community Coun., 1970-76, Ariz. Jewish Hist. Soc.; chmn. Meml. Hosp. Found., 1980-82; bd. dirs., chmn. coun. trustees, mem. exec. com. Ariz. Hosp. Assn., 1981-87, chmn. 1986-87, Ariz. del. to nat. conf. governing bds.; chmn. PMH Health Resources, Inc., 1983-89, Ariz. Voluntary Hosp. Fedn., 1984-88; chmn. Phoenix chpt. Am. Jewish Com., 1989-91; legal advisor Salt River Pima-Maricopa INdian Cmty. Police Commn., 1997-2002. 2d lt. USAF, 1952-53. Mem. Ariz. Bar Assn., Maricopa County Bar Assn., State Bar Ariz. (chmn. com. civil practice and procedure 1971-74, chmn. long-range com. 1980, peer rev. com., sole practitioner com. sect., alternate dispute resolution sects., mentor-mentee com.), Univ. Club Phoenix (pres. 1971-72), Phi Beta Kappa, Phi Delta Phi. Democrat. Jewish. Address: 2110 Encanto Dr SW Phoenix AZ 85007-1526 E-mail: alfeinstein@cox.net.

FEINSTEIN, DIANNE, senator; b. San Francisco, June 22, 1933; d. Leon and Betty (Rosenburg) Goldman; m. Bertram Feinstein, Nov. 11, 1962 (dec.); 1 child, Katherine Anne; m. Richard C. Blum, Jan. 20, 1980. BA History, Stanford U., 1955; LLB (hon.), Golden Gate U., 1977; D Pub. Adminstrn. (hon.), U. Manila, 1981; D Pub. Service (hon.), U. Santa Clara, 1981; JD (hon.), Antioch U., 1983, Mills Coll., 1985; LHD (hon.), U. San Francisco, 1988. Fellow Coro Found., San Francisco, 1955-56; with Calif. Women's Bd. Terms and Parole, 1960-66; mem. Mayor's com. on crime, chmn. adv. com. Adult Detention, 1967-69; mem. Bd. Suprs., San Francisco, 1970-78, pres., 1970-71, 74-75, 78; mayor City of San Francisco, 1978-88; senator from Calif. U.S. Senate, Washington, 1992—. Mem. exec. com. U.S. Conf. of Mayors, 1983-88; Dem. nominee for Gov. of Calif., 1990; mem. Nat. Com. on U.S.-China Rels.; mem. judiciary com., appropriations com., rules and adminstrn. Com., energy and natural resources com. Mem. Bay Area Conservation and Devel. Commn., 1973-78; mem. Senate Fgn. Rels. Com. Recipient Woman of Achievement award Bus. and Profl. Women's Clubs San Francisco, 1970, Disting. Woman award San Francisco Examiner, 1970, Coro Found. award, 1979, Coro Leadership award, 1988, Pres. medal U. Calif., San Francisco, 1988, Scopus award Am. Friends Hebrew U., 1981, Brotherhood/Sisterhood award NCCJ, 1986, Comdr.'s award U.S. Army, 1986, French Legion of Honor, 1984, Disting. Civilian award USN, 1987; named Number One Mayor All-Pro City Mgmt. Team City and State Mag., 1987. Mem. Trilateral Commn., Japan Soc. of No. Calif. (pres. 1988-89), Inter-Am. Dialogue, Nat. Com. on U.S.-China Rels. Democrat. Office: US Senate 331 Hart Senate Office Bldg Washington DC 20510-0001*

FEINSTEIN, FRED IRA, lawyer; b. Chgo., Apr. 6, 1945; s. Bernard and Beatrice (Mines) Feinstein; m. Judy Cutler, Aug. 25, 1968; children: Karen, Donald. BSC, DePaul U., 1967, JD, 1970. Bar: Ill. 1970, U.S. Supreme Ct. 1977. Ptnr. McDermott, Will & Emery, Chgo., 1976—. Lectr. in field. Contbr. articles to profl. jours. Pres. Skokie/Evanston (Ill.) Action Coun., 1981—84; bd. dirs. Temple Judea Mizpah, Skokie, 1982—84, Deborah Goldfine Meml. Cancer Rsch., 1968—, YMCA of Chgo.1985, 1985—. Mem.: Am. Coll. Real Estate Lawyers, Ill. Bar Assn., Blue Key, Union League, Beta Alpha Psi, Beta Gamma Sigma, Lambda Alpha, Pi Gamma Mu. Office: McDermott Will & Emery 227 W Monroe St Ste 3100 Chicago IL 60606-5096

FEINSTEIN, FREDERICK LEE, lawyer; b. N.Y.C., June 27, 1947; s. Alan and Mary (Kotick) F.; m. Karen E. Collins, Sept. 13, 1981; children: Emma Collins, Samuel Collins. BS, Swarthmore Coll., 1969; JD, Rutgers U., Newark, 1974. Bar: N.Y. 1975. Tchr. N.Y.C. Pub. Schs., 1969-71; staff dir., chief counsel labor-mgmt. rels. subcom. U.S. Ho. of Reps., Washington, 1977-94; field atty. NLRB, Winston-Salem, N.C., 1975-77, gen. counsel Washington, 1994-99, ret., 1999; sr. fellow, vis. prof. U. Md. Grad. Sch. Pub. Affairs, College Park, 2000—. Pres. Takoma Park (Md.) Elem. Sch. PTA, 1991-93; coach Takoma Park Soccer, 1995—. Mem. ABA. Avocations: music, playing in cajun band with wife. Home: 7114 Sycamore Ave Takoma Park MD 20912-4639 Office: U Md Van Munching Hall College Park MD

FEINSTEIN, MARTIN, performing arts consultant, art director; b. N.Y.C., Apr. 12, 1921; BSS, CCNY, 1942; MA, Wayne State U., 1943; MusD (hon.), Cath. U. Am., 1980, Shenandoah Coll. & Conservatory, 1983; LHD (hon.), Am. U., 1991; DFA, U. Md., 1995. Publicity dir. Hurok Concerts, N.Y.C., 1945-50, v.p., 1950-71; vis. prof. Yale U., New Haven, 1971-73; exec. dir. performing arts John F. Kennedy Ctr., Washington, 1972-80; pres., CEO Nat. Symphony, Kennedy Ctr., Washington, 1980-81; gen. dir. Washington Opera, 1980-95, cons., 1995—; sr. cons. U. Md. Performing Arts Ctr., College Park, 1995-2000, artistic dir., 1998-99, adj. prof., 2000—. Decorated commendatore Republic of Italy; cross of officer Order Arts and Letters (France); Grand Decoration of Honor for Svcs. (Austria), officer Order of Merit (Germany); recipient medal Nat. Soc. Lit. and the Arts, 1977, award of Contbns. in Field of Dance Am. Assn. Dance Cos., 1979, Townsend Harris medal CCNY, 1977, John Cranko medal, Stuttgart, 1979, Myrtle Wreath award Washington Hadassah, 1982, Amphion award Memphis Symphony, 1983. E-mail: martfein@msn.com.

FEINSTEIN, MILES ROGER, lawyer; b. Camden, N.J., June 25, 1941; s. Louis Emory and Sylvia K. (Jacobs) F.; m. Margaret Bott, Oct. 3, 2000; children: Bari, Matthew, Elizabeth. BA, Rutgers U., 1963; JD, Duke U., 1966. Bar: N.J. 1966, U.S. Dist. Ct. N.J. 1966, U.S. Ct. Appeals (3d cir.) 1967, U.S. Ct. Appeals (2d cir.) 1971. Pvt. practice, Clifton, N.J., 1967—. Mem. Passaic Criminal Justice commn.; mem. com. on drugs and cts. N.J. Supreme Ct.; mem. speedy trial com. N.J. Supreme Ct.; expert commentator Nat. Courtroom TV; lectr. N.J. Inst. of Continuing Legal Edn., Trial Lawyers Assn., and other bar groups and civic assns. Author: Historical Development of Pineys of Southern New Jersey. Trustee Passaic County Heart Fund, 1970-93, Passaic County Cancer Soc.; chmn. Passaic County March of Dimes, 1989. Named Man of Yr., Passaic County Heart Fund, 1976, Passaic County Cancer Soc., 1978, Passaic County coun. Boy Scouts Am., 1978, Passaic County Bad Guys Charitable Orgn., 1974; recipient award Passaic Civic Orgn., Humanitarian award Unico, 1976, Nationwide Bail Bonds award Policeman's Benevolent Assn., Disting. Svc. award, 1980, 84, 85, History prize Soc. Colonial Wars; subject of numerous legal articles. Mem. ABA, Assn. Trial Lawyers Am., Nat. Assn. Criminal Def. Lawyers, Fed. Bar Assn., N.J. Bar Assn. (criminal law com. 2000-2002), N.J. Assn. Criminal Def. Lawyers (former trustee, treas., v.p., pres. 1990-91; lectr.), N.J. Assn. of Trial Lawyers (bd. govs. 1992-93), Passaic County Bar Assn. (chmn. criminal law com. 1990-93), Phi Beta Kappa, Phi Delta Phi, Phi Alpha Theta (Henry Rutgers scholar). Avocations: sports, theatre, collecting stamps. Office: 1135 Clifton Ave Clifton NJ 07013-3642

FEINSTEIN, NATHAN B. lawyer; b. Phila., Nov. 13, 1929; s. Oscar and Donia (Weiner) F.; m. Joanne S. Polk, Jan. 5, 1959; children: Elliot Abraham, Michael Joel. BA in Polit. Sci., Pa. State U., 1951; LLB, Yale U., 1954. Bar: Pa. 1955, Md. 1988, D.C. 1988, U.S. Ct. Appeals (3d and 4th cirs.), U.S. Supreme Ct. 1981. Law clk. to Hon. T. McKean Chidsey Pa. Supreme Ct., Phila., 1956-57; assoc., ptnr. Cohen, Shapiro, Polisher, Sheikman and Cohen, Phila., 1957-83; ptnr. Dilworth, Paxson, Kalish and Kauffman, Phila., 1984-87, Piper & Marbury LLP, Washington, 1987-2000, ptnr. emeritus, 2000—, Piper Marbury Rudnick & Wolfe LLP, Washington, 2001—. With U.S. Army, 1954—56. Fellow: ABA (chair bus. bankruptcy com. 1989—93, chair joint com. on bankruptcy ct. structure 1993—97), Am. Coll. Bankruptcy; mem.: Phila. Bar Assn. (chair profl. guidance com. 1980—81), D.C. Bar Assn., Md. Bar Assn., Pa. Bar Assn. (chair com. on legal ethics and profl. responsibility 1983—84). Democrat. Jewish. Office: Piper Marbury Rudnick & Wolfe LLP 1200 19th St NW Fl 7 Washington DC 20036-2430 E-mail: natefein@yahoo.com.

FEINSTEIN, ROBERT NORMAN, retired biochemist; b. Milw., Wis., Aug. 10, 1915; s. Jacob Feinstein and Jennie Cohen; m. Betty Jane Greenbaum; children: Ann E. Levis, Jean L. Feinstein-Lyon. BS in Chemistry, U. Wis., 1937, MS in Biochemistry, 1938, PhD in Biochemistry, 1940. Asst. scientist toxicity lab. U. Chgo., 1945—49; sr. scientist Argonne (Ill.) Nat. Lab., 1959—80; ret. Contbr. scientific papers to profl. jours., poetry to anthologies. Capt. U.S. Army, 1941—45. Recipient Guggenheim fellowship, 1959—60. Democrat. Jewish. Achievements include patents in field. Avocation: writing light verse. Home: 250 Village Dr Downers Grove IL 60516

FEINSTEIN, ROBERT P. dermatologist; b. N.Y.C., July 31, 1941; s. Jerome and May (Wolpin) F.; m. Diane Marla Gutstein, Oct. 25, 1969; children: Steven, Michelle, Suzanne, Gary, Lori. AB in Biology, NYU, 1963, MD, 1967. Diplomate Am. Bd. Dermatology. Intern Kings County Hosp. Ctr., Bklyn., N.Y., 1967-68; resident in dermatology Columbia U., N.Y.C., 1968-71, assoc. clin. prof. dept. dermatology; chief of dermatology, innoculations and phys. exams. Navy Regional Med. Clinic, Washington, 1971-73; pvt. practice in dermatology Mineola, N.Y., 1973-99, Smithtown, N.Y., 1983-2000. Author: (book) Dermatology, 1975, (monograph) Rosacea, 1998; contbr. articles to profl. jours. Lt cmmdr. USNR, 1971-73. Fellow Am. Acad. Dermatology (mem. managed care com., 1995-99, mem. com. physician practice, professionalism study group program for dermatology in 21st cent., vice chmn. adv. bd. 2001—), Am. Soc. for Dermatologic Surgery; mem. AMA, N.Y. State Soc. of Dermatology (pres. 1997-99), L.I. Dermatology Soc. (pres. 1996-98), Suffolk County Dermatology Soc. (pres. 1982-84), Atlantic Dermatology Soc. (bd. dirs. 1995); N.Y. State Med. Soc. (health care delivery sys.). Avocation: golf.

FEINSTEIN, ROCHELLE, artist, educator; BFA, Pratt Inst., 1975; MFA, U. Minn., 1978. Represented by Max Protetch Gallery, N.Y.C.; tchr. Bonnington Coll., 1979—94; assoc. prof. painting, printmaking Yale U., 1994—98, prof. painting and printmaking, 1998—. Participant pub. arts project CETA/N.Y. Artists Program, 1978—79. Represented in permanent collections Mus. Modern Art. Nat. Endowment for the Arts grantee, 1990, Joan Mitchell Found. grantee, 1994, John Simon Guggenheim Meml. Found. fellow, 1996. Office: Yale U Sch Art PO Box 208339 New Haven CT 06520-8339

FEINSTEIN, ROSALIND DEBORAH, social worker; b. N.Y.C., July 20, 1935; d. Julius J. and Jeanette (Silberman) Sobelman; m. Howard Marvin Feinstein, June 24, 1956; children: Jonathan, Eric, Roger. BA, Sarah Lawrence Coll., 1957; MSW, Syracuse U., 1972. Cert. diplomate social worker; cert. social worker, N.Y. Staff social worker Tompkins County Mental Health Clinic, Ithaca, N.Y., 1972-81, supervising social worker, 1981-84; pvt. practice clin. social work Ithaca, 1975—. Cons. Suicide Prevention and Crisis Svc., Ithaca, 1983-87. Avocation: pianist. Office: 103 Dewitt Bldg 215 N Cayuga St Ithaca NY 14850-4329

FEINTUCH, HENRY PHILIP, public relations executive; b. Bklyn. BA, Bklyn. Coll. TV and Radio, 1976. Anchorperson, reporter Stas. WMTR and WDHA-FM, N.J.; news editor Sta. WCBS-TV, N.Y.C.; pub. rels. sr. acct. exec. Paul Kaufman Assocs., N.Y.C., Booke and Co., N.Y.C.; dir. corp. comm. Ring Group N.Am., N.Y.C., 1985-86; mng. ptnr. KCSA Pub. Rels., N.Y.C., 1987—. Office: KCSA Pub Rels 800 2nd Ave New York NY 10017-4709 E-mail: hfeintuch@kcsa.com.

FEIRSON, STEVEN B. lawyer; b. Bklyn., June 6, 1950; s. Aaron M. and Gertrude Feirson. BA, U. Pa., 1972; JD, U. Chgo., 1975. Bar: Pa. 1975, U.S. Dist. Ct. (ea. dist.) Pa. 1975, U.S. Ct. Appeals (3d cir.) 1976, U.S. Supreme Ct. 1980, U.S. Ct. Appeals (2d and 9th cirs.) 1990, U.S. Ct. Appeals (8th cir.) 1992, U.S. Ct. Appeals (6th cir.) 1994, U.S. Dist. Ct. (ea. dist.) Mich. 1996. Assoc. Dechert LLP, Phila., 1975-83, ptnr., 1983—. Mem.: Phila. Bar Assn. Office: Dechert LLP 4000 Bell Atlantic Tower 1717 Arch St Lbby 3 Philadelphia PA 19103-2713

FEISEL, LYLE DEAN, retired dean, electrical engineer, educator; b. Tama, Iowa, Oct. 16, 1935; s. Clyde Edward and Clara Maria (Ehlers) F.; m. Dorothy Evelyn Stadsvold, June 15, 1957; children: Patricia, Margaret, Kenneth. BSEE, Iowa State U., 1961, MSEE, 1963, PhDEE, 1964. Registered profl. engr., S.D. Engr. Honeywell, Mpls., 1961-62; staff engr. IBM Corp., Poughkeepsie, N.Y., 1963, Burlington, Vt., 1967; mem. faculty of elec. engring. S.D. Sch. of Mines, Rapid City, 1964-83, head elec. engring. dept., 1975-83; dean Watson Sch. SUNY, Binghamton, 1983—2001. Vis. prof. Cheng Kung U., Tainan, Taiwan, 1969-70; rsch. engr. Northrop Corp., L.A., 1974; Wachmeister prof. engring. Va. Mil. Inst., 1982; mem. engring. accreditation commn. Accreditation Bd. Engring. and Tech., 1987-92, bd. dirs., 1992-97. Nat. Def. fellow, 1961-64; recipient profl. achievement citation Iowa State U., 1984, Ednl. Achievement award N.Y. State Soc. Profl. Engrs., 1989, Nat. Soc. Profl. Engrs. award, 2002. Fellow IEEE (pres. edn. soc. 1978-79, v.p. ednl. activities 2000-2002, Meritorious Svc. award, Ben Dasher award 1983, Centennial medal 1984, Ronald J. Schmitz award 1989, achievement award Edn. Soc. 1999, Third Millennium medal 2000), Am. Soc. Engring. Edn. (bd. dirs. 1982-83, 94-99, pres. 1997-98); mem. S.D. Renewable Energy Assn. (pres. 1979-81, N.Y. State Engr. of Yr. 2000), Tau Beta Pi (Disting. Alumnus award 2002). Democrat. Lutheran. Address: PO Box 839 Saint Michaels MD 21663 E-mail: l.feisel@ieee.org.

FEISEL, LYLE DEAN, lawyer; b. Boston, Dec. 14, 1918; s. Edward Barton and Jeannette (Thomas) C.; m. Elizabeth Ann Parker, Sept. 6, 1940; children: Allan M., Elizabeth M. BA, Yale U., 1940; JD, Harvard U., 1943. Bar: Mass. 1943. Of counsel Warner & Stackpole LLP now Kirkpatrick & Lockhart LLP, Boston, 1954—. Chmn. bd. dirs. H.B. Smith Co., Inc.; pres., trustee emeritus Phillips Acad.; chmn. emeritus, trustee Mass. Eye and Ear Infirmary and Found. Hon. dir. Chewonki Found. Inc.; chmn. Yale U. Planned Giving; trustee Sturbridge Village; mem. leadership coun. New Bedford Whaling Mus.; mem. state adv. com. Salvation Army; v.p. Polly Hill Found. Fellow Am. Bar Found., Mass. Bar Found.; mem. ABA, Boston Bar Assn., Mass. Bar Assn., Internat. Bar Assn., Edgartown Yacht Club. Home: 15 Traill St Cambridge MA 02138-4738 Office: 75 State St Fl 6 Boston MA 02109-1808 E-mail: mchapin@kl.com.

FEISS, GEORGE JAMES, III, financial services company executive; b. Cleve., June 24, 1950; s. George James Jr. and Bettie (Kalish) F.; m. Susan Margaret Cassel, May 30, 1981; children: Kalish Ilana Cassel-Feiss, Nika Catherine Cassel-Feiss. BA in Social Studies, Antioch Coll., 1973; MBA in Internat. Fin., Am. Grad. Sch. Internat. Mgmt., Phoenix, 1975. Registered investment advisor, Wash.; CFP Coll. Fin. Planning, Denver. Ptnr. Healthcare Cons., Seattle, 1976-80; pres. M2 Inc., Seattle, 1980—. Pres., CEO, Vivid Image Co., San Diego, 1994—; cons. Sta. KRAB, Seattle, 1988-89, Zion Christian Acad., Seattle, 1990—. Author: Mind Therapies/Body Therapies, 1979, Hope & Death in Exile - The Economics and Politics of Cancer in the United States, 1981. Bd. dirs. B'nai Brith, Seattle, 1988-91; mem. fin. com. Univ. Child Devel. Sch., Seattle, 1989—; mem. social action com. Am. Jewish Com., Seattle, 1992. Mem. Eastside Estate Planning Coun., Inst. for CFPs, Social Investment Forum, Social Venture Network. Avocations: sailing, skiing, travel, writing, sculpture. Office: M2 Inc 1122 E Pike St Seattle WA 98122-3916

FEISS, HUGH BERNARD, priest, religious educator; b. Lakeview, Oreg., May 8, 1939; s. Sherman H. and Margaret I. (Furlong) F. Licentiate in Sacred Theology, Cath. U. Am., 1967, Lic. in Philosophy, 1972; STD, Anselmianum, Rome, 1976; MA, U. Iowa, Iowa City, 1987. Ordained priest Roman Cath. Ch., 1966. Asst. dean of men Mt. Angel Seminary, St. Benedict, Oreg., 1967-72, prof. philosophy, 1967-74, prof. humanities and theology, 1976-96; dir. Mt. Angel Abbey Libr., St. Benedict, 1987-96. Translator: Works of Pierre de Celle, 1988, Supplement to Life of Marie d'Oignies, 1986, Hildegard of Bingen, Explanation of the Rule of Benedict, 1990, Life of Holy Hildegard, 1996, Essential Monastic Wisdom, 1999, Works of Achard of St. Victor, 2001; contbr. articles to profl. jours. Mem. Am. Acad. Religion, Am. Benedictine Acad., Cath. Theol. Soc. Am., Am. Cath. Philos. Assn. Home and Office: Monastery of the Ascension 541 E 100 S Jerome ID 83338-5655 E-mail: hughf@idahomonks.org.

FEISSEL, GUSTAVE, former international organization official; b. July 11, 1937; s. Rene Felix and Marthe (Wild) F.; m. Sharon Lynn Hoover, July 31, 1966; children: Jennifer, John. BA, Hunter Coll., 1959; postgrad., NYU, 1963; Cycle Superieur d'Etudes Politiques, Nat. Found. Polit. Scis., Paris, 1962; Cycle d'Initiation Rech Africaniste, Paris, 1962. Country desk officer Bur. Tech. Assistance Ops., UN, N.Y.C., 1963-67, spl. asst. to assoc. commr. for tech. coop., 1967-69, spl. asst. to under sec.-gen. for econ. and social affairs, 1970-75, assoc. dir. Ctr. Transnational Corps., 1975-84, dir. dept. spl. polit. affairs, 1984-91, dir. planning and early warning sys., 1991-92, dir. Europe divsn., dept. polit. affairs, 1992-93, asst. sec.-gen., chief of mission UN Operation in Cyprus Nicosia, 1993-98, ret., 1998. Internat. cons., Santa Rosa, Calif., 1999—. With USMCR, 1955-61. Recipient scholarship Alliance Francaise, 1961-62. Mem. Coun. Fgn. Rels., Pacific Coun. Internat. Policy, Cyprus Am. Archeol. Rsch. Inst. (bd. trustees 2000—, treas.). Avocations: nature photography, digital photo processing, hiking, reading. Home: 5791 Trailwood Dr Santa Rosa CA 95404 E-mail: feissel@sonic.net.

FEIST-FITE, BERNADETTE, international health education consultant; b. Sept. 28, 1945; d. John K. and Cecilia Feist; m. William H. Fite. BS in Dietetics, U. N.D., Grand Forks, 1967; MS in Edn., Troy (Ala.) State U., 1973; EdD, U. So. Calif. Commd. officer USAF, 1965, advanced through grades to maj., 1983; prof. health and fitness Nat. Def. U., Ft. McNair, Washington, 1989—. Pres. Feist Assocs., instr. internat. edn. programs, seminars and workshops. Decorated Air Force Commendation medal, Dept. Def. Meritorious Svc. medal. Mem. NAFE, VFW, Soc. Internat. Edn., Tng. and Rsch., Am. Dietetic Assn., Japan-Am. Soc. Washington, Dieticians in Bus. and Industry, Sports and Cardiovasc. Nutritionists, Nutritional Entrepreneurs, S.W. Writers, Wash. Ind. Writers, Andrews Officers Club. Home and Office: Ste 312 2442 Cerrillos Rd Santa Fe NM 87505

FEIT, BARBERI PAULL, composer, lyricist, psychotherapist, author; b. N.Y.C., July 27, 1947; d. S. Paull and Alyce (Togniere) Platt; m. Glenn M. Feit, May 24, 1975. Diploma, Juilliard Sch. Music, N.Y.C., 1972; BS, NYU, 1979, MS, 1980. Dir. Barberi Paull Musical Theatre, 1969-75; pvt. practice psychotherapy N.Y.C., 1980—. Studied with Pulitzer prize winning composers Charles Wuoninen and Jacob Druckman; gen. asst. to Mme. Koussevitzky at Tanglewood and asst. condr. to Leonard Bernstein, 1972—74; founder Illumina, Inc.; pub., author, dir.; creator thewhitenotebook.com (web libr. original titles); co-founder The Barberi Paull Feit and Glenn Martin Feit Charitable Trust. Composer, lyricist: songs The American Dream, I Have a Dream, Believe, composer: theatre pieces, mixed media events including Celebration, Angel Music, electronic ballets, : concert and choral works and music for young people (showcased A Christmas Carol and Close to the Sky on Broadway), piano concert tours: U.S., Eng., France, Switzerland, 1952—63; author: Le Petit Foret, The Angel Chronicles, Love and Dreams. Named "Meet the Composer" honoree and internat. Tours, 1972—80, scores and memorabilia selected for inclusion in the Am. Heritage Archive, 1975—; recipient Lehman Engles BMI Musical Theatre Workshop fellow, 1972—73, Dellus award, 1979; Nat. Endowment for the Arts fellow, 1982. Mem.: ASCAP (awards 1980—), The Century Assn., Hist. Soc. N.Y. (vice-chmn.), The Met. Opera Club, Mus. City of N.Y. (vice-chmn.), The Doubles Club. Avocations: interior design, yachting, gardening, French culture and language. Home: PO Box 1906 Bridgehampton NY 11932-1906 Office: Apt 33K One Lincoln Plz New York NY 10023

FEIT, GLENN M. lawyer; b. Elizabeth, N.J., Oct. 16, 1929; s. Charles Theodore and Beatrice (Esther) F.; m. Rona F. Gottlieb, June 14, 1953 (div. 1974); children: Glenn M., John Paul, Adam Gibbs (dec.), m. Barberi Platt Paull. BS in Econ., U. Pa., 1951; JD magna cum laude, Harvard U., 1957. Bar: N.Y. 1958, U.S. Dist. Ct. (2d dist.) 1959). Assoc. Cravath, Swaine & Moore, N.Y.C., 1957-64; ptnr. London, Buttenwieser & Chalif, N.Y.C., 1965-70, Feit & Ahrens, N.Y.C., 1970-88, Feit & Shor, N.Y.C., 1988-89, Proskauer Rose LLP, N.Y.C., 1989—. Bd. dirs. Blair Industries, Inc., Scott City, Mo.; sec. Charterhouse Group Internat., Inc., N.Y.C. Mem. editl. bd. Harvard Law Rev., 1955-57. Bd. dirs. Friends of the IDF, N.Y.C. Lt. USN, 1951-54. Mem. ABA, Assn. Bar City N.Y., Aircraft Owners and Pilots Assn., Exptl. Aircraft Assn., Tailhook Assn., Harvard Club, Seaplane Pilots Assn., N.Y. Yacht Club, Doubles. Office: Proskauer Rose LLP 1585 Broadway New York NY 10036-8299 E-mail: gfeit@proskauer.com.

FEITELSON, MARK ALAN, biomedical scientist, educator; b. Bklyn., Dec. 27, 1952; s. Seymour and Ann (Papper) F.; m. Rene Joyce Hoffman, July 8, 1979; children: Arielle Schulamit, Solomon Noah, Adena Michelle. BS, U. Calif., Irvine, 1974; PhD, U. Calif., L.A., 1979. Pre-doctoral fellow U. Calif., L.A., 1974-79; postdoctoral fellow Stanford (Calif.) U., 1979-82; rsch. assoc. Fox Chase Cancer Ctr., Phila., 1982-87, assoc. mem., 1988-91; assoc. prof. pathology and cell biology, dir. molecular microbiology (diagnostic) lab. Thomas Jefferson U. Sch. Medicine, Phila., 1991—. Author: (monographs) Molecular Components of Hepatitis B, 1985, Hepatitis C Virus: From Laboratory to Clinic, 2002; contbr. articles to Jour. Virology, EMBO Jour., Gastroenterology, Cancer Research, Oncogene, Neoplasia, Hepatology. Am. Cancer Soc. fellow Stanford U., 1979-82, Regents scholar, 1973-74. Mem. AAAS, Am. Soc. for Microbiology, Am. Soc. for Virology, N.Y. Acad. Scis., Am. Soc. Investigative Pathology, Am. Assn. Cancer Rsch., Assn. for Molecular Pathology. Achievements include discovery that Hepatitis B virus chronic carrier-like state and associated liver disease are established in HBV transgenic immunodeficient mice; research on structural and functional characterization of Hepatitis B X and polymerase associated polypeptides, role of X antigen in virus replication and hepatocarcinogenesis, on characterization of anti-X and anti-pol markers during hepatitis B infections, discovery of X region mutants of hepatitis B. E-mail: Mark.Feitelson@jefferson.edu.

FEITH, DOUGLAS JAY, federal agency administrator; b. Phila., July 16, 1953; s. Dalck and Rose (Bankel) F.; m. Tatyana Belenky, July 8, 1979; children: Daniel J., David J., Dafna Miriam, Dore Lev. AB magna cum laude, Harvard Coll., 1975; JD magna cum laude, Georgetown U., 1978. Bar: D.C. 1978. Assoc. Fried, Frank, Harris, Shriver and Kampelman, Washington, 1978-81; staff mem. Nat. Security Coun., Washington, 1981-82; spl. counsel to asst. sec. def. for internat. security U.S. Dept. Def., Washington, 1982-84, dep. asst. sec. def. for negotiations policy, 1984-86; mng. atty. Feith and Zell, P.C., Washington, 1986—2001; under secy. policy U.S. Dept. Def., Washington, 2001—. Bd. dirs. Chas. E. Smith Jewish Day Sch., Rockville, Md., 1993—, Ctr. for Security Policy, Washington, 1988—. Mem. Coun. Fgn. Rels. Office: US Dept Def Under Secy Policy 2000 Defense Pentagon Washington DC 20301-2000*

FEITLOWITZ, MARGUERITE, writer, literary translator; b. Hagerstown, Md., July 14, 1953; d. Robert Daniel and Virginia (Giancola) F.; m. David L. Anderson, Feb. 19, 1984. Student, U. Dijon, France, 1974; BA, Colgate U., 1975. Preceptor expository writing program Harvard U., Cambridge, Mass., 1993-99; prof. lit. Bennington (Vt.) Coll., 2002—. Author: A Lexicon of Terror: Argentina and the Legacies of Torture, 1998; editor, translator: Information for Foreigners: Three Plays by Griselda Gambaro, 1992; translator: Theatre Pieces: An Anthology by Liliane Atlan, 1985; contbr. articles to newspapers, mags. and profl. jours. Mary Ingram Bunting fellow, 1992-93; Fulbright scholar, Argentina, 1990, 98-99; grantee Marion and Jasper Whiting award, Boston, 1995; Fulbright Sr. Scholar, Argentina, 1999; Harvard Faculty Rsch. grantee, 1998. Mem. PEN, Authors Guild, Am. Literary Translators Assn., Latin Am. Studies Assn., Amnesty Internat. Democrat. Jewish. Office: Bennington Coll One College Dr Bennington VT 05201

FEITO, JOSE, architect; b. Havana, Cuba, Jan. 30, 1929; came to U.S., 1961; s. Jose and Hermina (Mayo) F.; m. Bertha A. Abascal, Oct. 7, 1995; children: Patricia Maria, Maria Esther, Jose Alfonso, Sergio P. (dec.). MArch, U. Havana, 1954. Registered architect, Fla. Prin. J. Feito Architects, Havana, 1954-60; assoc. J. DeHaro Architects, Madrid, 1960-61; ptnr. Ferendino et al, Miami, Fla., 1966-79; prin. F&F Architects and Planners, Miami, 1979-80, F&F Fraga and Feito Architects, Miami, 1980—. Pres. Professio Inc., Miami, 1983-84. Bd. dirs. Dade Co. Shoreline Com., 1986—; chmn. Gov.'s com. for Handicapped, Miami, 1973-75; trustee United Way, Miami, 1979-84. Recipient Meritorious Svcs. citation Gov.'s Com. for Handicapped, 1975. Fellow AIA (pres. Miami South chpt. 1977, Honor award 1985); mem. Fla. Assn. AIA (bd. dirs. 1978, Excellence award 1985), Interam. Businessmen's Assn. (pres. 1978-80), Cuba Soc. Architects (Gold medal 1957), Cuban Mus. Arts and Culture (founder), Greater Miami C. of C. (mem. bd. govs. 1978-83). Republican. Roman Catholic. Avocations: history, tennis, sailing. Office: F&F Fraga & Feito Architects 2151 NW 93rd Ave Miami FL 33172-4804 E-mail: ffarchit.@bellsouth.net.

FEJER, T. WILLIAM, pianist, composer, architect, furniture designer; b. L.A., Sept. 18, 1940; s. Andrew A. and Edith (Behal) F.; divorced; children: Tony (Stephen), Andrew. BS in Architecture, Ill. Inst. Tech., 1964, MS, 1967. Exhibit designer 20th century Art Inst. Chgo., 1962-67; archtl. draftsman Mies Van de Rohe, Chgo., 1964-66; design architect Skidmore, Owings & Merrill, Chgo., 1966-68; mng. dir. Evanston (Ill.) Art Ctr., 1970-72; instr. architecture Ill. Inst. Tech., Chgo., 1967-74; nat. designer, advt. mgr. Plastofilm, Chgo., 1974-84; creative dir. Design Prodns., Chgo., 1984-87; staff pianist Nordstrom, Schaumburg, Ill., 1993—97; CEO Live From Chgo., 1968—. Co-dir., chief composer Anderson/Fejer Musicals, Round Lake, Ill., 1996—; ofcl. pianist Boy Scouts Am., Chgo., 1990—; entertainment coord. Internat. Press Club Chgo., 1992-96; theme composer Little City Found., Chgo., 1997. Designer contemporary furniture; composer: (musical comedy) Menage A Trois, 1997. Spl. occasion pianist Unitarian Ch., Chgo., 1987—97; vol. entertainment chair Woodfield Area Charitable Orgn., Schaumburg, 1994—97. Recipient Outstanding Archtl. Design award Women's Archtl. League, 1963. Mem. Internat. Press Club Chgo. (cartoonist), Gulf Jazz Soc., Phi Gamma Delta. Avocations: art collecting, photography, skiing, sailing, golf. Office: Box 124 14700 Front Beach Rd Panama City Beach FL 32413 E-mail: ruthswritings@aol.com.

FEKETE, GEORGE OTTO, judge, lawyer, pharmacist; b. Budapest, Hungary; s. Bela and Ilona (Mehr) F.; m. Amy Zheng; children: Jacqueline Kim, Jeanette Lee. BS in Psychology, Wayne State U., 1954; PhD, U. So. Calif., 1960; postgrad. in psychology, Calif. State U., Long Beach; JD, Pepperdine U., 1973. Bar: Calif. 1973, U.S. Dist. Ct. (so. dist.) Calif. 1973, U.S. Supreme Ct. 1980, U.S. Dist Ct. (no. dist.) Calif. 1986. Chief pharmacist Hylo Drug Co., Huntington Beach, Calif., 1970; pres. G.O. Fekete Law Corp., Anaheim, Calif., 1973-86; lead trial lawyer Melvin Belli Law Offices, San Francisco, 1986-88; ind. trial specialist, superior ct. apptd. arbitrator San Francisco and Bay Area, 1988—; judge pro tem. Served to maj. USAF, 1954-59. Mem. ABA, Assn. Trial Lawyers Am., Calif. Trial Lawyers Assn. (legis. com. 1976-78), Orange County Trial Lawyers Assn (bd. dirs. 1977). Fax: 707-552-4672. E-mail: gofesq@earthlink.net.

FELBINGER, CLAIRE LOUISE, research administrator; b. Joliet, Ill., Jan. 9, 1956; d. Theodore C. and Mary Ann F.; m. Richard John Martin Jr., May 27, 1978 (div. Mar. 1980); m. Richard Donnelly Bingham, Oct. 23, 1982. BA in Polit. Sci., Pub. Adminstrn., Augustana Coll., Rock Island, Ill., 1977; MA in Polit. Sci., U. Wis., Milw., 1979, PhD in Polit. Sci., 1986. Rsch. asst. NSF, Washington, 1981-82; asst. prof., rsch. assoc. No. Ill. U., DeKalb, 1986-88; acad. coord., asst. prof. Cleve. State U., 1988-92, dir., assoc. prof., 1992-98; editor pub. works mgmt., policy Sage Publs., Thousand Oaks, Calif., 1995—; chmn., assoc. prof. Am. U., Washington, 1998—2003; rsch. adminstr. Nat. Acad. Scis., Washington, 2003—. Rsch. asst., U. Wis., Milw., 1978-85; bd. dirs. Accreditation Bd. Engring. Tech., Balt., 1998. Author: Evaluation in Practice, 1989; editor Pub. Works Mgmt. Policy, 1995—. Bd. dirs. St. Clair Superior Coalition, Cleve., 1992-98, Pub. Works Hist. Soc., 1995—. Mem. NAS (bd. infastructure and the constructed environment), ASPA (chpt. pres, N.E. office, nat. coun. 1996-98, Nat. Svc. award), Am. Pub. Works Assn. (Excellence Edn. award 1993), Sect. Women Pub. Adminstrn. (bd. dirs. 1995—), Pi Alpha Alpha (pres. 1999-01). Avocations: traveling, fly fishing, gourmet cooking. Home: Apt 913 4200 Massachusetts Ave NW Washington DC 20016-4735 Office: Nat Acad Scis 500 5th St NW Washington DC 20001 E-mail: cfelbinger@nas.edu.

FELCH, JAMES WALTON, ophthalmologist; b. Ashland, Wis., Aug. 8, 1946; s. Robert W. and Janet I. (Anderson) F.; m. Barbara Anne Minkoff, Aug. 9, 1969; children: James W., Thomas G. BS in Chemistry, U. Del., 1968; PhD in Microbiology, Vanderbilt U., 1973, MD, 1977. Diplomate Am. Bd. Ophthalmology. Ophthalmologist Eye Assoc. of Middle Tenn., Franklin, Nashville, 1981—. Tissue typing for kidney transplants Vanderbilt Univ., 1970-73; adv. bd. Prevent Blindness Tenn., 1983-86, Lupus Found. Am., 1990-91; medical adv. com. Prevent Blindness Tenn., 1996-98. Den leader Boy Scouts, Nashville, 1984-91; asst. scoutmaster, 1987-93, scoutmaster, 1993-99. Lt. Army, 1973-74. Fellow ACS, Am. Acad. Ophthalmology; mem. AMA, Tenn. Med. Assn., Tenn. Acad. Ophthalmology (sec./treas. 1990-98, pres.-elect 1996-98, pres. 1998-2000), Franklin C. of C., Nashville C. of C. Republican. Presbyterian. Avocations: scouts, gardening, church liturgy team. Home: 117 Abbottsford Nashville TN 37215-2439 Office: Eye Assocs Middle Tenn 100 Covey Dr Ste 107 Franklin TN 37067-5603 also: 2010 Church St Ste 608 Nashville TN 37203-2086

FELCH, WILLIAM CAMPBELL, internist, editor; b. Lakewood, Ohio, Nov. 14, 1920; s. Don Harold Willison and Beth (Campbell) Felch; m. Nancy Cook Dean, Aug. 4, 1945; children: Patricia, William Campbell, Robert Dean. BA, Princeton U., 1942; MD, Columbia U., 1945. Diplomate Nat. Bd. Med. Examiners, Am. Bd. Internal Medicine. Intern St. Luke's Hosp., N.Y.C., 1945—46, resident in internal medicine, 1948—51; pvt. practice specializing in internal medicine Rye, NY, 1951—88; chief staff United Hosp., Port Chester, NY, 1975—77; med. dir. Osborn Home, Rye, NY, 1979—88; exec. v.p. Alliance for Continuing Med. Edn., 1978—91. Author: Aspiration and Achievement, 1981, Decade of Decision, 1989, Vision for the Future, 1992, The Secrets of Good Patient Care, Thoughts on Medicine for the 21st Century, 1996, Alliance for Continuing Medical Education: The First 20 Years, 1996; editor: The Internist, 1975—86, ACME Almanac, 1978—91, Jour. of Continuing Edn. in Health Professions, 1992—95; co-editor: Continuing Med. Edn.: A Primer, 2d edit., 1991. Trustee N.Y. Med. Coll., Valhalla, 1971—73. Capt. U.S. Army, 1946—48. Named Internist of Distinction, Internal Medicine Soc. N.Y. County, 1973; recipient award of merit, N.Y. State Soc. Internal Medicine, 1976, Disting. Svc. award, Alliance for Continuing Med. Edn., Founder's medal, 1995. Mem.: AMA (chmn. coun. on legislation 1977—79), ACP, Inst. of Medicine NAS, Am. Soc. Internal Medicine (pres. 1973—74), Alliance for Continuing Med. Edn. (exec. v.p. 1978—91). Republican. Home: 8545 Carmel Valley Rd Carmel CA 93923

FELD, ALAN DAVID, lawyer; b. Dallas, Nov. 13, 1936; s. Henry R. and Rose (Scissors) F.; m. Anne Sanger, June 1, 1957; children: Alan David, Elizabeth S., John L. BA, So. Methodist U., 1957, LL.B., 1960. Bar: Tex. 1960. Since practiced in Dallas; from ptnr. to chmn. bd. Akin, Gump, Hauer, Strauss & Feld, Dallas, 1960-96, sr. exec. ptnr., 1996—. Lectr. Southwestern U. Med. Sch.; chmn. Tex. State Securities Bd.; bd. dirs. Clear Channel Comms., Inc., Ctr. Point Properties, Inc. Contbr. articles to legal jours. Trustee AMR Advaantage Funds, So. Meth. U.; bd. dirs. Dallas Day Nursery Assn., Timberlawn Found., Dallas Symphony Orch. Mem.: ABA, Dallas Bar Assn., D.C. Bar Assn., Tex. Bar Assn., Dallas Country Club, Royal Oaks Country Club (corr.), Salesmanship Club, Phi Delta Phi. Home: 4235 Bordeaux Ave Dallas TX 75205-3717 Office: Akin Gump Strauss Hauer & Feld 1700 Pacific Ave Ste 4100 Dallas TX 75201-4675

FELD, ELIOT, dancer, choreographer; b. Bklyn., July 5, 1942; s. Benjamin Noah and Alice (Posner) Feld. Student, High Sch. Performing Arts, N.Y.C., 1954-58; DFA (hon.), Juilliard Sch., 1991. Dancer child prince The Nutcracker, N.Y.C. Ballet, 1954, West Side Story, 1958, Donald McKayle Co., Sophie Maslow Co., Pearl Lang Co., Mary Anthony Co., I Can Get It for You Wholesale, 1962, Fiddler on the Roof, Am. Ballet Theatre, 1963, Les Noces, Wind in the Mountains, Dark Elegies, Fancy Free, Billy the Kid, Helen of Troy, Giselle, choreographer Am. Ballet Theatre, , Royal Danish Ballet, Nat. Ballet of Can., N.Y.C. Ballet, Harbinger, 1967, At Midnight, 1967, Meadowlark, 1968, Intermezzo, 1969, Cortege Burlesque, 1969, Pagan Spring, 1969, Early Songs, 1970, Cortege Parisien, 1970, Consort, 1970, A Poem Forgotten, 1970, Romance, 1971, Theatre, 1971, The Gods Amused, 1971, A Soldier's Tale, 1971, Eccentrique, 1971, Winters Court, 1972, Jive, 1973, Sephardic Song, 1974, Tzaddik, 1974, The Real McCoy, 1974, Mazurka, 1975, Excursions, 1975, Impromptu, 1976, Variations on 'America', 1977, A Footstep of Air, 1977, Santa Fe Saga, 1978, La Vida, 1978, Danzon Cubano, 1978, Half-Time, 1978, Papillon, 1979, Circa, 1980, Anatomic Balm, 1980, Scenes, 1980, Play Bach, 1981, Song of Norway, 1981, Over the Pavement, 1982, Straw Hearts, 1983, Summer's Lease, 1983, Three Dances, 1983, Adieu, 1984, The Jig Is Up, 1984, Moon Skate, 1984, Intermezzo No. 2, 1985, Against the Sky, 1985, The Grand Canyon, 1985, Aurora I, 1985, Aurora II, 1985, Medium: Rare, 1985, Echo, 1986, Bent Planes, 1986, Skara Brae, 1986, Embraced Waltzes, 1987, A Dance for Two, 1987, Shadow's Breath, 1987, Petipa Notwithstanding, 1988, Kore, 1988, The Unanswered Question, 1988, Asia, 1988, Love Song Waltzes, 1988, Ah Scarlatti, 1989, Mother Nature, 1989, Contra Pose, 1990, Charmed Lives, 1990, Ion, 1990, Fauna, 1990, Common Ground, 1991, Savage Glance, 1991, Clave, 1991, Evoe, 1991, Endsong, 1991, Wolfgang Strategies, 1992, To the Naked Eye, 1992, Hello Fancy, 1992, Frets and Women, 1992, Hadji, 1992, Blooms Wake, 1993, The Relative Disposition of the Parts, 1993, Doo Dah Day, 1993, MRI, 1993, Doghead & Godcatchers, 1994, 23 Skidoo, 1994, Gnossiennes, 1994, Ogive, 1994, Chi, 1994, Ludwig Gambits, 1995, Tongue and Groove, 1995, Meshugana Dance, 1996, Paean, 1996, Paper Tiger, 1996, Shuffle, 1996, Industry, 1996, Evening Chant, 1996, Jukebox, 1997, Re:X, 1997, Yo Shakespeare, 1997, Joggers, 1997, Umbra Rumba, 1997, Yo Johann, 1997, The Last Sonata, 1997, Simon Sez, 1998, Cherokee Rose, 1999, Mending, 1999, Felix: the ballet, 1999, Apple Pie, 1999, Nodrog Doggo, 2000, Coup de Couperin, 2000, Organon, 2001, Pacific Dances, 2001, Skandia, 2002, Pianola: Raven, 2002, Lincoln Portrait, 2002, Behold the Man, 2002, (ballets) Pianola: Indigo, 2002, Mr. XY2, 2003, French Overtures, 2003. Recipient Dance Mag. award, 1990. Office: Ballet Tech 890 Broadway Fl 8 New York NY 10003-1211

FELD, HARVEY JOEL, pathologist; b. St. Petersburg, Fla., Mar. 16, 1949; s. Harold and Mona Feld; m. Karen Wendy Markman, June 2, 1973; children: Howard, Shari. BS in Chemistry, U. Fla., 1971, postgrad., 1971-73; MD, U. East Coll. Medicine, Manila, 1977. Diplomate Am. Bd. Pathology. Clin. clerkship L.I. Coll. Hosp., Bklyn., 1978; resident in pathology Mt. Sinai Sch. Medicine, N.Y.C., 1978-82; fellow in cytopathology MD. Anderson Cancer Ctr., Houston, 1982-83; pathologist Pasco Cmty. Hosp. (formerly Dade City (Fla.) Hosp.), 1983—, East Pasco Med. Ctr., Zephyrhills, Fla., 1983—. Sec./treas. med. staff East Pasco Med. Ctr., 1991. Contbr. articles to profl. jorus. Trustee, past treas. Suncoast chpt. Leukemia Soc.; trustee Chesed Shel Emes of Greater Tampa; chmn., med. adv. com. Mus. of Sci. and Industry, Tampa, 1998-2000; program sponsor "Cornerstones of the Cmty.: the Jewish Presence in Ybor City", Ybor City Mus., Tampa, 1999. Recipient Ralph Colp award for journalistic excellence Mt. Sinai Jour. Medicine, 1982-83, Brooks Bros. Man of Yr. award Leukemia Soc., 1995. Fellow Coll. Am. Pathologists, Am. Soc. Clin. Pathologists; mem. Am. Pathology Found., Fla. Soc. Pathology, So. Med. Assn., Philippine Med. Soc. (West Coast chpt., Sunsine & Scholarship com.), Pasco Co. I.P.A. (v.p., sec. 1999), Tampa Palms Country Club. Jewish. Avocations: rock collecting, reading. Home: 16111 Ancroft Ct Tampa FL 33647-1041 Office: Pasco Cmty Hosp (Lab) 13100 Fort King Rd Dade City FL 33525-5294

FELD, JOSEPH, construction executive; b. N.Y.C., June 25, 1919; s. Morris David and Golda (London) F.; m. Doris Rabinor (dec.); 1 child, Elaine Susan; m. Mairuth Hirsch Maloney, July 25, 1999. Student, CCNY, 1946-47. Builder housing, apt. projects, L.I., N.Y.C., N.J., 1948-54; pres. Kohl and Feld, Inc., builder housing devels., Rockland County, N.Y., 1955-57, Feld Constrn. Corp., New City, N.Y., 1957—, Birchland Constrn. Corp., 1957-70, Ramapo Towers, Inc., 1963-83. Vice-chmn. People's Nat. Bank Rockland County, Monsey, N.Y., 1974-85. Mem. Clarkstown Bldg. Code Com., 1959; mem. indsl. devel. adv. com. Rockland County Bd. Suprs., 1969-71; chmn. housing adv. coun. Rockland County Legislature, 1976-86; chmn. Housing Task Force, 1979-80; mem., past pres. Men's Club; mem. Rockland County coun. Jewish War Vets., past commdr. New City post. Staff sgt. AUS, 1941-45. Mem. Rockland County Assn., Inc. (former bd. dir.), Rockland County Home Builders Assn. (past pres., bd. dirs., chmn. rental housing com.), Nat. Assn. Home Builders (past bd. dirs., mem. rental housing com.), N.Y. State Assn. Home Builders (past bd. dir., mem. rental housing com.), Rockland County Apt. Owners Assn. (pres., bd. dirs. 1971-94), Rockland County Bd. Realtors, N.Y. State Assn. Realtors (past dirs.), Masons, Lions (local pres. 1959-60, zone chmn. 1961-62). Home: 901 E Camino Real Apt 6C Boca Raton FL 33432-6344

FELD, KAREN IRMA, columnist, journalist, broadcaster, public speaker; b. Washington, Aug. 23; d. Irvin and Adele Ruth (Schwartz) F. BA, Am. U. Columnist, reporter Roll Call Newspaper, Washington; nat. pub. rels. coord. Ringling Bros./Barnum & Bailey Circus, Washington; publicist Twentieth Century Fox, L.A.; pub. rels. account exec. Harshe, Rotman & Druck, L.A.; freelance writer, broadcaster; corr. People mag., Washington, 1980-85; adj. instr. Kent State U. Pol. Campaign Mgmt. Inst., 1981; broadcaster Voice of Am., 1984; columnist, contbg. editor Capitol Hill mag., Washington, 1980-89; columnist Washington Times, 1986-87, Universal Press Syndicate, 1988-89, Creators Syndicate, 1989-90; syndicated columnist Capital Connections, 1990—; Prodigy polit. columnist, 1990-93. Radio/TV commentator syndicated radio segment Radio America, 1993—; syndicated columnist Nat. Post, 1998-99; Washington editor Delta Shuttle Sheet, 2000—; lectr. in field, 1990—. Contbr. articles to Parade mag., People mag., Money mag., Time mag., Vogue mag., George, USA Weekend, Family Circle, Others. Recipient Health Journalism award Am. Chiropractic Assn., 1991. Mem. AFTRA/SAG, Nat. Fedn. Press Women (Excellence in Journalism awards 1984-2003), Capital Press Women (v.p. 1985-91, Excellence in Journalism awards 1984-2003, Entrepreneur/Communicator of Yr. award 1995), Am. Soc. Journalists and Authors, N.Am. Travel Journalists Assn., Nat. Assn. of Travel Journalists Am., Nat. Press Club, Capitol Hill Club, Woodmont Country Club (Rockville, Md.), U.S. Senate Press Gallery, White House Corr. Assn., Sigma Delta Chi (bd. dirs.). Jewish. Office: 1698 32nd St NW Washington DC 20007-2969 E-mail: news@karenfeld.com.

FELD, MICHAEL STEPHEN, physics educator; b. N.Y.C., Nov. 11, 1940; s. Albert and Lillian R. Norwalk; children: David A., Jonathan R., Alexandra A. SB in Humanities and Sci., SM in Physics, MIT, 1963; PhD in Physics, M.I.T., 1967. Postdoctoral fellow MIT, Cambridge, 1967-68, asst. prof., 1968-73, assoc. prof., 1973-79, prof. physics, 1979—, dir. George R. Harrison Spectroscopy Lab., 1976—, dir. Laser Research Ctr., 1979—; dir. Laser Biomed. Research Ctr., 1985—. Co-editor: Fundamental and Applied Laser Physics, 1973, Coherent Nonlinear Optics, 1980. Alfred P. Sloan rsch. fellow, 1973; recipient Disting. Svc. award MIT Minority Cmty., 1980, Gordon Y. Billard award, 1982, Thomas award Spectrochimica Acta, 1991, Vinci d'Excellence, France, 1995, Disting. Baltzer Colloquim spkr. Princeton U., 1996, Lamb medal Physics of Quantum Electronics Soc., 2003. Fellow AAAS, Am. Optical Soc., Am. Phys. Soc., Am. Soc. Laser Medicine and Surgery (bd. dirs.), Sigma Xi. Home: 66 Dunster Rd Jamaica Plain MA 02130 Office: MIT George R Harrison Spectroscopy Lab 77 Massachusetts Ave Cambridge MA 02139-4307

FELDBAUM, CARL, biotechnologist; B in Biology, Princeton U.; grad. in Law, U. Pa. Asst. spl. prosecutor, Washington, 1973; chief of staff to Senator Arlen Specter (Rep.-Pa.); pres., founder Palomar Corp., Washington; asst. to Sec. of Energy; insp. gen. for def. intelligence U.S. DOD; pres. Biotech. Industry Orgn., Washington. Author: Looking the Tiger in the Eye: Confronting the Nuclear Threat, 1988 (Christopher medal, 1988, N.Y. Times Notable Book of Yr., 1988). Recipient Disting. Civilian Svc. medal, Def. Sec. Harold Brown, 1979. Office: Biotech Industry Orgn Ste 400 1225 Eye St NW Washington DC 20005

FELDBERG, CHESTER BEN, banker, lawyer; b. N.Y.C., Dec. 16, 1939; s. William and Janet (Mesh) F.; m. Lynn Lea Uebelhack, Sept. 17, 1963; children: Gregory Howard, Suzanne. AB, Union Coll., Schenectady, 1960; LL.B., Harvard, 1963. Bar: N.Y., 1963. Atty. Fed. Res. Bank of N.Y., N.Y.C., 1964-68, asst. counsel, 1968-73, sec., 1969-73, v.p., 1975-83, sr. v.p., 1984-89, exec. v.p., 1989-2000. Sec. bd. govs. Fed. Res. System, 1973-74; chmn. Barclays Americas, 2000—. Office: Barclays Bank PLC 200 Park Ave New York NY 10166 E-mail: chester.feldberg@barcap.com.

FELDBERG, MEYER, university dean; b. Johannesburg, Mar. 17, 1942; s. Leon and Sarah (Kretzmer) F.; m. Barbara Erlick, Aug. 9, 1965; children: Lewis Robert, Ilana. BA, Witwatersrand U., Johannesburg, 1962; MBA, Columbia U., 1965; PhD, Cape Town (South Africa) U., 1969. Product mgr. B.F. Goodrich Co., Akron, Ohio, 1965-67; dean Grad. Sch. Bus., U. Cape Town, 1968-79; assoc. dean J.L. Kellogg Sch. Mgmt., Northwestern U., Evanston, Ill., 1979-81; prof., dean Sch. Bus., Tulane U., New Orleans, 1981-86; pres. Ill. Inst. Tech., Chgo., 1986-89, chmn. bd. govs. Rsch. Inst.; dean Grad. Sch. Bus. Columbia U., N.Y.C., 1989—. Bd. dirs. Federated Dept. Stores, UBS Funds, Revlon, Inc., Primedia Inc.; vis. prof. MIT, 1974, Cranfield Inst. Tech., 1970, 76. Author:

Organizational Behaviour: Text and Cases, 1975; contbr. articles to profl. jours. Named Jaycee Young Man of Yr., 1972 Mem. Univ. Club (N.Y.C. and Chgo.). Econ. Club (N.Y.C. and Chgo.). Office: 101 Uris Hall Columbia U Grad Sch Bus 3022 Broadway New York NY 10027-6945

FELDBERG, MICHAEL SVETKEY, lawyer; b. Boston, May 21, 1951; s. Sumner Lee Feldberg and Eunice (Svetkey) Cohen; m. Ruth Lazarus, Sept. 23, 1978; children: Rachel, Jesse, Ben. BA, Harvard U., 1973, JD, 1977. Bar: N.Y. 1978, U.S. Dist. Ct. (ea. and so. dists.) N.Y. 1978, U.S. Ct. Appeals (2d cir.) 1983, U.S. Supreme Ct. 1994. Assoc. Orans, Elsen, Polstein & Naftalis, N.Y.C., 1977—80; asst. U.S. atty. So. Dist. of N.Y., N.Y.C., 1981—84; ptnr. Shea & Gould, N.Y.C., 1985—91, Schulte Roth & Zabel, N.Y.C., 1991—2003; head U.S. Litig. Allen & Overy, N.Y.C., 2003—. Bd. dirs. 92d St. YMCA, N.Y.C., Child Devel. Rsch., N.Y.C., 1988—. Mem. Assn. Bar City N.Y. (criminal law com., com. on the judiciary, com. on profl. responsibility). Office: Allen & Overy 122 Avenue of the Americas New York NY 10020 E-mail: michael.feldberg@newyork.allen.overy.com.

FELDBLUM, SANDRA FAYE NEUMAN, communal worker, nurse; b. St. Paul, Apr. 18, 1946; d. Joseph and Dorothy (Rifkin) Lipschultz; m. Richard Neuman, Apr. 7, 1941 (div. Aug. 1988); children: Jennifer, Marc; m. Stephen Feldblum, Aug. 19, 2001. AS, St. Mary's Coll., Mpls., 1967; student, U. Minn., 1967—. RN, Minn. Operating rm. nurse U. Minn. Hosps., Mpls., 1967-68; staff nurse Twin Cities Airport Med. Clinic, Mpls., 1968; mem. fin. staff Durenberger for Senate, Mpls., 1987-88; asst. dir. maj. gifts United Jewish Appeal, Fedn. of Jewish Philanthropies of Greater N.Y., N.Y.C., 1988-89; dir. east coast region The Jerusalem Found., N.Y.C., 1989-91; Ea. regional dir. Israel Tennis Ctrs., N.Y.C., 1991—. Nat. officer, chair women's young leadership cabinet United Jewish Appeal, N.Y.C., 1985-86; owner Back Door Art Studio. Mem. exec. coun. Am. Israel Pub. Affairs Com., Washington, 1985-86; mem. nat. com. Joint Action Com. for Polit. Affairs, Chgo.; trustee Temple Shalom, Naples, Fla. Recipient Outstanding Young Leadership award Coun. Jewish Fedns., 1981. Mem. Nat. Soc. Fund Raising Execs., Nat. Coun. Jewish Women, Women in Fin. Devel. Home: 24030 Copperleaf Blvd Bonita Springs FL 34135-8169 E-mail: sandyneuman@email.msn.com.

FELDER, FRANKIE OTTOWIESS, academic administrator; b. Nuremburg, Germany, Aug. 19, 1950; d. Tyree Preston and Muriel Diggs Felder; 1 child, Ayesha Chevelle Apryl. EdM, U. of Vt., 1972—74, Harvard U., 1982—84, EdD, 1982—86. Counselor, spl. services Va. Commonwealth U., 1978—79; dir. of upward bound Kans. State U., 1979—82; asst. dir. McKnight Programs in Higher Edn. in Fla., Tampa, Fla., 1984—87; assoc. dean of the grad. sch. Clemson U., SC, 1987—, assoc. dean for internat. programs and services, 1987—2003. Consulting/seminar/presentations on issues related to minorities in higher edn. (mentoring, grantwriting, pursuing grad. edn., univ. rsch.) various universities across the country, 1979—. Author: (poetry book) As a Family Thinketh. Mem. Lions Internat., Clemson, SC, 1987—90; dir., African Heritage Day State Fair of Va., Richmond, 1978—78; pres. (then v.p.) Westside H.S. PTSA, Anderson, SC, 1997—2000; leadership trainer Fifth St. Bapt. Ch., Richmond, Va., 1978—79; mem. Richmond Urban League, Va., 1978—79; chairperson Douglas Cmty. Ctr., Manhattan, Kans., 1981—82; mem. and current chairperson Houston Ctr., Clemson, 1988—2003; initiator Boys Club, Clemson, SC, 1988—90. Recipient Positive Image Award, S.E. Region U.S./Newspaper Group, 1992, Academic Affairs Adminstr. of the Yr. for State of SC, S.E./South Regional Assn. of Academic Affairs Administrators, 1996. Mem.: S.C. Women in Higher Edn. (univ. rep.), Nat. Assn. of State Universities and Landgrant Colleges, Assn. of Internat. Edn. Administrators (editor, newsletter 1989—92), Nat. Assn. of Fgn. Student Affairs (regional rep. 1992—94), Nat. Phys. Sci. Consortium, Coun. of So. Grad. Schools (chair, internat. com. 1998—2000). Baptist. Avocations: reading, writing, art, genealogy, music. Office: Clemson U E106 Martin Hall Clemson SC 29634 Office Fax: 864-656-5344. E-mail: frankie@clemson.edu.

FELDER, MYRNA, lawyer; b. N.Y.C., Apr. 19, 1941; BA magna cum laude, Brown U., 1961; JD cum laude, NYU, 1971. Bar: N.Y. 1971, U.S. Dist. Ct. (so. and ea. dists.) N.Y. 1974, U.S. Ct. Appeals (2nd cir.) 1977, U.S. Supreme Ct. 1978. Ptnr. Raoul Lionel Felder P.C., N.Y.C., 1972—. Lectr., cons. in field; mem. N.Y. State Civil Practice Adv. Com., chair subcom. on matrimonial procedures, 1983—. Editor-in-chief: The Matrimonial Strategist, 1985-89; bimonthly columnist New York Law Jour.; contbr. chpts. to books. Mem. ABA, N.Y. State Bar Assn. (chair cts. of appellate jursidiction com. 1988-92), Assn. Bar City of N.Y., Women's Bar Assn., State N.Y. (dir. 1980-85, chmn. com. on matrimonial law 1984-85, pres. 1986-87), N.Y. Women's Bar Assn. (pres. 1976-77), Order of the Coif, Phi Beta Kappa. Home: 60 Sutton Pl S Apt 19as New York NY 10022-4168 Office: Raoul Lionel Felder PC 437 Madison Ave New York NY 10022-7001

FELDER, RAOUL LIONEL, lawyer; b. N.Y.C., May 13, 1934; s. Morris and Millie (Goldstein) F.; m. Myrna Felder, May 26, 1963; children: Rachel, James. BA, NYU, 1955; JD, NYU, Switzerland, 1959; postgrad., U. Bern, Switzerland, 1955-56; hon. degree of fellow in jurisprudence, Oxford U., 1995. Bar: N.Y. 1959, U.S. Dist. Ct. (so. and ea. dists.) N.Y. 1962, U.S. Ct. Appeals (2d cir.) 1962, U.S. Supreme Ct. 1970. Pvt. practice, N.Y.C., 1959-61, 64—; asst. U.S. atty., 1961-64. Mem. faculty Practicing Law Inst., 1979, Marymount Coll., 1982-85, Ethical Culture Sch., 1981, 82; moderator Nat. Conf. on Child Abuse, 1989; apptd. to N.Y.C. Cultural Affairs Adv. Commn., 1995-2001, State Commn. on Child Abuse, 1996; bd. dirs. Kidney and Urology. Author: Divorce: The Way Things Are, Not the Way Things Should Be, 1971, Lawyers Practical Handbook to the New Divorce Law, 1981, Raoul Felder's Encyclopedia of Matrimonial Clauses, 1990, updated, 1991, Getting Away with Murder, 1996, Restaurant Guide to Los Angeles and New York, 1996, Survival Guide to New York, 1997, Bare Knuckle Negotiations, 2003; columnist Fame mag., 1988-92, Am. Women Mag., 1994, N.Y. Daily News Sundays, 1995; contbr. articles on law to profl. jours. and N.Y. Times; editorials to Newsweek mag., Harper's Bazaar mag., Newsday newspaper, N.Y. Post, The Guardian (London), Jerusalem Post, Penthouse mag., Cosmopolitan mag., N.Y. Times; columnist Am. Spectator Mag, 1999-2001, Washington Times, 1999-2002; commentator Cable News Network, 1989, BBC World Wide, 1994, 95, 97, Crossing the Line (pub. TV series), 1997-99, The Felder Report (pub. TV series), 1998-99, guest commentator Court TV, 1992, bd. advisors, 1992-95, editl. contbr.; (documentary) Survival Guide to New York, 1998; host (TV series) Metrolaw, 1995-97; host (radio talk show) The Felder Report, 1997-2002, TalkAmerica. Mem. Gov.'s Commn. on Child Abuse, 1989; chmn. Nat. Kidney Found. Auction, N.Y. Fund; chmn. dinner Jerusalem Reclamation Project; bd. dirs. Big Apple Greeters, 1997—99, Cop Care, Hosp. Audiences Inc., Nat. Kidney Found., N.Y.C. Econ. Devel. Corp., 2000—, Kidney and Urology Found. Am., N.Y. Cops Found.; hon. police commr. N.Y. City Police Comms., 2000—; grand marshall U.S.A. Day Washington, Israel Day Parade, N.Y.C.; apptd. Cultural Adv. Commn., N.Y.C., 1994—2001, 2001—02. Named Man of Yr. Bklyn. Sch. for Spl. Children, Met. Geriatric Ctr., Shield Inst., 1997; recipient Defender of Jerusalem medal, 1990, Crimebusters award Take Back N.Y., 1996, Child Abuse Prevention Svc. award, Child Safety Inst. 1998. Mem. ABA (judge nat. finals client counseling competition), Assn. of Bar of City of N.Y. (spl. com. matrimonial law 1975-77), N.Y. State Trial Lawyers Assn. (past chmn. matrimonial law 1974-75), Am. Arbitration Assn., N.Y. Women's Bar Assn., Minion of the Stars (chmn. bd. 1993). Home: 60 Sutton Pl S New York NY 10022-4168 Office: 437 Madison Ave New York NY 10022-7001 E-mail: raoulfelder@raoulfelder.com.

FELDER-HOEHNE, FELICIA HARRIS, librarian; b. Knoxville, Tenn. d. Henry Thomas and Luvilla Tate Harris. BS in English, Knoxville Coll., 1958; MS in Libr. Sci., Atlanta U., 1966; postgrad., U. Tenn., 1972—78; grad., Knoxville (Tenn.) Police Dept. English tchr. McMinn County Schs., J.L. Cook Sch., Athens, Tenn., 1958—60; adminstrv. asst. Adminstrv. Offices Knoxville (Tenn.) Coll., 1960—63, adminstrv. asst. to the dir. pub. rels., 1963—65; grad. libr. asst. Trevor Arnett Libr., Atlanta U., 1965—66; head circulation and reserve svcs. Alumni Libr. Knoxville Coll., 1966—69; tchr., libr. summer study skills program Union Presbyn. Ch., Bd. Nat. Missions, Knoxville Coll., 1967—68; prof., reference libr. John C. Hodges Libr. U. Tenn., Knoxville, 1969—. Founder, dir. Larks: Linking Librs. with At-Risk Students, Knoxville, 1997—. Author: A Subject Guide to Basic Reference Books in Black Studies; co-author: (online ency.) Project TAPP: Tennesse Authors Past and Present, 1999—; contbr., ;, author poems; contbr. articles to profl. jours. Notary pub. at-large State of Tenn., Nat. Notary Assn., 1992—; adv. bd. Mentoring Acad. for Boys, Knoxville, 1997—; sec. to bd. Ctr. for Neighborhood Devel., Knoxville, 2000—; dir. pub. rels. Concerned Assn. Residents East, Knoxville, 1988—90; active Tenn. Valley Energy Coalition, Knoxville, 1988—90, Town Hall East, Knoxville, 1988—, Save Our Cumberland Mountains, Tenn., 1988—; mem. religious task force World's Fair, Knoxville Internat. Energy Exposition, 1982; pres. Spring Place Neighborhood Assn., Knoxville, 1980—; others; bd. dirs. Ctr. for Neighborhood Devel., Knoxville, 1998—, Knoxville Opera Co., 1999—, UT Fed. Credit Union, Knoxville, 1984—89. Named Outstanding Young Women of Am., 1967; recipient Cert. of Merit for Contbns. to Edn., Jack and Jill, Inc., 1976, Plaque of Appreciation, Interdenominational Concert Choir, 1976, Religious Svc. award, Nat. Conf. Christians and Jews, 1976, Citizen of the Yr. award, Order of the Ea. Star Prince Hall Masons, 1979, Cert. of Appreciation, Knoxville's Internat. Energy Exposition, 1982, Pub. Svc. award, U. Tenn. Nat. Alumni Assn., 1984, Cert. of Merit for Disting. Svc. to the Cmty., Dictionary of Internat. Geography, 1985, Habitat for Humanity award, 1992, The Humanitarian Libr. Spirit award, 1994, Citation for Svc., Knoxville Police Dept., 1998, The Knoxville News-Sentinel Cmty. Cornerstone award, 1998, The Miles 500 Libr. Spirit award, 1999, Harold B. Love Outstanding Cmty. Involvement award, 2003. Mem.: YWCA, YMCA, ALA, NAACP, Nat. Mus. Women in the Arts (charter), East Tenn. Libr. Assn., Tenn. Libr. Assn., Citizens Police Acad. Alumni Assn., Beck Cultural Exch. Ctr. (charter), Met. Opera Assn., Knoxville (Tenn.) Opera Guild, Alpha Kappa Alpha. Avocations: community service, music, drama, writing poetry. Office: 145 John C Hodges Libr 1015 Volunteer Blvd Knoxville TN 37916-3109

FELDERMAN, LENORA I. physician; b. N.Y.C., July 17, 1952; d. Ephraim Jacob and Sylvia (Farber) F.; m. Arnold Komisar, Dec. 23, 1984; children: Alexandra Danielle, Johnathan Reed. MD, N.Y. Med. Coll., 1981. Diplomate Am. Bd. Dermatology. Resident in dermatology Albert Einstein Med. Ctr., Bronx, 1982-85; resident in internal medicine Montefiore Hosp., Bronx, N.Y., 1981-82, assoc. attending dermatologist, 1985-97, Lenox Hill Hosp., N.Y.C., 1985—; asst. prof. medicine/dermatology Albert Einstein Coll. Medicine, N.Y.C., 1985-97, Cornell U. Med. Coll., 1998—. Speaker on dermatology and skin care. Contbr. articles to profl. jours. Recipient Am. Women's Med. Assn. award, 1985, Pathology award N.Y. Med. Coll., 1985. Fellow Am. Acad. Dermatology, Internat. Soc. Dermatology, Soc. Pediatric Dermatology; mem. AMA, Dermatology Soc. Greater N.Y., Med. Soc. State N.Y., New York County Med. Soc., Alpha Omega Alpha. Avocations: reading, design, skiing, parenting, dance. Office: 1317 3rd Ave New York NY 10021-2995

FELDER-RODRIGUEZ, MONICA LEE, lawyer; b. Vallejo, Calif., Aug. 20, 1968; d. Kenneth Doyle Allen and Barbara Jean Felder. BA in Internat. Rels., Tulane U., 1989; JD, Duke U., 1992, LLM in Internat. Law, 1995. Bar: Fla. 1993. Sr. atty. Agy. for Health Care Adminstrn., State of Fla., Tallahassee, 1993-96; asst. atty. gen. Fla. Office Atty. Gen., Ft. Lauderdale, 1996-98; assoc. Dresnick & Ellsworth, PA, Miami, Fla., 1998—99; ptnr. Dresnick, Ellsworth & Felder, P.A., 1999—. Mem. Am. Health Lawyers Assn., Fla. Bar Assn. (mem. exec. coun. health law sect.), Fla. Hosp. Assn., Dade County Bar Assn. Office: Dresnick & Rodriguez PA 201 Alhambra Cir Ste 701 Coral Gables FL 33134-5108

FELDER-WRIGHT, PAMELA THERESA EVANS, education educator; b. Natchez, Miss., Aug. 1, 1956; d. Albert and Yvonne Evans; m. Marion Earl Wright, June 14, 2003; children: D'Antwanette Felder, Crystal Wright, Demetric Felder, Brandon Wright. BSc, Alcorn State U., 1974—78, MSc, 1979—80; D, Kans. State U., 1980—82. Asst. prof. edn. Winston-Salem (N.C.) State U., 1984—90; dir. med. ctr. child care Bowman Gray Sch. Medicine, Winston-Salem, 1993—96; coord. spl. edn. Alcorn State U., Lorman, Miss., 1999—. Pres. Pam's Unique Technique, Natchez, Miss.; mem. Oxford Round Table, London, 2003. Author: (books) Dream.but Dream Big, I'm Black and Beautiful, (poetry) I Looked at You Today (Internat. Poet of the Yr., 2002). Recipient Internat. Soc. of Poets Disting. Mem. award, Internat. Soc. of Poets, 2002, Editor's Choice Award for Outstanding Poetry, Internat. Libr. of Poetry, 2000, Hon. Appointment to the Profl. Women's Adv. Bd., Am. Biog. Inst., Inc., 2000, Medallion and Silver Cup Trophy -Poet of Merit award, Internat. Soc. of Poets, 2002, Plaque of Appreciation, Am. Reads-Mississippi, 2002. Mem.: Miss. Assn. of Tech., Miss. Assn. of Educator, Nat. Assn. of Edn. for Young Children, Coun. for Exceptional Children, Phi Delta Kappa. Baptist. Achievements include research in Sped Tech SMCET. Avocations: reading, writing, travel. Office: Alcorn State University 1000 ASU Dr Alcorn State MS 39096 Office Fax: 601-877-6211. E-mail: pfelder@lorman.alcorn.edu.

FELDHAUS, STEPHEN MARTIN, lawyer; b. Lawrenceburg, Tenn., Jan. 12, 1945; s. Lawrence Bernard and Margaret Martha (Holthouse) F.; m. Allis Rennie, Aug. 18, 1968 (div. 1980); 1 child, Rennie Elizabeth; m. Marcia Virginia Hughes, Dec. 30, 1980; stepchildren: Matthew Rankin FitzSimmons, Ryan Ford FitzSimmons. AB, U. Notre Dame, 1967; JD, Stanford U., 1973. Bar: Tex. 1973, D.C. 1984. Law clk. to Hon. Eugene A. Wright U.S. Ct. Appeals (9th cir.), Seattle, 1972-73; assoc. Fulbright & Jaworski, Houston, 1973-76, London, 1976-79, ptnr., 1979-81, Washington, 1981—. Bd. dirs. Foundation, Vaduz, Liechtenstein. Bd. dirs. D.C. Downtown Partnership, Washington, 1988-92 Mem.: ABA, D.C. Bar, Internat. Fiscal Assn., Internat. Bar Assn., City Club of Washington. Republican. Avocations: tennis, squash, skiing, chess, reading. Office: Fulbright & Jaworski 801 Pennsylvania Ave NW Fl 3-5 Washington DC 20004-2623 E-mail: sfeldhaus@fulbright.com.

FELDHUSEN, HAZEL JEANETTE, elementary education educator; b. Camp Douglas, Wis., Feb. 20, 1928; d. Vincent O. and Helen (Johnson) Artz; m. John F. Feldhusen, Dec. 18, 1954; children: Jeanne V., Anne M. B, U. Wis., 1965; M, Purdue U., 1968; postgrad., U. Wis. Tchr. Suldal Sch., Mauston, Wis., 1947-50, Lake Geneva (Wis.) Schs., 1950-55, West Lafayette (Ind.) Schs., 1965-91. Presenter World Conf., Hamburg, 1985, Juneau (Alaska) Schs., 1986, Vancouver (B.C., Can.) Schs., 1990, Norfolk (Va.) Schs., 1991, Taiwan Nat. U., 1992, U. New South Wales, Sydney, Australia, 1993, New Zealand Schs., Auckland, 1993; 2d Nat. Conf. Gifted, Taiwan, 1992, Sarasota, Fla., 1998. Author: Individualized Teaching of the Gifted, 1993, 2d edit., 1997; contbr. articles to profl. jours., chpts. to books, 1981-2002. Mem. Tchr. of Yr. Com., West Lafayette, 1988. Recipient Outstanding Tchr. award Elem. Tchrs. Am., 1974, Appreciation award U. Stellenbosch, 1984, Appreciation award Australian Assn. for the Gifted, 1987; winner Golden Apple Tchg. award Greater Lafayette C. of C., 1989, Disting. Alumnus award Purdue U., 1996. Mem. NEA, Ind. State Tchrs. Assn., West Lafayette Edn. Assn. (Outstanding Achievement award 1984), Phi Delta Kappa, Delta Kappa Gamma (v.p 1983-85). Avocations: reading, interior decorating. Home: Sarasota Bay Club 1301 N Tamiami Apt 205 Sarasota FL 34236 E-mail: feldhusenjf@aol.com.

FELDMAN, ALLAN MAURICE, economist; b. Paterson, N.J., Jan. 9, 1943; s. Jacob and Rachel (Eisen) F.; m. Barbara Ellen Moses, June 19, 1965; children: Paula, Elizabeth, Jacob. BS in Math., U. Chgo., 1965, MA in Anthropology, 1967; PhD in Econs., Johns Hopkins U., 1972. Asst. prof. econs. Brown U., Providence, 1971-78, assoc. prof. econs., 1978—. Cons., expert witness, Providence, 1975—. Author: Welfare Economics and Social Choice Theory, 1980. Treas. Common Sense, Providence, 1983-84. Recipient fellowship, Johns Hopkins U., 1970, Richard D. Irwin fellowship, Richard D. Irwin Found., 1971. Mem. Nat. Assn. Forensic Economists, Am. Economic Assn., Nat. Assn. Watch and Clock Collectors, Phi Beta Kappa (treas. R.I. Alpha chpt. 1999--). Avocations: antique clocks, hiking, nature study. Office: Brown U Dept Econs Providence RI 02912-0001

FELDMAN, ALLAN ROY, corporate development and marketing executive; b. Chgo., June 2, 1945; s. Michael and Sophie (Grossman) F.; m. Micki McCabe, Sept. 21, 1984. BS, Roosevelt U., 1968; postgrad., U. Louvain, Belgium, 1969-71; MBA, U. Chgo. Asst. to dir. gen. Rank-Xerox, S.A., Brussels, Belgium, 1969-71; dir. new bus. ventures graphic sys. group Rockwell Internat. Corp., Chgo., 1971-73, dir. mktg., consumer ops., 1973-75, gen. mgr. microwave oven divsn., 1975-78; group v.p. Chromalloy Am. Corp., N.Y.C., 1978-80; mng. ptnr. Mktg. Trademark Cons., N.Y.C., 1980-85; CEO, pres. Leveraged Mktg. Corp. Am., N.Y.C., 1986—. Bd. dirs. Alimansky Venture Group, Inc., N.Y.C., ITC Integrated Sys., Inc., N.Y.C., Growthtech Corp., N.Y.C., Indsl. Computer Corp., Farmington, Conn., Intellectual Property Mgmt. Inst., Lic. Industry Merchants Assn.; guest lectr. Columbia U.; spkr. trademark licensing and brand bldg., orgns. including Internat. Trademark Assn. and Licensing Execs. Soc., various U.S. and European confs. Bd. dirs. 329108 Owners Corp., N.Y.C., 1993. Mem. Licensing Industry Merchants Assn. (officer bd. dirs. 2001—). Avocations: master carpenter, photography, motorcycle riding. Office: Leveraged Mktg Corp of Am 156 W 56th St New York NY 10019-3800 E-mail: allanf@lmca.net.

FELDMAN, ARLENE BUTLER, aviation industry executive; BA cum laude in Polit. Sci., U. Colo., 1975; JD, Temple U. Sch. Law, 1978. Supervising atty. U.S. Railway Assn., Phila., 1977-82; dir. divsn. aeronautics N.J. Dept. Transp., Trenton, 1982-84; from acting dir. to dep. dir. tech. ctr. FAA, Atlantic City, N.J., 1984-86, dep. dir. Western-Pacific region Exec. Sch. L.A., 1986-87, dep. dir. Western-Pacific region, 1986-87, regional adminstr. N.Eng. Region Burlington, Mass., 1988-94, exec. sch., 1986-87, eastern regional adminstr. Jamaica, N.Y., 1994—. Panelist, guest spkr. Women in Aviation Conf., 1992, 93; vice-chair N.Y. Fed. Exec. Bd.; chairperson regional airport sys. planning adv. com. Delaware Valley Regional Planning Commn.; founder rotorcraft R&D forum FAA. Chairwoman Boston Federal Exec. Bd. Saving Bond, 1993; mem. adv. bd. U. So. Calif. Recipient Presdl. Meritorius Rank award Sr. Exec. Svc., Disting. Svc. award N.J. Aviation Hall of Fame, Amelia Earhart medal; inducted N.J. Aviation Hall of Fame, 1997. Mem. ABA, Ninety-Nines Internat. Orgn. (Earhart medal), Lawyer/Pilot Bar Assn., Air Traffic Control Assn. (dir., exec. bd., conf. panel moderator 1993, 91, spkr. 1993, chmn. bd. 1996, chmn. elect 1997), Am. Assn. Airport Execs., Am. Assn. State Hwy. and Transp. Ofcls., Am. Helicopter Soc., Helicopter Assn. Internat. (hon.), Nat. Assn. State Aviation Ofcls., Nat. Coun. Women in Aviation Aerospce, Internat. Aviation Women's Assn., Profl. Women Contrs., Inc. (1st hon. mem.), Wings Club N.Y.C. (bd. govs. 1996), Pi Sigma Alpha. Office: FAA 1 Aviation Plz Jamaica NY 11434

FELDMAN, ARNOLD H. lawyer; b. Yonkers, N.Y., Aug. 22, 1931; s. Joseph and Minnie Sarah Feldman; m. Carole Linzer, Jan. 29, 1956; children: Tamar Miller, Deena Altman, David, Nathan. BA, Yeshiva U., 1953; JD, Rutgers U., 1981. Bar: Pa. 1981, N.J. 1981, U.S. Dist. Ct. (ea. dist.) Pa. 1981, U.S. Dist. Ct. N.J. 1981, U.S. Ct. Appeals (3d cir.) 1981, U.S. Tax Ct. 1981; ordained as rabbi, 1956. Atty. Ballen Gertel and Feldman, Camden, NJ, 1982—89, Feldman and Hildebrand P.C., Cherry Hill, NJ, 1989—2001, Feldman, Hildebrand & Blaker, LLC, Cherry Hill, NJ, 2001—. Office: Feldman, Hildebrand & Blaker LLC 800 Kings Hwy N Cherry Hill NJ 08034-1512

FELDMAN, ARTHUR M. cardiologist; m. Susan Boochever; children: Emily Kate, Elizabeth Willa. BA, Gettysburg Coll., 1970; MS, U. Md., 1973, PhD, 1974; MD, La. State U., 1981. Diplomate Nat. Bd. Med. Examiners, Am. Bd. Internal Medicine, Sub-Bd. Cardiovascular Disease. Intern, resident fellow in cardiology Johns Hopkins Hosp., Balt., 1981-86, from asst. prof. to assoc. prof. medicine, 1986-94; Harry S. Tack prof. medicine, prof. cell biology/physiology U. Pitts., 1994—2002, chief divsn. cardiology, dir. Cardiovasc. Inst., 1998—2002; Magee prof., chmn. dept. medicine Jefferson Med. Coll., Phila., 2002—. Mem. editl. bd. Heart Failure, Jour. Cardiac Failure, Jour. Cardivasc. Pharmacology & Therapeutics, Jour. Cardiovasc. Pharmacology, Clin. Cardiology, Jour. Am. Coll. Cardiology, Cardiac Failure. Trustee Gettysburg Coll. Grantee, NIH, 1989—94, 1999—2003. Fellow: Am. Coll. Cardiology, Coun. Clin. Cardiology (exec. com. 1996—2000, basic rsch. coun.), Am. Heart Assn. (heart failure com.); mem.: Assn. Univ. Cardiologists (councilor 1999—2001), Heart Failure Soc. Am. (founding mem. 1995, sec. 1996—98, pres. 1998—2000), Assn. Profs. Cardiology (treas. 2000—01, pres 2002—), Assn. Subsplty. Profs., Internat. Soc. Heart Rsch., Assn. Am. Physicians, Am. Soc. Clin. Investigation. Home: 136 Knightsbridge Wynnewood PA 19096 Office: Jefferson Med Coll Coll Bldg Rm 822 1025 Walnut St Philadelphia PA 19096 E-mail: arthur.feldman@jefferson.edu.

FELDMAN, BRUCE ALLEN, otolaryngologist; b. Washington, Mar. 22, 1941; s. Irvin and Miriam Thelma (Rothstein) F.; m. Sharon Lee Pearlman, Dec. 25, 1966; children: Kathryn Ellen, Michael Aaron. AB, Dartmouth Coll., 1962, B Med. Sci., 1963; MD, Harvard U., 1965. Diplomate Am. Bd. Otolaryngology. Intern Hosp. of U. Pa., Phila., 1965-66, resident in surgery, 1966-67; resident in otolaryngology Mass. Eye and Ear Infirmary-Harvard U., Boston, 1967-70; pvt. practice Washington, 1972—; clin. prof. surgery (otolaryngology), pediatrics/hlth. care George Washington U., Washington, 1990—; clin. prof. otolaryngology Georgetown U. Sch. Medicine, Washington, 1995—. Pres. med. staff Children's Hosp. Nat. Med. Ctr., Washington, 1994-96; bd. dirs. Children's Hosp., Washington, 1994--, vice chmn. bd. dirs., 1999-2001. Contbr. articles to med. jours., chpt. to book. Lt. comdr. M.C., USNR, 1970-72. Mosby scholar, 1963; recipient Physician's Recognition award Children's Hosp. Washington, 1991. Fellow ACS, Am. Laryngol., Rhinol. and Otol. Soc. (Mosher award 1981), Am. Acad. Pediatrics; mem. AMA, Acad. Medicine Washington, Med. Soc. D.C., Jacobi Med. Soc. (pres. 1986-87), Washington Met. Ear, Nose and Throat Soc. (pres. 1978-79), Woodmont Country Club (Rockville, Md.), Phi Beta Kappa, Alpha Omega Alpha, Phi Delta Epsilon (pres. grad. club 1979-80). Jewish. Office: 5454 Wisconsin Ave Chevy Chase MD 20815

FELDMAN, CECILE ARLENE, dentist; b. N.Y.C., Oct. 8, 1959; d. Melvin and Claire (Halpern) F.; m. Harry Kenneth Zohn, Aug. 19, 1984. BA, U. Pa., 1980, DMD, 1984, MBA, 1985. Adj. sr. fellow Leonard Davis Inst. Health Econs., Phila., 1985—; dean, prof. N.J. Dental Sch., Newark. Cons. in field. Fellow Acad. Gen. Dentistry, Internat. Coll. Dentists, Am. Coll. Dentists; mem. Am. Assn. Dental Schs., Internat. Assn. Dental Rsch., Am. Assn. Pub. Health Dentistry, Am. Dental Assn., Am. Med. Informatics Assn., N.J. Dental Assn. Office: NJ Dental Sch 110 Bergen St Newark NJ 07103-2400

FELDMAN, CLARICE ROCHELLE, lawyer; b. Milw., Dec. 2, 1941; d. Harry and Beatrice (Hiken) Wagan; m. Howard J. Feldman, July 11, 1965; 1 child, David Lewis. BS, U. Wis., 1963, LL.B., 1965. Bar: Wis. 1965, D.C. 1969, Md. 1984. Appellate atty. NLRB, Washington, 1965—69; co-counsel to Joseph A. Yablonski, Washington, 1969; atty. Washington research project Clark Coll., 1970-72; asso. gen. counsel United Mine Workers Am., Washington, 1972-74; partner Becker, Channell, Becker & Feldman, Washington, 1974-76, Becker & Feldman, 1976-77; gen. counsel Ams. for Energy Independence, Washington, 1978-80; atty. Office of Spl. Investigations, Dept. Justice, 1980-84; pvt. practice law Washington, 1984-98; atty. pro bono, 1999—. Trustee Washington Internat. Sch., 1987-98; advisor Assn. Union Democracy. Mem. Wis., D.C., Md. bar assns. Democrat. Jewish. Home: 4455 29th St NW Washington DC 20008-2307

FELDMAN, DANIEL CHARLES, adult education educator; b. Lowell, Mass., Mar. 7, 1951; s. Harry Louis and Shirley Ruth Feldman. BA, U. Pa., 1972; MA, Yale U., 1974, PhD, 1976. Instr. adminstrv. scis. Yale U., New Haven, Conn., 1975-76; asst. prof. indsl. rels. Indsl. Rels. Ctr. U. Minn., Mpls., 1976-77; asst. prof. orgn. behavior Kellogg Sch. Mgmt. Northwe. U., Evanston, Ill., 1977-81; assoc. prof. mgmt. Grad. Sch. Bus., U. Fla., Gainesville, 1981-86, prof. mgmt., 1986-89; disting. found. prof. mgmt. Darla Moore Sch. Bus., U. S.C., Columbia, 1989—. Chmn. careers divsn. Nat. Acad. Mgmt., N.Y.C., 1992-93, mem. exec. com. organizational behavior divsn., 1986-88; chmn. univ. tenure and promotion com., U. S.C., Columbia, 1996-97; dir. doctoral program mgmt. U. S.C., 1993-96. Author: Coping with Job Loss, 1992; contbr. articles on career devel. to profl. publications; cons. editor Jour. Organizational Behavior, Detroit, 1996—; editl. bd. Acad. Mgmt. Jour., 1984-87, Human Resource Mgmt. Jour., 1991—. Recipient Addison Wesley Best Paper award Acad. Mgmt., 1997; vis. Sloan scholar MIT, 1987; Eli Lilly Sr. Tchg. fellow U. S.C., 1992-95. Fellow So. Mgmt. Assn.; mem. Phi Beta Kappa (exec. com. mem. coun. 1996—). Avocations: biking, reading, swimming. Office: U SC Darla Moore Sch Bus Columbia SC 29208-0001 E-mail: defeldman@darla.badm.sc.edu.

FELDMAN, DAVID EDWARD, playwright; b. Yonkers, NY, Feb. 8, 1939; s. Samuel and Edith Ruth Feldman; m. Tina Marie Feldman, Jan. 17, 2003; m. Norma Jane Schonfeld, Aug. 28, 1964 (div.); 1 child, Jessica Beth. BA, SUNY, 1960; MA, Syracuse U., 1966; MFA, Brandeis U., 1970. Asst. editor The Life Ins. Courant, New York, NY, 1960—61; asst. prof. English SUNY, Cortland, NY, 1963—67; lectr. English Leslie Coll., Cambridge, Mass., 1970—71; asst. dir. residence halls Brandeis U., Waltham, Mass., 1971—72; prof. English, journalism Onondaga C.C., Syracuse, NY, 1972—2001, dir. journalism program, 1980—2001, prof. emeritus, 2001—. Theater critic WCNY-TV, Syracuse, 1974—78, Syracuse Guide Mag., 1975—78, WONO-FM, 1975—79; arts auditor NY State Coun. Arts, NYC, 1979—80, grants panelist, 1983—84; regional corr. Stages Mag., Morristown, NJ, 1984—87; artistic dir. new plays

program Contemporary Theater, Syracuse, 1984—97; grants panelist Upper Catskill Arts Coun., NY State Coun. Arts, Utica, NY, 1995—96; artistic dir. Armory Sq. Playhouse, Syracuse, 1996—. Author: (plays) Georgie Porgy, 1970, Steinberg, 1977, Smile F, Hotel de Dream, 1981, Lisa in Syracuse, 1986, Erie Canal Afternoon, 1989, Sitting Quietly Doing Nothing, 1990, Steinberg in Scarsdale, 1993, Bill and Mary! Right Now, 1996, He and She, 1996, Fade to Black, 2001, The Fifty Year Game of Gin Rummy, 2002, The Wonder of It, 2002; contbg. editor Syracuse New Times, 1972—88; contbr. columns in newspapers. Recipient Profl. Recognition award, Syracuse Press Club, 1980, 1981, 1982, 1984; fellow, Brandeis U., 1968—72; grantee Spl. Oportunity, NY State Coun. Arts, 1996; Coll. Tchg. fellow, Regents of SUNY, 1961—63. Mem.: Dramatists Guild. Personal E-mail: dfeldman@twcny.rr.com. E-mail: feldmand@sunyocc.edu.

FELDMAN, DAVID HENRY, psychologist, educator; b. Pitts., Nov. 1, 1942; s. Rudolph Abraham and Deborah Ruth (Appleman) F.; m. Ann Cheryl Benjamin, July 2, 1990; children: Keffie, Betsy, Daniel, Anne Catherine. BA, U. Rochester, 1964; MA in Tchg., Stanford U., 1965; EdM, Harvard U., 1966; PhD, Stanford U., 1969. Asst. prof. U. Minn., Mpls., 1969-71, Yale U., New Haven, 1971-74; assoc. prof., then prof. Eliot Pearson dept. child study Tufts U., Medford, Mass., 1974—, chmn. Eliot Pearson dept. child devel., 1984—86, 1995—96. Fulbright vis. prof. Tel Aviv U., 1980-81; vis. scholar Harvard U., Cambridge, Mass., 1987-88, 2001-02, U. Calif., San Diego, 1995. Author: Nature's Gambit, 1986 (Scholar of Yr. award 1988), Changing the World, 1994, Beyond Universals in Cognitive Development, 1994; contbr. over 150 articles to profl. publs. Chair com. on devel., learning and giftedness Social Sci. Rsch. Coun., N.Y., 1980-90; mem. Mozart Bicentennial Smithsonian Instn., Washington, 1991; mem. nat. policy com. Javits program USOE, Washington, 1993. Named Disting. Scholar Nat. Assn. for Gifted Children, 1988; Fulbright scholar, 1980-81; grantee Rockefeller Found., 1990-93, Spencer Found., 1984-88. Fellow APA; mem. Soc. for Rsch. in Child Devel.

FELDMAN, DONNA B. literature educator; b. St. Joseph, Mich., Mar. 6, 1956; d. Harold and Pearl Phyllis Goldenberg; m. David J. Feldman; children: Jon, Eric, Caren, Sara, Mike. BA in Econs. and Psychology, Brandeis U., 1976. Cert. tchr. Mich., Ohio. History tchr. Cleve. City Schs.; secular tchr. Hebrew Acad., Cleveland Heights, Ohio; 7th grade tchr. Shaarey Zedek Sch., Southfield, Mich.; v.p. FLD Software Services, Inc., Southfield; test rsch. analyst Detroit; English tchr. Cleveland Heights and University Heights, Ohio, 2002. Spkr., intro to computers Nerim, Southfield, Mich., 1998; spkr., parenting and tchg. ld, ad / hd and gifted children U. Mich., Dearborn, Mich., 1998—98, Wayne State U., Detroit. Contbr. articles to profl. jours. Leader Girl Scouts U.S., Cleve., 2000—02; cubmaster, den leader Boy Scouts Am., Southfield; bd. dirs. Akivn PTA, Southfield, 1988—98. Recipient Student Tchr. of the Yr. award, Mich. Assn. Tchr. Educators, 1999, Cantor Disting. Educator award, Shaarey Zedek Sch., Southfield, 1995, Shofar award, Boy Scouts Am., 1995. Mem.: Amit. Home: 23957 Greenlawn Ave Beachwood OH 44122-1434

FELDMAN, DOUGLAS A. anthropologist; b. N.Y.C., Jan. 29, 1947; s. Samuel C. and Sylvia (Libin) F. AA, Bronx C.C., 1966; BA, CCNY, 1968; MA, New Sch. for Social Rsch., N.Y.C., 1972; PhD, SUNY, Stony Brook, 1981. Asst. contract adminstr. N.Y.C. Dept. Parks & Recreation, Flushing, 1979-81; prin. writer, editor N.Y.C. Dept. Fin., 1983-86; exec. dir. AIDS Ctr. Queens County, Rego Park, N.Y., 1986-88; rsch. assoc. prof. U. Miami Sch. Medicine, 1989-94, 97-00, dir. AIDS Social Rsch. Program, 2000; prof., dir. Nova Southeastern U., Ft. Lauderdale, 1995-96; pres. D.A. Feldman & Assocs. Inc., Ft. Lauderdale, 1995-98; dir. grants and devel. The Village, Miami, 2001; vis. rsch. prof. Fla. Internat. U., 2001; chmn. SUNY, Brockport, 2001—02, prof., 2002—. Adv. com. Inst. Medicine Internat. Forum AIDS Rsch., Washington, 1990—91; HIV cons. USIA, 1988; adj. prof. U. Miami Sch. Medicine, 2001. Editor: The Social Dimensions of AIDS: Method and Theory, 1986, Culture and AIDS, 1990, Global AIDS Policy, 1994, The AIDS Crisis: A Documentary History, 1998. 1st v.p., bd. dirs. Health Crisis Network, Miami, 1990-91; bd. dirs. Cure AIDS Now, Miami, 1989-95. Rsch. awards include Rwanda, 1985, Uganda, 1988, Senegal, 1992, U.S., 1995, 98, Zambia, 1989, 92-93, 97-2000. Fellow Am. Anthropol. Assn. (mem. nominations com. 2001—), Soc. Applied Anthropology; mem. APHA, AIDS & Anthropology Rsch. Group, Soc. Med. Anthropology (Solon T. Kimball award 1996), Nat. Assn. for the Practice of Anthropology (treas. 2002—).

FELDMAN, EDMUND BURKE, art critic; b. Bayonne, N.J., May 6, 1924; s. Lucian Theodore and Bertha (Seldin) F.; m. Lailah G. Link, Mar. 15, 1953; children: Eva Jeanne, Jessica Marion. B.F.A., Syracuse U., 1949; MA, UCLA, 1951; Ed.D., Columbia U., 1953. Curator painting and sculpture Newark Mus., 1953; assoc. prof. art Livingston (Ala.) State U., 1953-56, Carnegie Inst. Tech., 1956-60; head art div. State U. Coll., New Paltz, N.Y., 1960-66; vis. prof. art Ohio State U., 1966; prof. art U. Ga., Athens, 1966-91, Alumni Found. disting. prof. art, 1973-91, prof. emeritus, 1991—. Vis. prof. aesthetic edn. U. Calif., Berkeley, 1974; bd. govs. Pitts. Plan for Art, 1964-66; mem. U.S. Office Edn., Art TV Project, Whitney Mus., 1967, Ednl. Testing Svc., N.Y.C., 1969-70, Coll. Entrance Exam Bd., Princeton, N.J., 1969-70, Nat. Instructional TV Ctr., Bloomington, Ind., 1969-71; editorial cons. art Prentice-Hall, Inc. (arts and humanities Canfield Press subs. Harper & Row); advisor Ga. Coun. for arts, 1973-74, Nat. Faculty for Arts and Humanities, 1986; cons. J. Paul Getty Trust, 1981-85. Author: Art as Image and Idea, 1967, Varieties of Visual Experience, 1971, 4th edit., 1992, The Artist, 1982, 2d edit., 1994, Thinking About Art, 1985, Practical Art Criticism, 1993, Philosophy of Art Education, 1995; editor Art Bull., Ea. Arts Assn., 1957-60, Art in American Institutions, 1970; mem. editorial bd. Rev. Rsch. in Visual Arts Edn., 1975-77; mem. editorial adv. bd. Jour. Aesthetic Edn., 1976-80; chmn. editorial bd. Ga. Rev., 1977. Served with USAAF, 1942-46. Recipient Roswell Hill prize in painting Syracuse U., 1948 Fellow Nat. Art Edn. Assn. (pres. 1981-83, Disting. 1984), Royal Soc. Arts; mem. Coll. Art Assn., U.S. Soc. for Edn. Through Art, Tau Sigma Delta, Kappa Delta Pi, Kappa Pi, Phi Kappa Phi. Jewish. Home: 140 Chinquapin Pl Athens GA 30605-3314 Office: U Ga Sch Art Athens GA 30602

FELDMAN, ELAINE BOSSAK, medical nutritionist, educator; b. N.Y.C., Dec. 9, 1926; d. Solomon and Frances Helen (Fania) Nevler Bossak; m. Herman Black, Dec. 23, 1951 (div. 1957); 1 child, Mitchell Evan; m. Daniel S. Feldman, July 19, 1957; children: Susan, Daniel S. Jr. AB magna cum laude, NYU, 1945, MS, 1948, MD, 1951. Diplomate Am. Bd. Internal Medicine, Nat. Bd. Med. Examiners; cert. in Clin. Nutrition. Rotating intern Mt. Sinai Hosp., N.Y.C., 1951-52, resident in pathology, 1952, asst. resident, 1953, fellow in medicine, resident in metabolism, 1954-55, rsch. asst. in medicine, 1955-58, clin. asst. physician Diabetes Clinic, 1957; asst. vis. physician Kings County Hosp., Bklyn., 1958-66, assoc. vis. physician, 1966-72; asst. attending physician Maimonides Hosp., Bklyn., 1960-68; spl. fellow USPHS Dept. of Physiol. Chemistry U. of Lund, Sweden, 1964-65; attending physician Eugene Talmadge Meml. Hosp., Augusta, Ga., 1972-92, Univ. Hosp., Augusta, 1972-92, cons., 1973; prof. medicine Med. Coll. Ga., Augusta, 1972-92, prof. emeritus, 1992—, chief sect. of nutrition, 1977-92, chief emeritus, 1992—, acting chief sect. of metabolic/endocrine disease, 1980-81, prof. physiology and endocrinology, 1988-92, prof. emeritus physiology and endocrinology, 1992—; instr. medicine SUNY Downstate Med. Ctr., 1957-59, asst. prof. medicine, 1959-68, assoc. prof. medicine, 1968-72. Tchg. fellow dept. zoology U. Wis. Grad. Sch., 1945-46, dept. biology NYU Grad. Sch., 1946 47; cons. N.Y.-N.J. Regional Ctr. for Clin. Nutrition Edn., 1983-92; vis. prof. and Harvey lectr. Northeastern Ohio Sch. Medicine, Youngstown, 1985; cons., vis. prof. U. Nev. Sch. Medicine (NCI grant), 1989-94; mem. nat. adv. com. nutrition fellowship program Nat. Med. Fellowship Inc., 1988-95; dir. Ga. Inst. Human Nutrition, 1978-92, dir. emeritus, 1992—; dir. Clin. Nutrition Rsch. Unit, 1980-86; mem. med. nutrition curriculum initiative adv. bd. U. N.C., Chapel Hill, 1992-2001; advisor ednl. materials Am. Inst. Cancer Rsch., 1997—. Author: Essentials of Clinical Nutrition, 1988; (with others) Conference on Biological Activities of Steroids in Relation to Cancer, 1969, Nicotinic Acid, 1964, The Menopausal Syndrome, 1974, Hyperlipidemia, Medcom Special Studies, 1974, Medcom Famous Teaching in Modern Medicine, 1979, Harrison's Principles of Internal Medicine, 1980, Health Promotion: Principles and Clinical Applications, 1982, The Encyclopedic Handbook of Alcoholism, 1982, The Climacteric in Perspective, 1986, Selenium in Biology and Medicine, Part A., 1987, Medicine for the Practicing Physician, 1988, Clinical Chemistry of Laboratory Animals, 1989, Ency. Human Biology, 1991, Laboratory Medicine: The Selection and Interpretation of Clinical Laboratory Studies, 1993, Modern Nutrition in Health and Diseases, 1994, Nutrition Assessment-A Comprehensive Guide for Planning Intervention, 1995, The Women's Complete Healthbook, 1995, The American Medical Women's Association's Guide to Nutrition and Wellness, 1996, Normal Nutrition and Therapeutics, 1996, Handbook of Nutrition and Food, 2001; editor: Nutrition and Cardiovascular Disease, 1976, Nutrition in the Middle and Later Years, 1983 (paperback edit. 1986), Nutrition and Heart Disease, 1983, Handbook of Nutrition and Food, 2001, Human Nutrient Needs in the Life Cycle, 2001; mem. editl. adv. bd. Contemporary Issues in Clin. Nutrition, 1980-92; mem. edit. bd. Am. Jour. Clin. Nutrition, 1983-91, 92-98, Jour. Clin. Endocrinology and Metabolism, 1984-88, MidPoint: Counseling Women through Menopause, 1984-85, Jour. Nutrition, 1985-89; cons. editor Jour. Am. Coll. Nutrition, 1982-94; mem. edit. bd. Complementary Med. for the Physician, 1996-2000; contbg. editor Nutrition Rev., 1997-2002; mem. editl. bd. Nutrition Today, 1999—; reviewer Jour. Lipid Rsch., Biochm. Pharmacology, Sci., The Physiologist, Jour. Am. Acad. Dermatology, Israel Jour. Med. Scis., N.Y. State Jour. Medicine, Jour. of Nutrition Edn., Jour. Am. Dietetic Assn., Am. Jour. Medicine, Am. Jour. Med. Sci., So. Med. Jour., Jour. AMA, Jour. NCI; author 176 published articles in field, numerous abstracts and presentations. Mem. tech. adv. com. for sci. and edn. Rsch. Grants Program, Human Nutrition Grants Peer Panel, USDA, 1982, mem. bd. sci. counselors human nutrition; Community Svc. Block Grant Discretionary Program Panel; vice chmn. Urban and Rural Econ. Devel. Panel, Dept. HHS, 1982, grant reviewer, 1983; mem ad hoc and spl. rev. coms. and groups NIH, 1979-93, mem. nutrition study sect., 1976-80; mem. Rev. Panel Nat. Nutrition Objectives, Life Scis. Rev. Office, Fed. Am. Socs. Exptl. Biology, 1985-86; mem. subcom. Women's Health Trial Nat. Cancer Inst., 1987, mem. bd. sci. counselors cancer prevention and control program, 1990-94; mem. adv. com. Clin. Nutrition Rsch. Unit, U. Ala., 1986-94, Ga. Nutrition Steering Com., 1974-75, Ctrl. Savannah River Area Nutrition Project Coun. 1974-75, ednl. adv. com. Health Central, 1980; mem. geriatrics and gerontology rev. com. Nat. Inst. on Aging, 1986-90; breast cancer initiative peer rev. Dept. of Def., 1997, 98. N.Y. Heart Assn. rsch. fellow, 1955-57. Fellow Am. Heart Assn. Coun. on Atherosclerosis (nominating com. 1978, chmn. nominating com., mem. exec. com. 1979-80, Spl. Recognition award 1995), Am. Inst. Nutrition (grad. nutrition edn. com. 1980-83, 89-93); mem. Am. Coll. Nutrition (chmn. com. pub. affairs), Am. Soc. for Clin. Nutrition (com. on nutrition edn. 1982, chmn. subcom. on nutrition edn. in med. schs. 1983-84, chmn. com. on med./dental residency edn., 1985-87, com. on subsplty. tng. 1988-92, nominating com. 1982, 90, chair nominating com. 1994, com. on clin. practice issues in health and disease 1989-92, Nat. Dairy Coun. award 1991, rep. coun. acad. socs. 1990-96, membership com. 1996—, chair 1999, 2000), Fedn. Am. Socs. Exptl. Biology. Am. Oil Chemists Soc., Am. Physiol. Soc., Endocrine Soc., Soc. Exptl. Biology and Medicine, So. Soc. Clin. Investigation, Am. Diabetes Assn., Am. Fedn. Clin. Rsch., Am. Gastroent. Assn., AMA (Joseph B. Goldberger award 1990), Am. Med. Women's Assn. (profl. resources com. 1975-76, med. edn. and rsch. fund com. 1976-79, chmn. 1978-90, chmn. student liaison subcom. of membership com. 1981-84, pres. Br. 51, Augusta 1977-80, treas. 1980-97, Calcium Nutrition Edn. award 1991, CSRA Girl Scout Women of Excellence award 1994), Am. Soc. Parenteral and Enteral Nutrition, Am. Heart Assn. (Ga. affiliate, nutrition com., chmn. sci. session for nutritionists, 1978, chmn. nutrition com. 1979-90, mem. long range planning com. 1980-81, rsch. com. 1980-83, bd. dirs. 1987-90, profl. edn. task force, 1988-89), Richmond Country Med. Assn., Augusta Opera Assn. (bd. dirs. 1973—, recording sec. 1973-74, pres. 1974-75, coord. audience devel. 1975-77, at-large exec. com. 1994-96, chair nominating com. 1994-96, corr. sec. 1998-99, 1st v.p. 1999-2000, chair search com., gen. dir. 2002), Augusta Sailing Club (women's com. 1973), Greater Augusta Arts Coun. (Arts Festival Collage 1982 chmn. promotion and publicity com., Festival coms. 1983-86, 89-93, 95, 96, 98, 99, bd. dirs. 1984-94, Vol. of the Yr., 2001), Gertrude Herbert Inst. Art (bd. dirs. 1987-92), Authors Club Augusta, Philomathic Club (sec. 1999—), Phi Beta Kappa, Sigma Xi (chpt. sec. 1982-83, pres. elect 1983-84, pres. 1984-85), Alpha Omega Alpha. Avocations: opera, wine tasting, travel. Home: 2123 Cumming Rd Augusta GA 30904-4333 E-mail: efeldman7@comcast.net.

FELDMAN, ELDA BEYLERIAN, lawyer; b. Beirut, Nov. 14, 1966; d. Hagop Garbis and Jacqueline Beylerian. BA, Yale U., 1988; JD, Rutgers U., Newark, 1991. Bar: N.J. 1991, U.S. Dist. Ct. N.J. 1991, N.Y. 1992, U.S. Dist. Ct. (so. and ea. dists.) N.Y. 1996. Clk. Hon. Geoffrey Gaulkin presiding judge of N.J. Superior Ct.-Appellate Divsn., Jersey City, 1991-92; assoc. Varet Marcus & Fink, N.Y.C., 1992-93, Budd Larner Gross Rosenbaum Greenberg & Sade, Short Hills, N.J., 1993-96; first liaison to Republic of Armenia ABA Ctrl. and East European Law Initiative, Washington, 1996-97; assoc. LeBoeuf Lamb Greene & MacRae, Newark, 1997—2002; v.p., assoc. gen. counsel Everest Reinsurance Co., Liberty Corner, NJ, 2002—. Editor-in-chief Women's Rights Law Reporter, 1990-91. Armenian Apostolic. Office: Everest Reinsurance Co PO Box 830 477 Martinsville Rd Liberty Corner NJ 07938-0830 Fax: 908-604-3450.

FELDMAN, EVA LUCILLE, neurology educator; b. N.Y.C., Mar. 30, 1952; d. George Franklin and Margherita Enriceta (Cafiero) F.; children: Laurel, Scott, John Jr. BA in Biology and Chemistry, Earlham Coll., 1973; MS in Zoology, U. Notre Dame, 1975; PhD in Neurosci., U. Mich., 1979, MD, 1983. Diplomate Am. Bd. Neurology; lic. med. practitioner, Mich. Instr. dept. neurology U. Mich., Ann Arbor, 1987-88, asst. prof. neurology, 1988-94, mem. faculty Cancer Ctr., 1992-2000, assoc. prof. neurology, 1994-2000, prof., 2000. Mem. faculty neurosci. program U. Mich., Mich. Diabetes Rsch. and Tng., Ann Arbor, 1988—; dir. JDRF Ctr. for the Study of Complications in Diabetes. Author (book chpts.) Diabetes in the New Millenium, 1999, Cecil's Textbook of Medicine, 2000; contbr. articles to profl. jours. Grantee, NIH, 1989, 1994, 1997, 1998, 2001, Juvenile Diabetes Inst., 1994, 1997, 1999, 2001. Avocation: research on the elucidation of the role of growth factors in the pathogenesis of human disease. Office: Dept Neurology U Mich 200 Zina Pitcher Pl Rm 4144 Ann Arbor MI 48109-2205

FELDMAN, FRANKLIN, lawyer, printmaker; b. N.Y.C., Nov. 12, 1927; s. Reuben and Anne (Schulman) F.; m. Naomi Goldstein, June 3, 1956; children: Sarah, Eve, Jacob. BA, NYU, 1948; LLB, Columbia U., 1951. Bar: N.Y. 1952. Mem. office Gen. Counsel, USAF, Dept. Def., Washington, 1951-53; atty. office gen. counsel to gov. State of N.Y., Albany, 1954; assoc. Stroock & Stroock & Lavan, N.Y.C., 1955-64, ptnr., 1965-88, counsel, 1989—. Cons. Temp. N.Y. Commn. on Constl. Conv., 1967; lectr. in law Columbia Law Sch., 1979-2001. Editor-in-chief Columbia U. Law Rev., 1950-51; author: (with Stephen E. Weil) Art Works: Law, Policy and Practice, 1974, Art Law, 1986 (Best Law Book Published in 1986, Scribes); contbr. articles to profl. jours. Trustee Am. Jewish Hist. Soc., Waltham, Mass., 1987-96. 1st lt., USAF, 1951-53. Yaddo Fellow, Saratoga Springs, 1983. Fellow Am. Bar Found. (life); mem. N.Y. State Bar Assn., Assn. of Bar of City of N.Y. (chmn. art com. 1968-71), Internat. Found. Art Rsch. (pres. 1971-76, bd. dirs. 1976-96), Ltd., Soc. Am. Graphic Artists, Century Assn., Pvt. Art Dealers Assn., Inc. (counsel, dir. 1993—), Grolier Club. Jewish. Home: 15 W 81st St New York NY 10024-6022 Office: Stroock & Stroock & Lavan 180 Maiden Ln Fl 17 New York NY 10038-4937 E mail. feldmanf@aol.com.

FELDMAN, FRIEDA, physician; m. Rubem Pochaczevsky. MD, NYU. Diplomate Am. Bd. Radiology. Prof. radiology & orthopedics Columbia U. Coll. Physicians and Surgeons, N.Y.C., 1962—; attending radiologist N.Y. Presbyn. Med. Ctr., N.Y.C., 1962—. Contbr. articles to profl. jours. Fellow Am. Coll. Radiology; mem. Radiologic Soc. N.Am., Am. Roentgen Ray Soc., N.Y. Acad. Medicine, N.Y. State Radiol. Soc., Internat. Skeletal Soc. (charter). Office: NY Presby Med Ctr Dept Radiology 622 W 168th St New York NY 10032-3720

FELDMAN, GARY MARC, nutritionist, consultant; b. Bklyn., Dec. 3, 1953; m. Debra Lynn Bieler, Sept. 21, 1984. Diploma in Sci. of Nutritional Cons., Am. Nutrition Cons. Assn., 1986. Pres. Steps In Health, Ltd., Douglaston, N.Y., 1986-88, Margate, Fla., 1988-90, Nesconset, N.Y., 1990—. Educator for children in sci. of food and nutritional supplementation. Developer: Steps in Health Ltd.'s Catalogue of Vegetarian Name-Brand Nutritional Supplements and Health Products; author nutrition newsletter. Vol. listen to children program Mental Health Assn. and Vol. Program Broward County (Fla.) Pub. Schs., 1989; arbitration participant Better Bus. Bur. South Fla., 1989-90. Mem. AAAS, Am. Nutrition Cons. Assn., Life Extension Found., Pub. Citizen Health Rsch. Group, People for Ethical Treatment of Animals, Doris Day Animal League, Humane Soc. Broward County, Ctr. for Sci. in the Pub. Interest, Internat. Platform Assn., N.Y. State Sheriffs Assn., L.I. Assn. Inc., Herb Rsch. Found., Vegetarian Resource Group, N.Am. Vegetarian Soc., Nutritionists Health Am. (nutrition edn. program com.), Ctr. Sci. Pub. Interest (edn. com.), Feingold Assn., U.S. Co-op Am. Bus. Network, N.Y. Acad. Scis. Avocations: reading and data collection in health field, bodybuilding. Office: PO Box 220123 Great Neck NY 11022-0123

FELDMAN, HELAINE, editor, public relations associate; b. Brooklyn, NY, June 22, 1937; d. Joseph H. and Ruth Levine; m. Chester Feldman, Aug. 6, 1961; children: Jeffrey, David. BS, Syracuse Univ., Syracuse, NY, 1958. Assoc. editor Dick Moore & Assoc., Inc., New York, NY, 1966—, sr. assoc., 1966—. Contbg. editor: (newsletter) Equity News, 1975, Aftra Mag., 1990. Mem.: Drama Desk, Coalition of Profl. Women in the Arts & Media, League of Profl. Theatre Women. Home: 144-09 Coolidge Ave Briarwood NY 11435 Office: Dick Moore & Assoc 165 W 46th St New York NY 10036

FELDMAN, HOWARD WILLIAM, lawyer; b. Chgo., July 18, 1946; s. Nathan and Sylvia (Greenberg) F.; m. Beryl Dale Fruchter, July 12, 1970; children: Neal J. (dec.), Stephen D., Shira B. BS, Purdue U., 1968; JD, Ind. U., 1973. Bar: Ill. 1973, U.S. Dist. Ct. (cen. dist.) Ill. 1975, U.S. Ct. Appeals (7th cir.) 1975, U.S. Supreme Ct. 1977. Asst. atty. gen. Office Ill. Atty. Gen., Springfield, 1973-79; gen. counsel Capital Deve. Bd., 1979-82; pvt. practice, 1982-86; ptnr. Feldman & Wasser, 1987-95, Feldman, Wasser, Draper & Benson, 1996—. Mem. Springfield Human Rights Commn., 1986—93, Ill. Devel. Fin. Authority, 1999—2002; chmn. Springfield Fair Housing Bd., 1986—93. Mem.: ABA, Ill. State Bar Assn. (bd. govs. 1999—, sec. 2003—). Jewish. Avocations: amateur radio, woodworking. Office: Feldman Wasser Draper & Benson 1307 S 7th St Springfield IL 62703-2460

FELDMAN, IRVING, poet; b. Bklyn., Sept. 22, 1928; m. Carmen Alvarez del Olmo, 1955; 1 son, Fernando R. Ed., CCNY, Columbia U. Formerly prof. English U. P.R., Rio Piedras, Kenyon Coll., Gambier, O.; disting. prof. English State U. N.Y., Buffalo, 1964—. Author: Works and Days, 1961, The Pripet Marshes, 1965, Magic Papers, 1970, Lost Originals, 1972, Leaping Clear, 1976, New and Selected Poems, 1979, Teach Me, Dear Sister, 1983, All of Us Here, 1986, The Life and Letters, 1994, Beautiful False Things, 2000; contbr. to periodicals. Recipient poetry prize Jewish Book Coun. Am., 1962, award Nat. Inst. and AAAL, 1973; Ingram Merrill Found. grantee, 1963, N.Y. State Creative Artists Pub. Svc. grantee, 1980; Guggenheim fellow, 1973, Acad. Am. Poets fellow, 1986, MacArthur fellow, 1992; grantee Nat. Endowment for the Arts, 1987. Home: 284 Richmond Ave Buffalo NY 14222 Office: SUNY Dept English Buffalo NY 14260-0001

FELDMAN, JACK L. neurobiology educator; b. Bklyn., Jan. 6, 1948; s. Norman Feldman; m. Courtney Heckman, June 15, 1977; children: Ion Isaac, Ilya Björn, Dylan Jacob. BS, Poly. Inst. Bklyn., 1968; PhD, U. Chgo., 1973. Rsch. assoc. U. Paris VI, 1973-74; instr., then asst. prof. Yeshiva U. Albert Einstein Coll. Medicine, Bronx, N.Y., 1975-78, asst. prof., assoc. prof., then prof. dept. physiology Northwestern U., Chgo., 1978-86; prof. dept. physiol. sci. UCLA, 1986—2002, Edith Agnes Plumb prof., chmn. dept. neurobiology, 1996—2001, prof. dept. neurobiology, 1996—, chmn. dept. physiol. sci., 1991-97. Vis. scientist Karolinska Inst., Stockholm, 1982-83. Mem. Soc. for Neurosci., Am. Physiol. Soc. E-mail: feldman@ucla.edu.

FELDMAN, JAY NEWMAN, lawyer, telecommunications executive; b. N.Y.C., Nov. 11, 1936; s. Morris Kenneth and Della (Newman) F.; m. Nancy Tobias, Dec. 7, 1963; children— Nina Cheryl, Karen Elise. AB with high honors in History magna cum laude, Colgate U., 1958; JD, Harvard U., 1961. Bar: N.Y. 1962, U.S. Dist. Ct. (so. and ea. dists.) N.Y. 1962. Assoc. Jacobs Persinger and Parker, N.Y.C., 1961-68; sec., treas., gen. counsel Lynch Corp., N.Y.C., 1968-69; counsel Allied Artists Industries, Inc., N.Y.C., 1970-80, sec., 1970-76, v.p., 1975-76, v.p. adminstrn., 1976-77, group v.p., 1977-80, dir., 1973-80; sec. Allied Artists Pictures Corp., 1973-74, dir., 1974-80; v.p., sec., dir. Allied Artists Video Corp., 1978-80; resident counsel Lorimar Prodns., Inc., N.Y.C., 1980-83; gen. corp. atty. NYNEX Corp., White Plains, N.Y., 1983-94; sec. NYNEX Devel. Co., White Plains, N.Y., 1984-87, NYNEX Internat. Co., White Plains, N.Y., 1985-87, Data Group Corp., White Plains, N.Y., 1985-87, NYNEX Info. Solutions Group Inc., White Plains, N.Y., 1987, NYNEX Sci. & Tech., Inc., White Plains, N.Y., 1991, NYNEX Venture Co., White Plains, N.Y., 1992-94. Sec., counsel, dir. PSP, Inc., 1970-76; sec., dir. D. Kaltman & Co., Inc., 1970-79, v.p., 1977-79; sec., dir. Vitabath, Inc., 1970-72, Apollo Motor Homes, Inc., 1970-80, v.p., 1977-80; sec., dir. Westwood Import Co., Inc., 1972-79, v.p., 1977-79; sec., dir. Paul-Marshall Products Inc., 1972-75, Adstat Co., 1972-74; v.p., dir. Palmland Fashions, Inc., 1971-78; mem. com. on criminal cts. Legal Aid Soc., 1969-72. Trustee Temple Beth Israel, Port Washington, N.Y., 1981-83, 87-89, rec. sec., 1983-85, fin. sec., 1985-87. Mem. ABA, N.Y. State Bar Assn., Am. Law Inst., Corp. Bar Assn. Westchester-Fairfield (co-chmn. SEC corp. and fin. com. 1989-90, bd. dirs. 1991-93, chmn. major program com. 1991, co-chmn. 1992-93), Phi Beta Kappa. Home: 61 Roger Dr Port Washington NY 11050-2527 *Dare to be different - the path to success is the road least travelled.*

FELDMAN, JEFFREY MARC, lawyer; b. Providence, Nov. 8, 1949; s. Samuel and Shirley (Halpern) F.; m. Marjorie Burrows, Aug. 15, 1971; children: Peter, James. BA, Northeastern U., Boston, 1972, JD, 1975. Bar: Alaska 1976, U.S. Dist. Ct. Alaska 1976, R.I. 1976, U.S. Dist. Ct. R.I. 1976, U.S. Ct. Appeals (9th cir.) 1976, U.S. Supreme Ct. 1980. Law clk. Alaska Supreme Ct., Anchorage, 1975-76; asst. pub. defender Alaska Pub. Defender Office, Anchorage, 1976-78; mem. Gilmore & Feldman, Anchorage, 1978-90, Young, Sanders & Feldman, 1991—; mem. Supreme Ct. Com. on Pattern Jury Instrns., 1979-85, Alaska Com. Bar Examiners, 1981-86; chmn. Supreme Ct. on Criminal Rules, 1984-90; atty. rep. Jud. Conf. 9th Cir. Ct. Appeals, 1983-87; reporter Dist. of Alaska Adv. Group for Civil Justice Reform Act of 1990, 1991—. Contbr. articles to profl. jours. Mem. ABA, Am. Judicature Soc., Assn. Trial Lawyers Am., Am. Bd. Trial Advocates, Nat. Assn. Criminal Def. Lawyers, Alaska Acad. Trial Lawyers, R.I. Bar Assn., Alaska Bar Assn. (mem. bd. govs. 1986-92, pres. 1989-90), Anchorage Bar Assn. Home: 1014 H St Anchorage AK 99501-3431 Office: Young Sanders & Feldman 500 L St Ste 400 Anchorage AK 99501-5911

FELDMAN, JEROME IRA, lawyer, patent development executive; b. N.Y.C., July 17, 1928; s. George and Tanya (Rubenstein) F.; m. Terry Jean Harmon, Oct. 23, 1964; children: Rebecca Page, Michael Dana, Kyra Joelle, Sarah Allison. BA, Ind. U., 1949; LLB, JD, NYU, 1951, PhD (hon.), 1990. Bar: N.Y. 1951. Ptnr. Feldman & Pollak, N.Y.C., 1953-60; pres., CEO Nat. Patent Devel. Corp., N.Y.C., 1959—; bd. dirs. GP Strategies Corp., N.Y.C. Chmn., bd. dirs. Global Simulation and Engring. Sys. Inc.; chmn. bd. 5 Star Products. Chmn. New Eng. Colls. Fund.; trustee No. Westchester Hosp. Mem. N.Y State Bar Assn. Office: GP Strategies Corp 9 W 57th St Ste 4170 New York NY 10019-2795

FELDMAN, JOEL MARTIN, magistrate judge; b. Atlanta, Jan. 2, 1941; s. Louis Aaron and Rosalie (Bach) F.; m. Debora A. Kirkpatrick; children: Lawrence A., Allison R. AB in Law, Emory U., 1962, JD, 1964. Bar: Ga. 1963, U.S. Dist. Ct. (no. dist.) Ga. 1963, U.S. Ct. Mil. Appeals 1964, U.S. Ct. Appeals (5th cir.) 1963, U.S. Ct. Appeals (11th cir.) 1981, U.S. Supreme Ct. 1967. Asst. legis. counsel Gen. Assembly Ga., Atlanta, 1964-66; asst. atty. gen. State of Ga., Atlanta, 1966-68; asst. dist. atty. Atlanta Jud. Cir., 1968-72, 74; legis. asst., legal counsel Sen. Sam Nunn of Ga., 1973-74; magistrate U.S. Dist. Ct. (no. dist.) Ga., Atlanta, 1974—; cert. mil. judge Naval-Marine Corps Trial Judiciary, 1982-92. Former chmn. North Fulton Citizens Mental Health Adv. Coun.; pres. Temple Sinai Synagogue, Atlanta, 1994-96; chmn. Met. Atlanta 50th Ann. WWII Commemorative Cmty. With USAFR, 1964, capt. USNR, 1964-92. Mem. Fed. Bar Assn., State Bar Ga., Atlanta Bar Assn., Naval League U.S. (pres. Atlanta coun. 1985-86), Naval Res. Assn. (pres. 6th Dist. 1982-83), Fed. Magistrate Judges Assn. (dir. 11th cir. 1982-83), Atlanta Lawyers Club, Navy League (Atlanta dir., pres.), Naval Order (Atlanta pres., dir.). Office: 2027 US Courthouse 75 Spring St SW Atlanta GA 30303-3309

FELDMAN, JOEL SHALOM, mathematician; b. Ottawa, Ont., Can., June 14, 1949; s. Keiva and Anna (Ain) F. BS, U. Toronto, Ont., 1970; AM, Harvard U., 1971, PhD, 1974. Rsch. fellow Harvard U., Cambridge, Mass., 1974-75; Moore instr. MIT, Cambridge, 1975-77; prof. U. B.C., Vancouver, Can., 1977—;

Aisenstadt chair lectr., Ctr. Rsch. Math. U. Montréal, 1999—2000. Assoc. editor Revs. Math. Physics, 1988—, Can. Jour. Math., 1994-98, Can. Math. Bull., 1994-98, Math Phys. EJ, 1995—, Ann. Henri Poincaré, 2000—; contbr. articles to profl. jours. Recipient Killam Rsch. prize U. B.C., 1988; Woodrow Wilson fellow, 1970. Fellow Royal Soc. Can. (John L. Synge award). Office: U BC Dept Math Vancouver BC Canada V6T 1Z2

FELDMAN, LEONARD CECIL, physicist; b. N.Y.C., June 8, 1939; s. Milton and Minnie (Schulman) F.; m. Elizabeth Gecsey, July 5, 1964; children: Gregory, Dana. MS, Rutgers U., 1963, PhD, 1967. Mem. tech. staff radiation physics rsch. dept. AT&T Bell Labs., Murray Hill, N.J., 1967-83, supr. materials interfaces, 1983-84, dept. head materials interfaces and ceramics, 1984-87, dept. head thin film semicondr. rsch., 1987-90, dept. head silicon device rsch., 1990-92, dept. head silicon materials rsch., 1992-96; Stevenson prof. physics Vanderbilt U., Nashville, 1996—. Guest scientist Aarhus (Denmark) U., 1970-71; vis. prof. Cornell U., Ithaca, N.Y., 1981, 82, 88; cons. Livermore (Calif.) Nat. Lab., 1989—; chmn. Gordon Conf. on Particle Solid Interactions, 1978, Gordon Conf. on Defects in Semicondrs., 1994; chmn. internal sci. coun. Danish Microelectronics Ctr.; mem. adv. com. N.J. Inst. Tech., Colo. Sch. Mines, Livermore Nat. Labs.; disting. vis. scientist Oak Ridge Nat. Lab., 1996—. Co-author: Materials Analysis by Ion Channeling, 1982, Fundamentals of Surface and Thin Film Analysis, 1986 (transl. into Japanese 1988, Russian, 1989), Electronic Thin Film Science, 1992; editor Applied Surface Sci., 1985-96; contbr. over 300 articles on semiconductor interface sci. to sci. jours. Recipient Disting. Merit award in material sci. and engring. U. Ill., 1989, sci. alumni award Drew U., 1995. Fellow Am. Phys. Soc. (David Aller award 1999), Am. Vacuum Soc.; mem. IEEE, Materials Rsch. Soc., Am. Ceramic Soc., Danish Acad. Arts and Scis. Achievements include patent on semiconductor heterostructures having GexSi1-x layers, 20 others in thin films; discovery of structure of clean silicon surfaces; first demonstration of preservation of surface structures at buried interfaces; developement of technique of Rutherford Scattering for surface and interface analysis. Home: 510 Belgrave Park Nashville TN 37215-2450 Office: Vanderbilt Univ Dept Physics and Astronomy Nashville TN 37235

FELDMAN, LES J. finance educator; b. Miami, Aug. 25, 1946; s. Sidney Feldman and Sophie Suda; children: Joshua, Jessie, Amy. AA, Miami Dade North Jr. Coll., 1969; BS in Sci., Fla. Atlantic U., 1971; MBA, Nova Southeastern U., 1991, Doctorate in Bus. Adminstrn., 1996. Cert. tchr. Fla., purchasing mgr. Purchasing mgr. Motorola, Inc., Ft. Lauderdale, Fla., 1981—; instr. Everglades Coll., Ft. Lauderdale, 2002, Fla. Atlantic U., Ft. Lauderdale, 1996—2001. Contbr. articles to profl. jours., chapters to books. Mem.: Acad. Mgmt. Home: 1780 SW 55th Ave Fort Lauderdale FL 33317

FELDMAN, LILLIAN MALTZ, early childhood education consultant; b. N.Y.C. d. Jacob and Ida (Burko) Maltz; m. Harry A. Feldman (dec. Jan. 1985); children: Ronald, Donna Feldman Weisman, Jeffrey, Robert. AB, George Washington U., 1937, MA, 1939; EdD in Early Childhood Edn., Syracuse U., 1987; HLD (hon.), SUNY, 1993. Cert. tchr., guidance counselor, sch. adminstr., N.Y. Elem. sch. guidance counselor Syracuse (N.Y.) Sch. Dist., 1963-65, Kindergarten tchr., 1957-63, dir. early children edn., 1965-83; dir. Syracuse Head Start, summers 1968-70; cons. early childhood edn. Syracuse, 1985—. Adj. instr. child, family and community studies Syracuse U., 1988-89, adj. prof. child and family studies, 1990-91. Author invited papers in early child devel. and care, 1988, 89, 95, 96. Adv. com. network adv. bd. Dr. Martin Luther King Jr. Cmty. Sch., Syracuse, 1988—. Named Woman of Achievement in Edn., Post-Standard, Syracuse, 1969; recipient Hannah G. Solomon Award Nat. Coun. Jewish Women, Syracuse, 1979, Honoree Na'amat USA 1988, Friend of Children award Women's Commn. Task Force on Children, 1992. Mem. Syracuse Assn. for Edn. Young Children (Outstanding Early Childhood Educator award 1984), Consortium for Children's Svcs. (Silver Dove award 1985, Friend of Family award 1992), Onondaga County Child Care Coun. (Community Svc. award 1983, Friend of Children award 1992), Delta Kappa Gamma, Phi Delta Kappa. Democrat.

FELDMAN, MARION, musician, music educator; b. Bklyn., Mar. 17, 1940; d. Benjamin and Sadie Goldberg Feldman. BS, Juilliard Sch. Music, 1960, MS, 1962. Cello and chamber music prof. Bklyn. Coll., CCNY, N.Y.C., 1972—; cello faculty City Univ. Grad. Ctr., N.Y.C., 1980—; cello and chamber music faculty Manhattan Sch. Music, N.Y.C., 1982—, NYU, N.Y.C., 1998—, dir. Summer String Quartet Program, 2001—. Instr. master classes in cello Korea Dae Jin U., Republic of Korea, 1998—, Taiwan Am. Sch., 1998—, Shanghai Conservatory Music, 2002—, Beijing Ctrl. Conservatory, 2003. Leader Soka Gakkai Internat./USA Peace Orgn./V.I.C.P., 1973—. Recipient Soka Edn. award, Soka Gakkai Internat./USA, 2000—; fellow, Aspen Festival, 1960—; scholar, Juilliard Sch., N.Y.C., 1956—. Mem.: Violincello Soc. (bd. mem. 1995—). Avocations: coin collecting, instrument collecting, photography. Home: 248 W 88th St #9B New York NY 10024 Office: Manhattan Sch Music 120 Claremont Ave New York NY 10027

FELDMAN, MARK, lawyer; b. Bklyn., Aug. 28, 1940; s. James and Beatrice Irene (Borowick) Feldman; m. Barbara L. Lifton, June 15, 1963; children: James, David. AB, Columbia Coll., 1962; LLB, Columbia U., 1965. Bar: N.Y. 1965, U.S. Dist. Ct. (so. dist.) N.Y. 1976. Asst. state atty. gen., NYC, 1968—. With Tchrs. Ins. And Annuity Assn.-Coll. Retirement Equities Fund, NYC, 1968—, assoc. gen. counsel, 1979—. Contbr. chapters to books, articles to profl. jours. Mem.: ABA (life ins. com. of TIPS sect. 1978—), Assn. of Life Ins. Counsel, Nat. Assn. Coll. and Univ. Attys., N.Y.C. Bar Assn., N.Y. State Bar Assn. (com. on life, health and accident ins. of INCL sect. 1971—), U.S. Power Squadrons (squadron comdr. 1985—86), Sheldrake Yacht Club (Mamoroneck, N.Y.). Home: 93 Rose Ave Tuckahoe NY 10707-3835 Office: 730 3rd Ave New York NY 10017-3206

FELDMAN, MARK B. lawyer; b. Rochester, N.Y., Oct. 3, 1935; s. Edward P. and Grace Feldman; m. Marcia Smith, Nov. 23, 1963; children: Ilana, Rachel. AB, Wesleyan U., 1957; LLB, Harvard U., 1960. Bar: N.Y. 1961, D.C. 1974. Assoc. Kaye, Scholer, Fierman, Hays & Handler, N.Y.C., 1960-65; with Office Legal Adviser, Dept. State, 1965-81, dep. legal adviser, 1974-81, acting legal adviser, 1981; of counsel Donovan, Leisure, Newton & Irvine, Washington, 1981-84, ptnr., 1984-87; mem. Feith & Zell, P.C., 1988—2001; of counsel Garvey, Schubert & Barer, 2002—. Adj. prof. Georgetown U., Washington, 1982—89. Mem.: ABA, Am. Soc. Internat. Law, Coun. Fgn. Rels. Address: 4010 48th St NW Washington DC 20016-2318

FELDMAN, MARVIN HERSCHEL, financial consultant; b. East Liverpool, Ohio, Dec. 1, 1945; s. Ben and Freda (Zaremberg) F.; m. Vicki Jo Smith, Mar. 18, 1967; children: Terri Nicole, Barbi Lynn. BS, Ohio State U., 1967. CLU, chartered fin. cons. Agt. N.Y. Life Ins. Co., Columbus, Ohio, 1967-69, 74—, asst. mgr., 1969-74; ptnr. Feldman Agy., East Liverpool, 1974—; corp. sec., v.p. Fremar Corp., East Liverpool, 1974—; pres. Fremar Mgmt. Co., Youngstown, 1975-89, Fremar Fin. Group, East Liverpool, 1983—; mng. exec. Royal Alliance Assocs., Inc., East Liverpool, 1983—2003; reg. rep. Valmark Securities, Inc., 2003—. Foundding dir. 1st Nat. Community Bank, East Liverpool, Ohio, 1987—; mem., sec. agt. adv. coun. N.Y. Life, N.Y.C., 1985-86; speaker in field. Contbr. articles to profl. jours. Chmn. United Jewish Appeal, East Liverpool, 1976—, v.p., sec. Temple Beth Shalom, East Liverpool; mem. Econ. Devel. Com., East Liverpool; bd. dirs. East Liverpool City Hosp., 1992-2001, chmn., 1998-99. Mem. Nat. Assn. Ins. and Fin. Advisors, Am. Soc. Fin. Svc. Profls., Fin. Planners Assn., Assn. Advanced Life Underwriters, Million Dollar Round Table (life, v.p. divsn. 1985-86, ann. meeting chmn. 1998, exec. com. 1998-2003, pres. 2002), Top of the Table (bd. dirs. 1982-87, chmn. 1985-86). Republican. Avocations: golf, reading, sports car racing, boating. Office: The Feldman Agy PO Box 30 16569 Saint Clair Ave East Liverpool OH 43920-9123 E-mail: tfa@financialprtnr.com.

FELDMAN, MAX, insurance executive; b. Newark, Jan. 24, 1935; s. Daniel J. and E. Ruth (Fast) F.; m. Bernita Braha, June 14, 1959; children: Alan, Renee. BBA cum laude, U. Miami, Coral Gables, Fla., 1956; MA, Western Mich. U., 1958. Ins. agt. The Feldman Agy., Bloomfield, N.J., 1958—. Owner Rotisserie baseball team. Sec. Congregation Ahawas Achim B'nai Jacob and David, West Orange, N.J., 1963-93, dir. emeritus 1993—, pres. Men's Club, 1970-80; chmn. Israel Bond Campaign, West Orange, 1971-80; mem. West Orange Dem. Com., 1974-82. Master sgt. USAR, 1952-59, Korea. Mem. Profl. Ins. Agts., Ind. Ins. Agts., N.J. Ins. Brokers Assn., N.J. U. Miami Alumni Assn. (pres. 1972-74), West Orange Current Affairs Club, Huntington Lakes Tennis Club, B'nai B'rith. Avocations: tennis, travel, reading, golf. Home: 10 Wessman Dr West Orange NJ 07052-2809 Office: The Feldman Agy Inc PO Box 1069 1246 Broad St Bloomfield NJ 07003-3031 E-mail: feldins@comcast.net.

FELDMAN, MICHAEL SAUL, cardiologist, educator; b. Phila., Dec. 25, 1941; s. Jack and Faye Leah (Romisher) F.; m. Nini R. Feldman. BS, Temple U., 1963; MD, Hahnemann U., 1967. Diplomate Am. Bd. Internat. Medicine, subspecialty in cardiovascular disease. Intern medicine Hahnemann U., Phila., 1967-68, resident in internal medicine, 1968-70, fellow in cardiology, 1970-72; clin. asst. prof. medicine dept. medicine U. Pa. Sch. Medicine, 1972-79, clin. assoc. prof. medicine dept. medicine, 1979—; prof. medicine Med. Coll. Pa. and Hahnemann U., 1996—. Cons. in cardiology Dept. Medicine Meml. Hosp. Roxborough, Phila., 1972-80, Einstein So. Divsn., Phila., 1972-89, Met. Hosp., Phila., 1972-89; dir. non-invasive cardiac lab. Presbyn. Med. Ctr., Phila., 1972-80; dir. divsn. cardiology Grad. Hosp., Phila., 1974-78, 2001—, dir. med. edn., 2001—; dir. electrocardiography and electrophysiology Mid-Atlantic Heart and Vascular Inst., Presbyn. Med. Ctr., Phila., 1980-84, dir. cardiology svcs., 1984-86, dir. atherosclerotic cardiovascular laser rsch., 1983-86; dir. cardiology svcs. Phila. Heart Inst., Presbyn. Med. Ctr., Phila., 1986-95; dir. atherosclerotic cardiovascular laser rsch. Phila. Heart Inst., 1986-91; investigator in field. Fellow Am. Coll. Cardiology, Am. Fedn. Clin. Rsch., Coun. on Cardiology, Coun. on Atherosclerosis, Coun. on Circulation, Laennec Soc., Am. Heart Assn.; mem. Phila. Acad. Cardiology (founder). Address: 1800 Lombard St # 802 Philadelphia PA 19146-1498 Office: # 802 1800 Lombard St Philadelphia PA 19146-1498

FELDMAN, MIRIAM BERNICE, social worker; b. N.Y.C., May 16, 1933; d. Louis Leon and Rose (Berkowitz) Reiner; m. Samuel (Mitchell) Feldman, Sept. 16, 1954 (div. 1978); children: Lee Stephen, David Saul. BA, U. Pa., 1954; MSW, McGill U., Montreal, Can., 1958. Diplomate in clin. social work, Am. bd. examiners. Asst. dir. group homes Abbott House, Irvington, N.Y., 1974-77; adminstrv. supr. Jewish Bd. of Family & Child Svcs., N.Y.C., 1978-79; instr. field work NYU Sch. Social Work, N.Y.C., 1978-79; asst. dir. of svcs. to developmentally disabled Jewish Child Care Assn., N.Y.C., 1980-82; supr. Louise Wise, N.Y.C., 1982-83; social worker Mamaroneck (N.Y.) Bd. Edn., 1983-85; family social worker George Jr. Republic, Freeville, N.Y., 1986-87; social worker N.Y. Assn. for New Ams., N.Y.C., 1988-89; psychotherapist Family Inst., Albuquerque, 1989-90; social worker St. Joseph's Rehab. Ctr., Albuquerque, 1990-92; clin. social worker, instr. family therapy U. N.Mex. Children's Psychiat. Hosp., 1992-98; social worker pvt. practice, 1999—. Mem. NASW, Acad. Cert. Social Workers. Home: 5211 Ironwood Dr NW Albuquerque NM 87114-4627 E-mail: miriambill@webtv.net.

FELDMAN, MYER, lawyer; b. Phila., June 1917; s. Israel and Bella (Kurland) F.; m. Adrienne Arsht, Sept. 28, 1980; children by previous marriage: Jane Margaret, James Alan. Student, Girard Coll., Phila., 1922-31; BS in Econs., U. Pa., 1935, LL.B. (fellow 1938-39), 1938. Bar: Pa. 1938, D.C. 1965, U.S. Supreme Ct. 1965. Pvt. practice, Phila. and D.C., 1939-42, 65—; spl. counsel, exec. asst. to chmn. SEC, 1946-54; mem. counsel armed svcs. com. U.S. Senate, 1954-55, counsel banking and currency commn., 1955-57; legis. asst. to Senator John F. Kennedy, 1958-61; dep. spl. counsel to Presidents Kennedy and Johnson, 1961-64; counsel to Pres. Johnson, 1964-65; founder, ptnr. Ginsburg Feldman & Bress, Washington, 1965-98; pres. Ardman Broadcasting Corp., 1992—. Pres. S.W. Fla. Broadcasting, KEFCO Apparel Corp.; lectr. law U. Pa., 1941-42; prof. law Am. U., 1955-56; pres. Radio Assocs., Inc., 1959-81; dir. Music Fair Group, Inc.; chmn. bd. Fin. Satellite Corp.; partner Key Stas., 1960-79; chmn. bd. Speer Publs., 1972-77, Capital Gazette Press, Inc., 1972-77, Bay Publs., 1972-77; bd. dirs. Nat. Savs. & Trust Co., Flame Hope, Inc., Media and Art Svcs., Inc., WSSH, Inc., Internat. Fusion Energy Systems Co., Inc., WLLH Broadcasters, WLAM Broadcasters, Capitol Broadcasting Inc., Lazare Kaplan, Inc., Trade Nat. Bank; chmn. bd., CEO Totalbank Corp.; pres. Les Amis Constrn., 1997; v.p. Crystal Galleria LLC, 2000—. Author: Standard Pennsylvania Practice, 4 vols., 1958; prodr. various broadway musicals and plays; prodr. Am. Forum TV show; contbr. articles to profl. jours. Pres. N.Y. Art Festival, Inc., 1972-80; del. Democratic Nat. Conv., 1968; pres. McGovern for Pres. Com., 1971-72; vice chmn. Congl. Leadership for Future, 1970; finance chmn. Bayh for Pres. Com., 1975-76; bd. dirs. Weitzman Inst., 1963-84; chmn. exec. com. Spl. Olympics, Inc.; trustee Eleanor Roosevelt Meml. Found., 1963—, Jewish Publ. Soc., 1966-78, Declaration of Independence, House and Library, 1965-75; bd. dirs. Henry M. Jackson Found., 1984-92, trustee; mem. exec. com. Hollings for Pres. Com., 1984; bd. dirs. John F. Kennedy Library, 1983— ; bd. overseers V.I. U., 1962—; dir. U. Minn. Freeman Ctr., 1991—. Served with USAAF, 1942-46. Mem. U. Pa. Law Alumni Assn. Washington (pres. 1952-58), Potomac Tennis Club, Tau Epsilon Rho (pres. 1938) Office: 10608 Stapleford Hall Dr Potomac MD 20854-4447 *Using your sense of humor will diffuse any problem.*

FELDMAN, NANCY JANE, health organization executive; b. Green Bay, Wis., July 6, 1946; d. Benjamin J. and Ellen M. Naze; m. Robert P. Feldman, Aug. 24, 1968; 1 child, Sara J. BA, U. Wis., 1969, MS, 1974. Supr. EPSDT program Minn. Dept. Human Svcs., St. Paul, 1974-80, supr. healthcare programs, 1980-84; team leader human resources budget Minn. Dept. Fin., St. Paul, 1984-87; asst. commr. Minn. Dept. Health, St. Paul, 1987-91; team leader CORE program Minn. Dept. Adminstrn., St. Paul, 1991-93; dir. state pub. programs Medica, Allina Health Sys., Mpls., 1993-95; CEO UCare Minn., St. Paul, 1995—. Mem. Minn. Coun. Health Plans, Mpls., 1995—; bd. dirs. Stratis Health. Bd. dirs. Vols. Am. Health Svcs., 1994—, chair, 1999—; vice chair bd. dirs. Ctr. for Victims of Torture, 1997—. Mem. Women's Health Leadership Trust. Avocations: distance swimming, bicycling, travel. Home: 4124 Burton Ln Minneapolis MN 55406-3638 Office: UCare Minn PO Box 52 Minneapolis MN 55440-0052 E-mail: nfeldman@ncare.org.

FELDMAN, PETER DYLAN, pharmaceutical executive; b. Nagoya, Aichi, Japan, Sept. 18, 1958; s. Harvey Julien Feldman and Carolina Johanna Borja. PhD, U. Mich., 1987. Biol. technician NIH, Bethesda, Md., 1978—78; rsch. specialist U. Pa. Coll. Medicine, Phila., 1980—82; rsch. asst. U. Mich. Sch. Medicine, Ann Arbor, 1982—87; postdoctoral assoc. U. Iowa Sch. Medicine, Iowa City, 1987—90; asst. prof. pharmacology La. State U. Med. Ctr., New Orleans, 1990—97; documentation mgr. Universal Imaging Corp., West Chester, Pa., 1997—99; sr. sci. comm. assoc. Eli Lilly and Co., Indpls., 1999—2002, assoc. sci. comm. cons., 2002—. External reviewer Am. Heart Assn., La. Affiliate, New Orleans, 1993—95, The Wellcome Trust, London, 1995—95; external reviewer com. for the study of rsch. doctorate programs in the U.S. NRC, Washington, 1996—96. Contbr. chapters to books, articles to profl. jours. Treas. Boy Scouts Am., Cub Scout Pack 520, Indpls., 2002. Recipient F.I.R.S.T. award, NIH, NIMH, 1990—95; Dean's scholar, U. Pa., 1976—77, 1979—80, Dean's fellow, U. Mich. Sch. Grad. Studies, 1985—86, Instl. Rsch. fellow, U. Iowa Cardiovasc. Ctr., 1987—90. Mem.: Internat. Coll. Geriatric Psychoneuropharmacology, Am. Acad. Neurology, Am. Med. Writers Assn., Soc. for Neuroscience. Achievements include research in the pharmacology of brainstem mechanisms of blood-pressure regulation; atypical antipsychotics in the treatment of schizophrenia, bipolar disorder, agitation, and anxiety. Home: 9426 Moorings Blvd Indianapolis IN 46256 Office: Eli Lilly and Company Lilly Corporate Center Indianapolis IN 46285 Home Fax: 317-585-4809. Personal E-mail: pdfeldman@earthlink.net. E-mail: pdfeldman@lilly.com.

FELDMAN, PHILLIP, lawyer; b. N.Y.C., Apr. 26, 1932; BS, Calif. State U., 1956; MBA, U. So. Calif., 1963, JD, 1966. Bar: Calif. Expert witness Law Offices of Phillip Feldman, Sherman Oaks, Calif., 1967—. Fellow Am. Bd. Profl. Liability Attys. (chair cert. com. legal). Office: 15250 Ventura Blvd Ste 610 Sherman Oaks CA 91403-3218

FELDMAN, ROBERT C. public relations executive; b. N.Y.C., Oct. 22, 1956; BA, Syracuse U., 1978. Gen. mgr. Sta. WPNR-FM Utica Coll. Syracuse U., 1976-78; from asst. acct. exec. to sr. v.p., group mgr. Burson-Marsteller, 1978-88; sr. v.p. Ketchum Pub. Rels., N.Y.C., 1988-97; pres., CEO GCI Group, 1997—. Office: GCI GROUP INC 777 3rd Ave New York NY 10017-1401

FELDMAN, ROGER BRUCE, government official; b. Bklyn., Sept. 21, 1939; s. Jacob and Rose (Doodlesack) F.; m. Gilda Weinstock, June 19, 1960; children— Hadley, Scott, Mitchell AB, Brown U., 1960; postgrad., NYU Grad. Sch. Pub. Adminstrn., 1962-64. Mgmt. intern USIA, Washington, 1964-65, budget officer, 1965-70, chief programming, planning, 1970-73; dir. budget and fin. U.S. Consumer Product Safety Commn., Washington, 1973-74, dir., adminstrn., 1974-75; dep. dir. office budget Dept. State, Washington, 1975-76, dir. budget, 1976-78, dep. asst. sec. budget and fin., 1978-79, comptroller, 1979-89, cons. fin. and mgmt. systems, 1989—. Pres.'s award of Meritorious Exec., 1981, 87, Pres.'s award of Disting. Exec., 1986, Joint Fin. Mgmt. Improvement Program Scantlebury award, 1984. Mem. Assn. Gov. Accts. (chmn. nat. awards com.), U.S. Chief Fin. Officers Coun., Internat. Consortium on Fin. Mgmt. Home: 10466 NW 66th St Parkland FL 33076-2912 Office: PO Box 84 Grantham NH 03753-0084 E-mail: rfeldman@gate.net.

FELDMAN, ROGER DAVID, lawyer; b. N.Y.C., Apr. 7, 1943; s. Louis and Dora (Goldsmith) F.; m. Gail Steg, May 31, 1969; children: Rebecca, Seth. AB, Brown U., 1962; LLB, Yale U.; MBA, Harvard U. Bar: N.Y. 1966, D.C. 1977. Ops. rsch. analyst Office Asst. Sec. Def., Washington, 1967-68; staff asst. Office of Pres. U. S., Washington, 1968-69; assoc. LeBoeuf Lamb Leiby & MacRae, 1969-75; ptnr. Le Boeuf Lamb Leiby & MacRae, 1977-83; dep. asst. adminstr. FEA, Washington, 1975-77; mng. ptnr. project fin. group Nixon Hargrave Devans & Doyle, Washington, 1983-89; head ptnr. project fin. group McDermott Will & Emery, Washington, 1989-97; chair project fin. group Bingham McCutchen LLP, 1997—. Mem. fin. adv. bd. EPA, 1989-92; bd. dirs. R.J. Rudden & Assocs. Inc., Cogeneration Inst., pub.-pvt. venture divsn. Am. Road and Transp. Builders, 1991-93, Water Industry Coun.; bd. dirs. N.E. Energy and Commerce Assn., also chair fin. com.; pres. Nat. Coun. for Pub. Pvt. Partnerships, 1983-88, chair, 1998—; v.p. Internat. Pvt. Water Assn. Author: (with others) Infrastructure Finance: Tools for the Future, 1988, Public-Private Ventures in Transportation, 1990, Comprehensive Guide to Water and Wastewater Finance, 1991, Privatization of Public Utilities, 1995, Privatization, 1995; mem. bd. editors Yale Law Jour., 1964-65, Jour. Structured and Project Fin., 1995—, Constrn. Bus. Rev., 1992—; Washington editor Cogeneration Monthly Letter, 1987-98, Mcht. Power Monthly, 1998—, Strategic Planning for Energy and the Environment, 1992— (Author of the Yr. 1998), Power Marketers Assn. On Line Mag., 1999—, Power Exec., 2002—; contbr. articles to profl. jours. Mem. ABA (chmn. energy law com. 1980-83, alt. energy sources com. 1981-84, 86-90, chmn. environ. values com. 1983-89, com. on privatization 1985-90, chmn. energy fin. 1990-91), Fed. Energy Bar Assn. (chmn. cogeneration com. 1981-82), Nat. Coun. for Pub.-Pvt. Partnerships (Outstanding Contbn. to Privatization award), N.Y. Bar Assn., D.C. Bar Assn. (chair internat. fin. and investment com. 1998—), Assn. Energy Engrs. (Cogeneration Profl. of Yr. 1990), Phi Beta Kappa. Office: Bingham Dana LLP 1120 20th St NW Ste 800 Washington DC 20036-3406 E-mail: r.feldman@bingham.com.

FELDMAN, ROGER LAWRENCE, artist, educator; b. Spokane, Wash., Nov. 19, 1949; s. Marvin Lawrence and Mary Elizabeth (Shafer) Feldman; m. Astrid Lunde, Dec. 16, 1972; children: Kirsten B., Kyle Lawrence. BA in Art Edn., U. Wash., 1972; postgrad., Fuller Theol. Sem., Pasadena, Calif., 1972-73, Regent Coll., Vancouver, B.C., 1974; MFA in Sculpture, Claremont Grad. U., 1977. Teaching asst. Claremont (Calif.) Grad. U.; prof. art Biola U., La Mirada, Calif., 1989-2000, Seattle Pacific U., 2000—. Adj. instr. Seattle Pacific U., 1979, 80, 82, 83, Linfield Coll., 1978, Edmonds C.C., 1978-80, Shoreline C.C., 1978; guest artist and lectr. One-man shows include Art Ctr. Gallery, Seattle Pacific U., 1977, 83, 84, Linfield Coll., McMinnville, Oreg., 1979, Blackfish Gallery, Portland, 1982, Lynn McAllister Gallery, Seattle, 1986, Biola U., 1989, 93, Coll. Gallery, La. Coll., Pineville, 1990, Gallery W, Sacramento, 1991, 96, Aughinbaugh Gallery, Grantham, Pa., 1992, Riverside Art Mus., 1994, Azusa Pacific U., 1995, Cornerstone '96, Bushnell, Ill., 1996, Davison Gallery, Roberts Wesleyan Coll., Rochester, N.Y., 1997, Concordia U., Irvine, Calif., 1999, Northwestern Coll., St. Paul, 2000, Union U., Jackson, Tenn., 2001, F. Schaeffer Inst., St. Louis, 2001, Seattle Pacific U., Seattle, 2002, G. Fox U., Newberg, Oreg., 2002; group shows include Pasadena Artists Concern Gallery, 1976, Libra Gallery, Claremont, 1977, Renshaw Gallery, McMinnville, 1978, Cheney Cowles Mus., Spokane, 1979, 80, 83, Lynn McAllister Gallery, Seattle, 1985, Bumbershoot, Seattle, 1985, 86, 87, Pacific Arts Ctr., Seattle, 1987, Grand Canyon U., Phoenix, 1990, Connemara, Dallas, 1991, West Bend (Wis.) Gallery, 1992, L.A. Mcpl. Satellite Gallery, 1990, 93, Greenbelt 93, Northamptonshire, Eng., 1993, Claremont Sch. Theology, 1994, Queens Coll. Cambridge U., Eng., 1994, Jr. Arts Ctr. Gallery, Barnsdall Park, L.A., 1994, Bade Mus. Pacific Sch. of Religion, Berkeley, Calif., 1995, Ctrl. Arts Collective, Tucson, 1995, L.A. Mcpl. Gallery Barnsdall Art Park, 1996, Reconstructive Gallery Santa Ana, Ct., 1997, Guggenheim Gallery, Chapman U., Orange, Calif., 1997, Weaver Art Gallery, Bethel Coll., Mishawaka, Ind., 1998-, Concordia U. Art Gallery, Mequon, Wis., 1999, Palos Verdes Art Ctr., Calif., 1999, Grand Canyon U.,Phoenix, 2000, Tryon Ctr. Visual Arts, Charlotte, N.C., 2001, U. Dallas, 2001, Weaver Gallery, 2001, John Brown U., Siloam Springs, Ark., 2001, Sweetwater Ctr. for the Arts, Sewickley, Pa., 2002, Ind. Wesleyan U., Marion, 2002, others; comms. Wheaton, Pasadena, Calif., 1999, Renton Vocat. Tech Inst., 1987-89. Recipient King County Arts Commn. Individual Artist Project award, Seattle, 1988, Natl. Endowment for the Arts Individual Artist fellowship in Sculpture, 1986, David Gaiser award for sculpture Cheney Cowles Mus., 1980, Disting. Award for Harborview Med. Ctr. "Viewpoint", Soc. for Tech. Comm., 1987, Design award for "Seafirst News", Internat. Assn. Bus. Comm., 1987, Pace Setter award, 1987, others; Connemara Sculpture grant, 1990, Biola U., 1991. Office: Seattle Pacific U 3307 Third Ave West Seattle WA 98119 E-mail: rakfeldman2@attbi.com.

FELDMAN, RONALD ARTHUR, social work educator, researcher; b. Buffalo, Jan. 17, 1938; s. David Jacob and Clara (Spector) F.; m. Dina Cohen Feinstein, Dec. 23, 1962; children: Daniel, Deborah, Darrah. BA, U. Buffalo, 1960; MSW, U. Mich., 1963, PhD, 1966. Cert., Acad. Cert. Social Workers. Asst. prof. U. Calif., Berkeley, 1966-68; Fulbright lectr. Social Services Acad., Ankara, Turkey, 1968-69; assoc. prof. Washington U. Sch. Social Work, St. Louis, 1969-72, prof., 1972-86, acting dean, 1973-74; dir. Ctr. for Study of Youth Devel., Boys Town, Nebr., 1974-78, Ctr. for Adolescent Mental Health, St. Louis, 1983-87; assoc. dean Columbia U. Sch. Social Work, N.Y.C., 1985-86, prof., dean, 1986—2001, Ruth Harris Ottman Centennial prof., 1995—, dir. Ctr. for Study of Social Work Practice, 2002—. Cons. NIMH, Rockville, Md., 1980-91; bd. dirs. Ednl. Inst., Jewish Bd. Family and Children's Svcs., N.Y.C., 1986—, William T. Grant Found., Bd. Behavior and Mental Disorders, Inst. Medicine. Sr. author: Contemporary Approaches to Group Treatment, 1975, The St. Louis Conundrum: The Effective Treatment of Antisocial Youths, 1983, Children at Risk: In the Web of Parental Mental Illness, 1987; sr. editor: Advances in Adolescent Mental Health, vols. 1-4, 1986—. Citizen leader Clayton (Mo.) Bd. Edn., 1981-82; mem. profl. rev. bd. Mo. Dept. Mental Health, Jefferson City, 1981-86; trustee Wm. T. Grant Found., 1993—. Recipient Disting. Faculty award Washington U., St. Louis, 1984; research grantee NIMH, Rockville, Md., 1970-75, 80-84, Office of Human Devel. Services, Washington, 1983-87. Fellow NASW, Soc. for Rsch. in Child Devel.; mem. Coun. on Social Work Edn. (bd. dirs. 1992-95), Am. Sociol. Assn., Internat. Assn. Child and Adolescent Psychiatry and Allied Professions (v.p. 1995—). Avocations: swimming, tennis. Office: Columbia U Sch Social Work 622 W 113th St New York NY 10025-7982

FELDMAN, SAMUEL MITCHELL, neuroscientist, educator; b. Phila., Sept. 26, 1933; s. Boris and Fannie B. (Shrager) F.; children— Lee Stephen, David Saul. BA, U. Pa., 1954; MA, Northwestern U., 1955; PhD, McGill U., 1959. Fellow in physiology U. Wash., Seattle, 1958-60; from instr. to asso. prof. physiology Albert Einstein Coll. Medicine, 1960-71; prof. psychology N.Y. U., 1971—, head dept., 1972-76, prof. neuroscience, 1988—, dir. grad. studies neural sci., 1989—; mem. psychol. sci. study sect. NIMH, 1968-72, chmn., 1970-72, mem. biol. sci. tng. grant rev. com., 1977-83. Cons. in field. Contbr. articles to profl. jours. Fellow USPHS, 1958-60; recipient Career award, 1969-71, research grantee, 1963— Mem. Am. Physiol. Soc., Soc. Neurosci., Sigma Xi. Home: 336 Ctrl Pk W New York NY 10025 Office: New York Univ Ctr for Neural Science New York NY 10003

FELDMAN, SANDRA, labor union executive; b. N.Y.C. m. Arthur Barnes. M in English Lit., NYU. Tchr. Pub. Sch. 34, N.Y.C.; field rep. United Fedn. Tchrs., 1966-83, exec. dir., 1983-86, sec., 1983-86, pres., 1986-97, Am. Fedn. Tchrs., 1997—. Exec. com. Edn. Internat.; exec. coun. AFL-CIO, 1997—. Active Coun. on Competitiveness, Internat. Rescue Com., Freedom House, A. Philip Randolph Inst., Jewish Labor Com., Coalition Labor Union Women, Nat. Coun. Ams. to Prevent Handgun Violence, N.Y. Urban League, Women's Forum,

Women's Commn. on Refugee Children; co-chair Child Labor Coalition; nat. bd. mem. Profl. Tchg. Stds.; chair AFL-CIO Com. on Social Policy; mem. U.S. com. UNICEF Named one of N.Y.C. 75 Most Influential Women, Crain's New York Bus. Avocations: collecting african art, jazz, reading. Office: Am Fedn Tchrs 555 New Jersey Ave NW Washington DC 20001-2029 E-mail: online@AFT.org.

FELDMAN, SCOTT MILTON, lawyer; b. N.Y.C., July 31, 1942; s. Abe and Lilian F.; m. Susan Lauer, July 13, 1968; children: James W., Mark A. BA, Amherst Coll., 1964; JD, Harvard U., 1967. Bar: NY 1968, Ill. 1978. Instr. UCLA Law Sch, 1967-68; lt. Judge Advocate Gen's. Corp. U.S. Navy, Washington, 1968-71; assoc. Sullivan & Cromwell, N.Y.C., 1971-77; ptnr. Winston & Strawn, Chgo., 1978-2001; assoc. gen. counsel Bank of Am. N.A., Chgo., 2001—. Trustee Village of Glencoe, Ill., 1983-91. Mem. ABA, Chgo. Bar Assn., Assn. Bar City N.Y., Amherst Alumni Assn. Office: Bank of America NA Mail Code ILI-231-07-17 231 S LaSalle St 7th Fl Chicago IL 60697 E-mail: scott.m.feldman@bankofamerica.com.

FELDMAN, STANLEY GEORGE, lawyer; b. N.Y.C., N.Y., Mar. 9, 1933; s. Meyer and Esther Betty (Golden) F.; m. Norma Arambula; 1 dau., Elizabeth L. Student, U. Calif., Los Angeles, 1950-51; LL.B., U. Ariz., 1956. Bar: Ariz. 1956. Practiced in, Tucson, 1956-81; ptnr. Miller, Pitt & Feldman, 1968-81; justice Ariz. Supreme Ct., Phoenix, 1982—2002, chief justice, 1992-97; of counsel Haralson, Miller, Pitt Feldman & McAnally. Lectr. Coll. Law, U. Ariz., 1965-76, adj. prof., 1976-81, 2000, 03. Bd. dirs. Tucson Jewish Community Council, U. Ariz. Found., 1999—. Mem. ABA, Am. Bd. Trial Advocates (past pres. So. Ariz. chpt.), Ariz. Bar Assn. (pres. 1974-75, bd. govs. 1967-76), Pima County Bar Assn. (past pres.), Am. Trial Lawyers Assn. (dir. chpt. 1967-76), U. Ariz. Law Coll. Assn. Democrat. Jewish. Office: 1 S Church Ave Tucson AZ 85701-1620

FELDMAN, STEPHEN, academic administrator; b. N.Y.C., Sept. 11, 1944; s. Harry and Mae (Morris) F.; m. Constance M. Lerudis, June 1, 1969; children—Jennifer Dawn, Timothy Richard. BBA, CCNY, 1966, MBA, 1968, PhD (fellow), 1971. Chmn. dept. banking, fin. and investments Hofstra U., Hempstead, N.Y., 1969-77, assoc. prof., 1974-77; dean Ancell Sch. of bus. Western Conn. State U., Danbury, 1977-81, pres., 1981-92, Nova Southeastern U., Ft. Lauderdale, Fla., 1992-94; v.p. real estate Ethan Allen Inc., Danbury, 1995-96; v.p. univ. rels., devel. Calif. State U., Long Beach, 1996-99; pres. Astronaut Meml. Found., Kennedy Space Ctr., Fla., 1999—. Bd. dirs. Ethan Allen Inc., Sci. Horizons Inc.; cons. IBM, N.Y. Telephone Co. Editor: Credit Unions, 1974, Handbook of Wealth Management, 1977, Smarter Money, 1985; contbr. articles to profl. jours. Trustee Danbury Hosp., United Way. Mem. Am. Assn. State Colls. and Univs. (chmn. corp. coll. rels.), Greater Ft. Lauderdale C. of C. Office: Astronaut Meml Found Ctr Space Mail Code Amf Kennedy Space Center FL 32899-0001 E-mail: sfeldman@amfcse.org.

FELDMAN, SUSAN ELEANOR, technology analyst; b. N.Y.C., Feb. 14, 1947; d. Bernard and Ruth (Gold) Goodman; m. Robert Larry Feldman, June 25, 1967; children: David, Elana. BA, Cornell U., 1967; AM in Libr. Sci., U. Mich., 1968. Lic. libr., Calif., N.Y. Tech. info. specialist Nat. Tech. Info. Svc., Springfield, Va., 1968-70; audio-visual coord. South Ctrl. Rsch. Libr. Coun., Ithaca, N.Y., 1970-71; young adult svcs. libr. Tompkins County Pub. Libr., Ithaca, 1972-75; adj. prof. Syracuse U. Sch. Info. Studies, 1975; reference libr. Cuesta C.C., San Luis Obispo, Calif., 1976-79, instr., 1977-78, mgmt. intern, 1978-79; asst. to dir. Ithaca Coll. Libr., 1980-81; pres. Datasearch, Ithaca, 1981—2000, rsch. v.p. for content mgmt. and retrieval software, 2000—. Pres. LAMP, San Luis Obispo, 1978-79; mem. reference com. South Cen. Rsch. Libr. Coun., 1984-89; mem. program. coms. Search Engines, Joint Com. on Digital Librs. Author: The Internet at a Glance, 1993, 94, 95; contbr. articles to profl. publs., chpt. to book. V.p., pres.-elect Children's and Young Adults Svcs. sect. N.Y. Libr. Assn., 1974-75; violist San Luis Obispo Orch., 1976-79, Beaux Eaux Quartet, Ithaca, 1981—, Cornell U. Orch., Ithaca, 1989-95; instr. Gifted and Talented Program, 1983-90. Mem. Assn. Ind. Info. Profls. (ethics com. 1986-87, v.p., pres.-elect 1992-93, pres. 1993-94, dir. 1995—), Assn. Computing Machinery, Am. Soc. Info. Sci. and Tech. Avocations: music, reading, hiking, skiing, travel. Office: IDC 5 Speen St Framingham MA 01701

FELDMANN, EDWARD GEORGE, pharmaceutical chemist, pharmacologist; b. Chgo., Oct. 13, 1930; s. Edward Louis and Vera (Arnesen) F., stepmother Helen E. Whitney; m. Mary J. Evans, Aug. 30, 1952; children: Ann Marie Whittington, Edward William, Robert George, Karen Lynn Zaragoza. BS in Chemistry, Loyola U., Chgo., 1952; MS in Pharmacy (research fellow Am. Found. Pharm. Edn. 1953-55), U. Wis., 1954, PhD in Pharm. Chemistry-Biochemistry, 1955; postgrad., Northwestern U., 1956, U. Chgo., 1958. Teaching asst. Loyola U., Chgo., 1951-52; research asst. U. Wis., 1952-53; sr. chemist Am. Dental Assn., 1955-58, dir. div. chemistry, 1958-59; assoc. dir. sci. div. Am. Pharm. Assn., 1959-60, dir., 1960-85, assoc. editor sci. edit. assn. jour., 1959-60, editor, 1960—97, assoc. exec. dir. for sci. affairs, 1970-83, v.p. sci. affairs, 1983-85, project dir. Handbook of Non-Prescription Drugs, 1985—89, mng. editor, 1989-90, project cons. Handbook on Non-Prescription Drugs, 1991—93, mem. adv. panel, 1994-95; exec. sec. Acad. Pharm. Scis., 1983-85; mem. adv. panel Am. Pharm. Assn., 1994-98; pvt. pharm. cons., 1985—; assoc. dir. revision Nat. Formulary, 1959—60; dir. revision Nat. Formulary, 1960-70. Mem. adv. panel dental drugs Nat. Formulary, 1955-60, Am. Pharm. Assn. Handbook of Non-Prescription Drugs, 1994-95; reviewer Internat. Pharmacopeia, WHO, 1958; spl. lectr. drug standards George Washington U., 1960-64; del. conf. on fellowships Nat. Health Council, 1960; mem. coordinating com. Nat. Conf. Antimicrobial Agts., Soc. Indsl. Microbiology, 1960-63; mem. adv. panel pharm. nomenclature A.M.A.-Am. Pharm. Assn.-U.S. Pharmacopeia, 1961-66, mem. nomenclature com., 1962-66; sec. U.S. Com. Internat. Drug Standards, 1964-65; adv. panel food chems. codex Nat. Acad. Scis.-NRC, 1961-71, liaison rep. to drug research bd., 1968-76; spl. liaison rep. to Commn. of Life Scis., NAS-NRC, 1973-85; mem. lab. com. Am. Pharm. Assn. Found., 1961-75; mem. com. Ebert prize, 1961-75; judge Lunsford-Richardson Pharmacy Awards, 1962-69; cons. Council on Drugs, A.M.A., 1962; vis. scientist Am. Assn. Colls. of Pharmacy, NSF, 1963-66; mem. expert adv. panel on internat. pharmacopeia and pharm. preparation World Health Orgn., 1963-75; drug abuse cons. to Office of US Pres., Lyndon B. Johnson, 1965, drug cons. Office Sec., U.S. Dept. Health, Edn. and Welfare, 1967-70; nomenclature cons. to Commr., U.S. Food and Drug Adminstrn., 1968-71; mem. expert working group Indsl. Devel. Orgn., UN, 1969; mem. organizing com. 31st Internat. Congress Pharm. Scis., 1970-71; mem. NRC, 1971-85; del. U.S. Pharmacopeia, 1970-85, 90-95; mem. Nat. Council on Drugs, 1976-83; mem. scientific adv. bd. Biodecision Labs., Inc., 1987-90; scientific cons. Am. Assn. Pharmaceutical Scientists, 1986-93; pharm. scis. cons. ERGO Sci. Inc., 1992—; mem. steering com. Japan-U.S. Pharmaceutical Scis. Congress, 1987; expert witness congressional drug legis. hearings and civil litigation cases, Drug quality specifications, Fed. legal requirements, Clinical pharmacology and Toxicology, 1965-; lectr. in field. *Dr. Feldmann's professional achievements encompassed four broad areas: conducted laboratory research, most notably to experimentally determine relative duration of action of dental local anesthetic agents; subsequently, coordinated and directed development and adoption of official standards of quality for numerous pharmaceutical products; concurrently, edited leading pharmaceutical research journals broadly fostering major advances in medicinal research, while editing numerous drug reference books thereby facilitating transfer of new pharmaceutical information from research laboratories into clinical practice; lastly, served as frequent consultant to government agencies and Congressional committees, helping to shape public policy, regulations, and legislation on various pharmaceutical issues, e.g., generic drug equivalency.* Assoc. editor Drug Standards, 1959-60, editor, 1960; chmn. (1960-70) Nat. Formulary Bd.; editor Jour. Pharm. Scis., 1961-75, cons. editor, 1975-85, 87-89, interim editor, 1991, editor in chief, 1991-94, emeritus editor 1994-95; editor APS Accd. Reporter, 1983-85; author more than 420 articles in field, editor or co-editor 24 ref. books; mem. editorial adv. bd. Index Chemicus, 1968-71; med. contbr. World Book Ency., 1986-88. Mem. membership com. Ravenwood Park Citizens Assn., Falls Church, Va., 1962, mem. nominating com., 1971-72; mem. Lake Barcroft Community Assn., 1975-97. Recipient Man of Yr. award Nat. Assn. Pharm. Mfrs., 1970, G.A. Bergy Lectr. award U. W.Va., 1975, Pres. award Am. Assn. Pharm. Scis., 1993, Disting. citation U. Wis., 1971, Commr.'s citation FDA, 1975, Spl. Recognition award U.S. Pres. Lyndon Johnson, 1965. Fellow Acad. Pharm. Scis.; mem. Am. Pharm. Assn. (life), Am. Chem. Soc. (emeritus), Am. Assn. Pharm. Scis. (charter mem., fellow, fellows selection com. 1989, Pres.'s award 1993), N.Y. Acad. Scis., Nat. Soc. Med. Rsch. (coun. 1961-69), Am. Testing Materials, Coun. Biology Editors, AMA (affiliate), Fedn. Internat. Pharm., U.S. Tennis Assn., Mid-Atlantic Tennis Assn., Fla. Tennis Assn., Sleepy Hollow Bath and Racquet Club (Falls Church, Va.), Arlington Tennis and Squash Club, 4-Seasons Tennis Club, Fairfax Golden Racquets Club, Venice (Fla.) Golf and Country Club (bd. mem. tennis assn. 1998—, pres. 2002—, mem. sports and health com. 2002—), K.C., Sigma Xi, Rho Chi, Lambda Chi Sigma. Roman Catholic. Home and Office: 316 Wild Pine Way Venice FL 34292-4624

FELDMANN, FRANK NEIL, chemistry educator; b. N.Y.C., July 7, 1954; s. Robert Joseph and Kay Constance (Wasserman) F. BS, Johns Hopkins U., 1976; MS, U. Houston, 1980, PhD, 1985. Postdoctoral rsch. assoc. Adelphi U., Garden City, N.Y., 1985-86, Miss. State U., 1987; acad. assoc., dir. chemistry labs. Poly U., Farmingdale, N.Y., 1988-92; asst. prof. dept. life scis. N.Y. Inst. Tech., Old Westbury, 1996—. Contbr. articles to profl. jours.; patentee in field. Robert A. Welch predoctoral fellow, 1982-83, Nat. Eye Inst. postdoctoral fellow, 1985. Mem. Am. Chem. Soc. Avocations: chess, classical music. E-mail: franknf@ix.netcom.com.

FELDMANN, JUDITH GAIL, language professional, educator; b. Grenova, N.D., Feb. 10, 1938; d. Jule and Evelyn (Hagen) F.; children: Robert, Carole Elizabeth. BA magna cum laude, Minot State Tchrs. Coll., 1962; MA, Mich. State U., 1971; postgrad, U. Oslo, 1980, U. London, 1982, 85; postgrad., Western Mich. U., 1987, Eastern Mich. U., 1992-93, Harvard U., 1994. Cert. tchr., secondary adminstrn., Mich. English tchr. Minot Pub. Schs., N.D., 1961, Charlotte Pub. Schs., Mich., 1962; grad. asst. instr. Mich. State Univ., East Lansing, Mich., 1963; reading specialist, English educator Jackson (Mich.) Pub. Schs., 1964—2003, English educator, 1964—2003. Mem. Internat. Reading Assn., Mich. Reading Assn. (presenter Grand Rapids 1995), Assn. for Supervision and Curriculum Devl., Jackson Edn. Assn. (v.p.). Home: 2791 Brookside Blvd Jackson MI 49203-5532 E-mail: jfeldman2456@aol.com.

FELDMANN, SHIRLEY CLARK, psychology educator; b. Niagara Falls, N.Y., Apr. 14, 1929; d. Franklin T. and Mildred L. (Payne) Clark; m. Robert Feldmann, June, 1952 (dec.); m. Horace S. Bush (dec.). BA, Barnard Coll., 1951; MA, Columbia U., 1952, PhD, 1961. Asst. prof. edn. SUNY, Fredonia, 1958-60; asst. research prof. psychiatry N.Y. Med. Coll., N.Y.C., 1960-63; prof. sch. edn. City Coll., CUNY, N.Y.C., 1963-98; prof., PhD program in edn. psychology CUNY Grad. Sch., N.Y.C., 1974-98, exec. officer, 1976-85; ret., 1998. Contbr. articles to profl. jours. Mem. Am. Psychol. Assn., Am. Ednl. Research Assn. Home: 11 Cedar Lake Rd Chester CT 06412-1009

FELDSTEIN, JAY HARRIS, lawyer; b. Elizabeth, Pa., June 23, 1937; s. Norman George and Gladys Shirley (Goldstein) F.; m. Judith Mae Stern, Sept. 8, 1963; children: Wendy Shawn, David Eric, Marc Howard. BA, Pa. State U., 1959; JD, Yale U., 1962. Bar: Fla. 1963, Pa. 1963, U.S. Dist. Ct. (we. dist.) Pa. 1963, U.S. Supreme Ct. 1967. Sole practice, Pitts., 1963-65; ptnr. Feldstein, Grinberg, Stein & McKee and predecessors, Pitts., 1965—. Chmn. Pa. Lottery Commn., Harrisburg, 1980-82; pres. Southview Apts. for Sr. Citizen Housing, Mt. Lebanon, 1980-84, State U. Nat. Alumni Assn., 1979-81; v.p. Am. Jewish Com., Pitts., 1984—. Served with USAF, 1963-69. Recipient Outstanding Young Man in Pitts. Area award Jr. C. of C., 1969. Mem. Pa. Trial Lawyers Assn. (bd. govs. 1984—), Allegheny County Acad. Trial Lawyers, Nat. Bd. Trial Advocacy (cert.). Democrat. Jewish. Club: Harvard, Yale, Princeton. Lodge: Masons (master 1972). Home: 592 Sandrae Dr Pittsburgh PA 15243-1733

FELDSTEIN, JOSHUA, educational administrator; b. Russia, Apr. 12, 1921; arrived in U.S., 1939, naturalized, 1944; s. Cemach and Fania B. Feldstein; m. Miriam Myzel, Dec. 24, 1944; children: Theodore Lee, Daniel Ethan. BS, Delaware Valley Coll., 1952; MS, Rutgers U., 1956, PhD, 1962. Instr. horticulture Delaware Valley Coll., Doylestown, Pa., 1952—56, asst. prof. horticulture, 1956—60, assoc. prof. horticulture, 1960—65, prof. horticulture, 1965—, chmn. dept., 1959—69, chmn. plant sci. divsn., 1966—73, assoc. dean, 1969—73, dean, 1973—75; pres. Delaware Valley Coll. Sci. and Agr., Doylestown, Pa., 1975—87, pres. emeritus, 1987—, interim pres., 1995—97. Coord. nat. tchg. fellowships, student fin. aid, chmn. admissions, curriculum, athletics, student affairs, acad. std. coms. Delaware Valley Coll. Sci. and Agr. Author (with N.F. Childers): Effect of Irrigation on Fruit Size and Yield of Peaches in Pennsylvania, 1957; author: Peach Irrigation in a Humid Region, 1964, Effects of Irrigation on Peaches in Pennsylvania, 1965. Recipient Legion of Honor, Chapel of Four Chaplains, Phila., 1974, award, Pa. Future Farmers Am., 1980. Mem.: Commn. of Ind. Colls. and Univs., Pa. Assn. Colls. and Univs., Soil Conservation Soc. Am., Ea. Assn. Coll. Deans and Advs. to Students, Am. Inst. Biol. Scis., Am. Soc. Hort. Sci. Jewish.

FELDSTEIN, KATHLEEN FOLEY, economist, consultant; b. Boston, Feb. 3, 1941; d. Charles Joseph and Eleanor (Croxon) Foley; m. Martin Feldstein, June 19, 1965; children: Margaret, Janet. BA, Radcliffe Coll., 1962; PhD, MIT, 1977. Pres. Econs. Studies, Inc., Belmont, Mass., 1987—. Bd. dirs. Bank Am. Corp., Ionics Corp., Knight-Ridder, Bell South Corp. Contbr. articles to nat. and internat. newspapers. Corp. mem. Winsor Sch., Boston, 1985-97, Simmons Coll., Boston, 1986-96; bd. overseers Mus. Fine Arts, Boston, 1990-92, trustee, 1992—, treas., 1998; trustee Com. for Econ. Devel., 1990—, McLean Hosp., 1993—. Home: 147 Clifton St Belmont MA 02478-2603 Office: Econs Studies Inc 147 Clifton St Belmont MA 02478-2603

FELDSTEIN, MARTIN STUART, economist, educator; b. N.Y.C., Nov. 25, 1939; s. Meyer and Esther (Gevarter) Feldstein; m. Kathleen Foley, June 19, 1965; children: Margaret, Janet. AB summa cum laude, Harvard U., 1961; MA, Oxford U., 1964, DPhil, 1967; LLD (hon.), Rochester U., 1984; LLD (hon.), Marquette U., 1985. Research fellow Nuffield Coll., Oxford U., 1964—65, ofcl. fellow, 1965—67, lectr. pub. fin., 1965—67; asst. prof. econs. Harvard U., 1967—68, assoc. prof., 1968—69, prof., 1969—, George F. Baker prof., 1984—; pres. Nat. Bur. Econ. Research, 1977—82, 1984—; chmn. Council Econ. Advisers, 1982—84. Bd. dirs. AIG, HCA, Eli Lilly; mem. internat. adv. coun. J.P. Morgan, Daimler-Chrysler, Robecco. Bd. contbrs.: Wall St. Jour. Fellow: Am. Philos. Soc., Nat. Assn. Bus. Economists, Econometric Soc. (coun. 1977—82), Nuffield Coll. (hon.), Brit. Acad. (corr.), Am. Acad. Arts and Scis.; mem.: Trilateral Commn. (exec. com. 1987—), Coun. on Fgn. Rels. (bd. dirs. 1998—), Inst. Medicine-NAS, Austrian Acad. Scis. (fgn.), Corp. Mass. Gen. Hosp., Am. Econ. Assn. (exec. com. 1980—82, v.p. 1988, pres.-elect 2003, John Bates Clark medal 1977), Phi Beta Kappa. Home: 147 Clifton St Belmont MA 02478-2603 Office: Nat Bur Econ Rsch Inc 1050 Massachusetts Ave Cambridge MA 02138-5317 E-mail: mfeldstein@harvard.edu.

FELDSTEIN, PAUL JOSEPH, management educator; b. N.Y.C., Oct. 4, 1933; s. Nathan and Sarah Feldstein; m. Anna Martha Lee, Dec. 24, 1968; children: Julie, Jennifer. BA in Econs., CCNY, 1955; MBA in Fin., U. Chgo., 1957, PhD in Econs., 1961. Dir. divsn. rsch. Am. Hosp. Assn., Chgo., 1961-64; prof. Sch. Pub. Health U. Mich., Ann Arbor, 1964-87; prof. Grad. Sch. Mgmt. U. Calif., Irvine, 1987—. Author: Health Care Economics, 5th rev., 1998, Health Policy Issues: An Economic Perspective on Health Reform, 3d edit., 2003, The Politics of Health Legislation, 2nd edit. rev., 2001; contbr. articles to profl. jours. 1st lt. inf. U.S. Army, 1955-57. Mem. Am. Econ. Assn. Avocations: jogging, biking. Office: U Calif Grad Sch Mgmt Irvine CA 92697-0001 E-mail: pfeldste@uci.edu.

FELDSTEIN, STANLEY, psychologist; b. Bklyn., Dec. 13, 1930; s. Mark and Dora (Kruger) F.; m. Joyce Lister, Sept. 27, 1964; children: Heather M. Quay, Judd Thomas Markham. BA, CUNY, 1953; MA, Columbia U., 1954, PhD in Clin. Psychology, 1961. Cert. psychologist, N.Y. Teaching fellow English dept. Bklyn. Coll. CUNY, 1954; rsch. asst. Columbia U., N.Y.C., 1957-60, rsch. assoc. in psychiatry, 1964-68; clin. intern Franklin D. Roosevelt VA NP Hosp., Montrose, N.Y., 1957-58, East Orange (N.J.) VA GM&S Hosp., 1958-59, Newark VA Mental Health Clinic, 1959-60; rsch. psychologist rsch. dept. William Alanson White Inst., N.Y.C., 1961-67, mem. faculty, 1964-69; assoc. prof. psychiatry div. biol. psychiatry N.Y. Med. Coll., 1964-72; prof. psychology U. Md., Baltimore County, 1971—, assoc. chmn. dept. psychology, 1971-75, 75-78, acting chmn., 1975. Rsch. and clin. cons. drug addiction svcs. Beth Israel Med. Ctr., 1961-68; rsch. cons. bur. rsch. in neurology and psychiatry N.J. Neuropsychiat. Inst., Princeton, 1965-68; vis. prof. Clarke Inst. Psychiatry, U. Toronto, Ont., Can., 1978-79; lectr. coll. physicians and surgeons Columbia U., 1984—; vis. scholar dept. psychology Brigham Young U., Provo, Utah, 1986; cons., presenter in field; vis. scholar German Acad. Exch. Svc. at U. Giessen, Fed. Republic Germany, 1980. Co-author: Rhythms of Dialogue, 1970, Computer Aided Interactive Psychiatric Diagnosis Programs, 1971, Nonverbal Behavior and Communication, 1978, Rhythms of Dialogue in Infancy, 2001, others, also books chpts.; sect. editor Clin. Psychologists, 1967-71; cons. editor Profl. Psychology, 1969-76; mem. editorial bd. Jour. Psycholinguistic Rsch., 1976—, Jour. Lang. and Social Psychology, 1982—, Jour. Comm. Disorders, 1984-91, Jour. Asian Pacific Comm., 1988—; reviewer, contbr. to publs. in field/ Chmn. bd. trustees, acting pres. Blue Bird Sch., Ruxton, Md. 1977-78, chmn. bd. dirs., 1979-80. Grantee NIMH, Laidlow Found., Nat. Heart, Lung and Blood Inst. of NIH, March of Dimes Birth Defects Found., Md. Psychiat. Rsch. Ctr., DRIF Fund, others. Mem. AAAS, Am. Psychol. Soc. (charter), Soc. Personality and Social Psychology, Internat. Soc. for Infant Studies, Soc. for Rsch. in Child Devel., N.Y. Acad. Scis., Acoustical Soc. Am., Ea. Psychol. Assn., Sigma Xi, Kappa Delta Pi. Home: 244 Blenheim Rd Baltimore MD 21212-1703 Office: U Md Baltimore County Dept Psychology Baltimore MD 21228

FELDT, LEONARD SAMUEL, university educator and administrator; b. Long Branch, New Jersey, Nov. 2, 1925; s. Harry and Bessie (Doris) F.; m. Natalie Ruth (Fischer), Aug. 29, 1954; children: Sarah Feldt Roach, Daniel C. BS in Edn., Rutgers Univ., 1950, EdM, 1951; PhD, U. Iowa, 1954. Asst. prof. to prof. U. Iowa, Iowa City, 1954-94, dir. testing programs, 1981-94, Lindquist prof. ednl. measurement, 1981-94, prof. emeritus, 1994. Pres. Iowa Measurment Rsch. Found., Iowa City, 1978—; editor standardized tests, Iowa Tests Ednl. Devel., 1960—. With U.S. Army, 1943—46. Recipient Disting. Svc. Award Rutgers U., 1999; Disting. Achievement Award, Nat. Ctr. for Rsch. on Evaluation Stds. and Student Testing, 1999. Mem.: Am. Stats. Assn., Psychometric Soc., Nat. Coun. on Measurement in Edn. (Career Contbns. award 1994), Am. Ednl. Rsch. Assn. (E.F. Lindquist award 1995), Sigma Xi, Phi Beta Kappa. Avocation: golf. Home: 810 Willow St Iowa City IA 52245-5438 Office: Univ Iowa Lindquist Ctr Iowa City IA 52242 E-mail: leonard-feldt@uiowa.edu.

FELDT, ROBERT HEWITT, pediatric cardiologist, educator; b. Chgo., Aug. 3, 1934; s. Robert Hewitt and Frances (Swanson) F.; m. Barbara Ann Fritz, Aug. 17, 1957; children: Christine, Susan, Kathryn. BS, U. Wis., 1956; MD, Marquette U., 1960; MS, U. Minn., 1965. Diplomate: Am. Bd. Pediatrics, Am. Bd. Pediatric Cardiology. Intern Miller Hosp., St. Paul, 1960-61; resident in pediatrics cardiology Mayo Found., Rochester, Minn., 1961-65; cons. pediatrics Mayo Clinic, Rochester, Minn., 1966—, chmn. dept. pediatrics, 1980-85, prof. pediatrics; ret. Mem. Am. Bd. Pediatrics; chmn. sci. coun. Am. Heart Assn. Author numerous sci. articles, book chpts., monographs. Fellow Am. Acad. Pediatrics, Am. oll. Cardiology; mem. Minn. Heart Assn. (pres. 1982), Midwest Soc. Pediat. Rsch., Am. Pediatric Soc. Congregationalist. Home: 1804 Walden Ln SW Rochester MN 55902-0903

FELGAR, RAYMOND E(UGENE), pathologist, medical educator; b. Mt. Pleasant, Pa., Mar. 2, 1963; s. Samuel Hurst and Anna June (Stull) F. BS in Microbiology with honors, Pa. State U., 1985; PhD in Pathology, U. Pitts., 1990, MD, 1992. Diplomate Am. Bd. Pathology in Anatomic and Clin. Pathology, Am. Bd. Pathology, cert. subspecialty in Hemotology Am. Bd. Pathology. Resident in anatomic and clin. pathology U. Pa. Med. Ctr., Phila., 1992-96; fellow in hematopathology dept. pathology Vanderbilt U., Nashville, 1996-98; dir. hematopathology and clin. flow cytometry Hahnemann Hosp., Phila., 1998; asst. prof. dept. pathology and lab medicine MCP-Hahnemann Sch. Medicine, Phila., 1998; dir. clin. flow cytometry lab., hematopathologist and dir. hematopathology Strong Meml. Hosp., Rochester, N.Y., 1998—; asst. prof. Dept. Pathology & Lab. Medicine U. Rochester Sch. Medicine & Dentistry, 1998—. Co-dir. Course on T-cell lymphomas, ASCP Nat. Meeting. Contbr. articles to profl. jours., chpt. to book. NIH med. scientist tng. fellow, 1987-92. Mem. AMA, Coll. Am. Pathologists, Am. Soc. Clin. Pathologists (co-dir. course t-cell lymphomas nat. mtg.), Am. Soc. Hematology, U.S. and Can. Acad. Pathology, Soc. for Hematopathology, European Assn. for Hematopathology, Eastern Coop. Oncology Group (pathology com.), Southwestern Oncology Group, Children's Oncology Group, Pa. State U. Alumni Assn., Phi Beta Kappa.

FELGER, RALPH WILLIAM, educator, retired military officer; b. Hamilton, Ohio, Oct. 14, 1919; s. Edward Lewis and Blanche Esther (House) F.; m. Bernice Regina Moeller, Dec. 28, 1944 (dec.); 1 child, Mary Karen. BA, Whitworth Coll., 1950; MBA, U. Denver, 1952; MS, Trinity U., 1954. Cert. instr. bus. and psychology, Calif. Commd. 2d lt. U.S. Army, advanced through grades to 1st lt., pers. tng. officer, 1942-46, relieved from active duty, 1946; commd. 1st lt. USAF, 1951, advanced through grades to col., edn. and pers. officer, 1951-67, ret., 1967; asst. prof. Bakersfield (Calif.) Coll., 1967-68; dean continuing edn. Lincoln Land C.C., Springfield, Ill., 1968-72; dir. corp. tng. Sangamo Electric Co., West Union, S.C., 1972-74; asst. campus dir. Ohio State U., Marion, 1974-79, asst. to v.p. Columbus, 1979-83; exec. v.p. Internat. Mgmt. Inst., Westerville, Ohio, 1983-84; dir. continuing edn. N.Mex. Inst. Mining and Tech., Socorro, 1984-85; part-time cons. edn. and mktg. Midwest Human Resource Sys., Columbus, Ohio, 1985-89; acad. counselor Franklin U., Columbus, 1990-91; edn. program mgr. Jr. Achievement of Ctrl. Ohio, Columbus, 1991-92; v.p. Career Mgmt. Ctrs., Inc., Columbus, 1991-92; ret., 1992. Ill. divsn. chmn. United Way, Springfield, 1972; mem. Police Human Rels. Com., Springfield, 1970-72; bd. dirs. ARC, Oconee, S.C., 1973; edn. chmn. Marion (Ohio) Econ. Coun., 1975-79, Marion County chpt. Am. Heart Assn., 1975-79. Decorated Legion of Merit, U.S. Joint Chiefs of Staff Badge, 3 USAF Commendation medals; recipient 2 commendations United Way Community Service. Mem.: U.S. Ret. Mil. Officers Assn., Am. Biog. Inst. (rsch. bd. advisors), Pers. Mgrs. Club (v.p. 1972—74), Delta Sigma Pi (life). Avocations: fishing, camping, travel, cooking, reading. Home: 1300 O Ave #106 Anacortes WA 98221

FELGRAN, STEVEN DAVID, economist, educator; b. N.Y.C., July 1, 1953; s. Howard H. and Ilse H. (Sturm) F.; m. Hilary Ann Macht, June 13, 1999; 1 child, Harry Max. BA, U. Pa., 1975; MA in Econs., MPhil in Econs., Yale U., 1978, PhD in Econs., 1982. Analyst Congl. Budget Office, Washington, 1975-76; cons. Arthur D. Little, Inc., Cambridge, Mass., 1981-83; economist Fed. Res. Bank of Boston, 1983-89; prof. Coll. Bus. Adminstrn. Northeastern U., Boston, 1989-93; sr. mgr. Economic Cons. Svcs./KPMG, N.Y.C., 1993-97, ptnr., 1997—. Contbr. articles to profl. jours. Mem. ABA, Am. Econ. Assn., Phi Beta Kappa. Avocations: theater, musical comedy, historic preservation and restoration, civil war era, travel. Office: KPMG 345 Park Ave Fl 36 New York NY 10154-0004 E-mail: sfelgran@kpmg.com.

FELHOFER, MARYLOUISE KATHERINE, nursing administrator; b. Milw., June 30, 1952; d. Charles Walter and Tillie Elizabeth (Hrymnak) Tomasicyk; m. Paul Robert Felhofer, Aug. 12, 1977. BSN, Alverno Coll., Milw., 1974; MS in Nursing Adminstrn., U. Md., Balt., 1991. RN, Md.; cert. profl. in healthcare quality. Commd. ensign USN, 1972, advanced through grades to capt., 1997; staff and charge nurse Naval Regional Med. Ctr., Orlando, Fla., 1974-77; instr., adminstrv. officer Naval Officer Indoctrination Sch., Newport, R.I., 1977-81; charge nurse, relief dept. head, supr. Naval Hosp., Great Lakes, Ill., 1981-86, head command quality assurance dept., 1986-89; head command quality assessment dept. Nat. Naval Med. Ctr., Bethesda, Md., 1991-93; head orgnl. performance improvement customer support br. Navy Bur. Medicine and Surgery, 1994-95, head tricare quality br., 1995-96; dir. nursing adminstrv. matters, quality mgmt. specialist Office of Naval Med. Insp. Gen., 1996-99; head clin. ops. Mil. Med. Support Office, 1999—2001; ret. USN, 2001; case mgr. Vista Health Emergency Svcs., Waukegan, Ill., 2002; performance improvement coord. Clement V. Zablocki, VAMC, Milw., 2002—. U.S. Navy Medicine fellow Joint Commn. on Accreditation of Healthcare Orgns., 1993-94. Decorated 3 Commendation medals USN, 3 Meritorious Svc. medals; recipient various awards. Mem. Nat. Assn. for Healthcare Quality, Assn. Mil. Surgeons U.S., Navy Nurse Corps Assn., Nurses Alumnae Assn. U. Md., Sigma Theta Tau, Delta Epsilon Sigma, Kappa Gamma Pi, Phi Kappa Phi. Avocations: reading, cooking, gardening, traveling.

FELICETTA, JAMES VINCENT, endocrinologist, educator; b. Seattle, Mar. 1, 1949; s. Vincent Frank and Alice Marie (Felton) F.; m. Susan Marie Roman, Aug. 3, 1985. BS, U. Wash., 1970, MD, 1974, postgrad., 1977-80. Intern U. Utah, Salt Lake City, 1974—75, resident, 1975—77; fellow in endocrinology and metabolism U. Wash., 1977—80; asst. prof. medicine U. Mich., Ann Arbor, 1980—84; chief endocrinology Wayne County Gen. Hosp., Westland, Mich., 1980—84; from asst. prof. medicine to vice chief endocrinology Wayne State U., Detroit, 1984—87; chief endocrinology VA Med. Ctr., Allen Park, Mich., 1985—87; chief medicine Phoenix VA Med. Ctr., 1997—; assoc. clin. prof. medicine U. Ariz., Tucson, 1988—95, prof. clin. medicine, 1995—. Adj. prof. Coll. of Liberal Arts, Ariz. State U., Tempe, 1991—; dir. Phoenix Citywide Endocrinology and Metabolism Fellowship Prog., 1994—. Contbr. many articles and abstracts to profl. jours. Fellow Am. Coll. Physicians; mem. Am. Fed. for Clin. Research, Am. Diabetes Assn., Am. Soc. Hypertension, The Endocrine Soc. Roman Catholic. Avocations: hiking, films. Home: 5543 E Sheena Dr Scottsdale AZ 85254-2961 Office: VA Med Ctr 7th St Phoenix AZ 85034

FELICETTI, DANIEL A. academic administrator, educator; b. N.Y.C., Apr. 25, 1942; s. Ernest and Rose (DiAdamo) F.; m. Barbara D'Antonio, July 13, 1969. BA in Polit. Sci., Hunter Coll., 1963; MA in Polit. Sci., NYU, 1966, PhD in Polit. Sci., 1971. From asst. to assoc. prof. Fairfield (Conn.) U., 1967-77, chmn. dept. politics, 1973-76, spl. asst. to pres., 1977; acad. v.p., acad. dean Wheeling (W.Va.) Coll., 1977-80; sr. v.p. for acad. affairs Coll. New Rochelle, N.Y., 1980-81, Southeastern U., Washington, 1982-84; v.p. acad. affairs U. Detroit, 1984-89; pres. Marian Coll., Indpls., 1989-99, Capital U., Columbus, Ohio, 1999-2001; founder Higher Edn. Leadership Projects Consulting Svc., 2001—. Participant Am. Coun. on Edn., Washington, 1976-77, vis. assoc., 1984-85; intern Inst. for Ednl. Mgmt. program Harvard U., 1981; cons. Coun. for Ind. Colls., Washington, 1986. Trustee Am. Heart Assn., Mich.; bd. dirs. Am. Heart Assn., Ind., Mental Health Assn. Marion County, Econ. Club Indpls., Coun. Ind. Colls.; mem. health and substance abuse com. New Detroit, Inc., 1986-89; mem. Greater Indpls. Progress Com.; mem. Pub. Safety Task Force Ind.; mem. Colls. Ind. Found.; mem. Indpls. delegation to Pres.'s Summit for Am.'s Future, 1997. Trustee Am. Heart Assn., Mich.; bd. dirs. Am. Heart Assn., Ind., Mental Health Assn. Marion County, Econ. Club Indpls., Coun. Ind. Colls.; mem. health and substance abuse com. New Detroit, Inc., 1986-89; mem. Greater Indpls. Progress Coml; mem. Pub. Safety Task Force Ind.; mem. Colls. Ind. Found.; mem. safety vision coun. United Way Columbus. Named to Hunter Coll. Hall of Fame, Hunter Coll. Alumni Assn., 1986; recipient Cert. of Recognition Sen. Lugar, 1994; Lilly Found. vis. faculty fellow Yale U., 1975; named Sagamore of the Wabash Gov. of Ind., 1990. Mem. Indpls. Athletic Club, received hon. doctoral degree from Marian Coll., 1999, Columbus C. of C. (pub. rels. com.), Rotary, Alpha Sigma Nu (hon.), Beta Gamma Sigma (hon.). Democrat. Roman Catholic. Avocations: baseball, reading, antiques.

FELICIANO, JOSÉ, entertainer; b. Larez, P.R., Sept. 10, 1945; s. Jose and Hortencia (Garcia) F.; m. Susan Feliciano; children: Melissa, Jonathan, Michael. Pres. Feliciano Enterprises. Folk singer in Greenwich Village, N.Y.C., 1962, rec. artist for Universal Records; TV appearances Feliciano—Very Special, 1969, Monsanto Night Presents Jose Feliciano, 1972, Statue of Liberty Celebration, 1984, Absolutely the Best, 2000, Feliciano, A Legend in Concert, 2000, over 100 others; has performed with major symphonies worldwide; composer some of own material including: Affirmation, Rain, Chico and the Man, Feliz Navidad, Ay Carino, Como tu Quieres; composer: guitar concerto Concerto de Paulinho, Mozartean Influence. Recipient 6 Grammy awards, including award in 1990, 11 Grammy nominations, Best Folk Guitarist award Guitar Player Mag. 1973, Best Pop Guitarist award 1973-77; more than 40 Gold albums; star in his name implanted on Hollywood Blvd., 1987. Achievements include having José Feliciano Sch. Performing Arts, East Harlem, N.Y., dedicated in his honor, 1987, DHL (hon.), 2001. Address: World Entertainment Assocs 8815 Conroy Windermere Rd Ste #407 Orlando FL 32835 *The greatest tragedy for many so-called handicapped people is that they let others convince them that there are limits to what they can accomplish. It's just not so.*

FELICIANO, JOSÉ CELSO, lawyer; b. Yauco, P.R., Mar. 7, 1950; s. Santiago and Cielo (Rodríguez) F.; m. Mary Colleen Dempsey; children: José, Rebecca, Marisa. BA, John Carroll U., 1972; JD, Cleve. State U., 1975; MBA, 1984. Bar: Ohio 1975, U.S. Dist. Ct. (no. dist.) Ohio 1975, U.S. Supreme Ct. 1979, U.S. Ct. Appeals (6th cir.) 1981, Staff atty. Legal Aid Soc., Cleve., 1975-78; asst. county pub. defender Cuyahoga County, Cleve., 1978-80; chief police prosecutor City of Cleve., 1980-84; White House fellow, Washington, 1984-85, ptnr. Baker & Hostetler, Cleve., 1985—. Contbr. articles to legal jours. V.p., gen. counsel Neighborhood Housing Svc., Cleve., 1977-80; v.p. United Way Svcs., Cleve., 1981-84, Fedn. for Community Planning, Cleve., 1981-84; bd. dirs. ARC, Cleve., 1981-84; chmn. vis. com. Case Western Res. U. Law Sch., Cleve., 1983-84; pres., founder Hispanic Community Forum, Cleve., 1984; bd. dirs. St. John's Hosp., 1986—; trustee Cleve. Ballet, 1986—. Book reviewer for Cleve. Plain Dealer. Recipient Disting. Svc. award Cleve. Jaycees, 1982, Disting. Alumni award Cleve. State U., 1990; named One of Outstanding Young Men of Ohio Ohio Jaycees, 1983, One of Outstanding Young Men. of Am. U.S. Jaycees, 1985; named Pub. Adminstr. of Yr. Am. Soc. Pub. Adminstrn., 1983. Mem. ABA (sec. alternate dispute resolution sect.), Am. Bar Found., Ohio State Bar Assn. (mem. del. assembly), Ohio Hispanic Bar Assn. (founder, trustee, v.p. 1983-84), Cleve. Bar Assn. (trustee 1982-84). Democrat. Roman Catholic. Avocations: travel, reading, sports. Home: 46 Wolfpen Dr Chagrin Falls OH 44022-4268 Office: Baker & Hostetler 3200 Nat City Ctr 1900 E 9th St Ste 3200 Cleveland OH 44114-3475

FELIG, ELLIOT MILES, lawyer; b. New Haven, Conn., Mar. 9, 1966; s. Philip and Florence Farber F. BA, Brandeis U., 1988; JD, NYU, 1992. Bar: N.Y., Conn. Asst. dist. atty. N.Y. County Dist. Atty.'s Office, N.Y.C., 1996—. Office: NY County Dist Atty's Office One Hogan Pl New York NY 10013

FELIX, CHERYL A. air transportation executive; b. St. Paul, Aug. 31; d. Lawrence J. and Beverly J. McGuinn; m. Guy J. Felix, May 20, 2000. AA, Normandale C.C., Bloomington, Minn.; AAS in Exec. Secretarial, Inver Hills C.C., Inver Grove Heights, MN; BA in Polit. Sci., BA in Pub. Adminstrn., St. Cloud State U., 2000; postgrad., Embry-Riddle Aero. U., 2001—. Customer svc., tech. support adminstr. Shadin Co., Inc., St. Louis Park, Minn., 1995—98; materials mgr. Dallas Airmotive, Mpls., 2000—01; engring. adminstr./master planner/scheduler Shadin Co., Inc., St. Louis Park, Minn., 2001—. Grad. rsch. asst. Embry-Riddle Aero. U. Mem.: Am. Soc. Pub. Adminstrn., Women Aviation, Internat., Exptl. Aircraft Assn., Aircraft Owners and Pilots Assn., Internat. Aerobatic Club. Avocations: aerobatics, politics, pool. Personal E-mail: Little_scrapper@msn.com.

FELIX, DAVID, retired economics educator, consultant; b. N.Y.C., June 10, 1918; s. Oscar and Jenny Felix; m. Gretchen Schafer, Aug. 20, 1945; children: Tonia, Gianna. BA, U. Calif., Berkeley, 1942; MA, U. Calif., 1947, PhD, 1955. Vis. asst. prof. econs. U. Wash., Seattle, 1950-52; prof. econs. Wayne State U., Detroit, 1954-63, Washington U., St. Louis, 1964-88; prof. emeritus, 1988—. Vis. rsch. fellow Ctr. U.S.-Mex. Studies, U. Calif., 1984, vis. rsch. assoc. Ctr. Internat. Affairs, Harvard U., 1967-68; cons. UNDP, 1994-96, UN Econ. Commn. L.Am., 1974. Editor: Debt and Transfiguration, 1990; contbr. ove 26 articles to profl. jours. Lt., USN, 1942-46. Fulbright fellow, 1967, 91. Mem. Am. Econ. Assn., Econ. History Assn. (editl. bd. 1978-84), L.Am. Studies Assn. (editl. bd. 1970-72), Washington U. Prof. Emeritus Assn. (coun. 1990-91, pres. 1992). Avocations: tennis, gardening, travel. Office: Washington U Dept Econs One Brookings Dr Saint Louis MO 63130 E-mail: felix@wueconc.wustl.edu.

FELIX, PATRICIA JEAN, steel company purchasing professional; b. Baptistown, N.J., Dec. 13, 1941; d. Dmitri and Rosalia (Hryckowian) F. Student, Pratt Inst., 1960-61, Moravian Coll., Bethlehem, Pa., 1961-63. Cert. purchasing mgr. Pricing analyst Riegel Paper Co., N.Y.C., 1966-69; placement mgr. Gardner Assocs., N.Y.C., 1969-72; buyer Bethlehem Steel Corp., 1973-78, buyer exempt, 1978-84, sr. buyer, 1984, purchasing supr., 1984-94, raw materials team, 1994-97, sr. sourcing specialist, 1997—. Sec. coun. St. Nicholas Russian Orthodox Ch., Bethlehem, 1982-85, mem. coun., 1985-91, bldg. com., 1992-93, 97, icon com., 1996-97; bldg. com. 1998— Bethlehem-Tondabayashi Sister City Commn., 1988-91, sec., 1989-90, chmn., 1991-93. Mem. Nat. Assn. Purchasing Mgrs. Home: 1721 Millard St Bethlehem PA 18017-5142 Office: 1170 8th Ave Bethlehem PA 18016-7699

FELIX, ROBERT LOUIS, law educator; b. Detroit, Apr. 7, 1934; s. Camille Auguste and Rosalie (Le Floch) F.; m. Judith Joan Grossman, Aug. 25, 1962; children: Marie, Bridget, Robert, Conan. AB, U. Cin., 1956, LLB, 1959; MA, U. B.C., 1962; postgrad. Oxford U. 1962-63; LLM, Harvard U., 1967. Asst., assoc. prof. law Duquesne U., Pitts., 1963-67; assoc. prof. law U. S.C., 1967-72, prof., 1973—; chair James P. Mozingo III prof., 1984—; faculty assoc. U.S.C. Inst. Internat. Studies. With U.S. Army, 1960. Ford fellow Harvard Law Sch., 1966-67; Fulbright vis. lectr. U. Clermont-Ferrand, France, 1975-76; lectr. Program on Internat. Legal Coop., Free U., Brussels, Belgium, 1976. Mem. Assn. Am. Law Schs. (sect. on Conflict of Laws), Fulbright Alumni Assn. Roman Catholic. Author: (with R. Leflar, L. McDougal) Cases and Materials on American Conflicts Law, 1982, 2d edit., 1989, (with L. McDougal, R. Whitten) 3d edit., 1998, American Conflicts Law, 4th ed., 1986, (with L. McDougal, R. Whitten) 5th ed, 2001; (with F.P. Hubbard) The South Carolina Law of Torts, 1990, 2d edit., 1997; (with others) New Directions in Legal Education, 1969, (with others), The Vanity Fair Gallery, 1979. Contbr. articles to profl. jours. Home: 6233 Macon Rd Columbia SC 29209-2016 Office: U SC Law Sch Main & Greene St Columbia SC 29208-0001

FELIX, SUSAN DUHAN, consultant, community development specialist, artist; b. Queens, N.Y., July 23, 1937; d. Eliot Mendel and Evelyn Silverman Duhan; m. Morton Neil Felix, June 16, 1957; children: Lisa Anne. BA, Queens Coll., 1958; MA, U. Conn., 1961. Cert. Corp. Tng., 1992., lifetime Jr. Coll. tchg., Calif., 1969; instr. credential Cmty. Coll., Calif., 1982. Ceramics instr. Art Co-Op, Berkeley, Calif., 1968-78, class coord., 1972-79; reader/cons. UC Press, Berkeley, 1982; instr. Vista Coll., Berkeley, 1983; exec. dir. UA Housing, Inc., Berkeley, 1979-99; devel. cons. KPFA, Berkeley, 1984-85; cmty. specialist Resources Cmty. Devel., Berkeley, 1999—2001. Panelist Women of Vision, Washington, 1994; task force Art Dist. City of Berkeley, 1995-98; mem. adv. com. Berkeley (Calif.) Cultural Plan, 2002—. Bd. dirs. Berkeley Richmond Jewish Cmty Ctr., 1975—79; art liaison Mayor for City of Berkeley, 1989—92; pres. Berkeley Art Commn., 1985—89; mem. Berkeley Waterfront Commn., 1997—2001, Berkeley Cultural Trust, 2001—; art amb. City of Berkeley, Calif., 2003—; bd. dirs. Berkeley Art Festival, 2001—. Recipient Maxwell award, Fannie Mae Found., Washington, 1994, Cert. of Congl. Recognition, Washington, 1999, Outstanding Berkeley Woman award, City of Berkeley, 1993, 1st prize New England Ceramics Show, 1963, Excellence in Design award, 1986, Ford Found. scholar, McAuley Inst., Houston, 1998, named "Art Ambassador of Berkeley", 2003. Mem.: Jewish Arts Cmty. Bay (exec. dir. 1980—91, founder), Pacific Rim Sculptural Group, Assn. Ceramic and Glass Artists. Avocations: family, swimming, dancing, reading poetry. . Home and Office: 1436 Berkeley Way Berkeley CA 94702-1520 E-mail: sdfelix@aol.com.

FELIX, TED MARK, accountant; b. Bklyn., Apr. 23, 1947; s. Jack and Shirley (Starr) F.; children: Randi Sue, Jennifer Lynn. BS in Acctg., L.I. U., 1968, MBA in Fin., 1976. CPA, N.J., N.Y. Sr. auditor KPMG Peat Marwick, N.Y.C., 1968—71, 1975—80; mgr. tech. standards Clarence Rainess & Co., N.Y.C., 1971—75; ptnr. Trien, Rosenberg, Felix, Rosenberg, Barr & Weinberg, N.Y.C., Morristown, 1980—95, Lazar Levine & Felix LLP, N.Y.C. and Parsippany, NJ, 1995—2002, mng. ptnr., 2002—. Adj. prof. acctg. Ocean County Coll., Toms River, N.J., 1976-79, Rutgers U., New Brunswick, N.J., 1981-83; bd. dirs. Internat. Group Acctg. Firm, N.Y.C., London, Hong Kong. Contbr. articles to profl. jours. Bd. dirs. JCC of Metrowest, Whippany, N.J., 1989-99, v.p., 1992-99. Mem.: AICPA (dir. quality control rev. divsn. 1975—80, numerous coms.), N.J. Soc. CPAs (v.p. 1993—94, trustee 1989—90, numerous coms.), N.Y. Soc. CPAs (numerous coms.), B'nai B'rith (pres. West Morris 1987—89, bd. govs. Dist. 3 1988—92, treas. No. N.J. coun. 1989—90, v.p. 1990—92, pres. Tri-State region 1997—, internat. bd. govs. 1998—). Avocations: personal computers, first day covers, model railroading. Office: Lazar Levine & Felix LLP 350 5th Ave New York NY 10118-0110

FELKEL, CHARLENE CAMPBELL, family nurse practitioner, nursing educator; b. Belton, SC, Aug. 8, 1953; d. Charles G. and Billie Jo Campbell; m. John A. Felkel Jr., July 19, 1975; children: Preston, Warren. BSN, Med. U. S.C., Charleston, 1975; MSN, U. S.C., Columbia, 1978, family nurse practitioner certificate, 1995. Cert. family nurse practitioner, ANCC. Coronary care staff nurse Providence Hosp., Columbia, 1975-76; tchg. assoc. U. S.C. Coll. Nursing, Columbia, 1976-78; clin. nurse specialist Bapt. Hosp., Columbia, 1978-81; sr. pub. health nurse S.C. Dept. Health Environ. Control, Aiken, 1990-91; asst. prof. nursing U. SC, Aiken, 1991—2003; family nurse practitioner Aiken Med. Specialties Practice, Aiken, 1995—. Author patient edn. pamphlets and booklets, 1978, 79, 95; author, dir., prodr. video hosp. orientation for student nurses, 1994, nursing recruitment video, 1999; contbr. articles to profl. jours. including Jour. Nursing Edn. Mem. bd. Am. Lung Assn., Columbia, 1980-81. Mem. ANA, Am. Lung Assn., Am. Heart Assn., Habitat for Humanity, S.C. Nursing Assn., Sigma Theta Tau. Baptist. Avocations: family, reading, furniture refinishing, gardening. Office: 191 Centre South Blvd Aiken SC 29803

FELKER, GERALD LEE, music educator, musician; b. Canastota, NY, May 8, 1963; s. James Neil and Shirley Jean Felker; m. Erika Ingrid DeMilo, Feb. 2, 1969; children: Emily, Alexander. MusM, Potsdam Coll., 1991; postgrad., SUNY, Stony Brook, 2002—. Cert. tchr. NY. Band dir. Farmingdale (NY) Pub. Schools, 1991—. Profl. bass trombonist, L.I. and N.Y.C. With U.S. Army, 1981—84. Mem.: Farmingdale Fedn. Tchrs. Liberal. Roman Catholic. Avocations: reading, travel. Home: 3 Rhonda Terr Farmingdale NY 11735 Office: Farmingdale Pub Schs 101 Albany Ave North Massapequa NY 11758-2199 Office Fax: 516-752-7039. Personal E-mail: mr_felker@hotmail.com.

FELKER, WILLIAM H. (B. C. STUVINSKI), filmmaker, videomaker; b. Rockford, Ill., Oct. 14, 1953; s. Robert Hugh and Suzanne (Billig) F.; m. Janell Ann Schwartz, Sept. 20, 1975; children: Sage Brook, Ruth Rama, Alexandra Alta. BFA, Mpls. Coll. Art and Design, 1976. Owner B.C. Stuvinski Prodns., Mpls., 1976-78; with prodn. dept. EMCOM, Mpls., 1978-79; owner House of Cinemagraphics, Mpls., 1979—; gaffer Feature, Comml. and Indsl. Prodn. Svcs., 1975—; dir. photography Private Public, 2000—. Prodn. mgr. Paisely Pk. Enterprises, 1992-93; dir. photography Godfathers Pizza, 1995—; lighting dir. ITVA Awards, 1995, SmithKline Beecham, IBM, SuperValue, Bell Mus., 40 Muscular Dystrophy Assn. Telethons, 2002. Filmmaker: Voices, 1970, Field Animation Series, 1972, The Cave, 1974, What??, 1975, Phenomena 24, 1976, Dialetic Complex, 1976, Pink Movie, 1976, Turn Off After Viewing, 1976, Bridge, 1977, Five Bridge Installation Allusions, 1977, Factors of Six by David Means, 1979, L.A.S.E.R., 1979; (with Janell Felker) A Matter of Time, 1976, Cloud Gel, 1977, Sand Animation, 1977, Green Movie, 1977, The Circus is Kinder, 1977, Nine States of Motion, 1977, Landscape, 1978-90, Scrim Film, 1978, Desert, 1979, Bucolics, 1979, Homage to the 41 Sperm Whales That Beached on the Eve of the Signing of the Strategic Arms Limitation Treaty (SALT II), 1980; (with Jack Becker and Janell Felker) Upsidedownandbackwards, 1976; electric dept. Purple Rain, 1984, Here on Earth, 1999, Drop Dead Gorgeous (1st a/c B camera 1998, 1st A/C gaffer NFL films 1998-2001); dir. photography: Breakfast on Broadway, 1988, Target, 1998, Select Comfort, 1998-99, Pillsbury Spots, 1999, The Private Public, 2000; dir. lighting and sound Letter Press Printing, 1978, Picasso, 1980; dir. lighting Too Far, Too Fast, 1989, Swedish TV in American, 1993, Marraige Day, Mall of America, Dr. John Grey, 1996, Bell Live, 1995-2000; 1st asst. camera 2nd unit Home Town Boy Makes Good, 1989, The Come Back, Get Off, 1991, Organ Grinder, 1991; 2d asst. Divine Madness, 1980; dir., cameraman, editor AT&T Mpls. Tower: Time Lapse Documentary, 1989-91; dir. spl. effects photography, assoc. producer Resident Alien, 1990-91; lighting dir. Violet the Organ Grinder, Housestyle, 1991, Mayo Clinic, Infection Control, 1995-2000, Bankers Systems, 1998-2000, Children's Home Society Korea and U.S., 1996; assoc. producer What About Bob, 1991-92; lighting dir., camera operator Meantime, 1990, Prince concerts and videos, 1991-92; prodn. mgr. Sacrifice of Victor, 1992; post prodn. mgr. Three Chains o' Gold, 1992, Undertaker, 1992; co-dir., dir. photography, editor Stu and Bink, 1993-97; editorial svcs., Simple Plan, 1998, Sugar and Spice, 1999; camera operator, gaffer The Visionary, 1995; camera operator, 1st asst. camera 2d unit Mallrats, 1995; helicopter camera operator In the Line of Duty, 1995; electrician Feeling Minnesota, 1995; 2d asst. camera Mighty Ducks, 1995; 2d unit gaffer, video colorist Grumpier Old Men, 1995; gaffer Psychic Friends Network, Mall of America, 1996, Through the Window, 1998, Target, 1998, United Way, 1998, Mall Masters, 2000, ABC News, Nightline, Good Morning America, 1999-2002: cinematographer NBA Jam, 1993; dir. of photography, Private Public, 2001, Kwik Stop, 2001, Jel, Gaffer, 2001, Best Buy Campus Timelapse, 2001-03, Von Maur, 2002; lighting dir. Bell Live, 1996-2000, MDA, 2001. Recipient Jerome Found. grant, 1978, Minn. State Arts Bd. grant, 1978, NEA grants, 1978, 92. Mem. Assn. Ind. Comml. Prodrs. (bd. dirs. 2002, sec.), Ind. Feature Project North. Home and Office: 4802 Quail Ave N Minneapolis MN 55429-3739 E-mail: film@visi.com., houseofcinema@netscape.net.

FELKNOR, BRUCE LESTER, editorial consultant, writer; b. Oak Park, Ill., Aug. 18, 1921; s. Audley Rhea and Harriet (Lester) F.; m. Joanne Sweeney, Feb. 8, 1942 (div. Jan. 1952); 1 child, Susan Harriet Felknor Pickard; m. Edith G. Johnson, Mar. 1, 1952; children: Sarah Anne, Bruce Lester II. Student, U. Wis., 1939-41. Reporter Dunn County News, Menomonie, Wis., 1937-39; freight brakeman Pa. R.R., N.Y.C., 1941, asst. yardmaster, 1942; prodn. coordinator Hwy. Trailer Co., Edgerton, Wis., 1943; radio officer U.S. Maritime Service, 1944-45; flight radio officer Air Transport Command, 1945; mem. pub. relations dept. Am. Airlines, 1945; writer pub. relations dept. ITT, 1946; Southeast regional pub. relations dir. Ford Motor Co., Chester, Pa., 1946-48; free lance pub. relations N.Y.C., 1948-49; pub. relations exec. Foote, Cone & Belding, Inc., N.Y.C., 1950-53; v.p. Market Relations Network, N.Y.C., 1954-55; exec. dir. Fair Campaign Practices Com., Inc., N.Y.C., 1956-66; asst. to William Benton (chmn. and pub. Ency. Brit.), 1966-70; dir. mktg. info. internat. div. (Ency. Brit.), 1970-73, dir. advt. and promotion, 1973, dir. pub. info., 1974-76, exec. editor, 1977-83; dir. yearbooks Ency. Brit., 1983-85; editorial cons., 1985—. Vis. lectr. Hamilton Coll., 1966, 75, 82; history editor Mcht. Marine internet web site www.usmm.org, 1999—. Author: Fair Play in Politics, 1960, State-by-State Smear Study, 1956, You Are They, 1964, (with C.P. Taft) Prejudice & Politics, 1960, Dirty Politics, 1966, reprinted, 1975, 2001, (with Frank Jonas et al) Political Dynamiting, 1970, How to Look Things Up and Find Things Out, 1988, Political Mischief: Smear, Sabotage, and Reform in U.S. Elections, 1992, The Highland Park Presbyterian Church: A History 1871-1996, 1996 (Robert Lee Stowe award 1997), The U.S. Merchant Marine at War 1775-1945, 1998, The Great Witch Hunt of the Presbyterian Left, 2001; editor: The U.S. Government: How and Why it Works, 1978; also various newspaper, jour. and yearbook articles on politics; contbg. editor (with Clifton Fadiman) The Treasury of the Encyclopaedia Britannica, 1992; contbr. Encyclopedia of the American Presidency, 1993. Chmn. Citizens Com. for Sch. Centralization in Armonk, N.Y., 1957-61; ruling elder, chmn. com. religion and race Presbytery Hudson River, 1963-67, mem. nat. coun. on ch. and soc., 1966-72; bd. dirs., mem. exec. com. Fair Campaign Practices Com.; mem. nat. adv. bd. Amigos de las Americas, 1982-89, Am. U., Washington, 1982—; mem. Ill. Literacy Coun., 1984-86; mem. bd. advisors, acad. adv. coun. Nat. Strategy Forum, 1987—, mem. bd. edn. Lake Forest (Ill.) H.S. Dist., 1989-93. Republican. Presbyterian. Home and Office: 509 Trinity Ct Evanston IL 60201-1908 E-mail: brucefelk@cs.com. *Man's greatest gifts are empathy and the ability to penetrate balderdash.*

FELL, CHERYL COOKMEYER, artist, art educator; b. New Orleans, Feb. 2, 1969; d. Eugene Napolean and Jo Ann (Karl) Cookmeyer; m. Shane Michael Fell, Dec. 21, 1996 (div.); 1 child, Joshua. BA in Art Edn., U. Southwestern La., 1995; MFA in 3d Animation, Savannah Coll. Art and Design, 2001; postgrad., U. New Orleans, 1996-98. Cert. tchr. K-12 in art edn. Tchr. art and English Brother Martin H.S., New Orleans, 1995-99; media tech. instr. Pooler (Ga.) Elem. Sch., 2000—01; prof. computer art Savannah Coll. Art and Design, 2001—. Site leader, team tchr. web design Urban Arts Summer Tng. Program, Arts Coun. of New Orleans, 1998-99; lab. asst., cage monitor Computer Art Dept., Savannah Coll. Art and Design, 2000-01; guest lectr. dept. art U. Southwestern La., Lafayette, 1999. One-woman shows Cheryl Fell paintings, 1999, 2001, 03; exhibited in group shows at Ark. Arts Ctr., Little Rock, 1998, d.o.c.s. gallery, New Orleans, 1999, 2001, Mobile (Ala.) Mus. Art, 1999, La. Open Juried Exhbn., Southeastern Juried exhbn., 1999, Artlink, Inc., 2000, Savannah (Ga.) Art Assn., 2000, Exhibit A Gallery, Art of the New Faculty, Savannah, 2001. Southeby's, Savannah, Ga., 2002, Internat. Young Artists, N.Y.C., 2002; represented in permanent collection d.o.c.s. gallery, New Orleans, 1999—. Vol. curator Neutral Ground Coffee House, New Orleans, 1998-99. Recipient The Power of Art award Robert Rauschenberg Found. and the Lab Sch. of Washington, 1999. Mem. Savannah Arts Assn. Home: 202 W 37th St Apt D Savannah GA 31401 E-mail: cheryl@cherylfell.com.

FELL, ELIZABETH P. education educator; b. Jackson, Ala., Nov. 28, 1942; d. Alvin Curtis and Annie Mae Paul; m. George Ray Fell, Dec. 18, 1965; children: Ashley, Allison, Kirk. BS in Edn., Livingston U, 1964, ME, 1968; Ed.D. in Elem. Edn., U. Ala., 1985; A. Cert. Elem. Edn. U. of Ala., 1975. Elem tchr. elem. sch., Ga., 1964—81, 1964—81, 1964—81; asst. prof. Mobile (Ala.) Coll., 1981—89; prof., chair, Curriculum and Instrn. Troy State U, Dothan, Ala., 1989. Nat. Scholastic Judge Am. Jr. Miss, Mobile, 1986—89; SACS Facilitator and Review Chmn. So. Assn. of Ala. Pub. Coll. and Sch. Ala. Elem. and Middle Sch., 1982—. Mem.: AACTE, Nat. Council for the Social Studies, Nat. Council for Tchr. of English, Phi Delta Kappa (hon.), Kappa Delta Pi (Counselor). Office: Troy State U Dothan PO Box 8368 Dothan AL 36304-0368

FELL, FREDERICK VICTOR, publisher; b. Bklyn., May 21, 1910; s. Samuel and Victoria (Greenhut) F.; m. Selma Shampain, May 18, 1975; children: Linda Fell Firestein, Nancy. Student, NYU, 1928-31; LLB, Bklyn. Law Sch., 1935. Pres. Frederick Fell Pubs., N.Y.C., 1943-81; prin. Frederick Fell & Assocs., Inc., Literary Agts., Hollywood, Fla., 1981—. Author: (pseudonym Vic Fredericks) Crackers in Bed, 1953, More for Doctors Only, 1953, Just Married, 1958, For Golfers Only, 1964, Wit and Wisdom of Presidents, 1966, others; editor and publisher: The Hillcrest Hotline, 1993—. Trustee Long Beach (N.Y.) Library, 1948-50; councilman City of Long Beach, 1950-54, pres. city council, 1950-52; pres. Long Beach Hosp. Club, 1949, 59; chmn. book pubs. div. crusades N.Y.C. div. Am. Cancer Soc., 1977-81. Mem. Assn. Am. Pubs., Am. Booksellers Assn., Book Group South Fla. Clubs: Hillcrest Country, Hollywood (Fla.). Democrat. Jewish. Home: 3800 Hillcrest Dr Apt 1120 Hollywood FL 33021-7940

FELL, JENNIFER ANNE, writer; b. Columbus, Ohio, Nov. 6, 1968; d. James Frederick Fell and Mary Elizabeth Kelly McColl. BA in English, Santa Clara U., 1990. Pub. rels. asst. de Saisset Mus., Santa Clara, Calif., 1987—90; tech. writer Rational Software Corp., Santa Clara, 1990—94; sr. tech. writer ParcPlace-Digitalk, Inc., Sunnyvale, Calif. and Austin Tex., 1994—97; mem. tech. staff Neometron, Austin, Tex., 1997; tech. writer Expert Support, Mountain View, Calif., 1997—99; sr. tech. writer NativeMinds, Inc., San Francisco, 1999—, dir. tech. comms., 1999—, v.p. engring., 1999—2003. Vol. Planned Parenthood, Calif. and Idaho, 1993-96. Mem. NOW, Planned Parenthood, Soc. for Tech. Comm., HTML, Writers Guild, KQED, CLCV, Alpha Sigma Nu, Sigma Tau Delta, Phi Sigma Tau. Avocations: dogs, softball.

FELL, SAMUEL KENNEDY (KEN FELL), infosystems executive; b. Wilmington, Del., Oct. 6, 1944; s. S. Kennedy and Anna Elizabeth (Alford) F.; m. Diana Marie Dickson, May 8, 1965; children: Melissa Ann, Michael Kennedy. BSBA, Oklahoma City U., 1983; postgrad. in bus., John F. Kennedy U.; grad. exec. mgmt. program, Duke U., 1991. Mgmt./data processing sys. designer/implementor Gen. Motors Corp., Detroit and Oklahoma City, 1967-81; v.p. info. systems Totco Divsn. Baker Internat., Norman, Okla., 1981-85; v.p. computer info. Cleve. Pneumatic subs. Pneumo Abex Corp. div. IC Industries, 1985-88; sr. dir. systems devel. Sprint, Kansas City, Mo., 1988-95; exec. v.p. product devel., exec. bd. mem. SynQuest, Inc., A Warburg Pincus Co., 1995-2000; CIO NYISO, Schenectady, N.Y., 2000—. Mem. Data Processing Mgrs. Assn., Oracle Users Group, Soc. Info. Mgrs. Office: NY ISO 3890 Carman Rd Schenectady NY 12303

FELLA, MARIE ANN, intelligence analyst, drug enforcement administration; b. New London, Conn., Dec. 9, 1956; d. Rosario Joseph and Mildred Mae (Carlins) F.; m. Thomas Boles, Sept. 10, 1975 (div. 1979). Associate's, U. Cinti and No. C.C., Annandale, Va., 1997. Clk., stenographer Gen. Svcs. Adminstrn., Cin., 1978-79, Drug Enforcement Adminstrn., Cin., 1979-82, office asst. V.p. Joint Task Force Miami, Fla., 1982-83, adminstrv. support specialist Marseille, France, 1983-93, chief sec. Arlington, Va., 1993-95, program analyst internal affairs, 1995-99, intelligence analyst, 1999—. Mem. World View Internat. T.V., Kennedy Ctr. Roman Catholic. Avocations: golfing, tennis.

FELLEGI, IVAN PETER, statistician; b. Szeged, Hungary, June 22, 1935; immigrated to Can., 1957. s. Andor and Barbara (Partos) F.; m. Marika Gulyas, Dec. 27, 1958; children— Nicolette, Vivien. BSc, U. Budapest, Hungary, 1956;

MSc, Carleton U., Ont., Can., 1958, PhD, 1961; PhD (hon.), Simon Fraser U., 1995; LLD (hon.), McMaster U., 1997; PhD (hon.), Carleton U., 1999; D (hon.), U. Que., 2001, U. Montreal, 2002. With Statistics Can., Ottawa, Ont., 1957—, asst. chief statistician, 1973-84, dep. chief statistician, 1984-85, chief statistician of Can., 1985—. Contbr. articles to profl. jours. Bd. govs. Carleton U., 1989—, chmn. bd. govs., 1995-97; chair Conf. European Statisticians, 1993-97. Named to Order of Can., 1992, officer, 1998; recipient Robert Schuman medal, European Cmty., 1997, Outstanding Achievement award, Pub. Svc. Can., 2002. Fellow AAAS, Am. Statis. Assn., Royal Statis. Soc. (hon.); mem. Internat. Statis. Inst. (hon., pres. 1987-89), Statis. Soc. Can. (pres. 1982), Internat. Assn. Survey Statisticians (pres. 1985-87). Home: 16 Larchwood Ave Ottawa ON Canada K1Y 2E3 Office: Statistics Canada RH Coats Bldg Tunney's Pasture Ottawa ON Canada K1A 0T6

FELLENSTEIN, CORA ELLEN MULLIKIN, retired credit union executive; b. Edwardsville, Ill., June 2, 1930; d. Russell K. and Elberta Mable (Rheude) Mullikin; m. Charles Frederick Fellenstein, Feb. 24, 1951; children: Keith David, Kimberly Diane. Student, Cmty. Coll., 1980-83. Teller, loan officer, office mgr. Credit Union of Johnson County, Olathe, Kans., 1976-84, 1st. v.p., supr. lending, collection and Mastercard depts. Lenexa, Kans., 1984-86, exec v.p., 1987-94. Vol. Cerebral Palsey, 1957—66, Olathe Cmty. Hosp., 1976—92, Shawnee Mission (Kans.) Med. Ctr., 1986—90, Caring For Others, Amigos de Los Ninos de Mexico, 1996—, Mex. Children's Refuge, 1998—, HOSTS (Help One Student to Succeed) Program, San Juan, Tex.; Precinct committeewoman Johnson County Reps., Olathe, Kans., 1976—92; bd. dirs. Consumer Credit Counseling Svc., Kansas City, Mo., 1992—94. Mem. NAFE, Internat. Assn. Credit Card Investigators, Internat. Credit Assn., Kans. Credit Assn., Credit Profls. (dir. 1983-92, Exec. of Yr. Johnson county chpt.), DAR (treas. 1966-86), Daus. Am. Colonists (treas. 1976-86), Friends of Historic Mahaffie Farmstead, Soroptomist Internat., Beta Sigma Phi. Mem. Christian Ch. Avocations: genealogy, camping, travel. Home: 800 FM 495 Lot 689 Alamo TX 78516-6932 E-mail: cokefell2@aol.com.

FELLER, BENJAMIN E. actuary; b. Bronx, N.Y., Mar. 4, 1947; s. Morris and Beatrice (Wolff) F.; m. Debra May Morane, June 1973 (div. 1983); children: Amy; m. Sue Ann Kaufman, Sept. 23, 1984; children: Meredith; stepchildren: Stefanie McCoy, Alison McCoy. BS in Math., Clarkson U., Potsdam, N.Y., 1968; MA in Math., Ind. U., 1971. Enrolled actuary. Actuarial asst. U.S. Life Ins. Co., N.Y.C., 1971-75; assoc. actuary The Wyatt Co., Washington, 1975-76; cons. actuary Buck Cons., N.Y.C., 1976-85; ptnr. Chernoff Diamond & Co., Williston Park, N.Y., 1985-92; pres. Pension Rev. Svcs., Plainview, N.Y., 1992—. Contbr. articles to profl. jours. Fellow Soc. Actuaries; mem. Am. Soc. Pension Actuaries, Am. Acad. Actuaries, Bklyn. Tech. H.S. Alumni Assn. (dir.). Republican. Jewish. Home: 10 Allison Dr Old Bethpage NY 11804-1602 Office: Pension Rev Svcs 45 Executive Dr Plainview NY 11803-1737

FELLER, LLOYD HARRIS, lawyer; b. New Brunswick, N.J., Aug. 27, 1942; s. Alexander and Freda (Kaminsky) F.; m. Susan Sydney Weinberg, Aug. 6, 1967; children: Jennifer, Andrew. BS in Econs., U. Pa., 1964; LLB, NYU, 1967. Bar: N.Y. 1967, D.C. 1980. Assoc. Rubin, Wachtel, Baum & Levin, 1967—70; trial atty. organized crime sect., divsn. enforcement SEC, Washington, 1970—72, legal asst. Commr. A. Sydney Herlong, Jr., 1972—73, legal asst. Commr. A.A. Sommer, Jr., 1973—76; chief counsel Office of the Chief Acct., 1976—77; assoc. dir. divsn. market regulation Office of Market Structure and Trading Practices, 1977—79, of counsel, 1979—81; ptnr. Morgan, Lewis & Bockius LLP, Washington, 1981—99, mem. governing bd., 1996—99, mem. exec. com., 1989—99, mem. allocations com., 1999—; sr. v.p., sec., gen. counsel SoundView Tech. Group, Inc., San Francisco, 1999—. Office: SoundView Tech Group Steuart Twr One Market Plaza San Francisco CA Home: 419 S Lee St Alexandria VA 22314-3815

FELLER, MIMI, newspaper publishing executive; BA cum laude, Creighton U.; JD, Georgetown U. Asst. dir. congl. rels. Gen. Svcs. Adminstrn., 1975-77; legis. asst. Environ. and Pub. Works Com. U.S. Senate, 1977-81; from legis. dir. to Washington chief of staff Sen. John Chafee (Rep.), R.I., 1981-83; dep. asst. sec. legis. affairs U.S. Dept. Treasury, 1983-85; from v.p. govt. rels. to sr. v.p. Gannett Co., 1985—. Bd. dirs. Nat. Ct. Apptd. Spl. Advs. Assn. Bd. dirs. Creighton U. Recipient Disting. Alumnus award Creighton U., 1987. Office: Gannett Co Inc 7950 Jones Branch Dr Mc Lean VA 22107

FELLER, ROBERT LIVINGSTON, chemist, art conservation scientist; b. Newark, Dec. 27, 1919; s. William Henry and Edna (Buckelew) F.; m. Ruth M. Johnston, Mar. 31, 1975. AB, Dartmouth Coll., 1941; MS, Rutgers U., 1943, PhD, 1950. Sr. fellow Nat. Gallery Art Research Project, Mellon Inst., Pitts., 1950-76; dir. Research Ctr. on Materials of Artist and Conservator, Carnegie-Mellon Rsch. Inst., Pitts., 1976-88, dir. emeritus, 1988—. Vis. scientist Conservation Ctr., Inst. Fine Arts, NYU, 1961; pres. Nat. Conservation Adv. Council, 1975-79 Co-author: On Picture Varnishes and their Solvents, 2d rev. edit., 1985, Evaluation of Cellulose Ethers for Conservation, 1990, Accelerated Aging: Photochemical and Thermal Aspects, 1994; editor: Artists' Pigments: A Handbook of Their History and Characteristics, Vol. I, 1986. Served with USN, 1944-46. Recipient Coll. Art Assn.-Nat. Inst. for Conservation Joint award, 1992, Univ. Products award for disting. achievement in conservation of cultural property, 2000. Fellow Internat. Inst. Conservation Hist. and Artistic Works (hon.), Am. Inst. Conservation Hist. and Artistic Works (hon.), Illuminating Engring. Soc.; mem. AAAS, Am. Chem. Soc. (Pittsburgh award 1983), Internat. Coun. Museums (pres. conservation com. 1969-78), Fedn. Socs. Coatings Tech., Inter-Soc. Color Coun., Am. Inst. Conservation. Clubs: Cosmos (Washington); Univ. (Pitts.). Achievements include research on deterioration of varnishes, paper, pigments and dyes used by artists. Office: Carnegie Mellon U Artists Materials Rsch Ctr 700 Technology Dr Pittsburgh PA 15219-3124

FELLER, ROBERT WILLIAM ANDREW, baseball team public relations executive, retired baseball player; b. Van Meter, Iowa, Nov. 3, 1918; s. William and Lena (Forrett) F.; m. Anne Morris Gilliland, Oct. 1, 1974. Pub. rels. exec. Cleveland Indians Baseball Team, 1936-56. Played first major league game Cleve. vs. St. Louis Browns, 1936; pitched 3 no-hitters Cleve. vs. Chgo., 1940, Cleve. vs. N.Y., 1946, Cleve. vs. Detroit, 1951; member 9 all-star teams. Author: Strikeout Story, 1947, How to Pitch, 1948, Now Pitching Bob Feller, 1990, Bob Feller's Little Black Book of Baseball Wisdom, 2000. CPO USNavy, 1941-45, PTO. Inducted to Baseball Hall of Fame, Cooperstown, N.Y., 1962; named Greatest Living Right-Hand Pitcher Profl. Baseball Centennial Celebration, 1969. Mem. Green Berets (hon.). Republican. Episcopalian. Avocation: restoring caterpiller tractors. Fax: 440-423-3248.

FELLER, THOMAS RICHARD, JR., music educator; b. Elmhurst, Idaho, Dec. 17, 1976; s. Thomas Richard and Loretta Kay Feller; m. Melissa Joy Eilers, Jan. 15, 2002. MusB, Palm Beach (Fla.)Atlantic Coll., 1995. Cert. tchr. Fla., 1999. Music tchr. West Riviera (Fla.) Magnet Sch., 1999—. Singer Lost Tree Chapel, North Palm Beach, Fla., 2000—. Men's leadership Maranatha Ch., Palm Beach Gardens, Fla., 2001. Grantee Handbell Grant, Palm Beach Graham-Eckes Found., 2000. Mem.: Christian Educators Assn. Internat. (assoc.), Profl. Educators Network of Fla. (assoc.), Gordon Inst. for Music Learning (assoc.), Nat. Music Educators Assn. (assoc.), Fla. Elem. Music Educators Assn. (assoc.), Fla. Music Educators Assn. (assoc.), Parent Tchr. Assn. (assoc.; sec. 2002—03), U.S. Achievement Acad. (hon.), Kappa Delta Epsilon (hon.). Independent. Avocations: bicycling, travel, reading, bible study, photography. Office: West Riviera Magnet School 1057 W 6th St Riviera Beach FL 33404 Office Fax: 561-840-3215. E-mail: feller_t@firn.edu.

FELLER, WINTHROP BRUCE, physicist; b. Cleve., Nov. 1, 1950; s. Robert William and Virginia Adele (Winther) F.; m. Lydia M. Conca, Aug. 14, 1988; 1 child, Daniel James. SB, MIT, 1974; postgrad., Yale U., 1974-75. Lectr. in physics and astronomy Northwestern U., Evanston, Ill., 1977-83; sr. scientist Galileo Corp., Sturbridge, Mass., 1984-92; v.p., chief scientist Nova Sci., Inc., 1993—. Assoc. Nat. Inst. Sci. and Tech. Contbr. articles to profl. jours. Recipient R&D 100 award R&D mag.; grantee NASA, ARPA, NIH, NSF, Dept. Energy, Dept. Def., Dept. Commerce. Mem. AAAS, Am. Phys. Soc., Am. Philos. Assn., Optical Soc. Am., Soc. Photo-Optical Instrumentation Engrs. (session co-chmn. detector conf.), Fedn. Am. Scientists, Union Concerned Scientists, Am.-Scandinavian Found. Achievements include patents in microchannel plate field; development of low noise, conductively cooled, neutron-, hard x-, and gamma ray sensitive microchannel plate detectors, microsphere plates, lobstereye x-ray telescope optics, electron-beam lithography sources, x-ray lithography optics, x-ray and neutron focusing microchannel lens, others; research on detectors for x-ray astronomy, homeland security space plasma detectors, mass analysis of biomolecules, philosophy of science and religion. Home: 50 Shanda Ln Tolland CT 06084-3951 E-mail: bfeller@novascientific.com.

FELLERS, RHONDA GAY, lawyer; b. Gainesville, Tex., July 20, 1955; d. James Norman and Gaytha Ann (Sanders) F.; m. Bruce C. Hinton, Oct. 15, 1981 (div. Oct. 1985). BA, U. Tex., 1977, JD, 1980; LLM in Taxation, U. Denver, 1987. Bar: Tex. 1981, Colo. 1981, U.S. Dist. Ct. (no. dist.) Tex. 1982, U.S. Dist. Ct. Colo. 1985, U.S. Tax Ct. 1985, U.S. Ct. Appeals (5th cir.) 1986, U.S. Ct. Appeals (10th cir.) 1989, U.S. Supreme Ct. 1993, U.S. Ct. Claims 1993. Assoc. Walters & Assocs., Lubbock, Tex., 1981-83; gen. counsel Security Nat. Bank, Lubbock, 1983; sole practice Lubbock, 1983-87; assoc. Melvin Coffee & Assocs., P.C., Denver, 1984-85, 87-90; atty. adviser U.S. Tax Ct., Washington, 1990-94; pvt. practice Pinehurst, Tex., 1994-98; with Arthur Andersen LLP, Houston, 1998—2002; sole practice, 2002—. Mem. ABA, State Bar Tex., Colo. Bar Assn., Houston Bar Assn. Avocations: golf, tennis, photography. E-mail: rgfellers@starband.net.

FELLHAUER, DAVID E. bishop; b. Kansas City, Mo., Aug. 19, 1939; Student, Pontifical Coll. Josephinum; D in Canon Law, PhD, St. Paul U., Ottawa, Can. Ordained priest Roman Cath. Ch., 1965. Former prof. Holy Trinity Sem., Dallas; judicial vicar Diocese of Dallas, 1990; bishop of Victoria Tex., 1990—. Bd. govs. Canon Law Soc. Am. Recipient Role of Law award, Canon Law Soc., 1998. Office: PO Box 4070 Victoria TX 77903-4070*

FELLINGHAM, WARREN LUTHER, JR., retired banker; b. Chgo., Dec. 28, 1934; s. Warren Luther and Dorothy Eaton (Park) F.; m. Judith Cutler, Sept. 14, 1962; children: Warren III, Margo, Victoria. AB, Dartmouth Coll., 1956; MBA, Northwestern U., 1968. Cert. bank compliance officer. Auditing asst. The Northern Trust Co., Chgo., 1956-61, asst. cashier, 1962-71, 2d v.p., 1972-77, v.p., 1978-96, consumer compliance officer, 1988-96. Pres. Chicagoland Compliance Assn., Chgo., 1988—92. Village pres., mayor Village of Golf, Ill., 1981-85, village trustee, clk., 1973-81; bd. dirs. United Way of Glenview-Golf, 1983-92; unit commr. N.E. Ill. coun. Boy Scouts Am., 1996—; treas. Glenview Area Hist. Soc., 1998—. Recipient Dist. award of Merit, 1989, N.E. Ill. Coun. Boy Scouts of Am., 1989, William H. Spurgeon III award, 1998, Silver Beaver award, Vigil Honor, Order of Arrow, Boy Scouts Am., 2001. Mem. Glenview Area Hist. Soc. (treas. 1998—), Dartmouth Club Chgo., Order of Arrow. Avocation: bicycling. Home: 37 Overlook Dr Golf IL 60029

FELLMAN, GERRY LOUIS, lawyer, arbitrator; b. Omaha, May 22, 1932; s. Charles and Rose Mae Fellman; m. Jane Hallock, July 25, 1964. BS in Law, U. Nebr., 1954, JD, 1956; MA, U. Minn., 1959. Bar: Nebr. 1956, Calif. 1964, U.S. Supreme Ct. 1982; cert. Mediator. Field atty. NLRB, L.A., 1959-63; atty. div. labor law enforcement State of Calif., L.A., 1964-66; sole practice L.A., 1967-83; assoc. Ibanez & Fellman, L.A., 1968-75; sole practice Pasadena, Calif., 1984—. Arbitrator labor mgmt. disputes Am. Arbitration Assn., 1967—, Fed. Mediation and Conciliation Svc., 1968—, Calif. State Mediation and Conciliation Svc., 1967—, UCLA, 1977-89, L.A. City Employee Rels. Bd., 1973—, E.E.O.C. Mediation Panel, 1996—. Contbr. numerous articles to legal jours. Bd. dirs. Legal Aid Found. L.A., 1974-83, pres., 1981-82. With U.S. Army, 1956-58. Mem. Nat. Acad. Arbitrators (chmn. So. Calif. region 1980-82, bd. dirs. 1997-2000), Indsl. Rels. Rsch. Assn. (past pres. So. Calif. chpt. 1976-77), ABA, Calif. Bar Assn., L.A. County Bar Assn. (exec. com. labor and employment sect.), Nebr. Bar Assn., Soc. for Profl. in Dispute Resolution, So. Calif. Mediation Assn. Jewish.

FELLMETH, ROBERT CHARLES, law educator; b. Lake City, Fla., Sept. 21, 1945; s. Robert Butler and Jane Zenith F.; m. Jill D. Heiman, Dec. 17, 1967; children: Michael Q., Aaron X.; m. Julianne Barbara D'Angelo, Aug. 4, 1995. BA, Stanford U., 1967; JD, Harvard U., 1970. Bar: Calif. 1971, U.S. Dist. Ct. (so. dist.) Calif. 1979, U.S. Ct. Appeals (9th cir.) 1984, U.S. Supreme Ct. 1985. Assoc. Ctr. for Study of Responsive Law, Washington, 1969-73; dep. DA, asst. U.S. Atty. Offices of D.A. and U.S Atty., San Diego, 1973-82; Price prof. pub. interest law U. San Diego, 1977—, dir. Ctr. Pub. Interest Law, Children's Adv. Inst., 1980—. State bar discipline monitor separate office, Calif., 1987-92. Author: The Politics of Land, 1972, Child Rights and Remedies, 2002, California Children's Budget, annually 1993-2003; co-author: Interstate Commerce Omission, 1970, California White Collar Crime, 1996, 2000, 02. Chair, bd. dirs. Pub. Citizen Found., Washington, 1992—; bd. dirs. Consumer's Union, 1981-85, Calif. Common Cause, 1986-91; cmty. champion Civil Justice Found., Ill., 1998; chmn. athletic comm. State of Calif., 1977-81. Mem. Nat. Asn. Child Advocates (bd. dirs., counsel to bd. 1992—), Nat. Assn. Counsel for Children (bd. dirs. 1991—). Avocations: native american artifacts and art, whaling and nautical artifacts, parrots. Office: Children's Advocacy Inst 5998 Alcala Park San Diego CA 92110-2492 E-mail: cpil@acusd.edu.

FELLNER, ERIC, film producer; b. Oct. 10, 1959; Formed Working Title Films (with Tim Bevan), 1982-; Prodr. (films) Sid & Nancy, 1986, Straight to Hell, 1987, Pascali's Island, 1988, Hidden Agenda, 1990, Liebestraum, 1991, Wild West, 1992, Romeo is Bleeding, 1993, No Worries, 1993, The Hawke, 1993, Four Weddings and a Funeral, 1994, French Kiss, 1995, Moonlight & Valentino, 1995, Fargo, 1996, Bean, 1997, The Matchmaker, 1997, The Borrowers, 1997, The Hi-Lo Country, 1998, Elizabeth, 1998 (Alexander Korda Awd, ALFS Awd, 1999), What Rats Won't Do, 1998, Solo, 1999, Plunkett & MaCleane, 1999, Bridget Jones Diary, 2001, Captain Corelli's Mandolin, 2001, 40 Days and 40 Nights, 2002, About A Boy, 2002, The Guru, 2002, Johnny English, 2003, Love Actually, 2003, The Calcium Kid, 2003; exec. prodr.: The Rachel Papers, 1989, Year of the Gun, 1991, A Kiss Before Dying, 1991, Posse, 1993, Romeo is Bleeding, 1993, The Hawk, 1993, Four Weddings and a Funeral, 1994, The Hudsucker Proxy, 1994, Panther, 1995, Dead Man Walking, 1995, Loch Ness, 1995, Fargo, 1996, The Big Lebowski, 1998, Notting Hill, 1999, O Brother, Where Art Thou?, 2000, The Man Who Cried, 2000, The Man Who Wasn't There, 2001, Long Time Dead, 2002, My Little Eye, 2002, Thirteen, 2003, The Shape of Things, 2003, Ned Kelly, 2003, The Italian Job, 2003; prodr. TV; Frankie's House, 1992, Underbelly (exec.), 1992 Recipient ShowEast's Kodak award for excellence in filmmaking (with Tim Bevan), 2003. Office: Working Title Films 8 Kensington Gardens London W11 3HO England*

FELLOWS, ALICE COMBS, artist; b. Atlanta, Sept. 14, 1935; d. Andrew Grafton III and Wilhelmina Drummond (Jackson) Combs; m. Robert Ellis Fellows Jr., Aug. 20, 1957 (div. 1978); children: Ariadne Elisabeth Fellows-Mannion, Kara Suzanne. BFA, Syracuse U., 1957; M in Clin. Psychology, Antioch U., 1992. Guest artist Yaddo, Saratoga Springs, N.Y., 1991; artist-in-residence Dorland Colony, Temecula, Calif., 1983; guest lectr. psychology seminar UCLA, 1990. Exhibited works in numerous group and one-woman shows including Hiromi Gallery, Santa Monica, Otis Gallery, Otis Coll. Art and Design, L.A., 2000, L.A. Mcpl. Art Gallery, C.O.L.A. Fellows Exhbn., 1998, El Camino Coll., 1997, Hunsaker-Schlesinger Gallery, 1996, The Armory Ctr. at Pasadena, 1996, Barnsdall Mcpl. Gallery, 1995, Claremont Grad. Sch. Gallery, 1991, Saxon-Lee Gallery, L.A., 1989, Santa Monica Coll. Gallery Art, 1988, J. Rosenthal Gallery, Chgo., 1986, The Biennial at the Hirshhorn Mus. and Sculpture Garden, Washington, 1986, Kirk de Gooyer Gallery, L.A., 1984, 85, many others; works represented in numerous collections including The Norton Collection, Santa Monica, Broad Found., Santa Monica, Mint Mus., Charlotte, N.C., N.C. Mus. Raleigh, N.C., Security Pacific Corp., L.A., Ft. Lauderdale Mus.; others. Arts commr. City of Santa Monica Arts Commn., 1995—99; mem. Pub. Art Com., Santa Monica, 1996—2000; mem. artists adv. bd. L.A. Mcpl. Art Gallery at Bransdall, 1998—2001. Recipient Durfee Found. award; grantee Dale Chihuly grant for Srs. Making Art Workshops, 1996; painting fellow Western States Arts Fedn./NEA, 1990, painting fellow Getty Trust, 1990, NEA fellow in painting, 1991, City of L.A. Individual Artist's fellow, 1998. Home: 18880 Melvin Ave Sonoma CA 95476 E-mail: alice@alicefellows.com.

FELLOWS, CHRISTOHPER CHARLES, information scientist; b. Hilsdale, Ill., Jan. 20, 1979; s. Richard Charles and Raejean Mary Fellows. BA, U. Calif., San Diego, 2001. Web cons. Fellowsplacement, Novato, Calif., 1998—2001; pub. New-Atlantis, San Diego, 2000—01. Mem.: Golden Key Honor Soc. Avocations: scuba diving, rugby, golf, computers. Home: 4384 W Pont Loma Blvd # C San Diego CA 92107

FELLOWS, ESTHER ELIZABETH, musician, music educator; b. Miami, Ariz., Nov. 5, 1952; d. John Wilmont and Flora Elizabeth (Eyestone) Walker; m. James Michael Fellows, Aug. 20, 1976; children: Joy Christine, Rachel Lindsay, Daniel Matthew, Jessica Grace. B in Music Edn., U. Colo., 1975. Co-dir. Children's Piano Lab. U. Colo., Boulder, 1975-76; instr. So. Calif. Conservatory Music, Sun City, 1976-78; pvt. instr. Ft. Lauderdale, 1978-84; instr. Ft. Lauderdale Christian Sch., 1981-83; sect. violinist Signature Symphony Tulsa Ballet, 1984—, Bartlesville (Okla.) Symphony, 1990—; pvt. instr. Broken Arrow, Okla., 1984— Pvt. instr. Ft. Lauderdale, 1978-84. Mem. Music Tchrs. Nat. Assn. (cert. piano, violin and viola), Am. String Tchrs. Assn., Am. Viola Soc., Okla. Music Tchr. Assn., Suzuki Assn. Am., Hyechka Music Club Tulsa, Tulsa Accredited Music Tchrs. Assn. (chair scholarship com.). Avocation: biking. Home: 19821 S Harvard Ave Mounds OK 74047-5049

FELLOWS, HENRY DAVID, JR., lawyer; b. N.Y.C., Dec. 17, 1954; s. Henry D. Sr. and Mary (Stecko) F.; m. Pam Neal Fellows, May 15, 1982; children: Christopher, Suzanne, Thomas. BSBA, Bucknell U., 1975; JD, Georgetown U., 1978. Bar: Ga. 1978, U.S. Dist. Ct. (no. dist.) Ga. 1978, U.S. Ct. Appeals (11th cir.) 1978, U.S. Supreme Ct. 1997. Law clk. to hon. judge Charles A. Moye Jr. U.S. Dist. Ct. (no. dist.) Ga., Atlanta, 1978-80; assoc. Hurt, Richardson, Garner, Todd & Cadenhead, Atlanta, 1981-87, ptnr., 1987-92, Fellows, Johnson & LaBriola, LLP (and predecessor firm), Atlanta, 1993—. Mem. ABA, Ga. Bar Assn., Atlanta Bar Assn. (chmn. ct. com. 1992-98, bd. dirs. litigation sect. 1999—, CLE com. bd. dirs. 2001—, bd. dirs. 2002—, chair 2003—), Lawyers Club of Atlanta, Indsl. Rels. Rsch. Assn. (bd. dirs. Atlanta chpt.), Fulton Indsl. Bus. Assn. (gen. counsel). Avocations: tennis, piano. Office: Fellows Johnson & LaBriola LLP Peachtree Ctr # 2300 South 225 Peachtree St NE Atlanta GA 30303-1701 E-mail: hfellows@fjl-law.com.

FELLOWS, JERRY KENNETH, lawyer; b. Madison, Wis., Mar. 19, 1946; s. Forrest Garner and Virginia (Witte) F.; m. Patricia Lynn Graves, June 28, 1969; children: Jonathon, Aaron, Daniel. BA in Econs., U. Wis., 1968; JD, U. Minn., 1971. Bar: U.S. Dist. Ct. (no. dist.) Ill. 1971. Ptnr. McDermott, Will & Emery, Chgo., 1971—2002; with Bell, Boyd & Lloyd LLC, Chgo., 2002—. Speaker Bur. Nat. Affairs, Washington, 1985—. Contbr. articles to profl. jours. Bd. dirs. Midwest Benefits Coun., 1998. Mem. U. Minn. Law Alumni Assn. (bd. visitors), Gamma Eta Gamma. Avocations: coaching track, basketball, baseball. Home: 4541 Middaugh Ave Downers Grove IL 60515-2761 Office: Bell Boyd & Lloyd LLC 70 West Madison St Ste 3100 Chicago IL 60602-4207 E-mail: jfellows@bellboyd.com.

FELLOWS, ROBERT ELLIS, medical educator, medical scientist; b. Syracuse, N.Y., Aug. 4, 1933; s. Robert Ellis and Clara (Talmadge) F.; m. Karlen Kiger, July 2, 1983; children: Kara, Ari. AB, Hamilton Coll., 1955; MD, CM, McGill U., 1959; PhD, Duke U., 1969. Intern N.Y. Hosp., N.Y.C., 1959—60, asst. resident, 1960—61, Royal Victoria Hosp., Montreal, Canada, 1961—62; asst. prof. dept. medicine Duke U., Durham, NC, 1966—76, asst. prof. dept. physiology and pharmacology, 1966—70, assoc. prof. dept. physiology and pharmacology, assoc. dir. med. scientist tng. program, 1970—76; prof., chmn. dept. physiology and biophysics U. Iowa Coll. Medicine, 1976—2002, dir. med. sci. tng. program, 1976—97, dir. physician sci. program, 1984—88, dir. neurosci. program, 1984—88. Mem. Nat. Pituitary Agy. Adv. Bd.; mem. NIH Population Rsch. Com., 1981-86, VA Career Devel. Rev. Com., 1985-88; cons. NIH, NSF March of Dimes. Mem. editorial bd.: Endocrinology, Am. Jour. Physiology. Mem. AAAS, Am. Chem. Soc., Am. Fedn. Clin. Rsch., Am. Physiol. Soc., Am. Soc. Biol. Chemists, Am. Soc. Cell Biology, Assn. Chairmen Depts. Physiology, Biochem. Soc., Biophys. Soc., Endocrine Soc., Internat. Soc. Neuroendocrinology, N.Y. Acad. Scis., Soc. for Neurosci., Assn. Neurosci. Depts. and Programs (pres. 1995-96), Sigma Xi, Alpha Omega Alpha. Home: 135 Pentire Cir Iowa City IA 52245-1575 Office: 5-660 Bowen Sci Bldg Iowa City IA 52242 E-mail: robert-fellows@uiowa.edu.

FELLRATH, RICHARD FREDERIC, lawyer; b. Dearborn, Mich., Nov. 30, 1940; s. Jerome John and Jane Elizabeth (Ayers) F.; m. Barbara Ann Osani, Oct. 14, 1966; children: Richard F., Jr., Christina Joyce Devlin. BA, U. Notre Dame, 1963; JD, U. Detroit, 1966. Bar: Mich. 1967, D.C. 1969, U.S. Ct. Mil. Appeals 1967, U.S. Supreme Ct. 1970, U.S. Ct. Appeals (6th cir.) 1984, U.S. Ct. Claims 1987. Judge adv. U.S. Army, Balt., 1967-71; ptnr. Milmet & Vecchio P.C., Detroit, 1971-85; sr. atty. Miller, Canfield, Paddock & Stone, Detroit, 1985-91, Fitzgerald & Dakmak, P.C., Detroit, 1991-96; pvt. practice Detroit, 1996—. Contbr. articles to profl. jours. Capt. U.S. Army, 1967-71. Mem. Fed. Bar Assn. (Detroit bankruptcy chmn. 1985-87), SAR, Sons Union Vets Civil War. Republican. Roman Catholic. Avocations: stamps, windsurfing, ancient coins, military miniatures, genealogy. Home: 4056 Middlebury Dr Troy MI 48085-3620 Office: 600 Ford Bldg 615 Griswald Detroit MI 48226 Fax: 313-961-3132.

FELMAN, YEHUDI M. dermatologist; b. Bridgeport, Conn., July 11, 1938; s. Meir and Helen (Kleter) F.; m. Brenda Ruth Wishengrad, Oct. 10, 1962; children: Nahum, Hillel. BA, Yeshiva U., 1959, MD, 1963; MA, Columbia U., 1966, MPhil, 1975. Cert. Am. Bd. Dermatology. Intern Mount Sinai Hosp., N.Y.C., 1963-64; dermatology resident Columbia Presbyn. Med. Ctr., N.Y.C., 1964-66; pvt. practice dermatology Downstate Med. Ctr., Bklyn., 1967—. From asst. instr. to clin. prof. SUNY, Downstate Med. Sch., Bklyn., 1967—; prof. dermatology Touro Coll. Health Scis., N.Y.C., 1973-85; dir. Bur. Venereal Disease Control, N.Y.C. Health Dept., 1975-85; cons. physician dermatology Maimonides Hosp., Bklyn.; attending physician dermatology Downstate U. Hosp., Bklyn., Kings Hwy. Hosp., Bklyn.; mem. med. bd. Ohel Children's Home, Planned Parenthood N.Y.C., 1993—; lectr. in field. Contbg. editor Jour. Dermatologic Surgery and Oncology, 1987-92; mem. editl. bd. Jour. Am. Acad. Dermatology, Sexually Transmitted Diseases, Cutis; mem. editl. adv bd. Sexual Medicine Today; manuscript cons. Jour. AMA, Annals of Internal Medicine, Archives of Dermatology; contbr. chpts. to books and numerous articles to profl. jours. Recipient Disting. Svc. award Pharm. Soc. N.Y., 1979, Disting. Alumnus award for achievements in health care Yeshiva U., 1983; N.Y. State Regents Med. Sch. scholar, 1959-63. Fellow ACP, Am. Acad. Dermatology (task force on infectious diseases 1981-89, com. on sexually transmitted diseases 1986-91, Continuing Med. Edn. award 1978-81, 81-84, 84-87, 87-90, 90-93, 93-96, 96-2002), Am. Soc. for Dermatologic Surgery, Am. Venereal Disease Assn. (chair membership com. 1979-80), Internat. Soc. Tropical Dermatology, N.Y. Acad. Medicine; mem. AMA, Am. Social Health Assn., Dermatologic Radiotherapy Soc., Med. Soc. for the Study of Venereal Disease (London), Med. Soc. State N.Y., N.Y. Acad. Scis., N.Y. State Med. Soc. (first prize for sci. exhibit 1978), N.Y. State Soc. Dermatology, Soc. for Investigative Dermatology, Bklyn. Dermatologic Soc. (sec. 1974-75, v.p. 1975-76, pres. 1976-77, treas. 1981—), Kings County Med. Soc. (trustee 1974-84, chmn. pub. health com. 1976-84, mem. publs. com. 1978-85, mem. dermatology com. 1978-85, mem.-at-large Comitia Minora 1979-80). Jewish. Avocations: reading, Jewish studies. Office: 8100 Bay Pkwy Brooklyn NY 11214-2548

FELNER, RICHARD M. real estate consultant, lawyer; b. N.Y.C., Mar. 27, 1936; s. Theodore I. and Sylvia L. Felner; m. Linda Marks Vogel, Dec. 15, 1963 (div. May 1994); children: Andrew, David, Julie. AB, Cornell U., 1958; LLB, Columbia U., 1961. Bar: N.Y. Supreme Ct. 1962. Intern Senator Jacob Javits U.S. Senate, Washington, 1958, spl. asst. to Senator Jacob Javits N.Y.C., 1958-61; assoc. Hays, Sklar & Hertzberg, N.Y.C., 1961-62, Cole and Dietz, N.Y.C., 1962-65; assoc. counsel N.Y. State Joint Legis. Com. to Revise the Banking Law, N.Y.C. and Albany, 1962-65; co-chief exec. The Fabric Tree Ind., N.Y.C., 1966-77; gen. counsel, sec. Brooks Fashion Stores, Inc., N.Y.C., 1978-85; exec. v.p., dir. Worths Stores, Inc., N.Y.C. and St. Louis, 1985-91; chmn. Richard M. Felner Assocs., N.Y.C., 1991—. Bd. dirs. Ames Dept. Stores, Inc., Rocky Hill, Conn. Active Westchester (N.Y.) County Rep. Com., 1968-85; mem. various adv. coms. Town of Mamaroneck, N.Y., 1970-85. Mem. Internat. Coun. Shopping Ctrs., Assn. Bar City N.Y. Office: 200 E 57th St New York NY 10022-2860

FELNER, ROBERT DAVID, psychology educator, researcher, consultant; b. Norwich, Conn., June 3, 1950; s. Joseph and Roslyn (Aptaker) Felner. BA, U. Conn., 1972; MA, U. Rochester, 1975, PhD, 1977. Lic. psychologist. Clin. psychology intern Convalescent Hosp. for Children, Rochester, NY, 1973—74, Center for Cmty. Studies, Rochester, 1974—75, U. Rochester Med. Ctr., 1975—76; asst. prof. psychology Yale U., New Haven, 1976—81; assoc. prof., dir. doctorlal program in clin./cmty. psychology Auburn U. (Ala.), 1981—86; prof. psychology U. Ill., Champaign, 1986—90, prof. pub. policy edn., social welfare, 1990—96, dir. doctoral program in clin./cmty. psychology, dir. clin. tng., 1986—90; prof., dir. sch. edn. and Nat. Ctr. on Pub. Edn. and Social Policy U. R.I., Kingston, 1996—. Mem. NIMH Small Grants Panel, 1978—82, NIMH Child/Family/Prevention Panel, 1983—87; NSF grants reviewer, 1983; cons. Conn. Bar Assn., 1978—82, Charles Henderson Child Health Ctr., 1981—86, Office for Prevention, NIMH, 1973—90, Alcohol, Drug and Mental Health Adminstrn., 1981—82, Office of Substance Abuse Prevention, Office of Health and Human Services, 1986—88. Author: Preventive Psychology: Theory Research and Practice, 1983, A Multidisciplinary Approach to Prevention, 1987; contbr. chapters to books, articles to profl. jours. in field; mem. editl. bd. Jour. Clin. Child Psychology, Jour. Divorce, Am. Jour. Cmty. Psychology, Jour. Social and Clin. Psychology, Profl. Psychology: Theory and Research, Suicide and Life Threatening Behavior, Jour. of Consulting and Clin. Psychology, Jour. Primary Prevention. Grantee, NIH, 1976—77, Edward W. Hazen Found., 1978—81, NSF rsch. grantee, 1980—82, 1983—85, Carnegie Corp. of N.Y., 1989—, Lilly Endowment, 1993—98, Kellogg Found., 1994—98, E.M. Kaufmann Found., 1995—99, R.I. Dept. Edn., 1997—. Fellow: APA, Am. Orthopsychiat. Assn.; mem.: Am. Assn. Sociology (bd. dirs. 1988—92, chair Council of Community Psychology Program Dirs. 1983), Soc. for Research in Child Devel. Republican. Jewish. Office: Univ RI Sch Edn 705 Chafee Hall Kingston RI 02818 E-mail: rfelner@uri.edu.

FELPER, DAVID MICHAEL, lawyer; b. Springfield, Mass., Dec. 17, 1954; s. Lawrence Allen and Edith Charlotte (Flesher) F.; m. Kimberlee White, May 19, 1979; children: Andrew Martin, Evan Matthew, Scott Tyler. BA in Polit. Sci., George Washington U., 1976; JD cum laude, Western New Eng. Coll., 1980. Bar: Mass. 1980, U.S. Dist. Ct. Mass. 1981, U.S. Ct. Appeals (1st cir.) 1987. Assoc. Michelman & Feinstein, Springfield, 1980-82; asst. regional counsel Dept. Social Services, Commonwealth of Mass., Springfield, 1982-83; labor relations counsel Sprague Electric Co., Lexington, Mass., 1983-87; assoc. Bowditch & Dewey, Framingham, Mass., 1987-92, ptnr., 1992—. Lectr. various human resource orgns. throughout U.S., 1984—; pres. Valley Tech. Ednl. Found. Inc., 1998—; corporator Milford-Whitinsville Regional Hosp. Bd. dirs. Horace Mann Ednl. Assocs., Inc. Mem.: Worcester County Bar Assn., Mass. Bar Assn. (labor law com.), Blackstone Valley C. of C. (dir.). Avocations: golf, running, reading. Office: Bowditch & Dewey 311 Main St Worcester MA 01608 E-mail: DFelper@bowditch.com.

FELS, GERHARD, economist; b. Baumholder, Germany, June 17, 1939; s. Karl Ludwig and Frieda (Schug) F.; m. Waltraut Endres, Mar. 31, 1962; children: Joachim, Florian, Katrin. Diploma in Econs., U. Saarbrücken, Fed. Republic Germany, 1965; D. in Econs., U. Saarbrücken, 1969. Economist Inst. für Weltwirtschaft, Kiel, Fed. Republic Germany, 1969-71, head dept. I, 1971-83, v.p., 1976-83, dir., prof., 1978-83; mng. dir. Inst. der deutschen Wirtschaft, Cologne, Fed. Republic Germany, 1983—. Mem. German Coun. Econ. Experts, 1976-82; mem. Com. for Devel. Planning, UN, 1978-82, Group of Thirty, 1988—. Contbr. articles to profl. jours. Lt. Germany Army, 1959—60. Mem. Aufsichtsrat Swiss Re Germany, Aufsichtsrat Oppenheim Kapitalanlagegesellschaft, Aufsichtsrat VHV Hommoversche Veisidrerung O.G., Beirat der MZM Nestlé. Office: Inst der deutschen Wirtschaft Gustav Heinemann Ufer 84-88 D 50968 Cologne Germany E-mail: gerhard.fels@iwkoeln.de.

FELS, NICHOLAS WOLFF, lawyer; b. White Plains, N.Y., Mar. 19, 1943; s. Lawrence P. and Fredricka (Gaines) F.; m. Susan T. McEwan, Dec. 28, 1968; 1 child, Sarah. BA, Harvard U., 1964; MA, U. Calif., Berkeley, 1965; LLB, Harvard U., 1968. Bar: N.Y. 1968, Calif. 1970, U.S. Dist. Ct. (cen. dist.) Calif. 1970, D.C. 1971, U.S. Dist. Ct. D.C. 1971, U.S. Ct. Appeals (10th cir.) 1976, U.S. Ct. Appeals (D.C. cir.) 1977, U.S. Supreme Ct. 1978, U.S. Ct. Appeals (4th cir.) 1979, U.S. Ct. Appeals (8th cir.) 1981, U.S. Ct. Appeals (5th cir.) 1982. Law clk. to Hon. John Minor Wisdom U.S. Ct. Appeals, New Orleans, 1968-69; atty. OEO Legal Services, Los Angeles, 1969-70; assoc. Covington & Burling, Washington, 1970-76, ptnr., 1976—. Mem. Nat. Com. on U.S.-China Relations, N.Y.C., 1982—. Contbr. articles to profl. jours. Mem. Energy Bar Assn., D.C. Appleseed Ctr. (bd. dirs. 1994—, pres. 1996-2000). Home: 3534 Edmunds St NW Washington DC 20007-1431 Office: Covington & Burling 1201 Pennsylvania Ave NW Washington DC 20004-2401 E-mail: nfels@cov.com.

FELS, RENDIGS, economist, educator; b. Cin., June 11, 1917; s. Clifford George and Estella Luella (Rendigs) F.; m. Beatrice Carmichael Baker, Dec. 27, 1941, (dec.); children: Charles Wentworth Baker, Carmichael (dec.); m. Marilyn W. Whiteman, July 15, 2001. AB, Harvard U., 1939, PhD, 1948; AM, Columbia U., 1940. Mem. faculty Vanderbilt U., 1948—, prof. econs., 1956-82, prof. emeritus, 1982—, dir. grad. program econ. devel., 1956- 57, chmn. dept. econs. and bus. adminstrn., 1962-65, 77-79. Chmn. Univs.-Nat. Bur. Com., 1962-67 Author: American Business Cycles, 1865-1897, 1959, Challenge to the American Economy, an Introduction to Economics, 1961, 2d edit, 1966, (with C. Elton Hinshaw) Forecasting and Recognizing Business Cycle Turning Points, 1968; Editor: (with Stephen Buckles) Casebook of Economic Problems and Policies, 5th edit, 1981. Served with USAAF, 1942-46. Mem. Am. Econ. Assn. (sec.-treas. 1970-75, treas. 1976-87), Midwest Econ. Assn. (pres. 1984-85), So. Econ. Assn. (pres. 1967-68) Home: Apt 109 4400 Belmont Park Ter Nashville TN 37215-3643

FELS, ROBERT ALAN, psychotherapist; b. Phila., Apr. 24, 1954; s. Joseph and Lenore F. BS, Pa. State U., 1974; MA, John F. Kennedy U., 1980; MS, Miami Inst. of Psychology, 1998, PsyD, 2000. Lic. marriage and family therapist; cert. by the Biofeedback Cert. Inst. of Am. Probation officer Broward County Probation, Ft. Lauderdale, Fla., 1979; family counselor Child Protective Svcs., State of Fla., Plantation, Fla., 1981-84; psychotherapist Jewish Family Svc., Boca Raton, Fla., 1984-88, Ctr. for Psychol. Svcs., Boca Raton, 1987-90; dir. biofeedback svcs. Lake Hosp., Lake Worth, Fla., 1990-92; pvt. practice psychotherapy Boca Raton, Fla., 1990—. Facilitator Stop Smoking Clinic, Am. Cancer Soc., Boca Raton, 1987-93. Fellow Am. Bd. Vocational Experts, Am. Acad Pain Mgmt.; mem. Am. Assn. for Marriage and Family Therapy, APA, Assn. for Applied Psychophysiology and Biofeedback. Jewish. Avocation: eastern philosophy and practice. Office: 20423 State Road 7 Ste 231 Boca Raton FL 33498-6797 E-mail: drfels@clinicalbiofeedbacktherapy.com.

FELSENSTEIN, FRANK ARJEH, educator; b. London, July 28, 1944; came to U.S., 1998; s. Ernest Maurice and Vera Lotte F.; m. Carole Alison Jaffe, Dec. 22, 1985; children: Kenny, Joanna. BA with honors, U. Leeds, England, 1966, PhD, 1971. Asst. lectr. English U. Geneva, Switzerland, 1968-70; lectr. English U. Leeds, England, 1971-86, sr. lectr. English, 1986-96, reader 18th century studies, 1996-98; vis. prof. book history Drew U., Madison, NJ, 1998—; dir. honors program Yeshiva Coll., N.Y.C., 1998—2001; Reed D. Voran honors disting. prof. Ball State U., Muncie, Ind., 2002—. Vis. prof. English Vanderbilt U., Nashville, 1989-90. Author: Anti-Semitic Stereotypes, 1995; editor: Travels Through France and Italy, 1979, A Practical Treatise of Flowers, 1985, English Trader, Indian Maid, 1999, Ann Yearsley and the Politics of Patronage, 2002-03 Mem. Am. Soc. 18th Century Studies. Avocation: antiquarian books and prints. Home: 8 Manor Dr Morristown NJ 07960-2611 Office: Ball State U Dept English Muncie IN 47306 E-mail: felsenstein@bsu.edu.

FELSENTHAL, GERALD, physiatrist, educator; b. N.Y.C., Aug. 27, 1941; s. Richard and Fay (Braunspiegel) F.; m. Diane Shretter, June 6, 1964; children: David, Steven, Suzann. BA, NYU, 1963; MD, Albany Med. Coll., 1967. Diplomate Am. Bd. Phys. Medicine and Rehab., Am. Bd. Electrodiagnostic Medicine. Rotating intern USPHS Hosp., Seattle, 1967-68; resident in phys. medicine and rehab. Bronx Mcpl. Hosp. Ctr., Albert Einstein Coll. Medicine, 1970-73; assoc. physiatrist Sinai Hosp., Balt., 1973-76, assoc. chief, 1976-86, chief dept. rehab. medicine, 1986-2001, chmn. emeritus rehab. medicine, 2001—; head divsn. rehab. medicine Levindale Hebrew Geriatric Ctr. and Hosp., Balt., 1983-2001. Dir. residency tng. program in phys. medicine and rehab. Sinai Hosp., 1986—2002; assoc. prof. U. Md. Coll. Medicine, Balt., 1987—92, prof., 1992—; assoc. prof. Johns Hopkins U. Sch. Medicine, 1989—. Editor of book Rehab of Aging and Elderly Patient and articles to profl. jours. Surgeon USPHS, 1967-70. Mem. Phys. Medicine and Rehab (residency review com. 1990, vice chmn. 1994, chmn. 1996-99), Am. Bd. Phys. Medicine and Rehab. (bd. dirs. 1993—, treas. 1998—), Am. Assn. Electrodiagnostic Medicine (bd. dirs. 1990-93), AMA, Am. Geriat Soc., Am. Acad. Phys. Med. and Rehab., Assn. Acad. Physiatrists. Avocation: horticulture. Office: Sinai Hosp Dept Rehab Med 2401 W Belvedere Ave Baltimore MD 21215-5269 E-mail: gfelsent@lifebridgehealth.com.

FELSENTHAL, STEVEN ALTUS, lawyer, educator; b. Chgo., May 21, 1949; s. Jerome and Eve (Altus) F.; m. Carol Judith Greenberg, June 14, 1970; children: Rebecca Elizabeth, Julia Alison, Daniel Louis Altus. AB, U. Ill., 1971; JD, Harvard U., 1974. Bar: Ill. 1974, U.S. Dist. Ct. (no. dist.) Ill. 1974, U.S. Ct. Claims 1975, U.S. Tax Ct. 1975, U.S. Ct. Appeals (7th cir.) 1981. Assoc. Levenfeld, Kanter, Baskes & Lippitz, Chgo., 1974-78; ptnr. Levenfeld & Kanter, Chgo., 1978-80, Levenfeld, Eisenberg, Janger, Glassberg & Lippitz, Chgo., 1980-84; sr. ptnr. Sugar, Friedberg & Felsenthal, Chgo., 1984—. Lectr. Kent Coll. Law, Ill. Inst. Tech., Chgo., 1978-80. Mem. ABA, Ill. Bar Assn., Chgo. Bar Assn., Chgo. Coun. Lawyers, Harvard Law Soc. Ill., Standard Club, Harvard Club, Phi Beta Kappa. Office: Sugar Friedberg & Felsenthal 30 N La Salle St Ste 3000 Chicago IL 60602-3327 E-mail: saf@sff-law.com.

FELSON, RICHARD BARNET, educator; b. Cin., Oct. 10, 1950; s. Benjamin and Virginia (Raphaelson) F.; m. Sharon Weber, June 10, 1976; children: Jacob, Benjamin. BA, U. Cin., 1972; MA, Ind. U., 1974, PhD, 1977. Prof. SUNY, Albany, N.Y., 1976-99, Pa. State U., State College, 1999—. Author: Violence, Aggression & Coercive Action, 1994, Violence and Gender Reexamined, 2001; editor: Aggression: A Social Interactiionist Approach, 1993, Psychological Perspectives on Self & Identity, 2000. Avocations: tennis, squash. Office: Pa State U Oswald Tower University Park PA 16802 E-mail: rbf7@psu.edu.

FELSTED, CARLA MARTINDELL, librarian, travel writer; b. Barksdale Field, La., June 21, 1947; d. David Aldenderfer Martindell and Dorthe (Hetland) Horton; m. Robert Earl Luna, Aug. 24, 1968, (div. 1972); m. Hugh Herbert Felsted, Nov. 2, 1974. BA in English, So. Meth. U., 1968, MA in History, 1974; MLS, Tex. Woman's U., 1978. Cert. secondary tchr., Tex.; cert. learning resources specialist, Tex. Tchr. Bishop Lynch High Sch., Dallas, 1968-72, Lake Highlands Jr. High Sch., Richardson, Tex., 1972-75; instr. Richland Coll., Richardson, Tex., 1973-76; library asst. So. Meth. U., Dallas, 1977-78; librarian Tracy-Locke Advt., Dallas, 1978-79; corp. librarian Am. Airlines, Inc., Ft. Worth, 1979-84; research librarian McKinsey & Co., Dallas, 1984-85; reference librarian St. Edward's U., Austin, Tex., 1985—2002, assoc. prof., 1994—2002. Ptnr. Southwind Info. Svcs. and Southwind Bed-Breakfast, Wimberley, Tex., 1985-92. Editor, compiler: Youth and Alcohol Abuse, 1986; co-editor Mexican Meanderings, 1991-99; contbr. Frommer's travel guides, 1991-96. Mem. adv. bd. Sch. Libr. and Info. Scis., Tex. Women's U., Denton, 1982-84; mem. curriculum com. Wimberley Ind. Sch. Dist., 1986; bd. dirs. Hays-Caldwell Coun. on Alcohol and Drug Abuse, San Marcos, Tex., 1986-88, Inst. Cultures for Wimberley Valley, 1989-91, Tex. Alliance Human Needs, 1992-96; Tex. Team Survivor, Danskin Triathlon, 1998-2002, co-capt. 1997-99; vol. Breast Cancer Resource Ctr., 1998-2000. Grantee St. Edward's U., 1986-89, 96. Mem. ALA, Tex. Libr. Assn. (dist. program com., membership com. 1986-88, Tex.-Mex. rels. com. 1992-2002), Wimberley C. of C. (bd. dirs. 1987-88). Unitarian Universalist. Avocations: health issues research and advocacy, regional and ethnic cooking, physical fitness, art history, travel. Home: 205 Sunset Dr 23 Sedona AZ 86336 E-mail: cfelsted@earthlink.net.

FELSTINER, JOHN, literature educator, literary translator; b. Mount Vernon, Ny, July 5, 1936; s. Louis John and Gertrude (Shiman) F.; m. Mary Lowenthal; children: Sarah, Aleksandr. BA, Harvard Coll., 1958; PhD, Harvard U., 1965. Fulbright-hays prof. in am. lit. U. Of Chile, Santiago, Chile, 1967—68; vis. prof. of english The Hebrew U., Jerusalem, Israel, 1974—75; vis. prof. of comparative lit. Yale U., New Haven, Conn., 1990—90; vis. faculty Ny State Summer Writers Inst., Saratoga Springs, NY, 1997—99; vis. prof. of english Yale U., New Haven, Conn., 2002—02; prof. of english Stanford U., Stanford, Calif., 1965—. Cons./evaluator Forty (40) Publishers, Journals, U. Departments, Foundations, 1965—; judge Am. PEN, MLA, helen and kurt wolff lit. prize, 1980—2003; vice-president Ctr. For Art In Transl., San Francisco, 2000—; bd. of directors Paul Celan Soc., Amsterdam, Netherlands, 1998—. Author: (non-fiction) The Lies Of Art: Max Beerbohm's Parody And Caricature, (poem) Twenty Questions I Wish I'd Asked My Father (Mass. rev.), The Runners In The Luxembourg Gardens (paris rev.), (scholarly study) Translating Neruda: The Way To Macchu Picchu (Calif. commonwealth club gold medal, 1981), (biography) Paul Celan: Poet, Survivor, Jew (truman capote award for lit. criticism, 1997); translator: (literary translation) The Dark Room And Other Poems By Enrique Lihn, (anthology) Selected Poems And Prose Of Paul Celan, 2001 (PEN, MLA, and ATA prizes for lit. transl., 2001), (bibliophile edition) Heights Of Macchu Picchu/alturas De Macchu Picchu, deathfugue/todesfuge; co-editor: (anthology) Jewish American Literature: A Norton Anthology, 2000. Bd. of directors Holocaust Ctr. Of No. Calif., San Francisco, Calif., 1979—2003. Recipient fellowship Guggenheim, Rockefeller, NEH, NEA, Gold medal Calif. Commonwealth Club, 1981, Truman Capote award for lit. criticism, 1997, Translation prize Brit. Comparative Lit. Assn.; finalist Nat. Book Critics Cir. award, 1996, MLA James Russell Lowell prize, 1997, MLA, ATA, and Pen West Transl. prizes, 2001. Democrat-Npl. Jewish. Avocations: book and map collecting, a capella singing, hiking, running. Office: English Department Stanford University Building 460 Stanford CA 94305-2087 Office Fax: 650-725-0755. E-mail: felstiner@stanford.edu.

FELT, JULIA KAY, lawyer; b. Wooster, Ohio, Apr. 8, 1941; d. George Willard and Betty Virginia F.; m. Lawrence Roger Van Til, May 31, 1969. BA, Northwestern U., 1963; JD, U. Mich., 1967. Bar: Ohio 1967, Mich. 1968. Tchr. Triway Local H.S., Wooster, Ohio, 1963-64; assoc. Dykema, Gossett, Detroit, 1967-75, ptnr., 1975—; adj. asst. prof. dept. cmty. medicine Wayne State U., Detroit, 1974—. Contbr. articles to profl. jours., chpts. to books. Trustee Rehab. Inst., Detroit, 1971-2001, sec., 1974-77, 91—99, vice chmn., 1978-83, 85-90, chmn. bd., 1983-85; trustee Detroit Med. Ctr. Corp. 1984-85; bd. dirs. Travelers Aid Soc., Detroit, 1974—90, v.p., 1978-81, United Way Cmty. Svc. Detroit, bd. dirs., 1981—; vis. com. U. Mich. Law Sch., Ann Arbor, 1972—, nat. vice chmn. law sch. fund, 1984-86, bd. dirs. Detroit Assn. U. Mich. Women, 1968-72, pres., 1971-72, Mich. Women's Found., trustee, 1993—02, bd. dirs. Med. Ethics Resourse Netro of Mich., 2002— Planned Giving Round table Southeatern Mich., chmn., 1993-94; chmn. Leave a Legacy Southeastern Mich., 1996-98. Campbell Competition winner U. Mich. Law Sch., 1967; recipient Svc. award Mich. League Nursing, 1977, Alumna-in-Residence U. Mich. Alumnae Coun., 1986, Disting. Svc. award Mich. Bus. and Profl. Assn., 1998. Fellow Am. Bar Found., Mich. Bar Found.; Educator of the Yr. award Mich. Hospice and Pallistive Care Orgn., 2002, mem. Am. Acad. Health Care Attys. of Am. Hosp. Assn. (pres. 1985-86, bd. dirs. 1980-87), Mich. Soc. Hosp. Attys. (pres. 1975-76, bd. dirs. 1975-77), Cath. Health Assn. U.S. (legal services adv. com. 1980-84), Gov's. Commn. on End Life Care,1999-2002, Adv. Com. Pain and Symptom Mgmt.1999-2002, ABA, Ohio State Bar Assn., State Bar Mich. (comm. medicolegal problems 1973-81, adminstrv. rule making com. 1978-79, awards com. chmn. 1989-99, disabilities com. Open Justice Commn., 1999—), Am. Hosp. Assn., Detroit Bar Assn., Women Lawyers Mich., Am. Soc. Law and Medicine, Am. Health Lawyers Assn. Presbyterian. Office: Dykema Gossett 400 Renaissance Ctr Detroit MI 48243-1668

FELTENSTEIN, HARRY DAVID, JR., chemical executive; b. St. Joseph, Mo., Nov. 6, 1920; s. Harry David and Isabel (Rosenbaum) F.; m. Rosalie Goldstein, Jan. 18, 1945 (dec. Sept. 1977); children: Andrew, Martha; m. Carmen Archabala Fernandez, Aug. 24, 1979; 1 son, Henry. BS, Harvard U., 1942. Engaged in book pub., 1946-50; with Merrill Lynch, Pierce, Fenner & Smith, 1951-57, Lithium Corp., Am. Inc., N.Y.C., 1957-69, financial v.p., treas., 1957-58, exec. v.p., treas., 1958-60, pres., treas., 1960-69; pres., dir. Beryllium Metals & Chems. Corp., 1962-69, Gt. Salt Lake Minerals and Chems. Corp., 1967-69; exec. v.p., dir. Gulf Resources & Chem. Corp., 1967-69; pres., bd. dirs. Fuel Mgmt. Corp., Washington, 1970-94, chmn., 1995—; pres., bd. dirs. Internat. Wine Investors, Ltd., 1972-86, Wildenstein & Co., 1972-74; European rep. C & K Coal Co. divsn. Gulf Resources & Chem. Corp., 1981-82; cons. to Spanish govt. cos., 1990—. Served with USNR, 1942-46. Address: Calle Lerez 4 Madrid 2 Spain E-mail: harry8@teleline.es.

FELTER, BRIAN ALBERT, sales executive; b. Washington, Nov. 27, 1948; s. Walter Thomas Felter and Betty Francis Thomas; m. Bonnie Nadine Weiss; children: Kiersten, Eric. BS Mgmt./Criminal Justice, U. Md., 1979. Spl. ops. divsn. - K-9 Prince Georges County Police, Forrestville, Md., 1972—86; dir. tng. Sigarms, Inc., Herndon, Va., 1986—89. East regional sales mgr. Beretta USA Corp., Accokeek, Md., 1989—98; nat. sales mgr. Sigarms, Inc., Exeter, NH, 1998—99; curriculum and mktg. dir. NRA, Fairfax, 1999—2001; nat. sales dir. Beamhit L.L.C., Columbia, Md., 2001—. Author: (college textbook) Police Defensive Handgun Use and Encounter Tactics, 1988, Police Shotguns and Carbines, 1991. Staff sgt. USAR, 1969—75. Curtis Bay, MD. Mem.: Internat. Assn. Chiefs of Police, Internat. Assn. Law Enforcement Firearms Instrs., Am. Soc. Law Enforcement Trainers, NRA, Fraternal Order of Police, Lodge 89. Conservative. Presbyterian. Avocation: writing, spelunking, martial/oriental arts, hiking. Home: 4210 Christiana-Parran Rd Chesapeake Beach MD 20732 Home Fax: 410-414-5040. Personal E-mail: bfmarket@aol.com.

FELTER, EDWIN LESTER, JR., judge; b. Washington, Aug. 11, 1941; s. Edwin L. Felter and Bertha (Peters) Brekke; m. Yoko Yamauchi-Koito, Dec. 26, 1969. BA, U. Tex., 1964; JD, Cath. U. of Am., 1967. Bar: Colo. 1970, U.S. Dist. Ct. Colo. 1970, U.S. Ct. Appeals (10th cir.) 1971, U.S. Supreme Ct. 1973, U.S. Tax Ct. 1979, U.S. Ct. Claims 1979, U.S. Ct. Internat. Trade 1979. Dep. pub. defender State of Colo., Ft. Collins, 1971-75; asst. atty. gen. Office of the Atty. Gen., Denver, 1975-80; state adminstrv. law judge Colo. Divsn. of Adminstrv. Hearings, Denver, 1980-83, chief adminstrv. law judge, 1983-98, sr. adminstr., law judge, 1998—. Disciplinary prosecutor Supreme Ct. Grievance Com., 1975-78; mem. faculty Nat. Jud. Coll., 1999—; mem. Coun. Can. Adminstrv. Tribunals, 2002--. Contbg. editor Internat. Franchising, 1970. Mem. Colo. State Mgmt. Cert. Steering Com., 1983-86; No. Colo. Criminal Justice Planning Coun., Ft. Collins, 1973-75; bd. dirs., vice chmn. The Point Cmty. Crisis Ctr., Ft. Collins, 1971-73; mem. Denver County Dem. Party Steering Com., 1978-79, chmn. 12th legis. dist., 1978-79; bd. dirs., pres. Denver Internat. Program, 1989-90. Mem.: Colo. Bar Assn. (chmn. grievance policy com. 1991—94, interprofl. com. 1995—), Nat. Assn. Adminstrv. Law Judges (pres. Colo. chpt. 1982—84, chair fellowship com. 1996—, Fellowship winner 1994), Denver Bar Assn., Arapahoe County Bar Assn., Nat. Conf. Adminstrv. Law Judges (chair 2000—01), ABA, Am. Inns of Ct. (master level 1996—). Office: Colo Divsn Adminstrv Hearings 1120 Lincoln St Ste 1400 Denver CO 80203-2140 Fax: 303-764-1401. E-mail: ed.felter@state.co.us.

FELTER, JOHN KENNETH, lawyer; b. Monmouth, NJ, May 9, 1950; s. Joseph Harold and Rosanne (Bautz) F. BA magna cum laude, MA in Econs., Boston Coll., 1972; JD cum laude, Harvard U., 1975. Bar: Mass. 1975, N.Y. 2003, D.C. 2002, U.S. Dist. Ct. Mass. 1976, U.S. Ct. Appeals (1st cir.) 1977, U.S. Ct. Appeals (2nd cir.) 2002, U.S. Supreme Ct. 1982, U.S. Tax Ct. 1993. Assoc. Goodwin, Procter LLP, Boston, 1975-83, ptnr., 1983—. Spl. asst. gen. Commonwealth of Mass., 1982-84, 94-95; spl. counsel Town of Plymouth, Mass., Town of Salisbury, Mass., Town of Edgartown, Mass.; spl. outside counsel City of Boston, 1990-92; mem. devel. com. Greater Boston Legal Svcs., 1980-99, bd. dirs., 1982—, mem. exec. com., 1989-93; mem. faculty Mass. Continuing Legal Edn., Inc., Boston. Mem. adv. com. The Boston Plan for Excellence in Pub. Schs.; mem. elem. edn. com. Blue Ribbon Commn. on Cmty. Learning Ctrs.; VIP panelist Easter Seals Telethon, Boston, 1978-79. Fellow: Am. Coll. Trial Lawyers; mem.: ABA (litigation sect., mem. personal rights litigation com., mem. ABA-Am. Law Inst. com. on cont. edn.), Greater Boston C. of C. (mem. edn. com., mem. health care com.), Boston Bar Assn. (bd. dirs. law firm resources project 1985—, mem. coll. and univ. law com. 1986—, chmn. fed. rules com. litigation sect. 1994), Mass. Bar Assn., Am. Arbitration Assn. (comml. arbitrator). Office: Goodwin Procter LLP Exchange Pl 53 State St Ste 17 Boston MA 02109-2881

FELTHEIMER, JON, entertainment company executive; Pres. Columbia Tristar TV; exec. v.p. Sony Pictures Entertainment Inc.; CEO Lion Gate Entertainment. Office: Sony Pictures Entertainment Inc 10202 Washington Blvd Culver City CA 90232-3119

FELTHOUS, ALAN ROBERT, psychiatrist; b. San Francisco, Oct. 16, 1944; s. Robert Alan and Agnetta Wilhelmena (Blindheim) F.; m. Mary Louise Wilkins, Aug. 6, 1971; children: Erik Alan, Emily Anna, Elizabeth Ashley. BS, U. Wash., 1967; MD, U. Louisville, 1971. Diplomate Nat. Bd. Med. Examiners, Am. Bd. Psychiatry and Neurology added qualifications in forensic psychiatry, Am. Bd. Forensic Psychiatry (v.p. 1992-93, pres. 1993-94). Intern Roosevelt Hosp., N.Y.C., 1971-72; resident in psychiatry McLean Hosp./Harvard Med. Sch., Belmont, Mass., 1972-75; staff psychiatrist Naval Regional Med. Ctr., Oakland, Calif., 1975-77; psychiatrist, sect. chief The Menninger Found., Topeka, 1977-83, dir. adult divsn., 1993—; chief forensic svc. dept. psychiatry and behavioral scis. U. Tex. Med. Br., Galveston, 1984—, assoc. prof. dept. psychiatry and behavioral scis., 1984-89, prof. dept psychiatry and behavioral scis., 1989-98, Marie B. Gale centennial prof. psychiatry, 1994-98; prof. dept. psychiatry, dir. forensic psychiatry So. Ill. U. Sch. Medicine, Springfield, 1998—; med. dir. Chester (Ill.) Mental Health Ctr., 1998—; prof. sch. law Carbondale, 2001—. Cons., mem. expert panel on psychiat. disorders and comml. drivers U.S. Dept. Transp., Fed. Hwy. Adminstrn., Washington, 1990; prof. law So. Ill. U., 2001—. Author: The Psychotherapist's Duty to Warn or Protect, 1989; newsletter editor: Am. Acad. Psychiatry and the Law, 1988-93; co-editor (forensic sect.) Current Opinion in Psychiatry, 1993-2001, Behavioral Sciences and the Law, 1997-2001, sr. editor, 2002-; contbr. articles to profl. jours. Capt. Y, 1969. Recipient Wood-Prince award for sci. pubs. The Menninger Found., 1978-82, Outstanding Achievement award Gulf Coast Mental Health and Mental Retardation, Galveston, 1991, Exemplary Psychiatrist award for 1993 Nat. Alliance for the Mentally Ill, Outstanding Svc. award Am. Acad. Psychiatry and the Law, 1994. Fellow Am. Acad. Forensic Scis. (sect. sec. psychiatry and behavioral sci., chmn. 1997-2000, dir. 2000-03, mem.-at-large exec. com. 2002-03, Maier I. Tuchler award 2000), Am. Psychiat. Assn. (disting. fellow); mem. German Soc. for Psychiatry, Psychotherapy and Neurology, Naval Res. Assn. (life). Achievements include research in abnormal aggressive behaviors. Office: Chester Mental Health Center PO Box 31 Chester IL 62233-0031 E-mail: DHSC6624@dhs.state.il.us.

FELTHOUSE, PATRICIA MAE AVRIT, librarian; b. Tillamook, Oreg., Mar. 28, 1924; d. Roy Calvin and Louise (Morgan) Avrit; m. James Whitman Felthouse, May 10, 1944; children: Timothy Roy, Daphne Diane. Student, Oreg. State U., 1941-44; BA in Elem. Edn., U. Wash., 1960. Libr. Tehama County Libr., Red Bluff, Calif., 1965-85; organist United Meth. Ch., Red Bluff, 1985—. Contbr. hist. articles to profl. jours. Bd. dirs. Tehama County Mus. Found., 1980—. Mem. AAUW (pres. Red Buff-Tehama County 1974-75), Calif. Conf. Hist. Socs. (regional v.p. 1981-84). Assn. No. Calif. Records and Rsch. (bd. dirs. 1983-86), Colusi County Hist. Soc. (bd. dirs. 1983-90, pres. 1984-85), Bus. and Profl. Women's Club (pres. 1977-78, Woman of Yr. 1987), Tehama County Geneal. and Hist. Soc. (pres. 1986-90). Republican. Methodist. Avocation: quilting. Home: 1140 Wetter Way Red Bluff CA 96080-4123

FELTON, JEAN SPENCER, physician; b. Oakland, Calif., Apr. 27, 1911; s. Herman and Tess (Davidson) F.; m. Janet E. Birnbaum, June 27, 1937 (dec.); children: Gary, Keith, Robin; m. Suzanne E. Colvin, Sept. 2, 1990. AB, Stanford U., 1931, MD, 1935. Diplomate: Am. Bd. Preventive Medicine, Am. Bd. Indsl. Hygiene. Intern Mt. Zion Hosp., San Francisco, 1934-35, resident in surgery, 1935-36, Dante Hosp., San Francisco, 1936-38; practice medicine San Francisco, 1938-40; guest lectr. indsl. sociology U. Tenn. at Knoxville, 1946-53; med. dir. Oak Ridge Nat. Lab., 1946-53; cons. dept. medicine, prof. dept. preventive medicine, pub. health U. Okla. Med. Sch., 1953-58; cons. indsl. hygiene Okla. State Dept. Health, 1953-58; past cons. VA, St. Louis area; prof. occupational health U. Calif. Schs. Medicine and Pub. Health, Los Angeles, 1958-68; dir. occupational health service Dept. Personnel, County Los Angeles, 1968-74; med. dir. occupational health Naval Regional Med. Center, Long Beach, Calif., 1974-78; clin. prof. community medicine U. So. Calif., 1968-82, clin. prof. emeritus, 1982—; clin. prof. medicine U. Calif., Irvine, 1975—. Cons. occupational health NASA, USN, VA, AEC, USPHS, Social Security Adminstrn., 1955-62; Fellow through Distinction faculty occupational medicine Royal Coll. Physicians, London, 1997—. Author: (with A. H. Katz) Health and Community, 1965, Man, Medicine, and Work, 1965, Occupational Medical Management, 1990; bd. dirs. Excerpta Medica, Sect. XXXV, The Netherlands; mem. editl. panel Occupational Medicine, London, 1994—; contbr. articles to med. jours. Past mem. youth svc. com. Oak Ridge Welfare Coun., 1946-53; past

mem. Tenn. Commn. on Childen, Welfare Svcs. Dept.; chmn., mem. adv. bd. Oak Ridge; past mem. Gov.'s Com. on Utilization Physically Handicapped Pres.'s Com. on Employment People with Disabilities, 1947-94. Lt. col. M.C., 1940-46. Decorated Army Commendation Ribbon, 1946; recipient Citation for Excellence in Med. Authorship by Am. Assn. Indsl. Physicians and Surgeons, 1948; Knudsen award Indsl. Med. Assn., 1968; Physician of Yr. award Calif. Gov.'s Com. on Employment of Handicapped, 1979; Physician of Yr. award Pres.'s Com. on Employment of Handicapped, 1979 Fellow Am. Coll. Preventive Medicine (pres. 1966-67), Am. Acad. Occupational Medicine, Am. Occupational Med. Assn. (Meritorious Svc. award 1965, Health Achievement in Industry award 1983), Am. Pub. Health Assn., Collegium Ramazzini (coun. of fellows 1994—); mem. AMA (sec., vice chmn. sect. preventive and indsl. medicine and pub. health 1949-53, chmn. sect. 1953), Am. Indsl. Hygiene Assn., Nat. Rehab. Assn. So. Calif. (dir.), So. Calif. Ind. Hygiene Assn. (past pres.), Am. Coll. Occupational Medicine (Robert A. Kehoe award 1989), New Eng. Occupational Med. Assn. (Harriet F. Hardy award 1989), Soc. Occupational Medicine (hon.). Unitarian Universalist. Achievements include preparing standard operating procedure of U.S. Army indsl. med. program at San Francisco Port of Embarkation (adopted by the U.S. Army Chief of Transp. for use by all Ports of Embarkation). Home: PO Box 246 45150 Cypress Dr Mendocino CA 95460-9796 E-mail: jfelton@mcn.org. *Irrespective of the occupation or professional ladder one ascends, skills in basic written and spoken communication are mandatory. It is essential in this period of frequent misquotation by overeager media that one's ideas are correctly conveyed and that one's feelings are accurately transmitted.*

FELTON, JULE WIMBERLY, JR., lawyer; b. Macon, Ga., July 22, 1932; s. Jule Wimberly and Mary Julia (Sasnett) F.; m. Kate Gillis, May 15, 1965; children— Jule Wimberly III, Mary Katherine, Laura Borden Student, Emory U., Atlanta, 1949-50; AB, U. Ga., Athens, 1954, LL.B, 1955. Bar: Ga. 1954. Assoc. Hansell & Post, Atlanta, 1955-59, mng. ptnr., 1959-89; sr. of counsel Jones Day Reavis & Pogue, Atlanta, 1989-92; ptnr. Ford & Felton, 1993-95, Proctor, Felton & Atkinson, Atlanta, 1995-96, Proctor, Felton & Chambers, Atlanta, 1996-99. Bd. dirs. dept. cmty. affairs Ga. State, vice chair, 2002—03. Mem. Ga. Gen. Assembly, Atlanta, 1969-72; mem. ofcl. bd. dirs. Northside United Meth. Ch., Atlanta, 1974-85, 88; mem. U. Ga. Bd. Visitors, 1986, 87, 91, chmn., 1987-88, 93-94; bd. dirs. Ga. Dept. Cmty. Affairs, 1999—. 1st lt. JAGC, U.S. Army, 1955-56. Fellow Am. Bar Found.; mem. ABA, Ga. Bar Assn. (pres. 1973-74), Nat. Conf. Bar Pres., Am. Coll. Trial Lawyers, Ga. Bar Found., Am. Judicature Soc., U. Ga. Law Sch. Assn. (pres. 1984-85), Lawyers Club Atlanta, Old War Horse Lawyers Club (pres. Atlanta chpt. 1983), Piedmont Driving Club, Capital City Club. Avocations: piano, golf, boating. Home: 1061 Arbor Trce NE # 34 Atlanta GA 30319-5381 Office: Peterson & Harris Lennox Towers Ste 1725 3400 Pete St Rd Atlanta GA 30326 Fax: (404) 239-0132. E-mail: info@petersonharris.com.

FELTON, ROBERT O'NEIL, II, secondary education educator; b. Akron, Ohio, May 2, 1955; s. Robert O. and Jean S. Felton; children: Kalan, Neill, Skylar, Raymond. BA, Malone Coll., 1978. Cert. tchr., Ohio. Tchr. Ravenna (Ohio) City Schs., 1981—. Lectr. Cultwatch, Akron, 1980-88. Precinct person Portage County Dems., Kent, 1982-2000; apptd. to Kent Ohio City Coun., 1994, re-elected, 1995, re elected, 1999; grad. Leadership Portage County, 1994. Mem. NEA (conv. del.), Ohio Edn. Assn. (conv. del.), No. Ohio Edn. Assn., Ravenna Edn. Assn. (v.p. 1985-86), NAACP. Democrat. Avocations: music, chess, entrepreneurship. Home: 1482 Stratford Dr Kent OH 44240-4659 Office: Ravenna High Sch 345 E Main St Ravenna OH 44266-3194 E-mail: feltonrobert@lycos.com.

FELTS, JOHN WINFRED, JR., school librarian, educator; b. Bluefield, W.Va., May 3, 1961; s. John Winfred Felts, Betty Joann Felts; m. Cathy Mary Connolly; children: Sydney, John Felts III. MLS, U. N.C., Greensboro, 1996. Libr. U. N.C., Greensboro, NC, 1992—96; project mgr. Keystone Sys., Raleigh, NC, 1996; electronic resources libr. Averett Coll., Danville, Va., 1996—98; curriculum specialist U. N.C., 1999—. Presenter in field; adj. asst. prof. Avarett Coll., Danville, 1997—2001. Contbr. articles. With U.S. Army, 1987—90. Mem.: Libr. and Info. Tech. Assn. Office: Univ NC Greensboro 1000 Spring Garden St Greensboro NC 27402-6175 Office Fax: 336-334-5399. Business E-Mail: jwfelts@uncg.edu.

FELTS, MARGARET "GEORGE" CLEMEN, environmental engineer, consultant; b. Ft. Worth, Tex., Dec. 16, 1950; d. Arthur Taylor and Jane Jolliffe Clemen; m. Robert Louis Felts; children: Shane, Jonathan, Julia. BA Orgn. Communications, Eckerd Coll., St. Petersburg, Fla., 1973; BS Petroleum Engring., La. Tech., Ruston, La., 1977; MS Energy Engring., LaSalle U., 1989; JD, U. Pacific, 2000. Registered environ. assessor II, Calif.; registered environ. mgr., Nat. Registered Environ. Profls.; lic. gen. contractor, Calif. Engr. AMOCO Oil Co. Refinery, Yorktown, Pa., 1977-80; process engr. Celanese, Vernon, Tex., 1980-82; energy spl. Calif. Energy Commn., Sacramento, 1982-84; energy cons., owner Clemen Co., Sacramento, 1984-89; chief engring. divsn. Environ. Mgmt., McClellan AFB, Sacramento, 1985-89; owner, mgr. Clemen Environ. Svcs., 1989-92; pres. Invictus Corp., Wilton, Calif., 1992—; dir. Calif. Superfund Program Calif. Dept. Toxic Substances Control, 1993-95; chmn. bd., CEO, M.C. Felts Corp., 1995—; pres., CFO Calif. Tel. Assn., 2002—. Litigation cons. Pvt. Attys. in Calif.; CEO Oil-Gasoline.com., Inc., 1999—; expert witness FERC; expert witness natural resources and utilities coms. Calif. State Assembly; cons., expert witness Calif. Pub. Utilities Commn., Calif. Energy Commn. Author: Studies and Testimonies for Calif. Pub. Utilities Com., FERC, Citizen's Energy Coun., 1984-89; article, Oil & Gas Jour., 1985; paper, Soc. of Petroleum Engring., 1986. Recipient Lee Community Leadership Award, Eckerd Coll., 1973. Mem. Soc. Petroleum Engrs. (assoc.), Calif. Telephone Assn. (pres.). Presbyterian. Office: MCFelts Corp 9156 Tavernor Rd Wilton CA 95693-9659 also: Calif Tel Assn 1851 Heritage Ln Ste 255 Sacramento CA 95815

FELTUS, ALAN EVAN, artist; b. Washington, May 1, 1943; s. John Randolph Feltus and Anne Eve Winter; m. Toni Travis, May 1968 (div. 1974); m. Lani Helena Irwin, Dec. 10, 1978; children: Tobias, Joseph. Student, Tyler Sch. Fine Arts, Phila., 1961-62; BFA, Cooper Union, 1966; MFA, Yale U., 1968. Instr. painting and drawing Sch. of Dayton Art Inst., 1968-70; asst. prof. art dept. Am. U., Washington, 1972-84; artist, 1984—. One-person shows include Forum Gallery, NYC, 1976, 80, 83, 85, 87, 91, 94, 96, 98, 2002-03, Ann Nathan Gallery, Chgo., 1994, 98, 2000, 03, Huntington (W.Va.) Mus. Art, 2000, Wichita (Kans.) Art Mus., 1987, Hemphill Fine Arts, Washington, DC, 2001. Mem.: NAD (nat academician 1994—). Avocations: lectures, workshops. Office: Forum Gallery 745 Fifth Ave New York NY 10151 Fax: 212-355-4547.

FELTY, KRISS DELBERT, lawyer; b. Cleve., May 5, 1954; s. John Gilbert and Stephanie (Kriss) F. BA in Psychology, Case Western Res. U., 1976; postgrad., Cleve. State U., 1977-79; JD, U. Akron, Ohio, 1983. Bar: Ohio 1983, Tex. 1988, Wis. 1989, U.S. Dist. Ct. Ohio 1983, U.S. Ct. Appeals (6th cir.) 1984, Fla. 1985, U.S. Supreme Ct. 1986. Assoc. Dennis Reimer Co., LPA, Twinsburg, Ohio, 1983-87; mng. ptnr. Shapiro & Felty, Independence, Ohio, 1987—. Mem. ABA, Fla. Bar Assn., Ohio Bar Assn., Greater Cleve. Bar Assn., Cuyahoga County Bar Assn., Mortgage Bankers Assn. Am., Ohio Mortgage Bankers Assn., Mortgage Bankers Assn. Met. Cleve., Phi Kappa Theta (trustee 1973-74). Avocations: golf, swimming, reading, music, leaded glass lamps. Office: Shapiro & Felty 1500 W 3d St Ste 400 Cleveland OH 44113

FELTY, WAYNE LEE, chemist, educator; b. Harrisburg, Pa., Aug. 27, 1943; s. David Felix Nissley and Eva Ruth Felty; m. Joan L. Lindemuth, Sept. 16, 1967; children: Colleen Lenore Reynolds, Hope Michelle. BS in Chem, Lebanon Valley Coll., 1965; MS, Ohio State U., 1968, PhD, 1971. From grad. tchg. asst. to post-doctoral rsch. asst. Ohio State U., Columbus, Ohio, 1965—71, post-doctoral rsch. assoc., 1971; post-doctoral rschr. Pa. State U., Univ. Pk., Pa., 1971—72; asst. prof. of chemistry Mansfield (Pa.) State Coll., 1972—73, Pa. State U., Lehman, Pa., 1973—. Supr. and judge Chem Lab Event NE PA Regional Sci. Olympiad, 1991—2003; judge PA Jr. Acad. of Sci. Region II, 1995—2002. Reviewer: Jour. Chem. Edn., 1975—88, four general chemistry texts, 1977—90, College Chemistry, 1980, General Chemistry, 1987, Introduction To College Chemistry, 1988, Engineer-In-Training Reference Manual, 1990. Recipient Sophomore Achievement award in Chemistry, Lebanon Valley Coll., 1963. Mem.: Am. Chem. Soc., Assn. for Retarded Citizens, Nat. Arbor Day Found., Pa. Trappers Assn. (life), Nat. Trappers Assn. (life). Methodist. Avocations: fur trapping, hunting, camping, trombone, gardening. Office: Penn State Univ Wilkes Barre PO Box PSU Lehman PA 18627-0217 Office Fax: 570-675-9268. E-mail: fh0@psu.edu.

FEMAN, STEPHEN S. ophthalmologist; b. Aug. 3, 1940; BA, Franklin and Marshall Coll., 1962; MD, U. Pa., 1966. Intern Harvard Surg. Svc., Beth Israel Hosp., Boston, 1966-67, resident in surgery, 1967-68; fellow in ophthalmic pathology Jules Stein Eye Inst., UCLA, 1968-69, resident in opthalmology, 1969-72, fellow in retinal diseases, 1972-73, Wilmer Ophthalmol. Inst., Johns Hopkins Hosp., Balt., 1973-74; asst. prof. ophthalmology Albany (N.Y.) Med. Coll., 1974-78; assoc. prof. ophthalmology Vanderbilt U., Nashville, 1978-88, prof. ophthalmology, 1988-98; dir. retinal svcs. Vanderbilt U. Med. Ctr., 1978-98; Dr. Walter F. and Sharon Ryan Davisson prof. ophthalmology St. Louis U., 1998—, chair dept. ophthalmology Sch. Medicine, 1998—2000. Attending physician Vanderbilt U. Med. Ctr., 1978—98, VA Hosp., Nashville, 1978—98; mem. nat. exec. com. collaborative study of retinopathy of prematurity NIH, 1986—87; mem. perinatal adv. panel Tenn. Dept. Health and Environ., 1985—88; dir. St. Louis U. Eye Inst., 1998—2000; mem. adv. bd. Vanderbilt Health Plan, 1994—96; mem. surveillance com. diabetes prevention and control program State of Tenn. Dept. Health, 1994—98, chair, 1995—98; dir. Fundus Photo Reading Lab. Vanderbilt U., 1984—98; cons. drug adv. com. FDA, U.S. Dept. Health, 2003; cons., spkr. in field. Contbr. chpt. to textbook, numerous articles to sci. and med. jours.; sci. editl. reviewer Am. Jour. Ophthalmology, Investigative Ophthalmology and Visual Scis., Retina, Current Eye Rsch. Bd. dirs. Found. for Macular Diseases, 1998—. Lt. USNR, 1963-68. Recipient Charles H. Best medal Am. Diabetes Assn., 1994; fellow NIH, 1968, Heed Found., 1972, Seeing Eye Found., 1973. Mem.: ACS, AMA, Assn. for Rsch. in Vision and Ophthalmology, St. Louis Ophthalmol. Soc. (exec. sec. 2002—), Retina Soc., Am. Ophthalmol. Soc. (chmn. sci. program 2000—), Macula Soc., Mo. Soc. Eye Physicians and Surgeons (bd. dirs. 1999—2000), Tenn. Med. Assn. (chair coun. med. specialty socs. 1997—98), Tenn. Acad. Ophthalmology (pres. 1992—94), Am. Acad. Ophthalmology (mem. coun. 1996—98, Sr. Honor award 2001). Address: 1755 S Grand Blvd Saint Louis MO 63104-1540

FEMMINELLA, CHARLES JOSEPH, JR., real estate appraiser, tax assessor, broker; b. Bklyn., Aug. 10, 1938; s. Charles J. and Rose L. Femminella; m. Mary Ann DeCaro, Sept. 11, 1965; children: Cindy L., Christy J. BS, Fairleigh Dickinson U., 1966. Cert. gen. real estate appraiser, tax assessor, N.J. Pres. Cert. Valuations, Inc., Randolph, N.J., 1974—. Advisor Tax. Ct. N.J., 1995—; instr. real estate Rutgers U.; expert witness real estate affairs; cert. green acres, farm, condemnation, right of way, development rights and local property tax appraiser; apptd. by N.J. to appraise all propetry in Newark for local property tax purposes; lectr., cons. in field. Author: Real Property Appraisal, 1974 (Presdl. Citation 1978, 95). Pres. Randolph Rep. Club, 1980, Pla. 447 Condominium Assn., 1986—, also bd. dirs. Cpl. USMC, 1958-64. Named to Hon. Order of Ky. Cols. Mem. Soc. Profl. Assessors, Pocono Forestry Assn., Randolph C. of C. (v.p., dir. 1972), Am. Legion, Marine Corps League, DAV (life), NRA (life). Lodges: Kiwanis, KC. Avocations: real estate teaching, development and investing. Office: Cert Valuations Inc Rte 10 Ste 8 Randolph NJ 07869

FENCHEL, GERD H(ERMAN), psychoanalyst; b. Berlin, Mar. 29, 1926; arrived in U.S., 1940; s. Eric Otto and Rosa (Goldschmidt) F.; children: Karen Fenchel Spiler, Erich; m. Leslie Spitz, June 30, 1991. BSS, CCNY, 1949, MS in Edn., 1950; PhD, NYU, 1959; cert., Washington Sq. Inst., 1970. Cert. psychologist, N.Y., Pa. Pvt. practice psychoanalysis, N.Y.C., 1949—; asst. dean Alfred Adler Inst., N.Y.C., 1955-73; psychotherapist, supr. and dir. group psychotherapy L.I. Cons. Ctr., Forest Hills, N.Y., 1953-60; mem. faculty Inst. for Analytic Psychotherapy, N.J., 1960-71; exec. dir., dean Washington Sq. Inst., N.Y.C., 1960—. Co-author: Development of Ego and Emergence of the Self in Group Psychotherapy, 1979; editor: Psychoanalysis at 100, 1994, The Mother-Daughter Relationship, 1998; contbr. articles to profl. jours. Fellow Coun. Psychoanalysts and Psychotherapists (pres. 1966-67), Am. Group Psychotherapy Assn., Pa. Psychol. Assn.; mem. APA. Avocations: travel, stamps, photography. Office: Washington Sq Inst 41 E 11th St Fl 4 New York NY 10003-4678 E-mail: ghfenchel@hotmail.com.

FENDEL, DAN, mathematician, educator; b. New York, Apr. 30, 1946; s. Irvin and Ruth Fendel; m. Nina G. Galerstein, Nov. 8, 1981; children: Joseph Brian, Rebecca Samara, Benjamin Jacob. AB, Harvard U., 1966; PhD, Yale U., 1970. Prof. math. San Francisco State U., 1973—. Dir. Interactive Math. Program, Sausalito, Calif., 1989—. Author: (curriculum) Interactive Math. Program (Exemplary rating by U.S. Dept of Edn., 1999). Bd. dirs. Namaste, Berkeley, Calif., 1985—2003. Grantee, NSF, 1992—98. Mem.: Nat. Coun. Suprs. of Math., Am. Math. Soc., Nat. Coun.Tchrs. of Math. Jewish. Home: 20 Greenbank Ave Piedmont CA 94611 Office: San Francisco State U 1600 Holloway San Francisco CA 94132 Home Fax: 510-653-7761. Personal E-mail: fendel@math.sfsu.edu.

FENDERSON, CAROLINE HOUSTON, psychotherapist; b. East Orange, N.J., June 17, 1932; d. George Cochran and Mary Bullard (Saunders) Houston; m. Kendrick Elwell Fenderson, Jr.; 1 child, Karen Sibley. BA, Vassar Coll., 1954; MA, U. So. Fla., 1973. Lic. mental health counselor, Fla.; diplomate Am. Bd. Cert. Managed Care Providers, diplomate Am. Psychotherapy Assn.; cert. Nat. Bd. for Cert. Clin. Hypnotherapists, Inc.; cert. trainer, devel. of human capacities Found. for Mind Rsch.; ordained to ministry of edn. Unitarian Universalist. Dir. of religious edn. Unitarian Universalist Ch., St. Petersburg, Fla., 1960-80, min. of religious edn. Clearwater, Fla., 1981-83; counselor and staff devel. cons. Pinellas County (Fla.) Schools, 1973-83; pvt. practice Clearwater and Palm Harbor, Fla., 1983—. Author: Life Journey, 1988; (with Kendrick Fenderson Jr.) Magnets, 1961, Southern Shores, 1964; (with others) Man the Culture Builder, 1970, U.U. Identity, 1979; contbr. articles to profl. jours. Pub. affairs chmn. St. Petersburg Jr. League, 1960; founder Childbirth and Parent Edn. League of Pinellas County, 1960-70, pres., v.p., com. chair, tchr.; v.p. Child Guidance Clinic, St. Petersburg, 1960. Mem. ACA, Liberal Religious Edn. Dirs. Assn. (v.p. 1980-81), Assn. Transpersonal Psychology, Assn. Humanistic Psychology, Internat. Transpersonal Assn., Unitarian Universalist Assn. (com. mem. 1975-79), Phi Beta Kappa, Kappa Delta Pi. Home: 29 Freshwater Dr Palm Harbor FL 34684-1106 Office: 25 400 US 19 N Ste 172 Clearwater FL 33763

FENDLER, JANOS HUGO, chemistry educator; b. Budapest, Hungary, Aug. 12, 1937; came to U.S., 1964; s. Janos and Vilma (Csiky) F.; m. Eleanor Johnson, june 15, 1965 (div. 1975); children: Michael, Lisa; m. Ann Fendler, Feb. 15, 1976 (div. 1997); children: Peter, Monika; m. Eliza Hutter, Sept. 15, 1997; children: Veronika Isabelle, David Viktor. BSc, U. Leicester, Eng., 1960; Diploma in Radiochemistry, Leicester Coll. Tech., 1961; PhD, U. London, 1964, DSc, 1978; DSc (hon.), U. Szeged, Hungary, 1999. Postdoctoral fellow U. Calif., Santa Barbara, 1965 66; fellow Mellon Inst., Pitts., 1966-70; assoc. prof. chemistry Tex. A&M U., College Station, 1970-75, prof., 1975-81; prof. chemistry Clarkson Coll., Potsdam, N.Y., 1982-85; disting. prof. chemistry, dir. Ctr. Membrane Engring. & Sci. Syracuse U., 1985-97; disting. Camp prof. chemistry Clarkson U., 1997— Adj. prof. U. Montreal, 1967—94; indsl. cons., vis. prof., Japan, 1975, Switzerland, 79, Sweden, 81, France, 85, Germany, 92, Israel, 97, Paris, 2001—. Author: Catalysts in Micellar and Macromolecular Systems, 1975, Membrane Mimetic Chemistry, 1982, Membrane Mimetic Approach to Advanced Materials, 1994; rsch., numerous publs. in field; N.Am. editor Colloid and Polymer Sci.; mem. editl. bd. Jour. Organic Chemistry, 1978-82, jour. Colloid and Interface Sci., 1981-87, Langmuir, 1985-87, Bull. Chem. Soc. France, 1986-92, Magyar Kèmiai Folyoirat, 1992—, Advanced Materials, 1994—, Chemistry of Materials, 1997—. Recipient Sr. Humboldt Rsch. award, 1992. Mem. Am. Chem. Soc. (Kendall award 1982), Royal Chem. Soc., Internat. Assn. Colloid and Interface Scientists. Home: 608 Swan St Potsdam NY 13676-1147 Office: Clarkson U Ctr Adv Material Processing PO Box 5814 Potsdam NY 13699-0001 E-mail: fendler@clarkson.edu.

FENDLER, SHERMAN GENE, lawyer; b. Alexandria, La., Jan. 22, 1947; s. Ben and Rae (Kaplan) Fendler; m. Sarah Linda Dantzler, Dec. 26, 1976; children: Julia Kathleen, Abigail Leigh, Benjamin Brooks. BA, U. Va., Charlottesville, 1969; JD, La. State U., 1973. Bar: La. 73, U.S. Dist. Ct. La. 74, U.S. Ct. Appeals (5th and 11th cirs.) 75, U.S. Supreme Ct. 80. Law clk. U.S. Dist. Ct. (ea. dist.) La., New Orleans, 1973—74; ptnr. Liskow & Lewis, New Orleans, 1994—, mng. ptnr., 2003—. Capt. AUS, 1973—79. Mem.: ABA, Maritime Law Assn., La. Bar Assn., Order of Coir. Home: 1102 Metairie Rd Metairie LA 70005-3301 Office: Liskow & Lewis One Shell Sq 50th Fl New Orleans LA 70139

FENDRICK, ALAN BURTON, retired advertising executive; b. Bronx, N.Y., Mar. 22, 1933; s. Louis and Esther (Silberberg) F.; m. Beverly R. Schoenfeld, June 12, 1960; children: Sarah Shifrin, Lisa Rubinstein. AB with honors in Econs, Columbia U., 1954; MBA, Harvard U., 1958. Asst. sales mgr. splty. divsn. Hankins Container Co., 1958-60; mgr. bus. adminstrn., ops. and engring. NBC, 1960-67; exec. v.p., sec., treas. Grey Advt. Inc., N.Y.C., 1967-89, exec. v.p., chmn. fin. com., 1990-93. Trustee Woodlands H.S. Scholarship Fund, Greenburgh, N.Y., pres., 1977-78; trustee Jewish Child Care Assn. N.Y., 1985-97, hon. trustee, 1997—; trustee SAG Producers Pension and Health Plans, 1993—; mem. sch. bd. Mt. Plesant Cottage Sch., 1985-99; bd. dirs. Columbia Coll. Alumni Assn., 1989-96. With AUS, 1954-56. Mem. Am. Assn. Advt. Agys. (chmn. com. on fiscal control 1979-81), Advt. Agy. Fin. Mgmt. Group (chmn. exec. com. 1980-82, pres. 1982-84), Otis Woodlands Club Inc. (bd. dirs. 1985-89, treas. 1984-88), Columbia U. Alumni Club of Sarasota (pres. 1997—). Jewish (trustee temple). Home: 5880 Midnight Pass Rd Sarasota FL 34242-4106 E-mail: bevalan711@aol.com.

FENDT, GENE J. poet, philosopher, educator; s. Eugene James Fendt and Mary Virginia Lorbecki. BA magna cum laude, Marquette U., 1974—77; MA, The U. of Chgo., 1978—79; PhD, The U. of Tex., 1983—87. Prof. philosophy U. NE Kearney. Author: (book) Is Hamlet a Religious Drama?: An Essay on a Question in Kierkegaard, Works of Love?: Reflections on Works of Love, For What May I Hope?: Thinking with Kant and Kierkegaard, Platonic Errors: Plato, A Kind of Poet, (poetry) Theology Today, Anglican Theological Review, Nimrod, Aethlon, Puerto del Sol, Hurakan; actor: (plays) Shakespeare at Winedale; contbr. articles to profl. jours., chapters to books. Recipient Faculty award for rsch., Pratt-Heins Found., 2002, Invited scholar, U. of Copenhagen, 1996, Nat. Poetry Competition, Commendation, Chester H. Jones Found., 1997, Individual Artist fellowship, Nebr. Arts Coun., 1999; Seminar fellowship, Nat. Endowment for the Humanities, 2001, Rsch. grant, U. of Nebr., 1988, 1990, 1992, 1997. Mem.: Internat. Plato Soc., Soc. for Ancient Greek Philosophy, Am. Cath. Philos. Assn. (life). Home: 929 N Astor St #1005 Milwaukee WI 53202 Office: University of Nebraska 905 W 25th St Kearney NE 68849

FENECH, DANIEL THOMAS, cartoonist; b. Garden City, Mich., June 8, 1957; s. Carmel John and Elizabeth Frances (Borg) Fenech; m. Linda M. Speegle, Dec. 7, 1992. BA, U. Mich., 1979. Coll. intern WXYZ-TV, Southfield, Mich., 1978—79; tech. on-air dir. WEYI-TV, Flint, Mich., 1979—80; cartoonist Daniel Fenech Prodns., Saline, Mich., 1980—. Contbr. Best Editorial Cartoons of the Year 2001, Best Editorial Cartoons of the Year 2002. Pres. bd. of trustees Saline Dist. Libr., 1998—2001. Avocations: reading encyclopedias, reading, swimming, running, travel.

FENECH, JOSEPH CHARLES, lawyer; b. London, May 28, 1930; came to U.S., 1953; s. Carmel John and Elizabeth Frances (Borg) F.; m. Cynthia A. Rennie, June 14, 1980 (div. 1998); children: Paul C., Peter J., Elizabeth F. BA with honors, Mich. State U., 1972; JD, U. Mich., 1975. Bar: Mich. 1975, U.S. Dist. Ct. (ea. dist.) Mich. 1975, U.S. Ct. Appeals (6th cir.) 1977, Ill. 1980, U.S. Dist. Ct. (no. dist.) Ill. 1980, U.S. Dist. Ct. (ctrl. dist.) Ill. 1993, U.S. Dist. Ct. (ea. dist.) Wis. 1993, U.S. Ct. Appeals (7th cir.) 1980, U.S. Supreme Ct. 1993, U.S. Tax Ct. 1993. Law clk. Washtenaw Cir. Ct., Ann Arbor, Mich., 1975-76; asst. atty. gen. State of Mich., Detroit, 1976-80; labor rels. counsel McDonald's Corp., Oak Brook, Ill., 1980-82, sr. internat. atty., 1982-84; sr. mem. Fenech & Assoc., Oak Brook, Ill., 1985—. Contbr. articles to profl. jours. Bd. dirs. Cath. Charities Diocese of Joliet, Ill.; active Family Focus, Mich., 1979-80, Internat. Found. Employee Benefit Plans, Brookfield, Wis., 1980-83, Chmns. Club Ctrl.; mem. bd. govs. DuPage Hosp., Ctrl. DuPage Hosp. Tree Life, Ctrl., Glen Oaks Med. Ctr., Tree of Life, Rep. Campaign Coun., 1995; supt. adv. com. Naperville Cmty. Sch. Dist. 203; improvement com. Mill St. Sch., Naperville; charter mem. Marklund Children's Home Endowment; bd. govs. Ctrl. DuPage Hosp. Named Regents scholar U. Mich., 1973, 74, 75, Trustees scholar Mich. State U., 1969-72. Mem. ABA, Ill. State Bar Assn., Mich. Bar assn., DuPage Estate Planning Coun., U. Mich. Lawyers Club, Ill. Bankers Assn., Ill. Mortgage Bankers Assn., Internat. Platform Assn. Am. Hosp. Assn. (sr. mem.), Am. Acad. Healthcare Attys. (sr. mem.). Office: Fenech & Pachulski PC PO Box 5996 Naperville IL 60567

FENELON, JAMES V. sociologist, educator, poet, advocate; b. Fargo, Nd., Mar. 29, 1954; s. Vincent E. Fenelon and Barbara Jean Johnson; m. Sandra Luz Jimenez, May 6, 1995; children: Mikhael Joaquin, James Dean. Masters 2 (MAT & MIA), Sch. Internat. Tng., Brattleboro, Vt., 1979—83; CAS, Harvard (HGSE), 1990—91; PhD, Northwestern U., 1991—95. Leader edn. group Danish Expt. Int'l Living, Copenhagen & Vejen, Denmark, 1979; educator / tchr. Haitian-American Inst., Port-au-Prince, Haiti, 1982; lectr. (fgn. expert) Internat. Studies U., Shanghai, 1983—84; lectr. / educator SUMITOMO / Newport U., Tokyo & Kashima, Japan, 1984—85; lectr. U. Md./ITM, Kuala Lumpur (Kelanajaya), Malaysia, 1985—86; project dir. Standing Rock Coll., Fort Yates, ND, 1987—88; trainer-consultant Midwest BEMRC Resource Ctr., Des Plaines, Ill., 1989—91; prof. John Carroll U., University Heights, Ohio, 1995—99; assoc. prof. Calif. State U., San Berandino, Calif., 1999—. Workshop dir. Chambre-de-Commerce, Fort-de-France, Martinique, FWI, 1983. Author: (poetry, photography) Indigenous Images and Words (Best Show, Hon. Mention, 1st Pl.), (book) Culturicide, Resistance and Survival of the Lakota 'Sioux Nation', (formal research publications) American Indian Culture & Research Journal, Humboldt Journal of Social Relations, Journal of World Systems Research, etc. Ceremonial participant Cheyenne River Reservation, SD, 1989—94; chair and mem. First Nations Edn. Ctr., San Berandino, Calif., 1990—2002, Am. Indian Econ. Devel., Chgo., 1990—2002. Petty officer USN, 1973—76, San Diego, Chgo., Newport News. Mem.: Am. Sociol. Assn. (coun. & com. (elected) 1999—2003). Democrat-Npl. Christian, Lakota Spirituality, Buddhist. Achievements include research in Identified Culturicide Models for Analyzing Indian Nations. Avocations: indigenous peoples travels, climbing sacred mountains, learning about the land, languages & cultures. Office: California State U 5500 University Blvd San Bernardino CA 92407 Personal E-mail: jfenelon@charter.net. E-mail: jfenelon@csusb.edu.

FENET, ROBERT WICKLIFFE, lawyer; b. Lake Charles, La., Dec. 16, 1947; m. Sally Elizabeth Gamblin, Aug. 26, 1972; children: Charles, Lydia, Andrew, Hilary. BSc in Indsl. Engring., Ga. Inst. Tech., 1969; JD, La. State U., 1972; Cert. de Langue Francaise, U. Paris Sorbonne, 1972; Cert. Pratique de Langue Francaise, U. Grenoble, France, 1973. Law clk. 3d Circuit Ct. Appeals, Lake Charles, La., 1973-74, 14th Jud. Dist. Ct., Lake Charles, La., 1973-74; ptnr. Woodley, Williams, Fenet, Boudreau, Norman & Brown, Lake Charles, La., 1974-97; spl. counsel internat. affairs Breazeale, Sachse & Wilson, Baton Rouge, 1997—2000; mng. dir. Fenet & Anderson, 2000—. Spl. counsel City of Lake Charles, 1977—83; Impartial Hearing Officer State of La., 1978—83, spl. dep. atty. gen., 1998—. Mem. vestry Episc. Ch. Good Shepherd; bd. dirs. Am. Cancer Soc.. With USNR, 1965-70. Named Hon. Ins. Commr. State of La. Mem. ABA, S.W. La. Bar Assn., La. Bar Assn., Am. Assn. Average Adjusters, Brit. Assn. Average Adjusters of U.S., Maritime Law Assn. U.S., Southeastern Admiralty Law Inst., Union des Avocates Internat., Nat. Assn. Profl. Surplus Lines Offices, Ltd., La. Surplus Lines Assn., France Amerique (pres.), Rotary, S.W. La. C. of C. (mem. legis. affairs com.), City Club Baton Rouge, Country Club Lake Charles. Camelot Club, City Club Baton Rouge, Country Club Lake Charles. Avocation: golf. Home: 7522 Rienzi Blvd Baton Rouge LA 70809-1122 Office: Fenet & Anderson Ste 200 8641 United Plaza Blvd Baton Rouge LA 70809

FENG, ALBERT, science educator, researcher; b. Bandung, Java, Indonesia, Feb. 10, 1944; s. Shu-San and Yi (Chow) F.; m. Phoebe Lifei Wang, Oct. 14, 1974; children: Jeffrey Thomas, Jacqueline A. BSEE, U. Miami, 1968, MSc, 1970; PhD, Cornell U., 1975. Reliability engr. Singer Corp. Kearfott Div., Little Falls, N.J., 1970; asst. rsch. neuroscientist U. Calif. at San Diego, La Jolla, 1974-76; postdoctoral fellow Washington U., St. Louis, 1976-77; asst. prof. U. Ill., Urbana, 1977-83, assoc. prof., 1983-89, prof., 1989—, head dept. molecular and integrative physiology, 1992-97. Mem. adv. bd. Parmly Hearing Inst., Chgo., 1982-88; mem. review panel NSF, Washington, 1986-88, chmn. neuro-

sci. program U. Ill., Urbana, 1987-90; mem. hearing rsch. study sect. NIH, Washington, 1991-95, chmn., 1993-95. Contbr. articles to profl. jours. including Jour. Neurophysiology, Jour. Comparative Physiology, Science, Jour. Comparative Neurology, Jour. Acoustical Soc. Am., Jour. Neurosci. Fellow AAAS, Acoustical Soc. of Am.; mem. Assn. for Rsch. Otolaryngology, Internat. Soc. Neuroethology (treas. 1992-98, pres.-elect 1998-2001, pres. 2001—), Soc. of Neurosci. Achievements include research in neural mechanisms of sound localization and sound pattern recognition. Home: 1209 Wilshire Ct Champaign IL 61821-6916 Office: U Ill 405 N Mathews Ave Urbana IL 61801-2325

FENG, BAO QI (PAO CHI) (EDWARD), mathematician, educator; b. Hong Kong, China, Oct. 1, 1938; arrived in U.S., 1989; s. Chanson Feng and Ping Yun Feng-Chang; children: Zhi Min, Zhi Xin (Louis). BS, Nanjing (China) U., 1963; MSc, Youngstown (Ohio) State U., 1996; PhD in Math., Kent (Ohio) State U., 2001. Math. tchr. Harbin (China) First HS, 1963—78; assoc. prof. Harbin (China) Normal Coll., 1978—89; asst. prof. Kent (Ohio) State U., New Phila., Ohio, 2001—. Author: Key to the mathematics exercise (3), 1979, Methods of proof of trigonometric identities, 1982, Methods of proof of Algebraic identities, 1984. Mem.: Math. Assn. of Am., Am. Math. Soc.

FENG, GEN-SHENG, medical educator, researcher; b. Sept. 8, 1961; BSc in Biology, Hangzhou U., China, 1981; MSc in Immunology, 2d Med. Sch. of Army, Shanghai, China, 1984; PhD in Molecular Biology, Ind. U., 1990. Rsch. assoc. in molecular genetics 2d Med. Sch. of Army, Shanghai, 1985—86; assoc. instr. dept. biology Ind. U., Bloomington, 1987—90; postdoctoral fellow in molecular biology U. Toronto, 1990—94; with Rsch. Inst. The Hosp. for Sick Children, Toronto, 1990—91, Rsch. Inst. Mt. Sinai Hosp., Toronto, 1991—94; asst. prof. dept. biochemistry and molecular biology, dept. med. and molecular genetics, asst. mem. Walther Oncology Ctr. Ind. U., Indpls., 1994—; assoc. prof. oncogenes and tumor suppression program Burnham Inst., 2000—. Ad hoc reviewer: Jour. Biol. Chemistry, Jour. Cell. Sci., Oncogene, Leukemia; contbr. articles to profl. jours.; reviewer of rsch. grants: Internat. Human Frontier Sci. Program, 1994, 1995, U.S. Vets. Affairs Med. Rsch. Sys., 1996; spkr. in field. Recipient Silver prize for Achievement of Health Sci. and Tech., China, 1986, Carrie E. Wolff award, Am. Heart Assn. Ind. Affiliate, Inc., 1995. Mem.: AAAS, Soc. Chinese Biologists Am., Am. Soc. Microbiology, Am. Diabetes Assn. (career devel. award 1995—). Office: Ind U Sch Medicine Dept Biochemistry and Molecular Biology 1044 W Walnut St Rm 302 Indianapolis IN 46202-5254 also: The Burnham Inst 10901 N Torrey Pines Rd La Jolla CA 92037-1005

FENG, PAUL YEN-HSIUNG, lawyer, chemist; s. Chih-Chung and Pao-Ru Hu Feng; m. Marie Rose Rysiejko, Feb. 14, 1976; m. Mary Stella Pao-Ching Pai, Oct. 2, 1947 (dec. May 25, 1975); children: Joseph, Dorothy Feng Hamamura, Alphonso. BS, Fu-Jen Cath. U., Beijing, 1947; grad. fellow, Nat. Beijing U., 1947—48; PhD, Wash. U., 1954; JD, DePaul U., 1986; MBA, U. Chgo., 1991. CPA U. of Ill. Bd. Examiners, 1996; bar: U. S. Dist. Ct. (no. dist.) Ill. 1986, U. S. Tax Ct. 1994, U. S. Patent and Trademark Office 1989, U. S. Ct. Appeals (7th cir.) 1986, U. S. Supreme Ct. Tchr. Wen-Hua H.S., Beijing, 1945—47; tech. dir. Manu-Mine R & D Co., Reading, Pa., 1953—55; mgr. IIT Rsch. Inst. (formerly Armour Rsch. Found.), Chicago, 1955—66, sci. advisor, 1962—66; assoc. prof. Marquette U., Milw., 1966—70, prof., 1970—88; of counsel Lamet Kanwit & Davis, Brezina & Ehrlich, Chicago, Ill., 1990—2000; fulbright lectr. Nat. Taiwan U., Taipai, 1965; nrc prof. and dean Nat. Tsinghua U., Hsinchu, Taiwan, 1973—74; pvt. practice Wilmette, Ill., 1986—. Tech. advisor U. S. Del. to 2nd UN Conf. Peaceful Uses Atomic Energy, Geneva, 1958; cons. U.S. Army Natick Labs., Natick, Mass., 1966—74, Apollo Program - NASA, Washington, 1968, Chung Shan Inst. Tech., Taoyuan, Taiwan, 1970—74; sr. advisor NRC, Taipai, Taiwan, 1973—74; pres. North Suburban Bar Assn., Glenview, Ill., 1996—97. Contbr. articles, chapters to books; author: (book) Dividend Reinvestment Handbook. Dir. Chinese Refugee Relief, Washington, 1962; mem. Chinese Adv. Com. Cultural Rels. in Am., Washington; dir. Neighborhood Assistance Found., Chgo., 1992—96. Recipient Achievement award, Nat. Youth Commn., Taiwan, 1971; Rsch. grantee, USAF, U. S. Army, U.S. AEC, 1955 - 74. Mem.: Phoenix Soc., ACS (career cons. 1992—), Overture Soc., Elliott Soc. (life), Sigma Xi (pres., marquette chpt. 1973—74). Achievements include patents for method of making fluorinated compounds; a hot-atom cation defixation method for the production of high specific activity isotopes; research in method for specific tritiation of organic compounds. Avocations: linguistics, musicology, geographic archaeology. Mailing: PO Box 424 Kenilworth IL 60043 Personal E-mail: paulfeng@att.net.

FENG, TSE-YUN, computer engineer, educator; b. Hangchow, China, Feb. 26, 1928; s. Shih-ching and Lin Shao; m. Elaine Hu, Jan. 28, 1965; children: Wu-chun, Wu-chi, Wu-che, Wu-chang. BS, Nat. Taiwan U., 1950; MS, Okla. State U., 1957; PhD, U. Mich., 1967. Asst. engr. Taiwan Power Co., 1950-56; sr. designer Ebasco Services, N.Y.C., 1957-60; teaching fellow U. Mich., 1962-65, research asst., 1965-66, asst. research engr., 1966, research asso., 1967; asst. prof. elec. and computer engring. Syracuse U., 1967-71, asso. prof., 1971-75; prof. elec. and computer engring. Wayne State U., Detroit, 1975-79; prof. computer sci. Wright State U., Dayton, Ohio, 1979-80, chmn. dept., 1979-80; prof. computer and info. sci. Ohio State U., 1980-84; Binder prof. computer engring. Pa State U., University Park, 1984—, dir. computer engring. program, 1984-88; program dir. NSF, Arlington, Va., 1993—97, 2000—02. Cons. Transidyne Gen., Syracuse U., Pattern Analysis and Recognition Corp., N.Y. State Bd. Edn., NSF, Arlington, Va., 2000; chmn. Internat. Conf. on Parallel Processing, 1975—, Internat. Conf. on Computers and Applications, 1983-87; dir. N.E. Consortium for Engring. Edn., 1976-80; participant U.S. Technol. Policy Conf., 1978; leader del. U.S. Sr. Experts to China, 1985; cons. USAF. Contbr. numerous articles to others; patentee in field Recipient ABCD award NSF, 2001. Fellow Assn. Computing Machinery, IEEE (chmn. computer soc. standards com. 1974-78, mem. numerous other coms., presiding officer computer soc. governing bd. 1979-80, computer soc. disting. visitor 1973-78, pres. 1979-80, chmn. nominations com. 1981-83, chmn. disting. visitors program, 1987-93, Best Paper award 1975, Honor Roll award 1978, Spl. award 1981, Centennial medal 1984, Richard E. Merwin Disting. Service award 1985, Meritorious Service award, 1986, 2000, Millennium medal 2000, mem. del. to Chinese Electronics Soc. 1978, leader del. 1980, del. to Popov Soc. Congress, USSR 1978, editor-in-chief Trans. on Computers 1982-86, Trans. on Parallel and Distributed Systems, 1989-93, Tech. Achievement award and Outstanding Contbn. award, 1991); mem. Am. Fedn. Info. Processing Socs. (dir. 1979-80, 82-87, nominating com. 1979-80, 83-85, chmn. publs. com. 1984-86, exec. com. 1986-87, mem. numerous other coms.), Am. Nat. Standards Inst. (info. systems standards mgmt. bd. 1974-78), Sagamore Computer Conf. (chmn., editor proc. 1972-75), Pa. State Engring. Soc. (Outstanding Rsch. award 1989), Internat. Assn. Computers and Comms. (pres. 1995—), Hon. Order of Ky. Cols., Sigma Xi, Phi Kappa Phi, Tau Beta Pi, Eta Kappa Nu, Phi Tau Phi. Home: 319 Christopher Ln State College PA 16803-1261 Office: U Pa Dept Computer Sci & Enging Pond Lab University Park PA 16802 E-mail: feng@cse.psu.edu., t.feng@computer.org.

FENG, XIAHONG, geochemist, educator; b. Shanghai, July 1, 1957; arrived in came to U.S., 1985; d. Leyun Feng and Yiwen Wu. BS, Peking U., Beijing, 1982, MS, 1985; PhD, Case Western Reserve U., 1991. Rsch. assoc. Calif. Inst. Tech., Pasadena, 1991—94; asst. prof. Dartmouth Coll., Hanover, NH, 1994—2000, assoc. prof., 2000—. Recipient Career award, NSF, 1996. Office: Dartmouth Coll 6105 Fairchild Hanover NH 03755

FENGLER, JOHN PETER, television producer, director, advertising executive; b. Leipzig, Germany, Dec. 29, 1928; came to U.S., 1939; naturalized, 1952; m. Jessica M. Atkins, Dec. 7, 1961; 1 child, John Mark. BA in Radio and TV, NYU, 1952. Producer, dir. NBC, N.Y.C., 1950-58; exec. producer N.W. Ayer Co., N.Y.C., 1958-65; dir., exec. producer radio and TV dept. Doyle, Dane, Bernbach, 1965-70, Kurtz and Symon Inc., N.Y.C., 1970-73; v.p., dir. comml. prodn. dept., exec. producer D'Arcy-MacManus & Masius, N.Y.C., 1974-75; pres. U.S. TV Co., N.Y.C., 1975-90, Boca Raton, Fla., 1990-94. With U.S. Army, 1950-52. Mem. NATAS (Emmy award best children's program 1957, 58). Office: 6309 NW 25th Way Boca Raton FL 33496-3624 E-mail: jfengler@adelphia.net.

FENICHEL, ALVIN HENRY, financial executive; b. Lakewood, N.J., Sept. 28, 1944; s. Lester and Rose (Raisen) F.; m. Evelyn Friedman, Sept. 5, 1971; children: Rebecca, Marc. BS in Acctg., Rider U., 1966; MBA with distinction, Pace U., 1981. CPA. Acctg. supr. Coopers & Lybrand, N.Y.C., 1966-71; group v.p. fin. CBS Inc., N.Y.C., 1971-86; CFO publishing Harcourt Brace, Orlando, Fla., 1986-87; sr. v.p., contr. Equitable Co., N.Y.C., 1987-90, AXA Fin., 1990—. Mem. Fin. Execs. Internat. (chmn. ins. com. N.Y.C. chpt.). Home: 5 Paradise Dr Scarsdale NY 10583-1521

FENICHEL, RICHARD LEE, retired biochemist; b. N.Y.C., July 23, 1925; s. Irving and Dorothy (Rothchild) F.; widowed; children: Gladys, Marilyn. Student, Bucknell U., 1941-43; AB, NYU, 1947; MS, Poly. Inst. Bklyn., 1951; PhD, Wayne U., 1956. Commonwealth fellow for rsch. Poly. Inst. Bklyn., 1948-50; biochemist med. dept. Chrysler Corp., Highland Park, Mich., 1951-54; grad. tchg. asst. Wayne U. Med. Ctr., 1954-56; investigator Aviation Med. Acceleration Lab., Johnsville, Pa., 1957-59; group leader Ortho Rsch. Found., Raritan, N.J., 1959-63; sr. rsch. fellow biochemistry and pharmacology Wyeth-Ayerst Labs., Princeton, N.J., 1963-95. Contbr. numerous articles to profl. jours.; patentee in field. Served with U.S. Army, 1943-45. Recipient Angus McClear Rsch. award Wayne U., 1956, Superior Accomplishment award USN Med. Lab., 1966; Legion of Honor, Chapel of Four Chaplains, 1982. Mem. Am. Chem. Soc., N.Y. Acad. Scis., AAAS, Am. Soc. Biol. Chemists, Sigma Xi. Home: Apt A219 1400 Waverly Rd Gladwyne PA 19035-1257

FENIGER, JEROME ROLAND, JR., broadcast executive; b. Peoria, Ill., June 16, 1927; s. Jerome Rol and Marie Dorothy (Miller) F.; m. Marian Laura Schwartz, June 24, 1951; children: Robin Jean, Bruce David. BA, U. Iowa, 1948; postgrad., Columbia U., 1948, N.Y. U., 1949-50; D.Bus. in Sci. (hon.), St. John's U., 1984. Advt. account exec. Biow Co., N.Y.C., 1949-50; chief advt. time buyer Cunningham & Walsh, N.Y.C., 1950-51, v.p., 1954-60; sales exec. CBS, N.Y.C., 1952-54; exec. Cowles Comm. Co., N.Y.C., 1960-65; v.p. Grey Advt. Inc., N.Y.C., 1965-70; pres. Horizons Comm. Corp., N.Y.C., 1970-83; mng. dir. Sta. Reps. Assn., Inc., N.Y.C., 1983—2002; life bd. dirs. Advt. Coun., 1984—2002. Pres. Louise Wise Svcs., 1986-89; mem. pvt. sector commn. USIA/Voice of Am. Trustee Columbia Grammar and Prep Sch., 1965-77, treas., 1970-77; bd. dirs. UJA Fedn. on Domestic Affairs. Sgt. USAF, 1946—47. Recipient Disting. Alumnus award, U. Iowa, 2002. Mem. Internat. Radio and TV Soc. (pres. 1975-77), Friars Club, Dutch Treat Club, Yale Club of N.Y.C. Democrat. Home: 16 W 77th St New York NY 10024-5126

FENIK, VICTOR BORISOVICH, neurobiologist, researcher; b. Stariy Oskol, Russia, Nov. 30, 1960; came to U.S., 1994; s. Boris Stepanovich and Galina Grigorievna F.; m. Polina Vasilievna Motuzna, Mar. 2, 1991; children: Vasil, Pavlo. MSc in Biophysics, Kiev (Ukraine) State U., 1983; PhD in Physiology, Bogomolets Inst. of Physiology, Kiev, 1991. Technician Cancer Rsch. Inst., Kiev, 1977-81; rsch. fellow I, II Bogomolets Inst. of Physiology, Kiev, 1981-94; postdoctoral fellow U. Pa., Phila., 1994-98, rsch. assoc., 1998—2001, sr. rsch. investigator, 2001—. Contbr. articles to profl. jours. Mem. Soc. of Neurosci. Avocations: computer programming, traveling, tennis. Office: U Pa 3800 Spruce St Philadelphia PA 19104-6046 E-mail: vfenik@vet.upenn.edu.

FENIMORE, GEORGE WILEY, management consultant; b. Bertrand, Mo., 1921; BBA in Fin., Northwestern U., 1941; LLB, Harvard U., 1947; postgrad., UCLA, 1955; LLD (hon.), Southwestern U., 1992. Bar: Mich. 1948. Asst. to dir. planning Ford Motor Co., Dearborn, Mich., 1947-48; exec. to v.p. and gen. mgr. Hughes Aircraft Co., Culver City, Calif., 1948-53; adminstrv. mgr. tech. products Packard Bell Electronics Co., 1954-55; with TRW, Inc., Los Angeles, 1955-64; v.p., gen. mgr. TRW Internat., Los Angeles, 1959-64; v.p. internat. ops. Bunker Ramo Corp., Los Angeles, 1964-65; dir. public relations, then corp. sec. Litton Industries, Inc., Beverly Hills, Calif., 1965-73, v.p., corp. sec., 1973-81, sr. v.p., corp. sec., 1981-86, mgmt. cons., 1986—; sr. v.p. Peck Jones Constrn., Beverly Hills. Past chmn. bd. Southwestern U. Sch. Law; mem. Calif. Tchrs. Retirement Bd.; cons. Northrop Grumman Corp. Bd. dirs. Children's Bur. L.A., Child Shelter Homes a Rescue Effort; sec. French Found. for Alzheimer's Rsch.; mem. Calif. Fair Polit. Practices Commn., 1986-91; mem. United Way Emergency Food Sys. Study Task Force; elder, chmn. fin. com. Westwood Presbyn. Ch.; past trustee Sheldon Jackson Coll., Sitka, Alaska; mem. Beverly Hills Mayor's Econ. Adv. Com. and MOVE com. Maj. USAAF, WW II. Recipient Citizen of Yr. award, Beverly Hills Lions Club, 1976, Spirit Honoree, Beverly Hills Edn. Found., 1986, Beverly Hills YMCA, 1988, Brentwood/San Vicente C. of C., 1987, Hon. Citizen award, Beverly Hills City Coun., 1986, Guardian Angel award, Child S.H.A.R.E., 1989, Lifetime Achievement award, 2001, Highest award for Livetime Svc. to Cmty., Key to City of Beverly Hills, 1990, State Gold award, Calif. Tchrs. Assn., 1993. Mem. Am. Soc. Corp. Secs. (dir., past nat. dir., past pres. Los Angeles Group), Beverly Hills C. of C. (past pres., Citizen of Yr. award 1979, chmn. edn. com., bd. dirs., David Orgell Meml. award 1990), Mandeville Canyon Assn. (past pres.), Bar Assn. Mich., L.A. Country Club, Rotary (past pres. Beverly Hills, Paul Harris fellow, William C. Ackerman trophy 1986), Shriners. Presbyterian. Office: 1061 Cloverfield Blvd 400S Santa Monica CA 90404 Fax: 310-998-8703. E-mail: fenimore98@aol.com.

FENINGER, CLAUDE, industry management services company executive; b. Cairo, Jan. 15, 1926; came to U.S., 1960; s. Paul and Therese (DeRogatis) F.; m. Jill Ellis, Nov. 26, 1986; children from previous marriage: Paul Gordon, Eric. Student, Lausanne (Switzerland) Sch. Hotel Mgmt., 1948, Am. U., Cairo, 1945, Lincoln Sch., 1943, Lycee Francais, 1935. With Hilton Internat., 1955-67; product line mgr. ITT, 1967-68; pres. Sheraton Internat., 1968-74; chmn. bd., chief exec. officer Omni Internat. Hotels, Inc., Atlanta, 1974-80; pres. Aramark Internat., Phila., 1980—. Cons. in field, 1960— ; dir. VS Services, Can., Traulsen Refrigeration Co., N.Y.C. Mem. Am. Mgmt. Assn., Am. Hotel Assn. Home: 2045 Yellow Springs Rd Malvern PA 19355-8702 Office: Aramark Corp ARA Svcs Inc 1101 Market St Ste 45 Philadelphia PA 19107-2988 E-mail: cfeninger@aol.com.

FENN, JOHN BENNETT, chemist, educator; b. N.Y.C., June 15, 1917; s. Herbert Bennett and Jeanette Clyde (Dingman) F.; m. Margaret Elizabeth Wilson, June 6, 1939; children: Margaret Marianne, Barbara Leigh, John Bennett. AB, Berea Coll., 1937; PhD, Yale U., 1940. Research chemist (Monsanto Chem. Co.), Anniston, Ala., 1940-43, Sharples Chems., Inc., Wyandotte, Mich., 1943-45; v.p. Experiment, Inc., Richmond, Va., 1945-52; dir. Project SQUID, Princeton, 1952-62, prof. mech. engring., 1959-63, prof. aerospace scis., 1963-66; prof. applied sci. and chemistry Yale U., 1967—80; pres. Relay Devel. Corp., 1975—; prof. of engineering Yale U., 1980—87, prof. emeritus, 1987—; prof. of analytical chem. Virginia Commonwealth U., 1993—. Vis. scientist N.Am. Aviation Sci. Center, 1965-66; vis. prof. U. Trento, Italy, 1976, U. Tokyo, 1979, U. of China, 1987; dir. Thermal Research & Engring. Corp., 1952-59; sci. liaison officer Office Naval Research, London, 1955; dir. Aero Chem. Research Labs., 1956-60; cons. UN Author: Engines, Energy and Entropy, 1982; editor: (with A.B. Cambel) Transport Properties in Gases, 1958, Dynamics of Conducting Gases, 1960. Recipient Sr. Scientist award Alexander von Humboldt Found., 1983-84, Disting. Alumnus award Berea Coll., 1987, Nobel Prize in Chemistry, 2002. Mem. Am. Chem. Soc., AAAS, Am. Inst. Chem. Engrs., Internat. Soc. Mass Spectrometry (sec. 2000), Sigma Xi. Office: VCU Dept of Chemistry 1001 W Main St PO Box 842006 Richmond VA 23284-2006

FENN, ORMON WILLIAM, JR., furniture company executive; b. Tyler, Tex., Mar. 13, 1927; s. Ormon William and Madonna (Muphree) F.; m. Lucille Adrianne Kelley; children: Andrea Lee, Miles Linton, Kelly Sue, Michael Thomas. Student, U. Minn., 1945, Okla. U., 1945, Imperial U., 1946; BS, Yale U., 1949. Asst. dist. mgr. Armsrong Cork Co., Lancaster, Pa., 1949-59, asst. gen. sales mgr., 1959-70; v.p., gen. sales mgr. Thomasville (N.C.) Furniture Industries, Inc., 1970-74, sr. v.p., gen. sales mgr., 1974-77; exec. v.p. sales and mktg. Stanley Furniture Co. Mead Corp., Stanleytown, Va., 1977-78, pres., 1978-79; pres. CEO Stanley Furniture Co., 1979-82; vice chmn. LADD Furniture Co., High Point, N.C., 1982-92, dir., 1982-98. Chmn. emeritus N.C. furnishings export coun. N.C. Dept. Commerce, High Point, 1993—; chmn. N.C. Home Furnishing Coun., 1995-97; past chmn. bd. govs. Western Mdse. Mart, San Francisco; past chmn. market adv. bd. High Point So. Furniture Market Center; past dir. N.C. Furniture Export Office; past chmn. Internat. Home Furnishings Mktg. Assn.; past bd. dirs. Furniture Info. Coun.; past bd. dirs./exec. com. Home Furnishing Coun.; bd. dirs. Am. Furniture Mfrs. Hall of Fame; apptd. by Gov. of N.C. to nat. adv. bd. HandMade in Am.; bd. dirs. Vaughn Bassett Furniture Co., Galax, Va. Past adv. bd. Bryan Sch. Bus. and Econs., U. N.C., Greensboro; appt. hon. consul gen. Japan, 1999. 1st lt. U.S. Army, 1944-52, PTO. Recipient The Order of the Long Leaf Pine award (NC) Gov. Hunt (N.C. highest civilian honor), 1995. Mem. String and Splinter Club (past bd. dirs.). Episcopalian. Avocations: golf, hunting, physical fitness. Home: 510 Emerywood Dr High Point NC 27262-2812

FENN, RAYMOND WOLCOTT, JR., retired metallurgical engineer; b. Torrington, Conn., Feb. 4, 1922; s. Raymond W. and Josephine (Mueller) F.; m. Beatrice Myra Christian, Jan. 19, 1946; children— Carol Louise, Ralph Christian. B.Metall. Engring., Rensselaer Poly. Inst., 1943; M.Engring., Yale, 1947, D.Engring., 1949. Registered profl. engr., Calif. Metall. engr. Gen. Electric Co., West Lynn, Mass., 1943-44; supr. testing lab., chief testing and instrumentation sect. Metall. Lab., Dow Chem. Co., Midland, Mich., 1949-61; cons. scientist, sr. mem. research lab., mgr. materials and prodn. systems engring., mgr. mfg. research, mgr. material and process control ctr. Lockheed Missiles & Space Co., Sunnyvale, Calif., 1961-87. Bd. dirs. Rancho San Antonio Retirement Housing Corp., Cupertino, Calif. Contbr. articles to profl. jours. Served with USNR, 1944-46. Fellow Am. Soc. Metals (trustee 1969-71, chmn., mem. exec. com. Santa Clara Valley chpt. 1966-69); mem. Am. Soc. Testing Materials (dir. 1966-69, R.E. Templin award 1961), Am. Inst. Mining and Metall. Engrs., Research Soc. Am., Am. Welding Soc., Soc. Mfg. Engrs., Soc. for Advancement of Material and Process Engring. (chmn. No. Calif. chpt. 1973-74, nat. dir. 1974-76, 2d v.p. 1976-77, 1st v.p. 1977-78, pres. 1978-79), Nat. Mgmt. Assn., Sigma Xi. Home: The Forum 522F 23500 Cristo Rey Dr Cupertino CA 95014-6503

FENNEBRESQUE, KIM SAMUEL, investment banker; b. N.Y.C., Mar. 20, 1950; s. John Drouet and Frances Jane (Campbell) F.; m. Deborah Anne Johnson, Sept. 8, 1979; children: Quincy Campbell, John Drouet II, Madeleine Aubrey. AB, Trinity Coll., 1972; JD, Vanderbilt U., 1975. Bar: Conn. 1975, N.Y. 1977. Assoc. Day, Berry & Howard, Hartford, Conn., 1975-76, Simpson, Thacher & Bartlett, N.Y.C., 1976-77, The First Boston Corp., N.Y.C., 1977-81, v.p., 1981-85, mng. dir., 1985-90; gen. ptnr. Lazard Freres & Co., N.Y.C., 1991—; pres., CEO SG Cowen Securities, N.Y.C. Mem. Piping Rock Club, Racquet and Tennis Club, Links Club, St. Anthony Hall Lodge. Republican.

FENNEL, MELODY H. federal agency administrator; Grad., Vassar Coll. Legis. rep. Nat. Coun. State Housing Agys., 1988—90; legis. dir. Nat. Assn. Home Builders, 1990—95; profl. staff mem., chief housing advisor to Senator Phil Gramm U.S. Senate Com. on Banking, Housing and Urban Affairs, 1995—2001; asst. sec. for congl. and intergovernmental rels. Dept. HUD, Washington, 2001—. Office: Dept HUD Congl and Intergovernmental Rels 451 7th St SW Washington DC 20410-9000

FENNELL, CHRISTINE ELIZABETH, healthcare system executive; b. Providence, July 14, 1948; d. Edmond John and Geraldine Mary (Goodenough) F. BS cum laude, Nat. Coll, Denver, 1983. Activity dir. Turtle Creek Convalescent Centre, Ft. Wayne, Ind., 1974-76; co-owner, operator Trail Ridge Welding, Estes Park, Colo., 1976-77; accounts mgr. Mayfair Women's Clinic, Denver, 1977-80; asst. adminstr. Ob-Gyn. Assocs., Aurora, Colo., 1980-82; admissions supr. St. Anthony Hosp. Sys., Denver, 1982-86; adminstr. Parkside Lodge of Colo., Thornton, 1986-89; ops./fin. mgr. Colo. Biodyne, Inc., Denver, 1989-90; adminstr. Kimberly Quality Care, Denver, 1990-93; br. mgr. Preferred Home Health Care, Inc., Lafayette, Ind., 1993-95; regional v.p. Arcadia Health Svcs., Inc., Southfield, 1995—. Part-time instr. Nat. Coll., Denver, 1983-84. Contbr. articles to profl. jours. Bd. dirs. S.W. Denver Community Mental Health Svcs., 1986. Mem. Denver Bus. Women's Network (pres. 1986-87), Colo. Coun. Hosp. Admitting Mgrs. (v.p. 1985-86), Rotary Club. Avocations: target shooting, horseback riding, tennis. Office: Arcadia Health Svcs Inc 26777 Central Park Blvd Southfield MI 48076-4162 E-mail: cefinc@aol.com.

FENNELL, DIANE MARIE, marketing executive, process engineer; b. Panama, Iowa, Dec. 11, 1944; d. Urban William and Marcella Mae (Leytham) Schechinger; m. Leonard E. Fennell, Aug. 19, 1967; children: David, Denise, Mark. BS, Creighton U., Omaha, 1966. Process engr. Tex. Instruments, Richardson, 1974-79; sr. process engr. Signetics Corp., Santa Clara, Calif., 1979-82; demo lab. mgr. Airco Temescal, Berkeley, Calif., 1982-84; field process engr. Applied Materials, Santa Clara, 1984-87; mgr. product mktg. Lam Rsch., Fremont, Calif., 1987-90; dir. sales and mktg. Ion & Plasma Equipment, Fremont, Calif., 1990-91; pres. FAI, Half Moon Bay, Calif., 1990-96; v.p. mktg. Tegal Corp., Petaluma, Calif., 1997-99; v.p. mktg. and sales Semicaps, Inc., Santa Clara, Calif., 1999—2001; exec. dir. Ctr. for Internat. Devel., Santa Clara, 2001—. Founder, coord. chmn. Plasma Etch User's Group, Santa Clara, 1984-87; tchr. computer course Adult Edn., Half Moon Bay, Calif., 1982-83. Founder, bd. dirs. Birth to Three program Mental Retardation Ctr., Denison, Tex., 1974-75; fund raiser local sch. band, Half Moon Bay, 1981-89; community rep. local sch. bd., Half Moon Bay, 1982-83. Mem. Am. Vacuum Soc., Soc. Photo Instrumentation Engrs., Soc. Women Engrs., Material Rsch. Soc., Commonwealth Club. Avocations: hiking, reading, gardening. Home: 441 Alameda Ave Half Moon Bay CA 94019-5337

FENNELL, RICHARD ARTHUR, artist; b. Ridgeland, S.C., Mar. 24, 1947; s. Joseph Edward and Mary Elizabeth (Jenkins) F.; m. Dorothy Hooper, Aug. 6, 1977; 1 child, Sarah Katherine. BFA, E. Carolina U., 1977; MFA, U. N.C., Greensboro, 1982. Part-time instr. U. N.C., Greensboro, 1987-88, Alamance C.C. Solo shows include Gilliam and Peden Art Gallery, 1989, Somerhill Gallery, Chapel Hill, 1990, 93, 96, 99, 2002, Hodges Taylor Gallery, Charlotte, 1991, 94, 97, 99, 2002, Cmty. Arts Coun., Goldsboro, N.C., 1991, Marita Gilliam, Inc., Gallery, Raleigh, 1992, Elon Coll., N.C., 1992, Greenville Mus. Art, 1993-94, Green Hill Ctr. for N.C. Art, 1995, City Art Gallery, Greenville, 2000, 02, ERL Originals, Inc., Winston Salem, N.C., 2000, 03, others; group shows include erl Originals, Inc., Winston-Salem, 1995, Fayetteville (N.C.) Mus. Art, 1995, Marita Gilliam Gallery, Raleigh, 1994, Somerhill Gallery, 1994, Weatherspoon Gallery of Art, 1987, 86, Hickory Mus. Art, 1986, Green Hill Ctr. for N.C. Art, 1980-2002, others; works in permanent collections at N.C. Mus. Art, Raleigh, Montgomery (Ala.) Mus. Fine Art, U. N.C., Chapel Hill, Duke U., Durham, N.C., Alamance Art Soc., Graham, N.C., East Carolina U., Elon Coll., Ctr. for Creative Leadership, Greensboro, Greenville (N.C.) Mus. of Art; corp. collections include Miller Breweries Corp., Phillip Morris Co., N.Y.C., No. Telecom, R.J. Reynolds, Winston-Salem, IBM, Raleigh, Dillard Paper Co., Greensboro, Interstate Securities, Charlotte, Coca-Cola Ent., Atlanta, Glaxo Pharm., Washington, Reagan Bldg., Inst. of Free Enterprise, Washington, others. Mayor-pro-tem Town of Whitsett, N.C., 1991-93, councilman, 1993-97. Recipient numerous purchase awards, best-in-show awards. Home and Office: 816 Hwy 61 Whitsett NC 27377

FENNELL, THOMAS EDWARD, JR., engineering educator; b. N.Y.C., June 18, 1940; s. Thomas Edward and Marjorie Adelaide (Deveraux) Fennell; m. Ellen Monica Fleming, Sept. 10, 1966; children: Heather, Marcus, Kieran. BEE, Manhattan Coll., N.Y.C., 1962; MEE, NYU, 1969. Registered profl. engr., N.Y. Engr. N.Y. Telephone Co., N.Y.C., 1962—92; instr. Tech. Career Insts., N.Y.C., 1993—. Math tutor, Bronx, 1956—58, Lentz & Lentz, New City, NY, 1990—2000. Mem. Bd. Elections, Ridgewood, NJ, 1988—. With U.S. Army, 1963—65. Roman Catholic. Avocations: baseball, hockey, bridge, chess, crossword puzzles. Home: 316 N Van Dien Ave Ridgewood NJ 07450 Office: Technical Career Insts 320 W 31st St New York NY 10001 Business E-Mail: tfennell@tcicollege.net.

FENNELL, TRACY LEE, music educator, composer; b. Canonsburg, Pa., July 21, 1961; d. Clyde Calvin and Nancy (Davidson) F. BM in Music Edn., Mansfield State Coll., 1983; MS in Music, Mansfield U. Pa., 1986. Cert. music tchr., Del., N.Y. Music tchr. Sussex Acad. Arts and Scis., Georgetown, Del., 2000—; composer Kallisti Music Press, Phila. Composer keyboard, instrumental, and choral music. Opportunity grantee Del. Divsn. Arts, 1999. Mem. ASCAP.

FENNELL ROBBINS, SALLY, writer; b. Greensburg, Pa., Feb. 17, 1950; d. Clifford Seanor and Charlotte Louise (Hoffman) Fennell; m. John W. Robbins, Sept. 22, 1984. BS in Journalism cum laude, Ohio U., 1972; MA in Journalism magna cum laude, Marshall U., 1974. Intern, reporter Tribune-Rev., Greensburg, Pa., 1972; prodn. asst. Harper's Bazaar, N.Y.C., 1972; reporter UPI, Birmingham, Ala., 1972-73; reporter, dept. editor Home Furnishings Daily, Fairchild Pubs., N.Y.C., 1974-77; acct. exec. supr., client svc. mgr., v.p. Burson-Marsteller, N.Y.C., 1977-83; group mgr., v.p. pub. rels. divsn. Ketchum

Comm., 1983-84; freelance writer, editor, 1984-89; dir. comm. Deloitte & Touche Retail Svcs. Group, NY, 1989-93; writer and author, 1993—; grad. teaching asst. Sch. Journalism/Reporting, Marshall U., Huntington, W.Va., 1973-74. Home and Office: 237 E 20th St New York NY 10003-1805 E-mail: sally.robbins@att.net.

FENNELLY, JANE COREY, lawyer; b. N.Y.C., Dec. 12, 1942; d. Joseph and Josephine (Corey) F. BA, Cornell U., 1964; MLS, UCLA, 1968; JD, Loyola U., L.A., 1974. Bar: Calif. 1974, U.S. Dist. Ct. (ctrl. and so. dists.) Calif. 1974, U.S. Dist. Ct. (ea. dist.) Calif. 1977, U.S. Dist. Ct. (no. dist.) Calif. 1980, N.Y. 1982, Colo. 1993, Ariz. 1995. Ptnr. Graham & James, 1976-83; with legal dept. Bank of Am., L.A., 1973-76, Wyman, Bautzer, Kuchel & Silbert, L.A., 1983-87, Dennis, Shafer, Fennelly & Creim (merged with Bronson & McKinnon), L.A., 1987-96; with Squire, Sanders & Dempsey, Phoenix, 1996—98; prin. Jane C. Fennelly, P.C., Phoenix, 1998—; of counsel Creim, Macias & Koenig LLP, L.A., 1999—. Mem. ABA, Am. Bankruptcy Inst., Calif. Bankruptcy Forum, L.A. County Bar Assn. (bd. dirs., mem. exec. com. comml. law and bankruptcy sect. 1989-92), Maricopa County Bar Assn., Fin. Lawyers Conf. (pres. bd. dirs. 1983-84, mem. bd. govs. 1984—). Home: 15356 W Pasadena Dr Surprise AZ 85374 Office: #610 Ste 101 15508 W Bell Rd Surprise AZ 85374 E-mail: jane.fennelly@azbar.org.

FENNELLY, PAUL F. chemist; s. Earl L. and Emma H. Fennelly; m. Katharine D. Fennelly, Aug. 15, 1970; children: Maura, Jeffrey, Eileen, Kevin. BS in Chemistry, Villanova U., 1967; MA in Chemistry, Brandeis U., 1968, PhD in Chemistry, 1972. Mgr. environ. measurements GCA Corp., Bedford, Mass., 1980—83, dir. mktg., 1983—85; mgr. air toxics ERT Inc., Concord, Mass., 1985—88; regional v.p. ENSR Corp., Acton, Mass., 1988—95, sr. v.p. corp. devel., 1995—98, pres. internat. ops. Westford, Mass., 1998—. Contbr. articles to profl. jours. Active Arlington (Mass.) Town Meeting, 1985—94; mem. adv. com. Congl. Sci. Panel, Denver, 1987; mem. sci. adv. com. Arlington/Cambridge Advisor, 1990. Democrat. Roman Catholic. Avocations: tennis, golf, gardening. Home: 97 Gray St Arlington MA 02476 Office: ENSR Internat 2 Technology Park Westford MA 01886

FENNELLY, WILLIAM, basketball coach; b. Davenport, Iowa., May 14, 1957; m. Deborah fennelly; children: Billy, Steven. BBA and Econs., William Penn Coll., 1979. Women's basketball coach William Penn Coll., Fresno State U., Notre Dame (Ind.) U.; head women's basketball coach U. Toledo, Ohio, Iowa State U., Ames, 1994—. Office: Iowa State Univ Jacobson Athletic Bldg 1800 S 4th St Ames IA 50011-0001

FENNEMA, OWEN RICHARD, food chemistry educator; b. Hinsdale, Ill., Jan. 23, 1929; s. Nick and Fern Alma (First) F.; m. Ann Elizabeth Hammer, Aug. 22, 1948; children: Linda Gail, Karen Elizabeth, Peter Scott. BS, Kans. State U., 1950; MS, U. Wis., 1951, PhD, 1960; PhD of Agrl. and Environ. Scis. (hon.), Wageningen Agrl. U., The Netherlands, 1993. Project leader for R&D, Pillsbury Co., Mpls., 1953-57; asst. prof. food sci. dept. U. Wis., Madison, 1960-64, assoc. prof., 1964-69, prof., 1969-96, chmn. dept., 1977-81, interim chmn. dept. landscape architecture, 1994-96, prof. emeritus, 1996—. Cons. Grand Metropolitan, Mpls., 1979-99; pub. mem. Internat. Life Scis. Inst.-Nutrition Found., 1987-90; mem. food adv. com. U.S. FDA, 1995-99, mem. sci. bd., 2000-02. Author: Low Temperature Preservation of Foods, 1973; editor: Principles of Food Science, 2 vols., 1976, Proteins at Low Temperatures, 1979, Food Chemistry, 3d edit., 1996, mem. editl. bd. Cryobiology, 1966-82, Internat. Jour. Food Sci. and Nutrition, Jour. Food Sci., 1975-77, Jour. Food Processing Preservation, 1977-2002, Jour. Food Biochemistry, 1977-80, Nutrition Rsch. Newsletter, 1983-98, Acta Alimentaria (Budapest, Hungary), 1990-98, South African Jour. Food Sci. and Nutrition, 1991-2002; editor-in-chief Jour. Food Sci., 1999-2003, Jour. Food Sci. Edn., Comprehensive Revs. in Food Sci., Food Safety. Served to 2d lt. U.S. Army, 1951-53. Recipient Excellence in Tchg. award U. Wis., Madison, 1977, Dir.'s Spl. Citation award Ctr. Food Safety and Nutrition, FDA; Fulbright disting. lectr., Spain, 1992. Fellow Am. Chem. Soc. (Agrl. and Food Chemistry Divsn. award 1995), Inst. Food Technologists (pres. 1982-83, treas. 1994-99, Excellence in Tchg. award 1978, Carl R. Fellers award 1988, Nicholas Appert award 1988); mem. Internat. Union Food Sci. and Tech. (del. 1983-88, exec. com. 1988-99, v.p. 1992-95, founding fellow Internat. Acad. Food Sci. and Tech. 1997, pres. 1999-2001. Home; 3023 Old Creek Rd Middleton WI 53562 Office: U Wis 1605 Linden Dr Madison WI 53706-1519 Fax: 608-262-6872. E-mail: ofennema@facstaff.wisc.edu.

FENNER, PETER DAVID, communications executive; b. Newark, Apr. 18, 1936; s. John David and Janice (Gleason) F.; m. Nancy Carrell Royce, Aug. 1958; children: Guy David, Karl Gleason, James Andrew. BS in Indsl. Engring., Lehigh U., 1958; MSBA, MIT, 1975. Field engr. Factory Mut.Engring., Montclair, N.J., 1958-61; assignments in engring., d.p., and software devel. Western Electric Co., Inc., N.J., N.Y., Mo., Colo., Calif., Mass., 1961-82; regional v.p. AT&T Network Systems (now Lucent Techs.), Balt. and Bethesda, Md., 1982-85; v.p. product planning, Morristown AT&T Network Systems, Balt. and Bethesda, Md., 1986-88, pres. Transmission Systems, 1989-92; mgmt. cons., 1993-95; CEO, COM 21, Milpitas, Calif., 1996-2001. Bd. dirs. SBS Techs., Albuquerque, BitMicro, Fremont, Calif., Active Strategies, Pa. Sloan fellow MIT, Cambridge, 1974-75. Mem. Westhampton Yacht Squadron, Westhampton Country Club. Avocations: sailing, tennis. Home and Office: 215 Hanna Way Menlo Park CA 94025-3583

FENNER, SUZAN ELLEN, lawyer; b. Grand Junction, Colo., Dec. 5, 1947; d. Harry J. and Louise (Bain) Shaw; m. Michael Lee Riddle, Apr. 24, 1969 (div. Feb. 1976); m. Peter R. Fenner, Nov. 24, 1978; children: Laura Elizabeth, Adam Lyle. BA, Tex. Tech U., 1969, JD, 1971. Bar: Tex. 1972, U.S. Dist. Ct. (no. dist.) Tex. 1972. Assoc. Smith & Baker, Lubbock, Tex., 1971-72; law clk. to presiding judge U.S. Dist. Ct., Dallas, 1972-73; assoc. Gardere Wynne Sewell LLP, Dallas, 1973-78, ptnr., 1978—, chair retirement com., 1973—, chair tax practice., 2001—, mem. ptnrs. bd., 1991—94. Bd. dirs. Tex. Lawyers Ins. Exch., 1985—, S.W. Benefits Assn. (formerly S.W. Pension Conf.), 1987—92, pres., 1990—91. Bd. dirs. East Dallas Devel. Ctr., 1982—91; Lone Star coun. Camp Fire USA, 1995—2001, v.p. outdoor programs, 1996—98, pres.-elect, 1997, pres., 1998—2000; bd. dirs. Episcopal Ch. Women of the Diocese of Dallas, 1992—, pres., 1996—2000; del. to triennial nat. conv. Episcopal Diocese of Dallas, 1994, 1997, 2000, asst. chancellor, 1994—, exec. coun., 1995—2000, standing com., 2001—; pres. Episcopal Ch. Women for Episcopal Ch. of Ascension, 1992, bd. dirs., 1992—94; pres. Province VII Episcopal Ch. Women, bd. dirs., 1999—2002; exec. coun. Province VII of the Episcopal Ch., 1999—2002. Mem. ABA, Tex. Bar Assn. (chmn. bar. jour. com. 1982-88), Dallas Bar Assn. (treas. employee benefits com. 1998, sec. 1999, v.p. 2000, pres. 2001), Dallas Bus. League (pres. 1986), 500 Club. Episcopalian. Avocation: sailing. Home: 600 Goodwin Dr Richardson TX 75081-5603 Office: Gardere Wynne Sewell LLP 1601 Elm St Ste 3000 Dallas TX 75201-4761 E-mail: sfenner@gardere.com.

FENNESSY, JOHN JAMES, radiologist, educator; b. Clonmel, Ireland, Mar. 1933; s. John and Ann (McCarthy) F.; m. Ann M. O'Sullivan, Aug. 20, 1960; children— Deirdre, Conor, Sean, Emer, Rona, Nial, Ruairi M.B., B.Ch., BAO, Univ. Coll., Dublin, Ireland, 1958. Assoc. prof. U. Chgo., 1971-74, prof., 1974—, chief chest and gastrointestinal radiology, 1971-73, acting chief diagnostic radiology, 1973-74, chmn. dept. radiology, 1974-84, assoc. chair ..n., 1990—. Fellow: Am. Coll. Radiology, Royal Coll. Surgeons Ireland (hon.); mem.: NRA, Fleischner Soc., Am. Gastroent. Soc., Radiology Soc. N. Am., Thoracic Radiology Soc., Chgo. Radiol. Soc., Am. Assn. Univ. Radiologists, Irish Am. Cultural Inst., County Tipperary Hist. Soc., Trout Unltd., Chgo. Art Inst., Alpha Omega Alpha, Sigma Xi. Republican. Roman Catholic. Office: U Chgo Dept Radiology 5841 S Maryland Ave Chicago IL 60637-1463

FENNING, LISA HILL, lawyer, mediator, former federal judge; b. Chgo., Feb. 22, 1952; d. Ivan Byron and Joan (Hennigar) Hill; m. Alan Mark Fenning, Apr. 3, 1977; 4 children. BA with honors, Wellesley Coll., 1971; JD, Yale U., 1974. Bar: Ill. 1975, Calif. 1979, U.S. Dist. Ct. (no. dist.) Ill., U.S. Dist. Ct. (no., ., so. & cen. dists.) Calif., U.S. Ct. Appeals (6th, 7th & 9th cirs.), U.S. Supreme Ct. 1989. Law clk. U.S. Ct. Appeals 7th cir., Chgo., 1974-75; assoc. Jenner and Block, Chgo., 1975-77, O'Melveny and Myers, L.A., 1977-85; judge U.S. Bankruptcy Ct. Cen. Dist. Calif., L.A., 1985-2000; mediator JAMS, Orange, Calif., 2000-01; ptnr. Dewey Ballantine LLP, L.A., 2001—. Bd. govs. Nat. Conf. Bankruptcy Judges, 1989-92; pres. Nat. Conf. of Women's Bar Assns., N.C., 1987-88, pres.-elect, 1986-87, v.p., 1985-86, bd. dirs.; lectr., program coord. in field; bd. govs. Nat. Conf. Bankruptcy Judges Endowment for Edn., 1992-97, Am. Bankruptcy Inst., 1994-2000; mem., bd. advisors Nat. Jud. Edn. Program to Promote Equality for Women and Men in the Cts., 1994—. Mem., bd. advisors: Lawyer Hiring & Training Report, 1985-87; contbr. articles to profl. jours. Durant scholar Wellesley Coll., 1971; named one of Am's. 100 Most Important Women Ladies Home Jour., 1988, one of L.A.'s 50 Most Powerful Women Lawyers, L.A. Bus. Jour., 1998. Fellow Am. Bar Found., Am. Coll. Bankruptcy (bd. regents 1995-98); mem. ABA (standing com. on fed. jud. improvements 1995-98, mem. commn. on women in the profession 1987-91, Women's Caucus 1987—, Individual Rights and Responsibilities sect. 1984—, bus. law sect. 1986—, bus. bankruptcy com.), Nat. Assn. Women Judges (nat. task force gender bias in the cts. 1986-87, 93-94), Nat. Conf. Bankruptcy Judges (chair endowment edn. bd. 1994-95), Am. Bankruptcy Inst (nominating com. 1994-95, bd. steering com. stats. project 1994-96), Calif. State Bar Assn. (chair com. on women in law 1986-87), Women Lawyers' Assn. L.A. (ex officio mem., bd. dirs., chmn., founder com. on status of women lawyers 1984-85, officer nominating com. 1986, founder, mem. Do-It-Yourself Mentor Network 1986-96), Phi Beta Kappa. Democrat. Office: Dewey Ballantine LLP 333 S Grand Ave 26th Fl Los Angeles CA 90071 E-mail: Lfenning@deweyballantine.com.

FENNO, RICHARD FRANCIS, JR., political scientist, educator; b. Winchester, Mass., Dec. 12, 1926; s. Richard Francis and Mary Brooks (Trendennick) Fenno; m. Nancy Davidson, Sept. 10, 1948; children: Mark Richard, Craig Pierce. Student, Williams Coll., 1944-46; AB, Amherst Coll., 1948, LLD (hon.), 1986; PhD, Harvard U., 1956; LHD (hon.), Union Coll., 1989. Instr. govt. Wheaton (Mass.) Coll., 1951-53; instr. polit. sci. Amherst Coll., 1953-56, asst. prof., 1956-57; mem. faculty U. Rochester, NY, 1957—, prof., 1964—, Don Alonzo Watson prof. polit. sci., 1971-78, William R. Kenan prof. polit. sci., 1978—, Disting. Univ. prof., 1985—. Author: (book) The President's Cabinet, 1959, The Power of the Purse, 1966, Congressmen in Committees, 1973, Home Style: U.S. House Members in Their Districts, 1978 (Woodrow Wilson Found. award, 1979, D. B. Hardeman prize, 1980); author: (with F. Munger) National Politics and Federal Aid to Education, 1962; author: The Making of a Senator: Dan Quayle, 1989, The Presidential Odyssey of John Glenn, 1990, Watching Politicians, 1990, The Emergence of a Senate Leader: Pete Domenici and the Reagan Budget, 1991, Learning to Legislate: The Senate Education of Arlen Specter, 1991, When Incumbency Fails: The Senate Career of Mark Andrews, 1992; editor: The Yalta Conf., 1956, 1973, (book) Senators on the Campaign Trail: The Politics of Representation, 1996, Learning to Govern: An Institutional View of the 104th Congress, 1997, Congress at the Grassroots: Represntational Change in the South, 1970-1998, 2000, Going Home: Black Representatives and Their Constituents, 2003. With USNR, 1944—46. Rockefeller Found. fellow, 1963—64, Ford fellow, 1971—72, Guggenheim fellow, 1976—77, Russell Sage Found. grantee, 1978, 1980—85. Mem.: Am. Philos. Soc., Am. Acad. Arts and Scis., Social Sci. Rsch. Coun. (dir. 1973—75, fellow 1960—61), Nat. Acad. Scis., Am. Polit. Sci. Assn. (coun. 1971—73, v.p. 1975—76, pres. 1984—85), Phi Beta Kappa. Home: 108 Farm Brook Dr Rochester NY 14625-1519

FENNOY, ILENE, pediatrician, endocrinologist; b. Texarkana, Ark., Apr. 11, 1947; d. David Henderson and Thelma (Rand) F.; m. Daulton Joseph Lewis, June 23, 1979; 1 child, Ilene Castille. AB, Stanford U., 1968; MD, U. Calif., San Francisco, 1973; MPH, Columbia U., 1993. Bd. cert. pediatric endocrinologist. Chief pediatrics and endocrinology Harlem Hosp. Ctr., N.Y.C., 1979-90, assoc. dir. pediatrics, chief pediatrics and endocrinology, 1990-93, v.p. clin. affairs, 1993-94; acting sr. v.p. med. and prof. affairs Health & Hosp. Corp., N.Y.C., 1994-95; assoc. chief staff, med. dir. ambulatory care Bklyn. Hosp. Ctr., 1995-99; chief pediatric endocrinology St. Luke's Hosp. Ctr., N.Y.C., 1999—2003; assoc. attending in pediatric endocrinology Children's Hosp. of N.Y. Presbyn., N.Y.C., 2003—. Bd. dirs. Pub. Health Assn. N.Y.C., 1995-99, N.Y. Assn. Ambulatory Care, N.Y.C., 1998—; mem N.Y. Forum Child Health, N.Y.C., 1997—. Contbr. articles to profl. jours. Lt. comdr. USPHS, 1972-79. Fellow Am. Acad. Pediatrics, Am. Coll. Endocrinologists, N.Y. Acad. Medicine; mem. Susan Smith McKinney Steward Med. Soc. (pres. 1999—). Office: Children's Hosp of NY Presby 630 168th St PH-SE-522 New York NY 10032 E-mail: Ifl@columbia.edu.

FENOGLIO-PREISER, CECILIA METTLER, pathologist, educator; b. N.Y.C., Nov. 28, 1943; d. Frederick Albert and Cecilia Charlotte (Asper) Mettler; m. John Fenoglio Jr., May 27, 1967 (div. 1977); 1 child, Timothy; stepchildren: Johanna, Andreas, Nicholas; m. Wolfgang F.E. Preiser, Feb. 16, 1985. Ach, Coll. St. Elizabeth, 1965; MD, Georgetown U., 1969. Diplomate Am. Bd. Pathology. Intern Presbyn. Hosp., N.Y.C., 1969-70; dir. Central Tissue Facility Columbia-Presbyn. Med. Ctr., N.Y.C., 1976-83; co-dir. div. surg. pathology Presbyn. Hosp., N.Y.C., 1978-82, div. div. surg. pathology, 1982-83; dir. Electron Microscop. Lab. Internat. Inst. Human Reprodn., 1978-85; assoc. prof. pathology Coll. Physicians and Surgeons, Columbia U., 1981-82, prof., 1982-83, attending pathologist, 1982-83; dir. lab. services Albuquerque VA Med. Ctr., 1983-90; prof. pathology U. N.Mex. Sch. Medicine, Albuquerque, 1983-90, also vice-chmn. dept. pathology; MacKenzie prof., chmn. dept. pathology and lab. medicine U. Cin. Sch. Medicine, 1990—, dir. cancer programs, 2001—. Mem. com. gastrointestine cancer WHO. Author: General Pathology, 1983, Gastrointestinal Pathology, An Atlas and Text, 1999, 2nd edit., 1999, Tumors of the Large and Small Intestine, 1990; editor: Advances in Pathobiology Cell Membranes, 1988-92, Advances in Pathobiology: Aging and Neoplasia, 1976, Progress in Surgical Pathology, vols. I-XIV, 1980-87, Advances in Pathology, vols. I-V, 1988-89. Grantee NIH, 1973, 79-82, 84-87, 85-2003, Cancer Rsch. Ctr., 1975-83, Population Coun., 1977-83, Nat. Ileitis and Colitis Found., 1979-80, Am. Cancer Soc., 1987-94. Fellow AAAS (life); mem. U.S. and Can. Acad. Pathology (edn. com. 1980-85, coun. 1984-87, exec. com. 1987-91, v.p. 1987, pres.-elect 1988, pres. 1989, fin. com. 1998-2001), Internat. Acad. Pathology (N.Am. v.p. 1990-94, pres. 1996-98, exec. com. 1990-2000, edn. com. 1998—), Nat. Surg. Adj. Breast Project (sci. adv. bd.), Am. Assn. Pathologists, Armed Forces Inst. Pathology (sci. adv. bd. 1990—), N.Y. Acad. Sci., N.Y. Acad. Medicine, Fedn. Am. Scientists for Exptl. Biology, Gastrointestinal Pathologist Group (founding mem. edn. com. 1983-85, sec.-treas. 1993-96, pres.-elect 1996, pres. 1997), S.W. Oncology Group (chmn. GI tumor biology com., chmn. pathology com., chmn. correlative sci. com.), Arthur Purdy Stout Soc. (coun. 1987-90). Office: U Cin Sch Medicine 231 Bethesda Ave Cincinnati OH 45229-2827 E-mail: cecilia.fenogliopreiser@uc.edu.

FENSELAU, CATHERINE CLARKE, chemistry educator; b. York, Nebr., Apr. 15, 1939; d. Lee Keckley and Muriel (Thomas) Clarke; m. Allan Herman Fenselau, 1962 (div. 1980); children: Andrew Clarke, Thomas Stewart; m. Robert James Cotter, 1984. AB, Bryn Mawr Coll., 1961; PhD, Stanford U., 1965. Research scientist U. Calif.-Berkeley, 1965-67; instr. to prof. Johns Hopkins U., Balt., 1967-87; chmn. chemistry, biochemistry U. Md., Balt. County, 1987-98, prof. dept. chemistry and biochemistry College Park, 1998—; chmn. dept. chemistry and biochemistry, 1998-2000. Cons. NIH, NSF, USDA, U.S. Army, FDA, others. Editor: Biomed. Environ. Mass Spectrometry, 1973—89; editor: (assoc. editor) Analytical Chemistry, 1990—; contbr. articles to profl. jours. Fellow: AAAS; mem.: Am. Soc. Pharmacology and Exptl. Therapeutics, Am. Chem. Soc. (Garvan medal 1985, Md. Chemist award Md. sect. 1989), Am. Soc. Mass Spectrometry (pres.). Office: U Md Dept Chemistry Biochemistry College Park MD 20742-0001

FENSKE, JERALD ALLAN, minister; b. Wausau, Wis., Sept. 29, 1960; s. Martin W. and Whynona B. (Ramthun) F.; m. Kay A. Lang, Aug. 17, 1985; children: Kiersten, Deena. BA, Lakeland Coll., 1983; MDiv, United Theol. Sem. of the Twin Cities, 1988. Ordained to ministry United Ch. of Christ, 1991. Pastor Congl. Ch. of Excelsior United Ch. of Christ, Excelsior, Minn., 1998—. Mem. Excelsior Masons, Western Clergy Cluster United Ch. of Christ, Excelsior Ministerial Assoc. Mem. Lakeland Coll. Alumni Assn. (Zeta Chi chpt.). Home: 17411 Creek Ridge Pass Minnetonka MN 55345-6230 Office: Congl Ch of Excelsior United Ch of Christ 471 3rd St Excelsior MN 55331-1945

FENSTER, FRED A. lawyer, educator; b. Hartford, Conn., Oct. 8, 1946; s. Albert J. and Eleanor S. (Meyers) F.; m. Andrea Reifman, Jan. 2, 1972; children: Amanda Susanne, Monica Danielle. BA, U. So. Calif., 1968, JD, 1971. Bar: Calif. 1972, U.S. Dist. Ct. (cen. and so. dists.) Calif. 1972. Assoc. Richards, Watson & Gershon, L.A., 1971-76, ptnr., 1977-94, Heenan Blaikie, 1995—; adj. prof. U. So. Calif., L.A., 1977—. Campaign organizer Democratic Party, L.A.. Recipient 4 Am. Jurisprudence awards U. So. Calif., 1968-71; Asso. Men's Student's Scroll of Honor, 1968; scholar Cambridge U., Eng., 1967. Mem. Los Angeles County Bar Assn., Calif. Bar Assn., ABA, Order of Coif, Phi Beta Kappa, Phi Kappa Phi, Phi Eta Sigma, Pi Sigma Alpha. Office: Richards Watson & Gershon 333 S Hope St Bldg 38 Los Angeles CA 90071-1406

FENSTER, HERBERT LAWRENCE, lawyer; b. N.Y.C., Mar. 29, 1935; s. Oscar Samuel and Bessie Estelle (Schafran) F.; m. Gail Frances Meier, Apr. 18, 1964; children— Christopher Lawrence, Jennifer Gail, Jonathan Adam; m. Jane Porter Elam Allen, Dec. 31, 1993. A.B., U. Pa., 1957, M.A., 1958; J.D., U. Va., 1961. Bar: Va. 1961, D.C. 1962, U.S. Supreme Ct. 1967, Colo., 1993. Assoc., Sellers, Conner & Cuneo, Washington, 1961-66, ptnr., 1967-78, sr. ptnr., 1978-80; sr. ptnr. McKenna, Conner & Cuneo, 1980-90, McKenna & Cuneo, 1990-2002, McKenna, Long & Aldridge, 2002--. Author treatise Anti Deficiency Act, ABA, 1979. Litigation counsel Reagan-Bush Campaign Com., Washington, 1980-83, pres.'s pvt. sector survey Grace Commn., 1982— ; bd. dirs. Nat. Chamber Litigation Ctr., Washington, 1983— ; bd. dirs. Keewaydin Found., Middlebury Vermont, 1982—, also trustee, corp. dir. Fellow Assn. Trial Lawyers Am.; mem. ABA, Fed. Bar Assn., D.C. Bar Assn., Am. Law Inst. Republican. Episcopalian. Clubs: Metropolitan, University. Home: 845 6th St Boulder CO 80302-7418 Address: 1875 Lawrence St Denver CO 80202-1370

FENSTER, MARVIN, lawyer, department store executive; b. Bklyn., Jan. 19, 1918; s. Isaac and Anna (Greenman) F.; m. Louise Rapoport, Nov. 13, 1953; children: Julie, Mark. AB, Cornell U., 1938; LLB, Columbia U., 1941. Bar: N.Y. 1942. Assoc. Lauterstein, Spiller, Bergerman & Dannett, N.Y.C., 1941-42, 46-48; atty., asst. gen. atty. R.H. Macy & Co., Inc., N.Y.C., 1948-60, sr. v.p., gen. counsel, sec., 1960-84, sr. v.p. spl. counsel, sec., 1984-87, dir., sr. v.p., spl. counsel, sec., 1987—, pres., dir. Macy's Bank, 1981—; sr. v.p., sec. Macy Credit Corp., N.Y.C., 1961-86, pres., dir., chief exec. officer, 1986—; pres., chief exec. officer Macy Receivables Funding Corp., N.Y.C., 1989—. 1st lt. U.S. Army, 1943-46. Mem. Assn. of Bar, City of New York (corp. law depts. post-admission legal edn., council jud. adminstrn. 1983), Am. Coll. Real Estate Lawyers, Harmonie Club, Beach Point Club, Phi Epsilon Pi. Jewish. Office: R H Macy & Co Inc 151 W 34th St New York NY 10001-2180

FENSTER, ROBERT DAVID, lawyer; b. N.Y.C., Sept. 25, 1946; BA, Queen's Coll., 1968; JD, Bklyn. Law Sch., 1973. Bar: N.Y. 1974, U.S. Dist. Ct. (so. and ea. dists.) N.Y. 1974, U.S. Supreme Ct. 1977. Investigator, prosecutor N.Y. Stock Exch., N.Y.C., 1972-73; ptnr. law firms Rockland County, 1974—80; prin. Robert D. Fenster, Atty. at Law, P.C., 1980—2001; ptnr. Fenster & Kurland LLP, New City, 2002—. Bd. dirs. Brit. Pub. Corp., various other corps. Advisor Clarkstown Youth Ct., New City, NY, 1982; bd. dirs. Legal Aid Soc., Rockland County, 1974—78, Nyack Hosp. Found., 1995—2000, Good Samaritan Hosp. Found. Mem. ABA, N.Y. State Bar Assn., Rockland County Bar Assn., Am. Arbitration Assn. (arbitrator), Police Chiefs Found., Internat. Bus. Network of Greater N.Y. Office: Fenster & Kurland LLP Attys at Law 337 N Main St Ste 11 New City NY 10956-4310 Fax: 845-638-4767.

FENSTER, SAUL K. university president emeritus; b. N.Y.C., Mar. 22, 1933; s. Samuel and Rose (Glass) F.; m. Roberta Schamis, Jan. 11, 1959; children: Deborah, Lisa, Jonathan. Student, Bklyn. Coll., 1949-51; B of Mech. Engring., CUNY, 1953; MS, Columbia U., 1955; postgrad., NYU, 1955-56; PhD, U. Mich., 1959; LLD, Rutgers U., 2002, William Paterson U., 2002; DHL (hon.), N.J. Inst. Tech., 2002. Lectr. mech. engring. CUNY, 1953-56; teaching fellow engring. mechanics U. Mich., 1956-57, with univ. Rsch. Inst., 1957-58; rsch. engr. Sperry-Rand Corp., 1959-62; prof. engring. Fairleigh Dickinson U., Teaneck, N.J., 1962-78, chmn. dept. physics, 1962-63, chmn. dept. mech. engring., 1963-70, grad. adminstrv. asst. to dean, 1965-70, assoc. dean, 1970-71, exec. asst. to pres., 1971-72, provost Rutherford campus, 1972-78; pres. N.J. Inst. Tech., Newark, 1978—2002, N.J. Inst. Tech. (Found.), 1978—2002. Bd. dirs. various Prudential Mut. Funds, IDT Corp.; vice-chmn. Bus.-Higher Edn. Forum, 1992; cons., 1962—. Author: (with Wallace Arthur) Mechanics, 1969, (with A. Cahit Ugural) Advanced Strength and Applied Elasticity, 1975, 87, 94; contbr. chpts. to books, tech. papers. Mem. Hudson River Waterfront Study and Planning Commn., 1979-80; bd. dirs. N.J. Assn. Colls. and Univs., 1980-2002, N.J. Alliance for Action, 1982-2002, R&D Coun. N.J., 1994-2002, Regional Bus. Partnership, 1994-95, Prosperity N.J., Inc., Soc. Mfg. Engrs. Edn. Found., 1998—; trustee Newark Boys Chorus Sch., 1980-84, Newark Acad., 1984-86; mem., vice chmn. N.J. Water Supply Authority, 1981-88; mem. N.J. Commn. on Sci. and Tech., 1985—; bd. govs. Union County Coll.; mem. Commn. Def. Conversion and Cmty. Assistance, 1993; mem. Commn. on Jobs, Growth and Econ. Devel., 2003—; mem. N.J. Coun. on Job Opportunities; bd. visitors Air U., 1993-98. Shell fellow U. Mich., 1957-58. Fellow ASME, Am. Soc. Engring. Edn.; mem. AAAS, Assn. Ind. Colls. and Univs. N.J. (chmn. bd. 1978-80, bd. dirs. 1980-96), Greater Newark C. of C. (bd. dirs. 1980-91), N.J. State C. of C. (bd. dirs. 1987-2002), Coun. on Competitiveness, Sigma Xi, Tau Beta Pi, Omicron Delta Kappa, Pi Tau Sigma. Home: 524 Bernita Dr Westwood NJ 07675-5902 Office: NJ Inst Tech Office of Pres University Heights Newark NJ 07102

FENSTERSTOCK, BLAIR COURTNEY, lawyer; b. N.Y.C., Aug. 20, 1950; s. Nathaniel and Gertrude (Isaacson) F.; children: Michael Bayard, Evan Steele, Laurel Sage. AB summa cum laude, Bowdoin Coll., 1972; JD, Columbia U., 1975. Bar: Ind. 1976, N.Y. 1976, U.S. Dist. Ct. (so., ea. and no. dists.) 1976, U.S. Ct. Appeals (2d cir.) 1976, U.S. Customs Ct. 1976, U.S. Ct. Internat. Trade 1976, U.S. Supreme Ct. 1980. Assoc. Simpson, Thacher & Bartlett, N.Y.C., 1975-79, Dewey, Ballantine, Bushby, Palmer & Wood, N.Y.C., 1979-83; v.p., assoc. gen. counsel, asst. sec. Reliance Group Holdings, Inc., N.Y.C., 1983-91; sr. v.p., gen. counsel, sec. Frank B. Hall & Co., Inc., 1987-92; ptnr. Sutherland, Asbill & Brennan, 1993-95, Brock, Fensterstock, Silverstein & McAuliffe, LLC, N.Y.C., 1995-98, Fensterstock & Ptnrs., LLP, N.Y.C., 1998—. Mem. bd. visitors Columbia U. Sch. Law, 1988—. Bd. dirs. Safety Nat. Casualty Corp., 1990-93; bd. regents Ctr. for Security Policy, 2003. Harlan Fiske Stone scholar Columbia U., 1975. Mem. ABA, N.Y. State Bar Assn., Assn. Bar City N.Y., Coun. N.Y. Law Assocs. (bd. dirs. 1979-82), Lawyers Com. for Internat. Human Rights (bd. dirs. 1979-80), Am. Arbitration Assn. (panel of arbitrators), Internat. Peace Acad. (sec. 1977-79), Univ. Club (N.Y.C.), Ctr. for Security Policy (bd. regents 2003—), Aspetuck Valley Country Club (Weston, Conn.) (bd. govs. 1993-97), Palmas del Mar Country Club (P.R.), Pinehurst Country Club (N.C.), Phi Beta Kappa. Republican. Jewish. Home: 10 West St New York NY 10004- Office: Fensterstock & Ptnrs LLP 30 Wall St New York NY 10005-2201

FENTON, ALEXANDER, writer; b. 1929; Sr. asst. editor Scottish Nat. Dictionary, Edinburgh, 1955-59; asst. keeper Nat. Mus. Antiquities Scotland, Edinburgh, 1959-75, dep. keeper, 1975-78, dir., 1978-85; rsch. dir. Nat. Mus. Scotland, 1985-89; dir. European Ethnological Rsch. Ctr., 1989—; lectr. U. Edinburgh, 1958-60, 74-80; prof. Scottish ethnology, dir. Sch. Scottish Studies, 1990-94; hon. prof. Royal Scottish Acad., 1996—. Editor The Review of Scottish Culture, 1984—. Author: The Various Names of Shetland, 1973, 2d edit., 1977, Scottish Country Life, 1976, 3d edit., 1999, A Guide to the Black House at 42 Arnol, Lewis, 1978, The Northern Isles: Orkney and Shetland, 1978, new edit., 1997, Continuity and Change in the Building Tradition of Northern Scotland, 1979, (with Bruce D. Walker) The Rural Architecture of Scotland, 1981, The Shape of the Past, 2 vols., 1985-86, Wirds an' wark 'e seasons roon on an Aberdeenshire Farm, 1987, Country Life in Scotland: Our Rural Past, 1987, The Turra Coo, 1989, Scottish Country Life, 1989, On Your Bike: Thirteen Years of Travelling Curators, 1990; author: (with others) Studies in Folk Life, 1969, The Scottish Tradition, 1974, The Union of 1707: Its Impact on Scotland, 1974, Folklore Today: A Festschrift for Richard M. Dorson, 1976, The Making of the Scottish Countryside, 1980, From the Stone Age to the 'Forty-Five: Studies Presented to R. B. K. Stevenson, 1983, The Fishing Culture of the World, 1984, Farm Servants and Labour in Lowland Scotland, 1984, Fermfolk and Fisherfolk, 1990, Essays on the Music, Poetry and History of Scotland and England, 1990, Scottish Culture, 1991, Loch Ness and Thereabouts, 1992, Scotland and the Sea, 1992, Creativity and Tradition in Folklore, 1992; editor (with Alan Gailey), contbr.: The Spade in Northern and Atlantic Europe, 1970; editor (with Hermann Pálsson), contbr.: The Northern and Western Isles in the Viking World: Survival, Continuity, and Change, 1984; editor (with Geoffrey Stell), contbr.: Loads and Roads in Scotland and Beyond:

Road Transport Over Six Thousand Years, 1984; editor (with Eszter Kisbán), contbr. Food in Change: Eating Habits from the Middle Ages to the Present Day, 1986; editor (with Janken Myrdal), contbr.: Food and Drink and Travelling Accessories: Essays in Honour of Goesta Berg, 1988; editor (with others), contbr.: Land Transport in Europe, 1973, Building Construction in Scotland: Some Historical and Regional Aspects, 1976; contbr., section editor: Manual of Curatorship: A Guide to Museum Practice, 1992, Craiters...or Twenty Buchan Tales, 1995, The Terminology of Food for Personal Occasions, Food and Celebration From Fasting to Feasting, 2002. Office: care Nat Mus Scotland Chambers St European Ethnol Rsch Ctr Edinburgh EH1 1JF Scotland E-mail: a.fenton@nms.ac.uk.

FENTON, CLARENCE ASA, healthcare facility administrator; b. Warren, Ohio, Sept. 11, 1950; s. Calvin A. and Betty (Miller) F. AAS in Nursing, Youngstown (Ohio) State U., 1976; BS in Occupational Edn., U. So. Maine, 1988, M in Nursing Adminstrn., 1996. RN, Maine, Ohio, Mass., N.J., Calif.; CNOR. Staff nurse operating rm. Mercy Hosp., Portland, Maine, preceptor operating rm.; clin. nurse educator Brighton Med. Ctr., Portland; dir. surg. svcs. Parkview Hosp., Brunswick, Maine, 1995-98; perioperative nurse cons. Higman Healthcare, St. Petersburg, Fla., 1998—2000; nurse mgr., O.R. New Eng. Med. Ctr., Boston, 2000—02; perioperative nurse cons. Maine Med. Ctr., Portland, 2002—. Mem. Nat. Cert. Bd. for Perioperative Nursing Inc., treas., 1995—2001. With USN, 1969-70. Mem. Maine Assn. Oper. Rm. Nurses (pres. 1992-94), Nat. Nursing Staff Devel. Orgn., Assn. Nurses in AIDS Care, Nursing Alumni Assn. Youngstown State U., Sigma Theta Tau, Kappa Zeta (cmty. counselor 1995-97). Home: 705 Riverside St Portland ME 04103-1030 Office: Maine Med Ctr 22 Bramhall St Portland ME 04102

FENTON, CLIFTON LUCIEN, investment banker; b. Bryan, Ohio, May 11, 1943; s. Gibson Lucien and Elizabeth (Newcomer) F.; m. Judith Todd Wallis, June 23, 1973; children: Gregory, Eric, Alyssa. AB, Princeton U., 1965; JD, Ohio State U., 1968; MBA, Columbia U., 1970; grad., Kellog Grad. Sch. Mgmt., 2001. Bar: Ohio 1968. Assoc. Bank N.Y., N.Y.C., 1970-72, Morgan Guaranty Trust Co., N.Y.C., 1972; v.p. Kidder, Peabody, N.Y.C., 1972-84; mng. dir. Prudential-Bache Securities, N.Y.C., 1984-89; v.p., nat. mgr. John Nuveen & Co., Chgo., 1989-95, v.p. and mgr. Investment Banking Divsn., 1995-99; mng. dir. and co-head pub. fin. U.S. Bancorp Piper Jaffray, Chgo., 1999-2000. Trustee Ravinnia Festival, Associated Colls. of Ill. and Good City. Mem. Met. Club (N.Y.C.), Univ. Club Chgo. Avocations: water and snow skiing, sailing, piano. Home: 808 Sunset Rd Winnetka IL 60093-3850 E-mail: cliffenton@comcast.net.

FENTON, DONALD MASON, retired oil company executive; b. L.A., May 23, 1929; s. Charles Youdan and Dorothy (Mason) F.; m. Margaret M. Keehler, Apr. 24, 1953; children: James Michael, Douglas Charles. BS, U. Calif., L.A., 1952, PhD, 1958. Chemist Rohm and Haas Co., Phila., 1958-61; sr. rsch. chemist Union Oil Co., Brea, Calif., 1962-67, rsch. assoc., 1967-72, sr. rsch. assoc., 1972-82, mgr. planning and devel., 1982-85; mgr. new tech. devel. Unocal, Brea, 1985-92. Cons. AMSCO, 1967-73; co-founder, 1st chmn. Petroleum Environ. Rsch. Forum; chmn. bd. dirs. Calif. Engring. Found., 1991-92. With U.S. Army, 1953-55. Inventor in field. Fellow Am. Inst. Chemists, Alpha Chi Sigma; mem. Am. Chem. Soc. Achievements include more than 100 patents in field; co-invention of unisulf process. Home: 2861 E Alden Pl Anaheim CA 92806-4401

FENTON, ELLIOTT CLAYTON, lawyer; b. Oklahoma City, Nov. 26, 1914; s. Edgar R. and Mary (Gaddo) F.; m. LeNoir Massey, July 6, 1939; children: Mike, Ann Wallis; m. Ruby L. Simpson, Aug. 21, 2002. BA, U. Okla., 1935, LLB, 1937. Bar: Okla. 1937, U.S. Dist. Ct. (no., ea. and we. dists.) Okla., U.S. Ct. Appeals (10th cir.), U.S. Supreme Ct., U.S. Ct. Mil. Appeals. Atty. Looney & Fenton, Oklahoma City, 1937—38; atty., claims rep. Nat. Mut. Casualty Co., Tulsa, 1938-40, Hartford Ins. Group, Oklahoma City, 1940-47; atty. Fenton & Fenton, Oklahoma City, 1947—. Chmn. bd. trustees United Meth. Found., Oklahoma City, 1973-83; chancellor United Meth. Found., Oklahoma City, 1983-89. Ret. comdr. USNR. Fellow Am. Bar Found; mem. Internat. Assn. Def. Counsel, Def. Research Inst. (state chmn. 1978-83), Okla. Assn. Def. Counsel (pres. 1972), Okla. County Bar Assn. (bd. dirs.). Republican. United Methodist. Avocation: golf. Home: 14901 N Penn Ave Duplex 4A Oklahoma City OK 73134-6079 Office: Fenton Fenton Smith et al 1 Leadership Sq Ste 800 Oklahoma City OK 73102 E-mail: elbeau88@cox.net., ecfenton@fentonlaw.com.

FENTON, HOWARD NATHAN, III, lawyer, educator; b. Toledo, May 6, 1950; s. Howard Nathan, Jr. and Maxine Claire (LaFountaine) F.; children: William Carl, Margaret Claire, Andrew Scimeca, Julie Marie, Christopher Howard; m. Beth Anne Kostic, Mar. 9, 2001. BS with honors, U. Tex., 1971, JD with honors, 1975. Bar: Tex. 1975, D.C. 1976, Ohio 1990, U.S. Dist. Ct. D.C. 1976, U.S. Ct. Appeals (D.C. cir.) 1976. Assoc. Williams & Jensen PC, Washington, 1975-77; ptnr. Swift & Swift PC, Washington, 1978; supervisory compliance officer office antiboycott compliance Internat. Trade Adminstrn./U.S. Dept. Commerce, Washington, 1979-80, dir. compliance policy, 1981-84; assoc. prof. Miss. Coll. Sch. Law, Jackson, 1984-87, prof., 1987-88, Ohio No. U. Coll. Law, Ada, 1988—, assoc. dean, 1988-93, interim dean, 1995—96. Cons. adminstrv. law reform to govts. of Ukraine, Georgia, Armenia, 1996—; chief of party US AID Rule of Law Project, Tbilisi, Georgia, 2001-02; cons. Adminstrv. Conf. U.S., 1989-91, 93-94; fellow Nat. Ctr. for Export/Import Studies, Georgetown U., Washington, 1983-86; adj. faculty Cath. U. Law Sch., Washington, spring 1984; mem. U.S.-Can. Free Trade Agreement Dispute Panel, 1993-94, N.Am. Free Trade Agreement Dispute Panel, 1994-2001. Contbg. editor: Boycott Law Bull, 1984—92. Mem. ABA, Ohio State Bar Assn. (chair internat. law com. 2002—), Am. Soc. Internat. Law. Democrat. Office: Pettit Coll of Law Ohio Northern U Ada OH 45810 E-mail: h-fenton@onu.edu., fentonhoward@hotmail.com.

FENTON, JONATHAN E. osteopath; b. NYC, Sept. 14, 1956; s. Paul E. Fenton and Alexandra F. Markoff; m. Judith Jorgensen, June 29, 1984 (div. Dec. 1992); m. Lori B. Lustberg, Aug. 30, 1997; 1 child, Liam A. Lustberg. BA, NYU, 1983; DO, N.Y. Coll. Osteo. Medicine, 1988. Diplomate Am. Acad. Phys. Medicine and Rehab., Am. Acad. Osteopathy. Resident phys. medicine and rehab. St. Vincent's Hosp., NYC, 1989-92; attending physician Champlain Sports Medicine, Essex Junction, Vt., 1992—2002; chief rehab. Ctr. for Musculoskeletal Medicine, Essex Junction, 1996-99, Green Mountain Phys. and Occupl. Medicine, Essex Junction, 1999—2002; pvt. practice Burlington, Vt., 2002—. Contbg. author: An Osteopathic Approach to Diagnosis and Treatment, 1998. Merit scholar N.Y. Coll. Osteo. Medicine, 1995. Fellow Am. Acad. Phys. Med. and Rehab.; mem. Am. Acad. Osteopathy, Am. Acad. Med. Acupuncture, Am. Coll. Osteo. Rehab. Medicine (cert.). Avocations: downhill skiing, hiking, bicycling. Office: 321 Main St Winooski VT 05404 E-mail: jefenton@sover.net.

FENTON, LAWRENCE JULES, pediatric educator; b. Chgo., June 1, 1940; s. Arthur S. Fenton and Dorothy (Schochet) Wade; m. Gayle Ann Yeager, Apr. 10, 1965; children: Lori Ann Novak, Scott L. BS, U. Mich., 1962; MD, U. Cin., 1966. Diplomate Am. Bd. Pediatrics, Sub-bd. Neonatal and Perinatal Medicine. Intern U. Cin. Med. Ctr., 1966-67, jr. and sr. resident, 1967-69, chief pediatric resident, 1969-70, fellow neonatal, perinatal medicine, 1972-74; asst. prof. pediatrics U. Ariz. Health Scis. Ctr., Tucson, 1974-78; assoc. prof. pediatrics U. S.D. Sch. Medicine, Sioux Falls, 1978-84, head sect. of neonatal, perinatal medicine, 1979-88, prof. pediatrics, 1984—, chmn. dept. pediatrics, 1988—. Dir. newborn intensive care unit Sioux Valley Hosp., 1980-88; chmn. pharmacy and therapeutics com. Sioux Valley Hosp., 1982-97, bd. dirs., 1997—; v.p. children's med. svcs. Sioux Valley Hosp. and U. S.D. Med. Ctr., 2000-02. Author: (with others) Current Therapy in Neonatal and Perinatal Medicine, 1989, Conn's Current Therapy, 1989, 90; contbr. articles to profl. jours. Chmn. rsch. funding group Am. Heart Assn., Dakota Affiliate, 1986-88; mem. allocations com. Childrn's Miracle Network Telethon, Sioux Falls, 1986-87; bd. dirs. Childrens Miracle Network, 1996-99; chmn. Health Svcs. Adv. Com., State of S.D., 1991-93. Maj. U.S. Army, 1970-72. Rsch. grantee Nat. Inst. Child Health and Human Devel., Tucson, Sioux Falls, 1976-79, Am. Heart Assn., Sioux Falls, 1984; recipient Army Commendation medal, 1991-93, Pioneer award S.D. Perinatal Assn., 1993; inductee Hall of Honor Children's Hosp. U. Cin. MEd. Ctr., 1993. Fellow Am. Acad. Pediatrics; mem. Society for Pediatric Rsch., Midwest Soc. for Pediatric Rsch., Assn. Med. Sch. Pediatric Dept. Chmn., S.D. States Med. Assn. Avocations: water skiing, boating, hiking, cross country skiing, classical music. Office: 1305 W 18th St Sioux Falls SD 57117-5039

FENTON, LEWIS LOWRY, lawyer; b. Palo Alto, Calif., Aug. 20, 1925; s. Norman and Jessie (Chase) F.; m. Gloria J. Palmieri, Aug. 21, 1978; children: Lewis Lowry, Juanita F. Donnelly, Daniel Norman, Pamela Chase. BA, Stanford U., 1948, LL.B., 1950. Bar: Calif. 1950, U.S. Dist. Ct. (no. dist.) Calif. Atty. Calif. Dept. Pub. Works, 1950-52; chmn., bd. dirs. Hoge, Fenton, Jones & Appel, Inc., Monterey, San Luis Obispo and San Jose; counsel Fenton & Keller, P.C., Monterey, 1993—, Hoge, Fenton, Jones & Appel, Inc., San Jose, 1993—. Bd. dirs. 1st Nat. Bank Monterey County, 1984—, chmn., 1987-90, Mem. bldg. com. Community Hosp. Monterey Peninsula, Carmel, 1961-62; found. dir. Monterey Jazz Festival, 1958; trustee Monterey Peninsula Coll., pres. 1971-72, Monterey Inst. Fgn. Studies; past pres. and bd. dirs. York Sch., Monterey, Calif., 1960-74, chmn. bd., 1992—; founding bd. dirs. Monterey Bay Aquarium; bd. dirs. Community Found. Monterey County, chmn., 1998—; bd. visitors Stanford Law Sch. Served to 2d lt. USAAF, 1942-46. Fellow Am. Coll. Trial Lawyers, Internat. Acad. Trial Lawyers; mem. ABA, Calif. Bar Assn., Santa Clara Bar Assn., Monterey County Bar Assn. (pres. 1963, 1st Chief Justice Gibson award), Assn. Def. Counsel (pres. 1969), Nat. Bd. Trial Advocacy, Nat. Assn. R.R. Counsel, Internat. Assn. Def. Counsel, Def. Research Inst., Am. Judicature Soc., Am. Acad. Hosp. Attys., Am. Bd. Trial Advs. (adv., mem. exec. bd.), Stanford U. Alumni Assn. (pres. 1966-67), Calif. Med. Legal Nat. Health Lawyers Assn. Episcopalian (vestryman, sr. warden 1956-58). Clubs: Cypress Point, Old Capital, Pacheco, Pacific Union. Home and Office: PO Box 791 Monterey CA 93942-0791 E-mail: LFenton@fentonkeiler.com., llf@hogefenton.com.

FENTON, MATTHEW JOHN, immunologist, molecular biologist; b. New Hartford, Conn., Dec. 2, 1956; s. John Frederick and Antoinette Louise (Mitchell) F.; m. Gillian Carter Magee, Oct. 27, 1984. BS with honors, U. Conn., 1979, PhD, Boston U., 1984. Postdoctoral fellow MIT, Cambridge, Mass., 1984-86; postdoctoral assoc. Harvard U.-MIT Div. Health Scis. and Tech., 1986-88; asst. prof. medicine and biochemistry Boston U. Sch. Medicine, 1988-95, assoc. prof. medicine and pathology, 1995-2001, prof. medicine and pathology, 2001—03; prof. medicine, microbiology and immunology U. Md. Sch. Medicine, Balt., 2003—, dir. pulmonary rsch., 2003—. Rsch. grant and fellowship reviewer Am. Heart Assn., NSF, U.S. VA; mem. exptl. immunology study sect. NIH, 1998; cons. in field. Mem. editl. bd. Jour. Immunology, Jour. Interferon and Cytokine Rsch., Cytokine and Growth Factor Revs.; contbr. articles. Arthritis Found. fellow, 1984; NIH rsch. grantee; recipient Aid for Cancer Rsch. Young Investigator award, 1988. Mem. Soc. Leukocyte Biology (coun. 2001—), Am. Assn. Immunologists, Internat. Cytokine Soc. (treas. 1998-2001, councilor 2001—), Sigma Xi. Democrat. Avocations: scuba diving, sailing, kayaking, blues music. Office: Divsn Pulmonary Crit Care Medicine MSTF-800 826 W Baltimore Baltimore MD 21201 E-mail: mfenton@medicine.umaryland.edu.

FENTON, MICHAEL I. artist, educator; b. Bklyn., May 22, 1942; s. Al and Selda Fenton; m. Diana Lee Silverman, July 1, 1967; children: Kimberly, Ryan. BS, Ohio State U., 1965; MFA, Cranbrook Acad. Art, 1967. Instr. Cooper Sch. Art, Cleve., 1967—70; sr. instr. Art Acad. Cin., 1971—74; asst. prof. art Skidmore Coll., Saratoga Springs, NY, 1974—78; pres. MDF Enterprises Corp., Troy, 1983—88; tchr. art Niskayuna High Sch., Schenectady, 1989—97. Instr. Cuyahoga C.C., Cleve., 1969—70; vis. instr. Kent State U., 1970—71; vis. asst. prof. Adirondack C.C., Glens Falls, NY, 1979; adj. prof. Russell Sage Coll., Troy, 1980, 2000; vis. asst. prof. The Hyde Mus., Glens Falls, 1981—82; instr. SUNY, Albany, 1981—82; vis. asst. prof. art Ind. U., Indpls., 1982—83; tchr. art Rensselaer Columbia-Green BOCES, Troy, 1989. One-man shows include Cin. Art Mus., 1971, Cooper Sch. Art, 1972, Massilon Mus. Art, Ohio, 1972, Michael Wyman Gallery, Chgo., 1973, Hawthorn Gallery, Saratoga Springs, 1976, Saks Fifth Ave., N.Y.C., 1981, Viridian Gallery, 1981, Miss. Mus. Art, Jackson, 1982, Rensselaer Coun. Arts, 1985, Anne Grey Gallery, Saratoga Springs, 1986, Nisk Art Gallery, Schenectady, 1990, Dome Gallery, N.Y.C., 1991, Albany Ctr. Galleries, Albany, 2002, exhibited in group shows at Cleve. Mus. Art, 1967, Gallery Eight, Erie, Pa., 1968, Karamu Ho., Cleve., 1968, Shirley Aly Campbell Gallery, 1969, Cuyahoga C.C., 1970, Kent State U., 1971, Lantern Gallery, Ann Arbor, Mich., 1974, Cin. Mus., 1974, Hawthorn Gallery, 1975, Canton Art Inst, Ohio, 1981, Blossom Music Ctr., Akron, Ohio, 1981, Viridian Gallery, N.Y.C., 1981, 1982, 2000, The Gallery at Saratoga, 1988, Agora Gallery, 1995, Adirondack C.C., 1996, Creiger Dane Gallery, Boston, 1996, Copley Soc., 1997, Riester-Greenberg Gallery, New Preston, Conn., 2000, Represented in permanent collections Cleve. Mus. Art, Canton Art Inst, Phillips-Born Collection, Chgo., Fin. Internet Network Corp. Collection, N.Y.C., Temple Sinai, Saratoga Springs, Karamu Ho., Cleve. Home: 216 Church St Saratoga Springs NY 12866 E-mail: michael@fentonarts.com.

FENTON, NOEL JOHN, venture capitalist; b. New Haven, May 24, 1938; s. Arnold Alexander and Carla (Mathiasen) F.; m. Sarah Jane Hamilton, Aug. 14, 1965; children: Wendy, Devon, Peter, Lance. BS, Cornell U., 1959; MBA, Stanford U., 1963. Research asst. Stanford (Calif.) U., 1963-64; v.p. Mail Systems Corp., Redwood City, Calif., 1964-66; v.p., gen. mgr. products div. Acurex Corp., Mountain View, Calif., 1966-72, pres., chief exec. officer, dir., 1972-83, Covalent Systems Corp., Sunnyvale, Calif., 1983-86; mng. gen. ptnr. Trinity Ventures Ltd., 1986—. Bd. dirs. Requisite Tech., Inc., LoopNet, Inc., SciQuest, Inc., Fuego, Inc., ChipData, Inc., ID Analytics, Inc. Chmn. adv. coun. resource Ctr. for Women, chmn. bd. dirs. 1987-88; mem. San Jose Econ. Devel. Task Force, 1983, Young Pres.'s Orgn., 1976-88, Pres. Reagan's Bus. Adv. Panel; mem. World Pres.'s Orgn., 1988—, dir., 1994-2000; mem. athletic bd. Stanford U., 2003—. Lt. (j.g.) USN, 1959-61. Mem. Am. Electronics Assn. (chmn. 1978-79, dir. 1976-80), Santa Clara County Mfrs. Group (dir. 1980-83), Chief Execs. Orgn., Stanford Bus. Sch. Alumni Assn. (pres. 1976-77, dir. 1971-76), Stanford Alumni Assn. (exec. bd. 1985-89). Republican. Episcopalian. Home: 247 Mapache Dr Portola Valley CA 94028-7354 Office: Trinity Ventures Bldg 4 3000 Sand Hill Rd Ste 160 Menlo Park CA 94025-7113

FENTON, ROBERT EARL, electrical engineering educator; b. Bklyn., Sept. 30, 1933; s. Theodore Andrew and Evelyn Virginia (Brent) F.; m. Alice Earlyn Gray, Dec. 13, 1934; children: Douglas Earl, Andrea Leigh. BEE, Ohio State U., 1957, MEE, 1960, PhD in Electrical Engring., 1965. Registered profl. engr., Ohio. Engr. rsch. N. Am. Aviation, Columbus, Ohio, 1957; instr. electric engring. Ohio State U., Columbus, 1960-65, prof., 1965-95, prof. emeritus, 1995—. Cons. transp. sys. divsn. GM, Warren, Mich., 1974-80, Battelle Meml. Inst., Columbus, Ohio, 1991-93. Inventor kinesthetic-tactile display; contbr. articles to profl. jours. Capt. USAF, 1957-60. Recipient Outstanding Tchr. award Eta Kappa Nu, 1963, Neil Armstrong award Ohio Soc. Profl. Engrs., 1971, Pioneering Rsch. award Nat. Automated Hwy. Systems Consortium, 1997, Significant Achievement award Intelligent Vehicle Hwy. Sys. Ohio, 1993. Fellow IEEE (IEEE Millennium medal 2000), Radio Club Am., IEEE Vehicular Tech. Soc. (pres. 1985-87, v.p. 1983-85, treas. 1981-83, prize paper 1980, Stuart F. Meyer Meml. award 1998), NAE, Sigma Xi. Avocations: bicycling, swimming, classical music. Home: 2177 Oakmount Rd Columbus OH 43221-1229 Office: Ohio State Univ Dept Elec Engring 2015 Neil Ave Dept Elec Columbus OH 43210-1210 E-mail: fenton.2@osu.edu.

FENTON, ROBERT LEONARD, lawyer, literary agent, movie producer, writer; b. Detroit, Sept. 14, 1929; s. Ben B. and Stella Frances (Saffir) F.; children: Robert L. Jr., Cynthia R. AB, Syracuse U., 1952; LLB, U. Mich., 1955. Bar: Mich. 1955. Asso. Marks, Levi, Thill & Wiseman, Detroit, 1955-60; ptnr. Fenton, Nederlander, Tracy & Dodge, Detroit, 1960-85; pvt. practice Detroit, 1985—. Adj. prof. U. Mich. Law Sch., Marygrove Coll., Detroit, 2002-03; lectr. Flint and Lansing Real Estate Bds., 1966-68; spl. counsel Detroit Fire Dept., 1975—, Mich. Motion Picture and TV Commn., 1978-82; producer Universal Studios, Calif., 1983-86, 20th Century Fox, 1986-87; guest lectr. U. Mich. Law Sch., 1998; presenter entertainment law seminar, U. Mich., Apr. 1998, writer's workshop Holland Am. Cruise Lines, Feb. 1999; conductor writer's workshops. Author: (novels) Black Tie Only, 1990, Blue Orchids, 1992, Royal Invitation, 1995; producer NBC movie of week Double Standard, 1988, Woman on the Ledge, 1993. Treas. Oakland County Dem. Com., 1960-64; mem. Dem. State Fin. Com., 1966-69, Nat. Fin. Com., 1962-74, Dem. Pres.'s Club, 1962-74; fin. adviser to Mayor Roman S. Gribbs, 1969-73, Mayor Coleman A. Young, 1974-94; chmn. State of Mich. Film and TV Commn.; bd. dirs. Detroit Bicentennial Commn., Rivers and Harbour Congress of U.S.; mem. adv. bd. NAACP, U. Mich. Pres.'s Club. Served with USAF, 1950-52. Recipient Distinguished Pub. Service medal City of Detroit, 1973, Letter of Commendation USAF, 1953; named Man of the 60's City of Detroit, 1964; decorated Order of St. Johns of Jerusalem, 1980. Mem. ABA, Mich., Detroit bar assns., Econs. Club, Acad. Magical Arts, Soc. Preservation Variety Arts, Franklin Hills Country Club, Variety Club of Detroit (bd. dirs.), Variety Clubs Internat., Recess Club (Detroit), St. James Club (L.A., N.Y.C., London, Paris), Mt. Kenya Safari Club (Nairobi), Masons, Shriners. Office: Village Park Bldg 31800 Northwestern Hwy Ste 390 Farmington Hills MI 48334-1604 E-mail: fenent@msn.com.

FENTON, THOMAS CONNER, lawyer; b. Cin., Feb. 9, 1954; s. William Conner and Virginia (Rawnsley) F.; m. Karen Lois Haswell, Oct. 20, 1979; children: Margaret Lois, Rebecca Conner, Robert Ellis. BA, Centre Coll., 1976; JD, Ohio State U., 1979. Bar: Ky. 1979, U.S. Dist. Ct. (we. dist.) Ky. 1979, U.S. Ct. Appeals (D.C. cir.) 1981, U.S. Dist. Ct. (ea. dist.) Ky. 1985, U.S. Ct. Appeals (6th cir.) 1986. Assoc. Greenebaum, Treitz, Brown & Marshall, Louisville, 1979-85, ptnr., 1985-88; v.p., counsel Nat. City Bank Ky., Louisville, 1989-93; counsel Nat. City Corp., Cleve., 1989-93; v.p. human resources Nat. City Processing Co., Louisville, 1993-95; of counsel Morgan & Pottinger PSC, Louisville, 1996-2001, mem., 2001—. Lectr. Ohio Bankers Assn. Sch. of Human Resources Adminstrn., 1989-91. Author: Affirmative Action Relevant to Bankers, 1996. Bd. trustees St. Matthew's United Meth. Ch., 2001—, chmn., 2002—; bd. dirs. Elder Serve Inc., Louisville, 1983—91, 1995—2001, sec., 1984—86, v.p., 1986—87, pres., 1987—90; bd. dirs. Louisville Youth Choir, Inc., 1996—2002, chmn., 1997—2002. Mem. Ky. Bar Assn. (chmn. labor rels. law sect. 1981-83), Louisville Bar Assn. Methodist. Home: 11003 Fox Moore Ct Louisville KY 40223-5531 Office: Morgan & Pottinger PSC 601 W Main St Louisville KY 40202-2976

FENTON, THOMAS TRAIL, journalist; b. Balt., Apr. 8, 1930; s. Matthew Clark and Beatrice (Trail) F.; m. Simone France Marie Lopes-Curval, Jan. 10, 1959; children: Ariane France, Thomas Trail. AB, Dartmouth Coll., 1952; PhD (hon.), U. Balt., 1999. Mem. staff Balt. Sun, 1961-70, chief Rome bur., 1966-68, chief Paris bur., 1968-70; reporter-producer Rome bur. CBS News, 1970-73, corr. Tel Aviv bur., 1973-77, corr. Paris bur., 1977-79, chief European corr., 1979-94, 1994-96, London, 1996—. Assignments include 1967 Middle East War, 1968 Paris Peace Talks, 1971 Indo-Pakistan War, 1973 Middle East War, 1979 takeover of the Am. Embassy in Tehran, 1985 Geneva Summit, 1989-90 Revolution in Ea. Europe, 1990 Gulf Crisis, Moscow Coup, 1991, Collapse of Communism and the Soviet Union, German Nationalism, 1992, War in Former Yugoslavia, 1992, War in Chechnya, 1995, 1991 Persian Gulf War, 1991 Balkans War, 1999, Death of Princess Diana, 1997, War Against Terrorism Pakistan, 2001, Afghanistan, 2002, War in Iraq, 2003, second Gulf War, 2003 Served with USN, 1952-61. Recipient Overseas Press Club awards for articles from Paris, 1968, for coverage Indo-Pakistan War, 1971, Mid. East War, 1973 Sadat visit to Jerusalem, 1977, Mountbatten funeral, 1980, hunger in Africa 1981, radio documentary series, 1992, Emmy awards NATAS for bombing of Marines in Beirut, 1983, for assassination in Indira Gandhi, 1984, 2 Emmy awards for death of Princess Diana, 1998, DuPont award, 1990, Weintal award Georgetown U., 1999. Mem. Soc. the Cin., Internat. Inst. Strategic Studies. Assn. Am. Corrs. London, Assn. de la Presse Presdl. Paris. Office: care Fgn Desk CBS News 524 W 57th St New York NY 10019-2902 E-mail ttfenton@yahoo.com.

FENTON, WAYNE S. psychiatrist; b. Mar. 24, 1953; BA in Exptl. Psychology Bard Coll., 1975; MD, George Washington U., 1979. Cert. Am. Bd. Medica Examiners, 1980; cert. Md., Conn., Va.; Diplomate in Psychiatry. Rotating internship, dept. internal medicine Norwalk Hosp., Conn., 1979-80; resident post doctoral fellow psychiatry Yale U., 1980-83; fellow Inst. Social and Policy Studies, Yale U., 1983-84; staff psychiatrist Yale Psychiat. Inst., Yale U., New Haven, 1983-84, Chestnut Lodge, Rockville, Md., 1984-85; rsch. assoc Chestnut Lodge Rsch. Inst., Rockville, Md., 1984-90; clin. adminstrv. psychiatrist Chestnut Lodge Hosp., Rockville, Md., 1985-90; dir. rsch. Chestnut Lodge Rsch. Inst., Rockville, Md., 1990—; asst. clin. dir. Chestnut Lodge Hosp. Rockville, Md., 1990—, med. dir., CEO, 1994—; assoc. clin. prof., psychiatry and behavior scis. George Washington U., D.C., 1990—; mem. faculty Washington Sch. Psychiatry, 1991—; dep. dir. clin. affairs NIMH, 1999— acting dep. dir., 2002. Cons. Montgomery County Pub. Defender, Md., 1984— McAuliffe House, Md., 1990—. Editl. cons. Schizophrenia Bulletin, 1986— assoc. editor, 1994—; editl. cons. Jour. of Nervous and Mental Disease, 1986— Am. Jour. Psychiatry, 1989—; contbr. to profl. jours. Recipient nat. rsch. svc award USPHS, 1983-84, young investigator award NIH, 1989, Nat. Alliance fo Rsch. in Schizophrenia and Depression, 1989, Gralnick award Am. Suicid Found., 1992, Md. Schizophrenia Sci. award, 1995. Mem. Am. Psychiat. Assn Wash. Psychiat. Sopc., Nat. Alliance for Mentally Ill (exemplary psychiatris 1996), NAPPH. Office: NIMH 6001 Exec Blvd Rm 6216 MSC 9621 Washington DC 20013-1101

FENTON, WILLIAM NELSON, anthropologist, anthropology educato emeritus; b. New Rochelle, N.Y., 1908; s. John William and Anna Bell (Nourse) F.; m. Olive Louise Ortwine, 1936 (dec. 1986); children: Elizabet Fenton Snyder, John W., Douglas Bruce, Harry (dec.). AB, Dartmouth Coll 1931; PhD, Yale U., 1937; LLD, Hartwick Coll., 1968. Cmty. worker U.S Indian Service (N.Y. Agency, in charge Tonawanda and Tuscarora Reservations), 1935-37; instr. sociology and anthropology St. Lawrence U., 1937-3 asst. prof., 1938-39; instr. (summers) Allegany Sch. Natural History, U. Buffal 1938, St. Lawrence U., 1938; vis. prof. Northwestern U., 1947, U. Mich., 195 U. Ariz., 1963. Lectr. Johns Hopkins U., 1949-50, Cath. U. Am., 1950-5 assoc. anthropologist Bur. Am. Ethnology, Smithsonian Instn., 1939-43, s ethnologist, 1943-51, mem. and sec., war com., 1942-44; research asso Ethnogeographic Bd., 1943-45; exec. sec. div. anthropology and psycholog NRC, 1952-54; dir., asst. commr. N.Y. State Mus. and Sci. Service, 1954-6 research prof. anthropology State U. N.Y., Albany, 1968-74, Disting. prof 1974-79, Disting. prof. emeritus, 1979— ; U.S. del. IV Internat. Congres Anthrop. and Ethnol. Sci., Vienna, 1952; co-chair Am. del. VII Interna Congress on Anthropology and Ethnology, Moscow, 1964; ethnol. field trips Iroquois Indian Reservations; Nat. Endowment Humanities fellow Huntingto Library, 1978-79; mem. Iroquois Documentary History Project, Newberr Library, 1979-81 Author: Area Studies in American Universities, 1947, Iroquo Eagle Dance, 1953, Indian and White Relations to 1830, 1957, Parker on th Iroquois, 1968, The Little Water Medicine Society of The Senecas, 200 co-editor, transl.: Customs of the American Indians (J.F. Lafitau) 2 vols, 197 76, The False Faces of the Iroquois, 1987, The Great Law and the Longhous A Political History of the Iroquois Confederacy, 1998; contbr. numerous articl to profl. jours. Mem. com. on lang. and areal implications Commn. o Implication of Armed Svc. Ednl. Programs, Am. Coun. Edn., 1946; trustee Mu Am. Indian-Heye Found., 1976-80, 82-89; mem. adv. com. Adirondack Fore Preserve, 1993-95. Recipient Cornplanter medal for Iroquois Rsch., 196 Citizen Laureate award SUNY Found., 1978, Dartmouth Class of 1930 awar 1979, 50th Anniversary award, 1995 Conf. Iroquois Rsch., Wilbur Cross med Yale U. Grad Sch., 1999, Rothbaum Prize U. Okla. Press, 2000, John C. Ewe award Western History Assn., 2000; named Dean in Perpetuum of Iroquoi Studies, 1979; Fulbright-Hays rsch. fellow to N.Z., 1975, NEH sr. fello 1982-83. Fellow Am. Folklore Soc. (pres. 1959-60), Am. Anthrop. Assn. (exe bd. 1963-65, Disting. Service award 1983), Am. Ethnol. Soc. (pres. 1959), A Soc. Ethnohistory (pres. 1962), Anthrop. Soc. Washington (former sec., v. pres.), Keene Valley Library Assn. (trustee 1970-73), Sigma Xi. Clubs: Tro Unltd. (pres. Clearwater chpt. 1979-81). Episcopalian. Home: 44 Lakeview N Cooperstown NY 13326-3001 E-mail: wnfenton@yahoo.com.

FENVES, ANDREW ZOLTAN, nephrologist; b. Budapest, Nov. 29, 195 came to U.S., 1969; s. Ervin Jeno and Vera (Lippai) F.; m. Saralynn Busch, Ju 28, 1981; children: Carla, Diana. BS, Stanford U., 1975; MD, U. Tex., Dalla 1979. Diplomate in Internal Medicine, Am. Bd. Nephrology. Intern Jewi Hosp. St. Louis, 1979-80, resident in internal medicine, 1980-81, Baylor Med. Ctr., Dallas, 1981-82, fellow in nephrology, 1982-84; ptnr. Dal Nephrology Assocs., 1984—; clin. prof. U. Tex., Dallas, 1996—; prof. medici Baylor U. Med. Ctr., Dallas, 1996—. Dir. nephrology divsn. Baylor U. Me

Ctr., Dallas. Contbr. articles to profl. jours. Fellow ACP; mem. Nat. Kidney Found. (past pres. Region IV), Nat. Kidney Found. Tex. (pres.). Office: 3601 Swiss Ave # 200 Dallas TX 75204-6225

FENWICK, JAMES HENRY, editor; b. South Shields, Eng., Mar. 17, 1937; came to U.S., 1965; s. James Henry and Ellen (Tinmouth) F.; m. Suzanne Helene Hatch, Jan. 27, 1968. BA, Oxford U., Eng., 1960. Freelance lectr., writer, 1960-65; assoc. editor Playboy mag., Chgo., 1965-71; planning and features editor Radio Times, BBC, London, 1971-77, U.S. rep. N.Y.C., 1978-87; sr. editor Modern Maturity mag., Lakewood, Calif., 1987-90, exec. editor, 1990-91, editor, 1991-98; contbg. editor Get Up and Go!, Age Wave Comm., Lakewood, Calif., 1998-99; editor Next Mag., Palm Springs, Calif., 2000—01, Desert Mag., Palm Springs, 2002—.

FENWICK, JUDITH L. oceanographer, researcher; b. Stamford, Conn., May 20, 1947; d. F. Leslie Fenwick, Jr. and Ethel Phippen Cheney Fenwick; m. Alan Forsyth Poole, Oct. 19, 1985 (div. July 0, 1993); 1 child, Phoebe Akin Poole. BA, Wesleyan U., Middletown, Conn., 1982; EdM, Harvard U., 1996. Admissions officer, bus. mgr. Sea Edn. Assn., Woods Hole, Mass., 1978—81; rsch. asst. Woods Hole Oceanog. Inst., Woods Hole, 1983—89; rsch. assoc. Woods Hole Oceanog. Instn., 1990—; tchr. English Falmouth (Mass.) H.S., 1997—98. Chmn. Woods Hole Sci. and Tech. Edn. Partnership, 2002—; mem. tech. adv. bd. Falmouth (Mass.) Pub. Schs., 1996—. Author: International Marine Science Funding Guide, 1990, International Profiles on Marine Scientific Research, 1992, (map) Maritime Claims and Marine Scientific Research Jurisdiction, 1992; contbr. articles, chapters to books. V.p. Falmouth Svc. Ctr./Food Pantry, 2001—03; mem. Falmouth Town Meeting, 2000—03, Falmouth Sch. Com., 2000—03; trustee Woods Hole Pub. Libr., 1993—2000, Woods Hole Cmty. Assn., 1984—93; dir. Children's Sch. Sci., Woods Hole, 2001—03, VNA Child Care Ctr., Falmouth, 1992—96. Recipient Hardin Craig Award, Munson Inst./Mystic Seaport, 1983, Morse-Porteous award for discovery and excellence, Woods Hole Oceanog. Instn., 1996. Mem.: AAAS, Oceanography Soc., Harvard Club (Cape Cod). Avocations: reading, travel, lacrosse and field hockey mom, weaving, gardening. Home: 18 Mill Rd Falmouth MA 02540 Office: Woods Hole Oceanographic Instn 11 School St Woods Hole MA 02543 E-mail: jfenwick@whoi.edu.

FENWICK, LEX, communications executive; With Bloomberg LP, N.Y.C., 1987—, mng. dir., bus. in Europe, Middle East, and Africa, 1996—2002, CEO, 2002—. Trustee Whitechapel Art Gallery, N.Y.C. Office: Bloomberg LP 499 Park Ave New York NY 10022*

FENWICK, LYNDA BECK, lawyer, writer; b. Great Bend, Kans., Oct. 24, 1944; d. Ralph George and Margaret Pauline (Hawk) Beck; m. Larry Dean Fenwick, Dec. 23, 1962. BS with distinction, Fort Hays State U., 1966; JD, Baylor U., 1975. Bar: Tex. 1975, Ga. 1989, N.C. 1993, U.S. Dist. Ct. (we. dist.) Tex. 1980, U.S. Dist. Ct. (no. dist.) Tex. 1986. Atty. VA, Waco, Tex., 1975-79; assoc. Pakis, Cherry, Beard & Giotes, Waco, 1979-81; sole practice Dallas, 1981-85; assoc. Taylor & Mizell P.C., Dallas, 1985-88. Adj. faculty law Baylor U., Waco, 1979-81; grader exams Supreme Ct. of Tex., 1981-85. Author: Should the Children Pray? Historical, Judicial, Political Examination of Public School Prayer, 1989, Private Choices, Public Consequences; Reproductive Technology and the New Ethics of Conception, Pregnancy, and Family, 1998; assoc. editor Baylor U. Law Rev., 1974-75. Docent Dallas Mus. Art., 1982-85. Named Ga. Author of Yr. for Nonfiction, 1990. Mem. ABA, Tex. Bar Assn., Ga. Bar Assn., Portrait Soc. Atlanta, Southeastern Pastel Soc., Phi Delta Phi.

FEOLA, DAVID CRAIG, secondary school administrator; b. Akron, Ohio, Oct. 14, 1954; s. Thomas and Mary (Koci) F.; m. Shellie Feola. BA in Edn., U. Akron, 1976, MA in Edn., 1979, PhD, 1999. Tchr. math. Akron Pub. Schs., 1976-86, asst. prin., 1986-95, Revere H.S., Richfield, Ohio, 1995-2001; prin. Buckeye Jr. High, Medina, Ohio, 2001—. Part-time prof. U. Akron, 1997-2000; math./computer cons. Assocs.: Programs for Learning, Akron, 1991—. Interviewer People to People, Akron, 1994—; vol. for homeless Gennesaret, Inc., Akron, 1997. Named Top Asst. Prin., Akron Edn. Assn., 1995. Mem. ASCD, Nat. Assn. Secondary Sch. Prins., Ohio Assn. Secondary Sch. Prins., Akron Adminstrs. Assn. (treas. 1986-95), Akron City Club, Pi Lambda Theta. Democrat. Congregationalist. Avocations: travel, computers, woodworking, reading, outdoor sports. Home: 4101 Timber Trl Medina OH 44256 Office: Buckeye Jr HS 3024 Columbia Rd Medina OH 44256

FEOLA, RALPH LEONARD, insurance agent; b. Cohasset, Mass., Aug. 24, 1946; s. Randolph Archibald and Marie (Dyson) F.; 1 child, Ralph L. Jr. BS in Bus. Mgmt., Fla. So. Coll., 1969. Mgr. retail sales J.M. Fields Dept. Stores, Winter Haven, Fla., 1970-78; ins. agt. Feola Ins. Agy., Lakeland, Fla., 1978-85, Allstate Ins. Co., Plant City, Fla., 1986-94; pres., CEO, Feola Ins. Agy., Plant City, 1994—. Fellow Life Underwriting Tng. Coun. (sgt. 1989); mem. Am. Sco. CLU and ChFC (v.p. 1991-92, pres. 1992-93, 93-96), Profl. Ins. Agts. Fla., Nat. Assn. Life Underwriters, Nat. Assn. Health Underwriters, Plant City C. of C., Estate Planning Coun. of Polk County, Elks, Moose. Democrat. Roman Catholic. Avocations: softball, fishing, golf, diving, travel. E-mail. Home: 5314 Woodhaven Ln Lakeland FL 33813-2656 Office: Feola Ins Agy 1003 S Collins St Plant City FL 33566-6507 E-mail: rlf824@aol.com.

FERA, STEVEN RAYMOND, internist, cardiologist, educator; b. Providence, R.I., Nov. 2, 1955; MD, Georgetown U., 1981. Diplomate Am. Bd. Internal Medicine, Am. Bd. Cardiology. From intern to resident Case Western Res. U., 1981-84; fellow in cardiology Brown U., Providence, 1984-86, asst. instr.; mem. med. staff, dir. ICU South County Hosp., Wakefield, R.I.; med. staff R.I. Hosp., Providence; pvt. practice Wakefield. Bd. dirs. R.I. affiliate Am. Heart Assn. Fellow Am. Coll. Cardiology (exec. coun. R.I. chpt.); mem. ACP, Alpha Omega Alpha. Office: So Co Cardiol Assocs Inc 70 Kenyon Ave Ste 103 Wakefield RI 02879-4239

FERARES, KENNETH, automobile executive; b. Bklyn., Jan. 29, 1957; s. William Harry and Elsie Marion (Millard) F.; m. Rosanne Misiti, Oct. 11, 1981; children: Jessica Lee, Michael Kenneth, Gina Michelle. Grad. high sch., Bayside, N.Y. Parts salesman Ed DiBenedetto Imports, Great Neck, N.Y., 1981-82, Penn Toyota, Roslyn, N.Y., 1982-83; mgr. Wantagh (N.Y.) Mitsubishi, 1983-88, Hassett Lincoln Mercury, Wantagh, 1988-91, Manhasset (N.Y.) Mitsubishi, 1991-96, Valley Stream (N.Y.) Mitsubishi, 1996-2000, Star Toyota, Bayside, NY, 2000—02; parts mgr. Huntington Audi, NY, 2002—. Recipient parts excellence award Mitsubishi Motor Sales Am., 1986-88, 91—. Mem. Mitsubishi Motors Excellence Soc., Metro N.Y. Parts and Svc. Mgrs. Guild (treas. 1991, pres. 1992-93, v.p. 1996—). Republican. Office: Huntington Audi 959 Jericho Turnpike Huntington NY 11743

FERBEL, THOMAS, physics educator, physicist; b. Radom, Poland, Dec. 12, 1937; arrived in U.S., 1949, naturalized, 1955; s. Joseph and Natalie (Gotfryd) F.; m. Barbara G. Goolnick, Apr. 20, 1963; children: Natalie, Peter Jordan. BS, Queens Coll., 1959; MS, Yale U., 1960, PhD, 1963. Research staff physicist Yale U., New Haven, 1963 65; asst. prof. physics U. Rochester, N.Y., 1965-69, assoc. prof., 1969-73, prof., 1973—, assoc. dean grad. studies, 1989-91; sci. assoc. CERN, Geneva, 1980-81. Vis. scientist cen. design group Superconducting Supercollider, Lawrence-Berkeley Lab., U. Calif., 1988-89; vis. prof. LAL, Orsay, France, 1995.U. Mainz, Germany, 2001. U. Freiburg, Germany, 2002; mem. program adv. com. Stanford Linear Accelerator Ctr., Calif., 1974-76, Brookhaven Lab., Upton, N.Y., 1981-84; exec. com. Users' Orgn. of Brookhaven Lab., 1972-74; exec. com. Fermi Nat. Accelerator Lab., 1973-75, chmn., 1986-87; sci. dir. Biennial Advanced Study Inst. on High Energy Physics, St. Croix. Author: (with A. Das) Introduction to Nuclear and Particle Physics, 1993; editor: Techniques and Concepts of High Energy Physics, Vol. 1-X, Silicon Detectors in High Energy Physics, 1982, Experimental Techniques in High Energy and Nuclear Physics, 1991; mem. edtl. bd. Phys. Rev., 1978-80, Zeitschrift fur Physik, 1981-85, Internat. Jour. Modern Physics, 1995—. Recipient Alexander von Humboldt prize, 1995; Alfred P. Sloan fellow, 1970, John S. Guggenheim fellow, 1971; Particle Physics and Astronomy Rsch. Coun. sr. fellow Imperial Coll., London, 2002-03. Fellow Am. Phys. Soc. (sec.-treas. divsn. particles and fields 1983-85, chmn. com. on internat. freedom of scientists 1990-92, mem. com. on internat. sci. affairs 1999-2001). Office: U Rochester Dept Physics Rochester NY 14627

FERBER, LINDA S. museum curator; b. May 17, 1944; BA cum laude, Barnard Coll., 1966; MA, Columbia U., 1968, PhD in Art History, 1980. Curator Am. Painting and Sculpture The Bklyn. Mus. Art, 1970-97, chief curator, 1985-99, Andrew W. Mellon Curator Am. Art, 1997—. Author: William Trost Richards (1833-1905): American Landscape and Marine Painter, 1980, Tokens of a Friendship: Miniature Watercolors by William T. Richards, 1982, (with others) The New Path: Ruskin and the American Pre-Raphaelites, 1985, Never at Fault: The Drawings of William T. Richards, 1986, (with others) Albert Bierstadt: Art and Enterprise, 1991, (with others) Masters of Color and Light: Homer, Sargent and the American Watercolor Movement, 1998, Pastoral Interlude: William T. Richards in Chester County, 2001, (with others) In Search of a National Landscape: William T. Richards in the Adirondacks, 2002; contbr. articles on 19th and 20th century Am. art history. Wyeth Endowment for Am. Art fellow, 1976-77; recipient Disting. Alumna award Barnard Coll., 2001, Fleischman award Smithsonian Archives of Am. Art, 2002. Mem. Coll. Art Assn., Am. Assn. Mus., Am. Studies Assn., Assn. Art Mus. Curators, Century Assn., Phi Beta Kappa. Office: Brooklyn Mus Art 200 Eastern Pkwy Brooklyn NY 11238-6052 E-mail: linda.ferber@brooklynmuseum.org.

FERBER, MARIANNE ABELES, economics educator; b. Mirkov, Bohemia, Czechoslovakia, Jan. 30, 1923; came to U.S., 1944; d. Karl and Elsa (Ornstein) Abeles; widowed; children: Don R., Ellen J. BA, McMaster U., 1944; MA, U. Chgo., 1946, PhD, 1954; LHD (hon.), Ea. Ill. U., 2002. Economist Standard Oil (N.J.), N.Y.C., 1944-46; lectr. Hunter Coll., N.Y.C., 1945-46; dir. women's studies U. Ill., Urbana, 1980-83, 91-93, from asst. prof. to full prof., 1954—. Matina S. Horner Disting. Vis. prof. Radcliffe Coll., 1993—95. Pres. LWV, Champaign County, Ill., 1954; chair Univ. YWCA, Urbana, 1957. Named Disting. Alumna, McMaster U., 1996; recipient Carolyn Shaw Bell award, Com. on Status of Women in Econs. Profession, 2002. Mem. Am. Econ. Assn. (com. status women 1975-78), Midwest Econ. Assn. (pres. 1987-88), Am. Stats. Assn. (chair com. status women 1979-90), Nat. Women's Studies Assn., Internat. Assn. Feminist Economists (pres. 1995-96). Jewish. Avocations: swimming, cooking. Home: 606 S Western Ave Champaign IL 61821-3735

FERBER, ROBERT RUDOLF, physics researcher, educator, science administrator; b. June 11, 1935; s. Rudolf F. and Elizabeth J. (Robertson) F.; m. Eileen Merhaut, July 25, 1964; children: Robert Rudolf, Lynne C. BSEE, U. Pitts., 1958; MSEE, Carnegie-Mellon U., 1966, PhD in Semiconductor Physics, 1967. Registered profl. engr., Pa. Mgr. engrng. dept. WRS Motion Picture Labs., Pitts., 1954-58, sec., 1959-76, v.p., 1976-79; sr. engr. Westinghouse Rsch. Labs., Pitts., 1956-67; mgr. nuclear effects group Westinghouse Elec. Corp., Pitts., 1967-71, mgr. adv. engr. energy projects East Pittsburgh, 1971-77; photovoltaic materials and collector rsch. mgr. Jet Propulsion Lab., Pasadena, Calif., 1977-85, SP100 Project contract tech. mgr., 1985-90, asst. project mgr. Spaceborne Imaging Radar, 1990-96, Earth Observing Sys. microwave limb sounder radiometer, 1995-99, mgr. Herschel HIFI project amplifier devel. task mgr., 2000—. V.p. Executaire Inc., Pitts., 1960-64; pres. Tele-Cam Inc., Pitts., 1960-78. Editor: Transactions of the 9th World Energy Conf. 1974, Digest of the 9th World Energy Conf., 1974. Contbr. articles to profl. jours.; patentee in field. Mem. Franklin Regional Sch. Dist. Bd., Murrysville, Pa., 1975-77. Fellow Buhl Found., 1965-66, NDEA, 1976-77. Mem. IEEE (sr.), ASME (chmn. 1986 Solar Energy divsn. conf.). Republican. Lutheran. Home: 5314 Alta Canyada Rd La Canada Flintridge CA 91011-1606 Office: NASA Jet Propulsion Lab 4800 Oak Grove Dr Pasadena CA 91109-8001 E-mail: robert.r.ferber@jpl.nasa.gov.

FERBER, SAMUEL, publishing executive; b. N.Y.C., June 6, 1920; s. Isidore and Sadie (Irgang) F.; m. Beatrice Ruth Ziman, June 18, 1944; children: Bruce Joseph, Joel David. BBA, CCNY, 1941; postgrad., Columbia U., 1946-48. Promotion dir. Nat. Advt. Service, Inc., N.Y.C., 1946-50, Boys' Life mag., N.Y.C., 1950-52; promotion dir. Esquire mag., N.Y.C., 1952-58, advt. mgr., 1959-65, sr. v.p., assoc. pub., 1965-70, advt. dir., 1970-74, pub., 1974-76; co-dir. Esquire mag. (Bus. and the Arts awards program), 1966-74; dir. Esquire mag. (Corp. Social Responsibility awards program), 1972-75; sr. v.p., prin. Altman, Stoller, Weiss Advt., 1976-80, exec. v.p., 1980-82; v.p. Nadler & Larimer Advt., 1982-84; owner Sam Ferber, Pub. Cons., 1984—. Mem. faculty econs. and advt. Latin Am. Inst., N.Y.C., 1946-49; lectr. on mag. pub. at various colls. and univs.; mem. bd. advisors Alliance Resident Theatres, N.Y.C., 1987—. Mem. Leader Gt. Books Discussion Group, Bd. Art/N.Y. Served with Adj. Gen.'s Dept. AUS, 1942-46. Home: 2210 Rutland Pl Thousand Oaks CA 91362 *I have always subscribed to the philosophy of my former colleague, Arnold Gingrich, that one should "never leave well enough alone" . When things are progressing smoothly is the precise moment to plan the evolutionary change that insures progress and vitality. In my time, I have seen pillars of industry and publishing fall by the wayside because their emphasis has been on self-preservation rather than innovation.*

FEREBEE, STEPHEN SCOTT, JR., architect; b. Detroit, July 30, 1921; s. Stephen Scott and Caroline (Cheatham) F.; m. Mary Elizabeth Cooper, July 7, 1945; children: Scott III, John, Caroline. B.Archtl. Engring., N.C. State U., 1948; D. Fine Arts (hon.), U. N.C., Charlotte, 1992. Job capt. A.G. Odell, Jr. & Assocs. (Architects), Charlotte, NC, 1948-53; ptnr. Higgins & Ferebee (Architects), Charlotte, 1953-59, Ferebee & Walters (Architects), 1959-64; pres. Ferebee, Walters & Assos. (Architects/Planners), Charlotte, 1964-86; chmn., CEO FWA Group (Architects & Planners), Charlotte, 1987-90. Dir. AIA Found., Washington, 1986-87, Prodn. Systems for Architects and Engrs., Inc., Washington, 1969-71, 77-78, Republic Bank & Trust Co., Charlotte, 1971-91, John Crosland Co., Charlotte, 1973-83. Prin. projects include Southpark Mall, Colonial Heights, Va., 1989, Tech. Center for Union Carbide Agrl. Products Co., Inc, Research Triangle Park, N.C., 1982, Sch. Vet. Medicine, N.C. State U., Raleigh, 1983, Charlotte Conv. Ctr., 1994, Coll. Architecture bldg., U. N.C., Charlotte, 1990. Bd. dirs. United Cmty. Svcs., Charlotte, 1977—82, Opera Carolina, Charlotte, 1988—91, Aldersgate, Charlotte, 1995—, Habitat for Humanity, Charlotte, 1999—2002; pres. N.C. Design Found., 1966—68, 1978—79. Capt. 101st Airborne Divsn. AUS, 1942—46, maj. gen. Res. (ret.). Decorated D.S.M., Bronze Star, Purple Heart, Croix de Guerre France and Belgium, Order of the Long Leaf Pine State of N.C.; recipient Watauga medal, N.C. State U., 2001. Fellow: AIA (pres. N.C. 1964, chmn. commn. profl. practice 1971, nat. pres. 1973, chancellor Coll. of Fellows 1987, Deitrick medal N.C. chpt. 1995), Internat. Union Architects (coun. 1975—81), Royal Archtl. Inst. Can. (hon.); mem.: Mex. Soc. Architects (hon.), N.C. State U. Alumni Assn. (pres. 1980—81), Charlotte C. of C. (v.p. 1975—76, bd dirs. 1989—91), Rotary (pres. Charlotte East 1997—98), Phi Kappa Phi. Methodist (past chmn. ofcl. bd.). Home: 5334 Sandtrap Ln Charlotte NC 28226-7978 E-mail: sferebee@bellsouth.net.

FERENCAK, MICHAEL NEILL, mathematician, educator; b. Uniontown, Pa., Feb. 22, 1964; s. Edmund Andrew and Faith Ann Ferencak; m. Carol Suchevits, June 4, 1993. BS in Secondary Math. Edn., California U. Pa., California, Pa., 1987; MS in Math., W.Va. U., 1989, PhD in Math., 1998. Vis. asst. prof. math. Carnegie Mellon U., Pittsburgh, Pa., 1998—99; asst. prof. math. U. of Pitts. at Johnstown, Johnstown, Pa., 1999—. Fellow: Inst. of Combinatorics and its Applications (assoc.); mem.: Math. Assn. Am. (dept. liaison 1999—2003), Am. Math. Soc. Avocations: amateur musician, bicycling, weightlifting, classic cars. Office: U Pitts at Johnstown Dept Math Johnstown PA 15904 E-mail: ferencak@stargate.pitt.edu.

FERENCE, HELEN MARIE, nursing consultant, consultant; b. Ohio, Sept. 1, 1946; d. Emery and Josephine Leona (Terlecki) F.; m. William Verill Nick. Diploma, Youngstown (Ohio) Hosp. Assn., 1967; BS, Youngstown U., 1970; MS, Ohio State U., 1972; PhD, NYU, N.Y.C., 1979. Cert. advanced cardiac life support; cert. nursing sci. Cons., pres. Nursing Cons. and Rsch., Pebble Beach, Calif., 1972—; dir. rsch. and programs Sigma Theta Tau, Indpls., 1986-88; dir. clin. evaluation, rsch. and nursing standards Mt. Sinai Hosp., N.Y.C., 1986-88. Asst. prof. Ohio State U., Columbus, 1972-80; cons. Battelle Meml. Inst., Columbus, 1972-81, VA, Chillicothe, Ohio, 1975-80; asst. prof. NYU, 1979-80; cons. McGraw-Hill, Monterey, Calif., 1981-85; bd. dirs. Mt. Sinai Hosp., N.Y., 1986-88. Editor Notes on Nursing Sci., 1986—. Bd. dirs. Monterey Health Inst. Recipient Laureate: Nightingale Prize, 1991. Fellow Nightingale Soc. (bd. dirs.); mem. Sigma Theta Tau. Home: PO Box 862 Pebble Beach CA 93953-0862 E-mail: webadmin@fnnf.com.

FERENCE, L.W. psychologist; b. Gary, Ind. s. Andrew and Mary Ference. BA, UCLA, 1963; MA, U. So. Calif., 1965, PhD, 1970. Rsch. psychologist City of Milw., 1971-74, pers. officer Chase Manhattan Bank, N.Y.C., 1974-76; pres. FBS Co., Westwood, N.J., 1976-85; v.p. Excorp Sys., Newark, 1985-97; pres. FBS Co., Kerrville, Tex., 1997—. Author numerous articles and rsch. papers in field. Mem. Am. Psychol. Soc., Am. Statis. Assn., Soc. for I/O Psychology. Avocations: computer design, precision knife grinding. Office: FBS Co PO Box 291347 Kerrville TX 78029-1347

FERENCE-VALENTA, MARY JEAN, osteopath, health facility administrator; b. Middletown, Pa., Nov. 26, 1969; d. Edward W. and Virginia J. Ference; m. Erik D. Valenta, Sept. 9, 1995; 1 child, Joseph Valenta. BS, St. Vincent Coll., 1992; DO, Chgo. Coll. Osteo. Medicine, 1996. Rsch. intern Pitts. Energy Tech. Ctr., 1991; chemistry analyst Allegheny Power Svc. Corp., Greensburg, Pa., 1992; intern St. Vincent Med. Ctr., Toledo, 1996-97; resident in family practice Toledo Hosp., 1997-99, chief resident, 1998-99; family practitioner Ulrich Profl. Group, 1999; pvt. practice, Kent, Ohio, 1999—; med. dir. Child Health Svcs. of Portage County, Ravenna, Ohio, 2001—; dir. Portage County Child Health Svcs., Ravenna, Ohio, 2001—. Grantee Chgo. Coll. Osteo. Medicine Alumni Assn., 1993-94, 94-95; scholar Pa. Osteo. Med. Assn., 1995; recipient Student Coun. Leadership award 1996. Mem. AMA, Am. Acad. Family Physicians, Am. Osteo. Assn., Am. Coll. Osteo. Family Physicians, Chgo. Coll. Osteo. Medicine Alumni Assn., Sigma Sigma Phi Alumni Assn. (sec.-treas. 1994-95, Am. Osteo. Assn. (conv. rep. 1994), Headache Soc. Avocations: jogging, reading, arts and crafts, antiques. Office: 401 Devon Pl Kent OH 44240-6482

FERENCZ, BENJAMIN BERELL, lawyer; b. Soncuta Mare, Romania, Mar. 11, 1920; arrived in U.S., 1921, naturalized, 1933; s. Joseph Ferencz and Sarah (Legman) Ferencz Schwartz; m. Gertrude Fried, Mar. 29, 1946; children: Carol, Robin Eve, Donald Martin, Nina Dale. BSS, CCNY, 1940; JD, Harvard U., 1943. Bar: N.Y. 1943, U.S. Supreme Ct. 1943, U.S. Dist. Ct. (so. and ea. dists.) N.Y. 1958. Exec. counsel U.S. Chief Counsel War Crimes, Nuremberg, Germany, 1946—48; dir. gen. Jewish Restitution Orgn., Franfurt, Germany, 1948—56; ptnr. Taylor, Ferencz & Simon, N.Y.C., 1956—. Adj. prof. Pace U. Sch. Law, N.Y.C.; dir. United Restitution Orgn., London, Frankfurt, N.Y.C., 1948—. Author: (book) Less than Slaves, 1979 (Nat. and Present Tense Lit. awards, 1980), Defining International Aggression, 2 vols., 1975, An International Criminal Court, 2 vols., 1980, Enforcing International Law, 2 vols., 1983, Common Sense Guide to World Peace, 1985. Mem. Human Rights Commn., New Rochelle, NY, 1975—. With inf. U.S. Army, 1943—45, ETO. Mem.: Internat. Law Assn., Am. Soc. Internat. Law (v.p. 1979—80), World Peace Through Law Ctr., Amnesty Internat., Internat. League Human Rights, Harvard Club (N.Y.C.), B'nai B'rith (local pres. 1960, counsel supreme lodge 1966 -70). Democrat. Jewish. Home: 14 Bayberry Ln New Rochelle NY 10804-3402 Personal E-mail: benferen@aol.com.

FERENCZ, CHARLOTTE, pediatrician, epidemiology and preventive medicine educator; b. Budapest, Hungary, Oct. 28, 1921; came to U.S., 1954; d. Paul Ferencz and Livia deFekete. BSc, McGill U., 1944, MD, CM, 1945; MPH, Johns Hopkins U., 1970. Cert. pediatrics Royal Coll. Physicians and Surgeons, Can., pediatric cardiology Am. Bd. Pediatrics. Demonstrator McGill U., Montreal, 1952-54; asst. prof. pediatrics Johns Hopkins U., Balt., 1954-58, U. Cin., 1959-60; asst. prof. SUNY, Buffalo, 1960-66, assoc. prof., 1966-73; assoc. prof. epidemiology and preventive medicine U. Md. Sch. Medicine, Balt., 1973-74, prof., 1974-98, prof. pediatrics, 1985—, prof. emeritus, 1998—. Prin. investigator population based study Etiology of Congenital Heart Disease, 1981-89; mem. epidemiology and disease control study sect. NIH, 1984-88; pres. Delta Omage Alpha chpt. Pub. Health Soc., 1990-92. Recipient M.E.S. Abbott scholarship McGill U., 1943-45, M.E.R.I.T. award Nat. Heart, Lung & Blood Inst., 1987, Fogarty Internat. Ctr. Health Sci. Exchange award NIH, 1988, Helen B. Taussig award Am. Heart Assn. Md. Affiliate, 1991, Achievement award Univ. Ctr. Life Scis., Balt., 1993, Johns Hopkins U. Disting. Alumnus award, 2001. Fellow Am. Acad. Pediatrics (Spl. Achievement award Md. chpt. 1994), Am. Coll. Cardiology; mem. Teratology Soc. Democrat. Office: U Md Sch Medicine 660 W Redwood St Baltimore MD 21201-1541

FERENCZ, ROBERT ARNOLD, lawyer; b. Chgo., Sept. 10, 1946; s. Albert and Frances (Reiss) F.; m. Marla J. Miller, May 20, 1973; children: Joseph, Ira. BS in Acctg., U. Ill., 1968; JD magna cum laude, U. Mich., 1973. Bar: Ill. 1973. From assoc. to ptnr. Sidley, Austin, Brown & Wood, Chgo., 1973—. Mem. ABA, Ill. Bar Assn. Office: Sidley Austin Brown & Wood Bank One Plz 10 S Dearborn St Chicago IL 60603-2000

FERENS, DANIEL VINCENT, civilian military employee; b. Oswego, NY, Feb. 26, 1948; s. Walter Frank and Sophie (Longeski) F.; m. Marcella Jean Spinner, Apr. 28, 2001. BS, Rensselaer Poly. Inst., 1969, MSEE, 1970; MBA, U. No. Colo., 1976. Satellite sys. engr. air def. co. USAF, Denver, 1971-75, computer software engr. Aeronaut. Sys. Ctr. Dayton, Ohio, 1976-77, program mgr. Aeronaut. Sys. Ctr., 1977-78; engrng. cost analyst civil svc. USAF Avionics Lab., Dayton, 1978-83; assoc. prof. civil svc. USAF Inst. Tech., Dayton, 1984-97; program dir., 1995-97; adj. assoc. prof. civil svc. USAF Inst. Tech., Dayton, 1998-2000; corp. affordability officer civil svc. USAF Rsch. Lab., Dayton, 1998-00, directorate rep. Corp. Affordability Coun., 1999—2001; tchr. software mgmt. NATO Officers, Belgium, 2000; dept. project mgr. USAF Rsch. Lab., Rome, NY, 2001—. Software estimating cons. Aeronautics Sys. Ctr., Dayton, 1984—2000, Electronic Sys. Ctr., Boston, 2000—02; adj. instr. SUNY Inst. Tech., Utica, 2003—. Author: Mission Critical Computer Software Management, 1987, Defense System Software Project Management, 1990; guest editor: Engineering Cost and Production Economics, 1988; contbr. 35 articles to profl. jours. Tchr. adult Sunday sch. Kirkmont Presbyn. Ch., Beaver Creek, Ohio, 1987—2000, chmn. edn. com., 1992; tchr. adult Sunday sch. Abiding Christ Luth. Ch., Fairborn, Ohio, 2000—01, mem., 2000—02, First Presbyn. Ch., Rome, Ohio, 2002—. Capt. USAF, 1969—78. Decorated Commendation Medal USAF, 1976. Mem. Internat. Soc. Parametric Analysts (bd. dirs. 1979-80, pres. Midwest chpt. 1993-94, Internat. Parametrician of the Yr. award 1990, Freiman Lifetime Achievement award 1999, keynote spkr. European Symposium, 1999, life), Internat. Function Point Users Group (univ. mem., mem. edn. com. 1999-2000), Soc. Cost Estimating and Analysis (mem. edn. com. 1992—), Soc. Logistics Engrs. (assoc. editor newsletter 1993), Toastmasters Internat. (area gov. 2003, Area Gov. of Yr. 1987, pres. 2003—), Polish Legion Am Vets. Avocations: running, computers, church activities, travel, games. Mailing: PO Box 386 Rome NY 13442-0386 Office: Air Force Rsch Lab (AFRL/IFEA) 32 Brooks Rd Rome NY 13441 E-mail: ferensd@rl.af.mil.

FERENTZ, KEVIN SCOTT, physician; b. New York, NY, Apr. 26, 1958; s. Leslie Benjamin and Sylvia F.; m. Lisa Roslyn Ettinger, Nov. 13, 1983; children: Jacob Avi, Zachary Daniel, Noah Samuel. MD, SUNY, Buffalo, 1983. Diplomate Nat. Bd. Med. Examiners, cert. Am. Bd. Family Practice. Assoc. prof. dept. family medicine U. Md. Sch. of Medicine, Balt., 1993—. Residency dir. Dept of Family Medicine, Balt., 1993—. Contbr. articles. Adv. bd. Tova Ho., Balt., 2002. Recipient Exemplary Tchr. of the Yr., Am. Acad. Family Physicians, Resident rsch. award, North Am. Primary Care Rsch. Group Nat. Meeting, 1986, Pub. Rels. award, Am. Acad. Family Physicians, 1991. Mem.: Soc. Tchrs. Family Medicine, Md. Acad. Family Physicians (pres. 1997—98), Am. Acad. Family Physicians (chair, com. on pub. rels. and mktg. 1995—96, Exemplary Tchr. of Yr. 1981, Pub. Rels. award 1991). Democrat. Jewish. Achievements include Regular host of weekly national radio show Sunday Rounds, heard on over 250 stations - for eight years; Organized Smoking Cessation program for Baltimore County High Schools, using medical students and residents as group leaders. Avocations: theater, music. Office: U Md Sch Medicine Lower Level 29 South Paca St Baltimore MD 21201 Office Fax: 410-328-0639. E-mail: kferentz@som.umaryland.edu.

FERET, ADAM EDWARD, JR., dentist; b. Newark, Mar. 5, 1942; s. Adam Edward and Bronislawa Anne (Szorc) F. BA (athletic scholar), Seton Hall U., 1963; DMD, U. Medicine & Dentistry of N.J., 1967. Pvt. practice, Westfield, N.J., 1972—. With USNR, 1967-70. Fellow Am. Acad. Gen. Dentistry; mem. ADA, N.J. Dental Assn., L.D. Pankey Study Club, Soc. Oral Physiology and Occlusion, Quest Study Club, Internat. Coll. Oral Implantologists, Am. Soc.

Oral Implantology, Central Dental Soc., Balloon Fedn. Am., Polish-Am. Guardian Soc., Polish Falcons of Am., Copernicus Soc. Am., Toastmasters, Psi Omega. Roman Catholic. Home and Office: 440 E Broad St Westfield NJ 07090-2124

FERGUS, GARY SCOTT, lawyer; b. Racine, Wis., Apr. 20, 1954; s. Russell Malcolm and Phyl Rose (Muratore) F.; m. Isabelle Sabina Beekman, Sept. 28, 1985; children: Mary Marckwald Beekman Fergus, Kirkpatrick Russell Beekman Fergus. AB, Stanford U., 1976; JD, U. Wis., 1979; LLM, NYU, 1981. Bar: Wis. 1979, Calif. 1980. Assoc. Brobeck, Phleger & Harrison, San Francisco, 1980-86, ptnr., 1986—2001, mng. ptnr. products liability, ins. coverage, environ. and antitrust/appellate practices, 1996-2000, sr. ptnr. e-commerce anti-trust group, 2000—01; founder law firm Fergus, San Francisco, 2002—. Mem. ABA. Home: 3024 Washington St San Francisco CA 94115-1618 Office: Fergus a law firm 595 Market St Ste 2430 San Francisco CA 94105 E-mail: gfergus@ferguslegal.com.

FERGUS, PATRICIA MARGUERITA, English language educator emeritus, writer, editor; b. Mpls., Oct. 26, 1918; d. Golden Maughan and Mary Adella (Smith) Fergus. BS, U. Minn., 1939, MA, 1941, PhD, 1960. Various pers. and editing positions U.S. Govt., 1943-59; mem. faculty U. Minn., Mpls., 1964-79, asst. prof. English, 1972-79, coord. writing program conf. on writing, 1975, dir. writing centre, 1975-77; prof. English and writing, dir. writing ctr., assoc. dean Coll. Mt. St. Mary's Coll., Emmitsburg, Md., 1979-81; dir. writing seminars Mack Truck, Inc., Hagerstown, Md., 1979-81; writer, 1964—. Editor, 1997—; vocal soloist, 1997—; editl. asst. to pres. Met. State U., St. Paul, 1984-85; coord. creative writing, writer program notes for Coffee Concerts, The Kenwood, 1992-94; dir. Kenwood Scribes Presentation, 1994; spkr. and cons. in field; dir. 510 Groveland Assocs.; bus. mgr. Eitel Hosp. Gift Shop; freelance manuscript editor, 1997-99; writer, reviewer Whittier Publs., Long Beach, N.Y., 1997; instr. Elderlearning Inst., 1999-2000, Univ. Coll., U. Minn., 1999-2000; poetry and prose reading, retirement cmtys., 2002-03. Author: Spelling Improvement, 5th edit., 1991; contbr. to Downtown Cath. Voice, Mpls., Mountaineer Briefing, ABI Digest, Women in the Arts The Penletter; contbr. poems to Minn. English Jour., Women in the Arts, Decatur Area Arts Coun. Newsletter, Mpls. Muse, The Moccasin, Heartsong and Northstar Gold, The Pen Woman, Midwest Chaparral, Rhyme Time, The Best of Rhyme Time, 1998, Fantasy, 1998; contbr. short stories to anthologies, including Seeking the Muses, Inspired Works of Creativity, 2000; musical works performed at St. Olaf Ch., 1997, Nat. League Am. Pen Women, 1998. Mem. spl. vocal octet St. Olaf Ch. Choir, 1977-79, 81-92, St. Olaf Parish Adv. Bd., 1982-84, Windmore Found. for the Arts., 1996. Recipient Outstanding Contbn. award U. Minn. Twin Cities Student Assembly, 1975, Horace T. Morse-Amoco Found. award, 1976; Golden Poet award World of Poetry, 1992; Ednl. Devel. grant U. Minn., 1975-76, Mt. St. Mary's Coll. grant, 1980; 3d prize vocal-choral category Nat. Music Composition Contest, Nat. League Am. Pen Women, poetry prize No. Dist. Women's Club, Va., 1996. Mem.: Midwest Fedn. Chaparral Poets (poetry judge numerous poetry prizes, numerous poetry prizes including 1st prize 1998, 1999, 2001, 2003), Mpls. Poetry Soc. (pres. 2000—02, numerous poetry prizes including 1st prize 1999, 2d prize 2003), World Lit. Acad., Nat. League Am. Pen Women (Minn. br. past pres., 1st pl. Haiku nat. poetry contest 1992), Minn. Coun. Tchrs. English (chmn. career and job opportunities comm., spl. com. tchr. licensure, sec. legis. com.), Nat. Coun. Tchrs. English (regional judge 1974, 1976—77, state coord. 1977—79), Mpls. Woman's Club (critic writers group). Roman Catholic. Home and Office: # 612 3535 Bryant Ave S Minneapolis MN 55408-4134

FERGUSON, A. H. poet, medical/surgical nurse; b. Bonne Terre, Mo., July 5, 1947; d. Orin W. Hana and Mildred Rebecca Jones; m. Joseph White Ferguson III, July 3, 1967; 1 child, Jody Suzanne. Completion diploma, Barretts Writers Course, 1976; degree in psychology, Am. Sch., 1967; degree in nursing, Buckeye Hills Career Coll., 1985. CNA, Ohio. Nurse Mental Retardation Assn.; pvt. duty nurse. Sec. French Art Colony, Gallipolis, Ohio, 1982; tchr. ch. sch., Gallipolis, 1982—89. Author: (poetry) Meditations in the Storm, 1984, At the Waters Edge, 1985, From Midnight Till Dawn, 2001, From Mourning Till Midnight, 2003; contbr. articles to newspapers. Mem. Am. Indian Relief Coun. Recipient award, Poetic License Mag., 1998; poetry grantee, Greater Cin. Writers League, 2002. Mem.: United Meth. Women, Ocean Conservancy, Am. Indian Relife Coun., Sierra Club, Defenders of Wildlife, United Animal Nations, Ohio Poetry Assn., Internat. Fund for Animal Welfare. Home: 1529 McCormick # 4 Gallipolis OH 45631-8688

FERGUSON, BRADFORD LEE, lawyer; b. Ottumwa, Iowa, May 29, 1947; s. G. Wendell and Virginia Sue (Baker) Ferguson. BA, Drake U., 1969; JD, Harvard U., 1972. Bar: Minn. 1972, Ill. 1980. Assoc. Dorsey, Marquart, Windhorst, West & Halladay, Mpls., 1972-75; legis. asst. Senator Walter F. Mondale, Washington, 1975-77; spl. asst. to asst. sec. tax policy U.S. Treasury Dept., Washington, 1977-78, assoc. tax legis. counsel, 1978-80; ptnr. Hopkins & Sutter, Chgo., 1980-96, Sidley & Austin, Chgo., 1996-2001. Fellow Am. Coll. Tax Counsel; mem. ABA (taxation sect., chair com. formation tax policy 1991-93, mem. coun. 1994-97), Chgo. Bar Assn., Nat. Tax Assn. (bd. dirs. 1994-97).

FERGUSON, CHARLES ALAN, lawyer; b. Fulton, Mo., Jan. 7, 1940; s. Charles Milton and Hazel A. (Jackson) F.; m. Janill Florene; children: Stacy Christine, Scot Alan. BA, So. Meth. U., 1962, JD, 1965. Bar: Tex. 1965, U.S. Dist. Ct. (we. dist.) Tex. 1967, U.S. Supreme Ct. 1976; CLU. Assoc. McGown, McClanahan & Hamner, San Antonio, 1965-69; atty. Govt. Personnel Mut. Life Ins. Co., San Antonio, 1969—; assoc. gen. counsel, asst. sec. Govt. Pers. Mut. Life Ins. Co., San Antonio, 1970-79, v.p., gen. counsel and sec., 1979-88, sr. v.p., gen. counsel, sec., 1988—, also bd. dirs., exec. com.; pres., bd. dirs. G.P.M. Fed. Credit Union, San Antonio, 1971-80; sec., bd. dirs. Greenwood Life Ins. Co., San Antonio, 1970-76. Mem. adv. com. on replacement, Tex. State Bd. Ins., 1981-82; mem. legis. com. Tex. Life Ins. Assn.; com. chmn. aero. med. divsn. and Wilford Hall USAF Hosp., San Antonio, 1972-73, Joint Jr. Officers Council, San Antonio, 1974, Brooks AFB, 1980-81; chmn. PAC com. Tex. Assn. Life and Health Insurers, 1997—; mem. legis. com. 2003—. Bd. dirs. Scenic Oaks Property Owners Assn., 1986—, pres. 1986-94. Fellow Life Mgmt. Inst.; mem. ABA, San Antonio Bar Assn., San Antonio Jr. Bar Assn. (v.p. 1973), State Bar Tex. (Coll.), Fiesta Men (v.p. 1974-76), Assn. Life Ins. Counsel, San Antonio C. of C., Phi Gamma Delta, Phi Alpha Delta. Clubs: Turtle Creek Country (bd. govs.), Diez y Seis Handball (sec.-treas. 1975), The Dominion. Home: 8601 Barn Swallow San Antonio TX 78255-3623 Office: 800 NW Loop 410 San Antonio TX 78216-5619

FERGUSON, CHARLES AUSTIN, retired newspaper editor; b. New Orleans, Mar. 16, 1937; s. Austin and Josephine Hayes (Gessner) F.; m. Jane Pugh, Dec. 21, 1961; children: Elizabeth Hayes, Caroline Pugh. BA, Tulane U., 1958, LL.B., 1961; DLitt (hon.), Dillard U., New Orleans, 1996. Bar: La. bar 1961. From reporter to editor States-Item, New Orleans, 1961-80; editor Times-Picayune/States-Item, New Orleans, 1980-90. Anchor TV program City Desk, New Orleans, 1971-78 Trustee Dillard U., New Orleans, 1972—, chmn. exec. com., 1978—, chmn. bd. trustees, 1992—; trustee Inst. Politics, Loyola U., New Orleans, 1968-75, pres., 1971-75; co-chmn. Louis Armstrong Meml. Park Com., New Orleans, 1971-79. Recipient Torch of Liberty award Anti-Defamation League of B'nai B'rith, 1981; Nieman fellow, 1965-66 Mem. La. Bar Assn., Interant. Lawn Tennis Club U.S.A. Clubs: New Orleans Lawn Tennis. Home: 1448 Joseph St New Orleans LA 70115-4263

FERGUSON, CLEVE ROBERT, lawyer, educator; b. Long Beach, Calif., Dec. 31, 1938; s. Frank H and Ruth S Ferguson; m. Kathryn Jane Weaver, Apr. 10, 1965 (div. June 25, 1995); children: Sharon Anne, Robert Timothy; m. Peggy Burke Daniell, Nov. 19, 1995. AB in Econs., U. So. Calif., 1961, JD, 1965. Bar: Calif 1966, US Dist Ct (cent dist) Calif 1966, US Ct Appeals (9th cir) 1987, US Supreme Ct 1975. Assoc. Musick, Peeler & Garrett, L.A., 1965-69, Hayes & Hume, Beverly Hills, Calif., 1969-74; pvt. practice Pasadena/Claremont, Calif., 1974—; adj. prof. physics and astronomy U. La Verne (Calif.), 1993—; pres., CEO Mars Manned Mission Corp.; adj. prof. Coll. Law U. La Verne (Calif.), 1994—2001. Mem. alcohol and drug abuse com. Calif. State Bar, 1990—91; instr. astronomy and bus. law Chapman U., 1992—93; arbitrator Am. Arbitration Assn., Nat. Arbitration Forum; lectr. in field; tchr. telescope use and telescope optics UCLA, U. Calif., Irvine. Editor: (book) Tall Tales and Memories, 1987. Mem. Stony Ridge Obs., 1985—, pres., 1994—97; co-founder, bd govs. Mt. Wilson Inst., Calif., 1987, co-founder, trustee, 2003—; lectr., cons. Mcpl. Officers for Redevel. Reform, Calif., 1996—; mem. L.A. Opera League; bd. dirs. Clan Fergusson Soc. N.Am., 1987—2000. With U.S. Army, 1961—62. Decorated Knights Templar of Jerusalem, Grand Priory of the Scots. Fellow: Soc. Antiquaries Scotland; mem.: SR, Univ. Club Claremont, Univ. Club Pasadena, Beta Theta Pi (past pres). Avocations: astronomy, mountaineering, dry fly fishing, skiing. Office: C Robert Ferguson Atty at Law 237 W 4th St Claremont CA 91711-4710 Office Fax: 909-624-7291. E-mail: crflawyer@earthlink.net., crf@marsmannedmission.org.

FERGUSON, DALLAS EUGENE, lawyer; b. Blackwell, Okla., Dec. 20, 1945; s. Clyde L. and Agnes Loree (Humphrey) F.; children: Erin Nicole, Dallas Scott, Robert Brent. BA, Cornell Coll., Mt. Vernon, Iowa, 1968; JD, Columbia U., 1971. Bar: Okla. 1971, U.S. Ct. Appeals (10th cir.) 1971, U.S. Dist. Ct. (we. dist.) Okla. 1971, U.S. Dist. Ct. (no. dist.) Okla. 1973, U.S. Dist. Ct. (ea. dist.) Okla. 1978, U.S. Supreme Ct. 1999. Law clk. to judge U.S. Ct. Appeals (10th cir.), Oklahoma City, 1971-72; assoc. Doerner, Saunders, Daniel & Anderson LLP, Tulsa, 1973-78, ptnr., 1978—. Pres. Legal Aid Svcs. Okla., 2002; bd. dirs. Planned Parenthood Ark. and E. Okla., 1994—, Nat. Multiple Sclerosis Soc., Okla., 2002—, Legal Aid Svcs. Okla., 2002—. Mem. ABA, Okla. Bar Assn., Tulsa County Bar Assn. (Outstanding Young Lawyer 1980). Democrat. Unitarian Universalist. Office: Doerner Saunders Daniel & Anderson LLP 320 S Boston Ave Ste 500 Tulsa OK 74103-3725 E-mail: dferguson@dsda.com.

FERGUSON, DENNIS EDWARD, music educator, musician; b. Memphis, Tenn., Feb. 19, 1949; s. Forest Edward and Marjorie (Snow) Ferguson; m. Colette Marie Scraggs, July 21, 1979; children: Arva, Darren, Keith. MusB, Rhodes Coll., Memphis, 1971; MusM, U. Memphis, 1990. Cert. Tchr. Mass., 1995, Kodaly music tchr. Kodaly Music Inst., Boston, 2002. Coll. tchr. Royal Irish Acad. of Music, Dublin, 1978—87; dir. of music Cathedral of Immaculate Conception, Memphis, 1988—92; tchr. of music Norton (Mass.) Pub. Schools, 1994—2000, Worcester (Mass.) Pub. Schools, 2000—; organist/dir. of music Murray Unitarian-Universalist Ch., Attleboro, Mass., 1998—; condr. Franklin (Mass.) Cmty. Chorale, 1999—. Tchr. of music Commonwealth-American Sch. of Lausanne, Lausanne Pully, Switzerland, 1973—75; condr. various musical socs., Ireland, 1975—87; co-founder and dir. Ensemble Sine Nomine (early music group), Bray, Ireland, 1979—85, Bray (Ireland) Music Co. V.E.C., 1981—84; founder and dir. Cathedral Music Sch., Memphis, 1989—92, Neverending Cadence (early music group), Franklin, Mass., 1995—99, Quartetto Sine Nomine (vocal quartet), Franklin, Mass., 1999—. Mem.: Orgn. Kodaly Educators, Nat. Assn. for Music Edn., Am. Guild of Organists (sub-dean southeastern Mass. chpt. 2002—03). Avocations: gardening, playing Medieval and Renaissance instruments. Home: 41 Prospect St Franklin MA 02038

FERGUSON, DONALD LITTLEFIELD, lawyer; b. Greenville, S.C., June 10, 1930; s. H. L. and Anne (Littlefield) F.; m. Barbara Wilson, May 20, 1961; children: Donald L. Jr., David Wilson, Robert Neil. BA, Furman U., 1951; LLB, Tulane U., 1954. Bar: S.C. 1954, U.S. Ct. Mil. Appeals 1955, U.S. Dist. Ct. S.C. 1957, U.S. Ct. Appeals (4th cir.) 1974. Assoc. Haynsworth, Marion, McKay & Guerard, Greenville, 1954-61, ptnr., 1961—, sr. ptnr.; ret. Capt. USAF, 1954-57. Mem. ABA, Am. Judicature Soc., S.c. Bar Assn., Poinsett Club, Phi Kappa Phi, Phi Delta Phi. Baptist. Home: 612 Roper Mountain Rd Greenville SC 29615-4227 Office: Haynsworth Sinkler & Boyd 75 Beattie Pl Greenville SC 29601-2130

FERGUSON, DOUGLAS EDWARD, financial executive; b. Bronx, N.Y., Apr. 21, 1940; s. Lawrence and Claire (Billingheimer) F.; m. Cynthia L. Kords, Jan. 29, 1966; children: Elisabeth, Keith, Jonathan. AB, Columbia Coll., 1962. Chartered fin. analyst. Security analyst Heritage Securities/Nat. Securities and Rsch. Corp., N.Y.C., 1963-68; asst. v.p. John W. Bristol & Co., Inc., N.Y.C., 1968-74; v.p. Van Cleef, Jordan & Wood, Inc., N.Y.C., 1974-75; portfolio mgr. Trustees of Columbia U., N.Y.C., 1975-76; mgr. investment svcs. Trascott, Alyson, Craig, Inc., Teaneck, N.J., 1977-84; v.p. portfolio mgmt. Swiss Bank Corp., N.Y.C., 1984-88; chmn. Ferguson Investment Cons., Inc., Sleepy Hollow, 1988—. Contbr. articles to profl. jours. and newspaper. Pres. Westchester ARC, 1991-95; mem. Estate Planning Coun., Westchester County. Mem. N.Y. Soc. Security Analsyts, Rotary Club of the Tarrytowns. Home and Office: Ferguson Investment Cons 528 Bellwood Ave Sleepy Hollow NY 10591-1336

FERGUSON, EARL WILSON, cardiologist, medical executive, telemedicine consultant; b. Lebanon, Pa., Aug. 29, 1943; s. Warren Earl and Norma Laura (Wilson) F.; m. Sun Hye Paik, May 1, 1998; children: Steven Mark, Matthew Earl, Erin Lee. BA in Chemistry, Baylor U., 1965; MD, PhD in Physiology, U. Tex., Galveston, 1970. Diplomate Am. Bd. Internal Medicine, Cardiovascular Disease, Am. Bd. Preventive Medicine. Grad. teaching asst. dept. physiology U. Tex. Med. Br., Galveston, 1967-70, intern medicine, 1970-71; resident medicine, then fellow cardiology Duke U. Med. Ctr., Durham, N.C., 1971-75, mem. assoc. faculty dept. medicine, 1974-75; research assoc. cardiology VA Hosp., Durham, 1974-75; commd. lt. USAF, 1966, advanced through grades to col., 1984-95; staff cardiologist, dir. coronary care Wilford Hall USAF Med. Ctr., Lackland AFB, Tex., 1975-76, chief cardiology, dir. cardiology tng. program, 1983-84; asst. prof. biochemistry, medicine and mil. medicine Uniformed Svcs. U. Health Scis., Bethesda, Md., 1976-80, assoc. prof. physiology, medicine and mil. medicine, 1980-84, asst. comdt., 1977-82, mem. faculty senate, 1979-80, adj. prof. physiology, 1984-93; dir. hosp. services USAF Med. Ctr., Scott AFB, Ill., 1984-86; comdr. USAF Hosp., Little Rock AFB, Ark., 1986-88; dep. command surgeon Mil. Airlift Command, Scott AFB, 1988-90; dir. Aerospace Medicine and Occupl. Health NASA, Washington, 1993-96; comdr. USAF Med. Ctr., Wiesbaden, Germany, 1990-93; CEO Sun Biomed. Techs., 2000—. Cons. to surgeon gen. for cardiology, medicine and physiology USAF, 1980-95; cons. N.J. State Police and N.J. Atty. Gen.'s Office, 1984—, Ind. Atty. Gen.'s Office, 1985-87, NASA, 1997—; mem. life scis. subcom. NASA, 1989-93, interagency working group on telemedicine, 1994-96; adj. assoc. prof. preventive medicine Uniformed Svcs. U. Health Scis., Bethesda, 1993-96; physician So. Sierra Med. Clinic, Ridgecrest, Calif., 1996—; advisor House/Senate Com. on telemedicine and health care, 1994-96; corp. bd. Ridgecrest Regional Hosp., 1997—, bd. dirs., 1998—; bd. dirs. Calif. Telemedicine/Telehealth Ctr., 1997—, chair, 2002—; chief of medicine Ridgecrest Reg. Hosp., 2001—; CEO Sun Biomedical Tech., 2000—. Mem. editl. bd.: Telemedicine and e-Health Jour., 1996—2003; contbr. articles to profl. jours. Rsch. grantee VA, 1974-75, Dept. Def., 1976-82, NASA, 1982-84, Cooperative R&D Agreement, Naval Air Warfare Ctr., China Lake, Calif., 2000—, Dept. Def. SBIR, 2002—; Cardiovascular Health fellow Health Forum/Am. Hosp. Assn., 1999-2000. Ashbel Smith Distinguished Grad., 1993 Fellow Am. Coll. Cardiology (bd. govs. 1985-88), ACP, Am. Coll. Preventive Medicine. Nat. Republican Congressional Com. Bus. Adv. Coun., 2002-. Unitarian Universalist. Avocations: physical fitness activities, flying. E-mail: earl@ridgecrest.ca.us.

FERGUSON, EMMET FEWELL, JR., surgeon; b. DeSoto, Ga., Mar. 28, 1921; s. Emmet Fewell Sr. and Emma Ruth (Smith) F.; Edith Geraldine Strozier, Nov. 26, 1954; children: Berrylin, Joann, Virginia, Fran, Emmet III. Student, U. Ga., 1938-40; BS in Elec. Engring., US Naval Acad., 1943; MD, Med. Coll. Ga., 1950. Diplomate Am. Bd. Surgery, Am. Bd. Colon-Rectal Surgery. Rsch. assoc. U.S. Naval Hosp., St. Albans, N.Y., 1950-51; surg. resident U. Fla., Jacksonville, 1951-53, 54-55, U. Ala., Brimingham, 1953-54; pvt. practice Jacksonville, 1955-93; pres. staff Meth. Hosp., Jacksonville, 1958-60, U. Hosp., Jacksonville, 1972-73; chief colon rectal surgery Bapt., Meth., and St. Vincents Hosps. Clin. prof. surgery coll. medicine U. Fla., 1960-93; mem. med. missions to Honduras, Costa Rica, Nicaragua, Ecuador; del., speaker Pan Am. Med. Meeting, Buenos Aires, 1967; mem. adv. com. coll. medicine U. Fla., Gainesville, 1976-82; chmn. bd. dirs. N.E. Fla. Health Svc. Agy., 1980-2000; mem. Statewide Health Coun., 1980-89, chair, 1980-82. Author: Commonly Memorized Verse, 1991, The Five Most Important Numbers in our World, 1995, Guide to the Major and Minor Springs of Florida, 1997; contbr. articles to profl. jours. Del., speaker from Jax C. of C. to Internat. Exhbn., Moscow, 1959; tchr. Sunday sch. Riverside Bapt. Ch., 1955—, deacon, 1960, 90; del. from Am. Cancer Soc. to Internat. Cancer Soc., Tokyo, 1966; mem. United Way Bd., Jacksonville, 1970-80, chmn. profl. divsn., 1980; chmn. Fla. host com. Pres. Carter's Inauguration, Washington, 1977; life mem. Jacksonville Hist. Soc., pres., 1986-88; mem. Jacksonville Indigent Care Com.; bd. regents Nat. Libr. Medicine, Washington, 1977-81; founder bd. dirs. Bapt. Towers, 1970—; trustee, pres. bd. trustees Riverside Bapt. Day Sch., 1971-75; trustee health sci. ctr. libr. U. Fla., 1972-93; trustee Bartram Sch., 1974-84, pres., 1976-77; mem. exec. com., mem. office state commn. rsch., profl. svc. Am. Cancer Soc. With USN, 1940-46, 50-51, capt. M.C. res. Decorated Am. Def. medal, Naval Res. medal; recipient Disting. Svc. award Fla. divsn. Am. Cancer Soc., Tampa, 1972, 75, Silver Beaver award Boy Scouts Am., 1986, Emmet Ferguson award U. Fla. Health Sci. Ctr. Fellow ACS (pres. Fla. chpt. 1968), Am. Soc. Surgery Alimentary Tract, Am. Soc. Colon Rectal Surgeons, Piedmont Soc. Colon Rectal Surgeons (pres. 1996-97), Fla. Soc. Colon Rectal Surgeons (pres. 1972-74, 76-78); mem. AMA, Fla. Med. Assn. (life), So. Med. Assn., Southeastern Surg. Congress (Best Motion Picture award 1975), Duval County Med. Soc. (life, editor bull. 1970-73, pres. 1975-76), Navy League (life, pres. Jacksonville coun. 1983-84, Commendation award 1984), Sons Confederate Vets., Rotary (bd. dirs. 1978-80, chmn. com. polio plus 1987-88, Commendation award 1989), St. John's Dinner Club (pres. 1975-78, Commendation award 1978), Fla. Yacht Club (life), River Club, Kappa Sigma. Democrat. Avocations: hunting, fishing, tennis, sailing, sculpture. E-mail: effjr@aol.com.

FERGUSON, ESTHER B. philanthropist; b. Sumter, S.C., Jan. 24, 1943; d. Norwood Fleming Baskin and Nan Richardson Rickenbaker; m. George William Moore (div.); m. James Larnard Ferguson. BA in Polit. Sci./Art History, U. S.C.; LLD, William Penn Coll., 1983; DHL, Dominican Coll., 1987, U. Pacific, 1990, Johnson and Wales U., 1996, Coker Coll., 1996. Founder Nat. Drop-Out Prevention Fund & Ctr., Clemson U., 1985—, Study Abroad Program, Trujillo, Spain, 1995; bd. dirs. Charleston Symphony Orchestra, S.C., 1990-2000; vice-chmn. Young Concert Artists, N.Y.C., 1982-2000; bd. dirs. Spoleto U.S.A., Charleston, 1983-2000, Internat. Found. for Edn. and Self-Help, Phoenix, 1980—, Monmouth (N.J.) Coll., 1985-89, Coke Coll., Hartsville, S.C., 1993-96; founder, chair Am. Mental Health Resources, 1999—. Contbr. articles to profl. publs. and newspapers. Episcopalian. Republican. Avocations: reading, skiing, shooting, internat. travel. Office: PO Box 1457 Charleston SC 29402

FERGUSON, EVA DREIKURS, psychologist, educator, researcher, author; d. Rudolf and Sadie (Ellis) Dreikurs; m. John A. Ferguson, Jan. 28, 1950 (div. 1969); children: Rodney, Beth, Bruce, Linda. BA with honors, U. Ill., 1950; MA with honors, Melbourne U., Australia, 1953; PhD, Northwestern U., 1956. Sociologist Lady Gowrie Child Ctr., Melbourne, 1951-52; intern in psychology Ill. Neuropsychiat. Hosp., Chgo., 1954-55; postdoctoral fellow Western Psychiat. Inst., Pitts., 1956-58, psychologist Craig House for Children, Pitts., 1959-62; asst. prof. psychology Melbourne U., 1962-65, assoc. prof. psychology So. Ill. U., Edwardsville, 1965-69, prof., 1969—. Mem. staff Alfred Adler Inst., Chgo., 1965—; vis. prof. U. Vt., 1970, 1971—72, Northwestern U., 1979; chair Internat. Com. for Adlerian Summer Schs. and Insts., 1978—; vis. scholar U. Calif., Berkeley, 1985—86, Berkeley, 1992—93, Berkeley, 1999, U. Tex., Austin, 1992; vis. prof. U. Calif., Berkeley, 2000. Author: Motivation: An Experimental Approach, 1976, 82, Adlerian Theory: An Introduction, 1984; author: Motivation: A Biosocial and Cognitive Integration of Motivation and Emotion, 2000; editor: Equality and Social Interest: Lectures of ICASSI in Chios, 1990; contbr. articles to profl. jours. Recipient award in sociology, Chi Omega, 1950, Rsch. Scholar award, Sigma Xi Club So. Ill. U., Edwardsville, 1980, 1995, 2001. Fellow APA, Am. Psychol. Soc.; mem. AAAS (life), N.Am. Soc. Adlerian Psychology, Psychonomic Soc., Sigma Xi. Office: Dept Psychology So Ill U Edwardsville IL 62026-1121 Fax: 618-650-5087. E-mail: efergus@siue.edu.

FERGUSON, GARY WARREN, retired public relations executive; b. Stockton, Kans., May 5, 1925; s. Richard and Nelle (McBee) F.; m. Doris Drisler, Oct. 2, 1948; children: Arthur Richard, Frances (Mrs. Gregory H. Gebhart), Robert Warren, Scott William. AB, Yale U., 1946; MS in Journalism, Columbia U., 1948. Reporter Providence Jour. Bull., 1948-49, Richmond (Va.) News Leader, 1949-52, St. Louis Post-Dispatch, 1954-55, spl. writer, 1955-60; counselor Fleishman-Hillard, Inc., St. Louis, 1961-62, sr. ptnr., 1962-71; pres. Gary Ferguson Assocs., Inc., 1971-93. Vice-chmn. Dorf and Stanton Comm., Inc., 1988-93; editorial cons., 1993-99. Mem. founding bd. Greater St. Louis Coun. Alcoholism, 1965, pres., 1966-69; pres. mental Health Assn., St. Louis, 1980-81; trustee World Affairs Coun. St. Louis, 1990-95. Recipient Bishop's award Episcopal Diocese Mo., 1965. Mem. Soc. Profl. Journalists. Home: 1 Colonial Village Ct Apt D Saint Louis MO 63119-2722

FERGUSON, GERALD PAUL, lawyer; b. Teaneck, N.J., Oct. 17, 1951; s. James Richard and Ilene Veronica (Meyer) F.; m. Nancy Ivers, Aug. 20, 1977; 1 child, James Ralph. BA, Fairleigh Dickinson U., 1974; JD, Capital U., 1979. Bar: Ohio 1979, U.S. Dist. Ct. (so. dist.) Ohio 1980, U.S. Ct. Appeals (6th cir.) 1986, U.S. Supreme Ct. 1990. Ptnr. Vorys, Sater, Seymour and Pease, Columbus, 1979—; mem. rules adv. com. Ohio Supreme Ct., Columbus, 1993. Mem. ABA (litigation sect., mem. trial evidence subcom. 1985-86), Ohio State Bar Assn. (mem. jud. adv. and legal reform com., unauthorized practice law com. 1985-90), Columbus Bar Assn. (chmn. juror subcom. 1979-86). Republican. Roman Catholic. Avocations: tennis, golf, fishing. Office: Vorys Sater Seymour & Pease 52 E Gay St Columbus OH 43215-3161 E-mail: gpferguson@vssp.com.

FERGUSON, GLENN WALKER, lecturer, author; b. Syracuse, N.Y., Jan. 28, 1929; s. Forrest Erwin and Mabel Gertrude (Walker) F.; m. Patricia Lou Head, June 22, 1950; children: Bruce Walker, Sherry Lynn, Scott Sherwood. BA, Cornell U., 1950, MBA, 1951; grad., U. Santo Tomas, Manila, 1953; student, U. Chgo. Law Sch., 1955-56; JD, U. Pitts., 1957; D.S. (hon.), Worcester Poly. Inst., 1973; LL.D. (hon.), Sacred Heart U., 1974; DHL (hon.), Am. U. Paris, 1995. Staff assoc. Govtl. Affairs Inst., Washington, 1954—55; asst. editor, asst. sec.-treas. Am. Judicature Soc., Chgo., 1955—56; asst. to chancellor and asst. dean Grad. Sch. Pub. Affairs, U. Pitts., 1956—60; with McKinsey & Co. (mgmt. cons.), Washington, 1960—61, Peace Corps, 1961—64, rep. Thailand, 1961—63, assoc. dir., 1963—64; dir. Vols. in Svc. to Am., Washington, 1964—66; U.S. ambassador to Kenya, 1966—69; chancellor L.I. U., 1969—70; pres. Clark U., 1970—73, U. Conn., 1973—78, Radio Free Europe/Radio Liberty, Munich, Canada, 1978—82, Lincoln Ctr. Performing Arts, N.Y.C., 1983—84, Equity for Africa, 1985—92, The Am. U. of Paris, 1992—95. Cons. govt. agys., 1959-64, TV moderator fgn. affairs, Pitts., 1957-60; USIS lectr. India, Sudan, Uruguay, Argentina, 1984-92; vis. prof. fgn. policy Conn. Coll., U. R.I., 1990-91; cons. Internat. Exec. Svc. Corps., Uruguay, 1992. Author: (aphorisms) Unconventional Wisdom, 1999, (essays) Americana Against the Grain, 1999, Tilting at Religion, 2003; contbr. articles to profl. jours. Human rights commr. City of Worcester, Mass., 1971-72; trustee Cornell U., 1972-76, former mem. corp. bds.; mem. French-Am. Commn. for Ednl. Exch., 1992-95. 1st lt. USAF, 1951-53, Korea. Recipient Arthur S. Flemming award, 1968; Asso. fellow Timothy Dwight Coll., Yale U. Mem.: Am. Birding Assn., ABA, Coun. Am. Ambs. (bd. dirs. 1996—2003), Fgn. Policy Assn. (bd. dirs. 1974—83), Coun. Fgn. Rels., Fed. Bar Assn., Nat. Press Club, Phi Delta Phi, Psi Upsilon, Phi Beta Kappa. Address: 1060 Governor Dempsey Dr Santa Fe NM 87501-1078

FERGUSON, HAROLD LAVERNE, JR., lawyer; b. Cleveland, Miss., Dec. 3, 1938; s. Harold Laverne and Allene Thompson (Burford) F.; m. Jamie Frances Flemming, Nov. 20, 1965; children: Harold Laverne III, Samuel Christopher, Julie Allene. BA in Pub. Adminstrn., U. Miss., 1960; JD, Samford U., 1973. Bar: Ala. 1973. Ptnr. Spain, Gillon, Riley, Tate & Etheredge, Birmingham, Ala., 1973-80, Dominick, Fletcher, Yeilding, Wood & Lloyd P.A., Birmingham, 1980-98, Ferguson, Frost & Dodson LLP, Birmingham, 1998—. Served with Miss. and Tenn. N.G., 1955-63. Mem. ABA, Ala. Bar Assn., Tenn. Bar Assn., Birmingham Bar Assn., Ala. Def. Lawyers Assn., Def. Rsch. Inst., Fedn. Def. and Corp. Counsel, Birmingham Ole Miss. Alumni Club (pres. 1985-86), Rotary. Republican. Baptist. Home: 440 Hillwood Dr Birmingham AL 35209-5346 E-mail: hlf@ffdlaw.com.

FERGUSON, J. BRIAN, chemicals executive; b. Lubbock, Tex., June 16, 1954; B in Chem. Engring., Ariz. State U., 1977. Rsch. and devel. staff Eastman Kodak Co., Longview, Tex., 1977, various mfg. and staff pos., various bus. and strategic planning pos. Kingsport, Tenn., 1989, Washington, 1992—94; v.p. industry and fed. affairs Eastman Co., Washington, 1994, mng. dir. for Gtr. China Hong Kong; mng. dir. Eastman Chem. Asia Pacific Pte., Ltd., Singapore; pres. Eastman Co. Polymers Group, 1999, Eastman Co. Chems. Group, 2001; chmn., CEO Eastman Chem. Co., Kingsport, Tenn., 2002—. Office: Eastman Chem Co PO Box 511 100 N Eastman Rd Kingsport TN 37662-5075

FERGUSON, J. SCOTT, quality management coordinator; b. Decatur, Ill., June 14, 1970; s. Robert Lynn Ferguson and Roxanne Joyce Van Buskirk. Student, So. U., 1988—90, U. Houston, 1996, U. Phoenix, 2000—. CNA. Quality improvement rep. MacGregor Med. Assn., Houston, 1995-97; quality mgmt. coord., data analyst CIGNA Healthcare, Houston, 1998-99; sr. info. analyst Tex. Children's Health Plan, 2000—. Mem. Nat. Assn. for Healthcare Quality. Avocations: architecture, outdoor fitness activities, computers, music. Home: Apt 501 7979 Westheimer Rd Houston TX 77063-4511 E-mail: jsfergus@texaschildrenshospital.org.

FERGUSON, JAMES, anthropologist, educator; b. L.A., Calif., June 16, 1959; s. James Gordon and Jane Hardin Ferguson; life ptnr. Liisa H. Malkki, Dec. 16, 1959; children: Aila Sophia, Elias William. PhD, Harvard U., 1985; BA, U. Calif. Santa Barbara, 1979; MA, Harvard U., 1985. Prof. Anthropology U. Calif. Irvine, 1998—, chair, dept. anthropology, 1999—, dir. Critical Theory Inst., 2001—. Author: (book) The Anti-politics Machine: 'Development', Depoliticization, and Bureaucratic Power in Lesotho; editor: Culture, Power, Place: Explorations in Critical Anthropology, Anthropological Locations: Boundaries and Grounds of a Field Science; author: Expectations of Modernity: Myths and Meanings of Urban Life on the Zambian Copperbelt. Recipient Hon. Simon Vis. Prof., U. Manchester, 1998; fellow, Social Sci. Rsch. Coun., 1982, 1985, Ctr. for Advanced Study in Behavioral Scis., 2000—01, Social Sci. Rsch. Coun., 1989; Fulbright fellow, US Internat. Comm. Agy., 1982. Fellow: Am. Anthrop. Assn.; mem.: African Studies Assn., Am. Ethnol. Soc. Office: Dept Anthropology Univ California Irvine Irvine CA 92697-5100

FERGUSON, JAMES CLARKE, mathematician, algorithmist; b. Spokane, Wash., June 23, 1938; s. James Forsythe and Dorothy Eileen (Dillon) F. MS in Math., U. Wash., 1963; PhD in Math., U. N.Mex., 1984. Sci. programmer Boeing, Seattle, 1960-64; staff mem. GE Tech. Mil. Planning Office, Santa Barbara, Calif., 1964-66; mathematician TRW, Inc., Redondo Beach, Calif., 1966-71, Teledyne-Ryan Aero., San Diego, 1971-77; staff mem. Los Alamos (N.Mex.) Nat. Lab., 1977-85; sr. scientist Tektronix, Beaverton, Oreg., 1985-87, BBN Systems and Techs. Corp., Bellevue, Wash., 1987-92; with Point Control, Eugene, 1993-94, Camax Mfg. Technologies, Eugene, 1994-95; mathematician SDRC/Camax, Eugene, 1995-2000, consulting mathematician, 2001—. Cons. in field, 1975-87. Co-author: Key Works in Geometric Modeling, 1991, Fundamental Developments of Computer Aided Geometric Modeling, 1992; contbr. articles to profl. jours. Recipient advanced study fellowship, Los Alamos Nat. Lab., 1981. Mem. Assn. Computing Machinery, Soc. Indsl. and Applied Math. Achievements include introduction of parametric curve and surface techniques into computer aided geometric design field; complete classification of parametric planar cubics; application of parametric curve techniques to problem of shape preservation. E-mail: dddjim@earthlink.net.

FERGUSON, JAMES EDWARD, II, obstetrician, gynecologist, maternal-fetal medicine specialist; b. Glendale, Calif., Oct. 25, 1951; m. Lynn Corpening, June 21, 1975; children: James Edward III, David Gregory, Joshua Scott. Student, USCG Acad., 1969-71; AB in History, Marquette U., 1973; MD, Wake Forest U., 1977. Diplomate Nat. Bd. Med. Examiners, Am. Bd. Ob-Gyn., Am. Bd. Maternal and Fetal Medicine. Intern USPHS Hosp., San Francisco, 1977—78; resident in ob-gyn. Stanford (Calif.) U. Sch. Medicine, 1978—80, fellow in ob-gyn., 1982—84, asst. prof. ob-gyn., 1984—87, chief divsn. maternal-fetal medicine dept. ob-gyn., 1985—87, dir. prenatal diagnosis program dept. ob-gyn., 1986—87; chief resident Wake Forest U. Bowman Gray Sch. Medicine, Winston-Salem, NC, 1980—81, clin. faculty, 1981—82; pvt. practice Pollak, Zammit, Ferguson, MD, P.C., Winston-Salem, NC, 1981—82; asst. prof. ob-gyn. U. Va. Sch. Medicine, Charlottesville, 1987—90, assoc. prof. depts. ob-gyn. and radiology, 1990—91, assoc. prof. dept. ob-gyn., assoc. prof. dept. radiology, 1991—96, dir. prenatal diagnosis and treatment unit dept. ob-gyn., 1989—2000, dir. divsn. maternal-fetal medicine dept. ob-gyn., 1990—2002, John Nokes prof. ob-gyn., 1996—2002, prof. dept. radiology, 1996—2002; med. dir. perinatal svcs. U. Va. Hosp., Charlottesville, 1990—96, med. dir. women's svcs., 1997—2002; John W. Green Jr. prof., chair dept. ob-gyn. U. Ky. Coll. Medicine, Lexington, 2002—. Attending staff mem. Chandler Med. Ctr., 2002—, U. Va. Hosp., 1987-2002, Va. Bapt. Hosp., 1996-2002, Stanford U. Hosp., 1982-87, Forsyth Meml. Hosp., Winston-Salem, 1981-82, Med. Park Hosp., Winston-Salem, 1981-82; assoc. staff mem. Va. Bapt. Hosp., Lynchburg, 1992-96, Santa Clara Valley Med. Ctr., San Jose, Calif., 1982-87; cons. Mid-Coastal Calif. Perinatal Outreach Program, Stanford U., 1982-87, San Joaquin Gen. Hosp., Stockton, Calif., 1985-87, Va. Bapt. Hosp., Lynchburg, 1992-2002; fellow Project Hope, maternal-fetal medicine program, Krakow, Poland, 1987, 89, others; mem. numerous coms. in field. Editl. referee Am. Jour. Ob-Gyn., Ob-Gyn. Jour., Clin. Chemistry Jour., Am. Jour. Human Genetics, Am. Jour. Perinatology, Jour. Reproduction, Fertility and Devel., Jour. Maternal-Fetal Medicine; obstet. editl. cons. Perinatal Continuing Edn. Program, 1991-2002; contbr. articles to profl. jours., chpts. to books in field. Hon. chmn. March of Dimes Walkathon, U. Va. Health Scis. Ctr., 1990; active task force on smoking and pregnancy, Am. Lung Assn. of Santa Clara-San Benito Counties, 1983; bd. dirs. Ednam Forest Owners Assn., Inc., 1993-96; vol. physician Camp Va., Goshen. Recipient numerous grants in field, including Dept. Mental Health, Retardation and Substance Abuse, Commonwealth of Va., 1992-93, Perinatal Nurse Liaison Contract, 1991-92, others. Fellow ACOG (examiner for specialty oral bds. 1995—, mem. health care partnerships adv. com. to DMAS Va. sect. 1995); mem. AAAS, Am. Gynecol. and Obstets. Soc., Am. Physiol. Soc., Am. Inst. Ultrasound in Medicine (sr.), Internat. Cytokine Soc., South Atlantic Assn. Ob-Gyn., Soc. Gynecologic Investigation, Soc. Pfor Maternal-Fetal Medicine and Perinatal Obstetricians (bd. dirs. 1996-99, sec.-treas. 2000—), Frank Lock Soc., Assn. Profs. Ob-Gyn., So. Ob-Gyn. Seminar, Va. Ob-Gyn. Soc., U. Va. Residents' Soc. (hon.), N.C. Ob-Gyn. Soc. (hon.), Phi Beta Kappa, Phi Alpha Theta. Achievements include research in prenatal diagnostic techniques, prostaglandins and cervical compliance, fetal-pelvic disproportion, preterm labor, control of parathyroid hormone-related protein (PTHrP) secretion in myometrial and human umbilical vein endothelial (HUVEC) cells in culture, expression of PTHrP and its receptor in human myometrium in pregnancies complicated by preterm labor, expression of PTHrP and its receptor in placental and umbilical vessels in pregnancies complicated by pregnancy-induced hypertension. Home: 236 Desha Rd Lexington KY 40502 Office: U Ky Coll Medicine Dept Ob-Gyn 800 S Rose St Rm C375 Lexington KY 40536 E-mail: jef@uky.edu.

FERGUSON, JO MCCOWN, lawyer; b. Central City, Ky., Apr. 5, 1915; s. Jo Marvin and Willie Mae (Cain) F.; m. Margarita Hauser, July 12, 1947; children— Rita, Diane, Jo Frances. AB, U. Ky., 1937, LL.B., 1939. Bar: Ky. 1938. Practiced in, Central City, 1939-42; asst. atty. gen., 1948-56; atty. gen., 1956-60; commr. econ. security, 1960-61; partner firm Harper, Ferguson & Davis. Mcpl. bd. counsel, 1961-91. Chmn. Gov.'s Com. on Constl. Revision, 1961-62; chmn. Gov.'s Task Force on Fin., 1976-77; pres. Ky. Hist. Soc., 1988-90; chief Property Control br. Mil. Govt., Bavaria, 1946-47. Capt. AUS, 1944-47, ETO. Decorated Brigadier d'Honneur 3eme Regiment Anjou, French Army. Mem. ABA, Ky. Bar Assn., VFW, So. Attys. Gen. (chmn. 1957-58). Democrat. Episcopalian. Home: 403 Duff Ln Louisville KY 40207-1524

FERGUSON, JOHN BARCLAY, biology educator; b. Balt., July 5, 1947; s. John Miller and Helen (Sucro) F.; m. Jane Hough, June 28, 1970 (div. 1987); children: Hallam H., Gillian D.; m. Valeri J. Thomson, July 1, 1988; children: Samantha T., Fiona T. BS, Brown U., 1969; PhD, Yale U., 1973. Asst. prof. Bard Coll., Annandale, N.Y., 1977-83, assoc. prof., 1983-92, prof., 1992—, health professions advisor, 1985—. Contbr. to Microsoft Encarta 97 CD-ROM, 1 book and articles to profl. jours. Bd. trustees Ch. St. John Evangelist, Barrytown, N.Y., 1988—. NIH Postdoctoral fellow, 1974-76. Mem. AAAS, Am. Soc. Microbiology, N.Y. Acad. Scis., Sigma Xi. Home: 1469 Annandale Rd Red Hook NY 12571-3200 Office: Bard Coll Dept Biology Annandale On Hudson NY 12504 E-mail: ferguson@bard.edu.

FERGUSON, JOHN LEWIS, state historian; b. Nashville, Ark., Mar. 1, 1926; s. Clarence Walter and Nannye Nell (McCrary) F.; m. Oris Brandon, June 9, 1956; children— Clay Walt, Ora Lee. B.A., Henderson State Tchrs. Coll., 1950; M.A., U. Ark., 1952; Ph.D., Tulane U., 1960. Head dept. social studies Conway Bapt. Coll., Ark., 1952-58; asst. prof. history Ark. Poly. Coll., Russellville, 1958-60; state historian Ark. History Commn., Little Rock, 1960— . Editor: Arkansas and the Civil War, 1965; author: Arkansas Lives, 1965; co-author: Historic Arkansas, 1966. Baptist. Home: 12 Pilot Point Pl Little Rock AR 72205-2856 Office: Ark History Commn 1 Capitol Mall Little Rock AR 72201-1049

FERGUSON, JOHN MARSHALL, retired federal judge; b. Marion, Ill., Oct. 14, 1921; s. John Marshall and Vessie (Widdows) F.; m. Jeanne Harmon, Sept. 23, 1950; children: Marcia Ferguson Velde, Mark Harmon, John Scott, Mary Sue Holley. Student, So. Ill. U., 1939-41, S.E. Mo. Tchrs. Coll., 1941; LLB, JD, Washington U., St. Louis, 1948. Bar: Ill. 1949, U.S. Ct. Appeals (7th cir.) 1956, U.S. Supreme Ct. 1960. Asst. mgr. I.W. Rogers Theaters, Inc., Anna, Ill., 1934-42; atty. U.S. Fidelity & Guaranty Co., St. Louis, 1948-51; assoc. Baker, Kagy & Wagner, East St. Louis, Ill., 1951-56, ptnr., 1956-59, Wagner, Conner, Ferguson, Bertrand & Baker, East St. Louis and Belleville, Ill., 1959-72; magistrate judge U.S. Dist. Ct. (so. dist.) Ill., 1990-94. Pres. bd. Arch Aircraft, Inc., 1966-68; disciplinary commr. Ill. Supreme Ct., 1957-90, mem. joint com. on revision disciplinary rules, 1972-74; mem. hearing bd. Ill. Registration and Disciplinary Commn., 1974-90; pres. 1st Dist. Fedn. Bar Assns. Precinct committeeman Stookey Twp., St. Clair County (Ill.) Republican Com., 1958-62; Bd. dirs., v.p. East St. Louis chpt. ARC. Capt. AUS, 1942-45. Mem. ABA, Ill. Bar Assn. (profl. responsibility com. 1975-86, chmn. 1983-84), St. Clair County Bar Assn., 7th Fed. Cir. Bar Assn. (bd. govs.), Ill. Club (govs., pres. 1966-67), East St. Louis City Club (pres. 1960-61), Ill. Club (gov. pres. 1966-67), St. Clair Country Club (Belleville, pres. 1972-73), Masons, Elks, Delta Theta Phi. Home: 12 Oak Knoll Pl Belleville IL 62223-1817 E-mail: jferg7@juno.com.

FERGUSON, JOHN PATRICK, medical center executive; b. Weehawken, N.J., Jan. 22, 1949; s. Donald George and Margaret (Rienzo) F.; m. Gene Marie Promersperger, Jan. 16, 1971; children: Adam, David, Kate. BS in Econs., St. Peter's Coll., 1970; MBA in Hosp. Adminstrn., George Washington U., 1973. Sr. v.p. St. Vincent's Hosp., N.Y.C., 1972-81; v.p. ops. Hackensack (N.J.) Univ. Med. Ctr., 1981-85, sr. v.p., 1985, acting pres., chief exec. officer, 1985-86, pres., chief exec. officer, 1986—. Adj. faculty New Sch. for Social Rsch. Grad. Sch. Mgmt. and Urban Professions, N.Y.C., 1978—84; pres. Met. Health Adminstrs., N.Y.C., 1977—78; chmn. bd. trustees Univ. Health Sys. (now N.J. Coun. Tchg. Hosps.), Trenton, 1999—2001, vice chmn., 2002—; rep. to coun. on tchg. hosps. Assn. Am. Med. Coll., 1994—97; abstract presenter China-U.S. Conf. on Managing Hosps., 1987; bd. dirs. Commerce Bank/North; trustee UMDNJ, 2002—; mem. jobs growth and econ. devel. commn. State of N.J., 2002—. Co-chmn. health transition team Gov.-elect Jim McGreevey, 2001; trustee Molly Found. for Diabetes Rsch., 1995—; commr. Econ. Devel. Commn. of City of Hackensack, 1996—2002; founding commr. Bergen County Econ. Devel. Corp., 1996—; mem., bd. govs. Greater N.Y. Hosp. Assn., 2000—; mem., trustee St. Peter's Coll., 2000—, QualCare Alliance Networks, Inc., 2000—, Martha's Vineyard Hosp., Inc., 2000—; mem. exec adv. com. State of N.J. Commn. on Cancer Rsch., 2000; chmn. bd. dirs. Martha's Vineyard Hosp., 2002—. Named Man of Yr., Nat. Burn Victim Found., 1994, One of Top 12 Up and Coming Healthcare Execs., Modern Healthcare mag., 1988, One of 50 Bus. People to Watch for the 1990's, N.J. Bus. Jour., 1990, Citizen of Yr., Meadowlands Regional C. of C., 1993, Humanitarian of Yr., Make A Wish Found., 1996, Disting. Citizen of N.J., Ramapo Coll. Found., 1998, Humanitarian of Yr., Boys' Towns of Italy, 1999; named to, Found. for Free Enterprise Hall of Fame, 2002; recipient Man of Yr. award, Tomorrow's Children's Fund, 1989, Medallion award, Bergen C.C., 1993, Disting. Cmty. Svc. award, Anti-Defamation League, 1995, Disting. Citizen award, Hackensack C. of C., 1995, Disting. Cmty. Health Svc. award, Bergen County Bd. of Chosen Freeholders, 1996, Pres.'s award, N.J. State Nurses Assn., 1999, Med. Exec. award, Acad. Medicine N.J., 2000, Good Scout award, No. N.J. Coun. Boy Scouts Am., 2000, Ellis Island medal of honor, 2002, Disting. Alumni award for profl. achievement, St. Peter's Coll., 2002, Humanitarian award, Nat. Conf. for Cmty. and Justice, 2003. Fellow: Am. Coll. Healthcare Execs. (regent, gov. dist. II 1994—99); mem.: Met. Health Adminstrn. Assn. (Distinction award 1997), Am. Fedn. for Aging Rsch. (bd. dirs. 1997—2000), Commerce and Industry Assn. N.J. (bd. dirs. 1996—, chmn.'s award for Outstanding Leadership 1997), Am. Heart Assn. (pres. Mid-Bergen divsn. 1992—93, bd. dirs. 1993—94), Cath. Hosp. Assn., Am. Hosp. Assn. Office: Hackensack U Med Ctr 30 Prospect Ave Hackensack NJ 07601-1912

FERGUSON, JULIE ANN, physical education educator; b. Maquoketa, Iowa, June 19, 1958; d. Donald Hayes and Bonnie Lea (Bullock) Maxey; m. John Stephan Ferguson, Aug. 10, 1985; children: Dawn Ann, John Ryan, John Scott. BS in Edn., U. Mo., 1980; MS in Athletic Adminstrn., U. Ill., 1982. Cert. tchr. Mo. Sub. tchr. Ritenour Dist., St. Louis, 1978-80; asst. women's basketball coach U. Ill., Champaign, 1980-82, instr. phys. edn., 1981-82, adminstrv. asst. Athletic Assn., 1982-83; dir. championships, supr. officials Big Eight Conf., Kansas City, Mo., 1983-90; instr. phys. edn., head volleyball and girls basketball coach Lee's Summit (Mo.) Sch. Dist., 1990—. Speaker, clin. coord. Fellowship Christian Athletes, Kansas City, 1986; selection com. U. Mo., Kansas City, 1987, 88; scholar athlete Kansas City Star, 1989; coach, tour adminstr. Athletes in Action Basketball Team to China and Far East, 1984; tour adminstr. Big Eight Conf. Basketball Tour to Czechoslovakia, 1990. Deacon Lee's Summit Christian Ch., 1990--. Named to, Ritenour H.S. Hall of Fame, 1998. Mem. (life) U. Mo. Columbia Alumni Assn., (life) U. Ill. Alumni Assn., Women's Basketball Coaches Assn., Am. Volleyball Coaches Assn., Coun. Collegiate Women Athletic Adminstrs., Am. Alliance Health, Physical Edn., Recreation and Dance Fellowship Christian Athletes (Tchr. of Yr. finalist Lee's Summit Sch. Dist. 1997—, Excellence in Tchg. award). Avocations: horseback riding, cross stitch, sports, family. Home: 4151 SE Paddock Cir Lees Summit MO 64082-4926

FERGUSON, KINGSLEY GEORGE, retired psychologist; b. Newcastle-on-Tyne, Eng., Apr. 13, 1921; emigrated to Can., 1927; s. William George and Isobel (Finnegan) F. BA in English and French, U. Western Ont., 1943; MA in Psychology, U. Toronto, 1951, PhD, 1956. Diplomate Am. Bd. Profl. Psychology. Staff psychologist Sunnybrook Vets. Hosp., Toronto, Ont., Can., 1949-50; chief psychologist Westminster Vets. Hosp., London, Ont., Can., 1950-61, Montreal Gen. Hosp., Que., Can., 1961-68; psychologist-in-chief Clarke Inst. Psychiatry, Toronto, 1968-86. Chmn. Ont. Bd. Examiners in Psychology, Toronto, 1972-77. Served to lt. Can. Navy, 1942-45 Fellow Can. Psychol. Assn.; mem. Am. Psychol. Assn., Ont. Psychol. Assn. (pres. 1959-60; Lifetime Achievement award 1994-97). Address: 694 Sammon Ave Toronto ON Canada M4C 2E4 E-mail: geordie614@sympatico.ca.

FERGUSON, KITTY GAIL, writer, lecturer; b. San Antonio, Dec. 16, 1941; d. Herman Alvin and Prestyne Norma (Hocker) Vetter; m. Yale Hicks Ferguson, Aug. 26, 1961; children: Colin Yale, Duff Christopher, Caitlin Christiana. BA, Juilliard Sch. of Music, 1965, MS, 1966. Freelance singer, N.Y.C., 1965-72; music dir. Cmty. Presbyn. Ch., Chester, N.J., 1974-77; music dir./founder Chester Ensemble, 1975-80; music dir. Brookside (N.J.) Cmty. Ch., 1977-82, Liberty Corner Presbyn. Ch., Liberty Corner, N.J., 1982-86. John Elbridge Hines lectr. sci. and religion Episcopal Diocese of Newark, 1994; bd. advisors John Templeton Found., 2001—; coord. St. Peter's-Kothapallimitta Companionship St. Peter's Episcopal Ch., Morristown, NJ, 2000—. Author: Black Holes in Spacetime, 1991, Stephen Hawking: Quest for a Theory of Everything, 1992, 1993, The Fire in the Equations: Science, Religion, and the Search for God, 1994, 1995, Prisons of Light: Black Holes, 1996, 1998, Measuring the Universe: Our Historic Quest to Chart the Horizons of Space and Time, 1999, 2000, Tycho and Kepler: The Unlikely Partnership That Changed Forever Our Understanding of the Heavens, 2002, 2003. Office: Rita Rosenkranz Lit Agy 440 W End Ave #15D New York NY 10024

FERGUSON, LARRY P. food products executive; BS, Okla. St. Univ. With Schreiber Foods Inc., Green Bay, Wis., 1975—, pres., CEO, 1999—. Office: Schreiber Foods Inc 425 Pine St Green Bay WI 54301*

FERGUSON, LEWIS LEROY, retired senior correspondent; b. Ponca City, Okla., Jan. 9, 1934; s. Luther LeRoy and Henrietta Marie (Mueller) F.; m. Sue Ann Thomson, June 5, 1958; children: John Michael, Diane Marie. BA in Journalism, U. Okla., 1956, MA in Journalism, 1964. Sports and wire editor Ponca City (Okla.) News, 1958-60; newsman The AP, Okla. City, 1960, Sioux Falls, S.D., 1960-62, night editor, sports editor Mpls., 1962-68, sports editor Kans. City, Mo., 1968-70, corr. in charge Topeka, 1970-99; ret., 1999; columnist Topeka Capital-Jour., 2001. Trustee Karl Menninger Lecture Series, 1982—, pres., 1988; trustee William Allen White Found., 1987-2000; cons. Dole Inst., 2002—. Cons. on cameras in the courtroom Kans. Supreme Ct., Topeka, 1987-88; mem. Kans. Gov.'s Task Force on Sch. Finance, 2000; bd. dirs. Workforce of Kans., 2002-03; cons. Kans. Press. Assn., 2002; acive Kans. Bd. Regents, 2001—, Washburn U. Bd. Regents, 2003—. Capt. USAR, 1956-64. Recipient Outstanding Journalism Grad. award Sigma Delta Chi, U. Okla., 1956, AP Staffer of Yr. award Kans. City Star, 1992, Kans. Justice award Kans. Supreme Ct., 1993, Disting. Alumnus award Herbert Journalism Sch., U. Okla., 1996; featured in 1984 AP promotional film "One of a Kind" narrated by former NBC anchor John Chanselor. Mem. Kans. Bar Assn. (Bar-Media 2002). Lutheran. Avocations: internet, statistics, fishing. E-mail: lferguson@networksplus.net.

FERGUSON, LLOYD ELBERT, retired manufacturing engineer; b. Denver, Mar. 5, 1942; s. Lloyd Elbert Ferguson and Ellen Jane (Schneider) Romero; m. Patricia Valine Hughes, May 25, 1963; children: Theresa Renee, Edwin Bateman. BS in Engring., Nova Internat. Coll., 1983. Cert. hypnotherapist, geometric tolerance instr. Crew leader FTS Corp., Denver, 1968-72; program engr. Sundstrand Corp., Denver, 1972-87, sr. assoc. project engr., 1987-90, sr. liaison engr., 1990-93; sr. planning engr. Hamilton Sundstrand Corp., Denver, 1990-2000; ret., 2000. V.p. Valine Corp. Lic. practitioner of religious sci. United Ch. of Religious Sci., L.A.; team capt. March of Dimes Team Walk, Danver, 1987; mem. AT&T Telephone Pioneer Clowns for Charity. Recipient recognition award AT&T Telephone Pioneers, 1990 Mem. Soc. Mfg. Engrs. (chmn. local chpt. 1988, zone chmn. 1989, achievement award 1984, 86, recognition award 1986, 90, appreciation award 1988), Nat. Mgmt. Assn. (cert., program instr. 1982—, honor award 1987, 90), Am. Indian Sci. and Engring. Soc., Colo. Clowns. Mem. United Ch. of Religious Sci. Home: 10983 W 76th Dr Arvada CO 80005-3481

FERGUSON, MARGARET ANN, tax consultant; b. Steuben County, Ind., Mar. 24, 1933; d. Leo C. and Ruth Virginia (Engle) Wolf; m. Billy Hugh Ferguson, Feb. 15, 1955 (dec. Oct. 1971); children: Theresa Ruth, Scott Earl, Wade Leo, Luke, Angela, Cynthia, Brenda. AA in Psychology/Social Svs., Palomar Coll., San Marcos, Calif., 1977; BA in Behavioral Sci., Nat. U., Vista, Calif., 1980. Enrolled agt. Office mgr., adminstr. asst. Better Bus. Bur., San Diego, 1979-82; tax technician IRS, Oceanside, Calif., 1982-84, problem resolution tax specialist, 1985-87, revenue agt., 1987-90; pvt. cons. Vista, Calif., 1991—. Instr. adult edn. Vista Unified Sch. Dist., 1990-99; mem. adv. com. of nat. cemetery sys. Dept. Vet. Affairs, 1991-98, adv. coun. IRS, 1999-2001. Mem. AAUW (treas.), Calif. Assn. Ind. Accts., Calif. Soc. Enrolled Agts. (dir. Palomar chpt. 1993-95, 2000-01, 1st v.p. 1998-2000), Inland Soc. Tax Cons., Assn. Homebased Bus., Gold Star Wives Am., Inc. (regional pres. 1989-90, chpt. pres. 1992-93, 96-97, nat. pres. 1993-95). Avocations: lace making, needle work, gardening, writing. Home and Office: 1161 Tower Dr Vista CA 92083-7144 E-mail: gswtax@aol.com.

FERGUSON, MARGARET GENEVA, writer, publisher, real estate broker; d. James B. and Dollie (McCloud) F. Student, Kansas City Jr. Coll., 1949, YMCA Real Estate Inst., 1960, Bryant and Stratton Bus. Coll., 1962, Ill. Inst. Tech., 1969, 70, 72. pub. spkr. Sec. Cook County Grand Jury, 1979; acting mgr. internal svc. dept. Xerox Corp., 1985-86, fin. specialist, 1984-87. Tutor reading and math., 1988; instr. sociology Chgo. State U., 2001-2002; host Black Image Prodn. Cable 19, 1989; interviewed on various TV shows, including PM Mag., 1983; active pub. rels. newspapers, Chgo., Detroit, Kansas City, St. Louis, 1970-91; conductor workshops in field; participant Pan Meth. Pilgrimage to Eng., 1984, World Meth. Conf., Nairobi, Kenya, 1986; spkr. in field. Author, pub.: The History of St. Paul CME Church 1907-1988, 1989, Books in Print, 1989-90, This Is Your Life Dr. Owens, 1991. Co-treas. fund raiser Citizens for Mayor Harold Washington, Chgo., 1987; treas. St. Paul Mortgage Fund, 1984; vol. Am. Cancer Soc., Salvation Army, Lighthouse for the Blind, 1982, Dem. Nat. Conv., 1996, Olympic Torch, Nat. Coun. State Legis.; dist. pres. Christian Methodist Episcopal Ch. Nat. Women's League, 1980-86, nat. fin. sec., 1980-92; officer St. Paul Christian Methodist Episcopal Ch., 1983—; v.p. lay ministry, 1987-92, pres. 1992-99; 2d v.p. Ann. Conf. Lay Ministry, 1996-99; sec. Christian Methodist Episcopal Long Range Planning Commn., 1982-86; mem. Chgo. State Street Women's Coun.; judge Chgo. City Elections Bur., 1997; mem. State Street Woman's Coun., 1976, Du Sable Mus., 1990. Recipient PUSH Prison Min. award, 1970, Vol. of Yr. award Chgo. Lighthouse, 1982, Gold Coaster award Kiwanis Club, 1983, Black on Black Love award, 1988, History Writing award Christian Meth. Episcopal Ch., 1990, 1st Lady award V-103FM, 1991, Key to City, Ft. Smith, Ark., 1992, Lifetime Achievement Culture Ctr. award, Citizens award V-103FM, 1994, Bishop's award C.M.E. Ch., 1996; named to Cultural Citizens Found. Hall of Fame, 1990. Mem. NAACP, Nat. Coun. Negro Women, People United to Serve Humanity (prison ministry award 1991, Fred Davis award 1994, Steward of Yr. award 1999), Chgo. Bd. Realtors, S.W. Suburban Bd. Realtors, Hyde Park Co-op Soc. (bd. dirs. 1994-95), Internat. Platform Assn., Am. Assn. Ret. Persons (55 Alive instr. 1996—), DuSable Mus., Lambda Kappa Mu. Home: 727 E 60th St Apt 808 Chicago IL 60637-2592

FERGUSON, MARY CARFAGNO, artist; b. N.Y.C., July 15, 1948; d. Francis John and Edith (Leno) Carfagno; m. John Dunn Ferguson, July 3,1982 (div. Nov. 1997); children: Rebecca, Sarah, Eveylon. Student, N.Y.U., 1966-67; BA, Bklyn. Coll., 1975; MFA, Md. Inst. Coll. Art, 1981. Prin. works include pub. murals The Garden Wall, 1994, The Magic Theatre, 1995, The Riverbank, 1996, My Sisters Garden, 1997, The Marble Shooters, 1997, Baltimore Skyline, 1998, The Train, 1998, The Horseshoe Players, 1999, The Skaters' Mural, 1999, The Corner at Barre Circle, 1999, Between Two Houses, 2000; exhibited works in shows at Larson Dulman Gallery, New Hope, Pa., 1988, 89, Henri Gallery, Washington, 1993, 819 Gallery, Balt., 1994, Resurgam Gallery, Balt., 1996, 97, 98, Ridgefield (Conn.) Guild of Artists, 2001. Co-founder, artistic dir. The Women's Mural Project, Baltimore, 1995-97. Recipient citation Office of Mayor, Balt., 1994, 96, 98, 99; grantee Md. State Arts Coun., 1995, 97, Mayor's Adv. Com. for Art and Culture, Balt., 1995, 97; Open Soc. Inst. fellow Soros Found., 1999, 2000. Mem.: Ridgefield Guild Artists (bd. dirs.), Nat. Soc. Mural Painters. Home: 269 Kitchawan Rd South Salem NY 10590 E-mail: mcmars@optonline.net.

FERGUSON, MICHAEL, congressman; b. Ridgewood, NJ, July 22, 1970; m. Maureen: 3 children. BA in govt., U. Notre Dame; M in pub. policy, Georgetown U. Founder, pres. edn1. con. firm; history tchr. Mount St. Michael Acad., Bronx; mem. U.S. Ho. Reps. from 7th N.J. dist., 2001—. Mem. Congress Energy & Commerce com., adj. prof. Brookdale Cmty. Coll., Lincroft, NJ; exec. dir. Better Sch. Found., Catholic Campaign for Am. Mem. Nat. Fedn. Independent Bus., NJ Chamber Commerce, Epilepsy Found. NJ, Delbarton Sch., Friendly Sons of St. Patrick, Nat. Italian-Am. Found., Sierra Club, KC. Republican. Office: 214 Cannon House bldg Washington DC 20515-3007 also: 792 Chimney Rock Rd, Ste E Martinsville NJ 08836*

FERGUSON, MICHAEL JOHN, electronics and communications educator; b. Toronto, Ont., Can., May 7, 1941; s. John Albert and Dorothy (Bracewell) F.; m. Virginia Louise Boardman, June 15, 1969; 1 child, Margaret Elizabeth. BASc, U. Toronto, 1962; MS, Calif. Inst. Tech., 1963; PhD, Stanford U., 1966. Engring. specialist Ford Aerospace Co., Palo Alto, Calif., 1966-68; prof. McGill U., Montreal, Que., Can., 1968-76; rsch. assoc., mgr. Aloha system U. Hawaii, Honolulu, 1974-76; rsch. scholar Internat. Inst. Applied Systems Analysis, Laxenburg, Austria, 1976-78; mgr. systems analysis Bell Northern Rsch., Montreal, Que., 1978-82; Cyrille Duquet prof. comm. software INRS-Telecomm., Verdun, Que., 1985-98; prof. emeritus INRS Telecomms., 2001—. Recipient Erskine fellowship, U. Canterbury, 2001. Fellow IEEE; mem. Assn. for Computer Machinery (chmn. spl. interest group on communications 1985-87), Tex User Group (bd. dirs. 1991-96), Sigma Xi. Avocation: bicycle touring. Home: 4336 King Edward Ave Montreal QC Canada H4B 2H5 E-mail: mike@inrs-telecom.uquebec.ca., mjf_ferguson@yahoo.ca.

FERGUSON, MILTON CARR CARR, JR., lawyer; b. Washington, Feb. 10, 1931; s. Milton Carr and Gladys (Emery) F.; m. Marian Evelyn Nelson, Aug. 21, 1954; children: Laura, Sharon, Marcia, Sandra. BA, Cornell U., 1952; LL.B., 1954; LL.M., N.Y. U., 1960. Bar: N.Y. 1954. Trial atty. tax div. Dept. Justice, Washington, 1954-60, asst. atty. gen., 1977-81; asst. prof. law U. Iowa, 1960-62; assoc. prof. N.Y.U., 1962-65; prof. N.Y. U., 1965-77; vis. prof.

law Stanford (Calif.) U., 1972-73; of counsel Wachtell, Lipton, Rosen & Katz, N.Y.C., 1969-76; ptnr. Davis Polk & Wardwell, N.Y.C., 1981—2001, sr. counsel, 2002—. Spl. cons. to Treasury Dept., Commonwealth P.R., 1974 Author: (with others) Federal Income Taxation Legislation in Perspective, 1965, Federal Income Taxation of Estates and Beneficiaries, 1970, 2d edit., 1994. Trustee NYU Law Ctr. Found., Lewis and Clark Coll. Mem. ABA (chmn. tax sect. 1993-94), N.Y. State Bar Assn., Soc. Illustrators. Home: 32 Washington Sq W New York NY 10011-9156 Office: Davis Polk & Wardwell 450 Lexington Ave New York NY 10017-3982

FERGUSON, NANCY L. social worker, psychotherapist; b. Milw., Jan. 8, 1947; d. Earl Wayne and LaVerne Caroline Ferguson; children: Nathan J. Rosnow, Katherine Ann Rosnow. BA, U. Wis., Madison, 1971; MSW, U. Wis., Milw., 1983. Lic. ind. clin. social worker; cert. alcohol and drug counselor. Adminstr. McMahon Residential Ctr., Milw., 1973-79; children's program coord. Horizon House, Milw., 1980-84; family therapist Elmbrook Meml. Hosp., Brookfield, Wis., 1984-97; sch. social worker Greendale (Wis.) Schs., 1987—2002; psychiat. social worker Greenbriar Hosp., Milw., 1991-95; psychotherapist Acacia Clinic, White-Leonard Clinic, Lighthouse Clinic, Milw., 1993—; asst. prof. Cardinal Stritch U., Milw., 1997—. Cons., trainer, spkr. Nancy L. Ferguson & Assocs., LLC, Milw., 1997—. Co-author: Community Living Guide, 1976; author: Adolescent Post-Treatment Support: A High School Substance Recovery Course, 2001. Mem. NASW. Unitarian Universalist. Home: 2424 S Wentworth #6 Milwaukee WI 53207 Office: 2577 N Downer Ave #215 Milwaukee WI 53211 E-mail: nfergus@execpc.com.

FERGUSON, PAMELA ANDERSON, mathematics educator, educational administrator; b. Berwyn, Ill., May 5, 1943; d. Clarence Oscar and Ruth Anne (Stroner) Anderson; m. Donald Roger Ferguson, Dec. 18, 1965; children: Keith, Amanda. BA, Wellesley Coll., 1965; MS, U. Chgo., 1966, PhD, 1969. Asst. prof. Northwestern U., Evanston, Ill., 1969—70, U. Miami, Coral Gables, Fla., 1972—77, assoc. prof., 1978—81, prof. math., 1981—91, dir. honors program, 1985—87, assoc. provost, dean Grad. Sch., 1987—91; pres. Grinnell Coll., Iowa, 1991—97, prof. math., 1991—2003, Breid McFarland prof. of sci., 2003—. Mem. Nat. Sci. Bd., 1998—2004; vis. com. phys. scis. divsn. U. Chgo., 1996—. Contbr. articles to profl. jours. Mem. Iowa Rsch. Coun., 1993—97. Grantee NSF grantee. Mem.: Am. Women in Math., Am. Math. Soc., Wellesley Club, Phi Beta Kappa, Omicron Delta Chi, Sigma Xi. Lutheran. Avocations: hiking, reading, skiing. Office: Grinnell Coll Dept Math PO Box 805 Grinnell IA 50112-0805

FERGUSON, PAULA IRENE, nursing administrator; b. Worcester, Mass., Aug. 7, 1954; d. Richard R. and Patricia I. (Gilbert) Wood; m. George F. Ferguson, Oct. 12, 2001; children from previous marriage: Andrew, Brian. Diploma summa cum laude, David Hale Fanning Sch., 1974; BS in Computer Sci. summa cum laude, Clark U., 1986; AAS summa cum laude, SUNY, Albany, 1988; BSN, Barry U., 1996, MSN summa cum laude, 1998; PhD summa cum laude, Columbus U., 1999. Cert. nursing adminstrn. ANA, dir. nurses Nat. Assn. Dirs. Nursing Adminstrn./Long Term Care, nursing adminstrn. Head nurse Seven Hills Adolescent Program, Worcester, 1985-88; coord. utilization rev. Worcester County Hosp., 1988-90, 45th St. Mental Health Ctr., West Palm Beach, Fla.; nurse mgr. N.Medico Neurol. Rehab. Ctr. of Palm Beach (Fla.), 1990-91; dir. nurses Edgewater Pointe Estates, Boca Raton, Fla., 1991-93; DON Empathy Care, Boca Raton, 1993-96; owner Traditional Home Health Svcs., Inc., Lake Worth, Fla., 1996-99; nurse mgr. Genesis Eldercare Network, Laconia, N.H., 1998-99; DON Hollywood Hills Nursing Home, 1999-2001; adminstr. Physician's Choice Home Health Svcs., 2001—; case mgr. OASIS Home Care, 2003—. Trustee Fla. Nurse Found., 2003—; mem. content expert panel ANCC Nurse Adminstrn., 2002—. Trustee Fla. Nurse Found. Mem.: ANA, Nat. Assn. Dir. Nursing Adminstrn. (chairperson home health coun., cert.), Fla. Nurses Assn. (Quality and Unity in Nursing coun. mem., dist. XI bd. mem.), Fla. Orgn. Nursing Execs., Sigma Theta Tau. Home: 16 S Lakeshore Dr Hypoluxo FL 33462 E-mail: docpaula54@yahoo.com.

FERGUSON, R. NEIL, computer systems consultant; b. Dallas, June 22, 1952; s. Roy and Hellon Ferguson; m. L. Jean Ferguson, Aug. 12, 1977; 1 child, Rheachel Claire. BA in Psychology, U. Tex., 1976; grad., Winfield Sch. Race Driving, 1984. Systems engr. EDS, Dallas, 1976-77; systems programmer Collins Radio/Rockwell Internat., Richardson, Tex., 1977-78; systems programmer/analyst Moore Bus. Systems, Denton, Tex., 1978-79; supr., computer graphics Atlantic Richfield Co., Dallas, 1979-85; software engring. specialist E-Systems, Inc., Garland, Tex., 1986-90; dir. product mgmt., graphics and database systems MPSI, Inc., Irving, Tex., 1990-92; pvt. practice computer cons. Lewisville, Tex., 1990—; owner Computer Sys. Svc. & Cons. Co. Tech. program dir. Internat. Microcomputer Exposition, Dallas, 1978. Vol. computer sys. adminstr. Trinity Presbyn. Ch., 1997-2000. Recipient Golden Eagle award Am. Acad. Achievement, Tymshare award Tymshare Corp., Panasonic Sci. Achievement award Matsushita Electric Corp. of Am. and Jr. Engring. Tech. Soc., NASA award, Dallas County Med. Soc. award, 1st Place award in math. and computers 21st Internat. Sci. Fair; featured in Grolier's Sci. Ency. supplement, 1967; named Regional Class Champion, Sports Car Club of Am. Mem. Assn. for Computing Machinery, Spl. Interest Group on Computer Graphics, Am. Congress Surveying and Mapping, Am. Soc. Photogrammetry and Remote Sensing. Avocations: exotic sportscar restoration, stamp collecting, scale model car construction, wrist and pocket watch collecting and restoration. Home and Office: 1097 Holly Ln Lewisville TX 75067-5711

FERGUSON, ROBERT BRUCE, minerals company executive; b. Vancouver, B.C., Can., June 24, 1946; came to U.S., 1994; s. Robert Dixon and Elsie Patricia (Chappell) F.; m. Faye Diane Ferguson, Aug. 28, 1971; children: Spencer William Stuart, Colin Thomas Andrew. BS in Metallurgical Engring., U. B.C., 1970. Registered profl. engr. Yukon, N.W. Terrs., Province of Saskatchewan. Devel. engr. Cominco Ltd., Trail, B.C., Can., 1970-72; mill engr. Eldorado Nuclear, Uranium City, Sask., Can., 1972-75; chief metallurgist Cyprus Anvil Mining Corp., Faro Yukon, Can., 1975-79, Heath Steele Mines Ltd., Miramichi, N.B., Can., 1979-84; sr. metallurgist Mount Pleasant Tungsten, St. George, N.B., Can., 1984-85; mineral process engr. Billiton BV, Leidschendam, Netherlands, 1985-87; mill supt. Echo Bay Mines, Lupin, NWT, Can., 1987-94, Republic, Wash., 1994—. Inventor cyanide neutralization process. Mem. Pine Grove (Wash.) Water Coop., 1995—. Mem. Fraternal Order of Eagles. Avocations: downhill and cross country skiing, trapshooting, gardening, fishing, hunting. Office: Echo Bay Minerals Co 363 Fish Hatchery Rd Republic WA 99166-9787

FERGUSON, ROBERT BURY, mineralogy educator; b. Cambridge, Ont., Can., Feb. 5, 1920; s. Alexander Galt and Harriet Henrietta (Bury) F.; m. Margaret Irene Warren, Dec. 29, 1948; children: Evelyn Bury, Robert Warren, Marion Galt. BA, U. Toronto, 1942, MA, 1943, PhD, 1948. Asst. prof. mineralogy U. Man. (Can.), Winnipeg, 1947-50; assoc. prof. U. Man, Winnipeg, Can., 1951-59; prof. U. Man.(Can.), Winnipeg, 1959-85, disting. prof., 1983, prof. emeritus, 1985—. Fellow Royal Soc. Can., Mineral Soc. Am.; mem. Mineral Soc. Great Britain, Mineral Assn. Can. (Hawley award 1981). New Democratic Party. Unitarian. Home: 184 Wildwood Park Winnipeg MB Canada R3T 0E2 Office: U Man Dept Geol Scis Winnipeg MB Canada R3T 2N2 E-mail: ferguson@ms.umanitoba.ca.

FERGUSON, ROBERT L., JR., lawyer; b. Cambridge, Mass., Mar. 31, 1945; s. Robert L. and Mary Jane (Campbell) F.; m. Pamela Gail Fuller, Apr. 20, 1968; children: Colleen B. Ferguson Driscoll, R. Christopher, P. Scott, Elizabeth E. BS in Elec. Engring., U. Md., College Park, 1968; JD, U. Md., Balt., 1972. Bar: Md., D.C. 1985. Assoc. engr. Bethlehem Steel Corp., Balt., 1968-69, Balt. Gas & Electric, 1969-73, engr., 1971-73; assoc. Allen, Thieblot & Alexander, Balt., 1973-77, ptnr., 1977-88, Thieblot, Ryan, Martin & Ferguson, Balt., 1988-96, Ferguson, Schetelich & Ballew, P.A., Balt., 1996—. Pres. Balt. Coalition Against Substance Abuse, 1991-96; v.p. Balt. Prevention Coalition, 1995-96. Recipient Spl. award for legal excellence Md. Bar Found., 1995. Fellow: Md. Bar Found., Am. Coll. Trial Lawyers, Am. Bar Found.; mem.: Govs. Trial Cts. Jud. Nominating Commn., Bar Assn. Balt. City (pres. 1998—99), Md. State Bar Assn. (past chmn. litig. sect. 1991, bd. govs. 1999—2001). Roman Catholic. Avocations: reading, sports, music. Office: Ferguson Schetelich & Ballew PA 1401 Bank of Am Ctr 100 S Charles St Baltimore MD 21201-2725

FERGUSON, ROGER W., JR., bank executive; b. Washington, Oct. 28, 1951; m. Annette L. Nazareth; two children. BA in Econs. magna cum laude, Harvard U., 1973, JD cum laude, 1979, PhD in Econs., 1981. Atty. Davis Polk & Wardwell, N.Y.C., 1981-84; assoc. and ptnr. McKinsey & Co., Inc., N.Y.C., 1984-97; mem. bd. govs. Fed. Res. Sys., Washington, 1997—, v.chmn. Wash., 1999—. Past treas. Friends of Edn.; past mem. trustees' com. Mus. Modern Art, N.Y.C.; bd. overseers Harvard U. Frank Knox fellow Pembroke Coll., Cambridge U., 1973-74. Office: Fed Res Sys Office of the Vice Chmn 20th & C Sts NW Washington DC 20551-0001

FERGUSON, RONALD EUGENE, reinsurance company executive; b. Chgo., Jan. 16, 1942; s. William Eugene and Elizabeth (Hahnneman) F.; m. Carol Jean Chapp, Dec. 27, 1964; children: Brian, Kristin. BA, Blackburn Coll., 1963; MA, U. Mich., 1965. Statistician Lumbermans Mut. Casualty Co., Long Grove, Ill., 1965-69; actuary Gen. Reins. Corp., Greenwich, Conn., 1969-70, asst. v.p, 1972-74, v.p., 1974-77, sr. v.p., 1977-82, exec. v.p., 1982, dir., 1983, chmn., 1985—, CEO, bd. dirs., 1987—2002; ret., 2002. V.p., group exec. Gen. Re Corp., Stamford, 1981, pres., COO, 1983—87, chmn., pres., CEO, 1987—2002; chmn., bd. dirs. Colgate-Palmolive Co., 2001; bd. dirs. Blue Flame Data Corp.; cons. Gen. Re Corp. Contbr. articles to profl. jours. Served with USPHS, 1966-68. Fellow Casualty Actuarial Soc. (bd. dirs. 1978-81); mem. Am. Acad. Actuaries (dir. 1981—). Clubs: Patterson. Congregationalist. Office: Gen Re Corp Financial Ctr PO Box 10351 Stamford CT 06904-2351

FERGUSON, RONALD MAX, chemistry educator, researcher; b. Beaver Twp., Pa. s. Myrrel Delbert and Nellie M. (Boyer) F.; m. Dorothy Smith, Mar. 16, 1964; children: Clifford Scott, Laura Gail. BS, Clarion (Pa.) U., 1958; MS, Temple U., Phila., 1962, U. Conn., 1982. Tchr. Crafton H.S., Pitts., 1958-60, Moses Brown Sch., Providence, R.I., 1961-65; prof. Ea. Conn. State U., Willimantic, Conn., 1965—, dir. Can. studies program. Mem. adv. coun. Environ. Health Ctr., Storrs, Conn., 1986—; mem. adv. com. Air, Space & Environ. Edn., Willimantic, 1995—; chair solid waste mgmt. com. Town of Coventry, Conn., 1989-94; hydro power, thermal and nuclear power analysis Ea. Conn. State U., Willimantic, 1991—. Mem. editl. bd. Jour. Ecol. Chem., 1993—; reviewer science and tech. CHOICE-Am. Libr. Assn., 1993—. Recipient Exeter Rsch. award Oxford Energy, Sterling, Conn., 1991. Mem. Am. Chem. Soc., New England Assn. Chemistry Tchrs., Coll. Chemistry Can., Assn. Canadian Studies in Am. Univs. Avocations: photography, writing, swimming, gardening. Home: 91 Northfield Rd Coventry CT 06238-1421 E-mail: fergusonm@eastern.et.edu.

FERGUSON, STEVEN EDWARD, lawyer; b. Oklahoma City, Apr. 26, 1955; m. Shelly J. Smith, Aug. 5, 1977; children: Steven E. Jr., Cicely J. BA, U. Okla., 1977; JD, Oklahoma City U., 1980. Bar: Okla. 1980, U.S. Dist. Ct. (we. dist.) Okla. 1980. Sole practice Crabb, Ferguson & Riesen, PA, Oklahoma City, 1980—. Office: Crabb Ferguson & Riesen 5101 N Classen Blvd Ste 404 Oklahoma City OK 73118-4433

FERGUSON, TAMARA, clinical sociologist; b. The Hague, Netherlands; came to U.S., 1955; d. Simon and Sonia (Pokrowska) Van den Bergh; m. John D.A. Ferguson, Sept. 12, 1958. MA in Sociology, Columbia U., 1962, PhD, 1970. Asst. prof. U. Detroit, 1960-71; from asst. prof. to assoc. prof. U. Windsor, Ont., Can., 1971-78; adj. assoc. prof. sociology Wayne State U. Med. Sch., Detroit, 1978-99; assoc. med. staff dept. psychiatry Harper Hosp., Detroit, 1982-99. Co-author: The Young Widow: Conflict and Guidelines, 1981; contbg. author: Clinical Sociology in Mental Health Setting, 1991, Qualitative Analysis in Human Sciences: New Perspectives in Methodology, 1996. 2d lt. Free French armed forces, 1944-45, ETO. Mem. Am. Sociol. Assn., Found. Thanatology, Sociol. Practice Assn. (bd. dirs. 1990-96). Avocations: reading, music, swimming. Office: UPC Jefferson 2751 E Jefferson Ave Detroit MI 48207-4166

FERGUSON, THOMAS GEORGE, retired healthcare advertising agency executive; b. Newark, Oct. 14, 1941; s. George Francis and Dorothy Marie (Stinson) F.; m. Roberta Chiaviello, Jan. 27, 1967; children: Thomas, Jr., Michael, Cathleen, Margaret. BS in Bus. Mgmt., Fairleigh Dickinson U., 1965. Product mgr. Bard-Parker div. Becton Dickinson & Co., Lincoln Park, N.J., 1965-70; acct. exec. L.W. Frolich, Inc., 1970-71; v.p., acct. group supr. Sudler & Hennessey, Inc., N.Y.C., 1971-74; chmn., pres. Thomas G. Ferguson Assocs., Inc., Parsippany, N.J., 1974—; chmn. Ferguson Common Health USA. Mem. Hemophilia Assn. N.J., 1981-98, ret., 1998; bd. dirs. Tri-County Scholarship Fund, Paterson, N.J., 1982—; pres., bd. trustees Epilepsy Found. N.J., Trenton, 1982—; past pres., bd. mem. Delbarton Sch. Fathers & Friends, Morristown, N.J. Served with USNG, 1971. Recipient Humanitarian award Hemophilia Assn. N.J., 1985, Disting. Svc. award Epilepsy Found. N.J., 1987. Mem. Pharm. Advt. Club, Pharm. Mfrs. Assn., Midwest Pharm. Advt. Club, Nat. Wholesale Druggists' Assn., Bus. Publication Audits, Fairleigh Dickinson U. Alumni Assn. Republican. Roman Catholic. Clubs: Morris County Golf (bd. dirs. 1975—), Baltusrol Golf. Avocation: golf. Office: Ferguson Common Health USA 30 Lanidex Plz W Parsippany NJ 07054-2717

FERGUSON, THOMAS GLEN, internist; b. Chgo., Nov. 7, 1947; s. Thomas Glen and Mildred C. (Barrios) F. BS, Northwestern State U., Nachitoches, La., 1969, MS, 1970; MD, U. Tenn. Ctr. for Health Scis., 1974. Diplomate Am. Bd. Internal Medicine and Critical Care Medicine; cert. spl. competency in electrocardiography Am. Coll. Cardiology, spl. competency in echocardiography Am. Soc. Echocardiography. Chief of medicine, dir. critical care, noninvasive cardiol. S. La. Med. Assocs. and Leonard J. Chabert Med. Ctr., Houma, La., 1978—; med. dir. Leonard J. Chabert Med. Ctr., Houma, 1997; CEO and med. dir. S. La. Med. Assocs., 1997, also bd. dirs., 1978—. Contbg. author (book) Proceedings of the International Vascular Surgical Soc., 1993; also articles to profl. jours. Cons. La. State Legislature, Baton Rouge, Dept. Health and Hosps., State of La., Baton Rouge; participant Downtown on Bayou Festival Com., Houma, La., 1995—. Recipient Commendation VA, Memphis, 1978, Tchr. of Yr. award Alton Ochsner Med. Found., New Orleans, 1982, Best Drs. in Am. award, 1998, 99, 2000. Fellow ACP, Am. Coll. Critical Care (Pres. award 1997); mem. AMA, Am. Soc. Echocardiography, Soc. Critical Care Medicine, La. State Med. Soc., Terrebone Parish Med. Soc., Houma C. of C., Alpha Omega Alpha. Avocations: travel, finance, sports, music. Home: 1 Dandra Cir Houma LA 70360-6002 Office: S La Med Assocs 1978 Industrial Blvd Houma LA 70363-7055

FERGUSON, WARREN JOHN, judge; b. Eureka, Nev., Oct. 31, 1920; s. Ralph and Marian (Damele) Ferguson; m. E. Laura Keyes, June 5, 1948; children: Faye F., Warren John, Teresa M., Peter J. BA, U. Nev., 1942; LLB, U. So. Calif., 1949; LLD (hon.), Western State U., San Fernando Valley Coll. Law. Bar: Calif. 1950. Mem. firm Ferguson & Judge, Fullerton, Calif., 1950—59; city atty. for cities of Buena Park, Placentia, La Puente, Baldwin Park, Santa Fe Springs, Walnut and Rosemead, Calif., 1953—59; mcpl. ct. judge Anaheim, Calif., 1959—60; judge Superior Ct., Santa Ana, Calif., 1961—66, Juvenile Ct., 1963—64, Appellate Dept., 1965—66; U.S. dist. judge Los Angeles, 1966—79; judge U.S. Circuit Ct. (9th cir.), Los Angeles, 1979—86; sr. judge U.S. Ct. Appeals (9th cir.), Santa Ana, 1986—; faculty Fed. Jud. Ctr., Practising Law Inst., U. Iowa Coll. Law, N.Y. Law Jour. Assoc. prof. psychiatry (law) Sch. Medicine, U. So. Calif.; assoc. prof. Loyola Law Sch. With U.S. Army, 1942—46. Decorated Bronze Star. Mem.: Theta Chi, Phi Kappa Phi. Democrat. Roman Catholic. Office: US Courthouse 411 W 4th St Ste 10-80 Santa Ana CA 92701-4500 E-mail: judge_ferguson@ca9.uscourts.gov. *Having been born and raised in Nevada, I have adopted an old prospector's philosophy: "Live today; look every man in the eye; and tell the rest of the world to go to hell."*

FERGUSON, WENDELL, private school educator; b. Sandersville, Ga., May 6, 1954; d. Isadore and Willie Mae (Roberts) Jordan; m. Larry Brown Sr., May 28, 1971 (div. Dec. 1985); children: Larry Brown Jr., Dwyne Lamont Brown, Anthony Patrick Brown; m. Jerry Lang Ferguson, Sept. 28, 1992 (div.). Diploma, Alphena C.C., 1972; student, Ga. State U., 1983-87. Sales clk. U.S. NAS, Albany, Ga., 1972-74, 76-77; substitute tchr. Ga. Dept. Edn., Houston County, 1976-77; nutritionist (nursery) Howard AFB, Panama Canal, 1980; joined Sweet Adelines, Inc., Tulsa, 1981; data entry operator dept. budget mgmt. Atlanta City Hall, 1982; mgr., operator Atlanta Connections, 1982-83; asst. supr. micro-film Ga. Dept. Revenue, Atlanta, 1986-88; promotional sales rep. RG Clothier/L.B. Holyfield, Atlanta, 1992-95; substitute tchr. Old Nat. Christian Acad., College Park, Ga., 1995—; loan broker Cherokee Funding Inc., Thomaston, Ga., 1989—; owner, wholesale dist. Dells' Clevor Enterprises, 2000. Libr. YWCA, Rochester, N.Y., 1999; co-prodr., writer, owner Jeri-Del Prodns., Atlanta. Actress, singer, dancer various prodns. (Irving Berlin award 1982); author: Times In Life, 1996. Vol. persona bus. broker Asst. Sec. of State, Atlanta, 1994, J.D. Sims Recreation Ctr., 2000, Atlanta; Gospel Fest judge, 1995, coord. nominees judgeship position Fayette, Pike, Upson & Spaulding Counties, Ga., 1992; surveyor for st. lights, Atlanta, 1982; vol. Fulton County Dept. Parks and Recreation, Burdett Gym, 1996—; active We Are Today and Tomorrow; founder Steadfast Children Learning Systems Atlanta Coalition of Chs., 1997. Recipient Gold Citizens Acheivement award Mayor William Campbell, 1997, Outstanding People of 20th Century, Internat. Biog. Assn. Democrat. Avocations: horseback riding, chess, painting, cooking, tennis. Home: Fergusons' Entertainment PO Box 492383 College Park GA 30349 E-mail: dellthangs@aol.com.

FERGUSON, WHITWORTH, III, pastor; b. Buffalo, Aug. 16, 1954; s. Whitworth and Elizabeth Ferguson Jr.; m. Patricia Pierson, May 5, 2000. BA in Econs., St. Lawrence U., Canton, N.Y., 1976; MBA in Fin., U. Pa., 1978; JD, Cornell U., 1981; MDiv, Princeton Theol. Sem., 1999. Bar: Ill. 1981, N.Y. 1983. Assoc. McDermott, Will & Emery, Chgo., 1981—82, Damon & Morey, Buffalo, 1982—84; officer fin. planning Key Trust Co., Buffalo, 1984—86; pres. Alpine Sports, Ltd., Williamsville, NY, 1986—90, Buffalo Consulting Co., Buffalo, 1990—94; editor The Economist Intelligence Unit, N.Y.C., 1994—96; pastor The First Presbyn. Ch., 2000—. Mng. dir. The NORAM Group, Ltd., Buffalo, 1990-94. Contbg. editor Knowledge@Wharton, 1999—. Bd. dirs. Senecare Corp., 1983-88, YMCA Greater Buffalo, 1985-94, vice chmn., 1988-90; ho. of dels. United Way Buffalo and Erie County, 1984-94; chmn. campaign for creativity Creative Edn. Found.; advisor ctr. entrepreneurial leadership Sch. Mgmt., SUNY, Buffalo, 1991-94; dir. Western N.Y. Venture Assn., 1991-94; mem. Westminster Presbyn. Trustees, 1989-91, chmn. stewardship, 1989, ruling elder, 1992; advisor Ctr. for Entrepreneurship, Canisius Coll., 1992-94; bd. gov.'s Stony Point Conf. Ctr., 2001—.

FERGUSON, WILLIAM MCDONALD, rancher, writer, banker, retired lawyer, former state official; b. Wellington, Kans., Dec. 2, 1917; s. William McDonald and May (Deems) F.; m. Harriet Shelden, Sept. 12, 1939; children—Joan, William McDonald III. AB, U. Kans., 1938; LL.B., Harvard U., 1941. Bar: Kans. 1946. City atty., Wellington, 1948-57; gen. practice law, 1948-73; atty. gen., 1961-65; pres. Security State Bank, Wellington, 1958-74, chmn. bd., 1974-85, chmn. emeritus, 1985—. Co-mgr. Ferguson Ranch, Ferguson Cattle Co., 1965—, Spur Cattle Co., 1980-96; pres. Ferguson Ranch, Inc., 1993—. Author: (with John Q. Royce) Maya Ruins of Mexico in Color, 1977, Maya Ruins in Central America in Color, 1984; (with Arthur H. Rohn) Anasazi Ruins of the Southwest, 1986, Mesoamerica's Ancient Cities, 1990, 2d edit. (with R.E.W. Adams), 2001, Anasazi of Mesa Verde and the Four Corners, 1996. Mem. Kans. Ho. of Reps. 69th Dist., 1949-57. Served to lt. (s.g.) USNR, 1942-46. Mem. ABA (ho. dels. 1961-62), Kans. Bar Assn. (exec. council 1952-61, v.p. 1961, pres. 1963), Am. Legion, Sigma Alpha Epsilon. Lodges: Elks. Republican. Home: PO Box 236 101 N Washington Wellington KS 67152-3813 E-mail: wmferg@frontier.net.

FERGUSON, YALE HICKS, political science educator; b. Austin, Tex., May 28, 1940; s. Phil Moss and Marion (Hicks) Ferguson; m. Kitty Gail Vetter, Aug. 26, 1961; children: Colin Yale, Duff Christopher, Caitlin Christiana. BA magna cum laude, Trinity U., 1960; PhD, Columbia U., 1967. Lectr. CUNY, Bklyn., 1965; instr. Rutgers U., Newark, 1966-67, asst. prof. polit. sci., 1967-71, assoc. prof. polit. sci., 1971-77, prof. polit. sci., 1977-98, chmn. dept. polit. sci., 1985-90, 96-01, prof. II polit. sci., 1998—, co-dir. Ctr. for Global Change and Governance, 2002—. Hon. prof. U. Salzburg, Austria, 2002—; rschr. Fgn. Svc. Inst. U.S. Dept. State, Washington, 1979; mem. adv. bd. European Jour. Internat. Rels., 1995—2000, Internat. Studies Quar., 1998—2003. Co-author (with R.W. Mansbach): The Web of World Politics: Nonstate Actors in the Global System, 1976; co-author: The Elusive Quest: Theory and International Politics, 1988, The State Conceptual Chaos and the Future of International Relations Theory, 1989, Politics: Authority, Identities and Change, 1996, The Elusive Quest Continues: Theory and Global Politics, 2003; co-editor: Continuing Issues in International Politics, 1973, Political Space: Frontiers of Change and Governance in a Globalizing World, 2002; editor: Contemporary Inter-American Relations, 1972; contbr. Named Fulbright prof., U. Salzburg, 1992—93; recipient Bd. Trustees award Excellence in Rsch., Rutgers U., 1999; fellow, Norwegian Nobel Inst., 1996; scholar, U. Padova, 2001—02; Ctr. of Internat. Studies fellow, Cambridge U., 1986—87, 1991. Mem.: AAUP, Commn. of History Internat. Rels., Mid Atlantic Coun. L.Am. Studies (exec. com. 1988—90), Brit. Internat. Studies Assn., Internat. Studies Assn. (NE bd. dirs. 1996—2000), Clare Hall (life). Episcopalian. Avocations: tennis, swimming, photography. Office: Rutgers U Ctr for Global Change and Governance 123 Washington St Ste 510 Newark NJ 07102 E-mail: yhfergus@andromeda.rutgers.edu.

FERGUSSON, FRANCES DALY, college president, educator; b. Boston, Oct. 3, 1944; d. Francis Joseph and Alice (Storrow) Daly. BA, Wellesley Coll., 1965; MA, Harvard U., 1966, PhD, 1973; DLitt, U. Hartford, 2000, U. London, 2001. Asst. prof. Newton Coll., Mass., 1969—75; assoc. prof. U. Mass., Boston, 1974—82, asst. chancellor, 1980—82; provost, prof. Bucknell U., Lewisburg, Pa., 1982—86; pres. Vassar Coll., Poughkeepsie, NY, 1986—. Bd. dirs. HSBC Bank N. Am., 1990—. bd. dirs., Foreign Policy Assn. Bd. overseers Harvard U., 2002—; trustee Mayo Found., 1988—2002, chair, 1998—2002; trustee Ford Found., 1989—2001, Historic Hudson, 1990—99. Recipient Founder's award Soc. Archtl. Historians, 1973, Eleanor Roosevelt at Val-Kill medal, 1998, Centennial medal Harvard Grad. Sch. of Arts and Scis., 1999. Fellow: Am. Acad. Arts and Scis.; mem.: Fgn. Policy Assn. (bd. dirs. 2003—). Avocation: piano. Office: Vassar Coll PO Box 1 Poughkeepsie NY 12604-0001

FERK, FRANC, information technology executive; PhD in Bus. and Leadership Studies, Clermont Coll., 2002; DSc (hon.), U. Berkley, 2002. Pres. Stonediver, N.Y.C., 1992—. Writer (tech. lit.) Pay per Click Search Engines.

FERKOL, THOMAS WILLIAM, medical educator, pediatrician; b. Wurzburg, Germany, June 15, 1959; s. Thomas William Sr. and Judith Ann Ferkol; m. Sandra Ann Obrzut, July 23, 1983; children: Thomas Joseph, Katherine Lynn. BA, Case Western Res. U., 1981; MD, Ohio State U., Coll. of Medicine, 1985. Cert. Pediatrics Am. Bd. of Pediat., 1989, Pediatric Pulmonology Am. Bd. of Pediat., 1994. Chief resident U. of NC, Coll. of Medicine, Pediat. Dept., 1988—89; pediat. pulmonology divsn. instr. to asst. prof. Rainbow Babies and Children's Hosp., Case Western Res. U. Sch. of Medicine, Cleveland, 1992—2000; assoc. prof. Wash. U. Sch. of Medicine, St. Louis, 2000—, dir. Cystic Fibrosis Ctr. dept. pediat., 2000—, dir. dept. pediat., 2000—. Recipient LeRoy Matthews Physician-Scientist award, Cystic Fibrosis Found., 1989, Edward Livingston Trudeau scholar, Am. Lung Assn., 1994; grantee, NIH, 1994—99, 2001—, Therapeutic Devel. Ctr. award, Cystic Fibrosis Found., 2003—; rsch. grantee, March of Dimes, 2003—. Mem.: Am. Acad. of Pediat., Soc. for Pediatric Rsch., Am. Thoracic Soc. (program com.). Achievements include patents for compacted nucleic acids and their delivery into cells; fusion proteins for protein delivery; bifunctional molecules for delivery of therapeutics; serpin enzyme complex receptor-mediated gene transfer. Office: Wash U Sch of Medicine One Children's Pl Saint Louis MO 63011

FERLAND, E. JAMES, electric power industry executive; b. Boston, Mar. 19, 1942; s. Ernest James and Muriel (Cassell) F.; m. Eileen Kay Patridge, Mar. 9, 1964; children: E. James, Elizabeth Denise. BSME, U. Maine, 1964; MBA, U. New Haven, 1979; postgrad., Harvard U. Grad. Sch. Bus. Adminstrn. Electric utility engr. HELCO, New London, Conn., 1964-67; supt. nuclear ops. NNECO, Waterford, Conn., 1967-78; dir. rate regulation N.E. Utilities, Berlin, Conn., 1978-79, v.p., CFO, 1980-83, pres., COO, 1983-86; chmn., pres., CEO Pub. Svc. Enterprise Group Inc., Newark, 1986—; chmn., CEO Pub. Svc. Electric and Gas Co., 1986—; also bd. dirs. all Pub. Svc. Enterprise Group subs. Office: Pub Svc Enterprise Group Inc 80 Park Plz # 4B Newark NJ 07102-4194

FERLING, JOHN E. history educator; b. Charleston, W.Va., Jan. 10, 1940; s. Ernie Leroy and Ruth (McCracker) Ferling; m. Carol Millette Ferling, Sept. 5, 1965. BA, Sam Houston State U., 1961; MA, Baylor U., 1962; PhD, W.Va. U., 1971. Tchr. Luther Stark H.S., Orange, Tex., 1962—64; prof. Morehead (Ky.) State U., 1965—68, West Chester (Pa.) State U., 1970—71, State U. West Ga., Carrollton, 1971—. Author: The First of Men: A Life of George Washington,

1988, John Adams: A Life, 1992, Setting the World Ablaze, 2000, A Leap in the Dark, 2003. Recipient George Washing Dist Prof. award, Nat. Soc. Cinn., 1999, 2000, 2001. Lutheran. Avocations: photography, swimming. Office: Univ West Ga Dept History 3207 TLC Bldg Carrollton GA 30118

FERLINGHETTI, LAWRENCE, poet; b. Yonkers, N.Y., 1919; s. Charles and Clemence (Mendes-Monsanto) F.; children: Julie, Lorenzo. AB, U. N.C.; MA, Columbia U., Doctorat de l'Université, mention très honorable, Sorbonne, 1950. Founder (with Peter D. Martin), first all paperbound bookstore in U.S., City Lights Books, San Francisco, City Lights Rev., firm also publishes works of modern poets and writers; widely traveled poetry reader, also painter; participant (with Allen Ginsberg), Pan Am. cultural conf., U. Concepcion, Chile, 1960; participant, One World Poetry Festival, Amsterdam, 1981, Internat. Poetry Festival of Rome, 1979-85, World Congress of Poets, Florence, Italy, 1986; author: poetry Pictures of the Gone World, 1955, A Coney Island of the Mind, 1958, Starting from San Francisco, 1961, The Secret Meaning of Things, Open Eye, Open Heart, 1973, Who Are We Now?, 1976, Landscapes of Living and Dying, 1979, Endless Life: Selected Poems, 1981, Over All the Obscene Boundaries, 1984, These Are My Rivers: New and Selected Poems, 1955-1993, 1993; novel Her, 1960, Routines; plays Back Roads to Far Places; (poetry) A Far Rockaway of the Heart, 1997; poetry and prose jour. Northwest Ecolog, 1978, (with Nancy J. Peters) Literary San Francisco: A Pictorial History, 1980; Seven Days in Nicaragua Libre, 1984, novel Love in the Days of Rage, 1988, How to Print Sunlight, 2001; performed in literary events Winter Olympic Games, Calgary, 1988; one-man exhbns., paintings: Butler Inst. Am. Art, Youngstown, Ohio, 1993, Retrospective Painting Exhbn. Palazzo delle Esposizioni, Rome, 1996. Lt. comdr. USNR, World War II, Normandy. A San Francisco street named in his honor, 1994; recipient poetry prize City of Rome, 1993; Premio Internazionale Flaiano, Italy, 1999, di Ostia, Italy, 99, Premio Internazionale di Camaiore, Italy, 1999, Premio Cavour, Italy, 2000, Poet Laureate of San Francisco, 1998-2000, L.A. Times Book Festival Lifetime Achievement award, 2001, Am. Civil Liberties Union award, 2001, elected to the Am. Acad. of Arts and Letters, 2003, Authors Guild Lifetime Achievement award, 2003. Fellow: Poetry Soc. of Am. (Robert Frost medal 2003). Address: City Lights Bookstore 261 Columbus Ave San Francisco CA 94133-4519

FERLINZ, JACK, cardiologist, medical educator; b. Marburg, Austria, Feb. 18, 1942; came to U.S., 1957. s. Anthony and Maria (Nachtigall) F. AB, Harvard U.; MBA, Northeastern U., 1965; MD, Boston U., 1969; doctorate (hon.), U. Maribor, Slovenia, 1990. Diplomate Am. Bd. Internal Medicine, Am. Bd. Cardiovascular Diseases. Intern. U. Hosp. Boston U., 1969-70; jr. resident M. Hitchcock Hosp. Dartmouth Med. Sch., Hanover, N.H., 1970-71; sr. resident Jackson Meml. Hosp., U. Miami, 1971-72; NIH rsch. fellow cardiology P.B. Brigham Hosp., Harvard U., Boston, 1972-74; dir. cardiac cath. lab., asst. chief cardiology V.A.M.C., Long Beach, Calif., 1974-82; asst. prof. medicine U. Calif., Irvine, 1975-81, assoc. prof. medicine, 1981-82; chmn. adult cardiology Cook County Hosp., Chgo., 1982-88; prof. medicine Chgo. Med. Sch., North Chicago, Ill., 1984-88; chmn. dept. of internal medicine Providence Hosp., Southfield, Mich., 1988-92; clin. prof. medicine Wayne State U. Sch. Medicine, Detroit, 1989-92; dir. med. edn. & rsch., prof. medicine & cardiology Hamad Med. Ctr., Doha, Qatar, 1992-94; chief dept. medicine Aleda E. Lutz VA Med. Ctr., Saginaw, Mich., 1994—; clin. prof. medicine Mich. State U. Coll. Human Medicine, 1994—. Vis. prof. numerous U.S., Canadian and European med. schs., 1980—. Mem. editl. bds. Am. Jour. Cardiology, 1989—, Am. Jour. Noninvas Cardiology, 1987—, Jour. Am. Coll. Cardiology, 1984-88, 89-93; contbr. over 300 book chpts. and sci. papers. Named to Begg's Soc. Boston U. Sch. Medicine, 1969. Fellow Am. Coll. Cardiology, Am. Coll. Chest Physicians (chmn. coronary sect. 1983-85), Am. Heart Assn., Am. Coll. Physicians, Am. Coll. Angiology; mem. Am. Fedn. Clin. Rsch., Am. Soc. Clin. Pharm. Therapy. Avocations: mountain climbing, skiing, tennis, scuba diving. Office: VA Med Ctr 1500 Weiss St Saginaw MI 48602-5251 E-mail: jack.ferlinz@med.va.gov.

FERM, DAVID G. magazine publisher; BS in Mktg., Loyola U. With Chgo. Tribune, 1969-80, dir. Eastern divsn. advt. sales, mktg., circulation dir., 1977-80; dir. mktg. N.Y. Times, 1980-82; group v.p. N.Y. Times Mag. Group, 1982; exec. v.p., gen. mgr. Family Circle Mag., 1982; pub. Golf Digest Mag., Trumbull, Conn., 1992-93, Bus. Week, N.Y.C., 1993-99; pres., CEO bus. to bus. group Primedia Inc., 2000—03, exec. v.p., 2000—02, pres., mag. and media group, 2002—. Office: Primedia Inc 745 5th Ave Fl 21 New York NY 10151-2100

FERM, ROBERT LIVINGSTON, religion educator; b. Wooster, Ohio, Jan. 2, 1931; s. Vergilius Ture Anselm and Nellie Agnette (Nelson) F.; m. Fleur Kinney, June 28, 1952 (div. 1968), children: Eric, Alison; m. Sonja Olson. BA, Coll. Wooster, 1952; BD, Yale U., 1955, MA, 1956, PhD, 1958. From instr. to assoc. prof. religion Pomona Coll., Claremont, Calif., 1958-67, prof., 1967-69, acting chmn. dept. religion, 1960-63, chmn. dept. religion, 1963-69; prof., chmn. dept. religion Middlebury (Vt.) Coll., 1969-94, Pardon E. Tillinghast prof. religion, 1988-2000, Tillinghast prof. religion emeritus, 2000. Author: Jonathan Edwards The Younger 1745-1801: A Colonial Pastor, 1976, Piety, Purity Plenty: Images of Protestantism in America, 1991; editor Readings in the History of Christian Thought, 1964, Issues in American Protestantism, 1969. Mem. Am. Acad. Religion. Presbyterian. Home: PO Box 752 Middlebury VT 05753-0052

FERM, VERGIL HARKNESS, anatomist, embryologist; b. West Haven, Conn., Sept. 13, 1924; s. Vergilius T.A. and Nellie (Nelson) F.; m. Ruth Eleanor Rowe, June 5, 1948; children— Daniel W., David V., Judith N., Susan C. AB, Coll. Wooster, 1946; MD, Western Res. U., 1948; MS, U. Wis., 1950, PhD, 1955; MA (hon.), Dartmouth, 1967. Asst. prof. Ind. U., 1955-57; asso. prof. U. Fla., 1957-61; asso. prof. pathology Dartmouth Med. Sch., Hanover, N.H., 1961-66, prof. anatomy and embryology, 1966-94, also chmn. dept. anatomy. Cons. on environ. effects of heavy metals. Mem. Am. Assn. Anatomists, Am. Soc. Human Genetics, Teratology Soc. Exptl. Pathology, Phi Beta Kappa, Sigma Xi. Research, publs. on environ. and genetic factors causing birth defects. Home: 202 Dogford Rd Etna NH 03750-4307

FERMANICH, MARK LEON, education researcher, consultant; b. Fremont, Wis., May 16, 1957; s. Leon Charles and Betty Jane Fermanich; m. Nora Ellen Flood, July 17, 1990. BS, U. Wis., Oshkosh, 1979; MA, U. Wis., 1982, postgrad., 1998—. Rschr./analyst Minn. Dept. Revenue, St. Paul, 1983-89; fin. mgr. Am. Internat. Sch. Rotterdam, South Holland, The Netherlands, 1989-90; legis. analyst Senate Counsel and Rsch., St. Paul, 1990-95; mgr. intergovtl. rels. Mpls. Pub. Schs., 1995-97; program coord. St. Paul Pub. Schs., 1997-98; Spencer fellow CPRE, U. Wis., Madison, 1998—. Contbr.: Economic Report to the Governor, 1987. Mem. Sierra Club, Madison. Mem. Am. Edn. Fin. Assn., Delta Tau Kappa. Avocations: travel, bicycling, sailing, photography. Home: 610 Hintze Rd Madison WI 53704 Office: CPRE Univ Wis 1025 W Johnson St Madison WI 53706

FERMANIS, ERNEST GEORGE, urologic surgeon; b. N.Y.C., May 15, 1944; s. George Anastasios and Georgia Martha Fermanis; m. Pauline Angelique Papageorgopoulos Moore, Feb. 20, 1982; children: Nicole Elaine, Alexis Georgette. BS cum laude, CUNY, 1966; MA cum laude, Columbia U., 1969; MD, Vanderbilt U., 1974. Diplomate Am. Bd. Urology, Nat. Bd. Med. Examiners. Intern Albert Einstein Med. Sch. Montefiore Med. Sch., N.Y.C.; resident NYU Med. Ctr.; assoc. clin. prof. urology, urologic surgeon Crawford Long Hosp. of Emory U., Atlanta, 1982—. Columbia U. scholar, 1966-69. Mem. AMA, AMA Southeastern Sect., Am. Urol. Assn., Am. Urol. Assn. Southeastern Sect., Ga. Urol. Assn., Med. Assn. Ga., Atlanta Urol. Assn., Med. Assn. Atlanta, Am. Hellenic Ednl. Progressive Assn., Lions Club, Phi Beta Kappa. Greek Orthodox. Avocations: reading, pets, swimming, fishing. Home: 3056 Slaton Dr NW Atlanta GA 30305-2007

FERME, VALERIO CRISTIANO, language educator; b. Milan, July 6, 1961; arrived in US, 1980; s. Roberto and A. Patricia (Cicogna) Ferme; 1 adopted child, Michael. BA, Brown U., 1984; MA, Ind. U., 1992; PhD, U. Calif., Berkeley, 1998. Rowing coach US Naval Acad., Annapolis, Md., 1984—86, Brown U., Providence, 1986—90; asst. prof. U. Colo., Boulder, 1998—, assoc. chmn., dir. grad. studies dept. French and Italian, 2002—. Author: Diario Italo-Americano 1989-1996, 1997, Tradurre è Tradire, 2002. Recipient Coach award, U.S. Jr. Nat. Team, 1988, 1989. Mem.: MLA (del. Mountain Region 2003—), Am. Assn. Italian Studies (del. Western region 2003—), Am. Assn. Tchrs. Italian (del. Mountain Region 2003—), Sinclair Lewis Soc. Avocation: rowing. Home: 2520 Carr Ct Lakewood CO 80215 Office: Univ Colo Dept French & Italian Campus Box 238 Boulder CO 80309 Office Fax: 303-492-8338. Business E-Mail: ferme@spot.colorado.edu.

FERN, ALAN MAXWELL, art historian, retired museum director; b. Detroit, Oct. 19, 1930; s. Martin and Rose F.; m. Lois Ann Karbel, Mar. 17, 1957. AB, U. Chgo., 1950, MA, 1954, PhD, 1960; Fulbright scholar, Courtauld Inst., U. London, 1954-55. Asst., instr., asst. prof. humanities The Coll., U. Chgo., 1952-61; asst. curator prints and photographs div. Library of Congress, Washington, 1961, curator fine prints, 1962-64, asst. chief, 1964-73, chief, 1973-76, dir. research dept., 1976-78, dir. spl. collections, 1978-82; dir. Nat. Portrait Gallery, 1982-2000; ret. Author: A Note on the Eragny Press, 1957, (with others) Art Nouveau, 1960, (with M. Constantine) Word and Image, 1968, Leonard Baskin, 1970, (with M. Constantine) Revolutionary Soviet Film Posters, 1974; introductory essay Lasansky: Printmaker, 1975, Eichenberg, The Wood and the Graver, 1977, People and Power, 1985, Arnold Newman's Americans, 1992, (with H. Wright) Prints at the Smithsonian, 1996; contbr. articles to profl. jours. Bd. dirs. Smart Mus. Art, Chgo. Cosmos Club Foundation, Wash. D.C. Decorated chevalier Ordre de la Couronne (Belgium); Ordre des Arts et Lettres (France); comdr. Royal Order of Polar Star (Sweden). Mem. Print Coun. Am. (past pres.), Coll. Art Assn. Am., Am. Antiquarian Soc., AIA (hon.), Double Crown Club (hon.), Cosmos Club (Washington), Grolier Club (N.Y.C.). Home: 3605 Raymond St Chevy Chase MD 20815-4151

FERNALD, HAROLD ALLEN, publishing executive; b. Haverhill, Mass., June 1, 1932; s. Harold Allen and Leona Swan (Horton) F.; m. Sally Camilla Carroll, June 23, 1956; children: Robert Arthur, Melissa Anne, Thomas Allen. BA in Psychology, U. Maine, 1954; MBA, NYU, 1964; PhD, U. Maine, 2002. Trainee Nat. Shawmut Bank, Boston, 1954—55; sales Carter's Ink Co., Cambridge, Mass., 1955—56; sect. chief Western Electric Co., Andover, Mass., 1956—60, buyer N.Y.C., 1960—64; corp. devel. Holt Rinehart & Winston, N.Y.C., 1964—66, pers. dir., 1966—68, mgr. adminstrn., 1968—70; v.p. adminstrn. CBS, Inc. Pub. Group, 1970—77, v.p., gen. mgr. coll. pub. divsn., 1971—77; pub. Down East mag., Fly Rod and Reel mag., Fly Tackle Dealer Mag., Shooting Sportsman Mag., Fishing Tackle Trade News; pres. Down East Enterprise, Inc., Camden, Maine, 1977—2002, chmn., 2002—; pres. Twin City Printery, Inc., Lewiston, Maine, 1978—80, Fernald-Spahn Enterprise, Inc., Rockport, Maine, 1978—80; pres., treas. Hanson Energy Products, Inc., Newcastle, Maine, 1981—85; co-chmn., treas. Global Info. Inc., N.Y.C., 1987—95; pub., CEO Fishing Tackle Trade News, 1995—99. Bd. dirs. John Wiley & Sons., Inc., N.Y.C., United Publs., Inc., Wayfarer Marine, Foreside Co., Inc., Sun Jour., Inc., U. Maine Press; chmn. Performance Media, LLP, 2000—. Vice chmn. Maine Gov.'s Coun. Vacation Travel, 1979-81; bd. dirs. N.E. Health Found., 1982-89, 91-99; bd. dirs. U. Maine-Orono Devel. Found., 1982—, vice chair, 1991, chmn., 1992 93; mem. U. Maine Pres.'s Coun., 1995-97, bd. visitors, vice chmn., 2000-2002, chmn., 2003—; bd. dirs. Maine Cmty. Found., 1989-99, Bay Chamber Concerts, Inc., 1981-85, U. Maine Alumni Coun.; v.p. Farnsworth Mus., 1985-88, pres., 1988-93; chair Knox County Fund, 1996-99, Expansion Arts Fund, 1995-99; mem. Maine Gov.'s Bus. Adv. Com., 1985-86; v.p. Maine Tourism Commn., 1981-89; pres. 1st Congl. Ch., Camden, 1985-86; dir. The Camden Conf., 1987-92. Mem. Assn. Am. Pubs., Internat. Regional Mag. Assn. (dir., pres. 1988-89), Camden-Rockport C. of C. (dir. 1977-85), Alpha Tau Omega, Sigma Mu Sigma. Clubs: Camden Outing (dir. 1979). Lodges: Masons, Rotary (Camden pres. 1986).

FERNANDER, KAREN GENEINE, secondary school educator; b. Ft. Lauderdale, Fla., Feb. 18, 1957; d. Wilbur Franklin and Gloria Elaine (Chunn) Fernander. BA, Wesleyan Coll., Macon, Ga., 1978; MS, Nova U., Ft. Lauderdale, Fla., 1987. Cert. tchr. Fla. Author: (book) Hired Help, 1996. Charter mem. Dem. Women's Club of Ctrl. Broward, Ft. Lauderdale, 1990—91; mem. Dem. Exec. Com., Broward County, 1995—96; bd. dirs. Gwen Cherry Polit. Caucus, Ft. Lauderdale, 1988—90. Recipient Plaque for Svc./MAC chair, Broward Tchrs. Union, Tamarac, Fla., 1990. Mem.: Fla. Edn. Assn. (minority leadership cert. trainer 2001—), Broward Tchrs. Union (area v.p. 1985—, mem. exec. bd. 1985—). Democrat. Baptist. Avocations: travel, snorkeling, theater. Home: 27 SW 7th Ave Dania FL 33004

FERNANDES, DAVID RICHARD, physician; b. N.Y.C., Oct. 28, 1946; m. Donna Marie Catapano, July 21, 1991; children: Justin, Rachel, Julia, Brandon. BS, Fordham U., 16658; MPA, NYU, 1980; MD cum laude, SUNY, Bklyn., 1972. Intern in pediats. and pediatric pathology to resident Kings County Hosp., Bklyn., 1972-74; chief resident Northshore Univ. Hosp., Manhasset, N.Y., 1974-75; fellow in pediatric ambulatory care Bellevue (N.Y.) Hosp., 1975-76; dir. ambulatory care N.Y.C. Dept. Health, 1976-78; tchr. SUNY, Bklyn., 1978-81; physician pvt. practice, Bklyn., 1980—. Mem. Am. Acad. Pediatrics, Brooklyn Pediatric Soc. Avocations: magic, music. Office: 126 95th St Brooklyn NY 11209-7203

FERNANDES, JANE, academic administrator, educational consultant, sign language professional; b. Worcester, MA, Aug. 21, 1956; d. Richard Paul Kellecher and Mary Kathleen (Cosgrove) Kelleher; m. James John Fernandes; children: Sean William, Erin Frances. BA comparative lit., Trinity Coll., Hartford, CT, 1978; MA comparative lit., U of Iowa, Iowa City, IA, 1980, PhD comparative lit., 1986. Acting dir. (ASL prog.) Northeastern U., Boston, 1986—87; chmn. (sign comm.) Gallaudet U., Wash., DC, 1987; coord. (interp. tng.) Kapiolani C.C., Honolulu, 1988—90; dir. Statewide Ctr., Dept. of Ed., Honolulu, 1990—95; VP Gallaudet U, Wash., DC, 1995—2000, provost, 2000—. Edit. rev. bd. Perspectives in Ed. & Deafness, Wash., DC, 1994—97. Co-author: (novels) Signs of Eloquence, 2003. Chair State Commn. Persons with Disabilities, Honolulu, 1993—95, mem., 1988—95; mem. (bd. of dir.) Goodwill Indust. of Honolulu, Honolulu, 1992—95. Recipient Alice Cogswell, Gallaudet U, 1993; fellow alumni, U of Iowa/ IA, 2001. Mem.: Nat. Assoc. of the Deaf. Office: Gallaudet Univ 800 Florida Ave NE Washington DC 20002-3695

FERNANDES, JEANNE MARY, human resource administrator; b. Nairobi, Kenya, May 21, 1948; came to U.S., 1984; d. John Joseph and Joan Bertha (Correya) Athaide; m. Leonard Maurice Fernandes, Oct. 17, 1970; children: Donna Michelle, Nigel Leonard. Royal Soc. arts Diploma, Kenya Poly., 1965. Sec. East African Community, Nairobi, Kenya, 1966-67; exec. sec. East African Airways, Nairobi, 1968-69; adminstrv. asst. to M.D. Cadbury Schweppes, Nairobi, 1969-73; exec. sec. Pfizer Africa Middle East M.C., Nairobi, 1973-79, pers. adminstr., 1979-84; internat. pers. specialist Pfizer, Inc., N.Y.C., 1984-87, sr. pers. assoc., 1987-91, assoc. pers. mgr., 1991-92, pers. mgr., 1992-98, dir. employee resources and comms., 1999-2001, dir. human resources, values and global diversity, 2001—. Mem. NAFE, Am. Fedn. Police, Am. Mgmt. Assn., N.Y. Personnel Mgmt. Assn., Nat. Fgn. Trade Coun. (immigration com.). Roman Catholic. Avocations: music, dancing, reading. Home: 27 Dallaro Dr Shelton CT 06484-2424 Office: Pfizer Pharmaceuticals 42nd St New York NY 10017 E-mail: jeanne.fernandes@pfizer.com.

FERNANDES, JOHN, physician; b. Bombay, June 1, 1959; came to US, 1984; s. Fabian and Grace Fernandes; m. Rohini Fernandes, Nov. 9, 1991; children: Gabriella, Daniel, Stephanie. MBBS, St. Johns Med. Coll., Bangalore, India, 1983; MD, Hahnemann U., Phila., 1988. Resident in pediatrics Hahnemann U. Hosp., Phila., 1985-88; fellow in pediatric cardiology NYU Med. Ctr., N.Y.C., 1988-91; clin. assoc. prof. pediatrics and pediatric cardiology NYU, N.Y.C., 1991—; pediatric cardiology cons., dir. Pediatric Cardiology Cons. N.J., Livingston, 1996—. Fellow Am. Coll. Cardiology, assist. clin. prof. pediatrics/ped. cardiology, Columbia Univ., Coll. of fPhys. & Surgeons, 2002; attending phys., children Hosp. of NY Presbyterian, 2002/ Avocations: outdoor/wildlife recreation, hunting, fishing, cooking. Office: 349 E Northfield Rd Livingston NJ 07039-4802

FERNANDEZ, ALBERTO ANTONIO, security professional; b. Santiago de Cuba, Oriente, Cuba, May 21, 1945; came to the U.S., 1962; s. Carlos and Lydia (Sotera) F.; m. Alexis Quesada, July 19, 1968 (div. July 1984); children: Gyselle, Alexander; m. Rebeca Perez, Sept. 7, 1984; 1 child, Yanelle. Computer programmer, Fla. Computer Coll., 1968; police officer, Metro Dade Police Acad., 1970; AA, Miami (Fla.) Dade C.C., 1973; BS in Criminology, Fla. Internat. U., 1994; drug enforcement spl. agt., DEA Spl. Tng. Sch., 1977. Lic. pvt. investigator, Fla. Police officer Metro Dade Police, Miami, 1969-75; spl. agt. Drug Enforcement Adminstrn., 1976-88; ret., 1988; chief security advisor A.P.A. Internat. Airline, Miami, 1995-96, Faucett Internat. Airline, Miami, 1995-96, Servivensa Internat. Airline, Miami, 1996. Author (movie script) The Challenge, 1993, (screenplay) Between Two Worlds, 1997. Recipient Recognition award for fighting against drugs Dominican Govt., 1987, Outstanding Law Enforcement award U.S. Dept. Justice, 1988; named Police Officer of Yr., Kiwanis Club, Miami, 1971. Mem. Assn. Former Fed. Narcotic Agts., Fla. Internat. U. Alumni. Avocation: reading.

FERNANDEZ, BERNARDO B., JR., physician; b. Havana, Cuba, July 21, 1961; came to U.S., 1973; s. Bernardo B. and Magaly D. Fernandez; m. Rosa Monte, Dec. 28, 1985; children: Steven, Cristina. BS in Biology, U. Miami, 1983; MD, Ponce (P.R.) Sch. Medicine, 1987. Diplomate Am. Bd. Internal Medicine. Resident in internal medicine Cleve. Clinic Found., 1987-90, fellow in vascular medicine, 1990-91, dir. non-invasive vascular lab. & anticoagulation clinics Cleve. Clinic Fla., Ft. Lauderdale, Fla., 1991—2000, chmn. divsn. medicine, 2000—. Sect. head vascular medicine dept cardiology Cleve. Clinic Fla.; asst. prof. clin. medicine Ohio State U. Coll. Medicine. Contbr. articles to profl. jours. Fellow ACP, Soc. Vascular Medicine, Am. Coll. Angiology; mem. Am. Venous Forum. Office: Cleve Clinic Fla Vascular Medicine 2950 Cleveland Clinic Blvd Fort Lauderdale FL 33331

FERNANDEZ, FERDINAND FRANCIS, federal judge; b. 1937; BS, U. So. Calif., 1958, JD, 1963; LLM, Harvard U., 1963. Bar: Calif. 1963, U.S. Dist. Ct. (cen. dist.) Calif. 1963, U.S. Ct. Appeals (9th cir.) 1963, U.S. Supreme Ct. 1967. Elec. engr. Hughes Aircraft Co., Culver City, Calif., 1958-62; law clk. to dist. judge U.S. Dist. Ct. (cen. dist.) Calif., 1963-64; pvt. practice law Allard, Shelton & O'Connor, Pomona, Calif., 1964-80; judge Calif. Superior Ct. San Bernardino County, Calif., 1980-85, U.S. Dist. Ct. (cen. dist.) Calif., L.A., 1985-89, U.S. Ct. Appeals (9th cir.), L.A., 1989—2002, sr. judge, 2002—. Lester Roth lectr. U. So. Calif. Law Sch., 1992. Contbr. articles to profl. jours. Vice chmn. City of La Verne Commn. on Environ. Quality, 1971-73; chmn. City of Claremont Environ. Quality Bd., 1972-73; bd. trustees Pomona Coll., 1990—. Fellow Am. Coll. Trust and Estate Counsel; mem. ABA, State Bar of Calif. (fed. cts. com. 1966-69, ad hoc com. on attachments 1971-85, chmn. com. on adminstrn. of justice 1976-77, exec. com. taxation sect. 1977-80, spl. com. on mandatory fee arbitration 1978-79), Calif. Judges Assn. (chmn. juvenile cts. com. 1983-84, faculty mem. Calif. Jud. Coll. 1982-83, faculty mem. jurisprudence and humanities course 1983-85), L.A. County Bar Assn. (bull. com. 1974-75), San Bernardino County Bar Assn., Pomona Valley Bar Assn. (co-editor Newsletter 1970-72, trustee 1971-78, sec.-treas. 1973-74, 2d v.p. 1974-75, 1st v.p. 1975-76, pres. 1976-77), Estate Planning Coun. Pomona Valley (sec. 1966-76), Order of Coif, Phi Kappa Phi, Tau Beta Pi, Eta Kappa Nu. Office: US Ct Appeals 9th Cir 125 S Grand Ave Ste 602 Pasadena CA 91105-1621

FERNANDEZ, FERNANDO LAWRENCE, aeronautical engineer, research company executive; b. N.Y.C., Dec. 31, 1938; s. Fernando and Luz Esther (Fortuno) F.; m. Carmen Dorothy Mays, Aug. 26, 1962; children: Lisa Marie, Christopher John (dec.). ME, Stevens Inst. Tech., 1960, MS in Applied Mechanics, 1961; PhD in Aeronautics, Calif. Inst. Tech., 1969. Engr. Lockheed Missiles & Space Co., Sunnyvale, Calif., 1961-63; div. mgr. The Aerospace Corp., El Segundo, Calif., 1963-72; program mgr. R & D Assocs., Santa Monica, Calif., 1972-75; v.p. Phys. Dynamics, Inc., San Diego, 1975-76; pres. Arete Assocs., San Diego, 1976-93, AETC Inc., San Diego, 1994-98; dir. Def. Advanced Rsch. Projects Agy., Arlington, Va., 1998-2001; disting. rsch. prof., dir. inst. tech. initiatives, Stevens Inst. Tech., Hoboken, NJ, 2001—. Mem. Chief Naval Ops. Exec. Panel, Washington, 1983-98. Editor Jour. AIAA, 1970; contbr. articles to Fluid Mechanics. Office: Stevens Inst Tech Castle Point on the Hudson Hoboken NJ 07030 E-mail: ffernand@stevens-tech.edu.

FERNANDEZ, HAPPY CRAVEN (GLADYS FERNANDEZ), academic administrator; b. Scranton, Pa., Mar. 3, 1939; d. Orvin William and Florence (Waite) Craven; m. Richard Ritter Fernandez, June 10, 1961; children: John Ritter, David Craven, Richard William. BA, Wellesley Coll., 1961; MA in Teaching, Harvard U., 1962; MA, U. Pa., Phila., 1970; EdD, Temple U., 1984. Social studies tchr. various pub. schs., 1961-64; from vis. asst. prof. to prof. Sch. Social Adminstrn. Temple U., Phila., 1974—92; exec. dir. Parents Union for Pub. Sch., Phila., 1980-82; dir. The Child Care and Family Policy Inst., Phila., 1988-92; city councilwoman Phila., 1992-98; candidate for mayor City Phila., 1998-99; pres. Moore Coll. of Art and Design, Phila., 1999—. Cons. Nat. Com. for Citizens in Edn., Columbia, Md., 1982—87, Phila. Youth Study Ctr., 1988—90; commr. Phila. Gas Commn, 1992—97; trustee Edn. Law Ctr., Phila., 1983—; bd. dirs. Cultural Fund, 1996—98; chair Select Com. on Bus. Taxes, 1992—98, Select com. on Land Reuse, 1997—98; pres. Delaware Valley Child Care Coun., 1988—90. Author: Parents Organizing to Improve Schools, 1976, The Child Advocacy Handbook, 1980, Elder Care and Child Care Policies of Philadelphia Area Businesses, 1991. Chair bd. dirs. Am. for Dem. Action, Phila., 1980—92; chair Children's Coalition, 1982—86; bd. dirs. Phila. Citizens for Children and Youth, 1986—93; Greater Phila. Cultural Alliance, 2000—; Rock Sch. Ballet, 2000—01; Pa. Women's Forum, 2000—; founder Parents Union for Pub. Schs., 1972—, chair, 1972—75, 1978—80; del. Dem. Nat. Conv., Atlanta, 1988, N.Y.C., 1992, Chgo., 1996. Recipient Women in Edn. award Womens Way, 1989, Pub. Citizen of Yr. award NASW, 1991, Local Elected Ofcl. award Pa. Citizens for Better Librs., 1993, Pub. Svc. award Homeowners Assn. Phila., 1994 Phila. Op. Smile award, 1999, Woman of Yr.-Ivy Willis award, 2000, Fleisher Art Meml. Founders award 2001; named Outstanding Adv., Health Promotions Coun., 1994, 2002, Dist. Daughter of Pa., 2002; Wellesley Coll. scholar, 1961. Fellow: Nat. Assn. Orthopsychiatry; mem.: Nat. Assn. Ind. Colls. and Univs. (bd. dirs. 2003—), Greater Phila. C. of C., Assn. Ind. Schs. of Art and Design (nat. sec. 2001—, nat. bd. dirs.). Mem. United Church of Christ. Avocations: tennis, gardening. Home: 3400 Baring St Philadelphia PA 19104-2076 Office: Moore College 20th & Parkway 4 Philadelphia PA 19103 E-mail: hfernandez@moore.edu.

FERNANDEZ, HELEN AGNES, municipal official; b. Mansfield, La., Jan. 15, 1944; d. Arthur and Tommie Lee (Sabbath) Brown; m. Lamar Green (div. Nov. 2, 1973); 1 child, Marla elena Green McNear; m. David C. Fernandez, Dec. 9, 1995. BA in Edn., Ariz. State U., 1968; doctoral postgrad., Arizona State Univ. Sch. of Pub. Affairs, 1992—2003; MEd, No. Ariz. U., 2001. Cert. coll. tchr. Ariz. Jr. H.S. tchr., Phoenix, 1968—76; math. tchr. Job Corps, Phoenix, 1976—78; retail buyer Broadway S.W., Mesa, Ariz., 1978—84; real estate adminstr. City of Phoenix, 1984—91, elections adminstr., 1991—; tchr. Glendale (Ariz.) C.C., 1997. Candidate Valley Leadership Inst., Phoenix, 2003; tchr., chmn. vacation bible sch. Bapt. Ch.; campaign worker Terry Goddard for Mayor, Phoenix, 1982; chmn. Bapt. Women's Day. Mem.: Nat. Forum for Black Pub. Adminstrs. (bd. dirs. 2001—, membership chmn. 2002—), Internat. City County Mgmt. Assn., Toastmasters, Delta Sigma Theta. Avocations: collecting dolls, biographies, skiing, study of Black History, genealogy, travel. Office: City of Phoenix City Clk Dept 200 W Washington St Phoenix AZ 85003

FERNANDEZ, HERMES A., III, lawyer; b. Queens, N.Y., Aug. 22, 1955; s. Hermes Alexander and Helen Gloria (Hall) F.; m. Theresa Anne Dehm, Sept. 10, 1977; children: Holly Kathryn, Amy Elizabeth, Daniel Dehm. BA with honors, LeMoyne Coll., 1977; JD magna cum laude, Syracuse U., 1981. Bar: N.Y. 1982, U.S. Dist. Ct. (no. dist.) N.Y. 1991, U.S. Ct. Appeals (2d cir.) 1991, U.S. Ct. Appeals (5th cir.) 1984. Jud. clk. Hon. John MacKenzie U.S. Dist. Ct. (ea. dist.) Va., Norfolk, 1981-82; trial atty. civil divsn. U.S. Dept. Justice, Washington, 1982-86; asst. counsel to gov. State of N.Y., Albany, 1986-90; assoc., ptnr. Bond, Schoeneck & King, LLP, Albany, 1990—. Author articles. Mem. Citizens Budget Adv. Com., Albany, 1996-99; past pres. Homeless and Travelers Aid Soc., Albany; chair legis. com. MS Soc. N.E. N.Y., Albany, 1997-2000, mem. clin. adv. com., 2000—; past mem. bd. dirs. Capitol Region chpt. N.Y. Civil Liberties Union. Mem. N.Y. State Bar Assn. (health law sect., chair profl. discipline com., legis. policy com.), Am. Health Lawyers Assn., Univ. Club., Pine Haven Country Club. Avocations: golf, history. Office: Bond Schoeneck & King PLLC 111 Washington Ave Albany NY 12210-2202 E-mail: fernanh@bsk.com.

FERNANDEZ, JAMES, anthropology educator; b. Chgo., Nov. 27, 1930; m. Renate Helene Lellep, Oct. 18, 1958; children: Lisa Oyana, Luke Oliver, Andrew McClintock. BA, Amherst Coll., 1952; postgrad. in cultural anthropology, Northwestern U., 1953—54; postgrad., U. Madrid, 1954—55, Museo Etnologico Barcelona, 1955; PhD, Northwestern U., 1962. Tchg. asst. North-

western U., 1955—57, grad. rsch. fellow in program of African studies, 1956—57; instr. sociology and anthropology Smith Coll., 1961—62, asst. prof. anthropology, 1962—64; area program dir. Gabon Peace Corps trainees, 1962—63; cons., lectr. Fgn. Svc. Inst., Washington, 1964—70; prof. anthropology Dartmouth Coll., 1969—75, chmn. dept. anthropology, 1971—75; prof. anthropology Princeton U., 1975—86, chmn. dept. anthropology, 1978—82; prof. anthropology U. Chgo., 1982—. Lectr. and cons. in field. Recipient Guggenheim fellowship, 2003, Carnegie Fund Grant for African Rsch., 1955, Ford Found. fellowship, 1957, Ford Found. Ext. fellowship, 1959, Social Sci. Rsch. Coun.-Am. Coun. Learned Socs. African Rsch. fellowship, 1965, NSF grant, 1970, 1971, Spanish-N.Am. Joint Com. fellowship, 1977, NEH grant, 1988—89. Fellow: African Studies Assn., Am. Anthropol. Assn., Am. Acad. Religion, Am. Acad. Arts and Scis.; mem.: Northeastern Anthropol. Assn., Sigma Xi. Office: U Chgo Dept Anthropology 1126 E 59th St Chicago IL 60637

FERNANDEZ, JOSE WALFREDO, lawyer; b. Cienfuegos, Cuba, Sept. 19, 1955; arrived in U.S., 1967; s. Jose Rigoberto and Flora (Gomez) Fernandez; m. Andrea Gabor, June 22, 1985. BA, Dartmouth Coll., 1977; JD, Columbia U., 1980. Bar: N.Y. 1981, N.J. 1981, U.S. Dist. Ct. (so. dist.) N.Y. 1981, U.S. Dist. Ct. N.J. 1981. Assoc. Curtis, Mallet, Prevost, Colt & Mosle, N.Y.C., 1981-84, Baker & McKenzie, N.Y.C., 1984-89, ptnr., 1989-96, O'Melveny & Myers, L.L.P., N.Y.C., 1996—, mng. ptnr. N.Y. office, 2002—. Adj. prof. N.Y. Law Sch., 1984—87. Contbr. Bd. dirs. Ballet Hispanico, Ceiba Prodns., WBGO-FM Newark Pub. Radio; mem. adv. bd. Coun. of Ams., 2001—; bd. of trustees Dartmouth Coll., 2002—. Mem.: ABA (Inter-Am. law com. 1955—, Ctrl. Am. task force 1985—92, presdl. commn. L.Am. 1986—91), N.Y.C. Bar Assn. (fgn. and comparative law com., Inter-Am. affairs com. 1996—98, city bar fund 1999—), Brazilian-U.S. C. of C. (bd. dirs. 1994—99,), U.S.-Spain C. of C. (bd. dirs.). Avocation: Avocations: sports, non-fiction writing, travel. Home: 508 E 87th St New York NY 10128-7602 Office: O'Melveny & Myers LLP Citicorp Ctr 153 E 53rd St Fl 53D New York NY 10022-4611

FERNANDEZ, JOSEPH JACOB, sportscaster, basketball announcer; b. Red Bluff, Calif., Feb. 27, 1978; s. Joe Garcia and Barbara Jean Fernandez. BA magna cum laude, Humboldt State U., 2000. Announcer, play-by-play voice Humboldt State U., Arcata, Calif., 1998—2000; sportscaster KRFH/KHSU, Arcata, Calif., 1998—2000; radio sportscaster McCarthy Broadcasting, Redding, Calif., 1999, KHTK Sports 1140, Sacramento, 1999; TV sportscaster KAEF ABC 23, Eureka, Calif., 2000, KNVN North Valley News, Chico, Calif., 2000—. Mem.: Kappa Tau Alpha. Avocations: sports, surfing, fishing, running, volunteering. Home: PO Box 154 Cottonwood CA 96022

FERNANDEZ, KATHLEEN M. cultural organization administrator; b. Dayton, Ohio, Oct. 8, 1949; d. Norbert Katzen and Yenema Vermeda (Bermingham) F.; m. James Robert Hillibish, Oct. 1, 1977. BA, Otterbein Coll., 1971. Edn. asst. Ohio Hist. Soc., Columbus, 1971, vol. coord., 1971-74, interpretive specialist Zoar, 1975-88, site mgr., 1988—. Author: A Singular People: Images of Zoar, 2003. Bd. dirs., newsletter editor Ohio & Erie Canal Corridor Coalition, Akron, 1989—. Mem. Am. Assn. State and Local History, Nat. Trust Hist. Preservation, Zoar Cmty. Assn., Communal Studies Assn. (pres. 1981, editor newsletter 1981-86, 97—, bd. dirs. 1995—), Am. Assn. Mus. (surveyor mus. assistance program 1999—). Office: Zoar Village State Meml PO Box 404 221 W 3d St Zoar OH 44697

FERNANDEZ, MARY JOE, retired professional tennis player; b. Dominican Republic, Aug. 19, 1971; d. Jose and Sylvia F. 3rd ranked woman USTA; winner women's doubles (with Patty Fendick) Australia Open, 1991; gold medalist women's doubles Olympic Games, Barcelona, Spain, 1992, Atlanta, 1996; winner (with Davenport) French Open doubles Paris, 1996; mem. winning U.S. Fed Cup Team Atlantic City, N.J., 1996. Ranked # 8 World Tennis Assn. Tour, 1995, # 1 USA Women, 1995.

FERNANDEZ, MIKE, healthcare company executive; b. Long Beach, Calif., Aug. 31, 1956; s. Emilio and Starr Fernandez; m. Patricia Hamilton; children: Laura, Will. BA in Govt., Georgetown U., 1978, MS in Acctg., 1983. Rschr. Dem. Study Group, Washington, 1975-76; asst. treas. Nat. Com. for Effective Congress, Washington, 1976-79; press sec. U.S. Senator Ernest F. Hollings, Washington, 1980-87; dir. bus. presentations Eastman Kodak Co., Rochester, N.Y., 1987-93, dir. exec. comm., 1993-96; v.p. pub. rels. U.S. West Inc., Denver, 1996-2000; sr. v.p. comm. and pub. affairs CIGNA, Phila., 1999-2000. Dir. Pub. Rels. Seminar, N.Y.C., 2000—. City councilman, Rochester, 1994—96; dep. Coalition Affordable Quality Healthcare, 2000—; chmn. Nat. Sch. Bds. Found., Alexandria, Va., 1999—2000; chmn. corp. bd. advisors Nat. Coun. La Raza, Washington, 1997—2000; dir. Pub. Edn. and Bus. Coalition, Denver, 1999—2000; nat. bd. dirs. Vols. of Am.; commr. Bd. Edn., Rochester, 1990—94; bd. dirs. Pa. Econ. League, 2002—; mem. seminar com. Pub. Rels. Seminar. Named one of Most Influential Hispanics in Corp. Am., Hispanic Bus. Mag., 1997, 1998, 1999, 2000, 2001, Pub. Rels. All Star for Strategic Comm., Reputation Mgmt. Mag., 1999, Communicator of Yr., Denver chpt. Internat. Assn. Bus. Communicators, 1999; recipient Silver Anvil award, Pub. Rels. Soc. Am., 1995, 1996, Mktg. Rsch. award, Am. Mktg. Assn., 1999. Mem.: Am. Assn. Health Plans, Health Ins. Assn. Am. (policy com. 2000—01), Arthur W. Page Soc. (pub. affairs coun.). Home: 222 Broughton Ln Villanova PA 19085 Office: CIGNA 1650 Market St One Liberty Pl Philadelphia PA 19103

FERNANDEZ, RAMONA ESTHER, adult education educator; b. Elizabeth, N.J., Nov. 26, 1947; d. Domingo Fernandez and Irene Csertan. BA, SUNY, Old Westbury, 1970; MA, U. Ariz., 1973; PhD, U. Calif., Santa Cruz, 1995. Prof. Sacramento City Coll., 1975-97; asst. prof. Mich. State U., E. Lansing, 1998-99. Co-author: From Mouse to Mermaid: The Politics of Film, Gender, and Culture, 1995; author: Imagining Literacy, 2001. Fellow Ford Found., 1989-95, Smithsonian Instn., 1992-94. Office: Mich State U Am Thought and Lang 235 Bessy Hall East Lansing MI 48823

FERNANDEZ, RENÉ, aerospace engineer; b. Havana, Cuba, Oct. 2, 1961; came to U.S., 1967; s. Ramon and Emma (Fumero) F. Student, Broward Community Coll., Ft. Lauderdale, Fla., 1979-80; BS in Engring., Case Western Res. U., 1986, MSc in Engring., 1993, postgrad., 1993—. Registered profl. engr., Ohio. Rsch. fellow Univ. Space Rsch. Assn., Cleve., 1986; grad. teaching asst. Case Western Res. U., Cleve., 1986-87; rsch. engr. NASA Lewis Rsch. Ctr., Cleve., 1987—. Mem. speaker's bur. NASA Lewis Rsch. Ctr., 1988—; sci. fair judge Ohio Acad. Sci., Columbus, Ohio, 1988, 90. Pilot Search and Rescue Civil Air Patrol USAF, 1st lt. Civil Air Patrol USAF. Mem. AIAA (chmn. No. Ohio sect. 1991-92, dep. dir. for young mem. programs region III), ASTM, ASME, AAAS, IEEE, Optical Soc. Am., Aircraft Owners & Pilots Assn., Soc. Photo-optical Instrumentation Engrs., Ohio Acad. Sci., NASA Ski Club, NASA Karate Club. Roman Catholic. Avocations: scuba diving, skiing, dancing, astronomy, flying. Office: NASA Lewis Rsch Ctr 21000 Brookpark Rd Cleveland OH 44135-3191 E-mail: renedeb@prodigy.net.

FERNANDEZ-MARTINEZ, JOSE, physician; b. San Juan, P.R., Apr. 2, 1930; s. Telesforo and Luisa (Martinez) Fernandez; m. Carmen Dolores Noya, Dec. 26, 1954. BS, Villanova U., 1951; MD, U. Pa., 1955. Diplomate Am. Bd. Internal Medicine, Sub-Bd. Cardiovascular Diseases. Intern U. Pa. Hosps., Phila., 1955-56, resident in internal medicine, 1956-59, fellow in hypertension and cardiovascular diseases, 1956-57; practice medicine specializing in cardiovascular diseases Santurce, P.R., 1961—; attending physician in internal medicine San Juan City Hosp., 1961—; assoc. prof. medicine U. P.R., 1978-88, prof. Sch. of Medicine, 1988—. Served to capt. U.S. Army, 1959-61. Fellow ACP, Am. Coll. Cardiology; mem. P.R. Med. Assn. (pres. sci. coun. 1968), Alpha Omega Alpha. Office: Ashford Med Ctr Ste 208 29 Washington St San Juan PR 00907-1510

FERNANDEZ-VELAZQUEZ, JUAN RAMON, university chancellor; b. San Juan, P.R., Aug. 9, 1936; s. Ramon Fernández-Serrano and Elena Velazquez; m. Norah Moran, 1960 (div. 1967); children: Lynnette, Yasmin; m. Sonia M. Ramirez, Aug. 12, 1971 (div. 1992); 1 child, Juan Ernesto. BS, U. P.R., 1957, M in Pub. Adminstrn., 1963; PhD, CUNY, 1978; D honoris causa, U. Nacional, Piura, Peru, 1987. Adminstrv. tech. II Dept. Labor, San Juan, 1960; asst. to dir., lectr. Sch. Pub. Adminstrn., U. P.R., Río Piedras Campus, 1961-64, asst. prof., 1969-72, 79-80, assoc. prof., 1980-85, prof., 1984—, also chancellor, 1985-92; acad. senator faculty of social scis. U. P.R., 1983-85, mem. univ. bd., rep. Río Piedras Campus Acad. Senate, 1984-85; spl. asst. to Gov. of P.R., 1965-68; prof. Bklyn. Coll., CUNY, 1973-76; prof. sch. of pub. affairs Baruch Coll., CUNY, 1994—. Vis. assoc. rschr. Bildner Ctr. CUNY Grad. Sch., 1993-95; participant Fifth Ann. Conf. Caribbean Studies Assn., Curacao, 1980 and ann. meeting, 1981, seminar P.R. Planning Bd., 1979, symposium P.R. Found. for the Humanities, 1979, panel discussion Inst. Policy Scis. Ctr. for Study of State Policy, Duke U., 1981, seminar for grad. students Grad. Sch. Edn., Harvard U., 1981, Fifth Hispanic-Am. Conf., U. Mich., Ann Arbor, 1983, other confs., seminars; lectr. in field, 1975—; cons. Tchr.'s Assn., Hato Rey, P.R., 1984; hon. prof. U. Iberoamericana Sto. Do., Dominican Republic; lectr., bd. dirs. Ralph Bunche Inst. on the UN, 1986; vis. scholar, Bildner Ctr. for Western Hemisphere Studies, CUNY, 1993, adv. to the pres., Interam. U. P.R., 1996-97; founder Consenso Nacional Puertorriqueno, 1999; coodr. Com. for Devel. of Vieques Island, P.R., 1999; spl. commr. for Vieques and Culebra, Gov. P.R., 2001. Contbr. chpts. to books and articles to profl. jours. Mem. Puerto Rico's delegation to UNESCO World Conf. on Higher Edn., Paris, 1998; del. to Internat. Sem. on Evaluation and Accreditation Models for Higher Edn. Instns. in Latin Am. and the Caribbean/sponsored by IESALC-UNESCO, San Juan, 1999 Named Most Disting. Grad. Class 1953, Ctrl. High Sch. P.R.; Ford Found. grantee, 1981; recipient Disting. Alumni award CUNY, 1988. Mem. Acad. Arts, History and Archeology of P.R., Acad. for the Humanities and Scis., Caribbean Studies Assn.

FERNBERGER, MARILYN FRIEDMAN, events organizer, consultant, civic leader; b. Phila., Aug. 13, 1927; d. David and Edith (Rosen) Friedman; m. Edward Fernberger, June 21, 1947; children: Edward Jr., Ellen, James. BA, U. Pa., 1948. Promoter, developer, executor major events for cmty. orgns. and instns. on local, nat. and internat. basis, Pa., 1958—. Co-chmn. U.S. Pro Indoor Tennis Championships, 1967-92; co-chmn. Phila. Women's Tennis Championships, 1970-79; cons. tennis promoters throughout U.S., creats new events and expands markets for existing events; staged profl. women's tennis tournament, Phila., 1970-79; cons. Internat. Mgmt. Co. for Advanta Women's Tennis Championships; cons. on fundraising and art adminstrn.; former event coord. U. Pa. Inaugural Centenary Tennis Hall of Fame dinner; bd. dirs. Phila. Internat. Indoor Tennis Corp., Nat. Jr. Tennis League, Am. Tennis Assn., Phila. Tennis Patrons Assn., Phila. Youth Tennis & Edn. Benefit, Arthur Ashe Youth Tennis and Edn. Bd.; mem. Middle States Patrons Assn.; chmn. Middle States Devel. Com., Nat. Arthur Ashe Day; publ. com. U.S. Tennis Assn.; mem. Phila. Women's Interclub Bd.; founder, mgr. Ea. Pa. Boy's Championships; active Phila. Gold Cup; founder, chmn. People to People Sports Jr. Exhbns Contbr. to nat. and internat. publs., including World Tennis mag., Tennis South Africa, Tennis Italiano, Tenis Espanol, Algeman Dagblad, Royal Tennis, Japan, Tennis Australia, Tennis de France, Brit. Lawn Tennis Jour. of Lawn Tennis Assn., Eng. Trustee Phila. Mus. Art; mem. adv. com. Phila. Mus. Art Assocs.; mem. bd. or officer Rodin Mus., United Way, Nat. Coun. Jewish Women, Fairmount Park Assn. for Hist. Sites, Phila. Sports Congress, Nat. Art Mus. Sport, Internat. Tennis Hall of Fame and Mus.; dir. Tennis N.Am.; active Pa. Ballet, Emergency Aid, Albert Einstein Med. Ctr., Drama Guild, Ctr. for Internat. Visitors, Festival Theatre New Plays, U. Arts, Inst. Contemporary Art; pres. Rodin Mus.; bd. dir. Phila. Mus. Art, Internat. Tennis Hall Fame; mem. mus. devel. gala 2004 50th anniversary celebration; chmn. Phila. City of Yr. 1996 Dinner, ITHF. Recipient Marlboro award, Humanitarian Svc. award Phila. Bd. Edn., Kelly award Pa. Parks and Recreation Commn., Cmty. Svc. award Big Bros.-Big Sisters, Police Athletic League, Coren award Nat. Jr. Tennis League Phila., YWCA, Phila., Mangan Svc. award USTA/Mid. States, Pub. Svc. award City of Phila., 8 times, Appreciation award Orange Bowl Com. Rotary Club, Phila., Phila. Bd. Edn., Chmn.'s award Internat. Tennis Hall of Fame and Mus., Pres.'s award ITHF, 2002; named to USTA/Mid. States Hall of Fame. Mem. U.S. Tennis Writers Assn. (bd., officer), Internat. Tennis Tournament Dirs. Assn. (bd., officer), Assn. Tournament Dirs. (bd., officer), U. Pa. Alumni Assn. (bd., officer), Internat. Tennis Club USA (hon.). Home and Office: 1112 Penmore Pl Rydal PA 19046-1239

FERNER, DAVID CHARLES, non-profit management and development consultant; b. Rochester, N.Y., Mar. 14, 1933; s. John Theodore and Dorothy Flora (Seel) F.; m. Ursula Milda Thieme, Sept. 6, 1958, (dec. Nov. 12, 2002). BA, Amherst Coll., 1955; MEd, U. Rochester, 1957; postgrad., Columbia U., 1961. Dir. student activities U. Rochester, N.Y., 1956-58; asst. to provost Tchrs. Coll. Columbia U., N.Y.C., 1959-60; asst. dir. devel. St. Lawrence U., Canton, N.Y., 1961-62; dir. devel. Sarah Lawrence Coll., Bronxville, N.Y., 1962-66; cons., v.p. Frantzreb & Pray Assocs., Inc., N.Y.C., 1966-72, v.p., sec. Arlington, Va., 1972-75; pres. Frantzreb, Pray, Ferner & Thompson, Inc., Arlington, 1975-77, David C. Ferner & Assocs., Annandale, Va., 1977-80; v.p., dir. devel. Minn. Orchestral Assn., Mpls., 1980-87; mng. ptnr. Currie, Ferner, Scarpetta & DeVries, Mpls., 1987-99, cons., 2000—. Contbr. articles to profl. publs. Bd. dirs. Madeline Island Mus. Camp, 1992-98. Amherst Coll. scholar, 1951-55. Mem. Assn. Fundraising Profls. (bd. dirs. Minn. chpt. 1995-97), Nat. Com. Planned Giving, Am. Symphony Orch. League, Opera Am. Home: 245 Wekiva Cv Destin FL 32541-4763

FERNHABER, STEPHANIE ANN, grant administrator; b. Greenville, Mich., Apr. 16, 1975; d. Steven Paul and Trudy Ann Bosman; m. Ethan Daniel Fernhaber, Aug. 26, 2000. BA in Bus. Mgmt. and Spanish, Ripon Coll., Ripon, Wis., 1997; MBA, Marquette U., 1999; postgrad. in PhD in Entrepreneurship program, Ind. U., 2002—. Project mgr. Comml. Credit Consultants, Waukesha, Wis., 1997—2000; ERP bus. process analyst Brady Corp., Milw.; grant adminstr. Inst. for Entrepreneurship, Appleton, Wis., 1999—. Mem.: Women's Exch. Milw. (com. 2001—02), Nat. Assn. Women Bus. Owners (cmty. outreach Met. Milw. chpt. 2000—01), Acad. Mgmt. Home: 2301 North Dunn St Bloomington IN 47408-1326 Office: Indiana U Kelly Sch Bus 1309 East 10th St Bloomington IN 47405-1701 Personal E-mail: sfernhaber@hotmail.com. E-mail: sfernhab@indiana.edu.

FERNHOLZ, ERHARD ROBERT, investment executive; b. Princeton, N.J., Mar. 27, 1941; s. Erhard and Mary (Briganti) F.; m. Luisa Turrin, June 4, 1970; children: Daniel, Ricardo. AB, Princeton U., 1962; PhD, Columbia U., 1967. Rsch. dir. Met. Securities, N.Y.C., 1980-87; chief investment officer Enhanced Investment Techs., Princeton, 1987—. Author: Stochastic Portfolio Theory, 2002; contbr. articles to profl. jours.; patentee in field. NSF grantee, 1963-69. Home: 12 Dogwood Ln Princeton NJ 08540-5629 Office: Enhanced Investment Techs One Palmer Sq Princeton NJ 08542

FERNHOLZ, LUISA TURRIN, statistician, educator; arrived in U.S., 1970; d. Vanilio Turrin and Augusta Scian; m. E. Robert Fernholz, June 4, 1970; children: Daniel Turrin, Ricardo Turrin. Licenciada en Matematicas, U. Buenos Aires, 1968; MS in Stats., Rutgers U., 1977, PhD in Stats., 1979. Asst. prof. stats. U. Pa., Phila., 1979—80; lectr. stats. Princeton (N.J.) U., 1980—83; asst. prof. stats. Temple U., Phila., 1987—94, assoc. prof. stats., 1994—2002, prof. stats., 2002—; dir. Minerva Rsch. Found., Princeton, NJ, 1993—. Mem. adv. coun. dept. math. Princeton U., 1996—. Author: (book) Von Mises Calculus for Statistical Functionals, 1983; co-editor (with Brillinger and Morgenthaler): The Practice of Data Analysis, 1997; co-editor: (with Morgenthaler and Stahel) Statistics in the Sciences : Environmetrics, Genetics, and Related Fields, 2001; contbr. articles to profl. jours. Mem.: The Bernoulli Soc., Am. Statis. Assn., Inst. Math. Stats. Office: Temple Univ Stats Dept 13th St (Speakman Hall) Philadelphia PA 19122 E-mail: fernholz@temple.edu.

FERNIANY, ISAAC WILLIAM, health system administrator; b. Mobile, Ala., Mar. 15, 1951; s. Joe Michael and Vivian Elizabeth (Farah) F.; m. Dana Brownell Hardy, Apr. 19, 1978; children: Dylan Hardy, Glennie Brownell. BS, U. Ala., 1973; MS, U. Ala., Birmingham, 1975, PhD, 1984. Asst. adminstr. Bryce Hosp., Tuscaloosa, 1975—77; dir. resource devel. S.W. Health Systems Agy., Mobile, 1977—79; owner Mgmt. Resources, Birmingham, 1981—83; faculty U. Ala., Birmingham, 1982—83; v.p. devel. Health Care Services Am., Birmingham, 1983—87; CEO Hill Crest Hosp., Birmingham, 1987—88; exec. adminstr. U. Ala., Birmingham, 1988—90, assoc. adminstr. strategic planning and market devel., 1990—; sr. v.p. and chief adminstrv. officer U. Pa. Health System, Phila., 1992—. Mem. faculty U. Ala., Birmingham, 1987-92, lectr., 1993—; adj. faculty Wharton Sch. Bus., 1993—; sr. fellow Leonard Davis Inst., 1993—. Author: Bay Area Directory, 1979. Mem.: Am. Mktg. Soc. Episcopalian. Avocations: bike riding, walking, kayaking. Office: U Pa Health System 21 Penn Tower Philadelphia PA 19144-1407 E-mail: wferniany@yahoo.com.

FERNSLER, JOHN PAUL, lawyer; b. Lebanon, Pa., Dec. 24, 1940; s. K. Paul and Elizabeth M. (Snyder) F.; m. Christine Joan Chester, July 31, 1965; children: Euan, Scott. AB, Dickinson Coll., 1962; JD, U. Mich., 1965. Bar: Pa. 1965, U.S. Dist. Ct. (ea. and we. dists.) Pa., U.S. Ct. Appeals (3d cir.). Assoc. Snyder, Balmer & Kershner, Reading, Pa., 1965-66; dep. atty. gen. Commonweatlh of Pa., Harrisburg, 1968-70; chief counsel HUD, Pitts., 1970-81; ptnr. Reed Smith Shaw & McClay, Pitts., 1981-97; corp. counsel Weis Markets, Inc., Sunbury, Pa., 1997—2002. Lectr., spl. cons. Mortgage Bankers Assn., 1985-92; solicitor Mt. Lebanon Parking Authority, 1990-91; mem. Mt. Lebanon Commn., 1992-96, pres. 1993; bd. mem., treas. Med./Rescue Team South Authority, 1995-97. Contbr. articles to profl. jours. Mem. Mt. Lebanon Zoning Hearing Bd., 1981—88, sec., 1982—82, chmn., 1983—88; pres. Linn Conservancy; chmn. Mt. Lebanon Rep. Com., 1990—92; bd. dirs., counsel Coun. for Luth. Campus Ministry in Gt. Pitts., 1979—82. Decorated Commendation medal; recipient Spl. Cert. Pa. Dept Community Affairs, 1970. Mem. ABA (urban state and local law sect. coun. 1984-87), Pa. Bar Assn., Allegheny County Bar Assn. (real property sect., chmn., 1988), Am. Coll. Real Estate Lawyers (elected). Republican. Episcopalian. Avocations: bicycling, walking, photography. Home: 20 Brown St Lewisburg PA 17837-2104 Office: Weis Markets Inc 1000 S 2nd St # 471 Sunbury PA 17801-3399 E-mail: jjfern@jdweb.com.

FERO, LESTER KNIFFIN, aerospace engineer, consultant; b. Beaver Dams, N.Y., Feb. 28, 1919; s. Ray L. and Bertha (Kniffin) F.; m. Margery G. Wilde, Sept. 11, 1944; children: Gregory G. (dec.), Leslie Kay. BS in Aerospace Engring., U. Mich., 1940. Structures engr. Curtiss-Wright, Buffalo, 1940-46; v.p. Dansaire Corp., Dansville, N.Y., 1946-47; chief structural engr. Bell Aircraft, Niagara Falls, N.Y., 1947-56; program mgr. Martin Co., Balt., 1956-63, NASA Hdqrs., Washington, 1963-70; staff asst. NASC/Exec. Office of Pres., Washington, 1970-72; dir. space transp. plans NASA Hdqrs., Washington, 1972-82; pres., chief engr. Fero Enterprises, Inc., Bowie, Md., 1984-87, Loudon, Tenn., 1987—. Guest lectr. U. Mich., Ann Arbor, 1953. Pres. Community Assn., Lutherville, Md., 1960. Recipient Achievement awards NASA, 1969, 75, 82. Assoc. fellow AIAA (chmn. Balt. sect. 1961).

FEROZ, EHSAN HABIB, accounting educator, researcher, writer; b. Chittagong, Bangladesh, Jan. 9, 1952; came to U.S., 1979, permanent resident, 1983, naturalized, 1990; s. Mohammad Obaidul and Sabera (Begum) Hakim; m. Kishwar Sultana Beg, Oct. 16, 1982; children: Rubens, Jonas, Amran. BA with honours, U. Dacca, 1972, MA first class first, 1974; MA, Carleton U., 1978; PhD, U. Chgo., 1982. Cert. fraud examiner; cert. govt. fin. mgr. Asst. prof. acctg. SUNY, Buffalo, 1983-86; asst. prof. acctg. CUNY, Baruch, 1986-89; vis. asst. prof. acctg. Carlson Sch. of Mgmt. U. Minn., 1989-91, assoc. prof. acctg., assoc. mem. grad. faculty, 1991-93, prof. acctg., assoc. mem. grad. faculty, 1993—. Invited guest Ctr. For Internat. Studies, MIT, 1979; disting. faculty mentor U. Minn., 1990, 91; faculty mentor sch. bus. and econs., mem. honors and awards com., dean search com., outcome measures com., student behavior judiciary com., libr. policy com. U. Minn., Duluth, spl. project assoc. of vice-chancellor for acad. adminstrn., spring, 1995; invited presenter Jour. Acctg. Rsch. Conf., 1991; invited nominator Seidman Disting. Award in Polit. Economy, 1991, 92. Contbr. numerous articles to profl. jours., including Advances in Acctg., Acctg. Horizons, Australian Jour. Mgmt., Acctg. Orgns. and Soc., Acctg. Rev., Jour. Acctg. Rsch., Jour. Bus. Fin. and Acctg., Pub. Adminstrn. Quarterly, Fin. Accountability and Mgmt., Jour. Acctg. Abstracts, IEEE Transactions on Neural Networks, Encyclopedic Dictionary of Acctg.; mem. editl. bd. Internat. Jour. Acctg., Internat. Jour. Acctg. and Bus. Soc., Rsch. in Govtl. and Non Profit Acctg. Bd. dirs. Duluth Children's Mus., 1996—; mem. affirmative action rev. com. Minn. Edn. Assn., 1996-98. Mem. Assn. Govt. Accts., Assn. Cert. Fraud Examiners, Acad. Internat. Bus., Am. Acctg. Assn. (rsch. com. GNP sect. 1982-93, fin. com. 1992), Minn. Coun. Acctg. Educators. Avocations: walking, swimming, classical music. Office: U Minn-Dept Acctg 125 Sch Bus and Econs 10 University Dr Duluth MN 55812-2403

FERRAN, JAIME M. language educator; b. Hamilton, N.Y., Feb. 18, 1962; s. Jaime Ferrán and Carmen Rodríguez de Velasco. BArch, Syracuse U., N.Y., 1987; MA, Syracuse U., 1997; PhD, U. N.C., 2003. Architect Taller de Arquitectura, Barcelona, 1990; archtl. translator Gustavo Gili, Barcelona, 1993—94; tchg. fellow in Spanish U. N.C., Chapel Hill, 1997—. Lectr. confs. in field; tchg. assoc. Syracuse U., 1995—97. Illustrator Cuaderno de musica, 1983, translator Complete Works of Alver Aelto, 1995. Mem. YMCA, Chapel Hill. Named Best Tchg. Asst. in Spanish, Syracuse U., 1996; recipient Best Composition and Layout for Children's Book award, Graphical Industries of Spain, 1983. Fellow: MLA. Democrat. Roman Catholic. Avocations: drawing, swimming, political debating. Home: 306 N Estes Dr #16B Carrboro CA 27510

FERRAND, LOUIS GEORGE, lawyer; b. East Grand Rapids, Mich., Apr. 12, 1942; s. Louis George and Margaret Louise (LaBour) F.; m. Mary Eleanore Braseth, Oct. 25, 1969; children: Anne Elizabeth, Gregory Louis, Jacqueline Louise. BA, Alma Coll., 1964; JD, U. Mich., 1971. Bar: Mich. 1971, D.C. 1974, U.S. Supreme Ct. Pres., co-founder Cornerstone Project, Inc., Bklyn., 1966; vol. Peace Corps., Dominican Republic, 1966-68, trainer, 1968; dir. manpower programs Grand Rapids CAP, Mich., 1969-70; trial atty. Dept. Justice, Washington, 1971-76; counsel for civil rights Dept. Labor, Washington, 1976-81, dep. assoc. solicitor for civil rights, 1981-87, dep. assoc. solicitor for mine safety and health, 1987-88; of counsel Newman & Newell, 1988-89; sr. atty. Orgn. of Am. States, 1990-94, prin. atty., 1994—. Bd. dirs. Ayuda, Inc., 1988—, chair legal affairs and pers. coms., exec. com.; officer at large, bd. dirs. Parklawn Recreation Assn., Alexandria, Va., 1982-84, No. Va. Meml. Soc., 1991-95, Arlington Retirement Housing Corp., 1988-93; chmn. social responsibilities com. Unitarian Ch., Arlington, Va., 1981, co-chmn. capital fund dr., 1993-94; co-founder, bd. dirs. Fondo Quisqueya Found., Inc., 1993—, treas., 1993—; co-founder, bd. dirs. Friends of Williamsburg Rowing, Inc., 1993-97, treas. 1993-95; leader cub scout pack George Washington dist. Boy Scouts Am., 1984-86; basketball coach Recreational League, 1983-89; trustee Unitarian Ch. of Arlington, 1984-87, chmn. bd. trustees, 1986-87; bd. dirs. T.C. Williams H.S. Track Boosters, 1992-97, treas. 1992-95, co-pres. 1995-96; bd. dirs. MOAS Found., 1997—, treas. 1999—; bd. dirs. I-A Bar Found., 1995—; incorporator, bd. dirs. Young Americas Bus. Trust, Inc., 1999—, vice chair, 1999—; incorporator, bd. dirs. The Am.'s Endowment, Inc., 2003—. Mem. Fed. Bar Found. (adv. 1994-99), Fed. Bar Assn. (bd. dirs. D.C. chpt. 1986—, officer 1988-94, pres. 1993-94, nat. cir. officer 1993-97, nat. coun. mem. 1993-99, chair fed. career svc. divsn. 1996-99, co-chmn. nat. conv. com. 1989), D.C. Bar Assn., Mich. Bar Assn., Inter-Am. Bar Assn. (asst. sec. 1989-91, co-chmn. labor law sect. 1986-91, asst. treas. 1993-94, sec. gen. 1995—, mem. exec. com. 1995—, coun. mem. 1995—, mag. editor 1999—), Fed. Am. Inns of Ct. (charter mem., master 1989—, program chmn. and counselor, 1998-99, pres. 1999-2000). Avocations: reading, hiking, swimming, bicycling, travel. Office: Orgn of Am States Office Sec Gen Legal Svcs Washington DC 20006 E-mail: lferrand@oas.org.

FERRANTE, F. MICHAEL, anesthesiologist, internist; b. Bronx, Oct. 5, 1954; s. Francis Michael and Theo Algae (Glover) F. BS, Tulane U., 1976; MD, N.Y. Med. Coll., 1980. Diplomate Am. Bd. Anesthesiology with subspecialty in pain mgmt., Am. Bd. Internal Medicine. Intern Emory U. Affiliated Hosps., Atlanta, 1980-81, resident in internal medicine, 1981-83; fellow in infectious diseases Barnes-Washington U., St. Louis, 1983-84; resident in anesthesiology Emory U. Affiliated Hosps., Atlanta, 1984-86; fellow in pain Brigham Women's Hosp./Harvard U., Boston, 1986-87, staff physician, 1987-95, U. Pa. Hosp., Phila., 1995—2001; asst. prof. anesthesiology Harvard Med. Sch., Boston, 1990-95; assoc. prof. anesthesiology and internal medicine U. Pa., Phila., 1995-99, prof. anesthesiology and internal medicine, 1999—2001; prof. clin. anesthesiology and medicine UCLA, 2001—, staff physician, 2001—. Editor: Postoperative Pain Management, 1993, Patient-Controlled Analgesia, 1990. Mem. AMA, Am. Soc. Anesthesiologists, Am. Soc. Regional Anesthesia, Internat. Assn. for Study of Pain. Office: Pain Medicine Ctr Ste 660 200 UCLA Med Plz Los Angeles CA 90095

FERRANTE, JOAN MARGUERITE, language educator, literature educator, writer; b. N.Y.C., Nov. 11, 1936; d. Nicholas Henry and Josephine (Pisacane) Ferrante; m. R. Carey McIntosh. Student, Brearley Sch., 1950-54, Radcliffe Coll., 1954-55; BA, Barnard Coll., 1958; MA, Columbia U., 1959, PhD, 1963. Asst. prof. English and comparative lit. Columbia U., N.Y.C., 1966-70, assoc. prof., 1970-74, prof., 1974—, chmn. English and comparative lit., 1988-91, dir. Ctr. Italian Studies, 1977-80. Lectr. modern langs. Swarthmore (Pa.) Coll.,

1968; lectr. medieval studies Fordham U., N.Y.C., 1976; Andrew Mellon prof. humanities Tulane U., 1984. Author: (book) The Conflict of Love and Honor, 1973, Guillaume d'Orange, Four Twelfth Century Epics, 1974, Woman as Image in Medieval Literature from the Twelfth Century to Dante, 1975; author: (with Robert Hanning) The Lais of Marie de France, 1978; author: The Political Vision of the Divine Comedy, 1984, To the Glory of Her Sex: Women's Roles in teh Composition of Medieval Texts, 1997; editor (with George Economou): In Pursuit of Perfection, Courtly Love in Medieval Literature, 1975; editor: (with Robert hanning) The Challenge of the Medieval Text, 1985; editor: Database: Epistolae, Correspondence of Medieval Women Texts and Translations; mem. adv. bd. Spectrum, 1975—78, cons. editor Records of Civilization, 1975—. Am. Coun. Learned Socs. fellow, 1969—70, NEH fellow, 1980—81. Fellow: Medieval Acad. Am. (councillor, 2d v.p. 1998—99, 1st v.p. 1999—2000, pres. 2000—01); mem.: MLA (exec. coun. 1986—90), Internat. Courtly Lit. Soc., Internat. Arthurian Soc., Dante Soc. Am. (councillor, v.p. 1978—83, pres. 1985—91), Phi Beta Kappa (senator 1979—97, v.p. 1988—91, pres. 1991—94). Office: Columbia U 616 Philosophy Hall New York NY 10027

FERRANTE, OLIVIA ANN, retired educator, consultant; b. Revere, Mass., Nov. 9, 1948; d. Guy and Mary Carmella (Prizio) F. BA, Regis Coll., 1970; MEd, Boston Coll., 1971, postgrad., 1977-81, Middlebury Coll., 1974, Lesley Coll., 1982. Cert. history tchr., tchr. of blind. Chmn. Braille dept. Nat. Braille Press, Boston, 1971-74; tchr. of visually impaired, spl. needs dept. Revere H.S., 1974-92. Steven J. Rich scholarship com., 1993—; cons. Revere PTA, 1984—. Contbr. articles to profl. jours. Vol. Morgan Meml., Boston, 1983—, tchr. braille, 1993—, tchr. literacy program, 1993—; mem. Revere Com. for Handicapped Affairs, 1985—, Everett (Mass.) Chorus, 1974-76, Adult Music Ministry, 1989, Revere First Com., 1993, publicist; soloist Revere Music Makers, 1977-79; mem. partnership com. Internat. Year Disabled, 1980-81; mem. adult choir Immaculate Conception Ch., 1966—, lectr., 1995—, cantor, 1997; publicist Revere Commn. on Disabilities, 1985—, Revere Hist. Commn., 1996—, Cath. Daus., SHARE, 1995—, A Woman's Concern, 1996; mem. adv. bd. Mass. Commn. of Blind, 1988—, governing bd. on ind. living, 1989; access monitor Mass. Orgn. on Disability, 1988—; mem. adv. bd. Radio Reading Svc. for Blind, 1989; mentor Nat. Braille Literacy Project, 1992, Braille Lib., 1995—; mem. Friends of the Sick Children's Trust, 1992; vol. Birthright, 1992, ProLife Office, 1992; active Arts Coun. Coop, 1992—; mentor Vision Found., 1993—; friend Wang Ctr., 1993—, Boston Pub. Garden and Common, 1993—, Boston Pops, 1992—; mem. mobility adv. bd. Mass. Com. for Blind, 1994—; mem. Historic Mass., 1994—, Cath. League, 1994—; friend Paul Revere House, 1994—; mem. Peregrine Fund, 1994—, Ctr. for Marine Preservation, 1994—; sponsor Rite of Cath. Initiation for Adults, 1995—; publicist Next Door Theater Group, 1996; mem. access task force Revere Pub. Libr., 1996; mem. Revere 2000 Com., 1998-99. Mem. NEA, Internat. Soc. for Endangered Cats, Mass. Tchrs. Assn. Revere Tchrs. Assn., Nat. Space Soc., Nat. Cath. Assn. for Persons with Visual Impairment, Cath. Daus. of Am. (publicist), Soc. Bl. Kateri Tekakwitha, 1997, Friends of Revere Pub. Libr., Friends of Librs. for Blind, Friends of Boston Symphony Orch., Nat. Writers Union, Amnesty Internat., Soc. Creative Anachronism, Women Affirming Life, Michael Crawford Internat. Fan Assn., Revere Soc. for Cultural and Hist. Preservation (publicist, life mem., v.p. 1998—, chmn. grants com. 1998, 2000 com., 1998), Chelsea Hist. Soc., Mass. Aviation Hist. Soc., Brian Boitano Fan Club, Barry Manilow Fan Club, Michael Feinstein Fan Club, Feregrine Fund, Paul Revere House, Greater Lynn Arts and Crafts Soc.. Roman Catholic. Avocations: travel, music, swimming, ice skating, crafts. Home: 115 Reservoir Ave Revere MA 02151-5825 Office: Revere High Sch Spl Needs Dept 101 School St Revere MA 02151-3099

FERRARA, DOMINICK JOHN, IV, music educator; b. Newark, Mar. 19, 1967; s. Dominick John Ferrara, III and Phyllis Ferrara; m. Susan Lynne Strouse; children: Christopher Edward children: Dominick John, V. BA in Music Edn., Montclair State U., 1990; MAT in Music, Rutgers U., 1997. Cert. supr. instrn. N.J., music tchr. N.J. Music tchr. Clifton (N.J.) Bd. Edn., 1990—96; dir. bands Lenape Valley Regional H.S., Stanhope, NJ, 1996—; dir. wind ensemble Montclair State U./Stokes Forest Music Camp, NJ, 1997—; band dir. Fairleigh Dickinson U., 2003—. Mem.: Nat. Assn. Music Edn., Soc. Rsch. Music Edn., World Assn. Symphonic Bands and Ensemble, Assn. Supervisional Curriculum Devel., Nat. Band Assn., Nat. Eagle Scout Assn., Lenape Valley Edn. Assn. (pres. 2001—03, v.p. 2003—), Bloomfield Fedn. Music (exec. coun. 1989—2003, v.p. 1999—2003), Sussex County Music Educators Assn. (pres. 1998—2002, v.p. 2001—), Kappa Delta Pi. Roman Catholic. Office: Lenape Valley Regional H S Box 578 Sparta Rd Stanhope NJ 07874 Personal E-mail: ferraras@att.net. Business E-Mail: djf4@lvhs.org.

FERRARA, DONNA, state legislator; b. N.Y.C., June 22, 1959; m. Robert Gregory; children: Kathleen Lillian, Brendan Baron. BA, Albany U.; JD, St. John's U. Rep. Dist. 15 N.Y. State Assembly, 1992—. Office: NY Assembly Legis Office Bldg Rm 322 Albany NY 12224 also: 150 Post Ave Westbury NY 11590-3172

FERRARA, JAMES LAWRENCE MICHAEL, medical educator, physician, scientist; b. N.Y.C., Dec. 17, 1952; s. Lawrence Andrew and Mary Theresa (Fichter) F.; m. Flora Eleanor Viola Watson, June 27, 1981; children: Andrew, David, Michael. Diploma d'etudes, La Sorbonne, Paris, 1973; AB summa cum laude with honors, Xavier U., 1974; MA, Oxford U., 1976; MD cum laude, Georgetown U., 1980. Diplomate Am. Bd. Pediat. Intern in pediatrics Children's Hosp., Boston, 1980, resident in pediatrics, 1981; fellow pediatric hematology/oncology Children's Hosp. and Dana-Farber Cancer Inst., Boston, 1982, rsch. fellow pediatric hematology/oncology, 1983; rsch. fellow pediatrics Harvard Med. Sch., 1982, clin. instr. pediatrics, 1980, 85, asst. prof. pediatrics, 1987, assoc. prof. pediatrics, 1993; pediat. oncologist Dana Farber Cancer Inst., 1985-98; prof. medicine and pediatrics U. Mich. Med. Sch., 1998; dir. bone marrow transplant program U. Mich. Cancer Ctr., 1998. Lectr. Sydney, 1992, Munich, 1993, Chustchuch, New Zealand, 1993, Okayama, Japan, 1996, Innsbruck, Austria, 1997, Geneva, 1997, Bologna, 2000, Stockholm, 2001, Beijing, 2001, Seoul, 2002, Rio de Janiero, 2002. Author (with others): Graft Versus Host Disease, 1990, 2nd edit., 1996; editor Hematology Revs. and Comm., 1985, Transplantation, 1988, Jour. Immunology, 1993, Transplantation Immunology, 1993, Bone Marrow Transplantation, 1994; contbr. numerous articles to profl jours., chpts. to books. Recipient Physician Sci. award NIH, 1985, Stohlman scholar Leukemia Soc. Am., 1997, Alexander von Humoldt award, 1998, Doris Duke Disting. Clin. Scientist award, 2002; Am. Cancer Soc. Rsch. grantee, 1991, NIH grantee, 1992, 93. Mem. NIH (study sect. 1996), Am. Assn. Immunologists, Am. Soc. Hematology, Am. Soc. Clin. Investigation, Soc. Pediat. Rsch., Transplantation Soc., Am. Acad. Pediat., Am. Assn. Physicians. Avocations: opera, antique books and maps. Office: U Mich Cancer Ctr 1500 E Medical Center Dr Ann Arbor MI 48109-0005 E-mail: ferrara@umich.edu.

FERRARA, JEFFREY FRANCIS, electronics engineer; b. Bklyn., Jan. 11, 1953; s. Frank and Irene Ferrara. AA in Bus., AS in Engring., Coll. of DuPage, 1985; BS in Computer Engring., U. Ill., 1989. Electronics engr. NASA, Greenbelt, Md., 1989—. Election judge DuPage County (Ill.) Election Bd., 1980; sci. fair judge St. Joseph Sch., Beltsville, Md., 1991, 92, 93, 94; mentor Nat. Space Club, 1993; mentor summer program High Tech H.S., 2000. Recipient Space Act award for disclosure of an invention, 2000. Mem. IEEE, Assn. for Computing Machinery. Avocations: art and music composition, computer programming. Office: NASA Goddard Space Flight Ctr Code 584 Greenbelt MD 20771-0001

FERRARA, LEE, graphic designer, artists, art educator; b. Somerville, Mass. d. Joseph Charles and Mary Rose (Macalini) F. BFA, Mass. Coll. Art, 1951; postgrad., Yale U., 1951; MFA in Visual Comms., Syracuse U., 1976. Sr. designer Montgomery Ward, Chgo., 1956-61; graphic designer Raymond Loewy and Assocs., Chgo., Chapman, Goldsmith, and Yamasaki, Chgo., 1961-63; design dir. Family Products, Inc., Tyngsboro, Mass., 1972—82; founder, graphic designer Lee-Graphics, Santa Monica, Calif. Sr. designer Container Corp. Am., Boston, Walter Dorwin Teague, N.Y.C., 1971-72; mem. Winc Arts Coun., 1997-2000; freelance designer cos. including Max Factor of Hollywood, Pacific Air Inc., Metric Sys., Pacific Game Co., Chicken Delight, Joyce Chen, Sunbeam Corp., Teladyne, numerous others. Exhibns. include New Eng. Watercolor Soc., 1994, 95, Plymouth Art Assn., 1996, Dedham Art, 1996, Haverhill Art, 1997, Andover Art, 1997, Sharon Art Ctr., N.H., Copley Soc., Boston, 1996, Concord Art Assn., 1997, Lexington Arts and Crafts, Springfield (Mass.) Art League, 1998, Captured Wildlife 5th Annual, 1998, Andover Art in the Park, 1998, Internat. Nature Fine Arts Competition Bennington Art Complex, 1998, Arts Coun. S.E. Mo., Faulkner Centennial U. Mus., Acad. Artists Assn., 1998, Nat. Park Acad. Arts Top 200, 1998, Catharine Lorillard Wolfe Nat. Arts Club, 1998, 2001, Cambridge Art Assn., numerous others; author poems; contbr. articles to mags. publication, Art Of Color Printing On Pressure-Sensitve Lables. Participant advanced project mentor program Lincoln Sch., 1993, mem. arts lottery coun., 1998-2000; bd. dirs. Civic Symphony, 1982-88. Recipient Cert. of Appreciation, Lincoln Sch., 1993, Editor's Choice award Nat. Libr. Poetry, 1994, awards 3 categories Dedham Art, 1996, 2nd Place award Haverhill Art, 1997, 2nd Place award Andover Art, 1997, 1st prize mixed media Andover Art in the Park, 1998, Wilkins Art Cons. award Acad. Artists Assn. Nat. 1998, 2nd Place 25th Annual Winter Show Duxbury Art Assn. Mem. Am. Inst. Graphic Arts (N.Y.C.), Am. Artists Profl. League, New Eng. Watercolor Soc., Soc. Typographic Art (exhibn. chmn.), Artists Guild (Chgo.), Art Dirs. Club L.A., Concord Art Assn. (Mixed Media Collage award, Watercolor award 1999, 2002, Disting. Artist 2002), Copley Soc. (past bd. dirs.), North Shore Art Assn. (bd. dirs.), Allied Artists Am., Lexington Arts and Crafts (Rogowitz award, Most Creative award 2001, 2002). sig. mem., New England Watercolor Soc. Achievements include pioneer design of fabric overlay for plastic cap; Clio finalist. Avocations: acting, writing, tennis, folk music, mycology. Home: 41 Franklin Rd Winchester MA 01890 E-mail: leeferraradesigns@yahoo.com.

FERRARA, RALPH C. lawyer; b. Gloversville, N.Y., June 16, 1945; s. Rufus Ferrara and Clara F. Riccitiello. BSBA, Georgetown U., 1967; JD, U. Cin., 1970; LLM in Corp. Law summa cum laude, George Washington U., 1972. Bar: D.C. 1970, U.S. Ct. Appeals, U.S. Supreme Ct.; cert. ind. assessor Ins. Marketplace Stds. Assn. Profl. asst. to law libr. Nat. Law Ctr., Washington, 1970-72; mem. faculty George Washington U. Nat. Law Ctr., Washington; atty. divsn. enforcement SEC, Washington, 1971-72, trial atty. divsn. trading and markets, 1972-73, spl. counsel to chief enforcement atty., 1973-74, supervisory trial atty., 1974-75, spl. counsel to chmn., 1975, asst. gen. counsel, 1975-76, exec. asst. to legal counsel, 1976-77, exec. asst., 1977-78, gen. counsel, 1978-81; ptnr. Debevoise & Plimpton, Washington, 1981—. Co-chmn. PLI Ann. Inst. on Securities Law, 1994-98; mem. bd. visitors U. Cin. Coll. Law, 1995—, bd. advisors, D & O Advisor, 2003—; dir. Park Pl. Entertainment. Author: Takeovers II: A Strategists' Manual for Business Combinations in the 1990s, 1993, Shareholder Derivative Litigation: Beseiging the Board, 1995, Ferrara on Insider Trading the Wall, 1995, Managing Marketeers: Supervisory Responsibilities of Broker-Dealers and Investment Advisors, 2000, Takeovers: A Strategic Guide to Mergers and Acquisitions, 2001; contbr. articles on topics related to fed. securities law to profl. jours. With USAR. Recipient John L. Sayler award, Am. Jurisprudence award, Judge Alfred Mack award. Mem. ABA (planning rev. com. sect. on corp. and banking bus. law, fed. regulation of securities com.), FBA (exe. coun. securities law com., nat. coun., gen. counsels' com.), Southwestern Legal Found. (adv. com.). Office: Debevoise & Plimpton 555 13th St NW Ste 1100E Washington DC 20004-1163 Address: 919 3rd Ave New York NY 10022

FERRARI, DANIEL JOSEPH, business development manager; s. Theresa Marie and Daniel Lawrence Ferrari; m. Margaret Suzette Songy, Nov. 26, 1988; m. Yolanda Susan Greene, Mar. 19, 1977 (div. Nov. 6, 1986); children: Daniel Joseph, Brendan Alexander, Gabrielle Elaine. BS in engring., US Mil. Acad., 1976; MA in bus. mgmt., Ctrl. Mich. U., 1984. Facilities planning supr. Martin Marietta, New Orleans, 1981—86, bus. develop. mgr. Lockheed Martin, New Orleans, 1986—. Lt. Transp. Corps., 1981—98, cpt. Corps of Engrs., 1976—81. Mem.: AIAA. Avocations: swimming, golf, painting. Office: Lockheed Martin Space Sys Co Dept 3040 PO Box 29304 New Orleans LA 70189 Office Fax: 504-257-4482. E-mail: daniel.j.ferrari@maf.nasa.gov.

FERRARI, GARY JOHN, lawyer; b. Ill., Oct. 14, 1958; s. John Joseph and Geraldine May F. AA, Ill. Valley C.C., 1978; BA, U. Ill., 1980, JD, 1983. Bar: Ill. 1983, U.S. Ct. Mil. Appeals 1986, U.S. Dist. Ct. (cen. dist.) Ill. 1987, U.S. Dist. Ct. (no dist.) Ill. 1990. Atty. Goldsworthy, Fifield & Hasselberg, Peoria, Ill., 1987-90, John E. Mitchell Law Offices, Peoria, Ill., 1990—. Pres. Peoria Italian-Am. Soc., 1998-2000; sec. Peoria Area Ethnic Assn., 1997-2001. Lt.USNR, 1983 86. Mem. KC, Am. Legion. Roman Catholic. Home: 6710 N Fawndale Dr Peoria IL 61615-2315 Office: Law Offices John Mitchell 415 NE Jefferson Ave Peoria IL 61603-3725 E-mail: gjf445peo@aol.com., wclaw@mtco.net.

FERRARI, L. KATHERINE, speaker, consultant, entrepreneur; b. Chgo. d. August and Aurora (Lenzi) Puccinelli; m. Charles Wasserman; children: Michael John, Alexandra Marie; m. Gordon Wharton Holt Jr. MA in Architecture, MS in Engring., Stanford (Calif.) U., 1972; BA in Polit. Sci., Northwestern U.; M in Hypnotism, Hypnotism Tng. Sch. L.A., 1989. Educator Moreland Sch. Dist., San Jose, Calif., 1961-65; pres. Ferrari Design, Los Gatos, Calif., 1970—; project dir. AIA Energy Conservation Retrofit, San Jose, Calif., 1978—81, AIA/N.A.S.A. tech. house of future, Moffet Field, 1982—85; pres. Internat. Laughter Soc. Inc., Los Gatos, 1983—, Ferrari Communications, Los Gatos, 1989—. Bd. dirs. Pacific We. Bank, San Jose; bldg. cons. & design in field; product designer Internat. Laughter Soc. Inc., Los Gatos, 1983—; trainer non-profit groups. Contbr. articles to profl. jours. Mem. Advanced Tech. Advancement Com., Moffett Field, Calif., 1977-89; pres., v.p. League of Eastfield Children's Ctr., Campbell, Calif., 1964-66; pres., treas. Triton Mus. of Art, Santa Clara, Calif., 1979-81; bd. dirs. Coun. Environ. & Econ. Improvement, San Jose, Calif., 1976-79. Art Inst. scholar. Mem. AIA (hon. assoc., bd. dirs. San Jose chpt.), A.S.I.D., Nat. Speakers Assn., Am. Coun. Hypnotists, Nat. Guild Hypnotists. Avocations: travel, reading. Office: Ferrari Communications 16000 Glen Una Dr Los Gatos CA 95030-2911

FERRARI, LEONARDO, small business owner; b. Mendoza, Argentina, Nov. 14, 1952; s. Celestino Alejandro Ferrari and Ana Gonzalez; 1 child, Diana Christina. Degree, Nat. U. Cuyo, Mendoza, 1978; cert. parapsychology asst., Am. Inst. Parapsychology, Buenos Aires, 1982. RN Argentina. Owner The Shoe Svc., Miami, Fla., 1989—. Avocations: photography, reading, walking, writing, meditation. Office: The Shoe Svc 115 South Miami Ave Miami FL 33130

FERRARI, MICHAEL RICHARD, JR., university administrator; b. Monongahela, Pa., May 12, 1940; s. Michael Richard and Lillian Ann (Cristina) F.; m. Janice Bjurstrom, Sept. 5, 1964; children: Elizabeth Anne, Michael, III. BA, Mich. State U., 1962, MA, 1963, DBA (Ford Found. fellow), 1968; D of Pub. Svc. (hon.), Bowling Green State U., 1991. Asst. to dean men U. Cin., 1965-66; asst. to dir. residence life, resident hall head advisor Mich. State U., 1966-68; acting chmn. dept. adminstrv. scis. Kent (Ohio) State U., 1970-71; mem. adminstrv. staff Bowling Green (Ohio) State U., 1971-73, v.p. resource planning, 1973-78, provost, exec. v.p., 1978-81, interim pres., 1981-82; vis. scholar U. Mich., 1982-83; prof. mgmt., provost Wright State U., Dayton, 1983-85; pres. Drake U., Des Moines, 1985-98; chancellor Tex. Christian U., Ft. Worth, 1998—2003, chancellor emeritus, 2003—; pres. Ferrari and Assocs., 2003—. Bd. dirs. Pier One Imports; mgmt. cons., 1968—. Author: Profiles of American College Presidents, 1970, Measuring the Quality of Universities, 1970, National Study of Student Personnel Manpower Planning, 1972. Research fellow Am. Coll. Testing Program, 1970 Mem. Acad. Mgmt., Omicron Delta Kappa, Phi Kappa Phi, Beta Gamma Sigma, Pi Gamma Mu, Alpha Tau Omega. Episcopalian. Office: 570 Greenway Dr Lake Forest IL 60045

FERRARI, ROBERT JOSEPH, business educator, former banker; b. Bklyn., Dec. 3, 1936; m. Patricia A. Cantalupo, Sept. 6, 1958; children: Robert Joseph, James G., Judith A., Thomas A. BS in Econs, Villanova U., 1958; MBA, N.Y. U., 1962; grad. certificate, Brown U., 1969, Henry George Sch. Social Sci., 1961; D.Sc., London Inst., 1973. With arbitrace dept. Goodbody & Co., 1957-60; bank auditor Fed. Reserve Bank, N.Y.C., 1960-65; v.p. fin. Am. Savings Bank, N.Y.C., 1965-81; prof., chair dept. econs. and bus. Marymount Coll. of Fordham U., Tarrytown, 1981—. Cons. LaCorte Agy., Inc., 1963—65. Vice pres. Better Bklyn. Com.; v.p., bd. dirs. Kensington Flatbush Preservation Assn.; treas. Boy Scouts Am. Mem. Flatbush/Flatlands Republican Assn., Am. Econ. Assn., Am. Finance Assn., Am. Statis. Assn., Nat. Assn. Bus. Economists, Nat. Economists Club, N.Y. State, Met. econ. assns., Am. Acad. Polit. and Social Sci. Clubs: University (N.Y.C.). Office: Marymount Coll of Fordham Univ 100 Marymount Ave Tarrytown NY 10591-3704 Home: 425 River Rd Pipersville PA 18947

FERRARI, ROBERTO C. librarian; b. Saddle Brook, N.J., Apr. 10, 1970; s. Alfredo Ferrari and Kathleen Margaret Pape. BA in English and Creative Writing, U. South Fla., 1992, M of Liberal Arts in Humanities, 1994, MA in Libr. & Info. Sci., 1997. Adj. prof. Hillsborough C.C., Tampa, Fla., 1994—97; libr., adj. prof. Art Inst. Ft. Lauderdale, Fla., 1997—99; asst. libr. Fla. Atlantic U. Libr., Boca Raton, 1999—. Webmaster (internet research archive) Simeon Solomon Research Archive (Worldwide Books Electronic Publ. award, 2002); contbr. articles to profl. jours. Mem.: ALA, Art Libr. Soc. N.Am. (pres. S.E. chpt. 2002—02, H.W. Wilson Found. Rsch. award 2002), The William Morris Soc., Queer Caucus for Art, Coll. Art Assn. (assoc.), Pre-Raphaelite Soc. Office: Florida Atlantic Univ Library 777 Glades Rd Boca Raton FL 33431 Office Fax: 561-338-3863. E-mail: rferrari@fau.edu.

FERRARI, VICTOR ALFRED, cardiologist; BS in Elec. Engring., Drexel U., Phila., 1982; MD, U. Pa., Phila., 1986. Diplomate Am. Bd. of Internal Medicine, 1991. Staff echocardiographer U. Pa. Hosp., Phila., 1992—, assoc. dir., echo lab, 1993—; asst. prof., medicine U. Pa. Sch. Medicine, Phila., 1993—2002, asst. prof., medicine in radiology, 1993—2002, assoc. prof., medicine, 2002—, assoc. prof., medicine in radiology, 2002—. Contbr. articles to profl. jours. Recipient Best Doctors in Am. Award, Cardiac MRI, Best Doctors, Inc., 2001—02. Fellow: Am. Coll. Cardiology; mem.: Soc. for Cardiovasc. Magnetic Resonance (founding mem. 1995, sci. program com. 2002—, mem. editl. bd. 2000—), Am. Heart Assn. Office: Univ Pa Hosp 3400 Spruce St 9014 E Gates Philadelphia PA 19104 Office Fax: 215-349-8190. E-mail: ferrariv@mail.med.upenn.edu.

FERRARIO, LARRY, history and literature educator; b. Berkeley, Calif., Mar. 26, 1943; s. George Louis Ferrario and Virginia Maxine Stafford; m. Joan Inez Wilson, June 13, 1965; children: Jeffery Steven, Stephanie Ann. BA in English, San Jose State U., 1965, MA in English, 1970; MA in Rhetoric, U. So. Calif., L.A., 1985, PhD in Rhetoric and English, 1989. Cert. secondary tchg. credential Calif. Tchr. Campbell (Calif.) Union H.S. Dist., 1967—72, Lassen C.C., Susanville, Calif., 1972—84; bus. sch. prof. U. So. Calif., L.A., Calif., 1987—96; English prof. Calif. State U. Dominguez Hills, Carson, 1996—. Pvt. bus. comm. cons., 1986—. Avocations: fly fishing, fly tying, camping, skiing, travel. Home: 4158 Elizabeth Ct Cypress CA 90630 Office: Calif State Univ Dominguez Hills 1000 E Victoria St Carson CA 90747-0005

FERRARO, BETTY ANN, state senator, corporate administrator; b. Newport, Vt., Mar. 3, 1925; d. Clarence John and Mauretta Rowena (Potter) Morse; m. Dominic Thomas Ferraro, Oct. 8, 1964; children: Deborah, David, Susan, Barbara. Student, Mary Hitchcock Hosp. Sch. Nursing, Coll. St. Joseph, Rutland, Vt. Exec. sec. to asst. treas. Ctrl. Vt. Pub. Svc. Corp., Rutland, 1943-44; sec. to dean N.Y. Med. Coll., N.Y.C., 1944-46; model G. Fox Co., Hartford, Conn., 1947; corp. sec., office mgr. John Russell Corp., Rutland, 1970-80; exec. dir. Rutland Area Coordinated Child Care Com., Washington, 1977-79; adminstrv. asst. Hilinex of Vt., Rutland, 1981-83; owner Classic Connection Gift Shop, Rutland, 1983-87; adminstr. Vicon Recovery Sys., Inc., Rutland, 1987-90. Owner, operator nursery sch., 1973—77; mgr. Day Care Ctr., 1978—80; mem. Rutland City Bd. Aldermen, 1984—86, 2001—03; resource dir. Rutland City Emergency Mgmt. Team for State of Vt., 1984—90; mem. Vt. State Cmty. Devel. Commn., 1986. Chmn. Rutland City Rep. Com., 1991-93; county committeewoman State Rep. Com., 1984-86, rep.; rep. Rutland County Rep. Com.; state del. Rep. Nat. Conv., 1992; Rep. campaign coord. State of Vt., 1997-98; county co-chair Jim Douglas for Gov., 2001-02; mem. Vt. Ho. Reps., 1990-92; mem. Vt. Senate, 1992-94, 95-97; mem. jud. nominating bd. Human Resource Investment Coun., 1995-96, Vt. Student Assistance Corp. Bd., 2003; mem. Amtrak Study Commn., 1995-96; bd. dirs. Vt. Physicians Coun., 1997—, Coll. St. Joseph, 1996-2000, Marble Valley Transit, 1996—; mem. adv. bd. Paramount Theatre, 1997—; sec., receptionist Orton Family Found., 1999-2000; sec., receptionist Eddy Enterprises, Inc., 2000-01; county co-chair Jim Douglas for Gov., 2002; mem. Vt. State Transp. Bd, 2003-. Fleming Inst. fellow, 1995; named Woman of Yr. Green Mt. Coun. of Boy Scouts. Mem. Nat. Assn. Women in Constrn. (chartered, past pres.), Rutland County Rep. Women. Republican. Roman Catholic. Avocation: flower arranging. Home and Office: Condo 17 155 Dorr Dr Rutland VT 05701-3853 E-mail: b.m.ferraro@verizon.net.

FERRARO, F(RANCIS) RICHARD, psychologist, educator; b. Amsterdam, N.Y., Sept. 7, 1959; s. Richard and Mary (Palma) F. BA, SUNY, Potsdam, 1982; MA, U. Kans., 1986, PhD, 1989. Postdoctoral fellow psychology dept. Washington U., St. Louis, 1989-92; asst. prof. psychology U. N.D., Grand Forks, 1992-98, assoc. prof. psychology, 1998-2001, prof., 2001—. Mem. APA, Nat. Acad. Neuropsychology, Psychonomic Soc. Office: U ND Dept Psychology Grand Forks ND 58202-8380 E-mail: f_ferraro@und.nodak.edu.

FERRARO, GERALDINE ANNE, lawyer, former congresswoman; b. Newburgh, N.Y., Aug. 26, 1935; d. Dominick and Antonetta L. (Corrieri) F.; m. John Zaccaro, 1960; children: Donna, John, Laura. BA, Marymount Manhattan Coll., 1956, hon. degree, 1982; JD, Fordham U., 1960; postgrad., NYU Law Sch., 1978, hon. degree, 1984, Hunter Coll., 1985, Plattsburgh Coll., 1985, Coll. Boca Raton, 1989, Va. State U., 1989, Muhlenberg Coll., 1990, Briarcliffe Coll. for Bus., 1990, Potsdam Coll., 1991. Bar: N.Y. 1961, U.S. Supreme Ct. 1978. Pvt. practice, N.Y.C., 1961-74; asst. dist. atty. Queens County, N.Y., 1974-78; chief spl. victims bur., 1977-78; mem. 96th-98th Congresses from 9th N.Y. Dist.; sec. House Democratic Caucus; 1st woman vice presdl. nominee on Democratic ticket, 1984; fellow Harvard Inst. of Politics, Cambridge, Mass., 1988; mng. ptnr. Keck Mahin Cate & Koether, N.Y., 1993-94. Appointed Amb. to UN Human Rights Commn., 1994-95; co-host Crossfire, CNN, 1996-97; pres. G&L Strategies Golin Harris Internat., 1999—, Fox News Nightly, 1999—. Author: Ferraro, My Story, 1985, Changing History: Women, Power, and Politics, 1993, Framing a Life, 1998. Chair Dem. Platform Com., Bertarelli Found.; Dem. candidate U.S. Senate, 1992, 98; U.S. President Clinton's appointee to UN Human Rights Commn. Conf., Geneva, 1993, World Conf., Vienna, Austria, 1993, World Conf. on Women, 1995; bd. dirs. Fordham Law Sch. Bd. Visitors; bd. advocates Planned Parenthood Fedn. Am.; bd. dir. Nat. Women's Health Rsch. Ctr., Nat. Dem. Inst. Mem. Queens County Women's Bar Assn. (past pres.), Coun. Fgn. Rels., Internat. Inst. Women's Polit. Leadership (former pres.), Assn. Bar City NY. Roman Catholic.

FERRARO, JAY, psychologist, consultant; b. Bklyn., Nov. 25, 1962; s. William and Sharon Ferraro; m. Julie Kent, Dec. 19, 1998; children: Austin, Jayda, Zoe. BS, Oral Roberts U., 1984; MS, Northeastern State U., 1987; PhD, Kent State U., 1998. Nat. cert. psychologist NAMP, lic. profl. counselor Okla.; master cert. coach Inst. for Life Coach Tng., cert. corp. coach trainer Corp. Coach U. Counselor Shadow Mountain Inst., Tulsa, 1982—84; psychiat. counselor St. John Med. Ctr., Tulsa, 1984—87, mem. crisis intervention team, 1985—87, edn. coord. adolescent programs, 1985—87, program dir. Collinsville Youth Ctr., 1987—89; therapist Comprehensive Psychology, Tulsa, 1988—90; tchg. fellow Kent (Ohio) State U., 1990—93, grad. asst., 1990—91; family therapist, custody evaluator Family Svcs. Summit County, Akron, Ohio, 1990—92; clin. psychology intern Kevin Coleman Ctr., Kent, 1991—92, program dir. partial hosp. programs Ravenna, Ohio, 1992—95; assoc. Franklin Mills Consultants, Kent, Ohio, 1992—94; CEO, founder Empowerment Techs., Tulsa, Okla., 1995—; clin. psychology intern Children's Med. Ctr., Tulsa, 1995—96, staff psychologist, 1996—99; assoc. psychologist Consulting Svcs. Network, Santa Barbara, Calif., 1997—99; assoc. The Berrywood Group, Tulsa, 1999—, Jeff MaGee Internat., Tulsa, 1999—. Clin. staff Little Light House, Tulsa, 1982—83; cons. Tough Love Parenting Group, Tulsa, 1984—86; adj. instr. psychology dept. Tulsa Jr. Coll., 1988—90; corp. cons. Brookhaven Hosp., Tulsa, 1989—90. Mem.: Am. Psychotherapy Assn. (cert. diplomate in psychotherapy), Rotary Club. Avocations: martial arts, weightlifting. Home and Office: 2626 E 21st St 3 Tulsa OK 74114

FERRARO, JOANNE M. humanities educator; b. LA, May 22, 1951; d. Corrado and Jennie Grace Ferraro. BA, UCLA, 1973, MA, 1975, PhD, 1983. Asst. prof. history San Diego State U., 1984—89, assoc. prof. history, 1989—93, prof. history, 1993—. Author: Family and Public Life in Brescia 1580-1650, 1993, Marriage Wars in Late Renaissance Venice, 2001 (Helen and Howard R. Marraro Book prize Soc. for Italian Hist. Studies, 2002, Book award Soc. for Study Early Modern Women, 2002); contbr. articles to profl. jours. Fellow Mabel Wilson-Richards fellow, UCLA, 1978, NEH, 1988; grantee, Gladys Krieble Delmas Found., 1979, 1984, 1992, 2001, Am. Coun. Learned

Soc., 1984—85, 1993, NEH, 1986, San Diego State U., 1987, 1989—90, 1992; Rsch. scholar, 1990, 1992, 1995. Office: San Diego State Univ History Dept San Diego CA 92182 Office Fax: 619-594-2210. Business E-Mail: ferraro@mail.sdsu.edu.

FERRARO, JOHN FRANCIS, business executive, financier; b. N.Y.C., Jan. 3, 1934; s. John Anthony and Angelina (Figliola) F.; children: Elizabeth Ann, John Robert, Laura Marie, Rosemary. BS in Indsl. Engring. with honors and distinction, NYU, 1962. With United Technologies Corp., Windsor Locks, Conn., 1962-66; sr. project engr. United Techs. Corp., Windsor Locks, Conn., 1962-64, chief research and devel. promotion, 1964-66; founding ptnr. P.M.C. Corp., 1966-78; chmn. bd., chief exec. officer Thermodynetics, Inc.; pres. Spectrum Inc., 1966—, also dir.; pres. Pioneer Capital Corp.; mng. dir. Pioneer Ventures Assocs. L.P., Capital Mgmt. Ptnrs. LLC. Bd. dirs. Turbotec Products, Inc., Xtec Corp., Am. Interactive Media, Inc., Fidelity First Fin. Corp., Am. Shopping Mall, Inc. Contbr. numerous articles on bus., fin. and stock market to fin. publs., 1966-81; contbg. editor: Handbook of Wealth Management, 1977. Trustee Birth Right, Conn., 1970—80; chmn. Congl.. Com. for Apointees USAF Acad., 1980; commr. Develop Agy., Enfield, Conn., 1981; mem. Gov.'s task force for mfg. State of Conn., 1989—91; mem. exec. com. Holy Family Retreat League, 1984—88; mem. bd. advisors St. Joseph's Residence, Conn., 1991—; trustee Suffield Acad., Conn., 1980—93, chair budget and fin. com., 1987—92; trustee Western New Eng. Coll., 1997—2003. 1st lt. USAF, 1954—58. Decorated Meritorious Service medal. Mem. Psi Upsilon, Suffield Country Club. Home: 86 Berkshire Ave Southwick MA 01077-9642 Office: 651 Day Hill Rd Windsor CT 06095-1719 E-mail: jigfox@earthlink.net.

FERRARO, LINDA ANN, veterinarian; b. Summit, N.J., Feb. 20, 1946; d. Thomas John and Doris Pfluger Ferraro. BS, U. Del., 1968; MS, U. R.I., 1973; VMD, U. Pa., 1979; student in homeopathy, Allen Acad., Wilmington, Del., 2000—. Lic. vet., Pa., Md., Del. Rsch. aquatic biologist U.S. EPA, Narragansett, R.I., 1969-75; assoc. vet. Easton Vet. Clinic, Md., 1979—80; assoc. vet Animal Clinic Talbot, 1981; owner, vet. St. Michaels (Md.) Vet. Clinic, 1981—; tchr. Chesapeake Coll., 2001—; vet. Del. Humane Assn., 2001. Bd. dirs., mem. Talbot County Humane Soc., 1981-83. Scholar R.I. Kennel Club, 1973-76. Mem. Am. Vet. Med. Assn., Am. Animal Hosp. Assn., Assn. Avian Vets., Md. Vet. Med. Assn., N.Y. Acad. Scis., Beta Beta Beta. Avocations: canoeing, automobiles, marine biology, animal rescue, homeopathy. Home: 933 Riverview Terr Saint Michaels MD 21663 Office: St Michaels Vet Clinic 915 S Talbot St Saint Michaels MD 21663

FERRARO, MARIE, dental hygienist; b. Jamaica, West Indies, Mar. 12, 1937; arrived in U.S., 1964; d. Louis Ezekel and Uta Doreen Ferraro; m. Lionel Cunningham, Dec. 13, 1957; children: Sonia Francis, Karel. AS, N.Y.C. Tech. Coll., 1970; BS, Lehman Coll., 1986; MS, Columbia U., 1988. Registered dental hygienist N.Y. Dental hygienist Montefiore Med. Ctr., Bronx, NY, 1970—. Dental health coord. N.Y.C. Pub. Schs., Bronx, 1970—87. Mem.: Am. Dental Hygienists Assn., Columbia Alumni Assn. Democrat. Baptist. Home: 1311 Morris Ave Bronx NY 10456

FERRARO, RONALD LOUIS, health facility administrator; b. Washington, Pa., Apr. 14, 1943; s. Michael A. and Rose (Marino) F.; m. Lilyan McConomy, June 28, 1980; children: Suzanne Marie Schultz, Lynaia Lorraine Schultz. BA, Juniata Coll., 1965; MSW, W.Va. U., 1967. Diplomate Am. Bd. Examiners in Clin. Social Work; LCSW Pa., quality certified social worker. Supr. social work Embreeville State Hosp., Coatesville, Pa., 1967-72; from chief social worker to dir. mental health The Consortium, Phila., 1972-88, dir. base svc. unit, 1988-91; asst. dir. Resources for Human Devel., Phila., 1991—2002; dir. quality mgmt. COMHAR Inc., 2002—. Bd. dirs. Big Bros./Big Sisters Bucks County, Doylestown, pa., 1986-91. Mem. NASW (cert., diplomate, bd. dirs. 1973-86). Home: 40 New Pond Ln Levittown PA 19054-3822

FERRAZ, FRANCISCO MARCONI, neurological surgeon; b. Floresta, Pernambuco, Brazil, Aug. 14, 1951; arrived in U.S., 1976; Student, Colegio Nobrega, Recife-Brazil, 1967—69; MD, Faculdade de Medicine da Universidade Federal de Pernambuco-Brazil, 1975. Diplomate Am. Bd. Neurol. Surgery. Intern Jamaica Hosp., N.Y.C., 1976—77; resident Georgetown U. Med. Ctr. and Affiliated Hosps., Washington, 1977—82; pvt. practice medicine specializing in neurol. surgery Washington, 1982—; mem. staff Georgetown U. Hosp., 1982—, Arlington Hosp., 1982—; chief divsn. neurosurgery, faculty clin. instr. Georgetown U. Sch. Medicine, 1982—; faculty clin. assoc. prof. George Washington Sch. Medicine, 1994—. Cons. in health care fin., internat. health care. Contbr. articles to profl. jours. Fellow: ACS, Internat. Coll. Surgeons; mem.: AMA, Congress of Neurol. Surgery, Washington Acad. Neurosurgery, Neurosurg. Soc. of D.C., Arlington Med. Soc., Am. Assn. Neurol. Surgeons. Office: 611 S Carlin Springs Rd Ste 105 Arlington VA 22204-1061 E-mail: fferraz@starpower.net.

FERRE, ANTONIO LUIS, newspaper publisher; b. Ponce, P.R., Feb. 6, 1934; s. Luis A. and Lorenza (Ramirez de Arellano) F.; m. Luisa Rangel, Feb. 23, 1963; children: Maria Luisa, Antonio Luis, Luis Alberto, Maria Eugenia, Maria Lorenza. AB magna cum laude, Amherst Coll., 1955, PhD in Humanities (hon.), 1995; MBA, Harvard U., 1957; student, Inst. for Sr. Mgmt. and Govt. Execs., Dartmouth Coll.; PhD in Comm. Sci. (hon.), U. Turabo, 1992; HHD (hon.), Amherst Coll., 1994. Vice chmn. Banco Popular; pres., editor El Nuevo Dia, 1968—. Chmn. P.R. Conservation Trust. Author: (essays) Un Alto en el Camino; Pan, Paz y Palabra; also numerous newspaper editorials. Pres. P.R. Coun. on Higher Edn., 1966-68, Gov.'s Adv. Coun., 1968-72; mem. Gov.'s Labor Adv. Coun., 1975; pres. Com. for Econ Devel. P.R.; vice chmn. Ponce Mus. Art. With U.S. Army, 1958. Recipient Presdl. citation, 1976. Mem. P.R. Mfrs. Assn. (pres. 1965-66), Am. Mgmt. Assn. (President's Assn. 1963—), Coun. of Fgn. Rels., Inter-Am. Dialogue, P.R. C. of C., Dorado Beach and Golf Club, Bankers Club P.R., Club Deportivo de Ponce, Phi Beta Kappa. Roman Catholic.

FERRÉ, JOHN PATRICK, communications educator; b. Charlottesville, Va., Oct. 29, 1956; s. George Allan and Patricia (Wigglesworth) F.; m. Gweneth Anne Dunleavy, May 4, 1985; children: Megan Dunleavy, Ian Dunleavy. BA in Religion, Mars Hill (N.C.) Coll., 1977; MA in Comm., Purdue U., 1978; MA in Divinity, U. Chgo., 1982; PhD in Comm., U. Ill., 1986. Vis. instr. English and philosophy Purdue U. Calumet, Hammond, Ind., 1979-80; asst. prof. comm. U. Louisville, 1985-90, assoc. prof. comm., 1990—98, prof. comm., 1998—. Author: A Social Gospel for Millions, 1988; co-author: Good News, 1993 (Religious Speech Comm. Assn. Book award 1993); co-compiler: Public Relations and Ethics, 1991; editor: Channels of Belief, 1990. Mem. Am. Journalism Historians Assn., Assn. for Edn. in Journalism and Mass Communication (Krieghbaum Under-40 award for outstanding achievement in rsch., tchg., and pub. svc. 1996). Democrat. Presbyterian. Office: Univ Louisville Dept Comm Louisville KY 40292

FERRE, LUIS A. political organization administrator; b. Feb. 17, 1904; m. Tiody de Jesus, 1980. BA, MIT, 1924, MA, 1925; LLD (hon.), Harvard U., Amherst Coll.; LHD (hon.), NYU; D in Internat. Law (hon.), Fla. Internat. U.; D in Music, New Eng. Conservatory Music. Pres., CEO PR Cement Co., Inc.; mem. P.R. House Repr, 1953—56; gov. Puerto Rico, 1969-72; senator P.R. Legis., 1976-85; pres. Senate, 1977—80; chmn. P.R. Rep. Party, 1975—. Sr. adv. UN Edn., Scientific and Cultural Orgn., 1982-83; mem. Rep. Nat. Com.; del. Rep. Nat. Conv., 1968, 72, 76, 80, 84. Contbr. articles to profl. jours. Decorated Knight of the Holy Sepulchre Pope John XXIII, 1959, Order of Vasa, 1963. Fellow ASME, Am. Soc. Arts and Scis., Elks, Met. Opera; mem. AIA. Address: 502 Hostos Ave Hato Rey PR 00918 also: PO Box 266108 San Juan PR 00936-6108*

FERRÉ, MAURICE A. entrepreneur; b. Ponce, P.R., June 23, 1935; s. Jose Antonio and Florence (Salichs) F.; m. Maria Mercedes Malaussena; children: Mary Isabel, Jose Luis, Carlos Maurice, Maurice Raymundo, Florence, Francisco Antonio. BS in Archtl. Engring., U. Miami, 1957. Mem. Fla. Ho. of Reps., 1967; commr. City of Miami, 1968, mayor, 1968-85; prin. Ferré Holdings, Miami. Author: Metro-Miami Destination 2000, 1996. Chair Transp. Com., Miami, 1995-96, Dem. Nat. Com., 1994-95, Aviation Com., Miami, 1997-98; bd. dirs. ICARE Bay Point Schs.; chair Mimai Dade County Commn., 1993-96. Roman Catholic. Home: 3900 Poinciana Ave Coconut Grove FL 33133-6424 Office: Ferré Holdings 2655 Le Jeune Rd #504 Miami FL 33134 E-mail: jafarre2002@aol.com.

FERREE, CAROLYN RUTH, radiation oncologist, educator; b. Liberty, N.C., Jan. 29, 1944; d. Numer Floyd and Mary Isabel (Glass) Black; m. Richard C. Sanders, June 5, 1999. BA, U. N.C., Greensboro, 1966, DSc (hon.), 1998; MD, Bowman Gray Coll., Winston-Salem, 1970. Diplomate Am. Bd. Radiation Oncology. Intern medicine N.C. Bapt. Hosp., Winston-Salem, 1970-71, resident in radiation oncology, 1971-74; instr. radiation oncology Bowman Gray Sch. Medicine, Winston-Salem, 1974-75, asst. prof., 1975-80, assoc. prof., 1980-87, prof., 1987—. Contbr. articles to profl. jours. Mem., v.p. County Bd. of Pub. Health, Winston-Salem, 1985-92; bd. dirs. U. N.C.-Greensboro Excellence Found., 1988-94; med. dir. Forsyth County chpt. Am. Cancer Soc., 1975-90; bd. dirs. Hospice, 1990—. Recipient Disting. Svc. award U. N.C.-G Alumni, 1997, Disting. Achievement award Wake Forest U. Sch. Medicine, 1999; named Disting. Woman of N.C. in Professions, Gov.'s award, 1998. Fellow Am. Coll. Radiology; mem. AMA (N.C. del. to AMA), Pediat. Oncology Group (radiotherapy coord.), N.C. Med. Soc. (2d v.p. 1990-91, sec.-treas. 1991-95, pres.-elect 1996, pres. 1997), Am. Soc. Therapeutic Radiologists Orgn. Office: Wake Forest U Sch Medicine Med Center Blvd Winston Salem NC 27157-0001 E-mail: cferree@wfubmc.edu.

FERREE, DAVID CURTIS, horticultural researcher; b. Lock Haven, Pa., Feb. 9, 1943; s. George H. and Ruth O. (McClain) F.; m. Sandra J. Corman, Aug. 31, 1968; children: Curtis P., Thomas A. BS, Pa. State U., 1965; MS, U. Md., 1968, PhD, 1969. From asst. to assoc. prof. Ohio State U., Wooster, 1971—76, prof., 1981—. Contbr. numerous articles to profl. jours. Capt. U.S. Army, 1969-71. Recipient sr. scientist disting. rsch. award Ohio Agrl. Rsch. and Devel. Ctr., 1997, Disting. Svc. award Ohio Fruit Growers Soc., 1998. Fellow Am. Soc. Hort. Sci. (assoc. editor 1983-86, v.p. 1988-89, J.H. Gourley award 1982, Stark award 1983), Am. Pomological Soc. (editor 1985-2002), Internat. Dwarf Fruit Tree Assn. (Disting. Rschr. award 1989), Gamma Sigma Delta (Rsch. award 1981). Lutheran. Office: Ohio Agrl R & D Ctr Dept Horticulture Crop Sci Wooster OH 44691 E-mail: ferree.1@osu.edu.

FERREE, JOHN NEWTON, JR., fundraising specialist, consultant; b. Wadesboro, N.C., Nov. 21, 1946; s. John Newton and Mary Cleo Ferree. AA, Bluefield (Va.) Coll., 1966; BA, Baylor U., 1968; JD, Samford U., 1975. Bar: Ala. Contr. Aetna Life Ins. Co., Seattle, 1972; atty. Ferree & Armstrong, Alabaster, Ala., 1975-82; exec. dir. Northwest Bapt. Found., Portland, Oreg., 1982-84; asst. v.p. Harris Trust Co. of Ariz., Scottsdale, 1984; v.p. Bapt. Found. of Ariz., Phoenix, 1985-89; dir. planned giving Phoenix Children's Hosp., 1989-91; pres. Scottsdale (Ariz.) Healthcare Found., 1991—; bd. dir. Nat. Com. Planned Giving, 1994-96. Bd. dirs. FBI Citizen's Acad. Found., 1994—, v.p. 1994-96, 98-99, Charitable Accord, v.p., 1996-1998; instr. Cannon Sch. Found. Mgmt., 1995-2000; adj. prof. Ariz. State U., 1998-2000; cons. in field. Named Ariz. Profl. Fundraiser of Yr., 1996. Mem. Assn. Fundraising Profls. (pres. greater Ariz. chpt. 1991), Planned Giving Roundtable of Ariz. (pres. 1992, 97), Assn. for Healthcare Philanthropy. Republican. Baptist. Office: Scottsdale Healthcare Found 10001 E 92d St Ste 121 Scottsdale AZ 85258-4530 E-mail: jferree@shc.org.

FERREE, PATRICIA ANN, case management specialist and trainer; b. Middletown, N.Y., Oct. 5, 1947; d. William Harry and Florence Arlene (Sarr) Krenrich; m. Daniel Milton Ferree, Feb. 13, 1972; children: Patricia Ann, Daniel Milton Jr. AS, Ctrl. Fla. C.C., Ocala, 1969; BS in Nursing, Va. Commonwealth U., 1985. Cert. cardiac nurse therapist. Critical care nurse Fla. Hosp., Orlando, 1969-76, cardiac nurse therapist, 1976-80, head nurse cardiac rehab., 1980-82; nurse adminstrn., rsch. nurse Va. Heart Inst., Richmond, 1982-86; coord. health care cost containment Cir. City Stores, Inc., Richmond, 1986, mgr. health and safety, 1986-89, corp. mgr. workers' compensation and safety, 1989-94, corp. sr. analyst for managed care unit in risk mgmt. dept., 1994-97; case mgmt. specialist and trainer Concentra, Tampa, 1997—. Choir dir. Courthouse Rd. Seventh-Day Adventist Ch., Richmond, 1983-89, min. music, 1989-94; curriculum com. Richmond Acad. Home and Sch. Leader; chmn. cardiovascular task force Am. Heart Assn., 1984-85; youth leader Tampa 1st Seventh-Day Adventist Ch., 1998—. Recipient svc. plaque cardiology dept. Fla. Hosp., 1982; Peggy Gibson Meml. nursing scholar, 1967, Fla. Bd. Edn. nursing scholar, 1967-69. Mem. NAFE, Am. Assn. Occupational Health Nurses, Am. Soc. Safety Engrs., Soc. Nursing Profls., Am. Assn. for Cardiovascular and Pulmonary Rehab. (founding), Richmond Met. Soc. for Cardiac Rehab. (founding), West Coast Regional Case Mgmt. Assn., Phi Kappa Phi, Sigma Zeta. Republican. Avocations: music, water sports, computer art. Office: Concentra 5130 Eisenhower Blvd Tampa FL 33634

FERREIRA, ANTONIO MARIO, chemist, educator; b. Pittsfield, Mass., Sept. 25, 1968; s. Louis Baldo and Anna Paladino Ferreira; m. Mary Elizabeth Crabtree, June 27, 1998; 1 child, Lindsay Elizabeth. BA in Math., Syracuse U., Utica, N.Y., 1993; PhD in Phys. Chemistry, U. of Memphis, 2000. Vis. asst. prof. of chemistry U. of Memphis, 2001—; adj. prof. of pharm. sci. U. of Tenn. Health Sci. Ctr., Memphis., 2002—. Postdoctoral rsch. assoc. Kans. State U., Manhattan, 2000—01. Contbr. Mem. St. Vincent DePaul Soc., Memphis, 2002—03. With USN, 1986—87. Grantee Travel grant, NATO Advanced Study Inst., Erice, Italy, 2000; scholar Half-Tuition scholar, Utica Coll. of Syracuse U., 1990—93. Mem.: AAAS, Am. Math. Soc., Am. Phys. Soc., Am. Chem. Soc. Republican. Roman Catholic. Achievements include patents pending for Composition of matter for novel cannabinoid derivatives. Avocations: sailing, stargazing, trumpet (performing). Home: 1675 Estate Dr Memphis TN 38119 Office: Department of Chemistry Univ of Memphis Memphis TN 38152 Office Fax: 901-678-3447. E-mail: a-ferreira@memphis.edu.

FERREIRA, ARMANDO THOMAS, sculptor, educator; b. Charleston, W.Va., Jan. 8, 1932; s. Maximiliano and Placeres (Sanchez) F.; children: Lisa, Teresa. Student, Chouinard Art Inst., 1949-50, Long Beach City Coll., 1950-53; BA, UCLA, 1954, MA, 1956. Asst. prof. art Mt. St. Mary's Coll., 1956-57; mem. faculty dept. art Calif. State U., Long Beach, 1957—, prof., 1967—, chmn. dept. art, 1971-77, assoc. dean Sch. Fine Arts, acting dean Coll. Arts. Lectr., cons. on art adminstrn. to art schs. and universities, Brazilian Ministry Edn. One-man shows include, Pasadena Mus., 1959, Long Beach Mus., 1959, 69, Eccles Mus., 1967, Clay and Fiber Gallery, Taos, 1972; exhibited in group shows at L.A. County Art Mus., 1958, 66, Wichita Art Mus., 1959, Everson Mus., 1960, 66, San Diego Mus. Fine Arts, 1969, 73, Fairtree Gallery, N.Y.C., 1971, 74, L.A. Inst. Contemporary Art, 1977, Utah Art Mus., 1978, Bowers Mus., Santa Ana, Calif., 1980, No. Ill. U., 1986, Beckstrand Gallery, Palos Verdes (Calif.) Art Ctr., 1987, U. Madrid, 1993; permanent collections include Utah Mus. Art, Wichita Art Mus., Long Beach (Calif.) Mus. Art, State of Calif. Collection, Fred Jones Jr. Mus. Art U. Okla., U. Okla. Art Mus.; vis. artist, U. N.D., 1974. Fulbright lectr. Brazil, 1981 Fellow: Nat. Assn. Schs. Art and Design (bd. dirs.). *I suppose much of my own life has been shaped by my experience as a first generation American. What modest success I may have had in my work is considerably due to that sense of ambition with which immigrant parents imbue their children. My vision as an artist is also shaped by the strong sense of Spanish culture that was part of my upbringing.*

FERREIRA, DONNA BLAIR, interior designer; b. Columbus, Ohio, Apr. 23, 1947; Student, Phoenix Coll., 1965-69, Minn. Sch. Art, 1961-65. Cert. interior designer, Calif. Preliminary draftsman Paddock Pools, Phoenix, 1968; visual merchandising designer Goldwaters Fashion Stores, Ariz. and, N.Mex., 1970-75, Diamonds and Rhodes, Ariz., 1967-69; owner D.J. Sanchez Interiors, Phoenix, 1973-83; mem. design staff Lou Regesters, Phoenix, 1983—. Tchr. visual merchandising Phoenix Coll. and Mesa Community Coll. Fellow Internat. Furnishings and Design Assn., Internat. Soc. Interior Designers, Ariz. Design Coun., Interior Designers for Ariz. Legislature (bd. dirs., sec.). Office: PO Box 22061 Phoenix AZ 85028

FERREIRA, JO ANN JEANETTE CHANOUX, time-definite transportation industry executive; b. Dec. 3, 1943; d. John W. and June B. Chanoux; m. G. Dodge Ferreira, Apr. 21, 1979 (div. Dec. 1993). BS, Purdue U., 1965, MS, 1969. With sys. devel. rsch. IBM, San Jose, Calif., 1965-67; asst. dir. mgmt. info. sys. edn. Union Carbide Corp., N.Y.C., 1969; mgmt. cons. Touche Ross & Co., N.Y.C., 1974-75; dir. corp. devel. strategy cons. A.T. Kearney-Mgmt. Cons., Chgo., 1975-83; dir. Computer Devel. Ctr. United Airlines, 1983-88; pres. WSG Designs Inc., Northbrook, Ill., 1988-92; gen. mgr. acoustic rsch. divsn. Internat. Jensen, Inc., Lincolnshire, Ill., 1993—, v.p. bus. plans and export ops., 1994—, v.p. emerging markets, 1994-97; mng. dir. market planning and analysis Fed Express holding co. for Fed Ex, RPS, 1998. Lectr. Purdue U., 1969, 73-74; guest lectr. Northwestern U., 1981; spkr. in field. Contbr. articles to profl. publs. NSF fellow, 1969. Mem. Inst. Mgmt. Cons. (cert. mgmt. cons.), am. Arbitration Assn., Japan Am. soc., Phi Kappa Phi.

FERREIRA, LINDA DOREEN, long term, acute care and rehabilitation nurse; b. Elmhurst, Ill., Apr. 10, 1948; d. Louis S. and Clarice J. Grupe; m. Arthur M. Ferreira, Nov. 26, 1979; children: Scott Allen, Curtis Paul. ADN, U. Hawaii, Hilo, 1983; student, Kennedy Western U. LPN, Hawaii, RN, Hawaii, Alaska, Nev.; cert. gerontological nurse; cert. rehab. nurse. Nurse mgr. long term care, supr. Kona Hosp., Kealakekua, Hawaii, 1986-88; dir. long term care South Peninsula Hosp., Homer, Alaska, 1988; evening supr. Our Lady of Compassion Care Ctr., Anchorage, 1989-91; Alaska Psychiat. Inst., Anchorage, 1991-92; dir. nursing svc. Hillhaven-Kona Health Care Ctr., Kailua-Kona, Hawaii, 1993-95; evening charge nurse Fairbanks Meml. Hosp./Denali Ctr., Fairbanks, Alaska, 1995-97; subacute mgr. Washoe Progressive Care Ctr., Sparks, Nev., 1998; nurse mgr. Health South Rehab. Hosp., Reno, 1998-99; clin. leader rehab., nursing supr., dir. nursing svcs. Washoe Village Med. Ctr., Reno, 1999—2002; charge nuse rehab. Providence Alaska Med. Ctr., Anchorage, 2002—. Mem. ANA, Assn. Rehab. Nurses, Nat. Gerontol. Nurses Assn. E-mail: alferreira@msn.com.

FERRELL, CHARLES MADISON, retired nuclear engineer, health physicist; b. Clarksburg, W.Va., Apr. 30, 1928; s. Benjamin Franklin and Mary Ethlyn (Selby) F.; m. Donnie Sue Thompson, Aug. 30, 1957; children: Donald Franklin, Jeffrey Madison, Kimberly Marilyn. BS, Salem (W.Va.) Coll., 1950; postgrad., Vanderbilt U., 1954-55, W.Va. U., 1955-56, U. Md., 1959-61. Phys. scientist U.S. Army Chem. Corps, Edgewood, Md., 1951-52, physicist Frederick, Md., 1953-54; radiol. physicist U.S. AEC, Oak Ridge, 1956-57, Germantown, Md., 1957-74; nuclear engr. U.S. NRC, Bethesda and Rockville, Md., 1974-95; cons., 1995—. Co-author 5 U.S. Nuclear Regulatory publs. Dist. advancement chmn., unit commr. Seneca Dist. coun. Boy Scouts Am., 1993-2001. With U.S. Army, 1950-52. U.S. AEC radiol. physics fellow, 1954-55; recipient Silver Beaver award Boy Scouts Am., 1998, numerous vol. svc. awards including Nat. Assn. of Retired Fed. Employees State of Md. award, 1997, City of Gaithersburg,Md. People of Character award, 1997, Md. Sr. Citizens Hall of Fame, 2001. Mem. Health Physics Soc., Shriners. Methodist. Achievements include design of instrumentation to measure thermal radiation from nuclear tests; evaluation of radioactive sealed sources and devices for AEC licenses; evaluation of shipping casks for spent reactor fuel; tech. asst. to AEC office of Hearing Examiner on Contract Appeal cases and nuclear power reactor licensing; evaluation of power reactor site safety and design basis accidents. Home: 227 Rolling Rd Gaithersburg MD 20877-2041 E-mail: eagle1928@starpower.net.

FERRELL, CONCHATA GALEN, actress, acting teacher and coach; b. Charleston, W.Va., Mar. 28, 1943; d. Luther Martin and Mescal Loraine (George) F.; m. Arnold A. Anderson; 1 dau., Samantha. Student, W.Va. U., 1961-64, Marshall U., 1967-68. Actor: (NY theater appearances) The Hot L Baltimore, 1973, The Sea Horse, 1973—74 (OBIE award and Drama Desk award, 1974), Battle of Angels, 1975, (L.A. plays) Getting Out, 1978, Here Wait, 1980; (TV series) The Hot L Baltimore, 1975, B.J. and the Bear, 1979, McClain's Law, 1981, E.R., 1984, A Peaceable Kingdom, 1989, L.A. Law, 1991, Hearts Afire, 1993—94, Townies, 1996, Teen Angel, 1997, Push, Nevada, 2002, (movies) Network, 1975, Dangerous Hero, 1975, Heartland, 1981, Where the River Runs Black, 1986, For Keeps, 1987, Mystic Pizza, 1987, Witches of Eastwick, 1987, Chains of Gold, 1990, Edward Scissorhands, 1990, Family Prayers, 1993, True Romance, 1993, Samurai Cowboy, 1993, Heaven and Earth, 1993, Freeway, 1995, Touch, 1996, My Fellow Americans, 1996, Erin Brokovich, 2000, Crime and Punishment-High School, 2000, Stranger Inside, 2001, K-Pax, 2001, Mr. Deeds, 2002, (TV movies) A Girl Called Hatter Fox, 1977, A Death in Canaan, 1977, The Orchard Children, 1978, Before and After, 1979, Bliss, 1979, Reunion, 1980, The Rideout Case, 1980, The Great Gilley Hopkins, 1981, Life of the Party, 1982, Emergency Room, 1983, Nadia, 1984, Miss Lonely Hearts, 1985, Samaritan, 1986, Northbeach and Rawhide, 1986; actor, actor: Picnic, 1986, Eye on the Sparrow, 1987, Runaway Ralph, 1987, Goodbye Miss Liberty (Disney Channel), 1988, Running Mates, 1990, Deadly Intentions, Again, 1990, Back Field in Motion, 1991, 120 Volt Miracle, 1992, Forget Me Not, 1996, Sweetdreams, 1996, Amy and Isabelle, 2001. Recipient Wrangler award Nat. Cowboy Hall of Fame, 1981, Most Promising Newcomer award Theatre World, 1974, Emmy award nomination, 1991-92. Mem. AFTRA, ACLU, NOW, Actors Equity Assn., Screen Actors Guild, Women in Films, Circle West. Democrat. Office: Paradigm 10100 Santa Monica Blvd Los Angeles CA 90067-4003

FERRELL, DAVID STANLEY, aerospace company executive; b. South Charleston, W.Va., Nov. 24, 1946; s. Erastus Carden and Ella Belle (Stanley) F.; m. Lynda Ann Snodgrass, Jan. 25, 1969; children: Holley Elizabeth, Eric Carden. BA, Marshall U., Huntington, W.Va., 1969; MA, Webster U., St. Louis, 1983. Lic. comml. pilot. Commd. lt. U.S. Army, Washington, 1969-94, mgr. digitization, 1994-98; mgr., dir. Aviation Activities, Washington, 1998-2000; mgr. Washington ops. Sys. Studies and Simulations, Washington, 2000—. Recipient Bronze Star, U.S. Army, 1971, Legion of Merit, 1994, Combat Air Medals for Valor, 1971, others. Mem. Am. Helicopter Soc. (pres. 1994—), AHS Internat. (pres. membership 2000—), Crystal City Rotary (sec. 1994-96), Assn. U.S. Army (v.p. at large 1995-97). Lutheran. Avocations: outdoor activities, reading, computers.

FERRELL, DOROTHY DOBRANSKY, social worker; b. St. Louis, Nov. 28, 1922; d. Jacob and Bessie (Herman) Dobransky; m. James K. Ferrell, Mar. 19, 1943; children: Janet M., John K. BA, U. Mo., 1943; MSW, U. N.C., 1964. Cert. clin. social worker, marriage and family therapist, N.C. Exec. dir. Wake County Family Svc.-Travelers Aid, Raleigh, 1950-54; social worker Dorothea Dix Hosp., Raleigh, 1954-56; supr. social wk. Lynchburgh (Va.) Tng. Sch., 1958-60; social worker Family Svc. Agy., Lynchburg, 1960-62, Dorothea Dix Hosp., Raleigh, 1962-63; social wk. supr. John Umstead Hosp., Butner, N.C., 1964-65, Dept. Mental Health, Raleigh, 1965-73; pvt. practice Raleigh Psychiatric Assocs., 1973-88; pvt. practice psychiatric social wk. Raleigh, 1988—. Recipient Isabell Carter Social Wk. award, N.C. Assn. Social Workers in Mental Health, 1976; named Social Worker of the Yr., Nat. Assn. Social Workers, N.C. chpt., 1990, Clin. Social Worker of Yr., 1999. Avocations: swimming, antiques, travel, geneology. Home: 4205 Rowan St Raleigh NC 27609-5660

FERRELL, HENRY CLIFTON, JR., historian, educator; b. Greensboro, N.C., July 28, 1934; s. Henry Clifton and Mary Louise Ferrell; m. Martha Smith, Sept. 6, 1958; children: Mary Elizabeth, Martha Ann, Henry Clifton Ferrell III. AB, Duke U., 1956, MA, 1957; PhD, U. Va., 1964. Prof. History East Carolina U., Greenville, 1961—. Planner East Carolina U., Greenville, 1980—85, univ. historian, 2001—. Author: Claude A. Swanson of Virginia, 1986. Spec 4 U.S. Army, 1959—65. Democrat. Methodist. Home: 2010 Fern Dr Greenville NC 27858

FERRELL, HOWARD HULEN, retired petroleum engineer; b. Shreveport, La., Apr. 11, 1929; s. Bun Oliver and Eva Cotton Ferrell; m. Marianne Shea Shea; children: Karen Ferrell Young, H. Shea, Helen Ferrell Lundeen. BSME, Okla. State U., 1951; MSME, Okla. State U., 1957; PhD in Petroleum Engring., Tex. A&M U., 1959. Lic. profl. engr., Okla. From rsch. engr. to sr. staff engr. Conoco Inc., Ponca City, Okla., 1959—85; sr. cons. engr. Keplinger & Assoc., Tulsa, Okla., 1985—89; project engr. K&A Inc., Tulsa, Okla., 1989—93. Contbr., articles to profl. jours. Active Rep. Party. Comdr. USN, 1952—77, Korean. Mem.: Soc. Petroleum Engrs. (life; Senior Member, Pioneer in Improved Oil Recovery award 2002), Ret. Officers Assn. (President. Oklahoma Council 2001—03). Baptist. Achievements include invention of oil recovery. Avocations: travel, musicals, fishing. Home: 5813 S Lakewood Ave Tulsa OK 74135 Personal E-mail: howardferrell@worldnet.att.net.

FERRELL, JAMES T. sculptor; b. Clayton, NJ; Degree in painting, sculpture, graphics, Pa. Acad. Fine Arts, 1963; degree in art, Barnes Found. on Merion. Artist Phila. Evening Bull., 1963—69; monitor Profl. Artists' Graphics Work-

shop, Pa.; medallic artist Franklin Mint, Phila., 1969—89, US Mint, Phila., 1989—. Sculptor 1991 Mt. Rushmore Commemorative Half Dollar, 1991 Korean War Mem. Silver Dollar, 1992 Olympic $5 Gold, 1992 Christopher Columbus Quincentennial Half Dollar, 1992 Bill of Rights Silver Half Dollar, 1993 Thomas Jefferson 250 Anniversary Half Dollar, 1993 World War II 50th Anniversary Half Dollar and Five Dollar Gold, 1994 Women in Mil. Svc Silver Dollar, 1994 Civil War Battlefields Clad Half Dollar, 1995 Spl. Olympics World Games Silver Dollar, 1995 Centennial Olympic Basketball, Baseball, Rowing and Tennis Half Dollars, 1995 Centennial Olympic One Dollar, 1996 Centennial Olympic Cauldron Gold $5, 1996 Smithsonian Instn. 150th Anniversary Gold $5, 1997 Jackie Robinson 50th Anniversary Silver Dollar, 1997 Franklin D. Roosevelt Mem. Gold $5, 1999 Ga. and Conn. State Quarters, 2001 Vt. and Ky. State Quarters, 2001 Am. Buffalo Silver Dollar and 2002 US Mil. Acad. Bicentennial Silver Dollar, Rep. Medal Sculpting for, Ruth and Billy Graham, Mother Teresa, Nelson Mandela, John Paul II, Gen. Matthew Ridgeway & Navajo Code Talkers. Recipient Charles Toppan prize, Lux prize, Woodrow prize. Office: The US Mint 801 9th St NW Washington DC 20220*

FERRELL, MILTON MORGAN, JR., lawyer; b. Coral Gables, Fla, Nov. 6, 1951; s. Milton M. and Annie (Blanche) Bradley; m. Lori R. Sanders, May 22, 1982; children: Milton Morgan III, Whitney Connolly. BA, Mercer U., 1973, JD, 1975. Bar: Fla. 1975. Asst. state's atty. State's Atty.'s Office, Miami, 1975-77; ptnr. Ferrell & Ferrell, Miami, 1977-84; sole practice Miami, 1985-87; ptnr. Ferrell & Williams, P.A., Miami, Fla., 1987-90, Ferrell & Fertel, P.A., Miami, 1990-98, Ferrell Schultz Carter & Fertel P.A., 1999-2000, Ferrell Schultz Carter Zumpano & Fertel, P.A., 2000—. Bd. dir. Isotag Tech., Inc. Trustee Mus. Sci. and Space Transit Planetarium, 1977-82, Am. Red Cross of Greater Miami & The Keys (mem., Bd. of Dir., 2001-present); mem. Ambs. of Mercy, Mercy Hosp. Found., Inc., 1985-94, ARC, 2001; trustee, mem. legal com., chair com. U. Miami Project to Cure Paralysis, 1985-94; trustee Eaglebrook Sch., 1995-98, ARC Greater Miami and The Keys, mem. bd. dir., 2001-, Robinson Charitable Found., 1993—, Mount Sinai Med. Ctr. Found., The Funders, Founder, 2002-present; United Way of Miami-Dade, 2000—; bd. dir. Jackson Meml. Found., 1999—, Greater Miami and the Keys chpt. ARC, 2001—, Performing Arts Ctr. Found., 1998—. Fellow Nat. Assn. Criminal Def. Lawyers, Am. Bd. Criminal Lawyers (bd. gov. 1981-82, sec. 1983-84, v.p. 1984-86, pres. 1987-88); mem. ABA (grantee 1975), Am. Bar Found., Fellow, 2003; Fla. Bar Assn. (jury instrns. com. 1987-88, chmn. grievance com. 11-L 1989-91), Internat. Bar Assn., 2003-; Dade County Bar Assn. (bd. dir. 1977-80), Assn. Trial Lawyers Am., Bath Club (bd. gov. 1992-95), Miami City Club, Univ. Club, Banker's Club, Cat Cay Yacht Club, Inc. (bd. dir. 1997-2000, treas. 1998-99, pres. 1999-2000), Am. Bar Found., Internat. Bar Assn., Indian Creek Country Club, LaGorce Country Club, Fisher Island Club, Univ. Club, Farmington Country Club. Home: Bay Point 4511 Lake Rd Miami FL 33137-3372 Office: Ferrell Schultz Carter Zumpano & Fertel PA 201 S Biscayne Blvd Fl 34 Miami FL 33131-4332 E-mail: mmf@ferrellschultz.com.

FERRELL, PAUL CLEVELAND, writer; b. Morehouse, Mo., Aug. 17, 1943; s. Sherman Gentry and Virginia Irene (Brawley) F.; m. Wanda Darlene Jones, Nov. 27, 1963. Student, Mineral Area Jr. Coll., Flat River, Mo., 1965—66, U. Mo., S.E. Mo. State U. Registered technologist Am. Radiol. Soc. Head radiology dept. Madison Meml. Hosp., Fredericktown, Mo., 1965-66; ambulance attendant Pub. Emergency Svc., Sikeston, Mo., 1970-73; tchr. math. Sikeston Pub. Schs., 1978-80, vocat. instr., 1980-85; ghost writer Sikeston, 1981-84; author Bloomfield, Mo., 1985—. Mem. adv. bds. Vocat. Edn., Sikeston, 1980-85; lectr. in math., health and philosophy. Author: Diet and the Cardiovascular Condition, 1995, The Utopian Cause, 1996, Night Reader I, 1997, Night Reader II, 1997, Morehouse Missouri, 1997, vol. 3, 2001, Night Reader III, 1998, Good Son/Bad Son, 1999, The Songs and Dreams of the Iconoclast and the Misanthrope, 2000, others; ghost writer, editor: The Headlee Anthology, 1984; author cultural newsletter The Plow and the Stars, 1992-93; inventor game Choice and Chance, 1992. Served with USN, 1966—70, Vietnam. Mem. Am. Registry Radiol. Technologists. Avocations: local history, visual and performing arts. Office: The Plow and the Stars 21212 County Road 510 Bloomfield MO 63825-8500 E-mail: starplow@hotmail.com.

FERRELL, ROBERT HUGH, historian, educator; b. Cleve., May 8, 1921; s. Ernest Henry and Edna Lulu (Rentsch) F.; m. Lila Esther Sprout, Sept. 8, 1956 (dec. Jan. 2002); 1 dau., Carolyn Irene. BS in Edn., Bowling Green State U., 1946, BA, 1947, LLD (hon.), 1971; MA, Yale U., 1948, PhD, 1951. Intelligence analyst U.S. Air Force, 1951-52; lectr. in history Mich. State U., 1952-53; asst. prof. history Ind. U., 1953-58, asso. prof., 1958-61, prof., 1961-74, Disting. prof., 1974-88, emeritus, 1988—. Vis. prof. Yale U., 1955-56, Am. U. at Cairo, 1958-59, U. Conn., 1964-65, Cath. U. Louvain, Belgium, 1969-70, Naval War Coll., 1974-75, U.S. Mil. Acad., 1987-88. Author: Peace in Their Time, 1952, American Diplomacy in the Great Depression, 1957, American Diplomacy: A History, 1959, 4th edit., 1987, Frank B. Kellogg and Henry L. Stimson, 1963; (with M.G. Baxter and J.E. Wiltz) Teaching of American History in High Schools, 1964, George C. Marshall, 1966; (with R.B. Morris and W. Greenleaf) America: A History of the People, 1971; (with others) Unfinished Century, 1973, Harry S. Truman and the Modern American Presidency, 1983, Truman: A Centenary Remembrance, 1984, Woodrow Wilson and World War I, 1985, Harry S. Truman: His Life on the Family Farms, 1991, Ill-Advised, 1992, Choosing Truman: The Democratic Convention of 1944, 1994, Harry S. Truman: A Life, 1994, The Strange Deaths of President Harding, 1996, The Dying President: Franklin D. Roosevelt, 1998, The Presidency of Calvin Coolidge, 1998, Truman and Pendergast, 1999, Harry S. Truman, 2003; editor: Off the Record: The Private Papers of Harry S. Truman, 1980, The Autobiography of Harry S. Truman, 1980, The Eisenhower Diaries, 1981, Dear Bess: The Letters from Harry to Bess Truman, 1983; (with Samuel Flagg Bemis) American Secretaries of State and Their Diplomacy, 10 vols., 1963-85, Banners in the Air: The Eighth Ohio Volunteers and the Spanish-American War, 1988, Monterrey is Ours!, 1990; Truman in the White House: The Diary of Eben Ayers, 1991, (with L.E. Wikander) Grace Coolidge: An Autobiography, 1992, Holding the Line: The Third Tennessee Infantry 1861-64, 1994; Truman and the Bomb, 1996, (with Joan Hoff) Dictionary of American History Supplement, 2 vols., 1996, FDR's Quiet Confidant: The Autobiography of Frank C. Walker, 1997, The Kansas City Investigation, 1999, A Youth in the Meuse-Argonne: A Memoir of World War I, 1917-1918, 2000, A Colonel in the Armored Divisions: A Memoir (1941-1945), 2001, In the Philippines and Okinawa: A Memoir (1945-1948), 2001. Served with USAAF, 1942-45. Mem. Soc. Historians Am. Fgn. Rels., Am. Hist. Assn. Home: 3496 Daleview Ann Arbor MI 48105

FERRELL, ROBERT E. writer, educator; b. Memphis, Dec. 31, 1940; s. Robert E. and Evelyn W. Ferrell; m. Yvonne Qiansong, June 20, 1993; 1 child, Robert. BA, NTSU (now UNT), Denton, Tex., 1966; MA, UTEP, El Paso, Tex., 4989. Adj. lectr. UTEP, El Paso, Tex., 1990—2003; prof. EPCC, El Paso, Tex., 1989—2003. Contact coord. Philosophy Dept., EPCC, El Paso, Tex., 2003. Author: (jour.) Philosophic Invest., 1999. Seamam USN, 1961—63, No. Atlantic, Carbn., Med. Recipient Honors Soc., EPCC, 1995. Mem.: Philosophic Soc., New Mexico and W. Texans. Democrat. Buddhist. Avocations: table, golf, skiing, mahjong, Wei Qi. Home: 6617 Pino Real El Paso TX 79912 Office: EPCC El Paso TX 79902

FERRELL, SUSAN R. lawyer; b. Muncy, Pa., Jan. 13, 1959; d. Robert Walton and Lorma Rae (Egli) Ferrell; m. David Edward Troller, Aug. 31, 1985; children: Katharine Troller, Andrew Troller, Robert Troller. BA, Pa. State U., 1980; JD, Coll. William and Mary, 1983. Bar: Pa. 1983, Ohio 1986. Assoc. Mitchell, Mitchell & Gray, Williamsport, Pa., 1983-85; asst. dist. atty. Lycoming County, Williamsport, 1984; assoc. Hollingsworth & Sunderland, Cin., 1986-89; law clk. to judge U.S. Dist. Ct. (so. dist.) Ohio, Cin., 1990—. Adj. prof. U. Dayton Sch. Law, 1997, Chase Sch. Law, N. Ky. U., 2001—03. Pres. Jr. League Cin., 2000—01; bd. sec. Family Nurturing Ctr. Ky., Edgewood, 1993—96; bd. dirs. Village Views, Terrace Park, Ohio, 1994—98; mem. outreach coun. Armstrong Chapel United Meth. Ch., Cin., 2002—. Mem.: ABA. Avocations: volunteer work, music, writing. Office: 801 Potter Stewart US Courthouse 100 E 5th St Cincinnati OH 45202-3927 E-mail: sftroller@aol.com., susan_ferrell@ohsd.uscourts.gov.

FERREN, BRAN, graphics designer; Student, MIT, 1970. Pres. Assocs. & Ferren, 1978—93; exec. v.p. creative tech., R&D Walt Disney Imagineering, 1993—99; co-chmn., co-founder and chief creative officer, pres. Applied Minds, Glendale, Calif., 1999—. Mem. adv. coun. Nat. Reconnaissance Office; tech. adv. group mem. Senate Select Com. on Intelligence; mem. sci. adv. bd. NSA; mem. external/indsl. adv. com. Ctr. for Advanced Tech., NYU; bd. dirs. Internat. Design Conf., Aspen, Colo., 1992—. Recipient Outstanding Achievement in Theater, Drama-Logue Critics, 1980, Circle award, L.A. Critics, 1980, Ann. Theater Design award, Maharam Found., 1984, N.Y. Drama Desk award, 1984, Spl. Gold Jury award, Houston Film Festival, 1989, Wally Russell Lifetime Achievement award in entertainment tech., LDI, 1998. Mem.: Acad. Motion Picture Arts and Scis. (Oscar nominee for best visual effects, Little Shop of Horrors 1987, Tech. Achievement award for laser synchro-cue system 1987, Tech. Achievement award for computer controlled lightning effects system 1983, Sci. and Engrng. award for advanced concept digital optical printer 1987), Acad. TV Arts and Scis., Theatrical Sound Designers Assn. Office: Applied Minds Inc 1209 Grand Central Ave Glendale CA 91201

FERREN, JOHN MAXWELL, judge; b. Kansas City, Mo., July 21, 1937; s. Jack Maxwell and Elizabeth Anne (Hansen) Ferren; m. Ann Elizabeth Speidel, Sept. 4, 1961 (div.); children: Andrew John, Peter Maxwell; m. Linda Jane Finkelstein, June 17, 1994. AB magna cum laude, Harvard U., 1959, LLB, 1962. Bar: Ill. 1962, Mass. 1967, D.C. 1970. Assoc. Kirkland, Ellis, Hodson, Chaffetz & Masters, Chgo., 1962—66; dir. Neighborhood Law Office Program, Harvard U. Law Sch., Cambridge, Mass., 1966—68; tchg. fellow, dir. Neighborhood Law Office Program, Harvard Law Sch., Cambridge, 1968—69, lectr. law, dir., 1969—70; ptnr. Hogan & Hartson, Washington, 1970—77; assoc. judge D.C. Ct. Appeals, 1977—97, sr. judge, 1999—, disciplinary bd., 1972—76; corp. counsel D.C., 1997—99; fellow Woodrow Wilson Internat. Ctr. for Scholars, 2000—01; exec. com., bd. dirs. Council on Legal Edn. for Profl. Responsibility, 1970—80. Exec. com. Washington Lawyers Com. for Civil Rights Under Law, 1970—77. Contbr. articles to profl. jours. Exec. com. of legal adv. com. Nat. Com. Against Discrimination in Housing, 1974—77; steering com. Nat. Prison Project ACLU Found., 1975—77; legis. subcom. on consumer credit Chgo. Commn. on Human Rels. Com. on New Residents, 1964—66; originator, chmn. Neighborhood Legal Advice Clinics, Ch. Fedn. Greater Chgo., 1964—66; treas., bd. dirs. Firman Neighborhood House, Chgo., 1964—66; bd. dirs. Frederick B. Abramson Meml. Found., 1991—97, People's Devel. Corp., Washington, 1970—74, George A. Wiley Meml. Fund, 1974—84, Nat. Resource Ctr. for Consumers of Legal Svcs., 1973—77, Ctr. for Law and Edn., Cambridge, Mass., 1989—94. Fellow: Am. Bar Found.; mem.: ABA (commn. on nat. inst. justice 1972—80, consortium on legal svcs. and pub. 1972—73, 1976—79, chmn. 1979—82, chmn. spl. com. on pub. interest practice 1976—78), Am. Law Inst., Phi Beta Kappa. Presbyterian. Office: Dist Columbia Ct Appeals 500 Indiana Ave NW Washington DC 20001-2131

FERRENDELLI, JAMES ANTHONY, neurologist, educator; b. Trinidad, Colo., Dec. 5, 1936; s. Alex and Edna Ferrendelli; children: Elisabeth, Cynthia, Michael AB cum laude in Chemistry, U. Colo., Boulder, 1958; MD, U. Colo., Denver, 1962. Diplomate Am. Bd. Psychiatry and Neurology. Intern U. Ky. Med. Ctr., 1962-63; resident in neurology Cleve. Met. Gen. Hosp., 1965-68; research fellow in neurochemistry Washington U. Sch. Medicine, St. Louis, 1968-70, asst. prof. neurology and pharmacology, 1970-74, assoc. prof., 1974-77, prof., 1977-95, Seay prof. clin. neuropharmacology in neurology, 1977-95; prof., chmn. dept. neurology, prof. pharmacology U. Tex., Houston, 1995—, Kraft-Eidmann prof., 1995—. Contbr. numerous articles to profl. jours. Served to capt. M.C., U.S. Army, 1963-65 Recipient rsch. career devel. award USPHS, 1971-76, Founders Day award Washington U., 1981, Disting. Tchr. award, 1993, 94, Disting. Prof. of Yr. award, 1993, NIH grantee, 1971—. Mem. Am. Acad. Neurology, Am. Neurol. Assn., Am. Soc. for Pharmacology and Exptl. Therapeutics (Epilepsy award 1981), Am. Epilepsy Soc. (Lennox lectr. 1991, pres. 1995, William G. Lennox award 2002), Assn. Univ. Prof. Neurology (pres. 2002—), Am. Soc. Exptl. Therapeutics (pres.-elect 2002—). Avocations: fly-fishing, numismatics. Office: U Tex-Houston Med Sch Dept Neurology 6431 Fannin St Ste 7044 Houston TX 77030-1501

FERRER, ADELARDO MANUEL, physician; b. Havana, Cuba, May 16, 1956; s. Adelardo Jose and Maria Concepcion F. MD, U. Colo., 1982. Bd. cert. in child psychiatry and gen. psychiatry. Resident/tng. programs participant San Mateo (Calif.) County Psychiat. Residency Tng. Program, 1982-85, St. Mary's Hosp. and Med. Ctr., San Francisco, 1985-87; pvt. practice child and gen. psychiatry So. San Francisco, 1987-96, Millbrae, Calif., 1996—; child psychiatry cons. Westside/Bayview Mental Health Clinics, San Francisco, 1988-95; staff psychiatrist, adult team North County Mental Health, Daly City, Calif., 1987-94; med. chief, youth mental health svcs. San Mateo County Mental Health, 1994-98, child psychiatrist access team, 1998—. Vol. psychiatrist Homeless Advocacy Project, San Francisco, 1996—. Recipient Comm. Svc. award, Bar Assn. of San Francisco, 1996, Outstanding Vol. in Pub. Svc. award, Vol. Legal Svcs. of Bar Assn. San Francisco, 2001, 2002. Fellow Am. Orthopsychiat. Assn.; mem. Am. Psychiat. Assn., No. Calif. Psychiatric Soc., Union of Am. Physicians and Dentists, Phi Beta Kappa. Avocations: travel, chess set collecting, swimming. Office: 510 Broadway Ste 201 Millbrae CA 94030-1966

FERRER, MIGUEL ANTONIO, brokerage firm and investment bank executive; b. Ithaca, N.Y., May 18, 1938; s. Miguel and Conchita (Bolivar) F.; m. Suzan Nudelman, Aug. 1962 (div. 1973); children: Miguel Antonio, Ilena Christine; m. Lizette Gratacos, Sept. 4, 1980 (div. 2000); children: Alejandro Miguel, Augusto Miguel. BA, Cornell U., 1959, MBA, 1961. Account exec. Merrill Lynch Pierce Fenner Smith, San Juan, P.R., 1961-65; br. mgr. Eastman Dillon Union Securities, San Juan, 1965-71, ptnr., 1971-73; sr. v.p. Blyth Eastman Dillon & Co., Inc., San Juan, 1973-80, PaineWebber Inc., San Juan, 1980—; pres., CEO PaineWebber Inc. of P.R., Hato Rey, 1983—; chmn. PaineWebber Latin Am., 1993-98; pres., CEO PaineWebber Trust Co. of P.R., 1997—. Bd. dirs. P.R. Investors Tax Free Fund; dir. consultive bd. U. P.R., Rio Piedras, 1989-92; mem. governing bd. P.R. Strategy Project. Bd. dirs. P.R. Aqueducts and Sewer Authority, San Juan, 1986-88, P.R. Pub. Broadcasting Corp., 1990-92, P.R. Mus. Architecture, San Juan; Rafael Hernández Colon Found., 1993-2000, U. P.R. Found., 1995, 2001; pres. fund raising ARC, Rio Piedras, 1990-91; bd. dirs., treas. Casa del Libro, San Juan; founding dir. Found. Friends of P.R. Acad. of Spanish Lang., 1996—; bd. trustees Cornell U. Recipient Top Mgmt. award in fin. Sales and Mktg. Execs. Assn., 1980. Mem. Securities Industry Assn. (founding mem., bd. dirs., past pres.), P.R. Fin. Analysts Assn. (founding mem., past pres.). Banker's Club. Avocations: gymnasiums, art collecting, philanthropy. Home: K-22 St Villa Caparra Guaynabo PR 00966 Office: UBS PaineWebber Inc PR American International Plz Penthouse Fl Hato Rey PR 00918

FERRER, RAFAEL DOUGLAS PAUL, lawyer; b. Seattle, Apr. 12, 1957; s. Rafael George and Barbara (Gould) F. BA in Acctg., U. Wash., 1979; JD, U. Puget Sound, 1982. Bar: Wash. 1985, U.S. Ct. Appeals (9th cir.) 1986. Acct. Lallman & Feldman, Ketchum, Idaho, 1980; tax profl. Touche Ross & Co., Seattle, 1981-82; securities syndicator Brouner Securities, Seattle, 1983; legal intern Davies Pearson, Tacoma, Wash., 1984; Ferrer Law Offices P.C. Seattle, 1985—. Bd. dirs. Paisans on First, Seattle, Ferrer Law Offices. Mem. Poncho Arts Found., Seattle, 1982, Madrona Community Group, Seattle, 1985; bd. dirs. Westboro Assn., Federal Way, Wash., 1981. Served with U.S. Marine Corps, 1975 80. Recipient Mr. Seattle 1st Place award IFBB Affiliate, 1978, Mr. Wash. 2d Place award IFBB Affiliate, 1978. Mem. ACLU, Wash. State Bar Assn., Assn. Trial Lawyers Am., Seattle King County Bar Assn., Wash. State Trial Lawyers Assn., Constrn. Fin. Mgmt. Assn., Phi Delta Phi. Republican. Congregationalist. Avocations: skiing, skydiving, scuba diving, mountain climbing, sailing. Home: 157 Yesler # 606 Seattle WA 98104 Office: Interurban Bldg Ste 606 157 Yesler Way Seattle WA 98104

FERRER, ROBERTO O. surgeon; b. Rosario, Argentina, Sept. 30, 1937; MD, U. Nat. Litoral Rosario, 1963. Diplomate Am. Bd. Surgery; cert. nutrition support physician. Intern St. Francis Gen. Hosp., Pitts., 1965-66; resident gen. surgery St. Joseph Hosp., Towson, Md., 1966-70, staff physician, 1970—, Greater Balt. Med. Ctr., Towson, 2000—. Fellow ACS, Am. Coll. of Gastroenterology; mem. AMA, ASPEN. Office: 7600 Osler Dr Ste 304 Towson MD 21204-7702

FERRER, THOMAS JOHN, surgeon; b. Manila, Philippines, Jan. 22, 1965; s. Feliciano N. and Paz M. (Morales) F. MS in Microbiology, U. Mich., Ann Arbor, 1987; MD, Washington U. Sch. Medicine, St. Louis, 1991. Cert. general surgeon. Surg. intern Barnes Hosp., St. Louis, 1991-92; gen. surgery residency U. Ark. Med. Scis., Little Rock, 1992-96, instr. in surgery, 1996-98; fellow in trauma and critical care U. Md. Med. Ctr., 1998-99; asst. prof. surgery U. Ark. for Med. Scis., 1999—. Named James B. Angell scholar U. Mich., Ann Arbor, 1987; recipient Dean's Letter of Recognition Washington U., St. Louis, 1991. Mem. Ark. Med. Soc., Phi Beta Kappa. Roman Catholic. Avocations: camping, running, hiking. Office: U Ark for Med Scis 4301 W Markham St Little Rock AR 72205-7101

FERRERA, ARTHUR ROCCO, food distribution company executive; b. Boston, Feb. 1, 1916; s. James F. and Mary (Mangini) F.; m. Mildred Grace Rugg, Sept. 9, 1944; children: Kenneth Grant, James Howard. AB, Harvard U., 1938. Co-founder James Ferrera & Sons, Inc., 1945—, pres., 1945-57, chmn. bd., 1957-89, chmn. emeritus, cons., 1989-91, ret., 1991. Chmn. emeritus, cons. James Ferrera & Sons, Inc.; dir. Commonwealth Bank of Boston, 1966-70; past dir. Romi Foods, Toronto; chmn. food divsn. CD, Mass., 1966. Served with AUS, 1942-46; to lt. col. USAFR (ret.) Name to Mass. Food Assn. Hall of Fame, 1993; recipient Cert. of Recognition, U.S. Dept. Def., 2000. Mem. New Eng. Wholesale Food Distbrs. Assn. (dir., past pres.), Nazareth Food Assn. (dir.), Mass. Food Assn. (Hall of Fame 1993), DAV (life). Clubs: Officers (Bedford, Mass.). Republican. Roman Catholic. Home: 5 Longfellow Rd Winchester MA 01890-2209

FERRETTI, JEFFREY JOHN, real estate broker, mortgage broker; b. Bklyn., Jan. 20, 1958; s. John Salvatore and Madeline Susan Ferretti; m. Susan K. Abrams (div.); m. Shari Karen Ferretti, Oct. 16, 1993; children: Ross, Jesse. Student, Bklyn. Coll. Sales agt. Fillmore Real Estate, Bklyn., 1984-86; owner Nat. Brokerage, Bklyn., 1986—; pres. Nat. Abstract of N.Y. Inc. Pres. Bklyn. Bd. of Realtors; v.p. Mid County Multiple Listing Svc.; sec. South Shore Multiple Listing Svc. Mem. Lions Club (v.p. Mill Basin Bergen Beach 1999), Lions. Democrat. Roman Catholic. Avocations: boating, swimming, singing, running, tennis. Office: Nat Brokerage 5122 Avenue N Brooklyn NY 11234-3808 E-mail: Jeffrey@NationalBrokerage.com.

FERRETTI, MADDALENA F. humanities educator; d. Luigi Funiciello and Carmela Minozzi; m. Aldo Ferretti, Oct. 6, 1956; children: Victoria Monica Ferretti-Aceto, Louise Emily Ferretti-Ohrbach. PhD in Chemistry, U. Rome, 1947—53. Asst. prof. U. Milan, 1956—57; rsch. asst. State Water Survey, Urbana, Ill., 1958—59; instr., Italian Internat. Ctr. for Lang. Studies, Washington, 1975—85, Casa Italiana, Cultural Ctr. of Italian-Americans, Washington, 1975—88, Fgn. Svc. Inst., U.S. Dept. Sch. Langs., Rosslyn, Va., 1976—78; lectr., inorganic chemistry and toxicology Am. U., Washington, 1982—85; Italian instr. for editl. bd. Wash. Post, 1982—90; adj. prof., Italian Montgomery Coll., Rockville, Md., 1985—90; lectr., Italian George Wash. U., Washington, 1984—87, adj. prof., Italian, 1987—93. Dir., Italian program George Wash. U., Washington, 1993—. Sec. Italian Cultural Soc., Washington, 2001—03. Fellow: Coun. for Promotion of Italian Lang. in Am. Schs. (assoc.; sec. 1998); mem.: MLA, Nat. Italian Am. Found., Am. Assn. Tchrs. Italian, Order of Sons of Italy (hon.). Roman Catholic. Avocations: travel, swimming, cooking. Home: 8516 Howell Rd Bethesda MD 20817 Office: George Washington Univ 801 22nd St NW Washington DC 20052 Office Fax: 202 994-9126. E-mail: ferretti@gwu.edu.

FERRETTI, SILVIA, dean; MD, DO, Phila. Coll. Osteo. Medicine, cert. phys. medicine and rehab., 1977. With Phila. Coll. Osteo. Medicine, 1981—87; dean acad. affairs Lake Erie Coll. Osteo. Medicine, 1992—. Chmn. dept. phys. medicine and rehab. Millcreek Cmty. Hosp. Office: 1858 West Grandview Blvd Erie PA 16509

FERRI, DAVID, lighting designer; b. Bethlehem, Pa. BFA in Photography, Rochester Inst. Tech. Resident lighting designer, tech. dir. PS 122, 1988—91; lighting design/tech. dir. Hollins, N.Y.C., 1993—. Mgr. prodn. Pina Bausch's Am. West Coast Tours, 1996, 98, Am. Dance Festival, 1996—. Recipient Bessie award for Outstanding Lighting Design and Sustained Achievement, 1987—88, 2002. Office: Hollins PO Box 20760 New York NY 10009

FERRI, RONALD DOMENICO, artist, painter; b. Providence, Aug. 20, 1932; s. Domenico and Francesca (DeVona) F.; m. Monique Paulette Dutto, June 15, 1963 (div. Apr. 1991). Student, R.I. Sch. Design, 1948-49; AAS, Rochester Inst. Tech., 1959; BS in Art Edn., NYU, 1962, MFA, 1965. Exhibited in shows at Mus. Modern Art, N.Y.C., Smithsonian Mus., Washington, Chgo. Art Inst., Phila. Mus., Whitney Mus., N.Y.C., Mus. Modern Art, St. Etienne, France, Gallery Binotti, N.Y.C., Protfolio Gallery, Miami, Fla., Country Bazaar Gallery, Watermill, N.Y., R.V.S. Fine Art Gallery, Southampton, L.I., N.Y., 1998, Findlay Gallery, East Hampton, L.I., 1999. With USAF, 1952-56.

FERRIER, JOSEPH JOHN, atmospheric physicist; b. Weehawken, N.J., Jan. 28, 1959; s. Henry Pierre and Josephine (Logalbo) F. BS, Columbia U., 1980; MS, NYU, 1983. Sci. programmer Sigma Data Svcs. Corp., N.Y.C., 1980-81; programmer/analyst M/A-Com Info. Systems, Inc., N.Y.C., 1981-86; atmospheric physicist, planetary group mgr. Centel Fed. Svcs. Corp., N.Y.C., 1986-89, Hughes Aircraft Co., 1989-94; atmospheric physicist, planetary group mgr., interdisciplinary group mgr. S.S.A.I., N.Y.C., 1994-2000; atmospheric physicist, sr. group mgr. SGT, Inc., N.Y.C., 2000—. Mem. AAAS. Office: NASA/GISS 2880 Broadway New York NY 10025-7848

FERRIER, RICHARD BROOKS, architecture educator, architect; b. Ft. Worth, Mar. 29, 1944; s. Samuel Foster and Opal Birtha (Brooks) F.; m. Lynna Gail Elmore Mindlin; 1 child, Sean Brooks. BA, Tex. Tech U., 1968; MA in Art, U. Dallas, Irving, Tex., 1973. With planning dept. City of Lubbock, Tex., 1962-63; with Atcheson, Atkinson and Cartwright: Architects, Lubbock, 1963-65, Engrng. Assocs., Lubbock, 1966-68; mem. faculty U. Tex., Arlington, 1968—, prof. architecture, assoc. dean, 1980-95; prin. Richard B. Ferrier, AIA, architect, Arlington, 1982-91, Firm X Richard B. Ferrier, FAIA, architect, Arlington, 1991—. With Ralph Kelman, architects, Dallas, 1969-70; assoc. William S. Austin, Architect, Arlington, 1976-80; with Comm. Cons., Arlington, 1970-82; mem. architecture adv. bd. Dallas County C.C., 1983-88; architecture critic Ft. Worth Star Telegram, 1989; lectr., juror in field. Contbr. articles and revs. to profl. jours.; prin. works includeNat. Compact House Design Competition, 1990 (First Place), EML House, 1991, Nat. Cowboy Hall of Fame Addition, 1992, DMA Tower, 1993, Nara Toto, 1994, Bar K R Ranch, 1994, Compact House III, 1996, New Lighthouse Ch., 1997; exhibited in numerous group shows, 1968—, including Dallas Mus. Art, 1991-99, Arlington Mus. Art, 1992-2002, Tex. Fine Arts Assn., Austin, 1992-98, Archtl. Gallery, Chgo., 1994. Named Alumni of Yr., Tex. Tech U. Coll. Architecture, 1993; recipient numerous awards Am. Soc. Architecture Perspectivists, 1986—, 12 awards Tex. Architect Graphics Competition, 1988—, amateur animated film award Cannes Internat. Film Festival, 1973, Romieniec award Tex. Soc. Archs., 1997. Mem. AIA (elected to Coll. Fellows 1993, recipient 12 Dallas design awards 1991-97, 50 Dallas graphic awards 1980—, including 17 honor awards). Democrat. Episcopalian. Home: Firm X 1628 Connally Ter Arlington TX 76010-4516 Office: U Tex Sch Arch PO Box 19108 Arlington TX 76019-0001 Fax: 817-469-1856. E-mail: firmx@aol.com.

FERRILLO, PATRICK J., JR., academic dean, endodontist; b. St. Louis, Mar. 4, 1941; s. Patrick J. Ferrillo Sr. BS, Georgetown U., 1973; DDS, Baylor U., 1976, cert., 1978. Instr. Baylor Coll. of Dentistry, Dallas, 1976-78; clin. asst. prof. Sch. Dental Medicine So. Ill. U., Alton, 1978-79, asst. prof. Sch. Dental Medicine, 1979-84, sect. head Sch. Dental Medicine, 1979-87, dir. current affairs Sch. Dental Medicine, 1982-87, acting chmn. Sch. Dental Medicine, 1984-85, chairperson Sch. Dental Medicine, 1985-87, acting dean Sch. Dental Medicine, 1986-87, dean Sch. Dental Medicine, assoc. prof., 1987—2002; pres. Am. Assoc. Dental Schs., Washington, 1999—2000; dean Univ. of Nevada Sch. of Dentistry, Las Vegas, 2002—. Fellow Am. Coll. Dentists, Internat. Coll. Dentists; mem. Omicron Kappa Upsilon (v.p. 1988-89, pres. 1989-91), Phi Kappa Phi. Office: University of Nevada School of Dentistry 4505 Maryland Parkway Box 453055 Las Vegas NV 89154

FERRINI, JAMES THOMAS, lawyer; b. Chgo., Jan. 14, 1938; s. John B. and Julia (Marre) F.; m. Jeanne Marie Fontana, June 8, 1963; children: Anthony, Mary Caren, Emily, Joseph, Danielle. JD, Loyola U., 1963. Bar: U.S. Supreme Ct. 1963, U.S. Ct. Appeals (7th cir.) 1967, U.S. Ct. Appeals (8th cir.) 1969, U.S. Ct. Appeals (3d cir.) 1975, U.S. Ct. Appeals (6th cir.) 1982, U.S. Ct. Appeals

(10th cir.) 1984, U.S. Ct. Appeals (4th cir.) 1987, U.S. Ct. Appeals (9th cir.) 1989. Sr. ptnr. Clausen Miller Gorman Caffrey & Witous, P.C., Chgo., 1963—. Mem. pattern jury instructions Ill. Supreme Ct. Commn., Chgo., 1978-94. Contbr. articles to profl. jours. Mem. Mary Seat of Wisdom Parish, Park Ridge. Fellow Am. Acad. Appellate Lawyers; mem. ABA, Ill. Bar Assn., Chgo. Bar Assn. (chmn. civil practice com.), Ill. Assn. Def. Trial Counsel, Appellate Lawyers Assn. (pres. Chgo. chpt. 1978, 79), Justinian Soc. Roman Catholic. Avocations: handball, sailing, skiing, cooking. Office: Clausen Miller PC 10 S La Salle St Ste 1600 Chicago IL 60603-1098

FERRIS, ALAN RUSSEL, psychology educator; b. Columbus, Nebr., Dec. 11, 1964; s. Russel Duane and Kay Rochelle Feris; m. Dawn Marie Hardesty, Jan. 7, 1989; children: Lindsay, Natalie. BS, U. Nebr., Kearney, 1988; MS, Kans. State U., 1990, PhD, 1992. Grad. tchg. asst. Kans. State U., Manhattan, 1988-92; asst. prof. psychology Mt. Marty Coll., Yankton, S.D., 1992-99, assoc. prof., 1999—. Mem. adv. bd. Yankton Area Adjustment Tng. Ctr., 1996—, Yankton Regional Mental Wellness Conf., 1998—; sec. Mt. Marty Coll. Faculty Orgn., Yankton, 1998-2000. Pres. Christ the King Luth. Ch., Yankton, 1996-2000; mem. S.D. Synod coun. Evang. Luth. Ch. of Am., 1998-2002; treas. Mo. River Br. Luth. Brotherhood, 1999-2001. Mem. APA, Soc. for Tchg. Psychology, Midwest Psychol. Assn. Avocations: sailing, model railroading, gardening. Home: 44006 306th St Yankton SD 57078-6008 Office: Mt Marty Coll 1105 W 8th St Yankton SD 57078-3725 E-mail: aferris@mtmc.edu.

FERRIS, GEORGE MALLETTE, JR., investment banker; b. Washington, Mar. 11, 1927; s. George Mallette and Charlotte (Hamilton) F.; m. Nancy Strouce, Jan. 25, 1964; children: George Mallette III, Willard Bradley, Kimberly Anne, David Hamilton. BS in Engring. magna cum laude, Princeton U., 1948; MBA, Harvard U., 1950. Chmn. Ferris, Baker Watts, Inc., Washington, 1971—. Commr. Md. Aviation Commn.; mem. exec. com. Fed. City Coun.; vice chmn. bd. dir. Smithsonian Nat. Mus. Am. History; past bd. govs. NY Stock Exch.; past chmn. Pres.'s Commn. on Mgmt. Aid Programs; past pres. Washington Soc. Investment Analysts. Past gen. campaign chmn. United Givers Fund, 1966; past gen. chmn. sustaining fund drive Nat. Symphony Orch.; past mem. Pres.'s Task Force Internat. Pvt. Enterprise; past chmn. investment adv. bd. AID. Recipient Princeton in Nations's Svc. award, Washingtonian award Jaycees, Order Red Triangel award YMCA Greater Washington, Silver Beaver award Boy Scouts Am. Mem. Harvard Bus. Sch. Club Washington (past pres.), Met. Club, Chevy Chase Club (Md.), Burning Tree Club (Md.), The Ctr. Club (Balt.), Phi Beta Kappa, Tau Beta Phi. Home: 5601 Kirkside Dr Bethesda MD 20815-7113 Office: Ferris Baker Watts Inc 1700 Pennsylvania Ave NW Washington DC 20006-4704 E-mail: g.ferris@fbw.com.

FERRIS, JAMES LEONARD, academic administrator; b. Bellingham, Wash., Jan. 15, 1944; s. Gerald Durward and Esther Evelyn (Larson) F.; m. Virginia Marie Dowde, June 23, 1972; children: Eric, Heidi. BSChemE, U. Wash., 1966; MS in Pulp and Paper Sci., Lawrence U., Appleton, Wis., 1969, PhD in Pulp and Paper Sci., 1974; Advanced Mgmt. Program, Harvard Bus. Sch., 1992. Mill engr. Weyerhaeuser Paper Co., Everett, Wash., 1966-67, scientist R & D dept., 1974-75, mgr. tech. svcs. pulp div. Tacoma, 1975-80, dir. R & D, 1980-85, mgr. mfg. pulp div., 1985-88, v.p. rsch., 1988-96; pres. Inst. Paper Sci. and Tech., Atlanta, 1996—. Bd. dirs. Albany Internat. Corp.; dir. Atlanta Consortium for Higher Edn., 1998—. Lt. (j.g.) USN, 1970-72, Vietnam. Mem. TAPPI. Office: Inst Paper Sci and Tech 500 10th St NW Atlanta GA 30318-5794

FERRIS, JAMES PETER, chemist, educator; b. Nyack, N.Y., July 25, 1932; s. Richard B. and Mabel G. (Collier) F.; m. Joan E. Herrlich, Sept. 3, 1955 (div. 1985); children: Alison R., Laura J.; m. Susan Shipherd, Mar. 7, 1992. BS, U. Pa., 1954; PhD, Ind. U., 1958. Postdoctoral researcher MIT, 1958-59; asst. prof. Fla. State U., 1959-64; research assoc. Salk Inst., 1964-67; assoc. prof. chemistry Rensselaer Poly. Inst., Troy, N.Y., 1967-73, prof., 1973-97, chmn. dept. chemistry, 1980-83, rsch. prof., 1997—. Dir. N.Y. Ctr. for the Study of the Origins of Life, a NASA NSCORT, 1998—; vis. prof. Lab. Organic Chemistry, Swiss Fed. Inst. Tech., Zurich, 1985-86, Salk Inst., 1995; mem. life scis. adv. com. NASA, 1987-88, chair adv. panel on exobiology, 1995—; mem. task force on life scis. of space sci. bd. NRC, 1984-86, mem. space studies bd., 1990-94, past vice chair subcommn. F3 com. space rsch., sci. com. oceanic rsch. working group on hydrothermal sys., 1989-92; mem. panel on exobiology Am. Inst. Biol. Scis., 1984-90. Mem. editl. bd. Biosystems. Recipient Career Devel. award USPHS, 1969-74; NRC fellow, 1976 Fellow AAAS; mem. Am. Chem. Soc., Internat. Soc. for Study Origins of Life (treas. 1980-89, editor Origins Life and Evolution of Biosphere 1982-99, pres. 1993-96, Oparin medal 1996), Univ. Space Rsch. Assn. (bd. trustees), Clay Minerals Soc., Inter-Am. Photochem. Soc. Home: 10 Saddlehill Rd Wynantskill NY 12198-7616 Office: Rensselaer Poly Inst Dept Chemistry Troy NY 12180 E-mail: ferrij@rpi.edu.

FERRIS, RITA BERNADETTE, social worker; b. New Haven, Aug. 9, 1918; d. John B. and Olympia (D'Orio) Affinito; m. Edward A. Ferris, Aug. 8, 1942 (dec. Jan. 1987); 1 child, Miles. AB, Albertus Magnus Coll., 1940; postgrad., McGill U., 1940-41; MS, Fordham U., 1942; postgrad., Yale U., 1945. Caseworker Cath. Family Agy., Norfolk, Va., 1944, sr. caseworker New Haven, 1944-46, 50-52; social worker Psychiat. Clinic VA, Hartford, Conn., 1947-48; case workers, sr. citizen coord. Asnuntuck C.C., Enfield, Conn., 1978-79; tutor young children primary grades Broward County, Fla., 1983—. Vol. adult handicapped and retarded, 1986; v.p. Rep. Women's Club, Suffield, Conn., 1985, Ch. Guild Orgn., Suffield, 1986, Newcomers Club; pres. Coll. Alumnae, Milford, Conn., 1970; chief checker polls, Suffield, Conn.; vol. I'm a Listener program. Mem. NASW, AAUW (v.p. Fla. Broward Count. 1992—). Republican. Roman Catholic. Avocations: singing in a choral group, western line dancing, bocci, art courses, political discussion groups. Home: Garfield Bldg A208 1601 SW 128th Ter Pembroke Pines FL 33027-2149

FERRIS, ROBERT ALBERT, lawyer, venture capitalist; b. N.Y.C., May 11, 1942; s. Albert Gerard and Helen Elizabeth (Jones) F.; m. Evelyn T. Jarvis; children: Robert C., Kathleen J. AB, Boston Coll., 1963; JD, Fordham U., 1966; grad. Advanced Mgmt. Program, Harvard U., 1974. Bar: N.Y. 1967, Calif. 1973. Assoc. Carter Ledyard & Milburn, N.Y.C., 1966-71; v.p., sec., gen. counsel Arcata Corp., Menlo Park, Calif., 1972-82; ptnr. Sequoia Assocs., Menlo Park, 1982-98; mng. dir. Caxton-Iseman Capital Inc., N.Y.C., 1998—. Bd. dirs. Buffets, Inc., Anteon Corp., Clayton Group, Inc. Served with AUS, 1966-67. Home: 77 Elena Ave Atherton CA 94027-4025 E-mail: raferris@worldnet.att.net.

FERRIS, ROGER PATRICK, architect; b. Buffalo, Jan. 3, 1952; s. Herbert Parkhill and Dolores (Murphy) F.; m. Yvonne DeHaas, May 20, 1995; children: Wren, Georgia. BA, La Salle Coll., 1974; postgrad., Columbia U., 1977-78; M in Design, Harvard U., 1982. Registered arch., Conn., N.Y., Mass., Vt., Maine, N.H., Ill., Tex., N.Mex., Washington, Va., N.C., Pa., R.I., N.J., Fla., S.C., N.C.; cert. Nat. Coun. archtl. Registration Bds. Arch. Victor Christ-Janer & Assocs., new Canaan, Conn., 1974-78; prin. Landworks Assocs., Southport, Conn., 1978-80, Ferris Franzen Assoc., Southport, 1980-82, Ferris Architects, Westport, Conn., 1982-98, Roger Ferris & Ptnrs., Westport, Conn., 1998—. Co-editor: Architectural Practices in the Nineties, 1996. Recipient Progressive Architecture Citation award, 1991, Outstanding Design award James Beard Found., 1997; Loeb fellow in advanced environ. design Grad. Sch. Design Harvard U., 1991, 92. Mem.: AIA (New Eng. regional award of excellence in arch. 1985, Design award Conn. 1985—86, Builders Nat. Design and Planning award 1988, 1988—92, Design award Conn. 1989, 1993—94, New Eng. regional award of excellence in arch. 1994, Builders Nat. Design and Planning award 1994, Design award Conn. 1996—98, New Eng. regional award of excellence in arch. 1997, Builders Nat. Design and Planning award 1998, New Eng. regional award of excellence in arch. 1999, 2000, New Eng. regional award for excellence in arch. 2001, Design award Conn. chpt. 2002, cert.), Conn. Trust Hist. Preservation (Conn. Preservation Design award 1994), Royal Inst. Brit. Archs., Am. Planning Assn. Office: Roger Ferris & Ptnrs 90 Post Rd E Westport CT 06880-3409 E-mail: ferris@ferrisarch.com.

FERRIS, RONALD CURRY, bishop; b. Toronto, Ont., Can., July 2, 1945; s. Herald Bland and Marjorie May (Curry) F.; m. Janet Agnes Waller, Aug. 14, 1965; children: Elisa, Jill, Matthew, Jenny, Rani, Jonathan. Grad., Toronto Tchrs. Coll., 1965; BA, U. Western Ont., London, 1970; MDiv, Huron Coll., London, 1973, DD (hon.), 1982; DMin, Pacific Sch. of Religion, Calif., 1995; STD (hon.), Thorneloe U., 1995. Ordained to ministry Anglican Ch., 1970. Tchr. Pape Ave. Sch., Toronto, 1965-66; prin. Carcross Elem. Sch., Y.T., 1966-68; incumbent St. Luke's Ch., Old Crow, Y.T., 1970-72; rector St. Stephen's Ch., London, Ont., 1973-81; bishop Diocese of Yukon, Whitehorse, 1981-95, Diocese of Algoma, Sault Sainte Marie, Can., 1995—. Author: (poems) A Wing and a Prayer, 1990. Home: 134 Simpson St Sault Sainte Marie ON Canada P6A 3V4 Office: Diocese of Algoma Box 1168 Sault Sainte Marie ON Canada P6A 5N7 E-mail: dioceseofalgoma@on.aibn.com.

FERRIS, RUSSELL JAMES, II, freelance writer; b. Rochester, N.Y., June 11, 1938; s. Russell James and Phyllis Helen (Breheny) F.; m. Ilma Maria dos Santos, June 29, 1968. Student, St. Bonaventure U., 1956-59; BS, U. Rochester, 1967; MS, Emerson Coll., 1989; PhD, Universal Life Ch., 1983. Cert. social worker. Film inspector City of Rochester, 1962-67; social worker Tulare County, Visalia, Calif., 1967-69, Alameda County, Oakland, Calif., 1969-71; ghostwriter self-employed, San Francisco, 1971—. Author: Crescendo, 1972 and 14 other novels. With USAR, 1956-68. Recipient Botany fellowship Emerson Coll., 1989. Mem.: United Macanese Assn., Inc., Am. Mensa Inc., Air Force Assn., Assn. U.S. Army, Res. Officers Assn. (life), Mil. Officers Assn. Am. (life). Libertarian. Roman Catholic. Avocation: aviculture. Home and Office: 202 Font Blvd San Francisco CA 94132-2404

FERRIS, WILLIAM REYNOLDS, humanities organization administrator, folklore educator; b. Vicksburg, Miss., Feb. 5, 1942; s. William Reynolds and Shelby Gibbs (Flowers) F.; 1 child, Virginia Louise. BA, Davidson (N.C.) Coll., 1964; MA in English, Northwestern U., 1965; MA in Folklore, U. Pa., 1967, PhD in Folklore, 1969. Asst. prof. English Jackson State U., 1970-72; assoc. prof. Am. and Afro-Am. Studies Yale U., 1972-79; prof. anthropology U. Miss., University, 1979-97; chmn. Nat. Endowment for Humanities, Washington, 1997—2001; prof. of history, adj. prof. in folklore curriculum, sr. assoc. dir. Ctr. for Study of Am. South Univ. N.C., Chapel Hill, NC, 2002—. Dir. Ctr. for Study So. Culture, U. Miss., Oxford, 1979-2001; nat. advisor U. Pa. Black Lit. Ctr., Phila., 1989—; mem. history and memory group DuBois Inst., Harvard U., Cambridge, Mass., 1987—; vis. fellow Stanford U. Humanities Ctr., Palo Alto, Calif., 1989-90; pub. policy fellow Woodrow Wilson Internat. Ctr. for Scholars, 2002—. Author: Local Color, 1982, Blues from the Delta, 1984; editor Afro-Am. Folk Arts and Crafts, 1983; co-editor Ency. of Southern Culture, 1989, You Live and Learn, And Then You Die and Forget It All, Ray Lum's Tales of Horses, Mules, and Men, 1992. Decorated chevalier des arts et des lettres (France), 1985, Officer in Order of Arts and Letters, 1994; named Disting. Alumnus, Rotary Found., 1989, One of Top 10 Tchrs. in Nation, Rolling Stone, 1991; recipient Charles FRankel prize in the Humanities, 1995. Mem. Am. Folklore Soc. (exec. bd. 1987—), Am. Studies Assn. (nat. coun. 1991). Office: Univ NC Dept History CB #9127 Chapel Hill NC 27599-9127

FERRISS, ABBOTT LAMOYNE, sociology educator emeritus; b. Jan. 31, 1915; s. Alfred William Overby and Grace Chiles (Mitchell) F.; m. Ruth Elizabeth Sparks, Dec. 21, 1940; children: John Abbott, William Thomas. BJ, U. Mo., 1937; MA, U. N.C., 1943, PhD, 1950. Asst. prof. sociology Vanderbilt U., 1949-51; rsch. social scientist Human Resources Rsch. Inst. Air U., 1951-54; chief unit effectiveness br. Air Force Pers. and Tng. Rsch. Ctr., 1954-57; chief health survey br. Bur. of Census, 1957-59; supervisory survey statistician Outdoor Recreation Resources Rev. Commn., 1959-62; asst. study dir. NSF, 1962-67; rsch. sociologist Russell Sage Found., 1967-70; prof. sociology Emory U., 1970-82, prof. emeritus, 1982—, chmn. dept., 1970-76, Heilbrun disting. emeritus rsch. fellow, 2002—03. Lectr. George Washington U., 1958-59, U. Md., 1959-61, No. Va. Ctr. of U. Va., 1960-70; guest prof. ZUMA, Mannheim, Fed. Republic Germany, 1989. Author: National Recreation Survey, 1962, Indicators of Trends in the Status of American Women, 1971, Indicators of Change in the American Family, 1970, Indicators of Trends in American Education, 1969, Attitudes of Far Eastern Air Force Personnel Toward Natives, 1953; editor: Research and the 1970 Census, 1971, (with J.C. Glidwell) Reducing Traffic Accidents by Use of Group Discussions-Decision: An a priori Evaluation, 1957; editor, pub.: SINET (Social Indicators Network News), 1984-95, editor emeritus, 1995—; assoc. editor: Social Forces, 1976-79; editor: SINET Selections, Social Indicators Research, 1990—; editor (with Dennis Peck) The Sociology of Civility, thematic issue of Sociol. Inquiry, 2002; mem. editl. bd.: Social Indicators Research, 1980—. With USAAF, 1942-46; CBI. NSF grantee, 1976-78. Fellow Internat. Soc. Quality of Life Studies (bd. dirs. 2003—, disting. scholar award 1997); mem. Am. Sociol. Soc., Sociol. Rsch. Assn., So. Sociol. Soc. (pres. 1986-87, editor The So. Sociologist 1981-84), Population Assn. Am. (sec.-treas. 1968-71, editor PAAAffairs), Ga. Sociol. Assn. (cert. of merit 1989), D.C. Sociol. Soc. (sec.-treas. 1965-68, pres. 1969-70, Stuart Rice award 1984), Midsouth Sociol. Assn., Cosmos Club. Democrat. Episcopalian. Home: 1273 Oxford Rd NE Atlanta GA 30306-2426 E-mail: aferris@emory.edu.

FERRIS-WAKS, ARLENE SUSAN, compliance officer; b. N.Y.C., Apr. 4, 1954; d. Jack Charles and Marcia (Berman) Ferris; m. Robert Gilman Waks, Sept. 20, 1981; 1 child, Jason Lowell. BA cum laude, SUNY, Buffalo, 1977; M. of Libr. and Info. Sci., CUNY, 1981. Rsch. analyst Zimmerman & Assocs., Washington, 1981-83; sr. mkt. analyst Am. Stock Exch., N.Y.C., 1983-84; prin. mkt. analyst N.Y. Stock Exch., N.Y.C., 1984-97; sr. compliance officer J.W. Genesis Securities Corp., Boca Raton, Fla., 1996-99; assoc. dir. compliance Dalton Kent Securities Group, Inc., N.Y.C., 1999—2001; cons. J.B. Hanauer, Parsippany, NJ, 2001—. Lectr./demonstrator N.Y. Stock Exch., 1989-96; cons. in compliance bus. info., 2001-. Mem. Nat. Soc. Compliance Profls. Home: 601 Kensington Dr Westfield NJ 07090-3604 Office: JB Hanauer 4 Gatehill Dr Parsippany NJ 07094- E-mail: afwaks@lycos.com.

FERRITER, MAURICE JOSEPH, lawyer; b. Holyoke, Mass., Aug. 14, 1930; s. John J. and Aldea F.; m. Margaret; children: Maurice J., John J., Mary M., Joseph P. AA, Holyoke Jr. Coll., 1952; BA, U. Mass., 1979; JD, Western New Eng. Law Sch., Springfield, Mass., 1957. Bar: Mass. 1957, U.S. Dist. Ct. Mass. 1960, U.S. Supreme Ct. 1967, U.S. Ct. Appeals (1st cir.) 1980. Of counsel Lyon, Ferriter & Fitzpatrick, LLP, Holyoke, 1957—. Chmn. bd. dirs. emeritus Ferriter, Scobbo, Sikora, Singal, Caruso & Rodophele, P.C., Boston; gen. counsel emeritus Mass. Mcpl. Wholesale Electric Co.; arbitrator AAA. Pres. emeritus Holyoke Heritage Park R.R.; trustee Providence Health Sys., former chmn. bd. Holyoke C.C., Providence Ministries Needy; former city solicitor, Holyoke. With U.S. Army, 1948-51. Recipient Outstanding Servant of Pub. award Springfield TV Sta. WWLP Channel 22, 1976, Spl. Svc. award Mcpl. Electric Assn. Mass., 1981, award of merit Bur. Exceptional Children, 1979, Cmty. Svc. award YMCA, 1989, Disting. Alumni award Holyoke C.C., 1987, Disting. Svc. award, 2002, Outstanding Significant Achievement award Rotary, 1996; named Person of Yr., N.E. Pub. Power Assn., 1992, Peace and Justice award Providence Ministries, 1999. Fellow Mass. Bar Found.; mem. ATLA, Am. Pub. Power Assn. (Individual Achievement award 1998), Mass. Bar Assn., Hampden County Bar Assn., Holyoke Bar Assn., Mass. Acad. Trial Lawyers, Holyoke C. of C. (past pres., Bus. Man of Yr. award 1990, Appreciation award 1975). Home: 31 Longfellow Rd Holyoke MA 01040-1290 Office: Whitney Place 14 Bobala Rd Holyoke MA 01040-9632 E-mail: mferriter@lyonferriter.com.

FERRITOR, DANIEL E. chancellor; b. Kansas City, Mo., Nov. 8, 1939; m. Patricia Jean Ferritor; children: Kimberly Ann, Kristin Marie, Sean Patrick. BA, Rockhurst Coll., 1962; MA, Washington U., St. Louis, 1967, PhD, 1969. Tchr. grade sch., Raytown, Mo., 1962-64; program assoc., asst. dir. Nat. Program on Early Childhood Edn., 1970-71; asst. program dir. CEMREL Inc., St. Ann, Mo., 1969-70, assoc. dir. instrnl. systems program, 1970-71; asst. prof. sociology U. Ark., Fayetteville, 1967-68, assoc. prof., 1973-79, prof., 1979-85, chmn. dept., 1973-85, vice chancellor for acad. affairs, provost, 1985-86, chancellor, 1986-97, prof., 1997—, chancellor emeritus, 1998—. Author: (with Robert L. Hamblin, D. Buckholdt, M. Kozloff and L. Blackwell) The Humanization Processes, 1971; contbr. articles to profl. jours. Office: Dept Sociology Social Work Criminal Justice U Ark Fayetteville AR 72701 E-mail: def@uark.edu.*

FERRO, ELIZABETH KRAMS, lawyer; b. Cheverly, Md., Oct. 14, 1948; d. Harry Francis and Jeanne Elizabeth (Edwards) Krams; children: Stephen Christopher, Elizabeth Juliet, Alexander Eli; m. Jose M. Ferro, Oct. 7, 1994. BS magna cum laude, U. Md., 1977; JD, George Washington U., 1982. Bar: D.C. 1983. Adminstr. Raleigh Stores Corp., Washington, 1973-83; atty. Lansfam Mgmt. Corp., Balt., 1983-2000, corp. sec., 1986-2000. V.p., dir. Sidney Lansburgh III Found., 1989—; bd. dirs. Debel Foods Corp., Elizabeth, N.J., 1986. Mem.: D.C. Bar Assn., Phi Kappa Phi, Alpha Sigma Lamda. Roman Catholic. Home: 10210 Riggs Rd Hyattsville MD 20783-1213 Office: Elizabeth K Ferro Esq 300 E Lombard St Ste 1800 Baltimore MD 21202-6739 E-mail: eferro1048@aol.com.

FERRO, VINCENT ANTHONY, elementary school educator, music educator; b. Carnegie, Pa., Dec. 11, 1956; s. Leonard and Jane Philomena Ferro; m. Kathy Ann Philbin-Ferro, June 29, 1985; children: Amanda Danhires, Vincent L. B in Music Edn., Baldwin Wallace, 1978, Puquesne U., 1991. Music tchr. Carlyntor Jr. Sr. High, Carnegie, Pa., 1992—96; elem. music tchr. Carnegie (Pa.) Elem., 1996—2002. Musician Full Gospel Ch. Carnegie, 1992—2002. Home: 639 Edward Dr Carnegie PA 15106

FERRO, WALTER, artist; b. N.Y.C., Oct. 6, 1925; s. Joseph Salvador and Mary Elizabeth (Potezna) F.; m. Lore Gausmann, Sept. 20, 1966; children—Elizabeth, Paula. Certificate, Bklyn. Mus. Art Sch., 1952. Art cons. One-man exhbns. include Wakefield Gallery, N.Y.C., 1960, Dominican Coll., Racine, Wis., 1962, Kings Coll., Briarcliff, N.Y., 1967, Hiram Malle Meml. Library, Pound Ridge, N.Y., 1988, Gallery L 9, Oberursel, Fed. Republic Germany, 1991; group exhbns. include Bklyn. Mus., 1953, U. Okla., 1959, Jersey City Mus., 1966, Phila. Mus., 1966; represented in permanent collections Met. Mus. Art, Nat. Mus. Am. Art, Smithsonian Instn. Served with USNR, 1942-44. Recipient Kenneth Hayes Miller Meml. award Audubon Artists, 1953; Kate W. Arms Meml. award Soc. Am. Graphic Artists, 1959; Guggenheim fellow, 1972 Address: PO Box 304 Pound Ridge NY 10576-0304

FERRY, DAVID KEANE, electrical engineering educator; b. San Antonio, Oct. 25, 1940; s. Joseph Jules and Elizabeth (Keane) F. m. Darleen Heitkamp; Aug. 25, 1962; children: Lara Annette, Linda Renee. BSEE, Tex. Tech U., 1962, MSEE, 1963; PhD, U. Tex., 1966. Lectr. U. Tex., Austin, 1966; postdoctoral fellow U. Vienna, Austria, 1966-67; asst. prof., then assoc. prof. Tex. Tech U., Lubbock, 1967-73; sci. officer Office Naval Rsch., Arlington, Va., 1973-77; prof., head elec. engring. Colo. State U., Ft. Collins, 1977-83; Regent's prof., dir. Ctr. for Solid State Electronics Rsch. Ariz. State U., Tempe, 1983-89, Regent's prof., chair elec. computing engring., 1989-92, Regent's prof., 1992—. Mem. microelectronics panel NRC, Washington, 1977-79; mem. materials rsch. coun. Def. Advanced Rsch. Projects Agy., Arlington, 1982-98; mem. supercomputer adv. group NSF, Washington, 1981-87. Author: (with D. R. Fannin) Physical Electronics, 1971; (with L. A. Akers and E. W. Greeneich) Ultra Large Scale Integrated Microelectronics, 1988, Semiconductors, 1991, (with R.O. Grondin) Physics of Submicron Devices, 1991, Quantum Mechanics, 1995, 2d edit., 2000, (with S.M. Goodnick) Transport in Nanostructures, 1997, Semiconductor Transport, 2000, (with J.P. Bird) Electronic Materials and Devices, 2001, Semiconductor Transport, 2001; numerous pub. sci. articles; editor: GaAs Technology, 1985, GaAs Technology II, 1989; (with J. R. Barker and C. Jacoboni) Physics of Nonlinear Transport in Semiconductors, 1979, (with J.R. Barker and C. Jacoboni) Granular Nonelectronics, 1991, (with C. Jacoboni) Quantum Transport in Semiconductors, 1992, (with C. Jacoboni, A.P. Jauho, H.L. Grubin) Quantum Transport in Ultrasmall Devices, 1995; patentee in field. Fellow IEEE (Cledo Brunetti prize for advancements in nanoelectronics 1999), Am. Phys. Soc.; mem. Sigma Xi. Avocations: photography, skiing. Office: Ariz State U Elec Dept Tempe AZ 85287

FERRY, JOAN EVANS, school counselor; b. Summit, N.J., Aug. 20, 1941; d. John Stiger and Margaret Darling (Evans) F. BS, U. Pa., 1964; cert., Coll. of Preceptors, London, 1966; EdM, Temple U., 1967; postgrad., Villanova U., 1981. Cert. elem. sch. tchr., elem. sch. counselor; cert. vol. Dale Carnegie. Indsl. photographer Bucksco Mfg. Co., Inc., Quakertown, Pa., 1958-59; math. and German tutor St. Lawrence U., Canton, N.Y., 1959-61; research asst. U. Pa., Phila., 1963; tchr. elem. sch. Pennridge Schs., Perkasie, Pa., 1964-74, 75-77, elem. sch. counselor, 1981—2001; pvt. practice counselor, real estate partnership Perkasie, 1981—; chair child study team Perkasie Elem. Sch., 1988-94; editor Princeton (NJ) Pub. Group, 2000—. Tutor math., German, St. Lawrence U., Canton, N.Y., 1959-61; supervisory tchr. East Stroudsburg U., Pennridge Schs., 1971-74; research asst. U. Pa., Phila., 1963; mem. acad. coms. for Pennridge Schs.; adj. faculty Bucks County Community Coll., 1983—; instr. Am. Inst. Banking, 1982—; notary pub., 1986—; mcpl. auditor, sec. bd. auditors, 1984-90, mcpl. auditor 1990—, chmn. bd. auditors 1990—; cons. in field. Author (with others) Life-Time Sports for the College Student: A Behavioral Objective Approach, 1971, 3d rev. edit. 1978, Elementary Social Studies as a Learning System, 1976. Vol. elem. sch. counselor Perkasie, 1979-80; mem. Hilltown Civic Assn., 1965-70, 92—; exec. com. chairperson Hilltown PTO, 1965-73; soloist Good Shepherd Episcopal Ch. Choir, Hilltown, 1964-77; steering com. Perkasie Sch., 1989-95; poll watcher, 1993; med. vol. Olympics, Atlanta, 1996; vol. Dublin Ambulance Squad, 1996—, House Rabbit Soc., Chadds Ford, Pa., 1998—, Special Olympics World Games, Summer, North Carolina, 1999, Silverdale Quick Response Med. Svc., 1999; mem. Dublin Vol. Fire and Ambulance Co., Silverdale Fire Co., Silverdale, Pa.; mem. prin.'s round table Perkasie (Pa.) Sch., 1997; vol. House Rabbit Soc. Southeastern Pa./Del. Foster Home and Sanctuary, Chadds Ford, Pa., 1998—; vol. marshal First Union USPro Championship Cycling Race, Phila., 1999, 2000; vol. spl. driver Bush Family and Friends at Rep. Nat. Conv., Phila., 2000, Bucks County Crisis Response Team, 2001-; mem. Nat. Arbor Day Found., Best Friends Animal Sanctuary. NSF grantee, Washington, 1972-73, Philanthropic Edn. Orgn. grantee, Doylestown, Pa., 1982; recipient Judith Netzky Meml. Fellowship award B'nai B'rith, Phila., 1979; Durning scholar Delta Delta Delta, Arlington, Tex., 1981, Am. Mgmt. Assns. scholar, N.Y.C., 1983, Statesman's award World Inst. Achievement, 1989, Achievement award Women's Inner Circle, 1990, Golden Acad. award for lifetime achievement, 1991; named to Internat. Tennis Hall of Fame, 2000 Notable Am. Women Hall of Fame, 1989, Cmty. Leaders of Am. Hall of Fame, 1990, Internat. Book of Honor Hall Of Fame, 1990, Internat. Bus. & Profl. Women's Hall of Fame, 1994, Lifetime Achievement Acad. Humane Soc. of U.S., Internat. Honor Soc. In Edn., Certificate of appreciation in recognition and acknowledgement for outstanding service and dedication as a member of the 1996 Atlanta Olympics Med. Team, 1997, Certs. of Appreciation Spring Mountain Ski Patrol, 1997, Honorary Educator certificate, St. Joseph's Indian Sch., 1996, ARC, 1986, Cert. Achievement in Recognition of Contbn. as Med. Svcs. Vol. at 1996 Centennial Olympic Games, 1996, Honor Award for Svc. to Edn. and Tchg. Profession, 1996, 99, award for Outstanding Svc. to Edn. Pennridge Schs., 1999, Certificate of appreciation for dedication to the success of the 1999 Special Olympics World Summer Games, 1999. Fellow Internat. Biog. Assn.; mem. AAUW, NEA, NAFE, Humane Soc. U.S., World Inst. Achievement, Pa. State Edn. Assn. (polit. action com. for edn., chair Pennridge Schs. 1986—, del. leadership conf. 1987, 89, Honor award for svc. to edn. and tchg. profession, 1996, 99), Pennridge Edn. Assn. (faculty rep. 1986-88, exec. coun. 1986—, negotiations resource com. 1987-89, 1990-93, steering com. Perkasie Sch. 1989-95, chairperson Child Study Team, 1988-94, Instructional Support Team, 1992—, selection com. for asst. supt. Pennridge Schs. 1993, selection com. for prin. Perkasie Sch. 1994, prin. round table 1997—), Am. Inst. Banking (chairperson 1987), U.S. Tennis Assn. (hon. life), Pa. and Mid. States Tennis Assn. (hon. life), U.S. Profl. Tennis Registry, Mid. States Profl. Tennis Registry, Women's Internat. Tennis Assn., Nat. Ski Patrol (Svc. Recognition award 1994), Spring Mountain Ski Patrol (Outstanding Aux. 1993, MOM Dedication award 1995, Outstanding Svc. and Dedication award 1996, 98, certificate of appreciation, 1997, svc. award, Nat. Ski Patrol, 1999), Pa. Elected Women's Assn., Bucks County Assn. Twp. Ofcls., Bucks County Sch. Counselors Assn., Pa. Sch. Counselors Assn., Pa. Assn. Notaries, Am. Soc. Notaries, Internat. Fedn. Univ. Women, Internat. Platform Assn., World Inst. Achievement, Am. Biog. Inst. Rsch. Assn. (rsch. bd. advisors, bd. govs. 1989—), World Inst. of Achievement, Lifetime Achievement Acad., Rails-to-Trails Conservancy, World Wildlife Fund, Bucks County Sch. Counselors Assn., Highpoint Athletic Club, Pennridge Cmty. Rep. Club. (recording sec. 1986-91, publicity chmn. 1991-92, Pen care chmn. 1992—), Assn. Tennis Profls. Tour Tennis Ptnrs., Sierra Club, The Nature Conservancy, Nat. Wildlife Fedn., John Wayne Found., Mediterranean Club, Philadelphia Sports Club, Delaware Valley Jaguar Club, Jaguar Clubs of North Am., Nockamixon Boat Club, Peace Valley Yacht Club, Kappa Delta Pi. Episcopalian. Avocations: land and water sports, flying, music, parasailing, photography. Home and Office: 834 Rickert Rd Perkasie PA 18944

FERRY, MARTHA MORTON, nonprofit executive; b. Amherst, Mass., Apr. 5, 1945; d. Edward Morrison and Dorothy Mae (Beck) F. AB, Mt. Holyoke Coll., 1966; MBA, Harvard U., 1968. Asst. mgmt. sci. officer Bankers Trust

Co., N.Y.C., 1968-71; v.p. Am. Express Internat. Bank Corp., N.Y.C., 1971-82; sr. v.p. Nat. Westminster Bank USA, N.Y.C., 1982-88; CFO Cmty. Svc. Soc. of N.Y., 1989—2002; dir. fin. and adminstrn. Assn. Jr. Leagues Internat., 2002—. Bd. dirs., N.Y. Women's Found., 2001—, treas., 2002—, bd. dirs., N.Y.C. YWCA, 1986-99, bd. trustees, 1st Presbyn. Ch., N.Y.C., 1997-99. Mem. Fin. Womens Assn. N.Y., Alumnae Assn. Mt. Holyoke Coll. (treas. 1983-86), Harvard Club, Mt. Holyoke Club (pres. 1974-75, bd. dirs. 1988-98). Democrat. Presbyterian. Avocations: travel, reading, performing arts. Office: 132 W 31st St New York NY 10001

FERRY, MILES YEOMAN, state legislator; b. Brigham City, Utah, Sept. 22, 1932; s. John Yeoman and Alda (Cheney) F.; m. Suzanne Call, May 19, 1952; children: John, Jane Ferry Stewart, Ben, Helen, Sue Ferry Thorpe. BS, Utah State U., 1954. Rancher, Corinne, Utah, 1952; pres. J.Y. Ferry & Son, Inc.; mem. Utah Ho. of Reps., 1965-66, Utah Senate, 1967-84, minority whip, 1975-76, minority leader, 1977-78, pres. senate, 1979-84; mem. presdl. advisor commn. on intergovtl. affairs, 1984; mem. governing bd. Council State Govts., 1983-84. V.p. Legis./Exec. Consulting Firm, 1994—; chmn. Corinne Cemetery Dist., 1989—. Pres. Brigham Jr. C. of C., 1956-61, Nat. Conf. of State Legislators, 1984, v.p., 1982, pres.-elect, 1983, pres., 1984; v.p. Utah Jr. C. of C., 1960-61; nat. dir. Utah Jaycees, 1961-62; pres. Farm Bur. Box Elder County, 1958-59; food and agr. commr. USDA, commr. agr. State of Utah, 1985-93. Recipient award of merit Boy Scouts Am., 1976, Alumnusi of Yr. award Utah State U., 1981, award of merit Utah Vocat. Assn., 1981, Friend of Agr. award Utah Farm Bur., 1988, Cert. Appreciation USDA, 1988, Contbn. to Agr. award Utah-Idaho Farmers Union, 1989, Disting. Svc. award Utah State U., 1993, 94; named Outstanding Young Man of Yr., Brigham City Jr. C. of C., 1957, Outstanding Nat. Dir. U.S. Jaycees, 1963, Outstanding Young Man in Utah, Utah Jr. C. of C., 1961, Outstanding Young Farmer, 1958, One of 3 Outstanding Young Men of Utah, 1962, Rep. Legislator of Yr., 1984, One of 10 Outstanding Legislators of Yr., 1984. Mem. SAR, Sons Utah Pioneers, Gov.'s Cabinet, Utah Commn. Agr., Fed. Rsch. Com., Nat. Assn. State Depts. Agr. (bd. dirs. 1989), Western Assn. of State Depts. of Agr. (v.p. 1990-91, pres. 1991-92), Western U.S. Agr. Trade Assn. (sec. treas- elect 1987-88, pres. 1989-90), Utah Cattlemen's Assn., Nat. Golden Spike Assn. (dir. 1958—), Phi Kappa Phi, Pi Kappa Alpha. Republican. Address: 815 N 6800 W Corinne UT 84307-9737 E-mail: leg.ex.con@worldnet.att.net.

FERRY, RICHARD MICHAEL, executive search firm executive; b. Ravenna, Ohio, Sept. 26, 1937; s. John D. and Margaret M. (Jenny) F.; m. Maude M. Hillman, Apr. 14, 1956; children: Richard A., Margaret L., Charles Michael, David W., Dianne E., Ann Marie. BS, Kent State U., 1959. CPA. Cons. staff Peat, Marwick, Mitchell, Los Angeles, 1965-69, ptnr., 1969; founder chmn. Korn/Ferry Internat., Los Angeles, 1969—. Bd. dirs. Mellon/1st Bus. Bank, L.A., Avery Dennison, Pasadena, Calif., Dole Food Co., Calif., Pacific Life Ins. Co., Newport Beach, Calif. Trustee St. John's Health Ctr., Santa Monica, Calif.; bd. dirs. Calif. Cmty. Found., Hugh O'Brian Youth Leadership; pres. Cath. Edn. Found., L.A. Republican. Roman Catholic. Office: Korn/Ferry Internat 1800 Century Park E Ste 900 Los Angeles CA 90067 1512

FERRY, ROBERT JEAN, JR., pediatric endocrinologist; b. Chgo., July 16, 1969; s. Robert Jean Ferry sr. and Margarita Beatriz Guzman-Lopez. BS, Yale U., 1989; MD, U. Tex. Health Sci. Ctr., San Antonio, 1994. Diplomate Am. Bd. Pediatrics. Resident in pediats. U. Tex. Health Sci. Ctr., 1994-97, chief resident pediats., 1996-97; fellow in pediat. endocrinology Children's Hosp. of Phila., 1997—2000; asst. prof. pediats UCLA Sch. Medicine, 2001—02; rsch. and tng. dir. pediat. endocrinology U. Tex. Health Sci. Ctr., San Antonio, 2002—. Ad hoc reviewer Pediats., 1999—, Growth Hormone & IGF Rsch., 1999—; presenter in field. Contbr. articles to profl. jours., chpts. to books. Recipient Caroline Duncan award So. Pediat. Neurology Soc., 1996, UCLA Stein-Oppenheimer award, 2001; Maurice Attie Meml. lectr. Phila. Endocrine Soc.; grantee Ross Products, 1996, U. Tex. Health Sci. Ctr., 1996, U. Pa. Sch. Medicine, 1998-99, Ethel Brown Foerderer Fund for Excellence, 1998-99, Genentech Found., 1998-2000, Endocrine Fellows Found., 1999-2000, NIDDK, 1999-2000, Lawson Wilkins Pediat. Endocrine Soc., 1999. Mem. AMA, Am. Acad. Pediats., Endocrine Soc. (mwm. assocs. coun. 1998—, chmn. assocs. coun. 2002-03), Am. Diabetes Assn., Internat. Soc. Insulin-like Growth Factor Rsch., Lawson Wilkins Pediat. Endocrine Soc. (Pharmacia Upjohn rsch. fellow 1999), Pa. Med. Soc. Avocations: philately, numismatics. Office: 533-F MSC 7806 7703 Floyd Curl Dr San Antonio TX 78229-3900 E-mail: bob@uthscsa.edu.

FERSHEE, SUSAN JOYCE, lawyer; b. Battle Creek, Mich., Apr. 20, 1947; d. James Fershee and Marian (Paden) Metcalf; m. Daniel Bernard Keating, Aug. 29, 1970 (div. Apr. 1974); m. George Frederick Wolfgang Hauck, Sept. 7, 1974. BA in Fgn. Langs., Maryville Coll., 1969; postgrad., U. Tuebingen, Germany, 1969-70; MA in German Lit., Ohio State U., 1972; JD, U. Mo.-Kansas City, 1988. Bar: Mo. 1988. Instr. German & French Tri-State U., Angola, Ind., 1972-74; self employed translator Angola, 1974-75; adminstrv. asst. Faultless Starch/Bon Ami Co., Kansas City, Mo., 1976-85; assoc. Law Office of Dennis W. Jennings, Kansas City, Mo., 1990-92; ptnr. Budesheim, Schlegel & Fershee and predecessor, Kansas City, Mo., 1993-95; of counsel Boyd & Kenter, P.C., Kansas City, Mo., 1995—. Judge moot ct. competition U. Mo.-Kansas City Sch. Law, 1990. Active Country Club United Meth. Ch., Kansas City, Mo., 1976—; rep. Cuban detainees Project Due Process, Leavenworth, Kans., 1988. Fulbright Found. fellow, 1969-70. Mem. Assn. Women Lawyers (treas. 1993-95), Kansas City Metro. Bar Assn., Mo. Assn. Trial Attys., Nat. Orgn. Social Security Claimants Reps. Democrat. Avocations: choral singing, piano, reading, theater, symphony. Home: 5724 McGee St Kansas City MO 64113-2130 Office: 1150 Grand Blvd Ste 700 Kansas City MO 64106-2309

FERSHTMAN, JULIE ILENE, lawyer; b. Detroit, Apr. 3, 1961; d. Sidney and Judith Joyce (Stoll) F.; m. Robert S. Bick, Mar. 4, 1990. Student, Mich. State U., 1979-81, James Madison Coll., 1979-81; BA in Philosophy and Polit. Sci., Emory U., 1983, JD, 1986. Bar: Mich. 1986, U.S. Dist. Ct. (ea. dist.) Mich. 1986, U.S. Ct. Appeals (6th cir.) 1987, U.S. Dist. Ct. (we. dist.) Mich. 1993. Assoc. Miller, Canfield, Paddock and Stone, Detroit, 1986-89; assoc. Miro, Miro & Weiner P.C., Bloomfield Hills, Mich., 1989-92; pvt. practice, Bingham Farms, Mich., 1992—; of counsel Zausmer, Kaufman August & Caldwell, P.C., Farmington Hills, Mich., 2002—. Adj. prof. Schoolcraft Coll., Livonia, Mich., 1994—; lectr. in field. Author: Equine Law & Horse Sense, 1996, More Equine Law and Horse Sense, 2000; contbr. article to Barrister Mag. Bd. dirs. Franklin Cmty. Assn., 1989-92, sec., 1991-92; mem. Franklin Planning Commn., 1993-94. Recipient Nat. Ptnr. in Safety award Assn. for Horsemanship Safety and Edn., 1997, Outstanding Achievement award Am. Riding Instrs. Assn., 1998, Catalyst award, 2002; named one of Crain's Detroit Bus. "40 Bus. Leaders Under 40", 1996. Mem. ABA (planning bd. litigation sect. young lawyers divsn., honoree Barrister mag., 1995, FBA (courthouse tours com. Detroit chpt., featured in Barrister mag. in 21 Young Lawyers Leading US and the 21st Century 1995), State Bar Mich. (exec. coun. young lawyers sect. 1989-96, chmn. 1995-96, bd. commrs. 1994-96, 1999-2002, grievance com. 1997-99, structure and governance com. 1997-98, strategic planning action group 2001, rep. assn. 1997—, chmn. rep. assembly 2001-2002), Oakland County Bar Assn. (profl. com. 1995—, chmn. 1998-99 Inns of Ct. com. 1995—, chair 1998-99, bd. dirs. 2001—, Professionalism award 2000), Markel Equestrian Safety Bd., Women Lawyers Assn., Soc. Coll. Journalists, Phi Alpha Delta, Omicron Delta Kappa, Phi Sigma Tau, Pi Sigma Alpha. Avocations: horse showing, writing, music, art. Bus. Office: 31700 Middlebelt Rd Ste 150 Farmington Hills MI 48334 Home: 31700 Briarcliff Franklin MI 48025 E mail: fershtman@aol.com.

FERSKO, RAYMOND STUART, lawyer; b. Newark, Dec. 6, 1947; s. Seymoure Arnold and Hannah Judith (Geffner) F.; children: Stacey Michelle, Madeline Poses. BA, Am. U., 1969; JD, 1972. Bar: N.Y. 1973, U.S. Ct. Appeals (D.C. cir.) 1973, U.S. Dist. Ct. (so., ea. and we. dists.) N.Y. 1975, U.S. Ct. Appeals (2nd cir.) 1975, U.S. Supreme Ct. 1982. Trial atty. CAB, Washington, 1972-75; assoc. Demov Morris Levin & Shein, N.Y.C., 1975-76; assoc. Walsh & Levine, N.Y.C., 1976-80, ptnr., 1980-82; ptnr. Shapiro Shiff Beilly Rosenberg and Fox, N.Y.C., 1982-84, Tanner Propp Fersko & Sterner, N.Y.C., 1984— ; cons. World Aviation Services, Ltd., London, 1982—, Internat. Joint Ventures, Ltd., London, 1983— ; sec. Tradewinds Express Inc., N.Y.C., 1982-86; pres. Cornwell Corp., N.Y.C., 1986-88. Treas., Paine Heights Orgn., New Rochelle, N.Y., 1978—; dir. conservation of chimpanzees com., Sierre Leore, West Africa, 1988, Austria, 1987, U.S., 1989—. Mem. Assn. of Bar of City of N.Y. (mem. com. on state legis. 1976-78), N.Y. County Bar Assn., ABA (mem. anti-trust sect. civil practice and procedure com. 1973—, mem. adminstrv. law sect. aviation com. 1973-77), N.Y. State Bar Assn., Internat. Bar Assn., Argentine U.S. C. of C., Spain U.S. C. of C., Phi Alpha Delta. Jewish. Club: Harmonie (N.Y.C.). Office: Tanner Propp Fersko & Sterner 99 Park Ave Ste 25th New York NY 10016

FERSTENFELD, JULIAN ERWIN, internist, educator; b. Des Moines, Sept. 5, 1941; m. Sharon Rukas, Mar. 8, 1975; children: Megan Ann, Adam Justin. B.A., U. Iowa, 1963, M.D., 1966. Intern Milwaukee County Gen. Hosp., Milw., 1966-67, resident in internal medicine, 1969-71, fellow in infectious diseases, 1972-73; instr. internal medicine Med. Coll. Wis., Milw., 1974-75, asst. prof. medicine, 1975-78, asst. clin. prof. medicine and family practice, 1978-83, assoc. clin. prof. family practice and medicine, 1983—, internal medicine dir. Waukesha family practice residency, 1978— ; practice medicine specializing in infectious diseases, Milw., 1974— ; mem. staff Waukesha Meml. Hosp. (Wis.), West Allis Meml. Hosp. (Wis.), Elmbrook Meml. Hosp., Brookfield, Wis., Froedtert Meml. Hosp., Milw. Served as capt. M.C., U.S. Army, 1967-69; Korea. Fellow ACP; mem. Wis. Thoracic Soc., Am. Fedn. Clin. Research, Phi Beta Kappa. Contbr. articles, abstracts to profl. jours.

FERTEL, RUTH U. restaurant owner; b. 1927; Pres. Ruth's Chris Steak House, New Orleans, 1965-97, chmn., founder, 1997—. Office: 711 N Broad St New Orleans LA 70119-4206

FERTIG, HOWARD, publisher, editor; b. N.Y.C. s. Benjamin and Rose (Mallman) F.; m. Ellen C. Bandler (div. 1993); children: Paul, Daniel. BA, NYU. Asst. editor Commentary mag., N.Y.C., 1960; editor Alfred A. Knopf, Inc., N.Y.C., 1961-62; chief editor Univ. Library Paperbacks, Grosset & Dunlap, Inc., N.Y.C., 1962-65; pres., editor-in-chief Howard Fertig, Inc., N.Y.C., 1966—. Mem. MLA, P.E.N., Am. Hist. Assn., Friends of Columbia Library. Home: 49 E 10th St New York NY 10003-6153 Office: Howard Fertig Inc 80 E 11th St New York NY 10003-6000

FERTIG-DYKES, SUSAN BEATRICE, communications executive, human resources professional, community and civil society facilitator; b. Panay, The Philippines, Jan. 9, 1944; d. Claude Edward and B. Laverne (Shockley) Fertig; m. George Middleton Dykes III, Sept. 18, 1965; children: George M. Dykes IV, Dirk Fertig Dykson. BA in Comm., U. Mo., 1982. Cert. trainer in Technologies of Participation. Freelance writer, dir. producer, Kansas City, Mo., 1981-83; dir. pub. svc. Sta. KSHB-TV, Kansas City, Mo., 1982-83; dir. broadcast svc. VA, Washington, 1983-86; pres., CEO Victoria Prodns., Ltd., Alexandria, Va., 1986-89; dir. media info. Bicentennial Presdl. Inaugural com., Washington, 1988-89; resume review Office Presdl. Personnel The White House, Washington, 1989; dir. policy, spl. projects Office Human Resources & Adminstrn. Dept. Vets. Affairs, Washington, 1989; dir. pub., visual comm. USDA, Washington, 1989-93; pres., CEO Fertig Comms., Alexandria, Zagreb, Croatia, 1993-96; CEO, bd. dirs. Fertig & Assocs. Internat., Zagreb, Croatia, 1993-96; dir. Inst. Cultural Affairs, Zagreb, Croatia, 1993-96, Inst. Cultural Affairs: Bosnia & Herzegovina, Sarajevo, 1996-97; internat. bd. dirs. ICA Internat., Brussels, 1994-98; mgr., pub. rels., human resource devel., civil soc. initiatives World Vision Internat., Bosnia and Herzegovina, 1997-99, internat. recruiter Washington, 1999—2002; sr. Balkans desk officer for Bosnia and Herzegovina US AID, Washington, 2002—. Chmn. Philippine Festival Commn., Washington, 1992; 1st v.p. Nat. Assn. Govt. Communicators, 1994, pres.-elect, 1995; pres.-elect, chmn. Internat. Gold Screen Film/Video Competition, 1994; talent, script cons., writer/prodr. Hrvatska Radio-Televizija, 1994-96; script cons. Jadran Film, Zagreb, 1994-96; dep. head ICA observer delegation to UN Internat. Conf. on Women, Beijing, 1995; participant numerous confs.; presenter in field. Ofcl. U.S. observer XVI Internat. Film Competition, Berlin, 1990; judge XVII Internat. Film Competition, Berlin, 1992, Internat. Contest Agrarian Cinema & Video, Zaragosa, 1992; judge Golden Eagle awards Coun. Internat. Non-Theatrical Events (CINE), 1992—, adv. coun., 1993—; judge Festival Internat. du Court Metrages de Mons, Belgium, 1994; precinct chmn., poll worker George W. Bush Campaigns in Va. Primaries, 1999-2001; vol. Bush/Cheney Transition & Virginia Victory, 2000. Active Christ Ch., Alexandria, Va., 1983—; chmn. coord. George Bush for Pres., Alexandria, 1987-88; surrogate speaker women's groups Bush/Quayle and Victory 88, Washington; campaign tours N.H. primaries, 1988; mem. Pres.'s Club Rep. Nat. Com., Washington, 1984; bd. dirs. Found. for Aid to the Philippines, 1991-92; precinct chair George W. Bush for Pres., Alexandria, 2000; del. 8th dist. and state Rep. Convs., 2000. Mem. NATAS (D.C. chpt.), Assn. Philippine Am. Women (life, pres. 1991-93), Women in Film & Video, Alexandria Rep. City Com., Coun. Filipino-Am. Reps., Rep. Nat. Com. (life). Episcopalian. Fax: 202-547-0973; 703-751-7626.

FERTIS, DEMETER GEORGE, civil engineering educator; b. Athens, Greece, July 25, 1926; s. George P. and Athanasia (Papazacharia) F.; m. Vaslike J.Beltsos, July 26, 1953; children: Athanasia, Evaggelia; m. Anna Kapetanaki, Apr. 9, 1993. BS, Mich. State U., 1952, MS, 1955, DEng, 1964; diploma in engineering, Nat. Tech. U., Athens, 1962. Planner-in-charge Ohio, Army C.E., Greece, 1948-50; research engr. Mich. Hwy. Dept., Lansing, 1952-57; asst. prof. mechanics dept. Wayne State U., Detroit, 1957-63; vis. prof. Nat. Tech. U., 1963-64; asso. prof. U. Iowa, 1964-66; prof. civil engring. U. Akron, Ohio, 1966—. Cons. in field. Author: Transverse Vibration Theory, 1961, Deflection and Vibration of Engineering Structures, 1964, Notes on Structural Dynamics, 1966, Dynamics of Structural Systems, Vol. 1, 1971, Vol. 2, 1972, Dynamics and Vibration of Structures, 1973, Nonlinear Mechanics, 1993, Advanced Engineering Mechanics, 1994, Mechanical and Structural Vibrations, 1995, Advanced Mechanics of Structures, 1996, Infrastructure Systems, 1997, Historical Evolutions of Infrastructure, 1998, Nonlinear Mechanics, 2nd edit., 1999; contbr. articles to profl. publs. Mem. ASCE, Am. Soc. Engring. Edn., Ohio Planners-in-Charge, Am. Concrete Inst., Indsl. Math. Soc., N.Y. Acad. Scis., Contemporary Authors. Greek Orthodox. Office: U Akron Dept Civil Engring Akron OH 44325-3905

FERVENZA, FERNANDO C. nephrologist, educator; b. Livramento, R.S., Brazil, Nov. 21, 1958; s. Fernando E. and Lorena C. Fervenza; m. Ivete Martinez. MD, PUCRS, 1982; PhD, Oxford U., 1991. Diplomate Am. Bd. Internal Medicine and Nephrology. Sr. house officer, registrar Renal Unit Oxford U., England, 1986—91; asst. prof. Medicine PUCRS, Porto Alegre, Brazil, 1991—93; fellow Nephrology divsn. Stanford U., Calif., 1993—97; resident Internal Medicine Mayo Clinic, Rochester, Minn., 1997—99; asst. prof. Mayo Med. Sch., Rochester, 1999—. Cons. Nephrology Mayo Clinic, Rochester, 1999—. Office: Mayo Clinic 200 First St SW Rochester MN 55905*

FERZLI, GEORGE SALEM, surgeon; b. Lebanon, Jan. 10, 1955; came to U.S., 1979; s. Salem and Milia Ferzli; m. Berthe Ferzli, Aug. 25, 1983; children: Georgina, Christina, George Jr., Christopher. MD, St. Joseph U., Beirut, 1979. Lic. physician, France, N.J., N.Y.; diplomate Am. Bd. Gen. Surgery, Am. Bd. Surg. Critical Care. Resident gen. surgery S.I. (N.Y.) U. Hosp., 1979-84, dir. surg. ICU, assoc. dir. surgery, 1984—, dir. laparoendoscopic surgery, 1991—; prof. surgery SUNY Health Sci. Ctr., Bklyn., 1999—. Vis. and oper. surgeon NYU, Cornell U., Columbia Presbyn. Hosp., Beth Israel Hosp., Maimonides Med. Ctr., Montefiore Hosp., L.I. Coll. Hosp., St. Mary's Hosp., Valley Hosp., St. Peter's Hosp., U. Medicine and Dentistry N.J. Children's Hosp., Newark, Overlook Hosp., L.I. Coll. Hosp., China, South Africa, France, Russia, Bahrain, Kuwait, Kazakhstan, Greece, Egypt, Lebanon, Uzbekistan Portugal, Belgium, Can., Japan, Singapore, Italy, Dominican Republic; vis. prof. Spain, Portugal, Norway, Singapore, Italy, Belgium, Turkey, Japan, France, Can. Reviewer Jour. ACS, Surg. Endoscopy, Am. Jour. Surgery, Archives of Surgery, Jour. Laparoendoscopic Surgery, contbr. over 100 articles to profl. jours., chpts. to books; patentee in field. Fellow ACS, Am. Coll. Gastroenterologists; mem. Soc. for Surgery Alimentary Tract, Am. Soc. Bariatric Surgery, N.Y. Surg. Soc., Soc. Internat. de Chirurgie, Soc. Am. Gastrointestinal Endoscopic Surgeons, Assn. Francaise de Chirurgie, Soc. Critical Care Medicine, Am. Soc. Parenteral and Enteral Nutrition, Richmond County Med. Soc., Med. Soc. State N.Y., European Assn. Endoscopic Surgery, Internat. Fedn. Surg. Colls. Office: 65 Cromwell Ave Staten Island NY 10304-3933 Fax: 718-667-6280. E-mail: info@drferzli.com.

FESHBACH, MURRAY, demographer, educator; b. N.Y.C., Aug. 8, 1929; s. Benjamin and Lilly (Harfenist) F.; m. Muriel Joan Schreiner, Dec. 30, 1956; children: Michael Lee, David Steven. AB in History, Syracuse U., 1950; MA in History, Columbia U., 1951; PhD in Econs., Am.U., 1974. Rsch. asst. Nat. Bur. Econ. Rsch., N.Y.C., 1955-56; economist U.S. Bur. Census, Washington, 1957-67; chief USSR population, employment, rsch. and devel. br., 1967-81; sr. rsch. scholar Georgetown U., Washington, 1981-84, rsch. prof. demography, 1984-2000; sr. scholar Woodrow Wilson Internat. Ctr. for Scholar, Smithsonian Instn., Washington, 2000—. Rsch. emeritus prof., 2000—; bd. dirs. Internat. Rsch. and Exch. Bd., program com., 1975-94; cons. Rand Corp., Santa Monica, Calif., 1981-90, U.S. Dept. Def., 1981-90, U.S. Dept. State, 1982-83, NSF, 1987, World Bank, 1992-93, Health Found. of Russia, 1992, Russian Winter Campaign, 1992; sr. advisor CH2M Hill on Environ. Policy and Tech. in Russia; vis. prof. Columbia U., N.Y.C., 1983-84; Sovietologist-in-residence Office of Sce. Gen., NATO, Brussels, 1986-87; internat. adv. bd. Fernand Braudel Inst. World Econs., Sao Paulo, Brazil; disting. vis. lectr. U.S. Dept. State. Author: Ecological Disaster: Cleaning Up the Hidden Legacy of the Soviet Regime, 1995, Russian Population Meltdown, 2001; (with Alfred Friendly Jr.) Ecocide in the USSR: Health and Nature Under Siege, 1992; editor-in-chief Environmental and Health Atlas of Russia, 1995; editor National Security Issues in the USSR, workship held at NATO, Nov. 6-7, 1986, Brussels, Dordrecht, Nijhoff, 1987; contbr. articles to profl. jours. Mem. Coun. on Fgn. Rels. Served to sgt. U.S. Army, 1951-55. Recipient Silver medal Dept. Commerce, Washington, 1979; Woodrow Wilson Internat. Ctr. for Scholars fellow Smithsonian Instn., 1979. Mem. Assn. Comparative Econ. Studies (pres. 1985), Am. Assn. for Advancement of Slavic Studies (pres. Washington chpt. 1974-78, bd. dirs. 1979-82, v.p. 1984-85, nat. pres. 1985-86), Internat. Union for Sci. Study of Population, Internat. Instn. Strategic Studies, Ctr. for Strategic and Internat. Studies (adv. coun.), Cosmos Club. Democrat. Jewish. Home: 11403 Fairoak Dr Silver Spring MD 20902-3136 Office: Woodrow Wilson Internat Ctr for Scholar Smithsonian Instn 1300 Pennsylvania Ave NW Washington DC 20004-3027

FESHBACH, ORIOLE FARB, artist; b. N.Y.C., Oct. 28, 1931; d. Louis L. and Nettie S. (Silverstein) Horch; m. Peter Farb, Feb. 27, 1953 (dec. Apr. 1980); childen: M. Daniel, Thomas F.; m. Sidney Feshbach, Sept. 20, 1981. BA in Painting and Art History, Sarah Lawrence Coll., 1953; MFA in Painting, U. Mass., 1976. Asst. dir. Master Inst. United Arts, Inc., Riverside Mus., N.Y.C., 1953-63, dir., 1963-70. Lectr. U. Mass., Amherst, 1975-81, 2001; vis. prof. fine arts Amherst Coll., 1977-78. Author: Illumninations, 1991; co-author: Parallels: Artists/Poets, 1993; art, photography editor The Mass. Rev., 1975—; one-woman shows include Ctr. Gallery, Bucknell U., Lewisburg, Pa., 1978, Mead Art Mus., Amherst Coll., 1979, Westfield (Mass.) State Coll., 1979, Albright Coll., Reading, Pa., 1979, Greenfield (Mass.) C.C., 1981, Mary Ryan Gallery, N.Y.C., 1984, Wood-Ridge (N.J.) Meml. Libr., 1987, Jersey City State Coll., 1988, Womens Artists Series, Douglass Coll., Rutgers U., New Brunswick, N.J., 1988, Trenton (N.J.) State Mus., 1992, Wesleyan U., Middletown, Conn., 1992, William Carlos Williams Ctr. for the Arts, Rutherford, N.J., 1993, U. Mass. Med. Ctr. Gallery, Worcester, 1994, R. Michelson Galleries, Amherst, Mass., 1998, Springfield (Mass.) Sci. Mus., 2000-01, Hampden Gallery, U. Mass., Amherst, 2002; represented in permanent collections Mus. Modern Art, N.Y.C., Hartford (Conn.) Atheneum, Zimmerli Art Mus., New Brunswick, Newark Mus., Mus. Fine Arts, Boston, Smith Coll. Mus. Art, Northampton, Mass., New Britain (Conn.) Mus. Am. Art, Rose Art Mus., Waltham, Mass., Lehigh U., Bethlehem, Pa., Harry Ranson Rsch. Ctr., U. Tex., Austin, Worcester (Mass.) Art Mus. Fellow N.J. State Coun. of the Arts, 1983, 86. Democrat. Jewish. Home: 39 Pokeberry Rdg Amherst MA 01002-1514

FESKOE, GAFFNEY JON, management consultant; b. N.Y.C., Feb. 21, 1949; s. George Jon and Mary Margaret (Gaffney) F.; children: Gregory, Alexandra, Julia, Elizabeth. BS, Boston Coll., 1971; MBA, Fordham U., 1976. With Mfrs. Hanover Trust, N.Y.C., 1971-75; asst. treas. European-Am. Bank, N.Y.C., 1975-77; asst. v.p. Citibank, N.A., N.Y.C., 1977-80; asst treas. U.S. Filter Corp., N.Y.C., 1980-82; v.p. Bank of N.Y., N.Y.C., 1982-84; cons. Arthur D. Little, Inc., N.Y.C., 1986-88; exec. v.p. Madison One Group, N.Y.C., 1988-93; mng. ptnr. Horton Group Internat., N.Y.C., 1994-95; pres. Halifax Assocs., LLC; ptnr. Handy Assocs. Corp., N.Y.C. Advisor Halifax Ship Yard, 1997-99. Trustee Yale Libr. Assocs., 1983—; mem. Darien (Conn.) Cable TV and Comm. Commn., 1985-87; mem. steering com. Friends of Yale Ctr. for Brit. Art, 1989-95; mem. London Libr. Mem. Bibliog. Soc. (London), Bibliog. Soc. Am., Boston Athenaeum (propr.), Can. Soc. N.Y., Club of Odd Vols. (Boston). Roman Catholic. Office: 420 Lexington Ave New York NY 10168-0002 E-mail: gfeskoe@handypartners.com.

FESQ, JACQUELINE, education educator; b. Camden, N.J., Mar. 11, 1952; d. Natalie Fesq; m. Bruce Haislip, Dec. 27, 1975; children: Alison Haislip, Greg Haislip. EdD, Rutgers U., New Brunswick, NJ, 1995. Cert. tchr. cert. math. NJ, 1974. Tchr. of math. North Plainfield H.S., North Plainfield, NJ, 1974—80; instr. of math. Rutgers U., New Brunswick, NJ, 1981—85; prof. of math. Raritan Valley C.C., Somervilles, NJ, 1986—. Reader of ap calculus exams Ednl. Testing Svc., Princeton, NJ, 1996—. Mem.: Nat. Coun. of Tchr. of Math. Office: Raritan Valley Cmty Coll PO Box 3300 Somerville NJ 08876 Personal E-mail: jfesq@raritanval.edu. E-mail: jfesq@raritanval.edu.

FESSEL, WALFORD JEFFREY, rheumatologist; b. London, June 20, 1932; came to U.S., 1957; s. Jack Isaac and Alma (Yarmolinski) F.; m. Nicole J. Noble, Sept. 11, 1957; 1 child, Jason N. MB, BS, U. London, 1955. Diplomate Am. Bd. Internal Medicine. Intern U. Coll. Hosp., London, 1955; resident Can. Red Cross Hosp., Taplow, England, 1956, U. Calif., San Francisco, 1963, 64; rheumatologist Kaiser-Permanente, San Francisco, 1965—, chief of medicine, 1979-89, dir. internal medicine residency tng. program, 1979-89, dir. HIV rsch. unit, 1989—; clin. prof. medicine U. Calif., San Francisco, 1983-97, mem. clin. faculty promotion com., 1986—, emeritus clin. prof. medicine, 1997—. Chmn. regional chiefs of medicine No. Calif. Permanente Med. Group, 1980-89. Contbr. articles to profl. jours. Fellow ACP, Royal Coll. Physicians, Am. Coll. Rheumatology (founder). Jewish. Avocations: gardening, art, music, travel, languages. Office: Kaiser Permanente 2200 Ofarrell St San Francisco CA 94115-3394

FESSLER, RAYMOND R. metallurgical engineering consultant; b. St. Nazianz, Wis., May 6, 1939; BS, Carnegie Inst. Tech., 1961; PhD in Metallurgy, MIT, 1965. Staff mem. Battelle Columbus Divsn., 1965-68, assoc. mgr. ferrous metallurgy sect., 1968-77, mgr. phys. metallurgy sect., 1977-82, assoc. dir. programs corp. tech. devel., 1982-83, mgr. transp. and structure dept., 1983-85, mgr. advanced materials dept., 1985-86; dir. basic indsl. rsch. lab. Northwestern U., Evanston, Ill., 1987-96; prin. cons. BIZTEK Cons., Inc., Evanston, Ill., 1997—. Fellow Am. Soc. Metals Internat. Achievements include research in physical metallurgy of steels, high temperature alloys and nonferrous metals; fracture toughness; metal physics; optical and electron metallography; advanced ceramics; process and physical metallurgy; polymers; corrosion; electrochemistry; mechanics. Address: 820 Roslyn Ter Evanston IL 60201-1724

FESTA, ROGER REGINALD, chemist, educator; b. Norwalk, Conn., Sept. 6, 1950; s. Reginald and Rosemary (Chappa) F. BA in Biology and Chemistry magna cum laude, St. Michael's Coll., 1972; MA in Agr., U. Vt., 1979; cert. in Adminstrn., Fairfield U., 1981; PhD in Edn., U. Conn., 1982. Tchr. Cen. Cath. High Sch., Norwalk, 1975-79, Brien McMahon High Sch., Norwalk, 1979-82; asst. prof. chemistry Truman State U. (formerly N.E. Mo. State U.), Kirksville, 1983-89, dir. Chem. Comm. Devel. Ctr., 1983-90, assoc. prof., 1989-97, prof., 1997—, coach men's volleyball, 1991-2000, dean frats., 1991-92. Adj. prof. U. Conn., 1983. Author: National Curriculum Development Programming for Teachers of High School Chemistry, 1981, Fairfield County High School Chemistry Curriculum Handbook, 1982. Sec. Diocese Bridgeport (Conn.) Edn. Assn., 1978-79, sci. cons. schs. office, 1979, exec. adminstr., 1979; bd. dirs. Norwalk Community Services Agy., 1980-81. Named one of Ten Outstanding Young Men of Mo., Mo. Jaycees, 1986. Fellow Am. Inst. Chemists (pub. edn. com. 1980-83, edn. editor The Chemist Jour. 1981-95, mem. editl. bd. The Chemist 1986-91, bd. dirs. 1982-99, chmn. nat. meetings com. 1982-91, 94-95, history com. 1982-99, archivist 1983-2002, sec. 1991-93, pres.-elect 1994-95, pres. 1996-97); mem. Am. Chem. Soc. (founding editor The Fairfield Chemist 1978-79, assoc. editor Jour. Chem. Edn. 1980-89, vice chmn. edn. com. Western Conn. sect. 1979-81, chmn. elect Mark Twain sect. 1985, chmn. 1986, exec. bd. 1984-95, program chair 1984-95), St. Louis Inst. Chemists (founder 1984, pres. 1985-87, sec.-treas. 1987—), Acad. Sci. St. Louis, Assn. Frat. Advisors, Coll.

Frat. Editors' Assn., Kirksville Jaycees (bd. dirs. 1983-86, sec. 1984-85, chair ret. sr. vols. com. 1985-87), Order of Omega, Delta Epsilon Sigma, Alpha Chi Sigma (assoc. editor The Hexagon 1984-99), Sigma Phi Epsilon (bd. govs. 1994—, advisor Truman State U. chpt. 1991—). Democrat. Roman Catholic. Home: 114 E Mcpherson St Kirksville MO 63501-3570 Office: Truman State U 100 E Normal Ave MG 202 Kirksville MO 63501-4200

FESTINGER, RICHARD, music educator, composer; b. Newton, Mass., Mar. 1, 1948; s. Leon and Mary (Ballou) F.; m. Karen Cummings Rosenak; stepchildren: Jacob Rosenak, Max Rosenak. Student, Stanford U., 1965-68; student jazz arrangement and composition, Berklee Coll. Music, 1970-72; BM magna cum laude, San Francisco State U., 1976; MA in Music, U. Calif., Berkeley, 1978, PhD in Music, 1983; postgrad., Calif. State U., Hayward, 1984-85; postgrad. studies in Computer Engring., Calif. State U., San Jose, 1985; postgrad. studies in Computer Sci., Stanford U., 1985-86, 91. Lectr. music theory U. Calif., Berkeley, 1982-83, Davis, 1989-90; assoc. prof. music San Francisco State U., 1990—, dir. theory and composition, dir. Electronic Music Studio, 1992—. Asst. conductor U. Calif. Symphony Orch., 1980-82; vis. asst. prof. music Dartmouth Coll., 1984; rsch. affiliate Ctr. for Computer Rsch. Music and Acoustics, Stanford U., vis. scholar, 1996, 97; pres. bd. dirs., artistic dir. music ensemble EARPLAY, San Francisco, 1987-91, 94; resident Edward Macdowell Colony, 1983, 85; music panelist New England Found. for Arts, 1983, dir., Composition program, Summer Arts Festival, Calif. State U., 1996, 97. Published music includes Triptych for solo flute, 1979, Impromptu for clarinet and piano, 1985, Septet for flute, clarinet, violin, viola, violoncello, percussion and piano, 1987, Variations for Piano, 1988, Two Little Piano Pieces, 1992, A Serenade for Six for flute, clarinet/bass, clarinet, violin, violoncello, percussion and piano, 1993, Twinning for violin and piano, 1994, String Quartet for two violins, viola and violoncello, 1994, Violuminescence for violin solo and chamber orchestra, 1995, Windsongs for flute, oboe, clarinet, horn and bassoon, 1996, Trionometry for flute, clarinet/bass clarinet and piano, 1996, Tapestries for violin, violoncello and piano, 1997, After Blue for flute/piccolo, clarinet/bass clarinet, violin, violoncello, percussion and piano, 1998; recordings and include Triptych for unaccompanied flute, Live at Pangaea Improvisations, vols. I and II, 1996, Richard Festinger Chamber Music, Septet, 1996, A Serenade for Six, 1998; commissions include Alter Ego Ensemble, Rome, Italy, 1999-2000, San Francisco Contemporary Music Players, Barlow Found., 2000-01, N.Y. New Music Ensemble, 1999-2000, Cygnus Ensemble, 2000-01, others. Recipient George Ladd Grand Prix de Paris, 1978, Nicolo di Lorenzo prize in music composition, 1981, Roslyn Schneider Eisner award, 1982, Prometheus Orch. Composition Competition award for piano concerto, 1982, Walter Hinrichsen award Am. Acad. Arts and Letters, 1993; Composition Assistance grantee Am. Music Ctr., 1982, Regents fellow U. Calif., 1976; Meet the Composer grantee, 1984, 91, Rsch. and Profl. Devel. grantee San Francisco State U., 1991, 93-94, Alfred Hertz Meml. fellow, 1977, Edward MacDowell Colony Norlin/MacDowell fellow, 1982, Wellesley Composers Conf. fellow, 1993, June in Buffalo Conf. fellow, 1994; Jerome Found. commn., 1990, San Francisco Contemporary Music Players commn., 1992, N.Y. New Music Ensemble commn., 1993, Alexander String Quartet commn., 1994, Fromm Found. commn., 1995, City Winds commn., 1996, Laurel Trio commn., 1997, Koussevitzky Music Found. commn., 1997, Left Coast Ensemble commn., 1998, Calif. Assn. Profl. Music Tchrs. commn., U. Calif. Davis commn. Office: San Francisco State U 1600 Holloway Ave San Francisco CA 94132-1722 Fax: 415-338-3294. E-mail: raf@sfsu.edu.

FETCHERO, JOHN ANTHONY, JR., otorhinolaryngologist; b. Jeannette, Pa., June 4, 1951; s. John Anthony Sr. and Cleda (Byerly) F.; m. Wynona Ann Kestler, Feb. 26, 1982; children: John Anthony III, Christopher Jason, Dominic Vincent, Victor Thomas. BS in Biology, St. Vincent Coll., 1973; DO, Coll. Osteo. Medicine, Des Moines, 1976. Intern Des Moines Gen. Hosp., 1976-77; Flight surgeon Naval Aero. Med. Inst., Pensacola, Fla., 1977-78; resident Nat. Naval Med. Ctr., Bethesda, Md., 1980-84; otorhinolaryngologist, oro-facial plastic surgeon Am. Co. Osteo. Opthalmology and Otorhinolaryngology, 1987; otolaryngologist Am. Coll. Otolaryngology, 1988; pvt. practice, Orange Park, Fla., 1988—. Capt. USNR, 1973—2001, ret. Med. Sch. scholar USN, 1973-76. Mem. Fla. Osteo. Assn., Osteo. Acad. Otorhinolaryngology, Am. Acad. Otolaryngology, Am. Osteo. Assn., Fla. Med. Assn., Clay County Med. Soc. Republican. Roman Catholic. Avocations: running, photography, boating, bowling. Home: 2862 Country Club Blvd Orange Park FL 32073-5728

FETHERSTON, BRIAN LLOYD, artist, painter, sculptor; b. Milw., Jan. 26, 1955; s. William Charles and Marynell (Lloyd) F.; 1 child, Sean Levis; m. Marianne Desmeules, Oct. 19, 1981. Student, Ont. Coll. Art, Toronto, 1980—82. Artist Fetherston & Fetherston, 1990—. Exhbns. include Galerie Cluny Geneva, 1986, 87, 89, Circulo Bellas Artes, Salon de Otono Palma de Mallorca, Spain, 1987, Galerie Bearn Palma de Mallorca, 1988, Galerie Jaime III Palma de Mallorca, 1988, Dresdner Bank Geneva, 1990, Les Amis de L'Atelier, Geneva, 1990, Galerie Ramko Istanbul, Turkey, 1990, Forum Des Grotte Geneva, 1991, Galerie Du Vieux Chene, Chene-Bourg, Switzerland, 1991, Finans Bank SA, Geneva, 1991, UN Exhbn., Geneva, 1995, Gallery Montserrat, N.Y.C., 1996, Mus. Internat. Art, Carnac, France, 1996, UN Exhbn., Geneva, 1996, Biennale Du Japon, Grnad Prix De Sapporo, 1997, Societe Generale Bank Trust, Zurich, 1997, Gallery Ballard-Fetherston, Seattle, 1998, Art Expo, N.Y.C., 1999, Barcelona Art Fair, 1999, DTW Gallery, Geneva, 2000.

FETHERSTON, MARIANNE RENEE, artist, painter; b. Alexandria, Egypt, Aug. 14, 1959; parents Swiss citizens; d. Jean-Jacques Alois and Eva Desmeules; m. Brian Lloyd Fetherston, Oct. 19, 1981; 1 step-child, Sean Lewis Fetherston. Student, Ont. Coll. of Art, Toronto, 1981—82. Artist Fetherston & Fetherston, 1990—. One-woman shows include Galerie Cluny, Geneva, 1986, Gallery Montserrat, N.Y., 1996, Six Tech S.A., Geneva, 1997, Ballard-Fetherston Gallery, Seattle, 1998, Designer Workteam Gallery, Geneva, 2000; exhibited in group shows at Circulo de Bellas Artes, Palma de Mallorca, Spain, 1987, Peintures d'Europe, Lille, France, 1987, Galerie Art & Vie, Paris, 1987 (Grand prize), Galeria Bearn, Palma de Mallorca, 1988, Finansbank S.A., Geneva, 1991, UN, Geneva, 1995, 96, Mus. Internat. Art, Carnac, France, 1996, Red Cross, Geneva, 1996, Biennial of Japan (Grand Prize of Sapporo (Japan), 1997, Société Generale and Trust Zurich, 1997, ART Expo, N.Y., 1999, Barcelona Art Fair, 1999. Studio: 8 Rue de Fribourg 1201 Geneva Switzerland

FETKOVICH, JOHN G. physics educator; b. Aliquippa, Pa., June 9, 1931; s. Michael and Anna (Klacik) F.; m. Anna Marie Argenziana, Dec. 13, 1958; children: Anne Marie, John G. BS, Carnegie Mellon U., 1953, MS, 1955, PhD, 1959. From postdoctoral rschr. to prof. physics Carnegie Mellon U., Pitts., 1959-2000, prof. emeritus. Vis. scientist Argonne (Ill.) Nat. Lab., 1970-71, Rutherford High Energy Lab., England, 1971-72; spl. asst. to pres. acad. affairs Carnegie Mellon U., 1990-98, assoc. head physics dept., 1990-95. Lt. Signal Corps U.S. Army, 1953—61. Fellow Am. Phys. Soc.; mem. AAAS, Penn Arts Assn., Pitts. Soc. Artists, Pitts. Ctr. Arts, Sigma Xi, Phi Kappa Phi. Avocations: furniture design and construction, art. Home: 113 Yorkshire Dr Pittsburgh PA 15238-2417 Office: Dept Physics Carnegie Mellon U Pittsburgh PA 15213 E-mail: jf5e@andrew.cmu.edu.

FETLER, ANDREW, author, educator; b. Riga, Latvia, July 24, 1925; came to U.S., 1939, naturalized, 1944; s. Basil Andreyevitch and Barbara (Kovalevski) Fetler-Malof; m. Carol J. McMahon, Aug. 29, 1960; 1 son, Jonathan. Student, U. Chgo., 1946-48; BA, Loyola U., Chgo., 1959; M.F.A., U. Iowa, 1964. Tchr. Master Fine Arts Program in English, U. Mass., Amherst, 1964-89. Author: The Travelers, 1965, To Byzantium, 1976, Norton Anthology of Short Fiction, 5th edit., 1994; contbr. fiction to lit. quars. Served with AUS, 1944-46. Recipient grants for fiction writing Iowa Industries, 1962-63; grantee Mass. Arts and Humanities Found., 1976, Nat. Endowment for Arts, 1976-77, 83-84, Guggenheim Found., 1978-79; recipient O. Henry awards, 1977, 84

FETLER, PAUL, retired composer; b. Phila., Feb. 17, 1920; s. William Basil and Barbara (Kovalevski) Fetler-Malof; m. Ruth Regina Pahl, Aug. 13, 1947; children: Sylvia, Daniel, Beatrix. MusB, Northwestern U., 1943; MusM, Yale U., 1948; PhD, U. Minn., 1956. From instr. to prof. music theory and composition U. Minn., Mpls., 1948—91, ret., 1992. Vis. composer, condr. and lectr. various colls. and univs. Composer: Symphonic Fantasia, 1941, Passacaglia for orch., 1942, Dramatic Overture, 1943, Prelude for orch., 1946, Orchestral Sketch, 1949, A Comedy Overture for Orchestra, 1952, Gothic Variations for Orchestra, 1953, Contrasts for orch., 1958, Sing Unto God for mixed voices, 1958, Nothing but Nature for mixed voices and orchestra, 1961, Soundings for orch., 1962, Jubilate Deo for voices and brass, 1963, Te Deum for mixed voices, 1963, Four Symphonies, 1948-67, Cantus Tristis for orch., 1964, Five Pieces for guitar, 1964; opera Sturge Maclean, 1965, A Contemporary Psalm for chorus, organ and percussion, 1968, Prayer for Peace for mixed voices, 1969, Hosanna for mixed voices, 1970, Cycles for percussion and piano, 1970, The Words From the Cross for mixed voices, 1971, First Violin Concerto, 1971, Four Movements for guitar, 1972, Dialogue for flute and guitar, 1973, Six Pastoral Sketches for guitar, 1974, Lamentations for chorus, narrator, percussion and flute, 1974, Three Venetian Scenes for guitar, 1974, Dream of Shalom for mixed voices, 1975, Songs of the Night for voices, narrator and flute, 1976, Three Poems by Walt Whitman for narrator and orch., 1975, Pastoral Suite for piano trio, 1976, Celebration for orch., 1976, Three Impressions for guitar and orch., 1977, Five Piano Games, 1977, Sing Alleluia, 1978, Song of the Forest Bird for voices and chamber orch., 1978, Six Songs of Autumn for guitar, 1979, Second Violin Concerto, 1980, Missa de Angelis for three choirs, orch., organ and handbells, 1980, Serenade for chamber orch., 1981, Rhapsody for violin and piano, 1982; song cycle The Garden of Love for voice and orch., 1983, Piano Concerto, 1984; Capriccio for chamber orch., 1985; Frolic for Flute, Winds and Strings, 1986, Three Excursions, A Concerto for Percussion, Piano and Orchestra, 1987, String Quartet, 1989, Toccata for Organ, 1990, numerous sacred and secular choral works, 1949-93, Twelve Sacred Hymn Settings, 1993, Divertimento for Flute and Strings, 1994, December Stillness for Flute, Harp and Voices, 1994, Suite for Woodwind Trio, 1995, Up the Dome of Heaven, Three Pieces for Mixed Voices and Flute, 1996; The Raven for basso, clarinet, percussion and string, 1998, Saraband variations for guitar, Folia Lirica,, 1999 . Served with AUS, 1943-45. Recipient Guggenheim awards, 1953, 60, Soc. for Publ. Am. Music award, 1953, Yale U. Alumni Assn. cert. of merit, 1975, NEA award, 1975, 77, 87; Ford Found. grantee, 1958. Mem. ASCAP (ann. award 1962—), Sigma Alpha Iota (nat. arts assoc.) Home: 174 Golden Gate Pt Apt 32 Sarasota FL 34236-6602 Office: U Minn 100 Ferguson Hall Minneapolis MN 55455 E-mail: pf-tonus8@webtv.net. *Ultimately there is no way to explain a new work of art if it does not explain itself.*

FETNER, ROBERT HENRY, radiation biologist; b. Savannah, Ga., Feb. 22, 1922; s. William Westcott and Lucille Fedora (Goodrich) F.; m. Mary Carolyn Guiney, July 8, 1972; 1 dau., Amber. BS, U. Miami, Fla., 1950, MS, 1952; PhD, Emory U., 1955. Mem. faculty Ga. Inst. Tech., Atlanta, 1955—, prof. radiation biology, 1963—; dir. Ga. Inst. Tech. (Sch. Biology), 1964-70. Cons. in field. Contbr. articles in field to profl. jours.; patentee computer digitizer. Served with AUS, 1942-45. Decorated Combat Inf. badge. Mem. Ga. Acad. Sci. (editor bull. 1960-64), Sigma Xi, Phi Kappa Phi. Presbyterian. Address: 2219 Walker Dr Lawrenceville GA 30043-2473 *My most rewarding career experience has been as a participant in the search for knowledge in science.*

FETNER, SUZANNE, small business owner; b. Fowlerville, Mich., May 4, 1929; d. Clayton Charles and Ferne Marie (Abbey) Fenton; m. William Clyde Peters, June 1950 (div. Aug. 1971); children: Randall Ray, Gregory Kim, Melinda Jane Peters Jones, Kelly Sue Peters Raymond; m. Eugene Macelee Fetner, Apr. 10, 1977. BS, Ea. Mich. U., 1967. Cert. early childhood edn., Fla. Tchr. kindergarten Fowlerville (Mich.) Pub. Schs., 1949-50, Horsebrook Sch., Lansing, Mich., 1950-51, Grand Ledge (Mich.) Pub. Schs., 1951-52, Manchester (Mich.) Pub. Schs., 1952-56, Holy Trinity Episcopal Sch., Melbourne, Fla., 1967-72; owner, tchr. Country Adventure, Inc., Melbourne, 1973-77; owner, dir. Woodlake Wonderland, Inc., Palm Bay, Fla., 1978-89, Country Beginnings, Inc., Palm Bay, 1985-93. Mem. Presch. Adminstrv. Cons., Palm Bay, 1985-96; mem. adv. bd. Dist. Interagy. Coun. for Early Childhood Svcs., Brevard County, 1990-96, South Brevard H.S. Child Care, Melbourne, 1980-93. Author: (booklet) Stepping Stones, 1984. Founder, coord. Read to Your Child Week, Melbourne, Palm Bay, 1988-92. Named Unforgettable Lady of 80's Soroptomist Club, Melbourne, 1989. Mem. Nat. Assn. Child Care Profls., Brevard Assn. Children Under Six (pres. 1981-82), Fla. Assn. Children Under Six, So. Assn. Children Under Six. Republican. Methodist. Home and Office: 567 Birch St West Melbourne FL 32904-2541 E-mail: genesue6@juno.com.

FETRIDGE, BONNIE-JEAN CLARK (MRS. WILLIAM HARRISON FETRIDGE), civic volunteer; b. Chgo., Feb. 3, 1915; d. Sheldon and Bonnie (Carrington) Clark; m. William Harrison Fetridge, June 27, 1941; children: Blakely (Mrs. Harvey H. Bundy III), Clark Worthington. Student, Girls Latin Sch., Chgo., The Masters Sch., Dobbs Ferry, N.Y., Finch Coll., N.Y.C. Bd. dirs. region VII com. Girl Scouts U.S.A., 1939-43, nat. program com., 1966-69, nat. adv. bd., 1972-85, internat. commr.'s adv. panel, 1973-76, Nat. Juliette Low Birthplace Com., 1966-69; bd. dirs. Girl Scouts Chgo., 1936-51, 59-69, sec., 1936-38, v.p., 1946-49, 61-65, chmn. Juliette Low world friendship com., 1959-67, 71-72; mem. Friends Our Cabana Com. World Assn. Girl Guides and Girl Scouts, Cuernavaca, Mexico, 1969—, vice chmn., 1982-87; founder, pres. Olave Baden-Powell Soc. of World Assn. Girl Guides and Girl Scouts, London, 1984-93, bd. dirs., 1984—, hon. assoc., 1987; asst. sec. Dartnell Corp, Chgo., 1981-91, sec., 1991-98, bd. dirs. 1989-98; vice chmn. Dartnell Found., 1990-2000, Ravenswood Found., 2001—; bd. dirs. Jr. League of Chgo., 1937-40, Vis. Nurse Assn. Chgo., 1951-58, 61-63, asst. treas., 1962-63; women's bd. dirs. Children's meml. Hosp., 1946-50; v.p. parents coun. Latin Sch. Chgo., 1952-54, bd. dirs. alumni assn., 1964-69; Fidelitas Soc., 1979, 96; mem. women's bd. U.S.O., 1965-75, treas., 1969-71, v.p., 1971-73; mem. women's svc. bd. Chgo. Area coun. Boy Scouts Am., 1964-70, mem. nat. exploring com., 1973-76; staff aide and ARC Motor Corps, World War II. Recipient Citation of Merit Sta. WAIT, Chgo., 1971, Juliette Low World Friendship medal Girl Scouts U.S.A., 1989; 1st recipient Medal of Recognition World Assn.Girl Guides and Girl Scouts, London, 1993; Baden-Powell fellow World Scout Found., Geneva, 1983. Mem. Nat. Soc. Colonial Dames Am. (life, Ill. bd. mgrs. 1962-65, 69-76, 78-82, v.p. 1970-72, corr. sec. 1978-80, 1st v.p. 1980-84, state chmn. geneal. info. svcs. com. 1972-76, corr. sec. 1978-80, hist. activities com. 1979-83, mus. house com. 1980-83, house gov. 1981-82), Chgo. Dobbs Alumnae Assn. (past pres.), Nat. Soc. DAR, Conn. Soc. Genealogists, New Eng. Hist. Geneal. Soc., N.Y. Geneal. and Biog. Soc., Newberry Libr. Assocs., Chgo. Hist. Soc. (life), Casino Club, The Racquet Club Chgo., Onwentsia Club, Union League Club. Republican. Episcopalian. Home: 1100 Pembridge Dr Apt 215 Lake Forest IL 60045

FETRIDGE, CLARK WORTHINGTON, business executive; b. Chgo., Nov. 6, 1946; s. William Harrison and Bonnie-Jean (Clark) F.; m. Jean Hamilton Huebner, Apr. 19, 1980; children: Clark Worthington II, William Hamilton. BA, Lake Forest Coll., 1969; MBA, Boston Coll., 1971. Money market specialist Continental Ill. Nat. Bank, Chgo., 1971-73; with Dartnell Corp., Chgo., 1973-98, sr. v.p., 1977-78, pres., CEO, 1978-98, chmn. bd., CEO, 1995-98; pres. The Ravenswood Corp., Chgo., 1998—2002; mng. ptnr. Michigan Ave. Ventures, Chgo., 2002—. Bd. dirs. Clin. Resources Internat., Inc., M.R. Mead & Co. LLC., Prolam, Inc., United Pet Ltd., Applimaxx, Can., Old People's Home of Chgo. Author: Office Administration Handbook, 1975. Trustee Lake Forest Coll., 1977-85, 91-95, Jacques Holinger Meml. Found., 1983-95; pres. Dartnell Found., 1989—; trustee Latin Sch. Chgo., 1990-94; internat. commr. Boy Scouts Am., 1992-95, mem. nat. exec. bd., 1986-96, mem. internat. com., mem. Chgo. coun.; pres. U.S. Found. Internat. Scouting 1991-95; chmn. 1200 Club Ill., 1975-84; Rep. candidate for Congress, 1972; del. Rep. Nat. Conv., 1976; bd. dirs. Rep. Fund of Ill.; mem. pres.'s coun. Mus. Sci. and Industry, Chgo., 1986-94. Mem. Ill. Mfrs. Assn. (bd. dirs. 1990-96), Latin Sch. Chgo. Alumni Assn., St. Andrews Soc. (bd. dirs. 1994-97, 98—), Nat. Eagle Scout Assn. (chmn. 1985-88), Chgo. Pres. Orgn. (bd. dirs. 1998-2001), Tau Kappa Epsilon. Republican. Episcopalian. Office: Michigan Avenue Ventures 30 N Michigan Ave Ste 1412 Chicago IL 60602-3404 Fax: 312-236-1343.

FETTER, ALEXANDER LEES, theoretical physicist, educator; b. Phila., May 16, 1937; s. Ferdinand and Elizabeth Lean Fields (Head) F.; m. Jean Holmes, Aug. 4, 1962 (div. Dec. 1994); children: Anne Lindsay, Andrew James. AB, Williams Coll., 1958; BA, Balliol Coll., Oxford U., 1960; PhD, Harvard U., 1963. Miller rsch. fellow U. Calif., Berkeley, 1963-65; mem. faculty dept. physics Stanford U., 1965—, prof., 1974—, chmn. dept. physics, 1985-90, assoc. chmn. dept. physics, 1998-99, asso. dean undergrad. studies, 1976-79, assoc. dean humanities and sci., 1990-93, dir. Hansen Exptl. Physics Lab., 1996-97, dir. lab. for adv. materials, 1999—2002; vis. prof. Cambridge U., 1970-71; Nordita vis. prof. Tech. U., Helsinki, Finland, 1976. Author: (with J.D. Walecka) Quantum Theory of Many Particle Systems, 1971, Theoretical Mechanics of Particles and Continua, 1980. Alumni trustee Williams Coll., 1974-79. Rhodes scholar, 1958-60; NSF fellow, 1960-63; Sloan Found. fellow, 1968-72; Recipient W.J. Gores award for excellence in teaching Stanford U., 1974 Fellow Am. Physics Soc. (chmn. div. condensed matter physics 1991), AAAS; mem. Sigma Xi. Home: 904 Mears Ct Palo Alto CA 94305-1029 Office: Stanford U Physics Dept Stanford CA 94305-4045

FETTER, ROBERT BARCLAY, retired administrative sciences educator; b. Berwyn, Ill., May 6, 1924; s. Russell M. and Dorothy (Dupuis) F.; m. Audrey Louise Lillard, Feb. 7, 1951; children: Sarah Anne, Robert Alan, Martha Sue. BS, Va. Poly. Inst., 1947; MBA, Ind. U., 1949, D.BA, 1952; MA (hon.), Yale U., 1963. Instr., asst. prof. Ind. U., 1949-53; asst. prof. Mass. Inst. Tech., 1953-58; asso. prof. Yale U., 1958-63, prof. adminstrv. scis., 1963-86, Harold H. Hines Jr. prof. health care mgmt., 1986-89, chmn. adminstrv. scis., 1969-72; dir. Health Systems Mgmt. Group, Sch. Orgn. and Mgmt., 1976-89, Instn. Social and Policy Studies, 1969-89. Cons. Rand Corp., 1963-71, E.I. duPont de Nemours & Co., Inc., 1960-72, McKinsey & Co., Inc., 1960-89, 3M, 1990-97; cons. editor R.D. Irwin, Inc., Homewood, Ill., 1960-90, WHO, 1972-73; v.p. Puter Assocs., Inc., 1971-77, chmn., 1977-82; v.p., dir. Health Systems Internat. Inc., 1982-90; dir. Dead River Co., 1984-94. Served with USNR, 1944-46. Recipient Baxter Found. prize Assn. Univ. Programs in Health Adminstrn., 1992; Ford Found. fellow, 1964. Fellow Acad. of Mgmt., Decision Scis. Inst.; mem. Ops. Research Soc. Am., Inst. Mgmt. Scis. (Franz Edelman prize 1990). Home: 427 Indies Dr Vero Beach FL 32963-9552 E-mail: BobFet@aol.com.

FETTER, TREVOR, healthcare industry executive; b. San Diego, Jan. 16, 1960; married; 2 children. BS in Econs., Stanford U., 1982; MBA, Harvard U., 1986. With investment banking divsn. Merrill Lynch Capital Mkts.; sr. v.p. MGM/UA Comm. Co., 1988; exec. v.p., CFO Metro-Goldwyn-Mayer, Inc.; exec. v.p. Tenet Healthcare Corp., Santa Barbara, Calif., 1995—96, exec. v.p., CFO, 1996—2000; chmn., CEO Broad Ln., Inc., San Francisco, 2000—02; pres. Tenet Healthcare Corp., Santa Barbara, Calif., 2002—03, pres., acting CEO, 2003, pres., CEO, 2003—. Chmn. bd. Santa Catalina Island Conservancy; trustee Santa Barbara Zool. Garden; bd. dirs. iVillage Corp. Office: Tenet Healthcare Corp 3820 State St Santa Barbara CA 93105*

FETTERLY, LYNN LAWRENCE, real estate broker, developer; b. Ogdensburg, N.Y., Oct. 21, 1947; s. Keith C. and Florence E. Fetterly; m. Melody Bulriss, July 23, 1971; children: Kim Marie, Adam Lynn. AAS, Canton (N.Y.) Coll., 1967; BS, SUNY, Albany, 1969; MA, U. Detroit, 1972; cert. in mgmt., U. So. Calif., L.A., 1984. Auditor Arthur Andersen & Co., Rochester, N.Y., 1969-70; asst. v.p. Security Pacific Nat. Bank, L.A., 1972-75, Security Pacific Corp., L.A., 1976-77, Citibank, N.A., Rochester, 1977-81; v.p. regional mgr. Security Pacific Nat. Bank, N.Y.C., 1981-84; pres., CEO Security Pacific EuroFinance, Inc., London, 1984-88; vice chmn. Security Pacific Fin. Svcs. Sys., Inc., San Diego, 1988-90; pres., COO Security Pacific Fin. Svcs. System, Inc., San Diego, 1991-92; ind. real estate broker/developer, gen. contractor, 1993—. With USAR, 1969-75. Republican. Presbyterian. Avocations: golf, tennis.

FETTERLY, MARY E. counseling administrator; b. Wenatchee, Wash., Aug. 9, 1960; d. Jesus Gonzalez Pliego, Anita Maria Castillo; m. Roger Dale Fetterly, Aug. 14, 1982 (div. Nov. 20, 2000). Grad. H.S., Burien, Wash. Cert. completion fgn. credentials analysis. Internat. admissions evaluator U. Wash. Office Grad. Admissions, Seattle, 1980—91, internat. admissions counseling svcs. coord., 1991—. Recipient Cert. Appreciation to Region 1 Conf., Nat. Assn. for Fgn. Student Affairs, 1997. Mem.: Nat. Assn. for Fgn. Student Affairs (nat. com. on edn. and tng. 2001—), Nat. Assn. Grad. Admissions Profls., Assn. Wash. State Internat. Student Affairs, Seattle Athletic Club. Roman Catholic. Avocations: Karate, travel, collecting thimbles, bicycling, skiing. Office: U Wash Grad Admissions #301 Loew Hall Box 352191 Seattle WA 98195-2191

FETTERMAN, JAMES CHARLES, lawyer; b. Charleston, W.Va., Apr. 13, 1947; s. Kenneth Lee and Sara Jane (Shaffer) F.; children: Janet, Paula, Kenneth, David. BA, Miss. State U., 1969, MA, 1970; JD, U. Miss., Oxford, 1972; MBA, St. Louis U., 1985. Bar: Miss. 1972, Sarasota County, U.S. Dist. Ct. (no. dist.) Miss. 1972, U.S. Ct. Mil. Appeals 1972, U.S. Dist. Ct. (mid. dist.) Fla. 1986, U.S. Tax Ct. 1986, U.S. Ct. Appeals (11th cir.) 1986. Staff atty. First Miss. Corp., Jackson, 1976-77; cert. of need adminstr. Office of Gov. State of Miss., Jackson, 1977-78; adminstrator, prin. investigator Miss. Bd. Nursing, Jackson, 1978-79; asst. prof., head dept. fin. Jackson State U., 1979-82; asst. prof. dept. mgmt sci. St. Louis U., Mo., 1982-86; ptnr. Borza Fetterman, Sardelis, Chartered, Sarasota, 1986-89, James C. Fetterman, P.A., Sarasota, Fla., 1989-2000; pres., ptnr. Fetterman & Zitani, P.A., 2001—03; prin., owner James C. Fetterman Chartered, 2003—. Sr. res. adviser to gen. counsel and assoc. gen. counsel Def. Logistics Agy., 1993-94; assoc. prof. U. Sarasota, 1987—; judge advocate I.M.A. USAF, 1987; spl. master for zoning and code enforcement Sarasota County, 1991-2000; vol. counsel Am. Radio Relay League, 1995—; legal advisor Family Forum, CompuServe, 1996—. Editor Midwest Law Review U. Kans., 1984-86, also textbooks. Asst. scoutmaster Boy Scouts Am., 1991—95, 1999—, scoutmaster, 1995—98, scoutmaster nat. jamboree troop, 1998, dist. com., 1998—, venture crew advisor, 2001—, Boy Scouts Am. Aquatics Inst., 2003—; mem. sch. adv. coun. McIntosh Mid. Sch., 1999—2000; mem. Sarasota chpt. Eagles Club, 1999—, chaplain, 2001—02, v.p., 2002—03; active Incarnation Ch. Folk Group, 1986—90, 2000—; bd. dirs., v.p., chaperone Sarasota Boy's Choir, 1992—93; bd. dirs. Fla. Inst. Traditional Chinese Medicine, 1998—2002, chmn. bd. dirs., 1998—2002. Capt. USAF, 1972—76, ETO, col. res. USAF, 1972—. Named one of Outstanding Young Men of Am., Jaycees, 1982; recipient award of merit Boy Scouts Am., 1998, Order of the Bronze Pelican, Nat. Cath. Com. on Scouting, 2001, Silver Beaver award Boy Scouts Am., 2003. Mem. Am. Bus. Law Assn., Res. Officer Assn. (Sarasota chpt. pres. 1989-91, v.p. 1991-92), Fla. Bar (vice chmn. mil. law com. 1991-94, chmn. 1994-95), Ret. Officer's Assn. (bd. dirs. Sarasota chpt. 1991-93), Am. Legion, Nat. Eagle Scout Assn., Loyal Order Moose. Republican. Roman Catholic. Avocations: running, swimming, ham radio. Office: 4521A Bee Ridge Rd Sarasota FL 34233-2517 E-mail: jfetterman@compuserve.com.

FETTEROLL, EUGENE CARL, JR., human resources professional; b. Hartford, Conn., Mar. 8, 1935; s. Eugene Carl and Gladys Marion (Crilley) F.; m. Barbara Ann Meeker, June 15, 1957; children: Eugene Carl III, Douglas Alan, Steven Joseph, Gary Michael. BA, U. Conn., 1957; MEd, Suffolk U., 1973. Supt. customer svc., mgr. pers. svcs., dir. tng. Boston Gas Co., 1957-76; dir. Ea. Enterprises, Boston, 1977-81, Associated Industries of Mass., Boston, 1981-87, v.p. human resources, 1987-89; pres. Fetteroll Assocs., South Portland, Maine, 1989—. Tng. cons. Associated Industries of Mass., Boston. Author: Growing Teams, 1993, (e-book) The Sage's Secrets of Successful Supervision, 2002; editor: Trainer's Resource, 1989. Vol. United Way, Mass. and R.I., 1965—; vice-chmn. bd. trustees Medfield (Mass.) Pub. Libr., 1966-70; chmn. Sch. Land Acquisition Com., Medfield, 1963-65; bd. dirs. Growth Opportunity Alliance Lawrence/Quality Productivity Competitiveness, Salem, N.H. Mem. ASTD (pres. Mass. chpt. 1972-73, Bay Colonies chpt. 1981-82, nat. ethics com. 1986—, Torch award 1979), Mass. Coalition for Adult Edn., Mass. Arms Collectors. Republican. Roman Catholic. Avocations: collecting antique powder flasks, photography, travel. Home and Office: Fetteroll Assocs PO Box 2887 South Portland ME 04116 Fax: 207-741-9031. E-mail: genefett@maine.rr.com.

FETTERS, NORMAN CRAIG, II, banker; b. Pitts., Aug. 27, 1942; s. Karl Leroy and Hazel (Lower) F.; m. Linda Wood, Aug. 14, 1965; children— Eric Craig, Kevin Edward, Brian Allan AB, Westminster Coll., 1964; MBA, U. Pitts., 1965. Various positions to v.p. Security Pacific Nat. Bank, Los Angeles, 1965-66, 69-74, v.p., 1974-82; sr. v.p. Security Pacific Bank Washington, Seattle, 1982-92, SeaFirst Bank, Seattle, 1992-93; sr. v.p., dir. Security Pacific Savs. Bank, Seattle, 1993-94; v.p. Key Bank of Wash., Seattle, 1994-96, sr. v.p., 1996-99; v.p., credit officer Fed. Home Loan Bank of Seattle, 1999—. Served to lt. U.S. Army, 1966-69 Mem. Risk Mgmt. Assocs., Lions Club (pres. 1988-89). Presbyterian (elder). Avocations: cross-country skiing, travel, hiking, photography. Office: Fed Home Loan Bank of Seattle 1501 4th Ave Ste 1900 Seattle WA 98101-1693 E-mail: CraigF@Fhlbsea.com.

FETZER, DEREK, industrial engineer, consultant; b. Lima, Peru, Dec. 6, 1967; s. Erwin Fetzer and Christine Jaskowski; m. Veronica Noriega, Nov. 27, 1998; 1 child, Dominic Alexander. MBA, Purdue U., MS in Indsl. Engring., 2000. Six Sigma Black Belt, Six Sigma Qualtec, 2002. Ops. mgr. IPRELSA, Lima, 1993—94; mktg. rsch. cons. Michelsen Cons.; ops. rsch. analyst ZS

Associates, Evanston, Ill., 1995—96; rsch. asst. Purdue U., West Lafayette, Ind., 1998—2000; market inetlligence mgr. Owens Corning, Toldedo, Ohio, 2000—. Recipient winner Burton Morgan Entrepreneurial Competition, Purdue U., 2000; fellow, Am. Heart Assn., 1983; scholar, Purdue U., 1999. Achievements include Entrepreneurial competition winner. Office: Owens Corning 1 OC Pky Toledo OH 43659 Personal E-mail: maxfetzer@hotmail.com.

FETZER, JAMES HENRY, philosopher, educator; b. Pasadena, Calif., Dec. 6, 1940; s. Henry Jr. and Eleanor Atwood (Waterhouse) F.; m. Janice Elaine Morgan, June 12, 1977. AB in Philosophy magna cum laude, Princeton U., 1962; MA in History and Philosophy of Sci., Ind. U., 1968, PhD in History and Philosophy of Sci., 1970; postgrad., Columbia U., 1968-69. Asst. prof. U. Ky., Lexington, 1970-77; vis. assoc. prof. U. Va., Charlottesville, 1977-78, U. Cin., 1978-79, vis. NSF rsch. prof., 1979-80; vis. lectr. U. N.C., Chapel Hill, 1980-81; vis. assoc. prof. New Coll. of U. South Fla., Sarasota, 1981-83, MacArthur vis. disting. prof. arts and scis., 1983-84; adj. prof. U. South Fla., Tampa, 1984-85; vis. prof. U. Va., Charlottesville, 1984-85; postdoctoral fellow Wright State U., Dayton, Ohio, 1986-87; prof. philosophy U. Minn., Duluth, 1987-96, dept. chmn., 1988-92, disting. McKnight prof., 1996—. Rsch. scholar New Coll. U. South Fla., Sarasota, 1985-86; Landsdowne lectr. U. Victoria, Can., 1992. Author: Scientific Knowledge, 1981, AI: Its Scope and Limits, 1990, Philosophy and Cognitive Science, 1991, 2d edit., 1996, Portuguese translation, 2000, Philosophy of Science, 1993, Computers and Cognition, 2001; co-author: Glossary of Cognitive Science, 1993, Glossary of Epistemology/Philosophy of Science, 1993; editor: Principles of Philosophical Reasoning, 1984, Sociobiology and Epistemology, 1985, Aspects of AI, 1988, Probability and Causality, 1988, Epistemology and Cognition, 1991, Foundations of Philosophy of Science, 1993, Assassination Science, 1998, Science, Explanation, and Rationality, 2000, Murder in Dealey Plaza, 2000, The Philosophy of Carl G. Hempel, 2001, Consciousness Evolving, 2002, The Great Zapruder Film Hoax, 2003; co-editor: Philosophy, Language, and AI, 1988, Philosophy, Mind and Cognitive Inquiry, 1990, Definitions and Definability, 1991, Program Verification, 1993, The New Theory of Reference, 1998; co-editor Synthese, 1990-99; founder, book series editor: Studies in Cognitive Systems, 1986—, Explorations in Philosophy, 1994—; founder, editor: Minds and Machines, 1989-2002; founder, editor Assassination Rsch., 2002—. With USMC, 1962-66. Recipient Dickinson prize Princeton U., 1962, Medal of U. Helsinki, Finland, 1990. Mem. AAUP, AAAS, Am. Philos. Assn., Internat. Soc. for Human Ethology, Soc. for Machines and Mentality (founder), Philosophy of Sci. Assn., Assn. Computing Machinery, Human Behavior and Evolution Soc. Office: U Minn Dept Philosophy Duluth MN 55812 E-mail: jfetzer@d.umn.edu.

FEUER, CY, motion picture and theatrical producer, director; b. N.Y.C., Jan. 15, 1911; s. Herman and Ann (Abrams) F.; m. Posy Greenberg, Jan. 20, 1946; children: Robert, Jed. Student, Inst. Mus. Art Julliard Found., 1928-32. Head music dept. Republic Pictures, 1938-42, 45-47; partner Feuer and Martin Prodns., N.Y.C., 1947—; mgr.-dir. San Francisco Civic Light Opera Assn., 1975-80. Pres. The League of Am. Theatres and Producers, 1989—. Theatrical prodns. include Where's Charley, 1948, Guys and Dolls, 1950, Can-Can, 1953, The Boy Friend, 1954, Silk Stockings, 1955, Whoop-Up, 1958, How To Succeed in Business Without Really Trying, 1961 (Pulitzer prize for drama), Little Me, 1962, Skyscraper, 1965, Walking Happy, 1966, The Goodbye People, 1968, The Act, 1977; producer: motion pictures Cabaret, 1972 (winner 8 Acad. awards), Piaf, 1975, Chorus Line, 1985; author: (autobiography) I Got the Show Right Here, 2003. Inducted into the Theater Hall of Fame, 1994. Office: Feuer and Martin 630 Park Ave New York NY 10021-6544

FEUER, HENRY, retired chemist; b. Stanislau, Austria, Apr. 4, 1912; arrived in U.S., 1941, naturalized, 1946; s. Jacob and Julia (Tindel) Feuer; m. Paula Berger, Jan. 19, 1946. MS, U. Vienna, Austria, 1934, PhD, 1936. Postdoctoral fellow U. Paris, 1939; with dept. chemistry Purdue U., Lafayette, Ind., 1943-79, prof. chemistry, 1961-79, prof. emeritus, 1979—. Vis. prof. Hebrew U., Jerusalem, 1964, Indian Inst. Tech., Kanpur, India, 1971, Peking (China) Inst. Tech., 1979. Pres., contbr. Organic Electronic Spectral Data, Inc., 1962—89; mng. editor: Organic Nitro Chemistry Series, 1982—; mem. adv. bd. Turkish Jour. Chemistry, mem. editl. bd. Chimica Acta Turcica. Fellow: AAAS; mem.: Royal Soc. Chemistry, Am. Chem. Soc., Sigma Xi, Phi Lambda Upsilon. Achievements include research in organic nitrogen compounds; discovery of new methods for syntheses nitro compounds, cyclic hydrazides; research in mechanism of nitro compounds reactions. Home: 726 Princess Dr West Lafayette IN 47906-2036 Office: Purdue U Dept Chemistry Lafayette IN 47907

FEUER, MARSHALL ZEV, import/export company executive; b. N.Y.C., Dec. 13, 1941; s. Menkes and Rose Feuer; m. Judith Fern Rosenberg, Dec. 18, 1966; children: Menachem (Matthew), Ronald. BS, Columbia U., 1963; MS in Ops. Rsch., Johns Hopkins U., 1965. Engr. Martin-Marietta Corp., Balt., 1965; sr. engr. Ford Instrument Co. div. Sperry Rand Corp., N.Y.C., 1965—66, Lockheed Electronics Co.-Lockheed Aircraft Corp., Plainfield, NJ, 1965—68; tech. support Chamy Tan Processing Corp., Gloversville, NY, 1968—71; leather mcht. Trans-Am. Leather Co. Inc., Gloversville, 1971—77; leather mcht., pres. Interamerica Leather Co. Inc., Gloversville, 1977—90; dir. Safety Leather Co., Johnstown, NY, 1991—. Mem. B'nai Brith, N.Y.C., 1985—2002; hon. state chmn. Nat. Rep. Congl. Com., N.Y.C., 2002; congregant Knesseth Israel Synagouge, Gloversville, 1968—2002. Recipient Walter M. Rautenstrauch award, Columbia U., 1963; fellow, Rockefeller Inst., 1959; NASA fellow, Johns Hopkins U., 1963—65. Mem.: Alpha Pi Mu, Tau Beta Pi. Conservative. Jewish. Avocations: physical fitness, travel, sailing.

FEUER, MARVIN C. political scientist, educator; b. Cleve., Oct. 15, 1950; s. Henry and Gita Feuerwerger; m. Debra S. Lichtman, Dec. 1, 1974; children: David, Rachel, Danny. BA, Columbia U., 1971; MA, Harvard U., 1974, PhD, 1977. Dep. sr. advisor to pres. and sec. of state Carter Adminstrn., Washington, 1978-80; dir. for policy planning Office of Asst. Sec. of Def. for Internat. Security Affairs, Washington, 1984-85; dep. asst. sec. of def. for policy analysis Office of Sec. of Def., Washington, 1985-86; first sec. Am. Embassy, Tel Aviv, 1986-89; prof. lectr. in internat. rels. The Johns Hopkins U. Sch. of Advanced Internat. Studies, Washington, 1990—; asst. dep. undersec. for policy analysis Office of the Sec. of Def., Washington, 1990; sr. strategic fellow Washington Inst. for Near East Policy, 1990-92; dir. for def. and strategic issues Am. Israel Pub. Affairs Com., Washington. Cons. Nat. Pub. Radio, Washington, 1991. Author: (book) Congress and Israel, 1979, (monographs) The Arrow Next Time?, 1992, Restoring the Balance: U.S. Strategy and the Gulf Crisis, 1991. Mem. nat. adv. coun. Am. Jewish Com., Washington, 1992—, Johns Hopkins U. Strategoi, Washington, 1996—. Recipient Alumni Achievement award Am. Friends of the Hebrew U., Jerusalem, 1996; Found. fellow Nat. Found. for Jewish Culture, 1975-76. Office: AIPAC 440 1st St NW Ste 600 Washington DC 20001-2028 E-mail: marvin_feuer@aipac.org.

FEUER, MICHAEL, office products superstore executive; With Fabri-Centers, Cleveland, Ohio, 1970—88; co-founder OfficeMax, Shaker Heights, Ohio, 1988—, chmn., CEO. Office: OfficeMax 3605 Warrensville Center Rd Shaker Heights OH 44122-5203

FEUERMAN, CAROLE A. sculptor, artist; b. Hartford, Conn., Sept. 21, 1945; d. Milton and Doris Sue Ackerman; div.; m. Ron Cohen; children: Lauren, Craig, Sari. Student, Hofstra U., 1963, Temple U., 1964, Sch. Visual Arts, 1967. Pres. Feuerman Studios, Inc., N.Y.C., 1967—. One-woman shows include Art 10 '79 Basel Art Fair, Switzerland, 1979, O.K. Harris, Scottsdale, Ariz., 1982, Ackland Art Mus., Chapel Hill, N.C., 1985, Queens Mus., Flushing, N.Y., 1987, Arnesen Gallery, Vail, Colo., 1990, Internat. Swimming Hall of Fame, Ft. Lauderdale, Fla., 1993, So Alleghenies Mus. Art, Loretto, Pa., 2000, Lobby Gallery, N.Y.C., 2001, Queensborough C.C. Mus. and Art Gallery, Bayside, N.Y., 2003, Frederick R. Weisman Mus. Art, Malibu, Calif., 2003, Pepperdine U., 2003, exhibited in group shows at Isetan Mus. Art, Tokyo, ACA Gallery, Harkone Open-Air Mus., Parrish Art Mus., Whitney Mus. Am. Art, Nat. Sculpture Soc., Riverside Art Mus., West Chelsea Arts Festival, N.Y.C., 1998, Frederick R. Weisman Mus. Art, Pepperdine U., Malibu, Calif., 1998, Biennale Internat. dell'ARTE Contemporanea, Florence, Italy, 2001 (Lorenzo di Medici award, 2001), So. Alleghenies Mus. Art, 2002, Queensborough C.C. Mus. and Art Gallery, 2002, Nat. Biennale fur Bildende Kunst, 2002 (Honor prize), Austria Biennale (Honor prize), Represented in permanent collections Lowe Art Mus., Fla., Tampa Mus. Art, So Alleghenies Mus. Art, Brandeis U., CUNY, Bayside, NY, Bass Mus., Miami, Fla., Sen. Hilary Rodham Clinton, Pres. Bill Clinton, Dr. Henry Kissinger, Bass Mus., Fla., Ft. Lauderdale (Fla.) Mus. Art, Boca Raton Mus., Fla., Caldic Collection, Rotterdam, The Netherlands, Pres. Mikael S. Gorbachov, Moscow. Recipient Betty Parsons Sculpture award 1970, Charles D. Murphy Sculpture award 1981, Amelia Peabody award for sculpture 1982, 1st prize U.S. Nat. Fine Arts Competition 1984. Mem.: Internat. Women's Forum (N.Y.), Solomon R. Guggenheim Mus., Met. Mus. Art, Mus. Modern Art, Internat. Sculpture Ctr., Nat. Assn .Women Artists, Am. Women's Econ. Devel. Corp., Pro Arts, Nat. Women Caucus for Art, SVA Alumni Assn., UNESCO. Home: 200 Mercer St Apt 1F New York NY 10012-1510 Studio: Feuerman Studios Inc 350 Warren St 8th fl Jersey City NJ 07302-1101 Business E-Mail: caroljf@mindspring.com.

FEUERSTEIN, ALAN RICKY, lawyer; b. Buffalo, Oct. 24, 1950; s. Aaron Irving and Doris Jean (Davis) F.; m. June, 1973 (div. Jan. 1984); children: Marni Lauren, Jami Lynn; m. Susan T. Skop, Dec. 31, 1986; children: Christopher Borkowski, Philip Borkowski. BS cum laude, SUNY, Buffalo, 1974; LLB, U. Toledo, 1977. Bar: N.Y. 1978, Territorial and Dist. Ct. V.I. 1989, U.S. Supreme Ct. 1992, Fed. Ct. Puerto Rico 1993. Assoc. Law Offices of Salvatore Martoche, Buffalo, 1977-79; ptnr. Martoche & Feuerstein, Buffalo, 1979-81; lectr. Erie County Cen. Police Svcs. Acad., Buffalo, 1981-82; pvt. practice Buffalo, 1981-93; ptnr. Feuerstein & Santapia, Buffalo, 1993-94; prin. Law Offices of Alan R. Feuerstein, Buffalo, 1994-97; ptnr. Feuerstein & Smith, LLP, Buffalo, 1998—. Lectr. Daemen Coll. Consortium, Buffalo, 1980-81; cons. in field. Mem. Erie County Reps., Buffalo, 1979—. Mem. Niagara Club, St.Thomas Yacht Club, The Buffalo Launch Club, Confrérie de la Châine des Rôtisseurs (chevalier). Republican. Jewish. Office: 17 St Louis Pl Buffalo NY 14202-1502 also: Woods & Woods 1 Comptroller Plz San Juan PR 00917 also: PO Box 502008 Saint Thomas VI 00805-2008

FEUERSTEIN, BURT GARY, medical educator, geneticist; b. Buffalo, May 7, 1949; s. Aaron Irving and Doris Jeanne (Davis) F.; m. Janet Carol Shalwitz, June 20, 1976; children: Jesse S., Samuel S., Jeanne S. Student, Conservatory City of Vienna, 1971-72; BA in Music, Wesleyan U., 1972; MD, SUNY, Buffalo, 1979, PhD, 1980. Lic. physician, Calif. Resident in pediat. U. Calif., San Francisco, 1979-82, fellow in hematology/oncology dept. pediatrics, 1982-85, asst. rsch. physician dept. neurol. surgery, 1982-86, asst. prof. dept. lab. medicine and pediatrics, 1987-94, assoc. prof. dept. lab. medicine and neurol. surgery, 1994-2000, prof. dept. lab. medicine and neurol. surgery, 2000—. Prin. investigator Brain Tumor Rsch. Ctr./U. Calif., San Francisco, 1989—; adhoc reviewer and cons. in field. Mem. editl. bd. Cancer Genetics and Cytogenetics; contbr. articles to profl. jours; patentee therapeutic polyamines, genetic gain and loss in gliomas. NIH grantee, 1987—. Mem. AAAS, Am. Assn. for Cancer Rsch., Soc. for Neuro-oncology. Jewish. Avocations: piano, skiing. Home: 100 Kensington Way San Francisco CA 94127-1104 Office: U Calif San Francisco San Francisco CA 94143-1631 E-mail: feuer@cc.ucsf.edu.

FEUERSTEIN, DONALD MARTIN, lawyer; b. Chgo., May 30, 1937; s. Morris Martin and Pauline Jean (Zagel) F.; m. Dorothy Rosalind Sokolsky, June 3, 1962 (dec. Mar. 1978); children: Eliza Carol, Tony David; m. Summer Donna Berben, May 25, 1987; 1 child, Ashley Paul. BA magna cum laude, Yale U., 1959; JD magna cum laude, Harvard U., 1962. Bar: N.Y. 1962. Assoc. firm Cleary, Gottlieb, Steen & Hamilton, N.Y.C., 1962-63; law clk. to U.S. dist. judge N.Y.C., 1963-65; assoc. firm Saxe, Bacon & Bolan, N.Y.C., 1965; asst. gen. counsel, chief counsel instl. investor study SEC, Washington, 1966-71; ptnr., counsel Salomon Bros., N.Y.C., 1971-81, mng. dir., sec., 1981-91; exec. v.p., chief legal officer Salomon, Inc., 1991; spl. asst. U.S. Dept. Edn., Washington, 1993-94, sr. advisor, 1994-99; pres. New Am. Schs., Arlington, Va., 1999-2000, sr. advisor, 2000-2001, Imaging Acceptance Corp., 2001—02, Nat. Coun. Accreditation of Tchr. Edn., Washington, 2001—. Spl. cons. Intersch. Group, N.Y.C., 1991-93; mem. bus. policy coun. com. on excellence in edn. Nat. Alliance of Bus., 2000-2001. Editor Harvard Law Rev., 1960-62; mem. editl. adv. bd. Securities Regulation Law Jour., 1973-90; bd. editors Nat. Law Jour., 1978-90. Mem. vis. com. Northwestern U. Law Sch., 1975—78; bd. dirs. 1st All Children's Theatre, 1976—85, chmn., 1976—82; mem. long-range planning and capital campaign coms. Brearley Sch., N.Y.C., 1981—83; mem. adv. bd. Solomon R. Guggenheim Mus., 1984—91, chmn. bus. com., 1988—91, mem. internat. coun., 1991—; bd. dirs. Arts and Bus. Coun., 1980—85, v.p., 1985—88; trustee, v.p., mem.e xec. com. Dalton Sch., 1983—89, trustee, v.p., mem. exec. com., 1990—93; mem. dean's adv. coun. Harvard U. Law Sch., 1988—95, mem. steering com. and capital campaign, 1991—95; mem. com. on univ. resources Harvard U., 1988—; mem. vis. com. Harvard Grad. Sch. Edn., 1993—99, mem. tech. adv. coun., 1996—2001; chmn. tech. com. Georgetown Day Sch., 1997—2000, trustee, 1997—2003, mem. exec. com., 2001—02, chmn., trusteeship commn., 2001—02, chmn. fin. aid com., 2002—03; mem. Brookings Coun., 1998—2001. Mem. ABA, Phi Beta Kappa, Pi Sigma Alpha. Home: 6430 Bradley Blvd Bethesda MD 20817-3246 E-mail: dfeuer13@cs.com.

FEUERSTEIN, HOWARD M. lawyer; b. Memphis, Sept. 16, 1939; s. Leon and Lillian (Kapell) F.; m. Tamra Lynn Saperstein, May 19, 1968; children: Laurie, Leon. BA, Vanderbilt U., 1961, JD, 1963. Bar: Tenn. 1963, Oreg. 1965. Law clk. to justice U.S. Ct. Appeals (5th cir.), Montgomery, Ala., 1963-64; teaching fellow Stanford U., 1964-65; assoc. Davies, Biggs et al (now Stoel Rives LLP), Portland, Oreg., 1965-71; ptnr. Stoel Rives LLP, Portland, 1971—. Mem. Oreg. Gov.'s Task Force on Land Devel. Law, 1974; bd. realtors Condominium Study Com., Oreg., 1975-76. Editor-in-chief Vanderbilt Law Rev., 1962-63. Trustee Congregation Beth Israel, Portland, 1977-83; bd. dirs. Jewish Family & Child Service, Portland, 1975-81, Young Musicians and Artists Inc., 1991-96. Recipient Founder's medal Vanderbilt Law Sch., 1963. Mem. ABA, Oreg. State Bar, Community Assn. Inst. (bd. dirs. Oreg. chpt. 1980-86), Am. Coll. Real Estate Lawyers. Office: Stoel Rives LLP 900 SW 5th Ave Ste 2600 Portland OR 97204-1268 E-mail: hmfeuerstein@stoel.com.

FEUERSTEIN, PAUL BRUCK, social services agency executive; b. Jersey City, Dec. 22, 1947; s. Charles Philip and Helen Lydia (Bruck) F.; m. Kathleen Olivia Pasco, May 30, 1970 (div. June 1979); children: Kristin, John Mark; m. Rebecca Ruth Eddy, Sept. 15, 1979; 1 child, Martha. BA in Philosophy, Concordia Sr. Coll., 1969; MA in Comm., NYU, 1971; M of Sacred Theology, Gen. Theol. Seminary, N.Y.C., 1973; MSW, Hunter Sch. Social Work, 1982; grad. Inst. Non-Profit Mgmt., Columbia U., 1997. Cert. social worker, N.Y.; ordained Episcopal priest. Mem. youth team Diocese of N.Y. Region II, 1973-74; asst. St. Mary's Episcopal Ch., Chappaqua, N.Y., 1973-74; assoc. rector Ch. of Holy Trinity, N.Y.C., 1974-76; assoc. chaplain St. Albans Sch., Washington, 1976-77; assoc. dir. Project Outward Bound Fedn. of Handicapped, N.Y.C., 1978-80; pres., CEO Barrier Free Living, N.Y.C., 1981—. Founder, first chairperson N.Y.C. Coalition on Housing for People with Disabilities, 1979-81; mem. exec. com. Fedn. Mental Health Mental Retardation and Alcoholism Svcs., N.Y.C., 1993—, chmn. exec. com., 2001—; mem. N.Y.C. Domestic Violence Task Force, 1993—, Traumatic Brain Injury Housing Task Force, 1994-97, N.Y.C. Medicaid Managed Care Task Force, 1995-2002; bd. dirs. Coalition of Vol. Mental Health Agys., N.Y.C., 1995-2003, Integrated Behavioral Health Sys., 1996-2002, Citywide Behavioral Network, 1998-2002; co-chair Disability Network of N.Y.C.; founder, vice chairperson Disability Network N.Y.C., 2002—. Author: Women and Children with Disabilities and Domestic Violence, 1997. Mem. Manhattan Borough Pres. Adv. Com. on Persons with Disabilities, 1987—; priest assoc. Ch. of the Holy Trinity, 1978—; bd. dirs. Open Congregation, 1990—; vice chairperson Episcopal Diocese of N.Y. Commn. on Ministry with Persons with Disabilities. Fellow Brookdale Ctr. on Aging, Am. Orthopsychiat. Assn.; mem. Harlem Yacht Club. Avocations: sailing, model boat building, hiking, cross country skiing, painting. Home: 431 E 118th St New York NY 10035-4318 Office: Barrier Free Living 270 E 2nd St New York NY 10009-7815 E-mail: pbfbflnyc@aol.com.

FEUERWERKER, ALBERT, history educator; b. Cleve., Nov. 6, 1927; s. Martin and Gizella (Feuerwerker) F.; m. Yi-tsi Mei, June 11, 1955; children: Alison, Paul. AB, Harvard U., 1950, PhD, 1957. Lectr. history U. Toronto, Ont., Can., 1955-58; rsch. fellow Harvard U., Cambridge, Mass., 1958-60; assoc. prof. history U. Mich., Ann Arbor, 1960-63, prof., 1963-96, chmn. dept., 1984-87; dir. U. Mich. Ctr. for Chinese Studies, Ann Arbor, 1961-67, 72-83; A.M. and H.P. Bentley prof. of history U. Mich., Ann Arbor, 1986-96, prof. emeritus, 1996—; dir. d'études École des Hautes Etudes en Scis. Sociales, Paris, 1981; vis. scholar Acad. Social Scis., Shanghai, China, 1981, 88, Sichuan U., Chengdu, China, 1988. Joint com. on contemporary China, Social Sci. Research Council-Am. Council Learned Socs., 1966-78, 80-83, chmn., 1970-75; mem. com. on scholarly comm. with the People's Republic of China, Nat. Acad. Scis.-Social Sci. Rsch. Coun.-Am. Council Learned Socs., 1971-78, 81-83, vice-chmn., 1975-78 Author: China's Early Industrialization, 1958, History in Communist China, 1968, The Chinese Economy 1870-1911, 1969, Rebellion in 19th Century China, 1975, The Foreign Establishment in China, 1976, Economic Trends in the Republic of China, 1977, Chinese Social and Economic History from the Song to 1900, 1982, Studies in the Economic History of Late Imperial China, 1996, The Chinese Economy, 1870-1949, 1996; co-editor: Cambridge History of China, vol. 13, 1986; mem. editl. bd. Am. Hist. Rev., 1970-75, The China Quar., 1967-91, Comparative Studies in Soc. and History, 1964-2001. Served with AUS, 1946-47. Fellow NEH, 1971-72, Social Sci. Research Council-Am. Council of Learned Socs., 1962-63, Guggenheim Found., 1987-88. Fellow AAAS; mem. Assn. for Asian Studies (v.p. 1990, pres. 1991), Nat. Com. on U.S.-China Rels. Home: 827 Asa Gray Dr Apt 356 Ann Arbor MI 48105 Office: U Mich Ctr for Chinese Studies 1080 S University Ave Ste 3668 Ann Arbor MI 48109-1106 E-mail: afeuer@umich.edu.

FEUERWERKER, ELIE, secondary school educator; b. Paris, Dec. 2, 1948; arrived in U.S., 1989; s. David Feuerwerker and Antoinette Gluck. BSc in Biology, U. Montreal, Que., Can., 1971, MSc in Biology, 1976, PhD in Biology, 1983. Postdoctoral fellow Harvard U., Cambridge, Mass., 1985—87; rsch. assoc. Boston U., 1987—88; rsch. fellow McGill U., Montreal Neurol. Inst., 1987—89; mem. I-V team The Mount Sinai Med. Ctr., N.Y.C., 1990—94; tchr. biology Lycee Française de N.Y., N.Y.C., 1994—2000; tchr. N.Y.C. Bd. Edn., 2000 . Presenter in field. Contbr. articles to profl. jours. and newspapers. Grantee, The Hannah Inst. for the History of Medicine, NSF, The Rockefeller U.; Rsch. grantee, N.Y. Acad. Scis. Jewish. Avocation: photography. Home: 1617 Cherry St Highland Park NJ 08904

FEUERZEIG, HENRY LOUIS, lawyer; b. Chgo., Dec. 12, 1938; s. Samuel Alexander Feuerzeig and Esther Fleeger; m. Penny Zweigenhaft, Apr. 8, 1967; children: Paul Lawrence, Darcy Elizabeth. BS, U. Wis., 1962; JD, George Washington U., 1970. Bar: D.C., V.I., Fla., Md. Reporter various newspapers, Dubuque, Iowa, Chgo., Madison, Wis., Cin. and Washington, 1962-64, 65-67; assoc. Sachs, Greenebaum, Frohlich & Tayler, Washington, 1970-72; asst. atty. gen. V.I. Dept. Law, St. Thomas, 1972-73, chief civil and adminstrv. law divsn., 1973-74, 1st asst. atty. gen., 1974; ptnr. Feuerzeig & Zebedee, St. Thomas, 1974-76; judge Territorial Ct. V.I., St. Thomas, 1977-87; del., chmn. jud. powers and functions com. 4th V.I. Constl. Conv., 1981; ptnr. Dudley, Topper and Feuerzeig, St. Thomas, 1987—. Mem. supervisory bd. V.I. Law Enforcement Planning Commn., 1978-87, Juvenile Justice and Delinquency Prevention, 1988—; mem. V.I. Juvenile Code Revision Task Force, 1978-83, V.I. Criminal Code Revision Task Force, 1978-87. Mem. Montgomery County (Md.) Dem. State Ctrl. Com., 1970-72; mem. V.I. Indsl. Devel. Commn., 1976; bd. dirs. Environ. Studies Program, St. Thomas, 1977-80, United Way, 1986-92; bd. reps. Hebrew Congregation of St. Thomas, 1983-90, 96-2002, co-chair Bicentennial Campaign com., 1993-97; trustee Antilles Sch., St. Thomas, 1983-91; mem. adv. coun. Youth Multi-Svc. Ctr., 1989-94; dir. Cmty. Found. of V.I., 1992—, pres., 1993-94. Sigma Delta Chi scholar, 1962; Congressional fellow Am. Polit. Sci. Assn., 1964-65; named Person of Yr. Hebrew Congregation of St. Thomas, 2003. Mem. ABA (lawyers conf. jud. performance and conduct com. 1984—), D.C. Bar Assn., Fla. Bar Assn., V.I. Bar Assn. (pres. 1976), Am. Law Inst. (life, cons. group for principles of family dissolution, 1992-2000, cons. group for restatement of law governing lawyers, 1992-99), Am. Judicature Soc., Assn. Trial Lawyers Am., Internat. Soc. of Barristers, Order of Coif, Sigma Delta Chi, Phi Delta Phi. Lodges: Rotary, Harmonic Lodge No. 356, E.C. Jewish. Office: Dudley Topper and Feuerzeig 1A Frederiksberg Gade PO Box 756 Charlotte Amalie VI 00804-0756 E-mail: hfeuerzeig@dtflaw.com., hfeuer@attglobal.net.

FEUILLE, RICHARD HARLAN, lawyer, director; b. Mexico City, June 10, 1920; s. Frank and Margaret (Levy) F.; m. Louann Johnston Hoover, Oct. 20, 1948; children: Louann H., Richard H., Robert R., Joseph L. (dec.), James M., Patrick F. (dec.), Margaret J. BA, U. Va., 1947, LL.B., 1948; JD, 1970. Bar: Tex. 1948. Assoc. Jones, Hardie, Grambling & Howell, El Paso, Tex., 1948-53; ptnr. Hardie, Grambling, Sims & Feuille, El Paso, 1953-57; sr. ptnr. Scott, Hulse, Marshall & Feuille, El Paso, 1957—. Bd. dirs. El Paso Nat. Bank (now known as Chase Bank of Tex., N.A.), 1964-93. Active United Fund El Paso, 1963—, founder, v.p. trust fund, 1969—, pres., 1968, 75—, bd. dirs., 1966-72; pres. El Paso Cmty. Concert Assn., 1961-67; mem. adv. coun. U. Tex. at El Paso, 1968—, mem. exec. com., 1968-70; bd. dirs. Providence Meml. Hosp., 1986-92; bd. dirs. St. Clement's Episcopal Parish Sch., El Paso, pres., 1993-95; trustee YWCA, El Paso; bd. dirs. El Paso Cmty. Found., 1980—, pres., 1983-84. Served to maj. USAAF, 1941-46, PTO, participant in invasion of Iwo Jima. Decorated bronze star; recipient Disting. Svc. award City of El Paso and Rotary Club, 2002. Mem. ABA (estate and gift tax com.), El Paso County Bar Assn. (pres. 1972-73), Tex. Bar Assn., Greater El Paso Tennis Assn. (bd. dirs.), Rotary Club of El Paso, Order Coif, Phi Beta Kappa, Omicron Delta Kappa. Episcopalian (vestryman, sr. warden). Clubs: Coronado Country (El Paso), El Paso Tennis (El Paso) (pres. 1973). Home: 1021 Broadmoor Dr El Paso TX 79912-2003 Office: Scott Hulse Marshall & Feuille 201 East Main Dr 1100 Chase Tower El Paso TX 79901 E-mail: rfeu@scotthulse.com.

FEULNER, EDWIN JOHN, JR., research foundation executive; b. Chgo., Aug. 12, 1941; s. Edwin John and Helen J. (Franzen) F.; m. Linda C. Leventhal, Mar. 8, 1969; children: Edwin John III, Emily V. BS, Regis Coll., 1963; MBA, U. Pa., 1964; PhD, U. Edinburgh, 1981; hon. degree (hon.), Nichols Coll., 1981, Universidad Francisco Marroquin, Guatemala City, 1982, Hanyang U., Seoul, Korea, 1982, Bellevue Coll., Nebr., 1987, Gonzaga U., 1992, Grove City Coll., 1994, Pepperdine U., 2000, St. Norbert Coll., 2002. Richard Weaver fellow London Sch. Econs., 1965; fellow Ctr. for Strategic and Internat. Studies, 1965—66; pub. affairs fellow Hoover Instn., 1966—68; rsch. analyst Rep. Conf. U.S. Ho. of Reps., 1968-69; confidential asst. to sec. def. Melvin Laird, 1969-70; campaign mgr. Crane for Congress Com., 1972; adminstrv. asst. to U.S. Congressman Philip M. Crane, 1970-74; exec. dir. Rep. Study Com., Ho. of Reps., 1974-77; pres. Heritage Found., Washington, 1977—; chmn. Inst. European Def. and Strategic Studies, 1977-96; counselor to v.p. candidate Jack Kemp, 1996. U.S. adv. com. pub. diplomacy USIA, 1982—94, chmn., 1982—91; nat. adv. bd. Ctr. Edn. and Rsch. in Free Enterprise Tex. A&M U.; disitng. fellow mobilization concepts Devel. Ctr. Nat. Def. U., 1983—89; disting. vis. prof. Hanyang U., Seoul, 2001—; mem. Pres.'s Commn. White House Fellows, 1981—83. Author: Congress and the New International Economic Order, 1976, Looking Back, 1981, Conservatives Stalk the House, 1983, The March of Freedom, 1998, Intellectual Pilgrims, 1999, Leadership for America, 2000; pub. Policy Rev., 1977-2001; contbr. articles to profl. jours., newspapers, chpts. to books. Sec. Korea-U.S. Exch. Coun.; chmn. Citizens for Am. Edn. Found., 1985—89; mem. coun. advisors Bryce Harlow Found.; trustee Nat. Chamber Found., 1998—; mem. exec. coun. Am.'s Future Found., 1998—; trustee Lehrman Inst., 1981—90, Sarah Scaife Found., 1988—, St. James Sch., 1990—98, Sequoia Nat. Bank, 1987—99, Regis U., 1991—2001, Internat. Rep. Inst., 1995—2001, Acton Inst., 1995—2002; vice chmn. bd. Aequus Inst., 1989—, Intercollegiate Studies Inst., 1979—, chmn., 1989—93; vice-chmn. bd. dirs. Roe Found., 1983 ; mem. exec. com. Coun. Nat. Policy, 1993—2001; trustee Am. Coun. Germany, NY, 1982—92, Found. Francisco Marroquin, Inst. Rsch. Econs. Taxation, 1980—87; vice chmn., trustee Manhattan Inst. Policy Studies, 1977—86; mem. bd. visitors George Mason U., 1996—; mem. Multimedia Supercorridor Internat. Adv. Coun., Malaysia, 2001—. Decorated Order of Brilliant Star with Grand Cordon Republic of China, Order of Diplomatic Svc. Merit-Gwanghwa medal Republic of Korea; named Free Enterprise Man of Yr., Tex. A&M U., 1985, Man of Yr., Wharton Sch., 1993; recipient Washington award, Freedom Found., 1979, 1980, Disting. Alumni award, Regis U., 1985, Superior Pub. Svc. award, Dept. of Navy, 1987, Presdl. Citizens medal, 1989, Dir.'s Svc. award, USIA, 1992, Thomas Jefferson Servant Leadership award, Coun. Nat. Policy, 1996, Am. Eagle award, Invest-in-Am. Nat. Coun., 1983. Mem. Am. Econs. Assn., Internat. Inst. Strategic Studies, U.S. Strategic Inst., Inst. d'Etudes Politques, Phila. Soc. (treas. 1964-79, pres. 1982-83), Mont Pelerin Soc. (treas. 1979-96, pres. 1996-98), Internat. Com. of the G.K. Chesterton Soc. (chmn. 1989-92), Belle Haven Country Club, Union League (N.Y.C.), Met. Club, Reform Club (London), Bohemian Club (San Francisco), Old. Dominion Boat Club (Alexandria, Va.), Knights of Malta, Knights of the Holy Sepulchre, Alpha Kappa Psi. Republican. Roman Catholic. Office: The Heritage Found 214 Massachusetts Ave NE Washington DC 20002-4958

FEVURLY, KEITH ROBERT, educational administrator; b. Leavenworth, Kans., Oct. 30, 1951; s. James R. Fevurly and Anne (McDade) Barrett; m. Peggy L. Vosburg, Aug. 4, 1978; children: Rebecca Dawn, Grant Robert. BA in Polit. Sci., U. Kans., 1973; JD, Washburn U. of Topeka Sch. Law, 1976; postgrad., U. Mo. Sch. Law, 1984; MBA, Regis U., 1988; LLM, U. Denver, 1992. Bar: Kans. 1977, Colo. 1986; cert. fin. planner. Pvt. practice, Leavenworth, 1977; atty. estate and gift tax IRS, Wichita and Salina, Kans., Austin, Tex., 1977-83; atty., acad. assoc. Coll. for Fin. Planning, Denver, 1984-91, program dir., 1991-95, v.p. edn., 1995-98; COO, U. St. Augustine (Fla.) for Health Scis., 1998-2000; exec. dir. fin. planning edn. program Kaplan Coll., Denver, 2000—. Adj. prof. taxation Met. State Coll., Denver; adj. faculty in retirement planning and estate planning Coll. Fin. Planning. Contbg. author tng. modules, articles on tax mgmt., estate planning. Mem. Colo. Bar Assn., Toastmasters Internat., Rotary Internat., Delta Theta Phi, Pi Sigma Alpha. Republican. Presbyterian. Avocations: softball, racquetball. Home: 3007 E Otero Pl Littleton CO 80122-3666 Office: Kaplan Coll 1401 19th St Denver CO 80202 E-mail: KFevurly@KaplanCollege.edu.

FEWELL, CHARLES KENNETH, JR., lawyer; b. Washington, Jan. 26, 1943; s. Charles Kenneth and Mary Amanda (Hunt) F.; m. Christine Baker Huff, Jan. 23, 1971; children: Anna Catherine, John Maenner. BA magna cum laude, Dartmouth Coll., 1964; JD, Harvard U., 1967. Bar: N.Y. 1968, U.S. Dist. Ct. (so. dist.) N.Y. 1970, U.S. Ct. Appeals (2d cir.) 1975. Law clk. U.S. Dist. Ct. (so. dist.) N.Y., N.Y.C., 1967-68; assoc. White & Case, N.Y.C., 1968-75; v.p., counsel Nat. Westminster Bank, N.Y.C., 1975-80; sr. counsel, sr. v.p. Deutsche Bank AG, N.Y.C., 1980-92; chief counsel, mng. dir. Deutsche Bank N.Am., 1992-97; ptnr. Eaton & Van Winkle, N.Y.C., 1998—. Bd. dirs. Deutsche Bank Trust Co., Deutsche Fin. Svcs. Can. Corp.; v.p., sec. Deutsche Bank Fin., Inc., N.Y.C., 1980-97; v.p. DB Alumni Inc., 2003—. Mem. mediation panel U.S. Dist. Ct. (so. dist.) N.Y., 2001—; mem. vestry Grace Episc. Ch., Hastings-on-Hudson, N.Y., 2000-02. Mem. ABA (banking com. 1980—, co-chair internat. banking and fin. com. 1995-98), Am. Fgn. Law Assn. (v.p. 2000—), Inst. Internat. Bankers (legis. and regulatory com. 1988-97), German Am. Law Assn. (dir. 1982—), N.Y. State Bar Assn. (internat. banking and securities markets 1987—, internat. employment law 1992—, publ. com., editl. bd. 2001—), Assn. Bar City N.Y. (banking law sect. 1992-95), Phi Beta Kappa. Office: Eaton & Van Winkle Three Park Ave New York NY 10016-2078 E-mail: cfewell@evw.com.

FEWELL, CHRISTINE HUFF, psychoanalyst, alcohol counselor; b. Ancon, Canal Zone, Oct. 12, 1942; d. Maenner B. and Antoinette (Baker) Huff; m. Charles K. Fewell, Jr., Jan. 23, 1971; children: Anna C., John M. BA, Antioch Coll., Yellow Springs, Ohio, 1965; MSW, U. Chgo., 1967; student, NYU Sch. Social Work, 1999. Cert. social worker; cert. psychoanalyst; credentialed alcohol and substance abuse counselor. Social worker Ill. Children's Home and Aid Soc., Chgo., 1967-68, Bronx (N.Y.) State Hosp., 1968-70; field work instr. Columbia Sch. Social Work, 1973-75; social worker in alcoholism treatment ctr. St. Lukes/Roosevelt Hosp., N.Y.C., 1970-75; pvt. practice Hastings-on-Hudson, 1976—, N.Y.C., 1976—. Mem., chair N.Y. State Bd. Social Work, 1993-03, extended mem. 2003—; adj. prof. NYU Sch. Social Work, 1995—; faculty advisor NYU Sch. of Social Work, 1996—. Editor: Social Work Treatment of Alcoholism 1984, Pychosocial Issues in the Treatment of Alcoholism, 1985, Alcoholism Treatment Quar., 1986; editorial adv. bd. Social Casework, 1978; asst. editor Jour. Social Work Practice in the Addictions, 1999—; contbr. articles to profl. jours. Mem. NASW (N.Y.C. chpt. alcoholism com. 1971—, chairperson 1975, 98-99, editl. com. 1978-86, peer consultation com. for impaired social workers chairperson 1976—, cons. Com. on Inquiry), Internat. Psychoanalytical Assn., Inst. for Psychoanalytical Tng. and Rsch. (mem.), Acad. Cert. Social Workers (diplomate), N.Y. State Soc. Clin. Social Workers (Westchester chpt. fellow 1981—, referral com. 1983-86), Employee Assistance Profls. Assn. (N.Y. and mid-Hudson chpt. 1983—). Home: 4 Nichols Dr Yonkers NY 10706-3525 Office: 1651 3rd Ave Ste 201 New York NY 10128-3679

FEX, CECILIA, lawyer; b. Stockholm, Dec. 23, 1957; d. Jorgen and Harriet (Carlson) Fex; m. Dane Galloway, June 7, 1997. AD, Montgomery Coll., Sch. Nursing, Takoma Park, Md., 1982; BA summa cum laude, U. Md., College Park, 1988; JD, Harvard Law Sch., Cambridge, 1991. Bar: Md., D.C. Assoc. Koonz McKenney, Washington, 1991—94; tchr. The Cath. U. Law Sch., Washington, 1994—96; assoc. Proskauer Rose, Washington, 1996—98; mem. The Ackerson Group, Washington, 1998—2002; dir. Sommer Barnard Ackerson, PC, Washington, 2002—. Contbr. articles to profl. jours. Mem.: ABA, Wash. Agrl. Roundtable, Supreme Ct. Hist. Soc., U.S. Ct. Appeals for Fed. Cir. Bar Assn., Assn. Trial Lawyers of Am., U.S. Ct. of Fed. Claims Bar Assn., Harvard Law Sch. Assn. Avocations: running, movies, reading, painting. Office: Sommer Barnard Ackerson PC 1666 K St NW Ste 1010 Washington DC 20006

FEY, JOHN THEODORE, retired insurance company executive; b. Hopewell, Va., Mar. 10, 1917; s. Raymond B. and Ruth (Fultz) F.; m. Jane K. Gerber, Apr. 5, 1947 (dec.); 1 child, John Theodore; m. Deborah F. Fitzgerald, Dec. 6, 1986. Student, Washington and Lee U., 1935-37, LL.D., 1978; LL.B., U. Md., 1940; MBA, Harvard U., 1942; J.S.D., Yale U., 1952; LL.D., Middlebury Coll., Alma Coll., 1961, U. Vt., 1967, Washington and Lee U., 1980, St. Augustine Coll., 1981. Bar: Md. 1940, D.C. 1953, Vt. 1959, N.Y. 1977. County atty., Md., 1947-49; faculty Law Sch., George Washington U., 1949-53, dean, 1953-56, professorial lectr., 1956; clk. Supreme Ct. U.S., 1956-58; pres. U. Vt., 1958-64, U. Wyo., 1964-66, Nat. Life Ins. Co., 1966-74, also dir., 1966-74; chmn. bd. Equitable Life Assurance Soc. U.S., N.Y.C., 1974-82, Nat. Westminster Bank U.S.A., N.Y.C., 1982-85, Fidelity Union Life Ins. Co., Dallas, 1982-85. Bd. dirs. Sara Lee Corp., Certain-Teed Co., Norton Corp.; chmn. bd. dirs. Saint-Gobain Corp.; mem. Md. Legislature, 1946-50 Trustee Getty Mus., Malibu, Calif., 1979-92. Served to col. USMCR, 1942-46. Mem. Am. Coll. Life Underwriters, Order of Coif. Home: PO Box 4529 Tubac AZ 85646-4529 E-mail: fitzfey@aol.com.

FEY, WILLARD, global environmental researcher, educator; b. Cin., Ohio, June 29, 1935; s. Russell Richard and Irene Emma Fey; m. Mary Elizabeth Foley, June 21, 1958 (div. July 18, 1974); children: Lorenne Elizabeth, Leanne Susan, Erik Richard. BSEE, MIT, 1953—57, BS in Mgmt., 1957, MSEE, 1961. Instr. Sloan Sch. Mgmt. MIT, Cambridge, Mass., 1961—64; lectr. indsl. engring. dept. Northeastern U., Boston, 1963—68; asst. prof. Sloan Sch. Mgmt. MIT, Cambridge, 1964—67, dir. undergrad. sys. program, 1964—67; tech. staff The MITRE Corp., Bedford, Mass., 1967—68; assoc. prof. Indsl. and Sys. Engring. Sch. Ga. Inst. Tech., Atlanta, 1969—99; CEO Ecocosm Dynamics Ltd., Tucker, Ga., 2000—. Cons. The MITRE Corp., Boston, 1962—67, Reynolds, Smith & Hills, Jacksonville, Fla., 1969—71, Guyana Mining, Ltd., Georgetown, Guyana, 1980—83, Coca Cola Co. USA, Atlanta, 1981—83; prin. rsch. investigator U.S. Law Enforcement Assistance Adminstrn., Washington, 1972—74, USAF, Tyndall AFB, Panama City, Fla., 1979—80, U.S. Forest Svc., U. Ga. Office, Athens, Ga., 1981—88. Contbr. book; co-author (Luis Gutierrez): (book) Ecosystem Succession, 1980; co-prodr. Ann Lam : (video presentation) Pie in the Sky: A System Dynamics Perspective of Sustainability, 1998; co-prodr. The Bridge to Humanity's Future, 2000; contbr. reports and articles to profl. publs. Voting dep. Episcopal Ch., Detroit, 1988; bd. dirs. Episcopal Diocese Atlanta, 1983—85; mem. standing com. Episcopal Ch., Atlanta, 1986—88; sr. warden Episcopal Ch. of the Holy Cross, Decatur, Ga., 1986—88. Named to Leadership Atlanta, 1977. Mem.: Soc. Christian Ethics, Am. Schs. Oriental Rsch., Internat. Soc. for Sys. Scis., Sys. Dynamics Soc. (charter mem.), Bibl. Archaeology Study Group of Greater Atlanta, Inc. Episcopalian. Achievements include research in system dynamics philosophy and practice; dynamics of higher education, dynamics of Atlanta criminal justice system, forest management dynamics; development of environmental research that identified Ecocosm Paradox. Avocations: Biblical research, classical music, opera, sustainable architectural design, gardening. Office Fax: 770-908-9447. E-mail: fey@ecocosmdynamics.org.

FHANKS, HERSHEL, editor, writer; b. Sharon, Pa., Mar. 8, 1930; s. Martin and Mildred (Freedman) S.; m. Judith Alexander Weil, Feb. 20, 1966; children: Elizabeth Jean, Julia Emily. BA, Haverford (Pa.) Coll., 1952; MA, Columbia, 1953; LLB, Harvard, 1956. Bar: D.C. 1956. Trial atty. Dept. Justice, 1956-59; pvt. practice Washington, 1959-88; ptnr. Glassie, Pewett, Beebe & Shanks, 1964-88; editor Bibl. Archaeology Rev., Washington, 1975—. Pres. Bibl. Archaeology Soc., 1974—, Jewish Ednl. Ventures Inc., 1987—. Author: The Art and Craft of Judging, 1968, The City of David, 1973, Judaism in Stone, 1979, Jerusalem--An Archaeological Biography, 1995, The Mystery and Meaning of the Dead Sea Scolls, 1998, also articles; co-author: (with Ben Witherington III) The Brother of Jesus, 2003; co-editor: Recent Archaeology in the Land of Israel, 1984; editor: Ancient Israel, A Short History, 1988, revised edit., 1999, Christianity and Rabbinic Judaism, 1992, Understanding the Dead Sea Scrolls, 1992; editor Bible Rev., 1985—, Moment mag., 1987—, Archaeology Odyssey, 1998—; contbr. articles to profl. jours. Fellow Royal Asiatic Soc.; mem. ABA, D.C. Bar Assn., Am. Schs. Oriental Rsch., Soc. Bibl. Lit., Cosmos Club, Phi Beta Kappa. Home: 5208 38th St NW Washington DC 20015-1812 Office: Bibl Archaeology Soc 4710 41st St NW Washington DC 20016-1706 E-mail: hshanks@bib-arch.org. *I try to take time to identify what is important in my life, to focus on that and ignore the rest when it conflicts. It takes conscious effort not to dissipate energy on activities and attitudes that don't matter in the big picture of my priorities. Free to concentrate on what I value most, I try to accomplish something each day in a regular, habitual way.*

FIALA, DENNISON FAIRCHILD, technical consultant; b. Duluth, Minn., Apr. 18, 1935; s. Martin Josef and Grace Ingersoll (Fairchild) F.; m. Beverly Alice Ward, Dec. 28, 1957 (div. May 1984); children: Josef Ward, James Dennison. BME, Cornell U., 1958. Registered profl. engr., Conn. Rocket engr. Thiokol Chem. Corp., Elkton, Md., 1958-65; tech. rep. DuPont, Wilmington, Del., 1966-69; v.p. U.S. Grout Corp., Fairfield, Conn., 1970-84; pvt. practice cons. Danbury, Conn., 1985-92; pres. Cemtech, Inc., Yorktown Heights, N.Y., 1993. Cons. Lone Star Industries, Houston, 1985, CTS Cement, L.A., 1987-90, Blue Cir. Cement, Stamford, Conn., 1994. Chmn. Town Charter Commn., Ridgefield, Conn., 1978; candidate for U.S. Congress, 1980. Mem. ASTM. Achievements include design of first American object to land on the moon; patents for rapid setting patching materials; development of non shrink grouts, mortars, flooring materials and concrete admixtures.

FIALKOW, STEVEN, accountant; b. Bklyn., July 24, 1943; s. Irving and Ida (Berglass) F. m. Arlene Michele Klein, Oct. 19, 1963 (div. Oct. 1985); children: Cheri Ann, Laura Beth; m. Frances Theresa Miller, Apr. 15, 1986; 1 stepchild, Francis Joseph Miller. BBA, CUNY, 1965, MBA, 1970. CPA, N.Y. Profl. staff Price Waterhouse & Co., N.Y.C., 1965-69; asst. treas., contr. Anglo Am. Corp., N.Y.C., 1969-72; treas., contr. Video Playbacks, Inc., N.Y.C., 1972-75; adminstrv. mgr. Kenneth Leventhal & Co., N.Y.C., 1975-77; instr. N.Y. Inst. Tech., N.Y.C., 1975-79; ptnr. Herzig, Blumenfeld & Fialkow, CPAs, N.Y.C., 1979-81; assoc. dir. nat. acctg. and audit profl. edn. Touche Ross & Co., N.Y.C., 1981-83; mng. ptnr. Steven Fialkow & Co., CPAs, Coram, N.Y., El Paso, Tex., 1983—. Cons. Banis Securities Corps. N.Y.; chmn. fin. com. CCHOA, U.S. Virgin Islands, St. Croix. Bd. dirs. outreach program YMCA, L.I., N.Y. Mem. AICPA, N.Y. State Soc. CPAs, Nat. Conf. of CPA Practitioners, Mensa, Masons. Republican. Home: 368 Woodland Ct Coram NY 11727-3657 Office: Fialkow Bldg 976 Skyline Dr Coram NY 11727-3670 also: 4800 N Stanton St Unit 48 El Paso TX 79902-1219 E-mail: steve@fialkow.com.

FIALKY, GARY LEWIS, lawyer; b. Lawrence, Mass., July 24, 1942; s. Paul James and Estelle F. (Gottlieb) F.; m. Elaine N. Scotch, Aug. 19, 1967; children: Jeffrey, Joshua. BA, Am. Internat. Coll., Springfield, Mass., 1964; JD, Suffolk U., Boston, 1967; LLM in Taxation, Boston U., 1968. Bar: Mass. 1967, U.S. Dist. Ct. Mass. 1969, U.S. Dist. Ct. Conn. 1975. Ptnr. Alpert & Fialky, Springfield, Mass., 1968-75, Bacon & Wilson, P.C., Springfield, 1975—. Bd. trustees Naismith Meml. Basketball Hall of Fame, 2003—, Am. Internat. Coll., Springfield, 1984—88, Wibraham & Monson Acad., 1986—; mem. adv. bd. Western new Eng. Coll. Tax Adv. Bd. Mem. Estate Planning Coun. of Hampden County (pres. 1973, 74, 75), Springfield Tax Club (pres. 1985), Springfield C. of C. (pres. 1998-2000). Avocations: skiing, tennis, reading, running. Office: Bacon & Wilson PC 33 State St Springfield MA 01103-2003

FIBICH, HOWARD RAYMOND, retired newspaper editor; b. Oak Park, Ill., Jan. 6, 1932; s. Raymond Clarence and Vivian (Barrie) F.; m. Carrol Jean Anderson, June 5, 1954; children: Linda, Steven, Barbara. BS, Northwestern U., 1954, MS, 1955; postgrad., Columbia U., 1966. Reporter Kokomo (Ind.) Tribune, 1955-56; copy editor Milw. Jour., 1956-64, telegraph editor, 1964, asst. news editor, 1964-67, news editor, 1967-84, asst. mng. editor, 1984-86, dep. mng. editor, 1986-93; ret., 1994. Freelance writer, 1959-63; chmn. Mid-Am. Press Inst.; producer, host Jazz for the Quiet Hours, WYMS, Milw. Bd. dirs. Friends of WYMS. Named Milw. Media Hall of Fame, 1994. Mem. Mid.-Am. Press Inst. (bd. dirs. 1976-86, chmn. 1980-81), Wis. History Found., AP Mng. Editors Assn. (new tech. com.), Milw. Press Club, Kappa Tau Alpha. Home: 17800 Caribou Pass Unit B Brookfield WI 53045-2041

FIBIGER, JOHN ANDREW, life insurance company executive; b. Copenhagen, Apr. 27, 1932; came to U.S., 1934, naturalized, 1953; s. Borge Rottboll and Ruth Elizabeth (Wadmond) F.; m. Barbara Mae Stuart, June 22, 1956; children: Karen Ruth McCarthy, Katherine Louise. BA, U. Minn., 1953, MA, 1954; postgrad., U. Wis. With Lincoln Nat. Life Ins. Co., Ft. Wayne, Ind., 1956-57; with Bankers Life Ins. Co. Nebr., Lincoln, 1959-73, sr. v.p. group, 1972-73; with New Eng. Mut. Life Ins. Co., Boston, 1973-89, vice chmn., pres., chief operating officer, 1981-89; with Transam Life Cos., 1991-94; exec. v.p., CFO, then pres. Transamerica Occidental Life Ins. Co., L.A., 1994-95, chmn., 1995-97. Past vice chmn. Actuarial Bd. for Counseling and Discipline. Life trustee, past chmn. Mus. Sci., Boston, 1989-91; past overseer New Eng. Med. Ctr., Boston Symphony Orch.; past bd. dirs. Menninger Found., past v.p.; bd. dirs. L.A. Chamber Orch.; past chmn. Menninger Fund; bd. dirs. U. So. Calif. Sch. Gerontology; past trustee Calif. Mus. Sci. and Industry. Fellow Soc. Actuaries (past bd. dirs.); mem. Nat. Acad. Social Ins. (founding mem.), Am. Acad. Actuaries (past pres.), Assn. Calif. Life Cos. (past bd. chmn.).

FICARRA, BERNARD JOSEPH, former surgeon, legal medicine and bioethics consultant; b. N.Y.C., Jan. 1, 1914; s. Humphrey and Rose Marie (D'Ambra) F.; m. Jean Alice Augustine, Aug. 31, 1966; 1 son, Bernard Thaddeus. BA magna cum laude, St. Francis Coll., 1935, ScB, 1936; MD, Georgetown U., 1939; ScD, U. Steubenville, 1950; LLD, St. Francis Coll., N.Y.; PhD, Minerva U., Milan, Italy, 1960. Diplomate Am. Bd. Surgery. Surg. intern Kings County Hosp. Med. Ctr., Bklyn., 1939-41, resident pathology, 1941-42, resident surgery, 1942-44; fellow surgery Lahey Clin. Found., Burlington, 1946-48; practice medicine specializing in surgery N.Y.C., 1948-60, Greenvale, N.Y., 1953-80; mem. vis. surg. staff Kings County, St. Peters, Holy Family, St. Mary's hosps. Dir. surg. rsch. Ficarra Found., Inc., 1949-69; prof. physiology St. Francis Coll., 1948-51; prof. rsch. physiology St. John's U. Postgrad. Sch., 1951-61; professorial rsch. assoc. L.I. U., Postgrad. Sch., 1961-73; dir. Somerset Enterprises, Ltd., Doric Corp. Author: Diagnostic Synopsis of Acute Surgical Abdomen, 1950; Emergency Surgery, 1953; Thyroid and Parathyroid Diseases, 1958; Surgical and Allied Malpractice, 1968; Medicolegal Handbook, 1983; Medicolegal Examination Evaluation and Report, 1986, Abortion Analyzed, 1989, Feudal Chateau, 1990, Church on The Hill, 1990, Virtue Lost: Virtue Found, 2000, Evolution: Fact, Fiction, or Fancy, 2001, Real Property: A Perilous Possession, 2001, Bioethics Rise, Decline, and Fall, 2001, Virtue Lost: Virtue Found, 2002, Royal Religious Revolutionaries, 2002, Stem-cell Research, 2003, Endless Battle Between Good and Evil, 2003; mem. emeritus adv. bd. jour. Med. Malpractice Prevention; mem. editl. bd. Jour. Contemporary Health Law and Policy; contbr. 270 articles to profl. jours. Trustee L.I. Ednl. TV Coun. Inc., Sta. WLIW; pres. Cath. Acad. Scis. U.S.A.; cons. Holy Land Christian Charity. Recipient Golden Anniversary Alumni citation, Georgetown U., 1989, Recognition award N.Y. Acad. Sci., N.Y. Acad. Sci.; named to Alumni Hall of Fame St. Francis Preparatory Sch., N.Y., 1990; received Silver Palm of Jerusalem, His Beatitude Archbishop Michele Sabbah, Latin Patriarch of Jerusalem, 1988, Gold medal for Svc. to Holy Land, His Patrimony Rev. Joseph Nazzaro, OFM Custos of the Holy Land, Archbishop Boyle Archdiocesan medal James Cardinal Hickey, 1998, Knight of Merit with Star Sacred Mil. Constantinian Order St. George, Spain. Fellow Am. Coll. Gastroenterology (com. for legal matters), Am. Coll. Legal Medicine (edn. com.), Am. Coll. Angiology (achievement honor award 1964-65); mem. AMA (Physicians Recognition award 2001), N.Y. State Med. Soc., N.Y. Acad. Medicine, N.Y. Acad. Scis., N.Y. Soc. Med. Jurisprudence, Acad. Templars (Bologna, Italy), Greenvale C. of C., Lahey Clinic Alumni Assn. (coun.), Cath. Acad. Scis. (.U.S. pres.), Alpha Omega Alpha, Pi Alpha, Phi Chi. Lodges: Lions (hon., pres. 1976-78, Knight of Malta, Knight Cmdr. of St. Gregory the Great), Equestrian Order of the Holy Sepulchre of Jerusalem (sect. rep. southeastern lieutenancy Washington, So. Md., No. Va., lt. mid. Atlantic lieutenancy Del., Md., Va., W.Va., Tenn., N.C., Washington, mil. svcs. of USA, Knight Grand Cross, lt. by grand magisterium, lt. of honor Equestrian Order Holy Sepulchre of Jerusalem conferred by Grand Master of Order, Carlo Cardinal Furno, 1998, Vatican City State). Office: PO Box 9611 Washington DC 20016-9611 Fax: 301 963-6049.

FICCAGLIA, LESLIE M. psychologist, portrait artist; b. Huntington, NY, Oct. 3, 1943; d. Sewall M. and L. Lillian (Bartok) Pastor; m. Anthony W. Ficcaglia, Nov. 4, 1968; children: Jeremy Clinton, Linnet Kyung. BA in Psychology, NYU, 1965; MA in Psychology, Western Wash. U., Bellingham, 1971; cert. sch. psychologist, Rowan Coll., Glassboro, N.J., 1984. Cert. sch. psychologist. Clin. psychologist Eastern Diagnostic and Evaluation Ctr., Phila., 1968; staff clin. psychologist Vineland State Sch., NJ, 1970—74; staff psychologist Cumberland County Hosp., Hopewell Twp., NJ, 1974—81; sch. psychologist Downe Twp. Bd. Edn., Newport, NJ, 1981—2000, grantswriter, 1990—2000; portrait artist Minnamuska Creek Studio, Port Elizabeth, NJ, 1995—. Devel. ecotourism website; author newspaper articles. Mem. Maurice River Twp. Planning Bd., 1979-98, chair, 1990-98; mem. Cumberland County Planning Bd., Bridgeton, NJ, 1982—, vice chair, 1988—; mem. NJ State Pinelands Commn., New Lisbon, 1996—; trustee Assn. NJ Environ. Commns., Mendham, 1995-99, adv. bd., 2000—; trustee Citizens United to Protect the Maurice River and Its Tributaries, 1999—; mem. Del. Bayshore adv. bd. Nature Conservancy, 1998—; founding chmn. Riverfront Renaissance Ctr. Arts, Millville, NJ, bd. dir., 1999—. Recipient Outstanding Svc. award Cumberland County Bd. Freeholders, 1991; EPA Region 2 Environ. Qualtiy Award for Individuals, 2003. Mem.: Portrait Soc. Am., Am. Soc. Portrait Artists., Nat. Assn. Sch. Psychologists, NJ Planning Ofcl., Phi Delta Kappa. Avocations: land use planning, environmental issues. Home: Minnamuska Creek Farm and Studio Box 27 Port Elizabeth NJ 08348

FICEK, VINCE H. lawyer; b. Dickinson, N.D., Feb. 24, 1949; s. Vince F. and Emily L. (Kralicek) F.; m. Roxanne Herberholz, Apr. 23, 1994; children: Mariah Kelsey, Delanie Chelsey. BA in Social Sci., U. N.D., 1971, JD, 1976. Bar: N.D. 1976, U.S. Dist. Ct. N.D. 1979. Trust officer 1st Nat. Bank & Trust, Dickinson, 1976-77; pvt. practice Dickinson, 1978-92; ptnr. Reichert Buresh Herauf & Ficek, P.C., Dickinson, 1992-96, Ficek & Buresh, P.C., Dickinson, 1997—2001; prin. Ficek Legal Svcs., Dickinson, 2002—. City atty. City of Dickinson, 1980-91; petroleum landman, Dickinson, 1979-81. Candidate for N.D. Ho. of Reps., 1989, 91. Mem. N.D. Trial Lawyers Assn. (bd. govs., 1997-2003, sec., treas., v.p., 1990-94, pres. elect 1994-95, pres. 1995-96), Stark-Dunn County Bar Assn. (pres. 1980-81), S.W. Jud. Dist. Bar Assn. (sec.-treas. 1994-96, pres. 1996-98), State Bar Assn. (bd. govs. 1996-98). Democrat. Roman Catholic. Avocations: snow skiing, trout fishing, reading, golfing, fishing. Office: Ficek Legal Svcs PO Box 866 Dickinson ND 58602-0866 E-mail: vhf@ndsupernet.com.

FICHANDLER, ZELDA, director; m. Thomas C. Fichandler (separated); children: Hal, Mark. BA in Russian Lang. and Lit., Cornell U., 1945; MA in Theater Arts, George Washington U., 1950, Doctor in Humane Letters (hon.), 1974, Smith Coll. Co-founder, producing dir. Arena Stage, Washington, 1950-97. Former vis. prof. U. Tex.; former prof. theater arts Boston U.; former artistic cons. Huntington Theater Co.; former artistic dir. The Acting Co.; chmn. grad. acting program Tisch Sch. of the Arts, NYU. Dir. at Arena Stage: (plays) A Doll House, The Three Sisters, Death of a Salesman, An Enemy of the People, Six Characters in Search of an Author, Duck Hunting, Ascent of Mt. Fuji, Screenplay, Inherit the Wind, After the Fall, The Crucible. Recipient Artistic Founder award Cultural Alliance of Greater Washington, 1989, Common Wealth award, John Houseman award The Acting Co., The Margo Jones award, Washingtonian of the Yr. award, Brandeis U. Creative Arts award, Tony award, 1976, Nat. Medal of Arts award, 1997;Inducted to The Theatre Hall of Fame, 1999. Office: Tisch School of the Arts Graduate Acting NYU 721 Broadway Fl 5 New York NY 10003-6807

FICHENBERG, ROBERT GORDON, newspaper editor, consultant; b. Phila., Jan. 1, 1920; s. Samuel Harrison and Katherine (Gordon) F.; m. Ruth Pollard, Sept. 14, 1947; children: Ruth Ann, Kathryn Leigh. BS, Syracuse U., 1940. City editor Adirondack Daily Enterprise, Saranac Lake, N.Y., 1940-42; reporter, copy editor, asst. city editor Binghamton (N.Y.) Press, 1942-57; mng. editor Knickerbocker News, Albany, N.Y., 1957-66, exec. editor, 1966-78; chief Washington bur. Newhouse Newspapers, editor Newhouse News Svc., 1979-91; writer, cons. Nat. Dist. Attys. Assn., Washington, 1991—. Bd. dirs. Nat. Press Found. Served to 1st lt. Signal Corps AUS, 1942-46; to capt. U.S. Army, 1951-52. Mem. Am. Soc. Newspaper Editors, N.Y. State Soc. Newspaper Editors (pres.), AP Mng. Editors Assn., White House Corrs. Assn., N.Y. State AP Assn. (past pres.), Soc. Profl. Journalists, Nat. Press Club, Army and Navy Club, Fed. City Club, Univ. Club Washington, Gridiron Club (Washington). Home: 1605 Mason Hill Dr Alexandria VA 22307-1930 Office: Nat Dist Attys Assn 99 Canal Center Plz Ste 510 Alexandria VA 22314-1588 E-mail: robert.fichenberg@ndaa-apri.org.

FICHERA, LEWIS CARMEN, lawyer; b. Woodbury, N.J., July 16, 1949; s. Paul Benjamin and Mary (Cristaudo) F. BSBA, Villanova U., 1971; JD, Widener U., 1982. Bar: N.J. 1984, Pa. 1984. Cost analyst Catalytic, Inc., Phila., 1974-76, field cost analyst Balt., 1976-77, cost analyst London, 1977-78, chief cost analyst Phila., 1978-82; ptnr. Cristaudo & Fichera, West Deptford, N.J., 1984-86; pvt. practice West Deptford, 1987—. Pres. Diversified Funding Svcs., Inc. Active Cristaudo for N.J. Ho. of Reps. campaign, 1988. With USANG, 1971-77. Mem. Am. Cash Flow Assn., Cash Flow Profls. Network (sec.), N.J. State Bar ASsn., Pa. Bar Assn., Gloucester County Bar Assn., Fitness Unltd., Nat. Orgn. of Social Security Claimant's Reps., Nat. Orgn. of Vet.'s Advocates, Cherry Hill Regional C. of C. Republican. Roman Catholic. Home: 773 Atlantic Ave Sewell NJ 08080-1502 Office: 773 W Atlantic Ave Sewell NJ 08080-1502 Fax: 856-468-3089. E-mail: lcfichera@yahoo.com.

FICHTEL, RUDOLPH ROBERT, retired association executive; b. N.Y.C., Dec. 12, 1915; s. Paul Gotthard and Helen (Szapka) F.; m. Elsie E. Terebesy, Dec. 24, 1942; children: Nancy Lynn, Robert Paul, Richard John. BBA cum laude, Coll. City N.Y., 1938; cert., Am. Inst. Banking, 1941; diploma fin. pub. relations, Northwestern U., 1950; MBA, NYU, 1951; diploma banking, Rutgers U. Stonier Grad. Sch. Banking, 1954. Tchr. N.Y.C. Pub. Schs., 1938-39; adminstr. East River Savs. Bank, 1939-42; dir. pub. relations, editor, asst. sec. Savs. Banks Assn. N.Y. State, 1945-53; dir. pub. relations counsel, savs. and mortgage div. Am. Bankers Assn., N.Y.C. and Washington, 1953-64; nat. dir. Am. Inst. Banking, 1964-78; regional v.p. United Student Aid Funds, Inc., N.Y.C., 1978-87. Mem. lender relations com. Higher Edn. Loan Programs; mem. faculty Am. Inst. Banking, Stonier Grad. Sch. Banking; contbg. editor Am. Inst. Banking textbooks; speaker. Contbr. articles to profl. jours. Vol. tutor Literacy Program, N.Y.C.; income tax counsellor Am. Assn. Retired Persons. Served to capt. AUS, 1942-45, ETO. Recipient highest award citation Internat. Council Indsl. Editors, 1948, Dr. Marcus Nadler award for excellence in finance; N.Y. U., 1951 Mem. Beta Gamma Sigma. Home: 65-19 170th St Flushing NY 11365-1949 *Success in my life has been the result of hard work, continuing search for knowledge, constant effort to understand and relate to people, and total dedication to excellence in full partnership with a loving family.*

FICHTER, DAVID HARRY, conservationist, environmentalist; b. Englewood, N.J., Jan. 18, 1941; s. Harry Charles and Mary Louise (Kay) F. BS, Ariz. State U., 1966; BFT, Am. Grad. Sch. Internat. Mgmt., 1967. Cert. hazardous materials mgr., registered environ. mgr. Dir. environ. affairs Chgo. Bridge & Iron Co., 1967—2001. Elected commr. Oak Brook (Ill.) Park Dist., 1995-99, pres. 1998-99; pres. Mayslake Landmark Conservancy, 1994-2002. Mem. Sigma Lambda Chi. Home: 3804 Washington St Oak Brook IL 60523-2749

FICHTHORN, FONDA GAY, gifted and talented educator, retired principal; b. Jamestown, Ohio, Sept. 4, 1949; d. Robert William and Evelyn Elizabeth (Schmitt) Fichthorn. BS, Otterbein Coll., 1970; MEd, Wright State U., 1983. Cert. tchr., prin., supr., elem. music, gifted edn. Ohio. Elem. tchr. Groveport (Ohio) Madison Schs., 1970-71, Miami Trace Schs., Washington Court House, Ohio, 1971-92, prin., 1992-2000, ret., 2000. Part-time gifted coord. Clark County Schs., Ohio; part-time intervention coord. Miami Trace Schs., Ohio. Bd. dirs. Scioto Paint Valley Mental Health Ctr., crisis vol. Recipient Class Act award Sta. WDTN-TV, 1990. Mem. AAUW, Phi Delta Kappa, Delta Kappa Gamma. Republican. Avocations: piano, flute, travel, gardening. Home: 7313 State Route 729 NW Washington Court House OH 43160-9526

FICHTNER, MARGARIA, journalist; b. Lakeland, Fla., May 4, 1944; d. August Albert and Margaret Louise (Kelly) F. BA, Fla. So. Coll., 1966. Book critic Miami Herald. Recipient First Place criticism award Green Eyeshade, Am. Assn. Sunday and Feature Editors, 1996, First Place criticism award Fla. Soc. Newspaper Editors, 1997, First Place Criticism Sunshine State award Soc. Profl. Jour., 2003. Office: The Miami Herald Pub Co One Herald Plz Miami FL 33132-1693 E-mail: mfichtner@herald.com.

FICK, GARY WARREN, agronomy educator, forage crops researcher; b. O'Neill, Nebr., July 10, 1943; s. Walter Henry and Doris Marie (Parks) F.; m. Mae Ellen Ruddell, June 29, 1969; children— Joseph, David, Charles BS, U. Nebr., 1965; diploma Agr. Sci., Massey U., 1968; PhD, U. Calif., Davis, 1971. Asst. prof. Cornell U., Ithaca, N.Y., 1971-76, assoc. prof., 1976-84, prof., 1984—, acting chair dept. soil crop and atmospheric scis., 1993, 95, tchg. leader soil crop and atmospheric scis., 1994—99; vis. scientist Lincoln Coll., N.Z., 1977-78; tchg. leader crop and soil scis. Cornell U., Ithaca, NY, 2002—. Assoc. editor Agronomy Jour., 1978-81. Assoc. editor Jour. of Prodn. Agr., 1987-93; mem. editl. bd. Jour. of Sustainable Agr., 1996—; contbr. articles to profl. jours. and monographs. Fellow Crop Sci. Soc. Am., Am. Soc. Agronomy (tchg. award N.E. br. 1991); mem. Am. Forage and Grassland Coun. (Merit cert. 1989), Sigma Xi, Gamma Sigma Delta (Cornell pres. 1992-93), SUNY Chancellor's tchg. award 1995. Office: Cornell U Dept Crop and Soil Scis Ithaca NY 14853 E-mail: gwf2@cornell.edu.

FICK, HERBERT J. chemist, consultant; b. Rice County, Jan. 4, 1937; s. Herbert Bernhard and Alice Minnie Fick; m. Lola Marie Nordin, Apr. 20, 1960 (div.); children: Herbert Blaine, Heidi Marie, John Martin; m. Patricia Gail Fick, June 18, 1988. BA, St. Olaf Coll., 1959; MS, U. Chgo., 1960. Self employed, Northfield, Minn.; scientist Bergquist Co., Chanhassen, Minn., Sheldahl Co., Northfield. Dir. Stafford Blaine Design and Ltd., Mpls. Named Disting. Alumni, Northfield Pub. Schs., 2003. Mem.: Guild Metalsmiths (dir. 2003). Lutheran. Achievements include 16 U.S. patents, principally electrical insulation and heat transfer, 1962-2000. Avocations: diving, skiing, ballroom dancing. Home: 519 E Eighth St Northfield MN 55057

FICKENSCHER, GERALD H. chemicals company executive; b. Buenos Aires, 1943; Graduate, Cath. U. Argentina, Buenos Aires, 1967; Post-Graduate, Cath. U. Argentina, 1970. V.p., CFO Uniroyal Chem. Corp., Middlebury, Conn.; v.p.-Europe, corp. officer Crompton Corp., Middlebury, 1994—. Home: 3200 Park Ave Unit 6b1 Bridgeport CT 06604-1147 Office: 199 Benson Rd Middlebury CT 06749 E-mail: gerald_fickenscher@cromptoncorp.com.

FICKETT, EDWARD HALE, architect, planner, arbitrator; b. L.A., 1923; s. George Edward and Marguerite (Hale) F.; m. Joyce Helen Steinberg, Apr. 8, 1982. BArch, grad. studies in engrng and archaelogy, U. So. Calif.; M in City Planning, M in City Planning, M in Arch, MIT. Registered architect, 50 states. Pvt. practice architecture, L.A., 1950—. Archtl. advisor to Pres. Dwight D. Eisenhower, 1957-60; cons. to Federal Govt. on Housing; wrote guidelines and specifications for HUD, VA, FHA; Calif. Housing Bd. under Gov. Edmund G. Pat Brown; honored with fellowship in AIA, 1969; archtl. commr. City of Beverly Hills, Calif., 1977-86, chmn. Archtl. Commn., 1979-82; guest lectr., vis. prof. UCLA, U. Calif., Berkeley, MIT, Stanford U., U. So. Calif., U. Fla., Calif. Poly. State U.-San Luis Obispo, Rensselaer Poly. Inst., N.Y., U. Chgo.; arbitrator Nat. Panel Arbitrators, 1961—, Am. Arbitration Assn., 1963—. Archtl. works include L.A. Harbor (Port of L.A.) Cargo and Passenger Terminals, San Pedro, Sands Hotel, Las Vegas, Nev., La Costa Resort and Condominiums, Carlsbad, Calif., Las Cruces Resort Hotel, La Paz, Mex., Hacienda Hotel, Cabo San Lucas, Mex., Ocotillo Lodge Hotel, Palm Springs, Calif., Mammoth Mountain Inn, Mammoth, Calif., Murietta Hot Springs Resort, Murietta, Calif., Stallion Springs Resort, Tehachapi, Calif., Bistro Gardens Restaurant, Beverly Hills, Calif., Spago Restaurant, Beverly Hills, Scandia Restaurant, West Hollywood, Calif., Nicks Fishmarket Restaurant, West Hollywood, Univ. High Sch., UCLA Faculty Ctr., L.A. Police Acad., L.A., master plans for Edwards AFB, Calif., Norton AFB, Calif., Murphy Canyon Heights Naval Base, Calif., Los Alametos Naval Base, Calif., San Pedro Naval base, Calif., L.A. City Hall Hist. and Seismic Renovation, Nethercutt Antique Car Mus., Dodger Stadium, others; comml. devels., master planned communities, office bldgs., restaurants, resorts, hotels, homes, condominiums, shopping ctrs., air force bases, naval bases, schs., renovation of hist. bldgs., historic & seismic rehab, designed over 60,000 homes. Mem. Gov. Pat Brown's Housing Bd. for Calif.; U.S. del. to Internat. Congress of Archs. Lt. comdr. Sea Bees, USN. Recipient Merit of Honor award by Pres. of U.S., L.A. Conservancy Preservation Arch. award, 1999, National Progressive Architecture Design awards, city beautification awards from L.A., Beverly Hills, Reno, Seattle, numerous Nat. Assn. Home Builders awards, Sunset Magazine and House and Home awards, Better Homes and Gardens House of Yr. awards, Nat. Assn. Home Builders awards, Los Angeles Conservancy Archtl. Design Award, 1999, Nat. Hist. Monuments Archtl. Design Award, 1999, Housing Hall of Fame, other awards. Fellow AIA (AIA First Honor Awards, numerous AIA merit of honor awards, pres. So. Calif. chpt. 1958-62, pres. Calif. chpt. 1962, chmn. Nat. Ethics Com., featured speaker nat. convs., lectr., formulated and participated in AIA Univ. Lecture series, fellow 1969), Nat. Commn. for Bldg. Industry (chmn. 1962-72), Nat. Assn. Home Builders (speaker nat. convs.), Calif. Coun. Architects (sec. 1960), Am. Archtl. Found. Octagon Soc. (charter mem.), U. So. Calif. Archtl. Guild (charter mem.). Avocations: tennis, golf. Office: 7421 Beverly Blvd Los Angeles CA 90036-2703 Fax: 323-939-8060.

FICKINGER, WAYNE JOSEPH, communications executive; b. Belleville, Ill., June 23, 1926; s. Joseph and Grace (Belton) F.; m. Joan Mary Foley, June 16, 1951; children: Michael, Joan, Jan, Ellen, Steven. BA, U. Ill., 1949; MS, Northwestern U., 1950. Overnight editor United Press, Chgo., 1950-51; spl. project writer Sears-Roebuck & Co., Chgo., 1951-53; account exec. Calkins & Holden Advt. Agy., Chgo., 1953-56; account supr. Foote, Cone & Belding Advt. Agy., Chgo., N.Y.C., 1956-63; sr. v.p. J. Walter Thompson Co., Chgo., 1963-72, exec. v.p., dir. U.S. Western div., 1972-75, pres. N.Am. divsn., 1975-78; pres., chief operating officer J. Walter Thompson Co. Worldwide, 1978-79; pres. JWT Group, Inc., 1979-82, trustee retirement fund, dir., mem. exec. com., 1980-82; mng. dir. Spencer Stuart & Assocs., 1982-83; vice chmn., dir. Bozell, Jacobs, Kenyon & Eckhardt Inc., Chgo., 1984-89; pres. Mid-Am. Com., Chgo., 1989-93; exec. v.p., dir. Monroe Comm. Corp., 1992—; v.p., dir. Adams Comm., 1994—. Mem. adv. bd. Phase One Inc.; bd. dirs. Alford Group, Inc. Fundraising cons. Nat. Mental Health Assn., 1970; comm. counselor Cook County (Ill.) Rep. Orgn., 1970; bd. dirs. Off-the-Street Club, Chgo., 1974-77, Mundelein Coll., 1985-91, United Cerebral Palsy, 1986, Chgo. Conv. and Tourists Bur., 1986-90, Columbia Coll., Chgo., 1990-95, Fermi Inst. Hadron Therapy, 2000-02; chmn. Chgo. Funding Statue of Liberty, 1986, March of Dimes, 1987, Mayor's Chgo. Tourism Com., 1990-92; mem. steering com. El Valor, 1997-98. With USNR, 1943-46. Recipient Five-Year Meritorious Service award A.R.C., 1963, Service award Mental Health Assn., 1970 Mem. Am. Assn. Advt. Agys., Council on Fgn. Relations (Chgo. com.), Sigma Delta Chi, Alpha Delta Sigma. Clubs: Exmoor Country (Highland Park, Ill.); N.Y. Athletic; Mid-Am. (Chgo.), Internat. (Chgo.). Office: 350 S Beverly Dr Ste 300 Beverly Hills CA 90212-4817 E-mail: bignoise3@hotmail.com.

FICKLER, ARLENE, lawyer; b. Phila., Apr. 21, 1951; BA cum laude, U. Pa., 1971, JD cum laude, 1974. Bar: Pa. 1974, D.C. 1980, U.S. Supreme Ct. 1989. Ptnr. Hoyle Fickler Herschel & Mathes LLP, Phila. Staff atty. Commn. on Revision of Fed. Ct. Appellate System, 1974-75; exec. asst. Bicentennial Com. Jud. Conf. of U.S., 1975-76. Comment editor U. Pa. Law Rev., 1973-74; contbr. articles to law jours. Pres. U. Pa. Law Sch. Alumni Bd. Mgrs., 1997-99; trustee Jewish Fedn. of Greater Phila., 1981-88, 89-93, 94-98, 99—, Phila. Bar Found., 1993-98, Jewish Cmty. Rels. Coun. Greater Phila., 1983-94, 98-00; trustee Jewish Cmty. Ctrs. of Phila., 1997—, chair, 2003—; trustee HIAS Immigration Svcs. Phila., 1998—; mem. United Jewish Appeal Nat. Young Women's Leadership Cabinet, 1982-87; v.p. Phila. chpt. Am. Jewish Congress, 1995-2001; co-chmn. Phila. Maccabi Games, 2001. Recipient Mrs. Isidore Kohn Young Leadership award Jewish Fedn. Greater Phila., 1981, Next Generation Leadership award Jewish Cmty. Ctrs. Assn., 2000, award of merit U. Pa. Law Sch. Alumni, 2001. Mem. ABA, Am. Law Inst., Am. Bar Found., Pa. Bar Assn., D.C. Bar, Phila. Bar Assn. (chmn. fed. cts. com. 1992), Fed. Bar Coun. of Second Cir., U. Pa. Am. Inn of Ct. Office: Hoyle Fickler Herschel & Mathes LLP One South Broad St 1500 Philadelphia PA 19103 E-mail: afickler@hoylelawfirm.com.

FICKLIN, ROBERT LEE, soil scientist, research scientist; b. Warrensburg, Mo., May 30, 1968; s. Donald Lee and Connie Lynn (Spears) Ficklin; m. Darla Hope Christopher, Nov. 3, 1987 (div. Apr. 2000); 1 child, Robert Scot. BS in Forestry, U. Mo., 1992, MS in Forestry, 1997, PhD in Soil Sci., 2002. Energy conservation cons. City of Columbia, Mo., 1993-99; instr. agrl. econs. U. Mo., Columbia, 1998, rsch. specialist, 1999—2002; asst. prof. U. Ark., Monticello, 2002—. Activities and rsch. coord. Prairie Fork Conservation Area, Williamsburg, Mo., 1999—2002. Contbr. articles to profl. jours. Asst. scout master Boy Scouts Am., Columbia, 1998—99. Rsch. grantee, Mo. Dept. Conservation, 1997. Mem.: Soil Sci. Soc. Am., Soc. Am. Foresters, Sigma Xi, Xi Sigma, Gamma Sigma Delta. Avocations: horticulture, website development, bicycling. Home: #12 Hickory St Monticello AR 71655 E-mail: ficklinr@finclinsoils.net.

FICKLING, KARL FREDERICK, church consultant, educator; b. Sacramento, Calif., Dec. 22, 1957; s. Robert Mitchell and Grace Reddick Fickling; m. Dana Lori Terry, Oct. 3, 1981; children: Ryan Stuart, Chase Garrison. BA, Baylor U., 1980; MDiv, Southwestern Bapt. Theol. Sem., Ft. Worth, 1984, PhD, 1990. Pastor Pk. Forest Bapt. Ch., Dallas, 1989—99; intentional interim specialist Bapt. Gen. Conv. of Tex., Dallas, 2000—. Mem. Tarrant County Interfaith Network, Ft. Worth, 2002—, Lunch Bunch, Ft. Worth, 2001—; adj. prof. pastoral care Southwestern Bapt. Theol. Sem., Ft. Worth, 1996—2000; adj. prof. adult edn. Dallas Bapt. U., 1993—. Contbr. articles to profl. jours. Trustee Dallas Bapt. U., 1994—2003. Mem.: Tarrant Bapt. Assn. Intentional Interims (pres. 2002). Baptist. Avocations: guitar, travel. Home and Office: 4720 Lincolnshire Dr Grand Prairie TX 75052

FIDDICK, PAUL WILLIAM, government official, broadcasting executive; b. St. Joseph, Mo., Nov. 20, 1949; s. Lowell Duane and Betty Jean (Manring) F.; m. Julie Hanna Lorms, July 31, 1983; children: Lea Elizabeth, Hanna Manring. BJ, U. Mo., 1971. Account exec. Sta. KCMO-KFMU, Kansas City, Mo., 1971-72, Sta. WEZW, Milw., 1972-74, dir. sales mktg., 1974-76, v.p., gen. mgr., 1976-81; sr. v.p. Multimedia Broadcasting Co., Milw., 1981; pres. Multimedia Radio, Cin., 1982-86, Radio Group, Heritage Communications, Inc., Des Moines, 1986-87, Radio Group, Heritage Media Corp., Dallas, 1987-98; dir, vice chmn. RadioWave.com, Inc., Schaumburg, Ill., 1998-99, acting pres., 1999; asst. sec. USDA, Washington, 1999-2001, dir. USDA Grad. Sch., 2000—; dir. Nat. Assn. of Broadcasters, Washington, 1994-98; pres. Emmis Internat., Wash., 2002—; dir. pres. Democracy Radio Inc., Wash., 2002—. Dir. Radio Advt. Bur., N.Y.C., 1983—99, chmn., 1993—94; trustee Washington Chorus, 2000—; mem. acad. staff U. Wis., Milw., 1978—81; mem. adv. bd. Advanced Microbial Solutions LLC, Pilot Point, Tex., 2002—. Elder Westminster Presbyn. Ch., Dallas, 1997-99. Named one of 40 Most Powerful People in Radio, Radio Ink Mag., 1996, Fifth Estater, Broadcasting Mag., 1990, Up and Coming Radio Exec. of Yr., Radio Only mag., 1983, recipient Pub.'s Profile, Radio and Records mag., 1998. Mem. Phi Eta Sigma, Kappa Tau Alpha.

FIDDLER NICHOLS, BARBARA DILLOW, sales and marketing professional; b. Decatur, Ill., Sept. 2, 1940; s. N. Eugene and Ruth (Kirchhoff) Dillow; children: John Eugene, Thomas Crawford. BA, U. Vt., 1963. Grad. registrar Troy State U., European divsn., Wiesbaden, W. Ger., 1977-79; adminstrv. asst. Mt. Mansfield Co. Mktg. Dept., Stowe, Vt., 1980-84; asst. dir. promotions and advt. Rossignol Ski Co., Tennis divsn., Williston, Vt., 1984-85; project mgr. Birch Hill Devel. Co., Stowe, 1985-86; asst. to dir. of devel. Johnson State Coll., Johnson, Vt., 1986-89; asst. dir. devel. The Trustees of Reservations, Beverly, Mass., 1989-91, adminstr. Epsilon Inc., Burlington, Mass., 1991-94; group sales mgr. Topnotch at Stowe, Vt., 1994-98. Bd. dirs., pres. Robert Alden Ellsworth Trust, Johnson, Vt., 1991—. Trustee Fund for Johnson (Vt.) State Coll.; bd. dirs. United Way of Lamoille County, Hyde Park, 1988-92, 1994-2000, pres., 1998-99; mem. Stowe (Vt.) Planning Commn., 1988-92; bd. dirs., chmn. fin. and fundraising com. Johnson Friends of Arts, 1986-88; regional trustee Vt. Symphony Orch., 1995-2000. Mem. Women in Devel. in Greater Boston, Lamoille Valley C. of C. (bd. dirs.). Republican. Episcopalian. Avocations: skiing, knitting, reading, creative cooking. Home and Office: 227 Upper Baird Rd Stowe VT 05672-4203

FIDEL, RAYA, library science educator; b. Tel Aviv, Jan. 18, 1945; came to U.S., 1977; BSc, Tel Aviv U., 1970; MLS, Hebrew U., Jerusalem, 1976; PhD, U. Md., 1982. Tchr. Adult Edn. Ctr., Jerusalem, 1971-72; br. libr. Hebrew U., Jerusalem, 1972-77; asst. prof. libr. sci. U. Wash., Seattle, 1982-87, assoc. prof. libr. sci., 1987-2000, prof. Info. Sch., 2000—, head Ctr. Human-Info. Interaction The Info. Sch., 2003—. Vis. libr. Duke U. Libr., Durham, N.C., 1992-93. Author: Database Design, 1987; editor Advances in Classification, 1991-94 (award 1992-94); contbr. articles to profl. publs. Recipient Research award Am. Society for Information Science, 1994 Mem. AAUP (chair U. Wash. chpt. 1990-92, pres. state conf. 1992-97), Assn. Computing Machinery, Am. Soc. Info. Sci. (dir.-at-large 2000-02). Home: 5801 Phinney Ave N Seattle WA 98103-5862

FIDLER, CAROL ANN, accountant; b. Sharon, Pa., Apr. 28, 1942; d. Thomas Daniel and E. Geraldine (Boyer) Bracken; m. Michael Lawrence Fidler, Aug. 23, 1969 (div. 1991); 1 child, Michael Lawrence Jr. Diploma, Akron City Hosp. Sch. Nursing, 1963; BS in Chemistry, Kent State U., 1967; MS in Preventive Medicine, Ohio State U., 1972, MBA, 1979. CPA, Ohio; RN, Ohio; cert. valuation analyst, Nat. Assn. Cert. Valuation Analysts. Rsch. assoc. dept. preventive medicine Ohio State U., Columbus, Ohio, 1969-70; dir. Riverside Meth. Hosp. Sch. Nursing, Columbus, 1973-77; dir. nursing devel. Ohio Hosp. Assn., Columbus, 1977-79; sr. bus. analyst Borden Inc.-Chem. Divsn., Columbus, 1979-81; fin. adminstr. Bank One, Columbus N.A., 1981-84; pres. Northwest Tax Svc., Columbus, 1984-86; sr. cons. Peat, Marwick, Mitchell, Columbus, 1985-86; pvt. practice Columbus, 1986-90; controller The Wood Co's., Columbus, 1987-88; co-owner Clem & Fidler CPAs, 1991-94; owner Carol A. Fidler & Assocs., CPAs, Columbus, 1994-97; with Whalen & Co., CPAs, Columbus, 1997-2000; sr. mgr. Am. Express Tax and Bus. Svcs., Columbus, 2000—02; owner C.A. Fidler & Assocs., Inc., Columbus, 2002—. Instr. Newton Becker CPA Rev., Columbus, 1988-90; dir., treas. Donovan Prodns. Inc., Columbus, 1989-01; bd. dirs. Dominican Home Health Agy., 1995-03, treas., 1997-99, pres., 1999-02. Vol. Arthritis Assn., Columbus, 1978-84; treas. Northside Child and Family Devel. Ctr., Columbus, 1987-95, bd. dirs., 1986-97; bd. dirs., treas. Friends of the Arts in Upper Arlington, 2001—. Mem. Nat. Assn. Cert. Valuation Analysts (Ohio chpt. treas. 1999—), Ohio Soc. CPAs (chair MAP com. Columbus chpt. 1991-93, mem. MAP com. 1992-96, Cert. award 1986, Silver medal 1986), Inst. Mgmt. Accts. (dir. member attendance Columbus chpt. 1988-89, dir. tech. programs 1989-90, dir. student and acad. affairs 1990-91, dir. CMA program 1991-93, treas. 1993-95, lead instr. CMA rev. course 1991-94), Planning Forum (pres. Columbus chpt. 1986-87, v.p. fin. com. 1985-86, v.p. programs 1984-85, dir. 1987-90). Republican. Home: 4138 Winfield Rd Columbus OH 43220-4606 E-mail: cf@coil.com.

FIDLER, CHARLES ROBERT, electrical engineer; b. Park Ridge, Ill., July 7, 1964; s. Charles Ezra and Shirley Ann (Skerce) F.; m. Mary Beth Olson, Mar. 16, 1991; children: Ashley Paige, Charles Robert Jr. BSEE, Ill. Inst. Tech., 1986. Registered profl. engr., Ill. Commd. ensign USN, 1986, advanced through grades to lt., 1990, student Navy nuclear power sch., 1986, student Navy nuclear prototype Idaho Falls, Idaho, 1986-87, student surface warfare officer sch. San Diego, 1987-88; anti-submarine warfare officer USS Cushing, San Diego, 1988-90; reactor plant shift supr. USS Enterprise, Norfolk, Va., 1990-91; prin. engr. ABB Impell Corp., Chgo., 1991-93; sr. engr. Vectra, Chgo., 1993-96; supr. maintenance planning and support Nebr. Pub. Power Dist. Cooper Nuc. Sta., 1996, sr. rector ops. cert., 1996, plant performance supr., 1998, asst. maintenance mgr., 1998, asst. to plant mgr., 2000—, maintenance mgr., 2000, engrng. mgr. (rotation), 2002; recalled to active duty USN, 2003, mgr. NAVSEA, 2003—. Contbr. articles to profl. jours. Acolyte in Cath. Ch., 2000. Mem. IEEE, Am. Nuclear Soc., Naval Inst., Naval Reserve Assn., Am. Soc. Naval Engrs. Home: 2581 Holly Manor Dr Falls Church VA 22043 Office: Naval Sea Sys Command 1333 Issac Hull Ave SE Stop 1200 Washington Naval Yard DC E-mail: fidlercr@navsea.navy.mil.

FIDOCK, DAVID ARMAND, microbiology educator; b. Paris, Dec. 8, 1965; s. Dean Henwood Fidock and Joan Frazer; m. Benedicte Therese Mullier, June 4, 1994; children: Jeremy, Emilie. BSc in Math., U. Adelaide, 1985, BSc with honors, 1986; PhD in Microbiology, U. Paris, 1994. Rsch. asst. Biotech. Australia, Sydney, 1987-89; rsch. scientist Pasteur Inst., Paris, 1989-99; asst. prof. Albert Einstein Coll. of Medicine, Bronx, N.Y., 2000—. Vis. fellow U. Calif., Irvine, 1995-96, NIH, Bethesda, 1996-99; referee Whitehead Found., N.Y.C., 1998; grants reviewer Nat. Inst. of Allergy and Infectious Diseases, Bethesda, 1999. Author: Malaria: Molecular and Clinical Aspects, 1998, Malaria: Parasite Biology, Pathogenesis and Protection, 1999; contbr. numerous articles to sci. and profl. jours.; ad hoc reviewer Am. Jour. Tropical Medicine and Hygiene, Molecular and Biochem. Parasitology, Procs. Nat. Acad. Sci. U.S.A. Mem. AAAS, Am. Soc. Tropical Medicine and Hygiene. Avocations: violin, piano, literature. Office: Albert Einstein Coll Medicine Dep Microbiology Immunology 1300 Morris Park Ave Bronx NY 10461-1926

FIEBACH, H. ROBERT, lawyer; b. Paterson, N.J., June 7, 1939; s. Michael M. and Silvia Irene (Nadler) F.; m. Elizabeth D. Carlton, Mar. 17, 1984; children: Michael, Emma; children by previous marriage: Jonathan, Rachel. BS, U. Pa., 1961, LLB cum laude, 1964. Bar: Pa. 1965, U.S. Supreme Ct. 1971. Law clk. to Chief Judge Biggs U.S. Ct. Appeals for 3d Cir., 1964-65; assoc. Wolf, Block, Schorr and Solis-Cohen, Phila., 1965-71, ptnr., 1971-79, sr. ptnr., 1979-95; sr. mem., shareholder Cozen O'Connor, Phila., 1995—. Permanent mem. U.S. Jud. Conf. for 3d cir., 1967—; mem. Pa. Supreme Ct. Adv. Com. on Appellate Rules, 1987-93, Commn. on Jud. Elections, 1997-98; arbitrator, mediator U.S. Dist. Ct. (ea. dist.) Pa., 1966—. Contbg. author: Business and Commercial Litigation in the Federal Courts, 1998; rsch. editor U. Pa. Law Rev., 1964-65; contbr. articles to legal jours. Past mem. Phila. adv. bd. Anti-Defamation League of B'nai Brith, Greater Phila. Regional Commn. on Law and Social Action, Am. Jewish Congress; bd. dirs. Greater Phila. chpt. ACLU, past chmn. criminal justice and police practices com.; past bd. dirs. Pa. chpt. ACLU; bd. dirs. Congregation Rodeph Shalom. Fellow: Am. Coll. Trial Lawyers; mem.: ABA (past chmn. jud. performance and conduct com., jud. adminstrn. divsn. 1986—91, nat. conf. bar pres. 1991—95, ho. of dels. 1991—2000, pres. nat. caucus state bar assns. 1994—95, chmn. standing com. on lawyers profl. liability 1994—95, bd. govs. 1997—2000, ho. of dels. 2001—, state del. 2001—, litigation sect., 1988 and 2002 midyear meeting host com.), Am. Bar Found., Soc. of Fellows, Phila. Trial Lawyers Assn. (bd. dirs. 1989—90, past chmn. bus. litig. com.), Am. Judicature Soc. (state membership chmn. 1988), Defender Assn. Phila. (bd. dirs.), Pa. Bar Inst. (pres. bd. dirs. 1984—90, 2000—), Phila. Bar Assn. (chmn. spl. com. on ins. 1983—84, bd. govs. 1983—87, past chmn. fed. cts. com., spkr. various panels, past vice-chmn. arbitration com., civil jud. procedures com., past mem. spl. com. to study appellate cts.), Pa. Bar Assn. (past vice-chmn. jud. selection com., chmn. jud. retention election com 1980—83, chmn. polit. action com. for merit retention of judges 1980—83, ho. of dels. 1983—, chmn. com. on profl. liability 1984—87, bd. govs. 1987—95, pres.-elect 1992—93, pres. 1993—94, Pa. Bar Trust 1996—, Spl. Achievement award 1986), Order of Coif (past dir. U. Pa. chpt.). Home: 301 Delancey St Philadelphia PA 19106-4208 Office: Cozen & O'Conner 1900 Market St Fl 3 Philadelphia PA 19103-3572 E-mail: rfiebach@cozen.com.

FIEBERT, MARTIN STEPHEN, psychology educator, psychologist; b. N.Y.C., June 6, 1939; s. Max and Grace F.; m. Paula Barbara Schwartz, June 1, 1963 (div. 1999); children: Bryan, Deirdre; m. Margo Law Kasdan, Jan. 4, 2000. PhD, U. Rochester, 1965. Lic. psychologist, Calif. Prof. psychology Calif. State U., Long Beach, Calif., 1965—. Contbr. over 35 articles to profl. jours. Mem. Am. Psychol. Soc., Calif. Faculty Assn. (pres. chpt.). Avocations: tennis, travel, sculpting, meditation. Office: Calif State U 1250 Bellflower Blvd Long Beach CA 90840 Fax: 562-985-8004. E-mail: mfiebert@csulb.edu.

FIECHTNER, JUSTUS JOHN, rheumatologist, consultant; b. Bismarck, N.Dak., Dec. 11, 1946; s. Gottlieb Henry Fiechtner and Elfriede Louise Lazar; m. Karlene J. Gehler, June 24, 1953; children: Lauren Gehler, Benjamin Gehler. BS in Chemistry and Medicine, U. of N.Dak., 1970; MD, Boston (Mass.) U., 1972; MPH, U. of Wash., 1981. Diplomate. Intern USN, 1973—77; resident Marshfield Clinic U of Wis., 1978—79; fellow in rheumatology U. Wash., 1980; assoc. prof. of medicine U. of ND, Fargo, ND, 1981—90; pvt. practice Fiechtner Rsch., Lansing, Mich., 1990—. Assoc. prof. Mich. State U., East Lansing, Mich., 1990—. Chmn. bd. dirs. Arthritis Found., Mich., 1980—2000. Lt. comdr. USN, 1972—75. Fellow: ACP, Am. Coll. of Rheumatology. Office: Fiechtner Research 3394 E Jolly Road Suite C Lansing MI 48910 Office Fax: 517-272-9706. E-mail: jfiechtner@pol.net.

FIEDEROWICZ, WALTER MICHAEL, lawyer; b. Hartford, Conn., Aug. 23, 1946; s. Michael and Sylvia Christine (Ramunno) F.; m. Gerry Prattson, June 1, 1968; children: Michael, Catherine. BA, Yale U., 1968; JD (DuPont fellow), U. Va., 1971. Bar: Conn. 1971, U.S. Supreme Ct. 1977. Mem. firm Cummings & Lockwood, Stamford, Conn., 1971-76, ptnr. firm, 1979-88, of counsel, 1989-91; pres. Covenant Mut. Ins. Co., Hartford, 1985-92; White House fellow U.S. Dept. Justice, Washington, 1976-77; spl. asst. to Atty. Gen., Dept. Justice, Washington, 1976-77; assoc. dep. Atty. Gen., 1977-79. Bd. dirs. Photronics, Inc., First Albany Corp., Hematech; chmn. CDT Corp., Meacock Capital, Omega Underwriting Holdings, Ltd. Mem. editl. Va. Law Rev., 1969-71. Mem. grad. coun. Loomis-Chaffee Sch. Bd.; trustee Conn. Trust for Hist. Preservation. Mem. ABA, Conn. Bar Assn., Order of the Coif, Hartford Golf Club, Univ. Club. Roman Catholic. Home: 102 North St PO Box 939 Litchfield CT 06759-0939 E-mail: fiederowicz@juno.com.

FIEDLER, HANS KARL, network analyst, consultant; b. Milw., Dec. 26, 1955; s. Leon Dale and Wilma Pauline (Mercer) F.; m. Teresa Cox. AAS, U. Louisville, 1980, BS, 1983. Dir. Bus. Sch. Microcomputer Lab. U. Louisville, 1983-85, programmer, analyst, 1985-88, systems programmer, 1988-94, comm. analyst, 1994-2000; network analyst Comms. Svcs. Info. Tech., U. Louisville, 2000—. Owner HF Cons., Louisville, 1983—. Mem. ACM, NRA, IEEE, Digital Equipment Computer Users Soc., Order Ky. Cols., Sports Car Club of Am., Ohio Falls Sports Car Assn. Republican. Methodist. Avocations: sailing, road rallying, target shooting, amateur radio. Home: 10201 Cambrie Ct Louisville KY 40241-1187 Office: Comms Svcs Info Tech U Louisville Louisville KY 40292-0001 E-mail: hans@hermes.louisville.edu., hans@hfconsulting.com.

FIEDLER, HAROLD JOSEPH, electrical engineer, consultant; b. Detroit, Apr. 29, 1924; s. Oscar Emil and Frances (Majczak) F.; m. Ruth Irene Ciesielski, Aug. 20, 1949; children: Charles Steven, Susan Allison Fiedler Gobat, James Brian. BEE, U. Detroit, 1951. Application engr. GE, Schenectady, N.Y., 1951-67, sr. application engr., 1967-70, mgr. system automation operation, communication and control, 1970-73, sr. application engr., 1973-86, cons. elec. utility communication and control, 1986—. Chmn. automated distbn. systems GE Task Force, 1980-81; expert advisor Conference Internationale des Grands Reseaux Electriques Study Com. 35, Schenectady, 1973-92. Co-author: EPRI RP3158-1 HVDC Handbook, 1991-92; contbr. over 35 tech. articles on electric utility application to profl. jours., 1952-86. Pres., bd. dirs. Mohawk Opportunities in Mental Health, Inc., Schenectady, 1990-94, fund distbn. com. United Way, 1988-96; fin. officer sect. II Marriage Encounter, Schenectady, 1987-89. 1st class petty officer USN, 1943-46, PTO Recipient prize paper AIEE N.E. Dist., 1957. Fellow IEEE (chmn. Schenectady sect. 1961-62, chmn. power system communication com. 1965-67, mem. adminstrv. com. 1978-82, Centennial medal 1983); mem. NSPE (registered profl. engr.), IEEE Power Engrng. Soc. (chmn. chpts. dept. 1972-82), Mayfield Yacht Club (open class racing 1980-81), Eta Kappa Nu, Tau Beta Pi. Republican. Roman Catholic. Avocations: sailing, photography, electronics. Home: 22 Beechwood Dr Ballston Lake NY 12019-2650 E-mail: hfie368611@aol.com.

FIEDLER, JAY, football player; b. Dec. 29, 1971; Postgrad in engrng. sci., Dartmouth Coll. Quartback Miami Dolphins, 2000—, Minn. Vikings, 1998—99. Mem. bd. dirs. Reach for the Stars Found. Recipient Dick Steinberg Good Guy award. Office: Miami Dolphins 2269 NW 199th St Miami FL 33056

FIEDLER, JOHN AMBERG, marketing scientist; b. Evanston, Ill., Nov. 14, 1941; s. George and Agnes Zoe (Amberg) F.; m. Frances Eudora Murphy, June 18, 1966 (div. 1983); children: Margaret, Neil; m. Lesley A. Bahner, Dec. 28, 1986. BA, U. Wis., 1965; MBA, U. Chgo., 1969; MPS, Loyola U., New Orleans, 2000. V.p. Leo Burnett Co., Inc., Chgo., 1969-72, 74-79; mgr. decision systems Market Facts, Inc., Chgo., 1972-73; exec. v.p. Ted Bates Co., Inc., N.Y.C., 1980-84; prin., founder POPULUS, Inc., Boise, Idaho, 1985—; v.p., co-founder 12 Americans, Inc., Boise, 1999—; pres. Oreon Inc., Boise, 1999—. Co-author: (book) Psychological Effects of Advertising, 1985; contbr. articles to

profl. jours. and confs.; inventor Ballot Box (TM) communication assessment system, 1985. Rsch. dir. Reagan-Bush '84, Wash., 1984, bd. dirs. Childreach, U.S.A., 1986-98, mem. exec. com.; bd. dirs. Cath. Charities Idaho, 2003--. Democrat. Roman Catholic. Office: Oreon Inc 195 Wilderness Way Boise ID 83716-3383

FIEDLER, JOSEPH ROBERT, mathematician, educator; b. Dayton, Ohio, Aug. 26, 1948; s. Otto E and Winifred Cochran Fiedler. AB in Math., Harvard U., Cambridge, Mass., 1970; MS in Math., The Ohio State U., 1972, PhD in Math., 1988. Program assoc. Dept. of Math., The Ohio State U., Columbus, 1980—85; asst. prof. Dept. of Math., Calif. State U., Bakersfield, 1989—93, assoc. prof., 1993—99, prof., 1999—. Vis. assoc. prof. math. Ohio State U., 1995; co-dir. math. preparation initiative Calif. State U. Co-author (textbook) Calculus Laboratories with Maple: A Tool, not an Oracle, Calculus: Mathematics and Modeling. Grantee Prin. Investigator, Math. Profl. Devel. Inst., U. of Calif., 1001—, 2002—. Mem.: Am. Math. Assn. of Two Yr. Colls. (referee, amatyc rev. 1988), Assn. for Women in Math., Calif. Math. Coun. of Cmty. Colls., Bakersfield Math. Coun. (interim pres. 2000—02, Tchr. of the Yr. 2002), Calif. Math. Coun., Nat. Coun. Tchrs. Math., Teachers Tchg. with Tech. (coll. short course instr.), Am. Math. Assn. of Two Yr. Colleges, Nat. Coun. of Teachers of Math. (mem. math. tchr. adv. panel 2001—02), Math. Assn. of Am. (chair subcom. on svc. courses 1995—98). Home: 6513 S Half Moon Dr Bakersfield CA 93309 Office: California State University Bakersfield 9001 Stockdale Hwy Bakersfield CA 93311-1099 Office Fax: 661-664-2039. Personal E-mail: jfiedler@csub.edu. E-mail: jfiedler@csub.edu.

FIEDLER, ROBERT MAX, management consultant; b. Midland, Mich., June 19, 1945; s. Edward Louis and Lenora Margaret Fiedler; m. Carol Ann Raddatz, Nov. 28, 1981; children: Katy, Christa. BS in Packaging Sci., Mich. State U., 1967, MS in Packaging Sci., MBA, Mich. State U., 1971. Grad. rsch. asst. Mich. State U., East Lansing, 1969—71; divsn. mgr. MTS Systems Corp., Mpls., 1971—80; cons. Robert Fiedler & Assocs., Mpls., 1980—2000; v.p. engring. develop. The Packaging Dept., Inc., Mpls., 2000. Adj. prof. dept. engring. U. Minn., Mpls., 1990; mem. adv. bd. ad-hoc com. on packaging U. Minn., 1985-2000; seminar lectr. in field, Brazil, Mex., China, Italy, The Netherlands, Tunisia. Contbg. editor: Fundamentals of Packaging Dynamics, 1985; editor: Distribution Packaging Technology, 1995, The Best of Transpack, 1966; contbr. articles to profl. jours. Lt. USNR, 1967-69. Recipient Diamond Wing award U.S. Parachute Assn., 1974. Fellow ASTM (chmn. subcom. 1986-93, divsn. chmn. 1993-2001), Inst. Packaging Profls. (cert. profl. in packaging, past chmn. cons. coun., chmn. tech. com. 1993-97, v.p. coun. of specialists 1997-2000, Mem. of Yr. 1997). Office: The Packaging Dept 10901 Nesbitt Ave S Minneapolis MN 55437 E-mail: bobfiedler@aol.com.

FIEDLER, TOM, editor-in-chief; Degree in engring., Merchant Marine Acad.; M in Journalism, Boston U., 1971. Fellow profl. journalism Duke U., 1984—85; polit. editor, columnist, White Ho. corr., war corr. Miami Herald, editl. page editor, 1999—2001, v.p., exec. editor, 2001—. Author: Florida Institute of Government's Almanac of Florida Politics. Recipient Bronze Medallion, Soc. Profl. Journalists, 1988, Pulitzer prize reporting polit. influence extremist group, 1991, Pulitzer prize coverage Hurricane Andrew disaster, 1993. Office: Miami Herald One Herald Plz Miami FL 33132*

FIEGELMAN, RICHARD PAUL, sales consultant, freelance writer; b. Phila., Pa., Nov. 5, 1957; s. Marvin Louis and Beverly Jane Fiegelman; m. Ruthann Claudia Brink, Aug. 2, 1992; children: Zachary, Derek, Alexander, Jared. BS in comm., Northeastern U., Boston, Mass., 1980. Lic. Real Estate Pa. Corp. sales cons. Legion Industries, Dallas, Pa., 2000—; land devel., sales Eagle Rock Resort, Valley of Lakes, Pa., 1999—; sales cons. Colo. Prime Foods, Wilkes-Barre, Pa., 1993—99. Author short story, numerous poems; contbr. articles to jours. Vol. Defend Our Watershed, Wyoming Valley, Pa., 2001—, ALS Found., 2002—. Recipient outstanding achievement, Nat. Libr. of Poetry, Maryland, 1995. Home: 19 Country Pine Dallas PA 18612 E-mail: rsiegelman@epix.net.

FIEGER, GEOFFREY NELS, lawyer; b. Detroit, Dec. 23, 1950; s. Bernard Julian and June Beth (Oberer) F.; m. Kathleen Janice Podwoiski, June 25, 1983. BA, U. Mich., 1974, MA, 1976; JD, Detroit Coll. Law, 1979. Bar: Mich. 1979, U.S. Dist. Ct. (ea. dist.) Mich. 1979, Fla. 1980, U.S. Dist. Ct. (mid. dist.) Fla. 1980, Ariz. 1980. Ptnr. Fieger Fieger Kenney & Johnson, P.C., Southfield, Mich., 1979—. V.p. Orgn. United to Save Twp., West Bloomfield, Mich., 1987; dem. nominee for gov. of Mich., 1998. Mem. ABA, Detroit Bar Assn., Assn. Trial Lawyers Am. Unitarian Universalist. Avocations: running, swimming. Office: Fieger Fieger Kenney & Johnson PC 19390 W 10 Mile Rd Southfield MI 48075-2463

FIEL, MAXINE LUCILLE, journalist, behavioral analyst, lecturer; b. N.Y.C. d. William Jack and Rowena (Burton) Stempel; m. David H. Fiel; children: Meredith Susan, Lisa Beth. Student in psychology and humanities, NYU. Nat. columnist, contbg. editor Mademoiselle Mag., N.Y.C., 1972—2001; nat. columnist Womens World, Englewood, N.J., 1979-89; contbg. editor Overseas Promotions, N.Y.C., 1979—; articles and features editor Japanese Overseas Press, 1976—; feature editor N.Y. Now, N.Y.C., 1980-91; contbg. editor Woman's World mag., 1979-89, Bella mag., Eng., 1987-89; nat. columnist First mag. for women, 1989-91; founder Starcast Astrological Svcs., Floral Park, N.Y., 1993—; columnist Borderland Mag., Japan, 1995—2000, IM Mag., Japan, 1997—2000. Cons. legal profession jury selection, 1984—; mktg. cons. Imperial Enterprises, Tokyo and Princeton, N.J., 1983—; cons. spokesperson Rowland Co., N.Y.C., 1972-81, Allied Chem. Co., N.Y.C., 1972-75; lectr., cons. Atlanta and Fla. Bar Assns., 1986—; creator Touch Game Parker Bros., Salem, Mass., 1971-76; behavior analystand communications advisor multi-nat. bus. corps.; cons. Chesebrough-Ponds, Footwear Coun., Grand Marnier Liquor; founder Starcast Astrological Svcs., 1993; pres. Interglobal Mktg. Co., 1999. Pioneer field of polit. body lang., 1969; author: Lovescopes, 1998, The Little Book of Body Language, 1998; contbr. articles to News Am., L.A. Times, Newhouse News Svc., Newspaper Enterprise Assocs., King Features, Borderland Mag.; adv. bd. mem. Writers Digest Mag., 2002; TV appearances on morning and afternoon shows including A Current Affair, The Regis Philbin Show, Eyewitness News, Cable News Networks, Tonight Show, Today Show, Good Morning Am., Joan Rivers Show, Jenny Jones, Entertainment Tonight, Hard Copy, Inside Edition, BBC Breakfast Show, Good Morning Japan, Fox News Channel, MSNBC, many others; appears in daily segment Good Morning Japan; own daily TV show on Nippon Network, Japan, 1989—. Active Sister Cities, Tokyo and N.Y.C.; charter mem. Elem. Sch. Cultural Exchange, Toyko and N.Y.C., Ctr. Environ. Edn.; bd. dirs. Periwinkle Prodns. Anti-Drug Abuse, N.Y.C., Adirondacks Save-A-Stray. Recipient Achievement award field behavioral sci. and photojournalism, Tokyo, 1974, Outstanding Rsch. award field psychology of gesture, Tokyo, 1976, Outstanding Achievement award Internat. Conf. Soc. Para-Psychology, 1974-75; honored guest at award dinner for involvement and support in the merging of Eye Rsch. Inst. Boston and Harvard Med. Sch., 1991. Mem. AFTRA, Internat. Found. Behavioral Rsch. (past v.p.), Nat. Writers Assn. (profl.), Profl. Writers Assn., Authors Guild, Authors League, World Wildlife Fund, Whale Protection Fund, Environ. Def. Soc., Nature Conservancy, Greenpeace, People for Ethical Treatment Animals, Humane Assn. U.S., Sea Shepherd Conservation Soc., Defenders of Wildlife, Guiding Eyes for Blind, Braille Camps for Blind Children, Save the Children, Lotos Club (N.Y.C.), East End Yacht Club (Freeport, N.Y.). Office: 338 Northern Blvd Ste 3 Great Neck NY 11021-4808

FIEL, STANLEY BRUCE, internist, pulmonogist, educator, researcher; b. Aug. 9, 1948; children: Jami Marissa, Seth Jordan, Marla Anne. BS, U. Conn., 1969; MD, Med. Coll. of Pa., 1973. Diplomate Am. Bd. Internal Medicine, Pulmonary Bd. Internal Medicine; lic. physician, Pa. Intern Temple U. Hosp., Phila., 1973-74, resident, 1974-76; pulmonary disease fellow Hosp. of U. Pa., Phila., 1976-78; attending physician Temple U. Sch. Medicine, Phila., 1978-91, Am. Oncologic Hosp., Phila., 1982-92, St. Christopher's Hosp. for Children, Phila., 1988—, Med. Coll. Pa., Phila., 1991—; asst. prof. medicine, assoc. prof. Temple U. Sch. Medicine, Phila., 1978-89, prof. medicine, 1990—, Med. Coll. Pa., Phila., 1991—, Allegheny U. Health Scis., Phila., 1994—. Chief pulmonary disease and critical care medicine sect. Drexel U. Coll. Medicine, 1991—, v.p. medicine, chief medicine, 2001; attending physician, chief pulmonary unit Drexel U. Coll. Medicine, 1991—, dir. fellowship tng. program, 1991—, dir. Adult Cystic Fibrosis Program, 1991—, dir. Respiratory Care Svcs., 1991—, exec. com. of faculty, 1992—, mem. utilization com., 1992—, chmn. search com. Cmty. and Preventive Medicine, 1992-93, sec. Exec. Faculty Com., 1993—. Mem. editl. bd. Clin. Respiratory Medicine, 1993—, Jour. of Asthma, 1993—; assoc. editor New Insights into Cystic Fibrosis, 1993—; contbr. articles to profl. jours. and chpts. to books. Recipient Lange Book award in Medicine, 1973, Rittenhouse Book award, 1973, Mosby Book award, 1973, Golden Apple Teaching award, 1985, 88; named Finalist for Lindbach Teaching award, 1990; grantee NIH, 1978-83, 89-91, Maternal and Child Health Care, 1984-88, Cystic Fibrosis Found., 1987-89, 93, Rorer Pharms., 1991-92,Am. Lung Assn., 1989-90, Glaxo Pharm. Co., 1991-93, G.H. Besselaar Assocs., 1991-93, ICI Pharm. Group, 1991-2000, Cortech Pharm. Group, 1993-2000, Genentech, Inc., 1993. Mem. Am. Thoracic Soc., Am. Coll. Chest Physicians, Assn. Am. Med. Colls., Am. Coll. Physicians, Soc. Clin. Decision Making, Am. Fedn. Clin. Rsch., ASTE, Phila. County Med. Soc., Pa. Med. Soc., Pa. Thoracic Soc. Home: 132 Adrienne Ln Wynnewood PA 19096-1227 Office: Drexel U Coll Medicine Pulmonary Disease Sect 3300 Henry Ave Philadelphia PA 19129-1191

FIELD, ALEXANDER JAMES, economics educator; b. Boston, Apr. 17, 1949; s. Mark George and Anne (Murray) F.; m. Valerie Nan Wolk, Aug. 8, 1982; children: James Alexander, Emily Elena. AB, Harvard U., 1970; MS, London Sch. Econs., 1971; PhD, U. Calif., Berkeley, 1974. Asst. prof. econs. Stanford (Calif.) U., 1974-82; assoc. prof. Santa Clara (Calif.) U., 1982-88, acad. v.p., 1986-87, prof., chmn. dept. econs., 1988-93, assoc. dean Leavey Sch. Bus. and Adminstrn., 1993-96, dean, 1996-97, Michel and Mary Orradre prof. econs., 1992—. Mem. bd. trustees Santa Clara U., 1988-91. Author: Educational Reform and Manufacturing Development in Mid-Nineteenth Century Massachusetts, 1989, Altruistically Inclined: The Behavioral Sciences, Evolutionary Theory and the Origins of Reciprocity, 2001; author, editor: The Future of Economics, 1995, assoc. editor: Jour. Econ. Lit., 1981—98, 1999—; editor: Rsch. in Econ. History, 1993—; mem. editl. bd.: Explorations in Econ. History, 1993—, Jour. Econ. History, 2001—. Recipient Nevins prize Columbia U., 1975; NSF rsch. grantee, 1989. Mem. Phi Beta Kappa, Beta Gamma Sigma. Home: 3762 Redwood Cir Palo Alto CA 94306-4255 Office: Santa Clara Univ Dept Econs Santa Clara CA 95053-0001

FIELD, ARTHUR NORMAN, lawyer; b. N.Y.C., Sept. 28, 1935; s. Harry and Rose (Lemberg) F.; m. Doris Helen Rabbiner, Sept. 1, 1957; children: Michael, Karen. BBA, CCNY, 1955; LLB, Harvard U., 1958. Bar: (N.Y.) 1959, (Fla.) 1975. Assoc. Shearman & Sterling, N.Y.C., 1959-68, ptnr., 1968-2000; pres. GXG Mgmt., LLC, N.Y.C., 2000—; mem. Field Cons. LLC; of counsel Shearman & Sterling, N.Y.C., 2001. Author: Legal Opinions in Business Transactions, 2003; co-editor (with M. Moskin): Transactional Lawyers Deskbook, 2001. Chmn., bd. dirs. Community Action for Legal Svcs., 1972-77 (chair 78-79); bd. dirs. Brookdale Found., 1983—, Wave Hill Inc., N.Y.C., 1968-80, Washington Square Legal Svcs., 1979-95, Historic House Trust of N.Y., 2000-; trustee Ramapo Trust, 1983; bd. dirs. Preservation League N.Y., 2003-, Brookdale Inst. on Aging, 2003-. Fellow Am. Bar Found., NY Bar Found., NY County Lawyers Assn. (pres. 1990-92); mem. ABA (ho. of dels. 1990-92), NY State Bar Assn. (v.p. 1992-97), Assn. Bar City NY, Am. Law Inst., Assn. of Arbitrators, NYC, (dir. 1998-2002), chair Tribar Opinion Com.1985-90, chair ABA Bus. Sect. Opinion Com. 2002—). E-mail: anfield@igxg.com.

FIELD, BARRY ELLIOT, internist, gastroenterologist; b. Hartford, Conn., Apr. 21, 1947; s. Arnold and Selma (Nechrich) F.; m. Julie Farr, Jan. 6, 1991; children: Rachel Elizabeth, Hannah Margaret, Miles Jay. BA (scholar), Harvard U., 1968; MD, Albert Einstein Coll. Medicine, 1972. Intern in pediat. Montefiore Hops., Bronx, N.Y., 1972-73; intern in medicine Met. Hosp., N.Y.C., 1973-74, resident in medicine, 1974-76; fellow in gastroenterology Harbor Gen. Hosp., Torrance, Calif., 1976-78; pvt. practice in internal medicine and gastroenterology North Tarrytown, N.Y., 1978—. Dir. medicine Phelps Meml. Hosp., North Tarrytown. Mem. Am. Gastroenterol. Assn., Alpha Omega Alpha. Office: 777 N Broadway Ste 305 Tarrytown NY 10591-1040

FIELD, CHARLES TWIST, artist, retired art educator; b. Van Nuys, Calif., Oct. 17, 1936; s. Edward Winter and Enid (Twist) F.; m. Germaine E., Dec. 27, 1961; children: Michele, Caroline, Mark Charles. BA, Stanford U., 1958; MFA, U. Wash., 1965. Instr. art Western Ill. U., Macomb, 1965-67; asst. prof. art U. Tex., Austin, 1967-72; assoc. prof. art U. N.Mex., Albuquerque, 1972-74; prof. dept. of art and art history U. Tex., San Antonio, 1974—2002, prof. emeritus, 2002—. Capt. USAF, 1958-62. Ballinglen Arts Found. fellow Republic of Ireland, 1999—. Roman Catholic.

FIELD, DANIEL, history educator; b. Boston, July 26, 1938; s. Richard Hinckley and Caroline (Crosby) F.; m. Harriet Beecher, June 26, 1959; children: Richard Henry, Jonathan Beecher. BA, Harvard U., 1959, MA, 1962, PhD, 1968. Lectr. Harvard U., Cambridge, Mass., 1968-70; asst. prof. Barnard Coll., N.Y.C., 1970-76; prof. Syracuse (N.Y.) U., 1976—2001, prof. emeritus, 2001—. Vis. prof. Harvard U., Cambridge, 1981-82; Fulbright lectr. Moscow State U., 1996. Author: The End of Serfdom, 1976, Rebels in the Name of the Tsar, 1988; editor: Quantitative Studies in Agrarian History, 1993; editor Russian Rev., 1982-89. Fulbright Hays fellow U.S. Govt., 1964, 78, 81, Sr. fellow Harriman Inst., Columbia U., N.Y.C., 1990-91. Fellow Davis Ctr. for Russian Studies-Harvard U. Democrat. Office: Syracuse Univ Dept History 145 Eggers Hl Syracuse NY 13244-0001 E-mail: dxfield@syr.edu.

FIELD, DAVID ELLIS, lawyer; b. Washington, Feb. 3, 1953; s. Ellis Arrington and Phyllis Martina (Anderson) F. BA, U. Va., 1975, MEd, 1976; JD, George Mason U., 1983. Bar: Va. 1983, D.C. 1990, Md. 1991, U.S. Dist. Ct. (ea. dist.) Va. 1984, U.S. Ct. Appeals (4th cir.) 1985. Assoc. Law Offices Alphonse Audet, Fairfax, Va., 1984; asst. commonwealth's atty. Office of Fairfax County, Va., 1984-87; assoc. Miller & Bucholtz, P.C., Reston, Va., 1987-89, Falcone & Rosenfeld, Ltd., Fairfax, 1989, Lewis, Dack, Paradiso, O'Connor & Good, Wasington, 1989-91, Deckelbaum, Ogens & Fischer, Wasington, 1991-92; atty. Alan S. Toppelberg & Assocs., Washington, 1992-94; ptnr. Field & Cram, Fairfax, Va., 1994-98; pvt. practice Fairfax, Va., 1998-99; staff counsel AllState, Falls Church, Va., 1999—. Asst. city atty. City of Fairfax, 1988-89. Mem.: Fairfax Bar Assn., Delta Theta Pi. Democrat. Presbyterian. Office: 3141 Fairview Park Dr Ste 175 Falls Church VA 22042-4507

FIELD, ELLEN, marketing professional; b. Marlinton, W.Va., Dec. 26, 1952; d. George S. and Vivienne W. Sharp; m. John A. Field, May 7, 1977 (div.); children: Margaret Elaine, George William Butler. BS, W.Va. U., 1974; MA, Coll. Grad. Studies, 1976. Rsch. assoc. Nat. Gov.'s Assn., Washington, 1978-80; mem. presdl. pers. Reagan-Bush Transition Team, Washington, 1980; vice chmn. McLean (Va.) Cmty. Ctr., 1987-90; spl. asst. Office Drug Control Policy, Washington, 1990-93; vol. coord., dir. spl. events Tom Davis Campaign, Springfield, Va., 1994-95; exec. dir. McLean (Va.) C. of C., 1995-98; dir. mktg. and bus. devel. Decision Strategies/Fairfax Internat., Falls Church, Va., 1999; sr. analyst Rep. Nat. Com., 2000—; mem. Bush-Cheney Transition Team, 2000-01; dir. comms. Peace Corps, Washington, 2001—. Field dir. Bobbie Kilberg for Lt. Gov., McLean, 1993, George Allen for Gov., McLean, 1993; legis. dir. Congressman Tom Davis, Washington, 1995. Author: Governing the American States, 1978; editor: Governor's Policy Initiatives, 1980, Reflections on Being Governor, 1981. Treas. Dranesville Rep. Party, McLean, 1994-98, mem. Fairfax County Rep. Commn., 1994—; mem. Greater McLean Republican Women's Club, 1983—, pres., 1987. Mem. Nat. Fedn. Rep. Women, Va. Fedn. Rep. Women (exec. com., chmn. bylaws). Presbyterian. E-mail: efield@peacecorps.gov.

FIELD, HAROLD GREGORY, lawyer; b. Feb. 27, 1923; s. Harold Gregory and Catherine (Crowley) F.; m. Nancy L. Kesecker, Sept. 30, 1977. BS, Ariz. State U., 1948; LLB, Chgo. Kent Coll. Law, 1952. Bar: Ill. 1953. Ptnr. Burek & Field, Wheaton, Ill., 1960-86; pvt. practice Wheaton, Ill., 1986-96; ptnr. Schiller, Du Canto & Fleck, 1996—. Home: 979 Creekside Cir Naperville IL 60563-2472 Office: 311 S County Farm Rd Ste G Wheaton IL 60187-2438

FIELD, HELEN, soprano; b. Wales; Attended, Royal Coll. Music, London. Prin. artist Welsh Nat. Opera. Singer: (Operas) Welsh Nat. Opera, Met. Opera, Deutsch Opera Berlin, Covent Garden, numerous others; operatic roles Mimi, Musetta, Gilda, Marenka, Vixen, Jenufa, Tatyana, Desdemona, Butterfly, Salome, Governess (Turn of Screw) numerous others; performer (numerous concerts): major European and Am. orchs. Address: c/o Heol Isaf Radyr Cardiff CF15 8DZ Wales

FIELD, HENRY AUGUSTUS, JR., lawyer; b. Wisconsin Dells, Wis., July 8, 1928; s. Henry A. and Georgia (Coakley) F.; m. Patricia Ann Young, Nov. 30, 1957 (dec. 1980); children: Mary Patricia (dec. 1992), Thomas Gerard, Susan Therese (Mrs. Thomas Hempel); m. Molly Kelly Martin, Apr. 13, 1985. Student, Western Mich. Coll., 1946-47; PhB, Marquette U., 1950; LLB (cum laude), U. Wis., 1952. Bar: Wis. 1952, U.S. Dist. Ct. (we. and ea. dists.) Wis. 1952, U.S. Ct. Appeals (7th cir.) 1957, U.S. Supreme Ct. 1980. Asst. U.S. atty. Western Dist. of Wis., 1956-57; assoc. Roberts, Boardman, Suhr, Bjork & Curry, 1957-62; jr. ptnr. Roberts, Boardman, Suhr & Curry, 1962-70; ptnr. Boardman, Suhr, Curry & Field, Madison, Wis., 1970—. chmn. exec. com., 1985-95; mem. Wis. Jud. Council, 1974-79. Dir. Family Service Soc., 1969-75, treas., 1971-72, pres., 1973-74; trustee Dane County Bar Pro Bono Trust Found., 1995-99. Served with C.I.C., AUS, 1952-55. Fellow: Wis. Bar Found., Am. Bar. Found., Am. Coll. Trial Lawyers (state chmn. 1982—83); mem.: ABA (Wis. chmn. legis. com. 1975—76), Wis. Law Found. (trustee 2003), Wis. Bar Assn. (chmn. litigation sect. 1971—72), Milw. and Dane County Bar Assn. (pres. 1971—72), 7th Fed. Cir. Bar Assn., Madison Club, Order of Coif, Sigma Tau Delta, Phi Delta Phi. Republican. Roman Catholic. Home: 3310 Valley Creek Cir Middleton WI 53562-1988 Office: Boardman Suhr Curry & Field 1 S Pinckney St Madison WI 53703-2892

FIELD, JAMES BERNARD, internist, educator; b. Fort Wayne, Ind., May 28, 1926; s. Abraham and Clara (Ridner) F.; m. Dorothy Spivey, Sept. 25, 1954; children: Carolyn, Nancy, Douglas, Susan. Student, Harvard Coll., 1944, student, 1946—47; MD cum laude, Harvard Med. Sch., 1951. Diplomate: Am. Bd. Internal Medicine. Intern internal medicine Mass. Gen. Hosp., Boston, 1951-52, asst. resident internal medicine, 1952-53, resident internal medicine, 1953-54; practice medicine specializing in endocrinology Pitts., 1962-78, Houston, 1978-89. Med. officer USPHS, Nat. Inst. Arthritis and Metabolic Diseases, Bethesda, Md., 1954, sr. asst. surgeon, 1954-58, sr. investigator, 1958-60, surgeon, 1958-60, sr. surgeon, 1960-61; asst. in medicine diabetic dept. Kings Coll. Hosp., London, 1957-58; med. officer Nat. Inst. Metabolic Disease, Bethesda, Md., 1961-62; head divsn. endocrinology and metabolism U. Pitts. Sch. Medicine, 1962-78, assoc. prof. medicine, 1962-66, prof. medicine, 1966-78, dir. clin. research unit, 1962-78; Rutherford prof. medicine Baylor Coll. Medicine, Houston, 1978-89, head div. endocrinology and metabolism, 1978-87; vis. prof. dept. exptl. medicine Univ. Coll. Med. Sch., London, 1985-86; dir. Diabetes and Endocrinology Rsch. Ctr., Baylor Coll Medicine, 1980-89; med. adv. bd. Nat. Pituitary Agy., 1967-69; research collaborator Brookhaven Nat. Lab., 1972-85; mem. nat. diabetes adv. bd. HEW, 1977-83, chmn., 1982-85, mem. endocrinology study sect. USPHS, 1965-69, chmn., 1968-69, endocrinology and metabolism tng. grant com., 1970-74, gen. clin. rsch. ctr. rev. com., 1976-79; mem. panel clin. scis. com. study nat. needs biomed. and behavioral rsch. pers. Nat Rsch. Coun., 1976-80; mem. VA merit rev. com. on endocrinology and metabolism, 1982-85; lectr. medicine Harvard Med. Sch., 1992—; mem. honors com. Harvard Med. Sch., 1993-2001. Editor (assoc. editor): Metabolism, 1959—69; editor: (editor-in-chief), 1969—; editor: (contbg.) Clin.Thyroidology, 1988—2000; contbr. numerous research articles on endocrinology to profl. jours. Bd. dirs. Gen. Clin. Research Centers, 1977-79; mem. Physician Vols. in Medicine, Hilton Head Island, S.C., 2001—. Served with U.S. Army, 1944-45. Decorated Purple Heart, Bronze Star; recipient Van Meter prize award Am. Goiter Assn., 1961, Prize Boylston Soc., 1951. Mem. Assn. Am. Physicians, Endocrine Soc. (mem. coun. 1972-75, internat. liaison com. 1972-75, mem. pub. affairs com. 1972-75, mem. awards com. 1972-75, chmn. 1974-75, nominating com. 1982-84, chmn. 1984), Am. Diabetes Assn. (dir. 1968-74, vice chmn. com. on rsch. 1972-73, chmn. com. rsch. 1975-77, mem. established investigator rev. bd. 1975-77, Eli Lilly award 1958), Am. Fedn. Clin. Rsch., Am. Clin. and Climatol. Assn., Am. Physiology Soc., Am. Soc. Clin. Investigation, Mass. Med. Soc. (chmn. com. on ret, physicians 1993—, Prize 1951, Vol. of Yr. 2001), Quechee Lakes Club (Quechee, Vt.), Harvard Med. Alumni Assn., (treas. 1997-2000), Sea Pines Country Club (Hilton Head), Alpha Omega Alpha. Home: 50 Stoney Creek Rd Hilton Head Island SC 29928

FIELD, JOHN LOUIS, architect; b. Mpls., Jan. 18, 1930; s. Harold David and Gladys Ruth (Jacobs) F.; m. Carol Helen Hart, July 23, 1961; children: Matthew Hart, Alison Ellen. BA, Yale U., 1952, MArch, 1955. Individual practice architecture, San Francisco, 1959-68; v.p. firm Bull, Field, Volkmann, Stockwell, Architects, San Francisco, 1968-83; ptnr. Field/Gruzen, Architects, San Francisco, 1983-86, Field Paoli Architects, San Francisco, 1986—. Guest lectr. Stanford, 1970; chmn. archtl. council San Francisco Mus. Art, 1969-71; mem. San Francisco Bay Conservation and Devel. Commn., Design Rev. Bd., 1980-84; founding chmn. San Francisco Bay Architects Review, 1977-80 Co-author, producer, dir.: film Cities for People (Broadcast Media award 1975, Golden Gate award San Francisco Internat. Film Festival 1975, Ohio State award 1976); film The Urban Preserve (Calif. Council AIA Commendation of excellence 1982); co-design architect: design for New Alaska Capital City (winner design competition). Recipient Archtl. Record award, 1961, 1972; AIA, Sunset mag. awards, 1962, 64, 69; No. Calif. AIA awards, 1967, 82; Calif. Council AIA award, 1982; certificate excellence Calif. Gov.'s Design awards, 1966; Homes for Better Living awards, 1962, 66, 69, 71, 77; Albert J. Evers award, 1974, Best Bldg. award Napa (Calif.) C. of C., 1987, Design award Internat. Council Shopping Ctrs., 1988, Stores of Excellence award Nat. Mall Monitor, 1989, 92, 93, Pacific Coast Builders Gold Nugget award, 1989, 91, Urban Design award Calif. Coun. AIA, 1991, 93. Fellow AIA (com. on design); mem. Nat. Coun. Archtl. Registration Bds., Urban Land Inst. (Design award 1995), Yale Club, Lambda Alpha. Office: Field Paoli Architects 1045 Sansome St Ste 206 San Francisco CA 94111-1315 E-mail: jlf@fieldpaoli.com.

FIELD, JOHN MCCABE, medical educator; b. Phila., Pa. BS, Villanova U., 1969; MD, Pa. State U., 1973. Prof. medicine and surgery Pa. State Coll. Medicine, Hershey, 1984—. Office: Pa State U Coll Medicine 500 University Dr Hershey PA 17033 Office Fax: 717-531-1793. E-mail: jfield@psu.edu.

FIELD, JONATHON HUGH, theater director, theater educator; b. Chgo., Feb. 27, 1953; s. William Hugh Wylie and Dolores Filman Field; m. Tracey Komoski, Apr. 13, 1985. MFA, U. of Wash., 1976. Composer Empty Space Theater, Seattle, 1973—78; stage dir./stage mgr. Seattle Opera, 1976—95; stage dir. Ariz. Opera, Tucson & Phoenix, 1985—93, West Bay Opera, Palo Alto, Calif., 1988—2000, Chgo. Lyric Opera, 1992—95; assoc. prof./dir. of opera Oberlin Conservatory of Music, Oberlin, Ohio, 1997—; artistic dir. Lyric Opera Cleve., Cleveland, Ohio, 2000—. Composer: (theatrical musicals) Gertrude, or Would She Be Pleased to Receive It?; translator (choreographer): (theater/ballet) Pulcinella; dir.: (opera) Don Giovanni (Hon. Mention - No. Ohio Live Awards of Achievement, 2002). Mem.: Opera Am. Achievements include first to Began using video projected and computer generated scenery in opera productions, 1988. Office: Lyric Opera Cleveland PO Box 93046 Cleveland OH 44101 Office Fax: 216-685-5988. E-mail: lyric@core.com.

FIELD, JOSEPH HOOPER, judge; b. Weston, Mass., Dec. 28, 1946; s. Edward Olsen and Harriet Margaret (Jacobs) F.; m. Georgina Munson Ducey, Aug. 1, 1970; children: Charles H., Elizabeth M., William O. AB, Harvard U., 1969; JD, U. Maine, 1976. Bar: Maine, 1976, U.S. Dist. Ct. Maine 1976, U.S. Ct. Appeals (1st cir.) 1984, Mass. 1977, U.S. Dist. Ct. Mass. 1977, U.S. Supreme Ct. 1982. Asst. dist. atty. Maine Prosecutorial Dist. VI, Bath, Maine, 1976-80; ptnr. Loyd, Bumgardner & Field, Brunswick, Maine, 1980-90; judge Maine Dist. Ct., Bath, 1990—. Chmn. Coastal Waters Commn., Freeport, Maine, 1980-88. Comdr. USCG Res., 1973-93. Mem. Wolf Neck Club (pres. 1987-89, 91-93, 99-2001), Harraseeket Yacht Club. Avocations: sailing, music, farming. Office: Maine Dist Ct 147 New Meadows Rd Bath ME 04530-9704

FIELD, JUDITH JUDY, librarian; b. Bucyrus, Ohio, Sept. 30, 1939; d. William Harrison and Eva Gertrude (Miller) Judy; m. Nathaniel Lamson Field III, Jan. 25, 1959. BBA, U. Mich., 1961, M.L.S., 1963, MBA, 1969. Library mgr. Western Electric Bell Telephone Labs., Indpls., 1962-65; asst. librarian Natural Sci. Library, Ann Arbor, Mich., 1965-66; assoc. librarian Sch. Bus. Adminstrn., Ann Arbor, Mich., 1966-69; library mgr. Inst. Internat. Commerce, Ann Arbor, 1969-71, research assoc., 1971-72; head gen. reference Flint Pub. Library, Mich., 1972-86; dir. Legis. Ref. Libr., St. Paul, 1987; mgmt. cons., 1988—; sr. lectr. libr. and info. sci. Wayne State U., 1989—. Pres. Mich. Interorgn. Council on Continuing Library Edn., Lansing, Mich., 1983-85; bd. dirs. Continuing Library Edn. Network and Exchange, Washington, 1979-81. Editor: International Finance Bibliography, 1971, Apprentice and Training

Program, 1972, Beginning Positions and Training Program, 1973, Michigan Legal Literature, 1991; editl. bd. The One-Person Lib. Mem. LVA. Mem. ALA (com. accreditation 1993-97, task force adv. com. White House Conf. 1990-92), Friends of Detroit Pub. Libr., Spl. Librs. Assn. (dep. conf. chmn. 1983, chmn. libr. mgmt. divsn. 1983-84, pres. Mich. chpt. 1981-82, bd. dirs. 1975-77, 86-89, 96-99, pres. 1997-98, conf. chair 1994), Am. Soc. Info. Sci. (pres. Mich. chpt. 1991-93), ARMA Internat. Edn. Found. (bd. trustees 1998-2002). Republican. Avocations: archaeology, backgammon. Home: 20500 Clement Rd Northville MI 48167-1334 Office: Wayne State U 106 Kresge Lib Detroit MI 48202

FIELD, JULIA ALLEN, planner, strategist, writer; b. Boston, Jan. 5, 1937; d. Howard Locke and Julia Wright (Field) Allen. BA cum laude, Harvard U., 1960; postgrad., Harvard Grad. Sch. Design, 1964-65, Pius XII Grad. Art Inst., Florence, Italy, 1961; MA, PhD fellow, Walden U. Inst. Adv. Studies, 1983-89. Appointments Joint Harvard Karachi Univ. Expdn. to Baluchistan, Pakistan, 1957; cons. to archtl. and environ. firms, 1964—70; cons. Forestry Dept. of Simla, India, 1969—70; founder, v.p. Black Grove, Inc., Miami, Fla., 1970-80; founder, pres. Amazonia 2000, Bogota, Colombia, 1970—79; leader Task Force Amazonia 2000, DAINCO, 1977-78; elected pres. New Found. Amazonia 2000 in Gen. Assembly, Leticia, Colombia, 1979—. Acad. Arts and Scis. of the Ams., Miami, Fla., 1979—. Mem. Presdl. Com. on Innovative Tech. Devel. Group of Yr. 2000, Colombia, 1971-74; mem. survey U.S.S.R. Zoos for Internat. Union for Conservation of Nature, Morges, Switzerland, 1964; advisor Techno-Update Jour., Simla, 1969-70; mem. Man and Biosphere com. UNESCO, Colombia, 1972-78; mem. Task Force on Colonization Report to Pres. of Colombia, 1973; cons. So. Unified Command, Republic of Colombia, 1981-86; Hon. Nat. Insp. resources and environment Republic of Colombia, 1982—; mem. bd. visitors Duke U. Primate Ctr., 1979-82; prin. spkr. at internat. seminars and congresses; keynote spkr. World Jungle Conf., U. Sci. Ctr. Penang, Malaysia, Dec. 1979, HSUS Nat. Leadership Conf. Wildlife Exploitation, Saddlebrook, N.J., 1968, II symposium and forum tropical biology, Leticia, Amazonas, Republic of Colombia, 1969; participant Only One Earth Forum, UN Environ. Programme, Rene Dubos Ctr., N.Y.C., 1987, internat. seminar econ. coop. future Amazon Basin, Leticia, 1970; lectr. in field. Author: Man and Nature, the Integral Concept, 1965, Amazonia 2000, 1978, Amazonia as a World Model, 1972, (film) Man Against Nature, 1966; editor Man and Nature Series, 1969-73, Game and Wildlife Preserves in U.S.S.R., 1969, Conservation in the USSR, 1972, Amazon Wildlife Exploitation Report for Nature Editor, Life Mag., 1968; created exhbn. Writing on the Wall for internat. conf., Cities in Context U. Notre Dame, 1968; contbr. articles to profl. jours and popular mags. including Nature, Life. Mem. City of Miami Bicentennial Com., 1975-76; coord. Cmty. of Man Task Force, Miami, 1975-76; mem. Blueprint for Miami 2000, 1982-85; adv. Tech. Jour., Delhi, India, 1985-86; founder Amacayacu Nat. Park, Amazonia, Colombia, 1975; creator, builder with other scientists Villa Ciencia, Rio Cotuhe, Colombia, 1975; signed Third Amazon World Model Accord for Amazonia 2000 with IGAC and DAINCO, Colombia, 1988-93. Fellow Royal Geog. Soc. (London) (life); mem. Internat. Assn. Hydrogen Energy, EarthJustice Legal Def. Fund, Nature Conservancy, Friends of Earth, Friends of Worldwatch, Nat. Resources Def. Coun. Home and Office: 9450 Old Cutler Rd Miami FL 33156-2242 Fax: 305-663-5600.

FIELD, KAREN ANN (KAREN ANN SCHAFFNER), real estate broker; b. New Haven, Conn., Jan. 27, 1936; d. Abraham Terry and Ida (Smith) Rogovin; m. Barry S. Crown, 1954 (div. 1969); children: Laurie Jayne, Donna Lynn, Bruce Alan, Bradley David; m. Michael Lehmann Field, 1969 (div. 1977); m. Ronald E. Schaffner, Apr., 1998. Student, Vassar Coll., 1953-54, Harrington Inst. Interior Design, 1973-74, Roosevelt U., 1987—. Cert. residential specialist. Owner Karen Field Interiors, Chgo., 1970-86, Karen Field & Assocs. Realtors, Chgo., 1980-81; pres., ptnr. Field-Pels & Assocs. Realtors, Chgo., 1981-86; with top sales volume Sudler-Marling, Inc., Chgo., 1989; sales broker Koenig & Strey GMAC, Chgo., 1992—. Mem. Women's Coun. Camp Henry Horner, Chgo., 1960; bd. dirs., treas. Winnetka Pub. Sch. Nursery (Ill.), 1961-63; pres. Jr. Aux. U. Chgo. Cancer Rsch. Found., 1960-66, mem. exec. com. women's bd., 1965-66; bd. dirs., sec. United Charities, Chgo., 1966-68, Victory Gardens Theatre, Chgo., 1979; co-founder, pres. Re-Entry Ctr., Wilmette, Ill., 1978-80; mem. br. Child Abuse Svcs., Chgo., 1981-89, Stop AIDS Real Estate Divsn., 1988, AIDS Walkathon Com., 1990; bd. dirs. The Chgo. Ctr. for Self-Taught Art, 1993-96. Recipient Servian award Jr. Aux. of U. Chgo. Cancer Rsch. Found., 1966, Margarite Wolf award Women's Bd., U. Chgo. Cancer Rsch. Found., 1967, Founder's award, 1997, WAIT Woman of Day. Mem. Chgo. Real Estate Bd., Chgo. Assn. Realtors, Chgo. Coun. Fgn. Rels., English Speaking Union (jr. bd. 1958-59), Art Inst. Chgo., Field Mus., Union League Club, Pres.'s Club, Founders Club, Confrerie de la Chaine des Rotisseurs (Dame de la Chaine), Fulton River Dist. Assn. Office: Koenig & Strey GMAC 900 N Michigan Ave Ste 830 Chicago IL 60611-1514

FIELD, LARRY, paper company executive; b. June 2, 1939; BS, U of Illinois. CEO Field Container, Elk Grove Village, Ill. Office: Field Container 1500 Nicholas Blvd Elk Grove Village IL 60007-5575

FIELD, MARGARET M. retired librarian; b. Washington, Sept. 16, 1928; d. Samuel Weis and Catherine Reel (Hawley) Mendum; m. Rodney Wayne Lancaster, Aug. 12, 1950 (div. Jan. 1969); children: Barbara Lynn, Margaret Susan; m. Jack Field, Jan. 26, 1980. BA, U. Wis., 1950; MLS, Rutgers U., 1971. Hazlet br. libr. Monmouth County Libr., Manalapan, N.J., 1971-73, br. libr., Ocean Twp., 1973-79, br. coord., 1980-93, asst. dir., 1993—2002; ret., 2002. Mem. Monmouth Librs. Assn. (pres. 1979-80). Unitarian Universalist. Avocations: medieval times, repair work, sewing, exploring, local history.

FIELD, MARSHALL, business executive; b. Charlottesville, Va., May 13, 1941; s. Marshall IV and Joanne (Bass) F.; m. Joan Best Connelly, Sept. 5, 1964 (div. 1969); 1 child, Marshall; m. Jamee Beckwith Jacobs, Aug. 19, 1972; children: Jamee Christine, Stephanie Caroline, Abigail Beckwith. BA, Harvard Coll., 1963. With N.Y. Herald Tribune, 1964-65; pub. Chgo. Sun-Times, 1969-80, Chgo. Daily News, 1969-78; dir. Field Enterprises, Inc., Chgo., 1965-84, dir., mem. exec. com., 1965-84, chmn. bd., 1972-84, The Field Corp., 1984—, Cabot, Cabot & Forbes, 1984—, chmn. exec. com., 1985-89, sr. dir., chief exec. officer, 1989—; pub. World Book-Childcraft Internat. Inc., 1973-78, dir., 1965-80. Bd. trustees Art Inst. Chgo., Chgo. Pub. Libr. Found., Rush-Presbyn.-St. Lukes Med. Ctr., Chgo. Cmty. Trust; vice-chmn. bd. trustees Field Mus. Natural History; chmn. bd. Terra Mus. Am. Art; adv. bd. Brookfield Zoo; mem. charitable adv. coun. Office of Atty. Gen. of State of Ill.; active Chgo. Orchestral Assn.; mem. bd. visitors, vice chair Nicholas Sch. of the Environment, Duke U.; bd. dirs. First Nat. Bank Chgo., 1970—85, Field Found. Ill., Lincoln Park Zool. Soc.; chmn. Nat. Coun. of the World Wildlife Fund; bd. dirs. Atlantic Salmon Fedn. Mem. Nature Conservancy, River Club, Chgo. Club, Comml. Club, Harvard Club, Racquet Club, Onwentsia Club, Jupiter Island Club, Shore Acres Club. Office: 225 W Wacker Dr Ste 1500 Chicago IL 60606-1235

FIELD, MICHAEL JAY, education educator; b. NYC, May 1, 1943; s. Nathan H. and Sylvia (Froman) F.; m. Diane Patricia Hoffman, June 28, 1964; children: Valerie, Carolyn, Joshua. BA, SUNY, Stony Brook, 1964; MA, Cornell U., 1963, PhD, 1970. Asst. prof. Temple U., Phila., 1968-72, Bemidji (Minn.) State U., 1972-78, assoc. prof., 1978-81, prof., 1981—99, provost Shawnee State U., 1999—, interim pres., 2001—03. Dir. honors program Bemidji State U., 1974-99, ctr. profl. devel., 1986-99; cons., evaluator North Cen. Assn. Schs. and Colls. Contbr. articles to profl. jours. NEH fellow, 1979-80. Fellow Soc. Values Higher Edn., Am. Coun. on Edn.; mem. Assn. Integrative Studies (bd. dirs. 1985-97, pres. 1989-90), Nat. Coun. Tchrs. English (bd. dirs. 1979-81). E-mail: mfield@shawnee.edu.

FIELD, NOEL MACDONALD, JR., lawyer; b. Providence, May 15, 1934; s. Noel Macdonald and Ellen DeWolf (Preston) F.; m. Phyllis Campbell, Nov. 10, 1962; children: Ellen, Noel III, Campbell, Margaret. AB summa cum laude, Brown U., 1956; LLB cum laude, Harvard U., 1961. Bar: R.I. 1962. Ret. ptnr. Hinckley, Allen & Snyder and predecessors, Providence, 1961—. Former v.p. and sec. bd. dirs. U.S. Yacht Racing Union, Newport, R.I.; former trustee Rocky Hill Sch., Providence Country Day Sch.; v.p., trustee Lincoln Sch., Providence; bd. dirs., former mem. Arthritis Found. (Southern New Eng. chpt.). Fellow Am. Coll. Trust and Estate Counsel (state chmn. 1986-91); mem. Phi Beta Kappa (pres. R.I. Alpha). Avocations: sailing, bicycle riding. Office: Hinckley Allen & Snyder LLP 1500 Fleet Ctr Providence RI 02903-2319

FIELD, RICHARD CLARK, lawyer; b. Stanford, Calif., July 13, 1940; s. John and Sally Field; m. Barbara Faith Butler, May 22, 1967 (dec. Apr. 1984); 1 child, Amanda Katherine; m. Eva Sara Halbreich, Dec. 1, 1985. BA, U. Calif., Riverside, 1962; JD, Harvard U., 1965. Bar: Calif. 1966, U.S. Supreme Ct., 1971, U.S. Ct. Appeals (9th cir.) 1979. Assoc. Thompson & Colegate, Riverside, 1965-69; ptnr. Adams, Duque & Hazeltine, Los Angeles, 1970-89, mem. mgmt. com., 1981-84, chmn. litigation dept., 1985-89; ptnr. Cadwalader, Wickersham & Taft, Los Angeles, 1989-97, Bingham McCutchen LLP, Los Angeles, 1997—. Bd. dirs. ARC, L.A., 1984-93, 97—. Mem. ABA (litigation, torts and ins. practice sects., bus. torts com., products, gen. liability and consumer law com.), Los Angeles County Bar Assn. (trial lawyers sect.), Assn. Bus. Trial Lawyers (bd. govs. 1978-82). Episcopalian. Office: Bingham McCutchen LLP 355 S Grand Ave Ste 4400 Los Angeles CA 90071-3106

FIELD, ROBERT EDWARD, lawyer; b. Chgo., Aug. 21, 1945; s. Robert Edward and Florence Elizabeth (Aiken) F.; m. Jenny Lee Hill, Aug. 5, 1967; children: Jennifer Kay, Kimberly Anne, Amanda Brooke. BA, Ill. Wesleyan U., 1967; MA, Northwestern U., 1969, JD, 1973. Bar: Ill. 1973, U.S. Dist. Ct. (no. dist.) Ill. 1974, U.S. Supreme Ct. 1979. Exec. dir. Winnetka (Ill.) Youth Orgn., 1969-73; assoc. Seyfarth, Shaw, Fairweather & Geraldson, Chgo., 1973-79, ptnr., 1979-93, Field & Golan, Chgo., 1993—. Bd. dirs. Gt. Lakes Fin. Resources, Matteson, Ill., 1983—, vice chmn., 1988-91, chmn. 1991—; bd. dirs. Gt. Lakes Trust Co., 2001--, chmn., 2001--; bd. dirs. Chgo. chpt. Ill. Wesleyan U. Assocs., Great Lakes Ins. Svcs., Alsip, Ill., 2001--; chmn. bd. dirs. 1st Nat. Bank of Blue Island, 1989-2001, Great Lake Bank, 2001—, Bank of Homewood, 1988-2001; bd. dirs. Winchester Mfg. Co., Wood Dale, Ill., Ludell Mfg. Co., Milw., Comml. Resources Corp., Naperville, Ill., 1984-93; dir., sec. Ellis Corp., Itasca, Ill., 1980—; chmn. bd. dirs. Cmty. Bank of Homewood-Flossmoor, Ill., 1983-92, Bank of Matteson, Ill., 1992-99; bd. dirs. Grand Prairie Svcs., Inc., 1999--, sec., 2001--; mem. State Banking Bd. Ill., 1993-97. Bd. dirs. Ctr. for New Beginnings, 1997—, Svcs. Exch., 1998—, Family Svc. Ctrs. Cook County, Matteson, 1979-99, treas., 1981-82, pres., 1986-88, chmn., 1988-93; pres. Lakes of Olympia Condominium Assn., 1987-89; trustee Village of Olympia Fields, Ill., 1981-89, pres., 1991-97; trustee Ill. Wesleyan U., 1990—, treas., 1994—; bd. dirs. Northwestern U. Sch. Law Alumni Assn., 1990-94. Mem. ABA, Ill. Bar Assn., Am. Bankers Assn., Ill. Bankers Assn., United Meth. Bar Assn. (v.p. Chgo. chpt. 1989), Chgo. Bar Assn., Bankers Club Chgo., Union League Club Chgo., Calumet Country Club. Office: Field & Golan 3 1st National Plz Ste 1500 Chicago IL 60602 E-mail: refield@fieldgolan.com.

FIELD, SALLY, actress; b. Pasadena, Calif., Nov. 6, 1946; m. Steve Craig, Sept. 1968 (div. 1975); children: Peter, Eli; m. Alan Greisman, Dec. 1984 (div. 1994); 1 son, Samuel. Student, Actor's Studio, 1973-75. Starred in TV series Gidget, 1965, The Flying Nun, 1967-69, The Girl With Something Extra, 1973; film appearances include The Way West, 1967, Stay Hungry, 1976, Heroes, 1977, Smokey and the Bandit, 1977, Hooper, 1978, The End, 1978, Norma Rae, 1979 (Cannes Film Festival Best Actress award 1979, Acad. award 1980), Beyond the Poseidon Adventure, 1979, Smokey and the Bandit II, 1980, Back Roads, 1981, Absence of Malice, 1981, Kiss Me Goodbye, 1982, Places in the Heart, 1984 (Acad. award for best actress 1984), Murphy's Romance (also exec. producer), 1985, Surrender, 1987, Punchline, 1987 (also prodr.), Steel Magnolias, 1989, Soapdish, 1991, Not Without My Daughter, 1991, Homeward Bound: The Incredible Journey, 1993 (voice only), Mrs. Doubtfire, 1993, Forrest Gump, 1994; TV movies include Maybe I'll Come Home In the Spring, 1971, Marriage: Year One, 1971, Home for the Holidays, 1972, Bridges, 1976, Sybil, 1976 (Emmy award 1977), A Woman of Independent Means, 1994; prodr. Dying Young, 1991, Eye for an Eye, 1995, Homeward Bound II: Lost in San Francisco, 1996, Merry Christmas George Bailey, 1997, From The Earth to the Moon, 1998, A Cooler Climate, 1999.

FIELD, STEPHEN IRA, dermatologist, educator; b. Detroit, Sept. 22, 1949; s. Elliott and Frieda Rose (Lasser) F.; m. Ellyce Rochelle Field, July 15, 1973; children: Jordan, Andrew, Garrett. BA, U. Mich., 1971, MD, 1975. Diplomate Am. Bd. Dermatology. Intern St. Joseph Mercy Hosp., Ann Arbor, Mich., 1975-76; resident U. Mich. Med. Ctr., Ann Arbor, Mich., 1976-79; pvt. practice St. Clair Shores, Mich., 1979—. Clin. asst. prof. dermatology U. Mich., Ann Arbor, 1979-86, Wayne State U., Detroit, 1979—. Contbr. article to Jour. Am. Acad. Dermatology. Mem. AMA, Mich. State Med. Soc., Mich. Dermatol. Soc. (pres. 1990-91), Phi Beta Kappa. Office: 28333 Harper Ave Saint Clair Shores MI 48081-1687

FIELD, STEVEN PHILIP, medical educator; b. Newark, Feb. 21, 1951; s. Irving and Florence (Engel) F. BA, Yale U., 1973; MD, NYU, 1977, cert. in Bioethics and Med. Humanities, 2003. Diplomate Am. Bd. Internal Medicine, Am. Bd. Gastroenterology; cert. psychodynamic psychotherapy NYU Psychoanalytic Inst., Bioethics, Montefiore, NYU. Intern in internal medicine Bellevue Hosp., N.Y.C., 1977-78, resident in internal medicine, 1978-81; instr. in medicine Mt. Sinai Hosp., N.Y.C., 1981-83, NYU Sch. of Medicine, N.Y.C., 1983—, clin. asst. prof. medicine, 1991—. Contbr. articles to med. jours., chpts. to med. textbooks. Recipient John Addison Porter Prize Yale U., 1973. Mem.: ACP, Crohn's and Colitis Found. Am. (sci. adv. coun.), N.Y. State Med. Soc., N.Y. Acad. Gastroenterology (v.p. 1995—96), Am. Gastroent. Assn., Yale Club Ctrl. N.J. (alumni schs. com.), Alpha Omega Alpha. Office: 245 E 35th St New York NY 10016-4283

FIELD, TED (FREDERICK FIELD), film and record industry executive; b. Chgo. s. Marshall Field IV and Katherine W. Fanning; 6 children. Student, U. Chgo., Pomona Coll. Former race car driver; chmn., CEO Radar Pictures, 2002—; chmn., CEO Artistdirect, Inc.; chmn., CEO Artistdirect Recs.; founder Interscope Communications, Interscope Records; former co-owner Field Enterprises, Chgo.; owner Panavision, 1985-87. Co-producer (films) Critical Condition, 1987, Outrageous Fortune, 1987, Three Men and a Baby, 1987, Revenge of the Nerds II, 1987, Cocktail, 1988, The Seventh Sign, 1988, An Innocent Man, 1989; co-exec. producer (films) Bill and Ted's Excellent Adventure, 1989, Renegades, 1989; producer Revenge of the Nerds, 1984, Turk 182, 1985, Three Men and a Little Lady, Class Action, Jumanji, 1995, Mr. Holland's Opus, 1996, Runaway Bride, 1999; exec. producer The First Power, 1990, Bird on a Wire, 1990, What Dreams May Come, 1998, Very Bad Things, 1998; exec. producer Hand That Rocks The Cradle, 1992; co-exec. producer (TV films) The Father Clements Story, Everybody's Baby: The Rescue of Jessica McClure, A Mother's Courage. Avocations: chess, martial arts. Office: Radar Pictures 10900 Wilshire Blvd Ste 1400 Los Angeles CA 90024-6532

FIELD, THOMAS HAROLD, software design engineer; b. Flint, Mich., May 13, 1951; s. Harold Franklin and Evelyn Agnus (DeHate) F.; m. Sharon Deborah Patronis, Dec. 11, 1982 (div. May 1999); 1 child, Gabriel. BSE, U. Mich., Dearborn, 1973; MS in Computer Sci., Fla. Inst. Tech., 1986. Sr. software design engr. Gen. Dynamics Def. Systems, Pittsfield, Mass., 1974—. Roman Catholic. Avocations: photography, gardening, woodworking. Office: General Dynamics Def Sys PO Box 246 Cape Canaveral FL 32920-0246 Address: PO Box 320405 Cocoa Beach FL 32932-0405 E-mail: thfield@mpinet.net.

FIELDEN, C. FRANKLIN, III, early childhood education consultant; b. Gulfport, Miss., Aug. 4, 1946; s. C. Franklin and Georgia (Freeman) F.; children: Christopher Michaux (dec.), Robert Michaux, Jonathan Dutton. Student, Claremont Men's Coll., 1964-65; AB, Colo. Coll., 1970; MS, George Peabody Coll. Tchrs., 1976, EdS, 1979. Tutor Proyecto El Guacio, San Sebastian, P.R., 1967-68; asst. tchr. GET-SET Project, Colorado Springs, Colo., 1969-70, co-tchr., 1970-75, asst. dir., 1972-75; tutor Early Childhood Edn. Project, Nashville, 1975-76; pub. policy intern Donner-Belmont Child Care Ctr., Nashville, 1976—77; asst. to urban min. Nashville Presbytery, 1977; intern to prin. Steele Elem. Sch., Colorado Springs, 1977-78, tchr., 1978-86; resource person Office Gifted and Talented Edn. Colorado Springs Pub. Schs., 1986-87; tchr. Columbia Elem. Sch., Colorado Springs, 1987-92; tchr., pre-sch. team coord. Helen Hunt Elem. Sch., Colorado Springs, 1992-93; validator Nat. Acad. Early Childhood Programs, 1992—, mentor, 1994—, commr., 1996-2000, 2001—; cons. Colo. Dept. Edn., Denver, 1993—96, sr. cons., 1996—2001, state coord. Even Start Family Literacy Program, 1997—, prin. cons., 2001—. Lectr. Arapahoe C.C., Littleton, Colo., 1981-82; instr. Met. State Coll., Denver, 1981; cons. Jubail Human Resources Devel. Inst., Saudi Arabia, 1982; mem. governing bd. GET-SET Project, 1969-79, 91-93. Ad hoc bd. trustees Tenn. United Meth. Agy. on Children and Youth, 1976-77; mem. So. Regional Edn. Bd. Task Force on Parent-Caregiver Relationships, 1976-77; day care com. Colo. Commn. Children and Their Families, 1981-82; active Nashville Children's Issues Task Force, 1976-77, Tenn. United Meth. Task Force on Children and Youth, 1976-77, Citizens' Goals Leadership Tng., 1986-87, Child Abuse Task Force, 4th Jud. Dist., 1986-87, First Impressions (Colo. Govs. Early Childhood Initiative) Task Force, 1987-88, El Paso County Placement Alternatives Commn., 1990-96, White Ho. Summit on Early Childhood Cognitive Devel., 2001; proposal rev. team Colo. Dept. Edn., 1992—; co-chair City/County Child Care Task Force, 1991-92; charter mem. City/County Early Childhood Care and Edn. Commn., 1993-96; bd. dirs. Colo. Office of Resource and Referral Agys., 1996-99; appeals panel Divsn. Child Care, Colo. Dept. Human Svcs., 2002—. Recipient Arts/Bus./Edn. award, 1983, Innovative Tchg. award, 1984; fellow NIMH, 1976. Mem.: ASCD, Pikes Peak Assn. Edn. Young Children, Nat. Assn. Early Childhood Specialists in State Depts. of Edn. (v.p. 1997—99, pres. 1999—2001, past. pres. 2001—03), Colo. Assn. Edn. Young Children (legis. com. 1979—84, governing bd., sec., exec. com. 1980—84, rsch. conf. chmn. 1982, tuition awards com. 1983—86, governing bd. 1985—86, chmn. tuition awards com. 1985—86, governing bd. 1989—95, pub. policy com. 1989—96, exec. com., treas. 1993, primary grades conf. chmn. 1994), Nat. Assn. Edn. Young Children (founding mem. primary-grades caucus 1992—2001, co-chair Western States Leadership Network 1993, Membership Action Group grantee 1993, panel profl. ethics in early childhood edn. 1993—97, nominating panel 2000—02, co-facilitator primary-grades interest forum 2001—), Nat. Trust Hist. Preservation, Huguenot Soc. Gt. Britain and Ireland., Phi Delta Kappa. Presbyterian. Home: PO Box 7766 Colorado Springs CO 80933-7766 Office: 201 E Colfax Ave Denver CO 80203-1704

FIELDER, CHARLES ROBERT, oil industry executive; b. Lubbock, Tex., Mar. 9, 1943; s. Clarence Daniel and Ola Marie (Sewell) F.; m. Mary Ruth Wills, May 31, 1964; 1 child, Sara Elizabeth. BBA, Tex. Tech. U., 1965, MS in Acctg., 1972. C.P.A., Tex. Staff acct. Peat, Marwick, Mitchell & Co., Dallas, 1965-66, Arthur Andersen & Co., Dallas, 1968-69; treasury acct. Halliburton Co., Dallas, 1969-71, treasury supr., 1971-72, asst. treas., 1972-78, treas., 1978-89, v.p., treas., 1990-96, ret., 1997. Mem. AICPA, Fin. Execs. Inst., Tex. Soc. CPAs, Phi Eta Sigma, Beta Alpha Psi, Beta Gamma Sigma, Phi Kappa Phi. Republican. Mem. Ch. of Christ. Office: PMB 189 6757 Arapaho Rd Ste 711 Dallas TX 75248-4073

FIELDER, DOROTHY SCOTT, retired postmaster; b. Detroit, Apr. 20, 1943; d. William Lacy and Gertrude Elizabeth (Coddington) Davis; m. Douglas Stratton Fielder, July 13, 1968; 1 child, William Todd. AB, Randolph-Macon Woman's Coll., 1965; MA, Kent State U., 1968. Lab. instr. Mary Baldwin Coll., Staunton, Va., 1965-66, Hartwick Coll., Oneonta, N.Y., 1969-70; rsch. and teaching asst. Kent (Ohio) State U., 1966-68; high sch. tchr. biology Fairfax County Pub. Schs., Va., 1968-69; postal clk. U.S. Postal Svc., Maryland, N.Y., 1978-80, rural carrier, 1980-81, postmaster Schenevus, NY, 1981—2003. Coord. Benjamin Franklin Stamp Club, U.S. Postal Svc., Albany, N.Y., 1982-93. Author: Pictorial History of the Town of Maryland, N.Y., 1990, Otsego County Postal History, 1994, (with others) Time Once Past Never Returns, 1996. Vice chmn. Maryland Planning Bd., 1989-93, chmn., 1993-2001. Recipient Otsego County Local History award, 1995. Mem. AAUW, Nat. Assn. Postmasters U.S., Town of Md. Hist. Assn. (pres. 1982-2001), Tri-County Postmasters Assn. (pres. 1990-94), Empire State Postal History Soc., Am. Philatelic Soc., Rotary. Methodist. Avocations: stamp collecting, gardening, local history, photography. Home: 112 Stevens Rd Maryland NY 12116-3302 Office: US Postal Svc 97 Main St Ste 2 Schenevus NY 12155-9998 E-mail: scottfielder@stny.rr.com.

FIELDER, WILLIAM JAMES, III, electrical engineer, consultant; b. Cordele, Ga., Dec. 19, 1940; s. William James, Jr. Fielder and Ruth Emma Barendsz; m. Mary Virginia Cole, Dec. 23, 1976; children: Tiffany Lynn Monhollen, Elizabeth Cole. BSEE, U. of Fla., Gainesville, FL, 1967—69. EIT State of Fla., 1973, Certified Energy Manager, Energy Engring. Soc.; U.S., 2002, EIT State of S.C., 1973, State of Ga., 1973, State of Va., 1973, State of N.C., 1973. Design engr. The Bechtel Corp, San Francisco, 1969—71; chief elec. engr. Black, Crow, & Eidsness, Inc., Gainesville, 1972—74; pres. Aries Consulting Engineers, Inc., Gainesville, 1974—86; chief elec. engr. CRS Sirrine, Inc., Savannah, 1986—91; elec. dept head Piedmont Olsen Hensley, Inc, Raleigh, NC, 1991—94; elec. dept. head Beaufort Engring. Services, Inc, Beaufort, 1994—. Author: (textbook) The Lit Interior. With USN, 1959—62. Mem.: Energy Engineers Assoc., Illuminating Engring. Soc. Achievements include design of State Energy Office Design Award for lighting Design. Home: 54 Estill Beach Cir Bluffton SC 29910 Office: Beaufort Engineering Services Inc 31 Professional Village Ct Beaufort SC 29902 Home Fax: 843-757-4832; Office Fax: 843-522-2096. Personal E-mail: wfielder@hargray.com. E-mail: wfielder@besbeaufort.com.

FIELDHAMMER, EUGENE LOUIS, civil engineer; b. N.Y.C., Feb. 11, 1925; s. Louis and Agda Elvira (Anderson) F.; m. Genevieve Mullin, Aug. 26, 1950; children: Keith A., Michael D., Nancy H. Welsh. BCE, Kans. State U., 1950. Registered profl. engr., Mo., Ill., N.Y. Design engr. Edwards and Kelcy, Newark, 1950, D.B. Steinman, N.Y.C., 1952; project engr. Goodkind and O'Dea, Inc., Hamden, Conn., 1956, project/office mgr. Chgo., 1959; from sect. chief to pres. Booker Assocs. Inc., St. Louis, 1963-85; pres. Fieldhammer Inc., St. Louis, 1985-92; cons. in field St. Louis, 1992—. Mem. Ferguson (Mo.) Pers. Bd., 1965-72, Ferguson Archtl. Rev. Bd., 1985—. With USNR, 1943-46, ETO, PTO. Inducted into Engring. Hall of Fame Kans. State U., 1990. Mem. ASCE (life), Nat. Soc. Profl. Engrs., Mo. Soc. Profl. Engrs., Engrs. Club St. Louis (life), Soc. Am. Mil. Engrs. (pres. St. Louis chpt. 1982-83). Achievements include design and design management of bridges over Mackinac Straits, Hudson, Mississippi, and Missouri Rivers. Home and Office: 153 S Clay Ave Ferguson MO 63135-2447

FIELDING, ALLEN FRED, oral and maxillofacial surgeon, educator; b. Paterson, N.J., Jan. 22, 1943; s. Fred W. and Emily Claire (Boehm) F. BS, Fairleigh Dickinson U., 1959, DMD, 1963; postgrad. in oral surgery, N.Y. U., 1965-66; MD, U. Health Sci. Antigua, 2001; MBA, U. Phoenix, 2003. Diplomate Am. Bd. Oral and Maxillofacial Surgery (adv. bd. 1983-86), Am. Bd. Forensic Medicine, Dental Nat. Anesthesia Bd. Intern in oral surgery Roosevelt Hosp., N.Y.C., 1966-67; resident in oral surgery Phila. Gen. Hosp., 1967-69; practice dentistry specializing in oral-maxillo facial surgery Phila., 1969—; prof., chmn. dept. oral and maxillofacial surgery Temple U., Phila., 1983-88, staff prof., chief dept. oral and maxillofacial surgery univ. hosp., 1982-87. Cons. VA Hosp., Wilmington, Del.; staff St. Christopher's Hosp. for Children, Phila., Northeastern Hosp.; staff, chief divsn. oral and Maxillofacial surgery Epics. Hosp.; sect. chief oral and maxillofacial surgery Quakertown (Pa.) Hosp., Lawndale Hosp., Phila.; cons. Gt. Lakes Naval Hosp., Ill., Brandywine Hosp.; lectr. in field. Contbr. articles to profl. jours. Mem. Chapel of Four Chaplains, Valley Forge, Pa. Served to capt. USAF, 1963-65. Fellow Am. Dental Soc. Anesthesiology, Royal Soc. Health, Am. Soc. Oral and Maxillofacial Surgeons (Pa. del.), World Affairs Coun. (Phila. chpt.), Am. Coll. Dentistry (editor local chpt.), Internat. Coll. Dentists, Internat. Assn. Oral and Maxillofacial Surgeons, Am. Assn. Oral and Maxillofacial Surgeons, Am. Coll. Oral and Maxillofacial Surgeons, Internat. Assn. Oral Maxillofacial Surgery; mem. AAUP, ADA, Pa. Dental Soc., Phila. County Dental Soc., Assn. Mil. Surgeons, Am. Assn. Dental Schs., Del. Valley Soc. Oral Surgeons (com. resident tng. 1973-85, exec. com., pres. 1985), Am. Assn. Hosp. Dentists (sec.-treas. Del. County chpt. 1972-74, v.p. 1974, pres. 1976), Great Lakes Soc. Oral Maxillofacial Surgeons, Mid-Atlantic Soc. Oral Maxillofacial Surgeons, Temple U. Oral Surgery Honor Soc. (advisor), Pa. Soc. Oral and Maxillofacial Surgeons (exec. com., govt. affairs com., pres. 1995-96), Coll. Physicians and Surgeons Phila., Dental Assts. Nat. Bd. (adv. bd.), Internat. Assn. Oral Implantologists, Del. Valley Acad. Osseointegration, Pierre Fauchard Soc. (elected mem.), Omicron Kappa Upsilon (pres. 1985, Temple chpt.). Home: 1203 Rodman St Philadelphia PA 19147-1129 Office: 3223 N Broad St Philadelphia PA 19140-5007 also: County Line Med Ctr Lincoln Hwy Gap PA 17527

FIELDING, ELIZABETH BROWN, education educator; b. Ligonier, Ind., Feb. 17, 1918; d. Herbert Benjamin and Roberta (Franklin) B.; m. Frederick Allan Fielding, May 23, 1942 (wid. July 1962); children: Elizabeth Enndriss Fielding, Frederick Allan Fielding, Jr. BA, Smith Coll., 1939; MA, U. San Francisco, 1975. Cert. tchr. com. colls., Calif. Field staff mem. San Francisco Bay Girl Scout Assn., 1963-69; exec. dir. Tri-City Project on Aging, Rodeo,

Calif., 1970-73; tchr., cons. various univs., 1974—. Mem. curriculum com. U. Calif., Berkeley, 1979-80; chair edn. programs Diablo Valley Found. on Aging, Walnut Creek, Calif., 1980s. Author: The Memory Manual: 10 Simple Things You Can Do to Improve Your Memory After 50, 1999, Teacher's Guide to The Memory Manual, 2000; contbr. articles to profl. jours. Chair Mental Health Task Force, County Coun. for Aging, Contra Costa County, 1974-76; mem. Sr. Svcs. Commn., City of Lafayette, Calif., 1981—; pres. bd. dirs. Calif. Specialists on Aging, Calif., 1976-79. Mem. Western Gerontol. Assn. (now Am. Soc. on Aging), Internat. Transactional Analysis Assn., Nat. Coun. on the Aging, Authors Guild, Calif. Writers Club. Avocations: writing fiction, genealogy, art appreciation, bird watching. Home: 1824 Stanley Dollar Dr 4A Walnut Creek CA 94595

FIELDING, FRED FISHER, lawyer; b. Phila., Mar. 21, 1939; s. Fred P. and Ruth Marie (Fisher) F.; m. J. Maria Dugger, Oct. 21, 1967; children: Adam Garrett, Alexandra Caroline. AB, Gettysburg Coll., 1961; LL.B, JD, U. Va., 1964; LittD (hon.), U. Detroit, 1986, Pepperdine U., 1986. Bar: Pa. 1965, D.C. 1974. Assoc. Morgan, Lewis & Bockius, Phila., 1964-65, 67-70, ptnr. Washington, 1974-81; asst. counsel to Pres. of U.S. The White House, Washington, 1970-72, dep. counsel, 1972-74, counsel to Pres. of U.S., 1981-86; ptnr. Wiley, Rein & Fielding, Washington, 1986—; pres. Gilmore Broadcasting Corp., 1988-90. Mem. Jud. Conf. D.C. Cir. Ct., 1976—; mem. internat. adv. bd. Credit Internat. Bank, 1990-96; bd. dirs. Gilmore Broadcasting Corp., Coun. for Excellence in Govt.; spl. counsel Adminstrv. Conf. U.S., 1982-86, pub. mem., 1987-94, chmn. spl. com. on ethics in govt., 1988-92, com. on regulation, 1992-94; presdl. appointment to panel arbitrators Internat. Ctr. for Settlement Investment Disputes, 1987-95, 2002-; mem. CPR panel Disting. Neutrals, 2000—, bd. dirs. Pediat. AIDS Foundn, 1998—, mem. standing com. Fed, Judiciary ABA, 1996-2002; bd. dirs., vice chmn. Nat. Legal Ctr., 2002—; clearance counsel Bush-Cheney transition team, 2000-2001; commr. Nat. Commn. on Terrorism Attacks, 2002—. Mem. Commn. on White House Fellowships, 1981-86, Pres.'s Commn. for German-Am. Tricentennial, 1983-84; mem. presdl. del. to observe Philippine presdl. elections, 1986, pres.'s personal rep. Australia/Am. Friendship Week, 1986; spl. counsel to Rep. vice presdl. campaign, 1988, sr. legal advisor Bush-Quayle campaign, 1992; conflict-of-interest counsel Office of Pres.-Elect, 1980; gen. counsel 50th presdl. inaugural, 1984-85; dep. dir. presdl. transition, 1988-89; mem. Pres.'s Commn. on Fed. Ethics Law Reform, 1989; U.S. designated arbitrator Arbitration Tribunal on U.S.-U.K. Air Treaty Dispute, 1989-94, Sec. of Transp. Task Force on Air Disaster Victims, 1996-98; mem. bd. visitors Sch. Law Pepperdine U., 1989-92; bd. dirs. Coun. for Excellence in Govt., 1989-95; bd. fellows Gettysburg Coll., 1992—, also trustee; bd. dirs. USAir Shuttle, 1992—, Ethics Resource Ctr., 1993; sec.-treas., bd. dirs. Arlington Va. Hosp. Found., 1994—; mem. commn. on selection fed. judges U. Va. Miller Ctr., 1994-97; bd. dirs. Washington Scholarship Fund, 1994-97, Ctr. Democracy, 1995-98, vice-chmn. 1996-97, chmn., 1997; commr. Nat. Commn. Terrorism Attack, 2002-. Served to capt. AUS, 1965-67. John McKee Found. fellow. Fellow ABA (life, standing com. on fed. judiciary), CEELI, FBA, D.C. Bar Assn. (bd. govs. 1996-98), Pa. Bar Assn., Am. Arbitration Assn. (nat. panel), Lawyer's Club of Washington, Fed. City Club, Washington Golf and Country Club, 1925 F Street Club, Univ. Club, Phi Gamma Delta, Pi Delta Epsilon, Omicron Delta Kappa, Pi Lambda Sigma, Phi Delta Phi. Republican. Lutheran. Office: Wiley Rein & Fielding 1776 K St NW Washington DC 20006-2304

FIELDING, INEZ VICTORIA BROWN, community health nurse; b. Lewisburg, St. Mary, Jamaica, July 12, 1933; came to the U.S., 1968; d. Stanley J. and Nora (Facey) Thomas; m. Wynford Brown, Mar. 14, 1958 (dec. 1968); children: Laurel, Seymour; m. Clay Burton, Aug. 15, 1981. Diploma in nursing, Wolverhampton Sch. Nursing, England, 1960; BS in Spl. Studies, St. Francis Coll., Bklyn., 1978. RN, N.Y., Fla.; cert. effective mgmt. for suprs.; cert. phys. health assessment; cert. legal nurse cons. Nursing supr. Wilson Hosp., Mitcham Surrey, England, 1966-68, Far Rockaway Nursing Home, NY, 1968-69; staff nurse Down State Med. Ctr., Bklyn., 1968-70; asst. head nurse Kingsbrook Jewish Med. Ctr., Bklyn., 1970-82, St. Albans Vets. Hosp., NY, 1982-83; paramedic examiner Insurex Corp., 1983-85; vis. nurse Trico Home Visit Svc., 1984-86; area nurse Visiting Nurse Assn. Indian River County, Vero Beach, Fla., 1985-87; sr. cmty. health nurse, specialist, coord. Indian River County Health Unit, Vero Beach, Fla., 1987—. Supr. Fellsmere Outreach Clinic, Gifford Health Ctr., 1964—99; bd. dirs. Mental Health Assn., Vero Beach, 1988, Am. Cancer Soc., Vero Beach, 1990; active Sebastian (Fla.) Property Owners Assn.; mem. Sebastian Charter Rev. Com., 1999; ombudsman Dist. 9, 1998; mem. Sebastian 75th Anniversary Com., 2000; v.p. AARP, 1998—2000; bd. dirs. Ret. Sr. Vol. Program Indian River County, 2001—03; vol. counselor Serving Health Ins. Needs of Elders, State of Fla. Dept. Elder Affairs. Mem.: AAUW (healthy start coalition rep., Nurse of Yr. Dist. #17 1989, Mary Cash award 1994, Barbara Lumpkin award 2001, Nurse of Yr. Dist. # 17 1998), ANA (coun. cultural diversity 1991, Nurse Excellence award 1991), Fla. Pub. Health Assn., Fellsmere Health CareCoalition, Fla. Nurses Assn. (conv. del. 1988—97, pres. dist. 17 1996—97, bd. dirs. 1999—, treas.). Democrat. Methodist. Avocations: travel, dancing, social entertainment, community involvement, reading. Home: 1197 Gardenia St Sebastian FL 32958-8215 Office: Indian River County Pub Health Dept 1900 27th St Vero Beach FL 32960-3383

FIELDING, STUART, psychopharmacologist; b. Bronx, N.Y., Oct. 31, 1939; s. Harry and Ethel (Weisberg) Feinblatt; m. Maralyn J. Lowy, Aug. 26, 1962; children: Kimberly Ellen, Bradford Scott. BA, Monmouth Coll., 1962; MS, Howard U., 1964; PhD, U. Del., 1968. Mgr. psychopharmacology rsch. Ciba-Geigy Corp., Summit, N.J., 1967-75; assoc. dir. pharmacology Hoechst-Roussel Pharms., Inc., Somerville, N.J., 1975-76, assoc. dir. biol. sci., mgr. pharmacology, 1977-84, dir. pharmacology, 1984-86, dir. biol. rsch., 1987-89; v.p. R & D, dir. Interneuron Pharms., Inc., Lexington, Mass., 1989-92; chmn., CEO Bio-Enhancement Systems Corp., Morris Plaines, N.J., 1992—. Editor: (book) Psychopharmacology of Clonidine, 1981, (book series) Industrial Pharmacology: A Monograph Series, 1974-79, (jour.) Drug Devel. Rsch., 1980-92; contbr. articles to profl. publs. Fellow Am. Psychol. Assn.; mem. Am. Chem. Soc., Am. Soc. Pharmacology and Exptl. Therapeutics, Soc. Neurosci. Home and Office: 16 Bromleigh Way Morris Plains NJ 07950-1642

FIELDS, ALLEN, artistic director; b. Pinehurst, N.C. Student, N.C. Sch. Arts, Am. Ballet Theatre Sch., N.Y.; studied with Patricia Wilde, Wilhelm Burman, David Howard, Ivan Nagy, Melissa Hayden. Performer with Cynthia Gregory, Gwen Verdon, Samuel Ramie, Madonna, Geena Davis; guest appearances in South Am., Europe, Can., Mex.; dancer with Ohio Ballet, Eglevsky Ballet, Ballet du Nord, France, Atlanta Ballet, Newport News Ballet, Phoenix Ballet, Hubbard St. Dance Co.; prin. dancer Cleve. San Jose Ballet; artistic dir. Minn. Ballet, 1992—. Office: Minn Ballet Ste 800 301 W 1st St Duluth MN 55802

FIELDS, ANTHONY LINDSAY AUSTIN, health facility administrator, oncologist, educator; b. St. Michael, Barbados, Oct. 21, 1943; arrived in Can., 1968; s. Vernon Bruce and Marjorie F.; m. Patricia Jane Stewart, Aug. 5, 1967. MA, U. Cambridge, 1969; MD, U. Alta., 1974. Diplomate Am. Bd. Internal Medicine. Sr. specialist Cross Cancer Inst., Edmonton, Alta., Can., 1980-85, dir. dept. medicine, 1985-88, dir., 1988-2000; v.p. med. affairs and cmty. oncology Alta. Cancer Bd., 2000—. Asst. prof. medicine U. Alta., Edmonton, 1980-84, assoc. prof., 1984-98, prof., 1998—, dir. divsn. med. oncology, 1985-89, dir. divsn. oncology, 1988-93; v.p. Nat. Cancer Inst. Can., 2000-02. pres., 2002--. Fellow ACP, Royal Coll. Physicians and Surgeons Can. (specialist cert. med. oncology, internal medicine); mem. Can. Assn. Med. Oncologists (pres. 1994-96), Am. Soc. Clin. Oncology, Am. Fedn. Clin. Rsch., Can. Soc. for Clin. Investigation, Can. Med. Assn. Avocation: photography. Office: # 1220 10405 Jasper Ave Edmonton AB Canada T5J 3N4

FIELDS, BERTRAM HARRIS, lawyer; b. LA, Mar. 31, 1929; s. H. Maxwell Fields and Mildred Arlyn (Ruben); m. Lydia Ellen Minevitch, Oct. 22, 1960 (dec. Sept. 1986); 1 child, James Eldar; m. Barbara Guggenheim, Feb. 21, 1991. BA, UCLA, 1949; JD magna cum laude, Harvard U., 1952. Bar: Calif. 1953. Practiced in, LA, 1955—; assoc. firm Shearer, Fields, Rohner & Shearer, and predecessor firms, 1955—57, mem. firm, 1957—82; ptnr. Greenberg, Glusker, Fields, Claman, Machtinger and Kinsella, 1982—. Mem. bd. editors: Harvard Law Rev., 1953—55; author (as D. Kincaid): The Sunset Bomber, 1986; author: The Lawyer's Tale, 1992; author: (as B. Fields) Royal Blood Richard III and the Mystery of the Princes, 1998. Bd. dirs. U. So. Calif. Annenberg Sch. Comm. 1st lt. USAF, 1953—55, Korea. Mem.: ABA, Coun. Fgn. Rels., LA County Bar Assn. Achievements include being the subject of profiles Calif. Mag., Nov. 1987; Avenue Mag., Mar. 1989; Am. Film Mag., Dec. 1989; Vanity Fair Mag., Dec. 1993; Harvard Law Sch. Bull., spring 1998; London Sunday Telegraph, June 1999; Sunday New York Post, July 1999; W Mag., Apr. 2002; L.A. Times, Apr. 2003; London Sunday Times, Apr. 2003. Office: Greenberg Glusker Fields Claman & Machtinger Ste 2000 1900 Avenue Of The Stars Los Angeles CA 90067-4590

FIELDS, CARL VICTOR, food company executive; b. Lima, Ohio, Apr. 26, 1951; s. John Cecil and Baby Doll (Harris) F.; m. Charlean Annett Hartsfield, Oct. 3, 1981. BA, U. Calif., Irvine, 1973; MA, Yale U., 1975. Mktg. officer Wells Fargo Bank, San Francisco, 1975-77; bus. planner Dart Industries, L.A., 1977-80; mgr. bus. rsch. Amfac Foods, Portland, Oreg., 1980-83, v.p. mktg. Monterey Mushrooms, Watsonville, Calif., 1983—. Fruits and vegetables adv. com. USDA. Mem. Mushroom Coun. (vice-chmn.), Am. Mushroom Inst. (bd. dirs.), U. Calif. at Irvine Alumni Assn. (pres.), UCI Found. (bd. ambs.), Yale Club (San Francisco). Baptist. Home: PO Box 1210 Capitola CA 95010-1210 Office: Monterey Mushrooms Inc 260 Westgate Dr Watsonville CA 95076-2452 E-mail: carlfieds@aol.com.

FIELDS, CLEO, state legislator; b. Nov. 22, 1962; m. Debra Horton; 1 child, Cleo Brandon. BA, Southern U., 1984, JD, 1987. Mem. La. State Senate from Dist. 14, 1987-92, 97—, 103d-104th Congresses from 4th La. Dist., 1993-96. Founder Young Adults for Positive Action. Named Outstanding Young Men in Am., 1987. Democrat. Baptist.

FIELDS, DAISY BRESLEY, human resources specialist, writer; b. Bklyn., 1915; m. Victor Fields, Aug. 2, 1936; 1 child, Barbara Fields Ochsman. Student, Hunter Coll., 1932-35, Am. U., 1949-53. Pers. officer USAF Base, Norfolk, Va., 1942-45; asst. pers. officer Dept. Agr., Phila., 1945-47; asst. dir. pers. Smithsonian Instn., Washington, 1954-60; chief spl. programs NASA, Washington, 1960-67; spl. asst. Fed. Womans Program VA, Washington, 1967-70; sr. program assoc. Nat. Civil Svc. League, 1971-72; cons. Equal Employment Opportunity/Affirmative Action, 1978—90; exec. dir. Federally Employed Women, Washington, 1975-77. Pres. Fields Assocs., Silver Spring, Md., 1978—2000; exec. dir. The Womens Inst., Am. U.; instr. Mt. Vernon Coll., 1979-80, Am. U., 1982; cons. USAID, 1990-93; freelance writer. Author: A Woman's Guide to Moving Up in Business and Government, 1983; editor: Winds of Change: Korean Women in America, 1991; contbr. articles to profl. jours. Chair Montgomery County (Md.) Pers. Bd., 1972-78; chair legis. com. Com. for Women in Pub. Adminstrn., 1976-79; commr. Md. Commn. for Women, 1979-82; editor newsletter, past pres. Clearinghouse on Womens Issues; v.p., mng. editor Womens Inst. Press; bd. dirs. Nat. Womans Party, 1989-97. Reciipent UN Assn. U.S.A. award, 1980, Vet. Feminists Am. medal, 1998. Mem. NAFE, Nat. Coun. Career Women, Womens Equity Action League (pres. Md. 1972-74, award 1978), Federally Employed Women (pres. 1969-71, editor newsletter 1972-77, award 1974, 78), Nat. Press Club, Am. News Womens Club, Internat. Womens Writing Guild, Washington Ind. Writers, Capital Press Women, Fedn. Orgns. Profl. Women (exec. coun. 1976-77, 80-82), Nat. Assn. Women Bus. Owners, Freelance writer. Home and Office: #404 3005 S Leisure World Blvd Silver Spring MD 20906-8305 E-mail: dbresley@aol.com.

FIELDS, DAN, newspaper editor; b. Kankakee, Ill., Apr. 23, 1975; s. John B. and Susan L. Fields. BA in Journalism, Ea. Ill. U., 1997. Reporter City News Bur. Chgo., 1996, Peoria (Ill.) Jour. Star, 1996, Decatur (Ill.) Herald and Review, 1997-99, The Times of N.W. Ind., Munster, 1999-2000; newspaper editor The Times-News, Twin Falls, Idaho, 2000—01; mng. editor Austin (Minn.) Daily Herald, 2001—. Recipient Peter Lisagor award Chgo. chpt. Soc. Profl. Journalists, 1999, 2d pl. award non-deadline news reporting Ind. AP Mng. Editors, 1999, 2d pl. issues reporting Ind. SPJ chpt. 1999, 1st pl. enterprise reporting Howard Publs., 1999, 3d pl. award investigative reporting Idaho Press Assn., 2001.

FIELDS, DOUGLAS PHILIP, building supply wholesale company executive; b. Jersey City, May 19, 1942; s. M. Emanuel and Priscilla (Wagner) F.; m. Paulette Susan Titko, Dec. 15, 1970 (div. Feb. 1990); children: Douglas Philip, Priscilla Wagner, Jessica Elizabeth; m. Maureen Virginia Hanmer, June 12, 1993; 1 child, Jacob Wagner. BS summa cum laude, Fordham U., 1964; MBA with distinction, Harvard U., 1966. Investment analyst Lehman Bros., N.Y.C., 1966-67; asst. to pres. Talley Industries Inc., Mesa, Ariz., 1967-69; CEO, pres. TDA Industries Inc., N.Y.C., 1969—; founder Unimet Corp., N.Y.C., 1970-73; pres., chmn. Westcalind Corp., R.I., 1971-87; CEO Acqueren, Inc., 1995-98. Chmn. bd. TDA Industries, Inc., N.Y.C., 1970—, Westco Corp., Boston, 1970—79, Cooper Flooring Internat., Inc., Miami, 1972—98; chmn. bd. dirs., CEO Eagle Supply, Inc., Tampa, Fla., 1973—; CEO JEH/Eagle Supply, Inc., Dallas, 1997—; CEO, chmn. MSI/Eagle Supply Inc., Dallas, 1998—2000, Eagle Supply Group, Inc. (NASDAQ:EEGL), N.Y.C., 1996—; chmn. Northeastern Plastics, Inc., NY, 1986—98; cons. U.S. Office Edn., 1973—74, Fed. Energy Adminstrn., 1974—75. Outside dir. NYU Grad. Sch. Bus., Mgmt. Decision Lab., 1973-78; mem. N.Y. State adv. com. U.S. Civil Rights Commn., 1974-85; bd. dirs. YMHA-YWHA of So. Westchester, Mt. Vernon, N.Y., 1981-92, Associated YMHA-YWHA of N.Y.C., Inc., 1989-91; mem. Young Pres.'s Orgn., 1973-92. Mem. Chief Execs. Orgn., Met. Pres. Orgn., World Pres. Orgn., Belle Haven Club.

FIELDS, FREDDIE, producer, agent; b. Ferndale, N.Y., July 12, 1923; s. John Jacob and Jeanette (Sewal) F.; m. Polly Bergen; children: Kathy, P.K., Peter; m. Corinna Tsopei (Miss Universe 1968); children: Andrew, Steven, Paris. V.p. MCA Inc., N.Y., 1946-59; pres. Freddie Fields Assocs., N.Y., 1959-60; founder, pres., chief exec. officer Creative Mgmt. Assocs. Inc., Internat. Creative Mgmt. Agy., Los Angeles and worldwide, 1960-75; pres., chief exec. officer Freddie Fields Prodns., Los Angeles and N.Y.C., 1975-78; pres., chief operating officer MGM Film Co., Los Angeles, 1980-82; pres. worldwide prodn. MGM/UA Entertainment, Los Angeles, 1982-84; pres., chief exec. officer The Fields Orgn., Los Angeles, 1984—. Chmn. programming Network Event Theatre, 1995. Prodr.: (films) Looking for Mr. Goodbar, American Gigolo, Citizens Band, Victory, Fever Pitch, Poltergeist II, Lipstick, Crimes of the Heart, Millenium, Glory; executive prodr.: The Montel Williams Show. Recipient Creativity awards, 1970, 71, 72, Soc. Illustrators awards, 1969, 70, 71. Recipient Prodr. of Yr. NAACP award, 1991.

FIELDS, HARRIET GARDIN, counselor, educator, consultant; b. Pasco, Wash., Feb. 25, 1944; d. Harry C. and Ethel Jenell (Rochelle) Gardin; m. Avery C. Fields; 1 child, Avery C. BS in Edn., S.C. State U., Orangeburg, 1966; MEd, U. S.C., 1974. Lic. profl. counselor and supr.; nat. bd. cert. counselor and career counselor. Tchr. Richaldn Sch. Dist., Columbia, S.C., 1966-67 73-76; counselor supr. S.C. Dept. Corrections, Columbia, 1971-73; counselor Techinal Edn. System, West Columbia, S.C., 1967-70; exec. dir. Bethlehem Community Ctr., Columbia, 1976-79; human rels. cons. Calhoun County Schs., St. Matthews, S.C., 1979-82; admission counselor Allen U., Columbia, 1982-83; pres., cons. H.G. Fields Assn., Columbia, 1973—. Exec. dir. Big Bros./Big Sisters, Columbia, 1984-87 Mem. Richland County Coun., Columbia, 1989-97, chair, 1993, 94, 95, 96, 97; 2d vice chair Richland County Dem. Party, Columbia, 1984-88; sec. Statewide Reapportionment Com., 1990-97; mem. Richland Lexington Immunization Com., Hope for Kids, The Lifeline: Mission to Families; commr. Midlands Tech. Coll., 2001—. Recipient inaugural Woodrow Wilson award Greater Columbia C. of C., 1994, Pres.'s Disting. Svc. award Nat. Orgn. Black County Ofcls., 1996, numerous human rels. and outstanding svc. awards. Mem. ACA (resolutions chair So. br. 1993-94, parlimentarian 1998, 99-2000), SC Counseling Assn. (chair govt. rels. 1985-97, 98-99, pres. 1982-83), Assn. Multicultural Counseling Devel. (v.p. for African Am. concerns 1999-2000, rep. to Am. governing coun. 2000-2003), SC Coalition Pub. Health, Nat. Assn. Counties (d. dir. 1996, bylaws and election cm. 1996, 97, employment steering com. 1997), Nat. Assn. Counties (employment steering com. 1993-97, chair youth subcom. employment steering 1995-97, vice chair 1993-94), Am. Bus. Women's Assn. (pres. Midlands chpt. 1998-99), Columbia C. of C. Democrat. Methodist. Avocations: travel, reading. Home and Office: HG Fields and Assocs 412 Juniper St Columbia SC 29203-5055

FIELDS, JAMES PERRY, dermatologist, dermatopathologist, allergist; b. Sherman, Tex., July 30, 1932; s. John Galloway and Alma (Goff) F.; m. Linda Hensley, May 30, 1958; children: Timothy Austin, Amy Elizabeth. BS, U. Tex., 1953, MS, 1957; MD, U. Tex., Galveston, 1958. Diplomate Am. Bd. Dermatology, Am. Bd. Allergy and Immunology, spl. competence cert. in dermatoapathology. Dir. dept. dermatology USPHS, S.I., N.Y., 1964-78; assoc. prof. medicine and pathology Vanderbilt U. Sch. of Medicine, Nashville, 1978-88; pvt. practice, Nashville, 1988—; dir. dermatopathology Lab. of the Mid-South, Nashville, 1988—. From instr. to assoc. clin. prof. dermatology and pathology Columbia-Presbyn. Hosp. and Coll. of Physicians and Surgeons, N.Y.C., 1968-88; assoc. clin. prof. medicine Vanderbilt U. Sch. Medicine, Nashville, 1988—. Author (with others): Mycobacterial Diseases, 1991, 2d edit., 2000; contbr. articles to profl. jours. Bd. dirs. Am. Leprosy Missions Internat., Greenville, S.C., 1974—; vol. med. missionary, United Meth. Vols. in Mission, 1984—. Capt. USPHS, 1958-79. Recipient citation for meritorious svcs. President's Com. on Employment of Handicapped, 1970, Meritorious Svc. medal USPHS, 1978, Good Samaritan award Nashville Acad. Medicine, 2002. Fellow ACP (Volunteerism and Cmty. Svc. award in Medicine, Tenn. chpt. 2000), Am. Acad. Allergy and Immunology, Am. Acad. Dermatology, Am. Coll. Allergy and Immunology, Am. Soc. Dermatopathology, Am. Soc. for Dermatologic Surgery, N.Y. Acad. Medicine (sec. 1976-77, chmn. sect. on dermatology 1977-78). Home: 411 Lynwood Blvd Nashville TN 37205-3434 Office: 4301 Hillsboro Rd # 222 Nashville TN 37215-3314

FIELDS, JERRI LYNN, foundation administrator; Human svcs. Horizons Cmty. Svcs., Chicago; exec. dir. Rape Victim Adv., Chicago; devel. and comm. dir. Fund for N.Y., V-Day: Until the Violence Stops, San Francisco, 2001—02, exec. dir., 2002—. Pres. Ill. Coalition Against Sexual Assault; mem. Gov.'s Commn. on Status of Women in Ill. Office: VDay Adminstrv Offices 388 Market St Ste 400 San Francisco CA 94111

FIELDS, JILL S. education educator; d. Valerie and Jerry Fields, Sandy Boxbaum. BA with honors in women's studies and hisotry, U. of Calif. at Santa Cruz; MA in history, PhD in history, Grad. Cert., Women's Studies, U. of So. Calif., 1997. Vis. asst. prof., am. studies Ariz. State U., West, 1998—99; asst. prof. of history Calif. State U., Fresno, 1999—. Historian Survivors of the Shoah Visual History Found., Burbank, 1998—99; prof. Smittcamp Family Honors Coll., CSU Fresno, 2000—; symposium dir. 30 Years of Feminist Art in Fresno and Beyond, 2000—01. Musician: (albums) (album) Let's Get Acquainted: The Holy Sisters of the Gaga Dada (Best Underground Band, LA, 1987), Gaga at the GoGo, author: (book) The Production of Glamour: A Social History of Intimate Apparel in the Twentieth Century; contbr. articles to profl. jours., chapters to books. Founding mem., steering com.,DBCP water standards project chair Fresno Com. Against the Misuse of Pesticides, 1999. Recipient U. Rsch. award, CSU Fresno, 2000—03; fellow All U. Predoctoral Merit fellowship, The Grad. Sch., USC, 1990—93; Feminist Art Symposium, Calif. Arts Coun., 2000—01, Haynes Found. fellowship, USC Grad. Sch., 1996—97, McVicar Dissertation fellowship, Dept. of History, USC, 1995, Sharon Tedesco fellowship, Gender Studies, USC, 1994, Feminist Art Symposium grant, Harry C. Mitchell Trust, 2001, Marshall Fishwick Travel to Popular Culture Collection grant, Popular Culture Assn. and Am. Culture Assn., 2000, Henry Du Pont fellowship, Hagley Mus. and Libr., 1999, Vis. Rsch. Scholar fellowship, Feminist Rsch. Inst., U. of N.Mex, 1999, Woodrow Wilson Dissertation grant in Women's Studies, Woodrow Wilson Fellowship Found., 1994, Veronika Gervers Rsch. fellowship, Royal Ont. Mus., 1993, Stella Blum Rsch. grant, Costume Soc. of Am., 1994—95. Mem.: Calif. Faculty Assn. (dept. of history rep. 2001), Am. Studies Assn., Western Assn. of Women Historians, Orgn. of Am. Historians, Am. Studies Assn., Am. Hist. Assn. Jewish. Avocations: yoga, music. Office: CSU Fresno Department of History M/S SS 21 Fresno CA 93740 Office Fax: 559-278-5321.

FIELDS, KATHY ANN, dermatologist; b. Waukegan, Ill., May 14, 1958; d. Maynard Bernard and Blanche Fields; m. Garry Rayant, Oct. 10, 1991; children: Richard, Mark. Student, Northwestern U., 1975-76; BS, U. Fla., 1979; MD, U. Miami, Fla., 1983. Diplomate Am. Bd. Dermatology. Intern in ob-gyn. Jackson Meml. Hosp., 1983-84; resident in dermatology Stanford (Calif.) U. Med. Ctr., 1984-87; laser specialist Sydney, Australia, 1987; pvt. practice San Francisco, 1988—; clin. instr. dermatology U. Calif., San Francisco, 1992—. Co-owner K-R Dermatologics, Inc.; creator Proactiv Solutions, internat. acne skin care line; co-owner Rodan and Fields; assoc. clin. prof. U. Calif., San Francisco; pres. Rodan and Fields; cons. in field. Fundraiser Am. Cancer Soc., San Francisco, 1988—, Child Abuse Prevention, United Jewish Appeal, Women's Young Leadership Cabinet, 1991—, mosaic counsel. Recipient award of excellence in cosmetic industry, Cosmetic Exec. Women, 2003; featured in People mag., 2002. Fellow: Am. Acad. Dermatology; mem.: AMA, San Francisco Med. Soc., Calif. Med. Assn. Avocations: aerobics, skiing, windsurfing, dance. Office: 2100 Webster St Ste 505 San Francisco CA 94115-2381

FIELDS, LEO, former jewelry company executive, investor; b. Wichita Falls, Tex., 1928; married. Student, U. Tex. With Zale Corp., Irving, Tex., 1942-87; pres. Fine Jewelers Guild divsn. Zale Corp., Irving, Tex., 1965-69; v.p. jewelry mdse. dir. Zale Corp., Irving, Tex., 1969-81, vice chmn., 1981-83, also bd. dirs.; co-chmn., investment advisor Weisberg & Fields, Inc. Bd. dir. CBL & Assoc. Properties Inc., M.B. and Edna Zale Found.; chmn. Trustee M.B. and Edna Zale Found.; pres. Dallas Home for the Jewish Aged Endowment Found.

FIELDS, POLLY STEVENS, educator, writer, researcher; b. Tenn. BA, Vanderbilt U., 1978; PhD, La. State U., 1992. Cert. tchr., Tenn. Tchr. U. Sch. Nashville, 1978—84, Miami Valley Day Sch., Dayton, Ohio, 1984—87; instr. U. Ala., Tuscaloosa, Ala., 1993—95; from asst. prof. english to prof. Lake Superior State U., Sault Ste. Marie, Mich., 1995—2003, prof. english, 2003—. Vis. scholar UCLA, 2000-01. Co-author: (with others) Compendious Conversations: Methods of Dialogue in the Early Enlightenment, 1993, Eighteen-Century Anglo-American Women Novelists, 1998, A Pilgrimage for Love: New Essays in Early Modern Literature, 2000; contbr. articles to profl. jours. Recipient MAGB Faculty award Mich. Assn. Governing Bds., 1998; Rsch. fellow La. State U., 1990, 91, 92, UCLA, 1997-98, 2000-01, NEH, 2002. Fellow: Am. Soc. Eighteenth-Century Studies, Canadian Soc. Eighteenth-Century Studies, The British Soc. Eighteenth Century Studies, The Voltaire Soc.; mem. AAUW, Nat. Coun. Tchrs. English, Assn. Literary Scholars and Critics, British and Am. Women Writers, Early Modern Studies Assn., Modern Lang. Assn., Ireland Soc., John Donne Soc., Milton Soc., Mich. Acad. Arts, Scis., and Letters, Shakespeare Soc., Seventeenth Century Soc., Rocky Mountain MLA, Aphra Behn Soc. Avocations: opera, fitness, yoga. Office: Lake Superior State U 650 West Easterday Ave Sault Sainte Marie MI 49783 Fax: 906-635-6678. E-mail: pfields@gw.lssu.edu.

FIELDS, RICHARD LAWRENCE, lawyer, consultant; b. Washington, May 3, 1948; s. Robert Arthur and Helen Elizabeth (Hasty) F.; m. Michele McDowell, Apr. 17, 1971; children— Lauren Michele, Lindsey Suzanne. A.B., Columbia U., 1970; disting. grad. Officers Tng. Sch., U.S. Air Force, 1971; honor grad. Criminal Investigator Sch., U.S. Treasury, 1973; M.A., U. Md., 1974, J.D., 1977. Bar: Md. 1977, U.S. Dist. Ct. D.C. 1978, U.S. Dist. Ct. Md. 1978, U.S. Ct. Appeals (D.C. and 4th cirs.) 1978. Position classification specialist U.S. Geol. Survey, Washington, 1971-73; chief position mgmt. Bur. Alcohol, Tobacco, and Firearms, 1973-78; sole practice, Md. and Washington, 1978-82; ptnr. Fields & Fields, Oxon Hill, Md., and Washington, 1982— ; cons. mgmt. and personnel adminstrn., 1978-80. Served to 1st lt. USAFR, 1971-72. Mem. ABA, Assn. Trial Lawyers Am., Md. Bar Assn., Prince Georges County Bar Assn. Democrat. Office: Fields & Fields Ste LL500 5620 Saint Barnabas Rd Oxon Hill MD 20745

FIELDS, RICKY EDWARD, counselor; b. Spartanburg, S.C., Jan. 15, 1964; s. Betty Jean Fields; 1 child, Ricky Edward Jr. BS, S.C. State U., 1986, M of Counseling Edn., 1998; A of Logistics, C.C. of Air Force, USAF, 1988. Student tchr. asst. S.C. State U., Orangeburg, 1985-86; counselor, case mgr. Camp White Pines (AMI), JOnesville, SC, 1991—. Sec., mem. Comprehensive Health Edn., Spartanburg, 1992-94; adv. mem. Bethlehem Ptnrs .Prevention, Spartanburg, 1996-99. Contbr. Spartanburg Herald Jour., 1994. Mem. S.C. Alliance of Black Edn., Columbia, 1997—; trustee Macedonia Bapt. Ch., Spartanburg. With USAF, 1986-90. Mem. ACA, Am. Sch. Counselor Assn., S.C. Sch. Counselors Assn., Macedonia Single Ministries (chmn. 1996—), Omega Psi Phi. Democrat. Baptist. Avocations: swimming, running, reading, writing. Home: 114 Delmar Ct Spartanburg SC 29302 Office: Spartanburg City Sch Dist # 7 610 Dupre Dr Spartanburg SC 29307-2980

FIELDS, STUART HOWARD, labor relations specialist; b. Chgo., Dec. 15, 1943; s. Albert B. and Cecelia (Kessler) Fields; m. Birgit Willeke, Dec. 5, 1971; children: Jessica N., Jascha D. BS, UCLA, 1965; MS, U. Calif., Northridge, 1968. Cert. tchr. and instr. Calif. Labor rels. specialist Hughes Tool Co., Culver City, Calif., 1970, Dept. of the Navy, Point Mugu, Calif., 1971-76; employee rels. specialist Agrl. Rsch. Svc., Hyattsville, Md., 1976-81, labor rels. specialist, 1981-84, Pub. Health Svc., Rockville, Md., 1985-86; employee rels. specialist Def. Nuclear Agy., Bethesda, Md., 1986-88, Consumer Product Safety Commn., Bethesda, 1988-89, U.S. Dept. Commerce, Washington, 1989-97; sr. paralegal Gagliardo & Zipin, Attys. at Law, Silver Spring, Md., 1997—; labor rels. specialist IRS, Washington, 1997—. Presdl. classroom instr.; cons. in field. Author: Requirements for Top Positions in Personnel Administration, 1968. Lt. U.S. Army, 1968—70. Mem.: Soc. Fed. Labor Rels. Profls., Mensa, Jewish Cmty. Ctr. Democrat. Avocations: classical music, numismatics, tax law, basketball. Home: 9449 Reach Rd Potomac MD 20854-2853 Office: IRS 5000 Ellin Road Lanham MD 20706

FIELDS, SUZANNE BREGMAN, syndicated columnist; b. Washington, Mar. 7, 1936; d. Samuel Holiday and Sadie (Hurwitz) Bregman; m. Theodore Martin Fields, June 16, 1957; children: Alexandra, Miriamne, Tobias. BA, George Washington U., 1957, MA, 1964; PhD, Cath. U., 1971. Freelance writer, Washington, 1965-71; editor Innovations Mag., Washington, 1971-79; columnist Vogue mag., Washington, 1982; author Like Father, Like Daughter (Little Brown), 1983; columnist Washington Times, 1984 ; syndicated columnist L.A. Times Syndicate, Washington, 1988-2001, Chgo. Tribune Media Svcs., 2001—. TV commentator, regular panelist CNN & Co. Mem. Phi Beta Kappa. Jewish. Home: 1934 Biltmore St NW Washington DC 20009-1510 Office: The Washington Times 3600 New York Ave NE Washington DC 20002-1996

FIELDS, THEODORE ROBERT, physician, rheumatologist; b. Bklyn., Nov. 25, 1951; s. Murray Arthur and Beatrice Leah (Ginsburg) F.; m. Randy Louise Gilbert, Sept. 23, 1984; children: Robin, Kara. BA cum laude, Bklyn. Coll., 1972; MD cum laude, Downstate Med. Ctr., 1976. Intern Nassau County Med. Ctr., East Meadow, N.Y., 1976-77, resident, 1977-79; fellow in rheumatology SUNY, Stonybrook, 1979-82; dir. rheumatology LaGuardia Hosp., Forest Hills, N.Y., 1982-86; physician Hosp. Spl. Surgery, N.Y.C., 1986—, dir. rheumatology faculty practice, 1994—. Assoc. prof. medicine Cornell Med. Coll.; coord. rheumatology fellowship program, Hosp. Spl. Surgery, 1999—, dir. rheumatology Internet edn. project, 1999—, mem. med. bd., 2003—. Co-editor: Advances in Clin. Rheumatology, 1992; contbr. chpts. to books, articles to profl. jours. Recipient svc. award, N.Y. Rheumatism Assn., 1988. Fellow ACP, Am. Coll. Rheumatology; mem. Am. Coll. Physician Execs., Phi Beta Kappa. Avocations: computers, literature, music. Office: Hosp Spl Surgery 535 E 70th St New York NY 10021-4872 E-mail: fieldst@hss.edu.

FIELDS, TINA RAE, artist, ecopsychologist; b. Paradise, Calif., Dec. 29, 1960; d. Henry C. Fields and Tilla M. Fields (Jacobs). BA in Humanities and Arts with honors, Old Coll., 1985; PhD, East-West Psychology, Calif. Inst. Integral Studies, 2001. Faculty Lesley U., Audubon Expdn. Inst., Cambridge, Mass., 1999—, Belfast, Maine, 1999—. Artist-in-residence Douglas Co. Sch. Dist., Nev., 1986, Alpine Co. Arts Commn., Calif., 1986—88. Social justice: Food Not Bombs, San Francisco; nuclear test site activist Nev. Fellow Calif. Grad., 1994—99; scholar Imagery in Healing Invitational scholar, Washoe Med. Ctr., Reno NV, 1988, CIIS, 1997—98. Mem.: N.Am. Assn. Environ. Edn., Soc. Anthropology of Consciousness (mem. exec. bd. 1998—2001). Green Party. Avocation: music.

FIELDS, VELMA ARCHIE, medical/surgical nurse; d. Charles and Ella Ruth Archie; m. Herrell Lee Fields Sr., July 29, 1972; children: Sherri Debnam, Herrell Jr., LaShonda Hairston. BSN, Winston-Salem State U., 1968. Cert. N. C. State Bd. Nursing. Nurse, oper. rm. nurse N.C. Bapt. Hosp., Winston-Salem, 1969—90; nursing instr. Forsyth Tech. Coll., Winston-Salem, 1990—93; client coord. Sr. Svcs. Meals-on-Wheels, Winston-Salem, 1993—96; nurse Nursefinders, Winston-Salem, 1997—. Actor: (plays, off-Broadway play) Crowns, 2002—03. Vol. cardiopulmonary instr. ARC, Winston-Salem, NC, 1980; deacon Emmanuel Bapt. Ch., Winston-Salem, NC. Recipient Race Progress Promotors Achievement award in healthcare, Effort Club, New Bethel Bapt. Ch., Winston-Salem, N.C., 2001. Baptist.

FIELDS, W(ADE) THOMAS, dental educator; b. McKenzie, Tenn., Oct. 15, 1942; s. Thomas N. and Rachel (Reynolds) Fields; m. Sherry J. Jolly, Aug. 12, 1966; children: Jeffrey Thomas, Susan Michele. DDS, U. Tenn., 1965; MPH, U. N.C., 1970. Clin. dentist N.C. State Bd. Health, Raleigh, 1966-69; asst. prof. U. Louisville, 1972-75, assoc. prof., dept. chmn., 1975-79, U. Tenn., Memphis, 1979-83, assoc. prof., divsn. dir., 1983-90, prof., 1990—, divsn. dir., 1990—, dept. chair, 1998-99. Faculty cons. Memphis (Tenn.) VA Hosp., 1981—; project cons. Am. Bd. Dental Pub. Health, Gainesville, Fla., 1984; cons. to asst. surgeon gen. and chief dental officer USPHS, Washington, 1985; presenter in field. Reviewer Jour. Acad. Gen. Dentistry, 1984—; author: 6 tchg. manuals; contbr. articles to profl. jours. Head coach Little League, Elizabeth City, NC, 1968—69, Peewee Baseball, Louisville, 1976—78; asst. den leader Boy Scouts Am., Louisville, 1978—79; pres. Germantown (Tenn.) HS Band Boosters, 1985—86, 1989—90. Recipient Traineeship, USPHS, 1969—71. Mem.: ADA (content cons. monographs 1983, 1986), Deans' Odontological Soc. (elected mem.), Am. Assn. Pub. Health Dentistry (sec.-treas. 1979—82, pres. 1982—84, abstract reviewer 1985, pres.-elect), Am. Dental Edn. Assn., Memphis Dental Soc. (editor newsletter 2002—), Tenn. Dental Assn. (cons. Coun. Dental Edn. 1984—87), Omicron Kappa Upsilon. Avocations: chess, golf. Home: 1536 Carr Ave Memphis TN 38104-4901 Office: Univ Tenn Coll Dentistry 875 Union Ave Memphis TN 38163-0001 E-mail: tfields@utmem.edu.

FIELDS, WARREN C. music educator, minister; b. York, Ala., Mar. 12, 1936; s. Travis Edward and Ada Beatrice Fields; m. Bobbie R. Richards; children: Karen Byrd, Kristi Warden. B in Music Edn., Samford U., 1958; MusM, Baylor U., 1963; PhD, U. Iowa, 1973. Tchr. Ensley H.S., Birmingham, Ala., 1958—66; prof. Ga. So. U., Statesboro, 1966—85; state missionary, dept. dir. Ga. Bapt. Conv., Atlanta, 1986—99; adj. prof. Atlanta Christian Coll., East Point, Ga., 2000—; min. of music Pky. Bapt. Ch., Duluth, Ga., 2000—. Conf. leader Lifeway Christian Resources, Nashville, 1986—99. Mem.: So. Bapt. Ch. Music Conf., Am. Choral Dirs. Assn., The Hymn Soc., Soc. for Am. Music. Avocations: woodworking, travel. Home: 2152 Plantation Ct Lawrenceville GA 30044-3743 Office: Atlanta Christian Coll 2605 Ben Hill Rd East Point GA 30344-1999

FIELDS, WILLIAM ALBERT, lawyer; b. Parkersburg, W.Va., Mar. 30, 1939; s. Jack Lyons and Grace (Kelley) F.; m. Prudence Brandt Adams, June 26, 1964. BS magna cum laude, Ohio State U., 1961; postgrad., Harvard Law Sch., 1961-64. Bar: Ohio bar 1964. Since practiced in, Marietta; city prosecutor, 1964-65; acting Judge Marietta Mcpl. Ct.; dir. elections Washington County, 1967-74; profl. bass-baritone soloist. Bd. dirs. Bank One, Marietta, N.A.; lectr. on estate planning and probate matters. Mem. editl. bd. Probate Law Jour. of Ohio. Chmn. Washington County Heart Assn., 1965-67; mem. dist. exec. com. Boy Scouts Am., 1967-74; Treas. County Republican Exec. Com., 1966—; trustee YMCA, Salvation Army; pres. bd. trustees Washington State Community Coll., Marietta; exec. com., trustee Coll. Adminstrv. Scis., Ohio State U.; trustee Appalachian Bible Coll., Bradley, W.Va., 1974-77, Marietta Meml. Hosp., also treas.; bd. dirs. Ohio Valley Port Authority. Recipient Wall St. Jour. award, 1961; named Outstanding Young Man of Marietta, 1968, Outstanding Citizen of Marietta, 1992; named to Ohio Valley Sports Hall of Fame, 2001. Fellow Am. Coll. Trust and Estate Counsel; mem. Ohio Bar Assn. (chmn., bd. govs., probate and trust law sect., mem. splty. bd. Ohio Supreme Ct.), Washington County Bar Assn., Marietta Area C. of C. (v.p., trustee), Am. Mensa, Nat. Soc. of Arts and Letters (bd. trustees), Sigma Chi, Beta Gamma Sigma. Clubs: Rotarian (pres. 1970-71), Marietta Country (trustee). Home: 129 Hillcrest Dr Marietta OH 45750-9321 Office: 217 2nd St Marietta OH 45750-2916 E-mail: WAF125@wirefire.com. *Without the light of Christ, all is darkness and vain machination.*

FIELDS-GOLD, ANITA, retired dean; b. Amarillo, Tex., Oct. 29, 1940; d. Dera and Mamie Maureen (Craig) Bates; m. Maurice Gold; 1 child, William Kyle. Grad. nursing, Jefferson Davis Hosp., 1962; BSN, Tex. Christian U., 1966; MSN, Northwestern State U. La., 1974; PhD, Tex. Women's U., 1980. C.E. coord., asst. prof. Northwestern State U., Shreveport; prof., dean McNeese State U., Lake Charles, La.; ret., 2000. Gov.'s appointee, chmn. S.W. La. Hosp. Dist. Commn., 1989—91. Mem. allocations com. and loaned exec. United Way, 1991—92, Am. Heart Assn.; Am. Cancer Soc.; ARC. Recipient Ben Taub award, 1962, Ann Magnussen award, ARC, 1977. Mem.: ANA (del.), Lake Charles Dist. Nurses Assn. (bd. dirs., Nurse of Yr. award 1972, 1980), La. Nurses Assn. (past pres. and 1st v.p., Spl. Recognition award 1993, Nightingale Hall of Fame award 2002), Phi Kappa Phi, Delta Kappa Gamma, Sigma Theta Tau (Image of Nursing award 1993). Home: 2339 21st St Lake Charles LA 70601-7946 E-mail: amgold@cox-internet.com.

FIELDS-HILL, VALERIE, journalist; b. Farmerville, La., Apr. 29, 1965; d. Elvadus and Mamie Marie (Harrison) F.; m. Clarence Edward Hill, Jr. BA in Liberal Studies, So. U. and A&M Coll., 1987; postgrad., Robert Maynard Inst. Jour. Edn, 1993, Maynard Inst. Journalism, 2000. Billing acct. rep. Sprint, Atlanta, 1987-88; reporter Daily Comml., Leesburg, Fla., 1988-90; urban affairs writer Ft. Worth Star-Telegram N.E., Bedford, Tex., 1990-94; advt. acct. rep. Ft. Worth Star-Telegram, 1994-95, religion writer, 1995-96; sr. writer, religion editor Arlington (Tex.) Morning News, 1996-98, copy editor, 1999-2001; asst. city editor The Dallas Morning News, 2001—. Media cons. One Church, One Child, Ft. Worth, 1997. Mem. Leadership Arlington, 1997; co-chmn. Urban H.S. Journalism Workshop, Dallas, 1996. Named Journalist of Yr., Duborma Liberian Women's Orgn., 1997. Mem. Nat. Assn. Black Journalists, Dallas-Ft. Worth Assn. Black Communicators (exec. bd. 1992-97), Soc. Profl. Journalists, Delta Sigma Theta. Democrat. Baptist. Home: 3628 White Birch Way Euless TX 76040-7171 Office: 508 Young St Dallas TX 75202-4893 E-mail: valeriefieldshill@hotmail.com., vfields@dallasnews.com.

FIELEKE, CAROL C. See KLEINSCHMIDT, CAROL

FIELEKE, NORMAN SIEGFRIED, economist, educator; b. Kankakee, Ill., Aug. 22, 1932; s. Lessly and Catharine M. (Nicholson) F.; m. Carol A. Curtiss, June 16, 1962 (div. Dec. 1985); children: Andrew, Eric, Michael. BA summa cum laude, Amherst Coll., 1954; AM, Harvard U., 1955; PhD, 1969. Economist, budget examiner Office Mgmt. and Budget, Washington, 1959-64; industry economist Office U.S. Trade Rep., Exec. Office Pres., 1964-65; v.p., economist Fed. Res. Bank of Boston, 1967-97. Dir. econ. rsch. U.S. Internat. Trade Commn., Washington, 1980; cons. IMF, Washington, 1993; adj. prof. Boston U., 1975-76, Brandeis U., 1988-90, Duke U., Durham, N.C., 1998-2000; lectr. Duke Inst. for Learning in Retirement, 2001—. Author: The Welfare Effects of Controls over Capital Exports from the United States, 1971, The International Economy under Stress, 1988; contbr. articles to profl. jours. Lt. USAF, 1955-57. Littauer fellow, NSF fellow Harvard U., 1969. Home: 101 Dundalk Dr Chapel Hill NC 27517-6583

FIELO, MURIEL BRYANT, interior designer; b. Bklyn., Dec. 11, 1921; d. Harry and Minnie (Dick) Bryant; m. Julius Fielo, June 17; 1 child, Michael Kenneth. Student, CCNY, 1938-41, Rutgers U., 1965-69; cert., N.Y. Sch. Interior Design, 1970. Gen. mgr. Fidelity Discount Corp., Irvington, NJ; advt. supr. Lincoln Loan Cos., Essex County, NJ, 1941-49; interior designer Alex Fielo Interior Decorators, Newark, 1942-49, prin., 1949-69, owner, 1969—. Designer, cons. space engr. MUDGE Interior Design Studios, East Orange, N.J., 1969—; mem. adv. panel Interior Design mag., 1977—. Clk. Essex County Bd. Freeholders, 1972-76; commr. East Orange Bus. Devel. Authority, 1977-86; mem. U.S. adv. coun. SBA-Region II, 1980-811 active LWV, 1950 55; organizer, 1st pres. South Orange chpt. Women's Am. ORT, 1952-54, mem. nat. spkrs. bur., 1952-65, parliamentarian No. N.J. coun., 1955-65; pres. Amity chpt. B'nai B'rith, Newark, 1946-48, v.p. No. N.J. coun., 1948-49, various nat. and state positions, 1948-80; mem. nat. com. on sect. fund raising Nat. Coun. Jewish Women, 1979-81, nat. tour chmn., 1979-81; trustee cmty. svcs. coun. Oranges and Maplewood, United Way Essex and West Hudson, 1981-83; bd. dirs. East Orange Central Avenue Mall Assn., 1979-83, chmn. new voter registration drive East Orange 2d Ward, 1955, entire city, 1969; pres. East Orange Dem. Club, 1957-58, campaign coord. for Dem. mayoral candidate, 1969; calendar coord. Essex County Dem. Com., 1970-76; mem. N.J. Bipartisan Coalition for Women's Appts., 1981. Named Outstanding Entrepreneur of 1984, Gov. of N.J., Outstanding Orgn. Pres., Kean Coll. Profl. Women's Assn., 1985, Wonder Woman of 1986, Bus. Jour. N.J., One of 8 Women To Watch, Jersey Woman mag., 1987, Bus. Person of Yr., East Orange C. of C., 1988; recipient various awards for civic svc. Mem. Internat. Soc. Interior Designers (bd. dirs. 1981-85), Nat. Home Fashions League (N.J. membership chmn. N.Y. chpt. 1981-82), Interior Design Soc., Internat. Interior Design Assn. (charter), N.J. Assn. Women Bus. Owners (state bd. dirs. 1979-82), Women Entrepreneurs N.J. (pres. 1981-85, CEO 1987—), N.J. Home Furnishings Assn. (bd. dirs. 1981-84, 86—), Constrn. Specifications Inst., N.J. Soc. AIA profl. affiliate), Guild Designer Woodworkers, Women Bus. Ownership Ednl. Coalition (N.J. pres. 1985-87, CEO 1987—, mem. steering com. interior designers for licensing in N.Y. 1985—), East Orange C. of C. (bd. dirs. 1977—, v.p. 1981-85), Bus. and Profl. Women's Club Oranges (bd. dirs. 1958-66). Jewish. Home and Office: Mudge Interior Design Studio 185 S Clinton St East Orange NJ 07018-3099 Fax: (973) 672-7287.

FIENBERG, LINDA DORIS, lawyer; b. Albany, July 7, 1942; d. Chester Leonard Fienberg and Marcia Shirley Doris Kartzman; m. Jeffrey D. Bauman, Mar. 2, 1980; children by previous marriage; Lane Blumenfeld, Shawn Blumenfeld. B.A., Cornell U., 1964; M.A.T., Wesleyan U., 1966; J.D.; Georgetown U., 1973. Bar: D.C. 1973, U.S. Supreme Ct., U.S. Ct. Appeals (various cirs.), U.S. Dist. Ct. D.C. 1974. Research analyst EEOC, Washington, 1968-69, U.S. Commn. on Civil Rights, Washington, 1969-70; assoc. Arnold and Porter, Washington, 1973-78; spl. counsel SEC, Washington, 1979-80, asst. gen. counsel, 1980-82, assoc. gen. counsel, 1982— . Mem. ABA, Women's Legal Def. Fund, Phi Beta Kappa. Office: SEC 450 5th St NW Washington DC 20001-2739

FIENBERG, STEPHEN ELLIOTT, statistician; b. Toronto, Ont., Can., Nov. 27, 1942; came to U.S., 1964; BS, U. Toronto, 1964; A.M., Harvard U., 1965, PhD, 1968. Asst. prof. dept. stats. and theoretical biology U. Chgo., 1968-72; asso. prof. dept. applied stats. U. Minn., St. Paul, 1972-76, prof., 1976-80, chmn. dept., 1972-78; prof. dept. stats. and social sci. Carnegie Mellon U., Pitts., 1980-85; Maurice Falk prof. Carnegie-Mellon U., Pitts., 1985-91, head dept. stats., 1981-84, dean Coll. Humanities and Social Scis., 1987-91; vice pres. acad. affairs York U., Toronto, 1991-93; chmn. com. on nat. stats. NRC, 1981-87; Maurice Falk prof. dept. stats Carnegie Mellon U., Pitts., 1992-97, Maurice Falk univ. prof., 1997—; prof. Stats and Ctr. Automated Learning and Discovery, 2000—, Ctr. for Computer and Communications Security, 2002—. Author: (with others) Discrete Multivariate Analysis: Theory and Practice, 1975, Analysis of Cross-classified Categorical Data, 1977, 2d edit., 1980, (with others) Beginning Statistics with Data Analysis, 1983, (with M. Anderson) Who Counts? The Politics of Census-Taking in Contemporary America, 1999, revised paperback edit., 2001; editor: (with A. Zellner) Studies in Bayesian Econometrics and Statistics, 1975, (with D.V. Hinkley) R.A. Fisher: An Appreciation, 1980, (with A.J. Reiss, Jr.) Indicators of Crime and Criminal Justice: Quantitative Studies, 1980, (with others) Sharing Research Data, 1985, (with W. Mason) Cohort Analysis in Social Research, 1985, (with A.C. Atkinson) A Celebration of Statistics, 1985, (with others) Statistics and the Law, 1986, The Evolving Role of Statistical Assessments as Evidence in the Courts, 1989, (with others) A Statistical Model: Frederick Mosteller's Contributions to Statistics, Science and Public Policy, 1990, (with M. M. Meyer) Assessing Evaluation Studies: The Case of Bilingual Education Strategies, 1992, (with others) Intelligence, Genes, and Success: Scientists Respond to The Bell Curve, 1997, (with others) The Polygraph and Lie Detection, 2003; editor: Jour. Am. Statistics Assn., 1977-79, Chance, 1987-92. statistics edit. Int. Encyl. Soc. Beh. Sci., 2001. Recipient Pres. award Com. Pres. Statis. Socs., 1982. Fellow AAAS, Am. Statis. Assn. (v.p. 1986-88, Wilks medal 2000), Inst. Math. Stats. (pres. 1998-99), Internat. Soc. Bayesian Analysis (pres.1996-97), Royal Statis. Soc.; mem. Nat. Acad. Sci. (elected), Biometric Soc., Internat. Statis. Inst., Psychometric Soc., Statis. Soc. Can. Office: Carnegie Mellon U Dept Stats Pittsburgh PA 15213

FIENNES, RALPH NATHANIEL, actor; b. Suffolk, Eng., Dec. 22, 1962; s. Mark and Jini Fiennes; m. Alex Kingston, 1993 (div. 1997). Student, Chelsea Coll. Art and Design, Royal Acad. Dramatic Art. Actor (theatre prodns.) with Royal Shakespeare Co., Broadway debut in Hamlet, 1995 (Tony award Lead Actor in a Play), Ivanov, 1997, Richard II and Coriolanus, 2000, The Talking Cure, 2002, Brand, 2003; (TV films) Prime Suspect, 1991, A Dangerous Man: Lawrence After Arabia, 1992, Wuthering Heights, 1992, The Baby of Macon, (films) Schindler's List, 1993 (Academy award nomination best supporting actor 1993, New York Film Critics Circle award best supporting actor 1993), Quiz Show, 1994, Strange Days, 1995, The English Patient, 1996 (Academy award nominee, Golden Globe award nominee), Oscar & Lucinda, 1997, The Avengers, 1998, Spider, 2002, The Good Thief, 2002, Red Dragon, 2002, Maid in Manhattan, 2002; exec. prodr.Taste of Sunshine, 1999, End of the Affair, 1999; voice Prince of Egypt, 1998, actor, prodr. Onegin, 1999

FIER, ELIHU, lawyer, educator; b. N.Y.C., Mar. 25, 1931; s. Charles H. and Helen N. (Nadel) F.; m. Jane Lee Saltser, Jan. 10, 1956 (dec. Jan. 1964); children— Jennifer, Michael, Carlyn. BA, Dartmouth Coll., 1952; LL.B., Harvard U., 1958. Bar: N.Y. 1959, U.S. Dist. Ct. (so. and ea. dists.) N.Y. 1960 U.S. Tax Ct. 1961, U.S. Ct. Appeals (2d cir.) 1961, Fla. 1997. Ptnr. Weil, Gotshal & Manges, N.Y.C., 1969-80, Morgan, Lewis & Bockius, N.Y.C., 1980-83, Finley, Kumble, Wagner, Heine, Underberg, Manley & Casey, Beverly Hills, Calif., 1983-88, N.Y.C., 1983-88; of counsel Pryor, Cashman, Sherman & Flynn, N.Y.C., 1988-93, Blum & Fier P.C., N.Y.C., 1993-97, Gillespie & Allison, P.A., Boca Raton, Fla., 1995-97; mgr. Realty Cons. LLC. Adj. assoc. prof. NYU, N.Y.C., 1969-76; lectr. N.Y. Law Jour., Law and Bus., Practicing Law Inst. Served to lt. (j.g.) USNR, 1952-60 Mem.: ABA (com. creditors' rights in real estate financing 1983—90). Home: 240 NW 70th St Boca Raton FL 33487-2391

FIERER, JOSHUA ALLAN, pathology educator; b. N.Y.C., Nov. 25, 1937; s. Norman and Evelyn (Bolstein) F.; m. Mary Ellen Bailey, June 14, 1959; children— Pamela, Robin, Jonathan, Lisa. BA, Alfred U., 1959; MD, SUNY-N.Y.C., 1963. Diplomate Am. Bd. Pathology; cert. Nat. Bd. Med. Examiners. Asst. in surgery U. Rochester, N.Y., 1964-65; instr. in pathology Columbia U., N.Y.C., 1969-70; guest investigator Rockefeller U., N.Y.C., 1969-70; asst. prof. pathology Columbia U., N.Y.C., 1970-75; prof., dir. divsn. anatomic pathology Creighton U., Omaha, 1975-78; prof., chmn. dept. pathology Coll. of Med., U. Ill., Peoria, 1978-86, dir. labs., 1978-86; pres., CEO U Pathology Assoc., Chgo., N.Y.C., North Palm. Dir. microbiology and immunopathology Francis Delafield Hosp., N.Y.C., 1970-75; asst. attending pathologist Presbyterian Hosp., N.Y.C., 1972-75; cons. Lenox Hill Hosp., N.Y.C., 1972-75, Omaha Vet.'s Hosp., 1976-78, Ill. Cancer Council, Chgo., 1981-86. Contbr. articles to profl. jours. Bd. dirs. Ill. div. Am. Cancer Soc., Chgo., 1981-86, pres. Peoria unit, 1982-84; med. adv. bd. ARC, Heart of Ill. region, Peoria, 1981-86; bd. dirs. Peoria Civic Opera Co., 1978-81. Served to capt. USAF, 1965-67. Fellow Am. Cancer Soc. 1968, NIH, 1969 Fellow Coll. Am. Pathologists; mem. Am. Soc. Clin. Pathologists, Am. Assn. Pathologists, Assn. Pathology Chmn., Ill. Soc. Pathologists, Am. Assn. Immunologists, Soc. Exptl. Biology and Medicine, Cul. Ill. Pathology Soc. (pres. 1981-82), Old Port Yacht Club (North Palm Beach, Fla.), Palm Beach Sailing Club. Office: 132 Lakeshore Dr Apt 1020 North Palm Beach FL 33408-3617

FIERHELLER, GEORGE ALFRED, corporate director; b. Toronto, Can., Apr. 26, 1933; s. Harold Parsons and Ruth Hathaway (Bauld) F.; m. Glenna E. Fletcher, Apr. 17, 1957; children: Vicki Elaine, Lori Ann BA, U. Toronto, 1955; LLD, Concordia U.; DSLitt, Trinity Coll., U. Toronto. With IBM, Toronto, 1955-58, account mgr., 1962-65, mktg. mgr., 1966-68; founder, pres. Sys. Dimensions Ltd., Ottawa, Ont., 1968-79; pres., CEO Rogers Cable TV Broadcasting Co. Ltd., Vancouver, B.C., Can., 1979-85, Cantel Inc., Toronto, 1985-90; chmn., CEO Rogers Cantel Mobile, Inc., 1990-93; vice chair Rogers Comm., Inc., Toronto, 1993-96; pres. Four Halls Inc., Toronto, 1997—. Bd. dirs. Extendicare Inc., Rogers AT&T Wireless, GBC N.Am. Fund Inc., Can. Inst. Advanced Rsch., Ont. Exports Inc.; pres. Bd. of Trade of Met. Toronto, 1996-97. Contbr. articles to profl. jours. Gen. chmn. United Appeal Campaign, Ottawa, 1972; chmn. campaign Carleton U., 1975-77, also chmn. bd. govs., 1977-79; mem. adv. com. Norman Paterson Sch. Internat. Affairs; bd. dirs., v.p. United Way Ottawa, 1975-79 (United Way of Can. highest award 1998); Opera Ottawa, 1970-71; trustee, mem. exec. com. Nat. Arts Ctr., 1973-79; trustee Royal Ottawa Hosp., 1978-79, Vancouver Gen. Hosp. Found., 1981-85, Can. Ctr. for Advanced Rsch, 2001—; mem. Vancouver Centennial Commn., 1983-84; bd. govs. Simon Fraser U., Vancouver, 1981-84; chmn. United Way Vancouver, 1981, B.C. Coun. of 80's, 1980-83, Vision 2000, 1990-91; chair United Way Met. Toronto, 1994-96, chmn. gen. campaign, 1991; trustee Sunnybrook Hosp. Found., 1993-99, chair Sunnybrook and Women's Health Scis. Ctr. campaign, 1999—, McMichael Can. Art Collection, 1993-99; chair Trinity Coll. Campaign, 1996-99; bd. dirs. Coun. for Bus. and the Arts, 2003--. Decorated mem. Order of Can., 2000; recipient Award of Merit, City of Toronto, 1991, Award of Excellence, Can. Wireless Ind. Assn., 1996, Queen's Golden Jubilee medal, 2002, Salute to City award Toronto, 2002; named to Can. Info. Tech. Hall of Fame, 1998, Outstanding Vol. of Yr., Assn. Fundraising Profls., 2001. Mem. Can. Info. Processing Soc. (pres. 1970-71), World Pres. Orgn., Chief Execs. Orgn., Can. Assn. Data Processing Svc. Orgns., Assn. Cert. Computer Profls. (founding com.), Can. Ctr. for Philanthropy (bd. dirs. 1987-91), Bus. Coun. on Nat. Issues, Coun. for Bus. and the Arts (bd. dirs.), Cellular Telecom. Industry Assn. (bd. dirs. 1986-94), Smart Toronto (chmn. 1996), Greater Toronto Mktg. Alliance (chair 1997-2003), Vancouver Club, Rideau Club, Granite Club, Nat. Club, Rosedale Golf Club, Toronto (Can.) Adventurers Club (chmn. 2003—). Home: 24 Pearwood Crescent Toronto ON Canada M3B 2C2 Office: Four Halls Inc 77 King St W Ste 4545 Toronto ON Canada M5K 1K2 Fax: 416-443-9360. E-mail: fierhel@attglobal.net.

FIERING, STEVEN, medical educator; b. Aug. 28, 1951; BS in Geology with distinction, U. Mich., 1975; BS in Microbiology, Eastern Mich. U., 1985; PhD in Genetics, Stanford U., 1990. Ptnr. food processing bus. Soy Plant, Ann Arbor, Mich., 1975—83; teaching asst. microbiology Eastern Mich. U., Mich., 1982—84, lectr. microbiology, 1985; teaching asst. Med. Sch. Stanford U., 1986—89; rsch. group leader AFRC Ctr. Genome Rsch. U. Edinburgh, Scotland, 1990—91; postdoctoral fellow Hutchinson Cancer Rsch. Ctr., Seattle, 1991—96; asst. prof. microbiology dept. Dartmouth Med. Sch., Lebanon, NH, 1997—. Contbr. articles to profl. jours. Recipient scholarship, Am. Soc. Hematology, 1995. Mem.: AAAS. Office: Dartmouth Coll Molecular & Cellular Biology Dept 7200 Vail Building Hanover NH 03755-3840

FIERKE, THOMAS GARNER, lawyer; b. Boone, Iowa, Nov. 12, 1948; s. Norman Garner and Mary Margaret (Mullen) F.; m. Susan Marie Butler, July 17, 1976 (div. Mar. 1983); m. Debra Lynn Clayton, Sept. 17, 1988; children: Veronica Helen, Caroline Margaret. BSMetE, Iowa State U., 1971; JD, U. Minn., 1974; LLM, Boston U., 1978; M in Strategic Studies, U.S. Army War Coll., 1999. Bar: Ill. 1974, U.S. Dist. Ct. Mass. 1976, U.S. Dist. Ct. (no. dist.) Ill. 1976, U.S. Ct. Appeals (1st cir.) 1976, U.S. Tax Ct. 1978, U.S. Supreme Ct. 1978, Mass. 1980, N.Y. 1981, U.S. Ct. Appeals (fed. cir.) 1989. Commd. 2nd lt. U.S. Army, 1971, advanced through grades to col., 1980, ret., 2002; trial ct. prosecutor Ft. Devens, Mass., 1974-77; group judge adv. 10th Spl. Forces Group, 1975-78; chief adminstrv. law sect., 1977-78; chief legal counsel, contracting officer U.S. Def. Rep., Am. Embassy, Tehran, Iran, 1979; chief adminstrv. law Ft. Devens, 1979-80; judge adv. gen. corps, 1974-80; atty.-advisor Army Materiel Command, 1980-82; mgr. contracts policy and review Martin Marietta Michoud Aerospace, Martin Marietta Corp., New Orleans, 1982; gen. counsel Lockheed Martin Manned Space Sys., Lockheed Martin Corp., New Orleans, 1984—. Apptd. to La. Gov.'s Mil. Adv. Commn., 1991; bd. dirs. La. Orgn. for Jud. Excellence, 1988—; mem. La. state com. Employer Support of Guard and Res., 1988—92, dep. state ombudsman, 1992—94, state ombudsman, 1994—2001, state chmn., 2001—; mem. Mil. Adv. Com. of Greater New Orleans, 1993—, vice chair internat. rels., 2002—. Recipient Most Valuable Employer Support for the Guard and Res. award, NASA Pub. Svc. medal, 1992, La. Cross Merit award State of La., 1994, 5 Outstanding Vol. Svc. medals Dept. Def., 1994, 96, 97, 99, 2001, Legion of Merit, 1998, 2001, USN Superior Pub. Svc. medal, 1999, USCG commendation, 2001. Mem. Am. Corp. Counsel Assn. (bd. dirs. New Orleans chpt. 1987—, v.p. 1989-90), Internat. Assn. Def. Counsel, New Orleans C. of C. (bd. dirs.), Metro-Vision Econ. Devel. Orgn. (bd. dirs., mayor's mil. adv. com. 1993—, vice chair internat. rels. 2002—), French-Am. C. of C. (bd. dirs.). Republican. Episcopalian. Avocations: snow skiing, reading, running. Office: Lockheed Martin Michoud Space Sys PO Box 29304 New Orleans LA 70189-0304 E-mail: tom.fierke@lmco.com.

FIERROS, RUTH VICTORIA, retired secondary school educator; b. McRoberts, Ky., Mar. 29, 1920; d. Willie A. and Harriet (Wright) Cornett; m. Jose Fernando Fierros, Nov. 22, 1945 (dec.); children: Cedric Joseph, Philip Alonso, Stephen Michael. BA in English, Berea Coll., 1942; MA in English and Edn., Tex. A&I U., 1954. Cert. tchr., Tex. Tchr. Jenkins Ind. Schs., McRoberts, 1942-43, Laredo (Tex.) Ind. Schs., 1951-87; ret., 1987. Editor: Class '42 Yearbook, 1982, 87, 92; author: Upon the Easel of My Heart, 1982, Love's Collage of Rose Petals, 1996, Welcome to my World, 2002; co-author: The Berea Experience of Class of '42, 1997; contbr. poems to anthologies. Chairperson 50th, 55th, 58th, and 60th anniversary reunions Berea Coll. Class of 1942; pres.Tuesday Music & Literature, 1986-88. With USN, 1943-46. Recipient Tchr. Excellence award U. Tex., 1987, Golden Apple award Alpha Delta Kappa, 1987, Golden Poet award, 1988, Cert. of Citation State of Tex. Ho. of Reps., 1987, Armed Forces award, 1988, Leadership award, 1988; inducted into edn. area Laredo Hall of Fame, 1998. Mem. AAUW (charter, 1st v.p. 1966-68), NEA, Gifted and Talented Assn., Nat. Coun. Tchrs. English, Tex. State Tchrs. Assn., So. Poetry Assn. (Critics Choice award), Nat. Libr. of Poetry, Webb County Unit Ret. Tchrs. Assn. (2d v.p. 1994-95), Charles T. Morgan Soc., Internat. Soc. Poets (Disting. mem.), Delta Kappa Gamma (pres. 1966-68), Internat. Poetry Assn. Democrat. Roman Catholic. Avocations: church choir, writing poetry, reading, walking, collecting dolls and figurines. Home: 1801 Fremont St Laredo TX 78043-2606

FIERS, JOHN ROBERT, church executive, police chaplain; b. Lafayette, Ind., Dec. 3, 1961; s. John Ludwig and Virginia Lee Fiers; m. Marlene Ann Hughes, July 30, 1993; 1 child, Amber Lynn. BS in Mgmt., Purdue U., 1983; MBA, Ind. Wesleyan U., 1990; degree, Inst. Fin. Edn., Chgo., 1988; DDiv (hon.), World Christianship, Fresno, Calif., 1997. Ordained to ministry World Christianship Ministries. Sr. loan officer First Fed. Savs. Bank, Lafayette, 1984-91; v.p. Tippecanoe Title Svcs., Lafayette, 1991-93; pastor Romney (Ind.) United Meth. Ch., 1991-93; assoc. pastor Trinity United Meth. Ch., Lafayette, 1993-94; pres. First Mortgage of Ind., Indpls., 1994-97; chaplain Marion County Sheriff's Dept., Indpls., 1997—; corp. treas. Electro Painters, Inc., Indpls., 1997-2000; contr. Bd. Ch. Ext. Christian Ch., 2000—02; bus. adminstr. Tabernacle Presbyn. Ch., Indpls., 2002—. Mem. pres.'s bd. U. Indpls., 1994-95; mem. lenders bd. State Student Assistance Commn., Indpls., 1987-90; treas. Ind. Student Lenders Assn., Indpls., 1989-90. Festival fin. mgr. Downtown Bus. Ctr., Lafayette, 1988-93, Greater Lafayette C. of C., 1988-93. Mem. Internat. Conf. Police Chaplains (treas. 2001-), York Rite, Pi Sigma Alpha. Republican. Avocations: reading, current events. Home: 8632 Mariesi Dr Indianapolis IN 46278-2213 Office: Tabernacle Presbyn Ch 418 E 34th St Indianapolis IN 46205 E-mail: JRFPM@aol.com.

FIERST, BRUCE PHILIP, lawyer; b. Chgo., Jan. 26, 1951; s. Robert Jay and Esther Toby (Kaplan) F. BA with honors, Tulane U., 1973; JD, U. Denver, 1975. Bar: Colo. 1976, U.S. Dist. Ct. Colo. 1976. Assoc. Epstein, Lozow & Preblud, P.C., Denver, 1976-79; pres. Bruce P. Fierst, P.C., Denver, 1979—. Co-author manual Handling the DUI case, 1981. Big Brother, Big Bros. of Colo., Denver, 1975-81. Mem. ABA, Colo. Bar Assn., Denver Bar Assn., Am. Trial Lawyers Assn., Colo. Trial Lawyers Assn. (lectr., bd. dirs. 1986-94). Democrat. Jewish. Avocation: sports. Home: 5431 S Dayton Ct Greenwood Village CO 80111-3633 E-mail: bruce1st@msn.com.

FIERSTEIN, HARVEY FORBES, playwright, actor; b. Bklyn., June 6, 1954; s. Irving and Jacqueline Harriet (Gilbert) F. Acting debut in Andy Warhol's Pork, N.Y.C., 1971; author: (plays) In Search of the Cobra Jewels, 1973, Freaky Pussy, 1975, Flatbush Tosca, 1976, Cannibals Just Don't Know Better, 1978, Spookhouse, 1984, Safe Sex, 1987, Forget Him, 1988; (book of musical) La Cage Aux Folles, 1983 (Tony award best book of musical 1984, Tony award best musical 1984, L.A. Drama Critics Circle award 1984, Dramatists Guild award 1984), (with Peter Allen and Charles Suppon) Legs Diamond, 1989; author and star: The International Stud, 1978, Fugue in a Nursery, 1979 (Villager award 1980), Widows and Children First!, 1979, (all three one-acts compiled into) Torch Song Trilogy, 1981 (Obie award 1982), (on Broadway), 1982 (Tony award best play 1982, Tony award best actor 1982, Drama Desk award best play 1982, Drama Desk award best actor 1982, George Oppenheimer-Newsday Playwrighting award 1982, Theatre World award 1983), (in London's West End), 1985 (Olivier Best Play award nominee 1985); screenwriter and star: Torch Song Trilogy, 1988, Tidy Endings, 1988 (ACE award best dramatic special 1988, ACE award writing 1988); actor: (off-Broadway) The Haunted Host, 1991, (films) Garbo Talks, 1984, The Harvest, 1992, Mrs. Doubtfire, 1993, White Lies, 1993, Bullets Over Broadway, 1994, Dr. Jekyl and Ms. Hyde, 1995, The Celluloid Closet, 1996, Independence Day, 1996, Everything Relative, 1996, Kull The Conqueror, 1997, Safe Men, 1998, Legend of Mulan, 1998, Playing Mona Lisa, Death to Smochy, 2002; (TV guest star appearances) Miami Vice, 1985, The Simpsons, Murder She Wrote, 1992, Cheers, 1992 (Emmy award nomination 1992), (narrator) The Times of Harvey Milk, (Sesame Street spl guest star) Elmo Saves Christmas, 1996, (spl. project) Am. Film Inst. TV or Not TV (Guest star HBO) Larry Sanders Show, 1996; audio CD This Is Not Going to Be Pretty, 1995, (Live Performance Plump Record) 1996; (wrote and starred in productions) (HBO's children's specials) The Sissy Duckling, 1999, (Showtime special film) Common Ground, 2000; returned to Broadway in Hairspray, 2002; monthly commentator POS' In the Life, 2002. Recipient Theater World award for Broadway debut, 1983, Fund for Human Dignity award, 1983. Avocations: aids activist, gay rights activist, painting, gardening, cooking. Office: c/o AGF Inc 30 W 21st St Fl 7 New York NY 10010-6905

FIES, JAMES DAVID, elementary education educator; b. Chgo., May 19, 1950; s. Arthur Herbert Sr. and Ruth Paulina (Rehm) F.; m. Ruth Elaine Carlson, June 24, 1972; children: Samuel Jacob, Sarah Rae. BA, Purdue U., 1972, MS, 1975. Cert. elem. edn. tchr., Ind. Tchr. math. Morton Elem./Mid. Sch., Hammond, Ind., 1972-82, Eggers Elem./Mid. Sch., Hammond, 1982-88, Gavit Jr./Sr. High Sch., Hammond, 1988—, interim asst. prin., 1992. Dept. chair Eggers Mid. Sch., 1983-86. Bldg. union rep. Hammond Tchrs. Fedn. Local 394, 1981-87; trustee Trinity Luth. Ch., Hammond, 1976-82, 86-87, bd. fin., 1993—. Mem. Nat. Coun. Tchrs. of Maths., Hammond Tchrs. Fedn., Am. Fedn. of Tchrs. Avocations: traveling, fishing, family activities. Home: 544 Hickory Ln Munster IN 46321-2409

FIESS, STEPHEN CHARLES EDWARD, musician, music educator; b. Stratford, Ont., Sept. 10, 1956; s. Philip Louis and Grace Phyllis Fiess. BMus with honors, U. Western Ont., 1978; MMus, Ind. U., 1980; D of Mus. Arts, U. Colo., 1989. Accompanist, composer-in-residence Ballet Images Studio, Boulder, Colo., 1983—88; piano continuing edn. instr. U. Colo., Boulder, 1985—88, part-time instr. piano, 1988—89; pvt. piano instr. Highlands Ranch Piano Instr., Highlands Ranch, Colo., 1989—. Organist Prince of Peace Luth. Ch., Denver, 1989—98, Good Shepherd Episc. Ch., Centennial, Colo., 1998—; accompanist Columbine Chorale, Denver, 1992—2001. Author: (book) The Piano Works of Serge Prokofiev, 1994; composer: (piano sonata) Sonata in Ragtime, 1985, (organ composition) Variations on Twas in the Moon of Wintertime, 1995, (piano composition) Northern Wilderness Suite, 2002. Recipient Rosie Robinow prize for piano, U. Western Ont., 1977, 3d prize sr. Kronek divsn., Joanna Hodges Internat. Piano Competition, 1989; fellow Postdoctoral fellow, U. Colo.-Boulder, 1987—88. Mem.: Music Tchrs. Nat. Assn., Nat. Guild of Piano Tchrs., Pi Kappa Lambda. Lutheran. Home and Office: 1837 W Mountain Daisy Ct Highlands Ranch CO 80129-6279

FIETSAM, ROBERT, JR., physician; b. Columbus, Ohio, Dec. 15, 1956; s. Robert and Mary E. (Maccombie) F.; m. Jill Courtney Brach, Nov. 6, 1993; children: Dominique, Desiree, Alexandra, Robert Mac, Elle, Paris. BSChem., U. Mich., 1978; MD, Wayne State U., 1986. Diplomate Am. Bd. Surgery, Am. Bd. Thoracic Surgery. Cardiac surgeon Southeastern Cardiovasc. Assn., Dothan, Ala., 1995-96; asst. prof. surgery Duke U., Durham, N.C., 1996-98; dir. cardiac surgery Village Surg. Assocs., 1998—2003; pres. Sandhills Heart Surgery P.A., Fayetteville, NC, 2003—. Contbr. chpt. Cardiac Issues, 1992; contbr. aritcles to profl. jours. Recipient Charles C. Guthrie award Vascular Surg. Soc., 1990, Charles Johnston award Detroit Surg. Assn., 1991. Mem. AMA, ACS, Soc. Thoracic Surgeons, Cumberland County Med. Soc. Office: Sandhills Heart Surgery PA 3419 Melrose Rd Fayetteville NC 28304 Fax: 910-323-9501. E-mail: dellnewjet@aol.com.

FIFE, BETTY H. retired librarian; b. Indpls., Mar. 31, 1925; d. Otho Cova and Mae Craddock (Paxton) Hay; m. James A. Fife, Aug. 30, 1945; children: Andrew, Marlie, John, Laurie. BS, Boston U., 1967, MS, 1969; student, Northeastern U. Classroom tchr., libr. Town of Hanover (Mass.); elem. libr. City of Newburgh (N.Y.); ret., 1999. Fellow Northeastern U. Mem. NCTE. Home: 174 Cedar Acres Rd Marshfield MA 02050-6036 Office: PO Box 115 Vails Gate NY 12584-0115

FIFE, DENNIS JENSEN, chemistry educator, air force officer; b. Brigham City, Utah, Feb. 10, 1945; s. Glen Shumway and June (Jenson) Fife; m. Metta Marie Gunther, June 20, 1972; children: Kimball, Kellie, Keith, Kurt, Katie, Kenton. BS in Chemistry, Weber State U., Ogden, Utah, 1969; MBA, Inter-Am. U., San German, P.R., 1973; MS in Chemistry, Utah State U., 1978, PhD in Phsy. Chemistry, 1983. Assoc. chemist Thiokol Chem. Corp., Brigham City, 1969; commd. 2d lt. USAF, 1969, advanced through grades to lt. col.; pilot, instr., flight examiner Hurricane Hunters, Ramey AFB, P.R. and Keesler AFB, Miss., 1971-76; test project pilot 6514th Test Squadron, Ogden, Utah, 1979-81; instr. chemistry USAF Acad., Colorado Springs, Colo., 1977-79, asst. prof., 1983-85, assoc. prof., 1985-90, prof., 1990; pres. Select Pubs., Inc., Colorado Springs, 1985-90, also chmn. bd. dirs., 1990; mgr. analytical labs. dept. Thiokol Corp., Brigham City, Utah, 1990—. Author: How to Form a Colorado Corporation, 1986; contbr. articles to profl. jours. Active Boy Scouts Am., 1981—, sustaining mem. Rep. Nat. Com., Washington, 1983— Decorated Air medal with oak leaf cluster: NSF research grantee, 1967-68. Mem. Internat. Union Pure and Applied Chemistry (affiliate), Am. Chem. Soc., Phi Kappa Phi. Republican. Mem. Lds Ch. Avocations: racketball, fly fishing, hunting. Office: ATK Thiokol Propulsion PO Box 707 Brigham City UT 84302-0707

FIFE, EDWARD H. landscape architecture educator; b. Mass., Oct. 18, 1942; s. Edwin Kenneth and Yvonne Barbara F.; children: Sarah Rodman and Mike Malcolm. BS in Landscape Architecture, R.I. Sch. Design, Providence, 1965; M in Landscape Architecture, Harvard U., 1967. Registered landscape architect, Ont. Designer Sasaki, Strong Assoc., Toronto, Ont., Can., 1964-66; asst. prof. landscape architecture Ohio State U., Columbus, 1967-69, U. of Toronto, 1969-73, assoc. prof., 1973—, asst. chmn., 1983-85, chmn. program in landscape architecture, 1985-89, 92-96; dir. Ctr. for Landscape Rsch. U. Toronto, 1987—89, 2001—03; prin. E. H. Fife Landscape Architecture, Toronto, 1979—. Mem. roster vis. educators Landscape Archtl. Accreditation Bd., 1986-96. Bd. dirs. Koffler Gallery, Toronto, 1986-95, Landscape Architecture Can. Found., 1987-88, 94—; mem. adv. com. Restoration of Monserrate Park, Portugal, 1988-90; mem. sci. and edn. com. Royal Bot. Garden, 1988-91, mem. property com., 1991-93; mem. acad. bd. governing coun. U. Tornoto, 1988-89. Fellow Can. Soc. Landscape Architects; mem. Internat. Fedn. Landscape Architects, Can. Soc. Landscape Architects (roster vis. educators), Ont. Assn. Landscape Architects (pres. 1987-88, bd. dirs. 1983-89, 2000-02). Avocations: painting, organic farming, canoeing, hiking. Home: 269 Waverley Rd Toronto ON Canada M4L 3T5 Fax: (416) 971-2094. E-mail: fife@clr.utoronto.ca.

FIFE, JONATHAN DONALD, higher education educator; b. Washington, Nov. 9, 1941; s. G. Donald and Marie (Wall) F.; m. Janice McKenna, Aug. 10, 1968 (div.); children: Patrick McKenna, Timothy Kingston, Brendan Martin; m. Ann Ferren, 1996. BBA, U. Mass., 1965; MS, SUNY, Albany, 1970; postgrad, U. Cin., 1965-67; EdD, Pa. State U., 1975. Asst. dir. student activities State U. Coll., Buffalo, 1967-69; rsch. asst. Pa. State U. Ctr. for Study Higher Edn., State College, 1970-72; assoc. dir. ERIC Clearinghouse on Higher Edn., George Washington U., Washington, 1972-77, dir., 1977-98, prof. edn., 1977-98; vis. prof. Va. Poly. Inst. and State U., Blacksburg, 1998—. Edn. pilot team evaluator Malcolm Baldridge Nat. Quality Award, 1994, sr. evaluator, 1995-96, bd. examiners, sr. examiner, 1996-97, alumni examiner, 1999-2000, examiner, VA Sen. Productivity & Quality Award, 2002. Mng. editor Rev. Higher Edn., 1980-86; cons. editor Change, 1981-2001. Bd. dirs. Nat. Ctr. for Higher Ednl. Mgmt. Systems, Boulder, 1980-82; cons. Rosenberg Commn., Md., 1975; pres., Wheaton Sq. East Condominium, Wheaton, Md., 1973-78; pres. High Meadows Owners' Master Assn., Radford, Va., 2000—. Mem. Assn. Study Higher Edn. (exec. sec. treas. 1978-87), Am. Ednl. Rsch. Assn. (sec. treas. spl. interest group postsecondary edn. 1977-81), Higher Edn. Group Washington (sec. 1979-81, v.p., 1997-98, pres. 1998-99), Assn. Instl. Rsch., Phi Kappa Phi. Avocations: tennis, golf, boating. E-mail: jfife@vt.edu.

FIFE, WILLIAM FRANKLIN, retired drug company executive; b. Buffalo, W.Va., Nov. 6, 1921; s. Alfred Charles and Grace (Pitchford) F.; children: Scott Franklin, Susan Elizabeth, Cindy Francine. AB, Berea Coll., 1949; MS, U. Wis., 1950. Operating mgr. McKesson & Robbins, Chgo. and Kansas City, Mo., 1950-56, Cleve. Wholesale Drug Co., 1956-58; with Owens, Minor & Bodeker, Inc., 1958-91; pres., exec. v.p., sr. v.p. Owens & Minor, Inc., Richmond, Va., 1981-87, chief oper. officer, 1987-91, exec. v.p., 1989-91, ret., 1991—, now cons., bd. dirs.emeritus, 1998—. Capt. C.E. U.S. Army, 1942-46. Home: 507 S Gaskins Rd Richmond VA 23233-5709 Office: Owens & Minor Inc 4800 Cox Rd Glen Allen VA 23060-6294

FIFER CANBY, SUSAN MELINDA, library administrator; b. Stockton, Calif., Jan. 23, 1948; d. Reginald Dekovan and Shirley Rae (Canaday) Fifer; m. Thomas Yellott Canby, Oct. 9, 1982. BS, U. Nebr., 1970; MLS, U. Md., 1974. Circulating libr. Nat. Geog. Soc., Washington, 1975-81, asst. libr., 1981-83, dir. libr., 1983-94, dir. libr. & indexing, 1994-99, dir. librs., 1999—, v.p. librs. and info. svcs., 2002—. Mem. mems. coun. OCLC, Dublin, Ohio, 1997-2003; literacy tutor; bd. dirs. Washington Lit. Coun., 1999-2001. Bd. dirs. tech. com. D.C. Coun. Govts., 1985-88, D.C. Libr. Coun., 1997-2003, Capital Area Libr. Network, 1989-95, 98—, chair, 1994-95; bd. dirs. Sandy Spring Mus., 2002—. Mem.: ALA (John Cotton Dana award 1985, 1989), Spl. Librs. Assn. (pres. DC Spl. Librs. 2003—, Innovations and Tech. award 2001). Avocations: gardening, reading. Home: 6855 Haviland Mill Rd Clarksville MD 21029-1308 Office: Nat Geog Soc Library 1145 17th St NW Washington DC 20036-4701 E-mail: sfiferca@ngs.org.

FIFFIE PROCTOR, JOANN, media and technology specialist; b. New Orleans; d. Joseph Paul Sr. and Elouise Marie Fiffie. BA in Comm., U. Southwestern, Lafayette, La., 1980; EdM, Minot State U., 1992; M of Libr. and Info. Sci., U. So. Miss., 1997. Tchr. St. James Sch. Bd., Lutcher, La., 1992-93, tchr. computers, 1994-96; spl. edn. tchr. Calif. Sch. Dist., Sacramento, 1993-94; instr. Southwestern U., Lafayette, La., 1997-98; media/tech. specialist St. John Sch. Bd., Reserve, La., 1998—; rschr. Lyndon Baines Johnson Presdl. Libr., 1996—2000. Dir. sta. WJLO-TV Magnet Sch., LaPlace, La., 2000. Founder mag. Tender Times, 2000. Active Parent-Tchr., St. James, La., 1994-96; pres./CEO House Hands & Hugs, Vacherie, La.; mem. adv. bd. Big Brothers & Sisters, Lafayette. Houma-Terabone grantee, 1998; Metrovision Sch.-To-Career grantee, 2002. Mem. ALA, AAUW, NEA, Libr. Info. Tech. Assn., Nat. Assn. Female Execs., Mothers of 21st Century Leaders. Office: John L Ory Magnet Sch 182 W 5th St La Place LA 70068-4501

FIFIELD, MARVIN G. psychologist, educator; BA in Music, Idaho State U., 1956, MEd in Ednl. Adminstrn., 1958; EdD in Counseling, Wash. State U., 1963. Lic. psychologist, Idaho; cert. sch. psychologist, Utah, Idaho; cert. sch. counselor, Utah, Idaho. Dir. rsch. and spl. svcs. Pocatello (Idaho) Sch. Dist., 1964-66; dir. Ctr. for MR Study Idaho State U., Pocatello, 1967-69; postdoctoral fellow Columbia Tchr. Coll., N.Y.C., summer 1970; chmn. dept. spl. edn. Utah State U., Logan, 1969-72, dir. Affiliated Devel. Ctr. for Handicapped Persons, 1972-86, dir. Affiliated Ctr. for Persons with Disabilities, 1987—, dir. Utah Assistive Tech. Program, 1989—, prof. dept. spl. edn. and psychology, 1989—; profl. staff mem. Com. on Labor and Human Resources U.S. Senate, Washington, 1986-87. Vocat. expert HEW/Social Security Adminstrn., Washington, 1968—; UAF liaison cons. HEW/OHDS Divsn. Devel. Disabilities, Washington, 1975-78; expert cons., tchr. trainer WHO Pan Am. Sanitary Bur., Santiago, Chile, 1979; cons. in evaluation tng. and psychol. svcs. Diné Ctr. for Human Devel., Navajo C.C., Ariz., 1980-86; curriculum and psychol. cons. Assn. Venezolena de Padres y Amigos de Ninos Excepcionales, Caracas, 1981-86. Contbr. articles to profl. jours.; author 18 books, chpts. in books, monographs. Vice chmn. Idaho Mental Retardation and Mental Health Planning Coun., 1963-65; adv. bd. Intermountain Regional Med. Program, 1972-76; mem. Utah Gov.'s Coun. for Persons with Disabilities, 1978—; chmn. Senator Hatch's Adv. Com. on Disability Issues, 1981—; chmn. bd. dirs. OPTIONS for Independence, No. Utah, 1987-91; exec. com. Utah Legis. Task Force on Svcs. for Persons with Handicaps, 1990-91; bd. dirs. Utah Legal Ctr. for Persons with Disabilities, 1991—; active ARC. Mem. APA (mem. divsn. counseling psychology, ednl. psychology and sch. psychology), Am. Assn. Univ. Affiliated Proglrams (pres. 1984-85, bd. dirs. 1995—), Rehab. Engring. Soc. N.Am. (co-chair ann. conv. 1996), Am. Assn. on Mental Retardation, Nat. Assn. Retarded Citizens, Utah Cerebral Palsy Assn., Phi Delta Kappa. Office: Utah State U Ctr Persons with Disabilities UMC 680C Logan UT 84322-0001 E-mail: marv@cpo2.usu.edu.

FIFIELD, SEAN C. lawyer; b. Monticello, Ill., Apr. 15, 1972; s. David H. and Margaret R. Fifield; m. Barbara Z. Fifield, Apr. 28, 2001. BS in Aero. Engring., U. Mich., 1993, JD, 1996. Ptnr. Lord, Bissell & Brook, Chgo., 1997—. Mem.: ABA, Licensing Exec. Soc., Am. Intellectual Property Law Assn. Office: Lord Bissell & Brook 115 S LaSalle St Chicago IL 60603

FIFIELD, WILLIAM O. lawyer; b. Crown Point, Indiana, May 25, 1946; BS(hon.), Purdue U., 1968; JD (hon.), Harvard U., 1971. Bar: Ill., 1971; Tex., 1998. Assoc. Sidley and Austin, Dallas, 1971-77, ptnr., 1977—, mng. ptnr. Dallas office, 1996—. Bd. dirs. Kimberly-Clark Corp., 1995—2003. Office: Sidley Austin Brown & Wood LLP 717 N Harwood St Ste 3400 Dallas TX 75201-6534

FIFLIS, TED JAMES, lawyer, educator; b. Chgo., Feb. 20, 1933; s. James P. and Christine (Karakitsos) F.; m. Vasilike Pantelakos, July 3, 1955; children: Christina Eason, Antonia Fowler, Andreanna Lawson. BS, Northwestern U., 1954; LLB, Harvard U., 1957. Bar: Ill. 1957, Colo. 1975, U.S. Supreme Ct. 1984. Pvt. practice law, Chgo., 1957-65; mem. faculty U. Colo. Law Sch., Boulder, 1965—, prof., 1968—. Vis. prof. NYU, 1968, U. Calif., Davis, 1973, U. Chgo., 1976, U. Va., 1979, Duke U., 1980, Georgetown U., 1982, U. Pa., 1983, Am. U., 1983, Harvard U., 1988; Lehmann disting. vis. prof. Washington U., St. Louis, 1991; cons. Rice U.; arbitrator AT&T divesture disputes, 1984-87. Author: (with Homer Kripke, Paul Foster) Accounting for Business Lawyers, 1970, 3rd edit., 1984, Accounting Issues for Lawyers, 1991; editor-in-chief Corp. Law Rev., 1977-88; contbr. articles to profl. jours. Mem. ABA, Am. Assn. Law Schs. (past chmn. bus. law sect.), Colo. Bar Assn. (mem. coun. sect. of corp., banking and bus. law 1974-75), Am. Law Inst. (chmn. com. on rsch. proposed fed. securities code), Colo. Assn. Corp. Counsel (pres. 1998-99). Greek Orthodox. Home: 1602 Columbine Ave Boulder CO 80302-7832 Office: Univ Of Colo Law Sch Boulder CO 80309-0001 E-mail: ted.fiflis@colorado.edu.

FIGA, PHILLIP SAM, lawyer; b. Chgo., July 27, 1951; s. Leon and Sarah Figa; m. Candace Cole, Aug. 19, 1973; children: Benjamin Todd, Elizabeth Dawn. BA, Northwestern U., 1973; JD, Cornell U., 1976. Bar: Colo. 1976, U.S. Dist. Ct. Colo. 1976, U.S. Ct. Appeals (10th cir.) 1980, U.S. Supreme Ct. 1980. Assoc. Sherman & Howard, Denver, 1976-80; ptnr. Burns & Figa, P.C., Denver, 1980-90, pres., 1988-90; pres., shareholder Burns, Figa & Will, P.C., Englewood, Colo., 1991—. Instr. U. Denver Law Sch., 1984, 86, Nat. Inst. Trial Advocacy, Rocky Mountain Region, 1992, 94; bd. dirs. Colo. Lawyers Com., Denver, 1984-89, vice chair 1987-88, treas. 1988-89; mem. model rules of profl. conduct Colo. Supreme Ct., 1987-92, com. lawyer regulation to revise Colo. discipline rules, 1997-98, com. group legal svcs. and advt., 1982-86; mem. U.S. Dist. Ct. Justice Reform Act. Adv. Com., 1994-97; active Colo. Commn. on Jud. Discipline, 1995—; chair nominating com. Faculty Fed. Advs., 1999, 2000; spl. dir. Colo. Jud. Inst., 1999—; presdl. nominee for fed. judgeship, U.S. Dist. Ct. for Dist. of Colo., 2003. Articles editor Cornell Internat. Law Rev., 1975-76; contbr. articles to legal jours. Bd. dirs. B'nai B'rith Anti-Defamation League, 1984—, regional bd. chair, 1996-98, co-chmn. civil rights com., 1988-90; trustee Rose Med. Ctr., 1987-95, exec. com., 1990-95, AMC Cancer Rsch. Ctr., 1993-95; trustee Rose Cmty. Found., 2002—; trustee Jewish Life Com., 2001—, co-chmn., 2002—. Evans scholar, 1969-73. Fellow Internat. Soc. Barristers, Am. Bar Found., Colo. Bar Found. (trustee 1999—, pres. Colo. Bar. Fellows 2001—); mem. ABA (standing com. on profl. discipline 1997-99), Am. Judicature Soc., Colo. Bar Assn. (mem. ethics com. 1978-93, chair ethics com. 1984-85, bd. govs. 1986-88, 89-91, pres. 1995-96, chair awards com. 1998-99, chair nominating com. 1999-2000), Denver Bar Assn., Arapahoe County Bar Assn., Phi Beta Kappa, Phi Eta Sigma. Home: 9928 E Ida Ave Greenwood Village CO 80111-3743 Office: Burns Figa & Will PC Ste 1030 6400 S Fiddlers Green Cir Englewood CO 80111-4950 E-mail: pfiga@burnsfigawill.com.

FIGARI, ERNEST EMIL, JR., lawyer, educator; b. Navasota, Tex., Feb. 18, 1939; s. Ernest Emil and Louise (Campbell) F.; children: Alexandra Caroline, Audrey Elizabeth. BS, Tex. A&M U., 1961; LLB, U. Tex., 1964; LLM, So. Meth. U., 1970. Bar: Tex. 1964, U.S. Ct. Appeals (5th cir.) 1965, U.S. Dist. Ct. (no. dist.) Tex. 1964, U.S. Supreme Ct. 1967. Law clk. to judge U.S. Dist. Ct. (no. dist.) Tex., Dallas, 1964-65; assoc. Coke & Coke, Dallas, 1965-70, ptnr., 1970-75, Johnson & Swanson, Dallas, 1975-86, Figari Davenport & Graves, Dallas, 1986—. Adj. prof. law So. Meth. U., Dallas, 1974-79, 81-82, U. Tex., 1980. Contbr. articles to profl. jours. Fellow ABA Found., Tex. Bar Found., Dallas Bar Found.; mem. State Bar Tex. Roman Catholic. Office: Figari Davenport & Graves Bank of Am Plz 901 Main St Ste 3400 Dallas TX 75202-3796

FIGLAR, ANITA WISE, retired banker; b. Camas, Wash., Oct. 7, 1950; d. William Hulon and Mary Wise (Adkisson) Ward; m. Richard Bould Figlar, Aug. 7, 1976; children: Richard Bould II, David Wise. Student, U. Wash., 1968-70; BA in Intercultural Studies, Ramapo Coll., 1974. Mktg. coord. power and control ops. Gen. Cable Corp., Union, N.J., 1975-76, mktg. analyst power and control ops., 1976-78; various positions Potters Industries, Inc., Hasbrouck Heights, N.J., 1971-75, with highway safety programs dept. Parsippany, N.J., 1981-82, mgr. highway safety programs dept., 1982-84, mgr. bus. devel., 1985-86, industry mgr. Highway Products div., 1986-89; with customer svc. United Jersey Bank, Hackensack, N.J., 1989, fin. svc. rep., 1989-90, asst. br. mgr., bank officer, 1990-91, bank officer retail sales, 1991-92, bank officer retail sales mgr., 1992-94; v.p., mgr. retail sales Summit Bank (formerly United Jersey Bank), Hackensack, N.J., 1994-97, market mgr., 1997-98, sr. regional mgr. New Canaan, Conn., 1998-99; v.p., dist. mgr. Summit Bank, New Canaan, Conn., 1999-2000; v.p., regional sales mgr. The Bank of N.Y., Nanuet, 2000—02, ret., 2002. Contbr. articles to many profl. and govtl. publs.

FIGLEY, MELVIN MORGAN, radiologist, physician, educator; b. Toledo, Dec. 5, 1920; s. Karl Dean and Margaret (Morgan) F.; m. Margaret Jane Harris, Mar. 16, 1946; children: Karl Porter, Joseph Dean, Mark Thompson. Student, Dartmouth, 1938-41; MD magna cum laude (John Harvard fellow), Harvard, 1944. Diplomate: Am. Bd. Radiology (trustee 1967-72). Intern, then resident internal medicine Western Res. U., 1944-46; resident radiology U. Mich., 1948-51, instr., asst. prof., asso. prof. radiology, 1950-58; practice specializing in radiology Seattle, 1958-86; prof. radiology, chmn. dept. U. Wash., 1958-78, prof. radiology and medicine, 1979-85, emeritus prof. radiology and medicine, 1986—. Mem. radiation study sect. NIH, 1963-67; mem. com. on radiology Nat. Acad. Scis.-NRC, 1964-69, chmn., 1968-69 Editor: Am. Jour. Roentgenology, 1976-85; contbr. articles profl. jours. Bd. dirs. James Picker Found., 1970-80. Served to capt. M.C. AUS, 1946-48. John and Mary R. Markle scholar, 1952-57 Fellow Am. Coll. Radiology (Gold medal 1987), Royal Coll. Radiologists (hon., London), Royal Australian Coll. Radiologists (hon.); mem. Royal Soc. Medicine (hon.), Assn. Univ. Radiologists (pres. 1966, Gold medal 1983), Am. Roentgen Ray Soc. (exec. council 1970-88, pres. 1983-84, Gold medal 1986), N. Am. Soc. Cardiac Radiology (pres. 1974), Fleischer Soc. (pres. 1986-87), Radiol. Soc. N.Am. (Gold Medal 1986), AMA, Boylston Med. Soc., Wash. Heart Assn. (past trustee), Soc. Chmn. Acad. Radiology Depts. (exec. council 1969-71), Phi Beta Kappa, Sigma Xi, Alpha Omega Alpha, Sigma Alpha Epsilon. Episcopalian. Home: PO Box 859 Grantham NH 03753-0859

FIGLIN, ROBERT ALAN, hematologist, oncologist; b. Phila., June 22, 1949; s. Jack and Helen Figlin; 1 child, Jonathan B. BA in Chemistry, Temple U., 1970, postgrad., 1972; MD, Med. Coll. Pa., 1976. Diplomate Am. Bd. Internal Medicine, sub-bd. Med. Oncology; diplomate Nat. Bd. Med. Examiners; lic. physician, Calif. Med. intern, resident in medicine Cedars-Sinai Med. Ctr., L.A., 1976-79, chief resident in medicine, 1979-80; fellow in hematology-oncology UCLA, 1980-82, asst. prof. medicine Sch. Medicine, 1982-88, assoc. prof. Sch. Medicine, 1988-94, prof. medicine Sch. Medicine, 1994—, chmn. instnl. rev. bd., human rsch. policy bd., 1998—; dir. Bowyer Oncology Ctr., dir. outpatient clin. rsch. unit Jonsson Comprehensive Cancer Ctr., 1990-92, dir. clin. rsch.

unit, 1993-98, dir. hematology/oncology fellowship program, 1995—; prof. urology, Sch. Medicine UCLA, 2001—, Henry Alvin and Carrie L. Meinhardt chair in urol. oncology, 2001—. Med. dir. thoracic oncology program Johnson Comprehensive Cancer Ctr., 1994—, genito uninary program, 1994—, solid tumor program, 1997—99, solid tumor translational rsch. program, 1999—; prin. investigator UCLA S.W. Oncology Group, 1992—2000; sci. founder Agensys, 1996—. Editor: Interferons in cytokines, 1988—90, Kidney Cancer Jour., 1993—94, Current Clin. Trials, 1992—96; UCLA Cancer Trials Newsletter, 1990—96, Seminars on Oncology-Kidney Cancer, 1995, Cancer Therapeutics, 1997, Cancer Biotherapy and Radio Pharms., 1997, contbr. articles and revs.; editor: Renal & Adrenal Tumors, 2002. Mem. med. adv. bd. Nat. Kidney Cancer Assn., 1993—; FDA cons., 1990-92. Recipient numerous awards. Fellow ACP; mem. Am. Soc. Clin. Oncology, Am. Fedn. Clin. Rsch., Am. Assn. for Cancer Rsch., Soc. for Biologic Therapy (chmn. ann. scientific meeting 1997, pres. cancer panel 1997, S.W. Oncology Group, Assn. Subsplty. Profs., Internat. Assn. for Study of Lung Cancer. Office: UCLA 10945 Le Conte Ave Ste 2333 Los Angeles CA 90024-2828

FIGNER, WILLIAM JAMES, instructional systems designer, consultant; b. Cheverly, Md., Feb. 5, 1968; s. James Alexander and Eleanor Rose Figner; m. Amelia Elizabeth Figner, Oct. 20, 1997. BA in History, U. Ctrl. Fla., Orlando, 1992—94, BA in Liberal Studies, 1992—95, MA in Instrnl. Sys. Design, 1992—96. Florida Professional Educator's Certificate Fla. Dept. of Edn., 1997. Instrnl. designer Carley Corp., Orlando, Fla., 1997—98; lead instrnl. designer Jardon & Howard Technologies, Inc., Orlando, Fla., 1998—2001; quality assurance dir. AERA, Inc., Orlando, Fla., 2001—, lead instrnl. designer, 2001—. Ofcl. town historian Mt. Dora Hist. Soc., Mount Dora, Fla., 1995—96. E-5 USAR, 1985—99, Eustis, FL. Decorated Meritorious Svc. Ribbon U.S. Army, Fla. N.G.; recipient Cold War Cert. of Recognition, U.S. Sec. of Def., 2000. Mem.: Army Aviation Assn. Am. Home: 26515 State Rd 19 Howey In The Hills FL 34737 Office: AERA Inc 11315 Corporate Blvd Ste 100 Orlando FL 32817 Office Fax: 407-382-6838. Personal E-mail: bfigner@msn.com. E-mail: bfigner@aera.com.

FIGUEIRA, THOMAS JOHN, classics educator; b. N.Y.C., Dec. 30, 1948; s. Charles Philip Figueira and Marion Catherine Gentile; m. Sarah George, Aug. 14, 1976; children: Elizabeth Anne, Julie Rose, Charles Francis. BA, Fordham U., 1970; PhD, U. Pa., 1977. Vis. asst. prof. classics Stanford U., Palo Alto, Calif., 1977-78; asst. prof. classics Dickinson Coll., Carlisle, Pa., 1978-79, Rutgers U., New Brunswick, N.J., 1979-85, assoc. prof. classics and ancient history, 1985-91, prof. classics and ancient history, 1991-99, prof. II classics and ancient history, 1999—. Author: Aegina, 1981, Athens and Aigina in the Age of Imperial Colonization, 1991, Excursions in Epichoric History, 1993, The Power of Money: Coinage and Politics in the Athenian Empire, 1998; co-author: Wisdom from the Ancients, 2001. Rsch. fellow Fulbright Found., Athens, Greece, 1976-77, Summer fellow NEH, Harvard U., 1981, Jr. Rsch. fellow Ctr. for Hellenic Studies, Harvard U., Washington, 1982-83, Rsch. fellow John Simon Guggenheim Found., N.Y.C., 1984-85. Roman Catholic. Home: 4 Barnett Rd Lawrenceville NJ 08648-3122 Office: Rutgers Univ Dept Classics 131 George St New Brunswick NJ 08901-1414 Fax: 732-932-9246. E-mail: figueira@rci.rutgers.edu.

FIGUEROA, LIZ, state senator; b. San Francisco; children: AnaLisa, Aaron. Ed., Coll. San Mateo. Owner, oeprator Figueroa Employment Cons., 1981-98; mem. Union Sanitary Dist., pres., 1985; mem. Calif. State Senate, 1998—, mem. bus. and professions com. Mem. Hispanic Cmty. Affairs Coun.; mem. Fermont Adult Sch. Adv. Bd.; bd. dirs. Legal Assistance for Srs.; local bd. dirs. Selective Svc. Sys.; mem. adv. bd. Peninsula Coll. Law. Named Outstanding Legislator by several orgns. Mem. Calif. Elected Women's Assn. for Edn. and Rsch. (bd. dirs.). Democrat. Office: Calif State Senate State Capitol Rm 2057 Sacramento CA 95814 also: 43271 Mission Blvd Fremont CA 94539-5826*

FIGUEROA, ORLANDO, federal agency executive; b. San Juan, P.R., Sept. 9, 1955; m. Josephine Cerra; children: Daniel, Alexis. BSME, U. P.R., 1978; postgrad., U. Md. Mgr. superfluid helium On Orbit Transfer shuttle experiment Goddard Space Flight Ctr., 1986—89, head cryogenics tech. sect., 1987—89, mgr. Small Explorers project, 1990—94, mgr. explorers program, 1994—97, dir. sys., tech. and advanced concepts directorate, 1997—2000; dep. chief engr. sys. engring. NASA, Washington, 2000—01, dir. Mars exploration program Office Space Sci., 2001—. Office: NASA Hdqrs Mail Code S 300 E St SW Washington DC 20546

FIGUEROA, TOMAS, internist; b. San Juan, P.R., Apr. 20, 1965; s. Tomas and Surin (Nieves) F.; m. Emma Diaz, June 15, 1991; children: Tomás Enrique, Andrés Eduardo, Javier Esteban. BS, Washington U., St. Louis, 1987; MD, U. P.R., 1991. Diplomate Am. Bd. Internal Medicine. Intern Emory U. Hosps., Atlanta, 1991-92, resident, 1992-94, VA Hosp. Atlanta, 1994-95, staff, 1997-99, Emory Clinic at Crawford Long Hosp., Atlanta, 1995-97; asst. prof. Emory U., Atlanta, 1995-99; mem. staff VA Med. Ctr., Decatur, Ga., 1997-99, Tampa, Fla., 1999-2001; pvt. practice, Tampa, 2001—. Mem. ACP, AMA, Am. Soc. Internal Medicine. Office: Primary Care Phys Alliance Ste 450 2727 ML King Jr Blvd Tampa FL 33607

FIGUEROA, YILE MARGARET HANNAH, writer, educator; b. Tucson, Ariz., July 15, 1948; d. Robert Monroy Figueroa and Mary Hortense (Preciado) Figueros; children: Taj Marie Maxedon, Joseph Christopher Jude Fereday, Alexandria Patience Moody. Universal Life Church Minister Universal Life Ch., Calif., 1991; cert. Clin. Hypnotherapist Wesland Hypnotherapy Inst., 1995, Reiki Master Usui Shiki Ryoho, Kellen L. Jones, 1995, Professional Psychic Counselor Am. Assn. of Profl. Psychics, Inc., 1991. Contbr. articles to jour. Achievements include Serving God and Country by selfless humanitarianism. Home and Office: AngelCoast 1108 E Harbor View Dr Gilbert AZ 85234-6063 Office Fax: 480-892-4067. E-mail: angelcoast@aol.com.

FIKE, EDWARD LAKE, newspaper editor; b. Delmar, Md., Mar. 31, 1920; s. Claudius Edwin and Rosa Lake (Pegram) F.; m. Rosa Amanda Drake, Apr. 1, 1952; children: Rosa, Evelyn, Amy, Melinda. *Remarkably, Edward and his three siblings are all represented in Who's Who in America. Brother Dr. Claude E. Fike (deceased) was a Professor of History and Dean of Arts and Sciences at Mississippi Southern University, Hattiesburg, Miss. Sister Evelyn's Husband Dr. William Laupus was the founding first Dean of the Medical School at Eastern Carolina University, Greenville, N.C. Sister Ruth's husband Robert Pittman was editor, Editorial Page at the St. Petersburg, Fla. Times.* BA, Duke U., 1941; postgrad., U. Cin., 1941-42. Editor, co-pub. Nelsonville (Ohio) Tribune, 1945-48; dir. bur. pub. info. Duke U., Durham, N.C., 1948-52; mem. U.S. del. N. Atlantic Council, Paris, 1952-53; assoc. editor Rocky Mount (N.C.) Evening Telegram, 1953-57; editor, pub. Fike Newspapers, Lewistown and Glendive, Mont., 1957-62, also Wilmington and Tujunja, Calif., 1957-68; assoc. editor Richmond (Va.) News Leader, 1968-70; dir. news and editorial analysis Copley Newspapers, 1970-77; editor editorial pages San Diego Union, 1977-90. Lectr. journalism San Diego State U., San Diego Evening Coll. Parole commr. San Diego County, 1993-94, pres. adv. coun. San Diego State U., 1988-93; bd. dir. Hubbs Seaworld Rsch. Inst. and Midway Aircraft/Carrier Mus. Grossmont Hosp. Found., Armed Svc. YMCA. Lt. USNR, 1942-45. Recipient George Washington award Freedoms Found., 1969-71, 73, 78, Editorial Writing awards N.C. Press Assn., 1954-55, Va. Press Assn., 1969, Calif. Newspaper Pubs. Assn., 1969, 80; Hoover Inst. Media fellow Stanford U., 1990-91. Mem. Omicron Delta Kappa. Republican. Methodist. Home: 17369 Plaza Maria San Diego CA 92128-2251

FIKRIG, EROL, rheumatologist, medical educator; b. Dec. 15, 1959; BA in Chemistry cum laude, Cornell U., 1981, MD, 1985. Diplomate Am. Bd. Internal Medicine, Am. Bd. Infectious Diseases. Resident in internal medicine Vanderbilt U. Hosp., 1985—88; fellow in infectious diseases and immunobiology Yale U., 1988—92, assoc. rsch. scientist in immunobiology, 1992, asst. prof. medicine sect. of rheumatology, 1992—96, assoc. prof. medicine sect. of rheumatology, 1996—. Contbr. articles to profl. jours.; ad hoc reviewer NIH study sect.: Bacteriology and Mycology I, 1994; spkr. in field. Recipient Young Investigator award, Nat. Found. Infectious Disease, 1991, award in vaccine devel., Infectious Disease Soc. Am., 1992, Young Investigator award, Am. Heart Assn., 1993, Investigator award, Arthritis Found., 1993, Apollo Kinsley award, State of Conn., 1993, NIH First award, 1994, Goodyear award, State of Conn., 1994, Established Investigator award, Am. Heart Assn., 1996; fellow NIH Clin. Investigation, 1990, Daland, Am. Philos. Soc., 1990; scholar Pew, 1993. Mem.: Phi Beta Kappa. Office: Yale U Sch Medicine Dept Rheumatology 333 Cedar St New Haven CT 06510-3289

FIKS, YEVGENIY, artist, critic; b. Moscow, Oct. 21, 1972; BFA, Bklyn. Coll., 1997; MFA, Sch. Visual Arts, 1999. Instr. Mercer County C.C., Trenton, NJ, 1999—2000, asst. prof., 2000—. Art critic Moscow Art Mag., 1994—, NY Arts Mag., 2002—. Exhibitions include Surikovskiy Inst., Moscow, 1992, Mural Art Gallery, Ohio, 1994, Bklyn. (N.Y.) Bridge Anchorage Mus., 1995, Bklyn. (N.Y.) Coll., 1996, 8th Fl. Gallery, NY, 1996, Soho Arts Festival, 1996, Visual Arts Gallery, 1999, Bronx (NY) River Art Ctr., 2000, Trenton (NJ) City Mus., 2000, Mercer Coll., NJ, 2000, Rhizome OpenMouse, NY, 2001, Fairleigh Dickinson U., NJ, 2002, Plug_and_Play, London, 2002, Mastel & Mastel Gallery, NY, 2002, Centro Cultural Pablo, Havana, Cuba, 2002, Kingsborough Coll., N.Y., 2003. Mem.: NEA, Trenton Artists' Workshop Assn. (Hon. Mention 2000), Coll. Art Assn.

FILA, JOHN CHARLES, psychoanalyst; b. Boston; s. John F. and Marion L. Fila. AB, Harvard U., 1992; PhD, U. Berkeley, Mich., 1995. Diplomate Am. Coll. Profl. Mental Health Practitioners. Pvt. practice, Wellesley, Mass., 1997—2000, Santa Monica, Calif., 2000—. Nat. bd. dirs. Internat. Acad. Philosophy, N. Hollywood, Calif. Contbr. articles to profl. jours. Vol. mentor for disadvantaged, 1995—; ombudsman/officer The Prometheus Soc.; mem. Nat. Com. on Am. Fgn. Policy, NY, Nat. Campaign for Tolerance, Montgomery, Ala. Mem.: AAAS, N.Y. Acad. Scis., Menninger Soc., Harvard Club (Boston, So. Calif., Palm Beach). Republican. Episcopalian. Achievements include research in post traumatic stress disorder and its comorbid relationship to a syndrome of mental health issues. Avocations: eclectic reading, sports, travel, theater, films. Home: 2928 4th St Apt 40 Santa Monica CA 90405 Office: 5155 Rosecrans Ave Ste 1215 Hawthorne CA 90250 E-mail: psychdr721@hotmail.com.

FILA, JOSEPH DUNCAN, marketing and sales executive, public relations executive, real estate broker, investor; b. Elizabeth, N.J., Jan. 2, 1950; s. Joseph Charles and Agnes McCallum (Muller) F.; m. Ann Therese Scott, Dec. 11, 1971; children: Dawn Nicole, Daniel Aaron. Comm. dir. Better World Inst., Miami, 1973-74; graphic designer ID Assoc., Miami, 1974-76; pres. Conceptum, Inc., Miami, 1976-87; assoc. Radian Realty Corp., Miami, 1982-85, Income Realty Corp., Miami, 1985-87; exec. v.p. Cervera Real Estate, Miami, 1987-91; v.p. Markets Abroad, Inc., Espoo, Finland, 1987-91; pres. Fila Assoc., Inc., Miami, 1987-96; v.p. mktg. and sales Bldg. Inspection Svcs., 1991-95; broker assoc. Cervera Real Estate, Miami, 1991—; dir. mktg. and sales Vidicomp, Miami, 1995-97; N.Am. sales dir. Aethra Telecomm., Miami, 1998-2000; COO, RealCast Corp., 2000—. Trustee So. Fla. Ctr. Theol. Studies, Miami, 1989-96; assoc. Bus. Coun. Internat. Understand., N.Y.C., 1989—; guest instr. U. Miami, 1986-88. Editor Rotary Caribbean Chronicle, 1985-88. Pres. Elephant Forum, Miami, 1990-92; del. White House Conf. Small Bus., Washington, 1986, Curacao (N.Am.) Symposium Free Enterprise Caribbean, 1984; spl. advisor Sec. Commerce Fla. VOICE Program, Miami, 1987-90; committeeman, membership chmn. Rep. Party Dade County, Miami, 1988-96; mem. Fla. del. Rep. Nat. Conv., 1992; scoutmaster Boy Scouts Am., 1973-85; mem. Am. Forum, 1993-98. Mem. Soc. Broadcast Engrs., Internat. TV Assn., Bldg. Industry Assn. South Fla., Fla. Motion Picture and TV Assn., Coral Gables C.C. (chmn. Caribbean rels. and pub. rels. coms. 1980-85), Finish Am. C. of C. (bd. dirs.), Rotary (pres. Miami West club 1987-88, chmn. dist. pub. rels. com. 1983-84, comm. dir. Fla./Caribbean project 1983-88, internat. pub. rels. consultative com. 1988-89, dist. comm. chmn. 2000—), Miami Club (dir. 1996-98). Avocations: archery, fishing, camping, travel, motorcycling. E-mail: jaddfila@att.net.

FILARDI, ELDONNA MARIE, music educator, accompanist; b. South Bend, Ind., July 19, 1957; d. Frank Dominick Massa and Emalou (Harshman) Massa; m. Robert Joseph Stephen Filardi, Nov. 9, 1996. BS in Music, Nyack Coll., 1980; postgrad., Westminster Choir Coll., Princeton, N.J., 1985-87. Pvt. tchr. piano, Bergen County, N.J., 1973—. Music dir. Vacation Bible Sch., Oakland, N.J., 1991-93, Curtain Up, Ridgewood, N.J., 1992; tchr. music St. Alban's Presch., Oakland, 1991-92, Saddle River (N.J.) Day Sch., 1992-93; music dir., Christian edn. asst. St. Alban's Ch., Oakland, 1991-93; dir. handbell choir Congl. Ch., Park Ridge, N.J., 1993-94; accompanist Canticum Sacrum, Wyckoff, N.J., 1993-94, Royal Acad. Dance classes and exams Robin Horneff Performing Arts Ctr., Waldwick, N.J., 1991-96; mem. adj. faculty music dept. William Paterson Coll., Wayne, N.J., 1994-96; asst. Summer Choir Sch., Ridgewood; mem. N.. Choral Soc., 1986-87, Pro Arte Festival Chorus, 1987-92. Performance with Bergen Philharm., John Harms Ctr., Englewood, 2001. Accompanist benefit concert Christ Ch., Pompton Lakes, N.J., 1996, Leukemia and Lymphona Soc., 2003; mem. choir St. Paul's Episcopal Ch., Englewood, N.J., 2000-01. Mem.: N.J. Choral Soc. Protestant. Avocations: cross stitch, crocheting, crafts, watercolor painting, writing. Home: 326 Faller Dr Apt C New Milford NJ 07646-5265 E-mail: emfpinao@yahoo.com.

FILCHOCK, ETHEL, education educator, poet; BS in Edn., Kent State U. Tchr. Cleve. Pub. Schs.; with EFC Creations, Solon, Ohio. Author: Voices in Poetics: Vol. 1, 1985 (Merit award), Hall of Fame, Ethel Filchock, Vol. 1, 1991, (book of poetry) Softer Memories Across a Lifetime, 1989, (poetry chapbook) A Glimpse of Love, 1991; composer: Praise God, The Lord is Coming; lyricist (songs) He Is Born, 1991, An Old-Fashioned Christmas, Let's Wave the Stars and Stripes Forever, 1991, Be There for Me Music of America, 1993, Christmas Joy, Happy Holidays, 1993, Beautiful Lady of Medugorje, 1993 (Harmonious Honor award), Christmas Joy, There is a Story, 1994, Hilltop Country, Love is Not a Game, 1994, High Country, Loving is Caring, 1995, Mistletoe and Holly, 1996, The Joy of Christmas, This Land is Called America, 1996, Together We Stand, 1996, Everyday, 1997, America Sounds of the Street, Music of America, 1997, Hilltop Country Songbook Songs, Just Love, Love is Not a Game, 1997, Hilltop Records, album, Christmas in My Heart Song, This Holy Morning, 1998, Christmas Songbook, Songs, Mistletoe and Holly, 1998, There Is a Story, 1998, This Holy Morning, 1998 (Award for Excellence, 2000), Adore Him Today, 2000, Christmas Time, 2000, Love Came Down, 2001, Santa Came to our House, 2001, This Land is Called America, 2001, We Will Remember September, 2001, I Will Be With You, 2002, America Is Our Land, 2002. Chmn. sch. United Way, 1985-86. Recipient Cert. of Achievement N.Y. Profl./Amateur Song Jubilee, 1986, Editor's Choice award Disting. Poets of Am., Outstanding Achievement in Poetry, Nat. Libr. of Poetry, 1993, Outstanding Poets of 1994, Interregnum Nat. Libr. of Poetry, Best Poets of 1995, Transformation, Nat. Libr. of Poetry, Editor's Choice award Outstanding Achievement in Poetry, 1996, 2000, 01, 02, Nat. Libr. of Poetry, 1995, 96, 2001, Outstanding Poets of 1998 for Magnanimous Beauty, Nat. Libr. of Poetry, 1998, Editor's Choice award for outstanding achievement in poetry, 1998. Mem. NAFE, Am. Fedn. Tchrs. Clubs: Akron Manuscript. Roman Catholic. Avocations: painting, traveling, dancing, fishing.

FILDES, RICHARD JAMES, lawyer; b. N.Y.C., Nov. 9, 1952; s. Edgar E. and Lucille (Sanna) F.; m. Deborah D. Davenport, June 21, 1979; children: Matthew, Melissa, Heather. BS in Psychology and Econs. magna cum laude, Duke U., 1974; JD cum laude, U. Fla., 1977. Bar: Fla. 1977. Ptnr. Lowndes, Drosdick, Doster, Kantor & Reed, Orlando, Fla., 1977—, also bd. dirs., mem. mgmt. com. Gen. counsel Fla. Citrus Sports; trustee, dir. at large Fla. Citrus Sports Found., Inc. Mem. Lake Nona Club. Democrat. Roman Catholic. Avocations: golf, working out, fishing, reading, running. Office: Lowndes Drosdick Doster et al 215 N Eola Dr Orlando FL 32801-2095

FILE, JOSEPH, research physics engineer; b. Lecce, Italy, May 6, 1923; s. Carlo and Laura (Nuzzi) F.; m. Dorothy Richards, Sept. 2, 1944; children: Joseph C., Laurel M., Jeannette. BME, Cornell U., 1944; MS, Columbia U., 1958, PhD, 1967; D in Physics, U. Lecce, Italy, 1978. Design engr. Petro Chem. Devel. Co., N.Y.C., 1946-56; rsch. sr. Princeton (N.J.) U., 1956—. Advisor N.E. region Fed. Lab. Consortium, 1992—; ofcl. U.S. rep. 2nd Atoms for Peace Conf., Geneva, 1958; Def. Dept. appointee Employer Support for the Guard and Res., 1995. Contbr. articles to profl. jours. Pres. Marine Corps Scholarship Found., 1965-75, chmn. bd. dirs., 1975-94, chmn. emeritus. Col. USMCR, 1942-74; PTO, Korea. Decorated comdr. Order of Italian Republic; Fulbright fellow, 1978. Roman Catholic. Achievements include patent on bending free D, shaped magnetic coils for fusion reactors, and fabrication and operation of world's first sixth order superconducting magnet now used on MRI imaging devices. Office: PPPL Princeton U Princeton NJ 08543

FILEK, ALLAN AUGUST, physician; b. Chgo., May 18, 1907; s. August and Jenny (Mikota) F.; m. Maurine Mary McCord, June 25, 1960; m. Meta Katherine Johnson, Feb. 11, 1934 (wid. Dec. 1955); 1 child, Suzanne Henderson. BS, U. Chgo., 1928; MD, Rush Med. Coll., 1932; MSPH, U. Mich., 1941. Pvt. practice, Musooda, Wis., 1934-36; dist. health officer Wis. Bd. of Health, Green Bay, 1936-43, dir. TB Divsn. Madison, Wis., 1943-46, dir. local adminstrn., 1946-58; regional health officer Ill. Dept. Health, Aurora, 1958-64; pub. health dir. Evanston-North Shore Health, Evanston, Ill., 1964-73; admitting officer VA Rsch. Hosp., Chgo., 1973-74; admitting chief VA Hosp., Phoenix, 1974-75; clinic physician Maricopa County, Phoenix, 1975-77; physician Rock Resorts, Jackson Lake, Wyo., 1976; examining physician Plasma Donor Ctrs., Phoenix, 1979-97. Chmn. Madison Human Rights Commn., 1957-58. Capt. Army Med. Corps, 1941-42. Mem. Sun Cities Physicians Club (past officer), Lions (pres. Madison club 1958, Evanston club 1972, Sun City West club 1980, Sun City, Ariz. club 1994), Alpha Omega Alpha, others. Home: 10101 W Palmeras Dr Apt 328 Sun City AZ 85373-2088 E-mail: hepa4@juno.com.

FILER, CRIST N. artist, chemist; b. Hartford, Conn., May 12, 1949; s. Charles Edward and Ann Filer; m. Lynn Robin Filer, Aug. 24, 1975; 1 child, Courtney Lauren. BS, Trinity Coll., 1971; PhD, MIT, 1975. Lectr. MIT, Cambridge, Mass., 1971—75; postdoctorate Northeastern U., Boston, 1975—78; group leader NEN Life Sciences, Boston, 1978—95; fellow scientist Perkin Elmer Life Sci., Boston, 1995—. Adv. bd. Internat. Isotope Soc., Cambridge, Mass., 1999—, Jour. of Labelled Compounds and Radiopharmaceuticals, Cambridge, Mass., 1995—. Contbr. articles to profl. jours. Cadet USAF, 1971—74. Mem.: New Eng. Watercolor Soc. (pres. 2002). Avocation: watercolor painting. Home: 14 Bow Street Pl Somerville MA 02143 Office: Perkin Elmer Life Scis 549 Albany St Boston MA 02118 Office Fax: 617-350-9696. E-mail: crist.filer@perkinelmer.com.

FILER, EMILY SYMINGTON HARKINS, retired foundation administrator, writer; b. Balt., May 12, 1936; d. Frank Fife and Grace (Cover) Symington; m. George Archer Harkins, June 21, 1958 (div. 1982); children: Montgomery Fox, Emily Harrison (dec. Apr. 1978); m. Robert Hoagland Filer, June 24, 1989. Degree, Villa Julie Med. Sec. Sch., Balt., 1955. Cert. vol. adminstr. Registrar Johns Hopkins Hosp., Balt., 1955-57, sec. hearing and speech ctr., 1957-58; pres. Distaff Wives, San Francisco, Boston, 1958-63; v.p., bd. dirs. The Planning Council, Tidewater, Va., 1969-78; pres. Jr. League of Norfolk (Va.)-Virginia Beach, 1972-74; founder, coord. Lee's Friends, Norfolk, 1978-86, exec. dir., 1986-2001; ret., 2001. Chmn. Tidewater dist. Va. Council Soc. Welfare, 1985-87, Va. Council Social Welfare, 1988; bd. dirs. Va. Wesleyan Coll., Norfolk, 1979-2001, Olde Huntersville Devel., Norfolk, 1985-87; mem. Glennan Geriat. Clerkship Faculty Ea. Va. Med. Sch., 1996-2001; nat. cons., trainer, vis. instr. Norfolk State U., Old Dominion U., Regent U., Tidewater C.C., Va. Wesleyan Coll. Lic. pastoral caregiver, lay reader The Ch. of Good Shepherd, 1992—, instr. adult Sunday sch., 1998, group leader Alpha program, 1999-2000, co-leader lay pastoral care, 2000—; bd. dirs., sec., exec. com. Westminster Canterbury of Virginia Beach, 1993-2001; mem. Mayor's Commn. on Aging, Virginia Beach, 1996-2000, vice chair, 1997-2000, chair, 1999-2001, mem. mayor's Census 2000 com.; bd. trustees Va. Wesleyan Coll., 1979-2001; mem., past pres. Tidewater dist. Va. Coun. on Social Welfare; steering com. Hampton Rds. Leadership Prayer Luncheon, 1999, co-chair prayer luncheon, 2001—; del. Episcopal Diocese of So. Va., 1999-2000, co-chair Diocese Gala, 2001; mem. profl. adv. group Clin. Pastoral Edn., 2001-; vol. assoc. chaplain Westminster Canterburg, 2003—. Named Gt. Citizen of Hampton Roads, 1987, Va. Vol. Adminstr. of Yr., Internat. Assn. for Vol. Adminstrn. Va. affiliates, 1992; recipient Women in Transition award YWCA of South Hampton Roads, 1989, Spl. award Outstanding Profl. Women of Hampton Roads, 1989, Disting. Merit citation NCCJ, 1992, Outstanding Cmty. Svc. award Delta Sigma Theta Norfolk Alumae chpt., 1997, Pub. Citizen of Yr. award NASW, Va. chpt., 1999. Mem. Internat. Assn. for Vol. Adminstrs. (cert. liaison, region IV 1986, profl. devel. liaison assn. 1987-88, region IV 1987-88, 93-94, recertification chair 1990-92, exec. planning com. Internat. Conf. on Vol. Adminstrn. 1997, chair subcom. peer assessment 2000—), Southeastern Va. Assn. for Vol. Adminstrs. (dep. sec. 1986-87, pres. 1987-89), Tidewater Cancer Network (assoc. 1986), Nat. Hospice Orgn. (profl.), Va. Assn. for Hospice Orgn. (assoc.), Jr. League of Norfolk-Va. Beach (hon., sustainer, past pres., 1st Outstanding Sustainer award 1981), Assn. for Jr. Leagues Internat. (Disting. Vol. Centennial Cookbook profile 1996). Episcopalian. Avocations: reading, walking, gardening, cooking. E-mail: emilyfiler@yahoo.com.

FILERMAN, GARY LEWIS, health educator; b. Mpls., Nov. 16, 1936; s. Joseph H. and Bonnie (Kobrin) F.; m. Jane Harding, Sept. 15, 1962; children: Amy Beth, Joseph Harding, Suzanne Louise. BA, U. Minn., 1959, M.Health Adminstrn. (Phillips Found. fellow 1959-60), 1961, MA (W.K. Kellogg fellow 1961-64), 1963, PhD (Milbank travel grantee 1964, Orgn. Am. States fellow 1964), 1970. Adminstrv. resident Johns Hopkins Hosp., 1961-62; acting dir. Minn. Hosp. Assn., 1965; pres. Assn. Univ. Programs in Health Adminstrn., Washington, 1965-93; exec. sec. Accrediting Commn. Edn. Health Services Adminstrn., 1968-80; assoc. dir. PEW Health Professions Commn., Washington, 1993-95; dir. David A. Winston Fellowship, 1986—, pres., 1998—2003. Mem. faculty George Washington U., chmn., prof. dept. health mgmt. and policy, 1998-2000, prof. and dir. health sys., Georgetown U., 2000—; guest scholar Brookings Instn., 1962; sr. health advisor Acae. Ednl. Devel., 1998-2000; cons. in field. Author: A Future of Consequence, 1989;, editor Jour. Health Adminstrn. Edn., 1982-93; author articles in field.; mem. editl. bds. profl. jours. Mem. nat. health professions adv. coun. HHS, 1983-87, coun. agy for health care policy and rsch., 1990-92; bd. dirs. Am. Refugee Commn., 1982—, Fairfax Audubon, 1989-93, Am. Internat. Health Alliance; chmn. Planned Parenthood Metro Washington, 1990-91, bd. dirs. 1989-92; bd. dirs. Ctr. for Transformational Leadership, 2000-02; internat. adv. bd. Vols. of Am., 2003—. Recipient Silver medal Leuven (Belgium) U., 1972, Disting. Contbn. award Assn. U. Programs Health Adminstrn., 1979, Outstanding Achievement award Regents of U. Minn., 1982, Outstanding Achievement award Ohio State U., 1992; Salzburg Seminar fellow, 2000. Fellow APHA, Am. Acad. Med. Adminstrn. (hon.), hon. alumni, Univ. Chgo.,1992, diplomate Am. Coll. of Health Care Execs., 1990—; mem. Royal Soc. Health, Assn. Am. Med. Colls., Assn. Acad. Rsch., Cosmos Club (Washington), Phi Beta Kappa. Home: 1322 Banquo Ct Mc Lean VA 22102-2707

FILERMAN, MICHAEL HERMAN, television producer; b. Chgo., May 4, 1938; s. Arthur Joseph and Anne Leah (Greenfield) F. BS in Communications, U. Ill., 1960. Gen. program dir. Sta. WGN-TV, Chgo., 1962-67; gen. program dir., dir. daytime programs CBS TV Network, N.Y.C., 1967-72; dir. series devel. Paramount TV, 1972-74; v.p. series devel. Lorimar Prodns., 1976-83; with 20th Century Fox, 1983-85, NBC Prodns., 1985-88. Exec. prodr.: Knots Landing, Falcon Crest, Flamingo Road, Secrets of Midland Heights, King's Crossing, Sisters, John Grisham's The Client, Four Corners, (Movie of the Week) Christmas Eve, Peyton Place: The Next Generation, A Letter to Three Wives, Assault and Matrimony, The Child Saver, Take My Daughters, Please, Turn Back the Clock, Coins in the Fountain, The Story Lady, The Return of Eliot Ness, Roommates, Deadly Family Secrets, Once You Meet a Stranger, Knots Landing: Back to the Cul-de-Sac, When Andrew Came Home; prodr.: (theatre) 24th Day, I Love You!, You're Perfect!, Now Change!, Lypsinska: The Boxed Set, Our Lady of 121st Street, Tea At Five.

FILI-KRUSHEL, PATRICIA, media company executive; b. Nov. 12, 1953; BA, St. John's U., Jamaica, NY, 1975; MBA, Fordham U., Bronx, NY, 1982. Dir. of prod. HBO, 1981—83, v.p. business affairs, 1984—88; senior v.p. programming & prod. Lifetime Television, 1988—89; group v.p. Hearts/ABC-Viacom Entertain. Services, 1990—93; pres. of ABC Daytime ABC TV, 1993—98, pres., 1998-2000; pres., CEO Web MD, 2000—01; exec. v.p. of administration AOL Time Warner, 2001—. Office: AOL Time Warner 75 Rockefeller Plz New York NY 10019

FILIMONOV, MIKHAIL ANATOLYEVITCH, investment company executive; b. Odessa, Ukraine, Oct. 26, 1956; came to the U.S., 1971; s. Anatoly M. and Ludmila G. (Yankelevitch) Filimonov; m. Natalia Baranova; 1 child, Nicholas M.;1 child from previous marriage, Alexandra K. AAS, N.Y. Tech. Coll., 1982; student, Baruch Coll., 1983. V.p. Arnhold & S. Bleichroder, N.Y.C., 1983, Cresvale Internat., London and N.Y.C., 1984; 1st v.p. Quadrex Securities, N.Y.C., 1985-87; v.p. Baring Securities, N.Y.C., 1987-90; first v.p. London

Investment Trust Am., Inc., N.Y.C., 1990-92; chmn., chief investment officer, CEO Alexandra Investment Mgmt. (formerly Hermes Capital Mgmt.), N.Y.C., 1992—. Bd. dirs. Alexandra Global Investment Fund, Brit. Virgin Islands. Republican. Office: Alexandra Investment Mgmt 767 3d Ave 39th Fl New York NY 10017

FILIPPINE, EDWARD LOUIS, federal judge; b. 1930; AB, St. Louis U., 1951, JD, 1957. Bar: Mo. 1957. Pvt. practice law, St. Louis, 1957—77; spl. asst. atty. gen. State of Mo., 1963—64; dist. judge U.S. Dist. Ct. (ea. dist.) Mo., St. Louis, 1977—, chief judge, 1990—95; U.S. sr. dist. judge U.S. Dist. Ct. for Ea. Dist. Mo., 1995—. Served with USAF, 1951-53 Mem. ABA, Mo. Bar Assn., Bar Assn. Met. St. Louis, Lawyers Assn. of St. Louis. Office: US Dist Ct Thomas F Eagleton US Cthse 111 S 10th St Rm 10 137 Saint Louis MO 63102

FILIPPINI, CHRISTINE MARIE, counselor; b. Norristown, Pa., Aug. 1, 1957; d. Nicholas John Caramenico and Christine (Dougherty) Stayton; m. Anthony John Filippini, May 26, 1989; children: Anthony, Christopher. AB, Muhlenberg Coll., 1979; MEd, Millersville (Pa.) U., 1980. Cert. counselor Nat. Bd. for Cert. Counselors, 2002, Profl. Counselor Commn. of Pa., 2002. Sch. counselor West Perry Sr. High Sch., Elliottsburg, Pa., 1980-84, READS Inc., Levittown, Pa., 1984-87, Methacton Sch. Dist., Fairview Village, Pa., 1987—. Co-chair Montgomery County Teen/Parent Task Force, Norristown, 1991-93. Presenter Chester County (Pa.) Intermediate Unit, 1989, 94, March of Dimes Conf., Phila., 1990, Pa. Dept. of Edn., State College, 1991—. Mem.: AACD (del. 1990), Pa. Counselors Assn. (exec. bd. 1989—94, 1996—97), Montgomery County Counselors Assn. (senator 1989—94, 1997—, treas. 1998—2001, sch. rep.-at-large 2001—03, pres. 2003—), Methacton Edn. Assn., Pa. Edn. Assn., Pa. Counseling Assn., Pa. Sch. Counselors Assn. Avocations: cooking, reading, writing, friends, basket making. Office: Methacton Sch Dist Kreible Mill Rd Fairview Village PA 19408

FILKINS, SUSAN ESTHER, small business owner; b. McCloud, Calif., Dec. 21, 1958; d. Donald Gene Ragan and Sandra Esther (Lange) Heron; m. Timothy John Filkins, Oct. 10, 1987; children: Erin Sue, Ann Lauren, Eric Timothy. Degree in Office Adminstrn., Moore's Bus. Coll., Sacramento, 1978; AS in Studio Art and Design summa cum laude, Cayuga C.C., Auburn, N.Y., 2001. Lic. real estate, broker. Adminstrv. asst. Sacramento Blood Ctr., 1979—83; convention coord. Calif. State Blood Banking Sys., Sacramento, 1982; supr. radiology Mercy Gen. Hosp., Sacramento, 1983—87; owner, pres. Rose Sparrows Agy., Skaneateles, NY, 1988—. Radiology computer software specialist Mercy Gen. Hosp., Sacramento, 1986; cons. Syracuse U. Ctr. Career Svcs., 2002—03. Photographer N.Y. State Fair Exhbn., 1996, 1997, 2002. Mem. planning bd. Village of Elbridge, 1990—91; team leader Jordan-Elbridge Site-Base Mgmt. Jordan-Elbridge Ctrl. Sch. Dist., 1993—; mem. Cayuga County Arts Coun., 2000—; alumni program coord. Syracuse U.; com. person Rep. Com., Elbridge, NY, 1998—. Mem.: Phi Theta Kappa. Baptist. Avocations: theater, writing, photography. Office: Rose Sparrows Agy PO Box 645 Skaneateles NY 13152

FILLBROOK, THOMAS GEORGE, telephone company executive; b. Detroit, Jan. 3, 1949; s. John Moyle and Marie Evelyn (Pelto) F. BA, Wayne State U., 1970. Cert. tchr., Mich. Substitute tchr. Van Dyke Pub. Schs., Warren, Mich., 1971-73; mgr. Ameron, Okemos, Mich., 1973-74; salesman F&E Check Protector, Detroit, 1974-76; ops. mgr. Loss Prevention Inc., Royal Oak, Mich., 1976-78; svc. rep. SBC Global Markets, Pontiac, Mich., 1979—; actor/clown Clowning Around Entertainment, Romeo, Mich., 1958—. Actor Holy Cow Show, WGPR Channel 62, Detroit, 1988; dir. Winter Magic, Harron Cable, Rome, 1991; on air analyst "Hockeytime" WBRW Channel 6, 1998—. Polit. and hist. columnist, polit. editor Mill Creek View Newspaper, Washington; mem. City of Hope 1994 Com. Mem. Rep. Nat. Com., Washington, Founders Soc., Detroit Inst. Arts. Recipient commendation Macomb County Bd. Commrs., 1991, 1st Place Clown Costume Competition and Group Act award Mich. State Fair and Exposition, 1995, Top Individual Fund Raiser City of Hope, 1997, 98, 99, 2000. Mem. Internat. Platform Assn., Finnish Ctr. Assn., Detroit Zool. Soc., Citizens Against Government Waste (charter), Elks (chmn. 1985). Episcopalian. Avocation: poetry. Home: 54723 Shelby Rd Shelby Township MI 48316-1441 E-mail: fillbrookme@aol.com.

FILLER, DANIEL M. law educator; s. Robert and Miriam Filler; m. Alisa H. Hoffman; 1 child, Deborah. BA, Brown U., 1984; JD, NYU, 1990. Bar: NY 1992, Pa. 1993, Ala. 1998. Jud. law clk. Judge J. Dickson Phillips, U.S. Ct. of Appeals for the Fourth Circuit, Durham, NC, 1990—91; assoc. Debevoise & Plimpton, N.Y.C., 1991—93; asst. pub. defender Defender Assn. of Phila., 1993—97; staff atty. The Bronx Defenders, 1997—98; asst. prof. U. Ala. Sch. Law, Tuscaloosa, 1998—2001; assoc. prof. U. of Ala. Sch. of Law, Tuscaloosa, 2001—. Chair sect. on law and humanities Assn. Am. Law Schs., 2002—03. Office: U of Ala Sch of Law Box 870382 Tuscaloosa AL 35487 E-mail: dfiller@law.ua.edu.

FILLER, RONALD HOWARD, lawyer; b. St. Louis, Apr. 11, 1948; s. Leon Isaac and Jeanette Frances (Sanofsky) F.; m. Paula; children: Stephen Paul, Lindsay Ann. BS, U. Ill., 1970; JD, George Washington U., 1973; LLM in Taxation, Georgetown U., 1976. Bar: D.C. 1973, Ill. 1976, N.Y. 1993. Atty. SEC, Washington, 1973-76; assoc. Abramson & Fox, Chgo., 1976-77; assoc. counsel Conti Cmty. Svc., Chgo., 1977-78, dir. mgmt. accounts, 1978-80; mng. ptnr. Filler Zaner & Assocs., Chgo., 1980-85; ptnr. Vedder, Price, Kaufman & Kammholz, Chgo., 1985-93, corp. practice leader, 1989-91, mem. exec. com., 1991-93; dir. futures adminstrn. Lehman Bros., Inc., 1993—. Dir. Commodities Law Inst., Ill. Inst. Tech./Chgo-Kent Law Sch., 1978-97, adj. prof. law, 1977-93, bd. overseers, 1982-97; lectr. Commodities Ednl. Inst., 1977-89; adj. prof. law Bklyn. Law Sch., 1994-96; vice chmn. Broker Tec Clearing Corp., 2002—. Contbr. articles to jours. and futures mags. Named one of top 315 lawyers State of Ill., 1991. Mem. ABA (chmn. sub futures commn. mchts. 1986—), Nat. Futures Assn. (bd. dirs. 1984-87), Am. Arbitration Assn. (arbitrator), Mid Am. Commodity Exch. (bd. dirs. 1984-86), Chgo. Bar Assn. (chmn. commodities law com. 1981-82, vice chmn. fin. and legal svcs. com. 1988-89, co-vice chmn. large law firm com. 1991-92), Nat. Assn. Futures Traders Assn., Futures Industry Assn. (bd. dirs. 1990-92, exec. com. Chgo. divsn. 1986-88, exec. com. Law and Comp. divsn. 1985-90, 92—, sec. 1995-98, pres. 1998-2000), N.Y. State Bar Assn., Ill. State Bar Assn. Democrat. Jewish. Home: 54 Collinwood Rd Maplewood NJ 07040-1038 Office: Lehman Bros Inc 745 7th Ave 5th Fl New York NY 10019 Office Fax: 212-526-6193. E-mail: RFiller@LEHMAN.com.

FILLER, SUSAN MELANIE, musicologist; b. Gary, Ind., July 18, 1947; d. Robert and Lael Carol (Rosenbloom) F. BA, U. Ill., Chgo., 1969; MusM, Northwestern U., 1970, PhD, 1977. Music editor and rschr., 1975—. Invited lectr., The Netherlands, Can., France, China. Author: Gustav and Alma Mahler: A Guide to Research, 1989; contbr. numerous articles, papers, edits., translations and reviews. Mem. Am. Musicol. Soc. (editor newsletter Midwest chpt. 1981-95, guest lectr. Midwest chpt. and nationwide 1975—), Internat. Musicol. Soc. (speaker Bologna meeting 1987), Coll. Music Soc., Internat. Gustav Mahler Soc., Gustav Mahler Soc. of N.Y. (adv. bd. 1998—), Gustav Mahler Soc. of Chgo. (editor newsletter 2002—), Midwest Jewish Studies Assn. Avocations: writing, walking, swimming, ethnic cooking.

FILLEY, CHRISTOPHER MARK, neurologist, researcher; b. Saranac Lake, N.Y., July 31, 1951; s. Giles Franklin and Mary Brown (Klinefelter) F. BA, Williams Coll., 1973; MD, Johns Hopkins U., 1979. Diplomate Am. Bd. Psychiatry and Neurology. Intern U. Conn., Farmington, 1979-80; resident in neurology U. Colo., Denver, 1980-83; behavioral neurology fellow Boston U., 1983-84; from instr. to asst. prof. neurology U. Colo. Sch. Medicine, Denver, 1984-91, assoc. prof. neurology, 1991-97, prof. neurology, 1997—. Prin. investigator studies in Alzheimers Disease NIH, Bethesda, Md., 1991-94. Author: Neurobehavioral Anatomy, 1995, Neurobehavioral Anatomy, 2d edit., 2001, The Behavioral Neurology of White Matter, 2001; contbr. articles to profl. jours. Health com. Denver Found., 1995-98. Mem. Am. Acad. Neurology, Am. Neurol. Assn., Internat. Neuropsychol. Soc., Soc. for Behavioral and Cognitive Neurology, Colo. Soc. Clin. Neurologists. Avocations: piano, hiking, reading, guitar, skiing. Office: Univ Colo Behavioral Neurology Sect 4200 E 9th Ave Denver CO 80220-3700 E-mail: christopher.filley@uchsc.edu.

FILLEY, WARREN VERNON, allergist, immunologist; b. Topeka, Kans., Oct. 27, 1950; MD, U. Kans. Sch. Medicine, 1976. Diplomate Am. Bd. Allergy and Immunology, Am. Bd. Internal Medicine. Intern U. Okla., 1976-77, resident in internal medicine, 1977-79; fellow allergy & immunology Mayo Clin., Rochester, 1979-81; with Presby. Hosp., Okla. City; clin. prof. medicine U. Okla. Mem. AMA, Am. Acad. Allergy, Asthma and Immunology,Am. Coll. Allergy, Asthma and Immunology, Okla. Med. Assn. Office: Okla Allergy and Asthma Clin 750 NE 13th St Oklahoma City OK 73104-5051

FILLINGER, MARK F. vascular surgeon, researcher; b. Columbus, Ohio, Oct. 7, 1957; s. Robert J. and Charlotte A. Fillinger; m. Mary C. Pawlinga, Jan. 1, 1989. BS in Mech. Engring., Ohio State U., 1979, MD, 1984. Diplomate Am. Bd. Surgery (Added Qualifications in Vascular Surgery), Nat. Bd. Med. Examiners; registered vascular technologist; lic. physician, N.Y., N.H. Resident in gen. surgery SUNY Health Sci. Ctr., Syracuse, 1984-91, rsch. fellow dept. surgery, 1987-89; fellow in vascular surgery Dartmouth-Hitchcock Med. Ctr., Hanover, NH, 1991—93, asst. prof. vascular surgery, 1993—99, assoc. prof., 1999—. Contbr. chpts. to books, articles to profl. jours. Recipient Peter B. Samuels award Soc. Clin. Vascular Surgery, 1989, Ralph A. Deterling award New Eng. Soc. for Vascular Surgery, 1993. Fellow ACS, Soc. Vascular Surgery, European Soc. Vascular Surgery, Internat. Soc. Endovascular Specialists; mem. AMA, Internat. Soc. for Applied Cardiovascular Biology, Soc. for Vascular Tech., Am. Inst. Ultrasound in Medicine, N.H. Med. Soc., Pi Tau Sigma. Avocations: golf, skiing, tennis, horseback riding. Home: 17 Mulherrin Farm Rd Hanover NH 03755-4907 Office: Dartmouth-Hitchcock Med Ctr Sect Vascular Surgery One Medical Ctr Dr Lebanon NH 03756

FILLIOS, LOUIS CHARLES, retired science educator; b. Boston, July 1, 1923; s. Charles Louis and Pagona (Kefalas) F.; m. Iphigenia Loomis, June 15, 1947; children: Despena, Diana, Hilary. AB, Harvard, 1948, MS, 1953, ScD, 1956. Rsch. assoc., then assoc. Harvard U., 1956-60; asst. prof. physiol. chemistry MIT, 1961-64, assoc. prof., 1964-66; assoc. rsch. prof. biochemistry and pathology Boston U. Sch. Medicine, 1966-68; prof. nutritional sci. Boston U., 1968-94; prof. biochemistry Boston U. Sch. Medicine, 1970-94; dir. divsn. basic sci. Boston U. Sch. Medicine (Sch. Grad. Dentistry), 1970-75, chmn. dept. nutritional scis., 1973-94; prof. biochemistry emeritus Boston U., 1994—. Chmn. Mass. Task Force Nutrition and Aging, 1970-71; cons. Mass. Office of Elder Affairs, 1971-73; co-chmn. nutrition sect. White House Conf. Aging, 1971-72; cons. VA, Bedford, Mass., 1982-87, mem. pres.'s adv. coun. Hellenic Coll., 1968-73. Author numerous research articles fields biochemistry, pathology and nutrition; contbr. sci. and profl. jours. 1st lt. USAAF, 1943-45. Decorated D.F.C., Air Medal with 3 oak leaf clusters (7 battle stars); recipient Outstanding Educator of Am. award Boston U., 1972, Spl. Honor, 1995. Fellow AAAS, Am. Heart Assn. (established investigator 1961-66); mem. Am. Inst. Nutrition (chmn. fellow award com. 1978-81), Am. Soc. for Nutritional Scis., Sigma Xi (Harvard chpt.), Omicron Kappa Upsilon (hon.). Home: 19 Eliot Rd Lexington MA 02421-5630

FILLMORE, JOHN DILLON, artist; b. Canoga Park, Calif., Nov. 24, 1951; s. Herbert Peter and Patricia Louise (Dillon) F. BFA, Art Ctr. Coll. Design, Hollywood, Calif., 1973. Fine artist, designer Chris O'Connell Inc./Ancient Echoes/Martex, Santa Fe, N.Mex., 1989-95; freelance fine artist Santa Fe, Tarzana, 1974—. Recipient Hubbard Art award for excellence, 1991. Republican. Roman Catholic. Avocations: art history, collecting art and books.

FILLMORE, MARY DINGEE, management consultant; b. Boston, Oct. 11, 1948; d. Richard Harold and Rebecca Watson (Dingee) F.; life ptnr. Joanna Marie Rankin. BA, Oberlin (Ohio) Coll., 1972. Editl. asst. Health, Edn. & Welfare, Washington, 1972-73; assoc. dir. Fedn. Am. Scientists, Washington, 1973-75; assoc. Environ. Policy Ctr., Washington, 1975-77; fed. women's program mgr. EPA, Washington, 1977-81; dir. Changing Work, Boston, 1981-94, Burlington, Vt., 1994—. Cons. Ctrs. Disease Control, Royal Inst. Pub. Adminstrn., London, U.S. Dept. Agr., Gardener's Supply Co., others. Author: Women MBAs: A Foot in the Door, 1987. Vol. Career Beginnings, Burlington, Boston Women's Health Book Collective, Vt. Businesses for Social Responsibility. Named Woman of Yr., Bus. and Profl. Women, Boston, 1989. Mem. AAUW, Orgn. Devel. Network, Am. Soc. Tng. and Devel., Federally Employed Women, Vt. Consultants Network. Home and Office: Changing Work 30 Adams St Burlington VT 05401-4611

FILLMORE, PETER ARTHUR, mathematician, educator; b. Moncton, N.B., Can., Oct. 28, 1936; s. Henry Arthur and Jeanne Margaret (Archibald) F.; m. Anne Ellen Garvock, Aug. 6, 1960; children: Jennifer Anne, Julia Margaret, Peter Alexander. B.Sc., Dalhousie U., 1957; MA, U. Minn., 1960, PhD, 1962. Instr. U. Chgo., 1962-64; asst. prof. math. Ind. U., 1964-67, assoc. prof., 1967-71, prof., 1971-72; vis. assoc. prof. U. Toronto, Canada, 1970-71; prof. math. Dalhousie U., Halifax, Canada, 1972-2001; Killam sr. fellow Dalhousie U., Halifax, 1972-73, Killam rsch. prof., 1973-78, chmn. dept. math., stats. and computer sci., 1987-91, prof. emeritus, 2001—. Sr. vis. fellow U. Edinburgh, 1977; mem. Math. Scis. Rsch. Inst., Berkeley, Calif., 1984-85, Fields Inst. Rsch. Math. Sci., 1994-95; vis. prof. U. Copenhagen, 1990. Author: Notes on Operator Theory, 1970, A User's Guide to Operator Algebras, 1996; mem. editl. bd. Jour. Integral Equations and Operator Theory, C.R. Math. Rep. Acad. Soc. Can.; contbr. articles to profl. jours. Fellow Royal Soc. Can.; mem. Can. Math. Soc. (council 1973-75, 77-79, v.p. 1975-77, pres. 1994-96), Am. Math. Soc. (council 1982-84). Office: Dalhousie U Math Dept Halifax NS Canada B3H 3J5 E-mail: fillmore@mathstat.dal.ca.

FILMON, GARY ALBERT, Canadian provincial premier, civil engineer; b. Winnipeg, Man., Can., Aug. 24, 1942; s. Albert and Anastasia (Doskcoz) F.; m. Janice Clare Wainwright, 1963; children: Allison, David, Gregg, Susanna. BSc in Civil Engring., U. Man., 1964, MSc, 1967. Registered profl. engr. Mcpl. design engr. Underwood McLellan and Assocs., Winnipeg, 1964-67, br. mgr. Brandon, Man., 1967-69; v.p. Success Bus. Coll., Winnipeg, 1969-71, pres., 1971-81. City councillor Queenston Ward, City of Winnipeg, 1975-77, Crescent Heights Ward, City of Winnipeg, 1977-79; mem. legis. assembly River Heights Constituency, Man., 1979-81, Tuxedo Constituency, Man., 1981—, minister consumer and corp. affairs and environment Man. Govt., 1981, leader of the opposition, 1983-88, 99—premier of Manitoba, 1988-99; chmn. com. of works and ops. City of Winnipeg, 1977-79. Recipient award of merit B'nai B'rith Can., 1991; honored for may yrs. of svc. to Jewish Cmty., Man.-Sask. region Jewish United Fund Can., 1996. Mem. Assn. Profl. Engrs. Province of Man., Assn. Can. Career Colls. (pres. 1974-75), U. Man. Alumni Assn. (pres. 1974-75). Conservative. Anglican. Office: Man Legis Assembly Legislature Bldg Rm 204 Winnipeg MB Canada R3C OV8

FILNER, BOB, congressman; b. Pitts., Sept. 4, 1942; m. Jane Merrill; children: Erin, Adam. BA in Chemistry, Cornell U., 1963; MA in History, U. Del., 1969; PhD in History, Cornell U., 1973. Prof. history San Diego State U., 1970-92; legis. asst. Senator Hubert Humphrey, 1974, Congressman Don Fraser, 1975; spl. asst. Congressman Jim Bates, 1984; city councilman 8th dist. City of San Diego, 1987-92, dep. mayor, 1992; mem. U.S. Congress from 51st Calif. dist. (formerly 50th), 1993—; mem. transp. and infrastructure com., vets. affairs com. Pres. San Diego Bd. Edn., 1982, mem.-elect 1979-83; chmn. San Diego Schs. of the Future Commn., 1986-87. Democrat. Office: US Ho of Reps 2428 Rayburn Hob Washington DC 20515-0001*

FILO, DAVID, Internet company executive; b. Moss Bluff, La. BS, Tulane U.; MSEE, Stanford U., 1990. Co-creator online navigational guide Yahoo!, Calif., 1994—; co-founder, chief Yahoo! Inc., Calif., 1995—. Office: Yahoo! Inc 701 First Ave Sunnyvale CA 94089*

FILORAMO, DOROTHY CHRISTINE, academic administrator; d. John Michael Filoramo and Lillian Cecilia Bracken; m. William Thomas Byrnes, Sept. 8, 1962 (div. Jan. 0, 1985); children: Christa Regina Brynes-O'Brien, John Anthony Byrnes, William Thomas Byrnes, Meghan Rita Byrnes-Coyle. BA, Marymount Manhattan Coll., N.Y.C., 1962. Dir. of mktg. Gurney's Inn Resort and Internat. Spa, Montauk, NY, 1983—89, Deer Run Ski Resort, Stamford, NY, 1989—90; mktg. cons. NY, 1990—93; dir. of mktg. Catskill Advt. Agy., Arkville, NY, 1991—92; v.p. for instl. advancement Dominican Coll., Orangeburg, NY, 1993—. Mem. Westchester Devel. Orgn., 1997—, Leadership Rockland, Inc., NY, 2002; pres. Leadership Rockland Alumni, NY, 2002; bd. dirs. People-To-People, Nyack, NY, 2000; chair of the bd. of trustees Dominican Acad., N.Y.C., 1998—2000, trustee, 1994—2000; first pres., founding mem. East End Women's Network, Riverhead, NY, 1981—83; chair New Directions for Women, Riverhead, NY, 1983—85; first pres. and founder Catskill Women's Network, Roxbury, NY, 1991—93; exec. bd. dir. Rockland Devel. Coun., NY. Named Woman of the Yr., East End Women's Network, 1990; recipient Nat. Silver award for mktg., ARRDA, 1985, 1987. Mem.: Women in Devel., Fund Raising Profls. Roman Catholic. Home: 18 Bon Aire Cir Suffern NY 10901 Office: Dominican College 470 Western Hwy Orangeburg NY 10962 E-mail: dorothy.filoramo@dc.edu.

FILOSA, GARY FAIRMONT RANDOLPH V., II, columnist, theater and film producer; b. Wilder, Vt., Feb. 22, 1931; s. Gary F.R. de Marco de Varra and Rosaline M. (Falzaran) F.; m. Catherine Moray Stewart (dec.); children: Marc Christian Bazire de Villadon III, Gary Fairmont Randolph de Varra III. Grad., Mt. Hermon Sch., 1950; PhB, U. Chgo., 1954; BA, U. Americas, Mex., 1967; MA, Calif. Western U., 1968; PhD, U.S. Internat. U., 1970. Sports reporter Claremont Daily Eagle, Rutland Herald, Vt. Informer, 1947-52; pub. The Chicagoan, 1952-54; account exec., editor house publs. Robertson, Buckley & Gotsch, Inc., Chgo., 1953-54; account exec. Fuller, Smith & Ross, Inc., N.Y.C., 1955; prodr./host Weekend KCET Channel 13, N.Y.C., 1955-67; editor Apparel Arts mag. (now Gentlemen's Quar.), Esquire, Inc., N.Y.C., 1955-56; chmn. bd., CEO, pres. Filosa Publs. Internat., N.Y.C., 1956-63; pub. Teenage, Rustic Rhythm, Teen Life, Mystery Digest, Top Talent, Rock & Roll Roundup, Celebrities, Stardust, Personalities, Campus monthly mags.; pres., chmn. bd. Teenarama Records, Inc., N.Y.C., 1956-62; chmn. bd., pres. Produciones Mexicanes Internationales (S.A.), Mexico City, 1957-68; assoc. pub. Laundromatic Age, N.Y.C., 1958-59; ptnr. with Warner LeRoy purchase of Broadway plays for Hollywood films, N.Y.C., 1958-61; pres. Montclair Sch., 1958-60, Pacific Registry, Inc., L.A., 1959-61; exec. prodr. Desilu Studios, Inc., Hollywood, Calif., 1959-61; exec. asst. to Benjamin A. Javits, 1961-62; propr. Gino's of Hollywood, 1961-70; dean admistrn. Postgrad. Ctr. for Mental Health, N.Y.C., 1962-64; chmn. bd., CEO Filosa Films Internat., Beverly Hills, Calif., 1962—; pres. Amateur Athletes Internat., Iowa City, Iowa, 1996-2000; chmn. bd., pres. Cinematografica Americana Internationale (S.A.), Mexico City, 1964-84; pres. Casa Filosa Corp., Palm Beach, Fla., 1982-87; dir. Cmty. Savs., North Palm Beach, Fla., 1982-87. V.p. acad. affairs World Acad., San Francisco, 1967-68; asst. to provost Calif. Western U., San Diego, 1968-69; assoc. prof. philosophy Art Coll., San Francisco, 1969-70; v.p. acad. affairs, dean of faculty Internat. Inst., Phoenix, 1968-73; chmn. bd. dirs., pres. Universite Universelle, 1970-73, 2000—; bd. dirs., v.p. acad. affairs, dean Summer Sch., Internat. C.C., L.A., 1970-72; chmn. bd., pres. Social Directory Calif., 1967-75, Am. Assn. Social Registries, L.A., 1970-76; pres. Social Directory U.S., N.Y.C., 1974-76; pres. Herbert Hoover Forum, Iowa City, 1996-2000; chmn. bd. dirs. Internat. Soc. Social Registers, Paris, 1974—; surfing coach U. Calif. at Irvine, 1975-77; v.p. Xerox-Systemic, 1979-80; CEO Internat. Surfing League, Palm Beach, 1987-95, Santa Barbara, Calif., 1996—; chmn., CEO Filosa Harrop Internat., Phoenix, 1987-89; pres. Amateur Athletes Internat., Iowa City, 1996-2000; nationally syndicated columnist Conservations with Am., 1997-. Editor: Sci. Digest, 1961-62; composer: (lyrics) The Night Discovers Love, 1952, That Certain Something, 1953, Bolero of Love, 1956; author: (stage play) Let Me Call Ethel, 1955, The Bisexual, 1961, Technology Enters 21st Century, 1966, (mus.) Feather Light, 1966, No Public Funds for Nonpublic Schools, 1968, Creative Function of the College President, 1969, The Surfers Almanac, 1977, The Filosa Newsletter, 1986-92, The Sexual Continuum, 1990, Traveltalk, 1991, God's Own Prince, 1995, Holy Hawai'i, 1996, (biography) A Plague on Paradise, 1994, (TV series) Danny Thomas Show, 1963, Surfing USA, 1977, Payne of Florida, 1985, Honolulu, 1991, The Gym, 1992, Sales Pitch, 1992, 80 Ocean Avenue, 1992, One Feather, 1992, Conversations with America, 1989, All American Beach Party, 1989, Riding High, 2000, Dreamsport, 2000, Icons, 2000; contbr. numerous articles, editorials, to profl. jours., newspapers, and encys., including Life, Look, Sci. Digest, Ency. of Sports, World Book Ency., New York Times, Cedar Rapids Gazete, L.A. Times, others. Trustee Univ. of the Ams., Pueblo, Mex., 1986-2000; candidate for L.A. City Coun., 1 959; chmn. Educators for Re-election of Ivy Baker Pirest, 1970; mem. So. Calif. Com. for Olympic Games, 1977-84. With AUS, 1954-55. Recipient DAR Citizenship awrd, 1959, Silver Conquistador award Am. Assn. Social Registers, 1970, Ambassador's Cup U. Ams., 1967, resolution Calif. State Legis., 1977, Duke Kahanamoku Classic surfing trophy, 1977, gold pendant Japan Surfing Assn., 1978, Father of Olympic Surfing award Internat. Athletic Union, 1995, Father of Surfing trophy Amateur Athletes Internat., 1997, Father of Surfing trophy Internat. Surfing Fedn., 2000; inducted into Rock & Roll Mus. & Hall of Fame, Cleve., 1995. Mem. NAACP, NCAA (bd. dels. 1977-82), AAU (gov. 1978-82), Am. Acad. Motion Picture Arts and Scis., Internat. Surfing Com., U.S. Surfing Com. (founder 1960—), Internat. Surfing League (founder, chmn., CEO 1988—), Internat. Surfing Fedn. (pres. 1960—), Am. Assn. UN, Authors League, Authors Guild, Alumni Assn. U. Ams. (pres. 1967-70), Surf Club of the Palm Beaches (pres. 1983-94), Sierra Club, Surfing Hui of Hawaii, Internat. Soc. Bibliotherapists (Paris, pres. 1997—), Lords Corybantes (Berlin) (life pres. 1966—), Commonwealth Club (San Francisco), Town Hall (L.A.), Calif. Club (L.A.), Palm Beach Surf Club, Sigma Omicron Lambda (founder, pres. 1965-92). Episcopalian. Office: PO Box 299 Beverly Hills CA 90213-0299 E-mail: garyfilosa@att.net.

FILSHIE, MICHELE ANN, editor; b. Hartford, Conn., Mar. 5, 1964; d. Joseph James Fitzgibbons and Judith Ann (Bennett) Small; m. Glenn Filshie, May 24, 1986 (div. 1997). BA in English, U. Western Ont., London, 1986. Asst. to the pub. Black Sparrow Press, Santa Rosa, Calif., 1991—2002. Pres., bd. dirs. Sonoma County People for Econ. Opportunity, Santa Rosa, Calif., 1999-2001; candidate West Sonoma County Union H.S. Dist. Sch. Bd., 1998, elected trustee, 2000. Recipient Write Women Back into History award Nat. Women's History Project, Windsor, Calif., 1995. Mem. NOW (pres. Sonoma County chpt. 1994-96), Nat. Women's Polit. Caucus, Sebastopol C. of C., Rotary Club of Sebastopol Sunrise (past dir.). Democrat. Avocation: dance.

FILSON, MARGUERITE B. lawyer; b. Feb. 22, 1935; d. Bernard and Ruth (Wallerstein) Filson; m. Daniel H. Filson, June 20, 1954 (dec.); children: Paul Eliot, Adele Janet; m. Abraham Spector, May 27, 1983. BA, UCLA, 1956; MA, Brandeis U., 1965; JD, Harvard U., 1969. Bar: N.Y. 1971, U.S. Dist. Ct. (so. and ea. dists.) N.Y. 1973, U.S. Ct. Appeals (2d cir.): 1974, U.S. Supreme Ct.: 1976. Law clk. to presiding judge U.S. Dist. Ct., Balt., 1969—70; assoc. Paul, Weiss, Rifkind, Wharton & Garrison, N.Y.C., 1970—73; sr. assoc. Patterson, Belknap, Webb & Tyler, N.Y.C., 1973—76, Schulte, Roth & Zabel, N.Y.C., 1976—77; atty. A T & T Technologies Inc., N.Y.C., 1977—84; counsel Internat. Paper Co.; counsel land utilization, 1984—86; v.p. Bader Rsch. Corp., N.Y.C., 1986—92; adj. instr. N.Y. Law Sch., N.Y.C., 1978—79; adminstrv. law judge N.Y.C. Dept. Health, Parking Violations Bureau; arbitrator N.Y. Stock Exchange, NASD, Am. Arbitration Assn., 1991; vol. atty. NAACP Legal Def. Fund, N.Y.C., 1979—81. Mem.: Harvard Law Sch. Assn., Assn. Bar City N.Y. Office: 808 Broadway Ph 612 New York NY 10003-4809

FILSON, RONALD COULTER, architect, educator, college dean; b. Chardon, Ohio, Dec. 11, 1946; s. Clifford Coulter and Mae Alice (Foster) F.; m. Susan Virginia Saward, Dec. 14, 1973 (div. May 1996); children: Timothy Coulter, Lily Virginia; m. Lea Ann Sinclair, Oct. 9, 1999. Diploma, Am. Acad. in Rome, 1970; B.Arch., Yale U., 1970. Registered arch., Calif., La., Mass., Ohio, Miss., Nat. Coun. Archtl. Registration Bds. Architect Atelier d'Etudes, Ghardaia, Algeria, 1971-73; asst. prof., asst. dean Sch. of Architecture UCLA, 1974-80; dean sch. architecture Tulane U., New Orleans, 1980-92, prof. sch. architecture, 1980—; prin. Ronald Filson, FAIA, Architects, New Orleans. Prin. works include Piazza d'Italia, New Orleans, 1978 (award 1976), Eola Hotel, 1980, Lee House, 1984, Hyatt Hotel, Poydras Plaza, 1987-88, Nat. Pk. Svc. Edn. Ctr., Nat. D-Day Mus., Trump Casino, L.A. Artists Guild, Natchez Visitors Ctr. Pres. Friends of the Schnidler House, L.A., 1978-80; bd. dirs. New Orleans Arts Coun., 1980-93, pres., 1989-92, Contemporary Arts Ctr., New Orleans, 1980-84, New Orleans Planning Commn., 1985-87. Recipient design citations Progressive Architecture mag., 1969, 76, Rome prize Am. Acad. in Rome, 1969 Fellow AIA (Design awards 1980, 81, 85, 87, 89, 92, 94, 98, 99, 2000, 01, Richardson medal 1992); mem. AIA La. (pres. 1998), New Orleans AIA (pres. 1994), Yale Alumni Assn. La. (pres. 1992-94), So. Yacht Club, New Orleans Lawn Tennis Club (bd. govs. 1998—). Avocations: sailing; watercolors. Office: 740 St Charles Ave New Orleans LA 70130

FILSTON, HOWARD CHURCH, pediatric surgeon, educator; b. NYC, Dec. 29, 1935; s. Howard Samuel and Marion (Church) F.; m. Nancy Lee Jameson, June 3, 1961 (dec. Nov. 2002); children: Scott Jameson (dec.), Timothy Howard, Megan Lee Johnson. AB, Harvard U., 1958; MD, Case Western Res. U., 1962. Diplomate Am. Bd. Med. Examiners. Intern in gen. surgery Univ. Hosps., Cleve., 1962-63, asst. resident in gen. surgery, 1963-64, 66-68, chief resident, 1968-69; asst. chief resident pediatric surgery Children's Hosp. Phila., 1969-70; instr. pediatric surgery U. Pa. Sch. of Medicine, Phila., 1969-71, chief resident pediatric surgery, 1970-71; asst. prof. pediatric surgery Case Western Res. U. Hosp., Cleve., 1971-76; assoc. prof. pediatric surgery and pediatrics Duke U. Med. Ctr., Durham, NC, 1976-82, chief pediatric surgery, 1976-90, prof. pediatric surgery and pediats., 1982—90, prof. pediatric surgery and pediatrics, U. Tenn. Med. Ctr., Knoxville, 1990-2000, chief pediatric surgery, 1990-2000, vice chmn. dept. surgery, 1992-2000; emeritus prof.of pediat. surgery, 2000—. Specialist site visitor, pediatric surgery, Accreditation Coun. Grad. Med. Edn., 1982-90, 1995—. Author: Surgical Problems in Children, 1982; author: (with others) The Surgical Neonate, 1978, rev. 1985; assoc. editor, Jour. Pediatric Surgery, 1985-2000; mem. editorial bd. Pediatrics, 1990-97; contbr. articles to profl. jours. Bd. dirs. Pediatric Family Ctr. of N.C. (Ronald McDonald House), Durham, 1980-90, Surgeon Gen.'s Workshop on Drunk Driving, chmn. Citizens Adv. Panel, 1988; mem. exec. bd. Met. Drug Commn., Knoxville, 1993-2000, v.p., 1997-2000, chair DUI task force, 1994-99. Served to capt. U.S. Army, 1964-66. Nat. scholar Harvard U., 1954-58. Fellow ACS (gov. 1992-98), Am. Acad. Pediatrics (surg., exec. com. 1984-91, chmn. 1989-90), Am. Pediatric Surg. Assn. (cdn. com. 1984-90, sec., bd. govs. 1994-97), Am. Surg. Assn., So. Surg. Assn.; mem. Alpha Omega Alpha. Republican. Presbyterian. Avocations: family activities, water sports, sailing. Office: Univ of Tenn Med Ctr Dept Surgery Box U-11 1924 Alcoa Hwy Knoxville TN 37920-6900 Fax: (865) 544-6898. E-mail: hnfilston@earthlink.net.

FILVAROFF, ELLEN H. research scientist; d. David Filvaroff and Joan Bailin. BA, MS, Stanford U., 1986; PhD, Yale U., 1992. Post-doctoral fellow U. of Calif. San Francisco, 1992—97; scientist Genentech, South San Francisco, 1997—. Cons. UCSF, San Francisco, 1997—2002. Author sci. articles. Recipient Phi Beta Kappa, 1985. Achievements include patents pending for Author on various pending patents.

FINA, PAUL JOSEPH, lawyer; b. Chgo., Mar. 1, 1959; s. Paul Emil and Vera Christiane (Mutzbauer) F.; m. Robyn Leann Hughes, May 24, 1986; 1 child, Paul George. BA in Econs., U. Ill., 1982, MA, 1983; JD, DePaul U., Chgo., 1987. Bar: Ill. 1988, U.S. Dist. Ct. (no. dist.) Ill. 1990, U.S. Ct. Appeals (7th cir.) 1990, U.S. Supreme Ct. 1991. Assoc. Haskin, Taylor & McDonough, Wheaton, Ill., 1988-90, Komessar & Wintroub, Chgo., 1990-94; pvt. practice Law Offices of Paul J. Fina, Chgo., 1994—2001, Law Offices of Fina & Huner, Chgo., 2001—. Mem. bus. faculty Coll. of DuPage, Glen Ellyn, Ill., 1986—, Aurora (Ill.) U., 1997—. Gen. counsel Housing Helpers, Inc., Riverside, Ill., 1991—. DePaul law grantee, 1985. Mem. ABA, Ill. Bar Assn., Assn. Trial Lawyers Am., DuPage County Bar Assn. (civil practice com.), Million Dollar Advocates Forum (life), Phi Alpha Delta. Roman Catholic. Avocations: music performance, athletics. Home: 509 Bent Tree Ct Oswego IL 60543-8734 Office: 940 W Adams St Ste 300 Chicago IL 60607 E-mail: pjfinalawyer@aol.com.

FINAISH, FATHI ALI, aeronautical engineering educator; b. Tripoli, Libya, July 22, 1954; came to U.S., 1981; s. Ali Finaish and Zuhra (Lamin) Mahfud; m. Deborah Lynn Demijohn, Dec. 28, 1984. BS in Aero. Engring., U. Al-Fateh, Tripoli, 1978; MS in Aerospace Engring., U. Colo., 1984, PhD in Aerospace Engring., 1987. Lic. pvt. pilot; FAA airframe and power plant cert. mechanic. Rsch. asst. U. Colo., Boulder, 1984-87, adj. asst. prof., 1987-88; asst. prof. aero. engring. U. Mo., Rolla, 1988-94, assoc. prof., 1994-2000, prof., 2000—, assoc. chair aerospace engring., 1999—. Dir. Mo. NASA Space Grant, 1999—; airworthiness engr. Dept. Civil Aviation, Tripoli, 1979-81; ground sch. instr. Tripoli Flight Ctr., 1980-81; rsch. fellow Naval Under Water Systems Ctr., Newport, R.I., 1991, NASA Langley Rsch. Ctr., Hampton, Va., 1992; lectr. various univs.; advisor Licking High Sch., St. James High Sch.; summer rsch. fellow U.S. Navy-Am. Soc. Engring. Edn., 1991, NASA-Am. Soc. Engring. Edn., 1992. Contbr. articles to profl. jours. Head coach Rolla Soccer Club, asst. to soccer head coach, 1997-99. Grantee U. Mo., Rolla, 1988-92, U. Mo. Systems, 1991-92, U. Mo. Rsch. Bd., 1994-95, Office Naval Rsch., 1991, NASA, 1993-95, Precision Environ. Sys., 1995-96, Ctr. Indoor Rsch., 1998—, ASHRAE, 1999—. Fellow AIAA (assoc., Outstanding Tchr. award U. Mo. chpt. 1993); mem. ASEE, ASHRAE (grantee 1992-93, 99). Achievements include development of several ednl. computer codes and courses in aerospace engring.; design and bldg. an exptl. system that generates and visualizes impulsive and accelerating motions and other unsteady airflow histories; designed and developed several wind tunnels for steady and unsteady aerodynamic testing at the University of Missouri-Rolla. Office: U Mo Dept Mech Engring Rolla MO 65401

FINAN, ELLEN CRANSTON, secondary education educator, consultant; b. Worcester, Mass., June 26, 1951; d. Thomas Matthew and Maureen Ann (Moulton) F. BA, U. San Francisco, 1973; MA, U. Calif., Riverside, 1978. ESL specialist U.S. Peace Corps, Finote Selam, Ethiopia, 1974-75; English instr. U. Redlands, Calif., 1977-79; mentor tchr. Jurupa Unified Sch. Dist., Riverside, 1979—; teaching supr. U. Calif., Riverside, 1993—. Tech. writer Callan Assocs., San Francisco, 1973-74, Wilshire Assocs., Santa Monica, Calif., 1976-77; English instr. U. Pa., Phila., 1979; writing cons. Inland Area Writing Project U. Calif., Riverside, 1980—; tchr., coordinator U. Calif., Riverside, 1982. Author: Prickley Pear, 1981, CAP Attack Handbook, 1987. NEH fellow, 1985, 92; Squaw Valley Community of Writers scholar, 1981, Carnegie Mellon fellow, 1987, NEH Inst. fellow, 1993, 97. Mem. Nat. Council English Tchrs., Assn. Supervision and Curriculum Devel., Alpha Sigma Nu, Phi Delta Kappa. Democrat. Avocations: writing, travel. Home: 22440 Mountain View Rd Moreno Valley CA 92557-2655 Office: Jurupa Unified Schs 4250 Opal St Riverside CA 92509-7251

FINAN, JOHN JOSEPH, hospital administrator; b. New Orleans, Nov. 26, 1946; married. B, U. New Orleans, 1968; M, Loyola U., 1970. Dir. acctg. Hotel Dieu Hosp., New Orleans, 1970-71, asst. administr., 1971-76; v.p. Good Samaritan Regional Health Ctr., Vernon, Ill., 1976-84, Barnes Hosp., St. Louis, 1984-86, exec. v.p., 1986-92, pres., 1992—. Mem. Ill. Hosp. Assn. (coms.). Home: 15410 Elk Ridge Ln Chesterfield MO 63017-5310 Office: Franciscan Missionaries Our Lady Health Sys Inc 4200 Essen Ln Baton Rouge LA 70809-2158

FINAN, MARCEL BASSIL, mathematics educator, researcher; s. Bassil Michel Finan and Therese Tarazi; m. Pallavi Subhash Ketkar, June 1, 1999. PhD, U. of North Tex., 1998. Vis. asst. prof. U. of Tex., San Antonio, 1998—99, vis. scholar Austin, 1999—2001; asst. prof. math. Ark. Tech U., Russellville, 2001—. Referee Electronic Jour. of Differential Equations, Tex., 1998—2000. Author: (manuscript) Fundamentals of Linear Algebra, Lecture Notes in Discrete Math., A Calculus Approach to Math. Modeling, A Problem Solving Approach to Coll. Algebra; contbr. articles to profl. jours. Mem.: Math. Assn. of Am., Am. Math. Soc. Office: Ark Tech U Dept of Math Corley 244 Russellville AR 72801 Office Fax: 479-968-0677. Personal E-mail: marcel.finan@mail.atu.edu.

FINAN, RICHARD H. b. Cin., Aug. 16, 1934; m. Joan L. Finan, 1956; children: Patrick, Nancy, Julie, Michael. BS, U. Dayton; LLB, U. Cin. Bar: Ohio. Pvt. practice, Sharonville, Ohio; mem. Ohio Senate from 7th dist., Columbus, 1978—2002; pres. Ohio Senate, Columbus, 1997—2002. Asst. pro tem, chmn. ways and means com., Senate legis. ethics com., fin. com., commerce and labor com., rules com., reference and oversight com., joint legis. com. on fed. funds, welfare oversight com., taxation rev. com., mem. Rep. campaign com.; chmn. fed. budget and taxation com. Nat. Conf. State Legislators; bd. dirs. Franklin Savs. & Loan; arbitrator Hamilton County Ct. Common Pleas, Am. Arbitration Assn. Councilman Evendale Village, Ohio, 1963-69, mayor, 1969-73; mem. Ohio Ho. of Reps., Columbus, 1973-78; exec. dir. Hamilton County Reagan-Bush Campaign, 1984; dir. Dole for Pres. Campaign, 1988; trustee U. Dayton; past trustee St. Rita's Sch. for Deaf; bd. dirs. Cath. Social Svcs. Southwestern Ohio, Carillon Funds, Rest Haven. Named Legislator of Yr., Ohio Trial Lawyers Assn., 1975, Twp. Clks. and Trustees Assn., 1976, Disting. Alumnus award U. Dayton, Andrew Carnegie award Oho Libr. Assn., 1993, Outstanding Merit award for statehouse preservation Ohio Hist. Soc. Mem. Ohio Bar Assn., Cin. Bar Assn., Sharonville Bus. Assn., U. Dayton Alumni Assn. (past pres. Cin. chpt.), U. Dayton Nat. Alumni Assn. (past pres.). Office: 3068 Stanwin Pl Cincinnati OH 45241-3360*

FINAURI, GRACIELA MARIA, foreign service professional; b. Buenos Aires, June 18, 1956; d. Gerardo and Norma Mercedes (Burich) F. Student in law, Cath. U. Buenos Aires, 1985. Adminstr. protocol dept. Ministry of Fgn. Affairs, Buenos Aires, 1979-85, pvt. sec. min., 1985-87; pvt. sec. amb. Embassy of Argentina, Rome, 1987-91; pvt. sec. min. Ministry of Internal Affairs, Buenos Aires, 1993-95; chief of protocol Senate of Argentina, Buenos Aires, 1995-98; pvt. sec. to v.p. Argentine Republic, Buenos Aires, 1995-98; attaché Mission of Argentina to UN, N.Y.C., 1998—2003; attache Promotion Ctr. and Consulate Gen. of Argentine Republic in N.Y., N.Y.C., 2003—. Named Cavalier of Hon. and Merit, Haiti Republic, 1983, Officer of Order of Merit, Italian Republic, 1985; recipient Insignia award, Mex. Order of Aztec Eagle, 1984. Roman Catholic. Office: Promotion Ctr and Consulate Gen of Argentine Republic NY 12 W 56th St New York NY 10019 E-mail: gmf@mrecic.gov.ar.

FINBERG, BARBARA DENNING, not-for-profit developer; b. Pueblo, Colo., Feb. 26, 1929; d. Rufus Raymond and Velma Aileen (Hopper) Denning; m. Alan R. Finberg, June 21, 1953 (dec. 1995). BA, Stanford U., 1949; MA, Am. U. Beirut, Lebanon, 1951. Intern U.S. Dept. State, Washington, 1949-50, fgn. affairs officer, Tech Coop. Adminstrn., 1952-53; program specialist, area chief Inst. Internat. Edn., N.Y.C., 1953-59; editorial assoc., program officer Carnegie Corp. N.Y., N.Y.C., NY, 1959-80, v.p. program, 1980-88, exec. v.p., 1988-97; v.p. MEM Assocs., Inc., 1997—. Vis. fellow Woodrow Wilson Nat. Fellowship Found., 1998. Bd. dirs. Parent Child Home Program, 2002—, Nat. Coun. Rsch. on Women, 2003—; trustee Stanford U., 1976—86, v.p. bd. dirs., 1981—85, vis. com. Stanford U. Librs., 1984—90, 1993—96, chmn., 1986—88; trustee N.Y. Found., 1979—91, vice chmn. bd. dirs., 1983—85, chmn., 1985—89; bd. dirs. Bard Musical Festival, 1995—, vice chair, 2003—; bd. dirs. Ednl. Equity Concepts., 2003—, U. Cape Town (South Africa) Fund, 1997—. High/Scope Ednl. Rsch. Found., 1998—, vice chair, 2003—; mem. adv. com. to govtl. studies program Brookings Instn., 1996—2000; bd. govs. New Sch. U., Eugene Lang Coll., 1997—2001; nat. adv. panel Inst. for Rsch. on Women and Gender, Stanford U., 1991—, Humanities and Scis. Coun., Stanford U., 1996—, chair, 2002—; nat. adv. com. Ctr. for the Comparative Study of Race and Ethnicity, Stanford U., 2001—; mem. Stanford in Washington Coun., 1998—, chmn., 2002—; bd. dirs. Hole in the Wall Gang Camp Fund, 1987—. Recipient Women of Vision award, N.Y. Women's Found., 1995, John Dewey award for disting. pub. svc., Bard Coll., 1998; fellow Rotary Found., 1950—51. Mem.: Coun. Fgn. Rels., Soc. Rsch. Child Devel., Century Assn., Cosmopolitan Club NY. Home: 165 E 72nd St Apt 19L New York NY 10021-4351 Office: MEM Assocs Inc 521 5th Ave 17th Fl New York NY 10175-0088

FINBERG, JAMES MICHAEL, lawyer; b. Balt., Sept. 6, 1958; s. Laurence and Harriet (Levinson) Finberg; m. Melanie Piech; children: Joseph, John. BA, Brown U., 1980; JD, U. Chgo., 1983. Bar: Calif. 1984, U.S. Dist. Ct. (no. dist.) Calif. 1984, U.S. Dist. Ct. (ea. dist.) Calif. 1987, U.S. Ct. Appeals (9th and fed. cirs.) 1987, U.S. Dist. Ct. Hawaii, 1988, U.S. Supreme Ct. 1994. Law clk. to assoc. justice Mich. Supreme Ct., 1983-84; assoc. Feldman, Waldman and Kline, San Francisco, 1984-87, Morrison and Foerster, 1987-90; ptnr. Lieff, Cabraser, Heimann & Bernstein, L.L.P., San Francisco, 1991—. Lawyer rep. to 9th Jud. Conf., 1999-2001 (chair No. Calif. del. 2000-01); adv. com. local rules for securities cases U.S. Dist. Ct., Calif., 1996. Exec. editor U. Chgo. Law Rev., 1982-83. Mem.: ACLU (bd. dirs. No. Calif. chpt. 1995), ABA (chmn. securities subcom. class and derivative action com. 1998—, plaintiff's program chair equal employment opportunity com. 1999—2001), Lawyers Com. for Civil Rights of San Francisco Bay Area (fin. chmn. 1992—95, bd. dirs. 1992—98, sec. 1996, co-chmn. 1997—98), Calif. Bar Assn. (mem. standing com. on legal svcs. to poor 1990—94, vice-chmn. 1993—94), Bar Assn. San Francisco (jud. evaluation com. 1994, bd. dirs. 1999—2000, sec. 2001—02, treas. 2002—03). Office: Lieff Cabraser Heimann & Bernstein LL 275 Battery St Fl 30 San Francisco CA 94111-3305

FINBERG, LAURENCE, pediatrician, educator, dean; b. Chgo., May 20, 1923; s. Joseph and Anne (Malkow) F.; m. Harriet Levinson, June 17, 1945 (dec. Jan. 1994); children: Robert, Jeanne, James; m. Joann Quane, Mar. 17, 1995. BS, U. Chgo., 1944, MD, 1946. Diplomate: Am. Bd. Pediatrics (examiner 1969-94, bd. dirs. 1974-79, 82-88, pres. 1978, chmn. 1987). Intern U. Chgo. Clinics, 1946-47; asst. resident pediatrics Balt. City Hosps., 1949-50, resident in pediat., 1950-51; practice medicine specializing in pediat. Balt., 1951-63, N.Y.C., 1963-94; asst. chief pediatrician Balt. City Hosps., 1951-61, dir. pediatric out-patient dept., 1951-63, dir. premature nursery, 1951-59, assoc. chief pediatrics, 1961-63; pediatrician Harriet Lane Home, 1951-63; chmn. dept. pediatrics Montefiore Hosp. and Med. Center, Bronx, N.Y., 1963-80, prof., 1995—; chmn. dept. pediatrics SUNY Health Sci. Ctr., Bklyn., 1982-95, prof. pediatrics, 1982-95, prof. emeritus, 1995—, dean, 1988-91; prof. clin. pediat. U. Calif., San Francisco, 1995—, Stanford U. Sch. Med., 1997—. Instr. pediatrics Johns Hopkins U., 1951-56; asst. prof., 1956-63; prof. pediatrics Albert Einstein Coll. Medicine, Yeshiva U., Bronx, 1963-82, chmn., 1968-80; cons. in field; mem. pediatric adv. com. N.Y.C. Dept. Health, 1970-94. Mem. editl. bd. Jour. Pediat., 1973-83, Am. Jour. Diseases of Children, 1984-94, named changed to Archives of Pediat. and Adolescent Medicine, 1994—, editor nutrition sect., 1995—; editor Saunders Manual of Pediat. Practice, 1997, 2002. Served with USPHS, 1947-49. Recipient Bela Schick medal, 1992, Nutrition award Am. Acad. Pediatrics, 1992. Mem. AAAS, AMA (Goldberger Clin. Nutrition award 1993), Am. Pediatric Soc., Soc. Pediatric Research, Am. Acad. Pediatrics (com. on environ. hazards 1968-83, chmn. 1979-83, com. nutrition 1983-89—, chmn. 1984-89), Am. Coll. Nutrition, Am. Soc. for Nutritional Scis., Nat. Cholesterol Edn. Program Coordinating Com. (panel on children and adolescents 1989-93), Ambulatory Pediatric Assn., Am. Soc. Clin. Nutrition, Am. Fedn. Clin. Research, Sociedad Peruana de Pediatria, Sociedad Dominica De Peditria, Harvey Soc., N.Y. Acad. Medicine (past chmn. pediatric sec.), Phi Beta Kappa, Sigma Xi, Alpha Omega Alpha. Achievements include research in electrolyte physiology. Home: 152 Lombard St Apt 602 San Francisco CA 94111-1134 E-mail: finberg@itsa.ucsf.edu.

FINCH, C. HERBERT, retired archivist, library administrator, historian; b. Boise City, Okla., Nov. 8, 1931; s. Cloyd Herbert and Gladys Erma (Fellows) F.; m. Joyce Ongelene Hamilton, May 23, 1954 (dec.); children: Douglas Hamilton, Philip Andrew, Diana Ruth; m. Elsie Thorp Freeman, Aug. 2, 1992. BA, Okla. Bapt. U., 1953; BD, So. Bapt. Theol. Sem., Louisville, 1957; MA, U.Ky., Lexington, 1959, PhD, 1965. Field rep. U. Ky., Lexington, 1961-64; assoc. archivist Cornell U., Ithaca, N.Y., 1964-67, archivist, 1967-72, asst. Univ. librarian, 1972-96, lectr., 1972-80. Mem. adv. coun. Nat. Archives, Washington, 1975-81, N.Y. State Hist. Records, Albany, 1976-85; cons. archives and libraries; cons. John A. Woods Appraisers, South Windsor, Conn. Author: Charter Day: Cornell University Centennial, 1965; Guide to Manuscripts-Charles Abrams: Papers & Files, 1975; contbr. articles to profl. jours. Fellow Soc. Am. Archivists. Democrat. Baptist. Home: 904 Coddington Rd Ithaca NY 14850-6022 E-mail: chf3@cornell.edu.

FINCH, CAROL ANNE, former secondary education educator; b. N.Y.C., Oct. 22, 1942; d. William George and Anna Frances (O'Connell) Simpson; m. Aug. 1, 1970 (div.); children: Robert A., James J. BA, William Paterson Coll., 1964, MA, 1968. Cert. English, reading and learning disabilities tchr., N.J. Tchr. Bridgewater-Raritan (N.J.) Sch. Dist., 1964-67, Ramsey (N.J.) Bd. of Edn., 1967-71; office mgr. Maywood (N.J.) Pub. Libr., 1985-86; tchr. Teaneck (N.J.) Bd. of Edn., 1987-88, Passaic County Tech. & Vocat. High Sch., Wayne, N.J., 1988-91, Elizabeth (N.J.) Bd. Edn., 1991-93; collections asst. Party Rental, Teterboro, N.J., 1994-98; adminstrv. asst. Randy Hangers, LLC, East Rutherford, N.J., 1998, Bryant Staffing, Emerson, NJ, 1999; shareholder rels. Mellon Investor Svcs., Ridgefield Park, NJ, 1999—. Mem. NEA, Internat. Reading Assn., N.J. Edn. Assn., N.J. Reading Assn. Avocations: reading, crocheting, ceramics, crewel work. Home: 279 Clark St Apt A15 Hackensack NJ 07601-1062 Office: Mellon Investor Svcs 85 Challenger Rd Ridgefield Park NJ 07660-2104

FINCH, EDWARD RIDLEY, JR., lawyer, diplomat, writer, educator; b. Westhampton Beach, N.Y., Aug. 31, 1919; AB with Atwater honors, Princeton U., 1941; JD, NYU, 1947; LLD (hon.), Mo. Valley Coll., 1963; DSc (hon.), Cumberland Coll., 1985. Bar: N.Y. 1948, U.S. Supreme Ct. 1953, D.C. 1978, Fla. 1980, Pa. 1992. Ptnr. Finch & Schaefler, N.Y.C., 1950-85; of counsel Le Boeuf, Lamb, Leiby & MacRae, N.Y.C., 1986-88; commr. City of N.Y., 1955-58. V.p. gen. counsel, dir. St. Giles Found., 1964—, Am. Internat. Petroleum Corp., 1988-92; U.S. del. 4th UN Congress, Geneva, 1970, 5th UN Congress, Japan, 1975; U.S. spl. ambassador to Panama, 1972; legal advisor, mem. U.S. Del. UNISPACE II, 1982, UNISPACE III, Vienna, Austria, 1999; lectr. in field. Author: Holes in Your Pockets, 3rd edit., Astro Business-A Guide to Commerce and Law of Outer Space, Judicial Politics; contbr. articles to profl. jours. Pres., bd. dirs. St. Nicholas Soc. N.Y., 1948—; past pres. N.Y. Inst. Spl. Edn., 1950—; bd. govs. Nat. Space Soc., 1984—; mem. faculty adv. com. dept. politics Princeton U.; treas. Jessie Ridley Found., N.Y.C., Finch Trusts; pres. Adams Meml. Fund Inc.; v.p. St. Giles Found.; trustee St. Andrew's Dune Ch., Southampton, Cathedral of St. John the Divine, 1989-92, Whittell Trust; bd. dirs. Am. Found. Cancer Rsch.; life trustee Met. Mus. of Art, N.Y.C.; mem. Coun. Am. Ambs. Col. JAG, USAFR, 1941-72. Decorated U.S. Legion of Merit with oak leaf cluster; order Brit. Empire; Knight Order St. John; officer French Legion of Honor, Disting. Eagle Scout, Coun. of Am. Ambassadors. Fellow Am. Bar Found. (chmn. aerospace coun. sect. sci. and tech 1986-92); mem. ABA (ho. of dels. 1971-72, chmn. corp. lawyers sr. lawyer divsn., chmn. aerospace law divsn. internat. law sect.1973-79), AIAA (sr.), Fed. Bar Assn., Inter-Am. Bar Assn. (Hallgarten telecommunications award 1991), N.Y. State Bar Assn. (internat. law and practice sec., chmn. arms control and nat. security com.), Pa. Bar Assn., Fla. Bar Assn., Bar City of N.Y., Internat. Bar Assn., Judge Advs. Assn. U.S. (past pres.), Am. Law Inst., Am. Judicature Soc. (sr.), Internat. Astronautical Acad. (full elected mem.), Internat. Inst. Space Law (Lifetim Disting. Svc. award 1997), Am. Arbitration Assn. (panelist), Univ. Clubs of Wash. and N.Y., Union League Club, Union Club, Princeton Club (bd. govs. 1982—), L.I. Club, Bathing Corp. of Southampton, Westhampton County Club, Hillsboro Club (sr.). Office: 862 Park Ave New York NY 10021-1831 Fax: 212-327-0593. E-mail: erfinchjr@aol.com.

FINCH, EVELYN VORISE, financial planner; b. Marietta, Ohio, Jan. 20, 1930; d. Richard Raymon Juantzee and Oreatha Fay (Carnes) Metcalf; m. Herman Frederick Ahrens, May 13, 1948 (div. Nov. 1957); children: Erick K.F. Ahrens, Hilda Kate Ahrens(dec.), Nicole Schwartz; m. James Derwood Finch, June 29, 1973 (dec. Oct. 1993). BS in Music Edn., Concord Coll., 1961; postgrad., U. Md., Am. U., Northeastern U., 1990. Registered Health Underwriter, Boston. Music tchr. Prince George's County (Md.) pub. schs., 1961—72; pvt. piano tchr. Washington, 1961—73; china and crystal sales rep. Quality Products Co., Washington, 1973—80; ins. agt. Mut. of Omaha Cos., Washington, 1980—92, Memphis, 1992—94; pvt. practice Alamo, Tenn., 1994—; tax assoc. H&R Block Inc., Jackson, Tenn., 2002—. Ind. assoc. Pre-Paid Legal Svcs., Inc., 2000—. Supporting mem. Nat. Mus. Women in Arts, Washington, 1990—, Women's Philharm., San Francisco, 1993—. Mem.: LWV (Memphis br.), AAUW (br. pres. 1994-96, Tenn. chair ednl. found. 1996-98, Nat. Diversity Resource Team 1997-2000), Internat. Assn. Fin. Planners, Nat. Assn. Health Underwriters (registered health underwriter), Nat. Assn. Ret. Fed. Employees, Chesapeake Bay Yacht Clubs Assn. (commodore 1982), Prince George's Yacht Club (commodore 1978), Potomas River Yacht Clubs Assn. (legis. chair 1978-87), Nat. Boating Fedn. (pres. 1985), Kappa Delta Pi, Pi Mu. Home and Office: 208 Finch Rd Alamo TN 38001-5923 E-mail: EvelynFinch@msn.com.

FINCH, LAWRENCE NELSON, II, computer scientist, consultant; b. Bklyn., June 26, 1943; s. Lawrence N. and Amelia Julia (Weiss) F.; m. Patricia Moldauer, June 20, 1976 (div. July 1980); m. Wanda Richards, Sept. 27, 1981; 1 child, Abigail Emily. BEE, NYU, 1966; MS in Computer Sci., Stevens Inst. Tech., 1978. Engr. Airborne Instruments Lab., Deer Park, N.Y., 1966-70, Republic Electronic Industries Corp., Farmingdale, N.Y., 1970-73; tech. staff Schering Pharm., Bloomfield, N.J., 1973-74; regional analyst mgr. computer div. Tex. Instruments, Clark, N.J., 1974-80; v.p., tech. dir. Prolifics, N.Y.C., N.J., 1980—. Recipient NSF rsch. grant, 1965. Achievements include patent for fixed compound lens scanning microwave antenna with moveable feed. Office: Prolifics 116 John St New York NY 10038-3300 E-mail: finches@bellatlantic.net., larry@prolifics.com.

FINCH, MELODY RENEE, nurse; b. Huntington, W.Va., Apr. 30, 1967; d. Donald P. Jr. and Ella Sue (Carter) Watkins; m. Andrew John Finch, Apr. 20, 1991. AS, Beckly Coll., 1988; diploma, Beckly County Sch. Nursing, 1991; student, Regents Coll., 1997—. Nurse Pine Lodge Healthcare, Beckly, W.Va., 1992-93, Appalachian Regional Hosp., Beckly, W.Va., 1993—2002, Hospice, Beckly, W.Va., 1995—97, Beckley VA Med. Ctr., 2002—. Mem.: Appalachian Bible Coll. Laudies Aux., Beckley Kennel Club. Baptist. Avocations: exercising, quilting, church activities. Home: 168 Canterbury Dr Beckley WV 25801-3104

FINCH, MICHAEL PAUL, lawyer; b. Galveston, Tex., Jan. 4, 1946; s. Albert Lynn and Ila Belle (Robertson) Finch; m. Rebecca Jean Minnear, Dec. 27, 1969; children: Michael Paul, Rachelle Jean. BA cum laude, MEE, Rice U., 1969; JD magna cum laude, U. Houston, 1972. Bar: Tex. 1973. Petroleum engr. Exxon Corp., Houston, 1969-72; assoc. Vinson & Elkins, Houston, 1972-79, ptnr., 1980—. Bd. dirs. Rice Engring. Alumni, 1994—98; dir. Houston Pops Orch., 1988—89. Master: Am. Contact Bridge League (life); mem.: ABA, Houston Bar Assn., Tex. Bar Assn. Republican. Methodist. Avocations: electronics, woodworking, skiing, piano. Home: 12531 Overcup Dr Houston TX 77024-4915 Office: Vinson & Elkins 2300 First City Tower 1001 Fannin St Houston TX 77002-6706

FINCH, RAYMOND LAWRENCE, chief judge; b. Christiansted, St. Croix, V.I., Oct. 4, 1940; s. Wilfred Christopher and Beryl Elaine (Bough) F.; m. Anne Marie Mohammed, May 8, 1996; children: Allison, Mark, Jennifer. AB, Howard U., 1962, JD, 1965. Bar: V.I. 1971, Third Circuit Ct. of Appeals 1976. Law clk. Judge's Municipal Ct. of V.I., 1965-66; partner firm Hodge, Sheen, Finch & Ross, Christiansted, 1970-75; judge Territorial Ct. of V.I., Charlotte Amalie, 1975-86, Ct. of Appeals, V.I., Charlotte Amalie, 1986-94, U.S. Dist. Ct. of V.I., 1994—, chief judge, 1999—. Instr. Grad. div., Coll. of V.I., Am. Inst. Banking, 1976— Bd. dirs. Boy Scouts Am., Boys Club Am. Served to capt. U.S. Army, 1966-69. Decorated Army Commendation medal, Bronze Star medal. Mem. Am. Judges Assn., Am., Nat. bar assns., Internat. Assn. Chiefs of Police. Democrat. Lutheran. Office: PO Box 24051 Christiansted VI 00824-0051

FINCH, ROB, photographer; b. Des Plaines, Ill., Apr. 7, 1976; Grad Hist., Notre Dame, South Bend, IN, 1998. Employed Copley Chgo. Newspapers, Aurora, Ill.; staff photographer The Oregonian. Recipient Newspaper Photographer of the Yr., Yr. Internat. Competition for Copley Chgo., 1999—2000, Yr. Internat. Competition for Copely Chgo., 2003, 2nd Pl. Newspaper Photographer of the Yr., Newspaper Photographer of the Yr., The Oregonian in the 60th Ann. Pictures of the Yr. Internat. Competition, 2nd and 3rd-Pl. honors in the portrait and sports photography div., The Oregonian. Mem.: Mt. Peoples Workshop (judge and spkr.), Flying Short Course (faculty mem., judge and spkr.), Wold Press Joop Swart Masterclass. Office: The Oregonian Photo Dept 1320 SW Broadway Portland OR 97201*

FINCH, ROBERT JONATHAN, communications engineering consultant; b. Chgo., Sept. 21, 1955; s. Herman Manuel and Frances (Gutlow) F.; m. Gayle Deborah Falk, Mar. 28, 1991; children: Layla Michelle, Grant Dillon. BA in Broadcast Mgmt., U. So. Calif., 1977. Engr.-in-charge LFI Prodns., Inc., Lafayette, Ind., 1990-92; comm. engring. cons., L.A., 1978-90, Lafayette, 1992—. Developer: ABC Hollywood's 1st satellite video-tape ctr., Saudi Arabia's 1st color TV studio, 1st digitally based pub. transponder in 2-way radio svc. in continental U.S., 1st large volume, pub. access and radio accessed computer database in U.S.; contbr. articles to pubs. Mem. Tippecanoe Amateur Radio Assn. (trustee), Hollywood (Calif.) Magic Castle, Pasadena Casting Club (instr.). Avocations: fly fishing, close-up magic. Home: 7530 Ridgeview Ln Lafayette IN 47905-9795

FINCH, ROGERS BURTON, association management consultant; b. Broadalbin, N.Y., Apr. 16, 1920; s. Cecil Clement and Olga Ulrika (Lofgren) F.; m. Barbara Ellen Hine, Jan. 3, 1942; children: David Rogers, John Richard, Steven Alan, Kathryn Ann, Elizabeth Gale. BS, Mass. Inst. Tech., 1941, MS, 1947,

Sc.D., 1950. Prof. Mass. Inst. Tech., 1946-53; dir. U.S. Fgn. Aid Mission, Rangoon, Burma, 1953-54; dir. research Rensselaer Poly. Inst., Troy, N.Y., 1954-61, v.p. planning, 1963-72; dir. univ. relations Peace Corps, Washington, 1961-63; exec. dir. ASME, N.Y.C., 1972-81; cons., 1987—; exec. v.p. Illuminating Engineering Soc. N.Am., 1982-87. Contbr. articles profl. jours. Served to maj. AUS, 1941-46; to brig. gen. U.S. Army Res.; ret. 1975. Decorated Army Commendation medal, Legion of Merit. Fellow ASME (life), AAAS; mem. Am. Soc. Assn. Execs. (life), Am. Soc. Engring. Edn. (life), Council Engring. and Sci. Soc. Execs. (emeritus past pres.), Illuminating Engring. Soc. N.Am., Sigma Xi, Tau Beta Pi. Home: 202 Brooksby Village Dr Apt 304 Peabody MA 01960

FINCH, SHEILA, writer; b. London, 1935; 3 children. Postgrad., Ind. U. Faculty creative writing El Camino Coll., Torrance, Calif. Author: Infinity's Web (Crompton Crook/Stephen Tall award 1985), 1985, Triad, 1986, The Garden of the Shaped, 1987, Shaper's Legacy, 1988, Shaping the Dawn, 1989, The Falcon and the Falconer, 1997, (series) Tiger in the Sky, 1999, No Brighter Sky, 1999, Nor Unbuild the Cage, 2000, (short fiction) Forkpoints, 2002. Winner 1998 Nebula award for novella: Reading the Bones. Avocations: travel, tai chi, hiking, 4-wheeling in the desert. Office: c/o Avon Books Harper Collins 10 E 53rd St New York NY 10022-5244

FINCH, SUSAN CHLOË, mediator, educator; b. Norfolk, Va., Apr. 24, 1962; d. Charles Warren Wagner and Patsy Ann (Barker) Carlin; m. Patrick Kenneth Finch, Aug. 10, 1985; children: Ryan Patrick, Hannah Chloë. BA in Psychology, San Diego State U., 1985; MA in Marital and Family Therapy, MA in Sociology, U. So. Calif., 1992, PhD, 2000. Cert. family life educator Nat. Coun. on Family Rels. Tchg. asst., asst. lectr. dept. sociology U. So. Calif., L.A., 1985-88, therapist trainee, 1987-89, academic advisor, 1988-91; lectr., 2000—; mediator intern Family Ct. Svcs./Conciliation Ct., L.A., 1989-90, family counselor, 1990-96, sr. family mediator, 1996—. Contbr. article to profl. jour., chpt. to book. Mem. Lancaster (Calif.) Child Abuse Task Force, 1996-97. Mem. Am. Assn. Marriage and Family Therapy, Am. Sociol. Assn., Nat. Coun. Family Rels. Episcopalian. Office: Mediation and Conciliation Svc 38256 N Sierra Hwy Rm 158 Palmdale CA 93550

FINCHEM, TIM, sports association executive; BA, U. Richmond, 1969; JD, U. Va., 1973. Dep. advisor econ. affairs White House, Washington, 1978—79; nat. staff dir. Jimmy Carter-Walter Mondale Presdl. Campaign, 1980; pres. Beckel, Finchem, Toricelli and Assocs., Washington, 1980—84; co-founder Nat. Strategies and Mktg. Group, Washington, 1984—87; v.p. bus. affairs PGA Tour, Ponte Vedra Beach, Fla., 1987—94, commr., 1994—. Co-founder World Golf Found., First Tee program; developer World Golf Hall of Fame, World Golf Village. Office: PGA Tour 112 PGA Tour Blvd Ponte Vedra Beach FL 32082

FINCHER, CAMERON LANE, psychology educator; b. Douglas County, Ga., Nov. 4, 1926; s. Andrew Jackson and Ada (Swafford) F.; m. Mary Frances Cutts, June 15, 1957; children: Marcel Andriette, Matthew Donnellan, Ada Amanda, Melissa Lane. B.C.S., Ga. State U., 1950; MA, U. Minn., 1951; PhD, Ohio State U., 1956. Lic. psychologist, Ga. Dir. testing and counseling Ga. State U., Atlanta, 1956-65; assoc. dir. Inst. Higher Edn., U. Ga., Athens, 1965-69, dir. Inst., 1969-99, prof. higher edn. and psychology, 1965—, Regents prof. higher edn. and psychology, 1981—. Cons. various indsl. and comml. cos., also state governing bds. colls. and univs., La., S.C., Ala., Tenn.; mem. Gov.'s Com. on Postsecondary Edn., Ga., 1978-83; mem. rsch. panel So. Edn. Found., 1978-86. Author: A Preface to Psychology, 1972, Challenge of Reform in Higher Education, 1991, Historical Development of the University System of Georgia, 1991, 2d edit., 2003, Administrative Leadership in Academic Governance and Management, 2003; co-author: One Hundred Classic Books in Higher Education, 2001; contbg. columnist: Athens Banner-Herald, 1970-90; editor: Planning Imperatives for the 1990s, 1989, Assessing Institutional Effectiveness in Higher Education, 1989, Defining and Assessing Quality, 1994, IHE Perspectives, 1999—; contbg. editor: Oryx Dictionary of Education, 2001; contbg. editor Rsch. in Higher Edn., 1978—; contbr. articles to profl. jours. Served with USNR, 1944-46. Recipient Disting. Achievement in Public Service medallion U. Ga., 1980, 2000, Ben W. Gibson award So. Regional Council, Coll. Bd., 1982; Ga. Ho. of Reps. and Senate Resolution recognizing contbns. to higher edn. and State of Ga., 1986, Abraham Baldwin award U. Ga. Alumni Assn., 1991. Mem. APA, Ga. Assn. Instnl. Rsch., Planning, Assessment and Quality (1st recipient Cameron Lane Fincher outstanding svc. award 1997), Assn. Study of Higher Edn. (Howard Bowen Disting. Career award 1991), So. Assn. Instl. Rsch. (James R. Montgomery award 1991), Am. Assn. Higher Edn., Assn. Instnl. Rsch. (Disting. Mem. 1983, Outstanding Svc. award 1980, AIR/Suslow award, 1995), So. Assn. Instnl. Rsch. (disting.), Alpha Kappa Psi, Phi Delta Kappa, Golden Key Office: U Ga Inst Higher Edn Meigs Hall Athens GA 30602

FINCHER, DAVID, film director, film producer; b. Denver, Colo., 1962; Co-founder Propaganda Films, 1986. Dir. videos for Don Henley, Sting, The Wallflowers, Paula Abdul, Aerosmith, Madonna, Michael Jackson, Rolling Stones (Grammy award for best music video Love is Strong 1995), Wallflowers; dir.:(films) Alien 3, 1992, Seven, 1995, The Game, 1997, The Fight Club, 1999, The Panic Room, 2002; prodr. Ambush, 2001, Chosen, 2001, The Follow, 2001, Star, 2001, Power Keg, 2001, The Ticker, 2002. Office: Propaganda Films 1746 Ivar Ave Los Angeles CA 90028*

FINCK, KEVIN WILLIAM, lawyer; b. Whittier, Calif., Dec. 14, 1954; s. William Albert and Ester (Gutbub) F.; m. Kathleen A. Miller, Oct. 7, 1989. BA in History, U. Calif., Santa Barbara, 1977; JD, U. Calif., San Francisco, 1980. Bar: Calif. 1980. Pvt. practice, Orinda, Calif. Lectr. Internat. Bar Assn., Learning Annex. Author: California Corporation Start Up Package and Minute Book, 1982, 9th edit., 1998; contbr. articles to various profl. jours. Avocations: hiking, golf, skiing. Office: Ste 1670 Two Embarcadero Ctr San Francisco CA 94111 E-mail: kevin@kevinfinck.com.

FINCKE, EDWARD MICHAEL (MIKE), astronaut; b. Pitts., Pa., Mar. 14, 1967; s. Edward and Alma Fincke; m. Renita Saikia; 1 child. BSc in Aero. & Astronautics, BSc in Earth, Atmospheric & Planetary Sci., MIT, 1989; MSc in Aero. & Astronautics, Stanford U., 1990; Msc in Physical Sci., U. Houston, 2001. Commd. 2d lt. USAF, 1989, advanced through grades to col., various assignments, 1990—94, mem. 39th flight test squadron, 1994—96, flight test liaison Gifu Air Base, Japan, 1996; astronaut NASA, Houston, 1996—. Astronaut Internat. Space Sta. Expedition, 2001. Decorated two Commendation medals USAF, Achievement medal. Mem.: Geological Soc. Am. Avocations: hiking, flying, travel, geology, astronomy. Office: Astronaut Office CB NASA Johnson Space Center Houston TX 77058

FINCKE, GARY W. writer, educator; b. Pitts., July 7, 1945; s. William A. and Ruth L. Lang F.; m. Elizabeth L. Locker, Aug. 17, 1968; children: Derek, Shannon, Aaron. BA, Thiel Coll., 1967; MA, Miami U., 1969; PhD, Kent State U., 1974. Tchr. English Freedom (Pa.) Area Schs., 1968-69; instr. English Pa. State U., Monaca, 1969-75; chair English dept. LeRoy (N.Y.) Ctrl. Sch., 1975-80; prof. English Susquehanna U., Selinsgrove, Pa., 1980—, coach men's tennis, 1980—; instr. fiction Pa. Govs. Sch. Arts, 1984. Cons. in field. Author of poems, short stories and creative nonfiction. Dir. Ea. Region Pa. Act 101 Program, Harrisburg, 1987-89. Recipient Bess Hokin prize Poetry Mag., 1991, Pushcart prize, 1996, 2000, PEN Fiction prize, 1984, Rose Lefcowitz prize, 1997; Artist fellow Pa. Coun. Arts, 1982, 85, 87, 91, 95, 2000, 03. Mem. Associated Writing Programs. Avocations: tennis, golf, music. Office: Susquehanna U Dept English Selinsgrove PA 17870

FINDER, JOSEPH ALAN, writer; b. Chgo., Ill., Oct. 6, 1958; s. Morris and Natalie Finder; m. Michele Souda, Aug. 27, 1989; 1 child, Emma Josephine Souda Finder. BA summa cum laude, Yale Coll., 1980; MA, Harvard U., 1984. Writer, novelist, Boston, 1982—; writing faculty Harvard Coll., John F. Kennedy Sch. Govt., Harvard U., Cambridge, Mass., 1988, Harvard Coll./Harvard Ext. Sch., Cambridge, 1984—90. Author: (nonfiction book) Red Carpet: The Connection Between the Kremlin and America's Most Powerful Businessmen, 1983, (novels) The Moscow Club, 1991, Extraordinary Powers, 1993, The Zero Hour, 1996, High Crimes, 1998; contbr. book revs. and articles to newspapers and publs. Mem.: SAG, PEN New Eng. (bd. dirs.), Boston Athanaeum, Harvard Club Boston, Yale Club Boston, Phi Beta Kappa. E-mail: joe@josephfinder.com.

FINDER, STUART GREGG, medical ethics educator; b. Pitts., Mar. 21, 1961; s. Moses J. and Laryn S. Finder; m. Cynthia N. Finder; children: Samuel, Sarah, Nathan. BS, Allegheny Coll., 1983; MA, U. Colo., 1986, U. Wis., 1988; PhD, U. Utah, 1991. Asst. prof. med. ethics Vanderbilt U., Nashville, 1991—. Clin. ethics cons. Vanderbilt U. Hosp., Nashville, 1991—, St. Thomas Hosp., Nashville, 1992-93; assoc. dir. Ctr. for Clin. and Rsch. Ethics, Nashville, 1992-2000, dir., 2000—. Contbr. chpt. to book and articles to profl. jours. Mem. Am. Soc. for Bioethics and Humanities, Can. Bioethics Soc., Hastings Ctr. Office: Ctr for Clin and Rsch Ethics 319 Oxford House Nashville TN 37232-4350

FINDER-STONE, PATRICIA ANN, nurse, health educator, volunteer; b. Platteville, Wis., Jan. 27, 1929; d. Arthur Charles and Marcella Mary Finder; m. Mark Henry Stone, Dec. 28, 1953 (dec. Nov. 1997); children: Teresa Kay Stone Gulyas, Susan Elizabeth Stone Crane, Mark Henry Jr., Matthew Riley. Grad., Columbia Sch. Nursing, 1950; BS, U. Wis., Green Bay, 1973; MS, U. Wis., Madison, 1975. RN; cert. in pub. health, Wis. Staff and adminstrv. nurse various hosps., 1980-95; DON San Luis Manor, Green Bay, 1967-68; asst. head nurse Bellin Meml. Hosp., Green Bay, 1968-69; instr. nursing Bellin Coll. Nursing, Green Bay, 1969-79; dir. Bellin Hospice Program, Green Bay, 1979-80; nursing cons. local law firms, Green Bay, 1984—87, 1999—2001; instr. ADN program N.E. Wis. Tech. Coll., Green Bay, 1980-96. Past chair Brown County Bd. of Health; ethics com. St. Mary's Hosp., Green Bay, 1987—, adv. bd., 1998—, chair legis. com., 1999—; mem. Wis. ethics com. network Med. Coll. Wis., Milw., 1988—; assoc. mem. Hastings Ctr. Inst. Soc., Ethics and Life Scis., N.Y., 1975—. Bd. dirs. Wis. divsn. Am. Cancer Soc., 1975-99, Midwest divsn., 1998-2000, pub. issues chair Wis. divsn., 1983-91, sec. bd. dirs.. 1990-91, chair bylaws, 1994-96, chair bd. dirs., 1996-97, chair advocacy com. 1998-2000, mem. midwest tactical team, 2000-2001; mem. Midwest Regional Leadership Group, 2001—; bd. dirs., pres., pub. affairs chair Brown County unit Am. Cancer Soc., 1976-2000; bd. dirs. Greater Green Bay Cmty. Found., 1991-97; bd. dirs. Bay Area Cmty. Coun., 1992—, chmn., 2001-03, Bay Area Cmty. Health Partnership, chair pub. policy, 2001—; bd. dirs. ASPIRO (formerly Brown County Assn. Retarded Citizens), 1996—, pres., 2002—, chair legis. com. 1998—; mem. Brown County Women's Cancer Coalition, 1994—; adv. bd. Brown County Planning Commn., 1992-98, mem. planning divsn. United Way, 1992-99, chair cmty. edn. com., 1997-2000, mem. planned givers adv. com., 2001-02, mem. health and wellness impact coun., 2002—; bd. dirs., legis. chair Start Smart, 1997-2002; past bd. dirs. Northeastern Wis. Health Systems Agys., Wis. Health Policy Coun., chair health svcs. to elderly com.; mem. Brown County Tobacco-Free Coalition, 1996—, chair, 1996-99; gov. appointee Wis. Tobacco Control Bd., 2000-03; mem. Wis. Supreme Ct. Commn. on Jud. Ethics and Elections, 1997-2000, mem. Wis. Bd. on Aging and Long Term Care, 2003—; bd. dirs. Brown County Commn. on Aging/Aging Resource Ctr., 1997—, Scholarships, Inc., 1998—, Wis. Dept. Health and Family Svcs. Turning Point, 1998-2002; Bay Area Agy. on Aging, 2002— (chair legislative com. 2001—), AARP State Coord. Coun., 2001—, AARP-Wis. Exec. Coun., 2002—; adv. com. Wis. Pub. TV Creating Health, 1999-2000, Wis. Coalition to Improve Palliative Care; bd. dirs., legis. com. Wis. Coalition of Aging Group, 1999—, dist. chair, 1999-2003, 1st v.p., 2003—. Lt. Nurse Corps, USAF, 1950-53; mem. USAFR, 1953-57. Named Woman of the Yr. Green Bay YWCA, 1977, Vol. of Yr., Greater Green Bay, 1997; recipient Tchr. of the Yr. award Wis. Vocat. Assn., 1983, J.C. Penney Golden Rule award for volunteerism, 1997, Disting. Svc. award U. Wis.-Green Bay Alumni Assn., 1998, Zonta award Sci. and Tech., 1999, Outstanding Cmty. Vol. award United Way, 1999, Woman of Vision award YWCA, 2002; grantee NEH, Marquette U., 1992-93; fellow Advocacy Inst., Washington, 1999. Mem. LWV (bd. dirs. Greater Green Bay chpt. 1992-94, pres. 1989-92, action chair 1992—, Wis. br. bd. dirs. 1993-94, legis com. 1994—), AAUW (pres. Greenbay area 1997-98, pub. policy chair 1998—, bd. dirs. 1995—, Wis. chpt. bd. dirs., voter edn. chmn. 1999-2000), Wis. Nurses Assn. (chair legis. commn. 1985-94, ethics commn. 1994-2001, pub. policy commn. 1995—, chair 2000-02, Polit. Nurse of Yr. 1996), N.E. Wis. Dist. Nurses Assn. (bd. dirs., pres. 1992-94, co-chair legis. com. 1994-2001, Nurses Leadership award 1992), Pi Lambda Theta, Sigma Theta Tau (past v.p.), Phi Delta Kappa. Avocations: hiking, cross country skiing, world travel. E-mail: stone@netnet.net.

FINDLAY, ANNETTE MARIE, information systems executive; b. Ft. Wayne, Ind., Aug. 9, 1958; d. Paul J. and Catherine Ann Findlay; 1 child, Jacqueline. AAS in Data Processing, U. Akron, Ohio, 1978, BS in Mgmt., 1980; MBA, U. Phoenix, Southfield, Mich., 1999. Systems programmer Diebold, North Canton, Ohio, 1980—81; mgr. systems software Ctrl. Nat. Bank, Cleve., 1981—85; mgr. tech. svcs. AAA Mich., Dearborn, 1985—96; divsn. info. officer, bus. svcs. Blue Cross Blue Shield Mich., Detroit, 1996—2001; divisional chief info. officer Blue Care Network, Southfield, 2001—. Dir. pub. rels. Northville Twp. Found. Parade, Northville, Mich., 1999, 2000; grad. Leadership Oakland, 1999; bd. trustees Generation of Promise Program, 1999-2002. Mem. Women's Econ. Club Detroit. Avocations: tennis, music, sports cars. Office: Blue Cross Blue Shield Mich MCB844 25925 Telegraph Rd Southfield MI 48086 E-mail: findlaya@aol.com.

FINDLAY, DONALD CAMERON, federal agency administrator, lawyer; b. Chgo., Sept. 7, 1959; s. Donald C. and Judith R. (Lilly) F.; m. Amy Scalera, July 9, 1988; children: Alexander B., James M. BA with highest distinction, Northwestern U., 1982; MA 1st class, Oxford (Eng.) U., 1984; JD magna cum laude, Harvard U., 1987. Bar: Ill. 1987, D.C. 1988. Law clk. to Judge Stephen Williams U.S. Ct. Appeals (D.C. cir.), Washington, 1987-88; law clk. to Justice Antonin Scalia U.S. Supreme Ct., Washington, 1988-89; counselor to sec. U.S. Dept. Transp., Washington, 1989-91; dep. asst. to the pres. The White House, Washington, 1991-92; assoc. Sidley & Austin, Chgo., 1992-95, ptnr., 1995—2001; dep. secy. U.S. Dept. Labor, Washington, 2001—. Adj. prof. Northwestern U., Evanston, Ill., 1994-96. Office: US Dept Labor 200 Constitution Ave NW Washington DC 20210-0001 Office Fax: 202-693-6143.

FINDLAY, MARGERY WALDO, retired librarian; b. Boston, Feb. 28, 1935; d. Allen Worcester and Cherrie Katherine (Malcolmson) Waldo; m. William Francis Findlay, Sept. 11, 1955; children— Wendy, Eric Steven, Heidi. B.A., Stanford U., 1957; M.L.S., San Jose State U., 1977; postgrad. Calif. State U., Sacramento, 1970-74. Librarian Rio Linda Union Sch. Dist., Calif., 1972-79, dist. librarian, 1979-96; instr. Calif. State U., Sacramento, 1979; reference librarian Cosumnes River Coll., Sacramento, 1981. Bd. dirs. Sacramento Lit. Symposium, 1980—94; medal com. Calif. Young Reader, 1994-97. Mem. Calif. Library Media Educators Assn. (state treas. 1987-93, treas. no. sect. 1982-86, regional rep. 1981-82), Calif. Reading Assn., Sacramento Area Libr. Orgn., Stanford Club, Phi Beta Kappa, Beta Phi Mu. Republican. Home: 8510 Walden Woods Way Granite Bay CA 95746-8152

FINDLAY, MICHAEL ALISTAIR, art dealer, poet; b. Innellan, Scotland, May 13, 1945; came to U.S., 1964; s. Robert John Findlay and Mary Beatrice (Duffy) Collins; m. Naomi Sims, Aug. 4, 1973 (div. Jan. 1990); children: Bob, Beatrice; m. Victoria Wolfe, July 24, 1999. BA, York U., Toronto, Ont., Can., 1963. V.p., dir. exhbns. Richard L. Feigen and Co., Ltd., N.Y.C., L.A., Chgo., 1964-70; founder, owner, dir. J.H. Duffy and Sons, Ltd., N.Y.C., 1970-77; dir. William Beadleston Gallery, N.Y.C., 1977-84; sr. v.p., sr. dir. Christie, Manson and Woods, N.Y.C., 1984-94, sr. dir., 1994-97, internat. dir., 1997—; dir. fin., 1997-2000; dir. Acquevella Galleries, N.Y.C., 2000—. Lectr. Moore Coll. Art, Phila., 1970-80; find arts advisor N.Y.C. Parks Dept., 1979-84; mem. art adv. panel GSA, N.Y.C., 1985; keynote spkr. Oxford U. Alumnae Assn., N.Y.C., Rotary Clubs Internat., Taipei, Taiwan, Credit Suisse, Singapore, Young Pres.'s Orgn., N.Y.C., 1993-96; sr. faculty Christie's Edn., 1994-2000; bd. dirs. Christie's Internat.; mem., bd. dirs. Christie's Fine Art, Inc. Contbr. poetry and articles on art criticism to Arts, Artnews, mags. Bd. dirs. Peacemaker Found., Inc., Santa Fe, 1975—, Lacoste Sch. Arts, Vaucluse, France, Christie's Internat. Fine Arts, 1998—; hon. sec., v.p. for grants Brit. Sch. and Univs. Found., Inc., N.Y.C., 1975-85, bd. dirs., 1985—; trustee Parrish Mus., Southampton, N.Y., 1993-95; mem. adv. coun. Shanghai Mus., China, 1996; mem. scholarship com. Jade Found., N.Y.C., 1999—. Mem. ACLU, Amnesty Internat. Roman Catholic. Office: Acquavella Galleries 18 E 79th St New York NY 10021-0106

FINDLER, HANS JOSEF, retired business executive; b. Vienna, June 16, 1920; s. Samuel and Margareta (Schwarz) F.; m. Helga Zweig, June 3, 1942 (div. 1944); m. Lucie Lederer, Jan. 11, 1946; children: Gideon, Uriel. Prodn. mgr. The Textile Dyers and Finishers Keshet Ltd., Ramat-Gan, Israel, 1940-59; comml. mgr. Nechushtan Lift Works, Tel-Aviv, 1959-85, ret., 1985. Mem. Planetary Soc., N.Y. Acad. Sci. Avocations: comparative philology, education, astrophysics, nuclear physics, cosmogony. Home: 27 Nitzana Str 53364 Givatayim Israel

FINDLEY, DELPHA YODER, retired public health nurse; b. Falls City, Nebr., Mar. 6, 1930; d. Ralph A. and Marguerite (Prior) Brackhahn; m. James E. Findley, Jan. 30, 1988; children: Kimberly Yoder Goff, Steven Amos Yoder. Diploma, Mo. Meth. Sch. Nursing, St. Joseph, 1950. RN, Nebr., Mo. Missionary sch. nurse and tchr. Meth. Bd. Missions, Iquique, Chile, 1957-61; dir. nurses Northview Care Center Nursing Home, Falls City, 1973-75; dir. nurses, asst. adminstr. Community Hosp. Inc., Falls City, 1975-88; pub. health nurse Clinton County Health Dept., Plattsburg, Mo., 1988-91; ret., 1991. Recipient Dist. V Nursing Leadership award Nebr. Orgn. Nurse Execs., 1986. Home: 8485 SE Highway 33 Osborn MO 64474-9148 E-mail: jfindley@cameron.net.

FINDLEY, DON AARON, manufacturing company executive; b. Gadsden, Ala., June 11, 1926; s. Royal Guy and Hattie Elizabeth (Walden) F.; m. Mary Elizabeth Abernathy, Oct. 22, 1947; children: Elizabeth Jane Findley Dever, David Walden. BS, Auburn U., 1950. Acct. Buckeye Cellulose Corp. Augusta, Ga., 1950-51; acct. Tenn. Eastman Co., Kingsport, 1951-59, gen. supr. standard cost and analysis dept., 1959-64, gen. mgmt. staff, 1964-67, asst. comptroller, 1971-73, comptroller, 1975-79, v.p. fin. and adminstrn., 1979-88; mng. dir. Ectona Fibres Ltd., Cumberland, Eng., 1967-71; asst. comptroller Eastman Chem. Products, Eastman Chem. Internat. Ltd., Kingsport, 1971-73, comptroller, 1975-79, v.p. fin. and adminstrn., 1979-88; asst. comptroller Eastman Chem. Internat. Co., Kingsport, 1971-73, comptroller, 1975-79, Holston Def. Corp.; asst. v.p. Ark. Eastman Co., Carolina Eastman Co., Tex. Eastman Co. Dir. 1st Am. Nat. Bank, Kingsport Bd. dirs. Holston Valley Hosp. and Med. Ctr., Kingsport, 1978-90, treas., 1978-83; dir. United Way of Kingsport, 1994-97. Recipient Achievment award Ala. Soc. C.P.A.s, 1950, Outstanding Acctg. Alumnus award Auburn U., 1981 Fellow Inst. Dirs. (U.K.); mem. Nat. Assn. Accts. (pres. East Tenn. chpt. 1963-64), Tenn. Mfrs. and Taxpayers Assn. (bd. dirs. 1978-86), Delta Sigma Pi, Phi Kappa Phi, Beta Alpha Psi, Greater Kingsport C. of C. (bd. dirs. 1975-77) Clubs: Ridgefields Country (Kingsport) (bd. dirs. 1984-86). Republican. Methodist. Avocations: photography; coin collecting; gardening; golfing. Home: 524 Lakewood Rd Kingsport TN 37660-3420

FINDLEY, JOHN ALLEN, JR., publishing executive; b. Fulton, Mo., Feb. 25, 1951; s. John Allen and Naomi Joan (Reker) F.; m. Oneida Lynn Blackwell, Dec. 4, 1993; children: John III, Hugh. Student, U. Mo., 1973; AB, Westminster Coll., 1973. Sales rep. Kingdom Daily News, Fulton, 1973-74; advt. dir. Colo. Daily, Boulder, 1973-74; advt. sales rep. Dallas Times Herald, 1976-77, advt. sales mgr., 1977-80, dir. consumer mktg., 1981-83, dir. circulation, 1983, dir. retail advt., 1983-84; regional sales mgr. Times Mirror Nat. Mktg., 1984-86; v.p. mktg. So. Conn. Newspapers, Stamford, 1986-88, sr. v.p. mktg. and prodn., 1989-93; pres. Charleston (W.Va.) Newspapers, 1993-97; pub., CEO Long Beach (Calif.) Press-Telegram, 1998—2001; v.p. newspaper rels. Parade Mag., L.A., 2002—03, sr. v.p., 2003—. Bd. govs. Calif. State U., Long Beach; bd. dirs. Long Beach Coun., Boy Scouts Am., Long Beach Found., Long Beach Venture Forum, Nat. Conf. Cmty. and Justice. Mem. Newspaper Assn. Am., Internat. Newspaper Promotion Assn., Sigma Chi. Office: 6300 Wilshire Blvd Los Angeles CA 90048

FINDLEY, JOHN SIDNEY, dentist; b. Bryan, Tex., Oct. 3, 1942; s. Sidney Albert and Leila Mae (Reading) F.; m. Patricia Ann Reep, June 10, 1967 (div. 1977); children: John Brett, Sidney Alan; m. Judith Ann Smith, May 22, 1981. Student, USAF Acad., 1961-62, N. Tex. State U., 1963-65; DDS, Baylor U. Coll. Dentistry, 1970. Pvt. practice, Plano, Tex., 1970—. Bd. dirs. Fin. Svcs. Inc. Contbr. articles to profl. jours. Formerly bd. dirs. Plano YMCA, United Way of Plano, Park Bd. City of Plano, Charter Rev. Commn. City of Plano; pres. Colleagues of the Plano Police, City of Plano; chmn. advancement com. North Trail Dist. Boy Scouts Am.; campaign chmn. Plano YMCA Fund Dr., 1978; councilman City of Cross Rds., Tex., 1988-89, mayor, 1992-94; chmn. bd. trustees Oak Grove United Meth. Ch.; gen. chmn. Dallas Midwinter Dental Clinic. Recipient Cert. of Recognition Am. Acad. Dental Radiology, 1970; Paul Harris fellow Rotary Internat., 1979. Fellow: Internat. Coll. Dentists, Am. Coll. of Dentists; mem.: ADA (mem. task force on governance 2000—01, mem. Future of Dentistry project 2001, trustee 2003), Acad. Gen. Dentistry, Dallas County Dental Soc. (gen. chmn. Dallas Mid-winter Dental Clinic 1992, pres.-elect 1992—93, pres. 1994, bd. dirs., editor DDS News, Dentist of Yr. 1995), Tex. Dental Assn. (pres.-elect 1996, pres. 1997—98, chmn. coun. on legis. and regulatory affairs 1999—2003, chmn. coun. govt. affairs, Pres. award 1994, 1995, 1996, 1999, 2000, 2001, 2003), Rotary (Plano, bd. dirs., pres. 1977—78). Methodist. Home: 3800 S Pottershop Rd Aubrey TX 76227-2587 Office: 1410 14th St Plano TX 75074-6359

FINDLEY, MARY BAKER, violinist; b. Norfolk, Va., May 9, 1943; d. Henry Givens and Virginia Marie (Bredenfoerder) Baker; m. David Francis Findley, Mar. 3, 1966. MusB, U. Cin., 1965, MusM, 1966, DMA, 1974; student, Staatlich Hoschschle Musik, Frankfurt/Main, Germany, 1966-68. Pvt. studio, Cin., 1972-75, Tulsa, 1976-80. Adj. asst. prof. violin Oral Roberts U., Tulsa, 1976-80; Arts Coun. Okla. artist-in-residence, 1977-81; concertmaster, soloist, founding mem., bd. dirs. Tulsa Little Symphony Orch., 1978-80; founder Tulsa Chamber Music Festival, 1980; founding mem. Washington Music Ensemble, 1981-89; concert soloist and recitalist; pvt. studio tchr., Washington, 1981—; adj. asst. prof. and co-coord. of strings George Washington U., Washington, Levine Sch. Music, Washington, 1981—; founder All-Okla. String Symposium, 1977, Summer Serenades, 1986; concert master, soloist, bd. dirs. Amadeus Chamber Orch., 1984-88. Mem. Am. String Tchrs. Assn. with Nat. Sch. Orch. Assn., Music Educators Nat. Conf., Music Tchrs. Nat. Assn., Chamber Music Am., Suzuki Assn. Ams., Internat. Alliance for Women in Music, Mortar Bd., Sigma Alpha Iota (Performance awrd 1972). Office: George Washington U Music Dept Washington DC 20052-0001

FINDLEY, PAUL, former congressman, author, educator; b. Jacksonville, Ill., June 23, 1921; s. Joseph S. and Florence Mary (Nichols) F.; m. Lucille Gemme; children: Craig Jon, Diane Lillian. AB, Ill. Coll., 1943, LLD, 1972; LHD (hon.), Lindenwood Coll., 1969, Lincoln U., 1988, MacMurray Coll., 1997; LLD, Sana'a U., Yemen, 1997. Mem. 87th-97th Congresses from 20th Ill. dist., mem. Fgn. Affairs com., mem. Agr. com.; chmn. factfinding mission to Paris, 1965; chmn. Rep. NATO Task Force, 1965-68; chmn. com. to investigate internat. problems caused by agrl. support policies Ditchley (Eng.) Conf., 1973; del. N. Atlantic Assembly, 1965-70, 72-79, Munich Conf. German Rels., 1969-71; Ditchley Conf. Atlantic Trade, 1967; European Parliament, 1974-76; mem. 7th Congl. Del. to People's Republic China, 1975; chmn. Ill. Trade Mission to, USSR, 1972, 1978. Mem. internat. food and agrl. devel. bd. AID, 1983-94; vis. prof. MacMurray Coll., 1994-96. Author: Abraham Lincoln: The Crucible of Congress, The Federal Farm Fable, They Dare to Speak Out: People and Institutions Confront Israel's Lobby, Deliberate Deceptions: Facing the Facts About the U.S.-Israel Relationships, Silent No More: Confronting America's False Images of Islam; contbr. numerous articles on fgn. policy and agr. to periodicals. Trustee emeritus Ill. Coll.; lectr. leadership program UN Leadership Acad., Amman, Jordan, 1987-88; chmn. Coun. for the Nat. Interest, 1989-2000. Served to lt. (j.g.) USNR, WWII. Named laureate Lincoln Acad., 1980; decorated Grand Cross Order of Merit Fed. Republic of Ger.; recipient Outstanding Svc. to Agr. citation So. Ill. U., Kefauver award for promoting Fedn. of Atlantic Nations; Hon. Am. Farmer degree FFA, Outstanding Achievement award FFA Alumni Assn., citation Nat. Assn. State Univs. and Land-Grant Colls., EAFORD Humanitarian award, 1986, Alex Odeh Human Rights award Am. Arab Anti-Discrimination Com., 1992, Disting. Svc. award Assn. for Internat. Agr. and Rural Development, 1995; Malcolm X award Muslim Assn., 2000. Mem. Assn. to Unite Democracies (bd. dirs.), Am. Legion, Phi Beta Kappa. Republican. Presbyterian. Home and Office: 1040 W College Ave Jacksonville IL 62650-2306

FINDLING, RHONDA BARBARA, psychotherapist; b. Bronx, N.Y., Aug. 13, 1954; d. Marvin Findling and Anita Weinstein. BA, Stonybrook U., 1975; MA, Roosevelt U., 1978. Cert. rehab. counselor Bd. Rehab. Cert., Chgo. Counselor Victims Info. Bur., Smithtown, NY, 1980—82; psychologist State of N.Y., 1982—85; psychotherapist Postgrad. Ctr. for Mental Health, 1985—2000; pvt. practice psychotherapist Forest Hills, NY, 1993—, N.Y.C., 1993—. Author:

(plays) The Psychic, 1996, Don't Call That Man: A Survival Guide to Letting Go, 1999, (novels) Mourning Losses, 2003. Mem.: N.Y. State Psychol. Assn., Am. Screenwriters Assn., Nat. Spkrs. Assn. Avocations: screenwriting, piano, writing, filmmaking.

FINDLING, ROBERT LAWRENCE, psychiatrist; MD, Med. Coll. Va., 1987. Dir. child/adolescent psychiatry Case Western Reserve U., Cleve., 1992—. Office: UHC Dept Psychiatry 11100 Euclid Ave Cleveland OH 44106-5080

FINDORFF, ROBERT LEWIS, retired air filtration equipment company executive; b. Mpls., Apr. 15, 1929; s. Hugo Clarence and Elfriede Louise (Schade) F.; m. Jocelyn J. Curtis, June 20, 1953; children— Robert H., Jean, Paul, Laura, Mary, Karl, John. BBA, U. Minn., 1952, MBA, 1956; JD magna cum laude, William Mitchell Coll. Law, 1962. Bar: Minn. bar 1962. Trust accounting mgr. No. Trust Co., Chgo., 1953-54; personnel mgr. purchasing dir. Donaldson Co., Inc., Mpls., 1955-62, plant mgr., v.p. mfg., v.p., gen. mgr. then sr. v.p., 1965-94, assoc. firm Oppenheimer, Hodgeson, Brown, Wolf & Leach, St. Paul, 1962-64. Bd. dirs. Exec. Svc. Corp. Tampa; instr. property law William Mitchell Coll. Law, 1981-89. Trustee William Mitchell Coll. Law, 1981-89. Served with AUS, 1947-48; USAF, 1962-68. Recipient Minn. State Bar Scholarship award 1962. Mem. Svc. Corp. Ret. Execs. Roman Catholic. Home: 6812 Paiute Dr Minneapolis MN 55439-1033

FINE, ANNE, author; b. Leicester, Eng., Dec. 7, 1947; d. Brian and Eileen Mary (Baker) Laker; m. Kit Fine, Aug. 3, 1968 (div. 1991); children: Ione, Cordelia. BA with honors, U. Warwick, Eng., 1968. Tchr. Cardinal Wiseman Secondary Sch., Coventry, U.K., 1968-69; info. officer Oxfam, Oxford, England, 1969-71; tchr. Saughton Prison, Edinburgh, Scotland, 1971-72. Author: (children's fiction) The Summer-House Loon, 1978, The Other Darker Ned, 1979, The Stone Menagerie, 1980, Round Behind the Ice House, 1981, The Granny Project, 1983, Scaredy-Cat, 1984, Anneli the Art Hater, 1986, Madame Doubtfire, 1987, Crummy Mummy an Me, 1987, A Pack of Liars, 1988, Goggle-Eyes, 1989, Bill's New Frock, 1989, The Book of the Banshee, 1991, Flour Babies, 1992, Step By Wicked Step, 1995, The Tulip Touch, 1996, Charm School, 1999, Bad Dreams, 2000, Up on Cloud Nine, 2002, The True Story of Christmas, 2003, others; (adult fiction) The Killjoy, 1986, Taking the Devil's Advice, 1990, In Cold Domain, 1994, Telling Liddy, 1998, All Bones and Lies, 2001, STories of Jamie and Angus, 2002. Decorated Order Brit. Empire; named Children's Author of Yr., Brit. Book Awards, 1990, 1993, U.K. nominee for Hans Christian Anderson Author award, 1998, Children's Laureate, 2001—03; recipient Children's Lit. award, The Guardian, 1990, Carnegie medal, Brit. Libr. Assn., 1990, 1993, Whitbread Children's Novel award, 1993, 1996, Horn Book award, Boston Globe, 2003; fellow, Royal Soc. Lit., 2003. Avocations: reading, walking. Office: David Higham Assocs 5-8 Lower John St Golden Sq London W1R 4HA England

FINE, ARTHUR I. philosopher, educator; b. Lowell, Mass., Nov. 11, 1937; s. David Fine and Rae (Silverberg) Mintz; m. Helene S. Feldberg, June 16, 1957 (div. May 1980); children: Dana S., Sharon D.; m. Micky Forbes, July 11, 1980. Student, Harvard U., 1955-56; BS, U. Chgo., 1958; MS, Ill. Inst. Tech., 1960; PhD, U. Chgo., 1963. Asst. prof. math and philosophy Ill. Inst. Tech., Chgo., 1961—63; asst. prof. philosophy U. Ill., Urbana, 1963—65; assoc. prof. philosophy Cornell U., Ithaca, NY, 1967—71, prof. philosophy, 1971—72, U. Ill., Chgo., 1972—82, Northwestern U., Evanston, Ill., 1982—85, John Evans prof. philosophy, 1985—2001; prof. philosophy U. Wash., Seattle, 2001—, adj. prof. physics, 2003—. Mem. nat. com. Internat. Union History and Philosophy of Sci. Nat. Acad. Sci., 1973-77; mem. adv. panel History and Philosophy of Sci. Nat. Sci. Found., 1975-77, 87-88, 92-93; adj. prof. physics U. Wash., Seattle, 2003—. Author: The Shaky Game, 1986, 2d edit., 1996; co-editor: Philosophical Review, 1969-71; editor: (with others) PSA: 1986, 88, 90, vols. I and II; subject editor: Philosophy of Science Routledge Encyclopedia of Philosophy, 1993-98; contbr. articles to profl. jours. NSF fellow, 1966-67; NSF grantee 1968, 73, 78, 80, 89; sr. fellow NEH, 1974-75; Guggenheim fellow, 1982-83; fellow Ctr. Advanced Study in Behavioral Scis. Stanford, 1985-86; vis. fellow Dibner Inst., MIT, 1996. Mem. Philosophy of Sci. Assn. (pres. 1986-88), Am. Philos. Assn. (ctrl. divsn. pres. 1997-98). Office: U Wash Philosophy Dept Box 353350 Seattle WA 98195-3550

FINE, BARRY KENNETH, lawyer; b. N.Y.C., May 15, 1938; s. Harry Harold and Annn Fine; m. Rho Joy Stengel, Sept. 3, 1965; children: Scott Jefferson, Jill Ashley. BS, SUNY Empire State Coll., 1986; JD, Touro Coll., 1990. Jr. civil engr. N.Y.C. Transit Authority, 1957-58; pres. Active Industries (formerl Active Steel Drum Co.), L.I., N.Y., 1958-93; founder, pres. Glass Tint Svcs., Inc., L.I., N.Y., 1985-93; founding ptnr. Fine Hummel, P.C., Huntington, NY, 1990—2002; founding mem. Fine, Fine & Berman, LLP, Melville, NY, 2003—. Patentee in field. Project bus. cons. Queens Jr. Achievement, Queens, N.Y., 1984-88. With USAR, 1957-63. Mem. ABA, Suffolk County Bar Assn. (former co-chair Environ. law com., lectr., environ. law writer Suffolk Lawyer), Nassau County Bar Assn., N.Y. State Bar Assn., Masons (past master). Republican. Jewish. Avocations: boating, cabinetmaking, gardening. Office: Fine Fine & Berman LLP 445 Broad Hollow Rd Ste 200 Melville NY 11747-3448 E-mail: bkf@ffbllp.com.

FINE, BOB, lawyer, real estate developer; b. Mpls., Mar. 29, 1949; s. Ralph I. and Beverlee (Rockler) F.; m. Sylvia Latarus, June 20, 1971; children: Jacob, Andy, Ellyn, Joe. BA, U. Minn., 1970; JD, Washington U., 1973. Bar: U.S. Dist. Ct. Minn. 1974, Minn. 1974, U.S. Supreme Ct. 1980, U.S. Ct. Appeals (8th cir.) 1995. Sole practice, Mpls., 1974-79; real estate developer, 1979-90; pres., commr. Mpls. Park and Recreation Bd., 1998—. Referee Hennepin County Conciliation Ct., Mpls., 1977—; mem. Mpls. Bd. Estimate and Taxation, 1998—. Commr. Mpls. Commn. Civil Rights, 1981—99; mem. Mpls. Zoning Bd. Admistrs., 1984—86; trustee Mpls. Inst. Art, 2000—01; mem. St. Anthony Falls Heritage Preservation Bd., 1999—. Avocations: swimming, basketball. Office: PO Box 24192 Minneapolis MN 55424-0192

FINE, CORY R. education educator, consultant; b. Queens, N.Y., Oct. 25, 1961; s. Roslyn Fine; m. Lisa C. Augustine, Jan. 24, 1993; 1 child, Tyler Marcus. M in Pub. Adminstrn., U. of N.Mex, 1992—94; PhD in Indsl. Rels., U. of Leeds, Eng., 1995—98. Prof. of mgmt. U. of North Fla., Jacksonville, 2000—. Mgmt. cons. www.LaborWise.com, Jacksonville, Fla., 2000—; vis. prof. Warsaw U., Poland, 2001—. Author: (rsch. article) Employee Rights and Responsibilities Jour., (book chapter) Ann. Editions: Mgmt.; member, editorial board (rsch. jour.) Mgmt. Devel. Forum; author: (rsch. article) Jour. of Intellectual Capital, Jour. of Labor Rsch., Labor Law Jour., Labor Studies Jour., Jour. of Collective Negotiations in the Pub. Sector, East European Quart., Pub. Adminstrn. Rev., Dispute Resolution Jour. Grantee Assoc. Sr. Rsch. Fellowship, Hungarian Acad. of Sci., Inst. of Polit. Sci., 2002-Present, Sr. Rsch. Assoc., U. of North Fla. Ctr. for Internat. Bus. Studies, 2002-Present. Mem.: Indsl. Rels. Rsch. Assn., Internat. Indsl. Rels. Assn., Soc. for Human Resource Mgmt., Acad. of Mgmt., River Club, Jacksonville. Avocations: travel, antiques. Home: 5336 Heronview Dr Jacksonville FL 32257 Office: U of North Fla CCB-MML 4567 St John's Bluff Rd South Jacksonville FL 32224 Office Fax: 708-575-2966. E-mail: cfine@unf.edu.

FINE, DEBORAH, publishing executive; V.p., advt. dir. Family Cir. Mag., 1991—93; v.p., assoc. pub. Mary Emmerling's Country, 1993—94; advt. dir. Glamour, 1994—95, assoc. pub., 1995—96; pub. Bride's Mag., 1996—99; v.p., pub. Glamour, 2000—01; pres. Avon Future, 2001—. Office: Avon Future 1345 Avenue of the Americas New York NY 10105-0196

FINE, GARY ALAN, sociology educator; b. N.Y.C., May 11, 1950; s. Bernard David and Bernice (Tanz) Fine; m. Susan Hirsig, June 9, 1972; children: Todd, Peter. BA, U. Pa., 1972; PhD, Harvard U., 1976. Asst. prof. sociology U. Minn., Mpls., 1976-80, assoc. prof. sociology, 1980-85, prof. sociology, 1985-90; head dept. sociology U. Ga., Athens, 1990-93, prof. sociology, 1993-97, Northwestern U., Evanston, Ill., 1997—. Author: With the Boys, 1987, Kitchens, 1996, Morel Tales, 1998, Gifted Tongues, 2001. Pres. Atlanta Writing Resource Ctr., 1993-94; bd. dirs. Nexus Ctr. Comtemporary art, Atlanta, 1993-97, Intuit Ctr. Self-Taught and Initiitive Art, Chgo., 1999—. Spencer Found. grantee, Chgo., 1991, NSF grantee, Washington, 1992-95. Mem.: Folklore Fellows Internat., Soc. Study Social Problems (pres. 2004—), Sociol. Rsch. Assn., Midwest Sociol. Soc., Am. Sociol. Assn., Am. Folklore Soc. Avocations: cooking, theater, art. Office: Northwestern U Dept Sociology 1810 Chicago Ave Evanston IL 60208 E-mail: g-fine@northwestern.edu.

FINE, GLENN, federal agency administrator; AB magna cum laude, Harvard Coll., 1979; BA, MA, Oxford U.; JD magna cum laude, Harvard U., 1985. Asst. states atty. U.S. States Attys. Office, Washington, Del., 1986—89; atty. Washington, Del.; spl. counsel Dept. Justice Office Inspector Gen., Alexandria, 1995—96, dir. spl. investifations and rev. unit, 1996—2000, inspector gen., 2000—. Scholar Rhoades scholar. Office: US Dept Justice 950 Pennsulvania Ave NW Washington DC 20530-0001

FINE, HOWARD ALAN, travel industry executive; BS, NYU, 1961, MBA, 1964. Internat. sales mgr. Pfaff, A.G., Fed. Republic of West Germany, 1964-67; regional sales dir. Brit. Transport Hotels, London, Eng., 1967-70; dir. internat. mktg. Sonesta Internat. Hotels, N.Y.C., 1970-71; dir. Pacific mktg. Forte Hotels, L.A., 1971-74, dir. Atlantic area and Latin Am. mktg. N.Y.C, 1974-75, v.p. sales and mktg., 1975-78, exec. v.p., 1978-81; pres. Norwegian Am. Cruise Line, N.Y.C, 1981-83; pres., chief exec. officer Costa Cruise Line, Miami, Fla., 1983-87; chmn., chief exec. officer Tourism Devel. Internat., Miami, 1987—. Bd. dirs. Bahamas Devel. Found., Nassau, Traveling Times, Los Angeles; speaker, presenter Young Pres.'s Orgn, World Pres.'s Orgn., 1987—. Contbr. articles to profl. jours. Mem. mayors adv. bd. City of Los Angeles, 1972-74; mem. senatorial commn. Rep. Senatorial Inner Circle, Washington, 1984—, Presdl. task force to Pres. Bush, 1989—; bd. dirs. Calif. Dept. Agr. Wine Bd., 1974-75, Ptnrs. for Liveable Places, Washington, 1978-83, NYU Ctr. for Study of Foodservice, 1978-83, Fla. Crime Prevention Commn., 1984—, Boys Town of Italy, 1986—. Served to capt. USAR, 1961-66. Named Hon. Order Ky. Cols., 1986; named Man of Yr. Am. Jaycees, 1983, Man of Yr. Internat. Hotel Industry, 1980; recipient Disting. Marker of Yr. Sales and Mktg. Mgmt. Mag., 1979, Christopher Columbus award Nat. Columbus Day Com., 1986, Spirit of Life Humanitarian award City of Hope, 1987; numerous hotel and travel industry awards and citations from fgn. govts., 1972-87. Fellow Inst. Cert. Travel Agts.; mem. Young Pres.'s Orgn. (chmn. 1978—), World Pres.'s Orgn., Hotelier of the World Com. (bd. dirs. 1978—), Italian C. of C. (bd. dirs. 1975—), Brit. C. of C. (bd. dirs. 1975—), Norwegian C. of C. (bd. dirs. 1975—), South African C. of C. (bd. dirs. 1975—), Greater Ft. Lauderdale C. of C. (bd. govs. 1986—), NYU Alumni Fedn., Sigma Alpha Mu, NYU Club (N.Y.C.), 110 Tower Club (bd. dirs. 1987—), Harbor Beach Club (bd. dirs. 1987—). Clubs: NYU (N.Y.C.); 110 Tower (bd. dirs. 1987—), Harbor Beach (Ft. Lauderdale) (bd. dirs. 1987—). Avocations: boating, travel, gardening, photography, flying. Office: Tourism Devel Internat PO Box 22323 Fort Lauderdale FL 33335-2323

FINE, J(AMES) ALLEN, insurance company executive; b. May 2, 1934; s. Samuel Lee and Ocie (Loflin) F.; m. Marie Nan Morris, Sept. 1, 1957 (dec. Apr. 1989); children: James A(llen), William. Student, Pfeiffer Coll., 1957—58; BS, U. N.C., 1961, MBA, 1965. Sr. acct. Haskins & Sells, CPAs, Charlotte, NC, 1961—62, Watson, Penry & Morgan, Asheboro, NC, 1962—64; instr. U. N.C., Chapel Hill, 1964—65; asst. prof. Pfeiffer Coll., Misenheimer, NC, 1956—66; treas., v.p. adminstrn. Nat. Lab. for Higher Edn. (formerly Regional Edn. Lab. Carolinas and Va.), Durham, NC, 1966—72; organizer, CEO, treas., dir. Investors Title Ins. Co., Inc., Chapel Hill, 1972—, Cpres., dir., 1976—; developer Carolina Forest Subdivsn., Chapel Hill, 1970—78, Springhill Forest Subdivsn., Chapel Hill, 1977—80, Stonycreek Subdivsn., 1978—. Lectr. acctg. U. N.C., Chapel Hill, 1967—70. Area officer ann. alumni giving U. N.C., Chapel Hill, 1968—69, 1971—73, 1975—. With USN, 1953—57. Recipient Haskins & Sells Found. award for excellence in accounting, 1961, N.C. Assn. CPAs award for most outstanding accounting student, U. N.C., 1961. Mem.: AICPA, CEDAR Bus. Mgrs. (chmn. nat. exec. com. 1971), U. N.C. Nat. Devel. Com., Nat. Assn. Ins. Commrs. (liaison com. 1987—88, 1994—), Am. Land Title Assn. (rsch. com. 1983—, membership com. 1984—85, recruitment, retention subcom. 1985, exec. com. underwriters sect. 1986, 2002—), Am. Accounting Assn., N.C. Assn. CPAs, Phi Beta Kappa, Beta Gamma Sigma (treas. 1961). Home: 112 Carolina First Chapel Hill NC 27516-9033 Office: 121 N Columbia St Chapel Hill NC 27514-3502

FINE, JAMES STEPHEN, physician; b. St. Paul, June 14, 1946; s. Ralph Irving and Beverlee Lois (Rockler) F.; m. Meredith Ann Blehert, June 20, 1970; children: Zachary, Esther, Gabriel. BA in Math., U. Minn., 1968, MD, 1972, MS in Biometry, Health Info. Systems, 1977. Intern in medicine St. Paul-Ramsey Hosp., 1972-73; residency U. Minn., Mpls., 1973-77; assoc. prof., dir. info. and specimen processing div. U. Wash. Hosp., Seattle, 1977-94, chmn. lab. medicine, 1994—. Mem. Am. Assn. Clin. Chemistry, Acad. Clin. Lab. Physicians and Scientists (Gerald T. Evans award 2001), Computer Soc. of IEEE, Am. Med. Informatics Assn., Wash. State Med. Assn., King County Med. Soc. Office: U Wash Hosp Box 357110 1959 NE Pacific Ave NW 120 Seattle WA 98195

FINE, JO RENÉE, management executive; b. June 19, 1943; d. Ruby Arthur and Tillie Fern (Goldman) F.; m. Edward Trieber, Apr. 12, 1981; 1 child, Jessica. BA, Smith Coll., 1965; MA, NYU, 1968, PhD, 1973. Probation officer N.Y.C. Office Probation, 1966; rsch. asst. NYU, N.Y.C., 1966-68; assoc. rsch. scientist Inst. Devel. Studies, N.Y.C., 1968-73, rsch. scientist, 1973-77; program analyst N.Y. State Dept. Mental Health, N.Y.C., 1977-78; pvt. practice psychotherapy N.Y.C., 1978-81; pres. CVM Prodns., Inc., N.Y.C., 1978-92; dir. Ctr. for Diversity and Quality Mgmt. Cicatelli Assocs., N.Y.C., 1992-96; exec. v.p., dir. tng. Harris Rothenberg Internat., N.Y.C., 1996—. Adj. asst. prof. dept. ednl. psychology, NYU, 1973-76, adj. asst. prof. ednl. comm. and tech., 1988-95; cons. to bds. edn., N.Y.C., also greater met. area, 1973-92, tng. cons., 1990-96. Co-author: The Synagogues of New York's Lower East Side, 1978. Co-chair bd. dirs. Project People Found. Mem. APA, ASTD, Am. Jewish Com. (v.p. N.Y. chpt., nat. bd. govs.). Home: 55 W 16th St New York NY 10011-6305 Office: Harris Rothenberg Internat 99 Wall St Fl 8 New York NY 10005-4389

FINE, LAURA I, language educator; b. Washington D.C., Oct. 21, 1963; d. Ron E and Joan (Cushman) Fine. PhD, U. of Calif., Davis, 1994. English prof. Clark Atlanta U., Atlanta, Ga., 1994—. Grad. coord. Clark Atlanta U., Atlanta, 2000—. Vol. tutor Renfroe Mid. Sch., Decatur, Ga., 1999—2003. Mem.: MLA (assoc.). Dfl. Avocation: soccer. Office: Clark Atlanta Univ 223 James P Brawley Dr SW Atlanta GA 30314 E-mail: lfine@cau.edu.

FINE, LAWRENCE B. lawyer; b. June 20, 1951; BA, BS, U. Pa., 1973; JD, U. Va., 1976. Bar: Pa. 1976. Ptnr. Morgan, Lewis & Bockius, Phila. Office: Morgan Lewis & Bockius 1701 Market St Philadelphia PA 19103-2903

FINE, MARJORIE BLANK, surgeon; b. N.Y.C., 1944; MD, UCLA, 1975. Diplomate Am. Bd. Surgery. Intern UCLA Hosps., 1975-76, resident in Surgery, 1976-80; sr. surgeon St. Johns Hosp., Santa Monica, Calif., 1980—; chief surgery Santa Monica (Calif.) Hosp., 1999—2001; assoc. clin. prof. UCLA, 1980—2001. Mem. ACS, Am. Med. Women's Assn., L.A. Surg. Soc., Alpha Omega Alpha. Office: Surg Assocs Santa Monica Ste 625E 2021 Santa Monica Blvd Santa Monica CA 90404-1240

FINE, MARJORIE LYNN, lawyer; b. Bklyn., Aug. 14, 1950; d. Percy and Sylvia (Bernstein) F.; m. John Kent Markley, May 6, 1979; children: Jessica Paige Markley, Laura Anne Markley. BA, Smith Coll., 1972; JD, U. Calif., 1977. Bar: Calif. 1977. Assoc. to ptnr. Donahue Gallagher Woods, Oakland, Calif., 1977-87; sr. counsel Bank of Am., San Francisco, 1987-89; assoc., gen. counsel Shaklee Corp., San Francisco, 1989-90; gen. counsel, v.p. Shaklee U.S., Inc., San Francisco, 1990-94, Shaklee U.S., Shaklee Technica, 1995-99, 1999—, Yamanouchi Pharma Techs., Inc., 1999-2001; gen. counsel, sr. v.p. Shaklee Corp., 2001—. Judge pro tem Oakland Piedmont Emeryville Mcpl. Ct., 1982-89; fee arbitrator Alameda Co. Bar Assn., 1980-87. Mem. ABA, Calif. Bar Assn., Calif. Employment Law Coun. (bd. dirs. 1993—). Jewish. Office: Shaklee Corp 4747 Willow Rd Pleasanton CA 94588-2740

FINE, MICHAEL JOSEPH, publishing company executive; b. N.Y.C., Jan. 30, 1937; s. William and Rosa F.; m. Marlene Rosen, Apr. 4, 1959; children: Anton Adeus, Kaethe Elizabeth. Student, U. Fla., 1953-54; BA, Bklyn. Coll., 1957; postgrad., State U. Iowa, 1959-60. Propr. Paper Place Bookstore, Iowa City, 1960-63; v.p. Paperback Affiliates, Inc., N.Y.C., 1963-74; mgr., co-owner The Paperback Forum Bookstore, N.Y.C.; mgr. The Manhattanville Book Forum, Manhattanville Coll., Purchase, N.Y.; asst. to pres. Simon & Schuster, Inc., N.Y.C., 1964-65, v.p. Assoc. Ednl. Svcs., 1966, assoc. dir. Washington Square Press, 1967-69, mem. editl. bd., 1968; founder, pub. trade paperback divsn. Simon & Schuster Clarion Books, N.Y.C., 1967-69; founder, exec. v.p. Bookthrift, Inc., 1971-78; pres. Bookthrift, Inc. div. Simon & Schuster, 1978-81; sr. v.p., exec. com. mem. Ingram Book Co., Nashville, 1981-83; pres., chief exec. officer Ingram Ventures, Inc., N.Y.C., 1981-83; chief exec. officer Feeling Fine Programs, Inc., 1984-86; co-founder, pres. Lynx Communications, Inc., N.Y.C., 1987-90; founder, pres. Fine Creative Media, Inc., N.Y.C., 1991—. Pub. MJF Books, Prod. Barnes and Noble Classics. Contbr. articles to profl. jours. Past chmn. bd. dirs. St. Michaels Montessori Sch., N.Y.C.; bd. dirs. Morningside Area Alliance, Inc., 1974-83. Mem. N.Y. Acad. Scis. (mem. publs. com. 1984-88), Nat. Arts Club. Office: Fine Comm MJF Books 322 8th Ave New York NY 10001 *The older I become the more I am struck by how uniquely independent each of us is, one from the other and, at the same time, how urgently connected we all are, one to each other. To publish is to navigate the time and the space between the two .*

FINE, MIRIAM BROWN, artist, educator, poet, writer; b. Vineland, N.J., Mar. 8, 1913; d. Abraham and Katie (Walidarsky) Brown; m. Irvin Fine, Nov. 3, 1935; children: Ruth Fileen Fine, Adele Aviva Fine Gross. BFA, The U. the Arts (formerly Indsl. Sch. Arts) and U. Pa., 1935; postgrad., Cheltenham (Pa.) Art Sch., 1968-77, Temple U., 1976-91. Tchr. art and watercolor painting Phila. Pub. Schs., 1953-60; lectr., watercolor tchr. Assn. Ret. Profls. Temple U., 1976-92. Pvt. tchr. art, Phila., 1952-77; geriatric poster contest judge and program cover design Pa. Podiatric Med. Assn., 1984-95; tchr., vis. artist Abington Friends Com., 1989-90; tchr. watercolor N.E. Cultural Art Coun. Phila., 1987-90; tchr. watercolor, speaker poetry forum David G. Neuman Sr. Ctr., Jewish Community Ctr. Phila., 1991—. Executed 7 murals at Spruance Elem. Sch., Phila., 1951, Holocaust oils and watercolors displayed in Temple Sholom Synagogue, Oxford Cir. Synagogue, UN Women's Conf., Nairobi, Kenya, 1985—, Libr. Nat. Mus. Women in Arts, Washington, 1992—; 16 one-person exhbns. John Wanamaker's Fine Art Gallery, The Hahn Gallery, Cida Art Gallery, First Pa. Bank, Revsin Art Gallery, Frankford Trust Co., Temple U. Ctr. City, Northeast Regional Libr., Phila., 1996, Spring Art Exhbn. N.E. Regional Libr., 1997, Printmaking Gallery U. of Arts, Phila., 1998; group shows include: U.N. Women's Conference, Nairobi, Phila. Art Show, Provident Nat. Bank, Cheltenham Art Ctr., Art Alliance, Pa. Acad. Fine Arts, Phila. Mus. Art, Camden County Hist. Soc., Rutgers Coll., Frankford Women's Art League, Pennock Art & Flower Show, Nat. Coun. Jewish Women, Immaculata Coll., Ocean City Art League, Artist Equity, Cape May Art Ctr.; author: (poetry and illustrations) Word and Drawings, 1984, (in braille) 1996, Mom I Didn't Know It Was Like That, Family History, 1984, The Full Moon Energises My Creativity, 1988, You Are in My Galaxy, 1990, That's Life, 1992, Flowers I, 1993 (Nat. Mus. Women in Arts, Washington), Treasures of Miriam Brown Fine for You, 1993; author, illustrator: My Bible, 1994; contbr. watercolor paintings on boxes and book covers Continental Box Co., 1995, Flower Book VII, 1996, Flower Book VIII, 1996, Flower Book IX, 1997, Flower Book X, 1998, Flower Book XI, 1999, Flower Book XII, 2000-02, cover (Passover prayer book) The Haggadah, 1998 (honored by Am. Jewish Congress, Pa. region, 1998); author: Poetry from My Soul, 1998. Did benefit for St. Christopher's Children's Hosp., Phila., 1984-87; mem. Torch of Life chpt. City of Hope, Phila., 1935—, mem. Herman chpt., 1992—; vol. Overbrook Sch. for the Blind, Phila., 1991—. Recipient Phila. Art Tchrs. award, 1956, Chapel of Four Chaplains Humanitarian award Torch of Life chpt. City of Hope, 1964, Nat. Synagogue Women's League award, Frankford Women's League award, 50 Yr. Svc. award 1981, 60 Yr. Svc. award 1991, Solomon Schector Illustrated Book award, City Coun. Citizen award City of Phila., 1996, award City of Hope, 1996; Bd. Edn. Art scholar, 1931; Citation in honor of Miriam Brown Fine for her artistic and literary contbn. to the life of the City of Phila. and N.E. Regional Libr., 1996. Mem. NOW, Artists Equity Inc., Phila. Watercolor Club (hon.), Women's Caucus for Art, Univ. Arts Alumni Assn., Acad. Am. Poets, Nat. Fedn. State Poetry Socs., Writers Cadence Crafters, Poets Study Group, Nat. Mus. of Women in Arts (charter mem.), Temple U. Assn. Ret. Profls. (pres. emeritus, award), Pa. State Poetry Socs., Fight for Sight. Republican. Jewish. Avocations: music, teaching, sharing knowledge, learning. Home: Brith Sholom House 3939 Conshohocken Ave Apt 820 Philadelphia PA 19131-5470

FINE, MORRIS EUGENE, materials engineer, educator; b. Jamestown, N.D., Apr. 12, 1918; s. Louis and Sophie (Berrington) F.; m. Mildred Eleanor Glazer, Aug. 13, 1950; children: Susan Elaine, Amy Lynn. B.Metall. Engring. with distinction, U. Minn., 1940, MS, 1942, PhD, 1943. Instr. U. Minn., 1942-43; mem. tech. staff Bell Telephone Labs., Murray Hill, N.J., 1946-54; prof. emeritus Northwestern U., Evanston, Ill., 1954—, prof., chmn. dept. metallurgy Tech. Inst., 1955-57, chmn. dept. materials sci., 1958-60, prof. and chmn. materials research center, 1960-64, Walter P. Murphy prof. materials sci., 1963-89, tech. inst. prof., 1985-89, dir. Am. Iron and Steel Inst. steel resource ctr., 1986-93, assoc. dean grad. studies and research Tech. Inst., 1973-85, prof. emeritus, 1989, mem. grad. faculty, 1989—. Vis. prof. dept. materials sci. Stanford U., 1967-68; JSPS vis. scholar, Japan, 1979; chmn., vis. prof. materials sci. and engring. U. Tex., Austin, 1984-95; assoc. engr. Manhattan Project, U. Chgo. and Los Alamos, N.Mex., WWII; mem. materials adv. bd. NRC, 1963-68; mem. com. geol. and materials scis. NRC, 1979-82; chmn. adv. bd. program on modular methods for tchg. materials Pa. State U., 1973-77; chmn. vis. com. metallurgy and materials Sci. and Materials Rsch. Ctr., Lehigh U., 1965-75; mem. vis. com. Lawrence Berkeley Lab., 1978-81, chmn., 1981, mem. vis. com. Ames Dept. Energy Lab., 1976-80, Materials Rsch. Ctr., Pa. State U., 1988-91, Colo. Sch. Mines, 1991-96; chmn., organizer numerous confs. in field. Author numerous tech. and sci. articles on mech. properties of metals and ceramics, fatigue of metals, phase transformations, high temperature alloys, and other subjects.; author: Introduction to Phase Transformation in Condensed Systems. Recipient Gilbert Speich award Iron and Steel Soc., 1993; named Chicagoan of Year in Sci., 1961 Fellow Am. Phys. Soc., Japan Soc. Metals (hon.), Am. Soc. Metals (chpt. chmn. 1963, Campbell lectr. 1979, chmn. seminar com. 1979, hon. mem. com. 1993-96, gold medal 1986), Metall Soc. of AIME (chmn. inst. metals div. 1966-68, bd. dirs. 1968-71, bd. dirs. inst. 1972-75, mem. Bardeen gold medals com. 1992-96, chmn. 1995-96, Mathewson gold medal for rsch. 1981, James Douglas gold medal 1982, Educator award 1993, hon. mem.), Am. Ceramic Soc. (keynote lectr. electronic materials div. 1972); mem. NAE (astronautics space engring. bd. 1973-77, membership com. 1974-79, chmn. 1977-78, mem. membership adv. com. 1991-94), AAAS, Scripta Met et Mat (Outstanding Paper award 1991), The Metals, Materials, Minerals Soc. (inst. metals lecture and R.F. Mehl gold medal 1996), Sigma Xi, Tau Beta Pi, Alpha Sigma Mu, Sigma Alpha Sigma. Home: 1101 Manor Dr Wilmette IL 60091-1026 Office: Dept Materials Sci and Engring Northwestern U Evanston IL 60208-3108 E-mail: m-fine@northwestern.edu.

FINE, PAM, newspaper editor; Mng. editor Mpls. Star Tribune. Office: Star Tribune 425 Portland Ave Minneapolis MN 55488-0002

FINE, ROBERT PAUL, lawyer; b. Buffalo, June 10, 1943; s. Leonard and Sylvia (Wagner) Finkelstein; m. Eileen Joyce Levitsky, Nov. 26, 1967; children: Lisa Robin, Julie Beth. BA, SUNY, Buffalo, 1965, JD, 1968. Bar: NY 1968, US Dist. Ct. (we. dist.) NY 1969, U.S. Tax Ct. 1973, Fla. 1985. Intern US Dept. Justice, Washington, 1967; law asst. appellate divsn. 4th jud. dept. NY Supreme Ct., Rochester, NY, 1968-69, chief law asst., 1969-70; assoc. Williams, Stevens, McCarville & Frizzell, P.C., Buffalo, 1970-74, ptnr., 1974-77; co-founder, sr. ptnr. Hurwitz & Fine, P.C., Buffalo, 1977—. Mem. Buffalo and Erie County Pvt. Industry Coun., 1988—95; exec. com., counsel local organizing com. World Univ. Games, Buffalo, 1993; adj. prof. SUNY Buffalo Sch. Law, 1996—; bd. dir. Roswell Pk. Cancer Inst., chair fin. com. Bd. dirs. United Jewish Fedn., 1979-84, treas., 1982-84, v.p., 1986-88; chmn. exec. bd. We. NY Israel Bonds, 1980-82; mem. Dean's Adv. Coun., SUNY Buffalo Law Sch., mem. dean search com., 1986-87; mem. dept. jud. screening com. 4th dept. appellate divsn. state of NY, 1999—, Magistrate Judge, merit selection panel we. dist. NY, 1990—, chair, 2000—. Mem. ABA, NY State Bar Assn. (exec. com. bus. law sect.), Fla. Bar Assn., Erie County Bar Assn. (chmn. tax com. 1978-81, chmn. corp. law com. 1981-84, bd. dirs. 1985-88)), Fin. Planning Counselors We. NY (pres. 1986-87), Estate Analysts We. NY, Nat. Health Lawyers Assn., SUNY Sch. Law Alumni Assn. (pres. 1976-77), Mid-Day of Buffalo Club, Westwood Country Club (Williamsville, NY), Buffalo Club (dir. 2001-). Office: Hurwitz & Fine PC 1300 Liberty Building Buffalo NY 14202-3670

FINE, ROGER SETH, pharmaceutical executive, lawyer; b. Bklyn., Sept. 22, 1942; s. Jack F. and Mildred (Perlmutter) F.; m. Rebecca Gold, June 14, 1964; children: David, Adam. BA, Columbia Coll., 1963; LLB, NYU, 1966. Bar: N.Y. 1966, U.S. Dist. Ct. (so. dist.) N.Y. 1967, U.S. Ct. Appeals (2d cir.) 1967. Assoc. Cahill, Gordon & Reindel, N.Y.C., 1966-74; gen. atty. Johnson & Johnson, New Brunswick, N.J., 1974-78, asst. gen. counsel, 1978-84, assoc. gen. counsel, 1984-91, v.p. adminstrn., mem. exec. com., 1991-95, v.p., gen. counsel, mem. exec. com., 1996—. Mem. ABA. Home: 26 Brook Dr Milltown NJ 08850-1932 Office: Johnson & Johnson 1 Johnson And Johnson Plz New Brunswick NJ 08933-0002*

FINE, SALLY SOLFISBURG, artist, educator; b. Aurora, Ill., July 20, 1948; d. Roy John Jr. and Edith Warrick (Squires) Solfisburg; m. Philip Clark Fine, May 5, 1973 (div. 1997); children: Alexander, Arielle. BFA, Ohio U., 1970; postgrad., Boston U., 1978-82, MFA, 1984. Graphic designer Mus. of Sci., Boston, 1970-72; teaching fellow Boston U., 1980-81; instr., lectr. U. Mass., North Dartmouth, 1993-95; sr. lectr. Bradford Coll., 1995-96, asst. prof., 1996-2000; assoc. prof. art. Regis Coll., Weston, Mass., 2000—. Prin. S.S. Fine Design, Boston, 1970—. Solo shows include Viridian Gallery, N.Y.C., Bradford Coll., Chapel Gallery; exhibited in group shows at DeCordova Mus., Lincoln, Mass., Danforth Mus. of Art., Framingham, Mass., Brockton (Mass.) Art Mus., Newport (R.I.) Art Mus., A.I.R. Gallery, N.Y.C., Cité Internationale Gallerie, Paris. Bd. dirs. Kendall Ctr. for the Arts, 1983-86. Visual Artists grantee Mass. Coun. for the Arts, 1995, Sculpture fellow New Eng., Found. for the Arts, 1995, others. Mem. AAUP, Coll. Art Assn. Avocations: swimming, gardening, biking. Office: Regis Coll 235 Wellesley St Weston MA 02493-1571 E-mail: sally.fine@regiscollege.edu.

FINE, TONI MICHELE, law educator; b. N.Y.C., Feb. 7, 1961; d. Seymour and Wilma Gangel Fine. BA, SUNY, Binghamton, 1983; JD, Duke U., 1986. Bar: Pa. 1986, D.C. 1988, U.S. Ct. Appeals (D.C. cir.) 1988. Assoc. Crowell & Moring, Washington, 1986-93; assoc. professorial lectr. in law George Washington U. Law Ctr., Washington, 1992-93; lawyering instr. NYU Law Sch., N.Y.C., 1993-93, coord. Master Comparative Jurisprudence program, 1995-98 assoc. dir. global law sch. program, 1998-2000, acting dir. LLM (CJ) program, 1999-2000; dir. grad. and internat. programs Benjamin N. Cardozo Sch. Law, 2000—. Author: Americal Legal Systems: A Resource and Reference Guide, 1997; contbr. articles to profl. jours. Mem.: Am. Assn. Law Schs. (chair sect. on grad. programs for fgn. students 2001, sect. internat. legal exch. chair 2002), Phi Beta Kappa, Pi Sigma Alpha. Office: Cardozo Sch Law 55 Fifth Ave New York NY 10003 Fax: 212-790-0232. E-mail: tfine@ymail.yu.edu.

FINE, WILLIAM IRWIN, real estate developer; b. St. Paul, May 26, 1928; s. Adolph and Ida (Cohen) F.; m. Bianca M. Fine, Apr. 10, 1994. BLS, U. Minn., 1949, LLB, 1950. Bar: Minn. 1950, Tex. 1950. Asst. dist. atty. Dallas County, 1950-52; judge adv. gen. USAF, Keesler AFB, Miss., 1952-53; ptnr., founder Fine, Simon & Schneider, Mpls., 1953-69; pres., co-founder Fine Properties Corp., Chgo., 1969-71; mng. gen. ptnr., co-founder Fine Assocs., Mpls., from 1972; co-founder VISTA Sci., Inc., 1991, DYUAR, Inc., 1992. Advisor Inst. Tech. U. Minn., Mpls., 1987—. Trustee Sci. Mus. Minn., St. Paul, 1989-94; co-founder/co-chmn. William I. Fine Theoretical Physics Inst. U. Minn., 1987; charter mem. indsl. liaison com. Materials Rsch. Lab. U. Chgo., 1993-97. Mem. AAAS, Am. Inst. Physics. Home: Minneapolis, Minn. Died May 18, 2002.

FINE, WILLIAM IRWIN, lawyer; b. Hammond, Ind., Feb. 2, 1951; s. Leonard and Sylvia (Appleman) F.; m. Adele Barbara Hult; children: Rachel, Sarah, Rebecca. AB, Ind. U., 1973, JD, 1976; MA, Purdue U., 1996. Bar: Ind. 1976, U.S. Dist. Ct. (no. dist.) Ind. 1987. Assoc. Efron, Efron & Komyatte, Hammond, 1977-79, Efron and Efron, Hammond, 1979-88; pvt. practice, Highland, Ind., 1988—. Fellow Anglo-Zulu War Hist. Soc.; mem. Ind. State Bar Assn., Lake County Bar Assn., Phi Beta Kappa. Home: 1341 Fitzgerald Dr Munster IN 46321-4203 Office: 2833 Lincoln St Ste F Highland IN 46322-1924

FINEBERG, HARVEY VERNON, professional society administrator; b. Pitts., Sept. 15, 1945; s. Saul and Miriam (Pearl) F.; m. Mary Elizabeth Wilson, May 16, 1975 AB, Harvard U., 1967, MD, M.P.P., Harvard U., 1972, PhD, 1980. Intern Beth Israel Hosp., Boston, 1972—73; asst. prof. Sch. Pub. Health, Harvard U., Boston, 1973—78, assoc. prof., 1978—81, prof., 1981—2002, dean Sch. Pub. Health, 1984—97; provost Harvard U., Cambridge, Mass., 1997—2001; physician East Boston Health Ctr., 1974—76, Harvard Street Health Ctr., 1976—84; pres. Inst. of Medicine, Washington, 2002—. Jr. fellow Harvard U., 1974—75; Mellon fellow, 1976. Co-author: Clinical Decision Analysis, 1980, The Epidemic That Never Was, 1983. Trustee Newton Wellesley Hosp., Mass., 1981-86; study sect. chmn. Nat. Ctr. Health Services Research, Rockville, Md., 1982-85; active Pub. Health Council, Mass., 1976-79; bd. dirs. Am. Found. AIDS Rsch., 1986-97. Mem.: Soc. Med. Decision Making (pres. 1980—81), Inst. Medicine (pres. 2002). Jewish. Home: 1812 Kalorama Sq NW Washington DC 20008-4022 Office: Inst of Medicine 500 5th St NW Washington DC 20001-2721

FINEBERG, ROBERT ALAN, lawyer; b. Portland, Maine, May 29, 1948; s. Samuel and Lillian (Smith) F.; m. Virginia June Brealey, Aug. 22, 1970; children: Cynthia Joy, Daniel Harwood. BA, U. Conn., 1970; JD, Temple U., 1975. Bar: Pa. 1976, N.J. 1976, U.S. Dist. Ct. (ea. dist.) Pa. 1976, U.S. Dist. Ct. N.J. 1976, U.S. Supreme Ct. 1981; cert. civil trial atty. Assoc. Charles Blasband, Norristown, Pa., 1975-76, Perskie & Callinan, Wildwood, N.J., 1976-79; sole practice Wildwood, 1979-81; ptnr. Fineberg & Rodgers, North Wildwood, N.J., 1981-89; sole practice Cape May Courthouse, 1989—. Solicitor Borough of Avalon, N.J., 1979-87, Borough of Wildwood Crest, N.J., 1985-89, Bd. of Edn. of City of Cape May, N.J., 1983-91, City of Cape May, 1991-99, City of Cape May Hist. Preservation Commn., 1999—. Bd. dirs. Assn. for Retarded Citizens of Cape May County, Rio Grande, N.J., 1982-87, Cape May Jazz Festival; pres. Wildwood Crest Civic Assn., 1985-87; mem. Bd. Edn. Middle Township, N.J., 1990—. Mem. ATLA, ABA, N.J. State Bar Assn., Assn. N.J. Trial Lawyers, Cape May County Bar Assn., N.J. Inst. Mcpl. Attys., Phi Beta Kappa, Phi Kappa Phi, Delta Sigma Rho, Pi Sigma Alpha. Clubs: Union League (Cape May County, N.J.). Lodges: Lions. Democrat. Jewish. Home: 24 Chestnut Ave Cape May Court House NJ 08210-2623 Office: 208 N Main St Cape May Court House NJ 08210-2122 E-mail: courtlaw@bellatlantic.net.

FINEGOLD, AMY BETH, elementary school educator, consultant; b. Bklyn., June 10, 1968; d. Ira and Barbara May Finegold. BA, Univ. Miami, 1990; MA, Ind. State U., 1992, N.Y.U., 1999. Cert. tchr. N.Y. Tchr. ESL N.Y. Bd. Edn., N.Y.C., 1997—. New tchr. staff devel. tchr.; elem. lang. trainer; geography cons. N.Y. Geographic Alliance; mem. spl. interest group N.Y. State Tchrs. Eng. to Spkrs. Other Langs., 1997—2001; presenter in field. Contbr. articles to newsletters. Vol., chair events for entertainment United Jewish Appeal Fedn. Young Leadership, 1995—98; mem. Make A Wish Found., NY, 1997. Grantee, Excell, N.Y., 1998, United Fedn. Tchrs., 1998; scholar, NYU, 1996—97. Mem.: Manhattan Soc., Kappa Delta Pi, Pi Lambda Theta (membership chair, historian). Republican. Jewish. Avocations: reading, dancing. Home: 309 East 49th St Apt 5B New York NY 10017

FINEGOLD, DAVID NEAL, medical educator; b. Pitts., Oct. 5, 1947; BS in Physics, U. Pitts., 1968, MD, 1972. Bd. cert. Am. Bd. Pediat., Am. Bd. Pediat. Endocrinology, Am. Bd. Med. Genetics. Intern and resident Children's Hosp. Pitts., 1972-75; postdoctoral rsch. fellow George S. Cox Med. Rsch. Inst., Hosp. U. Pa., Phila., 1975-77; JDF fellow Children's Hosp. Phila., 1977-78; rsch. assoc. dept. biochemistry and biophyics U. Pa., Phila., 1978-81, asst. prof. pediatrics, 1979-81, U. Pitts., 1981-88, asst. prof. medicine, 1981-88, assoc. prof. pediatrics, 1989-96, prof. pediatrics, 1996—, assoc. prof. medicine, 1989-96, prof. medicine, 1996—. Clin. assoc. dept. pediat. U. Pa., Phila., 1978-79; asst. physician dept. medicine, Divsn. Endocrinology and Diabetes, Children's Hosp. of Phila., 1978-81, animal rsch. and care com., 1986—, libr. com., 1986—, clin. lab. use com., 1988—, human rights com., 1990—; med. adv. bd. Biocontrol Tech., Inc., 1989—; lectr. and rschr. in field. Contbr. chpts. to books and articles to profl. jours. Mem. Am. Diabetes Assn. (bd. mem. Pa. affiliate 1990—, pres. Pa. affiliate 1990-91, vice chair-vol. devel. com. Pa. affiliate 1991—, chair affiliate rsch. com. 1992—, exec. bd. mem. western Pa. affiliate 1981-90, chmn. profl. edn. com. Pa. affiliate 1982-86, v.p. western Pa. affiliate 1987-88, pres. western affiliate 1988-90, Recognition award), Am. Fedn. for Clin. Rsch., Am. Soc. Nephrology, Am. Soc. Human Genetics, Am. Assn. Diabetes Educators, Endocrine Soc., Soc. for Pediat. Rsch., Soc. for Inherited Metabolic Disease, Lawson Wilkins Pediat. Endocrine Soc. Office: Divsn Endocrinology Childrens Hosp Pitts 3705 5th Ave Pittsburgh PA 15213-2524

FINEGOLD, MAURICE NATHAN, architect; b. Providence, Sept. 6, 1932; s. Samuel R. and Ruth (Marks) F.; m. Muriel Ann Savitz, Apr. 30, 1964; Jordan, Daniel Warren, Jonathan Eric, Michael Andrew. AB, Harvard Coll., 1954; MArch, Harvard U., 1958. Lic. architect. Mass., and 15 other states. Prin. Maurice N. Finegold & Assocs., AIA, Architect, Boston, 1964-69; ptnr. Finegold & Bullis, Architects, Boston, 1969-74; prin. Notter Finegold & Alexander, Boston, 1974-92; pres. Finegold Alexander & Assocs., Inc., Boston, 1992—. Chair Mass. Bd. of Registration of Architects, Boston, 1989-91. Bd. dirs. Downtown North Assn., Boston, 1990—, pres. 1997-99; mem. New Eng. Holocaust Meml. Com., Boston, 1990—; chair presdl. search com. Boston Archtl. Ctr., 1990-91, 96-97, bd. dirs., 1994—, vice chair bd. dirs., 1995-99, chair, bd. dirs., 1999-2003. Sgt. U.S. Army, 1958-64. Fellow AIA (numerous local and nat. design awards, Frey award 2002), Soc. for Arts, Religion and Contemporary Culture; mem. ALA, Boston Soc. Architects (chmn. several coms. 1961—), Soc. Coll. and Univ. Planning, Nat. Trust for Hist. Preservation, League Hist. Am. Theaters. Democrat. Jewish. Avocations: sailing, skiing, travel. Office: Finegold Alexander & Assocs Inc 77 N Washington St Boston MA 02114-1908 E-mail: mnf@faainc.com.

FINEGOLD, RONALD, computer services executive; b. Bklyn., Nov. 17, 1942; s. Herman Hearsch and Ethel (Kanner) F.; m. Ellen Carole Sehr, Mar. 22, 1964; children: Sherry Dawn, Edward Jon. BS, CCNY, 1963. Supr. programming Celanese Chem. Co., N.Y.C., 1962-66; v.p. mktg Automation Scis., Inc., N.Y.C., 1966-69; pres. Computer Horizons Corp., N.Y.C., 1969-82, chmn. bd., 1977-82, dir., 1969-82; chmn. bd. Stamford Assocs., Inc., N.Y.C., 1969-75; pres., dir. Rizons Brokerage, Inc., 1970-71, chmn. bd. dirs., 1972-75; chmn. bd. Custom Terminals Corp., 1976-82; pres. Skylane Corp., 1977—. Chmn. bd., dir. Starlex Systems & Svcs., Inc., 1983-89; bd. dirs. Atlantic Sports & Entertainment, Ltd., Exec. Sports Network, Inc. Mem. Data Processing Mgmt. Assn., Am. Mgmt. Assn., Young Pres.'s Orgn., Aircraft Owners and Pilots Assn., Tau Epsilon Phi. Home: 5686 NW 38th Ter Boca Raton FL 33496-2719

FINEGOLD, SYDNEY MARTIN, microbiology educator; b. N.Y.C., Aug. 12, 1921; s. Samuel Joseph and Jennie (Stein) F.; m. Mary Louise Saunders, Feb. 8, 1947 (dec. June 1994); children: Joseph, Patricia, Michael; m. Gloria Weiss, Feb. 18, 1996. AB, UCLA, 1943; MD, U. Tex., 1949. Diplomate: Am. Bd. Med. Microbiology (mem. bd. 1979-85), Am. Bd. Internal Medicine. Intern USPHS, Galveston, Tex., 1949-50; fellow in medicine U. Minn. Med. Sch., 1950-52, research fellow, 1951-52; resident medicine Wadsworth Hosp., VA Ctr., Los Angeles, 1953-54; instr. medicine U. Calif. Med. Ctr., Los Angeles, 1955-57, asst. clin. prof., 1957-59, asst. prof., 1959-62, assoc. prof., 1962-68, prof., 1968—2000, emeritus, 2000—, prof. microbiology and immunology, 1983—2000, emeritus, 2000—; chief chest and infectious disease sect. Wadsworth Hosp., 1957-61, chief infectious disease sect., 1961-86, assoc. chief staff for research and devel., 1986-92; staff physician infectious disease sect. VA Med. Ctr., L.A., 1992—. Mem. pulmonary disease rsch. program com. VA, 1961-62, infectious disease rsch. program com., 1961-65, merit rev. bd. (infectious diseases), 1972-74, med. rsch. program specialist, 1974-76, adv. com. on infectious disease, 1974-87; mem. NRC-Nat. Acad. Sci. Drug Efficacy Study Group, 1966-69; mem. subcom. on gram-negative anaerobic bacilli Internat. Com. on Nomenclature Bacteria, 1966—, chmn., 1972-78; mem. adv. panel U.S. Pharmacopoeia, 1970-75; chmn. working group on anaerobic susceptibility test methods Nat. Com. Clin. Lab. Standards, 1987-97, advisor, 1998-2002. Mem. editl. bd. Calif. Medicine, 1966-73, Applied Microbiology, 1973-74, Western Jour. Medicine, 1974-77, Am. Rev. Respiratory Disease, 1974-76, Jour. Clin. Microbiology, 1975-85, Infection, 1976—, Jour. Infectious Disease, 1979-82, 84-85, Antimicrobial Agts. Chemotherapy, 1980-89, Diagnostic Microbiology and Infectious Diseases, 1982-90; editor Revs. of Infectious Diseases, 1990-91, Clin. Infectious Diseases, 1992-2000; sect. editor: infectious diseases vols. Clin. Medicine, 1978-82, Microbiol. Ecology in Health and Disease, 1987-90; assoc. editor, consulting editor Anaerobe, 1994—, editor-in-chief, 1998—. Vice chmn. UCLA Acad. Senate, 1986-87, chair, 1987-88. Served with USMCR, with USNR, 1943-46, to 1st. lt. AUS, 1952-53. Co-recipient V.A. Williams S. Middleton award for biomed. rsch., 1984; recipient Profl. Achievement award UCLA, 1987, Mayo Soley award Western Soc. Clin. Investigation, 1988, Disting. Alumnus award U. Tex. Med. Br., 1988, UCLA Med. Alumni Assn. Med. Scis. award, 1990, Hoechst Roussel award Am. Soc. Microbiology, 1992, medal Helsinki U., Finland, 1996, Lifetime Achievement award Infectious Disease Assn. Calif., 1995, Wm. H. Oldendorf Lifetime Achievement awrd VA Med. Ctr., 1996, Lifetime Achievement award Internat. Soc. Anaerobic Bacteriology, 1998, Becton Dickinson award in Clin. Microbiology, 1999; organism named Finegoldia magna, 1999. Master ACP; fellow APHA, AAAS, Am. Acad. Microbiology, Infectious Diseases Soc. Am. (councilor 1976-79, pres.-elect 1980-81, pres. 1981-82, exec. com. 1980-83, Bristol award 1987, Soc. citation 1999); mem. Assn. Am. Physicians, Am. Soc. Microbiology (chmn. subcom. on taxonomy of Bacteroidaceae 1971-74, 1st annual Alex Sonnenwirth award 1986), Am. Thoracic Soc., Western Soc. Clin. Rsch., Western Assn. Physicians, Wadsworth Med. Alumni Assn. (past pres.), Anaerobe Soc. of the Ams. (interim pres. 1992-94, pres. 1994-96), Soc. Intestinal Microbiology Ecology and Disease (interim pres. 1982-83, pres. 1983-87), Va. Soc. Physician in Infectious Diseases (pres. 1986-88), Am. Fedn. Clin. Rsch., Sigma Xi, Alpha Omega Alpha. Democrat. Jewish. Office: Infectious Disease Sect VA Med Ctr Wilshire & Sawtelle Blvds Los Angeles CA 90073 Home: 13082 Mindanao Way #17 Marina Del Rey CA 90292 E-mail: sidfinegol@aol.com.

FINELSEN, LIBBI JUNE, lawyer; b. Encino, Calif., Apr. 14, 1968; BA in Polit. Sci. summa cum laude, U. Nev., 1990; JD magna cum laude, Lewis and Clark Coll., 1993. Bar: D.C. 1996, U.S. Ct. Appeals (9th, 11th and D.C. cirs.) 1996, U.S. Ct. Appeals (4th cir.) 1999, U.S. Ct. Appeals (fedl. cir.) 2001, Ct. Fed. Claims 2001. Jud. law clk. Gen. Svcs. Bd. Contract Appeals, Washington, 1993-94; assoc. McAleese & Assocs. P.C., McLean, Va., 1994-96; atty. USDA, Washington, 1996-99; trial atty. U.S. Dept. Air Force, Wright Patterson AFB, Ohio, 2000—01; atty./adv. U.S. Dept. Air Force, L.A. AFB, 2001—. V.p. edn. Hadassah Young Profls. Group, Washington, 1998-99; mem. hospitality com. Kesher Israel Synagogue, Washington, 1998-99. Mem. ABA, Phi Alpha Delta, Phi Kappa Phi. Avocations: cooking, handicrafts, travel, art exhibitions.

FINEMAN, JEANETTE KRULEVITZ, retired artist; b. Balt., Apr. 21, 1919; d. Jacob and Ruth Irene Krulevitz; m. Jerome Fineman, Jan. 4, 1947 (dec. Jan. 1978); children: David, Elliott, Mary. Degree in med. illustration, U. Md., 1940; BFA cum laude, Md. Inst. Coll. Art, 1970, MFA, 1972. Med. illustrator Sinai Hosp., Balt., 1940, Charleston (W.Va.) Gen. Hosp., 1941-43; head art dept. St. Timothy's Sch., Stevenson, Md., 1973-79; ret., 1979. One-woman shows include Johns Hopkins U., Balt., Villa Julie Coll., Balt., Oheb Shalom Temple, Balt., Balt. Hebrew Cong.; exhibited in group shows at Corcoron Gallery Art, Washington, Balt. Mus., Peale Mus., Balt. (prize), NY Acad. Design (prize); contbr. illustrations to profl. jours. Mem. Oakland (Calif.) Mus. Home: 8 Admiral Dr Apt # 425 Emeryville CA 94608-1567

FINERAN, DIANA LOU, association administrator; b. Rice Lake, Wis., Dec. 25, 1945; d. Earl Orin and Leona May (Steltzner) Frommader; m. John James Fineran, III, Apr. 28, 1979. Grad. high sch., Rice Lake. Tel. operator Wis. Tel. Co., Rice Lake, 1964-69; svc. rep. Gen. Tel. Co., Rice Lake, 1969-79, Dallas, Tex., 1979-80; founder, sec., treas. The Traditional Cat Assn. Inc., Jonesborough, Tenn., 1987-92, Alpharetta, Ga., 1992-96, Battle Ground, Wash., 1996—. Contbr. articles to mags. Leader 4-H, Jonesborough, 1990. Lutheran. Avocations: animal training, sewing, outdoor activities. Home and Office: Traditional Cat Assn Inc 18509 NE 279th St Battle Ground WA 98604-9717 E-mail: diana@traditionalcats.com.

FINERTY, MARTIN JOSEPH, JR., military officer, researcher, association management executive; b. Wilmington, Del., July 22, 1936; s. Martin Joseph and Jane Morris (McClenaghan) F.; m. Joan Eddleman, Dec. 3, 1960; children: Nancy Jane, Laura Tourison. BSE, U.S. Naval Acad., 1959; MS in Phys. Oceanography, U. Miami, Coral Gables, Fla., 1966; MS in Indsl. Mgmt., Coll. of the Armed Forces, 1979. Commd. ensign USN, 1959, advanced though grades to capt., 1985; head, polar programs Office of Oceanographer of Navy, Alexandria, Va., 1975-76; spl. asst. submarines Office of Asst. Sec. of Navy, Washington, 1976-77; spl. asst. ocean environ. Office of Chief of Naval Ops., Washington, 1977-78; commdg. officer Naval Polar Oceanography Ctr., Washington, 1982-85; program officer NAS, Washington, 1985-87; asst. dir. rsch. ASME, Washington, 1987-88; exec. dir., COO Marine Tech. Soc., Washington, 1988-99; sr. cons. editor Compass Publs., Arlington, Va., 1999—. Expert in ocean and hydro survey ops., polar programs and assn. mgmt. Author/editor tech. publs. Fellow Marine Tech. Soc.; mem. AAAS, Assn. of U.S. Naval Acad. Class of 1959 (sec. 1971-74), The Army Navy Club. Lodges: Masons. Avocations: reading, gardening. Home: 1841 Northbridge Ln Annapolis MD 21401-6576 E-mail: mjfjef@erols.com.

FINESILVER, ALAN GEORGE, rheumatologist; b. Hartford, Conn., Sept. 4, 1942; s. Merrill Joseph and Bernice Ruth (Kamerman) F.; m. Cynthia Ann Philbrook, Sept. 8, 1973; children: Matthew Phillip, Elizabeth Ann. AB, U. Rochester, 1964; MD, Yale U., 1968. Diplomate Nat. Bd. Med. Examiners, Am. Bd. Internal Medicine. Intern in surgery Beth Israel Hosp., Boston, 1968-69; fellow in radiation therapy Yale-New Haven Hosp., 1969-70; resident in internal medicine U. Mich. Med. Ctr., Ann Arbor, 1972-75; primary care physician Community Health Care Plan, New Haven, 1975-78; fellow in rheumatology U. Mo. Med. Ctr., Columbia, 1978-81, instr. medicine, 1981-82; rheumatologist Green Bay (Wis.) Clinic, 1982—2002, Aurora BayCare Health Ctr., Green Bay, 2002—. Lt. comdr. USN, 1970-72. Fellow Am. Coll. Rheumatology; mem. ACP. Avocations: sport fishing, tennis, photography. Office: Aurora BayCare Health Ctr 2253 W Mason St Green Bay WI 54303

FINESTONE, SHEILA, legislator, state official; b. Montreal, Que., Can., Jan. 28, 1927; d. Monroe and Minnie Abbey; m. Alan Finestone, June 9, 1947; children: David, Peter, Maxwell, Stephen. BS in Edn., McGill U. M.P. to Ho. of Commons for Mount Royal, 1984, 88, 93-99; critic for commn. and culture, 1985-93; Sec. of State Multiculturalism and the Status of Women, 1993-96; appt. Senate of Can., Ottawa, Canada, 1999—. Advisor to Parliament on eliminating anti-personal land mines. Pres. (hon.) Young Men and Young Women's Hebrew Assn.; mem. Nat. Coun. Jewish Women; hon. gov. Jewish Gen. Hosp.; mem. exec. com. Orgn. Jewish Parliament. Named Person of the Yr., McGill U., 2001; recipient Jackie Robinson Leadership award, 1996, Samuel Bronfinan Leadership award, 1995, O.R.T. Sophie Benett award, 1996. Mem. Orgn. Rehab. and Tng. Liberal.

FINGARETTE, HERBERT, philosopher, educator; b. Bklyn., Jan. 20, 1921; m. Leslie J. Swabacker, Jan. 23, 1945; 1 dau., Ann Hasse. BA, UCLA, 1947, PhD, 1949; LHD, St. Bonaventure U., 1993. Mem. faculty U. Calif.-Santa Barbara, 1948—, Phi Beta Kappa Romanell prof. philosophy, 1983—; William James lectr. religion Harvard U., 1971; W.T. Jones lectr. philosophy Pomona Coll., 1974; Evans-Wentz lectr. Oriental religions Stanford U., 1977; Gramlich lectr. human nature Dartmouth Coll., 1978; cons. NEH; Raphael Demos lectr. Vanderbilt U., 1985. Disting. tchr. U. Calif.-Santa Barbara, 1985, faculty research lectr., 1977. Author: The Self in Transformation, 1963, On Responsibility, 1967, Self Deception, 1969, Confucius: The Secular as Sacred, 1972, The Meaning of Criminal Insanity, 1972, Mental Disabilities and Criminals Responsibility, 1979, Heavy Drinking: The Myth of Alcoholism as a Disease, 1988, Rules, Rituals, and Responsibility: Essays Dedicated to Herbert Fingarette, 1991, Death: Philosophical Soundings, 1996. Washington and Lee U. Lewis law scholar, 1980; fellow NEH, NIMH, Walter Meyer Law Research Inst., Battelle Research Ctr., Addiction Research Ctr., Inst. Psychiatry, London; fellow Ctr. for Advanced Studies in Behavioral Sci., Stanford, 1985-86. Mem. Am. Philos. Assn. (pres. Pacific divsn. 1977-78). Home: 1507 APS Santa Barbara CA 93103 Office: U Calif Dept Philosophy Santa Barbara CA 93106

FINGER, HAROLD B. consultant; b. N.Y., Feb. 18, 1924; s. Beny and Anna (Perlmutter) F.; m. Arlene Karsch, June 11, 1949; children: Barbara Lynn Korengold, Elyse Sue Camozzo, Sandra Ruth Ciccarelli. BME, CCNY, 1944; MS in Aero Engring., Case Inst. Tech., 1950. With NASA and predecessor NACA, 1944-69; mgr. AEC-NASA Space Nuc. Propulsion Office, 1960-67; dir. nuc. sys. NASA, 1958-64, dir. space power and nuclear sys., 1964-67; dir. space nuc. sys. divsn. AEC, 1965-67; assoc. adminstr. for orgn. and mgmt. NASA, 1967-69; asst. sec. for rsch. and tech. HUD, 1969-72; mgr. electric utility engring. oper. GE, Schenectady, N.Y., 1972-74, gen. mgr. Ctr. for Energy Sys. Washington, 1972-80; staff exec. Power Sys. Strategic Planning and Devel., Fairfield, Conn., 1980-83; pres., CEO U.S. Com. for Energy Awareness, Washington, 1983-87, U.S. Coun. for Energy Awareness, Washington, 1987-91; cons. energy, space, nuc. energy, urban affairs, govt. mgmt. Recipient Manley Meml. award Soc. Automotive Engrs., 1958. Fellow: AIAA (James H. Wyld Propulsion award 1968), Nat. Acad. Pub. Adminstrn.; mem.: AAAS, AIA (hon.), NASA Alumni League (pres.), Nat. Housing Conf. (life trustee), Am. Nuc. Soc., Am. Soc. Pub. Adminstrn., Cosmos Club.

FINGER, IRIS DALE ABRAMS, elementary school educator; b. Ironton, Ohio, Jan. 22, 1939; d. Frank Abrams and Pearl (Moore) Schwab; m. Robert James Roderick Sr., July 20, 1957 (div. Nov. 1971); children: Robert James Roderick Jr., Elizabeth Ann Roderick Travis; m. Henry Waterman Bromley Jr., May 14, 1972 (div. June 1987); child: Henry Waterman Bromley III; m. Grover Cleveland Finger III, Apr. 1, 1989. Degree in early childhood and elem. edn., U. South Fla.; degree in design, Jackson Coll., Honolulu. Cert. middle sch. math. tchr.; cert. TESOL; cert. gifted edn. Children's libr. Ft. Myers (Fla.) Pub. Libr., 1955-57; workmen's compensation payroll adminstr. San Diego, 1964-66; permanent substitute tchr. Sigsbee Elem. Sch., Key West, Fla., 1968-70; part-time libr. Danielson (Conn.) Libr., 1970-71; residential design Bateman Homes, Leigh Acres, Fla., 1971-72; structural steel designer So. Machine and Steel, Ft. Myers, 1972-73; dir. Ft. Myers Bus. Coll., 1973-77; structural prestress concrete designer Southland Prestress, Dean Steel and Kirby MaCumber Steel, 1977-83; tchr. Lee County Sch. Bd., Ft. Myers, 1983—, team leader, math. coach, 1983, 94-95; with Bonita Spring Mid. Sch., 1994-96, equity coord., 1995-96. Pres. PTA, Key West, 1966-68, Fla. Art League, Ft. Myers, 1984-86; dir. Ft. Myers Bus. Coll., 1973-77; hosp. nurse ARC, 1964-66; med. evacuation for Vietnam wounded Philippine Islands Subic Hosp.; mem. Treasury of Island Coast Uni-Serve; rep. to Lee County Safety Com. Recipient Pres. Regan Achievement award, 1976, Pres. Johnson People to People award and plank award for sch. constrn. at San Meguel, the Philippines, 1960. Mem.: Am. Legion, VFW Aux., Navy Wives and Navy Relief Soc., Pioneer Club Ft. Myers, Lee County Math. Coun., Fla. Math. Coun., Rep. Assembly, Tchrs. Assn. Lee County, Fla. Tchrs. Profession, NEA, Phi Beta Kappa, Alpha Delta Kappa. Republican. Methodist. Avocations: arts and crafts, reading, vacationing at the beach, family socials, swimming. Home: PO Box 7068 Naples FL 34101-7068

FINGER, MICHAEL STEVEN, psychologist, educator, statistician, consultant; s. Louis and Janet S. Finger. BS, U. Ctrl. Fla., 1993; PhD, U. Minn., 2001. Asst. prof. psychology U. Kans., Lawrence, 2000—. Contbr., articles to profl. jours. Mem.: APA, Nat. Coun. on Measurement in Edn., Psychometric Soc., Am. Ednl. Rsch. Assn., Psi Chi (life). Office: Univ Kans 1415 Jayhawk Blvd Lawrence KS 66045 Personal E-mail: mfinger@ku.edu. E-mail: mfinger@ku.edu.

FINGER, ROBERT ROY, marketing executive; b. Lancaster, Pa., Jan. 28, 1952; s. John LeFever and Pauline Irene (Scott) F.; m. Denise A., May 22, 1971; children: Jennifer, Robert, Claire, Andrew. AA, Franklin & Marshall Coll., 1976; BS, Elizabethtown Coll., 1979; MBA, Lebanon Valley Coll., 1995; PhD in Internat. Mktg., Harrington Ctr. Internat. Studies, London, 2000. Dispatcher Pa. Power & Light, Lancaster, 1975-79, sr. residential cons., 1985-92, bus. cons, 1992-95; pres., fin. sec. Internat. Brotherhood Elec. Workmen, Allentown, Pa., 1979-85; dir. mktg. Superior Walls Am., New Holland, Pa., 1995-97, 1998—; pres. Superior Walls Systems, Oxford, N.C., 1997-98, dir. mktg., 1999-2001; v.p. mktg. Success Performance Solutions, Leola, Pa., 2001—; v.p. Smart Start Bldg. Sys., Marietta, Ga.; ptnr. GRT Energy Solutions, 2000—; v.p. terr. devel. Superior Walls of the Hudson Valley, Poughkeepsie, NY. Mem. Nat. Assn. Home Builders, Bldg. System Coun., Am. Concrete Inst., Precast Concrete Inst., Concrete Found. Assn., Sales and Mktg. Execs. (Command Performance award 1998), Ctrl. Penn Pub. Guild (pres.). Republican. Roman Catholic. Avocations: family, singing. Home and Office: 32 Greenfield Rd Lancaster PA 17602-3386 E-mail: Finger001@msn.com.

FINGER, SEYMOUR MAXWELL, political science educator, former ambassador; b. N.Y.C., Apr. 30, 1915; s. Samuel and Bella (Spiegel) F.; widowed; m. Annette S. Baslaw, June 12, 1988; 1 child, Mark. BS, Ohio U., 1935; postgrad., U. Cin., 1942, Littauer Sch. Pub. Affairs, Harvard U., 1953-54. Branch mgr. Photo Reflex Studios, Inc., 1935-37, 1938-40, regional supr., 1940-43, asst. to v.p., 1945-46; tchr. O'Keefe Jr. High Sch., 1937-38; vice consul Am. Consulate, Stuttgart, Fed. Republic of Germany, 1946-49; 2d sec. Am. Embassy, Paris, 1949-51; 2d sec., econ. officer Am. legation Budapest, Hungary, 1951-53; econ. def. officer Am. Embassy, Rome and Budapest, 1954-55; 1st sec. Vientane, Laos, 1955-56; sr. econ. adv. U.S. Mission to UN, 1956-65; min. counselor of mission to UN, 1965-67; ambassador, sr. adviser to permanent rep. U.S. Mission to UN, 1967-71; prof. govt. and internat. orgn. CUNY, Coll. of S.I., 1971-85; prof. polit. sci. Grad. Sch. CUNY, 1973-85, prof. emeritus, 1985—, adj. prof., 1986—; dir. Ralph Bunche Inst. on UN, 1973-85, dir. emeritus, 1985—; adj. prof. NYU, 1986—; exec. dir. Nat. Com. on Am. Fgn. Policy, 1986-88. Vis. prof. Georgetown U., Washington, 1993; sr. adviser policy studies UN Assn. of U.S.A., N.Y.C., 1971-73; mem. U.S. del. to UN Gen. Assembly, 11th-25th sessions, chmn. security council com. on sanctions in Rhodesia; mem. UN com. on contbrs.; spl. cons. to Brookings Instn., 1964; mem. Task Force for Nuclear Test Ban. Author: People, Politics and Bureaucracy in the Making of Foreign Policy, 1980, American Ambassadors at the UN, 1987, Bending with the Winds: Kurt Waldheim and the UN, 1990, Inside the World of Diplomacy, 2001; editor (with others): The New World Balance and Peace in the Middle East, 1975, Terrorism: Interdisciplinary Perspectives, 1978, American Jewry and the Holocaust, 1984; contbr. articles to nat. newspapers, mags. and jours. Bd. dirs. Travel Program for Fgn. Diplomats, South Nassau Communities Hosp., 1973-74. Served as staff sgt. AUS, 1943-45. Mem. Coun. on Fgn. Rels. (pres.), Inst. for Mediterranean Affairs (pres. 1971—), Am. Soc. Internat. Law, Commn. for Study Orgn. Peace, Phi Beta Kappa, Kappa Delta Pi. Office: CUNY Grad Ctr 365 5th Ave New York NY 10016-4309

FINGER, STEPHEN, otolaryngologist; b. Bklyn., 1943; BS in Physics, Bklyn. Coll., 1964; MD, U. Cin., 1972. Intern Lenox Hill Hosp., N.Y.C., 1972-73, resident surgery, 1973-74; resident ear, nose and throat Mt. Sinai Hosp., N.Y.C., 1974-77; otolaryngologist L.I. Coll. Hosp., Bklyn., 1977—, Kings Hwy. Hosp., 1977—; pvt. practice Bklyn., 1997—. Mem. Kings County ENT Soc. Office: 2256 Hendrickson St Brooklyn NY 11234-5131 E-mail: drstevefinger@aol.com.

FINGERHUT, MARILYN ANN, federal agency administrator; b. Bklyn., Oct. 3, 1940; d. Robert Vincent and Marion (Carroll) F.; m. David W. Haartz, May 14, 1988; children: Margot, D. Bradley. BS in Cell Biology, Coll. of St. Elizabeth, Convent Station, N.J., 1964; PhD in Cell Biology, Cath. U. Am., 1970; MS in Occupational Health, Harvard U., Boston, 1981. Tchr. elem. schs., Jersey City, 1961-62, East Orange, N.J., 1964-65; instr. Coll. of St. Elizabeth, 1970-71; rsch. assoc. N.J. Coll. Medicine and Dentistry, Newark, 1971-72; asst. prof. to assoc. prof. St. Peter's Coll., Jersey City, 1973-80; researcher St. Joseph Med. Ctr., Paterson, N.J., 1977-80; predoctoral fellow USPHS, 1966-69, commd. capt., 1989; epidemiologist Nat. Inst. for Occupational Safety and Health, Cin., 1981-88, br. chief, 1988-94, sr. scientist office of dir. Washington, 1994-95, asst. dir. ops., 1995-96, chief staff, 1996—99; coord. occup. and environ. health WHO, Geneva, 2000—02; internat. coord. NIOSH, Washington, 2003—. Contbr. articles to sci. jours. Founding mem. Women's R&D Ctr., Cin., 1987-95. Recipient disting. svc. medal, 2000, commendation medal USPHS, 1989, 92. Mem. APHA, Soc. for Epidemiologic Rsch. Democrat. Roman Catholic. Office: NIOSH 200 Independence Ave SW Washington DC 20201

FINGERMAN, MILTON, biologist, educator; b. Boston, May 21, 1928; s. Irving and Rose Lillian (Goodman) F.; children: Stephen Whitsell, David Clay; m. Maria Esperanza Espinosa, Dec. 17, 1994. BS, Boston Coll., 1948; MS, Northwestern U., 1949, PhD, 1952. Instr. Tulane U., New Orleans, 1954-56, asst. prof., 1956-60, assoc. prof., 1960-63, prof. dept. ecology, evolution and organismal biology, 1963—, chmn. dept., 1990-99, chmn. dept. ecology, evolution and organismal biology, 1990-99, prof. emeritus, 2000—. Mem. univ. senate Tulane U., 1995-96, pres.'s faculty adv. com., 1995-96; instr. invertebrate zoology Marine Biol. Lab., Woods Hole, Mass., 1958-60; Petrie chair vis. prof. Technion, Haifa, Israel, 1986; mem. adv. panel for regulatory biology NSF, 1966-69; mem. com. on marine invertebrates Inst. Lab. Animal Resources of NRC, 1976-81; cons. Food and Agr. Orgn. of UN, Cochin, India, 1986, U.S. Office Naval Rsch. project on biofouling, Goa and Aurangabad, India, 1990-97, Inst. Wood Sci. & Tech., Bangalore, India, 1997—; Ming Yu vis. scholar Chinese U. Hong Kong, 1997. Author: The Control of Chromatophores, 1963, Animal Diversity, 1969; assoc. editor Jour. Crustacean Biology, 1980-85, Pigment Cell Rsch., 1986-91; mem. editorial bd. Physiol. Zoology, 1976-84, Trends in Life Scis., 1986—, Indian Jour. Invertebrate Zoology and Aquatic Biology, 1989, 1998—; co-editor Recent Advance in Marine Biotech., 1997-2003. Served with U.S. Army, 1952-54 Recipient Excellence in Rsch. award The Crustacean Soc., 2000; NSF grantee, 1956-85; named to Hon. Order Ky. Cols. Fellow AAAS; mem. Am. Inst. Biol. Scis., Am. Soc. Zoologists (exec. com. 1981-95, mng. editor Am. Zoologist 1981-95), Sigma Xi (pres. chpt. 1972-73), Delta DX Assoc. (pres. 1983-84, 96-97, sec. 2002-03). Democrat. Jewish. Avocation: amateur radio. Home: 1730 Broadway St New Orleans LA 70118-5304 E-mail: miltonf@tulane.edu.

FINGERSON, LEROY MALVIN, engineering executive, mechanical engineer; b. Rochester, Minn., July 1, 1932; s. Malvin Ferdinand and Corolla Racelia (Sundet) F.; m. Ruth Anne Johnson, Nov. 26, 1960; children: Mark, Karin, Laura. BSME, U. Minn., 1954, MSME, 1955, PhDME, 1961. Chmn. bd. TSI, Inc., St. Paul, 1961-98, CEO, 1961-97, ret., 1998, chmn. emeritus. Contbr. articles to profl. jours. Mem. Nat. Acad. Engring. Lutheran.

FINGHAM, RICHARD FRANK, lawyer; b. Lafayette, Ind., Aug. 2, 1946; s. James R. and Loretta C. (Hoenigke) Kingham; m. Justine Frances McClung, July 6, 1968; 1 child, Richard Patterson Kingham. BA, George Washington U., 1968; JD, U. Va., 1973. Bar: D.C. 1973, U.S. Dist. Ct. D.C. 1974, U.S. Ct. Appeals (8th cir.) 1977, U.S. Supreme Ct. 1977, U.S. Ct. Appeals (5th cir.) 1980, registered: Law Soc. Eng. and Wales (fgn. lawyer) 1994. Edtl. asst. Washington Star, 1964-68, 69-70; assoc. Covington & Burling, Washington, 1973-81, ptnr., 1981—, mng. ptnr. London office, 1996-2000; mem. mgmt. com., co-head Life Scis. Industry Group, 2000—. Lectr. law U. Va., Charlottesville, 1977—90; mem. com. issues and priorities new vaccine devel. Inst. Medicine, NAS, 1983—86, Nat. Adv. Allergy and Infectious Diseases Coun. NIH, 1988—92; mem. adv. bd. World Pharms. Report, 1990—96; mem. WHO Coun. Internat. Orgns. Med. Scis. and Working Party in Pharmacovigilance, 1997—99; mem. com. on accelerating biowarfare countermeasures Inst. of Medicine, NAS, 2002—; lectr. grad. program in pharm. medicine U. Wales, 1999—; adj. prof. Georgetown U., 2003—. Contbr. articles to profl. jours. Pres. Am. Friends of St. Peter's Eaton Square, 2001—; treas., mem. parochial ch. coun. St. Peter's Ch. Eaton Sq., London, 1998—2001. With U.S. Army, 1968—69. Mem.: ABA, European Forum for Good Clin. Practice, Soc. Vertebrate Paleontology, Food Law Group (U.K.), European Soc. Pharmacovigilance, Food and Drug Law Inst., Drug Info. Assn., Brussels Pharm. Law Group, Reform Club (London), Order of Coif. Republican. Episcopalian. Avocation: vertebrate paleontology. Home: 4821 Dexter St NW Washington DC 20007 E-mail: rkingham@cov.com.

FINIFTER, ADA WEINTRAUB, political scientist, educator; b. NYC; d. Isaac and Stella (Colchamiro) Weintraub. BA, CUNY, Bklyn., 1959; MA, U. Mich., 1961; PhD, U. Wis., 1967. Prof. polit. sci. Mich. State U., East Lansing, 1967—. Author: Using Your IBM Personal Computer: Easywriter, 1984; editor: Political Science: The State of the Discipline, 1983, Alienation and the Social System, 1970, Political Science: The State of the Discipline II, 1993; editor Am. Polit. Sci. Rev., 1996-2001; contbr. articles to polit. sci. jours. Vol. U.S. Peace Corps, Venezuela, 1962-64. Rsch. grantee Russell Sage Found., 1979-82, NSF, 1977-78; fellow NSF, 1966, 73. Mem. Am. Polit. Sci. Assn. (v.p. 1983-84, program chmn. 1982), Midwest Polit. Sci. Assn. (pres. 1986-87). Office: Mich State U Dept Polit Sci 303 S Kedzie Hall East Lansing MI 48824-1032 E-mail: finifter@msu.edu.

FINK, AARON, artist; b. Boston, 1955;, Skowhegan Sch. Painting, 1976; BFA, Md. Inst. Coll. of Art, 1977; MFA, Yale U. Sch. of Art, 1979. One man shows include Galerie Barbara Farber, Amsterdam, The Netherlands, 1981, 82, 85, 87, 91, 94, Alpha Gallery, Boston, 1981, 83, 85, 87, 91, 92, 93, 95, 97,David Beitzel Gallery, N.Y.C., 1988, 90, 93, 95, 97, Magidson Fine Art, Aspen, Colo., 1994, Jaffe Baker Blau Gallery, Ft. Collins, Colo., 1994, Rockford (Ill.) Art Mus., 1995-96, Alpha Gallery, Boca Raton, Fla., 1995, Hatton Gallery Colo. State U., and numerous others; exhibited in group shows at Mus. Fine Arts, Boston, 1994, Olga Dollar Gallery, San Francisco, 1994, Galerie Mourlot, Boston, 1994, Karl Drerup Fine Arts Gallery, Plymouth, N.H., 1994, Art Complex Mus., Duxbury, Mass., 1997, and numerous others; represented in numerous pub. and pvt. collections. Recipient Skowhegan Scholarship award, Md. Inst. Coll. Art, 1976; grantee NEA, 1982, 1987; artists fellow Mass. Coun. Arts and Humanities, 1984. Home: 63 Maverick Sq Boston MA 02128-2312

FINK, ALMA, retired elementary education educator; b. Missoula, Mont., Sept. 2, 1934; d. Frederick James and Annabelle (Pearson) Gariepy; m. Millard Allen Fink, June 18, 1955 (dec. Sept. 1980); children: Melanie Ann, Laurie Jean. Diploma, Western Mont. Coll., Dillon, 1954; BA, U. Mont., 1968, MA, 1992. Cert. elem. and reading tchr., Mont. Tchr. 1st grade Granite County Elem. Sch., Phillipsburg, Mont., 1954-55, Missoula County Pub. Schs., Missoula, 1955-56, 68-99; ret. Mem. Five Valleys Reading Coun., Missoula. Editor state newsletter Chit Chat. Named Gold Star Tchr., KECI-TV, 1998. Mem. NEA (life), Missoula Elem. Edn. Assn. (polit. action com. for educators, mem. exec. bd.), Alpha Delta Kappa (Mont. state pres. 1988-90, pres. chpt., regional chmn., Violet award). Roman Catholic. Avocations: sewing, crafts, sports, reading, travel.

FINK, BRUCE, psychoanalyst, educator; b. Pt. Jefferson, N.Y., 1956; BA, Cornell U., 1976; MA in Philosophy, U. Paris VIII, 1985, PhD in Psychoanalysis, 1987. Lic. rsch. psychoanalyst Calif. Assoc. prof. Duquesne U., Pitts., 1993—97, prof., 1997—. Psycoanalyst Ecole Cause Frendienne, Paris, 1990—. Author: (book) The Lacanian Subject, 1995, A Clinical Introduction to Lacanian Psychoanalysis, 1997; translator: Ecrits: A Selection, 2002. Named Soc. for Humanities fellow, Cornell U., 1997—98; recipient Transl. Project grant, NEH, 1997—2000. Home: 350 Cobblestone Cir Silver Creek NY 14136 Office: Duquesne U 600 Forbes Ave Pittsburgh PA 15282 Fax: 412-859-3997. E-mail: fink@duq.edu.

FINK, CHARLES AUGUSTIN, behavioral systems scientist; b. McAllen, Tex., Jan. 1, 1929; s. Charles Adolph and Mary Nellie (Bonneau) F.; m. Ann Heslen, June 1, 1955 (dec. June 1981); children: Patricia A., Marianne E., Richard G., Gerard A. AA, Pan-Am. U., 1948, BS, Marquette U., 1950; postgrad., George Washington Med. Ctr., Walter Reed Army Med. Ctr., 1969-70, No. Va. C.C., 1973, George Mason U., 1974; MA, Cath. U. Am., 1979. Journalist UP and Ft. Worth Star-Telegram, 1950-52; commd. 2d lt. U.S. Army, 1952, advanced through grades to lt. col., 1966, various positions telecommunications, 1952-56, instr., 1956-58, exec. project mgmt., 1958-62, def. analysis and rsch., 1962-65, fgn. mil. rels., 1965-67, def. telecommunications exec., 1967-69, chief planning, budget and program control office Def. Satellite Communications Program, Def. Communications Agy., 1969-72, ret., 1972; pvt. practice cons. managerial behavior Falls Church, Va., 1972-77; pres. Behavioral Systems Sci. Orgn. (and predecessor firms), Falls Church, 1978—. Leader family group dynamics, 1958-67; home hemodialysis technician, 1969-81; pub (jour.) Circle, 1985—; computer program cons. Hubble Space Telescope Servicing Mission, NASA, 1993. Developer hierarchial theory of human behavior, 1967—, uses in behavioral, social and biol. sci. and their applications, 1972—, behavioral causal modeling research methodology, 1974—, computer-aided behavior systems coaching for persons and orgns., 1982—, telecoaching, 1989; microbiol. chromatographic profiling, 1989—; public domain Portable Personal Health Record, 1994; adv. for copyrighting computer graphics displays and multi-media communications in scis. Adv. bd. Holy Redeemer Roman Cath. Ch., Bangkok, Thailand, St. Philip's Ch., Falls Church, Va., 1971-73. Decorated Army Commendation medals, Joint Services Commendation medal; named to Fink Hall of Fame, 1982; recipient Behavior Modeling award Internat. Congress Applied Systems Rsch. and Cybernetics, 1980, Mission Pin award NASA, 1993. Mem. AAAS, SAR, Nat. Genealogical Soc., Internat. Soc. Systems Scis., Am. Soc. Cybernetics, Internat. Assn. Cybernetics, Internat. Network Social Network Analysis, Assn. U.S. Army, Ret. Officers Assn., Finks Internat. (v.p. 1981—), KC. Home: 3305 Brandy Ct Falls Church VA 22042-3705 Office: PO Box 2051 Falls Church VA 22042-0051

FINK, CONRAD CHARLES, journalism educator, communications consultant; b. Marquette, Mich., Sept. 16, 1932; s. Donald Ellsworth and Mary Ruth (Fox) F.; m. Sue Carol Henry, Sept. 4, 1954; children: Karen Sue, Conrad Stephan. BS, U. Wis., 1954. Reporter Bloomington (Ill.) Daily Pantagraph, 1956-57; various positions to night city editor AP, Chgo., 1957-60, writer fgn. desk N.Y.C., 1961, fgn. corr. Tokyo Bur., 1961-64, bur. chief South Asia, 1964—67; dir. AP-Dow Jones Econ. Report, London, 1967-70; asst. to pres. AP, N.Y.C., 1970, v.p., 1971-77, sec., 1974-77; 1st v.p., dir. Wide World Photos, Inc.; v.p. Press Assn., Inc.; v.p., dir. AP (Can.), Ltd.; sec., dir. N.Y.C. News Assn., Inc., 1974-77; exec. v.p. adminstrn., dir. Park Broadcasting, Inc., Ithaca, N.Y., 1977-81, Park Newspapers, Inc., 1977-81; disting. lectr. U. Ga. Sch. Journalism, Athens, 1982, prof. newspaper mgmt., 1983—; dir. James M. Cox Jr. Inst. for Newspaper Mgmt. Studies, Athens, 1990—, William S. Morris prof. newspaper strategy and mgmt., 1995—. Sr. fellow U. Ga., 1996—2001, mem. Univ. Coun., Univ. Tchr. Acad., 2000—. Author: Strategic Newspaper Management, 1988, Media Ethics, 1988, Inside the Media, 1990, Introduction to Professional Newswriting, 1992, Introduction to Magazine Writing, 1993, Writing Opinion for Impact, 1999, Bottom Line Writing, 2000, Sports Writing: The Lively Game, 2001, Writing to Inform and Engage, 2003. Served to 1st lt. USMCR, 1954-56. Named Nat. Journalism Tchr. of year, Freedom Forum, 2002; recipient Disting. Svc. award, U. Wis., 1969. Home: 116 S Stratford Dr Athens GA 30605-3024 Office: U Ga Sch Journalism Athens GA 30602 also: Alta Vista Farm 108 Pine Ridge Rd Cherry Valley NY 13320 E-mail: CFink@uga.edu.

FINK, DANIEL JULIEN, management consultant; b. Jersey City, Dec. 13, 1926; s. Joseph and Dorothy (Weisberger) F.; m. Tobie E. Weiss, June 21, 1951; children: Kenneth Wayne, Betsy Ilene, Karen Patrice. BS, MIT, 1948, MS, 1949. Registered profl. engr., Mass. Aeromechanics engr. Cornell Aero. Lab., 1948; chief aircraft dynamics Bell Aircraft Corp., Buffalo, 1949-52; v.p. Allied Rsch. Assocs., Inc., Concord, Mass., 1952-63; asst. dir. def. rsch. and engring. (def. systems) Dept. Def., 1963-65, dep. dir. def. rsch. and engring. (strategic and space sys.), 1965-67; with Gen. Electric Co., 1967-82, v.p., gen. mgr. space divsn., 1969-77, v.p., group exec. aerospace group, 1977-79, sr. v.p. corp. planning and devel. Fairfield, Conn., 1979-82; pres. D.J. Fink Assocs., Inc., 1982—. Bd. dirs. Titan Corp., Orbital Scis. Corp.; def. sci. bd. Dept. Def., 1968—72, sr. cons., 1979—98; nat. indsl. adv. coun. Opportunities Industrialization Ctrs., 1977—79; sci. adv. panel Dept. Army, 1971—74; adv. coun. NASA, 1978—79, chmn. adv. coun., 1982—88; corp. vis. dept. aero. and astronautics MIT, 1972—82, Sloan Sch., 1982—85; chmn. dept. adv. bd. dept. mech. engring. Rensselaer Poly. Inst., 1981—84; mem. Vice Pres.'s Space Policy Adv. Bd., 1992. Patentee vibration isolation, weapon systems mgmt., aerospace mgmt. and corp. planning. Recipient Disting. Pub. Svc. award Dept. Def., 1967, NASA Disting. Svc. medal, 1986, NASA medal for Outstanding Leadership, 1988; Collier trophy, 1974 Hon. fellow AIAA (pres. 1974-75, von Karman lectr. 1980); fellow AAAS; mem. NAE (chmn. space applications bd. 1976-81, chmn. telecomms. and computer applications bd. 1984-87, chmn. com. on U.S.-Japan linkages in transport aircraft 1993, chmn. com. on space facilitics 1994), Cosmos Club. Office: 8016 Matterhorn Ct Potomac MD 20854-4058

FINK, EDWARD MURRAY, lawyer, educator; b. N.Y.C., Mar. 11, 1934; s. Nathaniel and Elsa Charlotte (Lenrow) F.; divorced; children: Jeffrey Neil, Andrea Sue; m. Rita Toby Cohen, Aug. 11, 1985. BS in Chemistry, CCNY, 1955; JD, Georgetown U., 1959. Bar: D.C. 1960, U.S. Dist. Ct. D.C. 1960, U.S. Ct. Appeals (D.C. cir.) 1960, N.Y. 1962, N.J. 1970, U.S. Dist. Ct. N.J. 1970, U.S. Patent and Trademark Office 1960. Patent examiner U.S. Patent Office, Washington, 1955-60; atty. Bell Labs., Murray Hill, N.J., 1960-83, Bell Comm. Rsch. Inc., Livingston, N.J., 1984-91, Edward M. Fink, P.A., Edison, N.J., 1991—; v.p., gen. counsel Eastern R.R. Investment Corp., Bridgewater, N.J., 2000—, chmn. bd. dirs., 2001—, Somerset Terminal R.R. Corp., 2001—02. Adj. prof. torts, bus. law and civil litigation Middlesex County Coll., Edison, N.J., 1980-2000; adj. prof. partnerships and corps, contract law Montclair State U., Upper Montclair, N.J., 1984-2000. Mem. ABA, Am. Intellectual Property Assn., N.J. Patent Law Assn., N.J. State Bar Assn., Middlesex County Bar Assn., D.C. Bar Assn., N.Y. State Bar Assn. Democrat. Jewish. Home and Office: 51 Jamaica St Edison NJ 08820-3726 E-mail: patemf@aol.com.

FINK, ELOISE BRADLEY, educator, writer, editor; b. Decatur, Ill., Mar. 13, 1927; d. Keith and Eileen Bradley; m. John Fink, Aug. 8, 1949 (div.); children: Sara, Joel, Alison. BA in English with honors, U. Ill., 1949; student, Colo. Coll., 1951. Cert. tchr., Ill. Tchr. English, social studies Paxton, Decatur and Arlington Heights, Ill., 1949-56; freelance Scott Foresman, Ency. Brit. and SRA, 1956-80; dir. pub. rels. Rehab. Inst. Chgo., 1980-82; instr. creative writing and poetry Loyola U., Water Tower campus, Chgo., 1983-90; artist-in-residence Ill. Arts Coun., 1984-93; facilitator workshops in poetry, fiction and nonfiction New Trier Extension, 1974—. Founder, editor, pres. Thorntree Press, Winnetka, Ill., 1985—. Author: The Girl in the Empty Nightgown, 1986, Lincoln and the Prairie After, 1999. Recipient Friends of Lits. award (2), Gwendolyn Brooks award for Twenty Significant Ill. Poets; Breadloaf Writing Conf. fellow, 1986. Mem. Acad. Am. Poets, Poetry Soc. Am. Home: 547 Hawthorn Ln Winnetka IL 60093-4148

FINK, J. THEODORE, planner, consulting firm executive; b. Buffalo, Mar. 19, 1952; s. Theodore Rodney and Dorothy Marie F.; m. Ronnie Citron Fink, Aug. 20, 1983; children: Lainey, Benjamin. BA, SUNY, Buffalo, 1972-76; M in Urban Planning, U. Ill., Chgo., 1976-78. Cert. planner. Research assoc. Ctr. for Urban Affairs, Chgo., 1976-78; project mgr. Open Lands Project, Chgo., 1978-80; assoc. planner N.Y. State Dept. Environ. Conservation, New Paltz, 1980-83; v.p. Quepco, Inc., Pleasantville, NY, 1983-86; pres. EnviroPlan Assocs. Inc., Poughkeepsie, NY, 1986-91, GREENPLAN Inc., Rhinebeck, NY, 1991—. Prof. grad. program in environ. studies Bard Coll., 1995. Mem. Am. Inst. Cert. Planners. Roman Catholic. Avocations: scuba instructor, photography, kayaking, boat building. Office: GREENPLAN Inc 302 Pells Rd Rhinebeck NY 12572-3354

FINK, JAMES BREWSTER, geophysicist, consultant; b. Los Angeles, Jan. 12, 1943; s. Odra J. and Gertrude (Sloot) F.; m. Georgeanne Emmerich, Aug. 24, 1970; 1 child, Jody Lynn. BS in Geophysics and Geochemistry, U. Ariz., 1969; MS in Geophysics cum laude, U. Witwatersrand, Johannesburg, Transvaal, Republic of South Africa, 1980; PhD in Geol. Engring., Geohydrology, U. Ariz, 1989. Registered profl. engr., Ariz., N.Mex.; registered land surveyor, Ariz.; registered profl. geologist, Wyo.; cert. environ. inspector. Geophysicist Geo-Comp Exploration, Inc., Tucson, 1969-70; geophys. cons. IFEX-Geotechnica, S.A., Hermosillo, Sonora, Mex., 1970; chief geophysicist Mining Geophys. Surveys, Tucson, 1971-72; research asst. U. Ariz., Tucson, 1973; cons. geophysics Tucson, 1974-76; sr. minerals geophysicist Esso Minerals Africa, Inc., Johannesburg, 1976-79; sr. research geophysicist Exxon Prodn. Research Co., Houston, 1979-80; pres. Geophynque Internat., Tucson, 1980-90, hydro-Geophysics, Inc., Tucson, 1990—; cons. on NSF research U. Ariz., 1984-85, adj. lectr. geol. engring., 1985-86, assoc. instr. geophysics, 1986-87, supr. geophysicist, geohydrologist, 1986-88, bd. dirs. Lab. Advanced Subsurface Imaging, 1986—; v.p. R&D Alternative Energy Engring., Inc., Tucson, 1992—, also bd. dirs.; v.p. Reclamation Svcs., Inc., 1995—, also bd. dirs.; v.p. Catalina Marble Inc., 1996—. Lectr. South African Atomic Energy Bd., Pelindaba, 1979; cons. Argonne Nat. Lab., 1992-93, Los Alamos Nat. Lab., 1987—. Pacific N.W. Nat. Lab.; v.p. Rincon Stock Yard, 1997-2000. Contbr. articles to profl. jours. Served as sgt. U.S. Air NG, 1965-70. Named Airman of Yr., U.S. Air NG, 1967. Mem. Soc. Exploration Geophysicists (co-chair internat. meetings 1980, 81, 92, sr. editor monograph 1990, reviewer), Am. Geophys. Union (reviewer), Assn. Ground Water Scientists, Nat. Water Well Assn. (reviewer), Ariz. Geol. Soc., Ariz. Water Well Assn., Environ. and Engring. Geophys. Soc., Assn. State Dam Safety Ofcls., Pres.'s Club U. Ariz., Ariz. Hydrological Soc., Assn. Engring. Geologists. Republican. Avocations: reading, computers, natural sciences, genealogy. Home: 5865 S Old Spanish Trail Tucson AZ 85747-9487 Office: hydroGEOPHYSICS Inc 2302 N Forbes Blvd Tucson AZ 85745 E-mail: jim@hydrogeophysics.com.

FINK, JENNIFER NATALYA, publishing executive, educator; b. Washington, Aug. 28, 1966; d. Gerald Ralph and Rosalie Pamela Fink; m. Jon Keith Brunelle, Sept. 13, 1994. PhD, NYU, 1996. Asst. prof., writer Pratt Inst., Bklyn., 1997—2002; founder, exec. dir. The Gorilla Press, Bklyn., 2000—. Mem. editl. bd. Women & Performance, N.Y.C., 1993—; bd. visitors The Walnut Hill Sch., Natick, Mass., 2001—; juror Coun. of Lit. Mags. and Small Presses, N.Y.C. Author: (novel) The Mikveh Queen (The Dana Award for the Novel, 1997); editor: (book by gay & lesbian youth) Out on Fire (Billy Heekin Meml. Award from Stonewall Found., 2002); author: (novel) Burn (Edward Albee Ctr. for Creative Persons Artist's Residency, 2001), Veronica (Saltonstall Found. Artist's Residency, 2001), over 50 published short stories and novels; contbr. Recipient Georgetown Rev. Fiction award, Editors, Georgetown Rev., 1997, Artist's Residency, Blue Mountain Found. for Arts, 2002, Short Fiction award, Story Mag., 2000. Mem.: MLA (assoc.). D-Liberal. Jewish. Achievements include development of Created, designed, and implemented non-profit press that helps kids to write, illustrate, and publish their own works. Avocations: travel, reading, swimming, tutoring. Home: 105 Grand St #3 Brooklyn NY 11211 Personal E-mail: jfink@gorillapress.com.

FINK, JEROLD ALBERT, lawyer; b. Dayton, Ohio, July 16, 1941; s. Albert Otto and Marjorie Carolyn (Scheidt) F.; m. Mary Jo McHone, Dec. 31, 1961 (div. July 1978); children: Marjorie, Kathryn, Erick; m. 2d, Deborah Lynn Bailey, Dec. 25, 1980 (div. Oct. 1986); 1 child, Justin. AB, Duke U., 1963, LLB, 1966. Bar: Ohio 1966. Assoc. Taft, Stettinius & Hollister, Cin., 1966-73, ptnr., 1973—. Bd. dirs. The Wm. Powell Co., Cin., 1974—, Great Trails Broadcasting Co., Cin., 1974-79. Co-author: (with Judy Cohn) Power Defensive Carding, 1988, (with Joe Lutz) The American Forcing Minor Bidding System, 1995, (with Joe Lutz) Defensive Carding in the 21st Century, 2001. Pres. Cin. Musical Festival Assn., 1978-79; trustee Cin. Playhouse, 1976-95, New Life Youth Svcs., Cin., 1971—. Republican. Presbyterian. Office: 1800 Firstar Tower 425 Walnut St Cincinnati OH 45202-3923 E-mail: fink@taftlaw.com.

FINK, JOHN FRANCIS, retired newspaper editor, columnist, writer; b. Ft. Wayne, Ind., Dec. 17, 1931; s. Francis Anthony and Helen Elizabeth (Hartman) F.; m. Marie Therese Waldron, May 31, 1955; children: Regina Marie, Barbara Ann, Robert Paul, Stephen Lawrence, Therese Rose, David Francis, John Noll. BA, U. Notre Dame, 1953. Assoc. editor Our Sunday Visitor, Religious Pub. Co., Huntington, Ind., 1956-68; editor Family Digest, 1956-67; mktg. mgr., 1967-72; exec. v.p., 1972-76; pres., 1976-82; pub., 1982-84; chmn. Noll Printing Co., 1978-84; editor in chief The Criterion, Indpls., 1984-96, ret., 1996, columnist, editl. writer, 1984—; columnist The Indpls. Star, 1997—2002. Bd. dirs. Center for Applied Research in the Apostolate, 1978-85, Internat. Cath. Orgns. Center, 1979-85; mem. Cath. Com. for White House Conf. on Families, 1980; mem. communications com. U.S. Cath. Conf., 1981-84 Author: Moments in Catholic History, 1992, Traveling With Jesus in the Holy Land, 1998, The Mission and Future of the Catholic Press, 1998, Married Saints, 1999, The Doctors of the Church, 2 vols., 2000, American Saints, 2001, Letters to St. Francis de Sales: Mostly on Prayer, 2002, Memoirs of a Catholic Journalist, 2002. Chmn. United Fund Drive, 1963; pres. United Way of Huntington County, 1973-74, bd. dirs., 1971-74; bd. dirs. YMCA, Huntington, 1966-78, Cath. Journalism Scholarship Fund, Founds. and Donors Interested in Cath. Activities, 1977-84; trustee Huntington Coll., 1978-81; bd. dirs. Huntington Coll. Found., 1977-84, pres. bd., 1978-81; bd. dirs. Huntington Med. Meml. Found., 1978-84. Served as 1st lt. USAF, 1954-56. Decorated knight of Malta, knight of Holy Sepulchre; recipient Disting. Svc. award Huntington Jaycees, 1960; named Chief of Flint Springs Tribe, 1971, St. Francis de Sales award Cath. Press Assn., 1981, award of yr. Notre Dame Club of Indpls., 1994. Mem. Internat. Fedn. Cath. Press Assn. (v.p. 1974-80, pres. 1980-86), Internat. Cath. Union of the Press (coun. and bur. mem. 1974-86, hon. 1986—), Cath. Press Assn. (pres. 1973-75, dir. 1965-75, hon. 1997—), Indpls. Serra Club (pres. 1995-96). E-mail: mtfink@indy.net.

FINK, JOSEPH ALLEN, lawyer; b. Lexington, Ky., Oct. 4, 1942; s. Allen Medford and Margaret Ruth (Draper) F.; m. Marcia L. Horton; children: Alexander Mentzer, Justin McGranahan. Student, Wayne State U., 1960-61; BA, Oberlin Coll., 1964; JD, Duke U., 1967. Bar: Mich. 1968, U.S. Dist Ct. (ea. dist.) Mich. 1968, U.S. Dist. Ct. (we. dist.) Mich. 1974, U.S. Ct. Appeals (6th cir.) 1987, U.S. Supreme Ct. 1998. Assoc. Dickinson, Wright, McKean & Cudlip, Detroit, 1967—72, Lansing, Mich., 1972—75, ptnr. Dickinson Wright

PLLC, Lansing, 1976—. Instr. U.S. Internat. U. Grad. Sch. Bus., San Diego, 1971; adj. prof. trial advocacy Thomas M. Cooley Law Sch., Lansing, 1984-85; mem. com. on local rules U.S. Dist. Cts., 1985; chmn. trial experience subcom. U.S. Dist. Ct. (we. dist.) Mich., 1981; bd. dirs. Universal Holding Co.. Contbg. author: Construction Litigation, 1979, Legal Considerations in Managing Problem Employees, 1988, Michigan Civil Procedure During Trial, 2d edit., 1989; contbr. articles to profl. jours. Bd. dirs. Lansing 2000 Inc., 1985-92, Professionals Direct, Inc., Universal Holding Co.; bd. trustees Olivet (Mich.) Coll., 1985-94; mem. bd. advisors Mich. State U. Press, 1993-96. Lt. JAGC, USNR, 1968-72. Fellow Mich. State Bar Found.; mem. State Bar of Mich. (chmn. local disciplinary com. 1983—, com. for US Cts. 1984), Profls. Direct (bd. dirs.), Assn. Life Ins. Counsel, Internat. Assn. Ins. Episcopalian. Avocations: writing, reading, golf. Home: 6302 W Lake Dr Haslett MI 48840-8930 Office: Dickinson Wright PLLC 215 S Washington Sq Ste 200 Lansing MI 48933-1816

FINK, JOSEPH E. purchasing agent, finance educator; b. Alexandria, La. s. Joseph J. and Rosemary W. Fink; m. Carol W. Fink; children: Dinah C. Sandusky, Charles J. Bachelors, St. Louis U., 1967; MSc, U. So. Calif., L.A., 1968; MA, Webster U., 1981. Cert. sr. profl. in human resources Soc. for Human Resource Mgmt., 1997. Commd. lt. USAF, 1963, advanced through grades to col., ret., 1990; pvt. practice cons., ins. and retirement benefits Monterey, Calif., 1990—92; dir. procurement and svcs., product devel. Tanimura & Antle, Inc., Salinas, Calif., 1992—. Chmn., mem. bd. dirs. United Agribusiness League, Irvine, Calif., 1992—; prof. MBA program Golden Gate U., Monterey, 1996—. Pres. cmty. coun. Sacred Heart Cmty. Chapel, Ord Military Community, Calif., 2001; vice chmn, bd, dirs., sec. Steinbeck Credit Union, Salinas, 2001—; mem. acad. adv. bd. Heald Coll., San Francisco, 1996. Office: Tanimura & Antle Inc 1 Harris Rd Salinas CA 93908 E-mail: joe@taproduce.com.

FINK, JOSEPH LESLIE, III, law educator; b. Altoona, Pa., May 27, 1947; s. J. Leslie Jr. and Drucie Mardell (Stover) F.; m. Maureen Mae Malaney, Aug. 12, 1972; children: Joseph Leslie IV, Jonathan Morgan. BS in Pharmacy, Phila. Coll. Pharmacy and Sci., 1970; JD, Georgetown U., 1973. Bar: Pa. 1973, Ky. 1981, U.S. Dist. Ct. (ea. dist.) Pa. 1973, U.S. Ct. Appeals (3d cir.) 1973, U.S. Supreme Ct. 1977. From asst. prof. to prof. Phila. Coll. Pharmacy and Sci., 1973-81; exec. dir. Del. Pharm. Soc., Wilmington, 1976-78; prof. pharm. law U. Ky., Lexington, 1981—, asst. dean, 1981-88, assoc. vice chancellor for acad. affairs, 1988-96, asst. v.p. for rsch. and grad. studies, 1996—2001, assoc. v.p. for rsch., 2001—, v.p. for corp. rels. and econ. outreach, 2001—, exec. dir. UK coldstream rsch. campus, 2002—. Author: Manager's Guide to Third Party Programs, 1983; editor: Pharmacy Law Digest, 1981—; contbr. more than 250 articles to rsch. and profl. jours. Named to Nat. Fink Hall of Fame, Finks Internat., 1980; recipient Great Tchr. award U. Ky. Alumni Assn., 1984, 2000, Alumni Achievement award, U. Scis., Philadelphia, 2003; Am. Coun. on Edn. fellow, 1985-86. Fellow Am. Pharm. Assn., Am. Soc. for Pharmacy Law (Pres. award 1984, 94); mem. ABA, Am. Assn. Colls. Pharmacy, Ky. Bar Assn. Republican. Presbyterian. Avocations: gardening, household projects. Home and Office: 2011 Hart Rd Lexington KY 40502-2442 E-mail: jfink@uky.edu.

FINK, JOSEPH RICHARD, academic administrator; b. Newark, Mar. 20, 1943; s. Joseph Richard and Jean (Chorazy) F.; m. Donna Gibson, 1965 (div. 1986); children: Michael, Taryn; m. Christine Gaudenzi, oct. 4, 1992; children: Madison, Joseph. AB, Rider U., 1963; PhD in Am. History, Rutgers U., 1971; DLitt (hon.), Rider U., 1982, Coll. of Misericordia, 1992, Golden Gate U., 1994. Asst. then assoc. prof history Immaculata (Pa.) Coll., 1964-72, adminstrv. asst. to pres., 1969-72; dean of Arts & Scis. City Colls. Chgo., 1972-74; pres. Raritan Valley Coll., Somerville, N.J., 1974-79, Coll. Misericordia, Dallas, 1979-88, Dominican U of Calif, San Rafael, 1988—. Pres. Regional Planning Coun. Higher Edn., Region 3/Northeastern Pa., 1986-88. Mem. exec. com. Philharm. Soc. Northeastern Pa., 1986-89; bd. dirs. Marin Symphony, 1989-, San Francisco Ballet, 1994-97, Ind. Coll. No. Calif., 1992—, Marin Forum, 1991—, Guide Dogs for The Blind, 1994-97; bd. dirs. Am. Land Conservancy, 1995—, exec. com.; mem. campaign cabinet United Way San Francisco, 1990; bd. dirs. North Bay Coun., 1993—, chmn., 1996, exec. com. Mem. Nat. Assn. Ind. Colls. and Univs. (secretariat 1986), Nat. Assn. Intercollegiate Athletics (pres.'s adv. coun. 1986), Am. Coun. on Higher Edn. (commn. leadership devel. higher edn. 1978-82, commn. on internat. edn. 1993-96, acad. adminstrn. fellow 1974-75), Assn. Mercy Colls. (pres. 1985-87, exec. com. 1981-87), Coun. for Ind. Colls. (bd. dirs. 1989-92), Am. Hist. Assn., World Affairs Coun. No. Calif. (bd. dirs. 1990-96), Commonwealth Club Calif. (quar. chmn. 1989, chmn. Marin County chpt. 1989—, bd. dirs. 1992—, exec. com. 1997—, pres., 2003). Office: Dominican U Calif 50 Acacia Ave San Rafael CA 94901-2230

FINK, JUDY SMOLKA, social worker; b. N.Y.C., Aug. 20, 1951; d. Norman M. and Rose R. Smolka; m. Steven M. Fink, Dec. 5, 1981; children: Jeffrey, Samantha. BA, SUNY, Albany, 1973, MSW, 1975. Cert. social worker, N.Y. Hematology/oncology social worker Jewish Hosp. and Med. Ctr. Bklyn., 1979-82, Temple U. Hosp., Phila., 1975-79; social worker Am. Cancer Soc., Bklyn., 1980-82; socialworker Project Time Out Westchester Jewish Cmty. Svcs., White Plains, N.Y., 1995—. Mem. NASW, N.Y. State Soc. Clin. Social Work Psychotherapists. Home: 4 Revere Ln Purchase NY 10577-1814

FINK, MATTHEW E. health facility executive, educator; b. Phila., Jan. 15, 1951; m. Andrea Fink; children: Sarah, Daniel. BA cum laude, U. Pa., 1972; MD cum laude, U. Pitts., 1972-76. Diplomate Am. Bd. Critical Care Medicine, Am. Bd. Psychiatry and Neurology, Am. Bd. Internal Medicine, Nat. Bd. Med. Examiners. Intern then asst. resident in medicine Boston City Hosp., 1976-78, chief resident in internal medicine, 1978; asst. resident then chief resident in neurology Columbia-Presbyn. Med. Ctr., N.Y.C., 1978-82, chief neurology clin., 1982-84, dir. neurology ICU, 1983-93, co-investigator Coma Clin. Rsch. Ctr., 1986-90, dir. neurology and neurosurgery ICU, 1991-93; clin. fellow Coll. Physicians and Surgeons Columbia U., N.Y.C., 1978-82, assoc. in clin. neurology Coll. Physicians and Surgeons, 1982-83, from. asst. prof. to assoc. prof. in clin. neurology Coll. Physicians and Surgeons, 1983-90, dir. divsn. critical care neurology, 1988-93, assoc. prof. clin. neurology depts. neurology and neurosurgery, 1990; asst. attending neurologist Presbyn. Hosp., N.Y.C., 1982-90; chmn. dept. neurology and comprehensive stroke ctr. Beth Israel Med. Ctr., N.Y.C., 1993-97, co-dir. Inst. Neurology and Neurosurgery, 1996—99, pres., CEO, 1997—; pres. and CEO Continuum Health Prtnrs., Beth Israel Med. Ctr., N.Y.C., 1997—. Tchg. assoc. dept. medicine Sch. Medicine Boston U., 1979-80; emergency svcs. physician Health Ins. Plan N.Y., 1980-83; co-investigator Am. Critical Care, Inc., 1985, Nat. Inst. Neurol. and Communicative Disorders and Stroke, 1987-89, Nat. Inst. Neurol. Diseases and Stroke, 1991-95; sr. investigator Nat. Stroke Assn.; vis. prof. rounds Sch. Medicine Robert Wood Johnson U., New Brunswick, N.J., 1990, St. Vincent's Hosp. and Med. Ctr., N.Y.C., 1990, New Rochelle (N.Y.) Hosp., 1991, U. Med. and Dentistry NJ, Newark, 1992, Mt. Sinai Hosp., 1993, numerous others; vis. prof., grand rounds Yale-New Haven Med. Ctr., Sch. Medicine Yale U., 1990, Health Scis. Ctr. U. Oreg., Portland, 1991, Jersey Shore Med. Ctr., Neptune, 1993, others; course dir. neuro-critical care Child Neurology Soc., 1993, World Congress Neurology, Can., 1993, others; examiner Am. Bd. Psychiatry and Neurology, Inc., 1998; cons., lectr. and presenter in field. Ad hoc reviewer Archives Neurology, 1988—, Neurology, 1988—, Neurosurgery, 1988—, New England Jour. Medicine, 1988—; mem. editl. bd. Neurology Chronicles, 1991—; contbr. articles to profl. jours., chpts. to books. Nat. Inst. Neurol. Diseases and Stroke grantee, 1991-95; Nat. Stroke Assn. rsch. fellow, 1993-95. Mem. Am. Acad. Neurology (sec. sect. critical care and emergency medicine 1989, vice chmn. sect. critical care and emergency neurology 1991, chmn. sect. critical care and emergency medicine 1993), N.Y. County Med. Soc., World Fedn. Neurology (founding mem. rsch. group intensive mgmt. neurology 1989), Alpha Omega Alpha, Sigma Xi. Office: Beth Israel Med Ctr 1st Ave and 16th St New York NY 10003 Fax: 212-420-2881.

FINK, MATTHEW POLLACK, trade association executive, lawyer; b. N.Y.C., Jan. 8, 1941; s. Harry L. and Helen (Pollack) F.; m. Ellanor Thompson Stengel, June 22, 1945; children: Emily Pollack, Owen Thompson, Nina Pepper BA summa cum laude, Brown U., 1962; LLB cum laude, Harvard U., 1965. Asst. gen. counsel Investment Co. Inst., Washington, 1971-77; gen. coun., 1977-82, sr. v.p., 1982-91, pres., 1991—. Mem. adv. coun. SEC Hist. Soc., Boston Coll. Fin. Adv. Bd.; prin. Coun. of Excellence for Govt.; past mem. Dept. Commerce Industry Sector Adv. Com. on Svcs., SEC Emerging Markets Adv. Com. With U.S. Army, 1967-68. Mem. Fed. Bar Assn., Investment Co. Com. (past chmn.), Met. Club. Office: Investment Co Inst 1401 H St NW # 1200 Washington DC 20005-2110 E-mail: fink@ici.org.

FINK, NORMAN STILES, lawyer, educational administrator, fundraising consultant; b. Easton, Pa., Aug. 13, 1926; s. Herman and Yetta (Hyman) F.; m. Helen Mullen, Sept. 1, 1956; children: Hayden Michael, Patricia Carol. AB, Dartmouth Coll., 1947; JD, Harvard U., 1950. Bar: N.Y. 1951, U.S. Dist. Ct. (ea. and so. dists.) N.Y. 1954, U.S. Supreme Ct. 1964. Mem. legal staff Remington Rand, Inc., N.Y.C., Washington, 1949-54; ptnr. Lans & Fink, N.Y.C., 1954-68; counsel devel. program U. Pa., Phila., 1969-80; v.p. devel. and univ. rels. Brandeis U., Waltham, Mass., 1980-81; dep. v.p. devel., alumni rels., assoc. gen. counsel devel. Columbia U., N.Y.C., 1981-89; sr. counsel John Grenzebach & Assocs., Inc., Chgo., 1989-91. Cons. v.p. Engle Consulting Group, Inc., Chgo. Editor: Deferred Giving Handbook, 1977; author: (with Howard C. Metzler) The Costs and Benefits of Deferred Giving, 1982. V.p. Am. Australian Studies Found.; mem. bd. visitors Brevard (N.C.) Coll., 1995-99, life trustee, 1999; Warren Wilson Coll., 1997—, Killough Trustee, N.Y.C. With U.S. Army, 1945-46. Recipient Alice Beeman award for excellence in devel. writing Coun. Advancement and Support of Edn., 1984, Silver medal for fundraising comms., Coun. Advancement and Support of Edn., 1988; Lilly Endowment grantee, 1979-80. Master Mason; mem. ABA (mem. com. on exempt orgns. sect. taxation and com. estate planning and drafting, charitable givint), Coun. Advancement and support of Edn. (various coms.), Am. Arbitration Assn. (panelist), Assn. of Bar of City of N.Y.C. (com. on tax-exempt orgns. 1987-90), Dartmouth Lawyers Assn., Harvard Law Sch. Assn., Nat. Assn. Fundraising Profls. (Contbn. to Knowledge award 1985), Harvard Club Western N.C., Elks. Democrat. Jewish.

FINK, RAYMOND, medical educator; b. N.Y.C., Apr. 21, 1927; s. William and Yetta (Rales) F.; m. Ruth Ursula Gebhard, May 28, 1961 (div. 1982); children: William D., David S.; m. Louise Berenson, Jan. 27, 1983. BBA, CCNY, 1947; MA, U. Denver, 1949; PhD, Cornell U., 1956. Statistician Opinion Rsch. Ctr. U. Denver, 1949; survey statistician U.S. Bur. Census, Suitland, Md., 1949-50, 56; rsch. assoc. human resources rsch. George Washington U., Washington, 1952-53; rsch. assoc. Bur. Social Sci. Rsch., Washington, 1957-60; assoc. dir. drinking practices study Calif. State Dept. Pub. Health, Berkeley, 1960-62; v.p. rsch. and stats. Health Ins. Plan Greater N.Y., N.Y.C., 1962-78; prof. community and preventive medicine N.Y. Med. Coll., Valhalla, 1978-2000, dir. health policy mgmt., 1982-90, dir. health svcs. rsch., 1990-2000; dir. rsch. Mid-Hudson Family Health Inst., New Paltz, N.Y., 1999—. Chmn. social sci. adv. com. Planned Parenthood Fedn. Am., N.Y.C., 1966-71; chair task force on HMOs Nat. Inst. Mental Health, Rockville, Md., 1971-72. Contbr. articles to profl. jours. Trustee Health Svcs. Improvement Fund, N.Y.C., 1986-2000. Sgt. U.S. Army, 1950-52. Grantee Nat. Inst. Mental Health, 1968-72, Nat. Cancer Inst., 1972-78, Social Sci. Rsch. Coun., 1982-83, Robert Wood Johnson Found., 1990-94. Mem. APHA, Am. Assn. Public Opinion Rsch. (co-editor 1968-69), Med. and Health Rsch. Assn. (chair 1975-2002), Assn. for Health Svcs. Rsch., Herman Biggs Soc. (pres. 1994-98). Jewish. Office: Med Health Rsch Assn of NYC 40 Worth St Rm 720 New York NY 10013-2904 E-mail: raymond.fink@att.net.

FINK, RICHARD DAVID, chemist, educator; b. N.Y.C., July 14, 1936; s. Merwin Jesse and Claudia (Lowenthal) F.; m. Alice Christine Hovenden, Sept. 8, 1961; children: Rebecca Elisabeth, Johanna Hovenden. AB, Harvard U., 1958; PhD, MIT, 1962; MA (hon.), Amherst Coll., 1971; LHD (hon.), Doshisha U., Kyoto, 1988. NSF fellow in chemistry Yale U., 1962-63; NIH fellow, 1963-64; asst. prof. chemistry Amherst (Mass.) Coll., 1964-67, assoc. prof., 1967-71, prof., 1971—, Mellon prof., 1977-80, chmn. dept., 1970-73, 79-82, dean of faculty, 1983-88. Vis. prof. U. London, 1972-73, 76-77, 96-97, 99-2000; vis. scholar U.S. Army War Coll., 1992, MIT, 1988-90, 93-95; cons. Edn. Assocs., Inc. Contbr. articles to profl. jours. NSF fellow U. London, 1968-69, Sloan Found. fellow, 1970-74; Dreyfus Found. tchr.-scholar prize, 1971; NSF Profl. Devel. award, 1979 Mem. Am. Phys. Soc., Am. Chem. Soc., AAAS, Sigma Xi. Home: 30 Orchard St Amherst MA 01002-2516 Office: Amherst Coll Amherst MA 01002

FINK, ROBERT RUSSELL, music theorist, former university dean; b. Belding, Mich., Jan. 31, 1933; s. Russell Foster and Frances (Thornton) F.; m. Ruth Joan Bauerle, June 19, 1955; children: Denise Lyn, Daniel Robert. B.Mus., Mich. State U., 1955, M.Mus., 1956, PhD, 1965. Instr. music SUNY, Fredonia, 1956-57; instr. Western Mich. U., Kalamazoo, 1957-62, asst. prof., 1962-66, assoc. prof., 1966-71, prof., 1971-78, chmn. dept. music, 1972-78; dean Coll. Music U. Colo., Boulder, 1978-93; retired, 1994. Prin. horn Kalamazoo Symphony Orch., 1957-67; accreditation examiner Nat. Assn. Schs. Music, Reston, Va., 1973-92, grad. commr., 1981-89, chmn. grad. commn., 1987-89, assoc. chmn. accreditation commn., 1990-91, chmn., 1992. Author: Directory of Michigan Composers, 1972, The Language of 20th Century Music, 1975; composer: Modal Suite, 1959, Four Modes for Winds, 1967, Songs for High School Chorus, 1967; contbr. articles to profl. jours. Bd. dirs. Kalamazoo Symphony Orch., 1974-78, Boulder Bach Festival, 1983-90. Mem. Coll. Music Soc., Soc. Music Theory, Mich. Orch. Assn. (pres.), Phi Mu Alpha Sinfonia (province gov.), Pi Kappa Lambda. Home: 643 Furman Way Boulder CO 80305-5614 E-mail: Robert.Fink@colorado.edu.

FINK, ROBERT STEVEN, lawyer, writer, educator; b. Bklyn., Dec. 7, 1943; s. Samuel Miles and Helen Leah (Bogen) F.; m. Abby Deutsch, Mar. 20, 1980; children: Juliet Leah, Robin Rachel. Diploma, U. Vienna, 1962; BA, Bklyn. Coll., 1965; JD, NYU, 1968, LLM, 1973. Bar: N.Y. 1969, U.S. Dist. Ct. (so. and ea. dists.) N.Y. 1970, U.S. Tax Ct. 1970, U.S. Ct. Appeals (2d cir.) 1970, U.S. Supreme Ct. 1972, U.S. Dist. Ct. (we. dist.) N.Y. 1975, U.S. Ct. Claims 1984, U.S. Dist. Ct. (no. dist.) N.Y. 1985, U.S. Ct. Appeals (fed. cir.) 1990, U.S. Ct. Internat. Trade 1998. Assoc. Kostelanetz & Ritholz, N.Y.C., 1968-75, ptnr., 1975-87, Kostelanetez, Ritholz, Tigue and Fink, N.Y.C., 1987-94, Kostelanetz & Fink LLP, N.Y.C., 1994—. Lectr. in field; expert witness IRS; adv. com. tax divsn. Dept. Justice; chmn. IRS/Bar Liaison Com. N.E. Region, 1996-99; adj. prof. law NYU. Author: Tax Controversies: Audits, Investigations, Trials, 2 vols., 1980, 23d rev. edit., 2003; co-author: How to Defend Yourself Against the IRS, 1987, 2nd rev. edit., 1988; dept. editor Jour. Taxation, contbr. numerous articles to profl. jours. Fellow Am. Coll. Tax Counsel; mem. ABA (chmn. com. civil and criminal tax penalties 1983-85, chmn. task force for revision of tax penalties 1982), N.Y. State Bar Assn. (chmn. com. criminal and civil tax penalties 1982-85, 88-90, chmn. compliance and unreported income 1985-87, chmn. commodities and fin. futures 1987-88, chmn. com. compliance and penalties 1991-93, chmn. com. compliance practice and procedure 1993-2003, mem. house of dels. 1995-97), Fed. Bar Assn., N.Y. County Lawyers Assn. (chmn. com. taxation 1988-92, 96-97, bd. dirs. 1989-95), Assn. of Bar of City of N.Y., Am. Arbitration Assn. (arbitrator). Office: Kostelanetz & Fink LLP 530 5th Ave New York NY 10036-5101 E-mail: rfink@kflaw.com.

FINK, THOMAS MICHAEL, lawyer; b. Huntington, Ind., Oct. 6, 1947; s. Francis Anthony and Helen Elizabeth (Hartman) F.; m. Sheila Ann Jeffers, Aug. 11, 1973; children: Mark, Matthew, Megan. BBA, U. Notre Dame, 1970; JD, Northwestern U., 1973. Bar: Ind. 1973, U.S. Dist. Ct. (no. dist.) Ind. 1973. Assoc. Barrett & McNagny, Ft. Wayne, Ind., 1973-78, ptnr., 1979—. Speaker Estate Planning Coun., Ft. Wayne, 1987—. Pres. Bishop Luers H.S. Bd. Edn., Ft. Wayne, 1992-93; bd. dirs. Ft. Wayne Cmty. Found. Bus. Edn. Fund, 1990—; bd. dirs., treas. Planned Giving Coun. N.E. Ind., 1995—. Mem. Am. Coll. Trust and Estate Counsel, Ft. Wayne Country Club, Notre Dame Club of Ft. Wayne, Beta Gamma Sigma. Roman Catholic. Avocations: coaching basketball, golf, tennis, travel. Home: 1302 Sunset Dr Fort Wayne IN 46807-2952 Office: Barrett & McNagny 215 E Berry St Fort Wayne IN 46802-2705 E-mail: tmf@barrettlaw.com.

FINK, WILLIAM JAMES, retired surgeon; b. Washington, June 24, 1917; s. Gale J. and Elizabeth (Thomas) F.; m. Frances Kay Kerlin, Mar. 1945 (dec. Aug. 1985); children: Robert, Barbara, Barry; m. Arline Peeler, Jan. 1992. AB, DePauw U., 1939; MD, George Washington U., 1944. Diplomate Am. Bd. Surgery. Intern George Washington Hosp., Washington, 1944-45, resident in anesthesiology, 1948; resident in surgery Sibley Meml. Hosp., Washington, 1945-46, VA Hosp., Coral Gables, Fla., 1948-51, chief surg. svc. Fayetteville, Ark., 1951-79; advanced clin. assoc. prof. surgery to clin. prof. surgery U. Ark, 1967-80; ret., 1979. Pres. Universal Tongs, Inc., Fayetteville, 1979-90. Contbr. numerous articles to med. jours. Capt., M.C., AUS, 1946-48. Fellow ACS, S.W. Surg. Congress, Western Surg. Assn.; mem. Sigma Nu, Phi Chi. Republican. Methodist. Home: 1412 E Elmwood Dr Fayetteville AR 72703-3002

FINKBEINER, CARLTON S. (CARTY FINKBEINER), mayor; b. Toledo, 1939; BA, Dennison U. Tchr., football coach Maumee Valley Country Day Sch., St. Francis De Sales H.S., U. Toledo; city councilman City of Toledo, vice-mayor, mayor, 1994—; founder Toledo's Cmty.-Oriented Drug Enforcement program; co-sponsor City-wide Curfew; chair Coun.'s Housing, Neighborhood Revitalization and Natural Resources Com., Toledo. Mem. Econ. Opportunity Planning Assn. of Greater Toledo, Presidential Scholars Commn., U.S. Small Bus. Adminstrn. Adv. Commn. Northeastern and Northwestern Ohio, Internat. Gt. Lakes St. Lawrence Mayors Conf. Achievements include being appointed to the Presidential Scholars Commission by President Gerald Ford, 1975. Office: Office of the Mayor/City Coun One Goverment Ctr Ste 2200 Toledo OH 43604

FINKBOHNER, GEORGE WHEELER, JR., lawyer; b. Mobile, Ala., Mar. 30, 1935; s. George Wheeler Finkbohner and Rachel Elizabeth Norville; m. Beverly Ryan Finkbohner, Feb. 6, 1960; children: George W., Patricia, Patrick Ryan, Elizabeth F. Sayler. BA, U. Ala., 1957, LLB, 1960. Bar: Ala. 1960, U.S. Dist. Ct. (so. dist.) Ala. 1960, U.S. Ct. Appeals (5th and 11th cirs.) 1981. Assoc. Howell, Johnston, and Langford, Mobile, 1960-63; ptnr. Howell, Johnston, Langford, Finkbohner & Lawler, Mobile, 1964-82, Finkbohner, Lawler & Olen, Mobile, 1982-92; ptnr., mem. Finkbohner & Lawler, LLC, 1993—. Spkr. Cath. Charities for Archdiocese, Mobile, 1973-97; seminar spkr. Cath. Archdiocese of Mobile, 1970-71. Pres. St. Thomas Moore Cath. Lawyers Guild, Mobile, 1965; mem., pres. Bd. Cath. Edn., Mobile, 1974-76, Archdiocesan Bd. Cath. Edn., 1976-78; dist. chmn. Cath. Charities, Mobile, 1973-75, deanery chmn., 1976, archdiocesan chmn., 1978; rep. Diocesan Pastoral Coun., Evergreen, Ala., 1974-76; coun. pres. St. Mary's Parish. Mobile, 1970-71, 83-84, fin. coun., 1994—; bd. dirs., author of constitution Vol. Mobile, 1976-78, Jr. Tennis Patrons Assn., Mobile, 1976-78; mem., chmn. Mattei Meml. Endowment Fund, St. Mary's Sch., Mobile, 1994—; lector St. Mary's Parish, Mobile; bd. dirs. Little Sisters of the Poor, Mobile, 1979-80, mem. maj. gifts com. McGill-Toolen H.S., Mobile, 1994-95. Named Outstanding Cath. Alumnus, St. Mary's Sch./Nat. Cath. Edn. Assn. Cath. Social Svcs., Mobile, 1994; Recipient Valentine award Cath. Social Svcs., 1996. Mem. KC (3d and 4th deg., advocate 1967-74, knight of quar. 1964—), ABA, Ala. Bar Assn. (founding mem. bankruptcy and comml. law sect. 1983—, pres. bankruptcy sect. 1984), Mobile Bar Assn. (pres. young lawyer's sect. 1967-68, pres. 1990, nominating com. 1995—, constn. com. 1999, spkr.), Athelstan Downtown Men's Club (bd. dirs. 1987-89), Mardi Gras Orgns., KC (3rd, 4th degree, bd. advisors 1967-74, Knight of Quarter 1969). Roman Catholic. Avocations: tennis, golf, aerobic exercise, gardening, hunting. Home: 116 Ryan Ave Mobile AL 36607-3228

FINKE, LEONDA FROEHLICH, sculptor, educator; b. NYC; d. Herman and Evelyn (Praeger) Froehlich; m. Arnold I. Finke; children: David, Erica, Rachel. Student, Art Students League, N.Y.C., 1945. Instr. large bronze figure sculpture and samll art medals, Roslyn, N.Y., 1969-95; academician NAD, 1994—. One-woman shows include Oxford Gallery, Rochester, NY, others; exhibited in group shows at L.I. Mus., Stonybrook, NY, 2003, others; represented in permanent collections at Smithsonian Nat. Portrait Gallery (portrait of Georgia O'Keefe), Brit. Mus., Century Assn., Chrysler Mus., Butler Inst. Am. Art, CUNY, Bates Coll. Mus. Art, (outdoor sculpture) Brookgreens Gardens, S.C., Grounds for Sculpture, N.J.; commd. works include 3 life-size bronzes for park in Altlanta, Max Som medal for Albert Einstein Med. Coll., 1991, Brit. Art Med. Soc. commn. of Virginia Woolf medal, 1989, Royal Philharm. Orch. commn. for medal, 1995, Aiken award poetry, Sewanee Rev., Tenn.; exhibited medals FIDEM, Helsinki, 1990, Brit. Mus., London, 1992; slide talk FIDEM, London, 1992, Germany, 2000; guest lectr., exhibitor Brit. Art Medal Soc., Loughborough U., Eng. Recipient medal of Honor Nat. Assn. Women Artists, 1972, Alex Ettl award NAD, 1990, J. Sanford Saltus award Am. Numismatic Soc., 1997. Fellow Nat. Sculpture Soc. (sec. 1987—, Gold medal 1989, Bas Relief award 1991, Maurice Hexter award 1992, Agop Agapoff award 1993, Silver medal and John Cavanaugh prize 1994), Sculptors Guild, N.Y. Soc. Women Artist (sculptors guild exhbn. in Kyoto, Japan 1993), Medallic Sculpture Assn., Audubon Artists (pres. 1984-85, medal of honor 1979). Jewish. Home: 10 The Locusts Roslyn NY 11576-1724

FINKE, ROBERT FORGE, lawyer; b. Chgo., Mar. 11, 1941; s. Robert Frank and Helen Theodora (Forge) Finke. AB, U. Mich., 1963; JD, Harvard U., 1966. Bar: Ill. 1966, U.S. Dist. Ct. (no. dist.) Ill. 1966, U.S. Ct. Appeals (7th cir.) 1966, U.S. Supreme Ct. 1970, U.S. Ct. Appeals (9th cir.) 1980, U.S. Ct. Appeals (4th and 6th cirs.) 1982, (18th cir.), 1998. Law clk., 1966—67; assoc. Mayer, Brown Rowe & Maw LLP, Chgo., 1967—71, ptnr., 1972—. Pres., bd. dirs. Lyric Opera Guild; trustee Rush Presbyn. St. Luke's Med. Ctr. Mem. ABA (sects. litigation, bus., antitrust, legal edn. and admissions to the bar, vice chmn. 1974-75), Lawyers Club Chgo., Univ. Club, Econ. Club. Office: Mayer Brown Rowe & Maw 190 S La Salle St Ste 3100 Chicago IL 60603-3441

FINKEL, EUGENE JAY, lawyer; b. Phila., June 21, 1931; BA, Swarthmore (Pa.) Coll., 1952; MA, George Washington U., 1961, JD, 1965. Bar: U.S. Dist. Ct. D.C. 1966, U.S. Ct. Appeals (D.C. cir.) 1972, U.S. Supreme Ct. 1980. Various positions U.S. Dept. Treasury, Washington, 1952-74; dep. dir. Office Internat. Fin. Policy Coordination and Ops., Washington, 1963-67; dir. Office Latin Am., Washington, 1967-70, Multilateral Instns. Program Office, 1970-74, Developing Nations Fin., 1974-75; asst. exec. sec. World Bank-IMF Devel. Com., 1975-77; alt. U.S. exec. dir. Inter-Am. Devel. Bank, Washington, 1977-81; ptnr. Porter Wright Morris & Arthur, Washington, 1981—. Lt. comdr. USNR ret. Office: Porter Wright et al 1919 Pennsylvania Ave NW Washington DC 20006-3434 E-mail: jfinkel@porterwright.com.

FINKEL, GERALD MICHAEL, lawyer; b. N.Y.C., July 29, 1941; s. Abraham B. and Elizabeth B. (Michaels) F.; m. Beverly Lynne Jaffee, Aug. 26, 1962; children: Bruce Daniel, Judith Michelle. BA, NYU, 1962; JD, U. S.C., 1970. Bar: S.C. 1970, U.S. Dist. Ct. S.C. 1970, U.S. Ct. Appeals (4th cir.) 1973, U.S. Supreme Ct. 1973, D.C. 1973. Prin. Finkel & Altman, L.L.C. and predecessor firm, Columbia, S.C., 1970—. Adj. prof. trial advocacy and ins. law U. S.C.; mem. faculty fed. trial practice AM. Law Inst., ABA; lectr. S.C. Bar, S.C. Trial Lawyers Assn., Richland County Bar and Profl. Insts.; instr. S.C. Dept. Pub. Safety/Criminal Justice Acad.; spl. judge Richland County Family Ct., 1974-78, Ct. Gen. Sessions 5th Jud. Cir., 1976 Author: (with Ralph C. McCullough II) A Guide to South Carolina Torts, 1st edit., 1981, 2d edit., 1986, 3d edit., 1990, 4th edit., 1995, (with Elizabeth Rhodes) South Carolina Legal and Business Forms, Vols. 1 and 3, 1997. Hearing officer S.C. Dept. Health and Environ. Control, 1979-82; mem. S.C. Appellate Def. Commn., 1982-83, Gov.'s Sentencing Guidelines Commn., 1982-83. Served to capt. U.S. Army, 1962-67. Recipient Outstanding Alumni cert. Phi Alpha Delta, 1972 Mem. ABA, S.C. Bar Assn. (bd. govs. 1985-88, profl. responsibility com. and ethics adv. com.), Richland County Bar Assn., Assn. Trial Lawyers Am., Am. Law Inst. (consultative group for restatement of the law 3d unfair competition, consultative group restatement law 3d torts), S.C. Trial Lawyers Assn. (exec. bd. 1978-81, pres. 1982-83), Phi Alpha Delta (dist. justice 1976-78). Democrat. Jewish. Home: 156 Pelzer Dr Summerville SC 29485-9703 Office: Finkel & Altman 1201 Main St Ste 1800 Columbia SC 29201-3294 E-mail: jfinkel@finkellaw.com.

FINKEL, JAY, psychiatrist; b. N.Y.C., Nov. 19, 1952; s. Paul and Ruth Finkel. BS, Hobart Coll., 1974; MS, CUNY, 1976; MD, N.Y. Med. Coll., 1980. Diplomate Am. Bd. Psychiatry and Neurology. Unit chief Mt. Sinai Hosp., N.Y.C., 1988—95; pvt. practice in psychiatry N.Y.C., 1984—. Named one of N.Y. Top Drs., N.Y. Mag., 1998, 1999, Castle/Connelly Guide to N.Y. Physicians, 1993—. Mem.: APA, Alpha Omega Alpha. Avocations: music, maps. Office: 108 E 91st St New York NY 10128

FINKEL, MARION JUDITH, physician, pharmaceutical company administrator; b. N.Y.C., Nov. 2, 1929; d. Israel and Bella (Stillman) Finkel; m. Simon V. Manson, Sept. 12, 1954. Student, L.I. U., 1945-48; MD (Howard Sloan Meml. scholar), Chgo. Med. Sch., 1952. Intern Jersey City Med. Ctr., 1952-53; resident in internal medicine Bellevue Hosp., N.Y.C., 1954-56; med. editor Merck and Co., 1957-61; pvt. practice specializing in internal medicine, N.Y.C., 1956-57, 1961-63; with FDA, 1963-85, dir. divsn. metabolic and endocrine drugs, 1966-70, dep. dir. bur. drugs, 1970-71, 72-74, dir. office new drug

evaluation, 1971-72, 74-82, dir. office orphan products devel., 1982-85; exec. dir. R&D Berlex Labs., Inc., 1985-88; v.p. drug registration and regulatory affairs Sandoz Pharms., Inc., 1988-94, v.p. corp. regulatory compliance, 1994-95, cons. regulatory affairs, clin. R&D, 1995—. Contbr. chpts. to books, numerous articles to profl. jours. Recipient award of merit FDA, 1972, Superior Svc. award USPHS, 1976, 84, Fed. Woman's award Fed. Govt., 1976, Meritorious Exec. award, 1980; named Disting. Alumnus, Chgo. Med. Sch., 1977, L.I. U., 1980. Office: 21 Squirrel Run Morristown NJ 07960-6411

FINKEL, SANFORD NORMAN, lawyer; b. Troy, N.Y., Oct. 19, 1946; s. Max and Mildred (Fares) F.; m. Amy Lynn Gordon, Oct. 13, 1974 (div. July 1984); children: Marcy Jennifer, Melanie Gordon. BA, SUNY, Buffalo, 1968; JD, Union U., 1974. Bar: N.Y 1975, U.S. Dist. Ct. (no. dist.) N.Y. 1975. Tchr. sci. Enlarged City Sch. Dist. of Troy, N.Y., 1968-71; pvt. practice Troy, 1975—; counsel to dem. study group N.Y. State Assembly, Albany, 1977-78; instr. paralegal studies Jr. Coll. Albany divsn. Russell Sage Coll., 1977-81; dep. corp. counsel City of Troy, 1990-94. Mem. Rensselaer County Bar Assn. Avocations: reading, numismatics, philately, travel. Home: 19 Capitol Pl Rensselaer NY 12144-9658 Office: 68 2nd St Troy NY 12180-3932

FINKELDAY, JOHN PAUL, retail sales executive; b. Pleasantville, N.J., Nov. 20, 1943; s. Charles John Henry and Viola Sybilla (Eastlack) F.; m. Karen Lynn Mattoon, Nov. 16, 1963; 1 son, John Paul. Student, Glassboro State Coll., 1961-63, Rider Coll., 1965. With McGraw Hill Publ. Co., Hightstown, N.J., 1963-65; asst. controller Exel Wood Products Co., Inc., Lakewood, N.J., 1965-66, office mgr., 1966-82, mgr. data processing, 1970-78, v.p., dir. data processing, 1978-83, v.p. MIS, 1983-86, v.p. adminstrn., 1983-84; v.p. Amici Systems, Inc., Brick, N.J., 1986-88; data processing mgr. Hamilton Beach, Inc., Washington, N.C., 1988-90, Hamilton Beach/Proctor-Silex, Inc., Washington, N.C., 1990-91; owner J&L Enterprises d/b/a Karen's Gifts, Greenville, N.C., 1991—; pres. ESP plus Inc., Greenville, N.C., 1993—. Mem. Del. Valley Computer Users Group. Third v.p. exec. com. Adm. Farragut Acad. Parents Assn., 1980-81. Mem. Am. Mgmt. Assn., U.S. Golf Assn. (assoc.), N.C. Aquarium Soc., Greenville Country Club. Home: 3044 Dartmouth Dr Greenville NC 27858-6745 Office: ESP plus Inc 803A Red Banks Rd Greenville NC 27858-5834

FINKELMAN, PAUL, law educator; b. Bklyn., Nov. 15, 1949; s. Simon and Ella Finkelman; m. Byrgen Finkelman. BA, Syracuse U., 1971; MA, U. Chgo., 1972, PhD, 1976. Instr. history U. Calif., Irvine, 1976—77; Andrew W. Mellon faculty fellow Wash. U., 1977—78; asst. prof. history U. Tex., 1978—84, SUNY, Binghamton, 1984—90; vis. prof. Bklyn. Law Sch., 1990—92; assoc. prof. history Va. Tech., 1992—95; vis. prof. Chgo. Kent Law Sch., 1995; Charlton W. Tebeau rsch. prof. U. Miami, Fla., 1996; dist. vis. prof. Hamline Law Sch., St. Paul, 1997; Baker Hostetler vis. prof. Cleve. Marshall Coll. Law, 1997—98; John F. Sieberling prof. U. Akron Sch. Law, Ohio, 1998—99; Chapman dist. prof. U. Tulsa Coll. Law, Okla., 1999—. Project dir. lecture series on Bill of Rights N.Y. Bicentennial Commn., 1989; dir. seminar secondary sch. tchrs. NEH, 1986, 88, 89; mem. adv. com. N.Y. State Freedom Trails Program, 1998—2000; fellow in law and history Harvard U., Cambridge, Mass., 1983; pres. 1921 Tulsa Meml. Found., 2003—. Author: An Imperfect Union: Slavery, Federalism and Comity, 1981, Slavery in the Courtroom, 1985 (Joseph L. Andrews award Am. Assn. Law Libr., 1986), The Law of Freedom and Bondage: A Casebook, 1986, Slavery and the Founders: Race and Liberty in the Age of Jefferson, 2d edit., 2001; co-author: Baseball and the American Legal Mind, 1995, American Legal History: Cases and Materials, 1996, Impeachable Offenses: A Documentary History From 1787 to the Present, 1998, A Match of Liberty: A Constitutional History of the United States, 2002; co-editor: Toward A Usable Past: Liberty Under State Constitutions, 1991, Macmillan Encyclopedia of World Slavery, 1998, The Encyclopedia of American Political History, 2001, The Library of Congress Civil War Desk Reference, 2002; editor: A Brief Narrative of the Tryal of John Peter Zenger, 1997, Religion and American Law: An Encyclopedia, 2000, Encyclopedia of the United States in the Nineteenth Century, 2001, Documents of American Constitutional and Legal History, 2002; contbr. chapters to books; editor: (two chpts.) His Soul Goes Marching On: Respones to John Brown and The Harpers Ferry Raid, 1995; contbr. articles; editor: (two chpts.) Slavery and The Law, 1997; co-editor: (series) Studies in the Legal History of the South; editor: Controversies in Constitutional Law, American History Through Literature; assoc. editor: American National Biography, 1990—98, Jour. So. Legal History, 1990—95, guest faculty editor: Chicago-Kent Law Review, vol. 68, no. 3, 1993, Chicago-Kent Law Review, vol. 70, no. 2 and no. 3, 1994, mem. editl. bd.: Law and History Review, 1985—92, Jour. of the Early Republic, 1985—88. Mem. adv. bd. N.Y. State Local Govt. Records, 1989—90; mem. jud. records disposition adv. com. N.Y. State Unified Ct. Sys., 1985—88; bd. dirs. Miller Mus. Jewish Art, Tulsa, Okla., 2001—. Recipient Historian of Yr., Va. Social Sci. Assn., 1995; fellow, Am. Bar Found., 1979—80, Harvard Law Sch., 1982—83, Am. Coun. Learned Soc., 1982—83, Nat. Endowment for Humanities, 1986—87, Japan Soc. for Promotion of Sci., 2001; grantee, Am. Philos. Soc., 1979, 1994, N.J. Hist. Commn., 1986, N.Y. African-Am. Inst., 1986—87, N.Y. State Archives, 1987—88, Ind. Hist. Soc., 1990; J. Franklin Jameson fellow, Libr. of Congress, 1978—79, Writing fellow, ACLS/Am. Nat. Biography, 1995—96. Mem.: Phi Kappa Phi, Phi Alpha Theta, Phi Beta Kappa. Democrat. Jewish. Office: Univ Tulsa Coll Law 3120 E 4th Pl Tulsa OK 74104

FINKELSTEIN, ALLEN LEWIS, lawyer; b. N.Y.C., Mar. 19, 1943; s. David and Ella (Miller) F.; m. Judith Elaine Stutman, June 20, 1964 (div. Mar. 1980); children: Jill, Jennifer; m. Shelley Gail Barone, June 15, 1980; 1 child, Amanda. BS, NYU, 1964; JD, Bklyn. Law Sch., 1967; MBA, L.I. U., 1969. Bar: N.Y. 1968, U.S. Dist. Ct. (ea. and so. dists.) N.Y. 1973, U.S. Ct. Appeals (2d cir.) 1973, U.S. Supreme Ct. 1976, U.S. Tax Ct. 1979. Ptnr. Finkelstein, Bruckman, Wohl, Most & Rothman, N.Y.C., 1974-97; sr. ptnr. Pressman Finkelstein, N.Y.C., 1997-99; ptnr. Ganfer & Shore LLP, N.Y.C., 1999—. Asst. prof. L.I. U., N.Y.C., 1969-73, adj. assoc. prof., 1973-74; bd. dirs. Amyotrophic Lateral Sclerosis Assn. Mem. ABA (bus. law and family law sect.), N.Y. State Bar Assn., Assn. of Bar of City of N.Y., Queens County Bar Assn. Lodges: Masons. Jewish. Home: 425 E 63rd St New York NY 10021-7804 Office: Ganfer & Shore LLP 360 Lexington Ave New York NY 10017-6502 E-mail: afinkelstein@ganshore.com.

FINKELSTEIN, BERNARD, lawyer; b. N.Y.C., Jan. 21, 1930; s. Irving and Sadie (Katz) F.; m. Adele S. Levine, June 29, 1952; children: Sharon Ann, Marcia Lyn. BA, NYU, 1951; LLB, Yale U., 1954. Bar: N.Y. 1954, D.C. 1970. Assoc. Paul, Weiss, Rifkind, Wharton & Garrison, LLP, N.Y.C., 1956-64, ptnr., 1965-95, of counsel, 1996—. Mem. wills and trusts adv. com. Practicing Law Inst. Trustee, mem. Altman Found., N.Y.C., 1985—. Named one of the Best Lawyers in N.Y., N.Y. Mag., 1995. Fellow Am. Coll. of Trust and Estate Counsel (estate and gift tax com. 1987-93); mem. ABA (com. on pre-death planning, probate and trust div. of sect. on real property, probate and trust law 1985-88), N.Y. State Bar Assn. (chmn. gift and tax com. of tax sect. 1978-80), Assn. of Bar of City of N.Y. (trusts, estate and surrogate's ct. com. 1986-89), N.Y. Bar Found., Yale Law Sch. Assn. (exec. com. 1983-86), Phi Beta Kappa, Phi Alpha Delta, Order of Coif. Clubs: Elmwood Country (White Plains, N.Y.). Home: 1 Tory Ln Scarsdale NY 10583-2314 Office: Paul Weiss Rifkind Wharton & Garrison LLP 1285 Avenue of the Americas New York NY 10019-6064

FINKELSTEIN, DAVID, retired cardiologist; b. Phila., Apr. 27, 1911; MD, Temple U., 1935. Diplomate Am. Bd. Internal Medicine, Am. Bd. Cardiovascular Diseases. Ret., 1987; assoc. prof. medicine U. Pa.; staff physician Wilmington VA Hosp. With U.S. Army, New Guinea. Fellow ACP, Am. Coll. Cardiology; mem. AMA, Am. Heart Assn.

FINKELSTEIN, DAVID RITZ, physicist, educator, consultant; b. N.Y.C., July 19, 1929; s. Isidore and Esther (Rubinstein) F.; m. Helene Cooper, 1948 (div.); children: Daniel, Beth, Eve; m. Shlomit Ritz, 1981; 1 child, Aria. BS, CCNY, 1949; PhD, MIT, 1953. Asst., then assoc. prof. physics Stevens Inst. Tech., 1954-60; assoc. prof. Yeshiva U., then prof., chmn., dean, 1960-79; prof. physics Ga. Inst. Tech., 1979—. Vis. prof. Tougaloo Coll., 1965, Hebrew U. Jerusalem, 1974 Author: Quantum Relativity, 1996; editor Internat. Jour. Theoretical Physics; editl. bd. mem. Jour. Math. Physics, 1991-93. Co-chmn. Miss. Project Parents Com., 1965. Ford Found. fellow, 1958; NSF grantee, 1954-96. Fellow Lindisfarne Assn.; mem. AAAS, Am. Phys. Soc., Internat. Quantum Structures Assn. (sec. 1990-93). Jewish. Achievements include research in black holes, high energy physics, space-time quanta, topological physics, gravity, quantum logic, Clifford-algebraic quantum network dynamics, quantum computers. Office: Ga Inst Tech Physics Dept Atlanta GA 30332-0001 E-mail: david.finkelstein@physics.gatech.edu.

FINKELSTEIN, EDWARD SYDNEY, department store executive; b. New Rochelle, N.Y., Mar. 30, 1925; s. Maurice and Eva (Levine) F.; m. Myra Schuss, Aug. 13, 1950; children: Mitchell, Daniel, Robert. BA, Harvard U., 1946, MBA, 1948; DCS (hon.), N.Y.U., 1988. Successively trainee, buyer mdse. adminstr. Macy's, N.Y.C., 1948-62, sr. v.p., dir. merchandising, 1962-67, exec. v.p., merchandising and sales promotion, 1967-69, pres., 1969-74, pres., chmn., chief exec. officer, 1974-80; chmn., chief exec. officer R.H. Macy & Co. Inc., 1980-92; dir. R.H. Macy, Inc., 1971-92; chmn. bd. Finkelstein Assocs., N.Y.C., 1992-97; chmn., CEO CWT Specialty Stores, Inc. d/b/a/ Cherry & Webb, N.Y.C., 1997-99; chmn. Finkelstein/Eugene Assocs., Inc., N.Y.C., 1999—. Mem. adv. bd. Yale Sch. Mgmt., 1984-89. Mem. nat. adv. coun. Cystic Fibrosis Found., 1975-80, trustee, 1977-80, hon. trustee, 1980—; mem. adv. bd. Harvard Bus. Sch., 1983-91. With USN, 1943-46. Mem. Harvard Club. Jewish. Office: Finkelstein/Eugene Assoc Inc 19 W 44th St New York NY 10036-5902

FINKELSTEIN, JAMES ARTHUR, management consultant; b. N.Y.C., Dec. 6, 1952; s. Harold Nathan and Lilyan (Crystal) F.; m. Lynn Marie Gould, Mar. 24, 1984; children: Matthew, Brett. BA, Trinity Coll., Hartford, Conn., 1974; MBA, U. Pa., 1976. Cons. Towers, Perrin, Forster & Crosby, Boston, 1976-78; mgr. compensation Pepsi-Cola Co., Purchase, N.Y., 1978-80; mgr. employee info. systems Am. Can. Co., Greenwich, Conn., 1980; mgr. bus. analysis Emery Airfreight, Wilton, Conn., 1980-81; v.p. Meidinger, Inc., Balt., 1981-83; prin. The Wyatt Co., San Diego, 1983-88; pres., chief exec. officer W. F. Corroon, San Francisco, 1988-95; founder, CEO FutureSense, Inc., 1995—97, chmn., CEO, 2001—; founder TallyUp Software, 1996—; dir. En Wisen, Inc., 1996-98; ptnr. Andersen LLP, San Francisco, 1997-2001. Mem. regional adv. bd. Mchts. and Mfrs. Assn., San Diego, 1986-88; instr. U. Calif., San Diego, 1984-88. Mem. camp com. State YMCA of Mass. and R.I., Framingham, 1982-86; pres. Torrey Pines Child Care Consortium, La Jolla, Calif., 1987-88, Marin Football Club, Inc., 2003—; vice chmn. La Jolla YMCA, 1986-88; chmn. fin. com. YMCA, San Francisco, 1992-95, vice chmn., 1993-95, chmn., 1995-97, bd. dirs., 1988—; bd. dirs. San Domenico Sch., 1994-2000; trustee World Affairs Coun., 1998—; bd. dirs. Becket Chimney Corners YMCA, 1999—; treas. Ctrl. Marin Competitive Soccer Club, 2000—. Avocations: music, sports, camping. Home: 17 Bracken Ct San Rafael CA 94901-1587 Office: FutureSense Inc 369 B 3d St # 181 San Rafael CA 94901-3581 E-mail: jim@futuresense.com.

FINKELSTEIN, JAMES DAVID, physician, educator; b. N.Y.C., Oct. 16, 1933; s. Harry and Sylvia Z. (Bernstein) F.; m. Barbara Joan Eisenberg, Dec. 12, 1959; children: Donna Ilene, Laura Helene. AB, Harvard U., 1954; MD, Columbia U., 1958. Diplomate Am. Bd. Internal Medicine. Intern, resident in medicine Presbyn. Hosp., N.Y.C., 1971-73; chief med. svc. VA Med. Ctr., Washington, 1979-99, chief gastroenterology, 1970-79, assoc. chief staff for rsch., 1975-79, med. investigator, 1970-75, clin. investigator, 1965-68, chief biochemistry rsch. lab., 1965—, sr. clinician, 1999—. Cons. Children's Hosp., Washington, 1968-85; prof. medicine George Washington U., 1969—; clin. prof. medicine Georgetown U., 1981—, prof. medicine Howard U., Washington, 1983—; mem. Nutrition Study sect. NIH, 1972-78; hon. pres. 2d Internat. Conf. on Homocysteine Metabolism, Nijmegen, Netherlands, 1998. Contbr. articles on biochemistry and nutrition of methionine to profl. jours. Served as surgeon USPHS, 1963-65. Recipient F.P. Gay Rsch award Columbia U., N.Y.C., 1956, Arthur S. Fleming award Jr. C. of C., Washington, 1971, Disting. Rschr. medal George Washington U., 1999; NIH grantee, 1966-95. Mem. Am. Soc. for Clin. Investigation, Am. Gastroent. Assn., Assn. of Am. Physicians, Am. Inst. Nutrition, Am. Soc. Clin. Nutrition (Robert H. Herman award 2001), Am. Fedn. Clin. Rsch., Harvard Club. Office: VA Med Ctr 50 Irving St NW Washington DC 20422-0001 E-mail: james.finkelstein@med.va.gov.

FINKELSTEIN, JEROME, physicist, educator; b. Long Branch, N.J., Aug. 22, 1941; s. Saul and Anna F.; m. Helen Finkelstein, May 27, 1966; children: Erik, Malaika. BA, Columbia U., 1963; PhD, U. Calif., Berkeley, 1967. Vis. scientist CERN, Geneva, 1967-68, 70-71; asst. prof. physics Stanford U., Palo Alto, Calif., 1968-72, Columbia U., N.Y.C., 1972-79, San Jose (Calif.) State U., 1980-82, assoc. prof. physics, 1982-85, prof. physics, 1985—. NORDITA guest prof. U. Helsinki, 1974; participating guest Lawrence Berkeley Nat. Lab., Berkeley, Calif., 1980—. Editor: A Passion for Physics, 1985; contbr. articles to profl. jours. Recipient Postdoctoral fellowship NATO, 1967-68, fellowship Alfred P. Sloan Found., 1970-74; Rsch. grant NSF, 1984-88. Avocations: photography, canoeing, kayaking. Office: San Jose State U Dept Physics San Jose CA 95192-0106

FINKELSTEIN, JOSEPH SIMON, lawyer; b. Vineland, N.J., Feb. 28, 1952; s. Absalom and Goldie (Cukier) Finkelstein; m. Sara M. Green, May 30, 1976; children: Adam, Julia, Seth. BA, Rutgers U., 1973; JD, U. Pa., 1976. Bar: Pa. 1976, N.J. 1976, U.S. Supreme Ct. 1982. Assoc. Wolf, Block, Schorr and Solis-Cohen, Phila., 1976-85, ptnr., 1985—. Pres. Perelman Jewish Day Sch., 1996—99; mem. Wexner Heritage Found., 1991—95; mem. exec. com., bd. dirs., chair funds distbn. United Way Southeastern Pa., 1997—99; exec. bd. young leadership coun. bd. Fedn. Jewish Agys., Phila., 1986—88; mem. nat. young leadership cabinet United Jewish Appeal, 1987—91; bd. dirs. Temple Beth Hillel Beth El, Beth Am Israel; trustee Jewish Fedn. Greater Phila., 1996—2000; bd. dirs. State of Israel Bonds, Phila., SCRUB Found. Recipient New Life/New Leadership award, State of Israel, 1989, Hearts of Gold award, United Way Southeastern Pa., 1999. Mem.: ABA, Pa. Land Title Assn., Phila. Bar Assn., N.J. Bar Assn., Pa. Bar Assn., Internat. Coun. Shopping Ctrs. Home: 716 Oxford Rd Bala Cynwyd PA 19004-2112 Office: Wolf Block Schorr & Solis-Cohen LLP 1650 Arch St Fl 22D Philadelphia PA 19103-2097 E-mail: jfinkelstein@wolfblock.com.

FINKELSTEIN, NORMAN, literature educator; b. N.Y.C., May 30, 1954; s. Harry and Dora Lana Finkelstein; m. Alice West, May 10, 1997; m. Kathryn Wekselman (div.); children: Ann Kayla, Steven Max. BA, Binghamton U., 1975; PhD, Emory U., 1980. Prof. English Xavier U., Cin., 1980—. Author: (volume of poetry) Restless Messengers, Track, Columns: Track, Volume II, (book) The Utopian Moment In Contemporary American Poetry, The Ritual of New Creation: Jewish Tradition and Contemporary Literature, Not One of Them In Place: Modern Poetry and Jewish American Identity. Jewish. Office: Xavier Univ 3800 Victory Pkwy Cincinnati OH 45243-4446 Office Fax: 513-745-3065. Personal E-mail: finkelstein.norman@lycos.com. E-mail: finkelst@xu.edu.

FINKELSTEIN, NORMAN HENRY, librarian; b. Chelsea, Mass., Nov. 10, 1941; s. Sydney and Mollie (Fox) F.; m. Rosalind Brandt, July 4, 1967; children: Jeffrey, Robert, Risa. BS, Boston U., 1963, MEd, 1964; MA, Hebrew Coll., 1986. Dir. edn. Hebrew Coll. Sch. & Camp, Northwood, N.H., 1982-87; instr. Hebrew Coll., Brookline, Mass., 1982—; libr./media specialist Brookline Pub. Schs., 1970—. Author: Remember Not to Forget: A Memory of the Holocaust, 1985, The Other 1492: Jewish Settlement in the New World, 1989, The Emperor General: A Biography of Douglas MacArthur, 1989, Theodor Herzl: Architect of a Nation, 1991, Captain of Innocence: France and the Dreyfus Affair, 1991, Sounds in the Air: The Golden Age of Radio, 1993, Thirteen Days/Ninety Miles: The Cuban Missile Crisis, 1994, With Heroic Truth: The Life of Edward R. Murrow, 1997, Heeding The Call, 1997, Friends Indeed, 1998, The Way Things Never Were, 1999, Forged in Freedom, 2002.. CBE/NEH fellow, Washington, 1992; Study grantee Brookline Found., 1987; recipient study award Kennedy Presdl. Libr., 1987, Ford Presdl. Libr., 1996, Golden Kite Honor award, 1997, Nat. Jewish Book award, 1998, 2002. Mem. Mass. Sch. Libr./Media Assn. (com. chair 1977-82), Wayfarer's Club, Phi Delta Kappa. Office: Edward Devotion Libr 345 Harvard St Brookline MA 02446-2907 E-mail: nfinkelstein@hebrewcollege.edu.

FINKELSTEIN, RICHARD ALAN, retired microbiology educator, consultant; b. N.Y.C., Mar. 5, 1930; s. Frank and Sylvia (Lemkin) F.; m. Helen Rosenberg, Nov. 30, 1952; children: Sheri, Mark, Laurie; m. Mary Boesman, June 20, 1976; 1 dau., Sarina Nicole. BS, U. Okla., 1950; MA, U. Tex., Austin, 1952, PhD, 1955. Teaching fellow, research scientist U. Tex., Austin, 1950-55; fellow, instr. U. Tex. Southwestern Med. Sch., Dallas, 1955-58; chief bioassay sect. Walter Reed Army Inst. Research, Washington, 1958-64; dep. chief, chief dept. bacteriology and mycology U.S. Army Med. Component, SEATO Med. Research Lab., Bangkok, Thailand, 1964-67; assoc. prof. dept. microbiology U. Tex. Southwestern Med. Sch., Dallas, 1967-73, prof., 1973-79; prof., chmn. dept. microbiology Sch. Medicine U. Mo., Columbia, 1979-93, Curators' prof., 1990-2000, Millsap Disting. Prof., 1985-2000, prof. emeritus, 2000—. Mem. Nat. Com. for Coordination Cholera Rsch., Ministry for Pub. Health, Bangkok, 1965-67; cons. WHO, 1970—, commdg. gen. U.S. Army Med. R&D Command, 1975-79, Schwarz-Mann Labs., 1974-79, ICN Biomeds., 1979—, Wyeth-Ayerst, 1992—, Amgen, 1992, Molecular Pharms., 1993—; Microbiolog. and Infectious Diseases Rsch. Com. Nat. Inst. Allergy and Infectious Diseases, NIH, 1994-98; vis. assoc. prof. U. Med. Scis., Bangkok, 1965-67; vis. prof. U. Chgo., Med. Sch., 1977; vis. scientist Japanese Sci. Coun., 1976, Ciba-Geigy lectr. Waksman Inst., Rutgers U., 1975; vis. lectr. Nat. Sci. Coun., Taipei, Taiwan, 1995, others. Contbr. articles on cholera, enterotoxins, gonorrhea, and role of iron in host-parasite interactions to profl. jours. Recipient Robert Koch prize Bonn, Fed. Republic Germany, 1976; Chancellor's award for outstanding faculty rsch. in biol. scis. U. Mo.-Columbia, 1985, Sigma Xi Rsch. award U. Mo.-Columbia, 1986. Fellow Am Acad. Microbiology (bd. govs. 1990-93), Am. Soc. for Microbiology (pres. Tex. br. 1974-75, hon. Tex. br. divsn. councilor, chmn. program com. 1979-82, sec.-treas. Mo. br. 1985-87, v.p. 1987-89, pres. 1989-91, councillor, 1991-92, coun. policy com. 1992-95, Disting. Svc. award 1998), Am. Assn. Immunologists, Infectious Diseases Soc. of Am., Soc. Gen. Microbiology, Pathol. Soc. Gt. Britain and Ireland, Sigma Xi. Achievements include first purification of cholera enterotoxin; first purification of heat-labile enterotoxin from Escherichia coli; patent for living attenuated candidate cholera vaccine. Home: 3861 S Forest Acres Dr Columbia MO 65203-8608 Office: U Mo Sch Medicine Dept Molecular Microbiol Columbia MO 65212-0001

FINKELSTEIN, RONALD, assistant principal, director; b. New Brunswick, N.J., Nov. 22, 1962; s. Wallace and Cynthia Finkelstein; m. Andrea Sable, Oct. 17, 1993; children: Samuel Douglas, Dana Morgan. BA, SUNY, Binghamton, 1986; MEd, Coll. New Rochelle, N.Y., 1988, PDL, 1996; EdD, St. John's U., Jamaica, N.Y., 1999. Cert. tchr. handicapped learning disabilities N.J., tchr. cons. N.J., sch. prin. N.J., sch. adminstr. N.J. Tchr. spl. edn. N.Y.C. Bd. Edn., Bronx, 1986—95; sch. prin. Morris County Ednl. Svcs. Commn., Morristown, NJ, 1995—99, Mine Hill (N.J.) Twp. Bd. Edn., 1999—2000; asst. prin., dir. spl. svcs. Manchester Regional HS, Haledon, NJ, 2000—. Adj. prof. William Paterson U., Wayne, NJ, 2001—. Mem.: N.J. Prins. and Suprs. Assn. Avocation: auto restoration. Office: Manchester Regional HS 70 Church St Haledon NJ 07508 Office Fax: 973-956-8805.

FINKELSTEIN, SEYMOUR, business consultant; b. N.Y.C., July 14, 1923; s. Morris and Anna (Landin) F.; m. Hermine Yuder, June 19, 1948 (dec. Aug. 1989); children: Andrew, Charles, Robert, Adam. BS in Econs., U. Pa., 1946; student Wharton Sch., Univ. of Pa. Supr. Glemby Internat., N.Y.C., 1946-53, mktg. exec., 1953-58, account exec., 1958-62, v.p., 1962-64, pres., 1964-89, chmn., 1989-90. Cons. in field; mem. bd. overseers Inst. Contemporary Art, 1988—; trustee U. Pa., 1980-85; bd. dirs. Am. Crafts Mus., N.Y.C.; mem. pres.'s coun. U. Pa. Lt. USAAF, 1943-45. Mem.: Met. Pres.'s Orgn., Chief Execs. Orgn., Air Force Assn., Am. Numismatics Assn. (life), Am. Numismatics Soc., Scarsdale Hist. ., U. Pa. Club N.Y., Fairview Country Club (bd. dirs. 1982—84). Republican. Jewish. Avocations: numismatics, tennis, music, art.

FINKENBINE, ROY EUGENE, history educator; b. Sidney, Ohio, Sept. 9, 1953; s. Richard Roy and Joy Evelyn (Miller) F.; m. Barbara Therese Emley, July 31, 1982; children: Michael, Daniel, Lorah, Sarah. BS in Social Studies, Taylor U., 1975; MA in History, No. Ariz. U., 1976; PhD in Am. Culture, Bowling Green State U., 1982. Adminstrv. asst. grants and spl. projects River Corridor Project Shelby County, Sidney, Ohio, 1977-78; from asst. editor to assoc. editor Black Abolitionist Papers Project/Fla. State U., Tallahassee, 1981-91; asst. prof. history Hampton (Va.) U., 1992-96, U. Detroit Mercy, 1996-98, assoc. prof. history and African-Am. studies, 1998—, dir. Black Abolitionist Archives. Vis. asst. prof. history Murray (Ky.) State U., 1991-92; assoc. editor Am. Nat. Biography, 1990-98. Author: (with C. Peter Ripley et al) Witness for Freedom: African American Voices on Race, Slavery, and Emancipation, 1993, The Black Abolitionist Papers, 1830-1865, 1985-92, Sources of the African-American Past, 1997, 2003; contbr. articles to profl. jours. Grantee Fla. State U., 1986-88, 91, Rockefeller Archive Ctr., 1983, NEH, 2002--; Bowling Green State U. Dissertation fellow, 1980-81, Teaching fellow Bowling Green State U., 1978-80, Nat. Hist. Publ. and Records Commn. fellow, 1981-82; Victorian Soc. in Am. scholar, 1979; Princeton U. fellow, 1986. Mem. Am. Hist. Assn., Orgn. Am. Historians, Phi Kappa Phi. Democrat. Lutheran. Home: 30850 Puritan Livonia MI 48154-3253 Office: U Detroit Mercy History Dept 4001 W McNichols Rd Detroit MI 48219 E-mail: finkenre@udmercy.edu.

FINKLE, BERNARD J, biochemist, researcher; b. Chgo., Ill., Mar. 17, 1921; s. Nathan Ephraim and Lena Finkle; m. Evelyn Cohen Finkle; children: Wayne, Claudia. BS, U. of Chgo., 1942; PhD, UCLA, 1950. Biochemist Western Regional Rsch. Lab., U.S. Dept. of Agrl., 1957—83; retired; cons. U. of Calif., 1983—90; asst. to exec. dir. (vol.) Golden State Wildlife Fedn., Berkeley, Calif., 1991; asst. to program dir. (vol.) Nat. Tchr. Tng. Inst., 1992; editor and experimentalist (vol.) Climate Protection Inst., 1992—93; tech. adv. to dir. (vol.) San Francisco Baykeeper, 1993—94; docent U. of Calif. Bot. Garden, 1993; libr. specialist Calif. Inst. of Biodiversity, 1994. Cons. Column Waters, Albany, Calif., 1977—83; lab. dir. Atomic Rsch. Lab., Los Angeles, 1953—54. Author: (book) Phenolic Compounds and Metabolism Regulation, 1967; contbr. articles to profl. jours. Bd. dirs. Congl. Beth Israel, Berkeley, Calif., 1964—66; Berkeley Cmty. Chorus and Orch., 1998—2003. Mem.: TESOL, Internat. Bd. for Plant Genetic Resources, Nat. Coun. on Gene Resources (adv. bd.), Tissue Culture Assn., Soc. for Cryobiology, Am. Chem. Soc., Phytochemical Soc. of North Am. (pres. 1965—66), Am. Soc. of Plant Physiologists, Am. Soc. of Biol. Chemists, Berkeley Cmty. Chorus and Orch. Achievements include patents for; discovery of new plant enzyme; catechol-O-methyl transerase. Avocations: music, singing. Home: 6216 Estates Dr Oakland CA 94611

FINKLE, JEFFREY ALAN, professional association executive; b. Newark, Ohio, Apr. 22, 1954; s. Richard James and Margery (Orr) F.; m. Diane Elizabeth Letchford, Aug. 20, 1983 (div. July 1989). BSc cum laude, Ohio U., 1976; postgrad., Ohio State U., 1978-80. Legis. dir. Ohio Rep. Party, Columbus, 1976-78; legis. liason Ohio Dept. Mental Health, Columbus, 1978-80; mktg. dir. Systems 80, Bethesda, Md., 1980-81; exec. asst. HUD, Washington, 1981-83, dep. asst. sec., 1983-86; pres., CEO Coun. for Urban Econ. Devel., Washington, 1986—2001; pres, CEO Internat. Econ. Devel. Coun., 2001. Mem. adv. com., Ohio U. Inst. for Local Govt. Adminstrn. and Rural Devel., 1986—. Bd. dirs., pres. Bollinger Found., 1989—, Arlington County Va. Econ. Devel. Corp., 1999—, D.C. Mktg. Ctr., 1998-2000. Mem. Housing Rehab. Assn. (bd. dirs. 1986-90), Nat. Assn. Ind. Living Ctrs. (nat. adv. bd. 1987-89), Sr. Living Choices (bd. dirs. 1991-98), Ohio U. Alumni Assn. (past pres. Washington chpt., past bd. dirs. nat. assn.). Republican. Roman Catholic. Avocations: golf, genealogy. Office: Internat Econ Devel Coun 734 15th St NW Ste 900 Washington DC 20005 E-mail: jfinkle@iedconline.org.

FINKS, ROBERT MELVIN, paleontologist, educator; b. Portland, Maine, May 12, 1927; s. Abraham Joseph and Sarah (Bendette) F. BS magna cum laude, Queens Coll., 1947; MA, Columbia U., 1954, PhD, 1959. Lectr. Bklyn. Coll., 1955-58, instr., 1959-61; lectr. Queens Coll., CUNY, 1961-62, asst. prof., 1962-65, acting chmn., 1963-64, assoc. prof. geology, 1966-70, prof., 1971—2002, prof. emeritus, 2002—; geologist U.S. Geol. Survey, 1952-54, 63—; rsch. assoc. Am. Mus. Natural History, 1961—77, Smithsonian Instn., 1968—; rsch. assoc. in paleontology N.Y. State Mus.; rsch. prof. dept. geology Union Coll., Schenectady, NY. Doctoral faculty CUNY, 1983—; cons. in field. Author: Late Paleozoic Sponge Faunas of the Texas Region, 1960; Editor: Guidebook to Field Excursions, 1968; Contbr. articles profl. jours. Queens Coll. Scholar, 1947. Fellow AAAS, Geol. Soc. Am., Explorers Club; mem. AAUP, Paleontol. Soc. (vice chmn. Northeastern sect. 1977-78, chmn. 1978-79), Paleontol. Assn. Britain, Soc. Econ. Paleontologists and Mineralogists, Internat. Palaeontol. Assn., Geol. Soc. Vt. (charter mem.), Planetary Soc. (charter), Phi Beta Kappa (v.p. Sigma chpt. N.Y. 1993-95, pres. 1995-99), Golden Key (hon.), Sigma Xi (exec. sec. Queens Coll. chpt. 1982-85). Office: Queens Coll CUNY Sch Earth and Environ Scis Flushing NY 11367 Address: Geology Dept Union Coll Schenectady NY 12308 *Be humble in studying nature.*

FINLAY, BRIAN DEREK, federal agency administrator; b. London, Ont., Can., July 26, 1972; s. Alexander and Katherine Finlay; m. Susan Blanchard, Aug. 26, 2001; children: Lauren McLeod, Benjamin Charles. BA with honors, U. Western Ont., London, 1994; grad. cert., Johns Hopkins U., Bologna, Italy, 1997; MA in Internat. Affairs, Carleton U., Ottawa, 1996. Cons. Dept. Fgn. Affairs, Ottawa, 1996—97; program mgr. Health Can., Ottawa, 1997—99; sr. rschr. Brookings Instn., Washington, 1999—2001; program officer The Century Found., Washington, 2001—02; dir. Nuclear Threat Reduction Campaign, Washington, 2002—. Mem. Coun. on Emerging Nat. Security Affairs, Washington, 2000—. Mem.: New Analysts Internat. Soc. Office: Nuclear Threat Reduction Campaign 1725 Eye St Flr 4 Washington DC 20006

FINLAY, JAMES CAMPBELL, retired museum director; b. Russell, Man., Can., June 12, 1931; s. William Hugh and Grace Muriel F.; m. Audrey Joy Barton, June 18, 1955; children: Barton Brett, Warren Hugh, Rhonda Marie. BSc, Brandon U., 1952; MSc in Zoology, U. Alta., 1968. Geophysicist Frontier Geophys. Ltd., Alta., 1952-53; geologist, then dist. geologist Shell Can., Ltd., 1954-64; chief park naturalist and biologist Elk Island (Can.) Nat. Park, 1965-67; dir. hist. devel. and archives, dir. hist. and sci. service, dir. Nature Center, dir. interpretation and recreation City of Edmonton, Alta., 1967-92; founder Fedn. Alta. Naturalists, 1969. Author: A Nature Guide to Alberta, Bird Finding Guide to Canada; (with Joy Finlay) Ocean to Alpine-A British Columbia Nature Guide, A Guide to Alberta Parks. Recipient Order of the Bighorn, Govt. of Atla., 1987, Heritage award Environment Can., 1990, Loran Goulden award Fedn. Alta Naturalists, 1991, Can. 125th Anniversary award, 1993, Greenways Achievement award, B.C. Province Capital Commn., 2001; named to Edmonton Hist. Hall of Fame, 1976. Mem. Can. Mus. Assn. (pres. 1976-78), Alta. Mus. Assn. (founding mem., past pres.), Am. Mus. Assn. (past council), Am. Ornithol. Union. Home: 270 Trevlac Pl RR 3 Victoria BC Canada V9E 2C4 *I will walk but once on this earth. In this short time I hope to help my fellow man come to a greater awareness, appreciation and understanding of the world environment of which we are very much a part. I am trying to ensure that our descendants have a fit planet on which to live.*

FINLAY, ROBERT DEREK, food company executive; b. U.K., May 16, 1932; s. William Templeton and Phyllis F.; m. Una Ann Grant, June 30, 1956; children: Fiona, Rory James. BA with honors in Law and Econs, Cambridge (Eng.) U., 1955, MA, 1959. With Mobil Oil Co. Ltd., U.K., 1955-61, assoc. McKinsey & Co., Inc., 1961-67, prin., 1967-71, dir., 1971-79; mng. dir. H.J. Heinz Co. Ltd., U.K., 1979-81; sr. v.p. corp. devel. world hdqs. H.J. Heinz Co., Pitts., 1981-93, chief fin. officer world hdqrs., 1989-92, sr. v.p. corp. devel., area v.p., 1992-93. Chmn. Dawson Internat., 1995-98. Mem. London com. Scottish Coun. Devel. and Industry, 1979-03; trustee Mercy Hosp., Pitts., 1983-93; bd. dirs. Pitts. Symphony Soc., 1989-92, U.S.-China Bus. Coun., 1984-92, Pitts. Pub. Theater, 1988-92. Capt. Gordon Highlanders, 1950-61. Fellow Inst. Dirs., Royal Soc. Arts; mem. Inst. Mktg., Highland Brigade Club, Leander Club, Annabel's, Caledonian Club, Three Rivers Rowing Assn. (gov.).

FINLAY, SUSAN SPARLING, education educator; b. Sarasota, Fla., Sept. 5, 1963; d. Gerald Walker and Joan Highleyman Sparling; m. John Michael Finlay, Sept. 5, 1987; 1 child, Logan Spencer. BA, Eckerd Coll., 1981—85; MA, U. of South Fla., 1988—90. Assoc. prof. of sociology and psychology Suffolk C.C., Selden, NY, 1992—95, Manatee C.C., Venice, Fla., 1996—. Bd. mem. Vol. Ctr. South, Venice, Fla., 1998—99. Mem.: Am. Sociol. Assn. (corr.), Am. Psychol. Soc. (corr.), APA (corr.), Am. Assn. of Women in Cmty. Colleges (corr.). Office: Manatee CC 8000 South Tamiami Trail Venice FL 34293 Office Fax: 941-497-7698. E-mail: finlays@mccfl.edu.

FINLAY, TERENCE EDWARD, archbishop; s. Terence John and Sarah (McBryan) F.; m. Alice-Jean Cracknell, 1962; 2 daus. BA, U. We. Ont., London; BTh, Huron Coll., London, Ont.; MA, U. Cambridge, Eng.; DD (jure dignitatis), Huron Coll., 1987. Ordained deacon Anglican Ch., 1961, priest, 1962. Dean of residence Renison Coll., Waterloo, Can.; incumbent All Saints, Waterloo, 1964-66, St. Aidan's, London, Can., 1966-68; rector St. John the Evangelist, London, 1968-78; archdeacon of Brant, 1978-82; incumbent Grace Ch., Brantford, Can., 1978-82, St. Clement's, Eglinton, Toronto, Can., 1982-86; suffragan bishop Diocese of Toronto, 1986, coadjutor bishop, 1987, bishop, 1989—; archbishop Met. of Ecclesiastical Province of Ont. Anglican. Avocations: music, skiing, travel. Office: Diocese of Toronto 135 Adelaide St E Toronto ON Canada M5C 1L8

FINLAYSON, BRUCE ALAN, chemical engineering educator; b. Waterloo, Iowa, July 18, 1939; s. Rodney Alan and Donna Elizabeth (Gilbert) F.; m. Patricia Lynn Hills, June 9, 1961; children: Mark, Catherine, Christine BA, Rice U., 1961, MS, 1963; PhD, U. Minn., 1965. Asst. prof. to assoc. prof. U. Wash., Seattle, 1967-77, prof. dept. chem. engring. and applied math., 1977-82, Rehnberg prof. dept. chem. engring., 1983—, chmn. dept. chem. engring., 1989-98. Vis. prof. Univ. Coll., Swansea, Wales, U.K., 1975-76, Denmark Tekniske Hojskole, Lyngby, 1976, Universidad Nacional del Sur, Bahia Blanca, Argentina, 1980; Gulf vis. prof. Carnegie Mellon U., 1986; trustee Computer Aids to Chem. Engring. Edn., Austin, Tex., 1980-92; mem. bd. on chem. sci. and tech. NRC, 1990-92. Mem. editorial bd. Internat. Jour. Numerical Methods in Fluids, Swansea, 1980—, Numerical Heat Transfer, 1981-2002, Numerical Methods for Partial Differential Equations, 1984—, Chem. Engring. Edn., 1991—; author: The Method of Weighted Residuals and Variational Principles, 1972, Nonlinear Analysis in Chemical Engineering, 1980, Numerical Methods for Problems with Moving Prints, 1992. Lt. USNR, 1965-67. Mem. AIChE (CAST divsn. programming 1981-85, William H. Walker award 1983, bd. dirs. CAST divsn. 1984-86, vice chmn. 1987-88, chmn. 1989, bd. dirs. 1992-94, editorial bd. 1985-91, v.p. 1999, pres. 2000, past pres. 2001), Am. Chem. Soc. (bd. dirs. Petroleum Rsch. Fund 1998--), Am. Soc. Engring. Edn. (dir. Summer Sch. for Chem. Engring. Faculty 1997), Soc. Indsl. and Applied Math., Soc. Rheology, Nat. Acad. Engring., N.Am. Alliance of Chem. Engrs. (pres. 2001). Home: 6315 22nd Ave NE Seattle WA 98115-6919 Office: U Wash Dept Chem Engring PO Box 351750 Seattle WA 98195-1750 E-mail: ravenna@mindspring.com., finlayson@cheme.washington.edu.

FINLAYSON, JOHN SYLVESTER, biochemist; b. Phila., Sept. 19, 1933; s. Alexander Smeillie and Anna Eva (Sylvester) F.; m. Rasma Irēne Bramane; children: Mark Lars, Siglinda Erika Finlayson Beyeler. BA summa cum laude, Marietta Coll., 1953; MS, U. Wis., 1955, PhD, 1957. Rsch. fellow Inst. Radiophysics, Stockholm, Sweden, 1957-58; biochemist NIH, Bethesda, Md., 1958-72; rsch. chemist FDA, Bethesda, 1972-75, chief Lab. Plasma Derivatives, 1975-86, chief Lab. Hepatitis, 1986-89, chief Lab. Hemostasis & Thrombosis, 1988-89, acting dir. divsn. hematology, 1990-92, assoc. dir. sci. office blood rsch. and review, 1993—. Vis. prof., scientist Protein Rsch. Inst., Osaka, Japan, 1976; lectr. in biochemistry Found. Advanced Edn. in Sci., Bethesda, 1961-76, 86-96. Author: Basic Biochemical Calculations, 1969; co-editor: Immunoglobulins, 1980; contbr. articles to profl. jours. With USPHS, 1958-61. Mem. Internat. Soc. Thrombosis and Haemostasis (charter), Soc. Exptl. Biology and Medicine, Sr. Biomed. Rsch. Svc. Office: FDA Ctr Biol Eval & Rsch HFM-330 1401 Rockville Pike Rockville MD 20852-1448

FINLEY, CHANDLER R. lawyer; b. Miami Beach, Fla., Oct. 2, 1963; BA, B of Music Performance/Polit. Sci., Emory U., 1985, JD, 1988. Bar: Fla. 1988, U.S. Dist. Ct. (so. dist.) Fla. 1989. Ptnr. Stuber & Finley, West Palm Beach, Fla., 1988-92; talent agt. Miami Beach, Fla., 1992—; ptnr. Finley & Assocs., West Palm Beach, 1992—2001, Chandler Finley & Assocs., West Palm Beach, 2001—02, Finley & Bologna Internat., 2003—; sports agt. Internat. Polo & Equestrian Sports Agy., West Palm Beach, 1994—. Legal counsel, state bd. Fla. Motion Picture T.V. Assn., Palm Beach County, 1995-2000, Finley Music and Entertainment, 1998—. Legal counsel Palm Beach County Work Force Devel. Bd., 1988—, Workforce Alliance, Inc., 2002—; bd.dirs. Fla. Philharmonic, West Palm Beach, 1997-2000. Mem.: Am. Immigration Lawyers Assn., Nat. Italian Am. Bar Assn., Italy Am. C. of C. (treas/. bd. dirs. 2002—). Office: Finley & Bologna Internat Ste 460 1645 Palm Beach Lakes Blvd West Palm Beach FL 33401-2217 also: 150 SE 2d St # 1010 Miami FL 33131 also: 1515 N Federal Hwy Ste 300 Boca Raton FL 33432-1994 E-mail: finleybologna@aol.com.

FINLEY, GARY ROGER, financial company executive; b. Gays, Ill., June 3, 1940; s. Fred Forrest and Dena Maxine (Jeffris) F.; m. Ardeth Kay Clawson, June 12, 1960; children: Deborah Finley Fisher, Shari Finley Swiger. AB, Lincoln (Ill.) Christian Coll., 1964; MA, Lincoln Christian Sem., 1971. Lic. commodities broker, securities broker. Ministry work Christian Ch. of Christ, Cen. and Western Ill., 1959-74; personnel counselor Jamar Personnel, Rock Island, Ill., 1974-75; sales and dept. mgr. Commodity Trend Svc., Davenport, Iowa, 1975-79; co-founder, co-owner Valley Commodities, Orion, Ill., 1979-83; sales rep. FGL Commodity Svcs., West Des Moines, Iowa, 1983-85; commodity pool operator pvt. practice, Orion, 1979-89; commodity broker, equity raiser Farmers Commodities Corp., Inc., West Des Moines, Iowa, 1987-93; pres. FCC Investments, Inc. and FCC Ultra, Inc., West Des Moines, 1990-93, also bd. dirs.; v.p., treas. The Com-Pac Corp., Davenport, Iowa, 1989-94; founder, pres. Finley Fin. Svcs., Inc., Gays, Ill., 1993-2001; owner, pres. Value Fuel, Inc., Gays, Ill., 1995-97; pres., owner Alpha Filtration Systems, Inc., Mattoon, Ill., 2001—. Dir., assoc. Nat. Ch. Growth Rsch. Ctr., Washington, 1992—; elder Orion Christian Ch., 1986-91; v.p. Prayerhouse Warehouse Ministry, Des Moines, 1992—; chaplain Heartland Christian Village, Neoga, Ill., 1998—. Avocations: ministry, fishing, art, music, bldg. constrn. Home: RR 1 Box 17 Gays IL 61928-9700 Office: 309 S 21st St #5 Mattoon IL 61938

FINLEY, GEORGE ALVIN, III, wholesale executive; b. Aurora, Ill., Apr. 25, 1938; s. George Alvin, II, and Sally Ann (Lord) F.; m. Sue Sellors, June 20, 1962 (dec. 1995); m. Phyllis Ann Finley; children: Valerie, George Alvin IV. BBA, So. Meth. U., 1962; postgrad. Coll. Grad. Program, Ford Motor Co., 1963. Rep. for Europe Finco Internat., 1959-61; trainee Ford Motor Co., Dearborn, Mich., 1962-63; v.p. mktg. Internat. Motor Cars, Oakland, Calif., 1963-64, Sequoia Lincoln lease mgr., 1965; regional mgr. Behlen Mfg. Co., Dallas, 1965-67; pres. C C Distbrs., Corpus Christi, Tex., 1967—. Guest instr. Sch. Bus., So. Meth. U., pres., 1986-91, Nueces River Authority, 1975-2001; bd. dirs. Contract Svcs. Assn. Am. Sec. Bd. Washington, MD Anderson Hosp. U. Tex., Christus-Spohn Health Sys., McDonald Obs., U. Tex., exec. com.; mem. Del Mar Coll. Found. Mem. pres.'s coun. Tex. A&M U., Corpus Christi. Mem. Tex. Wholesale Hardware Assn. (pres. 1991-92), Nat. Assn. Wholesalers, Am. Supply Assn., Wholesale Distbrs. Assn. (bd. dirs. 1994—), Impact Industries Inc. (chmn. bd. Sandwich, Ill. 1986-93), N.Am. Bldg. Material Distbn. Assn., Rotary Internat., State Bar of Tex. (grievance com. 1995-2001), Phi Delta Theta. Democrat. Methodist. Achievements include assisted in design, engring., production, mktg. Apollo Automobile, 1963-64. Home: 3360 Ocean Dr Corpus Christi TX 78411-1457 Office: PO Box 9153 210 Mcbride Ln Corpus Christi TX 78408-2338

FINLEY, GLENNA, writer; b. Puyallup, Wash., June 12, 1925; d. John Ford and Gladys De Ferris (Winters) F.; m. Donald MacLeod Witte, May 19, 1951; 1 child, Duncan MacLeod. BA cum laude, Stanford U., 1945. Producer internat. divsn. NBC, 1945-49; film librarian March of Time, 1949; with news bur. Life Mag., 1950; publicity and radio writer Seattle, 1950-51; freelance writer, 1951-57; contract writer New Am. Library Inc., N.Y.C., 1970—. Author numerous books including Master of Love, 1978, Beware My Heart, 1978, The Marriage Merger, 1978, Wildfire of Love, 1979, Timed for Love, 1979, Love's Temptation, 1979, Stateroom for Two, 1980, Affairs of Love, 1980, A Business Affair, 1983, Wanted for Love, 1983, A Weekend for Love, 1984, Love's Waiting Game, 1985, A Touch of Love, 1985, Diamonds for My Love, 1986, Secret of Love, 1987, The Marrying Kind, 1988, Island Rendezvous, 1990, Stowaway for Love, 1992, The Temporary Bride, 1993. Named Matrix Table Woman of Achievement, 1976 Mem.: Women's Univ. (Seattle). Republican. Anglican. Home: 7868-F Rea Rd #312 Charlotte NC 28277 *I have always made a point of writing pleasant books that "turn out right"- believing that after readers have opened their wallets to purchase a book all suffering should cease.*

FINLEY, GORDON ELLIS, psychology educator; b. Evanston, Ill., July 30, 1939; divorced; 2 children. BA, Antioch Coll., 1962; MA, Harvard U., 1965, PhD, 1968. Asst. prof. U. B.C., 1967-69, U. Toronto, 1969-71; vis. asst. prof. U. Calif., Berkeley, 1971-72; assoc. prof. psychology Fla. Internat. U., Miami, 1972-76, prof., 1976—. Exec. sec. U.S. and Can. Interamerican Soc. Psychology, 1974-76; sec. gen. XVI Interamerican Congress Psychology, 1976. Editor 2 books; cons. editor Jour. Cross-Cultural Psychology, 1974-90, Internat. Jour. Intercultural Rels., 1988—; editor Revista Interamericana de Psicologia/Interamerican Jour. Psychology, 1977-82, cons. editor, 1983-99; mem. bd. editl. commentators Behavioral and Brain Scis., 1978-82; editor Adoption Quarterly, 2000-03, cons. editor, 2003—; contbr. chpts. to books, articles to profl. jours. Grantee U. Chgo., 1965, Ednl. Rsch. Inst. B.C., 1968-69, Can. Coun., 1969-71, Fla. Internat. U., 1972-76, NIMH, 1975-76, Fla. Internat. U. Found., 1975-80, Nat. Inst. Aging, 1977, Fla. Internat. U./Fla. Atlantic U., 1980-81, Fla. Internat. U. Latin Am. and Caribbean Ctr., 1981-84, Fla. Internat. U. Coll. Arts and Scis., 1981-92, AID, 1982-84, S.E. Fla. Ctr. for the Aging, 1985, William T. Grant Found., 1991-92. Mem. APA, InterAm. Soc. Psychology (v.p. for U.S. and Can. 1983-85, exec. sec. U.S. and Can. 1974-76, sec. gen. XVI Interam. Congress Psychology 1976), Internat. Assn. Cross-Cultural Psychology (treas. 1981-82), Soc. for Rsch. in Child Devel., Nat. Coun. on Family Rels. (chair adoption focus group 1997-2000), Evan B. Donaldson Adoption Inst. (ethics adv. com. 2001—). Office: Dept Psychology Fla Internat U Miami FL 33199-0001 E-mail: finley@fiu.edu.

FINLEY, JENNIFER ELLEN, physical medicine and rehabilitation physician; b. Omaha, Apr. 16, 1960; BS cum laude, U. Mo., 1981; MD, St. Louis U., 1985. Diplomate Am. Bd. Phys. Medicine and Rehab., Am. Bd. Ind. Med. Examiners. Intern U. Hawaii, 1985-86; resident East Carolina U., Greenville, N.C., 1992-95; assoc. med. dir. MidAm. Rehab. Hosp., Overland Park, Kans., 1995-98. Mem. Am. Acad. Phys. Medicine and Rehab. Office: 10770 El Monte Ste 102 Overland Park KS 66211

FINLEY, JOHN CLIFFORD, cardiologist; b. Oct. 26, 1946; AB, U. Mo., 1968; MD, Northwestern U., 1972. Diplomate Am. Bd. Internal Medicine; bd. cert. internal medicine, cardiovascular diseases, critical care medicine. Intern, resident in internal medicine U. Ky. Med. Ctr., Lexington, 1972-75; from staff internist to dep. chief internal medicine Alaska Native Med. Ctr., Anchorage, 1975-81; fellow in cardiology San Francisco VA Med. Ctr., 1981-83; clin. specialty cons. in cardiovasc. diseases Alaska Native Med. Ctr., 1983-95; mem. Alaska Heart Inst., Anchorage, 1996—. Capt. USPHS, 1975-95. Fellow Am. Coll. Cardiology; mem. Am. Soc. Echocardiography. Office: Alaska Heart Inst 3340 Providence Dr Ste 552 Anchorage AK 99508-4608

FINLEY, KATHERINE MANDUSIC, professional society administrator; b. Mansfield, Ohio, Nov. 8, 1954; d. Sam and Ann Julia (Konves) Mandusic; m. Edwin D. McDonell, Aug. 18, 1979 (div. Dec. 1994); m. Jeffrey A. Finley, June 12, 1999. BA, Ohio Wesleyan U.; MA in History and Mus. Studies, Case Western Res.; MBA, Ind. U. Rschr. Conner Prairie Mus., Fishers, Ind., 1978-82; exec. dir./rsch. historian Ind. Med. History Mus./Ind. Hist. Soc., Indpls., 1982-91; asst. dir. for comm. and mktg. Ind. U. Ctr. on Philanthropy, 1991-93; exec. dir. Roller Skating Assn. Internat., Indpls., 1993-2000, Assn. for Rsch. on Nonprofit Orgns. and Voluntary Action, 2000—; mem. faculty philanthropic studies Ind. U.-Purdue U., Indpls., 2001—. Author: (book) The Journals of William A. Lindsay, 1989; contbg. editor: The Encyclopedia of Indianapolis, 1994; contbr. articles to profl. jours. Pres. Altrusa Internat. Indpls., 1995—97, treas., 1998—99, chmn. svc. com., 1999—2000; pres. Altrusa Found. Indpls.; bd. dirs. Nat. Mus. Roller Skating, Lincoln, 1994—2000. Mem.: Ind. Soc. Assn. Execs. (chair edn. com. 1997—98, bd. dirs. 1999—2001, chair conv. com. 1999—2000, chair found. 2000), Nat. Soc. Fund Raising Execs. (cert.), Am. Soc. Assn. Execs. (cert., Assn. Exec. of Yr. 2002), Toastmasters (v.p. edn. 1998—99, 2000—02, v.p. pub. rels. 2000, gov. area 18 2001—02), Rotary Internat. of Indpls., Phi Beta Kappa, Sigma Iota Epsilon, Beta Gamma Sigma. Avocations: reading, walking, gourmet cooking. Office: Arnova 550 W North St Ste 301 Indianapolis IN 46202 E-mail: kmfinley@iupui.edu.

FINLEY, KERRY A. lawyer; b. Iowa CIty, Iowa, June 15, 1965; d. Thomas A. and Diane Deckard F.; m. Roger A. Dahl, Dec. 14, 1996; children: Beckett, Deckard. BA, Dartmouth Coll., 1987; JD, U. Iowa, 1990. Bar: N.Y. 1991, Iowa 1993. Assoc. Willkie, Farr & Gallagher, N.Y.C., 1990-93; ptnr., shareholder Finley, Alt, Smith, Scharnberg, Craig, Hilmes & Gaffey, Des Moines, 1993—. Mem. ABA, Iowa Bar Assn., Polk County Bar Assn., C. Edwin Moore Am. Inn of Ct. (barrister). Democrat. Office: Finley Alt Smith Scharnberg Craig Hilmes & Gaffey 604 Locust St Des Moines IA 50309-3705 Home: 475 N Shore Dr Clear Lake IA 50428-1374

FINLEY, LEWIS MERREN, financial consultant; b. Reubens, Idaho, Nov. 29, 1929; s. John Emory and Charlotte (Priest) Finley; m. Virginia Ruth Spousta, Feb. 23, 1957; children: Ellen Annette Finley Guldenzopf, Charlotte Louise Finley Kinney. Student pub. schs., Spokane. With Household Fin. Co., Portland, Oreg. and Seattle, 1953-56, Doug Gerow Fin., Portland, 1956-61; pres. Family Fin. Planners Inc., Portland, 1961—. Assoc. broker Peoples Choice Realty, Inc., Milwaukie, Oreg., 1977-82, Lewis M. Finley, Real Estate Broker, Inc., 1982—; standing trustee Chpt. 13, Fed. Bankruptcy Ct., Dist. of Oreg., 1979. Author: The Complete Guide to Getting Yourself Out of Debt, 1975. With U.S. Army, 1951-53. Mem. Oreg. Assn. Credit Counselors (past pres.), N.W. Assn. Credit Counselors (past treas.), Am. Assn. Credit Counselors (v.p. 1982-85), Authors Guild, Nat. Assn. Realtors, Masons (past master), Scottish Rite (32d degree), Shriners. Republican. Methodist. Home: 3015 SE Riviere Dr Portland OR 97267-5548 Office: PO Box 12287 Portland OR 97212-0287 E-mail: yelnif@msn.com.

FINLEY, MARGARET MAVIS, retired elementary school educator; b. Jackson, Mich., Dec. 2, 1927; d. Allen Aaron and Minnie Mavis (Graham) Lincoln; m. Duane Douglas Finley, Aug. 23, 1952; 1 child, Linda Louise. BS, Ea. Mich. U., 1960; postgrad., Pepperdine U., 1968-72. Cert. tchr., Mich., Calif. Tchr. Jackson Sch. Dist., 1960-67, Pomona (Calif.) Sch. Dist., 1967-88. Editor Calif. Ret. Tchrs. Assn. Divsn. 82 Newsletter; contbr. poetry and articles to profl. jours. Mem. AAUW, Calif. Ret. Tchrs. Assn., Calif. Tchrs. Assn. (life). Avocations: writing, reading, hiking, travel, theater. Home: 1072 Cypress Point Dr Banning CA 92220-5404

FINLEY, MARLYNN HOLT, elementary educator consultant; b. Columbia, Mo., Oct. 19, 1936; d. Robert McDonnell and Lorraine Isabelle (Miller) Holt; husband dec. BS in Edn., U. Mo., 1958, MS in Edn., 1965, PhD in Spl. Edn., 1978. Cert. elem. educator, elem. adminstr., spl. educator. Elem. tchr. Ferguson (Mo.)/Florissant Schs., 1958-59, 60-61; elem., jr. high tchr. Anniston (Ala.) Schs., 1959-60; univ. instr. U. Mo., Columbia, 1961-64; elem. tchr. Riverview (Mo.) Gardens Schs., 1964-65; lang. arts cons. St. Charles (Mo.) Schs., 1966-69, Parkway Schs., Chesterfield, Mo., 1969-73, reading specialist, 1973-95; ednl. cons. self-employed Town & Country, Mo., 1995—. Jefferson Club trustee chmn. Devel. Coun., U. Mo., Columbia, 1991—. Grantee, 1967-69, 70-71. Alumni adv. chmn. Coll. Edn. Alumni, U. Mo., 1969-89; Sunday sch. tchr. Ladue Chapel Presbyn., St. Louis, 1960-61, deacon, 1999—. Recipient Carter award U. Mo., 1965, Life Saving award, 1980. Mem. AAUW, Internat. Reading Assn. (treas. 1970-72), St. Louis Suburban Reading Assn. (Svc. award 1982), Order of Ea. Star (grand rep. of B.C. and Yukon 1999-00, assoc. conductress 1982, conductress 1983, assoc. matron 1984, worthy matron 1985, 00, sec. 1987-95), PEO, Pi Lambda Theta, Zeta Tau Alpha. Republican. Avocations: reading, swimming, walking, skating, bridge, travel. Home: 12 Summerhill Ln Chesterfield MO 63017-8408

FINLEY, MICHAEL VALTON, foundation executive; b. Medford, Oreg., Apr. 8, 1947; s. Valton Austin and Anne Elsie (Huebner) F.; m. Lillie Eiteneir, June 14, 1969; children: Devon, Laura. BS in Biology, So. Oreg. State Coll., 1969. With Nat. Park Service, 1970-2001; park ranger Big Bend (Tex.) Nat. Park, 1970, Pinnacles Nat. Monument, Paicines, Calif., 1972-73, Yosemite (Calif.) Nat. Park, 1974-76; exchange ranger Calif. State Park System-Big Bas State Park, 1973-74; law enforcement specialist Grand Teton Nat. Park, Moose, Wyo., 1976-78; staff park ranger, Washington, 1978-80; legis. affairs specialist, 1980-81; supt. Assateague Island Nat. Seashore Berlin, Md., 1981-83; assoc. regional dir. Anchorage, 1983-86; supt. Everglades Nat. Pk., Homestead, Fla., 1986-89, Yosemite Nat. Pk., Mammoth Hot Springs, 1989-94; pres. Turner Found., Atlanta, 2001—. Served to sgt. U.S. Army, 1968-70. Mem. Assn. Nat. Park Rangers (pres. 1980-82). Lodges: Rotary. Lutheran. Avocations: fishing, scuba, photography, hiking, skiing. Office: Turner Found Inc. 133 Luckie St NW 2nd Fl Atlanta GA 30303*

FINLEY, ROBERT VAN EATON, minister; b. Charlottesville, Va., May 2, 1922; s. William Walter and Melissa (Hoover) Finley; m. Ethel Drummond, Dec. 23, 1949; children: Deborah Ann, Ruth Ellen. BA, U. Va., 1944; postgrad., U. Chgo. Div. Sch., 1946-47; LittD, Houghton Coll., 1952. Ordained to ministry Bapt. Ch., 1957. Evangelist Youth for Christ Internat., Chgo., 1945-46, Inter-Varsity Christian Fellowship, Chgo., 1945-46, overseas, 1948-51; pastor Evang. Free Ch., Richmond, Calif., 1951-52; minister to fgn. students 10th Presbyn. Ch., Phila., 1952-55; founder, gen. dir. Christian Aid Mission, Charlottesville, 1953-70, chmn., CEO, 1970—; founder, gen. dir. Overseas Students Mission, Ft. Eire, Canada, 1954-68, pres., 1969-85; pastor Temple Bapt. Ch., Washington, 1965-66. Pres. Bible Evang. Fellowship, Washington, 1973—87; founder, pres. Christian Aid Mission Can., 1985—88, chmn. bd. dirs., 1989—2003, Internat. Congress Indigenous Missions, Harrisburg, Pa., 1988—. Editor: (book) Conquest for Christ, 1954—74, Christian Mission mag., 1974—; author: (book) The Future of Foreign Mission, 2002. Founder, pres. Internat. Students, Inc., Colorado Springs, 1952—67, chmn., 1968—70. Mem.: Assn. Christians Ministering Internats. (bd. dirs. 1995—99), Omicron Delta Kappa. Office: Christian Aid Mission PO Box 9037 Charlottesville VA 22906-9037 also: Christian Aid Mission 201 Stanton St Fort Erie ON Canada L2A 3N8 *To indulge myself, beyond actual need, with the benefits of material wealth leaves me the poorer. But when my surplus resources are used to uplift those who lack opportunity, I am enriched.*

FINLEY, SARA CREWS, medical geneticist, educator; b. Lineville, Ala., Feb. 26, 1930; m. Wayne H. Finley; children: Randall Wayne, Sara Jane. BS in Biology, U. Ala., 1951, MD, 1955. Diplomate Am. Bd. Med. Genetics; cert. clin. geneticist; cert. clin. cytogeneticist. Intern Lloyd Noland Hosp., Fairfield, Ala., 1955-56; NIH fellow in pediatrics U. Ala. Med. Sch., Birmingham, 1956-60; NIH trainee in med. genetics Inst. Med. Genetics, U. Uppsala, Sweden, 1961-62; mem. faculty U. Ala. Med. Sch., 1960-96, co-dir. lab. med. genetics, 1966-96, prof. pediatrics, 1975-96, occupant Wayne H. and Sara Crews Finley chair med. genetics, 1986-96, prof. emeritus, 1996—; Disting. Faculty lectr. Med. Ctr., U. Ala. at Birmingham, 1983; mem. staff Univ. U. Ala. Hosp., Children's Hosp. Ala. Mem. ad hoc com. genetic counseling Children's Bur., HEW, 1966; mem. ad hoc rev. panel for genetic disease and sickle cell testing and counseling programs, 1980; mem. genetic diseases program objective rev. panel Bur. Maternal and Child Health and Resources Div., HHS, 1989, mem. adv. group on lab. quality assurance, 1989; Birmingham bd. dirs. Compass Bank. Author papers on clin. cytogenetics, human congenital malformations, human growth and devel. Mem. White House Conf. Health, 1965; mem. rsch. manpower rev. com. Nat. Cancer Inst., 1977-81; mem. Sickle Cell Disease Adv. Com., NIH, 1983-87; chairperson physician's campaign bd. dirs. United Way, 1993-95. Recipient Disting. Alumna award U. Ala. Sch. Medicine Alumni Assn., 1989, Med. award Ala. Assn. for Retarded Children, 1969, Turlington award Planned Parenthood of Ala., 1982, Nat. Outstanding Alumnae award Zeta Tau Alpha, 1992, Disting. Alumna award U. Ala. Nat. Alumni Assn., 1994, Brother Bryan Prayer Point award Birmingham Women's Com., 2001, Gardner award Ala. Acad. Sci., 2002; co-recipient Will Holmes award Children's Aid Soc. Birmingham, 1999; named Top Ten Women in Birmingham, 1989, Top 31 Most Outstanding Alumnae U. Ala., Tuscaloosa, 1993, named to Ala. Health Hall of Fame, 2001, named to Birmingham Bus. Jour. Healthcare Hall of Fame, 2002. Finley-Compass Bank Genetics Conf. Ctr. with portrait opened, 2001, Recipient Gardner award, Ala. Acad. Sci., 2002. Fellow AMA (founding), Am. Coll. Med. Genetics; mem. Am. Soc. Human Genetics, Med. Assn. Ala. (Samuel Buford Word award 2003), Ala. Assn. Retarded Children (Ann. Med. awad 1969), Ala. Acad. Sci., Jefferson County Med. Soc. (pres. 1990), Jefferson County Pediatric Soc., Rotary Club of Birmingham, Phi Beta Kappa, Sigma Xi, Alpha Omea Alpha, Alpha Epsilon Delta, Omicron Delta Kappa, Phi Kappa Phi, Zeta Tau Alpha. Office: U Ala 3412 Brookwood Rd Birmingham AL 35223-2023

FINLEY, SARAH MAUDE MERRITT, social worker; b. Atlanta, Nov. 19, 1946; d. Genius and Willie Maude (Wright) Merritt; m. Craig Wayne Finley, Aug. 10, 1968; children: Craig Wayne Jr., Jarret Lee. BA, Spelman Coll., 1968; postgrad., Atlanta U., 1968-69. Cert. GPS/MAPP leader 2001. Job placement advisor Marsh Draughton Bus. Coll., Atlanta, 1971-72; child attendant Fulton County Juvenile Ct., Atlanta, 1972; social worker Fulton County Dept. Family and Children Svcs., Atlanta, 1972-2000, casework supr., 1976-98, Title VI customer svc. coord. Ctrl. City/North Area office, 1990-98; RTD Fulton County Govt., 1996—; counselor/asst. to the project dir. Right Way Home Project N.W. Area Office, 1998-99; social svcs. case mgr. Placement Resource Devel. N.W.

Area Office, 2000; social worker Clayton County Dept. Family and Children Svcs., Jonesboro, Ga., 2000—; co-leader GPS/MAPP, 2001—. Supr. Count on Me video Ga. Dept. Human Resources, 1987. Vol. coord. family support program Family Support Group of Atlanta Detachment of 2d Army Maneuver Tng. Commd.; vol. family support coun. 87th Maneuver Area Command (now 4th Brigade, 87th Divsn.), 1991-93; del. Ft. McPherson (Ga.) Army Family Symposium, 1992, 3d ann. worldwide USAR Family Support Conf., St. Louis, 1992. Mem.: Fulton County Ret. Employees Assn., Nat. Assn. Counties, Ga. County Welfare Assn., Nat. Alumnae Assn. Spelman Coll., Womens Aux. Ga. VFW. Baptist. Avocations: poetry, reading, volunteer work, stress mgmt. Office: Clayton County Dept Family & Children Svcs 877 Battlecreek Rd Jonesboro GA 30236

FINLEY, SKIP, media consultant, communications executive; b. Ann Arbor, Mich., July 23, 1948; s. Ewell W. and Mildred Virginia (Johnson) F.; m. Karen Michele Woolard, May 6, 1971; children: Kharma I., R. Kristin. Student, Northeastern U., 1966-71. Owner Skifin Gallery, Boston, 1970-71; floor dir. Sta. WHDH-TV, Boston, 1971; floor mgr., asst. dir., producer Sta. WSBK TV, Boston, 1971-72; account exec. Sta. WRKO-AM, Boston, 1972-73; account mgr. Humphrey, Browning, MacDougall Advt., Boston, 1973-74; sales mgr. Sta. WAMO-AM-FM Sheridan Broadcasting Corp., 1974-75, gen. mgr. Sta. WAMO-AM-FM, 1975-76, v.p. radio div., 1976-77; dir. of sales Sheridan Broadcasting Network, 1977-79, exec. v.p., gen. mgr., 1979-81, pres., 1981-82; gen. ptnr. Sta. KEZO AM-FM, Omaha, 1983-88, Sta. KDAB-FM, Salt Lake City and Ogden, Utah, 1985-90; pres., gen. mgr. Sta. WKYS-FM, Washington, 1988-95; pres., CEO, Albimar Communications, Washington, 1992-95; CEO, COO Am. Urban Radio Networks, Pitts., 1995-98; pres., CEO Answers, Solutions, 1999—2003; v. chmn. Inner City Broadcasting Group, 2003—. Contbr. numerous articles on media-related subjects to various publs. Testimony to House subcom. on Communications, 1977, Congl. Black Caucus, 1990; mem. bd. overseers, trustee Vineyard Open Land Found. Recipient Excellence in Media award Nat. Assn. Media Women, 1981, Communicator of Yr. award Washington Area Media Orgn., 1982, New Horizons award D.C. Gen. Hosp., Washington, 1990, Advocacy in Edn. award D.C. Pub. Schs., Washington, 1990, Radio Wayne award as best overall broadcaster Radio Ink Mag., 1994. Mem. Nat. Assn. Black Owned Broadcasters (bd. dirs. 1977-95), Radio Advt. Bur. (bd. dirs. 1990—, chair 1997-98), Nat. Assn. Broadcasters (bd. dirs., vice chair radio bd. 1990-94), Nat. Thespian Soc., The Advt. Coun., Inc. (bd. dirs. 1998—), Martha's Vineyard Rod and Gun Club, Lowes Island Golf Club (founding adv. bd. govs. 1992-97). Avocations: computers, model trains, shooting, automobiles, boating, fishing. Office: Inner City Broadcasting Group 3 Pk Ave 40th Flr New York NY 10016-4244 Office Fax: 212-252-0791.

FINLEY-MORIN, KIMBERLEY K. educator; b. San Angelo, Tex., Nov. 23, 1954; d. James Griffith Jr. and Imogene (Powers) Finley; m. Michael Morin, Feb. 15, 1986. BA cum laude, Pan Am. U., 1982. Cert. Acupressuriest. Tchr. Dallas Theatre Ctr., Greenfield (Mass.) Child Care Ctr.; site coord., tchr. Greenfield Girls Club; tchr. theatre/acting Shea Theatre, Turners Falls, Mass.; prof. theatre/speech Greenfield Com. Coll., 1996—. Resident dir. Fellowship Players of South Deerfield, 1996—. Pres. Arena Civic Theatre, 1992—. With USN, 1976-80. Mem. Tex. Ednl. Theatre Assn., Alpha Omega. Home: 62 High St Turners Falls MA 01376-1709

FINMAN, SHELDON ELIOT, lawyer, mediator; b. Tampa, Fla., Aug. 25, 1943; s. Oscar E. and Shirley F. Finman; m. Donnie I. Finman, Jan. 16, 1966 (div. Sept. 1976); 1 child, Seth; m. Lynn E. Finman, June 18, 1978; children: Jennilynn, Julia Lynn. BA, U. Fla., 1965, JD, 1971. Bar: Fla. 1971; cert. family law mediator and arbitrator, cert. marital and family lawyer Fla. Bar Assn. Assoc. Robinson, Ginsburg et al, Sarasota, Fla., 1971-73, Allen Knudsen et al, Ft. Myers, Fla., 1973-75, ptnr., 1975-77; pvt. practice Ft. Myers, 1977—. Family law mediator Sheldon E. Finman Mediation Svcs., Ft. Myers, 1983—; mem. family steering com. Fla. Supreme Ct., 2000—02. Pro bono atty. Guardian Ad Litem Program, Ft. Myers, 1996—; exec. bd. Lee County YMCA, Ft. Myers, 1976-80, S.W. Fla. Sports Assn., Inc., Ft. Myers, 1976-2000. Capt. U.S. Army, 1966-68. Master: Calusa Inn of Ct.; mem.: AFCLC (pres. Fla. chpt. 2003, bd. dirs. 2000—), Assn. of Family Law Profls. (charter pres. 1995—97, exec. bd.), Assn. for Conflict Resolution, Fla. Bar Assn. (advanced practitioner). Avocations: health and fitness, racquetball, hiking, reading. Office: 2215 1st St Fort Myers FL 33901-2901 E-mail: sfinman@attglobal.net.

FINN, CHESTER EVANS, retired lawyer; b. Dayton, Ohio, July 13, 1918; s. Samuel Lawrence and Lillian Rose (Evans) F.; m. Phyllis Muriel Kessel, Apr. 29, 1942 (dec. Oct. 30, 1987); children: Chester E. Jr., Natalie K., Samuel J.; m. Theodora K. Wilks, Sept. 18, 1988. BA, Yale U., 1940; LLB, Harvard U., 1946. Bar: Ohio 1947, U.S. Dist. Ct. (so. dist.) Ohio 1949, U.S. Ct. Claims 1949, U.S. Ct. Appeals (6th cir.) 1966, U.S. Supreme Ct. 1975, U.S. Ct. Internat. Trade 1984. Assoc. Estabrook, Finn & McKee, Dayton, 1947-53, ptnr., 1953-83, Porter, Wright, Morris & Arthur, Dayton, 1983-92, of counsel, 1992-99; ret., 1999. Pres. Dayton United Way, 1969; trustee various civic groups. Lt. USNR, 1942-45, PTO. Mem. ABA, Ohio Bar Assn., Dayton Bar Assn. (pres. 1969), Dayton Bicycle Club, Belfair Golf Club (Bluffton, S.C.). Avocations: golfing, traveling. Home: 23 Cedar Ln Hilton Head Island SC 29926-1052

FINN, DANIEL KEVIN, economics and theology educator, former dean; b. Rochester, NY, Apr. 30, 1947; s. George Elwood and Ruth Mary (Schwenzer) F.; m. Nita Jo Rush, June 17, 1978; children: Jacob, Stephanie. BS, St. John Fisher Coll., 1968; MA, U. Chgo., 1975, PhD, 1977. Asst. prof. econs. and theol. ethics St. John's U., Collegeville, Minn., 1977-84, assoc prof., 1984-91, prof., 1991—, dean sch. of theology, 1984-89, William E. and Virginia Clemens chair econ. and liberal arts, 1989—, prof. econ. and theol. ethics, 1991. Cons. in field. Author: (with others) Toward Christian Economic Ethic, 1980, Just Trading: On the Ethics and Economics of International Trade, 1996. Mem. Assn. for Social Econs. (pres. 1986), Am. Econs. Assn., Soc. Christian Ethics (bd. dirs. 1988-92, 2001-03), Catholic Theol. Soc. Am. (bd. dirs. 2002—), Midwest Assn. Theol. Schs. (pres. 1985-87), Minn. Consortium of Theol. Schs. (v.p. 1987-89), Minn. Econ. Assn. Avocations: woodworking, bridge, gardening.

FINN, DAVID, public relations company executive, artist; b. N.Y.C., Aug. 30, 1921; s. Jonathan and Sadie (Borgenicht) Finn; m. Laura Zeisler, Oct. 20, 1945; children: Kathy, Dena, Peter, Amy. BS, CCNY, 1943. Co-founder Ruder Finn, Inc., N.Y.C., 1948, pres., 1956 68, chmn. bd., CEO, 1968—2000, chmn., 2000—, also bd. dirs. Exhibited in (group shows) Met. Mus. Art, N.Y.C., L'Orangerie, Paris, others; author: Public Relations and Management, 1956, The Corporate Oligarch, 1969; photographer (books) Embrace of Life, 1969, As the Eye Moves, 1970, Donatello: Prophet of Modern Vision, 1973, Henry Moore Sculpture and Environment, 1976, Michelangelo's Three Pietas, 1975, Oceanic Images, 1978, The Florence Baptistry Doors, 1980, Sculpture at Storm King, 1980, Busch-Reisinger Museum, 1980, Canova, Giambologna, Donatello, Cellini, David by the Hand of Michelangelo, In the Mountain of Japan, others; contbr. articles articles and chpts. to profl. jours. and art publs.; editor (former editor-in-chief): Sculpture Rev. mag. Bd. dirs. Jewish Theol. Sem. Am.; mem. Nat. Trust for Humanities; treas. Bus. Com. for Arts. 1st lt. A.C. AUS, 1944. Mem.: Internat. Pub. Rels. Assn., Am. Inst. Graphic Arts (past dir.), Am. Fedn. Arts, AAAS, Kappa Tau Alpha (hon.). Office: Ruder Finn Inc 301 E 57th St New York NY 10022-2900

FINN, EDWIN A., JR., publishing executive; BA in English and Polit. Sci., Tufts U.; MA in Internat. Banking and Fin., Columbia U. Asst. mng. editor Blackstone Valley Tribune, 1970; mng. editor Southbridge (Mass.) Daily News, 1970; nat. copyreader The Wall St. Jour., N.Y.C., 1980—81, editor fgn. desk, 1981—84, banking and fin. reporter Dallas bur., 1984—85; sr. editor internat. bus. and fin. Forbes Mag., 1986—89, asst. mng. editor, 1989—90; editor Am. Banker, 1990—92; mng. editor Barron's, The Dow Jones Bus. and Fin. Weekly, NYC, 1993—95, editor, 1995—, pres., 1998, pub., 2000—01. Chmn., editor-in-chief SmartMoney, 2002—, Wall St. Jour. Mag. Personal Bus., 2002—. Office: Barron's 200 Liberty St New York NY 10281-1003

FINN, FRANCES MARY, biochemistry researcher; b. Pitts., May 6, 1937; d. Stephen B. and Geraldine H. (Weber) F.; m. Klaus Hofmann, Feb. 26, 1965 (dec. Dec. 25, 1995); m. Eric Reichl, July 19, 1999. BS in Chemistry, U. Pitts., 1959, MS in Biochemistry, 1961, PhD in Biochemistry, 1964. Asst. rsch. prof. biochemistry U. Pitts., 1969-73, assoc. rsch. prof., 1973-80, assoc. prof. medicine, 1980-88, prof., 1988-99, prof. emerita, 1999—. Mem. Am. Chem. Soc., Endocrine Soc., Am. Soc. for Biochemistry and Molecular Biology, Am. Peptide Soc., Protein Soc. Home: 150 Brooks Bnd Princeton NJ 08540-7545 E-mail: ffreichl@patmedia.net.

FINN, JOHN STEPHEN, lawyer; b. Chgo., Dec. 18, 1951; s. Matthew Thomas and Mary (Martin) F.; m. Sarah Sanderford, Nov. 27, 1982; children: Caitlin, Erin. BA with high honors, Lehigh U., 1973; JD, U. Denver, 1975. Bar: Colo. 1976, U.S. Dist. Ct. Colo. 1976, U.S. Ct. Appeals (10th cir.) 1986, U.S. Ct. Appeals (8th cir.) 1988. Assoc. Nelson and Harding, Denver, 1976-78, ptnr., 1979-88, Stettner, Miller & Cohn, P.C., Denver, 1989—. Instr. program for advanced profl. devel. U. Denver, 1984; lectr. various continuing legal edn. programs and profl. assn. lectures, Denver, 1985—. Mem. ABA, Colo. Bar Assn. (constrn. law forum), Colo. Contractors Assn., Denver Bar Assn., Constrn. Fin. Mgmt. Assn., Rocky Mountain Lehigh Alumni Assn., Met. Irish Counsellors Soc. (founding mem.). Avocations: tennis, golf, piano, jazz. Office: 1380 Lawrence St Ste 1000 Denver CO 80204-2058 E-mail: jfinn@stetmil.com.

FINN, MARIE FRANCES, artist; b. Phila., Sept. 5, 1938; d. John Joseph McCarthy and Helen Marie Emmons-Barrett; m. Thomas Michael Finn, May 21, 1966; children: Kathleen Mary, Rosemarie, Maryanne, Michael Sean, Thomas Patrick. AFA, Bucks County C.C., 1991; diploma, Pa. Acad. Fine Arts, 2000. Art tchr. St. Ignatius Sch., Yardley, Pa., 1986-87; owner, art tchr. Marie's Fine Arts Program, Yardley, 1993—. Reading instr. Doylestown (Pa.) Prison, 1995. One-woman shows include Lower Makefiled Soc. Performing Arts, Jayelin, LLC, Califon, N.J., Bristol Riverside Theater, exhibited in group shows at Bucks County C.C., Burlington, N.J., Spring Arts Festival, Flushing, N.Y., Langhorne Coun. Arts, New Hope Arts Festival, Mann Music Ctr., Heritage Conservancy, Aldie Manson, Doylestown, Cygnus Egg Harbor, N.J., Peddlers Village, Tinicum Art Festival, Phillips Mill Ann. Fall Exhbn., numerous others, Bianco Gallery, Del. River Gallery, Louisa Melrose Gallery, Canal Frame-Crafts Gallery, Rhinehart-Fischer Gallery, Coryell Gallery, Village Artworks Gallery, Barn Studio Gallery. V.p. New Hope Art League, Pa., 1998—2003. Recipient numerous awards. Mem.: Women in the Arts, Phila. Sketch Club, Trenton Artists' Workshop Assn., Artsbridge. Roman Catholic. Avocations: reading, travel, photography, genealogy. Home: 706 Chestnut Ln Yardley PA 19067-1804

FINN, MARVIN RUVEN, lawyer; b. Boston, Sept. 9, 1938; s. Max and Edith N. (Goldstein) F.; m. Norma R. Cadiff, July 4, 1965; children— Jonathan, Andrew. B.S. cum laude, Babson Coll., 1959; J.D., Boston Coll., 1962. Bar: Mass. 1962, U.S. Dist. Ct. Mass. 1964, U.S. Ct. Appeals (1st cir.) 1980. Assoc. Fox, Orlov & Cowin, Boston, 1962-63; atty. Mass. Crime Commn., Boston, 1963-65; spl. asst. atty. gen. Mass., Boston, 1965-69; ptnr. Spencer & Stone, Boston, 1969-82; chief trial dept. Fulman & Fulman, Malden, Mass., 1982— ; cons. civil litigation; rep. extradition proc. U.S. State Dept., Israel, 1968; speaker WBZ Radio, 1966. Coach, Youth Basketball Team, North Shore Jewish Community Ctr., 1976-81; mem. sch. com. Temple Beth El Sch., Swampscott, Mass., 1980. Mem. ABA, Mass. Bar Assn. (civil litigation com.), Boston Bar Assn., Assn. Trial Lawyers Am., Mass. Acad. Trial Lawyers, Am. Judicature Soc., Boston Coll. Alumni Assn., Babson Coll. Alumni Assn. Jewish. Lodges: K.P., Masons. Office: Fulman & Fulman 7 Dartmouth St Malden MA 02148-5103

FINN, MARY RALPHE, artist; b. St. Paul, Nov. 13, 1933; d. Wendell W. and Rose Marie (Arendt) Ralphe; m. H. Roger Finn, June 15, 1957; children: Mark W., Shelly, Scott R. BS, U. Ark., 1955; MS, U. Iowa, 1957. Workshop demonstrator and cons. in field. Exhibited in solo shows at Art Mart Gallery, 1973, 76, Brown's Gallery, Boise, 1977, 80, 85, 89, 94, St. Lukes Regional Med. Ctr., Boise, 1982, Piper Jaffray Hopwood, Boise, 1979, 85, St. Alphonsus Med. Ctr., Boise, 1981, 90, Bank of Idaho, Boise, 1975, 79, Morrison Knudsen, Boise, 1978; group shows include Browns Galleries, 1975-98, St. Lukes Regional Med. Ctr., 1976-90, Idaho State Capitol, 1978, Idaho Watercolor Soc., 1987, St. Alphonsus Hosp., 1990, Albertson Coll. Idaho, 1988-99, Boise State U., 1991; represented in permanent collections Morrison-Knudsen Corp., West One Bancorp, 1st Security Bank Idaho, Inc., St. Lukes Regional Med. Ctr., 1st Interstate Bank, Am.-Hydro Corp. Mem. Boise Art Mus., Phi Upsilon Omicron, Zeta Tau Alpha, Omicron Nu.

FINN, NITA ANN, social worker; b. N.Y.C., Jan. 2, 1936; m. Jerold G. Finn, Aug. 27, 1955; children: Bruce L., Betsy Finn-Dicarlo. BA in Psychology, Brandeis U., 1957; MSW, Simmons Coll., 1971. Lic. ind. clin. social worker. Co-dir. Families Extended, Family Counseling Svc., Newton, Mass., 1973-74; child and family psychotherapist Boston Childrens Svcs., 1975-76; project supr. adolescent and family svcs. Justice Resource Inst., Boston, 1976-77; social worker City of Newton, Mass., 1977-79; project dir. Dare Cape Cod, 1979-80; supr. of intake Dept. Social Svcs. Commonwealth of Mass., Cape Cod, 1980-82; pvt. practice, South Harwich, Mass., 1983—; clin. cons., group facilitator We Can Women's Empowerment Agy., Harwichport, 2001—. Home: PO Box 145 South Harwich MA 02661-0145 Office: 2 Brettwood Rd South Harwich MA 02661-0145 E-mail: jandncc@iopener.net.

FINN, PETER, public relations executive; b. N.Y.C., Mar. 31, 1954; s. David and Laura (Zeisler) F.; m. Sarah Duncan; children: Noah J., Emily M. BA, Brown U., 1976; MA, Columbia U., 1977. Researcher Research & Forecasts Inc., N.Y.C., 1977-79, dir. ops., 1979-81, chmn., 1981-84; chmn. fin. com. Ruder-Finn, Inc. (formerly Ruder, Finn & Rotman, Inc.), N.Y.C., 1984—, CFO, 1985-94, exec. v.p., 1986-87, chmn. exec. com., 1988—2001, CEO, 2001—. Chmn. Catskill Mt. Found., Inc., 1998—; bd. dirs. Hunter Found., Inc., 1998—. Office: Ruder-Finn Inc 301 E 57th St New York NY 10022-2900

FINN, PETER MICHAEL, television production executive; b. Milton, Mass., Feb. 19, 1936; s. Matthew Charles and Mary Germaine (Ireland) F.; m. Judith Mary Barry, Sept. 7, 1957 (div. Aug. 1996); children: Pamela Ann, Mary Kathryn, Matthew Ireland; m. Debra Jo McGraw, Oct. 18, 1997. AB, Holy Cross Coll., 1956; MBA, George Washington U., 1962; A.M.P., Harvard U., 1980. Account exec. J. Walter Thompson Co., N.Y.C., 1962-64, account supr., 1966-67; account exec. Foote Cone & Belding, N.Y.C., 1964-66, v.p., account supr., 1967-68, Doyle Dane Bernbach, N.Y.C., 1968-70; sr. v.p., dir. F.W. Free, N.Y.C., 1970-74; pres. Henderson Advt., Greenville, S.C., 1974-80, Bozell & Jacobs, Dallas, 1980-85, also dir.; sr. ptnr., div. pres. Whittle Communications, Knoxville, Tenn., 1985-92; pres., CEO Peter Matthew Prodns., NYC, 1992—. Mem. Greater Greenville Planning Council, 1976-79, Dallas Citizens Council. Served to lt. USNR, 1957-62. Mem. Am. Assn. Advt. Agys. (bd. govs.), Am. Advt. Fedn., Am. Mktg. Assn. Office: Peter Matthew Prodns 523 W 45th St New York NY 10036

FINN, ROBERT, writer, lecturer, broadcaster; b. Boston, July 13, 1930; s. Edward Anthony and E. Caroline (Seifert) F.; m. Mary Pacana, Oct. 12, 1957; children: Laurence, Elaine. BA, Boston U., 1952. Staff reporter, music-drama critic New Bedford (Mass.) Standard-Times, 1956-59, Akron (Ohio) Beacon Jour., 1959-64; music critic Cleve. Plain Dealer, 1964-92. Mem. guest faculty Rockefeller Found. project for tng. music critics, 1965, 66 Author: Exploring Classical Music, 2000, A Musical Journey, Con Amore, 2003; contbr. to Opera News mag., Am. Record Guide. Served with AUS, 1953-56. Co-recipient ASCAP-Deems Taylor award for, 1972, 74, 78, 80 Mem. Music Critics Assn. (life, exec. bd. 1975-83, v.p. 1983-85, pres. 1985-89). Roman Catholic. Home: 1211 Blanchester Rd Cleveland OH 44124-1325

FINN, ROBERT KAUL, retired biochemical engineering educator; b. Waukesha, Wis., May 3, 1920; s. Edward Albert and Myrtle (Kaul) Finn; m. Lucile Marie Rasmussen, Dec. 28, 1949; children: David T., Mary A.(dec.), Louisa M., John T., Helaina R. Sorey. B in Chemistry, Cornell U., 1941, Degree in Chem. Engring., 1942; PhD, U. Minn., 1949. Rsch. chem. engr. Merck & Co., Inc., Rahway, NJ, 1942—46; asst. prof. chem. engring. U. Ill., Urbana, 1949—55; assoc. prof. chem. engring. Cornell U., Ithaca, NY, 1955—61, prof. chem. engring., 1961—90, emeritus prof., 1990—. Vis. prof. U. Calif., Berkeley, 1969; vis. scientist Nuc. Rsch. Ctr., Julich, Germany, 1982—83, Julich, 1989. Editor: Biotechnology Focus, Vols. 1-3, 1978—81; co-author: (textbook) Microbiological and Biochemical Process Technology, 1985. Named vis. lectr., NSF, 1971; grantee, Fulbright Commn., 1961—62; rsch. fellow, Guggenheim Found., 1975—76. Mem.: European Fedn. Biotechnology (co-founder), Am. Inst. Chem. Engrs. (Divisional award 1985), Am. Soc. for Microbiology, Am. Chem. Soc. (divsn. chair 1960—61, Van Lanen award 1982). Democrat. Presbyterian. Achievements include patents for bacterial process to treat N-deficient wastewater; production of a biopolymer from methanol. Avocations: sports, church related activities. Home: 107 Oakwood Ln Ithaca NY 14850-2041 Office: Cornell Univ Sch Chem Engring 267 Olin Hall Ithaca NY 14853-5201

FINN, STEPHEN MARTIN, producer; b. Indpls., June 21, 1949; s. Martin Joseph and Theresa Diane (Mervar) F.; children: Shawn Marie, Stephanie Michelle, Rhyan Linthicum, Raimie Catherine (dec.). Pres. Equinox Systems, Grand Rapids, Mich., 1975-77, Solstice, Lake Helen, 1978—. Photographer Equitable Gallery, N.Y.C., 1978; contbr. articles profl. mags. Recipient Kinsa award Kodak Internat., N.Y.C., 1978. Mem. Am. Film Inst., Profl. Photographers Am., Aircraft Owners and Pilots Assn., Mensa, Fla. Motion Picture Theater Assn. Home and Office: PO Box 129 Lake Helen FL 32744-0129 E-mail: smfz@solsticeusa.com.

FINN, TERRENCE M. lawyer; b. Mpls., Feb. 13, 1948; BA, Yale U., 1970; JD, U. Pa., 1973. Bar: R.I. 1973, U.S. Dist. Ct. R.I. 1973, U.S. Ct. Appeals (1st. cir.) 1982, Mass. 1984. Mng. ptnr. Edwards & Angell, LLP. Mem. R.I. Bar Assn., Mass. Bar Assn., Fla. Bar., Boston Bar Assn. Office: Edwards & Angell 101 Federal St Fl 23 Boston MA 02110-1800

FINNBERG, ELAINE AGNES, psychologist, editor; b. Bklyn., Mar. 2, 1948; d. Benjamin and Agnes Montgomery (Evans) F.; m. Rodney Lee Herndon, Mar. 1, 1981; 1 child, Andrew Marshal. BA in Psychology, L.I. U., 1969; MA in Psychology, New Sch. for Social Rsch., 1973; PhD in Psychology, Calif. Sch. Profl. Psychology, 1981. Diplomate Am. Bd. Forensic Examiners, Am. Bd. Forensic Medicine, Am. Bd. Med. Psychotherapists and Psychodiagnosticians, Am. Bd. Disability Analysts, Am. Bd. Psychol. Specialties, Prescribing Psychologists Register; lic. psychologist, Calif. Rsch. asst. in med. sociology Cornell U. Med. Coll., N.Y.C., 1969-70; med. abstractor USV Pharm. Corp., Tuckahoe, N.Y., 1970-71, Coun. for Tobacco Rsch., N.Y.C., 1971-77; editor, writer Found. of Thanatology Columbia U., N.Y.C., 1971-76, cons. family studies program cancer ctr. Coll. Physicians & Surgeons, 1973-74; dir. grief psychology and bereavement counseling San Francisco Coll. Mortuary Scis., 1977-81; rsch. assoc. dept. epidemiology and internat. health U. Calif., San Francisco, 1979-81, asst. clin. prof. dept. family and cmty. medicine, 1985-93, assoc. clin. prof., dept. family and cmty. medicine, 1993—; active med. staff Natividad Med. Ctr., Salinas, Calif., 1984—2002, chief psychologist, 1984-96. Profl. adv. coun. Am. Bd. Disability Analysts; asst. chief psychiatry svc. Natividad Med. Ctr., 1985-96, acting chief psychiatry, 1988-89, vice-chair medicine dept., 1991-93, sec.-treas. med. staff, 1992-94; cons. med. staff Salinas Valley Meml. Hosp., 1991—, Mee Meml. Hosp., 1996-97; dir. tng. Monterey Psychiat. Health Facility, 1996-97, chief clin. staff, 1996-97; expert cons. Calif. Bd. Psychology. Editor: The California Psychologist, 1988-95; editor Jour. of Thanatology, 1972-76, Cathexis, 1976-81. Govs. adv. bd. Agnews Devel. Ctr., San Jose, Calif., 1988-96, chair, 1989-91, 94-95. Fellow Prescribing Psychologists Register (diplomate); mem. APA, Nat. Register Health Svc. Providers in Psychology, Calif. Psychol. Assn. (Disting. Svc. award 1989), Soc. Behavioral Medicine, Mid-Coast Psychol. Assn. (sec. 1985, treas. 1986, pres. 1987, Disting. Svc. to Psychology award 1993), Forensic Mental Health Assn. Calif., Western Psychol. Assn., Assn. Advancement Behavior Therapy, Am. Med. Writers Assn., Assn. Treatment Sexual Abuses, Soc. for Personality Assessment, Internat. Rorschach. Soc., Internat. Soc. Police Surgeons.

FINNEGAN, CYRIL VINCENT, retired university dean, zoology educator; b. Dover, N.H., July 17, 1922; emigrated to Can., 1958; s. Cyril Vincent and Hilda A. (McClintock) F.; children: Maureen A., Patrick S., Cathaleen C., Kevin S., Eileen D., Gormlaith R., Michaeleen S., Mairead B., Conal E. BS, Bates Coll., Lewiston, Maine, 1946; MS, U. Notre Dame, 1948, PhD, 1951. From instr. to asst. prof. St. Louis U., 1952-56; asst. prof. U. Notre Dame, South Bend, Ind., 1956-58; from asst. prof. to prof. zoology U. B.C., Vancouver, 1958-88, emeritus, 1988—, assoc. dean sci., 1972-79, dean sci., 1979-85, dean emeritus, 1988—, assoc. acad. v.p., 1986-88. Contbr. articles to sci. jours. Served to sgt F.A. and C.E. AUS, 1942-45, NATOUSA, CBI. Postdoctoral research fellow NIH, 1952-53; Killum sr. fellow, 1968-69 Mem. Soc. Devel. Biology, Can. Soc. Cell Biology, Tissue Culture Assn., Internat. Soc. Develop. Biology, Sigma Xi Roman Catholic. Office: U BC Dept Zoology Faculty of Science Vancouver BC Canada V6T 1Z4

FINNEGAN, EUGENE G. religious studies educator; b. N.Y.C., May 25, 1939; s. Eugene and Rose Finnegan; m. Margaret M. Klein, Oct. 9, 1971; 1 child, Joy F. Walton. BA, MA, Louvain U., Belgium, 1962—66; AB, Loyola U., 1962, MBA, 1976. Instr. Cath. Theol. Union, Chgo., 1969—71; mgr. Montgomery Ward, Franklin Oaks, Ill., 1971—96; instr. Prairie State, Chgo., 1996—98, South Suburban, S. Holland, Ill., 1997—98, St. Francis, Juliet, Ill., 1996—98; asst. prof. Calumet Coll. St. Joseph, Whiting, Ind., 1998—. Office: Calumet Coll St Joseph 2400 New York Ave Whiting IN 46394

FINNEGAN, HUGH PATRICK, lawyer; b. N.Y.C., May 7, 1958; s. Philip Joseph and Nora Mary (Kilkenny) F.; m. Peggy Donlon, Dec. 27, 1981; children: Philip James, Mary Kate, Conor John, Daniel Joseph. AB, Fordham U., 1980, JD, 1983. Bar: N.Y. 1984. Assoc. Sage, Gray, Todd & Sims, N.Y.C., 1983-86, DeForest & Duer, N.Y.C., 1986-87, Siller, Wilk, Mencher & Simkin, N.Y.C., 1987-90; spl. counsel Siller, Wilk & Mencher, N.Y.C., 1991, ptnr., 1992—. Bd. dirs. New Ground Inc. Mem. N.Y. State Bar Assn., Com. on Comml. Leasing and Litig. (real property law sect., environ. law sect.), Com. on Comml. Fin., Rural Resettlement (USA) Ltd. (pres.), New Ground Inc. (sec.), Ireland-U.S. Coun. Avocations: sports, charity. Office: Siller Wilk LLP 675 3rd Ave New York NY 10017-5704 E-mail: finnegan@sillerwilk.com.

FINNEGAN, JOHN D. insurance company executive; b. Jersey City; m. Kathleen Finnegan; 2 children. BA in Polit. Sci., Princeton U.; degree in Law, Fordham U.; MBA, Rutgers U. Mem. tax dept GMAC, 1976—86, dir. strategic planning, 1985, exec. v.p., CFO, 1992—95, pres., 1997—99, chmn., pres., 1999—2002; CFO GMAC Mortgage Corp., 1986; asst. treas. worldwide benefits compensation GM, 1987—89, asst. treas. internat. financing ops., 1989—92, v.p., treas., 1995—97, exec. v.p., 1999—2002; pres., CEO, dir. Chubb Corp., 2002—; chmn. bd. dirs., CEO Fed. Ins. Co., 2002—, chmn. Chubb & Son. Office: Chubb Group Ins Cos 15 Mountain View Rd Warren NJ 07059*

FINNEGAN, NEAL FRANCIS, banker; b. Boston, Mar. 28, 1938; s. Neal Francis and Mary Theresa (McNeil) F.; children: Theresa, Lynn, Neal, Wayne. BS, Northeastern U., 1961; MBA, Babson Coll., 1969. With Shawmut Bank of Boston, 1961-80, sr. v.p. in charge of OIC comml. banking, 1977-80; pres., chief exec. officer Worcester Bancorp Inc., Mass., 1980-82; chmn., chief exec. officer Worcester County Nat. Bank, 1980-82; sr. exec. v.p. Shawmut Corp., Boston, 1982-83, vice-chmn., 1983-86, dir., 1982-86; exec. v.p. Shawmut Bank of Boston, N.A., 1983-86; pres., chief operating officer, dir. Bowery Savs. Bank, N.Y.C., 1986-88; exec. v.p. Bankers Trust Co., N.Y.C., 1988-93; chmn. Citizens Bank of Mass., Boston, 2000—; chmn., CEO USTrust, Boston, 1993-99. Vice chmn. exec. com., chmn. bd. trustees Cath. Charities, Mass. chpt. Multiple Sclerosis Soc., vice-chmn.; chmn. bd. trustees Northeastern U., Boston, 1998; bd. dirs. Ireland C. of C. Office: Citizens Bank 28 State St Boston MA 02109

FINNEGAN, SARA ANNE (SARA LYCETT), publisher; b. Balt., Aug. 1, 1939; d. Lawrence Winfield and Rosina Elva (Huber) F.; m. Isaac C. Lycett, Jr., Aug. 31, 1974. BA, Sweet Briar Coll., 1961; MLA, Johns Hopkins U., 1965; exec. program, U. Va. Grad. Sch. Bus., 1977. Tchr., chmn. history dept. Hannah More Acad., Reisterstown, Md., 1961-65; redactor Williams & Wilkins Co., Balt., 1965-66, asst. head redactory, 1966-71, editor book div., 1971-75, assoc. editor-in-chief, 1975-77, v.p., editor-in-chief, 1977-81, pres. book div., 1981-88, group pres., 1988-94; editor Kalends, 1973-78, 89-92; exec. sponsor jour. Histochemistry and Cytochemistry, 1973-77. Dir. Passano Found., 1979-91. Editor Visions, Friends of Art of Sweet Briar Coll. Mag., 2001—. Trustee St. Timothy's Sch., Stevenson, Md., 1974—83; mem. adv. bd. Balt. Ind. Schs. Scholarship Fund, 1977—81; mem. adv. coun. grad. study Coll. Notre Dame of Md., 1983; mem. bd. overseers Sweet Briar Coll., 1987—88, bd. dirs., 1988—2000, chmn.-elect, 1994, chmn., 1995—2000; docent The Walters Art

Mus., 1994—; v.p. The Walters Art Mus. Docents, 2000—01, pres., 2001—02; bd. trustees The Walters Art Mus., 2001—02; bd. dirs. The Woman's Indsl. Exch., Balt., 1997—2000, v.p., 1998—2000; bd. dirs. Friends of Art of Sweet Briar Coll., 2000—. Mem. Assn. Am. Pubs. (exec. coun. profl. and scholarly pub. divsn. 1984-85), Internat. Sci., Tech. and Med. Pubs. Assn. (group exec. 1986-93, chmn.-elect 1988, chmn. 1989-92). Republican. Lutheran.

FINNELL, MICHAEL HARTMAN, corporate executive; b. LA, Jan. 27, 1927; s. Jules Bertram and Maribel Hartman (Schumacher) F.; m. Grace Vogel, Sept. 11, 1954 (div. June 1964); children: Lesley Finnell Blanchard, Carter Hartman, Hunter Vogel. Student, Asheville (N.C.) Sch., 1939-44; BA, U. Toronto, 1950; MBA, Harvard U., 1952; HHD (hon.), Capital U., Columbus, Ohio, 1980. Sec.-treas. Triad Oil Co. Ltd., 1952-62, v.p., dir., 1962-65; pres. Devon-Palmer Oils Ltd., 1966—70; v.p., dir. Can. Hydrocarbons, Ltd., 1970, pres., 1970—71, Montreal River Internat. Silver Mines Ltd., 1972—. Trustee Capital U., Columbus, 1982—94; life trustee Columbus Mus. of Art. Mem. Calif. Club, Annandale Golf Club, Ranchmen's Club, Calgary Petroleum Club, Calgary Golf and Country Club, La Grulla Gun Club, Nantucket Yacht Club. Home: 724 Holladay Rd Pasadena CA 91106-4115 Office: 625 Fair Oaks Ave Ste 288 South Pasadena CA 91030-2668

FINNEMORE, (ERHARDT) JOHN, civil engineer, educator; b. London, Jan. 27, 1937; came to U.S., 1965; s. Hubert John and Gerda Gertrud (Bloemeken) F.; m. Gulshan Gulamani, Aug. 7, 1962; children: (John) Riaz, Priya Jean. BSc in Engring., London U., 1960; MS, Stanford U., 1966, PhD, 1970. Registered profl. engr., Calif. Engr. J.D. and D.M. Watson, London, 1960-62, Found. Can. Engring. Corp. Ltd., Toronto, Ont., 1962-63; mcpl. engr. M.M. Dillon, Ltd., London, Ont., Can., 1963-65; rsch. engr. Metcalf & Eddy Engrs., Palo Alto, Calif., 1969-70; asst. prof. civil engring. Pahlavi U., Shiraz, Iran, 1970-71; sr. engr. Systems Control, Inc., Palo Alto, 1972-76; project mgr. Metcalf & Eddy Engrs., Palo Alto, Calif., 1977-79; assoc. prof. civil engring. Santa Clara (Calif.) U., 1979-94, prof., 1994—2002, prof. emeritus, 2002—. Cons. Tyndall & Cahners, Attys. at Law, San Jose, Calif., 1989-94, Wahler Assocs. Cons. Engrs., Palo Alto, 1990-91; chmn. tech. rev. com. on treatment plant issues, San Jose, 1981. Co-author: Fluid Mechanics with Engineering Applications, 1985, 1997, 2002; contbr. articles to profl. publs.; author govt. reports. European Engr. award European Fedn. Nat. Engring. Assns. Fellow ASCE; mem. Inst. Civil Engrs. U.K., Flamenco Soc. No. Calif. in San Jose (adv. bd., bd. dirs. 1985-87, chmn. 1986-87), Nat. Ground Water Assn., Universal Spiritual Brotherhood (pres. 1993—). Avocations: spiritual philosophy, flamenco guitar. Home: 22374 Riverside Dr Cupertino CA 95014-3982

FINNER, STEPHEN LAWRENCE, labor union administrator; b. Newark, May 4, 1938; s. Morris Abraham Finner and Dorothy Mendelson; children: Wendell, Wade. PhD, Brown U., 1963; degree in psychology and math., Colby Coll., 1960. Dir. chpt. svcs. AAUP, Washington, 1979—2002; coord. higher edn. svcs. United Professions of Vt., Burlington, Vt., 2002—. Composer: Live Life Well With Love, 1993, Chalice Lighting, 1996. Moderator All Souls Ch. Unitarian, Washington, 1993—2002. Recipient Layperson of The Yr. award, Greater Wash. Area Unitarian Universalist Congregations, 1991. Democrat. Unitarian Universalist. Home Fax: 802-813-1031. Personal E-mail: steve@stevefinner.net.

FINNERAN, KATIE, actress; b. Chgo., Jan. 22, 1972; Actor: (Broadway plays) On Borrowed Time, 1991—92, Two Shakespearean Actors, 1992, My Favorite Year, 1992—93, In the Summer House, 1993, The Heiress, 1995, Neil Simon's Proposals, 1997—98, The Iceman Cometh, 1999, Cabaret, 2000—01, Noises Off, 2001—02 (Tony award for Best Performance by a Featured Actor in a Play, 2002, Outer Critics Circle award, Drama Desk award nomination); (films) You've Got Mail, 1998, Liberty Heights, 1999, Night of the Living Dead; (TV series) Sex and the City, 1998, Frasier, 1999, Oz, 2001, Bram and Alice, 2002, Wonderfalls, 2003—. Office: CBS Studios May West Bldg Ste 30 5555 Melrose Ave Los Angeles CA 90023*

FINNERAN, KEVIN JOSEPH, editor; b. N.Y.C., June 4, 1949; s. Michael Joseph and Kathleen (Greally) F.; m. Kathleen Courrier, July 18, 1985; children: Anna Livia, Eamon Anders. BA in English, Villanova U., 1970; MA in English, Rutgers U., 1978; MA in Science Policy, George Washington U., 1988. Instr. Rutgers U., 1978-79; writer Counseling Soc., N.Y.C., 1979; editor Sun Times Mag., Washington, 1980-83; sr. researcher Solar Energy Industries Assn., Washington, 1984; cons. NAS, Washington, 1986-87; contbg. editor High Tech. Mag., Boston, 1986-87; sr. editor Issues in Science and Tech., Washington, 1987-91, editor-in-chief, 1991—. Author: The Federal Role in Research and Development, 1986; co-author: Cousteau Almanac of the Environment, 1980, Alternative Agriculture, 1988. Bd. dirs. Safe Energy Communications Coun., Washington, 1981-83; active Urban Forest Coun., Washington, 1991. Mem. NASW, AAAS, Am. Soc. Mag. Editors, D.C. Sci. Writers Assn.

FINNERAN, RICHARD J. literature educator; b. N.Y.C., Dec. 19, 1943; s. Maude F. Finneran; children: Richard E., Catherine A. PhD, U. N.C., 1968. Editor: The Poems of W. B. Yeats, 2nd ed., W. B. Yeats, _John Sherman and Dhoya_, Anglo-Irish Literature: A Review of Research, (scholarly jour.) Yeats: An Annual of Critical and Textual Studies. Mem.: South Atlantic MLA (hon.; pres. 1988—99). Office: Univ Tenn Dept English Knoxville TN 37996-0430

FINNERAN, THOMAS M. state legislator, lawyer; b. Boston, Jan. 27, 1950; m. Donna Kelley, 1975; children: Kelley, Shannon. BS, Northeastern U.; JD, Boston Coll., 1979. Ptnr. Finneran, Byrne & Lydon; rep. 13th Suffolk Dist. Mass. Ho. of Reps., 1979—, chmn. ways and means com., mem. fin. svc. commn., ho. speaker, 1996—. Office: State House Rm 356 Boston MA 02133*

FINNERTY, FRANCES MARTIN, medical administrator; b. Asheville, N.C., Dec. 23, 1936; d. Robert James and Elizabeth Howerton (Babbitt) Martin; m. Richard Phillip Caputo, Sept. 23, 1961 (div. 1974); m. Frank A. Finnerty Jr., July 26, 1975; children: Jonathan, Robert, Richard. Student, Mary Washington Coll., 1954-55, Croft Coll., 1955-57. Dist. mgr. Bus. Census Dept. Commerce, Suitland, Md., 1969-71; program coord. Georgetown U. D.C. Gen. Hosp., Washington, 1972-76; clin. mgr. Hypertension Ctr. Washington, 1976-82; project dir. PharmaKinetic Clin. Rsch. Labs., Balt., 1983; dir. mktg. Classic Glass, Alexandra, Va., 1984-86; office adminstr. Frank A. Finnerty Jr., M.D., Washington, 1987—. Cons. U.S. Census, U.S. Army, The Pentagon, Washington, 1969-70; cons. mapping ops. U.S. Census, Prince Georges County, Md., 1970; cons. paramedics pers. Merck Sharpe & Dohme, West Point, Pa., 1974. Contbr. articles to profl. jours. Recipient Cmty. Svc. award Dist. of Columbia, 1980. Mem. Am. Art League (Disting. Artist award 1993), Nat. Assn. Women in Arts, Dist. Med. Soc. Wives. Avocations: artist, landscape artist, reading. Home: 5 Eagle Circle Brevard NC 28712-4205

FINNERTY, JOHN DUDLEY, financial consultant; b. Glen Ridge, NJ, Apr. 23, 1949; s. John Patrick and Patricia (Conover) F.; m. Christine Watt, Dec. 29, 1973 (div. Jan. 1987); m. Louise Hoppe, May 21, 1988; 1 child, William Patrick Taylor. AB, Williams Coll., 1967-71; BA, U. Cambridge (Eng.), 1971-73, MA, 1977; PhD, Naval Postgrad. Sch., 1977. Adj. prof. Naval Postgrad. Sch., Monterey, Calif., 1973-77; sr. assoc. Morgan Stanley and Co. Inc., NYC, 1977-82; v.p. Lazard Frères and Co., NYC, 1982-86; exec. v.p., CFO Coll. Savs. Bank, Princeton, NJ, 1986-89, also bd. dirs.; gen. ptnr. McFarland Dewey & Co., NYC, 1989-95; dir. Houlihan Lokey Howard & Zukin, NYC, 1995-97; ptnr. PricewaterhouseCoopers LLP, NYC, 1997—2001; mng. prin. Analysis Group, Inc., NYC, 2001—03, Finnerty Econ. Cons., LLC, NYC, 2003—. Adj. prof. Fordham U., NYC, 1987-89, prof., 1989—. Author: Bond Refunding Analysts, 1984, Corporate Fin. Analysis, 1986, Fin. Mgr. Guide, 1988, Principles of Fin. with Corp. Applications, 1991, Yearbook of Fixed Income Investing, 1995, Project Fin., 1996, Corporate Fin. Mgmt., 1997, Principles of Fin. Mgmt., 1998, Debt Mgmt., 2001, Corp. Fin. Mgmt., 2d edit., 2004; assoc. editor Jour. of Corp. Fin., 1987-89, Fin. Mgmt., 1982-93; Jour. of Applied Fin., 1999-; mem. editl. bd. Jour. Portfolio Mgmt., 1990—, Jour. Fin. Engring., 1992-99; patentee Restructuring Debt Obligations, 1987, 88, Funding a Future Liability of Uncertain Cost., 1988, Insuring the Funding of a Future Liability of Uncertain Cost, 1989; editor: Fin. Mgmt., 1993-99, FMA Online, 2001-. Co-chmn. fund-raising in NJ for Williams Coll., 3d Century Campaign, 1990-93. Lt. USNR, 1973-77. Marshall Commn. scholar, London, 1971. Mem. Fin. Mgmt. Assn. (bd. dir. 1984-86, 91-99), Am. Fin. Assn., Western Fin. Assn., Fixed Income Analysts Soc. (program chmn. 1989-90, v.p. 1990-91, pres. 1991-92, bd. dir. 1990-92, 2001-), Williams Club (NYC), Spring Lake Bath and Tennis Club (NJ). Republican. Roman Catholic. Avocation: coin collecting. Home: 400 Park Ave Rye NY 10580-1213

FINNERTY, JOSEPH GREGORY, III, lawyer; b. Balt., Apr. 25, 1960; s. Joseph Gregory Jr. and Alice Ann (Fannon) F.; m. Amy Caroline Shull, Nov. 12, 1988 (div. 1999); children: Katherine Pagett, Alice Olivia. AB in English Lit., Hamilton Coll., 1982; JD, U. Md., Balt., 1987. Bar: N.Y. 1988. Assoc. Rogers & Wells, N.Y.C., 1988-94; prin. ptnr. McCarrick, Finnerty & Mayer, N.Y.C., 1994-96; ptnr. Piper & Marbury, L.L.P., N.Y.C., 1996-99, Piper & Rudnick LLP, 1999—. Mem. ABA, Assn. Bar City N.Y. Office: Piper and Rudnick 1251 Ave of Americas New York NY 10020-1104 E-mail: joseph.finnertyiii@piperrudnick.com.

FINNERTY, LOUISE HOPPE, beverage and food company executive; b. Alexandria, Va., Jan. 19, 1949; d. William G. and Ruth A. (Ehren) Hoppe; m. John D. Finnerty, May 21, 1988; 1 child, William Patrick Taylor. BA, Va. Commonwealth U., 1971; postgrad., Am. U., 1972-73. Staff asst. to Dr. Henry Kissinger NSC, Washington, 1971-73; adminstrv. asst. Nat. Petroleum Coun., Washington, 1973-75; profl. staff mem. Senate Armed Svc. Com., Washington, 1976-81; spl. asst. Office Legis. Affairs, U.S. Dept. State, Washington, 1981-84, dep. asst. sec. of state, 1984-88; mgr. govt. affairs PepsiCo, Inc., Purchase, N.Y., 1988-91; dir. govt. affairs PepsiCo Foods and Beverages Internat., Somers, N.Y., 1991-95; v.p. internat. govt. affairs PepsiCo, Inc., Purchase, N.Y., 1995—. Mem. Nat. Fgn. Trade Coun. (bd. dirs. 1991—), Spring Lake Bath and Tennis Club. Republican. Lutheran. Avocations: reading; gardening; cooking. Home: 400 Park Ave Rye NY 10580-1213 also: 506 2nd Ave Spring Lake NJ 07762-1107 Office: PepsiCo Inc 700 Anderson Hill Rd Purchase NY 10577-1444

FINNERTY, NANCY WELLS, family physician; b. Orlando, Fla., Dec. 2, 1953; d. Maxwell Warnock Wells Jr. and Dorothy Verne (Benz) Holte; m. John Joseph Finnerty III, Jan. 18, 1992; children: Lillian Ashley, John Joseph IV. BA, Vanderbilt U., 1975; PhD, Med. U. S.C., 1981; MD, U. Fla., 1985. Diplomate Am. Bd. Family Practice. Intern, then resident in family practice St. Vincent's Hosp., Jacksonville, 1985-88; physician Gary Dopson MD, PA, Macclenny, Fla., 1988-91, Fla. Med. Clinic, Zephyrhills, 1991—. Chief of medicine East Pasco Med. Ctr., Zephyrhills, 1994-95, 97-99, chief of staff elect, 1999-2000, chief of staff, 2000-02; team physician Baker County H.S., 1988-91, Zephyrhills H.S., 1992—; bd. dirs. Fla. KidCare Corp. Chmn. Am. Heart Walk, Am. Heart Assn., Zephyrhills, 1996. Lt. col. U.S. Army, 11982—. Decorated Bronze Star medal. Mem. Am. Acad. Family Practice, Fla. Acad. Family Practice (family practice amb. to state legis. 1994—, bd. dirs. 1999—). Republican. Episcopalian. Avocations: dance (ballet, tap, jazz). Office: Florida Med Clinic 38135 Market Sq Zephyrhills FL 33542-2505

FINNEY, BEN RUDOLPH, anthropologist, educator; b. San Diego, Calif., Oct. 1, 1933; s. Leon Howell Finney and Melba Regina Trefzger; m. Liudmila Alepko Finney; m. Ruth Elizabeth Sutherlin, Aug. 10, 1964 (div. Dec. 1985); children: Sean Tumoana, Gregory L. BA, U. Calif., Berkeley, Calif., 1955; MA, U. Hawaii, 1959; PhD, Harvard U., 1964. Sr. statistician Kaiser Steel, Fontana, Calif., 1956; mfg. analyst Convair Divsn. Gen. Dynamics, San Diego, 1956; aviation ground officer USNR, Pensacola, Fla., 1956—57; tchg. fellow Harvard U., Cambridge, Mass., 1960—64; asst. prof. U. Calif., Santa Barbara, Calif., 1964—67; sr. rsch. fellow Australian Nat. U., Canberra, Australia, 1968—70; assoc. prof. U. Hawaii, Honolulu, 1970—2000, prof. emeritus, 2001—, chmn. Dept. Anthropolgy, 1985—95. Rsch. assoc. East-West Ctr., Honolulu, 1972—76; vis. scholar Harvard U., 1979—80; nat. rsch. coun. assoc. Ames Rsch. Ctr. NASA, Mountain View, Calif., 1984—85; councillor sci. and cultural coun. French U. of Pacific Papeete, Tahiti, 1991—94; co-chmn. Dept. Space and Soc. Internat. Space U., Strasbourg, France, 1994—; rsch. assoc. Dept. Anthropology Bishop Mus., 1989—. Author: Polynesian Peasants and Proletarians, 1965, Big-Men and Business, 1973, Pacific Navigation and Voyaging, 1976, Hokulea, The Way to Tahiti, 1979, Interstellar Migration and the Human Experience, 1985, Business Development in the Highlands of Papua New Guinea, 1987, From Sea to Space, 1992, Voyage of Rediscovery, 1994, Surf Culture, The Art History of Surfing, 2002, Sailng in the Wake of the Ancestors, 2003; editor: News from the Pacific, 1958—59; author: Surfing, A History of the Ancient Hawaiian Sport, 1996; Polynesian Peasants and Proletarians, 1965; correspondant: Jour. of Pacific History, 1974—, assoc. editor: Space Power, Resources, Mfg. and Devel., 1987—95, mem. editl. bd.: The Contemporary Pacific, 1989—, adv. bd.: Space Energy and Trans., 1996—, adv. editor: Archaeostronomy, 1998—. Recipient medal, Royal Inst. Navigation, 1994, French U. of Pacific, 1995, Tsiolkovsky medal, Russia, 1995; grantee, Fulbright Found., 1956—57, NIH, 1961—64, NSF, 1965, 1974, NEA, 1976, NEH, 1979—80, Woods Hole Oceanographic Instn., 1979, NRC, 1984—85, NSF, 1985, 1992, Nat. Pk. Svc., Bishop Mus., Native Hawaiian Culture and Arts Program, 1995. Home: 2987 Kalakaua Ave Apt 401 Honolulu HI 96815 E-mail: bfinney@hawaii.edu.

FINNEY, CLIFTON DONALD, publishing executive; b. Dubuque, Iowa, Apr. 7, 1941; s. Clifton Monroe and Violet Irene (Snyder) F.; m. Kazuko Akiyama, Aug. 17, 1968; 1 child, Ann. BA in Chemistry, Austin Coll., 1964; PhD in Phys. Chemistry, Kans. State U., 1970. Postdoctoral fellow U. Toronto, Ont., Can., 1969-71; asst. prof. chemistry Drake U., Des Moines, 1971-75; pres. Natural Dynamics, Des Moines and Houston, 1975-86, Golf Physics Co., Baton Rouge, 1986-94, DeerStats, Houston and Baton Rouge, 1996—. Assoc. Ames (Iowa) Lab., U.S. AEC, 1971-75; instr. computer sci. U. Houston, 1984-86. Contbr. articles to Phys. Chemistry, Sci., Computers and Edn. Recipient energy rsch. grant Iowa Energy Policy Coun., 1975, USERDA, 1976. Mem. Am. Chem. Soc., N.Y. Acad. Scis. Achievements include patents in Inertial Weighting Systems for Golf Clubheads and a Superventuri Power Source. Home and Office: 17732 Glenn Knoll Ave Baton Rouge LA 70817-9567 Address: 11580 Perkins Rd Apt 221 Baton Rouge LA 70810-1846

FINNEY, ERNEST ADOLPHUS, JR., retired state supreme court chief justice; b. Smithfield, Va., Mar. 23, 1931; s. Ernest A. Sr. and Collen (Godwin) F.; m. Frances Davenport, Aug. 20, 1955; children: Ernest A. III, Lynn Carol (Nikky) Finney, Jerry Leo. BA, Claflin Coll., 1952; JD, S.C. State U., 1954, LHD (hon.), 1996; HHD (hon.), Claflin Coll., 1977; LLD, U. S.C., 1991, The Citadel, 1995, Johnson C. Smith U., 1995, Morris Coll., 1996; LHD (hon.), Coll. of Charleston, 1995; LLD, Morris Coll., 1996. Bar: S.C. 1954, U.S. Dist. Ct. S.C. 1957, U.S. Ct. Appeals (4th cir.) 1964. Pvt. practice law, Conway, S.C., 1954-60, Sumter, S.C., 1960-66; with Finney and Gray, Attys. at Law, Sumter, 1966-76; mem. S.C. Ho. of Reps., Columbia, 1973-76; judge SC Cir. Ct., Columbia, SC, 1976-85; assoc. justice SC Supreme Ct., Columbia, SC, 1985-94, chief justice, 1994-2000; interim pres. SC State U., 2003—. Chmn. S.C. Legis. Black Caucus, Columbia, 1973-75; chmn. bd. dirs. Buena Vista Devel. Corp., Sumter, 1967—; mem. S.C. State Elections Commn., Columbia, 1968-72; trustee Claflin Coll., Orangeburg, S.C., 1986—, chmn. bd. trustees, 1987-95; sch. law minority adv. com. U. S.C., 1988—. Recipient Disting. Alumni of Yr. award Nat. Assn. Equal Opportunity Edn., 1986, Achievement award C. of C., Sumter, 1986, Presdl. Citation Morris Coll., Sumter, 1986, Wiley A. Branton award NBA, 1998, Afro Am. Achievement award Turner Broadcasting Sys., 1998, Pub. Servant of Yr. S.C. C. of C., 1999, David P. Richardson Jr. Nation Builder award The Nat. Black Caucus of State Legislators, 1999; named 1987 Citizen of Yr. Charleston (S.C.) Med. Soc., 1987; inductee Nat. Black Coll. Alumni Hall of Fame, 1988. Mem. ABA, Am. Judges Assn., Am. Law Inst. (bd. dirs.), Conf. Chief Justices (bd. dirs.), Sumter County Bar, S.C. Bar, Assn. Trial Lawyers Am., Nat. Bar Assn. (appellate com.), S.C. Trial Lawyers Assn. (hon.), Masons, Shriners. Methodist. Avocations: reading, fishing, golf. Home: 24 Runnymede Blvd Sumter SC 29153-8742 Office: SC State U 300 College St NE Orangeburg SC 29117*

FINNEY, GRAHAM STANLEY, management consultant; b. Greenwich, Conn., Sept. 6, 1930; s. William Stanley and Sarah Margaret (Boswell) F.; m. Katharine Pillsbury Becker, June 22, 1957; children: Sarah Boswell Finney Johnston, Martha Becker, Samuel Warner, Garrett Stevens. Student, Washington and Lee U., 1948-49; BA, Yale U., 1952; MPA, Harvard U., 1954. Planning dir. City of Portland, Maine, 1957-60; asst. exec. dir. Phila. City Planning Commn., 1961-65; exec. dir. Phila. Coun. for Cmty. Advancement, 1965-66; dep. supt. schs. Phila., 1966-69; commr. addiction svcs. agy. City of N.Y.; mng. ptnr. Greater Phila. Partnership, 1975-76; dir. Phila. Partnership, 1973-75; pres. Corp. for Pub./Pvt. Ventures, Phila., 1977-80; sr. ptnr. The Conservation Co., Phila., 1980-87, pres., 1988-95; mgmt. cons.; pres. 21st Century League, 1997-2000. Dir. Exec. Svc. Corp. Delaware Valley; trustee Seybert Instn., Phila., 1978; dir. High Tech. High Charter Sch., Phila., 2001—. Author: Administering Catastrophe, 1975; (with others) Philadelphia: 1776-2076, 1975. Vol. exec. Internat. Exec. Svc. Corps., 2001—; chair Nat. Ctr. on Adult Literacy; trustee Inst. Pub. Adminstrn.; dir. Friends Phila. Parks, 2003—. With U.S. Army, 1954-56. Recipient The Phila. award, 1998. Mem.: Yale Club (N.Y.C.). Democrat. Presbyterian. Avocations: gardening, tennis, hiking. Home: 615 W Hortter St Philadelphia PA 19119-3650 E-mail: gkfinney@aol.com.

FINNEY, JAMES OWEN, JR., cardiologist; b. Gadsden, Ala., Feb. 3, 1938; s. James Owen and Margaret (Pride) F.; m. Pattie Perry Robinson, June 8, 1960; children: Margaret Carlisle, Pattie Perry, James Owen III, Mabel Pride. BA, Vanderbilt U., 1960, MD, 1965. Diplomate Am. Bd. Internal Medicine and Cardiovascular Diseases. Intern Univ. Ala., Birmingham, 1965-66, resident, 1966-68; fellow cardiology Univ. Chgo., 1968-69; fellow Univ. Ala., Birmingham, 1969-70, chief resident, 1970-71; pvt. practice Southview Med. Group, Birmingham, Ala., 1973—. Major USAF, 1971-73. Fellow ACP, Am. Coll. Cardiology, Coun. on Clin. Cardiology, Am. Heart Assn. (dir. Ala. alliance 1975—); mem. Vanderbilt Med. Alumni Assn. (v.p. 1992-94, pres. 1994-96). Avocations: gardening, boating. Office: Southview Med Group 833 Saint Vincents Dr Ste 300 Birmingham AL 35205-1612

FINNEY, JOHN EDGAR, III, food products executive; b. Hominy, Okla., Oct. 13, 1943; s. John Edgar and Ella Frances (Beckett) F.; m. Claudia Maddalena, Aug. 29, 1965 (div. Nov. 1979); children: Kristen, Eric; m. Tiare Richert, Oct. 18, 1980; children: Thomas Beckett, Elizabeth Stuart. BA, Okla. State U., 1965; JD, Stanford U., 1968. Bar: Colo. 1969, Hawaii 1969, U.S. Dist. Ct. Hawaii 1970, U.S. Ct. Appeals (9th cir.) 1970, Calif. 1974. Assoc. law Carlsmith, Carlsmith, Wichman Case, Honolulu, 1970-73; ptnr. law Augustine & Delafield, San Diego, 1973-75; pres., chief exec. officer Pentagram Corp., Honolulu, 1976-90; pres. Indsl. Income Property Inc., Honolulu, 1992—, also bd. dirs. Bd. dirs. Offshore Holdings Inc. Bd. dirs., bd. visitors Stanford (Calif.) U. Law Sch., 1986-93, USAF Pacific Adv. Bd., Hickam AFB, Honolulu, 1987-89, Hawaii Maritime Ctr., Honolulu, 1988-90. Capt. USMC, 1968-75. Named Okla. Ambassador, State of Okla., 1989; recipient Community Svc. award Aloha United Way, Honolulu, 1988, Community Svc. award Burger King Corp., San Francisco, 1987. Mem. Young Presidents' Orgn. (chmn. 1982-84), World Presidents' Orgn., Okla. Cattlemen's Assn., Stanford Univ. Assocs., Outrigger Canoe Club. Avocations: lit., canoe racing, rugby, skiing. Home: 155 Dowsett Ave Honolulu HI 96817-1109 Office: Indsl Properties Inc 6 Marin Lane Honolulu HI 96813-3107 E-mail: jefinneyhi@hotmail.com.

FINNEY, LEE, social worker, negotiator; b. Balt., Feb. 25, 1943; d. E. William and Mildred Lee (Refo) Carr; m. James Nathaniel Finney, Feb. 25, 1967 (div. Aug. 1970); 1 child, Karen Elizabeth. Student, Sweet Briar Coll., 1961-63; BA in Govt., George Washington U., 1965; MS in Counseling, Calif. State U., Hayward, 1986. Caseworker N.Y.C. Welfare Dept., 1966-68; probation officer N.Y.C. Probation Dept., 1968-74; dep. probation officer Alameda County Probation Dept., Oakland, Calif., 1974-78, child welfare social worker, 1979-80; children's svcs. social worker Contra Costa County Dept. Social Svcs., Richmond, Calif., 1980-87, social work supr. Antioch, Calif., 1987-88, dir. staff devel. Martinez, Calif., 1989-90; pay equity analyst Contra Costa County Pers. Dept., Martinez, 1988-89; labor rels. cons. Indsl. Employers and Distributors Assn., Emeryville, Calif., 1990—. Instr. edn. psychology dept. Calif. State U., Hayward, 1987-89; mem. exec. bd. Contra Costa Ctrl. Labor Coun., Martinez, 1987-89; no. v.p., chief negotiator Svc. Employees Internat. Union Local 535, Oakland, 1983-88; chair Coalition for Children and Families, Richmond, Calif., 1986-88. Author booklet: First Steps to Identifying Sex and Race Based Inequities in a workplace: A Guide to Achieving Pay Equity, 1989. Bd. dirs. YWCA, Contra Costa County, 1989-91; pres., acting dir. Comparable Worth Project, Inc., Oakland, 1984-87; mem. Adv. Com. on Employment and Econ. Status for Women Contra Costa, 1984-89, chair, 1987-89. Recipient Cmty. Svc. award Vocare Found., 1976, Golden Nike award Emeryville Bus. and Profl. Women, 1986, Woman of Yr. award Todos Santos Bus. and Profl. Women, 1989, Women Who Have Made a Difference award Coalition of Labor Union Women, 1989. Democrat. Avocations: sailing, travel, natural history. Home: 6 Commodore Dr # C336 Emeryville CA 94608-1649 Office: IDEA 2200 Powell St Ste 1000 Emeryville CA 94608-1869 E-mail: lee.finney@worldnet.att.net.

FINNEY, LINNEA RUTH, tailor, writer; b. Seattle, May 4, 1952; d. Donald Bruce and Ethel Ruth (Hagli) Deans; m. Raymond Howard Finney, Oct. 5, 1977; children: Sean Howard, Chelan Kimber. A of A of Arts and Scis., A of Applied Arts and Scis. in Acctg., Shoreline C.C., Seattle, 1995. Dental asst., technician Dr. Donald Bruce Deans, Seattle, 1966-74; dental technician Zundel Dental Lab., Seattle, 1976-79; tailor Carol McClellan Suedes & Leathers, Seattle, 1982, 84; wardrobe asst. Diana Ross on Tour, Seattle, 1982, Harry Belafonte on Tour, Seattle, 1987, Rod Stewart on Tour, Seattle, 1988, Dream Girls Nat. Tour, Seattle, 1988; home tchr. Mukilteo (Wash.) Sch. Dist., 1991-94, Stanwood (Wash.) Sch. Dist., 1995-96. Tailor Haute Couture, Bothell, Wash., 1964-74, 81-84, Seattle, 1977-80, Everett, Wash., 1984-95, Stanwood, Wash., 1995—. Vol. Habitat for Humanity, 1992. Avocations: reading, medicine. Home: 7719 274th St NW Stanwood WA 98292-5927

FINNEY, MICHAEL DOUGLAS, public safety consultant; b. Eatontown, N.J., June 10, 1968; s. Connie Douglas and Marion McCorkle Finney; m. Tory Lynn Stefonek, Mar. 9, 1967; children: Joshua Douglas children: Ashlyn Elizabeth. BA, U. S.C., 1994; MDiv, Columbia Internat. U., 1998; postgrad., Okla. State U., 1999. Coord., instr. S.C. Fire Acad., Columbia, 1990—99; curriculum mgr. Internat. Fire Svc. Tng. Assn./Fire Protection Publs., Stillwater, Okla., 1999—2001; dir. pub. safety svcs. Great Oaks Inst., Cin., 2002—. Contbr. articles to profl. jours. Scholar, Okla. State U., 2000—01. Mem.: Internat. Soc. Fire Svc. Instrs. (assoc.; bd. dirs. 2003). Achievements include research in Educational Technology For Fire And Emergency Services. Home: 1773 Continental Dr Cincinnati OH 45246 Office: Great Oaks Institute 3254 East Kemper Rd Cincinnati OH 45241 Personal E-mail: finneym@greatoaks.com.

FINNEY, PAUL DAVID, acupuncturist, Chinese herbologist, entrepreneur; b. Humboldt, Kans., Apr. 19, 1944; s. Robert Arthur and Gertrude (Leitzbach) F. BS in Indsl. Engring., Stanford U., 1968; Diplomate in Acupuncture, Medicina Alternativa, Colombo, Sri Lanka, 1988; Cert. in Chinese Herbology, Herbal Traditions, Boston, 1993. Mgmt. asst. Signet Sci. Co., Burbank, Calif., 1971; pres. Atlantic Coastal Cmtys., Cocoa Beach, Fla., 1972-81; lobbyist Am. Legion, Washington, 1982-83; legis. dir. Nat. Tax Limitation Com., Washington, 1983-84; pres. League for Ltd. Govt., Washington, 1985-86; intern Xi Yuan Hosp., Beijing, 1990; pvt. practice acupuncturist Humboldt, Kans., 1989—. Propr. Finney Enterprises, Humboldt, Finney Farms, Humboldt, 1994—, India Tours Internat., Humboldt, 1996—, Bailey Hotel, Humboldt, 1997—. Mem. staff Reagan for Gov., San Francisco, 1966; founding pres. Humboldt Hist. Preservation Alliance, 1992-97, 99-2003; founder Sathya Sai Baba Ctr. of Humboldt, pres., 1998—. Lt. Signal Corps USAR, 1968, comm. officer 2/12 Arty. Bn., 23d Arty. group U.S. Army, 1969—70, Vietnam. Decorated Bronze Star. Mem.: VFW (life), Acupunture Assn. Kans. (polit. dir. 1998—), Lotus Life Car Club, Humboldt Rotary Club. Libertarian. Presbyterian. Office: Finney Acupuncture Clinic 714 Bridge St Humboldt KS 66748-1708

FINNEY, ROY PELHAM, JR., urologist, surgeon, inventor; b. Gaffney, S.C., Dec. 7, 1924; s. Roy P. Finney Sr. and Mary Frances (Cannon) Woodard; m. Kay Harkness, Apr. 5, 1962; children: Wright C., James L., Joella R., Gray, Kevin. MD, Med. U. S.C., 1952. Diplomate: Am. Bd. Urology. Resident in urology Johns Hopkins U., Balt., 1952-57; prof. surg. urology U. South Fla., Tampa, 1972-84, dir. div. urology, 1972-84; ret. Designer and inventor implantable prostheses incontinence device inflatable penile prostheses treatment impotence, Double J ureteral stent, developer new surg. procedures treatment impotence; patentee in field. Fellow ACS; mem. Am. Urology Assn., Soc. Internationale D'Urologie, Internat. Continenece Soc., Urodynamic Soc. Republican. Home: 4382 Cortez Blvd Spring Hill FL 34607-1209

FINNIE, DORIS GOULD, investment company executive; b. Mpls., Sept. 2, 1919; d. Earl Chester and Marie Ethelee (McGulpin) Gould; m. Donald Johnstone Finnie, May 23, 1939; children: Dianne Elaine Boggess, Denise Finnie-Pascento. BA in Journalism, U. Denver, 1941. Office mgr. K&P, Inc., Golden, Colo., 1965-82; exec. dir. Rocky Mountain Coal Mining Inst., Lakewood, 1982—2000; conf. coord. Colo. Mining Assn., 2000—. Editor Procs. of Rocky Mountain Coal Mining Inst., 1982-2000. Founder City of Lakewood, 1968; dir. Alzheimer and Kidney Found., Denver, 1970-72. Recipient Ernest Thompson Seton award Camp Fire, Inc., 1963, St. Barbara's Day medal Colo. Mining Assn., 1999; named Woman of Yr. Denver Area Panhellenic, 1977; Paul Harris fellow Rotary Internat., 1998. Mem. Colo. Soc. Assn. Execs., Meeting Planners Internat. (Humanitarian award 1992), Profl. Conv. Mgmt. Assn., Mortar Board (Disting. Lifetime Mem. Achievement award 2001), Kappa Delta (Outstanding Alumnae award 1959, 74, Order of Emerald 1987). Avocations: gourmet cooking, playing bridge. Office: 11701 W 21st Pl Lakewood CO 80215-1101

FINNIE, IAIN, mechanical engineer, educator; b. Hong Kong, July 18, 1928; s. John and Jessie Ferguson (Mackenzie) F.; m. Joan Elizabeth Roth, July 28, 1969; 1 dau., Shauna. BS with honors, U. Glasgow, 1949; MS, MIT, 1951, M.E., 1952, Sc.D., 1954; D.Sc. (hon.), U. Glasgow, 1974. With Shell Devel. Co., 1954-61, engr., to 1961; mem. faculty dept. mech. engring. U. Calif., Berkeley, 1961—, prof., 1963—92. Vis. prof. Cath. U. Chile, 1965, Ecole Polytechnique, Lausanne, Switzerland, 1976, 87. Author: Creep of Engineering Materials, 1959; contbr. articles to profl. jours. Guggenheim Found. fellow, 1967-68 Mem. Nat. Acad. Engring., ASME (hon., Nadai award 1982). Home: 2901 Avalon Ave Berkeley CA 94705-1401 Office: U Calif 6179 Etcheverry Berkeley CA 94720-0001 E-mail: finnie@me.berkeley.edu.

FINNIGAN, ROBERT EMMET, retired small business owner; b. Buffalo, May 27, 1927; s. Charles M. and Marie F. (Jacobs) F.; m. Bette E. van Horn, Apr. 1, 1950; children: Michael, Patrick, Robert E. Jr., Joan, Shawn, Thomas, Matthew. BS, U.S. Naval Acad., 1949; MS, U. Ill., 1954, PhD, 1957. Commd. lt. USAF, 1949, advanced through grades to capt., 1954; sr. scientist Livermore Lab., U. Calif., 1959, U. Calif. Lawrence Livermore Lab., 1957-62; sr. rsch. scientist Stanford Rsch. Inst., Menlo Park, Calif., 1962-63; dir. Electronic Assocs. Inc., Palo Alto, Calif., 1963-67; founder, vice chmn., sr. v.p., chief strategic officer Finnigan Corp., San Jose, Calif., 1967-92, vice chmn. emeritus, cons., 1992—. Mem. panel NAS, Washington, 1986—89; bd. dirs. Pacific Nanotechnology, Inc., Santa Clara, Calif. Author: Identification and Analysis of Organic Pollutants in Water, 1976, Advances in Identification and Analysis of Organic Pollutants in Water, 1981. Chmn., co-founder U.S. Nat. Working Group on Pollution, Internat. Orgn. for Legal Metrology, Washington, 1982-87; mem. pres.'s coun., U. Ill., Urbana, 2002. Recipient Alumni Honor award Coll. of Engring., U. Ill., 1980, Winston Churchill medal of wisdom, 1999; named Pioneer in Analytical Instrumentation-Mass Spectrometry, Soc. for Analytical Chemists of Pitts. and Pitts. Conf. on Analytical Chemistry, 1994, Instrumentation Hall of Fame, Pitts., Conf. on Analytical Chemistry and Analytical Chem. Soc., 1999; named to Wisdom Hall of Fame, 1999; recipient Disting. Alumnus award, U. Ill. Dept. Elec. Engring. 1975; Robert Finnigan professorship established Keck Grad. Inst. Applied Life Sci., Claremont, Calif., 2002. Mem IEEE (sr.), Am. Soc. for Mass Spectrometry (bd. dirs.), Am. Electronic Assn. (bd. dirs. 1982-84, 87, chmn., co-founder environ. and occupational health com.), U.S. Naval Acad. Alumni Assn. (pres.'s cir. 1996—). Avocations: wine, hiking, snowshoeing.

FINO, MARIE GEORGETTE KECK, retired real estate broker; b. Greenville, Pa., Jan. 30, 1923; d. Harvey I. and Winifred L. (Fuller) Keck; m. Alex F. Fino, Sept. 27, 1947; children: Timothy A., Jeffrey J. Cert. in real estate, Pa. State U., 1980; grad., Realtors Inst., Harrisburg, Pa., 1981. RN, Pa.; lic. real estate broker, Pa. Broker, owner 305 Realty, North Warren, Pa., 1983-96; instr. Pa. State U., 1985-96, ret., 1996. Treas. Warren County Bd. Realtors, 1981-84, v.p., 1984-86, pres., 1988. Patentee fuel storage vent. Treas. Northwestern Pa. Regional Planning Commn., 1985-92, exec. com., 1988-92, treas., 1991; bd. dirs. Warren County Devel. Assn., Warren County Crime Stoppers, 1989-96. Named Woman of Yr. in Bus. and Industry, County of Warren, 1986, Citizen Amb. to China, 1994. Mem. Nat. Assn. Realtors, Pa. Assn. Realtors (bd. dirs. 1984-88, vice-chair comml.-indsl. com. 1984-88, bd. dirs. 1992-93), Soc. Indsl. and Office Realtors (nat. bd. dirs. 1992-95, dist. v.p. 1993-95), Warren County C. of C., Philomel Club (bd. dirs. 1978-80), Conewango Valley Country Club (Warren), Conewango Valley Kennel Club. Republican. Roman Catholic. Avocations: golf, bridge, showing and breeding maltese dogs. E-mail: keystonem@penn.com.

FINO, TERESA CRISTINA, legal secretary, business owner; b. Serra do Bouro, Portugal, Aug. 6, 1972; d. Antonio Jose Fino and Maria Rosa Jeronimo. AS, Ocean County Coll., Toms River, N.J., 1993; BS, St Peters U., Jersey City, 1995. CEO AmPort Constrn., Bayville, N.J., 1987-97; ins. coord. W. Hudson Chiropractic Ctr., Kearny, N.J., 1994-96; bus. owner Europa Constrn., Kearny, 1997—; legal sec. Cynthia M. Russo, Esq., Newark, 1996—. Mem. PALCUS, Washington, 1998—.

FINOCCHIARO, ALFONSO G. bank executive; b. Catania, Italy, Aug. 20, 1932; came to U.S., 1960; s. Giovanni and Giuseppina (Cavalier) F.; m. Diana Louise Cavagnolo, Jan. 19, 1936; children: John Paul, Carol Anne. D in Polit. Sci., U. Catania, 1958; MBA in Internat. Fin., Pace U., 1967. V.p. Chem. Bank, N.Y.C., 1966-77; pres., gen. mgr. Conn. Bank Internat., N.Y.C., 1977-78; exec. v.p., regional dir. Banco Portugues do Atlantico, N.Y.C., 1978-95; dir. BPA Futures Cayman, 1989-96, Internat. Strategy Svcs., 1990-96; vice-chmn. BPA Brazil, 1993-96; dir. BPA Overseas Ltd., 1993-96; advisor to bd. dirs. Banco Portugues do Atlantico, Lisbon, Portugal, 1996-97; chmn., CEO FINAB Internat. Corp. Svc. Ltd., 2000—. Bd. dirs. BPD Internat. Bank, N.Y.C., Alfie Internat., Inc., So. Fin. Bank, Warrenton, Va.; dir., Banif Fin. Scvs., Miami, Banif Mortgage Co.; advisor to bd. dirs. Banco Internat. do Funchal, Lisbon, Portugal, 1997—. Mem. Friends of Queen Catherine, Inc., chmn. fin. com., trustee, 1988-2001. Decorated comdr. Order Infante D. Henrique (Portugal). Fellow: Internat. Mgmt. and Devel. Inst. (Leadership award); mem.: European-Am. C. of C. in the U.S. (bd. dirs. 1991—98, v.p.), Internat. Mgmt. and Devel. Inst., Global Leadership Inst. (bd. dirs. 1991—2001), Am. Portuguese Soc. (v.p., bd. dirs. 1979—), Portugal C. of C. (bd. dirs., pres. 1978—98). Republican. Roman Catholic. Avocations: piano, music, travel, foreign affairs. E-mail: alfie333@yahoo.com.

FINOCCHIARO, PENNY MORRIS, secondary school educator; b. Glendale, Calif., Sept. 30, 1949; d. C. Harold and Margaret (Nelson) Morris; m. Paul D. Finocchiaro, Apr. 9, 1996; children from previous marriage: E. Pierce III, Hailey M. BA in Speech and English, Muskingum Coll., New Concord, Ohio, 1971; MA in Edn., Nat. U., Sacramento, 1991. Cert. multiple and single subject tchr. Assoc. prodr. Alhecama Players, Santa Barbara (Calif.) C.C. Dist., 1972-86; docent Santa Barbara Mus. Art, 1975-86; importer Cambridge Place Corp., Santa Barbara, 1974-86; promotions and fund raising Stewart-Bergman Assocs., Nevada City, Calif., 1986-89; travel columnist The Union, Grass Valley, Calif., 1987-90; tchr. drama and English Bear River H.S., Grass Valley, 1991-98, dept. chair visual and performing arts, 1993-98; tchr. English lit. Lycee Française La Perouse, San Francisco, 1999—, chair dept. English, 2001—. Art docent coord. Deer Creek Sch., Nevada City, 1986-90, pres. Parent Tchr. Club, 1987-88. Recipient award for valuable contbn. to schs. Nevada City Sch. Dist., 1990, Dir.'s award Santa Barbara C.C., 1982, Tchrs. Who Make a Difference award Assn. of Calif. Sch. Adminstrs., 1998. Mem.: No. Calif. Ednl. Theatre Assn., Calif. Ednl. Theatre Assn., Ednl. Theatre Assn., Calif. Assn. Tchrs. English, Nat. Coun. Tchrs. of English. Avocations: art and antique collecting, rollerblading, travel, biking, swimming, theatre. Home: 2123 Jones St San Francisco CA 94133-2582 Office: Lycee Francais Internat 755 Ashbury St San Francisco CA 94117-4013

FINORE HURD, DIANE, marketing executive, publisher; b. Abington, Pa., Aug. 11, 1950; d. Carmen George and Anna B. (Signore) F. AS, Tobe Coburn Sch., 1972; BA cum laude, Temple U., 1974; MA, NYU, 1984. Dir. spl. events Mus. Am. Folk Art (now Mus. Folk Art N.Y.C.), N.Y.C., 1982—85; pub. rep. Taxi Pub. Inc., N.Y.C., 1986-87; sales rep. CHILD Magazine, N.Y.C., 1986—87; dir. sales SALES, Inc., N.Y.C., 1987-88; pres. Finore Mktg. Svcs., Stone Harbor, N.J., 1989—. Founding pub./editor Seven Mile Times, Seven Mile Beach Party. Office: Finore Mktg Svcs PO Box 71 Stone Harbor NJ 08247-0071

FINS, JOSEPH JACK, internist, medical ethicist; b. NYC, Nov. 16, 1959; s. Herman and Ruth (Lovett) F.; m. Amy B. Ehrlich, July 2, 1989. BA with deptl. hons., Wesleyan U., 1982; MD, Cornell U., 1986. Diplomate Am. Bd. Internal Medicine. Intern in psychiatry N.Y. Hosp. Payne Whitney Clinic, N.Y.C., 1986—87; resident in medicine N.Y. Hosp., N.Y.C., 1987—89; instr. Cornell U. Med. Coll., N.Y.C., 1990; fellow in medicine N.Y. Hosp. Cornell Med. Ctr., N.Y.C., 1990—92; vis. assoc. for medicine Hastings Ctr., Briarcliff Manor, NY, 1990—92; instr. Cornell U. Med. Coll., N.Y.C., 1992—93; assoc. for medicine Hastings Ctr., Briarcliff Manor, 1992—; asst. attending physician N.Y. Hosp., 1992—98; asst. prof. medicine Cornell U. Med. Coll., N.Y.C., 1993—98; assoc. attending physician N.Y. Presbyn. Hosp., 1998—; assoc. prof. medicine and assoc. prof. medicine in psychiat. Weill Med. Coll. Cornell U., N.Y.C., 1998—; assoc. prof. program clin. epidemiology/health sci. rsch. Weill Grad. Sch. Med. Scis. Cornell U., N.Y.C.; assoc. prof. of pub. health Weill Med. Coll. of Cornell U., N.Y.C., 2001—, chief joint div. med. ethics/depts. medicine and pub. health, 2001—. Vis. scholar Hastings Ctr., Briarcliff Manor, 1989; ethics com. dept. medicine N.Y. Hosp., N.Y.C., 1991-94; dir. med. ethics The N.Y. Hosp., chmn. com., 1994—; physician, ethicist in residence The Healthcare Chaplaincy, N.Y.; temp. advisor Regional Bioethics Ctr. of Pan Am. Health Orgn., 1995; vis. fellow Woodrow Wilson Found., 1998—; faculty scholar Open Soc. Inst. Project on Death in Am., 1997-2000; bd. dirs. Fund for Modern Cts, mentor, adj. facutly, Rockefeller U., 2003, bd. mem., Fund for Modern Courts, 2003-. Mem. editl. bd. Jour. Am. Geriatrics Soc., 1991-92, The Oncologist; editor Bioethics, Cancer Investigation 1995-2000, Jour. Pain and Symptom Mgmt., 1997—; contbr. articles to profl. jours. Quality care at the end of life commn. N.Y. State Atty. Gen.'s Office, 1997-98; Predl. appt. commr. to White House Commn. on Complementary and Alt. Medicine Policy, 2000-02; bd. dirs. Partnership for Caring, 1999—; mem. Whit House Commn. on Complementary and Alternative Medicine Policy, 2000-02, nat. adv. com., Woodrow Wilson Nat. Fellowship Found., 2003-. Fellow ACP (vice-chmn. health and pub. policy com. NY chpt.), N.Y. Acad. Medicine; mem. Assn. of Bar of City of N.Y. (adj.), Am. Geriatrics Soc. (vice chair ethics com. 1994-96), Am. Soc. Internal Medicine. Office: Weill Med Coll Cornell U F-173 NY Presbyn Hosp Box 297 525 E 68th St Dept Medicine New York NY 10021-4870

FINSTAD, SUZANNE ELAINE, writer, producer, lawyer; b. Mpls., Sept. 14, 1955; d. Harold Martin and Elaine Lois (Strom) F. Student, U. Tex., 1973-74; BA in French, U. Houston, 1976, JD, 1980; postgrad., London Sch. Econs., 1980, U. Grenoble, France, 1979. Bar: Tex. 1981. Legal asst. Butler & Binion, Houston, 1976-78, law clk., 1978-81, assoc., 1982; spl. counsel Ad Litem in the Estate of Howard Hughes Jr., Houston, 1981; mng. ptnr. Finstad & Assoc., Houston, 1990—93. Author: Heir Not Apparent, 1984 (Frank Wardlaw award, 1984), Ulterior Motives, 1987, Child Bride, 1997, Sleeping With the Devil, 1991, Natasha: The Biography of Natalie Wood, 2001; co-prodr. (TV films) Sleeping with the Devil; exec. prodr.: (TV miniseries) Natasha, 2003. Named to Order of Barons, Bates Coll. Law, 1980; recipient Am. Jurisprudence award in criminal law. Office: care Alan Nevins 9465 Wilshire Beverly Hills CA 90210

FINSTER, JAMES ROBERT, library media specialist; b. Milw., Sept. 29, 1947; s. Milton Robert Finster and Eleonore B. (Worgull) Helvey; children: James Andrew, Nicholas William. BS in Edn., Dr. Martin Luther Coll., 1971; BS in Resource Mgmt., U. Wis., Stevens Point, 1976; MS in Edn. Media, U. Wis., LaCrosse, 1987. Cert. libr. media specialist, Wis., Minn. Ski instr. various ski clubs, resorts, Wis. and Colo., 1971—; elem. tchr. pvt. and pub. schs. Wis., 1971-73, 78-81; teaching asst. U. Wis., Stevens Point, 1975; park ranger Nat. Park Svc., various locations, 1976-77; ski. sch. dir. Whitecap Mountain, Montreal, Wis., 1982-83, Coffee Mill Ski Area, Wabasha, Minn., 1983-84; grad. asst. U. Wis., LaCrosse, 1986-87; libr. media specialist Chilton (Wis.) High Sch., 1987-93; libr. media specialist K-12 Rib Lake (Wis.) Pub. Schs., 1993-94, Elcho (Wis.) Pub. Sch., 1994-96; ski instr. Trollhaugen, 1997—. Mem. Wis. Ednl. Media Assn. Republican. Lutheran. Avocations: downhill skiing, travel, sports, games, music. Home: 200 Seminole Ave Lot 78 Osceola WI 54020-8076

FINSTON, SUSAN KLING, lawyer; b. Detroit, Mich., Feb. 21, 1961; d. Murray George and Minna Judith Kling; m. Matthew Arnold Finston, Aug. 13, 1989; children: Aaron Leo, Rachel Leah. BS with high honors, U. of Mich., 1978—82, JD, MPP, U. of Mich., 1982—86. Bar: State of Ill. 1987. Staff atty./motions clk. Fed. Ct. of Appeals for the Seventh Circuit, Chgo., 1986—88; u.s. fgn. svc. officer Dept. of State, Washington DC, 1988—99; assoc. v.p. Pharm. Rsch. and Manufacturers of Am. (PhRMA), Washington DC, 1999—. Cleared advisor to u.s. govt. (ifac-3) Dept. of Commerce, Washington, 2002—. Contbr. articles to profl. jours. Chair of grant working group Sulam, Silver Spring, Md., 2002—03. Decorated Meritorious Honor award Dept. of State; fellow Full Tuition for the Ford Sch. of Pub. Policy, U. of Mich., 1982—83. Mem.: Wash. Fgn. Law Soc. (bd. mem. 2001—03). Jewish. Avocations: swimming, travel, cooking, gardening. Office: PhRMA 1100 15th Street NW Washington DC 20005

FINTA, FRANCES MICKNA, secondary school educator; b. Stafford Springs, Conn., June 17, 1927; d. John Joseph Mickna and Mary Frances Breslin; m. Quinn Finta, Aug. 21, 1951; children: John Wright, Susan Frances Finta Phillips. BA in Math., Boston U., 1949; postgrad., U. Va., 1963—69, Prince George's C.C., Largo, Md., 1982, No. Va. C.C., Alexandria, 1982—84, postgrad., 1994, U. Va., Fairfax, 1988—89; MEd in Guidance and Counseling, George Mason U., 1975. Cert. tchr. Va. Food prodn. mgr., dining rm. mgr., waitress, field ops. rep., liaison to airlines Marriott Corp., Marriott In-Flight Svcs., Inc., Washington, 1950—62; tchr., guidance counselor Arlington (Va.) Pub. Schs., 1963—. Substitute tchr. Fairfax (Va.) Pub. Schs., 1972—73; substitute tchr. Arlington (Va.) County Pub. Schs., 1972—. Mem. Arlington County Scholarship Fund for Tchrs., Inc., 1995—, sec., 1996—2001, treas., 2002—; mem. Friends of Arlington Parks, 1995—, Maywood Cmty. Assn., 1966—; treas. Washington-Lee H.S. Band Booster Club, 1979—81, Evelyn Staples for County Bd., 1991; vol. coord. David Foster for Sch. Bd., 1994; Maywood del. Arlington County Civic Fedn., 1982—; mem. Arlingtonians for a Better County, 1999—2002; membership chmn. Arlington County Civic Fedn., 1984—, treas., 2000—; mem. Arlington County Rep. Com., 1994—, chmn. hdqrs., 2000—, mem. fin. com., 1994—95, canvass chmn., 2000—03, chmn. nominations com., 2000—01; mem. steering com. John Hager for Gov., 2000; del. to state conv. Rep. Party Va., 1996, 1998, 2000, Va. Fedn. Rep. Women, 1996—; mem. credential com. Va. 8th Dist. Rep. Conv., 1998; sec. adv. com. Commonwealth of Va., 1998—2002; mem. Organized Women Voters of Arlington, 1997—, mem. nominating com., 2000, treas., 2000—. Recipient Hon. Guardian of Srs.' Rights award, 60 Plus Assn., 1999, Vol. Svc. award, Arlington County Rep. Com., 1995—99, Hilda Griffith Lifetime Achievement award, 1999, Leon Delyannis Cmty. Involvement award, 1997, Cert. of Appreciation, Arlington County Civic Fedn., 1988, 1997, Jour. Newspapers trophy, 2001, Parent Vol. award, Washington-Lee H.S. Band Boosters Club, 1979, Appreciation award, 1981, Parent Vol. award, Woodmont Elem. Sch., 1975, Patrick Henry award, Commonwealth of Va., 2001, Disting. Meritorious Svc. award, Arlington Co. Civic Found., 2003. Mem.: AAUW (del. to Arlington County Civic Fedn. 1994—, co-1st v.p. programs 2001—03, exec. com. 2001—03, co-1st programs exec. com. 2001—03, 1st v.p. programs 2002—03), NEA, Arlington Ret. Tchrs. Assn., Arlington Edn. Assn., Va. Edn. Assn., Va. Ret. Tchrs. Assn. (life), Arlington County Taxpayers' Assn., Arlington Rep. Women's Club (auditor 1996, asst. treas. 1997, pres. 1998—99, newsletter editor 1998—99, chmn. achievement awards 2000, chmn. bylaws com. 2000, chmn. Barbara Bush literacy com. 2000, dir. 2000—01, chair fin. com. 2002—). Republican. Roman Catholic. Avocations: civic and political activities, reading. Home: 3317 23d St N Arlington VA 22201-4310

FINTEL, DAN JAMES, cardiologist; b. Petach Tikvah, Israel, Apr. 10, 1953; came to U.S., 1956; s. Mark and Slava (Zimmer) F.; m. Robin Randall, June 18, 1978; children: Bara Carrie, Joshua Seth, Zachary Noah. BS magna cum laude, Yale U., 1975; MD magna cum laude, Harvard U., 1979. Intern, then resident Mt. Sinai Hosp., N.Y.C., 1979-82; fellow cardiology Johns Hopkins U., Balt., 1982-85; assoc. dir. med. intensive care Northwestern U. Med. Ctr., Chgo., 1985—, assoc. in medicine, 1985-87, asst. prof. medicine, 1987—, dir. CCU, 1988—, assoc. prof. medicine, 1993—. Contbr. articles to profl. jours. Fellow Am. Coll. Cardiology, Am. Coll. Physicians, Am. Coll. Chest Physicians; mem. Am. Heart Assn., Am. Fedn. Clin. Research, Soc. Critical Care Medicine, Phi Beta Kappa, Sigma Xi. Democrat. Jewish. Avocations: tennis, snorkeling, bicycling, skiing. Home: 1868 N Orchard St Chicago IL 60614-5106 Office: Northwestern Meml Hosp Galter Ste 10-240 201 Ettuson St Chicago IL 60611 E-mail: dfintel@northwestern.edu.

FINZEN, BRUCE ARTHUR, lawyer; b. Mpls., Mar. 11, 1947; s. Floyd Arthur and Lorraine Jeannette (Offerdahl) F.; children: Margaret, Sara, Stephanie. BA, U. Minn., 1970; JD, U. Kans., 1973. Bar: Minn. 1973, U.S. Dist. Ct. Minn. 1973, Calif. 1988, U.S. Ct. Appeals (8th cir.) 1973, U.S. Ct. Appeals (7th cir.) 1983, U.S. Ct. Appeals (2d cir.) 1986, U.S. Ct. Appeals (4th cir.) 1994, U.S. Ct. Appeals (9th cir.) 1994, U.S. Supreme Ct. 1996. D.C., 2002, U.S. Dist. Ct. D.C. 2003. Law clk. to presiding justice Minn. Supreme Ct., St. Paul, 1973-74; assoc. Robins, Kaplan, Miller & Ciresi, Mpls., 1974-79; ptnr. Robins, Kaplan, Miller & Ciresi LLP, Mpls., 1979—. Mem. adv. bd. Ctr. for Pub. Integrity, 2001—; trustee Ho. of Hope Presbyn. Ch., 1988—94; bd. dirs. Union Gospel Mission, St. Paul, 1983—89; sec. bd. dirs. Boys and Girls Clubs St. Paul, 1984—91. Mem. ABA, Minn. Bar Assn., ATLA, Minn. Trial Lawyers Assn., Consumer Attys. Calif., Assn. Personal Injury Lawyers. Avocations: hunting, fishing. Office: Robins Kaplan Miller & Ciresi LLP 2800 LaSalle Plz 800 Lasalle Ave Ste 2800 Minneapolis MN 55402-2015

FINZER, CAROLYN LAUING, artist, speaker; b. Aurora, Ill., July 24, 1947; d. Royal Walter and Marcianna Julia (MIller) Lauing; m. Melvern Kent Finzer, July 26, 1969; children: Nicole Gabrielle, Deirdre Danielle. BS in Art Edn., Ill. State U., 1969; postgrad., Salzburg Coll., Austria, 1974. Cert. elem. and secondary tchr., Ill. Art tchr. Sch. Dist. # 90, Naperville, Ill., 1969-70; chmn. art dept. Sch. Dist. # 203, Naperville, Ill., 1970-75. Speaker, storyteller Native Am. enrichment programs.; tchr. weaving techniques, bead looming and quill embroidery, bookbinding workshops, 1990—; fashion model Marketplace Handwork of India Catalog. Illustrator Girl Scout field guide; featured in Birds and Blooms mag., 2000. Vol./amb. Morton Arboretum, Lisle, Ill., 1983—, docent Naper Settlement, Naperville, Ill.; leader, trainer Girl Scouts U.S., badge lab facilitator DuPage Coun.; charter bd. dirs. Naperville Area Clean Community, 1985—; mem. edn. com. Conservation Found.; mem. Wild Ones; Arboretum ambassador, 1997—, Women's Bd. Chgo. Art Inst. Naperville Assn. chpt. Recipient Disting. Svc. award Naperville Jaycees, 1985, Environ. Hero award Naperville Park Dist., 1991, Outstanding Alumnus award Ill. State U., 1992, Green Wood Environmentalist award Girl Scouts of DuPage County, Sts. Peter and Paul Disting. Grad. award Nat. Cath. Edn. Assn., 1999. Mem. Chgo. Art Inst. (historian, charter, women's bd.), Nature Conservancy, Ill. Storytellers Guild, Inc., DuPage Textile Artists Guild, Naperville Riverwalk Quilt Guild, United Air Lines Pilots Wives Friendship Club (historian 1989—). Roman Catholic (Eucharistic minister). Avocations: prairie gardening, weaving, cross county skiing, collecting native american dolls, antique, multi-cultural and gourd instruments. Home: 970 Sylvan Cir Naperville IL 60540-5532

FIONDELLA, ROBERT WILLIAM, insurance company executive; b. Bristol, Conn., May 19, 1942; s. Sisto William and Theresa (Nestico) F.; m. Carolyn Brozinski; children: Robert J., Jeffrey. AB, Providence Coll., 1964; JD, U. Conn., 1968. Computer programmer-analyst Travelers Ins. Co., Hartford, Conn., 1965; atty. Danaher, Lewis, Tamoney, Hartford, Conn., 1968-69; atty. law dept. Phoenix Mutual Ins. Co., Hartford, Conn., 1969-72, asst. counsel, officer, 1972-74, assoc. counsel, 1974-75, investment counsel, 1975-77, 2d v.p., counsel, 1977, v.p., gen. counsel, 1978-81, sr. v.p. gen. counsel, 1981-83, exec. v.p. individual ins., 1983-87, pres., 1987-89, bd. dirs., pres., COO, 1989-92, pres., prin. oper. officer, 1992-94; chmn. bd., CEO Phoenix Co. (formerly Phoenix Home Life Mutual Ins. Co.), Hartford, Conn., 1994—. Bd. dirs., pres. PML Internat. Ins. Ltd., Phoenix Investment Ptnrs. Ltd; bd. dirs. Life Ins. Coun. N.Y., The Advest Group, Phoenix Investment Ptnrs. Ltd., PXRE (formerly Phoenix Reins.), Phoenix Equity Planning Corp., Am. Phoenix; bd. dirs., pres. Phoenix Am. Life Ins. Co.; bd. dirs., chmn. bd. dirs. Phoenix Charter Oak Trust; bd. dirs. St. Francis Hosp. and Med. Ctr. Chmn. ea. regional fundraising Little League Ctr., Bristol; mem. Britol City Coun., 1969-71, Bristol Urban Renewal Commn., 1971-76; mem. steering com. Mayor Peter's Hartford AmeriCorps, 1995—; chmn. Bristol Retirement Bd., 1978-83; coach Edgewood Little League, Bristol, 1984-85; bd. dirs. St. Francis Hosp. and Med. Ctr., 1992—, Spl. Olympics World Summer Games, 1995—, Spl. Olympics Internat., 1996—, Barnes Group Inc., 1997—; mem. cabinet Conn. Children's Ctr. Campaign for Our Children, 1995—; mem. adv. bd. WKND Greater Hartford Initiative; co-chmn. Cmty. Cancer Ctr. Bldg. Fund, Johnson Meml. Mem. Conn. Bar Assn., Conn. Bus. and Industry Assn. (bd. dirs.), Greater Hartford C. of C. (bd. dirs., chmn. 1997—). Home: 29 Summerberry Cir Bristol CT 06010-2957 Office: Phoenix Home Life Mutual Ins Co PO Box 5056 Hartford CT 06102-5056

FIORAVANTI, JEFF, artist; b. Saugus, Mass., Feb. 21, 1958; s. Richard and Anne Fioravanti; m. Cathleen Martin, May 12, 1984; 1 child, Nicole. BSBA in Bus. Mgmt., Salem State Coll., 1982. Cert. graphics arts/web designer; cert. webmaster. Sr. materials planner Teradyne, Inc., Boston, 1984-96; prodn. scheduler Compensated Devices, Inc., Melrose, Mass., 1997-99; web specialist Attunity, Inc., Burlington, Mass., 2000-01; graphic designer, advt. copywriter T.K. Keith Co., Wakefield, Mass., 2001—; prin., owner Fioravanti Fine Art, 2003—. Tchg. asst. Clark U., Woburn, Mass., 2000. Exhibited in group shows at Art 3 Gallery, Manchester, N.H., 1996, Art Rsch. Assocs. Gallery, South Hamilton, Mass., 1997, Gallery 30, Gettysburg, Pa., 2003, Cape Cod Mus. Fine Art, 2003. Coach Saugus Youth Hockey, 1977-81, 93-94, Saugus Youth Soccer, 1977-79. Inducted into Saugus H.S. Athletic Hall of Fame, 1992; recipient Olympian Corp. award Pastel Soc. W. Coast Internat. Open Exhbn., 2000, Best in Show award Conn. Pastel Soc. Mem. Pastel Soc. Am. (signature), Degas Pastel Soc., Pastel Soc. Oreg., Conn. Pastel Soc. (signature), Pastel Painters Soc. Cape Cod (Dakota Art Store award 1999). Avocations: American Civil War reenacting, sports memorabilia collecting, walking, U.S. history. Home: 49 Pennybrook Rd Lynn MA 01905 Office: TK Keith Co 15 Edgewater Dr Wakefield MA 01880 E-mail: jfiorava@concentric.net., jfioravanti@tkkeithco.com.

FIORAVANTI, NANCY ELEANOR, retired banker; b. Gloucester, Mass., Apr. 10, 1935; d. Richard Joseph and Evelyn Grace (Souza) F. Grad. high sch. Various positions and depts. Bank of New Eng.-North Shore (formerly Cape Ann Bank and Trust Co., successor to Gloucester Safe Deposit & Trust Co.), Gloucester, 1953—, with trust dept., 1959-86, asst. trust officer, 1970-84, trust officer, 1984-86; trust officer Cape Ann Savs. Bank, 1986-97, corporator, 1992; ret., 1997. Past mem. and treas. art adv. com. Gloucester Lyceum and Sawyer Free Libr., mem. corp., 1989. Home: PO Box 1638 Gloucester MA 01931-1638

FIORE, CARMEN ANTHONY, writer; b. Trenton, N.J., Sept. 19, 1932; s. Ernest and Margaret Fiore; m. Catherine Marie Butera, Oct. 4, 1958; children: David, Lisa Fiore Childs. BS, Rider U., Trenton, N.J., 1954; MEd, Rutgers U., 1963. Cert. tchr. N.J., lic. real estate appraiser N.J. Social caseworker State of N.J., Trenton, 1957—60; tchr. Trenton Pub. Schs., 1960—61; with State of N.J., Trenton, 1961—87. Author: (novels) The Barrier, 1961, 1986, Little Oscar, 1988, Vendetta Mountain, 1987, (nonfiction) Voices of the Daughters, 1989, (novels) (juvenile novel) The Snakeskin, 1991, Searching, 2002, (screenplays) Vendetta Mountain, 1992, Manipulators, 1994, Little Oscar, 1993, Mixed Doubles, 2000, A Case in Principle, 1998, Avarice Can Be Deadly, 2000, Till Death Do Us Part, 1999, The Colored Kid, 1996, Italian Interlude, 1999, Prisoners of Love, 1999, Sweepstakes, 2000; contbr. With U.S. Army, 1955—57. Mem.: Poets and Writers, Civil War Round Table of Ctrl. Fla., Greater Orlando Civil War Round Table, Civil War Preservation Trust, Camp Olden Civil War Round Table. Roman Catholic. Home and Office: 1682 Keys Gate Dr Melbourne FL 32940-6317

FIORE, CAROLE DIANE, public library consultant for youth services; b. Philadelphia, May 5, 1946; d. Louis A. and Hortense (Menkes) Millendorf; m. Stanley Fiore, Jan. 2, 1980. BS in Edn., Temple U., 1969; MS in Library Sci., Drexel U., 1970; Cert. in Supr., Villanova U., 1977. Library page Free Library of Phila., 1962-63; library asst. Sch. Dist. of Phila., 1965-68, sch. librarian, 1969-82; dir. children's services Dunedin (Fla.) Pub. Library, 1982-85; head youth services cen. library Tampa-Hillsborough County (Fla.) Pub. Library System, 1985-90; pub. libr. cons. for youth svcs. State Libr. of Fla., Tallahassee, 1990—. Leader vacation reading club Free Libr. of Phila., 1975-78; advisor ea.

area br. div. sch. librs. Pa. Dept. Edn., 1976-82, cons. audio visual task force State Libr. of Fla., 1985-88; adj. instr. div. edn. U. Tampa, 1987-90; vis. instr. Sch. of Libr. and Info. Sci., Fla. State U., 1992—; cons. children's svcs. manual com. Fla. Dept. State Div. Libr. and Info. Svcs., Tallahassee, 1987-88; mem. coun. advisors for inst. proposal, Fla. State U. Sch. Info. Studies, 1997-98; nat. libr. adv. com., Grolier Pub., 1996—. Author: Bridging the Gap: Books for Transitional Readers, 1987, Programming for Introducing Adults to Children's Literature, 1994, Programming for Young Children: Birth through Age Five, 1996, Running Summer Library Reading Programs: A How-To-Do-It Manual, 1998, other manuals; exec. prodr. (video) Born to Read—Florida Style, 1999; host, dir. (TV program) Under the Story Tree, 1983; contbr. articles to profl. jours. Pers. review bd. City of Dunedin, Fla., 1989-90; mem. adv. bd., Trejo Foster Found. for Hispanic Libr. Edn., 1998-99. Recipient pub. rels. award John Cotton Dana Libr., 1994, Davis productivity award, 1996, 2000, contbn. to literacy award Leon County Reading Assn., 2001. Mem. ALA (Booklist editl. adv. bd. 1997—), Assn. Libr. Svcs. for Children (filmstrip evaluation com. 1987-90, chair filmstrip evaluation com. 1990-92, chair notable showcase 1990-91, Newbery com. 1985-86, membership liaison com. 1984—, Caldecott award com. 1992—, planning and budget com. 1996-97, priority group cons. 1997-99, rsch. and devel. com. 1998-00, dir. 1994-97), Nat. Assn. for Preservation and Perpetuation of Storytelling (v.p. 2000-01, pres. 2001-02), Assn. Specialized and Cooperative Libr. Agys. (state libr. sect. 1991—, discussion group leader cons. for svc. to children and young people 1997-98), Young Adult Libr. Svcs. Assn. (chmn. vision task force 1999-2000), Fla. Libr. Assn. (audio visual caucus steering com. 1986-87, children and schs. caucus steering com. 1987-90, awards and citations com. 1993-95, chair 1994-95, charter by-laws and manual com. 1989-94, chair intellectual freedom com. 1996-97), Early Childhood Assn. Fla., Fla. Reading Assn., Fla. Suncoast Puppet Guild, Internat. Reading Assn., Leon County Reading Assn., Leon Assn. Edn. of Young Children, Tallahassee Children's Lit. Cir., U.S. Bd. of Books for Young People, Young Adult Libr. Svcs. Assn. (serving the underserved II planning com. 1995), Beta Phi Mu (bd. dirs. Sigma chpt. 1978-81). Avocation: needlecraft. Office: State Libr of Fla RA Gray Bldg Tallahassee FL 32399 Home: 4651 Fledgling Dr Tallahassee FL 32311-1212

FIORE, COLLEEN MARY, meeting manager; b. Watertown, N.Y., May 4, 1969; d. Edward Francis Van Emmerik and Donna Roe Buske; m. James R. Fiore, Mar. 20, 1993; children: Mikaela, Miranda. BS, Roosevelt U., 1992. Cert. meeting profl. Program coord. Soc. Actuaries, Schaumburg, Ill., 1992-94, meeting coord., 1994-97, meeting mgr., 1997—2001, dir. meeting svcs., 2001—. Mem. Am. Soc. Assn. Execs., Profl. Conv. Mgmt. Assn. Office: Soc of Actuaries #800 475 N Martingale Rd Ste 800 Schaumburg IL 60173-2226

FIORE, JAMES LOUIS, JR., public accountant, educator, professional speaker, trainer consultant; b. Jersey City, Oct. 7, 1935; s. James Louis and Rose (Perrotta) F.; m. Alberta W. Pope, July 21, 1957; children: Carolyn Leigh, James Louis III, Toni Lynn. BS in Acctg., Seton Hall U., 1957; MBA, We. Colo. U., 1972; PhD, Calif. We. U., 1979. Lic. acct. Pa., N.J. Field auditor State of N.J., Trenton, 1958-60; supr. internal auditing Ronson Corp., Woodbridge, N.J., 1960-64; surp. gen. acctg. Electronic Assocs., West Long Branch, N.J., 1964-65; pvt. practice acctg., 1965—. Pres. Bucks County Rsch. Inst., Inc., 1972-79; mem. adj. faculty Allentown Coll. St. Francis de Sales, Ctr. Valley, Pa., 1979-81, Pa. Coll. Chriopractic, 1986-94, Holy Family Coll., Phila., 1995; sec.-treas. Cordian Group Internat., Inc. Bus. Cons., 2001— Author: (with others) Shareholder Loans, The National Public Accountant, 1988, Financial Problems and Your Profession, 1989, Non-Absorption of Nitrofurazone from the Urethra in Men, 1976, Comparative Bioavailability of Doxycycline, 1974; contbr. articles to profl. jours. Founder Brick Twp. (N.J.) Scholarship Fund, 1963-67; mem. adv. coun. Inst. for Accts., Pa. State U.; trustee Pa. Coll. Chiropractic, 1986-94; founder, treas. Cath. Acad. Sci. in U.S.A., Washington. Lt. U.S. Army, 1957. Named Jayce of Yr., 1962; recipient Legion of Honor, Chapel of Four Chaplains, 1979. Mem. Calif. We. U. Alumni Assn., We. Colo. U. Alumni Assn., Seton Hall U. Alumni Assn. (Crest and Centrury Clubs), Masons, Shriners, Scottish Rite, K.T. Home: 265 Thompson Mill Rd Newtown PA 18940-3105 E-mail: James.Fiore@speakerjim.com.

FIORE, JOSEPH ALBERT, artist; b. Cleve., Feb. 3, 1925; s. Salvatore Emmanuel and Gemma Marie (Cominelli) F.; m. Mary Falconer Fitton, Oct. 10, 1952; children: Thomas, Susanna. Student, Black Mountain Coll., 1946-48, 49, San Francisco Sch. Art Inst., 1948-49. Instr. painting, drawing Black Mountain (N.C.) Coll., 1949-56, chmn. art dept., 1951-56; free lance designer N.Y.C., 1958-61; instr. painting Phila. Coll. Art, 1962-70, Md. Inst. Coll. Art, Balt., 1970-75; instr. landscape painting Nat. Acad. Design, N.Y.C., 1979, Parson's Sch. Design Summer Program, Dordogne, France, 1980. Vis. artist-critic Artists for Environment Found., Walpack Center, N.J., 1972-83, Vt. Studio Sch., Johnson, Vt., 1987. One-man shows include Ten-Thirty Gallery, Cleve., 1944, 48, 50, Gallerie Parnass, Wuppertal, Germany, 1955, Round Top Ctr. for Arts, Damariscotta, Maine, 1997, 2002, Cathedral of St. John the Divine, N.Y.C., 1997, Black Mountain Coll. Mus. and Arts Ctr. at Zone One Contemporary, Asheville, N.C., 1995-96, Staempfli Gallery, N.Y.C., 1960, Robert Schoelkopf Gallery, N.Y.C., 1965, 69, Green Mountain Gallery, N.Y.C., 1973, John Bernard Myers Gallery, N.Y.C., 1974, Fischbach Gallery, N.Y.C., 1977, 81, Caldbeck Gallery, Rockland, Maine, 1988, Le Va-Tout Gallery, Waldboro, Maine, 1991, River Gallery, Damariscotta, Maine, 2002; exhibited in group shows Stable Gallery, N.Y.C., 1954, 55, Whitney Mus. Am. Art, 1959, U. Ill., Urbana, 1961, Am. Fedn. Art Travelling Exhbn., 1964, Corcoran Gallery Art, Washington, 1975, State Mus., Augusta, 1976, Cape Split Place, Addison, Maine, 1977, Am. Acad. Arts and Letters, N.Y.C., 1981, Landmark Gallery, N.Y.C., 1981, Jersey City Mus., 1982, Farnsworth Mus., Rockland, Maine, 1983, Artist's Choice Mus., 1983, Black Mountain Connection, Gilliam and Peden Gallery, Raleigh, 1987, Black Mountain Coll., Blum Art Inst., Bard Coll., N.Y.C., 1987, N.C. State Mus., Raleigh, 1987, Grey Art Ctr., NYU, 1987, Snyder Fine Arts, N.Y.C., 1992, Station Gallery, Katonah, N.Y., 1992, Anita Shapolsky Gallery, N.Y.C., 1997, Hofstra Mus., Hempstead, N.Y., 2001 Black Mountain Coll.: Experiment in Art Museo Nacional Centro De Arte Renia Sofia, Madrid, 2002-03, numerous others; represented in permanent collections Whitney Mus. Am. Art, N.Y.C., N.C. State Mus. Art, Raleigh, Corcoran Gallery, Art, Washington, Colby Art Mus., Waterville, Maine, Weatherspoon Gallery, Greensboro, N.C., NAD, N.Y., Chase Manhattan Collection, N.Y.C., Asheville Mus. of Art, N.C., Black Mountain Coll. Mus. and Art Ctr., Housatonic Mus. Art, Bridgeport, Conn. Served with AUS, 1943-46. Recipient prize for painting San Francisco Mus. Ann., 1949, 1st prize Met. Young Artists 1st Ann. Nat. Arts Club, N.Y.C., 1958, Adolph and Clara Obrig Prize, NAD 178th Ann., 2003; Artists for Environment Found. residence grantee, 1976; Nettie Marie Jones fellow Ctr. Music, Drama and Art, Lake Placid, N.Y., 1983, purchase award Am. Acad. Arts and Letters, 1998. Mem. NAD (cert. of merit 168th Ann. Exhbn. 1993, Edwin Palmer Meml. prize 170th Ann. 1995, Cannon prize 175th Ann. 2000, Andrew Carnegie prize 176th Ann. 2001, Adolph and Clara Obrig prize 178th Ann. 2003), Artists Equity Assn. N.Y., Nature Conservancy, Maine Audubon Soc., Natural Resources Coun. Maine. Home: 178 W 81 St New York NY 10024

FIORE, NICHOLAS FRANCIS, special components and materials company executive; b. Pitts., Sept. 24, 1939; s. William H. and Margaret (Scinto) F.; m. Sylvia M. Chinque, Aug. 13, 1960; children: Maria L., Nicholas F., Kristin M., Anthony T. BS, Carnegie-Mellon U., 1960, MS, 1963, PhD, 1964. Asst. prof. metall. engrng. and materials sci. U. Notre Dame, Ind., 1966-69, prof., 1969-81, chmn. dept., 1969-72, 80-81; v.p. Cabot Corp., Boston, 1982-89; mng. dir. materials and applied physics Arthur D. Little, Inc., Cambridge, Mass., 1989-90; v.p. Carpenter Tech. Corp., Reading, Pa., 1990-93, sr. v.p., 1993-2000; CEO Walsin USA, Waltham, Mass., 2000—. Vis. scientist Argonne (Ill.) Nat. Labs., 1974-75. Co-author: Binding of Solute to Dislocations, 1967, Hydrogen Related Embrittlement of High Temperature Materials, 1975; editor: (with B.J. Berkowitz) Advanced Techniques for Characterizing Hydrogen in Metals, 1982; contbr. articles to profl. jours. Trustee Albright Coll.; sci. and tech. edn. com. New Eng. Coun. Capt. U.S. Army, 1964-66. Fellow Am. Soc. Metals (trustee); mem. AIME, Alpha Sigma Mu. Office: Walsin USA 1601 Trapelo Rd Waltham MA 02451 E-mail: fiore@walsinusa.com.

FIORE, PETER AMADEUS, English educator, clergy; b. Sept. 8, 1927; MA in English, Catholic U., Washington, 1955; PhD in English, U. London, Eng., 1961. Entered Franciscan Order, 1950; ordained priest, 1955. Dean of arts Siena Coll., Loudonville, N.Y., 1966-72, chair English dept., 1962-67, 75-85, prof. English, 1971-85, prof. English, comm., 1996—2002, scholar in residence, 2002—. Office: Siena Coll 515 Loudon Rd Loudonville NY 12211-1459 E-mail: fiore@siena.edu.

FIORELLA, RUSSELL MICHAEL, pathologist; s. Russell and Flora Fiorella; children: Alex, Anna, Max. BA, Tulane U., 1977; MD, U. of Mo., Kansas City, 1982; MBA, Avila Coll., Kansas City, Mo., 1996. Diplomate cytopathology Am. Bd. of Pathology, anatomic and clin. pathology Am. Bd. of Pathology, Nat. Bd. of Med. Examiners. Clin. instr. of pathology U. of Kans. Med. Ctr., Kansas City, Kans., 1986—87; asst. prof. of pathology U. of Mo., Kansas City, 1991—95; dir. cytopathology dept. of pathology Truman Med. Ctr., Kansas City, Mo., 1991—93, dir. surg. pathology dept. of pathology, 1993—94; assoc. prof. of pathology U. of Mo., Kansas City, 1995—99; dir. anatomic pathology dept. of pathology Truman Med. Ctr., Kansas City, Mo., 1995—98, vice-chair dept. of pathology, 1996—98, interim chair, dept. of pathology, 1998—99; prof. of pathology U. of Mo., Kansas City, 1999—; chair dept. of pathology Truman Med. Ctr., Kansas City, Mo., 1999—. Pres., med. and dental staff Truman Med. Ctr., Kansas City, Mo., 2002—, mem. search com. for chief med. officer, 1999—2000, bd. of dirs., exec. com., 1999—2001; mem. legal com. Hosp. Hill Health Svcs. Corp., Kansas City, Mo., 1999—2001, mem. bd. nominating com., 1999—2002, mem. fin. com., 1999—2002, mem. compensation com., 1999—2002, mem. bylaws com., 1999—2002, bd. dirs.; mem. coun. on grad. med. edn. U. of Mo. Sch. of Medicine, Kansas City, 1999—, mem. acad. chairs, 1999—; bd. dirs. Truman Med. Ctr., Kansas City, Mo., pres.-elect med. and dental staff, 1998—2001, mem. coun. of chairs, 1998—, mem. joint profl. stds. com., 1998—2000, dir. pathology residency program, 1998—2002, sec.-treas. med. and dental staff, 1995—2002, mem. utilization com., 1994—98, mem. tissue com., 1994—96, dir. Sch. of Cytotechnology, 1993—96, mem. med. records com., 1993—94, mem. grievance com., 1992—93, mem. joint conf. and quality com., 2002—; dir. pathology course U. of Mo. Sch. of Medicine, Kansas City, 1991—98, mem. search com. for dean, 2003—03; mem. search com. for exec. dir. Hosp. Hill Health Svcs. Corp., Kansas City, Mo., 2001; mem. search com. for chief nursing officer Truman Med. Ctr., Kansas City, Mo., 2000; mem. search com. for med. dir. TMC Hosp. Hill Med. Pavillion, Kansas City, Mo., 2000—01; chair strategic planning com. Hosp. Hill Health Svcs. Corp., Kansas City, Mo., 2000—01; mem. med. and dental staff fin. com. Truman Med. Ctr., Kansas City, Mo., 2000—02, mem. info. svcs. bd. com., 1999—2001. Author: (book chpt.) Cytopathology in Laboratory Test Handbook; contbr. book rev., articles and abstracts to profl. jours.; jour. reviewer: Diagnostic Cytopathology. Fellow: Coll. of Am. Pathologists; mem.: Kans. City Soc. of Pathologists, Am. Coll. of Physician Execs., Am. Soc. of Cytology, Internat. Acad. of Pathologists, Nat. Com. for Clin. Lab. Stds., Am. Soc. of Clin. Pathologists, Assn. of Pathology Chairs. Office: Truman Med Ctr 2301 Holmes Kansas City MO 64108

FIORELLI, KAREN LYNN, registered nurse; b. Milw., Jan. 8, 1954; d. Enzo and Lydia Ann (Naspini) Fiorelli; children: Anthony P., Jack R. BSN, U. Wis., Milwaukee, 1978. RN. Nursing asst. St. Luke's Med. Ctr., Milw., 1974-75; nursing unit sec. St. Luke's Hosp., Milw., 1978-79, staff nurse IV, orthopedics, 1979-85, chmn. unit based quality assurance, 1984-85; employee health supervisor Aurora Health Care Inc., Milw., 1986-91, sr. quality mgmt. coord., 1991—2002; performance improvement coord. Ctr. Nursing Rsch and Practice, Aurora Health Care Inc., West Allis, Wis., 2002—. Roman Catholic. Avocations: music, art, theatre, sports. Home: 14132 Waters Way New Berlin WI 53151-4563 Office: West Allis Meml Hosp 8901 W Lincoln Ave West Allis WI 53227 E-mail: tjnikfio@execpc.com.

FIORENTINO, THOMAS MARTIN, transportation executive, lawyer; b. Washington, Aug. 4, 1959; s. Thomas Martin Sr. and Julia (Bray) F.; m. Mary Ann Hammer, June 12, 1983; children: Sara Elizabeth, Caroline McKay, Thomas Martin III. BA, U. Fla., 1980; JD, Mercer U., 1983. Bar: Fla. 1984. Claims rep. Seaboard System R.R., Evansville, Ind., 1983-84, atty. Jacksonville, Fla., 1984-86; dir. risk mgmt. CSX Corp., Jacksonville, 1986-87; asst. to pres. CSX Tech., Jacksonville, 1987-89; chief of staff Fed. R.R. Adminstrn., 1989-90; counselor to dep. sec. of transp. Office of the Sec., Dept. Transp., Washington, 1990-91; asst. v.p. pub. affairs CSX Transp., Jacksonville, 1991-94, v.p. govt. affairs, 1994-95, v.p. corp. comms. and pub. affairs, 1995-99, spl. counsel, 1999—; of counsel Holland & Knight LLP, Jacksonville, 1999—2002; pres. Fiorentino and Assocs., 2002—. Bd. dirs. St. Mark's Episcopal Day Sch., 1992—94; mem. bd. visitors The Bolles Sch., 1990—96; bd. dirs. Theatreworks, 1992—95, Boys and Girls Clubs of N.E. Fla., 1992—95, Mus. Sci. and History, 1993—96, Jacksonville Urban League, 1993—95, I.M. Sultzbacher Ctr. for the Homeless, 1994—95, Gov. Coun. Sustainable Devel., 1996—97, Children's Home Soc. of Jacksonville, 1996—98, James Madison Inst., 1997—2003, Fla. Theatre, 1997—99, Fla. Coun. Econ. Edn., 1999—, Ronald McDonald House, 1998—2001, Drug Free Am. Found., 2000—; chmn. Jacksonville Port Authority, 1999—, Bapt. Health Sys. Found., 1992—99; mem. Fourth Cir. Jud. Nominating Commn., 1988—89; bd. dirs. Gov.'s Mansion found., 2000—, Bapt. Beaches Hosp., 1999—, Jacksonville Symphony Orch., 2002—. Mem. Fla. Bar Assn., Fla. C. of C. (trustee 1995—), Jacksonville C. of C., First Coast Mfrs. Assn., River Club, Marsh Landing Country Club, Ponte Vedra Club, Fla. C. of C. (trustee 1996—), Jacksonville C. of C. (trustee 1995-98), Phi Delta Phi. Republican. Presbyterian. Avocations: golf, tennis. Home: 712 Great Egret Way Ponte Vedra Beach FL 32082-2155

FIORENZA, FRANCIS P. religion educator; b. Bklyn., Feb. 27, 1941; married, 1967; 1 child. AB, St. Mary's U., 1961, STB, 1963; ThD, U. Münster, Fed. Republic of Germany, 1972. Asst. prof. theology U. Notre Dame, Ind., 1971-77, Villanova (Pa.) U., 1977-79; assoc. prof. theology Cath. U. Am., Washington, 1979-87; now Charles Chauncey Stillman prof. Roman Cath. theol. studies Harvard U., Cambridge, Mass. Vis. scholar Union Theol. Sem., N.Y.C., 1974-75; vis. prof. Yale U., 1995. Author: Critical Social Theory and Christology, 1975, Political Theology as Foundational Theology, 1977, Religion und Politik, Christliche Glaube, 1982; translator: Schleiermacher: Open Letters on the Glaubenslehre, 1981, Foundational Theology: Jesus and Church, 1984; editor: Systematic Theology, Roman Catholic Perspectives, 2 vols., 1991; co-editor: (with Don Browning) Habermas, Modernity and Public Theology, 1992, Handbook of Catholic Theology, 1995, (with James Livingston) Modern Christian Thought: Vol. 2 The Twentieth Century, 2000; contbr. articles to religious jours. Fellow Div., U. Chgo., 1978-79; rsch. fellow Am. Assn. Theol. Schs., 1982-83, 89. Mem. Am. Acad. Religion, Cath. Theol. Soc. Am. (pres. 1985-86), Soc. Values Higher Edn., Coll. Theol. Soc., Hegel Soc. Roman Catholic. Office: Harvard U Div Sch 45 Francis Ave Cambridge MA 02138-1911

FIORENZA, JOSEPH A. bishop; b. Beaumont, Tex., Jan. 25, 1931; Student, St. Mary's Dem., LaPorte, Tex. Ordained to ministry Cath. Ch., 1954, consecrated bishop Cath. Ch., 1979. Bishop Diocese of San Angelo, Tex., 1979—85, Diocese of Galveston-Houston, Tex., 1985—. Office: Roman Cath Ch PO Box 907 Houston TX 77001-0907*

FIORI, DENNIS A. museum director; BA in Am. Studies, St. Michael's Coll.; postgrad., U. Vt. Asst. dir., head mus. programs Maine Arts Commn.; dep. dir. for programs Inst. Mus. and Libr. Svcs.; dir. Md. Hist. Soc., Balt. Vice chmn. Heritage Preservation; pres. Balt. History Alliance; chmn. Md. Mus. Assistance Program; mem. Govs. Tak Force on Md. Heritage; cons. com. Ladew Topiary Garens; overseer Strawberry Banke; trustee Balt. Conservatory Assn. Office: Md Hist Soc 201 W Monument St Baltimore MD 21201-4601 Fax: 410-385-2105.

FIORI, MICHAEL J. pharmacist; b. Brunswick, Maine, Nov. 25, 1951; s. Columbus H. and Marie Alice (Pelletier) F.; m. Anna Marie Robinson, Dec. 25, 1980 (div.); 1 child, Michela; m. Dora Anne Mills, Aug. 7, 1997; children: Anthony, Julia. BA in Biology, Bowdoin Coll., 1974; BS in Pharmacy, Mass. Coll. Pharmacy, 1977; MBA, U. Maine, 1987; cert. exec. mgmt., Cornell U., 1992; PhD in Bus. Mgmt., LaSalle U., 1995. Notary Public, Justice of the Peace; lic. auctioneer. Rsch. student Rsch. Inst. Gulf Maine, 1974-75; pharmacy intern Newton-Wellesley (Mass.) Hosp., 1977; pharmacist Allen Drug Store, Brunswick, 1977-78, cons. pharmacist Bangor, Maine, 1977-84; pres., COO, Downeast Pharmacy, Inc., Augusta, Maine, pres., cons. Pharmacists of New Eng. various cities, Maine, 1984—99, pres. Guardian Healthcare Augusta, 1990—99; pres. Omnicare Inc. divsn. Downeast Pharmacy Long Term Care, Augusta, 1996—99. Commr. Maine Commn. Pharmacy, 1985-90; pres. and CEO Vector Assocs., Inc. dba ODV, Inc., The E.Y.E. Found.; pres. New Maine Oppotunities, 2002—; mem. dist. adv. coun. Small Bus. Adminstrn. Exec. prodr. (film documentaries) The Forgotten Maine, Our Maine Democratic Heritage. Recipient president's award for svc. to medicine Maine Med. Assn., 1993; Earle S. Thompson scholar, 1971-73, Charles Lowery scholar, 1974. Fellow Am. Soc. Cons. Pharmacists; mem. Am. Soc. for Pharmacy Law, Narcotic Enforcement Officers Assn., Internat. Assn. for Identification, Internat. Assn. Chiefs of Police, Nat. Assn. Bds. of Pharmacy, Maine Pharmacy Assn., Health Care Providers, Inc., Nat. Assn. Retail Druggists, Nat. Fedn. Indp. Bus. (guardian adv. coun.), Internat. Platform Assn., Mass. Coll. Pharmacy Alumni Assn., Bowdoin Coll. Alumni Assn., LaSalle U. Alumni Assn., U. Maine Alumni Assn., Italian Heritage Soc., Gyro Internat., Maine Health Care Assn., NRA (life), KC, Elks, Beta Theta Pi (chpt. pres. 1972-73, ho. corp. pres. 1985—, ho. corp. dir. 1975—, dist. chief 1979-84, 88-89). Democrat. Roman Catholic. Home: Tallwood Dr PO Box 1016 Brunswick ME 04011-1016 Office: The EYE Found PO Box 1016 Brunswick ME 04011-1016

FIORI, PAMELA, publishing executive, magazine editor, writer; b. Newark, Feb. 26, 1944; d. Edward and Rita (Rascati) F.; m. Colton Givner. BA cum laude, Jersey City State Coll., 1966. Tchr. English Gov. Livingston High Sch., Berkeley Heights, N.J., 1966-67; assoc. editor Holiday Mag., N.Y.C., 1968-71, Travel & Leisure Mag., N.Y.C., 1971-74, sr. editor, 1974-75, editor-in-chief, 1975-80; editor-in-chief, exec. v.p. Am. Express Pub. Corp. (Travel & Leisure/Food & Wine), N.Y.C., 1980-89, editorial dir., exec. v.p., 1989-93; editor-in-chief Town & Country, N.Y.C., 1993—. Columnist: Travel & Leisure, 1976—89, Town & Country, 1993—; contbr. articles to periodicals. Bd. dirs. Jazz at Lincoln Ctr., East Side Houses Settlement. Recipient Chevalier de l'Ordre du Merite, 1985, Melva C. Pederson award for disting. travel journalism Am. Soc. Travel Afts., 1992, Outstanding Woman of the 90s award Found. for Neurosurg. Rsch., 1994, Bus. award Nat. Italian Am. Found., 1996. Office: Town & Country 1700 Broadway New York NY 10019-5905

FIORI-BLANCHFIELD, JOAN, artist, art historian; b. Tuxedo, N.Y., May 26, 1942; d. Anthony Justus Fiori and Janet Cynthia Pohl; m. William Charles Blanchfield; children: Lyn, Mark. BA, Coll. New Rochelle, 1964; MA in Studio Art, SUNY, Albany, 1972; MA in Art History with honors, Syracuse U., 1999; postgrad., CUNY, 2001—. Tutor in fine arts Empire State Coll., Saratoga Springs, N.Y., 1974-75; instr. in art Jewish Cmty. Ctr., Utica, N.Y.; adj. instr. Mohawk Valley C.C., Utica, 1976-83; instr. in art and fine art Herkimer (N.Y.) County C.C., 1979-80; dir. cultural exch. to Italy Utica Coll. of Syracuse U., Utica, 1988-89, lectr. in fine art, 1973, 82-93, dir. Edith Barrett Art Gallery, 1983-96; ind. scholar, artist, cons. Utica, 1996—. Contbr. articles to profl. publs.; executed sculpture at Museo d'Arte Moderna, Italy, Mostra Internazionale di Sculture all'Aperto, Italy, 1978, 79. Bd. dirs. Art Discovery Consortium, Oneida County, N.Y., 1985-87; dir. art-in-edn. program for Oneida County, N.Y. State Coun. on Arts, N.Y.C., 1985-96; art judge Munson Williams Proctor Inst. Art, Utica, 1992, Utica Pub. Libr., 1992-95; curator women's unit exhbn. Women's History Mus., Seneca Falls, N.Y., 1984; mem. upstate N.Y. com. Nat. Mus. Women in Arts, Washington, 1989-90. Recipient 1st prize Albany Inst. Art, 1966, Hon. Mention award Albany Inst. Art, 1967, Best in Show award Cooperstown Art Mus., 1981, 1st prize in sculpture, 1979, 80; Rettore's medal Università dell'Aquila, Italy, 1989; grantee Utica Coll. Syracuse U., 1988-91, N.Y. State Coun. Arts, 1983-89, N.Y. Coun. Humanities, 1984-85, others. Mem.: NOW, Assn. Historians Am. Art, Coll. Art Assn., Chamber Mus. Soc. Utica (sec. 2002—, bd. dirs.), Southeastern Medieval Assn. (sec., treas. 1989—96), Medieval Acad. Am. Avocations: piano, jogging. Home: 2610 Sunset Ave Utica NY 13502-6009

FIORILLA, JOHN LEOPOLDO, lawyer; b. Paterson, N.J., July 1, 1965; s. Giovanni and Maria Giuseppa (Mazzara) F. BS, Seton Hall U., 1987; JD, U. Pitts., 1990; LLM in Internat. Legal Studies, NYU, 1999. Bar: N.J. 1990, N.Y. 1991, D.C. 1991, U.S. Supreme Ct. 1995; master lic. USCG. Assoc. Sullivan & Cromwell, N.Y.C., London, 1990-94; prin., gen. counsel Elysium Group Inc., N.Y.C., 1994—; of counsel Studio Legale Vassalli, Milan, 1994-2001, Studio Legale Associato Caffie & Maroncelli, Bergamo and Milan, Italy, 1994—; fellow Fgn. Policy Assn. Bd. dirs. Elysium Group Inc. and affiliates; assoc. Brosio, Casati & Assocs., Milan, 1992-93; legal adviser to the nunciature, permanent observer Mission of the Holy See to the UN, 1997—, mem. Holy See Del. to the Gen. Assembly and other UN bodies, 1997—. Pres. standing com. Young Friends Save Venice, Inc., 1998—; bd. dirs. Internat. Cath. Orgns. Info. Ctr., 1999—, Save Venice Inc., 2001—. Decorated knight comdr. Equestrian Order Holy Sepulcher of Jerusalem, Sovereign Mil. Order of Malta, Order of Merit of Savoy. Mem.: Assn. Bar City N.Y. (spl. com. on UN), Circolo del Golf di Roma, Racquet Club of Phila., Players Club, Downtown Assn., Econ. Club N.Y., Met. Club. Roman Catholic. Home: 430 E 57th St New York NY 10022-3061 Office: Elysium Group Inc 641 Lexington Ave 26th Fl New York NY 10022-4503 Also: Via degli Omenoni 2 20121 Milan Italy E-mail: jlf@fiorilla.com.

FIORILLO, JOHN A(NTHONY), health care executive; b. N.Y.C., Jan. 20, 1943; s. John Albert and Matilda (Marotti) F.; m. Anita Daves Pitney, Dec. 6, 1969; 1 child, Alexandra. AB, NYU, 1963; AM, Brown U., 1965; postgrad., CUNY, 1972-74. Planning officer OEO, Washington, 1964-66; exec. asst. to commr. N.Y.C. Health and Hosps. Depts., 1966-69; sr. cons. Peat Marwick Mitchell and Co., N.Y.C., 1968-72; pres. Policy Planning Inc., N.Y.C., 1972-77; asst. v.p. Columbia U., N.Y.C., 1977-81; mng. dir. Am. Health Found., N.Y.C., 1981-82; pres. The Health Strategy Group, Inc., Chatham, N.Y., 1982—; sr. cons. The Robert Wood Johnson Found., 1999—2002. Mgmt. cons. NIH, Bethesda, Md., 1979-86; founding dir. People's Med. Soc., Emmaus, Pa., 1982-84. Author: (with others) Art Work, No Commercial Value, 1972; contbr. articles to profl. jours., chpts. in book. Mem. White House Task Force on Peace Corps, Washington, 1969, N.Y.C. Task Force on Employee Health Benefits, 1974-75; mem. advance team Sen. Robert Kennedy, 1964; asst. campaign dir. Congressman Jonathan Bingham, N.Y.C., 1964; bd. trustees Daytop Village Found., 1986-96; bd. dirs. The Shaker Mus., 1995-98, N.Y. Assn. for Ambulatory Care, 1997-2001, Performance Space for the 21st Century, 1999—. With USCG, 1965-71. Brown U. fellow, 1963-64. Mem. Austerlitz Club. Avocations: shooting sports, photography, modern jazz. Home: 275 Central Park W New York NY 10024-3015 Office: The Health Strategy Group Inc 46 River Rd Chatham NY 12037-3701 E-mail: J.fiorillo@earthlink.net.

FIORINA, CARLETON S. (CARLY FIORINA), computer company executive; b. Austin, Tex., Sept. 6, 1954; married. BA in Medieval History and Philosophy, Stanford U., 1976; MBA, U. Md., 1980; MSc, MIT, 1989; postgrad., UCLA. Account exec. Long Lines AT&T, 1980, sr. v.p. Global Mktg., pres. Atlantic and Canadian Region; v.p. Corp. Ops. Lucent Technologies, group pres. Global Svc. Provider; pres., CEO Hewlett-Packard, Palo Alto, 1999—, chmn. bd. dirs., 2000—. Bd. dirs. Cisco Sys., Power Up; elected U.S. China Bd. Trade. Named one of Fortune Mag. Most Powerful Women in Am. Bus., Hon. Fellow London Bus. Sch., 2001. Office: Hewlett-Packard 3000 Hanover St Palo Alto CA 94304-1181*

FIORINO, ANTHONY SAVERIO (TONY EITAN), research analyst; b. Bronxville, N.Y., Nov. 27, 1967; s. Francis Michael and Frances Rosemary (Campisi) F.; m. Deborah Alexandra Goldberg, May 23, 1994; children: Shoshana Elian, Netanel Moshe, Bentzion Azriel. BS in Biology, MIT, 1989; MS in Molecular Pharmacology, Yeshiva U., 1993, PhD in Molecular Pharmacology, 1995, MD, 1996. Intern internal medicine U. Pa., Phila., 1996-97, resident dermatology, 1997-98; rsch. analyst Paramount Capital, N.Y.C., 1998; assoc. JP Morgan Securities, N.Y.C., 1998-99, v.p., 2000, Citigroup Asset Mgmt., Stamford, Conn., 2000—. Contbr. articles to Drugs and Market Devel., Annals Internal Medicine, Brain Rsch., Ob-gyn., In Vitro, Cell Biology Internat., Leukemia, The Torah U Madda Jour., Jewish Action. Treas., bd. dirds. Albert Einstein Synagogue, Bronx, N.Y., 1992-96; mem. working group on cloning rsch., Jewish Law and Pub. Policy, Orthodox Union/Rabinnical Coun. Am. Mem. AMA, N.Y. Acad. Scis., Alpha Omega Alpha, Phi Beta Kappa, Sigma Xi. Jewish. Achievements include cloning a cell line useful in studying liver development. Office: Citigroup Asset Mgmt 100 First Stamford Pl Stamford CT 06902 E-mail: fiorino@alum.mit.edu.

FIORINO, JOHN WAYNE, podiatrist; b. Charleroi, Pa., Sept. 30, 1946; s. Anthony Raymond and Mary Louise (Caramela) F.; m. Susan K. Bonnett, May 2, 1984; children: Jennifer, Jessica, Lauren, Michael. Student, Nassau Coll., 1969-70; BA in Biology, U. Buffalo, 1972; Dr. Podiatric Medicine, Ohio Coll. Podiatric Medicine, 1978. Cert. primary podiatric medicine and podiatric surgery Am. Podiatric Med. Spltys. Bd.; diplomate Am. Bd. Med. Spltys. in Podiatry. Salesman E. J. Korvettes, Carle Place, N.Y., 1962-65; orderly Nassau Hosp., Mineola, N.Y., 1965-66; operating room technician-trainee heart-lung machine L.I. Jewish-Hillside Med. Center, New Hyde Park, N.Y., 1967-69; pharmacy technician Feinmel's Pharmacy, Roslyn Heights, N.Y., 1969-70; mgr., asst. buyer Fortunoffs, Westbury, N.Y., 1972-73; bd. certified perfusionist L.I. Jewish-Hillside Med. Center, New Hyde Park, N.Y., 1973-74; clin. instr. cardiopulmonary tech. Stony Brook (N.Y.) Univ., 1973-74; operating room technician Cleve. Met. Hosp., 1975; lab. technician Univ. Hosp., Cleve., 1976-78; surg. resident Mesa Gen. Hosp., 1978-79, staff podiatrist, 1979—; pvt. practice podiatry Mesa, 1979—. Staff podiatrist Sacaton (Ariz.) Hosp., 1979—, Mesa Gen. Hosp., 1979, Valley Luth. Hosp., Mesa, 1985, Chandler Community Hosp., 1985, Desert Samaritan Hosp., Mesa, 1986; podiatrist U.S. Govt. Nat. Inst., Sacaton, 1980-87, Indian Health Services, Sacaton, 1980-87; cons. staff Phoenix Indian Med. Ctr., 1985. Served with USN, 1966-67. Mem. Am. Podiatry Assn., Ariz. Podiatry Assn. (treas. 1984-86), Acad. Ambulatory Foot Surgery, Am. Coll. Foot Surgeons (assoc.), Mut. Assn. Profls., Am. Acad. Pain Mgmt. (cert.), Pi Delta, Alpha Gamma Kappa. Home: 2624 W Upland Dr Chandler AZ 85224-7870 Office: 5520 E Main St Mesa AZ 85205-8793

FIORITO, EDWARD GERALD, lawyer; b. Irvington, N.J., Oct. 20, 1936; s. Edward and Emma (DePascale) F.; m. Charlotte H. Longo; children— Jeanne C., Kathryn M., Thomas E., Lynn M., Patricia A. BSEE, Rutgers U., 1958; JD, Georgetown U., 1963. Bar: U.S. Patent and Trademark Office 1960, Va. 1963, N.Y. 1964, Mich. 1970, Ohio 1975, Tex. 1984. Patent staff atty. IBM, Armonk, N.Y., 1958-69; v.p. patent and comml. relations Energy Conversion Devices, Troy, Mich., 1969-71; mng. patent prosecution Burroughs Corp., Detroit, 1971-75; gen. patent counsel B.F. Goodrich Corp., Akron, Ohio, 1975-83; dir. patents and licensing Dresser Industries, Inc., Dallas, 1983-93. Alt. mem. Dept. Commerce Adv. Commn. on Patent Law Reform, 1991-92; spl. master, arbitrator, neutral evaluator, expert providing opinion testimony in intellectual property litigation, 1986—; U.S. del. to World Intellectual Property Orgn. Diplomatic Conf., 1991. Bd. dirs. Akron's House Extending Aid on Drugs, 1976. Mem. ABA (chmn. sci. and tech. sect. 1984-85, chair intellectual property law sect. 2000-2001), IEEE, Tex. Bar Assn. (chmn. intellectual property law sect. 1990-91), Internat. Assn. for Protection Indsl. Property (exec. bd. 1989—), Assn. Corp. Patent Counsel (exec. com. 1982-84), Tau Beta Pi. Roman Catholic. Avocations: music, running. E-mail: ipconsulting@msn.com. *Those of you who have received gifts in great abundance at the beginning of your journey here, should remember to use them before your journey ends in the service of your creator who gave them to you.*

FIORITO, JACK THOMAS, education educator; b. Chgo., Oct. 31, 1952; s. Isadore Thomas and Roberta Barbara (Gould) Fiorito; m. Susan Marie Syron, May 14, 1982; children: William, Roberta. BS in Econ. with honors, U. Ill., 1974, MA in Labor and Indsl. Rels., 1976, PhD in Labor and Indsl. Rels., 1980. Rsch. assoc. U. Ill., Urbana, 1975—76, 1978—79; asst. prof. Okla. State U,, Stillwater, 1979—82; from asst. prof. to prof. U. Iowa, Iowa City, 1982—90; from assoc. prof. to J. Frank Dame prof. Fla. State U., Tallahassee, 1990—. Cons. in field. Co-editor: State of the Unions, 1991; contbr. articles to profl. jours. Mem.: United Faculty Fla. (chpt. pres. 2002—). Office: Fla State Univ Coll Bus Tallahassee FL 32306-1110

FIOTO, GEORGE ANTHONY, chemist; b. N.Y.C., Nov. 22, 1933; s. George W. and Marie (Giafone) F.; m. Alice Dorothy Partridge, Oct. 13, 1956; children: Howard, George Jr., Jeanne. BS in Chemistry, Manhattan Coll., 1955; student, Poly. Inst. Bklyn., 1956-57. Assoc. dir. rsch. and devel. Revlon Rsch. Ctr., N.Y.C., 1956-68; sr. v.p. rsch. and devel. Noxell Corp., Balt., 1968-86; exec. v.p., pres., CEO Revlon Rsch. Ctr., Edison, N.J., 1986-93, pres. emeritus, 1994-98, pres., CEO, 1998—2001, pres. emeritus, 2001—. Mem. Soc. Cosmetic Chemists (chmn. N.Y. chpt. 1967-68, nat. dir. 1968-70, chmn. com. on sci. affairs 1975-78), Cosmetic Industry Assn. (chmn. exec. com. 1986-88, sci. adv. com. 1986-88, Cosmetic Industry Buyers and Suppliers award 1988). E-mail: gaftg33@aol.com.

FIRCHOW, EVELYN SCHERABON, German language and literature educator, writer; b. Vienna; came to U.S., 1951, naturalized, 1964; d. Raimund and Hildegard (Nickl) Scherabon; m. Peter E. Firchow, 1969; children: Felicity (dec. 1988), Pamina. BA, U. Tex., 1956; MA, U. Man., 1957; PhD, Harvard U., 1963. Instr. coll. math. Balmoral Hall Sch., Winnipeg, Man., Can., 1953-55; tchg. fellow in German Harvard U., Cambridge, Mass., 1957-58, 61-62; lectr. German U. Md. in Munich, 1961; instr. German U. Wis., Madison, 1962-63, asst. prof., 1963-65; assoc. prof. German U. Minn., Mpls., 1965-69, prof. German and Germanic philology, 1969—; vis. prof. U. Fla., Gainesville, 1973; Fulbright research prof. Iceland, 1966-67, 80, 94; vis. rsch. prof. Nat. Cheng Kung U., Tainan, Taiwan, 1982-83; permanent vis. prof. Jilin U., Changchun, People's Republic of China, 1987—. Vis. prof. U. Graz, Austria, 1989, 91, 2002, 03, U. Vienna, Austria, 1995, U. Bonn, 1996, Nat. U. Costa Rica, 2000. Editor and author: (under name E.S. Coleman) Taylor Starck-Festschrift, 1964, Stimmen aus dem Stundenglas, 1968, (under name E.S. Firchow) Studies by Einar Haugen, 1972, Studies for Einar Haugen, 1972, Was Deutsche lesen, 1973, Deutung und Bedeutung, 1973, Elucidarius in Old Norse Translation, 1989, The Old Norse Elucidarius: Original Text and English Translation, 1992, Notker der Deutsche von St. Gallen: De interpretatione, 1995, Categoriae, 2 Vols., 1996, De nuptiis Philologiae et Mercurii, 2 Vols., 1999, Notker der Deutsche von St. Gallen (950-1022): Ausführliche Bibliographie, 2000, De consolatione Philosophiae, 3 vols., 2003, Reluctant Modernists, Festschrift Peter Firchow, 2002; translator: Einhard: Vita Caroli Magni, Das Leben Karls des Grossen, 1968, 84, 95, Einhard: Vita Caroli Magni, The Life of Charlemagne, 1972, 85, Icelandic Short Stories, 1974, 87, East German Short Stories, 1979, (with P.E. Firchow) Alois Brandstetter, The Abbey, 1998; dir., editor Computer Clearing-House Project for German and Medieval Scandinavian; assoc. editor Germanic Notes and Revs., Am. Jour. Linguistics and Lit.; contbr. articles and book revs. to profl. jours. Fulbright scholar Tex., 1951-52; fellow Alexander von Humboldt-Stiftung, Munich, 1960-61, Tuebingen, 1974, Marburg, 1981, Goettingen, 1985, Tokyo, 1991, Marburg and Berlin, 1993, Bonn, 2001, Fulbright Found., Iceland, 1967-68, 80, 94, Austrian Govt., 1977, NEH, 1980-81, Am. Inst. Indian Studies, 1988, BUSH fellow, 1989, Thor Thors fellow, 1994, Mc Knight summer fellow, 1995, 96, 99, Deutscher Akademischer Austausdienst (DAAD) rsch. fellow, 2000; elected hon. mem. Multilingual Rsch. Ctr., Brussels, 1986. Mem. AAUP, MLA (chmn. div. German lit. to 1700 1979-80, 93-96, vice chmn. pedagogical seminar for Germanic philology 1979-86, 91-93, chair 1994), Medieval Acad. Am., Soc. German-Am. Studies (chair Linguistics I 1992), Internat. Comparative Lit. Assn., Soc. for Advancement Scandinavian Studies (chmn. Germanic philology 1979, text editing 1980, linguistics 1984, computers and Old Norse 1985), Assn. for Lang. and Linguistic Computing (founding mem.), Am. Comparative Lit. Assn., Midwest Modern Lang. Assn. (chmn. German I 1965-66, chmn. Scandinavian 1979), Internationale Vereinigung der Germanisten, Am. Assn. Tchrs. German, Modern Humanities Rsch. Assn., Mediävisten Verband, Soc. for Germanic Philology, Österreichische Germanisten-Gesellschaft. Office: U Minn Dept German Minneapolis MN 55455 E-mail: firch001@umn.edu.

FIRCHOW, PETER EDGERLY, language professional, educator, author; b. Needham, Mass., Dec. 16, 1937; s. Paul Karl August and Marta Loria (Montenegro) F.; m. Evelyn Maria Scherabon Coleman, Sept. 18, 1969; 1 dau., Pamina Maria Scherabon. BA, Harvard Coll., 1959; postgrad., U. Vienna, Austria, 1959-60; MA, Harvard U., 1961; PhD, U. Wis., 1965. Asst. prof. English U. Mich., 1965-67; asst. prof. English and comparative lit. U. Minn., Mpls., 1967-69, assoc. prof., 1969-73, prof., 1973—, chmn. Comparative Lit. Program, 1972-78. Disting. vis. prof. Nat. Cheng Kung U., Taiwan, 1982-83, Jilin U., Peoples Republic China, 1987, U. Munich, Germany, 1988, U. Graz, Austria, 1989, 2003; Fulbright prof. U. Bonn, Germany, 1995-96, Nat. U. Costa Rica, 2000. Author: Friedrich Schlegel's Lucinde and the Fragments, 1971, Aldous Huxley, Satirist and Novelist, 1972, The Writer's Place: Interviews on the Literary Situation in Contemporary Britain, 1974; (with E.S. Firchow) East German Short Stories: An Introductory Anthology, 1979; The End of Utopia: A Study of Huxley's Brave New World, 1984; The Death of the German Cousin: Variations on a Literary Stereotype, 1986; translator (with E.S. Firchow) The Abbey (Alois Brandstetter), 1998, Envisioning Africa: Racism and Imperialism in Conrad's "Heart of Darkness", 2000, W.H. Auden: Contexts for Poetry, 2002, Reluctant Modernists: Aldous Huxley and Some Contemporaries, 2002; contbr. articles on modern lit. subjects to profl. jours. Fellow Inst. Advanced Studies in Humanities, Edinburgh, 1977. Mem. Midwest Modern Lang. Assn. (v.p. 1977, pres. 1978), Am. Comparative Lit. Assn., Assn. Lit. Scholars and Critics, Internat. Aldous Huxley Soc. Home: 135 Birnamwood Dr Burnsville MN 55337-6814 Office: U Minn Dept English 310D Lind Hall 207 Church St SE Minneapolis MN 55455-0134 E-mail: pef@tc.umn.edu.

FIREBAUGH, FRANCILLE MALOCH, university official; b. El Dorado, Ark., July 15, 1933; d. Delton Verdis and Dorothy Lucille (Measeles) Maloch; m. John David Firebaugh, Dec. 28, 1970. BS, U. Ark., 1955; MS, U. Tenn., 1956; PhD, Cornell U., 1962. Instr. U. Tex., Austin, 1956-58; asst. prof. home econs. Ohio State U., Columbus, 1962-65, assoc. prof., 1965-69, prof., 1969-88; dir. Sch. Home Econs., 1973-82; acting v.p. agrl. adminstrn.; exec. dean of agr., home econs., natural resources, 1982-83; assoc. provost Office Acad. Affairs, 1983-84; vice provost for internat. affairs, 1984-88; acting provost, v.p. acad. affairs, 1985-86; dean coll. human ecology Cornell U., Ithaca, NY, 1988-99, dir. spl. projects office of pres. and provost, 2000—01, vice provost for land grant affairs, spl. asst. to the pres., 2001—. Mem. joint com. on agrl. research and devel. Bd. Internat. Food and Agr., 1982-87. Author: Home Management: Context and Concepts, 1975, Family Resource Management, 1981, 88. Bd. dirs. Columbus Coun. on World Affairs, 1987-88, Boyce Thompson Inst. for Plant Rsch., 1991-97; moderator First Baptist Ch., 1981-83; bd. dirs. Cayuga Med. Ctr., 1992-2001, Panamerican Agr. Sch., Zamorano, Honduras, 1994—, Kendal at Ithaca, 1995-2003; Families and Work Inst., N.Y.C., 1995—; trustee Ithaca (N.Y.) Coll., 2000—, Cmty. Found. of Tompkins County, 2000-02. Mem. Nat. Coun. Family Rels., AAAS, Am. Home Econs. Found. (bd. dirs. 1987-90), Am. Assn. of Family and Consumer Scis., Ohio State U. Faculty Club (pres. 1988), Assn. Women in Devel. (sec. 1988-89), Sigma Xi, Sigma Delta Epsilon, Kappa Omicron Nu, Phi Upsilon Omicron, Gamma Sigma Delta, Phi Kappa Phi, Epsilon Sigma Phi. Office: Cornell U Office of Provost 449 Day Hall Ithaca NY 14853-2801

FIREBAUGH, GLENN ALLEN, sociology educator; b. Charleston, W.Va., Oct. 23, 1948; s. George Lawrence and Rosanelle (Grose) Firebaugh; m. Judy Rae Thompson, Nov. 21, 1970; children: Heather, Joel, Rose Marie. BA, Grace Coll., 1970; MA, Ind. U., 1974, PhD, 1976. Prof. sociology Pa. State U., University Park, 1988—, head dept. sociology, 2001—. Author: The New Geography of Global Income Inequality, 2003; editor: (jour.) Am. Sociol. Rev., 1997—99; editor: (editl. bd.) Sociol. Quar., Sociol. Methods and Rsch., Social Forces, Am. Jour. Sociology; contbr. articles. Recipient Disting. Scholar award, Pa. State U., 2001; fellow, NIMH, 1972—76; grantee, NSF, 1983—84, 1988—2001. Office: Pa State Univ Dept Sociology 206 Oswald Tower University Park PA 16802

FIREBAUGH, MARCO ANTONIO, state official; b. Baja California, Mexico, Oct. 13, 1966; children: Ariana, Nicolas. BA, U. Calif., Berkeley, 1993; JD, UCLA, 1997. Prin. cons. Latino Legis. Caucus, 1990—95; mcpl. law analyst, 1995—98; state assembly mem. Dist. 50 Calif. State Assembly, 1998—. Democrat. Roman Catholic. Mailing: Rm 319 PO Box 942849 Sacramento CA 94249-0001 Office: Ste 104 8724 Garfield Ave South Gate CA 90280

FIREMAN, PAUL B. footwear and apparel company executive; b. Cambridge, Mass., Feb. 14, 1944; Student, Boston U. Pres., chmn., CEO Reebok Internat. Ltd., Stoughton, Mass. Founder The Reebok Found. Recipient Honored by Human Rights Law Group, numerous industry awards. Office: Reebok Internat Ltd 1895 JW Foster Blvd Canton MA 02021

FIREMAN, PHILIP, pediatrician, allergist, immunologist, medical association executive; b. Pitts., 1932; MD, U. Chgo., 1957. Diplomate Am. Bd. Allergy and Immunology (chmn. 1992-93). Intern Phila. Gen. Hosp., 1957-58; resident in pediatrics Children's Hosp., Pitts., 1958-60, resident pediatrician, 1964—; fellow in allergy and immunology NIH, Bethesda, Md., 1960-62; fellow allergist, immunologist Harvard Children's Hosp., Boston, 1962-64; prof. pediatrics, internal medicine U. Pitts. Med. Sch. Mem.: Am. Acad. Allergy, Asthma and Immunology (pres. 1997—98). Office: Children's Hosp 3705 5th Ave Pittsburgh PA 15213-2583 E-mail: philip.fireman@chp.edu.

FIRESIDE, HARVEY FRANCIS, political scientist, educator; b. Vienna, Dec. 28, 1929; came to U.S., 1940, naturalized, 1945; s. Norbert and Frances F.; m. Bryna Joan Levenberg, Dec. 12, 1959; children— Leela Ruth, Douglas Leonard, Daniel Ephraim. BA magna cum laude, Harvard U., 1952, MA, 1955; PhD, New Sch. Social Research, 1968. Info. specialist AEC, 1957-58; editor Palmerton Publishing Co., N.Y.C., 1959-60, Am. Cyanamid Co., N.Y.C., 1960-61, Fgn. Policy Assn., N.Y.C., 1961-62; freelance editor, 1962-64; asst. prof. polit. sci. N.Y. Inst. Tech., 1964-68; Charles A. Dana prof. politics Ithaca (N.Y.) Coll., 1968-96, prof. emeritus, 1998. Fulbright advisor Cornell U., 2003—; cons. in field. Author: Icon and Swastika: The Russian Orthodox Church under Nazi and Soviet Control, 1971, Soviet Psychoprisons, 1979, Brown vs Board of Education, 1994, Young People from Bosnia Talk About War, 1996, Plessy vs. Ferguson, 1997, The Fifth Amendment, 1998, New York Times vs. Sullivan, 1999, Nuremberg Trials of Nazi War Criminals, 2000, The Mississippi Burning Civil Rights Murder Conspiracy Trial, 2002; also articles. Group leader Amnesty Internat., Ithaca, 1973-80; co-chmn. Socialist Studies Com., Ithaca, 1977-83, Working Group Against Psychiat. Abuse, 1980-83; bd. dirs. Tompkins County chpt. ACLU, 1968-71, Ithaca Sanctuary Com., 1986-92, Tompkins County Mental Health Assn., 1986-89, 93-95, pres., 1995-96; bd. dirs. Com. on U.S.-Latin Am. Rels., 1990-92, Hillel Found., Ithaca Coll., 1991-93; coord. The Border Fund, 1989—, Bosnian Student Project, 1994-2000; Citizenship Project, 1997-99, Eleanor Roosevelt Loan Fund, 2000—, Ithaca City of Asylum, 2001-03. Recipient Tompkins County Human Rights award, 1992, 98; Harvard U. Russian Rsch. Ctr. fellow, summers 1975, 80; fellow Harvard U. Ukrainian Rsch. Inst., summer 1976; fellow Cornell U. Inst. for European Studies, 1995-98, Peace Studies Program, 1998-2001, Cornell Law Sch., 2001-03; grantee N.Y. Dept. Edn., 1965; vis. scholar Russian Inst., Columbia U., 1966; Nat. Endowment Humanities fellow, summer, 1983, 94. Mem. Am. Polit. Sci. Assn. Democrat. Jewish. Home: 202 Eastwood Ave Ithaca NY 14850-6239 Office: 322 N Aurora St Ithaca NY 14850-4202 E-mail: hfireside@juno.com.

FIRESTEIN, CECILY BARTH, artist; b. N.Y.C., Apr. 25, 1933; d. Sidney Monte and Esther (Schwartz) Barth; m. Stephen Kern Firestein; children: Conrad Elliot, Lesley Adam. BA, Adelphi U., 1953; MA, NYU, 1955, cert. in advanced study, 1958; cert., N.Y. Sch. of Interior Design, 1964. Cert. tchr., N.Y. State, N.Y.C. Art tchr., cons. Union Free Schs. Dist. #24, Valley Stream, N.Y., 1953-60; printmaker Phoenix Gallery, N.Y.C., 1962—; interior designer Firestein Interiors, N.Y.C., 1964—; instr., lectr. Mus. of the City of N.Y., 2001, The New Sch., N.Y.C., 1979, 80; tchr. Cooper Hewitt Mus., N.Y.C., 1980, South St. Seaport Mus., N.Y.C., 1981—2002, 2002, Parson's Sch. Design, N.Y.C., 1982, U. S.C., Columbia, 1989; freelance writer N.Y. Daily News Detroit News, 1977; with Montclair State U., N.J., 1993, U. S.C.; instr., lectr. Ctrl. Pk. Conservancy Mus. of the City of N.Y., 2000, Creative Ctr., N.Y.C., 2003. Art critic Art Speak, N.Y.C., 1983-91, Manhattan Arts Internat. mag. 1992, 93, Conn. Graphic Art Ctr.; cons. Miami (Fla.) Preservation League, 1980, Tarrytown (N.Y.) Hist. Soc., 1979; instr., lectr. Fordham U., N.Y., 1972, Bronx Mus. History, 1974-77, The New Sch., 1977-83. Author: Rubbingcraft, 1977, Making Paper & Fabric Rubbings, 1999; represented in permanent collections Corcoran Gallery of Art, Washington, Cin. Mus. Art, N.Y. Pub. Libr., Yale U. Art Gallery Mus., Newark Mus., Columbia (S.C.) Art Mus., Rose Art Mus., Cin. Art Mus., Bklyn. Mus., Jane Voorhees Zimmerli Art Mus., Mass. Art Mus., Fla. Internat. U., Del. Art Mus., Wilmington, Skirball Mus., L.A., So. St. Seaport Mus., B'nai Brith Klutznik Nat. Jewish Mus., Washington, Freud Mus., London, Freud Mus., Vienna; solo exhibitor at 20 galleries and mus.; author: Rubbing Craft, 1977. Recipient Artist-in-residence award Bronx Mus. of History; grant N.Y. State Council on the Arts, 1974. Mem. N.Y. Soc. Women Artists, Nat. Assn. Women Artists (Printmaking award 2000, Elizabeth Stanton Blake award 2000), Art Students League, Phoenix Gallery (pres. 1990—), Brandeis Club, Kappa Delta Pi, Pi Lambda Theta. Democrat. Jewish.

FIRESTONE, CHARLES MORTON, lawyer, educator; b. St. Louis, Oct. 16, 1944; s. Victor and Betty (Solomon) F.; m. Pattie Winston Porter, Apr. 19, 1975; children: Laurel, Asa. BA, Amherst Coll., 1966; JD, Duke U., 1969. Bar: D.C. 1969, U.S. Ct. Appeals (D.C. cir.) 1970, U.S. Ct. Appeals (5th cir.) 1972, U.S. Ct. Appeals (9th cir.) 1973, U.S. Ct. Appeals (2d cir.) 1975, U.S. Ct. Appeals (3d cir.) 1976, U.S. Ct. Appeals (8th cir.) 1977, U.S. Supreme Ct. 1977, Calif. 1983. Litigation atty. FCC, Washington, 1969-73; dir. litigation Citizens Comm. Ctr., Washington, 1973-77; adj. prof. law, dir. comm. law program UCLA, 1977-86; counsel Mitchell, Silberberg & Knupp, L.A., 1983-90; vis. lectr. UCLA Sch. Law, 1986-90; exec. dir. comm. and society program Aspen Inst., 1989—, exec. v.p. policy programs and internat. activities, 1998-2000. Adj. prof. Duke U., Terry Sanford Inst. Pub. Policy, 2003—; vis. prof. Duke U., Stanford Ctr. Pub. Policy, 2003—; faculty adviser Fed. Comm. Law Jour., L.A., 1977-86; counsel statewide TV debates LVW Calif., 1978-90, counsel Calif. media Dukakis-Bentsen Com.; co-cmmn. adv. com. LWC Calif. Speak Out 1988 Election Project; pres. Bd. Telecom. Commrs., City of L.A., 1984-86, mem. nat. adv. bd. Privacy and Am.Bus., 1993—; mem. Commn. on Radio and Tv Policy, 1996. Author: (with Ellen Mickiewiz) Television and Elections, 1992, (with Donald R. Browne and Mickiewicz) Television/Radio News and Minorities, 1994, (with Robert Entman, Dee Reid and Mickiewicz) Television, Radio & Privatization, 1998, (with Craig L. Lamay and Mickiewicz) Television Autonomy & the State, 1999, (with Mickiewicz Browne LaMay) Democracy on the Air, 2000; editor: Television for the 21st Century: The Next Wave, 1993, (with Jorge Reina Schement) Toward An Information Bill of Rights and Responsibilities, 1995, (with Amy Korzick Garmer) Creating a Learning Society: Initiatives for Education and Technology, 1996, (with Anthony Corrado) Elections in Cyberspace: Toward A New Era in American Politics, 1996, (with Garmer) Digital Broadcasting and the Public Interest, 1998; contbr. articles to profl. jours., chpts. to books. Bd. dirs. Corp. for Disabilities and Telecom., L.A., 1980-82; bd. dirs. KCRW Found., Santa Monica, Calif., 1982-90, vice chmn., 1987-90; trustee Ctr. for Law in Pub. Interest, 1988-89; mem. adv. com. campaign Mondale for Pres., L.A., 1984; mem. adv. com. Ctr. for Govtl. Studies, 2003—. Recipient cert. of commendation Mayor of L.A., 1986, resolution commendation award City Coun. L.A., 1986; Luther Ely Smith scholar and Andrew Laurie scholar Amherst Coll., 1965-66; Glocom fellow Japanese Inst. Global Comms., 2001—. Mem. ABA (chmn. broadcast and spectrum use com., sect. sci. and tech. 1981-83, chmn. electronic campaigning com. 1984-86), Fed. Comm. Bar Assn., Soc. Satellite Profls. (sec. bd. dirs. So Calif. chpt. 1984-87), Coun. Fgn. Rels., Cosmos Club. Jewish. Office: 1 Dupont Cir NW Ste 700 Washington DC 20036-1133 E-mail: firestone@aspeninstitute.org.

FIRESTONE, DEBORAH ILENE, publishing executive; b. Mpls., Mar. 2, 1954; d. Alan and Jeanne M. Firestone; m. Marc E. DesLauriers; 1 child, Anna Lise. BA, U. Colo., 1975; JD, U. Maine, 1981. Bar: Maine 1981, U.S. Dist. Ct. Maine 1981. Publisher, owner Commentaries, Inc., Portland, 1985-93; co-owner, exec. editor, pres. Maine Lawyers Rev., Portland, 1993—. Mem. Maine State Bar Assn. (mem. women's law sect.), Maine Women's Law Network. Office: Maine Lawyers Rev PO Box 6663 Portland ME 04103-6663 E-mail: dfirestone@mainelawyersreview.com

FIRESTONE, GARY, lawyer; b. Montreal, Quebec, Can., May 27, 1952; came to U.S., 1984; s. E. Harvey Firestone and Dorothy F. McCauley; m. M. Jane Burns, June 8, 1976; 1 child, Elliot T. BA, McGill U., 1974, MA, 1979; JD, U. Ariz., 1987. Bar: Oreg. 1987, Wash. 1994, U.S. Dist. Ct. Oreg. 1991, U.S. Dist. Ct. (We. Dist.) Wash. 1995, U.S. Ct. Appeals (9th and D.C. cirs.) 1990. Atty. Heller Ehrman White & McAuliffe, Portland, Oreg., 1989-93, Ramis, Crew, Corrigan & Bachrach, Portland, 1993—. Editor Ariz. J. Internat. Comp. Law, 1986-87. Office: Ramis Crew Corrigan & Bachrach 1727 NW Hoyt St Portland OR 97209-2226 E-mail: garyf@rccb.com.

FIRESTONE, MORTON H. business management executive; b. Chgo., Feb. 4, 1935; s. William and Lillian (Kliot) F.; m. Roberta (Bobbie) Schwartz, Feb. 3, 1957; children: Jeffrey, Scott, Dan. BS, U. Calif., Davis, 1957; MBA, U. So. Calif., 1971. V.p. Security Pacific Nat. Bank, Los Angeles, 1957-77; chmn. bd., chief fin. officer, corp. sec. Elixir Industries, 1977-87, also dir.; pres. Garden Ins., 1978-87, Club Wholesale Concepts, Inc., 1986-87; chmn. bd., chief exec. officer Rondure Industries, 1987-90; pres. Lin Mor Corp., Woodland Hills, Calif., 1990—. Bd. dirs. Robert Burns & Sons, Inc. Past chmn. Los Angeles-Eilat Sister City Com. Mem. Fin. Execs. Inst., Beta Gamma Sigma. Lodges: Optimist (past pres. Hollywood), Kiwanis (past pres. West Hollywood). Office: Lin Mor Corp PO Box 571025 Tarzana CA 91357-1025 E-mail: mort@linmorcorp.com.

FIRESTONE, RICHARD BARTLETT, lawyer; b. Jackson, Mich., July 13, 1934; s. Hubert M. and Elizabeth (Bartlett) F.; m. Isabelle Sherman, Oct. 9, 1985; children— Suzanne Lynne, Kathryn Jean. B.A., U. Mich., 1957; J.D., Detroit Coll. Law, 1960. Bar: Mich. 1960; mem. firm McInally, Rosenfeld & Firestone, Jackson, Mich., 1960-67; chmn. bd., pres. Camp Internat., Inc., Jackson, 1967— ; dir. Camp Ltd., Winchester, Eng., Camp Scandinavia AB, Helsingborg, Sweden, Camp Internat. Ltd., Trenton, Ont., Can., Comerical Bank-Jackson. Trustee Jackson Found., 1984, Ella Sharp Mus. Assn., 1984; mem. bd. edn. Jackson Pub. Schs., 1970-73. Mem. Jackson County Bar Assn., Mich. Bar Assn., Greater Jackson C. of C. (pres. 1984), LWV. Republican. Episcopalian. Clubs: Country of Jackson, Town. Home: 1004 Browns Lake Rd Jackson MI 49203-5669 Office: Camp Internat Inc 744 W Michigan Ave Jackson MI 49201-1909

FIRESTONE, RICHARD FRANCIS, chemistry educator; b. Canton, Ohio, June 18, 1926; s. Lester Ellis and Elizabeth Mary (Corkran) F.; m. Olwen Margaret Huskins, Aug. 21, 1954; children— William, Mark, Robert AB, Oberlin Coll., 1950; PhD, U. Wis., 1954. Resident rsch. assoc. Argonne Nat. Lab., Ill., 1954-56; instr. Internat. Sch. Nuc. Sci. and Engring., 1955—56; asst. prof. chemistry Western Res. U., Cleve., 1956-60; assoc. prof. chemistry Ohio State U., Columbus, 1961-66, prof., 1967-94, acting chair dept. chemistry, 1972 73, prof. emeritus, 1994—. Chair Gordon Conf. on Radiation Chemistry, 1978. Served with USNR, 1944-46 Fellow AAAS; mem. Am. Chem. Soc., Am. Phys. Soc. Address: 820 Old Woods Rd Columbus OH 43235-1248

FIRESTONE, ROGER MORRIS, computer scientist; b. Washington, Aug. 23, 1945; s. Linn Jacob and Regina Caroline (Steiner) F. AB summa cum laude, ScM, Brown U., 1967; MS, NYU, 1969, PhD, 1971; MBA, U. St. Thomas, St. Paul, 1976. Mgr. tech. planning Sperry Corp./Unisys Corp., St. Paul, then Blue Bell, Pa., 1969-86; mem. tech. staff MRJ Inc., Oakton, Va., 1987-92; assoc. dir. engring. svcs. Maden Tech. Cons. Inc., Arlington, Va., 1992-93; sys. engr. V Cray Rsch., Washington, 1995; sr. scientist Comm. Techs., Herndon, Va., 1996-97; software arch. Teknowledge, Fairfax, Va., 1997-2000; rsch. credit expert prin. MITRE Corp., McLean, Va., 2000—. Composer-in-residence Vienna (Va.) Cmty. Band, 2001—. Composer, arranger, performer orchestral, concert band, wind quintet and chamber music; contbr. articles to Scottish Rite Jour. (George Washington medal 1991). Rep. precinct capt. Devolites campaign, Fairfax County, Va., 1997. Mem.: Masons (dist. ednl. officer, dist. 4, Va. 2001—, past lodge master, past coun. grand master, 33d degree, gen. grand musician of Gen. Grand Coun. of Cryptic Masons Internat., grand cross of color), Sigma Xi, Phi Beta Kappa. Jewish. Avocations: theatre (acting), amateur astronomy. Home: 10159 Turnberry Pl Oakton VA 22124-2847 Office: MITRE Corp 7515 Colshire Dr Mc Lean VA 22102 E-mail: rfire@cais.net.

FIRETOG, THEODORE WARREN, lawyer; b. Bklyn., Sept. 18, 1950; s. Max E. and Ilene (Volk) F.; m. Kathleen Ann Neudecker, Feb. 21, 1980; children: Heather, Philip, Trevor. BS in Natural Resources, U. Mich., 1974, MS in Natural Resources, 1976; JD, SUNY, Buffalo, 1979. Bar: N.Y. 1980, U.S. Dist. Ct. (ea. dist.) N.Y. 1986, U.S. Dist. Ct. (so. dist.) N.Y. 1986. Dir. nature and conservation Nassau County coun. Boy Scouts Am., N.Y., 1967-73; teaching fellow dept. natural resources U. Mich., Ann Arbor, 1975-76; staff atty. Environ. Law Inst., Washington, 1979-80; atty., advisor EPA, Washington, 1980-85; sr. assoc. Rivkin, Radler, Dunne & Bayh, Uniondale, N.Y., 1985-87; environ. counsel Shea & Gould, N.Y.C., 1987-94; with Jaspen, Ginsberg, Schlesinger, Silverman & Hoffman, Garden City, N.Y., 1994-95; pvt. practice Farmingdale, N.Y., 1995—. Lectr. various environ. seminars. Contbr. articles to profl. jours. Mem. com. Nassau County Dem. Com., 1987—. Sea Grant Law

fellow U. Buffalo, 1977; recipient Cert. of award EPA, 1985. Mem. ABA (natural resources divsn.), Environ. Law Inst. (assoc.), N.Y. Bar Assn., Suffolk County Bar Assn. Jewish. Office: 111 Thomas Powell Blvd Farmingdale NY 11735-2251

FIREY, WALTER IRVING, JR., retired sociologist, educator; b. Roundup, Mont., Aug. 13, 1916; s. Walter Irving and Marie (Oveson) F.; m. Mary Lou Powell, Aug. 23, 1952; children: Paul, John. BA, Univ. Wash., 1938, MA, 1940; PhD, Harvard U., 1945. Asst. prof. Mich. State U., East Lansing, 1945-46; from asst. prof. to prof. emeritus Univ. Tex., Austin, 1946-85, prof. emeritus, 1985—. Author: Land Use in Central Boston, 1947, 3d edit., 1975, Man, Mind & Land, 1960, 3d edit., 1999, Law & Economy in Planning, 1965; contbr. numerous articles to profl. jours. Ctr. for Advanced Study in Behavioral Scis. fellow Stanford, Calif., 1959-60. Mem. Am. Sociological Assn., Rural Sociological Assn. (award of merit 1983), Sociological Rsch. Assn. (pres. 1972), Phi Beta Kappa. Presbyterian. Avocation: reading. Home: 1307 Wilshire Blvd Austin TX 78722

FIRKSER, ROBERT MICHAEL, lawyer; b. Phila., Mar. 16, 1953; s. Benjamin and Agnes V. Firkser; m. Judith J. Farrell, June 24, 1978; children: Stephen, Ryan, David, Carolyn. BA, St. Joseph's Coll., 1975; JD, U. Miami, 1978. Bar: Pa. 1979, U.S. Dist. Ct. (ea. dist.) Pa. 1979, U.S. Ct. Appeals (3rd cir.) 1981, U.S. Supreme Ct. 1982, Ct. Common Pleas. Assoc. Thomas R. Kimmel, Folcroft, Pa., 1978-80; ptnr. Kimmel & Firkser, Springfield, Pa., 1980-92, DelSordo, Firkser & Donze, Media, Pa., 1992-2000, DelSordo & Firkser, Media, 2000—. Editor: Del. County Legal Jour., 1985. Dir. Wallingford-Swarthmore (Pa.) Sch. Bd., 1991—, pres., 1996-97; founder, co-commr. daniel e. Murtaugh, Jr. Young Lawyers' Sect. Softball League; past bd. dirs. Child Guidance and Mental Health Clinic of Del. County, Inc., Del. County Immediate Unit. Mem. Pa. Bar Assn. (ho. of dels. 1983-86, real property and probate sect., civil litigation sect.), Pa. Trial Lawyers' Assn., Delaware County Bar Assn. (chmn. citizens' conf. com. 1985, jud. retention com. 1990, arbitration com. 1993—, civil trial practices com., civil rules com., civil justice adv. com., real estate practices com., civil legal edn. com., bd. dirs. 2001—), Delaware County Trial Lawyers Assn., Guy G. deFuria Am. in of Ct. (pres. 1993-94). Office: DelSordo & Firkser 333 W Baltimore Ave Media PA 19063-5625 Fax: 610-565-9853. E-mail: rfirkser@barristersclub.com.

FIRMIN, MICHAEL WAYNE, psychology educator; b. New Orleans, July 28, 1961; s. Lloyd John and Betty L. (Shepherd) F.; m. Karen Sue Tuttle, Aug. 4, 1984; children: Ruth, Sarah. BA, Calvary Bible Coll., 1983; MA, Calvary Theol. Sem., 1985; MS, Bob Jones U., 1987, PhD, 1988; MA, Marywood U., 1992; PhD, Syracuse U. Nat. cert. counselor; lic. psychologist, Ohio. Dir. counseling svcs. Bapt. Bible Coll. of Pa., Clarks Summit, 1988-98, assoc. prof., 1988-98, chmn. divsn. grad. studies, 1995-97; assoc. prof. psychology Cedarville (Ohio) U., 1998—; resident in psychology TCN: Behavioral Health Svcs., 2000—01; chmn. dept. psychology Cedarville U., 2000—. Cons. for psychol. svcs. Assn. Bapts. for World Evangelism, Harrisburg, Pa., 1991—94, 1999—; clin. assessment cons. Keystone City Residence, 1994—2000. Pastor Faith Fellowship Bapt. Ch., Danbury, Conn., 1991-94. Mem. Psi Chi. Republican. Home: 84 E Elm St Cedarville OH 45314-8513 Office: Cedarville Univ 251 N Main St Cedarville OH 45314-0601

FIRSCHEIN, SYLVIA, librarian, elementary education educator; b. Belleville, N.J., Apr. 8, 1933; d. Louis and Sonia (Osheroff) Haft; m. Hilliard E. Firschein, Apr. 12, 1964; children: Merry, Warren. BA, Brandeis U., 1955. Cert. K-8 tchr., ednl. media specialist, N.J., Calif., Mass. Tchr. Nutley (N.J.) Bd. Edn., 1959-65; tchr. learning disabled Wayne (N.J.) Bd. Edn., 1972-78, media specialist, 1986—97; libr. dir. YM & YWHA of North Jersey, Wayne, 1977-86, chair Judaica Libr., trustee, 1988—97; ret., 1997. Trustee Akiba Acad., L.A., 1969-72, Am. Labor Mus., Haledon, N.J., 1985-1997. Coun. mem. Assn. Jewish Libraries, chair, membership recruitment, 1984-1992; pres. Sch. Synagogue, Ctr. Divsn., 1984-86; founder, 1st pres. N.J. Assn. Jewish Libraries. Mem. Jewish Geneal. Soc., Pi Lambda Theta, Hadassah. Avocations: storytelling, genealogy.

FIRST, CRAIG PATRICK, composer, educator; b. Harrisburg, Pa., Mar. 16, 1960; s. William E. and Jeanette J. (Capalbo) F.; m. Jean Ann Harris, June 22, 1990; children: Craig Francis, Caroline Lauren. BMus, Am. Conservatory Music, 1982; MMus, Northwestern U., 1983, DMus, 1990. Instr. Am. Conservatory Music, Chgo., 1983-84; lectr. Northwestern U., Evanston, Ill., 1990-95; assoc. prof., coord. theory and composition U. Ala., Tuscaloosa, 1995—. Artistic dir. Chgo. 21st Century Music Ensemble, Chgo., 1992—. Composer: (piano trio) Intimate Voices, 1986, (League Composers award 1989, Padrone-Kantscheidt award 1990), (violin, piano) Black Sun, 1990 (Nat. Assn. Composers USA award 1990, ASCAP award 1990), (mandolin, tape) Tantrum, 1992, (World Music Days award 1998), String Quartet, 1996 (Octavo Concurso Internat. Musical Composition Spain 1997), Contrapuntal Variations, 1999 (World Music Days award 2000); commd. works include Contrapuntal Variations, Mosaics, String Quartet, Flights of Fantasy, The Eternal Return for four films and large ensemble, Chimera, Tantrum; recs. include Extended Resources, Of Time and Place; works published by MMB Music, European Am. Music Distbrs., Apoll Edits. Austria. Recipient Astral Composition award Nat. Found. Advancement Arts, Miami, 1998, ASCAP Stand awards, 1995--. Mem. ASCAP, Nat. Assn. Composers, Soc. Composers Inc., Coll. Music Soc. E-mail: cpfirst@comcast.net.

FIRST, HARRY, law educator; b. 1945; BA, U. Pa., 1966, JD, 1969. Bar: Pa. 1969, N.Y. 1979. Law clk. to justice Supreme Ct. Pa., 1969-70; atty. U.S. Dept. Justice, Washington, 1970-72; asst. prof. U. Toledo Coll. Law, 1972-76; vis. assoc. prof. NYU Law Sch., N.Y.C., 1976-77, assoc. prof., 1977-79, prof., 1979—; counsel Loeb & Loeb, N.Y.C. and Los Angeles, 1985-99; chief antitrust bur. N.Y. State Office of Atty. Gen., 1999-2001. Mem. editl. bd. Pa. Law Rev. Mem. Pa. Law Rev., Order of Coif, Phi Beta Kappa. Office: NYU Law Sch 40 Washington Sq S New York NY 10012-1099

FIRTH, EVERETT JOSEPH, timpanist; b. Winchester, Mass., June 2, 1930; s. Everett Emanuel and Rosemary (Scandura) F.; m. Olga Kwasniak, June 22, 1960; children— Kelly Victoria, Tracy Kimberly. Mus.B. with distinction, 1952. Faculty head New Eng. Conservatory, 1950—; mem. faculty Berkshire Music Center, 1956—. Pres., CEO Vic Firth Inc. (mfr. and distbr. worldwide drum sticks and mallets); CEO Vic Firth Mfg., Newport, Maine. Solo timpanist, Boston Symphony Orch., 1952—2002, Boston Pops Orch., 1952—2002, with, Boston Symphony Chamber Players; Recs. with, RCA Victor, Mercury, Columbia, Cambridge, Deutsche Grammophon. Mem. ASCAP, Phi Kappa Lambda, Phi Mu Alpha Sinfonia. Home: 3 Pinewood Rd Dover MA 02030-2521 Office: Vic Firth Inc 65 Commerce Way Dedham MA 02026-2953 E-mail: wwwvic@vicfirth.com.

FIRTH, PETER ALAN, lawyer; b. Rockville Center, N.Y., Jan. 7, 1943; s. Richard V. and Patricia (Gilmour) F.; m. Carol A. Smith, Aug. 21, 1965; children: Andrew, Marysusan, Patrick, James, William. AB in Econs., Georgetown U., 1964; LLB, Albany Law Sch., 1967. Bar: N.Y. 1967, U.S. Dist. Ct. (no. dist.) N.Y. 1967, U.S. Tax Ct. 1971, U.S. Ct. Appeals (2d cir.) 1985. Assoc. LaPann & Reardon, Glens Falls, N.Y., 1967-71; ptnr. LaPann, Reardon, FitzGerald & Firth, Glens Falls, 1971-86, LaPann, Reardon, Morris, Fitzgerald & Firth P.C., Glens Falls, 1986-90, Fitzgerald Morris Baker Firth PC, 1990—; asst. dist. atty. Warren County, Lake George, N.Y., 1972-74. V.p. Queensbury Econ. Devel. Corp., 1989-92. Assoc. editor Albany Law Rev., 1966-67. Mem. Albany Diocese Sch. Bd., 1989-91. Mem. ABA, N.Y. State Bar Assn., Warren County Bar Assn. (sec. 1969-72, treas. 1985-89, pres. 1993-94), Assn. Trial Lawyers Am., N.Y. State Trial Lawyers Assn., Am. Arbitration Assn. (arbitrator 1977-2000). Republican. Roman Catholic. Office: Fitzgerald Morris Baker Firth PC PO Box 2017 Glens Falls NY 12801-2017 E-mail: paf@fmbf-law.com.

FIRULLI, ANTHONY B. physiologist, educator; b. New Haven, Sept. 16, 1964; m. Beth Ann Tenseth; children: Nina, Emma. BS in Chemistry and Biology magna cum laude, Roger Williams Coll., Bristol, R.I., 1987; PhD in Molecular Biology, SUNY, Buffalo, 1993. Postdoctoral fellow M.D. Anderson Cancer Ctr., Houston, 1993—95, U. Tex. Southwestern Med. Ctr., Dallas, 1995—97; asst. prof. physiology U. Tex. Health Sci. Ctr., San Antonio, 1997—. Manuscript peer reviewer Developmental Bilology, Differentiation, Arteriosclerosis, Thrombobsis and Vascular Biology, Jour. Gerontology, Jour. Molecular and Cellular Cardiology; invited spkr. in field. Co-editor: Genetic Control of Heart Development, 1997; contbr. articles to profl. jours. Adv. bd. Northside Ind. Sch. Dist. Gifted and Talented Program, 2001—. Grantee NIH, 1999—. Mem.: AAAS, San Antonio Cancer Inst., Am. Heart Assn. (grantee 1998—2001). Office: U Tex Health Sci Ctr 7703 Floyd Curl Dr San Antonio TX 78284-7756

FISCH, EDITH L. lawyer; b. N.Y.C., Mar. 3, 1923; d. Hyman and Clara L. Fisch; m. Steven Ludwig Werner, Dec. 14, 1963 (dec.). BA, Bklyn. Coll., 1945; LLB, Columbia U., 1948, LLM, 1949, J.Sc.D, 1950. Bar: N.Y. 1948, U.S. Supreme Ct. 1957. Grad. asst. Columbia U. Law Sch., N.Y.C., 1948, fellow in law, 1949-50; assoc. firm Conrad & Smith, N.Y.C., 1951-57; pvt. practice N.Y.C., 1957-62, 65—. Asst. prof. law N.Y. Law Sch., 1963-65; counsel firm Brodsky, Lenett & Altman, N.Y.C., 1973-75; pres. Lond Publs., 1958—; ednl. dir. Found. for CLE, 1964-95; editor N.Y.C. Charter and Adminstrv. Code, 1965-81; presenter lectures, seminars and courses for profl. groups. Author: The Cy Pres Doctrine in the U.S., 1950, (with others) State Laws on the Employment of Women, 1953, Lawyers in Industry, 1956, Fisch on New York Evidence, 1959, 2d edit., 1977, supplements, 1978—, (with others) Charities and Charitable Foundations, 1974; contbr. numerous articles to legal publs. County committeewoman 7th Dist. N.Y. Dem. Party, 1949-52; bd. dirs., treas. nat. women's com. Brandeis U., 1964-68. Mem. AAUW, N.Y. Women's Bar Assn. (pres. 1970-71, bd. dirs. 1971-73, adv. coun. 1974—), Nat. Assn. Women Lawyers, Assn. Bar City N.Y. (chmn. libr. com. 1991-94), Bklyn. Coll. Lawyers Group (rec. sec. 1961-63, bd. govs. 1963-65), Am. Arbitration Assn. (nat. panelist), Acad. Polit. Sci., Alumni Assn. Columbia U., Bklyn. Coll. Alumni Assn. Home: 250 W 94th St New York NY 10025-6954 Office: PO Box D-3300 Pomona NY 10970

FISCH, GENE S. psychologist, researcher, statistician; b. N.Y.C., July 24, 1945; s. Joseph Fisch and Sylvia Pritzker. BA, CCNY, 1968; MS, Yeshiva U., 1976; PhD, CUNY, 1982. Rsch. scientist N.Y. State Inst. Behavioral Rsch., Staten Island, NY, 1983—88; dir. rsch. Kings County Hosp., Bklyn., 1988—97; assoc. clin. prof. psychology SUNY Health Sci. Ctr., Bklyn., 1988—97; sr. rsch. scientist Yale U., New Haven, 1997—2003; sr. rsch. statistician NS/LIJ Rsch. Inst., Manhasset, NY, 2002—. Editor: Genetics and Genomics of Neurobehavioral Disorders, 2003; editor, author (spl. jour. issue) Issues in Med. Genetics III, 2001; contbr. articles to profl. jours. Mem.: APA (fellow 2002), SSBP, AAMR, ASHG, Am. Statis. Assn. Achievements include research in longitudinal changes in cognitive-behavioral development in genetic disorders that produce cognitive deficits. Office: NS/LIJ Rsch Inst 1129 Northern Blvd Manhasset NY 11111

FISCH, JOSEPH, lawyer; b. N.Y.C., Apr. 7, 1939; s. Israel Ben Zion and Esther Leah (Spielvogel) F.; m. Norma Potter, Aug. 7, 1960; children: Adam Jeffrey, Jennifer Anne, Rachel Lynne. BA, Tufts U., 1960; JD, NYU, 1963, LLM in Taxation, 1969. Bar: N.J. 1964, U.S. Dist. Ct. N.J. 1964, U.S. Tax Ct. 1966, U.S. Supreme Ct. 1969, U.S. Ct. Appeals (3d cir.) 1971. Law clk. to judge N.J. Superior Ct., Jersey City, 1963-64; assoc. Hannock, Wiseman, Stern and Besser, Newark, 1964-65, Blume and Kalb, Newark, 1965-66; sole practice Somerset, N.J., 1966-87, Kendall Park, N.J., 1987—. Asst. prof. Rutgers U., New Brunswick, N.J., 1971-81; arbitrator Am. Arbitration Assn., 1969-97, N.J. Superior Ct., Somerville, 1985-89; atty. Franklin Twp. Rent Leveling Bd., Somerset, 1980-91; mem. malpractice panel N.J. Supreme Ct., 1980-84; atty. Franklin Twp. Bd. Adjustment, Somerset, 1991-2001. Contbr. articles to law jours. Pres. Franklin Twp. Jaycees, 1967-68, Franklin Housing and Neighborhood Devel. Corp., Somerset, 1975-78, Temple Beth El Men's Club, Somerset, 1971-72, trustee, 1970, 97—. Mem. ABA, N.J. Bar Assn. (chair gen. practice sect. 1990-91, Gen. Practitioner of Yr. 1992), Somerset County Bar Assn., Rotary (Franklin Twp. bd. dirs. 1987-88), Franklin Twp. Rep. Club (pres. 1999-2001). Republican. Jewish. Avocations: tennis, golf, skiing, sailing. Office: 3084 State Route 27 Ste 7 Kendall Park NJ 08824-1657 E-mail: fischjos@aol.com.

FISCH, NATHANIEL JOSEPH, physicist; b. Montreal, Quebec, Can., Dec. 29, 1950; s. Mandel and Helene (Greenfield) F.; m. Tobe Michelle Mann, Aug. 12, 1984; children: Jacob, Benjamin, Adam. BS, MIT, 1972, MS, 1975, PhD, 1978. Researcher Princeton (N.J.) Plasma Physics Lab., 1978-91, assoc. dir. for acad. affairs, 1993—; dir. program in plasma physics Princeton U., 1991—, prof. astrophys. scis., 1991—. Cons. Exxon Rsch. and Engring., Clinton, N.J., 1981-86; vis. scientist IBM, Yorktown Heights, N.Y., 1986. Recipient fellowship Guggenheim Found., 1985, 1992 APS award for Excellence in Plasma Physics, Am. Phys. Soc., 1992. Fellow Am. Phys. Soc. (vice chair divsn. of plasma physics 1996, chair-elect 1997, chair 1998). Achievements include patents in new ways to produce current in plasmas. Office: Princeton U Forrestal Campus PO Box 451 MS30 Princeton NJ 08543-0451 E-mail: nfisch@pppl.gov.

FISCH, ROBERT OTTO, medical educator; b. Budapest, Hungary, June 12, 1925; came to U.S., 1957. s. Zoltan and Irene (Manheim) F.; divorced; 1 dau., Rebecca A. Med. diploma, U. Budapest, 1951; study art, Acad. Fine Arts, Budapest, 1943, Mpls. Coll. Arts and Design, 1970-76. Gen. practice medicine, Hungary, 1951-55; pub. health officer, 1955; pediatrician Hosp. for Premature Children, Budapest, 1956; intern Christ Hosp., Jersey City, 1957-58; intern pediatrics U. Minn. Hosps., 1958-59, researcher, 1959-60, research fellow, 1961; instr. U. Minn. Sch. Medicine, 1961-63, asst. prof., 1963-72, assoc. prof., 1972-79, prof., 1979—, dir. phenylketonuric clinic, 1961-97. Author: Respiratory Diseases; PKU, Child Development (Best Cover Minn. Med. 1975), Light from the Yellow Star: A Lesson of Love from the Holocaust, 1994, The Metamorphosis to Freedom, 2000; contbr. articles to profl. jours.; exhibited art works in various one-man and group shows. Mem. Soc. Pediatric Rsch., Am. Physician Art Assn. (Best of Show award 2002, numerous others). Office: U Minn Mayo Hosp MMC 384 Minneapolis MN 55455 E-mail: fisch001@umn.edu.

FISCHBACH, CHARLES PETER, railway executive consultant, lawyer, arbitrator, mediator; b. Apr. 3, 1939; s. Howard C. and Pauline Lillian (Wasserman) F.; m. Paula Rae Steinhorn, July 15, 1973. BS, U. Wis., 1960, JD, 1967; MA, Rutgers U., 1962. Bar: Wis. 1967, U.S. Supreme Ct. 1974. Pvt. practice, Madison, Wis., 1967-68; labor rels. rsch. analyst and cons. N.Y.C., 1968-70; asst. to exec. officer labor rels. and pers. N.Y.C. Transit Authority, 1970; labor rels. rsch. analyst N.Y.C., 1970-72; exec. dir. Classified Mcpl. Employees Assn. Balt. City, 1972-74; labor rels. cons./arbitrator Balt., 1974-77; dir. labor rels., chief labor rels. officer, spl. labor counsel Chgo., Rock Island and Pacific R.R. Co., 1977-81, dir. pers. and employee rels., spl. labor counsel, 1981-84; dir. adminstrn. and human resources Chgo. Pacific Corp., 1984-85. V.p. Rock Island Improvement Co., 1984—85; dir. Peoria and Bur. Valley R.R. Co., arbitrator, mediator, 1985—; lectr. Am. Mgmt. Assn., Am. Arbitration Assn. Collective Bargaining Inst.; mem. editl. adv. panel Labor Rels. Bull. Aspen Pubs., Inc., 1999—2003. Contbg. editor: The Railway Labor Act, 1995; contbr. articles on labor rels. and arbitration to profl. jours. Mem. pub. sector labor rels. conf. bd. U. Md., 1973—77, Ill. Econ. Bd., 1988—90; mem. landlord-tenant law study commn. State of Md., 1976—77; mem. gov.'s commn. on sci. and tech. State of Ill., 1990—98; advisor Balt. City Charter Revision Commn., 1974—75, Balt. City Commn. on Aging, 1973—74; mem. Chgo. Workforce Bd. City of Chgo., 1999—; mem. coll. edn. adv. coun. Roosevelt U., 1990—93; mem. Chgo. postal customer adv. coun. U.S. Postal Svc., 1994—95; mem. bd. visitors dept. polit. sci. and LaFollette Sch. Pub. Affairs U. Wis., Madison, 2001—, vice chair, 2002—03; chair Com. on Support for Tchg. and Rsch., 2002—; mem. Mayor's Taskforce on Employment of People with Disabilities, City of Chgo., 2002—; chiar Employment Barriers and Model City Work Group, City of Chgo., 2002—. Recipient Am. Jurisprudence prize in corp. law Joint Pubs. of Annotated Reports Sys., 1966, cert. for encouragement of vol. dispute settlement procedures Am. Arbitration Assn., 1981-84; named hon. fellow Harry S. Truman Libr. Inst., 1976. Mem.: ABA, Nat. R.R. Adjustment Bd. (referee), Rutgers Alumni Assn., Wis. Alumni Assn., Am. Found. Automation and Employment, Friends of the Nat. Baseball Hall of Fame and Mus., Soc. Am. Baseball Rsch., Statue of Liberty -Ellis Island Found. (charter), Warner-Lambert (arbitration panel), Montgomery Ward Holding Corp. (alternative dispute resolutiion panel), Loewen Group Internat. (alternative dispute resolution panel), Herzog Transit Svcs./Transport Workers Union Am. (arbitration panel), Am. Airlines (Am. Eagle) and Air Line Pilots Assn. (mem. sys. bd. adjustment), United Air Lines and Internat. Assn. Machinists and Aerospace Workers Am. (mem. sys. bd. adjustment), Ill. Bd. Edn. Panel of Hearing Officers, Indsl. Rels. Rsch. Assn., Nat. Assn. R.R. Referees (regional v.p. 1996—2000), Ill. Pub. Employee Arbitration Mediation Panel, Nat. Mediation Bd. Register of Arbitrators, Fed. Mediation and Conciliation Svc. Roster of Arbitrators, State Bar Wis., Nat. Hist. Soc. Avocations: collecting commemorative coin series and first day medallic covers, collecting commemorative stamps, reading, baseball history and research, art. Office: 1122 N Clark St Ste 2303 Chicago IL 60610-2866 also: Ste 305-PMB 110 3455 Peachtree Industrial Blvd Duluth GA 30096-6501 Fax: 312-943-2539.

FISCHBACH, GERALD D. dean, neurobiology educator; b. New Rochelle, N.Y., Nov. 15, 1938; children: Elissa, Peter, Neal, Mark. AB, Colgate U., 1960; MD, Cornell U., 1965; MA (hon.), Harvard U., 1978. Intern U. Washington Hosp., Seattle, 1965-66; sr. surgeon, Pub. Health Svc., Lab. of Neurophysiology, Nat. Inst. Neurol. Diseases and Stroke NIH, Bethesda, Md., 1966-69; fellow Behavioral Biology Br. Nat. Inst. Child Health, 1969-73; assoc. prof. pharmacology Harvard Med. Sch., Boston, 1978-81, prof., 1978-81; Nathan Marsh Pusey prof. neurobiology, chair dept. neurobiology Harvard Med. Sch., Mass. Gen. Hosp., Boston, 1990-98; Edison prof. neurobiology, chmn. dept. anatomy and neurobiology Washington U. Sch. Med., St. Louis, 1981-90; dir. Neurol. Disorders and Stroke NIH, Bethesda, Md., 1998—2001; v.p. for health and biomed. sciences, dean Columbia U. Coll. of Physicians and Surgeons, NY, 2001—. Mem. exec. com. Program in Cell and Devel. Biology, Harvard Med. Sch., 1974-81; nonresident tutor Leverett House, Harvard Coll., 1974-77; clk. of corp. Marine Biol. Lab., Woods Hole, Mass, 1978-81, trustee, 1982—, exec. com., 1984-89; master Fuller Albright Acad. Soc., Harvard Med. Sch., 1979-81, faculty coun., 1980-81; chmn. Gordon Conf. on Molecular Pharmacology, 1983; dir. Ctr. for Cellular and Molecular Neurobiology, Washington U. Sch. of Med., 1983-90, dir. Jacob Javits Ctr. for Excellence in Neurosci., 1985-90, dir. Ctr. for Higher Brain Function, 1988-90, mem. Med. Ctr. Bd., 1989-90; dir. Neurosci. Ctr., Mass. Gen. Hosp., 1990—; mem. adv. bd. Nat. Spinal Cord Injury Assn., 1978—, Neurology B Study Sect., NIH, 1978-80, Alfred P. Sloan Found., 1984-89, Dept. Biology Adv. Coun., Princeton U., 1984-88, Fidia Rsch. Found., 1986—, McKnight Neurosci. Rsch. Awards Rev. Com., 1986—, Howard Hughes Med. Inst., 1988—, SUNY Health Sci. Ctr. at Bklyn, 1988—, Helen Hay Whitney Found., 1991, Children's Hosp., Boston, 1991; vis. prof. Dept. Pharmacology U. Calif. at San Francisco, 1978; lectr. Disting. Lecture Series in Pharmacology, U. Md. Sch. Medicine, 1978, 25th Ann. Bishop Lecture, Washington U. Sch. Medicine, 1980, Disting. Lecture Series, Dept. Zoology, U. Tex., 1981; invited speaker 5th Ann. Meeting European Neurosci. Assn., 1981 ; Alden Spencer lectr. Coll. Physicians and Surgeons, Columbia, U., 1981, Stephen W. Kuffler lectr. Harvard Med. Sch., 1990, numerous others; assoc. Neurosci. Rsch. Program, 1981—. Editor Jour. Cell Biolog, 1985-86; assoc. editor Devel. Biology, 1974-78, Jour. Neurophysiology, 1975-81, 1989—, Jour. Neurobiology, 1986—; corr. editor Proc. Royal Soc., Series B, London, 1989—; contbr. articles to profl. jours. Recipient Polk award Cornell U., 1965, Mathilde Solowey award Found. for Advanced Edn. in the Scis., NIH, 1975, W. Alden Spencer award Coll. Physicians and Surgeons, Columbia U., 1981; N.Y.State Regents scholar, 1956-60, N.Y. State med. scholar, Cornell U., 1962-65; Salk Inst. non-resident fellow, 1990. Mem. Soc. for Neurosci. (llth ann. lectr., pres.-elect 1982-83, pres. 1983-84), Soc. Gen. Physiologists, Am. Soc. Cell Biology, Phi Beta Kappa. Office: Columbia U Coll of Physicians and Surgeons 630 West 168th St P&S 2-401 New York NY 10032

FISCHBARG, ZULEMA F. pediatrician, educator; b. Buenos Aires, Mar. 22, 1937; arrived in U.S., 1962; d. Naun and Esther (Pollner) Fridman; m. Jorge Fischbarg; children: Gabriel Julian, Victor Ernesto. MD, U. Buenos Aires, 1960. Pediatric intern Children's Hosp., Louisville, 1962-63, resident in pediatrics, 1963, chief resident in pediatrics, 1964; fellow hematology Michael Reese Med. Ctr., Chgo., 1964-66, Presbyn. St. Lukes Hosp., Chgo., 1966-67; fellow pediatric hematology Children's Meml. Hosp., Chgo., 1967-68; asst. clin. pediatrician U. Chgo., 1968-69; instr. in pediatrics Cornell U. Med. Sch., N.Y.C., 1970-72, asst. prof. in pediatrics, 1972-76; assoc. prof. clin. pediatrics Weil Med. Coll., Cornell U., N.Y.C., 1978—; assoc. attending pediatrician N.Y. Hosp., Queens, N.Y.C., 1978—; attending in pediatrics St. John's Hosp./Cath. Med. Ctr., N.Y.C.; med. specialist, sch. health Dept. Health, N.Y.C., 1994—. Assoc. in pediat. Lenox Hill Hosp., N.Y.C.; instr. in medicine Ill. U., Chgo., 1967—68; assoc. attending physician N.Y. Hosp., N.Y.C., 1972—. Fellow: Am. Acad. Pediat. Democrat. Jewish. Home: 175 E 62nd St # 6D New York NY 10021-7626 Office: 37-51 72d St Jackson Heights NY 11372 Fax: 718-651-8225.

FISCHBEIN, CHARLES ALAN, pediatrician; b. Newark, June 5, 1945; s. Martin and Naomi (Litzky) F.; m. Ellen Ruth Niemtzow, Aug. 10, 1969; children: Melissa Paige, Neil Todd. BA in Biology, Case Western Reserve U., 1966; MD, SUNY, Buffalo, 1970. Diplomate Am. Bd. Pediatrics. Resident in pediatrics Children's Hosp. Med. Ctr., Cin., 1970-72, fellow in pediatric cardiology Boston, 1972-74; pvt. practice pediatrics, 1974—; pres. Pediatric Assocs. of Conn., Waterbury, 1982—; asst. clin. prof. U. Conn. Med. Sch., Farmington, Conn., 1974—, Yale U. Sch. Medicine, New Haven, Conn., 1974—; acting co-chief dept. pediatrics St. Mary's Hosp., Waterbury, Conn., 1995-97. Fellow Am. Acad. Pediatrics; mem. AMA, Am. Coll. Sports Medicine. Avocation: mountain biking. Office: Pediatric Assocs Conn PC 160 Robbins St Waterbury CT 06708-2652

FISCHEL, DANIEL NORMAN, publishing consultant; b. Bklyn., N.Y., Apr. 13, 1922; s. Joseph Louis and Liza (Herman) F.; m. Maxine Friedman, May 9, 1943; children: Anne, Jonathan, Lisa. BA, N.Y. U., 1943. Mng. editor Am. Water Works Assn., N.Y.C., 1946-55; editor Dodge Books, N.Y.C., 1955-61; with McGraw-Hill Book Co., N.Y.C., 1962-78, v.p., gen. mgr. profl. and reference books div., 1970-78; pres. Elsevier North-Holland, Inc., N.Y.C., 1978-81, Gordon & Breach Sci. Pubs., N.Y.C., 1982-85; pub. cons., 1981—. Mem. exec. com. tech., sci. and med. div. Am. Assn. Pubs., 1972-78, 79-81 Author: A Practical Guide to Writing and Publishing Professional Books: Business, Technical, Scientific, Scholarly, 1984 Served with AUS, 1943-45. Home and Office: 2200 N Central Rd Fort Lee NJ 07024-7557

FISCHEL, EDWARD ELLIOT, physician, educator; b. N.Y.C., July 29, 1920; s. Joseph L. and Lisa (Herman) F.; m. Pauline Dunieff, Dec. 26, 1943; children: Robert, Janet. BA, Columbia U., 1941, MD, 1944, Sc.D. in Medicine, 1948. Diplomate: Am. Bd. Internal Medicine. Intern Presbyn. Hosp., N.Y.C., 1944-45, asst. resident medicine, 1945-46; asst. in medicine Columbia U. Coll. Physicians and Surgeons, N.Y.C., 1947-50, asso. medicine, 1950-55, assoc. clin. prof. medicine, 1969-72, lectr. medicine, 1972-87; practice medicine specializing in internal medicine and rheumatology; asst. physician Presbyn. Hosp., N.Y.C., 1947-55; asso. clin. prof. medicine Albert Einstein Coll. Medicine, Yeshiva U., N.Y.C., 1957-69, prof. medicine, 1972-80, vis. prof. medicine, 1980-81; dir. dept. medicine Bronx-Lebanon Hosp. Center, Bronx, N.Y., 1954-80; chief dept. medicine Mt. Sinai Hosp., Hartford, Conn. and prof. medicine U. Conn., 1980-83; chief of staff VA Med. Ctr., Northport, N.Y., 1983-91; prof. medicine, assoc. dean vet. affairs SUNY, Stony Brook, 1983-91, prof. medicine emeritus, 1991—. Mem. exec. com. Health Rsch. Coun. City N.Y., 1966-75, chmn. allergy and infectious disease panel, 1968-75; mem. N.Y. State Coun. on Grad. Med. Edn., 1991-94. Contbr. articles to med. jours. Recipient Disting. Svc. award The Arthritis Found., 1978, Silver Medallion Bicentennial Awd., Columbia Univ., Coll. of Physicians, 1967. Fellow ACP, AAAS (past mem. coun.), N.Y. Acad. Medicine (past v.p., trustee 1972-80, plaque 1981); mem. Am. Soc. Clin. Investigation, Am. Assn. Immunologists, Am. Coll. Rheumatology (past pres.), Assn. Am. Med. Colls., Infectious Diseases Soc., Harvey Soc., Soc. Exptl. Biology and Medicine, Am.Fedn. Clin. Rsch., AMA, Bronx County Med. Soc., Am. Heart Assn. (past mem. rsch. com.), N.Y. TB and Health Assn. (past dir.), Phi Beta Kappa, Alpha Omega Alpha. Achievements include research in rheumatic fever—pathogenesis, treatment and prevention; effect of cortisone on antibody production and inflammation, serum complement in nephritis and non-specific (and nonimmunologic) inflammatory conditions, antiinflammatory and antirheumatic effects of aspirin. Home: 220 Little Neck Rd Centerport NY 11721-1145 E-mail: eefischel@aol.com.

FISCHEL, RICHARD JEFFREY, thoracic surgeon; b. L.A., Oct. 19, 1959; s. Maarna Rae Fischel; m. Lulu Fischel, July 18 1987; children: Rachel Marissa, Christina Jenelle, Ricky Jr. BS summa cum laude, U. Calif., Riverside, 1981; MD, UCLA, 1984; PhD, U. Minn., Mpls., 1995. Diplomate Am. Bd. Thoracic

Surgery, Am. Bd. Surgery. Intern in gen. surgery U. Minn., Mpls., 1984, resident in gen. surgery, 1985—92, fellow in thoracic surgery, 1992—95; dir. Lung Ctr. Chapman Med. Ctr., Orange, Calif., 1995—, attending thoracic surgeon, 1995—; assoc. dir. Lung Ctr. Cedars Sinai Med. Ctr., L.A., 1996—, attending thoracic surgeon, 1996—; clin. asst. prof. thoracic surgery UCLA, 1995—, U. Calif. Irvine, 1997—; chief surgery Chapman Med. Ctr., Orange, Calif., 2003—. Kolf young investigator ASAIO. Editor Video Assisted Surgery, 1995—; contbr. articles to profl. jours., chpts. to books; patentee in field. Dir. Chapman Found., Irvine, 1997—; vol. soccer ref. AYSO, Irvine, 1996, 97, 98, 99. Fellow in thoracic rsch. U. Minn., Mpls., 1987. Fellow ACS, Soc. Thoracic Surgeons, Am. Coll. Chest Physicians; mem. ACS Oncology Group, Am. Soc. Artificial Internal Organs, 21st Century Surg. Soc., Am. Soc. Artificial Internal Organs, Orange County Med. Assn., L.A. Med. Assn., Am. Youth Soccer Org. Avocations: skiing, snorkeling, hiking, biking, tennis. Office: 2601 E Chapman Ave Orange CA 92869 E-mail: cmclungctr@aol.com.

FISCHEL, WILLIAM ALAN, economics educator; b. Bethlehem, Pa., Apr. 10, 1945; s. John Jacob and Lois T. (Yerger) F.; m. Janice M. Goldberg, Aug. 5, 1973; 1 child, Joshua. BA, Amherst Coll., 1967; PhD, Princeton U., 1973. Prof. Dartmouth Coll., Hanover, N.H., 1973—, dept. chair, 2000—02, Patricia F. and William B. Hale prof. in arts and sci., 2002—. Vis. assoc. prof. U. Calif., Davis, 1980-81; vis. prof. U. Calif., Santa Barbara, 1985-86, U. Wash., Seattle, 1998-99; adj. prof. Vt. Law Sch., South Royalton, 1985, 87-92. Author: Economics of Zoning Laws, 1985, Regulatory Takings, 1995, Homevoter Hypothesis, 2001; mem. editl. bd. Land Econs. Jour., 1984—, Ea. Econ. Jour., 1992—. Mem. Zoning Bd., Town of Hanover, N.H., 1987-97, chmn., 1993-97. Olin fellow U. Calif., Berkeley, 1991-92. Mem. Phi Beta Kappa, Psi Upsilon. Home: 2 Read Rd Hanover NH 03755-1909 Office: Dartmouth Coll Dept Of Econs Hanover NH 03755 E-mail: Bill.Fischel@Dartmouth.Edu.

FISCHELL, ROBERT ELLENTUCH, physicist; b. N.Y.C., Feb. 10, 1929; s. Philip and Julia (Ellentuch) Fischell; m. Marian Standard; children: David R., Tim A., Scott J.S. BSMechE cum laude, Duke U., 1951; MS in Physics, U. Md., 1953, ScD (hon.), 1996. Physicist U.S. Naval Ordnance Lab., Silver Spring, Md., 1951—56; prin. staff engr. Emerson Rsch. Labs., Silver Spring, 1956—60; various staff positions Applied Physics Lab., Johns Hopkins U., Laurel, Md., 1959—97, prin. profl. physicist, 1962—, chief engr. space dept., 1972—80, chief tech. transfer space dept., 1978—88; pres., chmn. bd. MedInnovations, Inc., Dayton, Md., 1988—90; chmn. bd. MedInTec, Inc., Dayton, Md., 1990—; pres. Fischell Biomed. LLC, 2000—; prof. practice of engring. U. Md., 2002—. Chmn. bd., v.p. R & D Cathco, Inc., 1991—; pres., chmn. bd. IsoStent, Inc., Dayton, Md., 1993—; chmn. emeritus NeuroPace, Inc., Dayton, 1997—; cons. Cordis, a J&J Co., 1998—; expert witness Brown and Bain, Palo Alto, Calif., 1992—93; rsch. assoc. in medicine Johns Hopkins U. Sch. Medicine, 1983—95, Yale U. Sch. Medicine, 1988—95; mem. exec. panel Chief of Naval Ops., Washington, 1983—87; expert witness Fish and Neave, N.Y.C., 1986—92; field reviewer for orphan products FDA, 1984—90; mem. rsch. com. Md. affiliate Am. Heart Assn., 1985—87; mem. tech. com. on space guidance and control AIAA, 1972—75, chmn. nat. conf., 1973; mem. space com. Internat. Fedn. Automatic Control, 1970—75; mem., chmn. photovoltaic specialities com. IEEE, 1959—72; chmn., pres. Angel Med. Sys., Inc., 2002—, Neuralieve, Inc., 2002—. Author over 50 tech. publs.; assoc. editor: AIAA Jour Spacecraft and Rockets, 1972—75; holder 110 patents in field of biomed. engring., biomed. devices and spacecraft. Bd. visitors U. Md., 1997—; trustee U. Md. Found., 2000—. Named Disting. Citizen of Yr., "M" Club U. Md., 1984; named to Space Tech. Hall of Fame, U.S. Space Found., 1988; recipient Tech. Achievement award, ASME, 1962, Outstanding Young Engr. award, Washington Capitol area, 1963, awards for most significant inventions, Indsl. Rsch. mag., 1967, 1970, 1973, Inventor of Yr. award, Intellectual Property Owners Assn., 1984, Gold medal for contbn. to aerospace sci. and tech., N.Y. Acad. Sci., 1987, Exceptional Engring. award for MAGSAT satellite, NASA, 1980, Individual Achievement award for human tissue stimulator, 1982, Exceptional Engring. medal, 1984, Space Act prize, 1984, Disting. Engring. Alumnus award, Duke U., 1992. Mem.: NAE, N.Y. Acad. Scis., Internat. Soc. for Artificial Organs, Beta Omega Sigma, Pi Tau Sigma, Sigma Pi Sigma, Pi Mu Epsilon, Tau Beta Pi, Phi Beta Kappa. Avocations: tennis, sailing. Office: MedInTec Inc 14600 Viburnum Dr Dayton MD 21036-1247 E-mail: mfischell@aol.com.

FISCHELL, TIM ALEXANDER, cardiologist; b. Washington, Feb. 10, 1956; s. Robert Ellentuch and Marian (Standard) F.; m. Anne Elizabeth Arbetter, Sept. 23, 1984; children: Evan Daniel, Jonathan Morris. AB, Cornell U., 1977, MD, 1981. Diplomate Am. Bd. Internal Medicine (subspeciality cardiovas. disease and interventional cardiology). Intern internal medicine Harvard/Mass. Gen. Hosp., Boston, 1981-82, resident, 1982-84; fellow cardiology Stanford (Calif.) U., 1984-87, asst. prof. medicine, 1987-92; assoc. prof. medicine Vanderbilt U., Nashville, 1992-96; dir. Heart Inst.-Borgess Med. Ctr., Mich. State U., Kalamazoo, 1996—, prof. medicine, 1996—. Med. adv. bd. Scimed, Mpls., 1992—, Cardima, Inc., Fremont, Calif., 1993—, Isostent, Inc., San Carlos, Calif., 1995—. Patentee in field; contbr. articles to profl. jours., chpts. to books. Recipient Fischbach Residency Scholarship, 1986, Nat.Rsch. Svc. award grant NIH, 1986-87, clin. investigator award NIH, 1987-92, biomed. rsch. support grant NIH/Stanford U., 1988-90; Inventor of Yr. prize Thoraxcenter Course on Intracoronary Stenting, Rotterdam, The Netherlands, 1996. Fellow Am. Coll. Cardiology, Soc. Cardiac Angiography and Interventions, Andreas Gruntzig Soc., Am. Heart Assn. (coun. on circulation, advanced fellowship award Calif. affiliate 1987, grant in aid award 1988-90), Phi Beta Kappa, Phi Kappa Phi, Alpha Omega Alpha. Avocations: basketball, tennis, skiing, golf. Home: 701 Embury Rd Kalamazoo MI 49008 Office: Mich State U Heart Inst Borgess Med Ctr Kalamazoo MI 49001 E-mail: taf1@net-link.net.

FISCHER, A(LBERT) ALAN, family physician; b. Indpls., June 30, 1928; 4 children. MD, Ind. U., 1952. Diplomate Am. Bd. Family Practice. Intern St. Vincent Hosp., Indpls., 1952—53; pvt. practice, 1953—70; dir. family practice residency program St. Vincent Hosp., Indpls., 1969—75; prof. family medicine, chmn. dept. Ind. U., Indpls., 1974—90; med. dir. Lakeview Manor, Indpls., 1970—. Pvt. practice family medicine, 1953—. Mem.: AMA, Am. Acad. Family Physicians (v.p. 1971—72), Inst. Medicine-NAS (mem. nat. joint practicing commn.).

FISCHER, ALFRED GEORGE, geology educator; b. Rothenburg, Germany, Dec. 10, 1920; came to U.S., 1935; s. George Erwin and Thea (Freise) F.; m. Winnifred Varney, Aug. 26, 1939; children: Joseph Fred, George William, Lenore Ruth Fischer Walsh. Student, Northwestern Coll., Watertown, Wis., 1935-37; BA, U. Wis., 1939, MA, 1941; PhD, Columbia U., 1950. Instr. Va. Poly. Inst. and State U., Blacksburg, 1941-43; geologist Stanolind Oil & Gas Co., Kans. and Fla., 1943-46; instr. U. Rochester, N.Y., 1947-48; from instr. to asst. prof. U. Kans., Lawrence, 1948-51; sr. geologist Internat. Petroleum, Peru, 1951-56; prof. geology Princeton (N.J.) U., 1956-84, U. So. Calif., Los Angeles, 1984—. Co-Author: Invertebrate Fossils, 1952, The Permian Reef Complex, 1953, Electron Micrographs of Limestone, 1967; editor: Petroleum and Global Tectonics, 1975. Recipient Verrill medal Yale U. Fellow Geol. Soc. Am. (Penrose medal 1993), Geol. Soc. London (hon., Lyell medal 1992), Soc. Econ. Paleontologists (hon., Twenhofel medal); mem. AAAS, NAS, U.S. Nat. Acad. Sci., Am. Assn. Petroleum Geologists, Paleontol. Soc. (medal 1995), German Geol. Soc. (Leopold von Buch medal), Geol. Union (Gustav Steinmann medal 1992), Mainz Acad. Sci. Lit. (corr.), Lincei Acad. Rome (fgn.), Sigma Xi. Home: 1736 Perch St San Pedro CA 90732-4218 Office: U So Calif Dept Earth Scis Univ Park Los Angeles CA 90089-0001

FISCHER, ANGELA BROWN, business executive, civic volunteer; b. Providence, Mar. 8, 1938; d. John Nicholas and Anne (Kinsolving) Brown; m. Edwin Garvin Fischer, May 4, 1963; children: Olivia Fischer Fox, Edwin Garvin Jr., Chad B. BA, Harvard-Radcliffe Coll., 1960. Clk., dir., co-founder The Boston Cookery, Inc., 1979-84; dir. Le Dioyte Land Co., Omaha, 1978-88, Manisses Comms. Group, Providence, 1992-99, van Liew Capital, Providence, 1984—; mng. ptnr. Brown Land Co., Providence, 1979—; pres. Brown & Fischer Corp., Providence, 1979—. Trustee Hope Found., Providence, 1988—; v.p. Preservation Soc. Newport County, 1988—; dir. steering com. chair Redwood Libr. and Athenaeum, Newport, 1993—; treas., co-founder The J.N. Brown Ctr. for the Study of Am. Civilization, Providence, 1985-94; chair Gov.'s Commn. for Preserving the State House, Providence, 1993—; bd. govs. R.I. Commodores, Providence, 1987—; corp. mem. Brown U., Providence, 1980-93; bd. dirs., chair numerous coms. Preserve R.I., Inc., Providence, 1979-95, 97—. Recipient John H. Chaffee Meml. Svc. award R.I. Hist. Soc., 2000. Avocations: sailing, travel, reading.

FISCHER, AVRAHAM, software engineer; b. Ludus, Romania, Feb. 23, 1943; arrived in Israel, 1983; s. Herman and Edith (Genad) F.; m. Eva Jakobovits, Dec. 30, 1968; children: Robert, Ilan. MSc in Electronics, Politechnical Inst., Bucharest, 1967, postgrad., 1972, Haifa (Israel) U., 1992. Registered engr., Israel. Engr. Electromagnetica, Bucharest, 1967-73, software engr., 1973-75; sr. software engr. Ministry of Turism Computing Ctr., Bucharest, 1975-83; software engr. Elscint Ltd., Haifa, 1984-89; sr. software engr. Fibronics Ltd., Haifa, 1989-93, project mgr., 1993-99; prin. engr. Multiport Corp., Boston, 1999-2000; staff engr. Mobilian Corp., Yokne'am, Israel, 2000—02, Hillsboro, Oreg., 2002—03. Cons. for data bank design and implementation Haifa U. Rsch. Authority, Ctr. for Youth Policy, Haifa, 1985-88. Co-author: Optimizing Work Breakdown in Industry for Small Production Series, 1970. Lt. Romania Army, 1967-68. Achievements include development of interactive algorithm for calculating the spare parts and raw material requirements for a given technology and a product plan, suitable for poor computing configurations (only tape drives-no hard disks). Home: Albert Schweitzer 52/4 34991 Haifa 34995 Israel Office: Mobilian Corp 7431 NW Evergreen Pkwy Hillsboro OR 97124 E-mail: ady@mobilian.com.

FISCHER, BERND JURGEN, history educator; b. Bunde, Westphalen, Germany, Jan. 27, 1952; came to U.S., 1961; s. Emil and Gertrud (Einars) F. BA, U. Calif., Santa Barbara, 1973, MA, 1975, PhD, 1982. Asst. prof. European history Ctrl. Mich. U., 1982-83; instr., chair social sci. divsn. Wenatchee Valley Coll., 1983-86; asst. prof. Ea. European history U. Western Ont., London, Can., 1986-87, McGill U., Montreal, 1988, U. Hartford, Conn., 1989-93; prof., chair dept. history Ind. U., Ft. Wayne, 1993—, mem. exec. com. Russian and East European Inst., 1994-96. Mem. adv. bd. Ctr. for Albanian Studies, U. London. Author: King Zog and the Struggle for Stability in Albania, 1984 (transl. into Albanian 1996), Albania At War, 1939-1945, 2000 (transl. into Albanian 2000); contbg. author: Eastern European Nationalism in the 20th Century, 1995; editor: Albanian Studies: International Registry of Scholars and Research, 1998—; editor CLIO Jour. Lit., History and Philosophy of History, 1995—; also articles. Rsch. grantee Am. Coun. Learned Socs., 1989, NEH, 1992; travel grantee Mellon Found., 1995. Mem. Soc. for Albanian Studies (exec. com. 1990—, v.p. 1998—), Internat. Assn. for S.E. European Studies (exec. bd., U.S. com. 1993—). Avocations: travel, tennis, skiing. Home: 1517 Columbia Ave Fort Wayne IN 46805-5218 Office: Ind U Dept History Fort Wayne IN 46805 E-mail: fischer@1dfw.edu., bernd9@comcast.net.

FISCHER, CAREY MICHAEL, lawyer; b. Cleve., Apr. 4, 1950; s. Ernest and Kitty (Lehrer) F.; m. Ellen Schoenfeld, Aug. 17, 1975; children: Jordan, Douglas. BA, Tulane U., 1972; JD, U. Miami, 1975. Bar: Fla. 1975, U.S. Dist. Ct. (so. dist. 3L) Fla. 1976, U.S. Ct. Appeals (5th and 11th cirs.) 1981, U.S. Supreme Ct. 1986. Assoc. Ferrero, Middlebrooks & Houston, Ft. Lauderdale, Fla., 1975-77, Ferrero, Middlebrooks & Strickland, Ft. Lauderdale, 1977-82, ptnr., 1983-85, Ferrero, Middlebrooks, Strickland & Fischer, Ft. Lauderdale, 1985-90; pvt. practice Carey M. Fischer, P.A., Ft. Lauderdale, 1990—. Mem. long range planning and budget Jewish Fedn. of Ft. Lauderdale, 1989-90; bd. dirs. Jewish Community Ctr., 1987; pres. Temple Emanu El of Greater Ft. Lauderdale, 1987; exec. bd. Temple Bat Yam, East Ft. Lauderdale, 1996—; Broward trustee Performing Arts for Community Edn., 1992-94. Named Legal Exec. of Yr. Broward County Legal Secs. Assn., 1983. Mem. Fla. Bar (jud. selection and tenure com.), Broward County Bar Assn. (co-chmn. pub. rels. com. 1989-90, co-chmn. trial lawyers sect. 1990-92), Broward County Trial Lawyers Assn. (bd. dirs. 1985—, pres.-elect 1990, pres. 1991), U. Miami Sch. Law Alumnae Assn. (bd. dirs. 1990-94), Adopt-A-Family of Fla., Inc. (bd. dirs. Broward County chpt. 1990), Am. Bd. Trial Advocates (circuit civil mediator, qualified arbitrator). Avocations: music, writing. Address: 750 SE 3rd Ave Ste 300 Fort Lauderdale FL 33316-1153

FISCHER, CARL, graphic designer, photographer, actor; b. N.Y.C., May 3, 1924; s. Joseph Albert and Irma (Schwerin) F.; m. Marilyn Wolf, Oct. 30, 1949; children— Kim Alison Lloyd George, Douglas James, Kenneth Lee. BFA, Cooper Union Sch. Art, 1948; postgrad., Ctrl. St. Martins Coll. Art & Design, London, 1952. Designer Columbia Records, 1948, Look mag., 1949-51; asst. art dir. William H. Weintraub & Co., 1952-54; art dir. Sudler & Hennessey, 1954-56, Grey Advt., 1956-58; owner Carl Fischer Photography Inc., N.Y.C., 1960—. Vis. instr. art Cooper Union; TV, film dir.; William A. Reedy Meml. lectr. Rochester Inst. Tech. Exhibited Mus. Modern Art, 1965, Whitney Mus. Am. Art, 1974; represented in permanent collections, Met. Mus. Art, Rose Art Mus., Amherst, Mass., Internat. Ctr. of Photography, N.Y.C., Internat. Mus. Photography at George Eastman House, Rochester, Spencer Mus. Art, Lawrence, Kans.; contbg. editorial photographer various mags. including London Observer, London Sunday Times, Time, Life, Fortune, Esquire, New York. With AUS, 1942-45, PTO. Fulbright grant, 1951; recipient Profl. Achievement citation Cooper Union, 1966, St. Gaudens medal, 1969, Mark Twain Jour. award, 1971, Cleo award, 1980. Mem. Actors Equity Assn., SAG, Dirs. Guild, Art Dirs. Club (past pres., gold and silver medals), Century Assn. Office: 121 E 83d St New York NY 10028-0821 E-mail: fischerny@aol.com.

FISCHER, CARL ROBERT, retired health care facility administrator; b. Rahway, N.J., Nov. 15, 1939; s. Robert Carlton and Elsie Marie (Wolfarth) F.; m. Lynn Elaine Ekstrand, Mar. 12, 1966; children: Kristen, Leslie, Meredith, Kelly. BSN, Wagner Coll., 1964; MS, SUNY-Buffalo, 1966; MPH, Yale U., 1968. With Yale-New Haven Hosp., 1968-77, assoc. dir., 1975-77; exec. assoc. adminstr. U. Cin. Med. Ctr., 1977-80; exec. dir. clin. programs U. Ark. for Med. Scis., Little Rock, 1980-86; assoc. v.p. health scis., CEO Med. Coll. of Va. Hosps., Richmond, 1986-99; exec. v.p. corp. functions VCU Health Sys., 1999—2002; ret., 2003. Active Univ. Hosps., Richmond, 1986-2002; bd. dirs. Univ. Health Systems Consortium, 1986-2002, exec. com. 1994-2000, chmn. bd. dirs. 1997-98, chmn. supply and svcs. divsn., 1988-89, 95-96; mem. exec. com. Nat. Assn. Pub. Hosps., 1999-2002. Pres. Ctrl. Va. Health Planning Agy., 1991-93, mem.-at-large, 1997-2002, exec. com., 2000-2002; bd. dirs. Richmond Luth. Home, 2000-01. Mem. Am. Assn. Med. Colls., Am. Hosp. Assn., Va. Hosp. Assn. (bd. dirs. 1986-91, 99-2000, chmn. coun. on adminstrn. and health planning 1988, coun. on assn. devel. 1987-88, physician liaison com. 1989-90, chmn. ctrl. Va. regional planning coun. 1997-99). Lutheran. Office: VCU Health Sys Va Commonwealth U PO Box 980451 Richmond VA 23298-0451

FISCHER, CHARLOTTE FROESE, researcher, educator; b. Nikolajevka, Bachmut, Ukraine, Sept. 21, 1929; arrived in Can., 1930; came to U.S., 1974; d. John David and Helen (Thiessen) F.; m. Patrick Carl Fischer, Apr. 2, 1967; 1 child, Carolyn. BA, U. B.C., Vancouver, Can., 1952, MA, 1954; PhD, Cambridge U., England, 1957. Instr. math. to prof. U. B.C., 1957-68; prof. applied analysis, computer sci., & applied math. U. Waterloo, Ont., Can., 1968-75; prof. computer sci. Pa. State U., 1974-79; prof. computer sci., math., physics & astronomy Vanderbilt U., Nashville, Tenn., 1980-96, rsch. prof. computer sci., 1996—. Cons. Pacific Oceanographic Group, Nanaimo, B.C., Can., 1960-62; rsch. fellow Harvard Coll. Obs., Cambridge, 1963-64. Author: Introduction to Programming the IBM 1620, 1964, The Hartree-Fock Method for Atoms, 1977, Computational Atomic Spectroscopy, 1997; contbr. articles and papers to profl. jours.; editor Computing Reviews, 1968-78, Computer Physics Comm., 1968-2000. Fellow Alfred Sloan Found., 1964-68, Fulbright Found., 1998-99; grantee U.S. Dept. Energy, 1978—. Fellow Am. Phys. Soc.; mem. Royal Physiographical Soc. Lund. Home: 221 Burlington Pl Nashville TN 37215-1859 Office: Vanderbilt Univ Box 1679B Nashville TN 37235-1679 E-mail: Charlotte.F.Fischer@Vanderbilt.edu.

FISCHER, CLARE, composer; b. Durand, Mich., Oct. 22, 1928; s. Cecil Harold and Luella Blanche (Roussin) F.; children: Lee Clare, Brent Sean Cecil, Tahlia Georgienne Marguerite Bianca; m. Donna Van Ringelesteyn. MusB in Music Composition and Theory, Mich. St. U., 1952, MusM, 1955; MusD (hon.), Mich. State U., 1999. Arranger albums for Donald Byrd, George Shearing, Dizzy Gilespie, The Hi-lo's, Singers Unlimited, Cal Tjader, João Gilberto, Charles Lloyd, Chaka Khan, Prince, Michael Jackson, Robert Palmer, Paul McCartney, Paula Abdul, Earl Klugh, The Jacksons, Lembranças and Just Me-Solo Piano Excursions on Concord Records, Memento on Discovery, Rockin' in Rhythm on JVC Records, The Latin Side, Clare Fischer's Jazz Corps and Symbiosis, After the Rain, On a Turquoise Cloud, America The Beautiful; arranger movies for Prince; composer orchestral The Duke, Sweé Pea and Me, Tahlia, Sonatine for Clarinet and Piano, Time-piece, Suite for Cello and String Orch., others. E-mail: clarefischer@thegrid.net.

FISCHER, CRAIG LELAND, physician; b. Bklyn., Feb. 17, 1937; s. Emil Carl and Ruth Barbara (Minarcik) F.; m. Sandra Lucile Canfield, Feb. 17, 1962; children: Craig L. Jr., Emil Lewis, Lisa Anne. BS, Kans. State U., 1958; MD, U. Kans., 1962. Diplomate Nat. Bd. Med. Examiners, Am. Bd. Family Practice; cert. anatomic and clin. pathology, nuclear medicine. Intern in anatomic pathology Kansas U. Med. Ctr., 1962-63, resident in anatomic pathology, 1963-64, rsch. fellow in pathology (pub. health svc.), nuclear medicine, 1962-64, 1965-66; resident in clin. pathology, Meth. Hosp. Baylor U. Coll. Medicine, 1967-68; rsch. med. officer Manned Spacecraft Ctr., NASA, Houston, 1965-68, pathologist, chief clin. labs., 1968-71; chief med. ops. Johnson Space, NASA, Houston, 1980-82; assoc. dir. labs. to dir. labs. Eisenhower Med. Ctr., Rancho Mirage, Calif., 1971-78, dir. nuclear med., 1975-78; gen. practice medicine Palm Desert, Calif., 1978-80; dir. labs. J.F. Kennedy Hosp., Indio, Calif., 1982-99; gen. practice medicine Indio, Calif., 1982-99; dir. post grad. edn. J.F. Kennedy Hosp., 1982-92; dir. Fischer and Yao Cons. Pathologists, Indio, 1987-89; pres. Fischer Assocs., Cons. in Pathology, Indio, 1989-95; ptnr. Fischer and Starke Assocs., Indio, 1995-99; aviation med. examiner FAA, 1991-99; asst. dir. space medicine NASA Johnson Space Ctr., 1999—2001, chief, Space Medicine & health Care Systems Office, 2001—03, asst. dir. internat. space medicine, 2003—. Clin. prof. dept. preventive medicine and cmty. health U. Tex. Med. Br., Galveston, 2002-; asst. clin. prof. U. Calif., Irvine, 1986-99; mem. sci. adv. bd. Dept. Air Force, Washington, 1986-90, NAE, NRC; mem. Air Force Studies Bd., Washington, 1987-93; mem. aerospace med. adv. com. Office Space Scis. and Applications, NASA Hdqrs., Washington, 1988-93, chmn. operational medicine discipline working group, Life Scis. Directorate, 1988-92, mem. Shuttle-Mir Joint Sci. Working Group, 1993-94, mem. Adv. Coun. Task Force on the Shuttle-Mir Rendezvous and Docking Missions, 1995; mem. Mir Sci. Program Rev. Panel, 1993-98; mem. Internat. Space Sta. Task Force (Stafford Commn.), 1998—; chmn. multinat. med. ops. panel Internat. Space Sta., 2000-; cons. lab. medicine porject tektite U.S. Dept. Interior, 1969-70. Contbr. numerous articles to profl. jours. Capt. USAR, 1964-66, hon. discharge, 1966; lt. col. USAFR, 1983-97, hon. discharge, 1997. Recipient Group Achievement award NASA Manned Spacecraft Ctr., 1966, 69, 70, Group Achievement award Gemini support team NASA Manned Spacecraft Ctr., Apollo 7 Flight Ops. Team award NASA Manned Spacecraft Ctr., 1969, Sustained Superior Achievement award NASA Manned Spacecraft Ctr., 1969, Superior Achievement award, 1969, Skylab Group Achievement award NASA Johnson Space Ctr., 1974, Presdl. medal of Freedom Apollo 13 Mission Ops. Team, 1970, Group Achievement award NASA Space Shuttle Launch and Ops. Team NASA Manned Spacecraft Ctr., 1982, Meritorious Civilian Svc. award Dept. of Air Force, 1990. Fellow Am. Coll. Preventive Medicine, Am. Coll. Nuc. Physicians, Coll. Am. Pathologists, Am. Soc. Clin. Pathologists (CCE Commr.'s medal 1989), Aerospace Med. Assn., Riverside County Med. Assn. (councilor 1984-89, pres. 1990-91, alt. delegate 1991-96, councilor 1996-99, Outstanding Contbn. to Medicine award 1996), Palm Springs Acad. Medicine (pres. 1988-89). Republican. Avocations: sailing, tennis, flying. Home: 4402 N Pine Brook Way Houston TX 77059-3040 Office: NASA SD Johnson Space Ctr SD Houston TX 77058 E-mail: craig-L.fischer@nasa.gov.

FISCHER, DAVID JON, lawyer; b. Danville, Ill., July 27, 1952; s. Oscar Ralph and Sarah Pauline (Pomerantz) F. BA, U. Miami, 1974, JD, 1977. Bar: Fla. 1977, Iowa 1978, (mid. dist.) Fla. 1993, U.S. Ct. Appeals (8th cir.) 1978, U.S. Ct. Appeals (D.C. cir.) 1979, U.S. Ct. Appeals (llth cir.) 1984, U.S. Tax Ct. 1987, Ga. 1989, U.S. Dist. Ct. (no. dist.) Ga. 1990, U.S. Supreme Ct. 1990, U.S. Dist. Ct. (mid. dist.) Fla., 1993. Atty. Iowa Dept. Social Svcs., Des Moines, 1978; assoc. Parrish & Del Gallo P.C., Des Moines, 1978-79, Donald M. Murtha & Assocs., Washington, 1979-80; assoc. editor Lawyers Coop. Pub. Co., Washington, 1980-82; pvt. practice law Washington, 1982-83, Des Moines, 1983-84, Atlanta, 1984-93; pvt. practice Tampa, Fla., 1993; asst. dist. legal counsel Fla. Dept. Health and Rehab. Svcs., Largo, 1993-95; pvt. practice law Atlanta, 1995-2000; case law editor LexisNexis Group, 2001—. Part-time atty. Fla. Dept. of Children and Families, 1996-2000; prof. John Marshall Law Sch., Atlanta, 1986-88; instr. legal studies program dept. ins. and risk mgmt. Ga. State U., 1988-93, instr. aviation adminstrn. program Coll. Pub. and Urban Affairs, 1989-93; apptd. gen. counsel Techwerks, Inc., Mo., 1990-92; instr. Bridge the Gap seminar, Inst. CLE in Ga., 1993; presenter State of Fla. Dept. Health and Rehabilitative Svcs. Dist. Legal Counsel Workshop, 1994, 96, 97; spkr. Clearwater Bar Assn., 1993, 94, 95. Author: The Aeronaut's Law Handbook, 1986, (with others) Georgia Corporate Practice Forms for the Small Business Attorney, 1992; contbg. editor Balloon Life mag., 1986-96; editor: (suppl.) Georgia Corporate Forms, 1993—, Florida Criminal Sentencing, 1997-99; editor: Georgia Corporate Forms, 2d edit., 1999. Vol. liaison Atlanta Com. for the Olympic Games, 1991-92. Mem. ABA (sect. com. 1980-82), Fed. Bar Assn., Iowa Bar Assn., State Bar Ga., Atlanta Bar Assn., Fla. Bar Assn., D.C. Bar Assn., Polk County Bar Assn., Pros. Attys. Coun. Ga. (tech. editor Computer Crime Jour.), U. of Miami Alumni Assn., Balloon Fedn. Am. (chmn. com. 1986-91), Carolinas Balloon Assn., Ga. Balloon Assn. (chmn. com. 1985-90), Chesapeake Balloon Assn., Great Ea. Balloon Assn., Alpha Epsilon Pi (hon., faculty advisor). Jewish. Avocations: hot air balloon pilot, writing, competitive sports. E-mail: theschnauzers@yahoo.com., davidjon.fischer@lexisnexis.com.

FISCHER, DAVID SEYMOUR, internist, consultant; b. Bklyn., May 13, 1930; s. Simon and Charolotte Fischer; m. Iris Liquerman, June 1, 1958; children: Karen, Louise, Francie. AB, Williams Coll., 1951; MD, Harvard U., 1955. Diplomate Am. Bd. Internal Medicine, Am. Bd. Med. Oncology, Am. Bd. Hematology. Intern Kings County Hosp., 1955-56; resident U. Utah, 1956-57, Montefiore Hosp., Bronx, N.Y., 1957-58; fellow U. Wash., Seattle, 1958-59, Yale U., 1962-64; attending physician Yale New Haven Hosp.; emeritus attending physician Hosp. St. Raphael. Cons. Yale Comprehensive Cancer Ctr., New Haven, 1978—; clin. prof. medicine Yale U. Author: Cancer Chemotherapy Handbook, 6th edit., 2003, Follow-Up of Cancer, 4th edit., 1996; also articles; editor, author: Cancer Therapy, 1982. Pres. Conn. divsn. Am. Cancer Soc., 1981; pres. med. staff Hosp. St. Raphael, New Haven, 1980; pres. med. adv. bd. Jewish Home for Aged, 1983-85; mem. adv. bd. Leukemia Soc. South Cen. Conn., 1984—; pres. Congregation Bikur Cholim Sheveth Achim, 1983-85; pres. Hebrew Congregation of Woodmont, 1995—. Capt. U.S. Army, 1959-61. Recipient Harris award Yale New Haven Hosp., 1974, Bronze medal Am. Cancer Soc., 1982, Ptnrs. in Progress award Conn. Leukemia-Lymphoma Soc., 2002. Fellow ACP; mem. AMA, Am. Soc. Hematology, Am. Soc. Clin. Oncology (chmn. pub. issues), Conn. State Med. Soc., Conn. Oncology Assn. (pres. 1979-80), New Haven County Med. Soc., New Haven Med. Assn. (pres. 1990-91). Jewish.

FISCHER, DUNCAN KINNEAR, neurosurgeon; b. Chapel Hill, N.C., Sept. 14, 1957; s. Newton Duchan and Janet (Jordan) F.; m. Anne Holmes Billington, Sept. 10, 1983; children: Luke Duncan, Kent Billington, Duncan Newton II. AB, Princeton U., 1979; MPhil, Yale U., 1982, MD, PhD, 1986. Cert. in neurosurgery. Intern in surgery Baylor Coll. Medicine Affiliated Hosps., Houston, 1986-87, resident in neurosurgery, 1987-92; rsch. assoc. Baylor Coll. Medicine, Houston, 1988-92; neurosurgeon San Angelo (Tex.) Cmty. Med. Ctr. and Neurosurg. Ctr., 1992—. Contbr. numerous articles to profl. publs. Med. Scientist Tng. Program scholar NIH, ACS scholar. Fellow ACS; mem. Harvey Cushing Soc., Am. Assn. Neurol. Surgeons, Sigma Xi, Phi Beta Kappa. Republican. Episcopalian. Achievements include extensive experience in spinal microsurgery. Office: 3515 Executive Dr San Angelo TX 76904-6883

FISCHER, EDMOND HENRI, biochemistry educator; b. Shanghai, Apr. 6, 1920; arrived in U.S., 53; s. Oscar and Renée (Tapernoux) Fischer. Lic. es Sciences Chimiques et Biologiques, U. Geneva, 1943, Diplome d'Ingenieur Chimiste, 1944, PhD, 1947; D (hon.), U. Montpellier, France, 1985, U. Basel, Switzerland, 1988, Med. Coll. of Ohio, 1993, Ind. U., 1993, U. Bochum, Germany, 1994. Pvt. docent biochemistry U. Geneva, 1950—53; research assoc. biology Calif. Inst. Tech., Pasadena, 1953; asst. prof. biochemistry U. Wash., Seattle, 1953—56, assoc. prof., 1956—61, prof., 1961—90, prof. emeritus, 1990—. Mem. exec. com. Pacific Slope Biochem. Conf., 1958—59, pres., 1975; mem. biochemistry study sect. NIH, 1959—64; symposium

co-chmn. Battelle Seattle Rsch. Ctr., 1970, 73, 78; mem. sci. adv. bd. Biozentrum, U. Basel, Switzerland, 1982—86, Weizmann Inst. Sci., Rehovot, Israel, 1998—, bd. govs., 1997—; mem. sci. adv. bd. Principe Felipe Sci. Mus., Valencia, Spain, 1998—, Friedrich Miescher Inst., Ciba-Geigy, Basel, 1976—84, chmn., 1981—84; mem. bd. sci. govs. Scripps Rsch. Inst., La Jolla, Calif., 1987—; mem. scientific adv. bd. Basel Inst. for Immunology, 1996—2001; bd. sci. govs. Scripps Rsch. Inst., La Jolla, Calif. Contbr. Mem. sci. council on basic sci. Am. Heart Assn., 1977—80; sci. adv. com. Muscular Dystrophy Assn., 1980—88. Recipient Lederle Med. Faculty award, 1956—59, Guggenheim Found. award, 1963—64, Disting. Lectr. award, U. Wash., 1983, Laureate Passano Found. award, 1988, Steven C. Beering award, 1991, Nobel prize in Physiology or Medicine, 1992. Fellow: Am. Acad. Arts and Scis.; mem.: AAUP, NAS, AAS, Am. Chem. Soc. (editl. adv. bd. Biochemistry 1961—66, adv. bd. biochemistry divsn. 1962, assoc. editor 1966—91, exec. com. divsn. biology 1969—72, monograph adv. bd. 1971—73), fgn. acads. (hon.), Korean Acad. Sci. and Tech. (hon.), Japanese Biochem. Soc. (hon.), Spanish Royal Acad. Scis. (assoc.; fgn.), Venice Inst. Sci., Arts and Letters (assoc.; fgn.), Royal Acad. Medicine and Surgery (hon.; Cadiz, Spain), European Acad. Scis. (hon.), Am. Soc. Biol. Chemists (coun. 1989—93). Achievements include cellular regulation by phosphorylation/dephosphorylation cycle. Office: U Washington Med Sch PO Box 357350 Seattle WA 98195-7350 E-mail: efischer@u.washington.edu.

FISCHER, ELIZABETH (BETSY), television producer; b. New Orleans, Feb. 17, 1970; d. George Julius and Sally (Ford) Fischer; m. Gene Robert Raineri, Oct. 21, 1995; 1 child, Ella Elizabeth Raineri. BA cum laude, Am. U., 1992, MA, 1996. Polit. rschr. NBC News Meet the Press and Polit. Unit, Washington, 1992-94, assoc. prodr., 1995-96, prodr., 1997, sr. prodr., 1998—2002, exec. prodr., 2002—. Mem. Jr. League Washington. Nominee Emmy, Nat. Acad. TV Arts and Scis., 1997; recipient Walter Cronkite/USC Annenberg award. Mem.: Am. Women Radio and TV, Radio and TV News Dirs. Assn., Am. New Women's Club, Delta Gamma. Presbyterian. Avocations: racquetball, genealogy, reading, tennis. Home: 6525 Orland St Falls Church VA 22043-1865 Office: NBC News Meet the Press 4001 Nebraska Ave NW Washington DC 20016-2733

FISCHER, ERIC ROBERT, lawyer, educator; b. N.Y.C., Aug. 22, 1945; s. Maurice and Pauline (Pilcer) F.; m. Anita Ellen Cohen, July 31, 1977; children: Joshua, Lauren BA, U. Pa., 1967; MBA, JD, Stanford U., 1971; LLM in Taxation, Boston U., 1982. Bar: N.Y. 1975, Mass. 1977. Assoc. Fried, Frank, Harris, Shriver & Jacobson, N.Y.C., 1971-76; v.p., asst. gen. counsel, asst. sec. First Nat. Bank of Boston, 1976-86; exec. v.p., gen. counsel, corp. sec. UST Corp., Boston, 1986-2000; sr. counsel Goodwin Procter LLP, Boston, 2000—02, ptnr., 2002—. Lectr. on law Boston U. Law Sch., 1984— Trustee Boston Lyric Opera, Inc., 1989-2001; bd. dirs. Boston Area Youth Soccer, 1989-90, Spirit of Mass. Boys Soccer Club, 1991-97. Mem. ABA (banking law com., chmn. cmty. banking subcom., banking law com.), Bank Capital Markets Assn. (chmn. banking law subcom. 1984-90), UN Assn. Boston (treas. 1978-91), New Eng. Legal Found. (bd. dirs. 1990-92). Jewish. Home: 205 Waban Ave Waban MA 02468-2101 Office: Goodwin Procter Exchange Pl Boston MA 02109 E-mail: efischer@goodwinprocter.com. *The pursuit of an objective which you believe is meaningful and constructive (whether you are right or wrong) gives definition to your life and allows you to accept your own limitations.*

FISCHER, ERNST OTTO, chemist, educator; b. Munich, Nov. 10, 1918; s. Karl T. and Valentine (Danzer) Fischer. Diplom, Munich Tech. U., 1949, Dr. rer. nat., 1952, Habilitation, 1954, Dr. rer. nat. h.c., 1972, D.Sc.h.c., 1975, Dr. rer. nat. h.c., 1977, Dr.h.c., 1983. Assoc. prof. inorganic chemistry U. Munich, 1957—59, chair, 1959—64; prof. inorganic chemistry inst. Munich Inst. Tech., 1964—; prof. emeritus Tech. U. Munich, 1984—. Firestone lectr. U. Wis., 1969; vis. prof. U. Fla., Gainesville, 1971; Arthur D. Little vis. prof. MIT, Cambridge, 1973; vis. disting. lectr. U. Rochester, NY. Author: (with H. Werner) Metall-pi-Komplexe mit di- und oligoolefischen Liganden, 1963; transl. Complexes with di- and oligo-olefinic Ligands, 1966; Contbr. (with H. Werner) numerous articles in field to profl. jours. Recipient ann. prize Göttingen Acad. Scis., 1957, Alfred Stock Meml. prize Soc. German Chemists, 1959, Nobel Prize in Chemistry, 1973; Am. Chem. Soc. Centennial fellow, 1976 Mem. Bavarian Acad. Scis., Soc. German Chemists, German Acad. Scis. Leopoldina, Austrian Acad. Scis. (corr.), Accademia Nazionale dei Lincei, Italy (fgn.), Acad. Scis. Göttingen (corr.), Am. Acad. Arts and Scis. (fgn., hon.), Chem. Soc. (hon.) Achievements include special research in organometallic chemistry: metal pi complexes of arenes, olefins, carbene and carbyne complexes with metals, ferrocene type sandwich compounds, metal carbonyls. Office: Chemistry Inst Lichtenbergstrasse 4 D-85747 Garching Germany*

FISCHER, EUGENE, medical administrator, educator; b. Cheb, Czechoslovakia, June 9, 1948; came to U.S., 1952; s. David and Fanny (Kraus) F.; m. Klara Farkas, Nov. 25, 1978; children: Evelyn, Natalie. BS in Biology, L.I. U., 1971, MS in Biology, 1975; MS in Adminstrn. and Supervision, Queens Coll., 1988. Lic. tchr., N.Y. Med. dir. Robin Hood Country Day Sch., Brookville, N.Y., 1989-99; EMT Whitestone (N.Y.) Vol. Ambulance, 1977—, N.Y. state EMT, cert. instr. coord., 1982—. Pres. Whitestone Vol. Ambulance, 2002—. Author: (film strip) CPR. Recipient Meritorious Svc. award N.Y. State Vol. Ambulance and Rescue Assn., 1994. Mem. Nat. Assn. Notaries, N.Y. Vet. Police Assn. Home: 15504 Locke Ave Whitestone NY 11357-3250 E-mail: evzen@aol.com.

FISCHER, FRED WALTER, physicist, engineer, educator; b. Zwickau, Germany, June 26, 1922; s. Fritz and Louiska (Richter) F.; m. Yongja Kim, Oct. 1, 1970. BS in Mech. Engring., Columbia U., 1949, MS, 1950; MS in Physics, U. Wash., 1957; D in Elec. Engring., Tech. U. Munich, 1966. Analyst Boeing Co., Seattle, Germany, 1950—84, cons., 1984—88; owner Fischer Cons., 1984—88. Instr. physics, math., and engring. North Seattle Community Coll., 1973-93; guest tchr. Perkins Sch. Author: Analysis for Physics and Engineering, 1982, Renaissance Mathematics, 1992. First v.p., trustee Wedgwood Cmty. Coun., 1994-2000; mem. Wedgwood Elem. Sch. Site Coun., Eckstein Middle Sch. Site Coun. With AUS, 1943-46. Boeing scholar Max Planck Inst. Plasma Physics, 1964-65. Mem. AAAS, N.Y. Acad. Sci., Mercedes Benz Club (Seattle sect. bd. dirs.), Sigma Xi (life). Office: North Seattle CC 9600 College Way N Seattle WA 98103-3514

FISCHER, HARALD MAXIMILIAN, education educator, researcher; s. Katharina and Peter Hugo Fischer. PhD, U. of Wisc.-Madison, 1997—2003. All u. fellow U. of Wisc.-Madison, 2002—. Author: (jours.) The Role of Power and Politics in Repricing Exec. Stock Options, (book chptr.) Mobilizing Knowledge in Interorgnl. Alliances. Bd. mem. Morgridge Ctr. for Pub. Svc., Madison, Wis., 1995—97. Grantee Rsch. Grant, Ctr. for Internat. Bus. Edn. and Rsch., 2002. Mem.: Am. Sociol. Assn. (licentiate), Strategic Mgmt. Soc. (licentiate), Acad. of Mgmt. (licentiate).

FISCHER, JOEL, social work educator; b. Chgo., Apr. 22, 1939; s. Sam and Ruth (Feiges) F.; m. Renee H. Furuyama; children: Lisa, Nicole. BS, U. Ill., 1961, MSW, 1964; D in Social Welfare, U. Calif., Berkeley, 1970. Prof. sch. social work U. Hawaii, Honolulu, 1970—. Vis. prof. George Warren Brown Sch. Social Work, Washington U., St. Louis, 1977, U. Wis. Sch. Social Welfare, Milw., 1978-79, U. Natal, South Africa, 1982, U. Hong Kong, 1986; cons. various orgns. and univs. Author: (with Harvey L. Gochros) Planned Behavior Change: Behavior Modification in Social Work, 1973, Handbook of Behavior Therapy with Sexual Problems, vol. I, 1977, vol. II, 1977, Analyzing Research, 1975, Interpersonal Helping: Emerging Approaches for Social Work Practice, 1973, The Effectiveness of Social Casework, 1976, (with D. Sanders and O. Kurrem) Fundamentals of Social Work Practice, 1982, Effective Casework Practice: An Eclectic Approach, 1978, (with H. Gochros) Treat Yourself to a Better Sex Life, 1980, (with H. Gochros and J. Gochros) Helping the Sexually Oppressed, 1985, (with Martin Bloom) Evaluating Practice: Guidlines for the Helping Professional, 1982, (with Kevin Corcoran) Measures for Clinical Practice, 1987, (with Daniel Sanders) Visions for the Future: Social Work and Pacific-Asian Perspectives, 1988, (with Martin Bloom and John Orme) Evaluating Practice, 2nd edit., 1995, (with Kevin Corcoran) Measures for Clinical Practice, 2nd edit., vol. 1, 1994, Couples, Children, Families, vol. 2, 1994, Adults, 1994, East-West Connections: Social Work Practice Traditions and Change, 1992, (with Martin Bloom and John Orme) Evaluating Practice, 3d edit., 1999, (with Martin Bloom and John Orme) Instructor's Manual for Evaluating Practice, 1999; (with Kevin Corcoran) Measures for Clinical practice, 3d edit, vol. 1, 2000, Couples, Children and Families, Adults, vol. 2, 2000, (with Martin Bloom and John Orme) Evaluating Practice, 4th edit., 2003, Instructor's Manual for Evaluating Practice, 2d edit., 2003; mem. editl. bd. 12 profl. jours.; contbr. over 150 articles to profl. jours. Bd. dirs. U. Hawaii Profl. Assembly; precinct pres. Dem. Party. With U.S. Army, 1958. Mem. NASW, ACLU, Hawaii Com. for Africa, Coun. Social Work Edn., Acad. Cert. Social Workers, Nat. Conf. Social Welfare, AAUP, Unity Organizing Com., Hawaii People's Legis. Coalition, Bertha Reynold Soc., Amnesty Internat. Democrat. Home: 1371-4 Hunakai St Honolulu HI 96816-5501 Office: U Hawaii Sch Social Work Henke Hall Honolulu HI 96822-2217 E-mail: jfischer@hawaii.edu.

FISCHER, JOHN JULES, clergy member, theology educator, writer; b. Budapest, Hungary, May 27, 1946; came to U.S., 1949; s. George S. and Marianne (Komlos) F.; m. Patrice Eloise Pavka, June 4, 1972; children: Eve, Seth. BS in Bibl. Studies, Phila. Biblical U., 1970; MS in Comm., Temple U., 1970; MA in New Testament, Trinity Internat. U., 1972; B Judaic Studies, Spertus Coll. Judaica, 1978; PhD in Edn., U. So. Fla., 1987; ThD in Judaic Studies, Calif. Grad. Sch. Theology, 1989. Ordained by Union of Messianic Jewish Congregations, 1988. Dir. tng. Am. Messianic Fellowship, Chgo., 1973-74; v.p. The Watchmen Assn., Highland Park, Ill., 1975-78;; rabbi Congregation B'nai Maccabim, Highland Park, Ill., 1975-81; v.p. B'rit Shalom, Highland Park, 1978-81; dep. sec. N.Am. Internat. Messianic Jewish Alliance, Palm Harbor, Fla., 1981-84; rabbi Congregation Ohr Chadash, Clearwater, Fla., 1982—; exec. dir. Menorah Ministries, Palm Harbor, 1984—; v.p. acad. affairs St. Petersburg (Fla.) Theol. Sem., 1994—. Mem. vis. faculty Trinity Evangelical Div. Sch., Deerfield, Ill., 1975-81; v.p. Union Messianic Jewish Congregations, Washington, 1979-81; mem. exec. com. Internat. Messianic Jewish Alliance, Va. Beach, Va., 1994—; adv. bd. King of Kings Coll., Jerusalem, 1996—. Author: The Olive Tree Connection, 1983, Siddur for Messianic Jews, 1988, Messianic Svcs. for Festivals Holy Days, 1992, The Enduring Paradox, 2000. Dem. precinct com. man, Lake County, Ill., 1979-81. Mem. Am. Assn. Messianic Jewish Believers (pres. 1996—), Messianic Jewish Alliance Am. (treas. 1977-79), Messianic Jewish Alliance Chgo. (pres. 1974-78), Assn. Messianic Believers (pres. 1994—). Avocations: baseball, reading, playing games, tennis, physical fitness. Office: Menorah Ministries PO Box 669 Palm Harbor FL 34682-0669 E-mail: BetMidrash@aol.com

FISCHER, JOHN MARTIN, education educator, researcher; b. Cleve., Dec. 26, 1952; s. Joseph and Armeda F.; m. Tina Louise Astrolio, Feb. 2, 1991; children: Aja Marie Newton, Ariel Marton, Zoe Sigrid. BA, MA, Stanford U., 1975; MA, Cornell U., 1980, PhD, 1982; MA (hon.), Yale U., 1981. From asst. to assoc. prof. Yale U., New Haven, Conn., 1981-88; assoc. prof. U. Calif., Riverside, 1988-90, prof., 1990—. Dir. honors program U. Calif., Riverside, 1996—. Author: The Metaphysics of Free Will, 1994, Responsiblity and Control, 1998; editor: Moral Responsibility, 1986, The Metaphysics of Death, 1993. Faculty adv. Golden Key Nat. Honor Soc., 1999—; sec.-treas. Phi Beta Kappa, Riverside, 1999—; faculty rep. Rhodes, Marshall and Udall Scholarships, Riverside, 1998—. NEH fellow, 1983-84, 94-95, Residential fellow Nat. Humanities Ctr., Research Triangle Park, 1990-91, 93-94, Australian Nat. U. Rsch. Ctr., Canberra, Australia, 1994. Mem. Am. Philos. Assn. Home: 821 S University Dr Riverside CA 92507 Office: Univ Calif Dept Philosophy Riverside CA 92521 E-mail: john.fischer@ucrac1.ucr.edu.

FISCHER, KURT WALTER, education educator; b. Balt., June 9, 1943; s. Kurt Wilhelm and Irmgaard Louise (Funke) Fischer; m. Sandra Pipp (div.); 1 child, Seth; m. Jane Haltiwanger, Dec. 7, 1986; children: Johanna, Lukas, Kara. BA in Psychology summa cum laude, Yale U., 1965; MA in Soc. Rels., Harvard U., 1968, PhD in Soc. Rels., 1971. Asst. prof. Univ. Denver, 1972-78, assoc. prof., 1978-85, prof., 1985-87; prof. edn. Harvard U., Cambridge, Mass., 1986—, Charles Bigelow prof., chair human devel., 1989—92, 1994—95, 1999—2000, dir. mind, brain and edn., 1999—. Vis. scholar Univ. Geneva, 1978—79; vis. prof. U. Pa., Phila., 1985—86; master lectr. U. Groningen, The Netherlands, 1996; vis. prof. Nanjing Normal U., China, 2000. Author: Cognitive Development, 1981, Levels and Transitions in Cognitive Development, 1983; co-author: (with P. Shaver and A. Lazerson) Psychology Today: An Introduction, 2d and 3d edits., 1972, 75; co-author: Human Development from Conception to Adolescence, 1984, Development in Context, 1993, Human Behavior and the Developing Brain, 1994, Self Conscious Emotions, 1995, Development and Vulnerability in Close Relationships, 1996, Socioemotional Development across Cultures, 1998; contbr. articles to profl. jours. Fellow James McKeen Cattell Fund, 1985-86, Ctr. for Advanced Study, Palo Alto, Calif., 1992-93; grantee Carnegie Found., Nat. Inst. Child Health and Devel., 1994—, Sloan Found., Spencer Found., Rose Found., 1995—. Mem. Jean Piaget Soc. (pres. 1988-91), Phi Beta Kappa, Sigma Xi. Home: 29 Vincent Ave Belmont MA 02478-4418 Office: Harvard U Human Devel Grad Sch Edn Cambridge MA 02138 E-mail: kurt_fischer@harvard.edu.

FISCHER, LEROY HENRY, historian, educator; b. Hoffman, Ill., May 19, 1917; s. Andrew LeRoy and Effie (Risby) F.; m. Martha Gwendolyn Anderson, June 20, 1948; children: Barbara Ann, James LeRoy, John Andrew. BA, U. Ill., 1939, MA, 1940, PhD, 1943; postgrad., Columbia U., 1941. Grad. asst. history U. Ill., 1940-43; asst. prof. history Ithaca (N.Y.) Coll., 1946, Okla. State U. at Stillwater, 1946-49, assoc. prof. history, 1949-60, prof. history, 1960-73, Oppenheim Regents prof. history, 1973-78, Oppenheim prof. history, 1978-84, Oppenheim prof. emeritus, 1984—. Exec. sec. honors program, 1959-61; exec. council Emeriti Assn., 2000-2002. Author: Lincoln's Gadfly, Adam Gurowski, 1964; (with Muriel H. Wright) Civil War Sites in Oklahoma, 1967, The Civil War Era in Indian Territory, 1974, The Western States in the Civil War, 1975, Territorial Governors of Oklahoma, 1975, The Western Territories in the Civil War, 1977, Civil War Battles in the West, 1981, Oklahoma's Governors 1907-1979, 3 vols., 1981-85, Oklahoma State University Historic Old Central, 1988; co-author: A History of Governance at Oklahoma State University, 1992; editor: The History of the Oklahoma State University Centennial Histories Project, 1993; contbr articles to profl. jours. Vice chmn. Honey Springs Battlefield Park Commn., 1968-92, Okla. Civil War Centennial Commn., 1958-65; chmn. Old Ctrl. com. Okla. State U., 1971-98; mem. Okla. State Hist. Preservation Rev. Commn., 1978—, vice chmn., 1978-81, chmn., 1981-83, 97—; bd. dirs. Nat. Indian Hall of Fame, 1969-2002, YMCA, 1951-54, 83-85, 91—; bd. dirs. Assocs. Western History Collections, U. Okla., 1981-2002, pres., 1989-90; bd. dirs. Stillwater Mus. Assn., 1987-93, pres., 1990-91; mem. Okla. Chisholm Trail Centennial Commn., 1967-68; bd. dirs. Friends of Honey Springs Battlefield Park, 1991—, pres., 1994-97, sec. 1997-2000. With Signal Corps, AUS, 1943-45. Recipient Lit. award Loyal Legion U.S., 1963; named tchr. of Yr., Okla. State U.-Okla. Edn. Assn., 1969; inducted in Okla. Historians Hall of Fame, 1995, Centralia (Ill.) Hall of Fame, 1997, Okla. Higher Edn. Hall of Fame, 2002. Mem. Am. Hist. Assn., Southern Hist. Assn., Western History Assn., Am. Assn. State and Local History, AAUP, Okla. Heritage Assn. (Disting. Svc. award 1989), Okla. Hist. Soc. (bd. dirs. 1966—, treas. 1984-87), Ill. Hist. Soc., Orgn. Am. Historians, Omicron Delta Kappa, Pi Gamma Mu, Phi Alpha Theta, Alpha Kappa Lambda. Methodist (chmn. various coms. 1946—, adminstrv. bd. 1950-77, chmn. 1976-77, lay leader 1970-71). Home: 1010 W Cantwell Ave Stillwater OK 74075-4603

FISCHER, LINDA MARIE, nursing educator; b. Paterson, N.J., Sept. 26, 1959; d. William Jr. and Marie (Bilz) F. BSN cum laude, Coll. Misericordia, 1981; MSN magna cum laude, Bloomsburg U., 1996, clin. nurse specialist, 1996. RN, Pa.; CCRN-R. Staff nurse cardiac ICU Geisinger Med. Ctr., Danville, Pa., 1981-90, clin. nurse II cardiac ICU, 1987-90, clin. instr. cardiac ICU and cardiovasc. spl. care unit, 1990—, med. leave, 1990. Chair adv. group profl. pers. case record rev. subcom. Columbia-Montour Home Health/Vis. Nurses Assn., Inc. Contbr. articles to profl. jours. Active Montour-Riverside chpt. Am. Heart Assn., 1989-92. Mem. AACN, Sigma Theta Tau (nominating com. Theta Zeta chpt. 1995-97, 97-99, 99-01).

FISCHER, LUCY ROSE, gerontologist, researcher, artist; b. Wilmington, Del., Sept. 15, 1944; d. Henry Rose, Helen Rose; m. Mark Samuel Fischer; 1 child, Jeremy (Yirmi). PhD, U. Mass., 1979. Asst. prof. U. of Minn., Mpls., 1979—87; assoc. prof. St. Olaf Coll., Northfield, Minn., 1987—89; sr. rsch. scientist Wilder Rsch. Ctr., St. Paul, 1989—92; sr. rsch. investigator Health-Partners Rsch. found., Mpls., 1992—2002. Author: Linked Lives: Adult Daughters and Their Mothers, 1986, Older Volunteers, 1993 (NSFRE Research Prize, 1994); editor: Healthy Outcomes, 1994—2003; contbr. over 90 articles to profl. jours.; in one-woman and group exhbns., exhibitions include Creating and Connecting, Coll. of St. Catherine, 1997, Minn. State Fair Art Pavillion, 1999, Phipps Ctr. for Arts, 1999. Chair Aging Panel-Jewish Fedn, Minneapolis, 1983—86. Grantee Rsch. grant, Blandin Found., 1988, Nat. Inst. Aging, 1999—2002, MacArthur Found., 1999—2001. Fellow: Gerontol. Soc. Am. (chair qualitative interest gGroup 1995—98).

FISCHER, MARK ALAN, lawyer, law educator; b. Evanston, Ill, Sept. 28, 1950; s. Lee Earle and Zelda (Dlugo) F. BA magna cum laude, Emerson Coll., 1975; JD, Boston Coll., 1980. Bar: Mass. 1980, US Dist. Ct. Mass. 1980, US Ct. Appeals (1st cir.) Mass. 1985. Sole practice, Cambridge, Mass., 1980-83; mem. Cohen & Burg, Boston, 1983-86; ptnr. Wolf, Greenfield & Sacks, Boston, 1986-96, Palmer & Dodge, Boston, 1996—2002, Fish & Richardson, Boston, 2002—, co-chmn. media and entertainment sect. Lectr. copyright and trademark law Boston Coll. Law Sch., 1985—87; lectr. entertainment law New Eng. Sch. Law, Boston, 1983—93; assoc. prof. music law Berklee Coll. Music, 1989—90, 1994—95; lectr. intellectual property Northeastern Sch. Law, Boston, 1986; mem. adj. faculty advanced copyright law Suffolk U. Law Sch., 1999—2002. Contbr. articles to profl. jour.; columnist New Eng. Entertainment Digest, 1982-90; co-editor: Perle & Williams on Publishing Law, (3rd edit.). Mem. ABA, Mass. Bar Assn., Boston Patent Law Assn. (chmn. copyright law com., 1985-96), Copyright Soc. USA (trustee 1997-2000), Copyright Soc. New Eng. (co-founder). Office: Fish & Richardson 225 Franklin St Boston MA 02110

FISCHER, MARSHA LEIGH, civil engineer; b. San Antonio, May 9, 1955; d. Joe Henry and Ellen Joyce (Flake) F. BSCE, Tex. A&M U., 1977. Engring. asst. Tex. Dept. Hwys. and Transp., Dallas, 1977-79; outside plant engr. Southwestern Bell Telephone Co., Dallas, 1979-82, staff mgr. for budgets, 1982-84, area mgr., engring. design Wichita Falls, Tex., 1984-86, area mgr. Ft. Worth, 1986-88; dist. mgr., local provisioning application Bell Communications Rsch., Piscataway, N.J., 1988-91; dist. mgr. engring. Southwestern Bell Telephone, Ft. Worth, Tex., 1992-94, dir. customer svcs., 1994-95, dir. network engring., 1996-99, dir. OSP planning, 1999-2000, regional mgr. constrn., 2000—. Named one of Outstanding Women of Am., 1987. Mem. NSPE, Tex. Soc. Profl. Engrs., Tex. Soc. Civil Engrs., Profl. Engrs. in Industry, Tex. A&M Assn. Former Students. Republican. Avocations: tennis, travel, reading, cycling. Home: 4711 Ridge Dove San Antonio TX 78230-1192 Office: Southwestern Bell Telephone 1010 N St Marys San Antonio TX 78215-2109

FISCHER, MARY E. special education educator; b. Kansas City, Mo., July 7, 1948; d. Tom Earl and Sue Turner (Fitts) Walker; m. Timothy Montgomery Fischer, Sept. 4, 1971; children: Ethan David, Elizabeth Louise. AB, U. Mo., 1971; MSE, Cen. Mo. State U., Warrensburg, 1981; PhD, U. Wash., 1997. Occupl. therapy asst. Children's Therapy Ctr., 1971-73, tchr., 1976-78, psychometrist, 1978-79; program coord. United Cerebral Palsy, Camp Wonderland, Lake of the Ozarks, Mo., 1983; developmental presch. tchr. Children's Therapy Ctr., 1979-84, 75-76; project assoc. Early Childhood Follow Along Study, U. Wash., 1985-87; rsch. assoc. U. Wash., 1987-88; project assoc. Rsch. and Evaluation Network, U. Wash., 1989; project mgr. ChildFind project, Child Devel./Mental Retardation Ctr., Seattle, 1989-90; project coord. N.W. Insvc. Coop. for Transdisciplinary Teams U. Wash., Seattle, 1990-93; project coord. Choices, 1992-95; coord. Wash. Statewide Sys. Change Project, 1993-94; regional dir. Ctr. for Supportive Edn., Seattle, 1994-97; elem/early childhood spl. edn. and readiness to learn coord. Olympic Ednl. Svc. Dist. 114, Bremerton, Wash., 1997—. Adj. prof. Western Wash. U., 1999-2001; instr. Seattle Pacific U. Contbr. articles to profl. jours. Mem. Kitsap Infant Mental Health Coalition; pers. and tng. com. Infant/Toddler Early Intervention Program; family resource coord. tng. project; mem. Kitsap County Commn. on Children and Youth, 2002—; dir. children's choir Lake City Presbyn. Ch., 1999—2002. Mem.: ASCD, Assn. for Persons with Severe Handicaps, Coun. for Exceptional Children (sec. divsn. for early childhood 2001—), Nat. Assn. Edn. Young Children, Soc. Creative Anachronism, Bremerton Kiwanis Club, Pi Lambda Theta (Outstanding Mem. 1990), Phi Kappa Phi. Avocations: singing, camping. Home: 1514 N Montgomery Bremerton WA 98312

FISCHER, MAXIM, electronics engineer; b. Sibiu, Transylvan, Romania, June 14, 1946; s. Herman and Edita (Genad) F.; m. Aurelia Munteanu, Jan. 15, 1972; 1 child, Alina Christina. Diploma Engr., Poly. Inst., Bucharest, Romania, 1970. Prodn. engr. Electromagnetica, Bucharest, 1970-75; telecom. engr. Dept. Telecom., Beer Sheva, Israel, 1976-77; avionics engr. Tundra Tech. Industries, Edmonton, Alta., Can., 1978-82, chief engr., 1982-83; design engr. Northwestern Utilities, Edmonton, 1983-90, sr. engr. specialist, 1990-99; project leader Atco Pipelines, Edmonton, 1999—. Dir. Can Trade Rsch., Inc., Edmonton, 1992—, Trunked Wireless Technologies, Edmonton. Contbr. articles to profl. jours. Mem. Instrument Soc. Am., Assn. Profl. Engrs., Geologists and Geophysicists of Alta., Romanian Radio Assn. (v.p. 1991-92, 95-96, sec. 1993-94, pres. 2001-2002). Jewish. Avocations: tennis, chess, golf. E-mail: Max.Fischer@atcopipelines.com., maximf@telusplanet.net.

FISCHER, MICHAEL DAVID, civil engineer; b. N.Y.C., Aug. 27, 1944; s. Eduard and Anneliese (Buscher) F.; m. Rita Susan Weinberg, June 16, 1968; children— Adam Bruce, Jennifer Beth. B.C.E., Rensselaer Polytech. Inst., 1966; M.S. in Structural Engring., SUNY-Buffalo, 1968. Registered profl. engr., N.Y. Engr., hydrologist U.S. Geol. Survey, Albany, N.Y., 1964-66; structural engr. Frederick R. Harris, N.Y.C., 1966, Parsons, Brinkerhoff, Quade & Douglas, 1967; engr. mechanics of materials Gen. Electric Co., Schenectady, N.Y., 1968-82, project support mgr., 1982-84, signal processing facility mgr., 1984-86, steam generator project engr., 1986-89, prin. engr. generator inspection, 1989—; cons. structural engring., Clifton Park, N.Y., 1976—, MDF Cons., 2000—. Youth advisor Temple Gates of Heaven, Schenectady, 1969-74; v.p. Congregation Beth Shalom, Clifton Park, 1979-81, treas., 1984-88, fin. sec., 1988-1992; sec., Schenectady JCC, 1998-2003; mem. Elfun Soc., 1979—1993. Mem. Soc. Exptl. Stress Analysis, Nat. Soc. Profl. Engrs., Nat. Assn. Corosion Engrs., Nova Soc. Democrat. Jewish. Avocations: sailing; biking; kayaking; cross-country skiing; hiking. Office: Lockheed Martin Box 1072 Schenectady NY 12301-0010 Home: 28 Westbury Dr Saratoga Springs NY 12866

FISCHER, MICHAEL LUDWIG, environmental executive; b. Dubuque, Iowa, May 29, 1940; s. Carl Michael and Therese Marie (Stadler) F.; m. Jane Pughe Rogers; children: Christina Marie, Steven Michael. BA in Polit. Sci., Santa Clara U., 1964; M in City and Regional Planning, U. Calif., Berkeley, 1967; grad. exec. program in environ. mgmt., Harvard U., 1980. Planner City of Mountain View, Calif., 1960-65; planner assoc. Bay Area Govts., 1966-67; planner County of San Mateo, Calif., 1967-69; assoc. dir. San Francisco Planning and Urban Rsch. Assn., nonprofit civc orgn., 1969-73; exec. dir. North Cen. region Calif. Coastal Zone Conservation Commn., San Rafael, 1973-76; chief dep. dir. Gov.'s Office Planning and Rsch., Sacramento, 1976-78; exec. dir. Calif. Coastal Commn., San Francisco, 1978-85; sr. assoc. Sedway Cooke Assocs., environ. cons., San Francisco, 1985-87; exec. dir. Sierra Club, San Francisco, 1987-93; resident fellow John F. Kennedy Sch. Govt., Inst. Politics, Harvard U., Cambridge, Mass., 1993; sr. cons. Natural Resources Def. Coun., San Francisco, 1993-95; exec. officer Calif. Coastal Conservancy, Oakland, 1994-97; program dir. environ. William & Flora Hewlett Found., Menlo Park, Calif., 1997—2002, sr. fellow, 2002—03. Lectr. dept. city and regional planning U. Calif., Berkeley, 1984; mem., co-chair environ. com. adv. coun. Calvert Social Investment Fund, 1989—; mem. Harvard Commn. Global Change Info. Policy, 1993-95; mem. com. on impact of maritime facility devel. NAS/NRC, 1975-78; mem. nat. sea grant review panel NOAA, 1998-01; bd. dirs. High Country News Found., 2000—, Resources for Cmty. Collaboration, 1999—; mem. adv. bd. Sustainables Conservation, 2003—; mem. steering com. Indigenous Cmtys. Mapping Initiative, 2000—. Co-author Calif. state plan, An Urban Strategy for Calif., 1978, Building a New Municipal Railway, 1973, Oral History, Coastal Commn. Yrs., 1973-85, Oral History, Sierra Club Yrs., 1987-93; author intro. Ansel Adams: Yosemite, 1995; contbr. papers to profl. publs. Recipient Life Achievement award Assn. Environ. Profls., 1986, Disting. Leadership award. Am. Soc. Pub. Adminstrn., 1987, Outstanding Nat. Leadership award Coastal States Orgn., 1990, Exemplary Pub. Svc. award San Francisco Bay Conservation and Devel. Commn., 1997, Spl. Recognition award Calif. State Legis., 1998, Coastal Champion award, Calif., 2003. Mem. Calif. Planning and Conservation League (bd. dirs. 1970-76), Alliance Ethnic and Environ. Orgn. (founding bd. dirs. 1991-93), The Oceanic Soc. (bd. dirs.

1983-88), Am. Inst. Cert. Planners, Sierra Club, Friends of the Earth (bd. dirs. 1988-94), Am. Youth Hostels, Inc. (bd. dirs. 1985-87), Yosemite Restoration Trust (bd. dirs. 1990-97, pres. 1995-97), Lambda Alpha. E-mail: fischer@igc.org.

FISCHER, NORMAN CHARLES, music educator; b. Washington, May 25, 1949; s. Gerald John Fischer and Helen Beth Buckley; m. Jeanne Elaine Kierman, Aug. 28, 1971; children: Rebecca Jean, Abigail Elizabeth. MusB, Oberlin Coll., Ohio, 1971. Founding cellist Concord String Quartet, Hanover, NH, 1971—87; artist in residence Dartmouth Coll., Hanover, NH, 1974—87; coord. of string activities Tanglewood Music Ctr., Lenox, Maine, 1985—; assoc. prof. violoncello Oberlin Coll., Ohio, 1987—92; prof. violoncello Rice U., Houston, 1991—; cellist The Fischer Duo, Houston. Musician: (recording) Born in America in 1938, Charles Ives String Quartets (Grammy Nomination, 1975), Rochberg String Quartet #3 (Grammy Nomination, 1973), Am. Music in the 1990s, Robert Sirota Cello works. Independent. Office: Shepherd Sch of Music Rice U 6100 S Main St Houston TX 77005 Home Fax: 713-669-0200. Personal E-mail: nfischer@rice.edu.

FISCHER, PAMELA SHADEL, public relations executive; b. Harrisburg, Pa., Feb. 28, 1959; d. Richard Lee and Pauline Louise (Nies) S.; m. Charles J. Fischer Jr., June 11, 1983; 1 child, Zachary Joseph. BA in English, Lebanon Valley Coll., Annville, Pa., 1981. Cert. child passenger safety technician AAAA. Pub. relations coordinator Pa. Optometric Assn., Harrisburg, 1981-83; pub. relations dir. Morris Center YMCA, Cedar Knolls, N.J., 1983-85; pub. relations coordinator Delta Dental Plan of N.J., Parsippany, 1985-86; pub. relations mgr. AAA N.J. Automobile Club, Florham Park, N.J., 1986-91, mgr. mem. svcs. and pub. affairs, 1991-94, asst. v.p. pub. rels. & safety, 1994-96, asst. v.p. pub. affairs and fin. svcs., 1996—2002, v.p. pub. affairs and fin. svcs., 2002—. Corp. capt. United Way of Morris County, Cedar Knolls, 1985—90, chmn. publs. com., 1989—90, chmn. mktg. com., 1991—95, v.p. mktg., 1996; career counselor Lebanon Valley Coll., 1983—, bd. dirs. of exec. com., vol. v.p. mktg., 1996—99; mem. hwy. traffic safety policy adv. com. Gov.'s Office, 1998—; chair legis. com. Gateway Tourism Coun., 1997—2000; mem. Driver Edn. Commn. N.J., 1999—; mem. women's leadership initiative exec. com. United Way of Morris County, 1999—, vice chmn., 2002—03, chmn., 2003—; bd. dirs. First Night of Morris County, 1999—2002, chmn., 2003—; commr. NJ Motor Vehicle Commn., 2003—, mem., 2003—; bd. dirs. Morris Ctr. YMCA, 1992—94, Hist. Morris Vis. Ctr., 1999—2003, bd. pres., 2001—. Rotary Found. scholar, 1981; recipient Gold award United Way of Morris County, 1988. Mem. Pub. Rels. Soc. Am. (bd. dirs. 1995), N.J. Press Assn., N.J. Travel Industry Assn., Internat. Assn. Bus Communicators, Y's Club of Cedar Knoll (pres. 1986-91). Republican. Roman Catholic. Avocations: gardening, stenciling, reading, writing, photography. Office: AAA NJ Automobile Club 1 Hanover Rd Florham Park NJ 07932-1888

FISCHER, PATRICIA ANN, middle school educator; b. Cleve., Apr. 11, 1951; d. Norman Stanley and Teresa (Domagalski) Michaels; m. David Leland Stroh, June 1, 1973 (div. June 1977); m. Lawrence Joseph Fischer, June 14, 1986. BA in Edn., Ohio No. U., 1973; MBA in Edn., Mt. St. Joseph Coll., Cin., 1986; postgrad., Miami U., Oxford, Ohio, 1985—, Ohio State U., 1988. Cert. K-8 tchr., 7-12 history tchr., Ohio. Mid. sch. tchr. St. Gerard Sch., Lima, Ohio, 1973-79, Our Lady of Rosary Sch., Cin., 1980-89, Little Flower Sch., Cin., 1989—, coord. sci., 1989—. Recipient award Project Bus., Cin., 1986, 87, 88, 89, 98, 99 Civic Achievement award Burger King Corp., Cin., 1990, 91, 92, Sci. Tchr. award NSTA, 1993, 20-Yr. award for Cath. educator Diocese of Cin., 1994, Time Warner Cable Nat. Tchr. award, 2003. Mem. Nat. Cath. Edn. Assn., Ohio Edn. Assn., European Am. Study Ctr. Alumni Assn., Order Ea. Star, Alpha Omicron Pi. Roman Catholic. Avocations: painting, travel, needlework, reading. Home: 5450 Cecilia Ct Cincinnati OH 45247-7508 Office: Little Flower School 5555 Little Flower Ave Cincinnati OH 45239-6898

FISCHER, PATRICK CARL, computer scientist, retired educator; b. St. Louis, Dec. 3, 1935; s. Carl Hahn and Kathleen (Kirkpatrick) F.; m. Linda Loomis, Dec. 22, 1956 (div. Jan 1967); 1 child, Carl; m. Charlotte Froese, Apr. 2, 1967; 1 child, Carolyn. BS, U. Mich., 1957; MBA, 1958; PhD (Woodrow Wilson fellow, NSF fellow), Mass. Inst. Tech., 1962. Asst. prof. Harvard U., Cambridge, Mass., 1962-65; assoc. prof. Cornell U., Ithaca, N.Y., 1965-68; vis. assoc. prof. U. B.C., 1967-68; prof. computer sci. U. Waterloo, Ont., Can., 1968-74, chmn. dept. applied analysis and computer sci., 1972-74; prof. dept. computer sci. Pa. State U., State College, 1974-79, head dept., 1974-78; prof. dept. computer sci. Vanderbilt U., Nashville, 1980-98, chmn. dept., 1980-95, prof. emeritus, 1998—. Mem. computing and info. sci. grant selection com. Nat. Research Council Can., 1973-76; vis. prof. U. Calif., Berkeley, 1986, Ga. Tech., 1987 Editor in chief: spl. publs. Assn. Computing Machinery, 1971-88; assoc. editor: Jour. Computer and System Scis, 1968-74; editor, 1974-99, SIAM Jour. on Computing, 1974-84; mem. editorial bd.: Jour. Computer Lang, 1974-98; contbr. profl. jours. database theory. Research grantee, 1964-66, 66-68, 79-81, 82-84; Nat. Research Council Can. grantee, 1968-75 Fellow Soc. Actuaries; mem.IEEE, IEEE Computer Soc., Assn. Computing Machinery (founder, chmn. spl. interest group automata and computability theory 1968-73), Sigma Xi, Phi Beta Kappa, Phi Kappa Phi, Beta Gamma Sigma. Home: 221 Burlington Pl Nashville TN 37215-1859 Office: Vanderbilt U Station B Box 351679 Nashville TN 37235-1679 E-mail: Patrick.C.Fischer@Vanderbilt.edu.

FISCHER, R. M. sculptor; b. N.Y.C., Mar. 21, 1947; s. Bernard and Alva (Sherman) F.; m. Patti Paige, June 22, 1986; 1 child, Dena Paige. BA, L.I. U., 1971; MFA, San Francisco Art Inst., 1973. Numerous one-man shows, including Musee Ville Toulon, France, 1984, Whitney Mus. Am. Art, N.Y.C., 1984, Inst. Contemporary Art, Boston, 1985, Jay Gorney Modern Art, N.Y.C., 1989, Donald Young Gallery, Chgo., 1988, Sidney Janis Gallery, N.Y.C., 1991, Deitch Projects, N.Y.C., 1998, Sandra Gering Gallery, N.Y.C., 2002; exhibited in numerous group shows, including Mus. Modern Art, 1984, Whitney Mus. Am. Art, 1985, 88, 91, Aldrich Mus. Contemporary Art, 1988, Vienna (Austria) Seccession, 1990; represented in permanent collections Cin. Art Mus., Whitney Mus. Modern Art., Mus. Modern Art, Dallas Mus. Art, Carnegie Mus. Fine Arts, Pitts., Fundacao de Serrales Found., Oporto, Portugal; permanent pub. artworks include Kansas City Convention Ctr., Cleve. Gateway Plaza, Battery Park City, N.Y., Mass. State House, Boston, Seattle Tower, Sony Studios Fountain, Union Square, San Francisco. Studio: 390 Wythe Ave # 101 Brooklyn NY 11211

FISCHER, RICHARD SAMUEL, lawyer; b. Buffalo, July 31, 1937; s. Richard D. and Isabel B. (Van Dorn) F.; m. Malinda Berry, June 3, 1960; children: Richard B., Van D. AB, Harvard U., 1959, JD, 1963. Bar: N.Y. 1963, Okla. 1996. Law clk N.Y. Ct. Appeals, Albany, 1963-65; assoc. Nixon, Hargrave, Devans & Doyle, Rochester, N.Y., 1965-71, ptnr., 1972-95, mem. policy com., 1991-95, head Rochester office, 1992-95; mem. faculty Okla. State U., Stillwater, 1997—2002. Bd. dirs. Cowboy Golf, Inc. Past chair, trustee Highland Hosp.; past pres. Harley Sch.; past bd. dirs. Rochester Area Hosp. Corp., Primary Mental Health Project; bd. dirs. United Way, Stillwater; past pres. Friends of Music and Allied Arts, 2000-01, bd. United Way. Mem. ABA, N.Y. State Bar Assn. (past chmn. com. ins. programs and retirement plans), Monroe County Bar Assn., NYU Inst. Fed. Taxation (adv. com.), Okla. Bar Assn. Clubs: Genessee Valley, Country Club of Rochester (N.Y.), Stillwater Country Club, Karsten Creek Golf Club (dir.). Office: PO Box 1897 Stillwater OK 74076-1897

FISCHER, ROBERT BLANCHARD, university administrator, researcher; b. Hartford, Conn., Oct. 24, 1920; s. Charles Albert and Matilda (Nylen) F.; m. Mary Ellen Mitchell, June 29, 1946; children: Lois, Marcia, Philip, Vivian, Valerie. BS, Wheaton Coll., 1942; PhD, U. Ill., 1946. Rsch. chemist U.S. Army Atomic Bomb Project, Chgo., 1944-46; instr. chemistry U. Ill., Urbana, 1946-48; prof. chemistry Indiana U., Bloomington, 1948-63; dean sch. of sci. Calif. State U.-Dominguez Hills, Carson, 1963-79, dean emeritus, 1979—; provost, sr. v.p. Biola U., La Mirada, Calif., 1979-88, disting. prof., 1988-89, provost, disting. prof. emeritus, 1989—. Research assoc. Calif. Inst. Tech., Pasadena, 1959-60; cons. in field. Contbr. articles to profl. jours. Fellow AAAS, Am. Sci. Affiliation (nat. pres. 1965-66); mem. Am. Chem. Soc. (sect. and region chmn.). Republican. Avocations: theology, amateur radio, sports. Home: 860 Morningside Dr C302 Fullerton CA 92835

FISCHER, ROBERT LEE, engineering executive, educator; b. Huntington, W.Va., Feb. 4, 1947; s. Charles Lee and Frances Louise (Pennington) F.; m. Mona Lynn Reeser, Oct. 27, 1966; children: Robert Lee Jr., Amy Lynn, Cory Brandon. Cert. in electronics tech., Huntington East Vocat. Tech., 1965; BA in Physics and Gen. Sci., Marshall U., 1970, MS in Vocat. Tech. Edn., 1976; PhD in Elec. Engring., Kennedy-Western U., 1993. Registered profl. elec. engr., lic. master electrician, cert. plant engr., vibration analyst, IBEW Instrumentation and controls technician. Electrical engr. J.F. & M. Co., Huntington, 1970-71; electronics prodn. supr. polan ind. div. Wollensak, Inc., Huntington, 1971-72; electrical maintenance supr. ACF Industries, Inc., Huntington, 1972-76, electrical maintenance supt., 1976-78, sr. maintenance engr., 1978-80, plant engr., 1980-84, mgr. plant, prodn. and tooling engring., 1984-85; engr., prin. cons. Fischer Tech. Svcs., Huntington, 1979—; electrical, instrumentation and utilities mgr. Calgon Carbon Corp., Catlettsburg, Ky., 1985-93, maintenance mgr., 1993-94, maintenance svcs. mgr., 1994-2001; instrumentation and controls technician Pritchard Electric Co., Huntington, 2001—. Instr. robotics Marshall U. Cmty. and Tech. Coll, Huntington, 1986—99; mem. instrumentation and control engring. curriculum adv. com. Shawnee State U., Portsmouth, Ohio, 1995—2000. Patentee electronic height control device, robot safety mechanism. Elected to West Jr. High Sch. Hall of Fame, Huntington, 1988; recipient Sr.-Under Black Belt-Open 3d Place award United Fighting Arts Fedn. Nat. Karate Tournament, 1984; named W.Va. ambassador of sci. and engring. among all people, 1982. Mem. NSPE, W.Va. Soc. Profl. Engrs., W.Va., Acad. Sci., Ohio Valley Astron. Soc., Am. Radio Relay League, Six Meter Internat. Radio Club. Democrat. Avocations: ham radio, martial arts, amateur astronomy. Home: 4 Willowtree Dr Huntington WV 25704-9012 E-mail: fischertek@zoominternet.net.

FISCHER, ROBERT LEO, insurance agent, financial consultant; BA, St. Norbert Coll., 1970; postgrad. studies in Edn., U. Wis., Oshkosh; CLU, Am. Coll., Bryn Mawr, Pa., 1986, ChFC, 1989. Lic. ins. agt., Wis. Educator, De Pere (Wis.) Schs., 1970-80; ins. agt. Equitable Assurance Co., Green Bay, Wis., 1980—; assoc. RIA Midwest Profl. Planners Inc., WI and MN. Life Underwriters Tng. Coun. personal ins. and fin. planning instr.; guest lectr. U. Wis., Steven's Point; resource person for Small Bus. Devel. Ctr., U. Wis., Green Bay; seminar moderator and instr. Vol. Children's Hosp. VIP fund raising, Green Bay, 1990-94; bd. dirs. Children's Hosp. Found., 1993-94. Fellow Nat. Assn. Ins. and Fin. Advisors past pres. N.E. Wis. chpt.); Wis. Assn. Ins. and Fin. Advisors (past pres. N.E. Wis. chpt.), Estate Planning Coun. Green Bay (v.p.), Soc. Fin. Svc. Profls. (past pres.). Republican. Roman Catholic. Avocations: coin collecting, golf. Office: Axa Advisors LLC 1585 Allouez Ave Green Bay WI 54311-5639

FISCHER, RUSSELL LEONARD, public relations executive; b. East Orange, NJ, Feb. 4, 1958; s. Harold Martin and Annette Carol Fischer. BA, Boston U., 1980; JD, Antioch U., Washington, 1984. Importer, retailer, owner Fendi of Short Hills, N.J., 1982-92; pub. rels. dir., v.p. IME-Xaminations, Elizabeth, N.J., 1994—. Vol. World Trade Orgn., NYC, battered wives Unity Group, Short Hills, 1995-98; del. reform coun. Am. Jewish Congress, N.Y.C., 1991; adv. bd. Am. Assn. Reform Judaism, Washington, 1995-99; alumni advisor, pres. South Fla. chpt. Boston U. Alumni Assn., 2000-02; active Heritage Soc. Congregation Emanu-El, NYC. Recipient Meritorious and Outstanding Cmty. Svc. award Am. Nat. Red Cross, 1976. Mem.: N.J. Improters Assn., Ocean Point Beach Club, World Trade Ctr. Club, Williams Island Club, Crestmont Country Club. Avocation: sculpture.

FISCHER, SIBYLLE MARIA, literature educator; d. Christa and Hermann Fischer; m. Liam Murphy, July 17, 1992. MA in Latin Am. Studies, Philosophy, German, Free U., Berlin, 1987; PhD, Columbia U., 1994. Asst. prof. Duke U., Durham, NC, 1995—2003, assoc. prof., 2003—. Author: (cultural history, literary criticism) Modernity Disavowed: Haiti and the Cultures of Slavery. Office: Duke U Program in Lit Art Mus Durham NC 27708 E-mail: sfischer@duke.edu.

FISCHER, STANLEY, bank executive, economist, educator; b. Lusaka, Zambia, Oct. 15, 1943; came to U.S., 1966, naturalized, 1976; s. Philip and Ann (Kopelowitz) F.; m. Rhoda Keet, Dec. 12, 1965; children: Michael Adam, David Benjamin, Jonathan Phillip. BSc, London Sch. Econs., 1965, MSc, 1966; PhD, MIT, 1969. Fellow U. Chgo., 1969-70, asst. prof. econs., 1970-73; assoc. prof. MIT, 1973-77, prof., 1977—, Killian prof., 1992-94; chief economist, v.p. devel. econs. World Bank, 1988-90; 1st dep. mgr. dir. IMF, 1994—2001; vice chmn. Citigroup, N.Y.C., 2002—; pres. Citigroup Internat., 2002—. Vis. sr. lectr. Hebrew U. Jerusalem, 1972; fellow Ctr. for Advanced Studies Hebrew U., 1976-77; vis. fellow Hoover Instn., Stanford U., 1981-82; cons. on Israeli economy Dept. State, 1984-87, 91-94; cons. IMF, 1991-92. Author: Indexing Inflation and Economic Policy, 1986, (with R. Dornbusch and R. Schmalensee) Economics, 1988, (with O. Blanchard) Lectures in Macroeconomics, 1989, (with R. Dornbusch and R. Startz) Macroeconomics, 8th edit., 2001; editor Nat. Bur. Econ. Rsch. Macroecons. Ann., 1986-94; contbr. articles to profl. jours. Guggenheim fellow. Fellow Econometric Soc.; mem. Am. Acad. Arts and Scis., Coun. on Fgn. Rels. Office: Citigroup 399 Park Ave New York NY 10043

FISCHER, STEVEN THOMAS, writer, producer, director; b. Balt., June 10, 1972; s. Thomas William and Marjorie Lynne (Kadlec) F. BA Visual and Performing Arts, U. Md., Baltimore County, 1994—98. Prodr., dir., 1990—. Many film credits, including I.W.S., 1995, This is CLEARCorps, 1996, Mr. Lumpy, 1997, Water, 2000, (TV) Steve & Bluey: In a Minute, 1996—99, Silence of Falling Leaves, 2000 (Emmy nomination, Telly award, N.Y. Festivals finalist), (radio) Hole in My Hair, 1996, The Perfect Piece of Toast, 1996, A Night at the Soap Opera, 2000, The Big Bash at Baltimore Museum of Industry, 2000, The Big Bash at WOCV, 2001, author, illustrator There's a Blue Dog Under My Bed, 1991, The Wonderful, Happy, Cartoony World of Steve and Bluey, 2001. Avocations: music, writing. Office: Po Box 3866 Crofton MD 21114-3866

FISCHER, THEODORE DAVID, retired lawyer; b. Pitts., Pa., Oct. 21, 1933; s. Samuel M. and Beatrice (Stewart) Fischer; m. Joan F. Friedman, Aug. 29, 1954; children: Bruce, Steven, Sandra, Betsy. BA, U. Pitts., 1955, LLB, 1958, SJD (hon.), 1962. Bar: Pa. 1959, Fla. 1978, U.S. Dist. Ct. (we. dist.) Pa. 1959. Ptnr. Markel, Markel, Levenson & Fischer, Pitts., 1961—69, Motor Inn Investors, Pitts., 1971—91, Guren, Merritt, Fischer, Udell, Lasky, Sogg & Cohen, Miami, Fla., 1979—82; counsel Bercuson, Cahan, Weksler & Lasky, Miami, Fla., 1982—87; prin. In-Rel Group of Cos., 1987—2002; ret., 2002. Editor: U. Pitts. Law Rev., 1958; contbr. articles to profl. jours. Bd. dirs. Marion-Citrus Mental Health Ctr. and Mental Health Found. Mem.: Score, Order of Coif. Office: 3180 N Pinelake Village Pt Lecanto FL 34461-8139 E-mail: tfische2@tampabay.rr.com.

FISCHER, THOMAS COVELL, law educator, consultant, writer, lawyer; b. May 2, 1938; s. Vilas Uber and Elizabeth Mary (Holland) F.; m. Katherine Brenda Andrew, Sept. 29, 1972. AB, U. Cin., 1960; postgrad., U. Wash., 1960-62, Loyola U., Chgo., 1964-66; JD, Georgetown U., 1966. Asst. dir. U. Ill.-Chgo., 1964-66; asst. dean Georgetown U. Law Ctr., 1966-72; cons. Antioch Sch. Law, 1972-73; asst. exec. dir. Am. Bar Found., Chgo., 1974-76; assoc. dean, prof. law U. Dayton, 1976-78; dean, prof. law New Eng. Sch. Law, Boston, 1978—81, prof., 1981—2003, prof. emeritus, 2003—; disting. acad. in residence Seattle U. Law Sch., 2003—. Vis. scholar, Cambridge, 1991, Exeter, 91, Edinburgh, 91, Konstanz U., 1993, Muenster U., 1993; fellow Inst. Advanced Legal Studies, U. London; vis. fellow Wolfson Coll., Cambridge, England, 1997; vis. tutor LLM program U. Southampton Law Faculty, 2001, sr. vis. tutor, 02; sr. rsch. fellow Seattle U. Law Sch., 2003; cons. in field. Author: Due Process in the Student/Institutional Relationship, 1970; author: (with Duscha) The Campus Press: Freedom and Responsibility, 1973; author: (with Zenhle) Introduction to Law and Legal Reasoning, 1977, Legal Education, Law Practice and the Economy: A New England Study, 1990, The Europeanization of America: What Americans Need to Know About the European Union, 1996, The United States, the European Union, and the Globilization of World Trade: Allies or Adversaries?, 2000; author: (with Cox) Quick Review of Conflict of Laws, 4th edit., 2001. Project dir. Commn. on Legal Edn. and Practice and the Economy of New Eng. Recipient Elaine R. Maham award U. Cin., 1960; Pi Kappa Alpha Meml. scholar 1960-62, Fellow Inns of Ct.; mem. Delta Theta Phi, Pi Delta Epsilon, Phi Alpha Theta. Roman Catholic. Office: New Eng Sch Law 154 Stuart St Boston MA 02116-5616 *Every one of us is a teacher in some way; we are also students. May we teach truthfully, and learn well.*

FISCHER, VIOLETA PÈREZ CUBILLAS, Spanish literature and linguistics educator; b. Havana, Cuba, Nov. 20, 1923; came to U.S., 1959; d. Josè M. and Carmen (Reyes Pizey) Pèrez Cubillas; m. Rolando F. Fischer, Dec. 27, 1947 (dec. May 1994); 1 child, Violet Fischer Pack. PhD in Law, U. Havana, 1949; postgrad., U. N.C., 1967-68, MA in Romance Langs., 1975. Prin. Spl. Ctr. for English Teaching, Havana, Cuba, 1945—59; lawyer Havana, Cuba, 1949—59; asst. prof. East Carolina U., Greenville, NC, 1962—66; prof. Spanish lit. and linguistics Coastal Carolina Community Coll., Jacksonville, NC, 1970—96; ret., 1996. Speaker various civic, mil., ednl. assns., and community colls., 1963—. Bd. dirs. Onslow County Community Concerts, Jacksonville, N.C., 1987; chmn. CCCC Women's Assn., 1972-73. Recipient Josè de la Luz y Caballero award Cruzada Educativa Cubana Assn., 1987, Juan J. Remos award Cruzada Educativa Cubana, 1987, N.C. State Svc. award for 30 yrs. of svc., 1994; Paul Harris fellow Rotary Internat., 1996. Mem. MLA, Nat. Assn. Cuban Lawyers, Havana Bar Assn. in Exile, Nat. Cuban Tchrs. Assn., Nat. Assn. Cuban-Am. Educators, Count of Galvez Hist. Soc., Sigma Delta Mu (cofounder, state rep.), Delta Kappa Gamma (chmn. world fellowship com. 1982-84, 96-98, Wreath of Excellence ednl. award 1989, 2d v.p. Upsilon chpt. Jacksonville 1994-96). Roman Catholic. Home: 2107 Perry Dr Jacksonville NC 28546-1642

FISCHER, WILLIAM SAMUEL, composer, lecturer; b. Shelby, Miss., Mar. 5, 1935; s. Robert A. and Willye (Samuels) F.; m. Dolores Labrie, Feb. 14, 1934; children: Darius, Marc, Bryan, Paul. BS in Mus. Edn., Colo. Coll., 1956; MA in Music Theory and Composition, U. Southwestern La., 1961; postgrad., Vienna Acad. Music, 1965—66. Dir. band, choir Christianburg Inst., Cambria, Va., 1957-58, St. Landry Parish, Opelousas, La., 1958-62; faculty music Xavier U., 1962-66, High Sch. of Music and Art, N.Y.C., 1969-76; dir. music Atlantic Rec. Co., N.Y.C., 1967-71, record prodr., 1975—, Fantasy Rec. Co., Berkeley, Calif., 1976-79; freelance composer, arranger N.Y.C., 1967—. Lectr. N.Y.C.; cons. bd. of Edn., N.Y.C. Composer Jessea Simone, 1970, Touch Kiss, 1971, Dong Film Opera, 1977, Choral Music for a Saint in honor of Katharine Drexel, 1988, Gospel Spirit, 1966, Mass For a Saint, Concerto, The cross Bronx Concerto for Violin and Orch. Concert Music for Saxophone and Orch., 1996; musician: The Vatican, Rome, 1988, 2000; author: The Heart of Creativity, 1986, Mind to Music Theory of Music, 2000, Private Hours. Trilogy on Meditation and Trance, The LeBeau Mass, 1997. Mem. The LeBeau Mass com. for celebration 100 years of ch. established 1897 Immaculate Conception, St. Landry Parish, La. Served to corp. USMC, 1956-57. Recipient Deutsches Akademische Austaudienst award Fed. Republic of Germany, 1966; grantee Fulbright Found., 1965, Austrian govt., 1965, Pan Am. grantee, Tulane U., New Orleans, 1964-65. Mem. Internat. Platform Assn., ASCAP. Roman Catholic. Avocation: astronomy.

FISCHER, ZOE ANN, real estate and property marketing company executive, consultant; b. L.A., Aug. 26, 1939; d. George and Marguerite (Carrasco) Routsos; m. Douglas Clare Fischer, Aug. 6, 1960 (div. 1970); children: Brent Sean Cecil, Tahlia Georgienne Marguerite Bianca. BFA in Design, UCLA, 1964. Pres. Zoe Antiques, Beverly Hills, Calif., 1973—; v.p. Harleigh Sandler Real Estate Corp. (now Prudential-Jon, Douglas), 1980-81; exec. v.p. Coast to Coast Real Estate & Land Devel. Corp., Century City, Calif., 1981-83; pres. New Market Devel., Inc., Beverly Hills, 1983—. Dir. mktg. Mirabella, L.A., 1983, Autumn Pointe, L.A., 1983-84, Desert Hills, Antelope Valley, Calif., 1984-85; cons. Lowe Corp., L.A., 1985. Designer interior and exterior archtl. enhancements and remodelling; designed album cover for Clare Fischer Orch. (Grammy award nomination 1962). Soprano Roger Wagner Choir, UCLA, 1963-64. Mem. UCLA Alumni Assn., So. Calif. Restaurant Writers, Laguna Plain Air Painters Assn. Democrat. Roman Catholic. Avocations: skiing, designing jewelry, interior, landscape and new home design, antique collecting.

FISCHETTI, MICHAEL, public administration educator, arbitrator; b. Bklyn., Sept. 3, 1940; s. Michael A. and Marion T. (Vernola) Fischetti; m. Renate M. Winkler, Dec. 26, 1966; children: Peter N, Flori. BA, U. Md., 1965, MA, 1967, PhD, 1979; MPA, Am. U., 1971. Asst. to city mgr. City of Greenbelt, Md., 1966-67; rsch. assoc. Nat. League of Cities, Washington, 1967-68; div. dir. U.S. Dept. of Treasury, Washington, 1976-77; prof. and dir. Community Rsch. Svc. Montgomery Coll., Rockville, Md., 1968-2000, internat. edn. fellow, 1998-99. Consult Montgomery County Govt, Rockville, 1986—89, Pension Benefit Guarantee Corp, 1988—92. Editor: Pub Admin Rev, 1976—77, Pub Admin Quart, 1977—86. Vpres Montgomery County Coun PTA's, 1985—87; dir Project PEACE, 1998—2000. With U.S. Army, 1959—62. Recipient Mayor's Citation for Pub Serv, Mayor's Office, City of Baltimore, 1975, Pres's Citation for Outstanding Merit, pres City Coun, City of Baltimore, 1975. Mem.: Indust Relations Research Asn, Soc Fed Labor Relations Prof's, Soc Prof's Dispute Resolution, Am Arbit Asn, Am Soc Pub Admin (nat coun 1976—78). Roman Catholic. Avocations: swimming, softball. Home: 6017 Madawaska Rd Bethesda MD 20816

FISCHETTI, MICHAEL JOSEPH, accounting educator; b. Bklyn., Sept. 20, 1939; s. Anthony Joseph and Nicolina Rose (Marchitello) F.; m. Carlotta Theresa Cannarili, Sept. 25, 1960; children: Christine, Doreen, Clorissa, Diana. BBA, Pace U., 1968, MBA, 1970. CPA, N.Y. Audit mgr. Arthur Young & Co., N.Y.C., 1973-77, prin. Reston, Va., 1978-81; sr. mgr. Friedman & Fuller, Rockville, Md., 1982-86, Hoffman & Dykes, Vienna, Va., 1987-91; asst. dir. U.S. Gen. Acctg. Office, Washington, 1991—. Lectr. U. Md., Marymount U. Pace U. teaching fellow, 1967. Mem. AICPAs (chair computer edn. subcom. 1973-74), Christian Businessmen's Com. (chair 1988-91). Avocations: swimming, walking, bible study. Office: US Gen Acctg Office 441 G St NW Washington DC 20548-0001 E-mail: fischettim@msn.com.

FISCHHOFF, BARUCH, psychologist, educator; b. Detroit, Apr. 21, 1946; s. Henry and Shirley (Levine) F.; m. Andrea Marks, Dec. 22, 1968; children: Maya, Ilya, Noam. BS in Math., Wayne State U., 1967; MA in Psychology, Hebrew U., Jerusalem, 1972, PhD in Psychology, 1975. Rsch. assoc. Oreg. Rsch. Inst., Eugene, 1974-76, Decision Rsch., Eugene, 1976-85. Applied Psychology Unit Med. Rsch. Coun., Cambridge, Eng., 1981-82, Eugene Rsch. Inst., 1985-87; prof. Carnegie-Mellon U., Pitts., 1987—, Univ. prof., 1998—, Howard Heinz prof., 2002—. Vis. prof. U. Stockholm, 1982-83; mem. panels NRC; cons. in field. Author: Acceptable Risk, 1981, Mental Models, 2001; mem. editl. bd. Jour. Risk Uncertainty, Decision Analysis, Risk Analysis, also others; contbr. numerous articles to profl. jours . Mem. Eugene Commn. on Rights of Women, 1975-81; pres. Eugene Human Rights Coun., 1979-81. Fellow APA (Disting. Sci. award 1981, psychology in Pub. Interest award 1991), Soc. for Risk Analysis (Disting. Achievement award 1991), Soc. Judgment and Decision-Making (mem. coun. 1988-91, pres. 1990-91), Inst. Medicine, Phi Beta Kappa. Home: 1437 Denniston Ave Pittsburgh PA 15217 1332 Office: Carnegie Mellon U Dept Engring and Pub Policy Pittsburgh PA 15213-3890 E-mail: baruch@cmu.edu.

FISCHL, MARGARET A. education educator, researcher; MD, U. of Miami Sch. of Medicine, 1976. Cert. Am. Bd. of Internal Medicine, 1979. Prof. medicine U. of Miami Sch. of Medicine, 1990—, dir. aids clin. rsch. unit. Recipient Tchg. and Rsch. Award, Am. Coll. of Physicians, 1982—85, Woman of Vision award, Weuzmann Inst. of Sci., 2001, grantee Adult AIDS Clin. Trials Group, NIAID, NIH, 1986—96. Achievements include research in HIV/AIDS clinical trials. Office: Univ of Miami Sch of Medicine 1800 NW 10th Ave (R-60A) Miami FL 33136 Office Fax: 305-545-6705. E-mail: mfischl@med.miami.edu.

FISCHLER, ABRAHAM SAUL, educator, retired university president; b. Bklyn., Jan. 21, 1928; s. Morris and Esther P. Fischler; m. Shirley Balter, Apr. 9, 1949; children: Bruce Evan, Michael Alan, Lori Faye. BS in Soc. Sci., CUNY, 1951; MA in Sci. Edn., NYU, 1952; EdD, Columbia U., 1959; DSc (hon.), N.Y. Inst. Tech., 1981; LLD (hon.), Nova U., 1992. Sci. tchr., supr. Ossining (N.Y.) Pub. Schs., 1952-58; instr. Columbia U., N.Y.C., 1958-59; asst. prof. edn. Harvard U. Grad. Sch., Cambridge, Mass., 1959-62; assoc. prof. then prof. edn. U. Calif., Berkeley, 1962-66; dean grad. studies Nova U., Ft. Lauderdale, Fla., 1966-70, James Donn prof., 1966—, exec. v.p., 1969-70, pres., 1970-92; pres. emeritus, univ. prof., 1992—; mem. Broward County Sch.

Bd., 1994-98, chair, 1996-97. Vis. prof. nat. and internat. univs., 1963-65; cons. numerous sch. dists., Calif., 1962-67; advisor ednl. pubs.; mem. bus.-edn. adv. com. Alameda-Contra Costa Counties, Calif.; mem. Calif. Elem. Sci. Adv. Com., Sacramento; mem. Overseas Tchrs. Examining Team, Berkeley; bd. dirs. Cardio-Metrics, Inc., Inst. Learning Techs., Inc., Hollywood Med. Ctr., Fla. Med. Ctr., 2000— Author: Modern Science, Grades 7,8,9, 1963; (with others) Science: A Modern Approach, 1966, Modern Science, 1967, Modern Elementary Science: Grades 1 through 8, 1971, Nova U.'s Three National Doctoral Degree Programs: An Analysis and Formative Evaluation, 1977; contbr. numerous articles to profl. jours., author monograph and rsch. reports. Pres. United Way Broward County (Fla.), 1984-85, bd. dirs., 1973-2000, chmn. budget com., 1976-81; chmn. Broward County Overall Econ. Devel. Com., 1980-88, Broward Edn. and Tng. Coun., 1989—; pres. S.E. Fla. Holocaust Meml. Ctr., 1985-87, Temple Beth El, Hollywood, 1988-90; adv. bd. Leadership Broward; mem. 17th Jud. Nominating Commn., Broward County, 1982-86, Ft. Lauderdale Mus. Art, Fla. Philharm., Broward County Crime Commn., Broward Workshop Edn. Task Force, Town of Davie, Fla. Econ. and Indsl. Devel. Bd.; bd. dirs. Hollywood (Fla.) Med. Ctr., 1982—, chmn. bd. dirs., 1985—; pres. Health Care Rsch. and Edn. Found., 1988-89, United Ways Fla., 1990-91; bd. govs. Fla. Bar, 1991-95, Fla. Bar Found., 1996-01; chmn. Hollywood City Master Plan; mem. Broward Ctr. Performing Arts Authority, 1998; co-chair Sun Sentinel Diversity Fund, 2000—; chair Broward Edn. Found., 2002, South Fla. Cmty. Blood Ctrs., 2002. With USN, 1945-47. Recipient Outstanding Mgmt. and Leadership award Sales and Mktg. Execs., Ft. Lauderdale, 1978, Leader of Yr. award Leadership Broward, 1991, Humanitarian of Yr. award E.A.S.E. Found., 1991, Disting. Educator award Assn. Ind. Schs. Fla., 1992, Tree of Life award Jewish Nat. Fund, 1993, Spirit of Broward award, 1994, Lifetime Achievement award Urban League, 1994; named Broward Educator of Yr., Women's Am. ORT, 1997, Disting. Pub. Svc. award ADL, 1998, Sun Sentinel Cmty. Leader of the Yr., 1999, Sun Sentinel Cmty. Svc. award, 2000; DuPont fellow UCLA, 1958, Sci. Manpower fellow Columbia U., 1958-59. Fellow AAAS, Phi Delta Kappa; mem. ASCD, NSTA, Assn. for Edn. Tchrs. Sci. (past pres.), Nat. Assn. Research in Sci. Teaching, Soc. Advancement Edn., Soc. Research Adminstrs., Am. Assn. Higher Edn., Nat. Council Univ. Research Adminstrs., Com. of 100, Hollywood, Hundred Club Broward County (pres. 1985-86), Tower Club, Woodmont Country Club, Kappa Delta Pi. Avocations: running, golf, travel. Office: Nova U Office Pres Emeritus 3301 College Ave Fort Lauderdale FL 33314-7796 E-mail: fischler@nova.edu.

FISCHLER, ALAN BERNARD, communications educator; b. Bklyn., Sept. 3, 1952; s. Stanley and Miriam Fischler; m. Karen McDonold, June 25, 1995; m. Patricia Bonino, May 31, 1975 (div. Feb. 1, 1991); children: Stacey Noce, Stephanie Noce, Sonja Noce. BA in English, Cornell U., 1973; MA in English, PhD, U. of Rochester, 1987. Assoc. editor PTN Pub., Hempstead, NY, 1973; instr. in english Nazareth Coll., Rochester, NY, 1977—81; chair humanities and internat. studies Rochester (N.Y.) Inst. of Tech., Coll. of Continuing Edn.; mgr. tech. comm. Hartman Materials Handling Sys., Victor, NY, 1984—86; dir. of comm. program Le Moyne Coll., Syracuse, NY, 1988—91, assoc. prof. of english, 1991—97, prof. of english, 1997—. Cons. Gilbert and Sullivan documentary Power Productions, Ann Arbor, Mich. Author: Modified Rapture: Comedy in W.S. Gilbert's Savoy Operas. Green Party. Jewish. Avocations: travel, acting, directing. Home: 305 Dawley Road Fayetteville NY 13066 Office: Le Moyne College Salt Springs Road Syracuse NY 13214 Office Fax: 315-445-4540. E-mail: fischlab@lemoyne.edu.

FISCHLER, MARK STEVEN, physicist; b. N.Y.C., Aug. 28, 1953; m. Susan Ruth Robbins; children: Paula, Leanne. BS math and physics, Mass. Inst. of Tech., 1974; PhD in Physics, SUNY, Stony Brook, 1979. Scientist, assoc. head computational physics dept. Fermilab, Batavia, Ill., 1983—. Project leader for ACPMAPS supercomputer Fermilab, 1987—93. Patentee in field. Mem.: Am. Phys. Soc., Am. Contract Bridge League (life master 1988). Jewish. Office: Fermi Nat Accelerator Lab Kirk and Pine Sts Batavia IL 60510-0500

FISCHLER, SANDY LYNN, event producer; b. Anchorage, Alaska, Dec. 28, 1962; d. Joseph Michael Fischler and Sharon Leigh (Blodgett) Smith. Student, U. Alaska, 1980-83, Circle in Square Theatre Sch., 1983. Spl. event coord. Universal Studios Fla., Orlando, 1993-95; prodn. mgr. Headdress Ball, Orlando, 1994; assoc. prodr. Nickelodeon "Guts", Orlando, 1994; event mgr. First Night Providence, 1995; prodr. bike stunt segment 1997 Holiday Bowl Halftime Show, San Diego, 1997; event prodr. ESPN X Games, San Diego, 1995-98; ptnr. Avalanche Events Group, 1998—; owner 4th Wall Events, 1998—; event mgr. NFL Experience, Super Bowl XXXIII, 1999; broadcast mgr. NFL Experience, Super Bowl XXXIV, XXXV, XXXVI, XXXVII. Vol. Feral Cat Coalition, San Diego, 1998, Kisses for Kats Pet Rescue, 2000-01, Cat's Meow Cat Rescue, 2002--. Mem. Women in Sports and Events, Internat. Festival and Events Assn., Calfest, Nat. Sports Mktg. Network. Avocations: gardening, stained glass. Home: 5911 Cerritos Ave Long Beach CA 90805

FISCHLER, SHIRLEY BALTER, retired lawyer; b. Oct. 9, 1926; d. David and Rose (Shapiro) Balter; m. Abraham Saul Fischler, Apr. 9, 1949; children: Bruce Evan, Michael Alan, Lori Faye. BA, Bklyn. Coll., 1947, MA, 1951; JD, Nova U., 1977. Bar: Fla. 1977, D.C. 1980, U.S. Ct. Appeals (D.C. cir.) 1980. Tchr. N.Y.C. Bd. Edn., 1948-50, Richmond (Calif.) Pub. Schs., 1965-66; assoc. Panza, Maurer, Maynard, Platow & Neel, Ft. Lauderdale, Fla., 1977-95; pro bono atty. Broward Lawyers Care, 1982-86. V.p. Gold Cir. Nova Southeastern U., 1995-97, treas., 1997-2000; bd. govs. Nova U. Law Ctr., 1982-99; mem. Commn. on Status of Women, Broward County, Fla., 1982-87, vice chair, 1983-84, Entourage, Broward Ctr. for Performing Arts; bd. dirs. Hollywood (Fla.) Scholarship Found., 1999—. Mem. Fla. Bar Assn., D.C. Bar Assn., Broward County Bar Assn., Bklyn. Coll. Alumni Assn. (sec.-treas. So. Fla. chpt. 1997-2000), Close Encounters with Music (bd. dirs. 1998—). Home: 8640 Banyan Way Tamarac FL 33321-2645 E-mail: shirlb49@bellsouth.net.

FISCHMAN, MYRNA LEAH, accountant, educator; d. Isidore and Sally (Goldstein) Fischman. BS, Coll. City N.Y., 1960, MS, 1964; PHD, NYU, 1976. CPA N.Y. Asst. to contr. Sam Goody, Inc., N.Y.C.; tchr. accounting Ctr. Comml. H.S., N.Y.C., 1960—63, vicat. adviser, 1963—66; instr. acctg. Borough of Manhattan C.C., N.Y.C., 1963—66; self-employed acct. N.Y.C., 1960—; chief acct. investigator rackets Office Queens Dist. Atty., 1969—70, cmty. fels. coord., 1970—71; adv. prof. L.I. U., 1970—79, prof. acctg. taxation and law, 1979—, coord. grad. capstone courses, 1982—86, dir. Sch. Profl. Accountancy Bklyn. Campus, 1984—, dir. Ctr. Acctg. and Tax Edn., 1986—, chmn. acctg. dept. Editor: Ea. Bus. Educators Jour., 1988. Rsch. cons. pre-tech. program N.Y.C. Bd. Edn., mem., 1992—; acct.-advisor Inst. for Advancement of Criminal Justice; acct.-cons. Coalition Devel. Corp., Interracial Coun. for Bus. Opportunities; treas. Breakfree Inc., Lower East Side Prep. Sch.; mem. ednl .task force Am. Jewish Com., 1972—; mem. Chancellor Com. Against Discrimination in Edn., 1976—97; chmn. supervisory com. Fed. Credit Union # 1532, N.Y.C., 1983—; chmn. consumer coun. Astoria Med. Ctr., 1980—92; mem. subcom. on bus. edn. to the econ. devel. and mktg. com. Bklyn. C. of C., 1984—; mem. adv. bd. acctg. dept. burough of Manhattan C.C., 1997—; mem. Bus. Edn. Adv. Coun.; mem. steering com., youth div. N.Y. Dem. County Com., 1967—68; del. to Nat. Conv. Young Dems. Am., 1967, rep. assigned to women's activities com., 1967; mem. legis. adv. bd. N.Y. State Assemblyman Dennis Butler, 1979—97. Recipient award for meritorious svc., Cmty. Svc. Soc., 1969, Lifetime Achievement award, Soroptimist Internat. Bklyn., 1997. Mem.: NEA (bus. edn. assns.), AAUP, AICPA, Inst. Mgmt. Accts. (dir. N.Y. chpt. 1983—, dir. profl. devel. 1986—87, dir. pub. rels. 1987—88, dir. manuscripts 1991—92, dir. univ. rels. 1993—94), Tax Inst. L.I. U. (dir. Blyn. chpg. 1984—), N.Y. State Soc. CPAs (mem. com. on recruitment for CPA careers 1981—, auditing com. 1991—, gen. com. on edn. in colls. and univs. 1991—, pub. rels. com. 1992—, pres. Bklyn. chpt. 2001—02, Dr. Emanuel Saxe Outstanding CPA in Edn. award 1994—95), Fed. Credit Union (chmn. supervisory com. # 1532 n.Y.C. 1983—), Young Alumni Assn., Am. Assn. Jr. Colls., Doctorate Assn. N.Y. Educators (v.p. 1975—97), Assn. Govt. Accts. (dir. N.Y. chpg. 1983—, pres. elect n.Y. chpg. 1989—90, pres. N.Y. chpt. 1990—91), Fin. Execs. Inst., Grad. Students Orgn. NYU (treas. 1971—73), Internat. Soc. Bus. Edn., Nat. Eastern (co-chmn. ann. meeting 1967), Am. Acctg. Assn., Govt. Accts. (v.p. 1973—74, dir. rsch. and manuscripts 1985—, pres. elect N.Y. chpt. 1989—90, pres. 1990—91, bd. dirs. N.Y. chpt. 1994—), Emanu-El League Congregation Emanu-El, N.Y. (chmn. cmty. svcs. com. 1967—68), Jewish Guild for Blind, Jewish Braille Inst., Cmty. Welfare Com. Assn., Friends Met. Mus. Art, Friends Am. Ballet Theatre, Women's City Club (N.Y.), Delta Pi Epsilon (treas. 1976). Democrat. Jewish. Achievements include development of new bus. machine course and curriculum Borough Manhattan Bus. C.C. Office: LI U Sch Bus 1 University Plz Rm 700 Brooklyn NY 11201-5301

FISCHMAN, STANLEY EDWIN, psychiatrist; b. N.Y.C., Feb. 5, 1935; s. Irving and Libbie (Cohen) F.; m. Linda Zuckerman, Sept. 15, 1963; children: Ian Alexander, Seth Morrison. BA, Yeshiva U., 1956; MD, SUNY, Bklyn., 1960. Diplomate Am. Bd. Psychiatry and Neurology, Am. Bd. Child Psychiatry. Asst. prof. Stanford (Calif.) U., 1969-73; chief of psychiatry Children's Hosp. at Stanford, Palo Alto, 1973-76; pvt. practice in child psychiatry Mountain View, Calif., 1976—; chief dept. psychiatry El Camino Hosp., Mountain View, 2001—03. Assoc. clin. prof. Stanford U., 1975—. Fellow Am. Psychiat. Assn. (disting.); mem. Calif. Med. Assn., Santa Clara County Med. Assn., No. Calif. Psychiat. Soc., Am. Soc. for Clin. Psychopharmacology. Avocations: scuba diving, farming. Office: 2485 Hospital Dr Ste 351 Mountain View CA 94040-4103 E-mail: sef18@sprintmail.com.

FISCHOFF, GARY CHARLES, lawyer; b. Manhasset, N.Y., Nov. 23, 1954; s. Harold and Ann (Yablon) F.; m. Linda Lee Sacca, Nov. 22, 1985 (div. Nov. 2002); 1 child, Lisa Frances. BA, U. Buffalo, 1976; JD, St. John's U., Jamaica, N.Y., 1983. Bar: N.J. 1983, U.S. Dist. Ct. N.J. 1983, N.Y. 1984, U.S. Dist. Ct. (so. and ea. dists.) N.Y. 1985, U.S. Dist. Ct. (no. and we. dist.) N.Y., U.S. Ct. Appeals (2d cir.) 1988. Asst. treas. IAP, Inc., Lyndhurst, N.J., 1980-82; assoc. Hannoch Weisman, Roseland, N.J., 1983-85; ptnr. Fischoff Gelberg & Director, Garden City, N.Y., 1985-96, Fischoff & Assocs., Garden City, 1996—, Steinberg, Fineo, Berger, Barone & Fischoff, Garden City, NY, 2003—. Lectr. seminar Nat. Bus. Inst., Westbury, N.Y., 1990, 91, Practicing Law Inst., 1992, 93, N.Y. State Bar Assn., 1995. Rep. Greentree Homeowners Assn., Northport, N.Y., 1988-89; trustee Suffolk County Vanderbilt Mus., 1994-2002, corp. sec., 1995-97, treas. 1997-99, 1st v.p., 1999-2002. Mem. Am. Bankruptcy Bd. Cert. (cert. bus. bankruptcy and consumer bankruptcy), N.Y. State Bar Assn. (real property sect., seminar lectr. 1995, Practicing Law Inst., continuing legal edn. lectr. 1992, 93), Nassau County Bar Assn. (mem. bankruptcy com., jud. liaison 1988-89). Jewish. Avocations: bicycling. Office: Steinberg Fineo Berger Barone & Fischoff 1001 Franklin Ave Garden City NY 11530

FISCUS, LINDA KAY, music educator; b. Blackwell, Okla., Sept. 22, 1950; d. Howard Orris and Ella May Reusser; m. Terry Ray Fiscus, June 24, 1972; children: Sarah Elaine, Seth Howard. BA, Northwestern Okla. State U., 1972, ME, 1995. Vocal music instr. Freedom (Okla.) H.S., 1972—74, Lone Wolf (Okla.) Schs., 1974—76; choral accompanist Blackwell H.S., 1983—87; vocal music instr. Huston Elem., Blackwell, 1987—93, Deer Creek-Lamont (Okla.) Schs., 1993—97; prof. music No. Okla. Coll., Tonkawa, 1997—. Judge various piano contests, 1972—; pianist Victory Fellowship, Blackwell, 1981—. Active Music Boosters, Blackwell, 1993—, Basketball Boosters, Blackwell, 1999—; hostess Miss NOC Pageant, Tonkawa, 1998—. Avocations: sewing, reading, interior decorating. Office: No Okla Coll PO Box 310 Tonkawa OK

FISCUS, PHILIP WAYNE, underwriter; b. Hastings, Nebr., Nov. 8, 1955; BA, Calif. State U., Northridge, 1978. CPCU. Underwriter St. Paul Fire and Marine Ins. Co., 1978-80, sr. underwriter, 1980-84, underwriter dir., 1984-92; v.p. Reliance Nat., N.Y.C., 1992-94; sr. v.p. Minet, Inc., N.Y.C., 1994-95; v.p. Chubb Group of Ins. Cos., Warren, NJ, 1995—2002, sr. v.p., 2002—. Mem. adv. bd. Biolaw & Bus. Publ. Contbr. articles to profl. jours. Mem. AAAS, Biotechnology Industry Assn., Risk and Ins. Mgmt. Soc. (assoc.). Office: Chubb & Son Inc 202 Hall's Mill Rd PO Box 1650 Whitehouse Station NJ 08889 E-mail: pfiscus@chubb.com.

FISETTE, SCOTT MICHAEL, landscape and golf course architect; b. Orange, Tex., May 17, 1963; s. Roderick John and Addie Faye (Byrnes) F.; m. Keali'i Kane; children: Shane Roderick, Hayley Kaimalie. BS in Landscape Architecture, Tex. A&M U., 1985. Registered landscape architect, Tex., Hawaii, Commonwealth of No. Mariana Islands. Project architect Dick Nugent Assocs., Long Grove, Ill., 1985-90; prin., pres. Fisette Golf Designs, Kaneohe, Hawaii, 1991—. Mem. Golf Course Supts. Assn. Am., Am. Soc. Landscape Architects, Nat. Golf Found., Hawaii Turf Grass Assn. (bd. dirs. 1991-96), Donald Ross Soc. Avocations: golf, fishing, water skiing, softball. Office: Fisette Golf Designs PO Box 1433 Kaneohe HI 96744-1433

FISH, BARBARA JOAN, investor, small business owner; b. Seattle, June 12, 1936; d. George Francis Linehan and Maureece Shirley (Frederick) McCullough; m. Ralph Edwin Fish, July 14, 1956 (dec. Nov. 1986). Grad. high sch., Portland, Oreg. Owner Sea and Sand R.V. Park, Depoe Bay, Oreg., 1977—; real estate investor State of Oreg. Active St. Augustine's Ch. Mem. Lincoln City C. of C., Depoe Bay C. of C., Oreg. Sheriff's Assn. (hon.). Republican. Roman Catholic. Avocations: R.V. traveling, gardening. Home and Office: Sea and Sand RV Park 4985 N Highway 101 Depoe Bay OR 97341-9740

FISH, BRIAN R, music educator; b. Wilmington, Del., Nov. 19, 1963; s. Roger C. and Carol E. Fish; m. Beth Ann Steele, 1986; children: Kelsey, Thomas. MA in Music Edn., Ariz. State U., Tempe, AZ, 1987. Cert. 1985. Band dir./music tchr. Pendergast Elem. Sch. Dist., Phoenix, 1987—94; mid. sch. band dir. Berwick (Pa.) Area Sch. Dist., 1994—. Freelance musician, Berwick, Pa. Youth leader Bower Meml. Meth. Ch., Beriwck, Pa., 2001—02. Named Tchr. of the Yr., Pendergast Sch. Dist., 1992. Mem.: Music Educators Nat. Conf. Methodist. Avocations: outdoor activities, fishing.

FISH, CHESTER BOARDMAN, JR., retired editor; b. Worcester, Mass., June 30, 1925; s. Chester Boardman and Mary Elizabeth (Sheehan) F.; m. Claire Margaret Commo, Sept. 10, 1948; children: Craig Michael, Scott Kevin, Maribeth Ann, Andrea Dawn, Brian John. BA, Syracuse U., 1950, MA, 1952. Asst. editor Boys' Life mag., N.Y.C., 1951-53; assoc. editor Sports Afield mag., N.Y.C., 1953-55; copy chief Am. Home mag., N.Y.C., 1955-57; assoc. editor Outdoor Life mag., N.Y.C., 1957-63, article editor, 1963-67, mng. editor, 1967-73, editor in chief, 1973-76; sr. editor David McKay Co., Inc. book pubs., N.Y.C., 1976-80, Charles Scribner's Sons (pubs.), N.Y.C., 1980-81; pub. cons. The Competitive Edge, Greenlawn, N.Y., 1981-83; editorial dir. Stackpole Books, Harrisburg, Pa., 1983-85, exec. v.p., 1986-89, Stackpole Inc., Harrisburg, Pa., 1989-90; pub. Harness Horse mag., Harrisburg, 1989-91; pub. cons. and freelance writer Carlisle, Pa., 1990-94. Served with USNR, 1943-46, PTO. Mem. Carlindian Barbershop Chorus. Republican. Roman Catholic. Home: 709 Sutton Dr Carlisle PA 17013-3546

FISH, ELIZABETH ANN, physical education educator; b. Bryn Mawr, Pa., June 24, 1964; d. George David and Elizabeth Fish. BS in Health and Phys. Edn., U. Del., 1987; MS in Health Edn., Saint Joseph's U., Phila., 1990. Dept. head phys. edn. Springside Sch., Phila., 1987—. Coach Eastern Field Hockey Camp, Pottstown, Pa., 1983-93, Pvt. I's All-Star Field Hockey Team, Pa., 1990. Mem. Am. Alliance for Health, Phys. Edn., Recreation and Dance, U.S. Field Hockey Assn., Pa. Assn. for Health, Phys. Edn., Recreation and Dance, Phi Kappa Phi, Kappa Delta Pi. Avocations: woodworking, gardening, fitness, golf. Home: 279 Deerfield Ct New Hope PA 18938-1805 Office: Springside Sch 8000 Cherokee St Philadelphia PA 19118-4135

FISH, HOWARD MATH, aerospace industry executive; b. Melrose, Minn., Aug. 1, 1923; s. Nathaniel and Louise Magaret (Gaetz) F.; m. Jamie Katherine Tom, May 15, 1948; 1 child, Howard Math Jr. Student, Air Command and Staff Coll., 1954; MBA, U. Chgo., 1957; postgrad., Armed Forces Staff Coll., 1960, Air War Coll., Montgomery, Ala., 1964; MAIA, George Washington U., 1964. Enlisted USAF, 1942, commd. 2d lt., 1944, capt., 1950, col., 1965, advance through grades to lt. gen., 1974, retired, 1979; deputy asst. sec. defense internat. security affairs Dept. Defense, Washington; asst. vice chief of staff USAF, Washington; chmn. U.S. Mil. Delegation to UN; v.p. internat. LTV Aerospace and Defense Co., 1980-82, Loral Corp., 1992-96; sr. advisor Internat. Lockheed-Martin Missiles and Fire Control, Dallas, La., 1996—. Mem. Def. Policy Adv. Com. on Trade, Washington, 1987-94; chmn. Am. League for Exports and Security Assistance, Washington, 1986-94. Decorated Def. DSM, Air Force DSM, Legion of Merit, DFC, Air medal, Purple Heart, POW medal. Mem. Am. Def. Preparedness Assn. (chmn. internat. div. 1984-94), Army Navy Club, Air Force Assn., Washington Inst. Fgn. Affairs, Beta Gamma Sigma. Roman Catholic. Avocations: tennis, fishing. Home: 1192 County Rd 456 Thorndale TX 76577-5215 also: 1233 Capilano Dr Shreveport LA 71106-8286 E-mail: genhmfish@aol.com.

FISH, JANET ISOBEL, artist; b. Boston, May 18, 1938; d. Peter and Florence (Voorhees) F. BA, Smith Coll., 1960; postgrad., Skowhegan (Maine) Art Sch., summer 1961; BFA, MFA, Yale U., 1963; DFA (hon.), Lyme Acad., 2000. Represented by D.C. Moore Gallery, N.Y.C. One-woman shows D.C. Moore Gallery, N.Y.C., Columbus (Ga.) Mus., also others; represented in permanent collections Whitney Mus. Am. Art, N.Y.C., Met. Mus. Art, N.Y.C., Cleve. Mus. Art, Dallas Mus. Fine Arts, Am. Fedn. Arts, Am. Acad. Inst. Arts and Letters, Art Inst. Chgo., Kemper Mus., Kansas City,, Albright-Knox Gallery, Buffalo, N.Y., Newark Mus., Mpls. Mus. of Art, Nat. Gallery of Victoria, Melbourne, Australia, Powers Inst., Sydney, Australia, Colby Coll., Waterville, Maine, N.Y. Mus. of Fine Arts, Houston Art Ctr., RISD, Providence, Mus. Art, Providence, Va. Mus. Fine Arts, Richmond, Yale U., New Haven, Smith Coll. Mus. Art, Northampton, Mass., Albrecht Art Mus., St. Joseph, Mo., Milw. Art Mus., Hunter Mus. Art, Chattanooga, others. Bd. govs. Skowhegan Sch. Painting and Sculpture, Marie Walsh Sharpe Art Found. Recipient Harris award Chgo. Bienale award, 1974, Outstanding Woman Artist award Aspen Mus., 1992, Am. Acad. of Arts and Letters award, 1994, Henry Ward Ranger Purchase prize Nat. Acad. Design, N.Y., 2001; MacDowell fellow, 1968, 69, 72; Yale scholar, Australian Coun. for Arts grantee, 1975. Mem. Am. Acad. and Inst. of Arts and Letters (assoc.). E-mail: jfcp1@earthlink.net.

FISH, MARY MARTHA, economics educator; b. Albert Lea, Minn., July 17, 1930; d. Charles H. and Olga (Stennes) Thomassen; m. Donald C. Fish, Oct. 1954 (dec.); children: Jill S., Lynn M., Jason M. BBA, U. Minn., 1951; MBA in Econs, Tex. Tech. Coll., 1957; PhD (AAUW fellow 1960), U. Okla., 1963. Statis. asst. Iowa Bd. Control, 1951-53; pub. health analyst State of Calif., 1953-54; analytical statistician 46th Med. Gen. Lab., U.S. Army Forces, Tokyo, 1954-57; instr. econs. and bus. Odessa (Tex.) Coll., 1957-58; asst. prof., then assoc. prof. West Tex. State U., 1961-66; prof. econs. U. Ala., 1966-99, prof. emeritus, 1999 , prof. econs. Landegg Internat. U., Wienacht, Switzerland, 2000—02. Fulbright lectr. U. Liberia, 1974-75, Gambian Govt., 1978-79; cons. in field. Co-author: Convicts, Codes and Contraband, 1974; contbr. articles to profl. jours. Grantee U. Ala., 1967-68, 87-89, Dept. Labor, 1978-79; Fulbright rsch. fellow, Taiwan, 1995; Phifer Faculty Scholar, 1998. Mem. Am. Econ. Assn., So. Econ. Assn. Mem. Baha'i faith. Home: 1405 High Forest Dr N Tuscaloosa AL 35406-2153 E-mail: mfish@cba.ua.edu., mfish@landegg.edu.

FISH, PAUL WARING, lawyer; b. Ligonier, Pa., Apr. 12, 1933; s. Edmund R. and Catherine (McGuiggan) F.; m. Jacquelyn A. Shea, Sept. 19, 1959; children: Charles M., Edmund J., Catherine G., John H., Jacquelyn A. BS in Elec. Engring, Cath. U. Am., 1959, M.E.E., 1961; LL.B., George Washington U., 1965. Bar: D.C. 1965, N.Y. 1966, Mich. 1967, Wis. 1976, Ill. 1983, Pa. 1993. Patent agt., atty. Xerox Corp., Rochester, N.Y., 1965-66; patent atty., asst. dir. patent div. Burroughs Corp., Detroit, 1969, dir. patents, to 1976; asst. gen. counsel Jos. Schlitz Brewing Co., Milw., 1976-79, v.p., gen. counsel., sec., 1979-83; v.p., gen. counsel. Comdisco, Inc., Rosemont, IL, 1983-86, sr. v.p., gen. counsel, 1986-91, cons., 1991-93; of counsel Mason, Fenwick and Lawrence, Washington, 1992-94, Christie, Parker & Hale, Pasadena, Calif., 1994-97, Rader, Fishman & Grauer, Bloomfield Hills, Mich., 1997—. Mem. adj. faculty Cath. U. Am. Columbus Sch. of Law, 1994-99. With USN, 1951-55. Mem. Am. Intellectual Property Law Assn., D.C. Bar Assn., Pa. Bar Assn., Wis. Bar Assn., Ill. Bar Assn., Mich. Bar Assn. Roman Catholic. Home and Office: PO Box 239 Jones Mills PA 15646-0239 Fax: 724-593-6250. E-mail: fish@westol.com., pwf@raderfishman.com.

FISH, RICHARD VANCORTLANDT, JR., music educator; b. NY; s. Richard V. and Cynthia J. Fish. MusB, Ithaca Coll., 1990; MDiv, St. Joseph's Sem., Yonkers, NY, 1995; MS, Simmons Coll., Boston, 2001. Dir. performing arts Landmark Sch., Prides Crossing, Mass., 1999—; dir. music St. Mary Star of Sea Ch., Beverly, Mass., 2000—. Timpanist Cape Ann Symphony, Gloucester, Mass., 2000—; drum set player Hillyer Festival Orch., Marblehead, Mass., 1997—; guest lectr. Berklee Coll. Music, Boston Conservatory, Cath. U. Am. Dir.(producer): (compact disc) Music at Landmark School, Music at Landmark School: You Come Too., Landmark on Broadway!; musician: (compact disc) A Treasury of Sacred Music. Mem.: Percussive Arts Soc., Am. Choral Dirs. Assn., Music Educator's Nat. Conf. Avocations: kayaking, home improvement, bicycling. Home: 7 Longfellow Rd Wenham MA 01984 Office: Landmark Sch 412 Hale St Prides Crossing MA 01965 Office Fax: 978-921-0361. E-mail: rfish@landmarkschool.org.

FISH, ROBERT H. long term care industry executive; BA in sociology, Whittier Coll.; MPH, U. Calif. at Berkeley; postgrad., Ethel Percy Andrus Sch. Gerontology, U. So. Calif., L.A. CEO ValleyCare Health Sys., Calif.; pres. and CEO St. Joseph Health Sys./Sonoma County, Calif.; prtnr. Sonoma-Seacrest, LLC, Calif.; interim CEO Genesis Health Ventures, Inc., Kennett Square, Pa., 2002—. Office: Genesis Health Ventures Inc 101 E State St Kennett Square PA 19348

FISH, STANLEY EUGENE, university dean, English educator; b. Providence, Apr. 19, 1938; s. Max and Ida Dorothy (Weinberg) F.; m. Adrienne A. Aaron, Aug. 23, 1959 (div. 1980); 1 dau., Susan.; m. Jane Parry Tompkins, Aug. 7, 1982. BA, U. Pa., 1959; MA, Yale U., 1960, PhD, 1962. Instr. U. Calif., Berkeley, 1962-63, asst. prof., 1963-67, assoc. prof., 1967-69, prof., 1969-74; Kenan prof. English and Humanities Johns Hopkins U., Balt., 1978-85, chmn. dept., 1983-85; Arts and Sci. Disting. prof. English and prof. law Duke U., Durham, N.C., 1985-98, chmn. dept., 1986-92; exec. dir. Duke U. Press, Durham, 1994-98; dean U. Ill. Coll. Liberal Arts and Scis., Chgo., 1999—. Author: John Skelton's Poetry, 1965, Surprised by Sin: The Reader in Paradise Lost, 1967, 97 (Hanford Book award 1998), Seventeenth Century Prose: Modern Essays in Criticism, 1971, Self-Consuming Artifacts, 1972, The Living Temple: George Herbert and Catechizing, 1978, Is There a Text in This Class?, 1980, Doing What Comes Naturally, 1989, There's No Such Thing as Free Speech...And It's a Good Thing Too, 1994 (PEN/Spielvogel-Diamonstein award 1994), Professional Correctness: Literary Studies and Political Change, 1995, The Trouble with Principle, 1999, How Milton Works, 2001; mem. editl. bd. Milton Studies, Milton Quar. Recipient 2d place, Explicator prize, 1968; Am. Council Learned Socs. fellow, 1966; Guggenheim fellow, 1969 Mem. MLA, Am. Acad. Arts and Scis., Milton Soc. (hon. scholar 1991), Spenser Soc. Office: U Ill Chgo LAS Dean's Office M/C 228 601 S Morgan St Chicago IL 60607-7100

FISH, THOMAS EDWARD, English language and literature educator; b. Redbud, Ill., Aug. 1, 1952; s. Edward Charles and H. Grace (Thomas) F.; m. Kathryn Jane Griffith, Nov. 17, 1979; children: Dana Rose, Sally Kathryn. BA, Iowa State U., Ames, 1974; MA, U. Kans., 1976, MPhil, 1979, PhD, 1981. Asst. instr. in English U. Kans., Lawrence, 1974-81, staff mem. communications resource ctr., 1978, 80; adj. asst. prof. English Iowa State U., 1981-84; asst. prof. English Cumberland Coll., Williamsburg, Ky., 1984-86, assoc. prof. English, 1986-96, prof. English, 1996—. Dir., SACS self-study Cumberland Coll., 2003—09. Self-study editor SACS, 1992-95, 2002—, dir. re-accreditation, 2003—. Elder Corbin (Ky.) Presbyn. Ch., 1986, 90-92, 2002—. Lilly grantee Cumberland Coll., 1990, named Prof. for Excellence in Teaching, 1990; tchg. grantee Cumberland Coll., 1998; faculty-student rsch. grantee Appalachian Coll. Assn., 1999; recipient Cutting Edge award for Tchg. with Technology, Appalachian Coll. Assn., 1999. Mem. MLA, Nat. Coun. Tchrs. English, Popular Culture Assn., Browning Inst., South Atlantic MLA, Appalachian Coll. Assn. (Tchg. with Tech. coord. for English 2000-03), Phi Beta Kappa, Phi Kappa Phi. Democrat. Home: 260 Brush Arbor Rd Williamsburg KY 40769-1717 Office: 7193 College Station Dr Williamsburg KY 40769-1382 E-mail: tfish@cumberlandcollege.edu.

FISHBACH, MITCHELL HARVEY, cardiologist; b. Bklyn., 1951; s. William and Harriet (Zelefsky) F.; m. Valarie Overton, Mar. 26, 1977; children: Adam, Kim. MD, Albert Einstein Coll. Medicine, 1977. Diplomate Am. Bd. Internal Medicine, Am. Bd. Cardiovascular Disease. Intern Montefiore Hosp.,

Bronx, N.Y., 1977-78, resident in internal medicine, 1978-80, resident in cardiology, 1980-82; with Westchester Cardiology Assocs., 1982—; clin. asst. prof. Albert Einstein Coll. Medicine, Columbia U. Home: 688 White Plains Rd Ste 201 Scarsdale NY 10583-5059

FISHBACK, DAVID SIMON, lawyer; b. Oct. 20, 1947; s. Sam and Hilda (Barcan) F.; m. Barbara Helene Lewell, June 19, 1977; children: Michael Lawrence, Daniel Ross. BA with distinction, George Washington U., 1969; JD cum laude, Harvard U., 1973. Bar: D.C. 1973, U.S. Supreme Ct. 1977, U.S. Ct. Appeals (1st, end. 3rd, 4th, 5th, 7th, 9th, 10th, 11th, and D.C. cirs.). VISTA vol. Shelby County Penal Farm, Memphis, 1969-70; cons. Ctr. for Polit. Reform, Washington, 1971-72; atty. Appellate Ct. br. NLRB, 1973-83, Supreme Ct. br., 1977-79; atty., environ. and occupational disease lit., 1983—90; asst. dir. Environ. Torts Sect. Torts Br. Civil Divsn., 1990—. Adj. prof. law Georgetown U. Law Ctr., 1989—90. Mem. nat. bd. dirs. Am.for Democratic Action, Washington 1984-90; pres. Rosemary Hills Primary Sch. PTA, Silver Spring, Md., 1984-86; mem. Montgomery County Martin Luther King Commemorative Com., 1986-92; bd. trustees Temple Emanuel, Kensington, Md., 1986-90; pub. affairs dir., Gifted and Talented Assn. Montgomery County, 1991-94; exec. com. Richard Montgomery H.S. PTSA, 1996-99; mem. bd. dirs. Northeast Montgomery County Polit. Action Com., 2000-; mem. bd. dirs. Partnership Edn. Policy, 2001-, chair, Family Life and Human Devel. Adv. Com. Montgomery County Bd. Ed., 2003-. Mem. Phi Beta Kappa.

FISHBACK, ROBERT LAWRENCE, retired secondary education educator; b. Detroit, June 26, 1941; s. Anthony John and June Leona (Collins) F. BA, U. Mich., 1963; MA, Eastern Mich. U., Ypsilanti, 1969. Cert. tchr., Mich. Counselor Neuropsychiat. Inst., Ann Arbor, 1963-64; tchr. St. Timothy Sch., Trenton, Mich., 1964-67, Trenton H.S., 1967-94. Contbr.: Apex Curriculum, 1968, 71, 75. Mem. Nat. Coun. English Tchrs., Nat. Assn. Reading Tchrs., Mich. Reading Assn. (spkr.), U. Mich. Alumni Assn., U. Mic. Friends of Grad. Libr., John Monteith Soc., Detroit Inst. Arts, Smithsonian Inst. Democrat. Avocations: reading, travel, art collecting, music, theater. Home: 2501 Packard St Apt G Ann Arbor MI 48104-6807 E-mail: rfish@umich.edu.

FISHBEIN, LESLIE ELLEN, humanities educator; b. N.Y.C., N.Y., Apr. 7, 1947; d. Hyman and Fannie (Polakoff) Fishbein; m. Zoltan Kemeny, June 19, 1977; children: Alexander Joseph Kemeny, Sara Faye Kemeny. BA, CUNY, 1967; PhD, Harvard U., 1975. Tchg. fellow English Harvard U., Cambridge, Mass., 1971—72; asst. prof. history Simmons Coll., Boston, 1976—77; asst. prof. Am. studies Douglass Coll. Rutgers The State U. of N.J., New Brunswick, 1977—82, assoc. prof. Am. studies, 1982—, assoc. prof. Jewish studies, 2000—. Pub. spkr. Horizon Speakers Bur., N.J. Coun. for the Humanities, Trenton, NJ, 1999—; vis. lectr. history Rice U., Houston, 1975—76; vis. instr. Am. studies Occidental Coll., L.A., 1974—75; part-time vis. lectr. Am. history Hunter Coll. of CUNY, N.Y.C., 1970—71; sr. Fulbright lectr. history U. Haifa, Israel, 1986—87. Recipient Fulbright fellowship, Coun. for the Internat. Exch. of Scholars, 1986—87. Mem.: Orgn. Am. Historians, N.Y. State Hist. Assn. (mem. editl. bd. 1984—. Manuscript award 1976), Soc. for the History of the Gilded Age and Prog. Era, Am. Studies Assn. (mem. women's com. 2002—). Jewish. Avocations: film, cooking, travel. Home: 35 North 6th Ave Highland Park NJ 08904-2935 Office: Rutgers U Am Studies 131 George St New Brunswick NJ 08901-1414 Office Fax: 732-932-1169. Personal E-mail: fishbei@rci.rutgers.edu.

FISHBEIN, MICHAEL CLAUDE, physician, pathologist; b. Brussels, May 25, 1946, came to U.S., 1949; s. Fred F. and Celia (Feldman) F.; m. Astrid Lorette du Mortier, Aug. 11, 1974; children: Danielle Renee, Gregory Andrew. BS, U. Ill., 1967; MD, U. Ill., Chgo., 1971. Diplomate Coll. Am. Pathologists; cert. anatomic and clin. pathology. Intern UCLA/Harbor Gen. Hosp., 1971-72, resident, 1972-75; asst. prof. pathology Harvard U. Sch. Medicine, Boston, 1975-78; assoc. pathologist Peter Bent Brigham Hosp., Boston, 1975-78, Cedars-Sinai Med. Ctr., L.A., 1978-97, UCLA Med. Ctr., 1997—. Cons. Beth Israel Hosp., Boston, 1975-78, mem. faculty Harvard U.-MIT program in health scis., Boston, 1975-78; prof. UCLA Sch. Medicine, 1978—. Achievements include research in heart disease; contbr. over 300 articles to profl. jours. and 13 chpts. to books. Piansky scholar anatomy rsch.award, 1997—. Mem. Phi Beta Kappa, Alpha Omega Alpha. Jewish. Avocation: tennis. Office: UCLA Med Ctr A7-149 CHS 10833 Le Conte Ave Los Angeles CA 90095-3075 E-mail: mfishbein@mednet.ucla.edu.

FISHBEIN, MICHAEL ELLIS, technical director; b. Wheeling, W.Va., Mar. 6, 1950; s. Meyer and Marion (Gellis) F.; m. Gail Sherman, May 29, 1983; children: Jane, Jonathan. MA, Eastman Sch. of Music, 1982; MS, Rensselaer Polytechnic Inst., 1986, MBA, 1993; postgrad., Harvard U., 2000—. Dir. Fidelity Investments, Boston, 1997—2003; v.p. State St. Bank, Boston, 2003—. Chmn. fin. com. Town of West Boylston, Mass., 1998—2000. Office: State St Bank 1 Lincoln St Boston MA 02110-2900 E-mail: mike@fishbein.org.

FISHBEIN, PETER MELVIN, lawyer; b. N.Y.C., June 20, 1934; s. Arthur L. and Lotta (Chary) F.; m. Bette Klinghoffer, June 16, 1957; children: Stephen, Bruce, Gregory. BA magna cum laude, Dartmouth Coll., 1955; JD, Harvard U., 1958. Bar: N.Y. 1959, U.S. Supreme Ct. 1973. Note editor Harvard Law Rev., Cambridge, Mass., 1956-58; law clk. to Justice William J. Brennan, Jr. U.S. Supreme Ct., Washington, 1958-59; dep. sec. gen. Internat. Peace Corps., Washington, 1962-64; ptnr. Kaye, Scholer LLP, N.Y.C., 1967—2002, mng. ptnr., 1984-91; chief counsel N.Y. State Constl. Conv., Albany, 1967; mem. Presdl. Commn. to Nominate Candidates for Fed. Ct. of Appeals, N.Y.C., 1980. Adj. prof. constl. law NYU Law Sch., 1970-84. Contbr. articles to profl. jours. Trustee Goddard Coll., 1967—75, Fedn. Jewish Philanthropies, N.Y.C., 1975—81, Citizen's Budget Comm., 1995—99; mem. N.Y. State Gov.'s Bd. Pub. Disclosure, Albany, 1975—77; mgr. Justice Arthur J. Goldberg's Campaign for Gov., 1970; bd. dirs. Health Care Chaplaincy, 1993—99, Brennan Ctr. for Justice, 1995—, I Have A Dream Found., 2001—, White Plains Hosp., 2002—. Recipient Disting. Cmty. Svc. award Brandels U., Jurisprudence award Am. Ort. Fellow Am. Coll. Trial Lawyers, Am. Bar Found.; mem. ABA, Assn. of Bar of City of N.Y., Harvard Club (N.Y.), Beach Point Club (bd. govs. 1981-86), Phi Beta Kappa Home: 101 Woodlands Rd Harrison NY 10528-1423 Office: Kaye Scholer LLP 425 Park Ave New York NY 10022-3506

FISHBEIN, RONALD HARRISON, surgeon; b. Bklyn., Oct. 8, 1931; s. Herman J. and Mildred (Cohen) F.; m. Estelle Ackerman, June 10, 1956; children: Rand Harrison, Jonathan Marc. AB, Lafayette Coll., 1953; MD, Yale U., 1957. Diplomate Am. Bd. Surgery. Dean admissions Johns Hopkins Sch. Medicine, 1970-76; pre-med. advisor Johns Hopkins U., 1996—. Contbr. articles to profl. jours. Capt. U.S. Army, 1963-65. Fellow Am. Coll. Surgery; mem. Md. Acad. Sci. (bd. trustees 1992—). Avocation: sculpture. Office: Johns Hopkins U Garland Hall 3400 N Charles St Baltimore MD 21218-2680

FISHBERG, GERARD, lawyer; b. Bronx, May 23, 1946; s. Alfred and Sarah (Goldberg) F.; m. Eileen Taubman, Dec. 23, 1972; children: David, Dana. BA, Hofstra U., 1968; JD, St. John's U., Bklyn., 1971. Bar: N.Y. 1972, U.S. Dist. Ct. (ea. and so. dists.) N.Y. 1973, U.S. Ct. Appeals (2d cir.) 1975, U.S. Supreme Ct. 1976. Assoc. Cullen & Dykman, Garden City, N.Y., 1972-79, ptnr., 1980—. Assoc. editor St. John's U. Law Rev., 1970-71. Mem. legis. com. N.Y. Conf. of Mayors and Mcpl. Ofcls., Albany, 1976—; bd. dirs. Am. Heart Assn. L.I. region, 1995—, treas. 1997-98, vice chair, 1998-2000, chair, 2000-2002; bd. dirs. Heritage Affiliate 1999—. Capt. USAR, 1968-77. St. Thomas Moore scholar St. John's U. Sch. Law, 1969-71. Mem.: Rotacare (bd. dirs. 1992—, pres. 1993—99), Rotary (bd. dirs. 1988—94, treas. 1990—91, pres. 1992—93), Garden City C. of C., Nassau County Bar Assn. (chmn. mcpl. law com. 1981—83, 1985—87, chmn. labor law com. 1991-92 1991—92, bd. dirs. 1999—2002), N.Y. State Bar Assn. (mem. exec. com. 1978—, labor law sect. 1985, sec. 1985—87, mcpl. law 1985—, 1st vice chmn. 1989—91, chmn. 1991—93, mem. ho. of dels. 1993—). Jewish. Home: 1 Bucknell Dr Plainview NY 11803-1801 Office: Cullen & Dykman 100 Quentin Roosevelt Blvd Garden City NY 11530-4850

FISHBURNE, BENJAMIN P., III, lawyer; b. South Bend, Ind., Nov. 14, 1943; s. Benjamin Postell and Peggy (Gahan) F.; m. Edith E., Aug. 5, 1983. BA cum laude, U. Notre Dame, 1965; JD, U. Va., 1968. Bar: U.S. Ct. Mil. Appeals 1968, U.S. Army Ct. Mil. Rev. 1968, D.C. 1971. Capt. JAG Corps US Army, 1968-72; atty. Surrey & Morse, Washington, 1968, ptnr., 1975, mng. ptnr., 1981-84; ptnr. Jones, Day, Reavis & Pogue, 1986, ptnr.-in-charge Hong Kong office, 1986-91, ptnr., 1991-93, Winston & Strawn, Washington, 1993—. Gen. counsel Nat. Coun. U.S.-China Trade, 1981—87, assoc. coun., 1987—89, chmn. legal com., 1994—2001; mem. adv. com. China-U.S. Conciliation Ctr., 1993—; mem. Am. Arbitration Assn. spl. corp. com. East-West trade arbitration, 1973—79; mem. nat. coun. U.S.-China Trade Investment Del. to China; alt. mem. UN Assn.'s Nat. Policy panel study U.S.-China Rels., 1979; spkr. in field. Contbr. articles to profl. jours. Co-chmn. Am. C. of C. Hong Kong legal com., 1990, mem. bd. govs., 1991; mem. bd. advisors Johns Hopkins Nanjing Ctr., 1986-97. Mem.: Order of Coif. Home: 5535 Nevada Ave NW Washington DC 20015-1768 Office: Winston & Strawn 1400 L St NW Washington DC 20005-3508 E-mail: bfishbur@winston.com.

FISHBURNE, JOHN INGRAM, JR., obstetrician/gynecologist, educator; b. Charleston, S.C., Aug. 18, 1937; m. Jean Crawford, June 10, 1971; children: John Ingram III, Barron Crawford, Virginia Heyward. AB, Princeton U., 1959; MD, Med. Coll. S.C., 1963. Diplomate Am. Bd. Ob-Gyn. (sub. specialty maternal-fetal medicine). Surg. intern Duke U. Hosp., Durham, N.C., 1963 64; resident in ob-gyn. U. N.C., Chapel Hill, 1966-70, resident in anesthesiology, 1970-72, instr. dept. ob-gyn., 1970-71, asst. prof., 1971-74, assoc. prof., 1974-75, asst. prof. dept. anesthesiology, 1972-75; assoc. prof. dept. ob-gyn. Bowman Gray Sch. Medicine, Wake Forest U., Winston-Salem, N.C., 1975-78, prof., 1978-83, assoc. prof. anesthesiology, dept. anesthesiology, 1975-83; prof., chmn. dept. ob-gyn. U. Okla. Health Scis. Ctr., Oklahoma City, 1983-97, adj. prof. dept. anesthesiology, 1983-97, chmn. search com. for chair pathology dept., 1987-88, chmn. search com. for chair family medicine dept., 1993-94; residency program dir. dept. ob-gyn. Maricopa Med. Ctr., Phoenix, 1997—2001, chair dept. ob-byn., 1997—2000, vice chmn. dept. ob-gyn., 2000—, assoc. program dir. dept. ob-gyn., 2001—; prof. clin. ob-gyn. U. Ariz. Coll. Medicine, 1997—. Dir. maternal-fetal medicine dept. ob-gyn. Forsyth Meml. Hosp., Winston-Salem, 1977-83; vis. prof. U. W.I., Kingston, Jamaica, 1973-74, African-Health Tng. Instns. Project Nairobi, Kenya, 1975; cons. devel. mission U.S. AID, Dacca, Bangladesh, 1980, Assn. Vol. Surg. Contraception World Fedn. Health Agys., Manila, 1984, Singapore, 1986, Zhordania Inst., Tbilisi, Republic of Georgia, 1992, 93, 97, Ivanovo, Russia, 1994, Almaty, Kazakhstan, 1994, St. Petersburg, Russia, 1995, Khojand, Tahjikistan, 1995, Odessa, Ukraine, 1995, Chechenov, Moldova, 1996, L'viv Ukraine; oral examiner Am. Bd. Ob-Gyn, 1980—; chmn. Gov.'s Task Force on Perinatal Care, 1984-86; mem. steering com. Robert Wood Johnson Healthy Futures of Okla., 1988-92; trustee Am. Assn. for Gynecologic Laparascopists, 1980-81; presenter numerous sci. papers and lectures local, nat. and internat. profl. meetings. Author: (with others) The Prostaglandins, 1972, Endocrine-Metabolic Drugs, 1974, Gynecologic Laparoscopy: Principles and Techniques, 1974, Laparoscopy, 1977, Endoscopy in Gynecology, 1978, Clinics in Perinatology, 1982, Obstetric Anesthesia, 1982, Clinical and Diagnostic Procedures Obstetrics and Gyncecology, Part B, 1984, Advances in Clinical Obstetrics and Gynecology, Medical Economics Books, 1985, Clinical Obstetrics, 1987, Danforth's Obstetrics and Gynecology, 1994, 98, Bonica's Obstetric Analgesia and Anesthesia, 1995; contbr. update series Am. Coll. Obstetricians and Gynecologists; editorial bd. Obstetrics and Gynceology, 1985-89; author self instructional programs in field; contbr. numerous articles to profl. jours. Capt. USAFR, 1964-66. Clin. fellow Am. Cancer Soc. U. N.C., 1968-69, clin. fellow obstet. anesthesia Pub. Health Svc. U. Hosps. Case Western Res. U., 1969; tng. rsch. grantee NIH Med. U. S.C., 1961-62. Fellow ACOG (spl. interest rep. for obstet. anesthesia 1974-78, learning resources commn. 1981-82, mem. personal rev. of learning in ob-gyn. task force for obstetrics 1981-82, chair obs. IV, 1996-98, chair edn. commn. 1996-98, chair residency rev. com. ob/gyn. Accreditation Coun. for Grad. Med. Edn. 1994-97, dir., mem. exec. com. Accreditation Coun. for Grad. Med. Edn. 2000--, vice chair coun. of residency rev. com. chairs 1996, chair accreditation coun. for grad. med. edn. coun. res. rev. com. chairs, 1997-98, examiner 1980-2002), Am. Coll. Anesthesiologists (assoc. examiner 1974); mem. Am. Soc. Anesthesiologists, Maternal & Fetal Medicine Soc. (rep. liaison com. ob.-gyn. 1983-89, bd. dirs. 1981-84), S. Atlantic Assn. Obstetricians and Gynecologists (assoc.), Perinatal Rsch. Soc., Oklahoma City Ob-Gyn. Soc., Okla. County Med. Soc., Okla. Anesthesia Soc., Internat. Soc. Advancement Humanistic Studies in Medicine (pres. 1997), Cen. Assn. Obstetricians and Gynecologists, Continental Gynecol. Soc., So. Med. Assn., Am. Gynecol. and Obstet. Soc., Med. Alumni Assn., Med. U. S.C. (Disting. Alumnus award 1989), Alpha Omega Alpha. Episcopalian. Home: 7060 N Hillside Dr Paradise Valley AZ 85253-2813 Office: Maricopa Med Ctr Dept Ob-Gyn 2601 E Roosevelt St Dept Ob Phoenix AZ 85008-4973

FISHBURNE, LAURENCE, III, actor; b. Augusta, Ga., July 30, 1961; s. Laurence John Jr. and Hattie Bell Crawford F.; m. Majna Mass Fishburn, July 1, 1985; children: Langston Issa, Montana Isis. Appearances include (theatre) Section D, 1975, Eden, 1976, Short Eyes, 1984, Loose Ends, 1988, Urban Blight, 1988, Two Trains Running, 1992 (Best Featured Actor Tony award 1992), (films) Cornbread, Earl and Me, 1975, Apocalypse Now, 1979, Fast Break, 1979, Willie and Phil, 1980, Death Wish II, 1982, Rumble Fish, 1983, The Cotton Club, 1984, The Color Purple, 1985, Band of the Hand, 1986, Quicksilver, 1986, Gardens of Stone, 1987, A Nightmare on Elm Street 3: Dream Warriors, 1987, School Daze, 1988, Red Heat, 1988, King of New York, 1990, Cadence, 1991, Class Action, 1991, Boyz N the Hood, 1991, Deep Cover, 1992, What's Love Got To Do With It, 1993 (Academy award nominee, Best Actor, 1993), Searching For Bobby Fischer, 1993, Higher Learning, 1995, Bad Company, 1995, Just Cause, 1995, Othello, 1995, Fled, 1996, Hoodlum, 1997, Event Horizon, 1997, The Matrix, 1999, Once in the Life, 2000 (also dir., writer, prodr.), Osmosis Jones, 2001, Biker Boyz, 2003, The Matrix Reloaded, 2003, (TV movies) A Rumor of War, 1980, I Take These Men, 1983, 1983, The Father Clements Story, 1987, Decoration Day,1990, Miss Ever's Boys, 1997, Always Outnumbered, 1998; prodr. Miss Evers' Boys, 1997, Hoodlum, 1997, Always Outnumbered, 1998; TV guest appearances M*A*S*H, 1972, Hill Street Blues, 1981, Miami Vice, 1984, Spenser: For Hire, 1985, The Equalizer, 1985. Recipient Emmy award, 1993, 97, Image award, 1996, 98. Mailing: Landmark Artist & Mgmt 4116 W Magnolia Blvd, Ste 101 Burbank CA 91505*

FISHEL, ANDREW S. director, federal; b. Apr. 7, 1948; married, 1969. BA, Am. U., 1969; EdD of Am. Politics and Edn., Columbia U., 1975; MEd, Am. U., 1970. Legis. planning coord. U.S. Dept. HEW, Washington; mgmt. dir. Office for Civil Rights U.S. Dept. Edn., Washington; dir. fin. and resource mgmt. EEOC, Washington, 1982-89; mng. dir. FCC, Washington, 1989—. Co-author: (with Jan Pottker) Sex Bias in the Schools: The Research Evidence, 1977, National Politics and Sex Discrimination in Schools, 1977. Recipient Quality Improvement Prototype award Office Mgmt. and Budget, 1987, Outstanding Mgr. award ASTD, 1992, Disting. Svc. medal FCC, 1992. Office: Fed Comm Commn 445 12th St SW Washington DC 20554

FISHEL, PETER LIVINGSTON, accounting business executive; b. Chgo., Apr. 25, 1935; s. Philip W. and Dorothy B. (Livingston) F.; m. Donna Swift, Dec. 17, 1961; children: Pamela Leslie Fishel Saccocio, Patricia Jane Fishel Baquadano, Françoise Suzanne. BS, U. Pa., 1959. CPA, Pa., Fla. Agt.-in-charge investigation and civil rights divsn. Commonwealth of Pa. Dept. Justice, 1961-62; contr. Internat. Playtex Corp., 1962-70, BVD Knitwear, 1970-71; corp. contr. BVD Co., Inc., N.Y.C., 1971-73; v.p. fin. BVD Co., Inc. (BVD divsn.), N.Y.C., 1973; chief fin. officer Colebrook Mills, divsn. Bobbie Brooks, Inc., Hialeah, Fla., 1973-77; owner Gen. Bus. Svcs., 1978-86, regional dir. S.E. Fla., 1982-86; pvt. practice acctg., 1987—; mem. adv. com. Oceanmark Fed. Savs. & Loan, 1983-88. Mem. citizens adv. com. Met. Dade Police, Miami, Fla., 1981—, treas., 1985—; mem. fin. com. Metro-Dade Pig Bowl, 1985; mem. Andover Civic Assn., 1973—2001, v.p., 1986—91; mem. NMB Pride, 1989—93, bd. dirs., 1991—93, Dade Alumni Club, U. Pa., 1991—; mem., treas. Coalition for the Improvement of N.W. Dade, 1996—; mem. Aventura Mktg. Coun., 1991—. With M.P. U.S. Army, 1954—56. Mem. AICPA, Pa. Inst. CPAs, Fla. Inst. CPAs, Nat. Assn. Tax Practitioners, Mensa, N. Dade C. of C. (bd. dirs. 1978-97, v.p., Businessman of Yr. 1990, Mem. of Month, 1987, 91), N. Miami Beach C. of C. Home: 8119 S Savannah Cir Davie FL 33328-3033 Office: 2396 NE 172nd St Aventura FL 33160-2923 E-mail: plfishel@aol.com.

FISHER, A. JAMES, theater educator, director, actor; b. Long Branch, NJ, Nov. 8, 1950; s. Clarkson Sherman and Mae Shannon (Hoffmann) F.; m. Dana Kay Warner, Feb. 5, 1977; children: Daniel Clarkson, Anna Kathleen. BA, Monmouth Coll., 1973; MFA, U. N.C., 1976. Actor, dir. Parkway Playhouse, Burnsville, N.C., 1971-75; resident dir. Barn Theater, Greensboro, N.C., 1976-77, West Side Theater, Knoxville, Tenn., 1977-78; instr. U. N.C., Greensboro, 1976; from asst. to assoc. prof. Wabash Coll., Crawfordsville, Ind., 1978-94, prof., 1994—, chmn. theater dept., 1980—90, 1995—97. Author: The Theatre of Yesterday and Tomorrow: Commedia dell'arte on the Twentieth Century Stage, 1992, Al Jolson, A Bio-Bibiography, 1994, Spencer Tracy, A Bio-Bibliography, 1994, Eddie Cantor, A Bio-Bibliography, 1997, (plays) The Bogus Bride, 1983, The Theater of Tony Kushner: Living Past Hope, 2001, paperback, 2002; editor (book rev.): Jour. Dramatic Theory and Criticism, 1989—; contbr. articles to profl. jours. Newberry Libr. fellow, 1992, 2002, Pub. Humanities fellow Ind. Humanities Coun., 1991; recipient Rsch. award West European Ctr., Bloomington, Ind., 1986, Rsch. award Soc. for Theatre Rsch., London, 1992; named Ind. Theatre Person of Yr., 1996; scholar McLain-McTurnan-Arnold Rsch., 1999-2000. Mem. Assn. for Theatre in Higher Edn., Southeastern Theatre Conf., Am. Soc. for Theatre Rsch., Internat. Soc. for Theatre Rsch., Theatre Libr. Assn., Alpha and Delta Psi Omega (nat. bus. mgr. 1987—). Home: 103 Simpson St Crawfordsville IN 47933-1646 Office: Theater Dept Wabash College Crawfordsville IN 47933 Fax: 765-361-6341. E-mail: fisherj@wabash.edu.

FISHER, ALAN HALL, guidebook writer; b. Evanston, Ill., July 16, 1945; s. Howard Taylor and Marion Ethel (Hall) F.; m. Margaret Ellen Williams, July 3, 1974; children: Ellen Williams, Howard Williams. BA, Harvard U., 1967; JD, Boston U., 1977. Bar: Md. 1977. English tchr. Trinity-Pawling (N.Y.) Sch., 1967-68, Acton (Mass.)-Boxborough H.S., 1968-70; rsch. asst. Harvard U., Grad. Sch. Design, Cambridge, Mass., 1971-72; assoc. Venable, Baetjer and Howard, Balt., 1977-80; guidebook writer Balt., 1980—. Author: Country Walks Near Boston, 1976, 86, 2000, Country Walks Near Baltimore, 1981, 88, 93, 2001, Country Walks Near Philadelphia, 1983, Country Walks Near Washington, 1984, 96, Country Walks Near Chicago, 1987, Day Trips in Delmarva, 1992, 98, Country Walks and Bikeways in the Philadelphia Region, 1994, Country Walks in the Chicago Region, 2003. Home and Office: 1430 Park Ave Baltimore MD 21217-4230 E-mail: ramblerbooks@aol.com.

FISHER, ALAN J. otolaryngologist, plastic surgeon; b. Passaic, N.J., 1952; BA, Hamilton Coll., 1973; MD, U. Health Scis./Chgo. Med. Sch, 1976. Diplomate Am. Bd. Otolaryngology. Intern Rush-Presbyn. St. Luke's Hosp., Chgo., 1976-77, resident in otolaryngology, 1977-81; fellow in facial and plastic surgery Am. Acad. Facial Plastic and Reconstructive Surgery, Beverly Hills, Calif., 1981-82; pvt. practice Arcadia, Calif., 1985—; active staff Meth. Hosp. So. Calif., Arcadia, 1985—; cons. City of Hope Nat. Med. Ctr., Duarte, Calif., 1985—; courtesy staff Huntington Meml. Hosp., Pasadena, 1985—. Mem. ACS, AMA, Calif. Med. Assn., L.A. County Med. Assn., Am. Acad. Otolaryngology-Head and Neck Surgery, Am. Acad. Facial Plastic and Reconstructive Surgery. Office: 612 W Duarte Rd Ste 705 Arcadia CA 91007-9246 E-mail: nozedoc@aol.com.

FISHER, ALAN WASHBURN, historian, educator; b. Columbus, Ohio, Nov. 23, 1939; s. Sydney Nettleton and Elizabeth E. (Scipio) F.; m. Carol L. Garrett, Aug. 24, 1963; children: Elizabeth, Ann Christy, Garrett. BA, DePauw U., 1961; MA, Columbia U., 1964, PhD, 1967. Instr. history Mich. State U., East Lansing, 1966-67, asst. prof., 1967-70, assoc. prof., 1970-78, prof. Russian and Turkish history, 1978—2003, assoc. dean grad. studies and research, Coll. Arts and Letters, 1987-89, dir. Ctr. for Integrative Studies in Arts and Humanities, 1989-97, emeritus prof., 2003—. Author: Russian Annexation of the Crimea, 1772-1783, 1970, The Crimean Tatars, 1978, revised edit., 1987, Ottoman Studies Directory, I, 1979, II, 1981, III, 1983, Between Russians, Ottomans, and Turks: Crimea and Crimean Tatars, 1998, A Precarious Balance: Conflict, Trade and Diplomacy on the Russian-Ottoman Frontier, 1999. Am. Rsch. Inst. in Turkey fellow, 1969, 73, 76; Am. Coun. Learned Socs. grantee, 1976-77 Fellow Royal Hist. Soc., Turkish Hist. Assn. (corr.), Am. Rsch. Inst. Turkey (mem. bd. dels. 1990-99, v.p. 1995-99), Mid. East Studies Assn., Turkish Studies Assn. (pres. 1982-84, editor bull. 1984-87), Inst. Turkish Studies (dir. 1995-97, chmn. 1997-99). Office: Mich State U Dept History 301 Morrill Hall East Lansing MI 48824-1036 E-mail: fishera@msu.edu.

FISHER, ALLAN CAMPBELL, retired railway executive; b. Westerly, R.I., Aug. 9, 1943; s. Arthur Chester and Norma Jean (Campbell) F.; m. Ellen Tryon Roop, June 14, 1969; children: Bradford Booth, Thayer Everett. BA in Econs., St. Lawrence U., 1965; MS in Transp., Northwestern U., 1970. Rsch. economist GM Rsch. Labs., Warren, Mich., 1969; mgmt. trainee Penn. Ctrl., 1970, asst. trainmaster, 1970-71, trainmaster Toledo, 1971-72, terminal trainmaster Elkhart, Ind., 1972, trainmaster Cleve., 1972-74, asst. terminal supt., 1974, terminal supt. Balt., 1975-76, Conrail, Conway, Pa., 1976, supt. N.J. divsn. Elizabethport, 1977, supt. Lehigh divsn. Bethlehem, Pa., 1978, regional supt. ops. improvement ctrl. region Pitts., 1978-80, dir. budget control, 1980-82, regional supt. indsl. engring. So. region Indpls., 1982-83, sys. dir. oper. rules Phila., 1983-01. Membership sec. WW&F Ry. Mus., 2001—. Served with U.S. Army, 1966-67, Vietnam. Decorated Bronze Star medal; Urban Transp. fellow, 1969. Mem.: NAS, Norac Rules Com. (past chmn.), Oper. Rules Assn., Am. Assn. R.R. Supts. (bd. dirs.), Internat. Assn. Oper. Officers, Am. Inst. Indsl. Engrs. (sr.), Grange, Phila. Boys Choir and Men's Chorale (bd. dirs., Man of Yr. 1989—91, 1998, 2001), Soc. Mayflower Descs. (life), Masons, Sigma Chi. Home: 13 Pilot Cir PO Box 134 Nobleboro ME 04555-0134 E-mail: acfisher@midcoast.com.

FISHER, ALLAN MICHAEL, government official, educator; b. Bklyn., Apr. 9, 1955; m. Wendy Ellen Aronson, Nov. 11, 1979; children: Daniel Brian, Nicole Meredith. BBA, Baruch Coll., 1976; MPA, Am. U., 1988; PhD, Walden U., Mpls., 1993; diploma, Nat. Def. U., Washington, 1994; MS, Syracuse U., 1996. Cert. info. resource mgr., computing profl., sys. profl., office automation profl., govt. fin. mgr. Auditor U.S. Dept. Def., Washington, 1977-79; sr. auditor GSA, Washington, 1979-82; supervisory sys. acct. USDA, Washington, 1982-85; mgr. U.S. Dept. Treasury, Washington, 1985-91; dir. tactical programs U.S. Dept. Def., Ft. Meade, Md., 1991-97; asst ins. gen. U.S. Dept. Commerce, Washington, 1997-99; CFO U.S. Equal Opportunity Commn., Washington, 1999-2000; assoc. adminstr., CFO U.S. Dept. Transp., Washington, 2000—. Adj. prof. George Mason U., Fairfax, Va., 1994-96, Hood Coll., Frederick, Md., 1996-97, U. Md., 1999—, Johns Hopkins U., 2000—. Contbr. articles to profl. jours. Mem. coun. Montgomery County (Md.) Fiscal Affairs Com., 1984-86; coach Gaithersburg (Md.) Sports Assn., 1994—. Recipient Disting. Svc. award Montgomery County Coun., 1986. Mem. Nat. Assn. Hispanic Fed. Execs., Assn. Govt. Accts., Assn. Inst. for Cert. Computer Profls., Key Exec. Program Alumni Assn., Maxwell D.C. Alumni Assn., Syracuse U. Alumni Club Washington. E-mail: allan.fisher@fmcsa.dot.gov.

FISHER, ANDREW, management consultant; b. Richmond, Va., Dec. 17, 1920; s. Marion Nimmo and Sarah Randolph (Talcott) F.; m. Cornelia Johnson, Oct. 10, 1942; children: Peter R., Carolyn, Andrew R. BA, Amherst Coll., 1943; MBA, Harvard U., 1947; D.Sc. (h.c.), Albany Med. Coll. Dir. indsl. relations Internat. Braid Co., Providence, 1947; with N.Y. Times, 1947-71, v.p., 1963-70, exec. v.p., 1971; mgmt. cons., 1972-76; chmn., pres., pub. News Jour. Co., 1976-78. Mgmt. cons. Trustee emeritus Albany Med. Coll. Capt. AUS, 1943-46. Mem. Moorings Club. Home: 1780 Cedar Ln Vero Beach FL 32963-2621

FISHER, ANDREW, IV, newswriter, television producer; b. Richmond, Va., Jan. 15, 1944; s. Andrew III and Dorothy Dale (Crannis) Fisher; m. Sharon Mary Cozza, Aug. 16, 1969. BA, Columbia U., 1965. News anchor Sta. WIP Radio, Phila., 1965, investigative reporter, 1968-69; writer, editor WNEW News, N.Y.C., 1969-74; overnight news anchor Sta. WNEW-AM, N.Y.C., 1974-79; morning news anchor Sta. WNEW-FM, N.Y.C., 1979-81; radio news corr. NBC News, N.Y.C., 1981-89, prin. news writer Today Show, 1990-99; fin. journalist Business Center CNBC, Ft. Lee, NJ, 1999—. Guest lectr. NYU, 1978, 80, Rutgers U., New Brunswick, NJ, 1984, Ramapo Coll., Mahwah, NJ, 2002; adj. prof. journalism Columbia U., N.Y.C., 1989—90; judge TV Emmy Award, 2002. Reporter, prodr. Sunday News Closeup, 1969—79, corr. Source Report, 1981—88, host, prodr. Catch of the Day, 1985—88, Andy Fisher Reporting on Religion, 1986—89, network radio anchor Winter Olympics, Calgary, Can., 1988, Summer Olympics, Seoul, Republic of Korea, 1988; consulting editor: Joyful Noiseletter, 1988—, contbg. writer: Marketplace, Am. Publ. Radio, 1989, More Holy Humor, 1997, Dick Clark's American Bandstand: An Anniversary Celebration of Music and Dance, 1997, Holy Hilarity, 2000; writer (TV spls.) Christmas in Rockefeller Center, NBC-TV, 1999, Attack on America,

CNBC, 2001, Wall St. Responds, 2001. Clk. vestry St. Peter's Ch., Morristown, NJ, 1979; mem. various coms. Episcopal Diocese, Newark, 1982—87; lay reader Ch. of Savior, Denville, NJ, 1982—87; patron Flying Boat Mus., Foynes, Ireland, 1990—; mem. Denville Hist. Soc. With U.S. Army, 1965—68, spl. agt. U.S. Army, 1966—68. Decorated Disting. Mil. Svc. medal; recipient Headliner Reporting award, Nat. Headliners Club, 1985, Media award, Women in Radio & TV, 1985, N.Y. State Bar Assn., 1985, Gold medal, Internat. Radio Festival, 1989. Mem.: AFTRA, Writers Guild Am., N.Y. Acad. Scis., Actors Fund (life), Albany Acad. Alumni Assn., Boston St. Rlwy. Assn., Fellowship Merry Christians, Nat. Rlwy. Hist. Soc., N.Y.C. Transit Mus. (sustaining), Indian Lake Cmty. Club. Office: CNBC 2200 Fletcher Ave Fort Lee NJ 07024-5005

FISHER, ANDREW TAYLOR, computer software developer; b. Oakland, Calif., Nov. 22, 1950; s. Walter Dummer Fisher and Marjorie Catherine Lynis Smith. BA in Computer Studies, Northwestern U., 1988. Programmer Health Info. Reporting Co., Chgo., 1988-90; programming cons. Blue Cross and Blue Shield Assn., Chgo., 1990-91; programmer ACCO USA, Wheeling, Ill., 1992; programmer, tech. writer Healthcare Transformations, Hobart, Ind., 1992-93; programming cons. Abbott Labs., Abbott Park, Ill., 1993, tech. writing cons., 1995; programming cons. A.C. Nielson, Bannockburn, Ill., 1993-94; data mgmt. software devel. cons. Amoco, Chgo., 1995; programming contractor Northrop Grumman, Rolling Meadows, Ill., 1996; database programmer, tech. writer The Good Group, Inc., Evanston, Ill., 1997-2000; self employed contractor designing Websites, 2000—. Webmaster Nutrition for Optimal Health Assn. Recipient Steve Sutton Meml. award Chgo. Metro. Ski Coun., 1996; co-recipient Arthur B. Hanson Rescue medal Safety at Sea cCom. Nat. Gov. Body Sport of Sailing, 2000. Mem. Nutrition for Optimal Health Assn. (wood apple award 1998), Union of Concerned Scientists, Worldwatch Inst., Students for Ecological and Environ. Devel. of Northwestern U. (founder, 1st pres. 1986-88), Greenpeace, Sierra Club, Snowseekers Club (recording sec. 1995-96). Democrat. Mem. Unitarian Ch. Avocations: choral singing and acting, long distance biking, skiing, sailing, web site designing. Home: 1580 Sherman Ave Unit 1108 Evanston IL 60201-4494 E-mail: fisher.a@sbcglobal.net.

FISHER, ANITA JEANNE (KIT FISHER), language educator; b. Atlanta, Oct. 22, 1937; d. Paul Benjamin and Cora Ozella (Wadsworth) Chappelear; m. Kirby Lynn Fisher, Aug. 6, 1983; 1 child from previous marriage, Tracy Ann. BA, Bob Jones U., 1959; postgrad., Stetson U., 1961, 87, U. Fla., 1963, 87, 90; MAT, Rollins Coll., 1969; PhD in Am. Lit., Fla. State U., 197[illegible]; postgrad. U. Ctrl. Fla., 1978, NEH Inst., 1979, U. Ctrl. Fla., 1987, Disney U./U. Ctrl. Fla., 1996, Jacksonville U., 1996; student, Agnes Scot Coll. AP Inst., 1998, Duke Univ. AP TIP Summer Inst., 1999. Cert. English, gifted and adminstrn. supr., in ESOL. Chairperson basic learning improvement program secondary sch. Orange County, Orlando, Fla., 1964-65; chmn. composition Winter Park (Fla.) HS, 1978-80; chmn. English depts. Orange County Pub. Schs., Fla., 1962, 71; reading tchr. Woodland Hall Acad., Reading Rsch. Inst., Tallahassee, 1976; instr. edn., journalism, reading, Spanish, thesis writing Bapt. Bible Coll., Springfield, Mo., 1976-77; prof. English S.W. Mo. State U., Springfield, 1980-84, instr. continuing edn. music and creative writing, 1981-82, editor LAD Leaf; tchr. Volusia County Schs., Fla., 1984-88, 95-97, gifted students, 1986-88; tchr. Lee County Schs., 1988-95; gifted students Lake Mary HS, 1997; tchr. Seminole Pub. Schs., 1997—. Instr. Seminole CC; adj. prof. Edison CC, 1989—95, U. So. Fla., 1990—95, Barry U., 1993; mem. steering com. So. Assn. Colls. and Schs.; active Fla. Coun. Tchrs. English; assessor tchr. performance Nat. Bd. Profl. Tchg. Stds.; panel mem. PSAT/NMSQT Descriptive Score Report Ednl. Testing Svc.; spkr. in field.; chair advanced placement vertical team Lake Mary HS, 2000—01, chair dept. English, chair vertical team curriculum implementation, 2001—. Contbr. writings to publs. in field, papers to nat. profl. confs.; co-editor: Fla. English Jour., 1998—2000. Vol. Green County Action Com., 1977, Heart Fund, 1982; book reviewer Voice Youth Advs. Writing Program fellow U. Ctrl. Fla., 1978; mem. Rep. Nat. Com., 1994—; active Rep. Presdl. Task Force, 1998—2000. Named Lee County Tchr. of Distinction, 1994—95. Mem.: Seminole County Tchrs. English (chartered, pres. 1998—2000), Volusia Coun. Tchrs. English (pres. 1997), Fla. Coun. Tchrs. English (chair commn. ESL 1997—99, sch. adv. coun.), Nat. Count. Tchrs. English, Phi Delta Kappa (historian). Presbyterian.

FISHER, ANN BAILEN, lawyer; b. N.Y.C., Oct. 15, 1951; d. Eliot and Elise (Thompson) Bailen; m. John C. Fisher, Apr. 6, 1980. BA magna cum laude, Radcliffe Coll., 1973; JD, Harvard U., 1976. Bar: N.Y. 1977. Assoc. Sullivan & Cromwell, N.Y.C., 1976-80, 82-84, ptnr., 1984—, assoc. Paris, 1980-82. Mem. ABA, N.Y. State Bar Assn. Clubs: Cosmopolitan, Harvard (N.Y.C.). Episcopalian. Office: Sullivan & Cromwell 125 Broad St Fl 32 New York NY 10004-2400

FISHER, ANN LEWIS, judge; b. Reading, Pa., Mar. 31, 1948; d. William E. and Florence (Makowiecki) Lewis; m. Donald E. Fisher, Dec. 27, 1965 (div. July 1986); children: Caroline E., Catherine E., John Michael (dec.); m. David H. DeBlasio, May 28, 1988; 1 child, Michael Joseph DeBlasio. BS in Liberal Studies, Oreg. State U., 1975; JD, Willamette U., 1983. Bar: Oreg. 1984, U.S. Dist. Ct. Oreg. 1984, U.S. Ct. Appeals (9th cir.) 1984, Wash. 1987, U.S. Dist. Ct. (we. dist.) Wash. 1987, U.S. Dist. Ct. (ea. dist.) Wash. 1996, U.S. Ct. Appeals (fed. cir.) 1996. Atty. Spears, Lubersky, Portland, Oreg., 1983-85, Greene & Markley, Portland, Oreg., 1985-89; asst. gen. counsel Portland GE, 1988-93; atty. Schwabe, Williamson & Wyatt, Portland, 1993-96; founder Ann L. Fisher Legal and Consulting Svcs., Portland, 1996—. Pro tem judge Multnomah County Cir. Ct., Portland, 1995—; spkr. on corp. ethics, 1993-95; spkr. on energy issues, 1997—. Contbg. author: (treatise) ABA Year in Review, 1994, 95, Fed. Energy Bar Yr. Rev., 1997, 2000. Recipient Mem. of Yr. award, Bldg. Owners and Mgrs., Portland, 2001. Mem.: FBA (vice chair gas pipelines com. 1994—96, vice chair electric power com. sect. natural resources, energy and env), ABA, Disciplinary bd. Region 5, Builder Owners and Mgrs., N.W. Energy Assn. (sec.-treas. 1999—2000, Mem. of Yr. award 2001), Fed. Energy Bar Assn. (electric utility regulation com. 1996—99, ethics com. 1999—), Multnomah Bar Assn. (membership com. 1987—89, Multnomah Lawyer publ. com. 1994—96, chair 1995—96, professionalism com. 1997—99), Oreg. Bar Assn. (ins. and bar sponsored program com. 1985—87, sec. 1986—87, chair 1987—88, MCLE bd. 1991—94, Disciplinary bd. Region 5 1991—97, sec. 1992—93, chair 1993—94, 1996—97, ethics com. 1998—2001, chair utility sect. 2001—03), Oreg. State Bar (legis. exec. com. on adminstrv. law sect. 2002—03, exec. com. of utility sect. as past chair 2003—), Wash. State Bar Assn. Avocations: reading, writing, computers, golf, family activities. Office: Ann L Fisher Legal and Cons Svcs 1425 SW 20th Ave Ste 202 Portland OR 97201-2485 Fax: (503) 223-2305. E-mail: afisher1@qwest.net., annfisher@annfisherlaw.com.

FISHER, ANNA LEE, physician, astronaut; b. St. Albans, N.Y., Aug. 24, 1949; m. William Frederick Fisher; children: Kristin Anne, Kara Lynne. BS in Chemistry, UCLA, 1971, MD, 1976, MS in Chemistry, 1987. Physician, 1976-78; astronaut NASA Johnson Space Ctr., Houston, 1978—, mission specialist STS, 51-A, 1984. Mem. Sigma Xi. Office: NASA Johnson Space Ctr Astronaut Ofc Houston TX 77058

FISHER, ARTHUR, magazine editor; b. N.Y.C., Mar. 10, 1931; s. Abraham G. and Sadie (Gold) F.; m. Liliane E. Kowarsky, Aug. 18, 1951; 1 child, Anthony E. BA, NYU, 1951. Sr. rsch. aide NYU, 1954-56; mng. editor Dodge Books, 1957-62, Sci. World & Sr. Sci., 1962-68; sci. and tech. editor Popular Sci., N.Y.C., 1969-94, exec. editor, 1994-96, sci. editor emeritus, 1996—. Author: The Healthy Heart, 1981; co-author: (with Ernest V. Heyn) Century of Wonders, 1972, Fire of Genius, 1976; contbr. articles to mags. Recipient citations for excellence in sci. writing Deadline Club, 1973, 74, Claude Bernard Sci. Journalism award Nat. Soc. Med. Rsch., 1978, Sci. Writing award Am. Heart Assn., 1981, Am. Inst. of Phys. Sci. Writing award, 1985, Sci. Writing award AAAS, 1986, Grady-Stack Sci. Writing award Am. Chem. Soc., 1988, Writing award Ednl. Writers Assn., 1993, Journalism award Engring. Found., 1997. Mem. Nat. Assn. Sci. Writers, Coun. for Advancement of Sci. Writing (bd. dirs. 1989—). Home: 120 Cabrini Blvd New York NY 10033-3438

FISHER, BARBARA GAIL, writer, educator; b. N.Y.C., Dec. 10, 1940; d. David and Regina (Mandel) F.; m. Ernest Gene Perry, Sept. 24, 1967 (div. Oct. 1980); 1 child, Athelantis Thomas; m. Richard Alan Spiegel, June 21, 1983. BA, Hunter Coll., 1962; MS, Pace U., 1993; postgrad., The New Sch. for Social Rsch., Fordham U., Coll. S.I., others, 1988-93. Cert. high sch. fine arts tchr., sch. dist. adminstr. Staff Ten Penny Players, Inc., S.I., 1967—. Cons. N.Y. State Narcotics Addiction Control Commn., 1971-73, Insts. for the Achievement of Human Potential, Phila., 1974-76, Woodrock Project, Phila., 1975-76; poet in residence Hunter Coll. Elem. Sch., 1981, Canarsie Schs., 1982, Jefferson Market Libr., Greenwich Village, 1981-85; adj. prof. Nat. Acad. Alternative Edn., Fordham U., 1993—, Fordham U. Grad. Sch. Edn., 1993—; fundraiser, workshop presenter and lectr. in field. Author: Care Without Care, 1972, Davy Davy Dumpling, 1985, Coping With Your Baby's Frequent Hospitalizations Without Cigarettes, Alcohol, Prescription or Illegal Drugs, 1990, Death of Your Child, 1990, Parenting Teens Common Sense Survival Skills Manual, 1990, A Young Parent's Guide to Health and Sensible Eating, 1991, A Young Parent's Guide to Water: Good Health and Keeping Clean, 1991, Enabling the Family, 1991, others; contbr. numerous articles to profl. jours. and poetry to lit. publs. Youth program dir. St. Peter's Episcopal Ch., Chelsea, 1965-67; mem. The West Village Com., Inc., 1980—; bd. dirs. Ctr. for Independence of Disabled, N.Y.C., 1992-97; chmn. edn. subcom. Mayor's Office for People with Disabilities, 1992-93. Grantee N.Y. State Coun. on the Arts, 1987—, Learn & Serve Am. K-12, 1993—, Empire State Partnership Program, 1997—, Ctr. Arts Edn., 1998-2001—; recipient Pace/Promise/Nat. Acad. Alternative Edn. award for excellence in arts and edn., 1992, Mayor's N.Y.C. Very Spl. Arts award for lit., 1992, S.I. Cmty. TV award for bringing the best to cmty. access TV, 1992, Ednl. Adminstrn. and Supervision award for outstanding achievement Pace U., 1993, Disting. Svc. to the Arts in Edn. Field award, Assn. Tchg. Artists, 2003. Mem. United Fedn. Tchrs., Nat. Writers Union, Dramatist's Guild, Author's Guild. Avocations: raising birds, rescuing disabled and abandoned birds, designing petit point tapestries, music. Office: Ten Penny Players Inc 393 Saint Pauls Ave Staten Island NY 10304-2127

FISHER, BARRY ALAN JOEL, protective services official; b. N.Y.C., Sept. 11, 1944; s. George and Pearl (Newman) F.; m. Susan Joan Saperstein, Dec. 29, 1968; children: David, Michael. BS, CCNY, 1966; MS, Purdue U., 1969; MBA, Calif. State U., Northridge, 1973. With criminalistics lab. L.A. County Sheriff's Dept., 1969-79, chief sheriff's criminalistics lab., 1979-86, dir. Sci. Svcs. Bur., 1986—. Lectr. U. Calif., L.A.; adj. lectr. Calif. State U., 1996. Fellow Am. Acad. Forensic Scis. (disting. co-chmn. local arrangements com. 1981, chmn., sec. criminalistics sect. program 1981-82, sec., chmn. 1982-83, chmn. local arrangements com. 1991, chmn. sect. 1995—, pres.-elect 1997, pres. 1998-99); mem. Am. Soc. Crime Lab. Dirs. (chmn. forensic sci. ops. and program com. 1982-86, bd. dirs. 1986-89, pres. 1988-89, editor newsletter 1989-90), Forensic Sci. Found. (bd. dirs. 1985—, sec. 1988—), Forensic Sci. Soc., Internat. Assn. of Identification, Internat. Assn. Chiefs of Police, Internat. Assn. Forensic Scis. (pres. 1996-99), Consortium of Forensic Sci. Orgs. (chmn. 2000-01, vice chmn. 2001-01, vice chmn. 2001—). Republican. Jewish. Avocations: computers, reading, photography. Office: LA County Sheriffs Crime Lab 2020 Beverly Blvd Los Angeles CA 90057-2404 E-mail: bajfisher@earthlink.net.

FISHER, BENJAMIN CHATBURN, lawyer; b. Coos Bay, Oreg., Feb. 6, 1923; s. Benjamin S. and Catherine Selina (Chatburn) F.; m. Jean L. Whiting, June 30, 1951; children: John, Richard, Robert. AB with honors, U. Ill., 1948; JD magna cum laude, Harvard U., 1951. Bar: D.C. 1951. Law clk. to Hon. Learned Hand U.S. Ct. Appeals 2d cir., N.Y.C., 1951-52; with Fisher, Wayland, Cooper, Leader & Zaragoza, Washington, 1952-2000; sr. counsel Shaw, Pittman, Washington, 2000—. Mem. edn. appeal bd. U.S. Office Edn., 1973-83; mem. Adminstrv. Conf. U.S., 1970-76; U.S. del. Plenipotentiary Conf. Internat. Telecomm. Union, Nice, France, 1989, Geneva, 1992, Kyoto, Japan, 1994, Mpls., 1998, Marrakesh, Morocco, 2002; mem. U.S. del. World Radio Conf., Torremolinos, Spain, 1992, Geneva, 1995, 97; mem. nat. com. radio comm. sect., 1989—; chmn. bd. dirs. U.S. Internat. Telecomm. Union Assn., 2000—. Bd. dirs. Boys and Girls Clubs of Greater Washington, 1990—; bd. govs. Sigma Chi Found., 1991—. Mem. ABA (chmn. sect. adminstrv. law 1968-69, mem. ho. of dels. 1970-72, 73-75), Fed. Commn. Bar Assn. (pres. 1967-68), D.C. Bar Assn., Am. Law Inst., Soc. Satellite Profls. (chmn. 1983-85, bd. dirs. 1986-93, gen. counsel 1993—), Rotary (bd. dirs. Washington Club 1980-85, pres. 1983-84), Phi Beta Kappa, Phi Kappa Phi. Home: 5118 Cammack Dr Bethesda MD 20816-2902 Office: 2300 N St NW Washington DC 20037-1128 E-mail: ben.fisher@shawpittman.com.

FISHER, BERNARD, surgeon, educator; b. Pitts., Aug. 23, 1918; s. Reuben and Anna (Miller) F.; m. Shirley Kruman, June 5, 1947; children: Beth, Joseph, Louisa. BS, U. Pitts., 1940, MD, 1943; DSc (hon.), Mt. Sinai Sch. Medicine, CUNY, 1986; HHD (hon.), Carlow Coll., Pitts., 2003. Diplomate Am. Bd. Surgery. Intern Mercy Hosp., Pitts., 1943—44, resident in surgery, 1944—48; fellow in surg. research, resident in gen. surgery Harrison Dept. Dept. Surg. Research U. Pa., Phila., 1950—52; fellow London Postgrad. Med. Sch. Hammersmith Hosp., 1955—56; tchg. fellow in pathology U. Pitts., 1944—45, 1945—47, assoc. prof., 1956—59, prof. surgery, 1959—86, Disting. Svc. prof., 1986—; Fulbright Commn. award appointee to Peru, 1965; med. surg. staff Presbyn.-Univ. Hosp., 1953—98. Past mem. cons. staff Children's Hosp., Pitts.; mem. cons. staff Magee-Women's Hosp., VA Hosp., Pitts.; chmn. Nat. Surg. Adjuvant Breast and Bowel Project, 1967—94, sci. dir., 1995—; chmn. Adjuvant Therapy Ctr., 1973—94, Breast Care and Diagnostic Ctr., 1980—93, Pitts. Cancer Inst., 1985—, Comprehensive Breast Care Ctr., 1992—98; mem. spl. del. to China, 1977; mem. President's Cancer Panel, 1979—82, Nat. Cancer Adv. Bd., 1986—92, Inst. Medicine of NAS. Mem. editl. bd.: Transplantation, 1966—71, Cancer, 1969—71, 1975, Year Book of Cancer, 1973—85, Internat. Jour. Radiation Oncology Biology Physics, 1975—78, Cancer Clin. Trials, 1977, Invasion and Metastis, 1981—85, Cancer Metastasis Revs., 1981—85, Jour. Clin. Oncology, 1982—87, Internat. Jour. Breast and Mammary Pathology, 1982—84, Cancer Rsch., 1976, Seminars in Oncology, 1979, Breast Cancer Rsch. and Treatment, 1980, 1992—, Clin. and Exptl. Metastasis, 1980—94, Breast Diseases: Yr. Book Quar., 1989—95, Annals Surg. Oncology, 1993—94, Internat. Jour. Oncology, 1993—94, Advances in Oncology, 1992—96, Breast Disease: Internat. Jour., 1993—96, Cancer Jour., 1994—, Internat. Jour. Cancer, 1993—94, European Jour. Cancer, 1995—97; contbr. Named Fisher Breast Cancer lectureship established in his honor, U. Pitts., 1989; recipient Man of Yr. award in medicine, Pitts. Jr. C. of C., 1966, Philip Hench Disting. Alumnus award, U. Pitts. Sch. Medicine, 1976, McGraw medal, Detroit Surg. Assn., 1978, Lucy Wortham James Clin. Rsch. award, 1981, Heath Meml. award, 1982, Joseph H. Morton Meml. award, 1983, Julia Hudson Freund Meml. award, 1983, Albert Lasker Med. rsch. award, 1985, Hammer Cancer prize, 1988, Am. Cancer Soc. Medal of Honor, 1986, Milken Med. Found. Ctr. Rsch. award, 1989, Assn. Commn. Cancer Ctrs. award, 1990, Chancellors Dist. Rsch. award U. Pitts., 1992, Nat. Health Couns. Med. Rsch. award, 1992, Brinker Internat. Breast Cancer award, 1992, Durham N.C. City of Medicine award, 1992, Dr. Josef Steiner Cancer Rsch. prize, 1992, GM Cancer Rsch. Found. Kettering prize, 1993, Susan Komen Found. Sci. Distinction award, 1988, Bristol-Myers Squib award, 1993, James Ewing Lectr. award SSO, 1993, Gottlieb Meml. award, 1993, Sheen award, 1993, Claude Jacquillet award, 1995, Lifetime Achievement award in Breast Cancer Rsch., Senologic Internat. Soc., 1996, Health Care Lifetime Achievement award, Pitts. Bus. Times, 1998, Potamkin Found. award for breast cancer rsch., Pa. Breast Cancer Coalition, 1999, Celebrating Survival: A Century of Advancements in Early Breast Cancer award, 2000, Am. Surg. Assn. Medallion for Sci. Achievement, 2000, Flance-Karl award for contbns. to sci. of clin. surgery, 2001, St. Gallen Internat. Breast Cancer award, 2003; scholar Markle scholar in med. sci., John and Mary Markle Found., 1953—58. Fellow: AAAS, Am. Coll. Radiology (hon.); mem.: ACS, AAUP, Am. Italian Fedn. Cancer Rsch., Internat. Assn. Breast Cancer Rsch., Assn. Italiana per la Divulgaxione Sci. della Cancerologia Clinica, Italian Surg. Rsch. Assn., Pitts. Surg. Soc. (pres. 1979), Pitts. Acad. Medicine, Allegheny County Med. Soc. (Man of Yr. award 1983), Pa. Med. Soc., Am. Socs. for Exptl. Biology, Soc. Univ. Surgeons, Soc. Surg. Oncology, N.Y. Acad. Scis., Am. Surg. Assn. (v.p. 1996), Cell Kinetic Soc., Assn. Am. Med. Colls., Am. Physiol. Soc., Am. Soc. Clin. Oncology (pres. 1992-93, bd. dirs., Karnofsky award 1980, Disting. Svc. award for sci. achievement 1999), Am. Assn. Cancer Research (bd. dirs., 3d Jos. H. Burchenal Clin. Rsch. award 1998), Assn. Cancer Edn., Oncology Nursing Soc. (hon.), Peruvian Acad. Surgery (hon.), Am. Soc. Therapeutic Radiology and Oncology (hon.), Phi Beta Kappa, Alpha Omega Alpha. Office: 4 Allegheny Ctr Ste 602 Pittsburgh PA 15212-5234

FISHER, BERTRAM DORE, lawyer; b. N.Y.C., July 10, 1928; s. Samuel and Dorothy (Eisman) F.; m. Barbara Marks, Aug. 23, 1959; children— Beth Carlyle Cutler, Priscilla Brooke. Student Johns Hopkins U.; B.A., U. Miami, Fla., 1949; LL.B., Bklyn. Law Sch., 1951; postgrad. NYU Grad. Sch. Law. Bar: N.Y. 1951, D.C. 1981, U.S. Dist. Ct. (so. and ea. dists.) N.Y., U.S. Ct. Appeals (2d cir.), U.S. Supreme Ct. Sr. ptnr. Queller, Fisher & Wisotsky, N.Y.C.; mem. Supreme Ct. Com., 1985—, Med. Malpractice Jud. Panel, N.Y. State Supreme Ct., N.Y. County and Kings County, 1987—; Ind. Jud. Screening com., 1982—; lectr. N.Y. Acad. Trial Lawyers; frequent lectr. to profession on trial techniques, evidence, cross-examination. Bd. govs. Nat. Conf. for Furtherance of Jewish Edn., 1985—. With U.S. Army, 1951-53, Korea. Decorated Bronze Star. Recipient Man of Year award Nat. Com. for Furtherance of Jewish Edn., 1984. Mem. ABA, N.Y. State Trial Lawyers Assn. (bd. dirs. 1983—, mem. jud. screening com. 1978—), N.Y. State Bar Assn. (mem. ethics com. 1979-80, toxic waste com., negligence com. 1984—), Assn. of Bar of City of N.Y. (mem. judiciary com. Bklyn. chpt., 1987—, ethics com. 1978-80, Supreme Ct. com. 1985-86, tort com.), D.C. Bar Assn., N.Y. County Lawyers Assn. (com. on Supreme Ct. 1978—, forum com. 1983—), Assn. Trial Lawyers of City of N.Y., N.Y. Criminal and Civil Bar Assn., Bklyn. and Manhattan Trial Counsel Assn., Bklyn. Bar Assn. (mem. ethics com. 1978-80), Met. Women's Bar Assn., Jewish Lawyers Guild (corr. sec. 1979-81, 1st v.p. 1982-83, pres. 1984-87, chmn. bd. govs. 1988—), Assn. Trial Lawyers Am. (Roscoe Pound Found., M Club), Joint Bar Assn. (jud. screening com. 1983—), Internat. Assn. Jewish Lawyers and Jurists (bd. dirs. 1986, Merit award 1986), Bklyn. Law Sch. Alumni Assn., Am. Coll. Legal Medicine (assoc. in law 1986—), Network of Bar Leaders (com. of 26 N.Y. bar assns. 1982-88). Clubs: Downtown Athletic (N.Y.C.), Iota Theta; Dunes Racquet (Ammagamset, N.Y.). Office: Queller Fisher & Wisotsky 110 Wall St New York NY 10005-3801

FISHER, CALVIN DAVID, food manufacturing company executive; b. Nerstrand, Minn., June 10, 1926; s. Edward and Sadie (Wolf) F.; m. Patricia Vivian Capriotti, July 28, 1950; children: Cynthia, Nancy Joann, Michael. BS, U. Minn., 1950. Dairy specialist U.S. Dept. Agr., Mpls., 1950-54, chemist and dairy specialist Omaha, 1954-58; with Roberts Dairy Co., Omaha, 1958-80, sr. v.p., chief operating officer, 1967-70, pres., chief exec. officer, 1970-80, owner, chief exec. officer, 1975-80, Fisher Foods Ltd., Lincoln, Nebr., 1980—; pres., dir. Master Dairies, Indpls., 1968-80; bd. dirs. Internat. Assn. Ice Cream Mfrs. Milk Industry Found., 1973-80. Patentee spray-dried ice cream mix, pasteurized egg products. Bd. dirs., v.p. Omaha Safety Council, 1981; bd. dirs. Arthritis Found., 1972-81; mem. adv. council SBA; bd. dirs. Nebr. State Patrol Found., 1990—. With USN, 1944-47. Mem. Omaha C. of C. (pres.'s coun. 1976, 78), Internat. Food Scientists Assn., Inst. Food Tech., Nat. Ind. Dairies Assn., Rotary, Univ. Club (Lincoln), Firethorn Country Club. Republican. Methodist. Home: University Towers 128 N 13th St Ste 1001 Lincoln NE 68508-1501 Office: Fisher Foods Ltd 220 S 20th St Lincoln NE 68510-1007

FISHER, CHARLES HAROLD, chemistry educator, researcher; b. Hiawatha, W.Va., Nov. 20, 1906; s. Lawrence D. and Mary (Akers) F.; m. Elizabeth Dye, Nov. 4, 1933 (dec. 1967); m. Lois Carlin, July 1968 (dec. June 1990); m. Elizabeth Snyder Kiser, Nov. 29, 1991. BS in Chemistry, Roanoke Coll., 1928, ScD (hon.), 1963; MS in Chemistry, U. Ill., 1929, PhD, 1932; DSc (hon.), Tulane U., 1953. Tchg. asst. in chemistry U. Ill., Urbana, 1928-32; instr. Harvard U., 1932-35; rsch. group leader US Bur. Mines, Pitts., 1935-40; head carbohydrate divsn. Ea. Regional Rsch. Ctr. USDA, 1940-50; dir. So. mktg. and nutrition rsch. div. So. Regional Rsch. Ctr., USDA, New Orleans, 1950-72. Adj. rsch. prof. Roanoke Coll., Salem, Va., 1972—; established Elizabeth Snyder Fisher Scholarship, Roanoke Coll., 1992. Co-author: Profiles of Eminent American Chemists, 1988; contbr. over 200 articles to profl. jour. Co-inventor 72 patents. Pres. New Orleans Sci. Fair, 1967-69; bd. dir. Salem Hist. Soc., 1982-85, Salem Ednl. Found., 1991-99; established Lawrence D. and Mary A. Fisher Scholarship Roanoke Coll., 1978, Lois Carlin Fisher Scholarship, 1991. Recipient So. Chemists award, 1956, Herty medal, 1959; named Polymer Science Pioneer, 1981, Roanoke Coll. medal, 1996; named to Hall of Fame, Salem Ednl. Found., 1996; Charles H. Fisher Lectures established in his honor Roanoke Coll., 1990; Laboratory of Organic Chem. named in his honor Roanoke Coll., 2002. Mem. AAAS, Am. Inst. Chemists (hon., pres. 1962-63, chmn. bd. dir., Chem. Pioneer award 1966, Presdl. citation of merit 1986), Oil Chem. Soc., Am. Chem. Soc. (dir. region IV 1969-71), Chemurgic Coun. (dir.), Am. Assn. Textile Chemists and Colorists, Hidden Valley Country Club (Salem, Va.), Cosmos Club (Washington), Internat. House, Round Table Club (New Orleans); Chemists Club (NYC). Achievements include co-inventor of acrylic rubber. Office: Roanoke Coll Dept Chemistry 221 College Ln Salem VA 24153-3742 *I have worked hard as a physical scientist and research administrator because research is fun and offers the best way of benefiting humankind.*

FISHER, CHERYL SMITH, lawyer; b. Corning, N.Y., Sept. 4, 1951; d. Norman Albert and Betty (Manzella) Smith; 1 child: Daniel Terence. BA cum laude, SUNY, Oswego, 1973; JD cum laude, SUNY, Buffalo, 1976. Bar: N.Y. 1977, U.S. dist. Ct. (we. dist.) N.Y. 1977, U.S. Ct. Appeals (2d cir.) 1980, U.S. Supreme Ct. 1992. Assoc. Runfola, Birzon & Renda, Buffalo, 1976-77, Kavinoky Cook et al, Buffalo, 1977-79; asst. U.S. Atty. Western Dist. N.Y., Buffalo, 1979-84; assoc. Cohen Swados Wright Hanifin Bradford & Brett, Buffalo, 1984-86, Magavern & Magavern, Buffalo, 1986-87; ptnr. Magavern, Magavern & Grimm, 1988—. Spl. asst. U.S. atty. Dept. Justice, Buffalo, 1984. Pres. Cathedral Park Counseling Svc., Inc., Buffalo, 1979—83; mem. Civil Justice Reform Act, 1993—96, adv. panel, 1993—98; chmn. Lord of Life Adult and Child Svcs., 1999—2002; mem. vestry St. Paul's Cathedral, Buffalo, 1979—82, 1984—87, 2002—05; mem. bd. dirs. Child and Family Svc. Erie County, Buffalo, 1982—, chmn. bd. dirs., 1993—96; bd. dirs. Lord of Life Adult and Child Svcs., 1997—. Recipient Bishop Lauriston Scaife award, Episcopal Cmty. Svcs., 1999, John N. Walsh Jr. award, Child & Family Svcs. of Erie County, 2000. Mem. N.Y. State Bar Assn. (com. on profl. ethics), Erie County Bar Assn. (bd. dirs. 1996-99), N.Y. State Women's Bar Assn., Women Lawyers Assn., Alpha Psi Omega. Democrat. Episcopalian. Home: 306 Highland Ave Buffalo NY 14222-1751 Office: Law Offices 1100 Rand Building Bldg Buffalo NY 14203-1911 E-mail: cfisher@magavern.com.

FISHER, CLARKSON SHERMAN, JR., judge; b. Red Bank, N.J., Nov. 29, 1952; s. Clarkson Sherman and Mae Shannon (Hoffmann) F.; m. Carolyn Ann Sullivan, Aug. 27, 1977; children: Clarkson Sherman III, Caylan S., Cilloran S. BA, Villanova (Pa.) U., 1974; JD, Seton Hall U., 1977. Bar: U.S. Dist. Ct. N.J. 1977, N.J. 1978, U.S. Ct. Appeals (3d cir.) 1979, U.S. Ct. Appeals (2d and 5th cirs.) 1983, U.S. Supreme Ct. 1983, N.Y. 1984, U.S. Dist. Ct. (so. and ea. dists.) N.Y., 1984, U.S. Ct. Appeals (4th cir.) 1984. Law clk. N.J. Superior Ct., Newark, 1977-78; assoc. Robinson, Wayne & Greenberg, Newark, 1978-82, Evans, Koelzer, Osborne & Kreizman, Red Bank, 1982-85, ptnr., 1985-86, Ober, Kaler, Grimes & Shriver, Edison, N.J., 1986-93; judge Superior Ct. N.J., Freehold, 1993-97; presiding judge Superior Ct. Chancery Divsn., Freehold, 1997—. Mem. ABA, N.J. Bar Assn., Maritime Law Assn. Democrat. Roman Catholic. Home: 116 Bridgewaters Dr Oceanport NJ 07757-1316 Office: Monmouth County Court Freehold NJ 07728

FISHER, CRAIG BECKER, film and television executive; b. Manila, Jan. 19, 1932; s. Dale Davis and Francis Mary (Major) F.; m. Helen Rossi Ashton, Sept. 5, 1970; children: Christopher Ashton, Wenda Francis; children by previous marriage: Cathleen Anne, Dean Barnett. BA, U. Md., 1954. With Sta. WRC-TV, Washington, 1950, Sta. WTOP-TV, Washington, 1952, Sta. WMAL-TV, Washington, 1954; successively unit mgr., assoc. producer, film dir. CBS News, 1957-60; producer, dir., writer NBC News, 1960-70; pres. Osprey Prodns., Inc., N.Y.C., 1970-95, Fund for Arts & Scis. Films, Inc., 1981—, Kingfisher Prodns., 1996—. Adj. assoc. prof. film dept. St. John's U., NYU Film Sch.; dir. MFA Film Program, Rockport Coll.; instr. Maine Film & Video Workshops; Master Class instr. Boston Film and Video Found.; cons. Nat. Commn. Population Growth and the Am. Future; judge D.W. Griffith Film Festival; cons. TV, radio and film dept. U. Md.; bd. dirs., treas. Am. Friends of Brit. Acad. Film and TV Arts; mem. selection com. NEH; script cons. NEA; media cons. Green Peace, Am. Express, Office Pub. Responsibility; awards chmn. Sir Peter Ustin Writing Competition. Contbr. articles to profl. jours. and mags. Mem. exec. com. Scott Newman Drug Abuse Prevention Award. Served to capt. USAF, 1955-57, reserves, 1957-69. Recipient Thomas Alva Edison award, George Foster Peabody award, Freedoms Found. award, Wrangler award Western Heritage Ctr., Criss award, Golden Eagle award Council Internat. Nontheatrical Events, IFPA Cindy award., Best Documentary Script on Current Events award Writers Guild Am., Best Film award Nat. Press Photographers Assn., Emmy award, All Am. award Radio-TV Daily, Fame award TV Today and Motion Picture Daily, Blue Ribbon award Am. Film Festival, Silver Oscella La Biennale di Venezia, cert. Venice Film Festival, cert. Adelaide/Auckland (Australia) Internat. Film

Festival, Western Writers Am. Spur award . Fellow Explorers Club; mem. AAAS, Writers Guild Am. East (pres. 1977-79, exec. dir. found., del. internat. affiliation, Richard B. Jablow award for disting. svc.), Nat. Acad. TV Arts and Scis. (nat. trustee, chmn. Emmy awards), Internat. Acad. TV Arts and Scis. (assoc., awards chair Sir Peter Ustinov Writing Competition, judge Internat. Emmy awards), Internat. Interactive Comm. Soc., Assn. Am. Mus., Internat. Radio and TV Soc., Air Force Assn. (Charles Lindburgh chpt. v.p. comm.), Maine Film and Video Assn. (founding mem., vice chair), Overseas Press Club, Am. Alpine Club, Omicron Delta Kappa, Sigma Chi. Home: PO Box 681 Camden ME 04843-0681

FISHER, D. MICHAEL, state attorney general; b. Pitts., Nov. 7, 1944; s. C. Francis and Dolores (Darby) Fisher; m. Carol Hudak, Aug. 15, 1973; children: Michelle Lynn, Brett Michael. AB, Georgetown U., 1966; JD, Georgetown Law Ctr., 1969. Bar: Pa. 1970. Asst. dist. atty. Allegheny County, Pitts., 1970—74; rep. Pa. Ho. of Reps., Harrisburg, 1974—80; mem. Pa. Senate, Harrisburg, 1980—97; ptnr. Houston Harbaugh, Pitts., 1984—97; atty. gen. Commonwealth of Pa., Harrisburg, 1997—. Chmn. House Subcom. on Crime and Corrections, 1979—80, Senate Environ. Resources & Energy, 1981—90, Senate Majority Policy Com., 1988—90, Senate Rep. Caucus, 1992—; vice-chmn. Senate Jud. Com., 1981—90; mem. Majority Whip, 1990—96. Contbr. articles to profl. jours. Active Environ. Quality Bd., 1980—90, Pa. Commn. on Crime and Delinquency, 1979—; mem. Pa. Security Task Force, 2001—; chmn. Office of Nat. Drug Control Policy's Phila./Camden High Intensity Drug Trafficking Area, 2003—; mem. exec. working group for fed., state and local prosecutorial rels. U.S. Dept. Justice, 2001—; v.p. Nat. Assn. Attys. Gen. Exec. Bd., 2000—01; Rep. candidate for lt. gov. State of Pa., 1986; active Pa. Gov.'s Energy Coun., 1981—86, Pa. Energy Devel. Authority, 1984—86; del. Rep. Nat. Conv., 1988, 1992; Rep. nominee for gov. State of Pa., 2002; bd. dirs. Am. Legacy Found., 2003. Named Man of Yr., Upper St. Clair Rep. Club, 1980, Vector's Law & Govt., 1991; named one of Outstanding Young Men Am., 1977—79. Mem.: Pa. Bar Assn., Bethel Park Chamber, Rotary, Am. Legion, Elks. Republican. Roman Catholic. Avocations: golf, hockey, football. Office: Atty Gen 16 Strawberry Sq Harrisburg PA 17120*

FISHER, DALE DUNBAR, animal scientist, dairy nutritionist; b. Lewisburg, Pa., Feb. 13, 1945; s. Glenn Murray and Elsie May (Bryson) F.; divorced; children: Elsie Maria, Maria Vanessa. BS in Animal Sci., Pa. State U., 1967, MS in Animal Industry, 1978, PhD in Animal Industry, 1980. Vol. animal husbandry Peace Corps, Ciudad Quesada, Costa Rica, 1967-71; area animal husbandry-pasture specialist Costa Rican Ministry of Agr., Ciudad Quesada, 1971-73; vis. scientist Internat. Ctr. for Tropical Agr., Cali, Colombia, 1973-75; animal nutritionist Co-op. Feed Dealers, Inc., Chenango Bridge, N.Y., 1981—. Contbr. articles to profl. jours. Eva B. and G. Weidman Groff Meml. scholar Pa. State U., 1979. Mem. Am. Soc. Animal Sci., Am. Dairy Sci. Assn., Am. Soc. Agronomy, Am. Acad. Vet. Nutrition, N.Y. Acad. Scis., Am. Coll. Nutrition, Sigma Xi, Phi Kappa Phi, Gamma Sigma Delta. Democrat. Avocations: jogging, reading. Home: 578 Chenango St Binghamton NY 13901-2134 Office: Coop Feed Dealers Inc 380 Broome Corporate Pkwy PO Box 670 Conklin NY 13748 E-mail: nutrition@co-opfeed.com.

FISHER, DALE JOHN, chemist, instrumentation and medical diagnostic device investigator; b. Omro, Wis., June 4, 1925; m. Ruth J. Laird, Apr. 27, 1957; 1 child, Shelley Dale. BS, U. Wis., Oshkosh, 1947; PhD (Univ. fellow), Ind. U., 1951. Staff mem. Inst. Paper Chemistry, Appleton, Wis., summer 1945; chemist City of Oshkosh, Wis., summers 1946-48; chemist ionic analyses group Oak Ridge Nat. Lab., 1951-52, group leader analytical instrumentation group, 1952-72, mem. dir.'s staff, 1972-73; physicist (nuclear medicine) VA Hosp., Gainesville, Fla., 1973-74, tech. dir. nuclear medicine, 1974-76; grad. studies faculty U. Fla., Gainesville, 1974-76; physicist FDA, 1976-91, physicist divsn. in vitro diagnostic device standards, 1976-83, physicist Office Sci. and Tech., divsn. life scis., health scis. br., 1983-91; ret., 1991. Recipient Disting. Alumni award U. Wis., Oshkosh, 1982. Mem. ASTM (sr.), Am. Chem. Soc. (emeritus; nat. award chem. instrumentation), U. Wis. Oshkosh Alumni Assn. (life), Sigma Xi (emeritus), Phi Lambda Upsilon. Achievements include design and new applications of instrument systems and methods for analysis, process monitoring and research; creation electronic and mechanical designs and administration of research. Patentee in field. Research with computer-based nuclear medicine imaging instrumentation for the improvement of patient care. Development of med. device standards and performance requirements. Establish sci. basis for med. diagnostic and clin. lab. instruments. Improve safety and effectiveness of medical devices through toxicology and statistics research. Home: 6319 Golden Hook Columbia MD 21044-3710

FISHER, DARRYL, information services company executive; COO bus. info. svcs. Lexis-Nexis, Miamisburg, Ohio, 1996—98, pres. CEO, Reed Tech. & Info. Svcs., 1998—2000; pres., CEO Thomas Tech. Solutions, Inc., Horsham, Pa., 2000—. Office: Thomas Tech Solutions Inc 1 Progress Dr Horsham PA 19044-3502*

FISHER, DAVID BRUCE, land development executive; b. Glen Cove, N.Y., Oct. 22, 1954; s. David James and Margaret Virginia (Peters) F.; m. Janice Katherine Patterson, Oct. 25, 1980; children: Courtney Elizabeth, David Robert. BA in Geology, Susquehanna U., 1976; M in Cmty. Planning, U. Cin., 1979. Lic. profl. planner, N.J. Dir. environ. affairs and planning N.J. Builders Assn., Plainsboro, 1979-81, 83-87; project planner Ernst, Ernst & Lissenden, Toms River, N.J., 1981-83; v.p. forward planning N.J. div. Leisure Tech., Inc., Lakewood, N.J., 1987-91; dir. regulatory affairs, prin. planner Ernst, Ernst & Lissenden, Toms River, 1991-92; v.p. devel. Sammis Co./Gale & Wentworth, Florham Park, N.J., 1992-93; v.p. govtl. affairs Matzel & Mumford Orgn., Hazlet, NJ, 1993—. Chmn. N.J. Clean Water Coun., Trenton, 1985-89; mem. Citizen Com. of Permit Coord., Trenton, 1986-97; mem. N.J. State Planning Commn., 2000—; coach Toms River Soccer Assn., 1989-95; mem. vestry St. Raphael's Episcopal Ch., Brick, N.J., 1989-93. Recipient Bus. Watch award Bus. Jour. N.J., Vol. 5, No. 5, 1988; named to Builder Hall of Fame, 2001. Mem. Am. Planning Assn. (chartered), Am. Inst. Cert. Planners, N.J. Builders Assn. (bd. dirs. 1997—), N.J. Shore Builders Assn. (pres. 1998-2000, Bldr. of the Yr. award 1999). Avocations: skiing, tennis, soccer. Office: Matzel & Mumford Orgn 100 Village Ct Hazlet NJ 07730-1548

FISHER, DAVID ROBERT, forensic scientist; b. L.A., Feb. 15, 1975; s. Barry and Susan F.; m. Deena Garfinkel, Mar. 4, 2001. BS, U. Calif., San Diego, 1997. Instr. John Jay Coll. Criminal Justice, N.Y.C., 1999—2002; criminalist N.Y.C. Office of the Chief Med. Examiner, 2002—. Recipient Emerging Forensic Scientist award Forensic Sci. Found., 2000; John A. Reisenbach Found. scholar, 2000; Am. Soc. Crime Lab. Dirs. scholar, 2002. Mem. Am. Acad. Forensic Sci. (assoc.), Northeastern Assn. Forensic Scientists (assoc.). Republican. Jewish. Office: NYC Office of Chief Med Examiner Forensic Biology Lab 520 1st Ave New York NY 10016 E-mail: davidrfisher@hotmail.com.

FISHER, DAVID RUSSEL, government executive; b. Detroit, Mar. 23, 1946; s. Russel J. and Olive J. (Bilyea) F.; m. Janet I. Coolman; children: Christopher D., Autumn D., Matthew D. B of Bus. Adminstrn., Mich. State U., 1968, MBA, Fla. inst. Tech., 1984. Human resources dir. Omaha dist. U.S. Army Corps of Engrs., 1979-81; dir. recruitment and placement U.S. Army Missile Command Redstone Arsenal, Huntsville, Ala., 1981-85; human resources officer Def. Reutilization and Mktg. Svcs., Battle Creek, Mich., 1985-94, detailed v.p. reinvention, 1994, contr., 1994-95, v.p. resources, 1995-96, exec. v.p. corp. planning, 1996-98, dir. Army and Marine Corps cataloging ctr., 1998-99, dir. customer products and svcs. def. logistics info. svc., 1999—. Adj. prof. Fla. Inst. Tech., 1983-84; bd. dirs. Dept. of Def. Fed. Credit Union; sr. fellow JFK Sch. Govt., Harvard U., 2002. Bd. dirs., past v.p. human resources S.W. Mich. coun. Boy Scouts Am., Kalamazoo, Mich., 1991-2000; industry rep. dist. improvement com. Battle Creek Pub. Schs., 1994-2001; rep. Coun. Logistics Mgmt., Lansing, Mich., 1997-2000; deacon, elder, trustee United Presbyn. Ch. Decorated Bronze Star. Mem. Vietnam Vets. Am., Mich. State Alumni Assn., Battle Creek C. of C. (rep. 1995-99). Avocations: fitness, running, reading, sports. Office: Def Logistics Info Svc 74 Washington Ave N Battle Creek MI 49017-3085 Fax: 269-961-4715. E-mail: dfisher@dla.mil/dlis.

FISHER, DELBERT ARTHUR, physician, educator; b. Placerville, Calif., Aug. 12, 1928; s. Arthur Lloyd and Thelma (Johnson) Fisher; m. Beverly Carne Fisher, Jan. 28, 1951; children: David Arthur(dec.), Thomas Martin, Mary Kathryn. BA, U. Calif., Berkeley, 1950; MD, U. Calif., San Francisco, 1953. Diplomate Am. Bd. Pediat. Intern, resident in pediat. U. Calif. Med. Ctr., San Francisco, 1953—55; resident in pediat. U. Oreg. Hosp., Portland, 1957—58; Irwin Meml. fellow in pediatric endocrinology, 1958—60; from asst. prof. to assoc. prof. pediat. Med. Sch. U. Ark., Little Rock, 1960—67, prof. pediat., 1967—68, UCLA, 1968—73, prof. pediat. and medicine Med. Sch., 1973—91, prof. emeritus, 1991—; chief, pediat. endocrinology Harbor-UCLA Med. Ctr., 1968—75, rsch. prof. devel. and perinatal biology, 1975—85, chmn. pediat., 1985—89, sr. scientist Rsch. and Edn. Inst., 1991—, chmn. bd. Rsch. and Edn. Inst., 2001—02; dir. Walter Martin Rsch. Ctr., 1986—91; pres. Nichols Inst. Reference Labs, San Juan Capistrano, Calif., 1991—93; pres. acad. assocs., chief sci. officer Nichols Inst., San Juan Capistrano, Calif., 1993—94, Quest Diagnostics-Nichols Inst., San Juan Capistrano, Calif., 1994—97, sr. sci. officer, 1997—98, chief sci. officer, 1998—99; v.p. sci. and innovation Quest Diagnostics Inc., 1999—. Cons. genetic disease sect. Calif. Dept. Health Svcs., 1978—98; mem. organizing com. Internat. Conf. Newborn Thyroid Screening, 1977—88; examiner Am. Bd. Pediat., 1971—80, mem. subcom. on pediat. endocrinology, 1976—79. Co-editor: Pediatric Thyroidology, 1985, 8 other books; editor-in-chief: Jour. Clin. Endocrinology and Metabolism, 1978—83, Pediat. Rsch., 1984—89; contbr. over 400 articles to profl. jours., over 100 chpts. to books. Capt. M.C. USAF, 1955—57. Recipient Career Devel. award, NIH, 1964—68. Mem.: Clin. Ligand Assay Soc. (Disting. Scientist award 2001), Western Soc. Pediat. Rsch. (pres. 1982—83), Lawson Wilkins Pediatric Endocrine Soc. (pres. 1982—83), Assn. Am. Physicians, Am. Soc. Clin. Investigation, Am. Thyroid Assn. (pres. 1988—89, Disting. Lectr. 1982), Endocrine Soc. (pres. 1983—84, Leadership award 1998), Am. Pediat. Soc. (pres. 1992—93, John Howland medal 2001), Soc. Pediat. Rsch. (v.p. 1973—74), Am. Acad. Pediat. (Borden award 1981), Nat. Acad. Clin. Biochemistry, Inst. Medicine of NAS, Alpha Omega Alpha, Phi Beta Kappa. Home: 24582 Santa Clara Ave Dana Point CA 92629-3031 Office: Quest Diagnostics-Nichols Inst 33608 Ortega Hwy San Juan Capistrano CA 92675-2042

FISHER, DIERDRE DENISE, mental health nurse, administrator, educator; b. N.Y.C., Mar. 13, 1945; d. Horace Anderton and Alma (Ames) Taylor; m. Robert Fisher, Oct. 29, 1962 (dec. 1978); children: Sevareid, Pheon (dec.). AAS, Mercer County Coll., 1972; BS, Coll. N.J., 1979; MSN, U. Pa., 1982. Cert. clin. nurse specialist, nursing adminstr. Supr. Nursing Svcs. Trenton (N.J.) Psychiat. Hosp., 1979-81, program coord., 1981-84; cons. Pub. Health N.J. State Dept. Health, Trenton, 1984-87; psychiat. nurse cons. Div. Mental Health and Hosps., Princeton, N.J., 1987-89; asst. complex adminstr. Trenton Psychiat. Hosp., 1989-91; dir. edn. and practice N.J. State Nurses Assn., Trenton, 1991-96; dir. continuing edn. U. Tex. Health Sci. Ctr., San Antonio, 1996-98; owner, pres. Ames High, 1997—. Educator Ocean County Coll., Toms River, N.J., 1985-96; clin. instr. nursing Burlington County Coll., Pemberton, N.J., 1988-91; cons., educator Lake Area Health Edn. Ctr., Erie, Pa., 1988-96. Author nursing publs. Bd. dirs. Trenton YWCA, 1989-95. Recipient Care Givers award Delta Sigma Theta, 1991. Mem. Tex. Nurses Assn. (bd. dirs. Dist. 8, 1997-99), Sigma Theta Tau, Delta Sigma Theta. Home: 1918 Enero Park San Antonio TX 78230-0934

FISHER, DON CARLTON, toxicologist; b. May 13, 1954. BS, Okla. State U., 1985; MD, U. Okla., Tulsa, 1979; MS, U. Ariz., 1984. Diplomate Am. Bd. Preventive Medicine, Am. Bd. Toxicology. Intern family practice U. Okla., 1980-82; resident in family practice and occupl. medicine U. Ariz., 1982-84; med. dir. health venture St. Joseph Hosp., Tacoma, 1985-87, Presbyn. Occupl. Health Network, Albuquerque, 1987-98; pvt. practice toxicology and occupl. diseases, Albuquerque, 1998—. Asst. clin. prof. toxicology and internal medicine U. N.Mex. Office: 10400 Academy Rd NE Ste 380 Albuquerque NM 87111 E-mail: fishertox@earthlink.net.

FISHER, DONALD G. casual apparel chain stores executive; b. 1928; m. Doris Fisher. BS, U. Calif., 1950. With M. Fisher & Son, 1950-57; former ptnr. Fisher Property Investment Co.; co-founder Gap Stores, San Bruno, Calif., 1969; chmn. Gap Inc., San Bruno, Calif., 1969—, pres., 1969—83. Office: Gap Inc 2 Folsom St San Francisco CA 94105

FISHER, DONALD WAYNE, medical association executive; b. Pitts., Mar. 2, 1946; s. David H.W. and Jean K. F.; children by previous marriage: Kimberly Elizabeth, Jeffrey Wayne. AA, Hinds Jr. Coll., 1966; BS in Biology and Chemistry, Millsaps Coll., 1968; MS in Anatomy, U. Miss., 1970, PhD in Anatomy, 1973; postgrad. in assn. mgmt., U. Md., 1977-79. Cert. assn. exec. Instr. dept. chemistry and biology Hinds Jr. Coll., Raymond, Miss., 1968-74; instr. dept. anatomy U. Miss. Sch. Medicine, Jackson, 1973-74, co-dir. and exec. officer physician asst. program, 1972-74; asst. professorial lectr. George Washington U. Sch. Medicine, 1974—; exec. dir. Assn. Physician Asst. Programs, Arlington, Va., 1974-80, Am. Acad. Physician Assts., Arlington, 1974-80; pres., CEO Am. Med. Group Assn., Alexandria, Va., 1980—, Am. Med. Group Corp., Inc., Anceta, 1989, Am. Med. Group Data Warehouse; treas. polit. action com. Am. Med. Group, 1980—. Mem. Nat. Commn. on Allied Health Edn., 1977-80; mem. adv. com. for tng., devel. and utilization of physician extenders Systems Scis., Inc., 1975-80; pres. Am. Acad. Physician Assts. Ednl. and Rsch. Found., 1977-80; sec., treas. Am. Med. Group Found., 1980—; mem. Am. Express Health Care Faculty, 1985-88. Robert Wood Johnson Found. grantee, 1973-80 Mem. Am. Soc. Assn. Execs. (govt. rels. com. 1980—), Assn. Am. Med. Colls., AAAS, Am. Internat. Health Alliance (bd. dirs. 1992—, treas. 1995—), Greater Washington Soc. Assn. Execs., Fairfax County Hosp. Assn., Arlington (Va.) C. of C. Home: 3814 Ivanhoe Ln Alexandria VA 22310-2170 Office: Am Med Group Assn 1422 Duke St Alexandria VA 22314-3430

FISHER, DOUGLAS HOWARD, retail executive; b. Bridgeton, N.J., Apr. 28, 1947; BBA, Bryant Coll., Smithfield, R.I., 1969. Tchr. handicapped children Camden (N.J.) Pub. Schs., 1970-71; pres. Fisher's Food Ctr., Bridgeton, 1971—. Pres. Bridgeton Hist. and Cultural Commn., 1982—, Stop Coughin' Coffin, Bridgeton, 1985—, Congregation Beth Abraham, Bridgeton, 1986—, Bridgeton Cumberland Tourist Assn., 1983-86; dir. Bridgeton Tricentennial Com., 1986; commr. Bridgeton Mcpl. Port Authority, 1988—; bd. trustees Woodland Country Day Sch. Served as sgt. N.J. N.G., 1970-76. Recipient Medal of Merit City of Bridgeton, 1986. Mem. Nat. Assn. Specialty Food Mchts. (charter), Pa. Food Mchts., Am. Family Supermarkets. Jewish. Avocations: fishing, reading, antiques. Home: 421 Marlboro Rd Bridgeton NJ 08302-6716 Office: Bridgeton Meat Co Inc 654 Shiloh Pike Bridgeton NJ 08302-1469*

FISHER, EARL MONTY, utilities executive; b. Chgo., June 26, 1938; s. Harry George and Fannie (Feinberg) F.; m. Joyce Leah Bender, Mar. 14, 1959 (div. Dec. 1978); children: Jan Carol, Wendy Robin; m. Teri Jean Janssen, Jan. 27, 1979. Student, La. Trade Tech. Coll., 1961. Apprentice and journeyman Comfort Air Refrigeration Corp., L.A., 1955-64; contractor Bonanza Air Conditioning and Refrigeration Corp., Van Nuys, Calif., 1964—. Bd. dirs. Hidden Hills (Calif.) Homeowners Assn., 1982-84, vice chmn., v.p., 1990; chmn. Hidden Hills Rds. Com., 1984-85, Hidden Hills Gate Ops. Commn., 1988-91; commr. emergency svcs. City of Hidden Hills, 1986—; pres. Hidden Hills Cmty. Assn., 1991-93; mem. Hidden Hills City Coun., 1994, 2000—; mayor City of Hidden Hills, 1996-98, mayor pro-tem, 2001, mayor, 2002-03. Mem. Air Conditioning Sheet Metal Assn. (vice chmn. 1994-96, dir. 1996—, pres. 1999). Democrat. Avocations: scale model aircraft, horses. Office: Bonanza Air Conditioning Heating & Refrigeration Co 7653 Burnet Ave Van Nuys CA 91405-1081

FISHER, EDGAR JACOB, JR., religious organization administrator; b. Istanbul, Turkey, June 3, 1919; came to U.S., 1934; s. Edgar Jacob and Elisabeth Fehr Fisher; m. Mildred Anne Hill, Dec. 18, 1948 (dec. Oct. 1975); m. Constance Fleming Warwick, July 26, 1980; 1 child, Elisabeth Anne. BS, William and Mary Coll., 1942. Adminstrv. asst. Near East Coll. Assn., N.Y.C., 1945-48; dir. Va. Coun. on Health and Med. Care, Richmond, Va., 1948-84; v.p., treas., bd. dirs. Cross-Over Ministry, Richmond, 1982—. Vis. lectr. Ea. Va. Med. Sch., Med. Coll. Va./Va. Commonwealth U., U. Va. Sch. Medicine. Bd. mem., cons. Keep Virginia Beautiful, Richmond, 1960—; bd. mem. Needle's Eye Ministries, Richmond, 1980—, Med. Soc. Va. Found., Ctrl. Va. Health Edn. Ctr., Va. League for Nursing, Va. Thanksgiving Festival, Blue Cross Va., Richmond Area Rehab. Ctr.; sec., bd. mem. Westminster Presbyn. Homes; hon. bd. mem. Easter Seal Soc. Va.; mem. adv. com. Va. Assn. Women and Hwy. Safety Leaders, Va. Solicitation of Contbns. Law; cons. Ea. Va. Med. Sch.; ecumenical rels. divsn. Hanover Presbytery; mem. health info. com. Va. Lung Assn.; active Hunger Task Force for Hanover Presbytery, Engrs. Club Richmond; mem. task force com. on placement svcs. Nat. Health Coun., del.-at-large; mem. investigational rev. bd. Va. Heart Inst.; lay trustee Va. Recreation and Pks. Soc.; elder St. Giles' Presbyn. Ch.; others. Lt. USN, 1942-45. Recipient Disting. Svc. award Med. Soc. Va., Richmond, 1957, Disting. Svc. to Rural Va., Va. Farm Bur. Fedn., 1974, Friends of Nursing award Va. League for Nursing, Richmond, 1972, Cert. Appreciation, Va. Pharm. Assn., 1984, Cert. of Appreciation Am. Cancer Soc.-Va. Divsn., 1977. Mem. Va. Soc. Assn. Execs. (life), Richmond Pub. Rels. Assn. (treas., 2d v.p., 1st v.p., pres.), Kappa Alpha Order, Omicron Delta Kappa. Republican. Avocations: gardening, wood working. Home: 8008 Cameron Rd Richmond VA 23229-8402

FISHER, EDWARD ABRAHAM, cardiologist, educator; b. Honolulu, Apr. 30, 1958; s. Hyman Wendell and Rosalie (Joseph) F.; m. Vivian Degenszejn, Mar. 27, 1993; children: Rebecca, Alexander, Oliver. BA in Econs., U. Va., 1980; MD, Ea. Va. Med. Sch., 1984. Diplomate Nat. Bd. Med. Examiners, Am. Bd. Internal Medicine, Am. Bd. Cardiovascular Disease; lic. physician, N.Y. Intern Lenox Hill Hosp., N.Y.C., 1984-85, resident, 1985-87, adj. attending physician dept. medicine, 1987—; cardiology fellow Mt. Sinai Med. Ctr., N.Y.C., 1987-89, cardiology rsch. fellow, 1989-90, clin. asst. dept. medicine, 1990, asst. dir. echocardiography dept. medicine divsn. cardiology, 1990-98; asst. attending Mt. Sinai Sch. Medicine, N.Y.C., 1990-92, asst. clin. prof., 1992-97, assoc. clin. prof., assoc. attending, 1997—. Co-author: Effects of Estrogen and Progesterone on Blood Vessels, 1991, Restrictive Cardiomyopathy, 2001, Native Aortic Valve Endocarditis, 2003; author numerous articles concerning transthoracic and transesophageal echocardiography. Fellow ACP, Am. Coll. Cardiology, Am. Heart Assn. Avocation: marathon running. Office: 941 Park Ave New York NY 10028-0318 also: Mt Sinai Med Ctr Cardiovascular Inst #1030 1 Gustave L Levy Pl New York NY 10029-6500

FISHER, EDWIN R. pathologist; b. Pitts., Sept. 2, 1923; s. Reuben and Anna (Miller) F.; m. Carole Levy; children: Marjorie, Abbe Dava. BS, U. Pitts., 1945, MD, 1947. Staff pathology Cleve. Clin., 1953-54; prof. pathology U. Pitts., 1954; chief pathology VA Hosp., Pitts., 1954-70, Shadyside Hosp., Pitts., 1970-95. Mem. editorial bd. Breast Cancer Research and Treatment, European Cancer; chief pathologist Nat. Surg. Adj. Breast Project. Contbr. articles to profl. jours. Sr. surgeon USPHS, 1951-53. Recipient Parke-Davis award Soc. Exptl. Pathology, 1963. Mem. Am. Assn. Cancer Research, Am. Soc. Clin. Pathologists, Internat. Acad. Pathologists, Am. Thoracic Soc., Coll. Am. Pathology. Republican. Jewish. Avocations: golf, landscaping. Office: Allegheny Gen Hosp Human Oncology 320 E North Ave Pittsburgh PA 15212

FISHER, ELLEN ROOP, retired librarian, educator; b. Washington, Dec. 16, 1944; d. Robert Wendell and Katherine (Booth) Roop; m. Allan Campbell Fisher, June 14, 1969; children: Bradford Booth, Katherine Thayer. BA, Smith Coll., Northampton, Mass., 1966; MA, U. Chgo., 1974. Cert. library sci. edn., Pa. Rsch. asst. Indsl. Rels. Ctr. Library, U. Chgo., 1967-68; asst. sys. libr. U. Chgo. Libraries, 1968-71; reference asst. Toledo (Ohio) Pub. Libr., 1972; libr. Cleve. Orch. Chorus Library, 1973-74; reference libr. Harford County Library Sys., Bel Air, Md., 1975; computer tchr. Lawrence Twp. Sch. Dist., Indpls., 1982-84; music tchr. Hegvik Sch. of Music, Wayne, Pa., 1984-86; libr. Edn. Resource Ctr., Cabrini Coll., Wayne, Pa., 1986—87; libr. Radnor Twp. Sch. Dist., Wayne, Pa., 1987—94, head libr., 1994—2001. Author: Sources and Nature of Errors in Transcribing Bibliographic Data into Machine Readable Form, 1974; co-author: The University of Chicago Bibliographic Data Processing System, 1970. Singer St. Cecilia Chamber Choir, Newcastle, Maine, Tapestry Singers. La Verne Noyes scholar U Chgo., 1966. Mem.: ALA, Am. Recorder Soc. Unitarian Universalist. Avocations: travel, genealogy. Home: 13 Pilot Circle PO Box 134 Nobleboro ME 04555-0134

FISHER, ESTELLE MAUDE, retired artist; b. Battle Creek, Mich., Feb. 14, 1913; d. Clyde and Mabel (Blake) Clinefelter; m. Charles Fisher, Jan. 16, 1935 (wid. 1999); children: Charles, Norman, Virginia. Libr. asst. Coldwater (Mich.) Pub. Libr., 1966-68. Exhbns. include Mich. Art Exhibit, South Bend, Ind., 1987, U. Mich., 1962. Home: 150 Northshore Dr Apt 137 Coldwater MI 49036-1264

FISHER, EUGENE, marketing professional; b. Sept. 30, 1927; s. Morris and Sarah (Edelstein) Fisher; m. Joline Cobb, July 28, 1956 (dec.); children: Robin Downing, Amy Homer, Douglas; m. Penny Blanchard, Dec. 18, 1988. PhB, U. Chgo., 1945, MBA, 1948. With Brunswick Corp., Lake Forest, Ill., 1955-95, dir. mktg. planning bowling divsn., 1955-72, dir. corp. mktg. rsch., 1972-87, corp. mktg. dir., 1987-95; pres. Fisher Mktg. Intelligence, Inc., 1982—; chmn. Conf. Bd. Mktg. Rsch. Coun., 1988-89, mem. exec. com., 1989-95. Guest lectr. in field. Mng. editor: Profile Mag., 1988—98; prodr.: Maritime Festival, 1988—91, Brunswick 150th Anniversary Exhbn., 1995. Civic planning com. Ill. State Hist. Soc., 1994—2002; exec. dir. Diversey Harbor Lakeview Assn., 2000—; chmn., pres. Diversey Harbor Lakeview Preservation Assn., 2001—; bd. dirs. Park West Cmty. Assn., 2001—, pres., 2003—; bd. dirs. 2626 Lakeview Condominium Assn., 1995—2000, pres., 1996—2000; 50th reunion dinner chmn. U. Chgo. Alumni Assn., 1995; 55th reunion program chmn. U. Chgo. Class of 1945, 2000, vice chmn. emeritus, 2002—. Mem.: Nat. Bowling Coun. (mktg. com. 1975—83), Chgo. Maritime Soc. (bd. dirs. 1991—95), Am. Mktg. Assn., Phi Sigma Delta. Home and Office: Apt 4103 2626 N Lakeview Ave Chicago IL 60614-1832 Fax: 773-281-0822. E-mail: Fishermarketing@aol.com.

FISHER, FENIMORE, business development consultant; b. N.Y.C., 1926; s. Benn and Sadie (Cohan) F.; m. Marcia Obler, Nov. 9, 1952; children: Bennett G., Alan L., Karen Soo. BS in Physics, Columbia U., 1951; MBA, U. Pa., 1952. Staff physicist USN Rsch. Lab., Phila., 1951-52; ops. mgr., chief engr. instrument divsn. Thomas A. Edison Industries, West Orange, N.J., 1952-60; pres. Analogue Controls Inc., Hicksville, N.Y., 1960-67; corp. v.p. IMC Magnetics Corp., Jericho, N.Y., 1967-77, pres., CEO, 1977-89, also bd. dirs. Chmn. bd. Hansen Mfg. Co. Inc., Princeton Ind., IMC Ariz. Divsn., Tempe, IMC Fla. Divsn., Miami Lakes, IMC Tenn. Divsn., Camden, IMC Tex. Divsn., Mexia, IMC Western Divsn., Cerritos, Calif., New Eng. Alloys Inc., Lawrence, Mass., Pacific Propeller Inc., Kent Washington, Universal Magnetics Corp., Cerritos, 1989—; exec. v.p. Synergy Gas Corp., 1989-93; bus. devel. cons., 1993-96; v.p. bus. and fin. Dowling Coll., Oakdale, N.Y., 1996-98; exec. dir. Action Long Island, 1999—2001. Contbr. numerous articles on bus. econs., tech. edn., relation with the Far East. Bd. dirs. L.I. Philharm., West Suffolk YM & YWHA, United Way L.I.; chmn. L.I. Forum for Tech., Suffolk Cmty. Planning Coun., Old Westbury Coll. Found.; trustee Dowling Coll. Served to 1st lt. U.S. Army, 1944-46, PTO. Mem. Indian Hills Country Club (East Northport, N.Y.).

FISHER, FRANCES, actress; b. Milford-on-Sea, Eng., May 11, 1952; d. William I. and Olga (Moen) F.; 1 child, Francesca Ruth Fisher-Eastwood. Student, Lee Strasberg, Stella Adler, Marilyn Fried, Sandra Seacat, HB Studios. Appearances include (films) Can She Bake a Cherry Pie?, 1985, Tough Guys Don't Dance, 1986, Patty Hearst, 1987, Lost Angels, 1988, Pink Cadillac, 1989, Welcome Home Roxy Carmichael, 1989, L.A. Story, 1991, Unforgiven, 1992, Baby Fever, 1992, The Stars Fell on Henrietta, 1994, Molly and Gina, 1992, Female Perversions, 1993, Striptease, 1995, Wild America, 1996, Titanic, 1997, True Crime, 1998, The Big Tease, 1998, The Rising Place, 2002, Gone in 60 Seconds, 2000, (TV) Elysian Fields, 1987, Sudie & Simpson, 1988, Cold Sassy Tree, 1989, Promises to Keep, 1990, Lucy & Desi: Before the Laughter, 1991, Devlin, 1987, Crime and Punishment, 1989, Law and Order, 1990, Praying Mantis, 1992, Attack of the 50 Foot Woman, 1993, The Other Mother, 1994, Strange Luck, 1995, Becker, 2000, Audrey Hepburn, 1999, Titus, 2001, Jackie, 2000, Glory Days, 2001, (theater) Cat on a Hot Tin Roof, 1981, Hay Fever, 1981, The Chain, 1983, Desire Under the Elems, 1982, Still Life, 1983, Ruffian on the Stair, 1979, A Midsummer Night's Dream, 1981, Hunchback of Notre Dame, 1981, Orpheus Descending, 1986, The Hitchhikers, 1985, Crackwalker, 1987, Fool for Love, 1985, Three More Sleepless Nights, (Drama Logue award 1996), 1996, 1984, 1984, Jammed, 1997. Mem. Actors Studio. Office: Nevin Dolcefino Innovative Artists 1505 10th St Santa Monica CA 90401*

FISHER, FRANKLIN MARVIN, economist; b. NYC, Dec. 13, 1934; s. Mitchell Salem and Esther (Oshiver) F.; m. Ellen Jo Paradise, June 22, 1958; children— Abraham Samuel, Abigail Sarah, Naomi Leah. AB summa cum

laude, Harvard U., 1956, MA, 1957, PhD, 1960; PhD (hon.), Hebrew U., Jerusalem, 2001. Asst. prof. econs. U. Chgo., 1959-60; asst. prof. econs. MIT, 1960-62, assoc. prof., 1962-65, prof., 1965-2000, Jane Berkowitz Carlton and Dennis William Carlton prof., 2000—; chair Mid. East Water Project, 1992—. Cons. various law firms; dir. cons. Charles River Assocs., Inc., vice chmn., 1997—2002, chmn., 2002—; bd. dirs. Nat. Bur. Econ. Rsch. Editor: Econometrica, 1968-77. Trustee Combined Jewish Philanthropies, Boston, 1975—, bd. mgrs., 1979-92; trustee Beth Israel Hosp., Boston, 1979-97; chmn. faculty adv. cabinet United Jewish Appeal, 1975-77; bd. govs. Tel Aviv U., 1976-92, Acad. Coll. Tel Aviv-Yafo, 2000—; bd. dirs. New Israel Fund, 1983—, treas., 1984-96, pres. 1996-99; pres. Boston Friends of Peace Now, 1984-85, N.E. region Am. Jewish Congress, 1993-95; chmn. steering com. N.Am. Friends of Peace Now, 1986-88, bd. dirs., treas., 1988-91. NSF fellow, 1962-63; Ford Found. Faculty Research fellow, 1966-67; Guggenheim fellow, 1981-82; Erksine fellow U. Canterbury, N.Z., 1983. Fellow Econometric Soc. (council 1972-76, v.p. 1977-78, pres. 1979), Am. Acad. Arts and Scis.; mem. Am. Econ. Assn. (John Bates Clark medal 1973) Home: 130 Mt Auburn St Cambridge MA 02138-5757 Office: MIT 50 Memorial Dr # E52 359 Cambridge MA 02142-1347

FISHER, FREDERICK HENDRICK, oceanographer emeritus; b. Aberdeen, Wash., Dec. 30, 1926; s. Sam (Sverre) and Astrid K. Fisher; m. Julie Gay Saund, June 17, 1955 (dec. 1993); children: Bruce Allen, Mark Edward, Keith Russell, Glen Michael; m. Shirley Mercedes Lippert, Oct. 10, 1994 (div. 2003). BS, U. Wash., 1949, PhD, 1957. Tchg. asst. U. Wash., 1949-53; rsch. asst. UCLA, 1954-55; grad. rsch. physicist Marine Phys. Lab., Scripps Inst. Oceanography, 1955-57, rsch. physicist, rsch. oceanographer, 1958-91, assoc. dir., 1975-87, dep. dir., 1987-93, acting assoc. dir., 1993-94, rsch. oceanographer emeritus, 1997—; rsch. fellow acoustics Harvard U., 1957-58. Dir. rsch. in reverse osmosis and desalination Havens Industries, San Diego, 1963-64; prof., chmn. dept. physics U. R.I., Kingston, 1970-71; mem. governing bd. Am. Inst. Physics, 1984-90. Assoc. editor: Jour. Oceanic Engring., 2001—. Mem. San Diego County Dem. Ctrl. Com., 1956-57, 60-62. Midshipman U.S. Naval Acad., 1945-47, with USNR, 1945. NCAA nat. tennis doubles champion, 1949; named to U. Wash. Athletic Hall of Fame, 1989; recipient Disting. Svc. award IEEE Oceanic Engring. Soc., 1991, Disting. Tech. Achievement award IEEE/OES, 1996, 3d Millenium Medal IEEE, 2000. Fellow: Acoustical Soc. Am. (assoc. editor jour. 1969—76, v.p. 1980—81, pres. 1983—84, emeritus); mem.: IEEE (life; sr. editor Jour. Oceanic Engring. 1988—91, emeritus editor 2001—), Am. Geophys. Union, The Oceanographic Soc., Marine Tech. Soc., Seattle Tennis Club. Achievements include co-designer and project scientist ocean research platform FLIP, 355' long manned spar buoy with 300' draft in vertical position, 1960-62; co-discoverer of boric acid as cause of low frequency sound absorption in the ocean; measured effect of pressure on sound absorption and electrical conductivity of magnesium and calcium sulfate and other salts related to high frequency sound absorption in the ocean; conducted sound propagation measurements at long range 30-800 miles in the ocean. Home: # 106 291 Rosecrans St San Diego CA 92106 Office: Scripps Instn Oceanography Marine Phys Lab La Jolla CA 92093-0701 E-mail: fhf@mpl.ucsd.edu.

FISHER, FREDRICK LEE, lawyer; b. Charleston, W.Va., Nov. 12, 1952; s. Ahaz and Lois Mildred (O'Dell) F.; m. Roberta Lee Lane, Sept. 16, 1972; children: Jamie Elizabeth, John Fredrick, Jennifer Katherine. BA in Econs., Ohio State U., 1973; JD, Harvard U., 1976. Bar: Ohio 1976, U.S. Dist. Ct. (no. dist.) Ohio 1976, U.S. Claims Ct. 1978, U.S. Tax Ct. 1978. Assoc. Squire, Sanders & Dempsey, Cleve., 1976-80, Columbus, Ohio, 1981-85, ptnr., 1985-87, Schottenstein, Zox & Dunn, Columbus, 1987—. Trustee Players Theatre Columbus, 1982-93, pres., 1987-88; sec., treas., trustee The Bill and Edith Walter Found., Columbus, 1982—; trustee Meadow Park Ch., Columbus, 1985-88, 95-97, ctrl. Ohio chpt. Arthritis Found., 1988-89, Directions for Youth, Columbus, 1992-94. Mem. ABA, Ohio Bar Assn., Columbus Bar Assn., Phi Beta Kappa, Capital Club (Columbus). Republican. Avocations: reading, swimming, skiing, biking. Home: 6711 Elmers Ct Columbus OH 43085-2976 Office: Schottenstein Zox & Dunn 41 S High St Columbus OH 43215-6101 Fax: (614) 462-5135. E-mail: rfisher671@aol.com., ffisher@szd.com.

FISHER, GAIL FEIMSTER, government official; d. Maurice Blake and Sarah Estelle (Abell) Feimster; m. Eugene Joseph Fisher, Dec. 2, 1950 (dec.); children: Laurence Eugene, Robert Maurice. BA, U. Md., 1949, MA, 1951; PhD, U. N.C., 1976. Rsch. analyst Bur. of State Svcs., Dept. HHS, 1956-66; evaluation officer Bur. Health Svcs., Dept. HHS, 1966-68; planning officer Nat. Ctr. Health Stats.-Ctr. for Disease Control-Dept. HHS, Rockville, Md., 1968-93, assoc. dir. Hyattsville, Md., 1973-98; cons. epidemiologist, 1998—. Contbr. rsch. reports to profl. jours. and presentations. Avocation: antique vehicle restoration and preservation. Office: DHHS-CDC-Nat Ctr Hlth Stats PO Box 234 9685 Johnsontown Rd La Plata MD 20646 E-mail: gailfisher@aol.com.

FISHER, GARY ALAN, marketing professional; b. Akron, Ohio, Apr. 4, 1951; s. Paul McCray and Betty Elaine F.; m. Brianne Bremer, July 29, 2000. AB in History, Princeton U., 1973. Founder, pub. Courselector, Princeton, N.J. and Boston, 1973-75; bus. mgr. CBS Spl. Interest Mags., N.Y.C., 1976-78, dir. bus. ops., 1979; pub. Am. Photographer Mag., N.Y.C., 1980-84; CEO Spark Global Mktg. Solutions, N.Y.C., 1984—; pres. One World Global Mfg. Solutions, Hong Kong, 1995—. Bd. dirs. Marble Vision. Mem. Marble Collegiate Ch. Office: Spark Global Mktg Svcs 589 Eighth Ave New York NY 10018

FISHER, GENE JORDAN, retired chemical company executive; b. Quitman, Miss., Mar. 26, 1931; s. Ira R. and Gertrude (Jordan) F.; m. Christine Ann Hodges, May 28, 1954; children— Denise, Darrell BS, U. Tex., 1952. From research chemist to sr. research chemist Celanese Chem. Co., Corpus Christi, Tex., 1952-59, group leader, 1959-67, research mgr., 1967-77, dir. research, 1977-83, tech. dir., 1983-85, ret., 1985; tech. and mgmt. cons., 1985—. Contbr. articles to profl. jours.; patentee in field. Baptist. Home: PO Box 1944 Rockwall TX 75087-2044 E-mail: gfisher6@aol.com.

FISHER, GENE LAWRENCE, financial executive; b. Chillicothe, Ill., Nov. 15, 1929; s. Lawrence Hubert and Alyce Anne (Niggemeyer) F.; m. Sandra Kay Burns, Sept. 19, 1959; children— Kyle Butler, Kelley Anne. B.S., U. Ill., 1957. Staff acct. Inland Container Corp., Indpls., 1957-63, mgr. corp. acctg., 1964-65, asst. corp. controller, 1966-78, dir. fin. systems, 1979-93; ret., 1993. Chmn. fin. com.-exec. com. Winona Meml. Hosp., Indpls., 1979-81, chmn. bd. dirs., 1982-83. Served with U.S. Army, 1951-53. Mem. Beta Alpha Psi, Sigma Iota Epsilon. Republican. Avocations: fishing, swimming. Home: 5427 N Washington Blvd Indianapolis IN 46220-3027 E-mail: genofish@aol.com.

FISHER, GEORGE, gerontological educator; b. May 31, 1915; BS, U. Md., 1956; MBA, Western Mich. U., 1969, SpA, 1977; PhD, U. Mich., 1981. Mech. engr. Keystone Mfg., Boston, 1936-41; commd. C.E., U.S. Army, 1941, advanced through grades to col., ret., 1961; mgmt./computer sys. analyst Def. Logistics Svc., Battle Creek, Mich., 1962-77; prof. gerontology Western Mich. U., Kalamazoo, 1985—. Home: 2300 Portage St Apt 221 Kalamazoo MI 49001

FISHER, GEORGE ALEXANDER, JR., lieutenant general United States Army; b. Little Rock, Ark., July 1, 1942; BS, U.S. Mil. Acad., 1964; student Armor Officer Advanced Course, U.S. Army Armor Sch., Ft. Knox, Ky., 1968-69; MS in Ops. Rsch. and Analysis, U.S. Naval Post Grad. Sch., Monterey, Calif., 1970-72; student, U.S. Army Command & Staff Coll, Fort Leavenworth, Kans., 1972-73, U.S. Naval War Coll., Newport, R.I., 1983-84. Mortar platoon leader hdqtrs. co., 2d battalion, 508th infantry, 82d airborne divsn. U.S. Army, Fort Bragg, N.C., 1965-66, exec. officer Co. C to comdr. Co. C. 2d battalion, 508th, 1966-67; instr. U.S. Army Armor Sch., Ft. Knox, Ky., 1969; instr. to asst. prof. dept. math. U.S. Mil. Acad., West Point, N.Y., 1973-76; dep. inspector-gen. Berlin Brigade to battalion exec. officer 3d battalion Berlin Brigade U.S. Army Europe, Germany, 1976-79; ops. rsch./systems analyst Joint Strategic Planning Staff Strategic Air Command, Offutt AFB, Nebr., 1981-83; comdr. 3d battalion, 7th infantry divsn. U.S. Army, Fort Ord, Calif., 1981-83; G-3 (ops.) 7th infantry divsn. to comdr. 3d brigade 7th infantry divsn. U.S. Army, Fort Ord, Calif., 1984-88; chief tech. mgmt. office, Office Chief of Staff, U.S. Army, Washington, 1988-90; asst. comdr. 25th infantry divsn. (light), Schofield Barracks, Hawaii, 1990-91; comdr. joint readiness tng. ctr. U.S. Armed Forces, Little Rock, Ark. then, Ft Polk La, 1991-93; commanding gen. 25th infantry divsn. (light), Schofield Barracks, Hawaii, 1993-95; chief of staff U.S. Army Forces Command, Ft. McPherson, Ga., 1995-97; commanding gen. First U.S. Army, Ft. Gillem, Ga., 1997—. Decorated Defense Disting. Svc. medal, Disting. Svc. medal, Legion of Merit with 2 oak leaf clusters, Bronze Star medal, Defense Meritorious Svc. medal, Meritorious Svc. medal with oak leaf cluster, Air medal, Army Commendation medal with oak leaf cluster, Army Achievement medal. Office: Office of Commanding Gen First US Army Fort Gillem 4705 Wheeler Dr Forest Park GA 30297-5000

FISHER, GEORGE MYLES CORDELL, retired photographic imaging company executive, mathematician, engineer; b. Anna, Ill., Nov. 30, 1940; s. Ralph Myles and Catherine (Herbert) Fisher; m. Patricia Ann Wallace, June 18, 1965; children: Jennifer, Barcy, William. BS in Engring., U. Ill., 1962; MS in Engring., Brown U., 1964, PhD in Applied Maths., 1966. Mem. tech. staff Bell Telephone Labs., Murray Hill, NJ, 1965—67, supr. Holmdel, NJ, 1967—71, dept. head Indpls., 1971—76; dir. mfg. systems Motorola Inc., Schaumberg, Ill., 1976—77, asst. dir. mobile ops. Ft. Worth, 1977—78, v.p. portable ops. Ft. Lauderdale, Fla., 1978—81, v.p. paging divsn., 1981—84, asst. gen. mgr. comm. sector Schaumburg, 1984—86, sr. exec. v.p., 1986—88, pres., CEO, 1988—90, chmn., CEO, 1990—93; chmn., pres., CEO Eastman Kodak Co., Rochester, NY, 1993—97, chmn., CEO, 1997—99, chmn., 1997—2000; ret., 2000. Bd. dirs. GM, Delta Air Lines, Inc., Eli Lilly & Co.; chmn. Nat. Acad. Engring., 2000—; former mem. Pres.'s Adv. Com. for Trade Policy and Negotiation. Contbr. articles on continuum physics to profl. jours. Mem. U. Ill. Found. Recipient M. Eugene Merchant Mfg. medal, ASME, 1994. Mem.: IEEE, Internat. Acad. Astronautics. Achievements include patents for optical wave guides and digital communications. Office: Eastman Kodak Co 343 State St Rochester NY 14650-0229 E-mail: george.fisher@kodak.com.

FISHER, GORDON MCCRACKEN, program analyst; b. Washington, Mar. 4, 1946; s. F. McCracken and Constance (Clack) F. BA, Earlham Coll., 1968; MPA, U. Pitts., 1972. Program asst. U.S. Office Econ. Opportunity, Washington, 1968, program analyst, 1970-73, U.S. HHS, Washington, 1973—. Mem. Interagency Tech. Working Group to Improve Measurement Income and Poverty, Washington, 1997—. Unofficial historian U.S. poverty lines; contbr. articles to profl. jours. U.S. Presdl. scholar, Washington, 1964. Mem. Phi Beta Kappa. Office: US HHS Rm 404E Humphrey Bldg 200 Independence Ave SW Washington DC 20201-0004

FISHER, GORDON MCCREA, mathematician, educator; b. St. Paul, Oct. 5, 1925; s. Tully McCrea and Ione Adele (Brown) F.; m. (Helene) Dawn Smith, June 17, 1956; children: Andrea McCrea Rowland, Jennifer Ione Berger. BA in Math. and Philosophy, U. Miami, Coral Gables, Fla., 1951; MS in Computer Sci., U. Va., 1986; PhD in Math., La. State U., 1959. Instr. in math. Princeton (N.J.) U., 1959-62; sr. lectr. in math., history and philosophy of sci. U. Otago, Dunedin, New Zealand, 1962-65; sr. lectr. U. Waikato, Hamilton, New Zealand, 1965-67; prof. math. and computer sci. James Madison U., Harrisonburg, Va., 1967-91, prof. emeritus, 1991—. Contbr. articles to profl. jours. With USN, 1943-45, sgt. U.S. Army, 1947-49. Madison scholar, 1989. Mem. Am. Math. Soc.

FISHER, HANS, nutritional biochemistry educator; b. Breslau, Silesia, Germany, Mar. 4, 1928; s. George and Johanna (Gottheiner) F.; m. Ruth Hirschberg, July 24, 1950; children: Deborah M. Joseph, David E. Fisher, Daniel Z. Fisher. MS, U. Conn., 1952; PhD, U. Ill., 1954. Cert. Am. Bd. Nutrition. Asst. prof. Rutgers U., New Brunswick, N.J., 1954-57, assoc. prof., 1957-62, prof., 1962-72, dept. chair, 1966-88, assoc. provost, 1988-90, disting. prof., 1972—. Cons. food and pharm. industries, 1955—. Author: Rutgers Guide to Lowering Your Cholesterol, 1986; trans. (with Ruth H. Fisher Mendel) Rosenbusch, Tales for Jewish Children (from German into English), 1991; contbr. articles to profl. jours. Pres. Highland Park (N.J.) Temple Ctr., 1975-77; v.p. YMHA, Highland Park, 1958-70. Fellow AAAS, Am. Soc. Nutritional Scis., N.Y. Acad. Scis.; mem. Am. Chem. Soc. Jewish. Achievements include research in fiber lowering cholesterol, Tryptophan ameliorates neuroleptic side effects and supresses voluntary alcohol consumption. Discoverer novel treatment for alcohol withdrawal and craving, histamine and carnosine in wound healing and trauma amelioration. Home: 216 N 3rd Ave Highland Park NJ 08904-2412 Office: Rutgers U 96 Lipman Dr New Brunswick NJ 08901-8525 E-mail: fisher@aesop.rutgers.edu.

FISHER, HENRY, investment banker; b. Pitts., Feb. 17, 1936; s. Henry Clayton and Dorothea T. (Smith) F.; m. Ann Yeager, Aug. 6, 1960; children: Andrew Clayton, William Bradford. BA, U. Pitts., 1960; attended, Wharton Sch. Investment Bankin, 1967, 68. Gen ptnr. Singer Deane & Scribner, Pitts., 1961-69; exec. v.p. Chaplin McGuiness & Co., Inc., Pitts., 1969-74; mem. N.Y. Stock Exch., 1972-74. Pa. Gov.'s del. Southwestern Pa. Regional Planning Commn., 1995-98, Southwestern Pa. Devel. Commn., 1995-98; commr. Southwestern Pa. Commn., 1999—2003. Mem., Nat. Securities Traders Assn., Pitts. Mcpl. Analysts Soc., Pitts. Stock and Bond Assn., Pa. Boroughs Assn., Pa. League of Cities, Pa Twp. Assn., Pa. Mcpl. Authorities Assn., Pitts. Builders Exch., Sierra Club (co-founder Pitts. chpt.), Am. Youth Hostels, Inc. (past nat. v.p.), Pa. Soc. N.Y., Duquesne Club, Allegheny Club, Rivers Club. Office: 1317 Investment Building Bldg Pittsburgh PA 15222-1712

FISHER, HERBERT CALVIN, retired surgeon; b. Denver, July 7, 1910; MD, Cornell U., 1935. Intern St. Luke's Hosp., Denver, 1935-36; resident in surgery U. Minn.; fellow Mayo Found., Rochester, Minn., 1937-40; pvt. practice, 1946-75; ret., 1975. Chief of surg. svc. Children's Hosp.; chief of staff Denver Gen. Hosp., 1971-72; assoc. prof. surgery U. Colo. Sch. Medicine; chief exec. Colo. State Sci. Fair, 1970-75; pres. Internat. Sci. Fair, 1975; chief emergency rm. St Luke's Hosp., 1973-75; assigned Gen. MacArthur's hdqs. in the Philippine Islands, then chief of surg. svc. 315th Gen. Hosp. at Batangao, to 1946; chief surg. svc. Brook Gen. Hosp., 1941-45; county judge, Hinsdale County, 1977-80, 84—; co-founder Lake City Med. Ctr., 1976. Contbr. numerous articles and editls. to profl. jours. Dir. 1st Colo. Health Fair Colo. Md. Soc. Lt. col. M.C., U.S. Army, 1946. Recipient awards for bronze sculpture, 1950-75, Cert. Svc. Colo. Engring. Coun., 1962, 1st prize for bronze sculpture, N.Y.C., 1972. Fellow ACS (life); mem. AMA (life), Am. Bd. Surgery (diplomate, cert.), Cen. Surg. Assn. (elected, life), Am. Heart Assn. (life), Colo. Surg. Assn., Colo. Med. Assn. (life, 3 Top awards for pub. svc. 1950-75).

FISHER, HYMAN WENDELL, physician; b. N.Y.C., June 8, 1926; s. Emanuel and Reba (Jarmovsky) F.; m. Rosalie Joseph, June 28, 1953; children: Edward Abraham, Laura Lani, Naomi Deirdre Lakshmi, David Alexander, Andrea Maile, Daniel Clark, Jonathan Eliot Este. BS, MIT, 1947, MS, 1948; MD, NYU, 1954. Intern Bellevue Hosp., N.Y.C., 1954-55, resident, 1955-57, Queen's Hosp., Honolulu, 1957-58; practice medicine specializing in internal medicine Livingston, N.J., 1958—. Med. dir., sr. v.p. Sudler & Hennessey Inc., N.Y.C., 1972-80; dir., Intramed Comm. Inc., N.Y.C., 1974-80; pres. Hyman W. Fisher, Inc., cons. and health care comm., 1980—; pres. Northfield & Swan Press, 1982-95; dir. clin. lit. devel. Physicians World Comm. Group, 1996—; lectr. in cmty. medicine Mt. Sinai Med. Sch., N.Y.C., 1975—; clin. instr. medicine NYU Med. Ctr., 1975—; co-chmn. Livingston UN Com., 1975; mem. Livingston Rsch. Planning Panel, 1976-77. Contbr. articles to profl. jours. With U.S. Army, 1945-46, ATO, PTO. Fellow ACP, Soc. Advanced Med. Systems; mem. AMA, N.J. Heart Assn., Family Svc. W. Essex (v.p. 1969-71), Pharm. Advt. Coun., B'nai B'rith (gov. dist. Ill. 1971-78), Sigma Xi, Tau Beta Pi, Alpha Omega Alpha. Jewish. Office: 121 E Northfield Rd Livingston NJ 07039-4506

FISHER, JACOB ALEXANDER SHULTZ, retired clergyman; b. Wichita Falls, Tex., Apr. 22, 1925; s. Hiram Herbert Fisher and Mary Elizabeth Shultz; m. Nell Davidson, Aug. 13, 1949 (dec. June 2001); children: Michael D., Kelly Paige Fisher Matthews; m. Adelaide Boggs, Apr. 12, 2003. BA, Centenary Coll., 1950; MDiv, S.W. Bapt. Theol. Sem., 1953. Ordained to ministry Bapt. Ch., 1951. Commd. ensign USN, 1953, advanced through grades to lt. comdr., 1959, chaplain, 1953-72, ret., 1972; dir. pastoral care La. State U. Med. Ctr. (formerly Confederate Meml. Med. Ctr), Shreveport, 1972-95; ret., 1995. Founding pres. Ret. Srs. Vol. Program, Shreveport, 1976-78. With USNR, 1943-46, 47-55. Decorated Navy Letter of Commendation with combat star. Mem.: Greater Shreveport Ministerial Assn. (pres. 1980), La. Chaplains Assn. (pres. 1982, 1983), Assn. Profl. Chaplains, Masons. Democrat. Avocation: jogging. Home: 305 Baycliff Ln Shreveport LA 71105-4815 E-mail: jasfisher1@aol.com.

FISHER, JAMES AIKEN, industrial marketing consultant; b. Pitts., Mar. 15, 1920; s. Chester G and Margaret R (Aiken) Fisher; m. Edith C Hall, June 12, 1955; children: George S, Chester G III, James Aiken. BA, Yale, 1942. Engr. Alcoa Niagara Works, 1942-44; with Fisher Sci. Co., Pitts., 1944-85, sales staff, 1945-50, advt. staff, 1950-60, sr. v.p., dir., 1963-81; asst. to pres., 1981-85; chmn., pres. Kipling Corp., mktg. cons., 1985—. Bd dirs EFT Corp, Nat Sci Programs Inc, Optical Communications Corp. Trustee Carnegie Inst, Carnegie Mus Art, Carnegie Sci Ctr. Mem.: Am Mkt Asn, Sci Apparatus Makers Asn (past pres), Am Chemical Soc, Pittsburgh Golf Club, Rolling Rock Club, Duquesne Club, HYP-Pittsburgh Club. Home: 5414 Kipling Rd Pittsburgh PA 15217-1038 Office: 622 Oliver Bldg Pittsburgh PA 15222-2304

FISHER, JAMES CRAIG, lawyer; b. Cin., Dec. 23, 1942; s. James Donald and Helen Francis (Lineback) F.; m. Sara S. Godfrey, Apr. 21, 1964; children: Alicia Lynn, Bart Harry; m. Cynthia Hardy, Aug. 30, 1996. BA, Fla. State U., 1964; JD, Stetson U., 1967. Bar: Fla. Assoc. Billings, Frederick & Rumberger, 1967-69, Russell Troutman, 1969-70; ptnr. Mairs, Wood, Miller, Dorroughs & Fisher, 1970-72; prosecutor City of Longwood, 1971-76; pvt. practice Fisher & Matthews, P.A., Altamonte Springs, Fla., 1972-76, ptnr., 1976—. Counsel AFL-CIO, Seminole and Orange County, Fla., 1989-90; mem. bd. cert. commn. Fla. Bar; mem. unauthorized practice of law com. 18th Jud. Cir., 1988, vice chmn. grievance com., 1992-95. Co-author: Chapter 81 Liability of Attorneys Fla. Forms of Jury Instruction, 1989. Mem. ABA, ATLA (workers compensation sect.), Fla. Bar Assn., Nat. Bd. Trial Advocacy, Seminole County Bar Assn. (25 Yr. Outstanding Svc. award 1992). Democrat. Avocations: fishing, racquetball, reading. Office: 377 Maitland Ave Ste 107 Altamonte Springs FL 32701-5442

FISHER, JAMES LEE, lawyer; b. Akron, Ohio, Apr. 10, 1944; s. James Lee and Maxine (Sumner) F.; m. Nancy Lorenz, Dec. 20, 1980. BSCE, U. Akron, 1968, JD, 1971. Bar: Ohio 1971. Staff atty. Brunswick Mgmt. Co., Akron, 1972-77; prin. James L. Fisher Co., L.P.A., Akron, 1977-88, Buckingham, Doolittle & Burroughs, Akron, 1988—. City planner City of Akron, 1968-71, community devel. atty., 1971-73; mem. Metro Regional Transit Authority Bd., 1992—; sec.-treas. Summit County Planning Commn., 1978-99. Mem. ABA, Ohio Bar Assn., Akron Bar Assn., Home Builders Assn., Am. Planning Assn., Ohio Planning Conf., Copley Lions (pres. 1982). Republican. Mem. United Ch. of Christ. Home: 1135 Forest Pool Rd Akron OH 44333-1509 Office: Buckingham Doolittle & Burroughs PO Box 1500 Akron OH 44309-1500

FISHER, JAMES R. lawyer; b. South Bend, Ind., Apr. 15, 1947; s. Russell Humphries and Virginia Opal (Maple) F.; m. Cynthia Ann Winters, Aug. 14, 1971; children: Gabriel Christopher, Cory Andrew. AB in Psychology, Ind. U., 1969, JD summa cum laude, 1972. Bar: Ind. 1972, U.S. Dist. Ct. (so. dist.) Ind. 1972. Ptnr. Ice Miller, Indpls., 1971—. Co-author: Personal Injury Law and Practices vol. 23 of Indiana Practice series; contbr. articles to legal publs. Mem. ATLA, Ind. Bar Assn., Ind. Trial Lawyers Assn., Order of Coif. Office: Ice Miller 1 Am Sq PO Box 82001 Indianapolis IN 46282 E-mail: james.fisher@icemiller.com.

FISHER, JAMES W., JR., management consultant; b. Aug. 14, 1942; s.James W. and Virginia (Gustafson) F.; m. Hannelore enke, Aug. 15, 1966; children: Julia, Heidi, Michael, Elke. BA cum laude, Princeton U., 1964; MBA, Harvard U., 1966. With GM, Detroit, 1970-73, Ford Motor Co., Detroit, 1973-80; dir. compensation and benefits Air Products and Chems., Inc., Allentown, Pa., 1980-87, corp. dir. orgn. planning and human resources devel., 1987-92, dir. human resources rsch., 1992-94; pres. James Fisher Co., Ltd., Emmaus, Pa., 1991-98, Victoria Beach, N.S., Can., 1998—. Cons. on how to structure and manage large global orgns. Chair The King's Theatre Found., 2001—. Office: James Fisher Co Ltd Box 2294 Victoria Beach NS Canada B0S 1K0

FISHER, JAMES WILLIAM, medical educator, pharmacologist; b. Tucapau (now Startex), S.C., May 22, 1925; s. Ernest Amaziah and Mamie V. (Turner) F.; m. Carol Barbara Brodarick, June 5, 1947; children: Candis Loreen Fisher Rush Smith, Patricia Eileen Fisher Valladares, Richard W., William E., John C., Elaine Marie Fisher Spurr. BS, U. S.C., 1947; PhD in Pharmacology (USPHS fellow), U. Louisville, 1958. Devel. chemist Armour Pharm. Rsch. Labs., Chgo., 1950-53, Ayerst Pharm. Labs., Rouses Point, NY, 1953—54; pharmacologist Lloyd Bros. Pharm. Co., Cin., 1954-56; instr. pharmacology U. Tenn., 1958-60, asst. prof., 1960-62, assoc. prof., 1962-66, prof., 1966-68; prof., chmn. dept. pharmacology Med. Sch., Tulane U., 1968-96; Regents prof., chmn. pharmacology Tulane U., 1987—96, James W. Fisher Disting. Lectureship in Pharmacology, 1991—, Regents prof. emeritus, chmn., 1999—. Vis. prof. U. Zambia, Lusaka, 1987, Keio U., Tokyo, 1987, U. Nairobi, 1993; external examiner U. W.I., Trinidad, 1992; vis. scientist Christie Hosp. and Holt Radium Inst., Manchester, Eng., 1963-64; dir. Tulane-Universidad Nacional del Nordeste, Corrientes, Argentina, Pan Am. Health Orgn. Physiol. Scis. Tng. Program, 1972-77; lectr. in field; mem. Nat. Heart, Lung and Blood Inst. (erythropoietin com. 1971-74), mem. NIH hematology tng. grants com., 1977; mem. Cooley's Anemia Nat. Rsch. Com., 1974; pres. So. Blood Club, 1975-77; mem. Wellcome Professorships Com., 1976, 93, 94, 95; mem. pharmacology com. Nat. Bd. Med. Examiners, 1988-92; mem. ad hoc group med. rsch. funding AAMC, 1990-93. Author: Readings on the History of Pharmacology; editor: Kidney Hormones, Vol. I, 1971, Vol. II, 1977, Vol. III, 1986, Renal Pharmacology, 1971, Handbook of Pharmacology: Blood and Blood Forming Organs, 1992; co-editor: Erythropoiesis, 1975, Erythropoietin and Erythropoiesis, 1981; cons. editor: Erythropoietin, 1968; mem. editl. bd. Proc. Soc. Exptl. Biology and Medicine, 1971-86; contbr. articles to profl. jours. Served to lt. (j.g.) USNR, 1943-46, PTO. Recipient rsch. career devel. award USPHS, 1960-65, Purkinje medal Czechoslovakia Med. Soc., 1975, Golden Sovereign award, 1976, Aspet Exptl. Therapeutics award, 1992, U. Louisville Med. Sch. Alumni award, 1999; named Disting. faculty AOA Honor Med. Soc., 1993; Ann. Tulane Fisher Lectureship established in his honor, 1992. Mem. AAAS, AAUP, Am. Soc. Pharmacology and Exptl. Therapeutics (Sollman awards com. 1981, exptl. therapeutics award com. 1982, 94, alerting network 1986-90, ednl. affairs com. 1986-89, Krayer awards com. 1990, Exptl. Therapeutics award 1992, nominating com. 1997), Soc. Exptl. Biology and Medicine, Am. Soc. Nephrology, Am. Soc. Hematology (sci. affairs com. 1973-74, chmn. erythropoietin subcom. 1973), Assn. Med. Sch. Pharmacology (exec. com. 1979-82, nominating com. 1975, 86, 94, 96, 99, chmn. essential knowledge base in pharmacology com. 1984-95, pres. 1990-92), N.Y. Acad. Scis., Sigma Xi. Home: 4025 S Pin Oak Ave New Orleans LA 70131-8449 E-mail: jfisher@tulane.edu. *Creativity and brilliance are very important in science but in order to test one's ideas these qualities must be adequately supplemented by the necessary amount of work at the bench.*

FISHER, JANET WARNER, secondary school educator; b. San Angelo, Tex., July 7, 1929; d. Robert Montell and Louise (Buckley) Warner; m. Jarek Prochazka Fisher, Oct. 17, 1956 (div. May 1974); children: Barbara Zlata Harper, Lev Prochazka, Monte Prochazka. BA, So. Meth. U., 1950, M of Liberal Arts, 1982; student various including, Columbia U., U. Dallas, U. Colo., U. London and others. Cert. English, German and ESL tchr., K-12, Tex., N.Y. Bd. dirs., sec. Masaryk Inst., N.Y.C., 1968-71; with orphan sect. Displaced Persons Commn., Washington, 1950; fgn. editor Current Digest of the Soviet Press, N.Y.C., 1953-55; cable desk clk. Time, Inc., N.Y.C., 1955-56; tchr. of English and reading, langs. Houston Ind. Sch. Dist., 1975-80; tchr. Carmine Ind. Sch. Dist., Round Top, Tex., 1980-82; tchr. German Region IV Interactive TV, 1983-85; adj. prof. English U. Houston, 1983-87; tchr. Royal Ind. Sch. Dist., Brookshire, Tex., 1989-92, Hempstead Ind. Sch. Dist., Waller County, Tex., 1992-94. Adj. prof. English, U. Houston, Houston C.C., 1983-87, 1997—; tchr. Amnesty Program, Houston, 1988-90; adj. prof. English Blinn Coll., Brenham, Tex., 1995-97. Candidate sch. bd., South Orangetown, N.Y., 1962, state rep., Houston, 1980; del. Houston Tchrs. Assn., 1975-80; officer LWV, Nyack, N.Y., 1960-62; trustee, chair adminstrn. bd. Shepherd Drive United Meth. Ch., Houston, 1994-2003; del. Tex. ann. conf. United Meth. Ch., 1994-2001; del. Tex. State Dem. Conv., 1996, 2000, 02. Recipient award for Svc. to Missions, United Meth. Ch., Houston, 1985. Mem. AAUW, NOW, WILPF, Harris County Women's Polit. Caucus. Avocations: Russian and German literature, real estate development. Home: PO Box 66067 Houston TX 77266-6067 E-mail: jsufish@aol.com.

FISHER, JAY TODD, writer, educator; b. Lynn, Mass., Aug. 6, 1963; s. Martin and Elaine Fisher. BA, U. So. Calif., Los Angeles, CA, 1985; MFA, Emerson Coll., Boston, MA, 1998; MPW, U. So. Calif., Los Angeles, CA, 2001. Adj. faculty expository writing Emerson Coll., Boston, 1995—98; lectr. writing U. So. Calif., Los Angeles, Calif., 1998—; exec. prodn. cons. Twentieth Century Fox, Los Angeles, Calif., 1985—88. Learning assistance specialist Emerson Coll., Boston, 1995—98. Author: (screenplay) Finer Could Be Nothing (semi-finalist Chesterfield Film Co, Writers Film Project, 2000, 2002). Vol. Big Bros., Malden, Mass., 1980—81; fundraising chmn. Perkins Sch. for the Blind, Boston, 1980—81. Recipient Phi Beta Kappa, U. So. Calif., 1985, Outstanding Lectr., Ctr. for Excellence in Tchg., USC, 2001. Avocations: movies, sports, current events, literature, art. Home: 3288 1/2 Lowry Rd #2 Los Angeles CA 90027 Office: University Southern California University Park Los Angeles CA 90007 Personal E-mail: jtf63@hotmail.com.

FISHER, JEFF, professional football coach; b. Culver City, Calif., Feb. 25, 1958; m. Juli; children: Brandon, Trenton, Tara. Student, U. Southern California. Professional football player Chicago Bears, 1981-85; defensive backs coach Philadelphia Eagles, 1986-88, defensive coordinator, 1989-90, Los Angeles Rams, 1991; defensive backs coach San Francisco 49ers, 1992-93; defensive coordinator Tenn. Titans, 1994; head coach Tenn. Oilers/Titans, 1995—; exec. v.p. Tenn. Titans, 2000—. Avocations: fly-fishing, golf, sushi, travel. Office: Tennessee Titans Baptist Sports Park 460 Great Circle Rd Nashville TN 37228-1404*

FISHER, JEFFREY DAVID, cardiologist, educator; b. Bklyn., Jan. 11, 1951; s. Joseph and Marian (Traub) F.; m. Judy Essig, May 8, 1977 (div. June, 1981); m. Michelle Densen, Feb. 2, 1985; children: Katherine, James. AB, Cornell U., 1972; MD, Albert Einstein U., 1976. Intern, resident Bronx (N.Y.) Mcpl. Hosp. Ctr., 1976-79; fellow in cardiology Johns Hopkins Hosp., Balt., 1979-81; asst. prof. medicine Cornell U. Med. Coll., N.Y.C., 1981-87, assoc. prof. clin. medicine, 1987-89, clin. assoc. prof. medicine, 1989—2002, clin. prof. medicine, 2002—. Cons. cardiologist pvt. practice, N.Y.C., 1989—. Contbr. articles to Circulation, Am. Jour. Cardiology, Chest. Founder, pres. Inst. for Ednl. Achievement, New Milford, NJ. Fellow ACP, Am. Coll. Cardiology; mem. Am. Heart Assn. (gov. clin. coun.). Avocations: golf, gardening, fitness. Office: 311 E 72nd St New York NY 10021-4684

FISHER, JERID MARTIN, neuropsychologist; b. Houston, July 12, 1953; s. Seymour and Rhoda (Feinberg) Fisher. BS magna cum laude, Duke U., 1975; MS in Psychology, PhD in Clin. Psychology, U. Rochester, 1981. Diplomate Am. Bd. Profl. Neuropsychology, lic. psychologist N.Y. Clin. dir. neuropsychiatry lab. U. Rochester, 1982-83, asst. dir. neuropsychiatry unit, 1982-83, sr. instr. psychiatry and neurology, 1981-83; dir. Head Injury Ctr. at Highgate, Troy, NY, 1984; dir./developer Neurologic Ctr. at Highgate, Cortland, NY, 1985; pres., CEO Neurorehab Assocs., Inc., Rochester, 1985-93; pres. Comprehensive Rehab Network, Inc., Rochester, 1987-93, Brain Injury Consultants, Inc., Rochester, 1993—. Adj. asst. prof. SUNY, Albany, 1984—; developer brain injury rehab. program Our Lady of Victory Hosp., Buffalo, 1986—91, St. Mary's Hosp., Rochester, 1987—91; clin. asst. prof. neurology U. Rochester Med. Sch., 1988—95, adj. assoc. prof. psychiatry, 2002—. Co-author: (book) The Practice of Forensic Neuropsychology, 1997; contbr. articles to profl. jours. Adv. Compeer, Rochester 1978 . Fellow: Nat. Acad. Neuropsychology; mem.: APA, Am. Congress Rehab. Medicine, Am. Bd. Profl. Disability Cons., Internat. Nueropsychology Soc., Phi Beta Kappa. Republican. Jewish. Avocations: investing, boating, body building. Office: 6780 Pittsford Palmyra Rd Fairport NY 14450-3360 E-mail: braindoc12@aol.com.

FISHER, JOEL MARSHALL, political scientist, legal consultant, educator; b. Chgo., June 24, 1935; s. Dan and Nell (Kolvin) F.; children: Sara Melinda, Matthew Nicholas. AB, U. So. Calif., 1955; LLB, MA, U. Calif.-Berkeley; PhD in Govt., Claremont Grad. U., 1968. Orgn. dir. Republican Citizens Com. of U.S., Washington, 1964-65; dir. arts and scis. state legis. divs. Rep. Nat. Com., Washington, 1968-69; asst. dep. counsel to pres. U.S. White House, 1969-70; dep. asst. sec. econ. and social affairs U.S. Dept. State, Washington, 1969-71; vis. prof. comparative and internat. law Loyola U. Sch. Law, L.A., 1972-73; dir. World Bus. Inst., L.A., 1974-75; prof. constl. law Southwestern U. Sch. Law, L.A., 1974-76; dir. World Trade Inst. So. Calif., 1976-84; prof. internat. law, asst. dean Whitter Coll. Sch. Law, L.A., 1977-80; prin. Ziskind, Greene and Assocs., 1980-83; v.p. Wells Internat., 1983-84; pres. LawSearch Inc., 1984-91; v.p. Clarke Cos., 1991-93; pres. Fisher Group, 1993—; adj. prof. Calif. Internat. U., L.A., 1993-99. Spl. projects Hollywood Palace, 1998-2002, pub. affairs, 2002--; ofcl. visitor The European Communities, 1974, 76, wine instr., AILA/culinary arts, 1999—; mem. U.S. dels. UN confs., 1969-71; chmn. Strategy for Peace Conf. Panel on U.S. and UN, 1972—; coord. Series on the Contemporary Am. Presidency, 1972-73; cons. Robert Taft Inst., 1977-82, World Trade Inst. N.Y., 1977-80; chair Bid Renewal Steering Com., Hollywood Entertainment Dist.; bd. dirs., v.p. Vine St. Assn.; chair Hollywood United Neighborhood Coun.; chair Security Com., 2001-03, bd. dirs., treas. Hollywood Bus. Improvement Dist., 2001—. Co-author three books; contbr. articles to profl. jours. Mem. steering com. Calif. Com. for Reelection of Pres., 1972; nat chmn. Community Leaders for Ford, 1976; trustee Rep. Assocs., 1978—, exec. com., 1986—; mem. vestry, sr. warden St. Michael and All Angeles Ch., Studio City, Calif., 1983-86, 89-93, mem. diocesan coun. L.A., 1986-88, chmn. budget com. 1987; bd. dirs. Corp. of the Cathedral, 1988-91; mem. com. on constitution and canons, 1993—. Fellow Nobel Found., 1958; Falk fellow, 1961-62 Mem. Am. Polit. Sci. Assn. (state legis. fellow 1970-73). Home: 4358 Mammoth Ave Unit 26 Sherman Oaks CA 91423-3692 Office: 1735 Vine St Hollywood CA 90028-5248

FISHER, JOHN WILLIAM, civil engineering educator; b. Ancell, Mo., Feb. 15, 1931; s. Nevan August and Nettie (Miller) Fisher; m. Nelda Rae Adams, Oct. 11, 1952; children: John Timothy, Christopher Lee, Elizabeth Renee, Nevan Andrew. BSCE, Washington U., St. Louis, 1956; MS, Lehigh U., 1958, PhD, 1964, Swiss Fed. Inst. Tech., Lausanne, Switzerland, 1988. Registered Ill. Asst. bridge rsch. engr. Nat. Acad. Scis., Ottawa, Ill., 1958—61; from rsch. instr. to assoc. prof. Lehigh U., Bethlehem, Pa., 1961—69, prof. civil enging., 1969—, Joseph T. Stuart prof., 1988—2002, prof. emeritus, 2002—, assoc. dir. Fritz Engring. Lab., 1971—85, co-chmn. civil engring., 1984—85, dir. advanced tech. large structural sys. Engring. Rsch. Ctr, 1986—99, co-dir., 1999 -2001. Cons. Triborough Bridge and Tunnel Authority, 1991—, Weidlinger Assn., 2002—, T.Y. Lin Internat./WV Dept. Transp., 2000—01, Lichtenstein Engrs./WI Dept. Transp., 2000—01; civil col. eminent overseas spkr. Inst. Engrs. Australia, 1983; vis. prof. Swiss Fed. Inst. Tech., Lausanne, Switzerland, 1982, Lausanne, 99; sr. vis. scholar, lectr., China, 85; disting. lectr. Transp. Rsch. Bd., 1997, exec. com., 1997—2000; Portevin lectr. Internat. Inst. Welding, 1997. Author: Structural Steel Design, 1974, Guide to Design Criteria for Bolted Joints, 1974, 2d edit., 1987, Bridge Fatigue Guide, 1977, Fatigue and Fractures in Steel Bridges, 1984, A Fatigue Primer for Structural Engineers, 1998; contbr. articles to profl. jours. Directory council mem. Southside Ministries, Bethlehem, 1983—98; bd. dirs. New Bethany Ministries, Bethlehem, 1985—90. 2d lt. U.S. Army, 1951—53. Named Constrn. Man of Yr., ENR, 1987, Engr. of Yr., Rsch. Inst. for Bridge Integrity and Safety, 1989; recipient Alumni Achievement award, Washington U., 1987, John A. Roebling medal, Engrs. Soc. We. Pa., 1987, Frank P. Brown medal, Franklin Inst., 1992, Roy W. Crum Disting. Svc. award, Transp. Rsch. Bd., 2001. Mem.: NSPE, NAE (chmn. NAE/NRC com. internat. constrn. study 1987—88, internat. affairs adv. com. 1988—92, program adv. com. 1992—94), ASCE (hon.; world trade ctr. bldg. performance study team 2001—02, Huber Rsch. prize 1969, Ernest E. Howard award 1979, R.C. Reese Rsch. prize 1981, Cleve. sect. G. Brooks Earnest award 1997, United Engring. Found. John Fritz medal 2000), AASHTO/FHWA (Blue Ribbon Bridge and Tunnel Security 2002—03), Am. Inst. Steel Constrn. (specification com. 1976 -, T.R. Higgins lectr. 1977, Lifetime Achievement Educator award 2001), Internat. Assn. Bridge and Structural Engrs. (Laureate of Internat. Merit award 2001), Am. Welding Soc. (Adams mem.), Am. Ry. Engring. Assn. (steel structures com.), Am. Soc. Engring. Educators. Republican. United Methodist. Avocations: hiking, photography. Office: Lehigh U 117 Atlss St Bethlehem PA 18015-4728

FISHER, JOHN CROCKER, physicist; b. Ithaca, N.Y., Dec. 19, 1919; m. Jo Ann Johnson; children: Kelly, Mark, Holly. AB, Ohio State Univ., 1941; ScD, Mass. Inst. Tech., 1947. Rsch. engr. Battelle Meml. Inst., 1941-42; asst. & instr. mech. Mass. Inst. Tech., 1942-47; rsch. assoc. Gen. Elec. Co., 1947-51, mgr. phys. metall. sect., 1951-57; physicist, 1957-63; mgr. liaison & transition Rsch. Lab., 1963-64; mgr. physics sci. & info. disciplines Tech. Mil Planning Ops., 1964-68; cons. scientist Re-Entry & Environ. Systems Prod. Divsn., 1969-72; mgr. energy tech. Power Generation Bus. Group, 1972-78; cons. rsch. & devel. Corp. Rsch. & Devel., 1978-81; cons., 1981—; physicist, 1986—. Chief scientist USAF, Washington, 1968-69. Mem. Nat. Acad. Engring., AAAS, Am. Inst. Physics, Am. Phys. Soc., Am. Soc. Metals. Home: 600 Arbol Verde St Carpinteria CA 93013-2506

FISHER, JOHN HURT, English language educator; b. Lexington, Ky., Oct. 26, 1919; r. Bascom and Franke (Sheddan) F.; m. Jane Elizabeth Law, Feb. 21, 1942 (dec.); children: Janice Carol Fisher Craven, John Craig, Judith Law; m. Audrey A. Duncan, Aug. 28, 1997. BA, Maryville Coll., 1940; MA, U. Pa., 1942, PhD, 1945; L.H.D., Loyola U., Chgo., 1970; Litt.D., Middlebury Coll., 1970. Instr., English U. Pa., 1942-45, Yale U., summer 1944; instr. English NYU, 1945-48, asst. prof., 1948-55; lectr. U. So. Calif., summer 1955; instr. English U. Mich., summer 1956; assoc. prof. Duke U., 1955-58, prof., 1958-60; prof. English Ind. U., 1960-62, N.Y. U., 1962-72; John C. Hodges prof. English U. Tenn., 1972-88, chmn., 1976-78. Vis. prof. NYU, 1990, U. Tex., San Antonio, 1996. Author: John Gower: Moral Philosopher and Friend of Chaucer, 1964, The Importance of Chaucer, 1991, The Emergence of Standard English, 1995; editor: Tretyse of Loue, 1951, The Medieval Literature of Western Europe: A Review of Research, 1966, The Complete Poetry and Prose of Geoffrey Chaucer, 1977, 2nd edit., 1989; co-editor: The College Teaching of English, 1965, In Forme of Speche is Chaunge: Readings in the History of the English Language, 1973, An Anthology of Chancery English, 1984, The Essential Chaucer: An Annotated Bibliography of Major Modern Studies, 1987; contbr. articles on medieval lit., English linguistics, English edn. to profl. jours. Mem. U.S. Commn. to UNESCO, 1963-69; bd. dirs. Woodrow Wilson Nat. Fellowship Found., 1972-75, Maryville Coll., 1972-74. Nat. Endowment for Humanities sr. fellow, 1975-76 Fellow Medieval Acad. Am. (v.p. 1985-86, pres. 1986), Med. Acad. Soc. Fellows (pres. 1993-96); mem. Modern Lang. Assn. Am. (exec. sec. 1963-71, editor PMLA 1963-71, pres. 1974), New Chaucer Soc. (bd. dirs. 1978-90, exec. sec. 1981-89, pres. 1982-84), Linguistic Soc. Am., Nat. Coun. Tchrs. English, Fedn. Internationale des Langues et Littératures Modernes, UNESCO (Am. v.p. 1972-78), Phi Beta Kappa (senator-a-large 1977-83). Home: 1805 Chicadee Dr Knoxville TN 37919-8956

FISHER, JOHN MORRIS, association official, business executive, educator; b. Fairhaven, Ohio, Apr. 20, 1922; s. Marion Hays and Bessie (Morris) F.; m. Thelma Ison, Feb. 2, 1947; children: Steven, Roger, Linda Lucille. AB, Miami U., Oxford, Ohio, 1947; postgrad., Bklyn. Law Sch., 1950-51, Northwestern U., 1954-55; LLD (hon.), Nasson Coll., 1972. With Belden Mfg. Co., Richmond, Ind., 1941; spl. agt. FBI, 1947—53; exec. staff asst. to v.p. personnel and employee rels. Sears Roebuck & Co., Chgo., 1953—57, chmn. corp. security com., 1957—61; oper. dir. Am. Security Coun., 1956—57, pres., CEO, 1957—2002. Pres. Am. Rsch. Found., 1961-90; pres., CEO Am. Security Coun. Found., 1962-87, CEO, 1987-2002, chmn., 1992-2002; pres. Comm. Corp. Am., 1972-80, chmn., 1980—; pres. Am. Coalition Patriotic Socs., 1978-91; adminstrv. chmn. Coalition for Peace Through Strength, 1978-2002; dir. Cu. for Internat. Security Studies, 1977-83, organizer, pres. Fidelifax, Inc., 1956-57; chmn. merc. divsn. Nat. Safety Coun., 1959-60, 1st vice chmn. trades and svcs. sect., 1961-62. Chmn. Chgo. Retail Safety Conf., 1959-60; spl. adviser Ill. Supt. Pub. Instrn., 1963-64; cons. to Gov. Fla.; cons. to chmn. com. cold war edn. Nat Gov.'s Conf., 1962-65, Ill. CD Adv. Coun., 1965-68; pres. Am. Coun. World Freedom, 1971-72; mem. exec. com. Nat. Captive Nations Com., 1968-70; bd. visitors Freedoms Found., 1964-65; bd. dirs. Am. Fgn. Policy Inst., 1976-84, Security and Intelligence Fund, 1976-84, James Monroe Libr., 1977-85; pres. Culpeper Meml. Hosp. Found., 1984-86; exec. chmn. U.S. Congl. Adv. Bd., 1982-2002; chmn. Nat. Security Caucus Found., 1997-2002. 1st lt. USAAF, 1943-45. Decorated Air medal with clusters; recipient 10th Anniversary medal and scroll Assembly Captive European Nations, Order Lafayette Freedom award, 1973, Disting. Svc. award Chapel of 4 Chaplains, 1979, others. Mem. Am. Soc. Indsl. Security (dir. 1959-62), Phi Kappa Tau. Republican. Presbyterian. Home: 212 Richard Brewster Rd Williamsburg VA 23185-6532 Office: Comms Corp Am 13195 Freedom Way Boston VA 22713 E-mail: johnf@cca.net.

FISHER, JOHN RICHARD, engineering consultant, former naval officer; b. Columbus, Ohio, Dec. 28, 1924; s. Don Alfred and Katherine Buchanan (Galigher) F.; m. Kitson Overmyer, Oct. 2, 1946; children: Scott Owen, Lani Kitson. BS, U.S. Naval Acad., 1946; BCE, MCE, Rensselaer Poly. Inst., Troy, N.Y., 1950; grad. Advanced Mgmt. Program, Harvard, 1971. Registered profl. engr., S.C. Commd. ensign U.S. Navy, 1946, advanced through grades to rear adm., 1972; service in North Africa, Cuba, The Philippines, Antarctica, Vietnam, Australia; comdr. 30th Seabee Rgt., Vietnam, 1968-69; dep. comdr. Naval Facilities Engring. Command; also comdr. Chesapeake divsn. constrn. facilities U.S. Naval Acad. and Omega Nav. System, 1969-73; comdr. Pacific divsn. Naval Facilities Engring. Command, Constrn. Facilities Diego Garcia, 1973-77; ret., 1977; v.p. Raymond Internat., Inc., 1977-81, sr. group v.p., 1981-83, exec. v.p., 1983-86. Pres. Cmty. Hosp. Assn. Mid-Am., Scottsdale, Ariz., 1985-96; past sr. warden St. Anthony Episcopal Ch. Decorated DSM, Legion of Merit with combat V (2). Fellow Am. Soc. Mil. Engrs.; mem. ASCE, Navy League U.S. (nat. pres. 1999-2001), The Moles, Outrigger Canoe Club (Honolulu), Army-Navy Country Club (Arlington, Va.), Tau Kappa Epsilon (nat. pres. 1993-95), Navy League of U.S. (nat. pres. 1999-2001), Tau Beta Pi. Home: 10615 E Arabian Park Dr Scottsdale AZ 85258-6021 Office: PO Box 5585 Scottsdale AZ 85261-5585 E-mail: jFisher1947@aol.com.

FISHER, JOHN WELTON, II, law educator, magistrate judge, university official; b. Fisher, W.Va., Dec. 11, 1942; s. John Welton and Orrie (Shobe) F.; m. Susan Carol Vass, June 6, 1964; children: John Welton III, Jennifer Lynn. BA, W.Va. U., 1964, JD, 1967. Bar: W.Va. 1967, U.S. Dist. Ct. (no. and so. dists.) W.Va. 1967, U.S. Ct. Appeals (4th cir.) 1969. Law clk. to chief judge U.S. Dist. Ct. (no. dist.) W.Va., 1967-68; assoc. Farmer & Farmer, Morgantown, W.Va., 1968-71; mem. faculty W.Va. U. Coll. Law, 1971—, prof. law, 1977—, acting dean, 1981-82, 92-93, 97-98, dean, 1998—, exec. officer univ., 1982-86, magistrate judge U.S. Dist. Ct. No. Dist. W.Va., 1977-98. Reporter Speedy Trial Planning Group, No. Dist. W.Va. Reporter: Local Rules of Practice, Northern District of West Virginia, 1980. Fellow Am.Bar Found., W.Va. Bar Found.; mem. W.Va. State Bar, W.Va. Bar Assn., Fourth Cir. Jud. Conf., Order of Coif. Office: PO Box 6130 Morgantown WV 26506-6130 E-mail: John.Fisher@mail.wvu.edu.

FISHER, JOHN WESLEY, manufacturing company executive; b. Walland, Tenn., July 15, 1915; s. Arthur Justin and Rachel (Malott) F.; m. Janice Kelsey Ball, Aug. 10, 1940; children: Joan Fisher Woods, Michael J., James A., Jeffrey E., Judith Fisher Oetinger, John Wesley III, Jerrold M. BS, U. Tenn., 1938; MBA, Harvard U., 1942; LLD (hon.), Ball State U., 1972, Butler U., 1977, DePauw U., 1981, Ind. U., 1985. Field sec. Delta Tau Delta Frat., Indpls., 1938-40; trainee, various mfg., sales and adminstrv. positions Ball Corp., Muncie, Ind., 1941-70, pres., chief exec. officer, 1970-78, chmn. bd., chief exec. officer, 1978-81, chmn. bd., 1981-86, also dir., chmn. emeritus, 1986—. Bd. dirs. Kindel Furniture Co., Grand Rapids, Mich.; ptnr. Blackwood & Nichols Corp., Oklahoma City; chmn. CID Equity Ptnrs., Indpls., Nat. Trust Co., Muncie; pres. Nature's Catch, Inc., Clarksdale, Miss., Fisher Properties of Ind., Inc. State del. Rep. Party, Ind., 1950-70; mem. Rep. State Fin. Com., 1952-56, del. nat. conv., 1952, 54, 64, 68; chmn. bd. dirs. Ball Meml. Hosp.; pres. Cardinal Health Sys. Mem. NAM (chmn. 1979-80, bd. dirs.), Glass Packaging Inst. (trustee 1962-68, pres. 1965-67), Grocery Mfrs. Assn. (bd. dirs.), Ind. C. of C. (dir. 1959—, pres. 1966-68), Muncie C. of C. (past pres.), Conf. Bd., Ind. Acad., Delaware Country Club, Indpls. Athletic Club, Columbia Club (Indpls.), Royal Poinciana Country Club, Naples (Fla.) Yacht Club, Rotary, Naples Nat. Golf Club, Delta Tau Delta. Republican. United Methodist. Home: PO Box 832 Muncie IN 47308-0832 Office: Ball Assocs PO Box 1408 Muncie IN 47308-1408

FISHER, JOSEPH SAUL, endocrinologist, consultant; b. Phila., Oct. 29, 1942; s. Abraham and Sarah (Segal) F.; m. Judith Gayle Silverman, May 5, 1970; children: David, Craig, Caren. AB, Temple U., 1964; MS, Villanova U., 1966; MD (hon.), Jefferson Med. Coll., Phila., 1970. Diplomate Am. Bd. Internal Medicine, Am. Bd. Endocrinology and Metabolism. Intern in internal medicine Thomas Jefferson U. Hosp., Phila., 1970-71, resident in internal medicine, 1971-73, asst. clin. prof. medicine, 1977—; fellow in endocrinology UCLA Harbor Med. Ctr., Torrence, Calif., 1973-74, UCLA-San Fernando Valley Med. Program, L.A., 1976-77; chief endocrinology, diabetes and metabolism Holy Redeemer Hosp. and Med. Ctr., Meadowbrook, Pa., 1977—. Asst. clin. prof. medicine, U. Hawaii, Honolulu, 1974-76; Thomas Jefferson U. Hosp., 1977—; cons. in field. Rschr. in the field. Maj. U.S. Army, 1974-76. Recipient Legion of Honor, Chapel of Four Chaplains, 1983. Fellow ACP, Am. Coll. Endocrinology, Phila. Coll. Physicians; mem. Am. Diabetes Assn., Endocrine Soc., Phila. Endocrine Soc., Israel Med. Assn. (Am. div. World Fellowship), Internat. Diabetes Fedn., Am. Assn. Clin. Endocrinologists. Jewish. Office: 1650 Huntingdon Pike Ste 317 Jenkintown PA 19046-8007 Fax: 215-947-3458. E-mail: jsfishermd@aol.com.

FISHER, KATHLEEN V. lawyer; b. Aug. 9, 1948; AB, UCLA, 1971; JD, U. Calif., Davis, 1976. Bar: Calif. 1976. Extern to Hon. Raymond Sullivan Calif. Supreme Ct., 1975; mem. Morrison & Foerster, San Francisco. Mem. Order of Coif. Office: Morrison & Foerster 425 Market St San Francisco CA 94105

FISHER, LAURA LANI, physician, medical educator; b. East Orange, N.J., July 13, 1959; d. Hyman Wendell and Rosalie Jane (Joseph) F.; m. Adi Raviv; children: Micaela Sara, Jessica Alana, Gabriella Noa. BA in Biology and Biomed. Ethics, Brown U., 1981, MD, 1984. Intern in internal medicine N.Y. Hosp., 1984-85, resident in internal medicine, 1985-87, chief resident in medicine, 1989-90, dir. Lyme Disease Ctr., 1990—; from clin. to rsch. fellow in infectious diseases Mass. Gen. Hosp., Boston, 1987-89; dir. student health svc. Cornell Med. Coll., N.Y.C., 1990-93, asst. prof. medicine, 1990—. Contbr. articles to profl. jours. Mem. nat. cabinet Israel Bonds-Young Leadership, U.S., 1992-94, mem. city bd. dirs., 1993-94; mem. Anti-Defamation League, N.Y.C., 1993-94. Recipient Rsch. Scientist award NIH, 1988-89. Fellow ACP; mem. AMA, N.Y. Med. Soc., Mass. Med. Soc., Brown Med. Soc., Infectious Disease Soc. Am. Democrat. Jewish. Avocations: painting, sports, sculpture, reading, travel. Office: 1385 York Ave New York NY 10021-3904

FISHER, LAWRENCE EDGAR, market research executive, anthropologist; b. Los Alamos, N.Mex., Jan. 13, 1946; s. Leon H. and Phyllis (Kahn) F.; m. Valerie Joseph, Mar. 25, 1979; children: Lael Sharon, Jonathan Daniel, Matthew Joseph. AB, U. Calif., Berkeley, 1968; MA, Northwestern U., 1969; postdoctoral fellow, U. Chgo., 1973—74; PhD, Northwestern U., 1973; cert. in bus. adminstrn., U. Pa., 1982. Asst. prof. U. Ill., Chgo., 1974-83; dir. Ethnographic Field Sch. Northwestern U., Evanston, Ill., 1975-78, adj. assoc. prof., 1984-86; vis. scholar Stanford U., 1978; vis. asst. prof. U. Mich., Ann Arbor, 1979-80; account exec., sr. account exec., dir. client svc. MRCA Info. Svc., Northbrook, Ill., 1983-88; group mgr. Test Mktg. Group, Control Data Corp., Chgo., 1988-89; dir. client svc. Info. Resources, Inc., Chgo., 1989-90, v.p. client svc., 1991-94, sr. v.p., 1994-99, NFO WorldGroup, Chgo., 2000—. Mem. external adv. bd. A.C. Nielsen Ctr., Grad. Sch. Bus. U. Wis., Madison, 1991—, chmn. bd., 1998-99; founding bd. dir. Interactive Market Rsch. Org., 2000—. Author: Colonial Madness, 1985; also numerous articles; mem. edit. rev. bd., Jour. Online Rsch., 2001—. Fellow Woodrow Wilson Found., 1972-73, NIH, 1973-74, NEH, 1975. Mem.: Am. Mktg. Assn. (EXPLOR award com. 2001—03, conf. com. Exec. Insights Forum 2003). Home: 324 S Euclid Ave Oak Park IL 60302-3508 Office: NFO Interactive 500 W Monroe St Ste 2710 Chicago IL 60661-3629 E-mail: lfisher@nfow.com.

FISHER, LEONARD EVERETT, artist, writer, educator; b. N.Y.C., June 24, 1924; s. Benjamin M. and Ray Mera (Shapiro) F.; m. Margery Meskin, Dec. 21, 1952; children— Julie Anne, Susan Abby, James Albert BFA, Yale U., 1949, MFA, 1950. Dean Whitney Art Sch., New Haven, Conn., 1951-53; mem. faculty Paier Art Sch., Hamden, Conn., 1966-78; acad. dean Paier Coll. of Art, Hamden, 1978-82, dean emeritus, 1982—, vis. prof., 1982-87, Fairfield U., Conn., 1983-85. Del. at large White House Conf. on Library and Info. Services, Washington, 1979; lectr. in field, 1957— Author 88 childrens books; illustrator approximately 260 childrens books; author, illustrator: A Russian Farewell (Nat. Jewish Book award), 1981; designer 10 U.S. postage stamps including 1972 and 1977 U.S. Bicentennial Commemorative issues; paintings and illustrations represented in permanent collections Butler Art Inst., Youngstown, Ohio, Mt. Holyoke Coll., Mass., Union Coll., Schenectady, N.Y., Housatonic Mus., Bridgeport, Conn., New Britain Mus. Am. Art, U. Conn., Storrs, U. Minn., Mpls., U. Oreg., Eugene, U. So. Miss., Hattiesburg, Brown U., Providence, Libr. of Congress, Washington, N.Y. Pub. Libr., Mus. Am. Illustration, N.Y.C., Norwalk (Conn.) Transp. Ctr. Trustee Westport Pub. Library, Conn., 1982-89, v.p., 1985-86, pres. 1986-89; founding mem. Westport-Weston Arts Coun., 1969, pres., bd. dirs., 1973-74, trustee, 1969-76. With U.S. Army, 1942-46, NATOUSA, PTO. Recipient Premio Grafico Internat. Book Fair, Italy, 1968, Medallion, U. So. Miss., 1979, Christopher medal, 1980, Non-Fiction award Childrens Book Guild Washington and the Washington Post, 1989, Regina medal Cath. Libr. Assn., 1991, Kerlan award U. Minn., 1991, Arbuthnot Honor Lectr. citation ALA, 1995, New Eng. Booksellers award for children's lit., 2002, Pulitzer Art scholarship, 1950; Winchester fellow Yale U., 1949. Mem. Soc. Illustrators, Silvermine Guild (trustee 1970-74), Authors Guild N.Y., P.E.N. Home: 7 Twin Bridge Acre Rd Westport CT 06880-1028 E-mail: leonardoe1@aol.com.

FISHER, LESTER EMIL, zoo administrator; b. Chgo., Feb. 24, 1921; s. Louis and Elizabeth (Vodicka) F.; m. Wendy Fisher, Jan. 23, 1981; children: Jane Serrita, Katherine Clark. MDV, Iowa State U., 1943. Supr. animal care program Northwestern U. Med. Sch., 1946-47; attending veterinarian Lincoln Park Zoo, Chgo., 1947-62, zoo dir., 1962-92, dir. emeritus, 1992—; owner, dir. Berwyn (Ill.) Animal Hosp., 1947-68. Producer, moderator ednl. closed circuit TV for nat. vet. meetings, 1949-66; asso. prof. dept. biology DePaul U., 1968-98; adj. prof. zoology U. Ill., from 1972 Editor: Brit. Small Animal Jour. and Small Animal Clinician, 1958-72. Mem citizens com. U. Ill.; chmn. zoo and wildlife div. Morris Animal Found. Served to maj., Vet. Corps AUS, 1943-46. Recipient Alumni Merit award Iowa State U., 1968, Stange award Iowa State U., 1988, Chgo. Superior Pub. Svc. award Chgo. Park Dist., 1973, 92, Laureate Ill. Lincoln Acad., 1993. Mem. Am. Animal Hosp. Assn. (regional dir., outstanding Service award 1969), Am. Vet. Med. Assn., Nat. Recreation and Park Assn., Internat. Union Dirs. Zool. Gardens (v.p. 1980-83, pres. 1983-86), Am. Assn. Zoo Veterinarians (pres. 1966-69), Am. Assn. Zool. Parks and Aquariums (pres. 1972-73, chmn. gorilla species survival plan 1982-92), Chgo. Geographic Soc. (v.p.), Econ. Club Chgo., Theta Xi. Clubs: Adventures (pres. 1971-72), Execs. of Chgo. (bd. dirs. 1968-71), Arts. Assoc., Chgo. Econs. (membership com.) (Chgo.). Home: 3180 N Lake Shore Dr Apt 17H Chicago IL 60657-4868 Home (Summer): PO Box 656 Alexandria Bay NY 13607-0656

FISHER, LINDA ALICE, physician; b. Plainfield, N.J., Dec. 27, 1947; d. Alvin Edwin and Bertha Sophie (Steigmann) F. BA, Douglass Coll., New Brunswick, N.J., 1970; M in Med. Sci., Rutgers U., 1972; MD, Harvard U., 1975; MPH, St. Louis U., 1996. Fellow Am. Bd. Internal Medicine, Diplomate Am. Bd. Preventive Medicine. Intern, then resident Jewish Hosp. St. Louis, 1975-78; dir. ambulatory care St. Luke's Hosp., St. Louis, 1978-84; chief med. officer St. Louis County Dept. Health, Clayton, 1984-97, dir. rsch., 1997-2000; project dir. St. Louis STD/HIV Prevention Tng. Ctr., 1995-2000. Chief physician St. Louis Met. Police Dept., 1978-88; clin. instr. medicine Washington U., St. Louis, 1978-94, asst. clin. prof., 1994-2000; asst. clin. prof. medicine St. Louis U., 1979-95, assoc. clin. prof., 1996-2000; adj. faculty health svcs. mgmt. U. Mo., Columbia, 1996, St. Louis U. Sch. Pub. Health, 1993-2000; bd. overseers St. Louis Regional Med. Ctr., 1985-95; cons. Ill. Local Govtl. Law Enforcement Officers Tng. Bd., 1988; dir. Fairfax County Health Dept., 2000-2001. Contbr. articles to profl. jours.; author of short stories. Chmn. licensure com. Mo. Bd. Registration for Healing Arts, 1983-86; adv. coun. Greater St. Louis Coun. Girl Scouts U.S., 1986-2000. Recipient Disting. Alumni award Douglass Coll., 1992, Publ. award Mo. Pub. Health Assn., 1994, St. Louis Woman of Achievement award KMOX Radio and Suburban Jours., 1995. Fellow ACP; mem. AMA, APHA, Am. Med. Women's Assn. (chpt. pres. 1982-85, Cmty. Svc. award 1992), Am. Med. Writers Assn., Nat. Assn. Med. Communicators (Ken Alvord Cmty. Svc. award 1998), St. Louis Met. Med. Soc. (councilor 1982-84, sec. 1986, editor 1989-90), Fairfax County Med. Soc., Internat. Women's Forum. Lutheran. Office: Box 3927 Fairfax VA 22038-3927 E-mail: laf314@earthlink.net.

FISHER, LINDA J. federal agency administrator; b. Saginaw, Mich., June 26, 1952; BA, Miami U., Oxford, Ohio, 1974; MBA, George Washington U., 1978; JD, Ohio State U., 1982. Legis. asst. to Hon. Clarence J. Brown, Ohio, 1974-75, Hon. Ralph S. Regula, Ohio, 1976-80; special asst. to asst. adminstr. solid waste and emergency response EPA, 1983-84, chief staff to adminstr., 1985-87, asst. adminstr. policy and evaluation, 1988, asst. adminstr. pesticides and toxic substances, 1989—93, dep. adminr., 2001—03; of counsel Latham & Watkins, 1993—95; v.p. govt. and pub. affairs Monsanto, 1995—2000. Office Fax: 202-501-1470.

FISHER, LLOYD EDISON, JR., lawyer; b. Medina, Ohio, Oct. 23, 1923; s. Lloyd Edison and Wanda (White) F.; m. Twylla Dawn Peterson, Sept. 11, 1949 (dec. Apr. 1996); children: Karen S., Kirk P. BS, Ohio State U., 1947, JD, 1949. Bar: Ohio 1950. Mem. gen. hearing bd. Ohio Dept. Taxation, 1950-53; trust officer Huntington Nat. Bank, Columbus, 1953-62; ptnr. Porter, Wright, Morris & Arthur and predecessor firm, Columbus, 1962—. Adj. prof. law Ohio State U., Columbus, 1967-69, 84-91. Bd. dirs Wesley Glen Retirement Ctr., 1974-80, 88-95; bd. dirs. Grant/Riverside Hospice, 1997—. Served with AUS, 1943-45. Fellow Am. Coll. Trust and Estate Counsel; mem. ABA, Ohio Bar Assn., Columbus Bar Assn., Order of Coif. Home: 6478 Strathaven Ct E Worthington OH 43085-2985 Office: 41 S High St Columbus OH 43215-6101 E-mail: lfisher@porterwright.com.

FISHER, LOUIS MCLANE, JR., management consultant; b. Balt., July 25, 1938; s. Louis McLane and Betty Taylor (Griswold) F.; m. Sue Jane Roderick, Jan. 2, 1977; children: Kathy, Mark, Matthew, Andy; stepchildren: Rolf (dec.), Sonja, Kirsten. BA magna cum laude, Hampden-Sydney Coll., 1961; postgrad., U. Va., 1961-62; MBA, U. Oreg., 1963. Exec. trainee First Nat. Bank Oreg., Portland, 1963, investment analyst, 1964; owner. Bus. Consulting Svcs., Corvallis, Oreg., 1964-65; administrv. mgr. CH2M HILL, Denver, 1965-70, treas., 1970-75, exec. v.p., 1975-94; pres. Quaere, Littleton, Colo., 1995—. Guest lectr. Oreg. State U.; bd. dirs. Open Door Inc., Iotech Inc., OMI Inc., Indsl. Design Corp., Power Interests Holding Corp., Coleman Sperryn-Jones, Mariott Resort, Bahamas, GCSI Tissuscan Tech., Grand Masters of Lawrence, PSMA, Merrick Engring., Woodard & Curran Inc., Psomas Assocs. Contbr. articles to profl. jours. Bd. dirs. Corvallis Arts Ctr. Fellow Profl. Svcs. Mgmt. Assn. (cert. profl. svcs. mgr.; bd. dirs. 1975-78, pres. 1976-77, chmn. coll. fellows 1980—); mem. Am. Mgmt. Assn., Am. Cons. Engrs. Coun., Alliance Profl. Consultants, Nat. Assn. Corp. Dirs., Fin. Execs. Inst., Western Regional Coun. (treas. 1987-88), Denver C. of C., Corvallis Area C. of C. (bd. dirs., v.p. 1971), Met. Club, Châine de Rôtisseurs. Republican. Episcopalian. Home: 6093 S Bellaire Way Littleton CO 80121-3171 Office: Quaere 5250 E Arapahoe Rd Ste F7 Littleton CO 80122-2361

FISHER, LUCY, motion picture company executive; b. N.Y.C., Oct. 2, 1949; d. Arthur Bertram and Naomi (Kislak) F.; m. Douglas Z. Wick, Feb. 16, 1986; children: Sarah, Julia, Tessa. BA, Harvard U., 1971. V.p. prodn. 20th Century Fox, L.A., 1979-80; v.p. worldwide prodns. Zoetrope Studios, Burbank, Calif., 1980-81; v.p., sr. prodn. exec. Warner Bros. Pictures, Burbank, 1981-87, sr. v.p., 1987-89, exec. v.p. prodn., 1989-96; vice chmn. Columbia Tristar Motion Picture Co., Culver City, Calif., 1996-2000; producer Red Wagon Productions, Culver City, Calif., 2000—. Office: Red Wagen Entertainment Hepburn West 10202 Washington Blvd Culver City CA 90232-3119

FISHER, LYMAN MCARTHUR, retired clinical pathologist, hematologist; b. Appin, Ont., Can., Mar. 21, 1923; came to U.S., 1960; s. Clarence Andrew and Minnie (McArthur) F.; m. Dorothy Gwendoline Calvert, June 12, 1953; children: John Mark, Robert Paul, James Alexander, Ruth Anne. BA, U. Western Ont., 1951; MA, U. Sask., 1954, PhD, 1957, MD, 1960. Diplomate Am. Bd. Pathology. Asst. prof. pathology Med. Coll. Va., Richmond, 1960-66, assoc. prof. pathology, 1966-70; Fulbright prof. U. Tromsø, Norway, 1972-73; dir. hemostasis Med. Coll. Va. Hosps., Richmond, 1975-99; prof. pathology, clin. pathologist Va. Commonwealth U., Richmond, 1975-99; ret., 1999. Mem. adv. bd. Salvation Army, Richmond, 1988—. Fellow Am. Soc. Clin. Pathology; mem. Am. Assn. Blood Banks, Internat. Soc. Thrombosis and Haemostasis, Nat. Hemophilia Fedn. E-mail: Lymanmfish@aol.com.

FISHER, MARGARET, artist, researcher; b. Miami, Nov. 4, 1948; d. Gene Sapiro Fisher and Ethel Kott; m. Robert Grove Hughes, Feb. 29, 1996. BA, U. Calif., Berkeley, 1969, MA, 2001, PhD, 2003. Founder, dir. Cat's Paw Palace of Performing Arts, Berkeley, 1973—77, Ma Fish Co., Emeryville, Calif., 1983—; pub. Second Evening Art, Emeryville, Calif., 2003. Bd. dirs. Internat. Performance Network, Emeryville, Calif., 1974—. Author: (book) Ezra Pound's Radio Operas, 2002 (Ezra Pound Soc. award, 2002); dir.: (video) Faux Foreign Series, 1992—97; choreographer (dance) Ma Fish Co. Performing Group, 1977—94. Recipient Fulbright Rsch. award, Italy, 1981; Artist Exch. Fellowship, U.S. Japan Commn., 1983—84, Choreographers's Fellowship, NEA, 1981, 1982, 1988.

FISHER, MARGARET CATHARINE, pediatrician, epidemiologist, educator; b. York, Pa., Mar. 1, 1949; d. Robert Foster Fisher and Miriam Arlene (Miller) Coryell. BA summa cum laude, Susquehanna U., 1971; MD, UCLA, 1975. Diplomate Am. Bd. Pediats., sub-bd. pediat. infectious disease. Resident in pediat. St. Christopher's Hosp. for Children, Phila., 1975-78, fellow pediat. infectious disease, 1978-80, hosp. epidemiologist, 1980-99; asst. prof. pediat. Temple U., Phila., 1980-86, assoc. prof., 1986-94; assoc. prof. pediat. Drexel U. Sch. Medicine, Phila., 1994—97, prof., 1997—; mem. staff St. Christopher's Hosp. for Children, Phila., 1980-2000; mem. staff, chmn. dept. pediat. Monmouth Med. Ctr., Long Branch, N.J., 2000—. Cons. Temple U. Hosp., Phila., 1985-95. Contbr. articles to profl. jours. Pres. St. Christopher's Hosp. for Children Med. Staff, 1995-97. Fellow Am. Acad. Pediat. (editl. bd. Pediatric UPDATE 1993—, mem. com. on infectious diseases 1996-2002), Pediat. Infectious Disease Soc., Infectious Diseases Soc. Am.; mem. Am. Soc. Microbiology, Infectious Disease Soc. N.J. Avocations: reading, jigsaw puzzles. Office: Monmouth Med Ctr Dept Pediatrics 300 Second Ave Long Branch NJ 07740 E-mail: mfisher@sbhcs.com.

FISHER, MARGARET ELEANOR, psychologist, lawyer, arbitrator, mediator, educator; d. John T. and Mary (Worden) F. BS cum laude in Psychology, Seton Hall U., 1958; postgrad., U. Paris, 1958, Carl Jung Inst., Switzerland, 1958-59, NYU, 1959-60, U. Md., 1960-63; MA magna cum laude in Ednl. Psychology, San Diego State U., 1966; postgrad. (NDEA grantee), U. Alaska, 1965, MBA, MPA, 1991; Phd cum laude in Psychology, U. Wash., 1970; JD magna cum laude, La Salle U., 1993. Lic. pilot comml. helicopter, fixed wing, psychologist, Mass., Ind., Alaska. Resident counselor Children's Ctr., NYC, 1959-60; tchr. Am. Dependent's, Turkey, 1960—64, 1960—64, 1960—64, Am. Dependent's Sch., Japan, 1960-64; tchr. English as fgn. lang. Jean Giraudoux Lycée, Chateauroux, France, 1963-64; tchr. English and French Sweetwater Sch. Dist., Chula Vista, Calif., 1964-66; asst. to editor Rev. of Ednl. Rsch. Jour., Seattle, 1967-68; psychologist vocat. rehab. program Edmonds Sch. Dist., Lynnwood, Wash., 1968-70; cons. psychologist Charles Denny Youth Ctr., Everett, Wash., 1969-71; instr. psychology Seattle Cmty. Coll., 1971; asst. prof. dept.social sci., humanities and edn. Purdue U., Lafayette, Ind., 1971-72; lang. evaluation specialist Def. Lang. Inst., Monterey, Calif., 1972; rsch. psychologist U. Calif., San Francisco, 1972, asst. prof. psychology Santa Cruz, 1973, Mass. State Coll., 1973-76; pvt. practice psychology Mass., 1976-78; psychologist NY State Dept. Mental Hygiene, 1978, AK divsn. mental health Harborview Devel. Ctr., Valdez, 1978-79, AK Psychiat. Inst., Anchorage, 1979-95; psychologist, atty. AK Psychol., Arbitration & Mediation Svc., Inc., 1995—; with AK Civil Air Patrol, 1987. Adj. prof. law and psychology La Salle U. Contrb. articles to psychol. and law jour. Arbitrator, mediator forensic psychologist Am. Arbitration Assn.; pres. Internat. Coun. Psychologists, 1992, world area chairs coord.; mem. AK State Bd. Psychologists and Psychol. Assoc. Examiners, 1984—88; amb. to Mauritius Anchorage organizing com. 1994 Winter Olympics, 1988—. With Alaska Civil Air Patrol, 1987—. Recipient Internat. travel award Purdue U., 1972, scholarly support award Mass. State Coll., 1974, 75, 76. Fellow: Am. Coll. Forensic Examiners (cert. forensic examiner); mem.: DAR, Internat. Coun. Psychologists (past pres. 1992, diplomate), AK Psychol. Assn., Mensa. Home and Office: 7935 Hillside Way Anchorage AK 99516 Fax: (907) 345-6234.

FISHER, MARK JAY, neurologist, neuroscientist, educator; b. Bklyn., Aug. 23, 1949; s. Ralph Aaron and Dorothy Ann (Weissman) F.; m. Janeth Godeau, Aug. 5, 1994. BA in Polit. Sci., UCLA, 1970; MA in Polit. Sci., U. S.D., 1972; MD, U. Cin., 1975; JD, Loyola U., 1997. Diplomate Am. Bd. Psychiatry and Neurology. Intern UCLA Sepulveda VA Hosp., 1975-76; resident UCLA Wadsworth VA Med. Ctr., 1976-79, chief resident, 1979-80; faculty mem., dir. stroke rsch. program U. So. Calif. Sch. of Medicine, L.A., 1980-98, prof. neurology, 1995-98; dir. residency tng. program U. So. Calif. Sch. Medicine, L.A., 1992-96; chmn. dept. neurology U. Calif. at Irvine, Orange, 1998—, prof. neurology and anatomy and neurobiology, 1998—. Editor: Medical Therapy of Acute Stroke, 1989. Recipient Tchr. Investigator award NIH, Bethesda, Md., 1984-89, Program Project grantee, 1994-99. Mem. Am. Acad. Neurology, Am. Neurol. Assn., Am. Heart Assn. (stroke coun.), Internat. Soc. for Thrombosis and Haemostasis, State Bar of Calif. Office: U Calif Irvine Dept Neurology 101 The City Dr S Orange CA 92868-3201

FISHER, MICHAEL ELLIS, mathematical physicist, chemist; b. Trinidad, W.I., Sept. 3, 1931; m. Sorrel Castillejo; children: Caricia J., Daniel S., Martin J., Matthew P.A. BS with 1st class honors in Physics, King's Coll., London, 1951, PhD, 1957; DSc (hon.), Yale U., 1987, Tel Aviv U., 1992. Lectr. math. RAF, 1952-53; lectr. theoretical physics King's Coll., 1958-62, reader physics, 1962-64; prof. physics U. London, 1965-66; prof. chemistry and math. Cornell U., 1966-73, Horace White prof. chemistry, physics and math., 1973-89, chmn. dept. chemistry, 1975-78; Disting. prof. Inst. for Phys. Sci. and Tech. U. Md., 1987—, Regents prof. Inst. for Phys. Sci. & Tech., 1993—. Guest investigator Rockefeller Inst., 1963-64; vis. prof. applied physics Stanford U., 1970-71; Buhl lectr. theoretical physics Carnegie-Mellon U., 1971; Richtmyer Meml. lectr. Am. Assn. Physics Tchrs., 1973; S. H. Klosk lectr. NYU, 1975; 17th F. London Meml. lectr. Duke U., 1975; Walker-Ames prof. U. Wash., Seattle, 1977; Loeb lectr. physics Harvard U., 1979; vis.prof. physics MIT, 1979; Welsh Found. lectr. in physics U. Toronto, Ont., Can., 1979; 21st Alpheus Smith lectr. Ohio State U., 1982; Fairchild scholar Calif. Inst. Tech., 1984; Cherwell-Simon lectr., vis. prof. Oxford U., 1985; Schlapp scholar Edinburgh U., 1987; Marker lectr. Pa. State U., 1988, Nat. Sci. Coun. lectr., Taiwan, 1989; Hamilton Meml. lectr. Princeton U., 1990, 65th J. W. Gibbs lectr. Am. Math. Soc., 1992; E. U. Condon lectr. U. Colo., 1992; M. S. Green Meml. lectr. Temple U., 1992; R&B Sackler Disting. lectr. in solid state physics Tel Aviv U., 1992; 1st Lars Onsager lectr., Norway, 1993; Phi Beta Kappa vis. scholar, 1994; Lennard-Jones lectr. Royal Soc. Chemistry, 1995; Joseph O. Hirschfelder Prize lectr. U. Wis., 1995; Gilbert Newton Lewis Meml. lectr. U. Calif., Berkeley, 1995; George Fisher Baker lectr. chemistry Cornell U., 1997. Author (with d.M. MacKay): Analogue Computing at Ultra-High Speed, 1962; author: The Nature of Critical Points, 1964, The Theory of Equilibrium Critical Phenomena, 1967; assoc. editor Jour. Math. Physics, 1965—68, 1972—75, 1986—89, mem. adv. bd. Jour. Theoretical Biology, 1969—82, Chem. Physics, 1972—84, Discrete Math., 1971—78, Jour. Statis. Physics, 1978—81, mem. editl. bd. Comms. Math. Phys., 1984—2000. Recipient award in phys. and math. scis. N.Y. Acad. Scis., 1978, Guthrie medal and prize Inst. Physics, London, 1980, Wolf prize in physics, 1980, Michelson-Morely award Case Western Res. U., 1982, Boltzmann medal IUPAP, 1983, Hirschfelder prize U. Wis., 1995; Guggenheim fellow, 1970-71, 78-79. Fellow: AAAS, Kings Coll. London, Am. Phys. Soc., Phys. Soc. London, N.Y. Acad. Scis. (hon.), Royal Soc. Edinburgh (hon.), Am. Acad. Arts and Scis., Royal Soc. London (regional editor 1989—93, v.p. 1993—95); mem.: NAS (fgn. assoc.), Indian Acad. Scis., Brazilian Acad. Scis. (fgn. assoc.), Math. Assn. Am., Soc. Indsl. and Applied Math., Am. Philos. Soc., Am. Chem. Soc. Office: U Md Inst Phys Sci & Tech College Park MD 20742-0001

FISHER, MILES MARK, IV, education and religion educator, minister; b. Huntington, W.Va., Sept. 25, 1932; s. Miles Mark and Ada Virginia (Foster) F. BA, Va. Union U., 1954, M.Div., 1959; MA, N.C. Central U., 1968; D.Min., Howard U., 1978. Ordained to ministry Baptist Ch., 1961; tchr. pub. schs. Durham, N.C., 1959-67; assoc. min. White Rock Bapt. Ch., Durham, N.C., 1959-65; asst. prof. edn., counselor Norfolk (Va.) State U., 1967-69; cons. Model Cities Area of Recreation, Norfolk, 1968-69; exec.-sec., CEO Nat. Assn. Equal Opportunity in Higher Edn., Washington, 1969-78; spl. cons. Inst. for Services to Edn., Washington, 1969-70; vis. asst. prof. Sch. Divinity Howard U., 1978-80; staff dir., com. clk. Com. of Whole, Council of D.C., Washington, 1979-83; spl. asst. to v.p. acad. affairs U. D.C., Washington, 1983-84, dir. policy rev. and analysis Office of the Bd. of Trustees, 1985-88, exec. dir. Office of the Bd. of Trustees, 1989-90, interim pres., 1990-91, disting. U. prof., 1991—. Chaplain counselor Lincoln Hosp. Sch. Nursing, Durham, N.C., 1962-67; chaplain Fisher Funeral Parlor, Durham, 1963-67; mem. task force employment of minority populations Nat. Recreation and Park Assn., 1970-71; mem. task force on edn. and Vietnam Era vet. VA, 1971-72; mem. steering com. U.S. Office of Edn. Common Core Data for the 70's, 1971-78, Congl. Black Caucus Nat. Policy Conf. on Black Edn., 1972; mem. Nat. task force on Student Financial Aid Problems, 1974-75; bd. trustees Consortium of U. of the Washington Met. Area, 1990-91; bd. dirs. Washington Rsch. Libr. Consortium, 1990-91. Bd. dirs. Cooperative Coll. Registry, 1973-75; mem. adv. bd. Four-Year Servicemen's Opportunity Coll., 1974-77; mem. adv. com. to bd. dirs. Nat. Student Ednl. Fund, 1974-78; v.p. bd. dirs. Reading is Fundamental Program, 1977-79, Vis. Nurse Assn., 1974-80; bd. dirs. D.C. Citizens for Better Public Edn., 1977, pres., 1981-83; bd. dirs. Voice Informed Community Expression, pres., 1982-84; trustee Va. Union U., 1983-85, Shaw U. Div. Sch., 1982-88. Mem. ACA, Am. Assn. Higher Edn., Am. Acad. Polit. and Social Scis., Am. Acad. Religion, Assn. Multicultural Counseling and Devel., Assn. Spiritual Ethical and Religious Values in Counseling, Am. Soc. Ch. History, Internat. Alumni Assn. Va. Union U. (pres. 1983-85), Am. Tennis Assn. (life), Assn. for Study of Afro-Am. Life and History (life), Assn. for Study of Higher Edn., U.S. Tennis Assn. (life). Home: 4444 Connecticut Ave NW Apt 402 Washington DC 20008-2319 Office: PO Box 2340 Washington DC 20013-2340

FISHER, MORRIS ALAN, neurologist, medical educator; b. N.Y.C., Mar. 26, 1940; s. Joseph and Jeanette (Krotinger) F. m. Natalie Ellen Wilson, June 16, 1966; children: Bruce (dec.), Jeremy. BA magna cum laude, Yale U., 1961; MD, Harvard U., 1968. Diplomate Am. Bd. Psychiatry and Neurology, Am. Bd. Electrodiagnostic Medicine, Am. Bd. Neurology, with added qualificaitons in clin. neurophysiology. Rsch. asst. in neurophysiology Mass. Gen. Hosp., Boston, 1963-65; spl. grad. student in biology-neurophysiology MIT, Cambridge, Mass., 1964-65; med. intern Cleve. Met. Gen. Hosp., 1968-69; asst. resident in neurology Mass. Gen. Hosp., 1969-70, clin. fellow of Harvard U. in dept. of neurology, 1972-74, fellow in clin. neurophysiology, 1974-75; asst. prof. neurol. sci. Rush Med. Coll., Chgo., 1975-78, assoc. prof. neurol. sci., 1978-80; assoc. prof. neurology U. Chgo. Pritzker Sch. Medicine, 1980-89, U. Ill. at Chgo. Coll. Medicine, 1991-92; prof. neurology, Stritch Sch. Medicine Loyola U. Med. Ctr., Maywood, Ill., 1992—. Neurologist U.S. Army Med. Corps, Ft. Bragg, N.C., 1970-72; asst. attending in neurology Rush-Presbyn. St. Luke's Med. Ctr., Chgo., 1975-77, head sec. EMG and clin. neurophysiology, 1975-80, co-dir. MDA Clinic, 1978-80, cons. in neurology, 1980—; assoc. neurologist Michael Reese Hosp. and Med. Ctr., 1980-82, attending neurologist, 1982-92, dir. electromyography lab. 1980-82, dir. clin. neurophysiology, 1982-92, acting vice chmn. neurology, 1985-86, vice chmn. neurology, 1986-90, dir. low back pain program, 1988-89, acting chief of svc., dept. neurology, 1990-92; attending neurologist, Hines VA Hosp. and Loyala U. Med. Ctr., 1992—, dir. neuromuscular program, 1992—, dir. EMG Lab. Hines VA Hosp., 1992—; dir. clin. diagnostic neurophysiology labs., Hines VA Hosp., 1993—; dir. clin. neurophysiology fellowship Loyola U. Med. Ctr., 2002--. Contbr. numerous articles and revs. to profl. jours., chpts. to books; presenter and lectr. in field; editl. bd. Am. Soc. for Clin. Evoked Potentials, 1988-90, Electroencephalograph and Clin. Neurophysiology, 1997-98, Clin. Neurophysiology, 1999—; assoc. editor Neurology and Clin. Neurophysiology, 1999—. Major, U.S. Army, 1970-72. Fellow Am. Acad. Neurology, Am. Assn. Electrodiagnostic Medicine (examiner 1989—, exec. bd. 1985-88, extensive com. work); mem. AAAS, Am. Neurol. Assn., Am. Acad. Clin. Neurophysiology (exec. coun. 1993—, pres. elect 1997, pres. 1999-2001), Phi Beta Kappa. Office: Hines VA Hosp Dept Neurology 127 Hines IL 60141 E-mail: morris.fisher@med.va.gov.

FISHER, MORTON POE, JR., lawyer; b. Balt., Aug. 17, 1936; s. Morton Poe Sr. and Adelaide (Block) F.; m. Ann P. Fisher, Aug. 12, 1962; children: Stephen N., Marjorie P. AB, Dartmouth Coll., Hanover, N.H., 1958; LLB, Yale U., 1961. Bar: Md. 1961, D.C. 1961. Law clk. to presiding justice U.S. Dist. Ct. Md., Balt., 1961-62; assoc. Piper & Marbury, 1962-68; asst. gen. counsel Rouse Co., 1968-73; ptnr. Frank, Bernstein, Conaway & Goldman, Balt., 1973-92; mng. ptnr. Ballard Spahr Andrews & Ingersoll, Balt., 1992—2002. Faculty mem. U. Md. Law Sch., 1978-87. Mem. Balt. County Econ. Devel. Commn., 1988-90, Mayor's Adv. Commn., Balt. City, Risk Mgmt. Com. Balto City, 1999; bd. dirs. Balt. Downtown Partnership, 1998-2003, U. Md. Balt. Found., 2003, Johns Hopkins U. Real Estate Inst., 2003; dean U. of Shopping ctrs., 1998-99; bd. trustees U. of Md. Balt. Found., 2003—. Mem. ABA (vice chmn. real property divsn 1990-92, chmn. sect. real property, probate and trust law 1993-94), Am. Coll. Real Estate Lawyers (pres. 1988-89), Am. Coll. Constrn. Lawyers, Am. Law Inst., Anglo-Am. Real Property Inst., Internat. Coun. Shopping Ctrs. (co-chmn. law conf. 1995-97). Office: Ballard Spahr Andrews & Ingersoll LLP 300 E Lombard St Ste 1800 Baltimore MD 21202-6739 E-mail: fisher@ballardspahr.com.

FISHER, MYRON R. lawyer; b. Chgo., Aug. 13, 1935; BA, Calif. State U., Long Beach, 1964; JD, Southwestern U., 1969. Bar: Calif. 1970, U.S. Dist. Ct. (cen. dist.) Calif. 1970, U.S. Supreme Ct. 1974. Dep. pub. defender San Bernardino County (Calif.), 1970-71; assoc. Anderson, Adams & Bacon, Rosemead, Calif., 1971-74; sole practice San Clemente, Calif., 1974—. Judge pro tem South Orange County Mcpl. Ct., 1978— . Mem. State Bar Calif., South Orange County Bar Assn. (bd. dirs. 1978-83), Orange County Bar Assn., Los Angeles Trial Lawyers Assn., Orange County Trial Lawyers Assn., Calif. Trial Lawyers Assn., Assn. Trial Lawyers Am. Office: Fisher Profl Bldg 630 S El Camino Real San Clemente CA 92672-4200 Fax: 949-498-2673. E-mail: mrfisher@sbcglobal.net.

FISHER, NANCY, writer, producer, director; b. Oct. 21; d. Seymour and Tema Fisher; 1 child, Sarah Olivia. BA, Barnard Coll. Creative group head Benton & Bowles Advt., London, McCann Erickson Advt., N.Y.C.; creative dir. Norman, Craig & Kummel Advt., N.Y.C.; pres. Nancy Fisher Inc., N.Y.C., 1981—2002, Creative Programming Inc., N.Y.C., 1981-89. Author: Vital Parts, 1993, Side Effects, 1994, Special Treatment, 1996, Code Red, 1998, Code Blue, 2000; creator, writer, prodr. (TV series) Womanwatch, 1982—89, Celebrity Chefs, 1983—89, (numerous home video cassettes including) Look Mom, I'm Fishing (Parents Choice award), The Annapolis Book of Seamanship Video Series (Cindy award), The Christmas Carol Video, Video Dog, Video Cat, Video Baby; prodr.: (TV series) The Real Bottom Line. Sr. v.p., dir. comm. The Ch. Pension Group, N.Y.C., 2000—. Recipient 5 broadcast awards Network Documentary Series. Mem. Dirs. Guild Am., Authors Guild.

FISHER, NANCY DEBUTTS, library director; b. Pitts., Apr. 10, 1945; d. Jacob John DeButts and Marie Christine Grills; m. Bruce C. Fisher, May 29, 1971. BS, Cleve. State U., 1968; MSLS, Case Western Res. U., 1973. Reference libr. Cleveland Heights-University Heights Pub. Libr., 1968-79; mgr. Beachwood (Ohio) br. Cuyahoga County Pub. Libr., 1980-90; dir. Wickliffe (Ohio) Pub. Libr., 1990—. Mem. adv. coun. Wickliffe United Way, 1991—2001; key communicator Wickliffe City Schs., 1992; mem. comm. com. Lake County United Way, 2002—, mem. cabinet, 2003; mem. Wickliffe Cmty. Adv. Panel, 1995—; dir. Leadership Lake County, 2003; bd. dirs. Wickliffe Civic Ctr., Inc., 1999—; mem. adv. com. Holden Aboretum Warren H. Corning Libr., 1999—2002; mem. alumni planning com. Case Western Res. U. Libr. Sci., 1997—; mem. cmty. adv. panel Lake Hosp. Sys., 1997—, women's health adv. bd., 1999—. Mem.: ALA, Cleve. Area Met. Libr. Sys. (bd. dirs. 1994—96, mem. pers. com. 2003—), Ohio Libr. Coun., Lake County C. of C. Bd., Wickliffe C. of C. (v.p. 1998—99, pres. 2001—03, Civic Leader of Yr. 1999), Rotary (pres. 1992—94, cmty. adv. panel 1995—). Home: 939 Stuart Dr South Euclid OH 44121-3425 Office: Wickliffe Pub Libr 1713 Lincoln Rd Wickliffe OH 44092-2499 E-mail: fisherna@wickliffe.lib.oh.us.

FISHER, NEAL FLOYD, religious organization administrator; b. Washington, Ind., Apr. 4, 1936; s. Floyd Russell and Florence Alice (Williams) F.; m. Ila Alexander, Aug. 18, 1957; children: Edwin Kirk, Julia Bryn. AB, DePauw U., 1957, LHD (hon.), 1982; MDiv, Boston U., 1960, PhD, 1966; STD, MacMurray Coll., Jacksonville, Ill., 1991; DD, Coe Coll., 1994. Ordained to ministry United Meth. Ch., 1958; pastor 1st United Meth. Ch., Revere, Mass., 1960-63, North Andover, Mass., 1963-68; planning assoc. United Meth. Bd. Global Ministries, N.Y.C., 1968-73, dir. planning, 1973-77; assoc. dean, asst. prof. theology and society Boston U. Sch. Theology, 1977-80; pres., prof. theology and society Garrett-Evang. Theol. Sem., Evanston, Ill., 1980-2001, pres. emeritus, sr. scholar, 2001—. Mendenhall lectr. DePauw U., Greencastle, Ind., 1982, Willson lectr., Nashville, 1983, Voigt lectr. McKendree Coll., 1984, McKendree Blair lectr. MacMurray Coll., 1986, Henry Martin Loud lectr. U. Mich., Ann Arbor, 1987; Wright lectr. Morningside Coll., 1991, Bransford lectr., 1999; chaplain, preacher, Chautauqua, N.Y., 1984, 88, Lakeside, Ohio, 1996; mem. theol. edn. commn. United Meth. Ch., 1992-2000, former mem. univ. senate; mem. bd. of ordained ministry No. Ill. Conf. United Meth. Ch.; chmn. com. on acad. affairs DePauw U. Bd. Trustees. Author: Parables of Jesus: Glimpses of the New Age, 1979, rev. edit., 1990, Context for Discovery, 1980, Parables of Jesus: Glimpses of God's Reign, 1990; contbg. editor: Truth and Tradition: A Conversation about the Future of United Methodist Theological Education, 1995. Trustee DePauw U., Greencastle, Ind., 1996-2000; mem. bd. visitors Boston U. Sch. Theology, 2002—. Recipient Disting. Alumnus award Boston U. Sch. Theology, 1985, Disting. Alumni citation DePauw U., 1993; Jacob Sleeper fellow, 1960-61. Mem. Assn. United Meth. Scis., Assn. Chgo. Theol. Schs. (pres. 1985-87, 95-97). Mem. United Methodist Ch. Home: 2008 Elmore Pond Road Wolcott VT 05680 E-mail: nfisher@nwu.edu.

FISHER, PAUL CARY, writing supplies company executive; b. Lebanon, Kans., Oct. 10, 1913; s. Carey A. Fisher and Alice Bales-Fisher; children: Terry Hough, Cary Fisher, Pomm Hepner, Marteen Moore, Morgan Fisher, Scott Fisher. BS, Kans. State U., 1939. Gen. mgr. Butter-Nut Bakery, Cedar Rapids, Iowa, 1936-38, Aetna Ball Bearing Co., Chgo., 1952-45; pres. Fisher-Armour Mfg. Co., Chgo., 1945-50; owner Fisher Pen Co., Boulder City, Nev., 1950—. Dem. presdl. candidate, N.H. Primary, 1960. Named Small Bus. Person of Yr., State of Nev., U.S. Small Bus. Adminstrn., 1980, Exporter of Yr., Gov.'s Office State of Nev., 1995, 97, Inventor of Yr. Nev. Tech. Coun., 1998, Pres.'s Inventor award, Nev. Desert Rsch., 2001. Mem. Boulder city Rotary, Phi Kappa Phi. Achievements include invention of pressurized space pen for NASA. Avocations: handball, tennis, chess. Office: Fisher Pen Co 711 Yucca St Boulder City NV 89005-1905

FISHER, PETER R. federal agency administrator; b. 1956; 2 children. BA in History, Harvard U., 1980, JD, 1985. Mgr. sys. open market acct. Fed. Open Market Com.; exec. v.p. Fed. Res. Bank N.Y.; under sec. U.S. Treasury for Domestic Fin., Washington, 2001—, sr. advisor to treas. sec., 2001—, dep. sec. all aspects domestic fin., 2001. Bd. dirs. Securities Investor Protection Corp.; chair Advanced Counterfeit Deterrence Steering Com.*

FISHER, PHILIP CHAPIN, physicist; b. Rochester, N.Y., Aug. 3, 1926; s. Raymond Castle and Alice Chapin (Coggins) Fisher; m. Virginia Ruffner Ball, Aug. 18, 1948; 1 child, Christine Chapin Fisher Latham. BS in Physics, U. Rochester, 1947; MS in Physics, U. Ill., 1948, PhD in Physics, 1953. Staff mem. Los Alamos (N.Mex.) Sci. Lab., 1953-59; cons. scientist phys. sci. lab. Lockheed Missiles & Space Co., Palo Alto, Calif., 1959-74; physicist Ruffner Assocs., Menlo Park, Calif., 1975-77, 82-94; sr. physicist Rasor Assocs., Mountain View, Calif., 1976-77; sensor engring. mgr. Gas Tech, Inc., Newark, Calif., 1977-91; physicist Ruffner Assocs., Inc., Santa Fe, 1995—. Cons. Los Alamos Sci. Lab., 1959—64. Contbr. articles to profl. jours. Mem.: IEEE, Soc. Photo-Optical Instrumentation Engrs., Internat. Astron. Union, Am. Astron. Soc., Am. Phys. Soc., Am. Geophys. Union, Sigma Xi. Achievements include postulation and experimental proof that the apparently brightest non-solar x-ray sources would be in our galaxy and at low galactic latitude. Office: Ruffner Assocs Inc PO Box 1867 Santa Fe NM 87504-1867 E-mail: pcfisher@earthlink.net.

FISHER, PIERRE JAMES, JR., physician; b. Chgo., Oct. 29, 1931; s. Pierre James and Evelyn (Trevithick) F.; m. Carol Ann Walton, Mar. 16, 1951; children: James Walton, David Alan, Steven Edward, Teresa Ann. Student, Taylor U., 1949-51, Ball State U., 1951-52; MD, Ind. U., 1956. Diplomate Am. Bd. Surgery. Intern U.S. Naval Hosp., San Diego, 1956-57, resident in surgery, 1957-61; pvt. practice specializing in surgery Surgeons Inc., Marion, Ind., 1965—, pres., 1977—; mem. staff Marion Gen. Hosp., chief staff, 1970. Trustee Meth. Hosp., Indpls., 1972-94. Served with USN, 1956-65. Recipient Physicians Recognition award AMA, 1974, 77, 80, 83, 89; commd. Ky. Col., Gov. Ky., 1997. Fellow ACS; mem. AMA, Grant County Med. Soc. (pres. 1980),

Marion Area C. of C. (v.p. 1979-81), N.Am. Med. Golf Assn. (v.p. 1989-90, pres. 1991-93), Rotary (pres. Marion 1983-84, Dist. 656 Disting. Svc. award 1989), Kingsway Country Club (bd. dirs., pres. 1997-99). Methodist. Home: 11250 SW Essex Dr Lake Suzy FL 34269 Office: Surgeons Inc 330 N Wabash Ave Ste 450 Marion IN 46952-2600

FISHER, RAYMOND CORLEY, judge; b. Oakland, Calif., July 12, 1939; s. Raymond Henry and Mary Elizabeth (Corley) Fisher; m. Nancy Leigh Fairchilds, Jan. 22, 1961; children: Jeffrey, Amy. BA, U. Calif., Santa Barbara, 1961; LLB, Stanford U., 1966. Bar: Calif. 1967, U.S. Supreme Ct. 1967. Law clk. to Hon. J. Skelly Wright U.S. Ct. Appeals (D.C. cir.), Washington, 1966—67; law clk. to Hon. William J. Brennan U.S. Supreme Ct., Washington, 1967—68; ptnr. Tuttle & Taylor, L.A., L.A., 1968—88, Heller, Ehrman, White & McAuliffe, L.A., 1988—97; assoc. atty. gen. U.S. Dept. of Justice, Washington, 1997—99; judge U.S. Ct. Appeals (9th cir.), 1999—. Pres.: Stanford Law Rev., 1965—66. Dir. Constl. Rights Found., L.A., 1978—, pres., 1983—87, L.A. City Bd. Civil Svc. Commn., 1987—88; dep. gen. counsel Christopher Commn., L.A., 1991—92; pres. L.A. City Bd. Police Commrs., 1996—97; dir. Western Justice Ctr. Found., 2000—; spl. asst. to Gov. of Calif., 1975. With USAR, 1957—64. Fellow: Am. Bar Found., Am. Coll. Trial Lawyers; mem.: ABA, Am. Law Inst., L.A. County Bar Assn., Calif. State Bar, Fed. Bar Assn. (exec. com. 1990—96), Chancery Club, Order of Coif. Office: US Ct Appeals 125 S Grand Ave Rm 400 Pasadena CA 91105

FISHER, RICHARD, federal agency administrator; BS in Math., Grinnell Coll., 1961; PhD in Astrophysics, U. Colo., 1965. Mem. staff Inst. Astronomy U. Hawaii; staff astrophysicist USAF Sacramento Peak Obs.; sr. scientist Nat. Ctr. Astrospheric Rsch., Boulder, Colo.; project mgr., prin. investogator HAO; head solar physics br. Goddard Space Flight Ctr., 1991; sr. project scientist Living with A Star Project, chief lab. astronomy and solar physics NASA, dir. sun-earth connection divsn. Office Space Sci., 2002. Mem.: Phi Beta Kappa. Office: NASA Hdqrs Mail Code S 300 E St SW Washington DC 20546

FISHER, RICHARD B. investment banker; b. Phila., July 21, 1936; s. Ernest W. and Doris Virginia (Rans) F.; m. Emily Hargroves, Sept. 7, 1957 (div. 1994); children: R. Britton, Catherine Curtis, Alexander Dylan; m. Jeanne M. Donovan, May 31, 1997. AB, Princeton U., 1957; MBA, Harvard U., 1962. Mng. dir. Morgan Stanley & Co., Inc., N.Y.C., 1970—, pres., 1984-91, chmn., 1990-97; chmn. exec. com. Morgan Stanley Dean Witter & Co., N.Y.C., 1997-2000, chmn. emeritus, 2000—. Trustee Bard Coll.; chmn. Rockefeller U., Bklyn. Acad. of Music Endowment Trust, Urban Inst. Scholar Baker scholar with high distinction. Mem. Nat. Golf Links, Blind Brook Club, Lyford Cay Club, Mid Ocean Club, Meadow Brook Club, Golf Club Purchase, Waccabuc Country Club. Office: Morgan Stanley & Co 1221 Ave of Ams 30th Fl New York NY 10020

FISHER, RICHARD FORREST, research scientist, department chairman; b. Champaign, Ill., May 15, 1941; S. Richard Forrest Fisher and Hannah Elizabeth Ponath; m. Karen Dangerfield, Sept. 4, 1959; children: William Forrest, Marilu, Kevin Royden. BS, U. Ill., 1963; MS, Cornell U., 1967, PhD, 1968. Rsch. scientist Can. Forestry Svc., Sault Sainte Marie, Ont., 1968-69; asst. prof. forestry U. Ill., Urbana, 1969-72; assoc. prof. U. Toronto, Ont., 1972-77; prof. U. Fla., Gainesville, 1977-82; prof., head dept. forest resources Utah State U., Logan, 1982-90; prof., head dept. forest sci. Tex. A&M U., 1990-96, prof., 1996-99; dir. rsch. Temple-Inland, Diboll, Tex., 1999—. Author: (with others) Ecology and Management of Forest Soil, 3d edit.; contbr. articles to profl. jours. Fellow Soc. Am. Foresters, Soil Sci. Soc. Am. (co-editor in chief Forest Ecology and Mgmt.); mem. Internat. Soc. Tropical Foresters, Ecol. Soc. Am., Nat. Assn. Profl. Forestry Schs. and Colls. (pres. 1994-96), Internat. Assn. Round Dance Tchrs. (gen. chmn. 1997-99). Democrat. Avocations: round dance cuer, tchr. Home: 1004 Augusta Dr Lufkin TX 75901-7412 Office: Temple-Inland Forest PO Drawer N Diboll TX 75941 E-mail: dfisher@templeinland.com.

FISHER, RICHARD WELTON, investor, ambassador; b. L.A., Mar. 18, 1949; s. Leslie Welton and Magnhild (Andersen) F.; m. Nancy Collins, Sept. 8, 1973; children: Andersen, Alison, James, Texana. BA cum laude, Harvard U., 1971; student, Oxford (Eng.) U., 1972-73; MBA, Stanford U., 1975. Asst. to Robert Roosa Brown Bros. Harriman & Co., N.Y.C., 1975-77, sr. mgr., 1983-87; exec. asst. to sec. U.S. Treasury, Washington, 1977-79; mng. ptnr. Fisher Capital Mgmt., Dallas, 1987-98, Fisher Ewing Ptnrs. (Valve Ptnrs., Ltd.), Dallas, 1989-98; dep. U.S. trade rep. Exec. Office of the Pres., Washington, 1998-2001; mng. ptnr. Kissinger McLarty Assocs., Washington, 2002—. Chmn. Stanford U. Sch. Bus. Trust, Palo Alto, Calif., 1982-84; adj. prof. L.B.J. Sch., U. Tex., 1996-98; Weatherhead fellow Harvard U., 2001; mem. Latin Am. strategy Bd. Hicks, Muse, Inc. Bd. dirs., mem. exec. com. Dallas Mus. Art, 1985-89; bd. dirs. Goodwill Industries Dallas, 1989-98, treas., 1991-93, chmn., 1993-95; bd. dirs. Boys Club Dallas, 1984-84, Dallas Assembly, 1983-97, Russian Am. Enterprise Fund, 1993-98; active Dallas Com. Fgn. Rels., chmn., 1987-98; trustee Brookings Instn., 2001—, Eisenhower Fellowships, 2001—, Pacific Coun., 2002—; mem. Trilateral Commn., 2002—; Dem. candidate U.S. Senate, 1994. Decorated gran oficial Order of Bernardo O'Higgins (Chile); U.S.-Japan leadership fellow Japan Soc., 1989; recipient Outstanding Achievement award Stanford U. Assocs., 1986; named one of 10 Rising Stars of Tex., Tex. Bus. Mag., 1988; hon. fellow Hertford Coll., Oxford U., 2002; named Admiral of Tex. Navy, 1987. Fellow Am. Acad. Arts and Scis.; mem. Inst. Ams. (chmn. 1987-93), Inter-Am. Dialogue (exec. com. 1992), Am. Coun. on Germany (bd. dirs. 1985-94), Philos. Soc. Tex., Harvard Club, Petroleum Club, Met. Club (Washington). Presbyterian. Office: Fisher Family Fund 2200 Ross Ave Ste 4600W Dallas TX 75201-2790

FISHER, ROBERT, gastroenterologist, health facility administrator; b. Bklyn., July 28, 1939; married. BSE, Princeton U., 1960; MD, U. Pa., 1964. Intern Chgo. Wesley Meml. Hosp., 1964-65; resident in internal meedicine Temple U. Hosp., Phila., 1967-70; fellow in gastroenterology Hosp. U. Pa., 1970-72; from asst. prof. to assoc. prof. Temple U. Sch. Medicine, 1972-80, prof. medicine, 1980—; dir. Functional Gastrointestinal Disease Ctr. Temple U. Hosp., Phila., 1984—, chief gastroenterology sect., 1985—. Mem. Am. Coll. Gastroenterology, Am. Gastroent. Assn., Am. Soc. Gastrointestinal Endoscopy, Am. Fedn. Clin. Rsch., Rsch. Soc. Alcoholism. Office: Temple Univ 3400 N Broad St Philadelphia PA 19140-5104

FISHER, ROBERT ALAN, laser physicist; b. Berkeley, Calif., Apr. 19, 1943; s. Leon Harold and Phyllis (Kahn) F.; children: Andrew Leon, Derek Martin. AB, U. Calif., Berkeley, 1965, MA, 1967, PhD, 1971. Programmer Stanford (Calif.) linear accelerator Stanford U., Stanford University, 1965; staff mem. Granger Assocs., Palo Alto, Calif., 1966; lectr. U. Calif., Davis, 1972-74; physicist Lawrence Livermore Lab., Calif., 1971-74; laser physicist Los Alamos (N.Mex.) Nat. Lab., 1974-86. Cons. R.A. Fisher Assocs., Santa Fe, 1986—; instr. Engring. Tech., Inc., 1982—; mem. Air Force ABCD Panel, 1982; program com. mem. Internat. Quantum Electronics Conf., 1982, 86; vice chmn. Gordon Conf. on Lasers and Non-linear Optics, 1981; chmn. Soc. Photo-Optical Instrumentation Engrs. Conf. on Optical Phase Conjugation/Beam Combining/Diagnostics, 1987—; mem. Air Force Red Team for Space-Based Laser, 1983—86, HEDS II SDI Red Team, 1986, U.S. Ballistic Missile Office Options Team, 1986; mem. secretariat SDI Red/Blue Sensor Teams, 1986, SDI GBL Red/Blue Team Interaction, 1987—88; mem. architecture panel SDI SDS Phase I, 1990, Air Force Laser 21 Working Group, 1990, Program Com. CLEO Conf., 2003—04. Assoc. editor Optics Letters, 1984-86, Applied Optics, 1984-91, Topical Edit. Optics Letters, 2002—; editor: Optical Phase Conjugation, 1973; contbr. articles to profl. jours. Vol. coach elem. sch. chess team Pojoaque Elem. Sch. (winner nat. elem. championship 1984), Santa Fe, 1984. Fellow Optical Soc. Am. (guest editor jour. spl. issue on optical phase conjugation, Excellence award, 2003), SPIE (bd. dirs. 2002—); mem. IEEE (sr.), Scholarship Com., 2001-2003. Avocations: restoring old houses, skiing, music. Home and Office: 2996 Plaza Blanca Santa Fe NM 87507-5340

FISHER, ROBERT BRUCE, priest; b. Paragould, Ark., Feb. 6, 1937; s. Lawrence Bruce Fisher and Georgia M. (Paris) Kasper. BA, Divine Word Seminary, Techny, Ill., 1961, MA, 1965; STB, STL, Gregorian Univ., Rome, 1966; STD, Pont. Ateneo di Sant' Anselmo, Rome, 1969. Ordained priest Roman Cath. Ch., 1965. Adminstrv. attache Nunciature of Holy See, Accra, Ghana, 1982-83; pastor Good Shepherd Ch., Tema, Ghana, 1984-86; asst. pastor St. Matthias Ch., New Orleans, 1990-94; pastor St. Martin de Porres Ch., Prairie View, 1996-2000, St. Anthony's Ch., Lafayette, La., 2000—03, St. Bartholomew Ch., Little Rock, 2003—. Asst. prof. Xavier U., New Orleans, 1988-95; dir. studies A. Tolton House of Studies, New Orleans, 1991-96; dist. superior Divine Word Soc. New Orleans, 1990-96; promoter New African Cinema film series; instr. in ethics and critical thinking of Prairie View Tex. A&M U., 1998-2000; adj. prof. Prairie View A&M U., 1997-2000. Author: West African Religious Traditions: Focus on the Akan of Ghana, 1998; editor: (liturgical ordo) Ordo for the Philippines, 1972. Co-chmn. Cath. Returnee Crisis Com., Accra, 1982-83; mem. Cmty. Oriented Govt. Program, Lafayette.. Mem. Am. Soc. Missiology, Coll. Theology Soc., Am. Acad. Religion, KC (chaplain Met. chpt. 1993-96), African Assn. for Study of Religions, Divine Word Soc. (dist. coun.). Democrat. E-mail: africoco@aol.com.

FISHER, ROBERT CHARLES HARU, publishing company executive, editor; b. Burlington, Iowa, Mar. 3, 1930; s. Ray Erwin and Blanche Columbia (Brolin) Fisher. BA cum laude, Harvard U., 1955; postgrad., Columbia U. Law Sch., 1955-56, Tokyo U., 1957-59. Analyst, adjutant gen's. office U.S. Army, Kansas City, Mo., 1949-50, Washington, 1950-51, adv. Prime Minister Takeo Miki of Japan, 1957-64; Far Eastern rep. Fodor Travel Guides, Tokyo, 1959-64, exec. editor N.Y.C., 1964 66, 75-77, exec. v.p., 1975-77, pres., 1977-80, exec. editor, 1966-74; v.p. David McKay Co., N.Y.C., 1976-80; pres. Fisher Travel Guides, 1980-88; gen. editor Crown Insider's Travel Guides, 1988-89; editl. dir. Gault Millau Guides, 1989-90; cons. Simon & Schuster, N.Y.C., 1990-92; editl. dir. Maco Comm., N.Y.C., 1992-94; exec. editor Arthur Frommer, Inc., N.Y.C., 1995—2000; exec. editor, columnist www.frommers.com, N.Y.C., 2000—. Founder, dir. Kansas City Open Forum, 1949—50; bd. dirs. Internat. Assn. Med. Assistance to Travelers, 1972—, v.p., 1985—; chmn. Hotel and Restaurant Unsafe Food Labeling Action com., 1995—; pres. Fisher Publs. Inc., 1997—. Author: Picasso, 1967, Klee, 1967, Guide to Japan, 1981, Insider's Guide to Japan, 1986; co-author: Off-Season Riviera, 1997, Off-Season London, 1999. Served with CIC U.S. Army, 1952—54, Korea. Grantee for study in Japan, Balt. Scholarship Fund, 1956—59. Mem.: Soc. Am. Travel Writers Found. (pres. 1985—90), Brit. Guild Travel Writers (vice-chmn. 1970—71), N.Y. Travel Writers Assn. (pres. 1979—81), Soc. Am. Travel Writers (dir. 1978—80, v.p. 1981—83, pres. 1983—84), Internat. House of Japan, Japan Soc.N.Y., Am. Club of Japan, Harvard Club N.Y.C. E-mail: BobHaru@aol.com.

FISHER, ROBERT DALE, stockbroker, retired naval officer; b. Memphis, July 30, 1924; s. Hollis Welton and Anna Sue (Parrish) F.; m. Joy Lee Chandler, Mar. 30, 1946. BS, Am. U., 1957. Commd. ensign USN, 1944, advanced through grades to comdr., 1963; tng. officer Polaris Missile program, 1955-58, comdr. destroyer, 1959-61, ret., 1963; stockbroker, 1963—; v.p. investments Smith Barney, Washington, 1979—. Mem. Mil. Order Carabao, Kiwanis (pres. Falls Church, Va. 1969, McLean, Va. 1979-80), Nat. Capital Economists Club, Army-Navy Club, Masons, Shriners, Jesters. Republican. Methodist. Home: 6033 Chesterbrook Rd Mc Lean VA 22101-3213 Office: 1850 K St NW Ste 900 Washington DC 20006-2222 E-mail: robert.d.fisher@rssmb.com.

FISHER, ROBERT HENRI, physician; b. Auburn, NY, Jan. 5, 1955; s. Egon Fisher; children: Laura, Jessica, Deborah. BA, Haverford Coll., 1977; MD, U. Rochester, 1981; MS in Med. Adminstrn., U. Wis., 2000. Med. resident Washington U., St. Louis, 1981-84; instr. of medicine Deaconess Hosp., St. Louis, 1984-85; fellow clin. immunology Johns Hopkins U., Balt., 1985-88; asst. prof. medicine East Carolina U. Sch. Medicine, Greenville, N.C., 1988-93, Med. Coll. Wis., Milw., 1993-95; dir. allergy sect. Med. Assocs. Health Ctr., Menomonee Falls, Wis., 1995-2001; v.p. med. affairs Comty. Meml. Hosp., Menomonee Falls, Wis., 2001—. Chmn. subspecialty medicine Med. Assn. Health Ctrs., 1997—2001; clin. asst. prof. Med. Coll. of Wis., 1995—. Pres. Allergy Rsch. and Care, S.C. Rsch. grantee Am. Lung Assn. Wis., 1994-96; Davis fellow Am. Lung Assn. N.C., 1989-90. Fellow Am. Coll. Allergy and Immunology, Am. Acad. Allergy and Immunology; mem. ACP, Am. Thoracic Soc., Wis. State Med. Soc. (CME coun. 2000—), Wis. Hosp. Assn. (profl. coun.). Achievements include 2 patents for method of treating asthma using IL-8 and other cytokines; discovered that a group of protein cytokines improve bronchial hyperresponsivess and symptoms associated with asthma. Office: Comty Meml Hosp W 180 N8085 Town Hall Rd Menomonee Falls WI 53051 Fax: 262-257-2620. E-mail: rfisher7@wi.rr.com.

FISHER, ROBERT I. lawyer; b. Bklyn., July 10, 1939; s. Sidney B. and Jeanette (Talisman) F.; m. Debra Kram Fisher, June 30, 1974; children: Daniel I., Elizabeth R. BA, Columbia U., 1960; JD cum laude, Harvard U., 1963; LLM, N.Y.U., 1967. Bar: N.Y. 1964. Assoc. Dewey, Ballantine, Bushby, Palmer & Wood, N.Y.C., 1964-67, Sullivan & Cromwell, N.Y.C., 1967-72; ptnr. Greenbaum, Wolff & Ernst, N.Y.C., 1972—82, Katten Muchin Zavis Roseman, N.Y.C., 1982—. Lectr. Practicing Law Inst. Fulbright fellow, Israel, 1963-64. Mem. ABA, N.Y. State Assn., Assn. Bar. City of N.Y., Home: 150 Factory Pond Rd Locust Valley NY 11560-1416 Office: Katten Muchin Zavis Rosenman 575 Madison Ave Fl 11 New York NY 10022-2585 E-mail: robert.fisher@kmzr.com.

FISHER, ROBERT LLOYD, retired geologist, retired oceanographer; b. Alhambra, Calif., Aug. 19, 1925; s. Howard Bassett and Clara Elizabeth (Michalek) Fisher; m. Shirley Ann Chapman, Aug. 6, 1948 (div. 1968); 1 child, Carlos Andrew; m. Sarah Coburn Hills, July 18, 1986. BS in Sci., Calif. Inst. Tech., 1949; MS in Marine Geology, UCLA-SIO, La Jolla, 1953, PhD in Oceanography, 1957. Geologist U.S. Geol. Survey, St. Lawrence Island, Alaska, 1949; rsch. geologist Scripps Inst. Oceanography, U. Calif., San Diego, 1950-91, leader 16 maj. deep-sea oceanographic expdns., 1951-84, rsch. geologist emeritus, 1991—, assoc. dir., 1974-80. Expert, adviser, mem., chmn. U.S. and fgn. sci. panels and coms. UNESCO, Paris, Monaco, Washington, 1959—. Contbr. articles to profl. jours.; editor: Jour. Geophys. Rsch., others. With USN, 1944—46, PTO. Grantee, NSF, Office Naval Rsch., 1954—88. Fellow: Geol. Soc. Am., Am. Geophys. Union, Explorers Club (hon.); mem.: Oceanography Soc., Challenger Soc. U.K. (hon.), Sigma Xi. Avocations: travel, gardening, history (mainly marine). Office: U Calif San Diego Scripps Inst Oceanography Geosci Rsch Divsn La Jolla CA 92093-0220

FISHER, ROBERT MORTON, foundation administrator, university administrator; b. St. Paul, Minn., Oct. 15, 1938; s. S.S. and Jean Fisher; m. Elinor C. Schectman, June 19, 1960; children: Laurie, Jonathan. AB magna cum laude, Harvard Coll., 1960; JD, Harvard U., 1963; PhD, London Sch. Econs, Polit. Sci., 1967; LLD, West Coast U., L.A., 1981; DHL, Profl. Sch. Psychology, San Francisco, 1986; DPS, John F. Kennedy U., Orinda, Calif., 1988. Rsch. assoc. Mass. Mental Health Ctr., Cambridge, 1957-62; rsch. asst. Ctr. Study Juvenile Delinquency, Cambridge, 1961-63; spl. asst. to chief psychologist British Prison Dept. Home Office, London, 1963-67; prof. Sch. Criminology U. Calif., Berkeley, 1965-71; profl. race car driver, 1972-77; pres. John F. Kennedy U., Orinda, Calif., 1974-85; exec. dir. 92d St. YMHA, N.Y.C., 1984-85; dir., CEO The San Francisco Found., 1987-97. Mayor, councilman Lafayette, Calif., 1968-76; mem. Minn. and Calif. Bar Specialty: charitable gift planning; CEO Fisher Cos., 1997-2003; exec. dir. Alonzo King's Line Ballet, 2002—. Scholar-in-residence Rockefeller Found., Bellagio, 1994; Polit. Sci. vis. fellow London Sch. Econs. and Polit. Sci., 1994; named Outstanding Fundraising Exec. Nat. Soc. Fund Raising Execs. Home and Office: 85 Southwood Dr Orinda CA 94563-3026

FISHER, ROBERT PERRY, health effects scientist; b. Houston, May 30, 1945; s. George Robert and Brownie (Perry) F.; m. Cari Patrice Guritz, Sept. 6, 1969; children; William Robert, Jay Kenneth. BS in Chemistry cum laude, Centenary Coll., 1967; PhD in Analytical Chemistry, U. Fla., 1971. Postdoctoral rsch. assoc., asst. prof. U. Fla., Gainesville, 1971-72; rsch. chemist Nat. Coun. for Air and Stream Improvement, Gainesville, 1972-83, investigative programs mgr., 1983-88, regional mgr., 1988-92, program dir., 1992-95, v.p., 1995—. Chmn. methods com. APHA-Standard Methods, Washington, 1980—; co-chair, mem. tech. com. EPA Gulf of Mexico Program, 1999—. Contbr. articles to Analytical Chemistry, Jour. Tech. Assn. Pulp and Paper Industry, Pulp and Paper Canada and chpt. to ASTM Quality Assurance Monitoring. Leader Cub Scouts Boy Scouts Am., Gainesville, 1985—. Recipient Teaching award DuPont, U. Fla., 1969. Fellow Am. Inst. Chemists (Outstanding Chemistry Student 1967), Mem. ASTM (methods com. 1980—), Am. Chem. Soc., Am. Indsl. Hygiene Assn. Achievements include methodology for controlling sulfur gas releases from kraft pulp mills; 2 patents for methods of generating chlorine dioxide gas. Office: Nat Coun Air/Stream Improve PO Box 13318 Research Triangle Park NC 27709 E-mail: rfisher@ncasi.org.

FISHER, ROBERT SCOTT, lawyer; b. Detroit, July 16, 1960; s. Alvin Fisher and Beverly (Raider) Levin. BA, U. Mich., 1982; JD, U. Colo., 1985. Bar: Colo. 1985, U.S. Dist. Ct. Colo. 1985, Mich. 1987, U.S. Ct. Appeals (10th cir.) 1989, U.S. Supreme Ct. 1989, U.S. Ct. Appeals (D.C. cir.) 1999. Prin. Law Office of Robert S. Fisher, Colorado Springs, Colo., 1985—. Mem. Colo. Bar Assn., El Paso County Bar Assn., Criminal Def. Bar Assn., Phi Delta Phi. Avocations: scuba diving, ice hockey, skiing, racquetball. Home: 5185 Engleman Ct Colorado Springs CO 80906 Office: 924 N Wahsatch Ave Colorado Springs CO 80903-2915

FISHER, ROBERT WARREN, accountant; b. Springfield, Ohio, Sept. 17, 1952; s. Carl Arthur and Frances (Runyan) E.; m. Elizabeth Ann Davies, Dec. 11, 1982; children: Katherine Marie, Anne Margaret, Andrew Robert, David Carl. BA, Wittenberg U., 1974; MBA, U. Toledo, 1975. CPA; registered investment advisor; gen. securities rep.; lic. reinsurance. Mgr., acct. Price Waterhouse, Battle Creek, Mich., 1975-83, Deloitte, Haskins & Sells, Appleton, Wis., 1983-84; ptnr., acct. Wojahn & Fisher, S.C., Appleton, 1984-85; shareholder, v.p. Schumaker, Romenesko & Assocs., Appleton, 1985-97; pres., CEO Trade Winds Pizza, LLC, 1997-2000; fin. advisor, retirement planning specialist Morgan Stanley, 2000—. Treas., bd. dirs. Wis. Bus. Devel. Fin. Corp., Madison, 1983—; ind. cons. to CPA firms. Mem. fin. com. St. Mary's Ch., 1986—, Appleton Cath. Edn. System, 1986-90; mem. com. St. Paul Home. Mem. AICPA (PCPS peer rev. com. 1991-95), Wis. Soc. CPAs (exec. com., quality rev. com. 1989-95, assn. chmn. 1991, chmn. 1992-94), Nat. Assn. Accts. (v.p. 1982), Appleton C. of C. (small bus. com. 1984-94), Riverview Country Club (bd. dirs. 1986-96, treas. 1987-90, v.p. 1990-93, pres. 1993-94), KC, Rotary (membership dir. 1986, treas. 1988-94, Paul Harris fellow 1995). Home: 1027 E Rustic Rd Appleton WI 54911-8547 Office: Morgan Stanley 4545 W College Ave Appleton WI 54914-3967 Personal E-mail: rbtwfisher@aol.com. Business E-Mail: bob.w.fisher@morganstanley.com.

FISHER, ROGER DUMMER, lawyer, educator, negotiation expert; b. Winnetka, Ill, May 28, 1922; s. Walter Taylor and Katharine (Dummer) F.; m. Caroline Speer, Sept. 18, 1948; children: Elliott Speer, Peter Ryerson. AB, Harvard U., 1943, LLB magna cum laude, 1948; LHD, Conn. Coll., 1994; DHL, Bay Path Coll., 1999. Bar: Mass. 1948, D.C. 1950. Asst. to gen. counsel, then asst. to dep. U.S. spl. rep. ECA, Paris, 1948-49; with firm Covington & Burling, Washington, 1950-56; asst. to solicitor gen. U.S., 1956-58; lectr. law Harvard Law Sch., Cambridge, Mass., 1958-60, prof. law, 1960-76, Samuel Williston prof. law, 1976-92, prof. emeritus, 1992—, dir. Harvard negotiation project, 1980—. Vis. prof. internat. rels. dept. London Sch. Econ., 1965-66; cons. pub. affairs editor WGBH-TV, Cambridge, 1969; tech. adivsor Found. for Internat. Conciliation, Geneva, 1984-87. Originator, 1st exec. editor: (pub. TV series) The Advocates, 1969-70, moderator, 1970-71; co-originator, exec. editor: (pub. TV series) Arabs and Israelis, 1975; author: International Conflict for Beginners, 1969, Dear Israelis, Dear Arabs, 1972, International Mediation: A Working Guide, 1978, International Crises and the Role of Law: Points of Choice, 1978, Improving Compliance with International Law, 1981; co-author: Getting to Yes: Negotiating Agreement Without Giving In, 1981, 2d edit., 1991, Getting Together: Building Relationships as We Negotiate, 1988, Beyond Machiavelli: Tools for Coping with Conflict, 1994, Getting Ready to Negotiate: The Getting to Yes Workbook, 1995, Coping with International Conflict: A Systematic Approach to Influence in International Negotiation, 1997, Getting It Done: How to Lead When You're Not in Charge, 1998; co-author, editor: International Conflict and Behavioral Science--The Craigville Papers, 1964; lectr., contbr. articles on internat. rels., negotiation, internat. law and TV. Bd. dir. Coun. for Livable World; trustee Hudson Inst., 1962-95. 1st lt. USAF, 1942-46. Recipient Sziland Peace award 1981, Peace Advocate award Lawyers Alliance for Nuclear Arms Control, 1988, Spl. Contbn. award Ctr. Pub. Resources, 1993, Steve Brutschè award Assn. Atty. Mediators, 1994, D'Alemberte-Raven Outstanding Achievements and Contributions to Dispute Resolution award, 1995, Honorato Vasquez Nat. Order Insignia Great Cross Republic Ecuador, 1999, helping settle in 1998 the fifty-yr. boundary war between Ecuador and Peru, Lifetime Achievement award Am. Coll. Civil Trial Mediators, 1999, Pioneer award New Eng. Soc. Profls. Dispute Reolution, 1999, St. Thomas More award St. Mary's U. Law Sch., 1999; named Guggenheim fellow 1965-66. Fellow Am. Acad. Arts and Sci.; mem. ABA (sect. dispute resolution), Am. Soc. Internat. Law (exec. coun. 1961-64, 66-69, v.p. 1982-84), Mass. Bar Assn., Commn. to Study Orgn. of Peace, Coun. Fgn. Rels., Phi Beta Kappa. Clubs: Metropolitan (Washington); Harvard (NYC). Office: Harvard U Law Sch Harvard Negotiation Project Pound Hall # 525 Cambridge MA 02138 also: Conflict Mgmt Group 9 Waterhouse St Cambridge MA 02138-3607

FISHER, SALLIE ANN, chemist; b. Green Bay, Wis., Sept. 10, 1923; BS in Chemistry, U. Wis., 1945, MS, 1946, PhD, 1949. Instr. Mt. Holyoke Coll., South Hadley, Mass., 1949-50; asst. prof. U. Minn., Duluth, 1950-51; group leader Rohm & Haas Co., Phila., 1951-60; assoc. dir. rsch. Robinette Rsch. Labs., Berwyn, Pa., 1960-72; v.p. Puricons, Inc., Malvern, Pa., 1972-76, pres., 1976—. Mem. adv. bd. Internat. Water Conf., Pitts., 1976-91, Reactive Polymers, Netherlands, 1982-88. Contbr. chpts. to books and over 100 articles to profl. jours. Recipient award of merit Engring. Soc. Western Pa., Pitts., 1984. Fellow ASTM (vice-chmn. D-19 1972-78, award of merit 1974, Max Hecht award com. D-19 1975); mem. Soc. Chem. Industry (Ion Exchg. award, separations sci. sect. 2000), Am. Chem. Soc., Am. Waterworks Assn. Achievements include patent for regeneration of anion resins; research in process for the concentration and recovery of uranium; devel. of methodology for analyis of resins for nuclear industry. Office: Puricons Inc 101 Quaker Ln Malvern PA 19355-2480

FISHER, SANDRA IRENE, English educator; b. Massillon, Ohio, Aug. 7, 1947; d. Samuel Arnold and Pearl Irene (Wood) Sells; m. John Jay Fisher, July 23, 1978; children: Melissa Pearl, Benjamen Jay. BA in Edn., Harding U., Searcy, Ark., 1969; postgrad., Ohio U., 1980—; M in Tchg. and Tech., Nova Southeastern U., 2001. Cert. tchr. English grades 7-12, health/phys. edn. K-12, Ohio. Tchr. phys. edn. and health Shenandoah H.S., Sarahsville, Ohio, 1969-72; tchr. English grades 9-12 Belmont Career Ctr., St. Clairsville, Ohio, 1973—. Advisor Lit. Club, St. Clairsville, 1978-97, Skills-USA Vocat. Indsl. Clubs Am.; sec.-treas. Barnesville (Ohio) Track/Cross Country Orgn., 1993-2001; sec., charter mem. Mt. Olivet Water Trustees, Barnesville, 1994-96. Martha Jennings scholar, 1979-80. Mem. Belmont County Lang. Arts Coun. (v.p. 1998-2003), Ohio Coun. Tchrs. English Lang., Iota Lambda Sigma. Mem. Ch. of Christ. Avocations: singing, writing, reading, floral designing, traveling. Home: 36815 Morse Ln Barnesville OH 43713-9456 Office: Belmont Career Ctr 110 Fox Shannon Pl Saint Clairsville OH 43950-8751

FISHER, SARAH YOUNG, money manager, financial adviser; b. York, Pa., Aug. 26, 1953; d. John Paine and Lois Ann (Barnette) Young; m. Dallas R. Fisher Jr., June 20, 1975; children: Robert J., Mary Catherine. BS, Juniata Coll., 1974; cert., Northwestern U., 1985; ChFC, Am. Coll., Bryn Mawr, Pa., 1991; MSFS, Am. Coll., 2003. CFP; enrolled agt. Adminstrv. asst. York City DA's Office, 1974-78; paralegal Laucks and Monroe, York, 1978; v.p., sr. trust officer Fulton Bank, Lancaster, Pa., 1978-91; pvt. practice fin. cons., 1991—. Trust officer Hershey (Pa.) Trust Co., 1992-95. Officer Rape Crisis Ctr. of York, 1975-78; mem. fin. com. First United Meth. Ch., Lancaster, 1987, YWCA; pres., mem. Lancaster County Day Care Ctr. Bd.; bd. dirs. Dutch coun. Boy Scouts Am.; mem. bd. pensions Ea. Conf. United Meth. Ch. Mem. Lancaster County Estate Planning Coun. (pres.). Republican. Methodist. Home: 723 Farmingdale Rd Lancaster PA 17603-2310 Office: Ste 220 2137 Embassy Dr Lancaster PA 17603 E-mail: sarahyoungfisher@aol.com.

FISHER, SEAN MICHAEL, archivist; b. Reading, Pa., Dec. 20, 1966; s. Ronald Allen Fisher and Charlene Ann Ernesto; m. Anne Elizabeth Macdonald, Aug. 29, 1992. BA, Dickinson Coll., 1985—89; MA in History (Hist. Adminstrn.), Northeastern U., 1989—91; MLS, Simmons Coll., 1993—95. Editl. asst. The New Eng. Quar., Boston, 1989—91; rsch. asst./book editor The Bostonian Soc., Boston, 1990—92; archivist Met. Dist. Com., Boston, 1992—. Co-editor (book) The Last Tenement. Mem.: Mass. Com. for the Preservation of Archtl. Records, Orgn. of Am. Historians, Soc. of Am. Archivists, New Eng.

Archivists. Democrat. Roman Catholic. Avocations: historical research, genealogy. Office: Met Dist Com 20 Somerset St Boston MA 02108 Personal E-mail: sean.m.fisher@att.net. E-mail: sean.fisher@state.ma.us.

FISHER, SEYMOUR, psychologist, educator; b. N.Y.C., Nov. 4, 1925; s. George and Fannie (Hesselson) F.; m. Carmen Eldridge, June 20, 1959; children: Mark, Andrew. BA, NYU, 1948; PhD, U. N.C., 1952; postgrad., Washington Sch. Psychiatry, 1954-55. Diplomate Am. Bd. Examiners in Psychol. Hypnosis. Clin. psychologist trainee VA Hosp., Roanoke, 1950, psychology trainee, 1952; intern Psychol. Clinic, U. N.C., Chapel Hill, 1950-51; supervising clin. psychologist Walter Reed Army Inst. Rsch., Washington, 1952-58; rsch. psychologist Psychopharmacology Svc. Ctr., NIMH, Bethesda, Md., 1958-60; chief spl. studies unit Psychopharmacology Rsch Br., NIMH, Bethesda, 1960-63; prof. psychiatry (psychology), dir. rsch. tng., dir. psychopharmacology lab., divsn. psychiatry Boston U. Sch. Medicine, 1963-78; prof. dept. psychiatry and behavioral scis., U. Tex. Med. Br., Galveston, 1978—, prof. emeritus, 2000—, assoc. chmn. for rsch., 1978-80, rsch. advisor to chmn. dept., 1980-91, dir. Ctr. for Medication Monitoring, 1987-2000. Vis. prof. Harvard U., Boston U., May to Nov., 1988; cons. NIMH, Chevy Chase, Md., 1964-66, mem. clin. psychopharmacology rsch. rev. com., 1973-77, mem. treatment devel. and assessment rsch. rev. com., 1979-83; cons. Office Naval Rsch., Washington, 1964-66, Mass. Dept. Mental Health, 1969-78, FDA, 1973-77; pres. Boston Mental Health Found., Inc., 1970-72; mem. Commn. on Cmty. Care of Mentally Ill, chmn. tech. com. Hogg Found., 1987-90, planning com. for 50th anniversary rsch. conf., 1988-89 Mem. editl. bd. Psychopharmacology Svc. Ctr. Bull., 1959-63; assoc. editor Psychol. Record, 1960-66; sr. editor vol. on clin. and biobehavioral aspects of cocaine, Oxford U. Press, 1987; mem. adv. bd. Internat. Jour. Methods Psychiatry, 1998-2000; contbr. numerous articles to profl. jours., chpts. in books. Recipient Disting. Alumnus award U. N.C., 1981, Donald E. Francke award for best paper Drug Info. Jour., 1987. Fellow APA (mem. exec. coun. divsn. psychopharmacology 1979-82), Am. Coll. Neuropsychcopharmacology (life, pres. 1984, asst. sec.-treas. 1974-77, chmn. hon. awards com. 1985-87, mem. other coms. 1973-87, emeritus), Soc. Clin. and Exptl. Hypnosis, Internat. Coll. Psychosomatic Medicine, Collegium Internat. Neuro-Psychopharmacologicum (emeritus); mem. Am. Psychopathol. Assn. (exec. coun. 1970-72), Psi Chi, Sigma Xi, Beta Lambda Sigma. Office: U Tex Med Br Dept Psych Galveston TX 77555-0431 E-mail: sfisher@utmb.edu. *The difference between intelligence and wisdom: intelligence is knowing that half of what you hear or read is garbage; wisdom is knowing which half.*

FISHER, SHARON MARY, musician; b. Orange, N.J., Sept. 29, 1944; d. Stanley and Veronica Shirley (Conway) Cozza; m. Andrew Fisher IV, Aug. 16, 1969. B Music Edn., Westminster Choir Coll., 1966; postgrad., Acad. Vocal Arts, 1966-67, Temple U., 1967-69. Cert. music tchr., N.J. Chorister Westminster Choir, Princeton, N.J., 1964-66; music tchr. Phila. Pub. Schs., 1967-69; sect. leader Phila. Boys' Choir, 1969; performer Manhattan Light Opera Co., N.Y., 1969-70; soprano soloist St. Peter's Ch., Morristown, N.J., 1975-79; organist Ch. of the Saviour, Denville, N.J., 1981-84; performer, lectr., 1986—. Performer Scottish Games, Millington, N.J. Albums include Concert Memories, 1991, Ireland: Land of Harp and Song, 1998. Grand marshal Holiday Parade, Denville C. of C., 1991. Recipient Marietta MacLeod award An Comunn Gaidhealach, 1989, Scots award Scottish Club of Twinstates, 1988-89, Harp/Voice trophy O'Carolan Harp Festival, Keadue, Ireland, 1988, Merit award Passaic County Irish Am. Cultural Soc., 1995. Mem. Clarsach Soc. (Edinburgh), Scottish Harp Soc. Am. (Ellice MacDonald grantee 1987), Am. Harp Soc., Nat. Assn. Tchrs. Singing, Nat. Assn. Pastoral Musicians, Internat. Soc. Folk Harpers and Craftsmen, Comhaltas Ceoltoiri Eireann. Avocations: gardening, language study, study of pain management through music. Home: 46 W Shore Rd Denville NJ 07834-1520 E-mail: harpvoice@msn.com.

FISHER, STEVEN JAY, architect; b. N.Y.C., July 21, 1951; s. Norman and Shirley Fisher; m. Rosanna Ippolito, June 26, 1976; 1 child, Andrew David. BArch, Cooper Union, 1974; MArch, Harvard U., 1975. Registered arch., N.Y. Summer intern Michael Wurmfeld, Arch., N.Y.C., 1972-74; designer/constrn. supr. Irv Weiner, Arch., Atlanta, 1975-77; designer Carl Berger and Assocs., N.Y.C., 1977; assoc. Edward Larrabee Barnes/John M.Y. Lee, PC, N.Y.C., 1978-93, John M.Y. Lee/Michael Timchula Archs., N.Y.C., 1994-99; sr. assoc. Davis Brody Bond, LLP, N.Y.C., 2000—. Guest critic N.Y. Inst. Tech., N.Y.C., 1999, Harvard U., Cambridge, Mass., 2001. Author (anthology) Fisher Tales, 1993. Mem. AIA, Nat. Coun. Archtl. Registration Bds. Avocations: photography, writing. Fax: 212-633-4761.

FISHER, STEVEN KAY, neurobiology educator; b. Rochester, Ind., July 18, 1942; s. Stewart King and Hazel Madeline (Howell) F.; m. Dinah Dawn Marschall, May 2, 1971; children: Jenni Dawn, Brian Andrew, Steven William. BS, Purdue U., 1964, MS, 1966; postgrad., Johns Hopkins U., 1967-69; PhD, Purdue U., 1969. Postdoctoral fellow Johns Hopkins U., Balt., 1969-71; prof. U. Calif., Santa Barbara, 1971—, dir. Inst. Environ. Stress, 1985-88, dir. Neurosci. Rsch. Inst., 1989-2001. Cons. Ultrastructure Tech., Goleta, Calif., 1984—, Regeneron Pharms., Inc., 1993, 94, Amgen, Inc., 1994, 95; mem. NIH Visual Scis. A2 Study Sect. Contbr. numerous articles to profl. jours. Recipient Devel. award, NIH, 1980—84, M.E.R.I.T. award NIH, 1989—99, Ludwig von Sallmann prize for vision rsch., 2002; grantee, NIH, 1971—. Mem. Assn. Rsch. in Vision and Ophthalmology (mem. program com. 1979-80, K-12 edn. com. 1997-2001), Internat. Soc. for Eye Rsch., Soc. Neurosci. Avocations: music, gardening, literature, swing dancing, weight lifting. Home: 6890 Sabado Tarde Rd Goleta CA 93117-4305 Office: U Calif Neuroscience Research Institute Santa Barbara CA 93106-5060 E-mail: fisher@lifesci.ucsb.edu.

FISHER, STEWART WAYNE, lawyer; b. Phila., Mar. 5, 1950; s. Frederick and Evalyn (Wilson) F.; m. Melinda Ruley, Oct. 1, 1994; children: Henry J., Isabel Rose; children from previous marriage: Kira H., Amos N., Emily E. BA magna cum laude, Duke U., 1972; MA, Yale U., 1974; JD with honors, U. N.C., 1982. Bar: N.C. 1982, U.S. Dist. Ct. (ea. and ctrl. dists.) N.C. 1982, U.S. Dist. Ct. (we. dist.) N.C. 1997, U.S. Ct. Appeals (4th cir.) 1993, U.S. Supreme Ct. 1997, bd. cert. Civil Trial Advocate: Nat. Bd. Trial Advocacy 1998. Atty. Haywood, Denny & Miller, Durham, N.C., 1982-85; ptnr. Glenn, Mills & Fisher, PA, Durham, 1985—. Faculty Nat. Inst. for Trial Advocacy, Durham, 1988—. Coop. atty. ACLU, Raleigh, 1992—. Mem. ABA, ATLA, Nat. Employment Lawyers, N.C. Acad. Trial Lawyers, N.C. Bar Assn., Phi Beta Kappa. Democrat. Avocations: fishing, gardening. Office: Glenn Mills & Fisher PA PO Box 3865 Durham NC 27702-3865

FISHER, SYLVIA KAY, psychologist, researcher, consultant; b. Tampa, Fla., Sept. 27, 1962; d. Ronnie Herbert and Barbara (Turk) F.; life ptnr. Susan Easterly; 1 child, Elise Dolores Easterly Fisher. BA in Psychology, U. S. Fla., 1984, MA in Sch. Psychology, 1985, PhD in Edn. Measurement, 1994. Cert. behavior program specialist. Evaluation specialist Pinellas County Schs., Clearwater, Fla., 1987—93; counselor assoc. Inst. Living, Tampa, 1991—92; therapist I Mental Health Care, Tampa, 1992; cons., 1992—; sr. rsch. assoc. Miami (Fla.)-Dade C.C., 1993—95; rsch. psychologist Bur. Labor Stats., Washington, 1995—98, 2000—03; sr. study dir. Westat, Rockville, Md., 1998—2000. Adj. prof. Am. Sch. Profl. Psychology, Arlington, Va., 1996—; tng. developer Substance Abuse & Mental Health Svcs. Adminstrn., Rockville, 1998-99; presenter and reviewer in field. Contbr. articles to profl. jours. Vol. therapist Met. Cmty. Ch., Tampa, 1990-91; cmty. adv. bd. Lesbian Svcs. Program, Washington, 2000-; exec. bd. Prevent Child Abuse Md., 2001—. Mem. Am. Assn. Pub. Opinion Rsch., Am. Statis. Assn., Soc. Indsl. and Orgnl. Psychologists. Democrat. Avocations: writing haiku, pencil drawing, travel, ethnic cuisine. Office: U S Dept of Labor 200 Constitution Ave NE Washington DC 20212

FISHER, THOMAS EDWARD, lawyer; b. Cleve., Sept. 29, 1926; s. McArthur and Ruth Morgan (Dissette) F.; m. Virginia Moore, June 29, 1957; children: Laura, Linda, John. BS in Naval Sci. and Tactics, Purdue U., 1947, BS in Engring. Law, 1950; JD, Ind. U., 1950. Bar: Ohio 1951, U.S. Dist. Ct. (no. dist.) Ohio 1954, U.S. Supreme Ct. 1955, U.S. Ct. Appeals (Fed. cir.) 1973. Asst. to v.p. Lempco Products, Bedford, Ohio, 1950-51; house counsel Willard Storage Battery Co., Cleve., 1951-54; assoc. Schram & Knowles, Cleve., 1954-55; ptnr. Watts, Hoffmann, Fisher & Heinke Co. (predecessor firms), Cleve., 1955—. Mem. adv. bd. BNA Patent Trademark and Copyright Jour., 1972—; mem. adv. panel Franklin Pierce Law Sch., 1987—. Councilman Mentor (Ohio) on the Lake, 1955-57; chmn. ARC, Painesville, Ohio, 1956. Lt. USN, 1944. Mem. ABA (divsn. chair), Cleve. Bar Assn. (trustee), Am. Intellectual Property Law Assn. (chair com., bd. dirs.), Cleve. Intellectual Property Law Assn. (pres.), Cleve. World Trade Assn., Nat. Inventors Hall of Fame (pres.), Nat. Coun. Patent Law Assns. (chair). Avocations: woodworking, fishing, travel, gardening. Home: 617 Falls Rd Chagrin Falls OH 44022-2560 Office: Watts Hoffmann Fisher & Heinke Co 1100 Superior Ave Ste 1750 Cleveland OH 44114-2518 E-mail: tfisher@wattshoff.com.

FISHER, THOMAS GEORGE, lawyer, retired media company executive; b. Debrecen, Hungary, Oct. 2, 1931; came to U.S., 1951; s. Eugene J. and Viola Elizabeth (Rittersporn) F.; m. Rita Knisley, Feb. 14, 1960; children: Thomas G. Jr., Katherine F. Vaaler. BS, Am. U., 1957, JD, 1959; postgrad., Harvard U., 1956. Bar: D.C. 1959, Iowa 1977. Atty. FCC, Washington, 1959-61, 65-66; pvt. law practice, 1961-65, 66-69; asst. counsel Meredith Corp., N.Y.C., 1969-72, assoc. gen. counsel Des Moines, 1972-76, gen. counsel, 1976-80, v.p. gen. counsel, 1980-94, corp. sec., 1988-94, ret., 1994. Comml law liaison ABA Ctr. and East European Law Initiative, Krakow, Poland, 1994—95; atty. Iowa Legal Aid, 1996—. Contbr. articles to profl. jours. Bd. dirs. Des Moines Met. Opera Co., Indianola, 1980-94, pres., 1990-91; bd. dirs. Civic Music Assn., Des Moines, 1982-92, pres., 1987-88; chmn. legis. com. Greater Des Moines C. of C., 1976-77; bd. dirs. Legal Aid Soc. Polk County, 1986-93, pres., 1993. With U.S. Army, 1952-54. Mem. ABA, Iowa State Bar Assn. (chmn. corp. counsel subcom. 1979-82), Polk County Bar Assn., Embassy Club. Office: Iowa Legal Aid 1111 9th St Ste 380 Des Moines IA 50314-2527

FISHER, THOMAS GEORGE, JR., lawyer; b. Washington, June 1, 1961; s. Thomas George and Rita (Knisley) F.; m. Susan Jane Koenig, June 23, 1990. BA, Iowa State U., 1983; JD with high distinction, U. Iowa, 1986. Bar: Iowa 1986, U.S. Dist. Ct. (so. dist.), Iowa 1987, U.S. Ct. Appeals (8th cir.) 1987, U.S. Dist. Ct. (no. dist.) Iowa 1993. Jud. clk. Iowa Supreme Ct., Davenport, 1986-87; assoc. Duncan, Jones, Riley & Finley, P.C., Des Moines, 1987-91; asst. atty. gen. State of Iowa, Justice Dept., Des Moines, 1991-95; counsel Am. Mut. Life Ins. Co., Des Moines, 1995-96; ptnr. Hogan & Fisher, PLC, Des Moines, 1997—2003, Whitfield & Eddy, P.L.C., Des Moines, 2003—. Precinct chair Polk County Dem. Party, Des Moines, 1988-90, 94-96, 98-2000, 02--; candidate Iowa Ho. of Reps. Dists. 73, 1994; mem. Des Moines Leadership Inst., 1998-99; corp. bd. dirs., sec. Anawim Housing; bd. dirs., chair Metro Arts Alliance of Greater Des Moines. Mem. Blackstone Inn of Ct. Democrat. Roman Catholic. Office: Whitfield & Eddy PLC 317 6th Ave Ste 1200 Des Moines IA 50309-4195 E-mail: fisher@whitfieldlaw.com.

FISHER, THOMAS GRAHAM, judge; b. Flint, Mich., May 15, 1940; s. John Corwin and Bonnie Decou (Graham) F.; m. Barbara Alden Molnar, June 2, 1963; children: Anne Corwin, Thomas Molnar. AB, Earlham Coll., 1962; JD, Ind. U., 1965. Bar: Ind. 1965, U.S. Dist. Ct. (no. dist.) Ind. 1965, U.S. Supreme Ct. 1969. Assoc. John R. Nesbitt, Remington and Rensselaer, Ind., 1965-68; ptnr. Nesbitt & Fisher, Remington and Rensselaer, Ind., 1968-73, Nesbitt, Fisher & Daugherty, Remington and Rensselaer, Ind., 1973-78, Nesbitt, Fisher, Daugherty & Nesbitt, Remington and Rensselaer, Ind., 1978-82, Nesbitt, Fisher & Nesbitt, Remington and Rensselaer, Ind., 1982-83, Fisher & Nesbitt, Remington and Rensselaer, Ind., 1983-86; judge Ind. Tax Ct., Indpls., 1986—. Pros. atty. Jasper County, Ind., 1967-86; lectr. bus. law St. Joseph's Coll., Rensselaer, 1970-86; trustee Earlham Coll., 1995—. Recipient Eugene Feller award Ind. Pros. Attys. Assn., Indpls., 1986, Lawrence Lasser award, Nat. Conf. of State Tax Judges, 2001, rabb Emison award Ind. State Bar Assn., 2001. Mem. ABA, Ind. Bar Assn., Jasper County Bar Assn., Nat. Conf. State Tax Judges, Ind. Soc. Chgo., Columbia Club (bd. dirs. 1991-99, sec. 1992, treas. 1993, pres. 1997), Rotary (v.p. Indpls. chpt. 1998-99, pres. 2000-2001), Jaycees (Outstanding Young Man Am. 1975). Republican. Mem. Soc. Of Friends. Home: 4702 Mallard View Dr Indianapolis IN 46226-2187 Office: Ind Tax Ct 115 W Washington St Ste 1160S Indianapolis IN 46204-3418 E-mail: tfisher@courts.state.in.us.

FISHER, WESTON JOSEPH, economist; b. Glendale, Calif., Aug. 29; s. Edward Weston and Rosalie Eloise (Bailey) F. BS, U. So. Calif., 1962, MA, l965, MS, l97l, PhD, 1989. Sr. mgr. Naval Undersea Ctr., Pasadena, Calif., l964-69; chief exec. officer, prin. Ventura County, Ventura, Calif., l969-73; So. Calif. dir. County Suprs. Assn., L.A., l974-75; coord. govtl. rels. So. Calif. Assn. Govts., L.A., 1975-78; devel. dir. Walter H. Leimert Co., L.A., 1979-90. Bd. dirs. Gray Energy Corp., L.A., Mission Inn Group, Riverside, Calif., Coun. of Leaders and Specialists - UN, Peterson Oil and Gas. Mem. Gov.'s Adv. Coun. for Econ. growth, Channel Islands Conservancy. Mem. Medieval Acad. Am., El Dorado Country Club, Univ. Club, South Coast Yacht Club, Cave Creek Club, Lambda Alpha. Republican. Avocation: medieval and U.S. history. Home: 14373 Tawya Rd Apple Valley CA 92307-5545

FISHER, WILL STRATTON, illumination consultant; b. Nashville, June 27, 1922; s. Will Stratton and Estelle (Carr) R.; m. Patricia A. Fesco, Nov. 10, 1945; children: Patricia Jo, Will Stratton, Robert J. BSE.E., Vanderbilt U., 1947. Registered profl. engr., Ohio. With Lighting Bus. Group, Gen. Elec. Co., Cleve., 1947-87, mgr. advanced application engring., 1971-84, mgr. lighting edn., 1985-87; cons. lighting Moreland Hills, Ohio, 1987—. Cons. Lighting Research Inst. Contbr. articles, papers to profl. jours., symposia and internat. profl. meetings. Patentee parabolic wedge louver; developer concepts for utilizing heat from lighting systems to heat bldgs.; designer calorimeter; developer procedure for calculation contbn. of lighting to heating of bldgs. Served to 1st lt. C.E., AUS, 1943-46, Manhattan Project. Fellow Illuminating Engring. Soc. North Am. (pres. 1978-79, Disting. Service award 1980, Louis B. Marks award for exceptional service 1988); mem. SAR, Internat. Commn. Illumination (U.S. expert on tech. com., U.S. rep. to div. 3, interior lighting), ASHRAE, IEEE. Lodges: Kiwanis (pres. 1990-91). Methodist. Home and Office: 120 Meadowhill Ln Chagrin Falls OH 44022

FISHER, WILLIAM HENRY, sociologist, researcher, educator; b. Worcester, Mass., Sept. 4, 1947; s. Henry Frederick and Florence Fisher; m. Lynn Barbara Davidson, Aug. 26, 1973; children: Dana Lynn, Lesley Davidson. PhD, Northeastern U., 1980; BA, Clark U., 1969. Sr. rsch. assoc. Northeastern U., Boston, 1980—84; dir. policy rsch. group Mass. Dept Mental Health, Boston, 1984—88; post-doctoral fellow Harvard U., Cambridge, Mass., 1988—88; faculty mem. dept. psychiatry U. Mass. Med. Sch., Worcester, dir. ctr for mental health services rsch., 1993—98, dep. dir. ctr. for mental health services rsch., 1998—. Editor: (annual social science series) Research in Community and Mental Health; contbr. articles to profl. jours. Orgnl. oversight Worcester Cmty. HealthLink, 1991—94; mem., pres. Shrewsbury (Mass.) Cmty. Svcs., 1995. Christopher Walker fellow in Health Policy and Social Medicine, J.F. Kennedy Sch., Harvard U., 1988. Mem.: APHA (governing coun. and chair-elect 1997, chair-elect mental health sect. 2001—02, Mental Health Sect. award 2001), Phi Kappa Phi. Democrat. Avocation: traditional music. Home: 251 Prospect St Shrewsbury MA 01545 Office: Univ Mass Med Sch 55 Lake Ave North Worcester MA 01655 Office Fax: 508-856-8700. Personal E-mail: wdawgfish@aol.com. E-mail: bill.fisher@umassmed.edu.

FISHER, WILLIAM LAWRENCE, geologist, educator; b. Marion, Ill., Sept. 16, 1932; s. Henry Adam and Madge Lenora (Moore) F.; m. Marilee Booth, Dec. 18, 1954; children: Leah, Karl, Peter. BS, So. Ill. U., 1954, DSc, 1986; MS, U. Kans., 1958, PhD (Shell fellow), 1961; DEng, Colo. Sch. Mines, 2002. Research scientist Tex. Bur. Econ. Geology, Austin, 1960-68, assoc. dir., 1968-70, dir., 1970-75, 77-94, John A. and Katherine G. Jackson Sch. Geoscis., 2001—; asst. sec. for energy and minerals Dept. Interior, Washington, 1975-77; prof. dept. geol. scis. U. Tex., Austin, 1969—, Morgan J. Davis prof. petroleum geology, 1984-86, Leonidas T. Barrow chair in mineral resources, 1986—, chmn. dept. geol. scis., 1984-90, dir. Geology Found., 1984—. Bd. dirs. Pogo Producing Co.; geology assoc. bd. U. Kans., 1972-74, 83—; adv. coun. Gas Rsch. Inst., Tex. Energy and Natural Resource; mem. Tex. Sci. Adv. Coun., Gov.'s Energy Coun., White House Sci. Coun., Nat. Petroleum Coun., Pres.' Coun. of Advisors on Sci. and Tech. Panel on Energy R&D, and Sec. Energy Adv. Bd.; mem. Tex. 2000 Commn.; bd dir. Diamond Shamrock, 1987-98. Trustee Am. Assn. Petroleum Geologists Found., Southwest Rsch. Inst., Am. Geol. Inst. Found.; bd. dirs. Geol. Found. Tex., 1984—. With AUS, 1954-56. Recipient Hedberg medal Inst. for the Study of Earth and Man, 1995, Sidney Powers Meml. Medal award, Am. Assn. Petroleum Geologists 1994, Twenhofel medal Soc. for Sedimentary Geology, 2001, Boyd medal Gulf Coast Assn. Geological Socs., 2002. Fellow AAAS, Soc. Econ. Geology, Geol. Soc. Am. (councillor); mem. NRC (commn. on geoscis., environ. and resource, chmn. bd. mineral and energy resources, U.S. nat. com. on geology, chmn. bd. on earth scis. and resources, bd. on energy and environ. sys.), Nat. Acad. Engring., Nat. Assoc., Nat. Acad., Am. Inst. Profl. Geologists (pres. Tex. sect. 1979, pres. 1993, Parker medal, Pub. Svc. award), Assn. Am. State Geologists (hon. pres. 1981-82), Am. Assn. Petroleum Geologists (hon., pres. 1985-86), Am. Geol. Inst. (pres. 1991, Campbell medal, Heroy award), Austin Geol. Soc. (hon., pres. 1973-74), Gulf Coast Assn. Geol. Scis. (hon.; pres 1994), Tex. Ind. Prodrs. and Royalty Owners (Hats Off award 2002). Home: 8705 Ridgehill Dr Austin TX 78759-7342 Office: Univ Tex Dept Geological Scis Austin TX 78712 E-mail: wfisher@mail.utexas.edu.

FISHER, WILLIAM PIERRE, association executive; b. Ithaca, N.Y., Jan. 15, 1939; BS, Cornell U., 1960, MBA, 1965, PhD, 1968. Past. asst. prof. Sch. acctg., fin. and gen mgmt. courses Hotel Administrn. Cornell U., Ithaca, N.Y.; hospitality industry cons. Gaurnier Assocs., 1965-72; exec. v.p. Nat. Restaurant Assn., 1972-77; exec. v.p. fin. and adminstrn. Service Sys. Corp. (now Marriott Sodexho), Buffalo, 1977-84; exec. v.p. to pres. Nat. Restaurant Assn., 1984-96; pres., CEO Am. Hotel & Motel Assn., Washington, 1996—. Author: The Thinker's Guide to Management Action, 1999, Creative Marketing for the Food Service Industry, 1982, Lessons in Leadership, 1993. Served in USAF. Recipient Champion Edn. award Coun. Hotel Restaurant and Instl. Edn., 1996. Office: American Hotel and Motel Assn 1201 New York Ave NW Ste 600 Washington DC 20005-3931

FISHER, WILLIAM THOMAS, business administration educator; b. Central Falls, R.I., Mar. 15, 1918; s. William L. and Sarah (Foley) F.; m. Mary Rowena Donnelly, Dec. 26, 1949; 1 son, William Thomas. BS with high honors, Am. Internat. Coll., 1949; MEd in Econs. and Edn., Boston U., 1951; PhD, U. Conn., 1956; postgrad., Clark U., 1954, Columbia U., 1957, St. Thomas Sem., Bloomfield, Conn., 1970-73. Prodn. planner local industry, Putnam, Conn., 1938-42; prin. Templeton (Mass.) Sch., 1949-50, Tourtellotte High Sch., Thompson, Conn., 1950-57; instr. Becker Jr. Coll., Worcester, Mass., 1955-57; assoc. prof. State U. N.Y. at, Albany, 1957; asst. dean Sch. Ins., U. Conn., 1957-76; asst. dean adminstrn. U. Conn. Sch. Bus. Adminstrn., 1976-77; adminstrv. dir. (Hartford MBA program), 1957-64; vis. prof. Ohio U., summer 1962; dir. (IBM Advanced Ins. Industry Sch.), 1960-70; ednl. cons. IBM Corp., 1960-80; adminstr., asst. dir. Ctr. for Ins. Edn. and Rsch., Hartford, 1976-81; assoc. prof. mgmt. and adminstrv. scis. dept. Sch. Bus. Adminstrn., U. Conn., Storrs, 1976-81, assoc. prof. mgmt. and orgn. dept., 1981-89, assoc. prof. emeritus, 1989—, adj. prof., 1989-90, 92; ordained permanent deacon Roman Cath. Ch. for Archdiocese of Hartford, 1973; assigned St. Joseph Cathedral, Hartford, part-time 1973-83; rsch. fellow Divinity Sch. Yale U., New Haven, 1989-91, Theol. Opportunities Program Harvard U., Cambridge, Mass., 1994-95. Vis. scholar Divinity Sch., Duke U., Durham, N.C., 1995, 96, 98, 99, Divinity Sch., Vanderbilt U., Nashville, 1996-97, Emory U., Candler Sch. Theology, Atlanta, 1997; real estate broker, 1973-93; mem. Conn. State Ins. Com. and Conn. State Ins. Purchasing Bd., 1963-73, 75-91, chmn. bd., 1971-73; past pres., dir. Conn. Assn. Mcpl. Devel. Commns., 1963-91; mem. Conn. adv. coun. SBA, 1964-70, chmn., 1967; chmn. various coms. Greater Hartford Coun. Econ. Edn., 1958-81; mem. Thompson Bd. Fin., 1963-75; chmn. Thompson Indsl. and Devel. Com., 1964-70, 71-80, 81-91. Editor: Selective Readings in Human Resources Management, 1985, 87, 89; contbr. articles to profl. jours. Pres. Thompson Indsl. Found., 1965-66; mem. Gov.'s Conf. on Human Rights and Opportunities, 1967, Gov.s Conf. on Innovation, 1989; Organizer Conn. small bus. divsn. Businessmen for V.P. Humphrey, 1968; alumni dir. Am. Internat. Coll., 1961-63, 89-93, trustee, 1963-71, mem. corp., 1972—; chmn. adv. bd. govs. Conn. Libr. Svc. Ctr., Willimantic, 1964-68, mem. exec. com., 1968-70; bd. dirs., sec. Edn. and Rsch. Found. IMA-PIA for States N.Y., N.J. and Conn., Glenmont, N.Y., 1973-83; past trustee, past pres. Thompson Libr.; corporator Day Kimball Hosp., Putnam, Conn.; mem. region 3 adv. and planning coun. Conn. Dept. Mental Retardation, 1987-92; trustee Annhurst Coll., Woodstock, Conn., 1977-84; active Conn. Small Bus. Devel. Ctr., summer 1982, 83, 84, 85; bd. dirs. Norwich-Quinebaug unit Am. Cancer Soc. Served with AUS, 1942-45, 39.5 months continuous overseas svc. Recipient Yr. award Hartford Assn. Ins. Women, 1969; Presdl. Appreciation cert. Conn. Assn. Mcpl. Devel. Commns., 1968, Alumni Achievement award Am. Internat. Coll., 1999. Mem. NEA (life), AAUP, KC (hon. life), Am. Risk and Ins. Assn. (fellowship 1960, 62), Risk and Ins. Mgmt. Soc., Am. Soc. Personnel Adminstrn., Am. Acad. Mgmt., Am. Acad. Religion, Northeastern Indsl. Developers Assn., Conn. Hist. Soc., Nat. Trust Historic Preservatio, Am. Legion, Phi Delta Kappa, Delta Pi Epsilon. Home: Box 332 Thompson Hill Thompson CT 06277 also: 174 Valley View Rd Manchester CT 06040

FISHKIND, LAWRENCE, marketing consultant; b. N.Y.C., May 9, 1936; s. Samual and Fanny (Linkoff) F.; m. Lorraine Bernice Diamond, Oct. 23, 1960; 1 child, Paul Leslie. BA in Econs., Bklyn. Coll., 1959. V.p., gen. mgr. Mort N. Marton Corp., Ossining, N.Y., 1964-70; pres. Lawrence Fishkind Assocs., N.Y.C., 1970-77; v.p., gen. mgr. Italglass USA, N.Y.C., 1977-82; v.p. mktg. Crystal Clear Industries, Ridgefield Pk, N.J., 1982-84; pres., chief exec. officer Spl. Mkts., Yorktown Hts., N.Y., 1984—. Cons. in mktg. China, S.E. Asia; bd. dirs. Pacific Ave.-Thailand, N.Am. Mktg. Tom's Group U.S.A., Tom's Group Internat. Contbr. articles to profl. jours. With USMCR, 1958-74. Mem. Mensa, Alpha Mu Sigma. Jewish. Avocations: tennis, big game fishing, racquetball, golf, squash. Office: 2230 Palo Duro Blvd North Fort Myers FL 33917 E-mail: lfishkind@swfla.rr.com.

FISH-LACEY, HELEN THERESE, educator, author; b. Mpls., Mar. 17, 1944; d. John Howard and Helen Therese (Ochs) Berg; m. Ronald Bruce Fish, Oct. 13, 1967 (div. May 1994); children: Eric James, Angela Diane, Christine Ann; m. Richard Ellis Lacey, Feb. 1, 2003. BS, U. Minn., Mpls., 1966; postgrad., U. Minn., Mankato, 1969-70, U. Wis., Whitewater, 1970-72; MEd, Brenau Coll., 1986; EdS, U. Ga., 1992, EdD in Ednl. Leadership and Lifelong Learning, 2002. Cert. elem. tchr., Minn., Wis., Ill., Kans., Ga. Tchr. kindergarten Lincoln Hills Sch., Mpls., 1966-68, Mapleton (Minn.) Pub. Schs., 1968-69; tchr. 1st grade Hoover Sch., Mankato, 1969-70; kindergarten tchr. Todd Sch., Beloit, Wis., 1970-73; tchr. presch., K-1 Wilson Sch., Janesville, Wis., 1973-75; tchr. gifted and reading specialist (remedial) Lakewood Sch., Park Forest, Ill., 1975-77; tchr. kindergarten, 1st and 3d grades Sibley Sch., Albert Lea, Minn., 1977-82; tchr. kindergarten Most Pure Heart Sch., Topeka, 1983-85, Enota Sch., Gainesville, Ga., 1985-88, chronicler Danforth grant, 1988-91; tchr. kindergarten Centennial Sch., Gainesville, Ga., 1992—; adj. asst. prof. Brenau U., Gainesville, Ga., 1988—, U. Ga., 1990, 94—, Barton Coll., 2002. Cons. and field test tchr. Rsch. and Devel. Ctr. U. Wis., Madison, 1970-79, Ency. Britannica Edn. Corp.; workshop leader for adminstrs. and tchrs. in Pre-Reading Skills; demonstration tchr. Internat. Reading Assn. Conv., New Orleans, 1975; field rschr. U. Ga.2002, Ga. Dept. Edn., 2002. Author: Starting Out Well: A Parent's Approach to Exercise and Nutrition, 1989; editor Y's Menettes newsletter, 1971-75. Sec., treas. PTA, Mpls, Mankato, Albert Lea, Beloit, Janesville, Park Forest, Topeka, Gainesville; leader Girl Scouts U.S., Blue Birds, Topeka; asst. softball coach, Gainesville H.S. Recipient award for contbns. to edn. and participation in Tchr. in Space Program NASA, 1986; Cert. of World Leadership, Cambridge, Eng., 1990. Mem. Ga. Edn. Assn., Assn. for Supervision and Curriculum Devel., Ga. Presch. Assn., Internat. Platform Assn., Pi Lamda Theta (Hon. Teaching Soc. award). Roman Catholic. Avocations: writing, inventing, learning, teaching, sports. Home: 3650 Brown Well Ct Gainesville GA 30504-5774 Office: Enota Sch Gainesville GA 30501

FISHMAN, ALFRED PAUL, physician; b. N.Y.C., Sept. 24, 1918; s. Isaac Fishman and Anne (Tinter) Fishman; m. Linda Fishman, Oct. 7, 1984; children: Mark, Jay, Hannah Rae. AB, U. Mich., 1938, MS, 1939; MD, U. Louisville, 1943; MA (hon.), U. Pa., 1971. Diplomate Am. Bd. Internal Medicine, Nat. Bd. Med. Examiners. Intern Jewish Hosp., Bklyn., 1943—44; Dazian Found. fellow pathology Mount Sinai Hosp., N.Y.C., 1946—47, asst. resident, resident medicine, 1947—48; Dazian Found. fellow cardiovascular physiology Michael Reese Hosp., Chgo., 1948—49; Am. Heart Assn. rsch. fellow Bellevue Hosp., N.Y.C., 1949—50, established investigator Am. Heart Assn. cardiopulmonary lab., 1951—55; Am. Heart Assn. rsch. fellow in physiology Harvard U., Boston, 1950—51; instr. physiology NYU, 1951—53; assoc. in medicine Columbia Coll. Physicians and Surgeons, N.Y.C., 1953—55, asst. prof., 1955—58, assoc. prof., 1958—66; prof. medicine U. Chgo., 1966—69; dir. Inst. and Divsn. Cardiovasc. Disease Michael Reese Hosp., Chgo., 1966—69; prof. medicine U. Pa., Phila., 1969—72, William Maul Measey prof. medicine, 1972—, assoc.

dean Sch. Medicine, 1969—99, dir. cardiovasc.-pulmonary divsn., 1969—90, chmn. dept. rehab. medicine, 1990—97; steering com. of dept. chmn. U. Pa. Med. Ctr., 1992; assoc. dean program devel. U. Pa., 1998—99, sr. assoc. dean program devel., 1999—; mem. coun. on grad. med. edn. U. Pa. Med. Ctr., 1992—93. Dir. Robinette Found., Clin. Cardiovascular Rsch. Ctr., U. Pa. Med. Ctr., 1969—82; mem. steering com. dept. chmn. U. Pa. Med. Ctr., 1992, coun. on grad. med. edn., 1992—93; dir. Specialized Center of Rsch. (Lung), 1973—81; attending physician Hosp. U. Pa., 1969—, Presbyn. Hosp. Phila., 2000—; sr. attending physician Phila. Gen. Hosp., 1970—78; physician Mass. Gen. Hosp., 1979; cons. to chancellor U. Mo., Kansas City, 1973—78; vis. prof. Harvard U., 1970, Oxford (Eng.) U., 1972, Washington U., St. Louis, 1973, Johns Hopkins U., 1974, Ben Gurion U., 1975, Emory U., Atlanta, 1976, U. Porto Alegra, Brazilia, Brazil, 1976, U. Zurich, Switzerland, 1978, Duke U., 1986, U. N.C., 1986; vis. scientist for NIH to Peking, China, 1980, to USSR, 1985; cons. Exec. Office Pres., 1961—69, U. Athens, Greece, 1980; mem. WHO Expert Panel, Geneva, 1973—76, Nat. Adv. Heart and Lung Council, NIH, 1968—71, 1979—83, Steering Com. of Dept. Chmn U. Pa. Med. Ctr., 1992, Coun. on Grad. Med. Edn. U. Pa. Med. Ctr., 1992—93; coun. mem. Coll. of Physicians of Phila., 1993—; chmn. Gov.'s Com. for Rsch. on Respiratory Diseases in Coal Miners, 1974—90, Internat. Conf. on Lung, Titisee, Germany, 1976, Florence, Italy, 84, Prague, Czech Republic, 86, Prague, 89, NIH Conf. Proliferative & Obliterative Vascular Disease; chair steering com. Nat. Emphysema Treatment Trial, 1996—; U.S. chief del. Internat. Union of Physiol. Scis., Helsinki, Finland, 1989; cons. N.Y. State Bd. Health, 1987—91, Cleve. Found., 1984—; vis. com. Case Western Res. Sch. Medicine, Cleve., 1989—, Rsch Inst., Lankenau Hosp., Phila., 1990; chmn. Scientific Edn. Partnership U. Mo-U. Kans.-Merrill Dow, 1989—2001. Editor (with D.W. Richards): Circulation of The Blood-Men and Ideas, 1964; editor: (with H.H. Hecht) The Pulmonary Circulation and Interstitial Space, 1969; editor: Handbooks of Respiratory Physiology, Am. Physiol. Soc., 1967—72, 1979—87, Physiology in Medicine, New Eng. Jour. Medicine, 1969—79, Jour. Applied Physiology, 1981—89, 1989—99; editor: (with D.W. Richards) Circulation of the Blood Men and Ideas, 1982; editor: Merck Manual, 1972—80, Ann. Rev. Physiology, 1977—81, Heart Failure, 1979; editor: (with E. M. Renkin) Pulmonary Edema, 1979; editor: Pulmonary Diseases and Disorders, 1979, 2d edit., 1988, Classics in Biology and Medicine, 1989—97, The Pulmonary Circulation: Normal and Abnormal, 1990; ; 3d edit., 1998, Pulmonary Rehabilitation, 1994, Fishman's Pulmonary Diseases and Disorders, 3rd edit., 1998—, Fishman's Manual of Pulmonary Diseases and Disorders, 2002; contbr. articles to profl. jours.; reviewer Health Care Financing Adminstrn., 1995—97, Washington Adv. Group, 2000—. Bd. dirs. Polachek Found., Phila. Zool. Soc.; mem. Kansas City Life Scis. Inst., 2000—01. Recipient Disting. Alumni award, U. Louisville, 1984, Disting. award in nephrology, A.N. Richards, 1998. Fellow: ACP, Royal Coll. Physicians, Am. Coll. Chest Physicians (hon.); mem.: AAAS, NAS (com. on sci., edn. and pub. policy 1987—90, policy bd. complementary/alternative medicine 2003), Am. Thoracic Soc. (Trudeau medal 2001), Heart Assn. Southeastern Pa. (bd. dirs.), Coll. of Physicians of Phila. (coun. 1993—, pres.-elect 1994, pres. 1996—97), N.Y. County Med. Soc., Nat. Space Biomed. Rsch. Inst. (bd. dirs. 1999—), Health Care Financing Adminstrn. (mem. lung transplant ctr. rev. com. 1996—, NIH-HCFA nat. emphysema treatment trial 1996—, chair steering com.), Am. Coll. Cardiology (A.N. Richards Disting. Achievement award 1997), Fedn. Am. Socs. for Exptl. Biology (exec. bd. 1983—85), Internat. Union Physiol. Scis. (U.S. Nat. Com. 1982—89, chmn. 1986—89), N.Y. Heart Assn. (pres. 1965—67), Am. Heart Assn. (chmn. coun. on cardiopulmonary disease 1972—74, rsch. coun. 1974—79, sci. pub. com. 1986—88, bd. dirs. 1988—92, chmn. 1988—94, sci. adv. com. 1992—98, founder, Disting. Achievement award 1980, Merit award 1989, Gold Heart award 1992), Assn. Am. Physicians, Royal Soc. Medicine (London), Am. Acad. Arts and Scis., Am. Soc. Clin. Investigation, Am. Physiol. Soc. (chmn. publs. bd. 1974—81, pres. 1983, chmn. centennial celebration com. 1985—87, editor handbook 1986), Inst. Medicine of NAS (chmn. health scis. bd. 1990—95, com. on social and ethical impact of advances in biomedicine 1992—94), Interurban Clin. Club, Alpha Omega Alpha. Home: 2401 Pennsylvania Ave Apt 20a7 Philadelphia PA 19130-3004 Office: Hosp U Pa 3400 Spruce St Philadelphia PA 19104-4206

FISHMAN, BERNARD, mechanical engineer; b. Bklyn., June 26, 1920; s. Max and Mollie (Greenberg) F.; m. Sara Fishman, July 3, 1947; 1 dau., Carol Beth. Student, Bklyn. Coll., 1937-39; B.M.E., CCNY, 1942; M.M.E., Bklyn. Poly. Inst., 1951. Instr. CCNY Sch. Tech., 1942-44; design and mfg. engr. Star Auto Radio, 1944-45; rocket propulsion engr. M.W. Kellogg Co., 1946-53; chief hydro-mech. engr. Simmonds Precision Products, 1953-65; engring. specialist Reaction Motors div. Thiokol Corp., 1965-67; dir. research, dir. ops. exec. office ASME, N.Y.C., 1967-89; freelance consulting engr., 1989—. Contbr. articles to profl. jours.; patentee in field. Mem. Bd. Edn., Ft. Lee, N.J., 1968-72. Served with USAF, 1945-46. Fellow ASME; mem. Nat. Soc. Profl. Engrs., Tau Beta Pi, Pi Tau Sigma.

FISHMAN, BERNARD PHILIP, museum director; b. N.Y.C., July 25, 1950; m. Elizabeth Andersen, Jan. 8, 1983; 1 child, Philip. BA summa cum laude, Columbia U., 1972; MA, U. Pa., 1982. Rsch. fellow Mus. Applied Sci. Ctr. for Archaeology, U. Pa., Phila., 1976-79; Egyptologist Epigraphic Survey Oriental Inst., U. Chgo., Luxor, Egypt, 1979-82; dir. Fenster Mus. Art, Tulsa, 1982-85, Jewish Mus. Md., Balt., 1985-98, Lehigh County Hist. Soc., Allentown, Pa., 1998—2002, R.I. Hist. Soc., Providence, 2002—. Tchr., lectr. in field. Author, co-author, editor numerous books, exhibit catalogues, jours., articles; art critic World newspaper, Tulsa. Fellow R.I. Found.; mem. Phi Beta Kappa. Home: 499 Seven Mile Rd Hope RI 02831 Office: The RI Hist Soc 110 Benevolent St Providence RI 02906 E-mail: bfishman@rihs.org. *Without the study of history there can be no civilization; without the cultivation of the arts there can be no immortality.*

FISHMAN, BRIAN S. research analyst; BS in Packaging, Mich. State U., 1981; MS in Tech. and Human Affairs, Washington U., St. Louis, 1988; PhD in Urban Affairs and Pub. Policy, U. Del., 1997. Cert. packaging profl. Summer student assoc. IBM Corp., Lexington, Ky., 1980, indsl. engr. Rochester, Minn., 1981-83; staff assoc. Ctr. for Packaging Sci. and Engring., Piscataway, N.J., 1984-86; rsch. assoc. Disaster Rsch. Ctr., Newark, Del., 1990-91, Ctr. for Energy & Environ. Policy, Newark, 1988-96; rsch. assoc. (post-doc) Ctr. for Disabilities Studies, Newark, 1997; rsch. asst. Office Instl. Rsch. Coll. S.I. CUNY, Staten Island, NY, 1998-99; data base adminstr. III Tex. TWC/CDR, Austin, 1999—2002; rsch. analyst Purdue U., West Lafayette, Ind., 2002—03. Program adminstr. coop. ext. U. Del., 1991-92, adminstrv. asst. Coll. Urban Affairs, 1992-96, tchg. asst., 1990-92, rsch. asst., 1992-93; tchg. asst. in field. Author: Emergency Response to Toxic Chemical Releases in the Kanawha Valley of West Virginia, 1988, Tanker Oil Spills in the Delaware Estuary: September 1985- April 1989, 1990, Institutional Response to Oil-Polluting Incidents in the Delaware Estuary: 1967-1990, 1997. Named Packaging Sr. of Yr., 1981, Mich. State U. Outstanding Sr., 1981; recipient scholarship Packaging Edn., Found., 1980, Nat. Coun. Phys. Distbn. Mgmt., 1984, 85, N.J. Packaging Execs. Club, 1985, Rutgers U. Packaging scholarship, 1985, Washington U. fellowship, 1986, 87, U. Del. Pub. Svc. Assistantship, 1988, 89, 90 Mem. Assn. Instnl. Rsch., Ind. Assn. for Instnl. Rsch., Inst. Packaging Profls., Mortar Board, Alpha Zeta. Home: PO Box 2863 West Lafayette IN 47996-2863

FISHMAN, CHARLES LAWRENCE, internist; b. NYC, Oct. 13, 1961; s. Melvin Ivan and Alice Carol (Rheims) F.; m. Nancy Ellyn Mills, May 31, 1987; children: Alexa Simone, Kimberly Rose. BA, U. Pa., 1983; MD, Mt. Sinai Sch. Medicine, 1987. Diplomate Am. Bd. Internal Medicine, Pulmonary Diseases, Am. Bd. Critical Care Medicine. Intern, resident, chief resident Montefiore Med. Ctr., Bronx, N.Y., 1987-91; fellow pulmonary and critical care medicine NYU Med. Ctr., N.Y.C., 1991-94; pvt. practice, Bronx, N.Y., 1994—. Clin. asst. prof. medicine Albert Einstein Coll. Medicine, Bronx, 1994—; attending physician Montefiore Med. Ctr., Bronx, 1994—, Westchester Square Med. Ctr., Bronx, 1994—, Cmty. Hosp., Dobbs Ferry. Fellow Am. Coll. Chest Physicians; mem. ACP, Am. Thoracic Soc. Avocations: tennis, cooking, sailing. Home: 7 Northern Rd Hartsdale NY 10530-2106 Office: Pulmonary Medicine PC 1180 Morris Park Ave Bronx NY 10461-1925

FISHMAN, CHARLES M. literature educator, poet; b. Oceanside, N.Y., July 10, 1942; s. Morris Fishman and Naomi Ades; m. Ellen Haselkorn; children: Jillana Fishman Esposito, Tamara. BA in English, Hofstra U., 1964, MA in English, 1965; DA in Creative Writing, SUNY, Albany, 1982. Cert. secondary English N.Y., 1965. English tchr. Calhoun H.S., Merrick, NY, 1965—66, North Shore H.S., Glen Head, NY, 1966—67, Lindenhurst (N.Y.) H.S., 1967—70; disting. svc. prof. Farmingdale State U., NY, 1989—, dir. vis. writers program, 1979—97, dir. programs in the arts, 1987—90, dir. disting. spkrs. program, 2001—. Adj. prof. English Stony Brook U., NY, 1997—2001; mem. scholarship com. Hofstra U., Hempstead, NY; coord. H.S. partnership Vis. Writers-Farmingdale State, NY; lectr. in field. Author: Mortal Companions, 1977, The Death Mazurka, 1987, The Firewalkers, 1996; editor: Blood to Remember: American Poets on the Holocaust, 1991; author: (chapbooks) Aurora, 1974, Warm-Blooded Animals, 1977, Zoom, 1990, As the Sun Goes Down in Fire, 1992, Nineteenth-Century Rain, 1994, An Aztec Memory, 1997, Time Travel Reports, 2002, poetry, translations, articles, reviews and short stories; founding editor: Xanadu, 1975—78, series editor: Water Mark Poets of North America, 1980—83, poetry editor: Gaia, 1993—95, The Jour. of Genocide Rsch., 1997—99, The Cistercian Studies Quarterly, 1998—2000, assoc. editor: The Drunken Boat, 1999—. Surrogate father Big Bros. Am., Long Island, NY; online editor Clinton Position Papers, 1992; active Campaign for McGovern. Recipient Ann Stanford Poetry award, So. Calif. Anthology, 1996, Eve of St. Agnes Poetry award, Negative Capability, 1998; fellow in poetry, N.Y. Found. for the Arts, 1995, NEH, 1974, NEH, 1978, 1982. Mem.: Associated Writing Programs, Poetry Soc. Am. (Gertrude B. Clayton Meml. award 1987). Democrat. Jewish. Avocations: gardening, landscaping, photography, nature study, hiking. Office: SUNY Farmingdale Horton Hall Farmingdale NY 11735 E-mail: carolus@optonline.net.

FISHMAN, EDWARD MARC, lawyer; b. Cambridge, Mass., Apr. 28, 1946; s. Eli Manuel and Marian (Goldberg) F.; m. Barbara Ellen Stern, June 29, 1969 (div. Sept. 1982); children: Andrea Stern, Bradley Craig; m. Tracy Ann Lind, July 13, 1985; children: Alison Leigh, Kendall Paige. AB, Bowdoin Coll., 1968; JD, Columbia U., 1972. Bar: Tex. 1972. Assoc. Akin, Gump, Strauss, Hauer & Feld, Dallas, 1972-73, Luce, Hennessy, Smith & Castle, Dallas, 1973-76; corp. counsel Centex Corp., Dallas, 1976-78; from assoc. to ptnr. Brice & Barron, Dallas, 1978-82; v.p. Baker, Smith & Mills, Dallas, 1982-86; pres. Fishman, Jones, Walsh & Gray, Dallas, 1986-99; v.p. Clements, Allen, Fishman, Woods & Walsh, P.C., Dallas, 1999-2000; with Glast, Phillips & Murray, P.C., Dallas, 2000—. Bd. dirs. Space Found. Roundtable, Dallas, 1985-87, Hope Cottage, Dallas, 1990-96; officer local pub. TV sta., Dallas, 1976—. Mem. ABA, Tex. Bar Assn., Dallas Bar Assn. Avocations: reading, bicycling, swimming, running, skiing. Home: 4723 Stonehollow Way Dallas TX 75287-7525 Office: Glast Phillips & Murray PC Ste 2200 13355 Noel Rd Dallas TX 75240 6657 E-mail: efishman@gpm-law.com.

FISHMAN, ELLEN BETH, lawyer; b. Bklyn., May 19, 1953; d. Stanley Irving and Elizabeth Flynn Fishman. BA summa cum laude, MA, Tufts U., 1974; JD, U. Pa., 1978. Bar: N.Y. 1979. Asst. corp. counsel N.Y.C. Law Dept., 1978—86, asst. chief. appeals divsn., 1986—2000, sr. coun. appeals divsn., 2000—03; appellate coun. Martine Clearwater & Bell LLP, N.Y.C., 2003—. Pres. Epiphany Parish Coun., N.Y.C., 1988—89. Mem.: N.Y. Cir. Translators, N.Y. County Lawyers Assn., N.Y. State Bar Assn. (chair com. on appellate cts. 1992—94). Democrat. Roman Catholic. Office: Martine Clearwater & Bell LLP 220 E 42nd St New York NY 10017

FISHMAN, ELLIOT KEITH, medical educator, medical consultant, diagnostic radiologist; b. Bklyn., Feb. 13, 1953; s. Jerome and Pauline (Dubow) F.; children: Whitney and Torrey; m. Lori Meg Gottlieb, Feb. 26, 1995. BS with High Honors, U. Md., 1973; MD, U. Md., Balt., 1977. Diplomate Am. Bd. Radiology. Resident in diagnostic radiology Sinai Hosp. of Balt., Balt., 1977-80; fellow in computed body tomography The Johns Hopkins Hosp., Balt., 1980-81; asst. prof. Johns Hopkins U., Balt., 1981-86, assoc. prof. radiology, 1986-91, prof. radiology and oncology, 1991—, co-dir. divsn. of computed body tomography, 1982-85, dir. divsn. of abdominal imaging & computed body tomography, 1985—, dir. diagnostic imaging, 1996—. Bd. dirs. HipGraphics, Inc.; mem. adv. coun. Non-Ionic Contrast Agts. Amersham Imaging, Inc. (formerly Nycomed Pharms.), 1989—; mem. med. adv. bd. for computed tomography Siemens, 1993—; cons. divsn. oncology Burroughs Wellcome Co., 1995—; vis. prof. U. Toronto, 1996, U. Conn., 1997, U. South Fla., 1997, Dalhousie U., 1999, Mass. Gen. Hosp., 1999, Stanford U., 2000, Sloan Kettering, 2001, others; mem. adv. com. Nat. Geographic Soc., 1996—. Author: Spiral CT of the Chest, Abdomen and Pelvis: Case Studies, 1997, Spiral CT: Principles Techniques and Applications, 1995, 2d edit. 1998; editl. bd. Radiology, 1985-89, Radio Graphics, 1985-89, Investigative Radiology, 1989-94, Acad. Radiology, 1994—, Jour. of Computer Assisted Tomography, 1995—; editor Contemporary Issues, 1986-92; assoc. editor Body Computed Tomography, 1985-91; reviewer numerous jours.; contbr. over 800 articles to profl. jours. Co-founder Hip Graphics Inc., 1997. Fellow Am. Coll. Radiology, Am. Soc. Emergency Radiology; mem. Soc. of Computed Body Tomography and Magnetic Resonance, Radiol. Soc. of N.Am., Am. Roentgen Ray Soc., Assn. of Univ. Radiologists, Nat. Computer Graphics Assn., Soc. for Computer Applications in Radiology, Soc. of Gastrointestinal Radiology, Internat. Hepato-Pancreato-Biliary Assn., Internat. Soc. Optical Enging., Md. Radiol. Soc., Phi Eta Sigma. Jewish. Office: Johns Hopkins Hosp 601 N Caroline St JHDC Rm 3252 Baltimore MD 21287-0005 E-mail: efishman@jhmi.edu.

FISHMAN, FRED NORMAN, lawyer; b. N.Y.C., Aug. 21, 1925; s. Arthur Elihu and Frederica (Greenspan) F.; m. Claire S. Powsner, Sept. 19, 1948; children: Robert J., Nancy K. S.B. summa cum laude, Harvard U., 1946, LL.B. magna cum laude, 1948; postgrad., Yale U., 1945-46. Bar: N.Y. State 1950, U.S. Supreme Ct. 1954. Law clk. to Chief Judge Calvert Magruder, U.S. Ct. Appeals, 1st Circuit, Boston, 1948-49; to Assoc. Justice Felix Frankfurter, Supreme Ct. U.S., 1949-50; assoc. firm Dewey Ballantine LLP (and predecessors), N.Y.C., 1950-57; with Freeport Minerals Co., N.Y.C., 1957-61, asst. sec., 1958-59, asst. v.p., 1959-61; partner firm Kaye Scholer LLP, N.Y.C., 1962-92, mem. exec. com., 1970-87, chmn. exec. com., 1981-83, spl. counsel, 1993-95. Editor, officer: Harvard Law Rev. Chmn. Harvard Law Sch. Fund, 1977—79; mem. bd. overseers' com. to visit Harvard Law Sch., 1975—81, 1988—94; chmn. com. Harvard Law Sch. Class of 1948 Twenty-Fifth Anniversary Gift, Forty-Fifth Anniversary Gift; mem. bd. overseers' com. to visit Grad. Sch. Edn., Harvard U., 1971—77, bd. overseers' Com. on Univ. Resources, 1991—, permanent class com. Harvard Class of 1946; mem. bd. overseers' com. to visit Med. Sch. and Sch. of Dental Medicine Harvard U., 1997—2003; trustee Pub. Edn. Assn., N.Y.C., 1956—73, chmn. bd., 1970—71; dir. Harvard Alumni Assn., 1981—83; trustee Hosp. for Joint Diseases and Med. Ctr., 1971—73, Lawyers' Com. for Civil Rights under Law, 1979—, bd. dirs., 1983—, co-chmn., 1983—85; mem. steering com. Campaign for Harvard Law Sch., 1991—95; mem. dean's adv. bd. Harvard Law Sch., 2001—. Fellow: Am. Bar Found.; mem.: ABA, Harvard Law Sch. Assn. (trustee N.Y.C. assn. 1966—69, v.p. N.Y.C. assn. 1974—75, coun. 1978—82, exec. com. 1980—82, 1st v.p. 1984—86, pres. 1986—88, exec. com. 1988—90, pres. N.Y.C. assn. 1988—89), Legal Aid Soc. (bd. dirs. 1991—94), Am. Law Inst. (adviser corp. governance project 1980—92), Assn. of Bar of City of N.Y. (chmn. com. fed. legis. 1963—66, exec. com. 1966—70, chmn. com. corp. law 1980—82, treas. 1993—94), Harvard Club N.Y.C., Phi Beta Kappa. Home: 650 Park Ave Apt 3D New York NY 10021-6115 Office: Kaye Scholer LLP 425 Park Ave New York NY 10022-3598 E-mail: ffishman@kayescholer.com.

FISHMAN, GLENN I. medical educator; BA in Chemistry cum laude, Cornell U., 1978; MD, Stanford U., 1983. Diplomate Am. Bd. Internal Medicine, Am. Bd. Cardiovascular Diseases. Rschr. Syntex Rsch., Palo Alto, Calif., 1979—81; resident in internal medicine Mass. Gen. Hosp., Boston, 1983—86; clin. fellow in cardiology Columbia-Presbyn. Med. Ctr., N.Y.C., 1986—88, asst. in clin. medicine, 1988—89; postdoctoral rsch. fellow sect. molecular cardiology Albert Einstein Coll. Medicine, Bronx, 1988—90, asst. prof. medicine cardiology divsn., 1990—95, asst. prof. molecular genetics, 1991—95, assoc. prof. medicine cardiology divsn., assoc. prof. molecular genetics, acting dir. sect. molecular cardiology, 1995—98; cardiologist, prof. Mount Sinai Sch. Medicine, N.Y.C., 1998—. Recipient Physician Scientist award, NIH, 1990, Louis Katz Basic Sci. Rsch. prize, Am. Heart Assn., 1990, Established Investigator award, 1995. Fellow: Am. Coll. Cardiology; mem.: Phi Beta Kappa.

FISHMAN, JAY STEVEN, financial services executive; b. N.Y.C., Nov. 4, 1952; s. Edward and Shirley (Cantor) F.; m. Randy Lee Chapman, Sept. 25, 1976; children: Jordan Elliot, Scott Martin. BS in Econs. magna cum laude, MS in Acctg., U. Pa., 1974. CPA, N.Y. Audit supr. Coopers & Lybrand, N.Y.C., 1974-79; dir. mergers and acquisitions Am. Can Co., Greenwich, Conn., 1979-83; sr. v.p. Goergen & Sterling, Greenwich, 1983-86; sr. v.p. mcht. banking Shearson Lehman Bros., N.Y.C., 1986-89; exec. v.p., CFO Comml. Credit Co., N.Y.C., 1989-91; sr. v.p., treas. Primerica Corp., N.Y.C., 1991-94; sr. v.p. Travelers Group, N.Y.C., 1994—; vice chmn., CFO ins. group Travelers Inc., Hartford, Conn., 1994—. Mem. Wharton Club. Avocations: golf, running, skiing. Office: Travelers Group 388 Greenwich St Fl 39 New York NY 10013-2375

FISHMAN, JOAN ROSLYN, clinical information analyst; b. Cambridge, Mass., Sept. 1, 1945; d. Joseph and Tilla (Gerson) F.; m. Stephan B. Abramson, June 8, 1969 (div. 1983). BA, Wheaton Coll., Norton, Mass., 1967; MS, U. So. Calif., 1978. Research asst. Harvard U. Med. Sch., Boston, 1967-69; pulmonary technologist Peter Bent Brigham Hosps., Boston, 1969-71, Framingham (Mass.) Union Hosp., 1971-74; chief pulmonary physiol. lab. Los Angeles County-U. So. Calif. Med. Ctr., 1975-79; dir. pulmonary diagnostic lab. White Meml. Med. Ctr., Los Angeles, 1979-84; asst. dir. respiratory care Pacific Med. Ctr., San Francisco, 1984-85; asst. product mgr. Gould Med. Products, Dayton, Ohio, 1985-86; installation analyst Health Data Scis., San Bernardino, Calif., 1987-93; sr. clin. info. analyst Dartmouth-Hitchcock Med. Ctr., Lebanon, N.H., 1993—. Health profl. educator Am. Lung Assn., N.Y.C., 1977-78. Author: Programmed Gas Law for Cardiopulmonary Technology, 1979, Blood Gas Electrodes, 1984, (with others) Standards and Controversies in Pulmonary Function Testing, 1982. Mem. Nat. Soc. Cardiopulmonary Technology (regional dir. 1978-83), Nat. Bd. Respiratory Care (bd. dirs. 1983-92), Calif. Soc. Respiratory Care. Avocations: swimming, pottery, gardening, bicycling. Office: Dartmouth-Hitchcock Med Ctr Computer Svcs Lebanon NH 03756-0001

FISHMAN, JOSHUA AARON, sociolinguist, educator; b. Phila., July 18, 1926; s. Aaron S. and Sonia (Horwitz) F.; m. Gella Jeanne Schweid, Dec. 23, 1951; children: M. Manuel, David Elliot, Avrom Avi. BS, MS (Mayor Phila. competitive scholar 1944-48), U. Pa., 1948; PhD, Columbia U., 1953; Ped.D. (hon.), Yeshiva U., 1968; LittD (hon.), Free U. Brussels, 1986. Tchr. elem. and secondary Yiddish secular schs., 1945-50; ednl. psychologist, sr. research asso. dept. research and experimentation Jewish Edn. Com. N.Y., 1951-54; from lectr. to vis. prof. psychology CCNY, 1955-58; research assoc. to dir. research Coll. Entrance Exam. Bd., 1955-58; assoc. prof. human relations and psychology U. Pa., 1958-60; prof. psychology and sociology, dean Grad. Sch. Edn. Yeshiva U., 1960-66, disting. univ. research prof. social scis. Ferkauf Grad. Sch. Psychology, 1966-88, emeritus, 1988—, univ. v.p. acad. affairs, 1973-76; vis. rschr., vis. prof. Stanford (Calif.) U., 1990—. Cummings lectr. McGill U., 1979; Linguistics Soc. Am. prof. Linguistics Inst., 1980; disting. vis. prof. Monash U., Melbourne, Australia, summers 1985, 2000; mem. com. on sociolinguistics Social Sci. Rsch. Coun.; adviser, cons. Am. Jewish Congress, Nat. Scholarship Svc. and Fund for Negro Students, Coll. Entrance Exam. Bd., Am. Assn. Jewish Edn., Ministry of Fin., Republic of Ireland; cons. Ctr. for Applied Linguistics, Internat. Rsch. Ctr. on Bilingualism, Secretariat Linguistic Policy Basque Govt., 1986—, Maori Lang. Commn., 1995—; vis. prof. linguistics L.I. U., 2000, NYU, 1998—, Grad. Ctr. CUNY, 1999—; bd. dirs. Consortium for Study of Lang. Problems, 2001—. Author: Studies on Polish Jewry, 1974, Sociology of Bilingual Education, 1976, The Spread of English, 1977, Advances in the Study of Societal Multilingualism, 1978, Never Say Die: A Thousand Years of Yiddish in Jewish Life and Letters, 1981, Bilingual Education for Hispanic Students in the U.S., 1982, The Rise and Fall of the Ethnic Revival, 1985, Readings in the Sociology of Jewish Languages, 1985, Ethnicity in Action, 1985, The Fergusonian Impact (2 vols.), 1986, Ideology, Society and Language, 1987, Language and Ethnicity in Minority Sociolinguistic Perspective, 1988, Yiddish: Turning to Life, 1991, Reversing Language Shift, 1991, The Earliest Stage of Language Planning, 1993, Post-Imperial English, 1996, In Praise of the Beloved Language, 1997, The Multilinges Apple: Languages in New York City, 1997, Handbook of Language and Ethnic Identity, 1999, Can Threatened Languages Be Saved?, 2000, Llengua i identitat, 2001, Test Construction for Students of the Behavioral and Social Sciences, 2003, also numerous profl. publs. including Afn shvel, 1980—, Forverts, 1996—; assoc. editor: Jour. Ednl. Sociology, 1963-65, Yivo Ann., 1970-77, Yidishe Sprakh, 1970—; editor: Yivo Bleter, 1974-77; editor Jour. Social Issues, 1964-69; editor: (series) Contributions to the Sociology of Lang., 1971—, Internat. Jour. Sociology of Lang., 1973—, (series) Contributions to the Sociology of Jewish Languages, 1985-88. Pres.'s scholar E.C. Morris fellow Columbia Tchrs. Coll., 1952-53, postdoctoral rsch. tng. fellow Social Sci. Rsch. Coun., 1954-55, fellow Ctr. Advanced Study Behavioral Scis., 1963-64, Princeton Inst. Advanced Study fellow, 1975-76, fellow Netherlands Inst. Advanced Study, 1982-83, Israel Inst. Advanced Studies, 1983, Nat. Fgn. Lang. Ctr., 1995-96; NSF European Conf. grantee, 1960, Office of Edn. grantee, 1960-63, 66-68, 72-74, 79-80, Social Sci. Rsch. Coun. European Conf. grantee, 1961, NIMH grantee, Latin Am., 1963, 66, NSF grantee, Europe, 1966, 79-83, Ford Found. grantee, 1969-72, 75-76, Meml. Found. Jewish Culture grantee, 1970-71, 78-79, 82-83, Nat. Inst. Edn. grantee, 1978-79, 79-81; sr. specialist Inst. Advanced Projects, East-West Ctr., 1968-69; sr. assoc. Multicultural-Bilingual divsn. Nat. Inst. Edn., 1976-77. Fellow APA, Am. Sociol. Assn., Am. Anthrop. Assn.; mem. AAAS, Am. Ednl. Rsch. Assn., Linguistic Soc. Am., Yivo Inst. Jewish Rsch., Nat. Assn. Bilingual Edn. (Man of Yr. 1992), TESOL, Terralingua. Office: Yeshiva U Ferkauf Grad School Rousso Bldg/Einstein Coll of Med Campus 1300 Morris Park Ave Bronx NY 10461-1926 also: Stanford U Ctr Ednl Rsch at Stanford Stanford CA 94305 E-mail: jfishman@aecom.yu.edu., joshuaafishman@aol.com. *I have had the incredible good fortune to be exposed simultaneously to modern Western as well as both classical and modern Jewish thought, to secular and religious values, beliefs and ideals, and theoretical and applied emphases, to the comforts of a language of wider communication (English) and a language of ethnic intimacy (Yiddish), to the infinite world of science, the eternal land of my ancestors and the new world of democracy, opportunity and pluralism to which my parents came as immigrants. I have tried to combine all of these forces within myself and to contribute to them. I consider both the tensions and the creativity resulting from these varied stimuli to be a unique heritage: an American-Jewish heritage to be treasured, cultivated, improved and handed on.*

FISHMAN, KENNETH JAY, judge; b. Roslyn, N.Y., Nov. 12, 1950; s. George Norman and Eudys Sonia (Goldstein) F.; m. Nancy Ellen Santos, Sept. 22, 1984; children: Jason Edward, Hayley Alissa. BS in Econs., U. Pa., 1972; JD cum laude, Suffolk U., 1976. Bar: Mass. 1977, U.S. Dist. Ct. Mass. 1977, U.S. Dist. Ct. (no. dist.) Calif. 1982, U.S. Ct. Appeals (4th and 3rd cirs.) 1980, (6th cir.) 1982, (1st cir.) 1983, (5th and 10th cirs.) 1985, (8th cir.) 1985, U.S. Tax Ct. 1981, U.S. Ct. Mil. Appeals 1981, U.S. Dist. Ct. (ea. dist.) Wis. 1991, U.S. Ct. Appeals (2d cir.) 1993, U.S. Fed. Claims Ct. 1997, U.S. Supreme Ct. 1980. Assoc. Law Offices F. Lee Bailey, Boston, 1976-84; ptnr. Law Offices Bailey & Fishman, Boston, 1984-91, Law Offices Bailey, Fishman & Leonard, Boston, 1991-97, Law Offices Fishman, Ankner & Horstmann, Boston, 1997—2002; pvt. practice, 2002; assoc. justice Mass. Superior Ct., 2002—. Former instr. Met. Coll., Boston U. Note editor Suffolk U. Law Rev., 1975—76; co-author (with F. Lee Bailey): Bailey/Fishman Criminal Law Series, 1986—. Democrat. Jewish. Office: Commonwealth of Mass - The Superior Ct John W McCormack PO and Courthouse 90 Devonshire St Boston MA 02105

FISHMAN, LAWRENCE MARTIN, endocrinologist, educator; b. Bklyn., Dec. 20, 1933; s. Matthew and Ruth Janet (Frank) F.; m. Suzanne Marian Rubenstein, Oct. 16, 1955; children: Matthew Edward, Charles Neal, Betsy Rachel, Andrew Klein. AB magna cum laude, Harvard Coll., 1955; MD, Harvard U., 1960. Diplomate Nat. Bd. Med. Examiners, Am. Bd. Internal Medicine, subsplty. in endocrinology and metabolism. Intern Peter Bent Brigham Hosp., Boston, 1960-61, asst. resident in medicine, 1961-62; clin. assoc. endocrinology Nat. Cancer Inst., NIH, Bethesda, Md., 1962-65; fellow in diabetes and endocrinology Vanderbilt U. Sch. Medicine, Nashville, 1965-67; asst. prof. medicine U. Miami Sch. Medicine, 1967-72, assoc. prof., 1972-75, prof., 1975—. Chief endocrinology and metabolism sect. VA Med. Ctr., Miami, 1967-99, assoc. chief of staff for rsch., 1975—. Contbr. chpts. to books and articles to profl. jours. Fellow ACP; mem. Am. Fedn. Clin. Rsch., Endocrine Soc., So. Soc. Clin. Investigation, Phi Beta Kappa, Sigma Xi, Alpha Omega Alpha.

FISHMAN, LEN, state commissioner; BA in Polit. Sci., Antioch Coll., 1975; JD with honors, U. Md., 1981. Gen. counsel N.J. Assn. Non-profit homes for the Aging, 1991-94; commr. Dept. Health and Sr. Svcs., Trenton, N.J., 1994—;

CEO Am. Assn. Home and Svcs. for the Aging, Washington. Chair N.J. Health Care Financing Authority Named Person of Yr. Med. Soc. N.J., 1996. Achievements: created first cabinet-level dept. for srs.; initiated Worlds Aids Day of Learning for Youth, electronic birth cert. in hosps; developed consumer-oriented HMO rules, first report on mortality rates following coronary artery bypass surgery; expanded assisted living and alternate family care for elderly; published HMO report card. Office: Am Assn Home and Svcs for Aging 901 E St NW Washington DC 20004-2037

FISHMAN, LEWIS WARREN, lawyer, educator; b. Bklyn., Dec. 19, 1951; BA in Polit. Sci., Syracuse U., 1972; MPA, Maxwell-Syracuse U., 1973; JD, U. Miami, 1976. Bar: Fla. 1976, U.S. Dist. Ct. (so. dist.) Fla. 1977, U.S. Dist. Ct. D.C. 1978, U.S. Ct. Appeals (5th and 11th cirs.) 1981. Assoc. Simons & Fishman P.A. (and predecessor firm), Miami, 1976-80, ptnr., 1980-81; assoc. Wood, Lucksinger & Epstein, Miami, 1981—82; pres. Lewis W. Fishman, P.A., Miami, 1982—. Adj. prof. law Fla. Internat. U., 1981, 83, 84, 91; mem. bd. legal specialization and edn. Fla. Bar, 1999—. Mem. Fla. Acad. Healthcare Attys. (bd. dirs., sec. 1986-88, pres. 1990-92), Nat. Health Lawyers Assn. (lectr. 1983, 88-89), Fla. Hosp. Assn. (lectr. 1983, 88-89), Fla. Hosp. Assn. (lectr.), Fla.Med. Record Assn. (lectr. 1982, 83, 84), Am. Acad. Hosp. Attys. (lectr. 1989, 90, 91), Nat. Health Lawyers Assn., Cath. Health Assn., Fla. Bar Assn. (mem. exec. coun. health law sect. 1988-97, chmn. health law sect. 1988-97, chmn. health law sect. 1995-96, cert. health law atty., mem. health law cert. com. 1994-99, vice chmn. 1995-96, chmn. 1996-98, bd. legal specialization and edn. 1999—). Jewish. Home: 14140 SW 104th Ave Miami FL 33176-7064 Office: 9130 S Dadeland Blvd Miami FL 33156-7818 E-mail: lwfpa@aol.com.

FISHMAN, LOUIS, physicist, educator; b. Washington, Feb. 17, 1948; s. Fabius Samuel and Miriam (Helfand) F.; m. Ingrid Celeste Palmer, Aug. 18, 1974 (div. 1979); m. Shi Di, June 28, 1992; 1 child, Michael Di Fishman. BS in Chemistry, U. Rochester, 1969; AM in Chem. Physics, Harvard U., 1971, PhD in Physics, 1977. Postdoctoral fellow dept. chemistry U. Colo., Boulder, 1976-77; postdoctoral fellow dept. physics Vitreous State Lab., Cath. U. Am., Washington, 1978, sr. rsch. fellow dept. civil engring., 1978-83; prof. math. dept. math. and computer scis. Colo. Sch. Mines, Golden, 1987-93; sr. scientist Applied Math. Scis., Ames DOE Lab., Iowa State U., Ames, 1994-96; prof. physics U. New Orleans, 1997—2001; sr. scientist Naval Rsch. Lab., Stennis Space Ctr., Miss., 1997—2001. Adj. assoc. prof. dept. civil engring., The Cath. U. Am., Washington, 1983-87; vis. scientist in applied math. scis., Iowa State U., Ames DOE Lab., 1990; summer faculty fellow Naval Underwater Systems Ctr., New London, Conn., 1991; vis. prof. math. S.N. Bose Ctr. for Basic Scis., Calcutta, 1992; vis. Erskine fellow dept. math. and stats., U. Canterbury, Christchurch, New Zealand, 1999; pres. MDF Internat., 2001—; vis. prof. math. City U. of Hong Kong, 2002, Växjö (Sweden) U., 2002. Co-editor: Wave Splitting and Inverse Problems, 1999; editl. bd. Jour. Computational Acoustics, 1990—, Jour. Applied Sci. and Computation, 1992—; reviewer multiple jours. including Applied Mecsh. Rev., Jour. Acoustical Soc. Am., Jour. Optical Soc. Am., numerous others; contbr. numerous articles to sci. and profl. jours. Mem. AAAS, Am. Math. Soc., Math. Assn. Am., Soc. Indsl. and Applied Math., Am. Geophys. Union, N.Y. Acad. Scis., Acoustical Soc. Am., Internat. Union Radio Scientists, Electromagnetics Acad., Internat. Soc. for Analysis, its Applications and Computation (bd. dirs. 1997-2002). Office: MDF Internat Slidell LA 70461 E-mail: shidi53@aol.com.

FISHMAN, MARC JUDAH, physician, researcher, executive; b. Washington, June 14, 1960; s. Jacob Robert and Tamar (Hendel) F.; m. Ann Bruner, June 20, 1993; children: Samuel, Hannah, Yakov. BA, Columbia U., 1983, MD, 1988. Diplomate Am. Bd. Neurology & Psychiatry, Am. Soc. Addiction Medicine. Intern in internal medicine U. Md. Hosp., Balt., 1988-89; resident in psychiatry Johns Hopkins Hosp., Balt., 1989-92, fellow dept. psychiatry, 1992-93, attending physician, 1992—; v.p. Am. Healthcare Mgmt. LLC, 1999—. Med. dir. Mt. Manor Treatment Ctr., 1993—; med. dir. Md. Treatment Ctr., 1997—, chmn.; instr. Johns Hopkins U. Sch. Medicine, Balt., 1993-95, asst. prof., 1995—; bd. dirs. Potomac Healthcare Found., Balt., 1993—; prin. investigator, program evaluation grants Ctr. Substance Abuse Treatment. Co-editor: Patient Placement Criteria, Am. Soc. Addication Medicine; contbr. articles to profl. jours. Pres., bd. dirs. Chesapeake Youth Ctr. and Chesapeake Treatment Ctrs., 1997—; chmn. workgroup on adolescent patient placement criteria, Am. Soc. Addiction Medicine, 1997—.

FISHMAN, MARSHALL LEWIS, chemist; b. Phila., July 2, 1937; s. Harvey Abraham and Rose (Needleman) Fishman; m. Nanette Doris Hoffman, July 3, 1966 (dec. Sept. 1997); children: Harvey Abraham, Amy Lisa; m. Anne Austin, Oct. 14, 2001. AB, Temple U., 1959; MS, Villanova U., 1961; PhD, Poly. Inst. Bklyn., 1968. Postdoctoral fellow Poly. Inst. Bklyn., 1968-69; NRC/NAS postdoctoral fellow USDA, Phila., 1969-71; rsch. chemist R.B. Russel Ctr. USDA, Athens, Ga., 1971-80, USDA, Phila., 1980—. Editor: Chemistry and Function of Pectins, 1986, Polymers from Agricultural Coproduct, 1994; contbr. 70 articles to profl. jours. Mem. Am. Chem. Soc. (sec. Phila. sect. 1980, chmn. nutrition and food biochem. 1990-91, Agr. and Food divsn. fellow 1991), Chromatography Forum Delaware Valley (pres. 1985-86, exec. bd. 1983—, award 2000). Avocations: tennis, bicycling. Office: East Regional Rsch Ctr USDA 600 E Mermaid Ln Wyndmoor PA 19038 E-mail: mfishman@arserre.gov.

FISHMAN, MARVIN ALLEN, pediatrician, neurologist, educator; b. Chgo., Feb. 16, 1937; s. Joseph and Mary (Schneider) F.; m. Gloria Brenda Greenberg, Dec. 20, 1959; children: Bradley Steven, Patricia Ann. BS, U. Ill., 1959, MD, 1961. Diplomate Am. Bd. Pediatrics, Am. Psychiatry and Neurology. Intern, then resident in pediatrics Michael Reese Hosp. and Med. Center, Chgo., 1961-64; resident in neurology Mass. Gen. Hosp., Boston, 1966-67; fellow in pediatric neurology St. Louis Children's Hosp., 1967-70, dir. Birth Defects Ctr., 1971-79; prof. pediatrics, neurology and preventive medicine Washington U. Med. Sch., St. Louis, 1970-79, dir. Irene Walter Johnson Inst. Rehab., 1974-79; prof. pediatrics and neurology, dir. pediatric neurology tng. program Baylor Coll. Medicine, Houston, 1979—, vice chmn. dept. pediatrics, 1992—; chief neurology service Tex. Children's Hosp., Houston, 1979—. Mem. residency rev. com. for neurology Accreditation Coun. for Grad. Med. Edn., 1991-96, chmn., 1995-96; bd. dirs. Am. Bd. Psychiatry and Neurology, 1991-97, exec. com., 1995-97, v.p., 1996, pres., 1997, cons., 1999—; cons. Am. Bd. Pediat., 1999—. Conbr. articles in field, chpts. in books; mem. editorial bd. Jour. Pediatrics, 1980-87, Jour. Child Neurology, Pediatric Neurology, Annals of Neurology; editor textbook. With USAR, 1964-66. Grantee HEW; Grantee Grant Found.; Grantee Ga. Warm Springs Found.; Grantee Nat. Found.-March of Dimes Mem. Am. Soc. Neurochemistry (councilor 1977-79), Child Neurology Soc. (exec. com., councillor 1980-82, sec.-treas. 1984-86, pres.-elect 1986-87, pres. 1987-89, past pres. 1989-90, John B. Hower award 1999), Houston Neurol. Soc. (pres.-elect 1989-90, pres. 1990-91), Am. Acad. Pediatrics, Am. Acad. Neurology, Am. Neurol. Assn., Am. Pediatric Soc., Soc. for Pediatric Rsch., Soc. for Neuroscis. Home: 1523-B Potomac Dr Houston TX 77057-1925 Office: Tex Children's Hosp 6621 Fannin Houston TX 77030 E-mail: mfishman@bcm.tmc.edu.

FISHMAN, MITCHELL STEVEN, lawyer; b. N.Y.C., July 27, 1948; s. Abraham and Sylvia (Sher) F.; children: Danielle, Matthew, Jeremy. BA cum laude, Harvard U., 1970, JD cum laude, 1973. Bar: N.Y. 1974, D.C. 1984. Assoc. Breed, Abbott & Morgan, N.Y.C., 1973-74, Paul, Weiss, Rifkind, Wharton & Garrison, N.Y.C., 1975-81, ptnr., 1981-99. Exec. dir. Temp. State Commn. on Banking, Ins. and Fin. Svcs., N.Y., 1983-84; cons. Sirius Satellite Radio, Inc., N.Y.C., 2000-01. Mem. ABA, N.Y. State Bar Assn., Assn. of Bar of City of N.Y. (com. on corp. law 1976-79, mem. com. on securities regulation 1998-01). Democrat. Home: 10 Barnes Rd PO Box 1443 Washington CT 06793-0443 E-mail: mshishman@excite.com.

FISHMAN, RICHARD GLENN, lawyer, accountant; b. Orange, N.J., June 2, 1952; s. Irving and Eleanor (Tanenbaum) F.; m. Jean Goldhammer, Aug. 11, 1974; children: Neil Samuel, Peter Lawrence, Ellen Melissa. BA in Econs. with highest honors and highest distinction, Rutgers U., 1974; JD, Yale U., 1977; LLM in Taxation, NYU, 1980. Bar: N.Y. 1978, N.J. 1978, U.S. Dist. Ct. N.J. 1978, U.S. Ct. Claims 1978, U.S. Tax Ct. 1978, U.S. Dist. Ct. (so. dist.) N.Y. 1979, U.S. Ct. Appeals (3d cir.) 1994. Assoc. Stroock & Stroock & Lavan, N.Y.C., 1977-80, Roberts & Holland, N.Y.C., 1980-85; tax mgr. Spicer & Oppenheim (formerly Oppenheim, Appel, Dixon & Co.), N.Y.C., 1985-87, ptnr., 1987-88; from sr. tax. counsel to assoc. gen. tax counsel AlliedSignal Inc., Morristown, NJ, 1988—97, assoc. gen. tax counsel, 1997—99; dir. tax planning for bus. units, assoc. gen. tax counsel Honeywell Internat., Inc., Morristown, 1999—2001, dir. internat. & bus. tax planning, 2001—, assoc. gen. tax counsel, 2001—. Contbr. articles to profl. jours. Mem. ABA, AICPA, N.Y. State Bar Assn., N.J. State Bar Assn. Home: 6 Tilden Ct Livingston NJ 07039-2419 Office: Honeywell Internat Inc PO Box 1057 Morristown NJ 07962-1057 E-mail: richard.fishman@honeywell.com.

FISHMAN, ROBERT MICHAEL, lawyer; b. Bloomington, Ill., Dec. 28, 1953; s. Hank and Lucy (Moscovitch) F.; m. Victoria M. Swan, Aug. 12, 1979; children: Eric B., Samuel C., Matthew A. BA, U. Ill., 1972-76; JD, George Washington U., 1979. Bar: Ill. 1979, U.S. Dist. Ct. (no. dist.) Ill. 1979, (ea. dist.) Wis. 1998, U.S. Ct. Appeals (7th circuit) 1994. Atty. Office of Ill. Atty. Gen., Chgo., 1979-80; ptnr. Levit, Mason and Fishman, Ltd., Chgo., 1980-89, Ross & Hardies, Chgo., 1990-98; mem. Shaw Gussis Fishman Glantz Wolfson & Towbin LLC, Chgo., 1998—. Mem. adv. bd. BNA Bankruptcy Law Reporter. Mem. ABA (bus. bankruptcy sect.), Chgo. Bar Assn., Am. Bankruptcy Inst. (chmn., pres., bd. dirs., exec. com., mgmt. com.). Office: Shaw Gussis Fishman Glantz Wolfson & Towbin LLC 321 North Clark St Ste 800 Chicago IL 60610 E-mail: rfishman@shawgussis.com.

FISHTEIN, ELIZABETH (MARY BETH STONE), writer; b. N.Y.C., May 24, 1947; d. Oscar and Ruth (Cohen) F. Student, NYU, 1965-66, Baruch Coll., 1980-81. Lic. real estate salesperson, N.Y., tourguide, N.Y.C.; notary pub., N.Y. Owner Do the Write Thing!, N.Y.C.; pres. Signature Tours, Inc., N.Y.C.; owner Big Mama Music, N.Y.C., Stone Pulse Music. Composer, lyricist: (songs) Phoenix, 1989 (hon. mention Billboard Ann. Songwriter's Contest), She's Got It All, 2000 (top-ten finalist ASCAP/Lilith Fair Songwriting Contest), I Love When That Happens, 2000 (top-seven finalist NSAI Songwriting Contest); author: Focused or Dead: How to Live in Joy, 2001; What Would Love Do?, 2001 (finalist NSAI songwriting contest, 2001), It's Not Like You to Forget, 2002 (hon. mention NSAI songwriting contest, 2002); co-host : Brainline: In Search of Your Greatness. Mem. ASCAP, Nat. Acad. Rec. Arts and Scis., Songwriters Guild, Women in Music, Nashville Songwriters Assn. Internat. (regional coord.), Nat. Acad. Popular Music. Democrat. Jewish. Home and Office: Do the Write Thing 56 W 70th St New York NY 10023-4620 E-mail: stonepulse@aol.com.

FISHWICK, JOHN PALMER, retired lawyer, retired railroad executive; b. Roanoke, Va., Sept. 29, 1916; s. William and Nellie (Cross) F.; m. Blair Wiley, Jan. 4, 1941 (dec. June 1987); children: Ellen Blair (Mrs. Guyman Martin III), Anne Palmer (Mrs. Wesley Posvar), John Palmer Jr.; m. Doreen Allton, Nov. 17, 1989. AB, Roanoke Coll., 1937, DHL (hon.), 1971; LL.B., Harvard U., 1940; DL (hon.), Washington & Lee Univ., 2000. Bar: Va. 1939. Assoc. Cravath, Swaine & Moore, N.Y.C., 1940-42; asst. to gen. solicitor N. & W. Ry., Roanoke, Va., 1945-47, asst. gen. solicitor, 1947-51, asst. gen. counsel, 1951-54, gen. solicitor, 1954-56, gen. counsel, 1956-58, v.p., gen. counsel, 1958-59, v.p. law, 1959-63, sr. v.p., 1963-70, pres., chief exec. officer, 1970-80, chmn., chief exec. officer, 1980-81, also dir.; ptnr. Windels, Marx, Davies & Ives, N.Y.C., 1981-84; of counsel Fishwick, Jones and Glenn, Roanoke, Va., 1984-95; ret. Chmn., chief exec. officer Erie Lackawanna Ry. Co., 1968-70; pres., chief exec. officer Del. and Hudson Ry. Co., 1968-70; pres., dir. Dereco, Inc., 1968-81; chmn. investment com., bd. dirs. Norfolk So. Corp., 1981-89. Trustee Roanoke Coll., 1964-72; trustee Va. Theol. Sem.; former chancellor Diocese S.W. Va.; former bd. dirs. Va. Found. Humanities; former trustee Va. Mus. Fine Arts, Richmond. Served as lt. comdr. USNR, 1942—45. Mem. Met. Club (Washington). Episcopalian. Office: 110 Franklin Rd SE Roanoke VA 24042-0002

FISHWICK, MARSHALL W. education educator; BA, Univ. Va., 1944; MA history, Univ. Wis., 1946; PhD am. studies, Yale Univ., 1950; DLITT (hon.), Dhaka Univ., Bagladesh, 1983; PhD (hon.), Krakow Univ., Poland, 1967. Instr. Yale Univ., 1949; prof. Wash. and Lee Univ., 1950—62; vis. prof. Imov. Minn., 1957; dir., cons. Winerthur Mus., 1962—64; disting. vis. prof. Univ. Wyo., 1963; prof. Lincoln Univ., 1964—70, Temple Univ., 1970—76; vis. prof. Yale Univ., 1984; prof. Va. Tech., 1976—. Contbr. chapters to books;, editor to many profl. jour. Grantee Glenn Grant, Wash. and Lee Univ., 1955, Yale Almuni Grant, 1968, 8 Fulbright Grants, Denmark, Germany, Eng., India (2), Bangladesh, Korea, South-East Asia, 1959—85; Sterling Fellow, Rockfeller Found., N.Y., 1948—50. Mem.: Salzburg Adv. Faculty, Am. Culture Assn., Popular Culture Assn., Soc. of Achtl. Hist., Japenese-Am. Studies Assn., Conseils aux Assn., Centro Italiano di Studi Am., Guild to Scholars, Am. Studies Rsch. Ctr., India, European Am. Studies Assn., British Am. Studies Assn., So. Hist. Soc., Va. His. Soc., AAUP, Modern Language Assn., Ogrn. of Am. Hist., Am. Hist. Assn., Am. Studies Assn., Nat. Edn. Assn.

FISK, CHARLES CARROLL, retired civil engineer, consultant; b. St. Croix Falls, Wis., Jan. 7, 1918; s. Harry Abner and Emma Johanna (Anderson) F.; m. Micki Rennie, June 3, 1942; children: Terry, Cherie, Lucinda, Carolee. BS in Agr., U. Wis., 1941, BS in Civil Engring., 1942; profl. cert. in meteorology, U. Chgo., 1943. Hydraulic engr. Tenn. Valley Authority, Knoxville, Tenn., 1942; asst. chief river ops. U.S. Bur. Reclamation, Denver and Loveland, Colo., 1946-55; water supply engr. Denver Water Bd., 1955-61; cons. Fisk Engring., Denver, 1961-84; ret. Author, pub.: From Whence They Came, 1996, The Road From St. Croix Falls, 1997. 1st lt. U.S. Air Corps, 1942-46. Avocations: hiking, running, skiing, canoeing, chess. Home: 13691 E Marina Dr Apt 507 Aurora CO 80014-3731 E-mail: MickiFisk@webtv.net.

FISK, CHARLES JOHN, meteorologist, researcher, consultant; s. Everett Vincent Fisk and Florence Linnea Carlson. BSBA, U. Minn., 1968; MS in Meteorology, U. Wis., 1984; MBA, Mankato State U., 1973. Meteorologist/climatologist Naval Base Ventura County, Point Mugu, Calif., 1986—; fin. analyst IBM Corp., Rochester, 1974—79. Cons. long-range forecasting of so. Calif. temperatures and precipitation, 1996—2000. Author: The First Fifty Years of Continuous Recorded Weather History In Minnesota (1820-1869) - A Narrative Chronology; contbr. articles to profl. jours.; author procs. Pvt. U.S. Army, 1968—69. Mem.: Am. Statis. Assn., Am. Meteorol. Soc. Avocations: reading, travel, web publishing. Home: 590 Gilbert Street Newbury Park CA 91320 Office: Point Mugu CA 91342 Personal E-mail: cjfisk@worldnet.att.net.

FISK, DORIS ROSALIE SCANLAN, volunteer; b. Mpls., Aug. 20, 1915; d. Arthur William and Lea Marie (Beauchaine) Scanlan; m. Ellsworth William Fisk, Aug. 31, 1942; children: Gregory, Janine, Marilyn, Kathleen. Student, Mpls. Bus. Coll., 1935, U. Minn., 1940, San Antonio Jr. Coll., 1964. Hosp. vol. ARC, 1940-71; vol. Audie Murphy Vets. Hosp., 1972—; med. transcriber Radiology Assocs., San Antonio, 1962-64; nurse office mgr. for surgeon San Antonio, 1964-77; vol. Sr. Svc. Orgn., San Antonio, 1970—; vol., fund raiser Vis. Nurse Assn. S.W. San Antonio, 1992-97; vol. Quantum Brookhollow Med. Ctr., 1999—. Sec. vol. Demo-Ne Demos, San Antonio, 1960-64; pres. YWCA Wives, San Antonio, 1964-65, Espada Mission Aux., San Antonio, 1965-66; chair March of Dimes, San Antonio, ARC, 1940-1971, chmn. of vols.; vol. usher and seamstress Harlequin Theatre, from 1971; treas. altar soc. St. Mary's Cath.Ch., 1984-92; pres. flu shot prog. VNA, vol. Brookhollow Libr., 1995-96; chmn. Brooke Gen. Hosp. Vols. Recipient Golden Globe award Vol. Vis. Nurse of the Yr., San Antonio, 1993, Gold Key ring J.C. Penney; Letter of Congratulation, Pres. Clinton. Mem. AAUW, La Societé Francaise Canadian, Ret. Sr. Vols. (bd. mem. 1970—), Officers Wives Club (tour guide 1996-97, tel. chairperson 1999-2000, 2000-2001), Smithsonian Instn., Williamsburg, Met. Mus., Beta Sigma Phi (life), Kappa Kappa Gamma. Democrat. Roman Catholic. Avocations: travel, reading, sewing. Home: 7099 Beckett Rd Apt 1173 Austin TX 78749

FISK, EDWARD RAY, retired civil engineer, author, educator; b. Oshkosh, Wis., July 19, 1924; s. Ray Edward and Grace O. (Meyer) Barnes; married, Oct. 28, 1950; children: Jacqueline Mary, Edward Ray II, William John, Robert Paul. BCE, Marquette U., 1949; student, Fresno (Calif.) State Coll., 1954, UCLA, 1957-58. Registered profl. engr., Ariz., Calif., Colo., Fla., Idaho, Ky., La., Mont., Nev., Oreg., Utah, Wash., Wyo.; lic. land surveyor, oreg., Idaho; lic. gen. engring. contractor, Calif.; cert. arbitrator Calif. Constrn. Contract Arbitration Com. Engr. Calif. Div. Hwys., 1952-55, Bechtel Corp., Vernon, Calif., 1955-59; project mgr. Toups Engring. Co., Santa Ana, Calif., 1959-61; dept. head Perliter & Soring, Los Angeles, 1961-64; Western rep. Wire Reinforcement Inst., Washington, 1964-65; cons. engr. Anaheim, Calif., 1965; assoc. engr. Met. Water Dist. So. Calif., 1966-68; chief specification engr. Koebig & Koebig, Inc., Los Angeles, 1968-71; mgr. constrn. svcs. VTN Consol., Inc., Irvine, Calif., 1971-78; pres. E.R. Fisk Constrn., Orange, Calif., 1978-81; corp. dir. constrn. mgmt. James M. Montgomery Cons. Engrs., Inc., Pasadena, Calif., 1981-83; v.p. Lawrence, Fisk & McFarland, Inc., Santa Barbara and Orange, 1983—; pres. E.R. Fisk & Assocs., Orange, 1983—, Gleason, Peacock & Fisk, Inc., 1987-92. V.p. constrn. svcs. Wilsey & Hamm, Foster City, Calif., 1993-94; adj. prof. engring., constrn. Calif. State U., Long Beach, 1987-90, Orange Coast Coll., Costa Mesa, Calif., 1957-78, Calif. Poly. State U., Pomona, 1974; instr. U. Calif., Berkeley, Inst. Transportation Studies, 1978—, engring. prof. programs U. Wash., 1994—, internationally for ASCE Continuing Edn. Author: Machine Methods of Survey Computing, 1958, Construction Project Administration, 1978, 82, 88, 92, 97, 2000, Construction Engineers Complete Handbook of Forms, 1981, 92, Resident Engineers Field Manual, 1992; co-author: Contractor's Project Guide, 1988, Contracts and Specifications for Public Works Projects, 1992. With USN, 1942-43, USAF, 1951-52. Fellow ASCE (life, past chmn. exec. com. constrn. divn., past chmn. nat. com. inspection 1978—), Nat. Acad. Forensic Engrs. (diplomate); mem. Can. Soc. Civil Engring., Orange County Engring. Coun. (past pres.), Calif. Soc. Profl. Engrs. (past pres. Orange County), Structural Engrs. Assn. Calif. (engrs. joint contracts documents com. 1993-95), Am. Arbitration Assn. (nat. panel), U.S. Com. Large Dams, Order Founders and Patriots Am. (past gov. Calif.), Soc. Colonial Wars (dep. gov. gen. Calif. chpt.), S.R. (past dir.), Engring. Edn. Found. (trustee), Tau Beta Pi. Home: 1792 N Ridgewood St Orange CA 92865-4454 E-mail: fisk@uclink4.berkeley.edu., erfiskpe@worldnet.att.net.

FISK, FRANCINE JOAN, librarian; b. Tulsa, Okla., Mar. 3, 1953; d. Francis Charls and Alberta Joan (Fink) F.; m. Scott Franklin McClung, Nov. 30, 1991; 1 child, Miranda Fisk McClung. BS, U. Tulsa, 1974; MLS, U. Okla., 1976. Media specialist Moore (Okla.) Pub. Schs., 1976-85; coord. media svcs. U. Tulsa, 1985-87, head reference libr., 1987-89, coord. libr. info. svcs., 1989-92, coord. libr. info. svcs. and collections, 1992-93, coord. gen. svcs., 1993-98, library dir., 1998—. Bd. dirs., exec. bd. Okla. Coun. Acad. Libr., 1998—; adv. coun. Okla. Libr. Tech. Network, 2000—. Mem. ALA, Okla. Libr. Assn. (chair Adminstrn. Roundtable 1995-96, 99-2000, exec. bd. 2001-02, scholarship chair 2002-03), Tulsa Area Libr. Coop. (bd. dirs., vice chmn. 1991-92), Beta Phi Mu. Office: McFarlin Libr U Tulsa 2933 E 6th St Tulsa OK 74104-3121 E-mail: francine-fisk@utulsa.edu.

FISK, GAIL MARIE, music educator; b. Rochester, Minn., Mar. 9, 1958; d. Joseph Arthur and Jean Iris Anderson; children by previous marriage: Brian Patrick Liebl, Brittany Rose Liebl; m. Robert Benjamin Fisk, Sept. 28, 1996. BA, St. Olaf Coll., Northfield, Minn., 1980. Tchr. instrumental music Dawson (Minn.)-Boyd Pub. Schs., 1980-81; tchr. choir and classroom music Park Rapids (Minn.) Mid. Sch., 1986-87; pvt. tchr. Bud's Music Ctr., Hopkins, Minn., 1987-98, La Musique Music Studio, Minnetonka, Minn., 1996—; substitute tchr. Minnetonka Pub. Schs., 1987-98, tchr. classroom music, 1998—. Dir. vocal music groups Excelsior (Minn.) United Meth. Ch., 1990—. Mem. Minn. Music Tchrs. Assn. Methodist. Office: La Musique Music Studio 17724 Excelsior Blvd Minnetonka MN 55345-4109

FISK, IAN T. economic development consultant, publishing executive; b. Hyannis, Mass., Oct. 17, 1968; s. Bradley Jr. and Elizabeth (DeWolf) F.; m. Lorin Kleinman. BA in Polit. and Social Thought, U. Va., 1990; MBA in Pub. Mgmt., Yale U., 2001. Pub. The Yellow Jour., Charlottesville, Va., 1987-89; nat. office mgr. Tsongas for Pres., Boston, 1991-92; bus. mgr. Pub. Allies, 1993—95; CEO ITF Consulting, Inc., Washington, 1995—99; project mgr. Corp. for Nat. and Cmty. Svc., 1999—2003; dir. CitySort, Washington, 2003—. Mem. Minn. Chongus Theater Troupe, 2003—. Avocation: improv theatre. E-mail: itf@aol.com.

FISK, IRWIN WESLEY, financial investigator; b. Byers, Kans., Nov. 20, 1938; s. Walter Roleigh Fisk and Mae Pearle Irwin; m. Susie Bea Walters, Sept. 9, 1973; children: Mark Christopher, Paul Steven. Student, L.A. City Coll., 1958-60, Calif. State U., L.A., 1960-64, Pasadena C.C., 1987-88. Lic. pvt. investigator, Calif. Asst. exec. dir. Stores Protective Assn., L.A., 1962-66; sr. spl. investigator Calif. Dept. Corps., L.A., 1966-83, chief investigator, 1983-94; pres. Bus. and Fin. Investigations, Inc., La Crescenta, 1994—. Mem. Multi-State Law Enforcement Task Force of Fraudulent Telemarketing, L.A., 1987-94, Nat. Coun. Policy Advisors, 1994—, criminal justice adv. bd., Bethany Coll., 2002—. Contbr. articles to profl. publs. Mem. U.S. Chess Fedn. (life), Am. Radio Relay League (DXCC award 1993), Authors Guild, So. Calif. Fraud Investigators Assn., Masons, Nat. Coun. Policy Adv. for Inst. Law and Econ. Policy, 1994-, Criminal Justice Adv. Bd. Bethany Coll., 2002-. Republican. Avocations: chess, ham radio. Home: 701 Emerald Dr Lindsborg KS 67456-2004 Office: Bus and Fin Investigations Inc PO Box 8246 La Crescenta CA 91224-0246 E-mail: fisk@alltel.net.

FISK, LENNARD AYRES, physicist, educator; b. Elizabeth, N.J., July 7, 1943; s. Lennard Ayres and Elinor (Fischer) F.; m. Patricia Elizabeth Leuba, Dec. 28, 1966; children: Ian, Justin, Nathan. AB, Cornell U., 1965; PhD, U. Calif., San Diego, 1969. Postdoctoral fellow NASA/Goddard Space Flight Ctr., Greenbelt, MD., 1969-71, astrophysicist, 1971-77; assoc. prof. U. N.H., Durham, 1977-81, prof., 1981-87, dir. rsch., 1982-83, interim v.p./fin. affairs, 1983-84, v.p. rsch. and fin., 1984-87; assoc. administr. space sci. and applications NASA Hdqrs., Washington, 1987-93; prof. U. Mich., 1993—. Advisor NAS, NASA, 1980-87. Contbr. more than 120 articles to profl. jours. Recipient Space Science award Am. Inst. Aeronautics and Astronautics, 1994. Fellow Am. Geophys. Union; mem. Internat. Acad. Astronautics, Academia Europaea (fgn. mem.). Office: Univ of Michigan Atmos Oceanic & Space Scis 2455 Hayward St Ann Arbor MI 48109-2143

FISK, MARTIN H. lawyer; b. St. Paul, Apr. 11, 1947; BA, U. Minn., 1969; JD, Harvard U., 1976. Bar: Minn. 1976. Mem. Briggs and Morgan P.A., St. Paul. Mem. ABA, Phi Beta Kappa. Office: Briggs and Morgan PA 2200 1st Nat Bank Bldg Saint Paul MN 55101-3210

FISK, MERLIN EDGAR, judge; b. Great Falls, Mont., Mar. 18, 1921; s. Edgar Anson and Eleanor Sybil (Worden) F.; m. Margery Anne Hall, May 27, 1942; children: Mary Dana, Catherine, Anne, Elizabeth. BSChemE, Mont. State U., 1942. Tech. adminstr. Lago Oil & Transport Co., Ltd. subsidiary Exxon Corp., Aruba, Aruba Netherlands Antilles, 1942-62; v.p., gen. mgr. Antilles Chem. Co. subsidiary Exxon Corp., 1962-64; dir. mfg. Esso Pappas Indsl. Co., Athens, Greece, 1964-67; gen. mgr. Essochem, S.A. subsidiary Exxon Corp., Madrid, 1967-69, mgr. ops. and planning Brussels, 1969-71, ret., 1971; judge probate div. State of Conn., Newtown, 1979-91; ret., 1991. Pres. judge Conn. Probate Assembly, 1990-91. Mem. Commn. on Aging, Newtown, 1987-99; trustee Cyrenius H. Booth Libr., Newtown, 1975-95, 97-2003; bd. dirs. Newtown Meals on Wheels, Inc., 1974-93, Recording for the Blind, Inc. Conn. chpt., New Haven, 1975-92, Waterbury (Conn.) Ballet Co., 1987-97. Mem. Am. Arbitration Assn. (comml. panel 1991-98), Men's Literary and Social Club of Newtown (pres. 1984-85). Republican. Episcopalian. Avocations: golf, gardening, reading.

FISK, RAYMOND PAUL, marketing educator; b. Sept. 27, 1953; s. Elwin Lee and Verleen Thelma (Rafferty) F.; m. Jamie Tucker, Aug. 8, 1980. BS, Ariz. State U., 1976, MBA, 1977, PhD, 1980. Faculty assoc. Ariz. State U., Tempe, 1977-80; isntr. Am. Grad. Sch. Internat. Mgmt., Glendale, Ariz., 1978; asst. prof. mktg. Okla. State U., Stillwater, 1980-84, assoc. prof. mktg., 1984-89; mktg. analyst Nat. U. Teleconf. Network, 1983; dir. mktg. Teleconf. Consortium, 1984-85; faculty assoc. Ctr. for Internat. Trade Devel., 1986-89; assoc. prof. mktg. U. Cen. Fla., Orlando, 1989-96; prof., chair dept. mktg. U. New Orleans, 1996—. Guest prof. U. do Porto, Portugal, 1996. Author: (with Jamie T. Fisk) Airways: A Marketing Simulation, 1986, (with Stephen Grove and Joby John) Interactive Services Marketing, 2000; editor: (with Stephen W. Brown) Marketing Theory: Distinguished Contributions, 1984, (with Patriya S. Tansuhaj) Services Marketing: An Annotated Bibliography, 1985, (with Patriya S. Tansuhaj and Lawrence A. Crosby) Servmark: The Electronic Bibliography of Services Marketing Literature, 1987, (with Stephen Grove and Joby JHohn) Services Marketing Self-Portraits, 2000; cons. editor Mktg. News, 1981-82; editl. rev. bd. Jour. Health Care Mktg., 1983-89, Svc. Industries Jour.; contbr. articles to profl. jours. Fulbright scholar Klagenfurt U. of Edn. Scis., 1987;

dissertation rsch. grantee dept. mktg. Ariz. State U., 1980, Dean's excellence fund summer grantee Okla. State U., 1981-82, rsch. grantee Okla. State U./Asian Inst. Mgmt. Coop. Rsch. Program, 1983, summer bus. ext. grantee Okla. State U., 1983, 86, rsch. grantee Mktg. Sci. Inst., 1985-86, Ariz. State U., 1986-88. Mem. Am. Mktg. Assn. (doctoral consortium fellow 1979, editor mktg. newsletter 1984-86, dir. Svcs. Mktg. Spl. Interest Group 1993-95, sr. v.p. for Tchg./Info. Dissemination, Acad. Coun. 1994-96, pres. Ctrl. Fla. chpt. 1994-95, sr. v.p. mktg. 1998-99, pres. New Orleans chpt. 1998-99, pres. Acad. Coun. 2000-2001, editor AMA Mktg. Educator Online, 2002-03), Assn. Consumer Rsch., So. Mktg. Assn., Beta Gamma Sigma. Office: U New Orleans Coll Bus Admin Dept Mktg New Orleans LA 70148-0001 E-mail: rfisk@uno.edu.

FISKE, EDWARD B. editor, journalist, educational consultant; b. Phila., June 4, 1937; s. Edward R., Jr. and Jean F.; m. Dale Alden Woodruff, July 12, 1963 (div. May 1997); children: Julia F. Hogan, Suzanna F. Wilson; m. Helen F. Ladd, June 29, 1997. BA, Wesleyan U., Middletown, Conn., 1959; MA, Princeton Theol. Sem., 1963, Columbia U., 1965; LL.D. (hon.), Occidental Coll., 1991; and others. Religion reporter and editor N.Y. Times, 1964-74, edn. editor, 1974-91. Cons. Pew Forum on Edn. Reform, 1991-92, Bus. Roundtable Edn. Initiative, 1991-92, Dana Found., 1992-99, UNICEF Edn. Mission to Bangladesh, 1993, Internat. Rescue Com. in Cambodia, 1993-94, Acad. Ednl. Devel., 1993—, World Bank, 1995—, UNESCO, 1996—; edn. analyst Asian Devel. Bank, 1994; vis. scholar Victoria U. Wellington, New Zealand, 1998, U. Cape Town, South Africa, 2002. Author: Fiske Guide to Colleges, (annual) Smart Schools, Smart Kids, 1990, Basic Education, 1993, (with Bruce Hammond) Fiske Guide to Getting into The Right College, 1997, 2d edit., 1999, (with Helen F. Ladd) When Schools Compete, 2000; contbr. articles to nat. periodicals. Trustee Found. for Excellent Schs., 2000—, N.C. Ctr. for Internat. Understanding, 2001-, Central Park Sch. for Children, Durham, 2002—. Wolynsky-Joukowsky fellow Brown U., 1990, Montgomery fellow Dartmouth Coll., 1991. Mem.: Phi Beta Kappa. Home: 1723 Tisdale St Durham NC 27705-5631 E-mail: efiske@aol.com.

FISKE, JORDAN JAY, lawyer, retired prosecutor; b. Bklyn., Apr. 4, 1943; s. George Vlatofe and Pearl (Kalker) F.; m. Sandra Joyce Rappaport, June 22, 1974. BA, Brandeis U., 1963; JD, Fordham U., 1966. Bar: N.Y. 1967. Spl. agt. USAF Office of Spl. Investigations, Washington, 1966-71; trial atty. Dept. of Justice, N.Y.C., 1971-73; spl. asst. atty. gen. N.Y. State Office of the Spl. Prosecutor, N.Y.C., 1973-76; chief asst. dist. atty. Onondaga County Dist. Attys. Office, Syracuse, NY, 1976—2002; assoc. Syracuse Office of McGraw Law Firm, 2003—. Adviser Dist. Attys. Adv. Coun., Syracuse, 1976-2002; mem. Criminal Justice Adv. Bd., Syracuse, 1991. Capt. USAF, 1970-71, Vietnam. Mem. Jewish War Vets., Disabled War Vets., Vietnam Vets. Am. Office: 333 E Onondaga St Syracuse NY 13202

FISKE, ROBERT BISHOP, JR., lawyer; b. N.Y.C., Dec. 28, 1930; s. Robert Bishop and Lenore (Seymour) F.; m. Janet Tinsley, Aug. 21, 1954; children: Linda Goucher, Robert Bishop, Susan Williams. BA, Yale U., 1952; JD, U. Mich., 1955, LLD (hon.), 1997. Bar: Mich. 1955, N.Y. 1956, U.S. Ct. Appeals (2nd cir.) 1957, U.S. Supreme Ct. 1961. Assoc. Davis, Polk, Wardwell, Sunderland & Kiendl, 1955-57; asst. U.S. atty. So. Dist. N.Y., 1957-61; assoc. Davis Polk & Wardwell, 1961-64, ptnr., 1964—76, 1980—2002; U.S. atty. So. Dist. N.Y., N.Y.C., 1976-80; ind. counsel for Whitewater, Little Rock, 1994. Chmn. N.Y. State Jud. Commn. on Drugs and the Cts., 1999—2000; mem. Commn. for the Rev. of FBI Security Programs, 2001—02. Fellow Am. Coll. Trial Lawyers (pres. 1991-92); mem. ABA (chmn. standing com. on fed. judiciary 1984-87), Assn. of Bar of City of N.Y., Fed. Bar Coun. (pres. 1982-84), N.Y. State Bar Assn., Noroton Yacht Club, Wee Burn Country Club. Republican. Congregationalist. Office: 450 Lexington Ave New York NY 10017-3911

FISKE, SANDRA RAPPAPORT, psychologist, educator; b. Syracuse, N.Y., Sept. 25, 1946; d. Sidney Saul and Helen (Lapides) Rappaport; m. Jordan J. Fiske, June 22, 1974. BS, Cornell U., 1968; M.Ed., Tufts U., 1969; MA, Columbia U., 1971, PhD., 1974. Supervising sch. psychologist St. Elizabeth's Sch., N.Y.C., 1971-76; instr. clin. psychology Tchrs. Coll. Columbia, N.Y.C., 1973, clin. asst. dept. psychology, 1975-76; adj. prof. Syracuse U., 1976; sch. psychologist Syracuse Bd. Edn., 1976-77; prof. psychology Onondaga Community Coll., Syracuse, 1976-87, prof., 1988—, chair social sci. dept., 1993-99; pvt. practice psychology Syracuse, 1976—. NIMH fellow, 1969-72. Mem. APA, Ctrl. N.Y. Psychol. Assn., Sigma Xi, Psi Chi. Home: 2 Signal Hill Rd Fayetteville NY 13066-9674 Office: Onondaga Community Coll Dept Psychology Syracuse NY 13215 E-mail: fiskes@mail.sunyocc.edu.

FISKIN, ARTHUR MAX, JR., medical educator; b. Mt. Hope, Kans., Jan. 7, 1939; s. Arthur Monroe Fiskin and Mary Louise Armstrong-Fiskin; m. Joyce Elaine Buss, Dec. 22, 1957; children: Shawn Eugene, Shandin Cholena Klobe-Fiskin. BSc in Microbiology and Chemistry, Kans. State U., 1960; PhD in Biophysics, The Johns Hopkins U., 1966. Postdoctoral fellow U. of Groningen, Netherlands, 1966—67, VA Hosp. Rsch. Labs., Kans. City, Mo., 1967—68; prof. of microbiology U. of Kans., Kans. City, Kans., 1968—. Vis. prof. U. Delft, Netherlands, 1983—84; vis. scientist Inst. Cytological Investigations, Valencia, Spain, 1984; vis. prof. Mycology Ref. Lab. Case We. Res. U., Cleve., 1993—94; bd. dir. Childrens Internat., Kans. City, Mo.; chmn. and panelist biochemistry and strucutural biology fellowship panels Nat. Acad. of Sci., Washington, 1984—; contbr. Symposiums. Editor: European Jour. of Cell Biology, 1976—83. Co-chmn. project soar Shawnee Mission Sch. Dist., Overland Park, Kans., 1987—88; co-dir. intercity youth assistance project United Meth. Dist. Sister Chs., Kans. City, Kans., 1970—72; active Childrens Internat., Kansas City, Mo., 1984—. Fellow, NSF, 1958—59, Atomic Energy Commision, 1960, Johns Hopkins University-Biophysics, 1961—62, U.S. Pub. Health Svc., 1962—66, US Pub. Health Svc., 1966—67; grantee, U.S. Vets. Hosp. Rsch. Svc., 1968—88, NSF, 1981—83, U.S. Pub. Health Svc., 1991—94, Whittaker Found., 1995—98; scholar, Dow Chem. Corp., 1956, Gen. Electric Corp., 1957. Mem.: AAAS (corr.), N.Y. Acad. of Scis. (corr.), Internat. Soc. for Human and Animal Mycoses (corr.). Achievements include development of surface replica cytochemistry method. Avocations: swimming, music, theater, reading, writing. Office: Kasas University Medical Microbiology 3901 Rainbow Boulevard Kansas City KS 66103 E-mail: mfiskin@kumc.edu.

FISS, OWEN M. law educator, educator; b. 1938; BA, Dartmouth Coll., 1959; BPhil, Oxford U., 1961, LLB, Harvard U., 1964. Bar: N.Y. 1965. Law clk. to Judge Thurgood Marshall U.S. Ct. Appeals 2d Cir., 1964—65; law clk. to Justice Brennan U.S. Supreme Ct., 1965; spl. asst. atty. gen. civil rights divsn. U.S. Dept. Justice, Washington, 1966—67; acting dir. Office of Planning Coordination, 1968; prof. U. Chgo. Law Sch., 1968—74, Yale Law Sch., New Haven, 1974—84, Alexander M. Bickel prof. pub. law, 1984—92, Sterling prof., 1992—. Vis. prof. Stanford U., 1972; mem. Harvard Law Rev. Author: Injunctions, 1972, The Civil Rights Injunction, 1978; author: (with R.M. Cover) The Structure of Procedure, 1979; author: (with D. Rendleman) Injunctions 2d edit., 1984; author: (with Cover and J. Resnick) Procedure, 1988; author: (with Cover and Resnick) The Fed. Procedural Sys., 1988, The Fed. Procedural Sys. 3d edit., 1991, Holmes Devise Hist. of the Supreme Ct.: Troubled Beginnings of the Modern State, 1888-1910, 1993, Liberalism Divided, 1996, The Irony of Free Speech, 1996, A Cmty. of Equals, 1999, A Way Out, 2003; mem. edtl. bd.: Philosophy and Pub. Affairs and Found. Press, Yale Jour. Criticism, Yale Jour. Law and Humanities, Law, Econs. and Orgns.

FISTER, KATHERINE RENEE, mathematician, educator; d. Bennie Joe and Mildred Gayle Deaton; m. Kenneth William Fister, June 6, 1992; 1 child, Kristopher William Drew. BA, Transylvania U., 1990; MS, U. Tenn., 1992, PhD, 1996. Asst. prof. Murray (Ky.) State U., 1996—2002, assoc. prof., 2002—. Contbr. articles to profl. jours. Grantee, NSF, 2001– ; Presdl. Rsch. grant, Com. Instnl. Studies and Rsch. (CSIR), 2002—03. Mem.: Math. Assn. Am., Soc. for Indsl. and Applied Math., Assn. Women in Math. Roman Catholic. Avocations: reading, swimming. Office: Murray State Univ 6C Faculty Hall Murray KY 42071 Office Fax: 270-762-2314. Business E-Mail: renee.fister@murraystate.edu.

FISTER, MICHAEL J. music educator; b. Allentown, Pa., Feb. 13, 1958; s. William James and Marie Harding Fister; m. Barbara Jean Miller, Jan. 30, 1982; children: Sarah Elizabeth, Patricia Marie. BA in Music Edn., Moravian Coll., 1980; MS in Edn., Temple U., 1985. Dir. music St. Elizabeth Roman Cath. Ch., Whitehall, Pa., 1980—96; elem. music tchr. Northampton (Pa.) Area Sch. Dist., 1996—; chorus dir. Air Products & Chems., Inc., Trexlertown, Pa., 1984—. Chorus dir. Mcpl. Opera Co., Allentown, Pa., 1986—, bd. mem., 1989; dir. music St. Paul's Luth. Ch., Catasauqua, Pa., 1997—; musical dir. Catasauqua Area Showcase Theater, 1997—. Mem.: Music Educators Nat. Conf., Am. Guild Organists. Office: Lehigh Elem Sch 800 Blue Mt Dr Walnutport PA 18088 Home: 733 4th St Catasauqua PA 18032

FISZEL, GEOFFREY LYNN, investment banker, investment advisor; b. N.Y.C, Aug. 9, 1942; s. John Henry and Rebecca (Wexman) F.; m. Barbara Ann Foohey, Jan. 30, 1970; children: Sharon Lynn, Morgan Bernard, Austin Tyler, Alexander William. BS in Mgmt. and Ops. Rsch., NYU, 1974; MS in Acctg. and Tax (Seminar award), U. Hartford, 1976; grad. scholar program econs. of fin., Trinity Coll., 1980. Registered securities rep., gen. securities prin., investment adviser. Cost acct. O'Malley Cos., Phoenix, 1974; regional acct., asst. regional contr. Sanitas Svc. Corp., Hartford, Conn., 1974-75; asst. to corp. contr. Bristol (Conn.) Brass Corp., 1975-76; asst. contr. Security Ins. Co. of Hartford, 1976-80; contr. Chase Enterprises, 1980-81, v.p., contr., 1981, sr. v.p., contr., 1985, sr. v.p. corp. and real estate devel., banking, ins., telecom., and mergers and acquisitions, 1988-89; CEO, pres., chmn. Equity Investors Holding Co., Glastonbury, Conn., 1989—; v.p. investments Advest, Inc., Hartford, 1993-94, Tucker Anthony, Inc., Hartford, 1994-2000, first v.p. investments, 2000—01; v.p., fin. advisor Morgan Stanley, Hartford, 2001—. Tax and fin. cons. U. Conn.; lectr., cons. in field. Author: How to Start Your Own Private Investment Partnership, 1997; pub., author investment adv. newsletter Continuing Walks On The Wild Side. Mem. Juvenile Diabetes Found. Served with USMC, 1959-63. Mem. Real Estate Bd. N.Y., Fin. Execs. Inst. (mem. corp. fin. and taxation coms.), The Nature Conservancy. Home: 245 Farmcliff Dr PO Box 578 Glastonbury CT 06033-0578 Office: Morgan Stanley One City Pl Hartford CT 06103 E-mail: geoffrey_fiszel@msn.com.

FISZER-SZAFARZ, BERTA (BERTA SAFARS), research scientist; b. Wilno, Poland, Feb. 1, 1928; m. David Safars; children: Martine, Michel. MS, U. Buenos Aires, 1955, PhD, 1956. Lab. chief Cancer Inst. Villejuif, France, 1961-67; vis. scientist Nat. Cancer Inst., Bethesda, Md., 1967-68; lab. chief Institut Curie, Orsay, France, 1969—; vis. scientist Inst. Applied Biochemistry, Mitake, Gifu, Japan, 1986; gen. sec. dep. French-Israel Assn. Sci. Rsch. and Tech., 1994. Contbr. articles to profl. jours. Mem. European Assn. Cancer Research, Am. Assn. Cancer Research (corres. mem.), European Cell Biology Orgn., French Soc. Cell Biology. Office: Institut Curie-Biologie Bat 110 Centre Universitaire 91405 Orsay France

FITCH, COY DEAN, physician, educator; b. Marthaville, La., Oct. 5, 1934; s. Raymond E. and Joey (Youngblood) F.; m. Rachel Farr, Mar. 31, 1956; children: Julia Anne, Jaquelyn Kay. BS, U. Ark., 1956, MS, MD, U. Ark., 1958. Diplomate Am. Bd. Internal Medicine and Endocrinology. Intern U. Ark. Sch. Medicine, 1958-59, resident, 1959-62, instr. biochemistry, 1959-62, asst. prof. medicine and biochemistry, 1962-66, asso. prof., 1966-67; dir. U. Ark. Sch. Medicine (Honors Med. Student Research Program), 1965-67; asso. prof. internal medicine and biochemistry St. Louis U. Sch. Medicine, 1967-73, prof. internal medicine, 1973—, prof. biochemistry, 1976—, head sect. metabolism, 1969-76, dir. div. endocrinology and metabolism, 1977-85; chief med. service St. Louis U. Hosps., 1976-77, vice-chmn. dept. internal medicine, 1985-88, acting chmn. dept. internal medicine, 1985-88, chmn. dept., 1988-2000; practice medicine, specializing in internal medicine Little Rock, 1962-67, St. Louis, 1969—. Dir. Diabetic Clinic, U. Ark. Med. Ctr., 1962-67, head sect. metabolism and endocrinology, 1966-67; mem. nutrition study sect. div. research grants NIH, 1967-71 Assoc. editor: Nutrition Revs., 1964; contbr. articles to profl. jours. Served from capt. to lt. col., M.C. AUS, 1967-69. Recipient Lederle Med. Faculty award, 1966-67; Russell M. Wilder-Nat. Vitamin Found. fellow, 1959-62 Master ACP (gov. Mo. chpt. 1995-99); mem. Am. Inst. Nutrition, Am., Am. Soc. Biol. Chemists, Ctrl. Soc. Clin. rsch., Phi Beta Kappa. Office: 1402 S Grand Blvd Saint Louis MO 63104-1004 E-mail: fitchcd@slu.edu.

FITCH, FRANCES CONOVER, music educator; b. Boston, Apr. 29, 1951; d. Conover and Priscilla (Hall) Fitch; m. Gregory Robert Bover, Aug. 12, 1978; 1 child, Nicholas Fitch Bover. BA cum laude, Bard Coll., Annandale-on-Hudson, N.Y., 1973; MusM, New Eng. Conservatory of Music, Boston, 1976. Faculty New Eng. Conservatory, Boston, 1979—89; music dir. St. John's Episc. Ch., Gloucester, Mass., 1979—88; faculty, chair early music dept. Longy Sch. Music, Cambridge, Mass., 1979—. Faculty Leadership Program of Presiding Bishop's Diploma, 1996—99. Performer: (recording) O Ye Tender Babes, 2000, 12 recordings. Mem. liturgy and music commn. Episc. Diocese of Mass., 1993—96. Mem.: Am. Guild Organists (exec. com. 1990—93). Avocations: gardening, sailing. Home: 108 Magnolia Ave Gloucester MA 01930 Office: Longy Sch of Music Early Music Dept One Follen St Cambridge MA 02138-3502

FITCH, FRANK WESLEY, pathologist educator, immunologist, educator, administrator; b. Bushnell, Ill., May 30, 1929; s. Harold Wayne and Mary Gladys (Frank) F.; m. Shirley Dobbins, Dec. 23, 1951; children— Mary Margaret, Mark Howard. MD, U. Chgo., 1953, S.M., 1957, PhD, 1960; MD (hon.), U. Lausanne, Switzerland, 1990. Postdoctoral research fellow USPHS, 1954-55, 57-58; faculty U. Chgo., 1957—, prof. pathology, 1967—, Albert D. Lasker prof. med. sci., 1976—, emeritus prof., 1996, assoc. dean med. and grad. edn. div. biol. scis., 1976-85, dean acad. affairs, 1985-86, dir. Ben May Inst., 1986-95. Vis. prof. Swiss Inst. Exptl. Cancer Research, Lausanne, Switzerland, 1974-75. Editor-in-chief The Jour. of Immunology, 1997-2002; contbr. chpts. to books, articles to profl. jours. Recipient Borden Undergrad. Research award, 1953, Lederle Med. Faculty award, 1958-61; Markle Found. scholar, 1961-66; Commonwealth Fund fellow U. Lausanne (Switzerland) Institut de Biochimie, 1965-66; Guggenheim fellow, 1974-75 Mem. Fedn. Am. Socs. for Exptl. Biology (pres. 1993-94), Am. Assn. Immunologists (pres. 1992-93), Am. Soc. for Investigative Pathology, Am. Assn. for Cancer Rsch., Chgo. Path. Soc., Transplantation Soc., Sigma Xi, Alpha Omega Alpha. Home: 5449 S Kenwood Ave Chicago IL 60615-5312 E-mail: ffitch@uchicago.edu.

FITCH, LINDA BAUMAN, educator; b. Elmira, N.Y., Jan. 6, 1947; d. Floyd Theodore Bauman and Wilma Mildred Rennie; m. H. Taylor Fitch, Feb. 15, 1969; children: Trevor Andrew, Matthew Taylor. BS, Keuka Coll., Keuka Park, 1969. Elem. tchr. Penn Yan (N.Y.) Ctrl. Sch. Dist., 1972-73, tchg. asst. K-5, 1999—; computer coord. Fitch Auto Supply, Penn Yan, 1973-99. Com. chmn. troop 48 Boy Scouts Am., Branchport, N.Y., 1986-92; v.p. Penn Yan Cen. Sch. Bd., 1984-92, 95-97, pres., 1992-95; chmn. pub. rels. Yates Day Care Ctr., Penn Yan, 1980-82; mem. Bd. Coop. Ednl. Svcs., 1992-99. Mem. AAUW, Nat. Sch. Bds. Assn. (fed. rels. network 1988-99), N.Y. State Sch. Bds. Assn. (state legis. network 1991-99), Four County Sch. Bds. Assn. (legis. chmn., 2d v.p., 1st v.p., pres., mem. commr.'s adv. coun. sch. bd. mems. 1995). Republican. Presbyterian. Avocations: needlework, reading, swimming. Home: 3120 Kinneys Corners Rd Bluff Point NY 14478-9752

FITCH, MARY KILLEEN, human resources specialist; b. Carroll, Iowa, July 15, 1949; d. Michael Francis and Mildred (Pauley) Killeen; m. David Paul Fitch, July 3, 1971; 1 child, Emily Grace. BS, Iowa State U., 1971, MS, 1975; postgrad., U. Minn., 1982—. Pers. adminstr. Control Data Corp., Roseville, Minn., 1976-77; sr. compensation analyst/employee rels rep. Honeywell, Inc., Mpls., 1977-80; human resource mgr./compensation and benefits mgr. No. Telecom, Inc., Minnetonka, Minn., 1980-82; compensation cons. Gen. Mills, Wayzata, Minn., 1984-85; mgr. compensation Northwestern Nat. Life Ins., Mpls., 1985-87; prin. compensation specialist Conml. Bldgs. Group, Honeywell, Inc., Mpls., 1987-89; dir. compensation, HRIS, benefits, incentive design Nat. Car Rental Sys., Inc., Mpls., 1989—98; dir. compensation, HRIS, benefits, and pay system N.Am. Rental Group (combined Alamo and Nat. Car), Mpls., 1998—99; v.p. compensation, HRIS ANC Rental Corp., Ft. Lauderdale, Fla., 1999—. Cons. human resources compensation, Fitch, Fitch Assoc., 1986—, cons. human resources Les Kraus & Assocs., Edina, Minn., 1984; pres. Personnel Mgmt. Services of Twin Cities, St. Paul, 1983—; adj. instr., tchg. asst. Lakewood Cmty. Coll./U. Minn., Mpls., 1982-84. Author: (with Paul) Muchinsky) Organization Behavior and Human Performance, 1975; (with John Fossum) Personnel Psychology, 1985. Former chmn., bd. dirs. Kathadin, United Way Agy., Mpls., 1985-89; curriculum com. U. Minn., 1983-84. Georgie Catt Iowa State U. scholar, 1970. Mem. AAUW, Assn. Human Resources Systems Profls., Am. Compensation Assn., Psi Chi, Phi Kappa Pi. Avocations: dressage, Karate. Home: 9377 Olmstead Dr Lake Worth FL 33467-3616 Office: ANC Rental Corp 200 S Andrews Ave Fort Lauderdale FL 33301-1864 E-mail: mfitch@hotmail.com, fitchm@ancrental.com.

FITCH, MORGAN LEWIS, JR., intellectual property lawyer; b. Chgo., Nov. 21, 1922; s. Morgan Lewis and Marian (Ringer) F.; m. Helen Shearer, June 9, 1945; children: Ruth F. White, Mary F. White, Morgan Lewis, Frederick Shearer. BS in Chem. Engring., Ill. Inst. Tech., 1943; student, Princeton U., 1943, MIT, 1943-44; JD, U. Mich., 1948. Bar: Ill. 1948. Since practiced in Chgo.; partner Fitch, Even, Tabin, & Flannery, 1953—. Trustee emeritus Tri-State Coll., Angola, Ind.; trustee YMCA, Chgo.; bd. dirs. YMCA Found. Lt. USNR, 1943-46. Recipient Disting. Pub. Service award Sec. Navy, 1960, 65 Mem. ABA, Ill. Bar Assn., Chgo. Bar Assn., Intellectual Property Law Assn. of Chgo., Lawyers Club Chgo., Navy League U.S. (pres. 1965-67), U.S. Naval Sea Cadet Corps (pres. 1963-65), Naval Commandery, Naval Res. Assn., Soc. Mayflower Descs.. Home: 4640 Clausen Ave Western Springs IL 60558-1640 Office: 120 S La Salle St Chicago IL 60603-3403 E-mail: hsfmlf@aol.com.

FITCH, NANCY ELIZABETH, historian, educator; b. White Plains, N.Y., June 17, 1947; d. Robert Franklin and Nancy Elizabeth (Harvey) F. BA in Polit. Sci./English Lit., Oakland U., Rochester, Mich., 1969; MA in History, U. Mich., 1971, PhD in History, 1981. Danforth tchg. intern dept. history U. Mich., Ann Arbor, 1970; asst. prof. history and lit. Sangamon State U., Springfield, Ill., 1972-74; sr. social sci. rsch. analyst The Congl. Rsch. Svc. of Libr. of Congress, Washington, 1975-78; asst. to the chmn./historian U.S. EEO Commn., Washington, 1982-89; asst. prof. history Lynchburg Coll. of Va., 1989-91; asst. prof. African Am. studies Temple U., Phila., 1991-92; Jesse Ball Dupont vis. scholar Randolph-Macon Woman's Coll., Lynchburg, Va., 1992-93; assoc. prof. history U. N.C. at Asheville, 1993-95; hist. and assoc. prof. English, chair Coll. New Rochelle, N.Y., 1995—. Chmn.'s rep. White House Inst. on Hist. Black Colls. and Univs., U.S. Dept. Edn., 1985-89, EEO com.; pub. rels. vol. S. Africa Exhibit Project, Washington, 1986-88; mem. adv. com. DuPont Vis. Scholars Project, Va. Found. Ind. Colls., 1990-91; adj. prof. in history Shaw U., Asheville, 1994; lectr. Jesse Ball DuPont Found. Coll. Confs. on Diversity, The Aspen Inst., Queenstown, Md., 1995, 96; participating historian, spkr. Schomburg Ctr. for Rsch. in Black Culture, N.Y.C., 1994, Booker T. Washington Jr. Anniversary Commemoration. Anthology Editor: How Sweet the Sound: The Spirit of African American History, 1999; Editl. assoc.: Jour. S. Asian Lit., 1969-79; co-editor: Diversity: A Jour. of Multicultural Issues, 1995-98; mem. editl. adv. bd. Kente Cloth: African Am. Voices in Tex.; book reviewer Jour. S. Asian Lit., Lit. East and West, The Historian, Jour. Asian Studies; author: (series) Essays on Liberty, 1988; contbr. articles to profl. jours. Organizer, producer Ann. Dr. Martin Luther King Jr. Celebration prog., Washington, 1986-88; guest lectr. on history of Am. music Blue Ridge Music Festival, Lynchburg, 1991; participant Radio America African-Am. contbrs. to art and lit., 1990; vol./cons. The Holiday Project, Washington, 1986-88; mem. Widening Horizons Prog. of D.C. Pub. Schs., 1986-88; trustee Sister to Sister Internat. Recipient Achievement award Mt. Vernon Day Care Ctr., 1983, Spl. Commendation, U.S. EEO Commn., 1985, 89, Ft. Drum Sgt. Maj.'s medal for svc. 10th Mountain div. Light Inf., Ft. Drum, N.Y., 1992; fellow Ford Found., 1971-72, Nat. Def. Fgn. Lang., 1970, U. Mich., 1970-71, 78-79, John Hay Whitney Found., 1969-70; Faculty summer seminar fellowship Nat. Endowment for the Humanities, U. Kans., Lawrence, 1996; Alden B. Dow creativity fellow Northwood U., 1998; Millennium writer Westchester Libr. Sys. Inc., 2000. Fellow Soc. Values in Higher Edn.; mem. Assn. for Study African Am. Life and History, Orgn. Am. Hists., Phi Alpha Theta (faculty advisor 1990-91). Republican. Episcopalian/Buddhist. Avocation: photography. Home: 267 Bedford Ave Mount Vernon NY 10553-1517 Office: Coll New Rochelle 29 Castle Pl New Rochelle NY 10805-2338

FITCH, RACHEL FARR, health policy analyst; b. July 27, 1933; d. Allen Edward and Rosie Leola (Jones) Farr; m. Coy Dean Fitch, Mar. 31, 1956; children: Julia Anne, Jaquelyn Kay. Student, Little Rock U., 1965-67; BS, St. Louis U., 1974, MS, 1976, PhD, 1983. RN, Mo. Psychiat. staff nurse VA Ft. Root Hosp., North Little Rock, Ark., 1954-57; surg.-med. staff nurse St. Vincent Infirmary, Little Rock, Ark., 1957-65; acute care nurse Georgetown U. Hosp., Washington, 1968-69; pub. health nurse to adminstr. South office Vis. Nurse Assn. Greater St. Louis, 1970-73; cons. in edn. St. Louis City Health Dept., 1977-80; rsch. specialist Sen. John C. Danforth, St. Louis, 1980; owner RFF Assocs., 1983-86. Project dir. study of infant mortality in city of St. Louis, 1978. Mem. community health edn. com. Am. Heart Assn., 1977-87; bd. dirs. LWV of Mo., 1984-2001, editor newspaper, 1984-87, dir. health issues, 1987-99, 1st v.p. 1999-2001, 2003—; chmn. Mo. Consumer Health Care WATCH, 1996-2002; mem. adv. com. Mo. Medicaid Consumer, 1996-97; mem. Mo. Welfare Coord. Com., 1997-99; mem. healthcare mgmt. and policy adv. com. Maryville U., 2002—; mem. Mo. Found. for Health Advocates steering com., 2003—. Mem. Am. Pub. Health Assn., Healthcare Mgmt. Policy Adv. Com., Acad. Polit. Sci., Grand Jury Assn. St. Louis (bd. dirs.), Woman's Club (St. Louis U. Sch. Medicine, past pres.), Jr. League St. Louis, Sigma Theta Tau. Address: 23 Lenox Pl Saint Louis MO 63108-1901 E-mail: rachel.farr.fitch@sbcglobal.net.

FITCH, VAL LOGSDON, physics educator; b. Merriman, Nebr., Mar. 10, 1923; s. Fred B. and Frances Marion (Logsdon) Fitch; m. Elise Cunningham Fitch, June 11, 1949 (dec. 1972); children: John Craig(dec.), Alan Peter; m. Daisy Harper Sharp, Aug. 14, 1976. Bin Engring., McGill U., 1948; PhD, Columbia U., 1954, Princeton, 2000. Instr. Columbia, 1953; instr. physics Princeton, 1954—56, asst. prof., 1956—59, assoc. prof., 1959—60, prof., 1960—94, Class 1909 prof. physics, 1968—76, Cyrus Fogg Bracket prof. physics, 1977—84, James S. McDonnell Distinguished Univ. prof. physics, 1984—94, prof. emeritus, 1994—. Mem. Pres.'s Sci. Adv. Com., 1970—73. Trustee Assoc. Univ., Inc., 1961—67. Served with USAR, 1943—46. Recipient Rsch. Corp. award, 1967, E.O. Lawrence award, 1968, Wetherill medal, Franklin Inst., 1976, Nobel prize in Physics, 1980, Grad. Alumnus award, Am. Assn. State Colls. and Univs., 1984, Nat. medal of Sci., 1993; fellow Sloan, 1960. Fellow: Am. Phys. Soc. (pres. 1987—88); mem.: NAS, Am. Philos. Soc., Am. Acad. Arts and Scis. Office: Princeton U Dept Physics 391 Jadwin Hall Princeton NJ 08544-0001

FITCHEN, ALLEN NELSON, publisher; b. Syracuse, Aug. 8, 1936; s. John Frederick and Mary (Nelson) F. III; m. Jane Cady, June 13, 1959 (div. Feb. 1986); children— Anne Wheeler, Christopher Hardy, William Mills; m. Shirley Bergen, May 23, 1991. BA in English cum laude, Amherst Coll., 1958; MA in English, Cornell, 1960. Coll. traveler Macmillan Co., N.Y.C., 1960-62, editor, 1962-67; humanities editor U. Chgo. Press, 1968-82, sr. editor, 1971-82; dir. U. Wis. Press, 1982-98, ret., 1998. Mem. Psi Upsilon. Clubs: University (Madison). Home: 603 Eugenia Ave Madison WI 53705-3404 E-mail: afitchen@wisemail.wisc.edu.

FITCHEN, DOUGLAS BEACH, physicist, educator; b. N.Y.C., June 8, 1936; s. Paul R. and Eleanor B. Fitchen; m. Janet Mathews (dec. 1995); children: John, Katherine, Sylvia; m. Nancy Mathews, 1996 (dec. 2000); m. Karen Brazell, 2002. AB, Harvard U., 1957; PhD, U. Ill., 1962. Asst. prof. physics Cornell U., Ithaca, N.Y., 1962-65, assoc. prof., 1965-71, prof., 1971—, chmn. dept. physics, 1977-82, 86-91, 94-99. Vis. prof. Oxford U., 1968, U. Paris, Orsay, 1975 Alfred P. Sloan fellow, 1964-68 Achievements include research in optical studies of solids, Raman spectroscopy. Office: Cornell U Clark Hall Ithaca NY 14853

FITE, GILBERT COURTLAND, historian, educator, retired; b. Santa Fe, Ohio, May 14, 1918; s. Clyde Fite and Mary Jane McCardle; m. Alberta June Goodwin, July 24, 1941; children: James Franklin, Jack Preston. BA, MA in History, U. S.D., 1941, LittD (hon.), 1975; PhD, U. Mo., 1945, HHD (hon.), 1983; LittD (hon.), Seattle Pacific U., 1962. From asst. prof. to profl. U. Okla., Norman, 1945-68, George Lynn Cross prof. history, 1968-71; pres. Ea. Ill. U., Charleston, 1971-76; Richard B. Russell prof. history U. Ga., Athens, 1976-86, prof. emeritus, 1986—. Author: Peter Norbeck: Prairie Statesman, 1948, Mount Rushmore, 1952, George Peek & The Fight for Farm Parity, 1954, The Farmer's Frontier, 1865-1900, 1966, American Farmers: The New Minority, 1981, Cotton Fields No More, Southern Agriculture, 1865-1980, 1984, Richard B. Russell, Senator from Georgia, 1991, others; contbr. over 50 articles to profl. jours.

Trustee Phillips U., Enid, Okla., 1969-76, Lexington (Ky.) Theol. Sem., 1972-76. Fulbright scholar, 1962-63, 69-70; Guggenheim Found. fellow, 1964, Ford Fellow, 1954-55; named to S.D. Hall of Fame, 1990. Mem. Agrl. History Soc. (pres. 1960-61), So. Hist. Assn. (pres. 1974), Western History Assn. (pres. 1985-86), Phi Alpha Theta (pres. 1981-83). Methodist. Avocations: photography, golfing, traveling. Home: 4 Fite Cir Bella Vista AR 72714-5528

FITE, KATHLEEN ELIZABETH, education educator; b. Houston, June 26, 1948; d. Daniel Patrick and Edith Elizabeth (Burnett) F. BS in Edn., S.W. Tex. State U., 1969, MEd, 1970; EdD, N. Tex. State U., 1972. Cert. tchr., Tex. Prof. doctoral faculty S.W. Tex. State U., San Marcos, 1973—, dir. Ctr. for Study of Basic Skills, 1980, dir. Race Integration Tng. Inst., 1982-83, dir. elem. edn. dept., 1983-84, assoc. dir. sponsored projects, 1984-86, dir. sponsored projects, 1986-87. Cons. U.S. Dept. Edn., numerous pub. cos.; mem. adv. bd. Dushing Pub. Group, Inc. Author: Strutters: A few Favorites of the Total Teacher, The Super Ideas Book, Creative Art Ideas; asst editor SW Tex. U. Faculty Bull., 1977-78, editor, 1978-81; contbr. articles to profl. jours. Mem. sr. citizens adv. com. San Marcos City Coun., Commn. for Women; facilitator, dir. cmty. workshops; pres. Jr. Svc. League; activity chmn. Tex. Spl. Olympics. Named Ky. Col., 1975, named to Hall of Fame, San Marcos Commn. for Women, 1991; grantee U.S. Dept. Edn., L.B. Johnson Inst., 1988-89. Mem. ASCD, Nat. Assn. Edn. Young Children, Tex. Assn. Tchr. Educators, Kindergarten Tchrs. Tex., Tex. Computer Edn. Assn. (bd. dirs. 1984-87, publs. editor, state conf. asst. 1984-88), San Marcos Assn. for Edn. Young Children (treas.), S.W. Tex. State U. Alumni Assn. (Tchg. award of honor, Key of Excellence award, Strutter Hall of Fame), Golden Key, Phi Delta Kappa (pres. 1981, v.p., faculty advisor, ritual team 1986-89), Kappa Delta Pi (hon.). Methodist. Avocations: sewing, needle crafts, painting. Home: 602 Larue Dr San Marcos TX 78666-2410 Office: SW Tex State U Dept Curriculum & Instrn San Marcos TX 78666

FITILIS, THEODORE NICHOLAS, portfolio manager, financial analyst, retired; b. N.Y.C., July 6, 1937; s. Theris and Katherine Fitilis; children from previous marriage: Jennifer, Hillary. BA in Econs., NYU, 1959, MBA, 1965. Cert. fin. analyst, 1969. Fin. analyst Moody's Investment Service, N.Y.C., 1960-70; fin. analyst, sr. v.p. Alliance Capital Mgmt., L.P., N.Y.C., 1970-93. V.p. Printing and Pub. Analyst Group, N.Y.C., 1973-74. Served with U.S. Army, 1960-61. Mem. N.Y. Soc. Security Analysts, Media and Entertainment Analysts Assn. N.Y. Greek Orthodox. Avocations: tennis, travel, dancing. Mailing: 2600 S Ocean Blvd Apt 102N Palm Beach FL 33480-5418

FITOUSSI, JEAN-PAUL SAMUEL, economist, educator; b. Aug. 19, 1942; s. Joseph and Mathilde (Cohen) F.; m. Annie Krief, July 11, 1964; children: Lisa, David. Student, U. Paris, 1961-63; licencie in Econs., U. Strasbourg, 1966, D d'Etat in Econs., 1971, Agrege in Econs., 1973; D honoris causa, U. Buenos Aires. From asst. to hon. dean Louis Pasteur U., Strasbourg, France, 1968-77, hon. dean, 1977—; prof. European U. Inst., 1979-83, Inst. d'Etudes Politiques de Paris, 1983—. Cons. EEC, 1978-82, 84—; dir. Bur. Theoretical and Applied Econs., U. Strasbourg, 1974-82, rsch. dept. Observatoire Francais des Conjonctures Econs., 1982-89, pres. 1990—; adv. com. Econ. and Social Scis. Rsch. Coun., U.K., 1986; mem. French Nat. Com. Sci. Rsch., 1987-90; bd. dirs. GAN Ins. Co. Author: Inflation, Equilibre et Chomage, 1973, Le Fondement microeconomique de la theorie Keynesienne, 1974; co-author: (with E. Phelps) The Slump in Europe, 1988, Le débat interdit, 1995; (with P. Rosanvallon) Le Nouvel Age des Inégalités, 1996, (dir. Jean-Paul Fitoussi) Rapport sur l'État de l'Union Européenne, 1999-2000, 02, L'enseignement supérieur de l'économie en question, 2001, La Regle et le choix, 2002, (with J. Creel) How to Reform the ECB, 2002; editor: (with E. Malinvaud) Unemployment in Western Countries, 1980, Modern Macroeconomic Theory, 1984; (with M. de Cecco) Monetary Theory and Economic Institutions, 1986; (with P.A. Muet) Macrodynamique et déséquilibres, 1986, A L'est en Europe, 1991; (with others) Competitive Disinflation, 1993, Economic Growth, Capital and Labour Markets, 1995. Mem. Econ. Commn. of the Nation, 1996—, Coun. Econ. Analysis of the Prime Min., 1997—; pres. sci. coun. Inst. d'Etudes Politiques de Paris, 1997—; expert Commn. of the European Parliament, 2000—. Decorated chevalier Order of Nat. Merit, chevalier Legion of Honor (France); recipient prize Acad. Scis. Morales et Politiques, 1974. Mem. Internat. Assn. Applied Econometrics, Internat. Econ. Assn. (gen. sec. 1984, European chpt., French chpt. prize 1972, Am. chpt.). Office: Observatoire Francais des Conjonctures Economiques 69 quai d'Orsay 75007 Paris France E-mail: presidence@ofce.sciences-po.fr.

FITTERER, RICHARD CLARENCE, judge; b. Ellensburg, Wash., Jan. 22, 1946; s. L. George and Margeret H. (Lewis) F.; children: Christian C. (dec.), Zane I., Aaron G. BCS, Seattle U., 1968; JD, U. Puget Sound, 1975. Bar: Wash. 1976, U.S. Dist. Ct. (we. dist.) Wash. 1976, U.S. Dist. Ct. (ea. dist.) Wash. 1977. Assoc. Patrick R. Acres, Moses Lake, Wash., 1977; sole practice Moses Lake, 1977-79, 83-95; ptnr. Milne, Lemargie & Fitterer, Ephrata, Wash., 1979-1983; judge Grant County Dist. Ct., 1995—. Instr. Wash. State Jud. Coll. Bd. dirs. Columbia Basin Rodeo Assn. Moses Lake Roundup, 1984-91, United Way, Moses Lake, 1978-81, Moses Lake C. of C., 1979-83, 87-88. Mem. ATLA, ABA, Am. Judges Assn., Wash. State Dist. Judges Assn. (chair rules com. 1999—, bd. govs. 2001—, sec.-treas. 2003—), Grant County Bar Assn. (pres. 1993), Wash. State Trial Lawyers Assn., Moses Lake Golf and Country Club (bd. dirs. 1989-92, pres. 1991-92), Elks (bd. dirs. 1984). Avocations: skiing, boating, golfing, photography. Home: 322 N Crestview Dr Moses Lake WA 98837-1412 Office: PO Box 37 Ephrata WA 98823-0037

FITTERON, JOHN JOSEPH, gas industry executive, real estate company executive; b. Norwalk, Conn., Sept. 25, 1941; m. Leola Kellogg, Sept. 9, 1967; children: Derek, Deanne. BS, U. Conn., 1967. C.P.A., Conn. Mgr. Arthur Andersen & Co., N.Y.C. and Stamford, Conn., 1967-75; controller Beker Industries Corp., Greenwich, Conn., 1975-76, v.p., controller, 1976-78, sr. v.p. fin., treas., 1979-86, dir., 1984-86; sr. v.p., treas., CFO Getty Realty Corp. (formerly Getty Petroleum Corp.), Jericho, N.Y., 1986—. Served with USAF, 1959-63. Mem. Am. Inst. C.P.A.s, Conn. Soc. C.P.A.s (Scholastic award 1967), Fin. Execs. Inst. Office: Getty Realty Corp 125 Jericho Tpke Ste 400 Jericho NY 11753-1034

FITTING, MELVIN CHRIS, computer scientist, educator; b. Troy, N.Y., Jan. 24, 1942; s. Chris Philip and Herta Gertrude (Van Denburgh) Fitting; m. Greer Aladar Russell, Jan. 17, 1971 (div. July 1983); children: Miriam Amy, Rebecca Jo; m. Roma Simon, Jan. 11, 1992. BS, Rensselaer Polytechnic Inst., 1963; MA, PhD, Yeshiva U., 1968. Prof. computer sci., philosophy, math. CUNY, Bronx, 1969—. Author: (book) Intuitionistic Logic Model Theory and Forcing, 1969, Fundamentals of Generalized Recursion Theory, 1981, Proof Methods for Modal and Intuitionistic Logics, 1983, Computability Theory, Semantics and Logic Programming, 1989, First-Order Logic and Automated Theorem Proving, 1990, Types, Tableaus and Goedel's God, 2002; author: (with Greer Fitting) In Praise of Simple Things, 1975; author: (with Raymond Smullyan) Set Theory and the Contiuum Problem, 1996; author: (with Richard Mendelsohn) First-Order Modal Logic, 1998. Grantee, NSF, 1987, 1989, 1991. Democrat. Home: 11 Kings Ln Montrose NY 10548-1307 Office: Lehman Coll Math Dept Bedford Park Blvd W Bronx NY 10468-1589

FITTON, HARVEY NELSON, JR., former government official, publishing consultant; b. Washington; s. Harvey Nelson and Ada Hortense (Marshall) F.; m. Bernice Jeanette Sutton, Jan. 8, 1946 (dec. Sept. 1998). Student, Nat. Acad. Theater, 1940; degree in Am. Studies, George Washington U., 1949, MA in Am. Lit. and Cultural History, 1956; postgrad., Am. U., 1963. Editor, rsch. asst. Nat. Acad. Scis., Nat. Rsch. Coun., Washington, 1949-56; med. writer and editor NIH, Bethesda, Md., 1956-58; info. specialist farmer cooperative svc. USDA, Washington, 1958-61, publs. editor office of info., 1961-63, chief editorial br. office of info., 1963-66, head pub. divsn. office govtl. and pub. affairs, 1966-84, dep. dir. of info., office govt. and pub. affairs, 1984; cons. in writing, editing, publishing and continuing edn. Washington, 1985—. Instr. USDA Grad. Sch., Washington, 1962-92, chmn. editl. adv. com., 1976-85, mem. comm. skills adv. com., 1986-97. Editor, rsch. asst. Atlas of Tumor Pathology, 1949-56; editor NIH Record, 1956-58; contbr. articles to profl. jours. Pres. Clermont Woods Community Assn., Fairfax County, Va., 1968, No. Va. Family Svc., Falls Church, 1972-73; elder local Presbyn. Ch. With USN, 1942-45. Recipient Horace Hart award Edn. Coun. of Graphic Arts Industry, 1980; inductee Internat. Poetry Hall of Fame, 1996. Fellow Soc. for Tech. Comm. (pres. Washington chpt. 1972-73, asst. to pres. for recognition programs 1976-77); mem. Acad. Am. Poets, Internat. Soc. Poets, Haiku Soc. Am., Agrl. Communicators in Edn. (pres. Washington chpt. 1968, Spl. Achievement award 1986), Nat. Assn. Govt. Communicators (pres. Washington chpt. 1979, nat. pres. 1980, mem. editl. bd. Govt. Comm., 1994—, Communicator of Yr. 1984), St. Andrews Soc., Nat. Assn. Scholars, Assn. Lit. Scholars and Critics, Toastmasters (pres. Alexandria chpt. 1959-60), SAR. Avocations: gardening, tap dancing and singing, book collecting, writing poetry. Home and Office: 5624 Glenwood Dr Alexandria VA 22310-1323 E-mail: hnfitton@aol.com.

FITTRO, RONALD G., JR., healthcare executive, consultant; b. Charleston, W.Va., July 13, 1957; s. Ronald G. Fittro and Leona Gladys Craner. AS, C.C. Allegheny County, Pitts., 1981; BSN, U. Pitts., 1990, MSN, 1992. Assoc. chief nurse VA Med. Ctr., Pitts., 1992-95; DON, VA, Bklyn., 1995-97; mgr. United Healthcare, N.Y.C., 1997—99; CEO Genro LLC, 1999—. Mem. healthcare adv. bd. Covenant House, 1996-97. Coord. combined fed. campaign United Way. Mem. ANA, Sigma Theta Tau. E-mail: ron@genro.net.

FITTS, CATHERINE AUSTIN, investment advisor; b. Phila., Dec. 24, 1950; d. William Thomas Jr. and Barbara Kinsey (Willits) Fitts. AA, Bennett Coll., 1970; student, Chinese U., Hong Kong, 1971; BA, U. Pa., 1974, MBA, 1978; postgrad., MIT. With Dillon, Read & Co., Inc., N.Y.C., 1978-89, sr. v.p., 1984-86, mng. dir., 1986-89, also bd. dirs.; asst. sec. housing, urban devel., fed. housing commr. HUD, Washington, 1989-90; pres., chmn. Hamilton Securities Group, Inc., Washington, 1990-97, Solari, Inc., Tenn., 1998—. Bd. dirs. Student Loan Mktg. Assn. Sallie Mae, 1991—94; mem. adv. bd. Fedn. Nat. Mortgage Assn. Fannie Mae, 1992—93, Sanders Rsch., London; mem. emerging markets adv. com. SEC, 1990—93; columnist, The Real Deal Scoop Media, New Zealand. Author (columnist): Scoop Media. Mem. grad. adv. bd. Wharton Sch., U. Pa., Phila., 1986—95.

FITTS, DONALD DENNIS, chemist, educator; b. Concord, N.H., Sept. 3, 1932; s. Russell P. and Elisabeth (Reille) F.; m. Beverly Hoffman, July 11, 1964; children: Robert K., William R. AB, Harvard U., 1954; PhD, Yale U., 1957. NSF postdoctoral fellow U. Amsterdam, Netherlands, 1957-58; research fellow Yale U., 1958-59; mem. faculty U. Pa., 1959—, assoc. prof. chemistry, 1964-69, prof. chemistry, 1969—, asst. chmn. dept., 1965-72, assoc. dean grad. studies faculty arts and scis., 1978-82, 83-94, acting dean arts and scis., 1982-83. Cons. Am. Cyanamid Co., 1959-63 Author: Nonequilibrium Thermodynamics, 1962, Vector Analysis in Chemistry, 1974, Principles of Quantum Mechanics, 1999; also articles. Mem. Am. Phys. Soc. Achievements include research on theory of optical activity, statis.-mech. theory of transport processes, nonequilibrium thermodynamics, molecular quantum mechanics, theory of liquids, intermolecular forces, surface phenomena. Home: 634 Revere Rd Merion Station PA 19066-1008 Office: Dept Chemistry U Pa Philadelphia PA 19104-6323 E-mail: dfitts@sas.upenn.edu.

FITTS, JANET SUE, emergency nurse practitioner, educator, homeschool educator, cosmetics executive, consultant; b. Kansas City, Mo., Apr. 7, 1963; d. George Humphrey and Peggy Jean (Thompson) Jones; m. Thomas Allen Fitts, Oct. 14, 1989; children: Megan, Adam, Jacob. BSN, St. Louis U., 1989; cert. EMT-paramedic, St. John's Mercy Med. Ctr., St. Louis, 1991. RN, Mo.; cert. CEN, ACLS, BLS, pediatric advanced life support provider, neonatal resuscitation provider, basic trauma life support instr., pre-hosp. trauma life support instr., advanced burn life support provider; cert. trauma nurse specialist, ACLS instr., BLS instr. Firefighter, nurse, paramedic Eureka (Mo.) Fire Protection Dist., 1988-95; neonatal-obstetrics nurse Met. Med. Ctr.-West, Des Peres, Mo., 1989-90; paramedic supr. Medcor, Inc., Eureka, 1989-94; paramedic Meramec Ambulance Dist., 1991-93; nurse emergency dept. St. John's Mercy Hosp., Washington, Mo., 1990-2000, trauma nurse coord., 1994-97; nurse emergency dept. Mo. Bapt. Med. Ctr., St. Louis, 1991-93; owner, educator Emergency Med. Edn., Pacific, 1990-99; homesch. educator Fellowship Grace Acad., Pacific, Mo., 1994—; EMS program dir. East Ctrl. Coll., Union, Mo., 1999—2002; paramedic New Haven (Mo.) Ambulance Dist., Mo., 2000—02. Paramedic instr. East Ctr. Coll., Union, Mo., 1990-2002; instr. emergency nursing Forest Park C.C., St. Louis, 1992-2002; cmty./outreach educator Eureka Fire Protection Dist., 1990-94, dir. CPR program, 1991-94; beauty cons. Mary Kay Cosmetics, 2003—. Rev. textbooks; contbr. articles to profl. jours. Pianist Heritage Presbyn. Ch., Wildwood, Mo. Named Student Nurse of Yr., Mo. Student Nurses' Assn., 1987-88. Mem. ANA, Nat. Assn. EMS Educators (distributed learning com.), Mo. Nurses Assn. (membership com. 1990-91), Emergency Nurses Assn. (cert. trauma nurse core course provider), Nat. Assn. EMTs, Mo. Emergency Med. Svcs. Assn. (instr., coord., evaluator, sec. 1999-02), Firefighters Assn. Mo., Am. Heart Assn. (coun. on cardiopulmonary and critical care; regional faculty), Sigma Theta Tau, Sigma Alpha Iota. Avocations: computers, needlework crafts, classical musician (piano, bassoon, woodwinds), singing, rubber stamping. E-mail: jfitts911@yahoo.com.

FITTS, MICHAEL ANDREW, law educator, dean; b. Phila., Mar. 1, 1953; s. William Thomas Jr. and Barbara Kinsey (Willits) F.; m. Renee Judith Sobel, Jan. 2, 1982; children: Alexis, Whitney. AB, Harvard Coll., 1975; JD, Yale U., 1979; MA (hon.), U. Pa., 1991. Law clk. Hon. A. Leon Higginbotham, Jr., U.S. Ct. Appeals (3d cir.), Phila., 1979-81; atty. office legal counsel Dept. of Justice, Washington, 1981-85; asst. prof. law U. Pa., Phila., 1985-90, assoc. prof., 1990-92, prof., 1992—, assoc. dean acad. affairs, 1996-98, Robert G. Fuller Jr. prof. law, 1996-2000, Bernard G. Segal prof. law, 2000—, dean Sch. of Law, 2000—. Vis. prof. dept. polit. sci. Swarthmore Coll., 1999. Editor Yale Law Jour., 1978-79; contbr. articles to profl. jours. and chpts. to books. Harvard U. scholar, 1971. Mem. Am. Polit. Sci. Assn. (law and polit. process working group), Pa. Bar Assn., Com. of Seventy, Phi Beta Kappa. Mem. Soc. Of Friends. Office: U Pa Law Sch 3400 Chestnut St Philadelphia PA 19104-6204 Office Fax: 215-573-2025. Business E-Mail: mfitts@law.upenn.edu.

FITZALAN-HOWARD, BENNETT-THOMAS HENRY ROBERT, public administration and policy analyst, political theorist, theologian; b. Geneva, Oct. 10, 1955; came to U.S., 1959; s. S. and A. (Argyle-Campbel) FitzA.-H. BA, BS, Union Coll., Albany, N.Y., 1973; BA, Union Coll., 1973; MDiv, NBTS, 1978; MS, Rutgers U., 1980; MA, Russell Sage Coll., 1987; postgrad., NYU, 1989, Yale U., 1989. Cert. fin. analyst, broker, contractor in Nigeria, 1993-98; cert. min. Bride in the Light New Testament Ministry. Adminstrv. analyst Todd Logistics, Inc., NJ, Saudi Arabia, 1980—81; owner, cons. Fitz Co., Internat., Albany, 1981—; contractor Nigeria, 1994—98. Mem. N.Y. Merc. Exch.; insr. Gaton Sch., Yale U., 1987-89, NYU, 1987-89. Author: Expropriation Predictability and Politics, 1979, The Politics of the U.S. Budget, 1987, The Courts in a Democratic System, 1987, White House-Wall Street: The October 87 Crash and the Post Regan Persidency, 1987, The Politics of Deficits, 1988, Enemyless: Can We Survive?, 1989, Responsibility and Accountability: The Forgotten Cornerstones of Democracy, 1990, The Eagle and the UN: Is the US Mature Enough to be the Sole Super-Power?, 1998: contbg. author: Toward a Global Government, 1972, Conservetism: New World Order?, 1990, Tory vs. Labour: Tory: The New English Order, 1992, Hyperinflation, 1992, Eschatology Now, 1992, Eschatology and Current Events, 1992, Bride in the Light: New Testament Church, The Opened Seals of Revelation, How Bush Ambushed America, 2002. Active local ARC, RP Found. With U.S. Army, 1974-77. Mem. AIGA, AAAS, APA, SAR, VFW, Acad. Polit. Sci. (life), Am. Philatelic Soc. (life). Am. Vietnam Vets. Assn., Audubon Soc., Am. Numismatic Assn. (life), Fin. Analysts Fedn. (at large), Fin. Execs. Inst. (at large), Nat. Assn. Securities Dealers (at large), N.Y. Mercantile Exchange, Am. Enterprise Inst., Brookings Inst., Am. Legion, MENSA, Am. Soc. Internat. Law, Am. Bach Found., Am. Soc. Info. Sci., Blind Vets. Assn. (life), Am. Conservative Union, Nat. Press Club, Equestrian Club, Gideons, Mus. Modern Art, Barons of Magna Carta. Avocations: oriental antiques and silver, british stamps and coins, photography, reading, piano and cello. E-mail: Norfolk90@aol.com.

FITZ-CARTER, ALEANE, elementary education educator, composer; b. Council Bluffs, Iowa, July 24, 1929; d. Andrew Wilburt and Beatrice Mildred (Maddox) Fitz; m. James Benny Carter, Dec. 10, 1958 (wid. Aug. 1964); children: Angel Beatrix, Angel Sherrie. BSEd, U. Nebr., 1956. Elem. sch. tchr. Omaha Pub. Schs., 1956-69; instr. Black history and music U. Nebr., Omaha, 1970-74; nat. faculty mem. Gospel Music Workshop Am. Inc., 1986; music tchr. Ascension Luth. Sch., L.A., 1990-94; min. music Messiah Luth. Ch., L.A., 1996—2003; church musician Tamarind Seventh Day Adventist Ch., Compton, Calif., 1997—; performing artist Nebr. Arts Coun., Omaha, 1980—, Iowa Arts Coun., Des Moines, 1998—; tchr. adult edn. L.A. Unified Schs., 1998—; ednl. cons. Torrance (Calif.) Unified Schs., 1997—99; min. of music Olivet Luth. Ch., Hawthorne, Calif., 2003. Program prodr. KETV TV, Omaha, 1970-73; radio talk show host, KOWH Radio, Omaha, 1973-74; comms. cons. Mayor's Human Rels. Bd., Omaha, 1970-73; midwest bd. rep. Nat. Black Media Coalition, Washington, 1973-76, others; tchr. Black Awareness Opportunities Industrialization Ctr., 1969-74; instr. history of jazz, Oasis, L.A., 1997-2001; arranger, librettist, lyricist, elocutionist, storyteller, lectr. in field. Founder, dir. Omaha Gospel Choir, 1965—68, recs. include I Love Jesus, 1965, A Mighty Fortress, 1986; performer: (one-woman show) Rosa Parks, 1979—, Omaha Junior Theater, 1980—85; actress appearing in I Elvis, Hard Copy, 1992, Ice Cube video Dead Homie MTV, 1990, A Man Apart, 2003, music dir. (stage show) One Last Look, Marla Gibbs Theater, 1990; contbr. articles to profl. jours.; composer: One Child, 1993, (sacred hymns) Psalm 91, 1993—97, Children's TV workshop, Strawberry Square II: Take Time, NETV, 1983; invitee South African churches of KwaZulu Natal and African Enterprises to do a piano performance for country's celebration of 1st yr. anniversary freedom, Durban, S. Africa, 1995. Presentation vis. with Huell Howser, KCET; rschr. soul food history and cooking; min. music Olivet Luth. Ch., Hawthorne, Calif., 2003—. Nominee Best Supporting actress, Great White Hope Ctr. Stage, Omaha, Nebr., 1982; recipient Comty. Christian Leadership award, Salem Baptist Ch., Omaha, Nebr., 1987, Woman in Fine Arts award, Alyce Wilson Womens Ctr., Omaha, 1987, 5 yr. ACT-SO award, NAACP, Omaha, 1986, Outstanding Songwriter award, 1987—88, Psalm 91 Song of Yr. award, Thurston Frazier Chorale, 1987, Nebr. Chpt. GMWA award, 1987—88, Fine Arts award, Bethesda Seventh Day Adventist Ch., 1988, Comty. Guest Day, Bethesda Seventh Day Ch., Omaha, Nebr., 1988, Outstanding Svc. award, L.A. Union Seventh Day Acad., 1992, Creativity in music award, Thurston Frazier Chorale, GMWA, 1993, Svc. comty. award, Salem Baptist Mission, Norfolk, Nebr., 1995; grantee, L.A. Dept. of Cultural Affairs. Mem.: ASCAP, SAG, Rec. Acad., Profl. Musicians Union - Local 47, Nebr. Congress of Parents and Tchrs. (hon. life), Gold Star Wives Am., L.A. Pianist Club, VFW Ladies Aux., Sigma Gamma Rho (Gamma Beta Sigma chpt.). Seventh Day Adventist. Avocations: walking, swimming, cooking. Mailing: PO Box 90087 Los Angeles CA 90009 Home: Apt 1 200 E Hyde Pk Blvd #1 Inglewood CA 90302 Personal E-mail: Psalm91@mymailstation.com.

FITZ-ENZ, DAVID G. retired military officer, television producer; b. Aurora, Ill., Oct. 18, 1940; s. John Arthur and Kathryn M. Fitz-Enz; m. Carol J. Fitz-Enz, Aug. 12, 1961; children: David Scott, Timothy Robert, Jonathan Gregory. BA, Marquette U., 1963; postgrad., Command and Gen. Staff Coll., Ft. Leavenworth, Kans., 1974-75, U.S. Army War Coll., Carlisle, Pa., 1985-86. Comd. 2d lt. U.S. Army, 1963, advanced through grades to col.; ret., 1993, v.p. Cannonade Filmworks, Plattsburgh, N.Y., 1994—. Lectr. Brit. Nat. Army Mus., London, Eng., 2000—, U.S. Army War Coll. Author: Why a Soldier?, 2000, The Final Invasion, 2001, Nineteenth Century U.S. Army History (Disting. Writing award Am. Hist. Found. 2001); script writer: (film) The Final Invasion, 1999. Trustee Francis Scott Key Found., Frederick, Md., 1979-83, Battle of Plattsburgh Assn., 1999—. Named Knight, Sovereign Mil. Order of Temple of Jerusalem, 2003. Mem. Am. Mil. Retirees (nat. pres. 1994-98), Mil. Order St. Louis, Knights Templar, Naval and Mil. Club (Eng.). E-mail: coldfitzenz@earthlink.net.

FITZGEORGE, HAROLD JAMES, former oil and gas company executive; b. Trenton, N.J., June 15, 1924; s. George T. and Cecilia M. (Jansen) Fitzgeorge; m. Bette M. Weidel, June 23, 1945 (dec. May 1987); children: Barbara Marsh, Virginia Fisher, Patricia Boyle, Elizabeth Brown; m. Roberta Tefft, July 23, 1999. AB, Princeton U., 1948; M.B.M., MIT, 1964. Geologist Magnolia Petroleum Co., Oklahoma City, 1948; numerous positions with petroleum cos., 1948-60; with Mobil U.S. Exploration, N.Y.C., 1960-63; v.p. Mobil Exploration Can., 1964-66; mgr. Mobil Fgn. Exploration, N.Y.C., 1966-68; pres. Mobil de Venezuela, 1968-73; gen. mgr. Western U.S. Exploration & Prodn., Mobil Oil, Denver, 1973-77; cons. in field, 1977-78; pres. Pennzoil Exploration and Prodn., Houston, 1978-84, adv. dir., 1984—; now ret. Served with USMC, 1943-46, 50-52. Decorated Purple Heart, Bronze Star Combat V; Sloan fellow, 1963-64 Mem. Am. Assn. Petroleum Geologists, Assn. Profl. Engrs. and Geologists of Alta., Am. Petroleum Inst. Clubs: Princeton (N.Y.); Moorings; Hawksnest (Vero Beach, Fla.), Vero Beach Yacht Club. Republican. Roman Catholic.

FITZGERALD, ANTHONY PATRICK, criminal justice educator; b. Champaign, Ill., Apr. 17, 1957; s. Warren Walter Fitzgerald and Jean Harriet Huffmaster; m. Lucie Bruhn, Dec. 29, 1978 (div. Oct. 1, 1981); m. Lucie Bruhn, Mar. 18, 2003. AS, SUNY, Albany, 1985, BS, 1995; MPA, Jacksonville State U., 1998. Spl. agt. U.S. Army CID Command, Fort Huachuca, Ariz., 1984—86, Ft. Stewart, Ga., 1989—92, Baumholder, Germany, 1993—96; hwy. patrolman Ariz. Dept. of Pub. Safety, Phoenix, 1986—89; instr. U.S. Army Mil. Police Sch., Ft. McClellan, Ala., 1996—99; prof. criminal justice Abraham Baldwin Agrl. Coll., Tifton, Ga., 1999—. Sgt. U.S. Army, 1989—99. Decorated Bronze Star. Mem.: Acad. of Criminal Justice Scis. Avocations: travel, photography, history. Home: 310 Fulwood Blvd Tifton GA 31794 Office: Abraham Baldwin Agrl Coll 2802 Moore Hwy Tifton GA 31793 Personal E-mail: apf2925@msn.com. E-mail: afitz@abac.edu.

FITZGERALD, BETTY JO, artist, educator, curator; b. Colusa, Calif., Jan. 10, 1942; d. Richard Corwith and Wanda Eloise (Jones) Summerbell; m. James Edward Fitzgerald, Jan. 15, 1966. BS magna cum laude, U. No. Calif., 1963; MS in Botany, U. Wash., 1966. Tchg. asst. U. Wash., Seattle, 1963-66; instr. botany Seattle U., 1967-70; guest lectr. ecology Evergreen State Coll., Olympia, Wash., 1973, guest lectr. art, 1996, 97; artist Olympia, 1980—. Juror, tchr. regional arts workshops, Puget Sound area, Wash., 1990—97; chmn. S.W. Wash. Exhbn., Wash. State Capital Mus., Olympia, 1986—90. Contbr. articles to profl. publs. Fellow: Wash. Native Plant Soc. (hon.; bd. dirs. 1976—86, exec. sec.); mem.: N.W. Watercolor Soc. Found. (bd. dirs. 2000—), Women Painters Wash. (elected mem., pres. 1992—93, treas. 1999—2001), N.W. Collage Soc. (bd. dirs. 1987—99), N.W. Watercolor Soc. (exhbn. chmn. 1995—97, v.p. 1998—99, pres. 1999—2000, signature), Nat. Collage Soc. (signature). Republican. Avocations: hiking, bicycling, swimming. Studio: 3327 Windolph Ln NW Olympia WA 98502-3836 E-mail: bettyjoart@hotmail.com.

FITZGERALD, DANIEL R. artist, consultant; BS in Studio Art, U. So. Ind., 1984; MFA in Printmaking, So. Ill. U., Edwardsville, 1991. Exhibit preparer Evansville (Ind.) Mus. Arts and Sci., 1989—91, Henderson Arts Coun., Soaper Arts Ctr., Ky., 1991, Mus. Seminole County History, Sanford, Fla., 1995; artist, art dir., artist liaison Café Tu Tu Tango, Orlando, Fla., 1996—96; dir. artist rels., individual artist recognition program Arts Svcs. Coun., Seminole, Orange and Osceola counties, Fla., 1996; feature artist, art cons., art dir. Different Perspective Galleries, Winter Park, Fla., 1996—97; co-founder, dir. artist rels. Artist Advocacy Group & Artist Resource Cmty. Alliance, 1997; exhibit coord. The Blue Rm., Orlando, 1996—98; ind. art cons. Vgroove Gallery Lounge, Orlando, 1997; assisted performance artist Frenchy's U.S. Summer Tour, 1998; artist Frenchy and Fitz Collaborative Studios, New Orleans, 1998—99; exhibit coord., co-founder Evansville Artist Guild, 1999—2000; v.p., exhibit coord. Evansville Art Guild, 2000; represented by Davis Gallery, Ft. Lauderdale, Fla. In charge of hanging of permanent collection Evansville Mus. Art and Sci., 1997; asst. performance painting Frenchy's Summer Tour, 1998; asst., coord., exhibit coord. Evansville Art Guild, 1999; co-organizer, v.p. Art in the Park, Evansville, 2000; artist in reenactment as John James Audubon Wildlife Art Show, Henderson, Ky., 2000; organizer juror competition D.J. Arts Studio and Gallery, Evansville, 2002; organizer numerous art exhibits. Contbr. articles to profl. publs.; exhibitions include Evansvils Mus. Art and Sci., 1987 (Hon. Mention), 1991, Evansville Artists' Guild, 1988, Univ. Ctr., Evansville, 1988 (2 merit awards), Shelden Swope Art Mus., Terre Haute, Ind., 1989, 1991 (Purchase prize), 1992, Ind. U. S.E. Fine Art Gallery, New Albany, 1990 (Hon. Mention), Soaper Arts Ctr., Henderson, 1990, Office Pavilion of APG, Evansville, 1990, Krannert Gallery, U. Evansville, 1991, New Harmony Gallery Contemporary Art, 1991, Mark Twain Bank, Edwardsville, 1993, Club Firestone, Orlando, 1993, Orange County Adminstrn. Bldg., 1997, Jr. League Greater Orlando, 1997, A Different Perspective Galleries, Winter Park, Fla., 1997, The Blue Room, Orlando, 1997, Theater Downtown, 1997, Orange Ave., 1997, Harold & Maude's, 1998, Evansville Riverfest, 1999, Audubon State Park, Henderson, 2001, DJ Arts Gallery, 2001, Represented in permanent collections, Synchronicity, arts incubator, Evansville, Ind., 2003. E-mail: Drfitz2002@yahoo.com.

FITZGERALD, DESMOND J. philosopher, educator; b. Toronto, Ont., Can., Jan. 18, 1924; s. John Henry and Gertrude (Chadwick) FitzGerald; m. Evelyn Critelli FitzGerald, July 16, 1947; children: Cynthia Nieman, Brian. BA, U. Toronto, 1946, MA, 1947, U. Calif., Berkeley, 1950, PhD, 1954. Prof. philosophy U. San Francisco, 1948—98, prof. emeritus, 1998—, chmn. dept. philosophy, 1970—96. Scholar Rsch. scholar, Fulbright Found., 1966—67. Mem.: Am. Cath. Philos. Assn. (pres. 1975—76). Roman Catholic. Home: 270 Round Hill Rd Belvedere Tiburon CA 94920

FITZGERALD, DOROTHY STICKLE, librarian; b. Feb. 23, 1906; BA, Columbia U., 1928, MLS, 1937, MA, 1941. Libr. N.Y. Pub. Libr., N.Y.C., 1937, Glen Ridge (N.J.) Pub. Libr., 1937-43, Bloomfield (N.J.) Bd. Edn., 1943-72, Newtown (Pa.) Bd. Trustees, 1972-99. Home: 290 Winchester Ave Apt 216 Langhorne PA 19047-2230

FITZGERALD, EDMUND BACON, electronics industry executive; b. Milw., Feb. 5, 1926; s. Edmund and Elizabeth (Bacon) F.; m. Elisabeth McKee Christensen, Sept. 6, 1947; children: Karen, Kathleen, Edmund Greer, Rogers Christensen. BSEE, U. Mich., 1946. With Cutler-Hammer, Inc., Milw., 1946-78, v.p. in charge engring., 1959-61, adminstrv. v.p., 1961-63, pres., CEO, 1964-69, chmn., chief exec. officer, 1969-78; vice chmn. Eaton Corp., Cleve., 1978-79; mng. dir. Hampshire Assocs., Milw., 1979-80; pres., dir. No. Telecom, Inc., Nashville, 1980-82; pres. No. Telecom Ltd., 1982-84, chmn. bd. dirs., 1985-90; mng. dir. Woodmont Assocs., Nashville, 1990—. Adj. prof. mgmt. Vanderbilt U., Nashville, 1990—; former chmn., bd. dirs. Milw. Brewers Baseball Club, Inc.; former chmn. Com. for Econ. Devel.; mem. President's Nat. Security Telecom. Adv. Com. Capt. USMCR, 1943-46, 51-52. Named Man of Yr., Milw. Jr. C. of C., 1956 Mem. Nat. Elec. Mfrs. Assn. (pres. 1968). Office: Woodmont Assocs 3434 Woodmont Blvd Nashville TN 37215-1422

FITZGERALD, EDWARD FRANCIS, epidemiologist, educator; b. Bridgeport, Conn., Feb. 7, 1951; s. Edward Lewis and Felicia Mary (Zizzamia) F.; m. Patricia Lynn Chemeryinski, Oct. 13, 1973; children: Leigh Margaret, Edward Bryan. BA, U. Conn., 1973; MA, U. Toronto, 1974; PhD, Yale U., 1981. Rsch. scientist N.Y. State Dept. Health, Albany, 1981—; from asst. to assoc. prof. Sch. Pub. Health, SUNY, Albany, 1987—. Peer reviewer grant applications Nat. Inst Environ. Health Scis., Research Triangle Park, N.C., 1993, 96, 98, 99-2003; peer reviewer manuscripts Environ. Health Perspectives, 1993—; prin. investigator NIH, 1995, ATSDR, 1988—. Contbr. over 50 articles to profl. jours.. over 40 presentations. Grantee in field. Fellow Am. Coll. Epidemiology; mem. Soc. Epidemiologic Rsch. Achievements include research in field of health effects of exposure to toxic agents, especially polychlorinated biphenyls and dioxins. Office: NYS Dept Health 547 River St Troy NY 12180-2216

FITZGERALD, EDWIN ROGER, physicist, educator; b. Oshkosh, Wis., July 14, 1923; s. James C. and Edwina (Brown) F.; m. Carolyn H. Johnson, Aug. 30, 1946; children: Lucia Edwina, Margaret Mary, William Maurice, Alice Ann, Roger Edwin, Douglas Brendan, Thomas Michael, Jane Carolyn. BS in Elec. Engring, U. Wis., 1944, MS in Physics, 1950, PhD in Physics, 1951. Registered profl. engr., Md. Physicist Phys. Research Lab., B.F. Goodrich Co., 1944-46; Project asso. chemistry U. Wis., 1951-52; faculty Pa. State U., 1953-61, prof. physics, 1959-61; prof. dept. mechanics Johns Hopkins U., 1961—99; ret., 1999. Vis. prof. chemistry U. Wis., Madison, 1981. Author: Particle Waves and Deformation in Crystalline Solids, 1966; contbr. articles to profl. jours., sects. in books; patentee in field. Fellow: Am. Phys. Soc. (exec. com., chmn. high polymer physics 1958—59); mem.: Am. Chem. Soc. (poly. materials divsn.), Materials Rsch. Soc., Acoustical Soc. Am., Tau Beta Pi, Eta Kappa Nu, Sigma Xi, Phi Beta Kappa. Achievements include research in mechanical and dielectric properties solids including dynamic mechanical properties of violin wood in relation to tone qualities of violins and viscoelastic properties of marine mammal tissues, dynamic mechanical measurements during freezing and thawing of ice. Home: 2445 Traceys Store Rd Parkton MD 21120-9642

FITZGERALD, EUGENE FRANCIS, management consultant; b. Jersey City, Mar. 15, 1925; s. Arthur Gregory and Anna (O'Rourke) F.; m. Ellen M. O'Connor, Sept. 1, 1951; children— Timothy, Mary Ellen, Eugene Francis, Maura, John, Ann, Katherine. BS in Bus. Adminstrn, Georgetown U., 1949. Spl. agt. FBI, 1951-52; mgr. Prudential Ins. Co. Am., Newark, 1953-65; agy. v.p. K.C., New Haven, 1965-67; v.p. Minn. Mut. Life Ins. Co., St. Paul, 1967-70; pres., dir. North Star Equities Co., St. Paul, 1969-70; exec. v.p. Southland Life Ins. Co., Dallas, 1970-72, also dir.; exec. v.p. Equitable Life Ins. Co., Washington, 1972-73, also trustee; v.p. Liberty Life Ins. Co., Greenville, S.C., 1974-81; pres. Mountain View Orchard, Inc., 1981-85; mgmt. cons. Phillips Resource Group, Greenville, S.C., 1986—. Dir. Nathan Hale Life Ins. Co.; cons. Phillips Resource Group; bd. dirs. Nat. Peach Council, 1984-85 Chmn. bd. United Ministries, Greenville Free Med. Clinic; chmn. Greenville County Human Rels. Commn., 1991—; bd. dirs. Catholic Charities, Diocese of Charleston. Served with USMCR, 1943-45. Decorated Bronze Star. Mem. Nat. Assn. Life Underwriters, Sales and Mktg. Execs. Internat., Newcomen Soc. Clubs: Green Valley Country. Roman Catholic. Home: 305 Aberdare Ln Greenville SC 29615-2406 Office: Phillips Resource Group PO Box 5664 Greenville SC 29606-5664 E-mail: dadfitz@aol.com.

FITZGERALD, GERALD P. state agency executive; b. N.Y.C. m. Ellen Roche; 4 children. Student, Fordham U., 1962. With Port Authority of N.Y. and N.J., N.Y.C., gen. mgr. John F. Kennedy Internat. Airport, asst. dir. properties and fin., gen. mgr. mktg., econs. and fin., mgr. John F. Kennedy Airport ops.; asst. mgr. LaGuardia Airport, N.Y.C., supr. John F. Kennedy Airport maintenance, dep. dir., COO aviation dept., acting dir. aviation, 1995, dir. aviation, 1995-96; pres. Parsons Brinckerhoff Aviation Co., N.Y.C., 1996—. Bd. dirs. United Way N.Y.C.; pres. bd. trustees Cath. Charities for Bklyn. and Queens. Mem. Airports Coun. Internat. (chair internat. econs. com., mem. N.Am. econs. com.), Western European Airports Assn., Am. Assn. Airport Execs. (past chmn., mem. bd., exec. com.), Wings Club (mem. fin. com., chmn. membership com.). Office: Parsons Brinkerhoff Aviation Co 1 Penn Plz New York NY 10119-0002

FITZGERALD, HAROLD KENNETH, social work educator, consultant; b. Lakewood, Ohio, Apr. 28, 1921; s. Edward James and Julia Florence (Klell) F.; m. Caroline Lee Graham, May 31, 1951; children: Mark, Matthew, Mary, Maura, Kristin. AB, John Carroll U., 1942; MSSW, Cath. U. of Am., 1948, PhD, 1953. Social worker ARC, Cin., 1950-53, exec. dir. Cath. Social Svcs., Atlanta, 1953-56; dir. social services Muscular Dystrophy Assn. of Am., N.Y.C., 1957-58; regional cons., survey dirs. Am. Found. for the Blind, N.Y.C., 1958-66; assoc. dir. Commn. on Standards and Accreditation for the Blind, N.Y.C., 1963-66; prof. social work Syracuse (N.Y.) U., 1966-88, prof. emeritus, 1988—. Dir. internat. projects Coun. on Social Work Edn., N.Y.C., 1956-67; bd. dirs. Lighthouse, Syracuse, 1967-90, Cen. N.Y. Assn. for Hearing Impaired, Syracuse, 1976-90, Support, 1990-96, Aurora, 1991—; cons. Nat. Conf. Cath. Charities, Washington, 1966-80, UN, Teheran, Iran, 1975-76. Contbr. articles to profl. jours. Mem. Commn. on Peace and Social Justice, Diocese of Syracuse, 1989-91. Lt. USN, 1943-46. Mem. NASW, AAUP, N.Y. State Assn. Human Svcs. (bd. dirs. 1980-93), Internat. Assn. Schs. Social Work, Inter Univ. Consortium Internat. Social Devel. Roman Catholic. Avocation: swimming. Home and Office: 301 Greenwood Rd Syracuse NY 13214-2327

FITZGERALD, HELEN TERESA, grief therapist, writer; b. Jackson, Minn., Nov. 12, 1938; d. John Raymond and Mayme Mary (Benes) Cihak; m. Richard Carl Olson; stepchildren: Mark Albert Olson, Thomas Parker Olson, Jeffrey Paul Olson, Melissa Karen Franger; m. Jerald Charles Fitzgerald (dec. Apr. 1, 1974); children: Patti Ann Rauld, Sarah Jane Turosak, Charles Edwin, Mary Elizabeth. Diploma, Jackson HS, Jackson, MN, 1956. Cert. in thanatology Assn. for Death Edn. and Counseling, 2003. Creative therapist Fairfax Hosp., 1972—82; coord. grief program Mt. Vernon Ctr. for Cmty. Mental Health, Alexandria, Va., 1977—2000; dir. tng. Am. Hospice Found., Washington, 1996—. Bd. dir. Haven of No. Va., Annandale, Va. Author: (Book) The Grieving Child, 1992, The Mourning Handbook, 1994, The Grieving Teen, 2000, (tng. manual) Grief At School, 1998, Grief At Work, 1999. Recipient Outstanding Performance award, Cmty. Svcs. Bd. Fairfax County, 1998, Cmty. Svc. award, Social Work Assn. Fairfax County, 1999. Mem.: Assn. for Death Edn. and Counseling (bd. dirs. 1993—96, Clin. Practices award 1999), The Authors Guild. Avocation: painting. Home: 3601 Devilwood Ct Fairfax VA 22030 Office: Am Hospice Found Ste 200 2120 L St NW Washington DC 20037 Office Fax: 202-223-0208. Personal E-mail: helen38@cox.net.

FITZGERALD, JACK LYON, education educator, writer; b. Montgomery, Ala., Sept. 10, 1932; s. Everette Moore and Ruth Howard Fitzgerald. M. A., Middlebury Coll., Middlebury VT, 1960—61; B. A., Miss. State U., Starkville, MS, 1956—58; Assoc. Degree in Spanish, U. of Mex., Mexico City, Mexico, 1951—53; French Proficiency Cert., Sorbonne, U. of Paris, Paris, France, 1971—72; Linguistics Cert., Cambridge U., Cambridge, England, 1977—78. Prof. of English Colegio Oxford, Havana, Cuba, 1958—60; spanish tchr. Poly H.S., Riverside, Calif., 1962—69; jr. yr. abroad in S. Am. dir. SUNY, Plattsburg, 1969—71; pedagogical dir. Centre de Formation de la Profession Bancaire, Paris, France (incl. Monaco), 1972—79; acedemic counselor Woodbury U, Burbank, Calif., 1987—97. Author: Contessa (featured selection of Indian Wells Book Festival, 2002), (screenplays) Beyond Silence, Mindscape, (plays) Hotel Virginia (Festival du Tertre, 1973), (play) Cold Duck, Tijuana Lady (The Unesco Lit. Award in Drama, 1976), Apollo Experiment, Hell's Army (Moufetard Drama Festival, 1975), (tv series) Rainbow City; contbr. screenplay. Dir. of social, cultural and edn. inst. Desert Pride Ctr., Palm Springs, Calif., 2002—03; founder Paris English Theatre, 1972—79. Sgt. U.S. Army, 1953—56, USA and Okinawa. Scholar Spanish Govt. Scholarship for Grad. Studies in Spain, Govt. of Spain, 1960 to 1961. Mem.: Writers Guild of Am. Democrat-Npl. Meth. Avocation: travel. Home: 321 South Sunrise Way Apt #P-13 Palm Springs CA 92262 Home Fax: 760-416-6953. Personal E-mail: jlfitz@worldnet.att.net.

FITZGERALD, JAMES FRANCIS, cable television executive; b. Janesville, Wis., Mar. 27, 1926; s. Michael Henry and Chloris Helen (Beiter) F.; m. Marilyn Field Cullen, Aug. 1, 1950; children: Michael Dennis, Brian Nicholas, Marcia O'Loughlin, James Francis, Carolyn Jane, Ellen Putnam. BS, Notre Dame U., 1947. With Standard Oil Co. (Ind.), Milw., 1947-48; pres. F.-W. Oil Co., Janesville, 1950—, Total TV, Inc. (cable TV Systems), Wis., 1965-86. Bd. dirs. Milw. Ins. Co., Bank One, Janesville N.A.; chmn. bd. Golden State Warriors, Oakland, Calif., 1986-95, Total TV Calif., 1987-96. Bd. govs., chmn. TV com. NBA; chmn. bd., pres. S.P.A.C.E. Inc. subs. Milw. Bucks NBA team, 1976-85; chmn. Greater Milw. Open (PGA Tournament), 1985, Notre Dame Bus. Adv. Coun., 1989—. Served to lt. (j.g.) USNR, 1944-46, 51-53. Mem. Chief Execs. Forum, World Bus. Coun., Wis. Petroleum Assn. (pres. 1961-62), Janesville Country Club, Castles Pines Golf Club, Vintage Club (pres. 1989-91), San Francisco Golf Club, El Dorado Country Club. Roman Catholic. Home and Office: PO Box 348 Janesville WI 53547-0348

FITZGERALD, JAMES PAUL, lawyer; b. Binghamton, NY, Dec. 27, 1953; s. James J. and Dawn Woodrow Fitzgerald; m. Diane L. Fitzgerald, Aug. 8, 1980. BA cum laude, Marist Coll., 1976; JD, Bklyn. Law Sch., 1980. Bar: N.Mex., US Ct. Appeals (10th cir.). Asst. city atty. City of Albuquerque, 1980-85, 99—; dir. Rodey, Dickason, Sloan, Akin & Robb, P.A., Albuquerque, 1986-99. Chmn. Open Space Adv. Bd., Albuqueque, 1978-82. Author, editor: N.Mex. Environmental Law Handbook, 1998. V.p. Open Space Alliance, Albuquerque, 1999. Mem. Nat. Assn. of Indsl. and Office Properties (pres. 1997), Ronald McDonald House of New Mexico Charity, Bd. of Dir., 2003. Home: 14208 Turner Ct NE Albuquerque NM 87123-1836 Office: City Attys Office PO Box 9948 Albuquerque NM 87119-1048 Fax: 505-842-4278. E-mail: jfitzgerald@cabq.gov.

FITZGERALD, JANET ANNE, philosophy educator, retired academic administrator; b. Woodside, N.Y., Sept. 4, 1935; d. Robert W. and Lillian H. (Shannon) F. BA magna cum laude, St. John's U., 1965, MA, 1967, PhD, 1971, LLD (hon.), 1982. Joined Sisters of St. Dominic of Amityville, Roman Catholic Ch., 1953; NSF postdoctoral fellow Cath. U. Am., summer 1971; prof. philosophy Molloy Coll., Rockville Centre, N.Y., 1969—, pres., 1972-96. Trustee L.I. Regional Adv. Coun. on Higher Edn., 1972-96, chmn., 1981-84; trustee Commn. on Ind. Colls. and Univs., 1981-84, 89-92, Cath. Charities, Diocese of Rockville Centre, 1979-82; trustee Fellowship of Cath. Scholars, 1977—, v.p., 1977-80; invited expert peritus Vatican Internat. Conf. on Cath. Higher Edn., Rome, 1989; prof. S. John Neumann, Archdiocese of N.Y.; invited auditor St. Thomas Aquinas Pontifical U., Rome, 1999. Author: Alfred North Whitehead's Early Philosophy of Space and Time, 1979. Mem. bd. advisors Sem. of Immaculate Conception, 1975-80; mem. adv. bd. pre-theology program Dunwoodie Sem., Archdiocese of N.Y.; mem. pub. policy com. N.Y. State Cath. Conf., 1992-94; mem. N.Y. State Edn. Dept.-Blue Ribbon Panel on Cath. Schs., 1992-93; 1st woman grand marshal St. Patrick's Day Parade, Glen Cove, 1992. Recipient Disting. Leadership award L.I. Bus. News, 1988, plaque of recognition L.I. Women's Coun. for Equal Edn. Tng. and Employment, 1989, Pathfinder award Town of Hempstead, 1990, Disting. Long Islander in Edn. award Epilepsy Found. L.I., 1991, Educator of Yr. award Assn. Tchrs. N.Y., 1980, Spl. award for arts in edn. L.I. Arts Coun., 1994; honored by L.I. Cath. League for Religious and Civil Rights, 1989; named L.I.'s 100 Influentials, L.I. Bus. News, 1992, 93, 94, 95, 96. Mem. Soc. Cath. Social Scis. (bd. advisors). Office: Molloy College Philosophy Dept 1000 Hempstead Ave Rockville Centre NY 11570-1100

FITZGERALD, JOHN THOMAS, JR., religious studies educator; b. Birmingham, Ala., Oct. 2, 1948; s. John Thomas and Annie Myrtle (Walters) Fitzgerald; m. Karol Bonneaux, May 23, 1970; children: Kirstin Leigh, Kimberly Anne. BA, Abilene Christian U., 1970, MA, 1972; MDiv, Yale U., 1975, PhD, 1984. Instr. Yale Coll., New Haven, 1979, Yale Divinity Sch., New Haven, 1980-81; from instr. to asst. prof. U. Miami, Coral Gables, Fla., 1981—88, assoc. prof., 1988—, dir. honors program, master Hecht Residential Coll., 1987—91. Vis. assoc. prof. Brown U., Providence, 1992, Yale Div. Sch., New Haven, 1998—99. Author: Tabula of Cebes, 1983, Cracks in an Earthen Vessel, 1988; editor: Friendship, Flattery and Frankness of Speech, 1996, Christian Origins sect. Religious Studies Rev., 1994—2002, Greco-Roman Perspectitve on Friendship, 1997, Early Christianity and Classical Culture, 2003; contbr. articles to profl. jours. Judge for Silver Knight awards Miami (Fla.) Herald, 1988, 1990. Named Two Bros. fellow, Yale Div. Sch., 1974—75; recipient Max Orvitz Summer Rsch. award, U. Miami, 1985, 1987, 1994, 1995, 1998, 2002; fellow, Rotary, Tuebingen, Germany, 1974—76. Mem.: Soc. Bibl. Lit. (chmn. com. 1989—96, editor Texts and Translations Series: Greco-Roman Religion 1993—2000, editor Writings from the Greco-Roman World Series 2001—, chmn. com. 2003—, mem. coun. 2003—, rsch. grantee 1997—99), Golden Key Nat. Honor Soc., Iron Arrow Hon. Soc., Omicron Delta Kappa, Phi Kappa Phi (chpt. pres. 1988—89). Home: 15215 SW 78 Ct Palmetto Bay FL 33157-2349 Office: U Miami PO Box 248264 Coral Gables FL 33124-4672 E-mail: john.fitzgerald@miami.edu.

FITZGERALD, JOHN CHARLES, JR., investment banker; b. Sacramento, May 23, 1941; s. John Charles and Geraldine Edith (McNabb) F.; m. Mildred Ann Kilpatrick, June 26, 1965; children: Geraldine Kathrine, Erec John. BS, Calif. State U., Sacramento, 1964; MBA, Cornell U., 1965. Dir. corp. planning Bekins Co., L.A., 1966-73; mgr. corp. planning Ridder Publs., Inc., L.A., 1973-75; CFO City of Inglewood, Calif., 1975-77; treas./contr. Inglewood Redevel. Agy., 1975-77; v.p. mcpl. fin. White, Weld & Co., Inc., L.A., 1977-78; v.p. mcpl. fin. paine Webber Jackson & Curtis, L.A., 1978-79; v.p. and mgr. for Western region, mcpl. fin. dept. Merrill Lynch Capital Markets, L.A., 1979-82, mng. dir. Western region, mcpl. fin. dept., 1982-86; mng. dir. Seidler-Fitzgerald Pub. Fin., L.A., 1986—2002; sr. v.p. The Seidler Cos., Inc., L.A., 1986—2002; mng. dir. John C. Fitzgerald & Assocs., 2002—. Instr. fin./adminstrn. El Camino Coll., Torrance, Calif., 1977-80. Chmn. bd. dirs., exec. com., treas., chmn. fundraising com. L.a. chpt. Am. Heart Assn., 1977—; bd. dirs. Daniel Freeman Hosps. Inc., Corondelet Health Care corp.; trustee Mt. St. Mary's Coll., L.A., 1992-2001; bd. dirs. Tau Kappa Epsilon Ednl. Found., Indpls., 1995—; bd. dirs. Calif. Soc. for Biomed. Rsch., 1998; alumni coun. mem. Johnson Grad. Sch. Mgmt. Cornell U., real estate coun. Mem. Fin. Execs. Inst., Mcpl. fin. Officers, League Calif. Cities, So. Calif. Corp. Planners Assn. (past pres.), L.A. Bond, Lido Isle Yacht Club, Jonathan Club, The Calif. Club, Lake Arrowhead Country Club, Rotary, Beta Gamma Sigma. Address: PO Box 765 27447 Bayshore Dr Lake Arrowhead CA 92352

FITZGERALD, JOHN EDMUND, civil engineering educator; b. Revere, Mass., Sept. 29, 1923; s. John Valentine and Gertrude Margaret (Doyle) F.; m. Elaine Louise Ohlson, Feb. 24, 1945; children: Deborah Lee, Christine Louise, David John, John Paul (dec.). Student, Tufts U., 1941-42, 46; MCE, Harvard U., 1947; MS in Math.-Physics, Nat. U. Ireland, Cork, 1970, DSc, 1972. Registered profl. engr., Utah, N.D.; chartered physicist, U.K. Regional constrn. engr. Liberty Mut. Ins. Co., Dallas, 1947-48; assoc. prof. N.D. State U., Fargo, 1948-51; supr. structures and dynamics Armour Rsch. Found., Chgo., 1951-53; mgr. applied mechanics and med. physics Rsch. divsn. Am. Machine & Foundry Corp., Chgo., 1953-56; mgr. applied math. and mechanics Borg-Warner Ctr. Rsch. Labs., Des Plaines, Ill., 1956-59; dir. devel. br. Lockheed Propulsion Co., Redlands, Calif., 1959-66; prof. civil engring., chmn. dept. U. Utah, Salt Lake City, 1966-74, prof., assoc. dean, 1973-74; prof., dir. Sch. Civil Engring. Ga. Inst. Tech., Atlanta, 1975-89, prof. emeritus, 1991—, assoc. dean, 1989-91. Cons. numerous aerospace cos., govt. agys., 1966—; guest lectr. Trinity Coll., Dublin, Ireland, U. Bristol, U.K., U. Marseilles, France, NATO Advanced Study Inst., Italy, others., 1968—; bd. dirs. EFM Corp., Dublin. Author: Engineering Structural Analysis of Solid Propellants, 1971; editor Structural Integrity Handbook, 1972; contbr. over 100 articles to profl. jours.; 27 patents. Served with submarine service USN, 1942-46, ETO. Recipient U.S. Sr. Scientist award for teaching and research Alexander von Humboldt Found., 1973-74. Fellow Inst. Physics U.K., ASCE, AIAA (assoc., Outstanding Achievement in Solid Propulsion award 1987); mem. Soc. Rheology, Am. Acad. Mechanics, Structural Engring. Inst., Am. Phys. Soc., Irish Sailing Assn. Clubs: Royal Cork Yacht (Crosshaven, Ireland). Roman Catholic. Avocations: swimming, bicycling, sailing. Home: 2318 Ventana Crossing Marietta GA 30062-7747 Office: Ga Inst Tech Sch Civil Engring Atlanta GA 30332-0001 E-mail: jedmund72@aol.com.

FITZGERALD, JOHN EDWARD, III, lawyer; b. Cambridge, Mass., Jan. 12, 1945; s. John Edward Jr. and Kathleen (Sullivan) FitzGerald. BCE, U.S. Mil. Acad., West Point, N.Y., 1969; JD, M in Pub. Policy Analysis, U. Pa., 1975. Bar: Pa 1975, NY 1978, Calif 1983, US Supreme Ct 1991. Commd. 2d lt. U.S. Army, 1969, advanced through grades to capt., 1971, resigned, 1972; assoc. Saul Ewing Remick & Saul, Phila., 1975-77, Shearman & Sterling, N.Y.C., 1977-78; atty., dir. govt. rels. and pub. affairs Pepsico, Inc., Purchase, N.Y., 1978-82; sr. v.p., dept. head Security Pacific Corp., Los Angeles, 1982-83; ptnr. Schlesinger, FitzGerald & Johnson, Palm Springs, Calif., 1983-87; mng. ptnr. FitzGerald & Mulé, Palm Springs, 1987—. Judge pro tem Desert Jud. Dist. Chmn, pres United Way Desert; mem Comt 25, Palm Springs; trustee, vpres Palm Springs Desert Mus; pres exec bd Coachella Valley coun Boy Scouts Am; bd dirs, chmn Palm Springs Boys and Girls Club; treas. Desert Youth Found. Named Palm Springs Disting. Citizen of Yr., 1999; recipient Friend of Youth award, Boys and Girls Clubs, 1998, Disting. Eagle award, Boy Scouts Am., 1999, Jefferson award, 2003. Mem.: Am. Arbitration Assn. (arbitrator), Desert Bar Assn. (pres.), Calif. Bar Assn., Lincoln Club of the Coachella Valley (vice chmn. bd. dirs.), Desert Bus. Roundtable, O'Donnell Golf Club. Office: Ste 105 3001 Tahquitz Canyon Way Palm Springs CA 92262-6900 E-mail: jackfitzgerald3@aol.com.

FITZGERALD, JOHN MICHAEL, economist, educator; b. Dec. 9, 1955; s. Gerald and Ruth Fitzgerald; m. Susan Head, July 14, 1979; children: Jay, Elise. BA, U. Mont., 1978; MS, U. Wis., 1980, PhD, 1983. Prof. econs. Bowdoin Coll., Brunswick, Maine, 1983—. Contbr. articles to profl. jours. Office: Bowdoin Coll Dept Econs 9700 College Station Brunswick ME 04011

FITZGERALD, JOHN WARNER, law educator; b. Grand Ledge, Mich., Nov. 14, 1924; s. Frank Dwight and Queena Maud (Warner) F.; m. Lorabeth Moore, June 6, 1953; children: Frank Moore, Eric Stiles, Adam Warner. BS, Mich. State U., 1947; JD, U. Mich., 1954. Bar: Mich. 1954. Practiced in Grand Ledge, 1955-64; chief judge pro tem Mich. Ct. Appeals, 1965-73; justice Mich. Supreme Ct., 1974-83, dep. chief justice, 1975-82, chief justice, 1982; prof. law Thomas M. Cooley Law Sch., Lansing, Mich., 1982—. Mem. Mich. Senate from 15th Dist., 1958-64 Served with AUS, 1943-44. Mem. ABA, State Bar Mich. (bd. commrs. 1985-90), Am. Judicature Soc. Office: Thomas M Cooley Law Sch PO Box 13038 Lansing MI 48901-3038

FITZGERALD, JUDITH KLASWICK, federal judge; b. Spangler, Pa., May 10, 1948; d. Julius Francis and Regina Marie (Pregno) Klaswick; m. June 5, 1971 (div. Dec. 1982); 1 child; m. Barry Robert Fitzgerald, Sept. 20, 1986; 1 child. BSBA, U. Pitts., 1970, JD, 1973. Legal rschr. Assocs. Fin., Pitts., 1972-73; law clk. to pres. judge Beaver County (Pa.) Ct. Common Pleas, 1973-74; law clk. to judge Pa. Superior Ct., Pitts., 1974-75; asst. U.S. atty. U.S. Dist. Ct. (we. dist.) Pa., Pitts. and Erie, 1976-87, U.S. bankruptcy judge Pitts., Erie and Johnstown, 1987—, U.S. Dist. Ct. (ea. dist.) Pa., U.S. Dist. Ct. Del., 1997. Adj. prof. law U. Pitts., 1997. Co-author: Bankruptcy and Divorce, Support and Property Division, 1991; editor: Pennsylvania Law of Juvenile Delinquency and Deprivation, 1976; contbr. articles to profl. jours. Mem. Pitts. Camerata, 1978-80, Allegheny County Polit.-Legal Edn. Project, 1980, Mendelssohn Choir Pitts., 1982—; mem. coun. Program to Aid Citizen Enterprise, 1985-87. Recipient Spl. Achievement awards Dept. Justice, Spl. Recognition award Pittsburgh mag., Operation Exodus Outstanding Performance award Dept. Commerce, 1986. Mem. Internat. Women's Insolvency and Restructuring Conf., Allegheny County Bar Assn., Women's Bar Assn. of Western Pa., Nat. Conf. Bankruptcy Judges, Am. Bankruptcy Inst., Nat. Conf. Bankruptcy Clks., Comml. Law League of Am., Fed. Criminal Investigators Assn. (Spl. Svc. award 1988), Zonta. Republican. Lutheran. Avocations: singing, reading, traveling. Office: US Bankruptcy Ct 600 Grant St Ste 5490 Pittsburgh PA 15219-2805

FITZGERALD, KAREN MARIE, artist, art educator; b. Marathon County, Wis., Apr. 20, 1956; d. Gerald Patrick and Grace (Krieg) F.; m. Paul Baietto, June 16, 1984; children: Joseph, Daniel, Paul. BFA, U. Wis., Milw., 1979; MFA, Hunter Coll., N.Y.C., 1985; MEd, Columbia U., 1990. Arts-in-edn. coord. Jamaica Arts Ctr., Queens, N.Y., 1988-90, arts in edn. specialist, 1991—; artist-in-residence Tchrs. and Writers Collaborative, N.Y.C., 1989-91; adj. instr. Iona Coll.-Elizabeth Seton Sch., Yonkers, N.Y., 1989-91, St. John's U., Queens, 1991-92. Cons. Queens Mus., 1987-88, N.Y. State Dept. Edn., Albany, 1988; instr. staff devel. Tchrs. Ctr., Yonkers, N.Y., 1989; evaluation cons. N.Y. Found. for Arts, N.Y.C., 1991—; documentation cons. Fund for N.Y.C. Pub. Edn., 1991-93; edn. dir. Queens Symphony Orch., 1992—; workshop presenter various orgns.; project dir., Artist Cares, N.Y.C., 2001—. One-woman shows at Macy Gallery, N.Y.C., 1990, Daniel P. Quinn Gallery, 1992, Westchester Art Workshop, 1993, Jamaica Arts Ctr., 1994, Sunnen Gallery Soho, 1994, Interfaith Ctr., N.Y.C., 1999, Ctr. for Visual Arts, Wausau; two-person shows at U. Ariz., Tucson, Rotunda Gallery, 1997, Milw. Inst. Art and Design, 1998, Nese Alpan Gallery, 1998; exhibited in group shows at Columbia U., N.Y.C., 1989, La Mama Gallery, N.Y.C., 1989, Henry St. Settlement, N.Y.C., 1989, Dome Gallery, N.Y.C., 1989, Ctr. for Book Arts, N.Y.C., 1990, Pyramid Atlantic Gallery, Washington, 1991, Hunter Coll., N.Y.C., 1991, Gallery 124, Kemper Ctr., Kenosha, Wis., 1991, Cmty. Gallery, N.Y.C., 1992, Bklyn. Union Gas, U. Wis., Stevens Point, 1994, Reggio Gallery, N.Y.C., 1996, Gensler Arch., 1997, Chamot Gallery, 1998, Manhattan Transfer, 1998; represented in permanent collections N.Y. Pub. Libr., N.Y.C., also pvt. collections in Germany and U.S. Prodn. grantee Mysteries Lower East Side Print Shop, N.Y.C., 1988; grantee Women's Studio Workshop, 1999, Queen's Coun. on the Arts, 1998, 2000. Home: 2853 Hobart St Woodside NY 11377-7818

FITZGERALD, KATHLEEN M. communications company executive; BA, St. Peter's Coll.; MA in Journalism, Boston U. With Western Electric, 1973; mgr. media rels. computer bus. AT&T, pub. rels. dir. bus. comms. sys., pub. rels. dir. computer bus., 1989-91; v.p. pub. rels. and advt. network sys. Lucent Techs., Murray Hill, NJ, sr. v.p. pub. rels. and advt. Trustee St. Peter's Coll., Jersey City; bd. dirs. Winston Sch. Named Acad. of Women Achievers, YMCA, 1997, one of five pub. rels. All Stars, Inside PR, 1997. Office: Lucent Techs Inc 600 Mountain Ave Rm 6c-302 New Providence NJ 07974-2008

FITZGERALD, KEVIN GERARD, lawyer; b. Milw., Aug. 1, 1963; s. Raymond E. and Virginia L. Fitzgerald; m. Jill Ann Hussinger, 1997; 1 child, Zachary J. Mitschrich. BS, Marquette U., 1984; JD, U. Wis., 1987. Bar: Wis. 1987, U.S. Dist. Ct. (ea. and we. dists.) Wis. 1987, Fla. 1994. Ptnr. Foley & Lardner, Milw., 1987—. Bd. dirs. T.E. Brennan Co., Milw. Contbr. articles to profl. jours. Mem. ABA, Wis. Bar Assn., Milw. Bar Assn., Fedn. Regulatory Counsel. Office: Foley and Lardner 777 E Wisconsin Ave Milwaukee WI 53202-5367

FITZGERALD, KEVIN MICHAEL, lawyer, mediator; b. Kansas City, Kans., May 10, 1956; s. Thomas Francis and Theresa Ann (Grosdidier) FitzG.; m. Susan Patricia Parker, June 21, 1980; children: Kathryn Ann, Shannon Elizabeth, Erin Parker. BBA, U. Tex., Arlington, 1981; JD, U. Ark., 1985. Bar:

Mo. 1985, U.S. Dist. Ct. Mo. 1985, U.S. Ct. Appeals (8th cir.) 1985. Assoc. Taylor, Stafford, Woody, Cowherd and Clithero, Springfield, Mo., 1985-90; ptnr. Taylor, Stafford, Woody, Clithero and FitzGerald, Springfield, 1990-2000, Taylor, Stafford, Clithero, FitzGerald & Harris, Springfield, 2001—. Mediator, neutral U.S. Dist. Ct. (we. dist.) Mo. Atty. Roman Cath. Diocese of Springfield-Cape Girardeau. Mem. Mo. Bar Assn., Springfield Met. Bar Assn. (sec. 1997, chmn. alternative dispute com. 2000), Legal Aid Southwest Mo. (bd. dirs. 1993-96), Nat. Diocesan Attys. Assn. Office: Taylor Stafford et al 3315 E Ridgeview St Ste 1000 Springfield MO 65804-4083 E-mail: kfitzgerald@taylorstafford.com.

FITZGERALD, LAURINE ELISABETH, university dean, educator; b. New London, Wis., Aug. 24, 1930; d. Thomas F. and Laurine (Branchflower) F. BS, Northwestern U., 1952, MA, 1953; PhD, Mich. State U., 1959. Instr. English, dir. devel. reading lab., head resident-dir. Wis. State Coll., Whitewater, 1953-55; area dir. residence and counseling Ind. U., 1955-57; teaching grad. asst. guidance and counseling, then instr., counselor Mich. State U., East Lansing, 1957-59; asst. prof. psychology and edn., assoc. dean students U. Denver, 1959-62; asst. prof. counseling psychology, staff counselor for Carnegie Found. project U. Minn., 1962-63; assoc. dean, assoc. prof. Mich. State U., 1963-70, assoc. dean students. prof. adminstrn. and higher edn., dir. divsn. edn. and rsch., 1970-74; dean Grad. Sch., prof. counselor edn., dir. N.E. Wis. Coop. Regional Grad. Ctr. U. Wis.-Oshkosh, 1974-85; dean, dir. Ohio State U.-Mansfield, 1985-87, prof. edn. policy and leadership, 1985-93, dir. student pers. asst. program, edn. policy and leadership, 1989-92. Adj. prof. edn. policy and leadership Ohio State U., 1992-93; vis. lectr. U. Okla., Norman, 1961; vis. prof. Oreg. State U., 1977; cons. in field; vocat. expertwitness, 1962-95. Contbr. numerous articles to profl. jours.; co-author monographs, texts. Adv. bd. Mansfield Gen. Hosp., 1986-94; bd. dirs. Renaissance Theatre, 1986-87, New Beginnings, 1986-94; exec. com. Ohio Consortium on Tng. and Planning, 1985-87; trustee Mt. Carmel Coll. Nursing, chmn. acad. affairs com., 1988-96. Recipient Higher Edn. Rocky Mountain coun. Girl Scouts U.S., 1961, Evelyn Hosmer U. Denver, 1962, Merit award Northwestern Alumni Assn., 1993; named Old Master Purdue U., 1979, Most Disting. Women in Edn., Mich., 1973; Elin Wagner Found. fellow, 1963-64. Mem. AAUW, AAUP (chpt. treas. 1955-56), NEA, Am. Psychol. Assn., Mich. Psychol. Assn., Am. Pers. and Guidance Assn., Am. Coll. Pers. Assn. (sec. 1965-67, exec. bd. 1968-70, chmn. women's task force 1970-71, editor jour. 1976-82, Disting. Scholar award 1983, sr. scholars com. 1985-90, historian 1982-95, chmn. scholars com. 1986-87, sr. scholars diplomate 1990, awards and commendations com. 1988-89, pres.-elect 1989-90, pres. 1990-91, past pres. 1991-92, Esther Lloyd-Jones Disting. Svc. award 1997), Assn. Counselor Edn. and Supervision, Am. Assn. Higher Edn., Nat. Assn. Women Deans, Adminstrs. and Counselors (rsch., ednl. by-laws programs, publs., univ. coms. 1959-72, v.p. 1972-74, KSP Trust Commn. 1979-81, pres. 1980-81, editl. bd. 1991-2000), Mich. Assn. Women Deans, Adminstrs. and Counselors (pres. 1967-69), Ohio Assn. Women Deans, Adminstrs. and Counselors, Mich. Coll. Pers. Assn., Wis. Coll. Pers. Assn., Midwest Assn. Grad. Schs. (pres. 1980-82), Intercollegiate Assn. Women Students (editorial bd., nat. advisor), Women's Equity Action League (past pres. Mich., nat. sec.-treas. legal and edn. def. fund), Bus. and Profl. Women's Club (chpt. pres. 1980, state officer 1981, Lena Lake Forest fellow 1966-67), Wis. Soc. for Higher Edn. (Achievement award 1985, Pres. award 1982), Altrusa Internat. (mem. bd. dirs. 1986-94), Mortar Bd., Shi-Ai, Beta Beta Beta, Psi Chi, Alpha Lambda Delta, Delta Kappa Gamma, Zonta (pres. Lansing club, chmn. internat. status of women com. 1960-85). Home: 812 Wyman St New London WI 54961-1771

FITZGERALD, MARY EILEEN, museum program director; b. Dayton, Ohio, Dec. 21, 1944; d. William McAvoy and Irene Ann (Dougherty) F. BA in Studio Art, U. Dayton, 1966; MA in Art History, Ohio State U., 1970; PhD in Humanities, Syracuse U., 1986. Lectr. Colgate U., Hamilton, N.Y., 1984-85; asst. prof. Ithaca (N.Y.) Coll., 1987-89, Syracuse (N.Y.) U., 1989-90, Roanoke Coll., Salem, Va., 1990-96; curator of edn. Maier Mus. of Art, Lynchburg, Va., 1996—2002; head of edn. Art Mus. Western Va., Roanoke, 2002—. Vis. prof. Ohio U., Athens, 1986-87; adj. asst. prof. Sweet Briar (Va.) Coll., 2001—. Mem. editl. bd. Artemis, 1994-95. Grantee St. James Ch. (Italy), 1983, NEH, 1994; Mednick fellow Va. Found. Ind. Coll., 1991, Florence fellow Syracuse U., 1977-79. Mem. Artemis (pres. bd. dirs. 1994-98). Avocations: photography, hiking, yoga. Home: 2571 Brambleton Ave SW Roanoke VA 24015-4303 Office: Art Mus Western Va Roanoke VA 24011-1436 E-mail: mfitzgerald@artmuseumroanoke.org.

FITZGERALD, MARY JOAN, music educator; b. Chgo., Oct. 2, 1928; d. Arthur Frederick and Mary Naomi (Speidel) F. BA in Music Edn. and Liturgical Music, Alverno Coll. Music, 1965; MA equivalent in Ch. Music, DePaul U., 1980; BA in Theology, Loyola U. Chgo., 1982, MPS, 1987. Music edn. tchr. Cath. Sch. System, 1949-59; tchr. primary grades various parochial schs., 1959-67; piano/organ instr. Karnes Music Co., Des Plaines, Ill., 1967-78; pvt. music tchr. Glenview, Evanston, Ill., 1970-88; ch. musician St. Joseph Cath. Ch., Wilmette, Ill., 1973-76, St. Henry Cath. Ch., Chgo., 1981-88; ret., 1994. Author: Behold, Your Mother: Co-Redemptrix,(Marian sequences for the liturgical Yr.) 1994, Marian Sequences in the 21st Century, 1995, (religious poetry) Salvation in Christ Through Mary, 1995, To Live is Christ, 1996. Eucharistic min., min. of care St. Mary's Cath. Ch., Evanston, Ill; prof. mem. Secular Franciscan Order, N.W. Franciscan Cmty. of the Immaculate Heart of Mary. Mem.: St. Francis Xavier Fraternity. Roman Catholic. Avocations: reading, sewing. Home: 1615 Hinman Ave # 724 Evanston IL 60201-4509

FITZGERALD, MATTISON DALY, artist; b. San Francisco, Sept. 14, 1961; d. Daniel Joseph and Ann F. BA, U. Calif., Santa Cruz, 1985; postgrad. in Mus. Studies, John F. Kennedy U., 1993; postgrad., U. Calif., Berkeley, 2002. Cert. graphic design Univ. Calif., Santa cruz. Prin. M Gallery and M Landscape, San Jose, Calif., 1994—. Artist-in-residence Santa Fe Internat. Acad. of Art, 1998, San Jose Art League Beaux Artes Ball, 1996, CADartists Santa Clara County, 1996, Tamian Station Mural Project, San Jose, 1996, Santa Barbara Mus. Natural History, 1986. Paintings at exhbns. include: 29 East Main Street Gallery, Los Gatos, Calif., 1998, Kismet Galllery, San Jose, Calif., 1997, Works Gallery, San Jose, 1997, Los Gatos Arts Commn. Gallery, Los Gatos, 1996, San Jose Inst. Contemporary Art, San Jose, 1995, Popular Culture Libr., Bowling Green, Ohio, 1995, South First Street Gallery, San Jose, 1996, Cafe Q Gallery, Palo Alto, Calif., 1996, Period ARt Gallery, Omaha, Sirius Art Gallery, Santa Fe, M.Mex., 1999-2000, Gualala (Calif.) Art Ctr., 1999-2000, Imaginations Gallery, San Diego, 2000, Miami Mus. Art, 2001, Ft. Lauderdale (Fla.) Mus. Art, 2001, Triton Mus. Art, San Jose, Calif., 2001, Period Art Gallery, Omaha, 2001, others; commns. include NASA, Expoo Found.; work collected in numerous pvt. collections and represented at Ridgeway Gallery, Santa Fe, N.Mex., Studio One Gallery, Gualala, Calif., Arte Club Catania, Italy, Ceres Gallery N.Y., San Jose Art League, Mexica Art, San Jose; publs. include MS NBC Washington, Studio Notes Benicia, Calif., Sunset Mag., Bio Sci. Mag., others; short film Millenium, A Time of Happiness, Pulsart, 1998, shown at Canness Film Festival; monographs Calif. Acad. Scis.; contbr. revs. to profl. publs. Named to Outstanding Young Women of Am., 1998; recipient award Nat. Assn. Am. Penn Women, 1996; nominee Womens Fund Achievement awards, 1996, others. Mem. Art and Technology Soc. Internat., San Jose Jaycees, Calif. Assn. of Mus., Western Mus. Conf., Am. Assn. Museums, San Jose Mus. of Art, Santa Cruz County Mus. of Art, San Jose Inst. of Contemporary Art, Triton Mus. of Art, U.S. Jr. C. of C. (v.p. cmty. devel. 1998). Studio: M Art PO Box 2G San Jose CA 95109-0007 Fax: 903-673-1179.

FITZGERALD, MICHAEL FRANCIS, journalist; b. Bowling Green, Ohio, Feb. 16, 1964; s. Jon Michael and Linda Marie (Baldwin) F.; m. Lark Danielle Fitzgerald, Oct. 27, 1997; children: Jon Michael, Aedan Francis. AB in History, U. Chgo., 1986. Mng. editor Chgo. Computing, 1989-90; from midwest corres. to online editor Computer World, Framingham, Mass., 1990-96; sr. news prodr. ZDNet News, San Francisco, 1996-99; exec. editor news Red Herring, San Francisco, 2000—01; freelance journalist, 2001—. Recipient Best News Story or Series award Computer Press Assn., 1995, 2000, 1st place news series Am. Soc. & Bus. Press Editors, 1995, 2d place news series, 1995; named Most Prominent Cyberwriter, Press Access, 2000. Mem. Online News Assn. (chair membership com.). Presbyterian. Avocation: singing. E-mail: mikelark@juno.com.

FITZGERALD, MICHAEL STUART, history educator, researcher; b. Pueblo, Colo., Nov. 24, 1953; s. Robert Fulton and Lila Louise (Whiting) F.; m. Valerie Calistra Sandoval, Aug. 12, 1982; children: Joseph Sandoval, Alexandra Delphina. BS, U. So. Colo., 1976; MA, U. Chgo., 1979; PhD, Purdue U., 1990. Instr. history U. So. Colo., Pueblo, 1983-84, Pueblo C.C., 1984-85, Purdue U., West Lafayette, Ind., 1989-90; asst. prof. history Pikeville (Ky.) Coll., 1990-95, assoc. prof. history, 1995-2001, Franciscan U., Steubenville, Ohio, 2001—. Cons. Ky. Hist. Soc., 1998-99, James Monroe Papers project Nat. Hist. Publs. and Rsch. Commn., Washington, 1999-2003. Contbr. articles to profl. jours. David Ross fellow Purdue U., 1987-89, James Still fellow U. Ky., 1995, John B. Stephenson fellow Appalachian Coll. Assn., 1996-97; Mellon Student/Faculty rsch. grantee Appalachian Coll. Assn., 1994. Mem. Soc. for Mil. History Republican. Roman Catholic. Home: 224 Rockdale Rd Steubenville OH 43952 Office: Franciscan U 1235 University Blvd Steubenville OH 43952

FITZGERALD, PETER GOSSELIN, senator, lawyer; b. Elgin, Ill., Oct. 20, 1960; s. Gerald Francis and Marjorie (Gosselin) F.; m. C. Nina Kerstiens, July 25, 1987; 1 child, Jake Buchanan. AB, Dartmouth Coll., 1982; cert. of attendance, Aristotelian U., Salonica, Greece, 1983; JD, U. Mich., 1986. Bar: Ill. 1986, U.S. Dist. Ct. (no. dist.) Ill. 1986. Assoc. Isham, Lincoln & Beale, Chgo., 1986-88; ptnr. Riordan, Larson, Bruckert & Moore, Chgo., 1988-92; mem. Ill. Senate, 1993-98, chmn. state govt. ops. com., 1997-98; U.S. senator from Ill., 1999-. Counsel Harris Bankmont, Inc., 1992-96. Rotary Found. internat. grad. scholar, 1982-83. Mem. Econ. Club Chgo., Inverness Golf Club, Union League Club. Republican. Roman Catholic. Office: US Senate 555 Dirksen Bldg Washington DC 20510-0001 E-mail: senator_fitzgerald@fitzgerald.senate.gov.

FITZGERALD, ROBERT HANNON, JR., orthopedic surgeon; b. Denver, Aug. 25, 1942; s. Robert Hannon and Alyene (Webber) Fitzgerald Anderson; m. Lynda Lee Lang, Apr. 27, 1968 (div. 1984); children: Robert III, Shannon, Dennis, Katherine, Kelly; m. Jamie Kathleen Dent, Mar. 9, 1985; children: Brian, Steven. BS, U. Notre Dame, 1963; MD, U. Kans., 1967; MS, U. Minn., 1974; Magistri Artivum, U. Pa., 1995. Instr. orthop. surgery Mayo Med. Sch., Rochester, Minn., 1974-77, cons. orthop. surgery, 1974-89, asst. prof., 1977-82, assoc. prof., 1982-86, prof., 1986-89, chief adult reconstructive surgery, 1987-89, dir. orthop. rsch., 1988-89; prof. chmn. dept. orthop. surgery Wayne State U. Sch. Med., 1989-95, chief orthop. surgery Hutzel Hosp., 1989-95 Detroit Receiving Hosp., 1989-95; orthopedist-in-chief Detroit Med. Ctr., 1989-95, chmn. coun., specialist-in-chief, 1993-95; chmn. dept. orthop. surgery U. Pa. Sch. Med., Phila., 1995-99; chief orthop. surgery Hosp. U. Pa., Phila., 1995—2000; P.B. Magnuson prof. bone and joint surgery U. Pa. Sch. Med., Phila., 1996—2001; chief orthop. surgery Phila. Veterans Med. Ctr. Dir. Penn. Orthop. Inst., U. Pa. Health Sys., 1997—2001; cons. CDC, Atlanta, 1981—, NIH, 1987—93, chmn. orthop. study sect., 1989—91; cons. health care financing adminstrn. Ctr. of Excellence Program, 2001; cons. MMS, 2001, CMS, 2002—; chief orthop. surgery Bell Meml. Hosp., 2001—. Mem. editl. bd. Jour. Orthop. and Traumatology, 1978—, Jour. Bone Joint Surgery, 1982—88, Clin. Orthop. and Related Rsch., 1988—, Jour. Long Term Results Biomed. Devices, 1990; editor: Seminars in Arthoplasty, 1993—, Am. Acad. of Orthop. Surgery Ortho Knowledge Online, 2000—03; trustee Jour. Bone Joint Surgery, 1987—92, sec., 1988—92. Trustee Hutzel Hosp., 1989—95. Capt. USAF, 1968—70. Decorated Air Commendation medal; recipient Kappa Delta award for Musculoskeletal rsch., 1983. Fellow Am. Acad. Orthop. Surgeons, Phila. Coll. Physicians; trustee Lourdes H.S. Devel. Bd., Rochester, 1982-88; mem. AMA, Am. Orthopedic Assn., Rsch. Soc., Assn. Bone and Joint Surgeons, Interurban Ortho Soc., Internat. Soc. Microbiology, Zumbro County Med. Soc., Min-Da-Man Orthop. Soc., Minn. Orthopedic Soc., Am. Soc. Microbiology, N.Y. Acad. Scis., Am. Hip Soc. (Stinchfield award 1985, Charnley award 1986, 95, pres. 1993-94), Internat. Hip Soc., Am. Orthop. Assn. (N.Am. traveling fellow 1974, Am. Brit. Can. traveling fellow, 1981), Surg. Infection Soc. (charter mem.), Clin. Orthop. Soc., Internat. Soc. Orthop. Surgery and Traumatology, Mid-Am. Orthop. Soc. (bd. dirs. 1989-93, 94—, pres. elect 1994, pres. 1996), Detroit Acad. Orthop. Surgery, Mich. Orthop. Soc., Mich. State Med. Soc., Detroit Acad. Med., Pa. Orthop. Soc., Phila. Orthop. Soc. (bd. dirs. 1998-2001), Phila. Acad. Med., bd. devel. Mayo Clinic, 1984-87, St. John's Ch., 1988-89, bd. edn. St. John's Grade Sch./Jr. H.S., Rochester, 1983-87, Interurban Club, Sigma Xi, Kappa Delta, Alpha Epsilon Delta. Republican. Roman Catholic. Avocation: cross-country and downhill skiing. Home and Office: 97 South 4th St Ishpeming MI 49849 E-mail: drfitzgerald@bellmemorial.org.

FITZGERALD, ROBERT MAURICE, financial executive; b. Chgo., Jan. 8, 1942; s. James Patrick and Catherine (McNulty) Fitzgerald; children: Stephen, Peter, Susan, Martin. BS, Loyola U., Chgo., 1971; postgrad., U. Wis., 1974-76, Northwestern U., 1980. Sr. v.p. Fed. Reserve Bank, Chgo., 1979-85; pres. Chgo. Clearing House Assn., Chgo., 1985—. Cons. Currency Bd., Abu Dhabi, United Arab Emirates, 1979; past bd. dirs. Nat. Automated Clearing House Assn., Washington; advisor U.S. Coun. on Internat. Banking, N.Y.C. Pres. Coun. on Alcoholism, Ann Arbor, Mich., 1978, Diocesan Bd. Edn., Joliet, Ill., 1981—84; former dir. Frances Xavier Warde Sch.; vice chair. Chgo. Crime Commn.; trustee Union League Boys and Girls Clubs; sec. Civic and Arts Found.; former mem. adv. bd. St. Mary of Nazereth Hosp.; past pres., bd. dirs., vice chmn. exec. com. LaLalle St. Coun.; former chair, bd. trustees Old St. Patrick's Ch., Chgo.; bd. dirs. Concern Worldwide (U.S.), Inc. Mem.: City Club Chgo., Bankers Club Chgo. (sec., treas., exec. com.), Union League Club Chgo. (past pres.), Econ. Club Chgo., Execs. Club of Chgo. (bd. dirs., treas.). Democrat. Roman Catholic. Office: Chgo Clearing House Assn 230 S La Salle St Ste 700 Chicago IL 60604-1410 E-mail: fitz@chgo.org.

FITZ-GERALD, ROGER MILLER, lawyer; b. N.Y.C., July 13, 1935; s. Gerald Hartpence and Rovenia Francis (Miller) F.-G.; m. Martha Ann Odell, 1967 (div. 1985); children: Kathleen Odell, Maureen Roxanne, Arthur Thomas; m. Janice Evens, 1993. BS with honors, U. Ill., 1957, JD with honors, 1961. Bar: Ill. 1961, U.S. Dist. Ct. (no. dist.) 1961, U.S. Patent and Trademark Office, 1965, U.S. Ct. Customs and Patent Appeals, 1978, U.S. Ct. Appeals (fed. cir.) 1982, U.S. Dist. Ct. (so. dist.) Ill. 1992, U.S. Dist. Ct. (cen. dist.) Ill. 1994. Assoc. Kirkland, Ellis, Hodson, Chaffetz & Masters, Chgo., 1961-64; assoc. specializing in fgn. patent law Fitch, Even, Tabin & Luedeka, Chgo., 1964-72; patent atty. Bell & Howell Co., Chgo., 1972-74, sr. patent atty., 1974-75, group patent atty., 1975-76, group patent counsel, 1976-82, sr. patent counsel, 1982-85, sr. tech. law counsel, 1985-86, chief tech. law counsel, 1986-90; pvt. practice Urbana, Wilmette, Belleville, Ill., 1990—, St. Louis, 1990—. Author: (with Ferdinand J. Zeni) Precinct Captain's Guide, 1968; contbg. author: Materials on Legislation (Read, MacDonald, Fordham and Pierce), 1973 Constl. revision chmn. Ill. Young Republican Orgn., 1968-70. Served with AUS, 1957 Mem. ABA, Ill. Bar Assn., Chgo. Bar Assn., Champaign County Ill. Bar Assn., Intellectual Property Law Assn. Chgo., Am. Intellectual Property Law Assn., Assn. Corp. Patent Counsel, Computer Law Assn., Order of Coif, Phi Beta Kappa, Phi Eta Sigma, Phi Delta Phi, Delta Upsilon (province gov. 1969-75). Home: 906B E Colorado Ave Urbana IL 61801-6305 Office: 1104 S Orchard St Urbana IL 61801-4852

FITZGERALD, SUSAN HELENA, elementary educator; b. Ft. Washington, Pa., Sept. 28, 1953; d. John Robert and Helen Etta (Groscost) Payne; m. Richard Michael Fitzgerald, June 8, 1974 (dec. June 1998); children: Kevin Michael, Gregory Thomas, Wendy Elaine. BS in Edn., West Chester (Pa.) U., 1975, M, Reading Specialist, 1992. Cert. reading specialist, elem., spl. edn. tchr. Head start tchr. Chester County IU, Coatesville, Pa., 1987-89; intermediate spl. edn. tchr. Coatesville Sch. Dist., 1989-91, 5th grade tchr., 1991-92, 1st grade tchr., 1992-97, instrl. support tchr., 1997-99, title I reading splst., 1999—. Coach Spl. Olympics Coatesville Sch. Dist., 1989—91, mem. instn. support team, 1994—99; summer sch. tchr. Youth Writing Project, 1995—; part-time prof. West Chester U., 2001, site coord. young readers/young writers program, 2003—. Tchr. Pennington Presbyn. Ch., Atglen, Pa., 1992—93, Sunday sch. tchr., 2000—03, choir mem., 2000—, deacon, 2003—. Grantee Coatesville Sch. Dist., 1990, 92. Republican. Presbyterian. Avocations: reading, writing, gardening. Home: 175 Upper Valley Rd Christiana PA 17509-9771

FITZGERALD, THOMAS JOE, psychologist; b. Wichita, Kans., July 8, 1941; s. Thomas Michael and Pauline Gladys (Zink) F.; B.A., San Francisco State U., 1965; M.A., U. Utah, 1969, Ph.D., 1971. Dir. behavioral services programs VA Hosp., Topeka, 1971-73; pvt. practice as psychologist, Topeka, 1973-74, Prairie Village, Kans., 1974—; clin. instr. Menninger Sch. Psychiatry, Topeka, 1972-74; v.p. Preferred Mental Health Care Mgmt., Inc., 1986-90, pres., Preferred Mental Health, Inc., 1990—; sec.-treas. Kans. Bd. Psychologist Examiners, 1976-79, 79-80, chmn., 1980—, chmn. psychology examining com.; mem. Behavioral Scis. Regulatory Bd., 1980-82; pres. Psychol. Services Corp., Prairie Village, 1974—. Mem. Gov.'s Commn. on Criminal Adminstrn., 1974-76; vice-chmn. Gov.'s Com. on Med. Assistance, 1978-80; mem. Mid-Am. Health Systems Agy., 1979-82; mem. com. on utilization review orgns. Kansas Ins. Commr. Adv. Com., 1994—. Served with USMC, 1958-61. Mem. Kans. Psychol. Assn. (pres. 1980-81), Kans. Assn. Profl. Psychologists (pres. 1981-82, Outstanding Psychologist award 1979, 80, 81, 82), Greater Kansas City Soc. Clin. Hypnosis (pres. 1978-85). Office: Preferred Mental Health Inc PO Box 4404 Overland Park KS 66204-0404

FITZGERALD, THOMAS ROBERT, judge; b. Chgo., July 10, 1941; s. Thomas Henry and Kathryn (Touhy) F.; m. Gayle Ann Aubry, July 1, 1967; children: Maura, Kathryn, Jean, Thomas., Ann. Student Loyola U., Chgo., 1959-63; J.D., John Marshall Law Sch., Chgo., 1968. Bar: Ill. 1968, U.S. Dist. Ct. (no. dist.) Ill. 1968. Asst. state's atty. State's Atty. Cook County, Chgo., 1968-76, trial asst., 1968-72, felony trial supr., 1973-76; judge criminal div. Circuit Ct. Cook County, 1976—2000, justice Ill. State Supreme Ct., 2000-; adj. prof. law Chgo., Kent Coll. Law, 1977—2000, asst. coord. trial ad program, 1989-96, instr. Einstein Inst. for Sci., Health and Cts.; mem. faculty Nat. Inst. Trial Advs., Boulder, Colo., 1982, Ill. Jud. Conf., Chgo., 1982— . Pres. Sch. Bd. Queen of Universe Parish, Chgo., 1974-75. Served with USN. Recipient Outstanding Jud. Performance award Chgo. Crime Commn., Herman Kogan Media award for excellence in broadcast jour.; named Celtic Man of Yr. Celtic Legal Soc. Fellow Ill. Bar Found.; mem. Chgo. Bar Assn., Ill. Bar Assn., Ill. Judges Assn. (bd. dirs. 1981-84, treas. 1985, sec. 1986, 3d v.p. 1987, pres.). Office: 160 N LaSalle St Rm N-2013 Chicago IL 60601 Fax: 312-793-4579.

FITZGERALD, TIKHON (LEE R. H. FITZGERALD), bishop; b. Detroit, Nov. 14, 1932; s. LeRoy and Dorothy Kaeding (Higgins) F. AB, Wayne State U., 1958. Ordained deacon, 1971, priest, 1978, bishop Eastern Orthodox, 1987. Enlisted U.S. Army, 1954-57; commd. 2 lt. USAF, 1960, advanced through grades to capt., 1971; air staff, 1966-71; released, 1971; protodeacon Holy Virgin Mary Russian Orthodox Cathedral, L.A., 1972-78, rector, archpriest, 1979-87; bishop of San Francisco and the West Orthodox Ch. in Am., L.A., 1987—. Recipient Order of St. Vladimir II Class, Patriarch Aleksy of Moscow, 1993. Democrat. Russian Orthodox. Home: 649 Robinson St Los Angeles CA 90026-3612 Office: Orthodox Ch Am Diocese of the West 650 Micheltorena St Los Angeles CA 90026-3623

FITZGERALD, TIMOTHY K. writer, political organizer, non-profit administrator; b. San Jose, Calif., Jan. 3, 1946; *Tim is single, the oldest of three brothers. His grandfather Fitzgerald found his fortune as a baker in Nome, Alaska, during the Klondike gold rush. His mother's family date themselves to the Battle of King's Mountain in the American Revolution and further back to the early founding of Jamestown, Virginia in 1612. Tim himself pioneered first ascents in Yosemite Valley in its golden era of the sixties.* BA, San Jose State Coll., 1971, San Jose State U., 1980, MA, 1985, MA, 1997. Treas. Associated Students San Jose State Coll., 1969-70; camp bus. mgr. Boy Scouts Am., Sonora, Calif., 1973; co. budget analyst Allstate Equity Investments, 1980; adminstrv. asst. Summer Employment of Youth program CETA, San Jose, 1981; pres. Corp. for Shared Responsibility, San Jose, 1983-84; rschr. San Jose, 1992-96; owner/operator Raccoon Pubs., San Jose, 1991-92; freelance writer San Jose, 1986—; rschr., 1992-96. Sec. Discovery, Inc, 1991-93; adminstrv. trustee Inst. for Social Orgnl. Rsch., 1992-94, 98-2001, exec. dir., 2001—; instr. Cerro Coso C.C., Mammoth Lakes, Calif., 1998-2000. *Tim has been a civic leader in his community since his undergraduate days in the mid-sixties. As a student activist, he was first elected to office on a ticket with a militant black civil rights spokesperson in a campus party of ethnic pluralism in 1969. His first writings were published as letters in the campus daily. An advocate of issues of poverty, the disabled and disadvantaged, he has since become a facilitator in national and State issues in Green Party politics.* Author: Essays in Capitalism, 1986, Inner City, 1993, Twilight in the Afternoon, 1997, Critical Mass: Prologue to a New World Order, 1998, (memoir) The Quest, 3 vols., 2001, 2002, (narrative) Trail to Black Mountain, 1978, (poetry) Impressions from Idle Rock, 1981; corr.: Mono County Rev. Herald, 1997—98; talk show host KSJS Radio, San Jose, 1995—97. Mgr., candidate for State Assembly, San Jose, 1994, for San Jose City Coun., 1982, for Mono County Bd. Edn., 1998; delegate Green Party Nat. Conv., 2000; co-coord. State Green Party Platform, Calif., 1993, State Green Party campaigns and candidates, Calif., 1995-97; elected mem. Green Party County Coun., Santa Clara County, Calif., 1992-94, Mono County, 2000—; vol. Cmty. Companions, Inc., San Jose, 1990-91; commr. City of San Jose Disability Adv., 1993-97, vice chair, 1997; mem. task force on poverty Santa Clara County, 1995-97; mem. Mono County Mental Health Adv. Bd., 1998-2002, chair, 1999-2000. Advanced cadet U.S. Army ROTC, 1966-67. Mem. Am. Acad. Poets, Nat. Writers Union, Amnesty Interant., Fellowship of Reconciliation, Ams. for Dem. Action, Commonwealth Club, Sierra Club, Tau Delta Phi. Lutheran. Avocations: hiking, wilderness photography, chess, bridge. Office: Inst for Social Organizational Rsch PO Box 3504 Mammoth Lakes CA 93546-3504 E-mail: timkf@hotmail.com.

FITZGERALD, WALTER GEORGE, marketing consulting company executive; b. N.Y.C., Aug. 5, 1936; s. George Harold and Florence Mary (rank) F.; m. Welthie Kinney, Sept. 30, 1995; children: Pamela, Drew. BS, NYU, 1963. Mktg. rsch. analyst Ted Bates & Co., N.Y.C., 1956-59; sr. consumer analyst Lennen and Newell, Inc., N.Y.C., 1959-63; mgr. mktg. rsch. Nestle Co., White Plains, N.Y., 1963-67; mktg. dir. Y&S Candies divsn. Hershey (Pa.) Foods, 1967-79; gen. mgr. Ward Candies Fund Raising divsn. Terson, Inc., Chgo., 1979-82; v.p. mktg. John Middleton, Inc., King of Prussia, Pa., 1982-99; pres. Walt's Mktg. Wizardry, Inc., mktg. cons., Wayne, Pa., 1999—. Cons. Boyer Bros., Altoona, Pa., 1982. Contbr. numerous articles to profl. jours., 1967-79; patentee in field, 1986. Bd. dirs., devel. dir., co-dir. Strings for Schs., Phila. Fellow Am. Mktg. Assn.; mem. Am. Mgmt. Assn. Republican. Uniterian. Avocations: tennis, swimming, reading, carpentry, bicycling.

FITZGERALD, WILLIAM HENRY G. diplomat, corporation executive; b. Boston, Dec. 23, 1909; s. William Joseph and Mary Ellen (Smith) F.; m. Annelise Petschek, July 2, 1943; children: Desmond, Anne. BS, U.S. Naval Acad., 1931; postgrad., Harvard Law Sch., 1934-35; DSc (hon.), Adelphi U., 1962; LLD (hon.), Cath. U. Am., 1990; D in Pub. Svc. (hon.), Regis U., 1999. With Borden Co., N.Y.C., 1936-41; personal bus. interests Mexico, 1946-47; organized Metall. Research & Devel. Co., Washington, 1947, v.p., treas., 1947-56, pres., 1956-58, 60-82, chmn., 1960-82; chmn. bd. Nat. Metallizing Corp., Trenton, N.J., 1956-58; organizer FitzGerald Corp., 1959, pres., 1980—; chmn. bd. The Cottages, Ltd., Jamaica, 1960-70, Linden Corp., Washington, 1962-70, N.Am. Housing Corp., Washington, 1971-88; chmn. Supramar, Ltd., Lucerne, Switzerland, 1963-69, dir., 1970-75; pres. Nat. Media Analysis, Inc., Washington, 1968-70, chmn., 1970-72; ptnr. Hornblower & Weeks, Hemphill-Noyes, Inc., 1970-72, 1st v.p., 1972-77; vice chmn., dir., exec. com. Fin. Gen. Bankshares, Inc., 1977-82; vice chmn. African Devel. Found., 1990-92; U.S. amb. to Ireland, 1992-93. Dir., mem. exec. com. First Am. Bank (N.A.), Washington, 1977-83; dir., mem. exec. com., chmn. investment com. Avemco Corp., Washington, Frederick, Md., 1970-89; Cosmadent, Ltd., Zurich, Switzerland, 1964-75, Chase Fund of Boston, Chase Convertible Fund, Income & Capital Shares Inc., 1970-75, Pyrotector, Inc., Hingham, Mass., 1963-76; cons. to dir. ICA, Washington, 1957; dep. dir. for mgmt. ICA, Dept. State, 1958-60; U.S. conciliator Internat. Center for Investment Disputes, 1975-82; dir. Inst. Inter Am. Affairs, 1958-60; mem. President's Adv. Bd. on Internat. Investments, 1976-78; treas. Presdl. Inaugural Com., 1981; trustee Presdl. Inaugural Trust, 1981-89; mem. nat. adv. com. Internat. Edn., 1982-85. Trustee Fed. City Coun., 1962-90, Wash. Inst. Fgn. Affairs, 1966—; bd. dirs. Atlantic Coun. U.S., 1976—, treas., 1979-92, mem. exec. com., 1980—, vice chmn., 1993—; trustee Fgn. Student Svc. Coun., 1963—, Oblate Coll. (Cath. U.), 1966—; trustee Corcoran Gallery Art, 1977-90, also mem. exec. com., chmn. devel. com.; pres. Soc. for a More Beautiful Nat. Capital, Inc., 1974-77; bd. dirs., mem. exec. com., sr. v.p. Internat. Tennis Hall of Fame, 1964-92, 94—, hon. chmn., 2000—; nat. chmn. Yorktown Internat. Bicentennial Com., 1981; dir., mem. exec. com. Washington Tennis and Ednl. Found., 1987—; U.S. del. Atlantic Treaty Assembly, Reykjavik, Iceland, 1977, Washington, 1979, Rome, 1983, Istanbul,

Turkey, 1987, Brussels, 1989, Rome, 1996, sofia, 1997; grand officer Confrèrie des Chevaliers du Tastevin, 1979—; grand senechal Sous Commanderie de Washington, 1980-90; trustee White House Preservation Fund, 1979-89, chmn., 1982-89, chmn. emeritus, 1989-90; mem. Nat. Task Force on Prison Industries; trustee, mem. nominating com. U.D.C., 1982-87; mem. nat. com. Vatican Judaica Exhbn., 1987-89; mem. Bretton Woods com., 1992—; mem., dir. Coun. of Am. Ambassadors, 1992—. Ensign USN, 1931-34; from lt. (j.g.) to comdr., 1941-46. Decorated Orden Militar de Ayacucho Peru, knight grand cross honor & devotion in obedience Order Malta, knight grand cross Sovereign Mil. Order Malta, Equestrian Order Holy Sepulchre, Sacred Mil. Constantinian Order St. George; named to Mid-Atlantic Tennis Hall of Fame, 1997. Mem. Fed. Assn. in U.S.A. Sovereign Mil. Order of Malta (pres. 1975-79), Assn. for Diplomatic Studies and Tng. (dir. 1993—), Army-Navy Country Club (Washington), Univ. Club (Washington), Harvard Club (Washington), River Club (N.Y.C.), Met. Club (Washington), Essex Country Club (Manchester, Mass.), Portmarnock Golf Club (Dublin, Ireland), FitzWilliam Lawn Tennis Club (Dublin). Roman Catholic. Home: 2305 Bancroft Pl NW Washington DC 20008-4005

FITZGERALD-VERBONITZ, DIANNE ELIZABETH, healthcare executive; b. Tampa, Fla., July 11, 1943; d. James Gerald and Bernice Elizabeth (Creel) F.; children: Deborah Elizabeth Guilbault Starr, Fred Anthony Guilbault Jr. AA, Montgomery Coll., 1979; BS in Health Svcs. summa cum laude, No. Ariz. U., 1985, MEd, 1987. Nurse in Washington Internship, Advanced Internship. Pvt. practice counselor, Phoenix; mem. faculty C.V. Mosby Co., St. Louis; nurse clinician in orthopedics; mgr. orthopedic program Kimberly Quality Care; adminstr. Staff Builders Health Svcs., Phoenix, Cypress Health Care Svcs.; now exec. dir. Ariz. Psychol. Assn., Scottsdale. Bd. dirs. Valley of Sun Sch. and Rehab. Ctr., Arthritis Found.; mem. Am. Vol. Med. Team; med. vol. Habitat for Humanity. Named one of Top Ten Bus. Women in Managed Health Care, Today's Ariz. Woman, 1998. Mem.: State and Provincial Psychol. Assns., Am./Ariz. Soc. Assn. Execs. (bd. dirs.), Nat. Assn. Orthopedic Nurses (pres. 1989—90), Phi Kappa Phi (life).

FITZGERRELL SMITH, LEE, artist, illustrator; b. Hollywood, Calif., Sept. 11, 1946; d. Ray Hartley Jr. and Marcia (James) F.; m. Brian Rees Smith; children: Graham, Leslie, Lauren. BA, Occidental Coll., 1968; MFA, Instituto Allende, Mex., 1971. Illustrator L.A. Parks and Recreation, El Monte, Calif., 1970-71; staff artist Santa Barbara (Calif.) Pub. Library, 1972-74; tchr. Howard Sch., Montecito, Calif., 1972-73; instr. Santa Barbara Art Mus., 1971-74; freelance illustrator and muralist Placerville, Calif., 1974—. Illustrator: Indian Paintbrush, 1975, Comfort Clothes, 1981, Qué de gusta comer? El regalo de tía Gala, Los inventos de Nicolás, 1999, Inchelina Tabletop and Giftware Design, Blue Sky/Van Group, 2000—, internat. stationery and giftware products, 1994—, (TV comml.) Sacramento International Airport, 1996—, McGraw Hill Poetry Anthology, 1999, Giftware and ceramic design: Appletree Design, Inc., 2003—. Studio: 1815 Woodsman Ct Placerville CA 95667-8725

FITZGIBBON, DANIEL HARVEY, lawyer; b. Columbus, Ind., July 7, 1942; s. Joseph Bales and Margaret Lenore (Harvey) FitzG.; m. Joan Helen Meltzer, Aug. 12, 1973; children: Katherine Lenore, Thomas Bernard. BS in Engring., U.S. Mil. Acad., 1964; JD cum laude, Harvard U., 1972. Bar: Ind. 1972; U.S. Dist. Ct. (so. dist.) Ind. 1972, U.S. Tax Ct. 1977. Commd. 2d lt. U.S. Army, 1964, advanced through grades to capt., 1967, served with inf., resigned, 1969; assoc. Barnes & Thornburg, Indpls., 1972-79, ptnr., 1979-99, mem. mgmt. com., 1983-95, of counsel, 2000—. Speaker various insts; comml. law liaison, ABA-CEELI, Moscow, 1998-99. Mem. Sch. Bd. Met. Sch. Dist. Lawrence Twp., 1988-96, pres., 1990-91, 94-95; bd. advs. Eiteljorg Mus. Am. Indian and Western Art, 1993-2003. Capt. U.S. Army, 1964-69, Vietnam. Fellow Am. Coll. Tax Counsel, Am. Bar Found.; mem. ABA (internat. law sect.), Am. Law Inst., Ind. State Bar Assn. (tax sect.), Indpls. Bar Assn. (chmn. tax sect. 1982-83, coun. 1982-86), Lawyers Club, Woodstock Club. Home: 6460 Lawrence Dr Indianapolis IN 46226-1035 Office: Barnes & Thornburg 1313 Merchants Bank Bldg Indianapolis IN 46204-3506

FITZHUGH, DAVID MICHAEL, lawyer; b. San Francisco, Nov. 24, 1946; s. William DeHart and Betty Jean (Jeffries) F.; m. Jenny Lu Conner, Dec. 22, 1967; children: Ross DeHart, Cameron Hyatt, Michael Jeffries. Student, Carleton Coll., 1964-67; BA, Coll. William and Mary, 1972; JD, U. Va., 1975. Bar: D.C. 1975, U.S. Dist. Ct. D.C. 1979, U.S. Dist. Ct. Md. 1987, U.S. Ct. Claims 1980, U.S. Ct. Appeals (fed. cir.) 1982, U.S. Ct. Appeals (D.C. cir.) 1987, U.S. Ct. Appeals (4th cir.) 1989, U.S. Supreme Ct. 1982. Assoc. McKenna & Cuneo, Washington, 1975-80, ptnr., 1980-98, chmn. litigation dept., 1984-94; assoc. counsel Office of Counsel Naval Air Systems Command, 1999—. Mem. editl. bd. Nat. Contract Mgmt. Assn. Jour., 1975-2000; contbr. articles to legal pubs. Capt. USMC, 1967-71, Vietnam. Home: 11140 Beacon Way Lusby MD 20657-2442 Office: AIR-11 1 NAVAIRSYSCOM HQ Office Counsel Bldg 2272 Ste 257 47123 Buse Rd Unit Moffett Patuxent River MD 20670-1547 E-mail: fitzhughdm@navair.navy.mil.

FITZHUGH, WILLIAM, curator; BA in Anthropology, Dartmouth U., 1964; MA in Anthropology, Harvard U., 1967, PhD in Anthropology, 1970. Assoc. curator dept. anthropology Nat. Mus. Natural History/Smithsonian Instn., 1970—75, chmn. dept. anthropology, 1975—80, 2002—, curator dept. anthropology, 1980—; dir. Smithsonian Arctic Studies Ctr., Washington, 1988—. Robert L. Stigler lectr. U. Ark., 1988. Recipient Casebook award, 1984, Cine-Golden Eagle 2d prize for film Secrets of the Lost Red Paint People, Coun. on Internat. Non-theatrical Events, 1988, Smithsonian Disting.Lecture award, 2003. Office: Nat Mus Natural History Smithsonian Instn Washington DC 20560

FITZHUGH, WILLIAM WYVILL, JR., printing company executive; b. Bklyn., June 27, 1914; s. William Wyvill and Portia (Starr) F.; m. Florence Hardy, Dec. 13, 1941; children: William, Priscilla, John, Portia. AB, Dartmouth Coll., 1935; BA, Trinity Coll., Cambridge U., 1937, MA, 1938; M in Philosophy, Columbia U., 1977; JD, Pace U. Law Sch., 1980. Fellow Carnegie Endowment for Internat. Peace, 1938-39; sec. rapporteur Internat. Studies Conf., League of Nations, 1938-39; instr. govt. Columbia U., 1939-42; pres. William W. Fitzhugh, Inc., 1945-99, chmn. bd. dirs.; pres. New Haven Bd. & Carton Co., Inc., 1960-64; ptnr. Dalsemer, Fitzhugh & Catzen, N.Y.C., 1964-66; pres. Newspaper Preprint Corp., N.Y.C., 1966-75. Past chmn. Chappaqua Orchestral Assn. Lt. USNR. Mem. Gravure Tech. Assn. (past pres.), Folding Paper Box Assn Am. (past pres. met. N.Y. group), Label Mfrs. Assn. (past dir.), Bklyn. C. of C. (past dir.), Phi Beta Kappa, Sigma Chi. Republican. Episcopalian. Home: 253 Kendal at Hanover 80 Lyme Rd Hanover NH 03755-1225 Office: 148 Main St Montpelier VT 05602-2913 *A long life's enough, there's no need to be famous; just live, while you live: Dum Vivimus Vivamus!.*

FITZKEE, THOMAS L. education educator; s. Harry H. Fitzkee and Constance A. Paulson; m. Jill Stephenson, June 13, 1992; children: Lauren E., Rachel L. MS, Va. Tech, 1989—93; BS, Salisbury State U., 1985—89; PhD, George Wash. U., 1993—98. Support specialist Boeing Aerospace, Greenbelt, Md., 1986—98. Mem.: Math. Assn. of Am. Christian. Office: Francis Marion U POBox 100547 Florence SC 29501 Office Fax: 843-661-4616. E-mail: tfitzkee@fmarion.edu.

FITZMAURICE, GARRETT MARTIN, education educator, researcher; b. Dublin, June 1, 1962; s. Thomas Francis and Josephine Fitzmaurice; m. Laura Ellen Dobler; children: Kieran Patrick, Aidan Thomas. BA, Nat. U. of Ireland, 1983, MA, 1987; MSc, U. of London, 1986; DSc, Harvard U., 1993. Post-doctoral rsch. fellow Dept. of Biostatistics, Harvard U., 1993—94; rsch. fellow Nuffield Coll., Oxford U., 1994—97; asst. prof. Dept. of Biostatistics, Harvard U., 1997—99, assoc. prof., 1999—. Contbr. Recipient Elected Mem. of the Internat. Statis. Inst., Internat. Statis. Inst., 2002; Rsch. on methods for the analysis of longitudinal data, NIH, 2000—, Alumni scholarship, Harvard Sch. of Pub. Health, 1991. Fellow: Royal Statis. Soc., Am. Statis. Assn. Home: 1 Dana St Apt 20 Cambridge MA 02138 Office: Harvard School of Public Health 655 Huntington Ave Boston MA 02115

FITZMAURICE, LAURENCE DORSET, retired bank executive; b. Worcester, Mass., Aug. 7, 1938; s. John Vincent and Alice (Earle) F.; m. Ann McQuaid, Apr. 15, 1961; children: Laura, Peter, Meghan. BS in Mgmt., Babson Coll., 1959; postgrad. in law, Boston Coll., 1961. Prodn. control Sylvania, Needham, Mass., 1959-61; divsn. controller EG&G, Inc., Bedford, Mass., 1961-69; asst. corp. controller Tyco Labs., Waltham, Mass., 1970; corp. controller Analog Devices, Norwood, Mass., 1971-73; v.p. fin. Balco, Inc., Newton, Mass., 1974-75; comptroller Commonwealth of Mass., Boston, 1976-78, commr. of revenue, 1978; sr. cons. Am. Mgmt. Systems, Arlington, Va., 1979; prin. cons. Boston, 1980-81; v.p. State St. Bank & Trust Co., Boston, 1982—2002, ret., 2002; prin. Dorset Mgmt. Group, Wellesley, Mass., 2002—. Adj. prof. Northeastern U. Grad. Sch. Polit. Sci., Boston, 1977-78; mem. faculty New Eng. Coll. Fin., 1998—; mem. Bd. Bank Incorp., Boston, 1978; cons. Exec. Svc. Corps. of New Eng., 2003—. Commr. Mass. State Lottery, Braintree, 1976-78; sec. Mass. Housing Fin. Agy., Boston, 1978; pres. Human Rels. Svc., Wellesley, Mass., 1988-89, trustee, 1986-2000; bd. dirs. Social Policy Rsch. Group, Boston, 1981-92, Boston Mcpl. Rsch. Bur., 1985-2001, exec. com. 1999-2001; mem. allocations com. United Way of Mass. Bay, 1998, 2001-02, multi-yr. audit task force, 1999, 2000; bd. overseers USS Constitution Mus., 1999-2001, trustee, 2001—; mem. hearings com. Mass. Bd. Bar Overseers, 2002—. Cpl. USMCR, 1957-63. Democrat. Roman Catholic. Avocation: golf. E-mail: Dorsets4@comcast.net.

FITZMYER, JOSEPH AUGUSTINE, theology educator, priest; b. Phila., Nov. 4, 1920; s. Joseph Augustine and Anna Catherine (Alexy) F. AB, Loyola U., Chgo., 1943, AM, 1945; Licentiate in Sacred Theology, Facultés St. Albert de Louvain, Belgium, 1952; PhD, Johns Hopkins U., 1956; Licentiate in Sacred Scripture, Pontifical Bibl. Inst., 1957. Joined S.J., 1938, ordained priest Roman Cath. Ch., 1951. Asst. prof. N.T. and Bibl. langs. Woodstock (Md.) Coll., 1958-59, assoc. prof., 1959-64, prof., 1964-69; prof. Aramaic and Hebrew dept. Nr. Ea. langs.-civilizations U. Chgo., 1969-71; prof. N.T. and Bibl. langs. dept. theology Fordham U., Bronx, N.Y., 1971-74, Weston Jesuit Sch. Theology, Cambridge, Mass., 1974-76; prof. dept. Bibl. studies Cath. U. Am., Washington, 1976—. Tchr. Gonzaga H.S., Washington, 1945-48; Spkr.'s lectr. Bibl. studies Oxford (Eng.) U., 1974-75. Author: Essays on the Semitic Background of the New Testament, 1971, The Genesis Aprocryphon on Qumran Cave I, 1966, 2d edit., 1971; editor (with R.E. Brown and R.E. Murphy) The New Jerome Biblical Commentary, 1990; The Gospel According to Luke (Anchor Bible), vol. 28, 1981, vol. 28A, 1985, Romans (Anchor Bible), vol. 33, 1993, The Acts of the Apostles, vol. 31, 1998, The Letter to Philemon, vol. 34C, 2000. Mem. Cath. Bibl. Assn. (pres. 1970, editor Quar. 1980-84), Soc. Bibl. Lit. (pres. 1978-79, editor Jour. 1971-76), Studiorum Novi Testamenti Societas (pres. 1992-93). Home: Georgetown U Jesuit Cmty PO Box 571200 Washington DC 20057-1200 E-mail: fitzmyja@georgetown.edu.

FITZNER-ATCHINSON, JUDITH ANN, youth center director; b. Schenectady, N.Y., Sept. 28, 1941; d. Eugen A. Fitzner and Wanda Nowicki; m. Peter W. Jacobs, May 10, 1964 (div.); children: Dawn E. Jacobs, Beth R. Jacobs; m. Brian M. Oneil, Apr. 22, 1990. MusB, Hart Coll. Music, 1963, MFA, 1973. Founder, exec. dir. Quest Inc., Schenectady, 1994—. Artist in residence Skidmore Coll., Saratoga, NY, 1980—2000, Barnard Coll., N.Y.C., 1991—, Temple U., Phila., 1992—97, Union Coll., Schenectady, 1994—; composer, musician Don Wagoner Co., N.Y.C., 1991—93, Limon Co., N.Y.C., 1990—; artist, musician Bill T. Jones Co., N.Y.C., 1994—96; mem. adv. bd. Albany Med. Cmty. Outreach, 1999—, Carlisle Project, Phila., 1999—2002, Healthy Schenectady Families, 1999—. Composer (music): Documentary on Sculpture, 2002; composer: (score and script) Irish Nat. Ballet, 1999; composer: (installation) Smithsonian Mus., 1987. Mem. adv. bd. Proctors Theater, Schenectady, 2001—; mem. Internat. Dance Musicians, 1996 . Fellow, Pew Found., 1997; grantee, Nat. Endowment Assn., 1995, 1999, N.Y. Found. Arts, 1995, 1998, 2000. Democrat. Avocations: reading, travel, gardening, animal rights activist. Home: 1131 Van Antwerp Rd Schenectady NY 12309 Office: Quest Inc 801 Stanley St Schenectady NY 12307

FITZPATRICK, BRIAN, member of parliament; b. Assiniboia, Can., Nov. 18, 1945; m. Zinaida Fitzpatrick; 2 children. BA in History, Bemidji (Minn.) State U.; LLB, U. Saskatchewan, Can. Cert. tchr. Can. Mem. 37th parliament House of Commons, Ottawa, Canada. Ofcl. opposition's dep. industry critic House of Commons; trustee Nipawin Bd. Edn.; mem. Reform's Nat. Task Force on Criminal Justice, Dem. Populism and Provincial Party Involvement. Avocations: curling, fishing. Office: House of Commons Justice Bldg Ste 402 Ottawa ON K1A 0A6 Canada also: 200 28th St W Prince Albert SK S6V 4S9 Canada

FITZPATRICK, CHRISTINE MORRIS, legal administrator, former television executive; ret. b. Steubenville, Ohio, June 10, 1920; d. Roy Elwood and Ruby Lorena (Mason) Morris; student U. Chgo., 1943-44, U. Ga., 1945-46; m. T. Mallary Fitzpatrick, Jr., Dec. 19, 1942; 1 child, Thomas Mallary III. BA, Roosevelt U., 1947; postgrad. Trinity Coll., Hartford, Conn., 1970. Assoc. dir. Joint Human Rels. Project, City of Chgo., 1965-66; tchr. English, Austin Sch. for Girls, Hartford, 1966-70; promotion coord. Conn. Pub. TV, Hartford, 1971-72, dir. community rels., 1972-73, v.p., 1973-77; pub. rels./pub. affairs cons. Commonwealth Edison Co., Chgo., 1977-79; dir. spl. events Chgo. Public TV, 1979-84; v.p. Fitzpatrick Group, Inc., Chgo., 1986-88; adminstrv. dir. Fitzpatrick Law Offices, 1988-94, Fitzpatrick Eilenberg & Zivian, 1994-96; adminstrv. dir. Fitzpatrick Law Offices, Chgo., 1997-99, 2200 Ventures LLC, Chgo., 1999-2002; v.p. Pub. Rels. Clinic Chgo., 1980-81. Bd. advisers Greater Hartford Mag., 1975-77; bd. dirs. World Affairs Ctr., Hartford, 1975-77; mem. adv. coun. Am. Revolution Bicentennial Commn. Conn., 1975-77. Mem. Pub. Rels. Soc. Am. (dir. Conn. Valley chpt. 1976-77), Am. Women in Radio and TV (New Eng. chpt. pres. 1976-77), LWV (Chgo. chpt. pres. 1962-64, Hartford chpt. v.p. 1971-73). Home: 5518 S Harper Ave Chicago IL 60637-1830

FITZ-PATRICK, DAVID, endocrinologist, educator; b. Burnley, Lancashire, England, Sept. 1, 1951; came to U.S., 1975; s. Malcolm Milligan and Ada (Maguire) F.; m. Elizabeth Joaquin, Dec. 30, 1972; children: Ian Rodney, Claire Larissa. MB, BS, U. Newcastle-Upon-Tyne, England, 1974. House officer Newcastle (England) Gen. Hosp., 1974-75; resident in internal medicine U. Md. Hosp., Balt., 1975-77; fellow in endocrinology McGill U., Montreal, Que., Can., 1977-81; cons. physician Straub Clinic and Hosp, Honolulu, 1981-91, chief of endocrinology, 1986-91; asst. clin. prof. medicine John Burns Sch. Medicine, Honolulu, 1982-95, assoc. clin. prof., 1995—; med. dir. Diabetes and Hormone Ctr. of Pacific, Honolulu, 1990—, East-West Med. Rsch. Inst., 1999—. Mem. house of dels. Hawaii Med. Assn., 1987-90; med. adv. com. Bd. Med. Examiners, Hawaii, 1989—; founding mem., bd. dirs. Juvenile Diabetes Found., Honolulu, 1989-92 (Geraldine Fleming Meml. fellowship 1980-81); dir. East-West Med. Rsch. Inst., 1999—. Mem. editl. bd. Endocrine Practice, 2000—; contbr. articles to profl. jours.; founder, editor Diabetes & Endocrinology Home Page on Internet. Dir. The Straub Found., Honolulu, 1984-90. Rsch. scholar McGill U., 1979-80. Fellow Am. Coll. Physicians (mem. coun. 1990-93, Gov's. prize 1986), Am. Coll. Endocrinology; mem. Am. Diabetes Assn. (pres. 1984-86, 93-94), The Endocrine Soc., Am. Soc. Internal Medicine, Am. Assn. Clin. Endocrinologists (state chair 1992-96, 98—). Avocations: reading, family, tennis, golf. Office: 1585 Kapiolani Blvd Ste 1500 Honolulu HI 96814-

FITZPATRICK, DAVID J. electronics executive; b. 1954; BS in Acctg., U. Ill.; M in Mgmt., Northwestern U. CPA, Ill. With GM, 1977, chief acctg. officer; group v.p. fin. and adminstn. GMAC; contr., v.p. Eastmas Kodak Co., 1995; sr. v.p., CFO United Technologies Corp., Hartford, Conn., 1998—2002; exec. v.p., CFO Tyco Internat., 2002—. Bd. dirs. GMAC, GMAC Mortgage. Office: Tyco 1 Town Center Rd Delray Beach FL 33483

FITZPATRICK, GARRETT JOSEPH, lawyer; b. N.Y.C., Aug. 11, 1949; s. Daniel Edward and Lillian (Brown) F.; m. Karen Ann Chenault, Jan. 27, 1979; children— Michael, Brian. B.S., U. Dayton, 1970; J.D., St. John's U., 1973. Bar: N.Y. 1974. Sr. ptnr. Mendes & Mount, N.Y.C., 1973— . Mem. ABA (aviation and space law com.), Internat. Assn. Ins. Counsel. Roman Catholic. Home: 360 West St Harrison NY 10528-2509 Office: Mendea & Mount 750 7th Ave New York NY 10019-6834

FITZPATRICK, GEORGE E. research scientist, educator; b. Trenton, N.J., Oct. 7, 1946; s. George Edward and Mary Bisaha Fitzpatrick; m. Mary L. Lamberts, May 11, 1991; m. Donna L. Pruss, Aug. 23, 1969 (div. July 1987). BA, Trenton State Coll., 1968, MA, 1972; PhD, Rutgers U., 1975. Cert. profl. horticulturist Am. Soc. Horticultural Sci., 1991. Postdoctoral rsch. assoc. Miss. State U., Starkville, 1975—76; asst. rsch. scientist U. Fla., Ft. Lauderdale, 1976—79, asst. prof., 1979—84, assoc. prof., 1984—95, prof. environ. horticulture, 1995—, acting program dir. and prof., 2000—. Editor: (jour.) Proceedings of the Florida State Horticultural Soc., 2001; editor: (assoc.), 1986—95. Pres. Victoria Park Civic Assn., Ft. Lauderdale, 1981—82, 1987—89, Coun. of Ft. Lauderdale Area Civic Assns., 1982—83, 1988—89. Mem.: Fla. State Horticultural Soc., Am. Soc. Horticultural Sci., Internat. Soc.Horticultural Soc. Office: Univ Fla 3205 College Ave Fort Lauderdale FL 33314

FITZPATRICK, HAROLD FRANCIS, lawyer; b. Jersey City, Oct. 16, 1947; s. Harold G. and Anne Marie F.; m. Joanne M. Merry, Sept. 22, 1973; children: Elizabeth, Kevin, Matthew, Christopher. AB, Boston Coll., 1969; MBA, NYU, 1971; JD, Harvard U., 1974. Bar: N.J. 1974, U.S. Dist. Ct. N.J. 1974, U.S. Ct. Internat. Trade, 1986, U.S. Supreme Ct. 1994. Securities analyst Chase Manhattan Bank, N.Y.C., 1970-71, Brown Bros., Harriman & Co., N.Y.C., 1971; staff asst. U.S. Senate, Washington, 1972; law clk. to assoc. justice N.J. Supreme Ct., Trenton, 1974-75; assoc. Cleary, Gottlieb, Steen & Hamilton, N.Y.C., 1975-78; mng. ptnr. Fitzpatrick & Waterman, Secaucus, N.J., 1978—, Bayonne, N.J., 1978—. Gen. counsel Housing Authority City of Bayonne, 1976—, Color Pigments Mfrs. Assn., Alexandria, Va., 1978—, N.J. Assn. Housing and Redevel. Authorities, Brick, N.J., 1979—, Housing Authority Town of Secaucus, N.J., 1980-88, Rahway (N.J.) Geriatrics Ctr. Inc., 1981-92, Housing Authority City of Englewood, N.J., 1985-91, Housing Authority City of Rahway, 1986-2000, Edgewater Mcpl. Utilities Authority, 1986-93, Housing Authority City of Woodbridge, N.J., 1988-94, Housing Authority City of Asbury Pk., N.J., 1991-94, Bd. Edn. City of Rahway, 1994-97, N.J. Pub. Housing Authority Joint Ins. Fund, 1995-2001. Mem. ABA, N.J. Bar Assn., Hudson County Bar Assn. (trustee, officer 1984-92, pres. 1993), Beta Gamma Sigma. Office: Fitzpatrick & Waterman 333 Meadowlands Pkwy Secaucus NJ 07096-3159

FITZPATRICK, JAMES DAVID, lawyer; b. Syracuse, N.Y., Oct. 21, 1938; s. William Francis and Margaret Mary (Shortt) F. BS, Holy Cross Coll., Worcester, Mass., 1960; JD, Syracuse U., 1963. Bar: N.Y. 1963, U.S. Dist. Ct. (no. dist.) N.Y. 1965. Assoc. Bond, Schoeneck & King, Syracuse, N.Y., 1963-76, mem., 1976-88, ptnr., 1988—. Pres. Hiscock Legal Aid Soc., Syracuse, 1975-76; faculty Nat. Bus. Inst., Eau Claire, Wis., 1990—; del. Russian Conf. on Banking-The Kremlin, Moscow, 1992, 93; spkr. Internat. Conf. on Terrorism, Madrid, 2002. Mem. presdl. Roundtable, Washington, 1991-92; founding mem. pres.'s task force Nat. Coalition Against Pornography, Common Cause; chmn. adv. bd. Rep. Nat. Coms., 1994; mem. The Studio Mus. in Harlem, Am. Mus. Nat. History; founding mem. Am. Air Mus.; nat. adv. coun. USN Meml. Found. Recipient Afghanistan Freedom Fighter award Afghan Mercy Fund, 1989, Rep. Senatorial Medal of Freedom, Honored Friend of El Salvador award, 1991, Wisdom award of Honor, Wisdom Soc. for Advancement of Knowledge, Learning and Rsch. in Edn., named to Wisdom Hall of Fame, 1999. Mem. ABA, NAACP, N.Y. State Bar Assn., Onondaga County Bar Assn. (chmn. real estate com. 1990-96), Internat. Bar Assn., Am. Land Title Assn., UN Assn. of U.S.A., Habitat for Humanity Internat., Amnesty Internat. U.S.A., Nat. Audubon Soc., Ctr. for Nat. Independence in Politics, Smithsonian Nat. Assocs., Nat. Trust for Hist. Preservation, Navy League U.S., World Future Soc., Ams. Guild, Internat. Platform Assn. (spkr. Internat. Youth Ctr., New Delhi), Inst. Global Ethics, World Jurist Assn. Republican. Roman Catholic. Avocations: housing education, reading, walking. Home: 201 Croyden Rd Syracuse NY 13224-1917 Office: Bond Schoeneck & King 1 Lincoln Ctr Fl 18 Syracuse NY 13202-1324 E-mail: fitzpaj@bsk.com.

FITZPATRICK, JAMES FRANKLIN, lawyer; b. Bluffton, Ind., Jan. 18, 1933; s. Raymond North and Evelyn (Baughman) F.; m. Sandra McNear, July 22, 1961; children: Michael, David, Benjamin. AB, Ind. U., 1955, JD, 1959; postgrad., Cambridge U., 1956. Law clk. to chief judge U.S. Ct. Appeals, Chgo., 1959-61; assoc. Arnold & Porter, Washington, 1961-67, ptnr., 1967—. Adj. prof. law Georgetown U., Washington, 1971-75, 2003; acad. vis. London Sch. Econs., 1978-79; Trinity Coll., Dublin, Ireland, 1987-88; chmn., Internat. Human Rights Law Group, 1999—; vis. prof. law U. N.Mex., 1997. Author: Law and Roadside Hazards, 1975. Bd. dirs. ACLU, 1983-85, pres. Nat. Capital chpt., Washington, 1982-83; pres. Washington Project for the Arts, 1984-90; dir. Ctr. for Auto Safety, 1984—, The Phillips Collection, 1990—, The Shakespeare Theatre, 1991—, Site Santa Fe, 1997—, Ctr. for Arts and Culture, 1998—. Brit. Am. Arts Assn., 1999—; nat. chmn. Young Citizens for Johnson, 1964. Mem. ABA, Phi Beta Kappa Democrat. Presbyterian. Office: Arnold & Porter 555 12th St NW Washington DC 20004-1206

FITZPATRICK, JAMES WARD, JR., engineering technology educator; b. Birmingham, Ala., June 17, 1921; s. James Ward and Ellen Barbara (Vogtle) Fitzpatrick; m. Ruth Bertha Horn, June 19, 1948; 1 child, James Ralph (dec.). BS in Indsl. Engring., Auburn (Ala.) U., 1942, BS in Mech. Engring., 1947, postgrad., 1950, MIT. Registered profl. engr., Ala. Indsl. engr. O'Neal Steel, Birmingham, 1947-48; plant engr. Stockham Valves & Fittings, Birmingham, 1948-49; instr. mech. engring. Auburn U., 1950-53; structural engr. Decatur (Ala.) Iron & Steel Co., 1953-56, chief engr. jail and prison equipment, 1956-64; engring. and project mgr. Monsanto Co., St. Louis, 1964-72, engring. supt., 1972-82; v.p. personnel and ops. Continental Commodities, Inc., Charlotte, N.C., 1982-83; instr. York Tech. Coll., Rock Hill, SC, 1985-98, dept. mgr., indsl. and engring. tech. and constrn. trades, continuing edn. divsn., 1999-2001, cons. continuing edn. divsn., 2002—. Cons. Assn. Sys., Inc., Charlotte, NC, 1985—95; cons. textbook revs. various pubs., 1987—. Author: (software) Workplan, 1984. Capt. U.S. Army, 1942—46, ETO. Decorated Bronze Star. Mem.: Charlotte Philatelic Soc. (pres. 1985—89). Republican. Presbyterian. Avocations: fantasy baseball, stamp collecting. Home: 5006 Gamton Ct Charlotte NC 28226-7920 E-mail: ogoytc@att.net.

FITZPATRICK, JANE, entrepreneur; b. Cuttingsville, Vt., Nov. 18, 1923; m. John H. Fitzpatrick, Sept. 7, 1944; children: Nancy Jane, JoAnn Fitzpatrick Brown. HHD (hon.), N. Adams State Coll., Mass., 1978; LHD (hon.), U. Mass., 1987, Am. Internat. Coll., Springfield, Mass., 1994. Co-founder, chmn. bd. Country Curtains, Stockbridge, Mass., 1956—. Life trustee Boston Symphony Orch., trustee, 1982—96; trustee emerita The Norman Rockwell Mus., Stockbridge, Mass. Chmn. Berkshire Theatre Festival, Stockbridge, Mass, (bd. pres. 1977-98). Office: PO Box 954 Stockbridge MA 01262-0955

FITZPATRICK, JOAN MARIE, law educator; b. El Paso, TX, Sept. 14, 1950; d. Thomas Edward and Gabrielle Herman Fitzpatrick; m. Gary Hartman, Dec. 22, 1969 (div. June 30, 1981); 1 child, Devin Charles. BA History, Rice U, Houston, TX, 1972; JD, Harvard Law Sch., Cambridge, MA, 1975; Diploma Law, Oxford U, Oxford, UK, 1980. Bar: Mass. 1975, US Supreme Court: 1979. Atty. Fed. Trade Comm., Wash., DC, 1975—77, US Dept. of Justice, Wash., DC, 1977—79; assoc. prof. of law U of Ark., Fayetteville, Ark., 1980—83; vis. assoc. prof. U of Va., Charlottesville, Va., 1982—83; Brotman prof. of law U of Wash.. Seattle, 1984—. Vice chair Amnesty Internat. USA, New York, NY, 1986—88; bd. of editors Am. Jour. Internat. Law, Wash., DC, 2000—; vice pres. Proc. Aspects Internat. Law, Wash., DC, 2000—. Author: (novels) Human Rights in Crisis, 1994; co-author Internat. Human Rights, 2001; editor Human Rights Protection for Refugees, 2002. Recipient Spencer Short Award, U of Wash., 1994—95, Found. Scholar, 1995—97, Brotman Prof. of Law, 2000. Mem.: PAIL Institute (VP), Nijhoff Refugee and Human Rights. Avocations: hiking, birdwatching. Home: 6416 Francis N Seattle WA 98103-5534 Office: School of Law Univ of Wash 1100 NE Campus Parkway Seattle WA 98105-6617

FITZPATRICK, JOHN, poet; s. William Harry Fitzpatrick and Cecelia Schmidt. BA, U. Notre Dame, 1959; MS, Hofstra U., 1972; PhD, NYU, 2000. Cert. secondary edn., supr. secondary edn., secondary sch. prin. N.Y. English tchr. Hicksville (N.Y.) H.S., 1962—64, George W. Hewlett (N.Y.) H.S., 1964—94, coach speech-debate team, 1964—94. Pres. George W. Hewlett H.S. Faculty, 1968—70, L.I. Forensic Assn., 1976—78; sec., v.p. Hewlett-Woodmere (N.Y.) Faculty Assn. Retirees, 1994—99, 1999—2000. Author poetry. Dist. coord. Bicentennial Youth Debates Nassau County, L.I., 1975—76; bd. mem., officer Theatre Five, Dix Hills, NY, 1962—70, prodr., actor, publicity chairperson, 1962—70. Recipient Outstanding Educator award, U. Notre Dame, 1998. Mem.: Kappa Delta Pi, Pi Lambda Theta (Rho chpt.). Avocations: gardening, hiking. Home: 44 Creekside Rd Red Hook NY

FITZPATRICK, JOHN J. bishop; b. Trenton, Ont., Can., Oct. 12, 1918; s. James John and Lorena (Pelkey) F.. Student, Propaganda Fide Coll., Italy, Our Lady of Angels Sem.; BA, Niagara U., 1941. Ordained priest Roman Catholic

Ch., 1942. Titular bishop of Cenae and Aux. of Miami, Fla., 1968—71; bishop of Brownsville, 1971—91; bishop emeritus, 1991—. Roman Catholic. Office: 1904 Barnard Rd Brownsville TX 78520-8247

FITZPATRICK, JOSEPH MARK, lawyer; b. Jersey City, May 27, 1925; s. Joseph Francis Stephen and Meave (Wilson) F.; m. Elizabeth Anne Keane, June 18, 1949; children: Elizabeth A., Susan E., Christopher M., Stephen R. ME, Stevens Inst. Tech., 1945; JD, Georgetown U., 1951. Bar: Va. 1950, U.S. Patent Office 1950, N.Y. 1954. Trial atty. anti-trust divsn. Dept. Justice, 1951-53; mem. firm Ward, McElhannon, Brooks & Fitzpatrick, N.Y.C., 1954-70, Fitzpatrick, Cella, Harper & Scinto, N.Y.C., 1970—. With USNR, 1943-46. Fellow Am. Coll. Trial Lawyers; mem. ABA, Va. Bar Assn., N.Y. Bar Assn., Assn. of Bar of City of N.Y., Am. Intellectual Property Law Assn., N.Y. Intellectual Property Law Assn., Manasquan River Yacht Club. Home: 17 Oak Ln Scarsdale NY 10583-1628 Office: Fitzpatrick Cella Harper Scinto 30 Rockefeller Plz Fl 38 New York NY 10112-3800

FITZPATRICK, KATHLEEN G. education educator, accountant; b. Nashua, New Hampshire, July 7, 1955; d. Joseph Leo and Gertrude Meunier; m. Thomas Joseph Fitzpatrick, Dec. 29, 1978; children: Brendan, Kyle, Rachel. BS in Acctg., Syracuse U., 1977; MBA in Computer Sys., U. of Toledo, 1983. Cert. mgmg. acct., cert. fin. mgmt., Inst. of Mgmt. Accountants. Staff acct. U. Engineers Cons., Seabrook, NH, 1977—79; fiscal officer Criminal Justice Coordinating, Toledo, Ohio, 1979—84; acctg. supr. Omni Source Corp., Toledo, 1984—85; asst. contr. Bostwick Braun Co., Toledo, 1985—87; part-time instr. U. of Toledo, 1988—98, vis. prof., 1998—2000, asst. prof., 2000—. Mem.: Inst. of Mgmt. Accountants.

FITZPATRICK, KRYSTAL L. protective services official; d. William O. and Colleen L. Koch; m. Timothy M. Fitzpatrick, July 10, 1978. MS, Ea. Ill. U., Charleston, Ill., 2001. Police capt. U. Ill. Police Dept., Urbana, Ill., 1978—. Guest lectr. Police Tng. Inst., Russian-American Officer Exch., Champaign, Ill., 1998—98; trainer human resources office U. Ill., Champaign, 1996—, trainer provost office sexual harassment investigation, 1998. Contbr. articles. Mem. Champaign County Children's Advocacy Ctr., Urbana, Ill., 2000—, U. Ill. Networkers, Champaign, Ill., 1998—2001. Recipient Officer of the Yr., Champaign-Urbana Optimist Club, 1978, Medallion of Honor, U. of Ill. Mother's Associatiaon, 2000, Disting. Grad. Award, Ea. Ill. U., 2001, Officer of the Yr., Champaign Jaycees Officer of the Yr., 1978, Recognition, Ill. Coalition Against Sexual Assault, 1997. Mem.: Ill. Chiefs of Police, Internat. Assn. Chiefs of Police, Internat. Assn. Campus Law Enforcement Adminstrn., Nat. Assn. Women Law Enforcement Execs., FBI Nat. Acad. Assocs. Ill. (pres., railsplitters divsn. 1998—99), FBI Nat. Acad. Assocs. Office: U Ill Police Dept 1110 W Springfield Urbana IL 61801 Office Fax: 217-244-1979. E-mail: kfitzpat@uiuc.edu.

FITZPATRICK, LOIS ANN, library administrator; b. Yonkers, N.Y., Mar. 27, 1952; d. Thomas Joseph and Dorothy Ann (Nealy) Sullivan; m. William George Fitzpatrick, Jr., Dec. 1, 1973; children: Jennifer Ann, Amy Ann. BS in Sociology, Mercy Coll., 1974; MLS, Pratt Inst., 1975. Clk. Yonkers Pub. Libr., 1970-73, libr. trainee, 1973-75, libr. I, 1975-76; reference libr. Carroll Coll. Libr., Helena, Mnt., 1976-79, acting dir., 1979, dir., 1980—; asst. prof. Carroll Coll., Helena, 1979-89, assoc. prof., 1989-99, prof., 2000—. Bd. dirs. Mont. Shares; chmn. arrangements Mont. Gov.'s Pre White House Conf. on Libraries, Helena, 1977-78; mem. steering com. Reference Point coop. program for librs., 1991; mem. adv. com. Helena Coll. of Tech. Libr., 1994—; adv. coun. Mont. Libr. Svcs., 1996-2000; mem. Networking Task Force, Laws Revision Task Force; pres. elect Helena Area Health Sci. Libraries Cons., 1979-84, pres., 1984-88; bd. dirs. Mont. FAXNET. Co-chmn. interst group OCLC; chmn. local arrangements Mont. Gov.'s Pre White House Conf.; mem. adv. bd. Helena Coll. Tech., Mont. Race for the Cure; bd. dirs. ACLU-MT, 1999—. Mem. Mont. Libr. Assn. (task force for White House conf. 1991, chair govt. affairs com. 1997-2003, EdLINK-MT 1997-99, 2000-01), Soroptimist Internat. of Helena (2d v.p. 1984-85, pres. 1986-87). Home: 1308 Shirley Rd Helena MT 59602-6635 Office: Carroll Coll Jack & Sallie Corette Libr 1601 N Benton Ave Helena MT 59625-0001 E-mail: lfitzpat@carroll.edu.

FITZPATRICK, LORRAINE, accountant; b. Belmont, Mass., June 20, 1935; d. John F.X. Fitzpatrick and Mary J. MacDonald. AS in Acctg., Bentley Coll., 1963. Cashier Coward Shoe, Boston, 1953-59; acct. H & W Agy. Inc., Boston, 1959-85; asst. v.p. tax dept. Freedom Capital Mgmt., Boston, 1985-97; tax acct. Paul K. Hennessey Tax Svcs., Mansfield, Mass., 1997—. Mem. Inst. Mgmt. Accts. Avocations: reading, travel.

FITZPATRICK, M. LOUISE, dean, nursing educator; b. South River, N.J., May 24, 1942; d. John Francis and Bettina (Galassi) F. Diploma in nursing, Johns Hopkins U., 1963; BSN, Cath. U. Am., 1966; MA, Columbia U., 1968, MEd, 1969, EdD, 1972; cert., Harvard U., 1985. Former assoc. prof., dept. nursing edn. Tchrs. Coll., Columbia U., N.Y.C.; dean, prof. Villanova (Pa.) U. Coll. Nursing, 1978—. Cons. Mid. States Assn., Phila.; cons. to numerous univs., also univs. in Morocco, Egypt, Jordan, West Bank, Sultanate of Oman; cons., reviewer USPHS; bd. dirs. Nurses Ednl. Funds, Inc., N.Y.C. Author: The National Organization for Public Nursing, Development of a Practice Field, 1975; editor: Present Realities/Future Imperatives, 1977, Historical Studies in Nursing, 1978, Nursing in Society: A Historical Perspective, 1983; also 21 articles in profl. jours. Recipient Disting. Alumni award Columbia U. Tchrs. Coll., 1966, Cath. Univ. McManus medal, 1992; WHO fellow, Scandinavia and U.K., 1974; Am. Acad. Nursing fellow, 1978. Mem. Am. Nurses Assn. (past chmn. cabinet on nursing edn.), Am. Assn. Colls. Nursing, Nat. League for Nursing (bd. of govs.). Democrat. Roman Catholic. Avocations: music, theater, cooking, international travel. Home: 80 Woodstone Ln Villanova PA 19085-1425 Office: Villanova U Coll Nursing Villanova PA 19085

FITZPATRICK, NANCY HECHT, editor; b. Dec. 29, 1942; d. Ira Youngwood and Bettie Jane (Van Cleave) Hecht; m. Alan Rush Fitzpatrick, Dec. 15, 1973 (dec.). Student, Upsala Coll., 1960-62, New Sch. Social Rsch., 1962-64, Johns Hopkins U., summer 1987, Bennington Coll., summer 1988, Union Inst., 2002—. Asst. copyeditor Am. Home mag., N.Y.C., 1964-68; v.p. Creative Comms. Assocs., Newark, 1968-70; sr. editor Family Circle mag., N.Y.C., 1970-77; corp. sec., v.p. mktg. Alternative Telecom. Corp., N.Y.C., 1977-92; exec. editor Meeting News mag., N.Y.C., 1993-95; assoc. news editor, book and art reviewer The Vineyard Gazette, 1997—. Editor various publs. Mem.: LWV, NOW, Eastern Bedford Environ. Assn. (treas.), Empire women in Telecom. (pres.), N.Y. Women in Comms.

FITZPATRICK, PAUL FREDERICK, biochemistry educator; b. Chgo., Aug. 16, 1953; s. Frederick William and Joan Catherine Fitzpatrick; m. Susan Colette Daubner, Aug. 23, 1980; children: Andrew, Eileen. AB, Harvard U., 1975; PhD, U. Mich., 1981. NIH postdoctoral fellow Pa. State U., State College, 1982-86; asst. prof. Tex. A&M U., College Station, 1986-92, assoc. prof., 1992-96, prof., 1996—. Assoc. head biochemistry Tex. A&M U., 1998-2001; cons. NSF, Washington, 1992-96, U.S. Dept. Vet. Affairs, Washington, 1996-99. Established investigatorship grantee Am. Heart Assn., 1992. Mem. Am. Chem. Soc. (treas. divsn. biol. chemistry 1996-99), Am. Assn. Biochemistry and Molecular Biology. Office: Tex A&M U Ms 2128 College Station TX 77843-2128

FITZPATRICK, PHILIP J. probate judge, retired lawyer; b. Bronxville, NY, Aug. 21, 1945; s. Francis J. Fitzpatrick and Florence I. Tompkins; m. Gene F. Rybicki, July 25, 1970 (div. July 1985); 1 child, Matthew. BA cum laude, Georgetown U., 1967; JD cum laude, Boston U., 1973. Pvt. practice, Jeffersonville, Vt., 1974-90, 2000—02; probate judge Lamoille County, Vt., 1988—; sr. ptnr. Fitzpatrick & Hobart, Jeffersonville, 1990-2000; ret., 2002. Mem.: Vt. Probate Judges Assn. (pres. 1998—2002). Avocations: reading, landscaping, writing poetry. Home: PO Box 368 Hyde Park VT 05655-0368

FITZPATRICK, ROBERT, psychologist; b. Cin., Aug. 26, 1924; s. John Joseph and Helen (Collins) F.; m. Joanne Gehring Knauss, Aug. 12, 1952 (dec. Mar. 1970); children: John R., Janet E. Asbury, Jean A.; m. Dorothy G. Kail, Jan. 31, 1976; 1 stepson, Matthew A. Kail. BS, U. Pitts., 1947, MS, 1948, PhD, 1953. Project dir. Am. Inst. for Research, Pitts., 1948-54, program dir., 1954-59, 64-71; human factors unit supr. Boeing Co., Seattle, 1959-61; operational design group supr. System Devel. Corp., Lexington, Mass., 1961-62; mgr. psychol. dept., humetrics div. Thiokol Chem. Corp., L.A., 1963-64; pvt. practice indsl. psychology Pitts., 1971—. Dir. rsch. Psychol. Service, Pitts., 1976-78; lectr. U. Pitts., 1977-89; assoc. prof. St. Francis Coll., Pitts., 1979-85; grad. lectr. European div. U. Md., 1985-86. Served with USMC, 1943-46, 51-53. Mem. APA, Nat. Coun. Measurement in Edn., Pa. Psychol. Assn. Home: 334 Norman Dr Cranberry Township PA 16066-40 E-mail: rfitz@zoominternet.net.

FITZPATRICK, RUTH ANN, education educator; b. Brockton, Mass., July 12, 1941; d. Lenard Burton and Alva D.M. (Goranson) Parent; m. Richard Noll Fitzpatrick, July 9, 1966; 1 child, Elizabeth Ann. BS in Edn., Bridgewater State Coll., 1963, MEd, 1966, cert. advanced grad. study, 1985. Cert. elem. tchr. and prin., reading tchr. and supr., Mass. Tchr. Sharon Pub. Sch., Mass., 1963-72, 79-81; assoc. prof. edn., tchr. Bridgewater State Coll., Mass., 1982-98. Presenter in field. Contbr. articles to The Reading Tchr., NALS Jour., The Edn. Digest. Chair gifts and memls. com. 1st United Meth. Ch. Stoughton, 1968—, supt. ch. sch., 1968-74, liturgist, 1976-86, 95-2002, chair pastor/staff/parish com., 1994-97; tutor, bd. dirs. Literacy Vols. Am., Stoughton, 1998—. Mem. Nat. Assn. Lab. Schs. (life, chmn. N.E. conf. 1990, 95, exec. bd. dirs. 1991—, audit com. 1992-01, nominating com. 1993-94, 97, 2003, pres.-elect 1996, pres. 1997, historian 1998—, Disting. Svc. award 1999), Mass. Reading Assn. (mem. editl. bd. 1990-94), Delta Kappa Gamma (Alpha Beta chpt. corr. sec. 1985-92, treas. 1992—, presenter N.E. conf. Stockholm 1997), Phi Delta Kappa (charter mem. Bridgewater chpt., found. chair 1998-2000).

FITZPATRICK, THOMAS MARK, lawyer; b. Anaconda, Mont., June 12, 1951; s. Marcus Leo and Natalie Stephanie (Trbovich) F. BA, U. Mont., 1973; JD, U. Chgo., 1976. Bar: Ill. 1976, Wash. 1978. Asst. to pres.-elect ABA, Chgo., 1976-77, asst. to pres., 1977-78; assoc. Karr, Tuttle, Campbell, Seattle, 1978-85, ptnr., 1985-89, Stafford, Frey, Cooper, Seattle, 1989-99; asst. chief civil divsn. Snohomish County Prosecuting Atty.'s Office, Everett, Wash., 1999—. Editor: ABA: A Century of Service, 1979. Fellow Am. Bar Found.; mem. ABA (chmn. lawyer and media conf. 1985-88, profl. discipline com. 1988-94, LRIS com. 1994-97, ethics com. 2001—, chmn. nat. conf. groups 1982-85, ho. of dels. 1990—, state del. 1993-98, bd. govs. 1998-2001), Wash. Bar Assn. (pres. young lawyer divsn. 1986-87), Snohomish County Bar Assn., Seattle-King County Bar, U. Chgo. Law Sch. Alumni Assn. (bd. dirs., Seattle regional pres. 1980-86). Roman Catholic. Home: 7345 13th Ave NW Seattle WA 98117-5306 Office: Snohomish County Civil Divsn Prosecuting Attys Office 2918 Colby Ave Ste 203 Everett WA 98201-4011

FITZPATRICK, VINCENT DE PAUL, JR., retired gynecologist; b. Balt., Mar. 24, 1920; s. Vincent de Paul Sr. and Marie Anita (O'Conor) F.; m. Margaret Josephine Schanberger, Oct. 16, 1948 (dec. Apr. 1993); children: Vincent de Paul III, James Lawrence. BA, Loyola Coll., 1942; MD, U. Md., Balt., 1945. Resident Mercy Hosp., Balt., 1948-51; pvt. practice ob-gyn. Balt., 1951-93; head dept. ob-gyn. St. Joseph Hosp., Balt., 1987-98; ret., 2000. Pres. Mercy Hosp. Med. Staff, Balt., 1975-76; chmn. Cath. Health Care Consortium, Md., 1985-86. Contbr. articles to med. jours. Bd. trustees Loyola H.S., Balt., 1970-76. Capt. Army Med. Corps, 1943-48. Mem. AMA, Am. Coll. Ob-Gyn. (chmn. Md. sect. 1980-83), Balt. City Med. Soc. (bd. dirs.), So. Med. Assn., Knights of Malta (adm. com. 1991). Roman Catholic. Home: 2525 Pot Spring Rd Timonium MD 21093- Office: Mercy Ridge K301 2525 Pot Spring Rd Timonium MD 21093-2778

FITZPATRICK, WHITFIELD WESTFELDT, lawyer; b. New Orleans, Jan. 31, 1942; s. William Harry and Frances (Westfeldt) F.; m. Jean Phipps, July 6, 1984. BA, Washington & Lee U., 1964; JD, Tulane U., 1967; LLM, Grenoble U., France, 1969, Doctorate, 1972. Bar: La. 1967, Va. 1972, N.Y. 1974, U.S. Dist. Ct. (ea. dist.) La. 1974, D.C. 1975, U.S. Dist. Ct. (we. dist.) La. 1975, U.S. Ct. Appeals (5th cir.) 1975. Law clk. Supreme Ct. Commonwealth of Va., Norfolk, 1969-70; assoc. Coudert Bros., N.Y.C., 1972-74; sr. assoc. Phelps, Dunbar, Marks, Claverie & Sims, New Orleans, 1974-76; counsel Mobil Oil Corp., New Orleans, 1976-79, Mobil North Sea Ltd., London, 1979-82; gen. counsel The Hague, Netherlands, 1982; sr. counsel, asst. sec. Mobil Exploration and Producing U.S., Inc., Midland, Tex., 1987-89; asst. sec. Mobil Producing Tex. and N.Mex., Inc., Midland, 1987-89; with direction juridique Elf Aquitaine, Europe and U.S. coord., 1989-94; spl. advisor to dir. of comml. and lic. adminstrn. divsn. ELF Petroleum Norge, 1994-97; exec. v.p. and gen. counsel Fountain Oil Inc., 1997—99; of counsel The Silecky Firm, 1999—. Contbr. articles to profl. pubs. Named Mem. Soc. of the Friends of the Legion of Honor, Ordres de Chevalerie; Grenoble U. Law Sch. scholar, 1967-69; fellow Govt. of France, 1970-72. Mem. ABA, Maritime Law Assn., Internat. Bar Assn., La. Bar Assn., Va. Bar Assn., N.Y. Bar Assn., D.C. Bar Assn., chmn. Am. Coordinating Coun. of Norway, Boston Club of New Orleans, Racquet and Tennis Club of N.Y., Royal Auto Club of London, Soc. Colonial Wars, Societé des Amis du Musée National de la Légion d'Honneur. Avocations: golf, skiing, reading, tennis. Home: Camilla Collets vei No 8 0258 Oslo Norway

FITZRANDOLPH, CASEY, Olympic athlete; b. Verona, Wis., Jan. 21, 1975; Mem. U.S. Speedskating Team. Named U.S. Sprint Champion, 1995—97, 2001; recipient 500-Meter Gold medal, 2002 Olympic Games. Avocations: fishing, hunting, stock market. Address: US Speedskating PO Box 450639 Westlake OH 44145

FITZROY, NANCY DELOYE, engineering executive, mechanical engineer; b. Pittsfield, Mass., Oct. 5, 1927; d. Jules Emile and Mabel Winifred (Burr) deLoye; m. Roland Victor Fitzroy, Jr., Mar. 24, 1951. BChemE, Rensselaer Poly. Inst., Troy, 1949; DEng (hon.), Rensselaer Poly. Inst., 1990; DSc (hon.), N.J. Inst. Tech., 1987. Registered profl. engr., N.Y. Heat transfer engr. corp. R & D GE, Schenectady, NY, 1950-71, mgr. heat transfer consulting, 1971-74, strategy planner, 1974-76, mgr. program devel. gas turbine divsn., 1976-82, mgr. energy and environ. program, 1982-87. Dir. West Hill Devel. Corp., Rotterdam, NY, 1955—65; mem. adv. com. rsch. NSF, Washington, 1972—75; mem. transp. rsch. bd. coordinanting com. rsch. and tech. NRC, 1996—99; cons. in field; bd. dirs. ASME Found., 1989—95, 1997—, trustee, 1998—. Author, editor: book Heat Transfer and Fluid Flow, Data Books, 1955—75. Charter mem. Rensselaer Poly. Inst. Coun., 1972—. Named to Rensselaer Poly. Inst. Hall of Fame, 1999; recipient Demers medal, Rensselaer Poly. Inst., 1975, Achievement award, Fedn. Profl. Women, 1984, Disting. Alumna medal, Rensselaer Poly. Inst., 1996. Fellow: ASME (1st woman nat. pres. 1986—87, trustee Gear Rsch. Inst. 1987—89), Soc. Women Engrs. (Outstanding Achievement award 1972), Instn. Mech. Engrs. London (hon.); mem.: Assn. Engrings. Socs. (gov. 1987—89), Nat. Acad. Engring., Coral Ridge Yacht Club (Ft. Lauderdale, Fla.), Mohawk Golf Club, Whirly-Girls Club, Ninety-Nines Club. Republican. Episcopalian. Achievements include patents in field. Home: 2125 Rosendale Rd Niskayuna NY 12309-5418

FITZSIMMONS, JOSEPH JOHN, publishing executive; b. Newark, Nov. 10, 1934; s. Joseph A. and Frances E. (Baume) F.; children from previous marriage: Joseph John, Michael, Patricia, Susan, Thomas; m. Beth Berglund Duston, Nov. 30, 1996. B.Chem. Engring., Cornell U., 1957. With Xerox Corp., Rochester, N.Y., 1957-65; v.p., gen. mgr. Xerox Univ. Microfilms, Ann Arbor, Mich., 1974-75; pres. Univ. Microfilms Internat., Ann Arbor, 1976—, pres., chief exec. officer, 1987-94; v.p. Bell and Howell Co., 1987—; chmn. Univ. Microfilms Internat., Ann Arbor, 1994-95, ret., 1995; pres., CEO Nonprofit Enterprise at Work, 1999—2001. Bd. dirs. Nat. City Bank Mich./Ill., Bartech Inc., Nematron Corp. Gen. campaign chmn. Wastenaw United Way, 1977-78; mem. devel. com. St. Joseph's Hosp.; pres. Ann Arbor Hands-On-Mus., 1980; mem. adv. bd. for entrepreneurship Ea. Mich. Cen. U., 1986—; adv. bd. U. Pitts. Sch. Libr. and Info. Sci.; bd. dirs. Libr. Mich. Found., 1992, co-chair Capital Campaign, 1995—; trustee Dawn Farm, 1995, Siena Heights U., 1997; Rep. candidate U.S. Congress Mich., 1996. Mem. ALA, Info. Industry Assn. (bd. dirs. 1985, chmn. mktg. com. 1986, chmn. long range planning com. 1987, chmn. bd. elect 1988, chmn. 1989), The White House Conf. on Librs. and Info. Sci. (vice chmn. 1991). Home: 101 N Main St Apt 1005 Ann Arbor MI 48104-1475

FITZSIMONS, DENNIS JOSEPH, broadcasting executive; b. N.Y.C., June 26, 1950; s. Genevieve Theresa (English) F.; m. Ann Christie, Sept. 27, 1980; children: Matthew, Christine. BA, Fordham U., 1972. Account exec. Blair TV, N.Y.C., 1975-77; sales mgr. TeleRep, Inc., Chgo., 1977-78, N.Y.C., 1979-81, dir. spl. projects, 1978-79; dir. advt. sales Viacom Internat., N.Y.C., 1981; dir. sales and mktg. Sta. WVIT-TV, Hartford, Conn., 1981-82; dir. sales Sta. WGN-TV, Chgo., 1982-84, v.p., gen. mgr., 1987—92, Sta. WGNO-TV, New Orleans, 1984-85; v.p. ops. Tribune Broadcasting Co., Chgo., 1985-87; pres. Tribune Television, 1992—94, Tribune Broadcasting Co., 1994—2003; exec. v.p. Tribune Co., 2000—01, bd. of dir., 2000—, COO, 2001—03, pres., 2001—, CEO, 2003—. Vice chmn. United Negro Coll. Fund of Chgo. With U.S. Army, 1970-76. Mem. Ill. Assn. Broadcasters (bd. dirs.), INTV (bd. dirs.). Roman Catholic. Office: Tribune Co. 435 N. Michigan Ave. Chicago IL 60011*

FITZSIMONS, GEORGE KINSEY, bishop; b. Kansas City, Mo., Sept. 4, 1928; Student, Rockhurst Coll., Immaculate Conception Sem. Ordained priest Roman Cath. Ch., 1961. Aux. bishop, Kansas City-St. Joseph, Kans., 1975—84; bishop Salina, Kans., 1984—. Office: Chancery Office PO Box 980 Salina KS 67402-0980*

FIUME, BARBARA PARENTY, social worker; b. N.Y.C., Nov. 19, 1949; d. Louis J. (dec.) and Mary (Simonetti) Parenty; m. Orest Robert Fiume, Sept. 20, 1975; children: Christian Alexander, Michael Scott. BA, St. John's U., 1971; MSW, Fordham U., 1976. Bd. cert. diplomate in clin. social work; cert. English tchr., sch. social worker; lic. clin. social worker, N.J. Tchr. English Middletown (N.Y.) High Sch., 1971-73; social worker Pius XII, Middletown, 1973-75; social work therapist Family and Community Svcs., Fords, N.J., 1975-76; social worker Project Promise Presch., Belvidere, N.J., 1977-83, Project First Step, Washington, N.J., 1980-84; social work advocate Warren Arc, Washington, 1986-87; social work cons.; clin. social work therapist pvt. practice, 1991—. Adj. instr. Centenary Coll., Hackettstown, N.J., 1976-78; instr. Warren County Adult Edn. Mem. edn. input com. Lebanon Twp. Elem. Schs., Glen Gardner, N.J., 1988-90; mem. adv. bd. Warren CHADD; vol. counselor N.W. N.J. Women's Ctr., 1991—. Mem. NASW, Acad. Cert. Social Workers. Roman Catholic. Avocations: gardening, photography.

FIUMEFREDDO, CHARLES A. investment management company executive; b. Bayonne, N.J., May 12, 1933; s. Charles F. and Alice (Guiliana) F.; m. Joan Kuczynski, June 18, 1955; children— Joanne Fiumefreddo Lewicki, Charles M. BS, St. Peter's Coll., Jersey City, 1955; postgrad., NYU Sch. Bus. Adminstrn., 1955-57. Asst. v.p. First Jersey Nat. Bank, Jersey City, 1953-65; asst. v.p. investment mgmt. Anchor Corp., Elizabeth, N.J., 1965-69; from v.p. to pres., CEO Standard & Poor's/InterCapital, N.Y.C., 1969—77; pres. Morgan Stanley Investment Advisors Inc., N.Y.C., 1977—84, treas., 1977—82, chmn., 1982—98, CEO, 1977—98; pres. Morgan Stanley Investment Cos., N.Y.C., 1982—99, dir., trustee, 1991—, chmn., 1992—; exec. v.p., bd. dirs. Dean Witter Reynolds Inc., until 1998. Chmn. Morgan Stanley Trust FSB, Jersey City, 1989-98; bd. dirs., mem. exec. com. Investment Co. Inst., Washington, 1983-98; mem. investment co. com. SIA, N.Y.C., 1984-86. Bd. dirs. Bayonne Hosp., N.J., 1983-89. Mem.: K.C. (Bayonne, N.J.). Avocations: stamps; sport fishing.

FIX, DOUGLAS MARTIN, electrical engineer; b. Lincoln, Nebr., Oct. 20, 1953; s. Raymond Harold and Juliana Marie (Spatz) F. BSEE, BSCS, U. Colo., 1979; MSEE, Southern Meth. U., 1983. Registered profl. engr. Tex. Computer ops. Seismograph Svc. Corp., Denver, 1974-78, seismic analyst, 1978-80; design engr. Tex. Instruments, Dallas, 1980-85, sr. engr., 1985-88, lead engr., 1988—. Adj. prof., Eastfield Coll., Mesquite, Tex., 1983—; cons. Computers U2, Allen,Tex., 1990—. Contbr. article to profl. jours.; patentee digital video monitor interface arch., hardware ind. device interface. Elder, tchr. Zion Luth. Ch., Dallas, 1992—; crime watch council. Neighborhood Homeowners, Dallas, 1988. Recipient Sundstrand scholarship Sundstrand Corp., 1978. Mem. IEEE, Eta Kappa Nu (sec. 1978), Soc. Info. Display, Mensa, Tau Beta Pi. Republican. Lutheran. Achievements include electrical design of several types of consumer calculators, research in digital pll clocking for TV synch signal processor and preprocessor designs for 4 classified military projects. Home: 761 Livingston Dr Allen TX 75002-5229 Office: Texas Instruments 13510 N Central Expy Dallas TX 75243-1108

FIX, JOHN NEILSON, banker; b. Evanston, Ill., Apr. 10, 1937; s. John Leonard and Margaret (Neilson) F.; m. Linda Harris, Dec. 21, 1961; children: John, Christopher, David, Wendy. BS, U. Ill., 1959; grad., Stonier Sch. Banking, Rutgers U., 1971. Asst. cashier, v.p. No. Trust Co., Chgo., 1962-77; v.p., divsn. head Continental Ill. Nat. Bank & Trust Co., Chgo., 1977-80; sr. v.p., group head Continental Bank N.A., Chgo., 1980-83, sr. v.p., dept. head, 1983-94; sr. v.p, dir. corp. devel. global payment svcs. Bank of Am. N.T.S.A., Chgo., 1994-95, ret., 1995; mng. dir. Fixco, Inc., 1996—; prin. Treasury Strategies, Inc., Chgo., 1997—, dir., 2001—. Bd. dirs. Kenilworth Dist. 38 Sch. Bd., Ill., 1969-75; trustee, pres. Kenilworth Park Bd., 1981-89; mem. exec. com. Chgo. Area Boy Scouts, 1981-89; pres., treas. Kenilworth Baseball Assn., 1976-85; trustee Kenilworth Union Ch.., 1988-93; bd. dirs. Western Golf Assn., 1989—, audit com., 1992—. Lt. U.S. Army, 1959-61. Recipient George Huff award U. Ill., Champaign, 1955; Good Scout award Chgo. Area Boy Scouts Am., 1982 Mem. Bankers Club of Chgo., Ill. State C. of C. (bd. dirs., treas. 1980-82), Exec. Club of Chgo., Econ. Club of Chgo., U. Ill. Alumni Assn. (mem. bd. trustees 1987, exec. com. 1990-93, chmn. investment com. 1992-93), Nat. Corp. Cash Mgmt. Assn. (mem. publs. com. 1987-91, strategic planning com.), Indian Hill Club (bd. govs. 1984-87, 98-02, sec. 1999-2001, pres. 2001-03), Old Elm Club (Highland Park, Ill.), Western Golf Assn. (exec. com., par club chmn. 2000—). Clubs: Chicago; Minneapolis; Indian Hill (bd. govs. 1984-87). Avocations: golf, skiing, paddle tennis. E-mail: fixco@earthlink.net.

FIX, R. JOBE, plastic surgeon, reconstructive hand surgeon; b. Sterling, Colo., Dec. 14, 1956; m. Kathleen N. Neary; children: Alexander, Elizabeth, Andrew. BS, U. Nebr., 1978, MD, 1982. Diplomate, Nat. Bd. Med. Examiners, Am. Bd. Surgery, Am. Bd. Plastic Surgery, added qualification in hand surgery. Intern Valley Med. Ctr., Fresno, Calif., 1982-83, resident, 1983-87; resident in plastic surgery U. Ala., Birmingham, 1987-89; burn team instr. Valley Med. Ctr., Fresno, 1986-89; clin. instr. plastic surgery U. Ala., Birmingham, 1989, from asst. prof. to assoc. prof., 1990-2000, prof., 2000—; attending surgeon Children's Hosp., Birmingham, 1990—; chief of plastic surgery VA Med. Ctr., Birmingham, 1990—2001, attending surgeon, 1990—. Domestic vis. prof. Com. Plastic Surgery Ednl. Found., 1991, mem. vis. scholar com., 1995-96; mem. numerous coms. U. Ala. Birmingham. 1992—. Contbr. articles and abstracts to profl. jours., chpts. to books. Mem. Med. Mission to Ecuador Feb., 1996, 97, 98, 99, 2001, 02. Recipient Beach-Byer and Drier A&E Honor scholarship U. Nebr., 1976-77, Regent's scholarship, 1975-78. Mem. ACS (Ala. chpt.), Am. Soc. Maxillofacial Surgeons, Am. Soc. Plastic Surgeons, Am. Soc. Reconstructive Microsurgery, Am. Assn. Plastic Surgeons, Assn. Acad. Chmn. of Plastic Surgery, Plastic Surgery Rsch. Coun., So. Med. Assn., Am. Soc. for Surgery of the Hand, Ala. Soc. Plastic and Reconstructive Surgeons, Southeastern Soc. Plastic and Reconstructive Surgery, Med. Assn. Ala., Alpha Lamba Delta, Phi Eta Sigma. Office: U Ala Birmingham 510 20th St S FOT 1102 Birmingham AL 35294 E-mail: jobe.fix@ccc.uab.edu.

FIX, WILBUR JAMES, department store executive; b. Velva, N.D., Aug. 14, 1927; s. Jack J. and Beatrice D. (Wasson) F.; m. Beverly A. Corcoran, Sept. 20, 1953; children: Kathleen M., Michael B., Jenifer L. BA, U. Wash., 1950. Credit mgr. Bon Marche, Yakima, Wash., 1951-54, controller, ops. mgr. Boise, Idaho, 1954-58, sr. v.p. Seattle, 1970-76, exec. v.p., 1976-77, pres., chief exec. officer, 1978-87; chmn., chief exec. officer, sr. v.p. Allied Stores Corp., 1987-93; chmn. Fix Mgmt. Group, 1993—. Chmn. Wash. Retail Coun., 1983-84; bd. dirs. Bldg. Materials Holding Corp., Vans; mem. adv. coun. Inst. for Retail Studies, Col. of the Desert, Palm Desert, Calif., Corp. Coun. of the Arts, Seattle. Mem. pres.'s adv. com. Allied Stores Corp., N.Y., 1968-72; mem. citizens adv. com. Seattle Pub. Schs., 1970-71; v.p. Citizens Council Against Crime; chmn. Seattle King County Conv. & Visitors Bur., 1990. With AUS, 1946-47. Mem.: Mission Hills Country Club (Rancho Mirage, Calif.), Wash. Athletic Club, Wash. Round Table, Downtown Seattle Devel. Assn., Assn. Wash. Bus., Seattle C. of C., Western States Regional Controllers Congress, Fin. Execs. Inst., Seattle Retail Controllers Group, Controllers Congress, Nat. Retail Mcts. Assn., Phi Theta Kappa, Pi Kappa Alpha. Episcopalian. Office: The Bon Marché 3rd And Pine St Seattle WA 98181-0001 also: 5403 W Mercer Way Mercer Island WA 98040-4635 Address: 5403 W Mercer Way Mercer Island WA 98040-4635 E-mail: b2fix@aol.com.

FIXMAN, MARSHALL, chemist, educator; b. St. Louis, Sept. 21, 1930; s. Benjamin and Dorothy (Finkel) F.; m. Marian Ruth Beatman, July 5, 1959 (dec. Sept. 1969); children: Laura Beth, Susan Ilene, Andrew Richard; m. Branka Ladanyi, Dec. 7, 1974. AB, Washington U., St. Louis, 1950; PhD, MIT, 1954. Jewett postdoctoral fellow chemistry Yale U., 1953-54; instr. chemistry Harvard

U., 1956-59; sr. fellow Mellon Inst., Pitts., 1959-61; prof. chemistry, dir. Inst. Theoretical Sci., U. Oreg., 1961-64, prof. chemistry, research asso. inst., 1964-65; prof. chemistry Yale U., New Haven, 1965-79; prof. chemistry and physics Colo. State U., Ft. Collins, 1979-2000, prof. emeritus, 2000—. Mem. editorial bd. Jour. Chem. Physics, 1962-64, Jour. Phys. Chemistry, 1970-74, Macromolecules, 1970-74, Accounts Chem. Rsch. 1982-85, Jour. Polymer Sci. B, 1991-93; assoc. editor Jour. Chem. Physics, 1994—. Wwith U.S. Army, 1954-56. Fellow Alfred P. Sloan Found., 1961-63; recipient Governor's award Oreg. Mus. Sci. and Industry, 1964 Mem. NAS, Am. Acad. Arts and Scis., Am. Chem. Soc. (award pure chemistry 1964, award polymer chemistry 1991), Am. Phys. Soc. (high polymer physics award 1980), Fedn. Am. Scientists. Office: Colo State U Dept Chemistry Fort Collins CO 80523-0001 E-mail: mf@fibm.mfbl.colostate.edu.

FIXSEN, DALE J. physicist; b. Willmar, Minn., Jan. 14, 1956; s. Harold J. and Opal B. Fixsen; m. Elizabeth A. Penny, May 25, 1982; children: Benjamin, Sarah, Rachel. BS in Math. and Physics, Pacific Luth. U., 1977; PhD in Astrophysics, Princeton U., 1982. Postdoctorate U. Minn., Mpls., 1983—84; physicist Sperry/Unisys, St. Paul, 1984—90, Goddard Spaceflight Ctr., Greenbelt, Md., 1990—. Lutheran. Office: Goddard Spaceflight Ctr Code 685 Greenbelt MD 20771 Business E-Mail: fixsen@stars.gsfc.nasa.gov.

FIZDALE, RICHARD, advertising agency executive; b. Aug. 4, 1939; BA, U of Texas, Arlington. Copywriter BBDO Advt., 1967-68, Leo Burnett Co., Inc., Chgo., 1969-70, copy supr., 1970-72, assoc. creative dir., 1972-73, creative dir., 1973-74, v.p., 1974-78, v.p., exec. creative dir., 1978-79, sr. v.p., exec. creative dir., 1979, sr. v.p., mgr. creative ops., 1979-82, exec. v.p., dep. dir. creative svcs., 1982-85, pres., chief creative officer, bd. dirs., 1985-86, exec. com., 1986-87, pres., chief creative officer, 1987-92, chmn., CEO, chief creative officer, 1992-93, chmn., chief creative officer, 1993-97, chmn., CEO, 1997-2000; chmn. Leo Burnett Co., Inc. (The Leo Group), Chgo., 2000—; vice chmn. BDM Inc. (merger Leo Group & MacManus Group), Chgo., 2000—. Office: Leo Burnett USA 35 W Wacker Dr Ste 2220 Chicago IL 60601-1614

FJORDBOTTEN, ALF LEE, language educator; b. Camrose, Alta., Can., Apr. 26, 1952; arrived in U.S., 1960, naturalized, 1987; s. Alf Lee and Helene Josephine (Hansen) Fjordbotten; m. Beverly Elaine Lee, Oct. 22, 1983. BA in Religion, St. Olaf Coll., Minn., 1974; MDiv, Luther Northwestern Theol. Sem., 1978; MA in English and Comparative Lit., Fairleigh Dickinson U., 1989; PhD in English Lang. and Lit., Fordham U., 1999. Ordained to ministry Evang. Luth. Ch. Am., 1978. Vicar, chaplain Grace Luth. Ch., Good Shepherd Home, Allentown, Pa., 1976-77; pastor St. Mark's Luth. Ch., Ridge, NY, 1978-83, Holy Spirit Luth. Ch., Leonia, NJ, 1983—2002, Grace Luth. Ch., North Arlington, NJ, 2002—, First Luth. Ch., Kearny, NJ, 2002—; sr. editor Bishop Books, N.Y.C., 2000—. Adj. instr. Fairleigh Dickinson U., 1994—, Fordham U., 1999—2000, tchg. fellow, 1989—92. Recipient Charles J. Donahue prize, Fordham U., 1990. Home: 580 Gail Ct Teaneck NJ 07666-4128

FLAATEN, RUBY CHERYL, nurse manager; b. Mason City, Iowa, Dec. 12, 1944; d. Truman Almer and Truly Zeola (Ones) Flaaten. Diploma in nursing, Meth.-Kahler Sch. Nursing, 1965. Staff nurse Ear, Nose and Throat Rochester (Minn.) Meth. Hosp., 1965-67, asst. head nurse Ear, Nose and Throat, 1967-69; head nurse, nurse mgr. ear, nose and throat, plastic surgery, oral surgery, ophthalmology, gen. surgery Rochester (Minn.) Meth. Hosp./Mayo Med. Ctr., 1969-2001. Mem. ANA, AARP, Minn. Nurses Assn., 6th Dist. Minn. Nurses Assn. (sec.-treas., del.), Minn. Orgn. Leaders in Nursing, Dist. F. Orgn. Leaders in Nursing, Soc. Otorhinolaryngology and Head Neck Nurses, Am. Diabetic Assn., Am. Assn. for History Nursing, Meth.-Kahler Alumni Assn. (treas.), Sons of Norway. Republican. Lutheran. Avocation: reading. Home: 1929 3rd Ave NE Apt 4 Rochester MN 55906-4031

FLACCO, ELAINE GERMANO, computer programmer; b. Phila., June 20, 1959; d. William Joseph and Rose Angela (Ranelli) Germano; m. Dominick Albert Flacco, Oct. 27, 1984; 1 child, Dominick William. Assoc. in Computer Sci., Peirce Jr. Coll., 1985. Asst. supr. foreclosure Fidelity Bond & Mortgage Co., Phila., 1977-79; adminstrn. asst. multi family U.S. Dept HUD, Phila., 1980-81; computer programmer, analyst Reed & Stambaugh Co., Phila., 1982-86; computer programmer, residential coordinator, prop mgr. Linpro Co./LCOR, Inc., Phila., 1986—90, Tim Schaeffer Cmtys., 1999—, svc. mgr., 2002—. Democrat. Roman Catholic. Avocation: dancing. Home: 28 Briar Creek Rd Sicklerville NJ 08081-1304 Office: DayStar Constrn PO Box 560 Berlin NJ 08009-0560

FLACH, FREDERIC FRANCIS, psychiatrist; b. N.Y.C., Jan. 25, 1927; s. George Raymond and Margaret (Donovan) F.; m. Patricia Anne Kane, June 23, 1951 (div. 1966); children: Frederica, Christopher, Geraldine, Andrew, Winifred; m. Joyce Elizabeth Rasmussen, Sept. 9, 1971. BA summa cum laude, St. Peter's Coll., Jersey City, 1947; MD, Cornell U., 1951. Diplomate Am. Bd. Psychiatry and Neurology. Intern second med. div. Bellevue Hosp., N.Y.C., 1951-52; from resident to chief resident psychiatry Payne Whitney Clinic, N.Y.C., 1953-58; pvt. practice N.Y.C., 1958—; attending psychiatrist N.Y. Presbyn. Hosp., N.Y.C., 1962—, St. Vincent's Hosp., N.Y.C., 1974—. Adj. assoc. prof. psychiatry Cornell U. Med. Coll., N.Y.C., 1962—; program dir. Directions in Psychiatry, N.Y.C., 1981—; chmn. The Hatherleigh Co., Ltd., 1990—. Author: The Secret Strength of Depression, 1974, Choices, 1976, Fridericus, 1980, Resilience, 1988, Rickie, 1990, Take Command, 1994, The Secret Strength of Angels, 1998, Faith, Healing, and Miracles, 2000, others. Lt. (j.g.) USNR, 1945-46. Decorated knight comdr. Equestrian Order of the Holy Sepulchre of Jerusalem. Fellow Am. Psychiat. Assn. (life). Roman Catholic. Avocations: travel, swimming, reading. Office: 420 E 51st St New York NY 10022-8014

FLADUNG, RICHARD DENIS, lawyer; b. Kansas City, Mo., Aug. 1, 1953; s. Jerome Francis and Rosemary (Voeste) Fladung; m. Leslie Lynn Cox, June 1, 1985; children: Daniel Edwin, Erica Anne, Derek Richard. BSCE, U. Kans., 1976, postgrad., 1977; JD, Washburn U., 1980. Bar: Kans. 1980, U.S. Dist. Ct. Kans. 1980, Ind. 1981, U.S. Dist. Ct. (so. dist.) Ind. 1981, U.S. Patent and Trademark Office 1982, Mo. 1983, U.S. Dist. Ct. (we. dist.) Mo. 1983, Tex. 1984, U.s. Dist. Ct. (so. dist.) Tex. 1984, U.S. Ct. Appeals (fed. cir.) 1984, U.S. Ct. Appeals (5th cir.) 1987, U.S. Supreme Ct. 1987, U.S. Dist. Ct. (we. dist.) Tex. 1988, U.S. Dist. Ct. (ea. and no. dists.) Tex. 2000. Engr. Black and Veatch Cons. Engrs., Kansas City, 1975—80; corp. counsel CTB Inc., Milford, Ind., 1980—82; patent atty. Chase & Yakimo and predecessor firm, Kansas City, 1982—83, Bush, Moseley, Riddle and Jackson and predecessor firm, Houston, 1983—87, Pravel, Hewitt & Kimball, Houston, 1987—98, Akin, Gump, Strauss, Hauer & Feld LLP, Houston, 1999—. Contbr. articles to profl. ednl. programs. Com. chmn. Troop 1089 Boy Scouts Am., Houston, 2000—03; legal aide to spkr. Kans. Ho. of Reps., Topeka, 1980. Named one of Outstanding Young Men of Am., 1985. Fellow: Houston Young Lawyers Found. (founding mem.), Houston Bar Found., Tex. Bar Found. (charter); mem.: ASCE, ABA (vice chmn. patent, trademark sect. young lawyer divsn. 1988—89), Houston Intellectual Property Law Assn., Kansas City Bar Assn., Houston Young Lawyers Assn. (pres. 1987—88, exec. mem. bd. dirs. 1987—88, Outstanding Com. Chmn. award 1984—86), Ind. Bar Assn., Mo. Bar Assn., Tex. Young Lawyers Assn. (bd. dirs. 1988), Am. Intellectual Property Law Assn., Houston Bar Assn. (ex officio bd. dirs. 1987—88, vice chmn. profl. responsibility com. 1991—), Pi Alpha Kappa (treas. 1974—75). Roman Catholic. Avocations: tennis, jogging, bicycling, golf. Office: Akin Gump Strauss Hauer & Feld LLP 1900 Pennzoil Pl S Tower 711 Louisiana St Houston TX 77002-2716 E-mail: rfladung@akingump.com.

FLAGG, E(LOISE) ALMA WILLIAMS, educational administrator; b. City Point, Va., Sept. 16, 1918; d. Hannibal Greene and Caroline Ethel (Moody) Williams; m. J. Thomas Flagg, Jr., June 24, 1942 (dec. Apr. 1994); children: Thomas L., Lois Luisa. BS, Newark State Coll., 1940, LittD (hon.), 1968; MA, Montclair (N.J.) State Coll., 1943; EdD, Columbia U., 1955. Tchr., Washington, 1941-43; with Newark Pub. Schs., 1943-83, vice-prin., 1963-64, prin., 1964-67, asst. supt., 1967-78, dir., 1978-83; bd. dirs. Krueger-Scott Mansion Cultural Ctr., Share-N.J., v.p., 1996—; cons. edn., 1972—; adj. instr., spkr. in field, poet-in-residence various pub. schs. Author: (poetry) Lines and Colors, 1979, Feelings, Lines, Colors, 1980, Twenty More with Thought and Feeling, 1981, Lines, Colors, and More, 1998; editor: Cardiac Valve Bioprosthesis. Mem. Newark Bicentennial Commn. Recipient various profl. awards; E. Alma Flagg Sch. erected, 1984; E. Alma Flagg Scholarship Fund established, 1984. Mem. NAACP (life), LWV (pres. Newark 1982-84), AAUW, N.J. Hist. Soc., Nat. Assn. Negro Bus. and Profl. Women's Clubs (Truth award, 1985) Nat. Alliance Black Sch. Educators, Nat. Coun. Negro Women (life), Newark Sr. Citizen's Commn. (editl. cons. 1989—), Alpha Kappa Alpha (life), Kappa Delta Pi. Presbyterian. Home: 67 Vaughan Dr Newark NJ 07103-3470

FLAGG, MICHAEL JAMES, communications and graphics company executive; b. N.Y.C., Aug. 14, 1958; s. Wilbor Thomas and Sylvia (Kobitz) F. BA with highest distinction, U. Va., 1980. Intern, internat. economist U.S. Customs, Washington, 1979; mgmt. assoc. First Nat. Bank Atlanta, 1980-81, cash mgmt. officer, 1981-83, asst. v.p., group mktg. mgr., 1983-84; treasury mgr., asst. to chief exec. officer Contel Corp., Atlanta, 1984-89; v.p. fin. Contel Office Communications, Inc., St. Louis, 1989-91; v.p., treas. Am. Internat., Inc., Chgo., 1991-94; v.p. fin. Alliance Capital, N.Y.C., 1994; sr. v.p. corp. bus. devel. USL Capital, San Franciso, 1995; CFO InterCall, Chgo., 1995, COO, 1996-97; cons. Heidrich & Struggles, Inc., 1997—99, ptnr., 1999—2000, ptnr.-in-charge, 2000—. Instr. Am. Inst. Banking, 1982-83; chmn. Contel Profl. Devel. Assn., Atlanta, 1986. Assoc. editor Cash Mgmt. Forum, 1982-84; co-founder, co-editor First Word newsletter, 1983-84. Chmn. fundraising unit United Way, Atlanta, 1985—88, Atlanta unit Am. Cancer Soc., 1985—88, Atlanta Coll. Arts, 1985—88; governing mem. Brookfield Zoo, Chgo., 1992—99. Mem. Nat. Corp. Cash Mgmt. Assn. (bd. dirs. 1987-91, exec. com. 1988-91), Fin. Execs. Inst., Treasury Mgmt. Assn. Chgo., St. Louis Zoo Friends Assn. (bd. dirs. 1990-91). Avocations: sports, art, travel. Office: 1750 Tysons Blvd Ste 300 Mc Lean VA 22102 E-mail: mflagg@heidrick.com.

FLAGG, NORMAN LEE, retired advertising executive; b. Detroit, Jan. 21, 1932; s. Frank and Harriet (Brown) F.; m. Carolanne Flagg; children: James, Suzanne. BFA, U. Miami, Miami, Fla., 1958. Advt. supr. Smithkline Beckman, Phila., 1970-75, creative dir., 1975-80; owner Illusions Restaurants, Bryn Mawr, Pa., 1979—87, Illusions Restaurant, Tucson, 1984-88. Author: Shooting Blanks, 1994. With USMC, 1954-56. Recipient Diana awards Whlse Druggest Assn. 1977, Aesculapius award Modern Medicine 1978. Mem. Acad. Magical Arts. E-mail: nflagg@flash.net.

FLAGG, RAYMOND OSBOURN, biology executive; b. Martinsburg, W.Va., Jan. 31, 1933; s. Dorsey Slemons and Dorothy (Hobbs) F.; m. Ann Quinlan Birmingham, May 19, 1956; children: Richard Matthew, Elizabeth Ann, Catherine Garnett. BA with honors, Shepherd Coll., 1957; PhD in Biology, U. Va., 1961; diploma in advanced mgmt. program, U. N.C., Chapel Hill, 1994. Math tchr. Boonsboro (Md.) High Sch., 1957; rsch. asst. Blandy Exptl. Farm, Boyce, Va., 1957-61; rsch. assoc. U. Va., Charlottesville, 1961-62; dir. botany Carolina Biol. Supply Co., Burlington, NC, 1962-80, v.p., 1980-2000, exec. v.p., 2001—03; v.p. Wolfe Sales Corp., Burlington, 1985-97. Head Cabisco Biotech., Burlington, 1988-91; v.p. Found. for Ednl. Devel., Research Triangle Park, N.C., 1983-85; vice chmn. N.C. Plant Conservation Bd., Raleigh, 1984-88. Contbr. articles to profl. jours. Chmn. Beautification Commn., Burlington, 1976-80, Hist. Dist. Commn., 1981-82; bd. dirs. United Way of Alamance County, Burlington, 1984-88; vice chmn. Tree Adv. Com., Burlington, 1993-2000. Rsch. grant Am. Cancer Soc., 1960, rsch. equipment grant Va. Acad. Sci., 1961; recipient Community Leadership award No. Piedmont Devel. Assn., 1977. Mem. AAAS, Assn. Southeastern Biologists (pres. 1978-79), N.C. Acad. Sci. (pres. 1983-84), Va. Acad. Sci., Rotary (pres. Alamance A.M. 1988-89). Democrat. Presbyterian. Achievements include invention of instant drosophila medium, Carosafe, FlyNap, Sterigel, Planoslo, Vitachrome, Alga-Gro. Office: Carolina Biol Supply 2700 York Rd Burlington NC 27215-3398

FLAGG DAVIS, VIVIAN ANNETTE, librarian, researcher, public policy consultant; b. Milledgeville, Ga., July 18, 1960; d. Rufus and Sandra Ann (Seals) F.; m. Joe H. Davis Jr., Jan 16, 1993. BA, Ga. State U., 1982, MPA, 1988. Purchasing and sales clk. Reed Drugs, Atlanta, 1980-81; libr. assoc. Atlanta Jour. & Constn., 1981-84, libr. asst., 1984-89, assoc. libr., rsch. supr., 1989-91, systems libr., 1991—. Tutor Lit. Action, Atlanta, 1981-83, Alonzo Herndon Elem. Sch., 1999-2001; bd. dirs. Odyssey Family Counseling Ctr., Hapeville, Ga., 1983-85; mem. adv. coun. Vol. Atlanta, 1984-87, pres., 1983-85; vol. spl. projects Changed Living Recovery, 1994—; mem. svc. coun. Youth Devel. Allocations and Evaluation Com., Atlanta, 1987—, planning and allocations com. United Way, Atlanta, 1987—, co-chair Task Force for Homeless and Hungry, 1992—; chmn. social action com. social svcs. and human resources dir. Greater Piney Grove Bapt. Ch.; mem. Atlanta Ballet Assocs.; bd. dirs. Higher Plain Ministries, 1994—, chair adminstrn. com., 2003; co-chair edn. com. AJC in Action; founder reading program Will You Read To Me?, 2003. Recipient Outstanding Leader award Vol. Ga., 1984. Mem. ASPA, Nat. Young Profls. Forum, NAACP, Am. Soc. Info. Sci., Spl. Librs. Assn. Democrat. Avocations: piano, sewing, tennis, gardening, travel. Home: 3735 Landgraf Cv Decatur GA 30034-4775 Office: Atlanta Jour Constn 72 Marietta St NW Atlanta GA 30303-2804

FLAHARTY, GERALDINE, state representative; b. Parsons, Kans., Mar. 4, 1936; BS, Wichita State U., 1962, MEd, 1971. Elem. tchr. Wichita Pub. Schs., 1956—57; reading tchr. Oaklawn Elem., 1966—; mem. Kans. Ho. of Reps., 1995—. Precinct woman, 1988—. Mem.: AAUW, Kans. Nat. Edn. Assn., Internat. Reading Assn., Wichita State U. Alumni Assn. Democrat. Office: 279-W State Capitol 300 SW 10th Ave Topeka KS 66612 Address: 1816 Fernwood Wichita KS 67216-8039*

FLAHERTY, DANIEL LEE, prosecutor; b. Des Moines, Apr. 6, 1955; s. Jerry A. and Mary A. (Durlacher) F.; m. Kathleen L. Harrington, Aug. 10, 1980; children: Scott D., Amy K., Lacy A. BA, N.W. Mo. State U., 1978; JD, South Tex. Coll. Law, 1982. Bar: Tex. 1982, U.S. Dist. Ct. (so. dist.) Tex. 1983, U.S. Dist. Ct. (ea. dist.) Tex. 1985, U.S. Ct. Appeals (5th cir.) 1985, Iowa 1989, U.S. Dist. Ct. (no. dist.) Iowa 1991, U.S. Dist. Ct. (so. dist.) Iowa 1992, U.S. Ct. Appeals (8th cir.) 1992. Assoc. Newton Schwartz, P.C., Houston, 1982-83, George Chandler & Assocs., Baytown, Tex., 1983-85, Brack & Brack, Baytown, 1985-87, Margolin, Gildmeister, Willia, Mugan & Keane, Sioux City, Iowa, 1989-91; ptnr. Daniel L. Flaherty, Highlands, Tex., 1987-89; asst. county atty. Polk County Atty.'s Office, Des Moines, 1991—. Lectr. Iowa Judges Conf., Des Moines, 1993, 2001; panelist Iowa Magistrates Conf., Des Moines, 1997, Iowa Clks. Conf., Des Moines, 1997, Iowa County Attys. Spring Tng. Conf., 2000, Indigent Def. Advocacy Course, Des Moines. Contbr. articles to legal publs. Com. mem. troop 81 Boy Scouts Am., Baytown, 1983-89, chmn. membership com. Raven dist., 1987-89, scoutmaster troop 204, Sioux City, 1989-91, com. mem. troop 17, Des Moines, 1991-92, cubmaster pack 17, 1992-96, Webelos den leader 1993-96, scoutmaster troop 17, 1997-2000, advisor crew 350, 1999—2003, commr. Hawkeye dist. Mid-Iowa coun., 1994-96, asst. dist. commr., 1997—, mem. com., chmn. roundtable, 1990-92; precinct chmn. Iowa Dem. Party, Des Moines, 1993—; mem., elder Christian Ch. (Disciples of Christ). Recipient Scouters award Prairie Gold coun. Boy Scouts Am., 1990, dist. award of merit Hawkeye Dist., 1991, cubmaster's award, 1996, Webelos den leader award, 1996, Commr.'s Key, Hawkeye dist., 1997, Arrowhead award, 1997, Scouters Key, 2000, Silver Beaver award, 2001. Avocations: walking, swimming, boy scouting. Office: Polk County Atty's Office 111 Court Ave Rm 340 Des Moines IA 50309-2218 E-mail: dflah@aol.com., dflaher@attorney.co.polk.ia.us.

FLAHERTY, DAVID THOMAS, JR., lawyer; b. Boston, June 17, 1953; S. David Thomas Sr. and Nancy Ann (Hamill) F.; children: Alexandra Lynn, David Thomas III. BS in Math., German, U. N.C., 1974, JD, 1978. Bar: Mass. 1979, N.C. 1979, U.S. Dist. Ct. (we. dist.) N.C. 1979, U.S. Dist. Ct. (mid. dist.) N.C. 1981, U.S. Ct. Appeals (4th cir.) 1981, U.S. Tax Ct. 1982, U.S. Supreme Ct., 1987, U.S. Ct. Claims, 1992. Assoc. Wilson & Palmer, Lenoir, N.C., 1979-80, Ted West P.A., Lenoir, 1980-82; ptnr. Robbins, Flaherty & Lackey, Lenoir, 1982-85, Robbins & Flaherty, Lenoir, 1985-88, Delk, Flaherty, Swanson & Hartshorn, P.A., Lenoir, 1988-89, Delk, Flaherty, Robbins, Swanson & Hartshorn, P.A., Lenoir, 1989-90, Flaherty, Robbins, Swanson & Hartshorn, P.A., 1990-95; dist. atty. 25th prosecutorial dist. Office Dist. Atty., Lenoir, 1995—. Mem. N.C. Ho. of Reps., Raleigh, 1988-94, N.C. Cts. Commn., 1989—, N.C. Jud. Adv. Commn., 1997—. Mem. exec. com. Caldwell County Reps., Lenoir, 1985-86, 88—. Mem. N.C. Bar Assn., N.C. Conf. Dist. Attys., 25th Jud. Dist. Bar Assn. (mem. exec. com. 1987-88), Reps. Men's Club, Blue Key. Methodist. Avocations: water and snow skiing, motorcycling. Home: 228 Pennton Ave SW Lenoir NC 28645-4316 Office: Office of Dist Atty Caldwell County Courthouse PO Box 718 Lenoir NC 28645-0718

FLAHERTY, JOHN JOSEPH, quality assurance company executive; b. Chgo., Ill., July 24, 1932; s. Patrick J. and Mary B. Flaherty; m. Norrine Grow, Nov. 20, 1954 (dec. Sept. 1995); children: John, Bridgette, George, Eileen, Daniel, Mary, Michael, Amy; m. Rosemarie Clausen, Dec. 27, 2001. BEE U. Ill., 1959. Design engr. Admiral Corp., Chgo., 1959—60; project engr. Magnaflux Corp., Chgo., 1960—79, v.p., mgr. rsch. and engring., 1979—84, v.p., mgr. mktg. and sales, 1984—86, v.p., gen. mgr. electronic products, 1986—88; pres. Flare Tech., Chgo., 1988—. Served with AUS, 1951—53. Fellow: Am. Soc. Non-Destructive Testing; mem.: IEEE, Am. Soc. Metals. Roman Catholic. Achievements include patents and publications on nondestructive testing, including medical ultrasonic; laser scanning. Office: 401 Meadow Lark Rd Bloomingdale IL 60108

FLAHERTY, JOHN PAUL, JR., judge; b. Pitts., Nov. 19, 1931; s. John Paul and Mary G. (McLaughlin) F.; m. Linet Flaherty; 7 children, 2 stepchildren. BA, Duquesne U., 1953; JD, U. Pitts., 1958; LLD (hon.), Widener U., 1993. Bar: Pa. 1958. Pvt. practice, Pitts., 1958-73; mem. faculty Carnegie-Mellon U., 1958-73; judge Ct. Common Pleas Allegheny County, 1973-79, pres. judge civil divsn., 1978-79; justice Supreme Ct. Pa., 1979-96, chief justice, 1996—2001. USIA speaker in Far East, 1985-86. Mem. Pa. Hist. Soc.; chair Pa. County Records Com. Recipient Medallion of Distinction U. Pitts., 1987, Judicial award Pa. Bar Assn., 1993, Pres. award Pa. Bar Assn., 1999; Chief Justice John P. Flaherty award, Pa. Bar Assn. Conf. of Bar Leaders, 2001; named Man of Yr. in law and govt., Greater Pitts. Jaycees, 1978, named to Century Club of Disting. Alumni, Duquesne U., 1994. Mem. Pa. Acad. Sci. (chmn. hon. exec. bd. 1978-89, Disting. Alumnus award 1977), Am. Law Inst., Pa. Soc., Pa. Bar Assn. (award 2001), Mil. History Soc. Ireland, Friendly Sons St. Patrick, Am. Legion. Office: Pa Supreme Ct Rm 810 City County Bldg Pittsburgh PA 15219 *The law is the energy of the living world, and although developed and defined by the judiciary in our Anglo-American society, it is applied and is derived by and from the people. It exists only to protect one person from being hurt, physically or economically, by another. Serious problems face our age. In the final analysis, the judiciary must accomodate the various solutions which will be forthcoming. I hope that my brothers have the foresight and the stamina to accommodate what might be quite novel innovations in the law, which is the living energy, to make this world a place in which it's worth living, since that is the function of the law. Every case involves people. There is no such thing as a small case.*

FLAHERTY, LOIS TALBOT, editor, psychiatrist, educator; b. Nashville, Apr. 28, 1942; BA, Wellesley Coll., 1963; MD, Duke U., 1968. Diplomate Nat. Bd. Med. Examiners. Intern D.C. Gen. Hosp., 1968-69; resident in psychiatry Georgetown U. Hosp., 1969-71; resident in child psychiatry Johns Hopkins Hosp., 1971-73; pvt. practice Cross Keys, Md., 1973-81; dir. tng. divsn. child and adolescent psychiatry U. Md., 1981-89, assoc. prof. med. sch. divsn. child and adolescent psychiatry, 1982-93, dir. divsn. child and adolescent psychiatry, 1984-92, adj. assoc. prof., 1994—; clin. assoc. prof. psychiatry U. Pa., 1997-2000; pvt. practice Blue Bell, Pa., 1994-99; editor Adolescent Psychiatry, 2000—; lectr. Harvard U., 2002—. Instr. depts. psychiatry and pediatrics Johns Hopkins U. Sch. Medicine, 1973-92; attending staff psychiatrist family, child and adolescent divsn. Sinai Hosp. Balt., 1974-77; staff child psychiatrist Walter P. Carter Ctr., 1977-78, dir. child and adolescent svcs., 1978-92, acting dir. impatient adolescent unit, 1979-80; clin. asst. prof. U. Md., 1977-81; lectr. psychiatry Harvard U., 2002—; cons. Northwest Drug Alert Sinai Hosp. Balt., 1971-72, St. Vincent's Child Care Ctr., 1973-78, Children's Guild, Inc., 1975-82, SSA, Balt., 1985, many others. Contbr. chpts. to books and articles and book revs. to profl. jours. NIMH grantee, 1983-86. Fellow: Am. Soc. for Adolescent Psychiatry, Am. Psychiat. Assn.; mem.: Group for Advancement of Psychiatry, Am. Coll. Psychiatrists, Am. Acad. Child Psychiatry. Office: 4 Charlesgate East #605 Boston MA 02215-2369 E-mail: lflaher770@aol.com.

FLAHERTY, STEPHEN, composer, orchestrator; Composer songs including: Once On This Island (Tony nominee best score and best musical, 1995 Olivier award for London's Best Musical), My Favorite Year, Lucky Stiff, Anastasia (Acad. award nominee best score and best song, 2 Golden Globe nominations), composer incidental music for Neil Simon's play: Proposals, concert pieces include: Suite from Ragtime, Anastasia Suite. Recipient Tony award for original musical score "Ragtime", also Drama Desk award, Outer Critics Cir. award. Mem.: ASCAP, Drama Dept., Dramatists Guild. Office: c/o Songwriters Guild Found 1560 Broadway Rm 1306 New York NY 10036-1518

FLAHERTY, THOMAS JOSEPH, lawyer; b. Berwick, Pa., Oct. 1, 1943; s. Edward A. and Lucy (Simon) F.; m. Margaret Ann Broxton, Oct. 3, 1970; children— Jenifer, Thomas. B.S., St. Louis U., 1967, J.D., 1973. Bar: Mo. 1974, Oreg. 1974, U.S. Dist. Ct. Oreg. 1974, U.S. Ct. Appeals (9th cir.) 1977. Assoc., Lachman & Henninger, Portland, Oreg., 1974-78; sole practice, Lake Oswego, Oreg., 1979-84, Portland, 1986—; ptnr. Flaherty & Hall, Portland, 1984-86; staff Judge Advocate Marine Air Group-42, 4th Marine Aircraft Wing, U.S. Marine Corps Res., Naval Air Sta. Whidbey Island, Oak Harbor, Wash., 1982-85, asst. regional def. counsel, Pacific region, 1986-90, dep. chief def. counsel to the USMC, 1990-93. Scoutmaster Columbia council Boy Scouts Am., 1975; mem. parish council St. Matthews Ch., Hillsboro, Oreg., 1980— . Served to 1st lt. USMC, 1967-70, col. Res.; Vietnam. Decorated Purple Heart (2), Vietnamese Cross of Gallantry. Mem. Assn. Trial Lawyers Am., Oreg. Trial Lawyers Assn., Oreg. State Bar Assn. Republican. Roman Catholic. Office: 10300 SW Greenburg Rd Suite 490 Portland OR 97223

FLAHERTY, TINA SANTI, corporate communications executive, writer; b. Memphis; d. Clement Alexander and Dale (Pendergrast) Santi; m. William Edward Flaherty, Feb. 22, 1975. BA, U. Memphis, 1961; hon. doctorate, St. John's U., 1979. Commentator host interview program Sta. WMC-TV, Memphis, 1960-61; newscaster, commentator Sta. WHER, Memphis, 1961-62; cmty. rels. specialist Western Electric Co., N.Y.C., 1964-66; v.p. pub. rels. divsn. Grey Advt., N.Y.C., 1966-72; dep. dir. corp. rels. Colgate-Palmolive Co., N.Y.C., 1972-75, dir. corp. rels., 1975-76, corp. v.p., v.p. in charge of communications, 1976-84; v.p. pub. affairs GTE Corp., Stamford, Conn., 1984-86; pres., chief exec. officer Image Mktg. Internat., N.Y.C., 1986—. Author: The Savvy Woman's Success Bible, 1997 (one of Top Motivational Books of Yr., Books for a Better Life 1997), Talk Your Way to the Top, 1999. Former chmn. Bus. Coun. of UN Decade for Women; bd. dirs. Nat. Jr. Achievement, 1978—; mem. The White House Pub. Affairs Advisors, 1981-84; nat. bd. dirs. Animal Med. Ctr. Recipient Jr. Achievement Meml. award, 1984; named One of N.Y.C.'s Outstanding Women of Achievement, NCCJ, One of 100 Top Corp. Women, Bus. Week, One of 73 Women Ready to Run Corp. Am., Working Woman, Woman of Distinction, Birmingham So. Coll., One of 100 Amazing Ams., Am.'s Elite, 2000. Mem. DAR, Com. of 200, Internat. Women's Forum. Home and Office: Image Mktg Internat 1040 Fifth Ave New York NY 10028-0137 E-mail: imi1040@aol.com. *Persistence alone is omnipotent.*

FLAHERTY, WILLIAM E. chemicals and metals company executive; b. 1933; Formerly with GM Overseas Corp., Reynolds Metals Co.; with Gulf & Western, 1974-81, past COO zinc and chems. divsn.; now chmn. bd., CEO Horsehead Industries, N.Y.C.; chmn. bd. Great Lakes Carbon Corp. Office: Horsehead Industries 110 E 59th St New York NY 10022-1304

FLAKE, FLOYD HAROLD, former congressman; b. L.A., Jan. 30, 1945; m. M. Elaine McCollins; children: Aliya, Nailah, Rasheed, Hasan. BA in Psychology, Wilberforce U., 1967; D in Ministry, United Theol. Sem., Dayton, Ohio, 1995; postgrad., Northeastern U. Social worker, 1968-69; sales rep. Reynolds Tobacco Co., 1969; mktg. analyst Xerox Corp., 1969-70; assoc. dean students, dir. student activities Lincoln U., Pa., 1970-73; dean students, univ. chaplain, dir.Martin Luther King Jr. Afro-Am. Ctr. Boston U., 1973-76; mem. 101st-105th Congresses from 6th N.Y. dist., Washington, 1987-97, mem. banking and fin. svcs. com., mem. domestic & internat. monetary policy subcom., mem. small bus. com.; pastor Allen A.M.E. Cathedral, Jamaica, N.Y., 1976—; pres. Edison Charter Schs. Pres., Edison Charter Sch. 2000; sr. fellow Manhattan Inst., 1998—; pres., Wilberforce U., 2002-present, bd. dir. Fannie Mae Found. Columnist N.Y. Post, 1999; author: The Way of the Bootstrapper: Nine Action

Steps For Achieving Your Dreams. Pastor Allen A.M.E. Ch., Jamaica, N.Y., past chmn. affiliate corps. including Allen Sr. Citizen Complex, Allen Christian Sch. and Multi-Purpose Ctr., Allen Home Care Agy., Allen Housing Corp., So. Jamaica Multi-Svc. Ctr. Alfred Sloan fellow Northeastern U., Danforth fellow Payne Theol. Sem.; Gilbert H. Jones scholar Wilberforce U. 1986, Ebony Mag. Black Achievement award in Religion. Office: Allen AME Cathedral 11031 Merrick Blvd Jamaica NY 11433-3440

FLAKE, JEFF, congressman; b. Snowflake, Ariz., Dec. 31, 1962; m. Cheryl, 15 yrs.; 5 children. BA in Internat. Rels., MA in Polit. Sci., Brigham Young U. Worked in pub. rels., Wash., DC, 1987; exec. dir. Found. Democracy, Nambia, Goldwater Instit., Ariz., 1992; mem. U.S. Ho. Reps. from 1st Ariz. dist., 2001—. Mem. House Judiciary com.; serving on House Internat. Rels. com. Republican. Office: 424 Cannon House Office Bldg Washington DC 20515-0306*

FLAKES, LARRY JOSEPH, civil engineer; b. Birmingham, Ala., Jan. 27, 1947; s. John W. and Lurlene (Patton) F. BS in Civil Engring., Howard U., 1969; cert. Transp. Inst., Northwestern U., 1970. Registered profl. engr., Ga. Ala. Structural mass properties engr. Lockheed Ga. Co., Marietta, Ga., 1969-70; traffic engr. I, City of Atlanta, 1970-71; contract engr. Ala. Power Co., Birmingham, 1972-74; property tax engr. So. Ry. Co., Atlanta, 1976-81; project engr. Norfolk So. Corp., 1981-89; pres. Flakes Engring. Co., cons. engrs., 1983—. Mem. NAACP. Recipient Presdl. Merit award, 1982; Howard U. scholar, 1964-65. Mem. ASCE (Student Newsletter award 1967), Nat. Soc. Profl. Engrs., Am. Ry. Engrs. Assn. Baptist. Home and Office: 48 18th Ct S Birmingham AL 35205-6331

FLAKES, SUSAN, playwright, screenwriter, director; b. San Diego, July 9, 1943; d. Herbert Franklin and Dorothy Jean (Loafman) Barrows; m. Donald Lewis Flakes, Dec. 31, 1964; 1 child, Daniel Keith. BA, U. N.Mex., 1965; MA, San Diego State U., 1969; PhD, U. Minn., 1973. Asst., then assoc. prof. Tisch Sch. Arts NYU, 1973-76, dept. chair Tisch Sch. Arts, 1973-76; founder, artistic dir. Blue Tower Theatre, Stockholm, 1977-80, Strindberg's Intima Teater, Stockholm, 1981-83, Source Prodns., N.Y.C., 1984-90. Instr. U.S. Internat. Univ., San Diego, 1972-73; founder, artistic dir. 1st Strindberg Festival, Stockholm, 1977, mem. Women's Project and Prodns., N.Y.C., 1984-90; v.p. Ibsen Soc. Am., N.Y.C., 1986-99; coord. writers unit W. Coast Ensemble Theatre, Hollywood, Calif., 1991-93. Author plays, 1977, 92, 95-97, 98, 99, 2001, The Woman Will Play Strindberg's Christina, Laura, Silent Star, And Immortality, Marilyn's Rose, Portrait of Psyche, Daddy's Eyes, To Take Arms, Cafe L.A., (with Shirl Hendryx) 4F; (libretto with Galt MacDermot) Take It Higher, Maid of Lorraine, Any Saints Out There? (with Gabe Green), It Girls; (screenplays) To Take Arms, Stand the Storm, Hometown, Inc., Café L.A., Francois Poet/Thief, Lifetime Achievement, Daddy's Eyes; dir. Hughie, 1989, Mother Love, 1994; author: (book) Sing The Person; contbr. articles to profl. jours. and books in U.S. and Sweden; creator Exptl. Theatre Wing U.G. Drama Tisch Sch. Arts, NYU, 1975-76; contbr. play And Immortality to Baltic Seasons Mag., Russia. Ensign USN, 1965-67. Recipient honorable mention Writers Digest Writing Competition, 1999, winner Lamia Ink Internat. competition, 1991; fellow Am. Film Inst., 1990; grantee Nat. Endowment for Arts, 1972; travel grantee Am. Scandinavian Found., Norwegian and Swedish Govts., 1985, 86, 89, 94; finalist Susan Smith Blackburn prize, 1996-97, Nat. Playwrights Conf., 2000. Mem. Dramatists Guild, Actor's Studio (playwright/dirs. unit), Am. Film Inst. (finalist directing workshop for women 2003), Phi Beta Kappa. Address: 7552 Amazon Dr #1 Huntington Beach CA 92647 E-mail: sflakes@socal.rr.com.

FLAM, BERNARD VINCENT, retired secondary education educator; b. Bronx, N.Y., June 6, 1945; s. Abraham and Anna (Aptowitzer) F.; m. Lydia Esther Nieves, June 7, 1969 (div. Sept. 1989); children: Rachel, Elliot. BS in Psychology, CCNY, 1969. Registered jr. high sch. math. tchr., N.Y.C. Actuarial clk. Nat. Health & Welfare, N.Y.C., 1968-69; tchr. math. Intermediate Sch. 52X, Bronx, 1969-75, Intermediate Sch. 192X, Bronx, 1975—2002. Pres. Stratford Ave. Block Assn., Bronx, 1969-71; sec. Throgs Neck-Soundview Mental Health Ctr., Bronx, 1970; mem. 801 Bronx River Rd. Coop Bd., 2001-03. Recognized as Inspirational Tchr. Fordham Prep. Sch., 1995. Mem. United Fedn. Tchrs. (chpt. chmn. Intermediate Sch. 192X 1992-94), Am. Fedn. Tchrs. Jewish. Avocations: running (finished N.Y.C. marathon 1987), flood relief (St. Louis 1993), opera, rock and roll, supporting homeless shelter in N.Y.C. Home: 811 Bronx River Rd Bronxville NY 10708-8020

FLAM, JACK DONALD, art historian, educator; b. Paterson, NJ, Apr. 2, 1940; s. Max and Rose Leila (Silverberg) F.; m. Bonnie Suzanne Burnham, Oct. 7, 1972 (div.); 1 child, Laura Rose. BA, Rutgers U., 1961; MA, Columbia U., 1963; PhD, NYU, 1969. Instr. Rutgers U., Newark, N.J., 1962-66; asst. prof. U. Fla., Gainesville, 1966-69, assoc. prof., 1969-72, Bklyn. Coll., 1975-80, prof. grad. ctr., 1980-90, disting. prof., 1991—. Author: Matisse on Art, 1973, Bread and Butter, 1977, Robert Motherwell, 1983, Matisse, the Man and His Art, 1986, Motherwell, 1991, Richard Diebenkorn: Ocean Park, 1992, Matisse: The Dance, 1993, Western Artists/African Art, 1994, Robert Smithson: The Collected Writings, 1996, Judith Rothschild: An Artist's Search, 1998, Frankenthaler, 1999, The Modern Drawing, 1999, Matisse in the Cone Collections, 2001, Matisse and Picasso: The Story of Their Rivalry and Friendship, 2003, Primitivism and Twentieth-Century Art: A Documentary History, 2003; art critic Wall St. Jour., 1984-92. Guggenheim Found. fellow, 1979, NEH, 1986. Mem. Internat. Art Critics Assn., Internat. PEN, Coll. Art Assn. Am. Office: Bklyn Coll Art Dept Bedford Ave # H Brooklyn NY 11210-2889

FLAME, ANDREW JAY, lawyer; b. Phila, Apr. 4, 1968; s. Sheldon Paul and Rita Ann Flame; m. Lori Jill Bolno, Nov. 17, 1996; 1 child, Rachel Sara. BS in Mktg., Pa. State U., 1990; JD, Temple U., 1993. Bar: Pa. 1993, NJ 1993, US Dist. Ct. NJ 1993, US Dist. Ct. (sbt. dist.) Pa. 1993, DC 1994, US Dist. Ct. (mid. dist.) Pa. 1994. Law clk. to Hon. Louis Pollack US Dist. Ct. (ea. dist.) Pa., Phila., 1992-93, law clk. to Hon. Stuart Dalzell, 1994; ptnr. Drinker Biddle & Reath LLP, Phila., 1993—. Founder, Camp 4 Happy Days, Phila., 1985-86; trainer Youth Implemented Programs, San Francisco, 1988; trustee, v.p. Reform Congregation Keneseth Israel, Phila., 1994—; mem. Golden Slipper Club Charity, Phila., 1994-2000; mem. com. Cheltenham Twp. (Pa.) Drug/Alcohol Bd., 1979-86, 91-93. Avocations: sports, travel. Office: Drinker Biddle & Reath LLP 1100 N Market St Ste 1000 Wilmington DE 19801 Home: 118 Spyglass Dr Blue Bell PA 19422-3216 E-mail: andrew.flame@dbr.com.

FLAMM, LEONARD N(ATHAN), lawyer; b. Newark, May 23, 1943; s. Sydney Lewis and Lillian (Schreiber) F. Cert., London Sch. Econs., 1964; BA, Dartmouth Coll., 1965; JD, Harvard U., 1968. Bar: N.J. 1968, N.Y. 1970, U.S. Ct. Appeals (2d cir.) 1970, Fla. 1976, U.S. Dist. Ct. (so. and ea. dists.) N.Y. 1976, U.S. Ct. Appeals (7th cir.) 1986, U.S. Ct. Appeals (3d cir.) 1987, U.S. Supreme Ct. 1989. Assoc. Marshall, Bratter, Greene, Allison & Tucker, N.Y.C., 1968-70, Donovan, Leisure, Newton & Irvine, N.Y.C., 1970-72, Glass, Greenberg & Irwin, N.Y.C., 1972-75; ptnr. Hockert & Flamm, N.Y.C., 1975-90; pvt. practice N.Y.C., 1990—. Contbg. author Employee Rights Litigation: Pleadings and Practice, 1991. Named one of Best Lawyers in U.S., Town & Country Mag., 1985. Mem. Assn. Bar City N.Y. (legal referral panel 1975—), Nat. Employment Lawyers Assn. (v.p. N.Y. chpt., nat. co-chmn. Age Discrimination in Employment Act com.) Office: 880 3rd Ave Ste 1300 New York NY 10022-4730 E-mail: adealnf@aol.com.

FLANAGAN, BARBARA, journalist; b. Des Moines; d. John Merrill and Marie (Barnes) F.; m. Earl S. Sanford, 1966. Student, Drake U., 1942-43. With promotion dept. Mpls. Times, 1945-47; reporter Mpls. Tribune, 1947-58; women's editor, spl. writer Mpls. Star and Tribune, 1958-65; columnist Mpls. Star, 1965—. Author: Ovation, Minneapolis. Active Junior League Mpls., Womans Club Mpls. Mem. Mpls. Soc. Fine Arts (life), Mpls. Inst. Arts (founding mem. Minn. Arts Forum), Mpls. Club, Minikahda Club, Kappa Alpha Theta, Sigma Delta Chi. Episcopalian. Home: 3200 W Calhoun Pky Apt 301 Minneapolis MN 55416-4650 Office: Mpls Star Tribune 5th And Portland Sts Minneapolis MN 55488-0001

FLANAGAN, CLYDE HARVEY, JR., psychiatrist, psychoanalyst, educator; b. Louellen, Ky., Aug. 21, 1939; s. Clyde H. Sr. and Ruby M. Flanagan; m. Gloria Kay Glymph, June 1, 1961 (div. Feb. 1974); children: Clyde H. III, Christopher Shane; m. Carol Anne Ross, Apr. 13, 1974; children: Patrick Ross, Colleen Helen. BS, Maryville Coll., 1962; MD, U. Tenn. Med. Unit, Memphis, 1966. Cert. Am. Bd. Psychiatry and Neurology in Adult, Child, Adolescent Psychiatry; diplomate Nat. Bd. Med. Commd. 2d lt. U.S. Army, 1965, advanced through grades to col. MC, 1980; rotating med. intern U.S. Army Tripler Gen. Hosp., Honolulu, 1966-67; gen. psychiatry resident U.S. Army Walter Reed Gen. Hosp, Washington, 1967-69, child psychiatry resident, 1969-71; asst. chief child guidance svc. Walter Reed Army Med. Ctr., Washington, 1971-80; chief cmty. mental health activity Ft. Belvoir, Va., 1980-86; asst. head tri-svc. alcohol rehab. dept. Nat. Navy Hosp., Bethesda, Md., 1986-88, ret., 1988; dir. gen. psychiat. residency program W.S. Hall Psychiat. Inst., Columbia, S.C., 1988-92; prof. psychiatry dept. of psychiatry/behavioral sci. Sch. Medicine U. S.C., Columbia, 1988—, dir. divsn. psychoanalysis dept. psychiat./behavioral sci., 1992—. Candidate in psychoanalysis Washington Psychoanalytic Inst., 1978-88; tng. and supervising analyst U. N.C./Duke PSA Ednl. Program, Chapel Hill, 1991—. Contbr. chpt. to books in field. Recipient Tchr. Yr. award Resident's Gen. Psychiat. Rsch. Program William S. Hall Psychiat. Inst., 1995, Spl. Alumni citation Maryville Coll., 2000. Fellow Am. Psychiat. Assn. (disting. life fellow), Am. Coll. Psychiatrists (com. pub. edn. 1998-99, Laughlin fellow selection com. 2000-03, membership devel. com. 2003—), Am. Acad. Child and Adolescent Psychiatry (Franklin Robinson award 1975); mem. Am. Psychoanalytic Assn. (councilor 1989—, cert. in adult, adolescent, and child psychoanalysis Bd. Profl. Stds. 1991), N.C. Psychoanalytic Soc. (councilor 1989-98), S.C. Psychiat. Soc. (membership chmn. 1991—), Am. Group Psychotherapy Assn. (founder, cert. group psychotherapist), Internat. Psychoanalytic Assn., Am. Assn. Child Psychoanalysis. Avocations: fishing, boating. Office: U SC Sch Medicine Dept Neuropsychiatry 3555 Harden Street Ext Ste 104A Columbia SC 29203-6894

FLANAGAN, DENNIS, journalist; b. N.Y.C., July 22, 1919; s. John Richard and Nan (Apotheker) F.; m. Geraldine A. Lux, Jan. 9, 1948; children: Cara Louise, John Gerard; m. Ellen Raskin; Oct. 17, 1966; m. Barbara Grossman Williams, Sept. 11, 1999. AB, Mich., 1941. Staff writer Life mag., 1941-47; mng. editor Scientific Am., 1947-50, editor, 1950-84. Dir. Bull. Atomic Scientists, 1983-93; vis. and supernumerary fellow St. Cross Coll., Oxford, 1974-84; Marsh prof. U. Mich., 1985; Centennial prof. Wash. State U., 1989. Author: Flanagan's Version: A Spectator's Guide to Science on the Eve of the 21st Century, 1990. Trustee Marine Biol. Lab., Woods Hole, Mass. 1975-83, N.Y. Hall of Sci., 1965-99; mem. vis. com. for linguistics and philosophy MIT, 1984-86. Recipient Outstanding Achievement award U. Mich., 1961, Kalinga prize UN Ednl., Sci. and Cultural Orgn., 1982, Glenn T. Seaborg award Internat. Platform Assn., 1982, Olive Br. award Writers' and Pubs. Alliance for Disarmament, 1984; named to Mag. Editors' Hall of Fame, 1999. Fellow Am. Acad. Arts and Scis.; mem. Am. Soc. Mag. Editors (pres. 1977-79), Authors Guild, Century Assn., Sigma Xi. Home: 12 Gay St New York NY 10014-3538 E-mail: flanagand@earthlink.net.

FLANAGAN, EANNA EAMONN, physicist; b. Castlebar, County Mayo, Ireland, Dec. 1967; s. Michael and Finola Flanagan; m. Shelby Dietz, June 2, 2001. BSc, U. Coll. Dublin, Ireland, 1987, MSc, 1988; PhD in Theoretical Physics, Calif. Inst. Tech., 1993. Postdoctoral fellow Calif. Inst. Tech., Pasadena, 1993—94; Enrico Fermi postdoctoral fellow U. Chgo., 1994—96; asst. prof. physics Cornell U., Ithaca, NY, 1996—2001, assoc. prof. physics, 2001—. Fellow, Alfred P. Sloan Found., 1997—99, Radcliffe Inst., Harvard U., 2002—03. Office: Center for Radiophysics & Space Rsch Cornell Univ Ithaca NY 14853 E-mail: eef3@cornell.edu.

FLANAGAN, GARY LEE, librarian; b. Cincinnati, Ohio, Mar. 24, 1954; s. Roy Lee Flanagan and Ima Bernard; m. Evelyn Perez; 1 child, Shane Abimael Perez. BA, U. of Cin., 1976—82; MLS, U. of Ky., 1985—87. Libr. - cataloger Ky. State U., 1988—90, Morehead State U., Ky., 1990—96, libr. automation coord., 1996—. Mem.: IEEE Computer Soc., Libr. and Info. Tech. Assn., Assn. of Coll. and Rsch. Libraries, Am. Libr. Assn., ACLU, Sons of Union Veterans of the Civil War. D-Liberal. Muslim. Avocations: genealogy, herpetology, history, asian studies. Home: PO Box 263 Morehead KY 40351 Office: Camden-Carroll Library Morehead State U Morehead KY 40351 Personal E-mail: gflanagan@adelphia.net. E-mail: g.flanag@moreheadstate.edu.

FLANAGAN, HARRY PAUL, publishing executive; b. Columbus, Ohio, Dec. 8, 1933; m. Joan Dickas, June 23, 1956; children: Mary Beth, Kevin Hugh, Megan Joan. BS in Mktg., Ohio State U., 1956; Cert. in Mgmt., Capital U., Columbus, 1982, Advanced Mgmt. Cert., 1983. Pers. trainer For Lazarus Co., Columbus, 1960-61; supr. Wesleyan Press Co., Columbus, 1961-65; mgr. Xerox Ednl. Publs., Columbus, 1965-84, Field Publs., Columbus, 1984-89, ret., 1989; corp. dir. Highlights for Children, Columbus, 1989-94; ret., 1994—; pvt. practice bus. cons., freelance photographer, 1995—; with Metro Parks Blacklick Golf Course, 1997—. Chmn. Christ the King Sch. Bd., Columbus, 1975-80, mem. parish coun., 1968-78, 91-94, 96-2002, pres., 1994-96, 2000-02, chmn. golden jubilee com., 1995-96; bd. dirs. Multiple Sclerosis Soc., Franklin County, Ohio, 1980-83; mem. East Vicariate exec. com. Cath. Ch., 1998-2000. Recipient citation from Jr. Achievement, Columbus, 1966, Vol. award Ohio Ho. of Reps., 1975. Mem. Am. Mgmt. Assn., Fulfillment Mgrs. Assn., Techs. User Assn., Direct Mail Assn., Customer Svc. Coun. Roman Catholic. Avocations: golf, tennis, photography. E-mail: subway12@juno.com.

FLANAGAN, JAMES HENRY, JR., lawyer, writer, business educator; b. San Francisco, Sept. 11, 1934; s. James Henry Sr. and Mary Patricia (Gleason) F.; m. Charlotte Anne Nevins, June 11, 1960; children: Nancy, Christopher, Christina, Alexis, Victoria, Grace. AB in Polit. Sci., Stanford U., 1956, JD, 1961. Bar: Calif. 1962, U.S. Dist. Ct. (no. dist.) Calif. 1962, U.S. Ct. Appeals (9th cir.) 1962, U.S. Dist. Co. (so. dist.) Calif. 1964, U.S. Dist. Ct. (ea. dist.) Calif. 1967, Oreg. 1984. Assoc. Creede, Dawson & McElrath, Fresno, Calif., 1962-64; ptnr. Pettitt, Blumberg & Sherr and successor firms, Fresno, 1964-75; pvt. practice, Clovis, Calif., 1975—92, North Fork, Calif., 1992-98; counsel for Standing Chpt. 13 Trustee, 2003—. Instr. Humprey's Coll. Law, Fresno, 1964-69; instr. bus. Calif. State U., Fresno, 1986—; instr. MBA program Coll. of Notre Dame, Belmont, 1990-91; instr. Nat. U., 1991—, Emerson Inst., 1998—; judge pro tem Fresno County Superior Ct., 1974-77; gen. counsel Kings River Water Assn., 1976-79; founder, CEO Bus. and Non-profit Devel. Ctr. Author: California Water District Laws, 1962; columnist. Choir mem. Our Lady of Sierra, 1998—; exec. com. parish coun. St. Helen's Ch., 1982-85, chmn. exec. com., 1985; pres. parish coun. St. John's Cathedral, 1974-82; pres. bd. dirs. 3d Floor Ctrl. Calif.; bd. dirs. Fresno Facts Found., 1969-70, Fresno Dance Repertory Assn., St. Anthony's Retreat Ctr., Three Rivers, Calif.; sec. Coarsegold Resource Conservation Dist.; co-founder Clovis Big Dry Creek Hist. Soc.; chmn. Sierra Vista Nat. Scenic Byway Assn.; judge advocate Mountain Detachment, Marine Corps League. Recipient President award Fresno Jaycees, 1964. Mem. Calif. Bar Assn., Fresno County Bar Assn., Calif. Trial Lawyers Assn. (chpt. pres. 1975, 83, state bd. govs. 1990-94), Fresno Trial Lawyers Assn., Am. Arbitration Assn., Stanford Alumni Assn. (life, svc. award), Fresno Region Stanford Club (pres. 1979-80), Celtic Cultural Soc. Ctrl. Calif. (pres. 1977-78), Fresno County and City C. of C. (chmn. natural resources com. 1977-78), Clovis C. of C., North Fork C. of C. (pres. 1993-96, sec. 1998-2000, exec. dir. 2000—), Serra Club (pres. Fresno chpt. 1980-81, v.p. 1986-87), Rotary, Elks, KC (4th degree grand knight), Superchex, Western Assn. Chamber Exec. Republican. Roman Catholic. Avocations: writing, music, gardening, sailing, fishing. Office: PO Box 1555 North Fork CA 93643-1555 E-mail: jayflanagan@netptc.net.

FLANAGAN, JAMES LOTON, electrical engineer, researcher, engineering educator; BSEE, Miss. State U., 1948; SMEE, MIT, 1950, ScDEE, 1955; PhD (hon.), U. Madrid, 1992, U. Paris, 1996. Elec. engring. faculty Miss. State U., 1950-52; tech. staff Bell Labs., Murray Hill, N.J., 1957-61, head dept. speech and auditory rsch., 1961-67, head dept. acoustics rsch., 1967-85, dir. info. prins. rsch. lab., 1985-90; dir. ctr. for advanced info. processing Rutgers U., Piscataway, NJ, 1990—, v.p. for rsch. Piscataway, NJ, 1993—. Evaluation panel Nat. Bur. Standards/NRC, 1972—77; adv. panel on White House tapes U.S. Dist. Ct. for D.C., 1973—74; sci. adv. bd. Callier Center, U. Tex., Dallas, 1974—76; sci. adv. panel on voice comm. Nat. Security Agy., 1975—77. Author: Speech Analysis, Synthesis and Perception, 1972; contbr. articles to profl. jours. Recipient Disting. Svc. award in sci., Am. Speech and Hearing Assn., 1977, L.M. Ericsson Internat. prize in telecomms., 1985, Nat. Medal Sci., Nat. Medal Sci. Com., Pres. Clinton, 1996, N.J. R&D Coun. Sci. and Tech. medal, 2000; fellow, Marconi Internat., 1992. Fellow: IEEE (selection com. 1979—81, Edison medal 1986), Am. Acad. Arts and Scis., Acoustical Soc. Am. (assoc. editor Speech Comm. 1959—62, exec. coun. 1970—73, v.p. 1976—77, pres. 1978—79, Gold medal 1986); mem.: NAS (chmn. engring. sect. 1996—99), NAE, Acoustics, Speech and Signal Processing Soc. (v.p. 1967—68, pres. 1969—70, Achievement award 1970, Soc. award 1976), Eta Kappa Nu. Achievements include patents in field. Office: Rutgers U Advanced Info Processing Piscataway NJ 08854-8088 E-mail: jlf@caip.rutgers.edu.

FLANAGAN, JOANNA SCARLATA, lawyer; b. Pitts., Oct. 10, 1967; d. Charles Francis and Antonia (Lynch) Scarlata; m. Michael Joseph Flanagan, Aug. 10, 1996; children: Madelyn, Jack. BA in English, Cath. U. Am., 1989; JD, Duquesne U., 1994. Bar: Pa. 1994. Jud. law clk. to Hon. Bernard L. McGinley Commonwealth Ct. of Pa., Pitts., 1994-97; assoc. atty. Burns, White & Hickton, Pitts., 1997-98, Houston Harbaugh, Pitts., 1999—. Treas. young leadership bd. Girls Hope, Pitts., 1996—2001. Avocations: skiing, biking, walking, aerobics. Office: Houston Harbaugh 2 Chatham Ctr Fl 12 Pittsburgh PA 15219-3465

FLANAGAN, JOHN ANTHONY, lawyer, educator; b. Sioux City, Iowa, Nov. 29, 1942; s. J. Maurice and Lorna K. (Fowler) F.; m. Martha (Lang), May 8, 1982; children: Sean, Kathryn, Molly. BA, Iowa State U., 1964; JD, Georgetown U., 1968. Bar: Iowa, 1968; D.C., 1975; Ohio, 1977. Law clk. to judge U.S. Tax Ct., Washington, 1968-70; trial atty. U.S. Dept. Justice, Washington, 1970-74; prof. law U. Ohio, Cin., 1974-78; sr. tax ptnr. Graydon, Head, and Ritchey, Cin., 1978—. Adj. prof. U. Ohio, (Cin.), 1978—. Contbr. articles to profl. jour. Corp. mgr. United Way, Cin., 1988; head lawyers div. Fine Arts Fund, Cin., 1987-88; mem. Downtown Cin. Inc., 1995-2000. Mem. D.C. Bar Assn., Cin. Bar Assn.; Order of Coif. Roman Catholic. Avocations: gardening, golf, fly fishing. Home: 5 Walsh Ln Cincinnati OH 45208-3435 Office: Graydon Head & Ritchey 1900 5th-3rd Ctr PO Box 6464 Cincinnati OH 45202

FLANAGAN, JOSEPH PATRICK, advertising executive; b. Chgo., Jan. 6, 1938; s. Charles Larkin and Helen Mary (Sullivan) F.; children: Charlotte Ahern, Joseph P. Jr., Michael S., Larkin S., Brian A.; m. Carol Perkins, Nov. 6, 1999. BA, Mich. State U., 1959; MBA, U. Chgo., 1961. Dist. mgr. sales Time mag., Pitts. and Chgo., 1961-69; gen. mgr. Ctr. Advanced Research in Design, Chgo., 1969-75; v.p., dir. client services BBDO, Chgo., 1975-77; sr. v.p. IMPACT subs. Foote, Cone & Belding Comm. Co., Chgo., 1977-85, pres., 1985-99; corp. dir. sales promotion Foote, Cone & Belding Comm. Co., Chgo., 1987-99; pres. Flanagan Mktg., 1999—. Pres. Coun. of Sales Promotion Agys., 1986-89, also bd. dirs. Mem. governing bd. Chgo. Symphony Orch., 1974; v.p. Lyric Opera Guild, Chgo., 1974; trustee Loyola Acad.; bd. dirs. Count Theater; dir. arts and letters bd. Nat. Adv. Coun., Mich. State U.; bd. dirs. Total Focus Leo Burnett, Root-Lowell Mfg; client relationship exec. Diamond Cluster Internat., 1999—. Named Sales Promotion Profl. of Yr., Coun. Sales Promotion Agys., 1989; recipient Disting. Alumni award Mich. State U., 1991. Mem. Am. Assn. Advt. Agencies (chmn. sales promotion com.), Assn. of Promotion Mktg. Agys. Worldwide (Hall of Fame award 1998), Creek Club (Locust Valley, N.Y.). Roman Catholic. Avocations: classical music, opera. Home and Office: Flanagan Mktg 369 South Lake Dr Palm Beach FL 33480 Home (Summer): 334 Yacht Club Rd Oyster Bay NY 11771 E-mail: jpflanagansr@aol.com.

FLANAGAN, JOSEPH PATRICK, JR., lawyer; b. Wilkes-Barre, Pa., Sept. 18, 1924; s. Joseph P. and Grace B. F.; m. Mary Elizabeth Mayock, Aug. 5, 1950; children: Maureen Elizabeth, Joseph P. III. BS, U.S. Naval Acad., 1947; JD, U. Pa., 1952. Bar: Pa. 1953, U.S. Dist. Ct. (ea. dist.) Pa. 1953, U.S. Ct. Appeals (3d cir.) 1953, U.S. Supreme Ct. 1997. Assoc. Saul, Ewing, Remick & Saul, Phila., 1952-56; ptnr. Ballard, Spahr, Andrews & Ingersoll, Phila., 1956-94, chmn. pub. fin. dept., 1961-90. Editor: Practicing Law Inst., Health Facilities Financing, 1976; co-author: In Search of Capital-A Trustee's Guide to Hospital Financing; reviewing editor Disclosure Roles of Counsel in State and Local Government Securities Offerings. editor-in-chief: U. Pa. Law Rev., 1951-52; contbr. articles to profl. jours. Bd. dirs. Phila. Com. of 70, 1952-56; former trustee Wyoming Sem., Kingston, Pa.; former mem. bd. visitors U. Pa. Law Sch.; bd. dirs. John Bartram Assn.; adv. coun. of federalism Nat. Govs. Assn., 1988. Served to lt. (j.g.) USN, 1946-49. Fellow Am. Bar Found.; mem. ABA (past chmn. urban, state and local govt. sect.), Nat. Assn. Securities Dealers (regulation arbitrator 1998—), Phila. Bar Assn. (past chmn. bus. law sect., bd. govs., past founding chmn. tax exempt fin. com., past chmn. profl. edn. com., client's security fund com., fee disputes com.), Pa. Bar Assn., Pa. Bar Inst. (pres. 1983, chmn. curriculum and course planning com. 1976-88), Phila. Club, Racquet Club, Phila. Cricket Club, Chesapeake Bay Yacht Club, Army Navy Country Club of Va. Republican. Roman Catholic. Home: 401 E Mill Rd Flourtown PA 19031-1631 Office: Ballard Spahr Andrews & Ingersoll 1735 Market St Fl 49 Philadelphia PA 19103-7501

FLANAGAN, JUDY, special events professional, entertainment and marketing specialist, professional public speaker; b. Lubbock, Tex., Apr. 28, 1950; d. James Joseph II and Jean (Breckenridge) F. BS in Edn., Memphis State U., 1972; postgrad., Disney U., 1975-81, Valencia C.C., 1977-79, Rollins Coll., 1979; MS in Comm., U. Tenn., 2003. Cert. festival exec. Area/parade supr. Entertainment div. Walt Disney World, Orlando, Fla., 1972-81; parade dir. Gatlinburg (Tenn.) C. of C., 1981-85; entertainment prodn. mgr. The 1982 World's Fair, Knoxville, 1982; cons. Judy Flanagan Prodns./Spl. Events, Gatlinburg, 1982—, Miss U.S.A. Pageant, Knoxville, 1983; prodn. coord. Nashville Network, 1983; dir. sales River Terr. Resort, Gatlinburg, 1985-86; account exec. Park Vista Hotel, Gatlinburg, 1986-88; project coord. Universal Studios, Fla., 1988-90; dir. spl. events U. Tenn., Knoxville, 1990—. Dir. Neyland Stadium Expansion Dedication, 1996—; Vt. Bicentennial Events, 1994, 21st Century Campaign Major Events; prodn. mgr. 1984 World's Fair Parades and Spl. Events, New Orleans, Neil Sedaka rock video, Days of Our Lives daytime soap opera. Recipient Gatlinburg Homecoming award, 1986, World Lifetime Achievement award, 1993. Mem.: ASPCA, Tenn. Festivals and Events Assn. (bd. dirs.), Internat. Festivals and Events Assn. (cert. festival exec., found. bd.), Internat. Spl. Events Soc., Doris Day Animal League, Defenders of Wildlife, Humane Soc. U.S., U. Tenn. Soc. Pres. Club. Roman Catholic. Home: 350 Bruce Rd Gatlinburg TN 37738-5612 E-mail: judy-flanagan@utk.edu.

FLANAGAN, KATHLEEN THERESA, education educator; d. Robert and Elizabeth Flanagan; m. Randall Hendrick; 1 child. BA, Univ. N.C., Chapel Hill, N.C., 1976, MA, 1983, PhD, 1987. Lectr. Tunghai Univ., Taichung, Taiwan, 1979—81; prof. Longwood Univ., Farmville, Va., 1987—. Contbr. articles to profl. jour. Mem.: MLA.

FLANAGAN, LATHAM, JR., surgeon; b. Pitts., Dec. 2, 1936; s. Latham and Elizabeth Lansing (Bunting) Kimbrough; m. Elizabeth Ruth Losaw, June 26, 1961 (dec. May 1971); 1 child, Jennifer Ruth; m. Mary Jane Flanagan, Mar. 28, 1975; children: Sahale Ann, David Nooroa. MD, Duke U., 1961, student, 1957, MD, 1961. Diplomate Am. Bd. Surgery. Intern U. Calif., San Francisco, 1961-62; resident in surgery U. Oreg., Portland, 1962-66, chief resident in surgery, 1965-66; pvt. practice surgery Sacred Heart Hosp., Eugene, Oreg., 1968-84, 85—; clin. sr. instr. in surgery Oreg. Health Scis. U., Portland, 1968-84; assoc. prof. surgery U. Otago, Dunedin (New Zealand) Pub. Hosp., 1984-85; nat. surgeon Cook Islands, 1985; founder Oreg. Ctr. for Bariatric Surgery, Eugene, 1993—. Contbr. articles to profl. jours. Founder White Bird Clinic, Eugene, 1969-71; mem. adv. com. Planned Parenthood of Lane County, 1979-84, Lt. comdr. USNR, 1966-68, Vietnam. Fellow ACS (pres. Oreg. chpt. 1991-92); mem. AMA, Oreg. Med. Assn., Lane County med. Soc. (com. chair 1970s), Am. Soc. Bariatric Surgery (chair ins. com. 1991-94, councillor 1994-96, sec.-treas. 1996-98, pres. 1999-2000), North Pacific Surg. Soc., Eugene Surg. Soc. (pres. 1981). Republican. Avocations: mountaineering, photography, river running, scuba, raising llamas. Home: 31033 Foxridge Ln Eugene OR 97405-9589 Office: 655 E 11th Ave Ste 8 Eugene OR 97401-3621 *Honesty, sincerity and hard work gets you there. Not forgetting how to play - adventure -makes the journey worthwhile. Be not afraid to be different...to walk the less travelled path.*

FLANAGAN, MICHAEL BRENDAN, obstetrician/gynecologist; b. Ireland, 1917; s. Thomas Flanagan and Bridgid Conway; m. Vera Doreen Payne, Nov. 7, 1947; children: Michael Ashley, Amanda Jane, Veronica Margaret. MBBCh, Trinity Coll., 1942, MD, 1952. Diplomate Am. Bd. Obstetrics & Gynecology. Intern St. Mary's Hosp., San Francisco, 1953-54; resident in ob/gyn. Middlesex

County Hosp., London, 1948-52; staff St. Mary's Hosp., San Francisco, 1955-81, ret. honorary staff, 1981—. With Royal Navy, 1943-46. Fellow Am. Coll. Obstetrics & Gynecology, Am. Coll. Surgeons, Royal Coll. Obstetrics & Gynecology; mem. AMA. Home: 26317 Camino Real Carmel CA 93923-9241 E-mail: Flangan2@pacbell.net.

FLANAGAN, PATRICK SEAN LIAM, priest; b. Bethpage, N.Y., Dec. 16, 1964; s. Thomas Joseph Matthew and Claire Mary Agnes (Meiners) F. BS in Biology and Edn., Niagara U., 1987; MDiv in Theology, Sem. of Immaculate Conception, Lloyd Harbor, N.Y., 1992; postgrad., Loyola U. Cert. tchr., N.Y.; ordained priest, Roman Cath. Ch. Parish priest, dir. religious edn. Immaculate Conception Roman Cath. Ch., Phila., 1992-94; sci. tchr. Merion Mercy Acad., Merion Station, Pa., 1993-94; campus min., adj. prof. religious studies Niagara U., N.Y., 1994-98; adj. prof. theology St. John's U., Jamaica, NY, 2003—. Mem. Ancient Order of Hibernians (chaplain 1995-98). Republican. Avocations: computers, biking, travel. Office: St Johns Univ Vincentian Res 8000 Utopia Pkwy Jamaica NY 11439 E-mail: patrickflanagan@aol.com.

FLANAGAN, ROBERT JOSEPH, economics educator; b. New Haven, Dec. 16, 1941; s. Russell Joseph and Anne (Macauley) F.; m. Susan Rae Mendelsohn, Aug. 23, 1986. BA, Yale U., 1963; MA, U. Calif., 1966, PhD, 1970. Economist U.S. Dept. Labor, Washington, 1963-64; asst. prof. labor econs. Grad. Sch. Bus. U. Chgo., 1969-75; assoc. prof. labor econs. Grad. Sch. Bus. Stanford (Calif.) U., 1975-86; sr. staff economist Coun. of Econ. Advisors, Washington, 1978-79; sr. fellow The Brookings Instn., Washington, 1983-84; prof. labor econs. Grad. Sch. Bus., Stanford (Calif.) U., 1987-92, Matsushita prof. internat. labor econs. and econ. policy, 1993—, assoc. dean, 1996-99. Cons. OECD, Paris, 1988, U.S. Civil Rights Commn., Washington, 1982-83, NOAA, Washington, 1981; vis. scholar IMF, 1994, Australian Nat. U., 1990, 2000. Author: Labor Relations and Litigation Explosion, 1987; (with others) Unionism, Economic Stabilization and Income Policy, 1982, Economics of the Employment Relationship, 1989, numerous others; contbr. articles to profl. jours. Mem. Am. Econs. Assn., Indls. Rels. Rsch. Assn., Soc. Labor Economists. Office: Stanford U Grad Sch Bus Palo Alto CA 94305

FLANAGAN, TIMOTHY JAMES, criminal justice educator, university official; b. Pitts., May 16, 1951; s. Norman Patrick and Dorothy Helen (Hoffmann) F.; m. Nancy Ann Rosenbaum, Aug. 4, 1973; children: Erin E., Kevin C. BA, Gannon U., 1973; MA, SUNY, Albany, 1974, PhD, 1980. Asst. prof., then assoc. prof. Sch. Criminal Justice, SUNY Rockefeller Coll. Pub. Affairs and Policy, 1982—91; prof. criminal justice, dean Coll. Criminal Justice Sam Houston State U., Huntsville, Tex., 1991—98; provost SUNY, Brockport, 1998—. Presenter numerous papers to profl. meetings, also panel convenor, chmn., discussant; exec. dir. Michael J. Hindelang Criminal Justice Rsch. Ctr., Inc., Albany, 1981-83. Co-editor: Sourcebook of Criminal Justice Statistics - 1978-92; editor: Jour. Criminal Justice Edn., 1989-93; contbr. articles and book revs. to profl. jours., chpts. to books. Recipient Disting. Alumnus award SUNY Rockefeller Coll. Pub. Affairs and Policy, 1992. Fellow: Acad. Criminal Justice Scis.; mem.: Harvard U. Inst. for Ednl. Mgmt., Am. Coun. on Edn. (coun. fellows, leadership devel. fellow 1988—89), Am. Soc. Criminology, Pi Gamma Mu, Blue Key, Golden Key. Roman Catholic. Avocations: photography, bicycling, computers, sports, reading. Office: SUNY Brockport Brockport NY 14420-2914

FLANAGAN, VAN KENT, journalist; b. San Antonio, Sept. 20, 1945; s. Marquiss Monroe and Nina Louise (Fowler) F.; m. Janet Dorothy Robinson, Dec. 16, 1972. BA, Angelo State U., 1968. Reporter, editor San Angelo Standard-Times, Tex., 1966-68; copy editor Fort Lauderdale News, Fla., 1973-74; from news editor to editor Sun. Express-News, San Antonio, 1974-79; from newsman to bur. chief AP, Phila., 1979-80, Columbia, S.C., 1980-82, Bismarck, N.D., 1982-83, Nashville, 1983—. Served with U.S. Army, 1968-72, Vietnam. Decorated Bronze star. Mem.: Soc. Profl. Journalists (pres. Mid. Tenn. chpt. 1986—87, 2000—03). Presbyterian. Avocations: walking, hiking, reading novels and non-fiction. Home: 613 Riverview Dr Franklin TN 37064-5514 Office: AP 215 Centerview Dr Ste 110 Brentwood TN 37027-5246 E-mail: flana_k@bellsouth.net.

FLANAGAN KELLY, ANNE MARIE, academic administrator; b. North Kingstown, R.I., Apr. 13, 1954; d. John James Flanagan and Margaret Mary Ortstein; children: Timothy Kelly, Brigid Kelly. Cert. advanced studies, BA, SUNY; MEd, Pa. State U. Cert. sch. dist. adminstr., sch. adminstrv. supr., nursery, kindergarten and grades 1-6, spl. edn. K-12. Grade 4 tchr. Narrowsburgh Ctrl. Sch. Dist., Narrowsburgh, NY, 1976; spl. edn. tchr. Tompkins-Seneca-Tioga BOCES, Ithaca, NY, 1977—80; learning disabilities specialist Ithaca City Sch. Dist., Ithaca, NY, 1980—81; head tchr. Adolescent Day Sch./Cmty. Treatment Ctr., Worcester, Mass., 1981—83; resource/cons./remedial tchr. Onteora Ctrl. Sch. Dist., Boiceville, NY, 1986—93; supr. spl. edn. Ulster BOCES, New Paltz, NY, 1993—. Adv. bd. 21st Century Grant- Ulster BOCES and Ellenville CSD, New Paltz, NY, 2001—; mem. NY State Coun. of Admstrs. Spl. Edn., NY. Religious edn. tchr. St. Joseph's Ch., Kingston, NY, 1989—2000, eucharistic min., 1996—2003; merit badge counselor Boy Scouts of Am. Troop 20, Hurley, NY, 1999—2003; mem. Kingston H.S. Alumni Chior, 2002—. Fellow Spl. Edn., US Office Edn., 1976-1977; grantee VATEA, NY State Edn. Dept., 1995—97. Mem.: Regional Bd. N.Y. State Parent Tchr. Assn. (scholarship chairperson 1993—95, Hudson Valley chpt.), Sch. Administrator's Assn. of N.Y. State, N.Y. State United Tchrs., SUNY Cortland Alumni Assn., SUNY New Paltz Alumni Assn., Penn State U. Alumni Assn., N.Y. State Parent Tchr. Student Assn., Coun. for Exceptional Children, Assn. Supervision and Curriculum Devel. Roman Catholic. Avocations: reading, singing, church activities, athletic events. Home: 28 Village Ct Kingston NY 12401 Office: Ulster BOCES 175 Route 32 N New Paltz NY 12561 Personal E-mail: akelly342@aol.com. E-mail: akelly@mhric.org.

FLANARY, DONALD HERBERT, JR., lawyer; b. Texarkana, Ark., July 27, 1949; s. Donald Herbert and Tenney-Margaret (Webb) Flanary; m. Gina Lynn Rexrod; children: Donald Herbert III, Shannon Gail, Lauren Paige, David Tyler, John Paul, Noah Toliver. BS with honors, Tex. A&M U., 1971; JD, U. Houston, 1974. Bar: Tex. 1974, U.S. Dist. Ct. (no. dist.) Tex. 1975, U.S. Dist. Ct. (ea. dist.) Tex. 1976, U.S. Dist. Ct. (so. dist.) Tex. 1982, U.S. Tax Ct. 1982, U.S. Ct. Appeals (5th cir.) 1976, U.S. Ct. Appeals (11th cir.) 1984, U.S. Supreme Ct. 1983. Law clk. Hon. Mary Lou Robinson U.S. Dist. Ct., Amarillo, Tex., 1974—75; asst. dist. atty. Dallas County, Tex., 1975—76; ptnr. Henderson Bryant & Wolfe, Sherman, Tex., 1976—87, Vial Hamilton Koch & Knox, Dallas, 1988—99, Arter and Hadden, Dallas, 1999—2002, Flanary & Carter, Dallas, 2002—. Lectr. for bar assns. on tort law, 1981—84. Bd. dirs. Texoma Valley coun. Boy Scouts Am., Cancer Soc., Sherman. Named one of Outstanding Young Men Am., Jaycees, 1981. Fellow: Tex. Bar Found. (life); mem.: Am. Bd. Trial Advocates (cert.), Am. Bd. Profl. Liability Attys. (cert.), State Bar Assn. Tex. (bd. dirs. 1986—89, pres.-elect 1999), Nat. Bd. Trial Adv., Bd. Legal Specialization (civil trial law), Internat. Assn. Ins. Counsel (bd. cert. personal jury trial law), Grayson County Bar Assn. (pres. 1983—84), Tex. Assn. Def. Counsel (bd. dirs. 1981 1984, bd. dirs. 1986—88). Democrat. Roman Catholic. E-mail: dflanary@flanarycarter.com.

FLANDERS, DONALD HARGIS, manufacturing company executive; b. Memphis, Apr. 26, 1924; s. Henry Jackson and Mae (Hargis) Flanders; m. Phala Kathryn Davis, Dec. 15, 1946; children: Donald Hargis, Dudler Kennedy, Kathryn Cotten. Student, Tex. Christian U., 1943; BBA, Baylor U., 1947. Dir. cost acctg., purchasing agt. McCoy-Couch Furniture Mfg. Co., Benton, Ark., 1947-50, Garrison Furniture Co., Ft. Smith, Ark., 1950-54; pres., founder Flanders Mfg. Co., Ft. Smith, 1954-70, Flanders Industries, Inc., Ft. Smith, 1970—. Chmn. bd., CEO Lloyd/Flanders Industries, Inc., Menominee, Mich., bd. dirs. 1st Nat. Bank, Ft. Smith. Chmn. exec. com. Ft. Smith Freight Bur., 1960-61; chmn. furniture bd. govs. Dallas Mkt. Ctr., 1968; exec. com. Ark. Coun. on Econ. Edn., 1964-67; mem. Ark. Small Bus. Adv. Coun., 1966-68; chmn. Ft. Smith United Fund drive, 1962; dist. chmn. Boy Scouts Am., Ft. Smith, 1960-62, pres. Westark Area coun. 1963-65, regional exec. com., 1964-72, vice chmn. region 5, 1967-69, chmn. region 5, 1969-72, nat. exec. bd., 1969-77; Com. of 100, 1965—; exec. dir. Ark. Indsl. Devel. Commn., 1981-83; trustee, vice chmn. Sparks Regional Med. Ctr., Hendrix Coll., Westark Coll. Found., North Ark. Conf. 1986-95; bd. dirs. Meth. Ch. Served from apprentice seaman to lt. (s.g.) USNR, 1943-46. Recipient Silver Antelope, Silver Beaver, Silver Buffalo, Disting. Eagle Scout awards Boy Scouts Am., Free Enterprise award, 1964; named Industrialist of Yr. Ft. Smith Realtors Bd., 1965. Mem. SW Furniture Mfg. Assn. (pres. 1963), Ft. Smith C. of C. (dir. 1961-63, 73-75), Ark. Wood Products Assn. (dir. 1965-68), Summer Casual Furniture Mfrs. Assn. (pres. 1992-94, chmn. 1994-96), Masons (33 degree), Shriners, KT, Delta Sigma Pi. Methodist. Home: 1925 Jamaica Way Punta Gorda FL 33950-5176 Office: PO Box 1788 1901 Wheeler Ave Fort Smith AR 72902-1788 also: 20 Berry Hill Rd Fort Smith AR 72903-3501 E-mail: donf2@comcast.net., dhf@ipa.net.

FLANDERS, ELEANOR CARLSON, community volunteer; b. Spearville, Kans., Mar. 27, 1916; d. Carl Edward and Laura Rebecca (Pine) Carlson; m. Laurence Burdette Flanders, Jr., June 6, 1941; children: Laurel F. Umile, John C., Lynette F. Moyer, Paul L. BA, cert. journalism, U. Colo., 1938; family inst. cert., Vassar Coll., 1958. Examiner of credits U. Colo., Boulder, 1938-41; stock market analyst trust dept. First Nat. Bank, Longmont, Colo., 1970-85; landlady, investor St. Vrain Hist. Soc., Longmont, 1954—. Vice pres. elect, St. Vrain Valley Sch. Bd., 1978-84. Contbr. articles to profl. jours. Precinct worker, del. Rep. Party, Longmont and Boulder, 1941—; club leader 4-H Boulder County, 1947-63; pres., charter mem. Boulder County Mental Health Clinic, 1947-60; mem. PEO Sisterhood, 1948—; trustee, investment com. First Congl. Ch., Longmont, 1960-2001; North Colo. area rep. Am. Field Svc., Longmont, 1965-70; coord. tutoring program Boulder County Juvenile Ct., 1965-81; trustee, farm mgr. Carl and Laura Carlson Trust, Oberlin, Kans., 1971-85; trustee, dir. Colo. 4-H Youth Fund, Ft. Collins, 1973-86; trustee, investment counsel Am. Mothers Endowment Fund, N.Y.C., 1979-90; active St. Vrain Edn. Found. Endowment Fund, Longmont, 1985—; trustee, bd. dirs. Longmont Cable Trust, 1986-88; nat. treas. Am. Mothers, N.Y., 1988-90; elected 2-term dir. St. Vrain Valley Sch. Bd., 1978-86. Mem.: AAUW (charter), St. Vrain Edn. Found. (founder, dir., pres. 1984—), St. Vrain Hist. Soc. (dir., pres. 1970—), Sunshine Club, U. Colo. Alumni Assn. (dir., sec. 1950—58), Delta Kappa Gamma (hon.). Avocations: gardening, travel, duplicate bridge, reading, writing. Home: 917 W 3rd Ave Longmont CO 80501-5413

FLANDERS, HENRY JACKSON, JR., religious studies educator; b. Malvern, Ark., Oct. 2, 1921; s. Henry Jackson and Mae (Hargis) F.; m. Tommie Lou Pardew, Apr. 19, 1944; children: Janet Flanders Mitchell, Jack III. BA, Baylor U., 1943; BD, So. Bapt. Theol. Sem., 1948, PhD, 1950. Ordained to ministry Bapt. Ch., 1941. Asst. prof., assoc. prof. Furman U., Greenville, S.C., 1950-55, prof., chaplain, chmn. dept. religion, 1955-62; pastor First Bapt. Ch., Waco, Tex., 1962-69; prof. religion Baylor U., Waco, Tex., 1969-92, chmn. dept., 1980-83. Chmn., trustee Golden Gate Bapt. Theol. Sem., Mill Valley, Calif., 1966-76; chaplain Tex. Ranger Commn., 1965—; mem. exec. com. Bapt. Gen. Conv. Tex., Dallas, 1966-68. Author: (with R.W. Crapps and D.A. Smith) People of the Convenant, 1963, 73, 88, 96; (with Bruce Cresson) Introduction to the Bible, 1973; TV spkr. Lessons for Living, WFBC-TV, 1957-62. Trustee Baylor U., Waco, Tex., 1964-68; trustee Hillcrest Bapt. Hosp., 1963 64; chmn. Heart of Tex. Red Cross, 1967-68; narrator Waco Cotton Palace Pageant, 1970-80; chaplain Tex. Aero Commn., 1986—; pastor emeritus First Bapt. Ch., Waco, 1987; mem. grievance oversight com. Tex. Bar, 1979-87. Served to 1st. lt. USAAC, 1943-45, ETO. Named disting. alumnus Baylor U., 1986; grantee Furman U., 1960; grantee Baylor U., 1977, 82 Mem. Assn. Bapt. Profs. Religion (pres. 1958-59), AAUP (chpt. pres. 1973), Soc. Bibl. Lit., Am. Acad. Religion, Inst. Antiquity and Christianity, Waco Bapt. Ministerial Assn. (pres. 1967-68) Lodges: Rotary; Shriners. Home: 3820 Chateau Ave Waco TX 76710-7102 Office: Baylor U Religion Dept Waco TX 76798

FLANDERS, LAURENCE BURDETTE, JR., retired lawyer; b. Longmont, Colo., Feb. 7, 1917; s. Laurence Burdette and Harriet (Secor) F.; m. Eleanor Carlson, June 6, 1941; children— Laurel Flanders Umile, John C., Lynette Flanders Moyer, Paul L. B.S. with honors, U. Colo., 1938; J.D., 1940. Bar: Colo. 1940, U.S. Dist. Ct. Colo. 1965. Dep. dist. atty. Boulder County, Colo., 1948-52; ptnr. Flanders, Wood, Sonnesyn & Steinkamp, Longmont, Colo., 1946-89; pres., trustee Flanders Found., Inc. Bd. trustees Colo. Bar Found., 1967-87; mem. Longmont Charter Conv., 1961; mem. Longmont Water Bd., 1952-85, chmn. Longmont Long Range Planning Commn., 1971-72. Served with USNR, 1942-45. Fellow Am. Coll. Probate Counsel, Am. Bar Found.; mem. Colo. Bar Assn. (bd. of govs. 1963-67, v.p. bd. govs. 1967-68, chmn. probate and trust law sect. 1965-66), Boulder County Bar Assn., Am. Judicature Soc., Delta Sigma Pi, Order of Coif. Republican. Mem. United Ch. of Christ. Clubs: Rotary Internat., Boulder Country, Masons. Home: 917 3rd Ave Longmont CO 80501-5413

FLANDERS, MELANIE G. information architect; b. Agaña, Micronesia, Oct. 7, 1955; d. Mack H. and Rachel L. Flanders. BFA, U.S. Internat. U. SPVA, San Diego, 1977. Cert. User Info. Mapping, Inc., 1984. Engring. writer Gen. Dynamics Corp, WDSC, San Diego, 1979—81; software field engr. Gen. Dynamics Corp. Electronics Divsn., San Diego, 1981—84; stds. admin. Fed. Res. Sys., Dallas, 1984—86; sr. tech. writer Bus. Control Sys., Dallas, 1986—87, tech. writer, software tester, 1988—90; tech. writer BMC Software, Houston, 1991—95; info. arch. Dynasty Techs., Inc., Kingwood, Tex., 1995—98; chief info. arch. KnowledgeMasters, Inc., Houston, 1998—. Adj. instr. Houston C.C. Sys., 2000—01, curriculum adv. bd., 2002—; adj. lectr. U. of Houston-Downtown, 2002—. Author: (tech. book) Unleashing the Power of FrameMaker 6.0/7.0: Mastering the Basics, (book) More Than Melancholy, (tech. manual) Intro. to DYNASTY (Soc. for Tech. Comm. award of Merit, 1998), DYNASTY User's Guide (Soc. for Tech. Comm. award of Achievement, 1998). Recipient Disting. Chpt. Svc. award, Soc. for Tech. Communication, 2002. Mem.: Fedn. of Houston Profl. Women (women of excellence banquet program 1998—99), Am. Bus. Women's Assn. (newsletter editor 1997—98, Regional newsletter award 1998), Assn. of Authors and Publs. (bd. mem. 2002—), Soc. for Tech. Comm. (various coms. 1989, numerous Certs. of Appreciation 1994—2003). Avocation: travel. Office: KnowledgeMasters Inc 11850-G Bissonnet #203 Houston TX 77099 Personal E-mail: melanie_flanders@hotmail.com. E-mail: melanie@knowledgemastersinc.com.

FLANDERS, PAULA L. director public health; b. Bismarck, ND, Feb. 4, 1949; d. Hubert R. and Marian E. Freise; m. Marlow L. Flanders, June 9, 1971; children: Trevor Jay, Bridgette Lynn, Ian Turner. BSN Summa Cum Laude, Jamestown Coll., 1971. Dir. nursing, adminstr. Golden Manor, Inc., Steele, ND, 1971-74; home health nurse Home Med. Resources, Inc., Bismarck, ND, 1976-87; health facilities surveyor ND Dept. Health, Bismarck, ND, 1987-92, mgr. licensing and cert., 1992-98; dir. Bismarck-Burleigh Pub. Health, Bismarck, ND, 1998—. Environ. health practioner NDEHP Assn.; dir. Bridging the Dental Gap; mem. adv. bd. Joanne's Healthcare Clinic for Homeless, Bismarck/Mandan Local Emergency Planning Com.; adv. bd. Sch. Nursing U. Mary, United Tribes Tech. Coll.& Medcenter; mem. Interhosp. Bioterrorism Task Force, Bismarck Interagy. Task Force; adv. bd. United Tribes Tech. Coll. Sch. of Nursing, Bismarck Early Childhood Edn. Progrm. Cmty. health nurse, Pettibone, 1972—, 4-H leader, 1984-97. Mem. ND Nurses Assn., Childrens Svc. Coord. Cmty. (chair), Bd. of Dir., ND Pub. Health Assn., ND Pub. Health Adminstrs. Avocations: photography, travel, family. Home: 2190 47th Ave SE Pettibone ND 58475-9346

FLANDERS, RAYMOND ALAN, dentist, governmental health agency administrator; b. Bangor, Maine, Jan. 4, 1929; s. Carroll Benjamin and Mary (Watson) F.; m. Anne-Liss Teisen; children: Molly Olivia and Michael Benjamin (twins), Katherine Todd Mohan, James C. Todd. Student, Colgate U., 1948-50; BS, U. Miami, Fla., 1955; DDS, U. Md., 1959; MPH, U. Mich., 1979. Mem. faculty W.Va. U., Morgantown, 1964-65; program dir. Project Hope, Brazil, 1976-78; mem. faculty Coll. Dentistry U. Alagoas, Maceio, Brazil, 1976-78; regional dental dir. Va. State Health Dept., Richmond, 1970-76, 79-85; mem. faculty Med. Coll. Va., Richmond, 1980-85; state dental dir. Ill. Dept. Health, Springfield, 1985-96; mem. faculty Coll. Dental Medicine So. Ill. U., Alton, 1985-96; mem. faculty Coll. Dentistry Sch. Pub. Health U. Ill., Chgo., 1990-96; dental cons. Aetna U.S. Healthcare, 1998—2003. Cons. Project Esperanca, Amazon River, Brazil, 1981, Project HOPE/U.S.A.I.D., Grenada, West Indies, 1984, Project HOPE, Honduras, 1986, Am. Dental Assn., Brazil and Guyana, 1992. Contbr. articles to profl. jours. Served to capt. U.S. Army, 1946-47, 50-51, 60-63. Recipient Sec's Excellence in Health Promotion Award, 1990, Ranking 5th, Age Group 60-65, Western Tennis Assn., 1989, Gold Medal, Singles and Doubles Tennis, Ranked 4th Nat., Age Group 65-70, Sr. Olympics, 1991, Gold Medal, Singles Tennis, Age Group 70-75, 1999; fellow USPHS fellow, 1978—79. Mem. ADA (Preventive Dentistry award 1983, Cmty. Preventive Dentistry award 1990, 95), Ill. Dental Assn., Assn. State Territorial Dental Dirs. (exceptional achievement award 1998), Am. Assn. Pub. Health Dentists, Ill. Pub. Health Assn., Va. Dental Assn. Home: 5 Whittakers Mill Williamsburg VA 23185 E-mail: rafalt@aol.com.

FLANIGAN, JAMES J(OSEPH), journalist; b. N.Y.C., June 6, 1936; s. James and Jane (Whyte) F.; m. Patricia Quatrine, Nov. 28, 1997; children: Michael, Siobhan Jane. BA, Manhattan Coll., 1961. Fin. writer N.Y. Herald Tribune, 1957-66; bur. chief, asst. mng. editor Forbes Mag., 1966-86; bus. columnist, sr. econs. editor L.A. Times, 1986—. Office: LA Times 202 W 1st St Los Angeles CA 90012 E-mail: jim.flanigan@latimes.com.

FLANIGAN, LYNN FLOURNOY, nurse, social worker and administrator; b. Bklyn., Mar. 15, 1952; d. James Horner and Jacqueline Lockhart (Smith) Flournoy; m. Daniel Philip Flanigan, Sept. 22, 1984; children: Margaret Woodhull, James Keel, Ryan Howland. BSN, Hartwick Coll., 1975; MSW, U. Md., Balt., 1981. RN, Md.; lic. clin. social worker, Md.; cert. profl. in quality assurance. Clin. nurse Johns Hopkins Hosp., Balt., 1975-78, clin. psychotherapist, 1978-81; rehab. nurse cons. Linda Lee Cosby RN, BSN, PA, Balt., 1981-82; program coord. Sheppard and Enoch Pratt Hosp., Balt., 1982-85, quality assurance adminstr., 1985-89, clin. policy adminstr., 1989—91, dir. quality and evaluation svcs., 1992-96, dir. med. psychiatry, 1996-2000, regional dir. gen. hosp. managed svcs., 2000—. Author: (with others) Modern Hospital Psychiatry, 1988. Active Spl. Olympics. Avocations: sailing, skiing, travelling. Office: Sheppard Pratt Health Sys 6501 N Charles St PO Box 6815 Baltimore MD 21285-6815 E-mail: lflanigan@sheppardpratt.org.

FLANIGAN, RICHARD JOSEPH, retired career officer, company executive; b. Bangor, Maine, Oct. 5, 1948; s. Thomas Edmund and Mildred Marion (Myshrall) F.; m. Natalie Jean Rogers, Dec. 27, 1971; children: Nathan, Isaac, Bridget, Patrick. BSME, U. Maine, 1970; MS in Aero. Engring., Naval Postgrad. Sch., 1978; cert. environ. studies, Delaware Valley Coll., 1994; BS in Environ. Sci., Thomas Edison State Coll., Trenton, N.J., 1997; MS in Computer INfo. Sci., LaSalle U., 2002. Registered profl. engr., Va., Pa. Commd. ensign USN, 1972, advanced through grades to lt. commdr., 1981; program mgr. Vitronics, Inc., Eatontown, N.J., 1992-2001, Lockheed Martin Corp., Tinton Falls, N.J., 2001—. Mem. low level radio active waste adv. panel Pa. Dept. Environ. Regulation, 1993—. Twp. activist Day Care Home Assn., Newtown, Pa., 1989; meeting sponsor Suprs. Election Com., Newtown, 1988; coach Upper Makefield (Pa.) Soccer Assn., 1986-89; troop leader Bucks County Chpt. Boy Scouts Am., Upper Makefield, 1986-87. Mem. NSPE, Nat. Assn. Environ. Profls., Tau Kappa Epsilon. Avocations: skiing, tennis. Office: SFAE-C3S-AD-PLT Bldg 2705 Fort Monmouth NJ 07703-5402

FLANIGAN, ROBERT DANIEL, JR., academic administrator; b. Lithonia, Ga., Apr. 14, 1949; s. Robert Daniel and Maggie (Mabry) F.; m. Anne Butler, Dec. 12, 1970. BA, Clark Coll., 1970; MBA, Emory U., 1982. Auditor Arthur Andersen & Co., Atlanta, 1969-70; comptr. Spelman Coll., Atlanta, 1970-75, bus. mgr., 1975-81, exec. dir. bus. and fin. affairs, 1981-82, v.p. bus. and fin. affairs, 1982-94, v.p., treas., 1994—. Mem. Atlanta Bus. League, Inc.; bd. dirs. Managed Comp Ins. Co., The Common Fund. Bd. dirs. Leadership Atlanta, Paideia Sch., Childrens Sch.; mem. Leadership Atlanta. Mem.: Am. Mgmt. Assn., Nat. Assn. Coll. and Univ. Bus. Officers (fin. cons.), Nat. Assn. Coll. Aux. Svcs., Nat. Assn. Accts., 100 Black Men of Atlanta, Alpha Phi Omega. Democrat. Baptist. Office: 350 Spelman Ln SW Atlanta GA 30314-4399

FLANIGEN, EDITH MARIE, materials scientist, consultant; Rsch. fellow materials sci. UOP Tarrytown (N.Y.) Tech. Ctr., ret.; cons. White Plains, N.Y. Recipient Perkin medal, Soc. Chem. Ind., 1992, Francis P. Garvan-John M. Olin medal, Am. Chem. Soc., 1993. Home: 502 Woodland Hills Rd White Plains NY 10603-3136

FLANNAGAN, ROY CATESBY, JR., English literature educator, editor; b. Richmond, Va., Dec. 2, 1938; s. Roy Catesby Flannagan Sr. and Victoria (Iler) Hall; m. Julia Porter, June 8, 1962 (div. 1966); children: Roy Catesby III, Julia Wickham Flannagan; m. Anne Jacqueline Villers, Dec. 30, 1984; 1 child, Elisabeth Welsby Flannagan. BA, Washington & Lee U., 1960; MA, U. Va., 1961, PhD, 1966. Asst. prof. Va. Mil. Inst., Lexington, 1965-66, Ohio U., Athens, 1966-70, assoc. prof., 1970, prof., 1981—; scholar-in-residence U. S.C., Beaufort. Advisor Humanist Electronic Seminar, King's Coll., London, 1990—; advisor Text-Encoding Initiative, 1990—; editorial cons. Shakspeare-L, U. Toronto, Can., 1990—, Ficino Seminar, 1990—. Editor Milton Quar. Jour., 1966—, John Milton: Paradise Lost, 1993 (Irene Samuel award Milton Soc. of Am. 1994), Oxford Electronic Text Milton, 1992. Folger Shakespeare Libr. fellow, 1967; Fulbright grantee, 1969. Mem.: MLA, Internat. Milton Symposium, Milton Soc. Am. (pres. 1987—88, honoree scholar 2001), Renaissance English Text Soc. (bd. dirs. 2000—, bd. dirs. 2002), Renaissance Soc. Am. Avocations: newspaper writing, book designing, photography, tennis. Office: Univ SC Beaufort SC 29902 Home: 1201 King St Beaufort SC 29902 E-mail: roy@gwm.sc.edu.

FLANNAGAN, WILLIAM PATRICK, music educator; b. Bristol, Va., Dec. 25, 1952; s. Charles Bascom and Margaret Moore Flannagan; m. Della Elizabeth Luffman, Aug. 24, 1974; children: Mary Margaret, Charles Grady. BA in Psychology, King Coll., 1974; MusB in Ch. Music, Westminster Choir Coll., 1977, MusM in Choral Conducting, 1978; PhD in Musicology, Cath. U. Am., 1995. Min. music First United Meth. Ch., Ozark, Ala., 1978—82; prof. King. Coll., Briston, 1982—. Tenor soloist The Sophisticates, Johnson City, Tenn., 1999—; chorus master Kingsport Symphony Chorus, Tenn., 2001; music dir. Bristol Concert Choir, 2002—. Contbr. articles. Vol. Little League Baseball, Bristol, 1990—. Mem.: Am. Choral Dir. Assn., Rotary (Paul Harris fellow 1991). Avocations: bridge, reading, sports. Office: King Coll 1350 King College Rd Bristol TN 37620 Fax: 423-968-4456 E-mail: wpf@3wave.com.

FLANNELLY, KEVIN J. psychologist, research analyst; b. Jersey City, Nov. 26, 1949; s. John J. and Mary C. (Walsh) F.; m. Laura T. Adams, Jan. 10, 1981. BA in Psychology, Jersey City State Coll., 1972; MS in Psychology, Rutgers U., 1975; PhD in Psychology, U. Hawaii, 1983. Rsch. asst. dept. psychology U. Ill., Champaign, 1972-73; rsch. intern Alcohol Behavior Rsch. Lab. Rutgers U., New Brunswick, N.J., 1973-75; rsch. scientist Edward R. Johnstone Tng. and Rsch. Ctr., Bordentown, N.J., 1975-78; teaching asst. dept. psychology U. Hawaii, Honolulu, 1980-81, rsch. asst. Pacific Biomed. Rsch. Ctr., 1981-83, asst. prof. Bekesy Lab. Neurobiology, 1983-85; rsch. statistician, statewide transp. planning office Hawaii Dept. Transportation, Honolulu, 1986-89; researcher Office of Lt. Gov., Honolulu, 1989-93; legis. dir., policy analyst energy and environ. protection com. State House of Reps., 1994; with Office of Gov. of State of Hawaii, Honolulu, 1994-97; dir. rsch. Ctr. Psychol. Rsch., Honolulu, 1997 2001; assoc. dir. rsch. The HealthCare Chaplaincy, N.Y.C., 2001—. Instr. dept. social scis. Honolulu C.C., 1981; mem. State Ridesharing Task Force, 1987; staff mem. gov's. subcabinet on early childhood edn. and childcare, 1989, Hawaii task force on ednl. governance, 1991-92; mem. Gov's. Office State Planning, environ. scanning project, 1992-94; v.p. Ctr. Psychosocial Rsch., Honolulu, 1987—; ptnr. Flannelly Cons., 1991—; rsch. dir. Mktg. Rsch. Inst., 1992—; adj. prof. Hawaii Pacific U., 1998; mem. Gov. and Mayor Joint Waikiki Task Force, 1998. Editor: Biological Perspective on Aggression, 1984, Introduction to Psychology, 1987; reviewer 8 sci. and profl. jours., 1978—; grant reviewer NSF, 1984-92; contbr. numerous articles to profl. jours. Polit. survey cons., Honolulu, 1988—; transp. cons., Honolulu, 1989—; mktg. cons., Honolulu, 1990—. Grantee NIH, 1984, Fed. Hwy. Adminstrn., 1987; N.J. State scholar N.J. Dept. Higher Edn., 1968-72. Fellow Internat. Soc. Rsch. on Aggression; mem. AAAS, APA, Am. Psychol. Soc., Am. Statis. Assn., Internat. Soc. Comparative Psychology, N.Y. Acad. Scis., Psychonomic Soc., Sigma Xi. Achievements include research on aggression, educational testing, mental-health services, social and emotional behavior, transportation planning, stochastic models of decision-making. Home: 445 Kaiolu St Apt 1006 Honolulu HI 96815-2239 E-mail: kjflannelly@worldnet.att.net.

FLANNELLY, LAURA T. mental health nurse, nursing educator, researcher; b. Bklyn., Nov. 7, 1952; d. George A. Adams and Eleanor (Barragry) Mulhearn; m. Kevin J. Flannelly, Jan. 10, 1981. BS in Nursing, Hunter Coll., 1974; MSN, U. Hawaii, 1984, PhD in Ednl. Psychology, 1996. RN, N.Y., Hawaii. Psychiat.

nurse Bellevue Hosp., N.Y.C., 1975, asst. head nurse, 1975-77; psychiat. nurse White Plains (N.Y.) Med. Ctr., 1978-79; community mental health nurse South Beach Psychiat. Ctr., N.Y.C., 1979-81; psychiat. nurse The Queen's Med. Ctr., Honolulu, 1981-83; crisis worker Crisis Response Systems Project, Honolulu, 1983-86; instr. nursing U. Hawaii, Honolulu, 1985-92, asst. prof., 1992—, assoc. grad. faculty, 1998—; adj. instr. nursing Hawaii Loa Coll., Honolulu, 1988; assoc. prof. Am. Samoa Community Coll., Honolulu, 2000—, adj. instr. nursing, 1987, 89, 90. Mem. adv. bd., planning com. Psychiat. Day Hosp. of The Queen's Med. Ctr., Honolulu, 1981-82; program coord. Premenstrual Tension Syndrome Conf., Honolulu, 1984; dir. Ctr. Psychosocial Rsch., Honolulu, 1987—; program moderator 1st U.S-Japan Health Behavioral Conf., Honolulu, 1988; faculty Ctr. for Asia-Pacific Exch., 1995-99, Internat. Conf. on Transcultural Nursing, Honolulu, 1990; mem. bd. dirs. U. Hawaii Profl. Assembly, 1994-97; mem. Hawaii State Coun. Mental Health, 1997—. Contbr. articles to profl. jours. N.Y. State Bd. Regents scholar, 1970-74; NIH nursing trainee, 1983-84; grantee U. Hawaii, 1986, 91, Hawaii Dept. Health, 1990. Fellow Internat. Soc. Rsch. on Aggression; mem. AAAS, APA, Am. Ednl. Rsch. Assn., Am. Psychol. Soc., Am. Psychiat. Nurses Assn., Am. Statis. Assn., Nat. League for Nursing, N.Y. Acad. Scis., Sigma Theta Tau (rec. sec. chpt. 1995-97). Achievements include research on aggressive behavior, educational testing, learning styles, problem-based learning, cross-cultural differences, statistical modeling. Office: U Hawaii Sch Nursing Webster Hall Honolulu HI 96822 E-mail: flannel@hawaii.edu.

FLANNERY, ELLEN JOANNE, lawyer; b. Bklyn., Dec. 13, 1951; d. William Rowan and Mary Jane (Hamilla) Flannery. AB cum laude, Mount Holyoke Coll., 1973; JD cum laude, Boston U., 1978. Bar: Mass. 1978, D.C. 1979, U.S. Ct. Appeals (D.C. cir.) 1979, U.S. Dist. Ct. D.C. 1980, U.S. Ct. Appeals (4th cir.) 1981, U.S. Supreme Ct. 1983. Spl. asst. to commr. of health Mass. Dept. Pub. Health, Boston, 1973-75; law clk. U.S. Ct. Appeals D.C. cir., Washington, 1978-79; assoc. Covington & Burling, Washington, 1979-86, ptnr., 1986—. Lectr. ins. U. Va. Sch. Law, 1984—90, Boston U. Law Sch., 1993; bd. visitors Boston U. Sch. Law, 1995—; lectr. ins. U. Md. Sch. Law, 1994; mem. Nat. Conf. Lawyers and Scientists, AAAS-ABA, 1989—92; chair Fellows Adv. Rsch. Commn., 2002—. Contbr. to articles to profl. jours. Fellow: Am. Bar Found. (chair fellows adv. rsch. com. 2002—); mem.: ABA (chmn. life scis. divsn. 1982—84, chmn. com. med. practice 1987—88, chmn. life scis. divsn. 1988—91, vice chair food and drug law com. 1991—97, chmn. sect. sci. and tech. 1992—93, del. of sci. and tech. sect. to ho. of dels. 1993—, chmn. coordinating group on bioethics and the law 1998—2000, vice chair Ho. Tech. Com. 2002—), Cosmos Club. Office: Covington & Burling 1201 Pennsylvania Ave NW Washington DC 20004-2401

FLANNERY, HARRY AUDLEY, lawyer; b. New Castle, Pa., June 11, 1947; s. Wilbur Eugene and Ruth (Donaldson) F.; m. Maureen Louise Flaherty, June 28, 1969; children: Preston Wilbur, Courtney Lilyan. BA, Wesleyan U., 1969; JD, Ohio No. U., 1972; LLM in Taxation, Boston U., 1973. Bar: Pa. 1972, Ohio 2000, U.S. Tax Ct. 1973, U.S. Dist. Ct. (we. dist.) Pa. 1975, U.S. Supreme Ct. 1976, U.S. Ct. Appeals 1984. Sr. gen. svcs. specialist Pitts. Nat. Bank, 1973, asst. trust officer, 1974-75, trust legal officer, 1976; atty. Pa. Power Co., New Castle, 1977-98, FirstEnergy Corp., 1998—2002, FirstEnergy Svc. Co., 2002—; sec. fed. and state polit. coms. Pa. Power Co., New Castle, 1983-2000. V.p. and asst. treas. Euclid Manor Corp.; mem. panel arbitrators Bur. Mediation Dept. Labor and Industry. Assoc. editor Pitts. Legal Jour., 1981-99; contbr. numerous articles to legal publs. Bd. dirs. Lawrence County chpt. Pa. Assn. for Blind, 1st v.p., 1994-96, pres. 1996-98; mem. Highland Presbyn. Ch., New Castle, Estate Planning Coun. of Pitts., 1975-77; sec. Lil Maur Found., 1989—, v.p., 1999—; elected mem. sch. bd. dirs. Neshannock Twp. Sch. Bd. Lawrence County, Pa., 1993-01, v.p., 1997-99, pres., 1999-2001; mem. Pearson Park Commn., 1993-95; mem. oper. com. Lawrence County Area Vocat. Tech. Sch., 1997-2001; elected mem. Rep. Com., 3d Dist. Neshannock Twp., 2000. Mem. ABA (labor and employment law sect. com. on labor arbitration and law of collective bargaining agreements to 2002, tax sect. 1973-92, com. excise and employment taxes, subcom. payroll tax issues 1978-80), Pa. Bar Assn. (workmen's compensation sect., adminstrv. law sect., labor and employment law sect., pub. utility law sect., in house counsel com. 1995-98, 99-2000, dispute resolution com. 1989-91, 99-2000), Allegheny County Bar Assn. (coun., taxation sect. 1975-77, workmen's compensation sect., coun. labor and employment law sect. 2000-2001), Pitts. Legal Jour. Com., Lawrence County Bar Assn., Allegheny Tax Soc., Pennsylvania Soc. (life), The Supreme Ct. Pa. Hist. Soc. (life, trustee 1994—, sec. 1995-99, v.p. 1999-2002), Duquesne Club, Lawrence Club, New Castle Country Club, Lions (bd. dirs. 1982-91, tailtwister 1983-84, 3rd v.p. 1984-85, 2nd v.p. 1985, 1st v.p. 1986-87, pres. 1987-88), New Castle Lions Charities, Inc. (Lion of Yr. 1988-89), Iroquois Boating and Fishing Club, Phi Alpha Delta. Republican. Avocations: family, writing, tennis, boating. Home: 116 Valhalla Dr New Castle PA 16105-1037 Office: FirstEnergy Corp 76 S Main St Akron OH 44308-1425 E-mail: flanneryh@firstenergycorp.com.

FLANNERY, JAMES PATRICK, lawyer; b. Shenandoah, Pa., May 15, 1943; s. Anthony Joseph and Helen (Dorning) F.; m. Carol Lee Haddaway, July 12, 1970; children— Karen, Erin. B.A., St. Francis Coll., 1965; M.P.A., Am. U., 1967; J.D., Georgetown U., 1972. Bar: D.C. 1974, Pa. 1974, Minn. 1976. Mgr. Supreme Ct., Washington, 1970-73; cons. Arthur Young & Co., Washington, 1973-75, U.S. Dist. Ct., St. Paul, 1975-76; atty. Hugo Law Office, Minn., 1976— . Author: Speedy Trial, 1976. Chmn. Charter Commn., Lino Lakes, 1982— ; mem. Park Bd., Lino Lakes, 1981— ; chmn. Lino Lake Republican Com., 1984. Mem. ABA, Minn. Trial Lawyers (bd. govs. 1980), C. of C. (bd. dirs.). Republican. Roman Catholic. Office: 5669 147th St N Hugo MN 55038-9256

FLANNERY, JAMES WILLIAM, performing arts educator; b. Hartford, Conn., Nov. 8, 1936; s. James Joseph and Eileen Cotter Flannery; m. Ildiko Elizabeth Pokoly, Sept. 7, 1964; 1 child, Cieran Pokoly. BA, Trinity Coll., Dublin, 1958; MFA, Yale Sch. of Drama, 1961; PhD, Trinity Coll., 1970, DLitt (hon.), 1994, U. Ulster, Derry, Ireland, 2001. Dir. Eng. theater U. Ottawa, Canada, 1961—76; chair dept. theater U. R.I., Kingston, 1976—79, Emory U., Atlanta, 1982—89, prof. performing arts, 1989—, Winship prof. arts and humanities, 2001—. Exec. dir. Yeats Internat. Theatre Festival, Abbey Theatre, Dublin, 1989—93; founder, dir. W. B. Yeats Found., Atlanta, 1989—. Author: (book) W. B. Yeats and the Idea of Theatre; author/singer (book-recording) Dear Harp of My Country: The Irish Melodies of Thomas Moore. Named one of Top 100 Irish Americans, Irish-America Mag., NY, 1990, 1991, 1992, 1993, 1998; recipient Wild Geese Award for Outstanding Contbn. to Irish Culture, 1994, Award in the Humanities, Ga. Humanities Coun., Atlanta, 2002; Disting. Fulbright fellow, Fulbright Commn., UK, 2001. Mem.: Phi Beta Kappa. Roman Catholic. Home: 1342 Harvard Rd NE Atlanta GA 30306 Office: Emory Univ 1463 S Oxford Rd Atlanta GA 30322 Office Fax: 404-727-9536.

FLANNERY, JOHN FRANCIS, lawyer; b. Oct. 15, 1928; s. Edward J. and Ellie (Brennan) Flannery; m. Catherine E. Barden, Nov. 29, 1991; children: Colleen, John F., Erin, Kevin(dec.), Brian, Patrick, Michael. BSEE, U. Ill., 1950; postgrad., Northwestern U., 1953—55; JD, Loyola U., Chgo., Ill., 1959. Bar: Ill. 1959. Assoc. Fitch, Even, Tabin & Flannery, Chgo., 1957—61, ptnr., 1961—. Trustee Village of Lincolnwood, 1978—83. Served with AUS, 1951—53. Mem.: Am. Coll. Trial Lawyers, Am. Trial Lawyers Assn., Chgo. Patent Law Assn., Chgo. Bar Assn., ABA, Am. Legion, Eta Kappa Nu. Office: Fl 1600 120 S La Salle St Ste 1600 Chicago IL 60603-3402

FLANNERY, JOSEPH PATRICK, manufacturing executive, director; b. Lowell, Mass., Mar. 20, 1932; s. Joseph Patrick and Mary Agnes Egan F.; m. Margaret Barrows, June 1957; children: Mary Ann, Diane, Joseph, James, David, Elizabeth. BS in Chemistry, Lowell Tech. Inst., 1953; MBA, Harvard U., 1955; PhD, U. Lowell, Mass., 1981. Pres. Uniroyal Chem. Co., Naugatuck, Conn., 1975-77; exec. v.p. Uniroyal, Inc., Middlebury, Conn., 1977, pres., 1977—, chief exec. officer, 1980—, chmn. bd., 1982—; chmn., pres., chief exec. officer Uniroyal Holding, Inc., Naugatuck, Conn., 1986—. Bd. dirs. Newmont Mining Corp., The Scotts Co., ArvinMeritor. Mem.: Country Club of Fla., Oyster Harbors (Mass.), Vesper Country Club (Lowell), Country Club of Waterbury (Conn.), Knights of Malta. Roman Catholic. Office: Uniroyal Holding Inc 70 Great Hill Rd Naugatuck CT 06770-2224

FLANNERY, SUSAN MARIE, library administrator; b. Newark, Feb. 18, 1953; d. John Patrick Flannery and Assunta (Lardieri) Ege; m. Stephen A. Coren, Oct. 6, 1984. BA in History of Art, U. Pa., 1974; MLS, Simmons Coll., 1975. Dir. of libr. Newton Country Day, 1975-77, Am. Sch. in Switzerland, Montagnola, 1977-78; young adult libr. Somerville (Mass.) Pub. Libr., 1979-81; reference libr. Cary Meml. Libr., Lexington, Mass., 1981-83; asst. dir. Lucius Beebe Libr., Wakefield, Mass., 1983-87; dir. Reading (Mass.) Pub. Libr., 1987-91; assoc. dir. Cambridge (Mass.) Pub. Libr., 1991-1993, dir., 1993—. Steering com. Mass. delegation to White Ho. Conf. on Librs., 1990; corporator East Cambridge Savs. Bank. Reviewer Sch. Libr. Jour.; contbr. articles to profl. jours. Incorporator Cambridge (Mass.) Family YMCA, 1991—93; bd. dirs. Guidance Ctr., Inc., Cambridge, 1994—2000, sec., 2001—. Mem. ALA (Mass. councilor 1993-97, John Cotton Dana award 1989, Outstanding Libr. Adv. 20th Century 2000), ACLU Mass. (adv. bd. 1994-96, bd. dirs. 1996—), Mass. Libr. Assn. (pres. 1985-87, v.p. 1983-85), Rotary (bd. dirs. Cambridge 1993-99, v.p. 1995-96, pres. 1997-98, pres. Reading club). Office: Cambridge Pub Libr 449 Broadway Cambridge MA 02138-4125 E-mail: sflannery@ci.cambridge.ma.us.

FLANSBURGH, EARL ROBERT, architect; b. Ithaca, N.Y., Apr. 28, 1931; s. Earl Alvah and Elizabeth (Evans) F.; m. Louise Hospital, Aug. 27, 1955; children: Earl Schuyler, John Conant. BArch, Cornell U., 1954; MArch, MIT, 1957; S.C.M.P., Harvard U. Sch. Bus., 1982. Job capt., designer The Architects Collaborative, Cambridge, Mass., 1958-62; partner Freeman, Flansburgh & Assos., Cambridge, 1961-63; prin. Earl R. Flansburgh & Assocs., Cambridge, 1963-69, pres., dir. design, 1969—. Bd. dirs. daka, Inc.; exec. v.p. Environment Systems Internat., Inc.; vis. prof. archtl. design Mass. Inst. Tech., 1965-66; instr. art Wellesley Coll., 1962-65, lectr. art, 1965-69; cons. Arthur D. Little, Inc., Cambridge, 1964-70. Archtl. works include Weston (Mass.) High Sch. Addition, 1965-67, Cornell U. Campus Store, 1967-70, Cumnock Hall, Harvard U. Bus. Sch, 1973-75, Acton (Mass.) Elementary schs, 1966-68, 69-71, Wilton (Conn.) High Sch, 1968-71, 14 Story St. Bldg, 1970, Boston Design Ctr., 1985-86, Glenwood Sch., Dallas, 1985-88, New Univ. No. B.C., Prince George, Can., 1991—, Boston Coll. Law Sch., 1992—; exhibited works Light Machine I, IBM Gallery, N.Y.C., 1958, Light Machine II, Carpenter Center, Harvard, 1965, 5 Cambridge Architects, Wellesley Coll., 1969, Work of Earl R. Flansburgh and Assos, Wellesley Coll., 1969, New Architecture in New Eng, DeCordova Mus., 1974-75, Residential Architecture, Mead Art Gallery, Amherst Coll., 1976, works represented in, 50 Ville del Nostro Tempo, 1970, Nuove Ville, New Villas, 1970, Vacation Houses, 1970, Vacation Houses, 2d edit., 1977, Interior Design, 1970, Drawings by American Architects, 1973, Interior Spaces Designed by Architects, 1974, New Architecture in New England, 1974, Great Houses, 1976, Architecture Boston, 1976, Presentation Drawings by American Architects, 1977, Architecture, 1970-1980, A Decade of Change, 1980, Old and New Architecture, A Design Relationship, 1980, 25 Years of Record Houses, 1981, School Ways: The Planning and Design of American Schools, 1992, Elem. and Secondary Schs., 2001; Author: (with others) Techniques of Successful Practice, 1975. Chmn. architecture com. Boston Arts Festival, 1964, Downtown Boston Design adv. com.; bd. dirs. Cambridge Ctr. Adult Edn.; pres. Downtown North Boston, 1994—; trustee Cornell U., 1972—; chmn. bldgs. and properties com., 1976-87; mem. exec. com. acad. affairs com.; class sec. SCMP VII Harvard Bus. Sch., 1982-89. 1st lt. USAF, 1954-56. Recipient design awards Progressive Architecture, design awards Record Houses, design awards AIA, design awards City of Boston, design awards Mass. Masonry Inst., spl. design citations Am. Assn. Sch. Adminstrs., spl. 1st prize Buffalo-Western N.Y. chpt. AIA Competition., Walter Taylor award Am. Assn. Sch. Adminstrs., 1986, William Candill award Am. Coll. & Univ. Mag., 1993, Award of Honor, Boston Soc. Archs., 1999; Fulbright Rsch. grantee Bldg. Rsch. Sta., Eng., 1957-58. Fellow AIA, Nat. Acad. Design; mem. Royal Inst. Brit. Architects, Boston Soc. Architects (chmn. program com., 1969-71, commr. pub. affairs 1971-73, commr. design 1973-74, dir. 1971-74, pres. 1980-81), Boston Found. Architecture (treas. 1984-89), Cornell U. Coun., Quill and Dagger Soc., St. Botolph Club, Tau Beta Pi. Home: 3 Old Conant Rd Lincoln MA 01773 Office: 77 N Washington St Boston MA 02114-1908

FLASCHEN, EVAN DANIEL, lawyer; b. Summit, N.J., July 26, 1957; s. Steward Samuel and Joyce (Davies) F.; children: Reed Cromwell, Joan Steward, Thomas Bevan. BA, Wesleyan U., 1979; JD, U. Conn., 1982. Bar: Conn. 1982. Ptnr. Bingham McCutchen LLP, Hartford, Conn., 1982—. Adj. prof. U. Conn. Sch. Law, 1996—; lectr. in field. Co-editor: International Loan Workouts and Bankruptcies, 1989; mem. editorial bd. INSOL Internat. Jour., 1990—; contbr. articles to profl. jours. Mem. ABA (bus. bankruptcy com. sect. of bus. law 1984—, chmn. secured creditors subcom. 1993-96, vice chmn. 1988-89, vice chmn. Chpt. 11 subcom. 1989-93, internat. bankruptcy subcom. 1986-97), Internat. Bar Assn. (com. creditor's rights and insolvency 1986—), INSOL Internat. (co-chmn. cross-border insolvency project 1989—), Internat. Insolvency Inst., Am. Law Inst., Am. Bankruptcy Inst. (chmn. INSOL sect. 1988-92), Am. Coll. Bankruptcy. Home: 235 East River Dr Unit 605 East Hartford CT 06108 Office: Bingham McCutchen LLP One State St Hartford CT 06103 E-mail: eflaschen@email.com., evan.flaschen@bingham.com.

FLASKAMP, RUTH EHMEN STAACK, retired elementary education educator; b. Moline, Ill., Dec. 11, 1927; d. Henry Frederick and Tjiede Lena (Ehmen) Staack; m. Richard Kresse Flaskamp, June 10, 1950; children: Richard Henry, Thomas Marc. BA, Augustana Coll., 1949; MEd, Bowling Green State U., 1971. Tchr. elem. grades Lanark (Ill.) Consolidated Schs., 1949-50, Sylvania (Ohio) City Schs., 1956-93, ret., 1993; field supr. Coll. Edn., U. Toledo, 1994-99; tchr. U. Toledo, 1997-98. Part-time faculty dept. of curriculum and instrn. U. Toledo, 1997-99. Contbr. articles to profl. jours., various curriculum guides. Bd. dirs. Sylvania Pub. Libr., 1960-61; mem. ednl. adv. com. Toledo Edison, Toledo Zoo, 1986; active various polit. campaigns. Named Jennings scholar, 1982—83; recipient award for excellence in edn., NEA/Ladies Home Jour., 1990—91, award for outstanding contbns. to improve quality of life for young children, Toledo Asns. Young Children, 2002. Mem. NEA, Sylvania Edn. Assn. (sec. 1975-76, 89-90, pres. 1991), Ohio Edn. Assn. (rep.), N.W. Ohio Edn. Assn., Nat. Sci. Tchrs. Assn., Golden Emblem Club. Republican. Lutheran. Avocations: swimming, weaving, music, reading, baking. Home: 3129 Saint Bernard Dr Toledo OH 43606-2158 E-mail: rhf@buckeye-express.com.

FLASKERUD-RATHMELL, SUSAN MARIE, musician, music educator; d. Kenneth Alden and Joan Frances Flaskerud; m. Robert Jennings Rathmell, July 15, 1989. BFA in Piano Performance, U. Minn., 1980; MusM in Piano/Chamber Music Performance, Northwestern U., 1981; MusD Arts in Piano Performance, Ariz. State U., 1990. Asst. prof. piano Iowa State U., Ames, 1997—2000; artist/tchr. piano Hillsdale (Mich.) Coll., 2000—. Presenter in field. Sec. Hillsdale Natural Grocery, 2001—03. Mem.: Am. Musicological soc., Am. Liszt Soc., Music Tchrs. Nat. Assn. (collegiate chair Iowa Music Tchrs. Assn. 1999—2000), Scriabin Soc. Am., Coll. Music Soc. Avocations: yoga, swimming, foodie. Office: Hillside Coll Hillsdale MI 49242 Personal E-mail: susan.rathmell@hillsdale.edu. E-mail: susan.rathmell@hillsdale.edu.

FLATEN, ALFRED N. retired food and consumer products executive; b. 1935; With Nash-Finch Co., Mpls., 1861-98, mgr. Iowa divsn., 1983-86, v.p. S.E. divsn., 1986-89, v.p. retail ops., 1989-91, past exec. v.p., past pres., CEO, COO, also bd. dirs.

FLATEN, ROBERT ARNOLD, former ambassador; b. Mpls., May 21, 1934; s. Arnold Wangensten and Evelyn (Solberg) F.; m. Carroll Jean Johnson, Dec. 22, 1956; children: Kristin, Karen, Sonia, Arne. BA, St. Olaf Coll., Northfield, Minn., 1956; MA, George Washington U., 1961; LHD, Luther Coll., 2001. Vice consul Am. Consulate, Strasbourg, France, 1962-63, Peshawar, Pakistan, 1964-66; 2d sec. Am. Embassy, Tel Aviv, 1966-69, dep. chief mission, 1982-86; Fgn. Svc. insp., legis. mgmt. officer, office dir., dep. asst. sec. U.S. Dept. State, Washington, 1970-82, office dir., 1987-90; amb. to Rwanda Am. Embassy, Kigali, 1990-93. Chair exec. com. Nobel Peace Prize Forum, 1996; active St. Paul/Mpls. Com. on Fgn. Rels. 2d lt. USAF, 1956-59. Named disting. prof. of political sci., St. Olaf Coll., 2002, Disting. Alumnus, 2001. Mem. Am. Fgn. Svc. Assn., Minn. Internat. Ctr., Immortal Chaplains Found. (dir.), UN Assn./Minn. (v.p.), Rotary. Home: 5008 90th St E Northfield MN 55057-4349 E-mail: flaten@rconnect.com.

FLATER, MORRIS EUGENE, executive, lawyer; b. Augusta, Ga., Sept. 1, 1943; s. Morris E. Flater and Sue (Ransom) Bell; m. Susanne R. Flater (div. 1987); children: Lara, Morris E. III. BS, Tulane U., 1966; JD magna cum laude, Washington and Lee U., 1973; LLM, Georgetown U., 1997. Bar: Va. 1973, Mass. 1991. Of counsel Hunton and Williams, Norfolk, Va., 1973-84; pres. Channel Labs., Ltd., Norfolk, 1984-85, Hub Express Airlines, Boston, 1986-91; exec. dir., gen. counsel Am. Helicopter Soc., Alexandria, Va., 1991—. Pub. Vertiflite mag. Capt. USMC, 1966-70. Recipient Helicopter Assn. Internat. Excellence in Comm. award. Fellow Royal Aeronautical Soc., Order of Coif, Omicron Delta Kappa. Office: Am Helicopter Soc 217 N Washington St Alexandria VA 22314-2520 E-mail: rflater@vtol.org.

FLATLEY, LAWRENCE EDWARD, lawyer; b. Erie, Pa., May 24, 1950; s. Willard James and Loretta Grace (Moore) F.; m. Teresa Marie Kadunce, May 17, 1974; children: Daniel Lawrence, Steven James. BA, U. Pitts., 1972; JD, U. Pa., 1975. Bar: Pa. 1975, U.S. Dist. Ct. (we. dist.) Pa. 1975, U.S. Ct. Appeals (3d Cir.) 1975. Assoc. Reed, Smith, Shaw & McClay, Pitts., 1975-83, ptnr., 1983—. Contbg. author Foreign Policy, vol. 2, 1971, Mealey's Ins. Reports, 1990. Mem. Phi Beta Kapp. Democrat. Roman Catholic. Home: 2747 Shamrock Dr Allison Park PA 15101-3146 Office: Reed Smith Shaw & McClay Mellon Sq 435 6th Ave Ste 2 Pittsburgh PA 15219-1886

FLATO, WILLIAM ROEDER, JR., software development company executive; b. Apr. 20, 1945; s. William Roeder and Juanita Flato; m. Beatrice Pesl, Aug. 22, 1974; children: Amanda Leigh, William Roeder III. BBA, U. Houston, 1967. CPA, Tex. Acct. Hughes Tool Co., Houston, 1966-67, Milchem, Inc., Houston, 1967-72, accounting mgr., asst. contr., corp. contr., 1972-78; v.p. fin., sec., treas. Baker Performance Chems. Inc. (formerly magna Corp.), Houston, 1978-82, exec. v.p. fin. and planning, sec.-treas., 1982-93; CFO, v.p. fin. CoToCo Techs., Inc., Houston, 1993-97; founder, CFO, v.p. fin. Connective Techs., Inc., Houston, 1996—2001, CEO, pres., chmn. bd. dirs., 2001—. Active Country Village Civic Assn.; state chmn. Young Ams. for Freedom, 1964; precinct chmn. Harris County Rep. Exec. Com., 1966-67. With U.S. Army, 1968-69. Decorated Army Commendation medal. Mem. AICPA, Tex. Soc. CPA, Mensa. Presbyterian. Home: 11931 Drexel Hill Dr Houston TX 77077-3009 Office: 7676 Hillmont St Ste 120 Houston TX 77040-6468 E-mail: bflato@houston.rr.com., bflato@connective-edi.com.

FLATT, ADRIAN EDE, surgeon; b. Frinton, Eng., Aug. 26, 1921; came to U.S., 1956, naturalized, 1960; s. Leslie Neeve and Barbara F.; m. Judith Johnson. BA, Cambridge U., 1942, MA, 1945, MBBchir., 1946, MD, 1953, M. chir., 1972. Diplomate: Am. Bd. Orthopedic Surgery. Rotating intern, then resident in gen., plastic and orthopaedic surgery London (Eng.) Hosp., 1946-54, 55-56; mem. faculty U. Iowa Med. Sch., 1956-79; prof. orthopaedic surgery and anatomy, dir. div. hand surgery, chmn. dept. surgery Norwalk (Conn.) Hosp., 1979-82; clin. prof. Yale U. Med. Sch., 1979-82; chief dept. orthopaedics Baylor U. Med. Ctr., Dallas, 1982-92, coord. rsch. Tom Landry Sports Medicine Ctr., 1992-94, dir. edn. dept. orthopaedics, 1995—. Hunterian prof. Royal Coll. Surgeons, 1962; McIlrath guest prof. Royal Prince Alfred Hosp., Sydney, Australia, 1972; Sir R. Watson-Jones lectr. Brit. Orthopaedic Assn., 1986; cons. in hand surgery to surg. gen. U.S. Air Force, 1962— Editor in chief Jour. Hand Surgery, 1981-91; author textbooks, papers in field; patentee artificial wrist and finger joints. Served as officer RAF, 1948-50. Recipient Kappa Delta award Am. Acad. Orthopaedic Surgeons, 1972 Mem. Am. Soc. Surgery Hand, Brit. Hand Soc., Brit. Assn. Plastic Surgery (hon.), Group Etude de la Main, Am. Orthopaedic Assn., Am. Acad. Orthopaedic Surgeons, Am. Soc. Plastic and Reconstructive Surgery. Office: Baylor U Med Ctr George Truett James Orthopedic Inst 3500 Gaston Ave Dallas TX 75246-2096

FLATTAU, EDWARD, columnist; b. N.Y.C., May 18, 1937; BA, Brown U., 1958; postgrad., Columbia Law Sch., 1958-60. Polit. corr. UPI, Albany, N.Y., 1962-66, congrl. corr. Washington, 1967-69; legis. asst. Rep. Benjamin Rosenthal, Washington, 1969-71; asst. dir. of info. European Cmty., Washington, 1971-72; syndicated columnist Global Horizons Syndicate, Washington, 1972—. Author: Tracking the Charlatans, 1998, Evolution of a Columnist, 2003; contbr. articles to mags. Recipient Disting. Journalism citation Scripps Howard Found., 1978, Lorax award Global Tomorrow Coalition, 1985, Global Media award Population Inst., 1986. Avocations: tennis, golf, civil war buff. Home and Office: 1330 New Hampshire Ave NW Washington DC 20036-6350

FLATTAU, PAMELA EBERT, research psychologist, consultant; b. Chgo., Dec. 24, 1946; d. Raymond Clarence and Sylvia Anne (Jones) E.; m. Edward Samuel Flattau, Feb. 1, 1977; children: Jeremy Paul, Victoria Celeste. BSc with honors, U. Leeds, Eng., 1969; MS, U. Ga., 1972, PhD, 1974. Congrl. sci. fellow AAAS-APA, Washington, 1974-75; staff officer NAS/NRC, Washington, 1975-81, sr. staff officer, 1985-90, unit dir., 1990-95; policy analyst NSF, Washington, 1981-85; mgr. Flattau Assocs. LLC, Washington, 1995—. Mem. exec. com. Coun. Profl. Assns. for Fed. Stats., Washington, 1986-87. Editor: Research Doctorate Programs in U.S., 1995; author, editor series Biomed and Behavioral Research Personnel 1975-80, 1994; author, contbr.: Science and Engineering Indicators Series, 1981-85. Bd. dirs. Assn. Advancement Psychology, Washington, 1980-82. Mem. AAAS, APA (NSF travel grantee 1992, 2000, Young Psychologist travel award 1976), Am. Psychol. Soc., Soc. for Social Studies of Sci., Human Resources Planning Soc., Sigma Xi. Office: Flattau Assocs LLC 5335 Wisconsin Ave NW Ste 440 Washington DC 20015-2052 E-mail: pflattau@flattau.com.

FLATTÉ, STANLEY MARTIN, physicist, educator; b. Los Angeles, Dec. 2, 1940; s. Samuel and Henrietta (Edelstein) F.; m. Renelde Marie Demeure, June 26, 1966; children: Michael, Anne. BS, Calif. Inst. Tech., 1962; student, NYU, 1960-61; PhD, U. Calif.-Berkeley, 1966. Research particle physicist Lawrence Berkeley Lab., Calif., 1966-71; asst. prof. physics U. Calif.-Santa Cruz, 1971-73, assoc. prof., 1973-78, prof., 1978—; dir. Ctr. for Studies of Nonlinear Dynamics La Jolla Inst., 1982-86, dept. chmn., 1986-89. Cons. phys. oceanography and underwater sound U.S. Govt.; vis. researcher, Cern, Geneva, 1975, Scripps Inst. Oceanography, 1980, Cambridge U., Eng., 1981 Author: (with others) Sound Transmission Through a Fluctuating Ocean, 1979; contbr. (with others) articles profl. jours. Woodrow Wilson fellow, 1962; NSF fellow, 1962-66; Guggenheim Found. fellow, 1975 Fellow AAAS, Am. Phys. Soc., Acoustical Soc. Am., Optical Soc. Am.; mem. Am. Geophys. Union, Sigma Xi (pres. Santa Cruz chpt. 1999-2000). Achievements include discovery of cusp phenomenon in particle physics; developed methods for using sound and light waves to probe statis. atmosphere, ocean and earth processes. Office: Univ Calif Physics Dept Santa Cruz CA 95064 E-mail: sflatte@ucsc.edu.

FLATTERY, THOMAS LONG, lawyer, legal administrator; b. Detroit, Nov. 14, 1922; s. Thomas J. and Rosemary (Long) F.; m. Gloria M. Hughes, June 10, 1947 (dec.); children: Constance Marie, Carol Dianne Lee, Michael Patrick, Thomas Hughes, Dennis Jerome, Betsy Ann Sprecher m. Barbara J. Balfour, Oct. 4, 1986; Laura B. Lundquist, Linda B. Flint, William D. Balfour III. BS, U.S. Mil. Acad., 1947; JD, UCLA, 1955; LLM, U. So. Calif., 1965. Bar: Calif. 1955, U.S. Patent and Trademark Office 1957, U.S. Customs Ct. 1968, U.S. Supreme Ct. 1974, Conn. 1983, N.Y. 1984. With Motor Products Corp., Detroit, 1950, Equitable Life Assurance Soc., Detroit, 1951, Bohn Aluminum & Brass Co., Hamtramck, Mich., 1952; mem. legal staff, asst. contract adminstr. Radioplane Co. (divsn. Northrop Corp.), Van Nuys, Calif., 1955-57; successively corp. counsel, gen. counsel, asst. sec. McCulloch Corp., 1957-64; sec., corp. counsel Technicolor, Inc., Hollywood, Calif., 1964-70; successively corp. counsel, asst. sec., v.p., sec. and gen. counsel Amcord, Inc., Newport Beach, Calif., 1970-72; v.p., sec., gen. counsel Schick Inc., Calif., 1972-75; counsel, asst. sec. C.F. Braun & Co., Alhambra, Calif., 1975-76; sr. v.p., sec., gen. counsel Automation Industries, Inc. (now PCC Tech. Industries Inc. a unit of Penn Cen. Corp.), Greenwich, Conn., 1976-86; v.p., gen. counsel G&H Tech., Inc. (a unit of Penn Cen. Corp.), Santa Monica, Calif., 1986-93; temp. judge Superior. Ct. Calif. L.A. Jud. Dist. and Santa Monica Unified Cts., 1987—; settlement officer L.A. Superior Ct., 1991—; pvt. practice, 1993—. Panelist Am. Arbitration Assn., 1991—; jud. arbitrator and mediator Alternative Dispute Resolution Programs L.A. Superior Ct., 1993—, Calif. Ct. Appeals 2d Appellate Dist., 1999—; mem. L.A. Supr. Ct. Alternative Dispute Resolution com., 2001—. Contbr. articles to profl. jours. Served to 1st lt. AUS, 1942-50. Mem. ABA, Nat. Assn. Secs. Dealers, Inc (bd. arbitrators 1996, mediators 1997), State Bar Calif. (co-chmn. corp. law dept. com. 1978-79, lectr. continuing legal edn. program), L.A. County Bar Assn. (chmn. corp. law dept. com. 1966-67), Century City Bar Assn. (chmn. corp. law dept. com. 1979-80), Conn. Bar Assn., Santa Monica Bar Assn. (trustee 1999—, chmn. alt. dispute resolution sect. 2000—), N.Y. State Bar Assn., Am. Soc. Corp. Secs. (L.A.

regional group pres. 1973-74), L.A. Intellectual Property Law Assn., Am. Ednl. League (trustee 1988—, sec. 1998—), Am. Legion (life), West Point Alumni Assn., Army Athletic Assn., Friendly Sons St. Patrick, Jonathan Club (dir. 1996-99), Braemar Country Club, Phi Alpha Delta. Roman Catholic. Home and Office: 439 Via De La Paz Pacific Palisades CA 90272-4633 E-mail: flatterytl@earthlink.net.

FLAUCHER-FALCK, VELMA RUTH, retired special education educator; b. Hazleton, Iowa, Feb. 10, 1935; d. Amos Burdette and Florence Ella (Short) Flaucher; m. Kenneth Elgin Bienfang, Nov. 26, 1958 (div. Oct. 1975); children: Kende Sue Wynn, Victor Nolan Bienfang, Rodney Dean Bienfang; m. James Leo Falck, July 30, 1994. BA, U. No. Iowa, 1973, MA, 1977. Tchr. kindergarten Orange Ctr. Elem. Sch., Waterloo, Iowa, 1954—59; tchr. Van Eaton Elem. Sch., Waterloo, 1962; tchr. Headstart Exceptional Persons, Waterloo, 1967—68; tchr. kindergarten Hudson Sch. Dist., Hudson, Iowa, 1969—71; dir. activities Friendship Village, Waterloo, 1973—74; tchr. resource AEA7 Spl. Edn., Cedar Falls, Iowa, 1975—94; ret., 1994. Author: Whatever Became of LuAnn?, 2002; author: (poems) Internat. Libr. Poetry, 1999—. Mem.: Iowa Ret. Sch. Pers., Tues. Tourists Book Club of Oelwein. Avocations: writing, reading, music, oil painting. Home: 1111 1st St NE Oelwein IA 50662

FLAUM, JOEL MARTIN, judge; b. Hudson, N.Y., Nov. 26, 1936; s. Louis and Sally (Berger) Flaum; m. Delilah Brummet, June 4, 1989. BA, Union Coll., Schenectady, 1958; JD, Northwestern U., 1963, LLM, 1964; LLD, John Marshall Law Sch., 2002. Bar: Ill. 1963. Asst. state's atty. Cook County, Ill., 1965—69, 1st asst. atty. gen. Ill., 1969—72; 1st asst. U.S. atty. Chgo., 1972—75; judge U.S. Dist. Ct. (no. dist.) Ill., Chgo., 1975—83, U.S. Ct. Appeals (7th cir.), 1983—. Mem. Ill. Law Enforcement Commn., 1970—72; cons. U.S. Dept. Justice, Law Enforcement Assistance Adminstrn., 1970—71; lectr. DePaul U. Coll. Law, 1987—88; adj. prof. Northwestern U. Sch. Law, 1993—2000. Mem.: Northwestern U. Law Rev., 1962—63; contbr. articles to legal jours. Mem. vis. com. U. Chgo. Law Sch., 1983—86, Northwestern U. Sch. Law, 1983—; mem. adv. com. USCG Acad., 1990—93. Lt. comdr. JACG USNR, 1981—92. Fellow Ford Found. fellow, 1963—64. Fellow: Am. Bar Found. (licentiate); mem.: FBA, ABA, Am. Judicature Soc., Navy-Marine Corps Ret. Judges Advs. Assn., Maritime Law Assn., Chgo. Bar Assn., Chgo. Inn of Ct., 7th Cir. Bar Assn., Ill. Bar Assn., Chgo. Bar Found. (licentiate), Naval Res. Assn., Lawyers Club Chgo. Jewish. Office: US Ct Appeals 7th Ct 219 S Dearborn St Chicago IL 60604-1702

FLAUM, MARSHALL ALLEN, television producer, writer, director; b. Bklyn. s. Mayer and Ethel (Lamkay) P.; m. Gita Faye Miller; children: Erica, Seth Baruch. BA, U. Iowa, 1948; DFA (hon.), So. Ill. U., Edwardsville, 1974. Story editor, writer, assoc. producer TV series for 20th Century, 1957-62; producer, writer, dir. TV spls. for Wolper Prodns., 1962-65; founder Flaum-Grinberg Prodns., 1966; v.p. Metromedia Producers Corp., 1968-76; pres. Marshall Flaum Prodns., Inc., 1976—. Prodr., writer, dir.: TV spls. Day of Infamy, 1963, Hollywood: The Great Stars, 1963, The Yanks Are Coming, 1964, Battle of Britain, 1964, Berlin: Kaiser to Kruschev, 1964, Let My People Go, 1965 (Ohio State award, George Foster Peabody award), Miss Goodall and the Wild Chimpanzees, 1966 (Edinburgh Festival award), Bogart, 1967 (Melbourne Festival award) Hollywood: The Selznick Years, 1969 (Silver Lion award Venice film Festival), The Time of Man, 1969 (Silver Hugo award Chgo. Internat. Festival), Yabba Dabba Doo! The Happy World of Hanna-Barbera, 1977, Bing Crosby: His Life and Legend, 1978 (Christopher award), Playboy's 25th Anniversary Celebration, 1979, A Bing Crosby Christmas...Like the Ones We Used to Know, 1979, Bob Hope's Texaco Star Theatre, Life's Most Embarrassing Moments, 1984, Portrait of Dorothy Stratten, 1985, A Yabba Dabba Doo Celebration, 50 Yrs. of Hanna Barbera, 1989, Arts and Entertainment's Ancient Mysteries, 1996, Celebrate the Century, 1998-99, The Desilu Story, 1999-2000; prodr., writer TV spls. Killy Le Champion, 1969; exec. prodr., co-writer: (TV series) Undersea World of Jacques Cousteau, 1970-76, Jane Goodall and The World of Animal Behavior, 1972-76, The Wild Dogs of Africa, 1973 (Emmy award best documentary, Chgo. Internat. Festival Gold Hugo award), Baboons of Gombe, 1974, Hyena, 1975, Lions of Serengeti, 1976; prodr. Am. Film Inst. Salute to Bette Davis, 1977; prodr., co-writer (with others): TV spls. Ripley's Believe It or Not, 1982, Bob Hope's Who Makes the World Laugh, 1983. Recipient Emmy award as best documentary for A Sound of Dolphins, 1972, The Unsinkable Sea Otter, 1972, George Foster Peabody award for TV spls. for Miss Goodall and The Wild Chimpanzees, 1966, Monte Carlo Internat. TV Festival Golden Nymph award for TV spl. The Yanks are Coming, 1964, Silver medal Atlanta Film Festival for Wild Dogs of Africa, 1973, Octopus, Octopus, 1972, Chgo. Internat. Film Festival Silver Hugo award for Tragedy of the Red Salmon, 1971, Oscar nomination sfor best documentary feature for The Yanks Are Coming, 1964, Let My People Go, 1966, Golden Globe nomination for The Fogotten Mermaids, 1972, Writers Guild of Am. nomination for The Time of Man, 1969, 16 Emmy award nominations. Mem. Writers Guild Am., Dirs. Guild Am., Acad. Motion Picture Arts and Scis., Acad. TV Arts and Scis. Address: 301 S Rodeo Dr Beverly Hills CA 90212-4206

FLAUM, SANDER ALLEN, advertising and marketing executive; b. Apr. 5, 1937; s. Joseph and Rose (Deutsch) F.; children: Pamela, Jonathon; m. Mechele Plotkin, Apr. 25, 1990. BA, Ohio State U., 1958; MBA, Fairleigh Dickinson U., 1970. Mktg. dir. Lederle Labs. divsn. Am. Cyanamid Co., Wayne, NJ, 1964-84; exec. v.p. Klemtner Advt., N.Y.C., 1984-88; chmn., CEO Robert A. Becker, Inc., N.Y.C., 1988-98, 1998—. Vice chmn. Euro RSCG, Healthcare; chmn. Fordham Grad. Sch. Bus., NYU Stern Sch. Bus. Author: The Shortest Road to Success, Focusing Is for Tough Guys, The Leader's Edge, There's a Little Consumer in Every M.D., Great Is Better than Good, Hocus Focus, Darwin 2000; Survival of Fastest, Focus on the Future Direction: Outward. Trustee Hollins Coll. Comms. Rsch. Inst.; bd. mem. Atrix Labs., Neopharm Corp. With U.S. Army, 1959—61. Mem. Am. Mktg. Assn. Avocations: running, golf. Office: Robert A Becker Inc EURO RSCG 1633 Broadway Fl 27 New York NY 10019-6708

FLAUTZ, NANCY A. librarian; b. Akron, Ohio, Dec. 20, 1931; d. Roland and Ruth A. (Whitman) Page; m. John T. Flautz, June 26, 1951; children: Judy, Susan. BA, Cedar Crest Coll., 1967. Acquisitions libr. Cedar Crest and Muhlenberg Coll. Librs., Allentown, Pa., 1969-92. Mem. AAUW (booksale com. 1994-95, cmty. awards com., named outstanding woman 194). Home: 1413 Exeter Rd Allentown PA 18103-6314

FLAX, HERSCHEL, surgeon; b. Capetown, South Africa, Feb. 9, 1941; came to U.S., 1974; s. Alexander Elliah and Mary Freda (Pasvolsky) F.; m. Elana Yehudith Matzkin; children: Joshua, Daniel, Rachel, Alexander. MB ChB, U. Capetown, 1964; ChM, U. Capetown Med. Sch., 1974; MA, NYU, 1978. Diplomate Am. Bd. Surgery. Intern Groote Schuur Hosp., Cape Town, South Africa, 1965-66; surg. registrar U. Cambridge, London, Birmingham, Eng. and Cape Town, 1966-72; chief resident Albert Einstein Coll. of Medicine, Bronx, N.Y., 1974-75, attending surgeon, asst. clin. prof., 1975—, attending surgeon, 1975—, assoc. clin prof. surgery, 1989 97, prof. clin. surgery, 1997—; attending surgeon, specializing in diseases of the breast Mt. Sinai Hosp., N.Y.C., 2000—. Contbr. articles to profl. jours. Fellow ACS, Royal Coll. Surgeons (Eng.); mem. Med. Soc. State N.Y., N.Y. Surg. Soc., N.Y. Met. Breast Cancer Soc. Avocations: piano, photography, politics, travel, skiing. Office: 1115 Fifth Ave New York NY 10128 E-mail: hflax@hotmail.com.

FLAX, JANE, psychotherapist, educator; b. N.Y.C., Dec. 31, 1948; d. Seth and Nancy F.; m. Gene Frankel, Aug. 30, 1975 (dec. May 1986); one child, Gabe. BA, U. Calif., Berkeley, 1969; PhD, Yale U., 1974. Asst. prof. U. Mass., Amherst, 1974-77; pvt. practice Washington, 1977—; prof. Howard U., Washington, 1992—. Vis. assoc. prof. Stanford (Calif.) U., 1982-83; Harlan Fund lectureship Duke U., 1990. Author: Disputed Subjects, 1992, The American Dream in Black and White, 1998; mem. editl. bd. Feminist Studies, 1979-98, Am. Jour. Polit. Sci., 1981-85, Signs, 1988, Hypatia, 1989-99, Social Theory Practice, 1995, Studies Gender Sexuality, 2000; Contbr. articles to profl. jours. Kell fellow Mich. State, Vis. fellow Inst. Humanities, U. Mich., 1991, Inst. Human Scis., Vienna, Austria, 1999; Disting. Am. scholar Fulbright Found., 1998, Affiliated scholar Beatrice Bain Rsch. Group, U. Calif., Berkeley, 2000; Travel grantee Am. Coun. Learned Socs., 1990. Mem. Internat. Soc. Polit. Psychology, Internat. Assn. Women Philosophers, Am. Polit. Sci. Assn., Conf. Social Polit. Thought. Jewish. Avocations: exercise, theater, traveling, films, music. Office: Dept Polit Sci Howard U Washington DC 20059 Fax: (202)332-4731. E-mail: jane.flax@worldnet.att.net.

FLAX, MARTIN HOWARD, pathologist, retired educator; b. N.Y.C., Jan. 19, 1928; s. Abraham and Sadie (Finkel) F.; m. Ann E. Brockway, June 26, 1953; children: Adam, Jonathan, Elizabeth. AB, Cornell U., 1946; AM, Columbia U., 1948, PhD, 1951; MD, U. Chgo., 1955; MS in Health Mgmt., MIT, 1979. Intern Mt. Sinai Hosp., N.Y.C., 1955-56; fellow pathology U. Chgo., 1956-57; chief biophysics br. Armed Forces Inst. Pathology, Washington, 1957-59; clin. fellow Mass. Gen. Hosp., Boston, 1959-61, asst. pathology, 1961-66; fellow pathology Harvard U. Med. Sch., 1959-61, instr. pathology, 1961-63, assoc. pathology, 1961-66, asst. prof., 1966-69; prof., chmn. pathology dept. Tufts U. Sch. Medicine, 1970-97, chmn. pathology dept., 1985-96; pathologist-in-chief New Eng. Med. Ctr. Hosp., Boston, 1970-97; emeritus prof. pathology Tufts U., 1998—. Cons. pathology B study sect. NIH, 1970-74. Capt. M.C., USAF, 1957-59. Recipient Rsch. Career Devel. award NIH, 1966-69; Nat. Cancer Inst. fellow, 1959-61, Med. Found. fellow, 1963-65, Sloan fellow MIT, 1979. Mem.: Sigma Xi, Phi Beta Kappa. Home: 32 Gate House Rd Chestnut Hill MA 02467-1335

FLAXMAN, FRED, broadcast executive; b. N.Y.C., May 9, 1940; s. Philip and Helen F.; m. Annick Story, Sept. 10, 1963; children: Michel, Tana Flaxman Jencks. BA, Cert. in Journalism, U. Mich., 1962; MA, Stanford U., 1964; Cert. in French Studies, Sorbonne U. Paris, 1962. Founding mgr. WETA-FM (90.9), Washington, 1970-74; program dir. WETA-TV Channel 26, Washington, 1974-77; v.p. programming, 1977-78; pres. Pub. Broadcasting Internat., Paris, 1978-79; asst. gen. mgr., dir. programming and prodn. KUAT-TV Channel 6, Tucson, 1980-83; v.p. nat. programming WTTW, Chgo., 1984-89; v.p., gen. mgr. So. Oreg. Pub. TV, Medford, Oreg., 1990-91; pres., exec. prodr. Teleflax Prodns., Medford, 1991-98; v.p. devel. WXEL-TV-FM, W. Palm Beach, Fla., 2000—. Prodr., writer, host Compact Discoveries public radio program. Author: Doctors, Dentists, Teenagers & Other Demons of Modern Life, Sixty Slices of Life...On Wry; editor: The Timeless Tales of Reginald Bretnor, 1997; contbr. articles to newspapers and mags. Recipient Emmy award NATAS, 1989, First Place Nat. Soc. Newspaper Columnists, 1989, Put It in Writing award Placerville Creative Writing Conf., 1990. Avocations: classical music, writing, travel, reading. Home: 4732 Hunting Trail Lake Worth FL 33467 Office: WXEL-TV-FM PO Box 6607 West Palm Beach FL 33405 Fax: (561) 364-4473. E-mail: fred@fredflaxman.com., fflaxman@wxel.org.

FLAXMAN, KENNETH N. lawyer; b. N.Y.C., Apr. 30, 1948; s. Abraham A. and Muriel (Sussman) F.; m. Judith G. Safran, May 30, 1968; children: Abie, Joel, Seth. BE in Elec. Engring., CUNY, 1968; JD, Ill. Inst. Tech., 1972. Bar: Ill. 1972, N.C. 1978, U.S. Supreme Ct. 1975, U.S. Ct. Appeals (7th cir.) 1972, U.S. Ct. Appeals (D.C. cir.) 1973, U.S. Ct. Appeals (4th cir.) 1975, U.S. Ct. Appeals (3d cir.) 1976, U.S. Dist. Ct. (no. dist.) Ill. 1972. Staff atty. Bus. and Profl. People for the Pub. Interest, Chgo., 1972-73; pvt. practice law Chgo., 1973—. Home: 2310 Grant St Evanston IL 60201-2109 Office: 200 S Michigan Ave Chicago IL 60604

FLAY, BOBBY, food service executive; Diploma, French Culinary Inst., 1984. Exec. chef Miracle Grill, N.Y.C., 1984—91; chef, ptnr. Mesa Grill, N.Y.C., 1991—; ptnr. Bolo, N.Y.C., 1993—. Author: (cookbook) Bold American Food, 1994 (IACP award for design, 1995), From My Kitchen to Your Table, Boy Meets Grill; host (TV series) Grillin' & Chillin', The Main Ingredient, Hott Off the Grill. Office: Mesa Grill 102 Fifth Ave New York NY 10011 Office Fax: 212-989-0034.

FLAYHART, MARTIN ALBERT, lawyer; b. Williamsport, Pa., Mar. 1, 1950; s. William Henry and Naomi (Laux) F. BA with hons., U. Va., 1971; JD, U. Pa., 1974. Bar: Pa. 1974, U.S. Dist. Ct. (mid. dist.) Pa. 1976, U.S. Ct. Appeals (3rd cir.) 1985, U.S. Supreme Ct. 1986. Assoc. Smith & Williamson, Lock Haven, Pa., 1974-76; ptnr. Saxton & Flayhart, Lock Haven, 1977-83; dist. atty. Clinton County, Lock Haven, 1979; pvt. practice Jersey Shore, Pa., 1983-84; ptnr. Carpenter, Harris & Flayhart, Jersey Shore, 1984—. Lectr. Lock Haven U., 1981-85, 90, Lycoming Coll., Williamsport, Pa., 1993-94, State U. of Chernivtsi Law Sch., Ukraine, 1993. Pres. Jersey Shore Area C. of C., Pa., 1990, 2001-02; com. Lycoming County Dem. Party, 1988—. Mem. ABA, Lycoming County Bar Assn., Pa. Bar Assn., Rotary (pres. Lock Haven club 1991, Rotarian of Yr. 1990), Phi Beta Kappa. Methodist. Avocation: rare book collecting. Office: Carpenter Harris & Flayhart PO Box 505 128 S Main St Jersey Shore PA 17740-1810

FLECHNER, ROBERTA FAY, graphic designer; b. N.Y.C., June 7, 1949; d. Abraham Julius and Evelyn (Medwin) F. BA, CCNY, 1970; MA, NYU, 1972; cert., Printing Industries Met., N.Y., N.Y.C., 1974, 75, 79. Researcher, asst. editor Arno Press, N.Y.C., 1970-73; free-lance editor Random House, N.Y.C., 1973-74, graphic designer/compositor coll. dept., 1984-88; graphic designer Core Communications in Health, N.Y.C., 1974-76; prodn. mgr. Heights-Inwood News, N.Y.C., 1976-77; art dir., graphic designer Jour. Advt. Research, N.Y.C., 1976-81; prin., graphic designer/compositor W.W. Norton & Co., Inc., N.Y.C., 1977—, McGraw Hill, Inc., N.Y.C., 1990-94, 2000—; graphic design, layout artist, compositor R. Flechner Graphics, 1976—. Graphic designer, layout artist, compositor R. Flechner Graphics, 1976—; mech. artist Fawcett, N.Y.C., 1979-80; graphic designer Avon Internat., N.Y.C., 1982; art dir., compositor, layout artist Source: Notes in the History of Art, N.Y.C., 1982—; graphic designer John Wiley & Sons, Inc., N.Y.C., 1985. Designer stationery, 1979 (Art Direction mag., Creativity-cert. distinction 1979). Art dir. enviroNews, N.Y. State Atty. Gen.'s Environ. Protection Bur., N.Y.C., 1977-78. Mem. Graphic Artists Guild, NOW, Women's Nat. Book Assn. (cons.), NAFE, Women's Caucus for Art, Am. Inst. Graphic Arts, CCNY Alumni Assn., NYU Alumni Assn. Office: 10615 Queens Blvd Flushing NY 11375-4365

FLECK, BELA, country musician; Albums Deviation, 1985, Bela Fleck and The Flecktones, 1989, Drive, Places, Flight of the Cosmic Hippo, 1991, UFO Tofu, 1992, Three Flew Over the Cuckoo's Nest, 1993, Tabula Rosa, 1994, Tales from the Acoustic Planet, 1995, Live Art, 1996, Left of Cool, 1998. Recipient Grammy award Best Country Instrumental Performance, 1996. Office: Warner Bros Records 20 Music Sq E Nashville TN 37203-4344

FLECK, DAVID E. neuropsychologist; b. Cleve., Nov. 20, 1969; s. William George and Carol Ann Fleck; m. Adrienne Marie Ruez, Dec. 16, 1994; 1 child, Samuel Joseph. BA cum laude, Cleve. State U., 1992, MA, 1994; PhD, U. Cin., 1997. Postdoctoral asst. Dept. Psychiatry U. Cin., 1997—2000, postdoctoral fellow, 2000—. Cons. R.E.M. Consulting of Ohio, Inc., Cleve., 1993, Nova Rsch. Co., Cleve., 1993, numerous clin. drug trials, Cin., 1995—; presenter in field. Contbr. articles to profl. jours. Recipient Young Investigator award, Am. Neuropsychiat. Assn., 1999, Nat. Rsch. Svc. award, NIMH, 2000. Mem.: APA, Nat. Acad. Neuropsychology, Internat. Neuropsychol. Soc. (assoc. finalist Nelson Butters award 2000). Roman Catholic. Avocations: running, sports, fishing, hiking, camping. Office: Dept Psychiatry U Cin 231 Albert Sabin Way Cincinnati OH 45267-0559 E-mail: fleckde@email.uc.edu.

FLECK, GEORGE MORRISON, chemistry educator; b. Warren, Ind., May 13, 1934; s. Ford Bloom and Deloris Magdalene (Morrison) F.; m. Margaret Dyer Reynolds, June 27, 1959; children: Margaret Morrison, Louise Elizabeth. BS, Yale U., 1956; PhD, U. Wis., 1961. Asst. prof. Smith Coll., Northampton, Mass., 1961-67, assoc. prof., 1967-76, prof. chemistry, 1976-2000, prof. emeritus, 2001—. Author: Equilibria in Solution, 1966, Chemical Reaction Mechanisms, 1971, Carboxylic Acid Equilibria, 1973, Chemistry: Molecules That Matter, 1974, Patterns of Symmetry, 1977, Shaping Space: A Polyhedral Approach, 1987; contbr.: Nobel Laureates in Chemistry, 1993, Women in Chemistry and Physics, 1993, American National Biography, 1999, Chemistry: Foundation and Applications, 2003. Fellow Danforth Found., 1956-61; Dupont fellow, 1960; Danforth assoc., 1982— ; grantee NSF, NIH, U.S. Office Edn., Am. Philos. Soc. Mem. Am. Chem. Soc., Mass. Assn. Sci. Tchrs., New Eng. Assn. Chemistry Tchrs., Sigma Xi Office: Smith Coll Clark Sci Ctr Northampton MA 01063-0001 E-mail: gfleck@smith.edu.

FLECK, RAYMOND ANTHONY, JR., retired university administrator; b. Bklyn., Mar. 9, 1927; s. Raymond Anthony and Dorothy (Canavan) F.; m. Dorothy Marie Rossow, Aug. 22, 1970; children: Andrew Jerome, Casey Thomas. Student, Manhattan Coll., 1946-48; BS, U. Notre Dame, 1951, PhD, 1954; student Ins. Coll. and Univ. Adminstrs., Harvard U., 1959. Brother of Holy Cross, 1949-70. Prof. chemistry St. Edward's U., 1954-69, pres., 1957-69; assoc. research chemist dept. environ. toxicology U. Calif. at Davis, 1969-72; pres. Marygrove Coll., Detroit, 1972-79; acting dir. Food Protection and Toxicology Center, U. Calif., Davis, 1979-83; dir. research Calif. State Poly. U., Pomona, 1983-95; assoc. Anver Biosci. Design, Inc., Sierra Madre, Calif., 1995—. Cons. EPA, La. Bd. Regents, U. Wis., Eau Claire, NSF; dir. Monterey Basin Pilot Monitoring Project, 1971-72; pres. Our Lady of the Assumption Conf., St. Vincent de Paul Soc., Claremont, Calif., 1999—. Vice pres., bd. dirs. Harmony Village Home Corp. N.W., Detroit, 1977-79. Served with USN, 1945-46. NSF fellow, 1952, 1969; recipient U. Notre Dame Centennial of Sci. medal, 1965; sci. bldg. at St. Edward's U. named Fleck Hall. Home: 4273 Guava St La Verne CA 91750-3010 E-mail: raymonda2@aol.com.

FLECKENSTEIN, JAMES LAWRENCE, radiologist; b. Omaha, Mar. 18, 1957; BS in Biology, U. Washington, 1979, MD, 1984. Diplomate Nat. Bd. Med. Examiners, Am. Bd. Radiology. Intern U. Tex. Southwestern Affiliated Hosps., Dallas, 1984-85; resident in radiology U. Tex. Southwestern Med. Ctr., Dallas, 1985-89, fellow in musculoskeletal MRI and spectroscopy, 1987-88, fellow in neuroradiology, 1989-91, dir. neuroradiology magnetic resonance, 1991-94. Med. dir. Algur H. Meadows Diagnostic Imaging Ctr., U. Tex. Southwestern Med. Ctr., Dallas, 1991-94, acting med. dir. Aston Radiology, 1991, prof. radiology, 1999—. Fellow Am. Coll. Sports Medicine; mem. AMA, Am. Roentgen Ray Soc., Am. Soc. Neuroradiology, Radiol. Soc. N.Am., Tex. Med. Assn., Tex. Radiol. Soc., Internat. Soc. Magnetic Resonance in Medicine, Dallas County Med. Assn. Home: 4504 Tour 18 Dr Flower Mound TX 75022-6400 Office: U Tex SW Med Ctr Algur H Meadows Diagnostic Imaging Ctr 5171 Harry Hines Blvd Dallas TX 75235-7707

FLEDDERMAN, HARRY L. lawyer; Sr. v.p. Gen. Counsel; sec. Crown Zellerbach Corp., San Francisco. Office: James River Corp Nev 1 Bush St San Francisco CA 94104-4425

FLEDER, GARY, film director, producer; T.V. and motion picture dir., prodr. Dir. films Things to Do in Denver When You're Dead, 1995 (winner critics award and spl. jury prize Cognac Festival du Film Policier), Kiss the Girls, 1997, Don't Say a Word, 2002; (TV series) Tales from the Crypt, 1989, Homicide: Life on the St., 1993, L.A. Doctors, 1998, Falcone, 2000, The Shield, 2002; dir. T.V. movie The Companion, 1994, From Earth to the Moon, 1998; dir., prodr. Air Time, 1992, Impostor, 2002. Office: care David Wirtschafter William Morris Agy 151 El Camino Dr Beverly Hills CA 90212-3300

FLEEGER, DAVID CLARK, colon and rectal surgeon; b. Neubrucke, Germany, July 11, 1959; s. James Elliott and Madge Ellen (Iseminger) F.; m. Jamie Greenstreet, Aug. 16, 1984; 1 child, Lauren Ann. BS, Baylor U., 1981; MD, Tex. A&M U., 1985. Diplomate Am. Bd. Surgery, Am. Bd. Colon and Rectal Surgeons. Resident in gen. surgery Mayo Clinic, Rochester, Minn., 1985-90; fellow in colon and rectal surgery La. State U., Shreveport, 1990-91; ptnr. Austin (Tex.) Colon and Rectal Clinic, 1991—; chief surgery Columbia St. Davids. S. Hosp., 1996-97; co-chair St. Davids Med. Ctr. Pain Mgmt. Ctr., 2000—. Chmn. Cancer Ctr., St. David's Med. Ctr., 1997—. Fellow ACS, Am. Soc. Colon and Rectal Surgeons (socioecons. com. 2000-02), Tex. Soc. Colon and Rectal Surgeons (pres-elect 1994, pres. 1994-95); mem. AMA (alt. mem. ho. of dels.), Am. Soc. Gastrointestinal Endoscopy Surgeons, Am. Soc. Colon and Rectal Surgeons, Soc. Am. Gastrointestinal Endoscopy, Tex. Med. Assn. (chmn. young physician sect., mem. governing coun. 1992-99, chmn. com. on physician distbn. 1999-2002). Avocations: fishing, hunting, photography, kayaking. Office: 4208 Medical Pkwy Austin TX 78756-3310

FLEENER, TERRY NOEL, marketing professional; b. Ottumwa, Iowa, May 26, 1939; s. Lowell F. and Freda B. (Sparks) F.; m. Jane A. Bacon, Dec. 9, 1969; children: Clinton Todd, Clayton Scott. BSME, U. Iowa, 1963. Engr. Bendix Corp., Davenport, Iowa, 1963-67, Ball Aerospace, Boulder, Colo., 1967-74, bus. mgr., 1974-78; v.p. gen. mgr. Entropy Ltd., Boulder, 1978-80; pres. Energy Bank, Inc., Golden, Colo., 1980-82; program mgr. Ball Aerospace, Boulder, 1982-84, dir. mktg., 1984-99; mng. gen. ptnr. The Montane Group LLLP, 1999—. Pres. U.S. Rugby Assn., Colorado Springs, 1987-89, Pam-Am. Rugby Assn., Miami, 1991-93, 97-98. Mem. ASME, AIAA, Am. Astron. Soc., Cryogenic Soc. Am. Office: The Montane Group 2122 Montane Dr E Golden CO 80401-9126

FLEENOR, DEBRA L. biomedical researcher; b. Quincy, Ill., Aug. 12, 1961; d. Elvin D. and Virginia L. Starman. BS, Quincy Coll., 1983; PhD, U. North Tex., Ft. Worth, 2000. Rsch. technician Washington U., St. Louis, 1984-86; rsch. asst. U. Tex. Southwestern Med. Sch., Dallas, 1986-89; assoc. scientist Alcon Labs., Ft. Worth, 1989-90, scientist I, 1990-93, scientist II, 1993-97, sr. scientist I, 1998—2000, sr. scientist II, 2002—. Patentee in field of retinal neuroprotection. Mem.: Women in Neurosci., Soc. for Exptl. Biology and Medicine. Achievements include patent in field. Office: Alcon Rsch Ltd Glaucoma Rsch R3-24 6201 South Fwy Fort Worth TX 76134-2001 E-mail: debra.shade@alconlabs.com.

FLEENOR, GENEVA LUCILLE, retired elementary school educator; b. Kokomo, Ind., Mar. 25, 1923; d. Howard Burton and Jennie Pauline (Henderson) Benjamin; m. Gerald Howard Fleenor, Mar. 27, 1945; children: Sherri Lynn Fleenor Sebring, Roger Lee, Regina(dec.). BA in Edn., Ariz. State U., 1962, MA in Edn., 1964. Cert. edn. Ariz., 1962. Weather-map plotter U.S. Weather Bur., Washington, 1944—45; elem. sch. tchr. Roosevelt Dist., Phoenix, 1962—85; ret., 1985. Co-author (and co-editor): How Arizona Came to Life, 1968 (Thank You award, 1972). Vol. Women's Help of Ariz., Phoenix, Fountain of Hope, Phoenix; tchr., com. mem. Forest Lakes (Ariz.) Cmty. Ch., cmty. bible study leader. Recipient Golden Rule Cert., State of Ariz., 2003. Conservative. Home: 2234 W Vista Ave Apt 11 Phoenix AZ 85021-6925

FLEER, KEITH GEORGE, lawyer, former motion picture executive; b. Feb. 28, 1943; s. Samuel Robert and Sophia M. (Scherer) Fleer. BA in Govt., Am. U., 1964, JD, 1967. Bar: N.Y. 1968, D.C. 1968, Calif. 1976. Asst. dir. athletics Fordham U., 1967—68; assoc. Gettinger, Gettinger & Manheimer, N.Y.C., 1968—72, Kaye, Scholer, Fierman, Hays & Handler, N.Y.C., 1972—75; sr. counsel Avco-Embassy Pictures, Hollywood, Calif., 1976; assoc. Schiff, Hirsch & Schreiber, Beverly Hills, Calif., 1977; sr. v.p. bus. and legal affairs Melvin Simon Prodn., Inc., Beverly Hills, 1978—81; exec. v.p. Simon, Reeves, Landsburg Prodns., Beverly Hills, 1982—84; v.p. bus. affairs Warner Bros., Beverly Hills, 1984—88; ptnr. Denton Hall Burgin and Warrens, Beverly Hills, 1987—88, Sinclair Tenenbaum & Emanuel & Fleer, Beverly Hills, 1989—98, Loeb & Loeb, Century City, Calif., 1998—. Guest lectr. U. West LA Law Sch., 1979—80; legis. counsel N.Y. State Assemblyman, 1969—70; adj. prof. Law Ctr. U. So. Calif., 1995. Bus. editor: Am. U. Law Rev., 1966—67. Bd. trustees Am. U., 0920—1997. Recipient Bruce Hughes award, Am. U., 1964, Alumni award, Am. U. Law Sch., 1967, Stafford H. Cassell award, 1979. Mem.: ABA, Acad. Motion Picture Arts and Scis., LA Copyright Soc. (trustee 1983—90, pres. 1988—89), Beverly Hills (Calif.) Bar Assn. Office: 10100 Santa Monica Blvd Los Angeles CA 90010

FLEETWOOD, M. FREILE, psychiatrist, educator; b. Valparaiso, Chile, Nov. 20, 1915; d. Alfonso Larrea and Berta (Cordovez) Freile; children: Harvey Blake, Francis Freile. MD, U. Chile, 1941; PhD, Pedagogic Inst., Santiago, Chile, 1947; MD, U. of State of N.Y., 1950. Instr. biochemistry to asst. in pub. emergencies U. Chile, Santiago, 1937-41, resident in neurology at neurol. clinic, 1941-42, head of rsch. lab. in psychiatry, 1944-48; resident in psychiatry Henry Phipps Clinic, John Hopkins U., Balt., 1942-44; provisional asst. in psychiatry to out-patient psychiatrist N.Y. Hosp., N.Y.C., 1948-61; attending psychiatrist Gracie Square Hosp., N.Y.C., 1961—; clin. asst. prof. psychiatry Cornell Univ., N.Y. Hosp., N.Y.C., 1970-88, emeritus status, 1988—. Instr. psychiatry, Payne Whitney Clinic, Cornell U., N.Y. Hosp., N.Y.C., 1950-63; cons. Family Svc. of Patterson, N.J., 1955-56, East Harlem Project Community Svc. Soc., N.Y.C., 1960-61, Manhattan Family Svc. Ctr. Community Svc. Soc., N.Y.C., 1960-61; asst. psychiatrist NYU, U. Hosp., Bellevue Med. Ctr., N.Y.C.,

1954, psychiatrist 1954-55, and others. Contbr. articles to profl. publs. Recipient Rockefeller Found. grantee, 1942-43, 43-44, 44-45, Sagin Fund grantee, 1952-53, Squibb Fund grant, 1952-53. Mem. AAAS, Med. Soc. State and County of N.Y., Am. Med. Soc. on Alcoholism and Other Drug Dependencies, Am. Psychiat. Assn. (N.Y. county dist. br.), N.Y. Acad. Sci., Spanish Am. Med. Soc., Pan Am. Med. Soc., N.Y. Soc. for Adolescent Psychiatry, The N.Y. County Review Orgn., Women's Med. Assn. N.Y., Am. Med. Women's Assn. Office: PO Box 1955 28 Central Ave Amagansett NY 11930 also: 69 W 83rd St New York NY 10024-5248

FLEETWOOD, MARY ANNIS, education association executive; b. Winfield, Ala., July 31, 1931; d. George A. and Martha Ann (Perry) Sullivan; m. Lewis N. Fleetwood, Aug. 19, 1950; children: Juanita, Dexter Lewis, Melanie Louise. Student, HCC Community Coll., 1973-80. Gen. office staff Able Rose Mercentile Co., Birmingham, Ala., 1949-51; with auditing dept. Bank for Savs. & Trusts, Birmingham, Ala., 1951; account receivables clk. I.W. Phillips, Tampa, Fla., 1972-77; account clk. Sch. Bd. Hill County, Tampa, Fla., 1980, office mgr., 1981-90. V.p. PTA, 1961-62; pres. Woman's Missionary Union, Birmingham, 1963-64. Mem. DAR, Nat. Inst. Govt. Purchasing (cert. profl. buyer). Baptist. Avocations: photography, genealogy, travel.

FLEETWOOD, REX ALLEN, insurance company executive; b. Newton, Kans., Aug. 17, 1951; s. Milburn William and Edna Milton (Hughes) F.; m. Donna Kay Kurr, June 3, 1972. BS, Kans. Wesleyan U., 1973. Programmer First Nat. Bank, Salina, Kans., 1971-73, State of Kans., Topeka, 1973-74; project leader Blue Cross/Blue Shield, Topeka, 1974-77; asst. v.p. data systems Great Central Ins., Peoria, Ill., 1977-81; v.p. data systems Am. Universal Inc., Providence, 1981-84, Pa. Nat. Ins., Harrisburg, 1984-93; v.p. Am. Internat. Group, N.Y.C., 1993-94, Cigna Spl. Risk Facilities, Phila., 1994-99; sr. v.p. planning Internat. Software Cons. Inc., Princeton, NJ, 1999—2001; founder, COO NJRX, Inc., Mechanisburg, Pa., 2001—. Mem. Diamond Club, United Way, Harrisburg, 1988-92. Named Speaker of Yr., Data Processing Auditors Assn., Harrisburg, 1988. Mem. Pa. Assn. Mut. Ins. Cos. (chmn. data processing com. 1987-90). Republican. Baptist. Home: 276 Ridge Hill Rd Mechanicsburg PA 17050-1718 Office: Internat Software Cons Inc 100 Thanet Cir Ste 300 Princeton NJ 08540-3674

FLEEZANIS, JORJA KAY, violinist, educator; b. Detroit, Mar. 19, 1952; d. Parios Nicholas and Kaliope (Karageorge) F.; m. Michael Steinberg, July 3, 1983. Student, Cleve. Inst. Music, 1969-72, Cin. Coll.-Conservatory Music, 1972-75. Violinist Chgo. Symphony Orch., 1975-76; concertmaster Cin. Chamber Orch., 1976-80; violinist Trio D'Accordo, Cin., 1976-80; asst. prin. 2d violinist San Francisco Symphony Orch., 1980-81; assoc. concertmaster San Francisco Sympony Orch., 1980-89; acting concertmaster Minn. Orch., Mpls., 1988-89, concertmaster, 1989—; violinist Fleezanis-Ohlsson-Grebanier Piano Trio, San Francisco, 1984—; faculty mem. San Francisco Conservatory of Music, 1983-89, U. Minn., 1989—. Founder Chamber Music Sundaes, San Francisco, 1980-89, The Am. String Project, 2002; artist-in-residence U. Calif., Davis, 1995—; radio host St. Paul Sunday Show, Minn. Pub. Radio, 1998-2000; guest concertmaster, London Classical Players, L.A. Philharmonic, Sydney Symphony, Balt. Symphony. Performer World Premiere John Adams Violin Concerto with Minn. Orch., 1994, Nicholas Maw, Sonata for Solo Violin, commd. by Minn. Pub. Radio, 1997, Sir John Taverner's Ikon of Eros, commd. for her by Minn. Orch., 2002; commd. by Pub. Radio Internat. and Minn. Pub. Radio for world premiere of Nicholas Maw Sonata for Solo Violin, 1998; soloist Am. premier Benjamin Britten Double Concerto, 1998; rec. artist CRI and Koch Classical Records. Democrat. Avocations: photography, cooking. Office: Minn Orch 1111 Nicollet Mall Minneapolis MN 55403-2406

FLEG, JEROME LOUIS, physician, research cardiologist; b. Cin., June 15, 1945; s. Julian Francis and Elaine (Nelson) F.; m. Rosemarie T. Greyson, Sept. 20, 1977; children: Anthony, Jerome, Michael, Stephen. BS in Zoology, U. Cin., 1967, MD, 1970. Intern Balt. City Hosps., 1970-71; resident, internal medicine Barnes Hosp., St. Louis, 1973-75; fellow, cardiology Wash. Univ. Med. Sch., St. Louis, 1975-77; rsch. cardiologist Nat. Inst. Aging, Balt., 1977—; acting dir. Balt. Longitudinal Study of Aging, 1998—. Assoc. editor Medicine and Sci. in Sports and Exercise, 1996-98; mem. editl. bd. Am. Jour. Cardiology, Jour. Gerontology, Cardiology in the Elderly, Jour Am. Geriatrics Soc.; contbr. more than 140 articles to profl. jours. and chpts. to books. Capt. USAF, 1971-73. Fellow Am. Coll. Cardiology, Coun. on Geriatric Cardiology (v.p. 1988-90, pres. 1990-91); mem. Am. Heart Assn., Commd. Officers Assn., Am. Physiological Soc. Avocations: music, cycling. Office: Gerontology Rsch Ctr Eastern Ave Baltimore MD 21224-2735

FLEGLE, JIM L. lawyer; b. Paducah, Ky., Dec. 3, 1951; s. J.L. and Alice M. (Goodman) F.; m. Ophelia Flegle Camina; children: Lauren Tyler, Brittanie Len, James Brendan, Alexandra Carlisle, James Armand. BA, U. Ky., 1974; JD, U. Va., 1977. Bar: Tex. 1977, U.S. Dist. Ct. (so. dist.) Tex. 1977, U.S. Dist. Ct. (no. dist.) Tex. 1984, U.S. Dist. Ct. (we. dist.) Tex. 1988, U.S. Dist. Ct. (ea. dist.) Tex. 1989, U.S. Dist. Ct. Colo. 2002, U.S. Ct. Appeals (5th and 11th cirs.) 1981, U.S. Ct. Appeals (9th cir.) 1991, U.S. Ct. Appeals (fed. cir.) 1994, U.S. Supreme Ct. 1993. Assoc. Bracewell & Patterson, Houston, 1977-83, ptnr., 1983-89, Dallas, 1989—2002, head Dallas office, 1992-98; adv. com. Bracewell & Patterson, Dallas, 1996-98; ptnr. Loewinsohn & Flegle, LLP, 2002—. Mem. Coll. of the State Bar of Tex., 2003-, criminal justice act vol. atty. panel U.S. Dist. Ct. (no. dist.) Tex. Vol. Houston Pro Bono Program; active Tex. Lawyers and Accts. for Arts, Houston, 1982-85, St. Paul's Chamber Music Soc.; mem. corp. campaign com. Dallas Mus. Art, 1994-95, Dallas Hist. Soc., 1991-92. Mem. ABA, Tex. Bar Assn. (grievance com. 1996-99), Houston Bar Assn., Dallas Bar Assn., Houston Bar Found. (life fellow), Tex. Bar Found., Dallas Bar Found., Am. Bd. Trial Advocates (assoc.), Higginbotham Inn of Ct. (barrister), Coll. of the State Bar of Tex., Raven Soc., Phi Beta Kappa, Omicron Delta Kappa, Sigma Nu. Methodist. Office: Loewinsohn & Flegle 18383 Preston Rd ste 100 Dallas TX 75252-5476 E-mail: jimf@texasverdict.com.

FLEIFIL, MAHMOUD MOHAMED, acoustics engineer, researcher; b. El-Suez, Egypt, June 26, 1962; came to U.S., 1993; s. Mohamed Ahmed Fleifil; m. Nehad Omara, Mar. 25, 1999; 1 child, Salma Fleifil. BS in Engring., Ain Shams U., Cairo, 1985, MS in Engring., 1991, PhD in Engring., 1995. Trainee North Cairo Power Sta., 1983, South Helwan Power Sta., Cairo, 1984; tchg. asst. faculty engring. Ain Shams U., 1987-90, asst. lectr. faculty engring., 1991-93; vis. engr. MIT, Cambridge, 1993-95; asst. prof. faculty engring. Ain Shams U., 1996-98; postdoctoral assoc. MIT, 1996-99; acoustics engr. John Zink Co., Tulsa, Okla., 1999—. Investigator Shobera El-Khema Power Plant, Cairo, 1992-93; supr. grad. students MIT, 1996-99. Contbr. articles to profl. jours.; developed the first physically-based model of thermoacoustic instability. Mem. AIAA, ASME. Moslem. Avocations: reading scientific news, traveling, electronics. Home: 4857 S 73d Ave Apt 62-7 Tulsa OK 74145 Office: 11920 E Apache St Tulsa OK 74116-1309 E-mail: fleifilm@kochind.com., Fleifilm@yahoo.com.

FLEISCHAKER, MARC L. lawyer; b. Cin., Feb. 22, 1945; s. Leopold and Betty Jane (Spritz) F.; m. Phyllis S. Schmidt, June 16, 1969; children: Deborah, Julia. BS in Econs., Wharton Sch. U. Pa., 1967; JD, George Washington U., 1971. Bar: D.C. 1971, U.S. Dist. Ct. D.C. 1971, U.S. Supreme Ct. 1974, U.S. Ct. Mil. Appeals, U.S. Ct. Appeals D.C., U.S. Ct. Appeals (3d cir.) 1986, U.S. Ct. Appeals (4th, 5th and 11th cirs.). From assoc. to ptnr. Arent, Fox, Kintner, Plotkin & Kahn, Washington, 1971—78, head environ. practice, 1978—2000, chmn., 1997—, interim mng. ptnr., 1993, mng. ptnr., 2002, exec. com., 1983, vice chmn., 1986—96. Exec. com. Washington Lawyers Com. for Civil Rights and Urban Affairs, 1989—, co-chmn., 1990-91, 99—, chair fin. com. 1992-93; bd. dirs. Coun. for Ct. Excellence, Nat. Lawyers Com. Civil Rights Under Law, co-chmn. 1996-98; chmn. tech. com. legal sect. Am. Soc. Assn. Execs., 1995-96, bd. dirs. tchg., learning and tech. group; mentor U. Md. Sch. Pub. Affairs, 2002— Contbr. articles to profl. jours. Mem. Fed. City Coun., 2000—. With USNG, 1969-75. Recipient Triangle award, Motor and Equipment Mfrs. Assn., 1976. Mem.: ABA, Fed. Bar Assn., Econ. Club Washington. Avocations: politics, competitive running, golf, tennis. Home: 6308 Broad Branch Rd Bethesda MD 20815-3342 Office: Arent Fox 1050 Connecticut Ave NW Washington DC 20036-5339 E-mail: fleischaker.marc@arentfox.com.

FLEISCHER, ARTHUR, JR., lawyer; b. Hartford, Conn., Jan. 27, 1933; s. Arthur and Clare Lillian (Katzenstein) F.; m. Susan Abby Levin, July 6, 1958; children: Elizabeth, Katherine. BA, Yale U., 1953, LLB, 1958. Bar: N.Y. 1959. Assoc. Strasser, Spiegelberg, Fried & Frank, N.Y.C., 1958-61; legal asst. SEC, Washington, 1961-62, exec. asst. to chmn., 1962-64; assoc. Fried, Frank, Harris, Shriver & Jacobson, N.Y.C., 1964-67, ptnr., 1967—, chmn., 1989-97, sr. ptnr., 1997—. Vis. lectr. law Columbia U., N.Y.C., 1972-73; adviser to adv. com. Fed. Securities Code Project, Am. Law Inst., 1970-78; adviser to com. to consider new issue proposals Nat. Assn. Securities Dealers, 1973-75, mem. com. corp. financing, 1976-80; bd. dirs. Haleakala Inc. (The Kitchen), N.Y., 1987-2002; chmn. Ann. Inst. on Securities Regulation, Practising Law Inst., 1969-81; mem. indsl. issuers adv. com. SEC, 1972-73; mem. adv. com. corp. disclosure, 1976-77; bd. govs. Am. Stock Exch., 1977-83; legal adv. com, bd. dirs. N.Y. Stock Exch., 1987-91 Co-author: Tender Offers, 1978, 6th edit., 1995, Board Games, 1988; co-editor: Annual Institute on Securities Regulation, 1970-81; contbr. articles to profl. jours. Mem. adv. coun. Ctr. for study of fin. instns. U. Pa.; trustee, mem. photography com. of Whitney Mus.; trustee Ind. Curators Internat., 1990-2002. Recipient Disting. Cmty. Svc. award Brandeis U., 1983, Judge Learned Hand Human Rels. award Am. Jewish Com., 1983, Harold P. Seligson award Practicing Law Inst., 1988, Judge Joseph W. Proskauer award UJA Fedn., 1994. Mem. ABA (mem. com. on fed. regulation of securities regulation 1969—), Assn. Bar City N.Y. (mem. spl. com. on lawyers role in securities transactions 1973-77, chmn. com. securities regulation 1972-74), Century Country Club (N.Y.C.). Home: 1050 Park Ave New York NY 10028-1031 Office: Fried Frank Harris 1 New York Plz Fl 27 New York NY 10004-1980

FLEISCHER, ARTHUR C. medical educator, radiologist; b. Miami, Fla., May 15, 1952; s. Eugene and Lucille Fleischer; m. Leona Fleischer, May 25, 1975; children: Braden, Jared, Amy. BS in Biology, Emory U., 1973; MD, Med. Coll. Ga., 1976. Diplomate Am. Bd. Radiology. Prof. radiology Vanderbilt U. Med. Ctr., Nashville, 1987—, prof. ob-gyn., 1988—. Author: Principles and Practice of Ultrasonography in Ob/Gyn, 2001, books on diagnostic sonography. Fellow: Am. Inst. Ultrasound in Medicine (bd. govs. 1989—91, William Fry award 1999), Am. Coll. Radiology, Soc. Radiologists in Ultrasound (Larry Mack award 1999). Office: Vanderbilt Univ Med Ctr 21st & Garlands Sts Nashville TN 37212

FLEISCHER, CARL AUGUST, law educator, consultant; b. Oslo, Aug. 26, 1936; s. Carl Johan and Marie (Mathiesen) F.; m. Eva Sylvia Funder, Sept. 15, 1967. Legal exam. laudabilis, U. Oslo, 1960, LLD, 1964. 1st sec. legal divsn. Ministry Fgn. Affairs, 1960-61; spl. cons. internat. law, 1962—. Lectr. law U. Oslo Faculty Law, 1961-69, prof., 1969—; adviser in internat. law Ministry Fgn. Affairs, 1986—; lectr., cons., mem. dels. internat. confs.; mem. Internat. Council Environ. Law, Norwegian Petroleum Soc., Norwegian Soc. Int. Law. Author: Jurisdiction on Fisheries, 1963, International Law, 7th edit., 2000, Constitutional Limitations, 1969, The Law on Building and Regulation of Property, 4th edit., 1983, Commentary to the Act of Expropriation and Compensation, 1974, The Economic Zone, 1976, The Law of Expropriation, 1978, Expropriation Procedure, 1980, Application and Interpretation of Judgements, 1981, Petroleum Law, 1983, La pêche (The Fisheries), 1985; co-author: Traitè du Nouveau Droit de la Mer, 1985, Compensation to Fisheries for Offshore Devel. Report, 1986, The New Regime of Maritime Fisheries, 1989, Environment and Resources Management, 1991, 99; co-author: A Handbook on the Law New of the Sea, 1991, Environmental Law, 1992-96, Planning Building Law, 1992, Land-lease Contracts, 1992, Sources of Law, 1995, Private Law Subjects, 1995, Studies in International Law, 1997, Sources of Law and Legal Method, 1998; contbr. articles to profl. jours. Home: 13 Thomas Heftyes Oslo 2 Norway Office: U Oslo Karl Johans gt 47 Oslo N-0162 Norway

FLEISCHER, EVERLY BORAH, academic administrator; b. Salt Lake City, June 5, 1936; s. Arthur and Clare (Katzenstein) F.; m. Harriet Eve Perlysky, June 14, 1959; children: Deborah, Adam Joseph. BS, Yale U., 1958, MS, 1959, PhD, 1961. Asst. prof., then assoc. prof. chemistry U. Chgo., 1961-69; prof. U. Calif., Irvine, 1970-80, dean phys. sci., 1975-80; prof. chemistry, dean Coll. Arts and Scis. U. Colo., Boulder, 1980-88; exec. vice chancellor, prof. chemistry U. Calif., Riverside, 1988-94; program exec. Am. Acad. Arts and Scis., Western Ctr., 1996; project dir. NSF Math. Sci. Partnership Focus! grant, 2003—. Author articles on metalloporphyrins, bioinorganic chemistry. NSF fellow, 1959-61; Alfred P. Sloan fellow, 1962-66; recipient Univ. Svc. award U. Calif., Irvine, 1980. Fellow AAAS; mem. Am. Chem. Soc., Sigma Xi, Alpha Chi Sigma. Home: 8 Tivoli Ct Newport Beach CA 92657-1533 Office: Univ California Dept Chemistry Irvine CA 92697-0001 E-mail: ebfleisc@chem.ps.uci.edu.

FLEISCHER, LESLIE RAYMOND, cardiologist; b. Washington, Apr. 13, 1948; AB in History, Duke U., 1969; MD, Creighton U., 1975. Diplomate Am. Bd. Internal Medicine (fellow), Am. Bd. Cardiology. Cardiologist Conestoga Med. Assn., Lancaster, Pa., 1980-92, Carle Clinic Assn., Urbana, Ill., 1992-99, White-Wilson Med. Ctr., Ft. Walton Beach, Fla., 1999—, U. Ill. Coll. Medicine, Ft. Walton Beach. Fellow Am. Coll. Cardiology, Soc. Cardiac Interventions. Office: White Wilson Med Ctr 1005 Mar Walt Dr Fort Walton Beach FL 32547-6707 E-mail: lrfleischer@yahoo.com.

FLEISCHER, NORMAN SAMUEL, endocrinology administrator, medical educator; b. Springfield, Tenn., Jan. 24, 1936; s. Paul and Eva (Cohen) F.; m. Eva Lessy, Apr. 7, 1966; children: Deborah, Arlene. AB, Vanderbilt U., 1958, MD, 1961. Med. resident Albert Einstein Coll. of Medicine, Bronx, 1961-64; fellow in endocrinology Vanderbilt U., Nashville, 1964-66; dir. Endocrinology and Diabetes Ctr. Albert Einstein Coll. of Medicine, Bronx, 1976—, prof., 1978—; fellow in endocrinology Sch. of Medicine Vanderbilt U., Nashville, 1964-66; asst. prof. Coll. of Medicine Baylor U., Houston, 1966-71, assoc. prof. Sch. of Medicine, 1971-73; assoc. prof. Albert Einstein Coll. of Medicine, Bronx, 1973-77. Author chpts. in books; contbr. numerous articles to profl. jours. NIH grantee, 1966—. Fellow ACP; mem. Am. Fedn. Clin. Rsch., Am. Soc. Clin. Investigation, Am. Assn. Physicians, Am. Diabetes Assn., Endocrine Soc. Office: Yeshiva U Albert Einstein Coll Medicine 1300 Morris Park Ave Bronx NY 10461-1926

FLEISCHER, PETER, research geologist, oceanographer, educator; b. Coburg, Germany, Sept. 10, 1941; came to U.S., 1948; s. Heinrich Rudolf and Else Antonie (Kellersch) F.; m. Virginia Ann Thomas, Dec. 27, 1972. BA, U. Minn., 1963; PhD, U. So. Calif., 1970. Lectr. UCLA, 1970; postdoctoral fellow Duke U. Marine Lab., Beaufort, N.C., 1970-71; asst. prof. Inst. of Oceanography, Old Dominion U., Norfolk, Va., 1971-78; geologist Naval Ocean R&D Activity Naval Oceanogrpahic/Atmospheric Rsch. Lab., Stennis Space Ctr., Miss., 1978-91; geologist Naval Rsch. Lab., Stennis Space Ctr., 1992-99; oceanographer Naval Oceanographic Office, Stennis Space Ctr., 1999—. Contbr. articles to profl. jours. Mem. Am. Assn. Petroleum Geologists, Soc. for Sedimentary Geology, Sigma Xi. Achievements include research in marine sediments, side scan sonar applications, geoacoustics, clay minerology, coastal oceanography, marine geology. Home: 971 E 2nd St Pass Christian MS 39571-4719 Office: Naval Oceanographic Office Code N532 Stennis Space Center MS 39522-0001 E-mail: mudbug@sigmaxi.org., fleischerp@navo.navy.mil.

FLEISCHER, ROBERT LOUIS, physics educator; b. Columbus, Ohio, July 8, 1930; s. Leo H. and Rosalie (Kahn) F.; m. Barbara L. Simons, June 10, 1954; children: Cathy Ann, Elizabeth Lee. AB, Harvard U., 1952, AM, 1953, PhD, 1956. Asst. prof. metallurgy MIT, 1956—60; physicist GE Rsch. Lab., Schenectady, 1960—92; rsch. prof. earth and environ. scis. Rensselaer Poly. Inst., Troy, NY, 1992—97; rsch. prof. geology Union Coll., Schenectady, 1997—. Sr. rsch. fellow physics Calif. Inst. Tech., 1965-66; adj. prof. physics and astronomy Rensselaer Poly. Inst., 1967-68; adj. prof. geol. sci. SUNY, Albany, 1982-87; cons. U.S. Geol. Survey, 1967-70, GE R&D Ctr., 1992-93; vis. scientist Nat. Ctr. for Atmospheric Rsch., NOAA, 1973-74; adj. prof. applied physics and mech. engring. Yale U., 1984; vis. scientist Materials Rsch. Soc., 1995. Author: Nuclear Tracks in Solids, 1975, Tracks to Innovation, 1998; co-editor: Intermetallic Compounds: Principles and Practice, vols. 1 and 2, 1995, vol. 3, 2002, Crystal Structures of Intermetallic Compounds, Basic Mechanical Properties of Intermetallic Compounds, Magnetic, Electrical and Optical Properties, and Applications of Intermetallic Compounds, 2000, others; assoc. editor: 1st-4th Lunar Sci. Conf. Procs., 1970-73. Pres. Zoller Sch. PTA, 1968-69; mem. com. on candidates Schenectady Citizens Conv. for Sch. Bd., 1969-72, 82-83, chmn., 1969-70, 71-72, vice chmn. conv., 1977-78, chmn., 1978-79; mem. com. on priorities Schenectady Sch. Bd., 1974-75; bd. dirs. Schenectady Citizens' League, Freedom Forum, Inc; mem. Mayor's Com. on Transp. and Infrastructure, 2000. Recipient awards Indsl. Rsch., 1964, 65, 72, Spl. award Am. Nuc. Soc., 1964, Ernest O. Lawrence award AEC, 1971, Gen. Elec. Silver medallion Inventor's award, 1971, Gold Medallion Inventor's award, 1991, Golden Plate award Am. Acad. Achievement, 1972, Coolidge award Gen. Electric Rsch. and Devel. Ctr., 1972; NASA Exceptional Sci. Achievement award, 1973, spl. recognition, 1979; Disting. Career award Hudson-Mohawk chpt. AIME, 1991. Fellow: NAE, AAAS, Health Physics Soc., Am. Geophys. Union, Am. Phys. Soc., Am. Acad. Arts and Scis.; mem.; Sigma Xi. Achievements include research in charged particle tracks in solids and their use in several fields, including cosmic ray and meteorite sci., geochronology, nuclear physics, radiobiology, environmental radon, personal radon dosimetry, Hiroshima neutron dosimetry, mineral exploration; defects in solids and their effects on mech. properties and superconducting properties, high temperature materials. Home: 1356 Waverly Pl Schenectady NY 12308-2629 Office: Union Coll Dept Geology Schenectady NY 12308 E-mail: fleischr@union.edu.

FLEISCHER-RIEVESCHL, ELLEN LEE, real estate agent; b. Cin., Dec. 15, 1945; d. Leo Simon and Janet Fleischer; m. George Rieveschl, Jr. BA in Mgmt. Econs., U. Cin., 1968. Pub. rels. Cin. Gas and Electric CO., 1968-71; campaign coord. Taft for Senate, Cin., 1971-72; new bus. devel. profl. Fifth Third Bank N.A., Cin., 1973-77; mktg. mgr. Williamsburg Mgmt., Cin., 1984-86; real estate agt. Sibcy Cline Realtors, Ft. Mitchell, Ky., 1986-91, Re/Max Affiliates, Ft. Mitchell, 1992—. Artist, Cin., 1978-85; mem. Kenton Boone Bd. Realtors, Northern Ky. Exhibitor watercolor abstracts various galleries in Cin., Naples and Coral Gables, Fla., N.Y.C.; author essay, Congl. Record, 1st pl. award, 1968. Mem. steering com. Emery Soc. Childrens Hosp.; bd. dirs. Carnegie Arts Ctr. Mem. Ky. Assn. Realtors, Nat. Assn. Realtors, Million Dollar Club, Friends of Covington, No. Ky. Heritage League, Cin. Art Mus., Cin. Symphony Com., Forward Quest of Covington, Omicron Delta Epsilon. Avocations: horseback riding, walking, swimming, travel, painting. Home: 100 Riverside Pl Covington KY 41011-1718

FLEISCHHAUER, CARL-AUGUST, judge of international court of justice; b. Düsseldorf, Dec. 9, 1930; s. Kurt and Leonie (Schneider-Neuenburg) F.; m. Liliane Sarolea, 1957; 2 children. Student, U. Heidelberg, U. Grenoble, U. Paris, U. Chgo. Rsch. fellow Max-Planck Inst. Comparative Fgn. Pub. Law and Internat. Law, Heidelberg, 1960-62; with Fgn. Svc. of Germany, 1962-83, legal adviser fed. fgn. office, 1975, dir.-gen. legal dept., 1976; under-sec.-gen. legal affairs, legal counsel UN, 1983-94; judge Internat. Ct. Justice, 1994—2003. Contbr. articles to profl. jours. Recipient various decorations. Avocations: modern history, literature. Office: Internat Ct Justice Peace Palace 2517 KJ The Hague Netherlands

FLEISCHLI, GEORGE ROBERT, lawyer; b. Springfield, Ill., Aug. 23, 1940; s. Edward Constantine and Margaret Dorothy Fleischli F.; m. Ann Elizabeth Malmer, Nov. 5, 1966; children: Mary Elizabeth, Margaret Ann. BS, U. Ill., 1962, JD with honors, 1965, MA in Labor Rels., 1970. Bar: Ill. 1965, Wis. 1971. Rsch. asst. U. Ill., Urbana, 1965-66, 69-70; mediator, examiner employee rels. commn. State of Wis., Madison, 1970-75, gen. counsel employee rels. commn., 1976-81; pvt. practice Madison, 1981—. Guest spkr. U. Wis., Madison. Contbr. articles to profl. jours. Capt. USAF, 1966—69. Mem. Ill. Bar Assn., Wis. Bar Assn., Nat. Acad. Arbitrators (chmn. legal affairs com. 1978-90, bd. govs. 1990-93, chmn. com. profl. responsibility and grievance 1994-97, v.p. 1997-99), Order of Coif. Office: 131 W Wilson St Ste 1100 Madison WI 53703-3245

FLEISCHMAN, ALBERT SIDNEY (SID FLEISCHMAN), writer; b. Bklyn., Mar. 16, 1920; s. Reuben and Sadie (Solomon) F.; m. Beth Elaine Taylor, Jan. 25, 1942; children— Jane, Paul, Anne. BA, San Diego State Coll., 1949. Newspaper reporter San Diego Daily Jour., 1949-50; freelance screenwriter. Lectr. fiction writing UCLA. Author: (children's books) Mr. Mysterious & Company, 1962, By the Great Horn Spoon!, 1963, The Ghost in the Noonday Sun, 1965, Chancy and the Grand Rascal, 1966, McBroom and the Great Race, 1970, Longbeard the Wizard, 1970, Jingo Django, 1971, Kate's Secret Riddle Book, 1977, Me and the Man on the Moon-Eyed Horse, 1977, Jim Bridger's Alarm Clock and Other Tall Tales, 1978, Humbug Mountain, 1978, McBroom and the Beanstalk, 1978, The Hey Hey Man, 1979, McBroom and the Great Race, 1980, The Bloodhound Gang in the Case of the Cackling Ghost, 1981, The Bloodhound Gang in the Case of the Flying Clock, 1981, The Bloodhound Gang in the Case of the Princess Tomorrow, 1981, The Bloodhound Gang in the Case of the Secret Message, 1981, The Bloodhound Gang in the Case of the 264-Pound Burglar, 1982, McBroom's Zoo, 1982, McBroom's Ear, 1982, McBroom and the Big Wind, 1982, The Bloodhound Gang's Secret Code Book, 1983, McBroom's Almanac, 1984, The Whipping Boy, 1986 (John Newbery medal 1987), The Scarebird, 1988, The Midnight Horse, 1990, Jim Ugly, 1992, Here Comes McBroom, 1992, McBroom's Wonderful One-Acre Farm, 1992, The 13th Floor, 1995, The Abracadabra Kid, A Writer's Life, 1996, Mr. Mysterious & Company, 1997, Chancy and the Grand Rascal, 1997, The Ghost on Saturday Night, 1997, Bandit's Moon, 1998, McBroom's Ghost, 1998, McBroom Tells the Truth, 1998, McBroom the Rainmaker, 1999, McBroom Tells a Lie, 1999, A Carnival of Animals, 2000, Bo and Mzzz Mad, 2001, Disappearing Act, 2003; (screenplays) Blood Alley, 1955, Goodbye, My Lady, 1956, Lafayette Escadrille, 1958, The Deadly Companions, 1973, Scalawag, 1973, Prince Brat and the Whipping Boy, 1995. Served with USNR, 1941-45. Recipient Spur award Western Writers Am., Commonwealth Club award, Lewis Carrol Shelf award, Mark Twain award, Calif. Young Reader award, John and Patricia Beatty award. Mem. Writers Guild Am., Authors Guild, Soc. Children's Book Writers. Democrat. Jewish. Office: care Greenwillow Books 1350 Avenue Of The Americas New York NY 10019-4702

FLEISCHMAN, BARBARA GREENBERG, public relations consultant; b. Detroit, Mar. 20, 1924; d. Samuel J. and Theresa (Keil) Greenberg; m. Lawrence A. Fleischman, Dec. 18, 1948; children: Rebecca, Arthur, Martha. BA, U. Mich., 1944. Tchr. Detroit Pub. Schs., 1944-45; psychoanalyst's sec., 1947-49; sec. Greenberg Ins. Agy., 1947-49; customer/pub. rels. cons. Kennedy Galleries, N.Y.C., 1976—. Bd. dirs. Detroit Artists Market, 1958-66, Planned Parenthood, N.Y.C., 1990-96, Am. Craft Coun., 1980-83, Friends of Channel 13, 1968-80, pres., N.Y.C., 1975-79, chmn. auction, 1975, trustee, 1975-84; mem. women's com. Detroit Inst. Arts, 1957-66; pres. Friends of N.Y. Pub. Libr., 1979-84, trustee, 1980—, v.p., bd., 1987—; trustee The Acting Co., 1986-89, pres., 1988-89; mem. gov. bd. Off the Record Luncheons, Fgn. Policy Assn., 1978-85; assoc. prodr. Channel 13 Auction, 1978-80; trustee Mus. TV and Radio, 1988-92, Archives of Am. Art, 1997—, caryatids chmn., 1998-2003, chmn. bd., 2003—; vis. com. Am. Wing, Met. Mus., 1998—; commr. Art Commn. of the City of N.Y., 1995-98; hon. patron Brit. Mus., 1996—, Caryatids com., pres., 1998—, chmn.; v.p. Archives of Am. Art, pres.; mem. trustees com. Libr. Mus. Modern Art, 1998—; pres. Archives of Am. Art, 1998—; mem. Coun. Am. Mus. Nat. History, 1999—; mem. devel. trust Brit. Mus., 1999—; treas. Friends of the Art Commn., 1999—; trustee The Getty Trust, 2000—. Mem. Cosmopolitan Club. Office: Kennedy Galleries 730 5th Ave New York NY 10019-4105 E-mail: bgf324@aol.com.

FLEISCHMAN, EDWARD HIRSH, lawyer, consultant; b. Cambridge, Mass., June 25, 1932; s. Louis Isaac and Jean (Grossman) F.; m. Joan Barbara Walden, Dec. 27, 1953 (dec. 1993), m. Judy Vernon, Sept. 27, 1998. BA, Harvard U.; LLB, Columbia U., 1959. Bar: N.Y. 1959, U.S. Supreme Ct. 1980. Assoc. Beekman & Bogue, N.Y.C., 1959-67, ptnr., 1968-86; commr. SEC, Washington, 1986-92; ptnr. Rosenman & Colin, 1992-94; sr. counsel Linklaters, N.Y.C., 1994—. Bd. dirs. Soundview Tech. Group, Inc. (formerly Wit Capital Corp.), 1998—. Served with U.S. Army, 1952-55. Mem.: ABA (chmn. bus. law subcom. rule 144 1970—72, subcom. broker-dealer matters 1973—78, subcom. model simplified indenture 1980—83, adminstrv. law com. on securities, commodities and exchs. 1981—84, bus. law com. on devels. in bus. financing 1987—91, com. on counsel responsibility 1995—99, internat. law com. on internat. securities transactions 1999—2002), Security Traders Assn. (bd. govs. 1997—2000), Internat. Law Assn. (chmn. com. on internat. securities regulation 1998—), Internat. Bar Assn., Am. Soc. Corp. Secs., Am. Coll. Investment

Counsel (pres. 1990—91), Am. Law Inst. Republican. Jewish. Office: Linklaters 1345 6th Ave New York NY 10105-0302 Home: 897 Franklin Lake Rd Franklin Lakes NJ 07417-2115 E-mail: edward.fleischman@linklaters.com., edward@fleischman.org.

FLEISCHMAN, HERMAN ISRAEL, lawyer; b. Bklyn., Aug. 30, 1950; s. Boris and Bella (Weisbrot) F.; m. Francine Moskowitz, Feb. 3, 1973; children: Meredith, Brandon, Gary. BA, Bklyn. Coll., 1972; JD, Bklyn. Sch. Law, 1976; MPA, NYU, 1974. Bar: N.Y. 1977, U.S. Dist. Ct. (ea., so., we. and no. dists.) N.Y. 1977, U.S. Ct. Appeals (D.C. cir.) 1979, U.S. Tax Ct. 1982. Asst. counsel Amalgamated Ins. Fund, N.Y.C., 1976; spl. asst. atty. gen. State of N.Y., N.Y.C., 1977-79; asst. counsel N.Y. State Dept. Mental Hygiene, Staten Island, N.Y., 1979; assoc. Ackerman, Salwen & Glass, N.Y.C., 1979-80; sole practice N.Y.C., 1980—. Mem. Thomas Jefferson Dem. Club, Bklyn., 1983-85; chmn. B'nai Brith Youth Orgn., 1980-82; bd. dirs. Big Apple Region, vice chmn., 1986-88, bd. dirs. Nassau and Suffolk Counties, N.Y., 1990-2001. Recipient Citation, Town of Hempstead, 1986, Dist. Key award, B'nai B'rith Youth Org., 1979, Man of Yr. award, B'nai B'rith Youth Org., 1980; named Coach of Yr., North Merrick-North Bellmore Basketball League, 1998. Mem. ABA, N.Y. State Bar Assn., Bklyn. Bar Assn., United Mut. Industries, Inc. (pres. 1983—). E-mail: HFleischma@aol.com.

FLEISCHMAN, JOSEPH JACOB, lawyer; b. Jersey City, Mar. 10, 1946; s. Benjamin Emanuel and Esther (Robfogel) F.; m. Gloria Damast, May 31, 1975; children: Michael, Richard. BA with highest honors, Rutgers U., 1968; JD, Columbia U., 1972. Bar: N.J. 1972, U.S. Dist. Ct. N.J. 1972, U.S. Ct. Appeals (3d cir.) 1983, U.S. Ct. Appeals (9th cir.) 1986, U.S. Ct. Appeals (2d cir.) 1994, U.S. Supreme Ct. 1983. Assoc. Hannoch Weisman, Roseland, N.J., 1972-77, ptnr., 1977-99, Norris, McLaughlin & Marcus, P.A., Somerville, N.J., 1999—. Ptnr. Contbr. articles to legal publs. Mem. ABA, N.J. Bar Assn., Essex County Bar Assn., Phi Beta Kappa. Avocations: reading, golf. Home: 209 Lyncrest Rd Englewood Cliffs NJ 07632-2020 Office: Norris McLaughlin & Marcus PO Box 1018 Somerville NJ 08876-1018 E-mail: jjfleischman@nmmlaw.com., jjfleisch@aol.com.

FLEISCHMAN, KATHRYN AGNES, secondary education educator; b. Buffalo, Jan. 3, 1937; d. Charles Joseph and Catherine (Rydzynski) Baker; m. Jerome Joseph Fleischman, July 16, 1960. Student, Buffalo Sem., 1954; BA in Math., U. Buffalo, 1958; MS in Math., SUNY, Buffalo, 1964. Cert. secondary math. tchr., N.Y. Chmn. math. dept., tchr., enrichment coord. Amherst Cen. Schs., Snyder, N.Y., 1958-92; instr. Niagara C.C., Niagara Falls, N.Y., 1964-65. Cons. N.Y. State Edn. Dept., Bur. Math. Edn., 1962-64, 74, 84-86, Addison-Wesley Pubs., 1963-64; instr. U. SC Creative Retirement Ctr. Women's com. Buffalo Philharm. Orch. Soc., 1977-95, edn. com., 1986-90, bd. dirs., 1993-94; bd. dirs. World Hospitality Assn., 1987-88; active Encore Soc. Metropolitan Opera, N.Y.C., 1992—, Heritage Soc. Buffalo Seminary, 1992—, Women's Assn. Hilton Head Island, Women's Assn. Hilton Head Plantation, Low Key Piano, Scribblers. Jesse Ketchum scholar, 1950; recipient Citizenship award Am. Legion, 1950, George Washington medal Freedom Found. at Valley Forge, 1988. Mem. Assn. Math. Tchrs. of N.Y. State (pres. 1974-75, exec. com., speaker, coun., county chmn., corr. sec., rec. sec., 2d v.p., 1st v.p), Nat. Coun. Tchrs. of Math. (program com., speaker, nat. del. assembly, jour. referee, rep. to bd. govs. Mu Alpha Theta), Delta Kappa Gamma. Roman Catholic. Avocations: travel, piano, organ. Home: 15 Oyster Bay Pl Hilton Head Plantation Hilton Head Island SC 29926-2687

FLEISCHMAN, PAUL, children's author; b. Monterey, Calif., Sept. 5, 1952; s. Albert Sidney and Beth (Taylor) F.; m. Becky Mojica, Dec. 15, 1978; children: Seth, Diana. BA, Univ. of N.Mex., 1977. Author: The Birthday Tree, 1979, The Half-a-Moon Inn, 1980 (Silver medal Commonwealth of Calif. 1980, Golden Kite honor book Soc. Children's Book Writers 1980), Graven Images: Three Stories, 1982 (Newbery honor book 1983), The Animal Hedge, 1983, Finzel the Farsighted, 1983, Path of the Pale Horse, 1983 (Golden Kite honor book Soc. Children's Book Writers 1983, Parents' Choice award Parents' Choice Found. 1983), Phoebe Danger, Detective, in the Case of the Two-Minute Cough, 1983, Coming-and-Going Men: Four Tales, 1985, I Am Phoenix: Poems for Two Voices, 1985, Rear-View Mirrors, 1986, Rondo in C, 1988, Joyful Noise: Poems for Two Voices, 1988 (John Newbery medal 1989), Saturnalia, 1990, Shadow Play, 1990, Time Train, 1991, The Borning Room, 1991, Townsend's Warbler, 1992, Copier Creations, 1993, Bull Run, 1993, Ghosts' Grace: A Poem for Four Voices, 1996, Troy, 1996, A Fate Totally Worse than Death, 1997, Seedfolks, 1997, Whirligig, 1998, Weslandia, 1999, Mind's Eye, 1999, Cannibal in the Mirror, 2000, Big Talk: Poems for Four Voices, 2000, Lost!: A Story in String, 2000, Seek, 2001, Sidewalk Circus, 2003, Animal Hedge, 2003. Address: 1271 4th St Monterey CA 93940-3514 Office: Henry Holt & Co Inc 115 W 18th St New York NY 10011-4113*

FLEISCHMAN, PAUL ROBERT, psychiatrist, writer; b. Newark, N.J., Aug. 4, 1945; s. Martin L. and Etta G. Fleischman; m. Susan K., June 15, 1974; 1 child, Forrest. BA, U. Chgo., 1967; MD, Albert Einstein Coll. Medicine, N.Y.C., 1971. Diplomate Am. Bd. Psychiatry and Neurology. Seminar leader in psychiatry and religion Yale U., New Haven, 1981-87; pvt. practice psychiatry Amherst, Mass., 1975—. Keynote spkr. Highland Hosp., Asheville, NC, 1992, Albany Med. Coll., Coll. St. Rose, Albany Jewish Family Svcs., 1993, Values in Psychotherapy conf. Nashville Inst. Psychotherapy, 1995; 31st Williamson lectr. in religion and medicine U. Kans., 1995; cons. in psychiatry, Amherst, 1975—; lectr., spkr. U. Mass., Amherst, Hampshire Coll., Smith Coll., Amherst Coll., 1989—98, Med. Group Rounds Albany Med. Coll., 1990, Beth Israel, Boston, 1994; cons. Western Mass. Psychiat. Soc., 1994, Jaipur Med. Coll., India, 1994, Smith Coll. Chapel, 1995, Bombay Psychiat. Soc., India, 1996, Smith Sch. for Social Work, 1998, Antioch Coll., Seattle, 1998, U. Wash. Health Svc., 1998, N.W. Rehab. Facility, Seattle, 1998, Mich. Psychoanalytic Found., 1999, Vipassana in Prisons, 1999, Gujarati Sanagi South Mich., 1999, Vipassana, Addictions, Psychotherapy & Mental Health, 1999, U. Mass. Dept. Counseling, 1999, First Ch., Springfield, Mass., Unitarian Meeting, Amherst, Mass., Korf Found., N.Y.C., Johnson Meml. Hosp., Stafford Springs, Conn., 1999, Ctr. for Behavioral Health Holyoke Hosp., 1999, Biennial Jain Conf., Phila., 1999, Theosophical Soc., Seattle, 1999, Vancouver Pub. Libr., 1999, East Asian Studies, Wesleyan U., 2000, Barre Ctr. for Buddhist Studies, 2000, Medicine, Sci. and Spirtuality Conf., 2000, Brattleboro Retreat, 2001, MacAllister Coll., St. Paul, 2001, U.S. Psychiat. and Mental Health Congress, Boston, 2001, Dept. Religious Studies, McGill U., Montreal, 2001, CoPlanet Conf., Oaxaca, Mexico, 2002, Foros Univs., Oaxaca, Mexico, 2002, UNAM, Toluca, Mexico, 2002, Mex. City Hosp., 2002, Dharma Study Group, Mass., 2002, Wesleyan Coll., Conn., 2002, U. Mass. Sch. Nursing, Amherst, 2002, Evergreen State Coll., Olympia, Wash., 2002, U. Wash. Sch. Social Work, Seattle, 2002, U. Wash. Health Care Svcs., Seattle, 2002. Author: Therapeutic Action of Vipassana Meditation, 1986, The Experience of Impermanence, 1990, The Healing Spirit, 1990, Spiritual Aspects of Psychiatric Practice, 1993, Cultivating Inner Peace, 1997, Karma & Chaos, Collected and New Essays, 1999, Snowstorm in a Cabin in the Woods, 2001, Tapas, 2001, The Buddha Taught Nonviolence, Not Pacifism, 2002, New Buddha Taught Nonviolence, 2002; contbr. articles to profl. jours. Recipient Oskar Pfister award for important contbns. to spiritual and humanistic side of psychiatry Am. Psychiat. Assn., 1993. Mem. Phi Beta Kappa, Alpha Omega Alpha. Office: 1394 S East St Amherst MA 01002-3030

FLEISCHMAN, PHIL, radio news executive; b. Saxonburg, Pa., Jan. 8, 1965; Student, U. Pitts., 1984-86. News dir. WPIT, Pitts., 1984-86; prodr., editor Std. News, Washington, 1987-92, sr. editor, newsroom supr., religion editor; bur. chief SRN News, Washington, 1997—. Office: SRN News 1901 N Moore St Ste 201 Arlington VA 22209-1706 E-mail: pfleisch@srnnews.com.

FLEISCHMANN, ERNEST MARTIN, music administrator; b. Frankfurt, Germany, Dec. 7, 1924; came to U.S., 1969; s. Gustav and Antonia (Koch) F.; children: Stephanie, Martin, Jessica. B of Commerce, U. Cape Town, South Africa, 1950, MusB, 1954; postgrad., South African Coll. Music, 1954-56; MusD (hon.), Cleve. Inst. Music, 1987. Gen mgr. London Symphony Orch., 1959-67; dir. Europe CBS Masterworks, 1967-69; exec. v.p., mng. dir. L.A. Philharm. Assn. and Hollywood Bowl, 1969-98; artistic cons. L.A. Philharm. Assn., 1998—; pres. Fleischmann Arts, Intl. Arts Mgmt. Cons. Svc., 1998—. Mem. French Govt. Commn. Reform of Paris Opera, 1967-68; steering com. U.S. nat. commn. UNESCO Conf. Future of Arts, 1975; artistic dir. Ojai Festival, 1998-2003. Debut as condr. Johannesburg (Republic of South Africa) Symphony Orch., 1942; asst. condr. South African Nat. Opera, 1948-51, Cape Town U. Opera, 1950-54; condr. South African Coll. Music Choir, 1950-52, Labia Grand Opera Co., Cape Town, 1953-55; music organizer Van Riebeeck Festival Cape Town, 1952; dir. music and drama Johannesburg Festival, 1956; contbr. to music publs. Decorated officier Ordre des Arts et Lettres (France), comdrs. cross Order of Merit (Germany), knight 1st class Order of the White Rose (Finland); recipient award of Merit, L.A. Jr. C. of C., John Steinway award, Friends of Music award, Disting. Arts Leadership award U. So. Calif., 1989, L.A. Honors award, L.A. Arts Coun., 1989, Live Music award Am. Fedn. Musicians Local 47, 1991, Disting. Authors/Artists award U. Judaism, 1994, Treasures of L.A. award, Ctrl. City Assn. L.A., 1996, Los Amigos de Los Angeles award, L.A. Conv. and Vis. Bur., 1996; honored Mayor and City Coun. as First Living Cultural Treasure of L.A., 1998, Gold Baton award Am. Symphony Orch. League, 1999. Mem. Assn. Calif. Symphony Orchs., L.A. Philharm. Assn. (bd. dirs. 1984—), Salzburg Seminar/Alberto Vilar Conf. on Orch. Mgmt. (co-chmn. 2002). Office: Fleischmann Arts 2225 Maravilla Dr Los Angeles CA 90068 E-mail: artsernest@aol.com. *Progress in the arts involves taking risks. Safety and blandness go hand in hand and should be banished from the artistic experience: better to stick your neck out and fail than to err on the side of correctness and caution.*

FLEISCHMANN, GISELA EBERT, retired psychiatrist; b. Hamburg, Germany, Mar. 22, 1921; (parents Am. citizens); d. Carl A. and Clara (Hasenclever) E.; widowed; 1 child, Esther Fleischmann-Griffith. MD, Albert Ludwig U., Freiburg, Germany, 1944. Intern U. Polyclinic, Zurich, Switzerland, 1945-46; staff physician State Hosp., Yankton, S.D., 1946-47; resident St. Luke's Hosp., Chgo., 1947-48, Menninger Sch. Psychiatry, Topeka, 1948-50; staff psychiatrist Menninger Clinic, Topeka, 1950-51; clin. asst. Hillside Hosp., Glen Oaks, NY, 1963-66; pvt. practice Great Neck, NY, 1964—2002; attending psychiatrist St. Francis Hosp., Roslyn, NY, 1977-90; ret., 2002. Med. dir. Jewish Cmty. Svcs. L.I., Rego Park, N.Y., 1967-93. Fellow Am. Psychiat. Assn. (life); mem. Med. Soc. State N.Y., Greater L.I. Psychiat. Soc. Democrat. Avocations: collecting fine art, ecology, swimming, classical music. Home: 13801 York Rd Apt J-14 Cockeysville MD 21030-1824

FLEISCHMANN, PAUL, religious organization administrator, minister; b. June 20, 1946; s. Leonard and Viola (Tyler) F.; m. Anntoinette Jordan, June 14, 1973; children: Todd Paul, Tyler Jonathan. BA, Seattle Pacific Coll., 1968; MDiv, Western Bapt. Sem., Portland, Oreg., 1975; postgrad., Internat. Christian Grad. U., San Bernardino, Calif. Ordained to ministry, Conservative Bapt. Assn., 1981. Youth pastor Ballard Bapt. Ch., Seattle, 1965-67; campus staff Seattle Youth for Christ, 1967-68; high sch. ministry staff Campus Crusade for Christ, various locations, 1968-88; pres. Nat. Network of Youth Ministries, San Diego, 1982—. Home missionary, 1968—; youth ministry cons., 1974—; officer Bd. Deacons, 1980—82, 1988—93; mem. Bd. Christian Edn., 1980—82; ch. planter, 1988—93; adj. prof. Christian edn. Western Bapt. Sem., Portland, Oreg., 1981—83; chmn. Youth Ministry Exec. Coun., 1992—, Atlanta 96 Youth Leaders Conf., 1993—96, Campus Alliance. Author: Where to Turn for Help in Youth Ministry, 1996; contbg. author: Working with Youth, 1982, Magnet Effect, 1995—, Reaching a Generation for Christ, 1997, exec. editor: Insight for Student Discipleship, 1979—83, Network Mag., 1983—; editor: Discipling the Young Person, 1985; contbr. articles to profl. jours. Dir. Continental Singers Choir and Orch., 1977, Nat. Conv. on High Sch. Discipleship, 1979-83; asst. dir. Youth Congress '85, Washington. Recipient Gold Medallion, Evang. Christian Pubrs. Assn., 1986. Baptist. Office: Nat Network of Youth Min 12335 World Trade Dr Ste 16 San Diego CA 92128-3791

FLEISCHMANN, RUTH H. foundation executive; b. Cin. d. Hans and Hannah (Vogelsang) Sidon. BS in Bus. magna cum laude, Nazareth Coll., Rochester, N.Y., 1982. Exec. dir. Marie C. and Joseph C. Wilson Found., Rochester, 1982—. Bd. dirs. Martin Luther King Commn., Rochester, 1995—, Wilson Commencement Park, Rochester, 1988—. Recipient Career Achievement award Girl Scouts of Genesee Valley, 1995, Lena Gant Cmty. Svc. award Action for a Better Cmty., 1999. Office: MC JC Wilson Found 160 Allens Creek Rd Rochester NY 14618-3309

FLEISCHNER, THOMAS LOWE, conservation biologist, educator; b. Lakewood, Ohio, Aug. 24, 1954; s. Warren Edmund and Rose Marie (Myers) Fl; m. Edith Ann Dillon, Mar. 29, 1986; children: River Thomas Dillon Fleischner, Kestrel Edith Dillon Fleischner. BS in Field Biology, Evergreen State Coll., Olympia, Wash., 1977; MS in Biology, Western Wash. U., 1983; PhD in environmental stud., Union Inst., 1998. Interpretive naturalist/back county ranger (part-time) North Cascades Nat. Pk., Sedro Woolley, Wash., 1981-86; faculty Sierra Inst., U. Calif. Santa Cruz (part-time), 1983-88; program dir., co-founder North Cascades Inst., Sedro Woolley, 1986-88; prof. environ. studies Prescott (Ariz.) Coll., 1988—. Prin. Pacific Northwest Environ. Svcs., Bellingham, Wash., 1985-86; bd. dirs. North Cascades Inst., 1986-94, Four Corners Sch. Outdoor Edn., Monticello, Utah, 1990-92. Contbr. articles to profl. jours. Co-founder, bd. dirs. Granite Mountain Action, Prescott, 1990—. Recipient Nat. Wilderness Ednl. award U.S. Forest Svc./Izaak Walton League, 1990. Mem. Soc. for Conservation Biology (chair pub. lands grazing com. 1989—), Ecological Soc. Am., North Cascades Inst. (co-founder). Avocations: musician (percussionist), poet, wilderness travel. Office: Prescott Coll Environ Studies Program 220 Grove Ave Prescott AZ 86301-2912

FLEISHER, BETTY, artist, educator; b. Bklyn., June 7, 1932; d. Simon and Sadie Ellis; m. Harvey A. Fleisher, Oct. 30, 1955; children: Stephanie, Margaret. AA, Miami Dade C.C., 1972; BFA, Fla. Internat. U., 1974; MA, Goddard Coll., 1978. Adj. prof. Miami (Fla.) Dade C.C., 1974-76, Fla. Internat. U., Miami, 1978-88; instr. art Art Ctr. of South Fla., Miami. Lectr. in art Brandeis Women, Hollywood, Fla., 1985, Elders Inst. Fla. Internat. U., Miami, 1980. Exhibited in group shows at Soc. of the Four Arts, Palm Beach, Fla., 1974, 1976, 1987, Fla. Internat. U. Faculty Exhbn., 1983, Hollywood (Fla.) Art and Culture Ctr., 1987, Mus. Contemporary Art, North Miami, Fla., 1990, Art 800, Miami, Fla., 1997, 1998, 2000, 2002. Mem. panel Art in Pub. Places, Broward and Ft. Lauderdale, Fla., 1996-98. Mem. Nat. Assn. Women Artists. Jewish. Avocations: gourmet cooking, designing. Home: 21150 Point Pl Apt 1605 Miami FL 33180-4038

FLEISHER, ERIC WILFRID, retired foreign service officer; b. Washington, Jan. 31, 1926; s. Wilfrid and Greta Agda (Sundberg) F.; m. Elizabeth Fredrikson, Dec. 22, 1948 (div. 1974); children: Emily Susanne, Eric Torsten; m. Thale Gunneng, Aug. 5, 1974 (dec. Feb. 2000); 1 child, Arne Ericsson. Cert., U. Stockholm, 1948; BA, George Washington U., 1950; PhD, U. Lund, Sweden, 1953. Orientation officer U.S. Displaced Persons Commn., French Zone, Germany, 1950-51; program and ops. officer Refugee Relief Dept. State, Washington, 1954-55, intelligence rsch. analyst, 1955-58; polit. officer Am. Embassy, Copenhagen, 1959-63; consul Faroe Islands, 1959-63; polit. counselor Helsinki, Finland, 1964—69; dep. country dir., then dir. Nordic countries Washington, 1969—73; press attache Am. Embassy, Stockholm, 1974—76; spl. asst. human rights and refugee affairs Washington, 1977-80; fgn. affairs cons., sr. cons., 1980—. Author: Viking Times to Modern, 1953; translator, editor: Scandinavia in Great Power Politics, 1905-1908, 1958; contbr. articles to various publs. 1st lt. U.S. Army, 1944-47, Tokyo. Mem. Am. Fgn. Svc. Assn., Diplomatic and Consular Officers Ret., Am. Scandinavian Found. Avocations: hiking, hunting, photography. Home: 8300 Thoreau Dr Bethesda MD 20817-3164 Office: Rm 5121 SA2 Dept State Washington DC 20522-6001 E-mail: flycatcher26@comcast.net.

FLEISHER, GARY MITCHELL, employment industry and management consulting executive; b. Bklyn., July 10, 1941; s. Irving and Ccil F.; m. Grace M. Reynolds; children: Nina, Gwen Megan. Student Ogelthorpe U., 1959, U. Miami, 1960-61. Nat. ops. mgr. Staff Builders, Inc., N.Y.C., 1967-70; v.p., gen. mgr. Career Tempforce, East Meadow, N.Y., 1970-76; exec. v.p. Uniforce Temporary Services, New Hyde Park, N.Y., 1976-83; pres. G.M. Fleisher & Assocs., Inc., 1984-92, pres., dir. GMF Mgmt. Group., 1984-92; pres., dir. GMF Staffing Inc.; pres. Promax Staffing, 1990-92, ProMax Pers. Systems, 1991-92; ret. E-mail: gmfleish@optonline.net.

FLEISHER, HOMER LUTHER, III, surgeon; b. Chgo., Nov. 29, 1952; MD, So. Ill. U., 1980. Diplomate Am. Bd. Surgery; cert. in vascular surgery, gen. surgery. Intern So. Ill. U. Affiliated Hosps., Springfield, 1980-81, resident in gen. surgery, 1981-85; fellow in vascular surgery U. Ark. Med. Scis., Little Rock, 1985-87; pvt. practice Appleton, Wis., 1987-98, Conway, Ark., 1998—; mem. staff Conway Regional Med. Ctr., 1998—. Mem. AMA, Faulkner County Med. Soc. Address: 525 Western Ave Ste 203 Conway AR 72034-4980

FLEISHER, JERRILYN, financial planner; b. Phila., May 7, 1952; d. Earl D. and Bette (Romisher) F.; m. Steven M. Bierman, May 28, 1978; 1 child, Emily Larissa. BA, Dickinson Coll., 1973; MBA, Wharton Sch. U. Pa., 1975. Promotion analyst Gillette Co., Boston, 1975-77; product mgr. Chesebrough Ponds Co., Greenwich, Conn., 1977-80, Loreal Co., N.Y.C., 1980-81; account exec. Futterman Orgn., N.Y.C., 1981-83; fin. cons. Shearson Lehman Bros., Greenwich, 1983-92; pres. Fin. Views, Greenwich, 1992—. Mem. Internat. Bd. CFPs, Phi Beta Kappa. Home: 17 Ivanhoe Ln Greenwich CT 06830-3925 E-mail: Shanaraisa@aol.com.

FLEISHER, SEYMOUR, manufacturing company executive; b. Highland Park, N.J., Jan. 21, 1923; s. Benjamin Fleisher and Mary (Grossman) Kivitz; m. Estelle Uram, Aug. 12, 1944; 1 son, Bruce Michael. BS in Mech. Engring., Newark Coll. Engring., 1951. Rsch. engr. Eclipse Pioneer div. Bendix Corp., Teterboro, N.J., 1951-53; asst. gen. mgr. Wayne Engring. Corp., Hackensack, N.J., 1953-56; pres. Pilot Metal Fabricators, Inc., Wayne, 1956-89, chmn. bd., 1989-95, Pilot Technologies (now Chatham Technologies), 1995—. Patentee motorized bicycle with removeable fuel tank. Bd. dirs. YM and YWHa of Wayne, 1985-91, Kenneth L. Jordan Heart Fund, 1985—, Jewish Fedn. North Jersey, 1991—, Wayne Area C. of C., 1991—, United Way, 1990-93; trustee Found. for Handicapped, Wayne, 1986—, St. Joseph's Hosp. and Med. Ctr., Patterson, 1988—, Found. of St. Joseph's Hosp. and Med. Ctr., 1991—, exec. com., 1992—; mem. campaign cabinet United Way Passaic Valley, 1989-91; mem. adv. com. Sch. Indsl. Mgmt., N.J. Inst. Tech., 1990, chmn. athletic adv. bd., 1992-94; exec. bd. Passaic Valley Coun. Boy Scouts Am., 1992—; chmn. Wayne Township Indsl. Commn., 1994; bd. dirs. Am. Friends Tel Aviv U., 1993-2000; trustee Wash. Inst., 1990-2000. Capt. U.S. Army, 1942-46, PTO. Decorated Air medal; recipient Edward F. Weston medal for disting. svc. N.J. Inst. Tech., 1985, Benefactors award United Way of Passaic Valley, 1990, Wayne Twp. Corp. Citizen award, 1990; inducted into Athletic Hall of Fame, N.J. Inst. Tech., 1992. Mem. ASME, Precison Metalforming Assn., Soc. Mfg. Engrs., Aircraft Owners and Pilots Assn., Rotary (bd. dirs., past pres.), Masons, Shriners, Preakness Hills Country Club, Frenchman's Creek Yacht, Beach and Country Club, Pi Tau Sigma, Omicron Delta Kappa, Tau Beta Pi. Republican. Jewish. Avocations: flying, fly fishing, golf, jogging, exercise. Home: 3121 Monet Dr Palm Beach Gardens FL 33410 Office: Flextronics Enclosures 10 Pomeroy Rd Parsippany NJ 07054-3722

FLEISHER, STEVEN M. lawyer; b. Chgo., Feb. 5, 1945; s. Max M. and Meta J; m. Marilyn J. Eto, Sept. 2, 1984. AB cum laude, Yale U., 1966; JD cum laude, Harvard U., 1969. Bar: Calif. 1970, U.S. Ct. Appeals (9th cir.) 1970, U.S. Dist. Ct. (no. dist.) Calif. 1970, D.C. 1973, U.S. Ct. Appeals (D.C. cir.) 1973, U.S. Supreme Ct. 1973. Law clk. U.S. Dist. Ct., San Francisco, 1969-70; atty. Calif. Rural Legal Assistance, Gilroy, 1970-72; gen. counsel Food Advocates, Davis, Calif., 1973-74; dir. Drew Health Rights Project, San Francisco, 1974-76; counsel Calif. Dept. Consumer Affairs, Sacramento, 1976-78; ptnr. Fleisher & Neckritz, Oakland, Calif., 1978-82; shareholder Burnhill, Morehouse, Burford, Schofied & Schiller, Walnut Creek, Calif., 1982-87, ptnr. McNichols, McCann & Inderbitzen, Pleasanton, Calif., 1987-91, Hallgrimson, McNichols, McCann & Inderbitzen, Pleasanton, Calif., 1991-95, assoc. gen. counsel Calif. Med. Assn., San Francisco, 1995-2000; v.p., gen. counsel Medepass, Inc., San Francisco, 2000—02; prin. Fleisher & Assocs., 2002—. Bd. dirs. Nat. Health Law Program, L.A., 1988-94; arbitrator U.S. Dist. Ct., San Francisco, 1984-91. Contbg. author Advising California Partnerships, 1988, California Sole Proprietorships & Partnerships, 1992; contbg. editor Calif. Ltd. Liability Cos. Reginald H. Smith fellow Office Legal Svcs., Calif., 1970-72. Mem. ABA (bus. law sect., sci. and tech. sects. chair health info. privacy and security protection subcom. info. security com. 2000—), Am. Health Lawyers (health info. tech. com.), Am. Soc. Med. Assn. Counsel (pres. 2001), D.C. Bar Assn., Calif. State Bar (exec. com. bus. law sect. 1993-96, nonprofits orgn. com. bus. law sect. 1996-2000, chair 1998-99). Office: Fleisher & Assocs 35 Corwin Dr Alamo CA 94507-1906 E-mail: steven@fleisherlaw.com.

FLEISHER, THOMAS ARTHUR, physician; b. Rochester, Minn. s. Gerard and Gisela Fleisher; m. Mary Fleisher; children: Jeffrey, Jeremy, Matthew. BS, U. Minn., 1969, MD, 1971. Diplomate Am. Bd. Pediats., Am. Bd. Allergy and Immunology. Staff physician bone marrow transplant svc. Naval Med. Rsch. Inst., Bethesda, Md., 1975—77; commd. lt.comdr. USNR, 1975—77; commd. USPHS, 1977—80, advanced through grades to capt., 1983—2001; ret., 2001; clin. assoc. metabolism br. Nat. Cancer Inst., NIH, Bethesda, 1977—80; asst. chief allergy clin. immunology svc. Walter Reed Army Med. Ctr., Washington, 1980—83; chief immunology svc. Warren G. Magnuson Clin. Ctr., NIH, Bethesda, 1983—, chief dept. lab. medicine, 1998—. Tng. program dir. clin. lab. immunology NIH, Bethesda, 1992—; bd. dirs. Am. Bd. Allergy and Immunology, Phila., 1991—2001, chair, 1996. Editor Clin. Immunology, 1985—89, 1993—, Immunology, 1983—86, Clin. Diag. Lab. Immunology, 1993—, Cytometry, 1996—, contbr. numerous articles to sci. jours., —. House capt. Christmas in April, Montgomery County, Md., 1991—2000; deacon, elder St. Mark Presbyn. Ch., Rockville, Md., 1983—88; bd. dirs. Bethesda Soccer Club, 1987—95. Fellow: Am. Acad. Allergy, Asthma and Immunology (bd. dirs. 2003—); mem.: Clin. Immunology Soc., Clin. Cytometry Soc., Soc. for Pediat. Rsch., Am. Assn. Immunologists. Avocations: travel, skiing, woodworking. Office: NIH 10/2C306 9000 Rockville Pike Bethesda MD 20892-1508 E-mail: tfleisher@nih.gov.

FLEISHHACKER, DAVID, school administrator; b. San Francisco, May 30, 1937; s. Mortimer and Janet (Choynski) F.; m. Victoria Escamilla, Aug. 1965; children: William, Eleanor, Jeffrey. AB, Princeton U., 1959; MA, U. Calif., 1965. Tchr. Lick-Wilmerding High Sch., San Francisco, 1959-61, Peace Corps, Afghanistan, 1962-64, Marin Country Day Sch., Corte Madera, Calif., 1965, Town Sch., San Francisco, 1965-70; headmaster Katherine Delmar Burke Sch., San Francisco, 1970-95; ret.; interim head Hillbrook Sch., Los Gatos, 1997-98, South Peninsula Hebrew Day Sch., 1998-99. Pvt. ednl. cons. Author: (book) Lessons from Afghanistan, 2002; contbr. articles to profl. jours. Trustee Internat. Ho., Berkeley, Calif., 1987—95, pres. Fleishhacker Found., San Francisco, 1990—; bd. dirs. St. Joseph's Hosp./Queen of Angels, L.A., 1976—, San Francisco Youth Orch., 1981—, San Francisco Boys Chorus, 1997—, Educating Girls Globally, 2002—, Booker T. Washington Cmty. Ctr., 1995—. Mem. Nat. Assn. Prins. Schs. Girls. (bd. dirs. 1979-82), Elem. Sch. Heads Assn., Calif. Assn. Ind. Schs. (treas. 1978-81). Home: 3424 Jackson St San Francisco CA 94118-2021 E-mail: trampc@aol.com.

FLEISHMAN, LAZAR, literature educator; b. Ovrutch, Ukraine, May 15, 1944; arrived in U.S., 1984; s. Solomon and Pesja Fleishman; m. Irina Strelnikova Fleishman, Apr. 12, 1972 (div. Aug. 7, 1992); children: Raphael, Ella; m. Ekaterina Kozitskaia Fleishman, Oct. 16, 2002. PhD, Latvian U., 1966. From sr. lectr. to assoc. prof. depts. Russian and comparative lit. Hebrew U., Jerusalem, 1974—85; prof. Russian lit. Slavic dept. Stanford (Calif.) U., 1985—. Vis. prof. Slavic dept. U. Calif., Berkeley, 1978—79, 1980—81, 1999, Harvard U., Cambridge, Mass., 1984, Yale U., New Haven, 1984; vis. prof. Russian U. for the Humanities, Moscow, 1998. Author (in Russian): Boris Pasternak in the 20's, 1981; author: Boris Pasternak in the 30's, 1985; author: (in English) Boris Pasternak: The Poet and His Politics, 1990. Recipient Alexander von Humboldt Forschungspreis, Germany, 1994—95, 2000; fellow, Guggenheim Found., 1987. Home: 927 Mackenzie Dr Sunnyvale CA 94087 Office: Slavic Dept Stanford U Bldg 40-42 L Stanford CA 94305 Fax: 650-725-0011. Business E-Mail: Lazar.Fleishman@stanford.edu.

FLEISHMAN, PHILIP ROBERT, internist; b. Hartford, Conn., Apr. 17, 1935; s. Morris and Anna Lillian (Farber) F.; m. Anita Rose Coopersmith, Oct. 18, 1964; children: David, Beth, Rachael. BS, Trinity Coll., Hartford, 1957; MD, SUNY, Bklyn., 1961. Diplomate Am. Bd. Internal Medicine. Practice specializing in internal medicine East Islip, N.Y., 1967—; attending physician, dir. medicine Southside Hosp., Bay Shore, N.Y., 1993—; attending physician Good Samaritan Hosp., W. Islip, N.Y.; v.p. med. bd. Southside Hosp., 1986-89; pres., 1989—; clin. asst. prof. SUNY Med. Sch., Stony Brook, 1967—; asst. dir. medicine, 1988—; dir. med. sch., 1993—; founder, co-dir. diabetic clinic Southside Hosp.; also bd. dirs., 1999—. Bd. dirs. Southlake Hosp., 1998—.

Contbr. articles to profl. jours. Co-author, chmn. constn. and bylaws Pro-Arts Group Islips, 1979; asst. basketball coach Police Athletic League, 1979; v.p., trustee Bay Shore Jewish Ctr., 1979—, pres., 1988-90; bd. dirs. Southside Hosp., 1998—. Capt. M.C. U.S. Army, 1965-67. Fellow ACP; mem. AMA, Am. Diabetes Assn., N.Y. State Med. Soc., N.Y. State Soc. Internal Medicine (past chpt. pres.), Suffolk County Med. Soc.

FLEISHMAN, SUSAN NAHLEY, media consultant; b. Charlottesville, Va., Sept. 26, 1960; d. Richard and Mary Daniels Nahley; m. Eric Philip Fleishman, Dec. 28, 1995; 1 child, Henry Richard. BA Am. Lit., Middlebury Coll., Middlebury, Vt., 1978—82. Copywriter Macy's, New York, NY, 1984—86; dir. Interbrand, New York, NY, 1986—87; asst. v.p. Continental Ins., New York, NY, 1987—93; dir., pub. affairs Sony Corp. of Am., New York, NY, 1993—95; v.p. corp. comm. & pub. affairs Universal Studios, Los Angeles, Calif., 1995—2000, sr. v.p. corp. comm. & pub. affairs, 2000—. Mentor/tutor Eng. No. Hollywood HS, No. Hollywood, Calif., 2001—. Bd. mem. Workplace, Hollywood, Los Angeles, Calif., 2001—, St. Joseph's Hosp., Burbank, Calif., 2002—; bd. mem. - next generation coun. Motion Picture: TV Fund, Woodland Hills, Calif., 2003—. Democrat. Jewish. Avocations: running, reading, hiking, travel. Home: 3405 Blair Dr Los Angeles CA 90068 Office: Universal Studios LRW-14 100 Universal City Plaza Universal City CA 91608

FLEISIG, ROSS, aeronautical engineer, engineering manager; b. Montreal, Que., Can., Oct. 12, 1921; came to U.S., 1922, naturalized, 1922; s. Samuel and Ethel (Levy) F.; m. Marjorie M. Hall, June 6, 1943; children— Ann, Dale. BS in Aero. Engring., Poly. Inst. Bklyn., 1942, MS, 1955. Sr. aerodynamicist Chance Vought Aircraft Corp., Stratford, Conn., from 1942, Dallas, to 1950; engring. sect. head Sperry Gyroscope Co., Great Neck, N.Y., 1950-61; project mgr. Grumman Aerospace Corp., Bethpage, N.Y., 1961-84; pres. Therus Dynamics, Inc., 1984—95. Editor: Lunar Flight Programs, 1964, Lunar Exploration and Spacecraft Systems, 1962; contbr. articles to tech. jours. Fellow AAAS, BIS, AIAA (assoc., Disting. lectr. 1995-97), Am. Astronautical Soc. (pres. 1957-58, bd. dirs. 1958-68); mem. NSPE, Internat. Acad. Astronautics, Rotary (dir. local club). Home: The Bristal Ste 424 117 Post Ave Westbury NY 11590

FLEISSIG, ADRIAN R. economics educator, consultant; b. Johannesburg, Transvaal, South Africa, July 22, 1964; m. Sandra Fleissig. PhD in Econs. and Stats., N.C. State U., 1993. Prof. econs. U. Tex., 1993—95, St. Louis U., 1996—98, Calif. State U., Fullerton, 1999—. Rsch. assoc. Inst. Environ. and Econ. Studies Calif. State U., Fullerton, 1999—; guest spkr. U.S. Fed. Res. Bank St. Louis, 1994. Author: (developing econ. theory and methodology) A New PC Based Test for Varian's Weak Separability Conditions, 2003. Named World Ranking 757 out of 55,000 World Rankings of Economists and Econ. Depts., Tom Coupe, 2001. Mem.: Am. Econ. Assn. Office: Calif State U 800 N College Blvd Fullerton CA 92834

FLEMING, ALICE CAREW MULCAHEY, writer; b. New Haven, Dec. 21, 1928; d. Albert Leo and Agnes (Foley) Mulcahey; m. Thomas J. Fleming, Jan. 19, 1951; children: Alice, Thomas, David, Richard. Author: The Key to New York, 1960, A Son of Liberty, 1961, Doctors in Petticoats, 1964, Great Women Teachers, 1965, The Senator from Maine: Margaret Chase Smith, 1969, Alice Freeman Palmer: Pioneer College President, 1970, Reporters At War, 1970, General's Lady, 1971, Highways into History, 1971, Pioneers in Print, 1971, Ida Tarbell, The First of the Muckrakers, 1971, Nine Months, 1972, Psychiatry, What's it All About?, 1972, The Moviemakers, 1973, Trials that Made Headlines, 1974, Contraception, Abortion, Pregnancy, 1974, New on the Beat, 1975, Alcohol: The Delightful Poison, 1975, Something for Nothing, 1978, The Mysteries of ESP, 1980, What to Say When you Don't Know What to Say, 1982, The King of Prussia and a Peanut Butter Sandwich, 1988, George Washington Wasn't Always Old, 1991, What, Me Worry?, 1992, P.T. Barnum: The World's Greatest Showman, 1993, A Century of Service, 1997, Frederick Douglass From Slave to Statesman, 2003; editor: Hosannah the Home Run!, 1972, America Is Not all Traffic Lights, 1976; contbr. articles to mags. Nat. bd. dirs. Medic Alert Found. U.S., 1991-97, vice chmn., 1996-97, past chmn. N.Y. regional bd.; mem. pres.'s coun. United Hosp. Fund. Recipient Nat. Media award, Family Svc. Assn. Am., 1973, Alumnae Achievement award, Trinity Coll., 1979, Nat. Vol. of Yr. award, Medic Alert Found., 1991, 1993. Mem. PEN, Authors Guild. Address: 315 E 72nd St New York NY 10021-4625 E-mail: Fleming315@aol.com.

FLEMING, BRIAN ANTHONY, musician, educator; b. Bayshore, NY, Apr. 23, 1977; s. Richard Thomas and Frances Fleming. BFA, LI U., Brookville, NY, 1999; MusM, Johns Hopkins U., 2002. Founder, owner Brian Fleming Guitar Studio, Holbrook, NY, 1999—. Scholar, LI U., 1997—99, Merit Scholarship, Peabody Inst., Johns Hopkins U., 2000—02. Mem.: LI Classical Guitar Soc. (asst. dir. 2002—03), Music Tchrs. Nat. Assn., Music Educators Nat. Conf., NY State Sch. Music Assn.

FLEMING, CAROLYN ELIZABETH, religious organization administrator, interior designer; b. Sept. 24, 1946; d. Jerry J. and Mary Josephine (Korten) Maly; m. Roger Earl Fleming, May 26, 1974; children: Karl Joseph, Briana Danika. Student, Texarkana Jr. Coll., 1963-65, Okla. State U., 1965-66; BS in Interior Design, U. Tex., 1970. Asst. to designer Planning/Design Cons., Inc., Tulsa, 1970-72; pvt. cons. Texarkana, Tex., 1972-73; with Anchorage Neuro-Spinal Clinic, 1987-90, 91-96; sec. Nat. Tchg. Com. Bahais of Alaska, Anchorage, 1976—84, mem., 1989-92, Baha'i materials promotion com., Anchorage, 1987-89, Nat. Spirituality Assembly, Bahais of Alaska, 1992-97, sec. gen., CEO, 1994-96; chmn. Anchorage Bahais Local Spiritual Assembly, 1990-92; mem. Texarkana Bahai Local Spirituality Assembly, 1985, Oceanview (Alaska) Bahai Local Spiritual Assembly, 1986-87; rec. sec. Chena Valley (Alaska) Local Spiritual Assembly Bahais, 1997; mem. internat. goals com. Nat. Spiritual Assembly Bahais of Alaska, Inc., 1997-2000; adminstrv. asst. to treas. in corp. offices Alaska Comm. Sys. Group, Inc., 2000—, adminstrv. asst. to treas. and v.p., 2000, adminstrv. asst. to v.p. investor rels., 2000-2001, adminstrv. asst. to CFO and treas., 2001—, v.p. investor rels., 2001—, v.p. sales and mktg.-Corp. office, 2001—. Coord. Interdenominational Cultural Unity Conf. for Anchorage Area, 1986. Vol. Rural Comty. Action Program, 1986-87, Alaska Coun. on Prevention Alcohol and Drug Abuse, 1987, Spirit Days, 1987-88; trainee Parent and Youth Mediation Program, 1990; mem. Anchorage Local Spiritual Assembly, 1998; asst. aux. bd. for Bahai Oceanview Comty., 1989-92; mem. Arts Coun., Valdez, Alaska, 1974-76, Beyond Beijing Coalition, Anchorage, 1995-96. Mem. ACS (contbns. and donations com. 2000-2001), Assn. Interior Designers, Alaska Women's Network (chmn. 2001-02, vice-chmn. 2000-01, v.p. 2000—), Internat. Assn. of Adminstrv. Profls., Bus. and Profl. Women's Orgn., Beta Sigma Phi. Mem. Baha'I Faith. Office: PO Box 101997 Anchorage AK 99510-1997

FLEMING, CECIL, business executive; Exec. ptnr. BDO Dunwoody, Ward, Mallette, Toronto, Ont., Can., 1991-95; sr. ptnr. BDO Seidman, N.Y.C., 1995-97, CEO, pres., 1997—2002.*

FLEMING, CHRISTINA SAMUSSON, special education educator; b. Ft. Belvoir, Va., Dec. 20, 1950; d. Lewis Frew and Gayle Virginia (Pribnow) Samusson; m. Hal Alex Fleming, July 16, 1977; children: Hilary Anne, Alex Andrew. BS, Tex. Woman's U., 1972, MEd, 1974. Cert. tchr., Tex. Spl. edn. tchr. Richardson (Tex.) Ind. Sch. Dist., 1972-81; ednl. diagnostician Mental Health Mental Retardation, Plano, Tex., 1985-90; pre-kindegarten tchr. U. Gymnastics, Plano, 1987-90; spl. edn. tchr. Plano Ind. Sch. Dist., 1990—. Mem. spl. edn. task force Plano Ind. Sch. Dist., 1994-97; ednl. diagnostician Collin County Mental Health Mental Retardation, Plano, 1985-90; mem. Blue Ribbon Sch. Writing Team, 1996, 2000; master tchr. Tech. in Edn., 1998, mem. site based improvement coun., 1999—; math specialist TEXTEAMS, 2001—; Herman Method trainer, 2003—. Author: (manuals) Self Concept in the Primary Years, 1974, The Dick and Jane Guide to Paraeducators, 2002; (booklet) Heart to Heart: A Parent's Guide to Congenital Heart Disease, 1981. Exec. bd. Child Guidance Clinic, Plano, 1984-91, Shepard Elem. Sch. PTA, Plano, 1985-89, pres., 1987, life; exec. bd., founding mem. Heart to Heart, Dallas, 1980-86; leader Girl Scouts U.S.A., Tex., 1985-94; regional problem chair Destination Imagination, 2001--. Tech. in Edn. Fed. grantee, 1998, Plano Futures Found. grantee, 1998-99, 2002-03. Mem. Tex. Assn. Gifted and Talented, Richardson Learning Disabilities Assn. (exec. bd. 1974-87), Assn. Tex. Profl. Educators, Parent Tchr. Student Assn. (life), Destination Imagination (regional problem capt. 2001-). Republican. Methodist. Avocations: reading, creative problem solving. Home: 1217 Monterey Cir Plano TX 75075-7315 Office: Plano ISD Weatherford Elem 2941 Mollimar Dr Plano TX 75075-6306 E-mail: txfleming@comcast.net.

FLEMING, DORIS AVEN, mental health nurse; b. Pinehurst, N.C., Sept. 12, 1958; d. Robert Leslie and Margaret Louise F. AS in Nursing, Sandhills C.C., Pinehurst, 1985; BSN, U. N.C., 1995. Cert. biofeedback Biofeedback Cert. Inst. Am. Nurse, biofeedback therapist Moore Regional Hosp., Pinehurst, 1985—. Mem. ANA (cert. psychiat. and mental health nurse), N.C. Biofeedback Assn. Office: Moore Regional Hosp PO Box 3000 Pinehurst NC 28374-3000

FLEMING, DOUGLAS RILEY, journalist, publisher, public affairs consultant; b. Fairmont, W.Va., Jan. 25, 1922; s. Douglas Riley and Sarilda Artemes (Short) F.; m. Irene Stachowicz, Oct. 28, 1944 (dec. 1979); m. Nancy Evelyn Kincaid, May 30, 1992. BS, Georgetown U., 1953. Commd. ensign U.S. Navy, 1944, advanced through grades to comdr.; naval aviator; chief protocol NATO, Naples, Italy, 1962-67; ret. U.S. Navy, 1967; with Francis I. DuPont & Co., Investment Banking, Rome, 1968-70; exec. editor, gen. mgr. Daily American, Rome, 1970-75; pres. Stampa Generale, S.R.L., Pubs., Naples, 1975—; mng. dir. Italo-Am. Assn., Naples; dir. Am. Studies Ctr., Naples, 1975-80; pres. Gen. Press Svcs., Washington, 1979—. Dir. Va. Winery Coop., Inc., Culpeper, 1985-93; propr., operator Campicello Vineyards, Madison, Va., 1982-92. Active Nat. Trust Hist. Preservation, Smithsonian Assocs., Assn. Naval Aviation. Mem. Associazione della Stampa Estera in Italia, The Cogswell Soc., The Murray Clan Soc., St. Andrew's Soc. of Washington D.C., Georgetown U. Alumni ASsn. (pres. Italy 1972-80), Am. C. of C. in Italy, Ret. Officers Assn., Navy League of U.S., Nat. Press Club, Vinifera Wine Growers Assn., Jeffersonian Wine Grape Growers Soc., Va. Vineyards Assn., Naval and Mil. Club, Steering Wheel Club, Royal Aero Club (London), Circolo Canottieri (Naples), N.Y. Athletic Club, Dist. Yacht (Washington). Address: 400 Madison St Apt 1408 Alexandria VA 22314-1724

FLEMING, EDWARD J. priest, educator; b. Montclair, N.J., Mar. 29, 1924; s. Timothy Joseph and Agnes (Gannon) F. Student, Seton Hall Prep. Sch., South Orange, N.J., 1932-36; AB, Seton Hall U., 1940, MA, 1948, LL.D., 1970; student, Immaculate Conception Sem., Ramsey, N.J., 1936-40; S.T.L., Cath. U. Am., 1944; PhD, St. John's U., Bklyn., 1955; grad., Inst. Advanced Studies, N.Am. Coll., Rome, 1977; postgrad., Harvard Divinity Sch., 1980. Ordained priest Roman Catholic Ch., 1944, elevated to papal chamberlain, 1963, elevated to prelate to Pope John Paul II, 1983; priest St. Teresa's Ch., Summit, N.J., 1944-49; prof. ednl. psychology and theology Seton Hall U., 1949-51, dean student affairs, 1951-53, dean coll., 1953-59, exec. v.p., 1959-69, pres., 1969-70; pastor Our Lady of Blessed Sacrament Ch., Roseland, N.J., 1970-78; dean Archdiocese of Newark, 1975-77, mem. bd. of consultors; vis. scholar Oxford (Eng.) U., 1987-88; dir. devel. Seton Hall U. Seminary, South Orange, N.J., 1987—; dir. and lectr. Newman studies Univ. Coll., 1987—; dir. devel. Sch. Theology Seton Hall U., South Orange, 1987—. Mem. exam. bd. Archdiocesan Clergy and Sem., 1954-64; mem. Archdiocesan Commn. Parish Visitation, 1969—; Episcopal vicar Essex County Archdiocese; coord. dean Essex County, 1975—; pres. Roseland Coun. Chs.; mem. ethics com. N.J. Supreme Ct., 1979—; mem. Senate of Priests, Archdiocese of Newark, 1980—, Archdiocesan Sch. Bd., 1980; vis. scholar Oxford U., Eng., 1964-65; week-end asst. Our Lady Peace, New Providence, N.J., Holy Rosary, Elizabeth, N.J., St. Paul Agostle, Irvington, N.J., St. James, Springfield, N.J., Visitation, Brich, N.J., St. Michael's, Long Branch, N.J., St. Josephs, Rarilian, N.J., St. Peters, Pheasant Beach, N.J., Point Pleasant Beach, St. Theresa's, Kenilworth, N.J. Contbr. articles on higher edn. to ednl. periodicals and jours. Mem. Army Adv. Panel ROTC Affairs, 1961-70; mem. Edn. Commn. U.S.; mem. pres.'s council Caldwell Coll., N.J.; trustee Assumption Coll., Mendham, N.J., Greater Newark Black and White Opera Co., Tri-Hosp. Ecumenical Chaplaincy Council No. N.J., 1979. Recipient Alpha Epsilon Mu award, 1956; Sapientiae Christianae Humanitarian award, 1958; John J. Crecca Found. Humanitarian award, 1967; Irishman of Year award Friends of Brian Boru, Inc., 1967; Zionist Brotherhood award, 1979; named to Athletic Hall of Fame, Seton Hall U., 1986; N.Am. Coll. fellow, Rome, 1971—, fellow Weston Theol. Ctr., Cambridge, Eng., 1986-87. Mem. Eastern Assn. Coll. Deans and Advisers of Men, Nat. Cath. Edn. Assn. (pres. Eastern unit 1965-66), Middle States Accreditation Assn., N.J. Hist. Soc. (com. of 125), Cath. Theol. Soc. Am. Office: Seton Hall Univ 400 S Orange Ave South Orange NJ 07079 E-mail: fleminm5@shu.edu. *May I never stop reaching out to others. May I never stop loving. For I should have learned long ago that love is not love 'til I give it away.*

FLEMING, GEORGE MATTHEWS, lawyer; b. Houston, Mar. 26, 1946; s. George McMillian and Mary Kathryn (Matthews) F.; children: Matthew Joseph, Kathryn Nicole, Tyler James. BBA, U. Tex., Austin, 1968; JD, U. Tex., 1971. Bar: Tex. 1971, U.S. Dist. Ct. (so., no., we. and ea. dists.) Tex. 1976, U.S. Dist. D.C. 1973, U.S. Ct. Appeals (5th cir.) 1976, U.S. Ct. Appeals (7th cir.) 1979, U.S. Ct. Appeals (11th cir.) 1982, U.S. Ct. Appeals (D.C. cir.) 1974, U.S. Ct. Appeals (3d cir.) 2000, U.S. Supreme Ct. Tex. 1971, U.S. Supreme Ct. 1974. Trial atty. torts sect. U.S. Dept. Justice, Washington, 1972-76; ptnr. Byrd, Davis & Eisenberg, Austin, 1976-82, Fleming, Betts & Cooke, Houston, 1982-86; prin. Fleming & Assocs., L.L.P., Houston, 1986—. Lectr. South Tex. Coll. Law, Houston, Embry-Riddle Aero. U.,Orlando, Fla., So. Meth. U. Air Law Symposium; lectr. aviation accident law litigation N.Y. Law Jour. Seminar, N.Y.C. Contbr. articles to profl. jours. Served to lt. U.S. Army, 1972. Mem. D.C. Bar Assn., ABA (ins. and compensation law com., chmn. mil. aviation com.), Houston Bar Assn., Assn. Trial Lawyers Am., Tex. Trial Lawyers Assn., Fed. Bar Assn., Lawyer Pilots Bar Assn., Internat. Soc. Air Safety Investigators. Democrat. Roman Catholic. Home: 30 W Rivercrest Dr Houston TX 77042-2127 Office: 1330 Post Oak Blvd Suite 3030 Houston TX 77056

FLEMING, GEORGE ROBERT, psychologist; b. Detroit, July 24, 1947; m. Beinda Fleming (div. Feb. 1987); 1 child, Maisha Amira. BA, Hillsdale Coll., 1969; MA in Clin. Psychology, Mich. State U., 1972, PhD in Clin. Psychology, 1975. Lic. psychologist Mich., Am. Bd. of Profl. Disability Cons., Am. Bd. Specialists, Psychol. Am. Coll. of Forensic Examiners, Emergency Crisis Response, Am. Acad. of Experts in Traumatic Stress, cert. Profl. Qualification in Psychology, Assn. of State and Provincial Bd. Staff mem. Internat. Soc. Traumatic Stress Studies, Allied Health-Detroit Med. Ctr. Med. Staff; staff mem. dept. psychiatry and behavioral neuroscis. Harper Hosp. and Detroit Receiving Hosp., 1990—; ind. psychiatric examiner mental divsn. Wayne County Probate Ct., 1991—; psychologist risk mgmt. divsn. Detroit Police Dept., 1997—; psychologist dept. behavioral medicine St. John Detroit Riverview Hosp., 1998—; prof. med. staff Detroit Riverview Hosp. St. John Health Sys., 1998—; clin. dir. Wayne County Juvenile Assessment Ctr., Mich., 2002—. Cons. Sacred Heart Rehab. Ctr., Inc., Detroit, 1981-84, Detroit Pub. Schs., 1981, 86—, Southgate Regional Ctr. for Devel. Disabilities, Mich. Dept. Mental Health, Southgate, 1989-90, Detroit Med. Ctr., Dept. of Psychiatry and Behavioral Neurosciences, Harper Hosp. and Detroit Receiving Hosp., 1990-; cons./facilitator Morehouse Rsch. Inst., Morehouse Coll., Atlanta, 1990—; advisor African Am. Males at Risk, Rockefeller Found., N.Y.C., 1989-90; workshop panelist Congl. Black Caucus Found., Washington, 1988; asst. prof. Wayne State U. dept. cmty. medicine, 1991-. Fellow Am. Orthopsychiatric Assn.; mem. Am. Psychol. Assn., Assn. Black Psychologists (past pres. Mich. chpt. 1981—), Nat. Register Health Svc. Providers in Psychology, Am. Bd. Profl. Disability Cons. (bd. dirs. 1996-), Am. Coll. Forensic Examiners (Am. Bd. Specialists), Assn. State and Provincial Bds. (cert. profl. qualification in psychology 2002-), Nat. Black Child Devel. Inst., Am. Coll. of Forensic Examiners (diplomate 1997-), Am. Acad. of Experts in Traumatic Stress (diplomate 1999-, emergency crisis response), Internat. Soc. for Traumatic Stress Studies. Office: 3011 W Grand Blvd Ste 559 Detroit MI 48202 E-mail: gpsychdet@msn.com.

FLEMING, GRAHAM RICHARD, chemistry educator; b. Barrow-in-Furness, Lancashire, Eng., Dec. 3, 1949; came to U.S., 1979; s. Maurice Norman and Ena (Winter) F.; m. Jean McKenzie, Sept. 16, 1977; 1 child, Matthew. BS with honors, U. Bristol, Eng., 1971; PhD in Phys. Chemistry, U. London, 1974. Rsch. fellow Calif. Inst. Tech., Pasadena, 1974-75; univ. rsch. fellow U. Melbourne, Australia, 1975, Australian Rsch. Grants Commn. rsch. asst., 1976; Leverhulme fellow Royal Instn., London, 1977-79; asst. prof. U. Chgo., 1979-83, assoc. prof., 1983-85, prof., 1985-87, A.H. Compton Disting. Svc. prof., 1987-97, chmn. dept. chemistry, 1988-90; prof. U. Calif., Berkeley, 1997—, Melvin Calvin disting. prof., 2002—; dir. phys. bioscis. divsn. Lawrence Berkeley Nat. Lab., 1997—, assoc. lab. dir. for phys. sci., 2002—. Co-chmn. Ultrafast Phenomena V Meeting, Snowmass, Colo., 1986; co-dir. Inst. Bioengring., Biotech., Quantitative Biomedicine, U. Calif., Berkeley, San Francisco, Santa Cruz. Author: Chemical Applications of Ultrafast Spectroscopy, 1986; mem. editl. bd. Chem. Physics Letters, Jour. of Phys. Chemistry, Chem. Physics; contbr. 235 rsch. articles to profl. publs. Recipient Coblentz award, Coblentz Soc., 1985, Earle K. Plyler award, Am. Phys. Soc., 2002; fellow Alfred P. Sloan Found. fellow, 1981, J.S. Guggenheim fellow, 1987; scholar Dreyfus tchr.-scholar, 1982. Fellow Am. Acad. Arts and Scis., Royal Soc. London; mem. Optical Soc. Am., Inter-Am. Photochem. Soc. (award 1996), Royal Soc. Chemistry (Marlow medal 1981, Tilden medal 1991, Centenary medal 1996), Am. Chem. Soc. (Nobel Laureate Signature award for grad. edn. in chemistry 1995, Peter Debye award in phys. chemistry 1998, Harrison Howe award 1999). Avocation: mountaineering. Office: Univ of Calif-Berkeley Dept Chemistry B84 Hildebrand # 1460 Berkeley CA 94720-0001

FLEMING, HORACE WELDON, JR., educator, former university president; b. Elberton, Ga., Jan. 14, 1944; s. Horace Weldon Sr and Alma G (Dove) Fleming; m. Orene Stephens Greene, Feb. 8, 1970; children: Susan Renee, Patrick Weldon. BA, U. Ga., 1965, MA, 1966; PhD, Vanderbilt U., 1973. Mem. faculty Clemson (S.C.) U., 1971-87; chief economist U.S. Senate Judiciary Com., 1981; staff dir. Office of Pres. Pro Tem U.S. Senate, 1981-82; founding dir. Strom Thurmond Inst. Govt. and Pub. Affairs, Clemson, 1982-90; exec. v.p. U. of the Pacific, Stockton, Calif., 1990-92; exec. v.p., provost Mercer U., Macon, Ga., 1992-96; pres. U. So. Miss., Hattiesburg, 1997—2001. Consult to fed, state and local govt agys on fin, orgn and mgt, energy and water policy; frequent media columnist and speaker; bd dirs Miss Technology Inc, Inst Technology Develop. Charter trustee Dropout Prevention Fund, 1986—90, Palmetto Project, 1987—90; vpres Hill Found, 1982—96; mem SC Reorganization Commn., 1987—90, Stockton-San Joaquin Conv and Visitors Bur, Calif., 1990—92; mem Vision 2000 task force Stockton Bus Coun, 1990—92; bd visitors Air Univ, 1998—; mem Pres's Nat Vol Adv coun, 1986—89, Assembly Future SC, 1988, Gov's Transition Task Force Govt Reform, 1986—87. Capt U.S. Army, 1969—71, Vietnam. Recipient Order Palmetto, SC, 1990, Award of Merit, SC Water Resources Comn, 1990, Palmetto Pride Award, Palmetto Project, 1990; fellow Faculty, Leadership Hilton Head Island, 1989. Mem.: Tiger Brotherhood, Blue Key, Scabbard and Blade, Phi Kappa Phi, Omicron Delta Kappa, Sigma Phi Epsilon, Pi Sigma Alpha, Phi Mu Alpha.

FLEMING, JAMES DOUGAL, English educator, writer; b. Rochester, N.Y., Dec. 11, 1968; s. Donald George Fleming and Ruth Agatha Jacobsen; m. Cynthia Elizabeth von Ginkel, May 31, 1997. MA, U. Toronto, Can., 1997, Columbia U., 1998, PhD, 2001. Asst. prof. English,Simon Fraser U. Burnaby, Canada, 2000—. Recipient scholarship, U. Toronto, 1997, Doctoral fellowship, Social Sci. and Humanities Rsch. Coun. Can., 1997—2001, Pres.'s fellowship, Columbia U., 1998—2001, Pres.'s Rsch. grant, Simon Fraser U., 2001. Mem.: MLA, N-E MLA, Rocky Mountain MLA. Avocation: fitness. Office: Simon Fraser Univ Dept English 8888 University Dr Burnaby BC V5A 1S6 Canada

FLEMING, JAMES RODGER, science historian, educator; b. Windber, Pa., May 28, 1949; s. James Thomas and Ellen Jane (Rodger) Fleming; m. Miyoko Yamato, July 1, 1982; children: Jamitto, Jason Thomas. BS in Astronomy, Pa. State U., 1971; MS in Atmospheric Sci., Colo. State U., 1973; MA in History of Sci., Princeton U., 1984, PhD in History of Sci., 1988. Grad. rsch. asst. Colo. State U., 1971-73; meteorologist cloud physics divsn. U. Wash., 1973-74, Nat. Ctr. Atmospheric Rsch., 1973; cons. meteorologist pvt. practice, Fla. and N.Y., 1974-82; hist. cons., history editor Bull. Am. Meteorol. Soc., 1987-88, 2002—; prof. sci., tech. and soc. program Colby Coll., Waterville, Maine, 1988—2003, chair interdisciplinary studies divsn., 1997-99; vis. scholar dept. history sci. Harvard U., 1999-2000. Vis. prof. Pa. State U. Ctr. Global Change Sci., 1994; vis. scholar MIT Program Sci., Tech. and Soc., 1992—94; rsch. assoc. dept. history of sci. Harvard U., 1992—93; convener, pres. Internat. Commn. on History of Meteorology, 2000—; spkr. in field. Author: (book) Meteorology in America, 1800-1870, 1990, Science, Technology and the Environment: Multidisciplinary Perspectives, 1994, International Bibliography of Meteorology: From the Beginning of Printing to 1889, 1994, Historical Essays on Meteorology, 1919-1995, 1996, Historical Perspectives on Climate Change, 1998, Weathering the Storm: Sverre Petterssen, the D-Day Forecast, and the Rise of Modern Meteorology, 2001; editor (guest editor): Hist. Studies in the Phys. and Biol. Scis., 2000, Studies in the History and Philosophy of Modern Physics, 2000; contbr. chapters to books, articles to profl. jours. Recipient Bausch-Lomb Sci. award, 1967; fellow Predoctoral, Smithsonian Instn., 1985—87, Mellon Rsch., Am. Philos. Soc., 1991, Frederick W. Beinecke, Yale U., 1992, NEH, 1992—93, Ritter Meml., Scripps Instn. Oceanography, 2003; grantee Rsch. and Course Devel., Colby Coll., 1988—2003, NSF, 2001—; scholar Undergrad., Pa. State U., 1968—71. Mem.: AAAS (mem. nominating com. 2003—), History of the Earth Scis. Soc. (assoc. editor Earth Scis. History 2002—, program officer), Soc. History Tech., History of Sci.Soc. (spkr. 1986, 1987, 1992, 1995, 1997, 1999, 2003, adv. editor Isis, Schuman prize com.), Brit. Soc. History of Sci., Am. Meteorol. Soc. (hist. cons. 1996—, chair history com. 1996—2003, keynote spkr. 1999, history editor, Rsch. grantee 1987—88), Am. Geophys. Union (numerous offices), Internat. Union History and Philosophy Sci. Office: Colby Coll Sci Tech and Soc Program Waterville ME 04901 E-mail: jrflemin@colby.edu.

FLEMING, JAMES STUART, JR., retired pharmaceutical company manager; b. Buffalo, Sept. 1, 1936; s. James Stuart and Pauline (McClurg) F.; m. Marilyn Joyce Bartsch, June 7, 1960; children: Lois Vernette, James Stuart III. BA, Northwestern U., 1958; MS, U. Buffalo, 1962; PhD, Ohio State U., 1965; MBA, Syracuse U., 1983. Rsch. asst. Ohio State U., Columbus, 1962-65; rsch. scientist Bristol-Myers Co., Syracuse, N.Y., 1965-74, sr. rsch. scientist, 1974-82, mgr., 1982-85, assoc. dir. cardiovascular biology Syracuse and Wallingford, Conn., 1985-90; assoc. dir. project planning Bristol-Myers Squibb Co., Wallingford, Conn., 1990-2000. Author: (with others) Platelet Aggregation Inhibitors, 1974-82; editor: Drugs and the Delivery of Oxygen to Tissues, 1989. Cons., tchr. Jr. Achievement, Wallingford, 1988-90. Avocations: golf, tennis, hiking, skiing, gardening.

FLEMING, JANE WILLIAMS, retired educator, writer; b. Bethlehem, Pa., May 26, 1926; d. James Robert and Marion Pauline (Melloy) Groman; m. George Elliott Williams, July 2, 1955 (div. July 1965); children: Rhett Dorman, Santee Stuart, Timothy Cooper; m. Jerome Thomas Fleming, Sept. 25, 1980 (dec. 2002). BS, UCLA, 1951; MA, Calif. State U., Long Beach, 1969. Tchr. San Diego Unified Sch Dist., 1951-55, Costa Mesa (Calif.) Sch. Dist., 1955-56, Long Beach (Calif.) Sch. Dist., 1956-58, 62-87, 90-92; ret. Author: Why Janey Can't Teach, 2001. Mem. Phi Kappa Phi, Ret. Tchrs. Assn., UCLA Alumni Assn., Planetary Soc. (charter), Mus. of Tolerance. Avocations: theater, travel. Address: PO Box 13053 Belmont Shore CA 90803-8053 E-mail: jwilli5687@aol.com.

FLEMING, JON LEE, gastroenterologist; b. Charles City, Iowa, Sept. 7, 1952; s. Gilbert and Rose (Basuk) F. BS with distinction, Iowa State U., 1975; MD, U. Iowa, 1979. Diplomate Am. Bd. Internal Medicine, Am. Bd. Gastroenterology. Intern U. Kans. Hosps. and Clinics, Kansas City, 1979-80; resident in internal medicine U. Kans., Kansas City, 1980-83; fellow in gastroenterology Mayo Clinic, Rochester, Minn., 1983-86; gastroenterologist McFarland Clinic, Ames, Iowa, 1986—. Comprehensive rev. com. Iowa Found. for Med. Care, 1994-96, quality assessment com., 1990-93; adv. bd. Iowa Jewish Sr. Life Ctr., Des Moines, 1996—2002, Iowa State U. Athletic Dept., Ames, 1994-2000, corp. bd. dirs. Theta Chi, 1990—, devel. bd. dirs. WOI radio, 1997—, devel. bd. dirs. parks libr., 1991-96. Named Greek Alumnus of Yr., Iowa State U. Greeks, 1991, 97, Theta Chi Alumnus of Yr., 1996-97; Coll. Sci. and Humanities scholar, 1975. Fellow ACP, Am. Gastroenterology Assn.; mem. Iowa Crohns-Colitis Assn. (physicians adv. bd. 1990—), Phi Beta Kappa, Phi Kappa Phi, Phi Eta Sigma, Pi Mu Epsilon. Democrat. Jewish. Avocations: jogging, golf, sports, reading. Home: 417 Pearson Ave Ames IA 50014-7033 Office: McFarland Clinic PO Box 3014 Ames IA 50010-3014

FLEMING, JUANITA WILSON, nursing education, university official; BS, Hampton Inst., 1957; MA, U. Chgo., 1959; PhD, Cath. U. Am., 1969; D Pub. Svc., Berea Coll., 1994. From staff nurse to head nurse med.-surg. pediat. unit

Children's Hosp., Washington, 1957-58; pub. health nurse Bur. Pub. Health Nursing, 1959-60; instr. nursing children Sch. Nursing Freedmen's Hosp., Washington, 1962-65; cons. pub. health nursing dept. pediat. Child Devel. Clin., Howard U., 1965-66; from asst. prof. to assoc. prof. U. Ky. Coll. Nursing, Lexington, 1969-73; prof. U. Ky., Lexington, 1973—, spl. asst. to pres. for acad. affairs, 1991—2001, prof. emeritus, 2001—03; interim v.p. acad. affairs Ky. State U., Frankfort, Ky., 2003—. Mem. grad. faculty Coll. Nursing, U. Ky. 1971—, asst. dean grad. edn., 1975-81, assoc. dean, dir. grad. edn., 1982-86; prof. Coll. Edn. Edpt. Edn. Policy Studies and Evaln., 1979—; assoc. vice-chancellor acad. affairs Med. Ctr., 1984-91; prin. investigator nursing care high risk infants State Maternal and Child Health Divsn., 1972; project dir. advanced nurse tng. grant divsn. nursing Dept. Health Edn. and Welfare, 1977-80, prin. investigator high tech home care chronically ill children Bur. Maternal Child Health, 1989-93; prin. investigator healthcare and devel. status Children and Their Families MIRT Fogarty Ctr., 2001-2002; vis. prof. Case We. Res. U., Cleve., 1984, West Chester U., 1997; Martin Luther King/Rosa Parks/Cesar Chavez vis. prof. U. Mich., Ann Arbor, 1989, Elizabeth Carnegie endowed vis. prof. Howard U., 1995; Houston Endowed Minority Health and Rsch. Disting. vis. prof. Prairie View U., 1998; prin. investigator Am. Nurses Found., 1970-71; Faville lectr. Wayne State U., 1998. Recipient Ky. Nurses Assn. award, Marion E. McKenna leadership award, 1988, Disting. Svc. award ANA, 1994; Olhson scholar U. Ill., 1999, Robert A. Zumwinkle Student Rights award U. Ky. Student Govt. Assn., 2001. Mem. Am. Acad. Nursing, Nat. Acad. Scis., Inst. Medicine. Office: 316 Exum Court Frankfort KY 40601

FLEMING, JULIAN DENVER, JR., lawyer; b. Rome, Ga., Jan. 12, 1934; s. Julian D. and Margaret Madison (Mangham) F.; m. Sidney Howell, June 28, 1960; 1 dau., Julie Adrianne. Student, U. Pa., 1951-53; BChemE, Ga. Inst. Tech., 1955, PhD, 1959; JD, Emory U., 1967. Bar: Ga. 1966, D.C. 1967; registered profl. engr., Ga., Calif. Rsch. engr., prof. chem. engring. Ga. Inst. Tech., 1955-67; ptnr. Sutherland, Asbill & Brennan, Atlanta, 1967—. Contbr. articles to profl. jours.; patentee in field. Bd. dirs. Mental Health Assn. Ga., 1970-80; bd. dirs. Mental Health Assn. Met. Atlanta, 1970-80, pres., 1974-75; mem. coun. legal advisors Rep. Nat. Com., 1981-85. Fellow: Am. Bar Found., Am. Coll. Trial Lawyers, Am. Inst. Chemists; mem.: AIChE, AAAS, ABA (coun. sect. sci. and tech. 1980—82, vice chmn. 1982—84, chmn. 1985—86, ho. dels. 1990, bd. govs. 1994—95, ho. dels. 1994—96, chmn. spl. citation issues com. 1995—96, coord. commn. legal tech. 1995—97, standing com. tech. and info. sys. 1997—2001), Bleckley Inn of Ct. (master of bench), Nat. Conf. Lawyers and Scientists (chmn. ABA del. 1988—90, standing com. nat. conf. groups 1990, ABA liaison 1990—93, chmn. 1992—93). Achievements include patent for data apparatus. Home: 1248 Oxford Rd NE Atlanta GA 30306-2610 Office: Sutherland Asbill & Brennan 999 Peachtree St NE Ste 2300 Atlanta GA 30309-3996

FLEMING, JUNE HELENA, retired city manager; b. Little Rock, June 24, 1931; d. Herman Leroy and Ethel Lucille (Thompson) Dwellingham; m. Silas W. Cullins, June 5, 1956 (div.); m. Roscoe Lee Fleming, Jr., Mar. 11, 1966; children: Ethel Lucille, Roscoe Lee III. BA, Talladega Coll., 1953; MLS, Drexel U., 1954. Br. libr. Bklyn. Pub. Libr., 1954-55; HS libr. Little Rock Pub. Schs., 1955-56; assoc. prof. Philander Smith Coll., Little Rock, 1960-66; dir. librs. City of Palo Alto, Calif., 1968-79, asst. city mgr., 1980-92, city mgr., 1992-2000; ret., 2000. Mem. allocation com. Santa Clara United Way, San Jose, Calif., 1991—93; pres. search com. Foothill Coll., Los Altos Hills, Calif., 1994—; bd. dirs. Blackwater Regional Libr., 2001—, Paul D. Camp CC Found., 2001—. Mem.: Internat. City Mgrs. Assn., Rotary (bd. dirs.), Links, Inc., Delta Sigma Theta (corr. sec. 1993). Methodist. Avocations: walking, swimming, reading. Home: 121 Regency Ln Franklin VA 23851-2736

FLEMING, KATHLEEN GAIL, retired computer operations specialist; b. Staten Island, N.Y., Nov. 21, 1944; d. Fulton Lamont and Edna (Geist) Reid; m. Terry Lowell Fleming, Sept. 27, 1969; children: Heather Kathleen, Kevin Reid, Shannon Joy (dec.), Colin Martin. BS in Nursing, Wagner Coll., 1966. R.N., Oreg. Office nurse pvt. practice physician, Reno, 1972-73; staff nurse Green Valley Care Ctr., Eugene, Oreg., 1973-74, Good Samaritan Hosp., Portland, Oreg., 1974-75, Vet.'s Hosp., Portland, 1975, Woodland Park Hosp., Portland, 1975-78; office nurse pvt. practice physician, Beaverton, Oreg., 1978; staff nurse Forest Grove (Oreg.) Community Hosp., 1978-79; head maternity dept. Tuality Community Hosp., Hillsboro, Oreg., 1979-82; computer operator Transaction Recording Systems, Inc., Portland, 1982-93, Equitrac Corp., Portland, 1993-94; ind. computer operator, 1994—2003. Past bd. dirs. Washington County Assn. Retarded Citizens, Beaverton; parent contact, Pilot Parents, Washington County, 1986-91. Lt. USN, 1964-69. Mem. Oreg. Apt. Assn. Republican. Presbyterian. Avocations: horseback riding, scuba diving, travel, real estate investing, martial arts. Home: 14051 NW Grandview Pl Banks OR 97106-8880 E-mail: kgailf@yahoo.com.

FLEMING, KATHRYN ALICE, automotive executive; b. Detroit, Mar. 3, 1952; d. Albert Edwin and Alice May Fleming; m. Todd Gene Van Every, Feb. 25, 1978 (div. Sept. 1990); children: Allison Van Every, Todd Van Every. BS in Spl. Edn., Ea. Mich. U., 1979; MA, Marygrove Coll., 1999. With Ford Motor Co., 1977—; spl. edn. substitute tchr., 1981—82; songwriter Amerecord, Hollywood, Calif., 2000—, Hilltop Records, Hollywood, 2000—. Mem.: TAXI, Defenders Wildlife, Acad. Am. Poets. Avocations: piano, writing, gardening, Internet, songwriting. Home and Office: 3150 W Rattalee Lake Rd Rose Township MI 48442

FLEMING, KEN, publishing executive; Pres. Tulsa (Okla.) World, 1992—2000. Office: Tulsa World PO Box 1770 Tulsa OK 74102-1770

FLEMING, MACKLIN, judge, author; b. Chgo., Sept. 6, 1911; s. Ingram Macklin Stainback and Hazel (Caldwell) Fleming; m. Polly Naething, May 17, 1941; children: Penelope, Frances, Ingram. BA, Yale U., 1934, LLB, 1937; LLD, Pepperdine U., 1968. Bar: N.Y. 1938, Calif. 1946. Assoc. Sullivan & Cromwell, N.Y.C., 1937-39; atty. Bituminous Coal divsn. U.S. Govt., Washington, 1939-41; pvt. practice San Francisco, 1946-49; asst. U.S. atty. U.S. Atty.'s Office, San Francisco, 1949-53; assoc. Mitchell, Silberberg & Knupp, L.A., 1954-59; judge Superior Ct., L.A., 1959-64; justice Calif. Ct. Appeal, L.A., 1964-81; of counsel Troy and Gould, L.A., 1981-91; assigned judge Superior Ct., L.A., 1992-98. Author: The Price of Perfect Justice, 1974, Of Crimes and Rights, 1978, Lawyers, Money, & Success, 1997, Perfect Justice, 2001. Chmn. Far Eastern Art Coun., L.A. County Mus., 1967-69; v.p. Ctr. Theater Group, L.A., 1970. Pvt. to Capt. U.S. Army, 1941-46. Fellow Am. Bar Found.; mem. ABA, L.A. County Bar Assn., Bar of City of N.Y., Inst. of Jud. Adminstrn., Selden Soc. Democrat. Episcopalian. Avocations: skiing, tennis, gardening. Home: 331 N Carmelina Ave Los Angeles CA 90049-2701

FLEMING, MARCELLA, journalist; b. Paoli, Ind., Oct. 14, 1955; d. Kenneth Gale and Neva Louise (Thomas) F.; m. Brian D. Smith. AB in Journalism and English, Ind. U., 1978. Cert. tchr. Reporter Wabash Plain Dealer, 1978-80, Marion Chronicle-Tribune, 1980-83, city editor, 1990-91; city reporter, feature writer, copy editor, Sunday editor Ft. Wayne (Ind.) Jour.-Gazette, 1983-88; editor pubs. Children's Mus. Indpls., 1988-90; freelance writer Indpls. Monthly, 1989-91; nat. editor Indpls. CEO, Columbus (Ohio) CEO mags., 1991-92; writer state desk Indpls. Star & News, 1992—. Judge Thomas R. Keating Writing Competition, 1990. Recipient award of Excellence Nat. Down Syndrome Congress, 1988, Best Newsletter, Best Feature Story and Best News Story awards Editor's Forum, 1990, Best Ann. Report award Internat. Assn. Bus. Communicators, 1990. Mem. Ednl. Press Assn. (Breaking News Story Disting. Achievement award 1994). Office: Indpls Star 307 N Pennsylvania St Indianapolis IN 46204-1819

FLEMING, MICHAEL PAUL, lawyer; b. Orlando, Fla., June 25, 1963; s. Joseph Patrick and Therese (Eccles); m. Natalie Jackson, Oct. 15, 1988; children: Shannon Isabel, Nicholas Patrick, Patrick Edward, Michael Paul, Eamon John, Celeste Natalie. BA, U. St. Thomas, 1984; JD, U. Houston, 1987. Bar: Tex. 1987; U.S. Dist. Ct. (so. dist.) Tex. 1988; U.S. Ct. Appeals (5th cir.) 1988, U.S. Supreme Ct. 1991; cert. personal injury. Ptnr. Fleming & Fleming, Houston, 1987-91; asst. county atty. Harris County, Houston, 1991-96, elected Harris county atty., 1996-2001; ptnr. Bracewell & Patterson, Houston, 2001—02; gen. counsel LGI Devel., Conroe, Tex., 2002—; vice chair Harris County Housing Authority, 2003—. Bd. dirs. U. St. Thomas, 2002—. Named Irish Person of Yr., 2000. Mem. State Bar of Tex., Houston Bar Assn., Ancient Order of Hibernians, KC, KHS, Equestrian Order of Holy Sepulchre of Jerusalem, Phi Delta Phi, 100 Club of Houston, Irish Soc. Roman Catholic. Avocations: genealogy, castlemahon history. Home: 643 W Forest Dr Houston TX 77079-6915 Office: 19221 I-45 South Conroe TX 77385

FLEMING, NANCY MCADAM, landscape designer; b. Balt., July 24, 1940; d. Robert Martin and Jane Ellen (Weeks) McAdam; m. Samuel Crozier Fleming, Sept. 7, 1963; children: David McAdam, Timothy Crozier. BA, Mt. Holyoke Coll., 1962; cert. in Landscape Design, Radcliffe Coll., 1988. Tchr. The Harley Sch., Rochester, N.Y., 1962-63, Shady Hill Sch., Cambridge, Mass., 1965-67; flower show asst. Mass. Hort. Soc., Boston, 1986-88; pub., owner Country Pl. Books, Weston, Mass., 1995—; landscape designer Nancy Fleming, Inc., Weston, 1989—. Mem. landscape vis. com. U. Del., Newark, 1996—; mem. Cornell plantation com. Cornell U., Ithaca, N.Y., 1997—; com. mem. Weston Rds. Trust, 1997-2001, Weston Land Trust, 1998-2001; spkr., slide lectr. garden clubs, hort. orgns., Mass., N.H., N.Y., Del., Conn., 1988—. Author: Money, Manure and Maintenance, 1995; (booklet) Weston Town Common, 1988. Chmn. Park and Cemetery Commn., Weston, 1994-96; trustee Walnut Hill Sch., Natick, Mass., 1993-2001. Mem.: Baker Hill Golf Club, Weston Garden Club (pres. 1989—91), Chilton Club (Boston), Country Club (Brookline, Mass.). Republican. Episcopalian. Avocations: competitive golf, reading, bridge. Home and Office: Nancy Fleming Inc 61 Meadowbrook Rd Weston MA 02493-2407

FLEMING, NORMAN PATRICK, information scientist; s. Lindsey Fleming, Sr. and Laura D. Fleming; m. Yolanda Elisa Rocio, June 5, 1993. MBA, Devry U., Oak Brook Terrace, Ill., 1999; BS, So. Ill. U. Dir. client svcs. NY Times, NYC, 1999—2000; bus. sys. leader Kraft Foods, Inc., Northfield, Ill., 2000—. Specialist Army Nat. Guard, 1986—87, Ill. Recipient Pres.'s award, Chgo. Tribune Co., 1994. Mem.: Nat. Black MBA Assn. Inc. (life; chmn. 2001—03), Alpha Phi Alpha (pres. 2002—03), Mu Mu Lambda (pres. 2002—03, dir. edn. found. 1998—2003). Home: 2611 Lexington Ln Naperville IL 60540 Home Fax: 630-369-8105. Personal E-mail: nfleming@msn.com.

FLEMING, PATRICIA STUBBS, artist; b. Phila., Mar. 17, 1936; d. Fredrick Douglass Stubbs and Marion Turner Stubbs Thomas; m. Harold S. Fleming, June 1958 (div. Feb. 1971); children: Douglass, Craig, Gordon. BA, Vassar Coll., 1957; postgrad., NYU, 1958-60, U. Pa., 1957-58, Pa. Acad. Fine Arts, 1957-58. Legis. asst. to reps. U.S. Ho. of Reps., Washington, 1971-77; asst. to sec. HEW, Washington, 1977-78, dir. intergovtl. and legis. affairs Office Civil Rights, 1979-80; asst. to sec. U.S. Dept. Edn., Washington, 1979-80, dep. asst. sec. legis., 1980-81; sr. pub. policy assoc. James H. Lowry & Assocs., Washington, 1981-83; chief staff Rep. Ted Weiss U.S. Ho. of Reps., Washington, 1983-86, profl. staff mem. subcom. human resources & intergovtl. rels, 1986-93; spl. asst. to sec. HHS, Washington, 1993-94; dir. Office Nat. AIDS Policy The White House, Washington, 1994-97, cons. on govt. rels. and AIDS policy and programs, 1997—. Washington rep. Joint Co-sponsored UN Programme on HIV/AIDS; pres. Prevention Works Needle Exchange Program in the Nation's Capitol. One-person show NYU; exhibited in group shows in N.Y.C. and Washington; mem. Foundry Gallery, Washington.. Democrat. Episcopalian. Avocations: travel, music, reading. Home and Studio: 6009 Massachusetts Ave Bethesda MD 20816-2041

FLEMING, RENÉE L. opera singer; b. Indiana, Pa., Feb. 14, 1959; d. Edwin Davis Fleming and Patricia (Seymour) Alexander; m. Richard Lee Ross, Sept. 23, 1989 (div. 2000). BM in Music Edn., Potsdam State U., 1981; MM, Eastman Sch. Music, 1983; student, Juilliard Am. Opera Ctr., N.Y.C., 1983-84, 85-87. Rec. artist Decca Records, London, 1995. Debut engagements include Spoleto Festival, Charleston and Italy, 1986-90, Houston Grand Opera & N.Y.C. Opera, 1988, 89, San Francisco Opera, 1991, Met. Opera, Paris Opera at the Bastille, 1991, Covent Garden, London, 1989, Teatro Colon Buenos Aires, 1991, La Scala, 1993, Lyric Opera of Chgo., 1993, Paris Opera at Palais Garnier, 1996. Winner Met. Opera Nat. Auditions, 1988; recipient George London prize, 1988, Richard Tucker award, 1990, Solti prize l'Acad. du Disque Lyrique, 1996, Prize l'Acad. du Disque Lyrique, 1998; Fulbright scholar, Frankfurt, Germany, 1984-85; named Vocalist of Yr. Mus. Am., 1997; nominated 8 Grammy awards, 1997-99; recipient Grammy award, 1999, 2003, 3 gramophone awards, 1999, record of yr., opera award, recital award, Gift of Music award Orch. of St. Luke's, 2000; named one of top 10 classical singers of the 90s, AP, 2000; La Diva Renée dessert named in her honor by chef Daniel Boulud, 1999. Office: care ML Falcone Pub Rels 155 W 68th St Apt 1114 New York NY 10023-5817

FLEMING, REX JAMES, meteorologist; b. Omaha, Apr. 25, 1940; s. Robert Leonard and Doris Mae (Burrows) F.; m. Kathleen Joyce Ferry, Sept. 3, 1969; children: Thane, Manon, Mark, Noel. BS, Creighton U., 1963; MS, U. Mich., 1968, PhD, 1970. Commd. lt. U.S. Air Force, 1963, advanced through grades to capt., 1972; research scientist Offutt AFB, Nebr., 1963-67; sci. liaison to Nat. Weather Service for Air Weather Service, Suitland, Md., 1970-72; resigned, 1972; mgr. applications mktg. advanced sci. computer Tex. Instruments, Inc., Austin, 1972-75; dir. U.S. Project Office for Global Weather Expt., NOAA, Rockville, Md., 1975-80, Spl. Research Projects Office, 1980-82, Office of Climate and Atmospheric Research, 1983-84, Internat. Tropical Ocean and Global Atmosphere Project Office and Nat. Storm Program Office, 1984-86; pres. Tycho Tech. Inc., Boulder, Colo., 1986-87, Creative Concepts, Boulder, Colo., 1987-91; sr. mgr., coord. FAA rsch. Nat. Ctr. for Atmospheric Rsch., 1991-92, vis. scientist, 1987-88; NOAA, Boulder, 1993-2001; program mgr. U. Corp. for Atmospheric Rsch., 2001—. Contbr. articles to profl. jours. Recipient Gold Medal award Dept. Commerce, 1980 Fellow AAAS; mem. Am. Meteorol. Soc. (chmn. probability and statistics com. 1976-77), The Planetary Soc., Am. Geophys. Union (sec. atmospheric scis. sect. 1984-86). Republican. Home: 7225 Spring Dr Boulder CO 80303-5115 Office: NCAR PO Box 3000 Boulder CO 80307-3000 *One need only be inspired by its spring-morning freshness, stimulated by its magnificent variety of color and form, and humbled by the power of its ever-present energy, to be driven to unveil the secrets of our life-sustaining atmosphere.*

FLEMING, RHONDA, actress, singer, humanitarian; b. LA; d. Harold Cheverton and Effie (Graham) Louis; m. Ted (dec.); 1 child, Kent Lane. Student, pub. and pvt. schs., L.A., Beverly Hills. Appeared in 40 motion pictures, including Spellbound, 1945, Spiral Staircase, 1945, Out of the Past, 1947, A Connecticut Yankee in King Arthur's Court, 1949, The Great Lover, 1949, The Eagle and the Hawk, 1950, Cry Danger, 1951, Last Outpost, 1951, Hong Kong, 1952, Tropic Zone, 1953, Tennessee's Partner, 1955, Gunfight at OK Corral, 1956, Slightly Scarlett, 1956, Home Before Dark, 1958, Pony Express, 1953, The Nude Bomb, 1980; Broadway debut in The Women, 1973; appeared in musical and plays, including The Boyfriend, 1975, Marriage Go Round, 1960, Bell, Book and Candle, 1962, Kismet at Music Center, 1976; sang Gershwin concert in; 10-week tour, 1963; starred in Las Vegas, Nev., 1959, one-woman concert at Hollywood Bowl, 1964, numerous guest appearances on TV series and talk shows including MacMillan and Wife, Love Boat; TV movies include The Last Hours Before Morning, 1975; NBC's Legends of the Screen, 1980, Metromedia Spl. Road to Hollywood, 1983, Wildest West Show of the Stars, 1986. Founder Rhonda Fleming Mann Clinic and Resource Ctr. for Women's Comprehensive Care at UCLA, PATH (People Assisting the Homeless) Rhonda Fleming Family Ctr.; benefactor Music Ctr.; supporter Childhelp USA, Achievement Rewards Coll. Scientists; life assoc. Pepperdine U.; founding mem. French Found. for Alzheimer Rsch.; adv. bd. Olive Crest Treatment Ctrs. for Abused Children; supporter Freedoms Found. at Valley Forge, City of Hope, Excellence in Media, SPCA, Humane Soc. USA; patron of the arts Music Ctr. Blue Ribbon; bd. dirs. World Opportunities Internat., St. John's Med. Ctr. Recipient award NCCJ, Gold Angel award Excellence in Media, Woman of the World award Childhelp, USA, Eve award Mannequins of the Assistance League, 1986, Our Lady of Perpetual Inspiration award; named Woman of Year City of Hope, Oper. Children, 1991, honoree of the Music Ctr. Club 100, 1992, UCLA Alumni Assn. Disting. Contbns. award to UCLA Cmty., 2000; Rhonda Fleming Rsch. fellowship for women's cancer established at City of Hope, 2000.

FLEMING, RICHARD H. finance executive; b. Milw., July 22, 1947; s. David M. and Mildred (Codere) F.; m. Diana Loane, Mar. 21, 1970; children: Douglas Codere, Petria Anne. BA, U. Pacific, 1969; MBA, Dartmouth, 1971. Fin. analyst Graco, Inc., Mpls., 1971-72, mgr. banking and fgn. exchange, 1972-73; fin. analyst Masonite Corp., Chgo., 1973-74, mgr. capital investment, 1974-77, asst. treas., 1977-82, treas., 1982-84, v.p. fin., chief fin. officer, 1985-89; dir. corp. fin. and asst. treas. USG Corp., Chgo., 1989-90, v.p., treas., 1991-94, v.p., CFO, 1994-95, sr. v.p., CFO, 1995-99, exec. v.p., CFO, 1999—. Trustee USG Found., 1989—; bd. dirs. Columbus McKinnon Corp. Bd. dirs. Family Care Services Met. Chgo., 1977—, pres. 1983-86; bd. dirs. Child Welfare League Am., Washington, 1987—, pres. 1999-2000. Alumni fellow U. Pacific Sch. Bus. Adminstrn. and Pub. Policy, 1990. Office: USG Corp PO Box 6721 125 S Franklin St Chicago IL 60680-6721 Home: Apt 2802 195 N Harbor Dr Chicago IL 60601-7532

FLEMING, ROBBEN WRIGHT, retired educator; b. Paw Paw, Ill., Dec. 18, 1916; s. Edmunds Palmer Fleming and Emily Jeannette (Wheeler) Boutwell; children: Nancy Jo, James Edmund, Caroline Elizabeth. BA, Beloit Coll., 1938; LLB, U. Wis., 1941; hon. degree, Mich. State U., 1967, U. Mich., 1968, U. Wis., 1968, U. Ill., 1969, Ohio State U., 1972, Columbia U., 1974, Boston Coll., 1979. Sec., exch. com. lawyer Securities and Exchg. Commn., Washington, 1941-42; mediator Nat. War Labor Bd., Washington, 1942; with Nat. Housing Authority, Washington, 1946-47; asst. prof. U. Wis., Madison, 1947-52; dir. Inst. Lab. & Indsl. Rels., U. Ill., Urbana, 1952-58; prof. law U. Ill. Law Sch., Urbana, 1957-64; chancellor U. Wis., Madison, 1964-67; pres. U. Mich., Ann Arbor, 1967-79. Pres. Corp. for Pub. Broadcasting, Washington, 1979-81; chmn. bd. Nat. Inst. for Dispute Resolution, Washington, 1981-88; cons. to fed. judge on desegregation of pub. higher edn., Ala., 1994—. Author: The Labor Arbitration Process, 1965, Tempests Into Rainbows - Managing turbulence, 1996. Capt. U.S. Army, 1943-46. Mem. Rotary (Paul Harris fellow 1997). Avocations: reading, golf. Home: 827 Asa Gray Dr # Ann Arbor MI 48105 E-mail: rwf16@aol.com.

FLEMING, ROBERT, investment company executive; b. Sept. 18, 1932; s. Philip and Joan Cecil (Hunloke) Fl; m. Victoria Margaret Aykroyd, 1962; 3 children. Grad., Eton Coll., Eng., Royal Mil. Acad., Sandhurst, Eng. With The Royal Scots Greys, 1952-58, Robert Fleming, 1958—; dep. chmn. Robert Fleming Holdings, London, 1986-90, chmn., 1990-97; retired; chmn. Robert Fleming Holdings, 1999—. Bd. dirs. Robert Fleming Trustee Co., 1961—, chmn., 1985-91; bd. dirs. Robert Fleming Investment Trust, 1968—, Robert Fleming Holdings, 1974—, Glenshee Chairlift Co. Ltd., 1995—. High sheriff, 1980, Oxfordshire, Eng., dep. lt., 1990. Avocations: hunting, fishing, music. Office: Fleming Family and Ptnrs Ely House 37 Dover St London W15 4NJ England

FLEMING, ROBERT BURKE, law educator, lawyer; b. Pitts., Dec. 18, 1921; s. Pierce J. and Alice (Leufsted) Fleming; m. Jeanne C. Cullen, Apr. 7, 1947; children: Robert B., Michael, Molly, Andrew, Kate, Jane. BME, U. Minn., 1943; LLB, U. Buffalo, 1951. Bar: N.Y. Instr. Dean Pace Law Sch., White Plains, NY, 1976—82, prof., 1982—; of counsel Bleakley & Schmidt. Office: Pace Law Sch 78 N Broadway White Plains NY 10603-3710 Also: Bleakley & Schmidt 123 Main St White Plains NY 10601-3104

FLEMING, ROBERT WRIGHT, investment banker; b. Washington, Aug. 26, 1918; s. Robert Vedder and Alice Listen (Wright) F.; m. Martha Wills Schoenfeld, Nov. 21, 1942; children: Margaret Johanna, Robert Vedder II, Bruce Wright. BA, George Washington U., 1941. Washington rep. Pan. Am. Airways, 1946-48; became v.p., sec., dir. Folger Nolan Fleming Douglas Inc., Washington, 1950, now pres., dir. Bd. dir., mem. exec. com. Acacia Mut. Life Ins. Co.; bd. dirs. Security Storage Co.; cons. dir. emeritus Riggs Nat. Bank, Washington.; dir., chmn. audit com. Medlantic Healthcare Group, Inc. (formerly Washington Healthcare Corp.); mem. Washington Bd. Trade, N.Y., Am. stock exchanges.; chmn. endowment and investment com. Washington Hosp. Center; chmn. adv. com. Pub. Svc. Commn. D.C., 1967-70 Treas. Nat. Citizens for Eisenhower Congl. Com., 1953-55; Bd. dirs., treas. Easter Seals Soc. Disabled Children and Adult's, Inc.; chmn. bd. trustees endowment fund ARC; pres. Rotary Found., 1976-78; past bd. dirs. Washington Heart Assn., D.C. chpt. A.R.C.; trustee Boys Club of Washington. Served as lt. comdr. USNR, 1941-46. Mem. Friendly Sons St. Patrick, Nat. Assn. Security Dealers (bd. govs.), Assn. Stock Exchange Firms, Investment Bankers Assn., Phila.-Balt. Exchange, Nat. Geog. Soc. (finance com.), Kappa Alpha, Omicron Delta Kappa. Clubs: Burning Tree (Bethesda, Md.); Chevy Chase (Md.); Metropolitan (Washington), Alfalfa (Washington); Pine Valley Golf (N.J.); Rehoboth Beach Country (Del.). Lodges: Rotary. Home: 5106 Cammack Dr Spring Hill Bethesda MD 20816 Office: Folger Nolan Fleming Douglas Inc 725 15th St NW Ste 1 Washington DC 20005-2198

FLEMING, RONALD LEE, urban designer, arts administrator, preservation planner, environmental educator; b. L.A., May 13, 1941; s. Ree Overton and Elizabeth Ann (Ebner) F.; m. Renata von Tscharner, Nov. 9, 1978 (div. Nov. 1999); children: Severine von Tscharner, Siena Antonia von Tscharner, Reynolds Lombard von Tscharner BA cum laude, Pomona Coll., 1963; M of City Planning, Harvard U., 1967. Urban planner in Boston office of Marshall, Kaplan, Gans and Kahn, San Francisco, 1969-71; townscape designer Cambridge, Mass., 1971-78; pres. Townscape Inst., Cambridge, 1979—. Cons., lectr. townscape and planning issues throughout U.S.. Author: Saving Face: How Corporate Franchise Design can Respect Community Identity, 1994, 2d edit., 2002, Place Makers, 1981, 2d rev. edit. 1987, On Common Ground, 1982, Facade Stories, 1982; co-author: New Providence: A Changing American Cityscape, 1987; editor: Censored Laughter, 1976; contbr. articles to profl. jours. Founder, chmn. Cambridge Arts Coun., 1975-79; chmn. for Pub. Art, 1980-87; mem. adv. and standing com. Trustees of Reservations, Beverly, Mass., 1985-97; chmn. Boston chpt. Save Venice, 1993-96; chmn. bd. overseers Strawbery Banke, Portsmouth, N.H., 1980-84; bd. dirs. Victorian Soc. Phila., 1983-89; gov.'s appointee Mass. Hist. Com., 1986-90; co-founder Fleming Fellowships and Lecture Program on the built environment, Claremont Colls., 1985. Capt. Intelligence, U.S. Army, 5th Spec. Forces Group, 1966-68, Vietnam. State Dept. grantee, 1975; fellow Salzburg Seminars Am. Studies, Austria, 1978; recipient 1st prize Architecture and Planning, Columbia U. Urban Film Competition for Newburyport, A Measure of Change, 1975, Merit award Am. Soc. Landscape Architects, 1981, commendation NEA/Dept. Transp., 1981; nominated for Pulitzer prize Mass. Hist. Soc., 1982; winner EDRA/Places award for Urban Design, W. Radnor, Pa. Project, 1998, BSA award for urban design Radnor Pa. project, 1999. Fellow Royal Soc. Arts (London); mem. Mass. Hist. Soc., Soc. for Preservation New England Antiquities (past trustee), Mass. Hort. Soc. (past trustee), Inst. for Urban Design, Am. Inst. City Planners, Soc. Archtl. Historians, Scenic America (bd. dirs., sec. 1985-2002). Clubs: Somerset, Union Boat, Harvard (Boston), Club of Odd Volumes, Tavern (Boston); Century Assn., Knickerbocker (N.Y.C.), S.R.B.A. Newport Reading Room. Unitarian Universalist. Home and Office: 8 Lowell St Cambridge MA 02138-4726 Home: Bellevue House 304 Bellevue Ave Newport RI 02840-3518 E-mail: rfleming@townscape-inst.com.

FLEMING, SAMUEL CROZIER, JR., healthcare executive; b. Phila., Sept. 30, 1940; s. Samuel Crozier Sr. and Josephine Coverdale (Plowman) F.; m. Nancy Elizabeth McAdam, Sept. 7, 1963; children: David McAdam, Timothy Crozier. BChemE, Cornell U., 1963; MBA, Harvard U., 1967. Rsch. engr. DuPont Co., 1963; mgmt. cons. Arthur D. Little, Inc., 1967-90, v.p., 1977-83, sr. v.p., 1983-90; pres., CEO ADL Impact Svcs., 1976-79, Arthur D. Little Decision Resources, 1979-83, chmn. bd. dirs., 1983-90; CEO Decision Resources, Inc., Waltham, Mass., 1990—, also bd. dirs., chmn., 1990—. Mem. chem. engring. adv. coun. Cornell U., Ithaca, NY, 1989—96, mem. engring. coll. adv. com., 1996—, univ. trustee, 1997—, vice chmn. bd. trustees, 2002—; bd. dirs. Port Fin. Corp., Cambridgeport Bank, Cambridge, The Picker Inst., Boston, Charlesbridge Pub., Watertown, Mass., Commonwealth Fund, N.Y.C.; chmn. bd. dirs. Opinion Rsch. Corp., Princeton, NJ, 1984—88; trustee Standish-Mellon Mut. Funds, Boston. Vestry Trinity Ch., Boston, 1980-84; chmn. bd. dirs. New Eng. Bapt. Health Care Corp., 1984-90, New Eng. Bapt. Hosp., Boston, 1985-91; bd. dirs. CareGroup, Inc., 1996—, Pathway Health Network, Inc., Boston, 1994-96. 1st lt. U.S. Army, 1963-65. Mem. The Country Club (Brookline, Mass.), Harvard Club of Boston, Lake Sunapee Yacht Club, Baker Hill Golf Club, Cornell Club of N.Y. Episcopalian. Avocation: investments. Home: 61 Meadowbrook Rd Weston MA 02493-2407 Office: Decision Resources Inc 260 Charles St Waltham MA 02453 E-mail: sfleming@dresources.com.

FLEMING, SIDNEY HOWELL, psychiatrist, educator; b. Lubbock, Tex., May 22, 1938; d. McKinley and Wilna Adrian (Simer) Howell; m. J.D. Fleming, Jr., June 28, 1960; 1 child, Julie Adrianne. BA, Agnes Scott Coll., Decatur, Ga., 1959; MD, Emory U., 1964. Diplomate Am. Bd. Psychiatry and Neurology. Intern Emory U. Va. Hosp., Atlanta, 1964-65, resident in psychiatry, 1965-68; mem. faculty Emory U. Med. Sch., from 1968, assoc. prof. psychiatry, 1975—2002, prof. of medicine emerita, from 2002. Chmn. Pres.'s Commn. on Status of Women, 1984-85. Grantee NIMH, 1969-71. Mem.: Med. Assn. Ga., Ga. Psychiat. Assn., Assn. Acad. Psychiatrists, Am. Coll. Psychiatry, Am. Psychiat. Assn. (life; editl. bd. on curriculum on psychol. on women and men 1979—81, com. on women 1985—90), Druid Hills Club. Republican. Died Feb. 15, 2003.

FLEMING, STEVEN ROBERT, minister; b. San Bernardino, Calif., Apr. 30, 1951; s. Robert Ellsworth and Marie Claire (Kitzmiller) F.; m. Brenda Kay Cross, June 9, 1973. BA with honors, U. Md., 1972; D. Ministry, Union Theol. Sem., Richmond, Va., 1976. Ordained to ministry Presbyn. Ch. U.S.A., 1976. Assoc. pastor 1st Presbyn. Ch., Ft. Smith, Ark., 1976—79; pastor Shippensburg (Pa.) Presbyn. Ch., 1979-85; interim assoc. pastor Paxton Presbyn. Ch., Harrisburg, Pa., 1986-87; sr. pastor 1st United Presbyn. Ch., Westminster, Md., 1987-97; regional rep. bd. pensions Presbyn. Ch. USA, 1998—2002, edn. specialist bd. pensions, 2003—. Mem. Carlisle Presbytery; seminar leader; alumni bd. dirs., Union Theol. Sem. in Va., 1995-98. Contbr. articles to profl. jours.; contrbr. Abingdon Preaching Annuals. Bd. dirs. Shippensburg U. Campus Ministry, 1979-85. Recipient Common Ground award Shippensburg U., 1983. Mem.: Internat. Found. Employee Benefits, Am. Acad. Ministry. Republican. Avocations: photography, gardening, computers, travel, genealogy. Address: 975 Wayne Ave Ste 101 Chambersburg PA 17201-3895

FLEMING, SUSAN F. artist; b. L.A., 1944; d. Ree O. and Elizabeth E. Fleming. BA, Occidental Coll., 1966; BFA, U. Utah, 1974, MFA, 1976. Freelance artist, Salt Lake City. Exhibited paintings Utah Public Art Program Salt Lake City Courthouse, 1997-98, Utah Mus. Fine Arts; exhbns. murals Coll. Eastern Utah, Blanding, 1995-96, Utah Pub. Art Program, Utah Arts Coun.

FLEMING, SUZANNE MARIE, university official, chemistry educator; b. Detroit, Feb. 4, 1927; d. Albert T. and Rose E. (Smiley) F. BS, Marygrove Coll., 1957; MS, U. Mich., 1960, PhD, 1963. Joined Congregation of Sisters Servants of Immaculate Heart of Mary, Roman Catholic Commn. for Cmty., 1945. Chmn. natural sci. div. Marygrove Coll., Detroit, 1970-75, v.p., dean, 1975-78, acad. v.p., 1978-80; asst. v.p. acad. affairs Eastern Mich. U., Ypsilanti, 1980-82, acting assoc. v.p. acad. affairs, 1982-83; provost, acad. v.p. Western Ill. U., Macomb, 1983-86; vice chancellor U. Wis., Eau Claire, 1986-89; freelance writer, 1989—. Vis. scholar U. Mich., 1989-2000; pres. Mich. Coll. Chemistry Tchrs. Assn., 1975; councilor Mich. Inst. Chemists, 1973-77; bd. dirs. Nat. Ctr. for Rsch. to Improve Postsecondary Teaching and Learning, 1988-90. Contbr. articles to profl. publs. NIH research grantee, 1966-69 Home and Office: 2888 Cascade Dr Ann Arbor MI 48104-6659

FLEMING, THOMAS JAMES, writer; b. Jersey City, July 5, 1927; s. Thomas James and Katherine (Dolan) F.; m. Alice Mulcahey, Jan. 19, 1951; children: Alice, Thomas, David, Richard. AB, Fordham U., 1950; postgrad., Sch. Social Work, 1950-51. Reporter Yonkers (N.Y.) Herald Statesman, 1951; asst. to Fulton Oursler, 1951-52, lit. executor estate, 1953; asso. editor Cosmopolitan mag., 1954-58, exec. editor, 1959-61; writer, 1961—. Author: (book) Now We Are Enemies, 1960, All Good Men, 1961, The God of Love, 1963, Beat the Last Drum, 1963, One Small Candle, 1964, King of the Hill, 1966, A Cry of Whiteness, 1967, West Point, The Men and Times of the U.S. Military Academy, 1969, The Man from Monticello, 1969, Romans Countrymen Lovers, 1969, The Sandbox Tree, 1970, The Man Who Dared the Lightning, 1971, The Forgotten Victory, 1973, The Good Shepherd, 1974, 1776: Year of Illusions, 1975, Liberty Tavern, 1976, Rulers of the City, 1977, New Jersey, 1977, Promises to Keep, 1978, A Passionate Girl, 1979, The Officers' Wives, 1981, Dreams of Glory, 1983, The Spoils of War, 1985, Time and Tide, 1987, Downright Fighting: The Story of Cowpens, 1988, Over There, 1992, Loyalties: A Novel of World War II, 1994, Remember The Morning, 1997, Liberty! The American Revolution, 1997, The Wages of Fame, 1998, Lights Along the Way, 1998, Hours of Gladness, 1999, Duel: Alexander Hamilton, Aaron Burr and the Future of America, 1999, The New Dealers' War: FDR and the War Within World War II, 2001, When This Cruel War is Over, 2001, Conquerors of the Sky, 2003, The Illusion of Victory, America World War I, 2003, The Louisiana Purchase, 2003; editor: Affectionately Yours, George Washington, 1967, Benjamin Franklin, A Biography in His Own Words, 1972, The Living Land of Lincoln, 1980, The Secrets of Inchon, 2002; contbr. book., also various TV scripts, articles, short stories, book; cons. (movie) The American Revolution The History Channel, 1994, prin. commentator Long Journey Home - The Irish in America, 1998. Chmn. N.Y. Am. Revolution Round Table, 1970-81. Recipient achievement award in communication arts Fordham U., 1961, Encaenia award, 1965; Mass Media award NCCJ, 1963; Christopher award, 1970; Colonial Dames Am. ann. book award, 1970, 72; award of merit Am. Assn. for State and Local History, 1974; fiction award Nat. Cath. Press Assn., 1974; Best Book award Am. Revolution Round Table, 1975, 97, 99, award of recognition N.J. Hist. Commn., 1992, Best Magazine Award Army Historical Found. Fellow N.J. Hist. Soc., Soc. Am. Historians; mem. Am. PEN (pres. 1971-73), The Century Assn. Home: 315 E 72d St New York NY 10021-4625 E-mail: tflem37048@aol.com.

FLEMING, THOMAS J. editor, publishing executive; b. Superior, Wis., 1945; BA in Greek, Charleston Coll., 1967; PhD in Classics, U. N.C., 1973. Prof. classics Miami U., Charleston (S.C.) Coll., Shaw U., Raleigh, NC. Founding editor The Southern Partisan, 1979—83; mng. editor Chronicles, Rockford, Ill., 1984—85, editor, 1985—, pres., 1997—. Author: The Politics of Human Nature, 1987. Office: The Rockford Inst Chronicles 928 N Main St Rockford IL 61103-7061 E-mail: tri@rockfordinstitute.org.

FLEMING, TOMMY WAYNE, lawyer; b. Canyon, Tex., Nov. 13, 1941; s. Benjamin Dalby and Willie Mildred (Vineyard) F.; m. Sally Ann Moore, Nov. 30, 1968; children: Benjamin Dalby II, Hunter Leah. Student, West Tex. State U., 1960-61; BBA, U. Tex., 1964, JD, 1966. Bar: Tex. 1969, U.S. Dist. Ct. (so. dist.) Tex. 1971, U.S. Supreme Ct. 1978, U.S. Ct. Appeals (5th cir.) 1983. Asst. dist. atty. Office Dist. Atty., Amarillo, Tex., 1969-70; asst. criminal dist. atty. Cameron County Criminal Dist. Atty.'s Office, Brownsville, Tex., 1970-72; ptnr. Wiech, Lewis & Fleming, Brownsville, 1972-74, Wiech, Fleming, Hamilton & Uribe, Brownsville, 1974-82, Wiech & Black, Brownsville, 1982-89, Atlas & Hall, Brownsville, 1989-94, Fleming, Hewitt & Olvera, Brownsville, 1994-98, Fleming & Olvera, Brownsville, 1998-2001, Fleming & Hernandez, Brownsville, 2001—. Mem. Supreme Ct. Grievance Oversight Com., 1983-2000. Chmn. Brownsville Cmty. Health Clinic, 1978-79. 1st lt. U.S. Army, 1966-69. Fellow Tex. Bar Found. (life, bd. dirs. 1984-87); mem. Tex. Assn. Bank Counsel, State Bar Tex. (bd. dirs. 1981-84), Cameron County bar Assn. (bd. dirs. 1972-79, pres. 1979-80), Brownsville Hist. Assn. (bd. dirs. 1977-80). Home: 915 Santa Ana Ave Rancho Viejo TX 78575-9749 Office: Fleming & Hernandez 1650 Paredes Line Rd Ste 102 Brownsville TX 78521-1602

FLEMING, WENDELL HELMS, mathematician, educator; b. Guthrie, Okla., Mar. 7, 1928; s. James Lucian and Helen (Helms) F.; m. Florence Tatum, Apr. 4, 1948; children: Randall, Daniel, William. BS, Purdue U., 1948, MS, 1949, D honoris causa, 1991; PhD, U. Wis., 1951. Mathematician RAND Corp., 1951-55, cons., 1960-65; asst. prof. Purdue U., 1955-58; mem. faculty Brown U., 1958—, prof. math., 1963—, prof. applied math., 1969-95, chmn. dept., 1965-68, 82-85, 1991-94; prof. emeritus, 1995—. Author: Functions of Several Variables, 1965, (with R.W. Rishel) Deterministic and Stochastic Optimal Control, 1975, (with H.M. Soner) Controlled Markov Processes and Viscosity Solutions, 1992; editor SIAM Rev. NSF fellow, 1968-69; Guggenheim fellow, 1976-77 Mem. Am. Math. Soc. (chmn. com. on employment and ednl. policy 1975-77, Steele prize 1987), Soc. Indsl. and Applied Math. (Reid prize 1994), Am. Acad. Arts and Sci. Home: 9 Dolly Dr Bristol RI 02809-1578 Office: Brown U Div Applied Math Providence RI 02912-0001 E-mail: whf@cfm.brown.edu.

FLEMING, WILLIAM HARE, surgeon; b. Columbus, Ohio, May 1, 1935; s. William Bush and Charlotte (Hare) F.; m. Carolyn Etta Swift, June 25, 1959 (div. May 1978); children: Alice Fleming Guzick, William Swift, Edgar Hare; m. Pamela Anderton, Jan. 21, 1995. BA, Yale U., 1957; MD, Columbia U., 1961. Diplomate Am. Bd. Surgery, Am. Bd. Thoracic Surgery. Intern in surgery Presbyn. Hosp., N.Y.C., 1961-62, resident in surgery, 1962-66; resident in thoracic surgery Manhattan VA Hosp., N.Y.C., 1967, Harlem Hosp., N.Y.C., 1967, Presbyn. Hosp., N.Y.C., 1968; asst. prof. Emory U., Atlanta, 1971-76; chief thoracic surgery VA Hosp., Atlanta, 1971-76; adj. sr. research scientist Ga. Inst. Tech., Atlanta, 1974-76; assoc. prof. surgery U. Nebr. Med. Ctr., Omaha, 1976-80, prof. surgery, 1980-96, chief thoracic surgery, 1980-92. Pres. bd. dirs. Profl. Fees Office Nebr. Clinicians Group, Omaha, 1985-91. Contbr. over 100 articles. Served to maj. U.S. Army, 1969-70, Vietnam. Decorated Bronze Star. Fellow ACS, Am. Coll. Cardiology, Am. Acad. Pediatrics; mem. AMA (Physicians Recognition award 1988), Am. Assn. Thoracic Surgery, Soc. Thoracic Surgeons, Happy Hollow Club. Republican. Presbyterian. Avocations: tennis, sailing, windsurfing, waterskiing. Home: 2039 S 85th Ave Omaha NE 68124-2127 also: 34 Skipper Ln Salem SC 29676-4231 E-mail: stowaways@cox.net.

FLEMING, WILLIAM SLOAN, energy executive, computer company executive; b. Long Beach, Calif., Aug. 13, 1937; s. William Sloan and Helen Jean (Disler) Fleming; m. Jacquline M. Carrio, Mar. 9, 1960; children: Katherine A., Kimberly A. BSME, Calif. Maritime Acad., 1958; MBA, Syracuse U., 1970. Commd. ensign USN, 1958, advanced through grades to lt., 1967, attack pilot, 1958—67, disabled in the line of duty, ret., 1967; mech. engr. Carrier Corp., Syracuse, NY, 1967—70; regional sales mgr. Rheem Mfg., Atlanta, 1970—71; market devel. supr. Owens Corning Fiberglas, Toledo, 1971—73; pres. W. S. Fleming & Assocs., Inc., Syracuse, 1975—86, Fleming Group, Syracuse, 1986—87, CEO, chmn. bd., 1987—94; bus. devel. mgr., energy systems group Sci. Applications Internat. Corp. SAIC/Fleming Group, Syracuse, 1994—96; bus. devel. mgr. Sci. Applications Internat. Corp./Energy Sys. Group, 1996—97; exec. v.p. Jacwill Svcs. Inc., Cazenovia, NY, 1997—2000, pres. St. Petersburg, Fla., 2000—. Pres. Enterlog Sys., Inc., Syracuse, 1985—94; chmn. bd. Assn. Intelligent Sys. Tech., Inc., Syracuse, 1986—90. Contbr. articles to profl. jours.; author: singer energy simulation computer program. Recipient Energy awards, Ctrl. N.Y., 1981. Fellow: ASHRAE (life; chmn. tech. com. 6.7, solar energy utilization 1984—86, chmn. tech. com. 9.6, sys. energy utilization 1981—83, chmn. ad hoc com. 90, energy stds. 1983—84, chmn. nat. program com. 1985—86, mem. edit. coun. 1985—90, rsch. and tech. com. 1991—95, chmn. spl. publs. com. 1998—99, rsch. adminstrn. com. 2000—01, mem. handbook com. 2001—); mem.: DAV, Assn. Energy Engrs. (charter, 1 of 16 in Hall of Fame), Mil. Officers Assn., Am. Legion. Roman Catholic. Avocations: skiing, boating, homework. Office: JacWil Svcs Inc PO Box 8249 Saint Petersburg FL 33738-8249

FLEMING, WILLIAM WRIGHT, JR., pharmacology educator; b. Washington, Jan. 30, 1932; s. William Wright and Esme (Reeder) F.; m. Dolores D. Atchison, Sept. 1, 1952; children: Lisa Marie, Jennifer Amelia, David William. AB cum laude, Harvard U., 1954; PhD (Procter fellow), Princeton U., 1957. Mem. faculty W.Va. U. Med. Ctr., Morgantown, 1960—, prof. pharmacology, 1966—, chmn. dept., 1966-86, Mylan Chmn. of Pharmacology and Toxicology, 1986-99, prof. emeritus, 1999—. Vis. prof. U. Melbourne, Australia, 1969, St. George's Hosp. Med. Sch. U. London, 1978, Flinders U., Adelaide, Australia, 1985, 87, U. Adelaide, 1987; cons. Mead Johnson Rsch. Ctr., Evansville, Ind., 1970-77; mem. pharmacology-toxicology rsch. program. Nat. Inst. Gen. Med. Scis., NIH, 1973-77, chmn., 1975-77; mem. drug abuse rsch. rev. com. Nat. Inst. Drug Abuse, 1985-89; mem. pharmacology study sect., div. rsch. grants NIH, 1990-94. Mem. editl. bd. Jour. Pharmacology and Exptl. Therapeutics, 1966-85, Life Scis., 1978-90; contbr. articles to profl. jours. USPHS postdoctoral fellow Harvard U., 1957-60; Fogarty sr. internat. fellow, 1978; recipient P.L. MacLachlan award excellence in teaching W.Va. U. Med. Sch., 1964, 67, 78, 89, 92, 97, 99; named Outstanding Tchr., W.Va. U. Found., 1978. Mem. AAAS, Am. Soc. Pharmacology and Exptl. Therapeutics (councilor 1975-78, pres. 1981-82, chmn. bd publs. trustees 1984-90, Otto Krayer award 1986, Croker Meml. lectr. 1988, Torald Sollman award 1999), Assn. Med. Sch. Pharmacology (councilor 1977-79, treas. 1977-78, pres. 1986-88), Fedn. Am. Socs. for Exptl. Biology (dir. 1980-83), Internat. Union Pharmacology (del. 1980-83, 91-94, mem. internat. adv. com. for Congress of Pharmacology 1987, exec. com. 1994-98, 2002—, pres. 1998-2002, past pres. 2002—). Home: HC 3 Box 22 A Tionesta PA 16353 Office: WVa U Health Scis Ctr Dept Physiology & Pharmacology Morgantown WV 26506 E-mail: wfleming@hsc.wvu.edu.

FLEMINGS, MERTON CORSON, engineering educator, materials scientist; b. Syracuse, N.Y., Sept. 20, 1929; s. Merton C. and Marion (Dexter) F.; m. Elizabeth Goodridge, Sept. 7, 1956 (div. 1976); children: Anne, Peter; m. R. Elizabeth ten Grotenhuis, Feb. 20, 1977; children: Cecily, Elspeth. SB, MIT, 1951, SM, 1952, ScD, 1954. Mem. faculty MIT, Cambridge, Mass., 1956—, ABEX prof. Metallurgy, 1970-75, Ford prof. engring., 1975-81, dir. materials processing ctr., 1979-82, Toyota prof. materials processing, 1981-94, dept. head materials sci. and engring., 1982-95; dir. MIT-Singapore Alliance, 1999-2001, Lemelson-MIT Program, 2001—. Vis. prof. U. Tokyo, 1989, Ecole des Mines de Paris, 1996; bd. dirs. Hitchiner Corp., Metal Casting Tech., Inc., Silk Road Project, Inc. Author: Foundry Engineering, 1959; Solidification Processing, 1974. Contbr. numerous articles on metallurgy to profl. jours. Mem. Mass. Gov.'s Coun. Econ. Growth and Tech., 1994-2000. Recipient Simpson Gold medal Am. Foundrymen's Soc., 1961, Henri Sainte-Claire Deville medal Soc. Francaise de Metallurgie, 1977, Herbert J. Holloman award Acta Metallurgica, 1997, David Turnbull lectureship Materials Rsch. Soc., 1997. Fellow Metall. Soc. (Leadership award 1990, Bruce Chalmers award 1993, Educator award 1999), ASM Internat. (bd. trustees 1994-97, Henry Marion Howe medal 1973, 90, Edward DeMille Campbell Meml. lectr. 1990); mem. Am. Inst. Metall. Engrs. (Mathewson Gold medal 1969), Am. Acad. Arts and Scis., Japan Foundrymen's Soc. (hon.), Iron and Steel Inst. Japan (hon., Yukawa Meml. lectr. 1985, Tawara award 2000), Italian Metall. Assn. (Luigi Losana Gold medal 1986), Japan Inst. Metals (hon.), Nat. Acad. Engring., Fed. Materials Socs. (Nat. Materials Advancement award 1999), Korean Acad. Sci. and Tech. Home: 975 Memorial Dr Apt 605 Cambridge MA 02138-5803 Office: Dept Materials Sci and Engring MIT 4-415 Cambridge MA 02139 E-mail: flemings@mit.edu.

FLEMISTER, LAUNCELOT JOHNSON, physiologist, educator; b. Atlanta, Dec. 11, 1913; s. Launcelot Johnson and Willie (Moore) F.; m. Sarah Elizabeth Culbreth, Dec. 25, 1941 (dec. Feb. 1990); m. Mildred Beckham, Feb., 1993. AB, Duke, 1935, MA, 1939, PhD, 1941. Instr. Med. Sch. George Washington U., 1941-42; research asso. Sharp & Dohme, Phila., 1946-47; asst. prof. Swarthmore Coll., 1947-51, asso. prof., 1951-66, prof. zoology, 1966—. Vis. prof. Bryn Mawr Coll., 1959—60; cons. NSF, 1963—64. Lt. USNR, 1942—46. Fulbright fellow Peru, 1959-60 Fellow AAAS; mem. Am. Physiol. Soc., Am. Soc. Zoologists, Sigma Xi, Delta Tau Delta Address: 5154 Osceola Ave Saint Augustine FL 32080-7190

FLEMM, EUGENE WILLIAM, concert pianist, educator, conductor, chamber musician; b. Rahway, N.J., Jan. 16, 1944; s. Julius Eugene and Helen Frances (May) F. MusB, Coll.-Conservatory of Music, U. Cin., 1965, MusM, 1972, D in Mus. Arts, 1990. Music dir., condr. Cin. Civic Orch., 1979-83; assoc. prof., chmn. music dept. Mid. Ga. Coll., Cochran, 1983-90; concert pianist, studio tchr. Dunedin, Fla., 1990—. Founder, condr. Mid. Ga. Choral Union, 1983-90; chamber musician, founder, dir. The Omega soloists, Dunedin, 1987, Nuveau Ensemble piano quartet, It Takes Three; music dir., condr. Suncoast Symphony Orch., 1996—; ch. musician; bandmaster St. Petersburg Jr. Coll. Symphony Band; guest condr. Clearwater Cmty. Symphony Band; condr. Tampa Oratorio Soc., 1998—; faculty Clearwater Christian Coll. and Fla. Arts Sch. European concert tours include Amsterdam, Baden, Barcelona, Berlin, Brussels, Edinburgh, Geneva, Glasgow, The Hague, Innsbruck, London, Lüneburg, Lucerne, Milan, Monza, Munich, Oslo, Paris, Prague, Püttlingen, Rotterdam, Saarbrücken, Salzburg, Trier, Vienna; solo recitals include Carnegie Recital Hall, Lincoln Ctr., Atlanta-High Mus. Art, Dayton Art Inst., Tampa Bay Performing Arts Ctr., Anderson House, Washington. Mem. Fla. Hist. Soc., Pi Kappa Lambda. Republican. Lutheran. Avocations: cycling, tennis, jogging, training, boating. Home and Office: 1615 Santa Anna Dr Dunedin FL 34698-3722

FLEMMER, DAVID DUANE, clinical psychologist; b. Turtle Lake, N.D., Dec. 9, 1953; s. Walter Flemmer; 1 child, Michael. MS in Chemistry, S.D. State U., 1986; MA/CAS in Clin. Psychology, Loyola Coll., 1994; PsyD in Clin. Psychology, PhD in Pastoral Psychology, U. Oxford, 1998. Diplomate NDFE. Clin. psychologist D.C. Schs., Washington, 1994—. Asst. adj. prof. John Hopkins U., Balt., 1993—; adj. prof. Villa Julie Coll., Balt., 1991—. Contbr. articles to profl. jours. including Psychol. Reports, Nonverbal Assessment of Cognitive Ability: New Developments, Pharmacology, Biochemistry, and Behavior, Biological Psychiatry. Elder, deacon Redeemer Luth. Ch., Parkton, Md., 1996—. Univ. fellow U. Oxford, 1998. Mem. Am. Psychiat. Assn. Lutheran. Avocations: running, swimming, biking, gardening, softball. Address: PO Box 447 Hereford MD 21111-0447

FLEMMING, DAVID PAUL, biologist; b. Kittanning, Pa., Oct. 23, 1953; s. Paul Ross and Jeanne Marie (Seaton) F.; m. Diane Frances MacKenzie, Sept. 17, 1983; children: Daniel Robert, Peter David. BS in Biology, Grove City Coll., 1975; MS in Biology, Bowling Green State U., 1977. Child care worker George Jr. Rep., Grove City, Pa., 1978-79; park naturalist State of Pa.-McConnell's Mill State Park, Portersville, 1979; biologist sect. 7 U.S. Fish & Wildlife Svc., Washington, 1979-80, Atlanta, 1980-83, recovery coord. Denver, 1983-87, biologist endangered species Vero Beach, Fla., 1987-88, chief divsn. endangered species Atlanta, 1988-96, chief ecol. svcs., 1997-98, ecol. svcs. supr., 1998—. Contbg. author: Conservation and Resource Management, 1993. Asst. coach T-ball and soccer YMCA, Lawrenceville, Ga., 1991—92, premier soccer coach Snellville, Ga., 1995—2001; USS Ofcl., 1996—2003.

FLEMMING, STANLEY LALIT KUMAR, family practice physician, mayor, state legislator; b. Rosebud, S.D., Mar. 30, 1953; s. Homer W. and Evelyn C. (Misra) F.; m. Martha Susan Light, July 2, 1977; children: Emily Drisana, Drew Anil, Claire Elizabeth Misra. AAS, Pierce Coll., 1973; BS in Zoology, U. Wash., 1976; MA in Social Psychology, Pacific Luth. U., 1979; DO, Western U., 1985. Diplomate Am. Coll. Family Practice; cert. ATLS. Intern Pacific Hosp. Long Beach (Calif.), 1985-86; resident in family practice Pacific Hosp. Long Beach, 1986-88; fellow in adolescent medicine Children's Hosp. L.A., 1988-90; clin. preceptor Family Practice Residency Program Calif. Med. Ctr., U. So. Calif., L.A., 1989—; clin. instr. Sch. Medicine U. So. Calif., L.A., 1989-90; clin. instr. Western U. Health Sci., Pomona, Calif., 1989-90, clin. asst. prof. Family Medicine, 1987—; exam. commr., expert examiner Calif. Osteo. Med. Bd., 1987-89; med. dir. Cmty. Health Care Delivery System Pierce County, Tacoma, Wash., 1990—; mayor City of University Place, Wash. Clin. instr. U. Wash. Sch. Medicine, 1990—, bd. dirs. Calif. State Bd. Osteo. Physicians Examiners, 1989—, cons., 1989. Mayor, City of University Place, Wash. Col. M.C., U.S. Army, 1976—, Named one of Outstanding Young Men of Am., U.S. Jaycees, 1983, 85, Intern of Yr. Western U. Health Sci. Coll., 1986, Resident of Yr., Greater Long Beach Assn., 1988, Alumnus of Yr., Pierce Coll., 1993, 97; recipient Pumerantz-Weiss award, 1985. Mem. Fedn. State Bds. Licensing, Am. Osteopathic Assn., Am. Acad. Family Practice, Soc. Adolescent Medicine, Assn. Military Surgeons U.S., Assn. U.S. Army (chpt. pres.), Soc. Am. Military Engrs. (chpt. v.p.), Calif. Med. Assn., Wash. Osteopathic Med. Assn. (Physician of Yr. 1993), Calif. Family Practice Soc., Long Beach Med. Assn. (com. mem.), N.Y. Acad. Sci., Calif. Med. Review Inc., Sigma Sigma Phi, Am. Legion. Episcopalian. Home: 7619 Chambers Creek Rd W University Place WA 98467-2015 Office: Family Health Ctr University Place WA 98466

FLESCH, WILLIAM B. English educator; b. NYC, Nov. 7, 1956; s. Stephen and Alma Suzin Flesch; m. Laura Quinney, Sept. 6, 1987; children: Daniel, Julian. BA, Yale Coll., 1978; PhD, Cornell U., 1986. Prof. English Brandeis U., Waltham, Mass., 1985—. Chair English dept. Brandeis Univ., 1998—2001. Author: (book) Generosity and The Limits of Authority: Shakespeare, Herbert, Milton, 1992. Spkr. and writer Brandeis U. Nat. Women's Com., Boston Globe, Mass. Grantee fellowship, NEH, 1993—94. Mem.: MLA. Liberal. Avocation: fencing, travel. Office: Brandeis U Dept English MS 023 Waltham MA 02454 Office Fax: 781-736-2179. E-mail: flesch@brandeis.edu.

FLESH, HENRY, JR., writer, editor; b. Cin., Sept. 4, 1947; s. Henry Flesh III and Eleonor Jacob Wood. Student, Yale U., 1967. Editor People Mag., NYC, 1998—; editor, writer Paper Mag., NYC, 2002—. Panelist NY Found. Arts, NYC, 2002; judge NY Underground Film Fest., NYC, 2002. Author: (novels) Massage, 1999 (Lambda Lit. award, 1999), Michael, 2000. Mem.: Newspaper Guild, Authors Guild. Democrat. Home: 226 East 3rd Street Apt 2A New York NY 10009

FLESHER, DALE LEE, accounting educator, dean; b. Albany, Ind., June 27, 1945; s. Myron Lee and Deloris Rachel (Wright) F.; m. Tonya Kay Maloney, June 6, 1970; children: Flyn Lee, Felicity Kay. BS, Ball State U., 1967, MA, 1968; PhD, U. Cin., 1975. CPA, Cert. Govt. Fin. Mgr. Asst. mgr. Price's Food Market, Albany, 1960-66; asst. prof. Ball State U., Muncie, Ind., 1968-71; instr. U. Cin., 1971-73; assoc. prof. Appalachian State U., Boone, N.C., 1973-77; prof. accountancy U. Miss., Oxford, 1977—, assoc. dean, 1993—. Controller Am. Wicker, Inc., Boone, 1973-77; auditor Arthur Andersen & Co., New Orleans, 1978. Author 37 books, including: Accounting for Advertising Assets, 1978, CMA Examination Rev., 1984-87, 90, 92, 94, 96, 97, 99, 2001, 50 Years of Progress Through Sharing, 1991, The Third Quarter Century of the AAA, 1991, Auditing the Marketing Function, 1993, Internal Auditing Standards and Practices, 1996, Accountancy at Ole Miss, 1997, others; contbr. over 400 articles to profl. publs. Treas. Oxford-Univ. Meth. Ch., 1985—, mem. fin. com., 1985—; mem. sch. bd. Oxford-Univ. Sch., 1993-97, 1998-2002; pres. Meth. Men's Club, Oxford, 1980-81; treas. Oxford-U. Sch.-Parent Support Group, Oxford, 1989-90. Mem.: Acad. Acctg. Historians (pres. 1988, trustee), Miss. Soc. CPAs (Outstanding Educator award 1998), Assn. Cert. Fraud Examiners (cert. examiners), Inst. Internal Auditors (cert. mgmt. acct., cert. internal auditor, Leon Radde award 1990), Am. Acctg. Assn., Ind. Hist. Soc., Inst. Mgmt. Accts. (nat. bd. dirs. 1984—86, Cert. of Merit 1993, 1994, 1995, 1996), AICPA Found. (bd. dirs. 2002—). Avocations: softball, scripophily, writing, fishing, basketball. Office: U Miss Sch Accountancy University MS 38677 E-mail: acdlf@olemiss.edu.

FLESHER, MARGARET COVINGTON, communications consultant, writer; b. San Angelo, Tex., July 29, 1944; d. Charles C. and Helen Irene (Little) F.; m. Alexander Ribaroff, Dec. 11, 1976 (div. June 1988). BA in Polit. Sci., Vassar Coll., 1966. Assoc. editor Harcourt Brace Inc., N.Y.C., 1966-74; prodr. Guidance Assocs. subsidiary of Harcourt Brace, N.Y.C., 1974-76; freelance writer, editor London, 1976-81; sr. editor Franklin Watts, Inc., N.Y.C., 1981-85; pres. The Westport (Conn.) Pub. Group, 1985-89; coord. cmty. rels. Texaco Inc., White Plains, N.Y., 1989-91, sr. coord. media rels., 1991-93, contbg. editor, 1993-97; pursuit. cons. Deloitte & Touche, Wilton, Conn., 1998—. Author: Mexico and the United States Today: Issues Between Neighbors, 1985, New Leaves: A Journal for the Suddenly Single, 1987. Mem.: Internat. Women's Writing Guild, Fairfield County Pub. Rels. Assn. (bd. dirs. 1991—92), The Assn. for Women in Comm. (Fairfield County chpt. pres. 1986—88, v.p. profl. devel. 1994—95, Westchester chpt. bd. dirs., Clarion award 1995), Conn. Women's Forum (chair comm. com.), Conn. Press Club (v.p. programs 1998—99). Avocations: hiking, yoga, photography, gardening. Office: Deloitte & Touche 10 Westport Rd Wilton CT 06897-4522

FLESHMAN, LINDA EILENE SCALF, private investigator, writer, columnist, consultant, communications and marketing executive; b. Oklahoma City, Sept. 17, 1950; d. James Truman and Dortcha Virginia (Stiles) Scalf; children: Leatha Michele, Misty Dawn. AA, Tarrant County Jr. Coll., 1977; BA, North Tex. State U., 1979. Copywriter Advt., Graphics & Mktg., Ft. Worth, 1978-80; editor Ft. Worth mag. Ft. Worth C. of C., 1980-81; mktg. prodn. coord. City of Ft. Worth, 1981-83; dir. pub. rels. Circle T Coun. Girls Scouts U.S., Ft. Worth, 1983-85; mgr. corp. tng. Am. Airlines Direct Mktg., 1984-87; dir. corp. comms. LeasPak Internat., 1987-89; mgr. background svcs. AMR Svcs. (divsn. Am. Airlines), 1989-94; owner The Private Investigators, Ft. Worth; adminstr. internat. comm., editor Bell Helicopter News, 1997—2002; mem. pub. affairs staff Bell Helicopter Textron, 1997—2003. Owner mateinvestigate.com, ishopresale.com.; freelance writer, spkr. Author: Before You Say "I Do". Mem. Internat. Bus. Communicators. Democrat. Roman Catholic. Office: The Private Investigators PO Box 14807 Fort Worth TX 76117-0807

FLESSNER, PAUL, information technology executive; Degree in Computer Sci. & Bus. Adminstrn., Ill. State U. Sr. v.p. .NET enterprise servers divsn. Microsoft, Redmond, Wash., 1994—. Mem. bus. leadership team Microsoft, leader devel. & coord. combined enterprise bus. strategy plan. Office: One Microsoft Way Redmond WA 98052-6399

FLETCHER, ANDY, marketing professional; b. St. Joseph, Mo. ; BA in Journalism, U. Fla. With Barkley & Evergreen, Kansas City; with DDB/Needham, Della Femina, NY; pvt. practice as pres., CEO, 2002—. With nat. brands GE, First Data Corp., Learjet, The Kansas City Chiefs, Northwest Airlines, Sonic Drive-ins, Western Auto, NASCAR; dir. strategic vision launch campaign Atlanta Thrashers. Avocation: golf. Office: 303 Peachtree Ctr Ave Ste 625 Atlanta GA 30303

FLETCHER, ANTHONY L. lawyer; b. Washington, Dec. 12, 1935; s. Robert J. and Lyndell (Pickett) F.; m. Juliana Schump, Sept. 3, 1960 (div. 1977); children: Leigh Anne Grinstead, Kristin Marie Giffin, Julie Bowen Cimino; m. Zelda L. Fletcher, Mar. 30, 1986. BA, Princeton U., 1957; JD, Harvard U., 1962. Bar: N.Y. 1963, U.S. Ct. Appeals (2d cir.) 1966, U.S. Ct. Appeals (7th cir.) 1966, U.S. Supreme Ct. 1966, U.S. Ct. Appeals (3d cir.) 1969, U.S. Ct. Appeals (fed. cir.) 1972, U.S. Ct. Appeals (5th cir.) 1973, U.S. Ct. Appeals (1st cir.) 1981, U.S. Ct. Appeals (9th cir.) 1983. Assoc. Simpson Thacher & Bartlett, N.Y.C., 1962-71, Conboy, Hewitt, O-Brien & Boardman, N.Y.C., 1971-74, ptnr., 1974-86, Hunton & Williams, N.Y.C., 1986-97; prin. Fish & Richardson P.C., N.Y.C., 1997—2002, sr. counsel, 2003—. Editor-in-chief Trademark Reporter, 1982-84; contbr. articles to profl. jours. With U.S. Army, 1957-59. Mem. Internat. Trademark Assn. (bd. dirs. 1983-85), Princeton Club. Episcopalian. Office: Fish & Richardson PC 45 Rockefeller Plz Fl 28 New York NY 10111-0100

FLETCHER, BETTY BINNS, judge; b. Tacoma, Mar. 29, 1923; BA, Stanford U., 1943; LLB, U. Wash., 1956. Bar: Wash. 1956. Mem. firm Preston, Thorgrimson, Ellis, Holman & Fletcher, Seattle, 1956—79; judge U.S. Ct. Appeals (9th cir.), Seattle, 1979—, sr. judge, 1998—. Mem.: ABA (Margaret Brent award 1992), Fed. Judges Assn. (past pres.), Am. Law Inst., Wash. State Bar Assn., Phi Beta Kappa, Order of Coif. Office: US Ct Appeals 9th Cir 1010 5th Ave Ste 1000 Seattle WA 98104-1196

FLETCHER, BRADY JONES, vocational education career specialist; b. Natchitoches, La., Apr. 17, 1928; d. Louis Benjamin and Isadore Hannah (Stephens) Jones; m. Donald Greene Fletcher, Aug. 13, 1950; children: Donald Bruce, Nathan Louis, Debra Patrice. BA, Clark Coll., 1950; MA (fellow), Howard U., 1953; postgrad. (NDEA fellow), Ind. U., 1965; EdS in Guidance, George Washington U., 1967, EdD, 1977. Tchr. math. and sci. Fairmont Heights (Md.) High Sch., 1951-54; tchr. math. and sci. Douglas High Sch., Upper Marlboro, Md., 1955-57, Prince George's County (Md.) Pub. Schs., 1951-59, Banneker Jr. High Sch., Washington, 1959-63; chmn. guidance dept. Garnet/Patterson Jr. High Sch., 1963-67; counselor Lincoln Jr. High Sch., D.C. pub. schs., 1967-69, Kensington (Md.) Jr. High Sch., 1969-73, Banneker Jr. High Sch., 1975-77; career edn. specialist Montgomery County (Md.) Schs., 1973-75; counselor Frederic Douglass Middle Sch., Indpls., 1999—. Cons. Md. State Dept. Edn., 1973, Balt. City Pub. Schs., 1973, Balt. County Pub. Schs., 1973, D.C. Pub. Schs.; mem. adv. com. for spl. needs population Montgomery Coll., Rockville, Md., Am. Coll. Testing Bd., Washington, 1987—; project dir. InterAmerica Rsch. Assoc., Inc., Rosslyn, Va., 1977. Editor: Career Edn., 1973-75; Increasing Collaboration in Career Education (2 vols.). Rep. to Cmty. Action Bd. for Montgomery County Edn. Assn.; dir. D.C. Summer Youth Job Program, 1981; tech. cons., del. to Russia, Czech Republic and Poland with citizen amb. program People to People Internat., 1993. Inst. Ednl. Leadership fellow, summer 1984, Montgomery County Vocat. Assessment Ctr. (recipient dedicated service award 1987); recipient Educators award Clinton A.M.E. Ch., 1988, Multicultural Counseling award Founders of Orgn., 1987, award Montgomery County Coun., 1990; resolution in her honor Md. State Senate, 1990; Adminstr. of Yr. for I-Star Program, Ind. Say No to Drugs, 1994; named Alumnus of Yr. George Washington U., 1999, keynote spkr. opening conf. edn. and tech.; inducted into Hall of Fame, Englewood H.S., Chgo., 1999. Mem. AACD (Nat. award for govt. rels.), Am. Pers. and Guidance Assn. (Human Rels. Com. award 1974, editor conv. newsletter 1983), Am. Assn. Specialists in Group Work (nat. chairperson human rels. 1993, Recognition award 1993), Md. Pers. and Guidance Assn. (award 1975), Nat. Capital Pers. and Guidance Assn. (award 1975-76), Ind. Counseling Assn. (v.p. ctrl. chpt. 1992), Ind. Sch. Counselors Assn., Ind. Career Devel. Assn. (Ind. sch. counselor), Ind. Multicultural Assn., D.C. Assn. Counseling and Devel. (pres. 1986-87, del. to North Atlantic region assembly, recipient award disting. profl. leadership 1987, award for profl. devel. of assn. 1986, trustee 1988-89, co-chairperson govt. rels. com., Nat. awards Govt. Rels. Com. Boston 1989 and Cin. 1990), Nat. Vocat. Guidance Assn., Assn. Non-White Concerns, Nat. Assn. Career Edn., Nat. Sch. Counselor Assn., Internat. Platform Assn., Indpls. Urban League, Alpha Kappa Alpha, Phi Delta Kappa. Home: 7340 Steinmeier Dr Indianapolis IN 46250-2567 E-mail: dgflet1098@prodigy.net.

FLETCHER, COLIN, author; b. Cardiff, Wales, Mar. 14, 1922; s. Herbert Reginald and Margaret Elizabeth (Williams) F.; m. Sonia Savage, 1946 (div.); m. Thelma Brad, 1959 (div.). Student, West Buckland Sch., North Devon, Eng. Mfr.'s rep., Nairobi, Kenya, 1947; mgr. hotel Kitale, 1947-48; farmer nr. Nakuru, 1948-52; road builder on estate nr. Inyanga, So. Rhodesia, 1952-53; with mining cos., summers 1954-56; Santa Claus City of Paris Dept. Store, San Francisco, 1956; head janitor Polyclinic Hosp., San Francisco, 1957-58; writer Calif., 1958—. Author: The Thousand-Mile Summer, 1964, The Man Who Walked Through Time, 1968, The Complete Walker, 1968, The Winds of Mara, 1973, The New Complete Walker, 1974, The Man from the Cave, 1981, The Complete Walker III, 1984, The Secret Worlds of Colin Fletcher, 1989, River, 1997, (with Chip Rawlins) The Complete Walker IV; (audio tape) Learn of the Green World, 1991; contbr. articles to Life, Reader's Digest, Wilderness, other mags. in U.S., Can., Gt. Britain, Africa. Served to capt. Royal Marine Commandos, 1940-47. Office: Brandt & Hochman 1501 Broadway Ste 2310 New York NY 10036-5689

FLETCHER, COURTNEY VANCE, pharmacologist, educator; b. Greybull, Wyo., Mar. 25, 1955; s. John Cullen and H. Christene Fletcher; m. Jean Stanius Fletcher, Oct. 14, 1983. AS, Northwestern C.C., Powell, Wyo., 1975; BS in Pharmacy, Univ Wyo., Laramie, Wyo., 1978; DPharm, U. Minn., Mpls., 1982. Prof. and chmn. Dept of Clin. Pharmacy, Univ Colo. Health Sciences Ctr., Denver, Colo., 2002—; prof. Univ of Minn., Minneapolis, Minn., 1989—2001. Mem. antiviral drug adv. com. FDA, Rockville, Md.; mem. panel on clin. practices for treatment of HIV infection U.S. Dept. Health and Human Svcs., Washington. Contbr. articles to profl. jours. (Highest impact paper in clin. pharmacy infectious diseases, 1999). Fellow: Am. Coll. Clinical Pharmacy; mem.: ASM, AAAS, Am. Soc. for Clin. Pharm and Therapeutics, Soc. of Infectious Diseases Pharmacists. Office: U Colo Health Scis Ctr 4200 East 9th Ave C-238 Denver CO 80262 Office Fax: 303-315-4630. E-mail: courtney.fletcher@uchsc.edu.

FLETCHER, DANIEL A. adult education educator; PhD, Stanford U., Oxford U., U.K. Asst. prof. U. of Calif., Berkeley. Office: U Calif Berkeley 481 Evans Hall #1762 Berkeley CA 94720

FLETCHER, DAVID QUENTIN, civil engineering educator; b. Brisbane, Queensland, Australia, May 16, 1946; came to U.S., 1951; s. Quentin Henderson and Muriel Mary (Beeston) F.; m. Donna Elaine Worley, Sept. 1, 1968; children: Duncan Edward, Meredith Elaine. BS, U. Calif., Davis, 1967, MS, 1970, PhD, 1973. Registered profl. engr., Calif. Rsch. engr. U.S. Bur. Mines, Denver, 1971-73; asst. prof. civil engring. dept. U. of Pacific, Stockton, Calif., 1973-79, assoc. prof., 1979-82, prof., 1982—, dept. chmn., 1988—. Vis. lectr. U. Queensland, 1978, U. Calif., Davis, 1984. Author: Mechanics of Materials, 1985. Pres. Ctrl. Valley Youth Symphony Assn., Stockton, 1987-88; coach Valley Volleyball Club, Stockton, 1989, Stockton Volleyball Club, 1990-91. NDEA Title IV fellow, 1968. Mem. ASCE (pres. Ctrl. Valley 1978-80, nat. dept. heads coun. 1991-95), Am. Soc. Engring. Edn. Office: U Pacific Dept Civil Engring 3601 Pacific Cir Stockton CA 95211-0110

FLETCHER, DOROTHY, community health and primary home care nurse; b. Bklyn., June 10, 1939; d. John and Agnes (Burgio) Duffy; m. Richard Fletcher, May 19, 1962; children: Richard Derek, Leslie. Diploma, St. Anne's Sch. Nursing, Fall River, Mass., 1961; cert., Union Hosp. Sch. Anesthesia, Fall River, 1969. RN, Mass. Staff nurse ICU, Charlton Meml. Hosp., Fall River, nurse anesthetist; primary nurse Olsten Health Care, Braintree, Mass., Profl. Respite, Bridgeport, Mass.; nurse evaluator State of Mass.; nurse cons. Index Corp. Vis. nurse Roger Williams Hosp., Providence, Primary Nurse, Bridgewater, Mass.; case mgr. Primary Health Svcs., Brockton, Mass.; supt. field nurses, ventilator instr., nursing staff, dir. vent program, clin. supr., nursing adminstr., reg. dir. Former instr. CPR, Somerset (Mass.) Fire Dept.; youth leader South Swansea Bapt. Ch. Home: 85 Beach Ave Somerset MA 02726-2832

FLETCHER, DOUGLAS CHARLES, lawyer; b. Rockford, Ill., Mar. 5, 1943; s. Fred Leland and Dorothy Edwards Fletcher; children: Adrian, Lauren, Robin. *The Fletcher family settled in Virginia City, Nevada circa the 1860 Comstock Lode Silver boom. Douglas Fletcher's grandfather, Charles E. Fletcher, was a legendary Virginia City mining and electrical engineer who constructed the entire Northern Nevada power distribution system. Douglas' father, Fred L. Fletcher (Who's Who 1963), continued the family legacy as President of Sierra Pacific Power Company and was the driving force for the technology diversification of Northern Nevada. Douglas' son, Lauren, now continues with his pioneering work at the NASA Ames Research Center and Stanford University in the International Space Station program.* BA in Econs. and Engring., U. Nev., Reno, 1969, MBA in Fin. cum laude, 1972; JD, U. of Pacific, 1975; postgrad., Colo. State U., 1976. Bar: Nev. 1975, U.S. Ct. Appeals (9th cir.) 1976. Exec. v.p. PanWorld Engring., 1967-68; design engr. Nev. Bell, 1968-70; economist Sierra Pacific Power Co., 1970-72, gen. counsel, 1975-78; operating trustee William Lear Motors Co., 1978-79; ptnr. Leslie Gray & Assocs., 1979-81; oper. trustee Horseshoe Club Casinos, 1981-82, Mapes Hotel and Money Tree Casinos, 1982-85; owner, ptnr. Douglas C. Fletcher, Ltd., 1985—; operating receiver Echo Summit Tahoe Ski Resort, 1989-92. Advisor U. Nev. Grad. Bus. Sch., Reno, 1976-85; mem. U.S. Trustee Panel, 1978-95; judge pro tem Reno Mcpl. Ct., 1980-82. Author: Bond Reverse Yield Gaps of Public Utilities, 1972. Mem. ctrl. planning com. Republican Party of Washoe County, 1978-82; bd. dirs. Washoe County Youth Found., Reno, 1983-92, Eagles Nest Assn., Reno, 1998; founder, bd. dirs. Sierra League, Reno, 1989-99; bd. dirs., pres. ski team advisors U. Nev., Reno, 1982—. Mem. No. Nev. Bankruptcy Bar Assn. (founding mem.), Washoe County Bar Assn., State Bar Nev. (environ. law com. 1975—), Reno Tennis Club (pres., bd. dirs.), U.S. Ski Coaches Assn. (cert.), Reno Ski and Recreation Club (bd. dirs., pres. 1982—), Prospectors Club (bd. dirs.), Prof. Ski Instr. of Am. (cert.), Sigma Nu, Phi Kappa Phi, Beta Gamma Sigma. Office: 20 Sharps Cir Reno NV 89509-8009 E-mail: fletchlaw1@aol.com.

FLETCHER, EDWARD ABRAHAM, engineering educator; b. Detroit, July 30, 1924; s. Morris and Lillian (Protes) F.; m. Roslyn Silber, June 15, 1948; children— Judith Ellen, Deborah Gail, Carolyn Ruth. BS, Wayne State U., 1948; PhD (DuPont fellow, AEC fellow), Purdue U., 1952. Head propellant chemistry and flame mechanics sects. NASA, Cleve., 1952-59; assoc. prof. U. Minn., Mpls., 1959-60, prof., 1960—, dir. grad. studies, 1965-86. Vis. scientist Byellorussian Acad. Scis., 1964; vis. Fulbright prof. U. Poitiers, 1968; sr. Fullbright lectr. Weizmann Inst., Israel, 1989; vis. scientist, prof. Weizmann inst., 1991-97; cons. U.S. Dept. Commerce Study Waste Heat Mgmt., Minn. Energy Agy., No. States Power Co., Pub. Systems Rsch. Corp.; co-chmn. com. on fire resistant hydraulic fluids NRC-Nat. Acad. Scis. Nat. Materials Adv. Bd., 1977-78; Participant adv. group for aero. rsch. and devel. NATO Confs. on supersonic combustion, 1960, 61. Editor: Isotopes, 1958-59. Bd. dirs. Minn. Com. for Technion, New Friends of Chamber Music. Served with USNR, 1943-46. Recipient NASA Tech. Devel. award, 1961; Outstanding Ski Patrolman of Western Region award Nat. Ski Patrol, 1969-70 Mem. Combustion Inst. (bd. advisers, sec. Central States sect. 1967-78, vice chmn. 1978-79, chmn. 1979-82), Am. Chem. Soc., AAAS, Internat. Solar Energy Soc., Am. Solar Energy Soc., Sigma Xi, Tau Beta Pi, Pi Tau Sigma, Phi Lambda Upsilon. Home: 3909 Beard Ave S Minneapolis MN 55410-1042

FLETCHER, ERNIE (ROBERT FLETCHER), congressman; b. Mt. Sterling, Ky., Nov. 12, 1952; m. Glenna Foster; children: Rachael, Benjamin. BS, U. Ky., 1974, MD with distinction, 1984. Physician, Lexington, Ky.; CEO St. Joseph Med. Found., Lexington; mem. U.S. Congress from 6th Dist. Ky., 1999—. Mem. Ho. Budget Com., Agr. Com., Com. on Edn. and the Workforce (vice chmn. subcom. on Employer-Employee Rels.); elected freshman liaison to the Ho. Leadership. Elected state rep. for the 78th Dist. Ky., 1995-1996; served on numerous coms. including the Ky. Commn. on Poverty and the Task Force on Higher Edn.; chosen by gov. to play an important leadership role in reforming Ky.'s ailing health care sys.; lay min. Porter Meml. Baptist Ch.; vol. in cmty. With USAF, 1974—80. Republican. Office: 1117 Longworth HOB Washington DC 20515-1706*

FLETCHER, HARRY GEORGE, III, library director; b. Bklyn., Mar. 25, 1941; s. Harry G. and Helen T. (Dawson) F.; m. Toni A. Owen, 1966 (div. 1987); children: Alexandra, Thomas; m. 2d, Florence Sussman, 1987. AB, Fordham Coll., 1962, MA, 1970. Asst. editor, editor, dir. Fordham U. Press, 1966-91; Astor curator of printed books and bindings Pierpont Morgan Libr., N.Y.C., 1991-98; Brooke Russell Astor dir. spl. collections N.Y. Pub. Libr., N.Y.C., 1998—, acting dir. Humanities and Social Scis. Libr., 2003—. Adj. assoc. prof. NYU, 1996—. Author: Gutenberg and the Genesis of Printing, 1994, New Aldine Studies, 1988, In Praise of Aldus Manutius, 1995; co-author: The Art Deco Bookbindings of Pierre Legrain and Rose Adler, 2004; editor: The Heritage of New York, 1970, A Miscellany for Bibliophiles, 1979, The Wormsley Library, 1999; co-editor: Paradosis, 1976; contbr. articles to profl. jours., chpts. to books. Served with AUS, 1963-66. DAAD fellow, 1962-63. Mem. Baker Street Irregulars. Clubs: Grolier. Office: NY Pub Libr Fifth Ave and 42d St New York NY 10018-2788 E-mail: hgfletcher@nypl.org.

FLETCHER, HOMER LEE, librarian; b. Salem, Ind., May 11, 1928; s. Floyd M. and Hazel (Barnett) F.; m. Jacquelyn Ann Blanton, Feb. 7, 1950; children— Deborah Lynn, Randall Brian, David Lee. BA, Ind. U., 1953; MS in L.S, U. Ill., 1954. Librarian Milw. Pub. Library, 1954-56; head librarian Ashland (Ohio) Pub. Library, 1956-59; city librarian Arcadia (Cal.) Pub. Library, 1959-65, Vallejo (Calif.) Pub. Library, 1965-70, San Jose, Calif., 1970-90; ret., 1990. Contbr. articles to profl. jours. Pres. S. Solano chpt. Calif. Assn. Neurol. Handicapped Children, 1968-69; mem. Presbyn. Ch. Sunnyvale, 1997. Served with USAF, 1946-49. Mem. ALA (intellectual freedom com. 1967-72), Calif. Library Assn. (pres. pub. libraries sect. 1967), Phi Beta Kappa. Democrat. Presbyterian. Home: 7921 Belknap Dr Cupertino CA 95014-4973 *Standing up for what I believe regardless of the consequences. Accepting all human beings as important regardless of their circumstances. Emphasizing honest and forthright behavior in personal and professional life. Retaining a sense of humility and thankfulness.*

FLETCHER, JAMES WARREN, physician; b. Belleville, Ill., Oct. 6, 1943; m. Mary Bernadette Gatson; children: Michelle Marie, James W., Rebecca Lynn. MD, St. Louis U., 1968. Diplomate Am. Bd. Nuclear Medicine, lic. physician Mo. Intern in internal medicine St. Louis U. Hosp., 1968—69, asst. resident in internal medicine, 1969—70, resident in nuclear medicine, 1970—71; clin. fellow in radiology Harvard Med. Sch., Boston, 1971—72; sr. resident in nuclear medicine Peter Bent Brigham and Children's Hosp. Med. Ctr., Boston, 1971—72; asst. prof. medicine dept. internal medicine St. Louis U., 1972—75, assoc. prof. medicine dept. internal medicine, 1976—83, assoc. prof. radiology dept. radiology, 1977—84, assoc. dir. divsn. nuclear medicine, 1978—85, prof. medicine dept. internal medicine, 1983—, prof. radiology, 1984—, acting dir. divsn. nuclear medicine, 1985—88, dir. divsn. nuclear medicine, 1988—; staff physician nuclear medicine svc. VA Med. Ctr., St. Louis, 1972—76, med. dir. nuclear medicine network, 1972—79, asst. chief nuclear medicine svc., 1976—79, chief, 1979—, med. dir. AMA nuclear medicine technologist tng. program, 1983—, dir. opers. NMR program project, 1983—88; staff physician St. Louis U. Hosps., 1972—, dir. nuclear medicine dept., 1988—, dir. PET imaging ctr., 1991—; dir., program official nuclear medicine svc., dept. medicine and surgery VA Adminstrn. Ctrl. Office, Washington, 1986—89; dir. diagnostics svc. St. Louis VA Med. Ctr., 1997—99. Mem. tech. adv. com. to dir. nuclear medicine svc. VA Ctrl. Office, Washington, 1979—86, chmn. spl. interest user groups computer applications in nuclear medicine, 1984—85; spl. soc. liaison rep. Inst. Medicine Com. on Clin. Practice Guidelines, 1990—91; mem. residency rev. com. nuclear medicine Accreditation Coun. Grad. Med. Edn., 1992—97; interagy. NMR rask force Office Health Tech. Assessment, 1982; mem. Dept. Vet. Affairs Nat. Task Force on Tech. Assessment, 1992—97. Contbr. articles. 2d v.p. sch. bd. een of Peace Elem. Sch., Webster Groves, Mo., 1981, treas., 1982. Lt. comdr. USNR, 1966—77. Recipient Spl. Commendation award, Dept. Vets. Affairs, 1990. Mem.: AMA, Inst. for Clin. Positron Emission Tomography (bd. dirs. 1999—), Soc. Nuclear Medicine (bd. trustees 1988—92, chmn. health care policy com. 1991—92, vice chmn. commn. health care policy 1996—97, chmn. commn. health care policy 1997—98, pres., bd. dirs. 1998—99), Radiol. Soc. N.Am., Am. Bd. Nuclear Medicine (bd. dirs. 1990—93, vice chmn. 1992—93, chmn. 1994—95), Am. Coll. Radiology, Alpha Omega Alpha. Office: St Louis U Med Ctr PO Box 15250 3635 Vista Ave at Grand Blvd Saint Louis MO 63110-0250

FLETCHER, JEFFREY EDWARD, editor, medical writer; b. Toledo, Mar. 11, 1948; s. John Harper and Eleanore (Jackson) F.; m. Marcia Ruth Miller, Mar. 21, 1970 (div. Mar. 1977); m. Jeanne Claire Untied, Aug. 22, 1981; children: Katherine Ann, Lindsay Nicole, Sarah Jeanne. AA, Mohegan C.C., 1974; BA, Conn. Coll., 1976; PhD, U. Conn., 1981. Resident rsch. assoc. NRC, Washington, 1981-83; sr. instr. dept. anesthesia Hahnemann U., Phila., 1983-85, asst. prof., 1985-90, assoc. prof., 1990-95, prof., 1995-96; prof. dept. anesthesia Allegheny U. of Health Scis., 1996-98; v.p. sci. affairs Trinity Comms., Conshohocken, Pa., 1998-2001, sr. v.p. sci. affairs Media, Pa., 2001; clin. publs. lead AstraZeneca LP, Wilmington, Del., 2001—. Mem. editl. coun. sci. jour. Toxicon, 1991-98; contbr. articles to profl. jours. With USN, 1967-73, Vietnam. Conn. Coll. scholar, 1974-76. Mem. Am. Med. Writers Assn., Phi Beta Kappa, Sigma Xi, Rho Chi. Episcopalian. Avocations: classical guitar, photography, tennis, fishing, golf. Office: AstraZeneca LP DCC2-3E 1800 Concord Pike PO Box 15437 Wilmington DE 19850-5437 E-mail: jeffrey.fletcher@astrazeneca.com.

FLETCHER, JOHN C. physician; b. San Francisco, Apr. 16, 1933; s. Charles D. and Edith M. (Hirsch) F.; m. Judith G., Aug. 12, 1966; children: Steven, Scott. BS, U. Calif., Berkeley, 1954; MD, U. Calif., San Francisco, 1957. Intern U. Oreg. Hosp. and Health Ctr., Portland, 1957-58, resident, 1960-63; fellow in gastroenterology Mass. Gen. Hosp., Boston, 1963-64; physician pvt. practice. Lt. USN, 1958-60. Fellow Am. Coll. Physicians. Avocations: skiing, scuba diving, travel. Office: 3838 California St Rm 305 San Francisco CA 94118-1505

FLETCHER, JOHN CALDWELL, bioethicist, educator; b. Bryan, Tex., Nov. 1, 1931; s. Robert Capers and Estelle Collins (Caldwell) F.; m. Adele Davis Woodall, Sept. 4, 1954; children: John Caldwell, Page Moss, Adele Davis. BA, U. of South, 1953, DCL (hon.), 1993; M.Div. cum laude, Va. Theol. Sem., 1956; MDiv Fulbright scholar, U. Heidelberg, 1957; PhD, Union Theol. Sem., N.Y.C., 1969; DCL (hon.), U. of the South, 1993. Ordained priest Episcopal Ch., 1957-90. Curate St. Lukes Episc. Ch., Mountain Brook, Ala., 1957-60; rector R.E. Lee Meml. Ch., Lexington, Va., 1960-64; chaplain Cornell Med. Sch.-New York Hosp., 1964-66; assoc. prof. Va. Theol. Sem., 1966-71; dir. Interfaith Met. Theol. Edn., Inc., Washington, 1971—, pres., 1975-77; chief bioethics program Clin. Center, NIH, 1977-87; Emily Davie and Joseph S. Kornfeld prof. biomed. ethics U. Va., Charlottesville, 1987-97, prof. emeritus, 1999—. Co-investigator Internat. Survey Med. Geneticists, 1990. Author: (with Celia A. Hahn) Inter-Met: Bold Experiment in Theological Education, 1977, The Futures of Protestant Seminaries, 1983, Coping with Genetic Disorders, 1982; editor: (with Mark I. Evans et al) Fetal Diagnosis and Therapy, Science Ethics and the Law, 1988, (with Albert R. Jonson and Norman L. Quist) Ethics Consultation in Health Care, 1989, (with Franklin C. Miller, James Humler) The Nature and Prospect of Bioethics, 2003; editor and author: (with Dorothy Wertz) Ethics and Human Genetics: A Cross-Cultural Perspective, 1989, (with Mary F. Marshall, Franklin G. Miller and Paul A. Lombardo) Introduction to Clinical Ethics, 2d edit., 1997; translator: Creation and Fall, 1959; assoc. editor Ency. of Bioethics, 2d edit., 1995; contbr. articles to profl. jours. Recipient Lifetime Achievement award Am. Assn. Bioethics and Humanities, 2000; vis. fellow Inst. for Med. Genetics U. Oslo, 1984, Montgomery fellow Dartmouth Coll., 1997, Bellagio Ctr. fellow, Italy, 2000. Mem. Soc. Bioethics Consultation (founding, pres., bd. dirs.), Am. Soc. Human Genetics, Am. Soc. Bioethics and Humanities (Lifetime Achievement award 2000), Soc. for Advancement of Women's Health Rsch., European Soc. for Human Reprodn. and Embryology. Home and Office: 1454 Bremerton Ln Keswick VA 22947-9145 E-mail: jcf4x@virginia.edu. *My personal philosophy is that responsibility and accountability are the highest goals for human beings. Each situation can be saved from meaninglessness by the courage not to forsake these goals.*

FLETCHER, JOHN LYNN, psychology educator; b. Springdale, Ark., Apr. 18, 1925; s. Lynn Harrington and Elsie Irene (Jones) F.; m. Mary Lou Campbell, Aug. 21, 1949 (div. July 1974); children: Lynn Gray, Jana Lee. BA, U. Ark., 1950, MA, 1951; PhD, U. Ky., 1955. Commd. 2nd lt. U.S. Army, 1953, advanced through ranks to lt. col., 1968; chief audition br. Med. Rsch. Lab. Ft. Knox, Ky., 1953-70; ret. U.S. Army, 1970; prof. psychology Memphis State U., 1970-75; prof., dir. rsch. dept. otolaryngology U. Tenn. Ctr. for Health Sci., Memphis, 1975-81; prof., chair psychology dept. U. Mo., Rolla, 1981-87; lectr. psychology S.W. Tex. State U., San Marcos, 1987—. Cons. NASA Space Shuttle, Kennedy Space Ctr., 1972-76; mem. Commn. on Hearing and Bio Acoustics, 1956—. Editor: Effects of Noise on Animals, 1978; contbr. articles to profl. jours. Decorated Bronze Star. Fellow Acoustical Soc. Am., Am Speech, Lang. Hearing Soc.; mem. NAS, NRC, N.Y. Acad. Scis. (life), Human Factors Soc. Republican. Presbyterian. Achievements include patents for Acoustic Reflex Ear Defender. Home: PO Box 309 Martindale TX 78655-0309 Office: SW Tex State Univ Dept Psychology San Marcos TX 78666

FLETCHER, LAWRENCE FRANCIS, guidance counselor; b. Phila., June 9, 1946; s. Frank Louis and Lorraine Marie (Lawrence) F.; m. K. Star Yoham; children: Christopher Powell, Heather L., Michael L. BA, Villanova U., 1971, MA, 1973. Cmty. cons., counselor Sch. Dist. Phila., Pa., 1973-76; guidance counselor Delaware County Intermediate Unit, Media, Pa., 1976-83, Salesianum Sch., Wilmington, Del., 1983—, dir. guidance, 2003—. Poll watcher, Wilmington, 1992, poll greeter, 1994. Recipient 2d pl. Superstars in Edn., Del. State C. of C., 1994. Mem. ASCD, ACA, Del. State Counseling Assn., Coll. Bd. Avocations: reading, computers. Office: Salesianum Sch 1801 N Broom St Wilmington DE 19802-3891

FLETCHER, LELAND VERNON, artist; b. Cumberland, Md., Sept. 18, 1946; s. Kenneth L. and Marjorie L. (Benecke) F.; m. Janis Traub, July 19, 1978; children: Nathan Fletcher, Joshua Traub. BS, U. Minn., 1972. Artist-in-residence Lake County Arts Coun., Calif., 1998-99. Artist-in-residence Lake County Arts Coun., Calif., 1998-99, fine arts specialist, City of San Rafael, Calif., 1977-78. One man shows include U. Minn. Exptl. Gallery, 1972, La Mamelle Art Ctr., San Francisco, 1976, San Jose State U. Union Gallery, 1978, Place des Nations, Maubeuge, France, 1987, Univ. Art Gallery, Calif. State U., Hayward, 1989, McHenry County Coll. Art Gallery, Crystal Lake, Ill., 1991, Lake County Mus., Calif., 1995; group exhbns. include most recently Lake Co. Mus., 1995, Muscarelle Mus. Art, Coll. William and Mary, Williamsburg, Va., 1998, Mus. Internat. Contemporary Art, Florianopolis, Brazil, 1998, Manchester Met. U. Art Dept. Gallery, England, 1998, Helsinki Fine Arts Acad., Finland, 1998, The Sharjah Arts Mus., United Arab Emirates, 2000, Exit Art, N.Y.C., 2002, Free Gallery, Glasgow, Scotland, 2002, numerous others; represented in permanent collection at Mus. Contemporary Art, Sao Paulo, Mpls. Inst. Arts, Art Mus. of Calif. State U., Long Beach, deSaisset Mus., U. Santa Clara (Calif.), Art Inst. Chgo., Victoria and Albert Mus., London, Museen der Stadt Koln, Ludwig Mus., Cologne, Mus. Plantin-Moretus, Antwerp, Mus. de Arte Moderno, Barcelona, Bradford Mus., Eng., Kunsthalle, Hamburg, Galleria D'Arte Moderna, Trieste, Ecole des Beaux-Arts, Mus. Maubeuge, Musee de la Sculpture en plein Air, Maubeuge, Musee de Maubeuge, FMK Galeria, Budapest, Bur. for Artistic Exhibitions, Cracow, Poland, Kunsthalle Bremen, Germany, Museu de Arte da Universidad Federal de Mato Grosso, Brazil, Group Exibitions, 2002. Free Gallery, 2002, Exit Art, 2002, Permanent Collection Library of Congress, others. Address: 3288 Konocti Ln Kelseyville CA 95451-8209

FLETCHER, LEROY STEVENSON, mechanical engineer, educator; b. San Antonio, Oct. 10, 1936; s. Robert Holton and Jennie Lee F.; m. Nancy Louise McHenry, Aug. 14, 1966; children: Laura Malee, Daniel Alden. BS, Tex. A&M U., 1958; MS, Stanford U., 1963, Engr., 1964; PhD, Ariz. State U., 1968. Registered profl. engr., Ariz., N.J., Va., Tex., Australia; chartered engr., U.K. Rsch. scientist NASA-Ames Rsch. Ctr., Moffett Field, Calif., 1958-62, dir. aeronautics/aerospace, 1999—; instr. Ariz. State U., Tempe, 1964-68; prof. aero., engring. Rutgers U., New Brunswick, N.J., 1968-75, assoc. dean, 1974-75; prof., chmn. dept. mech. and aero. engring. U. Va., Charlottesville, 1975-80; dir. Ctr. Energy Analysis, 1979-80; assoc. dean Tex. A&M U., College Station, 1980-88, assoc. dir. Tex. Engring. Expt. Sta., 1985-88, Dietz prof.

mech. engring., 1988—, Regents prof., 1998—. Vis. prof. Tokyo Inst. Tech., 1993; hon. prof. Ruhr U.-Bochum, Germany, 1988—; disting. vis. prof. Am. U., Cairo, 1998, Am. U. Sharjah, U.A.E., 2000—; cons. to various industries, govt. labs. and univs.; mem. exec. com. Internat. Ctr. for Heat and Mass Transfer, Ankara, Turkey, 1994—(chmn., 1999—), fellow, 1998; disting. vis. scholar Hong Kong Polytechnic U., 2002. Author: Introduction to Engineering Including FORTRAN Programming, 1977, Introduction to Engineering Design with Graphics and Design Projects, 1979; editor: Aerodynamic Heating and Thermal Protection, 1978, Heat Transfer and Thermal Control Systems, 1978. Served to capt. USAF, 1958-61. Recipient Disting. Alumni award Ariz. State U., 1985, Exceptional Achievement medal NASA-Ames, 2002. Fellow ASME (bd. govs. 1983-87, pres. 1985-86, Charles Russ Richards award 1982, Heat Transfer Meml. award 1996, hon., medal 2002), AAAS (chair sect. M-engring. 1988-89, Internat. Scientific Coop. award 2003), Accreditation Bd. Engring. and Tech. (dir. 1979-89, 1991-94, 2003—, Linton Grinter award 2002), Am. Astron. Soc. (bd. dirs. 1993-96), Inst. Engrs. Australia, Inst. Mech. Engrs. U.K., Royal Aeronautical Soc. U.K., Am. Soc. Engring. Edn. (dir. 1974-77, v.p. 1978-80, George Westinghouse award 1982, Ralph Coats Roe award 1983, Donald E. Marlowe award 1986, Leighton W. Collins award 1993, Benjamin Garver Lamme award 2001), AIAA (dir. 1981-84, 1992-98, v.p. edn. 1992-95, pres. 1996-97, Lee Atwood award 1982, Energy Sys. award 1984, Thermophysics award 1992, Disting. Svc. award 2002), Internat. Astro. Fedn. (Frank J. Malina award 1997), Union Panamericana de Asociaciones de Ingenieros (Vector de Oro award 2000), Pan Am. Acad. Engring., Internat. Acad. Astronautics; mem. Sigma Xi, Tau Beta Pi, Pi Tau Sigma, Sigma Gamma Tau, Phi Kappa Phi. Office: Tex A&M Univ Dept Mech Engring College Station TX 77843-3123

FLETCHER, MARJORIE AMOS, librarian; b. Easton, Pa., July 10, 1923; d. Alexander Robert and Margaret Ashton (Arnold) Amos; A.B., Bryn Mawr Coll., 1946; m. Charles Mann Fletcher, May 14, 1949; children: Robert Amos, Elizabeth Ashton, Anne Kennard. Asst. to dir. rsch., then rsch. asst. to pres. Penn Mut. Life Ins. Co., 1946-49; officer A.R. Amos Co., Phila., 1949-66; part-time tchr., 1965-68; librarian Am. Coll., Bryn Mawr, Pa., 1968-77, archivist, 1973—, dir. oral history collection, 1975—, lectr. on archives, 1975—, asst. prof. edn., 1973-87, dir. archives and oral history, 1977—; pres. pub. rels. MAF Enterprises, 1987—. Author articles in field. Recipient awards Phila. Flower Show, 1965—; bd. dirs. Emergency Aid Found.. Mem. Spl. Librs. Assn. (pres. Phila. 1977-78), Soc. Am. Archivists (chairperson oral history sect. 1981-87, award of merit 1987), Oral History Assn., Hist. Soc. Pa., U.S. Pony Club, D.A.R., Nat. Soc. Colonial Dames in Commonwealth of Pa., Emergency Aid Pa. Found., Phila. Skating Club, Davis Creek Yacht Club, Bridlewild Pony Club (sponsor), Bridlewild Trails Club (Gladwyne). Republican. Episcopalian. Home: 1135 Norsam Rd Gladwyne PA 19035-1419 Office: Am Coll Bryn Mawr PA 19010

FLETCHER, MARY LEE, marketing professional; b. Farnborough, Eng.; d. Dugald Angus and Mary Lee (Thurman) F.; B.A., Pembroke Coll., Brown U., 1951. Ops. officer C.I.A., Washington, 1951-53; exec. trainee Gimbels, N.Y.C., 1953-54; head researcher Ed Byron TV Prodns., N.Y.C., 1954; copywriter Benton & Bowles, Inc., N.Y.C., 1955-63; creative dir. Alberto-Culver Co., Melrose Park, Ill., 1964-66; v.p. advt. and publicity Christian Dior Perfumes, N.Y.C., 1967-71; v.p. Christian Dior-N.Y., N.Y.C., 1972-78, exec. v.p., dir., 1978-85. Home: 12 Beekman Pl New York NY 10022-8059

FLETCHER, MICHAEL S. lawyer; b. Winchester, Va., Nov. 23, 1961; s. James William and Patty Jo (Stotler) F. BS, U. Tenn., Knoxville, 1984; JD, Seton Hall U., Newark, 1988. Bar: N.J. 1988, Pa. 1988, U.S. Dist. Ct. N.J. 1988, U.S. Dist. Ct. (ea. dist.) Pa. 1989. Law sec. to Hon. Donald G. Collester Jr. Superior Ct. N.J., Morristown, 1988-89; assoc. LaBrum and Doak, P.C., Phila., 1989-90; asst. dep. pub. defender State of N.J., Morristown, 1990—. Assoc. editor Seton Hall Law Rev., 1988. Shop steward Comms. Workers Am. Local 1037, Newark, 1991—; treas. Cornerstone Evang. Free Ch., 1994—. Office: Office of Pub Defender 25 Washington St Morristown NJ 07960-3950

FLETCHER, NORMAN S. state supreme court justice; b. July 10, 1934; s. Frank Pickett and Hattie Sears Fletcher; m. Dorothy Johnson, 1957; children: Mary Kiker, Elizabeth Coan. BA, U. Ga., 1956, LLB, 1958; LLM, U. Va., 1995. Assoc. Matthews, Maddox, Walton and Smith, Rome, Ga., 1958-63; pvt. practice LaFayette, Ga., 1963-90; city atty. City of LaFayette, 1965-89; county atty. County of Walker, 1973-88; spl. asst. atty. gen. State of Ga., Atlanta, 1979-89; justice Supreme Ct. of Ga., Atlanta, 1990—, now chief judge. Mem. State Disciplinary Bd., 1984-87, chair investigative panel, 1986-87. Ruling elder Peachtree Presbyn. Ch., Atlanta; former officer First Presbyn. Ch. of Rome, Ga., LaFayette Presbyn. Ch., Cherokee Presbytery; former commr. Presbyn. Ch. USA Gen. Assembly, 1984, 85; bd. visitors U. Ga. Sch. Law, 1992-95, chmn., 1994-95. Master Joseph Henry Lumpkin Inn of Ct.; fellow Am. Bar Found., Ga. Bar Found.; mem. State Bar Ga. (chair local govt. sect. 1977-78), U. Ga. Law Sch. Alumni Assn. (pres. 1977), Rotary. Office: Supreme Ct Ga 507 State Jud Bldg Atlanta GA 30334-9007

FLETCHER, OSCAR JASPER, JR., college dean; b. Bennettsville, S.C., Oct. 18, 1938; s. Oscar Jasper and Virginia (Baskin) F.; m. Sybil Morrison, June 3, 1962; children: John, Gregg. BS, Wofford Coll., 1960; DVM, U. Ga., 1964, MS, 1965; PhD, U. Wis., 1968. Asst. prof. U. Ga. Coll. Vet. Medicine, Athens, 1968-74, assoc. prof., 1974-79, prof., 1979-89, assoc. dean, 1975-82, head dept. avian medicine, 1982-89; dean Coll. Vet. Medicine Iowa State U., Ames, 1989-92, N.C. State U., Raleigh, 1992—. Mem. Am. Coll. Vet. Pathologist (cert., pres. 1990). Methodist. Office: NC State U Coll Vet Medicine 4700 Hillsborough St Raleigh NC 27606-1428 E-mail: Oscar_Fletcher@ncsu.edu.

FLETCHER, PAUL EDWIN, III, publishing executive, editor-in-chief; b. Asheville, N.C., Sept. 8, 1957; s. Paul Edwin Fletcher Jr. and Virginia Billingsley Fletcher; m. Jane Allen, Mar. 16, 1985; children: Kathleen C., Daniel C. JD, Washington & Lee U., 1985; MA, Emory U., 1980; AB, Coll. of William & Mary, 1979. Bar: Va. 1985. Tchr. Univ. Sch. Nova U., Ft. Lauderdale, Fla., 1981—82, adj. prof., 1981—83; assoc. White, Elliott & Bundy, Bristol, Va., 1985—88; news editor Va. Lawyers Weekly, Richmond, 1988—89, pub., editor-in-chief, 1989—. Editor: (books) Virginia Lawyers Weekly Research Library, 10 vols., 1994, Virginia Lawyers Weekly Trial Report Books, 1990, 1991, 1999, 2002. Mem. bd. trustees Richmond Montessori Sch., 1995—97. Recipient 2nd Pl. Cert. of Merit, Old Dominion Advt. Contest for In-Paper Feature, Va. Press Assn., 1999. Mem.: Soc. Profl. Journalists, Va. Trial Lawyers Assn., Va. Bar Assn. Home: 9509 Pine Shadow Dr Richmond VA 23233 Office: Va Lawyers Weekly Ste 701 801 E Main St Richmond VA 23219 Office Fax: 804-788-1242. Personal E-mail: PEFletcher@aol.com. Business E-Mail: pfletcher@va.lawyersweekly.com.

FLETCHER, PAUL GERALD, lawyer; b. Boston, Mar. 20, 1945; m. Susan Mary Beckerman, Aug. 11, 1968; children: Lynne, Michael, Allison. BAE, U. Fla., 1967; JD, U. Miami, 1970. Bar: Fla. 1970, U.S. Dist. Ct. (so. dist.) Fla. 1970, U.S. Ct. Mil. Appeals 1971, U.S. Supreme Ct. 1973, U.S. Ct. Appeals (11th cir.) 1982. Judge Adv. USAF, 1970-74; ptnr. Peskoe, Fletcher & Cahan, Homestead, Fla., 1974-77, Fletcher & Langer, Homestead, 1977-84, Paul G. Fletcher, P.A., Coral Gables, Fla., 1984—. Instr. bus. law No. Mich. U., Marquette, 1970-72; mem. adv. bd. Amerifirst Fla. Trust Co., 1987-91. Pres. Homestead ARC, 1975. Capt. USAF, 1970-74. Recipient Service award ARC, 1977, Leadership award Jewish Fedn., 1980; named in Leading Am. Attys. in Family Law, Fla., 1997—. Mem. Fla. Bar Assn. (family law, real property probate coms.), Homestead Bar Assn. (pres. 1980-81), ATLA, Am. Arbitration Assn. (arbitrator), Kendall-South Dade Bar Assn., Coral Gables Bar Assn., First Family Law Inns of Ct. (master 1993—), Attys. Real Property Coun., Kiwanis (v.p. 1980, pres. 1983), Tau Epsilon Phi. Avocations: photography, World War II history, baseball cards. Office: 1500 S Dixie Hwy Ste 200 Coral Gables FL 33146-3033 Fax: 305-661-6197. E-mail: pgflaw@earthlink.net.

FLETCHER, RAYMOND RUSSWALD, JR., lawyer; b. Schenectady, N.Y., June 7, 1929; s. Raymond Russwald and Elsie Dorothea (Hovemeyer) F.; m. Elsa Ellen Tillema, Dec. 20, 1949 (div. 1973); children— Raymond Russwald III, Nicholas H., Pamela L., William E., Catherine A. B.Ch.E., Rensselaer Poly. Inst., 1949; LL.B., Harvard U., 1956. Bar: N.Y. 1956. Vice-pres., gen. counsel Trans World Airlines, Inc., N.Y.C., 1969-78; ptnr. Chadbourne, Parke, Whiteside & Wolff, N.Y.C., 1978-84; counsel Gilbride, Tusa, Last & Spellane, N.Y.C., 1984—. Vice chmn. legal com. Internat. Air Transport Assn., Geneva, Switzerland, 1976-77 Served as lt. (j.g.) USN, 1949-53; Korea Decorated Air medal Mem. Harvard Club. Democrat. Presbyterian. Home: 453 Albany Hill Rd Rensselaerville NY 12147-2705 Office: Gilbride Tusa Last Et Al 420 Lexington Ave Rm 3005 New York NY 10170-0105

FLETCHER, ROBERT, retired lawyer, horologist; b. Birmingham, Ala., May 4, 1920; s. Robert Hall and Beatrice (Skelding) Jones; m. Florence K. Szuba, Sept. 12, 1942; children— Andrew R., William Alan. B.F.A., Ohio U., Athens, 1943; LL.B., JD, Case Western Res U., 1948. Bar: Ohio 1948. Asst. gen. counsel Cleve. Transit System, 1951-56; with firm Jamison, Ulrich, Johnson & Burt, Cleve., 1956-59, Meyers, Stevens & Rea, Cleve., 1959-61; pvt. practice Cleve., 1961-82; horologist Parma, Ohio, 1982—. Lectr. Am. Heart Assn. Served with AUS, World War II, Korea. Recipient Speakers Bur. award Am. Heart Assn., 1973-76 Mem.: Rosicrucian Order. Republican. Presbyterian. Home: 5801 Hollywood Dr Cleveland OH 44129-5220

FLETCHER, ROBERT HILLMAN, medical educator; b. Abington, Pa., Mar. 26, 1940; s. Stevenson Whitcomb and Wanda (Moss) F.; m. Suzanne Wright, June 15, 1963; children— John Wright, Grant Selmer BA, Wesleyan U., Middletown, Conn., 1962; MD, Harvard U., 1966; M.Sc., Johns Hopkins U., 1973. Diplomate Am. Bd. Internal Medicine. Intern, resident in medicine Stanford U. Hosp., Palo Alto, Calif., 1967-68; resident in medicine Baltimore City Hosp., 1971-73; asst. prof. faculty of medicine McGill U., Montreal, Canada, 1973-78; assoc. prof. medicine Sch. Medicine U. N.C., Chapel Hill, 1978-83, prof. medicine, clin. prof. epidemiology, 1983-90, dir. Robert Wood Johnson Clin. Scholars Program, 1983-90, co-dir. Clin. Epidemiology Resource and Tng. Ctr., Internat. Clin. Epidemiology Network, 1986-90; assoc. exec. v.p. ACP, Phila., 1990-92, sr. v.p., 1992-93; prof. Harvard Med. Sch., Boston, 1994—; assoc. med. dir. clin. edn. Harvard Pilgrim Health Care, Boston, 1998, dir. tchg. ctr., dept. ambulatory care and prevention, 1992—2002. Bd. dirs. INCLEN Inc., Boston, chmn., 1993-97. Sr. author: Clinical Epidemiology, The Essentials, 1982, 2d edit., 1988, 3d edit., 1996; co-editor: Jour. Gen. Internal Medicine, 1984-89, Annals of Internal Medicine, 1990-93; primary care editor UpToDate, 1997—. Served to maj. M.C., U. S. Army, 1968-71 Master ACP (master); mem. Am. Pub. Health Assn., Soc. Gen. Internal Medicine (pres. 1991-92), Phi Beta Kappa, Sigma Xi. Democrat. Mem. Soc. Of Friends. Home: 208 Boulder Bluff Chapel Hill NC 27516 Office: Dept Ambulatory Care/Prevention 133 Brookline Ave 6th Fl Boston MA 02215-3920 E-mail: robert_fletcher@hms.harvard.edu.

FLETCHER, ROBIN MARY, health care administrator; b. Waco, Tex., May 24, 1952; d. Arthur Hale Fletcher and Bersha Pauline (King) Gardner; 1 child, Jonathon Potter. AAS in Nursing, Tarraot County Jr. Coll., 1973; B of Liberal Studies in healthcare adminstrn., summa cum laude, St. Edwards U., 1996; M of Pub. Health in Cmty. Health, U. Tex., Houston, 1997. Staff/charge RN St. Joseph Hosp., Ft. Worth, 1973-75; staff RN/asst. head nurse Tarrant County Hosp. Dist., Fort Worth, Tex., 1975-76; staff/charge RN/asst. patient care coord. Med. Plaza Hosp., Ft. Worth, 1977-80; home health nurse Upjohn Health Care and Med. Pers. Pool, Fort Worth, 1981; med. care analyst, rev. supr. and mgr., dir. rev. Tex. Med. Found., Austin, 1981-83, 84-96; TQI coord. VA North Tex. Health Care Sys., Dallas, 1998-99; project dir. Tex. Med. Found., Austin, 1999—2002, dir. physician and hosp. quality improvement, 2002—. Bd. dirs., adv. bd. for med. record program Tex. Women's U., Dallas, 1989-90. Mem. ANA, Tex. Nurses Assn., Tex. Pub. Health Assn., Am. Diabetes Assn. (bd. dirs. local chpt. 1996-98), Health Care Compliance Assn., Alpha Sigma Lambda Nat. Honor Soc. Avocations: antiques, jogging, volkssports, rollerblading, travel. Office: Tex Med Found Barton Oaks Plz Two 901 Mopac Expy S Ste 200 Austin TX 78746

FLETCHER, RONALD DARLING, microbiologist educator; b. Foxboro, Mass., Jan. 18, 1933; s. Howard Wendel and Ada Louise (Darling) F.; m. Barbara Gundersen, Jan. 30, 1954; children: Deborah, Mark Ronald, Christopher Gary. BS, U. Conn., 1954, MS, 1959, PhD, 1963. Mule skinner U.S. Forest Svc., St. Maries, Idaho, 1952; instr. U. Conn., Storrs, 1959-63; rschr. Am. Cyanamid Co., Pearl River, N.Y., 1964-67; dir. microbiology McKeesport Hosp., Pa., 1971-79; prof., assoc. chair dept. microbiology U. Pitts., 1967—86, prof. microbiology dept. clin. lab. scis., 1989—; assoc. dir. Armed Forces Med. Intelligence Ctr. Dept. Def., Frederick, Md., 1984—85, sr. analyst Armed Forces Med. Intelligence Ctr., 1986—89; v.p. Affordable Tech., Inc., Pitts., 1990—91; exec. v.p. ATI Bioremediation, Inc., Pitts., 1991—92. Biotech. steering com. U.S. Dept. Def., 1987-89; cons. U.S. Army, Frederick, 1978-82, Mellon Inst., Pitts., 1981, Cons.'s Brokerage, Mountain View, Calif., 1981, Battelle Meml. Inst., Columbus, Ohio, 1989-90. Contbr. articles to prof. jours. Judge Internat. Sci. and Engring. Fair, Mpls., 1980, Milw., 1981, Dallas, 1982, Nat. Jr. Sci. and Humanities Symposium, West Point, N.Y., 1983, 85; dept. state lectr. med. schs. in Ankara and Istanbul, Turkey, 1982. Col. USA & USAR, 1954-85. USPHS fellow U. Zurich, Switzerland, 1963-64; grantee U.S. Army, Am. Cancer Soc., NIH; Postdoctoral fellow U. Saskatchewan, Can., 1965, Harvard Med. Sch., 1966, cert. of achievement in microbiology Surgeon Gen. U.S. Army, 1973. Fellow AAAS, Am. Acad. Microbiology (registered microbiologist, specialist microbiologist); mem. Internat. Assn. Dental Research (pres. Pitts. 1979-80), ADA, Assn. Mil. Surgeons, Am. Assn. Microbiologists, N.Y. Acad. Scis., Am. Soc. for Cell Biology, Nat. Mil. Intelligence Assn., Internat. Assn. Chiefs of Police, Am. Legion Office: U of Pitts 209 Pennsylvania Hall Pittsburgh PA 15261-1802 E-mail: fletchuconn@yahoo.com.

FLETCHER, SARAH LEE, retired elementary school educator; b. Webb, Ala., May 7, 1925; d. James Harvey and Emma Freddie (Scarborough) Lee; m. Gaston Maurice Fletcher, June 24, 1948; children: S. Daphne, Lee Maurice, Timothy J. Student, Bob Jones Coll., 1943-44, assoc. bus. cert., 1947; student, Calhoun Coll., 1968-70, Troy State U., 1970-72; BRE, Bethany Theol. Seminary, 1995, MRE, 1996. With Atlanta and St. Andrews Bay Rwy. Co., 1944-46; sec. to pub. Dothan (Ala.) Eagle, 1947-48; tchr. Morgan County Schs., Decatur, Ala., 1967-69, Newton (Ala.) Pub. Schs., 1969-72, Trinity Christian Schs., Oxford, Ala., 1972-73, Berachah Christian Acadamy, Huntsville, Ala., 1973-75; sec. Dominion Textile, Yarmouth, Nova Scotia, 1975-76; tchr. Mueller Christian Sch., Miami, 1976-79, Berean Christian Sch., Dothan, 1979-86, Grace Bible Acad., Dothan, 1987-90, Clinton Christian Acad., Upper Marlboro, Md., 1990-91. Cons. Mary Kay Cosmetics, 1982-99. Author: To Love Again, 1996, Love in Bloom, 2001; compiler, contbg. author: (book of short stories) The Set of the Sails, 1997; contbr. articles to Christian papers and mags. Active in ch. Mem. Troy State U. Creative Writing Club, Dothan Creative Writing Group. Baptist. Avocations: helping the elderly, writing, walking, speaking. Home: 1119 Garden Ln Dothan AL 36301-3407

FLETCHER, SUZANNE WRIGHT, physician, educator; b. Jacksonville, Fla., Nov. 14, 1940; d. Robert Dean and Helen (Selmer) Wright; m. Robert H. Fletcher; children: John Wright, Grant Selmer. BA, Swarthmore Coll., 1962; MD, Harvard Med. Sch., 1966; MSc, Johns Hopkins U., 1973. Diplomate Nat. Bd. Med. Examiners, Am. Bd. Internal Medicine. Intern Stanford (Calif.) U. Med. Ctr., 1966—67, resident, 1967—68; physician 22nd med. detachment U.S. Army, New Ulm, Germany, 1969—70; asst. prof. epidemiology and health Mc Gill U., Montreal, Canada, 1974—77, assoc. prof., 1977—78, asst. prof. medicine, 1973—78; dir. med. clinic dept. medicine NC Meml. Hosp., 1978—82; assoc. prof. medicine U. NC, 1978—83, co-chief divsn. gen. medicine and clin. epidemiology dept. medicine, 1978—86, rsch. assoc. health svcs. rsch. ctr., 1978—90, vice chmn. clin. svcs., 1981—84, prof. medicine, clin. prof. epidemiology, 1983—90, program dir. faculty devel. gen. medicine and gen. pediatrics, 1985—90, co-dir. internat. clin. epidemiology network program Rockefeller Found., 1986—90; prof. ambulatory care and prevention Harvard Med. Sch.; editor Annals of Internal Medicine, Phila., 1990—93. Adj. prof. medicine U. Pa., Phila., 1990—93, Jefferson Med. Coll., 1991—93, U. NC, 1994—; physician internal medicine; chmn. NIH Tech. Assessment Conf., 1992, Nat. Cancer Inst. Internat. Workshop, 1993; active World Bank Seminar on Preventive Strategies in Med. Edn., Hangzhou, China, 1986, Ad Hoc NCI Com. on BSE Cancer Detection Rsch. and Applications, 1986. Author: Clinical Epidemiology—The Essentials, 1982, 3d edit., 1995; contbr. chpts. to books, articles to profl. jours. Named rsch. grantee, Conseil de la Recherche en Sante du Quebec, 1975—77; recipient Can. Nat. Health Rsch. Scholar award, Can. Govt., 1975—78; grantee, Health and Welfare Can., 1976—78, Robert Wood Johnson Teaching Hosp. Gen. Medicine Group Practice Program, 1980—84, Nat. Ctr. Health Scis. Rsch. and Health Tech., 1985—89, Rockefeller Found. Clin. Epidemiology Resource and Tng. Ctr., 1986—90, NIH, 1987—90, 1997—. Master: ACP (med. knowledge self assessment program 1984—85, clin. practice subcom. 1987, pub. policy subcom. 1988—89); fellow: Coll. Physicians Phila., Am. Coll. Epidemiology (bd. dirs. 1990—93, chmn. pub. com. 1992—94); mem.: APHA, NCI Bd. Sci. Advisors, World Assn. Med. Editors (v.p. 1997—2001), Internat. Clin. Epidemiology Network (bd. dirs.), Inst. Medicine (coun. 1993—96, exec. com. 1993—96), Soc. Gen. Internal Medicine (counsellor 1978—81, pres.-elect 1982—83, pres. 1983—84, coeditor Jour. Gen. Internal Medicine 1984—89, mem. publs. com. 1990—, chmn. Glaser award com. 1991). Unitarian Universalist. Office: Harvard Med Sch Ambulatory Care/Prevention Dept 133 Brookline Ave Boston MA 02215-3920 E-mail: Suzanne_Fletcher@hms.harvard.edu.

FLETCHER, THOMAS D. psychologist, researcher; b. Atlanta, Jan. 12, 1971; s. Thomas D. Fletcher and Sarah C. Brownlee; life ptnr. Sarah L. Slaughter; children: Rachel D., Bryce P. MS, postgrad., Old Dominion U., 2002—. Ops. mgr. Justus Transport, Atlanta, 1998—2000; rschr. Old Dominion U., Norfolk, Va., 2000—. Mem.: Acad. Mgmt. (assoc.), Soc. for Indsl./Orgnl. Psychology (assoc.), Phi Kappa Phi. Office: Old Dominion Univ Dept Psychology Hampton Blvd Norfolk VA 23529 E-mail: tflet002@odu.edu.

FLETCHER, WILLIAM A. federal judge, law educator; b. 1945; BA, Harvard U., 1968, Oxford U., 1970; JD, Yale U., 1975. Law clk. to presiding justice U.S. Dist. Ct. Calif., San Francisco, 1975—76; law clk. to Justice William J. Brennan U.S. Supreme Ct., Washington, 1976—77; acting prof. law U. Calif., Berkeley, 1977—84, prof. law, 1984—98; judge U.S. Ct. Appeals (9th cir.), San Francisco, 1998—. Lieutenant USN, 1970—72. Office: 95 7th St San Francisco CA 94103*

FLETCHER, WINONA LEE, theater educator emeritus; b. Nov. 25, 1926; m. Joseph Grant; 1 child, Betty. BA, Johnson C. Smith U., 1947; MA, U. Iowa, 1951; PhD, Ind. U., 1968. Prof. speech and theatre Ky. State U., Frankfort, 1951-78; prof. theatre and afro-Am. studies Ind. U., Bloomington, 1978-94, prof. emeritus, 1994; assoc. dean COAS, 1981-84. Costumer, dir. summer theatre, U. Mo., Lincoln, 1952-60, 69. Recipient Lifetime Achievement award, 1993; Am. Theatre fellow, 1979. Mem. Am. Theatre for Higher Edn., Black Theatre Network, Nat. Assn. Dramatic and Speech Arts, Nat. Theatre Conf., Alpha Kappa Alpha. Home: 317 Cold Harbor Dr Frankfort KY 40601-3011

FLETTNER, MARIANNE, opera administrator; b. Frankfurt, Germany, Aug. 9, 1933; d. Bernhard J. and Kaethe E. (Halbritter) F. Bus. diploma, Hessel Bus. Coll., 1953. Sec. various cos., 1953-61, Pontiac Motor Div., Burlingame, Calif., 1961-63, Met. Opera, N.Y., 1963-74, asst. co. mgr., 1974-79; artistic adminstr. San Diego Opera, 1979—. Avocations: travel, hiking, swimming, cooking. Home: 4015 Crown Point Dr San Diego CA 92109-6270 Office: San Diego Opera 1200 Third Ave 18th Fl San Diego CA 92101-4112 E-mail: marianne.flettner@sdopera.com.

FLEURY, THEOREN, hockey player; b. Oxbow, Sask., Can., June 29, 1968; s. Wally and Donna Fleury; m. Veronica Fleury, 1995; children: Josh, Beaux. Hockey player Calgary Flames, Canada, 1987—98, Colo. Avalanche, Denver, 1998—99, N.Y. Rangers, N.Y.C., 1999—2002, Chgo. Blackhawks, 2002—. Named Man of Yr. N.Am., Juvenile Diabetes Found., 1992. Office: United Center 1901 W Madison St Chicago IL 60612

FLEXNER, JOSEPHINE MONCURE, musician, educator; b. Marion, Va., Oct. 11, 1919; d. Walter Raleigh Daniel and Harriet Ashby (Ogburn) M.; m. Kurt Fisher Flexner, Dec. 20, 1942; children: Thomas Moncure, Peter Wallace. BA, Univ. Richmond, 1941; tchr. cert. in piano, Peabody Conservatory, 1945; MS in piano, Juilliard Sch. Music, 1950. Class piano tchr. Balt. Pub. Sch., 1945-46; mem. piano faculty Peabody Conservatory Prep., Balt., 1945-46, Pius X Sch. Manhatanville Coll. Sacred Heart, N.Y.C., 1946-50, Henry Street Settlement Sch., N.Y.C., 1949-50; piano tchr. Bronxville, N.Y., 1950-54; mem. piano faculty Rhodes Coll., Memphis, Tenn., 1970-82; piano tchr. St. Mary's Episcopal Sch., Memphis, 1982-87. Judge for piano auditions, 1980-85, judge in Tenn. Nat. Guild Auditions, 1983-84. Contbr. articles to profl. jours. Den mother Boy Scouts Am., 1963-65, vice chmn., 1964-65; precinct worker, capt. Nat. Elections, Memphis, 1972, 74; mem. Memphis Arts Coun., 1977-79; area chmn. Westchester Soc. Performing Arts, 1964-66, chmn. cultural activities Sch. No. 8, Yonkers, N.Y., 1963-66; vice chmn. music dept. Bronxville Women's Club, 1964-66; pres. chancel choir Dutch Reformed Ch., Bronxville, 1963-66; program chmn. Seoul Internat. Women's Assn., Seoul, Korea, 1967-68, chmn. cultural activities Seoul Am. Schs., 1966-68, chmn. cultural seminars Am. Women's Club, Seoul, 1967-68; treas., pres. Greater Memphis Music Tchrs. Assn., 1975-79; bd. dirs. Young Peoples Piano Concerto Competition, 1979-85, Tenn. Music Tchrs. Assn., 1977-79. Named Tchr. of Yr., Greater Memphis Music, 1983, Tchr. of Yr., Tenn. Music Tchrs. Assn., 1985. Democrat. Presbyterian. Avocations: writing, reading, playing piano. Home: The Fountains at Millbrook 17 Crestview Rd Millbrook NY 12545

FLEXNER, KURT FISHER, economist, educator; b. Vienna, Sept. 26, 1915; arrived in U.S., 1928; s. Otto Gerard and Wilhelmine (Fisher) Flexner; m. Josephine Moncure, Dec. 20, 1942; children: Thomas Moncure, Peter Wallace. BS in Econs., Johns Hopkins U., 1946; PhD in Econs., Columbia U., 1954. From asst. prof. to prof. econs. NYU Grad. Sch. Arts and Scis., U. Coll. and Sch. Commerce, 1946-59; chief economist, dep. mgr. The Am. Bankers Assn., 1959-66; adj. prof. banking and fin. NYU, 1965-66, prof., chmn. dept. econs., 1968-78; prof. econs. U. Memphis, 1978-87, prof. emeritus, 1987—. Cons. U.S. Savs. and Loan League, 1955—59, N.Y. State Savs. and Loan League, 1955—59; P. K. Seidman vis. distin. prof. Christian Bros. U., Memphis, 1990—94; lectr. intergenerational seminars Bard Coll., Annandale on the Hudson, NY, 1987—, Ctr. for Life Studies, Marist Coll., Poughkeepsie, NY, 1995—; chief fin. instns. advisor U.S. Agy. for Internat. Devel., Seoul, Republic of Korea, 1966—68; spkr. in field; adv. com. to Chancellor Franz Vranitzky Prime Minister of Austria, 1991—93; guest lectr. Inst. USA and Can. Acad. Sci., Moscow, 1991—95; advisor to coun. Pres. Mikhail Gorbachev, 1990—91, Pres. Boris Yeltsin, 1991—94. Author: The European Payments Union 1950 to 1954, 1957, The Savings and Loan Associations in the State of New York, 1958, Mortgage Lending by Commercial Banks, 1964, The Enlightened Society: The Economy with a Human Face, 1989, The 21st Century-The Best of the Last, 2003; columnist Memphis Daily News, 1986—90, Comml. Appeal, 1980—87; contbr. articles to profl. jours. Trustee M. L. Seidman Town Hall Meml. Lecture Series, 1968—87; mem. Gov. Alexander's Action Team, 1980—85. With U.S. Army, 1944—45. Mem.: Econ. Club Memphis (exec. dir. 1973—85, pres. 1985—92). Home and Office: The Fountains at Millbrook 17 Crestview Rd Millbrook NY 12545

FLEYSHMAN, BENTSION, physicist, researcher, retired mathematician; b. Moscow, Nov. 21, 1923; s. Shimon and Nehama Fleyshman; m. Mira Etingof, June 19, 1955; 1 child, Simon. MS in Math., Moscow State U., 1947; PhD in Physics & Math., Russian Acad. of Sci., 1958, D in Physics & Math., 1966. Scientist Mil., Moscow, 1947—54; sr. scientist inst. radiotechnics & electronics Russian Acad. of Sci., Moscow, 1955—68, prin. scientist inst. oceanology, 1968—96; ind. cons. in risk analysis Bklyn., 1996—. Mem. of the interdisciplinary com. hon. pres. World Cultural Coun., Monterrey, NY, 1987—. Author: Constructive Methods of Optimal Coding for Channels with Noize (in Russian), 1963, Elements of Theory of Potential Efficiency of Complex Systems (in Russian), 1971, Fundamentals of Systemology (in Russian), 1982; contbr. ; author: The Choice is Yours (in Russian), 2000. Recipient Exceptional Work During WWII medal, Soviet Gov., 1945, City Com. Environ. Protection medal, Sofia, Bulgaria, 1991. Mem.: Soc. of Risk Analysis. Home and Office: 3093 Brighton 4th St Apt 5D Brooklyn NY 11235 Personal E-mail: daniel.fleyshman@verizon.net.

FLICK, ARNOLD L. retired physician, community activist; b. L.A., May 1, 1930; s. Samuel and Pearl Flick; m. Nancy Flick; children: Susan, Rachel, Sarah. BS, UCLA, 1950; MD, U. Chgo., 1954. Cer. Am. Bd. Internal Medicine, Am. Bd. Gastroenterology. Ret. clin. prof. medicine U. Calif., San Diego, 1968-91; med. dir. Smoking Rsch., San Diego, 1966-68; pvt. practice San Diego, 1961-98; cmty. activist Citizens for Fully Informed Vote, San Diego, 1999—. Jewish. Avocations: biking, hiking, tennis, violin.

FLICK, CARL, electrical engineer, consultant; b. Vienna, June 22, 1926; came to U.S., 1939; s. Henry Chaim Ber and Sofie (Dornhelm) F.; m. Frances Ethel Berman, July 4, 1954; children: Lawrence David, Susan Naomi, Jack Bennet. BEE, Poly. U. of N.Y., 1951; MEE, Poly. U., 1953. Registered profl. engr., Fla., Pa. Various engring. positions, adv. engr. Westinghouse Electric Corp., East Pittsburgh, Pa., 1952-84, adv. engr., Orlando, Fla., 1984-89; cons. Techno-Lexic, Orlando, 1989—. Co-author: Handbook of Electric Machines, 1987; contbr. articles to profl. jours.; patentee in field. With U.S. Army, 1945-47, PTO. Fellow IEEE (life; various coms., Centennial medal 1984, Outstanding Engr. award Orlando sect. 1989, Fla. coun. 1989, Region 3 1990, Nikola Tesla award 1994), Power Engring. Soc. (com. Disting. Svc. award, Millenium medal 2000); mem. B'nai B'rith. Democrat. Jewish. Avocations: writing, photography, painting.

FLICK, FERDINAND HERMAN, surgeon, prevention medicine physician; b. Bklyn., Feb. 19, 1925; s. Paul Albert and Elizebeth Kath (Herz) F.; m. Marie T. Flick, Apr. 7, 1945; children: Paul, Ferdinand, Annette Flick Riddle. BS, MS, Fordham U.; MD, Yale U., 1951. Diplomate Am. Bd. Preventive Medicine. Intern SUNY Downstate, 1951-52; resident in ob-gyn Coll. Physicians & Surgeons Columbia U., N.Y.C., 1952; asst. prof. Columbia U. Coll. Physicians & Surgeons, N.Y.C., 1959-62; surgeon 77th Divsn. USAR, N.Y.C., 1962-76; chief plant physician Fort Motor Co., Mahwah, N.J., 1976-80, Edison, N.J., 1980—. Asst. prof. U. Calif., Berkeley, 1946-47; trauma lectr. Middlesex C.C., 1984-85. Contbr. articles to profl. jours. including Nature and Am. Jour. Ob-gyn. Mem. smoking intervention team Am. Cancer Soc., New Brunswick, N.J., 1993-95. Col. USAR, 1946-76. Decorated Meritorious Svc. medal. Mem. Am. Coll. Occupl. and Environ. Medicine, Am. Coll. Preventive Medicine, Am. Soc. Abdominal Surgeons, Sigma Xi (Yale chpt.). Avocations: hunting, skiing. Home: 21 Miara St Parlin NJ 08859-1815

FLICK, JOHN EDMOND, lawyer; b. Franklin, Pa., Mar. 14, 1922; s. Edmond Leroy and Mary M. (Weaver) F.; m. Lois Anna Lange, Apr. 20, 1946; children: Gregory Allan, Scott Edmond, Lynn Ellen, Ann Elizabeth. Student, Northwestern U., 1941-44, U. Pa., 1945; LLB, Northwestern U., 1948. Bar: Ill. 1948, Calif. 1971, U.S. Dist. Ct. (ctrl. dist.) Calif. 1971, U.S. Ct. Appeals (9th cir.) 1971, U.S. Supreme Ct. 1974. Commd. 1st lt. Judge Adv. Gen. Corps U.S. Army, 1950, advanced through grades to lt. col. Res., 1968; ret., 1972; faculty U.S. Mil. Acad., 1954-57, Judge Adv. Gen. Sch., U. Va., 1960-61; counsel Litton Industries, 1963-67; sr. v.p., sec., gen. counsel, dir. Bangor Punta Corp., 1967-69; sr. v.p., gen. counsel Times Mirror Co., Los Angeles, 1970-87, cons., 1987-88. Past chmn. Los Angeles adv. bd. Salvation Army; mem. adv. bd., adult rehab. ctr. corps Santa Barbara, past mem. nat. adv. bd. Salvation Army. Recipient Am. Bar Assn. Acad. award, 1961 Mem. State Bars Calif. and Ill., Wigmore Club (life benefactor, Northwestern U. Law Sch.).

FLICK, LYNETTE LOWRY, piano teacher; b. Warren, Ohio, Mar. 17, 1942; d. Robert Iler and Ione Marguerite (Winbigler) F.; m. David Owens Flick, July 1, 1967; children: Gregory, Sharon, Carolyn. BS in Music Edn., Oberlin Coll., 1963; MS in Music Edn., Ohio State U., 1967. Tchr. elem. vocal music, supervising tchr. Akron (Ohio) Pub. Schs., 1963-70; adj. prof. U. Akron, 1968-72; ch. organist, choir dir., Akron, 1964-91; pvt. piano tchr., 1990—. Organist The Chapel, Akron, 1992—; freelance accompanist, Akron, 1990—; workshop presenter U. Akron, 1963-71. Chmn. fin arts fest Westside Neighbors Neighborhood Coalition, Akron, 1969 70; pres. Rankin Sch. PTA, Akron, 1988-90; co-chmn. after-prom party for high sch., 1993-97; leader Bible study The Chapel, 1995—. Mem. Music Tchrs. Nat. Assn., Internat. La Leche League (registered, accredited leader 1979—, counselor), Phi Kappa Lambda, Delta Kappa Gamma. Avocations: walking, reading, sewing, biking. Home: 617 Mineola Ave Akron OH 44320-1969

FLICK, THOMAS MICHAEL, mathematics educator, educational administrator; b. Covington, Ky., July 14, 1954; s. Thomas Lawrence and Crystel (Moore) F.; m. Jeanine M. Moran, Nov. 23, 1991. BS, No. Ky. U., 1976, MA, 1981; MEd, Xavier U., 1977; PhD, Southeastern U., 1979; EdD, U. Sarasota, 1989. Cert. secondary tchr., Ohio, Ky. Assoc. vice prin., dean, chmn. math., prin. summer sch. Purcell Marian High Sch., Cin., 1977-89; asst. prof. Xavier U., Cin., 1989-95, assoc. prof., 1995—. Lectr. astronomy Wilmington Coll., Ohio, 1977-78, engring. and nat. sci., U. Cin., 1979—. Author: Guidelines for Astronomy Courses, 1976, 1978; author: (with J. Ventre & J. Boothe) Astronomy Teaching Handbook, 1992; author: Introduction to the Universe, 1991, 1993, 2002, Eclipses: Presentations for Educators, 1999; contbr. articles to profl. jours. Guest lectr. Cin. Nature Ctr., Milford, 1976—; chmn. edn. Astron. League, Washington; tchr. Super Saturday Program for Gifted and Talented., Cin., 1983; commn. mem. Archdiocese Cin., 1986. Recipient Ohio NSF Presdl. Award for Excellence in Math. Edn., 1986, Greater Cin. Found./GE grantee, 1987. Mem. Ohio Coun. Tchrs. Math. (contest coord. 1983—, Outstanding Math. Tchr. award 1982), Nat. Astron. League (v.p. 1980-82, chmn. edn. 1975—), Nat. Coun. Tchrs. Math., Math. Assn. Am., Ohio Acad. Sci. (Jerry Acker Outstanding Math. Tchr. award 1986-87), Sigma Xi (Outstanding Math. Tchr. award 1985), Pi Mu Epsilon. Clubs: Midwestern Astronomers. Roman Catholic. Avocations: golf, piano, bicycling, model railroading. Office: Xavier U Dept Edn 3800 Victory Pkwy Dept Edn Cincinnati OH 45207-1035

FLICK, WILLIAM FREDRICK, surgeon; b. Lancaster, Pa., Aug. 18, 1940; s. William Joseph and Anna (Volkl) F.; m. Jacqueline Denise Phaneuf, May 21, 1966; children: William J., Karen E., Christopher R., Derrick W., Brian A. BS, Georgetown U., 1962, MD, 1966; MBA, U. Colo., 1990. Cert. Am. Bd. Surgeons, 1976. Self employed surgeon, Cheyenne, Wyo., 1973-84; pres., surgeon Cheyenne Surgical Assocs., 1984-94; med. dir. Blue Cross Blue Shield of Wyo., Cheyenne, 1994—. Trustee Laramie County Sch. Dist. #1, Cheyenne, 1988-92. Maj., chief of surgery USAF, 1971-73. Fellow ACS; mem. Am. Coll. Physician Execs., Nat. Assn. Managed Care. Republican. Roman Catholic. Office: Blue Cross Blue Shield Wyo 400 House Ave Cheyenne WY 82007-1468

FLICKER, ERIC LEE, civil engineer, consultant; b. Reading, Pa., Oct. 4, 1949; s. William L. and Doris L. (Rothermal) F.; m. Susan L. Stuart, Jan. 24, 1969 (div. 1983); children: Michael T., Scott E.; m. Gerry Ann Hopkins, Aug. 10, 1984. BS in Civil Engring. summa cum laude, Lehigh U., 1971, MBA, 1977. Registered profl. engr., Pa., Md., Del., Va., W. Va., Ohio; registered land surveyor, Pa. Engring. aide Spotts, Stevens and McCoy, Inc., Reading, 1966-71, civil engr., 1971 74, br. mgr., 1974-75, asst. to pres., 1975-81, sec.-treas., chief adminstrv. officer, 1981-86, pres., 1986-91; chief exec. officer, 1991; v.p. Woodward-Clyde Cons., Plymouth Meeting, Pa., 1991-94, Pennoni Assocs., Harrisburg, Pa., 1994-96, Phila., 1996-98, sr. v.p., 1998-99, sr. v.p.-treas., chief adminstrv. officer, 2000—02, CFO, treas., 2003—. Consistory pres., conf. del., chair bd. Christian edn. Community United Ch. Christ, Reading, 1977-83; mem. corp. adv. bd. Civil Engring. Rsch. Found., 1997—; Marksman Engring. News Record, 1991; treas. East Goshen United Ch. of Christ, 2000-01. Fellow Am. Coun. Engring. Cos. (bd. dirs. Rsch. and Mgmt. Found. 1996-2000, v.p. 1996-97, sr. v.p. 1997-98, chair-elect 2002-2003, chmn. 2003-); mem. Hazardous Waste Action Coalition (pres. 1990-91), Pa. Soc. Profl. Engrs. (state mathcounts coord. 1985-87, S.E. regional v.p. 1987-89, pres. 1990-91, Pa. State Disting. Svc. award 1987, Reading chpt. Engr. of Yr. 1988)., ACEC/PA (chmn. govt. affairs com. 1991—), Pa. Design Assoc. Ctr. (chmn. bd. dirs. 1996-97), Engrs. Club Phila. (bd. dirs. 1999—), Tau Beta Pi, Chi Epsilon. Republican. Avocation. golf. Home: 1355 Troon Ln West Chester PA 19380-6941 Office: Pennoni Assocs Inc One Drexel Plaza 3001 Market St Philadelphia PA 19104-2800 E-mail: eflicker@pennoni.com., elflicker@aol.com.

FLICKER, JOHN, foundation executive; With The Nature Conservancy, Great Plains dir., gen. counsel, chief legal officer, exec. v.p., Fla. state dir.; pres. Nat. Audubon Soc., N.Y.C., 1995—. Office: National Audubon Soc 700 Broadway New York NY 10003-9536

FLICKINGER, CHARLES JOHN, anatomist, educator; b. Bethlehem, Pa., July 13, 1938; s. Wilbur James and Verna (Diehl) F.; m. Agnes Elizabeth Dickel, Feb. 23, 1963; children: Laura Jill, David Paul. AB, Dartmouth Coll., 1960; MD, Harvard U., 1964. Rsch. fellow dept. anatomy U. Colo., Denver, 1964-65, Harvard Med. Sch., Boston, 1965-66; rsch. assoc. Inst. Developmental Biology, U. Colo., Boulder, 1966-67, asst. prof., 1967-70; assoc. prof. dept. anatomy Sch. Medicine, U. Va., Charlottesville, 1971-75, prof., 1975—, Harvey E. Jordan prof. anatomy, 1982—2002, chmn. dept. cell biology, 1982—2002. Mem. reproductive biology study sect. NIH, 1979-83; mem. anatomy test com. Nat. Bd. Med. Examiners, 1981-84 Author: (with Brown, Kutchai, Ogilvie) Medical Cell Biology, 1979; contbr. articles to profl. jours.; assoc. editor: Jour. Andrology, 1989-92; adv. editor: Internat. Rev. Cytology, 1974-98; mem. editl. bd. Biology of Reprodn., 1986-89, 2002-, Jour. Andrology, 1986-89, Anatomical Record, 1972-98. NIH rsch. career devel. award grantee, 1968-70. Mem. Am. Soc. Cell Biology, Am. Assn. Anatomists, Soc. Study Reprodn., Am. Soc. Andrology, Phi Beta Kappa, Alpha Omega Alpha. Home: 2009 Meadowbrook Rd Charlottesville VA 22903-1247 Office: University of Virginia Dept Cell Biology PO Box 800732 Charlottesville VA 22908-0732 E-mail: cjf@virginia.edu.

FLICKINGER, DON JACOB, patent agent; b. Massillon, Ohio, Dec. 31, 1933; s. John Jacob and Elizabeth Ann (Slinger) F.; m. Sonja Loy Jersild (dec. Aug. 1987); 1 child, Packy J. Flickinger. Student, Kent (Ohio) State U., 1951-54, U. Ariz., 1958; BA, Ariz. State U., 1963, MA, 1964. Bar: U.S. Patent and Trademark Office, 1973. Apprentice tool and die maker Spun Steel Corp., Canton, Ohio, 1951-54; staff Ariz. State U., Tempe, 1963-65; law clerk, paralegal Drummond, Cahill & Phillips, Phoenix, 1966-73; reg. patent agent Drummond, Nelson & Ptak, Phoenix, 1973-77, self employed, Phoenix, 1977-94; counsel Parsons & Goltry, Phoenix, 1995—2001. Lectr., instr. Patent Seminars & Courses, Phoenix, 1977—; staff Rio Salado C.C., Phoenix, 1982-84; intellectual property counselor SCORE Phoenix Chpt. 105, 2001. Patentee Collapsible Dust Pan, Hort. Growing Unit. Comdg. officer Poolee Enrichment Program, Family Marine Force, Poolee Assistance Co., Phoenix; sponsor Thunderbird Little League, Phoenix, 1985, 86, 87; big brother Valley Big Brothers, Phoenix, 1968-70; participant, staff Valley Big Bros./Big Sisters Fish-a-Ree, 1984-87; judge Crown Royal Kinetic Contraption Compeition, 1990. With USMC, 1954-57. Am. Soc. Tool. scholar, Tucson, 1960; recipient Disting. Svc. cert. Valley Big Brothers, Phoenix,1970, Honor award Westside Area Career Project, Glendale, 1981. Mem. BBB, NRA (endowment), Nat. Wildlife Fedn. (leaders club), Am. Legion, Ariz. Heritage Alliance, Wilderness Soc., Legal Defense Fund, Defenders of Wildlife, Am. Legion, Mensa, Svc. Corps. of Ret. Exec. (intellectual property counselor Phoenix chpt. 105 2001—), Kappa Delta Pi. Republican. Buddhist. Avocations: philosophy, reading, woodworking, arts and crafts. Office: Phoenix Score Chpt 105 2828 N Central Ave Ste 800 Phoenix AZ 85004

FLICKINGER, HARRY HARNER, organization and business executive, management consultant; b. Hanover, Pa., July 27, 1936; s. Harry Roosevelt and Goldie Anna (Harner) F.; m. Hsin Yang, May 30, 1961; children: Audrey Mae, Deborah Lynn. BS in Psychology, U. Md., 1958. Investigator U.S. Civil Service Commn., Washington, 1962-64; personnel specialist U.S. Naval Ordinance Lab., Silver Spring., Md., 1964-66; from asst. dir. to dir. personnel U.S. OMB, Washington, 1966-73; asst. dir. personnel AEC and Dept. Energy, Washington, 1973-78; dir. personnel U.S. Dept. Justice, Washington, 1978-79, dep. asst. atty. gen. adminstrn., 1979-85, assoc. asst. atty. gen., 1985-87, asst. atty. gen., 1987-92; exec. dir. Am. Consortium for Internat. Pub. Adminstrn., Washington, 1993; pres. Flickinger Enterprises, Gaithersburg, Md., 1994—. Recipient Presdl. Disting. Exec. Rank award, 1988. Office: 8730 Lochaven Dr Gaithersburg MD 20882-4464

FLICKINGER, JOE ARDEN, telecommunications educator; b. Cadillac, Mich., Feb. 4, 1949; s. Arden Henry and Stella Frances (Hurst) F.; m. Judith Marie Gardner, Sept. 18, 1971; children: Jan Elsa, Jill Kimberly. BA, Kalamazoo Coll., Mich., 1971; MA, U. So. Calif., 1975; AS, Clatsop Community Coll., 1985; PhD, U. Oreg., 1993. Asst. chief engr. Sta. KUSC-FM, L.A., 1972-74; sta. engr. Sta. KAST-AM-FM, Astoria, Oreg., 1974-75; studio operator, instr. Clatsop Community Coll., Astoria, 1975-88; grad. teaching fellow in telecommunications U. Oreg., Eugene, 1988-90; sr. mktg. cons. RKM Corp., Vancouver, Wash., 1990-93; vis. asst. prof. communications Lewis and Clark Coll., Portland, Oreg., 1991-92; assoc. prof. media studies Radford (Va.) U., Va., 1992—, dir. grad. program, corp. and profl. comm., 1996-98, chair media studies dept., 1998—. Session organizer on high definition TV, Northcon, 1989, IEEE and ERA Tech. Conf., 1989. Dir. TV muscular dystrophy telethon Astoria Jaycees, 1980, 81; canvasser Friends of Coll., Astoria, 1982; pres. bd. dirs. Sta. KMUN-FM Tillicum Found., Astoria, 1983-84. Mem. IEEE, IEEE Computer Soc., IEEE Comm. Soc., Am. Radio Relay League (life), Pacific Telecomm. Coun., Northcom Inner Circle, N.Y. Acad. Scis., Nat. Model R.R. Assn., Sunset Empire Amateur Radio Club (sec. 1978-81), Lions Club (region chair dist. 24-E 1999-2002). Democrat. Presbyterian. Avocations: amateur radio, golf, fishing, astronomy, cooking. E-mail: jflickin@radford.edu.

FLIER, MICHAEL STEPHEN, Slavic languages educator; b. L.A., Apr. 20, 1941; s. Albert and Bonnie F. BA, U. Calif., Berkeley, 1962, MA, 1964, PhD, 1968. Acting vis. asst. prof. Slavic langs. and lits. U. Calif., Berkeley, 1968; asst. prof. Slavic langs. and lits. UCLA, 1968-73, assoc. prof., 1973-79, prof., 1979-91, chmn. dept., 1978-84, 87-89. Vis. prof. Slavic langs. Columbia U., fall 1988, Harvard U., fall 1989; Oleksandr Potebnja prof. Ukrainian Philology Harvard U., 1991—, chmn. dept. Linguistics, 1994-99, chmn. dept. Slavic langs. and lits., 1999—, acting chmn. dept. linguistics, 2002; acting dir. Harvard Ukrainian Rsch. Inst., 2001. Author: Aspects of Nominal Determination in Old Church Slavic, 1974, Say It In Russian, 1982; editor: Slavic Forum: Essays in Slavic Linguistics and Literature, 1974, Am. Cont. to the Intl. Congress of Slavists, 1983, Ukrainian Philology and Linguistics, 1994; co-editor: Medieval Russian Culture, 1984, Issues in Russian Morphosyntax, 1985, The Scope of Slavic Aspect, 1985, Language, Literature, Linguistics, 1987, Medieval Russian Culture, vol. 2, 1994, For SK: In Celebration of the Life and Career of Simon Karlinsky, 1994, The Language and Verse of Russia: In Honor of Dean S. Worth on His Sixty-fifth Birthday, 1995; mem. editl. bd. Slavic and East European Jour., 1989—, Movoznavstvo, 1991—, Harvard Ukrainian Studies, 1991—, Russkii iazyk v nauchniom osveshchenii, 2000—. Vice chmn. Am. Com. Slavists, 1989-94, chmn., 1994—. Internat. Rsch. and Exchs. Bd. travel grantee Russia, Czechoslovakia, 1966-67, 71, 78, 93, 96; U. Calif. Pres.'s fellow, 1990, John Simon Guggenheim Meml. Found. fellow, 1990-91. Mem. Linguistics Soc. Am., Am. Assn. Tchrs. Slavic and East European Langs., Am. Assn. Advancement Slavic Studies, Western Slavic Assn., Coll. Art Assn., Am. Assn. for Ukrainian Studies (sec.-treas. 1989-93, bd. dirs.). Home: 76 Fresh Pond Ln Cambridge MA 02138-4641 Office: Harvard U Dept Slavic Langs and Lits Barker Ctr, 12 Quincy St Cambridge MA 02138

FLIGGE, JÖRG, librarian, library director; b. Königsberg, Germany, Dec. 1, 1940; s. Armin and Ursula (Schroeter) F.; m. Gabriele Edner, July 6, 1968; children: Christina, Claudia. PhD, U. Bonn, Germany, 1972. Cert. sci. libr. Jr. libr. U. Libr., Bonn, 1972-74, libr. adminstr. Duisburg, Germany, 1974-77, head libr. adminstr., 1978-79, dep. dir., 1979, libr. dir., 1980; dep. dir. City Libr., Duisburg, 1983-90; dir., ltd. libr. dir. Bibliothek der Hansestadt Lübeck, Germany, 1990—. Head commn. AV-media in librs. German Libr. Inst., Berlin, 1980-90; mem. German-Russian Libr. Commn. Restitution, Berlin, and St. Petersburg, Russia, 1993—. Author: Herzog Albrecht von Preussen und der Osiandrismus, 1972; author: (editor) Bibliotheca Baltica, 1994, Stadt und Bibliothek, 1997, Die Wissenschaftliche Stadtbibliothek, 2001; contbr. articles to profl. jours. Active Assn. zur Beförderung gemeinnützige Tätigkeit, Lübeck, 1991—. Mem. Verein Deutscher Bibliothekare, Verein der Bibliothekare an Öffentlichen Bibliotheken, Rotary, Heilige Drei Konige Bank zu Danzig/Lubeck. Lutheran. Avocations: music, studying cultural history. Home: Hermann-Lönsweg 24 23562 Lübeck Germany Office: Bibliothek der Hansestadt Lübeck Hundestr 5-17 23552 Lübeck Germany

FLINCHUM, RUSSELL ALAN, design historian; b. Winston-Salem, N.C., July 3, 1958; s. Russell Ray and Nancy Jacklyn (Dickerson) F.. BA in English, U. N.C., 1981, MA in Art History, 1985; PhD, CUNY, 1998. Guest curator Cooper-Hewitt Mus., N.Y.C., 1992-97; lectr. Mus. Modern Art, N.Y.C., 1992-98; archivist Century Assn. Archives Found., N.Y.C., 1998—; instr. Parsons Sch. Design, N.Y.C., 2003—. Adj. prof. Fashion Inst. Tech., N.Y.C., 1992-97, Cooper-Hewitt/Parsons Sch. Design, N.Y.C., 1993-96. Author: Henry Dreyfuss, Industrial Designer: The Man in the Brown Suit, 1997. Fellow Samuel H. Kress Found., 1992-93, Peter Krueger/Christie's fellow Cooper-Hewitt Mus., 1990-91. Democrat. Mem. Moravian Ch. Home: 1748 Virginia Rd Winston Salem NC 27104-3253 Office: Century Assn Archives Found 7 W 43rd St New York NY 10036-7402 E-mail: archives@thecentury.org.

FLINK, JANE DUNCAN, columnist; b. Atlanta, Feb. 17, 1929; d. James Archibald and Frances (Watkins) Duncan; m. Richard Albert Flink, Nov. 20, 1954; children: Jennifer, Elizabeth, Caroline, Charles Albert, James Duncan. Student, Carleton Coll., U. Mo. Reporter Tri-Town News, Greendale, Wis., 1958-61; reporter, photographer, feature writer, editor newspaper Ctrl. Mo. Fireside Guard, 1973-78; editor bus. briefs MFA Oil Co., Columbia, Mo., 1977; editor lifestyles Kingdom Daily News, Fulton, Mo., 1978-82; asst. editor Centralia (Mo.) Fireside Guard, 1982-83; editor Ctrl. Mo. Rural & Farm Life Mag.; assoc. editor Mo. Ruralist, Columbia, 1983-85; dir. external rels. Winston Churchill Meml. & Libr. Westminster Coll., Fulton, 1985-89, dir., 1989-90; owner, pub. Boone County Jour., Ashland, Mo., 1986-2001, columnist, 2001—; editl. cons. Greenways, Inc., Durham, NC, 2001—. Editor, pub.: Time and the River, 1993. Rep. committeewoman Ward 1, Centralia, 1972, 74, 76; Dem. committeewoman Cedar Twp., 2001--; mem. exec. bd. Friends of Winston Churchill Meml. and Libr., Fulton, 1978-97; mem. Boone County Commn. on Child Abuse, 1978-81, Boone County Hist. Soc.; bd. dirs., mem. pub. rels., devel., Maplewood coms., Walters-Boone County Mus. and Visitors Ctr., 1995—, 1st v.p. 1996-98, pres. 1998-2000; vice chmn. Endowment Trust, 2000—, chmn. 2003—; mem. Boone County Gov. Rev. Task Force, 1991-92, chair So. Boone County Sch. Budget Rev. Task Force, 1991-92; pres. Lake Champetra Homeowners Assn., 1993-95, v.p. 1995-96; vice chair Boone County Constn. Writing Commn., 1995-96; mem. ext. coun. U. Mo., 1995-97; co-chmn. Friends So. Boone County Fire Protection Dist., 1995-97; mem. steering com. Boone County Vision Plan, 2000-02; mem. dist. comms. com. United Meth. Ch., 2001—; trustee Ashland (Mo.) United Meth. Ch., 2001—; mem. Boone Hosp. Ctr. Found., 2002--. Mem. Nat. Fedn. Press Women (bd. dirs. 1991-93, 21st century com. 1992-93, Nat. Achievement award 1982), So. Boone County C. of C. (chmn. econ. devel. com. 1998—2002), Mo. Press Women (dist. v.p., v.p., treas. chmn. honors awards, pres. 1991-93. Communicator of Yr. award 1978, 79, 80, 81, 82, 83,85, 86, 95, Woman of Achievement award 1989), Mo. Press Assn. Home: 7230 E North Shore Dr Hartsburg MO 65039-9633 E-mail: jayscreen@aol.com.

FLINN, MICHAEL DE VLAMING, investment banker, former state legislator; b. Durham, N.C., June 15, 1941; s. Lawrence and Marion (de Vlaming) F.; m. Elizabeth Jamison Folk, Aug. 3, 1962 (div. Mar. 1985); children: William III, Michael de Vlaming, T. Rex, Randall E.; m. Ann G. Hanes, Feb. 14, 1993. BA magna cum laude, Yale U., 1962; JD, Harvard U., 1965. Bar: Conn. 1968. Ltd. ptnr. Ingalls & Snyder, 1970-96; mem. Conn. Ho. of Reps., Hartford, 1983-86; v.p. Spears, Benzak, Salmon & Farrell, Inc. (name now Victory, N.Y.C., 1996—, mng. dir., 1997. Mng. dir. Victory SBSF Capital Mgmt. Active Town Meeting, Greenwich, Conn., 1970-72; mem. Conn. Rep. Fin. Com., 1972; mem. Greenwich Rep. Town Com., 1980-85, exec. com., 1982-84; trustee Green-Wood Cemetery, 1983—; bd. dirs. Coldwater Conservation Fund, 2002—; pres., bd. dirs. Greenwich Boys Club Assn., 1977-92; pres., bd. dirs. Round Hill Assn., 1972-81; chmn. bd. dirs. Boys and Girls Club Greenwich, 1993-94. Capt. U.S. Army, 1966-68. Mem. ABA, Conn. Bar Assn., Greenwich Bar Assn., Hotchkiss Alumni Assn. (gov. 1979-83), Yale Alumni Assn. Greenwich (gov. 1982-85). Clubs: Links, Burning Tree Club. Home: PO Box 1309 Greenwich CT 06836-1309 Office: Victory SBSF Capital Mgmt 45 Rockefeller Plz New York NY 10111 E-mail: michaelf@sbsf.com.

FLINN, MICHAEL JAMES, lawyer; b. Pitts., June 9, 1949; s. George E. and Iris R. (Schartl) F.; m. Eileen McGrady, Aug. 7, 1971; children: Erin, Kevin. BA, U. Notre Dame, 1971; JD, U. Pitts., 1974. Bar: Pa. 1974, U.S. Dist. Ct. (we. dist.) Pa. 1974. Assoc. Moorhead & Knox, Pitts., 1974-81; ptnr. Buchanan Ingersoll, P.C., Pitts., 1981—. Dir. Buchanan Ingersoll Ltd., London. Pres. Nat. Aviary, 1992-97; mem. adv. bd. The Salvation Army, Southwestern Pa., 1993—; mem. Bd. Nat. Aviary, 1998—. Home: 728 Harden Dr Pittsburgh PA 15229-1107 Office: Buchanan Ingersoll PC 301 Grant St Ste 21 Pittsburgh PA 15219-1408 E-mail: flinnmj@bipc.com.

FLINN, PAUL ANTHONY, materials scientist; b. N.Y.C., Mar. 25, 1926; s. Richard A. and Anna M. (Weber) F.; m. Mary Ellen Hoffman, Aug. 20, 1949; children: Juliana, Margaret, Donald, Anthony, Patrick. AB, Columbia Coll., 1948, MA, 1949; ScD, MIT, 1952. Asst. prof. Wayne U., Detroit, 1953-54; research staff Westinghouse Research Lab., Pitts., 1954-63; prof. Carnegie-Mellon U., Pitts., 1964-78; sr. staff scientist Intel Corp., Santa Clara, Calif., 1978-95; cons. prof. dept. material sci. and engring. Stanford (Calif.) U., 1985—. Vis. prof. U. Nancy, France, 1967-68, U. Fed. do Rio Grand du Sol, Porto Allegro, Brazil, 1975, Argonne (Ill.) Nat. Lab., 1977-78, Stanford (Calif.) U., 1984-85. Contbr. sci. articles to profl. jours. Served with USN, 1944-46, PTO. Fellow Am. Phys. Soc.; mem. Metall. Soc., Materials Rsch. Soc., Phi Beta Kappa, Tau Beta Pi. Office: Stanford U Dept Material Sci & Engring Stanford CA 94305-2205

FLINN, ROBERTA JEANNE, management, computer applications consultant; b. Twin Falls, Idaho, Dec. 19, 1947; d. Richard H. and Ruth (Johnson) F. Student, Colo. State U., 1966-67. Cert. Novell netware engr. Ptnr. Aqua-Star Pools & Spas, Boise, Idaho, 1978—, mng. ptnr., 1981-83. Ops. mgr. Polly Pools, Inc., Canby, Oreg., 1983-84, br. mgr. Polly Pools, Inc., A-One Distributing, 1984-85; comptr., Beaverton Printing, Inc., 1986-89; mng. ptnr. Invisible Ink, Canby, Oreg., 1989—. Mem. Nat. Appaloosa Horse Club, Oreg. Dressage Soc., NetWare Users International (Portland chpt.). Home: 24687 S Central Point Rd Canby OR 97013-9743 E-mail: rjflinn@invisibleink.net.

FLINNER, BEATRICE JEFFREYS ALLAYAUD, retired library and media sciences educator; b. Uledi, Pa., Feb. 8, 1924; d. Charles Robert and Esther Marjorie (Sickles) Jeffreys; m. Donald Allayaud, May 18, 1944 (dec.); 1 child, Donald Allayaud; m. Lyle P. Flinner, June 27, 1947; 1 child, Carol Jean Flinner Dorough. *Parents Charles/Esther Jeffreys, Husband Dr. Lyle Flinner, AB 1949 GC; M.Div. 1952; ATS; M.Ed. 1960 U.Pgh; Ph.D 1967 U.Pgh; Professor SNU Religion, retired. Son Donald Allayaud, Assistantship MIT, MSAA MIT. Daughter-in-law Kathy Allayaud, CSU Greeley now Unc. Daughter Carol Dorough, BS 1974 BNC, BS 1991 SNU; MSM UTT 1997, 8 years teaching nursing, classes completed for Ed.D. Nova; Nursing professor, SNU 2003. Son-in-law Dr. James Dorough, BA 1973, BNC; M.Div. 19977, NTS; D.Min, 1998 TS. Grandson James Dorough, Jr; BA 2001 SNU; study, France, Army Reserves 2002. Granddaughter Stefanie Dorough, senior, psychology, SNU; Mortar Board.* AB summa cum laude, So. Nazarene U., 1974; MLS, U. Okla., 1977; MA in Social Studies, So. Nazarene U., 1978, MA in Early Childhood, 1981. Cataloging dept. Asbury Theol. Sem., Wilmore, Ky., 1949-52; aquisitions Geneva Coll., Beaver Falls, Pa., 1959-62, audio visual coord., 1965-68; assoc. prof., head pub. svcs. So. Nazarene U., Bethany, Okla., 1968-96, adj. prof. grad. edn., 1980-2000; ret., 1996. Adv. bd. Bethany Libr., rep. to bd. trustees, 1986-87. Book reviewer The Christian Librarian, 1980-94; indexer Christian Periodical Index, 1988-96; contbr. articles to profl. jours. Mem. AAUW (directory), Assn. Christian Librs. (v.p. 1991-93, program chair internat. conf. 1992), Univ. Women's Club, U. Okla. Sch. Libr. Info. Sci. Alumni Assn., Assn. Christian Librs. (conf. coord. 1992-95), Rsch. Interest Group, Acad. Sr. Profls. (libr. resources columnist, named one of 2000 Notable Am. Women), Phi Delta Lambda. Republican. Nazarene.

FLINT, DOUGLAS J. business executive; Chartered acct. Peat Marwick Mitchell & Co.; ptnr., 1988-95; group fin. dir. HSBC Holdings plc, London, 1995—. Bd. dirs. HSBC Holdings plc, HSBC Bank Malaysia Berhad, HSBC Bank USA, others. Office: HSBC Holdings plc 8 Canada Square London E14 5HQ England

FLINT, GEORGE SQUIRE, lawyer; b. Ft. Wayne, Ind., Oct. 28, 1930; s. A. Verne and Alberta (Minor) F.; m. Emily Gregg McLees, Nov. 23, 1968; 1 son, Alexander C.; children by previous marriage: Julia M., Melissa A., Anthony E. AB, U. Mich., 1952, JD, 1955. Bar: N.Y. 1956. Assoc., then sr. assoc. Fulton, Walter & Duncombe, N.Y.C., 1955-65; ptnr. Fulton, Duncombe and Rowe, 1983-89; with Tenneco Chems., Inc., 1965-82, v.p., sec., gen. counsel, 1969-82; counsel Jackson & Nash, N.Y.C., 1989—. Arbitrator Small Claims Part. Civil Ct., N.Y.C. With USN, 1955-57. Mem. N.Y. State Bar Assn., Assn. Bar City N.Y., Order of Coif. Clubs: Indian Harbor Yacht, Wadawanuck, Stonington. Home: 1185 Park Ave New York NY 10128-1308 Office: 330 Madison Ave New York NY 10017-5001

FLINT, H. HOWARD, II, printing company executive; b. Apr. 17, 1939; MBA, U of Penn Wharton Sch. With Flint Ink Corp., Detroit, Milw., 1960—, pres., 1985—92, chmn. bd., CEO, 1992—. Office: Flint Ink Corp 4600 Arrowhead Dr Ann Arbor MI 48105-2773*

FLINT, JOHN E. historian, educator; b. Montreal, Que., Can., May 17, 1930; s. Alfred Edgar and Sarah (Pickup) F.; m. Nezhat Sepanj, Sept. 19, 1975; children: Helen Sarah, Richard John. BA, U. Cambridge, 1952, MA, 1954; PhD, U. London, 1957. Asst. lectr., lectr., reader colonial history King's Coll., U. London, 1954-67; vis. prof., Fulbright fellow U. Calif., Santa Barbara, 1960-61; vis. prof., head history dept. U. Nigeria, Nsukka, 1963-64; prof. history Dalhousie U., 1967—, dir. African Studies Centre, 1967-92; prof. emeritus, 1993—. Mem. acad. panel Can. Council, 1967-68, Social Scis. and Humanities Research Council Can. Author: Sir George Goldie and the Making of Nigeria, 1960, Nigeria and Ghana, 1966, Cecil Rhodes, 1974; co-author: Oxford History of the British Empire, Vol. V, 1999; editor: Cambridge History of Africa, Vol. V, 1790-1870, 1977. Fellow Royal Hist. Soc., Royal Soc. Can.; mem. Canadian Assn. African Studies, Canadian Hist. Assn., Nigerian Hist. Assn., African Studies Assn. U.K. E-mail: jflint@chat.carleton.ca.

FLINT, LOU JEAN, retired state agency administrator; b. Ogden, Utah, July 11, 1934; d. Elmer Blood and Ella D. (Adams) F.; children: Dirk Kershaw Brown, Kristie Susan Brown Felix, Flint Kershaw Brown. BS, Weber State Coll., 1968; MEd, U. Utah, 1974, EdS, 1981. Cert. early childhood and elem. edn., Utah Bd. Edn., 1968, edn. adminstrn., 1981. Master tchr. Muir Elem., Davis Sch. Dist., Farmington, Utah, 1968-77; edn. specialist Dist. I Dept. Def., various locations, Eng., Scotland, Norway, 1977-79; ednl. cons. Utah Sys. Approach to Individualized Learning, various locations, Tex., S.C., Fla., Utah, 1979-81; acad. affairs officer Commn. Higher Edn. Office, State of Utah, Salt Lake City, 1982-98. Mem. Women's Politics Caucus; chair Women and Bus. Conf., 1985; mem. MHCS Centennial Com., 1995-96; welfare reform demonstration project State of Utah, 1992-96, foster care citizen rev. pilot project, 1993-99, Utah exec. bd. AARP, 1999-02; chmn. edn. workgroup U. Utah Grad. Sch. Social Work, 2001—. Author: The Comprehensive Community College, 1980. Bd. dirs. Utah YWCA; mem. nominating bd. Salt Lake YWCA. Recipient Appreciation award Gov. of Utah, 1983-85, 93, Woman of Achievement award Utah Bus. and Profl. Women, 1985, Pathfinder award C. of C., 1988, Outstanding Educator award YWCA, 1989, Silver Apple award Utah State U., 1992, award for svcs. Utah Mental Health Assn., 1996; named Exemplary Tchr., Utah State Bd. Edn., 1970-77, Outstanding Educator, London Ctrl. H.S., 1979. Mem.: AAUW (Edn. Found. award given in her honor 1986, named Woman Who Makes History 1994), Nat. Assn. Women's Work/Women's Worth (Disting. Woman award 1987), Women's Legis. Coun. (exec. bd. 2001—03, vol. 2002 Winter Olympics), Math. Sci. Network (chair Edn. Workgroup 2002—), Crones Coun., Utah Jaycee Aux. (past pres. Centerville), Women Concerned About Nuc. War, Utah Assn. Edn. Young Children (past pres.), Nat. Assn. Edn. Young Children, Women's Political Caucus (Susa Young Gates award 1987). Mem. Lds Ch.

FLINT, WILLIS WOLFSCHMIDT (WILLI WOLFSCHMIDT), artist, sculptor; b. Kenton, Ohio, Dec. 27, 1936; s. Wilbur Henry and Ilo Edna (Obenour) Flint. Student, Art Career Sch., N.Y.C., 1957-60, Ins. Allende, San Miguel Allende, Mex., 1961. Artist trainee Kossack Advt., Tucson, 1961; gen. boardman Mithoff Advt., El Paso, 1962-63; tech. illustrator Volt Tech. Corp., N.Y.C., 1967; gen. illustrator Salesvertising Advt., Denver, 1968; gen. boardman/cons. Burr-Brown Rsch. Corp., Tucson, 1969-71; musician, actor Paul Barons Harmonica Rascals, Bklyn., 1965-85; musician Wild Ones, Tucson, 1982-83; muralist San Diego, Tucson, N.Y.C., 1976-80; artist Tucson, 1985—; originator Fantasy-Expressionism, 1984; musician, comedian Desert Rats, Tucson, 1999-2000; founder Ragged Edge, 2003, Sch. Ragged Edge, 2003. Pvt. tchr. art, Tucson, 1981—85; cons. muralist Yaqui Indian-Pascua Ctr., Tucson, 1989; freelance muralist and graphic artist Wolfschmidt & Washburn, 1994—96. Co-author: (poems) Best-Loved Contemporary Poems, 1979, Famous Poems of Today, 1995, A Delicate Balance, 1996, Poetic Voices of America, 1996, Best Poems of the '90s, 1996, Best Poems of the 20th Century, 1996, Best Famous Poems of '96, 1997, Best Poems of '97, 1997, Soaring with the Wind, 1998, Ten Years Excellence, 1998; one-man shows include sculptor Old Pascua Village, Tucson, 1996, exhibited in group shows at United Way Fund Dr. Exhibit, United Servicemen's Orgn. Exhibit, Mobile, Ala., Student Union Exhibit, U. Ariz., Tucson, La Galeria Instituto, San Miguel de Allende, Margarita de Mena Gallery, N.Y.C., Represented in permanent collections So. Ariz. Hist. Soc., Tombstone, in pvt. collections; author: A Treatise on Fantasy—Expressionism from the School of the Ragged-Edge, 2003. With USN, 1954—57, with USN, 1979—81. Recipient award of merit, Latham Found., 1958, letter of commendation, U. Ariz. Family Practice, Tucson, 1978, U.S. Dept. Navy, San Diego, 1979; scholar, Latham Found., 1958. Mem.: Internat. Soc. Poets, Maverick Artists, Tucson Harmonica Club. Avocations: antique vehicles, travel, motorcycling. Home: 707 W Calle Progreso Tucson AZ 85705-6446

FLINTOFF, COREY ALAN, radio newscaster, writer; b. Fairbanks, Alaska, Apr. 8, 1946; s. Alan Dixon and Marjory Doris (Herman) F.; m. Diana Derby, June 24, 1990; 1 child, Claire Parnell. BA, U. Calif., Berkeley, 1970; MA, U. Chgo., 1971; DHL (hon.), U. Alaska, 2002. Freelance writer/reporter, Chgo., 1971-77; news dir., documentarian KYUK-AM/TV, Bethel, Alaska, 1977-84; host, prodr. Alaska Pub. Radio Network, Anchorage, 1984-89; newscaster NPR, Washington, 1990—. Assoc. prof. radio and TV, George Washington U., Washington, 1992-99. With USNR, 1966-68, San Diego. Recipient Reporting award Corp. for Pub. Broadcasting, 1989; Knight Internat. Press fellow to Mongolia, 2001. Mem. AFTRA. Office: NPR 635 Massachusetts Ave NW Washington DC 20001-3740

FLIPPEN, CHARLES CURTIS, neurologist; b. Flint, Mich., Jan. 23, 1965; s. Charles Curtis and Cecile Flippen; m. Jennifer Cecelia Haley, July 17, 1999; children: Charles Curtis III, Spencer Alexander. BA, Northwestern Univ., Evanston, Ill., 1981; MD, Univ. Mich., Ann Harbor, Mich., 1992. Diplomate Am. Bd. of Psychiatry and Neurology. Clin. instr. Ind. Univ. Sch. of Medicine, Indpls., 1997—99; asst. clin. prof. UCLA Sch. of Medicine, L.A., 1999—. Recipient Golden Hammer Tchg. award, UCLA Neurology residents/faculty, 2002. Mem.: Alpha Phi Alpha (chair com. on edl. activies 1999—). Office: Dept Neurology 14445 Olive View Dr Sylmar CA 91342-1437

FLIPPEN, EDWARD L. lawyer; b. Richmond, Va., Dec. 2, 1939; s. Hannie Thomas Flippen; m. Pearcy light, Feb. 14, 1970; children: Elizabeth Hunter, Margaret Harlan. BS, Va. Commonwealth U., 1965; MBA, Coll. of William and Mary, 1967, JD, 1974. Bar: Va. 1974, N.C. 1981. Gen. atty. Va. State Corp. Commn., Richmond, 1975-78, assoc. gen. counsel, 1978-80, dep. gen. counsel, 1980; asst. gen. counsel Duke Power Co., Charlotte, N.C., 1980-81, assoc., 1981-83; ptnr. Mays & Valentine, LLP, Richmond, 1983-99, McGuireWoods, LLP, Richmond, 1999—. Lectr. U. Va. Sch. Law, 1978-82; adj. law prof. Coll. William and Mary, 1996—, Washington and Lee U., 1997-99, U. Richmond, 2000—; vis. prof. George Mason Sch. Law, 2001-02; vis. fellow U. London, 1998-99; chmn. Gov.'s Blue Ribbon Commn. Higher Edn., 1998-2000, Atty. Gen.'s Task Force on Access to Higher Edn., 2003—. Author: Practical Networking: How to Give and Get Help with Jobs, 2001. Bd. visitors Va. Commonwealth U., Richmond, 1994-2002, rector, 2000-02; adv. bd. Va. Ctr. on Aging, Richmond, 1994-98; trustee River Rd. United Meth. Ch., Richmond, 1995-98; bd. VCU Health Sys., 2000-02. With U.S. Army, 1958-61. Mem. Va. State Bar (chmn. adminstrv. law sect., 1986-87), Soc. for Advanced Legal Studies (assoc. fellow). Republican. Avocations: writing, teaching, assisting others in job placements. Office: McGuireWoods LLP One James Ctr 901 E Cary St Richmond VA 23219-4057 E-mail: eflippen@mcguirewoods.com.

FLIPPEN, J. BROOKS, historian, educator; b. Norfolk, Va., Dec. 13, 1959; s. James Howard Flippen, Jr. and Nancy Schults Flippen; m. Celeste deLorge Flippen, Sept. 23, 1989; children: Maya Caroline, Emily Francis. BA, Washington and Lee U., 1982; MA, U. Richmond, 1988; PhD, U. Md., 1994. Secondary sch. tchr. The Hackley Sch., Tarrytown, NY, 1983—84, Trinity Episcopal H.S., Richmond, Va., 1984—86; asst. prof. Southeastern Okla. State U., Durant, 1995—99, assoc. prof., 1999—. Presenter in field. Author: Nixon and the Environment, 2000; contbr. articles to profl. jours. Rsch. grantee, Okla. Humanities Coun., 1987, 2001. Mem.: ACLU, Am. Hist. Assn., Am. Soc. for Environ. History, Orgn. Am. Historians. Democrat. Unitarian. Avocation: running. Home: 2803 Colonial Cir Mc Kinney TX 75070 Office: Dept Social Scis Southeastern Okla State Univ Durant OK 74701

FLIPPO, KAREN FRANCINE, social welfare administrator; b. Chgo., Nov. 19, 1947; d. Irving Albert and Ruth Goldie Feuerstadt; m. Charles Wayne Flippo, Aug. 6, 1978; 1 child, Ian David. BA in Govt., Am. U., 1969; M in Rehab. Adminstrn., U. San Francisco, 1981. Legis. aide Calif. Senate Subcom. on the Disabled, San Francisco, 1980-81; membership svcs. coord. Calif. Life Underwriters Assn., Oakland, 1981-84; project dir. U. San Francisco, 1984-90; sr. rsch. analyst InfoUSE, Berkeley, Calif., 1990-91, 2000; tng. assoc. Va. Commonwealth U., Richmond, 1991-96; dir. best practice initiative United Cerebral Palsy Assn., Washington, 1996-99, COO, 1999; rehab. program specialist Nat. Inst. on Disability and Rehab. Rsch., Dept. Edn., Washington, 2000; v.p. Brain Injury Assn., Alexandria, Va., 2001—03; exec. dir. Nat. Assn. Couns. on Devel. Disabilities, Washington, 2003—. Adv. bd. mem. InfoLines, St. Augustine, Fla., 1995—; bd. mem. Va. Coun. on Assistive Tech., Richmond, 1996-2001, CARF-The Accreditation Commn., Tucson, 1998-2000; dir. spl. projects Assn. for Persons in Supported Employment, Richmond, 1997-98. Lead editor: Assistive Technology: A Resource for School, Home and Community, 1995. Mem. Rehab. Engring. and Assistive Tech. Soc. N.Am., Assn. for Persons in Supported Employment (v.p. bd. dirs. 1993-95). Avocations: travel, reading, golf, community service. Office: Assn Couns on Devel Disabilities 1234 Massachusetts Ave NW Washington DC 20005

FLIPSE, JOHN EDWARD, naval architect, mechanical engineer; b. Montville, N.J., Feb. 4, 1921; SB, MIT, 1942; MME, NYU, 1948. Registered profl. engr., N.Y., Va., Tex. Sr. engr., ship stabilization dept. head, marine div. Sperry Gyroscope Co., Great Neck, N.Y., 1955-57; rsch. engr., dir. rsch., mgr. systems dept., asst. to pres. Newport News (Va.) Shipbuilding and Dry Dock Co., 1957-68; chmn., pres., chief exec. officer Deepsea Ventures, Inc., Gloucester, Va., 1968-77; pres., chief exec. officer Tex. A&M Rsch. Found., College Station, 1983-84; dep. dir. Tex. Engring. Experiment Sta., 1985-88; disting. prof. civil and ocean engring. Tex. A&M U., 1982-92, assoc. dean engring., 1984-88, assoc. dep. chancellor for engring., 1984-89, Wofford Cain prof. engring., 1988-91, dir. Offshore Tech. Rsch. Ctr., 1988-91, dir. emeritus, 1991—2000. Chmn. Nat. Adv. Com. on Oceans and Atmosphere, 1985-86; mem. marine bd. Nat. Rsch. Coun., 1979-84, chmn., 1982-84; mem. marine facilities panel U.S./Japan Coop. Program in Natural Resources, 1980-86; mem. marine petroleum and minerals adv. com. Dept. Commerce, 1974-75; expert mem. U.S. delegation to Law of the Sea Conf., UN, 1975-76; cons., lectr. in field. Contbr. articles to profo. publs., patentee in field. Mem. dean's adv. coun. Sch. Engring. & Applied Sci., U. Va., 1995-98. Fellow Marine Tech. Soc. (pres. 1985-87), Soc. Naval Architects and Marine Engrs. (past chmn. tech. and rsch. steering com.); mem. Nat. Acad. Engring. (membership policy com. 1987-90, membership com. 1987-90, peer rev. com. 1985-86), Va. Inst. Marine Sci. (vice chmn. bd. dirs. 1968-76).

FLISS, ALBERT EDWARD, JR., molecular biologist; b. Harrisburg, Pa., Nov. 8, 1959; s. Albert Edward and Irene (Pierlioni) F.; m. Makiko Suzuki Fliss, Sept. 10, 1994; children: Nicholas, Yuri. BS, U. Ctrl. Fla., 1982; MS, Mount Sinai Sch. Medicine, 1997, PhD, 1998. Rsch. assoc. USDA, Orlando, Fla., 1984-85; biol. scientist U. Fla., Gainesville, 1985-88, USDA, Gainesville, 1988-89; rsch. assoc. U. Fla., Gainesville, 1989, sr. biologist, 1989-92; sr. scientist BioNebraska, Inc., Lincoln, Nebr., 1992; rsch. assoc. Tex. A&M U., College Station, 1992—93; rsch. scientist Regeneron Pharm., Tarrytown, N.Y., 1993-95, U. Md. Sch. Medicine, 1998-2001; postdoctoral scientist Mt. Sinai/NYU Sch. Medicine, 2001—03; CEO, pres. Secregen Pharm. and Fipco Cons., 2001—03. CEO, pres. Designer Genes, Inc., Gainesville, 1990-93; dirs. biotech. rsch. lab. Taro Pharm. USA Inc., 1993—. Contbr. articles to profl. jours. Recipient Superior Accomplishment award U. Fla., 1990. Mem. Lambda Chi Alpha, Omicron Delta Kappa. Democrat. Roman Catholic. Home: 36 Senior Ave Mahopac NY 10541 E-mail: designdna1@cs.com.

FLITCRAFT, RICHARD KIRBY, II, former chemical company executive; b. Woodstown, N.J., Sept. 5, 1920; s. H. Milton and Edna (Crispin) F.; m. Bertha LeSturgeon Hitchner, Nov. 14, 1942; children: Alyce, Anne, Elizabeth, Richard. BS, Rutgers U., 1942; MS, Washington U., 1948. With Monsanto Co., St. Louis, 1942—, dir. inorganic rsch., 1960-65, dir. mgmt. info. and systems dept., 1965-67, asst. to pres., 1967-68, group mgr. electronics enterprises, 1968-69, gen. mgr. electronic products div., 1969-71; v.p. Monsanto Rsch. Corp., 1971-75; dir. Mound Lab., 1971-75, v.p. ops., 1975-76; pres. Monsanto Resh. Corp., Dayton, 1976-82, ret., 1982. Past chmn., bd. dirs. United Way, Dayton; bd. dirs. City-Wide Devel. Corp.; former trustee and chmn. bd. Miami Valley Hosp.; past bd. dirs. Pvt. Industry Coun., Srs., Inc.; chmn. bd. Headstart program Miami Valley Child Devel., Inc. Mem. AAAS, AICE, Am. Chem. Soc., Am. Inst. Chemists, Am. Mgmt. Assn., N.Y. Acad. Scis., Ohio Acad. Scis. (past exec. com.), Dayton C. of C. (past bd. dirs., chmn. small bus. adv. bd., mil. affairs com.), Engrs. Club of Dayton (past bd. dirs.), Engrs. Club Dayton Found. (bd. trustees, chmn.), Moraine Country Club, Dayton Racquet Club. Presbyterian.

FLITNER, ANDREAS HERMANN, education educator; b. Jena, Thuringen, Germany, Sept. 28, 1922; s. Wilhelm and Elisabeth (Czapski) F.; m. Sonia Christ, Aug. 14, 1950; children: Elisabeth, Margarete, Cornelia, Christine, Michael, Ursula, Gabriele. Tchr. degree, U. Hamburg, 1950; MA, PhD, U. Basle, 1951; Dr. habil., U. Tubingen, 1955. Lectr. dept. German lang. U. Cambridge, Eng., 1950-51; asst., lectr. Leibniz-Kolleg, U. Tubingen, 1951-53; prof. edn. U. Erlangen, 1956-58, U. Tubingen, 1958-88; hon. prof. U. Jena, 1991—. Author: Konrad...Uber Erziehung und Nicht-Erziehung, 1985, 10th edit., 2000, Für das Leben oder für die Schule? Pädagog u polit Essays, 1987, Reform der Erziehung - Impulse des 20 Jahrhunderts, 1992, 5th rev. edit., 2001; editor: Wilhelm von Humboldt: Werke in fünf Bänden, 5 vols., 2002; co-editor: Wege aus der Ausbildungskrise, 1999, Optik-Technik-Soziale Kultur: Siegfried Czapski, Weggefährte und Nachfolger Ernst Abbes, 2000. Mem. Akademie fur Bildungsreform Akademie gemeinn. Wissenschaften Erfurt, Academia Europaea, London. Home: Im Rotbad 43 72076 Tübingen Germany

FLITTIE, CLIFFORD GILLILAND, retired petroleum company executive; b. Brookings, S.D., Mar. 10, 1924; s. Theodore Ignatius and Grace Eliza (Gilliland) F.; m. Dawn Marie Lee, May 22, 1954. Student, Okla. State U., 1944, Colo. Sch. Mines, 1946; BS (Nat. scholar Am. Inst. Mining and Metall. Engrs.), S.D. Sch. Mines and Tech., 1948. Geologist Arabian Am. Oil Co., Dhahran, Saudi Arabia, 1948-57; v.p. exploration Conorada Petroleum Corp., N.Y.C., 1958-63, dir., 1963-65; v.p., mgr. Amerada Petroleum Corp. of U.K., London, 1964-65, Amerada Petroleum Corp. of Australia, Brisbane, 1966-69; exploration supr. Amerada Hess Corp., N.Y.C., 1970-73; v.p. Shaheen Natural Resources Co., Inc., N.Y.C., 1974-75, Macmillan Oil Co., N.Y.C., 1975-82, Natomas Co., San Francisco, 1982-86. Dir. Amerada Exploration Ltd., 1964-65 Served with USNR, 1944-46. Mem. Am. Assn. Petroleum Geologists, Soc. Exploration Geophysicists, Theta Tau, Sigma Tau. Episcopalian. Home: 46 San Jacinto Way San Francisco CA 94127-2033

FLOCH, MARTIN HERBERT, physician; b. N.Y.C., July 24, 1928; s. Samuel and Jean (Scheinman) F.; m. Gladys Wisser, Nov. 24, 1954; children: Jeffrey Aaron, Craig Lawrence, Lisa Suzanne, Neil Robert. BA, NYU, 1949; MS, U. N.H., 1950; MD, N.Y. Med. Coll., 1956. Diplomate: Am. Bd. Internal Medicine, Am. Bd. Gastroenterology Am. Bd. Nutrition. Intern Beth Israel Hosp., N.Y.C., 1956-57, resident in medicine, 1957-59; fellow in gastroenterology Seton Hall Coll. Medicine, South Orange, N.J., 1959-60; instr. medicine U. P.R., 1960-62; asst. attending physician Montefiore Hosp., N.Y.C., 1962-64; practice medicine specializing in gastroenterology Norwalk, Conn., 1962—; mem. staff Norwalk Hosp., 1964—, chmn. dept. medicine, 1970-94, chief gastroenterology and nutrition, 1970-98; clin. prof. medicine Yale U., New Haven, 1976—. Bd. dirs. Norwalk Bank, 1987. Editor Am. Jour. Gastroenterology, 1985-91, The Gastroenterologist, 1992-98; asst. editor Am. Jour. Clin. Nutrition; editor-in-chief Jour. of Clin. Gastroenterology, 1998—; contbr. articles in field to profl. jours. Trustee Aspetuck Valley Health Dist., 1974-76, Norwalk Hosp., 1972-78. Served with M.C. U.S. Army, 1960-62. Grantee, Conn. Digestive Disease Soc., 1974—76, NIH, 1975—78, Leslie Found., 1980, Ednl. Found. Am., 1989—92, 2001—03; U.S. Army Med. Rsch. grantee, 1964—67. Fellow ACP, Master Am. Coll. Gastroenterology (bd. trustees 1985-90), Am. Soc. Gastroendoscopy, Am. Coll. Nutrition; mem. Am. Soc. Clin. Nutrition, Am. Inst. Nutrition, Am. Gastroenterology Assn. (clin. counselor governing bd. 1997-2000), Am. Soc. Internal Medicine, Am. Fedn. Clin. Rsch., Fairfield County Med. Soc., Conn. Med. Soc. (pres. gastroenterology sect. 1972-74), Assn. Am. Med. Coll., Conn. Digestive Disease Soc. (pres. 1972-74). Home: 32 Woody Ln Westport CT 06880-2259 Office: Norwalk Hosp 30 Stevens St Norwalk CT 06850-3859

FLOCK, HOWARD, psychology educator; b. Phila., Nov. 24, 1924; s. Salomon and Della (Buschel) F. BA, Yale U., 1944; MA, Harvard U., 1958; PhD, Cornell U., 1962. Asst. prof. CUNY, 1961-64; assoc. prof. Dartmouth Coll., 1964-65, York U., Toronto, Ont., Can., 1965-70, prof. psychology, 1970—. Contbr. articles to profl. publs., chpts. to books, also to films. Lt. (j.g.) USN, 1943-45, ETO. Grantee NSF, NSERC, NRC Can., 1964-82. Fellow APA; mem. Psychonomic Soc., Ea. Psychol. Assn., Harvard Club. Avocations: skiing, travel, films, photography. Home: 20 W 64th St New York NY 10023-7180 Office: York U Dept Psychology North York ON Canada M3J 1P3 E-mail: hrflock@aol.com.

FLOCK, JEFFREY CHARLES, news bureau chief; b. Lakewood, N.J., Mar. 16, 1958; s. Byron Harry and Vicki Ruth (Macaulay) F.; m. Elizabeth Brack, Sept. 19, 1998; children: Elizabeth Kathryn, Emily Macaulay. BS in Broadcast Journalism, Boston U., 1980. Writer, producer Cable News Network, Atlanta, 1980-81, corr. Chgo., 1981-84, bur. chief, 1985—. Methodist. Avocations: running, antiques. Office: Cable News Network 435 N Michigan Ave Ste 715 Chicago IL 60611-4008

FLOCKHART, CALISTA, actress; b. Freeport, Ill., Nov. 11, 1964; d. Ronald and Kay F. BA in acting, Rutgers U. Actress Ally McBeal Twentieth Century Fox, L.A. Appeared in Broadway plays, including The Glass Menagerie, The Three Sisters; television work includes; The Guiding Light, 1978, Darrow, 1991, Ally McBeal, 1997-2002; film work includes; Quiz Show, 1994, Getting In, 1994, Naked in New York, 1994, Pictures of Baby Jane Doe, 1996, The Birdcage, 1996, Milk and Money, 1997, Drunks, 1997, Telling Lies in America, 1997, A Midsummer Night's Dream, 1999, Like a Hole in the Head, 1999, Jane Doe, 1999. Recipient Best Actress award Golden Globes, 1998 for her work on Ally McBeal. Office: Ally McBeal c/o David E Kelly Productions c/o Twentieth Century Fox 10201 W Pico Blvd Bldg 80 Los Angeles CA 90064-2606

FLOHR, CHARLES E. radiologist; b. Scottsbluff, Nebr., Dec. 18, 1950; s. Emanuel and Bertha Flohr; m. Diane Flohr, Nov. 2, 1974; children: Dana M., Jamie K. BS, U. Nebr., 1973, MD, 1977. Diplomate Am. Bd. Radiology. Intern and resident in diagnostic radiology U. Nebr. Med. Ctr., Omaha, 1977-81; radiologist St. Joseph's Hosp., Mitchell, S.D., 1981-89, Region West Med. Ctr., Scottsbluff, 1989-92; staff radiologist St. Luke's Regional Med. Ctr., Sioux City, Iowa, 1992-99, Mercy Hosp., Iowa City, 1999—2001; pvt. practice, Coralville, Iowa, 1999—2001, Sioux Falls, SD, 2001—. Office: Med X-Ray Ctr 1417 S Minnesota Ave Sioux Falls SD 57105

FLOM, EDWARD LEONARD, retired steel company executive; b. Tampa, Fla., Dec. 10, 1929; s. Samuel Louis and Julia (Mittle) F.; m. Beverly Boyett, Mar. 31, 1956; children— Edward Louis, Mark Robert, Julia Ruth. B.C.E., Cornell U., 1952. With Fla. Steel Corp., Tampa, 1954-93, v.p. sales, 1957-64, pres., dir., 1964-93, ret., 1993. Bd. dirs., mem. exec. com. Com. of 100, Tampa, United Fund Tampa; mem. adv. com. St. Joseph's Hosp., Tampa; bd. dirs. Family Svc. Assn. Tampa, Jewish Welfare Fedn. Tampa; bd. dirs. temple. With C.E., U.S. Army, 1952-54. Mem. Am. Iron and Steel Inst. (bd. dirs.), Fla. Engring. Soc., Young Pres. Orgn., Univ. Club, Palma Ceia Golf and Country Club, Tampa Yacht Club, Gasparilla Krewe, Rotary (bd. dirs. Tampa). Home: 4936 Saint Croix Dr Tampa FL 33629-4831

FLOM, GERALD TROSSEN, lawyer; b. Neenah, Wis., Feb. 6, 1930; s. Russell Craig and Lois Eva (Trossen) F.; m. Martha Herrington Benton, Aug. 21, 1954 (div. June 25, 1980); children— Katherine Simmons, Sarah Elizabeth Kiecker, Russell Craig. BA magna cum laude, Lawrence U., 1952; JD, Yale U., 1957. Bar: Minn. 1957, U.S. Dist. Ct. Minn. 1957. Assoc. Faegre & Benson LLP, Mpls., 1957-64, ptnr., 1964-95; retired, 1995. Adj. asst. prof. Law Sch., U. Minn., Mpls., 1966, bd. dirs., Old Republic Natl. Title Holding Co. and Old Republic Natl. Title Ins. Co., 1977-99. Mem. editorial bd. Yale Law Jour. Trustee Mpls. Soc. Fine Arts, 1970-76, Lawrence U., 1974-81, Plymouth Congl. Ch., 1978-81, William Mitchell Coll. Law, St. Paul, 1983-89; bd. dirs. Met. Med. Ctr. Research Found., Mpls., 1975-85. Served with U.S. Army, 1952-54 Mem. ABA, Minn. State Bar Assn., Hennepin County Bar Assn., Assn. Bar City of N.Y., Mace, Mpls. Club, Interlachen Country Club (Edina, Minn.), Phi Beta Kappa, Phi Delta Theta, Phi Alpha Delta. Congregationalist. Home: 3434 Zenith Ave S Minneapolis MN 55416-4663 Office: Faegre & Benson LLP 2200 Wells Fargo Ctr 90 S 7th St Minneapolis MN 55402-3901

FLOM, JOSEPH HAROLD, lawyer, director; b. Balt., Dec. 20, 1923; s. Isadore and Fannie (Fishman) Flom; m. Claire Cohen, Nov. 14, 1958; children: Peter Leslie, Jason Robert. Student, CCNY, 1948; LLB cum laude, Harvard U. Law Sch., 1948; LHD (hon.), Queens Coll., 1984; LLD (hon.), Fordham U., 1990. Practice of law, N.Y.C., 1949—. Spl. counsel subcom. on admisntrn. of internal revenue laws House Ways and Means Com. Editor Harvard Law Rev., 1947—48; co-editor: Disclosure Requirements of Public Corporations and Insiders, 1967, Texas Gulf Sulphur-Insider Disclosure Problems, 1968, Lawyer's Conflicts-The Evolving Case Law, 1991. Mem. N.Y.C. Mayor's Commn. on Status of Women, 1976—77, Mayor's Coun. Econ. Advisors, N.Y.C., 1990—93; co-chmn. task force on capital fin. and constrn. N.Y.C. Bd. Edn., 1987—89; chmn. N.Y.C. Commn. on Bicentennial of Constn., 1986—89; trustee Fedn. J ewish Philanthropies N.Y., 1977—89, Barnard Coll., 1983—93, N.Y. Hist. Soc., 1989—94; chair adv. com. Export-Import Bank of U.S., 1995; trustee Mt. Sinai-NYU Health Sys., 1978—99, Petrie Stores Liquidating Trust, Skadden Fellowship Found., Constl. Edn. Found., 1989—93, United Way N.Y.C., 1991—97; mayor's rep. Met. Mus. Art, 1990—93; mem. mayor's Mgmt. Adv. Task Force, 1991—93; chair Woodrow Wilson Internat. Ctr. for Scholars, 1994—98; mem. Archdiocesan Task Force on Crime Prevention and Youth, 1982—87. Mem.: Assn. Bar City N.Y. Office: Skadden Arps Slate 4 Times Sq Fl 41 New York NY 10036-6522

FLOOD, ANGELA, interior designer, artist; b. N.Y.C., Jan. 22, 1945; d. Americo Montes and Candace M. Hansen; m. Oscar William Rocafort, June 2, 1963 (div.); 1 child, Angélique Rocafort Ward; m. Steven Arthur Flood, June 12, 1988. Student, NYU, 1965—66, Pace U., 1973—76; AAS, Suffolk C.C., 1992. Artist, curator F.O.R.E., Bedford, NY, 1976—86; owner, designer A&S Interiors, Westhampton Beach, NY, 1992—. Exhibitions include Easthampton (N.Y.) Town Hall, 2001, Westhampton Beach Libr., 2002, Southampton RML Gallery, 2003, Southampton Guild Hall Mus., 2003. Counselor ARC, White Plains, NY, 1974—77. Republican. Avocations: horseback riding, kayaking, canoeing, sailing, skiing. Office: A&S Interiors PO Box 413 Westhampton Beach NY 11978 E-mail: lilly11967@yahoo.com.

FLOOD, DIANE LUCY, retired marketing professional; b. Plainfield, N.J., June 13, 1937; d. William Edward and Lucy (Dycker) Flood. BA, Vassar Coll., 1959; postgrad., Fontainebleau Sch. Fine Arts, France, 1961. Advt. prodn. aide indsl. chem. divsn. Am. Cyanamid Co., Wayne, N.J., 1959-62, prodn. supr., 1962-64, creative coord. organic chems. divsn. advt., 1964-66, design art and copy mgr., 1966-70, advt. rep., 1970-72, advt. rep. paper, process chems. and resins, indsl. chem. divsn., 1972-77, advt. coord. water treating, mining, paper, oil recovery chems., 1977-83, mgr. mktg. comms. indsl. products div., 1983—, mgr. mktg. comms. Venture Chems. divsn., 1986-87, Chem. Products and Indsl. Products divsn., 1987-89, mgr. mktg. comms. Chem. Products Indsl. Products and Interna, 1989-90, mgr. mktg. comms. Chem. Group, 1990-93; mgr. Global Mktg. Comms. Cytec Industries Inc., West Paterson, N.J., 1993-99, retired, 1999. Comms. cons. 1999—. Past dir., v.p., past pres. 103 Gedney St. Owners Co-op, 1985-92; mem. consistory First Reformed Ch., Nyack, N.Y. Mem. 1st Ref. Ch. Home: 103 Gedney St Apt 3C Nyack NY 10960-2227 Office: 103 Gedney St Lbby Office Nyack NY 10960-2227

FLOOD, DOROTHY GARNETT, neuroscientist; m. Paul David Coleman, Feb. 26, 1983. BA cum laude, Lawrence U., 1973; student, U. Ill., 1972-73; MS, PhD, U. Rochester, N.Y., 1980. Sr. instr. in anatomy U. Rochester, 1980-83, asst. prof. neurology, neurobiology and anatomy, 1984-90, assoc. prof. neurology, neurobiology and anatomy, 1990-94; sr. sci. Cephalon, Inc., West Chester,

Pa., 1994—. Contbr. to book chpts. and articles in field; mem. editl. bd. Neurobiology of Aging, 1989—. Recipient Fenn award U. Rochester, 1980; grantee NSF, NIH, Office of Naval Rsch., 1979-94. Mem. Soc. Neurosci. Office: Cephalon Inc 145 Brandywine Pkwy West Chester PA 19380-4249 E-mail: dflood@cephalon.com.

FLOOD, GREGORY CHARLES, human resources management specialist; b. Yonkers, N.Y., Sept. 4, 1946; arrived in Italy, 1980; s. Harold Austin and Anne Marie (Wallace) F.; m. Catherine Virginia Predham, Dec. 9, 1967. BS, SUNY, Albany, 1973. Personnel tech. Rensselaer County Civil Svc. Commn., 1974-77; from personnel adminstr. to assoc. program budget coord. N.Y. State Dept. Edn., Albany, 1977-80; establishments officer to chief human resources policy, planning and sys. svc. FAO, UN, Rome, 1980—, sec. fin. com., 1998—. Pres. East Greenbush (N.Y.) Rep. Club, 1974; vol. firefighter East Greenbush Fire Dept., 1974-80. With USN, 1966-70. Mem.: Assn. for Human Resources Mgmt. in Internat. Orgns., Internat. Pers. Mgmt. Assn., Am. Soc. Pub. Adminstrn., Am. Internat. Club Rome (treas. 1995—96, pres. 1996—98). Roman Catholic. Avocations: reading, computer programming, badminton, stage craft. Home: Via dei Pescatori 983/E/1 00125 Rome Italy Office: Food and Agriculture Orgn UN Via delle Terme di Caracalla 00100 Rome Italy E-mail: gregoryflood@mac.com ., gregory.flood@fao.org.

FLOOD, H(ULDA) GAY, editor, consultant; b. Plainfield, N.J., Aug. 14, 1935; d. William Edward and Lucy (Dycker) Flood. BA, Smith Coll., 1957. With picture dept. Sports Illustrated, Time Inc., N.Y.C., 1957-58, with letters dept., 1958-59, reporter, 1959-60, writer-reporter, 1960-71, assoc. editor, 1971-85, sr. editor, 1985-90. Mem. Greater Consistory First Reformed Ch., Nyack, NY. Mem.: Smith Coll. Students Aid Soc., Alumnae Assn. Smith Coll., Garden Club Nyack (chair cmty. flower show 2001), Smith Coll. Club N.Y. Office: 103 Gedney St Apt 3C Nyack NY 10960-2227

FLOOD, JAMES DUNCAN, music educator; b. Sanford, Maine, Jan. 14, 1946; s. Ernest Cecil Flood and Flood Evelyn (Avery); m. Donna Marie Reisdorf, Dec. 3, 1988; children: Heather, Deborah, Kelly, Christine. BA in Music, Syracuse U., N.Y., 1969. Pres. Poppenberg's Inc., Amherst, NY, 1976—88; dir. music First Bapt. Ch., Niagara Falls, NY, 1988—99; artistic dir. and prin. condr. Niagara Symphony Orch., Niagara Falls, 1991—; tchr. music and drama Villa Maria Acad., Buffalo, 2000—; minister of music Univ. Presbyn. Ch., Buffalo, 2001—. Organ recitalist, 1962—; piano and organ instr. Villa Maria Coll., Buffalo, 2002—. Condr. (cassette tape) Mendelssohn: St. Paul Oratorio, 1991; performer: (compact disc) The American Impressionist Organ, 1995. Fellow, Wessex Theol. Coll., 1989, Cambridge Soc. Musicians, 1992. Mem.: Organ Hist. Soc., Am. Guild of Organists, Phi Mu Alpha (life). Avocations: woodworking, book collecting, collecting organ historical materials. Home: Cantabile House 5010 Salt Rd Clarence NY 14031-1710 Office: University Presbyn Church 3330 Main St Buffalo NY 14214

FLOOD, JAMES TYRRELL, broadcasting executive, public relations consultant; b. L.A., Oct. 5, 1934; s. James Joseph and Teresa (Rielly) F.; m. Bonnie Carolyn Lutz, Mar. 25, 1966; children: Hilary C., Sean L. BA in Liberal Arts, U. Calif., Santa Barbara, 1956; MA in Comms., Calif. State U., Chico, 1981. Publicist Rogers & Cowan, 1959-60, Jim Mahoney & Assocs., 1960-61, ABC-TV, San Francisco, Hollywood, Calif., 1961-64; cons. pub. rels. Beverly Hills, Calif., 1964-72; pub. rels. and advt. dir. Jerry Lewis Films, 1964-72; dir. pub. rels. MTM Prodns., 1970-72; pub. rels. cons. Medic Alert Found. Internat., 1976-83; owner mgr. Sta. KRIJ-FM, Paradise, 1983-88; instr. Calif. State U. Sch. Comms., Chico, 1982-89; gen. mgr. KIXE-TV (PBS), Redding-Chico, Calif., 1991-92; media cons., 1993—. Represented numerous artists including Pearl Bailey, Gary Owens, Ruth Buzzi, Allen Ludden, Betty White, Celeste Holm, Jose Feliciano, Tom Kennedy, Shirley Jones, David Cassidy, others; pub. rels. dir. Warren Miller Prodns., 1967—, Mary Tyler Moore Prodns., 1971. Calif. media cons. Carter/Mondale campaign, 1976; mem. Calif. Dem. Fin. Com., 1982-83. Served with USNR, 1956-58. Mem. Calif. Broadcasters Assn. (bd. dirs. 1986-88). E-mail: xsh2oj@earthlink.net.

FLOOD, JOAN MOORE, paralegal; b. Hampton, Va., Oct. 10, 1941; d. Harold W. and Estalena (Fancher) M.; 1 child by former marriage, Angelique. B.Mus., North Tex. State U., 1963; postgrad., So. Meth. U., 1967-68, Tex. Women's U., 1978-79, U. Dallas, 1985-86. Clk. Criminal Dist. Ct. Number 2, Dallas County, Tex., 1972-75; reins. libr. Scor Reins. Co., Dallas, 1975-80; corp. ins. paralegal Assocs. Inc. Group, 1980-83; corp. securities paralegal Akin, Gump, Strauss, Hauer & Feld, 1983-89; asst. sec. Knoll Internat. Holdings Inc., Saddle Brook, N.J., 1989-90, 21 Internat. Holdings, Inc., N.Y.C., 1990-92; dir. compliance Am. Svc. Life Ins. Co., Ft. Worth, 1992-93; v.p., sec. Express Comm., Inc., Dallas, 1993-94; fin. transactions paralegal Thompson & Knight, Dallas, 1994-96; corp. transactions paralegal Jones, Day, Reavis & Pogue, Dallas, 1996-97, Weil, Gotshal & Manges, LLP, 1998—99; corp. paralegal PennCorp. Fin. Group, Inc., Dallas, 1999-2001; debt trade mgr. Patton Boggs LLP, Dallas, 2001—03, bus. transactions sr. paralegal, 2003—, sr. paralegal bus. transactions, 2003—. Mem. ABA, Tex. Bar Assn. Home: PO Box 190165 Dallas TX 75219-0165 E-mail: jflood@pattonboggs.com.

FLOOD, PATRICK CHRISTOPHER, business educator, researcher, corporate speaker; b. Drogheda, Leinster, Ireland, Apr. 22, 1961; s. Bartholomew and Catherine (Ellis) F.; m. Patricia Mary Quinn; children: Christopher, Patrick Ellis. B.Comm., U. Coll. Dublin, 1981, M.BS, 1982; PhD, London Sch. Econs., 1988; internat. tchrs. program cert., London Bus. Sch., 1998. Brit. coun. scholar London Sch. Econs., 1984-86; lectr., sr. lectr. U. Limerick, 1986-93, assoc. prof. orgnl. behaviour, human resource mgmt., 1997—2002, prof. orgnl. behavior, head joint rsch. program Irish Mgmt. Inst., 1994—; rsch. fellow in orgnl. behavior London Sch. Bus., 1994—; invited vis. assoc. prof. Australian Grad. Sch. of Mgmt. Mem. editl. bd. Bus. Strategy Rev., 1996—. Co-author: Pers. Mgmt. in Ireland, 1990, Continuity and Change in Employee Rels. in Ireland, 1994, Mng. Without Traditional Methods, 1996, The European Union and the Employment Relationship, 1997, Mng. Strategy Implementation, 2000, Attracting and Retaining Knowledge Workers, 2000, Effective Top Mgmt. Teams, 2001. Fulbright scholar, U. Md., 1993, Human Capital and Mobility scholar European Commn., London Bus. Sch., 1994-96; recipient Award for Excellence in Rsch. U. Limerick, 1998, Tchg. Distinction award, 1998. Mem. Strategic Mgmt. Soc., Acad. of Mgmt., Friends of LSE in Ireland (chair). Roman Catholic. Avocations: walking, oil painting, swimming, travel, gardening, fishing. Office: University of Limerick Plassey Park Limerick Ireland E-mail: patrick.flood@ul.ie.

FLOOD, PATRICK JAMES, political scientist, writer, retired diplomat; b. Zanesville, Ohio, July 1, 1939; s. Patrick Edward and Anita Helen (Norman) Flood; m. Anita Louise Rizzardi, Aug. 18, 1962; children: John, Mary-Catherine, Pauline, Anita, Patrick, Stephen. Student, Xavier U., 1955—57; AB, Providence Coll., 1959; MA in History, Georgetown U., 1964; PhD in Polit. Sci., U. Mass., 1995. Fgn. svc. officer Dept. of State, Washington, 1962—88; acad. advisor U. Mass., Amherst, 1993—94, lectr., 1996—; vis. lectr. Budapest (Hungary) Econs. U., 1994—95; lectr. Elms Coll., Chicopee, Mass., 1997—98. Author: The Effectiveness of UN Human Rights Institutions, 1998; contbr. chapters to books, articles to jours. and profl. publs. Vice chmn. Mass. Citizens for Life Polit. Action Com., 1998—2002; del. Rep. State Conv., Mass., 2002; mem. Rep. City Com., Holyoke, 1997—; del. Rep. State Conv., Mass., 1998; bd. dirs. Mass. Citizens for Life, 1997—2000, 2002—03. Mem.: Am. Assn. for Advancement of Slavic Studies, Am. Polit. Sci. Assn., Univ. Faculty for Life. Republican. Roman Catholic. Avocations: travel, political campaigning, hiking, swimming, golf.

FLOOD, SANDRA WASKO, artist, educator; b. N.Y.C., Mar. 12, 1943; d. Peter Edmund Wasko and Margaret Dalores Kubek; m. Michael Timothy Flood, June 28, 1969. BA in English, U. Calif., L.A., 1965; postgrad., Museo de Arte Moderno, Rio de Janeiro, 1970-73, U. Wis., 1977-78. Std. secondary tchg. credential L.A. State Coll., 1966. English, journalism instr. Nobel Jr. High, Northridge, Calif., 1967-69; ESL instr. U.S.-Brazil Inst., Rio de Janeiro, 1972-73; pvt. practice printmaking instr. Alexandria, Va., 1979—. Pub. rels. dir. Washington Women's Art Ctr., 1980; artist-in-residence U. Md., College Park, 1984; printmaking instr. St. Mary's City, St. Mary's City, Md., 1985; workshop coord. Lee Arts Ctr., Arlington (Va.) County Cultural Affairs, 1989—97; v.p. Gallery 10, Washington, 1995—97; program chair Women's Caucus for Art D.C. Chpt., 1998—99; founder The Labyrinth Soc. Internat. Orgn., 1998—99. Exhibitions include Phillips Collection, Washington, 1988, St. Peter's Ch., N.Y.C., 1989, Bookchamber Internat., Moscow, 1990, Montpelier Cultural Arts Ctr., Laurel, Md., 1992, Peninsula Fine Arts Ctr., Newport News, Va., 1995, Gallery 10, Washington, 1994, 1996, exhibited in group shows at Sch. 33 Installation Space, Balt., 1996, exhibitions include The Nat. Mus. Women in the Arts, Washington, 1996, Corcoran Gallery Art, 1999, Charles Sumner Sch. Mus., 2000, Millennium Ctr., 2001, Rockville (Md.) Arts Pl., 2002. Mem. Ylem Artists Using Sci. and Tech., Washington, 2002—03, Art Sci. Collaborative Inc., N.Y.C., 2002—03. Named Best of Show, Artists Equity D.C., Washington, 1997; Individual Artists fellow Va. Commn. for the Arts, Richmond, 1994; grantee Friends of the Torpedo Factory, Alexandria, Va., 1989. Mem.: Washington Project for the Arts, Md. Printmakers, N.Am. Print Alliance, Women's Caucus for Art (program chair), Washington Sculptor's Group. Avocations: creative writing, classical music, hiking. Home: 8106 Norwood Dr Alexandria VA 22309-1331 Studio: 57 N Street Fine Arts 57 N St NW Washington DC 20001-1254 E-mail: sandra@waskoart.com.

FLOOD, SUSAN J.A. marketing strategist; b. Yonkers, N.Y., Jan. 5, 1961; BA, Cornell U., 1983; postgrad., U. Calif., Davis, 1983—87. Scientist DNA Plant Tech., Berkeley, Calif., 1987—89, Cetus Corp., Emeryville, Calif., 1989—92; marketing scientist Applied Biosystems, Foster City, Calif., 1992—99; nat. marketing dir. MWG Biotech, High Point, NC, 1999—2000; marketing specialist SciQuest, Morrisville, NC, 2000—01; marketing mgr. SAS, Cary, NC, 2001—. Contbr. articles to profl. jours. Mem.: AAAS, Drug Info. Assn. Achievements include patents in field. Office: SAS Inst SAS Campus Dr Cary NC 27513 E-mail: susan.flood@sas.com.

FLOOR, RICHARD EARL, lawyer; b. Lynn, Mass., Aug. 3, 1940; s. Albert C. and Blanche (Goldthwait) F.; m. Elizabeth Wilson, Apr. 19, 1969; children: Amy, Lucy, Rebecca. AB, Fairfield U., 1962; JD, Harvard Law Sch., 1965. Bar: Mass. 1965, N.Y. 2001. Law clk. to Hon. C.P. O'Sullivan U.S. Ct. Appeals (6th cir.), 1965-66; assoc. Goodwin, Procter & Hoar, Boston, 1966-74, ptnr., 1974 , mem. mgmt. com., exec. com., 1987-93. Lectr. Harvard Bus. Sch., Cambridge, 1988-92; bd. dirs. Affiliated Mgrs. Group, Inc., New Am. High Income Fund, NYSE. Contbr. articles to profl. jours. Co-chmn. reverse investment com. internat. trade adv. bd. Commonwealth Mass., 1994; organizer Inst. Mgmt. Edn. Thailand; trustee Regis Coll., Wellesley, Mass., 1990-97, 99-; chmn. Harvard Ctr. Eating Disorders, 2000-01. Mem. ABA, Boston Bar Assn. Office: Goodwin Procter & Hoar LLP Exchange Pl Boston MA 02109-2803

FLOR, LOY LORENZ, retired chemist, corrosion engineer, consultant; b. Luther, Okla., Apr. 25, 1919; s. Alfred Charles and Nellie M. (Wilkinson) F.; m. Virginia Louise Pace, Oct. 1, 1946; children: Charles R., Scott R., Gerald C., Donna Jeanne, Cynthia Gail. BA in Chemistry, San Diego State Coll., 1941. Registered profl. engr., Calif. With Helix Water Dist., La Mesa, Calif., 1947-84, chief chemist, 1963-2001, supr. water quality, 1963-2001, supr. corrosion control dept., 1956-2001; ret. 1st lt. USAAF, 1941-45. Mem. Am. Chem. Soc. (chmn. San Diego sect. 1965—), Am. Water Works Assn. (chmn. water quality divsn. Calif. sect. 1965—), Nat. Assn. Corrision Engrs. (chmn. western region 1970), Masons. Republican.

FLORA, JAIRUS DALE, JR., statistician; b. Northfield, Minn., Mar. 27, 1944; s. Jairus Dale and Betty Ruth (Garvin) F.; m. Sharyl Ann Hughes, Aug. 18, 1967; 1 child, Edward Hughes BS magna cum laude, Midland Luth. Coll., 1965; postgrad., Tech. U. Karlsruhe, Fed. Republic Germany, 1965-66; MS, Fla. State U., 1968, PhD, 1971. Asst. prof. biostats Sch. Pub. Health U. Mich., Ann Arbor, 1971-73, asst. prof., asst. rsch. scientist Hwy. Safety Rsch. Inst., 1973-76, assoc. rsch. scientist Hwy. Safety Rsch. Inst., 1976-81, assoc. prof. biostats. Sch. Pub. Health, 1976-81, prof. biostats. Sch. Pub. Health, rsch. scientist Transp. Rsch. Inst., 1981-84; prin. statistician Midwest Rsch. Inst, Kansas City, Mo., 1984-90; sr. advisor for stats. Midwest Rsch. Inst., Kansas City, Mo., 1991-99, pres. coun. prin. scientists, 1986; clin. prof. biostats. Sch. Medicine U. Mo., Kansas City, 1984—; prin. statistician Ken Wilcox Assocs., Inc., Grain Valley, Mo., 1999, statis. cons., 1999—. Cons. statistician Nat. Burn Info. Exchange, 1971-76 Editorial collaborator Annals of Thoracic Surgery, Mathematical Bioscis., Biometrics, Accident Analysis and Prevention, 1979-90; contbr. articles to profl. jours.; patentee in field. Mem. adminstrn. bd. Valley View U. Meth. Ch., 1989-92; vol. leader Boy Scouts Am. Recipient CPS Enterprise award, 1985, Dir.'s award, 1987; German Acad. Exch. Svc. fellow, 1965-66; NASA trainee, 1966-69; NIH trainee, 1969-71; Nat Hwy. Traffic Safety Adminstrn. rsch. grantee, 1974-81. Mem. Am. Statis. Assn., Biometric Soc., Inst. Math. Stats., Masons, Scottish Rite, Blue Key, Sigma Xi (pres. Kansas City chpt. 1990-91, v.p. 1994-96). Republican. Home: 9921 Foster St Shawnee Mission KS 66212-2452 E-mail: jdflora@swbell.net.

FLORA, JOSEPH M(ARTIN), English language educator; b. Toledo, Feb. 9, 1934; s. Raymond D. F. and Frances (Ricica) Neumann; m. Glenda Christine Lape, Jan. 30, 1959; children: Ronald James, Stephen Ray, Peter Joseph, David Benjamin. BA, U. Mich., 1956, MA, 1957, PhD, 1962. Instr. U. Mich., Ann Arbor, 1961-62, U. N.C., Chapel Hill, 1962-64, asst. prof., 1964-66, assoc. prof., 1966-77, prof. English, 1977—, Atlanta prof. so. culture, 2001—, acting chmn. dept. English, 1980-81, chmn., 1981-91, asst. dean grad. sch., 1967-72, assoc. dean grad. sch., 1977-78. Author: Vardis Fisher, 1965, William Ernest Henley, 1970, Frederick Manfred, 1974, Hemingway's Nick Adams, 1982 (Mayflower Cup award 1982), Ernest Hemingway: A Study of the Short Fiction, 1989, Vardis Fisher: Centennial Essays, 2000; editor: The English Short Story, 1880-1945, 1985; co-editor: Southern Writers, 1979, Fifty Southern Writers Before 1990, 1987, Fifty Southern Writers After 1900, 1987, Contemporary Fiction Writers of the South, 1993, Contemporary Poets, Dramatists, Essayists, Novelists of the South, 1994, The Companion to Southern Literature, 2001; editorial bds. Mem. MLA, South Atlantic MLA (v.p. 1997-98, pres. 1998-99), Western Lit. Assn. (bd. dirs. 1978-81, 83-86, v.p. 1990, pres. 1992), Soc. for Study So. Lit., Thomas Wolfe Soc. (v.p. 1993-95, pres. 1995-97), Phi Beta Kappa, Phi Eta Sigma. Home: 505 Caswell Rd Chapel Hill NC 27514-2705 Office: UNC Dept Of English Chapel Hill NC 27599-0001

FLORANCE, DOUGLAS ALLAN, wholesale distributor; b. Johnson City, N.Y., Feb. 19, 1924; s. Joseph Elmer and Helen (Barton) F.; m. Shirley Rae Gravius, Feb. 10, 1945 (dec. Dec. 2002); 1 child, Deborah. Student, Syracuse U., 1946-49. V.p., asst. mgr. Florance Elec. Supply Co., Inc., Binghamton, NY, 1949—52, v.p., mgr., 1952—60, pres., CEO, 1960—84; chief estimator Gersh-Florance Elec. Supply, Binghamton, NY, 1984—88; tech. advisor Olsberg-Northeast, Syracuse, NY, 1988—93, William H. Posthill Co., Syracuse, NY, 1993—2002; pres. Flo-Root, Inc., Binghamton, 1957—2002; ret. Patentee in field. Bd. dirs. N.Y. State Industries for Blind Albany, 1981-87, chmn., 1987-88. Staff sgt. U.S. Army, 1942-46. Mem. IEEE (life), Nat. Assn. Elec. Distributors (hon. life), Internat. Assn. Elec. Inspectors, Elec Coun. So. Tier (treas. 1992-2001, dir. elec. coun. So. tier, 1970—), NRA (life). Office: Flo-Root Inc PO Box 123 Binghamton NY 13903-0123

FLORENCE, HENRY JOHN, lawyer; b. Rockville Centre, N.Y., Dec. 11, 1934; s. Henry Dulap and Mary (Hanley) F.; m. A. Jean Butler, June 13, 1959; 1 child, Henry John Jr. BS in Econs., Villanova U., 1956; JD, Fordham U., 1961. Bar: N.Y. 1962, Ariz. 1963, U.S. Dist. Ct. Ariz. 1967, U.S. Ct. Appeals (9th cir.) 1970, U.S. Supreme Ct. 1970. Advisor legal aid Navajo Indian Tribe, Window Rock, Ariz., 1962-63; asst. atty. Maricopa County, Phoenix, 1964-65, chief civil dep., 1965-67; ptnr. Stewart & Florence Ltd., Phoenix, 1967-73; sole practice Phoenix, 1973—. Pres. Ariz. Family, Phoenix, 1972-78. Served to lt. (j.g.) USN, 1956-58. Mem. Ariz. Bar Assn. (atty.), Nat. Assn. Criminal Def. Lawyers, Assn. Trial Lawyers Am., Calif. Attys. for Criminal Justice, Ariz. Attys. for Criminal Justice. Democrat. Roman Catholic. Avocation: philatelist. Office: 45 W Jefferson St Phoenix AZ 85003-2307 E-mail: sbellatty8@aol.com@.

FLORES, ALFINIO, mathematician, educator; b. Mexico City, July 7, 1953; BA in Math., UNAM, Mex., 1976, M in Math., 1978; PhD, Ohio State U., 1985. Prof. math. edn. Ariz. State U., Tempe, 1992—. Contbr. articles to profl. jours. Mem.: Nat. Coun. Tchrs. Math. (chair editl. bd. Tchg. Children Math. 2000—02).

FLORES, GEORGE H. obstetrician and gynecologist; b. Garapan, Saipan, Northern Marianas, Jan. 7, 1937; s. Francisco Aguon and Maria (Pangelinan) F.; m. Ursa Damian Flores, Aug. 27, 1960; children: George Jr., Nina June, Marybeth, Linda, Debra Jean. BS, St. Louis U., 1960, MD, 1964. Diplomate Am. Bd. Obstetrics and Gynecology. Commd. U.S. Army, 1965, advanced through grades to col., 1979, ret., 1985, chief ob-gyn. 5th Gen. Hosp., 1971-73, Ft. Knox, Ky., 1973-75, chief dept. surgery, 1975-79, chief ob-gyn. Gorgas Army Hosp. Panama Canal Zone, 1982-84; med. dir. Jefferson County Health Dept., Louisville, 1985-90; chief ob-gyn. dept. Hardin Meml. Hosp., Elizabethtown, Ky., 1994-95; pvt. practice ob-gyn. Elizabethtown, 1990—97; ret. Chmn. parish coun. St. Christopher Ch., Radcliff, Ky., 1977-81. Rotary Club of Guam scholar, 1957-60, Govt. of Guam Med. Sch. scholar, 1960-64. Fellow ACOG; mem. AMA, K.C. Republican. Roman Catholic. Avocation: volunteer work with church. Home: 884 Martin Ln Radcliff KY 40160 E-mail: geofloresmd@aol.com.

FLORES, J. ROBERT, federal agency administrator; m. Ingrid Flores; 3 children. BS in Bus. Adminstrn., JD, Boston U. Asst. dist. atty., Manhattan, NY; sr. trial atty., acting dep. chief child exploitation and obscenity sect. criminal divsn. U.S. Dept. Justice, 1989—97; v.p., sr. counsel Nat. Law Ctr. for Children and Families, 1997—2002; adminstr. Juvenile Justice and Delinquency Prevention U.S. Dept. Justice, Washington, 2002—. Apptd. mem. Child Online Protection Act Commn., 1999; lectr. and cons. in field. Office: US Dept Justice Juvenile Justice & Delinquency Preventio 810 7th St NW Washington DC 20531-0001

FLORES, JHONSON EDER, anesthesiologist; b. Cochabamba, Bolivia, Sept. 8, 1947; came to U.S., 1974; s. Teofanes and Neiza (Arteaga) F.; m. Elizabeth Herrera, July 7, 1973; children: Eliana, Esther. BS, U. Mayor de San Simon, Cochabamba, 1974. Diplomate in anesthesiology and in pain mgmt. Am. Bd. Anesthesiology. Intern Somerset Med. Ctr., Somerville, N.J., 1975; resident in anesthesiology Barnes Hosp. Washington U., St. Louis, 1976-78; head ob-gyn anesthesia St. Luke's Hosp. West, Chesterfield, Mo., 1979—. Fellow Am. Coll. Anesthesiology; mem. Am. Soc. Anesthesiology. Republican. Avocations: music, gardening. Office: St Whis Hosp 232 S Woods Mill Road Chesterfield MO 63011 Home: 1716 Stifel Lane Dr Town And Country MO 63017-8046 E-mail: j.flores442@aol.com.

FLORES, ROBIN ANN, social worker, social services administrator; b. Allentown, Pa., Oct. 6, 1949; d. Norman Henry and Ann May (Huff) F. BS in Edn., Kutztown U., 1971; MS in Adminstrn., U. Scranton, 1983. Exec. dir. Lehigh County Aging and Adult Svcs., Allentown, 1996—. Lectr. cmty. svcs., family care giving and on aging process, utilization cmty. resources, Lehigh County. Mem. adv. bd. Cmty. Acting Com. Lehigh Valley, 1979-82, Elder Well, 1987-90; Pa. del. White House Conf. on Aging, Hershey, Pa., 1981; bd. dirs. Vis. Nurse Assn. Lehigh County, 1982-98, Women Inc., 1983-87; mem. adv. bd. Homecare, Inc., 1982-91, Geriatric Edn. Modules, Allentown Osteo. Hosp., 1979; mem. profl. adv. com. Lehigh Valley Hospice, 1984-98; mem. utilization and rev. bd. Vis. Nurse Assn., 1979-98; consumer rep. Pa. Power and Light Co.; co-chmn. Human Svcs. Tng. Coop., 1975-81; bd. assocs. Lehigh Valley Hosp.; bd. trustees, Ethics Inst, Inc, Leigh County, TRIAD. Mem.: NAFE, Pa. Assn. Area Agys. on Aging, Nat. Assn. Area Agys. on Aging, Am. Soc. Aging, Allentown Art Mus., Quota Internat. Home: 2206 Overlook Ln Fogelsville PA 18051-1812 Office: Lehigh County Aging & Adult Svcs Govt Ctr 17 S 7th St Allentown PA 18101-2400

FLORES, WILLIAM VINCENT, Latin American studies educator; b. San Diego, Jan. 10, 1948; s. William J. and Velia (Aldrete) F.; m. Carole Mary Dische, July 3, 1973 (div. Jan 1986); children: Antonio Ramon, Diana Maria. BA, UCLA, 1970; MA in Polit. Sci., Stanford U., 1971, PhD in Social Theory/Pub. Policy, 1987. Teaching & rsch. fellow Stanford (Calif.) U., 1971-72; lectr. in polit. sci. Calif. State U., Hayward, 1972-75; program coord. Project Intercept, San Jose, Calif., 1976-78; assoc. dir. Gardner Cmty. Health Ctr., San Jose, 1979-84; lectr. U. Santa Clara, Calif., 1985-87; asst. dir. Inter Univ. Program for Latino Rsch., Stanford, 1987-88; chair dept. Chicano/Latin Am. studies Calif. State U., Fresno, 1988-92, assoc. dean Sch. of Social Scis., 1992-94, dean Coll. Soc. and Behavioral Scis. Northridge, 1996-2001; v.p., bd. trustees Arte Americas, 1995-96; provost N.Mex. State U., Las Cruces, 2001—, interim pres., 2003. Bd. dirs. N.Mex. State U. Arrowhead Rsch. Park Corp., Phys. Sci. Inst. Author: Latino Cultural Citizenship, 1997. Mem. CSU Northridge Found. Bd. CSUN pres.'s bus. coun., 1996-98, exec. com. Chicano/Latino Faculty Assn. Calif. State Univ. Sys., 1994-95; chair Com. for Hispanic Ednl. Equity, Fresno, 1990-92; mem. nat. adv. bd. U.S. Students Assn., Washington, 1991-93; v.p. Latino Agenda Coalition Calif., L.A., 1984-86; active Leadership N.Mex., 2003; bd. dirs. Nat. Hispanic Cultural Ctr., 2003—; co-chair Gov. Bill Richardson Transition Team, 2002-03. Chicano Fellows Program fellow Stanford U., 1971-72; Ford Found. fellow Stanford U., 1970-74; Compton-Danforth fellow Stanford U., 1984-85.; Rockefeller Humanities fellow, 1993-94; Am. Coun. on Edn. fellow, 1993-94. Mem. Am. Anthropol. Assn., Am. Studies Assn., Nat. Assn. Chicano Studies (co-chair polit. action com. 1986), Internat. Platform Assn. Democrat. Avocations: poetry, music, racquetball, hiking. Office: NMex State U Office Provost Box 3001 MSC 3445 Las Cruces NM 88003-8001 E-mail: bflores@nmsu.edu.

FLORES, YOLANDA, literature educator; b. Bakersfield, Calif., Mar. 2, 1962; d. Simon and Micaela Flores. BA, U. Calif., Berkeley, 1987; MA, U. Chgo., 1989; PhD, Cornell U., 1995. Lectr. Cornell U., Ithaca, N.Y., 1994-95; prof. Chapman U., Orange, Calif., 1995-99, U. Vt., Burlington, 1999—. Author: The Drama of Gender: Feminist Theater by Women of the Americas, 2000, 2d edit., 2002; contbr. articles to profl. publs. Mem. MLA, L.Am. Studies Assn., Am. Soc. for Theater Rsch., Feministas Unidas, Assn. Theater in Higher Edn. Democrat. Roman Catholic. Avocations: film, music, aerobics, travel. Office: Romance Langs and Lit Dept U Vt 517 Waterman Bldg Burlington VT 05405-0001 E-mail: yflores@200.uum.edu.

FLORESCU, RADU RADU, East European history educator; b. Bucharest, Romania, Oct. 23, 1925; s. Radu Alexander and Vera Marie Florescu; m. Nicole Elizabeth Michel, Dec. 2, 1951; children: Nicholas, John, Radu, Alexandra. BA, MA, BLitt, Oxford (Eng.) U., 1951; PhD, Ind. U., 1962. Instr. Boston Coll., Chestnut Hill, Mass., 1953-56, asst. prof., 1956-62, assoc. prof., 1962-89, prof., 1989-97, prof. emeritus, 1997—. Dir. East European Rsch. Ctr., Boston, 1968—; cons. US Embassy, Bucharest, 1969, Senator Edward Kennedy, Boston, 1989, U.S. Dept. State, Washington, 1953—; mem. consul of Romania, Boston, 1996. Co-author: In Search of Dracula, 1975, Dracula Prince of Many Faces, 1989, In Search of Dracula, 1994 (award Dracula Soc. 1997); author: Frankenstein, 1975, The Struggle Against Russia in Romania, 1989, Essays on Romanian History, 1999. Hon. sec. Oxford Soc., New Eng., 1968-88. Recipient Gladstone Meml. prize, 1948; Fulbright fellow, 1967, 68; sr. fellow St. Antony Coll., 1973-74. Fellow Romanian Acad. Soc. (sr.); mem. Soc. Romanian Studies (pres., bd. dirs. 1989). Democrat. Avocations: bicycling, tennis, table tennis, skiing. Home: James Landing 48 Ladds Way Scituate MA 02066-1901 Office: Consulate of Romania Harbor Tower I 85 East India Rowe 4H Boston MA 02110 E-mail: florescu@bc.edu.

FLORESTANO, DANA JOSEPH, architect; b. Inpls., May 2, 1945; s. Herbert Joseph and Myrtle Mae (Futch) F.; m. Peggy Joy Larsen, June 6, 1969. BArch, U. Notre Dame, 1968. Designer, draftsman Kennedy, Brown & Trueblood, architects, Indpls., 1965-69, Evans Woolen Assn., architects, Indpls., 1966; designer, project capt. James Assocs., architects and engrs., Indpls., 1969-71; architect, v.p. comml. projects Multi-Planners Inc., architects and engrs., 1972-73; pvt. practice architecture Indpls., 1973—; pres. Florestano Corp., constrn. mtmg., Indpls., 1973—. Co-founder, pres. Solargenics Natural Energy Corp., Indpls., 1975—; pres. Florestano Archery Co., 1985—, Star Archery Corp., Indpls., 1989—; prof. archtl. and constrn. tech. Ind. U.-Purdue U. at Indpls.; instr. in field. Tech. adviser hist. architecture Indpls. Model Cities program, 1969-70; mem. Hist. Landmarks Found. Ind., 1970-72; chmn. Com. to Save Union Sta., 1970-71, founder, pres. Union Sta. Found. Inc., Indpls., 1971—; dep. commr. and tournament dir. archery Pan-Am. Games, Indpls., 1987. Recipient 2d design award Marble Inst. Am., 1967, 1st design award 19th Ann. Progressive Architecture Design awards, 1972, Design award for excellence in devel. Marriott Inn, Indpls., Met. Devel. Commn.-Office of Mayor, 1977; 1st place award design competition for Visitor's Info. Ctr., Cave Run, Lake, Ky., 1978; 2d design award 1st Ann. Qualified Remodeler, Nat.

Competition for Best Rehab. Existing Structures in Am., 1979. Mem. U. Notre Dame Alumni Assn., Notre Dame Club Indpls., AIA (nat. com. hist. resources 1974—, commn. on cmty. svcs., Spkrs. Bur. Indpls. chpt. 1976—), Ind. Soc. Architects (chmn. historic architecture com. 1970—), Ind. Archery Assn. (founder, pres. 1985—, Overall Male State Champion 1987, 90, 94), No. Archery Assn. (bd. dirs. 1998—, pres. 1987—), Internat. Archery Ctr. (founder, exec. dir. 1992—), Ind. Kyudo Renmei (bd. dirs., 1998—, sec. 1999—, co-chmn. Am. Kyudo sem. 2000-04), Constrn. Specifications Inst., Constrn. Mgrs. Assn. Ind. (incorporator, dir. 1976—), World Archery Ctr. Home: PO Box 30089 Indianapolis IN 46230-0089 Office: 5657 Carvel Ave Indianapolis IN 46220

FLOREY, JERRY JAY, aerospace and management consultant; b. Geddes, S.D., Apr. 3, 1932; s. Henry Clifford and Lizzie M. Florey; m. Mary E. Richey, Sept. 17, 1955; children: Glenn David, Janet Renee. BSChemE, Oreg. State U., 1955. Cert. in electronics. From research engr. to engring. supr. Rockwell Internat., Canoga Park, Calif., 1955-66, sr. project engr. Downey, Calif., 1966-67, successively engring. mgr., engring. dir., chief engr. space sys. electronics divsn. Seal Beach, Calif., 1967-85, dir. advanced systems, rsch. and tech., 1985-89; propulsion sys. specialist, sr. staff mgr. strategic planning and market analysis McDonnell Douglas Space Co., Huntington Beach, Calif., 1989-95; cons. McDonnell Douglas, 1995-96; mgmt. cons., 1996—; cons. NASA Inst. for Advanced Concepts, 2001—. Participant on several industry workshop panels which advised USAF regarding its mil. space systems tech. planning activities. Mem. editl. bd. Aerospace Am. Scoutmaster Boy Scouts Am., Costa Mesa, Calif., 1970; mem. Republican Presdl. Task Force; del. at large Rep. Platform planning com. Recipient Astronaut Person Achievement award NASA, 1969, NASA Cert. Appreciation Marshall Space Flight Ctr., Huntsville, Ala., 1972, Skylab Achievement award NASA, 1973, AIAA and USAF Recognition of Svc. certs. AFSTC, 1985, Apollo Achievement award NASA, Washington, 1969. Fellow AIAA (assoc., bd. dirs., nat. space and missile systems tech. activities com., fin. and internat. membership coms.); mem. Nat. Mgmt. Assn., Nat. Mktg. Soc. Am., U.S. Space Found. Home: 2085 Goldeneye Pl Costa Mesa CA 92626-4770

FLOREY, KLAUS GEORG, chemist, pharmaceutical consultant; b. Dresden, Germany, July 4, 1919; came to U.S., 1947, naturalized, 1952; s. Friedrich Georg and Margarethe Käthe (Pick) F.; m. Anne Major, Nov. 22, 1956; children: Peter, Andrea. Ed., U. Munich, U. Heidelberg, Germany; PhD, U. Pa., 1954. Research asst. Bayer, Leverkusen, Germany, 1944-45; research asso. Merck & Co., Rahway, N.J., 1949-50; research chemist Squibb Inst. Med. Research, New Brunswick, N.J., 1954-59, dir. analytical research and devel., 1959-84, cons., 1984-90. Mem. com. revisions U.S. Pharmacopeia, 1970-95, hon. mem., 2000; mem. WHO Expert Adv. Panel Internat. Pharmacopeia, 1976-93; docent The Princeton U. Art Mus., 1991--. Editor: Analytical Profiles of Drug Substances, 22 vols., 1971—; contbr. articles to profl. jours.; patentee in field. Recipient Justin L. Powers award, 1987. Fellow AAAS, Acad. Pharm. Scis. (chmn. pharm. analysis and control sect. 1967-68, pres. 1980-81); mem. Am. Chem. Soc., Soc. Nuclear Medicine, Am. Assn. Pharm. Scientists (Disting. Svc. award 1990), Cosn. Sci. Soc. Pres. (chmn. 1983) Home: 151 Loomis Ct Princeton NJ 08540-3438

FLOREZ, DEAN R. state senator; b. Shafter, Calif., Apr. 5, 1963; m. Elsa Florez; children: Sean, Faith. BS in Polit. Sci., UCLA, 1986; MBA, Harvard Bus. Sch., 1993. Chair Banking, Commerce and Internat. Trade Com.; mem. Agriculture and Natural Resources Com., Health and Human Svcs. Com., Housing and Cmty. Devel. Com., Transp. Com., Joint Legis. Audit Com., 1998—2000, State Bd. Pub. Works, 1998—2000. Mem.: Hispanic C. of C., Bakersfield C. of C., Rotary (Shafter). Democrat. Roman Catholic. Mailing: State Capitol Rm 4090 Sacramento CA 95814 Office: 1800 30th St Ste 350 Bakersfield CA 93301*

FLOREZ-ESTRADA, NANCY B. language educator; b. Greensburg, Pa., June 14, 1941; d. Clarence William and Bernice M. Beck; m. J. Luis Flórez-Estrada, Aug. 5, 1972; children: Jaime, Krista. BA in Spanish, Grove City Coll., 1963; MA in Spanish Lit., Mich. State U., 1965; PhD of Spanish Applied Linquistics, U. Pitts., 1995. Instr. Spanish Purdue U. Calumet, Hammond, Ind., 1967—72; instr. ESL Gen. Foods, Madrid, 1973—78; asst. dir. SSDS Seton Hill Coll., Greensburg, Pa., 1979—82; assoc. prof. Hispanic Langs. and Lits. U. Pitts.-Greensburg, 1982—. Dir. Rossetti Internat. House U. Pitts.-Greensburg, 1999—; chmn. adv. bd. Spl. Student Svcs. Westmoreland County C.C., Youngwood, Pa., 1998—. Fellow: Am. Assn. Tchrs. Spanish and Portuguese, Am. Coun. Tchrs. Fgn. Lang., Modern Lang. Assn. Home: 109 University Dr Greensburg PA 15601 Office: Univ Pitts-Greensburg 1150 Mount Pleasant Rd Greensburg PA 15601

FLORI, ANNA MARIE DIBLASI, nurse anesthetist, educational adminstrator; b. Amsterdam, N.Y., Oct. 29, 1940; d. Tony and Maria (Macario) DiBlasi; children: Tammy, Tina, Toni; m. Gilberto Flori, May 24, 1986. Grad., Albany Med. Ctr. Sch. Nursing, 1962, Fairfax Hosp. Sch. Nurse Anesthetists, Va., 1972; BS in Anesthesia, George Washington U., 1979; M. in Bus. and Pub. Adminstrn., Southeastern U., Washington, 1982; PhD, Columbia Pacific U., 1983. Cert. registered nurse anesthetist. Staff nurse West Seattle Gen. Hosp., 1962-64; office nurse Filmore Buckner, M.D., Seattle, 1964-66; staff nurse anesthetist Fairfax Hosp., 1972-73; staff nurse anesthetist Potomac Hosp., Woodbridge, Va., 1973, chief nurse anesthetist, 1973—; dir. Potomac Hosp. Sch. for Nurse Anesthetists and Sch. for Nurse Anesthesia; faculty mem. Columbia Pacific U., 1973-90; chief nurse anesthetist No. Va. Anesthesia Assn., 1988—; guest lectr. No. Va. Community Coll., Inservice Potomac Hosp., George Washington U.; coord. Free Clinic Prince William County, Woodbridge, Va. Contbr. books on anesthesia. Mem. Am. Assn. Nurse Anesthetists, Va. Nurse Anesthesia Assn., Nat. Italian Am. Found. Home: 12954 Pintail Rd Woodbridge VA 22192-3831

FLORIAN, AGUSTIN MAX, thoracic and cardiovascular surgeon; b. Chiclayo, Peru, Apr. 20, 1938; came to U.S., 1966; s. Agustin M. and Rosa Adelina (Gavilano) F.; m. Ines Georgina Castro, June 15, 1966; children: Edgar, Michael, Kara, Kenneth, Keith, Kirk. BS, San Marcos U., Lima, Peru, 1958, MD, 1965. Clin. fellow in thoracic and cardiovascular surgery Hosp. Obrero, Lima, Peru, 1965-66; intern Springfield (Mass.) Hosp. Med. Ctr., 1967-68, asst. resident in surgery, chief resident in surgery, 1968-69, 70-71; sr. asst. resident in surgery Roswell Pk. Meml. Inst., Buffalo, 1969-70, Springfield (Mass.) Hosp. Med., 1969-70; assoc. resident in thoracic surgery, chief resident U. Md. Hosp., Balt., 1971-72, 72-73; rsch. fellow in thoracic and cardiac surgery Peter Bent Brigham Hosp. and Harvard Med. Sch., Boston, 1973-74; thoracic and cardiac surgeon VA Hosp., West Roxbury, Mass., 1974-75; thoracic surgeon Norwood (Mass.) Hosp. and Quincy (Mass.) Hosp., 1975-83; active staff thoracic and vascular surgery, courtesy staff Quincy (Mass.) Hosp., 1980-87, 88—; chief thoracic and cardiac surgery Norwood Hosp. and Southwood Hosp., Norwood and Norfolk, Mass., 1982—; mem. cardiothoracic surgeon St. Elizabeth Hosp., Boston, 1995—. Contbr. articles to profl. jours. Pres. Andes Relief Assn., Inc., Norwood, 1991. Fellow Am. Coll. Surgeons, Am. Coll. Chest Physicians; mem. U. Md. Surg. Soc., Am. Bd. Surgery, Mass. Med. Soc., Am. Bd. Thoracic Surgery, Soc. Thoracic Surgery, Boston Surg. Soc. Republican. Roman Catholic. Avocations: fishing, hunting, soccer. Home: 30 Grand Hill Dr Dover MA 02030-1704 Office: 825 Washington St Ste 115 Norwood MA 02062-3483

FLORIAN-LACY, DOROTHY, therapist, educator; b. Dearborn, Mich., Oct. 27, 1958; d. Raymond Joseph and Dorothy Mae Florian; m. Bill George Lacy, July 25, 1981; children: Jason M., Miles, Anderson. BS in Psychology and Edn., Eastern Mich. U., 1978, MA in Guidance and Counseling, 1979; EdD in Counselor Edn., Tex. Southeastern U., 1998. Lic. profl. counselor, Tex. Realtor Century 21, Ann Arbor, Mich., 1978-79; tchr. Adult Exception Ctr., Compton, Calif., 1979-81; owner, dir. Village Learning & Play Ctr., Houston, 1982-94; dept. chair spl. edn. Milby Sr. H.S., Houston, 1994-2000; therapist Houston Achievement Place, 1998—. Author: Fundamentals of Mathematics I, Fundamentals of Mathematics II, Consumer Math; co-author: Reference Manual for Special Education Department Chairpersons. Vol. Child Abuse Prevention, Houston, 1989-91, vol. coach YMCA, Houston, 1987-90. Recipient Adaptor grant Impact II, 1997, Study Group grant Impact II, 1998. Mem. Am. Counseling Assn., Children's Mus. Avocation: golf coach. Office: Houston Achievement Place 236 W 17th St Houston TX 77008-4002 E-mail: dflorian@houstonisd.org.

FLORIN, CYNTHIA, psychiatrist; b. Roslyn, N.Y., Apr. 6, 1954; d. Stanley and Doris (Kellman) F.; m. Andrey Shaw, June 25, 1983; children: Emily, Alex. BS, Grinnell Coll., 1976; MD, Columbia U. Coll. Phys. Surg., 1984. Diplomate Am. Bd. Psychiatry & Neurology. Resident Yale U. Sch. Medicine, New Haven, 1985-88, asst. prof., 1989-91; instr. Washington U. Sch. Medicine, St. Louis, 1991-96, clin. faculty, 1996—. Mem. Am. Psychiat. Assn., Am. Psychoanalytic Assn. Democrat. Office: 7750 Clayton Rd Ste 200D Saint Louis MO 63117-1342

FLORINE, JANE L. musicology educator; b. Waseca, Minn., July 22, 1953; d. Martin Clifford Florine and Alice Dorothy Ostergren. BA summa cum laude, U. Minn., 1975; MA, Lesley Coll., 1992; PhD, Fla. State U., 1996. Flutist Nat. Symphony Orch., Buenos Aires, 1975-83; bilingual asst. to the pres. Braun Argentina, Buenos Aires, 1983-86; fgn. student advisor Boston U., 1991-92; assoc. prof. ethnomusicology/musicology Chgo. State U., 1997—. Cons. Chgo. Symphony Orch., 1999-2001. Author: Cuarteto Music and Dancing from Argentina: In Search of the Tunga-Tunga in Cordoba, 2001; contbr. articles to profl. jours. Fulbright fellow, 1994, Dissertation fellow Fla. State U., 1995. Mem.: L.Am. Studies Assn., Coll. Music Soc., Argentine Musicology Assn., Soc. for Ethnomusicology (pres. Midwest chpt. 1999—2000), Internat. Assn. for Study Popular Music, Nat. Flute Soc. (life). Home: 5000 S Cornell Ave Apt 4C Chicago IL 60615 Office: Chgo State Univ Music Dept/HWH 331 9501 S King Dr Chicago IL 60628-1598

FLORIO, STEVEN T. magazine executive; b. N.Y.C., Apr. 19, 1949; s. F. Steve and Sophia (Masciale) F.; m. Marianne McNeill, June 1, 1974; children: Steven John, Kelly Anne. AA, NYU, 1970, BS, 1972. Rschr. Esquire mag., N.Y.C., 1972-73, New Eng. mgr., 1974-76, advt. dir., 1976-79, v.p., 1979-80; pub. Gentlemen's Quar., N.Y.C., 1980-85; pres., CEO New Yorker mag., N.Y.C., 1985-94, pub., 1985-88; pres. Condé Nast Publs., Inc., N.Y.C., 1994—, CEO, 1996—. Guest spkr. lecture series Harvard U., Rice U., NYU, Yale U. Chmn. Namesake Com. USS N.Y.C. USN. Mem.: Mag. Pubs. Assn. (chmn. conf. 1989), Men's Fashion Assn. Office: Conde Nast Publ 4 Times Sq New York NY 10036-6561*

FLORMAN, SAMUEL CHARLES, civil engineer; b. N.Y.C., Jan. 19, 1925; s. Arthur M. and Hannah (Weingarten) F.; m. Judith Hadas, Aug. 19, 1951; children: David A., Jonathan C. BS, CE, Dartmouth Coll., 1946; MA, Columbia U., 1947; DSc (hon.), Manhattan Coll., 1983, Clarkson U., 1986. Registered profl. engr., N.Y. Field engr. Hegeman Harris Co., Venezuela, 1948; asst. project mgr. Thompson-Starrett Corp., N.Y.C., 1949-54; project mgr. Jos. P. Blitz Inc., N.Y.C., 1954-56; prin., chmn. Kreisler Borg Florman Constrn. Co., Scarsdale, N.Y., 1956—. Author: Engineering and the Liberal Arts, 1968, The Existential Pleasures of Engineering, 1976, Blaming Technology, 1981, The Civilized Engineer, 1987, The Introspective Engineer, 1996, The Aftermath, A Novel of Survival, 2001; contbr. over 200 articles to profl. jours. Bd. overseers Thayer Sch. Engring., Dartmouth Coll., Hanover, N.H., 1971-77; trustee Hosp. for Joint Disease, N.Y.C., 1976—; bd. govs. Ethical Culture Fieldston Schs., N.Y.C., 1983-96; trustee N.Y. Hall of Sci., 1996—. Recipient Stevens award Stevens Inst. Tech., 1976, Ralph Coats Roe medal ASME, 1982, Robert Fletcher award Thayer Sch. Engring., 1983. Fellow AAAS, ASCE; mem. NSPE, Am. Soc. for Engring. Edn., Nat. Acad. Engring., Dartmouth Soc. Engrs. (pres. 1966-67). Home: 55 Central Park W New York NY 10023-6003 Office: 97 Montgomery St Scarsdale NY 10583-5104 E-mail: scf97@aol.com.

FLORMAN, SANDER SCOTT, transplant surgeon; b. N.Y.C., Sept. 20, 1967; s. Larry David and Phyllis Ehrlich Florman; m. Toby Jill Florman, June 28, 1998; children: Zachary, Frankie. BA, Brandeis U., 1989; MD, U. Louisville, 1994. Cert. bd. cert. gen. surgeon. Gen. surgery resident Tulane U., New Orleans, 1994—2000; transplant fellow Mt. Sinai, N.Y.C., 2000—02, asst. prof., 2002—. Adminstrv. chief resident Tulane Surgery, New Orleans, 1999—2000; rsch. resident Mt. Sinai Liver Transplant, N.Y.C., 1996—97. Author: (book chpt.) American College of Surgeons Surgery, 2002, Mastery of Surgery, 2000; contbr. articles to profl. jours. Mem.: ACS, Soc. for Surgery of the Alimentary Tract, Am. Soc. Transplantation. Office: Mt Sinai Liver Transplant Box 1104 1 Gustave Leng Pl New York NY 10029

FLORSHEIM, RENEE ANNE, marketing, educator, lawyer; b. L.A., Dec. 1, 1953; d. Warner Hanns and Eva (Herzberg) Florsheim. BS, Calif. State Poly. U., 1976; MBA, UCLA, 1979; PhD, Northwestern U., Evanston, Ill., 1989; JD, Loyola Law Sch., L.A., 1999. Bar: Calif. 1999. Asst. prof. U. Regina, Sask., Can., 1979-80; sessional lectr. U. B.C., Vancouver, Can., 1980-81; instr. Loyola U., Chgo., 1984-85; asst. prof. Temple U., Phila., 1985-89; assoc. prof., dept. co-chair Loyola Marymount U., L.A., 1989—. Contbr. articles to profl. jours. Mentor Big Sisters Phila., 1985-89, Big Sisters L.A., 1989-91, Fulfillment Fund, L.A., 1994-99. Mem. ABA, Am. Mktg. Assn. (v.p. acad. rels. 2000-01), Women Lawyers Assn. L.A. (mem. jail project 1999-2001), L.A. County Bar Assn., Beverly Hills Bar Assn. Home: 1851 Veteran Ave # 204 Los Angeles CA 90025 Office: Loyola Marymount U One LMU Dr Los Angeles CA 90045-8385 Office Fax: 310-338-3000. E-mail: rflorshe@lmu.edu.

FLORSHEIM, RICHARD STEVEN, lawyer; b. Milw., Apr. 2, 1949; s. Ernst Frederick and Ingeborg Miriam Florsheim; m. Neena B. Florsheim; children: Ali Brynn, David Ira, Rebecca Lynn. BS, MIT, 1971; JD magna cum laude, Marquette U., 1974. Bar: Wis. 1974, Fla. 1983. Assoc. Foley & Lardner, Milw., 1974-81, ptnr., 1981—, leader intellectual property litigation group, 1987-97, chair intellectual property dept., 1997—. Co-author: Biotechnology Patent Practice, 1994, Inside the Minds: Leading Intellectual Property Lawyers, 2001. Pres. North Shore Libr., Milw., 1985-87, Jewish Found. Econ. Opportunity, Milw., 1992-96; bd. dirs. Milw. Jewish Fedn., 1987-93, 96-2002, NCCJ Wis. region, 1990—, Ohr Hatorah Jewish Heritage Ctr., 2002--. Mem. ABA, Am. Intellectual Property Law Assn. (subcom. chmn. 1992-97), Fed. Cir. Bar Assn., Wis. Bar Assn., Milw. Bar Assn., Marquette Law Alumni Assn. (pres. 1985-86). Office: Foley & Lardner 777 E Wisconsin Ave Ste 3800 Milwaukee WI 53202-5367 Business E-Mail: rflorsheim@foleylaw.com.

FLORY, CURT ALAN, research physicist; BS in Physics with distinction, Stanford U., 1975; MS in Physics, U. Wash., 1977; PhD in Physics, U. Calif., Berkeley, 1981. R&D fellow, rsch. physicist Agilent Technologies, Palo Alto, Calif., 1984—; postdoc. SLAC, 1981-84. Recipient Indsl. Physics prize Am. Inst. Physics, 1993-94. Fellow Am. Phys. Soc. Office: Agilent Technolgies 3500 Deer Creek Rd # 26M Palo Alto CA 94304-1317 E-mail: curt_flory@agilent.com.

FLOSS, FREDERICK GEORGE, economics and finance educator, consultant; b. Buffalo, Feb. 12, 1957; s. Frederick H. and Mary (White) F.; m. Lauren Bodziak, July 26, 1986. BA in Econs. and English, SUNY, Oswego, 1979; MA in Econs., SUNY, Buffalo, 1982, PhD in Econs., 1986. Instr. econs. SUNY, Buffalo, 1980-85, asst. prof., 1986-90, mem. faculty senate, 1986-2000, assoc. prof., 1990-99, prof., 1999—, co-dir. Ctr. for Econ. Edn., 1997—. Rsch. assoc. Ctr. for Applied Rsch. in Urban and Regional Devel., 1983—; exec. bd. United Univ. Professions, 2000—; presenter in field. Contbr. articles to profl. jours. Committeeman Erie County Dem. Com., 1979—; mem. cmty. needs assessment com. United Way Western N.Y., 1987-92; mem. adv. coun. Erie-Niagara Planning Bd., 1987-92; chmn. bd. regional dirs. Young Dems. Am., 1988-90; bd. dirs. Literacy Vols. of Buffalo and Erie County, 1992-98, Summitt Edn.; sec. Literacy Vol. of Buffalo and Erie County, 1995-97. Regents scholar, 1975-79; fellow Ctr. for Devel. Human Svcs., 1987-88, 89-98. Roman Catholic. Home: 27 Landers Rd Buffalo NY 14217-2405 Office: SUNY Dept Econs and Fin 1300 Elmwood Ave Dept Econsand Buffalo NY 14222-1004 E-mail: flossfg@buffalostate.edu.

FLOSS, HEINZ G. chemistry educator, scientist; b. Berlin, Aug. 28, 1934; s. Friedrich and Annemarie F.; m. Inge Sauberlich, July 17, 1956; children: Christine, Peter, Helmut, Hanna. BS in Chemistry, Technische Universitat, Berlin, 1956, MS in Organic Chemistry, 1959; PhD in Organic Chemistry, Technische Universitat, Munich, W. Ger., 1961, Habilitation in Biochemistry, 1966; DSc (hon.), Purdue U., 1986; Dr. (h.c.), U. Bonn, 2001. Hilfsassistent Technische Universitat, Berlin, 1958-59; hilfsassistent Technische Hochschule, Munich, 1959-61, wissenschaftlicher asst. and dozent, 1961-66; on leave of absence at dept. biochemistry and biophysics U. Calif.-Davis, 1964-65; assoc. prof. Purdue U., 1966-69, prof., 1969-77, Lilly Disting. prof., 1977-82, head dept. medicinal chemistry, 1968-69, 74-79; prof. chemistry Ohio State U., Columbus, 1982-87, chmn. dept. chemistry, 1982-86; prof. chemistry U. Wash., Seattle, 1987—, adj. prof. medicinal chemistry and microbiology, 1988—, adj. prof. biochemistry, 1988-99, prof. emeritus, 2001—. Vis. scientist ETH Zurich, 1970; vis. prof. Tech. U. Munich, 1980, 86, 95; mem. bio-organic and natural products study sect. NIH, 1989-93; mem. internat. adv. Natural Product Reports, 1997—. Mem. editorial bd. Lloydia-Jour. Natural Products, 1971—2002, BBP-Biochemie und Physiologie der Pflanzen, 1971-84, Applied and Environ. Microbiology, 1974-84, Planta Medica, 1978-83, Jour. Medicinal Chemistry, 1979-83, Applied Microbiology and Biotech., 1984-88, Jour. Basic Microbiology, 1989—. Recipient Lederle faculty award, 1967, Mead Johnson Undergrad. Rsch. award, 1968, rsch. career and devel. award USPHS, 1969-74, Volwiler award, 1979, Humboldt sr. scientist, 1980, Newby-McCoy award 1981, award in microbial chemistry Kitasato Inst. and Kitasato U., 1988, White Magnolia Commemoration award and medal, Shanghai, 1995. Fellow Acad. Pharm. Scis. (Research Achievement award in natural products 1976), AAAS; mem. Am. Chem. Soc., Am. Soc. Biol. Chemistry and Molecular Biology, Am. Soc. Microbiology, Am. Soc. Pharmacognosy (Rsch. award 1988), Phytochem. Soc. N.Am., Sigma Xi (Faculty Research award 1976) Office: Univ Wash Box 351700 Seattle WA 98195-1700

FLOSS, MARK THADDEUS, civil engineer, computer scientist; b. Alexandria, Va., June 5, 1958; s. Charles Robert Jr. and Shirley Lee Ann (Bliss) F.; m. Alice LeeAnn Scholl, Aug. 10, 1985; children, Jennifer Ann, Johnathon Alexander. BSCE, The Citadel, 1980. Registered profl. engr., S.C.; cert. water distbn. operator, S.C. City engr. City North Charleston, S.C., 1985-92; constrn. insp. City of Savannah, Ga., 1993-94, facilities project coord., 1994; field engr. Town of Mt. Pleasant, S.C., 1994-95; asst. pub. works dir., city engr. City of Goose Creek, 1995—. Author road codes, computer macros. With USAFR, 1985. Avocations: military historical reenactments, wargaming. Home: 18 Briarcliff Dr Charleston SC 29407-6612 Office: City of Goose Creek Dept Pub Works PO Drawer 1768 Goose Creek SC 29445-1768 E-mail: mfloss@awod.com.

FLOURNOY, DAYL JEAN, clinical microbiologist, educator; b. San Antonio, Dec. 17, 1944; s. Dayl Jean Flournoy and Bonnie Allen; children: David, Michael, Michelle. BS, Southwest Tex. State U., 1965; AS, San Antonio Coll., 1966; MA, Incarnate Word Coll., San Antonio, 1968; PhD, U. Houston, 1973. Cert. med. technologist, specialist in microbiology Am. Soc. Clin. Pathologists; cert. clin. lab. dir. Am. Bd. Bioanalysis. Med. tech. automated chemistry Santa Rosa Med. Ctr., San Antonio, 1966-69; tchg. fellow U. Houston, Houston, 1969-72; med. tech., clin. lab. supr. St. Luke's Episcopal Hosp., Houston, 1972-73, postdoctoral fellow, 1975, microbiologist, med. tech., 1974-75; dir. clin. microbiology and serology VA Med. Ctr., Oklahoma City, 1975—; prof. pathology U. Okla. Health Sci. Ctr., Oklahoma City, 1987—, geriat. fellow, 1991. Manuscript reviewer Lab. Medicine, Med. Sci. Rsch., Can. Jour. Med. Tech., Mil. Medicine, Am. Jour. Infection Control, Infection Control Hosp. Epidemiology. Contbr. articles to sci. jours. Head soccer coach Tri-City Athletic Assn., 1979-83; teenline vol. Okla. Dept. Mental Health, 1989-90. Fellow Am. Acad. Microbiology; mem. Am. Soc. Microbiology, Soc. Hosp. Epidemiologists Am., Southwestern Assn. Clin. Microbiology, Toastmasters Internat. Avocations: physical fitness, automotive, gardening. Home: 2122 La Dean Dr Norman OK 73069-4255 Office: VA Med Ctr (113) 921 NE 13th St Oklahoma City OK 73104-5007 E-mail: dayl-flournoy@ouhsc.edu.

FLOURNOY, EDWARD BRIAN, financial consultant, consultant; b. Manhattan, N.Y., May 5, 1950; s. Julius Marshall and Hermie Starks; m. Lisa Diane Collier, Sept. 15, 1973; children: Siobhan Jasmil, Matthew Joshua. BA, Marist Coll., 1972; MPA, L.I. U., 1985. Assoc. mgr. Beneficial Fin. Svcs., Houston, 1982—84; P&L officer CitiCorp Houston, 1984—90; collections mgr. 1st City Tex., Houston, 1990—92; bank officer, mgr. Bank 1 Tex., Irving, 1992—93; exc. v.p. Comp-U-Check, Dallas, 1993—94; team leader, founder Spring PCS, Ft. Worth, 1996—2002; CEO, founder FmA Enterprise, Keller, Tex., 1993—. Recipient Martin Luther King scholarship, Marist Coll., 1968, Pepsi-Cola Music award, Pks. Dept., 1968. Mem.: North Tex.-Am. Soc. Pub. Adminstrs. (bd. dirs. 2002—), Am. Soc. Pub. Adminstrn., Nat. Assn. Urban Bankers (co-chmn. 1990, pres. Dallas chpt. 1994), Am. Note Network (life; exec. mem. 2001—). Avocations: sports, jazz, reading, dancing, speaking engagements. Home: 610 San Clemente Dr Keller TX 76248 Office: PO Box 1867 Keller TX 76244 Home Fax: 775-307-7684. E-mail: eflourno@fmadirect.net.

FLOURNOY, JACOB WESLEY, internal audit director; b. Odessa, Tex., June 18, 1956; s. Dan Dunn and Vonnie Rea (Morrow) F.; m. Tina Charlene Hargis, Jan. 5, 1980; children: Daniel Edward, Samuel Wesley. BBA, U. North Tex., 1978; MBA, U. Okla., 1984. CPA, cert. internal auditor; cert. info. sys. auditor; cert. fraud examiner. Asst. bank examiner Fed. Deposit Ins. Corp., Oklahoma City, Okla., 1978-80; internal auditor City of Oklahoma City, 1980-82; sr. internal auditor U. Okla., Norman, 1982-86; internal audit dir. U. Tex. Health Sci. Ctr., San Antonio, 1986-91, U. Ark. Sys., Little Rock, 1991—; instr. AICPA, 2000—. Fellow; AICPA (instr.); mem. Inst. Internal Auditors, Info. Sys. Audit and Control Assn., Assn. Coll. and Univ. Auditors, Assn. Cert. Fraud Examiners, Ark. Soc. CPAs. Office: U Ark 2404 N University Little Rock AR 72207-3608 E-mail: jwflournoy@uasys.edu.

FLOURNOY, JOHN CHARLES, SR., civilian military employee, retired military officer; b. Florala, Ala., Nov. 30, 1936; s. Q. P. and Alice Ruby (Cope) Flournoy; m. Charlene Reneé Lett, June 7, 1957; children: Jamie Lynn, John Charles Jr., Jeffrey Allan. BS, Auburn U., 1959. Commd. 2d lt. USAF, 1959, advanced through grades to col., dep. chief of staff for ops. 23rd Air Force, 1983—88; site mgr., tng. mgr. Raytheon Sys., Kirkland AFB, N.Mex., 1988-98, tng. analyst, Air Force Rsch. Lab. Albuquerque, 1998—99; cons. Air Force Rsch Lab, Mesa, 1999—. Decorated Legion Merit; recipient German Gratitude medal, Fed. Republic of Germany, 1962. Mem.: Air Rescue Assn. (pres.), Air Commando Assn., USAF Helicopter Pilot Assn., Tanker/Airlift Assn., Jolly Green Assn. (1st v.p. 1983—84, pres. 1985—86), Order of Daedalians (former flight capt.). Republican. Avocations: fishing, walking, coin collecting, Nascar. Home: 6817 Medinah Ln NE Albuquerque NM 87111-6419 E-mail: jflournoy2@comcast.net.

FLOURNOY, JOHN CRAIG, journalism educator; b. Shreveport, La., June 26, 1951; s. Camp Rogers and Carolyn (Clay) F.; m. Nina Planchard, May 21, 1977; children: Kathryn Helene, Louise, Emma. BA in History with honors, U. New Orleans, 1975; MA in History, So. Meth. U., 1986; PhD in Mass. Comm., La. State U., 2003. Freelance writer, landscaper The Courier, New Orleans, 1975; polit. reporter Houma (La.) Daily Courier, 1976; polit. reporter, columnist Shreveport Jour., 1977-78; investigative reporter Dallas Morning News, Dallas, 1978-2000; journalism prof. So. Meth. U., 2000—. Recipient First Place award Investigative Reporting Dallas Press Club, 1981, 82, 83, 85, 93, Pub. Svc. award Assn. Press Managing Editors Assn., N.Y.C., 1986, Silver Gavel award ABA, N.Y.C., 1986, Pulitzer Prize, N.Y.C., 1986, Outstanding Investigative Reporting award Investigative Reporters and Editors, 1989, Worth Bingham prize for investigative reporting, 1993, Edward Meeman award for environ. reporting, 1993. Avocation: gardening.

FLOURNOY, WILLIAM LOUIS, JR., landscape architect; b. Raleigh, N.C., May 6, 1945; s. William Louis and Flossie (Combs) F. Student, Gardner-Webb Jr. Coll., 1964-66; BS in Recreation and Parks Administrn., N.C. State U., 1969, M of Landscape Architecture, 1972. Cons. to City of Raleigh N.C. State U. Sch. Design, 1971-72; community planner Wake County Planning Dept., Raleigh, N.C., 1972-80; environ. analysis program mgr. Office Legis. & Intergovtl. N.C. Dept. Environment and Natural Resources, Raleigh, 1980—2002; sr. conservation specialist Office Conservation and Cmty. Affairs NC Dept. Environ. and Natural Resources, Raleigh, 2002—. Author reports, articles and conf. procs. Mem. N.C. bicycle com. N.C. Dept. Transp., 1974—83, chair, 1974—76, 1978—79; mem. nat. recreational trails adv. com. U.S. Dept. Transp., 1992—94; mem. steering com. Wake County Cmty. Assessment, 1992—94; mem. organizing com. N.C. Greenways Conf., 1986—95, conf. chair, 1992; mem. Triangle Open Space Network, 1997—99; bd. dirs. Southeastern U.S. Masters Track and Field, Inc., Raleigh, 1976—82, Triangle Land Conservancy, Rsch. Triangle Pk., NC, pres., 1991—94; bd. dirs. Triangle Greenways Coun., pres., 1989—91; bd. dirs. People for Parks, Wake County, NC, pres., 2002—. Fellow Am. Soc. Landscape Architects (treas. N.C. chpt. 1982-86, v.p. 1978-79, awards 1978, 86, 90, 95), mem. NCSU dept. Landscape Architecture (alum.

adv. bd. 1999—, chair 2003—), N.C. Trails Assn. (bd. dirs. 1977-82, acting pres. 1977), Landscape Architecture Founds., Landscape Architecture Urban Parks Honor Roll, others. Democrat. Methodist. Avocations: trail construction/maintenance, jogging, canoeing, hiking, bicycling. Home: 520 Polk St Raleigh NC 27604-1960 Office: NC ENR Office Conservation and Cmty Affairs 512 N Salisbury St Raleigh NC 27604-1170 E-mail: bill.flournoy@ncmail.net.

FLOWE, BENJAMIN HUGH, JR., lawyer; b. Durham, N.C., Feb. 8, 1956; s. Benjamin H. and Dorothy Amelia (Bell) F.; children: Samantha Kathleen, Andrew Benjamin. AB in Sociology and Psychology cum laude, Duke U., 1978; JD with high honors, N.C. U., 1981. Bar: U.S. Ct. Appeals (D.C. cir.) 1981, U.S. Supreme Ct. 1990. Assoc. Arent, Fox et al, Washington, 1981-84, Bowman, Conner & Touhey P.C., Washington, 1984-87, Verner, Liipfert, Bernhard, McPherson & Hand, Washington, 1987-89, ptnr., 1990-96; pvt. practice, Washington, 1996-97; ptnr. Berliner, Corcoran & Rowe, L.L.P., Washington, 1997—. Contbr. congl. testimony on export controls Ctr. for Stratetic and Internat. Studies; vice chair tech. adv. com. Commerce Dept. Author: Export Compliance Guide, 1995; contbr. articles to profl. jours. Mem.: ABA (chair export controls and econ. sanctions com.), Am. Electronics Assn. (co-chair export controls com.), Order of the Coif. Democrat. Presbyterian. Avocations: skiing, writing, golf, tennis. Home: 8120 Paisley Pl Potomac MD 20854-2748 Office: Berliner Corcoran & Rowe LLP 1101 17th St NW Ste 1100 Washington DC 20036-4798

FLOWE, CAROL CONNOR, lawyer; b. Owensboro, Ky., Jan. 3, 1950; d. Marvin C. Connor and Ethel Marie (Thorn) Smith; children: Samantha Kathleen, Andrew Benjamin. BME magna cum laude, Murray State U., 1972; JD summa cum laude, Ind. U., 1976. Bar: Ohio 1977, D.C. 1981, U.S. Dist. Ct. (so. dist.) Ohio 1977, U.S. Dist. Ct. Md. 1983, U.S. Dist. Ct. D.C. 1981, U.S. Supreme Ct. 1987, U.S. Ct. Appeals (2d, 3d, 4th, 5th, 7th, 9th and D.C. cirs.). Assoc. Baker & Hostetler, Columbus, Ohio, 1976-80, Arent Fox Kintner Plotkin & Kahn, Washington, 1980-87; deputy gen. counsel Pension Benefit Guaranty Corp., Washington, 1987-89, gen. counsel, 1989-95; ptnr. Arent, Fox, Kintner, Plotkin & Kahn, 1995—. Mem. ABA, D.C. Bar Assn., Order of Coif, Alpha Chi, Phi Alpha Delta. Avocations: computers, reading. Home: 8608 Aqueduct Rd Potomac MD 20854-6249 Office: Arent Fox Kintner Plotkin & Kahn 1050 Connecticut Ave NW Ste 500 Washington DC 20036-5339 E-mail: flowe.carol@arentfox.com.

FLOWER, WALTER CHEW, III, investment counselor; b. New Orleans, Mar. 3, 1939; s. Walter Chew II and Anne Elisa (Lusk) F.; m. Ella Smith Montgomery, Dec. 21, 1966; children: Anne Stuart, Lindsey Montgomery. BA in Econs., Tulane U., 1960; MBA in Fin., Harvard U., 1964. Cons. AID, State Dept., 1964-65; fin. analyst Delta Capital Corp., New Orleans, 1965-66; v.p., mng. partner Loomis Sayles & Co. Inc., New Orleans, 1967-78; pres. Walter C. Flower & Co., Investment Counsel, New Orleans, 1978—; dir. Starmount Cos.; chmn. Tulane U. Health Scis. Ctr.; bd. govs. Longue Vue Found., 1983—; dir GPOA Found., 1985—; vestryman, mem. parish coun. Trinity Ch., 1978—; dir fin. adv. Jr. League New Orleans, 1978-82; fin. adv. Beauregard House, 1979-2002, Metairie Park Country Day Sch., 1991—, New Orleans Mus. Art, 1998—. Lt. USNR, 1960-62. Mem. Boston Club, La. Club., Pickwick Club, New Orleans Lawn Tennis Club, So. Yacht Club (New Orleans), Fishers Island Yacht Club, Stratford Club, Lakeshore Club, Wyvern Club, N.Y. Yacht Club, Fishers Island Club, Confrerie Des Chevaliers Du Tastevin, Phi Beta Kappa. Office: 408 Magazine St New Orleans LA 70130-2435 E-mail: wcf@wfco.net.

FLOWERREE, ROBERT EDMUND, retired forest products company executive; b. New Orleans, Jan. 4, 1921; s. Robert E. and Amy (Hewes) F.; m. Elaine Dicks, Sept. 22, 1943; children: Ann D., John H., David R. BA, Tulane U., 1942. Vice pres. Georgia-Pacific Corp., 1956-63, exec. v.p. pulp, paper and chem. ops., 1963-75, pres., 1974-76, chmn., chief exec. officer, 1976-83, chmn., 1983-84, ret., 1984, Kilgore Corp. Past bd. dirs. Ga. Gulf Corp. Emeritus adminstr. Tulane U., New Orleans; life trustee Lewis and Clark Coll., Portland, Oreg. Served to lt. USNR, 1942-46. Recipient Disting. Alumnus award Tulane U., 1978; inducted into Paper Industry Internat. Hall of Fame, 2001. Mem.: Knights of Malta; Arlington (Portland), Waverley Country (Portland); Boston (New Orleans); Links (N.Y.C.). Office: 805 Broadway Ste 2290 Portland OR 97205

FLOWERS, CYNTHIA, investment company executive; b. N.Y.C., May 29, 1951; d. Bernard and Pearl (Davis) Heller; m. Robert Flowers, June 3, 1973; children: Perry, Lindsey. BS summa cum laude, Boston U., 1973; MBA with honors, NYU, 1976. Sr. mgr. portfolios Citibank NA, N.Y.C., 1973-82; v.p. Nat. Securities Corp., N.Y.C., 1982-87; pres. Stillrock Mgmt. Inc., N.Y.C., 1987-90; founder, pres. Flowers Capital Mgmt. Inc., N.Y.C., 1990—. Mem.: Westside Tennis Club, Beta Gamma Sigma. Avocations: tennis, antiques. Office: Flowers Capital Mgmt Inc 97 Groton St Forest Hills NY 11375-5956

FLOWERS, DAMON BRYANT, architect, facility planner; b. Detroit, May 16, 1952; s. Marrell Curtis and Mattie (Rice) F.; m. Adria Faye Burrows, July 28, 1979; children: Lee, Dadria, Damon Bryant II. BS in Architecture, Lawrence Inst. Tech., 1974; BA in Liberal Arts, Cen. Mich. U., 1982; MS in Fin., Ctrl. Mich. U., 1984; JD, Detroit Coll. Law, 1990. Bar: Mich. 1990; registered arch., Mich., Ill., Wis., Ohio, Fla., N.Y. Architect Wayne State U., 1983-85; construction project mgmt. dir. St. Joseph Hosp. and Health Ctrs., 1985-91; v.p. ops. Argus & Assocs., 1991-94; assoc. v.p. facilities devel. and ops. Washtenaw C.C., 1994—. Mem. AIA, APPA, BOCA, Constrn. Spec. Inst., NFPA. Mem. African Methodist Episcopal Ch. Avocation: photography. Home: 1706 Mountain Ash Dr West Bloomfield MI 48324-4003 Office: Washtenaw CC Ann Arbor MI 48106 E-mail: dflowers@wccnet.org.

FLOWERS, GLEN DALE, minister; b. Elberfeld, Ind., July 2, 1940; s. Otis Preston and Anna (Hollingsworth) F.; m. Naomi June Bruce, Aug. 13, 1943; children: Theresa Lynne Flowers Carr, Robert Preston. BA, Carson-Newman Coll., Jefferson City, Tenn., 1972; MDiv, So. Bapt. Theol. Sem., Louisville, 1976; real estate diploma, U. Indpls., 1982. Ordained to ministry So. Bapt. Conv., 1969. Driver United Parcel Svc., Evansville, Ind., 1962-69; pastor Mitchell Springs Bapt. Ch., Rutledge, Tenn., 1969-71, Broadway Bapt. Ch., Princeton, Ind., 1972-76, 1st Bapt. Ch., Mooresville, Ind., 1976-85; evangelist, Jefferson City, 1971-72; pastor Oakhill Bapt. Ch., Evansville, 1985—. Dir. BSU and ISUE, U. Evansville, 1974-75; mem. nat. steering com. Festival Religion and Rural Life, Home Missions Bd., State Conv. Bapts. in Ind., 1978, mem. exec. bd. and exec. com., 1978-80, 86-90, chmn. state exec. bd., 1979-80; mem. various coms. Cen. Ind. Bapt. Assn., Sunday sch. dir., 1978-79, 81-82; tchr. Boyce Bible Ctr., Monrovia, Ind., 1984-85; mem. com. on nominations So. Bapt. Conv., 1988-89; instr., ctr. dir. Extension Ctr. for Okla. Bapt. U., Evansville, 1991-94; numerous others. Contbr. to Ency. So. Bapts., Vol. IV, 1980. Chmn. Vol. Probation Officers for Juvenile Delinquents, Rutledge, 1971; bd. dirs. Mooresville Sr. Ctr., 1983—84, Morgan County Sr. Svcs., Martinsville, Ind., 1983—85; founder Ann. Ladies' Enrichment Day, Mooresville, 1980—85; chaplain Morgan County Sheriff's Office and Mooresville Police Dept., 1980—85; vol. chaplaincy program Mooresville H.S., 1983—84; bd. dirs. Morgan County Weekday Religious Edn., 1983—84; trustee internat. mission bd. So. Bapt. Conf., 1992—2000, mission trips to Antigua, Zambia, Kenya, Rwanda, Uganda, Malawi, Zimbabwe, South Africa, Swaziland, Guatemala and Ukraine; mem. State Conv. of Bapts. in Ind., 2000, pres., 2000—02. With USN, 1958—61. Mem. Southwestern Bapt. Assn. (bd. dirs. 1985—). Republican. Office: Oakhill Bapt Ch 4615 Oak Hill Rd Evansville IN 47711-2943 Home: 4128 Rosewood Ave Evansville IN 47711-3066 *Our generation has a need to be encouraged to express a sincere faith in God while the influences around them are teaching them to be so superficial about their feelings.*

FLOWERS, KENT GORDON, JR., lawyer; b. Aurora, N.C., Apr. 29, 1955; s. Kent Gordon Sr. and Shirley Temple (Deal); m. Debra Ann Henries, Aug. 21, 1981; children: Kent Gordon III, Rachel Ann. BA in Social Sci., U. N.C., Wilmington, 1976, BA in Secondary Edn., 1977; postgrad., Emmanuel Coll., 1977-78; JD, U. Ark., Little Rock, 1981. Bar: N.C. 1982, U.S. Dist. Ct. (ea. dist.) N.C. 1986. Staff atty. Craven County, New Bern, N.C., 1982—. Cons. Craven County Foster Parents, New Bern, 1982-92; com. chairperson Craven County Council for Children, New Bern, 1982-86; bd. dirs. Smart Start, 1999—; dist. comdr. Royal Rangers, 1994—. Mem. N.C. Bar Assn., N.C. Coll. of Advocacy, N.C. Assn. Social Service Attys. (sec. 1984-85). Democrat. Avocations: collecting antiques, home restoration. Home: PO Box 593 New Bern NC 28563-0593 Office: PO Box 12039 New Bern NC 28561-2039 E-mail: jr.flowers@ncmail.net.

FLOWERS, LANGDON STRONG, foods company executive; b. Thomasville, Ga., Feb. 12, 1922; s. William Howard and Flewellyn Evans (Strong) F.; m. Margaret Clisby Powell, June 3, 1944; children: Margaret Flowers Rich, Langdon Strong, Elizabeth Powell Flowers, Dorothy Howard Flowers Swinson, John Howard. BS, MIT, 1944, MS, 1947; H.H.D., Presbyn. Coll., 1984. Engr., Douglas Aircraft, Los Angeles, 1947; supr. Flowers Baking Co., Thomasville, 1947-50, sales mgr., 1950-58, v.p. sales, 1958-65; pres., chief operating officer Flowers Industries, Inc., Thomasville, 1965-76, vice chmn. bd., chief exec. officer, 1976-80, chmn. bd., 1980-85, ret., 1985. Past pres. Thomasville YMCA, 1958-62; past trustee Presbyn Coll., Clinton, S.C., Archbold Meml. Hosp., Thomasville. Served as lt. (j.g.) USNR, 1943-46. Named Man of Year, Thomas County C. of C., 1974 Mem. Am. Bakers Assn. (exec. com. 1974-75, chmn. 1975-76), So. Bakers Assn. (chmn. bd. 1969-70), NAM (dir., exec. com.), Thomasville C. of C. (pres. 1953-54), Sigma Alpha Epsilon. Presbyterian (chmn. bd. deacons 1952-56, elder 1956—, rep. Gen. Assembly 1966). Club: Rotarian. Home: 207 Fairways Dr Thomasville GA 31792-7626 Office: PO Box 997 Thomasville GA 31799-0997

FLOWERS, MARY E. state legislator; b. July 31, 1951; married. Ed., Kennedy-King C.C., U. Ill. Mem. from 21st dist. Ill. Ho. of Reps., 1985—, now asst. majority leader, mem. appropriations and pub. utilities coms. Co-chmn. Il. Conf. Women Legis.; spokesperson Com. on Ins.; mem. Healthcare and Human Svcs. Com., Fin. Instns. Com., Consumer Protection Com. Recipient Black Rose award League of Black Women, 1988, Kizzy award Black Women Hall of Fame Found., 1990, Friend of Labor award AFL-CIO, 1990. Home: 2539 W 79th St Chicago IL 60652-1729 Office: Ill Ho of Reps State Capitol 2048-j Stratton Bldg Springfield IL 62706-0001*

FLOWERS, ROBERT B. military career officer; b. Pa., July 9, 1947; m. Lynda F.; 4 sons. Grad., Va. Mil. Inst., 1969; M in Civil Engring., U. Va., 1976; grad., Command & Gen. Staff Coll., Nat. War Coll. Registered profl. engr., Va. Commd. 2nd lt. U.S. Army, 1969, advanced through grades to maj. gen., 1997, various positions, 1969-85, comdr. 307th Engr. Battalion, 1985-87, joint staff Nat. Mil. Command Ctr./Counternarcotics Divsn., 1987-90, comdr. 20th Engr. Brigade (Combat) (Airborne Corps) Ft. Bragg, N.C., 1990-92; dep. asst. commandant U.S. Army Engr. Sch., 1992-93, asst. commandant, 1993-95; dep. commdg. gen. U.S. Army Engring. Ctr., 1993-95; asst. divsn. comdr. 2nd Inf. Divsn. (Mechanized) Eighth U.S. Army; dep. chief staff engring. U.S. Army Europe, 1996; pres. Miss. River Commn. U.S. Army, comdr. Miss. Valley Divsn.; commandant U.S. Army Engr. Sch.; commdg. gen. U.S. Army Engr. Ctr. and Ft. Leonard Wood, 1997—. Joint task force engr. Joint Task Force, Somalia. Office: US Army Engr Ctr Fort Leonard Wood MO 65473

FLOWERS, SANDRA JOAN, elementary education educator; b. Newport, R.I., July 17, 1943; d. Joseph A. and Dolores A. (Martino) F. BA, Salve Regina Coll., 1965; MA in Teaching, R.I. Coll., 1968; postgrad., Salve Regina U., 1990—, cert. advanced grad. study, 1994. Cert. elem. tchr., R.I. Tchr. Newport Sch. Dept., 1965-95; ret., 1995; instr., edn. Salve Regina U., Newport, 1979—. Mem. adv. bd. Underwood Sch., Newport, 1986, mem. site-based mgmt. team, 1993—; mem. basic ednl. planning ream R.I. Dept. Edn., Barrington Pub. Schs., 1986; mem. planning team, reader Children's Reading Hour, Literacy Outreach, Newport. Mem. Funding and Expenditures Alternatives Strategic Planning, Newport, 1989—; mem. grad. student coun. Salve Regina U.; religious edn. tchr. St. Joseph's Parish, Newport, 1995—, chair liturgy com., 2000—, sec. parish coun., 2001—; bd. dirs. Aquidneck Collaborative for Edn., 1993—. Moore scholar Salve Regina Coll., 1961-65, R.I. State scholar, 1961-65; recipient Feinstein Enriching Am. award, 1999. Mem.: LWV, AAUW, ASCD, Newport County Ret. Tchrs. Assn., R.I. Ret. Tchrs. Assn., R.I. Assn. Tchr. Educators. Roman Catholic. Avocations: writing for children, reading, church work, drawing, painting. Home: PO Box # 114 16 Keeher Ave Newport RI 02840-2320 E-mail: flowerss@salve.edu.

FLOWERS, TERRY JAMES, headmaster; m. Gernise Flowers; children: Taylor, Taryn, Tia. My Childhood Edn., U. No. Iowa; M Curriculum and Instrn., M Ednl. Adminstrn., PhD, Columbia U. Exec. dir., headmaster St. Philip's Sch. and Cmty. Ctr., Dallas, 1983—. Office: St Philip's Sch and Cmty Ctr 1600 Pennsylvania Ave Dallas TX 75215

FLOWERS, V. ANNE, academic administrator emerita; b. Dothan, Ala., Aug. 29, 1928; d. Kyrie Neal and Annie Laurie (Stewart) F. BA, Fla. State U., 1949; MEd, Auburn U., 1958; EdD, Duke U., 1963. Teaching asst. Duke U., Durham, N.C., 1963; elem. and secondary sch. tchr., adminstr. Dothan and Dalton, Ga., 1949-61; assoc. prof., then prof. edn., head dept. Columbia (S.C.) Coll., 1963-68, assoc. dean, then dean, 1969-72; prof. edn. Va. Commonwealth U., 1968-69; teaching asst. Duke U., 1963; assoc. dean, asst. provost, acting dean, vice provost Trinity Coll. Arts and Scis., Duke U., 1972-74, prof. edn., chmn. dept., asst. provost ednl. program devel., 1974-80; dean Sch. Edn., Ga. So. Coll., Statesboro, 1980-85; asst. vice chancellor acad. affairs Univ. System of Ga., Atlanta, 1985-88, vice chancellor, 1988-90, vice chancellor emerita, 1990—. Ind. ednl. cons. Co-author: Law and Pupil Control, 1964, Readings in Survival in Today's Society, 2 vols, 1978; editorial bd.: Jour. Tchr. Edn, 1980-82, Ednl. Gerontology, 1979; ; contbr. articles to profl. jours. Bd. dirs., mem. exec. com. Learning Inst. N.C., 1976-80; mem. bd. visitors Charleston So. U., 1992-93; adv. trustee Queens Coll., Charlotte, N.C., 1976-78; vice chmn. continuing commn. on study of black colls. related to United Meth. Ch., 1973-76. Delta Kappa Gamma scholar Duke U., 1963, State of Fla. scholar Fla. State U., 1949. Mem. NEA, Am. Ednl. Rsch. Assn., So. Assn. Colls. and Schs. (mem. commn. on colls.), Am. Assn. Higher Edn., Am. Assn. Colls. of Tchr. Edn. (pres. 1983-84, bd. dirs., mem. exec. com. 1979-84), Nat. Orgn. Legal Problems in Edn., Kappa Delta Pi, Phi Delta Kappa. Home and Office: 41 Williamsburg Pl Dothan AL 36305

FLOWERS, VONETTA, Olympic athlete; b. Birmingham, Oct. 29, 1973; d. Jimmie and Barbara Jeffery; m. Johnny Mack Flowers. Olympic athlete, mem. U.S. bobsled team; grad. asst., men's track team U. Ala., 1997—99, asst. track coach, 1999—; placed 13th at the summer olympic trials Sacramento, 2000. Mem. U.S. Olympic Festival Team; chosen to compete in the World U. Games. Named U.S. push champion and record holder for boblsed start, 2002 Winter Olympics, 7-time NCAA All-Am.; named one of 50 most inspiring African-Am., 2002, 57 of the most intriguing blacks, Ebony Mag., 2002; recipient 4 World Cup medals, 2002 Winter Olympics, Gold medal for long jump, 1994 Olympic Festival, Citizen through Sports Alliance award, 2002, U.S. Olympic Spirit award, 2002, Victor award, 2002, Live the Dream award, 2002, 50 most beautiful people, People Mag., 2002, Wilma Rudolph Athlete of the Yr. award, 2002, Dodge Nat. Athletic Olympian award, 2003, U.S. Olympic Com. Team of the Yr. award, 2003. Achievements include 1st African-Am. to win a gold medal in the winter olympics, 1st person from Ala. to win a gold medal in the winter olympics, 2002 olympic champion. Office: U Ala-Birmingham 701 20th St S Birmingham AL 35294-010

FLOWERS, WILLIAM HAROLD, JR., lawyer; b. Chgo., Ill., Mar. 22, 1946; s. William Harold Sr. and Ruth Lolita (Cave) Flowers; m. Pamela Ann Mays, Sept. 13, 1980. BA, U. Colo., 1967, JD, 1971. Bar: Colo. 1973, U.S. Ct. Appeals (10th cir.) 1973, U.S. Dist. Ct. Colo. 1973, U.S. Supreme Ct. 1985, U.S. Ct. Appeals (4th cir.) 1994. Atty. Pikes Peak Legal Svcs., Colorado Springs, Colo., 1973; ptnr. Tate, Tate & Flowers, Denver, 1973-76; dep. dist. atty. Office Adams County Dist. Atty., Brighton, Colo., 1977-78; ptnr. Taussig & Flowers, Boulder, 1978-81; pvt. practice Boulder, 1981-89; ptnr. Holland & Hart, LLP, Denver, 1989-97, Hurth Yeager, Sisk & Blakemore LLP, Boulder, 1997—. Mem. Boulder County Cmty. Corrections Bd., 1985—90. Mem. Boulder Bd. Zoning Adjustment, 1973-78, chmn., 1977-78; mem. Boulder Growth Task Force, 1980-82; mem. exec. bd. Longs Peak coun. Boy Scouts Am., 1983-98; bd. dirs. Sta. KGNU, Boulder County Broadcasting, 1981-84, Coloradans Against the Death Penalty, 2001-; bd. trustees Nat. Coll. Advocacy, 2002—. Mem.: ATLA (chair Coun. of Pres. 2001—02, exec. com. 2001—03, bd. govs. 2002—, chair state dels. 2002—03), Colo. Bar Assn. (bd. govs. 2000, v.p. 2002—03), U. Colo. Found. (bd. dirs. 1995—2002), U. Colo. Boulder Alumni Assn. (bd. dirs. 1987—96, pres. 1994—95), Sam Cary Bar Assn. (pres. 1987), Boulder County Bar Assn. (civil litigation com. 1978—, criminal law com. 1979—, bd. dirs. 2003—04), Colo. Trial Lawyers Assn. (bd. dirs. 1989—, exec. com. 1996—2003, pres. 1999—2000), Colo. Criminal Def. Bar (bd. dirs. 1987—83), Nat. Bar Assn. (regional dir. 1983—86, bd. govs. 1983—96, v.p. 1990—91). Democrat. Methodist. Office: Hurth Yeager Sisk & BlakemoreLLP PO Box 17850 4860 Riverbend Rd Boulder CO 80308

FLOYD, ALTON DAVID, cell biologist, consultant; b. Henderson, Ky., July 17, 1941; s. Frank and Queen Tina (Melton) F.; m. Barbara Wilson, Aug. 18, 1962; children: Fara Alison, Heather Lynn. BS, U. Ky., 1963; PhD, U. Louisville, 1968. From lectr. to asst. prof. U. Mich., Ann Arbor, 1967-72; from asst. to assoc. prof. Sch. of Medicine Ind. U., Bloomington, 1972-83, assoc. prof. Sch. of Medicine Indpls., 1983-84; sect. head cell biology Miles Sci., Inc., Naperville, Ill., 1984-85; sr. staff scientist Miles, Inc., Elkhart, Ind., 1985 89; pvt. practice cons. Edwardsburg, Mich., 1989—; assoc. dir. Ctr. Light Microscope Imaging and Biotech. Carnegie Mellon U., Pitts., 1991. Bd. dirs. Endotech Corp., Indpls.; mem. subcom. immunohistochem. stains NCCLS, 1995-96; industry rep. adv. panel hematology and pathology devices FDA, 1996-99; trustee Biol. Stain Commn., 1997—. Mem. Am. Assn. Anatomists, Tissue Culture Assn., Soc. Analytical Cytology, Histochem. Soc., Soc. Quantitative Morphology, Soc. Histotech. Avocations: sailing, reading, wood and metal shopwork, computing. Home and Office: 23126 S Shore Dr Edwardsburg MI 49112-8502

FLOYD, ANGELEITA STEVENS, flutist; b. Concord, N.C., Aug. 6, 1952; d. William Russel and Elizabeth (Hopkins) Floyd. BMus, Stetson U., 1974; MMus, Fla. State U., 1979, MMus Edn., 1981, DMus, 1987. Music tchr., Rockhill, SC, Charlotte and Concord, NC; appearances with Charlotte Opera Assn., Charlotte Summer Pops Orch., Ice Capades, Ontario Singers; concert tours as soloist and with chamber groups Southeastern U.S., 1974—77; prin. flute Naples/Marco Philharm. Orch., 1984—85; vis. instr. U. Idaho, Moscow, 1984—85; asst. prof. flute U. Wis.-Eau Claire, 1985—86, also dir. flute choir; asst. prof. flute to assoc. prof. U. No. Iowa, Cedar Falls, 1986—97, prof., 1997—; prof. flute U. Karlstadt, Sweden, 2003—. Mem. Northwind Quintet; prin. flute Waterloo/Cedar Falls Symphony and Chamber Orch., Iowa; guest artist 5th, 6th and 11th Internat. Festival de Flautistas, Lima, Peru, 1990, 1st-13th Flute Festival, Quito, Ecuador, 1991, Mac Phall Ctr. for Arts, Fla. Flute Fair, Tenn. Tech. Flute Day, 1st Brazilian Flute Festival, Rio de Janeiro, 1995, 2d Brazilian Flute Festival, Porto Alegre, 1996, 1st and 2d Flute Festivals, Orebro, Sweden; owner, exec. dir. Winzer Press, splty. pub. flute methods. Author: The Gilbert Legacy Methods, Exercises and Techniques for the Flutist; contbg. author: Flute Talk, the Flutist Quar., NACWPI jour., Flute Forum-Emmerson, editor: Trevor Wye's An Extraordinary Man—Marcel Moyse. Home and Office: 3743 Beaver Ridge Cir Cedar Falls IA 50613-9447

FLOYD, JACK WILLIAM, lawyer; b. Columbia, S.C., May 14, 1934; s. Edward Immanuel and Edith Fletcher (Herlong) F.; m. Ruth Parker Matthews, Jan. 10, 1957; children: Connie, Cindy, Jay. BS, U. N.C., 1958, JD with honors, 1961. Bar: N.C. 1961, U.S. Supreme Ct. 1971. Assoc. Smith, Moore, Smith, Schell & Hunter, Greensboro, N.C., 1961-67, ptnr., 1967-87, Floyd, Greeson, Allen & Jacobs, Greensboro, N.C., 1988-90, Floyd, Allen & Jacobs, Greensboro, 1991-97, Floyd & Jacobs, Greensboro, 1998—. Lectr. acctg. U. N.C., 1960-61; lectr. bus. law Guilford Coll., 1962-64; speaker on jury trials Am. Bar Assn., Am. Patent Law Assn.; arbitrator U.S. Dist. Ct. Annexed Arbitration Program. Bd. editors: N.C. Law Rev. 1960-61. Mem. parents' bd. dirs. Meredith Coll., Raleigh, N.C., 1977-79, chmn., 1980-81. Served with USN, 1951-55. Mem. Am. Bar Assn., N.C. Bar Assn. (panelist on family law), Am. Law Inst., N.C. Assn. Trial Lawyers, Order of Coif. Clubs: Elks. Democrat. Baptist. Home: 1404 Valleymeade Rd Greensboro NC 27410-3938 Office: Floyd & Jacobs 401C N Eugene St Greensboro NC 27401-2644 E-mail: jackw.floyd@aol.com, jwf1404@aol.com.

FLOYD, JEANNE, professional society administrator; b. New Bedford, Mass. d. Alfred Oscar and Irene Fournier Morel; m. Harry Joseph Floyd Jr., Aug. 8, 1964; 1 child, Jason Alfred. BS, Coll. of Notre Dame of Md., 1982; MS, U. Md., 1984; PhD, Pa. State U., 1993. Asst. dir. Psychogeriatric Clin., Johns Hopkins Med. Instns., Balt., 1979-88; dir. programs and svcs. Pa. Nurses Assn., Harrisburg, 1988-95; exec. dir. Midwest Alliance in Nursing, Indpls., 1995-97; dir. rsch. and evaluation Sigma Theta Tau Internat., Indpls., 1997-2000; exec. dir. Am. Nurses Credentialing Ctr., Washington, 2000—. Contbr. articles to profl. jours., including Am. Jour. Gerontological Nursing, Reflections, Synergy. Mem. adv. bd. Friends of Strand Theater, York, Pa., 1994-95, Nursing 2000, Indpls., 1995-97. Lt. Nurses Corp., USAF, 1962-64. Mem. Am. Soc. Assn. Execs. (cert.), Ind. Soc. Assn. Execs. Roman Catholic. Avocations: gardening, exercising, antiquing. Home: 11 Third St NE Washington DC 20002 Office: Am Nurses Credentialing Ctr 600 Maryland SW Ste 100 W Washington DC 20024-2571 E-mail: jfloyd@ana.org.

FLOYD, JOHN ALEX, JR., marketing executive, editor, horticulturist; b. Selma, Ala., Feb. 21, 1948; s. John Alex Sr. and Louise (Johnson) F.; m. Pamela Lorene Billups, Aug. 14, 1982; children: Ryan Thomas, James Alex. BS, Auburn (Ala.) U., 1970; MS, Clemson (S.C.) U., 1972, PhD, 1975. Instr. Jefferson State Jr. Coll., Birmingham, Ala., 1975-77; sr. horticulturist So. Living Mag., Birmingham, 1977-84; editorial dir. Classics-So. Accents, Birmingham, 1985-87, Creative Ideas and Cooking Light, Birmingham, 1987-88; dir. mktg. svcs., editor So. Progress Corp, Birmingham, 1988-91; v.p., editor So. Living, 1991—. Author: (with others) Southern Living Trees & Shrubs, 1980, Southern Living Garden Guide, 1982, Southern Living Vegetable & Herbs, 1984. Mem. adv. com. Landscape Architecture Adv. Coun., Auburn U., 1988-93; bd. dirs. U. N.C. Botanical Gardens, Chapel Hill, 1988-90; program com. Brookgreen Gardens; bd. dirs. Ea. Health Found., Trussville Tree Commn.; vis. com. Longwood Gardens. Grantee NSF, 1977. Mem. Am. Soc. Hort. Sci., Garden Writers Am., Birmingham Bot. Soc. (pres. 1981, trustee 1984—), Am. Hort. Soc. (bd. dirs. 1991-94), The Club, Summit Club, Gamma Sigma Delta, Pi Alpha Xi. Methodist. Home: 369 Palace Dr Trussville AL 35173-1067 Office: So Progress Corp 2100 Lakeshore Dr Birmingham AL 35209-6721 E-mail: john_floyd@timeinc.com.

FLOYD, JOHN DAVID, theology educator, minister; b. Lockesburg, Ark., Sept. 28, 1934; s. William Chaney Floyd and Alice Thadine (Park) Trammell; m. Helen Nutt, June 3, 1955; children: Elizabeth Ann Stivers, John Paul. BA, Ouachita Bapt. U., 1952-56; BD, Southwestern Bapt. Theol. Sem., 1962, M in Div., 1969; PhD, Mid-Am. Bapt. Theol. Sem., 1976; post doctoral studies, Fuller Theol. Sem., 1980-81. Ordained to ministry Bapt. Ch., 1952. Pastor various So. Bapt. Chs., 1952-65; missionary Fgn. Mission Bd. So. Bapt. Conv., Philippines, 1965-75; v.p. adminstrn., prof. missions Mid-Am. Bapt. Theol. Sem., Memphis, 1975-84; dir. missionary enlistment Fgn. Mission Bd. So. Bapt. Conv., Richmond, Va., 1984-85; v.p., dir. of D of Ministry program Mid-Am. Bapt. Theol. Sem., Memphis, 1985-93; dir. fgn. mission bd. for Europe The Southern Baptist Convention, 1993 2000; v.p., chmn. missions dept. Mid-Am. Bapt. Theol. Sem., 2000—. Head Missions Dept. Mid-Am. Bapt. Theol. Sem., Memphis, 1977-84, cons. ch. growth, 1979-84, dir. sch. world missions, 1982-84. Editor: Inductive Bible Study Series, 1970, 1971 Church Growth Survey in the Philippines, 1972, Modern Cults, 1979; editor numerous articles Mid-Am. Bapt. Theol. Jour., 1976-86; editor Jour. Evangelism and Missions. Campaigner Rep. Party in Va., Richmond, 1984-85. Served as 1st lt. inf. U.S. Army, 1957-59. Recipient Eye of the Eagle award 101st Airborne Div. Ft. Campbell, 1984, Key to the City award Booneville City Govt., 1982. Mem. Am. Assn. Missiologists, Assn. Mission Profs., Internat. Missiological Soc., Nat. Planned Giving Assn., Am. Mgmt. Assn. Home: 2533 Brotherwood Cv Collierville TN 38017-8972 Office: Mid-Am Bapt Theol Sem 2216 S Germantown Rd Germantown TN 38138-3804 E-mail: jdfloyd@pobox.com.

FLOYD, JOHN EARL, economics educator; b. Moose Jaw, Sask., Can., May 6, 1937; s. Phineas John Earl and Marjory (Powell) F.; children— Laurie Marie, Ian Seth. B.Commerce, U. Sask., 1958, honors in econs., 1959; M.A., U. Chgo., 1962, Ph.D., 1964. Asst. prof. econs. U. Wash., Seattle, 1962-66, assoc. prof., 1966-69; prof. econs. U. Toronto, Ont., Can., 1970— . Author: World Monetary Equilibrium, 1985, (with Trevor J.O. Dick)Can. and the Gold Standard 1871-1913, 1992. Contbr. articles to prof. jours. Grantee in field. Mem. Am. Econ. Assn., Canadian Econ. Assn. Avocation: traditional jazz piano player. Home: 100 Quebec Ave # 1812 Toronto ON M6P 4B8 Canada Office: Univ Toronto Dept Econs Toronto ON Canada M5S 3G7

FLOYD, JOHN TAYLOR, electronics executive; b. Quincy, Mass., Jan. 17, 1942; s. John Taylor and Virginia Marie (Watts) F.; m. Denise Angela Dufault, Oct. 4, 1969; children: Jennifer, Aimee. BA, Northeastern U., 1965; MBA in Fin., Boston Coll., 1972. Product group controller Tex. Instruments, Attleboro, Mass., 1972-75; asst. to v.p. fin. Waters Assocs., Milford, Mass., 1975-76; group fin. mgr. Digital Equipment Corp., Maynard, Mass., 1976-82; v.p. mfg. Computer Devices, Burlington, Mass., 1982-83; dir. fin. and adminstrn. Wang Labs., Lowell, Mass., 1984-85; v.p. ops. Charleswater Products, Newton, Mass., 1985-90; v.p. Devon Group, Waltham, Mass., 1991—, also bd. dirs. Served to capt. U.S. Army, 1965-70, Vietnam. Mem. Fin. Execs. Inst., Am. Electronics Assn., Treas.' Club of Boston, Am. Legion. Republican. Home: 68 Longfellow Rd Sudbury MA 01776-1256 Office: Devon Group 800 South St Waltham MA 02453-1478

FLOYD, JULIET HENDRICKS, philosopher, educator; b. Boston, Mar. 12, 1960; d. William Beckwith and Margaret Boyle (Henderson) F.; m. Burton Dreben; 1 child, Margaux Sachi Floyd Kanamori. BA, Wellesley Coll., 1982; MA, PhD, Harvard U., 1990. Asst. prof. CUNY, N.Y.C., 1990—96; assoc. prof. Boston U., 1996—. Author chpts. and articles. ACLS Sr. grantee, 1998-99, Am. Philos. Soc., 2003—; Fulbright fellow, 2003. Fellow: Am. Philos. Assn. Office: Boston U Philosophy Dept 745 Commonwealth Ave Boston MA 02215-1401

FLOYD, RAYMOND LORAN, professional golfer; b. Ft. Bragg, N.C., Sept. 4, 1942; s. Loren B. and Edith (Brown) F.; m. Maria; children: Raymond Loran, Robert Loran, Christina Loran. Student, U. N.C., 1960. Profl. golfer PGA, 1961-92; profl. golfer Sr. PGA, 1992—; mem. Ryder Cup team, 1969, 75, 77, 81, 83, 85, 89, 91, 93; capt. Ryder Cup Team, 1989. Winner 2000 Ford Sr. Players Championship, Doral Ryder Open, 1992, GTE North Classic, 1992, Northville Long Island Classic Senior PGA, 1993, Sr. Tour Championship, 1994, Ford Sr. Players Championship, 2000; named Rookie of Year Golf Mag., 1963, 77, Player of Yr., 1976. Winner PGA tournament, 1969, 82 St. Petersburg Open, 1963, St. Paul Open, 1965, Jacksonville Open, 1969, Am. Golf Classic, 1969, Kemper Open, 1975, Masters, 1976, World Open, 1976, Byron Nelson Golf Classic, 1977, Pleasant Valley Golf Classic, 1977, Brazilian Open, 1978, Greater Greensboro Open, 1979, Canadian PGA, 1981, Vardon Trophy, 1983, Ryder Cup, 1969, 75, 77, 81, 83, 85, Doral Ea. Open, 1980, 81, Tournament Players Championship, 1981, Westchester Classic, 1981, Meml. Tournament, 1982, Memphis Classic, 1982, PGA Championship, 1982, $1Million Sun City Challenge, 1982, Houston Open, 1985, Chrysler Team Championship, 1985, U.S. Open, 1986, Walt Disney/Oldsmobile Classic, 1986, Skins Game, 1988, RMCC Invitational, 1990, Doral-Ryder Open, 1992, GTE North Classic, 1992, Ralph's Sr. Classic, 1992, Sr. Tour Championship, 1992, Thailand Srs., 1992, Northville L.I. Classic, 1993, The Tradition, 1994, Sr. Skins Game, 1994, 95, 96, 97, 98, Las Vegas Srs. Classis, 1994, Sr. Tour Championship, 1994, PGA Srs. Championship, 1995, Burnet Sr. Classic, 1995, Ford Sr. Players Championship, 1996; capt. Ryder Cup, 1989; inducted in PGA/World Golf Hall of Fame, 1989, winner father-son tourn. w/son Raymond Jr., 1995, 96, 97, w/son Robert, 2000, 01, winner Par 3 Shootout, 2000. Office: PO Box 2163 Palm Beach FL 33480-4349

FLOYD, ROSALYN WRIGHT, pianist, accompanist, educator; b. Charleston, S.C., Oct. 22, 1956; d. Reginald Abram and Dorothy (Brunson) Wright; m. Hernan Augustus Floyd, Nov. 27, 1987. BA, Talladega (Ala.) Coll., 1977; MusM in Piano Performance/Pedagogy, U S.C., 1981; D Musical Arts in Piano Performance, U. S.C., 1990. Music tchr. Charleston County Dist. 20, Charleston, 1977-78; grad. asst. U. S.C., Columbia, S.C., 1978-85; asst. prof. dept. music Benedict Coll., Columbia, SC, 1985—88; rehearsal accompanist Columbia Lyric Opera, 1983-86; prof. dept. fine arts Augusta (Ga.) State U., 1988—; rehearsal accompanist Augusta Choral Soc., 1994—2001. Bd. dirs. Augusta Choral Soc. Performer lectures and recitals; accompanist for Martina Arroyo and Myrtle Hall in their performances for Pope John Paul II, 1987. Evaluator, Arts Infusion program Greater Augusta Arts Coun., 1992, Music panel Ga. Coun. for the Arts, 1997-98. Black Am. Music Symposium scholar, 1985; Ambrose Headen scholar Talladega Coll., 1973-77. Mem. Augusta Music Tchrs. Assn. (v.p. for membership 1998—), Ga. Music Tchrs. Assn., The Links Inc. (v.p. Augusta chpt. 1999-2001, pres. 2001-03), Ctr. for Black Music Rsch. (pres. 2001-2003). Baptist. Avocations: crocheting, sewing, gardening, computing. Home: 2503 Larchmont Ct Augusta GA 30909-6567 Office: Augusta State U 2500 Walton Way Augusta GA 30904-4562 E-mail: rfloyd@aug.edu.

FLOYD, TIM, professional basketball coach; b. Hattiesburg, Miss. m. Beverly Floyd; 1 child, Shannon. BS, La. Tech. Univ., 1977. Coach Univ. El Paso, 1977-86, Idaho Univ., 1986-88, Iowa State Univ., 1994-98; head coach Chgo. Bulls, 1999—2001, New Orleans Hornets, 2003—. Named Coach of Yr.. Office: c/o New Orleans Hornets 1501 Girod St New Orleans LA 70113*

FLOYD, WALTER LEO, lawyer; b. St. Louis, May 29, 1933; s. Walter L. Sr. and Estelle E. (Kiess) F.; children: Michael W., Mary Ann, Mark L.; m. Patricia A. Knapko, Sept. 3, 1994. BS, St. Louis U., 1955, LLD, 1959. Bar: Mo. 1959, Ill. 1959, U.S. Dist. (ea. dist.) Mo. 1959. Owner The Floyd Law Firm P.C., St. Louis, 1959—. Contbr. articles to profl. jours. Fellow: Orgn. Nat. Bd. Trial Advocacy; mem. Mo. Assn. Trial Attys. (sec. 1961, v.p. 1962, 85), Am. Trial Lawyers Assn. (lectr.), Mo. Bar Assn., Ill. Assn., Phi Delta Phi. Democrat. Unitarian Universalist. Address: Floyd Law Firm 8151 Clayton Rd Ste 202 Saint Louis MO 63117-1111

FLOYD, WILLIAM R. health facility administrator; BA, MBA, U. Pa. Sr. mgmt. positions Pepsico, Pillsbury, Gillette; CEO Choice Hotels Internat.; pres., COO Beverly Enterprises Inc., 2000—, CEO/chmn., 2001—. Office: 1000 Beverly Way Fort Smith AR 72919 Office Fax: 479-201-1101.

FLOYD-HOOPER, CAROL ANN, musician, educator; b. N.Y.C. d. Frank Dallas and Marilyn Marcella Floyd; m. Dale B. Hooper; children: Christian Floyd Hooper, Sheila Rae Hooper. Bachelor of Music, Boise State U., 1990; Master of Music summa cum laude, Cin. Coll., 1993, Doctor of Music, 1994; diploma, Conservatoire de Musique, Fontainebleau, France, 1993. Pvt. instr. music, Boise, Idaho, 2000—. Chamber music coach and adviser Boise Tuesday Mus. Scholarships for Students, 1983—; spkr. in field. Musician (concert pianist): state, nat. and internat. performances. Fundraiser Cystic Fibrosis Found., Boise, 1994; mem. Am. Mothers, Inc. Recipient First Place award, Am. Mother's Inc., 2000. Mem.: Music Tchrs. Nat. Assn., Nat. Fedn. Music Clubs (judge). Avocations: gardening, weightlifting, reading.

FLUBACHER, JOSEPH FRANCIS, retired economics educator; b. Phila., Jan. 4, 1914; s. Gustave Edwin and Rose Mary (Ganz) F. AB, La Salle Coll., Phila., 1935; AM, Temple U., 1938, EdD, 1948; LHD (hon.), LaSalle U., 2000. Instr. econs. LaSalle Coll. (became Univ. 1984), 1938-41; asst. prof. La Salle Coll., 1941-45, assoc. prof., 1945-49, prof., 1949-88, prof. emeritus, 1988—, sec. corp., sec. bd. trustees, 1982—. Author: The Concept of Ethics in the History of Economics, 1950 (Phi Delta Kappa award). Mem. Am. Econ. Assn., Assn. for Social Econs. Democrat. Roman Catholic. Home: 309 Bridgeboro Rd Apt 3124 Moorestown NJ 08057-1440 Office: La Salle U PO Box 325 Philadelphia PA 19105-0325

FLUCK, ROBERT R., JR., respiratory therapy technician, educator; b. Pitts., May 14, 1950; s. Robert Roy Fluck and Betty Mae Lippman; m. Diane Marie Sullivan, Dec. 2, 1972; children: Robert R. III, Stephen Charles, Colleen Marie. BS in Biology, Rensselaer Poly. Inst., Troy, N.Y., 1972; Cert. in Respiratory Therapy, NYU/Bellevue Sch. Respiratory Therapy, N.Y.C., 1973; MS in Edn., Syracuse U., 1982. Registered respiratory therapist. Instr. NYU-Bellevue Respiratory Program, N.Y.C., 1973—74; staff therapist Bellevue Hosp. Ctr., N.Y.C., 1974—75; faculty SUNY-Upstate Med. Ctr., Syracuse, 1975—; staff therapist Crouse Hosp., Syracuse, 1990—. Cons. N.Y. State Dept. Health, Syracuse, 1983—98; mem. prof. adv. com. Loretto Geriatric Ctr., Syracuse, 1982—. Contbr. V.p. North Area Vol. Amb. Corps, North Syracuse, 1982—84, pres., 1988—91, bd. dirs., 1995—97. Recipient Onondaga Med. Instruments Rsch. award, 1983, Disting. Svc. award, N.Y. State Soc. Respiratory Care, 1983, Centrum award, 1988, Samuel Runyon Meml. award, 1989, Donald G. Goodman Faculty Devel. award, SUNY, 1999. Fellow: Am. Assn. Respiratory Care. Republican. Avocations: furniture refinishing, home repair. Office: SUNY-Upstate Med Univ 750 E Adams St Syracuse NY 13210

FLUG, JANICE, librarian; b. Mpls., Oct. 19, 1949; d. Albert William and Elberta Edna (Kimball) F.; m. William Raymond LeFevre, Jan. 2, 1982 (dec. June 1986). BA, Hamline U., St. Paul, 1971; MLS, U. Md., 1975; MPA, Am. U., 1980. Acquisitions searcher Am. U. Libr., Washington, 1972-75, asst. to the univ. libr., 1975-91, acquisitions libr., 1991—. Chmn. U. Libr. Faculty Coun., 1999—2003; mem. faculty senate Am. U., chmn. com. on instrl. budget and benefits, 2003—. Mem. bd. editors The Pub. Mgr., 1996—. Exec. bd. LOMS, 1997-99. Mem.: ALA (exec. bd. 1997—99, leadership devel. com. 1999—2003, chair 2001—03, budget and fin. com. 2003—, libr. orgn. and mgmt. divsn.), Libr. Adminstrn. Mgmt. Assn. (mem. exec. bd. 1997—99, mem. leadership devel. com. 1999—2003, chmn. leadership devel. com. 2001—03, budget and finance com. 2003—), Am. Soc. Pub. Adminstrn. (pres. Md. chpt. 1994—95, nat. coun. 1995—99, chair policy issues com. 1998—99, fin. com fin. vice chair 1999—2000, chair 2000—01, bd. ins. trustees 2001—, vice chair steering group 2002—03, chmn. steering group 2003—). Democrat. Lutheran. Avocations: swimming, church activities. Home: 2927 Mozart Dr Silver Spring MD 20904-6802 E-mail: jflug@american.edu.

FLÜGELMAN, MAXIMO ENRIQUE, financier, composer; b. Buenos Aires, Nov. 2, 1945; s. Cirilo and Matilde (Rhein) F. Lic. es Sci. Econ., U. Geneva; diploma in econ. policy, Cath. U., Buenos Aires; MBA, Harvard U.; BM, Manhattan Sch. Music; M in Composition, Juilliard Sch. Credit officer Citibank, Buenos Aires and N.Y.C., 1970; sr. investment officer World Bank Group Internat. Fin. Corp., Washington, 1972-77; internat. mgr., chief external funding, negotiator Nat. Devel. Bank, Buenos Aires, 1981-84; v.p. banker 1st Chgo. Internat. Capital Markets Group, Chgo. and N.Y.C., 1985-89; v.p., exec. com. Inter-Am. Investment Corp., Washington, 1989—94; prin. Corfina Global Advisors, LLC, 1995—. Mem. ofcl. Argentine del. to IMF/World Bank meetings, Inter Am. Devel. Bank gen. assemblies; lectr. Buenos Aires Nat. U., Cath. U., Washington. Author: Argentina and the Debt Crisis; composer: Symphonic Variants for orch., Concertino for woodwinds and orch., Sea Sonnets for soprano and orch., Sonatina for chamber orch., Rhapsody for Cello and Orch., Concerto for Piano and String orch., Dialogues for Orchestra, chamber works performed at Aspen Festival, Latin Am. Chamber Music Festival, Quinteto Rego, orchestral works performed Indpls. Symphony, Seattle Symphony, Interam. Festival Orch., Kennedy Ctr., Carnegie Hall, Northwestern U. Orch., Nat. Argentine Symphony, Buenos Aires Philharm. at Teatro Colon, Conn. Chamber Orch., Fla. Philharm., Am. Composers Orch.; contbr. articles. Bd. dirs. Am. Composers Orch. Recipient 14th ann. contemporary orchestral composition award Ind. State U./Indpls. Symphony; 1st prize LRA Argentine State Radio Chamber Orch. composition contest, Outstanding Young Musician of Yr. award Argentine Jr. C. of C.; Amigos de la Musica composition contest; finalist Nissim Orchestral Composition Competition, Plymouth Music Series award; fellow Bunge and Born Found. Mem. ASCAP (bd. dirs.), Am. Composers Org. (dir.), Argentine Coun. on Fgn. Rels., Teatro Colón Found. (trustee, founding), A. Ginastera Found. (dir.), Soc. Argentina de Autores y Compositores, Soc. Rural Argentina, Cosmos Club (Washington), Doubles, Harvard Club (N.Y.C.), Club Nautico San Isidro (Buenos Aires). Home: 2817 Dumbarton St NW Washington DC 20007-3366

FLUHARTY, DAVID ARTHUR, automotive executive, statistician, consultant; b. Steubenville, Ohio, Feb. 28, 1951; s. Ralph Osborn and Grace Elaine (Martin) Fluharty; m. Mary Margaret Reiter, Nov. 23, 1978; 1 child, Margaret Rose Elaine Fluharty-Reiter (dec.). BA, Wheeling (W.Va.)State U., 1973; MBA, U. Chgo., 1975, MA, 1978; grad. cert. in applied stats., Oakland U., Rochester, Mich., 1992; postgrad., Wayne State U., Detroit, Michigan, 1995. Loan guarantee analyst Maritime Adminstrn. U.S. Dept. Commerce, Washington, 1976—77; fin. analyst Ford Motor Co., Dearborn, Mich., 1977—85, statistician, 1985—88; program mgr., warranty/reliability mgr. Alcoa Fujikura Ltd., Allen Park, Mich., 1988—99, sr. statistician, 1999—2001; mgr. reliability and warranty adminstrn. Continental Teves, Auburn Hills, Mich., 2001—. Assoc. editor Stats Mag.; contbr. Mem. math. steering com. Macomb Intermediate Sch. Dist., Clinton Township, Mich., 1998; participant, intern in Ignatian spirituality Manresa SJ Retreat Ho., Bloomfield Hills, Mich., 1999. Mem.: Am. Statis. Assn. (various officer positions in the detroit chpt. 1990—2002, adv. com. on tchr. enhancement 2000—, chpt. svc. recognition award 1999). Roman Catholic. Office: Continental Teves One Continental Dr Auburn Hills MI 48126

FLUHARTY, GEORGE MARK, speech pathology/audiology services professional; b. Davenport, Iowa, Aug. 5, 1957; s. George Oliver and Roberta Bell Fluharty. BA in comm. disorders, U. No. Iowa, 1979, MA in comm. disorders, 1980; M in libr. and info. sci., U. Wis., 2002. Lic. speech pathology State of Iowa. Speech lang. pathologist United Rehab., Minneapolis, 1980—87, New Medico Rehab., Waterford, Wis., 1987—88, Lakefront Ctr. North West Rehab., Wis., 1988—90, Sacred Heart Rehab. Inst., Milwaukee, 1990—2002, Brain Injury Unit Mequon Healthcare Ctr., Wis., 2002—. Contbr. articles to profl. jours. Recipient Clinical Svc. award, Brain Injury Assn. Wis., 2003. Home: 3278 N Humboldt Blvd Milwaukee WI 53212 E-mail: fluharty@wi.rr.com.

FLUHARTY, JESSE ERNEST, lawyer, judge; b. San Antonio, Tex., July 25, 1916; s. Jesse Ernest and Gwendolyn (Elder) F.; m. Ernestine Gertrude Corlies, Oct. 25, 1945; 1 son, Stephen Robert. Student Calif. State U.-San Diego, 1935-36, Art Ctr. Sch. Design Los Angeles, 1938-39; J.D. with distinction, U. Pacific, 1951; grad. Nat. Jud. Coll. Adminstrv. Law 1982. Bar: Calif. 1952, U.S. Dist. Ct. (no. dist.) Calif. 1952, U.S. Ct. appeals (9th cir.) 1952, U.S. Dist. Ct. (cen. dist.) Calif. 1979, U.S. Supreme Ct. 1983. Sole practice, Sacramento, 1952-60; referee in charge Indsl. Accident Commn., Stockton, Calif., 1960-67; presiding referee so. Calif. Workers Compensation Appeals Bd., Los Angeles, 1967-71, workers compensation Judge, Los Angeles, 1971-79; presiding judge, Los Angeles, 1979-81, Long Beach, 1981-83; of counsel Law Office of Stephen Fluharty, Glendale, Calif., 1984-87; workers compensation judge., Van Nuys, Calif., 1987—. Pres. Family Service Agy., Sacramento, 1958, 59, Community Council Stockton and San Joaquin County, 1965, Service Club Council Los Angeles, 1973-74, Glendale Hills Coordinating Council, 1976-78, Chevy Chase Estates Assn., 1971-77; chmn. San Joaquin County Recreation and Park Commn., 1963-67. Served with U.S. Army, 1943-45. Decorated Bronze Star, Philippine Liberation medal; recipient Meritorious citation Calif. Recreation Soc., 1967. Mem. Calif. State Bar, Los Angeles County Bar Assn., Glendale Bar Assn., Lawyers Club Los Angeles (pres. 1980, Judge of Yr. 1982). Republican. Congregationalist. Clubs: Chevy Chase Country, Verdugo. Lodges: Lions (pres. Los Angeles 1971-72), Masons. Home: PO Box 9131 Glendale CA 91226-0131

FLUHR, HOWARD, consulting firm executive; b. Bklyn., Feb. 20, 1943; s. Morton and Evelyn (Cohen) F.; m. Margaret Appel, Sept. 7, 1963; children: Lisa Metaxas, Allison Kaufman. BS in Math. and Philosophy cum laude, NYU, 1964. Various actuarial positions Guardian Life Ins. Co., 1964-66, Eastern Life Ins. Co., 1966-69; various actuarial and mgmt. positions The Segal Co., N.Y.C., 1969-73, v.p., 1973-76, sr. v.p., 1976-87, exec. v.p., 1987-93, pres., CEO, 1994—. Contbr. articles to profl. jours.; speaker in field. Fellow Soc. Actuaries, Conf. Cons. Actuaries (bd. dirs. 1990-96, v.p. 1991-96), Can. Inst. Actuaries; mem. Internat. Actuarial Assn., Am. Acad. Actuaries (bd. dirs. 1989-95, v.p. 1993-95), Employee Benefit Rsch. Inst. (trustee 1994—, chmn. 2000-2002). Office: The Segal Co 1 Park Ave New York NY 10016-5895 E-mail: hfluhr@segalco.com.

FLUHR, STEVEN SOLOMON, lawyer; b. N.Y.C., Mar. 31, 1959; s. Irving Fluhr and Rita Shain; m. Elizabeth Ann Koehr, Oct. 1, 1988; children: Katherine Michelle, Alexandra Sophia. AB, Vassar Coll., 1981; JD, St. Louis U., 1984. Bar: Mo. 1984, Ill. 1985, U.S. Ct. Appeals (8th cir.) 1990, U.S. Dist. Ct. (ea. dist.) Mo. 1986. Staff atty. legal svcs. plan United Auto Workers, St. Louis, 1984-87; assoc. Dubail Judge P.C., Creve Coeur, Mo., 1987-89; ptnr. Rekowsi & Collins, Collinsville, Ill., 1989-90, Gourley Sallerson & Fluhr, St. Louis, 1990-95; mng. mem. Fluhr & Moore L.L.C., Clayton, Mo., 1995—. City atty., prosecuting atty., Hanley Hills, Mo., 1989—; prosecuting atty. Olivette, Mo., 1990—; city atty. Velda Village Hills, Mo., 2001—. Mem. Bar Assn. Metro. St. Louis, Lawyers Assn. St. Louis. Home: 530 Bonhomme Forest Dr Olivette MO 63132-3108 Office: Fluhr & Moore LLC 225 S Meramec Ave Ste 532T Clayton MO 63105-3598 E-mail: FluhrStl@aol.com.

FLUKE, LYLA SCHRAM (MRS. JOHN M. FLUKE SR.), publisher; b. Maddock, N.D. d. Olaf John and Anne Marie (Rodberg) Schram; m. John M. Fluke, June 5, 1937; children: Virginia Fluke Gabelein, John M. Jr., David Lynd. BS in Zoology and Physiology, U. Wash., Seattle, 1934, diploma tchg., 1935. H.S. tchr., 1935-37; tutor Seattle schs., 1980-84; pub. Portage Quar. mag. Hist. Soc. Seattle and King County, 1980-84. Author articles on history. Co-founder N.W. chpt. Myasthenia Gravis Found., 1953, pres., 1960-66; obtained N.W. artifacts for Navy destroyer Tender Puget Sound., 1966; mem. Seattle Mayor's Com. for Seattle Beautiful, 1962; sponsor Seattle World's Fair, 1962; charter and founding mem. Seattle Youth Symphony Aux., 1974; bd. dirs., benefactor Cascade Symphony, Salvation Army, 1981-87; benefactor U. Wash., 1982-01, nat. chmn. ann. giving campaign, 1983-84; benefactor Sterling Cir. Stanford U., MIT, 1984, Seattle Symphony, 1982—, Wash. State Hist. Soc., Pacific Arts Coun., Pacific Sci. Ctr. Twenty-Twelve Club, 1962—, Lyla A and John M. Fluke Chair, U. Wash. Coll. Engring., 1982; mem. condr.'s club Seattle Symphony, 1978—. Recipient Crystal plaque Coll. Engring. U. Wash., 2002; Seattle Pacific U. fellow, 1972. Mem. IEEE Aux. (chpt. charter mem., pres. 1970-73), Wash. Trust for Hist. Preservation, Nat. Trust for Hist. Preservation, N.W. Ornamental Hort. Soc. (benefactor, life, hon.), Nat. Assn. Parliamentarians (charter mem., pres. N.W. unit 1961-64), Wash. Parliamentarians Assn. (charter), Seattle C. of C. (women's divsn. 1965-66), Seattle Symphony Women's Assn. (life, charter, sec. 1982-84, pres. 1985-87), Hist. Soc. Seattle and King County (exec. com. 1975-78, pres. women's mus. league 1975-79, pres. Moritz Thomsen Guild of Hist. Soc., 1978-80, 84-87), Highlands Orthopedic Guild (life), Wash. State Hist. Soc., Antiquarian Soc. (v.p. 1986-88, pres. 1988-90, hon. mem. John Fluke Mfg. Co. 20 Year Club 1987—), Rainier Club, Seattle Golf Club, Seattle Tennis Club, U. Wash. Pres.'s Club. Republican. Lutheran. Address: 1206 NW Culbertson Dr Seattle WA 98177-3942 also: Vendovi Island PO Box 703 Anacortes WA 98221-0703

FLUKER, JAY EDWARD, middle school visual arts educator; b. Hackensack, N.J., Sept. 26, 1943; s. J. Edward and Betty B. (Berkey) Flucker; m. Eileen Elizabeth Owens, June 22, 1968; children: Colleen Sharon, Maureen Jaye. BA in Art Edn., William Paterson Coll. N.J., 1966, MEd in Art Edn., 1972, MA in Comm. Arts, 1974. Cert. art tchr., elem. tchr. Art tchr. South Plainfield (N.J.) Bd. Edn., 1966-67, Chester (N.J.) Bd. Edn., 1967—. Co-developer workshop instr. Visual Arts Gifted and Talented Consortium, NJ, 1990—2003; spkr. Nat. Conf. Sch. Restructuring, Atlanta, 1991, Phila., 93, Shore Consortium, Rumson, NJ, 1986; mem. Crayola Art Edn. Coun., 1998. Solo landscape painting exhibit Roxbury, N.J., 1989, 92, Chester, N.J., 1972; solo photograph exhibits Roxbury, N.J., 2000, Chester, N.J., 2001; creator of weaving, 1966 (pub. in Weaving Without A Loom). With U.S. Army Mil. Police, 1968-71, Vietnam. PTA grantee, 1991-97. Mem. NEA, N.J. Edn. Assn., N.J. Assn. for Mid. Level Edn. (conf. guest spkr. 1991-94, workshop presenter), Art Educators N.J. (presenter 1992, 94-99, 2001), Art Assn. in Roxbury (historian 1991-93, exhibitor 1989, 92, 2000), HUB Camera Club (Denville, N.J., 3 First pl. photo competition awards, 1 Second pl. award, 1 Hon. mention 2001-02). Roman Catholic. Avocations: painting, travel, avid sci. fiction Star Trek and Star Wars fan. Office: Black River Mid Sch Rte 513 Chester NJ 07930

FLUM, JOSEPH, lawyer; b. June 13, 1924; BS in Pre-Law, Temple U., 1947; cert. in fgn. svc., Georgetown U., 1949; JD, Temple U., 1951; PhD, Pacific Western U., 1977. Bar: Pa. Owner, operator Flum's Dept. Store, Newtown, Pa., 1950—; pvt. practice law Newtown, 1961—. Lectr. law-related edn., world travel, exploration, and cultures; author, lectr., prof. worldwide anthropol. film documentaries and travel logs; sch. bd. rep. from U.S. to mainland China. Author: The Weave and The Woven, 1989, The Flum Atlas, 1989. Bd. dirs. Council Rock Sch. Dist., Pa., 1967-79, pres., 1971-73; chmn. legis. com. Bucks County Sch. Dirs., 1967-79, chmn. Bucks County Sch.'s legis. com., 1972—; mem. com. revision state sch. code, mem. com. on law-related edn. Pa. Dept. Edn., 1974—, mem. global edn. adv. com., 1978—, apptd. to com. for revision of state sch. code, 1974—; others. Recipient Chapel of Four Chaplains Legion of Honor award, commendation Coun. Rock Edn. Assn., 1980. Fellow Explorers Club; mem. Pa. Bar Assn. (youth-edn. com.), Bucks County Bar Assn., ABA, Northeastern Bar Assn., Phila. Anthropol. Assn., Am. Anthropol. Assn., Smithsonian Instn., Am. Legion, Newtown Hist. Assn., others. Avocations: anthropology, archeology, international travel and exploration. Office: State St at Centre Ave Newtown PA 18940

FLUNO, JOHN ARTHUR, entomologist, consultant; b. Appleton, Wis., July 21, 1914; s. Arthur Swetland and Elsie (Younger) F.; m. Ruth Margaret Johnson, Aug. 15, 1942; children: Ruth Adaire, Jo Anne. BS, Rollins Coll., 1937; MS, Ohio State U., 1939. Field aide U.S. Dept. Agr., Orlando, Fla., 1937-38; entomologist Orlando, Fla., 1946-56, Beltsville, Md., 1956-72; asst. Ohio Biol. Survey, Columbus, 1938-40; instr. Rollins Coll., Winter Park, Fla., 1941; jr. entomologist USPHS, 1941-46. Served with AUS, 1943-46. Mem. Entomol. Soc. Washington, Rollins Coll. Alumni Assn. (past pres.), The Lepidopterists Soc., Am. Mosquito Control Assn. Home and Office: 1234 Lakeview Dr Winter Park FL 32789-5038

FLURY, JANE MADAWG, artist, educator; b. Furstenfeldbruk, Germany, May 31, 1955; d. Richard Benjamin and Cara Mae (Vondrack) McKee; m. Speed Coseboom, Jan. 11, 1986 (div. Dec. 1989); m. John Flury, Sept. 2, 1990; 1 child, Ty. AA, Bakersfield Coll., 1981; BA, U. Calif. Santa Cruz, 1992. Cert. adult edn. Dir. Robertson's Art & Antiques, Carmel, Calif., 1989-94; mgr. Collectors Framing, Pacific Grove, Calif., 1986-90; painting instr. Pacific Grove U.S.D., 1997—, Lyceum, City of Monterey, Monterey Mus. Art, Calif., 1997—, Monterey Bay Aquarium, 1997—. Intern Monterey Mus. Art, 1990—, docent Monterey Art & History Assn., 1994-96, open studio, Artist Equity, 1998—; owner Noble Savage Fine Art and Antiques, 1997—. Author: Jane Flury's Artists' Handbook, 2003. Mem. Ctrl. Coast Art Assn., Greenpeace. Home: PO Box 916 Pacific Grove CA 93950-0916 E-mail: artnants@aol.com.

FLUTH, JOHN ADAM, educational administrator; b. Beeville, Tex., May 19, 1954; s. John and Elouise (Perdue) F.; m. Martye René Glenn, June 22, 1991; children: Craig, Kent, Chad. PhD, Tex. A&M U., 1986; computer technician, Apple Computer, Inc., Culpertino, Calif., 1994. Cert. ednl. adminstr., Tex. Surrogate parent Coastal Bend Youth City, Driscol, Tex., 1977-78, dir. halfway house Corpus Christi, Tex., 1978; tchr. spl. edn. Robstown, Tex., 1978-81; grad. asst. Tex. A&M U., College Station, Tex., 1981-86; coord. assistive tech. Region 5 Edn. Svc. Ctr., Beumont, Tex., 1986-97; dir. Tex. Acad. Leadership in the Humanities, Beaumont, 1997-98. Peer reviewer U.S. Dept. Edn., Washington, 1995—; grant reviewer Entergy, Inc., Beaumont, Tex., 1995-98; fellow Perkins Sch. Theology So. Methodist U., Dallas, 1998—. Pres. Ptnrs. Resource Network, Tex., 1994-96, Cerebral Palsy Rehab. Ctr., 1994-96; mem. exec. bd. Boy Scouts Am., Beaumont, Tex., 1996-98. Olympic Torch Bearer Atlanta Com. for The Olympic Games, 1996; named Cmty. Hero, United Way, Beaumont, Tex., 1996; recipient Perkins-Prothro fellowship, Perkins Sch. of Theology, Dallas, 1998. Mem. Order of Eastern Star (worthy patron), Masons (worshipful master). E-mail: john@fluth.com.

FLUTIE, DOUGLAS RICHARD (DOUG FLUTIE), professional football player; b. Manchester, Md., Oct. 23, 1962; Student, Boston Coll. With N.J. Generals, L.A. Rams, 1985; quarterback Chgo. Bears, 1986—87, New Eng. Patriots, 1987—89, B.C. Lions, 1990—91, Calgary Stampeders, 1992—95, Toronto Argonauts, 1996—97, Buffalo Bills, 1998—2001, San Diego Chargers, 2001—. Named most valuable player, Grey Cup CFL championship game, 1992, 1996, Coll. Football Player of Yr., The Sporting News, 1984, quarterback coll. All-Am. first team, 1984, player, Grey Cup, 1993; recipient Heisman trophy, 1984. Office: San Diego Chargers PO Box 609609 San Diego CA 92160-9609 also: San Diego Chargers 4020 Murphy Canyon Rd San Diego CA 92123

FLYE, M. WAYNE, surgeon, immunologist, educator, writer; b. Tarboro, N.C., June 23, 1942; s. Charlie A. and Martha E. (Bullock) F.; m. Phyllis Webb, June 7, 1964; children: Christopher Warren, Brandon Reid. BS, U. N.C., 1964, MD, 1967; MA in Immunology, Duke U., 1972, PhD in Immunology, 1980; MA (hon.), Yale U., 1985. Diplomate Am. Bd. Surgery, Am. Bd. Thoracic Surgery, Am. Bd. Vascular Surgery. Intern. surg. Case-We. Res. U., Cleve., 1967-68, res. gen. and cardio-thoracic surgery, 1968-75; instr., teaching scholar, vascular and transplantation surgery Duke U. Med. Ctr., Durham, N.C., 1975-76; sr. investigator, chief thoracic surg. svc. NIH, Bethesda, Md., 1977-79; chief vascular surgery U. Tex. Med. Br., Galveston, 1979-82, assoc. prof. surgery and microbiology, 1980-82; dir. div. organ transplantation and immunology, prof. transplantation, dir. sect. gen. surgery Yale U. Sch. Medicine, New Haven, 1983-85; prof. surgery, molecular microbiology and immunology Washington U. Med. Sch., St. Louis, 1985—, prof. radiology, 2000—, mem. admissions

com., 2000—. Trustee New Eng. Organ Bank, Boston, 1984-85; com. mem. United Network Orgn. Sharing, Richmond, Va., 1986-89; mem. anesthesiology and trauma study sect. NIH Surgery, 1991-95; merit rev. com. for surgery VA, 1994-96, chmn., 1996—; merit rev. com. Am. Heart Assn. study sect., 2001--; chief of surgery St. Louis Regional Hosp., 1996; chief thoracic surgery St. Louis VA Hosp., 1996—. Editor: Principles of Organ Transplantation, 1989, The Thymus: Regulator of Cellular Immunity, 1993, Atlas of Organ Transplantation, 1994; mem. editl. bd. Clin. Transplantation, 1986—, Prospectives in Gen. Surgery, 1988-94, Transplantation, 1989-2000, Xanthus Intelligence Unit Reports, 1990—, Shock: Molecular, Cellular and Systemic Pathobiology of Injury, 1993-99, Transplantation Sci., 1993—, Jour. Surg. Rsch., 1995-2000, Surgery, 1997—, Graft, Jour. Organ and Cellular Transplantation, 1998—, New Surgery, 2000—; assoc. editor Jour. Immunology, 1996-99, Hepatology, 2003—. Lt. col. U.S. Army, 1976-78. Recipient James W. McLaughlin medal U. Tex.-Galveston, 1982. Fellow ACP, So. Thoracic Surg. Assn. (Best Sci. Paper award 1980); mem. Am. Assn. Immunologists, Internat. Cardiovascular Soc., N.Y. Acad. Sci., Soc. Thoracic Surgeons, Am. Soc. Transplant Physicians, Am. Soc. Transplant Surgeons (program com. 1984-86, Ethics Com. 1994-95), Brit. Soc. Immunology, Transplantation Soc., Mid Am. Transplant Assn. (bd. dirs. 1986-89), Am. Fedn. Clin. Rsch., Royal Soc. Medicine, AAAS, Surg. Infection Soc. (edn. and fellowship com. 1998-2002), Reticuloendothelial Soc., Soc. Univ. Surgeons, Soc. Clin. Vascular Surgery, Brit. Transplantation Soc., So. Assn. Vascular Surgery, Am. Coll. Chest Physicians, Soc. Surg. Oncology, Am. Assn. Thoracic Surgery, Surg. Biology Club I, Am. Assn. Study Liver Diseases, Am. Surg. Assn., So. Surg. Assn., Cen. Surg. Assn., Soc. Internat. de Chirurgie, Midwestern Vascular Surg. Soc., Soc. Vascular Surg., World Ann. Hepato-Pancreato-Bilary Surg., Soc. Surgery of Alimentary Tract, Shock Soc., Gen. Thoracic Surgery Club, Soc. Thoracic Surg., St. Louis Surg. Soc. (v.p. 2002-03, treas. 2003—), Sigma Xi, Alpha Omega Alpha., Chi Psi, Young Republicans N.C. Episcopalian. Avocations: sports, geneology, medical history. Home: 585 Coeur De Royale Dr Apt 402 Saint Louis MO 63141-6915 E-mail: flyew@msnotes.wustl.edu.

FLYNN, CARL FREDERICK, religious studies educator; b. El Paso, Tex., June 13, 1970; s. Carl Thomas Flynn and Joan Marie Mullikin; m. Chantal J.H. Giguere, Dec. 12, 1992. BA in Pub. Rels., Pepperdine U., 1992, MDiv, 1996; postgrad., Baylor U., 1996—. Campus ministry intern Malibu Ch. Christ, Calif., 1991—96; adj. faculty humanities and religion Pepperdine U., 1995—2001; asst. dir. residential networking Baylor U. Info. Tech. Services, Waco, Tex., 1999—2001; vis. lectr. religion Pepperdine U., 2001—. Co-author: God, Christ and Soteriology in Thomas Campbell's Declaration and Address; author: (book reviews) Various book reviews in Leaven Journal and Restoration Quarterly. Vol. Susan G. Komen Breast Cancer Found., Waco, 1999—2001, L.A., 2001—; preaching min. various congregations, 1991—. Grantee, Baylor U., 1996—, Pepperdine U., 1992—96; scholar J.P. Sanders scholar, 1992—96. Mem.: Am. Acad. Religion/Soc. Bibl. Lit. (assoc.), Karl Barth Soc. N.Am. (assoc.), Restoration Theol. Rsch. Fellowship (assoc.). Christian - Restoration Tradition (Churches Of Christ). Avocations: volleyball, computing, graphic design, basketball, reading. Home: 2472 Vista Wood Cir #28 Thousand Oaks CA 91362 Office: Pepperdine U 24255 Pacific Coast Hwy Malibu CA 90263-4352 Personal E-mail: carl_flynn@yahoo.com.

FLYNN, CHARLES P. lawyer; b. Chgo., Apr. 17, 1943; BA, Willamette U., 1965; LLB, Harvard U., 1968. Bar: Alaska 1968, U.S. Dist. Ct. Alaska 1968, U.S. Ct. Appeals (9th cir.) 1968. Lawyer Burr Pease & Kurtz, Anchorage, 1968-70, shareholder, 1970—. Office: Burr Pease & Kurtz 810 N St Anchorage AK 99501-3293 E-mail: cpf@bpk.com.

FLYNN, DUANE JAMES, entomologist; b. Pontiac, Mich., May 26, 1949; s. Eugene Robert and Helen Elizabeth Flynn; m. Shirley Sue Barker, Sept. 12, 1969 (div. Sept. 1977); children: David Paul, Andrew Douglas; m. Pamela Ann Moyer, May 8, 1978. BA in Biology cum laude, Olivet Coll., 1971; MS in Entomology, U. Ga., 1974; postgrad., Mich. State U., 1975-80. Tech. advisor Boland Bonded Pest Control, Athens, Ga., 1973; med. entomologist Ga. Dept. Human Resources, Atlanta, 1974-75; asst. curator entomology collection Mich. State U., East Lansing, 1975-78, teaching asst. biology & entomology depts., 1975-81; rsch. asst. Lee County Mosquito Control, Ft. Myers, Fla., 1981; pest & termite inspector Orkin Exterminating, Hampton, Va., 1983-84, Charlotte, NC, 1984; curator life scis. Schiele Mus. Natural History, Gastonia, NC, 1997—. Bd. dirs. Gaston County Humane Soc., 1985-89; vol. Crowder's Mountain State Park, Kings Mountain, N.C., 1985—. Mem. Entomological Soc. Am., Lepidopterist Soc., Coleopterists Soc., Gaston Audubon Soc. (pub. chmn. 1985, field trips chmn. 1987, 93, 94, v.p. 1986, pres. 1989, conservation chair 1990-94, chpt. rep. NC Audubon coun. 1987-94), Meth. Ch. Hist. Soc. (v.p. WNC Conf., 2003—), Gaston County Birding Club (founder, pres. 2002—), Phi Sigma Kappa. Democrat. Achievements include research in arthropod biodiversit, treehopper taxonomy (Hemiptera: Membracidae). Avocations: birding, insect collecting, nature walks, reading. Home: 209 Wrentree Ln Gastonia NC 28056 Office: Schiele Mus Natural History 1500 E Garrison Blvd Gastonia NC 28054 E-mail: dflynn49@yahoo.com.

FLYNN, ELIZABETH E. bank executive; m. Andy Flynn; children: Spencer, Grace. BA in Math., Providence Coll.; MBA, NYU. With Chase Manhattan Corp., 1982-1994, sr. v.p., 1994-97; exec. v.p. Chase Manhattan Corp. JP Morgan Chase, 1997—. Integration and support exec. Chase Nat. Consumer Svcs. businesses, 1996—; bd. dirs. Providence House. Office: The Chase Manhattan Corp 270 Park Ave Fl 12 New York NY 10017-2036*

FLYNN, GEORGE RICHARD, poet; b. Bklyn., Aug. 14, 1926; s. Francis Joseph and Mary Josephine Flynn; m. Catherine Mary Regan, Oct. 31, 1945 (div. 1975); children: Margaret, Christine, William. BS in English Edn., NYU, 1951. Ins. claims adjuster Gt. Am. Ins. Co., N.Y.C., 1951—59; poet, 1959—72. Author: Selected Poems, 1965, The High Ground: New Poems, 1972, Zingers: 25 Poems, 1978. Served with USN, 1943—45. Avocations: physical therapy, softball, swimming, films, theater. Home: 303 W 66th St Apt 8CE New York NY 10023

FLYNN, GEORGE WILLIAM, chemistry educator, researcher; b. Hartford, Conn., July 11, 1938; s. George William and Rose Margaret (Tummillo) F.; m. Jean Pieri, Oct. 3, 1970; children: David Kenneth, Suzanne MacKay BS, Yale U., 1960; A.M., Harvard U., 1962, PhD, 1965. Postdoctoral fellow MIT, Cambridge, 1965-67; asst. prof. chemistry Columbia U., N.Y.C., 1967-72, assoc. prof., 1972-76, prof., 1976—, Thomas Alva Edison prof. chemistry, 1986-92, Higgins prof. chemistry, 1994—, dir. lab., 1979-2000, chmn. dept. chemistry, 1994-96, co-chair dept. chem. engring. and applied chemistry, 1997-2000. Research collaborator Brookhaven Nat. Lab., Upton, N.Y., 1969-78, cons., 1978— Contbr. articles to profl. jours. Fellow Sloan Found., 1968-70, Guggenheim Found., 1974-75; A. Cressy Morrison award N.Y. Acad. Scis., 1983; recipient Advancement Basic and Applied Sci. award Yale U. Sci. and Engring. Assn., 1994, NAS, 2001. Fellow Am. Phys. Soc. (Herbert P. Broida prize 2003); mem. Am. Acad. Arts and Scis., Am. Chem. Soc. (chmn. divsn. phys. chemistry, 1996-97), N.Y. Acad. Scis., Sigma Xi Roman Catholic.

FLYNN, HARRY JOSEPH, bishop; b. Schenectady, N.Y., May 2, 1933; Ed., Siena Coll., Loudonville, N.Y., Mt. St. Mary's Coll., Emmitsburg, Md. Ordained priest Roman Cath. Ch., 1960, ordained coadjutor bishop Lafayette, La., 1986. Bishop of Lafayette, La., 1989—94; coadjutor archbishop, 1994—95; archbishop Diocese of St. Paul and Mpls., 1995—. Address: Chancery Office 226 Summit Ave Saint Paul MN 55102-2121*

FLYNN, JAMES O'DONNELL, statistician, educator; b. N.Y.C., Aug. 25, 1941; s. James Albert Flynn, Marguerite McManus. AB, UCLA, 1964; PhD, U. Calif., Berkeley, 1969. Cons. logistics dept. Rand Corp., Santa Monica, Calif., 1966—68; rsch. assoc. stats. dept. Stanford (Calif.) U., 1969—70; asst. prof. Grad. Sch. Bus. U. Chgo., 1970—76; assoc. prof. dept. mgmt. Wayne State U., Detroit, 1976—79; assoc. prof. quantitative bus. analysis dept. Cleve. State U., 1979—89, prof. ops. mgmt. and bus. statis. dept., 1989—. Contbr. articles to profl. jours. Mem.: INFORMS. Office: Cleve State U 1860 East 18 St Cleveland OH 44114 Business E-Mail: .flynn@popmail.csuohio.edu.

FLYNN, JOHN DAVID, writer, educator; b. Jackson, Tenn., Apr. 4, 1948; s. John Aloysius Flynn and Mary Evelyn Groom; m. Deborah Ann Coleman, Jan. 28, 1978 (div. Dec. 1989); 1 child, Caitlin Rose; m. Jennifer Leigh O'Saile, Jan. 2002. BA, B of Journalism, U.Mo., 1971; MA, U. Denver, 1972, Boston U., 1980; PhD, U. Nebr., 1984. Reporter Memphis Press-Scimitar, 1973-74; editor Chapin Pub. Co., Mpls., 1976-77; instr. Tenn. State U., Nashville, 1978-79, asst. prof., 1988-89, U. Hawaii, Honolulu, 1989-91; dir. English Hawaii Tokai Internat. Coll., Honolulu, 1992-93; assoc. prof. Vol. State C.C., Gallatin, Tenn., 1993—. Fulbright sr. specialist, Ukraine, 2002; cons. in field; with Japan Exch. and Tchg. Program, Osaka, 1987—88; adj. instr. Am. Intercontinental U. Online, 2002—. Author numerous poems, short stories and novels; writer-in-residence Millay Colony for the Arts, 1987, Tyrone Guthrie Ctr., Ireland, 1991, Israeli Ctr. for the Arts, 1992, Helene Wurlitzer Found., Taos, N.Mex., 1993, 97-98, 2002. Bd. dirs. Hawaii Literary Arts Coun., Honolulu, 1991-92; congrl. intern U.S. Congress, Washington, 1972. Fulbright scholar award Macedonia, 2001. Mem.: PEN, Poets and Writers, Acad. Am. Poets, Marion James Musicians Aid Soc. (pres. 2002, bd. dirs. 2001—), Music City Blues Soc. (bd. dirs. 1996—, v.p. 1999—2002, pres. 2002—), Am. Radio Relay League. Avocations: amateur radio, stained glass, astronomy, hiking. Office: Vol State C C 1480 Nashville Pike Gallatin TN 37066-3148 Home: 127 Brixworth Ln #11 Nashville TN 37205

FLYNN, JOHN J. museum curator; b. Wilkes-Barre, Pa., Aug. 10, 1955; s. John J. and Phyllis B. (Allen) F.; m. Alison L. Gold; children: Rachel S., Peter J. BS cum laude, Yale U., 1977; MA, Columbia U., 1979, MPhil, 1980, PhD, 1983. Lectr. dept. geology and geophysics Yale U., New Haven, 1982; asst. prof. geol. scis. Rutgers U., New Brunswick, N.J., 1982-88; assoc. curator dept. geology Field Mus. Natural History, Chgo., 1988-92, curator dept. geology, 1992—, chmn. dept. geology, 1993-2000, MacArthur curator dept. geology, 1995—. Rsch. assoc. Am. Mus. Natural History, N.Y.C., 1984-2000; co-chair Earth History and Global Change com. Systematics Agenda 2000, 1991-96; lectr. Com. on Evolutionary Biology, U. Chgo., 1990—, assoc. chair, 1995—; adj. prof. dept. biol. scis. U. Ill., Chgo., 1994—. Co-editor: Vertebrate Paleontology in the Neotropics: The Miocene Fauna of La Venta, Colombia, 1997, Mesozoic/Cenozoic Vertebrate Paleontology: Classic Localities, Contemporary Approaches, 1989; assoc. editor Jour. Vertebrate Paleontology, 1988-91, Systematic Paleontology, 2001—; contbr. articles to profl. jours. Grantee in field; recipient William R. Belknap prize, 1977, Best Mus. Curator award Chgo. Mag., 1995, Premio Roberto Araya award Sociedad Geologica de Chile, 2002; John S. Guggenheim fellow, 2001-02. Mem. Soc. Vertebrate Paleontology (chair affiliated soc. liaison 1986-93, mem. devel. com. 1987-89, chair collections computerization com. 1990-93, sec. 1993-96, v.p. 1996-98, pres. 1998-2000, past pres. 2000-02, Alfred Sherwood Romer prize 1982), Geol. Soc. Am., The Paleontological Soc., Soc. Systematic Biologists. Achievements include discovery of oldest S.Am. rodent, oldest well-preserved S.Am. monkey skull, oldest dinosaurs, work on geologic time scales. Office: Field Mus Natural History Dept Geology 1400 Lake Shore Dr Chicago IL 60605

FLYNN, KIRTLAND, JR., accountant; b. Orange, N.J., Aug. 27, 1922; s. Kirtland and Jane Elizabeth (Miller) F.; m. Lucy Jane Andrews, June 11, 1948 (dec. Oct. 2002); children: Patricia Carson Flynn Moore, Gail Miller, James Kirtland; m. Anne Blankenship Canter Jones, Apr. 26, 2003. BA, Colgate U., 1943. Enrolled agt. Acctg. staff Celnese Corp., Newark, Houston, Charlotte, N.C., 1947-65; sec.-treas. Little Constrn. Co., Inc., Charlotte, 1965-66; mem. contr.'s staff J.P. Stevens & Co., Inc., Charlotte, 1966-81, mgr. info. svcs. divsn. Charlotte and Greer, S.C., 1981-85; pvt. practice acctg., 1985-92; mem. staff Larry R. Swartz, CPA, 1993—. Bd. dirs., treas. Charlotte Exch. Student Program, 1979-83; chmn. Tryon Fire Protection Dist. Bd. Commrs., 1986—; bd. dirs. Tryon Fine Arts Ctr., 1987-89; bd. dirs., treas. Polk County Sheltered Workshop, 1987-91, exec. v.p., 1991-93, pres., 1994-96. 1st lt. USMCR, 1943-46. Decorated DFC, Air medals. Mem. Nat. Assn. Enrolled Agts., Inst. Mgmt. Accts. (chpt. pres. 1966-67, nat. dir. 1971-73, pres. Carolinas Coun. 1973-74, nat. v.p. 1978-79), Stuart Cameron McLeod Soc. (bd. govs. 1979-81, treas. 1981-82, sec. 1982-83, v.p. 1983-85, pres. 1985-86), Tryon C. of C. (bd. dirs. 1985-93, treas. 1985-90, v.p. 1990-92), Tryon Riding and Hunting Club (bd. dirs. 2000-03), Masons, Shriners, KT. Home: 390 Sourwood Ridge Rd PO Box 1138 Tryon NC 28782-1138 Office: 20 Jervey Rd Ste 103 Tryon NC 28782-3709

FLYNN, LAURA D, foundation administrator, consultant, educator; d. Augustus Earl and Lois Peal Drayton; m. James E Flynn, July 25, 1970; children: Jeanine Edwina, James Jr Edward. BS in Edn., Savannah State U., 1969; M in Christian Psychology, Jacksonville Theol. Sem., 1999, PhD in Christina Psychology, 2001. Cert. tchr. Ga., 1969. Tchr. various schools, Ga., 1969—2002; ret., 2002; founder/dir. Thanks Be To HUGS Found., Savannah, Ga., 1998. Author (redirective behavior specialist): (children's books) Little Sister Books. Mem. Internat. Fellowship of JTS Grads., Secred Heart Caholics, Chatham Assn. of Educators, Nat. Edn. Assoc., Savannah, Ga., EOA Thomas Austin Ho., 1996. Mem.: Jack & Jill of Am. (assoc.). Achievements include development of Family Literacy and Support (Non-profit) Org. Home: 28 Meriweather Dr (Dutch Island) Savannah GA 31406 Office: Thanks Be To HUGS Found PO Box 16241 Savannah GA 31406 E-mail: drldflynn@aol.com.

FLYNN, MARIE COSGROVE, portfolio manager, corporate financial executive; b. Honolulu, Jan. 1, 1945; d. John Aloysius and Emeline Frances Cosgrove; m. John Thomas Flynn, Jr., June 3, 1968; children: Jamie Marie, Jacqueline Elizabeth. BA, Trinity Coll., 1966. CFP, CFA. Analyst U.S. Govt., Washington, 1967-70; coord. nat. reading coun. F.X. Doherty Assocs., N.Y.C., 1970-71; security analyst Corinthian Capital Co., N.Y.C., 1971-73; portfolio mgr. Clark Mgmt. Co., Inc., N.Y.C., 1973-78; 1st v.p., sr. portfolio mgr. Lexington Mgmt. Corp., Saddle Brook, NJ, 1978-96; pres. Corinthian Capital Mgmt. Co., Inc., Morristown, NJ, 1996-99; v.p., mng. dir., sr. portfolio mgr. Glenmede Trust Co., 1999—. Bd. dirs., v.p. First Call for Help, 1996—2000; bd. trustees N.J. Pension and Annuity Fund, 1996—; elected mem. Somerset County Rep. Com., 1994—98; treas. Bernardsville Rep. Com., 1996—98, Bernardsville Planning Bd., 1996—98; elected to Bernardsville Borough Coun., 1998—; mayor Bernardsville, 2002; police commr. Bernardsville Police Commn., 2000—; pres. Women's Polit. Caucus N.J., 2001—03. Recipient Tribute to Women award, Patriots' Path Coun., 2002. Mem. Fin. Analysts Fedn., Inst. Chartered Fin. Analysts, N.Y. Soc. Security Analysts. Home: 50 Pickle Brook Rd Bernardsville NJ 07924-1909 Office: Carriage Ct II 264 South St Morristown NJ 07960-6078

FLYNN, MEGAN ALICE, librarian; b. Bronxville, N.Y., Oct. 30, 1967; d. Joseph Thomas and Dorothy Alice (Flood) F. BA, Boston Coll., 1988; MS, Simmons Coll., 1991. Ref. libr. Thomas Crane Pub. Libr., Quincy, Mass., 1993-97; ref. and collection devel. libr. Wellesley (Mass.) Free Libr., 1997—. Mem. ALA. Democrat. Roman Catholic. Home: 4 Chiswick Rd Apt 43 Brighton MA 02135-7173 Office: Wellesley Free Libr 530 Washington St Wellesley MA 02482-5916 Fax: 781-237-1354. E-mail: meganflynn@aol.com., mflynn@minlib.net.

FLYNN, MICHAEL, lawyer; b. Bklyn., Sept. 20, 1952; s. James Thomas and Catherine Marie (Fratello) F.; m. Janet Marie DiPaolo, Jan. 11, 1975; children: Michael Sean, Ashley Brooke, Thomas James. BA, Bklyn. Coll., 1970; JD, N.Y. Law Sch., 1978. Bar: N.Y. 1979, U.S. Dist. Ct. (so., ea., we. and no. dists.) N.Y. 1979, U.S. Ct. Appeals (2d cir.) 1979, U.S. Supreme Ct. 1985. Assoc. firm Elkind & Lampson, N.Y.C., 1979-83; sr. ptnr. Elkind, Flynn & Maurer, P.C., N.Y.C., 1983—2001; pvt. practice, 2001—. Cons. counsel United Transp. Union, Cleve., Brotherhood R.R. Signalmen, Cleve., Transport Workers Union N.Y., Brotherhood Locomotive Engrs. N.Y., Sheetmetal Workers N.Y., Internat. Brotherhood Elec. Workers, N.Y., Ind. Railway Supr's. Assn. Lodge #1, fireman and oilers S.E.I.U. ; judge (arbitration) Civil Ct., N.Y.C., 1980— ; cons. atty. Oceanside civil counsel (N.Y.), 1984, Oceanside Sch. Dist. Wide Com. site base mgmt., 1994-2000; judge N.Y. Law Sch., N.Y.C., 1978. Recipient Am. Jurisprudence award, 1976; Goodrich award Western New Eng. Sch. Law, Springfield, Mass., 1977. Mem. ATLA, N.Y. State Bar Assn., Civil Justice Found. (founding sponsor 1987), N.Y. State Trial Lawyers Assn., Acad. Rail Labor Attys., Trial Lawyers Care (pro bono campaign victims families 2001-). E-mail: FELAattorney@aol.com.

FLYNN, NORMA JEAN, librarian; b. Fitzhugh, Okla., Sept. 17, 1934; d. Marion Alfred and Rosa Lee (Brady) Sorrels; m. Robert L. Flynn, June 1, 1953; children: Deirdre Siobhan, Brigid Erin (dec.). BA, Baylor U., 1962; MLS, Our Lady of Lake U., 1976. Tchr. Waco (Tex.) Pub. Schs., 1962-63, Holmes High Sch., San Antonio, 1963-67, 71-76, Ursuline Acad., San Antonio, 1967-71; libr. Thunderbird Hills Elem., San Antonio, 1976-84, Sam Rayburn Mid. Sch., San Antonio, 1985-93. Libr. cons., presenter workshops, 1976—; guest speaker in schs., 1982—. Author: Jim Bowie: A Texas Legend, 1980, Stephen F. Austin: The Father of Texas, 1981, William Barret Travis: Victory or Death, 1982, James Walter Fannin: Remember Goliad, 1983, James Butler Bonham: The Rebel Hero, 1985, Lady: A Biogrpahy of Claudia Alta (Lady Bird) Johnson, 1992, Anson Jones: Last President of the Republic of Texas, 1997, Annie Oakley: Legendary Sharpshooter, 1998, Texas Women Who Dared to Be First, 1999; ednl. videos: Heroes of the Texas Revolution, 1995, The Spanish Mission of Texas, 1996. Vol. Dem. Party Campaigning, San Antonio, 1990; mem. San Antonio Conservation Soc. Named Woman of Yr. in Svc., San Antonio Express-News Corp., 1987. Mem. Tex. Libr. Assn., Bexar Libr. Assn., Tex. Folklore Soc. Democrat. Baptist. Avocations: travel, walking, reading. Home: 101 Cliffside Dr San Antonio TX 78231-1510

FLYNN, PATRICIA M. director, special education educator, gifted and talented educator; b. East Cleveland, Ohio, Sept. 11, 1952; d. Harry L. and Eleanore (Mahon) Flynn. BS in Edn. magna cum laude, St. John Coll., Cleve., 1974, MS in Edn., 1975; cert., Notre Dame Coll., 1992, Ursuline Coll., 2001. Cert. elem. edn., prin., edn. handicapped Ohio Detp. Edn. Reading specialist East Cleveland City Schs., 1974—98, reading coord., 1998—2000, curriculum specialist, 2000—01; dir. pupil svcs. Fairview Park (Ohio) Schs., 2001—. Local coord. Reading Is Fundamental Project, East Cleveland, 1996—2000; coord. East Cleveland Elem. Acad., East Cleveland, 1999. Scholar, St. John Coll., 1974. Mem.: Nat. Assn. Fed. Edn. Program Adminstrs., Internat. Reading Assn., Ohio Assn. Adminstrs. State and Fed. Edn. Programs, Ohio Assn. Pupil Svcs. Adminstrs., Irish Am. Club, City Club Cleve., Kappa Gamma Pi. Roman Catholic. Office: Fairview Park City Schs 20770 Lorain Rd Fairview Park OH 44126

FLYNN, PATRICIA MARIE, economics educator; b. Lynn, Mass. BA in Econs., Emmanuel Coll., 1972; MA in Econs., Boston U., 1973, PhD in Econs., 1980. Rsch. assoc. Inst. for Employment Policy, Boston U., 1975-83; prof. econs. Bentley Coll., Waltham, Mass., 1976—; sr. rsch. fellow New Eng. Bd. Higher Edn., Boston, 1980-82; vis. sch. Fed. Res. Bd., Boston, 1983-84; exec. dir. Inst. for Rsch. & Faculty Devel., Bentley Coll., Waltham, 1986-90; assoc. dean faculty Bentley Coll., Waltham, Mass., 1991-92, dean grad. sch., 1992—2002, Trustee prof. econs. and mgmt., 2002—. Mem. faculty Inst. in Employment and Tng. Adminstrn. Harvard U., Cambridge, Mass., summers, 1979-81; cons. U. Mo., Columbia, 1983-84, First Security Svcs. Corp., Boston, 1985, Devel. Alternatives, Inc., Jakarta, Indonesia, summer, 1987, ABT Assocs., Cambridge, 1987-89; bd. dirs. Fed. Savs. Bank, Waltham, Mass. Author: Technology Life Cycles and Human Resources, 1993; co-author: Turbulence in the American Workplace, 1991; contbr. articles to profl. jours. Adv. panel mem. Office Tech. Assessment, U.S. Congress, Washington, 1989-91; accreditation team mem. New Eng. Assn. Schs. and Colls., 1985—; mem. Newton (Mass.) Econ. Devel. Commn., 1984-87; bd. dirs. Big Sisters Assn., US Trust, 1998-2000, Boston Fed. Savs. Bank, 2000—, BostonFed Bancorp, Inc., 2000—; trustee Mass. Taxpayers Found., Sloan Found., 1995-98. Grantee Dept. Labor, 1982-84, 88-89, Nat. Inst. Edn., 1982-83, NSF, 1990-93, Sloan Found., 1995-98; recipient Gregory H. Adamian award for tchg. excellence Bentley Coll., 1986, Scholar of Yr., 1991, New Eng. Woman's Leadership award, 1998. Mem. Fin. Womens Assn., Am. Econ. Assn., Com. on the Status of Women in Econs. Professions, The Boston Club, The Boston Econ. Club. Office: Bentley Coll 175 Forest St Waltham MA 02452-4713

FLYNN, PATRICK, designer, programmer, consultant; b. Washington, Aug. 11, 1953; s. Walter L. and Virginia B. Flynn. BS in English, East Carolina U., 1977; AAS in Bus. Computer Programming, Coll. of the Albemarle, 1996. Disc jockey Sta. WBXB-FM, Edenton, N.C., 1976; copy coord. BDM Corp., McLean, Va., 1977-80; editor HBH Co., Arlington, Va., 1980-81; audio/visual technician Projection, Inc., Arlington, 1982; carpenter Sandalwood Construction Co., Kitty Hawk, N.C., 1983-86; ind. contractor Patrick Painting, Kitty Hawk, 1986-92; game designer TurnKey Design Group, Kitty Hawk, 1993-96; programmer Airline Tariff Publ. Co., Washington, Va., 1996-97, New Boston Sys., Vienna, Va., 1997-98, FC Bus. Sys., Falls Church, Va., 1998-2000; ind. game designer Paradise Games, Edenton, NC, 2000—. Media cons., 1973—; pub. SandTraveler, Kitty Hawk, 1992-93. Contbr. articles and editls. to mags. and newspapers; designer Cutthroat Chess (tm), 1993, Mighty Mutty Motor Mutts (tm), 2001, Poetry For Breakfast (tm), 2001, Waterbots (tm), 2001, Personal Space, Parking Place (tm), 2001, Pat Pendings and Sign Holder, 2001, Couch Potatoland (tm), 2002; appeared as extra Matlock series NBC-TV, 1989, (film) Toy Soldiers, 1990. Mem. Alpha Phi Gamma, Phi Theta Kappa. Republican. Avocations: chess, photography. Office: Paradise Games PO Box 16 Edenton NC 27932-0016 E-mail: patrickflynn@earthlink.net.

FLYNN, PAUL BARTHOLOMEW, foundation executive; b. Quincy, Mass., Sept. 17, 1935; s. Bartholomew Joseph and Katherine Marie (Coleman) F.; m. Aline Therese Nicholson, Feb. 11, 1961; children: Bonnie Marie, Laureen P., Elizabeth A., Bernadette J. AB, Stonehill Coll., 1957; LL.D. (hon.), Allentown Coll., 1985. Sportswriter The Patriot Ledger, Quincy, 1955-63, cmty. rels. dir., 1963-65; dir. pub. rels. Mass. Tchrs. Assn., Boston, 1965-66; asst. dir. pub. svc. Rochester (N.Y.) Democrat and Chronicle and The Times-Union, 1966-71, dir. pub. svc. and rsch., 1971-72; dir. advt. Huntington (W.Va.) Herald-Dispatch and Advertiser, 1972-74, Binghamton (N.Y.) Press and Sun-Bulletin, 1974-76; dir. mktg. services Gannett Co., Rochester, N.Y., 1976-77; gen. mgr. Jour.-News, Nyack, N.Y., 1977; pres., pub. Fort Myers (Fla.) News-Press, 1977-84; S.E. regional v.p. Gannett Co., 1981-83; exec. v.p. USA Today, Washington, 1983-84, pres., 1984; pres., pub. Pensacola News-Jour., Fla., 1984-87; v.p. Gannett South Newspaper Group, 1985-87; exec. v.p. Foster's Daily Democrat, Dover, N.H., 1989-93; dir. mktg. and pub. rels. Strawbery Banke Mus., Portsmouth, N.H., 1993-95; mktg. cons. Jour.-Transcript Newspapers, N.H., Maine, 1995-96; v.p. Susan Bennett Mktg. & Media, Fort Myers, Fla., 1996-97; exec. dir. Southwest Fla. Community Found., Ft. Myers, Fla., 1997—. V.p. Gannett Newspaper Advt. Sales, N.Y.C., 1976-77 Author: You Can Make News, 1996; co-editor: Promoting the Total Newspaper, 1977. Pres. Lend-A-Hand Fund S.W. Fla., S.W. Fla. coun. Boy Scouts Am., 1981, adv. bd., 1997—, commr. Daniel Webster coun., 1989-96, v.p., 1995-96; bd. dirs. Lee County United Way, 1979-84, campaign chmn., 1981; bd. dirs. Edison C.C. Endowment Fund, 1978-83, Sr. Friendship Ctrs., Inc., 1981-83, United Way Pensacola, Sacred Heart Hosp. Found., Pensacola Jr. Coll. Found.; mem. adv. bd. Stonehill Coll., 1984, trustee, 1987-92. With U.S. Army, 1957-58. Recipient Disting. Service award B'nai B'rith of Cape Coral, Fla., 1979; Gold medal for good citizenship SAR, 1980; disting. alumni award Stonehill Coll., 1984; Patriotism citation Freedom's Found., 1986, Legacy award ARC, 2003. Mem. Internat. Newspaper Promotion Assn. (bd. dirs. 1977-78), Greater Dover C. of C. (bd. dirs. 1989-93), Stonehill Coll. Alumni Assn., Rotary Ft. Myers. (bd. dirs. 2000-2002). Roman Catholic.

FLYNN, PETER ANTHONY, judge; b. Bronxville, N.Y., July 23, 1942; s. Ralph Harold and Caroline (Lindberg) F. BA magna cum laude, Harvard U., 1963; LLB, Yale U., 1966. Bar: Ill. 1969, U.S. Dist. Ct. (no. and so. dists.) Ill. 1969, U.S. Ct. Appeals (7th cir.) 1969, U.S. Supreme Ct. 1976, U.S. Dist. Ct. (ea. dist.) Wis. 1980, U.S. Ct. Appeals (2d and 5th cirs.) 1980, U.S. Ct. Appeals (9th cir.) 1987. Asst. lect. law U. Ife, 1967-69; assoc. Jenner & Block, Chgo., 1969-75; ptnr. Cherry & Flynn, Chgo., 1976-99; judge Cir. Ct. of Cook County, Ill., 1999—; adj. prof. The John Marshall Law Sch., 2002—. Adj. prof. John Marshall Law Sch., 2002—. Mem. Olympia Fields Plan Commn., Ill., 1979-83, chmn., 1983-85; trustee Village of Olympia Fields, 1985-89; pres. Touchstone Theatre, 1990-93; active U.S. Peace Corps, 1967-69. Mem. ABA, Ill. Bar Assn., Am. Law Inst., Yale Law Sch. Assn. (nat. exec. com. 2002-), Chgo. Lincoln Inn of Ct., Chgo. Bar Assn. (vice chair, comml. litigation com., 2003). Roman Catholic. Avocations: theater, piano, poetry, guitar, choral music, sailing, history.

FLYNN, ROBERT JAMES, electronic commerce executive; b. Detroit, Apr. 12, 1941; s. James Vincent and Rita Marie (Cloonan) F.; m. Marilyn Ann Webb, Nov. 21, 1964; 1 child, Sara Louise. BSc, St. John Fischer Coll., Rochester,

N.Y., 1964; MSc in Math., U. Windsor, Ont., Can., 1966; postgrad., U. Windsor-U. Mich., 1966-67. Systems engr. IBM, Detroit, 1967-69; applications devel. mgr. IBM/Svc. Bur. Corp., White Plains, N.Y., 1969-76; mktg. dir. Boeing Computer Svcs., McLean, Va., 1976-81; pres., owner Bus. Computer Corp. Am., Reston, Va., 1981-85; ptnr. Office Automation, Vienna, Va., 1985-87; tech. dir. Vanguard Rsch., Inc., Oakton, Va., 1987-93; pres. Ocean Thermal Energy, Inc., Oakton, 1993-95, X-Change Software, Inc., Oakton, 1994-97; exec. v.p., owner Electronic Bus. Svcs., Internet, Vienna, Va., 1997—2001, ind. cons., 2001—. Tech. cons. World Bank, Washington, 1985-87; software engring. cons. Nat. Test Facility, Colorado Springs, Colo., 1989-93. Inventor in field. Mem. KC (4th degree, grand knight 1993-94, state chmn. 1997-98). Republican. Roman Catholic. Avocations: gardening, piano, chess. E-mail: RJVFLYNN@ALDEPHIA.NET.

FLYNN, SCOTT D. lawyer; b. Washington, Iowa, Mar. 2, 1971; s. Daniel D. and Vickie L. Flynn. BS in Agrl. Engring., Iowa State U., 1994; JD, U. Iowa, 2000. Bar: Iowa, 2000. Rsch. asst. engring. ext. Iowa State U., Ames, 1991-92; laboror Carriage House Meats, Ames, 1993; tax asst. Neuzil & Sanderson, Iowa City, 1998-2000; legal clk. Garst Seed Co./Advanta USA, Inc., Slater, Iowa, 1998; assoc. Davis, Brown, Koehn, Shors & Roberts, P.C., Des Moines, 1999—; ptnr. Flynn Farms, Keota, Iowa. Reader, min. Newman Cath. Student Ctr., Iowa City, 1999-2000. Mem. ABA, Am. Numismatic Assn., Am. Farm Bur., Am. Agrl. Law Assn., Am. Soc. Agrl. Engrs., Iowa Numismatic Assn., Iowa Farm Bur., Iowa Bar Assn., Coun. for Agrl. Sci. and Tech., Polk County Bar Assn., Washington County Farm Bur., Ctrl. Iowa Alpha Gamma Rho Chpt., Iowa State U. Alumni Assn., Crohn's & Colitis Found. Am., Phi Delta Phi, Alpha Gamma Rho Ednl. Found. Eta Chpt. (sec. 2000-01, v.p. 2001-02, pres. 2002-03, treas. 2003-), Eta Alumni Corp. Alpha Gamma Rho (sec. 2000-01, v.p. 2001-02, pres. 2002--03, treas. 2003—). Avocations: numismatics, model trains. Home: 1917 NW Third St Ankeny IA 50021 Office: Davis Brown Koehn Shors & Roberts PC Ste 2500 666 Walnut St Des Moines IA 50309 E-mail: Scott.Flynn@lawiowa.com.

FLYNN, WILLIAM JOSEPH, JR., surgeon; b. Canton, NY, June 21, 1955; m. Nancy Skrobacz. BS, St. Bonaventure U., 1977; MS, SUNY, Buffalo, 1979; MD, Northwestern U., 1983. Intern SUNY, Buffalo, 1983—84, resident in gen. surgery, 1984—89; fellow trauma, critical care, burns U. Louisville, 1989—91; attending surgeon VA Med. Ctr., Louisville, 1990-91, Buffalo, 1991—. Attending surgeon, dir. surg./trauma ICU Erie County Med. Ctr., Buffalo, 1991—; assoc. prof. surgery SUNY, Buffalo, 1991—. Contbr. articles to profl. jours. and chpts. to books. Fellow ACS (assoc.); mem. Am. Burn Assn., ACS Regional Com. on Trauma, Am. Trauma Soc., Assn. Acad. Surgeons, Ea. Assn. for Surgery of Trauma, Med. Soc. Erie County, Microcirculatory Soc. Inc., NY State Com. on Trauma, Shock Soc., Soc. Am. Gastrointestinal Endoscopic Surgeons, Soc. Critical Care Medicine, Surg. Infection Soc., Soc. VA Surgeons, Cen. Surg. Assn. Office: Erie County Med Ctr 462 Grider St Buffalo NY 14215-3021

FLYNN-CONNORS, ELIZABETH KATHRYN, editor; b. Chgo., Aug. 17, 1939; d. Timothy Carver Flynn and Elizabeth Eleanor (Tait) Scanlon; m. Gerald Martin Connors, Dec. 30, 1978; children: Andrew, Kathryn, Elizabeth. Student, Monmouth Coll., Ill., 1957-59; BA in Journalism, U. Wis., 1961, postgrad., 1965-66. Cityside reporter Mpls. Tribune, 1961-62, Chgo. Daily News, 1962-66, UN/N.Y. corr., 1966-75, Washington corr., 1968; writer, press officer UN, N.Y.C., 1975-82; sr. writer UN Chronicle, N.Y.C., 1982-85, editor-in-chief, 1985-96; chief editor Yearbook of UN, N.Y.C., 1996-99; chief UN pubs., N.Y.C., 1999—. Troop leader Girl Scouts U.S., Tarrytown, N.Y., 1993-95. Russell Sage fellow U. Wis., 1965-66; recipient Investigative Reporting award Sigma Delta Chi, 1962, 1st Pl. Spot News award AP, 1970. Mem. UN Corrs. Assn. (alumni), Phi Beta Kappa, Kappa Delta. Avocations: reading, watching old movies. Home: 238 Hunter Ave Sleepy Hollow NY 10591-1317

FLYNT, CANDACE LAMBETH, writer; b. Greensboro, NC, Mar. 12, 1947; d. Ralph MacAulay Lambeth, Dorothea Elaine Patterson, James Hoyt Bray (Stepfather), Helen Marie Craven (Stepmother); m. John Franklin Kime; children: MacAulay, Charles, Elizabeth, Stuart Kime, Jordan Kime, Katherine Kime; m. Charles Homer Flynt (div. Dec. 3, 1991). Master of fine arts, University of North Carolina, Greensboro, 1969—74; bachelor of arts, Greensboro College, 1965—69. Reporter Greensboro Record, Greensboro, NC, 1969—73. Author: (novel) Mother Love, 1987, Sins of Omission, 1984, Chasing Dad, 1980. Trustee Greensboro College, Greensboro, NC, 1985—2002. Episcopalian. Avocation: photography. Home: 2005 Madison Avenue Greensboro NC 27403

FLYNT, JAMES WAYNE, history educator, researcher; b. Pontotoc, Miss., Oct. 4, 1940; s. James Homer and Mae Ellis (Moore) R.; m. Dorothy Ann Smith, Aug. 20, 1961; children: David Wayne, Sean Allen. AB, Howard Coll., Birmingham, Ala., 1961; MS, Fla. State U., 1962, PhD, 1965. From asst. prof. to prof. Samford U., Birmingham, 1965-77; prof., head dept. Auburn (Ala.) U., 1977-85, Hollifield prof., 1985-90, Disting. Univ. prof., 1990—. Author: Dixie's Forgotten People, 1979, Poor But Proud, 1989 (Lillian Smith prize for nonfiction, Acad. Book of Yr., Choice, James F. Sulzby award Ala. Hist. Soc., Nonfiction award ALA), also 9 other books. Recipient numerous teaching awards, Ala. Humanities Found. award, 1991; named to Ala. Acad. Disting. Authors, 1983, Clarence Cason Lifetime award for nonfiction writing, 2002, Hugo Black award for svc. to Ala. and nation; named Ala. Prof. of Yr., Coun. for Advancement and Support of Edn. Democrat. Baptist. Avocations: basketball, fishing. Home: 1224 Penny Ln Auburn AL 36830-2628 E-mail: flyntjw@auburn.edu.

FOALE, C. MICHAEL, astronaut; b. Louth, England, Jan. 6, 1957; s. Colin and Mary Foale; m. Rhonda R. Butler; 2 children. BA with hon. in Physics, Natural Sci. Tripos, Queen's Coll., Cambridge, Eng., 1978; PhD in Lab. Astrophysics, Cambridge U., 1982. With McDonnell Douglas Aircraft Corp., Houston, 1982—83; payload officer NASA, Houston, 1983—. Astronaut Atlas mission, 1992, Space Shuttle Atlantis, 1997; aboard Russian Space Sta. MIR, 1997; astronaut mission to upgrade Hubble Space Telescope, 1999. Avocations: wind surfing, private flying, soaring, scuba diving, writing children's software. Office: Astronaut Office CB NASA Johnson Space Center Houston TX 77058

FOARD, DOUGLAS W. educational association administrator; b. Balt., Oct. 23, 1939; s. George Winfield and Anna (Herrmann) F.; m. Janet Hess, Aug. 26, 1961; children: Wendy Lynn, Scott Douglas. BA, Randolph-Macon Coll., 1961; MA, U. Va., 1965; PhD, Washington U., 1972; LHD (hon.), Randolph-Macon Coll., 1992, Hampden Sydney Coll., 2001. Asst. to dir. pub. rels. Ferrum (Va.) Coll., asst. prof. history, 1965-70, chair social sci., 1970-79, prof. history, 1972-85, assoc. dean, 1979-81; program officer NEH, Washington, 1985-89; exec. sec. Phi Beta Kappa, Washington, 1989-2001; dir. Loudoun (Va.) County Mus., 2001—. Adj. prof. history George Mason U., Fairfax, Va. Author: The Revolt of the Aesthetes, 1989; contbr. articles to profl. jours.; guest editor Mag. of History, 1991. Bd. dirs. Nat. Humanities Alliance, 1994-2001, mem. exec. com., 1997-2000; bd. dirs. Nat. History Day, Washington, 1987-2001; bd. dirs. Va. Found. for Humanities and Pub. Policy, 1990-96, chmn., 1995-96. Grantee Ford Found. 1969-70; James Still fellow U. Ky. 1983, Nat. Defense Act fellow Washington U., 1967-70, Philip DuPont fellow U. Va., 1961-62, Ford Found. fellow Asian Studies, 1967, Nat. Meth. scholar Randolph-Macon Coll., 1960-61; NEH summer seminar Vanderbilt U., 1976. Mem. Soc. Spanish & Portuguese Hist. Studies (newsletter editor 1982-85) Va. Soc. History Tchrs. (pres. 1981-83), Phi Beta Kappa. Address: Phi Beta Kappa Society 4th Fl 1785 Massachusetts Ave NW Fl 4 Washington DC 20036-2111

FOARD, SUSAN LEE, editor; b. Asheville, N.C., Aug. 1, 1938; d. Carson Cowan and Anne (Brown) F. AB, Salem Coll., 1960; MA, William and Mary Coll., 1966. Asst. editor Inst. Early Am. Hist. and Culture, Williamsburg, Va., 1961-66, assoc. editor, 1966; editor U. Va. Press, Charlottesville, 1966—. Office: PO Box 400318 Charlottesville VA 22904-4318

FOBES, JOHN EDWIN, international organization official; b. Chgo., Mar. 16, 1918; s. Wilfred and Mable (Skogsberg) Fobes; m. Hazel Ward Weaver, June 7, 1941; children: Patricia Cleveland, John Geoffrey Weaver. BS cum laude, Northwestern U., 1939; MA, Tufts U., 1940; HHD (hon.), Bucknell U., 1973. With Bur. Budget, Washington, 1942, 1946—48; secretariat prep. commn. of UN London, 1945; exec. sec. UN advisory group of experts on adminstrn., pers. and budgetary questions, 1946; adviser Pan Am. Union, 1947—48; with ECA, Marshall Plan, 1948—52; attache U.S. del. to NATO and OEEC Paris, 1952—55; dir. Office Internat. Adminstrn. Dept. State, Washington, 1955—59, spl. asst. to asst. sec. state, 1959—60; asst. dir. Tech. Cooperation Mission to India, 1960—62; dep. dir. AID Mission to India, 1962—64; asst. dir. gen. UNESCO, Paris, 1964—70, dep. dir. gen., 1970—77. Vis. rsch. scholar Ind. U., 1970, Harvard, 1970; vis. scholar Duke U., Durham, 1978—82; vis. lectr. U. N.C., Chapel Hill, 1981—82; adj. prof. Western Carolina U.1, 1983—90; mem. adv. com. UN Gen. Assembly, 1955—60; chmn. U.S. Nat. Commn. for UNESCO, 1980—81. Pres. Am. Libr. in Paris, 1968—70. Served as maj. USAAF, 1942—46, ETO. Clarion Dewitt Hardy scholar, Northwestern U., 1939. Fellow: World Acad. Arts and Scis.; mem.: UN Assn. (nat. coun.), Ams. for Universality of UNESCO (founder, chmn.), Assn. for Promotion of Humor in Internat. Affairs (co-founder), World Futures Studies Fedn., Acad. Coun. on UN, Club of Rome, Phi Beta Kappa. Home: 28 Beaverbrook Rd Asheville NC 28804-1502

FOCH, NINA, actress, creative consultant, educator, director; b. Leyden, The Netherlands, Apr. 20, 1924; came to U.S. 1927; d. Dirk and Consuelo (Flowerton) F.; m. James Lipton, June 6, 1954; m. Dennis de Brito, Nov. 27, 1959; 1 child, Dirk de Brito; m. Michael Dewell, Oct. 31, 1967 (div.). Grad., Lincoln Sch., 1939; studies with Stella Adler. Adj. prof. drama U. So. Calif., 1966-68, 78-80, adj. prof. film, 1987—; creative cons. to dirs., writers, prodrs. of all media. Artist-in-residence U. N.C., 1966, Ohio State U., 1967, Calif. Inst. Tech., 1969-70; mem. sr. faculty Am. Film Inst., 1974-77; founder, tchr. Nina Foch Studio, Hollywood, Calif., 1973—; founder, actress Los Angeles Theatre Group, 1960-65; bd. dirs. Nat. Repertory Theatre, 1967-75. Motion picture appearances include Nine Girls, 1944, Return of the Vampire, 1944, Shadows in the Night, 1944, Cry of the Werewolf, 1944, Escape in the Fog, 1945, A Song to Remember, 1945, My Name Is Julia Ross, 1945, I Love a Mystery, 1945, Johnny O'Clock, 1947, The Guilt of Janet Ames, 1947, The Dark Past, 1948, The Undercover Man, 1949, Johnny Allegro, 1949, An American in Paris, 1951, Scaramouche, 1952, Young Man with Ideas, 1952, Sombrero, 1953, Fast Company, 1953, Executive Suite, 1954 (Oscar award nominee), Four Guns to the Border, 1954, You're Never Too Young, 1955, Illegal, 1955, The Ten Commandments, 1956, Three Brave Men, 1957, Cash McCall, 1959, Spartacus, 1960, Such Good Friends, 1971, Salty, 1973, Mahogany, 1976, Jennifer, 1978, Rich and Famous, 1981, Skin Deep, 1988, Sliver, 1993, Morning Glory, 1993, 'Til There Was You, 1996, Hush, 1998, Shadow of Doubt, 1998, How to Deal, 2003; appeared in Broadway plays including John Loves Mary, 1947, Twelfth Night, 1949, A Phoenix Too Frequent, 1950, King Lear, 1950, Second String, 1960; appeared with Am. Shakespeare Festival in Taming of the Shrew, Measure for Measure, 1956, San Francisco Ballet and Opera in The Seven Deadly Sins, 1966; also many regional theater appearances including Seattle Repertory Theatre (All Over, 1972 and The Seagull, 1973); actress on TV, 1947—, including Playhouse 90, Studio One, Pulitzer Playhouse, Playwrights 56, Producers Showcase, Lou Grant (Emmy nominee 1980), Mike Hammer; series star: Shadow Chasers, 1985, War and Remembrance, 1988, LA Law, 1990, Hunter, 1990, Dear John, 1990, 91, Tales of the City, 1993, Dharma and Greg, 1999, Just Shoot Me, 2000, recurring role Bull, 2000-01, State of Grace, 2003; many other series, network spls. and TV films; TV panelist and guest on The Dinah Shore Show, Merv Griffin Show, The Today Show, Dick Cavett, The Tonight Show; TV moderator: Let's Take Sides, 1957-59; assoc. dir. (film) The Diary of Anne Frank, 1959; dir. (nat. tour and on-Broadway) Tonight at 8:30, 1966-67, Family Blessings, 1997; assoc. producer re-opening of Ford's Theatre, Washington, 1968. Hon. chmn. Los Angeles chpt. Am. Cancer Soc., 1970. Recipient Film Daily award, 1949, 53. Mem. AAUP, Acad. Motion Picture Arts and Scis. (co-chair exec. com. fgn. film award, membership com., chair foreign lang. award com., 1998-99), Hollywood Acad. TV Arts and Scis. (bd. govs. 1976-77). Avocation: work. Office: PO Box 1884 Beverly Hills CA 90213-1884

FOCHLER, FRANCIS JOHN, surgeon; b. Altoona, Pa., Jan. 16, 1932; MD, U. Pa., 1962. Diplomate Am. Bd. Surgery. Intern Altoona Hosp., 1962-63; resident in gen. surgery SUNY Buffalo Affiliated Hosps., 1965-69; staff physician Hollidaysburg (Pa.) Vets. Home, 1993—. Mem. AMA. Home: 5825 Beale Ave Altoona PA 16601-5102

FOCHT, JOHN ARNOLD, JR., geotechnical engineer; b. Rockwall, Tex., Aug. 31, 1923; s. John Arnold and Fay (Goss) F.; m. Edith Rials, Aug. 8, 1950; children: John Arnold III, Judith Lynn Schweitzer. BSCE, U. Tex., 1944; MSCE, Harvard U., 1946. Soils engr. U.S. Waterways Expt. Sta., Vicksburg, Miss., 1947-50, 52-53; sr. soils engr. McClelland Engrs., Inc., Houston, 1953-55, v.p. engring., 1955-72, exec. v.p., 1972-87; v.p. TERA, Inc., 1965-85; chmn. bd. Fugro-McClelland Inc., 1987-90; cons., 1991-99, Focht Consultants, Inc., 1999—. Contbr. articles to tech. jours. Chmn. ofcl. bd. Grace Methodist Ch., 1960-62; bd. dirs. N.W. YMCA, 1957-59; chmn. vis. com. dept. civil engring. U. Tex., Austin, 1974. Served to capt. AUS, 1944-46, 50-52. Recipient Disting. Engring. Grad. award, U. Tex., Austin, 1964, Tech. Pioneer for Found. Design, Offshore Energy Ctr., 2001. Fellow: ASCE (pres. Tex. sect. 1970—71, nat. dir. 1980—83, nat. pres. 1989—90, Thomas A. Middlebrooks award 1957, James Laurie prize 1959, Civil Engring. State of the Art award 1971, Thomas A. Middlebrooks award 1976, Civil Engring. State of the Art award 1979, Terzaghi lectr. 1993, William H. Wisely Am. Civil Engr. award 1999, GeoInst. Hero 2002, Tex. Sect. Lifetime Svc. award 2002); mem.: NSPE, NAE, Instn. Engrs. Ireland, Inst. Profl. Practice (dir. 1996—99), Houston Engring. and Sci. Soc. (treas., dir. 1973—76), Tex. Coun. Engring. Labs. (dir. 1972—75), Cons. Engrs. Coun. Tex. (dir. 1965—67), Am. Cons. Engrs. Coun., Tex. Soc. Profl. Engrs. (Engr. of Yr. award 1987), Tau Beta Pi, Chi Epsilon (Nat. Honor Mem. 2000). Methodist. Home: 12226 Perthshire Rd Houston TX 77024-4244

FOCHT, MICHAEL HARRISON, health care industry executive; b. Reading, Pa., Sept. 16, 1942; s. Benjamin Harrison and Mary (Hannahoe) F.; m. Sandra Lee Scholwin, May 14, 1964; 1 child, Michael Harrison Archtl. estimator Caloric Corp., Topton, Pa., 1964-65, cost acct., 1965-66, indsl. engr., 1966-68, mgr. wage rates and standards, 1968-70; indsl. engr. Am. Medicorp. Inc., Fort Lauderdale, Fla., 1970-71, exec. dir. midwest region Chgo., 1977-78; asst. adminstr. Cypress Community Hosp., Pompano Beach, Fla., 1971-73, adminstr., 1975-77, Doctor's Hosp. Hollywood, Fla., 1973-75; v.p. Medfield Corp., St. Petersburg, Fla., 1978-79; v.p. ops. hosp. group Nat. Med. Enterprises, Inc., Los Angeles, 1979-81, regional sr. v.p. hosp. group Tampa, Fla., 1981-83, pres., chief exec. officer internat. group Los Angeles, 1983-86, pres. chief exec. officer hosp. group, 1986-91, sr. exec. v.p., dir. ops., 1991-93, pres., 1993-95; pres., COO Tenet Healthcare Corp., Santa Barbara, 1995—. Mem. Fedn. Am. Hosps. (bd. govs. 1983—), Fla. League Hosps. (bd. dirs. 1982-83) Republican. Roman Catholic. Home: PO Box 703 Santa Ynez CA 93460-0703 Office: Tenet Healthcare Corp 3820 State St Santa Barbara CA 93105-3112

FOCHT, THEODORE HAROLD, lawyer, educator; b. Reading, Pa., Aug. 20, 1934; s. Harold Edwin and Ruth Naomi (Boyer) F.; m. Joyce Gundy, Aug. 11, 1956; children: David Scott, Eric Steven. AB in Philosophy, Franklin and Marshall Coll., 1956; JD, Coll. of William and Mary, 1959. Bar: Va. 1959. Teaching assoc. Columbia U. Sch. Law, N.Y.C., 1959-60; atty. Office of Gen. Counsel SEC, Washington, 1960-61, legal asst. to Commr., Washington, 1961-63; mem. faculty U. Conn. Sch. Law, Hartford, 1963-71 (leave of absence, 1969-71); spl. counsel on securities legislation Interstate and Fgn. Commerce Com., U.S. Ho. of Reps., Washington, 1969-71; gen. counsel Securities Investor Protection Corp., Washington, 1971-94, pres., 1984-94; adj. prof. law American U. Sch. Law, Washington, 1979-84; mem. Fla. State Comptroller's Task Force on Regulatory DeCoupling, 1995. Mem. Va. State Bar, Phi Beta Kappa. Home: 8436 Pinafore Dr New Port Richey FL 34653-6739

FOCKLER, HERBERT HILL, foundation executive; b. Summersville, W.Va., Feb. 18, 1922; s. William Okey and Annie Lee (Fitzwater) Fockler; m. Mary Hildegarde Ziegler, May 15, 1950; 1 child, Herbert. BA, W.Va. U., 1947, MA, 1948; cert., Oxford (Eng.) U., 1948, Harvard U., 1949; MS in Libr. Sci., Cath. U. Am., 1952. Adminstr. libr. Princeton (N.J.) U., 1952-54, Library of Congress, Washington, 1956-58; advisor White House Confs., Washington, 1959-60; exec. NIH, Bethesda, Md., 1961-69; chmn. Sci. and Tech. Coms., Washington, 1969-70; exec. dir. Sci. Founds., Washington, 1971-72; trustee, chmn. Am. Arts Internat. Found., Washington, pres., 1984—, also bd. dirs.; trustee Nat. Mus. of Health and Medicine Found., 1989—. Adv. Nat. Coun. for Sci. and Environment, 2000—; chmn., trustee World Tech. Found., Washington, 1988-89; bd. dirs. Nat. Info. Tech. Ctr.; advisor NSF, 1975, White House Conf. on Bus., 1975, 78, Montgomery Coll., Rockville, Md., 1978, World Bank, 1986, Winston Churchill Found., 1988, IMF, 1991, others; adv. coun. Coolfont Found., Berkeley Springs, W.Va., 1980-87; mem. Presdl. Rsch. Group; assoc. Woodrow Wilson Internat. Ctr., 1988—; mem. Bd. on Sci. Edn.; advisor Global Internet, 2000-01; bd. dirs. Spectrum Access, Calif. Ctr. for Strategic Studies, 2001—. Editor: Contemporary South, 1968, also conf. records and newsletters; contbr. articles to profl. jours. Adv. Stanford U., 1967-69, Georgetown U., 1975-85; trustee Threshold Environ. Found., Washington, 1969-75, Nat. Mus. Health and Medicine Found., 1989-90, adv. coun., 1991—; mem. pres.'s coun. Shenandoah Coll., Winchester, Va., 1982-87; mem. Found. Advancement Edn. in Scis., 1980—, Joint Bd. Edn. in Sci. and Engring., 1991—; bd. dirs. Nat. Mus. of Lang., 1999—, Global Children's Health Fund, 1999—, Nat. Fgn. Lang. Ctr., 2000—; chmn. Sustainable Value Found., 2003—. Staff sgt. U.S. Army, 1941-45. Mem. AAAS, Acad. Polit. Sci., Am. Polit. Sci. Assn., Washington Acad. Scis. (bd. dirs.), U.N. Assn., Smithsonian Assocs., Am. Assn. Mus., Air and Space Mus., Nat. Trust Hist. Preservation, Libr. Congress Assocs., Colonial Williamsburg Found., SAR, Fgn. Policy Inst., World Affairs Coun., Policy Studies Orgn., Found. for Advancement Edn. in Sci., Internet Soc., Smithsonian Assocs., Am. Film Inst., Harvard Club, Princeton Club, W.Va. Club, W.Va. Acad. Sci., Nat. Press Club. Home and Office: 10710 Lorain Ave Silver Spring MD 20901-1512

FODA, RABIZ NASIR, industrial engineer, electrical engineer; b. Bombay, May 14, 1949; arrived in Can., 1994; s. Nasir Huseinibhai Foda and Amena (Yahya) Khairullah; m. Nermin Zoyeb Kantawala, Dec. 5, 1977; children: Maria, Zulqarnain, Farzeen. B Tech. with honors, Indian Inst. Tech., Bombay, 1973; grad. diploma in mgmt. studies, U. Bombay, 1981. Sr. asst. engr. Tata Electric Cos., Bombay, 1973-85; elec. engr. Sceco-Western Region, Jeddah, Saudi Arabia, 1985-92, corp. tech. mgmt. group for transmission dept., 1986-90, chief of sub-stations, 1990-92, acting dir. transmission, 1989-92; sr. engr. Indsl. Power Projects, Jeddah, 1993-94, Elecsar Engring. Ltd., Can., 1995-99, Atomic Energy Can. Ltd., Mississauga, Ont., Can., 1999—. Cons. for energy conservation Econ. Cons., Bombay. Contbr. articles to profl. jours. Mem.: IEEE (sr.), IEEE Engring. Mgmt. Soc. (Toronto), Inst. Elec. Engrs. U.K., Profl. Engrs. Ont. (experience requirements com.), Soc. Power Engrs. India, Project Mgmt. Inst., N.Y. Acad. Scis., Indian Inst. Tech. Alumni Assn. Can. (exec. bd. 1996—, treas. 2000—01, gen. sec. 2001—03, v.p. 2003—), Econ. Forum of Indian Expatriates (exec. com. 1987—88), India Forum, Embassy of India, Jeddah (mng. com. 1990—94). Avocations: painting, reading, music, tennis, swimming. Home: 1511 Hollywell Ave Mississauga ON Canada L5N 4P6 E-mail: foda@computer.org., fodar@aecl.ca.

FODERARO, ANTHONY HAROLDE, nuclear engineering educator; b. Scranton, Pa., Apr. 3, 1926; s. Edward and Myrtha (Bachman) F.; m. Rita Lacey, May 4, 1953; children— Anthony, John, Diana. BS in Physics, U. Scranton, 1950; PhD in Physics, U. Pitts., 1955. Supervisory scientist Westinghouse Atomic Power Div., Pitts., 1954-56; sr. nuclear physicist Gen. Motors Research, Warren, Mich., 1956-60; assoc. prof. nuclear engring. Pa. State U., University Park, 1960-63, prof., 1963-88; prof. emeritus, 1989—. Cons. on radiation protection govt. and industry. Author: The Elements of Neutron Interaction Theory, 1971, The Photon Shielding Manual, 1976; co-author: The Reactor Shielding Design Manual, 1956, The Engineering Compendium on Radiation Shielding, 1968; contbr. articles to pubs. in field. Served with U.S. Army, 1944-46. Fellow Am. Nuclear Soc. (chmn. radiation protection and shielding div. 1969-70); mem. Am. Phys. Soc., Am. Assn. Physics Tchrs. Home: 301 S Gill St State College PA 16801-3963 E-mail: tony@foderaro.com.

FODIMAN, AARON ROSEN, publishing executive; b. Stamford, Conn., Oct. 10, 1937; s. Yale J. and Thelma F. BS, Tulane U., 1958; LLB, NYU, 1960, MBA, 1961; grad., L'Academie de CuisineCanardier, Washington, 1977. Bar: N.Y. 1960, D.C. 1961, Va. 1965. With FTC, Washington, 1961-65; practiced in Arlington, Va., 1965-78; pres. Fast Food Operators, Inc., N.Y.C., 1978-84, Hampton Healthcare, 1984-91, Kapok Tree Restaurants, Tampa Bay Publs., 1986—. Author: Life is not an Illusion, it Just Looks That Way, 1998; pub., editor: Tampa Bay Mag.; TV host local sports show, Dine Line, Tampa Bay Mag. Bd. dirs. Tampa Players Inc., Washington Ballet, Manhattan Punch Line Theatre, Kent Jewish Cmty. Ctr., Mahaffey Theater Found., Outdoor Art Found., Clearwater Arts Found., pres., chmn., 2003; bd. advisors Fla. Orch.; pres. Dunedin Art Ctr., Bay Ballet Theatre; chmn. Pinellas County Arts Coun., Golda Meir Ctr., Bay Ballet Theatre, A Taste of Pinellas; cmty. advisor Clearwater Dunedin Jr. League; mem. adv. bd. Am. Film Inst.; chmn. Ford Presdl. Campaign, 1976; advisor Fed. Res. Bank Atlanta; participant Leadership Pinellas; participant, founder Leadership Tampa Bay, Nat. Conf. Christians and Jews; Pinellas County amb. to Ringling Mus. Art. Recipient Hyam Soloman Freedom award, 1974, Miniature Palette award Miniature Art Soc. of Fla., 1987, Order of Salvador medal Dali Mus., 1989, Lifetime Achievement award Internat. Restaurant and Hospitality Rating Bur., 2000; honoree award winner Friends of Arts Pinellas County, Svc. to Mankind award Sertoma Club; knighted as Baron Order of St. John of Jerusalem, 1999. Mem. Pinellas County Restaurant Assn. (pres.), Tampa Bay Restaurant Assn. (pres.), Fla. Restaurant Assn. (bd. dirs.), Tampa Bay Food and Wine Soc., Chaine des Rotisseurs (chpt. officer), Internat. Legal Frat., Phi Delta Phi, Barrister Inn Club (Washington, pres.), B'nai Brith (pres. Washington).

FODOR, IMOLA KATALIN, mathematician, researcher; b. Targu Mures, Romania, May 5, 1971; arrived in U.S., 1971; d. Ludovic Fodor and Katalin Maria Barbassy; BA, Rutgers U., 1994; MA, U. Calif., Berkeley, 1996, PhD, 1999. Statis. cons. Kwasha Lipton, Ft. Lee, N.J., 1994; sr. tech. assoc. AT&T Bell Labs., Murray Hill, N.J., 1994; statis. cons. U. Calif., Berkeley, 1995, 97, grad. student rschr., 1996-99, Livermore, 1997; postdoctoral rschr. Lawrence Livermore Nat. Lab., 1999-2000, computational mathematician, 2000—. Contbr. articles to profl. jours. Fellow, AT&T Bell Labs., 1994—99, Grad., NSF, 1994—97; scholar Rutgers Coll. Merit, Rutgers U., 1993. Mem.: AAAS, Inst. Math. Stats., Am. Statis. Assn., Nat. Ctr. Sci. Edn. Home: 8410E North Lake Dr Dublin CA 94568 Office: Ctr For Applied Sci Comptg 7000 East Ave Livermore CA 94550-9516 Office Fax: 925-422-6287. Business E-Mail: fodor1@llnl.gov.

FODOR, ISTVAN, molecular biologist, researcher; b. Ungvar, Hungary, Aug. 22, 1940; s. Istvan and Iren Fodor; m. Nadja Saveljeva; children: Iren, Kristina. BS, Uzhgorod U., Ungvar, Russia, 1962; PhD, USSR Acad. Scis., Moscow, 1968. Prin. investigator Inst. for Biochemistry and Protein Rsch. of the Agrl. Biotechnology Ctr., Godollo, Hungary, 1990—95; rschr., sr. rschr., head of lab. Inst. Biochemistry & Physiology of Microorganisms, USSR Acad. Scis., Pushchino, Russia, 1990—98; prof. Loma Linda U., Calif., 1995—. Scientist U. Calif., San Francisco, 1975—76. Contbr. articles to profl. jours. Grantee, NIH, 1997—2002. Mem.: AAUP. Avocations: running, soccer, swimming, hiking. Home: 1119 Via Barcelona St Redlands CA 92374 Office: Loma Linda Univ 11085 Campus St Loma Linda CA 92350 Office Fax: 909-558-0177. Personal E-mail: antheus@earthlink.net. E-mail: ifodor@som.llu.edu.

FODOR, SUSANNA SERENA, lawyer; b. Tg-Mures, Romania, Apr. 24, 1950; came to U.S., 1963; d. Bela Akos and Rachel (Rafira) F.; 1 child, Brooke Alexandra Bodoki-Fodor. BS, U. Wis., Milw., 1969; JD, U. Wis., Madison, 1972. Bar: Wis. 1972, N.Y. 1974. In ho. counsel Wis. Dept. Devel. Natural Resources, Madison, 1972-73, U.S. EPA, N.Y.C., 1973-74, Urban Devel. Corp., N.Y.C., 1975-77; assoc. Schulte, Roth & Zabel, N.Y.C., 1977-79; ptnr. Weil, Gotshal & Manges, N.Y.C., 1979-85, Shea & Gould, N.Y.C., 1985-89, Jones, Day, Reavis & Pogue, N.Y.C., 1989—. Editor chpt. to book; contbr. articles to profl. publs., chpt. to book. Mem. ABA (real property, probate and trust constrn. form com.), Am. Coll. Real Estate Lawyers, Profl. Women in Constrn., Real Estate Bd. N.Y. (owner labor coordinating com.), Am. Coll. Constrn. Lawyers, Am. Arbitration Assn. (large complex case panel), Comml. Real Estate Women N.Y. (editl. bd.), Urban Land Inst., CoreNet Global; CoreNet Learning Advisory Bd.; Wis. State Bar Assn., N.Y. State Bar Assn., Hungarian-Am. C. of C. of N.Y./N.J. Avocations: sports, art, languages. Home: 200 E End Ave Apt 14F New York NY 10128-7887 Office: Jones Day Reavis & Pogue 599 Lexington Ave Fl C1A New York NY 10022-6030 E-mail: ssfodor@jonesday.com.

FODREA, CAROLYN WROBEL, educational researcher, publisher, consultant; b. Hammond, Ind., Feb. 1, 1943; d. Stanley Jacob and Margaret Caroline (Stupeck) Wrobel; m. Howard Frederick Fodrea, June 17, 1967 (div. Jan. 1987); children: Gregory Kirk, Lynn Renee. BA in Elem. Edn., Purdue U., 1966; MA

in Reading and Lang. Devel., U. Chgo., 1973; postgrad., U. Colo., Denver, 1986—87. Cert. elem. tchr., Ind., Ill. Tchr. various schs., Ind., Colo., 1966-87; founder, supr., clinician Reading Clinic, Children's Hosp., Denver, 1969-73; pvt. practice in reading and lang. rsch. clinic Denver, 1973-87; pvt. practice in reading rsch. ctr. Deerfield, Ill., 1973—; creator of pilot presch.-kindergarten lang. devel. program Gary, Ind. Diocese Schs., 1987—, therapist lang. and reading disabilities, 1987—; pres. Reading Rsch. Ctr., Arlington Heights, Ill., 2000—. Conducted Lang. Devel. Workshop, Gary, Ind. 1988; tchr. adult basic edn. Dawson Tech. Sch., 1990, Coll. Lake County, 1991, Prairie State Coll., 1991—, Chgo. City Colls., 1991, R.J. Daley Coll., 1991, Coll. DuPage, 1991—; condr. adult basic edn. workshops for Coll. of DuPage, R.J. Daley Coll., 1992, Ill. Lang. Devel. Literacy Program; tchr. Korean English Lang. Inst., Chgo., 1996, Lang. Devel. Program for Minorities, 2000; dir. pilot study Cabrini Green Tutoring Ctr., Chgo., 2000; presenter in field. Author: Language Development Program, 1985, Presch. Kindergarten Lang. Devel. Program, 1988, A Multi-Sensory Stimulation Program for the Premature Baby in Its Incubator to Reduce Medical Costs and Academic Failure, 1986, Predicting At-Risk Babies for First Grade Reading Failure Before Birth A 15 Year Study, A Language Development Program, Grades 1 to Adult, 1988, 92; editor, pub.: ESL For Native Spanish Speakers, 1996, ESL for Native Korean Speakers, 1996. Active Graland Country Day Sch., Denver, 1981-83, N.W. Ind. Children's Chorale, 1988—; Ill. state chair Babies and You com. March of Dimes, 1999—. Mem. NEA, Am. Ednl. Rsch. Assn., Internat. Reading Assn., Am. Coun. for Children with Learning Disabilities, Am. Acad. Environ. Medicine (presenter pilot study at conf. 2002), Assn. for Childhood Edn. Internat., Colo. Assn. for Edn. of Young Children, Infant Stimulation Edn. Assn., Art Inst. Chgo., U. Chgo. Alumni Club (Denver area ann. fund, Pres. fund com. 1988—, numerous positions Denver area chpt. 1974-87). Roman Catholic. Avocations: sports, health and nutrition, literary and cultural activities, sewing. E-mail: cfodrea@readingresearch.com. *The ability to think, to read and to learn is dependent upon intact, internalized language system. It is this internalized language system that is dysfunctional in those who have not been successful students and who must have this language system rebuilt first if they are to become successful learners, productive workers and original thinkers capable of problem analysis and problem solutions.*

FOERST, JOHN GEORGE, JR., retired fundraising executive; b. Queens, N.Y., June 8, 1927; s. John George and Mary Elizabeth (McGinn) F.; m. Marion Theresa Cassidy, June 27, 1953; children: Gerard M., Kathryn J. BA, St. Johns U., Queens, 1950. Regional rep. Nat. Found. for Infantile Paralysis, N.Y.C., 1950-52; campaign dir., v.p. Cmty. Counselling Svc., N.Y.C., 1952-59, v.p., asst. to pres., 1965-69, pres., 1969-87, chmn., 1987-96, chmn. emeritus, 1997-2001; pres. John G. Foerst, Inc., N.Y.C., 1959-65. Special advisor to chmn. and bd. dirs. Changing Our World, Inc., 2001—. Contbg. author: complete Guide to Corporate Fund Raising, 1982. Trustee Pope John Paul II Libr. and Cultural Ctr., Washington, 1998—, Telecare, Uniondale, NY; chmn. Am. Assn. Fund Raising Counsel, N.Y.C., 1982; mem. Cardinal's Com. of Laity Roman Cath. Archdiocese N.Y., 1984—; bd. dirs. St. Francis Hosp., Roslyn, NY, 1972—2002, The Ctr. for Devel. Disabilities, Woodbury, NY, 1974—87, Nat. Ctr. for Disability Svcs. Inc., Albertson, NY, 1988—99, Cath. Health Sys. of L.I., 1998—99, Help for the Poor Found., 1998—99, Mid-Atlantic Hosp. Trust, Bermuda. Mem. Union League, Knights of Malta. Republican. Home: 77 Dover Rd Manhasset NY 11030-3717

FOERSTER, BARRETT JONATHAN, lawyer; b. Charleston, S.C., Oct. 20, 1942; S. Donald Madison Foerster and Margaret Jean (Barrett) Foerster Harkins; m. Susan Ruth Sibert, June 17, 1967; children: Andrea B., Bryn E. BA, U. Pa., 1964; JD, UCLA, 1967; LLM, U. San Diego, 2000. Bar: Calif. 1970, U.S. Dist. Ct. (so. and cen. dists.) Calif. 1970. Ptnr. Greer, Popko, Miller and Foerster, San Diego, 1970-75, Olins, Foerster and Hayes, San Diego, 1975—. Contbr. articles to legal jours. Served to capt. U.S. Army, 1967-69, Vietnam. Recipient Preservation award Save Our Heritage Orgn., 1983. Mem. Calif. Bar Assn., San Diego County Bar Assn., Calif. State Probate Referees Assn. (bd. dirs. 1984-85). Episcopalian. Avocation: jogging. Home: 4476 Ampudia St San Diego CA 92103-1046 Office: 2214 2nd Ave San Diego CA 92101-2020 E-mail: BFoerster@ofh.com.

FOERSTER, BERND, architecture educator; b. Danzig, Dec. 5, 1923; came to U.S., 1947, naturalized, 1954; s. Joseph and Martha (Brumm) F.; m. Enell Dowling, May 13, 1950; children: Kent, Mark (dec.). Student, Columbia U., 1948-49; BS in Architecture, U. Cin., 1954; MArch, Rensselaer Poly. Inst., 1957. Various positions Govt. The Netherlands, 1945-47; with various engrs. and architects offices, 1950-59; cons. Ch. bldgs., design cons., 1954—; instr. architecture U. Cin., 1954, Rensselaer Poly. Inst., Troy, N.Y., 1954-56, asst. prof., 1956-62, assoc. prof., 1962-65, prof., 1965-71; dean Kans. State U., Manhattan, 1971-84, prof., 1971—99; adjunct prof. Grad. Program in Hist. Preservation Goucher Coll., 1995—. Cons. archtl. and cmty. surveys N.Y. State Coun. Arts, 1962-71; chmn. Gov.'s Adv. Com. Hist. Preservation N.Y. State, 1968-71; cons. Albany Hist. Sites Commn., 1967-71, Independence (Mo.) Heritage Commn., 1975-77; leader U.S. del. Preservation Planning to China, 1982, USSR and Ea. Europe, 1989; leader faculty team Coll. Architecture and Design, Kans. State U. to Poland, The Czech and Slovak Republics, and Hungary, 1990; cons. selection of archs. and design cons. for Fed. projects U.S. GSA, 1994-96. Author: Man and Masonry, 1960, Pattern and Texture, 1961, Architecture Worth Saving in Rensselaer County, N.Y., 1965; (with others) Independence, Missouri, 1978, 2d printing, 1989; (films) Man and Masonry, 1961 (Am. Film Festival selection), What Do You Tear Down Next?, 1964, Earth and Fire, 1964, Assault on the Wynantskill, 1967; editorial adv. bd. Preservation Forum, 1987-93. Bd. dirs. Albany Inst. History and Art, 1967-71, Mohawk-Hudson Council on Ednl. TV, 1968-71, v.p., 1970-71; co-chmn. Conf. on Rensselaer County, 1966; pres. Rensselaer County Council for Arts, 1963-64, 66-67; trustee Olana Historic Site, 1969-71; pres. bd. trustees Riley County Hist. Mus., 1977; chmn. Manhattan Downtown Redevel. Adv. Bd., 1979-85, City Fountain Restoration Com., 1983-86; mem. coun. Drayton Hall, Charleston, S.C., 1985-93; mem. Hist. Dist. Rev. Bd. Manhattan, 1997-99; mem. Manhattan Hist. Resources Bd., 1999—, vice chmn., 1999-2001; mem. planning bd. Riley County, Kans., 1997-99; chair Road and Bridge Adv. Com. Riley County, 1997-98; chair steering com. Downtown Tomorrow, Manhattan, 1998-2000. Named Disting. prof. Assn. Collegiate Schs. Architecture, 1988; recipient Kans. Gov.'s award for historic preservation, 1995, James Marston Fitch Lifetime Achievement award Nat. Coun. for Preservation Edn., 2000. Fellow AIA (com. hist. resources 1977-92, vice chmn. 1986, chmn. 1987, state preservation coordinator 1979-92); mem. AIA Kans. (sec. 1975, exec. com. 1975-80, pres. 1979), Nat. Trust Hist. Preservation (bd. advs. 1979-81, trustee 1981-90, trustee emeritus 1990—), AAUP (chpt. pres. Rensselaer Poly. Inst. 1963-64, Kans. State U. 1987-88, v.p. Kans. conf. 1988-90, pres. 1990-92), The Land Inst. (bd. dirs. 1976-87), Manhattan Arts Coun. (bd. dirs. 1973-78, pres. 1976-77), LWV of Manhattan-Riley County (2d v.p. 1988-91, pres.-elect 91-92, pres. 92-93), Kans. Preservation Alliance (bd. dirs. 1979-85, hon. trustee 1999—), Nat. Council Preservation Edn. (bd. dirs. 1980-93, vice-chmn. 1981-85), Nature Conservancy, Audubon Soc., Scarab, Tau Sigma Delta, Phi Kappa Phi. Lodges: Rotary (Paul Harris fellow). Home: 920 Ratone St Manhattan KS 66502-5136 *Some places are so important, so fragile, or so beautiful that we must leave them alone.*

FOERSTER, CONRAD LOUIS, project engineer; b. Balt., Jan. 19, 1938; s. George Leroy Sr. and Jane Ruth (Carson) F.; m. Tina M. Capone, Sept. 20, 1964; children: Christopher C., George A. AS in Engring. Sci., Nassau C.C., 1971; BS in Engring. Sci., L.I. U., 1975; postgrad., Poly. Inst., N.Y.C., 1978, U.S. Partical Accelerator Sch., 1992. Vacuum technician Veeco Instrument Corp., Plainview, N.Y., 1959-68; electronic technician Gen. Instrument Inc., Hicksville, N.Y., 1968, eqipment supr., 1973; mfg. engr. Deutsch Relays Inc., East Northport, N.Y., 1968-73, product engr., 1973-79; project engr. Brookhaven Nat. Lab., Upton, N.Y., 1979-86, vacuum group leader, 1986—. Contbr. articles to profl. jours. With USAF, 1955-59. Achievements include research in vacuum science. Office: Brookhaven Nat Lab Nsls Bldg 725C Upton NY 11973

FOERSTER, JAMES FREDRICK, urban planning educator, university administrator; b. Chgo., Jan. 4, 1951; s. Fredrick William and Genevieve Catherine (Wych) F.; m. Patrice Narret, June 1984; children: Mary, Elizabeth. BA in Sociology, Northwestern U., 1973; M of Regional Planning, U. N.C., 1975, PhD, 1977. Rsch. assoc. U. N.C., Chapel Hill, 1975—77; asst. prof. U. Ill., Chgo., 1977—83, dir. grad. studies, 1980—89, assoc. prof., 1983—, coord. PhD program, 1983—88, coord. Master plan, 1988—91, assoc. dir. planning and policy devel., 1991—92, assoc. dir. capital planning, 1992—93; dir. Facility Planning and Space Mgmt., U. Ill., Chgo., 1993—97, asst. vice chancellor for adminstrn., 1997—99, assoc. vice chancellor for capital programs, 1999—, interim dep. vice chancellor for adminstrn., 2003—. Contbr. articles to tech. jours. Mem. Am. Inst. Cert. Planners, Am. Planning Assn., Soc. Coll. and Univ. Planners, Transp. Rsch. Bd. (Outstanding Paper award 1988, Disting. Svc. award 1989), Urban Land Inst. Office: U Ill 1140 S Paulina M/C 892 Chicago IL 60612-7215 E-mail: foerster@uic.edu.

FOERSTER, RICHARD ALFONS, editor, poet; b. N.Y.C., Oct. 29, 1949; s. Alfons Foerster and Elizabeth Zakrzewicz; m. Valerie Elizabeth Malinowski, Oct. 28, 1972 (div. 1986). BA in English, Fordham Coll., 1971; MA in English, U. Va., 1972. Asst. editor Clarence L. Barnhart Inc., Bronxville, N.Y., 1973-76; lang. arts editor Prentice Hall Inc., Englewood Cliffs, N.J., 1976-79; assoc. editor Chelsea mag., N.Y.C., 1978-94, editor, 1994—2001, Chautauqua (N.Y.) Lit. Jour., 2003—. Freelance ednl. writer, editor, York Beach, Maine, 1979—93; freelance typesetter, York Beach, 1993—; mem. prize com. The Poets' Prize, N.Y.C., 2001—; internat. writer-in-residence, Hobart, Tasmania, Australia, 2002. Author: (poetry books) Sudden Harbor, 1992, Patterns of Descent, 1993, Trillium, 1998 (Poets' prize hon. mention, 2000), Double Going, 2002. Recipient Discovery award The Nation mag., 1985, Bess Hokin prize Poetry mag., Chgo., 1992; Writers fellow Nat. Endowment for Arts, 1995, Individual Artist fellow Maine Arts Commn., 1997; Traveling scholar Trust under the Will of Amy Lowell, 2000-01. Fellow Soc. for Arts Religion and Contemporary Culture. Democrat. Episcopalian. Home: PO Box 1040 York Beach ME 03910

FOGARTY, CHARLES JOSEPH, lieutenant governor; b. Providence, Sept. 15, 1955; s. Charles Joseph and Martha Jane (Hague) F. BA, Providence Coll., 1977; MPA, U. R.I., 1980. Policy assoc. Office Gov., Providence, 1978-84; spl. asst. to commr. R.I. Dept. Edn., Providence, 1985; town councilman Glocester, R.I., 1985-91; sr. policy analyst Office Gen. Treas., Providence, 1985-88; dir. policy Office Lt. Gov., Providence, 1989-91; state senator R.I., Providence, 1991-99; majority whip R.I. Senate, 1993-95, pres. pro tem, 1995-99; lt. gov. State of R.I., 1999—. Chmn. Glocester Dem. Town Com., 1979-85, R.I. Longterm Care Coord. Coun., 1996—; del. Dem. Nat. Conv., N.Y.C., 1980, 96, 2000; bd. dirs. N.W. Cmty. and Nursing Health Svc., 1994-2001, R.I. chpt. ARC, 1994— Mem. Lions (pres. Glocester chpt. 1991—). Democrat. Roman Catholic. Home: 230 Paris Irons Rd Harmony RI 02829 Office: Rm 116 State House Providence RI 02903*

FOGARTY, EDWARD MICHAEL, lawyer; b. Woonsocket, R.I., Feb. 25, 1948; s. Raymond Henry and Mary (Hogan) F.; m. Gail Higgins, Jan. 8, 1977. BA, Providence Coll., 1969; JD, Georgetown U., 1972. Bar: R.I. 1972, D.C. 1973, U.S. Supreme Ct. 1977. Law clk. U.S. Dist. Ct. R.I., Providence, 1972-73; assoc. Wilkinson, Cragun & Barker, Washington, 1973-79, ptnr., 1979-82, Baenen, Timme, De Reitzes & Middleton, Washington, 1982-83; counsel Spriggs & Hollingsworth, Washington, 1983-98. Legal counsel to speaker R.I. Ho. of Reps., Providence, 1987-93; legal counsel to majority leader R.I. Senate, Providence, 1993-2003, legal counsel to pres., 2003-; arbitrator R.I. Superior Ct., 1989—. Trustee Festival Ballet Providence, 1988—, pres., 1994—96. Mem.: ABA, Am. Arbitration Assn. (nat. panel of arbitrators 1985—96), D.C. Bar, R.I. Bar Assn. (ho. dels. 1992—94), Univ. Club Providence, Univ. Club Washington. Democrat. Roman Catholic. Home: 488 Lloyd Ave Providence RI 02906-4550 Office: 309 State House Providence RI 02903

FOGARTY, JOHN PATRICK CODY, lawyer; b. Washington, Sept. 12, 1958; m. Sarah Shiffert, Jan. 20, 1989. BA, George Washington U., 1981; JD cum laude, New Eng. Sch. Law, 1984; postgrad., Georgetown U., 1985-87. Bar: Mass. 1985, D.C. 1985. Sr. atty. NLRG, Inc., Charlottesville, Va., 1984-85; atty., editor Environ. Law Inst., Washington, 1985-87; atty. office of toxic substances EPA, Washington, 1987-89, atty. office of enforcement, 1989-91; spl. counsel Office of Regulatory Enforcement, 1994—95; sr. atty. office of enforcement EPA, Washington, 1991-92, asst. enforcement counsel Superfund, 1992-94; assoc. dir. RCRA Enforcement Divsn., Washington, 1995-98; dep. dir. Office of Planning and Policy Analysis, Washington, 1998-2001; dir. site remediation & enforcement staff Fed. Facilites Enforcement Office, 2001—; dep. dir. FDA Title IV Taskforce, 2003—. Cons. in field; speaker on environ. issues. Co-author: The Clean Water Desk Book, 1988, Environmental Law and Practice, 1992, 94; editor, co-author: Law of Environment Protection, 1987, 90-91, 95-97; contbr. articles to profl. publs. Bd. trustees Sandy Spring Friends Sch., 1998—. New Eng. scholar, 1982. Mem. D.C. Bar Assn. (steering com., environ. energy and naval resources sect. 2000—), Environ. Law Inst. (assoc.). Mem. Soc. Of Friends. Home: 4408 Fairfield Dr Bethesda MD 20814-4743 Office: EPA 1200 Pennsylvania Ave NW Washington DC 20004-2403

FOGARTY, ROBERT STEPHEN, historian, educator, editor; b. Bklyn., Aug. 30, 1938; s. Michael Joseph and Marguerita (Carmody) F. BS, Fordham U., 1960; PhD, U. Denver, 1968. Instr. Mich. State U., 1963-67; asst. prof. Antioch Coll., Yellow Springs, Ohio, 1968-73, chmn. humanities area, 1973-74, 78-79, assoc. prof., 1974-80, prof. history, 1980—; prof. Advanced Internat. Studies, Ctr. for Chinese-Am. Johns Hopkins U., 1986-87; editor Antioch Rev., 1977—; dir. Associated Colls. Midwest/Gt. Lakes Coll. Assn., Program in Humanities, Newberry Library, 1978-79; cons. Nat. Endowment for Arts, 1975-81, U. Waterloo, Ont., Can., 1981. Vis. fellow NYU Inst. for Humanities, 1992—93; Darwin lectr. human biology Galton Inst., London, 1994. Author: Dictionary of American Communal and Utopian History, 1980, The Righteous Remnant-The House of David, 1981, All Things New: Communes and Utopian Movements, 1860-1914, 1990, Special Love/Special Sex, 1994, Desire and Duty at Oneida: Tirzah Miller's Intimate Memoir, 2000; editor Antioch Rev., 1977—; contbr.: American Encyclopeida of American Culture, 2001; contbr. essays to The Nation, TLS, Mo. Rev. Recipient Martha K. Cooper award for editl. achievement, 1981, Nora Magid Award for Editing PEN Am. Ctr., 2003; grantee Am. Philos. Soc., 1976, Am. Coun. Learned Socs.; fellow NEH, 1980, All Souls Coll., Oxford U., 1988, Lloyd Lewis fellow Newberry Libr., 1995, Galton Inst. fellow, 1995; Fulbright Disting. Lectr. to Korea, 2000, Gilder Lehrman fellow 2001. Mem.: PEN/Am. Ctr., Orgn. Am. Historians, Nat. Hist. Communal Sites Assn. (exec. com. 1975—2002), Am. Studies Assn. (bibliography com. 1981—). Office: Antioch Rev Inc PO Box 148 Yellow Springs OH 45387-0148

FOGED, LESLIE OWEN, mathematician, educator; b. Cheyenne, Wyo., Sept. 26, 1953; s. Leif Clifford and Darlene Ann (Lutz) F.; m. Robyn Rachel Gilliom, May 30, 1981 (div. 1984); 1 child, Leif Erik. BA in Math., Midland Luth. Coll., 1974; PhD in Math., Washington U., St. Louis, 1979. Asst., assoc. prof. U. Tex., El Paso, Tex., 1979—, chmn. dept. math., 1987-88. Dir. U. Tex. H.S. Math. Contest, 1990—. Contbr. articles to profl. jours. Recipient Master Tchr. award Midland Luth. Coll., 1991. Achievements include discovery of an internal characterization of topological spaces which are closed images of metric spaces, constrn. of a consistent example of a quotient space of a separable metric space which is not stratifiable; construction of open-compact image of metric space with no point countable closed quasibase. Office: U Tex at El Paso Dept Math El Paso TX 79968-0001

FOGEL, DANIEL MARK, administrator, English language and American literature educator, author; b. Columbus, Ohio, Jan. 21, 1948; s. Ephim and Charlotte Edith (Finkelstein) F.; m. Rachel Kahn, June 24, 1973; children: Nicholas Alden Kahn-Fogel, Rosemary Luttrell.. BA in English magna cum laude, Cornell U., 1969, MFA in Creative Writing, 1974, PhD in English, 1976. Tchr. English East Lyme (Conn.) High Sch., 1969-71; asst. prof. English La. State U., Baton Rouge, 1976-80, assoc. prof. English, 1980-84, prof. English, 1984—2002, assoc. dean grad. sch., 1990-92, assoc. vice chancellor acad. affairs, dean grad. sch., 1992-97, exec. vice-chancellor and provost, 1997—2002, prof. emeritus, 2002—; pres. Univ. of Vermont, 2002—. Tchr. poetry writing workshops, Baton Rouge, 1980-87; instr. creative writing and lit. Instituto Allende, San Miguel de Allende, Guanajuato, Mex., 1972; mem. adv. com. Publs. MLA, 1986-90. Author: Henry James and the Structure of the Romantic Imagination, 1981 (Pulitzer prize nomination), Daisy Miller: A Dark Comedy of Manners, 1990, Covert Relations: James Joyce, Virginia Woolf, and Henry James, 1990, A Companion to Henry James Studies, 1993; author: (with others) The Aspern Papers Souvenir Book, 1988, The World Book Encyclopedia, 1991; author (poetry): A Trial of Resilience, 1975; author foreword: The Henry James Encyclopedia, 1989; editor/co-editor, author introduction: American Letters and the Historical Consciousness, 1987, New Essays on the Portrait of a Lady, 1987; editor: The Princess Casamassima, The Tragic Muse, The Reverberator, 1989; editor, founder Henry James Rev., 1979-95; mem. editorial staff Epoch, 1974-76; poetry editor Epoch, 1974, Nat. Forum 1981-86; editorial cons. Nat. Forum, 1980-84; consulting editor UMI Rsch. Press, 1983-89; author articles in field; contbr. poems to anthologies and periodicals. NEH summer stipend, 1977, 87; grantee La. Endowment for Humanities, 1990, Manship rsch. grantee, 1991-92. Mem. MLA, Henry James Soc. (exec. dir. 1979-2000). Democrat. Jewish. Office: Univ Vermont President's Office Room 350B Waterman Bldg 85 South Prospect St Burlington VT 05405-0160 E-mail: daniel.fogel@unm.edu.

FOGEL, ESTHER MARIAN (ESTHER MARIAN ROSEIG), veterinary researcher; b. Bklyn., July 23, 1917; d. Chone and Rebecca (Kaplan) Fogel; m. Seymour Roseig, Jan. 21, 1967. Cert., Med. Assts. Sch., N.Y.C., 1967; student, Orange County Community Coll., Middletown, N.Y., 1967-68. Cert. clin. lab. technician, N.Y. Gen. lab. technician Arden Hill Hosp., Goshen, N.Y., 1967-68; tech. rsch. asst. Lamont-Doherty Geol. Obs., 1968-70. Democrat. Achievements include research on the organism saccharomyces cerevisiae in its inactive dry state as brewers yeast or bakers yeast, and its ability to repel the parasites, fleas and ticks from domestic pets through a biochemical process of metabolism in conjunction with meat protein: the end product as CO(NH2)2 in solution in sweat; a coincidental process of coat pigment losses in both dogs and cats fed the initial Yeast was resolved by adjusting the B, A, D Vitamins and Calcium.

FOGEL, HENRY, orchestra administrator; b. N.Y.C., Sept. 23, 1942; s. Julius and Dorothy (Levine) F.; m. Frances Sylvia Polner, June 12, 1945; children—Karl Franz, Holly Dana Student, Syracuse U., 1960-63. Program dir., v.p. Sta. WONO, Syracuse, N.Y., 1963-78; orch. mgr. N.Y. Philharm., N.Y.C., 1978-81; exec. dir. Nat. Symphony Orch., Washington, 1981-85; pres. Chgo. Symphony Orch. Assn., 1985—. Record reviewer Fanfare Mag., 1979—; contbr. to Contemporary Composers. Mem. music panel NEA, 1986-90; past pres. U. Ill. Arts Alliance, 1988-94. Mem. NARAS, Am. Symphony Orch. League (bd. dirs. 1988—), Assn. Recorded Sound Collections (record reviewer jour. 1978). Office: Chgo Symphony Orch 220 S Michigan Ave Chicago IL 60604-2596

FOGEL, IRVING MARTIN, consulting engineer; b. Gloucester, Mass., Apr. 15, 1929; s. Jacob and Ethel (David) F.; children: Ethan, Ronit. BS, Ind. Inst. Tech., 1954, D of Engring. (hon.), 1982. Registered profl. engr., 20 states, Israel. Civil engr. Ill. Hwy. Dept., Peoria, 1954-55; field engr. Peter Kiewit Sons Co., East Gary, Ind., 1955, field engr., progress engr., cost engr. Ogdensburg, N.Y., 1955-56; supt. grading and paving Merritt, Chapman & Scott, Binghamton, N.Y., 1956; cost engr. Drake-Merritt, Goose Bay, Labrador, 1956-57; constrn. mgmt. engr. Mil. Estimating Corp., Madrid, Spain, also P.I., 1957-58; project mgr. Ministry of Def., State of Israel, 1958-59, Frederic R. Harris (Holland) N.V., The Hague, also Tehran, Iran, 1959-61, Solel Boneh & Assocs., Addis Ababa, Ethiopia, 1961-63; asst. to tech. dir. Frederic R. Harris, Madrid, 1963-64; chief engr. McKee-Berger-Mansueto, Inc., N.Y.C., 1964-65, v.p. constrn. mgmt., 1965-69; pres. Fogel & Assocs., Inc., N.Y.C., 1969—. Lectr. Author guides and handbooks on constrn. bus., latest being Construction Owner's Handbook of Property Development, 1992; contbr. articles to profl. jours. Fellow ASCE (life); mem. NSPE, Am. Arbitration Assn. Home: 404 E 79th St #28D New York NY 10021-1404 Office: 168 Fifth Ave New York NY 10010-5910 E-mail: fogeleng@pangulf.com.

FOGEL, JENNIFER LYNN, technical associate, researcher; b. L.A., Apr. 15, 1976; d. Kenneth L. and Marcia Fogel. BS in Zoology, U. Tex., 1998; postgrad., Calif. State U., Northridge. Tech. assoc. US Borax Inc., Valencia, Calif., 1999—. Spkr. in field. Contbr. rsch. papers to profl. jours. Mem. AAAS, Internat. Rsch. Group, Forest Products Soc., U.S. Olympic Assn. Avocations: running, travel, reading, playing piano, singing. Office: US Borax Inc 26877 Tourney Rd Valencia CA 91355-1847 Office Fax: 661-287-6014. E-mail: jennifer.fogel@borax.com.

FOGEL, JEREMY DON, judge; b. San Francisco, Sept. 17, 1949; s. Daniel and Gladys (Caplan) F.; m. Kathleen Ann Wilcox, Aug. 20, 1977; children: Megan, Nathaniel. AB, Stanford U., Palo Alto, Calif., 1971; JD, Harvard U., 1974. Bar: Calif. 1974, U.S. Dist. Ct. (no. dist.) Calif. 1974. Atty. Smith, Johnson, Fogel and Ramo, San Jose, 1974-78; dir. atty. Mental Health Advocacy Project, San Jose, 1978-81; exec. dir. Santa Clara County Bar Assn. Law Found., San Jose, 1980-81; judge Santa Clara County Mcpl. Ct., San Jose, 1981-86, Santa Clara County Superior Ct., San Jose, 1986-98, U.S. Dist. Ct. (no. dist.) Calif., 1998—. Lectr., Stanford Law Sch., 2003—; faculty Calif. Continuing Jud. Studies Prog., Berkeley, 1987—; trainer of judges and lawyers in case mgmt. and mediation, Jordan, Bangladesh, Hong Kong, Israel, 1989-2001. Contbr. articles to profl. jours. Recipient Service award, Mental Health Assn., Santa Clara County, 1980, Honors award Legal Advocates Children and Youth, 1997, Spl. award for exemplary leadership and professionalism Santa Clara County Bar Assn., 2002; named Judge of Yr., Consumer Attys. Calif., 1997. Mem. Calif. Judges Assn. (v.p. 1990-91, exec. bd. 1988-91, chair jud. ethics com. 1987-88, discipline and disability com. 1991-93, jud. discipline adv. panel 1992-98, Pres.'s award 1997). Office: US Dist Ct 280 S 1st St Rm 4050 San Jose CA 95113-3095 Business E-Mail: jeremy_fogel@cand.uscourts.gov.

FOGEL, JOSHUA, psychologist, researcher; BA, Bklyn. Coll., 1993; MA, Yeshiva U., 2000, PhD, 2002. Intern Queen Elizabeth II Health Sci. Centre, Halifax, Canada, 2001—02; fellow Johns Hopkins U., Balt., 2002—. Contbr. chapters to books. Recipient Dr. H. Ralph Philips Award in Clin. Hypnosis, Dalhousie U. Sch. of Medicine, 2002. Mem.: APA (Dissertation Rsch. award 2001). Office: Johns Hopkins Univ 624 N Broadway Ste 861 Baltimore MD 21205 E-mail: joshua18@att.net.

FOGEL, NORMAN, retired chemistry educator; b. Chgo., May 20, 1924; s. Jacob and Gussie (Leone) F.; m. Joane Patricia Moran, Dec. 9, 1960; children: Nancy Fogel McAnarney, Dara Fogel. BS, U. Ill., 1950; MS, U. Wis., 1952, PhD, 1956. Instr. U. Wis. Extension, Wausau, 1952-53; teaching asst. U. Wis., Madison, 1953-55; rsch. asst. U. Wis. Ext., Madison, 1955-56; asst. prof. U. Okla., Norman, 1956-61, assoc. prof. chemistry, 1961-68, prof., 1968-88, prof. emeritus, 1988—. Contbr. articles to profl. jours. With U.S. Army, 1942-45. Mem. AAAS, Am. Chem. Soc., Royal Soc. Chemistry, Sigma Xi. Office: Univ of Okla 620 Parrington Oval Norman OK 73069-8813

FOGEL, PAUL DAVID, lawyer; b. Santa Monica, Calif., Sept. 19, 1949; s. Phillip and Betty (Distler) Fogel; m. Yvette Chalom, Feb. 11, 1981; 1 child, Daniele. AB, U. Calif.-Berkeley, 1971; postgrad., U. Paris II, 1972-73; JD, UCLA, 1976. Bar: Calif. 1976, U.S. Dist. Ct. (crtl. dist.) Calif. 1977, U.S. Dist. Ct. (no. dist.) Calif. 1987, U.S. Supreme Ct. 1990, U.S. Ct. Appeals (9th cir.) 1981. Grad. fellow Ctr. for Law in Pub. Interest, L.A., 1976-77; dep. state pub. def. State Pub. Defender, L.A., 1977-79; Fulbright fellow U. Paris II Law Sch., 1979-80; dep. state pub. def. State Pub. Def., San Francisco, 1980-82; sr. supervising atty. Calif. Supreme Ct., San Francisco, 1982-87; assoc. Hinton & Alfert, Walnut Creek, Calif., 1987-88, Crosby, Heafey, Roach & May, San Francisco, 1988-89, ptnr., 1990—2002, Reed Smith Crosby Heafey, San Francisco, 2003—. Lectr. Am. law USIA, Washington, 1980, 87, 99; lectr. U. Calif. Berkeley Boalt Hall Sch. Law, 1995, practitioner-advisor, 1991-94, 96—. Mem. Am. Acad. Appellate Lawyers, Calif. Acad. Appellate Lawyers (sec., treas. 2003-), Calif. State Bar Assn. (chmn. appellate cts. com. 1990-91), Bar Assn. San Francisco (chair appellate practice sect. 1999-2000, 9th cir. rules com. 1999-, appellate rules task force 1998--), Amnesty Internat. Office: Reed Smith Crosby Heafey 2 Embarcadero Ctr Ste 2000 San Francisco CA 94111-4191 E-mail: pfogel@reedsmith.com.

FOGEL, RICHARD, lawyer, educator; m. Sheila Feldman; children: Bruce, Lori Ellen. BA, York Coll., CUNY, 1971; JD, N.Y. Law Sch., 1974. Bar: N.J. 1976, U.S. Dist. Ct. N.J. 1976, N.Y. 1981, U.S. Dist. Ct. (so. dist.) N.Y. 2000, U.S. Tax. Ct. 1977. Tax law specialist IRS, Newark, 1975-77; sr. pension cons., atty. N.Y. Life, N.Y.C., 1977-81; pvt. practice Franklin, N.J., 1981-85, Wayne, N.J., 1985-88, McAfee, N.J., 1988—. Lectr. Inst. for Continuing Legal Edn., Newark, 1977—; mem. adj. faculty Upsala Coll., East Orange, N.J., 1978-88; presenter 34th ann. meeting. Internat. Soc. for Systems Scis., Portland State U., 1990. Recipient Certs. of Appreciation, IRS, Newark, 1977, Inst. Continuing Legal Edn., Newark, 1981 82, 84, Cert. in Recognition of Accomplishments,

Coop. Extension Cook Coll., Rutgers U., 1982, Disting. Grad. award York Coll., 1984, Founder's Day Dist. Alumni award, 1992. Home: 28 Elizabeth Dr Sussex NJ 07461-3402 Office: Vernon Colonial Pla PO Box 737 Rt 94 Mc Afee NJ 07428

FOGEL, ROBERT WILLIAM, economist, educator, historian; b. N.Y.C., July 1, 1926; s. Harry Gregory and Elizabeth (Mitnik) Fogel; m. Enid Cassandra Morgan, Apr. 2, 1949; children: Michael Paul, Steven Dennis. AB, Cornell U., 1948; AM, Columbia U., 1960; PhD, Johns Hopkins U., 1963; MA (hon.), U. Cambridge, Eng., 1975, Harvard U., 1976; DSc (hon.), U. Rochester, 1987, U. de Palermo, Argentina, 1994, Brigham Young U., 1995. Instr. Johns Hopkins U., 1958—59; asst. prof. U. Rochester, 1960—64; Ford Found. vis. research prof. U. Chgo., 1963—64, asso. prof., 1964—65, prof. econs., 1965—69, prof. econs. and history, 1970—75; prof. econs. U. Rochester, 1968—71, prof. econs. and history, 1972—75; Taussig research prof. Harvard U., Cambridge, Mass., 1973—74, Harold Hitchings Burbank prof. polit. economy, prof. history, 1975—81; Charles R. Walgreen Disting. Svc. prof. Am. instns. U. Chgo., 1981—. Pitt prof. Am. history and insts. U. Cambridge, 1975—76; chmn. com. math. and statis. methods in history Math. Social Sci. Bd., 1965—72; rsch. assoc. Nat. Bur. Econ. Rsch., 1978—; dir. DAE program, 1978—91; dir. Ctr. for Population Econ., Chgo. Author: The Union Pacific Railroad: A Case in Premature Enterprise, 1960, Railroads and American Economic Growth: Essays in Econometric History, 1964, Ten Lectures on the New Economic History, 1977, Without Consent of Contract: The Rise and Fall of American Slavery, Vol. 1, 1989, The Fourth Great Awakening and the Future of Egalitarianism, 2000, The Slavery Debates, 1952-1990: A Retrospective, 2003; author: (with others) The Reinterpretation of American Economic History, 1971, Dimensions of Quantitative Research in History, 1972, Without Consent of Contract: The Rise and Fall of American Slavery, Vols. 2-4, 1992; author: (with S.L. Engerman) Time on the Cross: The Economics of American Negro Slavery, 1974; author: (with G.R. Elton) Which Road to the Past? Two Views of History, 1983. Co-recipient The Bancroft prize, 1975, Gustavus Myers prize, 1990, Nobel prize, Nobel Found., 1993; recipient Arthur H. Cole prize, 1968, Schumpter prize, 1971, Disting. Alumnus award, Johns Hopkins U., 2000; fellow, Gilman, 1957—60, Social Sci. Rsch. Coun., 1960, Ford Found. Faculty Rsch., 1970, grantee Faculty Rsch., 1966, NSF, 1967, 1970, 1972, 1975—76, 1978, 1992—96, Fulbright, 1968, NIH, 1991—. Fellow: AAAS, Royal Hist. Soc., Econometric Soc., Brit. Acad. (corr.); mem.: NAS, Am. Philos. Soc., Internat. Union for Sci. Study of Population, Population Assn. Am., Am. Acad. Arts and Scis., Agrl. History Soc., Social Sci. History Assn. (pres. 1980—81), Assn. Am. Historians, Am. Hist. Assn., Econ. History Soc., Econ. History Assn. (trustee 1972—81, pres. 1977—78), Royal Econ. Soc., Am. Econ. Soc. (pres. 1998), European Acad. Arts, Scis. and Humanities, Phi Beta Kappa. Office: U Chgo Grad Sch Bus Ctr for Population Econ 1101 E 58th St Chicago IL 60637-1511

FOGELMAN, ANN FLORENCE, nutritionist, consultant; b. Reading, Pa., Oct. 12, 1924; d. George Franklin Fogelman and Ruth Amelia Swartley Fogelman. BS, U. Del., 1950; MPH, U. Calif., Berkeley, 1957. Registered dietitian Am. Dietetic Assn., lic. dietitian Tex. Cook Art Camp, Cragsmoor, NY, 1948; asst. dir. YWCA Camp Otonka, Dagsboro, Del., 1949; asst. dietitian Meml. Hosp., Wilmington, Del., 1950—51; dietetic intern Frances Stern Food Clinic, Boston, 1952; clinic and tchg. dietitian Vanderbilt U. Hosp., Nashville, 1953—56; nutritionist Charlotte (N.C.)-Mecklenburg Health Dept., 1957—60; nutrition cons. Md. State Dept. Health, Balt., 1960—63; nutritionist dept. ob-gyn. U. Tex. Med. Br., Galveston, 1963—91; ret. Dietary dir. Tex. Nutrition Survey, 1968—69; liaison Tex. Home Econs. Assn. Tex. Dietetic Assn. Exec. Bd., 1968—69; pres., other offices South Tex. Dietetic Assn., Houston, 1969—70; pres., various other offices and coms. Tex. State Nutrition Coun., 1976—78; Tex. del. Am. Home Econs. Assn. Nat. Conv., 1971, 73; rec. sec. Houston Area Home Econs. Assn., 1967—68; pres. South Tex. Dietetic Assn., 1969—70. Contbr. chapters to books, articles to profl. jours. Vol. Clear Lake Regional Med. Ctr., Webster, Tex., 1992—96, Meml. Hermann S.E. Hosp., Houston, 1994—, Vitas Healthcare, Friendswood, Tex., 1994—, Sr. Learning Ctr., Webster, 1997—; active Clear Lake Presbyn. Ch., 1992—, deacon, 1996, Stephen min., 2000. With WAVES, 1944—46. Named one of 10 Most Outstanding Students, 9th Home Econs. U. Delaware, 1962. Mem.: Houston Area Home Econs. Assn. (rec. sec. 1967—68), Bay Area Writers League, U. Tex. Med. Br. Retirees, Sr. Friends (Clear Lake chpt.), The Women's Meml. (charter), Beta Sigma Phi (pres. Charlotte chpt. 1959—60, pres. Pasadena chpt. 1974—75, Dickinson chpt. Girl of Yr. 1966—67, Girl of Yr. 1974—75). Avocations: travel, dancing, reading.

FOGELMAN, MARTIN, lawyer, law educator; b. N.Y.C., Mar. 16, 1928; s. Herman and Fanny (Abramowitz) F.; m. Suzanne Stern, Dec. 21, 1952; children: Henry Jonathan, Jeffrey Scott, Martin, Jr., Douglas Edmund. AB cum laude, Syracuse U., 1948, JD magna cum laude, 1950. Bar: N.Y. 1950, U.S. Dist. Ct. (no. dist.) N.Y. 1953, U.S. Supreme Ct. 1956, U.S. Dist. Ct. (so. dist.) N.Y. 1957, U.S. Dist. Ct. (ea. dist.) N.Y. 1958. Confidential law clk. to chief judge N.Y. Ct. Appeals, Albany, 1950-54; assoc. Saxe, Bacon, O'Shea & Bryan, N.Y.C., 1955-58; adj. prof. Fordham Law Sch., N.Y.C., 1956-58, prof. law, 1958-62, Arthur A. McGivney prof. law, 1982—. Pres. univ. senate, 1980-83, chmn. athletic bd., 1980-93, bd. dirs. Univ. Press, 1978—, chmn. 1987—, also past mem. univ. trustees acad. affairs com.; arbitrator Nat. Assn. Security Dealers, 1981—; mem. complaint mediation panel appellate div., 1st dept. N.Y. Supreme Ct. Co-author: Cases and Materials on Mortgages, 1963; author: West's Forms and Text, New York Business Corporation Law, 1965, 2d edit., 1984 and ann. supplements; West's Forms and Text, New York Not-For-Profit Corporation Law, 1972, 2nd edit., 1990, and ann. supplements. Mem. ABA, N.Y. State Bar Assn., Assn. of Bar of City of N.Y. (com. on profl. discipline), Assn. Trial Lawyers Am., N.Y. State Trial Lawyers Assn., Assn. Am. Law Schs. (ho. of dels. 1969-91), Phi Delta Phi. Home: 21 Brookside Dr Huntington NY 11743-2642 Office: Fordham U Sch Law 140 W 62nd St New York NY 10023-7407

FOGELSON, BRIAN DAVID, educational administrator; b. Newton, N.J., Sept. 25, 1953; s. Edwin Malcolm and Marylyn Jean (Post) F. MusB, Westminster Choir Coll., 1975; EdM, Stetson U., 1989; EdD, Fla. State U., 1992. Cert. music tchr. grades K-12, N.J., tchr. class VIII, N.S., Can.; cert. music tchr., tchrs. K-12, adminstr., ednl. leader, Fla.; cert. elem. and secondary prin., Pa.; cert. prin., sch. adminstr., N.J. Tchr. Lunenburg County Dist. Sch. Bd., Bridgewater, N.S., 1975-90; grad. asst., coord. alt. tchr. preparation program Stetson U., Deland, Fla., 1988-89; grad. asst., coord. tutors for at risk students Fla. State U., Tallahassee, 1989-92, rsch. assoc., asst. prof., 1992-93; program adminstr. Fla. Acad. for Excellence in Teaching and the Fla. League Tchrs., Fla. State Univ., Tallahassee, 1992-93; asst. prin. Key West (Fla.) H.S., 1993-95, Catasauqua (Pa.) H.S., 1995-97, prin., 1997-2000, Delaware Valley Regional H.S., Frenchtown, N.J., 2000—. Cons. Fla. Sch. Dists., 1989-95, Fla. Dept. Edn., Tallahassee, 1991-95. Vol. asst. conductor Steton U. Children's Chorus, Deland, 1988-89; mem. sect. leader, soloist Tallahassee (Fla.) Community Chorus, 1989-93; dir. Tallahasse Civic Chorale, 1993. Mem. ASCD, NASSP, Nat. Assn. Multicultural Edn., Nat. Coun. of the States, Internat. Soc. for Tchr. Edn., N.J. Prins. and Suprs. Assn., N.J. Assn. Sch. Adminstrs., Kappa Delta Pi, Phi Delta Kappa (newsletter editor 1992-93), Free and Accepted Masons (past master), Order of the Ea. Star (past worthy patron). Avocations: reading, singing, golfing. Office: Delaware Valley Regional HS 19 Senator Stout Rd Frenchtown NJ 08825-3721 E-mail: brian.fogelson@DVRHS.K12.NJ.US.

FOGELSON, ROBERT MICHAEL, history educator, writer, consultant; b. N.Y.C., May 19, 1937; s. Nathan B. and Gussie L. (Richman) F. BA, Columbia U., 1958; MA, Harvard U., 1959, PhD, 1964. Asst. prof. history Columbia U., N.Y.C., 1964-68; assoc. prof. urban studies and history MIT, Cambridge, Mass., 1968-74, prof. urban studies and history, 1974—. Cons. Pres.'s Commn. on Law Enforcement and Adminstrn. Justice, Washington, 1966; cons. Nat. Adv. Commn. on Civil Disorders, Washington, 1968-69; cons. O'Melveny & Myers, L.A., 1986-87, Mfrs. Hanover Trust Co., N.Y.C., 1990-91. Author: The Fragmented Metropolis: Los Angeles, 1850-1930, 1967, Violence As Protest: A Study of Riots and Ghettos, 1971, Big-City Police, 1977, America's Armories: Architecture, Society, and Public Order, 1989, Downtown: Its Rise and Fall, 1880-1950. Frederick Sheldon traveling fellow, 1961-62, Samuel Stouffer fellow, Harvard-MIT Joint Ctr. Urban Studies, 1962-64, Guggenheim fellow, 1973-74; recipient award Graham Found. Advanced Study in Fine Arts, 1984-85, Lewis Mumford prize Soc. for Am. City and Regional Planning History, 2001, Best Book in No. Am. Urban History, Urban History Assoc., 2002. Home: 41 Linnaean St Cambridge MA 02138-1542 Office: MIT 77 Massachusetts Ave 9 639 Cambridge MA 02139-4301 E-mail: foge@mit.edu.

FOGELSONG, ROBERT H. military officer; BS in Chem. Engring., W.Va. U., 1968, MS in Chem. Engring., 1969, PhD in Chem. Engring., 1971; grad., Nat. War Coll., 1989; PhD in Strategic Intelligence (hon.), Joint Mil. Intelligence Coll. Commd. 1st lt. USAF, 1972, advanced through grades to gen., 2001—; dep. chief of staff air and space ops. Hdqrs. US Air Force, Washington, 2000—01, vice chief of staff, 2001—. Contbr. articles to profl. jours. Decorated Meritorious Svc. medal with three oak leaf clusters, Aerial Achievement medal with two oak leaf clusters, Air Force Commendatio nmedal with two oak leaf clusters, Air Force Achievement medal, Mil. Outstanding Vol. Svc. medal. Mem.: Arnold Air Soc. (hon. nat. commdr.), Coun. Fgn. Rels. Office: 1670 AF Pentagon Washington DC 20330*

FOGG, JOSEPH GRAHAM, III, investment banking executive; b. Cleve., Oct. 22, 1946; s. Joseph G. Fogg; m. Leslie Kirk Solbert, Jan. 23, 1971; children: Nathaniel, Elizabeth Piper, Whitney Solbert. BA, Yale U., 1968; MBA, Harvard Bus. Sch., 1970. Advt. dir. Morgan Stanley & Co., N.Y.C., 1970—; chmn., CEO Westbury Capital Ptnrs., LLP, Westbury, NY, 1991—. Bd. dirs. Maxspeed Corp., Sunnyvale, Calif., 407 ETR Ltd., Toronto, Can., Pardee Resources Inc., Phila., QPass Inc., Seattle, Kennexa Corp., Phila., Yale U. Art Gallery, Keewayden Found., Rutland, Vt. Office: JG Fogg & Co Inc 1400 Old Country Rd Westbury NY 11590-5156

FOGG, RICHARD LLOYD, food products company executive; b. Boston, Jan. 22, 1937; s. Lloyd Clark and Mildred Ann (Cass) F.; m. Carolyn Ann Kane, Feb. 12, 1966; children— Amanda C., Jennifer S., Timothy L. AB, Bowdoin Coll., Brunswick, Maine, 1959; MBA, Cornell U., 1961. With brand mgmt. dept. Procter & Gamble Co., Cin., 1961-66; dir. mktg. mgmt. Hunt-Wesson Foods, Fullerton, Calif., 1967-76; sr. v.p. Amfac Food Group, Portland, Oreg., 1977; pres. subs. Fisher Cheese Co., Wapakoneta, Ohio, 1978-83; group v.p., COO Land O'Lakes Dairy Foods, Mpls., 1983-93; pres., CEO Orval Kent Food Co., Wheeling, Ill., 1991-96; pvt. investor, 1997—. Mem. Am. Mktg. Assn. Fax: (707) 939-7859. E-mail: sonomafogg@aol.com.

FOGIEL, MAX, publishing executive; b. Magdeburg, Germany, Aug. 29, 1929; came to U.S., 1940; s. Abram and Sara (Pergericht) F. BME, Cooper Union U., N.Y.C., 1952; MME, Poly. Inst., Bklyn., 1954; PhD in Elec. Engring., Tech. U., Munich, Germany, 1965. Bar: U.S. Patent Office, 1958; registered profl. engr., N.Y., N.J. Sr. engr. Ford Instrument, Long Island City, N.Y., 1952-56, Control Instrument, Bklyn., 1956-59; rsch. engr. Loral Electronics, Bronx, N.Y., 1959-61; project engr. RCA, N.Y.C., 1961-64; pres., CEO, Rsch. & Edn. Assn., Piscataway, N.J., 1964—, dir. engring. seminars, 1964-66. Instr. in elec. engring. N.J. Inst. Tech., 1965-66. Author: Microelectronics, 1968, 1973, Life Insurance, 1972, Beauty Care, 1993, AIDS and HIV, 1995, Handbook of Electrical Engineering, 1996, Handbook of Chemical Engineering, 1998, Handbook of Mechanical Engineering, 1998; editor: Problem Solvers, 1973—, Calculus Textbook, 2002, series bus. and math. books, 1999; pub. H.S. and coll. study guides and handbooks in sci. and tech.; editor: Basic Electronics, 2003, (test preparation books for) No Child Left Behind series, 2003. Achievements include invention of in field. Avocation: oil painting. Home: 44 Maple Ct Highland Park NJ 08904-1922 Office: Rsch & Edn Assn 61 Ethel Rd W Piscataway NJ 08854-5963 E-mail: m.fogiel@rea.com.

FOGLE, JAMES LEE, lawyer; b. Doniphan, Mo., June 6, 1950; s. Carter Lemuel and Leatha Sue (Logan) F.; m. Pattylynn Raymond, Sept. 18, 1982; children: Kirsten Nicole, Ryan Christopher. BA, Whitman Coll., 1972; JD, Duke U., 1975. Bar: Mo. 1975, Ill. 1976. Assoc. Coburn, Croft & Putzell, St. Louis, 1975-79; ptnr. Coburn & Croft, St. Louis, 1979-96, mng. ptnr., 1980-84, mem. mgmt. com., 1985-89; ptnr. Thompson Coburn, LLP, St. Louis, 1996—. Bd. dirs. Life Skills Found., 1991—, pres. 1996-98; adj. prof. Fontbonne Coll., St. Louis, 1991-2000. Alumni admissions rep. Whitman Coll., Walla Walla, Wash., 1980—; mem. planned giving coun. DePaul Health Ctr. Found. Nat. Merit scholar Whitman Coll., 1968. Mem. ABA, Estate Planning Coun., Mo. Bar Assn. (tax com.), St. Louis Health Lawyers Assn., Mo. Athletic Club, Racquet Club Ladue (bd. govs. 2001—), Masons, Order of Coif, Phi Beta Kappa. Republican. Baptist. Avocations: tennis, snow skiing, golf, collecting polit. memorabilia. Office: Thompson Coburn LLP Ste 3500 One USBank Plz Saint Louis MO 63101-1623 E-mail: jfogle@thompsoncoburn.com.

FOGLEMAN, GUY CARROLL, physicist, mathematician, educator; b. Lake Charles, La., Dec. 29, 1955; s. Louis Carroll and Peggy Joyce (Trahan) F.; m. Jenny S. Kishiyama, Mar. 14, 1993; children: Elyssa Mayumi, Myles Masaru. BS in Physics, La. State U., 1977; MS in Physics, Ind. U., 1979, MA in Math., 1981, PhD in Physics, 1982. Rsch. assoc. Tri Univ. Meson Facility U. B.C., Vancouver, Canada, 1982—84; assoc. prof. San Francisco State U., 1984—87, adj. prof., 1987—; project scientist RCA Govt. Svcs., Moffett Field, Calif., 1987—88; prin. investigator Search for Extraterrestrial Intelligence Inst., Mountain View, Calif., 1988—89; mgr. advanced programs life scis. divsn. NASA Hdqrs., Washington, 1990—93; acting chief environ. sys. and tech. br. Life and Biomed Scis. and Applications divsn. NASA Hdqrs., Washington, 1993—95; program exec. human exploration and devel. of space advanced human support techs. program Life Scis. divsn. NASA, Washington, 1996—2000; acting dir. bioastronautics rsch. divsn. NASA Hdqrs., Washington, 2000—03, dir. bioastronautics rsch. divsn., 2003—. Vis. physicist Stanford (Calif.) Linear Accelerator Ctr., 1984-86. Contbr. articles to sci. jours. Travel grantee NSF and NATO, 1980; rsch. grantee NASA, 1988, 89. Mem. AIAA (sr. mem.), AAAS, Am. Phys. Soc., Prometheus Soc. (ombudsman 1998-99), Mega Soc., Sigma Xi (assoc.), Sigma Pi Sigma. Achievements include research in physics of particles in microgravity, theoretical elementary particle physics, technologies for the collection of cosmic dust particles, the origins of life and the philosophy of mind. Office: NASA Hdqrs Code UB Washington DC 20546-0001 E-mail: gfoglema@hq.nasa.gov.

FOGLEMAN, JOHN ALBERT, lawyer, retired judge; b. Memphis, Nov. 5, 1911; s. John Franklin and Julia (McAdams) F.; m. Annis Adell Appleby, Oct. 24, 1933; children: John Albert, Annis Adell Fogleman Anderson, Mary Barton Fogleman Williams. Student, U. Ark., 1927-31; LLB, U. Memphis, 1934. Bar: Ark. 1934, U.S. Supreme Ct. 1966. Dep. circuit ct. clk., Crittenden County, 1933-34; pvt. practice law, 1934-44; ptnr. Hale & Fogleman, Marion and West Memphis, Ark., 1944-66; dep. pros. atty. Crittenden County, 1946-57; assoc. justice Ark. Supreme Ct., 1967-79, chief justice, 1980; of counsel firm Gill Skokos Simpson Buford & Owen, Little Rock, 1981-86; of counsel Gill and Elrod, 1986-92, Gill, Wallace, Clayton, Fleming, Elrod and Green, Little Rock, 1992-93, Gill, Fleming & Elrod, Little Rock, 1993, Gill Law Firm, 1994-98, Gill, Elrod, Ragon, 1999—. Mem. State Bd. Law Examiners, 1960-63; chmn. Ark. Judiciary Commn., 1963-65; mem. Ark. Constl. Revision Study Commn., 1967, Fed.-State Jud. Council, Ark., 1971-75, Ark. Criminal Code Revision Com., 1972-74; lectr. Sch. Law, U. Ark., Little Rock, 1981; assoc. justice Delta Theta Phi, 1981-93, chief justice, 1993-95. Active Ark. and Crittenden County Democratic central coms., 1937-44. Served from pvt. to 1st lt. JAGD AUS, 1944-45. Fellow Am. Coll. Trial Lawyers, Am. Bar Found., Ark. Bar Found.; mem. Ark. Bar Assn. (past pres.), NE Ark. Bar Assn. (past pres.), Crittenden County Bar Assn. (past pres.), Pulaski County Bar Assn., Masons, Rotary (charter, past pres. Marion club). Home: 8700 Riley Dr Apt 205 Little Rock AR 72205 Office: Gill Elrod Ragon 3801 TCBY Bldg Capitol at Broadway Little Rock AR 72201

FOGLEMAN, JOHN NELSON, lawyer; b. Memphis, Jan. 2, 1956; m. Nancy Darlene Norris, Aug. 14, 1976; children: John Nelson Jr., Adam Barrett. BS in Edn., Ark. State U., 1978; JD, U. Ark., 1981. Bar: Ark. 1981, U.S. Dist. Ct. (ea. dist.) Ark. 1981. Assoc. Hale, Fogleman & Rogers, West Memphis, Ark., 1981-85, ptnr., 1985-94; cir. judge 2d Jud. Dist. Ark., 1995—. City atty. City of Marion, 1982-94; dep. pros. atty. 2d jud. dist. Crittenden County, Marion, Ark., 1983-94. Mem. sch. bd. Marion Sch. Dist., 1985-94; pres. Marion C. of C., 1982-83. Mem. ABA, Ark. Bar Assn., Assn. Trial Lawyers Am., Ark. Trial Lawyers Assn. (mem. Ark. sentencing commn. 1998—, chair jud. resources assessment com. 1998-2002). Methodist. Avocations: golf, jogging, reading, gardening. Home: 206 Rivertrace Dr Marion AR 72364-2602 Office: 116 Military Rd Marion AR 72364-1753

FOGLEMAN, JULIAN BARTON, lawyer; b. Memphis, Apr. 17, 1920; s. John Franklin and Marie Julia (McAdams) F.; m. Melba Margaret Henderson, Aug. 11, 1950; children: Margaret Elisabeth Heath, Julian Barton, John Nelson, Jennifer Leigh Vaughan, Frances Lorie Irwin. BS, U. Ark., 1941, LL.B., 1943, JD, 1969. Bar: Ark. 1943. Practiced in Marion, 1946-54, West Memphis, 1954—; pvt. practice, 1946-52; assoc. Hale & Fogleman, 1952-66, ptnr., 1967-73, Hale, Fogleman & Rogers, 1974—2001, Fogleman & Rogers, 2002—. City atty., Marion, 1951-81, dep. pros. atty., 1957-64 Chmn. fin. dir. Crittenden dist. Chickasaw coun. Boy Scouts Am., 1969, mem. exec. bd. coun., 1970-71, 75-80; bd. dirs. Crittenden County Charities, 1994-97, v.p., 1995; bd. dirs. Ark. Good Rds. Transp. Coun., 1976-96; mem. Ark. Cmty. Based Rehab. Commn., 1978-86, Crittenden County Bd. Edn., 1987-92. With inf. AUS, 1943-45, ETO. Fellow Am. Bar Found., Ark. Bar. Found. (bd. dirs. 1989-92); mem. ABA, Ark. Bar Assn. (ho. of dels. 1972-75, 81-84, exec. council 1972-75, 81-84, outstanding lawyer citizen award 1995-96), N.E. Ark. Bar Assn. (past pres.), Crittenden County Bar Assn. (past pres.), Phi Alpha Delta, Sigma Chi. Methodist. Home: 84 Turner Ave Marion AR 72364-1932 Office: PO Box 1666 123 W Broadway West Memphis AR 72301

FOGLEMAN, RONALD ROBERT, retired air force officer, consultant; b. Juniata County, Pa., Jan. 27, 1942; s. Harry R. and Sara (Landis) F.; m. M. Jane Lauver, June 22, 1963; children: Harry R., William E. BS, USAF Acad., 1963; MA, Duke U., 1971. Commd. 2d lt. USAF, 1963, advanced through grades to gen., 1992, fighter, mobility and command pilot; chief Tactical Forces Divsn., The Pentagon, Washington, 1979-81; vice comdr. 388th Tactical Fighter Wing, Hill AFB, Utah, 1981-82; dir. fighter ops. Hdqrs. Tactical Air Command, Langley AFB, Va., 1982-83; comdr. 56th Tactical Tng. Wing, MacDill AFB, Fla., 1983-84, 836th Air Divsn., Davis-Monthan AFB, Ariz., 1984-86; dep. dir. Programs and Procedure, Hdqrs. USAF, Washington, 1986-88, dir., 1988-90; comdr. 7th Air Force, 1990-92; comdr. in chief U.S. Transp. Command, 1992-94; comdr. Air Mobility Command, 1992-94; chief of staff USAF, Washington, 1994-97, ret. gen., 1997. Bd. dirs. Mesa Airgroup, N.Am. Airlines, Mitre Corp., World Airways, Rolls-Royce N.Am.; mem. Def. Policy Bd., 2001—. Bd. dirs. Ft. Lewis Coll. Found. Mem. Air Force Assn., USAF Acad. Assn. Grads., Daedalians (flight capt. 1983-84, 89-90), Coun. Fgn. Rels. Republican. Methodist. Avocation: rugby. Home: 406 Snow Cap Ln Durango CO 81302-2626

FOGLESONG, PAUL DAVID, molecular biology and microbiology educator; b. Marion, Va., June 24, 1949; s. Everett Paul and Thelma Broucelle (Conner) F.; m. Clare Maria Wright, July 1, 1978 (div. Jan. 1985). BS, Va. Tech., 1971; PhD, SUNY, Stony Brook, 1980. Cost analyst Irving Trust Co., N.Y.C., 1973; rsch. asst. SUNY, Stony Brook, 1973-80; fellow Albert Einstein Coll. of Medicine, Bronx, N.Y., 1980-82, rsch. fellow, 1982; rsch. asst. St. Jude Children's Rsch. Hosp., Memphis, 1982-86; dir. biochemistry Biotherapeutics Inc., Memphis, 1986-88; asst. prof. Memphis State U., 1988-89, Rutgers U., Camden, N.J., 1989-96, U. Incarnate Word, San Antonio, 1996-97, assoc. prof., 1997—; pres. Progressive Capital Svcs., 2002—. Cons. So. Rsch. Inst., Birmingham, Ala., 1989—. Contbr. articles to Jour. Virology, Cancer Immunol. Immunother., Anal. Biochem., Virology, Jour. Heredity, Virus Genes. Treas. Am. Guild Organists, Memphis, 1988-89; trustee St. Mark's Ch., Phila., 1993-96, treas., 1991-95, acctg. warden, 1995-96; asst. organist St. Mary's Cathedral, Memphis, 1984-89. Gov. Westmoreland Davis scholar, 1967-71. Mem. AAAS, Am. Soc. Microbiology, Am. Soc. Virology, Am. Assn. Cancer Rsch., Soc. Exptl. Biology and Medicine, Phi Kappa Phi. Achievements include characterization of the inhibition of type I DNA topoisomerase by ATP analogs, antibiotics, and antitumor drugs; characterization of DNA topoisomerase levels in tumor tissues by immunohistochemistry; development of an in vitro system for faithful transcription of vaccinia virus genes, map of Frog Virus 3 genome. E-mail: davidf@universe.uiwtx.edu.

FOGLESONG, ROBERT H. lieutenant general United States Air Force; b. W. Va. m. Mary Foglesong; children: David, Mark. BS in Chem. Engring., W. Va. U., 1968, MSc in Chem,. Engring., 1969, PhD in Chem. Engring., 1971; student, Nat. War Coll., Ft. Lesley McNair, Washington, 1989; participant, Seminar XXI MIT, on Fgn. and Internat. Rels., 1996. Commd. 2d lt. USAF, 1972, advanced through grades to lt. gen., 1997; instr. pilot 557th Flying Tng. Squadron USAF Acad., Peterson Field, Colo., 1973-76; aide de campe to comdr. Air Forces Korea, 314th Air Divsn., Osau Air Base, S. Korea, 1976-77; instr. pilot, comdr. ops. officer, spl. asst to NORAD region comdr. USAF, Malmstrom AFB, Mont., 1977-80; pilot, squadron scheduler, 9th tactical fighter squadron chief quality 49th figher wing, comdr repair squadron USAF, Holloman AFB, N. Mex., 1980-82; spl. asst. tactical issues, exec. officer dep. chief of rsch, devel. and acquisition Headqtrs USAF, Washington, 1983-85; spl. asst. to comdr., chief combat analysis divsn. Hdqs. Tactical Air Command, Langley AFB, Va., 1985-87; chief of staff of the air force, chair, prof. joint and combined warfare Nat. War Coll. Ft. Lesley McNair, Washington, 1988-90; pilot F-16, chief of maintenance, 347th Air Tactical Wing USAF, Moody AFB, Ga., 1990-91, comdr. 14 flying tng. wing Columbus AFB, Miss., 1993, cmdr. 51st fighter wing Osau Air Base, S. Korea, 1994-95; dep. dir. for politico-mil. affairs Joint Staff, Washington, 1995-97, dep. dir., 1997-99, asst. to chmn., 1999—. Contbr. 37 articles to mil. and profl. jours. Decorated Defense Superior Svc. medal, Legion of Merit with oak leaf cluster, Meritorious Svc. medal with 3 oak leaf clusters, Aerial Achievement medal with 2 oak leaf clusters, Air Force Commendation medal with 2 oak leaf clusters, Air Force Achievement medal, Korean Nat. Security medal (Samil), Korean Nat. Security medal (Cheon-Su). Office: ACC 12th Air Force 2915 S 12th Air Force Dr Davis Monthan AFB AZ 85707

FOGLIA, STEPHEN PHILLIP, musician, recording industry executive; b. San Jose, Calif., Apr. 14, 1957; s. Rudolf Foglia and Carmel de la Pena. BA in Music, San Jose State U., 1982, MA in Music, 1993. Guitarist, pianist, vocalist, songwriter, arranger, prodr. SPF, San Jose, 1992—; owner/CEO Ramblood Recon Records, San Jose, 1992—; music instr. The Musicians Warehouse, San Jose, 1997—. Prodr.: (cd release) SPF "Island in the Sound" (revised), 2002, Stephen Foglia "Island in the Sound", 1998, (album release) Stephen Foglia, 1988; musician: (jazz band) Stephen Foglia Jazz Ensemble, 1992, (rock group) Chain Lightning, 1985, (jazz-rock group) Fly with the Wind, 1978. Avocations: muscle car and 4x4 enthusiast, collecting guitars. Personal E-mail: ramblood@stephenfoglia.com. Business E-Mail: ramblood@stephenfoglia.com.

FOGLIETTA, THOMAS MICHAEL, former diplomat, former congressman; b. Philadelphia, Pa., Dec. 3, 1928; s. Michael and Rose (Buttari) F. BA, St. Joseph's Coll.; postgrad., Temple U. Bar: Pa., U.S. Supreme Ct. Pvt. practice law, Phila.; mem. 97th-105th Congresses from 1st Pa. dist., Washington, D.C., 1981-97, Phila. City Coun.; U.S. amb. to Italy U.S. Dept. State, Rome, 1997—2001. Mem. subcom. Mil. Constrn. Transp. Appropriations, Congl. Human Rights Caucus, Congl. Arts Caucus, Congl. Narcotics Caucus, Congl. Hispanic Caucus; founder and chmn., Congl. Urban Caucus, Congl. Black Caucus. Mem. Dem. Study group. Democrat. Roman Catholic.

FOGO, PETER C. educator, novelist, poet; b. Glendale, Calif., Nov. 27, 1946; s. Dominic Guy and Elizabeth Elaine (Komenich) Fogo; m. Sharon Lee Miller, June 15, 1968 (div. Apr. 1976); children: Credence Elizabeth, Renard Marie; m. Georgia Holliday, Dec. 5, 1981. BA, U. Nev., 1969; MA, No. Mich. U., 1972. Lectr. No. Mich. U., Marquette, 1971-72; tchr. social studies Channelview (Tex.) H.S., 1988—. Featured poet Houston Poetry Fest, S.W. Writers Inst., 1995. Author: (poetry) Single Again, 1980, A Language That Keeps Company with the Moon, 1992 (novels) Nightsong, 1998, Bitterroot, 2001. Mem. Green Party. Home: Box 7743 Pasadena TX 77508

FOGWELL, TED E. obstetrician and gynecologist; b. Sept. 4, 1946; BS, U. Tex., Austin, 1965; MD, U. Tex., Dallas, 1969. Clin. vice chmn. dept. ob-gyn. Presbyn. Hosp., Dallas, 1999—, interim chmn. dept. ob-gyn., 1998. Med. mission trips coord. First United Meth. Ch., Carrollton, Tex., 1990—. Office: Margot Perot Women and Children's Hosp 8160 Walnut Hill Ln Ste 220 Dallas TX 75231-4354

FOHL, TIMOTHY, consulting and investment company executive; b. Pitts., Apr. 21, 1934; s. Edward Zinn and Dorothy (Umbenhauer) F.; m. Nancy Lee Hattox, Apr. 15, 1961; children: Nicholas, Jeffrey, Peter. AB, Dartmouth Coll., 1956; MS, MIT, 1959, PhD, 1963; postgrad. exec. devel. program, Whittemore

Sch. Bus. and Econs., 1977. Rsch. scientist Itek Corp., Lexington, Mass., 1962-63, Mt. Auburn Rsch. Assos., Newton, Mass., 1963-68, prin. scientist, dir., 1968-72; with GTE Products Corp., Danvers, Mass., 1972—88, mgr. new product devel. lighting group, 1977-82, mgr. engring. devel., 1982-85, dir. engring. devel., 1985-88; scientist GTE Labs., Inc., Waltham, Mass., 1988-92; pres. Tech. Integration Group, Carlisle, Mass., 1992—; v.p. Light Time in Space, Inc., 1992—; treas. Qualume Corp., 2002—. Contbr. articles to profl. jours.; patentee in field. Pres., trustee Carlisle Conservation Found., 1972-79; v.p. Carlisle Trails Assn., 1975—; fin. chmn. Town Republican Com., 1980; dir., treas. Qualume Corp., 2002. Recipient Leslie H. Warner Tech. Achievement award, 1990. Mem. Mass. Bus. Roundtable. Home: 681 South St Carlisle MA 01741-1517 E-mail: tfohl@tigco.com.

FOK, THOMAS DSO YUN, civil engineer; b. Canton, China, July 1, 1921; came to U.S., 1947, naturalized, 1956; s D. H. and C. (Tse) F.; m. Maria M.L. Liang, Sept. 18, 1949. B.Eng., Nat. Tung-Chi U., Szechuan, China, 1945; MS, U. Ill., 1948; MBA Dr. Nadler Money Marketeer scholar, NYU, 1950; PhD, Carnegie-Mellon U., 1956. Registered profl. engr., N.Y., Pa., Ohio, Ill., Ky., W.Va., Ind., Md., Fla. Structural designer Lummus Co., N.Y.C., 1951-53; design engr. Richardson, Gordon & Assocs., cons. engrs., Pitts., 1956-58; assoc. prof. engring. Youngstown U., Ohio, 1958-67, dir. computing ctr., 1963-67; ptnr. Cernica, Fok & Assocs., cons. engrs., Youngstown, Ohio, 1958-64; prin. Thomas Fok & Assocs., cons. engrs., Youngstown, Ohio, 1964-65; ptnr. Mosure-Fok & Syrakis Co., Ltd., cons. Engrs., Youngstown, Ohio, 1965-76; cons. engr. to Mahoning County Engr. Ohio, 1960-65; pres. Computing Systems & Tech., Youngstown, Ohio, 1967-72; chmn. Thomas Fok and Assocs., Ltd., cons. engrs., Youngstown, Ohio, 1977—. Contbr. articles to profl. jours. Trustee Pub. Libr. of Youngstown and Mahoning County, 1973—; trustee Youngstown State U., 1975-84, chmn., 1981-83; mem. Ohio State Bd. Registration for Profl. Engrs. and Surveyors, 1992-96. Recipient Walter E. and Caroline H. Watson Found. Disting. Prof.'s award Youngstown U., 1966, Outstanding Person award Mahoning Valley Tech. Socs. Council, 1987. Fellow ASCE; mem. Am. Concrete Inst., Internat. Assn. for Bridge and Structural Engring., Am. Soc. Engring. Edn., Nat. Soc. Profl. Engrs., AAAS, Soc. Am. Mil. Engrs., Ohio Acad. Sci., N.Y. Acad. Sci., Sigma Xi, Beta Gamma Sigma, Sigma Tau, Delta Pi Sigma Lodges: Rotary. Achievements include development of a design method by computer for a solid-ribbed tied, through arch Ft. Duquesne Bridge; development of Analysis of Continuous Truss by Digital Computer. Home: 325 S Canfield Niles Rd Youngstown OH 44515-4020 Office: 3896 Mahoning Ave Youngstown OH 44515-3022

FOKIN, VALERY VALERIEVICH, chemistry educator, researcher; b. Nizhny Novgorod, Russia, May 31, 1971; came to U.S., 1992; s. Valery Ivanovich and Valentina Nicholaevna F. Diploma, U. Nizhny Novgorod, 1993; BSc, Calvin Coll., 1993; PhD, U. So. Calif., 1998. Rsch. assoc. Scripps Rsch. Inst., La Jolla, Calif., 1998-2000, asst. prof., 2000—. Contbr. articles to profl. jours. Mem. Am. Chem. Soc. Avocations: photography, travel, aquarium keeping. Office: Scripps Rsch Inst 10550 N Torrey Pines Rd BCC-315 La Jolla CA 92037 E-mail: fokin@scripps.edu.

FOLAND, KENNETH A. geological sciences educator; b. Frederick, Md., May 25, 1945; s. Austin Franklin and P. Lillian (Wachter) F.; m. Ellen Lee Spero, June 18, 1968. BS, Bucknell U., 1967; MSc, Brown U., 1969, PhD, 1972. Postdoctoral fellow U. Pa., Phila., 1972-73, from asst. prof. to assoc. prof., 1973-80; assoc. prof. Ohio State U., Columbus, 1980-87, prof. geological scis., 1987—. Cons. divsn. nuclear chemistry Lawrence Livermore Nat. Lab., 1982-86, adv. com. nuclear waste U.S. Nuclear Regulatory Commn., 1990-99; mem. indoor radon panel Am. Lung Assn. Ohio, mem. steering and rev. com. Columbus and Franklin County Radon Study, Columbus Health Dept. Assoc. editor Isotope Geosci., 1982-99, Jour. Geophys. Rsch., Solid Earth, 1992-98; adv. editor Jour. Geol. Soc.; reviewer rsch. papers, rsch. proposals; author, co-author numerous rsch. papers, abstracts, revs. Recipient numerous grants NSF, NIH, DAAD and NATO. Fellow Geol. Soc. Am.; mem. Am. Geophys. Union, Geochem. Soc., Sigma Xi. Home: 4090 Fenwick Rd Columbus OH 43220-4870 Office: Ohio State U 125 South Oval Mall 379 Mendenhall Lab Columbus OH 43210 E-mail: foland.1@osu.edu.

FOLBERG, HAROLD JAY, lawyer, mediator, educator, university dean; b. East St. Louis, Ill., July 7, 1941; s. Louis and Matilda (Ross) F.; m. Diana L. Taylor, May 1, 1983; children: Lisa, Rachel, Ross. BA, San Francisco State U., 1963; JD, U. Calif., Berkeley, 1968. Bar: Oreg. 1968. Assoc. Rives & Schwab, Portland, Oreg., 1968-69; dir. Legal Aid Service, Portland, 1970-72; exec. dir. Assn. Family and Conciliation Cts., Portland, 1974-80; prof. law Lewis and Clark Law Sch., Portland, 1972-89; clin. asst. prof. child psychiatry U. Oreg. Med. Sch., 1976-89; judge pro-tem Oreg. Trial Cts., 1974-89; dean, prof. U. San Francisco Sch. Law, 1989-99, prof. law, 1999—. Chair jud. coun. Calif. Task Force on Alternative Dispute Resolution and the Jud. Sys., 1998-99, Calif. Blue Ribbon Panel Experts on Arbitration Ethics, 2001-2002, chair jud. coun.; Rockefeller Found. scholar in residence Bellagio, Italy, 1996; vis. prof. U. Wash. Sch. Law, 1985-86; mem. vis. faculty Nat. Jud. Coll., 1975-88; mem. Nat. Commn. on Accreditation for Marriage and Family Therapists, 1984-90; cons. Calif. Jud. Coun., U.S. Dist. Ct. (no. dist.) Calif. Author: Joint Custody and Shared Parenting, 1984, 2d edit., 1991; (with Taylor) Mediation-A Comprehensive Guide to Resolving Conflicts without Litigation, 1984; (with Milne) Divorce Mediation-Theory and Practice, 1988; mem. editorial bd.Family Counts Rev., Jour. of Divorce, Conflict Resolution Quar.; contbr. articles to profl. jours. Bd. dirs. Internat. Bioethics Inst., 1989-95, Oreg. Dispute Resolution Adv. Coun., 1988-89. Recipient Bernard E. Witkin award, Jud. Coun. Calif., 2002. Mem. ABA (chmn. mediation and arbitration com. family law sect. 1980-82, chmn. ethics com. dispute resolution sect. 2002-), Oreg. State Bar Assn. (chmn. family and juvenile law sect. 1979-80), Am. Bd. Trial Advs., Multnomah Bar Assn. (chmn. bd. dirs. legal aid svc. 1973-76), Am. Arbitration Assn. (mem. panel of arbitrators), Assn. Family and Conciliation Cts. (pres. 1983-84), Assn. Marriage and Family Therapists (disting. mem.), Am. Assn. Law Schs. (chmn. alternative dispute resolution sect. 1988), Acad. Family Mediators (bd. dirs., pres. 1988), Assn. Conflict Resolution, World Assn. Law Profs. (sec.-gen. 1995-2000). Office: U San Francisco Sch Law 2130 Fulton St San Francisco CA 94117-1080 E-mail: folbergj@usfca.edu.

FOLCH-PI, WILLA BABCOCK, romance language educator; b. Milw., June 22, 1925; d. Charles Whitney and Helen Gertrude (Robinson) Babcock; m. Jordi Folch-Pi, June 23, 1945 (dec. Oct. 1979); children: Raphael, Diana, Frederic. BA, Barnard Coll., 1945; MA, Harvard U., 1963, PhD, 1969. Lectr. in English Pembroke, Brown U., Providence, 1945-46; teaching fellow Harvard U., Cambridge, Mass., 1968-69; curator of manuscripts Harvard Med. Sch., Boston, 1971-75; assoc. acad. dean, asst. prof. romance langs. Tufts U., Medford, Mass., 1975-85, assoc. dean, asst. prof. emerita, 1985—. Vis. lectr. MIT, Cambridge, fall 1973; seminar lectr. Radcliffe, fall 1975; coord. program abroad Tufts U., 1975-82, prelaw advisor, 1975-85. Author rsch. papers in field. Pres. Sandwich Woman's Club, Center Sandwich, N.H., 1990-92, N.E. Assn. Pre-law Advisors, 1984; mem. Squaw Lakes Assn., Holderness, N.H., 1962—. Friends of Sandwich Libr., Center Sandwich, 1985—, Sandwich Hist. Soc., Center Sandwich, 1985—. Travel grantee Am. Philos. Soc., 1967, Tufts Mellon Found., 1982; fellow Bunting Inst., Radcliffe, 1969-71. Mem. MLA, Medieval Acad. Am., Societe Internationale Arthurienne, Societe Rencesvals, N.Am. Catalan Soc., Harvard Club. Avocations: painting, sewing, reading. Home: 909 Holderness Rd Center Sandwich NH 03227-3108

FOLDA, JAROSLAV THAYER, III, art historian; b. Balt., July 25, 1940; s. Jaroslav T. Jr. and Rosalie M. (Gilbert) F.; m. Linda E. Whitham, July 25, 1964; children: Natasha K., Lisa K. AB, Princeton U., 1962; PhD, Johns Hopkins U., 1968. Instr. art history U. N.C., Chapel Hill, fall 1968, asst. prof., 1968-72, assoc. prof., 1972-78, prof., 1978-96, N. Ferebee Taylor prof., 1996—, chmn. dept. art, 1983-87. Author: Crusader Manuscript Illumination at St.-Jean d'Acre: 1275-1291, 1976, The Nazareth Capitals and the Crusader Shrine of the Annunciation, 1986, The Art of Crusaders in the Holy Land, 1098-1187, 1995. Rsch. grantee Fulbright Commn., Paris, 1966-67, jr. fellow, Dumbarton Oaks, 1967-68, NEH, 1974-75, 81-82, 98-99, John Simon Guggenheim Meml. Found., 1988-89; vis. scholar J. Paul Getty Mus., Malibu, Calif., 1995; fellow Nat. Humanities Ctr., 1988-89, 98-99, Ctr. for Advanced Study in Visual Arts, Nat. Gallery of Art, Washington, 2002. Fellow Medieval Acad. Am. (Haskins medal 1999); mem. Am. Soc. Oriental Rsch., Soc. Study of the Crusades (gen. sec. 1983-89), Coll. Art Assn. Am., U.S. Nat. Com. Byzantine Studies. Office: UNC Dept Art Chapel Hill NC 27599-3405 E-mail: jfolda@email.unc.edu.

FOLDBERG, MORTON FALK, ophthalmologist, educator; b. Lawrence, Mass., June 8, 1937; s. Maurice and Helen Janet (Falk) G.; m. Myrna Davidov, Apr. 6, 1968; children— Matthew Falk, Michael Falk AB magna cum laude, Harvard U., 1958, MD cum laude, 1962; Doctoris Honoris Causa, U. Coimbra, Portugal, 1995. Diplomate Am. Bd. Ophthalmology. Intern Peter Bent Brigham Hosp., Boston, 1962-63; resident Wilmer Inst. John Hopkins Hosp., Balt., 1963-67, head dept., dir. Wilmer Inst., 1989—2003; prof. and head ophthalmology Eye and Ear Infirmary U. Ill. Hosp., Chgo., 1970-89; Joseph Green prof. ophthalmology Johns Hopkins Med. Sch., 2003—. Author: (with D. Paton) Injuries of the Eye, the Lids and the Orbit: Diagnosis and Management, 1968, Management of Ocular Injuries, 1976; editor: Genetic and Metabolic Eye Disease, 1974, (with G.A. Peyman and D.R. Sanders) Principles and Practice of Ophthalmology (3 vols.), 1980; editor-in-chief Archives of Ophthalmology, Chgo., 1984-94; contbr. articles to profl. jours. Lt. comdr. USPHS, 1967-69 Recipient award for outstanding contbns. in the field of vision rsch. Alcon Research Inst., 1987, Univ. Scholar award U. Ill.-Chgo., 1986, Michaelson medal Isreal Acad. Scis. and Humanities, 2000, Greatest Living Ophthalmologists award Ophthalmology Times, 1999, Mildred Weisenfeld Lifetime Achievement award Fight for Sight, Inc., 2001 Fellow: Am. Acad. Ophthalmology (sr. honor award 1985), Royal Australian Coll. Ophthalmologists (hon.); mem.: Internat. Academia Ophthalmologia, Academia Ophthalmologica Internationalis, Macula Soc. (pres. 1980—82, Patz medal 1999, David Paton medal 2002), Assn. Univ. Profs. Ophthalmology (trustee 1985—91, pres. 1990—91), Assn. Rsch. in Vision and Ophthalmology (trustee 1985—90, pres. 1989—90, Weisenfeld award 2000), Chgo. Ophthal. Soc. (pres. 1985—86), Am. Ophthal. Soc., Inst. Medicine-NAS. Avocation: snorkelling. Office: Johns Hopkins Med Insts Wilmer Eye Inst 600 N Wolfe St Baltimore MD 21287-0005 E-mail: mgoldberg@jhmi.edu.

FOLDEN, NORMAN C. (SKIP FOLDEN), information systems executive, consultant; b. San Francisco, July 28, 1933; BS in Math./English/Engring., U.S. Mil. Acad., 1956. With IBM, various locations, 1966-83, U.S. program mgr. I/S tech. Sommers, N.Y., 1983-86; owner Folden Mgmt. (Palladin Advocacy), Westchester, N.Y., 1986-91, Folden Mgmt., Las Vegas, 1991—. Author: Drug Criminalization: Organized Crime Cash Cow, Prime Cause of U.S. Victim Crime and Threat to National Sovereignty, 1996, Delegation of Legislative Authority, 1997, Payback to Lippo Group or Grand Coincidence at Grand Staircase, 1997, Kosovo Negotiations Provisions-Five by Five Plan, 1999, ICTY Charges and Submission, 1999. Mem. Assn. Grads. U.S. Mil. Acad., Little Big Horn Assocs., Calif. Scholarship Fedn., Team Marcus. Avocations: ancient history/teachings/exploration, organized crime and drug policy, antiquities, constitutional law. Home and Office: 4329 Silvercrest Ct North Las Vegas NV 89032-0116 E-mail: sfolden@ix.netcom.com.

FOLDES, LAWRENCE DAVID, film producer, director, writer; b. L.A., Nov. 4, 1959; s. George and Valerie (Keller) Foldes; m. Victoria Paige Meyerink, Apr. 24, 1983. Student, San Bernardino Valley Coll., 1975, UCLA, 1976, Calif. Inst. of the Arts, 1977; BA with hons., Brooks Inst. Photography, 1978. Pres. Star Cinema Prodn. Group, 1981-85; chmn. bd. Star Entertainment Group, Inc., 1985—. Faculty mem. UCLA, Internat. Film and TV Workshops, Internat. Coll., William Lyon U.; instr., film lectr. UCLA; exec. dir. Malibu Film and TV Workshops. Recipient Mayoral Proclamation for Outstanding Achievement, City of L.A., Cert. of Merit, Paris Internat. Film Festival, Outstanding Achievement award, Acad. of Family Films. Mem.: Fantasy and Horror Films (chmn. membership and direction coms., dir. Acad. film expn., Humanitarian award), Acad. Sci. Fiction, L.A. Film Tchrs. Assn., Acad. Motion Picture Arts and Scis. (acad. awards exec. com.). Avocations: scuba diving, travel, photography. Office: Star Entertainment Group Inc 13547 Ventura Blvd Sherman Oaks CA 91423-3825

FOLDES, LUCIEN PAUL, economics educator; b. Vienna, Nov. 19, 1930; s. Egon and Marta (Landau) F. B in Commerce, U. London, 1950, Diploma in Bus. Adminstrn., 1951, MSc., 1952. Asst. lectr. econs. London Sch. Econs., 1951-52, 54-55, lectr. econs., 1955-61, reader econs., 1961-79, prof. econs., 1979-96, prof. emeritus econs., 1996—. Author articles to profl. jours. Served to lt. British Army, 1952-54. Rockefeller Travelling fellow, 1962. Fellow Royal Econ. Soc., Royal Statistical Soc.; mem. Am. Econ. Assn., Inst. Math. Stats., London Math. Soc. Avocation: math. analysis. . Office: London Sch Econs Houghton St London WC2A 2AE England E-mail: l.foldes@lse.ac.uk.

FOLDI, ANDREW HARRY, retired singer, educator; b. Budapest, Hungary, July 20, 1926; came to U.S., 1939, naturalized, 1947; s. Alexis and Ann Foldi; children from previous marriage: David John, Nancy Susanne; m. Marta Justus. PhB, U. Chgo., 1945, MA, 1948; pvt. student singing and piano. Pvt. tchr. voice, 1949-61; cantor, mus. dir. Temple Isaiah Israel, Chgo., 1949-61, English-Speaking Jewish Community of Geneva, 1963-71; vis. prof. voice and music Cleve. Inst. Music, 1978-81; chmn. opera dept. Cleve. Inst. Mus., 1981-91; dir. Chgo. Lyric Opera Ctr. for Am. Artists, 1991-95; ret., 1995; mem. faculty U. Chgo., 1947-49, dept. adult edn., 1951-61; instr., dir. opera workshop DePaul U., 1949-57. Vis. instr. voice Augustana Coll., 1950-51; mem. faculty apprentice tng. program Santa Fe Opera, 1959, 64, 76, 77, also stage dir.; stage dir. Pa. Opera Festival, 1982, 83, Utah Opera, 1986, 88, 91, Wolf Trap Festival, 1987, Toledo Opera, 1987, 89, Atlanta Opera, 1989, Chgo. Opera Theater, 1990, Chgo. Lyric Opera Ctr., 1992. Author: recorded text An Introduction to Music, 1959; also criticism, program notes; contbr. articles to profl. pubs.; Leading bass, Met. Opera, N.Y.C., La Scala, Milan, Vienna Staatsoper, Teatro San Carlo, Naples, Vienna Festival, Grand Théâtre, Geneva, Théâtre Royale de la Monnaie, Brussels, Teatro Regio, Torino, Am. Nat. Opera, Cin. Opera, Stadttheater, Zurich, Teatro Comunale, Genoa, Nederlandsche Opera, Amsterdam, San Francisco Opera Co., Lyric Opera Chgo., Santa Fe Opera, Sociedad Pro Arte Mus., Havana, Cuba; guest soloist, Vienna Festival, Bavarian State Radio, Munich, Concertgebouw Orch., Amsterdam, Orch. de la Suisse Romande, Geneva, Nat. Orch. Monte Carlo, Pitts. Symphony Orch., Clarion Concerts, N.Y., Gulbenkian Found., Lisbon, Concerti sinfonici, Genoa, Atlanta Symphony Orch., Aldeburgh, Lucerne, Lausanne, Ravinia, Glyndebourne, Florence Maggio Musicale festivals, Chgo. Symphony Orch., N.Y. Philharmonic Orch., Boston Symphony, Cleve. Orchestra, San Francisco Symphony, Little Orch. Soc., N.Y., Rochester, Kansas City (Mo.) philharmonic orchs., Radio Sottens, Geneva, Radio Beromunster, Zurich, Grant Park Concerts, Chgo., Indpls. Symphony Orch., Internat. Soc. Contemporary Music, also numerous recitals, radio and TV appearances, recordings for Columbia, Vanguard, Concert Hall, La Voix d'Eglise.

FOLDY, SETH LEONARD, public health officer, family practice physician; b. Cleve., Sept. 3, 1955; s. Leslie Lawrance and Roma (Bisgyer) F; m. Joan Marie Bedinghaus, June 7, 1986; children: Benjamin, Eva. BA in Human Biology with distinction, Stanford U., 1977; MD, Case Western Res. U., 1982. Diplomate Am. Bd. Family Practice, Nat. Bd. Med. Examiners. Intern in family practice Cleve. Met. Gen. Hosp., 1982-83, resident in family practice, 1983-85, chief resident in family practice, 1984-85; family physician Great Brook Valley Health Ctr., Worcester, Mass., 1985-87; med. dir. MetroHealth Family Practice, Cleve., 1987-94, dir. cmty. health svcs., 1994-96; med. dir. City of Milw. Health Dept., 1996-98, health commr., 1998—. Asst. prof. family medicine Case Western Res. U., Cleve., 1987-96; assoc. clin. prof. family and cmty. medicine Health Policy Inst. Preventive Medicine, Med. Coll. Wis., Milw., 1996—, clin. prof. health adminstrn. and informatics, U. Wis., 2001—. Asst. editor: Urban Family Practice: A Resource Monograph, 1994; editor (newsletter) Urban Health News, 1990-96. Trustee Friends Sch. in Cleve., 1972-74; nat. com. War Resisters League, N.Y.C., 1970-74; mem. Nat. Health Policy Leadership Coun., Washington, 1991-92; mem. Ohio legis. adv. com. on environ. lead abatement, Columbus, 1994-95, Wis. Turning Point Transformation Team, 1998—; mem. Wis. pub. health system terrorism and pub. health emergencies legis. coun. com., 2002; mem. info. coun. U.S. CDC, 2000—; mem. mem. steering com. Rand Inst. Summits on Info. Tech. Infrastructure for Bioterrorism; bd. dirs. eHealth Initiative, 2002—, Greater Milw. Bus. Group on Health. Recipient award for Excellence in Info. Tech., Nat. Assn. County and City Health Officers, 1999. Fellow Am. Acad. Family Physicians; mem. AMA, APHA (gov. coun. 1992-94, 96-98, Roemer Award for Creative Local Pub. Health Wk. 2002), Nat. Assn. City and County Health Officers (various coms.), Wis. Med. Soc., Milw. Acad. Medicine, Milw. County Med. Soc. (chair pub. health com. 1996—, Cmty. Svc. award 1997), Phi Beta Kappa. Avocations: fishing, hiking, birding. Office: City of Milw Health Dept 841 N Broadway Milwaukee WI 53202-3613

FOLEY, CHARLES BRADFORD, university dean, music educator; b. Indpls., Jan. 30, 1953; s. Charles Lyman and Barbara Ann (Shaw) F.; m. Diane Ellen Berger, June 6, 1976; children: Carolyn Berger, David Bradford. BA with honors, Ball State U., 1975; MusM, U. Mich., 1977, D of Musical Arts, 1983. Grad. tchg. asst. U. Mich., Ann Arbor, 1975-77; instr. Stephen F. Austin State U., Nacogdoches, Tex., 1977-79, East Carolina U., Greenville, N.C., 1979-81, asst. prof., 1981-86, assoc. prof., 1986-92, prof., 1992—2002, asst. dean Sch. Music, 1984-95, dean Sch. Music, 1995—2002, mem. adv. bd. Friends of Music, 1984—2002, mem. adv. bd. Music Alumni Soc., 1985—2002; prof., dean sch. music U. Oreg., 2002—. Contbr. articles to profl. jours.; performer Brad Foley in Concert, 1984, soloist, chamber music, 1979—. Pres., bd. dirs. Greenville Choral Soc. and New Carolina Sinfonia, 1990—91; bd. dirs. Oreg. Bach Festival, 2002—. Grantee So. Arts Fedn., 1997-02, A.J. Fletcher Found., 1995-02, Presser Found., 1995-02, N.C. Arts Coun., 1997. Mem. N.Am. Saxophone Alliance (regional dir. 1982-88, treas. 1988-93, jour. editor 1989), N.C. Music Tchrs. Assn., Music Tchrs. Nat. Assn. Methodist. Avocations: reading fiction, swimming, travel. Home: 743 Brookside Dr Eugene OR 97405-4935 Office: Music Sch 1225 U Oreg Eugene OR 97403-1205 Fax: 541-346-0723.

FOLEY, DAVID, television and film actor; b. Toronto, Jan. 4, 1963; Appeared in films High Stakes, 1986, Three Men and a Baby, 1987, It's Pat, 1994, Hacks, 1997, A Bug's Life (voice), 1998, The Wrong Guy (aslo writer), 1998, Monkey Bone, 1999, Blast from the Past, 1999, Dick, 1999, (voice) South Park, 1999, (voice) Toy Story 2, 1999, Monkeybone, 2001, "Committed", 2001, On the Line, 2001, Stark Raving Mad, 2002, Fancy Dancing, 2002, Swindle, 2002, Kids in the Hall: Tour of Duty, (also writer), 2002, My Boss's Daughter, 2003; appeared in TV series Kids in the Hall (also writer, dir.), 1989, NewsRadio, 1995-99. Address: ICM 8942 Wilshire Blvd Beverly Hills CA 90211-1934

FOLEY, DAVID E. bishop; b. Worcester, Mass., Feb. 3, 1930; Student, St. Charles Coll., Catonsville, Md., St. Mary's Sem., Balt. Ordained priest Roman Cath. Ch., 1952, ordained titular bishop of Octaba, aux. bishop Richmond, Va., 1986. Aux. bishop of Richmond Roman Cath. Ch., Va., 1986—94; bishop Diocese of Birmingham, 1994—. Office: Chancery Office PO Box 12047 Birmingham AL 35202-2047*

FOLEY, DAVID W. career officer; b. Toledo, Mar. 28, 1947; Commd. officer U.S. Army, advanced through grades to brig. gen., commdg. gen. Criminal Investigation Command, 1998—. Office: US Army Criminal Investigation Comm 6010 6th St Ste 1 Fort Belvoir VA 22060-5585

FOLEY, DEBORAH ANN, civil engineer; b. Salem, Mass., July 21, 1954; d. Philip Douglas and Claire Joanne (Simoneau) Hussey; children: Joseph William, Michael Thomas. BCE, U. N.H., 1976; MS mgmt. tech., Vanderbilt U., 1994. Registered profl. engr., Minn. Ensign Nat. Oceanic & Atmospheric Adminstrn., Rockville, Md., 1976-77; civil engr. Wilmington (N.C.) Dist. C.E., 1977-79; project engr. Toltz, King, Duvall, Anderson, Inc., St. Paul, 1979-81; civil engr., software devel. St. Paul Dist. C.E., 1981-83, hydraulic engr., 1983-85, project mgr., 1985-89, 1989—2000; chief project mgr St. Louis Dist. C.E., 2000—. Contbr. articles to profl. jours. Active Turtle Lake Sch. PTA, Shoreview, Minn., 1990-96. Mem. ASCE, Soc. Am. Mil. Engrs. (Tudor medal 1990), Order of Engrs. Office: St Louis Dist Corps Engrs 1222 Spruce St Saint Louis MO 63103-2833

FOLEY, EUGENE ARTHUR, accountant, consultant; b. San Jose, Calif., May 6, 1953; s. Eugene Frank and Shirley Ann (Merrill) Foley; m. Elaine Syre, July 9, 1995; children: Eugene Welles, Patrick Michael, Brian Ross. BSBA, U. Hartford, 1976; MS in Taxation, Golden Gate U., 1979; MDiv, Princeton Theol. Sem., 1994; M in Acctg., Rutgers U., 2000. CPA Calif., N.J., cert. mgmt. acct., info. sys. auditor, internal auditor, govt. fin. mgr.; computer profl., networking specialist, info. tech. profl. Acct. J. K. Lasser et al, San Jose, 1976-79; internal auditor Carter Hawley Hale, L.A., 1979-81; lectr., asst. prof. Calif. State U., Sacramento, 1979-84; owner, cons. E. A. Foley Accountancy, Sacramento, 1981-84; corp. audit mgr. Emhart Corp., Farmington, Conn., 1984-86; controller Powers Mfg. div. Emhart Corp., Elmira, NY, 1986-88; owner, cons. Foley Cos., Elmira, 1988-92; asst. prof. Rider U., Lawrenceville, NJ, 1992-94; asst. Christian edn. Cold Spring Presbyn. Ch., 1993-96; pastor Court House Presbyn. Ch., 1996-2000; tchr. Cape May County Tech. Sch., 1999-2000; pvt. practice Camden, 2000—; dir. finance Parking Authority of City of Camden, 2003—. Bus. mgr. Calif. Polit. Rev., 1987—; lectr. Rutgers U., 2001—. Sec.-treas., exec. dir. Elmira YMCA, 1986—87; treas. Supreme Ct. Project, Calif., 1985—86; v.p. fin. Sullivan Trail Coun. Boy Scouts Am., 1987, treas., 1988, dist. commr. George Washington Coun., 1992—94, mem. So. N.J. Coun., 1994—96, dist. exec., 1996—99, mem. N.E. region religious com., 2001—, mem. N.E. region Sea Scout com., 2003—; treas. Calif. Pub. Policy Found., 1987—; commr. Learning Life/Venturing, 1999—2003; mem. Scoutreach com., Camden, 2000—, co-chair, 2003—; mcpl. auditor, contr. State of N.J., Camden, 2000—02; dir. fin. Parking Authority City of Camden, 2003—; mgr., CFO Lower Twp., NJ, 1994—97; ruling elder West Collingswood Presbyn. Ch., 2002—. Recipient Whitney M. Young Jr. Svc. award, Boy Scouts Am., 1989; Baden-Powell fellow, World Scout Found., 2002. Fellow: N.J. Soc. CPAs, AICPA Acad. Exempt Orgns.; mem.: AICPA, Nat. Assn. Comm. Sys. Engrs., Assn. Govt. Accts., Am. Numismatic Assn. (life), Info. Sys. Audit and Control Assn., Inst. Mgmt. Accts., Inst. Internal Auditors (cert.), Nat. Assn. Presbyn. Scouters (regional dir. 1995—), Am. First Day Cover Soc., Mensa, Am. Topical Assn. (life), Scottish Rite, Masons. Avocations: coin collecting, genealogy. Home and Office: 2985 Tuckahoe Rd Camden NJ 08104 E-mail: gfoley@snip.net.

FOLEY, GARY J. research chemical engineer, computer scientist, federal agency administrator; b. Staten Is.n, N.Y., Mar. 20, 1943; m. Barbara Ickes, 1986; children: William, Karen, Kevin, Ryan, Courtney. BChE, Manhattan Coll., 1964; MS, U. Wis., 1965, PhD in Chem. Engring., 1968. Engr. Am. Oil Co., 1968-73, EPA, 1973-76, 79-86; dir. Nat. Exposure Rsch. Lab., 1987-93, 95—, acting asst. adminstr. R&D, 1993-94. Mem. AiChE. Achievements include rsch. in air pollution, acid rain, emissions, transport and fate, human and ecosystem exposure and monitoring network design, total quality mgmt. in rsch. orgns.

FOLEY, HARRIET ELIZABETH, retired school librarian; b. Franklin, Ohio, Aug. 11, 1935; d. Milo A. and Nora Lucile (Babb) Fealy; m. Thomas R. Foley, Nov. 22, 1969. BA in Edn., Coll. of Mt. St. Joseph, Cin., 1957; MS in Libr. Sci., U. Ky., 1961; postgrad., Kent State U., 1965. Cert. tchr. elem. edn., libr. sci., Ohio. Elem. tchr. Carlisle (Ohio) Schs., 1957-61, tchr. secondary French, 1961-63, sch. libr., 1961-82. Editor: Carlisle, the Jersey Settlement in Ohio, 1980,90, Franklin in the Great Miami Valley, 1982, 2d edit., 2003; co-author: Foleys from County Clare, Ireland, 1994; editor Heir Lines, 1986—. Trustee, sec. Carlisle Fed. Credit Union, 1962—; mem. Bicentennial Com., Franklin, 1996; mem. various coms. Otterbein-Lebanon Retirement Com., 1990-98. Named to Franklin H.S. Hall of Fame, 2003. Mem. ALA, DAR (treas. 1988—), Ohio Assn. Sch. Librs. (sec./treas. 1970-75), Ohio Ednl. Libr./Media Assn., Ohio Ret. Tchrs. Assn. (life), Franklin Area Hist. Soc. (life, all offices, charter mem., editor newsletter 1986—, treas. 1999—). Warren County Geneal. Soc. (editor 1982—, treas. 1998—), Ohio Geneal. Soc., Plantagenet Soc., Magna Charta Dames, First Families Ohio, First Families Belmont County, First Families Clark County, Early Settlers of Warren County, Ohio. Republican. Roman Catholic. Avocations: genealogy, local history. Home: PO Box 345 Franklin OH 45005-0345 E-mail: hfoley@siscom.net.

FOLEY, JACK (JOHN WAYNE HAROLD FOLEY), poet, writer, editor; b. Neptune, N.J., Aug. 9, 1940; s. John Harold and Juana (Terio) F.; m. Adelle Joan Abramowitz, Dec. 21, 1961; 1 child, Sean Ezra. BA, Cornell U., 1963; MA, U. Calif., Berkeley, 1965. Exec. prodr.-in-charge poetry program Sta. KPFA-FM, Berkeley, 1988—; editor-in-chief Poetry USA, Oakland, Calif., 1990-95. Resident artist The Djerassi Program, 1994. Author: (poetry and prose) Letters/Lights-Words for Adelle, 1987, (poetry) Gershwin, 1991, Exiles, 1996, (prose) O Her Blackness Sparkles! The Life and Times of the Batman Art

Gallery, San Francisco, 1960-1965, 1995, O Powerful Western Star, 2000, Foley's Books: California Rebels, Beats and Radicals, 2000; editor, contbr. The Fallen Western Star Wars, 2001, (with Ivan Arquelles) New Poetry From California: Dead, Requiem, 1998, Advice to the Lovelorn, 1998, (translations from the French) Some Songs by Georges Brassens, 2001; contbr. (film jour.) Bright Lights; contbg. editor Poetry Flash, 1992—, performances of poetry with wife Adelle, 1985—, columnist Foley's books, The Alsop Rev., 1998—. Woodrow Wilson fellow U. Calif., 1963-65; Poetry grant Oakland Arts Coun., 1992-95. Mem. MLA, Poets and Writers, Nat. Poetry Assn. (sec. San Francisco 1989-95), PEN Oakland (program dir. 1990-97). Avocations: playing guitar, tap dancing, writing songs. Home and Office: 2569 Maxwell Ave Oakland CA 94601-5521 E-mail: JASFOLEY@aol.com.

FOLEY, JAMES DAVID, computer science educator, consultant; b. Palmerton, Pa., July 20, 1942; s. Marvin Winfield and Stella Elizabeth (Ziegler) F.; m. Mary Louise Herrmann, Aug. 22, 1964; children: Heather, Jennifer. BSEE, Lehigh U., 1964; MSEE, U. Mich., 1965, PhD, 1969. Group mgr. Info. Control Systems, Ann Arbor, Mich., 1969-70; asst. prof. U. N.C., Chapel Hill, 1970-76; sr. systems analyst Bur. of Census, Washington, 1976-77; assoc. prof. George Washington U., Washington, 1977-81, prof., 1981-90, chmn. dept. elec. engring. and computer sci., 1988-90; prof. Ga. Inst. Tech., Atlanta, 1991—, assoc. dean coll. computing, 2001—03; dir. Graphics Visualization and Usability Ctr., Atlanta, 1991-96, Mitsubishi Electric Rsch. Lab. (MERL), Cambridge, Mass., 1996-97; exec. v.p. Mitsubishi Electric Info. Tech. Ctr. Am., Cambridge, 1996-97, chmn., CEO, 1998-99; exec. dir. Ga.'s Yamacraw Mission, 1999—2000. Pres. Computer Graphics Cons., Washington, 1979-96; mem. industry program adv. com. NAS, 1997-99. Author: (with others) Fundamentals of Computer Graphics, 1982, (with others) Computer Graphics: Principles and Practice, 1990, (with others) Introduction to Computer Graphics, 1993; co-author (graphics standard) Core System, 1977. Bd. dirs. Patriot Trails coun. Girl Scouts. U.S., 1998-99. Fellow: IEEE, Computing Rsch. Assn. (bd. dirs. 1996—, treas. 1998—2000, chmn. 2001—), Assn. for Computing Machinery; mem.: Assn. for Computing Machinery/Computer-Human Interaction Acad. (Spl. Interest Group for Graphs Coons award 1997), Nat. Computer Graphics Assn. (bd, dirs. 1982—84), Spl. Interest Group for Graphics (vice chmn. 1973—75), Human Factors Soc. Avocations: skiing, sailing, model railroading. Office: Georgia Inst Tech College of Computing Atlanta GA 30332-0280 Home: 1588 Friar Tuck Rd Atlanta GA 30309 Business E-Mail: foley@cc.gatech.edu.

FOLEY, JAMES EDWARD, scientist, pharmaceutical company executive; b. Newburyport, Mass., Jan. 4, 1950; s. Everett James Foley and Jean Elizbeth (Wade) Doyle; m. Rosemary Ragozzine, June 3, 1972; children: Annarose, Ryan Seamus. BA in Biology, Merrimack Coll., 1972; PhD in Physiology, Dartmouth Med. Sch., 1976. Rsch. assoc. physiology and medicine Dartmouth Med. Sch., Hanover, N.H., 1976-77, postdoctoral fellow, 1977-79; guest scientist Panum Inst., Copenhagen, Denmark, 1979; lectr. physiology U. Århus, Denmark, 1979-80; rsch. asst., prof. medicine U. Tex., Phoenix, 1981; sr. staff fellow NIH/NIADDK, Phoenix, 1981-85; sr. scientist NIH, Phoenix, 1985-86; diabetes group leader Sandoz Rsch. Inst., E. Hanover, N.J., 1986, dir. diabetes, 1986-93, exec. dir. diabetes rsch., 1994-95, exec. dir. metabolic diseases rsch., 1995-96, exec. dir. diabetes pharmacology, 1997; sr. fellow new product mktg. and med. affairs Novartis Pharm. Corp., East Hanover, N.J., 1998-99, sr. sci. advisor med. affairs, 2000—, exec. dir. clin. R&D, 2001—. Contbr. articles to profl. jours. Mem. AAAS, Am. Diabetes Assn., N.Am. Assn. Study of Obesity, Am. Fedn. Clin. Rsch., Am. Jour. Physiology, European Assn. Study Diabetes, N.Y. Acad. Scis. Democrat. Avocation: skiing. Home: 73 Seneca Lake Rd Sparta NJ 07871-2825 Office: Novartis Pharmaceutical Corp One Health Plz East Hanover NJ 07936 E-mail: james.foley@pharma.novartis.com.

FOLEY, JANE DEBORAH, sr. v.p. b. Chgo., May 30, 1952; d. Colin Gray Stevenson and Bette Jane (Cullenbine) Coleman; m. George Edward Foley, Jan. 29, 1972; children: Sy Curtis, Shelly. BA, Purdue U., 1973, MS, 1977, PhD, 1992. Cert. elem. adminstr., Ind., cert. elem. adminstrn. and supervision. Tchr. phys. edn. and health Lafayette (Ind.) Jefferson H.S., 1973-74; tchr. music and phys. edn. Valparaiso (Ind.) Cmty. Schs., 1974-79, tchr. elem. phys. edn., 1979-90; prin. South Ctrl. Elem. sch., Union Mills, Ind., 1990-93, Flint Lake Elem. Sch., Valparaiso, 1993-98; v.p. Milken Family Found., Santa Monica, Calif., 1998—2003, sr. v.p., 2003—. Mem. panel of experts The Master Tchr., 1996-98; key note spkr., presenter state and nat. confs. Contbr. articles to profl. jours. Mem. Valparaiso Sch. Sys. PTA, mem. exec. bd., 1993-98; bd. dirs. Hold Onto Your Music, Wings Inc. Recipient Hoosier Sch. award, 1992, Ind. 2000 Designation award 1994, Outstanding Dissertation award Internat. Soc. Ednl. Planning, 1993, Nat. Educator award, Milken Family Found., 1994, Ind. Bell Ringer award Ind. Dept. Edn., 1994, Ind. 4 Star Sch. award, 1995, 96, 97, 98, Internat. Tech. Edn. Assn. award, 1995, Cmty. Improvement award Valparaiso C. of C., 1994, NCREL Pathways to Improvement Pilot Site, 1995, Ind. Sch. Improvement award, Ind. Dept. Edn., 1998, others; Ind. 2000 Planning grantee, 1993, Milken Educator Tech. Project leader, 1997, other grants. Mem. ASCD (assoc.), NAESP, Ind. Assn. Sch. Prins., Valparaiso Tchrs. Assn. (treas. 1989-90), Phi Kappa Phi. Avocations: running, reading, writing, computers. Office: Milken Family Found 1250 4th St Santa Monica CA 90401-1350 E-mail: jfoley@mff.org.

FOLEY, JOHN DONALD, physician; b. Rochester, NY, Jan. 2, 1944; s. J. Donald and Mary Margaret (Moran) F.; m. Patricia Susan Scaglione, June 6, 1970; children: Susan Mary, Karen Lynn. BS, U. Notre Dame, 1966; MD, SUNY, Buffalo, 1970. Diplomate Am. Bd. Pediats., Am. Bd. Adolescent Medicine. Intern in pediat. Buffalo (N.Y.) Children's Hosp., 1970-71, resident in pediat., 1971-73; asst. chief pediat. Eisenhower Army Med. Ctr., Augusta, Ga., 1973-82; chief of pediat. Martin Army Cmty. Hosp., Columbus, Ga., 1982-88; fellow in adolescent medicine William Beaumont Army Med. Ctr., El Paso, Tex., 1988-90, chief adolescent medicine, 1990-95; assoc. prof. pediat. Tex. Tech U. Health Sci. Ctr., El Paso, 1995—; commd. 1st lt. US Army, 1970, advanced through grades to col., 1985. Contbr. articles to profl. jours. Decorated Legion of Merit, Meritorious Svc. medal, Army Commendation medal. Fellow Am. Acad. Pediats., Soc. for Adolescent Medicine (treas. S.W. chpt. 1991-96); mem. El Paso Pediat. Soc., Notre Dame Club of El Paso (treas. 1990—). Avocations: hiking, jogging. Home: 5216 White Oak Dr El Paso TX 79932-2520 Office: Dept Pediat 4800 Alberta Ave El Paso TX 79905-2709

FOLEY, JOHN FRANCIS, retired judge, lawyer; b. Detroit, Feb. 10, 1928; s. Henry Michael and Rosemary (O'Neill) F.; m. Joan Marlow, Aug. 17, 1957; children: Sean, Patrick, Rosemary, Joan, Margaret, Ella. BS, Georgetown U., 1948; JD, U. Mich., 1957. Bar: Mich. 1957, U.S. Dist. Ct. (ea. dist.) Mich. 1961, U.S. Dist. Ct. (we. dist.) Mich. 1969, U.S. Ct. Appeals (6th cir.) 1983. Assoc. firm Wilson, Ingraham and Kavanagh, Birmingham, Mich., 1957-59; atty. NLRB, Detroit, 1959-61; ptnr. firm Swartz, O'Hare, Sharples & Foley, Detroit, 1961-66, Gergely & Foley, P.C., Vicksburg, Mich., 1969-85; judge Kalamazoo County Cir. Ct., Mich., 1985-98; ret. Commr. Mich. Ct. Appeals, Lansing, 1966-68. Mem. Dem. Exec. Com., Oakland City, Mich., 1961-64, Kalamazoo, 1980; bd. dirs. Kalamazoo ACLU, 1971-83. Lt. (j.g.) USN, 1951-55. Mem. ABA, Mich. Bar Assn., Kalamazoo County Bar Assn. Home: 2846 W Y Z Ave Schoolcraft MI 49087-9744

FOLEY, JOHN PATRICK, archbishop; b. Darby, Pa., Nov. 11, 1935; s. John Edward and Regina Beatrice (Vogt) Foley. BA summa cum laude, St. Josephs Coll., Phila., 1957; BA, St. Charles Borromeo Sem., Phila., 1958; PhL, U. St. Thomas Aquinas, Rome, 1964, PhD cum laude, 1965; MS magna cum laude, Columbia U., 1966; LHD (hon.), St. Joseph's U., Phila., 1985, Allentown (Pa.) Coll., 1990, Cath. U. Am., 1996, John Cabot U., 1998, St. John's U., 2001; DST (hon.), Assumption Coll., Worcester, Mass., 1997; D Journalism (hon.), Regis U., 1997. Ordained priest Roman Cath. Ch., 1962, archbishop 1984. Asst. pastor Sacred Heart Ch., Havertown, Pa., 1962—63; Rome corr. Cath. Standard & Times, Phila., 1963—65; asst. pastor St. John the Evangelist Ch., Phila., 1966; faculty Cardinal Dougherty H.S., Phila., 1966—67; assoc. prof. philosophy St. Charles Borromeo Sem., Phila., 1967—84; titular archbishop Neapolis in Proconsulari, 1984—. Vice-chmn. Pa. State Ethics Commn., 1979—84; apptd. pres. Pontifical Commn. for Social Comm., Vatican City, 1984; pres. Vatican TV Ctr., 1984—89; bd. govs. Internat. Eucharistic Congress, 1974—76; mem. Pontifical Coun. for Culture, 1993—, Commn. for L.Am., 1984—89; comm. com. U.S. Cath. Conf., 1979—82; news sec. gen. meetings Nat. Conf. Cath. Bishops, 1969—84. Author: Natural Law, Natural Right and the Warren Court, 1965; mem. editl. bd. Cath. Standard & Times, 1963, 1967—70; editor: Cath. Standard & Times, 1970—84. Regional bd. dirs. NCCJ, 1969—82. Decorated knight comdr. with grand cross Order the Holy Sepulchre, Order the No. Star (Sweden), comdr. with grand cross Order Bernardo O'Higgins (Chile); named hon. prelate, Pope Paul VI, 1976, Hon. chaplain with Grand Cross, Sovereign Mil. Order of Malta; recipient Sourin award, Cath. Philopatrian Lit. Inst., Phila., 1990, Pres.'s medal, Holy Family Coll., Phila., 1996, Shield of Loyola award, St. Joseph's U., Phila., 1997, Cath. Leadership award, Cath. Leadership Inst., Phila., 2001, Ignatian award, St. Joseph's Prep. Sch., Phila., 2003. Mem.: Cath. Press Assn. (St. Francis de Sales award 1984), Am. Cath. Philos. Assn., Am. Cath. Hist. Soc. (Barry award 1997). Roman Catholic. Home: Villa Stritch Via della Nocetta 63 00164 Rome Italy Office: Pontifical Coun Social Comm 00120 Vatican City Italy Fax: 011-39-06-6988-5373. *The most important reality in life is the existence of God, His love for every person exemplified in our redemption by His Son, Jesus Christ, and our eternal destiny to live with Him forever in heaven.*

FOLEY, JOSEPH LAWRENCE, sales executive; b. Albuquerque, June 14, 1953; s. Joseph Bernard and Joan Marie (Johnston) F.; m. Michelle Troglia, Jan., 1992; children: Joseph Louis, Kyle Benjamin. BS in Polit. Sci. & Mktg., Niagara U., 1975. Asst. retail buyer Lord & Taylor, N.Y.C., 1975, E.J. Korvette Co., N.Y.C., 1976-78, retail buyer, 1978-80, retail msde. mgr., 1980; import sales coord. Block Industries, N.Y.C., 1980-81; v.p. sales Sutton Shirt Co., N.Y.C., 1981-83; exec. v.p. V.I.P. Imports, N.Y.C., 1984-97; prin. Long-Term Care Cons., N.Y.C., 1998—. Mem.: Million Dollar Roundtable, Chi Are Racing Assn. Republican. Roman Catholic. Avocations: marathon running, baseball, tennis, skiing, golf. Home and Office: 225 Sunset Ridge Rd Willowbrook IL 60527-8406

FOLEY, JOSEPH PATRICK, public relations executive; married; two children. BA, Elon Coll., 1971; MA, Am. U., 1980. State heath and social worker Fla. Health Dept., 1971-74; legis. floor asst. U.S. Ho. Reps., Washington, 1974-80; dir. legis. affairs, progrm analyst, congrl. liaison officer Fed. Emergency Mgmt. Agy., Selective Svc. System, 1980-86; pres., sr. assoc. Foley Govt. and Pub. Rels. Inc., Potomac, Md., 1986—. Adj. prof. Sch. of Govt., Am. U. Office: Foley Govt and Pub Rels Inc PO Box 61303 Potomac MD 20859 E-mail: info@foley[illegible].com

FOLEY, KATHLEEN M. neurologist, educator, researcher; b. Flushing, N.Y., Jan. 28, 1944; d. Joseph Cyril and Catherine (Cribbin) Maher; m. Charles Thomas Foley, Aug. 10, 1968; children: Fritz, David. BA in Biology magna cum laude, St. John's U., N.Y.C., 1965; MD, Cornell U., 1969; DSc (hon.), St. John's U., N.Y.C., 1992. Diplomate Am. Bd. Psychiatry and Neurology (examiner 1980-), lic. physician N.Y. Intern, then resident in neurology The N.Y. Hosp., N.Y.C., 1969—74; asst. attending neurologist, neuology dept. Meml. Sloan-Kettering Cancer Ctr., N.Y.C., 1974—79, assoc. attending neurologist, 1979—88, chief-pain svc., 1982—, attending neurologist, 1988—, Manhattan (N.Y.) Eye & Ear Hosp., 1974—83; instr. in neurology, Med. Coll. Cornell U., N.Y.C., 1974—75, asst. prof., 1975—79, assoc. prof., 1979—89, assoc. prof. pharmacology, 1979—89, prof. neurology and neuroscience, 1989—, prof. clin. pharmacology, 1990—; rsch. assoc. lab. neuro-oncology Sloan-Kettering Inst. Cancer Rsch., N.Y.C., 1981—84. Vis. asst. physician, cons. in neurology Rockefeller U. Hosp., 1975—79, vis. assoc. physician, 1979—; cons. Calvary Hosp., 1982—; assoc. mem. Meml. Sloan-Kettering Cancer Ctr., 1985—88, mem., 1988—. Editor: Clin. Jour. Pain, 1985—87, Jour. Pain and Symptom Mgmt., 1987—, Palliative Medicine Jour., 1993—. Patient svcs. adv. group Am. Cancer Soc. Named Outstanding Woman Scientist, Women in Sci. Met. N.Y. chpt., 1987, A. Soriano Jr. Meml. Lectr., The Andres Soriano Cancer Rsch. Found. Inc., 1992; recipient Jr. Faculty award, Disting. Svc. award, Am. Cancer Soc., 1975—78, Disting. Svc. award, 1992, Nat. Bd. award, The Med. Coll. Pa., 1986, William M. Witter award, U. Calif. San Francisco, 1987, Annie Blount Storrs award, Calvary Hosp., 1988, Balfour M. Mount award, Am. Jour. Hospice Care, 1988, Disting. Oncologist award, Dayton Oncology Soc., 1990, Tenth Barbara Bohen Pfeifer award, Am. Italian Found. for Cancer Rsch., 1993; fellow Neuro-Oncology spl. fellow, Meml. Sloan-Kettering Cancer Ctr., 1975—78; grantee Genetic Tng. grantee, NIH, 1970—71, Program for Pain Rsch. grantee, Bristol-Myers, 1988—92. Mem.: NAS (Inst. Medicine), AMA (ad hoc adv. panel mgmt. chronic pain, DATTA reference panel), AAAS, Inst. Medicine NAS, Soc. for Neurosci., N.Y. Acad. Scis. (USP adv. panel on neurology 1990—), Internat. Assn. Study Pain (councilor 1984—90, edn. com. 1986—93, various other coms.), Harvey Soc., Eastern Pain Assn. (John J. Bonica award 1986), Assn. Rsch. in Nervous and Mental Diseases, Am. Soc. Clin. Pharmacology and Therapeutics, Am. Soc. Clin. Oncology (program com. 1991—92, com. on care at the end of life 1993—, other coms., David Karnosky award), Am. Pain Soc. (bd. dirs. 1980—82, pres. 1984—85, bylaws com. 1986—87, long range planning task force 1989—), Am. Neurol. Assn. (com. 1984—85, councilor 1984, 1994), Am. Med. Womens Assn., Am. Fedn. Clin. Rsch., Am. Acad. Neurology (chmn. long range planning com. 1990—, sci. program com. 1990, other coms.), Acad. Hospice Physicians, Cornell U. Med. Coll. Alumni Assn. (bd. dirs., nominating com.), Children's Hospice Internat., Children's Hospice, Alpha Omega Alpha. Office: Meml Sloan-Kettering Cancer Ctr Box 52 1275 York Ave New York NY 10021-6094

FOLEY, L(EWIS) MICHAEL, real estate executive; b. Detroit, Nov. 30, 1938; s. Raymond B. and Mabel F.; m. Pamela Wagner, June 16, 1962; children: Michael D., Kimberly B., Robin E. BS in Sci. Engring., U. Mich., 1960; MBA in Fin. and Mktg., Harvard U., 1964. Lic. real estate broker. Pres. Econ. Devel. Corp., Detroit, 1969-71; v.p. Chrysler Realty Corp., Troy, Mich., 1972-77; exec. v.p. Bell and Howell Video Group, Chgo., 1977-79; v.p. fin., chief fin. officer Bell and Howell Corp., Chgo., 1979-80; sr. v.p. Homart Devel. Co., Chgo., 1981-84, exec. v.p., 1984-93; sr. exec. v.p. Coldwell Banker Real Estate Group Inc., Chgo., 1986-93; chmn., CEO Sears Savs. Bank, Chgo., 1989-93; sr. v.p., CFO Coldwell Banker Corp., 1995-96. Chmn. Borrowers Choice Corp., 1992-93; bd. dirs. BRE Properties, Inc. Author: Management of Racial Integration in Business, 1965. Vestry, jr. warden St. James by the Sea Episcopal Ch. Mem. Internat. Council Shopping Ctrs. (v.p., trustee), Sigma Alpha Epsilon. Episcopalian. Office: 5824 Camino de la Costa La Jolla CA 92037-6551 E-mail: lfoley1@san.rr.com.

FOLEY, MARILYN LORNA, artist; b. Arlington, N.J., Aug. 30, 1929; d. Archibald and Mary Ellen (Hall) Lyon; m. William Edward Foley, June 19, 1954; children: Katherine Ann Hastings, William Edward III. BA, Wellesley Coll., 1950; postgrad., Rutgers U., 1950-52; postgrad studies Art Students' League, N.Y.C., 1953. Art instr. Wellesley (Mass.) Coll., 1953-54; chair artists com. Art Show: Bedford, 1985-92. One-woman shows include St. Mary's Gallery, N.Y.C., 1989, Northridge Art Gallery, Ridgefield, Conn., 1990, 1992, Kim Iocovozi Gallery, Savannah, Ga., 1997—99, 2000, 2002, 2003, exhibited in group shows at St. Peter's Gallery, 1997—2003, Salmagundi Club, N.Y.C., 1986, Nat. Arts Club, 1988, Knickerbocker Artists 40th Ann., 1990, Newington-Cropsey Gallery, Hastings on Hudson, N.Y., 1997 (1st prize watercolor), Broome St. Gallery, N.Y.C., 1997 (2d prize watercolor), Copley Soc. Mem. Show, 1982 (Juror's Choice prize), Art Show, Bedford, N.Y., 1983—87 (Emille Baker award, 1993), Landings Art Assn. Ann. Exhibitions (Best of Show 1996-2000), Mo. Nat. Winston Churchill Meml., 2003; author: The Artists Mag., 1998, Watercolor Basics, 2003. Mem. Hudson Valley Art Assn., Landings Art Assn., Catharine Lorillard Wolfe Art Club, Natl. Watercolor Soc. (signature mem.), Hilton Head Art League. Republican. Episcopalian. Avocations: travel, designer of church needlework. Studio: Foley Watercolors 2 Scotch Bonnet Ct Savannah GA 31411-2859 E-mail: mlfoley@bellsouth.net.

FOLEY, MARK ADAM, congressman; b. Newton, Mass., Sept. 8, 1954; Student, Palm Beach C.C. Owner, mgr. The Lettuce Patch Restaurant, 1975-81; real estate broker, pres. Foley-Smith & Assocs., Inc., 1975-94; commr. City of Lake Worth, 1977-79, commr., vice mayor, 1982-84; state rep. dist. 85 Fla., 1991—93; state senator dist. 35, 1993—95; mem. U.S. Congress from 16th Fla. dist., 1995—; mem. ways and means com.; dep. majority whip. Republican. Office: 104 Cannon Ho Office Bldg Washington DC 20515-0916*

FOLEY, MARTIN JAMES, lawyer; b. Nebr., Nov. 7, 1946; s. James Gleason and Mary Elizabeth (O'Brien) Foley; m. Linda Sivyer; children: James Gleason Foley II, Daniel Patrick, Ryan Edward, Michelle Sivyer. Cert. Completition, Cambridge U., 1967; BA in Philosophy, U. So. Calif., 1968, JD, 1974, MBA, 1975. Bar: Calif. 1975, U.S. Dist. Ct. (cen. dist.) Calif. 1980, U.S. Dist. Ct. (ea., so. and no. dists.) Calif. 1980, U.S. Ct. Appeals (9th cir.) 1980, U.S. Ct. Fed. Claims 1991, U.S. Supreme Ct. 1990. Acct. Ford Motor Co., San Jose, Calif., 1968, cost analyst, 1970-71; assoc. Adams, Duque & Hazeltine, 1975-80; sr. ptnr. Bryan, Cave, McPheeters & McRoberts, L.A., 1980-89, Sonnenschein Nath & Rosenthal, L.A., 1990—. Mem. bd. govs. Gen. Alumni Assn. U. So. Calif., 1982—84; ct. appt. settlement officer Calif. State, 1992—94, U.S. Dist. Ct. (cen. dist.), 1998—2001; lectr. groups and profl. confs. Contbr. Lt. j.g. USNR, 1968—70. Mem.: ABA (numerous coms.), L.A. County Bar Assn., Calif. Bar Assn. (conf. of dels. 1979—93), Annandale Golf Club Pasadena, Calif., Jonathan Club LA. Republican. Roman Catholic. Office: Sonnenschein Nath Rosenthal 601 S Figueroa St Ste 1500 Los Angeles CA 90017-5720 E-mail: mfoley@sonnenschein.com.

FOLEY, MAURA, picture editor; Picture editor People Mag., 1997; assoc. photo. editor Sports Illus., 1993; mgr. Duomo Photography, NY. Co-curator Newseum, Sports Illus. photos exhibit, NY; picture editor Sports Illus. Women Sport. Photographer (Olympic games) Lillehammer and Atlanta. Mem.: Eddie Adams Workshop (mem. of the Bd. of Dir.). She handled photographic coverage of the Olympic games including special features and Sportsman of the Yr. At Duomo Photgraphy she ran the on-site pecture desk at events in Calgary, Seoul, Albertville and Barcelona Olympics. Office: People Mag Picture Editor 1271 Ave of the Am New York NY 10020*

FOLEY, MAURICE BRIAN, federal judge; b. 1960; BA, Swarthmore Coll., 1982; JD, U. Calif., Berkeley, 1985; LLM in Taxation, Georgetown U., 1988. With Office of Chief Counsel, IRS, Washington, 1985-88; tax counsel, majority staff Com. on Fin., U.S. Senate, Washington, 1988-93; dep. tax legis. counsel U.S. Dept. Treasury, Washington, 1993-95; judge U.S. Tax Ct., Washington, 1995—. Mem. State Bar Calif. Office: US Tax Ct 400 2D St NW Washington DC 20217-0001

FOLEY, MIKE, state legislator; b. Rochester, N.Y., Apr. 5, 1954; m. Susan Foley; children: Laura, Matthew, Marie, Elizabeth, Peter. BS, SUNY, Brockport, 1976; MBA, Mich. State U., 1978. Cons. Kirschner Assn., 1978-79; dir. fin. analysis Nat. Assn. Regulatory Utility Commrs., 1979-97; corp. planning analyst Nebr. Pub. Power Dist., 1997—, mem. Nebr. Legislature from 20th dist., Lincoln, 2001—. Adv. neighborhood commr., Washington, 1984. Home: 6410 S 41st St Ct Lincoln NE 68516 Office: Rm 1101 State Capitol Lincoln NE 68509

FOLEY, PATRICIA JEAN, accountant; b. Bridgeport, Conn., Jan. 12, 1956; d. John Edward and Louise (Caselli) F. AA, Housantonic C.C., 1978; BS, Cen. Conn. State Coll., 1980; MBA, U. Hartford, 1996. CPA, Conn. Staff acct. Spitz, Sullivan, Wachtel & Falcetta, Hartford, Conn., 1981-82, client acct., 1982-85, sr. acct., 1985-87, supr., mgr., 1987-97; mgr. Falcetta Wachtel & Knochenhauer LLC, Bloomfield, Conn., 1997-98; prin. Patricia J. Foley, CPA, Newington, Conn., 1998—. Mem. Acctg. Del. to Russia, Ukraine & Estonia Citizens Amb., 1993. Pres. Woodsedge Condominium Assn., Newington, Conn., 1989—92, treas., 1985—92; bd. dirs. Friends of the Lucy Robbins Welles Libr., 1996—, membership co-chair, 2000—, v.p., 2001, pres., 2002—03. Mem. AICPA (mgmt. adv. svc. com. 1987—, info. tech. divsns., 1992—), Conn. Soc. CPAs, Am. Women Soc. CPAs, Cmty. Assn. Inst. (membership chair Conn. chpt. 1991-92), Nat. Assn. Women Bus. Owners (treas. 2001-03, mem. pub. policy com. 2000—). Home: 35 Woodsedge Dr Apt 1B Newington CT 06111-4271 Office: 35-1B Woodsedge Dr Newington CT 06111-4271 Fax: 860-594-8828. E-mail: pattyjfoley@pattyjfoley.com.

FOLEY, PAUL E. political scientist, educator; b. Detroit, Dec. 5, 1963; s. John C. and Elizabeth Marie Foley; m. Kimberly Anne Schuerger, May 7, 1994; 1 child, McKenna Louise. BA in Polit. Sci., Oakland U., 1988; MA in Polit. Sci., Am. U., 1991. Asst. prof., dept. chair St. Mary's Coll., Orchard Lake, Mich., 1992—2000; adj. prof. Mott C.C., Flint, Mich., 2000—. Visibility coord. Friends of Bob Carr, Waterford, Mich., 1988, polit. cons., 94; legis. aide U.S. Ho. Rep., Washington, 1989; adj. prof. Oakland C.C., Waterford, Mich., 1999—, Macomb C.C., Clinton Twp., Mich., 2000—. Asst. bd. dird. MH-STeCA, Lansing, Mich., 2000—03. Recipient Regional Coach of Yr., MH-STeCA, 1997, 1998, 1999, 2000 & 2001, Coach of Yr., MCTCA, 1997 & 1999, M.A.C., 1998-99 & 1999-2000. Mem.: NEA (assoc.), Mich. Edn. Assn. (assoc.), Am. Polit. Sci. Assn. (assoc.). Personal E-mail: p1k2foley@aol.com.

FOLEY, RIDGWAY KNIGHT, JR., lawyer, writer; b. Portland, Oreg., Oct. 7, 1937; s. Ridgway Knight and Eunice Alberta (Ammer) F. BS magna cum laude, Lewis & Clark Coll., 1959; JD, U. Oreg., 1963. Bar: Oreg. Assoc. Mautz, Souther, Spaulding, Kinsey & Williamson, Portland, 1964-71; gen. ptnr. Schwabe, Williamson & Wyatt (and predecessor firms), Portland, 1972-84, sr. ptnr., 1985-92; ptnr., shareholder Foley & Duncan, P.C., Portland, 1993-96; of counsel Greene & Markley PC, Portland, 1997—, med. office mgr., 1999—. Com. mem. Multnomah Lawyer Com., 1964-68, 90-93, chair, 1992-93. Contbr. more than 100 articles, essays to profl. jours., 1962—; lectr. profl. orgns., 1970—. Trustee Found. Econ. Edn., Inc., Irvington-on-Hudson, N.Y., 1974-91, 93-96; founding dir. Paulist Fathers Cath. Ctr., Portland, 1978-85. Mem. ABA, Oreg. State Bar, Multnomah County Bar (dir. 1993-97), University Club (Portland), Mt. Hood Philos. Soc. (founding trustee, officer 1972-85), Lang Syne Soc., Order of Colf. Episcopalian. Avocations: writing, lecturing, genealogy, publishing, history. Office: Greene & Markley PC 1515 SW 5th Ave Ste 600 Portland OR 97201-5449

FOLEY, THOMAS JOHN, lawyer; b. Detroit, July 3, 1954; s. Thomas John and Mary Catherine (Gluekert) F.; m. Virginia Lee, Aug. 20, 1977; 1 child, Kaitlin Shea. BA, Mich. State U., 1976, JD, 1979. Bar: Mich. 1980, Ohio 1992, U.S. Dist. Ct. (ea. and we. dists.) Mich. 1980, U.S.Ct. Appeals (6th cir.) 1980. Assoc. Kitch, Drutchas, Wagner, Denardis & Valitutti, Detroit, 1980—84, assoc. prin., 1984—87, prin., shareholder, 1987—2003; founder Foley, Baron & Metzger, PLLC, Farmington Hills, Mich., 2003—. Contbr. articles to profl. jours. Mem.: Food and Drug Law Inst., Def. Rsch. Inst., Internat. Assn. Def. Counsel. Avocations: business, private pilot. Office: Foley Baron and Metzger PLLC Ste 350 33533 W Twelve Mile Rd Farmington Hills MI 48331 Business E-Mail: tfoley@fbmlaw.com.

FOLEY, THOMAS STEPHEN, diplomat, former speaker House of Representatives; b. Spokane, Wash., Mar. 6, 1929; s. Ralph E. and Helen Marie (Higgins) F.; m. Heather Strachan, Dec. 1968. BA, U. Wash., 1951, LL.B., 1957. Bar: Wash. Ptnr. Higgins & Foley, 1957-58; dep. pros. atty. Spokane County, Spokane, 1958-60; asst. atty. gen. State of Wash., Olympia, 1960-61; spl. counsel interior and insular affairs com. U.S. Senate, Washington, 1961-64; mem. 89th-103rd Congresses from 5th Wash. dist., Washington, D.C., 1965-94, House majority whip, 1981-86, House majority leader, 1987-89; speaker U.S. Ho. of Reps., Washington, 1989-94; ptnr. Akin, Gump, Strauss, Hauer & Feld, Washington, 1995-97; chmn. Pres.'s Fgn. Intelligence Adv. Bd., 1995-97; U.S. amb. to Japan U.S. Dept. State, Tokyo, 1997—. Instr. law Gonzaga U., 1958-60; mem. bd. advisors Ctr. Strategic and Internat. Studies; mem. adv. council Am. Ditchley Found. Author: Honor in the House. Bd. overseers Whitman Coll.; bd. advisors Yale U. council; bd. dirs. Council on Fgn. Relations. Mem. Phi Delta Phi. Democrat. Office: US Embassy 1-10-5 Akasaka Minato-ku Tokyo 107-8420 Japan

FOLEY, VIRGINIA SUE LASHLEY, counselor, international training consultant; b. Richmond, Ind., May 1, 1942; d. Robert E. and Flora Rose (Johnson) Lashley; m. Laurence Michael Foley Sr., Jan. 28, 1968 (dec. 2002); children: Megan Leigh, Jeremie Beth, L. Michael Jr. BA, Hanover Coll., 1964; MS, San Francisco State U., 1969. Cert. profl. counselor and internat. mental health tng. cons.; nat. bd. cert. hypnotherapist; Myers Briggs Type indicator cert. specialist. Vol. Peace Corps, Danao City, The Philippines, 1964-66; counselor, tng. cons. In Touch Found., U.S. Peace Corps., Asian Devel. Bank, Manila, 1981-85, Internat. Sch., 1981-85; counselor, tng. cons. to Overseas Briefing Ctr. U.S. Dept. of State, Washington, 1988-90; counselor, mental health cons. U.S. State Dept./U.S. Peace Corps, La Paz, Bolivia, 1990-92; mental health coord. U.S. Embassy, Lima, Peru, 1992—96; counselor, preferred provider Aetna/HAI, Lima, Peru, 1994-96, mental health cons., internat. tng. cons. Harare, Zimbabwe, 1996-2000, Amman, Jordan, 2000—02; preferred provider AETNA-HAI, Peru, 1994—96. Archiving specialist USAID, Jordan, 2001—02. Author:

Leisure Time Activities for Families in Manila, 1983; (manuals) Career Development Manual, 1984; writer mags. What's On in Manila, 1983-85, Off Duty Mag., 1985, USAID Frontlines, 1991-94, Lima Times, 1994, Fgn. Svc. Jour., 1996; contbr. articles to mags. Mem. U.S. Embassy Mental Health Com.; chair Cmty. Morale Com. Recipient award of recognition Bukidnon State Coll., The Philippines, 1985. Mem.: ACA, Assn. Boliviana de Psicologia Humanista (founding), Internat. Assn. Marriage and Family Counselors (chair cmty. morale com.), Royal Soc. for Conservation of Nature, Am. Women's Assn. of Amman, Friends of Archeology, Am. Women's Club. Avocations: instrumental music, art, crafts, hiking, literature. Address: 1422 Varnum St NW Washington DC 20011 E-mail: virfoley@hotmail.com.

FOLEY, WILLIAM EDWARD, historian, educator, retired historian; b. Kans. City, Mo., Sept. 20, 1938; s. William Delbert and Lorene M. Foley; m. Martha A. Ellenburg, May 30, 1967; children: Laura Ann Sindhi, David Edward. BS in Edn., Ctrl. Mo. State U., 1960, MA in History, 1963; PhD in History, U. of Mo., 1967. Tchr. Consol. Sch. Dist. No. 2, Raytown, Mo., 1960—62; from asst. prof. to prof. emeritusof history Ctrl. Mo. State U., Warrensburg, Mo., 1966—2001, prof. emeritus of history, 2001—. Bd. dir. Friends of the Mo. State Archives; mem. Mo. Adv. Coun. on Hist. Preservation, 1991—, chmn., 1999—2001. Author: A History of Missouri, 1673-1820, 1971 (Merit award Am. Assn. for State and Local History), The Genesis of Missouri: From Wilderness Outpost to Statehood, 1989 (Best Book award Mo. Conf. on History, 1990); co-author: The First Chouteaus: River Barons of Early St. Louis, 1983, Missouri: Then and Now, 2001; editor: Mo. Biography Series, 1990—; co-editor: An Account of Upper Louisiana by Nicolas de Finiels, 1989, Dictionary of Missouri Biography, 1999; mem. editl. bd.: Mo. Hist. Rev., 1986—. Mem. Warrensburg R-6 Bd. of Edn., Warrensburg, 1977—83, pres., 1979—80; bd. of trustees Trails Regional Libr., Warrensburg, Mo., 2000—. Recipient Mo. Gov.'s award for Tchg. Excellence, Mo. Dept. of Higher Edn., 2000. Mem.: Johnson County Hist. Soc. (bd. dirs. 2001—, pres. 2002—), State Hist. Soc. Mo. (Disting. Svc. award 2002), Soc. for Historians of the Early Republic, Western History Assn., Orgn. of Am. Historians. Presbyn. Home: 1408 Kensington Court Warrensburg MO 64093

FOLEY, WILLIAM PATRICK, II, title insurance company executive; b. Austin, Tex., Dec. 29, 1944; s. Robert P. Foley; m. Carol J. Johnson, Nov. 15 1969; children: Lindsay, Robert P. II, Countney Diane, William P. III. BS, U.S. Mil. Acad., 1967; MBA, Seattle U., 1970; JD, U. Wash., 1974. Assoc. Streich, Lang, Weeks, Cardon & French P.A., Phoenix, 1974-76; ptnr., pres., dir. Foley, Clark & Nye P.A., Phoenix, 1976-84; pres. chief exec. officer Land Resources Corp., Scottsdale, Ariz., 1983-84; chmn. bd., pres., CEO Fidelity Nat. Title Ins. Co., Irvine, Calif., 1981—; also bd. dirs. Fidelity Nat. Title Ins., Irvine, Calif.; chmn. Checkers Drive-In Restaurants, Inc., Clearwater, Fl. Chmn. bd., dir., pres., chief exec. officer Fidelity Nat. Fin., Inc., Fidelity Nat. Title Ins. Co. of Calif., Fidelity Nat. Title Ins. Co. of Tenn., Fidelity Nat. Title Ins. Co. of Tex., So. Title Holding Co., Pacific Western Aviation, Inc., Western Am. Exch. Corp., Western Pacific Property & Casualty Agy., Inc., Fidelity Appraisal Group, Inc., Folco Devel. Corp., Western Pacific Acquisitions, Inc., Bristol Investment Corp.; chmn. bd., dir. Western Fin. Trust Co., Rocky Mountain Aviation, Inc.; chmn. bd. dir., chief exec. officer Fidelity Nat. Title Agy., Inc. Fidelity Nat. Title Agy. of Maricopa County, Inc., Fidelity Nat. Title Agy. of Pinal County, Inc., Fidelity Nat. Title Co. of El Paso, Fidelity Nat. Title Co. of Oreg., Ramada Inn Old Town Mgmt., Inc.; numerous other chairmanships and directorships in fin. industry. Office: Fidelity Nat Title Ins 2390 E Camelback Rd Phoenix AZ 85016-3448*

FOLGATE, CYNTHIA A. social services administrator; b. Chgo., Jan. 27, 1950; d. William C. and Cassie Edna (Sisemore) F. BA, No. Ill. U., 1974, MA, 1983. Sec. No. Ill. U., DeKalb, 1974—80, 1983—84, instr., 1984—92; outreach coord. Safe Passage, DeKalb, 1992—96, crisis intervention/outreach coord., 1996—97, systems advocacy coord., 1997—2002, cmty. edn. and tng. coord., 2002—. Instr. Waubonsee C.C., Sugar Grove, Ill., 1990—; mem. DeKalb County Domestic Violence Forum, 1990-91; family violence coord. coun. Ill. 16th Jud. Cir.; mem. adv. bd. Coop. Edn. Internship Office No. Ill. U. Speech cons. for various election campaigns DeKalb County, 1988—90; coord. DeKalb County Domestic Violence Initiative, 1998—2000; mem. bd. deacons 1st Congregational United Ch. of Christ, DeKalb, 1989—92. Mem. Friends of Barb City Manor. Office: Safe Passage PO Box 621 Dekalb IL 60115-0621

FOLK, FRANK ANTON, surgeon, educator; b. Chgo., Dec. 15, 1925; s. Frank A. and Anna (Pilisauer) F.; m. Lorna C. Hill, June 18, 1949; children: Laura, Lawrence, Patricia, Elizabeth, Thomas, James, Mary, Tracy Ann, William. BS, Northwestern U., 1945; postgrad., U. Wis., 1945-46; MD, U. Ill., 1949. Diplomate Am. Bd. Surgery, Nat. Bd. Med. Examiners; lic. Ill., Wis. Rotating intern Cook County Hosp., Chgo., 1949-51; resident in gen. surgery Cook County/Columbus Hosp., Chgo., 1951, Cook County Hosp., Chgo., 1954-57, surgeon, 1958-69, dir. of surgery, 1969-72; mem. faculty Stritch Sch. Medicine Loyola U., Maywood, Ill., 1958—, prof. surgery Stritch Sch. Medicine, 1972-96; prof. emeritus, 1997—; rsch. fellow Hektoen Inst., Chgo., 1959-64; asst. chief surgery VA Hosp., Hines, Ill., 1972-95, chief surg. svc., 1995-96. Mem. editl. bd.: The Am. Surgeon, 1984-92; contbr. articles to med. jours. including Am. Jour. Physiology, Jour. Occupl. Medicine, Annals of Surgery, Archives of Surgery, Jour. Trauma, Surg. Clinics of N.Am. Unit pres., exec. bd. Am. Cancer Soc., Chgo., 1972-89; mem. pres.'s adv. com. Benedictine U., Lisle, Ill., 1965-90. Lt. USN, 1951-53, Korea. Decorated Bronze Star, 1953. Fellow ACS (gov., chmn. gen. surgery Chgo. com. on trauma 1975-83, pres. met. chpt. 1977-78, mem. SESAP com. II and III, instr. ACS advanced trauma life support course 1980-87); mem. Am. Surg. Assn., Am. Assn. for Surgery of Trauma, Assn. Mil. Surgeons of U.S., Assn. for Acad. Surgery, Soc. for Surgery of Alimentary Tract, Assn. VA Surgeons, Collegium Internat. Chirurgiae Digestivae, Cen. Surg. Assn., Midwest Surg. Assn. (pres. 1974-75), Western Surg. Assn., Ill. Surg. Soc. (pres. 1971-72), Chgo. Surg. Soc. (pres. 1989-90), Inst. Medicine of Chgo. Roman Catholic. Avocations: medical history, civil war history, central american civilizations. Office: VA Hosp Surg Svc PO Box 5000 Hines IL 60141-1489 Fax: (708) 202-2180.

FOLK, JAMES CALVIN, ophthalmologist, researcher; b. Altoona, Pa., Mar. 11, 1954; s. Calvin Edward and Elizabeth Anne (Heiss) F.; m. Kathryn Hanelly, June 18, 1977; 1 child, Kate. BS with highest distinction, Pa. State U., 1973; MD cum laude, Thomas Jefferson Med. Coll., 1977. Diplomate Am. Bd. Ophthalmology. Asst. prof. ophthalmology U. Iowa, Iowa City, 1982-85, assoc. prof. ophthalmology, 1985-89, prof. ophthalmology, 1989— . Mem. exec. com., prin. investigator Macular Photocoagulation Study, Balt., 1983-94; mem. planning com., retina sect. Assn. Rsch. in Vision and Ophthalmology, Bethesda, Md., 1989-92; prin. investigator subretinal surgical trial, chair faculty practice plan com. ophthalmology, prin. investigator complications of AMD prevention trial U. Iowa, Iowa City, 1995—, exec. com. 2001. Author 3 book, 25 chpts. to books and over 135 articles to profl. jours. Sunday sch. tchr. Gloria Dei Luth. Ch., Iowa City, 1994—, mem. church coun., 1996— , pres. congregation, 1999—. Recipient Outstanding Med. Pub. Book award, Moody Pub., 1998. Mem. AMA, Am. Acad. Ophthalmology (Honor award 1990), Retina Soc., Vitreous Soc., Macula Soc., Iowa Acad. Ophthalmology (sec.-treas. 1985, pres. 1990), Alpha Omega Alpha. Lutheran. Avocations: writing, exercising, golf. Office: Univ Iowa 200 Hawkins Dr Iowa City IA 52242-1009

FOLK, MARIE GWYNN, library technician; b. Pelham, N.C., Dec. 9, 1955; d. Otis and Audrey Foster Gwynn; m. Hugh James Folk; children: Timothy, Thomas. AA, U. of S.C., 1998, BA in Edn., 2000. Libr. aide Perkins Libr. Duke U., Durham, NC, 1975; ammunition storage specialist US Army, various, SC, 1975—78; libr. technician Bad Toelz Am. Elem. Sch., Bad Toelz, Germany, 1981—82; adminstrv. asst. Detachment 1 15th Weather Squadron, Andrews Air Force Base, Md., 1988—89; sr. serials libr. technician Libr. of Congress, Washington, 1991—94; substitute tchr. Beaufort County Sch. Sys., Beaufort, SC, 1998—2000; libr. technician Nat. Libr. of Medicine, Bethesda, Md., 2000—03. Author: Follow Your Heart, Child, 2000, Uncle Sam is the Key, 2000. Active Mattaponi Elem. Sch. PTO, Upper Marlboro, Md., 2001—; mem. Opportunity Scholars Program, Beaufort, SC, 1998—2000, Antioch Bapt. Ch., Upper Marlboro, 2001—02. Specialist fourth class U.S. Army, 1975—78. Recipient Cert. of Appreciation, Bad Toelz Protestant Chapel, Bad Toelz, Germany, 1983, award, Opportunty Scholars Program, 1999—2000; scholar, Alcoa Found., 1997, Palmetto Fed. Savs. Bank, 1998, Mature Student scholarship, U. of SC., 1999. Mem.: Alpha Delta Kappa (scholarship 1998), Chi Delta Chi (sec. 1999—2000). Baptist.

FOLK, ROBERT LOUIS, geologist, educator; b. Cleve., Sept. 30, 1925; s. George Billmyer and Marjorie Marshall (Kinkead) F.; m. Marjorie Thomas, Sept. 7, 1946; children: Robert T., Jennifer Louise, Charles Marshall. BS, Pa. State Coll., 1946, MS, 1950, PhD, 1952. Research geologist Gulf Oil Co., Houston, 1951-52; mem. faculty U. Tex., Austin, 1952—, prof. geol. scis., 1960—, Dave Carlton prof. geol. scis., 1977-88. Vis. lectr. Australian Nat. U., Canberra, 1965, Tong-Ji U., Shanghai, China, 1980; vis. researcher Universita degli Studi, Milan, Italy, 1973 Author: Petrology of Sedimentary Rocks, 1980; contbr. articles to sci. publs. Neil Miner award Nat. Assn. Geology Tchrs., 1989, H.C. Sorby medal Internat. Assn. Sedimentologists, 1990. Fellow Geol. Soc. Am. (Penrose medal 2000); mem. Soc. Econ. Paleontologists and Mineralogists (hon., Twenhofel medal 1979). Methodist. Achievements include first discovery of mineralized nannobacteria on earth; the same-appearing organisms were discovered by NASA in Martian meteorite. Home: 1107 Bluebonnet Ln Austin TX 78704-2005 Office: U of Tex Dept Geol Scis Austin TX 78801 *My unique characteristic is that I run my life randomly. At home each day, I put all the things I have/want to do in a list. Then I roll dice to see which thing to do and do that immediately whether it be a painful or pleasureful choice. Since I adopted this method I get immeasurably more work done and much greater pleasure out of daily life. Try it.*

FOLK, THOMAS ROBERT, lawyer; b. Milford, N.J., Jan. 9, 1950; s. Conrad Frank and Isabella Ramsey (Sickels) F.; m. JoAnn Elizabeth Lo Pinto, June 21, 1975; children: Elizabeth Frances, Karina Marie. BS, U.S. Mil. Acad., 1972; JD, U. Va., 1978. Bar: Va. 1978, U.S. Ct. Mil. Appeals 1978, U.S. Ct. Appeals (4th cir.) 1978, U.S. Supreme Ct. 1983, U.S. Ct. Claims 1985, U.S. Ct. Appeals (9th and fed. cirs.) 1985, D.C. 1986., U.S. Dist. Ct. D.C. 1987, U.S. Dist. Ct. Md. 1987, U.S. Ct. Appeals (11th cir.) 2000. Commd. 2d lt. U.S. Army, 1972, advanced to maj., 1983, resigned, 1986, asst. to gen. counsel, 1980-82, atty. litigation, 1983-86; assoc. Hazel & Thomas, P.C., Fairfax, Va., 1986-88, owner, 1989-99; ptnr. Reed Smith LLP, Fairfax, 1999—. Contbr. articles to profl. jours. Mem. Com. Armed Svcs. and Vets. Affairs, 1985-88. Col. USAR, 1995, ret. Mem.: Fairfax Bar Assn. (bd. govs. 1993—97), Va. State Bar (bd. govs. constrn. and pub. contracts 1993—99). West Point Soc. D.C (bd. govs. 1993—99). Home: 4902 Asquith Ct Fairfax VA 22032-2102 E-mail: tfolk@reedsmith.com.

FOLKER, CATHLEEN ANN, business educator; b. West Allis, Wis., May 14, 1956; d. Norman Ralph and Lucille Catherine F. BA in Liberal Arts, Ambassador Coll., 1978; postgrad., U. Wis., Milw., 1986-91; MSBA, Tex. Tech. U., 1995, PhD, 1999. Customer rels. supr. Univ. Acctg. Svc., Milw., 1979-80; mktg. analyst Payco Am. Corp., Brookfield, Wis., 1980; controller West Allis Curtain & Drapery, 1980-92; mgmt. cons., 1992-93; tchg. asst. Tex. Tech U., Lubbock, 1994-97; lectr. U. Wis., Whitewater, 1998-99, U. Nebr., Lincoln, 1999-2000; asst. prof. entrepreneurship U. St. Thomas, St. Paul, 2000—. Freelance writer, Oconomowoc, Wis., 1989-93; tax preparer, 1991-93; grad. tchg. asst. U. Wis., Milw., 1989-90. Avocations: walking, reading, travel, singing, biking. E-mail: cafolker@stthomas.edu.

FOLKERS, CAY, economics educator; b. Luebeck, Germany, Dec. 24, 1942; s. Karl-Heinz and Gerda (Matthiessen) F.; m. Susanne Futterer, June 19, 1998. Diplom-Volkswirt, Free U. Berlin, 1967; D in Econs., U. Hamburg, Fed. Republic Germany, 1971; Habil. Econs., U. Hamburg, 1976. Asst. U. Hamburg, 1967-71, lectr. econs., 1971-77; prof. econs. and pub. fin. U. Hohenheim, Stuttgart, Fed. Republic Germany, 1977-90, U. Bochum (Fed. Republic Germany), 1990—. Author: Lineare Programmierung staatlicher Aktivität, 1971, Vermoegensverteilung und staatliche Aktivität, 1981, Begrenzungen von Steuern und Staatsausgaben in den USA, 1983; contbr. articles to profl. jours. Mem. Verein fuer Socialpolitik, Internat. Inst. Pub. Fin., Am. Econ. Assn., Pub. Choice Soc. Office: Ruhr Univ Bochum 44780 Bochum Germany E-mail: cay.folkers@ruhr-uni-bochum.de.

FOLKERS, KARL AUGUST, chemistry educator; b. Decatur, Ill., Sept. 1, 1906; married, 1932; 2 children. BS with honors, U. Ill., 1928; PhD in Organic Chemistry, U. Wis., 1931; ScD (hon.), Phila. Coll. Pharmacy and Sci., 1962, U. Wis., 1969, U. Ill., 1973; PharmD (hon.), U. Uppsala, Sweden, 1969; degree in medicine and surgery (hon.), U. Bologna, Italy, 1989, MD (hon.), 1990. Squibb & Lilly postdoctoral rsch. fellow Yale U., 1931—34; rschr. Merck & Co. Inc., 1934—38, asst. dir. rsch., 1938—45, dir. organic and biol. chemistry rsch. divsn., 1953—56, exec. dir. fundamental rsch., 1956—62, v.p. exploration rsch., 1962—63; pres., chief exec. officer Stanford Rsch. Inst., 1963—68; prof. chemistry, dir. Inst. Biomed. Rsch. U. Tex., Austin, 1968—, Ashbel Smith prof., 1973—; pres. Karl Folkers Found. for Biomed. and Clin. Rsch., 1990—95. Mem. divsn. 9 Nat. Def. Rsch. Com., 1943—46; Baker nonresident lectr. Cornell U., 1953; lectr. med. faculty Lund, Stockholm, Uppsala, Gothenburg univs., Sweden, 1954; chmn. conf. on vitamins and metabolism Gordon Rsch. Conf., 1956, trustee, 71; Strumer lectr., 57; mem. sci. adv. com. Inst. of Microbiology, Rutgers U., 1957—60; chmn. adv. coun. dept. chemistry Princeton U., 1958—64; Regent's lectr. UCLA, 1960; guest lectr. Am. Swiss Found. Sci. Exchange, 1961; Robert A. Welch Found. lectr., 63; courtesy prof. Stanford U., 1963—, U. Calif.-Berkeley, 1963—; Marchon vis. lectr. U. Newcastle, 1964; F.F. Nord lectr. Fordham U., 1971; mem. rev. com. U.S. Pharmacopoeia; chmn. NAS, 1975; mem. internat. adv. bd. 4th Intersci. World Conf. on Inflammation, Geneva, 1991; numerous invited lecture posts, 1953—. Bd. editors Internat. Jour. Vitamin Rsch., 1968, Rsch. Comm. in Chem. and Pharm. Pathology, 1969. Co-recipient Mead Johnson and Co. award, 1940, 1949; recipient Alexander von Humboldt-Stiftung award, Germany, 1977, Presdl. Cert. of Merit, 1948, award, Merck & Co., Inc., 1951, Spencer award, 1959, Perkin medal, 1960, Pres.'s Nat. Medal of Sci., NSF, 1990, Van Meter prize, Am. Thyroid Assn., 1969, Robert A. Welch Internat. award, 1972, Achievement award, Am. Pharm. Assn., 1974, Priestley medal, Am. Chem. Soc., 1986. Fellow: Am. Inst. Nutrition; mem.: Internat. Soc. Metabolic Therapy (bd. dirs. 1988), Am. Chem. Soc. (chmn. North Jersey sect., chmn. divsn. organic chemistry, pres. 1962, Harrison-Howe award and lectr. 1949, Spencer award Kansas City sect. 1959, Nichols medal N.Y. sect. 1967, Priestley medal 1986), Am. Inst. Chemists, Am. Soc. Biol. Chemistry, Soc. Italiana di Scienze Pharmaceutiche (hon.), NAS, AAAS, Royal Swedish Acad. Engring. Scis. (fgn.), Phi Lambda Epsilon (hon.). Office: U Tex Inst Biomed Rsch Welch Hall 4-304 Austin TX 78712

FOLKMAN, DAVID H. retail, wholesale and consumer products consultant; b. Jackson, Mich., Nov. 6, 1934; s. Jerome D. and Bessie (Schomer) F.; m. Susan Kleppner, June 22, 1958; children: Louis, Sarah, Karen, Jeffrey. AB, Harvard U., 1957, MBA, 1960. Mdse. mgr. Foley's, Houston, 1957-69; v.p. dir. stores Famous-Barr, St. Louis, 1969-74; sr. v.p., gen. mdse. mgr. Macy's Calif., San Francisco, 1974-82; pres., chief exec. officer Emporium Capwell, San Francisco, 1982-87; gen. ptnr. U.S. Venture Ptnrs., Menlo Park, Calif., 1987-90; venture ptnr., 1991-93; pres., chief exec. officer Laurel Burch, Inc., San Francisco, 1990-91; retail investor, cons., 1991-93; CEO Esprit de Corp, San Francisco, 1993-95; prin., Regent Pacific Mgmt. Corp., San Francisco, 1995—. Instr. U. Houston, 1968-69, Wash. U., St. Louis, 1970-73; bd. dirs. Regent Pacific Mgmt. Corp., Shoe Pavilion, Inc. Mem. Harvard Club (N.Y.C.). Office: Regent Pacific Mgmt Corp 425 California St Ste 1310 San Francisco CA 94104

FOLKMAN, MOSES JUDAH, surgeon, educator; b. Cleve., Feb. 24, 1933; s. Jerome D. and Bessie Folkman. BA, Ohio State U., 1953; MD, Harvard U., 1957; DSc (hon.), Mt. Sinai Sch. Medicine, 1996, Northwestern U., 1998; MD (hon.), Uppsala U., Sweden, 1998; DSc (hon.), Muhlenberg Coll., 1999, Albany Med. Coll., 1999; LHD (hon.), U. Mass., Lowell, 1999; MD (hon.), Göteborg U., Sweden, 2000; DSc (hon.), Thomas Jefferson U., 2001, U. Conn., 2002, Oberlin Coll., 2002, N.E. Ohio U., 2002, U. Mass., Dartmouth, 2003. From intern to asst. resident in surgery Mass. Gen. Hosp., Boston, 1957—60, sr. asst. resident in surgery, 1962—64, chief resident, 1964—65; chief resident in pediat. surgery Phila. Children's Hosp., 1969; instr. surgery Harvard U. Med. Sch., 1965—66, assoc. in surgery, 1967, prof. surgery, 1967—, Julia Dyckman Andrus prof. pediat. surgery, 1968—, prof. anatomy and cellular biology, 1989—. Asst. surgeon Boston City Hosp., 1965—66; assoc. dir. Sears Surg. Lab., 1966—67; sr. surgeon Children's Hosp. Med. Ctr., Boston, 1968—, surgeon-in-chief, 1968—81; dir Surg. Rsch. Labs., 1968—. With M.C. USN, 1960—62. Recipient Career Devel. award, NIH, 1966, Lila Gruber award, Am. Acad. Dermatology, 1974, Ledlie prize, Harvard U., 1987, Gairdner Found. Internat. award, Toronto, Can., 1991, Christopher Columbus Commemorative Sci. medal, U.S. Congress/NIH, Wolf award, Wolf Found., Jerusalem, 1992, Lucian award, Royal Coll. Surgeons Can., 1993, Steiner award, Josef Steiner Found., Switzerland, 1994, Bristol-Myers Cancer Rsch. award, 1995, Ernst Schering award, Germany, 1996, Gen. Motors Cancer Rsch. award, 1997, Ernst Jung Found. award, Germany, 1997, Med. prize, Keio (Japan) U., 1998, Chiron award in medicine, Italy, 1999, award in life sci., Benjamin Franklin Inst., Phila., 2001. Fellow: ACS (Sheen award 1989), German Surg. Soc. (hon.), Royal Coll. Surgeons (Ireland) (hon.); mem.: NAS (mem. Inst. Medicine), Assn. Am. Physicians, Mass. Med. Soc., Am. Pediat. Surg. Assn., Assn. Acad. Surgery, Am. Surg. Assn., Am. Acad. Arts and Scis., Am. Philos. Soc. Office: Children's Hospital Surgery/Hunnewell 103 300 Longwood Ave Boston MA 02115-5724 Office Fax: 617-739-5891.

FOLKS, CATHALIN BUHRMANN, English language educator; b. Aurora, Ill, Jan. 27, 1947; d. Donald C. and June D. Buhrmann; 1 child, Matthew A. BA, U. Calif., Santa Barbara, 1969; MA in Folklore, Ind. U., 1970, MA in English, 1974, PhD in English, 1989. Assoc. prof. English Cleve. State Cmty. Coll., Tenn., 1978-92; prof. English Pellissippi State Tech. Cmty. Coll., Knoxville, 1992—. Contbr. articles to profl. jour. Mem. New Chaucer Soc., Langland Soc., 2-Yr. Coll. English Assn., C.C. Humanities Assn., Smoky Mountains Hiking Club (hike leader conservation activities 1980—). Avocations: hiking, reading, gardening, travel. Office: Pellissippi State Tech CC PO Box 222990 Knoxville TN 37933-0990

FOLLET, DIANE W. music educator; b. Denver, Colo., Dec. 9, 1945; d. Edward G. and Helen Aldene Weber. MusB with highest honors, U. of Tex. at Austin, 1963—67; MusM, U. of Ariz., 1994—97; ArtsD, U. of No. Colo., 1997—2000. Asst. prof. of music Muhlenberg Coll., Allentown, Pa., 2000—; CPA Various acctg. firms, Tex. and Ariz. Composer: (opera) Echo; singer: (recital) A Celebration of Creative Women; composer: (choral work) Invocation; contbr. articles to jours. Faculty Summer grant, Muhlenberg Coll., 2002, 2003. Mem.: Nat. Assn. of Teachers of Singing, Internat. Alliance for Women in Music (bd.dirs.), Soc. for Music Theory, Coll. Music Soc. (pres. N.E. chpt. 2002—). D-Liberal. Episcopalian. Avocations: knitting, cooking, travel. Home: 218 S Fulton Allentown PA 18102 Office: Muhlenberg College 2400 Chew St Allentown PA 18104 Office Fax: 484-664-3633. Personal E-mail: musictheorydiva@aol.com. Business E-Mail: dfollet@muhlenberg.edu.

FOLLET, ROBERT EDWARD, music librarian; b. Syracuse, N.Y., Aug. 12, 1942; s. Robert Edward and Grace (Weymer) F.; m. Diane Weber, June 15, 1968 (div. Apr. 1997). MusB, Oberlin Coll., 1964; MusM, U. Ill., 1966; MLS, U. Tex., 1979. Asst. music libr. U. North Tex., Denton, 1980-89; music libr. Rice U., Houston, 1989-92; head music libr. U. Ariz., Tucson, 1992-95, Ariz. State U., Tempe, 1995—2002, Arthur Friedheim Libr., Peabody Conservatory, Balt., 2002—. Author: Albert Roussel: A Biobibliography, 1986; contbr. over 75 revs. to Am. Record Guide, L.Am. Music Rev. and Notes. Violist Tempe and Mesa Symphony Orch. Mem. Music Libr. Assn. (co-chmn. local arrangements for nat. meeting 1999-2002, chmn. Mountain Plains chpt. 1998-2000), Internat. Assn. Music Librs. (treas. U.S. br. 1991-98). Episcopalian. Avocations: reading, tennis. Address: 1733 E Pratt St Baltimore MD 21231

FOLLETT, CAROLYN BROWN, poet, artist; b. N.Y.C., Jan. 31, 1936; d. Lorne William and Helen Rudd (Swayze) Brown; m. Alan Lee Follett; children: Jeffrey Tredwell, Paul Seward, Lorne Hillary. BA in English, Smith Coll., 1958. Copy editor, proofreader dept. publs. Stanford U., Internat. Bus. Rels., San Francisco, McCann Erickson, San Francisco, Cunningham and Walsh; designer, creator, owner, bus. mgr. The Peaceable Kingdom; editor, pub. Arctos Press. Art bd. dirs. Sight and Insight, Mill Valley, Calif.; bd. dirs. Marin Poetry Ctr., Marin County, Calif., de Young Mus. Art Sch., San Francisco, Art Apprentice Program, San Francisco; leader workshops Internat. Women Writers Guild; numerous poetry readings. Author: The Latitudes of Their Going, 1993, Gathering the Mountains, 1995, Visible Bones, 1998, At the Turning of the Light, 2001 (Winner 2001 Nat. Poetry Book award); editor: Beside the Sleeping Maiden, Poets of Marin, 1997, GRRRRR, A Collection of Poems About BEARS, 2000; editor, pub.: Runes, A Review of Poetry, 2001, 02, 03; contbr. poetry to numerous jours.; two-person shows include O'Hanlon Gallery, Mill Valley, Calif., 1994; exhibited in group shows at Artisans Gallery, Mill Valley, 1989-2003, Signature Gallery, San Diego, 1990, 1994, O'Hanlon Gallery, Mill Valley, 1990-2003, Perception Gallery, Ft. Mason, San Francisco, 1991. Founding trustee San Francisco U. H.S., 1973-82; trustee, bd. chmn. Urban H.S., San Francisco, 1982-88; art vol. San Francisco Edn. Aux. Recipient numerous poetry awards; Marin Arts Coun. grant for poetry, 1995. Office: 1331 4th St #24 San Rafael CA 94901 E-mail: runes@aol.com.

FOLLETT, KENNETH MARTIN, author; b. Cardiff, Wales, June 5, 1949; s. Martin D. and Lavinia C. (Evans) F.; m. Mary Emma Ruth Elson, Jan. 5, 1968 (div. 1985); children: Emanuele, Marie-Claire; m. Barbara Broer, Nov. 8, 1985. BA, U. Coll., London, 1970. Reporter, music columnist South Wales Echo, 1970-73; reporter Evening News, London, 1973-74; editorial dir. Everest Books Ltd., London, 1974—76, dep. mng. dir., 1976-77. Pres. The Dyslexia Inst.; chair Nat. Year of Reading, 1998-99; mem. coun. Nat. Literary Trust. Author: The Shakeout, 1975, The Bear Raid, 1976, Secret of Kellerman's Studio, 1976, Eye of the Needle, 1978 (Edgar award Best Novel), Triple, 1979, The Key to Rebecca, 1980, The Man from St. Petersburg, 1982, On Wings of Eagles, 1983, Lie Down with Lions, 1985, The Pillars of Earth, 1989, Night over Water, 1991, A Dangerous Fortune, 1993, Pillars of the Almighty, 1994, A Place Called Freedom, 1995, The Third Twin, 1996, The Hammer of Eden, 1998, Code to Zero, 2000, Jackdaws, 2001, Hornet Flight, 2002; (as Martin Martinsen) The Power Twins and the Worm Puzzle, 1976; (as Symon Myles) The Big Needle, 1974, The Big Black, 1974, The Big Hit, 1975; (as Bernard L. Ross) Amok: King of Legend, 1976, Capricorn One, 1978; (as Zachary Stone) The Modigliani Scandal, 1976, Paper Money, 1977; screenwriter: Fringe Banking, 1978, A Football Star, 1979, Lie Down with Lions, 1987. Fellow U. Coll. London. Fellow Royal Soc. Arts. Office: PO Box 4 Stevenage SG3 6UT England

FOLLETT, PETER ARNOLD, entomologist, researcher; b. Burlington, VT, Dec. 27, 1957; s. Benjamin Branch Follett, Elsie Margaret Follett; m. Debra Lynn Checver, Mar. 24, 1995; 1 child, Fiona. BS cum laude, U. Vt., 1980; MS, Oreg. State U., 1983; PhD, N.C. State U., 1993. Postdoctoral fellow U. Md., College Park, 1993—94, faculty rsch. assoc., 1993—94; postdoctoral fellow U. Hawaii at Manoa, Honolulu, 1995—97; rsch. entomologist USDA, Hilo, Hawaii, 1997—. Affiliate grad. faculty U. Hawaii at Manoa, 1998; adj. prof. entomology U. Hawaii, Hilo, 1998. Editor: Nontarget Effects of Biological Control, 1999; contbr. articles to profl. jours. Coach St. Joseph's H.S., Hilo, 2001—02. Grantee, USDA Nat. Rsch. Initiative, 1993, USDA Nat. Rsch. Initiative, 1997. Mem.: Entomol. Soc. Am., Hawaiian Entomol. Soc. (pres. 1999—2001, editor procs. 1999—2003), Sigma Xi. Achievements include research in parasitoid drift after biological control inductions; accelerated development of quarantine treatments for insects on poor hosts; irradiation to ensure quarantine security for Cryptophlebia spp. (Lepidoptera: Tortricidae) in sapindaceous fruits; comparison of rambutan quality after hot-forced-air and irradiation quarantine treatments. Avocations: soccer, tennis, bicycling, kayaking, farming. Home: 27-699 Kaieie Rd Papaikou HI 96781 Office: USDA Agrl Rsch Svc PO Box 4459 Stainback Hwy/Kulani Rd Hilo HI 96720 Home Fax: 808-964-1364; Office Fax: 808-969-6967. Business E-Mail: pfollett@pbarc.ars.usda.gov.

FOLLETT, ROBERT JOHN RICHARD, publisher; b. Oak Park, Ill., July 4, 1928; s. Dwight W. and Mildred (Johnson) F.; m. Nancy L. Crouthamel, Dec. 30, 1950; children: Brian L., Kathryn R., Jean A., Lisa W. AB, Brown U., 1950; postgrad., Columbia U., 1950-51. Editor Follett Pub. Co., Chgo., 1951-55, sales mgr., 1955-58, gen. mgr. ednl. divsn., developer first multi-racial textbook program, first textbooks for disadvantaged, first beginning-to-read books, 1958-68, pres., 1968-78; chmn., dir. Follett Corp., 1979-94. Pres. Alpine Guild, Inc., 1977—; dir. Assn. Am. Pubs., 1972—79; chmn. Sch. Pubs., 1971—73; dir. Ednl. Sys. Corp.; mem. Ill. Gov.'s Commn. on Schs, 1972; pres. Alpine Rsch. Inst., Adv. Coun. on Ednl. Stats., 1975—77; chmn. Book Distbn. Task Force of Book Industry, 1978—81; adv. coun. Krannert Sch. of Mgmt., 1988—93; pres. Soda Creek Open Space Assn. Inc., 1994—; dir. Continental Divide Land Trust,

1996—; chmn. Rocky Mountain Resource Ctr., Inc., 1997—2002; lectr. Denver U. Pub. Inst., 1997—; mem. adv. bd. Ctr. for Living Democracy, 1997—2000; mem. Consortium on Renewing Edn., 1997—2000; chmn. Open Space for Summit, 1999; pres. Snake River Cmty. Assoc., 2001—, Continental Divide Land Trust, 2001—03. Author: Your Wonderful Body, 1961, What to Take Backpacking and Why, 1977, How to Keep Score in Business, 1978, The Financial Side of Book Publishing, 1982, rev. edit., 1988, Financial Feasibility in Book Publishing, 1988, rev. edit., 1996. Bd. dirs. Village Mgr. Assn., 1964-84, Cmty. Found. Oak Park and River Forest, 1959-86, Fund for Justice, 1974-77, For Character, 1983-93, Ctr. Book Rsch., 1985-88; trustee Inst. Ednl. Data Sys., 1965—, Rotary Found., 2000-; elected mem. Rep. State Com. from 7th dist. Ill., 1982-90, vice chmn., 1986-90; chmn. Ill. Reps. Strategic Planning Com., 1986-87; Presdl. Elector, 1988; pres. Keystone Citizens League, 1997—; mem. Keystone Mountain Responsibility Team, 1998-2000; hon. co-chair Colo. Mountain Coll. Campaign, 1998-99; mem. Wildlife/Wetlands Citizens Adv. Group, 2001-02. Served in AUS, 1951-53. Mem.: Soc. Midland Authors, Ill. C. of C. (chmn. edn. com. 1977—79), Am. Book Coun. (v.p. 1987—88), Rocky Mountain Book Pubs. Assn., Mid.-Am. Pubs. Assn. (mng. dir. 1987—88, dir. 1988—93), Chgo. Pubs. Assn. (pres. 1976—94), Rotary Club Summit County (trustee 2000—), River Forest Tennis Club, Sierra Club. Office: Alpine Guild Inc PO Box 4848 Dillon CO 80435-4848 Home: 0160 Kinnikinnik Rd Keystone CO E-mail: bob@alpineguild.com.

FOLLETT, RONALD FRANCIS, soil scientist; b. Laramie, Wyo., June 26, 1939; s. Roy Lawrence and Frances (Hunter) F.; m. Dorothy Mae Spangle, Jan. 1, 1967; children: William, Jennifer, Michael. BS, Colo. State U., 1961, MS, 1963; PhD, Purdue U., 1966. Rsch. soil scientist Agrl. Rsch. Svc., USDA, Mandan, N.D., 1968-75, nat. rsch. program leader Beltsville (Md.) and Ft. Collins (Colo.), 1976-86, rsch. leader soil-plant-nutrient rsch. unit Ft. Collins, 1986—; postdoctoral rsch. U.S. Plant-Soil-Nutrition Lab., Ithaca, N.Y., 1975-76. Co-author: The Potential of U.S. Cropland to Sequester Carbon and Mitigate the Greenhouse Effect, 1998; editor: Soil Erosion & Crop Productivity, 1985, Soil Fertility and Organic Matter as Critical Components of Production Systems, 1987, Nitrogen Management and Ground Water Protection, 1989, Managing Nitrogen for Ground Water Quality and Farm Profitability, 1991, Soil Processes & The Carbon Cycle, 1997, Soil Properties & Their Management for Carbon Sequestration, 1997, The Potential of U.S. Grazing Lands to Sequester Carbon and Mitigate the Greenhouse Effect, 2000, Nitrogen in the Environment, Sources, Problems and Management, 2001, Agricultural Practices and Policies for Carbon Sequestration in Soil, 2002; guest editor spl. issue Jour. Containment Hydrol.; contbr. over 150 articles to profl. jours. Officer 1st Presbyn. Ch., Mandan, then Ft. Collins; adult leader local Boy Scouts Am., Beltsville, then Ft. Collins. Capt. arty., U.S. Army, 1966-68; maj. Res. Recipient Disting. Svc. award USDA, 1984, 92, 2000, Superior Svc. award, 2000; cert. of merit, 1990, 99, 2001, 03, cert. of appreciation, 1992. Fellow Soil Sci. Soc. Am. (divsn. chmn. bd. dirs. 1985-88), Am. Soc. Agronomy, Soil and Water Conservation Soc. Am.(Colo. chpt. Presdl. citation 2002). Avocations: working with youth, skiing, fishing, gardening, woodworking. Office: USDA Agrl Rsch Svc Soil-Plant-Nutrient Rsch Unit PO Box E Fort Collins CO 80522-0470 E-mail: rfollett@lamar.colostate.edu.

FOLLICK, EDWIN DUANE, law educator, chiropractic physician; b. Glendale, Calif., Feb. 4, 1935; s. Edwin Fulfford and Esther Agnes (Catherwood) Follick; m. Marilyn K. Sherk, Mar. 24, 1986. BA, Calif. State U., LA, 1956, MA in Edn., 1961; MA in Social Sci., Pepperdine U., 1957, MPA, 1977; PhD, DTh, St. Andrews Theol. Coll., Sem. Free Prot. Episc. Ch., London, 1958; MS in LS, U. So. Calif., 1963, MEd in Instructional Materials, 1964, AdvMEd in Edn. Adminstrn., 1969; postgrad., Calif. Coll. Law, 1965; LLB, Blackstone Law Sch., 1966, JD, 1967; DC, Cleve. Chiropractic Coll., L.A., 1972; PhD, Academia Theatina, Pescara, 1978; MA in Orgnl. Mgmt., Antioch U., L.A., 1990. Tchr., libr. adminstr. L.A. City Schs., 1957-68; law librarian Glendale U. Coll. Law, 1968-69; coll. librarian Cleve. Chiropractic Coll., L.A., 1969-74, dir. edn. and admissions, 1974-84, prof. jurisprudence, 1975—, dean student affairs, 1976-92, coll. chaplain, 1985—, dean of edn., 1989—, rector, 2003—; assoc. prof. Newport U., 1982; extern prof. St. Andrews Theol. Coll., London, 1961; dir. West Valley Chiropractic Health Ctr., 1972-2000, West Valley Chiropractic Consulting, 2001—. Contbr. articles to profl. jours. Chaplain's asst. U.S. Army, 1958—60. Decorated cavaliere Internat. Order Legion of Honor of Immaculata (Italy); Knight of Malta, Sovereign Order of St. John of Jerusalem; Knight Grand Prelate, comdr. with star, Order of Signum Fidei; comdr. chevalier Byzantine Imperial Order of Constantine the Gt.; comdr. ritter Order St. Gereon; chevalier Mil. and Hospitaller Order of St. Lazarus of Jerusalem (Malta), Chaplain to the Order of St. Stanislas; numerous others. Mem. ALA, NEA, Am. Assn. Sch. Librarians, L.A. Sch. Libr. Assn., Calif. Sch. Libr. Assn., Assn. Coll. and Rsch. Librarians, Am. Assn. Law Librarians, Am. Chiropractic Assn., Internat. Chiropractors Assn., Nat. Geog. Soc., Internat. Platform Assn., Phi Delta Kappa, Sigma Chi Psi, Delta Tau Alpha. Democrat. Episcopalian. Home: 6435 Jumilla Ave Woodland Hills CA 91367-2833 Office: 590 N Vermont Ave Los Angeles CA 90004-2115 also: 7022 Owensmouth Ave Canoga Park CA 91303-2005 E-mail: follicke@cleveland.edu.

FOLLINGSTAD, CAROL C. psychologist, consultant, educator; b. Rantoul, Ill., Jan. 21, 1956; d. James Harvey and Ella May Watson; m. Eugene M. Follingstad; children: Alisha, Angela, Anita, Alayna, Arlyn, Arick. BA, Moorhead State U., 1990, MS, 1992. Lic. sch. psychologist, Minn., clin. psychologist, Minn. Med. sec. Korda Clinic, Pelican Rapids, Minn., 1974-77; news reporter KBRF Radio, Fergus Falls, Minn., 1981-84; rschr. Moorhead State U., 1986-92; sch. psychologist Sheyenne Valley SPED, Valley City, N.D., 1992-93; ind. sch. psychologist Rothsay, Minn., 1993-94, Cass County Spl. Svc., Fargo, ND, 1994—99; prof. psychology Moorhead State U., 1997—. Dir. After Sch. Program, Moorhead, 1997-99; cons. 4-H Vols., Breckenridge, Minn., 1996-2001. Editor Children's Works mag., 1990-91. Vol. coord. Wilkin County Ext., Breckenridge, 1996-2001; Blandin Leadership coord. Rothsay Br., Minn., 1996—; adv. bd. Bapt. Ch., Rothsay, 1992-2001; pres. PTO, Rothsay, 1994; dist. rep. Head Start, Moorhead, 1980-86; Sunday sch. supt. Bapt. Ch., Rothsay, 1988-90. Mem. APA (divsn. 16), Nat. Assn. Sch. Psychologists, N.D. Psychol. Assn., Minn. Sch. Psychol. Assn. Republican. E-mail: Cfollingstad@hotmail.com.

FOLMSBEE, PATRICIA HURLEY, reading and language arts consultant; b. Malden, Mass., Jan. 13, 1939; d. Patrick Francis and Maura Eileen (Earls) Hurley; m. Calvin Coolidge Folmsbee, June 29, 1968; 1 child, John Stephen. AB, Albertus Magnus Coll., 1960; MEd, U. Mass., 1962, postgrad., 1969; cert. in reading and lang. arts, Ctrl. Conn. State U., 1974. Cert. reading and lang. arts cons. Tchr. Chicopee (Mass.) Bd. Edn., 1960-62, 64-69, Air Force Deps. Sch., Toul-Rosieres, France, 1962-64; reading and lang. arts cons. East Windsor (Conn.) Bd. of Edn., 1970-95, English ESL coord., 1990-96, lead tchr. reading & lang. arts, 1995-96; retired. Town meeting mem. Town of So. Hadley Mass., 1961-67; treas. Enfield (Conn.) Cultural Arts Commn., 1989-99; reading edn. del. to China Citizen Amb. Program of People to People Internat., 1993. Mem. NEA, Conn. Edn. Assn., Internat. Reading Assn., Conn. Assn. Reading Rsch. Democrat. Avocations: world traveler, skiing, classical music, theatre, reading. Home: 9 Martin Ter Enfield CT 06082-4528

FOLSE, DEAN SYDNEY, retired pathologist; b. Kansas City, Mo., Dec. 19, 1921; s. Charles D. and Belle S. (Stewart) F.; m. Jean D. DeMasters, June 8, 1947. BS, DVM, Tex. A&M U., 1945; MS, Kans. State U., 1946; PhD, U. Tex. Med. Br., 1970, postgrad., 1969-91. From asst. to assoc. prof. Auburn (Ala.) U., 1948-52; assoc. prof. Kans. State U., Manhattan, 1952-66; pathologist Atomic Energy Commn., Vienna, 1966-69; pathologist, prof. emeritus U. Tex. Med. Br., Galveston, 1969—91. U.S. rep. to internat. food irradiation project U.S.-Atomic Energy Commn., Vienna, 1966-69; cons. Fla. Inst. Tech., Melbourne, 1979-81, Internat. Atomic Energy Agy., Budapest, Hungary, 1971, Vienna, 1970. Contbr. articles to profl. jours. Mem. Internat. Acad. Pathology (hon.), AAAS, Am. Vet. Medicine Assn. (hon.), Internat. Soc. Lymphologists, Am. Assn. Lab. Animal Sci. (hon.), Am. Assn. Pathologists, Sigma Xi, Masons, York Rite, Scottish Rite, Shriners. Avocation: stamp collecting. Home: 4302 Caduceus Pl Galveston TX 77550-8509

FOLSOM, LOWELL EDWIN, language educator; b. Pitts., Sept. 30, 1947; s. Lowell Edwin and Helen Magdalene (Roeper) Folsom; m. Patricia Ann Jackson, Aug. 30, 1969; 1 child, Benjamin Bradford. BA, Ohio Wesleyan U., 1969; MA, U. Rochester, 1972, PhD, 1976. Chmn. English dept. Lancaster (Ohio) H.S., 1969-70, 71-72; instr. Eastman Sch. Music, Rochester, NY, 1974-75; vis. asst. prof. SUNY, Geneseo, 1975-76; asst. prof. U. Iowa, Iowa City, 1976-82, assoc. prof., 1982-87, prof., 1987—, chair English dept., 1991-95, F. Wendell Miller disting. prof., 1997—2002, Carver prof., 2002—. Cons. Am. Coll. Testing Co., Iowa City, 1980—, Nat. Assessment Ednl. Progress, Denver, 1980—84; dir. Walt Whitman Centennial Conf., Iowa City, 1992, Walt Whitman Conf., Beijing, 2000; Fulbright sr. prof. U. Dortmund, Germany, 1996. Author: Walt Whitman's Native Representations, 1994 (Choice Best Acad. Book, 1995); editor: Walt Whitman: The Centennial Essays, 1994, Walt Whitman: The Measure of His Song, 1981 (Choice Best Acad. Book, 1982), rev. edit., 1998 (Ind. Publisher Book award, 1999), Walt Whitman and the World, 1995, (CD-ROM) Walt Whitman, 1997 (Choice Best Acad. Book, 1998), Walt Whitman Quar. Rev., 1983—, Whitman East and West, 2002; co-dir.: Walt Whitman Hypertext Archive, 1997—; editl. bd. Walt Whitman Encyclopedia, 1994—98, PMLA, 1999—2002, Profession, 2002—. Named Disting. Scholar, U. Rochester, 1995; recipient Rsch. award, NEH, 1991—94, Collaborative Rsch. award, 2000—, Faculty Excellence award, Iowa Bd. Regents, 1996. Mem.: MLA, Whitman Scholars Assn. (dir. 1992—), Am. Studies Assn., Am. Lit. Assn. Home: 739 Clark St Iowa City IA 52240-5640 Office: Univ Iowa Dept English 308 EPB Iowa City IA 52242 E-mail: ed-folsom@uiowa.edu.

FOLSOM, ROGER LEE, healthcare administrator; b. Hahira, Ga., May 17, 1952; s. Jesse Lee and Virginia (LeGette) F. BS in Biology, Valdosta (Ga.) State U., 1975; postgrad., U. Ga., 1975. From radiol. technologist to adminstrv. asst. Smith Hosp., Inc., Hahira, 1971-78; pharm. rep. The Upjohn Co., Dublin, Ga., 1979-85; cmty. rels. rep. Am. Med. Internat., Dublin, Ga., 1985-86; dir. mktg., pub. rels. Parkside Med. Svcs. Corp., Dublin, 1986-88, corp. mktg. dir. and pub. rels. S.E., 1988-94; owner, CEO Med1st Healthcare, Dublin, 1995—. Mem. adv. bd. Ga. Coop. Health Edn. Program, Dublin, 1987, pres., bd. dirs., 1992—95; apptd. to environ. adv. coun. State of Ga., 2001—; apptd. vice chair Govs. Environ. Adv. Coun., Ga.; chmn., Ga., 2003—. Friends of the Libr. Dublin, 1983—; coach Dublin Recreation Dept., 1986—, mem. adv. bd., 1986—; chmn. planning and devel. com. Laurens 2000; adminstrv. bd. Pine Forest United Meth. Ch., Dublin, fin. com.; mem. bd. dir. Ga. C. of C., mem. govtl. affairs com.; bd. dirs. Am. Heart Assn., Dublin, pres., 1989—90, chmn. bus. industry com.; bd. dirs. Ga. Assn. Med. Svcs., 1998—. Mem. Acad. Hosp. Mktg., Pub. Rels. and Planning/Am. Mktg. Assn., Dublin-Laurens C. of C. (charter leadership class 1989, mem. alumni com. 1990, bd. dirs. 1990, v.p. 1992, v.p. cmty. devel. 1992-93, pres. 1996—, chmn. bd. 1997-98, chmn. govtl. affairs com. 1999-2000), Ga. C. of C. (mem. govtl. affairs com.), Rotary (fund-raising chmn. Dublin 1986, bd. dirs. 1990-94, pres. Dublin club 1993-94, found. com. dist. 6920 gov.'s group rep., 1996—, lt. gov. 1997—), Dublin Country Club (bd. dirs., v.p. 1995—, pres. 1997). Democrat. Avocations: tennis, nature photography, reading, fly-fishing. Home: 506 Brookwood Dr PO Box 972 Dublin GA 31040-0972 Office: Med1st Healthcare 1204 Hillcrest Pkwy Dublin GA 31021 E-mail: med1st@NLAmerica.com.

FOLSOM, VIRGINIA JEAN, music educator; b. Oakland, Calif., Mar. 26, 1944; d. John Dixon Vincent and Marjorie Estelle Toothaker; d. Virginia J. Hansen; m. Robert Bruce Folsom, Oct. 19, 1970; children: Paul Dixon, Colleen Marie, Katherine Anne. BFA cum laude, U. Utah, 1973. Piano recitalist, 1960—; tchr. music, 1968—; lectr. music, 1972—; instr. piano U. Utah, Salt Lake City, 1982-83. Vol. Utah Pub. Schs., Salt Lake City, 1970-98. Mem. Music Tchrs. Nat. Assn. (tchr. v.p., Tchr.'s Enrichment grantee 2000), United Fedn. Music Clubs (chpt. treas.), Mu Phi Epsilon. Democrat. Mem. Lds Ch. Avocations: music, reading, cooking. E-mail: gfols@yahoo.com.

FOLTER, ROLAND, book historian, rare books company executive, bibliographer; b. Fulda, Germany, May 27, 1943; s. Heinz and Annemie (Bennewitz) F.; m. Siegrun Heinecke, Aug. 28, 1967 (dec. 1988); m. Mary Ann Kraus, Apr. 29, 1989; 1 child, Elizabeth. MA, Brown U., 1967, PhD, 1969. Rare books cataloger Yale U., New Haven, Conn., 1966-68; prof. U. Ill., Urbana, 1969-77; dir. H.P. Kraus Rare Books, N.Y.C., 1977—. Jury Internat. League Antiquarian Booksellers Prize for Bibliography. Author: Deutsche Dichterbibliotheken, 1975, The Gutenberg Bible in the antiquarian book trade, 1999; co-author: Bibliography: Its History, 1984; contbr. to ency. and articles to profl. jours. Violinist Frankfurt Youth Symphony Orchestra, Germany, 1960—65. Fellow Brown U., 1968, Faculty fellow U. Ill., 1970-75. Fellow Pierpont Morgan Libr.; mem. Bibliog. Soc. Am. (coun. 1982-90), N.Y. Philharm. Soc., Assn. Internat. de Bibliophilie, Maximilian Gesellschaft, Gesellschaft der Bibliophilen, Antiquarian Booksellers Assn. Am., Old Book Table (pres. 1995-97), Yale Libr. Assocs., Princeton Club. Avocations: violin, chamber music, book collecting, mountaineering. Office: H P Kraus Rare Books 16 E 46th St New York NY 10017-2404 E-mail: rolandfolter@hpkraus.com.

FOLTINY, STEPHEN VINCENT, special education educator; b. Syracuse, N.Y., Feb. 1, 1952; s. Stephen and Ilona T. (Kovacs) F. BA, Rutgers U., 1974; MA, Rider Coll., 1982; EdS, Rider U., 2002. Tchr. Princeton (N.J.) Child Devel. Inst., 1986-87; assoc. teaching parent devel. disabilities div. State of N.J. Human Svcs., Trenton, 1988-91; trainer Mercer County (N.J.) Assn. Retarded Citizens, 1991; tchr., job coach EDEN W.E.R.C., Montgomery Twp., N.J., 1991—; behavioral cons. N.J. Ctr. Outreach and Svcs. for Autism Cmty., Trenton, N.J., 1992. Assoc. teaching parent divsn. Youth and Family Svcs., Autism unit, State of N.J., 1988-91; respite cons. New Horizons in Autism, Cranbury, N.J., 1997-; intern presch. program Mercer County Sp; Sch. Dist., 1999; intern Ctr. for Innovative Family Achievement, 2001. Recipient N.J. State scholarship, 1970-74. Mem. ACA, Nat. Tchg. Family Assn. (cert.), Coun. Exceptional Children, Coun. Children with Behavioral Disorders, N.J. Assn. for Persons in Supported Employment, United Chess Fedn. (cert. chess coach 1998). Avocations: coaching, sports, reading, stamp and coin collecting.

FOLTZ, ELDON LEORY, neurosurgeon, educator; b. Ft. Collins, Colo., Mar. 28, 1919; s. Leroy Stwart and Emily Louise (Proctor) F.; m. Catherine Churchill Crosby, Oct. 18, 1943; children: Sally J., James. S., Janis A., Suzanne E., Patricia L. BS with honors, Mich. State U., 1941; MD, U. Mich, 1943. Diplomate Am. Bd. Neurol. Surgery. Intern U. Mich. Hosp., Ann Arbor, 1943-44, asst. resident surgery, 1946-47; neurosurg. resident Dartmouth Coll. Medicine, Hanover, N.H., 1947-49, U. Louisville, Ky., 1949-50; instr. neurosurgery U. Wash., Seattle, 1950-53, asst. prof. neurosurgery, 1953-58, assoc. prof. neurosurgery, 1958—64, prof. neurosurgery, 1964-69; prof., chmn. neurosurg. dept. U. Calif., Irvine, 1969-81, prof. neurosurgery, 1981-89, prof. emeritus, 1989—. Contbr. over 130 articles to profl. jours. Pres. and other offices Irvine Cove Cmty. Assn., 1994—. Lt. MC USN, 1944-46. NIMH postdoctoral fellow, 1950-51; Markle Med. Sci. scholar, Markle Found., N.Y.C., 1954-59; recipient Outstanding Alumnus award Mich. State U., 1980. Mem. Capistrano Bay Yacht Club. Avocation: competitive sailboat racing. Home: 2480 Monaco Dr Laguna Beach CA 92651-1007 E-mail: eldoulfoltzmd@aol.com.

FOLTZ, RODGER LOWELL, chemistry educator, mass spectroscopist; b. Milw., Feb. 10, 1934; s. Ross Milton and Ida Louise (Campbell) F.; m. Ruth Lynch Bilbe, June 9, 1956; children: Richard C., Camilla M. BS, MIT, 1956; PhD, U. Wis., 1961. Research chemist Battelle Meml. Inst., Columbus, Ohio, 1961-76, sr. research leader, 1976-79; adj. prof. pharmacy Ohio State U., 1972-76, adj. assoc. prof. pharmacology, 1976-79; assoc. dir. Center for Human Toxicology, U. Utah, Salt Lake City, 1979—; rsch. assoc. prof. dept. pharmacology and toxicology U. Utah, Salt Lake City, 1980-85, rsch. prof. pharmacology/toxicology dept., 1985—; pres. CHT, Inc., 1985-87; exec. v.p., lab. dir. N.W. Toxicology Inc., 1987-94; lab dir. Northwest Bioanalytical, 1994—99; tech. dir. Tandem Labs., 2000—. Contbr. articles to profl. jours.; editl. adv. bd. Biomed. Mass Spectrometry, 1979-87, 90-95. Pres. N.W. Area Human Relations Council, Columbus, 1968-70; deacon First Congregational Ch., 1971-75; trustee Denison U. Research Found., 1977-79. Mem. Am. Chem. Soc. (chmn.-elect Columbus chpt. 1978, award Columbus chpt. 1977), Am. Soc. Mass Spectrometry (chmn. nominating com. 1980, 82, bd. dirs. 1988-90), Calif. Assn. Toxicologists (bd. dirs. 1990-91, v.p. 1994, pres. 1995-96), Am. Acad. Forensic Scis. (Alexander O. Gettler award 2000), Am. Assn. Pharm. Scientists. Home: 2080 Belaire Dr Salt Lake City UT 84109-1409 also: NWT Inc 1141 E 3900 S Salt Lake City UT 84124-1215 E-mail: rodgerf@aol.com.

FOLZ, CAROL ANN, financial analyst; b. Cedar Rapids, Iowa, Dec. 28, 1951; D. Glenn Frederick and Ruth Frances (McIntosh) Rullman; m. Donald Harold McElderry, Oct. 3, 1970 (div. 1981); m. David Charles Folz, Mar. 19, 1983. AA, AS in Library Svcs., St. Louis Community Coll., 1973; BSBA, U. Mo., St. Louis, 1980. Libr. asst. Bloomfield (Iowa) Pub. Libr., 1968-70, Ferguson (Mo.) Pub. Libr., 1972-77; payroll clk. U. Mo., St. Louis, 1977-79, sr. sec., 1979-80, acct., 1980-82, sr. acct., 1982, sr. fiscal analyst, 1982-1989; payroll analyst Blue Cross and Blue Shield of Mo., St. Louis, 1990-91, sr. payroll acct., 1991; acct. Harris-Stowe State Coll., St. Louis, 1996-98, Accountemps, St. Louis, 1998; benefits specialist May Dept. Stores Co., St. Louis, 1998—. Methodist. Avocations: genealogy, music, reading, sports, needlework, crafts. Office: 611 Olive St Saint Louis MO 63101-1721 E-mail: cfolz21464@aol.com., carol_folz@may-co.com.

FOLZ, KATHLEEN LOUISE, elementary education educator; b. Chgo. d. Roman Louis and Dorothy Irene (Krueger) Salik; m. Thomas F. Folz. BS in Edn., Loyola U., Chgo., 1971; MS, St. Xavier U., 1997. Elem. tchr. St. Veronica Sch., Chgo., 1971-73, St. Robert Bellarmine Sch., Chgo., 1973-79; substitute tchr. St. Mary's Sch., Des Plaines, Ill., 1979-80, kindergarten and presch. tchr., 1980-86; kindergarten tchr. South Elem. Sch., Franklin Park, Ill., 1986-92, head tchr., 1989-90, tchr., 1992-93, 1992-93, tchr. kindergarten, 1993-97; tchr. North Elem. Sch., Franklin Park, 1997—. Master tchr. Archdiocese of Chgo., 1982-86. Creator/tchr. kindergarten program, 1975, perceptual-motor program, 1976-86; sold 2 ideas (Spl. Spiders and Little Sprouts to The Mailbox mag., 1995), Plant a Little Flower, 1997, others.

FOMBY, THOMAS BLAKE, economist, educator, consultant, researcher; b. Ashdown, Ark., July 5, 1947; s. Thomas Earl and Orpha Lee (Blake) F.; m. Nancy Ann May, Aug. 24, 1969; children: Elizabeth, Blake. BA in Math., Hendrix Coll., 1969; MA in Econs., U. Mo., 1973, PhD in Econs., 1975. Computer programmer Med. Ctr. U. Ark., Little Rock, 1969-71; teaching, rsch. asst. U. Mo., Columbia, 1971-75; asst. prof. dept. econs. So. Meth. U., Dallas, 1975-79, assoc. prof. dept. econs., 1979—2000, prof. dept. econs., 2000—, chmn. dept. econs., 1991-94; rsch. assoc., cons. Fed. Res. Bank Dallas, 1982—. Cons. Tex. Instruments, 1988—, Nations Bank, 1990—, Purolated Courier, 1980—, and others. Co-author: Advanced Econometric Methods, 1984; co-editor: Studies in the Economics of Uncertainty, 1989 (series) Advances in Econometrics, 1986-90, 93—; contbr. articles to profl. jours. Chair various coms. Lakewood United Meth. Ch., Dallas, 1982—, chair adminstrv. coun., 1989-90, 90-91, co-founder Devel. Learning Ctr., 1986. Mem. Am. Econ. Assn., Am. Statis. Assn., Econometric Soc. Avocations: reading, coaching youth sports, tennis, golf, hiking. Office: So Meth U Dept Econs Umphrey Lee Bldg Dallas TX 75275-0001

FOMEL, SERGEY, geophysicist; b. Novosibirsk, Russia, Jan. 3, 1968; PhD, Stanford U., 2000. Contbr. articles to profl. jours. Mem.: Soc. of Exploration Geophysicists (J. Clarence Karcher award for numerous contributions to seismology 2001). Office: University of Tex at Austin University Station Box X Austin TX 78713-8924 E-mail: sergey.fomel@beg.utexas.edu.

FOMON, SAMUEL JOSEPH, physician, educator; b. Chgo., Mar. 9, 1923; s. Samuel and Isabel (Sherman) F.; m. Betty Lorraine Freeman, Aug. 20, 1948 (div. Apr. 1978); children: Elizabeth Ann Fomon Seiberling, Kathleen Lenore Fomon Anderson, David Bruce, Christopher, Mary Susan Fomon; m. Louise G. Thomson, June 27, 1986. AB cum laude, Harvard U., 1945; MD, U. Pa., 1947; D (hons.), U. Catolica de Cordoba, Argentina, 1974. Diplomate Am. Bd. Pediatrics, Am. Bd. Nutrition. Intern Queen's Gen. Hosp., Jamaica, N.Y., 1947-48; resident Children's Hosp., Phila., 1948-50; research fellow Cin. Children's Hosp. Research Found., 1950-52; asst. prof. pediatrics U. Iowa, Iowa City, 1954-58, assoc. prof., 1958-61, prof., 1961-93, prof. emeritus, 1993—. Adj. prof. pediat. Baylor Med. Coll., Houston, 2002—; rev. com. child health and human devel. program project NIH, 1966-69, nutrition study sect., 1978-81; select com. GRAS-Generally Recognized as Safe substances Life Sci. Rsch. Office, 1974-80; expert to US Food and Agrl. Orgn. of UN and WHO, 2003—, mem. working group on infant formulas export to U.S., 2003. Author: Infant Nutrition, 1st edit., 1967, 2d edit., 1974, Nutrition of Normal Infants, 1993. Recipient Career Devel. award NIH, 1962-67, Rosen von Rosenstein award Swedish Pediatric Soc., 1975, McCollum award Am. Soc. Clin. Nutrition, 1979, F. Cuenca Villoro Found. award, Zaragosa, Spain, 1981, Commr.'s spl. citation FDA, 1984, Nutricia Found. award, Rotterdam, The Netherlands, 1991, Bristol-Myers Squibb/Mead Johnson award, 1992, Harry Schwachman award N.Am. Soc. Pediatric Gastroenterology and Nutrition, 1992, A.O. Atwater 2000 Lectureship, Spl. award L.Am. Nutrition Soc., 2000. Fellow AAAS; mem. Am. Inst. Nutrition (pres. 1989-90, fellow 1989, Conrad A. Elvehjem award 1990), Am. Acad. Pediatrics (chmn. com. nutrition 1960-63, Borden award 1956), Am. Soc. Clin. Nutrition (pres. 1981-82), Fedn. Am. Socs. Exptl. Biology, Midwest Soc. Pediat. Rsch. (pres. 1963-64, Founder's award 1986), Am. Dietetic Assn. (hon.), El Colegio de Pediat. de Jalisco (hon.). E-mail: samfomon@aol.com.

FONCILLAS, IGNACIO, lawyer; BA in Polit. Theory, U. Chgo., 1989, JD with honors, 1992. Atty. Gibson, Dunn & Crutcher LLP, N.Y.C., 1993—2000, ptnr., co-head Latin Am. practice, 2000—. Pro bono legal contbr. Sabera Found.; bd. patranos Museo del Prado, Madrid. Named one of 40 Under 40, Crain's N.Y. Bus., 2003. Mem.: Spain-US C. of C. (bd. dirs.). Office: 200 Park Ave 47th Fl New York NY 10166-0193 Office Fax: 212-351-5223. Business E-Mail: ifoncillas@gibsondunn.com.*

FONDA, PETER, actor, director, producer; b. N.Y.C., Feb. 23, 1939; s. Henry and Frances (Seymour) F.; m. Susan Brewer (div. Apr. 1974); 2 children. Student, U. Omaha. Film appearances include Tammy and The Doctor, 1963, The Victors, 1963, Lilith, 1964, The Young Lovers, 1964, The Trip, 1967, The Wild Angels, 1966, The Last Movie, 1971, Two People, 1973, Dirty Mary, Crazy Harry, 1974, Race With The Devil, 1975, 92 in the Shade, 1975, Killer Force, 1975, Fighting Mad, 1976, Futureworld, 1976, Outlaw Blues, 1977, High Ballin', 1978, Wanda Nevada, 1979, Open Season, Smokey and the Bandit II, 1980, Split Image, 1982, Certain Fury, 1985, Dead Fall, 1993, Nadja, 1994, Love and a .45, 1994, Painted Hero, 1996, Grace of My Heart (voice), 1996, Escape From L.A., 1996, Idaho Transfer, Spasm, 1983, Fatal Mission, 1990, The Tempest, 1998, The Passion of Ayn Rand, 1999, The Limey, 1999, Keeping Time, 1999, South of Heaven, West of Hell, 2000, Thomas and the Magic Railroad, 2000, Second Skin, 2001, Wooly Boys, 2001, The Laramie Project, 2002, The Maldonado Miracle, 2003; dir., actor in The Hired Hand, 1971, Two People, 1973; writer, co-producer, actor movie Easy Rider, 1969; TV movie appearances include The Hostage Tower, 1980, A Reason To Live, Don't Look Back, 1996, Ulee's Gold, 1997(won Golden Globe Award, Best Actor), Me and Will, 1998, South of Heaven West of Hell, 1999, The Passion of Ayn Rand, 1999, The Limey, 1999, Keeping Time, 1999; author Don't Tell Dad, 1998.*

FONDAHL, JOHN WALKER, civil engineering educator; b. Washington, Nov. 4, 1924; s. John Edmund and Mary (DeCourcy) F.; m. Doris Jane Plishker, Mar. 2, 1946; children: Lauren Valerie, Gail Andrea, Meredith Victoria, Dorian Beth. BS, Thayer Sch. Engring., Dartmouth, 1947, MSCE, 1948. Instr., then asst. prof. U. Hawaii, 1948-51; constrn. engr. Winston Bros. Co., Mpls., 1951-52; project engr. Nimbus Dam and Powerplant project, Sacramento, 1952-55; mem. faculty Stanford U., 1955—, prof. civil engring., 1966-90, Charles H. Leavell prof. civil engring., 1977-90, prof. emeritus, 1990—. Author reports in field. Served with USMCR, 1943-46. Recipient Golden Beaver award Heavy Constrn. Industry, 1976 Fellow ASCE (Constrn. Mgmt. award 1977, Peurifoy Constrn. Rsch. award 1990), Project Mgmt. Inst. (hon. life, Fellow award 1981); mem. Nat. Acad. Engring., Nat. Acad. Constrn., Phi Beta Kappa. Achievements include patent in field. Home and Office: 12810 Viscaino Rd Los Altos Hills CA 94022-2520 E-mail: fondahlj@aol.com.

FONDAW, RONALD EDWARD, artist, educator; b. Paducah, Ky., Apr. 25, 1954; s. Lex Alan and Rose Mary (Holley) Kilgore; m. Lynn S. Shepard, Oct. 7, 1987; children: Andrea Rose, Wyler S. BFA, Memphis Coll. Art, 1976; MFA, U. Ill., 1978. Instr. Ohio U., Athens, 1978; assoc. prof. art U. Miami, Coral Gables, Fla., 1978-95, prof., 1997—; prof. art Washington U., St. Louis, 1995—. Lectr., presenter workshops Ohio State U., Chgo. Art Inst., Tokyo U. Fine Art, Chautauqua Sch. Art. Exhbns. nat. and internat.; several public art commissions. Ford Found. fellow, 1977, Fla. Arts Coun. fellow, 1981, Guggen-

heim fellow, 1985, Pollack/Krasner fellow, 1997-98; grantee NEA, 1988; Kransberg award St. Louis Art Mus., 1998. Home: 7345 Elm Ave Saint Louis MO 63143-3216 Office: Wash U 721 Kingsland Ave Saint Louis MO 63130-3107 E-mail: refondaw@art.wustl.edu.

FONDURULIA, JULIE A. computer scientist; b. Gardner, Mass., Sept. 24, 1973; d. Michael and Janet L. Fondurulia. BS in Math., Worcester (Mass.) State Coll., 1996; MS in Applied Sci., Worcester (Mass.) Polytechnic Inst., 1999. Database mgr. Ctr. for Health Policy U. Mass. Med. Sch., Worcester, Mass., 1999—2001; sr. sys. programmer Mass. Divsn. Med. Assistance, Boston, 2001—. Mem.: Am. Math. Soc., Acad. Health Scis. Rsch. and Health Policy, Am. Statis. Assn. Avocations: needlepoint, reading, walking. Home: 86 West Main St Westminster MA 01473 Office: Divsn of Medical Assistance DMA IS 222 Maple Ave Chang Bldg Shrewsbury MA 01545 E-mail: j.a.fondurulia@verizon.net.

FONER, ERIC, historian, educator; b. N.Y.C., Feb. 7, 1943; s. Jack D. and Liza F.; m. Lynn Garafola, May 1, 1980. BA, Columbia U., 1963, PhD, 1969; BA, Oxford (Eng.) U., 1965. Prof. history City Coll., CUNY, N.Y.C., 1973-82, Columbia U., N.Y.C., 1982—; Pitt prof. Am. history and instns. Cambridge (Eng.) U., 1980-81. Harmsworth prof. Am. history Oxford (Eng.) U., 1993-94. Author: Free Soil, Free Labor, Free Men, 1970, Tom Paine and Revolutionary America, 1976, Politics and Ideology in the Age of the Civil War, 1980, Nothing But Freedom, 1983, Reconstruction: America's Unfinished Revolution, 1988, Readers' Encyclopedia of American History, 1991, Freedom's Lawmakers, 1993, The Story of American Freedom, 1998, Who Owns History?, 2002, Give Me Liberty!: An American History, 2004; editor: The New American History, 1990, The Reader's Companion to American History, 1991. Recipient Bancroft prize Columbia U., 1989, L.A. Times Book award, 1989, Parkman prize Soc. Am. Historians, 1989, Owsley prize So. Hist. Assn., 1989, Lit. Lion prize N.Y. Pub. Libr., 1994; named Scholar of Yr., N.Y. Coun. for the Humanities, 1995; fellow ACLS, 1972-73, NEH, 1983-84, Guggenheim fellow, 1974-76. Mem. Am. Hist. Assn. (pres. 2000), Orgn. Am. Historians (Avery O. Craven prize 1989, pres. 1993-94), Am. Antiquarian Soc., Am. Acad. Arts and Scis., British Acad. Home: 606 W 116th St New York NY 10027-7011 E-mail: ef17@columbia.edu.

FONER, NANCY, anthropologist, educator; d. Moe and Anne (Berman) F.; m. Peter Swerdloff; 1 child, Alexis. BA, Brandeis U., 1966; PhD, U. Chgo., 1971. Asst. prof. anthropology CUNY, York, 1970-73, SUNY, Purchase, 1973-77, assoc. prof., 1977-85, prof., 1985—. Author: Status & Power in Rural Jamaica, 1973, Jamaica Farewell, 1978, Ages in Conflict, 1984, New Immigrants in New York, 1987, revised edit., 2001, The Caregiving Dilemma, 1994, From Ellis Island to JFK, 2000, Immigration Research for a New Century, 2000, Islands in the City, 2001. Fellow Am. Anthrop. Assn. Office: SUNY Social Sci Divsn Purchase NY 10577 E-mail: nancy.foner@purchase.edu.

FONER, SIMON, research physicist; b. Pitts., Aug. 13, 1925; s. Newton F. Foner BS, Carnegie-Mellon U., 1947, MS, 1948, DSc, 1952. Research physicist Carnegie-Mellon U., Pitts., 1952-53; staff physicist Lincoln Lab. MIT, Lexington, 1953-61, Francis Bitter Nat. Magnet Lab., MIT, Cambridge, 1961-63, project leader, 1963-77, chief scientist, head research div., 1977—, assoc. dir., 1988-95; sr. rsch. scientist dept. physics MIT, Cambridge, 1982-95. Dir. NATO Advanced Study Insts. in Europe, 1970, 73, 76, 80; chmn. Internat. Cryogenic Materials conf., 1983-85; bd. dirs. Applied Superconductivity Conf., Inc., 1982-88, 92-94, hon. program chmn., 1992-94; bd. dirs. Cryogenic Engring. Conf., 1983-85; mem. Internat. Cryogenics Materials Conf., 1983-92; cons. editor Rev. of Sci. Instruments, 1979—; vis. scientist Francis Bitter Magnet Lab, MIT, 1995—. Editor 4 books in magnetism, superconductivity and applications; contbr. articles to profl. jours.; patentee magnetometers, superconducting materials. Served with USN, 1944-46. Named Disting. lectr. for Magnetic Soc. IEEE, 1982-83. Fellow AAAS, IEEE (3d Millennium medal 2000), Am. Phys. Soc. (exec. com. coun. 1983, chmn. publs. com. 1986-87, mem.-at-large exec. com. condensed matter physics div. 1970-72, chmn. 1978-81, councillor 1982-86, exec. com. magnetics group 1997, chair-elect 1999, chair 2000, Joseph F. Keithley award). Office: Francis Bitter Magnet Lab MIT 77 Massachusetts Ave Cambridge MA 02139-3529

FONG, BERNARD W.D. physician, educator; b. Honolulu, May 18, 1926; s. Leonard K. and Francis C. Fong; m. Roberta Wat, Aug. 14, 1950; children: Phyllis K., Jeffrey S., Camille K., Allison K. BS, Bucknell U., 1948; MD, Jefferson Med. Coll., 1952. Diplomate Am. Bd. Internal Medicine. Intern Germantown Hosp., Phila., 1952-53, chief med. resident, 1953-55; teaching fellow cardiology Jefferson Med. Coll. Hosp., Phila., 1955-56; attending physician Queen's Med. Ctr., Honolulu, 1956—2002, St. Francis Hosp., Honolulu, 1956-89; clin. prof. medicine U. Hawaii, Honolulu, 1982—; med. dir. medicare part B Aetna Ins. Co., Hawaii, Guam, 1988-97, Transamerica Occidental Life Ins. Co., Hawaii and Guam, 1997-2000, Noridian Adminstrv. Svcs., Hawaii and Guam, 2000—. Adv. coun. Nat. Heart, Lung and Blood Inst., NIH, Bethesda, Md., 1976-80, chmn. 3d forum on cardiovascular risk factors, 1985; adv. com. cardiovascular risk factors in minorities NIH, 1976-89; pres. Triple C, 1996-2001. Pres. Hawaii Heart Assn., Honolulu, 1962-63; bd. dirs. Am. Heart. Assn., N.Y.C., 1963-66; pres. Chung Shan Assn., Honolulu, 1969-70, United Chinese Soc. Hawaii, Honolulu, 1973-74; 1st v.p. Wong Leong Doo Benevolent Soc., Honolulu, 1973—; 1st v.p. Ocean View Cemetery, Honolulu, 1973—. With USNR, 1944-46, PTO. Fellow ACP (bd. govs. 1972-76, inaugural laureate internal medicine Hawaii chpt. 1986), Am. Coll. Cardiology (bd. govs. 1992-96, chairperson 1995-96, trustee 1997-2002), Am. Coll. Chest Physicians; mem. Am. Soc. Internal Medicine (pres. Hawaii chpt. 1980-82). Republican. Roman Catholic. Home: 97 Dowsett Ave Honolulu HI 96817-1107 Office: 1380 Lusitana St Ste 706 Honolulu HI 96813-2443 E-mail: Bernardfong@email.msn.com.

FONG, HIRAM LEONG, former senator; b. Honolulu, Oct. 15, 1906; s. Lum Fong and Chai Ha Lum; m. Ellyn Lo; children, Hiram, Rodney, Merie-Ellen Fong Gushi, Marvin-Allan (twins). AB with honors, U. Hawaii, 1930, LLD, 1953; JD, Harvard U., 1935; LLD, Tufts U., 1960, Lafayette Coll., 1960, Lynchburg Coll., 1970, Lincoln U., 1971, U. Guam, 1974, St. John's U., 1975, Calif. Western Sch. Law, 1976, Tung Wu (Soochow) U., Taiwan, 1978, China Acad., 1978; LHD, L.I. U., 1968. With supply dept. Pearl Harbor Navy Yard, 1924-27; chief clk. Suburban Water System, 1930-32; dep. atty. City and County of Honolulu, 1935-38; founder, ptnr. law firm Fong, Miho, Choy & Robinson, until 1959; founder, chmn. bd. emeritus Finance Factors, Grand Pacific Life Ins. Co.; founder, chmn bd. Finance Investment Co., Market City, Ltd., Fin. Enterprises Ltd.; pres. Ocean View Cemetery, Ltd.; owner, operator Sen. Fong's Plantation and Gardens, Honolulu. Dir. numerous firms, Honolulu; hon. cons. China Airlines. Mem. Hawaii Legislature, 1938-54, speaker, 1948-54; mem. U.S. Senate, 1959-77, Post Office and Civil Service Com., Judiciary Com., Appropriations Com., Spl. Com. on Aging; U.S. del. 150th Anniversary Argentine Independence, Buenos Aires, 1960, 55th Interparliamentary Union (World) Conf., 1966, Ditchley Found. Conf., 1967, U.S.-Can. Inter-Parliamentary Union Conf., 1961, 65, 67, 68, Mex.-U.S. Inter-Parliamentary Conf., 1968, World Interparliamentary Union, Tokyo, 1974; mem. Commn. on Revision Fed. Ct. Appellate System, 1975—; Active in civic and service orgns.; v.p. Territorial Constl. Conv., 1950; del. Rep. Nat. Conv., 1952, 56, 60, 64, 68, 72; founder, chmn. bd. Fin. Factors Found.; founder, pres. Hiram & Ellyn Fong Found.; founder, pres., chmn. bd. Market City Found.; hon. co-chmn. McKinley High Sch. Found., 1989; bd. visitors U.S. Mil. Acad., 1971—, U.S. Naval Acad., 1974—. Served from 1st lt. to maj. USAAF, 1942-44; ret. col. USAF Res. Recipient award NCCJ, 1960, Meritorious Svc. citation Nat. Assn. Ret. Civil Employees, 1963, Horatio Alger award, 1970, citation for outstanding svc. Japanese Am. Citizens League, 1970, award Am. Acad. Achievement, 1971, Outstanding Svc. award Orgn. Chinese Ams., 1973, award Nat. Soc. Daus. Founders and Patriots Am., 1974, cert. Pacific Asian World, 1974, Citizen Among Citizens award Boys & Girls Clubs of Hawaii, 1991, Disting. Alumnus award U. Hawaii Alumni Assn., 1991, Kulia I Ka Nu'u award Pub. Schs. Hawaii Found., 1992, Dedication and Support Svc. award McKinley Found., 1995, ABOTA-Hawai'i Ha'aheo award, 1997; named to Jr. Achievement Hawaii Bus. Hall of Fame, 1995; decorated Order of Brilliant Star with Grand Cordon Republic of China, 1976, Order of Diplomatic Svc. Merit, Gwanghwan Medal Republic of Korea, 1977; Univ. of Hawaii Colls. of Arts and Scis. Hiram L. Fong Endowment in Arts and Scis., 1995; recipient nat. Outstanding Citizen Achievement award Orgn. Chinese Ams., Inc., 1996, Disting. Svc. award Orgn. Chinese Am. Women, 1999; Outstanding Chinese Citizen award United Chinese Soc., 2001, Founders Lifetime Achievement award U. Hawaii Alumni Assn., 2002; named Model Chinese Father of Yr., United Chinese Soc., 1996. Mem. Am. Legion, VFW, Lambda Alpha Internat. (Aloha chpt.), Phi Beta Kappa. Republican. Congregationalist. Home: 1102 Alewa Dr Honolulu HI 96817-1507 Fax: 808-548-3367.

FONG, PHYLLIS KAMOI, federal agency administrator, lawyer; b. Phila., Oct. 16, 1953; d. Bernard W.D. and Roberta (Wat) F.; m. Paul E. Tellier, Nov. 25, 1978. BA, Pomona Coll., 1975; JD, Vanderbilt U., 1978. Bar: Tenn. 1978, D.C. 1982. Atty. U.S. Commn. on Civil Rights, Washington, 1978-81; asst. gen. counsel Legal Svcs. Corp., Washington, 1981-83; assoc. counsel to the insp. gen. U.S. Small Bus. Admin., Washington, 1983-88, asst. insp. gen. for mgmt. and policy, 1988-94, asst. insp. gen. for mgmt. and legal counsel, 1994-99, insp. gen., 1999—. Mem. ABA, Tenn. Bar Assn., D.C. Bar Assn. Office: Small Bus Admin Off of Insp Gen 409 3rd St SW Washington DC 20416 Office Fax: 202-205-7382.

FONKALSRUD, ERIC WALTER, pediatric surgeon, educator; b. Balt., Aug. 31, 1932; s. George and Ella (Fricke) F.; m. Margaret Ann Zimmermann, June 6, 1959; children: Eric Walter Jr., Margaret Lynn, David Loren, Robert Warren. BA, U. Wash., 1953; MD, Johns Hopkins U., 1957. Diplomate Am. Bd. Surgery, Am. Bd. Thoracic Surgery, Am. Bd. Pediatric Surgery. Intern Johns Hopkins Hosp., Balt., 1957-58, asst. resident, 1958-59, U. Calif. Med. Ctr., Los Angeles, 1959-62, chief resident surgery, 1962-63, asst. prof. surgery, chief pediatric surgery, 1965-68, assoc. prof., 1968-71, prof. LA, 1971—2001, emeritus prof., 2001—, vice chmn. dept. surgery, 1981-89; resident pediatric surgery Columbus (Ohio) Childrens Hosp. and Ohio State U., 1963-65; practice medicine specializing in pediatric surgery LA, 1965—. Mem. surg. study sect. NIH; James IV surg. traveller to, Gt. Britain, 1971 Mem. editl. bd. Jour. Surg. Rsch., Archives Surgery, Am. Jour. Surgery, Annals Surgery, Surgery, Current Problems in Surgery, Jour. Pediat. Surgery, World Jour. Surgery, Japanese Jour. Surgery, Turkish Jour. Pediat. Surgery, Med. Video Jour. Surgery; contbr. over 650 articles to profl. jours., chpts. to books. Recipient Golden Apple award UCLA Sch. Medicine, 1968; John and Mary R. Markle scholar, 1963-68; named Tree Farmer of Yr. Western Wash., 1998. Fellow ACS (surg. forum com., bd. govs. 1978-84, pres. So. Calif. chpt. 1995-96, Mead Johnson award 1963), Am. Acad. Pediat. (exec. bd., chmn. surg. sect. 1986-87, Salzberg award 2000), German Assn. for Surgery (hon.), Polish Assn. Pediat. Surgery (hon.), Japanese Pediat. Surgery Assn. (hon.), John Hopkins Soc. Scholars (hon.); mem. AMA, Am. Thoracic Surg. Assn., Am. Acad. Sci., Soc. Univ. Surgeons (pres. 1976, sec. 1972-76), Calif. Med. Assn., Crohns and Celitis Found. of So. Calif. (Man of Yr. 1999), Internat. Surg. Group (treas. 1993—), Lilliputian Surg. Soc. (chmn. 1989), L.A. County Med. Assn., Am. Surg. Assn., Pan Pacific Surg. Assn., Pacific Coast Surg. Assn. (recorder 1979-85, pres. 1989), Am. Pediat. Surg. Assn. (bd. govs. 1975-78, pres. 1989), Pacific Assn. Pediat. Surgeons (pres. 1983-84, Coe medal 1998), S.W. Pediatric Soc., L.A. Pediat. Soc., Soc. for Clin. Surgery, Transplantation Soc., Pediat. Surgery Biology Club, Bay Surg. Soc., L.A. Surg. Soc. (sec. 1988-90, pres. 1991), Town Hall (L.A.), Pithotomy Club (pres. 1956 57), Sigma Xi, Alpha Omega Alpha. Methodist. Home: 428 24th St Santa Monica CA 90402-3102 Office: U Calif Med Ctr Dept Surgery Los Angeles CA 90095 E-mail: efonkalsrud@mednet.ucla.edu.

FONKEN, GERHARD JOSEPH, retired chemistry educator, academic administrator; b. Krefeld, Germany, Aug. 3, 1928; came to U.S., 1930, naturalized, 1935; s. Henry A. and Wilhelmina Katerina (von Eyser) F.; m. Carolyn Lee Stay, Dec. 20, 1952; children: David, Katherine, Steven, Karen, Eric. BS, U. Calif., Berkeley, 1954, PhD, 1957. Chemist Procter & Gamble Co., 1957-58; chemist Stanford (Calif.) Research Inst., 1958-59; instr. U. Tex., Austin, 1959-61, from asst. to assoc. prof., 1961-72, prof. chemistry, 1972-94, asso. provost, 1972-75, acting v.p. acad. affairs, 1975-76, exec. asst. to pres., 1976-79, v.p. research, 1979-80, v.p. acad. affairs and research, 1980-85, exec. v.p., provost, 1985-94; retired, 1994. Contbr. articles to chemistry jours. Served with U.S. Army, 1946-49, 50-51, Korea. Decorated Order of the Crown, Kingdom of Belgium; grantee NIH, 1961-64, Robert A. Welch Found., 1962-79. Mem. Am. Chem. Soc. Home: 6612 Lost Horizon Dr Austin TX 78759-6116

FONNER, KELLY S. educational technologist, consultant; b. Harrisburg, Pa., Nov. 22, 1961; d. Richard L. and Frances (Szivos) Fonner. BS in Spl. Edn. cum laude, Millersville (Pa.) U., 1983; MS in Ednl. Tech. summa cum laude, Johns Hopkin's U., 1988; postgrad., U. Wis., Milw., 1995—. Asst. tchr. Bucks County Easter Seal Soc., Levittown, Pa., 1983-84; instructional media technologist Easter Seal Soc., Phila., 1984-87, ednl. technologist, 1987-90; assistive technology specialist Penn Tech, Harrisburg, 1990-95. Pvt. practice tech. cons., 1985—; instr. Johns Hopkins U., 1990, U. Wis., Milw., 1996—; presenter in field; edn. cons. Instrnl. Support Sys. Pa., 1997-99. Co-author: Getting off to a Great Start, Closing the Gap, 1994, Using Family Dreams to Develop Meaningful Goals, Closing the Gap, 1995. Cen. Dauphin Edn. Assn. scholar, 1979, 96. Mem. Coun. for Exceptional Children, Internat. Soc. for Augmentative and Alternative Comm., Internat. Soc. for Tech. in Edn. Democrat. Presbyterian. Avocations: sports, gardening, drum and bugle corps. Office: U Wisc Milwaukee Dept Occpl Therapy PO Box 413 Milwaukee WI 53201-0413

FONSECA, DANIEL J. engineering educator; b. San Jose, Feb. 18, 1969; s. Jose D. Fonseca and Lilia Alvarado; m. Lucia Torres-Ugarte, July 29, 1995; children: David, Daniel. BS in Indsl. Engring., U. Ala., 1992, MS in Indsl. Engring., 1994; MS in Engring. Sci., La. State U., 1997, PhD in Engring. Sci., 1998. Prof. engring. Monterrey Inst. Tech., Mexico City, 1994; sales mgr. Kimberly Clark, San Jose, 1994-95; asst. prof. U. Ala., Tuscaloosa, 1998-99; curricular dir. Monterrey Inst. Tech., Tampico, Mex., 1999-2000; asst. prof. U. Ala., Tuscaloosa, 2000—. Internat. cons. NASA, Inverlat, Cidsa, others, 1992—. Contbr. articles to profl. jours. Recipient H. Paul Hassel Jr. award U. Ala., 1993-94. Mem. Inst. Indsl. Engrs., Am. Soc. Engring. Edn., Mallet Assembly Hon. Soc., golden Rey Nat. Honor Soc., Alpha Pi Mu, Tau Beta Pi. Home: 3914 Watermelon Rd Northport AL 35473 Office: Dept Indsl Engring U Ala Tuscaloosa AL 35487 E-mail: dfonseca@roe.eng.ua.edu.

FONSECA, JOSEPH MOJICA, JR., financial analyst, educator; b. Seattle, Wash., Sept. 27, 1951; s. Joe Mojica Fonseca Sr. and Maria Flores Torres; m. Eva Rivas, Sept. 27, 1989; children: Monica, Frank Daniel, Jason, Nicole Jolene, Joseph Mojica Jr. and Jacob Matthew (twins). AA, San Antonio (Tex.) Coll., 1979; BA in Polit. Sci. and Psychology, St. Mary's U., 1998, MA, 2002. Adminstrv. aide Senator Glenn H. Kothmann, San Antonio, 1982-89; tax and mortgage analyst Bexar County Tax Office, San Antonio, 1989-95; fed., state and county process server Daniel Rivans Jr. owner, San Antonio, 1995-97; fin. analyst CitiGroup Investment Svcs., San Antonio, 1998—. Pres. SIMCONG leg. St. Mary's U., San Antonio, 1996-97, chair coll. dems., 1995-97, 1st pres. Mem. Bexar County Dems., San Antonio, 1995—; rape crisis vol. Rape Crisis Ctr. Seattle, 1973-74; spousal abuse vol. Spousal Abuse Ctr., Phoenix, 1973-74. Decorated 3 Purple Hearts, Silver Star for valor. Mem. Am. Legion, Acad. of Polit. Sci., K.C. (chancellor 1977-79), Rho Ki. Roman Catholic. Avocations: quarter horse racing, reading, football. Home: 2510 Village Pkwy San Antonio TX 78251-2539 Office: CitiGroup 100 Citibank Dr San Antonio TX 78245

FONSECA, PETER, surgeon; b. New Bedford, Mass., Mar. 9, 1956; s. George and Isabel Fonseca; m. Mary M. Fonseca, Dec. 30, 1985; children: Lauren, Peter, Philip, Margaret, Mary, Elizabeth, John, Paul, Thomas, Matthew, Marian. BS, U. Mass., 1978; PhD, Purdue U., 1983; MD, St. Louis U., 1987. Diplomate Am. Bd. Thoracic Surgery, Am. Bd. Surgery. Resident surgeon Wright State U., Dayton, Ohio, 1987-92, Med. Coll. Wis., Milw., 1992-94; surgeon St. Louis, 1998—. Contbr. articles to profl. jours. Comdr., attending physician USN, 1994-98. Fellow ACS, Am. Coll. Chest Physicians, Soc. Thoracic Surgeons; mem. Phi Beta Kappa, Sigma Xi. Roman Catholic. Avocations: sailing, reading, model railroading. Office: 10004 Kennerly Rd Ste 345A Saint Louis MO 63128

FONSECA, RAYMOND J. dental medicine educator; Prof. oral and maxillofacial surgery Sch. Dentistry U. Mich., 1989; dean Sch. Dental Medicine, U. Pa., Phila., 1989—. Office: U Pa Sch Dental Medicine 40th & Spruce Sts Philadelphia PA 19104-6003

FONSECA, VIVIAN ANDREW, physician; b. Nov. 29, 1952; m. Sarita Fonseca; children: Adam, Neil. MBBS, Armed Forces Medical Coll., Poona, India, 1974; MD, Bombay Univ., 1978; MRCP, Royal Coll. Physicians, London, 1980. Diplomate Am. Bd. Internal Medicine, Am. Bd. Endocrinology, Metabolism and Diabetes. Internship King Edward Meml. Hosp., Bombay, 1975-76; sr. house officer internal medicine Bombay Hosp., St. George's Hosp., J.J. Hosp., Bombay, 1976-77; registrar in gen. medicine King Edward Meml. Hosp., 1977-78; rsch. fellow Indian Coun. Medical Rsch. King Edward Meml. Hosp., Bombay, 1978-79; sr. house officer rotation internal medicine Oldchurch Hosp., Romford Essex, U.K., 1979-80; registrar in medicine and diabetes Queen Elizabeth Hosp., Welwyn Garden City, U.K., 1981-82; asst. prof. medicine & Endocrinology Riyadh Univ., Saudi Arabia, 1982-83; rsch. fellow Royal Free Hosp., London, 1983-85; sr. registrar medicine, diabetes, endcrinology Royal Free Hosp, London, 1985-92; assoc. prof. medicine divsns. endocrinology, staff physician Univ. Ark., Little Rock, 1992—; prof. Dept. Endocrinology Tulane U., New Orleans, La. Dir. Univ. Hosp. Diabetes Program, Diabetes Edn. Program; mem. promotions com. U. Ark. Med. Scis.; mem. outpatient clin. parctice com. Univ. Hosp. Contbr. numerous articles to profl. jours.; book chpts. Mem., bd. dirs. Am. Diabetes Assn. Recipient Bombay Univ. scholarship, 1976, Medical Edn. award Univ. Ark., 1995, rsch. grant Ednl. Trust Fund Delhi, 1979. Mem. The Endocrine Soc., Royal Soc. Medicine, British Diabetic Assn., European Assn. Study of Diabetes, Internat. Diabetes Fedn., Am. Assn. Clinical Endocrinologists, Am. Coll. Physicians. Office: Tulane U Med Dept PO Box SL53 1430 Tulane Ave New Orleans LA 70112-2699

FONT, CECILIO RAFAEL, biology educator, physician; b. San Sebastian, PR, Sept. 25, 1947; s. Cecilio Rafael Font and Juana N. Rios; m. Mercedes GArcia Font, Nov. 24, 1977 (div. July 3, 1995); m. Elisa Maria Baez, Apr. 2, 1998; children: Rafael, César. BS, Mayagüez (PR) A&M U., 1968; MD, U. Valencia, Spain, 1977; diploma in labor medicine, Nat. Sch. Labor Medicine, Madrid, 1980; postgrad., U. PR, San Juan, 1986—89. Asst. prof. physiology Ctrl. U. Caribbean, Bayamon, PR, 1978—79; gen. practice Nat. Health Sys., Castellon, Spain, 1979—81, Bilbao, Spain, 1981—82, Valencia, Spain, 1982—86; assoc. prof. physiology San Juan Bautista Sch. Medicine, 1986; prof. biology Coll. Philosophy and Edn., Bronx, NY, 1998—99; pres. Gluark Corp., Emax Corp., 2002—. Vis. fellow in physiology U. Copenhagen, 1980, King's Coll., London, 1983, Inst. Sur La Nutrition, Paris; adj. prof. biology Mercy Coll., NY, 1994—95. Author: 4 books in field; contbr. weekly column, over 40 articles to profl. jours. Recipient Hostos prize, Regular Dem. Club, Bronx, N.Y., 2003. Democrat. Avocations: photography, jogging, wine tasting, writing, music. Mailing: Hub Station PO Box 668 Bronx NY 10455-0668 Office: Hunts Point Multisvc 754E 151 St Bronx NY 10455 Fax: 718-742-9227. E-mail: font-membrane@juno.com., averroes661@hotmail.com., ceciliofl@aol.com.

FONTAINE, BERNARD LEO, JR., small business owner; b. Holyoke, Mass., Nov. 18, 1956; s. Bernard Leo and Claire Doris (Mathey) F.; m. Susan Eileen Scalia, Apr. 7, 1962. BS, Northeastern U., Boston, 1979; MS, U. Okla., 1983-84, Cert. Am. Bd. Indsl. Hygiene, Bd. Cert. Safety Profls.; registered indsl. hygiene profl., registered bldg. air quality counselor. Indsl. hygiene tech. U.S. Dept. Labor, OSHA, Springfield, Mass., 1976-79, indsl. hygienist Hartford, Conn., 1979-83; reg. indsl. hygienist U.S. Dept. Navy, Portsmouth, N.H., 1984-85; health and safety supr. Internat. Tech. Corp., Edison, N.J., 1985-87; corp. indsl. hygienist Atlantic Mut. Cos., Madison, N.J., 1987-90; founder, chief exec. officer The Windsor Group, Inc., Spotswood, N.J., 1990 97, Windsor Consulting Group, Inc., South River, 1997—. Contbr. articles to profl. jours. Mem. Am. Indsl. Hygiene Assn., Am. Soc. Safety Engrs., Am. Conf. Govt. Indsl. Hygienists, Am. Acad. Indsl. Hygiene, Council on Occupational Hearing Conservation. Republican. Roman Catholic. Avocations: golf, tennis, boating. Office: The Windsor Consulting Group Inc Ste 100 14 Sheinfine Ave South River NJ 08882-2526 E-mail: windsgroup@aol.com.

FONTAINE, EUDORE JOSEPH, JR., artist, art historian; b. Springfield, Mass., Aug. 5, 1929; s. Eudore Joseph and Antoinette Marie (Desautels) F.; m. Rose J. Brigada, June 28, 1952; children: Catherine, Christopher, Carolyn, Stephen, Thomas. BA magna cum laude, Tufts U., 1951; LLB, Harvard U., 1958. One-man shows include MIT, 1985, Crane Gallery, 1986, Babson Coll., 1987, Lily Pad Gallery, 1989, The Copley Soc. of Boston, 1989, David Findlay Gallery, N.Y.C., 1990, Mus. Fine Arts, Springfield, Mass., 1991, Elms Coll., 1991; exhibited in numerous galleries in New Eng. Lt. USN, 1951-55. Roman Catholic. Home: 73 Greylock Rd Wellesley MA 02481-1301

FONTAINE, KATHLEEN STUREY, human resources specialist; b. Balt., Mar. 22, 1962; d. Peter Sturey and Geraldine Marie Teodori; m. Mark Roselius Fontaine, Dec. 21, 1997; children: Elissa Anne Pedelty, Andrew Dylan Pedelty, Scott Gerald Pedelty, Michelle Rossi, Matthew. BS in Physics with Astrophysics Option, N.Mex Inst. Mining and Tech., 1984; MA in Sci. Tech. and Pub. Policy, George Washington U., 2002. Master trainer AchieveGlobal, 1999, MBTI (Myers Briggs Type Indicator) qualified Ctr. for Applications of Psychol. Type, 1998. Human resources devel. specialist NASAGSFC (Goddard Space Flight Ctr.) Office Human Resources, Greenbelt, Md., 1998—2002; sci. cmty. liaison NASA GSFC Global Change Data Ctr., Greenbelt, 2002—. Contbr. articles to profl. jours. Bd. dirs. Anne Arundel County Sch. Bd. Nominating Conv. Com., Annapolis, Md., 2001—; vol., leader Girl Scout Coun. of the Nation's Capitol, Bowie, Md., 1993—97; adult vol. Girl Scout Coun. Ctrl. Md., Annapolis, 1997—2002. Mem.: AIAA. Democrat. Avocations: music, travel, cooking, sailing. Office: NASA Goddard Space Flight Center Code 902 Greenbelt MD 20771 E-mail: kathleen.s.fontaine@nasa.gov.

FONTAINE, LAURA ANN, social worker; b. Elmhurst, Ill., Oct. 4, 1965; d. Lawrence Arthur and Lenita Ann (Marak) F. AA in Psychology, Ctrl. Fla. C.C., Ocala, 1994; BSW, BA in Psychology, U. South Fla., 1996; MSW, Fla. State U., 1998. Sec., receptionist Comml. Structures, Ocala, Fla., 1987-90, Frank Maio Gen. Contractor, Inc., Ocala, 1990-94; team mgr. asst. R.G.I.S. Inventory Specialist, Ocala, 1989-95. Vol. Rape Crisis, Domestic Violence, Ocala, 1996, Ocala Marion County Comty.-AIDS Network, 1997; mentor Take Stock in Children, 1997, Therapist, Ptnrs. for Children and Families, Ocala, 1998-2000, In-Home Counselor, Camelot Cmty. Care, Ocala, 2000-2001, Abuse Reactive Counselor, 2001-. Recipient Outstanding Svc. award Univ. S. Fla. Village Coun., Tampa, 1994-95. Mem. NOW, NASW, Psi Chi, Phi Alpha. Democrat. Home: 1746 SE 12th Ave Ocala FL 34471-5452

FONTANA, BERNARD LEE, retired anthropologist, writer, consultant; b. Oakland, Calif., Jan. 7, 1931; s. Bernard Campion and Hope Mary (Smith) F.; m. Hazel Ann McFeely, June 27, 1954; children: Geoffrey Earl Francis, Nicholas Anthony, Francesca Ann. BA, U. Calif., Berkeley, 1953; PhD, U. Ariz., 1960. Field historian U. Ariz., Tucson, 1960-62, 78-92; ethnologist Ariz. State Mus., Tucson, 1962-78; writer, cons. Tucson, 1992—. Lectr. anthropology dept. U. Ariz., 1962-78; expert witness Papago Tribe of Ariz., Sells, 1962-64; pres. Ariz.-Sonora desert Mus., Tucson, 1983-85; cons. San Xavier Dist. Tohono O'Odham Nation, Tucson, 1992-93, KUAT-TV, Tucson, 1996. Author: Tarahumara: Where Night Is The Day Of The Moon, 1979 (Border Regional Libr. Assn. award 1979), Of Earth and Little Rain: The Papago Indians, 1981 (Border Regional Libr. Assn. award 1981), Entrada: The Legacy of Spain and Mexico in the United States, 1994, A Guide to Contemporary Southwest Indians, 1999; editor: Before Rebellion, 1996, Trails to Tiburón, 2000. Active western regional adv. com. Nat. Pk. Svc., San Francisco, 1974-76; sheriff Tucson Corral of the Westerners, 1976; sec. Patronato San Xavier, Tucson, 1989—. Calif. Alumni scholar U. Calif. Alumni Assn., Berkeley, 1948; pre-doctoral fellow Wenner Gren Found. for Anthrop. Rsch., 1959; recipient Ben Avery award Ariz. Clean and Beautiful, 1994, Ariz. Gov. Hist. Preservation award Ariz. Heritage Found., 1995. Fellow Ariz. Nev. Acad. Sci.; mem. Soc. For Hist. Arch. (life, pres. 1970, J. C. Harrington medal 1992), Ariz. Arch. and Hist. Soc. (pres. 1960-61, editor 1958-60, Victor R. Stoner award 1990), Am. Soc. for Ethnohistory (pres. 1965, editor 1969-72), S.W. Pks. and Monuments Assn. (life, vice chmn. 1988, Edward Danson award 1989, Emil Haury award 1991). Avocation: philately. Home and Office: 7710 S Mission Rd Tucson AZ 85746-7143

FONTANA, JOHN ARTHUR, employee benefits specialist; b. N.Y.C., Feb. 24, 1955; s. Joseph and Gloria (Rosiello) F.; m. Patricia Ann Cooper, Nov. 10, 1979; children: Adam Vincent, Brian Patrick, Jennifer Ann. BA in Econs., Fordham U., 1977, MBA in Acctg., 1984. Pension analyst George Buck Cons.

Actuaries, N.Y.C., 1977-79; retirement plan analyst Sperry Corp., N.Y.C., 1979-80; ops. specialist Bankers Trust Co., N.Y.C., 1980-83; mgr. employee benefits Fidata Corp., N.Y.C., 1983-85; mgr. benefit plan devel. N.Y. Power Authority, White Plains, 1985-90; dir. employee benefits Random House, Inc., N.Y.C., 1990-98; dir. benefits and Human Resources Info. Sys. Polygram Holding, Inc., N.Y.C., 1998-99; sr. cons. Price-Waterhouse Coopers, N.Y.C., 1999—; pres. The Fontana Group, LLC, Montvale, N.J., 1999—. Bd. dirs. Monroe (N.Y.) Dem. Com., 1985-87; capt. United Way, N.Y.C., 1992—; musician Ch. of the Sacred Heart, Monroe, 1989—, fin. com.; team mgr. M-W Little League, 1987-90; mem. Orange County C. of C., Orange County Partnership. Mem. U.S. C. of C. (benefits com. 1987-89), Am. Mgmt. Assn. Republican. Roman Catholic. Avocations: music, golf, collecting baseball memorabilia. Home: 61 Peter Bush Dr Monroe NY 10950 Office: The Fontana Group LLC 110 Summit Ave Montvale NJ 07645-1712 E-mail: fontana@frontiernet.net.

FONTANA, MARIO H. nuclear engineer; b. West Springfield, Mass., Mar. 30, 1933; s. Remo and Sabina F.; m. Sue Janeway, Apr. 12, 1958; children: Richard, Edward. BS, U. Mass., 1955; MS, MIT, 1957; PhD, Purdue U., 1968. Registered engr., Tenn. Mem. rsch. staff Oak Ridge (Tenn.) Nat. Lab., 1957-63, 65-81, asst. dir. nuc. safety rsch., 1968-72, head advanced concepts devel. engring. tech. divsn., 1972-81, asst. to dir. engring. tech. divsn., 1990-92; group leader Advanced Concepts, 1993-94; instr. Purdue U., Oak Ridge, Tenn., 1964-65; dir. industry degraded core program Tech for Energy, Inc., Knoxville, Tenn., 1981-84; v.p. engring. Energex Oak Ridge, 1984-85; dir. nuclear safety tech. IT Corp. and Tenera, L.P., Knoxville, 1985-90; sr. scientist Avco Rsch. and Advanced Devel., Wilmington, Mass., 1963-64. Cons. AEC, Washington, 1972-73, Nuc. Regulatory Commn., Washington, 1979-81, 91—, U.S. Dept. Energy, Washington, 1986-89; adj. prof. U. Tenn., 1995—; mem. Adv. Com. on Reactor Safeguards, 1995-99. Author more than 100 reports and articles. Fellow Am. Nuclear Soc. (chmn. nuclear reactor safety divsn. 1972-73, 94-95); mem. ASME, Rotary Internat., Sigma Xi, Tau Beta Pi. Achievements include patents for method of arc synthesis of uranium carbide from UF6 and Graphite, others.

FONTANA, ROBERT EDWARD, electrical engineering educator, retired air force officer; b. Bklyn., Nov. 26, 1915; s. Valentino and Secondina (Lesca) F.; m. Victoria E. Mauriello, Dec. 2, 1945; children: Robert Edward, Thomas Paul, Mary Joan. B Elec. Engring, NYU, 1939; MS, U. Ill., 1947, PhD, 1949. Commd. 2d lt. USAAF, 1942; advanced through grades to col. USAF, 1959, ret., 1969; research scientist Sandia Corp., 1949-54; spl. asst. nuclear devel. Hdqrs. USAF, 1954-58; head nuclear applications (Air Research and Devel. Command), 1958-61; dir. (Aerospace Research Labs.), Wright-Patterson AFB, Ohio, 1961-66; chmn. dept. elec. engring. Air Force Inst. Tech., Wright-Patterson AFB, 1966-84, prof. emeritus, 1984—. Pres. Honors Seminars Met. Dayton, 1966-86. Decorated Legion of Merit with oak leaf cluster, Exceptional Civilian service award Dept. Air Force, 1985 Fellow IEEE (chmn. Dayton sect. 1971, editor edn. group newsletter 1970-81, meritorious service award 1983); mem. Am. Soc. Engring. Edn. (editor elec. engring. div. newsletter 1970-81, chmn. energy conversion com. 1978-80), Sigma Xi, Tau Beta Pi, Eta Kappa Nu. Home: 6534 Brook Lake Dr Dallas TX 75248-3915

FONTANA, SANDRA ELLEN FRANKEL, special education educator; b. N.Y.C., July 12, 1951; d. Robert Lowell and Mildred (Tropan) Sharoff; m. Jay Tommy Frankel, May 25, 1973 (div. 1993); children: Austin, Lauren; m. David Fontana, July 27, 2002; stepchildren: Troy, Tara. BS in Med. Tech., Rochester (N.Y.) Inst. Tech., 1973; MA in Linguistics, Gallaudet U., 1984. Cert. comprehensive permanent S.I.G.N. Nat. Assn. Deaf SIGN Instr. Guidance Network, 1985, profl. Am. Sign Language Tchr. Assn. (ASLTA), 1986. Coord. bus. affairs/sign lang. program dept. bus. affairs Gallaudet U., 1980-83; head tchr. dept. sign communication faculty retreat N000, winter 1981; instr. dept. interpreter/translator instruction Gallaudet U., 1981-84, instr. in sign lang. dept. sign communication, spring 1982, ASL instr. dept. sign communication, 1982-84, coord. NDC sign lang. program dept. sign communication, 1984-88, instr. dept. sign communication, 1984-88, head instr./trainer, ASL instr. dept. sign communication, 1988-89, ASL instr. Coll. Continuing Edn. extension/summer programs, 1988; assoc. prof. interpreting preparation program C.C. Balt. County, 1990—2002, Riverside (Calif.) C.C., 2002—. Evaluator Sign Instr. Guidance Network, Indpls., 1989-90; mem. Sign Instr. Guidance Network; bd. dir. State Md. Office Govr. Assistive Tech. Guaranteed Loan Program, 1999-2002. Mem. Am. Sign Lang. Tchr. Assn. (evaluator 1990-), Nat. Assn. of the Deaf, Metro. Wash. Assn. of the Deaf, Md. Assn. of the Deaf. Home: 1540 Highridge Rd Riverside CA 92506 Office: Riverside CC 4800 Magnolia Ave Riverside CA 92506

FONTANA, THOMAS MICHAEL, producer, scriptwriter; b. Buffalo, Sept. 12, 1951; s. Charles Louis and Marie Angelica (Internicola) Fontana. BA in Theater, State U. Coll., Buffalo, 1973; LittD (hon.), SUNY, 1997. Playwright in residence The Writers Theatre, N.Y.C., 1975-93; prodr., writer St. Elsewhere, NBC-TV, 1982-88; writer The Fourth Wiseman, MOW/ABC-TV, 1985; exec. prodr., writer Tattinger's NBC-TV, 1988-89, Nick and Hillary, 1989, Home Fires NBC-TV, 1991, Homicide: Life on the Street NBC-TV, 1993-99, Oz HBO-TV, 1997—2003; writer, exec. prodr. Homicide: Life Everlasting, MOW, NBC-TV, 2000, The Beat, UPN, 2000, Judas, MOW/ABC, 2003. Exec. prodr.: (TV films) The Press Secretary, PBS, 2001, Shot in the Heart, MOW, HBO, 2001, American Tragedy, CBS, 2000; author: (TV special) America: A Tribute to Heroes, 2001; contbr. articles to N.Y.Times, TV Guide, Esquire. Recipient Peabody Award, 1983, 1993, 1996, 1998, Humanitas Prize, 1984, Emmy Award for St Elsewhere, 1985, 1987, Emmy Award for Homicide-Life in the Street, 1993, Christopher Award, Nat Asn Cath Broadcasters, 1986, Autism Award, Nat Asn Autistic Children, 1986, Maggie Award, Planned Parenthood Asn, 1986, Distinguished Alumnus Award, State Univ Col, Buffalo, 1987, Founder's Award, VQT, 1995, Best Drama Series Award, 1996, Best Drama Series and Program of the Yr Award, TV Critics Asn, 1996, 1997, 1998, Nancy Susan Reynolds Award, 1996, Marylander of the Yr Award, Baltimore Sun, 1996, Best Drama Series Oz, Cable Ace Award, 1997, Prix Poula Meillevre Series Oz, 1997, Literacy in Media award for Oz, 1999, Caths in the Media Award, 1999, Lifetime Achievement Award, Casting Soc Am, 2000, Evelyn Burkey Lifetime Achievement Award, WGA, 2000, Fortune Soc. Award for Oz, 2000, award, Media Action Network for Asian-Ams., 2002. Mem.: Prodrs. Guild Am., Auths League Am, Writers Guild Am. East (Ann Award 1987, 1993, 1994), Dramatists Guild, West Side Rowing Club (Buffalo). Democrat. Roman Catholic. Office: Fatima Prodns 185 Broome St New York NY 10002

FONTANAZZA, FRANKLIN JOSEPH, accountant, business executive; b. Balt., Aug. 17, 1953; s. Emanuel Joseph and Mary Jane (Weese) F.; m. Hilda Mae Henry, May 18, 1980 (dec. Feb. 1982); m. Gina Louise De Deo, Sept. 3, 1983; 1 child, Gia. BS in Bus. Adminstrn., Towson (Md.) State U., 1975; MBA, U. Balt., 1988. CPA, Md. Field svcs. mgr. Mid-Atlantic Coun. on Compensation Ins., Towson, 1978-83; tech. svcs. mgr. Md. Casualty Co., Balt., 1983-84; sr. cost acct. Westinghouse Electric Co., Hunt Valley, Md., 1984-91; cost acctg. mgr. Beretta USA Corp., Accokeek, Md., 1991-94; plant contr. GAF Materials Corp., Balt., 1995-99; br. contr. interconnectors divsn. Framatome Connections USA, Inc., York, Pa., 1999-2000; chief fin. officer Cloverland Green Spring Dairy (now Two Farms, Inc.), Balt., 2000—. Mem. AICPA, Md. Assn. CPAs, Inst. Mgmt. Accts. Roman Catholic. Home: 4107 Sweet Air Rd Baldwin MD 21013-9623 Office: 3611 Roland Ave Baltimore MD 21211

FONTANIVE, LYNN MARIE, special education administrator; b. Detroit, June 29; d. Edward and Violet Fontanive; m. Paul Adasek Jr., Nov. 8, 1985; 1 child, Paul Fontanive. BA, Marygrove Coll., Detroit; MA, Mich. State U.; EdS, Wayne State U., Detroit; EdD, Wayne State U. Audiologist Plymouth (Mich.) Ctr. for Human Devel.; assoc. dir. Deaf Hearing & Speech Ctr.; from ednl. audiologist to dept. dir. ctr. programs Oakland Schs., Waterford, Mich., 1976—99; dir. presch. and assessment ctr. Macomb Intermed. Sch. Dist., Clinton Twp., Mich., 1999—. Lectr. in field. Adv. bd. Mich. Sch. for Deaf, Flint, 1986—91; pres. Suprs. for Programs for Hearing Impaired; bd. dirs. Career Leadership and Devel. Bd., 1987—90; bd. dirs., human svcs. coord. bd. HSCB, 1999—; pres. local coord. coun. LICC, 1999—; bd. dirs. State Spl. Edn. Adv. Com., 1994—98; adminstr. Macomb County Adminstrn. Spl. Edn., 1999—. Mem. Am. Speech and Hearing Assn., Mich. Speech, Lang., Hearing Assn. (v.p. 1986-90), Coun. for Exceptional Children Macomb County (membership chmn. 1988-90), Adminstrs. of Spl. Edn., Mich. Suprs. of Pub. Sch. Programs for Hearing Impaired (treas. 1996-97, pres. 1997-2000). Roman Catholic. Avocations: dance, aerobics, travel, biking, tennis. Office: Macomb ISD 44001 Garfield Rd Clinton Township MI 48038-1100

FONTENOT, ANDREA DEAN, communications executive; b. Drumright, Okla., Mar. 14, 1944; d. Howard G. and Ruby Jewell (Harvison) Harris; m. Lloyd John Culver, Aug. 12, 1962 (widowed Feb. 1966); m. Ronald Ray Fontenot. BS in Speech and Broadcasting, McNeese State U., Lake Charles, 1978, MFA in Creative Writing, 1985; ABD in English, Tex. Tech. U., Lubbock, 1997, PhD in English, 1998. Cert. Distance Educator. Jr. acct. exec. Harris & Weinstein Ad Agy., Atlanta, 1973-75; grad. teaching asst. McNeese State U., Lake Charles, La., 1981-85, adjunct prof., 1985-89, Davis Monthan Air Force Base, Pima CC Tucson, 1989-90; grad. teaching asst. Tex. Tech. U., Lubbock, Tex., 1990-96; rsch. asst. Distance Edn. College Engring., Lubbock, Tex., 1996; mgr. dir. CLEAR project Southwestern Bell Comms. Found., Lubbock, Tex., 1997—. Adv. bd. Teaching Learning and Tech. Ctr., Lubbock, Tex., 1996-98; teaching on internet ind. cons. Lubbock, Tex., 1993—; rsch. asst. Internet Cons. SCATE, Lubbock, Tex., 1996-97. Author: (short story) Minotaur, 1985, Hayden's Ferry Review, 1986; contbr. articles to profl. jours. Mem. Rural Assistance Initiative Task Force, 1998—; mem. Collaborative Cmty. Network Task Force, 1998—, Ctr. for Partnerships in Sci. and Tech.; mem. Svc. Learning Adv. Coun.; mem. High Plains Rural Broadband Network. Recipient Paul Whitfield Horn scholarship, 1995, Outstanding Grad. Tchr., 1993, 95, McNeese Award in Fiction, 1984, 85, Outstanding Classroom Practices award Conf. Coll. Composition and Comm., 1998. Mem. Nat. Coun. Tchrs. English, South Ctrl. MLA, Soc. for Tech. Comm., Assoc. Writing Program, Grad. English Soc., Tex. Learning Orgn., Tex. Alliance Minority Engrs. Home: 5020 Kenosha Ave Apt A Lubbock TX 79413-3948 Office: SBC CLEAR Program Southwestern Bell Comm COE Tex Tech Univ Lubbock TX 79409 E-mail: dean.fontenot@coe.ttu.edu.

FONTENOT, LYN, interior designer; b. Port Arthur, Tex., Mar. 3, 1942; d. William and Claudia Morton; children: William, Richard. BA, U. La., 1986; M, Somerset (Eng.) U., 1996; PhD, Pacific Western U., 1999. Lic. interior designer; lic. appraiser antique furniture. Pvt. practice, Ft. Worth, 1966-75; interior designer Groupe Harold Barnette, Paris, 1975-79, Lyn Fontenot Design Assn., Lafayette, La., 1979—. Author: French Furniture, 1983, Antique Furniture: How to Tell the Real Thing from the Fake, 1999. Bd. dirs. S.W. La. Ind. Ctr., 1993-96. Fellow Am. Soc. Interior Designers; mem. AIA, New Eng. Appraisers Assn. Office: Lyn Fontenot Design Assn 214 Clinton St Lafayette LA 70501 E-mail: lynfontenot@msn.com.

FONTES, J. MARIO F., JR., lawyer; b. São Paulo, Brazil, Jan. 17, 1964; m. Gladys Fontes, Jan. 7, 1995. BA cum laude in Econs. and Internat. Studies, Am. U., Washington, 1987; JD, Cath. U., Washington, 1992. Bar: Pa. 1993, Fla. 1995, U.S. Ct. Claims 1993, U.S. Ct. Internat. Trade 1993. Assoc. Porter, Wright, Morris & Arthur, Washington, 1992-93, Hughes Hubbard & Reed, Miami, Fla., 1993-96, Baker & McKenzie, Miami, 1996-2000, ptnr., 2000—. Mem. Phi Kappa Phi. Office: Baker & McKenzie 1111 Brickell Ave Miami FL 33131-3214

FONTES, PAULO A. surgeon, educator; b. Sao Paulo, Brazil, Jan. 20, 1962; came to U.S., 1991; s. Paulo B. and Mildred (Chaves) F.; m. Monica M. Mollerstrand, Sept. 9, 1991; children: Rafaella M., Karl Liam M. MD, Sao Paulo State U., 1985. Bd. cert. gen. surgery Brazilian Coll. Surgeons. Intern Sao Paulo State U. Sch. Medicine, Botucatu, Brazil, 1984-85; resident Prof. Edmundo Vasconcelos Hosp., Sao Paulo, 1986-88, mem. med. staff, 1990-91, supr. gen. surgery residents, 1990-91; rsch. fellow Sao Paulo Fed. U., 1990-91, U. Pitts. Med. Ctr., 1991-93, vis. asst. prof. surgery, 1993-96, clin. fellow, 1996-98, attending surgeon, asst. prof., 1998—. Dir. S. & Am. divsn. U. Pitts. Med. Ctr. Overseas Inc., 1998—, co-dir. liver transplant program. Contbr. articles to profl. jours. Recipient Bradesco Found. prize, 1988, 89; scholar Sao Paulo State Govt., 1980-85. Fellow: ACS. Avocations: sailing, biking, working out, surfing. Home: 522 Gettysburg St Pittsburgh PA 15206-4548 Office: U Pitts Med Ctr 4C Falk Clinic 3601 5th Ave Pittsburgh PA 15213-3403 Fax: 412-647-5480.

FONTES, RONALD HOGUE, writer; b. L.A., July 19, 1952; s. Ruben Paul and Lillian Pauline (Hogue) Fontes; m. Marie Elena Taft, Aug. 6, 1976 (div. Aug. 1981); m. Justine Hagen Korman, Nov. 24, 1998. BS, Austin Peay State U., Clarksville, Tenn., 1978. Art dir. The Art Factory, Nashville, 1976—78, McDonald/Seigenthaler Advt., Nashville, 1978—80; designer Whitman Comics, N.Y.C., 1980—82; prodn. supr. Marvel Comics Group, N.Y.C., 1982—85; graphic designer Nat. Law Jour., N.Y.C., 1985—86. Author (artist): Captain Fortune comic book series, 1995; author: Disney's American Frontier Series, 1991—93, Squanto, 1994, Mars Attacks!, 1996, Abraham Lincoln, Lawyer, Leader, Legend, 2001, George Washington, Soldier, Hero, President, 2001, How the Leopard Got its Spots, 1999, How the Zebra Got its Stripes, 2002, Peanuts Books, 2001—03, over 350 other children's books. Avocations: photography, filmmaking, painting, sculpture. Mailing: 70 Walker Rd Readfield ME 04355-3756

FONVIELLE, CHARLES DAVID, lawyer; b. Melbourne, Fla., Dec. 28, 1944; s. Charles David Fonvielle Jr. and Margaret Jordan Palmer; m. Deborah Konas, July 25, 1970; children: C. Caulley, D. Jordan. BA, U. Fla., 1968; JD, Fla. State U., 1972. Bar: Fla. 1972, U.S. Dist. Ct. (no., mid. and so. dists.) Fla. Asst. pub. defender Fla. Pub. Defender Assn., Tallahassee, 1972-74; pvt. practice Tallahassee, 1974-77; ptnr. Thompson, Wadsworth, Messer, Turner & Rhodes, Tallahassee, 1977-80, Green & Fonvielle, Tallahassee, 1980-84, Green, Fonvielle & Hinkle, Tallahassee, 1984-85, Fonvielle Hinkle & Lewis, Tallahassee, 1995—2002, Fonvielle Lewis Foote & Messer, 2002—. Bd. dirs. Fla. State U. Coll. Law, endowed prof. litigation. Mem. ATLA (sustaining), Tallahassee Bar Assn. (bd. dirs. 1978-79), Acad. Fla. Trial Lawyers (Eagle sponsor 1990—), Nat. Bd. Trial Advocacy (cert.), Fla. Bar Assn. (bd. legal specialization and edn. 1991—). Avocations: physical fitness, flying, spearfishing, sports cars. Office: Fonvielle Lewis Foote & Messer 3375 Capital Cir NE Ste A Tallahassee FL 32308-3778 E-mail: david@flfmlaw.com.

FOOLADI, MIKE M. physician, educator; b. Zolghadar, Iran, Feb. 22, 1937; arrived in U.S., 1960; m. Marjan Fooladi, Aug. 28, 1974; children: Michael, Mark. BS, Baylor U., 1965; MS, Tex. So. U., 1968; PhD, U. So. Miss., 1979; MD, Juarez Med. Sch., 1982; MPH, U. So. Miss., 1997. Lic. Iran, Mex. Prof. chemistry Miss. C.C., Gulfport; prof. biotechnology U. Tehran, Iran; cons. to min. Ministry Agr., Tehran; cons. Shaheed Modaress, Tehran; pres. Fuladi Rsch. Ins., El Paso, Tex., 1985—2001; v.p. Alpina Lab, Bay Minette, Ala.; corp. rsch. dir. Vicksburg (Miss.) & Vertac. Pres. Coosa Chem. Co., Childensburg, Ala., 1978—80. Author: (book) Tal Viva 2021, 1998; contbr. articles to profl. jours. Mem.: AMA, Am. Chem. Soc. Achievements include patents in field. Avocations: walking, horseback riding, reading, writing. Home: 2100 Sunset Dr Hattiesburg MS 39402 Office: Miss Gulf Coast Cmty 2226 Switzer Rd Gulfport MS 39507

FOORD, ROBERT LAVERNE, intelligence executive, consultant; b. Hillsboro, Oreg. s. Alton LaVerne and Mildred Louise F.; m. Susan Lelli, July 15, 1972; children: Shawna, Ryan. BS in Engring., U.S. Naval Acad., 1961. Divsn. chief, analyst CIA, Washington, 1965-85, inspector intelligence com. office of inspector gen., 1988-89; dir. sci. and weapons rsch. Offic, 1989-94; chmn. scientific and tech. intelligence com. U.S. Govt., 1980-85; sr. analyst Intec Inc., Arlington, Va., 1994-99, Centra Tech. Inc., Arlington, 1999—. CIA rep. Armed Forces Comms. and Electronics Assn., Washington, 1992-94. Contbr. articles to jours. Lt. USN, 1961-65. Recipient award Ladies Aux. VFW, 1961, Dir.'s award Def. Intelligence Agy., 1994. Avocations: golf, hiking, fishing. Home: 8100 Buckspark Ln E Potomac MD 20854-4267 E-mail: foordr@centrava.com.

FOOTE, AVON EDWARD, web developer/producer, communications educator; b. Sept. 24, 1937; s. Avon Ruble and Lila Frances (Broughton) F.; m. Dorothy Veronica Gargis, Mar. 15, 1960; children: Anthony E., Kevin A., Michele. Cert., NYU, 1961; BS, Florence State U., 1963; MS, U. So. Miss., 1968; PhD, Ohio State U., 1970. Announcer Sta. WJOI, Florence, Ala., 1958-60; prodn. mgr. Sta. WOWL-TV, Florence, 1960-64; advt. coord. Plough Inc., Memphis, 1964-66; faculty adviser Sta. WMSU, U. So. Miss., Hattiesburg, 1966-67; prodr.-dir. telecomm. Ohio State U., Columbus, 1967-69; assoc. prof. broadcasting U. Miss., Oxford, 1971-72; project dir. Ohio Valley TV Sys., Columbus, 1972-74; faculty, coord. grad. studies Sch. Journalism/Mass Comm. U. Ga., Athens, 1974-80; prof. broadcasting U. North Ala., Florence, 1980—. Prof., London, 1990, 91; awards judge Ohio State Awards, 1968-73; chmn. faculty screening com. Peabody Radio-TV Awards, 1976-79; jury chair, N.Y. Festivals TV awards, 2002—; founder Worldwide Web pages including Worldserver, 1995; Web cons. chotank.com, others, 1996—; collection developer: Gulf War Video Collection, 1992-2001, Libr. of Am. Broadcasting, U. Md., College Park, 2002—. Editor: The Challenges of Educational Communications, 1970, CBS and Congress: The Selling of the Pentagon Papers, 1972, Nat. Assn. Ednl. Broadcasters Broadcasting Rev., 1969-73 ; author: (with Koenig and others) Broadcasting and Bargaining, 1970, Chotankers, 1982; prodr. ednl. TV programs; editor ref. shelf materials Nat. Pub. Broadcasting Archives, U. Md., College Park, 2002. Bd. dirs. Florence YMCA, 1982-86. Recipient Cmty. Svc. award Florence Civitan Club, 1990, 1st pl. award Corp. Video Profl. Competition Nat. Broadcasting Soc., 1991, regional 1st pl. award, Nat. 3d pl. award Coll. Emmy award Hollywood Acad. TV Arts and Scsi., 1984, Honorable Mention Comedy awards Nat. Broadcasting Soc., 1987; Industry Faculty Seminar fellow Internat. Radio-TV Soc., 1987, NDEA fellow, 1967, NATAS Meml. fellow, 1970. Mem.: BBC Networking Club, Radio TV News Dirs. Assn. Republican. Anglican. Home: 222 Shirley Dr Florence AL 35633-1434 Office: Comm Bldg PO Box 5158 Florence AL 35632-0001 E-mail: chotank@aol.com.

FOOTE, CHANDRA JEANET, teacher educator; b. Rochester, N.Y., Jan. 20, 1970; d. Theron A. and Patricia M. Foote; m. Christopher A. Robins, July 3, 1999. BS, Syracuse U., 1992, MA, 1994, PhD, 1996. Cert. in elem. edn., N.Y. Tchg. assoc. Syracuse (N.Y.) U., 1994-96; assoc. prof. edn. Niagara U., N.Y., 1996—. Project dir. Niagara Falls (N.Y.) Bd. Edn., 1998-99. Co-author: (book) Constructionist Teaching Practices; contbr. chpt. to books, articles to profl.jours. Leadership rep. The Higher Edn. Task Force for Quality Inclusion, N.Y. State, 1998—; cmty. rep. LaSalle Mid. Sch. Quality Coun., 2001—. Recipient Golden Apple award Niagara Falls City Sch. Dist., 1998-99, Dean's award Coll. Edn. at Niagara U., 1998; Goals 2000 grantee N.Y. State Dept. Edn., 1998-99; Office of Vocat. and Ednl. Svcs. for Individuals with Disabilities grantee, 2000, 02,03. Mem. Am. Ednl. Rsch. Assn., Assn. Tchr. Educators. Avocations: reading, travel. Office: Niagara U Dept Edn B 11 O'Shea Hall Niagara University NY 14109-2042 Fax: (716) 286-8561. E-mail: cjf@niagara.edu.

FOOTE, CHRISTOPHER SPENCER, chemist, educator; b. Hartford, Conn., June 5, 1935; s. William J. and Dorothy (Bennett) F.; m. Judith L. Smith; children: Jonathan, Thomas. BS magna cum laude, Yale U., 1957; Fulbright scholar, U. Goettingen, 1957-58; AM, Harvard U., 1959, PhD, 1961. NSF predoctoral fellow Harvard U., 1958-61; instr. chemistry UCLA, 1961-62, asst. prof., 1962-66, assoc. prof., 1966-69, prof., 1969—, chmn. dept., 1978-81. Acad. adv. bd. Indsl. Rsch. Inst., 1997—2000. Sr. editor Accounts of Chem. Rsch., 1995—. Recipient Humboldt sr. scientist award, 1986-87; Sloane fellow, 1965-67; Guggenheim fellow, 1967-68. Fellow AAAS; mem. Am. Chem. Soc. (Baeklund medal, Tolman award 1996, Arthur C. Cope scholar 1994), Chem. Soc. London, Am. Soc. Photobiology (coun. 1978-81, pres. 1988-89, Rsch. award 2000), German Chem. Soc., Phi Beta Kappa, Sigma Xi, Phi Lambda Upsilon. Home: 930 Berkeley St Santa Monica CA 90403-2308 Office: U Calif Dept Chemistry & Biochemistry Los Angeles CA 90095-1569

FOOTE, EDWARD THADDEUS, II, university president, lawyer; b. Milw., Dec. 15, 1937; s. William Hamilton and Julia Stevenson (Hardin) F.; m. Roberta Waugh Fulbright, Apr. 18, 1964; children: Julia, William, Thaddeus. BA, Yale U., 1959; LLB, Georgetown U., 1966; LLD (hon.), Washington U., St. Louis, 1981, Barry U., 1991; hon. degree, Tokai U., Tokyo, 1984; LLD (hon.), Barry U., 1991. Bar: Mo. 1966. Reporter Washington Star, 1963-64, Washington Daily News, 1964-65; exec. asst. to chmn. Pa. Ave. Commn., Washington, 1965-66; assoc. Bryan, Cave, McPheeters & McRoberts, St. Louis, 1966-70; vice chancellor, gen. counsel, sec. to bd. trustees Washington U., St. Louis, 1970-73, dean Sch. Law, 1973-80, spl. adv. to chancellor and bd. trustees, 1980-81; pres. U. Miami, Coral Gables, Fla., 1981—. Mem. exec. com., bd. dirs. Am. Coun. Edn., 1986-88; chmn. citizens com. for sch. desegregation, St. Louis, 1980; chmn. desegregation monitoring and adv. com., St. Louis, 1980-81. Author: An Educational Plan for Voluntary Cooperation Desegregation of School in the St. Louis Met. area, 1981 Mem. Coun. on Fgn. Rels.; founding pres. bd. New City Sch., St. Louis, 1967-73; mem. gov.'s task force on reorganization State of Mo., 1973-74, steering com., chmn. governance com. Mo. Gov.'s Conf. on Edn., UN Assn. Greater St. Louis chpt., 1977-79, adv. com. Naval War Coll., 1979-82, Fla. Coun. of 100, Southern Fla. Metro-Miami Action Plan, exec. com. Miami Citizens Against Crime; founding chmn. Miami Coalition for a Drug Free Community, 1988—. Recipient Order of Sun (Peru). Democrat. Office: U Miami PO Box 248006 Miami FL 33124-8006

FOOTE, EVELYN PATRICIA, retired military officer; b. Durham, N.C., May 19, 1930; d. Henry Alexander and Evelyn Sevena (Womack) Foote. BA summa cum laude, Wake Forest U., 1953, LLD (hon.), 1989; student, U.S. Army Command & Gen. Staff Coll., Leavenworth, Kans., 1971-72, U.S. Army War Coll., Carlisle, Pa., 1976-77; MS in Govt. and Pub. Affairs, Shippensburg State U., 1977; student, U. Va. Sch. Bus. Adminstrn., 1980. Commd. 1st lt. U.S. Army, 1960, advanced through grades to brig. gen., 1986, platoon officer WAC, 1960-61, selection officer 6th recruiting dist. Portland, Oreg., 1961-64; comdr. WAC Co. U.S. Army Engr. Brigade, Ft. Belvoir, Va., 1964-66; student Adj. Gen. Officer Advanced Course, Ft. Benjamin Harrison, Ind., 1966; exec. officer, chief adminstrv. div. pub. affairs office U.S. Army, Vietnam, 1967; exec. officer, office personnel ops. WAC, Washington, 1968-71, plans and programs officer OFC, dir., 1972-74; personnel mgmt. officer U.S. Army Forces Command, Ft. McPherson, Ga., 1974-76; comdr. 2d basic tng. bn. U.S. Army Tng. Brigade and Military Police Sch., Ft. McClellan, Ala., 1977-79; faculty mem. U.S. Army War Coll., 1979-82; student Fgn. Service Inst., Dept. of State, Washington, 1982-83; comdr. 42d Mil. Police Group, Mannheim, Fed. Republic of Germany, 1983-85; spl. asst. to comdg. gen. 32d Army Air Def. Command Hdqrs., Darmstadt, Fed. Republic of Germany, 1985-86; dep., insp. gen. for inspections Hdqrs. Dept. of the Army, Washington, 1986-88; dep. comdg. gen. Mil. Dist. Washington, comdr. Ft. Belvoir, Va., 1988-89; ret. U.S. Army, 1989, recalled to active duty Sr. Rev. Panel, 1996-97, ret., 1997. Lectr. various U.S. Army and civilian groups. Contbr. articles to mil. jours. and books. Mem. Am Battle Monuments Commn., 1994—2001; bd. visitors Wake Forest U., 1991—2003, chmn. bd. visitors, 2001—03; trustee Fund for Peace, 2002—; bd. dirs. U.S. Army Women's Mus. Found., 1995—. Decorated DSM, Legion of Merit with oak leaf clusters, German Cross of Svc. 1st class; named Spokesperson of the Yr., Dept. Army, 1997—98; named to Disting. Fellows Hall of Fame, U.S. Army War Coll., 1996, Regimental Hall of Fame, U.S. Army MP Corps, 1998; recipient Disting. Pub. Svc. award, Wake Forest U., 1987, DSM, Am. Battle Monuments Commn., 2001. Mem.: Zonta. Democrat. Lutheran. Avocations: music, reading, hiking.

FOOTE, HORTON, playwright, scriptwriter; b. Wharton, Tex., Mar. 14, 1916; s. Albert Horton and Hallie (Brooks) Foote; m. Lillian Vallish, June 4, 1945; children: Barbara Hallie, Albert Horton, Walter Vallish, Daisy Brooks. Student, Pasadena Playhouse Sch. Theatre, Calif., 1933-35, Tamara Daykarhanova Sch. Theatre, N.Y.C., 1937-39. Actor, N.Y.C., 1939-42; mgr. prodn. co. Productions Inc., Washington, 1942-45; vis. disting. dramatist Baylor U., 2002—. Tchr. playwriting. Author: (plays) The Chase, 1956, (screenplays) Storm Fear, 1956, To Kill a Mockingbird, 1962 (Academy award best screenplay, 1962, Writers Guild Am. award, 1962), Baby, The Rain Must Fall, 1965, Hurry Sundown, 1966, Tomorrow, 1971, Tender Mercies, 1983 (Academy award best screenplay, 1983), 1918, 1984, On Valentine's Day, 1985, The Trip to Bountiful, 1985 (Academy award nomination best screenplay, 1985), Spring Moon, 1987, Convicts, 1991, Of Mice and Men, 1992, (plays) Texas Town, Out of My House, 1942, Only The Heart, 1944, Celebration, 1948, The Chase, 1952, The Trip to Bountiful, The Midnight Caller, 1953, A Young Lady of Property, 1954, The Traveling Lady, The Roads to Home, 1955, Harrison, Texas: Eight Television Plays, 1959, Tomorrow, 1960, Three Plays, Roots in a Parched Ground, 1962, Getting Frankie Married...and Afterward, 2002—, (musical adaption) Gone with the Wind, 1971, The Road to the Graveyard, 1985, Blind Date, 1986, Selected One Act Plays of Horton Foote, Habitation of Dragons, 1988, Dividing the Estate, 1989, Talking Pictures, 1990, Horton Foote: Four New Plays, 1994, The Young Man From Atlanta, 1994 (Pulitzer Prize for drama, 1995), Night Seasons, Laura Dennis, Talking Pictures, 1994, The Carpetbag-

ger's Children, also (play series) The Orphans' Home Cycle, 2001, The Last of the Thorntons, 2002, (TV films) Only The Heart, 1947, Ludie Brooks, 1951, The Travelers, 1952, The Old Beginning, The Trip to Bountiful, Midnight Caller, John Turner Davis, Young Lady of Property, The Oil Well, Rocking Chair, Expectant Relations, Death of the Old Man, Tears of My Sister, 1953, The Shadow of Wilie Greer, The Dancers, 1954, The Roads to Home, 1955, Flight, 1956, Drugstore: Sunday Noon, 1956, Member of the Family, Traveling Lady, 1957, Old Man, 1959, Tomorrow, 1960, 1971, The Shape of the River, 1960, The Night of the Storm, 1961, Gambling Heart, 1964, The Displaced Person, 1977, Barn Burning, 1980, Keeping On, 1983, The Habitation of Dragons, 1992, Mr. and Mrs. Loving, 1996; dir.: When They Speak of Rita, 2000. Recipient Evelyn Burkey award Writer's Guild, 1989, Nat. medal of Arts, 2000.

FOOTE, JOHN HOLLAND, lawyer; b. Birmingham, Ala., Aug. 4, 1946; s. John Elbert and Wanda Delashaw (Holland) F.; m. Rosamond P. Tompkins, July 26, 1980; children: Nathaniel Lucas, Samuel Tompkins. ADin Govt., La. State U., 1968; JD, U. Va., 1974. Bar: Va. 1974, DC 1976, U.S. Dist. Ct. (ea. dist.) Va. 1977, U.S. Ct. Appeals (2d. cir. 1977, U.S. Supreme Ct. 1979, U.S. Ct. Appeals (4th cir.) 1982, U.S. Dist. Ct. (we. dist.) Va., 1994, U.S. Ct. Appeals (11th cir.) 1996. Policy analyst Office of Policy and Planning U.S. Dept. Justice, Washington, 1974-77; assoc. gen. counsel Pres. Ford's Viet Nam Era Clemency Program, Washington, 1975-76; trial atty. criminal divsn. U.S. Dept. Justice, 1974—77; from dep. county atty. to county atty. Prince William County, Manassas, Va., 1977-89; owner Hazel & Thomas, P.C., Manassas, 1989-99, also bd. dirs.; prin. Walsh, Colucci, Lubeley, Emrich & Terpak, P.C., 1999—. Chmn. Prince William-Manassas Regional Jail Bd., 1978-82; bd. dirs. Hist. Manassas, Inc., 1992-96, Project Mend-a-House, 1995-97. Lt. U.S. Army, 1968-71, Vietnam. Mem. Va. State Bar (5th dist. com. disciplinary sys. 1992-95, faculty professionalism 1992-95), Prince William County Bar Assn. (pres. 1987-88), Local Govt. Attys. of Va. (pres. 1987-88). Democrat. Methodist. Avocations: reading, bicycling, guitar. Home: 10542 Knollwood Dr Manassas VA 20111-2834 Office: Walsh Colucci Lubeley Emrich Terpak P C 9324 West St Fl 3 Manassas VA 20110-5198

FOOTE, NATHAN MAXTED, retired physical science educator; b. Woodlawn, Pa., Oct. 8, 1913; s. Myron Tinkham and Ada May (Maxted) F.; m. Laura Belle Gruey, Sept. 5, 1936 (dec. June 2001); children: Jonathan W., L. Nadine, Frances C., Willard G. *Mr. Foote is the second of four sons of early American forebears. Nathaniel Foote, of Wethersfield, Conn. and James Cole of Plymouth, Mass. had been born in England during the sixteenth century. Foote's first ancestor born in America may have been Mary Foxwell born 8/17/1635 in Scituate, Mass. His wife died in June 2001.* AB, DePauw U., 1935; MS, Purdue U., 1939. Jr. chemist U.S. FDA, Phila., 1939-40; Rsch. engr. RCA, Camden, N.J., 1940-49; rsch. scientist Colgate Palmolive, Jersey City, N.J., 1950-52; rheologist B.F. Goodrich Chem. Co., Avon Lake, Ohio, 1953-58; acting head, Dept. Physics Baldwin Wallace Coll., Berea, Ohio, 1958-60; vis. asst. prof. Physics Pa. State U., University Park, 1960-61, asst. prof. Physics, Behrend Coll. Erie, 1964-78, ret., 1979; assoc. prof. Phys. Sci. SUNY, Geneseo, 1961-64. *Mr. Foote has suggested that high-flying aircraft have put water vapor where it reacts chemically with single oxygen atoms, forming two hydroxyl radicals, thereby reducing the formation of ozone. Ozone depletion probably altered climates. The magnetically active hydroxyl radicals contribute in the oxidation of nitrogen to nitric acid. The deterioration of the atmosphere is being caused by both the increase of energetic light at the ocean surface and by the increases of water in the stratosphere. Mr. Foote's preceptor R.F. Newton, was a student of G.N. Lewis, Who first saw that the atmosphere could "burn."* Author: Industrial and Engineering Chemistry, 1944, Industrial and Engineering Chemistry, 1947. Del. Ohio Coun. Am. Bapt. Men, 1955-58. Mem.: AAAS, Am. Chem. Soc. (50 Yr. award 1993), Sigma Xi. Avocations: stratospheric chemical change, lawn bowling. Home: 14 E Main St Lot B Mount Dora FL 32757-3470

FOOTE, RICHARD CHARLES, lawyer; 1 child, Elizabeth Ann. BA, Harvard U., 1973; JD, Case Western Reserve U., 1976. Bar: Ohio 1976, U.S. dist. Ct. (no. dist.) Ohio 1976, U.S. Ct. Appeals (6th cir.) 1982. Ptnr. Law Offices of Mark L. Hoffman and Richard C. Foote, Shaker Heights, Ohio, 1983—. Mem.: Bar Assn. Greater Cleve., Cuyahoga County Bar Assn. Office: Ohio Savs Bldg 20133 Farnsleigh Rd Cleveland OH 44122-3613

FOOTE, RICHARD VAN, lawyer; b. Feb. 5, 1930; s. Ernest Edward and Luva Gladys Foote; m. Lois Earlene Moore, Jan. 28, 1956; children: John Kevin, Christopher Lee. BS in Bus., Wichita State U., 1955; LLB, Washburn U., Topeka, 1958. Bar: Kans. 1958, U.S. Dist. Ct. Kans. 1958, U.S. Ct. Appeals (10th cir.) 1966. IBM operator IBM, Wichita, Kans., 1954—55, Kans. State Treasury, Topeka, 1955—57; law clk. Glen Cogswell, Topeka, 1957—58; ptnr. Matlack & Foote, Wichita, 1965—95; sole practice Wichita, 1958—64, 1995—. Dir. Bank Whitewater; Kans. bd. dir. Wichita Area Builders Assn., 1970—72. Sgt. USMC, 1951—54. Mem.: ABA, Wichita Bar Assn., Kans. Bar Assn. Republican. Episcopalian. Home: 7506 Norfolk Cir Wichita KS 67206-2108 E-mail: attnyfoote@hotmail.com.

FOOTE, ROBERT HUTCHINSON, animal physiology educator; b. Gilead, Conn., Aug. 20, 1922; s. Robert E. and Annie (Hutchinson) F.; m. Ruth E. Parcells, Jan. 12, 1946 (dec. Jan. 1992); children: Robert W., Dale H.; m. Barbara J. Johnson, Sept. 25, 1993. BS, U. Conn., 1943; MS, Cornell U., 1947, PhD Animal Physiology/Biochem. Genetics, 1950. Grad. asst. Cornell U., Ithaca, N.Y., 1946-50, asst. prof. animal physiology, 1950-56, assoc. prof., 1956-63, prof., 1963-93, Jacob Gould Schurman chair, 1980-93; emeritus, 1993—. Mem. study sect. NIH, 1974-78; cons. Shell Oil, 1985-89, EPA, 1988-96; program mgr. USDA competitive grants, 1986-87. Author: Animal Reproduction, 1954, AI to Cloning, 1998; mem. editl. bds. 5 jours., 1958-96, Cloning, 1999-2002, Reproductive Physiology, 1992-99, Cryobiology, 1991-94; contbr. some 500 articles to profl. jours., chpts. to books. Chmn. trustees Congregation Ch., Ithaca, 1955-60. Served to capt. inf. U.S. Army 1943-46, ETO. Recipient Sci. medal N.Y. Farmers, 1969, Nat. Physiology and Endocrinology award Am. Soc. Animal Sci., 1970, Casida Physiology Reprodn. award, 1991, JSPS award, 1996, SUNY Chancellor award, 1980, Superior Svc. award USDA, 1988, Alumni Merit award U. Conn., 1996; named hon. prof. Beijing Agrl. U., 1995. Fellow: AAAS; mem.: Internat. Embryo Transfer Soc. (Lifetime Pioneer award 2002), Am. Soc. Theriogenology (editl. bd. 1976—89, Robert H. Foote Symposium in his honor 1992), Am. Soc. Andrology (editl. bd. 1982—88, Outstanding Andrologist 1984, Upjohn physiology award 1985), Nat. Assn. Animal Breeders (Physiology award 1970), Soc. Study Reprodn. (bd. dirs. 1976—78, pres. 1985, Hartman Lifetime Rsch. award 2000), Am. Dairy Sci. Assn., Gamma Sigma Delta, Phi Kappa Phi, Sigma Xi. Republican. Home: 474 Savage Farm Dr Ithaca NY 14850-6508 Office: Cornell U Dept Animal Sci 204 Morrison Hall Ithaca NY 14853-4801 E-mail: rhf4@cornell.edu.

FOOTE, ROBERT LEONARD, oncologist, educator, researcher; b. Payson, Utah, Dec. 18, 1957; s. Leonard H. and Lauana (Whitaker) F.; m. Kally Rae Henderson, Apr. 20, 1979; children: Catherine Anne, Anthony Leonard, Robert Tyler, Ralph Andrew, Patrick Henderson, Thomas James. BS in Chemistry, Brigham Young U., 1980; MD, U. Utah, 1984. Diplomte Nat. Bd. Med. Examiners, Am. Bd. Radiology. Intern LDS Hosp., Salt Lake City, 1984-85; resident in radiation oncology Mayo Grad. Sch. Medicine, Rochester, Minn., 1985-88; Mayo Found. scholar U. Fla., Gainesville, 1988, clin. fellow in oncology, 1988; sr. assoc. cons. Mayo Clinic, Rochester, 1988-91, cons., 1991—; from instr. to assoc. prof. oncology Mayo Med. Sch., Rochester, 1988-99, prof., 1999—; vice-chair dept. oncology Mayo Clinic, Rochester, 2000—. Trustee Albert Lea (Minn.) Med. Ctr., 1997—. Contbr. articles to med. jours., including Jour. Neurosurgery, Cancer. Cubmaster, instnl. rep. Boy Scouts Am., Rochester, 1985—; bishop LDS Ch., Rochester, 1996-2002. Named Mayo Fellow Assn. Tchr. of Yr., Mayo Found., 1990, 95, 97, 2000, 02. Mem. Am. Soc. for Therapeutic Radiology and Oncology, Am. Coll. Radiology, Am. Soc. Clin. Oncology, Assn. Residents in Radiation Oncology (Tchr. of Yr. award 2002), Internat. Stereotactic Radiosurgery Soc., Internat. Soc. Intraoperative Radiation Therapy, Am. Radium Soc., Sigma Xi. Avocation: coin and rare book collecting. Office: Mayo Clinic 200 1st St SW Rochester MN 55905-0002

FOOTE, SHELBY, author; b. Greenville, Miss., Nov. 17, 1916; s. Shelby Dade and Lillian (Rosenstock) F.; m. Gwyn Rainer, Sept. 5, 1956; children: Margaret Shelby, Huger Lee. Student, U. N.C., 1935-37; DLitt (hon.), U. of the South, 1981, Southwestern U., 1982, U. S.C., 1991, U. N.C., 1992, Millsaps U., 1993, Notre Dame U., 1994, Coll. William and Mary, 1999, Loyola U., 1999. Novelist lectr., U. Va., 1963, playwright in residence, Arena Stage, Washington, 1963-64, writer in residence, Hollins Coll., Va., 1968; Author: (novels) Tournament, 1949, Follow Me Down, 1950, Love in a Dry Season, 1951, Shiloh, 1952, Jordan County, 1954, September September, 1978; history The Civil War, A Narrative: Vol. I, Fort Sumter to Perryville, 1958, Vol. II, Fredericksburg to Meridian, 1963, Vol. III, Red River to Appomattox, 1974; play Jordon County: A Landscape in the Round, 1964, Conversations with Shelby Foote, 1989; editor: Chickamauga and Other Civil War Stories, 1993, Correspondence of Shelby Foote and Walker Percy, 1997, Chekhov Stories, 3 vols., 2000, Tacitus Histories Annals, 2003. Mem. acad. adv. bd. U.S. Naval Acad., 1988-89. Recipient Disting. Alumnus award U. N.C., 1975, Dos Passos prize for Lit., 1988, Charles Frankel award 1992, St. Louis Literary award 1992, Nevins-Freeman award 1992, Ingersoll-Weaver award, 1997, Richard Wright award, 1997, N.Y. Pub. Libr. Literary Lion, 1994, 98, Cleanth Brooks medal, 1999; Guggenheim fellow, 1955-57, Ford Found. fellow, 1963-64. Mem. Am. Acad. Arts and Letters, Fellowship of So. Writers, soc. Am. Historians. Office: 542 E Parkway S Memphis TN 38104-4362

FOOTE, SHERRILL LYNNE, retired manufacturing company technician; b. Marshalltown, Iowa, Apr. 19, 1940; d. Howard Raymond and Lois Ellen Ellis; m. Terry D. Downey, July 27, 1958 (div. 1978); children: Patrick L., Holly L. Harrelson; m. Frank H. Foote, Nov. 17, 1979 (div. 1989); stepchildren: Lauri K., Christopher R. Student, Marshalltown C.C., 1981—. Receptionist Drs. Long & Clawson, Marshalltown, 1958-59; clk. Fisher Controls, Marshalltown, 1963-73, cost estimating analyst, 1974-82, sr. cost estimator, 1982-95. Contbr. limericks Des Moines Register (Contest Winner), 1976, Marshalltown Times Rep., 1986. Mem. Mensa (contbr. Bull. Wordplay 1981—, limerick editor M-Pressions Ctrl. Iowa newsletter 1989-91, local sec. 1991-93). Democrat. Methodist. Avocations: games, reading, movies, plays. Home: 702 Ratcliffe Dr Marshalltown IA 50158-3453

FOOTE, WARREN EDGAR, neuroscientist, psychologist, educator; b. Boston, Nov. 5, 1935; s. Warren Edgar and Edith Irene (Landry) F.; B.A., Hamilton Coll., 1958; M.A., Boston U., 1960; Ph.D., Tufts U., 1965; m. Cynthia Sue Hall, July 21, 1973; children: Pamela Fowler, Sarah Canby, Julia Landry, Christopher Warren. Research assoc. Harvard U. Med. Sch., 1966-67, vis. asst. prof. psychology, 1970-73, asst. prof., 1974-83, assoc. prof., 1983—; USPHS postdoctoral fellow Yale, 1967-69; research scientist Norwich (Conn.) State Hosp., 1969-70; sr. Fulbright scholar Max-Planck Inst., Munich, Germany, 1973-74; assoc. psychologist Mass. Gen. Hosp., Boston, 1974—, psychologist, 1984-95, sr. psychologist, 1995—; cons. Gen. Foods Corp., 1970-74, Neurotech Corp., 1987-88. Served with M.C., AUS, 1959-60. Recipient McCurdy prize Mass. Soc. Research in Psychiatry, 1962; sr. Fulbright fellow, 1973-74; Nat. Inst. Neurol. Disease and Stroke grantee, 1974-77; NIMH grantee, 1970-73; Nat. Eye Inst. grantee, 1979—; Wayland Pub. Sch. Found. advisor, 1982—; Nat. Inst. Communicative Disorders and Stroke grantee, 1983—. Mem. AAAS, N.Y. Acad. Scis., Soc. Neurosci., Am. Psychol. Assn., Sigma Xi. Club: Harvard (Boston). Contbr. articles, revs. to profl. jours. Home: 5 Hilltop Park Wilbraham MA 01095-1753 Office: Mass Gen Hosp PO Box 70 Boston MA 02114 E-mail: wfoote@partners.org.

FOOTE, WILLIAM CHAPIN, business executive; b. Milw., Mar. 15, 1951; s. Peter Chapin and Mary Jane (Manierre) F.; m. Kari H. Foote, July 27, 1969; children: Tracy, Leslie Suzanne. BA, Williams Coll., 1973; MBA, Harvard U., 1977. Asst. treas. Chase Manhattan Bank, N.Y.C., 1973-75; sr. engagement mgr. McKinsey & Co., Inc., Chgo., 1977-83; v.p. USG Corp., Chgo., 1984-94, pres., COO, 1994-99; pres. CEO L&W, USG Interiors Inc., 1994, chmn., pres., CEO, 1996-2000; now chmn. bd., pres., CEO USG Corp., Chgo., 1999—. Mem.: Economics Chgo.

FOOTMAN, GORDON ELLIOTT, educational administrator; b. L.A., Oct. 10, 1927; s. Arthur Leland and Meta Fay (Neal) F.; m. Virginia Rose Footman, Aug. 7, 1954; children: Virginia, Patricia, John. BA, Occidental Coll., 1951, MA, 1954; EdD, U. So. Calif., 1972. Tchr., Arcadia, Calif., 1952, Glendale, Calif., 1956; psychologist Burbank (Calif.) Schs., 1956-64, supr., 1964-70, dir. pupil pers. svcs., 1970-72; dir. divsn. ednl. support svcs. L.A. County Office Edn., Downey, Calif., 1972-91; cons. ednl. adminstrn., counseling and psychol. svcs., 1991—. Pres. Calif. Assn. Adult Devel. and Aging, 1994-95; lectr. ednl. psychology U. So. Calif., 1972-75, asst. prof. ednl. psychology, 1976-85. Pres. Coun. for Exceptional Children, 1969-70; pres. Burbank Coordinating Coun., 1969-70; mem. Burbank Family Svc. Bd., 1972-72. Served with AUS, 1945-47. Mem. ACA (senator 1983-86, gov. coun. 1989-93, exec. com. 1990-93, parliamentarian 1991-92, western region br. assembly publs. editor 1985-87, chair 1988-89, chair bylaws com. 1995-97), Am. Ednl. Rsch. Assn., Am. Assn. Humanistic Edn. and Devel. (bd. dirs., treas. 1996—), Calif. Assn. for Counseling & Devel. (pres. 1981-82, exec. coun. 1996—. bylaws chair 2000--), Calif. Assn. for Counseling and Devel. Found., Nat. Assn. Pupil Pers. Adminstrs., Calif. Assn. Pupil Pers. Adminstrs. (monograph editor 1977-80), Calif. Assn. Counselor Educators and Suprs. (trustee), Calif. Soc. Ednl. Program Auditors and Evaluators (sec. 1975-76, v.p. 1976-77, pres.), Calif. Assn. Measurement and Evaluation in Counseling and Devel. (sec. 1976, pres. 1979-80, 96-97, pres. 1997-98, cons. ednl. and pupil svcs. adminstrn. 1991—), Calif. Inst. Tech. Assocs., Assn. Humanistic Edn. and Devel. (bd. dirs. 1996-99, treas. 1996—, pres. 2000-2001. conv. coord. 1999--), Huntington Libr. Soc. Fellows, Phi Delta Kappa, Phi Beta Kappa, Phi Alpha Theta, Psi Chi. Republican. Presbyterian. Home and Office: 1259 Sherwood Rd San Marino CA 91108-1816

FORAN, CHRIS, poet, educator; b. Seattle, Wash., Nov. 6, 1959; s. Edward Michael Forhan and Ange Yvonne Peterson. BA in Comms., Wash. State U., 1982; MA in English, U. N.H., 1987; MFA in Creative Writing, U. Va., 2003. Tchr. English Clinton (N.C.) H.S., 1987—89; instr. English Trident Tech. Coll., Charleston, SC, 1989—99; prof. English N.Mex. State U., Las Cruces, 2000—01; mem. faculty MFA program for writers Warren Wilson Coll., Swannanoa, NC, 2000—. Author: (book) Forgive Us Our Happiness, 1999, (chapbook) X, 2000, Crumbs of Bread, 1993. Recipient Bakeless award, Bread Loaf Writers' Conf., 1998, residency, Yaddo, 2000, 2001, Hoyns fellowship, U. Va., 2001. E-mail: ccforhand@aol.com.

FORAN, DAVID JOHN, public relations consultant; b. Milw., July 15, 1937; BS in Journalism, Marquette U., 1959, postgrad., 1966-68. Reporter Cath. Herald Citizen, Milw., 1960, Milw. Jour., 1960-66; dir. news bur. Marquette U., Milw., 1966-74, assoc. dir. pub. rels., 1974-81, exec. dir., 1981-92, instr. journalism, 1975-81; dir. pub. rels. and advt. Milw. Pub. TV, Milw., 1994-99; moderator TV program Sta. WTMJ, Milw., 1982-83. Past mem. bd. dirs. Wis. Heart Assn., past chmn. pub. rels. com.; past bd. mem. Walnut Improvement Coun.; past pres. Human Rels. Radio and TV Coun. of Milw., Milw. Pen and Mike Club. With U.S. Army, 1959, 61-62. Mem. Soc. Profl. Journalists-Sigma Delta Chi (past pres., chmn., dir. Milw. chpt.), Milw. Press Club, Milw. Broadcasters Club. Home: 209 W Lexington Blvd Glendale WI 53217-5017 E-mail: forand@execpc.com.

FORBES, ALFRED DEAN, religious studies researcher; b. Pomona, Calif., Mar. 2, 1941; s. Paul Edward and Lela Irene Forbes; m. Ellen Moss, May 8, 1971. BA in Physics, Harvard Coll., 1962; MDiv, Pacific Sch. Religion, 1969. With U.S. Peace Corps, Nigeria, 1962—64; prin. med. dept. scientist Hewlett-Packard Labs., Palo Alto, Calif., 1971—98; vis. scholar U. Calif., San Diego, 1999—2002. Vis. scholar Stanford (Calif.) U., 1986-89, U. Calif., Berkeley, 2003—; adj. prof. Jewish studies Pa. State U., 1998-2003; lectr. Assn. Internat. Bible et Informatique, 2000; charter mem. Bibl. Colloquium West, 2002—. Author: (with F.I. Andersen) Spelling in the Hebrew Bible, 1986, The Vocabulary of the Old Testament, 1989; (with F.I. Andersen and D.N. Freedman) Studies in Hebrew and Aramaic Orthography, 1992, others; algorithms editor Jour. Clin. Monitoring and Computing, 1985-2001; contbr. articles to profl. jours. Trustee, v.p. Whitney Edn. Found., Los Altos, Calif., 1981—88. Mem. Soc. Bibl. Lit., IEEE (sr. mem.), Internat. Brotherhood of Magicians (Order of Merlin). Avocations: travel, magic. Home: 820 Loma Verde Ave Palo Alto CA 94303-4112 E-mail: adforbes@ix.netcom.com.

FORBES, CHRISTOPHER (KIP FORBES), publisher; b. Morristown, N.J., Dec. 5, 1950; s. Malcolm Stevenson and Roberta Remsen (Laidlaw) F.; m. Baroness Astrid Cornelia Mathilde Von Heyl Zu Herrnsheim, Sept. 7, 1974; 1 child, Charlotte Adelaide Mathilde. BA in Art History magna cum laude, Princeton U., 1972; LHD (hon.), N.H. Coll., Manchester, 1986. Curator Forbes Mag. Collection, N.Y.C., 1970-80; ad salesman Forbes Mag., N.Y.C., 1972-76, assoc. pub., v.p., 1978-89, sec., 1981-92, vice-chmn., corp. sec., 1989—, also dir. Pub. Nineteenth Century, Phila., 1976-78. Author books and catalogues, including: Victorians in Togas, Paintings by Sir Lawrence Alma-tadem from the Collection of Allen Funt, 1973; the Royal Academy (1836-1901) Revisited, 1975; (with Margaret Kelly) War a la Mode: Meisonier Detaille, de Neuville, and Berne-Bellecour, 1975; (with Hermione Waterfield) Faberge: Imperial Eggs and Other Fantasies, 1978; (with Dr. Armand Hammer) Faberge Eggs, 1980, (with Susan Casveras) Victorian Childhood, 1986; editor: Masterpieces from the House of Faberge, 1984, (with Robyn Trommeur Brenner) Faberge, 2000. Active Cultural and Hist. Commn. Somerset County, N.J., 1984-96; bd. dirs. Newark Mus., Prince of Wales Found.; vice-chmn., bd. advisers Princeton U. Art Mus., N.J., Bklyn. Mus. Art, Victorian Soc.; nat. trustee Balt. Mus. Art; chmn. bd. trustees Am. Friends of the Louvre. Decorated assoc. knight Venerable Order St. John Jerusalem. Mem. Grolier Club, Nat. Arts Club, Salmagundi Club, Century Club. Republican. Episcopalian. Office: Forbes Inc 60 5th Ave New York NY 10011-8882

FORBES, CYNTHIA ANN, small business owner, marketing educator; b. Richmond, Calif., Dec. 27, 1951; d. James Martin and Mary Jane (Clafferty) Forbes; m. Larry Charles Osofsky, Mar. 20, 1970 (div. 1980); 1 child, Anna; m. William Charles Ham, Aug. 30, 1986. BA, U. Calif., 1977; MS, Golden Gate U., 1981; AS, Butte Coll., 2002. Rsch. asst. U. Calif., Berkeley, 1975-77, Chevron Rsch., Richmond, 1977-79; specialist dealer affairs Chevron USA, San Francisco, 1979-80, sales rep. San Rafael, Calif., 1981-84, adminstrv. supr. San Ramon, Calif., 1984-85; advt. mgr. Chevron Chem. Co., San Francisco, 1986-88; assoc. prof. Golden Gate U., San Francisco, 1981-92. Vol., lectr. child abuse prevention; vol. children's theatre dir.; firefighter, paramedic, tng. dir. Downieville Fire Dept. Democrat. Avocations: mountaineering, bicycling. Home: PO Box 427 Downieville CA 95936-0427 E-mail: cynthiaforbes@excite.com.

FORBES, DAVID CRAIG, musician; b. Seattle, Feb. 12, 1938; s. Douglas James and Ruby A. (Niles) F.; m. Sylvia Sterling, Aug. 29, 1965 (div. Apr. 1973); 1 child, Angela Rose. Grad., USN Sch. Music, 1957; student, Western Wash. U., 1960-64. Prin. horn La Jolla (Calif.) Civic Orch., 1958-60, Seattle Worlds Fair Band, 1962, Seattle Opera Co., 1964—, Pacific Northwest Ballet, Seattle, 1964—; asst. prin. horn Seattle Symphony Orch., 1964—2003, ret., 2003; prin. horn Pacific Northwest Wagner Fest., Seattle, 1975—. Instr. horn Western Wash. State U., 1969-81, Cornish Inst., Seattle, 1964-78. Served with USN, 1956-60. Mem. NARAS, Internat. Horn Soc. Avocations: piano, golf, fishing. Home: 9050 15th Ave NW # 2 Seattle WA 98117-3429

FORBES, EDWARD JOHN, III, developmental psychologist, educator; b. Syracuse, NY; s. Edward John Forbes Jr. and Helen Frances Forbes; m. Eileen Paula Kuehnel, June 8, 1963; children: Kirsten Heather, Kip Pieter, Michael Ian, Courtney Anne. BS in Microbiology, Syracuse U., 1963; MA in Psychology, W.Va. U., 1973. Rsch. asst. in microbiology SUNY Med. Ctr. Upstate, Syracuse, 1961; pharm. microbiologist Parke, Davis & Co., Detroit, 1963—69; rsch. asst. in psychology W.Va. U., Morgantown, 1969—74, instr. in psychology, 1970—74; asst. prof. psychology Mansfield U. Pa., 1974—80, Lock Haven U. of Pa., 1980—85, assoc. prof. psychology, 1985—, chmn. dept. psychology, 1985—89, pres. faculty assn., 1997—99, 2001—03. Mem.: APA, American Psychological Soc. (APS), Jean Piaget Soc., Soc. for Rsch. on Adolescents, Soc. for Rsch. in Child Devel., Phi Kappa Phi, Psi Chi. Democrat. Home: 219 W Water St Lock Haven PA 17745 Office: Lock Haven U Dept Psychology 401 N Fairview St Lock Haven PA 17745

FORBES, GORDON MAXWELL, sports journalist, commentator; b. Bellport, N.Y., Feb. 6, 1930; s. Harlow Campbell and Grace Bain (DeVall) F.; m. June Lolita Cassidy, July 16, 1960 (dec. Jan. 1994); children— James Douglas, Christopher Bryan BA in English, Duke U., 1955. Sports writer Fla. Times Union, Jacksonville, 1957-62; pro-football writer Phila. Inquirer, 1962-82; pro-football editor USA Today, Rosslyn, Va., 1982—2002; sports commentator Home Box Office Cable TV, 1988, Sta. WIP Radio, Phila., 1992-95. Corr. Sports Illustrated, N.Y.C., 1963-89; selector Pro Football Hall of Fame, Canton, Ohio, 1975-87. Author: How to Win at the Trotters, 1966, Tales from the Eagles Sidelines, 2002; contbr. numerous articles to jours. and mags. Served to cpl. U.S. Army, 1952-54 Recipient Dick McCann award for outstanding pro football coverage, 1988; named to Suffolk County (N.Y.) Sports Hall of Fame, 2001. Mem. Duke U. Alumni Assn., Pro Football Writers of Am. Republican. Episcopalian. Avocations: jogging, tennis, weightlifting, thoroughbred horses (with Write Stuff Stable). Home and Office: USA Today 5 Summerlawn Dr Lakewood NJ 08701-7542

FORBES, J. RANDY, congressman; b. Chesapeake, Va., Feb. 17, 1952; BA, JD, U. Va. Mem. Va. Ho. Dels., 1990-98, Va. State Senate, 1998-2001, U.S. Congress from 4th Va. dist., 2001—; mem. armed forces com., sci. com.; mem. Judiciary Com. Chmn. Rep. Party Va. Republican. Baptist. Office: US Ho Reps 307 Cannon House Office Bldg Washington DC 20515 also: 524 Johnstown Rd Chesapeake VA 23322-5617*

FORBES, JOHN DOUGLAS, architectural and economic historian; b. San Francisco, Apr. 9, 1910; s. John Franklin and Portia (Ackerman) F.; m. Margaret Funkhouser, Feb. 4, 1937 (dec.); children: Pamela, Peter; m. Mary Elizabeth Lewis, July 26, 1980 and Dec. 24, 1999; 1 child, Michael. AB, U. Calif.-Berkeley, 1931; MA, Stanford U., 1932; A.M., Harvard U., 1936, PhD, 1937. Accountant J.F. Forbes & Co. (C.P.A.'s), San Francisco, 1937-38, 42-43; asst. to dir. fine arts, curator paintings San Francisco World's Fair, 1938-40; chmn. dept. fine arts U. Kansas City, Mo., 1940-42; faculty history Bennington Coll., 1943-46; assoc. editor Am. Enterprise Assn., 1944-46; assoc. prof. history and fine arts Wabash Coll., 1946-50, prof., 1950-54; prof. bus. history Darden Sch. U. Va., 1954-80; prof. emeritus U. Va., 1980—, lectr. art history sch. continuing edn., 1982—; adv. bd. Historic Am. Bldgs. Survey, 1974-78. Author: Israel Thorndike, 1953, Victorian Architect, 1953, Murder in Full View, 1968, Death Warmed Over, 1971, Stettinius, Sr., Portrait of a Morgan Partner, 1974, J.P. Morgan, Jr. (1867-1943), 1981, Death Among the Artists, 1993; editor: Jour. Soc. Archtl. Historians, 1953-58; adv. editor industry Ency. Britannica, 1956-58. 2d lt. AUS, 1942. Decorated officier Ordre des Palmes Académiques (France); cavaliere Ordine al Merito (Italy); named Hon. Alumnus Class of 1950, Assn. of Wabash Men, 1993. Mem. Am. Hist. Assn. (life), Coll. Art Assn. (life), Mystery Writers Am., Soc. Archtl. Historians (pres. 1962-64, life), Colonial Soc. Mass. (life), AAUP, AIA (hon.), Audubon Soc., Nat. Trust Historic Preservation, Wilderness Soc. (life), Sierra Club (life), Nature Conservancy (life), Mechanics Inst. (life), Victorian Soc. (life), Victorian Soc. in Am., Calif. Hist. Soc., Soc. Calif. Pioneers (life), Friends of Sea Otter (life), Tamalpais Conservation Club (life), Am. Kitefliers Assn. (life), Am. Soc. Dowsers (life), Save-the Redwoods League (life), Phi Beta Kappa. Clubs: Colonnade (Charlottesville) (life), Pacific-Union (San Francisco); Farmington Country (Charlottesville, life); Cambridge (Mass.) Boat. Home: PO Box 3607 Charlottesville VA 22903-0607 also: 1250 Jones St San Francisco CA 94109-4261

FORBES, JOHN EDWARD, financial consultant; b. Chgo., Sept. 18, 1925; s. Harry Charles and Jeanette Anne (Field) F.; m. Dorsey Connors, Aug. 10, 1961. Student, Rensselaer Poly. Inst., 1943-44, Franklin and Marshall Coll., Lancaster, Pa., 1943; BA, Monmouth Coll., 1949; postgrad., Northwestern U., 1949-50. Account exec. and commodity mgr. Merrill Lynch, Pierce, Fenner and Smith, Inc., Chgo., 1949-61; pres. San Jose Cigarette Co., Calif., 1958-68; account exec. Hornblower & Weeks, Hemphill, Noyes, Inc., Chgo., 1961-71, assoc. resident mgr., 1971-75, v.p., resident mgr., 1975-78; corp. v.p. Loeb, Rhoades, Hornblower & Co., Chgo., 1981—, Shearson Lehman Bros., Chgo., 1961—; sr. v.p. fin. cons. Smith Barney, Chgo., 1995—. Pres. 227 E. Delaware Corp, Chgo., 1980-86; bd. dirs. Trend Industries, Chgo. Lt. USN, 1943-46, PTO. Mem.: Econ., Chgo. Bond, Hundred Club of Cook County, Tavern (pres. 1981-82), Saddle and Cycle (bd. dirs. 1983-86), Soc. St. Andrew. Home: 227 E Delaware Pl Chicago IL 60611-7758 Office: Smith Barney Inc 10 S Wacker Dr Fl 2800 Chicago IL 60606-7438 E-mail: john.e.forbes@rssmb.com.

FORBES, JOHN MALCOLM, non-profit administrator; b. Orlando, Fla., May 12, 1932; s. John Malcolm Forbes and Ethel (Cummings) Amory; m. Ariadne Hallermund Politis, June 18, 1954; children: Cynthia, Anne, Rebecca, J. Malcolm Jr., Lydia. AB, Havard Coll., 1956; cert. advanced study, Harvard Grad. Sch. of Edn., 1979; MS, U. Wis., 1963. Cert. secondary sch. tchr., Mass. Tchr. history Park Sch., Buffalo, 1957-61, Choate Sch., Conn., 1961-64, Browne & Nichols Sch., Cambridge, Mass., 1966-74; founder, dir. Walden Earthnet, Concord, Mass., 1990-91; exec. dir. UN Assn. Greater Boston & Mass., 1974-77; founder, dir. Tchr.'s Ctr. Global Edn. Harvard Grad. Sch. Edn., Cambridge, 1977-79; co-founder, dir. Coun. for Nuclear Weapons Freeze, Cambridge, 1980-88; exec. dir. World Federalist Assn. New Eng., Cambridge, 1992—2002; mng. coord. Coalition for Strong UN, Cambridge, 1993-98. Chmn., bd. dirs. Cambridge Friends Sch., 1971-73; mem. nat. fin. com. McGovern for Pres. campaign, 1971-72; founding mem. Cambridge Peace Commn., 1982-94; mem., bd. dirs. Cambridge Civic Assn., 1993-95, N.E. regional office Am. Friends Svc. Com., Cambridge, 1996-2000. Mem. World Federalist Assn. (exec. com. 1994-2001, bd. dirs.), New Eng. History Tchrs. Assn. (chair 1971-72), UN Assn. Greater Boston (bd. dirs. 1978-99, adv. coun. 2000—), ACLU. Democrat. Religious Soc. Friends. Avocation: classical music. Home: 3 Gerrys Landing Cambridge MA 02138-5511

FORBES, JOHN RIPLEY, museum executive, educator, naturalist; b. Chelsea, Mass., Aug. 25, 1913; s. Kenneth Ripley and Ellen Elizabeth (Barker) F.; m. Margaret Sanders, Dec. 10, 1951; children: Ripley, Anne. Spl. student, U. Iowa, 1933-34, Bowdoin Coll., 1934-35, LHD (hon.), 1987. Founder, dir. Stamford (Conn.) Mus., 1935-37; ornithologist, taxidermist Lee Mus. Biology, Bowdoin Coll., MacMillan-Arctic Expdn., Labrador and Baffin Island, 1937; founder, dir. William T. Hornaday Meml. Found., N.Y., 1938-50; organizer, dir. Kansas City (Mo.) Mus., 1939-41; founder Nashville Children's Mus., 1944, acting dir., 1945-46, trustee for life, 1975; exec. dir. Jacksonville (Fla.) Children's Mus., 1945; founder Fernbank Children's Nature Mus., Atlanta, 1946; organizer, dir. Oreg. Mus. Sci. and Industry, Portland, 1947-49; founder Nat. Found. for Jr. Mus., N.Y., dir., 1951-60; founder Sacramento Jr. Mus., dir., 1951-53; co-founder, dir. ops. Nature Centers for Young Am., 1959-60; founder, pres., chmn. bd. Natural Sci. for Youth Found., Conn., 1961—, founder Conservancy Nature Ctr., Naples, Fla., 1959. Organizer Ft. Worth's Children's Mus., 1945. Founder, pres. William T. Hornaday Meml. Trust, Conn., 1961-77; founder Mid-Fairfield County Youth Mus., Westport, Conn., 1958, pres., 1963-66, trustee for life, 1966; founder Am. Assn. Youth Mus., 1964, hon. life mem., 1976; co-founder, v.p. Aspetuck Land Trust, Fairfield County; pres. St. John's on the Lake Assn., N.H., 1963-64; pres. emeritus, trustee John and Anna Newton Porter Found., N.H., 1974-89; founder Outdoor Activity Ctr., Atlanta, chmn., 1977-80; founder Chattahoochee Nature Ctr., Roswell, Ga., pres., 1977-78; founder Reynolds Arboretum and Nature Preserve Morrow, Ga., 1976; founder, pres. Lakes Region Conservation Trust, Meredith, N.H., 1977; founder Forbes Nature Ctr. on Ragged Island Lake Winnipesaukee, N.H., 1979; trustee Hilla Von Rebay Found., 1968; trustee Milford (Pa.) Reservation 1977, pres. 1977-82 1983; founder, pres. Natural Sci. Solar Ctr., Milford, Pa., 1983; founder, trustee Cochran Mill Nature Ctr. and Arboretum, Fairburn, Ga., 1987; founder Autrey Mill Nature Preserve and Heritage Ctr., Alpharetta, Ga., 1988; founder, pres. Big Trees Forest Preserve, Sandy Springs, Ga., 1984; founder Camp Whitley at Lake Careco, Nature Ctr., Austell, Ga., 1992; naturalist, lectr. on Bahia Paraiso, Argentine polar transport ship sunk near U.S. Palmer Base at Arthur Harbor, Antarctic Peninsula, 1989; bd. mem. Environ. Adv. Commn. State of Ga., 1992-94. With M.C., USAAF, 1942-45. Recipient merit award Calif. Conservation Coun., 1953, conservation award Am. Motors, 1971, William T. Hornaday gold medal, 1977, Founder's award Natural Sci. for Youth Found., 1979, Conservationist of Yr. award Ga. Wildlife Fedn., 1991, Nature Educator of Yr. award Roger Tory Peterson Inst., 1995, Cert. Merit, Garden Club of Ga., Inc., 2000, Spl. Appreciation award Friends of Preservation Oaks, 2000; named Hon. Tex. Citizen, Gov. Price Daniel, 1962. Mem. Am. Assn. Mus. (chmn. children's mus. sec. 1965), Nat. Audubon Soc. (life), Am. Nature Study Soc., Nature Conservancy, Wilderness Soc., Am. Ornithologist Union (life), N.Y. Zool. Soc., Am. Birding Assn. (life), Nat. Wildlife Fedn., Conn. Conservation Assn. (pres. 1969-70), Sierra Club, Audubon Soc. N.H. (pres. 1975) Clubs: Explorers (N.Y.C.); Mazamas (Portland, Oreg.). Home: 11 Wildwood Vly Atlanta GA 30350-4461 Office: Natural Scis for Youth Found 130 Azalea Dr Roswell GA 30075-4804

FORBES, JUDIE, university official; b. Fullerton, Calif., Sept. 27, 1942; d. James Franklin and Lois Virginia (Couse) F.; m. Ralph M. Hawk, Nov. 10, 1990; children: Laurel Alice Schader, James Joseph Resha, Edward John Resha III. BA in Physics, Calif. State U., Fullerton, 1974, MS in Engring., 1979; MBA, U. So. Calif., 1983; PhD in Exec. Mgmt., Claremont Grad. U., 1993. Engr. electromech. divsn. Northrop, Anaheim, Calif., 1975-80, project engr., mgr. electronic divsn. Hawthorne, Calif., 1981-87; mem. tech. staff TRW, San Bernadino, Calif., 1981; project mgr. Gen. Rsch. Corp., El Segundo, Calif., 1987-89; v.p. D.C. Caldwell & Co., Inc., Buena Park, Calif., 1987-91; European program mgr. TRW Technar, Irwindale, Calif., 1989-94; dir. engr. Thomas Lighting, L.A., 1995-96; COO MicroSeptic, Inc., Laguna Hills, Calif., 1997-98; v.p. for acad. affairs Northcentral U., Prescott, Ariz., 1998—2001; pres. Jandr Assocs., 1993—. Calif. State U. Found. grantee, 1974; named Disting. Alumni Calif. State U., 1986; recipient Engring. Merit award Orange County Engring. Council, 1985. Fellow: AIAA (assoc., pres. Orange County 1986—87), AAUW, nst. for Advancement Engring., Soc. Women Engrs. (pres. L.A. chpt. 1981—82, nat. v.p. 1983—84); mem.: Internat. Women Pilots Assn. Democrat. Home: 3333 E Murphy Way Prescott AZ 86303-5742 Office: Jandr Assocs 303 E Gurley # 515 Prescott AZ 86301 E-mail: drjforbes@commspeed.net.

FORBES, KENNETH ALBERT FAUCHER, urological surgeon; b. Waterford, N.Y., Apr. 28, 1922; s. Joseph Frederick (dec.) and Adelle Frances (Robitaille) Faucher; adopted s. James Peter Forbes; m. Jeanne Ann Bonacci, June 18, 1947 (dec.); 1 child: Michael; m. Eileen Ruth Gibbons, Aug. 4, 1956; children: Diane, Kenneth E., Thomas, Maureen, Daniel. BS cum laude, U. Notre Dame, 1944; MD, St. Louis U., 1947. Diplomate Am. Bd. Urology. Intern St. Louis U. Hosp., 1947-48; resident in urol. surgery Barnes Hosp., VA Hosp., Washington U., St. Louis. U. schs. medicine, St. Louis, 1948-52; asst. chief urology Letterman Army Hosp., San Francisco, 1952-54; fellow West Roxbury (Harvard) VA Hosp., Boston, 1955; asst. chief urology VA Hosp., East Orange, N.J., 1955-58; practice medicine specializing in urology Green Bay, Wis., 1958-78, Long Beach, Calif., 1978-85. Mem. cons. staff Fairview State Hosp. U. Calif. Med. Ctr., Irvine, VA Hosp., Long Beach; commr. State Med. Soc. Wisc., 1975—77, chmn. legal def. com., 1976—77; pres. Wis. Urological Soc., 1977—78; asst. clin. prof. surgery U. Calif., Irvine, 1978—85; cons. Vols. in Tech. Assistance, 1986—; locum tenens (cons. and surgery) 9 states, 1989—99. Contbr. articles to profl. jours. Served with USNR, 1944-46, ensign 1947-51; capt. U.S. Army, 1952-54. Named Outstanding Faculty Mem. by students, 1981. Fellow ACS, Royal Soc. Medicine, Internat. Coll. Surgeons; mem. AMA, AAAS, Calif. Med. Assn., Am. Urol. Assn. (exec. com. North Ctrl. sect. 1972-75, Western sect. 1980—), N.Y. Acad. Scis., Surg. Alumni Assn. U. Calif.-Irvine, Justin J. Cordonnier Soc. Washington U., Urologists Corr. Club, Notre Dame Club (Man of Yr. award 1965), Union League Club of Chgo., Miles City Club (Mont.), Phi Beta Pi. Republican. Roman Catholic. Mailing: 2951 Sage Ridge Dr Reno NV 89509-7044

FORBES, LEONARD, engineering educator; b. Grande Prairie, Alta., Can., Feb. 21, 1940; came to U.S., 1966; s. Frank and Katie (Tschetter) F. BSc with distinction in Engring. Physics, U. Alta., 1962; MS in Elect. Engring., U. Ill., 1963, PhD, 1970. Staff engr. IBM, Fishkill, N.Y., 1970-72, Manassas, Va., 1970-72; IBM vis. prof. Howard U., Washington, 1972; asst. prof. U. Ark., Fayetteville, 1972-75; assoc. prof. U. Calif., Davis, 1976-82; prof. Oreg. State U., Corvallis, 1983—; vis. prof. U. Calif., San Diego, 2000—01. With Hewlett-Packard Labs., Palo Alto, Calif., 1978; cons. to Telex Computer Products, D.H. Baldwin, Hewlett-Packard, Santa Rosa, Fairchild, United Epitaxial Tech., Naval Ocean Systems Ctr., Hewlett-Packard Corvallis, Micron Tech. Boise; organizer Portland Internat. Conf. and Exposition on Silicon Materials and Tech., 1985-87. Contbr. articles to profl. jours.; patentee in field (over 100 patents). Served with Royal Can. Air Force, 1963-66. Mem. IEEE. Home: 965 NW Highland Ter Corvallis OR 97330-9706 Office: Oreg State U Dept Elec Engring Corvallis OR 97331 E-mail: flf@ece.orst.edu.

FORBES, MARJORIE WEBSTER, volunteer counselor; b. Providence, July 25, 1930; d. George Wickliffe and Kathryn Craig (Annable) Webster; m. Richard Daniel Forbes, Aug. 4, 1951; 1 child, Richard Bruce. BA in Psychology, U. R.I., 1988; MA in Counseling, R.I. Coll., 1992. Vol. pres. Get Out and Live Successfully, Warwick, R.I., 1984—. Vocal tape Panic Disorder, 1987. Chairperson adv. coun. John A. Ferris Health Ctr., 1988—; vol. Samaritans, Providence, 1988. Recipient Jefferson award Am. Inst. for Pub. Svc., 1989, Community Svc. award U. R.I., 1989. Mem. Phobia Soc. R.I. (treas. 1987-91). Avocations: reading, musicals, visiting friends, travel..

FORBES, MICHAEL PATRICK, former congressman; b. Riverhead, N.Y., July 16, 1952; m. Barbara; children: Abby, Ted. BA, SUNY Albany, 1983. Coord. various local, state, fed. Rep. campaign, 1980-89; exec. asst. to U.S. Senator Alfonse D'Amato, 1981-84; adm. asst. to U.S. Rep. Connie Mack, 1985-87; owner small bus., 1985-89; regional administr. U.S. Small Bus. Administrn., 1989-92; legis. dir., regional mgr. U.S. C. of C., 1993-94; mem. 104th-106th Congress from 1st N.Y. dist., 1995-2001. Democrat.*

FORBES, MORTON GERALD, lawyer; b. Atlanta, July 12, 1938; s. Arthur Mark and Mary Dean (Power) F.; m. Eunice Lee Haynesworth, Jan. 25, 1963; children: John, Ashley, Sarah. AB, Wofford Coll., 1962; JD, U. Ga., 1965. Bar: Ga. 1965, U.s. Dist. Ct. (mid. dist.) Ga. 1965, U.S. Dist. Ct. (so. dist.) Ga. 1968, U.S. Dist. Ct. (no. dist.) Ga. 1993, U.S. Ct. Appeals (5th cir.) 1974, U.S. Ct. Appeals (4th cir.) 1972, U.S. Ct. Appeals (11th cir.) 1981. Assoc. Pierce, Ranitz, Lee, Berry & Mahoney, 1967-70; ptnr. Pierce, Ranitz, Berry, Mahoney & Forbes, 1970-76, Pierce, Ranitz, Mahoney, Forbes & Coolidge, 1976-81; ptnr., sec. Ranitz, Mahoney, Forbes & Coolidge, P.C., 1981-91, Forbes & Bowman, Savannah, Ga., 1991—. Gen. counsel Ga. Fed. Young Rep. Clubs, 1971-72; guest lectr. dept. dental hygiene Armstrong State Coll., 1970-72. Mem. Savannah (port Authority (now Savannah Econ. Devel. Authority), 1973-2003, chmn., 1979-81; mem. Chatham County Devel. Authority, 1973-80; nat. com. Nat. Fedn. Young Reps., 1973; econ. adv. coun. Coastal Area Planning and Devel. Authority, 1980—; bd. dirs. Savannah Symphony Soc., 1971-75; Ga. del. to Japan/Southeast Trade Mission, Kyoto, Japan, 1983, S.E. Asia U.S.A./Japan Assn. meeting, Birmingham, Ala., 1984. With USN, 1965-67. Recipient Outstanding Service award Savannah Port Authority, 1981. Mem. ABA, Internat. Assn. Defense Counsel, Fedn. Def. and Corp. Counsel, State Bar Ga., Ala. Def. Lawyer Assn. (hon.), Am. Judicature Soc., Nat. Assn. Bond Counsel, Ga. Def. Lawyers Assn. (v.p. 1987—, mem. exec. com. 1988, bd. dirs., exec. v.p. 1990-91, pres. 1991-92), Savannah Bar Assn. (exec. com. 1989-94, pres. 1992-93), Libel Def. Resource Ctr., Def. Rsch. Inst. (state chmn. 1992-99, bd. dirs. 1999-2002), Savannah Econ. Devel. Action Coun. (founding), Savannah Area Wofford Coll. Alumni Club (past pres.), Soc. of the Cincinnati (Va.), St. Andrews Soc. (bd. stewards), Soc. Colonial Wars, Sons of Revolution (sec. 1988-92), Chatham Club, Savannah Yacht Club, 1st City Club, The Landings Club. Republican. Presbyterian. Office: Forbes & Bowman PO Box 13929 Savannah GA 31416-0929

FORBES, PETER, architect; b. Berkeley, Calif., May 22, 1942; s. John Douglas and Margaret (Funkhouser) F.; m. Patricia Ann Marsh, Aug. 27, 1966 (div. 1982); children: Alexander John, Anne deMarken; m. Erica Longfellow deBerry, July 21, 1990; 1 child, Allegra Longfellow. BArch, U. Mich., 1966; MArch, Yale U., 1967; Dr. Engring. Tech. (hon.), Wentworth Inst. Tech., 1991. Registered architect, Mass., Va., Calif., Maine, R.I., N.Y., Mich., Conn., D.C.; cert. Nat. Council Archtl. Registration Bds. Project designer Skidmore, Owings & Merrill, Chgo., 1965-66; assoc. ptnr. PARD Team, Inc., Boston, 1967-71; pres. Forbes Hailey Jeas Erneman, Inc., Boston, 1972-80, Peter Forbes and Assoc., Inc., Boston, 1980-2000, Peter Forbes, FAIA Arch., Seal Harbor, Maine, 2000—. Mem. Commonwealth of Mass. Designer Selection Bd., 1986-89; mem. Spl. Commn. Concerning State and County Bldgs., 1978-81; bd. dirs. continuing edn. Boston Archtl. Ctr.; vis. critic U. Mich., 1980-82, Cath. U. Am., Rome, 1982; vis. lectr. Cath. U., Washington, 1997; lectr., vis. critic Va. Poly. Inst. and State U., 1989-92, 96, Columbia U., 1984; vis. critic N.C. State U., 1997; Thomas S. Monaghan Disting. vis. prof. U. Mich., 1987; vis. prof. Harvard U., 1989, 91, 94, G. Truman Ward vis. lectr. Va. Poly. Inst. and State U., 1996; vis. lectr. Lawrence Tech. U., 1996, Evergreen State Coll., 1996, U. B.C., 1996; guest lectr. Boston Mus. Fine Arts, 1997, Guido A. Binda vis. lectr. U. Mich., 1997, vis. prof. Wentworth Inst. of Tech., Gargonza, Italy, 2003 Author: Ten Houses: Peter Forbes and Associates, 1995; exhbns. include Cath. U. Am., 1982, 97, U. Mich., 1982, 87, 97, Va. Poly. Inst. and State U., 1983, Boston Athenaeum, 1986, Harvard U., 1986, Lawrence Tech. U., 1996; contbr. articles to profl. jours. Recipient Record House award, 1983, 86, 87, 89, New Eng. Design awrd, 1986, 87, 89, 91, 94, 96, 97, 98, Archtl. Excellence award Am. Inst. Steel Constrn., 1987, Tucker award Bldg. Stone Inst., 1987, 90, Best and Brightest award, 1995, Honor award Am. Wood Inst., 1989, Nat. Housing Design award, 1990, Silver award Indsl. Designers Soc. Am., 1993, 94, Am. Arch. award Chgo. Athenaeum Mus. Arch. and Design, 1999. Fellow AIA (nat. jud. coun. 1987—, Nat. honor award 1986, 92, New Eng. regional coun./design award 1986, 87, 89, 91, 94, 96, 97, 98, Washington D.C. merit award 1994; Excellence in Arch. award Maine chpt. 1995), Boston Soc. Archs. (bd. dirs., commr. pub. affairs, chmn. ethics com., v.p., pres. 1988-89, Excellence in Arch. award 1988-89, 91-94, 98, Honor award 1995, 97, 98, Excellence in Housing design award 1996, 98), Soc. Archtl. Historians (life), Century Club, Newport Reading Rm., Racquet and Tennis Club, Nat. Tennis Club, Yale Club, Boston Athenaeum. Home: Greenings Is Southwest Harbor ME 04679 also: Viale Giovanni Milton 65 50129 Florence Italy Office: 12 Main St Seal Harbor ME 04675 E-mail: pfamaine@acadia.net., pfafirenze@dada.it.

FORBES, RICHARD MATHER, biochemistry educator; b. Wooster, Ohio, Jan. 8, 1916; s. Ernest Browning and Lydia Maria (Mather) F.; m. Mary Medlicott, Feb. 26, 1944; children: Sally Allen, Anne Mather, Stephen Harding. BS, Pa. State Coll., 1938, MS, 1939; PhD, Cornell U., 1942. Instr. biochemistry Wayne State U., 1942; research fellow Cornell U., Ithaca, N.Y., 1942-43; asst. prof. U. Ky., Lexington, 1946-49; assoc. prof. U. Ill., Champaign-Urbana, 1949-55, prof. nutritional biochemistry, 1955-85, emeritus prof., 1985—. Contbr. articles to profl. jours. Served to capt. U.S. Army, 1943-46. Recipient H. H. Mitchell award U. Ill., 1981 Fellow AAAS, Am. Inst. Nutrition (Borden award 1984); mem. Am. Soc. Animal Sci. (Gustav Bohstedt award 1968), Sigma Xi. Democrat. Mem. United Ch. of Christ. Clubs: Nat. Exchange, Izaak Walton League . Home: 101 W Windsor Rd Apt 2105 Urbana IL 61802-6663

FORBES, SHARON ELIZABETH, software engineer; b. Lynn, Mass., Nov. 23, 1960; d. Leland James Brown and Vail (Wilkinson) Bartelson. BSChemE, U. Mass., 1983. Software engr. K&L Automation div. Daniel Industry, Tucson, 1983-86, 1986-87, asst. mgr. software systems, 1987; software mgr. Daniel Automation, Houston, 1987-91; sr. software engr. Praxis Instruments, Inc., Houston, 1991-93, Dresser Measurement, Houston, 1993-97, Dresser Roots Instruments Operation, Houston, 1997-98, Roots Meters and Instruments, Houston, 1999-2001, Dresser Inc., Houston, 2001; sr. softward engr. Omni Flow Computers, Inc., Stafford, Tex., 2001—02. Mem.: Instrument Soc. Am. Republican. Avocations: church, contemporary jazz, computers. Home: 5735 Henniker Dr Houston TX 77041-6589 Office: Omni Flow Computers Inc 10701 Corporate Dr Ste 300 Stafford TX 77477 E-mail: sforbes@omniflow.com.

FORBES, STEVE (MALCOLM STEVENSON FORBES JR.), publishing executive; b. Morristown, N.J., July 18, 1947; s. Malcolm and Roberta (Laidlaw) F.; m. Sabina Beekman, June 19, 1971; 5 children. BA, Princeton U., 1970; LHD (hon.), Lycoming Coll.; LHD, Jacksonville U., Kean Coll., Seton Hill U.; LLD (hon.), Lock Haven U., Westminster Coll., Sacred Heart U., Centenary Coll., Iona Coll., Pepperdine U., Lehigh U., New Hampshire U., Siena Coll.; LittD (hon.), Spring Arbor U.; ScD (hon.), N.Y. Inst. Tech., Lynn U.; SScD (hon.), U. Francisco Marroquin; D.P.S. (hon.), U. Rio Grande; PhD (hon.), Hillsdale Coll.; PhD (hon.), UEES Universidad Espiritu Santo, Ecuador; DBA (hon.), Lincoln Coll., New Bulgarian Univ.; AA (hon.), Raritan Valley C.C. With Forbes Inc., N.Y.C., 1970—, pres., COO, 1980-90, dep. editor-in-chief, 1982-90, editor-in-chief, pres., CEO, 1990—. Author: The Moral Basis of A Free Society, 1999; co-author (filmscript): Some Call It Greed, 1977, A New Birth of Freedom, 1999; editor: Fact and Comment, 1974. Pres. Somerset County Park Commn., 1981—91; mem. Bd. for Internat. Broadcasting, 1983—93, chmn., 1985—93; trustee Brooks Sch., North Andover, Mass., 1978—97; pres., bd. trustees Princeton U., 1992—2002, Freedom House, 1993—, Heritage Found., 2001—, Found. for the Def. Democracies, 2001—; bd. visitors Pepperdine U., 2002—; Ronald Reagan Presdl. Found., 1990; Rep. presdl. primary campaign candidate, 1995—96, 1999—2000; internat. adv. bd. Brit. Am. Bus. Coun., 2001—; pres. bd. trustees Brooks Sch., 1987—96; bd. overseers Meml. Sloan-Kettering Cancer Ctr., 1989—; chmn. bd. dirs. Empower Am., 1993—96, Ams. Soc., 1992—; chmn. bd dirs Nat. Endowment for Democracy, 1994—98; bd. dirs. Nat. Taxpayers Union, 1997, Jackie Robinson Found., 1996—; mem. Coun. for Nat. Policy, 1998; bd. dirs. Abraham Lincoln Presdl. Libr., 2001—. Republican. Office: Forbes Inc 60 Fifth Ave New York NY 10011-8882

FORBES, THAIS R. anthropologist, consultant; m. Michael B. Summers; children: Elijah D. Forbes-Summers, Athena N. Forbes-Summers. MA in Applied Anthropology, U. of South Fla.; BA in Geography, Anthropology, U. of So. Maine. Cert. Playground Safety Insp. Nat. Recreation & Pk. Assn., Va. Dir., CPR Health & Safety Edn., Tampa, 1989—2002; dir., mktg., cmty. edn. Vasectomy & Reversal Ctr. of Fla., Tampa, 2000—. Consulting anthropologist, mktg. cons. Vasectomy Support Found., Inc., Clearwater, 2000—02. First aid instr.-trainer Am. Safety & Health Inst., Tampa, 1999—2002; BLS instr.-trainer Am. Heart Assn., Fla. Affiliate, Tampa, 1990—2002; officer Lake Forest Homeowners' Assn., Tampa, 1996—99. Grantee Jesse Smith Noyes Found. Pub. Svc. Fellow, Ctr. for Human Ecology Studies, 1982, Master's Rsch. Fellow, Caribbean Studies Inst., InterAm. Found., 1988. Mem.: Phi Kappa Phi. Personal E-mail: trforbes@tampabay.rr.com.

FORBES, THEODORE MCCOY, JR., arbitrator, mediator, retired lawyer; b. Atlanta, Oct. 28, 1929; s. Theodore M. and Mary Beatrice (Christie) F.; m. Margaret Paty, Dec. 12, 1953; children: Theodore McCoy, Margaret Paty. BS in Chemistry, Ga. Inst. Tech., 1950; LLB, U. Va., 1953. Bar: Ga., 1952, D.C. 1973, U.S. Ct. Appeals (5th cir.) 1976, U.S. Ct. Appeals (11th cir.) 1981. Instr. Culver (Ind.) Summer Naval Sch., 1950; assoc. Smith, Gambrell & Russell, and predecessor firms, Atlanta, 1953-58, ptnr., 1958-91; solo practice, 1992-95. Bd. dirs. Travelers Aid Soc., Atlanta, 1974-90, pres., 1975-76, 86-89; bd. dirs., corp. sec. Shepherd Spinal Ctr., Atlanta, 1975-95; bd. dirs. Ga. Fund for Edn., 1986-89. Lt. (j.g.) USNR, 1950-62. Fellow Ga. Bar Found.; mem. ABA, Atlanta Bar Assn., State Bar Ga. (emeritus), Ga. C. of C. (bd. dirs. 1986-95), Capital City Club (life). Avocations: golf, american history, fishing. Home: 2520 Peachtree Rd NW Apt 202 Atlanta GA 30305-3617

FORBES, TIMOTHY CARTER, publisher; b. Morristown, N.J., Oct. 5, 1953; s. Malcolm Stevenson and Roberta (Laidlaw) F.; m. Anne Shepard Harrison, Mar. 4, 1983. AB with honors, Brown U., 1976, LHD (hon.), 1996. Prodr. Seven Seas Cinema, N.Y.C., 1977-81; prodr., screenwriter N.Y.C., 1981-85; v.p. Forbes Inc., N.Y.C., 1986—, COO, 1996, also bd. dirs. Dir., producer: (films) Some Call It Greed, 1977, Lost to the Revolution, 1979, Golden Age of Toy Boats, 1981, Happily Ever After?, 1992. Trustee N.Y. Med. Coll., 2000—; bd. fellows Brown U., 2000—; bd. dirs. United Hosp. Fund, 1992—, Margaret Thatcher Found., 1993—, Hist. House Trust N.Y.C., 1990—. Mem. Am. Antiquarian Soc. Office: Forbes Inc 60 5th Ave New York NY 10011-8882

FORBIS, BRYAN LESTER, state agency administrator; b. Jefferson City, Mo., Aug. 14, 1957; s. Lewis Wagner and Thelma Rose (Thompson) F.; m. Mary Beth Dobbs, Nov. 1987. BA in Polit. Sci. with honors, U. Mo., 1979, MA in Polit. Sci., 1981. Rsch. asst. Mo. Office of Lt. Gov., Jefferson City, 1980; teaching asst. U. Mo., Columbia, 1980-81; mgmt. analysis specialist I, Mo. Divsn. Family Svcs., Jefferson City, 1981-83; mgmt. analysis specialist II, Mo. Divsn. Med. Svcs., Jefferson City, 1983-85; asst. to dir. Mo. Divsn. of Aging, Jefferson City, 1985-89, dir., 1992-93, special asst. to dir., 1996—, dep. dir., 2000—; asst. dir. Mo. Dept. of Natural Resources, 1989, dir. program coordination, 1989-90, dir. policy devel., 1991-92; dep. dir. Mo. Div. Child Support Enforcement, 1993-95; spl. asst. Mo. Divsn. Aging, 1995-99, dep. dir., 1999—2001; commr. Mo. Pub. Svc. Commn., 2001—. Mem. Capital City Coun. on Arts, Jefferson City, 1985-89, Mo. Mansion Preservation Inc., Jefferson City, 1985-99; steering com. March of Dimes, Jefferson City, 1986; mem. Conservation Fedn. of Mo., 1992—; sec. U. Mo. Arts and Scis. Leaders, 1996-2000, Fund Distbn. Com., United Way, 1995—. Named One of Outstanding Young Men of Am., 1985, 86; curator scholar U. Mo., 1975, 77, 78, William Bradshaw scholar U. Mo., 1979. Mem. ASPA, Acad. Polit. Sci., Capital Area Mo. U. Alumni Assn. (exec. asst., pres. bd. dirs., dist. bd. dirs. 1992—), U. Mo. Arts and Scis. Alumni Orgn. (pres. 1999-2000), Phi Beta Kappa, Pi Sigma Alpha, Omicron Delta Kappa. Clubs: Pachyderms (Jefferson City). Republican. Lutheran. Avocations: chess, collecting polit. campaign buttons, football. Home: 2112 Whitney Woods Ct Jefferson City MO 65101-3544 Office: Missouri Public Svc Com Gov's Office Bldg Jefferson City MO 65101

FORBUSH, ROBERT RAYMOND, SR., financial consultant, small business owner, educator; b. Alhambra, Calif., Apr. 14, 1927; s. Robert Albert Forbush and Ellen Lucille Fullington; m. Peggy Ann Weber (div.); children: Robert Jr., Matthew Roger; m. Nelly Adela Roucaucio (div. Nov. 1991). BA, San Francisco State U., 1976; MA, Sonoma State U., Rohnert Park, Calif., 1981. Lic. Life, Health and Calif. Insurance Calif., 1968, Real Estate-Finance Calif., cert. Adult tchr. Real Estate Finance Calif., Nev; lic. C61 Contractor Calif. Owner, operator ABC Nursery Sch., San Rafael and Petaluma, Calif., 1960—65, Liceo Lynn Glenn, San Rafael and Petaluma, Calif., 1961—65, ABC Nursery Sch., San Rafael and Petaluma, Calif., 1966—91; pvt. bus. cons., 1991—. Treas. Pvt. Assn. Childhood Edn., 1983—86, accreditation com. chair. Author: (books) Investing Offshore Secrets of Asset Protection, 1989, Alone Again, 1999, Stop Identity Theft, 2003. Vol. Police Activities League, Palm Springs, Calif. Named an honored mem. ctr. for entrepreneurship creativity and innovative mgmt., Cal Poly U. Sch. Bus. Mem.: Palm Desert C. of C.

FORBUSH, SANDRA M. artist, educator; b. Garden City, N.Y., Jan. 14, 1940; d. John Herbert Jr. and Mary Elizabeth (Keeler) Mears; m. Wade Hampton Massie III, Mar. 27 (div. Aug. 1980); 1 child, Nancy Massie Wiley; m. Lloyd Augustus Forbush, Sept. 6, 1982. Student, Md. Inst. Art, Balt., 1957-59. Fashion model Garfinckel & Co., Washington, 1960-65; fashion freelance model, commls. and TV Washington, Balt., N.Y.C; ballet tchr. Wakefield Country Day Sch., Huntly, Va., piano tchr.; profl. portrait artist, art tchr. self-employed, Flint Hill, Va. Ofcl. artist The Va. Gold Cup, Great Meadow, 2002, $100,000 Grand Prix Jumper Classic, Great Meadow, 2002. One-woman shows include Montpelier, Va., Middleburg Libr., Fifth St. Gallery; exhibited in shows at Am. Acad. Equine Art, 1999, The Dog Mus., St. Louis, Farmington Hunt Club, Beresford Gallery, Saratoga Springs, N.Y., Mus. of Hounds and Hunting, At the Dog Show, Wichita, Kans., Somoza Gallery, Houston, 2000, others; offl. artist Va. Gold Cup, 2002, Grand Prix, Gt. Meadow, 2002; works include sporting art in oil, numerous portraits in oil; contbr. articles to profl. jours. Mem.: Am. Acad. Equine Art (assoc.). Episcopalian. Home: Foxhall Farm Box 149 Flint Hill VA 22627 E-mail: sforbush@rmaonline.net.

FORBY, GARY F. state representative; m. Angie Forby; 4 children. Farmer; owner Forby Excavating Inc., Benton, Ill.; mem. Ill. Ho. of Reps., 2001—. Past chmn. bd. Franklin County; bd. dirs. So. Ill. Workforce Man-Tra-Con. Mem.: Oper. Engrs. Laborers' Internat. Democrat. Office: 257-S Stratton Office Bldg Springfield IL 62706 Address: PO Box 1000 Benton IL 62812*

FORCE, ELIZABETH ELMA, retired pharmaceutical executive, consultant; b. Phila., Sept. 6, 1930; d. Harry Elgin and Loretta G. (Werner) F. BA, Temple U., 1952; postgrad., U. Pa., 1965-67; MPh, George Washington U., 1972, PhD, 1973. Cons. sr. scientist Booz-Allen Hamilton, Bethesda, Md., 1967-68; rsch. cons. scientist GEOMET, Inc., Rockville, Md., 1968-70; profl. assoc. div. med. scis. NAS-NRC, Washington, 1970-74; mgr. clin. adminstrn. dept. clin. rsch. and devel. Wyeth Labs., Radnor, Pa., 1974-77; exec. dir. regulatory affairs Merck Sharp and Dohme Rsch. Labs., West Point, Pa., 1977-88; cons. Clin. Regulatory Systems, Sarasota, Fla., 1988-91. Asst. professorial lectr. epidemiology and environ. health Sch. Medicine George Washington U., Washington, 1972-74; vis. assoc. prof. cmty. health and preventive medicine Med. Coll. Jefferson U., Phila., 1981-83. Editor Clin. Rsch. Practice and Drug Regulatory Affairs, 1983-85, Drug Info. Jour., 1984-88; contbr. 60 articles to profl. jours. Resident Coun., Abbey Delray South, 2003-05. Pres. Sterling Lakes Owners Assn., Boynton Beach, 1996-98, pres. Women's Resource Ctr., Sarasota, 1992-94; pres., bd. dirs. Siesta Tower Condominium Assn., Sarasota, 1990-92; vice chmn. Com. for Minority Contracts, Sarasota County, 1991; chmn. adv. coun. bd. trustees Ringling Mus. of Art, 1991-95, Coun. on Violence, Sarasota County, 1994; mem. steering com. Harid Conservatory Music, Lynn U., Boca Raton, 1999-2000. Pub. Health fellow U. Pa. Sch. Medicine, 1965-67, Ruhland

Pub. Health fellow George Washington U. Sch. Medicine, 1971-73. Mem. AAUW, Drug Info. Assn. (pres. 1986-87, Outstanding Dir. award 1985), Heritage Soc. of George Washington U. Avocation: collecting oriental antiques. Home: 1717 Homewood Blvd Apt 247 Delray Beach FL 33445-6801

FORCE, PIERRE MARIE, French language and literature educator; b. Toulon, France, Apr. 4, 1958; came to U.S., 1984; s. Louis Joseph and Marie (Hapette) F.; m. Christel Hollevoet, 1997; children: Charlotte, Eliot. BA, Sorbonne, Paris, 1979, MA, 1980, PhD, 1987, MBA, NYU, 1990. Fgn. svc. officer French Embassy, Mexico City, 1981-83; lectr. Yale U., New Haven, 1984-86, Johns Hopkins U., Balt., 1986-87; q.p. Banque Pallas France, Paris, 1990-91; asst. prof. French Columbia U., N.Y.C., 1987-90, assoc. prof., 1992—95, prof., 1995—2000, Nell Singer prof. of contemporary civilization, 2000—, chmn. dept. French, 1997—. Adv. bd. Maison Francaise; mem. governing bd. Soc. of Fellows. Author: Le Probleme Hermeneutique Chez Pascal, 1989, Moliere ou Le Prix des Choses, 1994, Self-Interest Before Adam Smith, 2003; mem. editl. bd. Romanic Rev. Fellow Ecole Normale Superieure, Paris, 1978-81. Mem. Societe des Amis de Port-Royal, Paris Am. Club. Democrat. Roman Catholic. Home: 35 Claremont Ave # 9N New York NY 10027-6802 Office: Columbia Univ 517 Philosophy Hall New York NY 10027

FORCE, ROBERT, law educator; b. Phila., Aug. 11, 1934; s. Charles and Dora (Woloshin) F.; m. Ruth Morris, Aug. 18, 1962; children: Joshua Simon, Seth Daniel. BS, Temple U., 1955, LL.B., 1958; postgrad., U. Adelaide, 1958-59; LL.M., NYU, 1960. Bar: Pa. 1961. Law clk. to presiding justice Pa. Ct. Common Pleas., Phila., 1960-61, U.S. Dist. Ct., Phila., 1961-62; instr. Temple U., Phila., 1960-61; assoc. Kleinbard, Bell & Brecker, Phila., 1963-64; asst. prof. Ind. U. Law Sch., Indpls., 1964-67, assoc. prof., 1968; prof. Tulane U., New Orleans, 1969—, Thomas Pickles prof. law, 1979-89, Niels F. Johnsen prof. maritime law, 1989—, acting dean, 1977-78. Dir. Tulane Maritime Law Ctr. Co-author: Hall's Criminal Law, 1993, Admiralty and Maritime Law: Cases, Notes and Text, vols. 1 and 2, 1997, Marine Pollution: Conventions, Statutes, Cases and Text, 1998. Fulbright fellow, 1958-59 Mem. ABA, Beta Gamma Sigma, Omicron Delta Kappa Home: 1038 Eleonore St New Orleans LA 70115-4311 Office: 6329 Freret St Ste 255 New Orleans LA 70118-6231 E-mail: rforce@law.tulane.edu.

FORCE, RONALD WAYNE, librarian; b. Sioux City, Iowa, Sept. 7, 1941; s. Robert N. and Madeline (Heine) F.; m. Jo Ellen Hitch, May 31, 1964; children: Emily, Alicia. BS, Iowa State U., 1963; MA, U. Minn., 1968; MS, Ohio State U., 1975. Asst. to head dept. librs. Ohio State U., Columbus, 1968-70, head engrng. librs., 1970-72, head edn./psychology libr., 1972-79; asst. dir. pub. svcs. Wash. State U. Librs., Pullman, 1979-82; asst. sci. libr. U. Idaho Libr., Moscow, 1982-84, pub. svcs. libr., 1984-85, humanities libr., 1985-88, assoc. dean libr. svcs., 1988-91, dean libr. svcs., 1991—. Mem. adv. coun. Libr. Svcs. and Constrn. Act. Author: Guide to Literature on Biomedical Engineering, 1972; contbr. articles to profl. jours. Mem. Sacajawea Coun. Campfire Bd., 1980-85, mem. Pullman Dist. Campfire Com., fin. com., 1980-82, chair, 1983-84, treas., 1985, Sacajawea County Self-Study Com., 1986; mem. adv. bd. N.W. Net Info. Resources, 1994-95, 2000—; mem. Idaho Network Adv. Com., 1993-95; mem. LSCA Adv. Coun., 1989-95; mem. Libraries Linking Idaho Bd., 2000—. Mem. ALA, Idaho Libr. Assn. (2d v.p. 1997-98, 1st v.p. 1998-99, pres. 1999-2000). Home: 343 N Blaine St Moscow ID 83843-3626

FORCHESKIE, CARL S. former apparel company executive; b. Shamokin, Pa., Feb. 3, 1927; s. John A. and Helen F.; m. Barbara Ann Pierz; children from previous marriage: Carl, Gail, Caroline Karen. BA, Pa. State U., 1951. Mgr. Coopers & Lybrand, 1951-62; cons. U.S. Dept. Treasury, 1962-63; chief fin. officer Loral Corp., 1963-69; exec. v.p. Salant Corp., N.Y.C., 1969-81, pres., chief exec. officer, 1981-85; ret., 1985. Mem. Planning Bd. Hastings-on-Hudson, N.Y. Served with AUS, 1945-46. Mem. AICPA, N.Y. State Soc. CPAs, Fin. Execs. Inst., Am. Apparel Mfrs. Assn., St. Andrews Golf Club, Union League, Paupack Hills Golf and Country Club. Roman Catholic. Home: 101 Beechwood Ln Greentown PA 18426-9052

FORCIER, RICHARD CHARLES, information technology educator, computer applications consultant; b. Chicopee, Mass., Feb. 17, 1941; s. Rudolph Joseph and Rachel Lena (Chagnon) F.; m. Peggy Jean Prosser, July 30, 1983; children: Laura, Andrea, Richard J. BSE, Westfield (Mass.) State Coll., 1962; MEd, U. Mass., 1964; postgrad., U. Colo, 1966; PhD, Mich. State U., 1969. Media cons. Mich. State U., East Lansing, 1967-69; prin. Lincoln County Sch. Dist., Newport, Oreg., 1969-70; instructional cons. U. Wis., Madison, 1970-72; prof. info. tech. Western Oreg. U., Monmouth, 1972-97, asst. dean Sch. Edn. Computer tech. cons. numerous cos., schs. and chs. Co-author: Computer: Tool for the Teacher, 1985; author: The Computer as a Productivity Tool in Education, 1996, The Computer as an Educational Tool: Productivity and Problem Solving, 1999, 4th edit., 2003; producer film Systems Analysis, 1971; contbr. numerous articles to profl. jours. Mem. Assn. Ednl. Comms. and Tech., Oreg. Ednl. Media Assn. Avocations: fishing, bowhunting. Home: 25335 SW Neill Rd Sherwood OR 97140-7301

FORCIER-DELGADILLO, JENNIFER LIBBY, Spanish language educator; b. Newport News, Va., Nov. 7, 1968; d. Barbara Libby and David Norman F.; m. Jorge Aaron Delgadillo-Osorio, May 13, 2000. BA, U. N.H., 1996, MA, MS, U. N.H., 1999. Tchr. Spanish, Exeter (N.H.) H.S., 2000—. Mem. Phi Beta Kappa, Sigma Delta Pi. Home: 322 Great Bay Woods Newmarket NH 03857-2409 E-mail: jenniferforcier@hotmail.com.

FORCINIO, HALLIE EUNICE, editor; b. Cleve., Aug. 25, 1952; d. Quentin L. and Bertha W. (Bolman) Schirch; m. Robert K. Forcinio, Jan. 24, 1981. BA cum laude, Baldwin-Wallace Coll., Berea, Ohio, 1974. Traffic mgr. Jaeger Advt., Berea, 1975; editorial asst. Arthur G. McKee & Co., Cleve., 1975-78; comm. asst. Work Wear Corp., Cleve., 1978-82; assoc. editor HBJ Publs. (name now Advanstar Comm.), Cleve., 1982-84, mng. editor, 1984-91, editor in chief, 1991-93; freelance writer, editor Cleve., 1993—. Mem. Friends Cleve. Pub. Libr. Mem. Internat. Assn. Bus. Communicators (sec., facilitator 1995-98, membership chair Cleve. chpt. 1998-2001), Am. Soc. Bus. Press Editors, Inst. Packaging Profls. (sec. 1993-95, v.p. 1995-97, pres. Cleve. chpt. 1997-99), Internat. Packaging Press Orgn., Cleve. Zool. Soc., Kappa Phi (editor 1976-83, pres. 1983-87, 89-91). Republican. Lutheran. Avocations: stamps, reading, Chinese cooking. E-mail: editorHal@cs.com.

FORD, ALMA REGINA, retired union official, educator; b. Owings, W.Va., Oct. 4, 1939; d. Charles Feathers and Pearl (Costello) F.; A.B., Fairmont (W.Va.) State Coll., 1960; M.A., W.Va. U., 1964; M.A., Ball State U., 1984; postgrad. Sorbonne. Cert. counselor. Tchr. in Ohio, W.Va., Turkey, England, France, Italy, W.Ger., 1961-78; v.p., dep. rep. for Dept. Def. Dependents Schs.-Europe, negotiator Overseas Fedn. Tchrs., 1978-80; tchr., Zweibrucken, W.Ger., 1980—, counselor, 1997; ret., 1999-2003; del. various internat. meetings. Recipient Sustained Superior/Performance award Dept. Army, 1972-76, Exceptional Performance award, 1984; NDEA fellow, 1968. Mem. AAUW, AARP, LWV, Nat. Assn. Ret. Fed. Employees, Nat. Council Tchrs. English, Nat. Assn. Ret. People, Speech Assn. Am., Am. Fedn. Tchrs., Overseas Fedn. Tchrs., W.Va. Sheriff's Assn., Marion County Ret. Tchrs. Assn., W.Va. Travelers Club, Am. Legion Ladies Aux., Eagles Ladies Aux., Ret. Eagles Club, VFW Ladies Aux., Elks, Moose, Fairmont State Coll. Alumnus Assn., Zweibrucken Alumnus Assn., Phi Delta Kappa, Alpha Psi Omega. Home: 13 Eldora St Fairmont WV 26554-7967

FORD, AMANDA MELODY, director; d. Robert Harry and Lenore Ann Dixon; 1 child, Jasmine Rue. MusM, Carnegie Mellon U., 1996. Faculty Carnegie Mellon U., Pitts., 1999—2000, Duquesne U., Pitts., 1998—, dir. career svcs., 2000—. Web content mgr. sch. music Duquesne U., Pitts., 2002—. Composer: (orchestral composition) Innovation (NY MetLife award, 1995), Fliegende Traume (Harry G. Archer Composition award, 1996), (music for documentary) Stephanie (Emmy award (Mid Atlantic Region), 2001). Grantee, Pub. TV, 1996, Race for the Cure, 2000. Mem.: ASCAP (life), Pitts. Musicians' Union (life). Avocations: reading, walking, billiards, songwriting. Office: Duquesne U Sch Musi 600 Forbes Ave Pittsburgh PA 15282 Office Fax: 412-396-5479. Personal E-mail: forda@duq.edu. E-mail: forda@duq.edu.

FORD, ANABEL, research anthropologist, archaeologist; b. LA, Dec. 22, 1951; d. Joseph B. Ford and Marjorie Henshaw; m. Michael A. Glassow, May 4, 1974. BA in Anthropology, U. Calif., Santa Barbara, 1974, MA in Anthropology, 1976, PhD in Anthropology, 1981. Teaching asst. dept. anthropology & environ. studies U. Calif., Santa Barbara, 1975-80, rsch. asst. archaeologist office of pub. archaeology, 1980-81, lectr. dept. archaeology, 1982—, asst. rsch. archaeologist Social Process Rsch. Inst., 1982-87, founding dir. MesoAmerican Rsch. Ctr., 1987, asst. rsch. archaeologist Community Orgn. Rsch. Inst., 1987-91, assoc. rsch. archaeologist, 1991-98, dir. MesoAm. Rsch. Ctr., 1991-98, rsch. archeologist Inst. Social, Behavioral and Econ. Rsch., 1998—; assoc. rsch. archaeologist Inst. Social, Behavioral and Econ. Rsch., 1991-98, rsch. archaeologist, 1998—. Vis. asst. prof. dept. anthropology UCLA, 1987-89; co-participant USIA, 1995-96; active commn. Centroamericana de Ambiente Y Desarrollo, 1996, Mac Arthur World Environment and Resources Program, 1997, Inst. for Internat. Edn., 1998; program initiator Ford Found., 1998; co-dir. Rsch. Across Disciplines, 1999; lectr., presenter in field. Contbr. over 50 articles to profl. jours. Supr. Vol. Lab. and Field Program, 1978—; pres. Exploring Solutions Past-the Maya Forest Alliance. Humanities fellow U. Calif., Santa Barbara, 1989-91; Fulbright rsch. scholar, 1986, 90; grantee U. Calif., Santa Barbara, L.S.B. Leakey Found., NSF, NEH, Heinz Found., Wenner-Gren, CIRMA, CIES/USIS, Univ. Rsch. Expeditions Program, Ford Found., Fulbright-Hays Found; recipient Rolex award for Enterprise, 2000, Outstanding Cmty. Svc. award U.S. Senate, 2000, certificate of recognition Amigos de El Pilar Belize/Guatemala, 2000; named Educator of Yr. Goleta Chamber, 2000, Calif. State Assembly, 2000, Calif. State Senate, 2000, Alumna of Yr., U. Calif., Santa Barbara, 2003. Mem. AAAS, Am. Anthropol. Assn., Soc. for Am. Archaeology, Assn. for Field Archaeology, Sociedad Mexicana de Antropologia, So. Calif. Mesoamerican Network, UCSB Affiliated Faculty Women, Assn. for Belizean Archaeology, Belize Ctr. for Environ. Studies, Sigma Xi. Office: U Calif Inst Social Behav & Econ Rsch Santa Barbara CA 93106-2150 E-mail: ford@marc.ucsb.edu., elpilar@btl.net.

FORD, ANDREW THOMAS, academic administrator; b. Cambridge, Mass., May 22, 1944; s. Francis Lawler and Eleanor (Vahey) F.; m. Anne M. Monahan, July 2, 1966; 1 dau., Lauren Elizabeth. BA, Seton Hall U., 1966; MA, U. Wis., 1968; PhD, U. Wis., 1971. Asst. prof. history Stockton State Coll., Pomona, N.J., 1971-72, asst. to v.p. for acad. affairs, 1972-74; acting dir. Nat. Materials Devel. Ctr. for French and Portuguese, Bedford, N.H., 1976-77; acad. programs coordinator N.H. Coll. and Univ. Council, Manchester, 1975-78; v.p. acad. affairs R.I. Sch. Design, Providence, 1978-81; dean Allegheny Coll., Meadville, Pa., 1981-93, provost, 1983-93; pres. Wabash Coll., Crawfordsville, Ind., 1993—. Mem. adv. bd. Marine Bank, 1987-93; founding mem. Commonwealth Partnership. Author: (with R. Chait) Beyond Traditional Tenure, 1982; mem. editl. bd. Liberal Edn., 2000—. Bd. dirs. Vis. Nurse Assn., Providence, 1979-81, Allegheny Summer Music Festival, Meadville, 1981-89, Meadville Med. Ctr., 1985-87; bd. incorporators Spencer Hosp., 1981-85; mem. Nat. Com. on U.S.-China Rels., 1986—; trustee Higher Learning Commn. North Ctrl. Assn. Schs. and Colls., 2002—; dir. Crawfordsville Main St. Program, 2001—.. Democrat. Home: 400 E Pike St Crawfordsville IN 47933-2520 Office: Wabash Coll Office of Pres Crawfordsville IN 47933

FORD, ASHLEY LLOYD, lawyer, retired consumer products company executive; b. Cin., Mar. 10, 1939; s. Starr MacLeod and Mary Lloyd (Mills) F.; m. Barbara Hill, Apr. 23, 1965; children: Christopher Ashley, Elizabeth Hill. AB, Princeton U., 1960; JD, Yale U., 1963. Bar: Ohio 1963. Assoc. Dinsmore & Shohl, Cin., 1965-69; counsel Procter & Gamble Co., Cin., 1969-71, divsn. counsel, 1971-89, sec., 1979-94; ret., 1994. Shareholder Cin. Mus. Assn.; dir. Hist. S.W. Ohio; mem. Cin. History Mus. Adv. Bd. Lt. USNR, 1966-72. Mem. Soc. Col. Wars, Cin. Country Club, Queen City Club, Univ. Club, Sailfish Pt. Country Club, Order of Coif, Phi Beta Kappa. Episcopalian.

FORD, BARBARA JEAN, library studies educator; b. Dixon, Ill., Dec. 5, 1946; BA magna cum laude with honors, Ill. Wesleyan U., 1968; MA in Internat. Rels., Tufts U., 1969; MS in Libr. Sci., U. Ill., 1973. Dir. Soybean Insect Rsch. Info. Ctr. Ill. Natural History Survey, Urbana, 1973-75; from asst. to assoc. prof. U. Ill., Chgo., 1975-84, asst. documents libr., 1975-79, documents libr., dept. head, 1979-84, acting audiovisual libr., 1983-84; asst. dir. pub. svcs. Trinity U., San Antonio, 1984-86, assoc. prof., assoc. dir., 1986-91, acting dir. librs., 1989, 91; prof., dir. univ. libr. svcs. Va. Commonwealth U., Richmond, 1991-98; asst. commr. Chgo. Pub. Libr., 1998—2002; dir., disting. prof. Mortenson Ctr. Internat. Libr. Programs, U. Ill., Urbana, 2003—. Mem. women's re-entry adv. bd. U. Ill., Chgo., 1980-82, student affairs com., 1978-80, student admissions, records, coll. rels. com., 1981-84, univ. senate, 1976-78, 82-84, chancellor's libr. coun. svcs. com. 1984, campus lectrs. com. 1982-83; admissions interviewer for prospective students Trinity U., 1987-91, reader for internat. affairs theses, 1985-91, libr. self-study com., 1985-86, internat. affairs com., 1986-91, inter-Am. studies com., 1986-91, faculty senate, 1987-90; with libr. working group U.S./Mex. Commn. Cultural Coop., 1990. Contbr. articles to profl. publs., papers to presentations. Bd. dirs. Friends of San Antonio Pub. Libr., 1989-91; adv. com. chair Office for Libr. Pers. Resources, 1994-95; mem. steering com. Virtual Libr. Va., 1994-98, chair user svcs. com., 1995-96. Celia M. Howard fellow Tufts U., 1969; sr. fellow UCLA Grad. Sch. Libr. and Info. Sci., 1993. Mem. ALA (conf. program com. 1985-91, libr. edn. assembly 1983-84, membership com. 1978-79, status of women in librarianship com. 1983-85, exec bd., 1996-99, Lippincott Award Jury 1979-80, Shirley Olofson Meml. award 1977), ALA Coun. (at-large councilor 1985-89, chpt. councilor Ill. Libr. Assn. 1980-84, com. on coms. 1987-88, spl. coun. orientation com. 1982-83, ALA exec. bd., 1996-99, pres.- elect 1996-97, pres. 1997-98), Assn. Coll. and Rsch. Librs. (bd. dirs. 1989-92, pres.-elect 1989-90, pres. 1990-91, publs. com. 1990-91, conf. program planning 1990-91), Nat. Assn. State Univs. and Land Grant Colls. (commn. info. tech. 1992-94), Internat. Fedn. Libr. Assns. and Instns. (sec. ofcl. pubs. sect., gen. info. com. 1985 conf., moderator Latin Am. seminar on ofcl. pubs. 1991, univ. and other rsch. librs. sect. standing com. 1999—), Spl. Librs. Assn. (program com. 1976-77, 80-82, publicity com. 1977-79, chair 1978-79, chair spl. projects com. 1981-82, sec./treas. divsn. social sci. internat. affairs sect. 1984-86), Assn. Libr. Info. Sci. Edn. (chair local arrangements conf. planning com. 1988, 92), Ill. Libr. Assn. (chair election com. 1976-77, exec. bd. 1978-79, 80-84, bd. govt. documents round table 1976-79, chair 1978-79, long range planning com. 1980-81), Tex. Libr. Assn. (pubs. com. 1985-87, legis. com. 1986-87, judge best of exhibits award 1987, task force Amigos Fellowship 1990, del. conf. on librs. and info. svcs., 1991), Va. Libr. Assn. (ad hoc. com. distance learning 1992), Va. State Libr. and Archives (Va. libr. and info. svcs. task force 1991-93, steering com. Arbuthnot lecture 1992-93, coop. continuing edn. adv. com. 1992-94), VIVA (steering com. 1994-98), Chgo. Libr. Club (2d v.p. 1983-84), Richmond Acad. Libr. Consortium (v.p. 1991-92, pres. 1992-93), Beta Phi Mu, Phi Kappa Phi, Phi Alpha Theta, Kappa Delta Pi. Office: Chicago Pub Libr Box 2033 400 S State St Chicago IL 60605-1216

FORD, BERNADETTE K. lawyer; b. Queens, N.Y., July 11, 1960; d. Alexander Stanley and Ita Angela F.; m. Michael G. Brisson, Apr. 19, 1986; 1 child. BA, St. John's U., 1981, JD, 1985. Bar: N.Y. 1986, N.J. 1987, U.S. Dist. Ct. (ea. dist.) N.Y. 1988. Asst. dist. atty. Queens Dist. Attys Office, Kew Gardens, N.Y., 1985—, dep. bur. chief, 1994-2000, sr. investigative asst. dist. atty., 2000—. Instr. Practicing Law Inst., N.Y.C., 1997; panelist St. John's U. Law Homecoming, 1997; faculty N.Y. Prosecutor's Tng. Inst., 1999. Mem. N.Y. Dist. Atty. Assn., Nassau County Bar Assn. Roman Catholic. Office: Queens Dist Attys Office 12501 Queens Blvd Kew Gardens NY 11415-1514

FORD, BETTY BLOOMER (ELIZABETH FORD), former First Lady of United States, health facility executive; b. Chicago, Apr. 8, 1918; d. William Stephenson and Hortence (Neahr) Bloomer; m. Gerald R. Ford (38th Pres. U.S.), Oct. 15, 1948; children: Michael Gerald, John Gardner, Steven Meigs, Susan Elizabeth. Student, Sch. Dance Bennington Coll., 1936, 37; LL.D. (hon.), U. Mich., 1976. Dancer Martha Graham Concert Group, N.Y.C., 1939-41; fashion dir. Herpolscheimer's Dept. Store, Grand Rapids, Mich., 1943-48; dance instr. Grand Rapids, 1932-48; co-founder Susan G/ Komen Foundation, 1982. Chmn. bd. dirs. The Betty Ford Ctr., Rancho Mirage, Calif. Author: autobiography The Times of My Life, 1979, Betty: A Glad Awakening, 1987. Bd. dirs. Nat. Arthritis Found. (hon.); trustee Martha Graham Dance Ctr., Eisenhower Med. Ctr., Rancho Mirage; hon. chmn. Palm Springs Desert Mus.; nat. trustee Nat. Symphony Orch.; bd. dirs. The Lambs, Libertyville, Ill. Recipient Congressional Gold Medal, 1999, Presidential Medal of Freedom, 1991, Woodrow Wilson Pub. Svc. award, 2003. Republican. Episcopalian. Home: PO Box 1560 Rancho Mirage CA 92270 Office: Betty Ford Center 39000 Bob Hope Dr Rancho Mirage CA 92270

FORD, CARL W., JR., federal agency administrator; b. Hot Springs, Ark., 1943; married. BA in Asian Studies, Fla. State U., 1968, MA in East Asian Studies. China analyst CIA, 1974—78, congl. fgn. affairs fellow, 1978; legis. asst. for arms control and fgn. policy Office of Senator John Glenn; staff mem. Senate Com. on Fgn. Rels., 1979—81; fgn. policy and def. issues dir. Office of Senator John Glenn, 1981—84; fgn. policy and def. advisor John Glenn Presl. Campaign, 1984; nat. intelligence officer for East Asia CIA, 1985—91; prin. dep. asst. sec. of def. for internat. security affairs U.S. Dept. of Def., 1989, acting asst. sec. of def., 1991, dep. asst. sec. of def. for Near East and South Asian affairs, 1991—93; ret. CIA, 1993; asst. sec. state for intelligence and rsch. U.S. Dept. of State, Washington, 2001—. With U.S. Army, 1963—66, Vietnam, with U.S. Army, 1969—74. Office: US Dept of State Intelligence and Rsch Bur 2201 C St NW Washington DC 20520-6510

FORD, CHARLES NATHANIEL, otolaryngologist, educator; b. N.Y.C., June 25, 1940; s. Charles Nathaniel and Marie (Casa) F.; children: C. David, Brian C.; m. Sharon L. James, Feb. 3, 1990; stepchildren: Scott James, Julie James. BA, SUNY, Binghamton, 1961; MD, U. Louisville, 1965. Intern and resident Henry Ford Hosp., Detroit, 1965-70, staff, 1970-71; with Gundersen Clinic, LaCrosse, Wis., 1973-81; chief otolaryngology Middleton VA Hosp., Madison, Wis., 1982-94; prof. otolaryngol. divsn. dept. surgery U. Wis., Madison, 1981-93, chmn. otolaryngol. divsn. dept. surgery, 1993—. Mem.-at-large med. bd. U. Wis. Ctr. for Health Scis., 1989-91, sec., 1992-93, v.p., 1994-95, pres. med. staff, chair med. bd. 1996-98; DeWeese lectr. U. Oreg., 1994; Manion Meml. lectr. Ind. U., 1995; Hough lectr. U. Okla., 1996; Sartian lectr. U. Tex., 1998; keynote lectr. Brit. Voice Assn., 2000, Voice Symposium Australia, 2002, G. Paul Moore lectr. Voice Found., Phila., 2003. Author, editor: Phonosurgery: Assessment and Surgical Management of Voice Disorders, 1991; mem. editl. bd.: Jour. Voice, Otolaryngol. Head and Neck Surgery, Laryngoscope, Microsurgery; author editor numerous sci. papers, chpts. and abstracts. Maj. USAF, 1971-73. Avalon Found. scholar, 1962-63; named to Best Drs. in Am., Woodward/White, Inc., 1991—. Fellow ACS, Am. Laryngol., Rhinol. and Otolog. Soc., Am. Bronchoesophical Assn. (pres.), Am. Laryngol. Assn., Am. Soc. for Head and Neck Surgery, Am. Acad. Otolaryngology, Head and Neck Surgery (honor award 1992); mem. AMA, Soc. Univ. Otolaryngologists-Head and Neck Surgeons (pres.), Internat. Assn. Phonosurgeons, Am. Speech-Lang.-Hearing Assn. Democrat. Unitarian Universalist. Avocations: tennis, golf, theater, art, music. Office: U Wis Ctr Health Sci 600 Highland Ave Madison WI 53792-0001

FORD, CHARLES REED, state legislator; b. Tulsa, Aug. 2, 1931; s. Juell Reed and Marzee (Lane) F.; m. Patricia Ann Ojers, 1951; children: Christopher Reed, Roger Howard, Karin Rebecca, Robyn Ann. Student, Okla. State U., 1949-51. Engr., aide U.S. Corps. Engrs., 1951-53; designer SunrayDX, 1953-55; asst. mktg. engr. Tidewater Oil Co., 1955-58; real estate investor Charles Ford Co., 1958—. Pres. Gothic Investments, Inc.,1963, mem. Okla. Ho. of Reps., 1967-81, minority floor leader, 1970-76, asst. minority leader, 1981; mem. Okla. Senate, 1981—, caucus chmn., 1982-83, caucus whip, 1984-86, asst. minority leader, 1987-88, minority leader, 1991-92; mem. Southwest region adv. com. Nat. Park Service, 1982-88. Trustee Tulsa Expn. and Fair Corp., 1955-67; vice chmn. Tulsa Met. Area Planning Commn., 1960-65; former officer Tulsa County Young Rep.; del. Rep. Nat. Conv., 1972, 84, 88; bd. govs. Spartan Sxh. Aeronautics, 1993—. Served with USNR, 1948-53. Named Legislator of Yr. Rep. Legis. Assoc., 1988, Outstanding Legis. Leader Nat. Conf. State Legislators, 1992. Mem. Jaycees (Okla. pres. 1959-60, U.S. v.p. 1960-61, internat. v.p. 1963, chmn. trustees War Meml. Fund 1963—), Nat. Petroleum Coun., Am. Inst. Architects (pres.'s award, 1998), Okla. Heritage (disting. svc. award, 1999, gov.'s Art award, 1999), Alpha Sigma Eta. Republican. Office: Okla Senate Rm 527A Oklahoma City OK 73105

FORD, CHARLES WILLARD, health science educator; b. Bloomsburg, Pa., Oct. 28, 1938; s. John Willard and Pauline Teresa (Rakocy) Ford; m. Barbara Marie Hanawalt, June 6, 1959; children: Lane(dec.), Lori, Lanae, Lanette. BA, Taylor U., 1960; BS, Pa. State U., 1961, MEd, 1962; PhD, SUNY, Buffalo, 1970; postgrad., U. Mich., 1976-77. HS tchr., 1961-64; mem. faculty Erie CC, 1965-70; fgn. svc. officer Peace Corps, Ghana, 1970-72; various positions Sch. Health Related Professions, SUNY, Buffalo, 1972-75, 77-79, assoc. dean Sch. Health Related Professions, 1978—79; with Grand Rapids (Mich.) Med. Edn. Ctr., 1975-77; dean U. Health Scis./Chgo. Med. Sch., 1979-81; dean undergrad. colls. U. New Eng., Biddeford, Maine, 1982-84, pres., 1984-91, prof. health sci., 1983—. Active in accreditation and curriculum program develop in 40 states and 6 countries; vis. prof. Israel, Tel Aviv, Jerusalem, Haifa, 1999—2003. Author (with M. K. Morgan): (book) Teaching in the Health Professions, Clinical Education for the Allied Health Professions; contbr. articles to profl jours. Pres. Maine Higher Edn. Coun., 1987—88, Maine Ind. Coll. Assn., 1988—89; bd. govs. Am. Assn. Coll. Osteo. Medicine, 1984—91. Recipient Study Exch., Rotary, Germany and Turkey, 1995. Mem.: NEA (life), Assn. Schs. Allied Health Profls. (life), Am. Assn. Higher Edn. (life). Office: U New Eng Biddeford ME 04005 E-mail: cford@une.edu.

FORD, CLARENCE QUENTIN, mechanical engineer, educator; b. Glenwood, N.Mex., Aug. 6, 1923; s. Clarence Noel and Elsie May (Jones) F.; m. Ruth Madge McKinney, June 11, 1950; children— Glenn Mac, Dabney Ann. BS, U.S. Mcht. Marine Acad., 1944; BS in Mech. Engrng., N.Mex. State U., 1949; MS in Mech. Engrng., U. Mo., 1950; PhD, Mich. State U., 1959. Registered profl. engr. Inst. U. Mo., 1949-50; instr. Wash. State U., 1950-53, asst. prof., 1953-56; instr. Mich. State U., 1956-59; prof. N.Mex. State U., Las Cruces, 1959-88, head dept. mech. engrng., 1960-70, assoc. dean engrng., 1974-80, 81-88, dean engrng., 1980-81, prof. and assoc. dean emeritus, 1988—; prin. Ford & Assocs., 1964—. Mem. N.Mex. Bd. Registration Profl. Engrs. and Land Surveyors, 1978-88, chmn., 1980-81, 86-87, mem. emeritus, 1989—; mem. N.Mex. State Hwy. Commn., 1989-95, sec., 1991-95. Editor: Space Technology and Earth Problems, Vol. 23 Sci. and Tech. Series, 1969 Served to lt. USNR, 1942-46 Fellow AAAS; mem. ASME, Am. Soc. Engring. Edn., Nat. Coun. Examiners for Engrng. and Surveying (v.p. 1986-88, Disting. Svc. award 1989, Disting. Svc. award with spl. commendation 1990), N.Mex. Soc. Profl. Engrs. (Outstanding Engr. 1964), Masons, York Rite, Kiwanis, Sigma Xi, Phi Kappa Phi, Pi Tau Sigma, Tau Beta Pi, Pi Mu Epsilon. Presbyterian. Home: 1985 Crescent Dr Las Cruces NM 88005-3300 E-mail: Chapace@aol.com.

FORD, DANIEL (DANIEL FRANCIS FORD), writer; b. Nov. 2, 1931; s. Patrick Joseph and Anne Theresa Ford; m. Sarah Lansing Paine; 1 child, Katharine Serena. BA, U. N.H., 1954; postgrad., U. Manchester, Eng., 1954-55. Reporter Overseas Weekly, Frankfurt, Germany, 1958; asst. editor N.H. Profiles mag., Portsmouth, 1959-60; publs. editor U. N.H., 1961-68; freelance writer Durham, N.H., 1969—. Corr. The Nation, South Vietnam, 1964; contbg. editor Air & Space/Smithsonian Mag., 1994—; pub. Warbird's Forum, 1997—. Author: Now Comes Theodora, 1965, Incident at Muc Wa (transl. in Dutch, filmed as Go Tell the Spartans), 1967, The High Country Illuminator, 1971, The Country Northward, 1976, Flying Tigers: Claire Chennault and the American Volunteer Group, 1991, Glen Edwards: The Diary of a Bomber Pilot, 1998, Remains, 2000, The Only War We've Got: Early Days in South Vietnam, 2001, Michael's War, 2003; editor: The Lady and the Tigers, 2002; contbr. Wall St. Jour., 2001—. With U.S. Army, 1956-57. Recipient award of excellence Aviation-Space Writers, 1992; Fulbright fellow U. Manchester, 1954-55, Verville fellow Nat. Air & Space Mus., 1989-90; Stern Found. Mag. Writers grantee, 1964; resident scholar U. N.H., 1996—. Mem. Authors guild, Met. Opera Guild, Phi Beta Kappa, Phi Kappa Phi. Office: 433 Bay Rd Durham NH 03824-3439

FORD, DANNY R. state representative; b. Berea, Ky, Apr. 25, 1952; m. Sue H. Ford; children: Danetta, Charles Matthew, Angela. CAT, Cert. Auctioneers Inst., 1987; BS, Ea. Ky. Univ., 1974. State Rep. House of Rep., Dist. 80, 1982—; dir. Monticello Banking Co., 2000; employed Cumberland Real Estate Investments, 1999; dir. Bank Mt. Vernon, 1997; mng. ptnr. Valley Oaks LLC, 1996; Auctioneer and Realtor Ford Bros., Inc., 1974. Bd. mem. Dix River, Somerset Bd. of Realtors; dir. Somerset-Pulaski County Bd. of Realtors, 1988—; (Rep.) fl. leader State House Minority, 1995—98; Rep. Whip State House, 1993—94;

mem. Nat./KY Auctioneers Assoc., Rockcastle County Young Rep. Club, Appropriations & Rev., Banking & Ins., Sr., Mil. Affairs & Pub. Safety, Rules Comm. caucuses: Mem., Fed. Corrd. & contact team Nat. Assoc. of Realtors, 1999-present. Republican. Baptist. Office: Capitol Capitol Annex, Rm 416A Frankfort KY 40601 also: Dist PO Box 1245 Mt. Vernon KY 40456*

FORD, DAVID CLAYTON, state senator, lawyer; b. Hartford City, Ind., Mar. 3, 1949; s. Clayton I. and Barbara J. (McVicker) F.; m. Joyce Ann Bonjour, Aug. 22, 1970; children: Jeff, Matthew, Kelly, Andrew. BA in Polit. Sci., Ind. U., 1973, JD, 1976; MBA in Internat. Trade, Ball State U., 1988. Bar: Ind. 1975, U.S. Dist. Ct. (so. dist.) Ind. 1976, U.S. Dist. Ct. (no. dist.) Ind. 1977, U.S. Tax Ct. 1988, U.S. Supreme Ct. 1983. City atty. City of Montpelier, Ind., 1977-79; town atty. Town of Shamrock Lakes, Ind., 1977—; mem. Ind. Senate from 19th dist., 1994—, chair econ. devel. and tech. com. Gen. counsel, internat. trade dir. Ind. Farm Bur., Inc., 1988—2002; chief dep. prosecutor Blackford County, 1979; pros. atty. 71st Jud. Cir., Blackford County, Hartford City, Ind., 1983—86; mem. com. on character and fitness State Bd. of Law Examiners. Mem. Ind. Agrl. Leadership Program, 1990-91; bd. dirs. Blackford County Young Reps., 1977-82, pres., 1977-78; chmn. Town of Shamrock Lakes Rep. Com., 1983, Ind. Lawyers for Bush and Quayle, 1988; vice chmn. Blackford County Rep. Ctrl. Com., 1978-82, chmn., 1993-2001; precinct committeeman Blackford County, Licking 7, 1980-93; mem. Ind. 10th Congl. Dist. Rep. Caucus, 1978-82, U.S. Edn. Appeals Bd., U.S. Dept. Edn., 1982-90, Nat. Def. Execs. Res., 1983-99; former mem. bus. adv. com. to Congressman Dan Burton; chmn. bus., industries and devel. com. Ptnrs. of Ams., Ind. chpt., 1983-84; mem. Blackford County Bd. Aviation Commrs., 1977-83, pres., 1979-83; bd. dirs. Dollars for Scholars, Blackford County, 1977-95, v.p., 1977-95; mem. St. John's-Riedman Meml. Sch. Bd., 1978-82, pres., 1978-82; mem. Blackford County Sheriff's Merit Bd., 1981-82. Named Man of Yr. Hartford City C. of C., 1978, Sagamore of the Wabash, Gov. Otis Bowen, 1978, Hon. Sec. of State Edwin J. Simcox, 1981; participant Rotary group study exch. to São Paulo, Brazil, 1981; named Outstanding Young Man of Am., U.S. Jaycees, 1982. Mem. ABA, ATLA, Ind. State Bar Assn., Blackford County Bar Assn., World Trade Club Ind., Mensa, Sigma Iota Epsilon. Home: 1023 N Walnut St Hartford City IN 47348-1553 Office: 210 W Main St Hartford City IN 47348-2209 E-mail: s19@in.gov.

FORD, DEBORAH HARDY, nursing administrator; b. Pineville, La., Apr. 3, 1960; d. Charles and Betty (Liggins) H.; m. Lyman T. Ford, Jr., June 12, 1982; children: April E., Myra R., Haylie E. Ford. AD, La. State U. at Alexandria, 1980; BSN, U. Southwestern La., 1985; MSN, Northwestern State U., 1992. Staff nurse Rapides Gen. Hosp., Alexandria, La., 1980-81; asst. head nurse Lafayette (La.) Gen. Med. Ctr., 1981-82, 1982-85, dir. orthopedics, 1985-92, dir. orthopedics and neurology, 1992-95, dir. nursing adminstrn., 1995-96, adminstr. home health, 1996—, emergency rm. dir., 2001—. Gov. apptd. rep. La. State Bd. Nursing Adminstrn., 1998—; mem. La. Blue Ribbon Task Force for Home Health, 1999; sec. La. Orgn. Hosp. Home Health, 1999—; project coord. for magnet excellence Lafayette Gen. Med. Ctr. Recipient Falgout Leadership Nursing award. Mem. ANA, La. State Nurses Assn. (bd. dirs. 2000—), La. Orgn. Nurse Execs. (bd. dirs. 2002--), Sigma Theta Tau. Home: 237 Beau Bassin Rd Carencro LA 70520-6315

FORD, DEXTER, retired insurance company executive; b. Utica, N.Y., Nov. 18, 1917; s. David E. and Anna Mae (Dexter) F.; m. Jean Brand McGowan, Nov. 1, 1944; children: David K., Dexter T., Nancy E. BS, St. Lawrence U., 1939. With Aetna Life & Casualty Co., Hartford, Conn., 1946—, v.p. mktg., 1968-76, v.p. personal ins. dept., 1976-80. Chmn. bd. mgmt. YMCA, 1978-80. Served to lt. (s.g.) USNR, 1941-45. Recipient St. Lawrence U. Alumni citation, 1978 Mem. St. Lawrence U. Alumni Assn. (pres. 1974-75) Republican. Congregationalist (chmn. bd. trustees 1970). Home: Apt 213 156 Lawrence St Saratoga Springs NY 12866-1351

FORD, DIANE, lawyer; b. Salem, Ill., Mar. 2, 1953; d. Robert Edwin and Mary Evelyn Ford; m. Zack Stamp, Oct. 23, 1983; children: Perry Ford Stamp, Nathan Ford Stamp. BA, Eastern Ill. U., 1975; JD, U. Ill., 1979. Bar: Ill. 1979. Legal counsel Ill. State Senate Republicans, Springfield, 1979-87, Gov. of Ill., Springfield, 1987-95; chief counsel Ill. Sec. of State, Springfield, 1995-99, Gov. of Ill., Springfield, 1999—2003; mem. Ill. Indsl. Commn., Chgo., 2003—. Republican. Methodist. Office: Ill Indsl Commn 100 W Randolph St Ste 8-240 Chicago IL 60601 E-mail: dkayford@aol.com.

FORD, DONALD HERBERT, psychologist, educator; b. Sioux City, Iowa, Aug. 15, 1926; s. Herbert Owen and Esther (Sanow) F.; m. Carol Clark, May 30, 1948; children— Russell, Martin, Douglas, Cameron. BS, Kans. State U., 1948; MS, 1951; PhD, Pa. State U., 1955. Counselor Kans. State U., 1948-52; asst. prof. psychology Pa. State U., University Park, 1955-64, assoc. prof., 1964-67, assoc. prof. human devel., 1967-72, prof. human. devel., 1972—, prof. biobehavioral health, 1992—. Asst. dir. div. counseling, 1956-59, dir., 1959-67; dean Coll. Human Devel., 1967-77, head dept. Communications Disorders, 1988-89, head biobehavioral health, 1992. Author: Systems of Psychotherapy; A Comparative Study, 1963, Humans as Self-Constructing Living Systems, 1987, 2d edit., 1992, Developmental Systems Theory, 1992, Contemporary Models of Psychotherapy, 1998. Served with USAAF, 1944-45. Mem. AAAS, Am. Psychol. Assn., Am. Psychol. Soc., Ea. Psychol. Assn. Home: 130 Slab Cabin Rd State College PA 16801-6971 Office: Penn State U Coll Health & Human Devel University Park PA 16802 E-mail: dhf6@psu.edu. *My basic values are rooted in the "teaching by example" of my parents, serving the objectives of being of service to others as well as to self, utilizing a strong, caring family unit as the best cornerstone of psychological, social, and economic health. My basic professional goal is to help harness the fruits of technological advances, resulting from the intensive application of the principle of specialization, to the evolution of humanistic societies designed to serve people as open, living systems. This requires a new scientific model of Man as a coherent unit, enabling us to synthesize the fruits of analytical science and to put "Humpty Dumpty" back together again as a person with purposes and values as well as productive potential.*

FORD, DONALD HERBERT, retired educator, consultant; b. Kansas City, Mo., Aug. 18, 1921; s. Horace Gridley and Gladys Evelyn (Newell) F.; m. Dorothy A. Ford, Aug. 5, 1944; 1 child, Linda Anne Summerall. BA, Wesleyan U., 1947, MA, 1949; PhD, Kans. U., 1952. Tchr. N.Y. Med. Ctr., Brooklyn, 1952—77. Rsch. dir. Coun. for Tobacco Rsch., N.Y.C., 1977-95. Author: Introduction to Basic Neurology, 1974, Review of Neuro-Anatomy, 1976; co-author: Intracranial Tumors, 1976; editor; Elsevier Rev. in Neurology, Mem. Floral Park Art League, treas., 1990—. Staff sgt. U.S. Army, 1942-45, ETO. Decorated Bronze Star. Mem. APA, Internat. Soc. Neuroendocrinology (past treas.), Am. Assn. Anatomy. Avocation: painting in watercolors. Home: 224 Verbena Ave Floral Park NY 11001-3047

FORD, E(MMA) JANE, public relations executive; b. Anderson, Ind., Mar. 25, 1918; d. Kenneth E. and Emma (Thomas) Griffith. BGS, Ind. U.-Purdue U. at Indianapolis, 1982. Advt. dir. Farm Bur. Ins., Indpls., 1956-73; pub. relations dir. Brulin & Co., Indpls., 1973-76; pub. info. dir. Ind. Arts Commn., Indpls., 1976-79, Indpls. Art League, Indpls., 1982-84; ret., 1984—. Talent coord., moderator Indy Internat. Cable TV, Indpls.; past vice chmn. Svc. Corps Ret. Execs.; panelist Ind. U., 1998. Author: (plays) An Evening With Zane Gray, 1985, In Bed with Education, 1998, Gillian Gilbrath; sculpture Indpls. Mus. Art; presenter monologues on Civil War wives, European and Asian travel; appeared in movie Back Home Again, 1999; vol. for Heartland Film Festival, 2003. Guide Eiteljorg Mus. Am. Indian and Western Art; nat. chmn. ann. conv. Women's Overseas Svc. League, 1994, pres., Ind. chpt., nat. nominations chmn.; panelist on advt. graduating srs. Ind. U., Bloomington, 1998; vol. Indpls. Mus. Art, 1974—; monthly spkr. Shepherd Ctr. Named Ad Woman of Yr. Ad Club of Ind., 1961; recipient cash award for poem, Writer's Ctr., 1998, 1st Pl. Brochure award, 2000. Mem. AAUW (assoc. editor), Nat. Soc. Arts and Letters (pres. Indpls. chpt. 1996-97, Indpls. schs. poetry chair), Women in Comm. (past sec.), Women's Press Club Ind. (past sec., edn. fund dir. 1996-97, 2d place winner for brochure Two Woman 1998), Pub. Rels. Soc. Am. (accredited), Ind. Filmmakers, Toastmaster's Club. Republican. Episcopalian. Avocations: painting, writing.

FORD, FORD BARNEY, retired government official; b. Norton, Va., Nov. 19, 1922; s. William Zachary and Annis Louvinia (Ford) Godbey; m. Norma Isabel Lentz, Jan. 16, 1945; children: Robert Barney, Jack T. (dec.). Student, Va. Mil. Inst., Lexington, 1942-43; BS, U. Calif., Berkeley, 1948; LLD (hon.), Huston Tillotson Coll., 1985. Registered indsl. and safety engr. Acting postmaster, Bishop, Calif., 1951-54; adminstrv. analyst Calif. Joint Legis. Budget Com., Sacramento, 1955-59; exec. dir. Calif. Senate Fact-Finding Com. on Natural Resources, Sacramento, 1959-67; dep. sec. Calif. Resources Agt., Sacramento, 1967-73; chmn. and mem. Calif. Occupl. Safety and Health Appeals Bd., Sacramento, 1973-78; v.p. Calif. Inst. Indsl. and Govtl. Rels., Sacramento, 1978-81; asst. sec. labor for mine safety and health Dept. Labor, Arlington, Va., 1981-83, undersec. Washington, 1983-85, acting sec., 1984-85; chmn. Mine Safety and Health Rev. Commn., 1985-92; ret., 1992. Rsch. publs. on fire prevention, geothermal devel. East Wilmington oil field. With U.S. Army, 1943-46, ETO. Decorated Combat Infantryman badge. Mem. DAV, SAR, VFW (comdr. Bishop, Calif. 1948-50), Elks, Masons, Shriners. Methodist. E-mail: fordbarneyford@cs.com.

FORD, FREDERIC HUGH, secondary school educator; b. Woonsocket, R.I., Feb. 5, 1939; s. Robert Saunders and Catherine Esther (Hudson) Ford; m. Kathleen Marie Hoffman, Oct. 12, 1968; children: Amy Meredith Ford Fitzgerald, Geoffrey Duncan. AB, Harvard Coll., 1960; MA in Music Edn., Harvard U., 1962, MA in Tchg.; MA in Music History, SUNY, Buffalo, 1969, PhD in Music History, 1990. Instr. U. Va., 1966—67; asst. prof. Wabash Coll., Crawfordsville, Ind., 1972—79, Rutgers U., New Brunswick, NJ, 1979—86; dir. N.J. State Teen Arts Program, New Brunswick, 1988—89; tchr. Bridgewater (N.J.)-Raritan Regional H.S., 1990—. Pres. Ea. divsn. Am. Choral Dirs. Assn., 1998—2000, chair 2000 divsn. conv., pres. N.J. chpt.; scorer Praxis exams for tchr. cert. Ednl. Testing Svc., Princeton, NJ. Lt. USNR, 1962—65. Mem.: NEA, Am. Musicol. Soc., Music Educators Nat. Conf. (condr. 1995, 2003). Unitarian Universalist. Home: 12 Melvin Ave East Brunswick NJ 08816 Office: Bridgewater-Raritan Regional HS PO Box 6569 Bridgewater NJ 08807

FORD, GAIL, library administrator; b. Sacramento, Mar. 5, 1952; d. R. Eugene and Jeanne P. Ford; m. Clive Matson, Jan. 15, 1993; 1 child, Ezra John Matson-Ford. AB in Philosophy, Stanford U., 1973. Adminstrv. analyst U. Calif. Berkeley Libr., 1984—; pub. Broken Shadow Publs., Oakland, Calif., 1993—. Pub.: (book) Emptiness That Plays So Rough, 1995, Under a Gibbous Moon, 1996, Squish Boots, 2002. Home: 472 44th St Oakland CA 94609-2136

FORD, GEORGE BURT, lawyer; b. South Bend, Ind., Oct. 1, 1923; s. George W. and Florence (Burt) F.; m. Charlotte Ann Kupferer, June 12, 1948; children: John, Victoria, George, Charlotte. BS in Engring. Law, Purdue U., 1946; LLB, Ind. U., 1949. Bar: Ind. 1949, U.S. Dist. Ct. (no. dist.) Ind. 1949. Assoc. Jones, Obenchain & Butler, South Bend, Ind., 1949-52; ptnr. Jones, Obenchain, Ford, Pankow & Lewis, South Bend, 1953-93, of counsel, 1994—. Co-author: Forms for Indiana Corporations, 1967, 2nd edit. 1977. With U.S. Army, 1943-45, ETO. Fellow Am. Coll. of Trust and Estate Counsel; mem. ABA, Ind. Bar Assn., St. Joseph County Bar Assn. (pres. 1976-77), Phi Gamma Delta, Phi Delta Phi. Presbyterian (trustee 1966-68, elder 1967-70). Office: Jones Obenchain LLP 600 Key Bank Bldg 202 S Michigan St Box 4577 South Bend IN 46634-4577

FORD, GERALD J. finance company executive; BA in Econs., So. Meth. U., 1966, JD, 1969. Bar: Tex. Chmn., CEO First Gibralter Bank, Tex., 1988-93; chmn. bd. dirs. First Madison Bank; pres., owner Madison Fin., Inc.; founder First United Bank Group, Inc.; chmn., CEO First Nationwide Bank, 1994, Calif. Fed. Bank, 1997, Golden State Bancorp, 1998—; bd. dirs. Freeport-McMokan Copper and Gold, 2000—. Named Among 40 Most Generous, Fortune Mag., 1998. Office: 1615 Poydras St New Orleans CA 70112*

FORD, GERALD RUDOLPH, JR., 38th President of the United States; b. Omaha, July 14, 1913; s. Gerald R. and Dorothy (Gardner) F.; m. Elizabeth Bloomer, Oct. 15, 1948; children: Michael, John, Steven, Susan. AB, U. Mich., 1935; LL.B., Yale U., 1941; LL.D., Mich. State U., Albion Coll., Aquinas Coll., Spring Arbor Coll. Bar: Mich. 1941. Practiced law at, Grand Rapids, 1941-49; mem. law firm Buchen and Ford; mem. 81st-93d Congresses from 5th Mich. Dist., 1949-74, elected minority leader, 1965; v.p. served under Pres. Richard Nixon U.S., U.S., 1973-74; pres. U.S., 1974-77. Del. Interparliamentary Union, Warsaw, Poland, 1959, Belgium, 1961, Bilderberg Group Conf., 1962; adv. dir. Am. Express Co.; mem. internat. adv. coun. Inst. Internat. Studies; bd. dir. Citigroup, Inc. Served as lt. comdr. USNR, 1942-46. Recipient Grand Rapids Jr. C. of C. Distinguished Service award, 1948; Distinguished Service Award as one of ten outstanding young men in U.S. by U.S. Jr. C. of C., 1950; Silver Anniversary All-Am. Sports Illustrated, 1959; Distinguished Congressional Service award Am. Polit. Sci. Assn., 1961, Medal of Freedom, 1999, Congressional Gold Medal, 1999, Profile in Courage award, 2001. Mem. Am., Mich. State, Grand Rapids bar assns., Delta Kappa Epsilon, Phi Delta Phi. Clubs: University (Kent County), Peninsular (Kent County). Lodges: Masons. Republican. Episcopalian. Office: PO Box 927 Rancho Mirage CA 92270-0927*

FORD, GORDON BUELL, JR., literature educator, writer; b. Louisville, Sept. 22, 1937; s. Gordon Buell Sr. and Rubye (Allen) F. AB summa cum laude in Classics, Medieval Latin, and Sanskrit, Princeton U., 1959; AM in Classical Philology and Linguistics, Harvard U., 1962, PhD in Linguistics, Slavic and Baltic Langs. and Lits., 1965; postgrad., U. Oslo, 1962-64, U. Sofia, Bulgaria, 1963, U. Uppsala, Sweden, 1963-64, U. Stockholm, 1963-64, U. Madrid, 1963. CPA. Yeager, Ford, and Warren Found. Disting. prof. Indo-European, Classical, Slavic, and Baltic linguistics, Sanskrit, and Medieval Latin Northwestern U., Evanston, Ill., 1965—; Lybrand, Ross Bros., and Montgomery Found. Disting. prof. English and linguistics U. No. Iowa, Cedar Falls, 1972—; sr. exec. v.p. for real estate acctg. fin. mgmt., bd. dirs. The Southeastern Real Estate Co., Inc., Louisville, 1976-93; sr. exec. v.p. reimbursement and rates acctg. fin. mgmt., hosp. acctg. divsn. Humana Inc., The Hosp. Co., Louisville, 1976-93; ret., 1993; bd. dirs. Southeastern Investment Trust, Inc., Louisville, 1976-93; ret., 1993; rsch. prof. The Southeastern Investment Trust, Inc. Rsch. Found., Louisville, 1976—. Vis. prof. Medieval Latin, U. Chgo., 1966—; vis. prof. linguistics U. Chgo., Downtown Ctr., 1966—; prof. English evening divs. Northwestern U., Chgo., 1968-69, prof. anthropology, 1971-72. Author: The Ruodlieb: The First Medieval Epic of Chivalry from Eleventh-Century Germany, 1965, The Ruodlieb: Linguistic Introduction, Latin Text with a Critical Apparatus, and Glossary, 1966, The Ruodlieb: Facsimile Edition, 1965, 3d edit. 1968, Old Lithuanian Texts of the Sixteenth and Seventeenth Centuries with a Glossary, 1969, The Old Lithuanian Catechism of Baltramiejus Vilentas (1579): A Phonological, Morphological, and Syntactical Investigation, 1969, Isidore of Seville's History of the Goths, Vandals, and Suevi, 1966, 2d edit. 1970, The Letters of Saint Isidore of Seville, 1966, 2d edit. 1970, The Old Lithuanian Catechism of Martynas Mazvydas (1547), 1971, others; translator: A Concise Elementary Grammar of the Sanskrit Language with Exercises, Reading Selections, and a Glossary (Jan Gonda), 1966, The Comparative Method in Historical Linguistics (Antoine Meillet), 1967, A Sanskrit Grammar (Manfred Mayrhofer), 1972; contbr. numerous articles to many scholarly jours. Appointed to Hon. Order Ky. Cols. (life). Mem. Linguistic Soc. Am. (life, Sapir life patron), Internat. Linguistic Assn. (life), Societas Linguistica Europaea (charter, life), Am. Philol. Assn. (life), Classical Assn. of the Atlantic States (life), Classical Assn. of the Middle West and South (life), Classical Assn. of N.Eng. (life), Medieval Acad. of Am. (life), Renaissance Soc. of Am. (life), MLA (life), Am. Assn. Tchrs. Slavic and East European Langs. (life), Am. Assn. Advancement Slavic Studies (life), Am. Coun. Tchrs. Russian (life), Assn. for Advancement Baltic Studies (life), Inst. Lithuanian Studies (life), Tchrs. of English to Speakers of Other Langs. (charter, life), SAR (life), Princeton Club (N.Y.C., Chgo.), Princeton Alumni Assn. (Louisville), Harvard Club (N.Y.C., Chgo., Louisville, Lexington, Ky.), Pres.'s Soc. Bellarmine Coll. (life), Louisville Country Club, KC (life), Phi Beta Kappa (life). Baptist. Home: 3619 Brownsboro Road Louisville KY 40207-1863 also: PO Box 2693 Clarksville Br Jeffersonville IN 47131-2693

FORD, HAROLD EUGENE, consultant, former congressman; b. Memphis, Tenn., May 20, 1945; s. Newton J. and Vera (Davis) F.; m. Dorothy Bowles, Feb. 10, 1969; children: Harold, Newton Jake, Sir Isaac. BS, Tenn. State U., 1967; AA, John Gupton Coll., 1969; MBA, Howard U. Mem. Tenn. Ho. of Reps., 1970-74; mem. 94th-106th Congresses from 9th Tenn. dist., 1975—96, edn. and workforce com., govt. reform and oversight com.; consult., founder The Harold Ford Group, Memphis, 2001—. Ways and means com., subcom. on oversight, mem. subcom. human resources, Dem. whip representing Tenn., La., Miss. during 99th Congress. Bd. dirs. Met. Memphis YMCA affiliated with Alpha Phi Alpha frat.; nat. adv. bd. St. Jude Children's Research Hosp. Named Outstanding Young Man of Year Memphis Jaycees, 1976, Outstanding Young Man of Year Tenn. Jaycees, 1977, Child Advocate of Yr. Child Welfare League Am., 1987. Democrat. Office: The Harold Ford Group 6060 Poplar Ave #150 Memphis TN 38119-0917

FORD, HAROLD EUGENE, JR., congressman; b. Memphis, Tenn., May 11, 1970; s. Harold E. Ford. BA, U. Pa., 1992; JD, U. Mich., 1996. Spl. asst. Econ. Devel. Adminstrn., 1993, Clinton & Gore Transition Team, 1992; mem. U.S. Ho. of Reps. from 9th Tenn. dist., 1997—. Aide Senate Budget Com.; mem. Blue Dogs, Com. Edn. & Workforce, Com. Fin. Svcs. Democrat. Baptist. Office: US Ho Reps Office Bldg 325 Cannon House Washington DC 20515-4209*

FORD, HARRISON, actor; b. Chgo., July 13, 1942; m. Mary Marquardt, 1964 (div. 1979); children: Willard, Benjamin; m. Melissa Mathison, 1983 (div. 2001); children: Malcolm, Georgia. Ed., Ripon Coll. Appeared in motion pictures including: Dead Heat on a Merry-Go-Round, 1966, Luv, 1967, The Long Ride Home, 1967, Getting Straight, 1970, Zabriske Point, 1970, American Graffiti, 1973, The Conversation, 1974, Star Wars, 1977, Heroes, 1977, Force 10 From Navarone, 1978, Hanover Street, 1979,More American Graffiti, 1979, The Frisco Kid, 1979, Apocalypse Now, 1979, The Empire Strikes Back, 1980, Raiders of the Lost Ark, 1981, Blade Runner, 1982, Return of the Jedi, 1983, Indiana Jones and the Temple of Doom, 1984, Witness, 1985, Mosquito Coast, 1986, Frantic, 1988, Working Girl, 1988, Indiana Jones and the Last Crusade, 1989, Presumed Innocent, 1990, Regarding Henry, 1991, Patriot Games, 1992, The Fugitive, 1993, Clear and Present Danger, 1994, Sabrina, 1995, A Hundred and One Nights, 1995, Devil's Own, 1996, Air Force One, 1997, Six Days Seven Nights, 1998, Random Hearts, 1999, What Lies Beneath, 2000, K-19: The Widowmaker, 2002, Hollywood Homicide, 2003; appeared in TV movies The Intruders, 1970, Judgement: The Court-Martial of Lt. William Calley, 1975, James A. Michener's Dynasty, 1976, The Possessed, 1977; numerous TV appearances including Ironside, The Mod Squad, The F.B.I., My Friend Tony, Gunsmoke, Kung-Fu, The Virginian, Young Indiana Jones Chronicles.*

FORD, JAMES CARLTON, human resources executive; b. Portland, Mar. 10, 1937; s. John Bernard and Margaret (Reynolds) F.; m. Carolyn Tadina, Aug. 22, 1959; children: Scott, Michele, Mark, Brigitte, Deidre, John. BA in History, U. Portland, 1960; MS in Edn., Troy State U., 1969; MPA, U. Puget Sound, 1976. Cert. sen. profl. in human resources. Commd. 2d lt. USAF, 1960, advanced through grades to lt. col., 1976, adminstr., tng. officer, 1960-70, personnel mgmt. officer, 1971-76; dep. inspector gen. U.S. Air Force Acad., Colorado Springs, Colo., 1977-80, ret., 1980; employment mgr. Western Fed. Savs. (name changed to Bank Western), Denver, 1980-82, v.p. human resources, 1982-88, sr. v.p. mgmt. svcs., 1988-92; dir. career mgmt. AIM Exec., Inc., Cons. Svcs., 1992-95; owner Orgn. Strategies, Inc., Cons., 1995—. Bd. dirs. Rocky Mountain chpt. Am. Inst. Banking, Denver, 1988-92; adj. prof. U. Colo., Colorado Springs, 1978-79, USAF Acad., Colorado Springs, 1978-80; adv. bd. U. Colo. Contemporary Mgmt. Program, Regis Coll. Career Svcs.; mem. faculty U. Phoenix, Colo., 1995—; mediator Pikes Peak Better Bus. Bur., 1995—. Mediator Neighborhood Justice Ctr., Colorado Springs, 1980; vol. allocations com. Pikes Peak United Way, Colorado Springs, 1978-79; vol. campaign exec. Mile Hi United Way, Denver, 1986-89; vol. mgmt. cons. Tech. Assistance Svc., Denver, 1991. Mem. Assn. for Mgmt. of Orgn. Design, Soc. for Human Resource Mgmt. (state dir. certification 1996-97). Republican. Roman Catholic. Office: Orgn Strategies Inc 975 Tari Dr Colorado Springs CO 80921-2256

FORD, JEAN ELIZABETH, former English language educator; b. Branson, Mo., Oct. 5, 1923; d. Mitchell Melton and Annie Estella (Wyer) F.; m. J.C. Wingo, 1942 (div. 1946; m. E. Syd Vineyard, 1952 (div. 1956); m. Vincent Michel Wessling, Feb. 14, 1983 (div. Dec. 1989). AA in English, L.A. City Coll., 1957; BA in English, Calif. State U., 1959; MA in Higher Edn., U. Mo., 1965; postgrad., UCLA, 1959-60, U. Wis., 1966, U. Mo. Law Sch., 1968-69. Cert. English tchr., real estate broker, Mo. Dance instr. Arthur Murray Studios, L.A., 1948-51; office mgr. Western Globe Products, L.A., 1951-55; pvt. dance tchr., various office jobs L.A., 1955-59; social dir. S.S. Matsonia, 1959; social worker L.A. County, 1959-61; 7th grade instr. Carmenita Sch. Dist., Norwalk, Calif., 1961-62; English instr. Leadwood (Mo.) High Sch., 1962-63; dance instr. U. Mo., 1963-66, SW Mo. State U., 1966-68, NW Mo. State U., 1970-76, Johnson County Community Coll., 1976-77; tax examiner IRS, Kansas City, Mo., 1978-80; tax acct. Baird, Kurtz & Dobson, Kansas City, Mo., 1981; dance tchr. Singles Program Village, Presbyn. Ch., Kans., 1981-96. Substitute tchr. various sch. dists., 1976-85; dance chmn. Mo. Assn. Health, Phys. Edn. and Recreation, 1965-66, 68-69, dance chmn. ctrl. dist. AAHPER, 1972-73; vis. author Young Author's Conf., Ctrl. Mo. State U., 1987, 88, 89; speaker Am. Reading Assn., Grandview, Mo., 1990; real estate sales agt., Kansas City, 1980-84; real estate sales broker, Mo., 1990—, Kans., 1990-2000; pvt. practice tax acct., dance tchr., 1984-2002. Author, pub.: Fish Tails and Scales, 1982, 2d edit., 2000; spkr. at librs. Mem. Am. Contract Bridge League, Kansas City Ski Club. Democrat. Presbyterian. Avocations: tennis, swimming, skiing, sailing, bridge. Home and Office: 142 Grandview Dr Bldg 4 #7 Branson MO 65616

FORD, JEREMIAH, III, architect; b. Phila., Apr. 22, 1932; s. Jeremiah II and Mary Sterling (Hewitt) F.; m. Judith Oakes Seidler, June 17, 1954 (div. 1973); children: Amanda Hewitt, Katherine Brewster; m. Elizabeth Dana Stewardson, Mar. 1, 1975; children: Elizabeth Connolly, Caroline Thornewill, Dana H. Stewardson. AB, Princeton U., 1954, MFA, 1959. Registered architect, N.J., Mass., Pa., Fla., Del. Designer Harrison and Abramovitz Architects, N.Y.C., 1960-61, Port of N.Y. Authority World Trade Ctr., N.Y.C., 1961-62; archtl. apprentice Kenneth Kassler Architect, Princeton, 1962-64; ptnr. Walker Sander Ford and Kerr Architects, Princeton, 1965-74, Short and Ford Architects, Princeton, 1974-93, Ford Farewell Mills and Gatsch Architects, Princeton, 1993—. Prin. works include Marriott Hotel and Conf. Ctr., Trenton, N.J. State House, Trenton, Summit (N.J.) City Hall, 1973, Morristown (N.J.) Libr., 1985, Princeton Cmty. Housing, 1982, Cranbury (N.J.) Sr. Housing, 1990, pvt. residences. Capt. USMC, 1954-57, Korea, Japan. Episcopalian. Avocations: painting, gardening. Home: 820 Pretty Brook Rd Princeton NJ 08540-7532 Office: Ford Farewell Mills Gatsch 103 Carnegie Ctr Ste 301 Princeton NJ 08540-6235 E-mail: jerryf@ffmg.com., jerryfiii@aol.com.

FORD, JERRY LEE, service company executive; b. Muncie, Ind., July 11, 1940; s. Robert Thomas and Thelma Adrien (Strickler) F.; m. Margaret Annette Bailey, Sept. 10, 1966; children: Duane A., Diana K., Brenda D. BS in Acctg., Ind. U., 1962. CPA, Ind. Sr. auditor KPMG Peat Marwick, Indpls., 1964-67; contr. Georgia Kraft Co., Rome, Ga., 1967-71; asst. dir. acctg. Gen. Mills, Inc., Mpls., 1971-75, sys. contr. foods group; v.p. fin., contr. Ship N Shore subs. Gen. Mills, Inc., Phila., 1979-80; v.p. fin., treas. Poppin Fresh Pies divsn. Pillsbury Co., Mpls., 1980-81; v.p. fin. foods group Pillsbury Co., Mpls., 1981-84, v.p. adminstrn. svcs., 1984-87; COO, exec. dir. Lindquist & Vennum, Mpls., 1988-93; chief operating officer Comdisco Network Svcs., Minnetonka, Minn., 1994-98; chief devel. officer and gen. mgr. western U.S. Jetways, Inc., 1998-2000; ind. bus. cons. Scottsdale, Ariz., 2000—. Instr. Def. Contract Audit Agy. Exec. Program, Memphis 1987; bd. dirs. Nash Finch Co., Western Horizon Resorts. Co-author: Controllers Handbook, 1984, 92. Bd. dirs. Min. Acctg. Aid Soc., 1986-88, 90-94, Mpls. YMCA, 1974-78. Mem. Fin. Execs. Inst. (chpt. pres., nat. bd. dirs.), Inst. Mgmt. Accts. (nat. v.p. 1984-85), Inst. Cert. Mgmt. Accts. (cert., chmn. bd. dirs. 1982-84), Ind. U. Alumni Assn. (bd. dirs. 1989-93). Republican. Methodist. Avocations: golf, racquetball.

FORD, JOE THOMAS, telephone company executive, former state senator; b. Conway, Ark., June 24, 1937; s. Arch W. and Ruby (Watson) F.; m. Jo Ellen Wilbourn, Aug. 9, 1959; children: Alison, Scott. BS, U. Ark., 1959. With Allied Telephone Co., Little Rock, 1959-83, v.p.-treas., 1963-77, pres., 1977-83, ALLTEL Corp., 1983-87, pres., chief exec. officer, 1987-91, chmn., pres., chief exec. officer, 1991-93, chmn., CEO, 1993—; now chmn. Alltel Corp., Little Rock, A.R. Mem. Ark. Senate, 1967-82; dir. Comml. Nat. Bank, 1970-85, Little Rock, Security Bank, Conway. Recipient Disting. Alumni cert. U. Ark., 1987. Baptist. Home: 2100 Country Club Ln Little Rock AR 72207-2040 Office: Alltel Corp PO Box 2177 1 Allied Dr Little Rock AR 72203

FORD, JOHN CHARLES, artist; b. Choudrant, La., Sept. 29, 1929; s. John Leon Ford and Jessie Faye Dugdale; m. Margaret Ann Preston, Sept. 1959 (div. Apr. 1964); 1 child, John Charles Jr. BFA, La. Poly. Inst., 1950; BDiv, Austin Pres. Theol. Sem., 1953; MFA, U. Oreg., 1960. One-man shows at Leicester Galleries, London, 1967, Otto Seligman Gallery, Seattle, 1962, 72, Francine Seders Gallery, Seattle, 1972, Avanti Gallery, N.Y., 1972, L.I. Painters Awards Exhbn., 1974, Country Art Gallery, Locust Valley, 1974, La. State U., Baton Rouge, 1974, Neuberger Mus., Purchase, N.Y., 1977, Sid Deutsch Art Gallery, N.Y., 1977, RR Gallery, N.Y., 1980, Jack Gallery, N.Y., 1982, Phillip Dash Gallery, N.Y., 1986, Ruston (La.) Art Assn., Piney Hills Gallery, Ruston, 1991, Shreveport (La.) Arts Coun., Centenary Gallery, Shreveport, 2001; two-man shows at Labette C.C., Parsons, Kans., 1998; represented in permanent collections at Solomon R. Guggenheim Mus., NYU, N.Y., Hirshhorn Mus. and Sculpture Garden, Washington, Corcoran Gallery of Art, Washington, Neuberger Mus., Purchase, N.Y., Herbert F. Johnson Mus., Ithaca, N.Y., Seattle Art Mus., Addison (Mass.) Gallery Am. Art, Nuffield Found., London, Birmingham (Ala.) Mus. Art, U. Oreg., Ark. Arts Ctr., Little Rock, Ea. Oreg. Coll., La Grande. Democrat. Presbyterian. Avocations: writing, gardening. Home: 1592 Highway 145 Choudrant LA 71227-3600

FORD, JOHN GILMORE, interior designer; s. John Gilmore and Marian Brunner (Mainhart) F.; m. Berthe Diana Hanover, Aug. 19, 1972. B.F.A., Md. Inst. Coll. Art. Founder, 1962; since pres. John Ford Assoc., Inc., Balt.; tchr. seminars Md. Inst. Coll. Art, Md.; lectr. Indo-Asian art Johns Hopkins U., Towson State Coll. Served with USCGR. Recipient citation of merit Md. Inst. Coll. Art, 1960 Fellow Am. Soc. Interior Designers (past nat. v.p., pres. Md. chpt.; Presdl. citation); mem. Internat. Chinese Snuff Bottle Soc. (pres., co-editor jour.), Asia Soc., Am. Soc. Appraisers (sr. mem.). Clubs: Masons (32 deg.). Office: 2601 N Charles St Baltimore MD 21218-4514 Home: 17 Roland Mews Baltimore MD 21210-1563

FORD, JOHN STEPHEN, treasurer; b. Clinton, Mass., Apr. 27, 1957; s. James Joseph and Rita (Hart) F.; m. Mary Andrejczyk, Apr. 15, 1978; children: Michelle, Amanda, William. BS, Lowell U., 1979. CPA, Mass.; notary pub., Mass. Staff acct. Main, Hurdman, Cranston, CPA's, Worcester, Mass., 1979; sr. acct. William S. Reagan & Co. CPA's, Fitchburg, Mass., 1979-82; treas. Peterborough Oil Co., Inc., Leominster, Mass., 1982—. Cons. in field. Active Lancaster (Mass.) Dem. Town Com.; former treas. Lancaster Soccer; former mem. Lancaster Recreation Com.; former coach Pop Warner football; former treas. Lancaster Baseball Assn.; bd. dirs. Worker's Credit Union, Fitchburg, Mass., Worker's Fin. Svcs., Inc. Fellow Mass. Soc. CPA; mem. AICPA (tax divsn.), Am. Turners, Elks. Roman Catholic. Avocations: sports, local politics, home improvements. Office: Peterborough Oil Co PO Box 787 665 N Main St Leominster MA 01453-1894

FORD, JOHN T., JR., art, film and video educator; b. Rotan, Tex., Feb. 17, 1953; s. John T. and Lala Fern (Shipley) F.; m. Betty Jean Crawford; children: Casey, Craig, Kirk. BA, U. Redlands, 1975. Cert. tchr. Calif. Tchr. art, film, video Yucaipa (Calif.) Joint Unified Sch. Dist., 1976-88; tchr. art and crafts Vacaville (Calif.) Unified Sch. Dist., 1990-92, tchr. video prodn., 1992—, sr. prodn. video, 1994—. Cons. Dist. Fine Arts Insvc., Yucaipa, 1987; co-sponsor Art Club, Will C. Wood High Sch., Vacaville, sponsor Video Club. Creator, coord. (conceptual art) Whole School Environments, Caves, Tubes and Streamers, Forest Edge, 1980-81; creator (comml. art prints) Toy Horse Series, 1982-83; prodr. ann. sr. video, 1994—. Mem. Yeoman Svc. Orgn., U. Redlands, 1972, Vacaville Sch. Dist. Tech. Com., Dist. Fine Arts Task Force, Yucaipa, 1984-87, Dist. Task Force for Vocat. Edn., 1992; interim dir. Hosanna House, Redlands, Calif., 1975; liaison Sch. Cmty. Svc./San Bernardino County (Calif.) Fire Dept., 1980-81. Recipient Golden Bell award Calif. Sch. Bd. Rsch. Found., 1987, Ednl. Svc. award Mason's, 1987-88; named one of Outstanding Young Men of Am., 1987, Tchr. of Yr. Calif. Continuation Edn. Assn., 1987-88; grantee Calif. Tchrs. Instructional Improvement Program, 1985; scholar U. Redlands, 1975. Mem. Am. Film Inst. Avocations: art, media fabrication, writing, collecting books, backpacking. Office: Buckingham Charter Sch 188 Bella Vista Dr Vacaville CA 95687-5735

FORD, JUDITH ANN TUDOR, retired natural gas distribution company executive; b. Martinsville, Ind., May 11, 1935; d. Glenn Leyburn and Dorotha Mae (Parks) Tudor; m. Walter L. Ford, July 25, 1954 (dec. 1962); children: John Corbin, Christi Sue. Student, Wichita State U., 1953-55; student, U. Nev.-Las Vegas. Legal sec. S.W. Gas Corp., Las Vegas, 1963-69, asst. corp. sec., 1969-72, corp. sec., 1972-82, v.p., 1977-82, sr. v.p., 1982-88, also bd. dirs., dir. 7 subs. Bd. dirs. NBA Svcs., Nev., residence for handicapped, 1989-97, treas., 1990-91, chmn., 1994-97; trustee Nev. Sch. Arts, Las Vegas, 1979-90, chmn. bd. dirs., 1985-86; trustee Disciples Sem. Found., Claremont Sch. Theology and Pacific Sch. Religion, San Francisco, 1985-91, 92-98, 99—, vice chmn., 1993-94, chmn., 1994-98; mem . Ariz. Acad., Ariz. Town Halls, 1986-92. Mem. Am. Soc. Corp. Secs., Greater Las Vegas C. of C. (bd. dirs. 1979-85), Pacific Coast Gas Assn. (bd. dirs. 1984-88), Ariz. Bus. Women Owners (exec. com. 1985-88). Democrat. Mem. Christian Ch. (Disciples Of Christ).

FORD, KATHLEEN MARIE, home health nurse, nursing administrator; b. N.Y., May 3, 1937; d. Gregory Henry and Mary Rose (Spinella) Kanellos; m. William Henry Ford, Jan. 8, 1958; children: William Henry Jr., Theresa Marie. AAS, Nassau C.C. RN, N.Y., N.Mex., Tex. Staff nurse ICU, CCU North Shore U. Hosp., Manhasset, N.Y., 1973; LIJ Hillside Med. Ctr., New Hyde Park, N.Y., 1974-75; utilization rev. coord., med. auditing asst. Terrace Heights Hosp., Jamaica, N.Y., 1975-76; utilization review coord., supr. Belen area, freelance discharge planning coord., key nurse for quality assurance program in N.Mex. Hosp. Home Health Care, 1976-78; utilization review coord. Huguley Meml. Hosp., Fort Worth, Tex., 1981-82; admissions nurse, acting supr., field RN Upjohn Healthcare Svcs., 1983-84; field nurse Med. Plz. Home Health Care, Fort Worth, 1984-86, PMI, Fort Worth, 1986-88, Fort Worth Osteopathic Med. Ctr., 1989; supr. Home Health of Tarrant County, 1989-91; patient care coord. Family Svc. Inc., Fort Worth, 1991-94; home health field trainer Total Home Health Svcs., Fort Worth, 1994-95; field supr. Vis. Nurse Assn., Ft. Worth, 1995—2000; ret., 2000. Host parent fgn. exch. student Aspect Found., San Francisco, 1989-90, 94-95. Roman Catholic. Avocations: sewing, crossword puzzles, reading, travel, photography. Home: 7525 Nutwood Pl Fort Worth TX 76133-7512 E-mail: kmford76133@yahoo.com.

FORD, KAY LOUISE, innovation consulting executive; b. Pontiac, Mich., Aug. 2, 1944; d. Norman Avery and Elsa Katherine (Wahlsten) F.; m. Billy Wayne Reed, Aug. 20, 1965 (div. Jan. 1979); children: Matthew Wayne Reed, Bradley Ford Reed. AB, U. Mich., 1965; MA, SUNY, Brockport, 1983. Speech therapist Cmty. Treatment Ctr., Bath, Maine, 1966-68; continuing edn. coord. SUNY, Brockport, 1974-78, grad. asst., 1978-79; contract tng. dir. Monroe C.C., Rochester, N.Y., 1979-86; exec. dir. Livingston Washtenaw Pvt. Industry Coun., Ann Arbor, Mich., 1986-91; dir. devel. McKinley Found., Ann Arbor, 1991-92; v.p. community rels. Regional Coun. Aging, Inc., Rochester, 1992-93; v.p. Drake Beam Morin, Inc., Rochester, 1993-96; cons. KLF Personal PR Assocs., 1993—; sector v.p. Idea Connection Sys., Inc., Rochester, 1996-2000; sr. v.p. Manchester, Inc., Phila., 1999—. Contract trainer Cornell U., Rochester, 1983-86, Learning Internat., Buffalo, 1984-87, Jannotta, Bray and Assocs., Chgo., 1992; field instr. U. Mich., 1988-92; adj. instr. SUNY, Brockport, 1993-98. Co-chmn. Internat. Spl. Olympics Ceremonies Com., Brockport, 1979-80, Washtenaw United Way Comm., Ann Arbor, 1987-91, Mich. Theatre Fund Raising, Ann Arbor, 1987-90; bd. dirs. Jazz for Life--On Stage for Kids, Ann Arbor, 1987-90, Peace Neighborhood Cu., 1991-92; mem. bus. and labor leaders adv. com. Washtenaw C.C.; fund drive and career svcs. coms. Rochester YWCA, 1996-99.. Mem. ASTD, Soc. Human Resource Mgmt., Finger Lakes SHRM (mem. strategic adv. bd.), Finger Lakes ASTD, Nat. Soc. Fund Raising Execs., Planned Giving Coun. Upstate N.Y., Ann Arbor Pers. Assn., Univ. Club Rochester, Rochester Women's Network, Union League of Phila. Avocation: collecting antiques.

FORD, KENNETH WILLIAM, physicist; b. West Palm Beach, Fla., May 1, 1926; s. Paul Hammond and Edith (Timblin) F.; m. Karin Stehnike, Aug. 27, 1953 (div. 1961); m. Joanne Baumunk, June 9, 1962; children: Paul T., Sarah E., Caroline A., Adam B., Jason L., Ian L.; 1 stepdau., Nina Tannenwald. Student, John Carroll U., 1945, U. Mich., 1945-46; AB, Harvard Coll., 1948; PhD, Princeton U., 1953. Rsch. asst. Los Alamos Sci. Lab., 1950-51; rsch. assoc. Princeton U., 1951-52; from rsch. assoc. to assoc. prof. Ind. U., 1953-58, asst. prof. physics, 1954-57; from assoc. prof. to prof. Brandeis U., 1958-64; prof. U. Calif., Irvine, 1964-70, chmn. dept. physics, 1964-68; prof. physics U. Mass., Boston, 1970-75; pres. N.Mex. Inst. Mining and Tech., Socorro, 1975-82; exec. v.p. U. Md., Adelphi, 1982-83; pres. Molecular Biophysics Tech. Inc., 1983-85; edn. officer Am. Phys. Soc., 1986-87; exec. dir. Am. Inst. Physics, 1987-93; tchr. Germantown Acad., 1995-98; sci. program dir. David and Lucile Packard Found., 1998-99; tchr. Germantown Friends Sch., 2000-2001. Mem. Commn. Coll. Physics, 1968—71; cons. in field. Author: The World of Elementary Particles, 1963, Basic Physics, 1968, Classical and Modern Physics, 3 vols., 1972-74; (with John Wheeler) Geons, Black Holes, and Quantum Foam: A Life in Physics, 1998; mem. editl. bd. Phys. Rev., 1960-62, The Physics Tchr., 2000—; contbr. articles to profl. jours. With USNR, 1944-46. Fulbright fellow Max Planck Inst., Germany, 1955-56, NSF sr. postdoctoral fellow Imperial Coll. London, 1961-62, MIT, 1962. Fellow AAAS (coun. del. physics electorate 1983-86), Am. Phys. Soc. (chmn. forum on physics and soc. 1981, councilor 1984-87, sec.-treas. forum on history of physics 2001-2004); mem. Am. Assn. Physics Tchrs. (pres. 1972, Disting. Svc. citation 1976), Fedn. Am. Scientists. E-mail: kwford@verizon.net.

FORD, LUCILLE GARBER, economist, educator; b. Ashland, Ohio, Dec. 31, 1921; d. Ora Myers and Edna Lucille (Armstrong) Garber; m. Laurence Wesley Ford, Sept. 1, 1946; children: Karen Elizabeth, JoAnn Christine. AA, Stephens Coll., 1942; BS in Commerce, Northwestern U., 1944, MBA, 1945; PhD in Econs., Case Western Res. U., 1967; PhD (hon.), Tarkio Coll., 1991, Ashland U., 1995. Cert. fin. planner. Instr. Allegheny Coll., Meadville, Pa., 1945-46, U. Ala., Tuscaloosa, 1946-47; personnel dir., asst. sec. A.L. Garber Co., Ashland, Ohio, 1947-67; prof. econs. Ashland U., 1967-95, chmn. dept. econs., 1970-75; dir. Gill Ctr. for Econ. Edn. Ashland Coll., 1975-86, v.p., dean Sch. Bus., Adminstrn. and Econs., 1980-86, v.p. acad. affairs, 1986-90, provost, 1990-92; exec. asst. to pres., 1993-95; pres. Ashland Comm. Found., 1995—. Bd. dirs. Peco II, Inc., Western Res. Econ. Devel. Coun., Morgan Freeport Corp., Ohio Coun. Econ. Edn.; lectr. in field; mem. govs. adv. com. on econ. devel. Author: University Economics-Guide for Education Majors, 1979, Economics: Learning and Instruction, 1981, 91; contbr. articles to profl. jours. Mem. Ohio Gov.'s Commn. on Ednl. Choice, 1992; candidate for lt. gov. of Ohio, 1978; trustee Stephens Coll., 1977-80, Ashland U., 1995—, North Cen. State Coll., 1998—; elder Presbyn. Ch.; bd. dirs. Presbyn. Found., 1982-88; chair, trustee Synod-Presbyn. Ch., 1994-2000; active ARC. Named to Ohio Women's Hall of Fame, 2001; recipient Outstanding Alumnus award, Stephens Coll., 1977, Outstanding Profl. award, Ashland U., 1971, 1975, Roman F. Warmke award, 1981, Women of Achievement award, 1998. Mem. Am. Econs. Assn., Nat. Indsl. Research Soc., Am. Arbitration Assn. (profl. arbitrator), Assn. Pvt. Enterprise Edn. (pres. 1983-84), North Ctrl. Assn. Colls. & Schs. (commr.), Omicron Delta Epsilon, Alpha Delta Kappa. Republican. Office: Ashland Comm Found PO Box 733 Ashland OH 44805-0733

FORD, MARK L. lawyer; b. Lexington, Ky., Nov. 7, 1960; s. Thomas Robert and Harriet (Lowrey) F.; m. Sue Thomas, May 17, 1986; children: Darian, Thomas, Caleb. BA, Ind. U., 1982; JD, U. Ky., 1985. Bar: Ky. 1985, U.S. Dist. Ct. (ea. dist.) Ky. 1987, U.S. Ct. Appeals (6th cir.) 1990, Ct. Vet. Appeals 1990, U.S. Supreme Ct. 1997. Rschr. Coun. State Govts., Lexington, 1984-85; assoc. Forester & Forester, Harlan, Ky., 1985-88; ptnr. Smith & Ford, Harlan, 1988-90; pvt. practice law Harlan, 1990—. Pres. Ea. Broadcasting Co., 1998—. Author: Hey, It Could Happen, 1999; co-author: Emergency Management in the States, 1984. Mem. Harlan (Ky.) County Pub. Libr. Bd. Trustees, 1990-94, pres. 2001-. Mem. Harlan County Bar Assn. (treas. 1990-97). Office: 105 Central St Harlan KY 40831

FORD, MARK LEE, aerospace engineer, scientist; b. Toronto, Ont., Can., Jan. 8, 1966; s. Jeffrey Theo Maurice and Elaine Joan Maude (de Lang) F. BSc, U. Toronto, 1989; MS, Boston U., 1993, PhD, 1996. Profl. engr. Grad. rsch. fellow Boston U., 1992-93, Am. Chem. Soc.-Petroleum Rsch. Fund fellow, 1993-96; U.S. Nat. Sci. Found. fellow Ministry Internat. Trade and Industry, Tsukuba, Ibaraki, Japan, 1996-98; strategy cons. Accenture (formerly Andersen Consulting), 2000—. Rsch. cons., sci. collaborator Mech. Enging. Lab., Tsukuba, 1994-98; investigator in field. Contbr. articles to profl. jours. and mags. Vol. Aijien Children's Home and Orphanage, Tsukuba, 1997—. Mem. AIAA, ASME, Am. Phys. Soc., Am. Astronautical Soc., Asiatic Soc. Japan (bd. dirs.), Am.-Japan Soc., Japan-Brit. Soc., Tau Beta Pi. Achievements include research and development of stratospheric airships as aerospace platforms; co-derivation of Ford-Nadim equation for thermocapillary migration of drops. E-mail: mozart@bu.edu.

FORD, MAUREEN MORRISSEY, civic worker; b. St. Joseph, Mo., July 1, 1936; d. Albert Joseph and Rosemary Kathryne (FitzSimons) Morrissey; m. James Henry Lee, Feb. 12, 1954; children: Kathryne Elizabeth, Maryellen, James Henry Lee III(dec.), William Charles, Maureen Lee. Student, U. N.Mex., 1953-54, U. Bridgeport, Conn., 1966-68; BS, Fairfield U., 1986, postgrad. in applied ethics, 1986—. Charity and sch. vol., 1959—; fundraiser for cmty. causes, mus., agys., 1964—; active presdl. campaign Barry Goldwater, 1963-64; congl. campaign Senator Lowell Weiker, 1968; pre-sch. tchr. Earth Place, 1966-68, trustee, v.p. bd. dir., 1968-75; assoc. program in applied ethics Fairfield U., 1986—. Author: (with Lisa H. Newton) Taking Sides: Controversial Issues in Business Ethics, 1990, 8th edit., 2003. V.p. Women's League, 1966-70; mem. exec. com. Rep. Women's Club, Westport, 1967-68; leader, trainer Troops on Fgn. Soil br. Girl Scouts US, Caracas, Venezuela, 1971-72; founding trustee, treas. Kara Mus., Norwalk, Conn.; mem. adv. coun. Fairfield County (Conn.) for spl. edn. Staples H.S.; bd. dirs. CLASP; mem. exec. com. Group Home Search; pres. Ind. Assocs. Cons. Firm, 1991—; cons., facilitator life planning workshops Merideth Assocs., Westport; v.p., bd. dirs. Isaiah 61:1, Inc., 1989—; active grants com. Bridgeport Pub. Edn. Fund and Devel. Commn., 1984—; mem. 1st selectmen's com. on recycling, 1974-75; bd. dirs. PTA, 1976-79; mem. YWCA of Bridgeport Com. of 100 and Task Force; v.p. bd. dirs. YWCA, 1980-87, pres., 1984-85; v.p. Conf. Women's Orgns., Bridgeport; founding mem. Concerned Women Colleagues of Bridgeport; pres. Jr. League Ea. Fairfield County, Inc., 1977-78; v.p., sec. J.H.L.F. Inc., Westport; mem. grants com. Conn. Cares Hartford Fund, 1995-97. Mem. Assn. Jr. League Am., Westport Tennis Assn. Roman Catholic. Home: 204 Stillson Rd Fairfield CT 06825

FORD, MICHAEL W. lawyer; b. Peoria, Ill., Dec. 9, 1938; s. Benjamin W. and Charlene (Oder) F.; m. Kristine L. Ford; children from a previous marriage: Sarah, Scott, Amy, Michael B. BA, U. Chgo., 1960; JD, Loyola U., 1965. Bar: Ill. 1965, Tex. 1997, U.S. Dist. Ct. (no. dist.) Ill. 1965, U.S. Dist. Ct. (ea. dist.) Wis. 1974, U.S. Dist. Ct. (mid. dist.) Ill. 1986, U.S. Dist. Ct. Nebr. 1987, U.S. Dist. Ct. (so. dist.) Tex. 1999, U.S. Ct. Appeals (7th cir.) 1965, U.S. Ct. Appeals (3d cir.) 1988, U.S. Ct. Appeals (6th dist.) 1989, U.S. Ct. Appeals (5th cir.) 1999, U.S. Supreme Ct. 1977. Mng. ptnr., sr. ptnr. in charge of gen. and corp. litigation Chapman and Cutler, Chgo., 1965-96; of counsel Jones, Day, Reavis & Pogue, Houston, 2001—. Contbr. numerous articles to profl. jours.; spkr. many seminars for legal or ednl. groups. Mem. nominating com. Riverwoods, Ill. Caucus, 1992-93. Mem. ABA (mem. trial evidence com. and other coms.), Tex. Bar Assn. Home: 4 Timberwood Ln Riverwoods IL 60015-2400 Fax: 713-223-0042.

FORD, NANCY LOUISE, composer, scriptwriter; b. Kalamazoo, Oct. 1, 1935; d. Henry Ford III and Mildred Wotring; m. Robert D. Currie, June 7, 1957 (div. 1962); m. Keith W. Charles, May 23, 1964. BA, DePauw U., 1957; D of Arts (hon.), Eastern Mich. U., 1986; D of Fine Arts (hon.), DePauw U., 2002. Composer (with Gretchen Cryer): (off-Broadway musicals) Now is the Time for All Good Men, 1967, The Last Sweet Days of Isaac, 1970, I'm Getting My Act Together and Taking It On the Road, 1978, The American Girls Revue, 1998, Circle of Friends, 2001; composer: (Broadway musical) Shelter, 1972; scriptwriter: TV daytime serials Love of Life, 1971—74, Ryan's Hope, 1975, Search for Tomorrow, 1981—82, Guiding Light, 1977—78, As the World Turns, 1978—80, 1987—95; performer: stage and cabaret; scriptwriter : (TV series) Ryan's Hope, 1983—84. Trustee DePauw U., 1988-97. Recipient Emmy awards, 1983, 84. Mem.: AFTRA, League Profl. Theatre Women N.Y. (bd. dirs.), Am. Fedn. Musicians, Actors Equity, Writers Guild Am., Dramatists Guild (mem. coun.).

FORD, PATRICK KILDEA, Celtic studies educator; b. Lansing, Mich., July 31, 1935; s. Oliver Patrick and Ina Mildred (Spence) F.; m. Carol Mae Larsen, June 20, 1959 (div. 1978); children: Anne Kristina, Paul Kildea, James Oliver; m. Chadine Pearl Bailie, Nov. 17, 1979. BA, Mich. State U., 1959; MA, Harvard U., 1966, PhD, 1969. Asst. prof. English Stanford U., 1968-70; asst. prof. Indo-European studies UCLA, 1970-71, asst. prof. English, 1971-74, assoc. prof., 1974-79, prof. English and Celtic studies, 1979-91, dir. Folklore and Mythology Ctr., 1979-84, chmn. Indo-European studies program, 1972-73, 74-75, 79-82, dir. writing programs, 1989-91; Margaret Brooks Robinson prof. Celtic Harvard U., Cambridge, Mass., 1991—; Wallace E. and Grace Connolly prof. Celtic Stanford U., 1986. Founder, pres. Ford & Bailie Pubs./Book Distbrs. Author: The Poetry of Llywarch Hen, 1974, The Mabinogi and Other Medieval Welsh Tales, 1977, Ystoria Taliesin, 1992, The Celtic Poets: Songs and Tales from Early Ireland and Wales, 1999, Math uab Mathonwy, 1999, Manawydan uab Llyr, 2000; editor, contbr.: Celtic Folklore and Christianity: Essays in Memory of William W. Heist, 1983; co-author: Sources and Analogues of Old English Poetry: Celtic and Germanic, 1984, The Irish Literary Tradition, 1992. With AUS, 1956-57. NEH fellow, 1972, UCLA fellow, 1973, Fulbright fellow, 1973-74; grantee Skaggs Found., 1981-83, Am. Council Learned Socs., 1985, NEH, 1986, 94, 96, 99, 2002; hon. fellow Ctr. for Advanced Welsh and Celtic Studies/U. Wales. Mem. MLA, Internat. Arthurian Soc. (pres. N.Am. br. 1981-83), Medieval Acad. Am., Celtic Studies Assn. N.Am. (v.p. 1984-86, pres. 1987-89). Office: Harvard U Dept Celtic Lang and Lit Barker Ctr 12 Quincy St Cambridge MA 02138-2030

FORD, PAUL B. lawyer; b. Augusta, Ga., Dec. 1, 1943; s. Paul Brendan Ford and Augustine Marie Roy; m. Nancy Young; children: Brendan, Ian, Hunter, Jade. BA magna cum laude, Boston Coll., 1965; JD, Duke U., 1968. Ptnr. Simpson Thacher & Bartlett, N.Y.C., 1976—. Contbr. articles to profl. jours. Active Nat. Com. on U.S. China Rels., N.Y.C., 1999—; chmn. U.S. Fgn. Policy Assn., N.Y.C., 1993—2000; dir. New Haven Symphony Orch., New Haven, 1992—. Mem.: ABA, Coun. Fgn. Rels., Japan Soc., Korea Soc., Inter Pacific Bar Assn., Internat. Bar Assn., Union Internat. des Avocats, Assn. Bar City of N.Y. Avocations: sailing, skiing. Office: Simpson Thacher & Bartlett Rm 2109 425 Lexington Ave New York NY 10017 Office Fax: 212-455-2502. Business E-Mail: pford@stblaw.com.

FORD, PAUL FRANCIS, theology studies educator, musician; b. Springfield, Mass., Apr. 8, 1947; s. Bernard William Ford and Theresa Marie Bourcier; m. Janice Daurio, June 29, 1985. PhD in Theology, Fuller Theol. Sem., 1987. Prof. theology and liturgy St. John Sem., Camarillo, Calif., 1988—. Author: (literary criticism) Companion to Narnia (Mythopoeic Soc. Award for Scholarship, 1982), (hymnal) By Flowing Waters: Chant for the Liturgy; composer (cd), Lord, By Your Cross and Resurrection: The Chants of Holy Week in English. Recipient Laudatus Award, Cardinal Roger Mahony, Archbishop of LA, 1995, Scholar Guest of Honor, C.S. Lewis Centenary Conf., Mythopoeic Soc., 1998. Mem.: So. Calif. C.S. Lewis Soc. (founder 1974). Roman Catholic. Office: St John Seminary 5012 Seminary Rd Camarillo CA 93012-2598 Office Fax: 805-482-3470. E-mail: paulfford@sjs-sc.org.

FORD, RICHARD, writer; b. Jackson, Miss., Feb. 16, 1944; s. Parker Carrol and Edna (Akin) F.; m. Kristina Hensley, 1968. BA in English, Mich. State U., 1966; MFA, U. Calif., 1970. Author: (novels) A Piece of My Heart, 1976, The Ultimate Good Luck, 1981, The Sportswriter, 1986 (PEN/Faulkner citation for fiction 1986), Wildlife, 1990, Independence Day, 1995, (short stories) Rock Springs, 1987, Women with Men: Three Stories, 1997, (play) American Tropical, 1983, (screenplay) Bright Angel, 1991; editor: (with Shannon Ravenel) The Best American Short Stories, 1990, The Granta Book of the American Short Story, (with Michael Kreyling), Eudora Welty: Complete Novels, 1998, Eudora Welty: Stories, Essays, and Memoir (Eudora Welty), 1998, The Granta Book of the American Long Story, 1999; contbr. articles to popular publs. Recipient Pulitzer prize for fiction, 1996, PEN/Faulkner prize for fiction, 1996; Guggenheim fellow, 1977-98, Endowment for the Arts, 1979-80, 85-86. Mem. U. Mich. Soc. Fellows, Am. Acad. Arts and Letters.*

FORD, RICHARD EDMOND, lawyer; b. Ronceverte, W.Va., May 3, 1927; s. Grady Williams and Hazel Loraine (Fry) F.; m. Sally Frances Alexander, June 14, 1952; children: Richard Edmond Jr., Sally Anne, Melinda J. Student, U. N.C., 1950; BS in Bus. Adminstrn., W.Va. U., 1951, LL.B., 1954. Bar: W.Va. 1954. Assoc. Holt & Haynes, Lewisburg, W.Va., 1954-55; ptnr. Haynes & Ford, Lewisburg, 1955-74, Haynes, Ford & Rowe, Lewisburg, 1975-96, The Ford Law Firm, Lewisburg, 1997—. Dir. W.Va. Power Co., First Nat. Bank Ronceverte, Greenbrier Cable Corp. Bd. dirs. W.Va. U. Found., Daywood Found., v.p., 1986—; bd. dirs. Faculty Merit Found. W.Va., W.Va. Legal Svcs. Plan, 1973—79; trustee Greenbrier Coll. for Women, 1960—73; mem. exec. bd. Buckskin Coun. Boy Scouts Am.; mem. adv. bd. Greenbrier C.C. Ctr.; mem. vis. com. Coll. Law W.Va. U., 1972—74; mem. W.Va. Legislature, 1961—64. Served as ensign U.S. Maritime Svc., 1945—47. Recipient Outstanding Alumnus award W.Va. U. Law Sch., 1980, W.Va. U., 88. Fellow Am. Bar Found., Am. Judicature Soc.; mem. ABA (ho. of dels. 1977-80), W.Va. Bar Assn. (v.p. 1965-66, 75-76, pres. 1978-79), Greenbrier County Bar Assn. (pres. 1964-66, 81-82), W.Va. Law Sch. Assn. (pres. 1966-67), Nat. Conf. Commrs. Uniform State Laws, Am. Coll. Real Estate Lawyers, W.Va. U. Alumni Assn. (pres. 1971), Phi Beta Kappa, Sigma Chi, Phi Delta Phi, Order of Vandalia. Clubs: Masons, KT, Shriners, Lewisburg Elks. Democrat. Methodist. Office: The Ford Law Firm 203 W Randolph St Lewisburg WV 24901-1023

FORD, ROBERT DAVID, lawyer; b. New Orleans, Oct. 30, 1956; s. Thomas Paul and Inez Mary (Rodriguez) F.; m. Jean Ann Burg, May 5, 1979; children: Robert David Jr., Charlene Elizabeth, Timothy Michael. BA, U. New Orleans, 1978; JD, Loyola U., 1983. Bar: La. 1983, U.S. Dist. Ct. (ea. dist.) La. 1983, U.S. Dist. Ct. (mid. dist.) La. 1997, U.S. Ct. Appeals (5th cir.) 1985. Claims rep. State Farm Mut. Auto Ins. Co., Metairie, La., 1978-80; assoc. Hammett, Leake & Hammett, New Orleans, 1983-86; ptnr. Thomas, Hayes & Beahm, New Orleans, 1986—95; mem. Chehardy, Sherman, Ellis, Breslin & Murray, Metairie, La., 1995-96; ptnr. Hailey, McNamara, Hall, Larmann & Papale, Metairie, 1996—2003, Mang, Batiza, Gaudin, Godofsky & Penzato, Metairie, 2003—. Mem. ABA (coms. on health law, profl. liability and products liability litigation 1992, subcoms. on hosp. and clinic med. devices and med. malpractice liability 1992), La. Bar Assn., La. Assn. Def. Counsel, Am. Soc. Law and Medicine, La. Soc. Hosp. Attys. of La. Hosp. Assn., Def. Rsch. Inst., Phi Kappa Theta, Pi Alpha Delta. Republican. Roman Catholic. Avocations: golf, softball. Home: 8 Caney Ct Kenner LA 70065-3944 Office: Mang Batiza Gaudin Godofsky & Penzato 1 Galleria Blvd Ste 700 Metairie LA 70001-7543 E-mail: rford@hmhlp.com.

FORD, ROBERT MACDONALD, III, architect, educator; b. Seattle, Apr. 4, 1934; s. Robert MacDonald Jr. and Nancy Elizabeth (McFate) F.; m. Ruth Evelyn Keene, 1957 (div. 1980); children: Karen, Judith, Robert IV; m. Martha Evelyn Cooper, Mar. 11, 1983 (div. 2000); m. Deborah Mahoney Nettles, Feb. 28, 2003. BArch, U. Wash., Seattle, 1962; MArch, U. Ill., 1963. Registered architect, Miss. Asst. prof. architecture U. Ill., Urbana, 1963-66, Wash. State U., Pullman, 1966-69, assoc. prof. architecture, 1969-74, prof. architecture, 1974-75, Miss. State U., Starkville, 1975-96, prof. emeritus architecture, 1996—. Vis. prof. Oreg. Sch. Design, Portland, fall 1982, U. P.R., San Juan, spring 1990; pres. Ford & Assocs., Architects, Miss., 1975-92; pres. Architecture/South, Miss., Tenn., 1992-97, Ford Properties, 1997—; Miss. commr. Clan Donald, 2002—. Councilman City of Pullman, 1969-74. With U.S. Army, 1953-56. Fellow AIA (bd. dirs. Miss. 1987, 90, 98, 2000--, sec.-treas. 1988, v.p. 1989, pres.-elect 1991, pres. 1992, state design awards 1981, 82, 83, 88, 99, regional design awards 1981, 84, 85, 91, 92), Archtl. Found., Tau Sigma Delta. Democrat. Avocations: sailing, genealogy, travel. Home and Office: 308 Mangrove Palm St Starkville MS 39759 E-mail: robmford3@hotmail.com.

FORD, SALLY J. physical education educator; b. Vincennes, Ind., July 2, 1950; d. Marion C. and Peggy A. (Clark) Ford; 1 child from previous marriage, Chanda D. BA, McKendree Coll., 1973; MS, Eastern Ill. U., 1980; PhD, So. Ill. U., 2000. Tchr., coach Effingham (Ill.) HS, 1974-80; head coach Bradley U., Peoria, Ill., 1980-83; exercise physiologist Curtiss Ave. Clinic, Sarasota, Fla., 1985-87; conditioning coord. Kansas City Royals, 1987-88; prof. Pima CC, Tucson, 1989—2001, Tusculum Coll., Greeneville, Tenn., 2001—. With U.S. Men's Sprint Com., 1982—86, Competitive Edge, Calif., 1993—95. Named to Sports Hall of Fame, McKendree Coll., 1991. Mem.: Clinics Speed Devel.,

Athletic Congress, Nat. Strength and Conditioning Assn., N.Am. Soc. Sport Mgmt., Am. Alliance Health, Physical Edn., Recreation and Dance. Avocations: running, weightlifting. Office: Tusculum Coll Erwin Hwy Greeneville TN 37743

FORD, STEVEN MILTON, insurance agent; b. Owensboro, Ky., Mar. 20, 1954; s. Wendell Hampton and Ruby Jean (Neel) F.; Sarah Whitley Ratliff, Aug. 28, 1976; children: Wendell Clay Hampton, Steven Neel, Morgan Ratliff. BBA, U. Ky., 1976. Agt., ptnr., mgr. E.M. Ford & Co., Owensboro, 1976-97; dir., organizer First Security Bank of Owensboro, 1997—. Bd. dirs. Owensboro-Daviess County Family-Y, 1977-85, Audubon Coun. Econ. Edn., Owensboro, 1986-92, Owensboro Symphony Orch., 1985-92, pres. 1991. Mem. Ind. Ins. Agts. Ky. (vice chmn. nat. young agts. 1987-88, chmn. 1988-89, treas. county bd. 1981-82, pres. 1983—, bd. dirs., state v.p. 1997-98, pres.-elect 1998-99, pres. 1999-2001, Outstanding Young Agt. award 1986), Owensboro C. of C. (bd. dirs., mem. leadership class 1984, v.p. adminstrn. 1999-2001). Democrat. Baptist. Avocations: golf, fishing, hunting. Office: EM Ford & Co PO Box 1677 Owensboro KY 42302-1677

FORD, TERRY LYNN, protective services official; b. Highland, Ill., June 4, 1953; s. Robert Elmer and Beverly June (Pashea) Ford; children: Carolyn M., Jacquelyn S., Laura L., Kaitlyn E. AAS, Lewis and Clark Coll., 1987. From firefighter to capt. Godfrey (Ill.) Fire Dept., 1976-87, fire chief, 1987-99; arson divsn. dir. Office Ill. State Fire Marshall, Springfield, 2000—. Chmn. bd. dirs. Madison County emergency Telephone Sys., Edwardsville, Ill., 1990—99; exec. fire officer Nat. Fire Acad., Emmitsburg, Md., 1993—97; mem. Ill. fire adv. bd. U. Ill., Springfield, 1996—; chmn. Ill. Firefighter Meml. Found., 2002—. Mem. Medal of Honor com. State of Ill., Springfield, 1992—; pres. Ill. Firefighter Meml. Found., 2001—. Mem.: Ill. Fire Svcs. Assn. (lobbyist 1990—), Madison County Firefighters (pres. 1997-99), Ill. Firefighters Assn. (v.p. 1992-96, pres. 1996—), Internat. Assn. Fire Fights, Internat. Assn. Fire Chiefs. Roman Catholic. Avocation: Avocations: coin collecting, golf, Cardinal baseball fan. Home: 1214 Douglas St Alton IL 62002-2221 Office: Ill State Fire Marshal 1035 Stevenson Dr Springfield IL 62706-0001

FORD, TIMOTHY ALAN, state representative; b. Oct. 22, 1951; m. Mary Cox Foose. BA, Univ. Miss., 1973, JD, 1977. State rep. dist. 18, Miss., 1980—; speaker of house, 1988—; ptnr. Riley, Ford, Caldwell & Cork, Tupelo, Miss. Presbyterian. Office: House of Representatives New Capitol Jackson MS 39205 also: Capitol Room 306-NC, PO Box 1018 Jackson MS 39215*

FORD, VICTORIA, retired public relations executive, writer, oral historian; b. Carroll, Iowa, Nov. 1, 1946; d. Victor Sargent and Gertrude Francis (Headlee) F.; m. John K. Frans, July 4, 1965 (div. Aug. 1975); m. David W. Keller, May 2, 1981 (div. Nov. 1985); m. Jerry W. Lambert, Mar. 30, 1991 (div. Aug. 2002). AA, Iowa Lakes Community Coll., 1973; BA summa cum laude, Buena Vista Coll., 1974; MA in Journalism, U. Nev., Reno, 1988. Juvenile parole officer Iowa Dept. Social Services, Sioux City, 1974-78; staff reporter Feather Pub. Co., Quincy, Calif., 1978-80; tng. counselor CETA, Quincy, 1980; library pub. info. officer U. Nev., Reno, 1982-84; pub. relations exec. Brodeur/Martin Pub. Relations, Reno, 1984-87; pub. relations dir. Internat. Winter Spl. Olympics, Lake Tahoe (Calif.) and Reno, 1987-89; owner Ford Factor Pub. Rels. cons. firm, Reno, 1989—2002. Staff writer Publs. and Pub. Info. Office Truckee Meadows C.C., 2001—. Author: Making Their Mark: Reno-Sparks YWCA History, 1997, (with R.T. King and Ken Adams) War Stories, 1995, Jean Ford: A Nevada Woman Leads the Way (oral history), 1998, Silver Peak Oral History Project, 2001, Never a Ghost Town: Silver Peak, Nevada, 2002; contbr. articles to profl. jours. Mem. adv. bd. Reno Philharm., 1985-87, Reno-Sparks Conv. and Visitors Authority, 1985-93; bd. dirs. Truckee Meadows Habitat for Humanity, 1992-93, half-time exec. dir., 1994; mem. Gov.'s Com. on Fire Prevention, 1991-92; mem. U. Nev. Reno Oral History Program, 1994; bd. dirs. Nev. Women's Archives, 1996; state sec. and roll of honor Nev. Women's History Project, 1998, 2001, com. Nev. Writers Hall of Fame, 1993-96; bd. dirs. Friends of the U. Nev. at Reno Libr., 1995-98. Mem.: NOW, Women Writing the West, Assn. Personal Historians, S.W. Oral History Assn. (bd. dirs. 2000—02, State Hist. Rec. adv. bd. 2002—), Pub. Rels. Soc. Am. (charter v.p. Sierra Nev. chpt. 1986—87, pres. 1987—88), Sigma Delta Chi. Democrat. Home and Office: The Ford Factor PO Box 33993 Reno NV 89533-3993

FORD, WILLIAM CLAY, automotive company executive, professional sports team executive; b. Detroit, Mar. 14, 1925; s. Edsel Bryant and Eleanor (Clay) F.; m. Martha Firestone, June 21, 1947; children: Martha, Sheila, William Clay, Elizabeth. BS, Yale U., 1949. Sales and advt. staff Ford Motor Co., 1949; indsl. relations, labor negotiations with UAW, 1949; quality control mgr. gas turbine engines Lincoln-Mercury Div., Dearborn, Mich., 1951, mgr. spl. product ops., 1952, v.p., 1953, gen. mgr. Continental Div., 1954, group v.p. Lincoln and Continental Divs, 1955, v.p. product design, 1956-80; dir., 1948—; vice chmn. bd., 1980-89; mem. fin. com. Ford Motor Co., 1987—; owner, chair Detroit Lions, 1964—. Mem. adv. coun. Tex. Heart Inst.; chmn. emeritus Edison Inst.; hon. life trustee Eisenhower Med. Ctr. Mem. Soc. Automotive Engrs. (asso.), Automobile Old Timers, Econ. Club Detroit, Masons, K.T., Phelps Assn., Psi Upsilon. Office: Ford Motor Co Design Ctr PO Box 6012 Dearborn MI 48121-6012 also: The Detroit Lions Inc 222 Republic Dr Allen Park MI 48101

FORD, WILLIAM CLAY, JR., automotive executive; b. May 3, 1957; married. BA, Princeton U., 1979; MBA in Mgmt., MIT, 1984. Prodn. planning analyst, advisor vehicle devel. design ctr., mfg. engr. auto assembly divsn., mgr. Ford Motor Co., N.Y., 1979-82, mem. nat. bargaining team Ford/UAW labor talks, mktg. strategy analyst No. Am. Auto Opns., advt. specialist, 1982-83, internat. fin. specialist, mem. fin. staff, 1984-85, planning mgr. car prodn. devel., 1985-86, dir. com. vehicle mktg. Europe divsn., 1986-87, chmn., mng. dir. Switzerland divsn., 1987-89, mgr. heavy truck engr. and mfg. Ford Truck Opns., 1989-90, dir. bus. strategy Ford Auto Group, 1990-91, exec. dir. bus. strategy Ford Auto Group, 1991-92, gen. mgr. climate control divsn., 1992-94, v.p. com. Trucking Vehicle Ctr. Ford Auto Ops., 1994-95, chmn. fin. com., 1995—2001, chmn. bd., 1998—, CEO, 2001—. Vice chmn. Detroit Lions; mem. fin. com., properties com. NFL. Chmn. bd. trustees Henry Ford Mus., Greenfield Village; trustee Henry Ford Health Sys., Detroit Renaissance; mem. World Econ. Forum's Global Leaders for Tomorrow. Alfred P. Sloan fellow MIT, 1983-84. Office: Ford Motor Co 1 American Rd Dearborn MI 48126-2798*

FORD, WILLIAM F. banker; b. Huntington, N.Y., Aug. 14, 1936; s. William and Margaret (Mueller) Freithaler; m. Diane McDonald, June 11, 1960; children: Eric W., Kristin E. BA in Econs. summa cum laude, U. Tex., 1961; MA, U. Mich., 1962, PhD, 1966; DSc (hon.), Fla. Inst. Tech., 1981; grad. sr. exec. program, Stanford U., 1983. Part-time teaching asst. U. Mich., 1962-63, instr., 1965-66; economist Rand Corp., 1966, cons., 1967-68, 70-71; asst. prof. econs. U. Va., 1967-69; assoc. prof. Tex. Tech. U., Lubbock, 1969-70; prof. econs., dean Transylvania Coll., Lexington, Ky., 1970-71; exec. dir., chief economist rsch. and planning group Am. Bankers Assn., 1971-75; sr. v.p., chief economist Wells Fargo Bank, San Francisco, 1975-80; pres., chief exec. officer Fed. Res. Bank Atlanta, 1980-83; pres., chief operating officer First Nationwide Savs., 1983-85; pres., chief exec. officer Broadview Savs. Bank, Cleve., 1986-89; dean coll. bus. U. Denver, 1990-91; prof. and chair fin. Mid. Tenn. State U., Murfreesboro, 1992—. Mem. faculty Stonier Grad. Sch. Banking, 1976—80; mem. fed. open market com. Fed. Res. Sys., 1982—83; sr. econ. advisor TeleCheck Svcs. Inc., 1992—2001; spkr. in field. Author: Mexico's Foreign Trade and Economic Development, 1968; also over 100 articles, revs., TV script. Bd. vis. Berry Coll., 1984—89. With USN, 1954—57. Woodrow Wilson fellow, 1961; NDEA fellow, 1961-63; Ford Found. fgn. area fellow, Mex., 1964-65; Rotary fellow, Chile, 1970; co-winner Fred M. Taylor Prize U. Mich. Mem. Stanford Grad. Sch. Bus. Adminstrn. Alumni Assn. (bd. dirs. 1985-86), Am. Econ. Assn., Nat. Assn. for Bus. Econs. (bd. dirs. 2002--), U.S. C. of C. (bd. dirs. 1989-91, chmn. econ. policy com. 1990-93), Phi Beta Kappa. Methodist. Office: Mid Tenn State U Coll Bus PO Box 27 Murfreesboro TN 37133-0027 E-mail: wfford@mtsu.edu.

FORD, WILLIAM FRANCIS, retired bank holding company executive; b. Albany, N.Y., Mar. 11, 1925; s. Patrick J. and Ellen M. F.; m. Marcia J. Whalen, Jan. 7, 1956; children: William Francis, Michael P., Timothy K., Daniel J., Cathleen A. BA in Acctg. with honors, St. Michaels Coll., 1950. V.p. Equitable Credit Corp., Albany, 1950-60, Am. Fin. Systems Inc., Silver Spring, Md., 1960-65, Gen. Electric Credit Corp., Stamford, Conn., 1965-74; chmn., chief exec. officer Security Pacific Fin. Corp., San Diego, 1974-81; exec. v.p., adminstr. specialized fin. services group Security Pacific Corp., Los Angeles, 1981-84, vice chmn., 1984-91. Bd. dirs., vice chmn. Ford Fin. Svcs., 1991—. Served with USN, 1943-46. Mem. Am. Fin. Svcs. Assn. (chmn., dir. emeritus exec. com.) Clubs: Stone Ridge Country.

FORDEMWALT, JAMES NEWTON, microelectronics engineering educator, consultant; b. Parsons, Kans., Oct. 18, 1932; s. Fred and Zenia (Chambers) F.; m. Suzan Lynn Hopkins, Aug. 26, 1958 (div. June 1961); m. Elizabeth Anna Hoare, Dec. 29, 1963; children: John William, James Frederick. BS, U. Ariz., 1955, MS, 1956; PhD, U. Iowa, 1960. Sr. engr. GE Co., Evandale, Ohio, 1959-60, U.S. Semcor, Inc., Phoenix, 1960-61; sect. mgr. Motorola Semiconductor Products Div., Phoenix, 1961-66; dept. mgr. Philco-Ford Microelectronics Div., Santa Clara, Calif., 1966-68; assoc. dir. R & D Am. Microsystems Inc., Santa Clara, 1968-71; assoc. rsch. prof. U. Utah, Salt Lake City, 1972-76; dir. microelectronics lab. U. Ariz., Tucson, 1976-87; assoc. prof., lab. mgr. Ariz. State U., Tempe, 1987—2001, prof. emeritus, 2001—, assoc. chair microelectronics, 1992—2001, asst. chair dept. electronic and computer tech., 1993—2001. Cons. Integrated Cirs. Engring., Scottsdale, Ariz., 1976—, Western Design Ctr., Mesa, Ariz., 1980—; mem. semiconductor com. United Techs. Corp., Hartford, Conn., 1978-87. Author: Silicon Wafer Processing Technology, 1979; editor: Integrated Circuits, 1965; contbr.: MOS Integrated Circuits, 1972. Mem. IEEE, Internat. Soc. for Hybrid Microelectronics (chpt. pres. 1982-83), Electrochem. Soc. Avocations: pilot, photographer. Home: 613 W Summit Pl Chandler AZ 85225-7798 E-mail: jfordemwalt@cox.net.

FORDEN, DIANE CLAIRE, magazine editor; b. N.Y.C., Apr. 6, 1951; d. Joseph Anthony and Helen (Nash) F. BA in English Edn. summa cum laude, Montclair (N.J.) State U., 1973. Fashion editor Seventeen Mag., N.Y.C., 1975-81; fashion and beauty dir. YM Mag., N.Y.C., 1981-85; fashion dir. Avon Fashions, N.Y.C., 1985-87, Prima Mag., N.Y.C., 1987-88; from fashion and beauty editor to editor in chief and v.p. Bridal Guide Mag., N.Y.C., 1989—. Author: How to Have an Elegant Wedding-Without Going Broke. Mem. Am. Soc. Mag. Editors, Fashion Group Internat., N.Y. Women in Comms. Avocations: piano, biking, skiing, photography. Home: 10 River Rd Apt F Nutley NJ 07110-3459 Office: Bridal Guide Mag 3 E 54th St New York NY 10022-3108

FORDHAM, CHRISTOPHER COLUMBUS, III, dean, academic administrator, medical educator; b. Greensboro, N.C., Nov. 28, 1926; s. Christopher Columbus and Frances Long (Clendenin) Fordham; m. Barbara Byrd, Aug. 16, 1947; children: Pamela Fordham Richey, Susan Fordham Crowell, Betsy Fordham Templeton. Student, U. N.C., 1943—45, student, 1946—47, cert. in medicine, 1949; MD, Harvard U., 1951. Diplomate Am. Bd. Internal Medicine. Intern Georgetown U. Hosp., 1951—52; asst. resident Boston City Hosp., 1952—53; sr. asst. resident N.C. Meml. Hosp., Chapel Hill, 1953—54; fellow in medicine U. N.C. Sch. Medicine, 1954—55, instr. medicine, 1958—60, asst. prof., 1960—64, assoc. prof., asst. dean, Sch. Medicine, 1964—68, prof., assoc. dean, 1968—69, prof. medicine, 1971—, vice chancellor for health affairs, 1977—80, chancellor, 1980—88, chancellor emeritus and prof. medicine, 1988—93, prof. medicine emeritus, 1993—, chancellor emeritus, dean emeritus, prof. medicine emeritus, 1993—; practice medicine, specializing in internal medicine Greensboro, NC, 1957—58; prof. medicine, v.p. for medicine, dean Sch. Medicine, Med. Coll. Ga., Augusta, 1969—71; dean Sch. Medicine U. N.C., 1971—79; acting asst. sec. for health Dept. HEW, Washington, 1977. Chair Gov.'s Com. on N.C. Awards, 1993—2000; chmn. N.C. Awards Com., 1993—2000; bd. dirs. Royal Soc. Med. Found., N.Y.C., 1990—95. Officer USAF, 1955—57. Master: ACP; fellow: AAAS; mem.: AMA (Spl. award 1990), AAUP, Elisha Mitchell Sci. Soc., Inst. Medicine NAS (coun. 1985—90), N.Y. Acad. Scis., Am. Assn. Med. Coll. So. Regional Deans (chmn. 1972—73, 1975—75, chmn. nat. coun. deans 1977), Am. Assn. Med. Colls. (exec. coun. 1975—78, rep. liaison com. med. edn. 1977—79), Soc. Health and Human Values, Am. Fedn. Clin. Rsch., Am. Soc. Nephrology, So. Soc. Clin. Investigation, N.C. Med. Soc., Nat. Assn. State Univs. and Land Grant Colls. (chair coun. univ. governance 1990—91), Order Golden Fleece, Alpha Omega Alpha, Sigma Xi. Office: Univ NC Sch Medicine Campus Box 7000 Rm 130 MacNider Bldg Chapel Hill NC 27514 E-mail: C.fordham@med.unc.edu.

FORDICE, KIRK (DANIEL KIRKWOOD FORDICE JR.), former governor, construction company executive, engineer; b. Memphis, Tenn., Feb. 10, 1934; s. Daniel Kirkwood and Clara Aileen (Augustine) F.; m. Patricia Louise Owens, Aug. 13, 1955 (div. 1999); children: Angela Leigh Fordice Roselle, Daniel K. III, Hunter L., James Owens; m. Ann Creson, Feb. 26, 2000 (div. 2003). BSCE, Purdue U., 1956, MS in Indsl. Mgmt., 1957. Registered profl. engr., Miss., La. Engr. Exxon, Baton Rouge, 1956-62; ptnr. Fordice Constrn. Co., Vicksburg, Miss., 1962-76, pres., chief exec. officer, from 1976; gov. State of Miss., 1992-2000. Bd. dirs. Mchts. Nat. Bank, Vicksburg, Miss., Taylor Energy; former vice-chmn. and chmn. So. Gov.'s Assn. Sec. Miss. Rep. Party, Jackson, 1981-88; vice-chmn. Vicksburg-Tallulah Dist. Airport Bd.; chmn. Econ. Devel. Found., Vicksburg, 1984. Served to col. C.E., USAR. Recipient Teddy Roosevelt award Cons. Engrs. Coun. Miss., 1992, Captain of Industry award Miss. Cystic Fibrosis Found., 1992; named one of Outstanding Young Men of Am., U.S. Jaycees, 1969, Vol. Laureate in Indsl. Devel., Gov. of Miss., 1985; achievement recognition Engineering News Record mag., 1982, 91, A Grade for Fiscal Policy award Cato Inst., 1994. Fellow ASCE (pres. Vicksburg br. 1982, Outstanding Civil Engr. of Yr. Miss. sect. 1992); mem. NSPE, NRA, Associated Gen. Contractors of Miss., (Outstanding Mem. of Yr. award 1992), Am. Inst. Constructors, Cons. Constructors Coun. Am., Soc. Am. Mil. Engrs., Assoc. Gen. Contractors Am. (nat. pres. 1990, nat. life dir., pres. Miss. Valley flood control br. 1970, Man of Yr. award 1992), Am. Constrn. Industry Forum (pres. 1991), Confederation Internat. Contractor's Assns. (v.p. 1990—), So. Govs. Assn. (chmn.), Aircraft Owners and Pilots Assn., Nat. Aero. Assn., Reserve Officers Assn., Quiet Birdmen, Am. Quarter Horse Assn., Safari Club Internat., Game Conservation Internat., Rivertown Club (Vicksburg), The Moles, Nature Conservancy, Sigma Chi (Significant Sig award 1993), Tau Beta Pi, Chi Epsilon. Republican. Methodist.

FORDYCE, JAMES GEORGE, physician; b. Detroit, Jan. 9, 1945; s. James Alexander and Stella Marie (Pakron) F.; m. Kathleen Marie Ray, June 17, 1967; children: James A., Jonathan A., Jared A. BS, Mich. State U., 1966, DVM, 1968; MD, Wayne State U., 1974. Diplomate Am. Bd. Pediats., Am. Bd. Allergy and Immunology. Intern, resident Children's Hosp. Mich., Detroit, 1973-76; fellow allergy and clin. immunology Henry Ford Hosp., Detroit, 1976-78; physician Dearborn (Mich.) Allergy and Asthma Clinic, PC, 1978—. Cons. Metro Med. Group, Detroit, 1979-95. Author: Asthma in Clinical Pulmonary Medicine, 1992. Bd. trustees Oakwood Healthcare, Inc., 1996-2000. Fellow Am. Acad. Pediats., Am. Acad. Allergy, Asthma and Immunology, Am. Coll. Allergy, Asthma and Immunology; mem. Mich. Allergy and Asthma Soc. (pres. 1991-92). Avocations: fishing, flying, sailing. Office: Dearborn Allergy & Asthma Clinic PC 20200 Outer Dr Dearborn MI 48124-2634

FORDYCE, THERESA ROSE, mental health nurse; b. Andrews AFB, Md., June 7, 1960; d. Robert David Sr. and Patricia Anne (Bahm) F. BA in Psychology, Belmont Abbey Coll., 1982; AAS, Mercer County C.C., Trenton, N.J., 1987; MA in Health Svcs. Adminstrn., Kennedy-Western U., 2001. RN, N.J., S.C. Nurse supr. Trenton Psychiat. Hosp., 1987-88; staff nurse Greenville (S.C.) Hosp. Systems/Marshall Pickens, 1988-91, Chestnut Hill Psychiat. Hosp., 1991-92; RN supr. Magnolia Manor, 1992-94; nurse lead clin. staff Boys Home of the South, Belton, S.C., 1994-95; RN nursing coord. SERV Ctrs. N.J., Inc., Trenton, 1996-2000; head nurse admissions Trenton Psychiat. Hosp., 2000—02; staff nurse Princeton (NJ) House at Med. Ctr. of Princeton, 2002—. Home: 446 Emory Ave Trenton NJ 08611-1030

FORE, ANN, counselor, educator, country dance instructor; b. Artesia, N.Mex., July 16, 1948; d. Stanley William and Jackie (Hightower) Blocker; divorced; 1 child Richard Todd. BS, Eastern N.Mex. U., Portales, 1971, MA, 1976. Instr. sociology Eastern N.Mex. U., Clovis, 1974; counselor, instr. So. Plains Jr. Coll., Plainview, Tex., 1975-76; drug and alcohol counselor U.S. Dept. Army, Ft. Hood, Tex., 1976-77; group leader Forest Svc., USDA, Estacada, Oreg., 1980-81; owner Women's Issues Counseling Svcs., Salem, 1985—. Tchr. country western ptnr. dancing and line dancing various ednl. settings, Salem, Oreg., Portland C.C., Salem Keizer Schs. Author: founder, adminstr. award-winning, nationally televised country dance team Country's What I Am; inventor laptop sound amplifier. U. N.Mex. rsch. dept. grantee, 1972; recipient Star award United Country/Western Dance Coun., 1998, Editor's Choice award Internat. Libr. Poetry, 2002. Mem. APGA, Willamette Writers Assn., Nat. Tchrs. Assn. for Country/Western Dance Instrs., Internat. Platform Assn. Republican. Christian. Avocations: reading, camping, photography, public speaking. Home and Office: PO Box 13851 Salem OR 97309-1851 E-mail: annfore@yahoo.com.

FORE, HENRIETTA HOLSMAN, federal agency administrator; m. Richard L. Fore. AB, Wellesley Coll., 1970; MA, U. No. Colo., 1975. Pres. Stockton Wire Products, Burbank, Calif., 1977-89; asst. adminstr. for pvt. enterprise AID, Washington, 1990-91, asst. adminstr. for Asia, 1991-93; Dir U.S. Mint Dept Treasury, Washington, 2001—. Mem. Com. of 200. Mem. Young Pres. Orgn., Wellesley Coll. Alumnae Assn. Address: 5401 Longley Ln # A11 Reno NV 89511-1818 Office: U S Mint Headquarters 801 9th Street NW Washington DC 20220

FOREHAND, JOSEPH W. finance company executive; b. Alexander City, Ala. m. Gayle Forehand; 2 children. BS in Indsl. Engring., Auburn U., 1971; MS in Indsl. Adminstrn., Purdue U., 1972. With Anderson Cons., 1972—, various positions with product group, regional dir. products industry, office mng. ptrn. Dallas, head Ams. products group, mng. ptrn. products, 1997-98, mng. ptnr. global comms. and high tech market unit; mng. ptrn., CEO Accenture(formerly Anderson), 2001—; chmn. bd. dirs. Accenture, 2001—. Spkr. in field. Recipient Most Influential Cons., Consulting Mag., 2001, Morgan Stanley Leadership award, 2003. Office: Accenture 100 S Wacker Dr Ste 1059 Chicago IL 60606*

FORELL, GEORGE WOLFGANG, religion educator; b. Breslau, Germany, Sept. 19, 1919; came to U.S., 1939, naturalized, 1945; s. Frederick J. and Madeleine (Kretschmar) F.; m. Elizabeth Jean Rossing, June 14, 1945; children: Madeleine Helene (Mrs. Gary Marshall), Mary Elizabeth (Mrs. Christopher Davis). Student, U. Vienna, 1937-38; BD, Luth. Theol. Sem., Phila., 1941; Th.M., Princeton Theol. Sem., 1943; ThD, Union Theol. Sem., N.Y.C., 1949; DD (hon.), Wartburg Theol. Sem., 1967; LHD, Gustavus Adolphus Coll., 1974; LLD, Luther Coll., 1983; LittD, Upsala Coll., 1983. Ordained to ministry Luth. Ch., 1941. Pastor Luth. Chs., N.J. and N.Y., 1941-47; asst. prof., then assoc. prof. philosophy Gustavus Adolphus Coll., St. Peter, Minn., 1947-54; asst. prof., then assoc. prof. theology U. Iowa, 1954-58, prof. religion, 1961-73, Carver prof., 1973-89, Carver Disting. prof. emeritus, 1989—, dir. Sch. Religion, 1965-71; prof. systematic theology Luth. Sch. Theology, Chgo., 1958-61. Vis. prof. U. Hamburg, Germany, 1957-58, All Africa Theol. Seminar, Marangu, Tanzania, 1960, Japan Luth. Coll., Tokyo, 1968, Gurukul Theol. Rsch. Inst., Madras, India, 1978, Luth. Coll., Hong Kong, 1980; Eli Lilly vis. prof. Berea Coll., Ky., 1979, 86, Pacific Luth. U., Tacoma, Wash., 1987, Luth. Theol. Sem., Phila., 1988-91, Luth. Sch. Theology, Chgo., 1991-92, China Evang. Sem., Taipei, Taiwan, 1993, Pacific Luth. Theol. Sem., Berkeley, Calif., 1995, Concordia U., Irvine, Calif., 1996-98, Trinity Luth. Coll., Seattle, 1999; cons. dept. studies Luth. World Fedn., Geneva, 1981-84. Author: Faith Active in Love, 1954, Ethics of Decision, 1955, The Protestant Faith, 1960, The Christian Year, 1964-65, Understanding the Nicene Creed, 1965, Christian Social Teachings, 1966, The Augsburg Confession, A Contemporary Commentary, 1968, Zinzendorf: Nine Public Lectures, 1973, The Proclamation of the Gospel in a Pluralistic World, 1973, The Christian Lifestyle, 1975, The Revolution at the Frontier: Reports from Moravian Missionaries Among the American Indians, 1976, History of Christian Ethics, Vol. I, 1979, The Luther Legacy, 1983, Martin Luther: Theologian of The Church, 1994. Mem. Ch. Coun. Evang. Luth. Ch. Am., 1987-91. Mem. Am. Philos. Assn., Am. Soc. Ch. History, Am. Soc. Reformation Research (pres. 1959), Omicron Delta Kappa. Democrat. Home: PO Box 2300 Iowa City IA 52244-2300 E-mail: gtroutl@aol.com.

FOREMAN, ALFRED G. theologian, philosopher; b. Sulfur, La., Mar. 19, 1960; s. Grover Foreman and Stella Kibodeaux. BA, U. La., Lafayette, 1987; MA, Liberty U., 1991. Founder S. La. Weather Sta., Crowley, 1986—; pastor Ch. of God, Crowley, 1986—2002; with Imam Al-Ruh-Al-Amin Masjid, Crowley, 2003—. Lectr. Islamic Ctr., Lafayette, La., 1983-84, La. Philos. Inst. Humanities, Crowley, 1993—. Author: The Ecclesiastic Order: The Apology, 2002, The Christian and Islamic Thesis in History, 2002; dir. South La. Weather Jour., 1986—. Mem. Internat. Palm Soc. (La. and Calif. ReUnion chpts.). Home: 130 Palms Rd Crowley LA 70526-1907 *I wish to dedicate this entry in part to my friend and associate Michael Scott Gietl, who has given me assistance and encouragement in these many endeavors.*

FOREMAN, EDWARD RAWSON, retired lawyer; b. Atlanta, May 15, 1939; s. Robert Langdon and Mary (Shedden) F.; m. Margaret Reeves, Oct. 19, 1968; children: Margaret Langdon, Mary Rawson BA, Washington & Lee U., 1962; JD, Emory U., 1965. Bar: Ga. 1965. Assoc. Jones, Bird & Howell, Atlanta, 1965-70, ptnr., 1970-82, Alston & Bird, Atlanta, 1982-99; ret., 1999. Chmn. McAliley Endowment Trust, 1978—; lectr. Inst. for Continuing Legal Edn. in Ga., 1989; panelist, moderator Bus. Atlanta's Office Leasing and Tenant Opportunities in 1990s. Mem. editl. bd. Comml. Leasing Law and Strategy, 1996-98. Bd. dirs. Ansley Park Beautification Found., Atlanta, 1984-99, Midtown Alliance, Atlanta, 1988-96, sec., chmn. fundraising com., 1989-91, v.p., 1991, pres., 1992; trustee Paidela Sch. Endowment Fund, Atlanta, 1980-99, Woodruff Arts Ctr., Atlanta, 1985-90; chmn. Emory U. Law Fund, Atlanta, 1981; chmn. legal divsn. United Way Met. Atlanta, 1984; chmn. strategic planning com. High Mus. Art, 1986-95, chmn., bd. dirs. 1998—, chmn. nominating com., 1993-95; vestryman, sr. warden St. Luke's Episc. Ch., 1975, 94, 2001, com. mem., 1975-90; pres. Atlanta Legal Aid Soc., 1975-76, Atlanta Preservation Ctr., 1986-91; trustee Miss Hall's Sch., Pittsfield, Mass., 1990-2001. Recipient Cmty. Svc. award Martin Luther King Jr. Ctr. Nonviolent Social Change, 1980, Outstanding Svc. award Atlanta Preservation Ctr., Inc., 1983. Mem. ABA (mem. comml. leasing com. 1987—), State Bar Ga. (chmn., panelist, moderator comml. leasing seminars 1979-86), Atlanta Bar Assn. (chmn., panelist, moderator leasing seminars 1979-86, chmn. hdqrs. search com. 1988-96), Lawyers Club Atlanta (chmn. long-range planning com. 1989-90), Atlanta Bar Found. (bd. dirs.), Old War Horse Lawyers Club, Nine O'Clocks Club (mem. centennial com. 1983), Highlands Country Club N.C. Democrat. Episcopalian. Home: 238 15th St NE House 16 Atlanta GA 30309-3594 Personal E-mail: mccoy10@mindspring.com.

FOREMAN, EDWIN FRANCIS, economist, real estate broker; b. Syracuse, N.Y., July 24, 1931; s. Herve Joseph and Ruth M. Foreman; m. Colleen Frances Tapp, July 7, 1962; children: Lisa C., Eric E. BAE in Econs. and Fgn. Trade, U. Fla., 1957; postgrad. in real estate, Fla. Internat. U., 1974-75. Owner, prin. Edwin F. Foreman, Mortgage Broker, Hollywood, Fla., 1974—; with Consol. Energy Corp., Hollywood, 1977—, pres., chmn. bd., 1977—; v.p. Ea. State Securities, Inc., 1977-92, J.S. Securities, 1994-97, Northridge Capital Corp., 1999—; owner, prin. Edwin F. Foreman, Real Estate Broker, 1978—. Pres., chmn. One-Fore-Devel., Inc., 1985, Three-Fore-Devel., Inc., 1985, L&E Comm. Inc., 1985; chmn., CEO Universal Traction, Hollywood, 1988—; gen. ptnr. Four-Fore Devel. Ltd., Five-Fore-Devel. Ltd., Six-Fore Devel., Ltd., 1987—, CCS Ventures, 1990—; mem. Funds Coordinating Group Internat., L.L.C., 1998—; econ. cons. Michael I. Warde de Colombia Ltd.; guest lectr. econs. Xavier U., Bogota, Colombia. Served with USAF, 1950-53. R.J. Reynolds fellow U. N.C., 1961; NSF fellow. Mem. Hollywood C. of C. (econ. devel. com.), Ft. Lauderdale World Trade Coun., Jockey Club (Miami), Grove Isle Club (Miami), Fisher Island Club. Democrat. Unitarian Universalist. Avocations: camping, fishing, bicycling, photography, travel. Office: PO Box 7570 Hollywood FL 33081

FOREMAN, GEORGE, former boxer, minister, boxing broadcaster; b. Marshall, Tex. s. J. D. and Nancy Foreman; children from previous marriages: Michi, Freeda, Natalie, George Jr., George 3d, George 4th. Profl. boxer, 1969-77, 87—; minister, 1977—; founder, minister Ch. Lord Jesus Christ, Houston, 1984—. Heavyweight champion 1968 Olympics; world heavyweight champion, 1973-74; WBA & IBF heavyweight champion, 1994, abandoned titles, 1994. Author: By George, 1995; boxing analyst HBO; numerous TV commercials and endorsements; owner George Foreman Grill. Founder George Foreman Cmty. Ctr., Houston. Achievements include being the oldest Heavyweight Champion in boxing history-45 yrs.

FOREMAN, JAMES LOUIS, retired judge; b. Metropolis, Ill., May 12, 1927; s. James C. and Anna Elizabeth (Henne) F.; m. Mabel Inez Dunn, June 16, 1948; children: Beth Foreman Banks, Rhonda Foreman Wittig, Nanette Foreman Love. BS in Commerce and Law, U. Ill., 1950, JD, 1952. Bar: Ill. Ind. practice law, Metropolis, Ill.; ptnr. Chase and Foreman, Metropolis, until 1972; state's atty. State of Ill., Massac County, asst. atty. gen.; chief judge U.S. Dist. Ct. (so. dist.) Ill., Benton, 1979-92, sr. status, 1992—. Pres. Bd. of Edn., Metropolis. With USN, 1945-46. Mem. Ill. State Bar Assn., Metropolic C. of C. (past pres.). Republican. Home: 38 Hilanoa-East Dr Metropolis IL 62960-2533 Office: US Dist Ct 301 W Main St Benton IL 62812-1362

FOREMAN, JOHN PATRICK, electrical engineer; b. Lake Charles, La., Aug. 16, 1954; s. John Calvin Foreman and Daisy Mae (Finley) Foreman Milsted; m. Nadine Rachelle Dudek, Nov. 10, 2001. BSEE, McNeese State U., 1976. Registered profl. engr., Tex., Calif., La., Oreg., Mass., Wash. Elec. engr. Fluor Engrs. & Contractors, Houston, 1977-83, Jacobs Engring. Group, Houston, 1983, Burgess & Niple, Ltd., Houston, 1984-86; project mgr. Turpin & Rattan Engring., San Diego, 1986-92, TH Rogers & Assocs., Oakland, Calif., 1993, Alfa Tech. Cons. Engrs., San Jose, Calif., 1994-99; assoc. TKG Cons. Engrs., San Diego, 2000—. Mem.: NSPE, IEEE, Tex. Soc. Profl. Engrs. Democrat. Roman Catholic. Avocations: darts, skiing, volleyball, softball, martial arts. Home: Apt 16 1233 22d St San Diego CA 92102-1954 Office: TKG Consulting Engrs 4370 La Jolla Village Dr San Diego CA 92122-1250 E-mail: jp816foreman@aol.com., nr211foreman@aol.com.

FOREMAN, JOHN WILLIAM, pediatrician, educator; b. Washington, June 23, 1947; s. William Roy and Elizabeth Roberts (McLean) F.; m. Linda Poffenberger, May 27 1973; children: Matthew John, Jennifer Lynne. BS, Duke U., 1969; MD, U. Md., 1973. Diplomate Nat. Bd. Med. Examiners, Pa., Va., N.C., Am. Bd. Pediatrics, subbd. pediatric nephrology. Intern, resident Montreal (Que., Can.) Children's Hosp., 1973-75; asst. chief resident pediatrics Children's Hosp. Phila., 1975-76, fellow pediatric nephrology, 1976-79, staff physician, 1979-86; instr. pediatrics U. Pa. Sch. Medicine, Phila., 1976-79, clin. asst. prof., asst. prof., 1979-85, assoc. prof., 1985-86; assoc. prof. pediatrics Med. Coll. Va., Va. Commonwealth U., Richmond, 1986-90, prof., 1990-93; prof., chief divsn. pediatric nephrology Duke U. Med. Ctr., Durham, N.C., 1993—. Cons. WHO, 1984; chmn. med. adv. bd. Nat. Kidney Found. Va., 1989-92, mem. exec. com. pediatric urology and nephrology coun.; mem. pediatric delegation to Chinese Med. Assn. of People's Republic of China. Contbr. articles to profl. jours., chpts. to books. Bd. dirs. Transplant Found., Richmond, 1991. Daland fellow Am. Philos. Soc., Phila., 1980-81; grantee Am. Heart Assn., 1984-88, NIH, 1988-91. Fellow Am. Acad. Pediat.; mem. Soc. Pediatric Rsch., Am. Pediatric Soc., So. Soc. Pediatric Rsch. (councillor 1989-91), Internat. Pediatric Nephrology Soc. (councillor 1993-98), Am. Soc. Pediatric Nephrology (coun. mem. 2002--), Am. Soc. Nephrology, mem. exec. com. sect. on Nephrology Am. Acad. of Pediatrics. Avocations: reading, bicycling. Home: 9 Streamley Ct Durham NC 27705-5396 Office: Duke U Med Ctr PO Box 3959 Durham NC 27710-0001 E-mail: forem001@mc.duke.edu.

FOREMAN, KELLY MARIE, anthropologist, music educator; b. Fridley, Minn., Aug. 13, 1969; d. Donald Sirola Foreman and Margaret Elizabeth Knight; m. Karl D. Braunschweig, June 18, 1994; 1 child, Katja Emmanuëlle Foreman-Braunschweig. BA, St. Olaf Coll., 1991; MA, Kent State U., 1994, PhD, 2002. Lectr. Rikkyo U., Tokyo, 1998—2000, Wayne State U., Detroit, 2000—. Recipient Prix Solfége/Theorie, Ville Fontainebleu, 1992. Mem.: Internat. Coun. Traditional Music, Japan Anthropology Workshop, Soc. Ethnomusicology (Thomas Tuttle prize 2002). Avocation: gardening. Office: Manoogian Hall Dept Anthropology Wayne State Univ Detroit MI 48202

FOREMAN, MICHAEL J. astronaut; b. Columbus, Ohio, Mar. 29, 1957; s. James W. and Nancy C. Foreman; m. Lorrie Lee Dancer; 3 children. BSc in Aerospace Engring., U.S. Naval Acad., 1979; MSc in Aeronautical Engring., U.S. Naval Postgraduate Sch., 1986. Commd. lt. USN, 1975, advanced through grades to capt., naval aviator, 1981—89, various assignments, 1990—93, chief engr., 1993—98; astronaut NASA, Houston, 1998—. Decorated Meritorious Svc. medal USN, Navy Commendation medal; recipient Adml. William Adger Moffett Aeronautics award, U.S. Naval Postgraduate Sch. Mem.: Assn. Naval Aviation, U.S. Naval Acad. Alumni Assn. Avocations: golf, running, skiing, home repair/improvement, time with family. Office: Astronaut Office CB NASA Johnson Space Center Houston TX 77058

FOREMAN, MICHAEL LOREN, lawyer; b. Sarasota, Fla., Mar. 13, 1944; s. Alexander Maynard and Edith Frances (Beck) F.; m. Alice Lynne Rodgers, Aug. 31, 1969; children: Laurie Kay, Gregory Michael. BSBA, U. Fla., 1966, JD, 1969. Bar: Fla. 1969, U.S. Dist. Ct. (mid. dist.) Fla. 1973, U.S. Ct. Appeals (5th and 11th cirs.) 1983. Assoc. Icard, Merrill, Cullis, Timm, Furen & Ginsburg, PA, Sarasota, 1969-78, sr. ptnr., 1978—. Contbr. articles to profl. jours. Bd. dirs. Big Bros./Big Sisters Found. of Sarasota, 1984-93, Fame Charities Inc., Sarasota. Mem. Fla. Bar (realtor-atty. jt. com. 1978-88, cir. rep. real property, probate and trust law sect. 1980-93, econs. of law practice sect. 1980-83, vice chmn. guardianship law com. 1990-91, chmn., 1992-2001, Durable Powers Atty. Com., 2001-, Real Property, Probate and Trust Law Sec. Ann. Svc. award 1995), Sarasota County Bar Assn. (econs. law practice sect. 1980-93, treas. 1981-84, v.p. 1984-85, pres. 1986-87), Kiwanis of Sarasota-Sunrise (pres. 1984). Home: 4917 Leatha Ln Sarasota FL 34232-2651 Office: Icard Merrill Cullis Timm Furen & Ginsburg PA 2033 Main St Ste 600 Sarasota FL 34237-6056 E-mail: mforeman@icardmerrill.com.

FOREMAN, RICHARD, theater director, playwright; b. N.Y.C., June 10, 1937; s. Albert and Claire (Levine) F. BA, Brown U., 1959, ArtsD (hon.), 1993; MFA, Yale U., 1962. Artistic dir. Ontological-Hysteric Theater, N.Y.C., 1968—. Dir.-in-residence N.Y. Shakespeare Festival, N.Y.C., 1975-76; artistic dir. Theatre O.H., Paris, 1973-85. Dir. Broadway and off-Broadway plays including 3-Penny Opera, 1976; author, dir. Dr. Sclavy's Magic Theater, 1972, Rhoda in Potatoland, 1976 (Obie award Village Voice 1976), Film Is Evil: Radio is Good, 1987 (Obie award Village Voice, 1987), Pearls for Pigs, 1997 (Obie award Village Voice, 1997), Benita Canova, 1998 (Obie award Village Voice, 1998); over 40 others; author: Unbalancing Acts, 1992 and others. Mem. panel theatre div. Nat. Endowment for Arts, Washington, 1976-79. Guggenheim fellow, 1972, Rockefeller fellow, 1974, Creative Artist's Pub. Svc. fellow, 1974, Creative Artist's Pub. Svc. fellow N.Y. State Arts Coun., 1971, MacArthur fellow, 1995-2000; recipient Lifetime Achievement award NEA, 1990, Am. Acad. Arts and Letters prize in lit., 1992, PEN/Laura Pels Master Am. Dramatist award, 2001; officer Order Arts and Letters, France, 2003. Mem. Dramatist's Guild, Soc. Stage Dirs., PEN. Jewish. Avocations: philosophy, psychoanalysis. Home and Office: 152 Wooster St New York NY 10012-5330 E-mail: mmeedwarda@earthlink.net.

FOREMAN, SPENCER, pulmonary specialist, hospital executive; b. Phila., Nov. 10, 1935; s. Samuel and Freda F.; m. Sandra Lee Finkelstein, June 10, 1961; children: Corinne, Todd, Cheryl, Andrea. BS, Ursinus Coll., 1957; MD, U. Pa., 1961. Diplomate in internal medicine and pulmonary disease Am. Bd. Internal Medicine. Intern Henry Ford Hosp., Detroit, 1961-62; med. officer USPHS, San Pedro, Calif., 1962-63; resident in internal medicine USPHS Hosp., New Orleans, 1963-65; fellow in pulmonary diseases Tulane U., 1965-67; asst. chief dept. internal medicine USPHS Hosp., Balt., 1967-68, chief dept. internal medicine, 1968-73, hosp. dir., 1971-73; CEO Sinai Hosp., Balt., 1973-86; pres. Montefiore Med. Ctr., Bronx, N.Y., 1986—. Prof. medicine, prof. social medicine and epidemiology Albert Einstein Coll. Medicine, Bronx; mem. Accreditation Coun. on Med. Edn., 1981-87, ProPAC (Prospective Payment Assessment Commn.) 1996. Contbr. articles to med. jours. Commr. Md. Health Resources Commn., 1982-86, Liaison Com. for Med. Edn., 1989-91; bd. dirs. Am. Jewish Joint Distbn. Com., Inc., Ursinus Coll., Collegeville, Pa.; chmn. Biomed. Rsch. Alliance N.Y., 1998-2000, chmn., 2000—; vice chmn. Ursinus Coll., 2002—. Capt. USPHS, 1962-73. Fellow ACP, N.Y. Acad. Medicine; mem. Inst. Medicine Nat. Acad. Scis., Assn. Am. Med. Colls. (rep. assembly, chmn. 1986, adminstrv. bd. Coun. Tchg. Hosps., chmn.-elect assembly 1991-92, chmn. 1992-93), Am. Hosp. Assn. (bd. dirs. 1995-98), Health Forum (bd. dirs. 1998-99), Greater N.Y. Hosp. Assn. (bd. dirs., vice chmn., chmn.), League Vol. Hosps. (bd. dirs., sec.-treas., chmn.), Soc. Med. Adminstrs. (pres. 2000-02). Office: Montefiore Med Ctr 111 E 210th St Bronx NY 10467-2401 E-mail: sforeman@montefiore.org.

FOREMAN, THOMAS ALEXANDER, dentist; b. Tionesta, Pa., Oct. 24, 1930; s. James Aura and May (Lanson) F.; m. Dorothy Jean Wolf, June 12, 1953; children: Bonnie Jean, Julie Marie, Mary Aleta, Lloyd George. Student, Grove City Coll., 1948-50; BS, Allegheny Coll., 1952; DDS cum laude, U. Pitts., 1957, DMD, 1970. Gen. practice dentistry, Clarion, Pa., 1961—. Mem. Clarion Hosp. Assn., 1965—; mem. exec. bd. Colonel Drake Council Boy Scouts Am., 1969-72, mem.-at-large French Creek council, 1972-73, vice chmn. Indian Trails dist., 1971-73; mem. governing coun. Alpha Christian Acad. Sch., 1977-81. Capt. with Dental Corps, USAF, 1957-61. Fellow Pierre Fauchard Acad. Fellow Acad. Dentistry Internat., Am. Coll. Dentists, Internat. Coll. Dentists, Royal Soc. Health; mem. ADA, Pa. Dental Assn. (dir. 8th dist. 1964-87, 91—, pres. 1974-76, trustee 1987-91), Acad. Gen. Dentistry (mem. 1977, fellow 1984, master 1988), AMA (affiliate), Clarion County Dental Soc. (pres. 1983-87), S.A.R. (pres. Capt. Samuel Brady chpt. 1970-71, 77-80), Soc. Mayflower Descs., Pilgrim Edward Doty Soc., Fedn. Dentaire Internationale, Pa. Soc., Western Pa. Conservancy, Cook Forest Ctr. for Arts, Clarion County Hist. Soc., Mason (Shriner), Phi Beta Phi, Omicron Kappa Upsilon, Delta Sigma Delta, Theta Chi. Presbyn. (pres. bd. trustees 1966-67, supt. Sunday sch. 1966-67, chmn. endowment trust fund dirs. 1980-84, elder 2001—). Home: 147 S 7th Ave Clarion PA 16214-2006 Office: 832 E Main St Clarion PA 16214-1168

FORER, ARTHUR H. biology educator, researcher, editor; b. Trenton, N.J., Dec. 17, 1935; arrived in Can., 1972; s. Bernard and Rose Ethel Forer; m. Alexandra Engberg Westengaard, Dec. 18, 1964; children— Michael, David. B.Sc., MIT, Cambridge, 1957; postgrad., U. Rochester, 1957-59, U. Wash.-Friday Harbor, summer 1959; PhD in Molecular Biology, Dartmouth Med. Sch., 1964. Postdoctoral fellow Am. Cancer Soc. Carlsberg Labs., Copenhagen, 1964-66; research asst. Cambridge U., Eng., 1966-67, Helen Hay Whitney Found. fellow, 1967-69, Duke U., Durham, N.C., 1969-70; lektor Odense U., Denmark, 1970-72; assoc. prof. biology York U., Toronto, Canada, 1972—75, prof. biology, 1975—2001, prof. emeritus, sr. scholar, 2001—. Mem. grant selection panel Natural Scis. and Engring. Rsch. Coun., 1976-78. Editor: Mitosis/Cytokinesis, 1981; mem. editorial bd. Jour. Cell Sci., 1972-84, Can. Jour. Biochemistry and Cell Biology, 1982-93, Cell Biology Internat. Reports, 1984—; contbr. articles to profl. jours. Active Amnesty Internat., Ottawa, Ont., 1980—, Cmty. Theatre Orchs., Toronto, A Pack-O-Lips Now Saxophone Quartet, Toronto. Fellow Royal Soc. Can., Acad. Scis.; mem. AAAS, Am. Soc. Cell Biology, Stankel Ben Soc. (charter mem. 1960—), Tarragon Theatre, Shaw Festival (supporting). Avocations: music, gardening, cycling, hiking. Home: 17 Michigan Dr Willowdale ON Canada M2M 3H9 Office: York U Biology Dept 4700 Keele St Downsview ON Canada M3J 1P3 E-mail: aforer@yorku.ca.

FORESE, JAMES JOHN, business machine company executive; b. Coatesville, Pa., Dec. 31, 1935; s. Samuel and Edith (Mastrangelo) Forese; m. Florine Skutnik, June 27, 1959; children: Laura Lee, James Anthony, Diane Edith, John Thomas. BSEE, Rensselaer Polytech. Inst.; MBA, MIT. With IBM, Armonk, NY, 1959—93; exec. v.p., COO Alco Std., 1996; exec. v.p., pres. internat. ops. IKON Office Solutions, Inc., 1997—98, pres., CEO, 1998—2000, chmn., 2000—. Bd. dirs. NUI Corp., Am. Mgmt. Sys., IBM Latin Am., IBM Credit Corp., Lexmark Internat. Trustee Rensselaer Polytech. Inst.; mem. CBA Found. adv. coun. Coll. Bus. Adminstrn.; mem. engring. found. adv. coun. Coll. Engring. U. Tex.-Austin. Office: IKON Office Solutions Inc 70 Valley Stream Pkwy Malvern PA 19355-1453

FORESMAN, JAMES BUCKEY, geologist, geochemist, industrial hygienist; b. Neosho, Mo., Apr. 8, 1935; s. Frank James and Helen Blackburn (Buckey) F.; m. Barbara Ellen Runkle, Aug. 13, 1961; children: James Runkle, Robert Buckey. BSBA, BS, Kans. State U., 1962; MS, U. Tulsa, 1970. From geologist, geochemist to staff dir. geology N.Am.-S.Am. Phillips Petroleum Co., Denver, Midland, Tex., Bartlesville, Okla., 1962-83; petroleum cons. Bartlesville, 1983-84; v.p. Mopro, Inc., Lyons, Mich., 1985-87; indsl. hygienist, asst. dir. phys. plant Pittsburg (Kans.) State U., 1987—. Geochemistry advisor Joint Oceanographic Instsn. for Deep Earth Sampling, 1974-75; ocean drilling advisor NSF, Washington, 1974-75; indsl. rep. for joint ventures with USSR, 1978; rep. Univ.-Indsl. Assoc. Programs, N.Y., Tex., Ariz., Mass., Calif., Cambridge (Eng.), 1981-83; citizen amb. programs Environ. Del. to Russia, Latvia, and Estonia, 1992. Contbr. articles to periodicals, jours., chpts. to books. Com. mem. Boy Scouts Am., Bartlesville, 1975-82; mem. Pitts. Planning and Zoning Commn., 1997-2000; bd. dirs. U.S. Little League, Bartlesville, 1975; smoke jumper Forest Svc., USDA. Sgt. USMC, 1954-57, Korea. Recipient Disting. Svc. award City of Bartlesville, 1977. Mem. Assn. Higher Edn. Facilities Officers, Kiwanis (past pres.), Kans. Kiwanis Found. (life). Republican. Presbyterian. Avocations: reading, collecting rare and antique books, ymca activities. Home: 1506 Woodland Ter Pittsburg KS 66762-5551

FOREST, EVA BROWN, songwriter, producer, performer, publisher; b. Ontario, Va., July 7, 1941; d. William Butler and Ruth Pauline (Simpson) Brown; m. Willie J. Forest Jr., Sept. 16, 1961; children: Gerald, Darryl, Angela. AA, Bismarck (N.D.) State Coll., 1981; BSN, U. Mary, Bismarck, 1984. RN, Colo. Charge nurse St. Alexius Med. Ctr., Bismarck, 1984-85, Cedars Health Care Ctr., Lakewood, Colo., 1989-90; staff devel. coord. Park Avenue Bapt. Home, Denver, 1990-91; supr., charge nurse Cedars Health Care Ctr., Lakewood, Colo., 1991—; charge nurse Villa Manor Health Ctr., Lakewood, Colo., 1991-93, Stovall Care Ctr., Denver, 1995-96, supr., 1997-98, supr., charge nurse, 1999—. Songwriter, prodr., 1999; recorded (CD) God Has Begun a Good Work in Me, 1999. Vol. for cultural exch. lang., culture and fashions YWCA, Kano, Nigeria; vocalist gospel music workshop, N.D.; pianist adult and children's choir, N.D.; mem. MADD, Habitat for Humanity Internat., HALT, Vols. of Am. Mem. Nat. Multiple Sclerosis Soc., DAV Commdrs. Club.

FOREST, HERMAN SILVA, biology educator; b. Chattanooga, Feb. 18, 1921; s. William Hirsh and Frances (Schutzer) Silva; m. Grace Marie Wyman, Apr. 5, 1963; children: Samuel, Benjamin. BA, U. Tenn., 1942; MS, Mich. State U., 1948, PhD with honors, 1951. Instr. biology Coll. William and Mary, Williamsburg, Va., 1953-54; instr. botany U. Tenn., Knoxville, 1954-55; asst. prof. U. Okla., Norman, 1955-58; research assoc. U. Tenn. Research Ctr., Knoxville, 1958-60; research asst. U. Okla. Med. Ctr., Oklahoma City, 1960-61; research assoc. U. Rochester, N.Y., 1961-65; mem. faculty SUNY, Geneseo, 1965-92, prof. biology, 1965-92; SUNY exchange prof. U. Moscow, 1979; vis. scholar SUNY, 1974-92; sr. scientist PAI Environ. Cons., 1995-2001. Prin. scientist Environ. Resource Ctr., Geneseo, 1968-80, dir., 1986; advisor N.Y. State Depts. Health and Environ. Conservation, 1965-74, Fedn. N.Y. Lake Assns., 1983-89, Monroe County Parks, 1984-86, Rochester City Water Supply Lakes, 1985-87; nat. lectr. Am. Inst. for Biol. Scis., 1970; mem. Monroe County Environ. Mgmt. Coun., 1971-74; assoc. herbarium Tenn. Tech. U., 1996-2001; advisor for stream water quality studies City of Cookeville, 2002-; cons. in field. Author: Handbook of Algae, 1954, The Limnology of Conesus Lake, in Lakes of New York State, 1978; chief editor Studies of Pollution Control in a Lake Front Community, 1982; co-author: Natural Survival and Reproduction of American Chestnut Trees, 1988; co-editor: Geology of the Genesee Valley Region since H.L. Fairchild, 1983, American Chestnut, a bibliography, 1990; editor, contbr. Prehistory of Lake Baikal Limnological Inst., Siberia, 1991; production editor: Translation of Fish Culture in Rice Fields (V.A. Meien), Bibl. Rice Field Ecology and Fish Culture C.H. Fernando, 1993, Aquatic Angiosperms of the Genesee Valley Region, Western N.Y., 1996; contbr. to Ency. Brit. Yearbook, 1986, articles to profl. jours. With U.S. Army, 1944-46, 51-53. Fellow Scientists Inst. for Pub. Info. (Nat. lectr.), 1974; fellow Rochester Acad. Sci., 1981; Nat. Acad. Scis. Exchange scholar, 1964, 80 Mem. Am. Inst. Biol. Scis., Internat. Congress Ecology, Internat. Great Lakes Research Assn. (conf. chmn. 1979), Ecol. Soc. Am., Bot. Soc. Am., Phycol. Soc. Am., Am. Soc. Plant Taxonomists, So. Appalachian Bot. Soc., Lucy Braun Forest Soc. (dir. 1998-2000), Sierra Club (Tenn. state dir. 1997-99), Save Our Cumberland Mountains. Jewish. Home: 215 Cherry Ave Cookeville TN 38501-2500 E-mail: hforest@usit.net.

FOREST, JAMES FRANZEN, university administrator; b. Pocatello, Idaho, Oct. 17, 1968; s. John Judson Franzen and Jeri Lynn Mallard. BS, Georgetown U., 1993; MA, Stanford U., 1994; PhD, Boston Coll., 1998. Policy analyst Mass. Bd. of Higher Edn., Boston, 1995—97; dir. tech. and rsch. Nat. Ctr. Urban Partnerships, N.Y.C., 1997—99; asst. to pres. Franklin Pierce Coll., Rindge, NH, 1999—2001; asst. dean acad. assessment U.S. Mil. Acad., West Point, NY, 2001—, asst. prof. polit. sci., 2001—. Ptnr. U. Strategies, 2000—. Author: (website) Higher Education Resource Hub, 1999; editor: University Teaching: International Perspectives, 1998, Higher Education in the United States-An Encyclopedia, 2002. Mem. Am. Edn. Rsch. Assn. (tech. facilitator 1997—), Assn. for Study of Higher Edn. (chair internat. coun. 1998-99), Am. Assn. Higher Edn. Avocations: website development, music. Office: US Mil Acad Office of Dean MAND-AAD Taylor Hall Rm 10 West Point NY 10996-5000

FORESTER, ERICA SIMMS, decorative arts historian, consultant, educator; b. N.Y.C., Feb. 13, 1942; d. Leon Marcus and Selma (Rosen) Simms; m. Bruce Michael Forester, Dec. 21, 1962; children: Brent Peter, Robin Ann, Russell Charles. BA, Cornell U., 1963; MA, Columbia U., 1964; cert., N.Y. Sch. Interior Design, 1973; AAS in Interior Design, Parsons Sch. Design, 1982. Owner Erica Forester, Interiors, Bronxville, N.Y., 1973—; mem. faculty Parsons Sch. Design, N.Y.C., 1982—. Lectr. Hudson River Mus., 1984, Eastchester Hist. Soc., 1989, Bartow Pell Mansion, 1990, Scarsdale Adult Sch., 1991, The Decorative and Fine Arts Soc. of N.J., 1995, 96, NYU, Christie's Decorative Arts Summer Sch., 1998; guest curator Scarsdale Hist. Soc., 1987; mem. adj. faculty NYU, 1997—. Author: (with others) At Home in Westchester: Style and Design, 1836-1886, The Evolution of Elegant Dining. Mem. adv. bd. Am. Field Svc. Rye Country Day Sch., 1984-88; mus. adv. bd. Scarsdale Hist. Soc.; mem. property coun. Lyndhurst, NY. Mem. Decorative Arts Trust. Home and Office: 55 Northway Bronxville NY 10708-2325

FORESTER, JEAN MARTHA BROUILLETTE, innkeeper, retired librarian, educator; b. Port Barre, La., Sept. 7, 1934; d. Joseph Walter and Thelma (Brown) Brouillette; m. James Lawrence Forester, June 2, 1957; children: Jean Martha, James Lawrence. BS La. State U., 1955; MA, George Peabody Coll. Tchrs., 1956. Libr. Howell Elem. Sch., Springhill, La., 1956—58; asst. post libr. Fort Chaffee, Ark., 1958; command libr. Orleans Area Command, U.S. Army, Orleans, France, 1958—59; acquisitions libr. Northwestern State U., Natchitoches, La., 1960; serials libr. La. State U., New Orleans, 1960—66, mem. faculty Eunice, 1966—85, asst. libr., 1972—85, assoc. libr., 1985—87, acting libr., 1987—88, dir. libr., 1988—89, libr. emeritus, 1989—, asst. prof., 1972—85, faculty senator, 1978—80, 1985—86, 1987—89; innkeeper Crown'n'Anchor Inn, Saco, Maine, 1989—. Co-author: Robertsons's Bill of Fare; contbr. articles to profl. jours. Active Eunice Assn. Retarded Children. Fellow Carnegie, 1955—56. Mem.: UDC, La. Libr. Assn. (sect. sec. 1971—72, coord. serials interest group 1984—85), Delta Kappa Gamma (chpt. parliamentarian 1972—74, rec. sec. 1984—86), Order Ea. Star, Phi Mu, Phi Gamma Mu, Alpha Beta Alpha. Democrat. Baptist.

FORESTER, JOHN GORDON, JR., lawyer; b. Wilkesboro, N.C., Jan. 14, 1933; s. John Gordon and Mary Hope (Hendren) F.; m. Georgina Ramirez, June 26, 1957; children: John Gordon III, Robert Raoul, Georgina Yasué, Richard Alexander. BS; in Indsl. Relations, U. N.C., 1955; LL.B., George Washington U., 1962. Bar: D.C. 1962, Md. 1993. Internat. economist Dept. Commerce, 1958-62; confidential asst. to dep. asst. sec. commerce, 1962-63; law clk. to U.S. Dist. Judge L.P. Walsh, 1963-64; pvt. practice Washington, 1964-80; ptnr. Pohoryles & Greenstein, P.C., Washington, 1980-89, Greenstein Delorme & Luchs, P.C., Washington, 1989-95; pvt. practice, 1995—. Mem. Jud. Conf. D.C. Cir., 1981, 82, 92, adv. com. Civil Justice Reform Act, U.S. Dist. Ct., 1991-93; pres. Lawyers Mut. Ins. Co. of D.C., 1990-92. Contbr. articles to profl. jours. Pres. Friendly Citizens Assn., 1963, Gonzaga Fathers Club, 1974-76; chmn. bd. dirs. Henson Valley Montessori Sch.; bd. dirs. Sursum Corda Neighborhood Center, 1975-77. Lt. comdr. USNR, 1955-58. Mem. ABA (mem. ho. of dels. 2000-2002), D.C. Bar Assn. (pres. 2001-02), Md. Bar Assn., Coun. for Ct. Excellence (chmn. ct. improvement com.), George Washington U. Law Alumni Assn. (pres. D.C. chpt. 1988-89), Counsellors (pres. 1984-85), Barrister Inn (pres. 1976-77), Order Golden Fleece, Kappa Alpha Order, Phi Delta Phi. Roman Catholic. Home: 10701 Laurel Leaf Pl Potomac MD 20854-1770 Office: 1914 Sunderland Pl NW Washington DC 20036 E-mail: jgfcadence@aol.com.

FORESTER, KARL S. chief district court judge; b. 1940; BA, U. Ky., 1962, JD, 1966. With Eugene Goss Esp., 1966—68; mem. firm Goss & Forester, 1968—75, Forester, Forester, Buttermore & Turner, P.S.C., 1975—88; judge U.S. Dist. Ct. (ea. dist.) Ky., Lexington, 1988—. Mem. Ky. Bar Assn., Harlan County Bar Assn., Fayette County Bar Assn. Office: US Dist Ct PO Box 2165 Lexington KY 40588-2165

FORGACS, JOSEPH, mycotoxicologist; b. Nokomis, Ill., Mar. 20, 1917; s. John and Elizabeth (Hallas) F.; m. Lillian Pearl Little, June 1, 1945; children: Theresa Maria, Joseph Alan, Lawrence David, Paul Axel, Lillian Pearl Maria. BS, U. Ill., 1940, MS, 1942, PhD, 1944. Dir. mycotoxicoses rsch. Fort Detrick, Frederick, Md., 1944-54; sr. rsch. fellow Am. Cyanamid Corp., Pearl River, N.Y., 1954-57; dir. lab. Spring Valley (N.Y.) Hosp., 1957-61; mycotoxicologist, staff microbiologist Good Samaritan Hosp., Suffern, N.Y., 1961-69; dir. clin. microbiology Rampo Gen. Hosp. and Automated Biochem. Labs., Spring Valley, 1969-78. Cons. mycotoxicologist Agrl. Rsch. Svc., U.S. Dept. Agr., food and feed industries, 1957—; cons. microbiologist N.Y. State Dept. Mental Hygiene, Letchworth Village, Thiells, 1973-95. Contbr. articles to profl. jours.; patentee in field. Served with AUS, 1944-46. Diplomate Am. Acad. Microbiology. Fellow AAAS, Am. Acad. Microbiology, Inst. Food Technologists; mem. N.Y. Acad. Scis., Am. Inst. Biol. Scis., N.Y. Med. Mycology Soc., Phi Sigma, Sigma Xi. Home and Office: 302 Highland Ave Pearl River NY 10965-1005

FORGER, ALEXANDER DARROW, lawyer; b. N.Y.C., Feb. 19, 1923; BA with honors, Princeton U., 1947; JD, Yale U., 1950. Bar: N.Y. 1951. Assoc. Milbank, Tweed, Hadley & McCloy, N.Y.C., 1950-57, ptnr., 1958—, chmn., 1984—92, spl. counsel, 1993—. Pres., Legal Svcs. Corp., 1994-97; bd. dirs. Oak Spring Farms, LLC Trustee Rockefeller U.; chmn. bd., Legal Aid Soc., 1984-92; v.p., Dorothea Leonhardt Found., Gerard B. Lambert Meml. Found., Inc. Fellow Am. Bar Found., N.Y. Bar Found., Am. Coll. Trust and Estate Counsel; mem. ABA (past state del. to ho. of dels.), N.Y. State Bar Assn. (past pres. ho. of dels.), Assn. Bar City of N.Y., Lawyers; Com. for Civil Rights Under Law. Office: Milbank Tweed Hadley & McCloy 1 Chase Manhattan Plz Fl 47 New York NY 10005-1413 E-mail: aforger@milbank.com.

FORGER, ROBERT DURKIN, retired professional association administrator; b. Norwalk, Conn., May 24, 1928; s. Alois John and Elsie Marie (Durkin) F.; m. Eleanor Marie Goddard, May 14, 1951; children: Gary Robert, Jeffrey Alois. BS, Norwich U., Northfield, Vt., 1949; grad., U.S. Army Command and Gen. Staff Coll., 1970. Research and devel. engr., mgr. tech. publicity Dorr-Oliver Inc., Stamford, Conn., 1949-59; conf. mgr., pub., exec. dir. Soc. Plastics Engrs., Brookfield, Conn., 1959-93; ret., 1993. Chmn. Westport (Conn.) Pub. Housing Authority, 1959-64; treas. Plastics Edn. Found., 1971-75; bd. dirs. Norwich U. Alumni Assn., 1981-86, pres., 1984-86; trustee Norwich U., 1987-92, Nat. Plastics Mus., 1983-93; mem. plastics engring. curriculum adv. com. U. Mass., Lowell, 1974-93. Lt. col. USAR. Named Conn. Assn. Exec. of Yr., 1983, elected to Plastics Hall of Fame, 1996; named Disting. Alumnus, Norwich U., 1999. Mem. Soc. Plastics Engrs. (disting. mem. 1984, pres.'s cup, 1992), Am. Soc. Assn. Execs. (life), Coun. Engring. and Sci. Soc. Execs. (bd. dirs. 1983-85, sec. 1985-86, v.p. 1986-87, pres. 1987-88), Plastics Pioneers Assn. Home: 42 DeForest Rd Wilton CT 06897-1909

FORGHANI-ABKENARI, BAGHER, virologist, researcher; b. Bandar-Anzali, Iran, Mar. 10, 1936;, s. Baba Forghani-Abkenari and Jahan Rahimi; m. Nikoo Alavi Forghani-Abkenari; children: Niki, Nikta. MS, Justus Liebig U., 1961, PhD, 1965. Postdoctoral fellow Utah State U., Logan, Utah, 1965—67; asst. prof. Nat. U. of Iran, Tehran, Iran, 1967—69; rsch. assoc. Utah State U., 1969—70; from post-doctoral tng. to chief viral immunoserology sec. State of Calif. Dept. Health Svc., Berkeley, Calif., 1970—82, chief viral immunoserology sec. Richmond, Calif., 1982—. Cons. The Nat. Registary of Microbiologists, Washington, 1976—; mem. sci. adv. bd. Varicella-Zoster Virus Rsch. Found., N.Y.C., 1991. Contbr. articles over 70 to profl. jours., chapters to books. Mem.: Am. Soc. Microbiology. Office: 850 Marina Bay Parkway Richmond CA 94804 E-mail: bforghan@dhs.ca.gov.

FORGIONE, DANA ANTHONY, healthcare accounting educator; BBA, U. Mass., 1975, MBA, 1977, MS in Acctg., 1980, PhD, 1987; Cert. in Christian Leadership with high honors, Heritage Bapt. Inst., 1979, Cert. in Ch. Ministries,

1983. CPA, Md., Tex., Fla.; CMA; cert. fraud examiner. Asst. prof. C.W. Post Ctr. Sch. Profl. Accountancy Long Is. U., Greenvale, N.Y., 1981-83; asst. prof. Sch. Bus. We. New Eng. Coll., Springfield, Mass., 1983-87; asst. prof. Coll. Bus. Adminstrn., Grad. Sch. Bus. Tex. A&M U., College Station, 1987-93; assoc. prof. Merrick Sch. Bus. U. Balt., 1993-2000, prof., 2000-2001, dir. profl. MBA program Merrick Sch. Bus., 1993-2000, advisor MBA specialization in healthcare mgmt., 1993-2001; affil. assoc. prof. Sch. Pharmacy U. Md., Balt., 1996-2000, affiliate prof., 2000-2001; dir., prof. Sch. Acctg. Fla. Internat. U., Miami, 2001—. Prin. Global Anti-Fraud Cons., Inc., Balt., 1998—2001; cons in field; cons. U.S. Dept. Vets Affairs, 1997. Author: Costly Reflections in a Midas Mirror, 1994, Costly Reflections in a Midas Mirror, 2d edit., 1999; co-author: Pet Polygon Mfg. Company Management Accounting Case, 1992, Pet Polygon Mfg. Company Management Accounting Case, 3d edit., Laser Logos, Inc., 1994, Laser Logos, Inc., 2d edit., 1997; editor: Rsch. in Healthcare Fin. Mgmt., 1994—2000, 2000—, chmn. editl. rev. bd. The White Paper, 1996—99, columnist Jour. Health Care Finance, reviewer Internat. Jour. Pub. Adminstrn., Govt. Accts. Jour., The Acctg. Rev., 1996, 2001—, Govtl. and Non Profit Acctg., 1992—, mem. editl. bd. Today's CPA, 1992—93, Jour. Econs. and Fin., 1992—95, Pub. Budgeting, Acctg. and Fin. Mgmt., 1994—, Jour. Health Care Fin., 1996, Rsch. in Govt. and Nonprofit Acctg., 1996—, rev. Issues in Acctg. Edn., 1997—, mem. editl. bd., 1998—, Fin. Accountability and Mgmt., 1994—, assoc. editor N.Am., 1998—; contbr. articles to profl. jours.; rev.: Internat. Jour. Pub. Adminstrn., 2001—. Litigation support, expert testimony, cons. Tex. Atty. Gen., 1992-93. Symposium fellow Office for Govt. Acctg. Rsch. and Edn. U. Ill. Chgo., 1984; recipient Hon. Mention Manuscript award Mass. Soc. CPAs, 1976, Manuscript award Nat. Assn. Accts., Black and Decker Rsch. Awd., Merrick Sch. Bus., U. Baltimore, 1995, 99, Top 10 List, Merrick Sch. of Bus., 1995, Curriculum Funds Development Awd., Merrick Sch. Bus., 1994, Outstanding Fac. Mem. Awd., Beta Alpha Psi (acctg. Hon. Fraternity), 1992, Incentive Grant for Tchg., Ctr. for Tchg. Excellence, Tex. A&M U., 1992, Chancellor's Citation for Undergrad. Instrs., U. Mass., 1973. Mem.: Inst. Pub. Sector Acctg. Rsch. U. Edinburgh (internat. assoc.), Assn. Cert. Fraud Examiners (bd. regents 1999—2000, regent emeritus 2001—), Internat. Soc. Rsch. in Healthcare Fin. Mgmt. (dir. 1994—, founder), Internat. Assn. Mgmt. (sr. editor jour. 1996—98, chmn. healthcare mgmt. divsn. 1997—98, Internat. Regional Publ. award 1996, Divsn. award 1998), Am. Acctg. Assn. (mem. exec. com. Mid-Atlantic region 1994—2001, pres. Mid-Atlantic region 1996—97, mem. nat. coun. 1996—97). Baptist. Avocations: computers, biblical chronology, woodworking. Office: Fla Internat U Univ Park Miami FL 33199 E-mail: forgione@fiu.edu.

FORGIONNE, GUISSEPPI ANTONIO, information scientis, educator; b. Jenkins Twp., Pa., July 9, 1945; s. William Feigo, Mary Susan Feigo. BS in Commerce and Fin., Wilkes U., 1966; MBA, U. Scranton, 1968; MA, U. Calif., Riverside, 1972, PhD, 1973. Prof. ops. mgmt. Calif. State Poly. U., Pomona, 1970—84; prof. mgmt. Bucknell U., Lewisburg, Pa., 1984—86; prof. info. sys. U. Md. Balt. County, Catonsville, 1986—. Cons. in field. Author: 25 Books; contbr. articles to profl. jours. Mem.: Assn. for Info. Sys., Decision Scis. Inst., Inst. Ops. Rsch. and Mgmt. Sci. Roman Catholic. Avocations: model railroading, sports. Office: Univ Md Baltimore County 1000 Hilltop Cir Catonsville MD 21250 Home Fax: 410-455-1073; Office Fax: 410-455-1073. Personal E-mail: forgionn@umbc.edu. Business E-Mail: forgionn@umbc.edu.

FORGO, FERENC, economics educator; b. Pècs, Hungary, Apr. 16, 1942; s. Ferenc F. and Margit (Kerènyi) Hetènyi; m. Erzsèbet Kiss, May 27, 1966; children: Ferenc, Erzsèbet. MS, U. Econs., Budapest, Hungary, 1965, PhD, 1974. From asst. prof. to assoc. prof. U. Econs., Budapest, Hungary, 1965-91, prof., 1992—. Vis. prof. Rutgers U., Camden, N.J., 1984-85, U. So. Calif., L.A., 1993-94; chmn. dept. math., computer sci. U. Econ., 1987-96, dept. ops. rsch., 1995—. Author: Nonconvex Programming, 1988; co-author: Einführung in die Spieltheorie, 1983, Introduction to the Theory of Games, Concepts, Methods, Applications, 1999. Mem. Hungarian Soc. for Econ. Modelling (pres. 1990-91), Math. Programming Soc., Econometric Soc. Avocations: tennis, chess. Home: Napviràg 19 1025 Budapest Hungary Office: U Econs Dept Ops Rsch Fövamtér 8 1093 Budapest Hungary E-mail: forgo@nero.bke.hu.

FORISTER, JEAN WHITBY, retired guidance counselor, consultant; b. Crowell, Tex., Oct. 31, 1935; d. Tom Mulry Whitby and Edith Catherine (Weatherall) Cogdell; m. Charles F. Russell, July 31, 1961 (div. 1966); m. Thomas Eugene Forister, Aug. 4, 1966; children: Thomas Eugene Jr., Jill. BA with honors, North Tex. State U., 1958; MEd with honors, U. Tex., 1966. Cert. tchr. and counselor, Tex.; lic. realtor, Tex.; lic. profl. counselor, N.Mex. Exec. sec. Humble Oil, Amarillo, Tex., 1958-59; tchr. Crowell Schs., Vernon and Dallas, 1959-65; psychol. and guidance counselor Houston Area Schs., 1966-75; owner TJs Ladies Store, Crowell, 1975-82; guidance counselor SEARCH, Amarillo, 1983-84, Humble (Tex.) Schs., 1984-87, Ruidoso (N.Mex.) Mcpl. Schs., 1990-96; ret. Co-owner Santana, Ltd., Ruidoso, 1992—. Mem. Crowell City Coun., 1976-80; vice chmn., bd. dirs. United Meth. Ch., Crowell, 1976-80. Grantee Nat. Fed. Edn. Act, 1965-66. Mem. NEA, Alpha Delta Pi. Avocations: art, cooking, gardening, animals.

FORKAN, PATRICIA ANN, foundation executive; b. N.Y.C., June 13, 1944; d. Robert James and Elaine May F. BA in Polit. Sci., Pa. State U., 1966; postgrad., Am. U., 1968-69. Manpower analyst Dept. Labor, Washington, 1967-69; nat. coord. Fund for Animals, N.Y.C., 1970-76; v.p. program and comms. Humane Soc. of U.S., Washington, 1976-86, sr. v.p., 1987-91, exec. v.p., 1992—. Weekly web-active commentator Soap Box, 1999—; bd. dirs. Solar Elec. Light Fund, 1990-2000; mem. U.S. del. Internat. Whaling Commn., 1978, 93, 94 Re-negotiation of Conv. for Regulation of Whaling, 1978, U.S. del. North Pacific Fur Seal Commn., 1985; mem. U.S. Public Adv. Com. to Law of the Sea, 1978-83; bd. dirs. Coun. for Ocean Law; advisor, contbr. weekly TV show Living with Animals, 1985-91; advisor Animal Polit. Action Com.; sr. v.p. Humane Soc. Internat., 1991-; coun. woman Friendship Heights (Md.) Village, 1993-2001; pres. Nat. Assn. Humane and Environ. Edn., 1994—; pres. Worldwide Network (Women in Devel. and Environ.), 1998; presdl. appointed mem. trade and environment policy adv. com. U.S. Trade Rep., 2000—. Contbr. articles to environ. and animal welfare publs.; co-host weekly radio show, 1986-87.. Office: Humane Soc of US 2100 L St NW Washington DC 20037-1596

FORKER, OLAN DEAN, agricultural economics educator; b. Kendallville, Ind., Aug. 18, 1928; s. Fred Forrest and Mary May (Butler) F.; m. Kathleen Rose Buuck, Apr. 21, 1951; children: Michael, Brent, Susan. BS, Purdue U., 1950; MS, Mich. State U., 1958; PhD, U. Calif., Berkeley, 1962. Fieldman Halderman Farm Mgmt. Service, Wabash, Ind., 1954-58; extension economist U. Calif. at Berkeley, 1961-65; assoc. prof. Cornell U., Ithaca, N.Y., 1965-70, prof., 1971-95, prof. emeritus, 1995—; chmn. dept. agrl. econs., 1976-85; fellow U. Manchester, 1981-82; dir. Universal Foods Corp., Inc., Milw., 1974-96. Cons. AID, Turkey, 1970-71, Ford Found., 1978, Nat. Dairy Promotion and Rsch. Bd., 1984-88; Naumes Family vis. prof. Santa Clara U., 1985-86; adj. prof. U. Fla., 1988-89; dir. Tompkins Co. Nutrition for Elderly, Inc. Author: (with Ron Ward) Commodity Advertising: The Economics and Measurement of Generic Programs, 1993; contbr. articles to profl. jours. Officer, council mem. Trinity Luth. Ch., Ithaca, 1967-69, 72— ; trustee Cornell U., 1984-88. Lt. col., ret., U.S. Army. Recipient award for profl. excellence for quality of discovery in pub. research Am. Agrl. Econs. Assn., 1975 Mem. Am. Agrl. Econs. Assn., Am. Agrl. Econs. Found. (pres. 1988-89), N.E. Agrl. and Resource Econs. Assn. (life, pres. 1991-92, Jour. award 1991, Disting. Mem. award 1994). Home: 13 Stormy View Rd Ithaca NY 14850-9774 Office: Cornell U 407 Warren Hall Ithaca NY 14853-7801 E-mail: oof1@cornell.edu.

FORLANO, FREDERICK PETER, lawyer; b. N.Y.C., July 12, 1947; s. Pasquale Genaro and Theresa Susan (Hartmann) F.; children: Christopher S., Jason D., Jennifer R.; m. Sharon S. Guinnup, 1995. AS, Suffolk Community Coll., 1968; BA in Math., Adelphi U., 1969; JD, U. Houston, 1975. Bar: Tex. 1975, U.S. Dist. Ct. (so. dist.) Tex. 1976, U.S. Ct. Appeals (5th cir.) 1976, U.S. Ct. Appeals (11th cir.) 1981, U.S. Tax Ct. 1977. Commd. 2nd lt. USAF, 1970, advanced through grades to maj., 1984; ptnr. Finger, Small, Cohen & Forlano, Houston, 1975-88; pvt. practice law Houston, 1988—. Advisor, legal v.p. Meadows Civic Assn., Stafford, Tex., 1977, pres., 1978-79; advisor Parents Without Ptnrs., Houston, 1987—; trustee The Wilhelm Schole, 1977—. With USAFR (ret.), 1970-92. Mem. Tex. Bar Assn., Houston Bar Assn., Ft. Bend Bar Assn., Ft. Bend County Criminal Def. Lawyers Assn., Res. Officers Assn. Republican. Roman Catholic. Avocations: golf, horses. Office: 3050 Post Oak Blvd Ste 1425 Houston TX 77056-6532 E-mail: fpforlano@aol.com.

FORLINI, FRANK JOHN, JR., cardiologist; b. Newark, Mar. 30, 1941; s. Frank Sr. and Rose Theresa (Parussini) F.; m. Joanne Marie Horch, July 19, 1969; children: Anne Marie, Victoria, Frank III, Anthony. BS in Biology, Villanova (Pa.) U., 1963; MD, George Washington U., 1967. Diplomate Am. Bd. Internal Medicine, Am. Bd. Cardiovascular Disease. V.p., bus. agt. Cooks, Countermen and Cafeteria Workers Union Local 399 AFL, 1960-61; intern Bklyn.-Cumberland Med. Ctr., N.Y., 1967-68, resident in internal medicine, 1968-70; fellow in cardiology Inst. Med. Sci. Pacific Med. Ctr. Presbyn. Hosp., San Francisco, 1970-72; practice medicine specializing in cardiology Rock Island, Ill., 1974—2000; sr. ptnr. Forlini Med. Speciality Clinic, Rock Island, 1974—2000. Owner Forlini Farm and Forlini Devel. Enterprises; assoc. prof. pharmacy L.I. U., Bklyn., 1969-70; pres., CEO U.S. Oil & Transp. Co., Inc., 1966-89; pres. Profl. and Execs. Ins. Assocs., 1973-89, Profls. Assocs., 1973-89; med. and exec. dir. Cardiovasc. Inst. Northwestern Ill., 1984—; exec. dir., owner Franksoft Pub., 1988—; Shelter for Abused Women and Children, Rock Island, 1992-94, pres., chmn., 1994, chmn. capital campaign com., 1994; bd. dirs. Rescue Missions and Christian Family Care Ctr., 1992-94, pres., 1994. Contbr. articles to profl jours. Dep. registrar County of Rock Island, 1985—; trustee South Rock Island Twp., Rock Island County, 1987—97, Twp. Intergovtl. Agy., 1993—97, Friends of Twp. Govt. of Rock Island County, chmn., 1995—; alderman City of Rock Island, Rock Island County, 1997—, mayor pro tem, 2000—01; mem. Rock Island Comml. Indsl. Revolving Loan Fund, 1998—, mem. health care com., 2001—; mem. exec. com. Rock Island County Rep. Cen. Com., 1992—94; chmn. fin. com. Life and Family Ednl. Trust, 2001—02; mem. Sunset Marina Steering Com., 2002—, Mayor's Quad City Transit Task Force, 2003—; mem. nat. com. Coll. Young Reps., 1965—66; mem. Physicians for Reagan-Bush, 1980, 1984; chmn. D.C. Coll. Young Reps., 1965—66; mem. exec. com. Rep. Cen. Com., Washington, 1965—66; vice chmn. Rock Island Reps., 1985—90, precinct committeeman, 1985—90, 1992—93; del. Ill. State Rep. Conv., 1992; pres. parish coun. St. Thomas Roman Cath. Ch., San Antonio; bd. dirs. Life and Family Ednl. Trust, 2000—. Maj. USAF, 1972—74. Nat. Inst. Heart Disease NIH-USPHS grantee, 1964-66, 70-72; Fellowship of Cath. Scholars, 1994—. Fellow: N.Am. Soc. Pacing and Electrophysiology, Am. Coll. Cardiology; mem.: KC (3d deg. 1994—), AMA, Soc. Cath. Social Scientists, Rock Island County Twp. Assn. (v.p. 1994, pres. 1994—95, mem. exec. com. 1994—97), Western Ill. Ind. Physicians Assn. (bd. dirs. 1995—2002, mem. exec. com. 1996—2002, sec. 1996—97, treas. 1997—2002), Rock Island County Med. Soc. (chmn. com. on ins. 1990—), Ill. State Med. Soc., Univ. Faculty for Life.

FORLITI, AMY MARIE, reporter; b. St. Paul, Feb. 2, 1973; d. Richard M. and Kathleen M. (Lethert) F. BA summa cum laude, U. St. Thomas, St. Paul, 1995. Pub. rels. intern Evans Larson Comm., Mpls., 1994—96; news prodr. Sta. WEAU-TV, Eau Claire, Wis., 1996—97; reporter Chippewa Herald, Chippewa Falls, Wis., 1997—98, ABC newspapers, Anoka, Minn., 1998; copy editor Star Tribune, Mpls., 1998; reporter AP, Indpls. and Providence, 1999—2002, supervisory corr. Providence, 2002—. Freelance writer, 1998—. Mem. Soc. Profl. Journalists. Avocations: running, reading. Office: AP 10 Dorrance St # 601 Providence RI 02903 E-mail: aforliti@ap.org.

FORM, FREDRIC ALLAN, accountant; b. Bklyn., Mar. 2, 1942; s. Milton and Tedde (Bilus) F.; m. Jo Ann August, Aug. 29, 1964; 1 child, Andrew. BBA, Pace U., 1970. Sr. acct. S.P. Cooper & Co., N.Y.C., 1963-69; pvt. practice pub. acctg. Levittown, N.Y., 1969—. Bd. dirs. Wantagh Cmty. Arts Program, Inc., 1980-84; bd. dirs., treas. Ctrl. Nassau County React, Inc., 1979-82; treas. Your, Ours, Mine Cmty. Ctr., Levittown, 1987-93, Levittown C.C., 1992—; v.p. Reli React, Inc., 1983-91, treas., 1983—. Named Small Businessman of Yr., Levittown C.C., 1993. Mem. Nat. Soc. Pub. Accts. (2d v.p. 1983-85, v.p. 1985-86, pres. 1986-87, bd. dirs. Nassau-Suffolk chpt. 1986-92, pres. 1992-94), Kiwanis (treas. Levittown club 1988-89, 97—). Office: 2950 Hempstead Tpke Levittown NY 11756-1383 E-mail: taxform@aol.com.

FORMAN, CHARLES WILLIAM, religious studies educator; b. Gwalior, India, Dec. 2, 1916; s. Henry and Sallie (Taylor) F.; m. Helen Janice Mitchell, Mar. 12, 1944; children: David, Sarah, Harriet. BA, MA, Ohio State U., 1938; PhD, U. Wis., 1941; BD, Union Theol. Sem., N.Y.C., 1944, STM, 1947. Ordained to ministry Presbyn. Ch., 1944. Prof. North India United Theol. Coll., Saharanpur, 1945-50; sec. program emphasis Nat. Coun. Chs., 1951-53; mem. faculty Divsn. Sch., Yale U., New Haven, 1953—; D. Willis James prof. missions Div. Sch., Yale U., New Haven, 1961-87, D. Willis James prof. missions emeritus, 1987—. Chmn. theol. edn. fund World Coun. chs., 1965-70, mem., 1970-77; mem. commn. ecumenical mission United Presbyn. Ch., 1962-71, chmn., 1965-71; chmn. Found. for Theol. Edn. in SE Asia, 1970-89, mem. 1966-69, 90—. Author: A Faith for the Nations, 1958, The Nation and the Kingdom, 1964, Christianity in the Non-Western World, 1967, The Island Churches of the South Pacific, 1982, The Voice of Many Waters, 1986. Mem. bd. edn., Bethany, Conn., 1957-66; bd. dirs. Community Action Agy., New Haven, 1978-81, Overseas Ministries Study Center, New Haven, 1979-2000. Home: 200 Leeder Hill Dr Hamden CT 06517-2726

FORMAN, DONALD T. biochemist, educator; b. N.Y.C., Feb. 27, 1932; s. Jack and Fannie (Jaffee) F.; m. Florence Sporn, Aug. 22, 1953; children: Joan Diane, Steven Lawrence, Debra Helene. BS, Bklyn. Coll., 1953; MS, Wayne State U., 1957, PhD, 1959. Clin. biochemist Mercy Hosp. Med. Center, Chgo., 1959—63; dir. clin. biochemistry, asso. prof. biochemistry and pathology Evanston Hosp./Northwestern U. Med. Sch., Chgo., 1963—78; rsch. prof. U. Stockholm and Royal Postgrad. Med. Sch., London, 1975; prof. pathology and biochemistry U. N.C., Chapel Hill, NC, 1978—2002, dir. clin. chemistry, 1978—2002, prof. emeritus pathology and biochemistry, 2002. Cons. clin. chemist, industry and govt., 1965— Editor: Clinical Chemistry, 1976. Served with AUS, 1953-55. Recipient Chgo. Clin. Chemists award, 1974, Sunderman award as clin. scientist for 1986, Spl. Recognition award for clin. chemistry Am. Chem. Soc., 2000; Mich. Heart Assn. fellow, 1957-59 Mem. AAAS, AAUP, Assn. Clin. Scientists (pres. 1973-74), Am. Assn. Clin. Chemistry (dir., award for outstanding contbn. to animal clin. chemistry 1995), Sigma Xi, Phi Lambda Upsilon. Jewish. Achievements include research on enzymology, inborn errors of metabolism, tumor-associated markers, atherosclerosis, human alcohol metabolism, clinical biochemistry and critical care chemistry. Home: 2559 Owens Ct Chapel Hill NC 27514-1737 Office: U NC Med Sch Dept Pathology Chapel Hill NC 27514 E-mail: dforman@nc.rr.com.

FORMAN, EDGAR ROSS, mechanical engineer; b. Camden, N.J., Oct. 5, 1923; s. Edgar Charles and Annie (Baragwanath) F.; m. Alma Kuppinger, Sept. 26, 1953; children: Bruce, Dianne. BSME, Drexel U., 1950, MBA, 1953. Registered profl. engr., Pa., 1955. Project engr. Penn Instrument div. Burgess Manning Co., Phila., 1950-55; application engr. Moore Products Co., Phila., 1955-59; chief instrument engr. Catalytic Co., Phila., 1959-67, mgr. mgmt. sys. dept., 1967-71; supervising instrument engr. United Engrs. & Constructors, Inc., Phila., 1971-78; mgr. instrument and controls dept. Day & Zimmermann, Inc., Phila., 1978—89; dir. Automation Tech., 1989-93; cons., 1993—. Guest lectr. U.S. Naval Acad., Sun Oil Co., U. Del. Contbr. articles to profl. jours. Past mem. Boy Scouts Am.; mem. pres. coun. Spring Garden Coll., 1979-83, chmn. indsl. adv. com., 1984-89; past pres. Erdenheim Civic Assn. Served with AUS, 1943-46. Fellow: Instrument Soc. Am. (Phila. sect. pres. 1960, v.p. dist 2 1982—84, chmn. food and pharm. divsn. 1986—87, nat. v.p. 1989—93, nat. honrs and awards com. 1993—96, China visitation team 1996, Engrs. Week liaison 1997—2001, founder Outstanding Tech. Achievement award 1998—2002, cert. instr. 1998—2002, Excom, FPID 2002, past chmn. edn. commn., Eckman award 1982, Man of Yr. 1987, Golden Achievement award 1989, Outstanding Svc. award 1990, Dist. 2 Svc. award 1999, Old Shoe award 2001); mem.: NSPE (pres. Valley Forge chpt. 1982—83, Engrs. Week coun. 1990—99, county Mathcounts coord. 1994—95, Man of Yr. award Del. Valley Engrs. 1990), ASME (life; past chmn. dynamic sys. and controls divsn., old guard com.), 94th Inf. Divsn. Assn. (pres. Delaware Valley chpt. 2003), Ea. Star, Commandry, Shriners, York Rite, Masons, Scottish Rite, Pi Tau Sigma (pres.), Pi Nu Epsilon, Alpha Phi Omega (nat. pres.). Episcopalian.

FORMAN, HOWARD IRVING, lawyer, former government official; b. Phila., Jan. 12, 1917; s. Jacob and Dora (Moses) F.; m. Ada Pressman, Aug. 2, 1938; children: Kenneth J., Harvey R. BS in Chemistry, St. Joseph's Coll., 1937; LLB, Temple U., 1944; MA, U. Pa., 1949, PhD, 1955. Bar: D.C. 1945, Pa. 1973. Rsch. chemist Frankford Arsenal, Dept. Army, Phila., 1940-44, patent atty., 1944-46, chief patents br., 1946-56; asst. dir. Pitman-Dunn Rsch. Labs., 1955-56; lectr. polit. sci. Temple U., 1956-63; from patent atty. to trademark and internat. corp. counsel Rohm and Haas Co., Phila., 1956-76; dep. asst. sec. U.S. Dept. Commerce, Washington, 1976-81; also dir. Office of Product Standards Policy; chmn. interagy. com. on standards policy Weiser, Stapler & Spivak, Phila., 1974-76; head. U.S. dels. to UN internat. confs., Geneva, 1976-81; sec., dir. Rohm & Haas Asia, Inc., 1973-76; v.p., gen. counsel, dir. Brilliant Internat., Inc., Bala-Cynwyd, Pa., 1974-83; sec., dir. Far East Chem. Services, Inc., Wilmington, Del., 1973-76, Rohm and Haas GmbH, Zug, Switzerland, 1975-76; dir. U.S. Pharm. Corp., 1975-83; pvt. practice Phila., 1981—. Advisor to asst. sec. for econ. affairs relative to internat. intellectual property matters Dept. State, 1968-72; orginator Internat. Lab. Accreditation world-wide biennial confs. (ILAC), 1977—; chmn. ANSI accredited stds. com., Z21, on performance and installation gas burning appliances and accessories, 1981-97. Author: Inventions, Patents and Related Matters, 1957, Patents-Their Ownership and Administration by the U.S. Government, 1957; Editor: Patents, Research and Management, 1961, The Law of Chemical, Metallurgical and Pharmaceutical Patents, 1967; author plays: The Birth of the American Patent System, 1976, The Birth of the American Patent and Copyright Systems, 1990.; contbr. to publs. in field. Bd. dirs. Lower Moreland Twp. Sch. Bd., Montgomery County, Pa., 1969-75; bd. dirs. Eastern Montgomery County Vocat.-Tech. Sch., 1969-75, sec., 1970-75; bd. dirs. Warminster (Pa.) Gen. Hosp., 1983-91; emeritus dir. Allegheny United Hosps., Inc., 1991-94; life trustee Med. Coll. Pa. and Hahnemann U. Hosps., 1994-98. Recipient Robert J. Painter Meml. award Stds. Engring. Soc.-ASTM, 1978, Leo B. Moore award Stds. Engring. Soc., 1981. Fellow Am. Inst. Chemists; mem. ABA, FBA, AAAS, ASTM (hon. life, bd. dirs. 1985-87), Internat. Assn. Protection Indsl. Property, Am. Nat. Stds. Inst. (bd. dirs. 1977-80, Finegan Stds. medal 1996), Nat. Coun. Patent Law Assn. (chmn. 1967-68), Am. Chem. Soc., Sci. Rsch. Soc. Am., Am. Assn. Lab. Accreditation (dir. 1983-91), Am. Patent Law Assn. (bd. mgrs. 1970-73), Am. Coll. Legal Medicine, Phila. Bar Assn. (sec. 1973-74, com. on jurimetrics, tech. and patents, v.p. 1975), Phila. Patent Law Assn. (pres. 1964-66), Licensing Execs. Soc., Stds. Engring. Soc. (Robert J. Painter Meml. award 1978, Leo B. Moore award 1981), Franklin Inst. (vice chmn. Futures Ctr. campaign), Nat. Lawyers Club, Gas Appliance Mfrs. Assn. (meritorious svc. award 1996), Am. Soc. Gas Engrs. (hon.), Sigma Xi. Achievements include being the principal draftsman, prime mover in devel. original OMB Circular A-119 which established nat. policy calling for primary dependence of Fed. Govt. on private sector standards orgns. for devel. of standards required for procurement and regulatory purposes by govt. agencies. Home: 1033 Corn Crib Dr Huntingdon Valley PA 19006-3335 Office: Albidale-Windmill Circle PO Box 66 Huntingdon Valley PA 19006-0066 Fax: (215) 947-5036. *My life has been a slow-but-sure progression in which patience, diligence and determination, mixed with a readiness to adapt myself to each new circumstance, have enabled me to overcome numerous obstacles and forge a useful career and a happy life as a husband, father and grandfather that have been personally gratifying and rewarding. My creed consists of truth, simplicity, candor, tolerance, genuine humility and faith in God and my fellow men and women.*

FORMAN, JAMES DOUGLAS, lawyer; b. Mineola, N.Y., Nov. 12, 1932; s. Leo and Kathryn F.; m. Marcia Fore; children: Karli, Elizabeth. AB, Princeton U., 1954; LLB, Columbia U., 1957. Bar: N.Y. 1958. Pvt. practice, Mineola, 1957—. Author: Cry Havoc, 1988, The Big Bang, 1989, The Scottish Dirk: Reality and Romance, 1991, Prince Charlie's Year, 1991, Becca's Story, 1992, The Blunderbuss 1500-1900, 1994, about 40 others. Bd. mem. Landmarks com., Sands Point, N.Y., 1987—. Mem. Ky. Rifle Assn., Co. Mil. Historians. Avocations: portrait painting, woodworking. Home: 2 Glen Rd Port Washington NY 11050-1207 Office: 800 Port Washington Blvd Port Washington NY 11050 E-mail: jamesdforman@aol.com.

FORMAN, J(OSEPH) CHARLES, chemical engineer, consultant, writer; b. Chgo., Dec. 22, 1931; s. Joseph O. and Marie (Smith) F.; m. Ursula Diane Weston, July 22, 1953; children: Stephen Charles, Diane Brigitte, Mary Erika. S.B., M.I.T., 1953; MS, Northwestern U., 1957, PhD, 1960. Registered profl. engr., Ill. Trainee chem. engring. Dow Chem. Co., Midland, Mich., 1953-54; from sr. chem. engr. to dir. mfg. ops. agrl. vet. div. Abbott Labs., North Chicago, Ill., 1956-77; assoc. exec. dir. Am. Inst. Chem. Engrs., N.Y.C., 1977-78; exec. dir., sec., pub. Am. Inst. Chem. Engrs. Jour., Internat. Chem. Engring., Biotech Progress, Plant/Ops. Progress, Energy Progress, Environ. Progress, 1978-87; pres. and prin. Forman Assocs. Cons. and Tech. Svcs., 1987—. Cons. in field, accreditation insp. chem. engring. curricula; mem. ednl. council MIT, 1961-74, 78-95; mem. chem. engring. consultor coun. Manhattan Coll., N.Y.C., 1985—. Mem. Lake Bluff (Ill.) Bd. Edn., 1967-73, pres., 1971-73; pres. Lake County (Ill.) Sch. Bd. Assn., 1969-71; mem. Lake Bluff Plan Commn., 1973-77, chmn., 1976-77; mem. Darien (Conn.) Pers. Adv. Commn., 1986-92, Darien Park and Recreation Commn., 1999—; dist. chmn. Boy Scouts Am., 1994-97. With USAF, 1954-56. Fellow Am. Inst. Chem. Engrs., AAAS; mem. Soc. Plastics Industry (profl. mem.), Am. Chem. Soc., Am. Soc. Assn. Execs., Coun. Engring. and Sci. Soc. Execs. (dir. 1980-83, sec. 1983-84, v.p. 1984-85, pres. 1985-86), Nat. Eagle Scout Assn., Sigma Xi, Tau Beta Pi, Phi Lambda Upsilon, Alpha Tau Omega. Achievements include patents in field. Home and Office: 77 Stanton Rd Darien CT 06820-5128 E-mail: jcforman@alum.mit.edu.

FORMAN, LORI ANN, federal agency administrator; b. Sioux Falls, S.D., Dec. 4, 1958; d. Richard William and Duaine Berenice (Erickson) F. BA, Augustana Coll., 1979; M in Pub. Policy, Harvard U., 1981. Cons. OILDECO, Sandvika, Norway, 1980; sr. polit. analyst Decision Making Info., Washington, 1981-83; spl. asst. U.S. Agy. Internat. Devel., Washington, 1983-87, sr. advisor, 1987-89, program officer, 1989-90; exec. v.p. Pacific Mgmt. Resources Inc., Honolulu, 1990; dir. Japan program Nature Conservancy, Arlington, Va., 1990—2001; asst. adminr. bur. for asia and near east USAID, Washington, 2001—. Lectr. in field. Reviewer; (book) Japan's Foreign Aid, 1990; contbg. reviewer (book) Yen for Development, 1990. Vol. Presdls. Youth for Ford, Kansas City, Mo., 1976, Saiki for Senate, Honolulu, 1992; vice chmn. Community Devel. Citizens Adv. Com., Sioux Falls, S.D., 1978-79; mem. internal audit com. Georgetown Luth. Ch., Washington, 1995. Harry S. Truman scholar Truman Found., 1979; ITT Internat. fellow Inst. Internat. Edn., 1980; named one of Ten Outstanding Young People Osaka Jr. C. of C., 1992. Mem. Soc. Internat. Devel., Japan-Am. Soc., Washington Area Bicycle Assn., Asia Soc., Sushi Club. Avocations: reading, cycling, scuba diving, sewing, travel. Office: USAID Bur for Asia and Near East RRB 1300 Pennsylvania Ave Nw Washington DC 20523-4900 Office Fax: 202-216-3386.

FORMAN, RICHARD T. T. ecology educator; b. U.S.A. BS, Haverford Coll., 1957; postgrad., Duke U., 1959-60; PhD, U. Pa., 1961; MA (hon.), Harvard U., 1985; LHD (hon.), Miami U., 1987; DSc (hon.), Fla. Internat. U., 2001. Vol. Am. Friends Svc. Com., Guatemala and Honduras, 1961-63; asst. prof. U. Wis., 1963-66; mem. faculty Rutgers U., New Brunswick, N.J., 1966-84, prof. botany, 1976-84, dir. grad. program, 1979-83; prof. landscape ecology Harvard U., Cambridge, Mass., 1984—; dir. Hutcheson Meml. Forest Ctr., N.J., 1972-84. Instr. field stas., Wis., Costa Rica, St. Croix, N.Mex., 1964-76; fellow Clare Hall, U. Cambridge, Eng., 1985—; hon. prof. Acad. Sinica, China, 1995. Author: Landscape Ecology, 1986, Land Mosaics, 1995, Landscape Ecology Principles for Landscape Architecture and Land-use Planning, 1996, Road Ecology, 2002; editor: Pine Barrens: Ecosystem and Landscape, 1979, 2nd edit., 1998, Changing Landscapes: An Ecological Perspective, 1990; mem. editl. bd. Ecology and Ecol. Monographs, 1973-77, Biosci., 1978-84, Landscape Ecology, 1987-2001; contbr. articles to profl. jours. Recipient award for excellence in tchg. Lindback Found., 1984, medal U. Florence, Italy, 1997, Charles U., Prague, Czech Republic, 1998; Fulbright scholar, Bogota, Colombia, 1970-71; chercheur CNRS, Montpellier, France, 1977-78; Miegunyah fellow U. Melbourne, 1999. Fellow AAAS; mem. Ecol. Soc. Am. (v.p. 1982-83), Torrey Bot. Club (pres. 1980-81, editorial bd. Bull. 1967-70), Nature Conservancy (bd. dirs. Mass. chpt. 2001—), Internat. Assn. Landscape Ecology (v.p. 1982-88, Disting. Landscape Ecologist award U.S. Sect., 1992, Disting. Scholarship award 1999), Societa Ecol. Paessagio Italiana (hon. mem.). Office: Harvard U Harvard Design Sch Cambridge MA 02138

FORMAN, SANDRA H. theater educator; b. Charlotte, N.C., July 9, 1944; d. Willis Edward Hopper and Mary Harriet Blackwell; m. Richard Charles Forman, Apr. 16, 1967; children: Rhyan Danette, Anna Regan, Daniel Edward. BA, U. N.C. Greensboro, 1966, MFA, 1971. Instr. Guilford Coll., Greensboro, NC, 1969—72; lectr., asst. prof., assoc. prof. U. N.C. Greensboro, 1977—89; prof. Theatre No. Ky. U., Highland Heights, 1990—. Dir. Va. Shakespeare Festival, Williamsburg, 2002. Author: Your Voice and Articulation, 1984, Public Speaking: Today and Tomorrow, 1989, Only Mystery: Lorca's Poetry etc., 1992; actor: Fox Rock Theatre Co., 2000, N.C. Shakespeare, 1988. Dist. pres.-Mid Atlantic Nat. Coun. Jewish Women, 1982—84. Mem.: Southeastern Theatre Conf., Internat. Hemingway Soc. (chair by-laws com.). Office: No Ky Univ Theatre Dept Nunn Dr Highland Heights KY 41099

FORMAN, WILLIAM HARPER, JR., lawyer; b. Houston, Aug. 13, 1936; s. William Harper and Ermaleen (Lukas) F.; m. Olive Goodwill Roberts, June 17, 1967; 1 child, William Harper III. BA, Tulane U., 1958, JD, 1961; postgrad., Coll. of William and Mary, 1965; MA in Govt., La. State U., 1970. Bar: La. 1961, U.S. Dist. Ct. (ea. dist.) La. 1982, U.S. Ct. Mil. Appeals 1989. Commd. 1st lt. USAF, 1961, advanced through grades to capt., 1967, judge adv., 1961-63; lt. col. USAFR, 1981-89; project leader Gulf South Rsch. Inst., La., 1968-69; atty. FTC, New Orleans, 1969-72, sec. consumer adv. bd., 1970-72, pub. info. officer, 1971-72, vice-chmn. consumer adv. bd., 1972-73; atty. City of New Orleans, Community Improvement Agy., 1972-79; pvt. practice New Orleans, 1977—; of counsel Law Office of Robert C. Evans, 1986-88; assoc. Law Offices of Inabnett, Suthon, Forman and Justrabo, New Orleans, 1989-95; adj. prof. dept. polit. sci. Tulane U., New Orleans, 1995-99. Lectr. mil. criminal law Tulane U., U. New Orleans, 1972-91; lectr. internat. law of war, mil. criminal law Tulane U., 1978-85; adj. prof. Naval War Coll., New Orleans, 2000—. Author texts for La. State Hist. Markers, Calumet Plantation and Jefferson City in New Orleans, 1971, 79; contbr. articles to profl. jours. Chmn. ROTC Awards Commn., 1975—87, ceremony commemorating birthday of George Washington, 1995—96; Counsel Downtown Devel. Dist., New Orleans, 1975—81; mem. La. State Consumer Adv. Bd., 1975—81; notary pub., 1975—; incorporator Preservation Resource Ctr. New Orleans, 1974; treas., 1974—76; trustee La. Landmarks Soc., 1978—79, 1981—83; corr. sec., 1979—81; v.p. La. SAR, 1981—87, 1997—2000; chpt. chmn. ROTC Awards Commn., 1987—; treas. La. Assn. Soc. of Cin., 1983—85, v.p., 1985, pres., 1987—89; vestry Christ Ch. Cathedral, 2000; bd. dirs. Jefferson City Improvement Assn. New Orleans, 1977—78; pres., 1975—77, 1978—79; bd. dirs. La. Consumers' League, 1970—72; pres., 1972—9173. Maj. USAR, 1981—89. Decorated Meritorious Svc. medal USAF, 1990; recipient Meritorious Svc. medals SAR, 1981, 87, 95, Patriot medal 1990, Bronze Good Citizenship medal, 1996, Silver Good Citizenship medal, 2001; George Washington Disting. Prof. La. Assn. Soc. Cincinnati. Mem. ABA, La. State Bar Assn. (pub. rels. com. 1970-72, chmn. consumer protection com. 1972-78). Home: 5301 Camp St New Orleans LA 70115-3035

FORMBY, BENT CLARK, immunologist; b. Copenhagen, Apr. 3, 1940; naturalized, 1991; s. John K. and Gudrun A. (Dinesen) F.; m. Irene Menck-Thygesen, June 28, 1963 (div. May 1980); children: Rasmus, Mikkel; m. Florence G. Schmid, June 28, 1980. BA in Philosophy summa cum laude, U. Copenhagen, 1959, PhD in Biochemistry, 1968, DSc, 1976. Asst. prof. U. Copenhagen, 1969-73, assoc. prof., 1973-79, prof., 1979-83; vis. prof. U. Calif., San Francisco, 1979-84; sr. scientist, dir. lab. of immunology Sansum Med. Rsch. Found., Santa Barbara, Calif., 1984-99; dir. rsch. The Rasmus Inst. Med. Rsch., Santa Barbara, Calif., 2000—; chmn., CEO Rasmus Pharms. Inc., 2002—. Cons. Cell Tech., Inc., Boulder, Colo., 1989—, Immunex Corp., Seattle, 1989—; med. adv. bd. Biocellular Rsch. Orgn., Ltd., London, Childrens Hosp. of Orange County, Lautenburg Ctr. for Gen. and Tumor Immunology, Hebrew U., Hadassah Med. Sch., Jerusalem, 1993—. Co-author: Lightsout, 2000, Sex, Lies and Menopause: The Choking Truth About HRT, 2003; editor: Fetal Islet Transplantation, 1988, 2d edit. 1995; contbr. articles to profl. jours.; patentee on non-invasive glucose measurement; BH55 Hyaluronidase. Grantee, Juvenile Diabetes Found., 1987, 1988, E.L. Wiegand Found., 1993, Santa Barbara Cottage Hosp. Rsch. Found., 1993—94, 2001—02, U. Calif. Breast Cancer Rsch. Found., 1995—98. Mem. N.Y. Acad. Scis., Am. Diabetes Assn. (grantee 1985, 86, 89, pres. Santa Barbara chpt. 1995), Am. Fedn. Clin. Rsch., European Assn. for the Study of Diabetes. Avocations: painting, swimming. Office: The Rasmus Inst Med Rsch 1620 Eucalyptus Hill Rd Santa Barbara CA 93103-2812 E-mail: bcformby@aol.com.

FORMELLER, DANIEL RICHARD, lawyer; b. Chgo., Aug. 15, 1949; s. Vernon Richard and Shirley Mae (Gruber) F.; m. Ann M. Paa, Aug. 17, 1974; children: Matthew Daniel, Kathryn Ann, Christina Marie. BA with honors, U. Ill., 1970; JD cum laude, DePaul U., 1976. Bar: (Ill.) 1976, (U.S. Dist. Ct. (no. and ctrl. dist.) Ill.) 1976, (U.S. Ct. Appeals (7th and 9th cirs.)) 1976, (U.S. Ct. Appeals (D.C. cir.)) 1995. Assoc. McKenna, Storer, Rowe, White & Farrug, Chgo., 1976-82, ptnr., 1982-86, Tressler, Soderstrom, Maloney & Priess, Chgo., 1986—. Editor: DePaul U. Law Rev., 1975—76. With USN, 1970—72, Vietnam. Mem. ABA, Ill. Bar Assn., Ill. Assn. Def. Trial Counsel (pres. 1994-95), Chgo. Bar Assn., Assn. Def. Trial Attys. (v.p. 2003). Office: Tressler Soderstrom et al 233 S Wacker Dr Chicago IL 60606-6306 E-mail: dformeller@mail.tsmp.com.

FORMENTO, DANIEL, radio company executive, writer; b. Pitts., Aug. 11, 1954; s. Stephen P. and Betty Jean (McCorkle) F.; m. Alison Ashley, Oct. 7, 1995; children: Alexander Daniel, Natalie Annette. Grad. high sch., Mt. Lebanon, Pa. Program mgr. The Source/NBC Radio Network, N.Y.C., 1979-82; prin. Dan Formento Prodns., N.Y.C., 1982-84; pres. Radio Today Entertainment, N.Y.C., 1984—, West Hill Studios, N.J., 1993—. V.p., creative dir. ABC Radio Network, 1998. Author: Rock Chronicle, 1982; producer radio programs including Flashback, 1984, Rock Stars, 1985—, Walter Cronkite's 20th Century, 1988, Pop Quiz, 1992—; radio comml. Grog Shop, 1976 (Aftra award 1976); announcer radio feature Today in Rock History, 1979—; TV comml. Short Cuts, 1989—; producer radio feature One Minute With, 1976 (Golden Quill award 1976), Pop Quiz, 1992— (Internat. Radio Festival of N.Y. grand award 1992). Democrat. Avocations: swimming, tennis, audio enthusiast. Office: ABC Radio Network 444 Madison Ave New York NY 10022-6903

FORMICHI, VIRGINIA JEANNE, retired social welfare administrator; b. San Francisco, Nov. 16, 1925; d. John and Marie F. BA, Dominican U. San Rafael, 1946; MSW, Cath. U., 1948; LLB-JD, U. San Francisco, 1952; postgrad., U. Calif., 1955. Cert. social worker. Asst. regional dir. Cath. Relief Svcs.; dir. adoption agy. Cath. Com. for Refugees; case worker, supr. Liason Cath. Social Svcs., San Francisco. Translated and edited Molino and Cataldi "Social Welfare in Italy". Scholarship com. Dominican U., 1972—, trustee, 1984—87; pres. Dominican U. Alumni Assn., 1984—87. Recipient Commendation, Govt. Malta Minister of Welfare, Pro Ecclesia Et Pontifice medal, Pope Paul VI, Order of Merit, Govt. Italy, Papal Order of the Holy Sepulchre. Mem. Acad. Cert. Social Workers, Nat. Assn. Social Workers (European chpt. pres.), Calif. Conf. Cath. Social Workers (v.p.), Met. Club (bd. dirs. 2001-2002), San Francisco Garden Club (bd. dirs. 2002-), Phi Delta Delta. Home: 3330 Pierce St # 204 San Francisco CA 94123-2036

FORMO, BRENDA TERRELL, travel company executive; b. Greensboro, N.C., May 18, 1946; d. Walter C. Terrell and Eunice W. Kirkman; m. Robert A. Formo, Oct. 14, 1978; 1 child, Eric Victor. BSBA, East Carolina U., 1968; MA in Bus. Adminstrn., Webster U., 1977; postgrad., 1970, 72, 77, 84, 87; grad., Army War Coll., 1990. Commd. 2d lt. U.S. Army, 1969, advanced through grades to col., 1991, ret., 1993; acctg. instr. U.S. Army Fin. Sch., Ft. Harrison, Ind., 1969-71; women's officer recruiter U.S. Army Kansas City Recruiting Main Sta., 1971-73; recruiting ops. officer U.S. Army SW Recruiting Command, San Antonio, 1973-75; area comdr. U.S. Army San Antonio Dist. Recruiting Command, 1975-77; chief pay and examination divsn. U.S. Army Fin. and Acctg. Office, Yongsan, Korea, 1977-78; asst. chief acctg. U.S. Army Mil. Dist. Washington Fin. and Acctg. Office, 1978-80; banking officer U.S. Army Europe Office of the Dep. Chief of Staff for Resource Mgmt., 1980-84; fin. and acctg. officer Def. Nuclear Agy., 1984-87; investigator Office of Dept. of the Army Inspector Gen., 1987-91; chief programs and analysis divsn. Dept. Army Office of Dep. Chief of Staff for Logistics, 1991-93; fin. mgmt. cons., 1993-96; co-founder, pres. BRE Travel, 1996—. Active Guilford Coll. United Meth. Ch., Greensboro. Decorated Legion of Merit with oak leaf cluster (2 awards), Meritorious Svc. medal with 3 oak leaf clusters (4 awards), Army Commendation medal with 4 oak leaf clusters (5 awards). Mem. Assn. U.S. Army, Cardinal Golf and Country Club (Greensboro). Address: 4116 Obriant Pl Greensboro NC 27410-8372

FORNAGE, BRUNO DENIS, radiologist, educator; b. Reims, France, July 2, 1949; came to U.S., 1987; s. Louis and Genevieve (Mercier) F.; m. Brigitte Wittmer, Oct. 18, 1991; 1 child, Louis Bruno. MD, Med. Sch. Reims, 1974. Diplomate French Bd. Radiology, French Bd. Oncology. Resident in oncology Inst. Jean-Godinot Regional Cancer Ctr., Reims, 1974-76, resident in radiology, 1976-79, asst. dept. biophysics and nuc. medicine, 1976-82, dir. dept. radiology, 1982-87; assoc. prof. radiology U. Reims, 1986-87; assoc. prof. radiology, chief sect. ultrasound U. Tex. M.D. Anderson Cancer Ctr., Houston, 1987-2000, prof. radiology, 1990—, prof. surg. oncology, 1999—. Author 5 textbooks; editor 2 textbooks; mem. editl. bd. various jours.; editor-in-chief Jour. of Clin. Ultrasound, 1997—; reviewer jours.; contbr. chpts. to books, articles to profl. jours.; patentee in field. Fellow Am. Inst. Ultrasound in Medicine, Soc. Radiologists in Ultrasound, Soc. Breast Imaging; mem. Am. Roentgen Ray Soc., Radiol. Soc. N.Am., Am. Coll. Radiology, Am. Soc. Breast Disease, Internat. Skeletal Soc., numerous others. Office: U Tex MD Anderson Canc Ctr 1515 Holcombe Blvd Houston TX 77030-4009 E-mail: fornage@swbell.net., bfornage@di.mdacc.tmc.edu.

FORNARA, CHARLES WILLIAM, historian, classicist, educator; b. N.Y.C., Nov. 19, 1935; s. Charles and Dorothy Mae (Stind) F.; 1 son, Charles William III. BA, Columbia U., 1956; MA, U. Chgo., 1958; PhD, UCLA, 1961. Instr. Ohio State U., Columbus, 1961-63; from asst. prof. to prof. classics and history Brown U., Providence, 1963—, David Benedict prof. classics, 1989—. Vis. prof. U. Tex., Austin, 1976; prof. Greek history Inst. Ancient History, Ann Arbor, Mich., summer 1977; vis. fellow Humanities Rsch. Ctr. Australian Nat. U., Canberra, spring 1983; lectr. Australian univs., 1983, English univs., 1987, U. Amsterdam, 1995. Author: Herodotus, An Interpretative Essay, 1971, The Athenian Board of Generals, 1971, Archaic Times to the End of the Peloponnesian War, 1977, 2d edit., 1983, The Nature of History in Ancient Greece and Rome, 1983, (with Loren Samons II) From Cleisthenes to Pericles, 1991 (commentary) Continuation of Felix Jacoby, Die Fragmente der griechischen Historiker III c, 1994; contbr. articles and revs. in field to profl. jours. John Simon Guggenheim fellow, 1988-89. Mem. Am. Philol. Assn., Soc. for Promotion Hellenic Studies. Clubs: Providence Art. Home: 527 Mooresfield Rd Saunderstown RI 02874-1208 Office: Brown Univ Dept Classics Providence RI 02912-0001

FORNARI, MARCO, physicist; b. Verbania, Italy, June 30, 1968; came to U.S., 1998; m. C. Pastorelli, May 16, 1998. Laurea in fisica, U. Pavia, Italy, 1992, specialista in scienza e tec. dei mat., 1995; dottorato di ricerca, U. Trieste, Italy, 1998. Rsch. scientist Inst. Nat. Fisica Della Materia, Trieste, 1997-98, Naval Rsch. Lab., Washington, 1998—2001; rsch. faculty George Mason U., Fairfax, Va., 1998—2001; asst. prof. Ctrl. Mich. U., Mt. Pleasant, Mich., 2001—. Recipient fellowship U. Pavia, 1993-94, fellowship Ministero U. Ricerca, 1995-98. Mem. AAAS, Am. Phys. Soc., Materials Rsch. Soc., Sigma Xi. Home: 117 N Fancher St Mount Pleasant MI 48858 Office: Ctrl Mich U Dept Phy Dow 228 Mount Pleasant MI 48859

FORNERIS, JEANNE M. lawyer; b. Duluth, Minn., May 23, 1953; d. John Domenic and Elva Lorraine (McDonald) F.; m. Michael Scott Margulies, Feb. 6, 1982. AB, Macalester Coll., 1975; JD, U. Minn., 1978. Bar: Minn. 1978. Assoc. Halverson, Watters, Bye, Downs & Maki, Ltd., Duluth, 1978-81, Briggs & Morgan, P.A., Mpls., St. Paul, 1981-83; ptnr. Hart & Bruner, P.A., Mpls., 1983-86; assoc. gen. counsel M.A. Mortenson Co., Mpls., 1986-90, v.p., gen. counsel, 1990-96; with Gen. Counsel, Ltd., Mpls., 1997-98; v.p., sr. counsel Medtronic, Inc., Mpls., 1999—. Instr. women's studies dept. U. Minn., Mpls., 1977-79. Author profl. edn. seminars; contbr. articles to profl. jours. Bd. dirs. Good Will Indusries Vocat. Enterprises, Inc., 1979-81; chmn. bd. trustees Duluth Bar Libr., 1981; mem. United Way Family and Individual Svcs. Task Force, Duluth, 1981. Nat. Merit Assn. scholar, 1971. Fellow Am. Coll. Constrn. Lawyers (bd. dirs.); mem. AMA, Am. Arbitration Assn. (mem. large complex case panel), Minn. State Bar Assn., Minn. Women Lawyers (bd. dirs.), U.S. Dist. Ct. Hist. Soc. (pres.). Democrat. Roman Catholic. Office: Medtronic Inc 7000 Central Ave NE Minneapolis MN 55432-3576

FORNESS, STEVEN ROBERT, educational psychologist; b. Denver, May 13, 1939; s. Robert E. and Rejeana C. (Houck) F. BA in English, U. No. Colo., 1963, MA in Ednl. Psychology, 1964; EdD in Spl. Edn., UCLA, 1968. Tchr. Santa Maria High Sch., Calif., 1964—66; counselor Sch. Edn. UCLA, 1966—68; spl. educator Neuropsychiat. Inst., 1968—2003, chief ednl. psychology child outpatient dept., 1970—2003, mem. mental retardation rsch. ctr., 1970—2003, prof. dept. psychiatry, 1972—2003, prin. inpatient sch., 1976—2003, dir. mental retardation and devel. disabilities tng. program, 1985—92, disting. prof. emeritus, 2003—. Grant rev. panelist U.S. Dept. Edn., 1974-2000; cons. Nat. Assn. Exceptional Children, Venezuela, 1974-2000; commn. ednl. psychology Calif. State Bd. Behavioral Scis. Examiners, 1977-99. Specialist in classroom observation tech. early identification of children with learning and behavior disorders; author publs. including (with Frank Hewett) Education of Exceptional Learners, 3d edit., 1984, (with K. Kavale) Science of Learning Disabilities, 1985, (with Kavale and Bender) Handbook of Learning Disabilities, vols. I, II and III, 1987, 88; (with K. Kavale) Nature of Learning Disabilities, 1995, Efficacy of Special Education, 1999, (with E. Sinclair) Learning Disabilites and Related Disorders, 2002; cons. editor various jours. Sr. scholar Shaklee Inst. on Spl. Edn., 1996-2001. Fulbright scholar Ministry of Edn., Portugal, 1976 Fellow Internat. Acad. Rsch. in Learning Disabilties, Am. Assn. Mental Retardation; mem. Tchr. Educators of Children with Behavior Disorders (pres. 1985-86), Coun. Children with Behavior Disorders (pres. 1987-88, Leadership award 1995), Am. Assn. Univ. Affiliated Programs in Developmental Disabilities (interdisciplinary coun. 1972-89), Internat. Coun. for Exceptional Children (del. Assembly 1988-91, Wallin award 1992, Excellence in Tchr. Edn. award 1995, honors com. 1999-2002), Acad. on Mental Retardation (exec. com. 1989-91), Nat. Mental Health and Spl. Edn. Coalition (co-chair of Definition Task Force 1987-2000), Am. Psychiat. Assn. (DSM IV subcom. on learning disorders 1988-94), Profl. Group for Attention and Related Disorders (com. profl. advisors 1990-91), Midwest Symposium on Behavioral Disorders (Leadership award 1993), Am. Acad. Child and Adolescent Psychiatry (co-chmn. practice parameters on learning disabilities 1996-98, Sidney Berman award on learning disorders 2000), Knights of Malta (Order of St. John 1994). Home: 11901 W Sunset Blvd Los Angeles CA 90049-4240 Office: UCLA Dept Psychiatry 760 Westwood Plz Los Angeles CA 90095-8353

FORNEY, G(EORGE) DAVID, JR., retired electronics company executive; b. N.Y.C., Mar. 6, 1940; s. George David Forney and Priscilla (Brush) Forney McDonnell; m. Harriett A. Bascom, June 9, 1962 (div. 1989); children: Mark Hamilton, Priscilla Jean, William McDonnell. BS in Engring., Princeton U., 1961; MSc, MIT, 1963, ScD, 1965. Mem. tech. staff Codex Corp., Watertown, Mass., 1965-70, v.p. rsch. Newton, Mass., 1970-75, v.p. R&D, 1975-78, v.p. rsch., 1978-82, v.p. tech. and bus. dept., 1986-89; v.p., dir. tech. and planning Motorola Info. Sys. Group, Mansfield, 1982-86; v.p. tech. staff Motorola, Inc., Mansfield, 1980-99. Vis. scientist Stanford (Calif.) U., 1971-72, vis. prof., 1990, mem. adv. coun., 1990-94; adj. prof. MIT, Cambridge, 1980-82, Bernard M. Gordon adj. prof., 1996—; mem. adv. coun. dept. elec. engring., Princeton (N.J.) U., 1977-99, Columbia, N.Y.C., 1986-93, Harvard U., Cambridge, 1995—. Author: Concatenated Codes, 1966; contbr. articles to profl. jours.; patentee in field. Bd. dirs. Am. Field Svc., N.Y.C., 1971-74, Aware, Inc., 1999—; trustee Lehrman Inst., N.Y.C., 1973-80, Mt. Auburn Hosp., Cambridge, 1986—; overseer Shady Hill Sch., Cambridge, 1980-86. Recipient Christopher Columbus award in Internat. Comm., 1996; Marconi Internat. fellow, 1997; named to Mass. Telecom Hall of Fame, 2001. Fellow AAAS, Am. Acad. Arts and Scis., IEEE (editor jour. 1970-73, Info. Theory Group award 1970, Browder J. Thompson prize paper award 1972, Centennial medal 1984, Donald G. Fink prize paper award 1990, Edison medal 1992, Shannon award 1995, Inf. Theory Golden Jubilee awards 1998); mem. NAE, NAS, IEEE Info. Theory Soc. (pres. 1992), Popov Soc. (Russia, hon.). Home and Office: 1010 Memorial Dr Apt 3G Cambridge MA 02138-4853 E-mail: forneyd@comcast.net.

FORNEY, ROBERT CLYDE, retired chemical industry executive; b. Chgo., Mar. 13, 1927; s. Peter Clyde and Hildur (Hoglund) F.; m. Marilyn Glenn, Apr. 3, 1948; children: Gerald Glenn, Barbara Dale, Robert C. BSChemE, Purdue U., 1947, MS, 1948, PhD, 1950. With E.I. DuPont de Nemours, Wilmington, Del., 1950—, asst. gen. mgr. textile fibers dept., 1970-75, v.p., gen. mgr., 1975-77, v.p. plastic products and resins, 1977-78, sr. v.p., 1979-81, exec. v.p., 1981-89, also bd. dirs., ret., 1989. Mem. AIChE, NAE, AAAS, Am. Chem. Soc., Sigma Xi. Republican. Lutheran. Home: PO Box 549 Unionville PA 19375-0549

FORNEY, RONALD DEAN, elementary school educator, consultant, educational therapist; b. Kearney, Nebr., June 28, 1954; s. Carl Roger and Florence Alyce (Gordon) F. Student, Community Coll. Denver, 1972-73; BA in Liberal Arts, Loretto Heights Coll., Denver, 1975; AS in Devel. Psychology, Arapahoe Community Coll., Denver, 1977; MBA, Calif. State Coll., San Bernardino, 1992; MS in Ednl. Adminstrn., Nat. U., 1993. Cert. tchr., English tchr., Calif.; cert. ednl. therapist. Tchr. Lake Elsinore (Calif.) Sch. Dist., 1985-87, Banning (Calif.) Unified Sch. Dist., 1987—, master tchr., classroom mgmt.-assertive discipline cons., 1990—, asst. prin. Ctrl. Elem. Sch., 1996-98. Cons. visual and performing arts, motivation and self-esteem bldg; ednl. therapist in pvt. practice, 1998—. Recipient cert. in affective domain Lake Elsinore Sch. Dist., 1986, Outstanding Tchr. award Hemmerling Sch., Banning, 1989. Avocations: theatre, reading, writing and reading haiku poetry.

FORNI, PATRICIA ROSE, dean, nursing educator; b. St. Louis, Feb. 14, 1932; d. Harold and Glenda M. (Keay) Brown. BSN., Washington U., St. Louis, 1955, MS (USPHS trainee), 1957; PhD (USPHS fellow), St. Louis U., 1965; postgrad. (USPHS scholar), U. Minn., summers 1968, 70. Staff nurse McMillan EENT Hosp., St. Louis, summer 1955, Renard Psychiat. Hosp., St. Louis, part-time 1955-57; rsch. asst. Washington U. Sch. Nursing, St. Louis, 1957-59, rsch. assoc., 1959-61, asst. prof., 1964-66, assoc. dean in charge grad. edn., assoc. prof. gen. nursing sci., 1966-68; assoc. prof. pub. health nursing Wayne State U., Detroit, 1968-69; asst. dir. for manpower and edn. Ill. Regional Med. Program, Chgo., 1969-71; project dir. Midwest Continuing Profl. Edn. for Nurses, St. Louis U., 1971-75; dean, prof. nursing So. Ill. U., Edwardsville, 1975-88; dean, prof. Coll. Nursing U. Okla., Oklahoma City, 1988—. Grant proposal reviewer Divsn. Nursing, USPHS, 1972-79, 88, 91, NSF, 1978, U.S. Dept. Edn., 1980; mem. Ill. Implementation Commn. on Nursing, 1975-77, Okla. State Health Plan Adv. Com., 1994—. Mem. peer rev. panel Nursing Outlook, 1987-91; mem. editl. bd. Health Care for Women Internat., 1984—, Jour. Profl. Nursing, 1988-90. Chairwoman articulation of nursing programs task force Okla. State Regents for Higher Edn., 1990-91; bd. dirs. Greater St. Louis Health Sys. Agy., 1976-81, Adult Edn. Coun. Greater St. Louis, 1973-76, Edwardsville unit Am. Cancer Soc., 1981-88. Fellow WHO, Sweden, Finland, 1985. Mem. Nat. League for Nursing (accreditation site visitor 1979—, nominating com. Coun. Baccalaureate and Higher Degree Programs 1979-82, pub. policy and legis. com. 1981-85, bd. dirs. 1991-93, treas. 1991-93, mem. fin. com. 1991-95), Nat. League for Health Care (trustee 1991-93), Nat. League for Nursing Accrediting Commn. (peer review panel, baccalaureate and higher degree programs 1997-2000, commr. 2000-, chmn. 2001-), Am. Nurses Assn. (chmn. continuing edn. publs. com. 1975-76), Mo. Nurses Assn. (chmn. edn. com. 1973-77), Greater St. Louis Soc. Health Manpower Edn. and Tng. (chmn. legis. com. 1974-75), Midwest Alliance in Nursing (1st governing bd. 1979-80, 93-96, chmn. nominations com. 1980, 81, mem. fin. com. 1993-94, chair fin. com. 1994-96, treas. 1994-96, pres. 1998-2000), Am. Assn. Colls. Nursing (program com. 1978-82, mem.-at-large, bd. dirs. 1990-92, chair rsch. com. 1990-92), Ill. Coun. Deans/Dirs. Baccalaureate and Higher Degree Programs in Nursing (chmn. 1979-81), Am. Acad. Nursing (treas., chairwoman fin. com., mem. gov. coun. 1989-93, editor Newsletter 1982-87), Ill. Nurses Assn. (commn. on adminstrn. 1983-87, commn. on edn. 1987-89), Okla. Nurses Found. (pres. bd. trustees 1990-93), Sigma Theta Tau Internat. (charter mem. Epsilon Eta chpt. 1980). Office: U Okla Coll Nursing PO Box 26901 Oklahoma City OK 73190-0001

FORNO, KARIN IDA, physician, educator; b. San Francisco, Calif., Dec. 27, 1958; d. Lysia Saxe and Bert Holck Forno. BS, Stanford U., 1977—81; MD, Med. Coll. Pa., 1981—85; MA in English Lit., CSU, Stanislaus, 1999—2002; MFA, CSU, Chico, 1999—2003. Diplomate Am. Bd. Family Practice, 1985. Family physician Contra Costa County Health Services, Martinez, Calif., 1988—91, Cornerstone Family Practice Med. Group, Modesto, Calif., 1991—99; family practice attending physician Scenic Faculty Med. Group, Modesto, Calif., 1999—; tchg. asst. CSU, Stanislaus, 2000—02, adj. instr., English, 2002—. Recipient Alpha Omega Alpha Med. Honors Soc. Membership, Alpha Omega Alpha, 1985; fellow Mary Stuart Rogers Grad. Fellowship, Mary Stuart Rogers Fellowship Com., 2001-2002. Avocations: knitting, handspinning, hiking.

FORNO, LYSIA S. neuropathologist; b. Hallund, Denmark, Feb. 14, 1918; arrived in US, 1954; d. Oluf Valdemar and Othilde Maria (Kousholt) Saxe; m. Bert Holck Forno, Jan. 15, 1954 (dec. July 1978). MD, U. of Copenhagen, Denmark, 1943. Intern to resident various Danish Hosp., Copenhagen, 1943—51; neuropathology fellow Mass. Gen. Hosp., Boston, 1951—52; instr. Stanford Med. Sch., Calif., 1957—69; staff physician Vet. Admin. Med. Ctr., Palo Alto, Calif., 1960—; asst. prof. to prof. Stanford Med. Sch., 1969—89; retired, 1989. Reviewer various med. jours., 1960—. Contbr. articles various profl. jours. Recipient Dedication to Neuropath. award, Am. Assoc. of Neuropath., 1991. Democrat. Achievements include research in experimental and human parkinsonism. MPTP-induced parkinsonism in squirrel monkeys. Nerve cell degeneration and Lewy body inclusions in human Parkinson's disease. Avocations: music, foreign languages, literature. Office: VA Palo Alto Health Care Sys 3801 Miranda Ave Palo Alto CA 94304

FORNOFF, ANN LYNETTE, secondary school educator; b. McCook, Nebr., June 17, 1962; d. Dale Arthur and Eva Marie (Sughroue) Hofman; m. Kevin Ray Fornoff, June 15, 1985; children: Kyle Ryan, Amanda Lynette. BA in English Lang. Arts and Bus., Kearney State Coll., 1984. Tchr. English Palco (Kans.) H.S., 1985; tchr. English, journalism Hayes Center (Nebr.) Schs., 1985—. Journalism advisor, Hayes Ctr. Schs., 1987—, sophomore class advisor, 1985—, sr. class advisor, 1996. Treas. Sacred Heart Ch. Altar Soc., Hayes Center, 1997—, catechism class coord., 1995—. Mem. NEA, NCTE, Nebr. Edn. Assn., Hayes Center Tchrs. Assn. (past pres., v.p., sec. and scholarship chmn.). Avocations: gardening, reading. Home: HC 62 Box 19 Hayes Center NE 69032-9609 E-mail: kfornoff@gpcom.net.

FORNOFF, FRANK J(UNIOR), retired chemistry educator, consultant; b. Mt. Carmel, Ill., Mar. 29, 1914; s. Frank and Ada (Arnold) F. AB, U. Ill., 1936; MS, Ohio State U., 1937, PhD, 1939. Asst. prof. Lehigh U., Bethlehem, Pa., 1942-44; chem. engr. Western Electric Co., N.Y.C., 1944-45; asst. prof. chemistry Lehigh U., 1945-47, assoc. prof., 1947-53, Kans. State U., Manhattan, 1953-56; lectr. Rutgers U., New Brunswick, N.J., 1956-84; sr. examiner Ednl. Testing Svc., Princeton, N.J., 1956-93, group head, 1956-83. Editor AP Chemistry newsletter, 1976-90; contbr. articles to profl. jours. Active Boy Scouts Am., Princeton, 1957-93. NRC fellow U. Calif., Berkeley, 1939-40; Procter and Gamble fellow Ohio State U., 1938-39. Mem. AAAS, Am. Chem. Soc. (chmn. local sect. assn. publs. 1960-70), Am. Soc. Engring. Edn., Nat. Sci. Tchrs. Assn., Nat. Council Measurements in Edn., N.J. Acad. Sci., N.Y. Acad. Sci. Methodist. Home: 110 E 7th St Mount Carmel IL 62863-2033

FORONDA, BARBARA ELAINE, professional organizer, writer; d. Walter Alexander Conway and Myttie Louise Terry; m. Elmer Ganuelas Foronda, Sept. 15, 1974; children: Raenee Elaine, Nicole Michele; m. Charles Vernon Brollier, May 7, 1962 (div. May 10, 1972); children: Karen Alane Brollier, Vernon Alexander Brollier. BA in Economics, San Jose State U., 1983—90. Cert. Netware Adminstr., Novell, 1993; Tech. Comm. De Anza Coll., Calif., 2001. Project mgr. City of San Jose, 1989—90; acctg. Coopers & Lybrand, San Jose, 1996—96; proposal adminstr. ABB, Santa Clara, 1997—2001. Mem.: (NAPO) Nat. Assn. of Profl. Organizers (treasurer-elect 2003—03), (SSG) Seizure Support Group. Independent. Roman Catholic. Avocation: exercise.

FORONDA, ELENA ISABEL, retired secondary school educator; b. Jan. 15, 1947; d. Severino Deliso and LaVerne (Ibanez) F. BS in Music, Hunter Coll., CUNY, 1969, MA in Music Edn., 1971. Permanent cert. tchr., N.Y. Tchr. vocal music Stuyvesant H.S., N.Y.C. Dept. Edn., 1970—2002, substitute vocal music

tchr. Asst. dir. tchr. placement Hunter Coll., City U. N.Y., summers 1971-72; examination asst. N.Y.C. Pub. Sch. System Bd. Examiners, 1987-89; music panelist Bklyn. Arts Coun., 2000—, auditor, 2001—; bd. dirs. Leif Ericson Day Sch., Bklyn., 2002—; asst. choral condr. Manhattan Arts Inst., summer 2003. Sponsor children in World Vision Internat., 1973-97; del. Asiam Am. Women's Caucus, 1977; mem. Hunter Coll. choirs, 1968-69, 71; pianist, min. of music Ch. of the Holy Spirit, Bklyn., 1988-90; lay reader, lay eucharist min. L.I. Diocese Episcopal Ch., 1993-99; bd. dirs. Leif Ericson Day Sch., Bklyn., 2002—; mem. chorus, VA Nat. Med. Group Flag Day Concert, Cannon Caucus Rm., Washington, D.C., 2003; mem. bd. edn. Manhattan Arts Inst., 2003. Dist. winner Nat. Piano Playing Auditions, 1965; grantee SPARC, 1999. Mem. Music Educators Nat. Conf., Music Educators Assn. N.Y.C. (adv. mem.), N.Y. State Sch. Music Assn., Amateur Chamber Music Players. Democrat. Office: 1037 72nd St Brooklyn NY 11228

FORREST, ALLEN WRIGHT, tax and financial services firm executive, accountant, financial planner; b. Quincy, Mass., Nov. 8, 1941; s. Edwin Wright and Sylvia (Locke) F.; m. Helen Frances Kolb, Nov. 10, 1962; children: Deborah, Teresa, Sandra, William. BBA, U. N. Fla., 1980, MS in Acctg., 1981. Enrolled agt., IRS; CFP. Enlisted USN, 1958, advanced through grades to sr. chief petty officer, 1972, resigned, 1977; treas., contr. Fla. Bonded Pools, Inc., Jacksonville, 1977-89; pvt. practice Jacksonville Beach, Fla., 1982-89; pres. Profl. Computer Support Inc., Jacksonville Beach, 1988-90, Forrest & Co., Inc., Jacksonville, Fla., 1989—. Treas. Beaches United Citizens, Jacksonville Beach, 1982. Recipient Carl Burger Meml. Manuscript Nat. Assn. Accts., 1982-83. Mem. Fin. Planning Assn., Fleet Res. Assn., Beaches Bus. Assn., Phi Kappa Phi, Beta Gamma Sigma. Avocations: jogging, weightlifting, microcomputers. Home: 259 Coral Way Jacksonville FL 32250-2911 Office: Forrest & Co Inc 1112 3d St Neptune Beach FL 32266 E-mail: allenforrest@bellsouth.net., aforrest@sigmarep.com.

FORREST, BRADLEY ALBERT, lawyer; b. Mpls., July 15, 1956; s. Vincent Clarence and Beverly (Malmrose) F.; m. Arlene Terry Clementson, Aug. 19, 1978; children: Kelsey, Whitney, Dylan. B in Elec. Engring., U. Minn., 1978, JD, 1981. Bar: Minn. 1981, U.S. Patent and Trademark Office, U.S. Ct. Appeals (fed. cir.) 1982, U.S. Supreme Ct. 1982. Atty. Rosemount Inc., Eden Prairie, Minn., 1981-84, IBM Corp., Rochester, Minn., 1981-93, trademark and copyright counsel Thornwood, N.Y., 1993-95; ptnr. Schwegman, Lundberg, Woessner & Kluth, P.A., Mpls., 1995—. Mem. Am. Intellectual Property Law Assn. (chair subcom. 1996-99, chair 2002-03), Minn. Intellectual Property Law Assn. (treas. 1996-97, sec. 1999-2000, v.p., pres. 2000—). Office: Schwegman Lundberg Woessner & Kluth PA 1600 TCF Tower 121 S 8th St Minneapolis MN 55402-2841

FORREST, DAVID VICKERS, psychiatrist, educator; b. N.Y.C., July 8, 1938; s. Melbourne Arthur and Cleo Florence (Garello); m. Lynne Putnam Stetson; children: Daniel Stetson, Susannah Nissly. AB summa cum laude, Princeton U., 1960; MD, Columbia U., 1964, cert. in psychoanalysis, 1974. Cert. in psychiatry Am. Bd. Psychiatry and Neurology. Intern in medicine St. Luke's Hosp., N.Y.C., 1964-65; resident in psychiatry N.Y. State Psychiat. Inst., Columbia Presbyn. Med. Ctr., N.Y.C., 1965-68; chief psychiatric clinic 935th Med. Det. (KO) 93d Evacuation Hosp., Long Binh, Vietnam, 1968-69; chief psychiatric consultation Letterman Army Med. Ctr., San Francisco, 1969-70; pvt. practice psychiatry N.Y.C., 1970—; mem. psychiatry faculty Columbia U., N.Y.C., 1970—; dir. edn. ednl. rsch. dept. N.Y. State Psychiat. Inst., 1970-77; assoc. prof. clin. psychiatry Columbia U., Coll. Physicians and Surgeons, N.Y.C., 1984—, faculty psychoanalytic ctr., 1974—, consultation-liaison psychiatrist neurology (movement disorders), 1977—, clin. prof. of psychiatry, 2000—. Lectr. psychiatry U. Saigon Med. Sch., Vietnam, 1968-69; lectr. abnormal psychology Far East div. U. Md., Long Binh, Vietnam, 1969. Author: Selected American Expressions, 1974, 76, 82; co-author: Treating Schizophrenic Patients, 1983, (video cassette series) Electronic Textbook of Psychiatry, 1972-77; co-author, pub: The Ballet Company Game, 1973; founding editor, pub. Spring: The Jour. of the E. E. Cummings Soc., N.Y.C., 1980—; editor: Neural Net News, N.Y. State Psychiat. Inst., 1989-91; technical cons. Star Trek TV series, 1997—; contbr. articles to profl. jours., textbooks. Psychiat. cons. N.Y.C. Ballet Co., 1973; first aid instr. Boy Scouts Am., 1983—. Capt. USAF, 1968-70, Vietnam. Decorated Bronze Star; Gen. Motors nat. scholar. Fellow Am. Psychiat. Assn., Am. Coll. Psychiatrists, Am. Acad. Psychoanalysis (program chair), Am. Coll. Psychoanalysts (program chair 1987-89, bd. regents 1989-92, v.p. 1993, pres.-elect 1994, pres. 1995), Explorers Club; mem. Am. Acad. Neurology (assoc.), N.Y. Clin. Soc. (v.p. 1995, pres. 1996). Episcopalian. Avocations: invention, discovery, magic. Office: 133 E 73rd St Ste 211 New York NY 10021-3556 also: 155 W 68th St Apt 1219 New York NY 10023-5818

FORREST, GEORGE PHILIP, physician; b. N.Y.C., Mar. 23, 1951; s. Lawrence Emanuel and Elaine (Cohen) F.; m. Nancy Schwebel, Feb. 15, 1987; children: Emily, Hilary. BA, Cornell U., 1973; MD, Med. Coll. Va., 1978. Intern Brookdale Hosp., Bklyn., 1978-79; resident SUNY, Buffalo, 1979-81; internist Health Care Plan, Buffalo, 1981-83; resident U. Wash., Seattle, 1983-85; attending physician Albany Med. Ctr., 1985-89, chmn. phys. medicine and rehab., 1989—. Mem. Am. Acad. Phys. Medicine and Rehab., Am. Assn. Electrodiagnostic Medicine, Med. Soc. State N.Y. Office: Albany Medical Ctr 47 New Scotland Ave Albany NY 12208-3412

FORREST, HERBERT EMERSON, lawyer; b. N.Y.C., Sept. 20, 1923; s. Jacob K. and Rose (Fried) F.; m. Marilyn Lefsky, Jan. 12, 1952; children: Glenn Clifford, Andrew Matthew. Student, CCNY, 1941, Ohio U., 1943-44; BA with distinction, George Washington U., 1948, JD with highest honors, 1952. Bar: Va. 1952, D.C. 1952, U.S. Supreme Ct. 1956, Md. 1959, U.S. Ct. Appeals (D.C. cir.) 1953, U.S. Ct. Appeals (1st cir.) 1992, U.S. Ct. Appeals (2d cir.) 1971, U.S. Ct. Appeals (3d cir.) 1957, U.S. Ct. Appeals (4th cir.) 1956, U.S. Ct. Appeals (5th cir.) 1981, U.S. Ct. Appeals (7th cir.) 1996, U.S. Ct. Appeals (8th cir.) 1991, U.S. Ct. Appeals (9th cir.) 1994, U.S. Ct. Appeals (11th cir.) 1981. Plate printer Bur. Engraving and Printing, Washington, 1942-43, 1946-52; law clk. to chief judge Bolitha J. Laws U.S. Dist. Ct., Washington, 1952-55; pvt. practice Washington, 1952-87; with Welch & Morgan, 1955-65, Steptoe & Johnson, 1965-85, of counsel, 1986-87; trial atty. fed. programs br. civil divsn. U.S. Dept. Justice, Washington, 1987—; chmn. adv. bd. D.C. Criminal Justice Act, 1971-74; sec. com. admissions and grievances U.S. Ct. Appeals, D.C., 1973-79; title-1 audit hearing bd. U.S. Office Edn. HEW, 1976-79; edn. appeals bd. U.S. Dept. Edn., 1979-82. Mem. Lawyer's Support Com. for Visitors Service Center, 1975-87 Contbr. articles to profl. jours.; mem. edit. bd. Duke Law Jour, 1969-75. Pres. Whittier Woods PTA, 1970-71. With F.A., Signal Corps U.S. Army, 1943-46. Recipient Walsh award in Irish history, 1952, Goddard award in commerce, 1952. Fellow Am. Bar Found. (life), ABA (council 1972-75, 1981-84, budget officer 1985-88, vice chmn. task force on sect. devel. 1987-89, chmn. com. on agy. rule making 1968-72, 1976-81, chmn. membership com. 1984-85, editor ann. reports 1973-88, adminstrv. law sect., fellow adminstrv. law and regulatory practice, mem. comm. com. public utilities law sect., vice chmn. industry regulation com. 1985-86, chmn. comm. subcom. 1983-85, antitrust law sect., internat. law sect., sec. judicial adminstrn., sect. sci. and tech., comm. forum); mem. George Washington Law Assn., Am. Judicature Soc., Va. State Bar Assn., Fed. Bar Assn. (chm. jud. rev. com. 1981-85, vice chmn. adminstrv. law sect. 1985-87), Fed. Comm. Bar Assn. (del. to ABA Ho. Dels. 1979-81, exec. com. 1967-71, 76-84, v.p. 1981-82, pres. 1982-83, chmn. telecomm. com. 1983-87), D.C. Bar Assn. (past sec., exec. com.), NAM, Nat. Conf. Bar Pres., Washington Council Lawyers, Legal Aid and Pub. Defender Assn., Am. Arbitration Assn. (comml. panel 1976-87), D.C. Unified Bar (bd. govs. 1976-79, chmn. com. on employment discrimination complaint service 1973-79, chmn. task force on services to public 1974-78, chmn. com. on appointment counsel in criminal cases 1978-88, co-chmn. com. on participation govt. employees in pro bono activities 1977-79), Broadcast Pioneers, Order of Coif, B'nai Brith, Phi Beta Kappa, Pi Gamma Mu., Artus, Phi Eta Sigma, Phi Delta Phi. Democrat. Home: 8706 Bellwood Rd Bethesda MD 20817-3033 Office: US Dept Justice 20 Massachusetts Ave NW Rm 7112 Washington DC 20530 E-mail: herbert.forrest@usdoj.gov.

FORREST, PAULA SUE, musician, music educator; b. Washington, June 10, 1951; d. Sidney and Faith Forrest; children: Erika Helmuth Saunders, Evan Helmuth. BA with high honors, U. Mich., 1973; MA in Musicology, U. N.C., 1978. Concert prodr. Libr. Congress, Washington, 1975—87; artistic dir. Ames (Iowa) Town and Gown Chamber Music Assn., 1997—; piano faculty Iowa State U., Ames, 2000—. Summer piano faculty Interlochen (Mich.) Ctr. for the Arts, 1993—. Mem.: Mortar Bd, Phi Beta Kappa. Avocations: photography, needlecrafts. Home: 3222 Oakland St Ames IA 50014 Office: Iowa State Univ Ames IA 50011

FORREST, ROBERT EDWIN, lawyer; b. Washington, July 31, 1949; s. Henry Smith and Jane (Witt) F.; m. Deirdre Loretto McGahey, Sept. 23, 1978; children: Matthew Henry, John Robert, Caitlin. BA, Northwestern U., 1971; JD, Georgetown U., 1974. Bar: D.C. 1975, Md. 1984, U.S. Ct. Appeals (D.C. cir.) 1976, U.S. Ct. Appeals (6th cir.) 1985, U.S. Ct. Appeals (11th cir.) 1991, U.S. Dist. Ct. D.C. 1976, U.S. Supreme Ct. 1980, U.S. Dist. Ct. (ea. and we. dists.) Mich. 1981. Law clk. to Hon. June L. Green U.S. Dist. Ct. D.C, Washington, 1974-75; tax div. trial atty. U.S. Dept. Justice, Washington, 1975-81; prin. ptnr. Raymond & Prokop, P.C., Southfield, 1981—. Adj. prof. U. Detroit/Mercy Sch. of Law, 1987—. Trustee Acad. of the Sacred Heart, 2002—. Fellow: Michigan Bar Furdhom; mem.: FBA (exec. bd. 1984—90, pres. 1989—90), Fed. Bar Found. (trustee 1995—), Oakland County Bar Assn. (tax com. 2001—02). Methodist. Home: 4861 Malibu Dr Bloomfield Hills MI 48302-2252 Office: Raymond & Prokop PO Box 5058 Southfield MI 48086-5058 Fax: 248-357-2720. E-mail: rforrest@raypro.com.

FORREST, ROBERT GILLILAND, mathematics educator; b. Norfolk, Va., July 15, 1929; s. James Randolph and Nancy Marie (Gilliland) F.; m. Violet Josephine Robertson, Mar. 23, 1957; children: Nancy, Beth, Scott. AB, Coll. William and Mary, 1955; MA, Ohio State U., 1960; DS, Washington and Jefferson Coll., 1996. Grad. asst. Ohio State U., Columbus, 1955-57; instr. Coll. William and Mary, Norfolk, Va., 1957-60; assoc. prof., dept. chmn. Frederick Coll., Portsmouth, Va., 1960-64; prof. Washington and Jefferson Coll., Washington, Pa., 1965-96, prof. emeritus, 1996—. Grad. fellow Vanderbilt U., Nashville, 1972-74. Mem.: AAUP, Math. Assn. Am., Kappa Alpha, Phi Beta Kappa. Episcopalian. Avocations: music, church music, travel. Home: 820 East Beau St 7L Washington PA 15301-2912

FORREST, SIDNEY, clarinetist, music educator; b. N.Y.C., Aug. 21, 1918; s. Paul and Esther Forrest; m. Faith Levine, Nov. 16, 1941; 1 child, Paula Forrest. Student, Juilliard Sch. Music, 1936-37; BA, U. Miami, Fla., 1939; MA, Columbia U., 1941; studied with Simeon Bellison, Otto Conrad, Alexander Williams. Prof. Peabody Conservatory of Music, Johns Hopkins U., Balt., 1946-85, prof. emeritus, 1985; dir. placement and career counseling Peabody, Balt., 1969-85. Clarinet soloist U.S. Marine Band and Symphony Orch., Washington, 1941-45; prin. clarinet Nat. Symphony, 1946-50; adj. prof. faculty Cath. U., 1954—; faculty Interlochen Ctr. for the Arts, Mich., 1959—, Am. U., 1961-81, Levine Sch. Music, Washington, 1980—; adjudicator Nat. Fulbright Commn., 1980-84, Que. Can. Nat. Conservatoire, 1969-84; former students mem. faculty major conservatories and univs. Editor and arranger clarinet solos including Nocturne No. 20: Chopin, Pastorale: Baermann, Twelve Fantasies for Solo Clarinet: Telemann, Variations on a Theme of Corelli: By Tartini, Four Hebraic Pictures (arranged by S. Bellison), Twelve Fantasies for Solo Saxophone: Telemann, Twelve Fantasies for Solo Oboe: Telemann, others; major full clarinet recitals include Carnegie Recital Hall, Bklyn. Mus., Nat. Art Gallery, Phillips Collection, Libr. Cong., Entrance March of the Boyars: Halvorsen, others; solo clarinet recordings and recitals with Galimir Quarter, Erno Balogh, Bernard Greenhouse, Carlton Cooley, Leonid Hambro, others; recs. include (clarinet quintet) Mozart, (trio with viola and piano) Mozart, (trio with cello and piano) Brahms, (clarinet) Sonata, (with piano) Grand Duo Concertant, Variations op. 33: Von Weber; contbr. articles to profl. jours.; former students in major Am. and overseas opera and symphony orchs.; co-designer (with J. Hall) of Sidney Forrest Signature Clarinet Mouthpiece. Mem. Internat. Clarinet Assn., Music Tchrs. Nat. Assn. Avocations: photography, gardening, stamps, travel. Home: 9611 Kingston Rd Kensington MD 20895-3521 Office: Cath U Rome Sch Music Harewood Rd NW Washington DC 20064-0001

FORRESTAL, ROBERT PATRICK, banker, lawyer; b. N.Y.C., Oct. 31, 1931; s. Patrick A. and Lillian D. (Moran) F.; m. Wilma Anderson, Sept. 29, 1956; 1 child, Renee Marie. BA, St. John's U., 1953; JD, Georgetown U., 1961. Bar: D.C. 1961, U.S. Supreme Ct. 1964. Atty. Spencer & Whalen, Washington, 1961-64, Fed. Res. Bd., Washington, 1964-68, asst. sec., 1968-70, v.p., gen. counsel Atlanta, 1970-74; sr. v.p., gen. counsel Fed. Res. Bank of Atlanta, 1974-79, 1st v.p., 1979-83, pres., 1983-95; ptnr. Smith, Gambrell and Russell, Atlanta, 1996—. Bd. dirs. ING Corp., Genuine Parts Co., Equifax Corp., ING Ins. Co. Bd. dirs. Leadership Atlanta, 1971-73, Child Svcs. and Family Counseling Ctr., Atlanta, 1974-81, Ga. Worlds Congress Inst., 1979-83, United Way of Met. Atlanta, 1984-90, So. Ctr. for Internat. Studies, 1986-94; bd. sponsors Atlanta Symphony Orch., 1973-75; divsn. chmn. United Way, Atlanta, 1980-81; bd. dirs., exec. com. Ga. State U., Atlanta, 1972-83, chmn. recognition fund, 1975, chmn. trustees, 1976-78, mem. bd. advisors Coll. Bus. Adminstrn.; bd. dirs. Ctrl. Atlanta Progress, Piedmont Hosp. Found.; trustee Atlanta Arts Alliance, Oglethorpe U.; mem. adv. bd. Atlanta Humanities Program; bd. visitors Emory U., 1986-89, Berry Coll., 1987-89, Ga. State U. Sch. Law; mem. bd. councilors Carter Ctr.; active Friends of Piedmont Hosp., Piedmont Med. Care Found. Lt. USN, 1953. Fulbright scholar, 1953 Mem. Atlanta C. of C. (bd. dirs. 1984-87, 93-94), Rotary (bd. dirs. 1985-88, 93—), World Trade Club of Atlanta. Home: 3949 Vermont Rd NE Atlanta GA 30319-1212 Office: Smith Gambrell & Russell 1230 Peachtree St NE Ste 3100 Atlanta GA 30309-3592

FORRESTER, ALFRED WHITFIELD, psychiatrist, educator; b. Springfield, Mass., May 15, 1953; s. Wallace Lomax and Alma Mae (Brooks) F. BA magna cum laude, Yale U., 1975; MD, Johns Hopkins U., 1979. Diplomate Nat. Bd. Med. Examiners, Am. Bd. Psychiatry and Neurology. Med. resident dept. medicine Mt. Auburn Hosp., Cambridge, Mass., 1979-82; psychiatry resident dept. psychiatry and behavioral scis. Johns Hopkins Med. Insts., Balt., 1982-85, research fellow, 1985-86, instr., 1986-93; clin. asst. prof. dept. psychiatry U. Md., Balt., 1987—; pvt. psychiat. practice, 1988—. Staff psychiatrist Cann Health Resources, Fallston, Md., 1987-88, The Sheppard and Enoch Pratt Hosp., 1988-97; dir. psychiat. svcs. Chase-Brexton Health Svcs., Balt., 1988-90, staff psychiatrist, 1985-2000; med. dir. Behavioral Sci. Assocs., Lutherville, Md., 1993-97, Nicotine Addiction Treatment Ctrs., Lutherville, 1997-2002; med. cons. Bon Secours Hosp., Balt., 1983-90; psychiat. cons. Shock-Trauma Ctr. U. Md. Hosp., 1987-90. Contbr. articles to profl. jours. Active Groton (Mass.) Sch. Bd. Govs., 1983-85, AIDS com., Med. and Chirurgical Faculty State of Md., 1988-91. Nat. Achievement scholar, 1971-75. Fellow APA; mem. Am. Coll. Physicians, Med. and Chirurgical Faculty State Md., AMA, Md. Psychiatric Soc., Md. Psychiat. Liaison Assn., Yale Alumni Assn. (fundraiser 1975—), Greater Balt. Bus. Profl. Assn. Clubs: Mory's Assn. (New Haven), Yale (Md.). Democrat. Episcopalian. Avocations: classical music, theater. Home: 115 Saint Dunstans Rd Baltimore MD 21212-3311 Office: 9515 Deereco Rd Ste 1001 Timonium MD 21093 E-mail: a.w.forrester@att.net.

FORRESTER, EUGENE PRIEST, former army officer, management marketing consultant; b. Watertown, Tenn., Apr. 17, 1926; s. Robert L. and Christine Elizabeth (Phillips) F.; B.S., U.S. Mil. Acad., 1948; M.A. in Internat. Relations, George Washington U., 1967; LL.D., Chung Ang U. (Republic of Korea), 1981; grad. Command and Gen. Staff Coll., Armed Forces Staff Coll., Brit. Staff Coll., Nat. War Coll.; m. Mary Louise Wagner, Dec. 28, 1953 (dec. 1971); children: Eugene Priest, II, Pamela Louise, Elizabeth Wagner. Commd. 2d lt. U.S. Army, 1948, advanced through grades to lt. gen., 1978; with Command and Gen. Staff Coll., Ft. Leavenworth, Kans., 1958-59; staff officer Supreme Hdqrs. Allied Powers Europe, 1961-63; dep. battle group comdr. 504th Inf., 82d Airborne Divsn., later asst. chief of staff for ops. 82d Airborne Divsn., Ft. Bragg, N.C., 1963-65; mil. asst. to Sec. Army, Washington, 1966; chief forces devel. U.S. Army, Vietnam, 1967-68, comdr. 3d Brigade, 4th Inf. Divsn., 1968; exec. officer to vice chief of staff Dept. Army, Washington, 1968-70; asst. divsn. comdr. 1st Cav. Divsn., Vietnam, 1970; dep. asst. chief of staff Civil Ops. and Rural Devel. Support, Hdqrs. Mil. Assistance Command, Vietnam, 1970-71; dir. officer personnel, later dir. procurement, tng. and distbn., then dir. plans, program and budget, Hdqrs. Dept. Army, 1971-73; comdr. U.S. Army Adminstrn. Center, Ft. Ben Harrison, Ind., 1973-75; comdr. U.S. Army Recruiting Command, Ft. Sheridan, Ill., 1975-78; comdr. 6th U.S. Army, Presidio, San Francisco, 1978-79; comdr. Combined Field Army, Korea, 1979-81; comdr. U.S. Army Western Command, Ft. Shafter, Hawaii, 1981-83; ret., 1983; mgmt. mktg. cons., corp. dir., 1983— . Trustee Nat. Def. U. Found., 1986—. Decorated D.S.M. with oak leaf cluster, Silver Star, Legion of Merit with 3 oak leaf clusters, D.F.C., Bronze Star with 2 oak leaf clusters, Air medal with 18 oak leaf clusters, Joint Svc. Commendation medal, Combat Inf. badge (2), Nat. Order Vietnam 4th-5th class, Gallantry Cross with 2 palms and gold star (Vietnam), Armed Forces Honor medal 1st class (Vietnam), Order of Nat. Sec. Merit Tong-Il medal (Korea), numerous others. Address: Apt 902 1101 S Arlington Ridge Rd Arlington VA 22202-1927

FORRESTER, JAMES RONALD, educator; b. Attleboro, Mass., July 7, 1935; s. Carolyn Kidd Forrester; m. Adelaide Emily Forrester, June 27, 1964; children: Suzanne, Carrie, Kimberly. PhD, W.Va. U., 1979. Prof. polit. sci. West Liberty (W.Va.) State Coll., 1969—. Author: (Book) Government and Politics in West Virginia: Readings, Cases and Commentaries 4th edit., 2000, 5th edit., 2002. Elections cons., 1988, 92. Sgt. U.S.M.C., 1954-57. Mem. Am. Polit. Sci. Assn., W.Va. Polit. Sci. Assn., Northeast Assn. Pre-Law Advisors, Pi Sigma Alpha. Avocation: sailing. Home: 103 Logan Ct Bethany WV 26032 Office: West Liberty State Coll WV Rte 88 West Liberty WV 26074 Fax: 304-336-8014. E-mail: forrestj@wlsc.edu.

FORRESTER, JAY WRIGHT, management specialist, educator; b. Anselmo, Nebr., July 14, 1918; s. Marmaduke M. and Ethel Pearl (Wright) F.; m. Susan Swett, July 27, 1946; children: Judith, Nathan Blair, Ned Cromwell. B.Sc., U. Nebr., 1939, D.Eng. (hon.), 1954; M.Sc., MIT, 1945; D.Sc. (hon.), Boston U., 1969, Union Coll., 1973; D.Eng. (hon.), Newark Coll. Engring., 1971, U. Notre Dame, 1974; D.Polit. Sci. (hon.), U. Mannheim, 1979; LHD (hon.), SUNY, 1988. Instr., X-ray equipment rschr. MIT, Cambridge, 1939-40, co-founder Servomechanisms Lab., 1940, devel. electric and hydraulic servomechanisms for gun mounts and radar, 1940-44, asso. dir. servomechanisms lab., also supr. Whirlwind I digital computer devel., 1944-51, founder Digital Computer Lab., dir., 1951-56, div. head Lincoln Lab. for Air Def., 1951-56, prof. mgmt. Sloan Sch. Mgmt., 1956-72, Germeshausen prof., 1972-89, Germeshausen prof. emeritus, sr. lectr., 1989—. Owner Forrester Cattle Ranch, Dunning, Nebr.; head System Dynamics Group, Sloan Sch., 1960-89. Lectures and tech. papers on digital computers and indsl. mgmt.; also dynamics indsl. and econ. behavior.; author: Industrial Dynamics, 1961, Principles of Systems, 1968, Urban Dynamics, 1969, World Dynamics, 1971, Collected Papers, 1975; patentee servomechanisms, digital info. storage, indsl. control. Recipient Inventor of Yr. award George Washington U., 1968, Valdemar Poulsen Gold medal Danish Acad. Tech. Scis., 1969, Outstanding Accomplishment award Systems, Man and Cybernetics Soc. of IEEE, 1972, Computer Pioneer award IEEE Computer Soc., 1982, Benjamin Franklin fellow Royal Soc. Arts, London, 1972, New Eng. award Engring. Socs. New Eng., 1973, Potts medal Franklin Inst., 1974; Harry Goode Meml. award Am. Fedn. Info. Processing Socs., 1977, Common Wealth award of Disting. Service, 1979, James R. Killain Jr. Faculty Achievement award MIT, 1987, Agricultura 2000 award, Italy, 1987, Info. Storage award IEEE Magnetics Soc., 1988, Lord Found. Leadership award, 1988, U.S. Nat. Medal of Tech., 1989, Pioneer award IEEE Aerospace & Electronic Systems Soc., 1990; named to Nat. Inventors Hall of Fame, 1979; Jay W. Forrester chair named in his honor, MIT. Fellow IEEE (medal of Honor 1972, Pioneer award 1990), Am. Acad. Arts and Scis., Acad. Mgmt.; mem. Nat. Acad. Engring., Inst. Mgmt. Scis., Soc. Mfg. Engrs. (hon.), Am. Phys. Soc., Assn. Computing Machinery, Eta Kappa Nu, Sigma Xi, Sigma Tau. Office: MIT Bldg E60-389 Cambridge MA 02139 E-mail: jforester@mit.edu.

FORRESTER, KEVIN KREG, lawyer; b. Beaver Dam, Wis., June 14, 1957; s. Roger Eugene and Gretchen Adeline (Yungclas) F.; m. Cheryl Kim Bahde, June 6, 1981; children: Courtney Kristine, Christopher Cody. BA, U. Calif., San Diego, 1980; JD, U. San Diego, 1986. Bar: U.S. Supreme Ct. Sales assoc. Century 21, Solana Beach, Calif., 1980-81; broker, assoc. Rand & Stewart Realtors, Rancho Santa Fe, Calif., 1981-83; law clk. Shernoff & Levine, San Diego, 1983-85; asst. to gen. counsel Pacific Scene, Inc., San Diego, 1985-87; atty. pvt. practice, Encinitas, Calif., 1987—. Ct. appointed mediator, bd. of arbitrators NASD Regulation, Inc.; San Diego County Superior Ct. pro tem judge. Pres. Colony of Olivenhain (Calif.) Town Coun., 1990, 91 Mem. Internat. Acad. Mediators, State Bar Calif., Calif. Assn. Realtors, San Diego County Bar Assn., North San Diego County Assn. Realtors, U. Calif. San Diego Alumni Assn. (gen. counsel 1992—, dir. 1985-92), William B. Enright Am. Inn of Ct. Republican. Avocation: running. Office: 4403 Manchester Ave Ste 205 Encinitas CA 92024-7903 E-mail: kforrester@psmkr.com.

FORRESTER, PATRICIA TOBACCO, artist; b. Northampton, Mass., 1940; Student, Yale Summer Sch. Music and Art, 1961; BA, Smith Coll., 1962; BFA, Yale U., 1963, MFA, 1965. Resident Yaddo Found., 1979, 81, The MacDowell Colony Residency, 1980, Hand Hollow Found., 1981, San Francisco Mus. Art, 1967. One woman shows include Trutton Gallery, San Francisco, 1968, Capper's Gallery, San Francisco, 1970, William Sawyer Gallery, San Francisco, 1974, 81, 83, Smith Coll. Fine Arts Bldg., Northampton, 1975, M. H. de Young Meml. Mus., San Francisco, 1977, Kornblee Gallery, N.Y.C., 1978, 79, 81, 82, 83, Fendrick Gallery, Washington, 1978, 79, 81, 88, 90, Sebastian Moore Gallery, Denver, 1981, Contemporary Art Ctr., Honolulu, 1984, Frick Gallery, U. Pitts., 1984, 87, U. Conn., 1984, New Orleans Acad. Fine Arts, 1984, 91, Mattingly-Baker Gallery, Dallas, 1985, Fischbach Gallery, N.Y.C., 1987, 89, 90, 92, Reynolds/Minor Gallery, Richmond, Va., 1987, Braunstein/Quay Gallery, San Francisco, 1987, 89, 91, 94, 98, 2001, Gail Severn Gallery, Sun Valley, Idaho, 1988, Sierra Nevada Mus., Reno, 1988, N.Y. Stock Exch. Bldg., N.Y.C., 1989, Luria Gallery, Bay Harbor Island, Fla., 1990, Kalamazoo Inst. Arts, 1991, Stephen Scott Gallery, Balt., 1992, 97, Addison/Ripley Gallery, Washington, 1993, 96, 99, Gerald Peters Gallery, Santa Fe, 1994; exhibited in group shows Mattingly-Baker Gallery, Dallas, 1982, Springfield (Mo.) Art Mus., 1983, Pa. Acad. Fine Arts, Phila., 1983, Art Inst. Chgo., 1983, Corcoran Gallery, Washington, 1984, Bklyn. Mus., N.Y.C., 1985, William Sawyer Gallery, San Francisco, 1985, 88, Coll. of Mainland, Texas City, Tex., 1985, William's Coll. Art Ctr., Williamstown, Mass., 1985-86, Akron (Ohio) Art Mus., 1985-86, Madison (Wis.) Art Ctr., 1985-86, San Francisco Mus. Art, 1985-86, DeCordova and Dana Mus. Art, Lincoln, Mass., 1985-86, Archer M. Huntington Art Gallery U. Evanston, Ill., 1985-86, William's Coll. Art Ctr., Williamstown, Mass., 1985-86, Akron (Ohio) Art Mus., 1985-86, Madison (Wis.) Art Ctr., 1985-86, Metro. Mus., Miami, 1986, Springfield (Mo.) Art Mus., 1986, Art Mus. Santa Cruz County, 1987, The Sierra Nevada Mus. Art, Reno, Nev., 1988, William Sawyer Gallery, San Francisco, 1988, Kohler Arts Ctr., Sheboygan, Wis., 1988, Grand Ctrl. Art Galleries, N.Y.C., 1989, Fendrick Gallery, Washington, 1989, Gallery K., Washington, 1989, The Palmer Mus. Art, Pa., 1990, Steven Scott Gallery, Balt., 1990, Am. Acad. and Inst. Arts and Letters, N.Y.C., 1991, The Gallery at Bristol-Myers Squibb, Princeton, N.J., 1991, The Noyes Mus., N.J., 1991, Ctr. Contemporary Arts, Miami, 1991, Nat. Mus. Women in the Arts, 1991-92, 2000, The Miyagi Mus. Art, Sendai, Japan, 1991-92, Sogo Mus. Art, Yokohama, Japan, 1991-92, Tokushima (Japan) Mod. Art Mus., 1991-92, Mus. Modern Art, Shiga, Japan, 1991-92, Kochi (Japan) Prefectural Mus. Folk Art, 1991-92; Kavesh Gallery, Ketchum, Idaho, 1993, Nat. Acad. Design, N.Y.C., 1993, Sewall Art Gallery Rice U., Houston, 1993, Gerald Peters Gallery, Santa Fe, N. Mex., 1993, Philbrook Mus., Davenport Mus., 2000, Meridian Internat. Ctr., Traveling to Vietnam, China, Singapore, Indonesia, 2000; represented in numerous pub. and pvt. permanent collections including The Achenbach Found., Art Inst. Chgo., Hawaii Arts Ctr., Indpls. Mus. Art., Meml. Art Gallery, Oakland Mus., N.Y. Pub. Lib., San Antonio Mus. Art, San Francisco Art Commn., Springfield Mus., The British Mus., The Brooklyn Mus., University Art Mus., Corcoran Gallery, Nat. Mus. Am. Art, Nat. Mus. for Women in the Arts; others. Guggenheim fellow in printmaking, 1967. Mem. Nat. Acad. Design, Phi Beta Kappa. Address: Addison Ripley Fine Art 1670 Wisconsin Ave NW Washington DC 20007

FORRESTER, PATRICK G. astronaut; b. El Paso, Tex., Mar. 31, 1957; s. Redmond V. and Patsy L. Forrester; m. Diana Lynn Morris; 2 children. BSc in Applied Sci. & Engring., U.S. Mil. Acad., West Point, 1979; MSc in Mech. & Aerospace Engring., U. Va., 1989. Commd. 2d lt. U.S. Army, 1979, advanced through grades to col., various assignments, 1980—89; flight test engr. Army Aviation Engring. Flight Activity, Edwards AFB, Calif., 1989—92; graduate USN Test Pilot Sch., 1992; engring. test pilot U.S. Army Aviation Tech. Test Ctr., Ft. Rucker, Ala., 1992—93; aerospace engr. NASA, Houston, 1993—, astronaut, 1996—. Astronaut Discovery mission to Internat. Space Sta., 2001. Decorated Meritorious Svc. medal with 2nd oak leaf cluster U.S. Army, Nat. Defense Svc. medal. Mem.: Am. Helicopter Soc., Army Aviation Assn. Am.,

Soc. Exptl. Test Pilots (Jack Northrop award 1996), West Point Soc. Greater Houston, U.S. Mil. Acad. Assn. Graduates, Order of St. Michael. Avocations: baseball, running. Office: Astronaut Office CB Johnson Space Center Houston TX 77058

FORROW, BRIAN DEREK, lawyer, corporation executive; b. N.Y.C., Feb. 6, 1927; s. Frederick George and Doris (Williams) F.; m. Eleanor Reid, Mar. 8, 1952; children: Lisa Coggins, Brian Lachlan, Catherine Frances, Derek Skylstead. AB, Princeton U., 1947; JD, Harvard U., 1950. Bar: N.Y. 1950, Conn. 1967, U.S. Supreme Ct. 1954. From assoc. to ptnr. Cahill, Gordon, Sonnett, Reindel & Ohl (and predecessors), 1950-68; v.p., gen. counsel Allied Chem. Corp., 1968-85, dir., 1969-85; sr. v.p., gen. counsel Allied-Signal Inc., 1985-92; pvt. practice, Greenwich, Conn., 1992—; of counsel Whitman Breed Abbott & Morgan, 1992-94. Bd. dirs. Union Tex. Petroleum, 1985-92. Contbr. articles to profl. publs. Mem. Greenwich Representative Town Meeting, 1993—; vestryman, former sr. warden, former diocesan rep., Episcopal Ch. Served to 1st lt. USAF, 1951-53. Mem. ABA, Am. Law Inst., Conn. Bar Assn., N.Y. State Bar Assn., Assn. Bar City of N.Y. (past chmn. com. corp. law depts.), Assn. Gen. Counsel, Am. Arbitration Assn. (bd. dirs. 1987-97), Corp. Bar Assn. Westchester-Fairfield (past pres., bd. dirs. 1986-91), Am. Corp. Counsel Assn. (bd. dirs. 1987-89), Assn. Corp. Counsel N.J. (past pres.), Indian Harbor Yacht Club (past bd. dirs.), Harvard Club N.Y., Ret. Men's Assn. Greenwich Conn. (officer, dir. 2003—). Republican. Home and Office: 704 Lake Ave Greenwich CT 06830-3361

FORRY, JOHN INGRAM, retired lawyer; b. Washington, Feb. 9, 1945; s. John Emerson and Marion Carlotta (MacArthur) F.; m. Carol Ann Micken, Jan. 12, 1980; children: Alicia Ann, Camilla Lorraine. BA, Amherst Coll., 1966; JD, Harvard U., 1969. Bar: Calif. 1970, D.C. 1998, N.Y. 1998, U.S. Tax Ct. 1977, U.S. Supreme Ct. 1975. Founding ptnr. Forry Golbert Singer & Gelles, L.A., 1973-80; sr. ptnr. Morgan, Lewis & Bockius, L.A., 1980-97, McDermott, Will & Emery, N.Y.C., 1997-98, Ernst & Young LLP, N.Y.C., 1999—2003; ret., 2003. Co-author, editor: A Practical Guide to Foreign Investment in the United States, 1979, 3d edit., 1989, Joint Ventures in the United States, 1988, Differences in Tax Treatment of Foreign Investors, 1984, others; contbr. more than 40 articles to profl. jours. Co-founder Fund in Philosophy and Sci., Amherst (Mass.) Coll., 1984—; mem. adv. group to U.S. Commr. of Internal Revenue, Washington, 1985-86. Mem. Internat. Bar Assn., Internat. Fiscal Assn., other bar assns. Republican. Roman Catholic. Avocations: philosophical implications of scientific developments, automobile racing, mountain climbing, scuba diving. E-mail: forryjo@aol.com.

FORRY, STEVEN, not-for-profit fundraiser; b. Bellflower, Calif., Aug. 30, 1952; s. Earl Forry and Darlys Gallagher; 1 child, Sarah Cathrine. BA French magna cum laude, BA English cum laude, U. Calif., Santa Barbara, 1978; MA English, Columbia U., 1984, PhD English, 1988. Dir. stewardship Columbia U., N.Y.C., 1987—89; sr. devel. officer Sharp Hosps. Found., San Diego, 1990—96; assoc. dir. devel. U. Calif., San Diego, 1996—99; dir. corp. rels. Orange County HS Arts, Santa Ana, Calif., 2000—01; dir. devel. Children's Hosp. of Orange County, 2001—. Author: (critical study) Hideous Progenies: Dramatizations of Frankenstein in the 19th Century, 1990, (screenplays) Squiggets, 2002. Recipient award for Best Essay on Theatre, Am. Theatre Assn., 1987, award for outstanding pub. speaking, Toastmasters Internat.; fellow, Columbia U., 1978—81, fellowship, 1982—83, English Dept. Tchg. fellowship, 1984—87; scholar Whiting scholar, 1984—86. Mem.: Assn. Fund-raising Profls., Nat. Soc. Fund Raising Profl. (chair Fund Raising Day San Diego chpt. 1993, chair fund raising day San Diego chpt. 1995, Orange Co. Chpt. 2001—02), Orange County Triathlon Club. Avocations: jogging N.Y.C. and LA marathons, men's over thirty baseball, sailing, tennis.

FORSBERG, C. ROBERT, retired minister, editor; s. Carl Harold and Naomi S. Forsberg; m. Joan Bates Forsberg (div. 1979); children: Larry, Barbara, Tim. BA, Coll. Wooster, 1946; BD, Yale U., 1953. Group ministry Oak St. Christian Parish, New Haven, 1950—57, Wider City Parish, New Haven, 1958—89; co-editor Sequoia News Mag., San Francisco, 1993—. Mem. justice, advocacy and caring com. Presbytery San Francisco; treas. Campaign to Abolish Poverty, San Francisco, 1994—; sec. No. Calif. Inter Religious Conf., Oakland, Calif., 1994—; clk. Mid. East Peace com. Am. Friends Svc. Com., San Francisco, 2001—. Editor: Wider City Parish News, 1950—89. Pres. Citizens for Humanizing Criminal Justice, New Haven, 1980. Recipient Burton Gross award, Campaign to Abolish Poverty, San Francisco, 2001. Democrat. Presbyterian. Avocation: computers. Home: 1280 Laguna St #10J San Francisco CA 94115

FORSBERG, PETER, professional hockey player; b. Ornskoldsvik, Sweden, July 20, 1973; Profl. hockey player MODO Hockey Swedish League, 1990-94, Swedish Olympic Team, 1994, Quebec Nordiques, Colo. Avalanche, 1994—. Office: c/o Colorado Avalanche Pepsi Center 100 Chopper Place Denver CO 80204-1743

FORSBERG, SUZANNE, humanities educator, speech professional; b. Salt Lake, Utah, May 16, 1940; d. J. Ernest and Maureen (Kendall) Forsberg; m. Raymond A. Joseph, Dec. 13, 1975; 1 child, André E.F. Joseph. MusB, U of UT, Salt Lake City, UT, 1962; MA, Harvard U, Cambridge, Mass., 1966; PhD, NYU, New York, NY, 1990. Inst. Brigham Young U, Provo, Utah, 1969—71; vis. instr. St. Francis Coll., Brooklyn, NY, 1975—76, adj. prof., 1976—91, prof., 1991—; instr. Newark Sch. of the Arts, Newark, 1997—. Con. NYC Bd. of Ed., New York, NY, 1990; spkr. NY Coun. for the Humanities, New York, NY, 2003—05. Author: (articles) music ency. and jour., 2000—01. Participant in Franciscan leadership pilgrimage to Assisi St. Francis Pilgrimages, Assisi, Italy, 1999. Grantee fellowship, Woodrow Wilson/Harvard U, 1962—63, German Academic Exch./ Munich, Germany, 1971—72. Mem.: Society for Eighteenth Century Music, American Bach Society, American Musicological Society, Phi Beta Kappa. Achievements include discovery of The symphonic output of the Bavarian composer Joseph Anton Camerloher. Avocations: travel, art history. Home: 865 W End Ave Apt 8C New York NY 10025-8405 Office: St Francis College 180 Remsen St Brooklyn NY 11201

FORSEE, GARY D. telecommunications industry executive; B in Engring., U. Mo., 1972. With Southwestern Bell Tele., 1972—80, AT&T, 1980—89; v.p., gen. mgr. govt. sys. divsn. Sprint Corp., 1989—91, pres.govt. sys., bus. svcs. group, 1991—93, sr. v.p. staff ops., 1993—95, interim CEO, 1995, pres., COO long distance divsn., 1995—98, CEO, 2003—; CEO, pres. Global One, Brussels, 1998—99, exec. v.p., chief staff officer Atlanta, 1999—2000; pres. Bell South Internat., 2000—03; vice chmn. Bell South Corp., Atlanta, 2000—03. Bd. dirs. Goodyear Tire & Rubber Co. Chmn. bd. trustees March of Dimes; adv. coun. sch. engring. U. Mo., Rolla. Office: Sprint Corp 6200 Sprint Pkwy Overland Park KS 66251*

FORSEE, JOE BROWN, library director; b. Fulton, Ky., Oct. 25, 1949; m. Carmen Anne E. V. Cosner; children: Amy, Matthew, Melanie. BSLS, Murray State U., 1971, MSLS, 1972. Assoc. regional libr. Barren River Regional Libr., Russellville, Ky., 1972-73; dir. interlibrary cooperation Ky. Dept. Libr. and Archives, Frankfort, 1973-76; libr. cons. Miss. Libr. Commn., Jackson, 1976, asst. dir. adminstrn., 1976-78, dir., 1978-80; dir. pub. libr. svcs. Ga. Dept. Edn., Atlanta, 1980-95; dir. N.W. Ga. Regional Libr., Dalton, 1995—. Co-chmn. Gov.'s Conf. Libr. and Info. Svcs.; past vice-chmn. White Ho. Conf. Libr. and Info. Svcs. Task Force; del. 1st and 2d White Ho. Confs. Libr. and Info. Scis.; libr. bldg. cons., mgmt. cons.; guest spkr. in field. Contbr. articles to profl. jours., fed. and state docs. Mem.: ALA, Ga. Libr. Assn., S.E. Libr. Assn. (past pres.). Home: 293 Floodtown Rd Chatsworth GA 30705 Office: NW Ga Regional Libr 310 Cappes St Dalton GA 30720-4123

FORSEN, HAROLD KAY, retired engineering executive; b. Sept. 19, 1932; s. Allen Kay and Mabel Evelyn (Buehler) F.; m. Betty Ann Webb, May 25, 1952; children: John Allen, Ronald Karl, Sandra Kay. AA, Compton Jr. Coll., 1956; BS, Calif. Inst. Tech., 1958, MS, 1959; PhD, U. Calif., Berkeley, 1965. Rsch. assoc. Gen. Atomic, San Diego, 1959-62; rsch. assoc., elec. engr. U. Calif., Berkeley, 1962-65; assoc. prof. nuclear engring. U. Wis., Madison, 1965-69, prof., 1969-73, dir. Phys. Sci. Lab., 1970-72; v.p. Exxon Nuc. Co., Bellevue, Wash., 1973-75, v.p., bd. dirs., 1975-80, exec. in charge of laser enrichment, 1981; exec. v.p. Jersey-Avco Isotopes, Inc., 1975-80, pres., 1981, dir., 1975-81; mgr. engring. and materials Bechtel Group, Inc., San Francisco, 1981-83, dep. mgr. rsch. and engring., 1983-84, mgr. advanced sys., 1984-85, mgr. R & D, 1986-91; sr. v.p. Bechtel Corp., San Francisco, 1986-95; mgr. Bechtel Tech. Group, 1992-93; v.p., dir. Bechtel Hanford Inc., 1994-95, ret., 1995. Mem. fusion power reactor sr. rev. com. U.S. Dept. Energy, 1977, mem. magnetic fusion adv. com., 1982-86, mem. fusion policy adv. com., 1990, mem. fusion energy adv. com., 1994-96; mem. tech. adv. com. Internat. Thermonuc. Exptl. Reactor, 1996-98; mem. Fusion Indsl. Coun., U.S., 1994-96; chmn. U.S. del. to former Soviet Union on ion sources AEC, 1972; mem. vis. com. dept. nuc. energy Brookhaven Nat. Lab., 1992-96; mem. external rev. com. accelerator ops. and tech. divsn. Los Alamos Nat. Lab., 1993-96, mem. indsl. adv. bd. Lawrence Livermore Nat. Lab., 1994-98, univ. rsch. assn. overseer-at-large Fermilab Bd., 1995—2000, Univ. Chgo. rev. com. tech. devel. divsn., Argonne Nat. Lab., 1996-2002; mem. adv. bd. Oak Ridge Nat. Lab. Spallation Neutron Source, 2000—; mem. burning plasma program adv. com., Dept. of Energy, 2003—. Mem. dean's vis. com. Coll. Engring., U. Wash., 1981—; bd. dirs. Plasma and Materials Tech., Inc., 1988-91, Pepco, 1998-99. Served with USAF, 1951-55. Named San Francisco Bay Area Eminent Engr., 1990. Fellow: Am. Nuc. Soc. (chmn. tech. group controlled nuc. fusion 1973, Arthur H. Compton award 1972), Am. Phys. Soc.; mem.: NAE (councillor 1993—95, fgn. sec. 1995—2003), NRC (mem. gov. bd. 1992—2003), Am. Acad. Arts and Scis., Sigma Xi, Tau Beta Pi. Address: Apt 201 4437 Lake Washington Blvd NE Kirkland WA 98033-7630 E-mail: hforsen@nae.edu.

FORSETH, WILLIAM J. retired education educator; b. Grand Forks, N.D., Feb. 11, 1922; s. Richard E. and Ruth Palm Forseth; m. Margie W. Anderson, Dec. 27, 1947; children: Catherine Ann, William(dec.), Thomas John. BBA, U. Minn., 1947; MEd, U. N.D., 1950, EdD, 1957. Cert. sch. adminstr., tchr. Minn. Prin. Audubon (Minn.) H.S., 1947—49, Stephen (Minn.) H.S., 1950—51, Wadena (Minn.) H.S., 1951—57; prof. edn. Bemidji (Minn.) State U., 1957—82, prof. emeritus, 1982—. Chair, dept. secondary edn. Bemidji State U., 1967—73, dir. Upward Bound Project, 1966—72. Contbr. articles to profl. jours. and periodicals. Bd. dirs. Bemidji Cmty. Arts Coun., 1985—87; Sunday sch. supt. Luth. Ch., Wadena, Minn., 1953—57. 2d lt. field arty. U.S. Army, 1943—46, Pacific. Mem.: NEA, Am. Legion (bd. dirs. 1999—), Bemidji Elks Club, Bemidji Lions Club (past pres.), Phi Delta Kappa. Democrat. Luth. Achievements include played an important role, state legel committee leadership, in establishment of Minnesota Board of Teaching, which gave classroom teachers a significant voice in education policy making. Avocations: oil painting, music, golf, fishing. Home: 3610 Birchmont Dr NE Bemidji MN 56601

FORSH, FREDERICK DOUGLAS, music educator; b. Canton, Ga., Oct. 3, 1954; s. Walter Roscoe and Mary Beatrice Forsh; m. Charolette McMickens; children: Kenya, Robbye. BS Music Edn., Berry Coll., 1976. Dir. vocal music M. A. Teasley Mid. Sch., Canton, 1986—, dir. instrumental music, 1986—91; pastor Liberty Hill A. M. E. Ch., Sharpsburg, Ga., 1998—, Gray's Chapel A. M. E. Ch., Adairsville, Ga., 1992—98, St. John A. M. E. Ch., Ringgold, Ga., 1990—92; ch. musician & choir dir. St. Paul A. M. E. Ch., Canton, 1970—98. Bd. dirs. Cherokee County Arts Coun., Canton, 1987—90. Composer: (music) Etowah High School Alma Mater, 1976. Mem. Blue Ribbon Com., Canton, GA., 2000—01. Named Outstanding Educator, Woodstock Jaycees, 2003. Mem.: Music Educators Nat. Conference/Georgia Music Educators Assn., ASCAP (Spl. Award 1988-1999). Democrat. Office: MA Teasley Middle School 8871 Knox Bridge Hwy Canton GA 30114 Business E-Mail: fred.forsh@cherokee.k12.ga.us.

FORSHEE, GLADYS MARIE, writer, insurance agent; b. Loveland, Colo., July 1, 1942; d. Henry William Hansen and Bird Marie Smith; m. Larry Bill Forshee, Aug. 27, 1960 (widowed Dec. 1992). Cert. ins. agt. Customer svc. rep., acct. mgr. various ins. agys., Denver, 1970-2000; owner Superior (Colo.) Janitorial Svc., 1975-2000, A Appletree Pub., Superior, Colo., 1991—. Author, pub.: (history book) Where Memories Linger, 1994, (cookbook) A Superior Centennial, Culinary Fest Cookbook, 1996, also 11 researched, published and updated family histories. Asst. organizer Superior Hist. Soc., 1998; town clk., recorder Town of Superior, 1970—73; cmty. svc. dir. Colo. State Grange, Aurora, 1992—99, Boulder county dep., 1999—2001; rsch. asst. Nat. Archives, Lakewood, Colo.; asst. organizer Superior (Colo.) Vol. Fire Dept., 1972—81; mem., vol. Adams County Hist. Soc., Henderson, Colo., 1991—2002; mem., vol. citizens adv. com. Boulder County Recycling and Composting Authority, 2000—01; mem. adv. bd. Boulder County Hist. Preservation, Boulder, 2002—03; mem. Boucler Country Resource Conservation Adv. Bd., 2002—03, Adams County Centennial Roundtable, 2002; mem. various state hist. and geneal. socs.; citizen adv. Town of Superior, Colo., 2003; event coord. Christian Clown Group, 2003. Mem.: Green Valley Grange. Avocations: gardening, crocheting, camping, reading, playing the stock market. Home: 404 S 3d Ave Superior CO 80027

FORSMAN, ALPHEUS EDWIN, lawyer; b. Montgomery, Ala., May 12, 1941; m. Greta Friedman, July 5, 1964; children: Ellen E., Jennifer Ann. BA with distinction, George Washington U., 1963, JD, 1967. Bar: Va. 1968, D.C. 1969, U.S. Supreme Ct. 1973, Mo. 1979. Trademark examiner U.S. Patent Office, Washington, 1967-69; atty. Marriott Corp., Washington, 1969-72; assoc. Roylance, Abrams, Berdo and Kaul, Washington, 1972-75, ptnr., 1975-78; trademark atty. Ralston Purina Co., St. Louis, 1978-81, trademark counsel, 1981-91, v.p., sr. trademark counsel, 1991-96; asst. v.p. Eveready Battery Co., Inc., St. Louis, 1986-98; asst. sec. Ralston Purina Co., St. Louis, 1999—2001, v.p., sr. counsel, 1996—2002; v.p. Eveready Battery Co., 1998-2000; v.p., sr. counsel Nestle Purina PetCare Co., 2001—02. Asst. sec. Continental Baking Co., 1990-95; adj. prof. law Washington U., 2000. Mem.: Bar Assn. Met. St. Louis. Republican. Episcopalian. Home: 417 Glan Tai Dr Manchester MO 63011-4067

FORSON, NORMAN RAY, controller; b. Port Arthur, Tex., July 12, 1929; s. Hollis G. and Annie (Butler) F.; m. Nancy McAnelly, Dec. 6, 1952; children: James Hollis, Diana Nancy. BA, Baylor U., 1952; MBA, U. Houston, 1961. CPA, N.Y. Sales engr. Magcobar, New Orleans and Houston, 1956-57; buyer Transcontinental Gas Pipe Line, Houston, 1957-61; supr. Ernst & Young, Houston, 1961-65; sr. v.p., treas. Gulf & Western Inc., N.Y.C., 1965-83; sr. v.p., chief fin. officer Hi-Shear Industries, Inc., North Hills, N.Y., 1984-85, Jonathan Logan Inc., Teaneck, N.J., 1985-97; sr. v.p., comptroller United Mchts. & Mfgrs., Inc., Teaneck, NJ., 1987-97; cons., 1997—. Served to 1st lt. USAF, 1952-56. Home: 7315 Marigold Dr Irving TX 75063-5501

FORST, EDMUND CHARLES, JR., communications educator, administrator, consultant; b. Chgo., June 25, 1961; s. Edmund Sr. and Patricia Ann (Dopek) Forst; m. Kelly Lee Globke; children: Morgan Mae, Shannon Rose, Maximillian. BA, Ea. Ill. U., 1983, MA, 1984; EdD, W. Va. U., 1994. Leader, mem. staff Neighborhood Boys Club, Chgo., summer 1975-84; instr. in communication DePaul U., Chgo., 1988-93; instr. Waubonsee C.C., Sugar Grove, Ill., 1993-94, assoc. dean comms. and humanities, 1994-98; dean arts & scis. Triton Coll., River Grove, Ill., 1998—. Cons. comm. for Leon Spinks, 1990; pres.-elect Ill. Coun. CC Adminstrs., 2003—. Contbr. articles to profl. jours. Eucharist minister Our Lady of Mercy, Chgo., 1989-90; bd. dirs. Neighborhood Boys Club, Chgo., 1988-92,; bd. dirs. St. Leonard Sch., Berwyn, Ill., 2000-2001, mem. parish coun., 2002, mem. fin. com. 2003. Mem. Aurora-Naperville Rotary, Forest Park C. of C. Republican. Roman Catholic. Avocations: sports, reading, movie collecting, model railroads. Home: 6509 Sinclair Ave Berwyn IL 60402-3737 E-mail: eforst@triton.cc.il.us.

FORST, MARION FRANCIS, bishop; b. St. Louis, Sept. 3, 1910; s. Frank A. J. and Bertha T. (Gulath) F. Grad., Kenrick Sem., Webster Groves, Mo., 1934. Priest Roman Cath. Ch., 1934. Pastor St. Mary's Cathedral, Cape Girardeau, Mo., 1949—60; vicar gen. Diocese of Springfield-Cape Girardeau, 1956—60; bishop Dodge City, Kans., 1960—76; aux. bishop Archdiocese of Kansas City, Kans., 1976—86; ret., 1986. Kans. chaplain KC, 1964—. With Chaplains Corps USNR, WWII. Roman Catholic.

FORSTADT, JOSEPH LAWRENCE, lawyer; b. Bklyn., Feb. 21, 1940; BA, CCNY, 1961; LLB, NYU, 1964. Bar: N.Y. 1965, U.S. Supreme Ct. 1968. Spl. legal counsel to bd. justices Supreme Ct. N.Y. County, 1965-67; dep. commr. N.Y.C. Dept. Licenses, 1967-68, acting commr., 1968-69, N.Y.C. Dept. Consumer Affairs, 1969; asst. adminstr. Econ. Devel. Adminstrn., 1969, assoc. Stroock & Stroock & Lavan, N.Y.C., 1969-75, ptnr., 1976—. Lectr. trial practice N.Y. County Lawyers Assn., Practising Law Inst., 1993-94, Title Ins. Litig.; mem. N.Y.C. Rent Guidelines Bd., 1984-97; arbitrator U.S. Dist. Ct. (ea. dist.) N.Y.; spl. counsel Appellate Div. First Dept., Disciplinary Com.; mem. Housing Ct. Adv. Bd., 2001-02. Contbr. articles to profl. jours. Dist. campaign mgr. John V. Lindsay for Mayor of N.Y.C., 1965; campaign mgr. Congressman Theodore Kupferman, 1966; chmn. N.Y.C. Young People for Nixon, 1968, pres. N.Y. State Assn. Young Rep. Clubs, 1970-72; pres. N.Y. Young Rep. Club, 1969-71; vice-chmn. N.Y. Com. to Re-elect Pres. Nixon, 1972. Judge Jacob Markowitz scholar NYU Law Sch., N.Y.C., 1964; recipient Brotherhood award NCCJ, 1987. Mem. Fed. Bar Coun., Am. Judicature Soc., Phi Alpha Delta. Office: Stroock & Stroock & Lavan 180 Maiden Ln Suite 32108 New York NY 10038-4937 E-mail: jforstadt@stroock.com.

FORSTER, ARNOLD, lawyer, author; b. N.Y.C., June 25, 1912; s. Hyman Lawrence and Dorothy (Turits) Fastenberg; m. May Kasner, Sept. 29, 1940; children: Stuart William (dec.), Jane Forster Berman. LLB, St. John's U., 1935. Bar: N.Y. 1935, U.S. Supreme Ct. 1949. Gen. practice law, 1935-40; dir. law dept. Anti-Defamation League of B'nai Brith, 1940-46; asso. dir. Anti-Defamation League of B'nai B'rith, 1946-78, gen. counsel, 1946—; of counsel Shea & Gould, N.Y.C., 1979-94, Baer Marks and Upham, N.Y.C., 1994—. Police justice N.Y. State, 1954-57 Author: Anti-Semitism in the United States, 1947, A Measure of Freedom, 1950, The Troublemakers, 1952, Cross-Currents, 1956, Some of My Best Friends, 1962, Danger on the Right, 1964, (with B.R. Epstein) Report on the Ku Klux Klan, 1965, Report on the John Birch Society, 1966, Radical Right: Report on the John Birch Society and Its Allies, 1967, Report From Israel, 1969, The New Anti-Semitism, 1974, Square One, 1988, Stubs-A Letter to His Children, 1994; author (TV/radio) Dateline Israel, 1967-83 Mem. bd. edn., New Rochelle, N.Y., 1962-66. Recipient Emmy award for film Avenue of the Just, 1980, Emmy award for film Zubin and the I.P.O., 1983 Home: 79 Wykagyl Ter New Rochelle NY 10804-3207 Office: Baer Marks and Upham 805 Third Ave New York NY 10022-7513 *In one's vintage years, it becomes unarguably clear that the only true satisfaction is in understanding that one's achievements, however small or large, made others happy and this earth a better place for living.*

FORSTER, CLIFFORD, lawyer; b. N.Y.C., July 6, 1913; s. Charles Von Foerster and Margaret (Buckwild) F.; m. Helene Gaubert, Sept. 9, 1972 (dec. 1976); m. Joan Smith, Sept. 20, 1981. BA, Yale U., 1935, LLB, 1938. Bar: N.Y. 1939, U.S. Dist. Ct. (so. dist.) N.Y. 1956, U.S. Ct. Appeals (2d cir.) 1973, U.S. Supreme Ct. 1980. Staff and spl. counsel ACLU, N.Y.C., 1940-54; counsel Internat. League Rights of Man, N.Y.C., 1955-65; assoc. Fitelson, Lasky, Aslan, Couture, N.Y.C., 1960-90. Bd. dirs. Internat. Rescue Com., N.Y.C., 1971—. Recipient Commemorative medal Assembly of Captive European Nations, 1964, Commdr. Order of Merit West German Gov., 1972. Mem. Assn. of Bar of City of N.Y. Roman Catholic.

FORSTER, DONALD R. vocational school educator; b. Denver, Colorado, Dec. 29, 1924; s. Clarence A. and Irene E. (Zwigard) Forster; m. Doris M. van Dragt, May 22, 1946; children: Diane C., Paul L., John R. Student, Hope Coll., Holland, Mich., 1943—44, U. Denver, 1946—47, BA indsl. arts (hon.), Mich. State U., 1949; MA edn, Colo. State U., 1968. Cert. teaching in Colo. 1953. Cabinet maker apprentice Denver Lumber Co., Denver, 1939—43; indsl. arts, vocat. tchr. Sch. Dist. 1, Laingsburg, Mich., 1949—52; shop tchr. No. Intermediate Sch., Saginaw, Mich., 1951—52; archtl. detailer Denver Lumber Co., Denver, 1952—55; ind. ins. adjuster various ins. companies, 1953—82; woodworking tchr. North H.S., Denver, 1954—58; drafting tchr. Denver Pub. Sch., 1954—82; tchr engring. and archtl. East H.S., Denver, 1958—59, George Washington H.S., Denver, 1960—82; Luthier self employed, Denver, 1960—; tchr. mech. drafting Opportunity Sch., 1955—77. Author: (syllabi) H.S. Engring. and Archtl. Drawing; has made and sold classical guitars, lutes, rihvulas, banjo. Precinct com., dist. 4 Colo. Dem. Party, Denver, 1960—65, dist. 4 capt., 1966—68; pres. Denver Fedn. of Teachers. Staff sgt. U.S. Army, 1943—46, PTO. Mem.: Am. Legion, VFW, Guild of Am. Luthiers. Democrat. Congregationalist. Achievements include patents for adjustable music stand. Avocations: trumpet, euphonium, reading, hunting, fishing.

FORSTER, FRANCIS MICHAEL, physician, educator; b. Cin., Feb. 14, 1912; s. Michael Joseph and Louise Barbara (Schmid) F.; m. Helen Dorothy Kiley, June 15, 1937; children— Denis, Susan, Kathleen, Mark, Gabrielle. Student, Xavier U., Cin., 1930-32, LL.D., 1955; BS, U. Cin., 1935, B.M., 1936, MD, 1937; D.Sc. hon., Georgetown U., 1982. Diplomate: Am. Bd. Psychiatry and Neurology (dir.). Rotating intern Good Samaritan Hosp., Cin., 1936-37; house officer neurology and neurosurgery Boston City Hosp., 1937-38, resident neurology, 1939-40; fellow psychiatry Pa. Hosp., Phila., 1938-39; asst. neurology Harvard Med. Sch., 1939-40; Rockefeller Found. research fellow physiology Yale Sch. Medicine, 1940-41; instr. neurology Boston U. Sch. Medicine, 1941-43; asst. prof. neurology Jefferson Med. Sch., 1943-47, assoc. prof. neurology, 1947-50; prof. neurology, dir. dept. Georgetown U. Sch. Medicine, 1950-58, dean Sch. Medicine, 1953-58; prof., chmn. dept. neurology U. Wis. Sch. Medicine, 1958-78; emeritus, 1978—; dir. Epilepsy Center, VA Hosp., Madison, Wis., 1977-82. Cons. neurology. Author: Synopsis of Neurology, 1962, 66, 73, 78, Reflex Epilepsy, Behavioral Therapy and Conditional Reflexes, 1977; editor: Modern Therapy in Neurology, 1957, Evaluation of Drug Therapy, 1961. Mem. AMA (chmn. nervous and mental diseases sect. 1952-53), AAAS, D.C. Med. Soc. (chmn. sect. neurology and psychiatry 1955-56, pres. 1958), Am. Acad. Neurology (chmn. survey com. 1948-51, pres. 1957-59), Am. Neurol. Assn. (chmn. com. internat. collaboration 1954-55), Am. Epilepsy League (pres. 1951-52), Assn. Rsch. Nervous and Mental Diseases, Am. Physiol. Soc., Am. Assn. Electroencephalographers, Med. Soc. Wis., Cosmos Club (Washington), Sigma Xi, Alpha Omega. Clubs: Cosmos (Washington). Home: 11120 Springfield Pike Cincinnati OH 45246 Office: U Wis Med Sch 600 Dept Neurology Madison WI 53792-0001 E-mail: fmforster@worldnet.att.net.

FORSTER, HAMISH, engineer; b. Blackburn, Lancashire, Eng., Sept. 7, 1969; came to U.S., 1999; s. William Toshach Forster and Eileen Barbara Walker. B in Engring., U. London, 1990, MSc, 1991; PhD, U. Leeds, Eng., 1996. Registered chartered engr. Rsch. fellow U. Leeds, 1996-97; biomaterials engr. Smith & Nephew Group Rsch. Ctr., York, Eng., 1997-99; sr. rsch. engr. Smith & Nephew Orthopaedics, Memphis, 1999—. Orthopaedic com. mem. Brit. Stds. Inst., London, Internat. Stds. Orgn., Geneva; biomaterials spl. interest group mem. Inst. Physics & Engring. in Medicine, York. Mem. Instn. Mech. Engrs., Inst. Materials, Inst. Physics and Engring. in Medicine. Avocations: Tae Kwon Do, mountain biking, snowboarding, adventure travel. Office: Smith & Nephew Orthopaedics 1450 E Brooks Rd Memphis TN 38116-1804 Fax: 901-399-6020. E-mail: hamish.forster@smith-nephew.com.

FORSTER, JULIAN, physicist, consultant; b. NYC, Aug. 31, 1918; s. Meyer Kivetz and Rose (Sommer) F.; m. Frieda Bain, July 2, 1941; children: Jeffrey M., Laura Gherman. BS in Physics, CCNY, 1940. Registered nuclear engr., Calif. Sr. physicist US Naval 4th Dist., Phila., 1941-56; sr. nuclear engr. GE, San Jose, Calif., 1956-70, sr. project mgr. nuclear energy dept., 1970-80; sr. mgmt. tech. Quadrex Corp., Campbell, Calif., 1980-85, cons., 1985-96, GE-NE, 1996—. Contbr. articles to profl. jours. Commr. Fine Arts, San Jose, 1987-95. Fellow IEEE (life, emeritus; standards bd. 1970—, computer soc. 1985—, nuclear scis. soc. 1963—, power engring. soc. 1975—, coord. pace divsn. IV 1993-2000, chmn. awards and recognition com. 1986-95, Divsnl. Profl. Achievment award 1994, Standards Bd. Spl. Achievement award 1995, Stds. Dist. Svc. award 2000, 3d Millennium medal of Honor 2000); mem. Internat. Electro Tech. Com. (nuclear power com. SC45A 1969—, R.F. Shea Svc. award 1992). Democrat. Jewish. Avocations: music, wine, fine arts, golf. Home: 6962 Castlerock Dr San Jose CA 95120-4704 Office: GE NE MC/334 175 Curtner Ave San Jose CA 95125-1014 Fax: 408-925-2923. E-mail: jay.forster@gene.ge.com.

FORSTER, MERLIN HENRY, foreign languages educator, writer, researcher; b. Delta, Utah, Feb. 24, 1928; s. Henry and Ila Almeda (Rawlinson) F.; m. Vilda Mae Naegle, Apr. 25, 1952; children: Celia Marlene, David Merlin, Angela, Daniel Conrad, Elena Marie. BA, Brigham Young U., 1956; MA, U. Ill., 1957, PhD, 1960. Instr. in Spanish U. Tex., Austin, 1960-61, asst. prof., 1961-62; asst. prof. Spanish and Portuguese U. Ill., Urbana, 1962-65, assoc. prof., 1965-69, prof., 1969-78, dir. Latin Am. studies, 1972-78; prof., chmn.

dept. Spanish and Portuguese, U. Tex., Austin, 1978-87; disting. prof. Latin Am. lit. Brigham Young U., Provo, Utah, 1987-98, chmn. dept. Spanish and Portuguese, 1989-93, prof. emeritus, 1998—. Dir. summer seminars NEH, 1978, 89, 90, 93, 96, 98. Author: Los Contemporáneos, 1964, Fire and Ice, 1976, Historia de la poesia hispanoamericana, 1981, The Committed Word: Studies in Spanish American Poetry, 2002; editor: Index to Mexican Journals, 1966, Tradition and Renewal, 1975, De la Crónica a la Nueva Narrativa, 1986, Vanguardism in Latin American Literature: An Annotated Bibliographical Guide, 1990, La vanguardia literaria en Mexico y la América Central, 2001. Rsch. grantee Social Sci. Rsch. Coun., Mexico City, 1965, Fulbright-Hays, Buenos Aires, 1971, NEH, Austin, 1986-87, Am. Coun. Learned Socs. and German Acad. Exch. Svc., 1993-94; fellow Ctr. for Advanced Study, Urbana, 1976-77. Mem. MLA, Latin Am. Studies Assn., Am. Assn. Tchrs. Spanish and Portuguese, Internat. Inst. Iberoam. Lit. (pres. 1981-83, 94-96). Mem. Lds Ch. Avocations: classical music, quartet singing, gardening, woodworking. Office: Brigham Young Univ Dept Spanish and Portuguese Provo UT 84602

FORSTER, ROBERT, history educator; b. N.Y.C., June 7, 1926; s. Theodore and Elise (Strobel) F.; m. Elborg Hamacher, July 8, 1955; children: Marc Richard, Thomas Theodore. BA, Swarthmore Coll., 1949; MA in Modern European History, Harvard U., 1951; PhD, Johns Hopkins U., 1956; D. honoris causa, U. Toulouse, France, 1985. Instr. modern European history Johns Hopkins U., 1956-57; Bissing fellow U. Toulouse, France, 1957-58; asst. prof. U. Nebr., 1958-62; assoc. prof. Dartmouth, 1962-65; prof. history Johns Hopkins, 1966-96, prof. emeritus, 1996—; fellow Inst. for Advanced Study, Princeton, N.J., 1975-76, Center for Advanced Study in Behavioral Scis., Stanford U., 1979-80; U.S. rep. Internat. Congress Hist. Scis., 1975-80. Author: The Nobility of Toulouse in the 18th Century, 1960, The House of Saulx-Tavanes: Versailles and Burgundy, 1700-1830, 1971, Seeds of Change: Peasants, Nobles, and Rural Revolution in 18th Century France, 1975; author: Merchants, Landlords, Magistrates: The Depont Family in 18th Century France, 1980; Author also articles.; Editor: (with Elborg Forster) European Society in the 18th Century, 1969, (with Jack P. Greene) Preconditions of Revolution in Early Modern Europe, 1970, (with Elborg Forster) European Diet from Pre-Industrial to Modern Times, 1975, (with Orest Ranum) Biology of Man in History, 1975, Family and Society, 1976, (with E. Carter and J. Moody) Enterprise and Enterpreneurs in 19th and 20th Century France, 1976, (with Orest Ranum) Rural Society in France, 1977, Deviants and the Abandoned, 1978, Food and Drink in History, 1979, Medicine and Society in France, 1980, Ritual, Religion, and the Sacred, 1981, (with Elborg Forster) Sugar and Slavery, Family and Race, 1996, European and Non-European Societies, 1450-1800, 2 vols., 1997. Served with AUS, 1944-46. Franch Govt. fellow, 1953-55; Social Scr. Rsch. Coun. fellow France, 1962, 64; Guggenheim fellow Paris, 1969-70; NEH fellow, 1983-84; recipient Prix Gaussail Acad. Toulouse, 1954, Chevalier de l'Ordre des Palmes Academiques award French Govt., 1994; named Hon. Citizen Vieillevigne, France, 1977; Doctor Honoris Causa, Toulouse, 1985. Mem. Internat. Commn. for Study of French Revolution, Soc. French Hist. Studies (pres. 1974), French Colonial Hist. Soc., Soc. Caribbean History, Am. Hist. Assn. (coun. 1985-88), Phi Beta Kappa. Home: 208 Oakdale Rd Baltimore MD 21210-2520

FORSTER, SUSAN H. ophthalmologist, educator; b. Phila., Dec. 11, 1950; d. William and Gail Forster; children: Alison, Jessica, William, Benjamin. AB, Harvard U., 1972; MD, Columbia U., 1976. Cert. Am. Bd. Ophthalmology. Physician, chief of ophthalmology Yale Health Plan, New Haven, 1983—; asst. prof. Yale U., New Haven, 1986—, dir. med. studies dept. ophthalmology and visual sci. Office: Yale Sch Medicine 330 Cedar St New Haven CT 06510

FORSTER, WILLIAM HULL, aerospace executive; b. Shelby, Miss., June 24, 1939; s. William Oskar Hermann and Amy B. (Hull) F.; m. Francine O'Neill, June 1999; children: William Hull Jr., Robert Brown. BS in Chemistry, U. Ala., 1960; PhD in Nuclear Chemistry, U. Calif., 1965; grad., Air Force War Coll., Navy Test Pilot Sch. Entered U.S. Army, 1965, advanced through grades to lt. gen.; comdr. Battery C, 6/56th Arty., Vietnam, 1965-66, 173d Assault Helicopter Co., Vietnam, 1971-72, 10th Combat Aviation Bn., Ft. Lewis, Wash., 1976-78; chief aviation systems div. hdqrs. U.S. Army, Washington, 1981-82; project mgr. Army Helicopter Improvement Program, 1982-85; dep. comdg. gen. Army Aviation Systems Command, 1985-86; program mgr. Apache Advanced Attack Helicopter, 1986-87; program exec. officer Combat Aviation, 1987-88; dir. requirements hdqrs. U.S. Army, Washington, 1988-91; comdr. Army Operational Test and Evaluation Command, Alexandria, Va., 1991-92; dep. asst. sec. rsch., devel., and acquisition U.S. Army, Washington, 1992-95; ret., 1995; now v.p. land combat systems Northrop G. Corp. Chmn. Nat. Acad. Sci. bd. Army Sci. and Tech., 1996—2001; sec. Am. Helicopter Soc., 2003. Decorated D.F.C., D.S.M. with oak leaf cluster, Bronze Star with oak leaf cluster, Legion of Merit with oak leaf cluster, Air medal (15 awards). Fellow Am. Helicopter Soc. (sec.-treas.); mem. Am. Phys. Soc., Russian Acad. Natural Sci., Army Aviation Assn., Nat. Aeronautic Assn. Presbyterian. Avocations: boating, automobile repair. Home: PO Box 106 Gibson Island MD 21056

FORSTOT, STEPHAN LANCE, ophthalmologist; b. N.Y.C., Aug. 19, 1943; s. Shepard and Edith Forstot; m. Lynne Rochelle Bitton, June 15, 1945; children: Michele, Jordan. AB, Princeton U., 1965; MD, Johns Hopkins U., 1969. Diplomate Am. Bd. Ophthalmology. Ophthalmologist Corneal Cons. of Colo., Denver, 1982—, U. Colo. Sch. of Medicine, Denver, 1976-82, clin. prof., 1982—. Contbr. articles to profl. jours. Recipient Honor award Am. Acad. Ophthalmology, Sr. Honor award Am. Acad. Ophthalmology. Mem. Contact Lens Assn. of Ophthalmology (bd. dirs. 1985-87), Internat. Soc. Refractive Surgery (bd. dirs. 1995-96). Avocation: tennis. Office: Corneal Cons of Colo 8381 Southpark Ln Littleton CO 80120-4508 E-mail: SL4STOT@aol.com.

FORSTROM, JUNE ROCHELLE, professional society administrator; b. Douglas County, Minn., June 24, 1932; d. George Dewey and Borghild Otillia (Sahl) Nelson; m. Keith William Forstrom, June 23, 1951; children: Mark William, Dawn Rochelle. Grad. high sch., St. Paul. Adminstr. rsch. grants, coord. comm. Geol. Soc. Am., Boulder, Colo., 1973—. Recipient Disting. Service award, Geological Soc. of Am., 1998. Republican. Lutheran. Avocations: reading, music, running, creative stitchery, travel. Home: 7705 Baseline Rd Boulder CO 80303-4707 Office: Geol Soc Am 3300 Penrose Pl Boulder CO 80301-1806

FORSYTH, BARBARA JEAN, elementary reading specialist, writer, poet; b. Detroit, Nov. 20, 1946; d. Henry Gurney and Alice Elaine Shreve; m. Sid H. Forsyth, May 28, 1966.; children: Janelle Forsyth Bauer, Linette Forsyth Donovan. BS in Edn., Taylor U., 1966; M in Edn., Calif. State U., L.A., 1980; adminstrv. credential, Calif. State U., Fullerton, 1997. Cert. tchr., reading specialist, Calif. Tchr. Rivera Elem. Sch., El Rancho Unified Sch. Dist., Pico Rivera, Calif., 1967-72; tchr. 3d and 4th grade LEP Class Hacienda La Puenta Unified Sch. Dist., Hacienda Hghts., Calif., 1979-80; reading specialist Monrovia Unified Sch. Dist., Monrovia, Calif., 1981-86, Alicia Cortez Elem. Sch., Chino, Calif., 1986—; cons. Houghton-Mifflin, San Jose, Calif., 1997—. Mentor Tchrs. of English Conf., San Diego, Calif., Calf. Reading Conf., Long Beach and Anaheim, Internat. Reading Assn., Albuquerque, N. Mex. Author: poetry, childrens' books; presenter How to Teach Reading using Readers' Theatre, 1996. Vol. Rep. campaign for state senate Chino, Calif., 1998. Recipient Editor's Choice award Nat. Libr. Poetry, Washington, 1997, 98, 99, 2000, 01. Fellow Internat. Soc. Poets; mem. ASCD, PTA, Internat. Reading Assn., Calif. Reading Assn., Foothill Reading Coun. Republican. Avocations: reading, writing plays, poetry, planning curriculum materials and weddings. Home: 3121 Genoa # G Ontario CA 91761 Office: Cortez Sch 12756 Carissa Ave Chino CA 91710-3701 E-mail: b4site@hotmail.com.

FORSYTH, BEN RALPH, academic administrator, medical educator; b. N.Y.C., Mar. 8, 1934; s. Martin and Eva Forsyth; m. Elizabeth Held, Aug. 19, 1962; children: Jennifer, Beverly, Jonathan. Attended, Cornell U., 1950-53; MD, NYU, 1957. Diplomate Am. Bd. Internal Medicine. Intern, then resident Yale Hosp., New Haven, 1957-60; postdoctoral fellow Harvard U. Med. Shc., Boston, 1960-61; rsch. assoc. NIH, Bethesda, Md., 1963-66; assoc. prof. med. microbiology, prof. med. coll. U. Vt., Burlington, 1966-90, assoc. dean div. health scis., 1971-85, assoc. v.p. acad. affairs, 1977-78, v.p. adminstrn., 1978-85, sr. v.p., 1985-90; sr. exec. asst. to pres. Ariz. State U., Tempe, 1990—2002, prof. health adminstrn. and policy, 1991—2002, interim v.p. adminstrv. svcs., 1991-93; interim provost Ariz. State U. West, Phoenix, 1992-93, Ariz. State U. East, Mesa, 1994-96; provost, v.p. Ariz. State U. West, Phoenix, 1993-96. Sr. cons. Univ. Health Ctr., Burlington, 1986-90. Contbr. articles to profl. jours. V.p., chmn. United Way Planning Com., Burlington, 1974—75, mem. ops. com., 1975—76, bd. dirs., officer, 1977—89; mem. New Eng. Bd. Higher Edn. Com., Burlington, 1985—89; chmn. U. Vt. China Project Adv. Bd., Burlington, 1989—90; trustee U. Vt., Burlington, 1996—2002. Lt. comdr. USN, 1962—63. Sinsheimer Found. faculty fellow, 1966-71. Fellow ACP, Infectious Diseases Soc. Am.; mem. Phi Beta Kappa, Alpha Omega Alpha. Avocations: hiking, gardening, travel. E-mail: forsyth@asu.edu.

FORSYTH, BEVERLY K. language educator, writer; b. Memphis, June 05; d. Marian Davidson Roy and Oakley Eugene Stover, Johnny Roy. AA in Mass Comm., Odessa (Tex.) Coll.; BA in Mass Comm., U. Tex., Odessa, MA in English, 1995; PhD in English, Union Inst., Cin., 2001. Author: (travel guide book) The Texas Monthly Guidebook to Texas, 3rd edition, 1993; co-author: (anthology) American Women Writers, 1900-1945, A Bio-Bibliographical Critical, 2000; author: (short stories) La Gringa Is My Name, 1999, Pontotoc Witch, 2000, Shadow's Edge, 2003; contbr. articles to profl. jours. Grantee Grace Mitchell/Learner Coun. Rsch. Travel, Union Inst., 2000; scholar, 2000, Agnes Rettig, 2000. Mem.: W. Tex. Writers, Tex. Assn. Creative Writing Tchrs., Tex. Coun. Tchrs. English (Pres.'s Classroom Rsch/Travel Study grantee 2001), Tex. C.C. Tchrs. Assn., Conf. Coll. Tchrs. English (exec. bd. councilors 2002—), S. Ctrl. MLA, Tex. Popular Culture Assn., S.W. Popular Culture Assn., Am. Culture Assn., Sigma Kappa Delta, Sigma Tau Delta (life). Office: Odessa Coll 201 W University Odessa TX 79764 Office Fax: 432-335-6846. Personal E-mail: bforsyth@cableone.net. Business E-Mail: bforsyth@odessa.edu.

FORSYTH, ILENE HAERING, art historian; b. Detroit, Aug. 21, 1928; d. Austin Frederick and Eleanor Marie (Middleton) H.; m. George H. Forsyth, Jr., June 4, 1960. AB, U. Mich., 1950; AM (univ. fellow), Columbia U., 1955, PhD (Fulbright, AAUW, Fels Found. fellow), 1960. Lectr. Barnard Coll., 1955-58; instr. Columbia U., 1959-61; mem. faculty U. Mich., Ann Arbor, 1961—, prof. history of art, 1974-97, prof. emerita, 1998—, Arthur F. Thurnau prof., 1984—; vis. prof. Harvard U., 1980; Mellon vis. prof. U. Pitts., 1981; vis. prof. U. Calif., Berkeley, 1996. Mem. Nat. Com. History Art, 1973-97, bd. dirs. Internat. Ctr. Medieval Art, 1970-95, v.p., 1981-85; mem. supervisory com. Woodrow Wilson Found., 1985-88; Rome prize juror Am. Acad. in Rome, 1986-88; bd. advisors Ctr. Advanced Study in the Visual Arts, Nat. Gallery Art, 1985-88; mem. vis. com. medieval dept. Met. Mus. Art, N.Y.C., 1990-95; Samuel H. Kress prof. Ctr. Advanced Study in the Visual Arts, Nat. Gallery Art, 1998-99, bd. advisors, 1999-2000. Author: The Throne of Wisdom, 1972 (Charles Rufus Morey Book award 1974), The Uses of Art: Medieval Metaphor in The Michigan Law Quadrangle, 1993 (Annie award for non-fiction 1994); co-editor: Current Studies on Cluny, 1988; contbr. articles to profl. jours. Rackham research grantee and fellow, 1965-66, 75-76; grantee Am. Council Learned Socs., 1972-73; mem. Inst. Advanced Study Princeton, 1977 Mem. Coll. Art Assn. (dir. 1980-84), Archaeol. Inst. Am., Medieval Acad. Am. (bd. advs. 1985-86, editorial bd. 1986-90), Medieval Club N.Y., Soc. francaise d'archéologie, Soc. Archtl. Historians, Acad. Arts, Scis. et Belles Lettres Dijon (France), Centre de recherches et d'études préromanes et romanes. Home: 5 Geddes Hts Ann Arbor MI 48104-1724 Office: U Mich Dept Art History Ann Arbor MI 48109

FORSYTH, RAYMOND ARTHUR, civil engineer, consultant; b. Reno, Mar. 13, 1928; s. Harold Raymond and Fay Exona (Highfill) F.; m. Mary Ellen Wagner, July 9, 1950; children: Lynne, Gail, Alison, Ellen. BS, Calif. State U., San Jose, 1952; MCE, Auburn U., 1958. Jr. engr., asst. engr. Calif. Divsn. Hwys., San Francisco, 1952-54; assoc. engr., sr. supervising, prin. engr. Calif. Dept. Transp., Sacramento, 1961-83, chief geotech. br., 1972-79, chief soil mechanics and pavement br., 1979-83; chief Transp. Lab., Sacramento, 1983-89. Cons., lectr. in field; geotech. engr. cons., 1989—. Contbr. articles to profl. jours. Served with USAF, 1954-56. Fellow ASCE (pres. Sacramento sect., chmn. Calif. coun. 1980-81); mem. Transp. Rsch. Bd. (chmn. embankments and earth slopes com. 1976-82, chmn. soil mechanics sect. 1982-88, chmn. group 2 coun. 1988-91), ASTM. Home: 5017 Pasadena Ave Sacramento CA 95841-4149 E-mail: slvrfox800@aol.com.

FORSYTH, ROSALYN MOYE, middle school educator; b. Pavo, Ga., Sept. 14, 1942; d. David Cody and Mary (Chapman) Moye; m. Jamos Floyd Forsyth, Aug. 7, 1965. AB, Wesleyan Coll., Macon, Ga., 1964. Cert. paraprofl. Tchr. edn. Dougherty County Bd. of Edn., Albany, Ga., 1965-70, substitute tchr., 1972-88, paraprofl., 1988—. Editor: Membership Roll and Register of Ancestors, 1986. Mem. at large exec. com. South Ga. conf. United Meth. Women, 1972-74, dist. pres. Thomasville dist., 1977-78, rec. sec., 1979-83, sec. publicity and pub. rels., 1983-87, mem. com. on nominations Southeastern jurisdiction 1988-92). Mem. Profl. Assn. Ga. Educators, Bus. and Profl. Woman's Club (pres. 1973-75, dist. dir. Ga. Fedn., state chmn. Young Careerist 1977-79, state chmn. nat. found. 1979-81), DAR (regent Thronateeska chpt. 1986-88, state chmn. Am. Heritage 1986-88, dist. dir. Ga. soc. 1988-90, state officer, historian 1990-92, state chmn. textbook study nat. soc. 1992-94, state officer, registrar 1994-96, state officer, libr. 1996-98). Methodist. Avocations: reading, jogging, georgia bulldog activities, basketball, football. Home: 1706 Pineknoll Ln Albany GA 31707-3770 Office: Alice Coachman Elem 1425 Oakridge Dr Albany GA 31707

FORSYTH, T. HENRY, plastic researcher; b. Pikeville, Ky., Nov. 8, 1942; s. Thomas H. Forsyth and Gearldean Absher Branham; m. Suzanne Reynolds Forsyth, May 24, 1963; children: Rebecca Lee, Thomas Patrick. BAChemE, U Ky., 1964; MS, Va. Poly. Inst, 1966; PhD, Va. Poly. Inst., 1968. EIT Reg. Profl. Engr., Ohio. Materials scientist Dow Chemical Co., Mid;land, Mich., 1967—70; assoc. prof. U Akron (Ohio), 1970—80; rsch. assoc. BF Goodrich, Avon Lake, Ohio, 1980—91, Noveon, Inc., Brecksville, Ohio, 1991—. Dir. 20 Masters and Doctoral Studies, 1970—80; participant Geon's CIM Bus. Team, 1984—90; participated TempRite's Bus. Segment Teams, 1991—. Contbr. articles. Recipient Engr of the Year, AIChE, 1980, Injection Molder of the Year, Injection Molding Soc. of Plast. Engr., 2000. Mem.: Soc. of Plastics Engrs. Presbyn./Bapt. Avocations: investing, reading, Am. History, Natural Sci.. Office: Noveon, Inc 9921 Brecksville Brecksville OH 44141 Home: 19980 Park Lane Dr Rocky River OH 44116

FORSYTHE, DENNIS M. biology educator; b. Toledo, Ohio, June 20, 1942; s. Glenn Luther Forsythe and Rowena Louise Kimmerlin; m. Neva Jean Vellenweth, Aug. 1, 1964 (div. Mar. 10, 1983); children: David Andrew, James Russell; m. Donna Wolfe, Mar. 24, 1990. BS in Zoology, Ohio U., 1964; MS in Zoology, Utah State U., 1967; PhD in Zoology, Clemson U., 1973. Upland game supr. Minn. Game & Fish, Madelia, 1967—68; from asst. to full prof. The Citadel, Charleston, SC, 1969—. Office: Biology Dept The Citadel 171 Moultrie St Charleston SC 29409

FORSYTHE, HENDERSON, actor; b. Macon, Mo., Sept. 11, 1917; s. Cecil Proctor and Mary Catherine (Henderson) F.; m. Dorothea Maria Carlson, May 26, 1942; children: Eric, Jason. Student, Culver-Stockton Coll., 1935-37; BA, State U. Iowa, 1939, M.F.A., 1940. Mem. faculty, dir. U. Iowa, summers 1953-55 Numerous appearances Broadway and off-Broadway plays, TV and film prodns., 1955—; sheriff in U.S. and London prodns. Best Little Whorehouse in Texas (Tony award); prin. role in TV series Eisenhower and Lutz, CBS, 1987-88, Nearly Departed, 1989; appeared in running role in daytime TV drama As the World Turns, 1960-91; prin. role in 110 in the Shade, N.Y.C. Opera, 1992; lead in Quarrel of Sparrows, 1993; TV comml./Col. Sanders for Kentucky Fried Chicken, 1994. Served with U.S. Army, 1941-46. Mem. Actors Equity Assn., AFTRA, Screen Actors Guild, ANTA. Presbyterian.

FORSYTHE, JANET WINIFRED, lawyer; b. L.A., May 12, 1957; d. John Winston and Madeleine S. (Henry) F. BA, George Washington U., 1979; JD, Georgetown U., 1982. Bar: Calif. 1983. Head atty. Pub. Defender's Office, City and County of San Francisco, 1983—97. Criminal law specialist, 1988-98. Bd. dirs. No. Calif. Svc. League, San Francisco, 1985-87, Black Coalition on AIDS, v.p., 1996-2001; founding mem. Women Across Generations, 1997—, pres., 1999—. Coro Found. City Focus fellow, 1989-90. Mem. Bar Assn. San Francisco (chmn. community law week 1988, jud. evaluation com. 1989-91, bd. dirs. Barristers Club 1987-88, Barrister of Yr. 1988, bd. dirs., 1992-93, criminal justice adv. com., 1992-96), Lawyers Club San Francisco. Democrat. Judeo-Christian. Avocations: biking, weight training, embroidery, crocheting. Office: PO Box 320115 San Francisco CA 94132-0115

FORSYTHE, ROBERT ELLIOTT, economics educator; b. Pitts., Oct. 25, 1949; s. Robert Elliott and Dolores Jean (Davis) F.; m. Lynn Maureen Zollweg, June 17, 1970 (div. July 1978); m. Patricia Ann Hays, June 20, 1981; 1 child, Nathaniel Ryan. BS, Pa. State U., 1970; MS, Carnegie-Mellon U., Pitts., 1972, MS, 1974, PhD, 1975. Ops. rsch. analyst PPG Industries Inc., Pitts., 1970-72; instr. Carnegie-Mellon U., Pitts., 1974-75; asst. prof. Calif. Inst. Tech., Pasadena, 1975-81; assoc. prof. U. Iowa, Iowa City, 1981-86, prof. econ., 1986-90, chmn. dept. econ., 1990-94, sr. assoc. dean Coll. Bus., 1994—, Cedar Rapids Area Bus. Chair, 1992-2000, Leonard A. Hadley Chair in Leadership, 2000—. Founder Iowa Polit. Stock Market; pres. Iowa Market Systems, Inc., 1993-2000. Author: Forecasting Presidential Elections: Polls, Markets, Models; assoc. editor Jour. Econ. Behavior and Orgn., Jour. Exptl. Econs., 1997—. Recipient State of Iowa Regents award for faculty excellence, 2002; Univ. faculty scholar U. Iowa, 1985-88. Mem. Econometric Soc., Am. Econ. Assn., Econ. Sci. Assn. (sect. head 1989-92, pres.-elect 1992-93, pres. 1993-95). Congregationalist. Home: 1806 E Court St Iowa City IA 52245-4643 Office: U Iowa Tippie Coll Bus 108 Pappajohn Bus Bldg Iowa City IA 52242-1000 E-mail: robert-forsythe@uiowa.edu.

FORSYTHE-ADAMSON, VELMA BROWN, accountant, consultant, English language educator; b. California, Pa., Apr. 27, 1928; d. Ernest and Anne Leyland Brown; m. Forrest Evans Forsythe, Aug. 6, 1950 (dec. Oct. 1982); children: Leslie Ann, Lynn Allyson; m. Robert E.L. Adamson, June 22, 2002. BS in Bus. Edn., Ind. (Pa.) U., 1950; student various univs. and colls., Pa. and Wis., 1952-96. High sch. tchr. bus. edn., Pa. and Ohio, 1954-58; v.p., tax preparer Kincaid Tax Svc., Akron, Ohio, 1968-74; pub. acct. Pitts. and Akron, 1974-82; controller Holiday Inn, Dubois, Pa., 1982-86; asst. controller Radisson Hotel, Lexington, Ky., 1986-87; asst. to pres. Petrolec Inc.-Jadel Inc., Clearfield, Pa., 1987-88; acct., cons. Forsythe Bus. Svcs., Dubois, 1982—; tchr. ELI Ulaanbartar, Mongolia, 1999—. Vol. Internat. Exec. Svc. Corps., Egypt, Ghana, Slovak Republic, Stanford, Conn., 1992—; lay missionary fin. and edn. United Meth. Ch. Uganda, Mozambique, 1991—; missionary amb. to Indonesia, 1998; vol. exec. Citizens Democracy Corps, Republic of Georgia, spring, 2000, Russia, summer and fall, 2000. Mem. AAUW (program chair 1997-99, Woman of Yr. award 1998), Kappa Delta Pi, Delta Sigma Epsilon. Republican. Methodist. Avocations: travel, reading, hiking, canoeing. Home and Office: 717 Treasure Lk Du Bois PA 15801-9019 E-mail: vel4sythe@webtv.net.

FORT, ARTHUR TOMLINSON, III, physician, educator; b. Lumpkin, Ga., Sept. 24, 1931; s. Thomas Morton and Gladys (Davis) F.; m. Jane Wilmer McClelland, June 15, 1957; children: Abby Lucinda, Arthur Tomlinson IV, Juliana Melody, Ernest Arlington, II. BBA, U. Ga., 1952; MD, U. Tenn., 1962. Diplomate: Am. Bd. Ob-Gyn, Am. Bd. Family Practice. Intern, then resident in ob-gyn U. Tenn.-City of Memphis Hosp., 1962-66; asst. prof. U. Tenn. Med. Sch., 1966-70; prof. ob-gyn, head dept. Sch. Medicine La. State U., Shreveport, 1970-73; prof. maternal-child health and family planning, head program family health Sch. Pub. Health Tulane U., 1973-74; prof. practice medicine specializing in rural family medicine Vacharie, La., 1974-79; prof. ob-gyn and family medicine, head dept. family medicine and comprehensive care Sch. Medicine La. State U., Shreveport, 1980—. Author articles in field. Adv. bd. mem. State of La. Dept. Health and Human Resources, 1986-88. With USAF, 1952-57. Recipient Golden Apple Teaching award Student AMA, 1969, Golden Apple Teaching award Western Interstate Commn. on Higher Edn., 1973 Fellow Am. Coll. Ob-Gyn, Am. Acad. Family Practice; mem. AMA. Office: PO Box 33932 Shreveport LA 71130-3932

FORT, DENISE DOUGLAS, law educator, former state official; b. Lexington, Ky., July 24, 1951; d. John Porter and Ruth (Chapin) Fort. BA, St. John's Coll., 1972; JD, Cath. U. Am., 1975. Bar: N.Mex. 1976, U.S. Supreme Ct. 1976, U.S. Ct. Appeals (9th and 10th cirs.) 1976. Atty. N.Mex. Pub. Interest Rsch. Group, Albuquerque, 1976-77, S.W. Rsch. and Info. Ctr., Albuquerque, 1977-79, Taxation and Revenue Dept., Santa Fe, 1979-83; sec. gov.'s cabinet Dept. Fin. and Adminstrn., Santa Fe, 1983-84, Environ. Improvement Dept., Santa Fe, 1979-83; prof. law U. N.Mex., Albuquerque, 1991—. Past mem. State Investment Coun., Santa Fe, 1983-84; exec. sec. N.Mex. Bd. Fin., Santa Fe, 1983-84; dir. water resources adminstrn. program, U. N.Mex., 1991-96; chair We. Water Policy Rev. Adv. Com., 1995-98; mem. water, sci. and tech. bd. NRC, 1997-2000; mem. N.Mex. Water Trust Bd., 2003—. Democrat.

FORT, JAMES TOMLINSON, lawyer; b. Albany, N.Y., Apr. 12, 1928; s. Tomlinson and Beatrice (Lawson) F.; m. Judith Anne Davis, May 9, 1959; children: Edward Tomlinson, Madeline Annabelle. AB, Allegheny Coll.; LL.B., Yale U. Bar: Supreme Ct. Assoc. Reed Smith Shaw & McClay, Pitts., 1954-62, ptnr., 1962—. Trustee Allegheny Coll., Meadville, Pa., 1975—; dir. Pitts. Dance Council, 1977-83, Pitts. Ballet Theatre Inc. With USMC, 1953-54. Mem. Bar Supreme Ct. U.S., Am. Coll. Trial Lawyers. Clubs: Duquesne (Pitts.), Rivers. Democrat. Presbyterian. Home: 204 Woodcock Dr Pittsburgh PA 15215-1546 Office: Reed Smith LLP 435 6th Ave Pittsburgh PA 15219-1886

FORT, JEFFREY C. lawyer; b. Burlington, Iowa, Oct. 10, 1950; s. Lyman R. and Lucille (Gibb) F.; m. Diane Locandro; children: Christopher Glen, Elizabeth Anne. BA, Monmouth, 1972; JD, Northwestern U., 1975. Bar: Ill. 1975, U.S. Dist. Ct. (no. dist.) Ill. 1976, U.S. Ct. Appeals (7th cir.) 1977, U.S. Ct. Appeals (D.C. cir.) 1985, U.S. Supreme Ct. 1980. Law clk. to John M. Karns, Jr. Appellate Ct., Belleville, Ill., 1975-76; assoc. Martin Craig Chester, et al, Chgo., 1976-83, ptnr., 1983-88, Gardner Carton & Douglas, Chgo., 1988-90, Sonnenschein Nath & Rosenthal, Chgo., 1990—. Adj. prof. Northwestern U. Sch. Law, Chgo., 1990-92; presenter in field. Author: Establishing an Effective Environmental Law Compliance Program, 1993—; editl. bd. Environmental Law for the Transactional Lawyer, 1991, rev. edit., 1994, 2001, Illinois Environmental Law, 1993, 2000; contbr. articles to profl. jours. Chair Lake Mich. States sect. Air and Waste Mgmt. Assn., Chgo., 1988-89; elder 1st Presbyn. Ch. Wilmette, Ill., 1990-93, 2001—. Mem. ABA, Chgo. Bar Assn. (chair environ. law com. 1987-88), Met. Club. Office: Sonnenschein Nath & Rosenthal 8000 Sears Tower Chicago IL 60606

FORT, JULIANA MELODY, psychiatrist; b. Memphis, Sept. 21, 1962; d. Arthur Tomlinson and Jane (McClelland) F.; m. William Dale Knox, Dec. 20, 1986; children: Eleanore, William, Clyde, Ernest. BS, La. State U., 1984, MD, 1986; MPH, U. South Fla., 2000; MBA, Centenary Coll., 2001. Diplomate in psychiatry, child and adolescent psychiatry, addiction psychiatry, geriatric psychiatry, forensic psychiatry Am. Bd. Psychiatry and Neurology. Resident in gen. psychiatry Tulane Med. Sch., New Orleans, 1986-90, fellow in child and adolescent psychiatry, 1989-91; clin. staff psychiatrist Schumpert Med. Ctr., Shreveport; clin. staff psychiatrist, med. dir. geriat. unit Minden (La.) Med. Ctr., 1995—2002; courtesy clin. asst. prof. psychiatry La. State U., Shreveport, 1991—2002; asst. prof. psychiatry and pediats. La. State U. Health Scis. Ctr., 2002—. Staff psychiatrist children and adolescents Shreveport Mental Healthcare; advisor La. Psychiat. Assn. Newsletter, 2000—. Founding chmn. 5O1C3 Red River Zooport, 1999; vol. Jr. League; hon. advisor African-Am. Tourism Commn. Mem. AMA (del. resident physician sect. 1987), La. State Med. Soc. (del. 1988, 99, mental health and substance abuse com. vice chmn. 1994, chmn. 1996), La. Assn. for Play Therapy (founding charter mem., bd. dirs., 1st treas.), Assn. for Play Therapy, Am. Acad. Child and Adolescent psychiatry, Shreveport Med. Soc., So. Med. Assn., Am. Psychiat. Assn. (Disting. fellow 2000), La. Psychiat. Assn. (com. on psychiatry and religion, pub. affairs com. 1998-99, com. on women, pres. N.W. chpt. 1994), Charity Hosp. House Staff Assn. (pres. 1987-88), Optimist Club, Phi Kappa Phi. Republican. Presbyterian. Office: LSUHSC Dept Psychiatry PO Box 33932 Shreveport LA 71130-3932

FORT, RANDALL MARTIN, investment banking executive; b. Richmond, Ind., July 4, 1956; Student, U. Cin., 1974-76; BA in Pub. Affairs with distinction, George Washington U., 1978. Various positions with rep. Willis D. Gradison Jr., Cin. and Washington, 1976-80; rsch. asst. office of hon. Roo Watanabe M.P., Tokyo, 1980-81; asst. dir., dep. exec. dir. Pres's. Fgn. Intelligence Adv. Bd., Washington, 1982-87; spl. asst. to sec. nat. security U.S. Dept. Treasury, Washington, 1987-89; dep. asst. sec. for functional analysis and rsch. U.S. Dept. State, Washington, 1989-93; dir. spl. projects TRW, Inc., Washington, 1993-96; v.p. Goldman Sachs, 1996—. Luce scholar Henry Luce Found., 1980. Mem. The Asia Soc., Phi Beta Kappa. Republican. Methodist. Office: Goldman Sachs 180 Maiden Ln Fl 15 New York NY 10038

FORT, ROBERT BRADLEY, minister; b. Portsmouth, Va., Dec. 27, 1948; s. Richard Gould and Hazel Naomi (McBride) F.; m. Esther Faith Hardin, June 10, 1967; children: Yvonne René, Nathan Michael. Ordained to ministry United Evang. Ch., 1973. Evangelist United Evang. Chs., Monrovia, Calif., 1966, nat. youth dir., 1968-70, asst. to the pres., 1970-73, Calif. dist. supt., 1973-75; evangelist Assemblies of God, Springfield, Mo., 1976-78; sr. pastor Lynden (Wash.) Assembly of God, 1978-81, County Christian Ctr., Bellingham, Wash., 1981-87, First Assembly of God, Salinas, Calif., 1988—. Exec. dir. Life Mgmt. Sems., Salinas, 1989—; pres. Ft. Ministries, Salinas, 1967—; exec. v.p., chmn. bd., CEO United Evang. Chs., Hollister, Calif., 1996—; faculty NY Coll. Advanced Studies, 2002—; plenary spkr. World Congress Evang. Chs., Nairobi, Kenya, Africa, 1993. Composer Love was the Color, 1980 (Grand prize Music City Songfest, Nashville, 1981); singer, musician 15 records. Chmn. resolutions com. NorCal/Nev. Dist. of the Assemblies of God, 1997-2000; mem. bd. adminstrn. Pentecostal/Charismatic Chs. N.Am., 2001—. Fellow: N.Am. Acad. Arts and Scis.; mem.: Am. Assn. Christian Counselors (charter mem.). Republican. Office: Fort Ministries PO Box 1000 San Juan Bautista CA 95045-1000

FORT, TOMLINSON, chemist, chemical engineering educator; b. Sumter, S.C., Apr. 16, 1932; s. Tomlinson and Madeline A. Kean (Scott) F.; m. Martha Kirby, Oct. 13, 1956; children: Tomlinson, III, Frances Clare; m. Nancy H. Blackwelder, Dec. 19, 1998. BS in Chemistry, U. Ga., 1952; MS, PhD in Phys. Chemistry, U. Tenn., 1957; A.E. and F.A.Q. Stephens postdoctoral fellow, U. Sydney, Australia, 1957-58; cert., Inst. Ednl. Mgmt., Harvard U., 1978. Instr. surface chemistry U. Sydney, 1957—58; rsch. chemist, then sr. rsch. chemist and project leader duPont Co., 1958—65; mem. faculty Case Western Res. U., 1965—73, prof. chem. engring., dir. surfaces research lab., 1971—73; prof. chem. engring. and chemistry, head dept. chem. engring. Carnegie-Mellon U., 1973—80, adj. prof., 1980—83; prof. chemistry and chem. engring., provost U. Mo., Rolla, 1980—82; v.p. acad. affairs Calif. Poly. State U., San Luis Obispo, 1982—83, provost, 1983—86, prof. chemistry and materials sci., 1986—89; Centennial prof. chem. engring., prof. materials sci. Vanderbilt U., Nashville, 1989—2002, Centennial prof. chem. engring. emeritus, 2002—, chair dept. chem. engring., 1989—96. Summer vis. prof. Nat. U. Mex., 1973, U. Copenhagen, 1978, 80; pres. Frances Fort Brown Realty Co., Chattanooga, 1970-94. Author papers on surface and colloid sci. Mem. AAAS, Am. Chem. Soc., Am. Inst. Chem. Engrs., Internat. Assn. of Colloid and Interface Scientists, KP, Sigma Xi, Phi Beta Delta, Gamma Sigma Epsilon, Alpha Chi Sigma, Sigma Chi. Home: 1015 Carlisle Ln Franklin TN 37064-4802 Office: Vanderbilt U Dept Chem Engring PO Box 1604 Station B Nashville TN 37235 E-mail: tomlinson.fort@vanderbilt.edu.

FORTADO, MICHAEL GEORGE, lawyer; b. Wichita Falls, Tex., Oct. 29, 1943; s. Antonio and Flossie Juanita (Bowers) F.; m. Avis Ann Smith, Mar. 12, 1964; children: Michael Scott, Angela Avis, Shannon Michelle. BBA, Midwestern U., Wichita Falls, 1965; LLB, U. Tex., Austin, 1968. Bar: Tex. 1968. Assoc. atty. firm McClure & Sharpe, Houston, 1968-69; atty. Enserch Corp. (and predecessor), Dallas, 1969-71, corp. sec., asst. gen. counsel, 1971-88, v.p., corp. sec., asst. gen. counsel, 1988-96; sr. v.p., gen. counsel, corp. sec. Enserch Exploration, Inc., Dallas, 1996-97; v.p., gen. counsel, corp. sec. Trinity Industries, Inc., Dallas, 1997—. Mem. ABA, Am. Soc. Corp. Secs. (bd. dirs. 1980-83), State Bar Tex., Dallas Bar Assn., DAC Country Club, Kappa Alpha Order, Delta Sigma Pi, Phi Alpha Delta. Office: Trinity Industries Inc 2525 N Stemmons Fwy Ste 1000 Dallas TX 75207-2400 E-mail: mike.fortado@trin.net.

FORTE, MARGARET LAYMAN, mathematics educator; b. Troutville, Va., Aug. 28, 1938; d. John Cline and Elsie Marie (Montgomery) Layman; m. Wesley Elbert Forte, July 29, 1961; children: Laura Jean, Scott Montgomery. BA, Longwood Coll., 1959; MA, So. Methodist U., 1975. Cert. math tchr., N.Y., reading specialist, Tex. Math tchr. Fairfax (Va.) Schs., 1959-61, The Baldwin Sch., Bryn Mawr, Pa., 1961-62, The Brearley Sch., N.Y.C., 1962-63, Lakehill Prep Sch., Dallas, 1977-78; adj. prof. math Westchester C.C., Valhalla, N.Y., 1989-93; adj. prof. edn. Iona Coll., New Rochelle, N.Y., 1994; adj. prof. math Coll. of New Rochelle, 1994-98, Concordia Coll., Bronxville, N.Y., 1994; asst. dir. learning support svcs. Coll. of New Rochelle, 1996-98. Bd. dirs. Friends of Bronxville (N.Y.) Pub. Libr., 1994-96. Mem. DAR (registrar 1985-87, 93-97, regent 1987-89), Kappa Delta Pi, Phi Delta Kappa. Avocation: collecting antique dolls. Home: 35 Green Meadow Ln East Falmouth MA 02536-6954 E-mail: margief@aol.com.

FORTE, STEPHEN FORREST, interior designer; b. Shreveport, La., Oct. 18, 1947; s. Forrest Lee and Alva (Clary) F. BA, Centenary Coll., Shreveport, 1971; postgrad., La. Tech U., 1971, Parsons Sch. Design, Paris, 1981. Lic. interior designer, La., Fla. Interior designer Interiors, Inc., Shreveport, 1974-75, Yarbrough Interior Designers, Shreveport, 1975-85; pres. Stephen Forte Interior Design, Shreveport, 1985—. Prin. works include: Strand Theatre Restoration, Shreveport, 1981-85, One Tex. Ctr., Shreveport, 1986, Southdown Retirement Ctr., Baton Rouge, 1988, Goodrich Oil Co., 1990, Caddo Parish Commn. Offices, 1993, Champion Lake Complex, Shreveport, La., 1995-96, Hummingbird & King, CPA, Shreveport, 1999, Ultimate Appearances Salon, Shreveport, 1999, Resneck Dermatology Offices, Shreveport, 2001, Iz and Max Botique, Shreveport, 2002; featured in The Designer, Designers West and So. Living mag. articles. Mem. Internat. Interior Design Assn., Internat. Soc. Interior Designers (chmn. membership). Democrat. Roman Catholic. Office: PO Box 52117 Shreveport LA 71135

FORTE, WESLEY ELBERT, former insurance company executive, lawyer; b. Worcester, Mass., Dec. 1, 1933; s. Elbert W. and Ethel M. (Lyons) F.; m. Margaret Ellen Layman, July 29, 1961; children: Laura Jean, Scott Montgomery. BBA, Clark U., 1956; JD, N.Y. U., 1959, LL.M., 1965. Bar: Pa. 1960, Ohio 1972, U.S. Supreme Ct 1972, Tex. 1974, D.C. 1975, N.Y. 1980. Atty. Dechert, Price & Rhoads, Phila., 1959-62; atty. corporate law dept. Standard Brands, Inc., N.Y.C., 1962-66; atty., foods div. counsel Borden, Inc., N.Y.C., 1966-71, sr. counsel domestic ops., 1971-72; sr. v.p. legal affairs Campbell-Taggart, Inc., Dallas, 1972-73, exec. v.p., gen. counsel, dir., 1973-79; sr. v.p. law USLIFE Corp., N.Y.C., 1979-85, exec. v.p., gen. counsel, 1985-97. Contbr. articles to profl. jours. Home: 35 Green Meadow Ln East Falmouth MA 02536-6954

FORTENBAUGH, SAMUEL BYROD, III, lawyer; b. Phila., Nov. 6, 1933; s. Samuel Byrod Jr. and Katherine Francisca (Wall) F.; children: Samuel Byrod IV, Cristina Fortenbaugh Alemany, Katherine Fortenbaugh-Silliman, Francesca Cowden; m. Sharon A. Swartz, Nov. 17, 2001. BA, Williams Coll., 1955; LLB, Harvard U., 1960. Bar: N.Y. 1961, U.S. Dist. Ct. (so. dist.) N.Y. 1961. Assoc. Kelley Drye & Warren, N.Y.C., 1960—69, ptnr., 1970—79, Morgan, Lewis & Bockius, 1980—2001, sr. counsel, 2001—02; atty. pvt. practice, 2002—. Bd. dirs. Baldwin Tech. Co., Inc., Shelton, Conn., Security Capital Corp., Greenwich, Conn.; bd. dirs., sec. Furgueson Capital Mgmt. Inc., N.Y.C.; chmn. bd. dirs., sec. Wall Industries, Inc., Kannapolis, N.C.; chmn. bd. dirs. Knight Textile Corp, Saluda, S.C.; trustee Patroni Scholastici, New Brunswick, N.J., 1978—, sec. 1985—; lectr. profl. seminars. Contbr. articles to profl. jours. Mem. ABA, Assn. of Bar of City of N.Y. (mem. Young Lawyers com. 1962-65, corp. law com. 1976-79, com. on securities regulation 1982-85, chmn. com. on issue distbn. of securities 1984-85), Univ. Club (N.Y.C.), N.Y. Yacht Club, Indian Harbor Yacht Club (Greenwich, Conn.) (bd. dirs.), Phi Beta Kappa. Office: 1211 Ave of Ams 27th fl New York NY 10036

FORTENBERRY, DELORES B. dean; b. McComb, MS, Jan. 31, 1933; d. Isaac and Maude Elma (Carmel) Brown; m. John Prowell, Jan. 22, 1956 (div. 1960); children: Dennis A. Prowell, Stevie G. Prowell; m. Fred D. Fortenberry, Dec. 3, 1971. BS, Jackson State U., 1963; MA, Ball State U., 1974, EdD, 1988. Sci. & math. tchr. McComb (Ms.) Pub. Schs., 1962-65; sci. tchr. Chgo. Pub. Schs., 1965-68; sci., art tchr. E. Chgo. Pub. Sch., Ind., 1968-80; sci. tchr. Ball State U. Lab Sch., Muncie, IL, 1980-81; sci., math. tchr., gen. edn. E. Chgo. Pub. Sch., Ind., 1981-89, dean, 1989—. Pres. Dist. Sci. Fair com., McComb, Miss., 1964-65; nat. chairperson Pike County Agrl. H.S. Alumni, Chgo., 1991-2000, Pike County Agrl. H.S. scholarship fund; chmn. sci. com. Nat. Alliance Black Sch. Educators, Washington, Chgo. Alliance Black Sch. Educators, 1984-86. Fellow NSF, 1963-64, Ball State U., 1980-81; sabbatical leave E. Chgo. Pub. Sch., 1980-81. Mem. AAUW, Nat. Alliance Black Sch. Educators, Chgo. Alliance Black Sch. Educators (certificate 1986), Afro-Am. History Club (chairperson 1999-2000), Pike County Agrl. H.S. Alumni (nat. chairperson 1991-2000, recipient plaques 1992-94, 96-98), Am. Fedn. Tchrs., Nat. Sci. Tchrs. Assn., Hoosier Assn. Sci. Tchrs., Assn. Supervision and Curriculum Devel., Kappa Delta Pi, Gamma Phi Delta (basilieus, 1968-73), Phi Delta Kappa. Avocations: reading, travel, collecting recipes, collecting black history materials, sports. Home: 831 E 192nd St Glenwood IL 60425-2005 Office: Ctrl High Sch 1100 W Columbus Dr East Chicago IN 46312-2582

FORTEZZA, VICTOR, writer; b. Bklyn., May 21, 1950; s. Vittorio and Gaetana Fortezza. BS, Western Mich.U., Kalamazoo, 1971. Author: (novel) Close to the Edge, 2000, (e-novel) Killing, (plays) The Last Laugh, numerous short stories and essays. Home: 2546 E 13th St #B-12 Brooklyn NY 11235 Office: NYMEX One North End New York NY 10001 Personal E-mail: chingame@flash.net.

FORTGANG, CHARLES, wholesale distribution executive; b. 1932; Grad., Syracuse U., 1953. With M. Fabrikant & Sons Inc., 1955—, CEO, now chmn.

FORTH, KEVIN BERNARD, beverage distributing industry consultant; b. Adams, Mass., Dec. 4, 1949; s. Michael Charles and Catherine Cecilia (McAndrews) F.; m. Alice Farnum (dec. 1994); children: Melissa, Brian; m. Deborah Newport. AB, Holy Cross Coll., 1971; MBA with distinction, NYU, 1973, Benjamin Levy fellow. Divsn. rep. Anheuser-Busch, Inc., Boston, 1973-74, dist. sales mgr. L.A., 1974-76, asst. to v.p. mktg. staff St. Louis, 1976-77; v.p. Straub Distbg. Co., Ltd., Orange, Calif., 1977-81, pres., 1981-93, chmn., CEO, 1986-93. Commr. Orange County Sheriff's Adv. Coun., 1988—; mem. adv. bd. Rancho Santiago C.C. Coll. Dist., 1978-80; bd. dirs. Children's Hosp. of Orange County Padrinos Found., 1983-85, St. Joseph's Hosp. Found., Orange County Sports Hall of Fame, 1980-89, Wilcox Health Found., 2003—; exec. com., bd. dirs. Nat. Coun. on Alcoholism, 1980-83; mem. pres. coun. Holy Cross Coll., 1987-91; bd. dirs., pres. Calif. State Fullerton Titan Athletic Found., 1983-85, 89-90; mem. Calif. Beer Wholesalers Assn., dir., 1978-89, v.p., 1984, chmn., 1985; bd. dirs. Freedom Bowl, 1984-93 (founders award, 1993), v.p., 1984-85, pres., 1986, chmn., 1986-87, Anaheim Vis. and Conv. Bur., 1989- 93,; bd. dirs. Orangewood Children's Found., 1988-93; mem. Calif. Rep. State Ctrl. Com., 1988-93, Orange County Probation Dept. Cmty. Involvement Bd., 1992-93. Recipient Vol. of Yr. award Calif. State U., Fullerton, 1990. Mem. Nat. Beer Wholesalers Assn. (bd. dirs. 1986-93, asst. sec. 1989-90, sec. 1989-91, vice-chmn. 1992, chmn. 1993; Lifetime Achievement Svc. award 2001), Holy Cross Alumni Assn., Sports Car Club Am. (Ariz. state champion 1982), Beta Gamma Sigma. Roman Catholic. Home and Office: 3636 Keoniana Rd Princeville HI 96722-

FORTI, LENORE STEIMLE, business consultant; b. Houghton, Mich., Sept. 9, 1924; d. Russell Nicholas and Agnes (McCloskey) Steimle; m. Frank Forti, May 29, 1950 (dec.). BBA summa cum laude, Northwood U., 1973, Dr.Laws, 1969. Asst. corp. sec., purchasing agt. Fed. Life & Casualty Co., Detroit, 1942-53; supr. sectl. J.L. Hudson Co., Detroit, 1953-57, adminstrv. asst. to exec. v.p., 1957-86; instr. Wayne State U. and U. Mich. Adult Edn., Detroit, 1958-71; creator, dir. Seminars for Profl. People, 1971—. Co-author: The Professional Secretary; contbr. articles to profl. jours. Asst. br. dir. planning City of Detroit for Civil Def.; chmn. bd. trustees PSI Rsch. and Ednl. Found., trustee PSI Retirement Home Complex, Albuquerque; elected dir. Property Owners and Residents Assn., Sun City West Mcpl. Govt., 1994—97; past pres. Women's Bd. Northwood U., Midland, Mich.; pres. parish coun. Our Lady of Lourdes Ch., Sun City West, Ariz., 1988, pres. ladies guild, 1990, 1995; 1st v.p. Vol. Bur. of Sun Cities, 1989; bd. dirs., pres. Sun City West Found., 2002—03; bd. dirs. Sun City West Cmty. Fund, 1998—99. Elected One of Detroit's Top Ten Working Women, 1969; elected to Exec. and Profl. Hall of Fame. Mem. Internat. Assn. Adminstrv. Profls. (internat. pres. 1967-69), Future Secs. Assn. (nat. coord.), Lioness Club (pres. 1991-92), Sun City West Singles Club (pres. 1988). Republican. Roman Catholic. Avocations: bridge, Mah Jongg, dancing. Home and Office: 12613 W Seneca Dr Sun City West AZ 85375-4635

FORTI, WILLIAM BELL, business executive, inventor; b. Washington, Dec. 6, 1941; s. Francis and Margaret Lee (Bell) F.; m. Martha Louise Goding; children: Scott, Jennifer, Meredith, Kimberly, Mark, Andrea. BS, U. Richmond, 1963, MComm., 1964. Fin. analyst SEC, Washington, 1964-66; economist Joint tax, House judiciary, Senate commerce coms. U.S. Congress, Washington, 1966-71; mgmt. positions in bus. planning and devel. Bendix Corp., Southfield, Mich., 1971-75, Internat. Paper Co., N.Y.C., 1975-78, Gen. Dynamics, St. Louis, 1978-92; founder, chmn. William Mark Corp., Claremont, Calif., 1992—. Patentee flying recreational products. Bd. visitors sch. ednl. studies Claremont Grad. U.; mem. World Affairs Coun., L.A., 2001; participant current strategy forum Naval War Coll., RI, 2003, nat. security forum Air War Coll., Maxwell AFB, Ala., 1997; trustee Naval War Coll. Found., 2001—; co-chmn. L.A. County Aerospace Task Force, L.A., 1992; chmn. internat. trade legislation working group Def. Planning Adv. Com. on Trade, 1986. Recipient Recognition of Dedicated Svc. County of L.A., 1992, Recognition of Contribution Naval War Coll. Found., 1997, Joint Civilian Orientation Conf., 1999. Mem.: NSTA, Def. Orientation Conf. Assn. (bd. dirs. 1999—2001), Claremont C. of C., Naval War Coll. Found. (trustee 2001—), Radio Controlled Hobby Trade Assn., Kite Trade Assn., Rotary, Claremont U. Club (asst. treas. 1994—). Republican. Avocations: travel, reading, hiking. Office: William Mark Corp 112 Harvard Ave Claremont CA 91711-4716

FORTIER, ALBERT MARK, JR., lawyer; b. Cambridge, Mass., July 22, 1936; s. Albert M. and Marie R. (Tagney) F.; m. Bente Mortensen, Nov. 10, 1964; children: John, Mark. AB, U. Chgo., 1955; LLB, Harvard U., 1958. Bar: Mass. 1958. Assoc. Richard S. Bowers, Boston, 1958-65; ptnr. Bowers, Fortier & Lakin, Boston, 1966-76, Rackemann, Sawyer & Brewster, Boston, 1976—. Contbr. articles to profl. jours. Mem. ABA, Am. Bar Found., Boston Bar Assn. (probate sect. former chair), Am. Coll. Trust and Estate Counsel (past state chair), Union Club (Boston, past bd. govs.). Republican. Methodist. Home: 90 Craftsland Rd Chestnut Hill MA 02467-2632 Office: Rackemann Sawyer & Brewster One Financial Ctr Boston MA 02111 E-mail: amf@rackemann.com.

FORTIER, L. YVES, barrister; b. Quebec City, Que., Can., Sept. 11, 1935; s. Francois and Louise (Turgeon) F.; m. C. Carol Eaton, Sept. 26, 1959; children: Michel, Suzanne, Margot. BA summa cum laude, U. Montreal, 1955; BCL, McGill U., 1958; BLitt, Oxford U., 1960, LLD (hon.), 1989, 92, 93, 99. Created Queen's counsel, 1976. Sr. ptnr., chmn. Ogilvy, Renault Advs., Barristers and Solicitors, Montreal, 1960—, on leave; Can. amb. to UN N.Y.C., 1988-92. Counsel Can. in Can.-USA, Gulf Maine Case in World Ct., 1984, Royal Commns., Commn. Inquiry War Criminals, Commn. Inquiry Lang. Air Tarffic Control, Commn. Inquiry R.C.M.P.; mem. Permanent Ct. Arbitration The Hague, 1984-1991; pres. London Ct. Internat. Arbitration, 1998-2001; chief negotiator Can.-France fishing dispute, 1987-89, Can.-U.S. Pacific Salmon Treaty dispute, 1993-98; Can.'s chief del. to 43d, 44th, 45th, 46th, sessions UN Gen. Assembly, Can. rep. UN Security Coun., 1989-90; v.p. UN 45th Gen. Assembly; gov. Hudson's Bay Co., Nortel Networks Corp.; bd. dirs. Royal Bank Can., Nova Chems. Corp., duPont Can. Inc.; chmn. bd. dirs. Alcan Inc. Bd. dirs. Can. Inst. Advanced Legal Studies, Internat. Peace Acad., UN Internat. Sch., Montreal Gen. Hosp. C.D. Howe Inst., Clin. Rsch. Inst., Can. Found. for AIDS Rsch.; trustee Internat. Acctg. Stds. Com. Decorated officer and companion Order of Can.; Rhodes scholar, 1960. Mem. ABA (hon.), Can. Bar Assn. (pres. 1982-83, founding dir. Law for Future Fund), Internat. Commn. Jurists (Can. sect.), Internat. Law Assn. (Can. br.), Am. Coll. Trial Lawyers (regent 1991-95), Internat. Assn. Permanent Reps. to UN (exec. bd.), Mount Royal Club (pres. 2002-03), Univ. Club, Montreal Indoor Tennis Club, Hermitage Country Club (pres. 1983-84), The Brook Club (N.Y.), The Toronto Club. Roman Catholic. Avocations: tennis, squash, skiing, golf. Home: 19 Rosemount Ave Westmount QC H3Y 3G6 Canada E-mail: yfortier@ogilvyrenault.com.

FORTIER, SAMUEL JOHN, lawyer; b. Spokane, Wash., Mar. 30, 1952; s. Charles Henry and Mary (Petersen) F.; m. Dagmar Christine Mikko, Sept. 15, 1983; children: Nova Marie, Matthew Theodore. BA cum laude, Boston U., 1974; JD magna cum laude, Gonzaga U., 1982. Bar: Alaska 1982, U.S. Dist. Ct. Alaska 1983, U.S. Ct. Appeals (9th cir.) 1987, U.S. Ct. Claims. 1999, U.S. Ct. Appeals (fed. cir.) 2000, U.S. Supreme Ct. 2002. Acting exec. dir. manpower Vista Bristol Bay Native Assn., Dillingham, Alaska, 1974-76; fin. analyst Alaska Fedn. of Natives, Anchorage, Alaska, 1976-78; loan analyst State of Alaska, Anchorage, 1978-79; law clk. consumer protection div., atty. gen.'s office State of Wash., Spokane, 1980-82; assoc. Cummings & Routh P.C., Anchorage, 1982-84; ptnr. Fortier & Mikko, Anchorage, 1984—. Adj. prof. U. Alaska, Anchorage, 1982-85; speaker workshop Small Bus. Adminstrn., Anchorage, 1982-85. Mem. ABA, Alaska Bar Assn. (Native law sect.), Anchorage Bar Assn. Democrat. Avocations: reading, writing, camping, skiing. Home: 6800 Sequoia Cir Anchorage AK 99516-3755 Office: Fortier & Mikko 101 W Benson Blvd Ste 304 Anchorage AK 99503-3936 E-mail: sfortier@fortmikk.alaska.com.

FORTINI, AMANDA PATRICIA, editor, writer; b. Iowa City, Iowa, Feb. 21, 1976; d. Patricia Marie Fortini. BA summa cum laude in English Lit., Harvard U., 1998. From editl. asst. to assoc. editor Health Mirabella Mag., N.Y.C., 1998—99, assoc. editor Health, 1999—2000; editl. asst. The N.Y. Review of Books, N.Y.C., 2000—. Contbr. ; assoc. editor: Lines of Fire: Woman Writers of WWI, 1998; contbr. articles to profl. jours. Recipient LeBaron Russell Briggs prize, Harvard U., 1998, Hoops prize, 1998. Mem.: Harvard Club N.Y.C., Young Lions, Phi Beta Kappa. Avocations: ballet, yoga. Office: The New York Review of Books 1755 South Broadway 5th Pl New York NY 10019

FORTIS, MARIE-JOSE, editor; b. Bayonne, France, Sept. 14, 1958; d. Albert Echeverria and Marianne Bérassatéguy; m. Pierre Noël Fortis, Sept. 22, 1978; 1 child, Maïa. BA in French, Clarion U. Pa., 1982, BA in Spanish, 1983, MA in English, 1986. Docent Musée Bonnat and Musée Basqe, Bayonne, 1976—77; dir. Voixde France Clarion (Pa.) U. Pa., 1978—81, ESL tutor English dept., 1983—86, temporary French instr. modern lang. dept., 1988, temporary Spanish instr. modern lang. dept., 1994, 1995; editor, founder Collages & Bricolages, Clarion, 1986—2002. Keynote spkr. AAUW, Clarion, 1994; guest poet Clarion U. Pa., 1995, Bridge Coffee House, Franklin, Pa., 1997. Editor: The Love Book, 2002, author poetry and short stories. Active P.E.A.C.E., Pa., 1988, 1997; vol. Rape Crisis Ctr., Clarion, 1989—91; sec. Alliance Française, Clarion. Recipient 1st place amateur Autumn Leaf Festival Art Show, Bi-County Artists Assn., Clarion, 2001, honorable mention for fiction, Writer's Digest 2001 Writing Competition, 2001; grantee, Sonia Raiziss Group Found., 1999—2001. Mem.: Clarion Art Coun., Amnesty Internat., Alpha Mu Gamma. Democrat. Home: PO Box 360 Shippenville PA 16254-0360

FORTMAN, MARVIN, law educator, consultant; b. Bklyn., Oct. 20, 1930; s. Herman and Bess (Smith) F.; m. Sorale Esther Elpern, Aug. 3, 1958; children: Brian E., Anita J., Deborah J. BS in Acctg., U. Ariz., 1957, JD magna cum laude, 1960; LLM, NYU, 1961. Bar: Ariz. 1960, N.Y. 1961, U.S. Tax Ct. 1962, U.S. Ct. Appeals 1962, U.S. Supreme Ct. 1962. Assoc. Aranow, Brodsky, Bolinger, Einhorn & Dann, N.Y.C., 1961-63, O'Connor, Cavanaugh, Anderson, Westover & Beshears, Phoenix, Ariz., 1963-65; prof. bus. law, bus. and pub. adminstrn. U. Ariz., Tucson, 1965—. Legal cons. various corps., 1963—. Author: Legal Aspects of Doing Business in Arizona, 1970; contbr. articles to profl. jours. Mem. legal com. Ariz. Coun. on Econ. Edn., Tucson, 1975—, Sabbar Shrine Temple, Tucson, 1978—, legal advisor, chmn. wills and gifts, 1981-84, 1990-00, 1990—. With U.S. Army, 1951-53; ETO. Kenneson fellow NYU, 1960-61. Mem. N.Y. State Bar Assn., Ariz. Bar Assn. (wills, trusts, estates sect.), Phi Kappa Phi, Beta Gamma Sigma (v.p., treas. 1972—), Beta Alpha Psi, Alpha Kappa Psi (v.p. treas. 1972-01). Home: 3844 E 15th St Tucson AZ 85711-4508 Office: U Ariz Coll Of Bus And Pub Adminstr Tucson AZ 85721-0001

FORTMANN, STEPHEN PAUL, medical educator, researcher, epidemiologist; b. Burbank, Calif., Oct. 13, 1948; s. Daniel John and Mary (Van Halteren) F.; married; children: Nicolas, Michele. AB, Stanford U., 1970; MD, U. Calif., San Francisco, 1974. Diplomate Am. Bd. Internal Medicine, Am. Coll. Epidemiology. Clin. instr. Stanford (Calif.) U. Sch. Medicine, 1979-83, asst. prof., 1983-90, assoc. prof., 1990-99, prof., 1999—. Advisor World Health Orgn., Geneva, 1980-86. Contbr. articles to profl. jours. Fellow ACP, Am. Heart Assn. (coun. on epidemiology and prevention), Am. Coll.Epidemiology, Soc. Behavioral Medicine. Avocations: photography, running. Office: Stanford U Sch Medicine 1000 Welch Rd Palo Alto CA 94304-1811 E-mail: fortmann@stanford.edu.

FORTNER, BILLIE JEAN, small business owner; b. Tarrytown, Ga. d. Willard and Sara (Beckworth) Burch; m. Randall Carroll; m. David Jones (div.); m. Robert F. Fortner, Jr., Sept. 20, 1981 (div.); children: Gina Sumner, Simone Dixon, Natalie Garner. AA summa cum laude, Brewton Parker Coll., 1970; BS, Ga. So. Coll., 1972, MEd, 1975, EdS, 1977. Math & sci. tchr. Toombs County Schs., Lyons, Ga., 1971-76, gifted tchr., 1976-81, Montgomery County Schs., Mt. Vernon, Ga., 1985-88; ptnr. Rabbit's Quik Stop, Vidalia, Ga., 1985—, Rabbit's Cargo Inc., Vidalia, 1987—, Fortner Rentals, Vidalia, 1988—, Rabbit On the Strip, Vidalia, 1988—, Fortner Farms, Vidalia, 1989—; artist-in-residence, ptnr. F.C.F. Investments, Vidalia, 1992—; ptnr. Kipling B. Collins. Artist-in-residence, Vidalia, Ga. Troup leader Girl Scouts, Vidalia, 1972-76; block coord. Ga. Heart Assn., Vidalia, 1976. Mem. Phi Beta Kappa. Baptist. Home: 404 Slayton St Vidalia GA 30474-4436 Office: Rabbit's Quik Stop Hwy 292 W Vidalia GA 30474

FORTNER, JOSEPH GERALD, surgeon, educator; b. Bedford, Ind., May 30, 1921; s. Everett Rex and Lula Alice (Robbins) F.; m. Roberta Olson, Nov. 4, 1948; children: Kathleen Alice Fortner, Joseph Jr. BS, U. Ill., 1944, MD, 1945; MSc in Immunology, Birmingham (Eng.) U., 1965. Diplomate: Am. Bd. Surgery. Intern St. Luke's Hosp., Chgo., 1945-46; resident in pathology Tulane U., New Orleans, 1948-49; surg. resident Bellevue Hosp., N.Y.C., 1949-51, Meml. Hosp., N.Y.C., 1952-54, clin. asst. surgeon, asst. to clin. dir., 1955-59, asst. attending surgeon, 1958-66, assoc. attending surgeon, 1966-69, attending surgeon, 1969-94, chief gastric and mixed tumor service, 1970-78, chief surg. research service, 1978-91, assoc. chmn. for lab. affairs dept. surgery, 1978-84, chief div. surg. research, 1968-77; chief Gen. Motors Surg. Rsch. Lab., 1977-92; instr. surgery Sloan-Kettering Inst., N.Y.C., 1954-58, asst. prof. clin. surgery, 1958-64; clin. asst. prof. surgery Cornell U. Med. Coll., N.Y.C., 1964-70, assoc. prof. surgery, 1970-72, prof., 1972—. Contbr. articles to profl. jours.; editor Accomplishments in Cancer Research. Pres. Gen. Motors Cancer Rsch. Found., 1978-96, pres. emeritus, 1996—, trustee. With U.S. Army, 1946-48. Recipient Alfred P. Sloan award Sloan-Kettering Inst. Cancer Research, 1963 Fellow ACS, N.Y. Acad. Scis., Royal Coll. Surgeons Edinburgh (hon.); mem. AMA, AAAS, Am. Assn. Cancer Research, Am. Gastroent. Assn., Am. Radium Soc., Am. Soc. Clin. Oncology, European Soc. Exptl. Surgery, Harvey Soc., Soc. Surg. Oncology, N.Y. County, N.Y. State med. socs., Am. Surg. Assn., N.Y. Surg. Soc., Soc. Univ. Surgeons, Hellenic Surg. Soc. (hon.), Chgo. Surg. Soc., Korean Surg. Soc., Am. Soc. Transplant Surgeons, Transplantation Soc., N.Y. Cancer Soc., Econ. Club of N.Y., Explorer Club N.Y., Met. Club N.Y., Madison Beach Club, Sigma Xi, Alpha Omega Alpha. Republican. Home: 131 E 66th St New York NY 10021-6129 E-mail: jgfortnermd@cs.com.

FORTNER, ROBERT STEVEN, mass communications educator, researcher; b. Baraboo, Wis., July 13, 1948; s. Donald Ray and Joyce Winifred (Buker) F.; m. Marcia Beth Knisley, June 27, 1970; children: Matthew Robert, Peter Nathaniel, Rachael Victoria. B.A. with distinction, Otterbein Coll., 1970; M.A., Ind. U., 1972; Ph.D., U. Ill., 1978. Asst. prof. Northwestern U., Evanston, Ill., 1978-79, Drake U., Des Moines, 1979-81; asst. prof. SUNY-Plattsburgh, 1981-84; assoc. prof. mass comm. George Washington U., Washington, 1984-89, dir. radio and TV, 1984-87; chmn. dept. communication, 1987-89; prof. communication arts and scis. Calvin Coll., Grand Rapids, 1989—, dir. grad. studies, 1994-98; chmn. dept. comms. arts and scis., 1995-97; dir. rsch. and tng. Words of Hope, Grand Rapids, Mich., 2000—; chmn. Cable Access Adv. Com., Plattsburgh, N.Y., 1981-84; editor The Pulse First Presbyn. Ch., Plattsburgh, 1981-84; rsch. cons. Far East Broadcasting Assn., 1989-90, Brit. Broadcasting Corp., 1991-2000, Ctr. for Strategic and Internat. Studies, 1991, Internat. Christian Media Com., 1991; lectr. U.S. Telecom. Tng. Inst., Washington, 1985-89, Acad. for Ednl. Devel., Washington, 1986-89, Inst. for Fgn. Journalists, Reston, Va., 1987-89, Meridian House Internat., 1987-89; faculty Enrichment grantee Can. Embassy, Washington, 1984, faculty rsch. grantee Inst. Advanced Christian Study, 1989-90; prin. investigator Worldwide Radio Receiver Population Analysis, 1986, International Communication, 1992; chmn. bd. dir. Far East Broadcasting Co., 1993—, chmn. 1994—; dir. rsch. InterSearch, 1995—; tng. coord. TWR Internat., 1994-2000. Deacon Silver Spring Christian Reformed Ch., Md., 1985-87. Mem. Assn. Reformed Communication (pres. 1985-88), Assn. Edn. in Journalism and Mass Communication, Can. Communication Assn., Internat. Communication Assn., Speech Communication Assn., Internat. Assn. Mass Communication Rsch., Nat. Rsch.

Coun. (panel Voice of Am. modernization, emergency preparedness and direct broadcast satellites 1987-89). Author: International Communication, 1993, Public Diplomacy and Internat. Politics, 1994. Democrat. Avocations: photography, biking, hiking. Home: 4316 Orchard Creek Dr SE Grand Rapids MI 49546-8263 Office: Calvin Coll Dept Comm Arts & Scis Grand Rapids MI 49546 E-mail: rfortner@speakeasy.net.

FORTNUM, DONALD H, chemistry educator, retired; s. Niels H. and Ruth Holly Fortnum; m. Emily Ann Waters, June 7, 1958; children: Holly, Timothy, Emily, Thomas. Bachelor sci., Carroll Coll., Waukesha, Wisconsin, 1950—54; phd, Brown Unversity, Providence, Rhode Island, 1954—58. Instr. Providence Coll., Providence, 1956—57; assitant prof. Ursinus Coll., Collegevill, Pa., 1958—65; assoc. prof. Gettysburg Coll., Gettysburg, Pa., 1965—72, prof., 1972—2000, prof. emeritus, 2001—. Contbr. articles to numerous jour. publ. Various offices United Meth. Ch., Norristown, Pa., 1959—65, Gettysburg, Pa., 1965—2002. Grantee summer undergrad. rsch. participation Am. Chem. Soc., Sigma Xi, 1968, Lab Equipment, Am. Chem. Soc., 1965. Methodist. Home: 161 Gordon Avenue Gettysburg PA 17325-3110

FORTUNA, WILLIAM FRANK, architectural engineer, architect; b. Paris, Ill., Apr. 3, 1948; s. William F. Sr. and Mary O. (Komatz) F. BArch, U. Ill., 1972, MS in Archtl. Engring., 1973. Lic. arch., Ill., Wis., Iowa, lic. structural engr., Ill., lic. profl. engr., Wis., lic. archtl. engr. specializing in crisis mgmt., Nat. Coun. Examiners for Engring. and Surveying, Nat. Coun. Archtl. Registration Bds. Designer Unteed Assocs. Ltd., Champaign, Ill., 1973-76; structural engr. Consoer Townsend, Chgo., 1976-79, Schmidt, Garden & Erikson, Chgo., 1979-83; sr. project structural engr. Skidmore Owings & Merrill, Chgo., 1983-87; pres. W.F. Fortuna Ltd., Archtl. Engring., Highland Park, Ill., 1987—. Project engr. World Trade Ctr., Cairo; structural engr. exhbn. ctr. McCormick Place Annex, Chgo., United Airlines terminal O'Hare Airport, Bishop's Gate, London; contract adminstr. One and Two Prudential Plaza, Chgo. (SEAOI Best Structure award and tallest concrete bldg. in the world). Active mem. Illinois Emergency Mgmt. Agency. Mem. AIA, NCARB, Structural Engrs. Assn. Ill., Nat. Coun. Examiners for Engring. and Surveying, Am. Concrete Inst., Am. Inst. Steel Constrn., Chgo. Hist. Soc., Nat. Trust His. Preservation. Home: WF Fortuna Ltd Archtl Engr 1420 Ridge Rd Highland Park IL 60035-2734 Office: Two Prudential Plz Chicago IL 60601 E-mail: bill42na@aol.com.

FORTUNATO, CHRISTOPHER R. lawyer; b. Garfield Heights, Ohio, Nov. 6, 1962; s. Ross J. and Agnes (Cosentino) Fortunato. AB, John Carroll U., 1984; JD, Cleve. State U., 1987. Bar: Ohio 87. Asst. prosecutor Lake County Prosecutor's Office, Painesville, Ohio, 1988; pvt. practice Cleve., 1989—90; assoc. Papandreas, Fahrer & Corso, Cleve., 1993—99, Maguire & Schneider LLP, Independence, Ohio, 1997—99, Edward M. Graham Co. LPA, Lakewood, Ohio, 2002—; asst. city prosecutor City of Cleve., 2000—02. Counsel Garfield Heights (Ohio) Little Theatre, 1989—, Sherwood Anderson Lit. Ctr., Elyria, Ohio, 2000—. Mem.: Cuyahoga County Bar Assn., Internat. Churchill Soc., Phi Alpha Delta (dist. justice 1990—92). Democrat. Avocations: stamps, books, Winston Churchill ephemera. Home: 1340 Shaker Blvd # 506 Cleveland OH 44120 Office: Edward M Graham Co LPA 13363 Madison Ave Lakewood OH 44107 Fax: 216-228-3484. E-mail: Blenheim@excite.com.

FORTUNATO, NANCY, artist; b. Highland Park, Ill., Nov. 29; d. Charles Fortunato and Virginia (Ashel) Niemuth; m. Donald William Anstedt. Student, Zhejiang Acad. Fine Art, Hangzhou, China. Bd. dirs. Nat. Arts Found., Ill. Author: So You Want to be An Artist, 1980, Watercolor Tips, 1982, reprinted 2001; exhibited in group shows Nat. Zool. Park, 1995, Midwest Watercolor Soc., Canton, Ohio, 2000, Mystic Maritime Gallery, Conn., 1995, Frye Art Mus., Seattle, 1996, Maritime and Yachting Mus., Stuart, Fla., 1997, Amsterdam (The Netherlands) Open Harbour Mus., 1999, Cape Mus. Fine Arts, Dennis, Mass., 2001, others. Fellow: Am. Art Profl. League (signature); mem.: Internat. Soc. Marine Artists (pres. 2002—), Western Fedn. Watercolor Soc., Acad. Artists Am., Ariz. Watercolor Soc. (Merit award 2002), Tex. Watercolor Soc. (signature, Excellence award 1999), Midwest Watercolor Soc. (v.p. 1995—97, pres. 1997—99, pres. emeritus 1999—), Coatimundi Honor Soc. (signature), Purple Sage Honor Soc. Avocations: photography, computer graphics, visiting lighthouses, birdwatching, travel. Studio: 249 N Marion St Palatine IL 60074-5470 Fax: 781-240-5630. E-mail: nanf@usa.com.

FORTUNE, ANNE E. social worker, educator; b. New Haven, June 27, 1945; d. Mark and Mary (Sutherland) F. Student, Am. Coll. in Paris, 1963-64; BA, U. Chgo., 1970, MA in Social Work, 1975, PhD, 1978. Action rsch. coord., rsch. asst. Woodlawn Exptl. Schs. Project, Chgo., 1968-71; tester Woodlawn Mental Health Ctr., Chgo., 1969; rsch. assoc. Looking Glass, vol. runaway ctr. Travelers Aids Soc. Metro. Chgo., 1971-73; rsch. asst. Ctr. Study of Welfare Policy U. Chgo., 1973-74, rsch. asst. Social Svcs. Fall-Outs Project, 1974-75, rsch. assoc., clin. supr. Task-Centered Treatment Project, 1974-77; asst. prof. George Warren Brown Sch. Social Work Washington U., St. Louis, 1977-82; assoc. prof. Sch. Social Work Va. Commonwealth U., Richmond, 1982-89; from assoc. prof. to prof. Sch. Social Welfare SUNY, Albany, 1989—99, assoc. dean, 2000—. Dir. Internship in Aging Project/SUNY, 1999—. Co-author: Research in Social Work, 1999, Teaching Research: An Instructor's Manual for Research in Social Work, 1999; editor: Task-Centered Practice with Families and Groups, 1985; co-editor: Multicultural Issues in Social Work, vol. II, 1998, Aging and Social Work, 2000; editor Social Work Rsch., 1997-2000; contbr. numerous articles to profl. jours., chpts. to books. Mem. NASW (comms. com. 1997-2000), Coun. Social Work Edn. (coms. edn. policy), Acad. Cert. Social Workers, Soc. for Social Work and Rsch. Office: Univ at Albany SUNY Sch Social Welfare 135 Western Ave Albany NY 12222-0001 E-mail: rfortune@albany.edu.

FORTUNE, ANNETTA, management educator, accountant; d. Joe H. and Evelyn K. Fortune. BBA, M in Acctg., U. N.C., 1994; PhD in Mgmt., Duke U., 2003. CPA, NJ, 1996. Tax cons. Ernst & Young LLP, Iselin, NJ, 1994—97; asst. prof. dept. mgmt. LeBow Coll. Bus. Drexel U., 2003—. Johnston scholar, U. N.C., Chapel Hill, 1989—93, Masters of Acctg. fellow, Kenan-Flagler Bus. Sch., U. N.C., 1993, Fuqua Sch. of Bus. fellow, Duke U., 1998—2003, GE Future Faculty fellow, 1998—2003. Mem.: AICPA, Acad. of Mgmt., NJ. State Soc. of CPAs.

FORTUNE, JAMES MICHAEL, computer support manager; b. Providence, Sept. 6, 1947; s. Thomas Henry and Olive Elizabeth (Duby) F.; m. G. Suzanne Hein, July 14, 1973. Student, Pikes Peak Community Coll., Colorado Springs, Colo., 1981-83; BSBA, BS in Computer Info. Systems, Regis Coll., 1991. Owner Fortune Fin. Svcs., Colorado Springs, Colo., 1975-79; ptnr. Robert James and Assocs., Colorado Springs, 1979-81; pres. Fortune & Co., Colorado Springs, 1981-88; sr. v.p. mktg. and editorial Phoenix Communications Group, Ltd., Colorado Springs, 1985-95, also bd. dirs.; sr. network analyst Coastal States Mgmt. Corp., 1995-99; mgr. computer support Colo. Interstate Gas, 1999—. Bd. dirs. Interstate Gas Credit Union, 1998-99, N.Am. Internet, LLC; talk show host Sta. KRCC, fin. commentator Wall Street Report, Sta. KKHT, 1983-84. Editor Fortune newsletter, 1981-85, The Can. Market News, 1981-83; editor, pub. Penny Fortune newsletter, 1981-95, The Low Priced Investment newsletter, 1986-87, Women's Investment Newsletter, 1987-95; pub. Internal Revenue Strategies, 1990, Tax and Investment Planning Strategies for Medical Professionals, 1991; contbr. articles to profl. jours. Cons. Jr. Achievement bus. project, Colorado Springs, 1985, 97-2000. Sgt. U.S. Army, 1968-70, Vietnam. Mem. Direct Mktg. Assn., Elks. Avocations: fly fishing, skiing, hiking, backpacking. Office: PO Box 1087 2 North Nevada Ave Colorado Springs CO 80944

FORTUNE, LOWELL, lawyer; b. Colorado Springs, Colo., Dec. 12, 1941; s. Benjamin Acres and Wilma E. (Henry) Fortune; m. Beverly Jane Sanborn, June 30, 1963; children: Sabrina Fortune Allen, Christina Fortune Howery. BA, U. Denver, 1963, JD, 1966. Bar: U.S. Dist. Ct. Colo. 1966, U.S. Ct. Appeals (10th cir.) 1966, U.S. Supreme Ct. 1976. Assoc. White & Steele, Denver, 1966—71, ptnr., 1971—75; pres. Lowell Fortune, P.C., 1975—79, Fortune & Lawritson, P.C., 1979—95, Fortune Law Firm, P.C., 1995—99, 2002—; spl. counsel Montgomery, Kolodny, Amatuzio, Dusbabek and Parker, L.L.P., 1999—2001. Author: (book) The Year 2000 Problem and the Economic Loss Rule, 1999. Mem.: Am. Bd. Trial Advs. Home: 5237 Bear Mountain Dr Evergreen CO 80439-5605 Office: 600 17th St Ste 2800 South Denver CO 80202-5402 E-mail: lowfort@mac.com.

FORTUNE, ROBERT RUSSELL, financial consultant; b. Collingswood, N.J., Nov. 22, 1916; s. Colin C. and Minnie M. (Brown) F.; m. Christine E. Dent, Nov. 10, 1956. BS in Econs., U. Pa., 1940. CPA, Pa. With Haskins & Sells (C.P.A.s), 1940-42, 46-48; with Pa. Power & Light Co., Allentown, 1948-84, v.p. fin., 1966-75, exec. v.p. fin., dir., 1975-84. Chmn., CEO Assoc. Electric and Gas Ins. Svcs. Ltd., 1984-93, Chestnut St. Exch. Fund, chmn., 1994—. Tech. adv. com. on fin. FPC, 1974-75. Treas. Allentown Sch. Dist. Authority, 1963-85, Lehigh-Northampton Airport Authority, 1985-94. With USN, 1942-46. Mem. Fin. Execs. Inst., Am., Pa. insts. CPAs. Clubs: Lehigh Country. Republican. Home: 2920 Ritter Ln Allentown PA 18104-2823

FOSCHIO, LESLIE GEORGE, judge; b. Oct. 29, 1940; s. Frank George and Sonia (Kaczynski) Foschio; m. Virginia Rose Kostur, June 27, 1964; children: John, Michael, Amy, Robert, Christa. BA cum laude, U. Buffalo, 1962; LLB cum laude, SUNY, Buffalo, 1965. Bar: N.Y. 1966, U.S. Ct. Appeals (7th cir.) 1973, U.S. Dist. Ct. (we. dist.) N.Y. 1975, U.S. Supreme Ct. 1975, U.S. Ct. Appeals (2d cir.) 1977, U.S. Ct. Appeals (DC cir.) 1977, U.S. Tax Ct. 1980. Law clk. to Hon. William B. Lawless, Jr. N.Y. State Supreme Ct., 1965; atty. Counsel's Office, SUNY, 1965-66; asst. dist. atty. Erie County, Buffalo, 1966-69; assoc. prof., asst. dean U. Notre Dame Law Sch., Ind., 1969-74; corp. counsel City of Buffalo, 1975-77; ptnr. Cohen Swados Wright Hanifin Bradford & Brett, Buffalo, 1978-80; commr. Dept. Motor Vehicles, State of N.Y., Albany, 1981-83; gen. counsel, sec., v.p. Barrister Info. Sys. Corp., Buffalo, 1983-91; U.S. magistrate judge U.S. Dist. Ct. (we. dist.) N.Y., 1991—. Lectr. law SUNY, Buffalo, 1966—68, Buffalo, 1978—80. Pres. Theodore Roosevelt Inaugural Nat. Hist. Site Found., Buffalo, 1978—87, trustee, 1978—; dist. chmn. Greater Niagara Frontier coun. Boy Scouts Am., Buffalo, 1980—82; dist. chmn. Eagle Scout; Dem. candidate Erie County N.Y. State Assembly, 1968; Dem. primary candidate for mayor Buffalo, 1977; trustee Theodore Roosevelt Assn., 1981—98. Recipient Character award, U. Buffalo, 1962, Disting. Pub. Svc. award, N.Y. Jaycees, 1976, Outstanding Svc. Hwy Safety award, N.Y. State Assn. Traffic Safety, 1982, Alumnus of the Yr. award, H. C. Tech. HS, 1997, Outstanding Young Men of America, 1970, 1977; T. R. McConnell Leadership scholar, U. Buffalo, 1962. Fellow: Am. Bar Found. (life), N.Y. State Bar Found. (life; Action Unit 5 1980—83); mem.: Bar Assn. Erie County (dir. 1988—91), N.Y. State Bar Assn., Fed. Magistrate Judges Assn., U. Buffalo Alumni Assn. (dir. 1995—99, v.p. membership 1988—89, Disting. Alumnus award 1983), U. Buffalo Law Sch. Alumni Assn. (pres. 1980—81, Disting. Alumnus award for pub. svc. 1987), Phi Alpha Delta (hon.). Roman Catholic. Home: 46 Woodley Rd Buffalo NY 14215-1321 Office: 424 US Courthouse 68 Court St Buffalo NY 14202-3405 E-mail: lesliefoschio@nywd.uscourts.gov.

FOSDICK, CORA PRIFOLD (CORA PRIFOLD BEEBE), management consultant; b. San Francisco, Nov. 3, 1937; d. George and Beatrice (Ehni) Prifold; m. Ronald Beebe, Jan., 1959 (div.); m. Donald James Fosdick, Oct. 12, 1997. Student, Hollins Coll., Va., 1955-57, Am. U., 1957-58; BA, U. Mich., 1959, MA, 1961; LHD (hon.), Southeastern U., 1993. Adminstrv. asst. Am. Polit. Sci. Assn., 1962-64; research assoc. Inst. Comparative Studies of Polit. Systems, Washington, 1963-65; program planning and evaluation specialist U.S. Office Edn., Washington, 1965-68, planning coordinator, 1968-73, dir. planning and budget div., 1973-80; prin. dep. asst. sec. for elem. and sec. edn. Dept. Edn., Washington, 1980-81; asst. sec. adminstrn. U.S. Treasury Dept., Washington, 1981-84; dir. office of policy, budget and program mgmt. OSWER, EPA, Washington, 1984-86; dir. office of planning, budget and evaluation Dept. Commerce, Washington, 1986-87; commerce & justice br. chief Office of Mgmt. and Budget, 1987-94, advisor to assoc. dir. gen. govt. and fin., 1994; exec. dir. adminstrn., chief fin. officer Office of Thrift Supervision, Washington, 1994-99; v.p. Jefferson Consulting Group, Washington, 1999—2002; ind. cons. Washington, 2002—. Mem. women's com. Washington Performing Arts Soc., 1983—; mem. Coun. for Excellence in Govt. Recipient HEW Superior Svc. award, Presdl. Rank award, 1989; Inst. World Affairs fellow, 1956, Am. Edn. Abroad former fellow, 1960. Fellow: Nat. Acad. Pub. Adminstrn. (bd. dirs., vice chair audit com.); mem.: Assn. Assn. Execs., Nat. Press Club, Exec. Women in Govt. Program and Budget Analysis. Home: 1501 Crystal Drive Arlington VA 22202 E-mail: corabeebe@aol.com.

FOSGATE HEGGLI, JULIE DENISE, producer; b. El Paso, Tex., Feb. 17, 1954; d. Orville Edward and Patricia (Ward) Fosgate; m. Bjarne Heggli, June 20, 1980; children: Elise Mai, Kristin April. BA in Broadcasting, U. So. Calif., 1976, MA in Journalism, 1978. On-board editor Royal Viking Line, San Francisco, 1978-80; editor Stentor, Trondheim, Norway, 1981; staff Grunion Gazette, Long Beach, Calif., 1981; news editor Nine Network Australia, Los Angeles, 1981-82; editor South Coast Metro News, Costa Mesa, Calif., 1981-82; v.p. The Newport Group, Newport Beach, Calif., 1982-85; exec. editor Orange County This Month, Newport Beach, 1985; exec. dir. mktg. Gen. Group Cos., Harbor City, Calif., 1985-87; sr. v.p. mktg. Automax Corp., L.A., 1987-88, Gen. Group Internat., Harbor City, Calif., 1988-90; assoc. producer Zoo Life TV Spls., L.A., 1991, NBC News, Burbank, Calif., 1992-94; v.p. mktg. Western Nat., Scottsdale, Ariz., 1994-99; sr. v.p. mktg. CNA Nat. (formerly Western Nat.), Scottsdale, 2000—. Mem. Phi Beta Kappa. Avocations: collecting, reading, art. Home: 9640 E Davenport Dr Scottsdale AZ 85260-1426 Office: CNA Nat 4150 N Drinkwater Blvd Scottsdale AZ 85251-3611

FOSHAY, MAXINE VALENTINE SHOTTLAND, civic worker, public relations executive; b. N.Y.C., Feb. 14, 1921; d. Maximillian Stanford and Violet Gertrude (Turner) Shottland; m. Robert Lethbridge Foshay, Mar. 16, 1956. BA, Royal Acad. Dramatic Arts, London, 1943. Field rep. Am. Cancer Soc., N.Y.C., 1967-68; dir. fund raising and pub. rels. Preventive Medicine Inst., Strang Inst., 1969-71, Fedn. Handicapped, N.Y.C., 1971-72; exec. dir. Irvington House, 1972-73; prin. Maxine V. Foshay & Assocs., N.Y.C., 1977—. Chmn. group affiliates Meml. Sloan Kettering, 1960—66; v.p. Meml. Sloan Kettering Soc., 1966—67; vol. Meml. Sloan Kettering Cancer Soc., 1956—77, 1987—; v.p. Victoria Home for Retired Men and Women, Ossining, NY, 1988—. Bd. dirs. Elder Craftsmen, N.Y.C.; bd. devel. Children's Asthmatic Found., N.Y. Mem. Daus. Brit. Empire State N.Y. (1st v.p. 1980-84, statewide pres. 1984-88, Medal Brit. Empire Her Majesty's Honours List 1987).

FOSHER, DONALD HOBART, marketing professional, inventor; b. St. Louis, Jan. 6, 1935; s. Hobart L. and Alby U. (Andrews) F.; m. Charlotte B. Reich, Oct. 6, 1956 (div. Dec. 1976); 1 child, Carey B.; Janet L. Leiber, Dec. 31, 1977. BSBA, Washington U., St. Louis, 1956. Copywriter Gen. Am., St. Louis, 1956-59; art dir. Artcraft, St. Louis, 1959-67; creative dir. Frank Block Assocs., St. Louis, 1967-69; account exec. Vangard/Wells, Rich, Green, St. Louis, 1969-74; ptnr., v.p. Vinyard & Lee, St. Louis, 1974-77; sr. v.p., creative dir. Hughes Advt., St. Louis, 1977-98; pres., owner Don Fosher, Inc., St. Louis, 1974—. Co-owner Stitches, and Sew On and Sew Forth, 1988, Brand Bank divsn. Don Fosher Inc., 1986—. Author: Art for Secondary Education, 1962; contbr. articles on cuisine to popular mags.; patentee sports, medicine, mech. design. Advisor, St. Louis County Spl. Sch. Dist., 1966-76; bd. dirs. Vocat. Schs., St. Louis, 1969-88; campaign designer St. Louis Better Bus. Bur., 1975, St. Louis Arts & Edn. Fund, 1984. Recipient Venice Biennial, Internat. Congress Designers, 1966, Package Design award Am. Fishing Tackle Mfrs. Assn., 1981, numerous Creative awards Art Directors, 1959-1998. Mem. Internat. Congress Designers, Soc. Communications Arts (pres. 1966-67, Art Dir. of Yr. 1967), Direct Mail Mktg. Assn., SAR. Mem. Christian Ch. Avocations: inventing, cooking, collecting primative art. Home: 5845 Nottingham Ave # 1 Saint Louis MO 63109-2736 Office: Brand Bank 5845 Nottingham Ave # 1 Saint Louis MO 63109-2736 E-mail: brandbnk@inlink.com.

FOSMIRE, MICHAEL, librarian, educator; b. Boston, Sept. 7, 1970; s. Gary James and Mary Ann Fosmire; m. Felicia Smith; children: Henry Clay, Cory Macoun. BS in Math., BS in Physics, Pa. State U., 1992; M in Physics, U. Wash., 1996, M in Libr. and Info. Sci., 1997. Pub. svcs. libr., asst. sys. libr. SUNY, Oswego, 1997—98; physics and earth and atmospheric scis. libr., asst. prof. Purdue U., West Lafayette, Ind., 1998—2000, head sci. librs., asst. prof., 2000—. Sect. editor: journal Issues in Science and Technology Librarianship; contbr. articles to profl. jours. Fellow, Achievement Rewards for Coll. Students, 1992; grantee, Learner Enabled Digital Learning Environment, 2001—04; scholar, Nat. Merit Scholarship Corp., 1988; Libr. Rsch. grantee, Purdue U. Librs., 2001. Mem.: ALA, Am. Phys. Soc., Spl. Librs. Assn. (treas. physics-astronomy-math. divsn. 2000—02, chair physics-astronomy-math. divsn. 2003—), Delta Alpha Theta, Sigma Pi Sigma, Phi Beta Kappa. Office: Purdue Univ Librs PHYS 504 West State St West Lafayette IN 47907-2058 E-mail: fosmire@purdue.edu.

FOSS, CHARLES R. contracting officer; b. Chgo., Nov. 1, 1945; s. Raymond C. and Marilyn (Halas) F. Assoc. in Transp., Davenport Coll., 1973, B in Mktg., 1985, BS in Mgmt., 1994. Cert. purchasing mgr., Nat. Assn. Purchasing Mgmt.; cert. profl. mgr., Inst. Cert. Profl. Mgrs.; cert. transp. and logistics profl., Am. Soc. Transp. Logistics. Yardmaster Chesapeake and Ohio Ry., Benton Harbor, Mich., 1963-66, ticket agt. Holland, Mich., 1969-71; freight agt., train dispatcher Penn Cen. Ry., Ft. Wayne, Ind., 1971-76; crew dispatcher Consol. Rail Corp., Grand Rapids, Mich., 1976-78; trainmaster Mich. No. Ry., 1978-85; customer service rep. Superior Brand Produce, Hudsonville, Mich., 1985; purchasing buyer U.S. Dept. Def., Dayton, Ohio, 1986-89, contract adminstr. Grand Rapids, Mich., 1989-94; transp. specialist, ops. CSX Transp. Inc., Grand Rapids, 1994-99; ops. inspector U.S. DOT-FRA, 1999-2000; contracting officer VA Nat. Acquisition Ctr., Hines, Ill., 2001—. Part-time sales rep. Foss Police Equipment and Communications, Battle Creek, Mich., 1978-85. Author: Evening Before The Diesel, 1980. Coord. Susquicentennial Commemorative Winchester Carbine, Byron Twp., Byron Ctr., Mich., 1985; hon. life mem. RR History Mus., Durand, Mich. With U.S. Army, 1966-69, Vietnam. Mem. NRA (life), Nat. Assn. Purchasing Mgmt. (cert. purchasing mgr.), Nat. Contract Mgmt. Assn., Am. Soc. Transp. and Logistics (cert. in transp. and logistics mgmt.), Chgo. and North Western Hist. Soc. (contbr.), So. Mich. R.R. Soc. (contbr.), Am. Truck Hist. Soc. (life). Republican. Avocations: firearms collection, antique cars and trucks, transp. art works collector.

FOSS, JEAN MITCHELL, school system administrator; b. Providence; d. Wendell Thornton and Mildred Irene (Stafford) Mitchell; children: Wendy Susan Foss Sweeney, David Cushing. BA, U. RI, 1960; MEd, U. Vt., 1981. Coord. of remedial programming Pine Ridge Sch., Williston, Vt., 1984—89, dir. of clin. tchg. and rsch., 1989—2002, edn. dir., 2002—. Contbr. articles to profl. jours. Recipient Alice H. Garside award, N.E. br. Orton Dyslexia Soc., 1998. Fellow: Acad. Orton-Gillingham Practioners and Educators (1st v.p. 1995—); mem.: Internat. Dyslexia assn. (nominating comm. 1991—93). Avocations: travel, golf. Home: 53 Twin Oaks Terr South Burlington VT 05403 Office: Pine Ridge Sch 9505 Williston Rd Williston VT 05495 E-mail: jfoss@pineridgeschool.com.

FOSS, JOHN FRANK, mechanical engineering educator; b. Washington, Pa., Mar. 24, 1938; s. Maurice Felker and C. Catharine (Reynard) F.; m. Jacqueline Kay Voss, July 24, 1960; children: Judith Kathleen, Janette Diane. Student, Wilmington Coll., 1956-58; BS, Purdue U., 1961, MS, 1962, PhD, 1965. Mem. faculty Mich. State U., East Lansing, 1964—, asso. prof. mech. engring., 1968-75, prof., 1975—; pres. Digital Flow Techs., Inc., Mich., 1994—. Dir. fluid dynamics & hydraulics program NSF, 1998-2000; cons. McDonnel Douglas Helicopter Co., Ford Motor Co., Bd. Water and Light, Lansing, Tranter Corp., United Techs. Rsch. Ctr., East Hartford, Conn. Author: (with M.C. Potter) Fluid Mechanics, 1975; N.Am. editor Measurement Sci. and Tech., 1995—. Mem. Oaks Recreation Program staff, 1976-78; moderator Edgewood United Ch., 1975-77. Sloan fellow John Hopkins U., Balt., 1970-71; Alexander von Humboldt fellow U. Karlsruhe, Fed. Republic Germany, 1978-79, U. Erlangen, Fed. Republic Germany, 1985-86, rsch. fellow U. Melbourne, Australia, 1995. Fellow ASME; mem. AIAA, AAAS, AAUP, Am. Soc. Engring. Edn., Am. Phys. Soc., Soc. Scholars Johns Hopkins U., Sigma Xi, Tau Beta Pi, Pi Tau Sigma. Mem. United Ch. of Christ. Home: 2353 Sapphire Lane East Lansing MI 48823 Office: Mich State U Dept Mech Engring East Lansing MI 48824 E-mail: foss@egr.msu.edu.

FOSS, LUKAS, composer, conductor, pianist; b. Berlin, Aug. 15, 1922; came to US from Paris, 1937, naturalized, 1942; s. Martin and Hilde (Schindler) F.; m. Cornelia Brendel, Sept. 1951; 2 children. Student, Paris Lycée Pasteur, 1932-37; grad., Curtis Inst. Music, 1940; spl. study, Yale U., 1940-41; pupil of, Paul Hindemith, Julius Herford, Serge Koussevitzky, Fritz Reiner, Isabelle Vengerova; hon. doctorate, Yale U., 1991; 15 other hon. doctorates. Former prof. UCLA (in charge orch. and advanced composition); faculty Harvard U., 1970-71; prof. of composition Boston U., 1992—. Founder Ctr. Creative and Performing Arts, Buffalo U.; vis. prof. Carnegie Mellon U., Pitts., 1987-90; composer in residence Tanglewood, 1989, 90; Mellon lectr. Nat. Gallery, Washington, 1987. Former condr., music dir., Buffalo Philharmonic; music dir., condr., Bklyn. Philharmonic, 1971-90, condr. laureate, 1990—; music dir., condr. Milw. Symphony Orch., 1981-86, condr. laureate, 1986—; orchestral compositions performed by many major orch.; best known works include (opera) Griffelkin, Baroque Variations (orch.), Echoi (4 instruments), Time Cycle (songs with orch.), Renaissance concerto (flute and orch.); orch., chamber music, ballets, works commd. by, League of Composers, Nat. Endowment for Arts, NY Arts Coun., NBC opera on TV, Am. Choral Condrs. Assn., Ind. U., 1979 Olympics, Boston Symphony, Chgo. Symphony; (recipient NY Critic Circle citation for Prairie 1944, Soc. for Pub. Am. Music award for String Quartet in G 1948, Rome prize 1950, Horblit award for Piano concerto #2 1951, Naumburg Rec. award for Song of Songs 1957, Creative Music grant Inst. Arts and Letters 1957, NY Music Critics Circle award for Time-Cycle orch. songs 1961, for Echoi 1963, Ditson award for condr. who has done the most for Am. music 1973, NYC award for spl. contbn. to arts 1976, ASCAP award for adventurous programming 1979, CRI rec. award for Thirteen Ways of Looking at a Blackbird 1979). Guggenheim fellow, 1945; Creative arts award Brandeis U., 1983; Laurel leaf award Am. Composers Alliance, 1983 Mem. Am. Acad. of Arts and Letters (Gold medal 2000).

FOSS, RALPH SCOT, mechanical engineer; b. Perth Amboy, N.J., Aug. 19, 1945; s. Frank Allen and Bessie Christine (Hopla) F.; m. Betsy B. See, Oct. 1, 1993. Student, Pa. State U., 1963-65; BME, Parsons Coll., Fairfield, Iowa, 1966; MBA in Bus., London Sch. Econs., 1970; postgrad., Heidelberg U., Fed. Republic Germany, 1970-71. Mgr. advanced facilities, compressed air Volkswagen GmbH, Wolfsburs, W.Ger., 1968-71; product mgr. Ingersoll Rand Co., East Brunswick, N.J., 1971-73; mgr. air compressor group Minn. Inst. Tech., Mpls., 1973-76; sales and mktg. mgr. Sullair Corp., Michigan City, Ind., 1976-81; sys. engring. mgr. Ingersoll Rand Co., Charlotte, N.C., 1982-88; pres. Plant Air Tech., Charlotte, 1988—, Winburn Assocs., Inc., Charlotte, 1989—. Bd. dirs. Amethyst Found., Charlotte, 1987-90. Author: Compressed Air Systems, 1989; inventor in field. Mem. Presdl. Task Force, Washington, 1982-88; pres.'s coun. Fla. Hosp. Found., Orlando, 1990—. With U.S. Army, 1966-68. Named to Hon. Order Ky. Cols., 1990. Mem. Am. Inst. Plant Engrs. (pres., corp. mems. coun. 1985-89, dir. 1989-90), Assn. Energy Engrs., Instrument Soc. Am., Internat. Platform Assn. Republican. Presbyterian. Avocations: golf, writing. Office: Plant Air Tech 7108 Seton House Ln Charlotte NC 28277-4515

FOSS, RICHARD JOHN, bishop; b. Wauwatosa, Wis., Dec. 27, 1944; s. Harlan Funston and Bernice Naomi (Lindaas) F.; m. Nancy Elizabeth Martin, June 21, 1969; children: Susan, Naomi Foss Welsh, Elizabeth, Peter, Andrew. BA, St. Olaf Coll., 1966; MDiv, Luther Theol. Seminary, 1971; ThM, Luther N.W. Theol. Seminary, 1984. Ordained to ministry Luth. Ch., 1971. Pastor St. Andrews Ch. and Ch. of Christ the Redeemer, Mpls., 1971-77; assoc. pastor First Luth., Fargo, N.D., 1977-79; sr. pastor Prince of Peace Luth., Seattle, 1979-86, Trinity Luth., Moorhead, Minn., 1986-92; bishop Ea. N.D. Synod, Fargo, 1992—. Soloist F-M Opera Co., Fargo, 1979; coach St. James Girls' Basketball Team, Settle, 1982-84; vol. Wash. State Patrol Crisis Chaplaincy, Seattle, 1983-86; bd. dirs. Discovery, Inc., Mpls., 1972-77, Highline Boys' and Girls' Club, Burien, Wash., 1980-81, Luth. Compass Ctr., Seattle, 1983-86, v.p., 1985-86; mem. Master Chorale, 1987-99; bd. regents Concordia Coll., 1992—; bd. dirs. Daily Bread, 1991-2000, Luth. Social Svcs. of N.D., 1992—, Oak Grove Luth. H.S., 1990—, Luth. Resources Network, 1994-97, Healthy Congregations Adv. Bd., 1997—, N.D. Conf. Chs., 1993—, Thrivent Fin. for Luths. Adv. Bd., 2000-, United Way Cmty. Bd., 2001-02; bd. regents Luther Seminary, 2002—. Lutheran. Avocations: golf, reading, travel, vocal performance. Home: 1510 2nd St S Moorhead MN 56560-4014 Office: Ea ND Synod 1703 32nd Ave S Fargo ND 58103-5936 E-mail: rick.foss@ecunet.org.

FOSS, WILLIAM OTTO, writer; b. Boston, Oct. 2, 1918; s. Hans Foss and Alma Josephine Sandstrom; m. Wilma Fehrs-Foss, June 3, 2000; m. Dulcie Elaine Daffer, Nov. 1, 1941 (dec. Dec. 23, 1991). Grad. h.s., Milton, Mass.

Transl. CIA, Washington, 1947—51; assoc. editor Navy Times, Washington, 1951—60; writer Beltsville, Md., 1960—62; writer, editor U.S. Dept. Commerce, Washington, 1962—67; pub. info. specialist U.S. Army ROTC Directorate, Ft. Monroe, Va., 1967—73. Co-author: (books) Coast Guard in Action, 1962, Helicopters in Action, 1962, Marines in Action, 1965, Skin Divers in Action, 1965, Oceanographers in Action, 1968; author: Here Is Your Hobby: Skiing, 1964, The Norwegian Lady and the Wreck of the Dictator, 1977, The United States Navy in Hampton Roads, 1984, It Happened First in Virginia, 1990, The Lives of Nine Cats, 1992, First Ladies Quotation Book, 1999; contbr. Chief yeoman USN, 1937—47. Mem.: U.S. Naval Inst., Authors Guild, Sons of Norway. Avocations: gardening, photography. Home: 813 Queen Elizabeth Dr Virginia Beach VA 23452

FOSSA, ANTHONY ANDREA, pharmacologist; b. Philadelphia, Pa., July 9, 1956; s. John Peter and Caroline Katherine Fossa; m. Katrina Ileen Mallery, Aug. 9, 1982; children: Mallory Nichole, Andrea Carina. PhD, Purdue U., 1983, MS, 1981; BS, U. N.Mex, 1979. Diplomate Am. Bd. Toxicology 1987. Rsch. advisor Pfizer, Inc., Groton, Conn., 1986—; rsch. toxicologist Squibb Inst. for Med. Rsch., New Brunswick, NJ, 1983—86. Founder (one of eight original) Safety Pharmacology Steering Com., Phila., 1992—2001; founder (original bd. of dirs.) Safety Pharmacology Soc., Phila., 2001—03. Editor: (drug development research) Spl. Issue - Safety Pharmacology. Mem.: Safety Pharmacology Soc. (pres. 1995—96). Achievements include discovery of Pfizer Achievement award for Synergistic effects of renin angiotensin system inhibitors used in combination for the treatment of hypertension and congestive heart failure; patents for Synergistic therapeutic compositions of angiotensin I converting enzyme inhibitors and angiotensin II antagonists and methods; Method of treating heart failure with corticotropin releasing hormone antagonists; Methods for treating congestive heart failure with phosphodiesterase type IV and the production of tumor necrosis factor. Home: 20 Niles Rd Mystic CT 06355 Office: Pfizer Global Rsch and Devel Eastern Point Rd Bldg 118 Groton CT 06340 Office Fax: 860-715-7636. E-mail: anthony_a_fossa@groton.pfizer.com.

FOSSATI, HUMBERTO MARIO, electrical engineer, researcher; b. Bryan, Tex., Nov. 16, 1965; s. Humberto and Nancy Miryam (Tejada) F. BS in Elec. Engring., Tex A&M U., 1987, MS, 1989; postgrad., Rice U. Staff engr. Space Sta., IBM, Houston, 1989—93; staff engr. LAMPS, IBM/Loral Fed. Systems, Owego, NY, 1993—95; with Compaq Computer Corp., Houston, 1995—2002, multimedia architect portable PC divsn., 1997—99, program mgr. advanced tech., 1999—2000; program mgr. microportable projects Access Bus. Group (ABG), Houston, 2000—02; solutions program mgr., personal workstas. Hewlett Packard Corp., Fort Collins, Colo., 2002—03, program mgr. Display Bus. unit Houston, 2003—. Rschr. Pleiades Rsch., 1989-96. Contbr. articles to profl. jours. Rice U. fellow, 1992; NSF grantee Tex. A&M U., 1987-89. Mem. IEEE, Sigma Xi. Republican. Roman Catholic. Avocations: collecting stamps, playing tennis, soccer, swimming. Home: 8206 Turnmill Ct Spring TX 77379 Office: 20555 SH 249 MS 070222 Houston TX 77070 E-mail: humberto.fossati@hp.com., fossati@highstream.net.

FOSSEEN, NEAL RANDOLPH, business executive, former banker, former mayor; b. Yakima, Wash., Nov. 27, 1908; s. Arthur Benjamin and Florence (Neal) F.; m. Helen Witherspoon, Sept. 26, 1936; children: Neal Randolph Jr., William Roger. BA, U. Wash., 1930; LD (hon.), Whitworth Coll., 1967. With Wash. Brick, Lime & Sewer Pipe Co., 1923-32, v.p., 1932-38; pres. Wash. Brick & Lime Co., 1938-58; dir. Securities Intermountain Co., 1954-71; v.p., dir. Old Nat. Bank Wash., 1958-68, Wash. Bancshares, 1968-71, vice chmn., 1971-72, chmn. bd., pres., 1972-73; dir. Utah-Idaho Sugar Co., 1968-79, 1st Nat. Bank Spokane, 1972-79. Dir. Spokane Indsl. Park, 1959-72, treas., 1959-66; dir. North Coast Life Ins. Co., 1965-76, Quarry Tile Co., 1965-68, Day Mines, Inc., 1968-81; chmn. emeritus, dir. Old Nat. Bancorp., 1973-77; pres. 420 Investment Co., 1982-84; hon. dir. Met. Mortgage Co., 1995-2001. Mem. exec. com. Expo '74; mem. adv. bd. Mus. Native Am. Culture, 1957-81; mayor City of Spokane, 1960-67, mayor emeritus, 1967—; mem. adv. bd. emeritus Spokane Intercollegiate Rsch. and Tech. Inst., 1993-96; past chmn. adv. bd. Wash. State Inst. Tech.; bd. dirs., past pres. coun. Boy Scouts Am.; bd. dirs. Wash. Rsch. Coun., sec., 1968-74; bd. dirs. YMCA, 1969-80, Pacific Sci. Found., 1970-73, Mountain States Legal Found., 1979-85; mem. adv. bd. Grad. Sch. Bus., U. Wash., 1974-81, emeritus, 1981—, mem. adv. bd. dept. history, 1981—; chmn. Regent Gonzaga U., 1948-61, emeritus, 1961—, benefactor, (hon.) LD, 1999; mem. adv. bd. Coll. Engring., Wash. State U., 1949-79; hon. trustee Found. N.W.; trustee Rockwood Cmty. Found., 1993-97, Gonzaga Dussault Found., Fosseen-Kusaka Disting. Professorship, Jackson Found. Scholarship, U. Wash., 1998; mem. adv. bd. Advanced Tech. Ctr., 1989-94, Mukogawa Fort Wright Inst., Whitworth Coll. Internat. Mgmt., City Innovation; founding. dir. Athletic Round Table. Col. USMCR, ret. Recipient Shrine award El Katif Temple, 1974, Non Sibi, Sed Patriae award Marine Corps. Res. Officers Assn., Outstanding Svc. award Fairchild AFB, Spokan Mcpl. League, Forward Spokane award Spokane County Hotel and Restaurant Coun., Liberty Bell award Spokane County Bar Assn., Book of Golden Deeds, Exchange Club, Sister City Outstanding Svc. award Town Affiliation Assn., Disting. Citizen award Ea. Wash. U., 1982, Founders Day award, 1994, Disting. Citizen award Air Force Air Mobility Command, 1995, Citizen League Lifetime Svc. award, 1997, Inland N.W. Philanthropy award Found. N.W., 1999; named hon. citizen Nishinomiya, Japan; inducted to Inland N.W. Hall of Fame. Mem. VFW, Ret. Officers Assn., Assn. Wash. Bus. (past pres.), Spokane C. of C. (v.0. 1946-51), Spokane-Nishinoniya Sister City Soc. (pres.), Srs. N.W. Golf Assn. (gov.), Mil. Order World Wars (Perpetual), Order of the Rising Sun (Japan), Balboa de Mazatlan Club (Mex.), Spokane Club (life), Spokane Country Club (life), Prosperity Club, Travellers Century Club, Spokane Ski Club, Rotary (Paul Harris fellow, benefactor), Beta Theta Pi (Oxford Cup award), Alpha Kappa Psi. Home: Rockwood Manor 701 2903 E 25th Ave Spokane WA 99223-7605

FOSSELLA, VITO JOHN, congressman; b. Staten Island, N.Y., Mar. 9, 1965; s. Vito John and Elizabeth Lucey Fossella; m. Mary Patricia Rowan, 1990. BS, U. Pa., 1987; JD, Fordham U., 1993. Mem. Cmty. Bd. 3, Staten Island, 1989-90; city councilman N.Y.C., 1994-97; U.S. Congressman 13th Dist. Staten Island, 1997—. Mem. commerce com., financial svcs. comm., telecomms. sub. com., capital mkts. subcom., environ. and hazardous materials subcom. U.S. Ho. of Reps. Mem. Phi Sigma Epsilon. Republican. Roman Catholic. Address: 4434 Amboy Rd Fl 2 Staten Island NY 10312-3858 Office: US House of Representatives 1239 Longworth Washington DC 20515-0001*

FOSSLAND, JOEANN JONES, professional speaker, personal coach; b. Balt., Mar. 21, 1948; d. Milton Francis and Clementine (Bowen) Jones; m. Richard E. Yellott III, 1966 (div. 1970); children: Richard E. IV, Dawn Joeann; m. Robert Gerard Fossland Jr., Nov. 25, 1982. Student, Johns Hopkins U., 1966-67; cert., Hogan's Sch. Real Estate, 1982. Cert. values coach, behaviors coach, 1998, GRI; master cert. coach. Owner Kobble Shop, Indiatlantic, Fla., 1968-70, Downstairs, Atlanta, 1971; seamstress Aspen (Colo.) Leather, 1972-75; owner Backporch Feather & Leather, Aspen and Tucson, 1975-81; area mgr. Welcome Wagon, Tucson, 1982; realtor assoc. Tucson Realty & Trust, 1983-85; mgr. Home Illustrated mag., Tucson, 1985-87; asst. pub., gen. mgr. Phoenix, Scottsdale, Albuquerque, Tricities Tucson Homes Illustrated, 1990-93; pres. Advantage Solutions Group, Cortaro, Ariz., 1993—. Power leader Darryl Davis Seminars Power Program, 1995—; personal and profl. coach.; instr. Women's Coun Realtors, 1999—. Designer leather goods (Tucson Mus. Art award 1978, Crested Butte Art Fair Best of Show award 1980); author: Personal and Professional Coaching: Coach University, Certified Training Program, 1996. Voter registrar Recorder's Office City of Tucson, 1985-91; bd. dirs. Hearth Found., Tucson, 1987-96, pres., 1994; bd. dirs. Ariz. Integrated Residential & Edl. Svcs., Inc., 1989-95, pres. 1994-95). Mem. NAFE, Internat. Fedn. Coaches (master cert. coach), Women's Coun. Realtors (leadership tng. grad. designation, pres. Tucson chpt. 1995, Ariz. state gov. 1997-98, v.p. Region IV, 2000, Tucson Affiliate of Yr. award 1991, Ariz. State Mem. of Yr. 1999), Tucson Assn. Realtors (Affiliate of Yr. award 1988). Democrat. Presbyterian. Avocations: tennis, gardening, reading, travel, public speaking. Office: Advantage Solutions Group PO Box 133 Cortaro AZ 85652-0133 E-mail: joeann@joeann.com.

FOSSUM, JERRY GEORGE, electrical engineering educator; b. Phoenix, July 18, 1943; s. George Clayton and Lillian Edith (McNeilis) F.; m. Mary Ellen; children: Kerry Ray, Kelly Lynn. AA, Phoenix Coll., 1963; BSEE, U. Ariz., 1966, MS, 1969, PhD, 1971. Mem. tech. staff Sandia Labs., Albuquerque, 1971-78; assoc. prof. elec. engring. U. Fla., Gainesville, 1978-80, prof., 1980—. Cons. Burr-Brown Rsch. Corp., Tucson, 1970-71, Jet Propulsion Lab., Pasadena, Calif., 1979, Harris Corp., Melbourne, Fla., 1984, Tex. Instruments, Inc., Dallas, 1988-89, 94-96, Ibis Tech. Corp., Danvers, Mass., 1995, Meta-Software, Campbell, Calif., 1995-96, Dynamics Rsch. Corp., San Diego, 1996-02; mem. adv. com. Semiconductor Rsch. Corp., 1991-95; mem. exec. com. IEEE SOI Conf., 1994-97. Contbr. articles to profl. jours.; assoc. editor: Solid-State Electronics, 1979—, IEEE Trans. Computer-Aided Design, 1988-91; patentee in field. Recipient Outstanding Rsch. award Am. Soc. Engring. Edn., 1979. Fellow IEEE (Best Paper award SOI Conf. 1992). Office: U Fla Dept Elec and Computer Engr Gainesville FL 32611-6130 E-mail: fossum@tec.ufl.edu.

FOSSUM, ROBERT H(EYERDAHL), retired English literature educator; b. Beloit, Wis., Mar. 19, 1923; s. Hans Martinius and Talma Irene (Heyerdahl) F.; m. Terry O'Brien Barker, Sept. 12, 1945 (div. Feb. 1951); m. Virginia Adelaide Hammond, June 7, 1952; children: Kristin, Robert Paul, Elizabeth. BA, Beloit Coll., 1948; MA, U. So. Calif., 1950; PhD, Claremont Grad. Sch., 1963. Tchg. asst., lectr. dept. English, U. So. Calif., L.A., 1948-50; instr., asst. prof., then assoc. prof. Beloit Coll., 1950-62; assoc. prof. Calif. State U., L.A., 1962-63; assoc. prof., then prof. Claremont (Calif.) McKenna Coll., 1963-87, Josephine Olp Weeks prof. lit., 1972-87, prof. emeritus, 1987—. Fulbright prof. Am. lit. U. Vienna and U. Graz, Austria, 1969-70, 76-77. Author: William Styron, 1968, Hawthorne's Inviolable Circle, 1972; co-author: Facing Mirrors, 1980, The American Dream, 1981; co-editor: American Ground, 1988. With inf. U.S. Army, 1943. Fellow Lilly Found., 1959-60, Shell Found., 1960-61 Mem. MLA, Phi Beta Kappa. Avocations: reading, spectator sports, theater, film. Home: 403 University Cir Claremont CA 91711-4251 E-mail: g_b_fossum@msn.com.

FOSSUM, ROBERT MERLE, mathematician, educator; b. Northfield, Minn., May 1, 1938; s. Inge Martin and Tina Otelia (Gaudland) F.; m. Cynthia Carol Foss, Jan. 30, 1960 (div. 1979); children: Karen Jean, Kristin Ann; m. Barbara Joel Mason, Aug. 4, 1979 (div. 1993); children: Jonathan Robert, Erik Anton; m. Robin Karyl Goodman, Aug. 10, 1997. BA, St. Olaf Coll., 1959; AM, U.Mich., 1961, PhD, 1965. Instr. U. Ill., Urbana, 1964-66, asst. prof., 1966-68, assoc. prof., 1968-72, prof., 1972—, elect. and computer engring., 2003—. Lectr. Aarhus U., Denmark, 1971-73, Copenhagen U., Denmark, 1976-77; vis. prof. U. Paris VI, 1978-79, Oslo U., 1968-69; prof. Beckman Inst., 2000-02. Contbr. articles to profl. jours. Recipient Disting. Alumni award Northfield H.S.; Fulbright grantee Oslos U., 1967-68. Fellow: AAAS; mem.: IEEE, Soc. Advancement Scandinavian Studies, European Math. Soc., Det Kongelig Norske Videnskabers Selskab (elected natural scis. sect.), Inst. Algebraic Meditation (sec.), Am. Math. Soc. (assoc. sec. cen. sect. 1983—87, sec. 1989—99), Soc. for Indsl. and Applied Math., Internat. Assn. Math. Physics, Assn. Computing Machinery, Nordmanns Forbundet, Heimskringla (Urbana), Sigma Pi Sigma (pres. coun. U. Ill.), Sigma Xi, Phi Beta Kappa. Democrat. Lutheran. Office: U Ill Dept Math 1409 W Green St Urbana IL 61801-2943 E-mail: rmfossum@uiuc.edu.

FOSSUO TALOM, PATRICK, research scientist; b. Yaounde, Cameroon, May 22, 1971; s. Lucien Fossuo Talom and Anne Marie Fonkwa Ngawa. B in Biology, Kean U., 2000; MBA in Pharm. Studies, Fairleigh Dickinson, 2003. Analyst Aventis Pharms., Bridgewater, NJ, 1999—2001; assoc. scientist Johnson and Johnson, Raritan, NJ, 2001—. Mem.: Am. Assn. Pharm. Scientists (assoc.).

FOSTER, ALAN HERBERT, financial consultant, educator; b. Somerville, Mass., Nov. 7, 1925; s. Herbert and Margaret J. (Griffin) F.; m. Cynthia Ann Brooks, June 26, 1954; children— Mark Brooks, Andrew Herbert. BS, BA, Boston Coll., 1951; MBA, Harvard U., 1953. With Sylvania Electric Products, Inc., 1953-63; with Am. Motors Corp., 1963-77, corp. dir. financial planning and analysis, 1963-67, treas., 1967-68, v.p., treas., 1968-77; pres. A.H. Foster & Co. (Cons. in Corp. Fin.), Ann Arbor, Mich., 1977—, Fin. Risk Mgmt. Inc., Ann Arbor, 1983—, ret., 2002—. Adj. prof. corp. strategy and internat. bus. Grad. Sch. Bus., U. Mich. Author: Practical Business Management, 1962, Treasurer's Handbook, also articles. Served with USNR, 1945-46. Mem. Commanderie de Bordeaux, Fin. Execs. Inst. (pres. Detroit chpt. 1972-73), Baker Street Irregulars, Speckled Band Boston, Inst. Mgmt. Scis. (past nat. chmn. coll. planning), U. Mexico Club, Samuel Pepys Club, Harvard Club N.Y.C., Harvard Faculty Club. Home: 810 Earhart Rd Ann Arbor MI 48105-2711

FOSTER, ARTHUR KEY, JR., retired lawyer; b. Birmingham, Ala., Nov. 22, 1933; s. Arthur Key and Vonceil (Oden) F.; m. Jean Lyles Foster, Jan. 7, 1967; children: Arthur Key III, Brooke Oden. BSE, Princeton U., 1955; JD, U. Va., 1960. Bar: Ala. 1960. Ptnr. Balch & Bingham, Birmingham, 1965-99. Trustee Episcopal Found. Jefferson County; bd. dirs. Met. YMCA, Downtown Club, Highlands Day Sch., Altamont Sch. Served to lt., USN, 1955-60. Mem. ABA, Ala. Bar Assn., Birmingham Bar Assn., Estate Planning Coun. of Birmingham, Nat. Assn. Bond Lawyers, Newcomen Soc. of U.S., Kiwanis (bd. dirs.). Republican. Episcopalian. Office: Balch & Bingham PO Box 306 Birmingham AL 35201-0306

FOSTER, ARTHUR ROWE, mechanical engineering educator; b. Peabody, Mass., Apr. 22, 1924; s. Francis Joel and Helen Almira (Rowe) F.; m. Nettie Claire Pease, July 12, 1947 (dec. Mar. 1997); children: Jackson Judd, Cynthia Grace. BS in Mech. Engring, Tufts U., 1945; M.Engring. in Mech. Engring, Yale, 1949. Registered profl. engr., Mass. Engr. material devel. lab. Pratt & Whitney aircraft div. United Aircraft Corp., 1947-48; mem. faculty Northeastern U., 1949—, prof. mech. engring., 1961-89, prof. emeritus, 1989—, chmn. dept., 1961-75; Latin Am. teaching fellow Escuela Politecnica Nacional, Quito, Ecuador, 1975-76; Fulbright lectr. solar engring. Colombia, summer 1979. Vis. prof. Escuela Politecnica Nacional, Quito, Ecuador, 1984 Author: (with R. L. Wright, Jr.) Basic Nuclear Engineering, 1968, 4th edit., 1983, (with Melvin Mark) Thermodynamics: Principles and Applications, 1979. Served to ensign USNR, 1945-46. Fellow ASME (life, Centennial medal 1980); mem. Am. Soc. Engring. Edn. (life), Delta Tau Delta, Pi Tau Sigma, Tau Beta Pi. Home: 10 Longwood Dr Apt 121 Westwood MA 02090-1131

FOSTER, BARRY ALAN, cultural organization researcher, educator; b. Tacoma, Wash., Dec. 11, 1956; s. Glen H. Foster and Selma Landers; m. Sue Rose Foster, July 20, 1954; children: Nathan M., Zachary A., Kristen B. BA in Theology, Southeastern Coll., Lakeland, Fla., 1994; MBA in Managerial Leadership, City U., Renton, Wash., 1996; MA in Orgnl. Devel., The Fielding Inst., Santa Barbara, Calif., 1998, PhD in Human and Orgnl. Sys., 2000. Orgnl. culture change leader The Boeing Co., Seattle, 1999—. Author: (organizational change model) Essential Foundations of the Engaged Organization. Dir. Lemonaid Fund, Chgo., 1999—2002. Mem.: Am. Sociol. Assn. (assoc.; cert.). Achievements include research in barriers to servant leadership and large scale organizational culture change. Avocations: mountain biking, racquetball, flag football. Office: The Boeing Co PO Box 3707 MS 5F-98 Seattle WA 98124 Home Fax: 646-607-3329. Personal E-mail: barryfoster777@comcast.net. E-mail: barry.a.foster@boeing.com.

FOSTER, BAYARD EVERSON, writer; b. Knoxville, Aug. 11, 1934; s. Bayard Collis and Zella Mae (Price) Foster; m. Virginia May Hall, Dec. 24, 1964 (dec. May 1998); children: Karla June, Rex David, Ronald Elliott, Beatrice Irene, Richard Lawrence. BA, Tex. Tech. U., 1955. Commd. 2d lt. USAF, 1955, adv. through grades to maj., ret., 1980; equipment sel. specialist Saudi Arabian Airlines, Jeddah, 1980—84; maintenance data analyst Scitek, Inc., St. Louis, 1988—89; v.p. ops. Aviation Logistics Systems, 1989—90; tech. writer Am. Elecs. Labs., Bethalto, Ill., 1990—92. Author: Mission Iorg, 2000, Reap the Whirlwind, 2002. Founder Angel Flights Min., Troy, Mo., 1998. Methodist. Avocations: writing, photography, travel. Home: 5403 Everhart Rd Corpus Christi TX 78411 Office: Rancho Pacifico Properties 5403 Everhart Rd PMB B Corpus Christi TX 78411

FOSTER, BENJAMIN, JR., educational administrator; b. Raleigh, NC, Mar. 30, 1946; s. Benjamin and Miriam Foster; children: Benjamin Bayete, Suliman Samuel; m. Walton L. Brown, Dec. 28, 1994. BA, Trinity Coll., Hartford, Conn., 1971; MA in Teaching with honors, Wesleyan U., Middletown, Conn., 1973; EdD, U. Mass., 1989, cert. advanced grad. study, 1984. Cert. social studies tchr., Mass., N.Y.; cert. intermediate adminstrn., Conn. Prin. planning analyst for human svcs. Conn. Office Policy and Mgmt., Hartford; rsch. fellow Ctr. for Study Pub. Policy, Cambridge, Mass.; staff rsch. asst. U. Mass., Amherst; asst. chief staff devel. Conn. Dept. Social Svcs., Hartford; asst. dir. A.I. Prince Regional Vocat. Sch., Hartford; prin. Bloomfield (Conn.) H.S.; dir. H.C. Wilcox Tech. Sch., Meriden, Conn., 1989-2000, E.C. Goodwin Tech. Sch., New Britain, Conn., 2000—02; dist. coord., adult edn., social studies and summer sch. New Britain Consol. Sch. Dist., 2002—. Vis. practitioner Harvard Grad. Sch. Edn., 1994—. Author: Looking for Payoff: A New Schooling for Inner-City Youth, 1990; contbr. numerous articles to profl. jours. Trustee Trinity Coll., Hartford. With U.S. Army, 1965-67. Nat. urban fellow, 1982-83. Mem. Inst. Ednl. Leadership (v.p. fellowship edn. policy program 1978-79), Nat. Dropout Prevention Network, Omega Psi Phi. Home: 6 Croydon Dr Bloomfield CT 06002-3446 E-mail: bfoster@hartnet.org.

FOSTER, BRIAN DUANE, biologist, consultant; b. Sacramento, 1961; s. Duane Ray and Loretta Margaret Foster. BA, Point Loma Coll., 1983; PhD, Vanderbilt U., 1991. Postdoctorate staff The Scripps Rsch. Inst., LaJolla, Calif., 1991-93; cons. San Diego, 1993—. Cons. endangered species monitoring Calif. Dept. Fish and Game, San Diego, 1993—97; ind. sci. advisors rev. panel N. San Diego County Multiple Species Conservation Plan, 2000—01. Contbr. articles to profl. jours. Spokesperson No on Proposition 4 Campaign, Calif., 1998. Recipient Grad. Rsch. assistantship Vanderbilt Grad. Sch., Nashville, 1988; grad. fellow Vanderbilt U., Nashville, 1984; rsch. grantee Am. Cancer Soc., Nashville, 1990, postdoctoral tng. grantee NIH, LaJolla, 1991. Mem. AAAS, Am. Ornithologists Union, Wilson Ornithological Soc., Cooper Ornithological Soc., Assn. Field Ornithologists, Colonial Waterbird Soc. Democrat. Avocations: birding, hiking, fishing. Home: 129 1/2 D Ave Coronado CA 92118-1334 E-mail: bfostern@hotmail.com.

FOSTER, C(HARLES) ALLEN, lawyer; b. Aug. 26, 1941; s. Charles Shearer and Bessie Lea (Long) F.; m. Susan Coomes; children: Charles Shearer Sanders II, Susan Elizabeth Coomes, Charles Henry Edward. BA summa cum laude, Princeton U., 1963; BA in Jurisprudence 1st class honors, Oxford (Eng.) U., 1965, MA in Jurisprudence, 1971; JD magna cum laude, Harvard U., 1967. Bar: N.C. 1967, D.C. 1994, U.S. Dist. Ct. (mid. dist.) N.C. 1968, U.S. Dist. Ct. (we. dist.) N.C. 1968, U.S. Dist. Ct. (ea. dist.) N.C. 1968, U.S. Tax Ct. 1970, U.S. Ct. Appeals (4th cir.), U.S. Ct. Appeals (5th cir.) 1970, U.S. Ct. Appeals (11th cir.) 1991, U.S. Ct. Appeals (10th cir.) 1993, U.S. Ct. Appeals (fed. cir.) 1995, U.S. Supreme Ct. 1971, U.S. Dist. Ct. D.C. 1985, U.S. Dist. Ct. (no. dist.) Tex. 1990, U.S. Dist. Ct. (so. dist.) Tex. 1991, U.S. Ct. Fed. Claims 1994. Assoc. McLendon, Brim, Brooks, Pierce & Daniels, Greensboro, N.C., 1967-72, ptnr., 1972-73; sec., dir., gen. counsel Spanco Industries, Inc., Greensboro and Sanford, N.C., 1973-75, Conestee, S.C., 1973-75; ptnr. Turner, Enochs, Foster, Sparrow & Burnley, Greensboro, 1975-81, Foster, Conner & Robson, 1983-88, Patton, Boggs LLP, 1988-99, Greenberg Traurig, Washington, 1999—. Sr. lectr. law Duke U., 1981-88; arbitrator Am. Arbitration Assn., mem. Nat. Acad. Arbitrators; pub. mem. N.C. Tax Rev. Bd., 1972-76; mem. N.C. Judicial Selection Study Commn., 1987 88; U.S. rep. Internat. Energy Agy. Dispute Resolution Ctr., Paris, 1984—; permanent panel arbitrator Martin Marietta and Atomic Trades and Labor Coun., others. Author: Construction and Design Law, 1984—, Construction and Design Law Digest, 1981—, Law and Practice of Commercial Arbitration in North Carolina, 1984; contbr. articles to profl. jours. Co-founder, sec., bd. dirs. Greensboro Day Sch.; exec. com. Princeton U. Alumni Assn.; exec. com. Harvard Law Sch. Assn. N.C., 1970; Rep. candidate for atty.-gen. N.C., 1984; spl. counsel Rep. Nat. Com., 1989—; spl. litigation counsel N.C. Rep. Cen. Com., 1987—. Named one of top 20 trial lawyers in D.C., 2003. Mem. ABA (litigation sect., labor and employment discrimination law sect., forum com. on constrn. industry), Am. Law Inst., Am. Arbitration Assn. (bd. dirs. 1980-83, nat. panels labor, constrn., internat. comml. arbitrators 1975—, chmn. N.C. regional adv. coun. 1979-83), Am. Coll. Constrn. Arbitrators (pres. 1983-84), Princeton U. Alumni Assn. (pres. alumni coun., exec. com. 1978-79, pres. mid. N.C. chpt. 1968-80), Phi Beta Kappa, Cap and Gown Club. Home: 3846 Cathedral Ave NW Washington DC 20016 E-mail: fostera@gtlaw.com.

FOSTER, CHARLES CRAWFORD, lawyer, educator; b. Galveston, Tex., Aug. 1, 1941; s. Louie Brown and Helen (Hall) F.; m. Marta Brito, Sept. 7, 1967 (div. Apr. 1986); children: John, Ruth; m. Lily Chen, Jan. 7, 1989; children: Zachary, Anthony. AA, Del Mar Jr. Coll., 1961; BA, U. Tex., 1963, JD, 1967. Bar: Tex. 1967, N.Y. 1969. Assoc. Reid & Priest, N.Y.C., 1967-69, Butler & Binion, Houston, 1969-73; ptnr. Tindall & Foster, Houston, 1973—. Hon. consul gen. Kingdom of Thailand, 1996—; adj. prof. immigration law U. Houston, 1985-89; bd. dirs. Greater Houston Partnership, 1997-2003, chmn. econ. devel. adv. bd., 2000 World Trade Adv. Bd., 1997; chmn. Asia Soc.-Tex., bd. trustees, 1990—; bd. dirs. Houston World Affairs Coun., 1990; chmn. Inst. Internat. Edn., The Houston Club, 1999—, Houston Ballet Found., Assn. of Cmty. TV, Houston Holocaust Mus.; mem. Mayoral Adv. Bd. for Internat. Affairs and Devel./Asia, 1999—; pres. Houston Forum, 2002. Contbr. articles to profl. jours. Chmn. immigration reform Gov.'s Task Force of Tex., 1984—87; mem. Bush-Cheney Transition Adv. Com., 2000—01. Admiral Texan Navy, 2003. Decorated comdr. 3d class Order of the Crown (Thailand), comdr. Exalted Order of White Elephant (Thailand); Rotary Internat. fellow U. Concepción, Chile, 1964; recipient Houston Internat. Svc. award Houston Jaycees, 1996, Disting. Friend of China award U.S. China Friendship Found., 2000; honoree Am. Immigration Law Found., 1998' commd. adm. Tex. Navy, Gov. Rick Perry, 2003. Mem. ABA (chmn. immigration com. internat. law and practice sect. 1982-90, chmn. coordinating com. on immigration and law 1987-89, fgn. rels. com. 2000—), Am. Immigration Lawyers Assn. (pres. 1981-82, Outstanding Svc. award 1985), Tex. Bar Assn. (chmn. com. law on immigration and nationality 1984-86), Tex. Bd. Legal Specialization (chmn. immigration adv. commn. 1979—), Houston Bar Assn., Asia Soc. (trustee 1992—, chmn. Houston Ctr. 1992—), Rotary, Houston Club (pres. 2001). Methodist. Avocations: mountain climbing, photography, travel. Home: 17 Courtlandt Pl Houston TX 77006-4013 Office: Tindall & Foster 2800 Chase Tower 600 Travis St Ste 2800 Houston TX 77002-3094

FOSTER, CHARLES HENRY WHEELWRIGHT, former foundation officer, consultant, author; b. Boston, Mar. 18, 1927; s. Reginald Candler and Frances Helen (Hoar) F.; m. Barbara Ann Duchaine, Sept 19, 1953; children: Frances H., Jonathan R., Susan Foster Swensen. BA, Harvard U., 1951; BSF, U. Mich., 1953, MS, 1956; PhD, Johns Hopkins U., 1969; DPA (hon.), Suffolk U., 1971; MA (hon.), Yale U., 1977. Exec. sec. Wildlife Conservation Inc., Boston, 1953-55; cons. Mass. Water Resources Commn., Boston, 1956-59; commr. Mass. Dept. Natural Resources, Boston, 1959-66; pres. Nature Conservancy, Washington, 1966-67; sr. staff mem. Conservation Found., Washington, 1967-68; chmn. bd. N.E. Natural Resources Ctr., Boston, 1969-70; sec. Mass. Exec. Office Environ. Affairs, Boston, 1971-75; sr. staff mem. A. D. Little, Inc., Cambridge, Mass., 1975-76; prof. environ. policy U. Mass., Amherst, 1975-76; dean Sch. Forestry and Environ. Studies Yale U., 1976-81; vis. scholar Stanford U., 1981-82; rsch. assoc. U. Calif., Santa Cruz, 1982; scholar in residence U. Va., 1983; pres. W. Alton Jones Found., Charlottesville, Va., 1983. Adj. prof. environ. studies Tufts U., 1984-85; vis. rsch. prof. Clark U., 1985-86; adj. rsch. fellow Harvard U., 1986—; vis. prof. environ. studies Brown U., 1987; cons., lectr. in field. Trustee of numerous natural resources and ednl. orgns. With U.S. Army, 1945-47. Bullard fellow Harvard U., 1969-70 Fellow AAAS; mem. Soc. Am. Foresters, Am. Water Resources Assn., Harvard Club (Boston). E-mail: charles_foster@harvard.edu.

FOSTER, DALE WARREN, political scientist, educator, management consultant, real estate broker, accountant; b. Bryan, Tex., Mar. 7, 1950; s. William Henry and Maysie Blanche (Hembree) F. BBA, Tex. A&M U., 1972, MA, 1979, Cert. in Profl. Teaching, 1987; BS, U. Houston, 1981, MEd, 1983; AAS, Houston C.C. Sys., 1982. Cert. in property mgmt. Dept. mgr. J.C. Penney Co., Bryan, 1973-74; shopper advt. mgr. Harte-Hanks Newspapers/Daily Eagle, Bryan, 1975-76; bus. mgr., contr. S.M. Hardee Enterprises, College Station, Tex., 1976-78; ops. mgr. Western Food Svcs., Inc., Pasadena, Tex., 1978-80; internal auditor Hermann Hosp., Houston, 1980-82; high sch. tchr. Cypress-Fairbanks Independent Sch. Dist., Houston, 1983-84; alternative sch. tchr. Alief Independent Sch. Dist., Houston, 1984-88; gov. prof. Houston C.C. System, 1980—, chmn. govt. dept. co-op program, 1992—; lead instr. Houston C.C. Sys., 1993—; supr. student tchr. U. Houston, 1989-90. Adj. instr. North Harris County Coll., Houston, 1983-96; fin. cons. Pro-Trac Econ. Planning Adv. Bd., Denver, 1985-86; Presdl. Scholars lectr. Minority Students Honors Program, Houston, 1986-89; coord. legis. practicum Harris County Congl. Internship

Program, 1988—; exch. tchr., The Netherlands, 1992. Co-editor textbook supplement, curriculum guide, departmental political reader; author classroom instructional project. Mem. adv. com. Hermann Affiliated Fed. Credit Union, Houston, 1980-82; mem. fin. coun. Harris County Dem. Com., 1991-93; mem. dean's coun. U. Houston, 1992-96; trustee, treas. Wilmington-Barnard Found., 1992—. Named Tchr. of Yr., Cy.-Fair H.S., 1984, Alief Individualized Study Ctr., 1987, Master Tchr. Nat. Leadership Inst. U. Tex., Austin, 1991, host tchr. Washington Week Intern Program, 1995; recipient Adj. Teaching and Comty. Svc. award North Harris County Coll. Dist., 1990, Teaching Excellence medal Nat. Inst. Staff and Orgn. Devel., 1991, 98; Fulbright scholar, 1992, 98; Robert A. Taft fellow L.B.J. Sch. Pub. Affairs, 1995, Fulbright-Hays fellowship U.S. Dept. Edn., 1998. Fellow Am. Bd. Master Educators; mem. Tex. Jr. Coll. Tchrs. Assn., Tex. Coun. Social Studies, Inst. Mgmt. Accts.,, Am. Fin. Assn., Fulbright Assn., Houston C.C. Sys. Faculty Assn. (treas. 1997-2000, v.p. 2000-01, pres.-elect 2001-02, pres. 2002-03, Outstanding Tchr. award 1991, Tchr. of Yr. 1997), Phi Theta Kappa, Alpha Phi Omega, Kappa Delta Pi. Democrat. Baptist. Avocations: travel, reading, bowling, water sports, outdoor activities. Office: Houston C C NW 1010 W Sam Houston Pkwy N Houston TX 77043 E-mail: corps1972@yahoo.com.

FOSTER, DAVID LEE, lawyer; b. Des Moines, Dec. 13, 1933; s. Carl Dewitt and Dorothy Jo (Bell) F.; m. Marilyn Lee Bokemeier, Aug. 12, 1957 (div. June 1978); children: Gwendolyn Foster Reed, Cynthia Foster Curry, David Lee Jr.; m. Kathleen Carol Walsh, Mar. 24, 1979; 1 child, John Wickersham. Student, Simpson Coll., 1951-52; BA, U. Iowa, 1954, JD, 1957. Bar: Iowa 1957, N.Y. 1958, Ohio 1964, U.S. Supreme Ct. 1975. Assoc. Cravath, Swaine & Moore, N.Y.C., 1957-63; from assoc. to ptnr. Jones, Day, Cockley & Reavis, Cleve., 1963-72; ptnr., counsel Willkie Farr & Gallagher, N.Y.C., 1972—. Lectr. So. Meth. U., 1979-84, U. Pitts., 1984, Practicing Law Inst., N.Y.C., 1984-85; mem. adv. bd. Civil RICO Report LRP Publs., 1988—; bd. govs. N.Y. Ins. Exch., 1987-96. Contbr. chpts. to book, articles to legal jours. Mem., bd. trustees Cardigan Mountain Sch., 1995—, v.p., 2002—. Served with USNR, 1952-60. Fellow Am. Coll. Trial Lawyers, Internat. Acad. Trial Lawyers (bd. dirs. 1987-92); mem. Am. Counsel Assn. (pres. 1994-95, bd. dirs. 1992-98), River Club, Order of Coif, Phi Beta Kappa. Office: Willkie Farr & Gallagher 787 7th Ave New York NY 10019-6099 E-mail: dfoster@willkie.com.

FOSTER, DAVID RAMSEY, soap company executive; b. London, May 24, 1920; (parents Am. citizens); s. Robert Bagley and Josephine (Ramsey) F.; m. Anne Firth, Aug. 2, 1957 (dec. June 1994); children: Sarah, Victoria; m. Alexandra Chang, May 24, 1996. Student in econs., Gonville and Caius Coll., Cambridge (Eng.) U., 1938. With Colgate-Palmolive Co. and affiliates, 1946-79; v.p., gen. mgr. Europe Colgate-Palmolive Internat., 1961-65, v.p., gen. mgr. household products divsn. parent co., 1965-68, exec. v.p., 1968-70, pres., 1970-75, CEO, 1971-79, chmn., 1975-79. Author: Wings Over the Sea, 1990. Trustee Woman's Sport Found. Served to lt. comdr. Royal Naval Vol. Res., 1940-46. Decorated Disting. Svc. Order, D.S.C. with bar, Mentioned in Despatches (2); recipient Victor award City of Hope, 1974, Herbert Hoover Meml. award, 1976, Adam award, 1977, Harriman award Boys Club N.Y., 1977, Charter award St. Francis Coll., 1978, Walter Hagen award, 1978, Patty Berg award, 1986, Commr.'s award LPGA, 1995. Mem. Soc. Mayflower Descs., Hawks Club (Cambridge U.), Royal Ancient Golf Club (St. Andrews, Scotland), Royal Cinque Ports Golf Club (life), Sunningdale Golf Club, Sankaty Head Golf Club, Racquet and Tennis Club (N.Y.C.), Mission Hills Country Club, Bally Bunion Golf Club (life). Home: 540 Desert West Dr Rancho Mirage CA 92270-1310

FOSTER, DAVID SCOTT, lawyer; b. White Plains, N.Y., July 13, 1938; s. William James and Ruth Elizabeth (Šeltzer) F.; m. Eleanore Stalker, Dec. 21, 1959; children: David Scott, Robert McEachron. BA, Amherst Coll., 1960; LLB, Harvard U., 1963. Bar: N.Y. 1963, D.C. 1977, Calif. 1978. Jud. law clk. U.S. Dist. Ct. (so. dist.) N.Y., 1963-64; assoc. Debevoise & Plimpton, N.Y.C., 1964-72; internat. tax counsel U.S. Treasury Dept., Washington, 1972-77; ptnr. Brobeck, Phleger & Harrison, San Francisco, 1978-90, Coudert Bros., San Francisco, 1990-91, Thelen, Reid & Priest LLP, San Francisco, 1991—. Mem. ABA, San Francisco Bar Assn., Internat. Fiscal Assn., Western Pension and Benefits Confs., St. Francis Yacht Club (San Francisco). Presbyterian. Office: Thelen Reid & Priest LLP 101 2nd St Ste 1800 San Francisco CA 94105-3659

FOSTER, DAVID SMITH, lawyer, arbitrator, private adjudicator; b. Wilmington, Del., May 20, 1927; s. David Smith and Mary Jeannette (Johnson) F.; m. Marie Elise Labbe, Nov. 10, 1956; children— Elise L., Chadford W., Donald Patch. B.A., U. Va., 1951; J.D., Tulane U., 1964. Bar: La. 1964. Landman Continental Oil Co., Lafayette, La., 1953-56, lease broker DS Foster Oil Proprs., Lafayette, 1956-61; ptnr. Voorhies & Labbe, Lafayette, 1964-71; pres. David S. Foster, P.C., Lafayette, 1971— ; judge pro tem 15th Jud. Dist. Ct., La., Lafayette Cir. Ct.; bd. dirs. Offshore Logistics, Lafayette, Billeaud Cos., Lafayette, Billead Marshlands, Lafayette. Past pres. Lafayette Parish Youth Council; past youth counselor Lafayette Juvenile and Young Adult Program; past bd. dirs. ADAPT Inc., Lafayette Mus. Natural History and Planetarium Assn.; past adv. bd. Mt. Carmel Cath. Sch., Acad. of Sacred Heart, Ascension Day Sch.; v.p. Faith House; past sec. Hamilton Sch. PTA; past mem. external services funding adv. council City of Lafayette, traffic planning commn.; Served as sgt. USAF, 1945-46, ETO. Mem. ABA, La. State Bar Assn., Lafayette Parish Bar Assn. (pres. 1977-78). Home: 242 Girard Park Cir Lafayette LA 70503-2043 Office: 242 Girard Park Cir Lafayette LA 70503-2043

FOSTER, DAVID WILLIAM, language educator, humanities educator; b. Seattle, Wash., Sept. 11, 1940; s. William Henry Foerster and Rosemond (Pépin) F.; m. Virginia María) Ramos, May 30, 1966; 1 child, David Raúl. PhD, U. Wash., 1964. Regents' prof. Spanish, women's studies, and interdisciplinary humanities Ariz. State U., Tempe, 1995—. Author books; contbr. numerous articles to profl. jours. Democrat. Avocation: acting. Home: 928 West Palm Ln Phoenix AZ 85007-1535 Office: Arizona State U Langs and Lits Tempe AZ 85287-0202 Home Fax: 480-965-3752; Office Fax: 480-965-0135. Personal E-mail: david.foster@asu.edu.

FOSTER, DOUGLAS TAYLOR, lawyer, investor; b. L.A., Oct. 30, 1927; s. James Taylor Foster and Irene Eve Ericksen; m. Nita Burt Peterson, July 3, 1951 (div. May, 1975); children: Jane Taylor Dickson, Stephanie Foster Abram. BA in Econ. and Bus., U. Wash., 1950; JD, Stanford U., 1956. Bar: Calif. 1957, U.S. Dist. Ct. (so. dist.) Calif. 1957, U.S. Ct. Appeals (9th cir.) 1959, U.S. Dist. Ct. (no. dist.) Calif. 1969, U.S. Supreme Ct. 1971, U.S. Dist. Ct. (ea. dist.) Calif. 1985. From assoc. to ptnr. Farrand, Fisher & Farrand, L.A., 1956-66; legal counsel McClatchy Newspapers and Broadcasting, Sacramento, Calif., 1967-81; ptnr. Diepenbrock, Wulff, Plant & Hannegan, Sacramento, 1981-84; pvt. practice, Sacramento, 1985—. Sec. bus. and corp. sect. L.A. County Bar Assn., 1966. Candidate L.A. County Rep. Ctrl. Com., San Marino, Calif., 1965. Lt. USN, 1950-53, Korean War. Mem. ABA, ATLA, Calif. State Bar, Sacramento County Bar Assn., Calif. Trial Lawyers Assn., Consumer Attys. of Calif., Capital City Trial Lawyers Corp., Consumer Attys. of Sacramento County, Rotary Club Arden-Arcade, Seattle Yacht Club, Sacramento Yacht Club, Sutter Club, Am. Trial Lawyers Am. Presbyterian. Achievements include succesful defense of cable television license, Lake of the Pines Development, No. Calif., involving first judicial interpretation and ruling under the Cable TV Act of 1984 in U.S. Dist. Ct. (ea. dist.) Calif., 1986. Office: 2625 Fair Oaks Blvd Ste 1 Sacramento CA 95864-4936

FOSTER, DUDLEY EDWARDS, JR., musician, educator; b. Orange, N.J., Oct. 5, 1935; s. Dudley Edwards and Margaret (DePoy) F. Student Occidental Coll., 1953-56; AB, UCLA, 1957, MA, 1958; postgrad. U. So. Calif., 1961-73. Lectr. music Immaculate Heart Coll., L.A., 1960-63; dir. music Holy Faith Episcopal Ch., Inglewood, Calif., 1964-67; lectr. music Calif. State U., L.A., 1968-71; assoc. prof. music L.A. Mission Coll., 1975-83, prof., 1983—, also chmn. dept. music, 1977—; mem. dist. acad. senate L.A. Community Colls., 1991-92; mem. acad. senate L.A. Mission Coll., 1993-97; dir. music 1st Luth. Ch., L.A., 1968-72. Organist, pianist, harpsichordist; numerous recitals; composer O Sacrum Convivium for Trumpet and Organ, 1973, Passacaglia for Brass Instruments, 1969, Introduction, Arioso & Fugue for Cello and Piano, 1974. Fellow Trinity Coll. Music, London, 1960. Recipient Associated Students Faculty award, 1988. Mem. Am. Guild Organists, Am. Musicol. Soc., Nat. Assn. of Scholars, Acad. Senate, Town Hall Calif., L.A. Coll. Tchrs. Assn. (pres. Mission Coll. chpt. 1976-77, v.p., exec. com. 1982-84), Mediaeval Acad. Am. Republican. Anglican. Office: LA Mission Coll Dept Music 13356 Eldridge Ave Sylmar CA 91342-3200 E-mail: fostermusic@eartlink.net., defoster@lamc.org.

FOSTER, EDWARD PAUL (TED FOSTER), process industries executive; b. Pawtucket, R.I., Aug. 23, 1945; s. Edward Francis and Vivian Adrienne (Davagne) F.; m. Barbara Philomena Cook, Dec. 17, 1965 (div. Apr. 1978); children: Edward Robert, Gwendolyn Lucy; m. Johanna Helena Klaassen, June, 1985 (div. 1988). BSChemE with distinction, U. R.I., 1967; MSChemE, Worcester Poly. Inst., 1970; MBA, Lehigh U., 1981. Mfg. melting engr. Corning Glass Works, Central Falls, R.I., 1966-67; group leader rsch. and devel. The Babcock & Wilcox Co., Alliance, Ohio, 1968-71, mgr. tampella process Barberton, Ohio, 1972-74; from comml. devel. engr. to dir. bus. devel. in gases, metallurgy, coal, energy, chems. and polymers, and environ. areas Air Products and Chem., Inc., Allentown, Pa., 1974—. Cons. U.S. Army Natick (Mass.) Lab., 1966-67. Contbr. articles to profl. jours.; patentee in field. Chmn. fin. Unitarian Ch., Bethleham, Pa., 1985, chmn. social, 1983-84. NDEA fellow HEW, 1967-69; ROTC scholar U.S. Army, 1965, Nat. Merit scholar, 1963. Mem. AIChE, Comml. Devel. Assn. (vice chmn. fall meeting 1996, nat. program chmn. 1997-99, bd. dirs.), Am. Chem. Soc., Comml. Devel. and Mktg. Assn. (bd. dirs. 2000—03), Phi Kappa Phi, Tau Beta Pi, Theta Chi. Avocations: tennis, downhill skiing, sailing. Home: 6023 Fairway Ln Allentown PA 18106-9610 Office: Air Products and Chems 7201 Hamilton Blvd Allentown PA 18195-1526

FOSTER, EDWIN POWELL, JR., educator, structural engineer; b. Louisville, May 7, 1942; s. Edwin Powell Sr. and Mary Alice (Thompson) F.; m. Joyce Ann Lane, June 25, 1966; children: Cathleen, Patricia, Michael. B in Engring., Vanderbilt U., 1964, MS, 1966, PhD, 1974; postgrad., U. Ill., 1966-67. Registered prof. engr. Tenn., Ga. Field engr. Am. Bridge, Cocoa Beach, Fla., 1964; stress analysis engr. Brown Engring., Huntsville, Ala., 1965-66; rsch. asst. U. Ill., Urbana, 1966-67; teaching asst. Vanderbilt U., Nashville, 1967-68; analysis engr. AVCO Aerostructures, Nashville, 1968; prof. engring. U. Tenn., Nashville, 1968-79, dir. civil engring. Chattanooga, 1979—. Rsch. engr. NASA-Langley Rsch. Ctr., Hampton, Va., 1977, 78, Combustion Engring., Chattanooga, 1979. Scoutmaster Boy Scouts Am. Troop 47, Chattanooga, 1987-90. NSF fellow, 1965, NASA fellow, 1977, 78. Mem. ASCE (pres. Nashville sect. 1978-79, v.p. Tenn. sect. 1993-94, pres.-elect 1995, pres. 1996), NSPE (treas. Chattanooga chpt. 1985, 86, sec. 1987), Am. Soc. for Engring. Edn. (chmn. civil engring. divsn. 1982, 86, 93, 94), K.C. Avocations: rebuilding mga sports cars, architecture, tennis, woodworking. Home: 507 Highbury Ln Hixson TN 37343-2822 Office: U Tenn 615 Mccallie Ave Chattanooga TN 37403-2504

FOSTER, ERIC HAROLD, JR., retail executive; b. Nov. 8, 1943; s. Eric H. Sr. and Dorothy (Schwarz) F.; married; children: Dawn, Eric III, Kimberly, Meredith. BS in Mgmt., Rutger's U., 1969; student grad. sch. acctg. and taxation, Farleigh Dickinson U., 1973-74. Computer and peripheral equipment operator N.J. Bell Tel. Co., 1965-66; mem. prodn. planning and scheduling 3M Co., St. Paul, 1966-68, data analyst, 1968-69; supr. customer and geog. info. ctr. McGraw-Hill Book Co., Hightstown, N.J., 1969-71, staff asst. to gen. mgr. distbn. ctr., 1971-75, 78, mgr. retail accounts receivable credit and collection dept., 1975-78, 79, responsible McGraw-Hill club and retail customer svc. depts., 1979, mgr., 1979-80, mgr. spl. svcs. and returns, 1980-82, gen. mgr. profl. pub. svcs., 1982-88. Councilman Borough of Freehold, pres., chmn. water and sewer dept., mem. planning bd., fin. and econ. devel. com.; bd. dirs. Freehold Presbyn. Nursery Sch.; chmn. bd. The Rugby Sch.; vice chmn. Freehold Borough Zoning Bd.; mem. vestry, bus. and pers. com., maintenance and repair com. St. Peter Episc. Ch., chmn. fin. com.; advisor Youth Group; charter mem., 1st pres., mem. founding group East Freehold Fire Co.; coord. troop 151 Boy Scouts Am. Recipient Bronze Palm award Eagle Scouts Am., 1960. Mem. Direct Mktg. Assn., Direct Mktg. and Credit Assn. (bd. dirs.), Internat. Consumer Credit Assn. (bd. dirs. region II N.Y./N.J. chpts.), N.J. Assn. Schs. and Agys. for the Handicapped, Internat. Credit Assn. (cert. consumer credit exec.). Episcopalian. Home: 35 Broadway Freehold NJ 07728-1864

FOSTER, FREDERICKA, artist; b. Seattle, Wash., June 14, 1944; d. Harold Frederick and Joann L. (Nelson) Fogman; m. Linn Philip Foster, Sept. 1963 (div. 1966); 1 child, Lisa; m. Bennett Michaels Shapiro, Mar. 13, 1982; children: Lise Sanders, Jon Shapiro. BA in Art, U. Wash., 1972. BA U. Ill. One-woman shows include Pelican Bay Gallery, Seattle, 1978, City Art Works, Seattle, 1981 (Second prize), Maison des Juenes et de le Culture, Nice, France, 1983, Equivalents Gallery, Seattle, 1985, Helen B. Smith Gallery/Green River C.C., Auburn, Wash., 1990, TSS Gallery, N.Y.C., 1992, Stover Mill Gallery, Bucks County, Pa., 1993, Riverrun Gallery, Lambertville, N.J., 1996, The Norbert Considine Gallery, 1996, From the Ground Up, Duvall, Wash., 1999, Fischbach Gallery, N.Y.C., 2002; exhibited in group shows at Arleri Ctr. Nicois de Photographie Documentaire, Nice, 1983-84, Tokyo Met. Art Mus., 1984, Pacific Luth. U., Tacoma, Wash., 1988-89, Tacoma Art Mus., 1989, Silver Image Gallery, Seattle, 1990, Mus. Am. Art of the Pa. Acad. Fine Arts, Phila., 1996, Soho 20, N.Y.C., 1999, The Limelight, N.Y.C., 1999, The Fables of La Fontaine, Aix-on-Provence, France, Rome, Italy, Ending at the Meyerhoff Gallery, Balt., Md., 2002—; represented in permanent collections Microsoft Corp., Artsbridge and Lambertville C. of C., Merck Corp.; contbr. articles: Art, Religion and Spirituality, 1999; (with Hilda O'Connell) Early Renaissance, a vol. in Art History Through Touch and Sound., 2001. Democrat.

FOSTER, GAYLA CATHERINE, musician; b. Oklahoma City, June 3, 1946; d. Jon B. and Betty Louise (Swidensky) Wagner; m. Bart Lewis Foster III, Mar. 9, 1974; children: Jason Scott (dec.), Jacob Bart, Joseph Matthew. MusB in Piano Performance, U. Okla., 1969, MusM in Piano Performance, 1971; postgrad., U. So. Calif., 1971-73; D of Musical Arts in Piano/Pedagogy, U. Okla., 1995. Cert. tchr. K-12, Okla., 1990. Grad. asst. in piano U. Okla., 1969-71, spl. instr. in piano, 1990, Okla. artist-in-residence, 1993-96; instr. music theory and chorus C.E. Donart High Sch., Stillwater, 1974-78; pvt. practice Stillwater, 1974—; dir. arts in edn. State Dept. Okla. State Dept. Okla., 1999—2001; v.p., dir. programs Okla. Arts Inst., 2001—. Instr. music theory Okla. State U., 1979, adj. keyboard faculty, 1993-95; team instr. keyboard skills, U. Okla., 1991; workshop leader, Okla. and Tex., 1991-97, Kans., 1991-2000; pianist Stillwater Chamber Singers, 1986-91, Okla. All-State Band, Oklahoma City, 1976, Thanksgiving Choral Festival Okla. State U., 1985, chorus mem. Pres. Masterworks Chorus, 1984, accompanist, 1985-89, accompanist for summer choir, 1982; adjudicator Okla. Fedn. Music Clubs, Okla. State U., Am. Coll. Musicians Piano Guild; specialist fine arts curriculum Stillwater Pub. Schs., 1996-99, Yukon and Moore Pub. Schs., 1996-99. Solo recitals include U. Okla., Norman, 1966-69, 71, 86, 89, 91, Okla. State U., Stillwater, 1971, 77, 84-85, 89, 91, 96, 99, Cameron U., Lawton, 1988, Tulsa Performing Arts Ctr., 1988, 90, Graz, Austria, 1992, So. Meth. U., Dallas, 1993, U. Nebr., 1995; ensemble recitals include Okla. State U., 1988-99, Composers Symposium U. Okla., 1991, St. Cecilia Music Club, Stillwater, 1975, 80-85, 88, Okla. Fedn. Music Club State Conv., Ponca City, 1977, Arts & Scis. Grad. Banquet Program Okla. State U., 1979. Dir. music Highland Park United Meth. Ch., Stillwater, 1976—; pianist St. Cecilia Christmas Choir, Stillwater, 1981-88, Town & Gown Community Theatre Prodns., Stillwater; performance pianist Cushing-Chandler Community Chorus, 1985 Recipient Outstanding Svc. award United Meth. Women, Stillwater, 1990, 3rd prize Mid-Am. Chopin Festival, 1990; named one of Outstanding Young Women of Am., 1981, 97, Okla. Musician of Yr., 1999. Mem. Music Tchrs. Nat. Assn. (cert., nat. chair-elect Nat. Arts Advocacy com. 1996—), Okla. Music Tchrs. Assn. (cert. bd. 1990—, state chair IMTF, Music Links Cmty. Outreach in Edn. 1990-2001, adjudicator), Stillwater Area Music Tchrs. Assn. (by-laws com. mem. 1984, exec. adv. bd. dirs. 1985-86, sec.-treas. 1986-89, v.p. 1993—, pres. 1997-99), Friends Music for Okla. State U. (exec. bd. dirs. 1983, sec.-treas. 1984-88), St. Cecilia Music Club (Stillwater coord. for N.W. dist. jr. festival 1985—, exec. bd. dirs. 1986-89, pres. 1982-84, 1st v.p. 1980-82, Outstanding Achievement Svc. award 1986), Okla. Fedn. Music Clubs (state exec. bd. 1982-87, state chmn. Nell Keaton Cook scholarship 1984-87), Chamber Music Soc. Palos Verdes, Pi Kappa Lambda, Sigma Alpha Iota (treas. 1969-70, Sword of Honor 1969). Home: 801 W 37th Ave Stillwater OK 74074-7307

FOSTER, GEORGE MCCLELLAND, JR., anthropologist, educator; b. Sioux Falls, S.D., Oct. 9, 1913; s. George McClelland and Mary (Slutz) F.; m. Mary Fraser LeCron, Jan. 6, 1938; children: Jeremy, Melissa Bowerman. BS, Northwestern U., 1935; PhD, U. Calif. at Berkeley, 1941; DHL (hon.), So. Meth. U., 1990. Instr. Syracuse U., 1941-42; lectr. UCLA, 1942-43; vis. prof. U. Calif.-Berkeley, 1953-55, prof. anthropology, 1955-79, prof. emeritus, 1979—, chmn. dept., 1958-61; acting dir. Mus. Anthropology, 1955-57; lectr. pub. health, 1955-64. Anthropologist Inst. Social Anthropology, Smithsonian Instn., 1943-52, dir., 1946-1952; field rsch. Calif. Indians, 1937, Spain, 1949-50, Mexico, 1940— ; adviser AID, India-Pakistan, 1955, Afghanistan, 1957, Zambia, 1961, 62, Nepal, 1965, Indonesia, 1973-74, WHO, Sri Lanka, 1975, Malaysia, 1978, India, 1979, 80, 81, Manila, 1983; adviser UNICEF, Geneva, 1976 Author: Traditional Cultures and the Impact of Technological Change, 1962, Tzintzuntzan: Mexican Peasants in a Changing World, 1967, Applied Anthropology, 1969, (with B. Anderson) Medical Anthropology, 1978, Hippocrates' Latin American Legacy, 1993, others, also monographs and articles. Recipient Berkeley citation, 1979; Guggenheim fellow, 1949; fellow Center for Advanced Study in Behavioral Scis., 1969-70 Fellow Am. Anthrop. Assn. (pres. 1970, Disting. Service award 1980); mem. Southwestern Anthrop. Assn. (Disting. Research award 1981), Nat. Acad. Scis., Am. Acad. Arts and Scis., Soc. Applied Anthropology (Malinowski award 1982) Clubs: Cosmos (Washington). Home: 790 San Luis Rd Berkeley CA 94707-2030 E-mail: foster@sscl.berkeley.edu.

FOSTER, HELEN R. language educator; b. Angleton, Tex., Oct. 19, 1950; d. C. Nolan and E. Lanore Ashley; m. Don L. Foster, Aug. 1, 1970; children: Thomas Blair, Mary Kathryn. BA, U. Tex., El Paso, Tex., 1990, MA, 1994; PhD, Purdue U., 2001. Ops. supr. Data Processing Divsn. Tex. Commerce Bank, Houston, 1975—84; adj. instr. U. Tex., El Paso, 1994—95; grad. instr. Purdue U., West Lafayette, Ind., 1995—97; vis. asst. prof. U. Tex., El Paso, 1998—99, asst. prof., 1999—. Instr. El Paso (Tex.) C.C., 1994; cons. Dept. Scis. U. Tex., 1994—95, instr., 1994; presenter in field; mem. various coms. U. Tex., 1997—. Contbr. articles to profl. jours. Mem.: AAUW, Internat. Reading Assn., Assn. Bus. Comm., Nat. Tchrs. Tech. Writing, Coll. Composition and Comm., Nat. Coun. Tchrs. English, Modern Lang. Assn., Coalition Women Scholars in History of Rhetoric and Composition, Sigma Tau Delta. Home: 6305 Los Altos Drive El Paso TX 79912 Office: U Tex English Dept 500 W University Ave El Paso TX 79968 0900

FOSTER, HENRY WENDELL, medical educator; b. Pine Bluff, Ark., Sept. 8, 1933; s. Henry Wendell and Ivie (Hill Watson) F.; m. St. Clair Anderson, Feb. 6, 1960; children: Myrna Faye, Henry Wendell. BS, Morehouse Coll., 1954; MD, U. Ark., 1958. Am. Bd. Ob-Gyn. Chief ob-gyn. John Andrew Hosp., Tuskegee, Ala., 1965-73; prof., chmn. dept. ob-gyn. Meharry Med. Coll., Nashville, 1973—, prof. emeritus; dir. maternal and infant care project Tuskegee Inst., Ala., 1970-73; sr. program cons. Robert Wood Johnson Found., Princeton, N.J., 1981-86. Chmn. ob-gyn. exec. com. Nat. Med. Assn., 1977—79; nominee for U.S. Surgeon Gen. Pres. Bill Clinton, 1995, sr. advisor on teen pregnancy, 1996—2001. Mem. editorial bd.: Jour. Med. Edn., 1974-77. Bd. dirs. Planned Parenthood Assn. Am., 1975-81; bd. dirs. Alan Guttmacher Inst., N.Y.C., 1975-81. Served to capt. USAF, 1959-61. Fellow Am. Coll. Obstetricians and Gynecologists; mem. Alpha Omega Alpha Democrat. Am. Baptist. Home: 4140 W Hamilton Rd Nashville TN 37218-1829 Office: Meharry Med Coll 1005 D B Todd Blvd Nashville TN 37208

FOSTER, JAMES CALDWELL, academic dean, historian; b. Madison, Wis., Apr. 10, 1943; s. Mark A. and Ruth C. (Caldwell) Foster; m. Diane L. Mohn, Sept. 3, 1966 (dec. Sept. 2001); children: Jeffrey, Justin, Joshua. BS, U. Wis., 1967; PhD, Cornell U., 1972. Assoc. dir. Wis. Humanities Commn., NEH, Madison, 1977-78; asst. prof. U. Alaska, College, 1971-74; dir. labor studies Ariz. State U., Tempe, 1974-81, Sch. for Workers, U. Wis., Madison, 1981-84; assoc. dean of campus Ohio State U., Newark, 1984-87; dean Coll. Arts, Scis. and Lit. U. Mich., Dearborn, 1987-92; dir. acad. affairs Pa. State U.-Fayette, Uniontown, 1993-95; v.p. acad. affairs Walsh U., Canton, Ohio, 1995-99, Mt. Senario Coll., Wis., 1999—2000; acad. dean Mount Marty Coll., Yankton, SD, 2001—. Author: The Union Politic, 1975, American Labor in the Southwest, 1982; newspaper columnist, Kenosha (Wis.) Labor, 1981— (1st, 2d and 3d best story awards for column Lest We Forget, AFL-CIO 1984); commentator Wis. Pub. Radio, Madison, 1981-84. Exxon Edn. grantee, Tempe, 1976, Rockefeller Found. grantee, Tempe, 1977, German Marshall Fund grantee, Madison, 1981. Mem. Indsl. Rels. Rsch. Assn., Am. Arbitration Assn. Home: PO Box 509 Yankton SD 57078 Office: Mt Marty Coll 1105 W 8th St Yankton SD 57078 E-mail: jcfoster@byelectric.com., jfoster@mtmc.edu..

FOSTER, JAMES FRANKLIN, professional sports management executive; b. Iowa; s. M. (Egerer) F.; m. Susan Jane Salsi, July 19, 1976. BGS, U. Iowa, 1972; postgrad., U. Pa., 1982. Retail advt. specialist Maytag Co., Newton, Iowa, 1972-78; founder, gen. mgr. Iowa Nite Hawks AAA Pro Football Club, 1974-78; founder, dir. Am. Pro Football Tour of Europe, 1977, 79; promotion mgr. NFL Properties, Inc., N.Y.C., 1979-82; asst. gen. mgr. Ariz. Wranglers Pro Football Club, 1982-83; exec. v.p. Chgo. Blitz Pro Football Club, 1983-84; v.p. Chgo. Sting Indoor Soccer Promotions-Burke Promo Mktg. Inc., 1984-85; founder, pres. Arena Football, Chgo., 1985-90, commr., 1985-92, spl. cons., 1992-94; founder, mng. owner Iowa Barnstormers Arena Football, Chgo., 1994—, Quad City Steamwheelers Arena Football, 1999—. Co-founder Arena Football 2 League. Patent holder Arena Football game sys. Active Davenport YMCA; bd. dirs. Iowa Hist. Found.; mem. Davenport (Iowa) One Chamber. Recipient Golden Helmet Excellence award NFL Properties, Inc., 1981-82; named Minor Pro Football Exec. of Yr., Pro Football Weekly, 1976, No. States League Gen. Mgr. of Yr., AAA Football, 1976, Exec. of Yr., Arena Football League, 1995-96; named to Minor Pro Football Hall of Fame, 1982, one of Inaugural Class, Arena Football Hall of Fame, 1998. Mem. Iowa State Hist. Soc., Antique and Classic Boat Soc., Boat Owners Assn. U.S., U. Iowa Alumni Assn., Aircraft Owners and Pilots Assn., Nat. Iowa Lettermans Club, Iowa Assn. R.R. Passengers, Commn. Airforce (Iowa unit), Coll. Football Hall of Fame Found., U. Iowa Kinnick Soc., Methodist. Home: 901 Mississippi Ave Davenport IA 52801-4418 Office: 200 W 3rd St Davenport IA 52801

FOSTER, JAMES HENRY, advertising and public relations executive; b. Kansas City, Mo., May 14, 1933; s. Wendell F. and Lillian M. (East) F. BA, Drake U., 1955, postgrad., 1957. Reporter, editor Des Moines (Iowa) Register, 1951-61; pub. rels. and advt. exec. J. Walter Thompson Co., N.Y.C., 1961-73, 79-99, v.p., 1970-73; sr. v.p., gen. mgr. Brouillard Comm. divsn., N.Y.C., 1979-81, exec. v.p., gen. mgr., 1981-84, pres., CEO, 1984-94; chmn., CEO Brouillard Comm., 1994-97, chmn., 1997-99, chmn. emeritus, 1999—; v.p. pub. affairs Western Union Corp., Uppper Saddle River, 1973-79; pres. Reputation Mgmt. Strategies, Durango, Colo., 1999—, Music in the Mountains, Inc., Durango, Colo., 2000—, also bd. dirs. Bd. dirs. Fort Lewis Coll. Found., 1999—. Mem. Union League Club (N.Y.C.), Petroleum Club (Durango). Presbyterian. Office: Reputation Mgmt Strategies 1472 E Third Ave Durango CO 81301-5244

FOSTER, JAMES REUBEN, travel company executive; b. Chgo., May 28, 1930; s. Reuben Aaron and Marion (Philipson) F.; m. Claire Lynn Block, Aug. 16, 1953; children: Kim Petracca, Craig James, Kyle Foster Weinstein. BA, Trinity Coll., 1952; JD, Yale U., 1955. Bar: Ill. 1955, U.S. Ct. Claims 1955, U.S. Ct. Mil. Appeals 1956, U.S. Ct. Customs and Patent Appeals, 1956. Trial atty. U.S. Dept. of Justice, Washington, 1955-57; v.p. L.B. Foster Co., Pitts., 1957-82; pres. Fosco Fabricators, Chgo., 1961-64; v.p., sec. Foster Industries, Inc., Pitts., 1977-97; gen. ptnr. Real Estate Partnerships, 1975-93; v.p., sec. Fostin Securities, Inc., 1978—; pres., 1994-98; chmn. bd., chief exec. officer Travel Profls. Inc., 1984—; v.p. Foster Holdings Co., Chgo., 1998—; also bd. dirs. Fostin Mgmt. Co., Chgo. Sec. United Comms. Sys. Inc., Chgo., 1993—; bd. dirs. Foster Industries, Inc., Pitts., Fostin Capital Co., Pitts., L.B. Foster Co., Pitts., Travel Profls., Inc., Chgo., Pelouze Scale, Evanston, Ill., 1990-94, United Comm. Sys., Inc., Chgo., Fostin Securities, Inc., Fostin Mgmt. Inc.; chmn. Foster Charitable Trust. Pres. Temple Jeremiah, Northfield, Ill., 1980-83; chmn. com. Chgo. Assn. Commerce and Industry, 1971-73; trustee, chmn. com. Lakeland Health Svcs./Highland Park Hosp., 1978-84, life trustee, 1985—; vice chmn., committeeman Lake County Reps. Ctrl. Com., Ill., 1964-74; bd. dirs., sec., treas. Groveland Health Svcs., Highland Park, 1982-90, sec., 1987-90; v.p. Am. Jewish Com., 1990-96, nat. coun., 1996—, exec. bd. Chgo. chpt. 1981—; mem., chmn., exec. bd. Am. Assocs. Ben Gurion U. of the Negev, 1991-95,2002; treas. collectors forum Mus. of Contemporary Art, Chgo., 1994-97.

Mem. ABA, Am. Inst. Mgmt. (pres. coun.), Std. Club (bd. dirs. 1985-92), Northmoor Country Club. Republican. Jewish. Avocations: art collector, travel, golf. Office: Travel Profls Inc 500 W Madison Ave Ste 411 Chicago IL 60611-4544

FOSTER, JEANNE O'CAIN, poet, fine arts educator; b. Portsmouth, Va., Sept. 10, 1931; d. James and Julia Sutton (Taft) O'Cain; m. Lue Raymond Haywood, July 13, 1951; children: Joy, Lee, Bonnie, Gregory; m. Charles Wilton Foster (div. 1988). BFA with honors, Columbia Coll., 1994; MFA (hon.), Mellen U., 1995; postgrad., U. Wales, U. London, Old Dominion U. Cons., educator, 1985—; cons., min. White Swan Ministries, Lake Ozark, Mo., 1995—. Actress CBN-TV, Va., 1980—85; scriptwriter PBS-TV, SC, 1990. Author: Dance the Divine, 1989 (Nat. Endowment Arts award, 89), (plays) Colony at Santee; editor: Annie's Gazette, 1988. Sec. Citizens Coun., Richmond, Va., 1958; educator Omega Inst., Rhinebeck, NY, 1989; founder Gifted Children, Va., 1965—67; first arts chmn. Edgar Cayce Found., 1968; founder ADRA sacred dance, 1968; sec. Bill Story for Gov., Richmond, 1962. Named Internat. Poet, 1989, Hon. Heirophant, Fellowship of Isis, Ireland, 1996; recipient Golden Poet award, World of Poetry, 1988, Editor's Choice award, Nat. Libr. Poetry, 1993, hon. award, Writers Digest, 1996. Mem.: Internat. Women's Writing Guild. Republican. Unitarian Universalist. Avocation: cross cultural dance. Home: 1029 College Park # 164 Virginia Beach VA 23464

FOSTER, JODIE (ALICIA CHRISTIAN FOSTER), actress, producer, director; b. L.A., Nov. 19, 1962; d. Lucius and Evelyn (Almond) F.; children: Charles, Kit BA in Lit. cum laude, Yale U., 1985. Acting debut in TV show Mayberry, R.F.D, 1969; numerous other TV appearances including My Three Sons, The Courtship of Eddie's Father, Gunsmoke, Bonanza, Paper Moon, 1974-75; TV spl. The Secret Life of T.K. Dearing, 1975; TV movies include Rookie of the Year, Smile, Jenny, You're Dead; motion picture appearances include Napoleon and Samantha, 1972, One Little Indian, 1973, Tom Sawyer, 1973, Alice Doesn't Live Here Anymore, 1974, Taxi Driver, 1976 (Acad. award nominee for Best Supporting Actress), Echoes of a Summer, 1976, Bugsy Malone, 1976, Freaky Friday, 1976, Moi, Fleur Bleue, 1977, Casotto, 1977, The Little Girl Who Lives Down the Lane, 1977, Candleshoe, 1977, Foxes, 1980, Carny, 1980, O'Hara's Wife, 1982, Hotel New Hampshire, 1984, The Blood of Others, 1984, Five Corners, 1987, Siesta, 1987, Stealing Home, 1988, The Accused, 1988 (Acad. award for Best Actress, 1989), Backtrack, 1989, The Silence of the Lambs, 1991 (Golden Globe award for Best Actress in Drama, 1992, Acad. award for Best Actress, 1992, BAFTA award for best actress, 1992), Shadows and Fog, 1992, Sommersby, 1993, Maverick, 1994, Contact, 1997, Anna and The King, 1999, Panic Room, 2002; dir., actress: Little Man Tate, 1991; prodr., actress: Mesmerized, 1986, Nell, 1994 (Acad. award nominee for Best Actress 1995); dir., prodr. Home For the Holidays, 1995; exec. prodr. (Showtime) Babydance, 1998, Waking the Dead, 2000, The Dangerous Lives of Altar Boys, 2002 Recipient Golden Globe award, 1989. Office: EGG Pictures Production Co Jerry Lewis Annex 5555 Melrose Ave Los Angeles CA 90038-3112

FOSTER, JOE B. oil company executive; b. Arp, Tex., July 25, 1934; s. William R. and Ruth D. (Knox) Foster; m. Harriet Foster; children: Warren, Ken, Jennifer. BS in Petroleum Engring., BBA, Tex. A&M U., 1957, Jr. petroleum engr. Tenneco Oil Co., Okla. City, 1957—59, petroleum engr. Lafayette, La., 1959—62, dist. engr., 1962—66, adminstrv. asst. to exec. com., 1966—68, chief econ. planning and analysis, 1968—70, mgr. exploration, 1970—72, v.p., 1972—74, sr. v.p., 1974—76, exec. v.p., 1976—78, pres. Tenneco Oil Exploration and Prodn., 1978—81; exec. v.p. Tenneco, Inc., Houston, 1981—89; chmn., CEO Newfield Exploration Co., Houston, 1989—2000; interim chmn., CEO Baker Hughes Inc., Houston, 2000. Bd. dirs. N.J. Resources, Meml. Hermann Hosp. Sys., McDermott Internat. Inc., Newfield Exploration. Bd. dirs. Houston Mus. Natural Sci., YMCA of Greater Houston; chmn. Nat. Petroleum Coun., 1989—99. 2nd lt. U.S. Army, 1958. Mem.: All Am. Wildcatters Com., Ind. Petroleum Assn. Am., Soc. Petroleum Engrs., AIME, Royal Oaks Country Club. Methodist. Office: 10000 Memorial Dr Ste 520 Houston TX 77024-3411 E-mail: j64foster@aol.com.

FOSTER, JOE C., JR., lawyer; b. Lansing, Mich., Feb. 5, 1925; s. Joe C. and Grace E. (McComb) F.; m. Janet C. Shanks, July 6, 1946; children: Cathy Foster Young, Susan Foster Ambrose, Thomas, John, Amy Foster Trenz. Student, Wabash Coll., 1943-44; JD, U. Mich., 1949. Bar: Mich. 1949, Fla. 1986. Assoc. Fraser, Trebilcock, Davis & Foster, and predecessors, Lansing, Mich., 1949-53, ptnr. and shareholder, 1954-2000; shareholder Foster Zack & Lowe, P.C., Lansing, Mich., 2001—. Co-author: Independent Probate Administration, 1980, 3d edit., 1995, Informal Estat Procs. in Mich., 2000. Trustee, sec. Renaud Found., Lansing, 1960-87; bd. dirs., sec. Abrams Found., Lansing, 1960—; bd. dirs., officer ACTEC Found., L.A., 1983-87, 98—; trustee Jr. League Endowment Found., Lansing, 1984-90; trustee, chmn. Sparrow Hosp., Lansing, 1970-84; trustee, pres. Okemos Bd. Edn., Mich., 1962-66; bd. dirs., pres. county unit Am. Cancer Soc., 1950-60; bd. dirs., pres. Community Nursing Bur., Lansing, 1956-57. Lt. USNR, 1943-46, PTO. Fellow Am. Coll. Trust and Estate Counsel (pres. 1985-86), Am. Coll. Tax Counsel, Am. Bar Found., Mich. Bar Found.; mem. ABA, Fla. Bar Assn., Mich. Bar Assn. (chmn. probate and estate planning sect. 1977-78), Internat. Acad. Estate and Trust Law (exec. coun. 1990-94), Joint Editl. Bd. for Uniform Probate Code 1991-2000, Rotary (bd. dirs. Lansing 1968-70), Phi Beta Kappa, Phi Gamma Delta. Avocations: sailing, running, tennis. Home: 1965 Yuma Trl Okemos MI 48864-2746 Office: Foster Zack and Lowe PC PO Box 27337 Lansing MI 48909-7337 E-mail: joe.foster@fosterzacklowe.com. *Honesty and kindness are two of our best precepts. They also are good business.*

FOSTER, JOHN BURT, JR., comparative literature educator and researcher; b. Chgo., Dec. 19, 1945; s. John Burt Foster and Jane Armour; m. Andrea Dimino, Mar. 28, 1970; 1 child, Sophia Maria Foster-Dimino. BA, Harvard Coll., 1963—67; PhD, Yale U., 1967—71. Asst. prof. English and comparative lit. Stanford U., Calif., 1972—81; Mellon faculty fellow in comparative lit. Harvard U., Cambridge, Mass., 1982—83; assoc. prof. English and European studies George Mason U., Fairfax, Va., 1983—92, prof. English and cultural studies, 1992—; vis. assoc. prof. comparative lit. NYU, 1986—87. Editor The Comparatist, Fairfax, Va., 1997—2003. Author: (scholarly book) Heirs to Dionysus; A Nietzschean Current in Literary Modernism, 1981, Nabokov's Art of Memory and European Modernism, 1993; editor: Thresholds of Western Culture: Identity, Postcoloniality, Transnationalism, 2003; contbr. articles to scholarly jour. Fellow, Deutscher Akademischer Austauschdienst, 1971-1972, Am. Coun. Learned Studies, 1981—82; Fellowship Coll. Teachers, Nat. Endowment Humanities, 1987-1988, 1997—98. Mem.: MLA, Am. Assn. Advancement Slavic Studies, Internat. Assn. Philosophy and Lit. (conf. organizer 1995—96), So. Comparative Lit. Assn. (bd. mem. 1993—95), Am. Comparative Lit. Assn. (bd. mem. 1998—99), Internat. Nabokov Soc. (pres. 1994—96). Unitarian Universalist. Avocations: swimming, travel, canoeing, nature walks. Home: 605 40th St Sarasota FL 34234 Office: MSN 3E4 (English) George Mason Univ 4400 University Dr Fairfax VA 22030-4444 Personal E-mail: jfoster@gmu.edu.

FOSTER, JOHN HORACE, consulting environmental engineer; b. Quincy, Mass., June 2, 1927; s. Horace Herbert and Alice Gertrude (Hatch) F.; m. Claire Alice Sabean, Aug. 31, 1952; children— Janet, Mark, David. BS, Tufts U., 1952; MS, Harvard U., 1953. Engr. Malcolm Pirnie Engrs., White Plains, N.Y., 1953-63; partner Malcolm Pirnie, Inc., 1963-70, pres., 1970-88, chmn. bd. dirs., 1988-95; chmn. emeritus, 1997—. Contbr. articles to profl. jours. Served with USN, 1945-47. Recipient Distinguished Service award Dept. Civil Engring. Tufts U., 1977 Mem. ASCE, Water Environment Fedn., Am. Water Works Assn., Am. Cons. Engrs. Coun. (v.p. 1989-91, pres. 1992-93), N.Y. Assn. Cons. Engrs. (v.p. 1987-92, Engr. of Yr. 1995). Clubs: Cedar Point Yacht (commodore 1975-76). Home: 53 Farrell Rd Weston CT 06883-2306 Office: Malcolm Pirnie Inc PO Box 751 104 Corporate Park Dr White Plains NY 10604-3335

FOSTER, JOHN MCNEELY, accounting standards executive; b. Denver, Mar. 7, 1949; s. Wallin G. and Marilyn Hope (Coxhead) F.; m. Bonnie McCune, Aug. 23, 1970 (div. 1978); m. Sharon Kay Sheffield, May 8, 1982 (div. 1991); children: Katherine McNeely, Matthew Thomas. BA in Econs., Colo. Coll., 1971. CPA, Tex. Treas. Meis and Co., Inc., Colorado Springs, Colo., 1971-73; sr. audit mgr. Price Waterhouse Co., Houston, 1973-81; v.p. fin. Krusen Energy Co., Houston, 1981-83; v.p., treas. Compaq Computer Corp., Houston, 1983-92; bd. dirs. Fin. Acctg. Standards Bd., Norwalk, Conn., 1993—. Mem. AICPA, Phi Beta Kappa. Libertarian. Episcopalian. Avocations: golf, fishing. Office: Fin Acctg Standards Bd 401 Merritt 7 Norwalk CT 06851-1000

FOSTER, JOHN ROBERT, lawyer; b. Long Beach, Calif., Feb. 13, 1940; s. Orlon c. and Catherine Rose Foster; m. Nancy Crandall, June 17, 1962; children: John Crandall, Christopher Peter, Blayney Robert, Courtland William. BA in History, San Jose State U., 1961; LLB, U. Calif., Berkeley, 1964. Bar: Calif. 1965, U.S. Dist. Ct. (no. dist.) Calif. 1965, U.S. Ct. Appeals (9th cir.) 1965; cert. specialist in probate, estate planning, and trust law. Dep. legis. counsel State of Calif., Sacramento, 1964-65; pres. Rusconi, Foster, Thomas & Wilson, APC, Morgan Hill, Calif., 1965—; asst. dist. atty. San Benito County, Hollister, Calif., 1967. Mem. Morgan Hill Unified Sch. Dist. Bd. Edn., 1967-74, 79-83, chmn. bd., 1969-71; councilman City of Morgan Hill, 1984-88, 97-98, mayor, 1984. Named Citizen of Yr., City of Morgan Hill. Mem. Calif. State Bar (past state bar exec. com. on estate planning, probate and trusts), Santa Clara County Bar Assn., Gilroy-Morgan Hill Bar Assn. (past pres.), Morgan Hill C. of C. (past pres.), Masons, Rotary (past pres. Morgan Hill). Republican. Methodist. Avocations: skiing, fly fishing, backpacking, camping. Home: 17630 Black Oak Ct Morgan Hill CA 95037-9442 Office: Rusconi Foster Thomas & Wilson 30 Keystone Ave Morgan Hill CA 95037-4325 E-mail: bob@rftw.com.

FOSTER, JOHN STUART, JR., physicist, former defense industry executive; b. New Haven, Sept. 18, 1922; s. John Stuart and Flora (Curtis) F.; m. Frances Schnell, Dec. 28, 1978; children: Susan, Bruce, Scott, John. BS, McGill U., 1948; PhD in Physics, U. Calif., Berkeley, 1952; DSc (hon.), U. Mon., 1979. Dir. Lawrence Livermore (Calif.) Lab., 1952-65; dir. def. rsch. and engring. Dept. Def., Washington, 1965-73; v.p. TRW Energy Systems Group, Redondo Beach, Calif., 1973-79; v.p. sci. and tech. TRW Inc., Cleve., 1979-88, also bd. dirs. Chmn. Def. Sci. Bd., 1989-93; chmn. Pilkington Aerospace; chmn. Tech. Strategies & Alliances. Decorated knight Comdr.'s Cross, Badge and Star of Order of Merit (Federal Republic of Germany); comdr. Legion of Honor (France); recipient Ernst Orlando Lawrence Meml. award AEC, 1960, Disting. Pub. Svc. medal Dept. Def., 1969, 73, 93, Crowell medal, 1972, Enrico Fermi Award, U.S. Dept. of Energy, 1992, Eugene Fubini award, U.S. Dept. Def., 1998. Mem. NAE (Founders award 1989), AIAA, Am. Def. Preparedness Assn., Nat. Security Indsl. Assn. Office: Northrop Grumman 1 Space Park Blvd Bldg E1-5010 Redondo Beach CA 90278-1071

FOSTER, JOSEPH KEVIN, IV, entertainer, scribe; b. Waterbury, Conn., Feb. 29, 1960; s. Joseph Adrian and Stella Lucia (Vicedomini) F. Prin., owner JK Enterprises, Kaweah Commonwealth, Calif., 1978—. Author: Cycling Castro's Country: The Tour de Cuba, 2000, (screenplay) 9 Dragon, 1999; photography featured in Outside Mag., Bicycling Mag., various newspapers worldwide; actor (Broadway) Go Home, Spec 5, 1983-85, (Off Broadway) various, 1980-83, (TV) Kane and Abel, 1985, (film) Friday 13th, Part 2, 1980, Daniel, 1983; active W. Thomas Littleton's Southbury (Conn.) Playhouse, 1974-78, HB Studio, N.Y.C., 1981, Stella Adler, N.Y.C., 1981, The Am. Acad. Dramatic Arts, N.Y.C., 1980-81, The Actor's Studio, N.Y.C., 1981-85; actor, writer, prodr., Septic Dreams, 2003. Recipient Guinness World Record award Guinness, London, 1989, Cyclist of Yr. award Cycling Industry Bicycling Mag., Emmaus, Pa., 1990. Mem. Internat. Press Assn., Highpointer's Club, Ch. at Kaweah. Office: JK Enterprises PO Box 72 Kaweah CA 93237 E-mail: captainamerica@kevin-foster.com.

FOSTER, JOY VIA, retired library media specialist; b. Besoco, W.Va., Aug. 11, 1935; d. George Edward and Burgia Stafford (Earls) Via; m. Paul Harris Foster, Jr., Dec. 8, 1956 (dec. Dec. 20, 1962); children: Elizabeth Lee, Michael Paul. BS, Radford Coll., 1971; MS, Radford U., 1979. Cert. pub. sch. libr., Va. Clk. Va. Tech. and State U., Blacksburg, 1955-57, Christiansburg (Va.) Primary Sch., 1971-72, libr., 1972-85, Auburn Mid. and High Sch., Riner, Va., 1985-00; ret., 2000. Meml. chmn. Am. Cancer Soc., Christiansburg, 1965-66; area chmn. Am. Heart Fund, Christiansburg, 1990-93, block worker, 1985-91; trustee Montgomery-Floyd Regional Libr. Bd., 2003—. Mem. NEA, ALA, Am. Assn. Sch. Librs., Montgomery County Edn. Assn. (v.p. 1988-89, sec. 1989-91, bldg. rep. 1991, sec. 1995-96), Va. Ednl. Media Assn. (Meritorious Svc. award 1999), Va. Ednl. Assn. Presbyterian. Avocations: reading, bowling, flea marketing, antique collecting.

FOSTER, JUDITH CHRISTINE, lawyer, writer; b. Columbus, Ohio, Nov. 25, 1952; d. Paul Marvel and Jean Harper (Uhland) F.; m. Sabah Amin Wali, Dec. 28, 1973; children: Samed Michel, Russeen Paul. BS in Natural Sci. and BA in Linguistics, Pa. State U., 1973; JD, Coll. William & Mary, 1979. Bar: Va. 1979, U.S. Ct. Appeals (4th cir.) 1979, U.S. Ct. Appeals (9th cir.) 1996, U.S. Supreme Ct. 1984. Pvt. practice, Fairfax, Va., 1980-90, Encino, Calif., 1991—. Mem. counsel U.S. Justice Found., Escondido, Calif., 1982-90; judge Internat. Moot Ct. Competition Assn. of Student Internat. Law Soc., 1984, 86. Author: (with Erich Pratt) Sanctuary: A People's Primer, 1986, monthly immigration newsletter, 1986-90. Del. Va. Reps., Fairfax, 1981, 85. Mem. Am. Immigration Lawyers Assn. (legis. com. 1985, D.C. chpt. 1980-90, L.A. chpt. 1992—). E-mail: jfoster_attorney_at_law@yahoo.com.

FOSTER, KATHRYN WARNER, newspaper editor; b. Charleston, S.C., Sept. 16, 1950; d. Jack Huntington Warner and Theodora (Warner) Miller; m. William Chapman Foster, Sept. 11, 1971; children: William Huntington, Jonathan Chapman. BA in English, Newberry Coll., 1972. Obituary writer, TV editor Greenville (S.C.) Piedmont, 1971-72; asst. lifestyle editor Greenville (S.C.) News-Piedmont, 1972-73, feature editor, 1973-78; Living Today copy editor Miami (Fla.) Herald, 1978-83, asst. weekend editor, 1984-86, asst. travel editor, 1986-91, 96-98, editor Getaways midweek travel page, 1993-94, editor Youth Only (YO), 1994, assoc. editor Health Beat, 1995-96, editor health page, 2000—, editor religion page, 2000—. Editor Miami Herald Dining Guide, 1988-91, Miami Book Fair Internat. tab, 1999; speaker S.W. Fla. Writer's Conf., Ft. Myers, 1992; mem. bri racial/tri ethnic adv. com., Dade County Pub. Schs., 1997-01; contbr. travel writing to Fodor's, newspapers. Sec. Palmetto Elem. PTA, Miami, 1990-91. Recipient Penney-Mo. 1st pl. award for feature sects. U. Mo. Sch. Journalism, Columbia, 1978. Lutheran. Avocations: bicycling, swimming, canoeing, reading, camping. Office: Miami Herald Features Dept 1 Herald Plz Miami FL 33132-1693

FOSTER, KENNARD P. magistrate judge; b. 1944; Student, Purdue U., 1962-64; BS, Ball State U., 1966; JD, Ind. U., 1970. Bar: Ind. Spl. agt. FBI, 1970-71; atty. Jones, Foster & Loveall, 1971-76; asst. U.S. Atty., 1976-86; magistrate judge U.S. Dist. Ct. (so. dist.) Ind., Indpls., 1985—2002, recalled magistrate judge, 2002—. Mem. Fed. Bar Assn., Johnson County Bar Assn., Fed. Magistrate Judges Assn. Office: US Courthouse Rm 269 46 E Ohio St Indianapolis IN 46204-1903

FOSTER, KENT B. information technology executive; BS in elec. engring., N.C. State U.; M in mgmt., U. S.C. Pres. Gen. Telephone Co. Northwest Inc., Everett, Wash.; bd. dirs. GIE Telephone Ops, Irving, Calif., 1992—99; vice chmn. bd. GIE Telephone Ops., Iriving, Tex., 1993—99, pres. Irving, Tex., 1995—99; chmn., CEO Ingram Micro Inc., Santa Ana, Calif., 2000—. Bd. mem. Campbell Soup Co., J.C. Penney Co., N.Y. Life Ins. Co., Dallas Symphony Orch., Dallas Opera. Capt. USAF, 1966—70. Office: PO Box 25125 1600 E St Andrew Pl Santa Ana CA 92705-4931*

FOSTER, KIM, art dealer, gallery owner; b. Washington, Nov. 22, 1956; d. James R. and Clair Lynn (Block) Foster; m. Antonio Petracca, Oct. 30, 1994. BA, Sarah Lawrence Coll.; MA, Johns Hopkins U. Lic. stockbroker, N.Y. Asst. treas. Bankers Trust Co., N.Y.C., 1980-83; asst. v.p. Marine Midland, N.Y.C., 1984-85; commodities credit mgr. Shearson Lehman, N.Y.C., 1985-86; v.p. Bayerische Vereinsbank, N.Y.C., 1988-94; pres. Kim Foster Gallery, N.Y.C., 1993—. Bd. dirs. Foster Holdings, Inc., Pitts. Speech writer Gov. James R. Thompson, Chgo., 1975. Mem. Mus. Modern Art., Whitney Mus. Am. Art. Republican. Jewish. Avocations: swimming, travel. Office: Kim Foster Gallery 529 W 20th St New York NY 10011-2800 E-mail: kimfoster1@hotmail.com.

FOSTER, LAWRENCE, concert and opera conductor; b. Los Angeles, 1941; Student, Bayreuth Festival Masterclasses; studied with, Fritz Zweig. Debut as condr., Young Musicians' Found., Debut Orch., 1960; condr., mus. dir., 1960-64, condr., San Francisco Ballet, 1961-65, asst. condr., Los Angeles Philharmonic Orch., 1965-68, chief guest condr., Royal Philharmonic Orch., Eng., 1969-75, guest condr., Houston Symphony, 1970-71, condr. in chief, 1971-72, music dir., 1972-78, Orch. Philharmonique of Monte Carlo, 1979, gen. music dir., Duisburg & Dusseldorf Opera (Ger.), 1982-86, former music dir. Lausanne Chamber Orch., 1991-96, Aspen (Colo.) Music Festival and Sch.; prin. guest condr. Orquestra Ciutat de Barcelona; music dir. Gulbenkian Orch., Lisbon; music adviser Jerusalem Symphony-Orch.; artistic dir. Bucharest Festival and Competition; guest condr. orchs. in, U.S., Europe, Australia and Japan; recorded, condr. world premiere Paul McCartney's Standing Stone, 1997; (Recipient Koussevitsky Meml. Conducting prize 1966, Eleanor R. Crane Meml. prize Berkshire Festival, Tanglewood, Mass. 1966); regular guest condr. Deutsche Opera, Berlin, L.A. Opera. Address: ICM Artists Ltd c/o Jenny Vogel 8942 Wilshire Blvd Beverly Hills CA 90211-1934

FOSTER, LESTER ANDERSON, JR., retired steel company executive; b. Apr. 4, 1929; s. Lester Anderson and Annie Lee (Swink) F.; m. Patricia White, July 9, 1955; children: Leslie Ann, Caroline Suzann, Lester Anderson, Samuel Timothy. Student, Elon Coll., 1947-50; BS, N.C. State U., 1952. With Bethlehem Steel Corp., Sparrows Point, Md., 1952-94, engr., 1956-57, med. foreman, 1957-59, asst. gen. foreman, 1959-61, asst. master mechanic, 1961-67, master mechanic, 1967-92, cons., 1992—. Pres. L&M Cons. Steel Plant Facilities, Inc. Pres. PTA, Sparrows Point, 1963—65; mem. exec. bd. nominating com. Balt. County Sch. Bd., 1964—65; dist. field svc. chmn. Boy Scouts Am., Balt., 1972—78, bicentennial show program chmn., 1976, dist. commr., 1979—83, dist. chmn., 1983—; lt. Md. Def. Force, Balt., 1995—2002; pres. 7th Dist. Rep. Club, 1969—72; mem. Md. Rep. State Ctrl. Com., 1980—90. With U.S. Army, 1952—54, lt. col. Md. Def. Force, 1995—99. Recipient Silver Beaver award Boy Scouts Am., 1975, award of Merit, 1984. Mem. SAR (pres. Md. Soc. 1993, v.p. gen. Mid-Atlantic, Silver Good Citizenship medal, Meritorious medal, Patriot meda, Minuteman medal 1999), Am. Inst. Iron and Steel Engrs., Soc. Mfg. Engrs., Am. Mgmt. Assn., Soc. Advancement Mgmt., Nat. Football Found. and Hall of Fame, Sparrows Point Country Club, Sparrows Point Engrs. Clubs, Masons, Shriners, K.T. (Grand Comdr.). Lutheran. Home: 3006 Dunmore Rd Baltimore MD 21222-5131 E-mail: lespatfoster@erols.com.

FOSTER, LINDA NEMEC, poet, educator; b. Garfield Heights, Ohio, May 29, 1950; d. John Joseph and Helen Agnes (Kumor) Nemec; m. Anthony Jesse Foster, Oct. 26, 1974; children: Brian Jesse, Ellen Kathleen. BA, Aquinas Coll., 1972; MFA, Goddard Coll., 1979. Social demographer Ctr. Environ. Study, Grand Rapids, Mich., 1971-74; clk. Jones & Laughlin Steel Corp., Detroit, 1974-77; lectr. art Ferris State U., Big Rapids, Mich., 1982-84; tchr. poetry and writing Mich. Coun. for Arts, Detroit, 1980—; prof. English, poetry workshops Aquinas Coll., 1999—. Bd. dirs. Mecosta County Coun. for the Humanities, Big Rapids, 1982-85; bd. dirs. Urban Inst. for Contemporary Arts, Grand Rapids, 1989-95, dir. lit. programming, 1989-96. Author: (poetry) A History of the Body, 1987, A Modern Fairy Tale: Baba Yaga Poems, 1992, Trying to Balance the Heart, 1993, Living in the Fire Nest, 1996, Contemplating the Heavens, 2001, Amber Necklance from Gdansk, 2001. Vol. East Grand Rapids H.S., 1994-98, Degage Homeless Shelter, Grand Rapids, 1995-97. Poetry fellow Arts Found. Mich., 1996, fellow for lit. achievement Nat. Writer's Voice, 1999; grantee Mich. Coun. for Arts and Cultural Affairs, Detroit, 1984, 90, Artserve Mich., 2001, named Poet Laureate of Grand Rapids, 2003. Mem. Detroit Women Writers, Urban Inst. for Contemporary Arts, Creative-Writers-In-Schs., Acad. Am. Poets, Poetry Soc. Am., Nat. Writers Voice Project. Roman Cath. Avocations: hiking, camping, boating, travelling. Home: 2024 Wilshire Dr SE Grand Rapids MI 49506-4014

FOSTER, LLOYD BENNETT, lawyer, musician; b. Wellman, Iowa, May 6, 1911; s. George Elliott and Lulu Nettie (Bennett) F.; m. Rowene Stevens, Sept. 1, 1940. BA cum laude in Commerce and Fin., Coe Coll., 1937; MS in Econs., Iowa State U., 1939; JD, De Paul U., 1952. Bar: Ill. 1952, U.S. Supreme Ct. 1980. Instr. Shenandoah Coll., Va., 1939-41; acct. McGladrey, Hansen, Dunn and Co., Cedar Rapids, Iowa, 1941-42; agt. Office of Dist. Dir., IRS, Chgo., 1946-52, pension plan reviewer, 1952-53, tech. advisor Appellate div., 1953-60; atty. Office of Chief Counsel, Washington, 1961-67; dep. asst. chief counsel Bur. of Pub. Debt, Chgo., 1967-71, atty., Washington, 1967; atty., income tax hearing officer, supr. regulations legis. rulings sect., litigation counsel, adminstrv. law judge Ill. Dept. Revenue, Chgo., 1971-87; of counsel McDermott, Will & Emery, Chgo., 1988. Mem., Chgo. Met. Symphony Orch., 1969—, Deerfield Park Dist. Community Band, 1968—. Served to comdr. USN, 1942-46. Mem. Fed. Bar Assn., Hammond Musicians Guild, Chgo. Fedn. Musicians, D.C. Fedn. Musicians, Naval Res. Assn., Retired Officers Assn.

FOSTER, LUCILLE CASTER, school system administrator, retired; b. Vallejo, Calif., Sept. 28, 1921; d. Lewis Caster and Mabel Estelle (Witt) Beidleman; m. Donald Foster, Nov. 21, 1942 (deceased). AB in History, U. Calif., Berkeley, 1943; MA in Elem. Edn., San Francisco State U., 1953; EdD, Stanford U., 1959. Cert. sch. adminstr., Calif. Elem. tchr. Alameda (Calif.) Unified Sch. Dist., 1948-55; curriculum cons. Laguna Salada Elem. Sch. Dist., Pacifica, Calif., 1955-60, asst. supt., 1960-81; ret., 1981. Fir br. Children's Med. Ctr. No. Calif. Co-author (handbooks) Selling Ventures, 2000, Grant Writing 4th edit., 2002, Fundraising, 2d edit., 2002, Resource Development, 2002; contbr. articles to Calif. Jour. Elem. Edn., 1957, 61. Mem. AAUW (Santa Rosa br.), Can. Fedn. Univ. Women (hon. life), Internat. Fedn. U. Women, Calif. Sch. Adminstrs. Assn. (life), Calif. Tchrs. Assn. (life), Calif. Sch. Personnel Commrs. Assn. (life), Nat. Assistance League, Assistance League Sonoma County (hon. life), Pi Lambda Theta, Delta Zeta. Avocations: community volunteer, bridge, travel. Home: 245 Mockingbird Cir Santa Rosa CA 95409-6245 Fax: 707-538-2584.

FOSTER, M. J., JR., (MIKE FOSTER), governor; b. Shreveport, La., July 11, 1930; married. BSCE, La. State U., 1952. Sugar cane farmer, La.; founder Bayou Sale, La.; pres. Sterling Sugars, Inc.; senator St. Mary/Assumption Parish Dist. La. State Senate, 1987, chmn. commerce com., 1991, gov. State of La., 1996—. Jr. warden St. Mary's Episcopal Ch.; pres. St. Mary Parish Farm Bur. With USAF, Korea. Mem. Am. Legion. Republican. Episcopalian. Avocations: hunting, fishing, tennis. Office: Office of the Governor PO Box 94004 Baton Rouge LA 70804-9004*

FOSTER, MARGARET ANNE, volunteer worker; b. Randolph County, Ind., Aug. 5, 1924; d. Jacob Calvin Streeter and Lura Alwylda Stick; m. Sherman Robinson Foster, Jan. 15, 1951; children: Mark, Christopher, Timothy, Jeff, Jenny. BS in Edn., Ball State Tchrs. Coll., 1948. Playground dir. Washington D.C. Parks and Recreation, 1946, Ft. Wayne (Ind.) Parks and Recreation, 1947-48; tchr. French Lick (Ind.) H.S., 1948-49; recreational dir. U.S. Army, Eschwege, Germany, 1949-51; vol. coord. Albuquerque Mus., 1975-77; tour guide Albuquerque, 1977-96; acting dir. The Storehouse, Albuquerque, 1992. Pres. German-Am. Club, Augsburg, Germany, 1962; organizer Last Three Graders Club for Wives of Lower Enlisted Men, 1954; bd. dirs. Officers' Wives Club, Germany, 1954-55, 62-63, Albuquerque, 1962; bd. dirs. Albuquerque Guild Santa Fe Opera, 1968-93, 96—, pres., 2002; bd. dirs. Meals on Wheels, 2000; presiding precinct judge Bernalillo County, N.Mex., 1970-80. Named to Order of Lioness, 1966; recipient Mil. Wife of Yr. award Kirtland Officers Wives Club, 1973, Silver Star for Volunteerism, Albuquerque Sr. Affairs Office, 1997. Mem. The Storehouse (bd. dirs., chair 1991, Silver Star 1997). Democrat. Methodist. Avocations: writing, cross-stitch, genealogy. Home: 704 Doe Ln SE Albuquerque NM 87123-3533

FOSTER, MARGERY SOMERS, educator; b. Boston, Mar. 27, 1914; d. L. Brent and Grace (Butler) F.; BA, Wellesley Coll., 1934; PhD, Radcliffe Coll., 1958; LittD, Russell Sage Coll., 1968. Asst. to actuary New Eng. Mut. Life Ins. Co., 1934-43; dep. comptroller and dir. devel. Wellesley Coll., 1946-54; lectr. econs. Harvard U. Sch. Bus. Adminstrn., 1956-58; lectr. econs., sec. coll. Mt Holyoke Coll., 1958-64; prof. econs., dean coll. Hollins Coll., 1964-67; prof. econs., dean coll. Douglass Coll. of Rutgers U., 1967-75. Univ. prof. econs. Rutgers, 1975-80, prof. emeritus, 1980— ; past dir. Prudential Ins. Co., Pub. Service Electric & Gas Co., N.J., 1973-85. Mem. commn. on tests Coll. Entrance Exam. Bd., 1966-70, trustee, 1969-72; mem. commn. on instl. affairs Assn. Am. Colls., 1971-74; mem. Harvard U. overseer's vis. com. for Warren Center in Am. History, 1973-79; trustee Middle States Assn. Colls. and Schs., 1973-79, Island Inst., 1984—. Served to lt. Women's Res., USNR, 1943-46. Mem. Am. Econ. Assn., Econ. History Assn., Econ. History Soc. Clubs: Appalachian Mountain, Cosmopolitan, Univ. Women's Club. Author: Out of

Smalle Beginnings, An Economic History of Harvard College in the Puritan Period, 1962. Spl. research on Am. colonial econ. history, history of edn., pub. fin. Office: PO Box 60 Francestown NH 03043-0060 also: Great Diamond Island Portland ME 04104

FOSTER, MARK STEPHEN, lawyer; b. Edgerton, Mo., Feb. 6, 1948; s. George Elliott and Annabel Lee (Bradshaw) F.; m. Camille Pepper, June 27, 1970; children: Natalie Ashley, Stephanie Ann. BS, U. Mo., 1970; JD, Duke U., 1973. Bar: Mo. 1973, U.S. Ct. Mil. Appeals 1974, Hawaii 1975, U.S. Dist. Ct. Hawaii 1975, U.S. Dist. Ct. (we. dist.) Mo. 1977, U.S. Ct. Appeals (8th cir.) 1986, U.S. Supreme Ct. 1994. Assoc. Stinson, Mag & Fizzell, Kansas City, 1977-80, ptnr., 1980—2002, mng. ptnr., 1987-90, chmn. bd. dirs., 2002—. Arbitration panelist Nat. Assn. Securities Dealers, N.Y.C., 1985—, Pvt. Adjudication Found., Durham, N.C., 1988—. Active Citizens Assn., Kansas City, 1982-92; pres. Spelman Med. Found., Smithville, Mo., 1984-88; bd. dirs. Alzheimers Assn. Metro. Kansas City, 1997—, 1st v.p., 1998, pres., 1999. Lt. comdr. USNR, ret. Mem. ABA, Hawaii Bar Assn., Mo. Bar Assn., Kansas City Met. Bar Assn., Am. Arbitration Assn. (panelist 1990—, large complex case adv. com. 1993—), Carriage Club (bd. dirs. 2000—, 2d v.p. 2001, 1st v.p. 2002, pres. 2003), Lawyers Edn. Assistance Program (bd. dirs. 2000—), Masons. Home: 1035 W 65th St Kansas City MO 64113-1813 Office: Stinson Morrison Hecker LLP PO Box 419251 1201 Walnut St Ste 2800 Kansas City MO 64106-2117

FOSTER, MARK WINGATE, lawyer; b. Bryn Mawr, Pa., Dec. 10, 1942; s. Frank Brisbon and Marion Reed (Keator) F.; m. Hope Schwarz, June 7, 1971; children— Victoria Reed, Noah Cary. B.A., Yale U., 1965; J.D., Harvard U., 1971. Bar: Conn. 1971, D.C. 1972, U.S. Supreme Ct. 1975, Md. 1985. Staff atty. Pub. Defender's Service, Washington, 1971-74, chief criminal trial div., 1974-75; assoc. Bierbower & Rockefeller, Washington, 1975-76; ptnr. Moore & Foster, P.C., Washington, 1976-83; ptnr., Zuckerman, Spaeder, Goldstein, Taylor & Kolker, Washington, 1983— , mem. Bd. Profl. Responsibility, D.C. Ct. Appeals, 1982-88, chmn., 1984-88. Contbr. articles to Dist. Lawyer, 1977-82. Home: 5068 Sedgewick St NW Washington DC 20016-1940 Office: Zuckerman Spaeder Goldstein Taylor & Kolker 1201 Connecticut Ave NW Washington DC 20036-2638

FOSTER, MARY CHRISTINE, motion picture and television executive; b. L.A., Mar. 19, 1943; d. Ernest Albert and Mary Ada (Quilici) F.; m. Paul Hunter, July 24, 1982. BA, Immaculate Heart Coll., Los Angeles, 1967; M of Journalism in TV News Documentary, UCLA, 1968. Dir. research and devel. Metromedia Producers Corp., Los Angeles, 1968-71; dir. devel. and prodn. services Wolper Prodns., Los Angeles, 1971-76; mgr. film programs NBC-TV, Burbank, Calif., 1976-77; v.p. movies and mini series Columbia Pictures TV, Burbank, 1977-81; v.p. series programs, 1981; v.p. program devel. Group W. Prodns., L.A., 1981-87; agt. The Agency, Los Angeles, 1988-90, Shapiro-Lichtman Agy., Los Angeles, 1990-99; ret., ind. prodr., 1999—. Lectr. in field, 1970—. Creator: (TV series) Sullivan, 1985, Auntie Mom, 1986. Trustee Immaculate Heart H.S., L.A., 1980—; mem. comty. devel. com. Immaculate Heart Cmty., 2001—; mem. vol. com., writer tour script, book, newsletter and website Cathedral of Our Lady of Angels, 2002; mem. exec. com. Humanitas Awards, Human Family Inst., 1985—, L.A. Roman Cath. Archdiocesan Comms. Commn., L.A., 1986-90; chmn. pastorial coun. St. Francis of Assisi, 2003—; bd. dirs., treas. Catholics in Media, 1992—. Mem. Women in Film (bd. dirs. 1974-78), Nat. Acad. TV Arts and Scis. Democrat. *Fidelity to God's will yields life's greatest satisfaction. Love of family and community gives life fulfillment.*

FOSTER, MARY KATHLEEEN, interior designer; b. Bklyn., June 16, 1947; d. John Frederick and Jane Margaret (Cahill) O'Connor; m. Charles A. Foster, Aug. 16, 1969 (div. Oct. 1995); children: Jeremiah John, Delaney Marie, Christian Anthony (dec.); m. Michael H. Nelson, Aug. 30, 1997. BA, Bklyn. Coll., 1969. Lic. interior designer, Fla. Tchr. Holy Family Elem. Sch., Bklyn., 1970-72; social coord. Palm Beach Polo and Country Club, Wellington, Fla., 1981-84; owner, interior designer Polo Interiors, Inc., Wellington, 1984-91; owner, designer K. Foster Designs, Inc., Wellington, 1991—. First elected ofcl. Acme Improvement Dist., Wellington, 1990, pres. bd. suprs., 1992; mem. nat. adv. bd. Adam Walsh Children's Fund, West Palm Beach, Fla., 1993—, exec. dir. 1999-2002, pres. Jr. Achievement of the Palm Beaches, 2002—; first mayor Village of Wellington, 1996. Mem. Palms West C. of C. (bd. dirs. 1994—), Exec. Women of Palm Beaches, Leadership Palm Beach. Democrat. Roman Catholic. Home and Office: K Foster Designs Inc 13650 Columbine Ave Wellington FL 33414-8164

FOSTER, MICHAEL KIRK, anthropologist, linguist; b. Athens, Greece, June 2, 1938; s. Andrew Brisbin and Barbara (Kirk) F.; m. Doris Elizabeth Wilkinson, Sept. 7, 1974; 1 child, Andrew Erskine. BA, Lawrence Coll., 1961; MAT, Harvard U., 1962; PhD, U. Pa., 1974. Instr. Ursinus Coll., Collegeville, Pa., 1964-66; ethnologist, curator Can. Mus. Civilization, Ottawa, Ont., Can., 1970-89; sessional lectr. Carleton U., Ottawa, 1975, 93; curator emeritus Can. Mus. Civilization, Ottawa, 1989—. Editor, co-editor 6 books; contbr. numerous articles on Iroquoian langs. and cultures to scholarly jours. and books. Grantee NSF, 1970-71, NEH, 1982-85, Am. Philos. Soc., 1990, 92, 97. Fellow Am. Anthrop. Assn.; mem. Can. Ethnology Soc., Soc. for Study of Indigenous Langs. of the Ams., Soc. for Linguistic Anthropology, Current Anthropology (assoc.). Home: 746 Pattrell Rd Norwich VT 05055-9479

FOSTER, MICHAEL WILLIAM, librarian; b. Astoria, Oreg., June 29, 1940; s. William Michael and Margaret Vivian (Carlson) F. BA in History, Willamette U., 1962; MA, U. Oreg., 1965; postgrad., So. Oreg. Coll., 1976. Tchr. Astoria High Sch., 1963-66, librarian, 1970-96; tchr. Am. Internat. Sch. of Kabul (Afghanistan), 1966-70. Bd. dirs. Astoria H.S. Scholarships, Inc., AG-BAG Internat. Ltd., Astoria Pacific Industries, Inc., Asta Ltd.; adv. bd. pacific region US Bank. Mem. Oreg. Arts Commn., Salem, 1983-91; commr. Oreg. Coun. Humanities, 1994—, chmn., 1995-97; commr. Oreg. Advs. for the Arts, 1994-97; bd. dirs. Am. Cancer Soc., Clatsop County, Oreg., 1980-87, Luth. Family Svcs., 1994-96, Oreg. Arts Advocates Found., 1994-98, Columbia Meml. Hosp. Found., 1992—, Edward Hall Scholarship Bd., pres. Clatsop C.C. Found.; bd. dirs. U. Oreg. Art Mus. Coun., 1991—, pres., 1993-95; bd. dirs., treas. Astoria Cmty. Concert Assn., 1964-88, pres., 1989—; bd. dirs., treas. Ed and Eda Ross Scholarship Trust; bd. dirs., pres. Clatsop C.C. Found., 1997-99, exec. dir., 1999—; mem. Oreg. Econ. Devel. Dept. Task Force, 1995-97; mem. adv. bd. Oreg. Symphony, 1992—; exec. dir. Clatsop Cmty. Coll. Found., 2000—. Mem. NEA, Oreg. Edn. Assn., Oreg. Edn. Media Assn., Clatsop County Hist. Soc. (bd. dirs., pres. 1983-87), Ft. Clatsop Hist. Assn. (treas. 1974-91, pres. 1991—, bd. dirs.), Astoria C. of C. (bd. dirs. 1982-88, George award 1985, pres. 1987), Lewis and Clark Trails Heritage Found., Rotary (pres. Astoria Club 1986), Astoria Golf and Country Club, Beta Theta Pi. Republican. Roman Catholic. Avocations: antique dealer, art collector, oil painter, golf, tennis. Home: 1636 Irving Ave Astoria OR 97103-3621

FOSTER, PAUL, playwright; b. Penn's Grove, N.J., Oct. 15, 1931; s. Elderidge M. and Mary (Manning) F. BA, Rutgers U., 1954; LLB, St. John's U., 1958. Pres. La Mama Theater Club, N.Y.C., 1962—; tchr. drama dept. NYU and U. Calif.-San Diego, 1983. Author: The Birthday Party Stories, 1962, Hurrah for the Bridge, 1963, The Recluse, 1964, Balls, 1964, Madonna In the Orchard, 1965, The Hessian Corporal, 1966, Tom Paine, 1967, Heimskringla, 1969, Satyricon, 1970, Elizabeth I, 1971, Silver Queen Saloon, 1972, Marcus Brutus, 1973-74, Murderers' Row, 1976, A Kiss is Just a Kiss, 1983, (stage trilogy) The Dark and Mr. Stone, 1985-87, (TV) The Tragedy of the Commons, 1979, The Vampyre and Dr. Frankenstein, 1980, Silver Saloon, 1992, (film) Andrew Mellon and the National Gallery of Art, 1980, Cop and the Anthem, 1982, Smile, 1983, Cinderella Story, 1984, (stage play based on Dickens) A Tale of Two Cities, 1988, Kisses, Bites and Scratches, 1990, Elizabeth Eins, 1992, Make Believe Musical Book and Lyrics, 1993, Murder in the Hollyhocks, 1995; translator: (Horvath) Back & Forth, Faith, Hope, Charity, 1983, Fritz Lang's M for stage, 1997, Masquerade, 1999-2000; contbr. e-zine series articles to Arts4All.com, 2000; donated collection of theatrical lit. to Rutgers U. Libr. Served to lt. (j.g.) USNR, 1955-57. Recipient Play award Irish Univs., 1967, 71, N.Y. Drama Critics award, 1968, Tony award nomination, 1973; Rockefeller Found. fellow, 1967-68; Creative Artists Pub. Service grantee, 1972; Nat. Endowment Creative Writing fellow, 1973; Guggenheim fellow, 1974. Mem. Eugene O'Neill Meml. Theater Found., New Dramatists, Dramatists Guild, Player's Club, Societe des Auteurs. Home: 115 Saint Marks Pl Staten Island NY 10301-1600 E-mail: caisby@aol.com.

FOSTER, RAYMOND ORVILLE, physics educator, priest; b. Hammond, Ind., Dec. 30, 1946; s. Raymond Orville and Dorothy Ann (Schilling) F. BA, Marquette U., Milw., 1969; MA, Washington Theol. Union, 1978; MA in Edn., Ball State U., 1995. Ordained priest, Roman Cath. Ch., 1973; joined Carmelite Order, 1964; cert. tchr. chemistry, physics, astronomy, Ill. Tchr. chemistry and physics Carmel H.S., Mundelein, Ill., 1974-84, Mt. Carmel H.S., Chgo., 1987-88, Joliet (Ill.) Cath. H.S., 1988-90, Joliet Cath. Acad., 1990—; regimental chaplain 3rd Marine Divsn., Okinawa, Japan, 1984-85; asst. command chaplain Naval Air Sta. Memphis, Millington, Tenn., 1985-87. Prior (superior) St. Elias Carmelites, Joliet, 1995-99; bd. dirs. Carmel H.S., Mundelein, Ill., 1998-2000; chaplain U.S. Naval Res., 1972-98. Contbr. articles to profl. jours. Mem. VFW, Am. Assn. Physics Tchrs., Cath. Assn. Scientists and Engrs., Naval Res. Assn., Am. Legion. Roman Catholic. Achievements include research on dialogue between religion and natural sciences. Home: 3506 Lake Shore Dr Joliet IL 60431-8819 Office: Joliet Cath Acad 1200 N Larkin Ave Joliet IL 60435-3484 E-mail: rfoster@carmelnet.org.

FOSTER, RICHARD, journalist; b. Chgo., Oct. 16, 1938; s. James Edward and Mary (Sebat) Foster; m. Susanne Elisabeth Hill, Sept. 28, 1996; children: Katherine Elisabeth, Arthur Edward. BA, Lawrence Coll., 1963. Reporter City News Bur., Chgo., 1963-64; reporter Chgo. Sun-Times, 1964-72, editorial writer, mem. editorial bd., 1972-78; editorial writer Des Moines Register & Tribune, 1978-82, Milw. Journal Sentinel, 1983—. Journalist-in-residence Colo. State U., spring 1982 Served with AUS, 1958-61. Recipient 1st place award, UPI, 1984, Inter-Am. Press Assn. award, 1988, 1st award (Group A), Wis. Newspaper Assn., 2000; fellow NEH Profl. Journalism, Stanford U., 1976—77. Mem. Nat. Conf. Editorial Writers, Nat. Press Club. Home: 4645 N Murray Ave Whitefish Bay WI 53211-1259 Office: 333 W State St Milwaukee WI 53203-1305 E-mail: rfoster@journalsentinel.com.

FOSTER, ROBERT CARMICHAEL, banker; b. Toledo, Ohio, Apr. 1, 1941; s. Robert Albert and Kate (Thompson) F.; m. Phyllis Lorainne Schmidt, Nov. 25, 1974; children: Brian Clinton, Suzanne Pamela, Robert Carmichael Jr. AB, Colo. Coll., 1963; MBA, U. Chgo., 1965; AMP, Harvard U., 1982. Analyst, programmer McDonnell-Douglas Corp., St.Louis, 1965-67; systems cons. Bristol-Myers Co., N.Y.C., 1967-70; comptroller Toledo Trust Co., 1970-73, sr. v.p., 1973-77, exec. v.p., 1977-87, also bd. dirs.; v.p. Trustcorp, Inc., 1975-86, exec. v.p., 1986-87; pres., dir. SeaGate Aviation Corp., Toledo, 1983-2000; pres., chief exec. officer, bd. dirs. West Mich. Nat. Bank & Trust, Frankfort, Mich., 1987—. Bd. dirs. Traverse Bay Econ. Devel. Corp., 1988—, exec. com. 1998—, treas. 2000-01, vice chmn. 2001—. Bd. dirs. Riverside Hosp., Toledo, 1978-85, Northcoast Health Sys., Inc., 1983-88, Lucas County Children Svcs., Toledo, 1981-85, Munson Healthcare Inc., 1990—, Traverse City, Mich.; trustee YMCA, Toledo, 1974-87; assoc. trustee Boys Club of Toledo, 1984-86, trustee, 1986-87; chmn. Lucas County U.s. Savs. Bond Program, Toledo, 1972-87; mem. planning commn. Crystal Lake Twp., 1988-97; sec.-treas. Paul Oliver Meml. Hosp., 1989-90, bd. dirs., pres., 1990-98 ; pres. Frankfort Indsl. Pk. Devel. Corp., 1989—; mem. Traverse Bay Cmty. Found., 1995-2000; chmn. Frankfort City-County Airport Authority, 1995—. Mem. Am. Inst. Banking, Bank Adminstrn. Inst., Toledo Area Govtl. Rsch. Assn. (pres., bd. dirs. 1974-79), Toledo C. of C. (aviation com.), Ottawa Skeet Club (treas.), Crystal Downs Country Club (treas. 1993-99), Rotary. Presbyterian. Avocations: airline transport-rated pilot; water and snow skiing; hunting; tennis. Home: 70 Thomas Rd Frankfort MI 49635-9538

FOSTER, ROBERT FRANCIS, communications executive; b. Chgo., June 4, 1926; s. William John and Anna Alice (O'Farrell) F.; m. Mary D. Palella, May 4, 1963; children: Sean Terence, Nancy Marie, Patrick Daniel. Student, Cath. schs., Chgo. and Evanston, Ill. News and sports writer Sta. WGN, Chgo., 1943-55; with Chgo. Pub. Rels. Counselors, 1955-60, WGN Continental Broadcasting Co., Chgo., 1960-82, news bur. chief Springfield, Ill., 1961-63, Washington news bureau chief Washington, 1964-82; press sec. to Ill. Congressman Philip M. Crane, 1982-96; reporter and analyst at 10 nat. polit. convs. WGN-TV and WGN-Radio. Chgo. Stadium announcer Chgo. Blackhawks, 1955-64. Goalie 78th Divsn. ice hockey team, 1946. With AUS, 1944-46. Decorated Combat Inf. badge, Bronze Star. Recipient award best pub. service news Am. Coll. Radio Arts, Crafts and Scis., 1961 Mem. Radio-TV Corr. Assn. Washington (pres. 1976), Broadcast Pioneers, Radio TV News Dirs. Assn., Am. Legion, Chgo. Press Vets. Assn. Roman Catholic. Home: 5718 Marble Arch Way Alexandria VA 22315-4037

FOSTER, ROBERT LAWSON, retired judge, deacon; b. Putnam, Okla., Nov. 17, 1925; s. Mark M. and Jessie Marie (Gregory) F.; m. Mary Jo Hull, July 1, 1949 (dec.); children: Candace Ann (Mrs. Dan Sebert), Martha Denise (Mrs. Gerald Speed), Karen Sue Greenfield, Robert L., John Michael (dec.), Cynthia Kay. BA, U. Okla., 1949, LL.B., 1950, JD, 1970. Bar: Okla. 1950; ordained deacon Roman Cath. Ch., 1979. Pvt. practice, Chandler, 1950-51; county judge Lincoln County, Okla., 1951-69; assoc. dist. judge 23d Jud. Dist., Chandler, Okla., 1969-86; ret., 1986. Chmn. dist. council Boy Scouts Am., 1968-69; chmn., an organizer Chandler Combined Appeal, 1954— ; sec., pres. Lincoln County Jr. League Baseball, 1960-68; county dir. Civil Def., 1953-70; mem. bd. Permanent Deacon Candidates for Okla., mem. deacon perceiver team, 1985-97; adv. to registrants Selective Svc., 1953—. Served with USAF, 1944-45. Mem. Lincoln County Bar Assn. (pres. 1965, sec. 1960-64, 67-69, 70-73), C. of C. (sec. 1964-68), Okla. Assn. County Judges (sec.-treas. 1964-67), Okla. Jud. Conf. Clubs: Chandler Parents. Lodges: Lion (dir. 1964-65, pres. 1967, treas. 1968-70, zone chmn. 1973-74, dep. dist. gov. 1974—, ret. 1990).

FOSTER, ROGER SHERMAN, JR., surgeon, educator, health facility administrator; b. Washington, Jan. 8, 1936; s. Roger Sherman and Genevieve Wakeman (Bartlett) F.; m. Joan Crile, June 25, 1960 (dec. Feb. 2000); children: Roger Sherman III, Charles Bartlett, Elizabeth Crile, Halle Crile Foster Moore. AB, Haverford Coll., 1957; MD, Case Western Res. U., 1961. Diplomate Am. Bd. Surgey, Nat. Bd. Med. Examiners; lic. Vt. Intern then resident in surgery Univ. Hosps., Cleve., 1961-66; research fellow Roswell Park Meml. Inst., Buffalo, 1966-68; asst. prof. surgery U. Vt., Burlington, 1970-73, assoc. prof. surgery, 1973-80, prof. surgery, 1980-92, dir. comprehensive cancer ctr., 1984-92; attending surgeon Med. Ctr. Hosp. of Vt., 1970-92; Wadley Glenn prof. surgery Emory U., Atlanta, 1992-99; chief surgical svcs. Crawford Long Hosp. of Emory U., 1992-99. Mem. cancer clin. investigation rev. com. NIH, 1987-92, chmn., 1991-92, chmn. various coms.; cons. Am. Internat. Health Alliance for Tblisi, Georgia Hosp., 1992-96. Assoc. editor: Clinical Surgery, 1987; co-editor: Essentials of Clinical Surgery, 1991; editor-in-chief: Breast Surgery: Index and Reviews, 1993-95; assoc. editor: Surgery: Problem-Solving Approach, 2d edit., 1995; co-editor: Q & A Review for Surgery, 1995; manuscript reviewer: Jour. AMA, Jour. Trauma, others; contbr. more than 100 articles to profl. jours. Trustee Univ. Health Ctr., Burlington, 1986-89; bd trustees, Vt. Ethics Network, 2001—. Served to maj. U.S. Army, 1968-69. Grantee NIH, 1971-92; summer rsch. fellow Josiah Macy Jr. Found., 1958-59. Fellow ACS (bd. regents 1991-2000, bd. govs. 1981-87, adv. coun. for gen. surgery 1989-92, 95-2000, sec./treas. Vt. chpt. 1979-80, v.p. 1980-81, pres. 1981-82), Am. Surg. Assn.; mem. AMA, AAAS, New Eng. Surg. Soc. (treas. 1986-89, exec. com. 1981-92, 2001-03, pres. 2001-02), Soc. Univ. Surgeons, So. Surg. Assn., Southeastern Surg. Congress, Soc. Surg. Oncology, Ea. Surg. Soc. (pres. 1994), Am. Endocrine Surg. Soc. (coun. 1992-95), Am. Soc. Clin. Oncology (pub. rels. 1989-91 and pub. issues coms. 1989-94), Transplantation Soc., New Eng. Cancer Soc. (treas. 1983-87, v.p. 1988-89, pres. 1989-90), Assn. Acad. Surgery, Newfoundland Club Am. (bd. dirs. 1976-78, 1st v.p. 1979), Nat. Surg. Adjuvant Breast Project, 1971-92 (exec. com. 1978-81). Avocations: white water canoeing, breeding newfoundland dogs, wilderness travel, chamber music. Home: 613 S Forty Dr Shelburne VT 05482-6492

FOSTER, S. THOMAS, JR., quality management educator, consultant, writer; b. Waynesville, Mo., Sept. 24, 1957; s. Stephen T. Foster and Jeanne L. Berridge; m. Casie L. Foster, May 11, 1979; children: Kimberlee, Amie, Stephen, Daniel, Matthew. BS, Brigham Young U., 1984; MBA, U. Mo., 1988; PhD, U. Mo., Columbia, 1993. Analyst Shell Oil Co., Houston, 1984-88; grad. asst. U. Mo., Columbia, 1989-93; prin. Foster Mgmt. Cons., Boise and Kansas City, 1988—; prof. quality mgmt. Boise State U., 1993—. Vis. prof. Pa. State U., University Park, 1999—; founder www.freequality.org., 2000—. Author: Handbook on Quality, 1998, Managing Quality, 2001; mem. editl. bd. Jour. Operatio Mgmt., 1998—, Quality Mgmt. Jour., 1997—; contbr. articles to profl. jours. Mem. Decion Scis. Inst. (various coms.), Am. Soc. for Quality (bd. dirs. 1992—), Idaho Total Quality Inst. (bd. dirs. 1994-96), Acad. of Mgmt., Prodn. and Ops. Mgnt. Soc. (coms. 1992—), North Cen. Assn. Colls. and Univs. (adv. bd. 1998—), Am. Prodn. and Inventory Control Soc., Beta Gamma Sigma. Republican. Mem. Ch. Latter Day Sts. Avocations: skiing, guitar playing, spending time with family. Home: 5795 W Barker Rd Kuna ID 83634 Office: Boise State U Dept CIS & PM Boise ID 83725

FOSTER, SALLY, interior designer; b. New Orleans, Nov. 6, 1927; d. Charles Shearer and Bessie Long Foster; m. Harold Barnett McSween, Dec. 21, 1948 (div. Mar. 1979); children: John Charles McSween, Robert Douglas McSween, Elizabeth McSween, Sally McSween Ward. BA, Tulane U., 1948. Interior designer, owner Sally Foster Designs, Alexandria, La., 1979—. Bd. dirs., past pres. Alexandria Mus. Art, 1988—92, 1999—, Kent Plantation House, Alexandria, 1964—67, 1998—; founding mem. bd. dirs. Rapides Symphony Orch., Alexandria, 1973. Mem.: Alexandria Jr. League (pres. 1963—64), Nat. Soc. Colonial Dames Am., Alexandria Golf and Country Club, Alexandria Rotary Club, Chi Omega. Republican. Episcopalian. Avocations: antiques, travel, food, reading. Office: Sally Foster Designs 1307 Windsor Pl Alexandria LA 71303-2751

FOSTER, SERRIN MARIE, non-profit organization executive; b. Washington, Sept. 17; d. William A. and Donna R. (Hayden) F. BA in Pub. Rels., Old Dominion U., 1977. Freelance pub. rels. specialist, Springfield, Va., 1978-82; program mgr., regional rep. St. Jude Children's Rsch. Hosp., Arlington, Va., 1982-89; dir. devel. Nat. Alliance for Mentally Ill., Washington, 1989-94; exec. dir. Feminists for Life of Am., Washington, 1994-99, pres., 1999—. Mem. adv. bd. Ivy League Coalition for Life, Harvard U., 1997—, Am. Collegians for Life, Washington, 1998. Author: (books) Pro-Women Answers to Pro-Choice Questions, 2003; author: (contbr.) Women's Rights, 2001—; editor-in-chief, contbr. The Am. Feminist mag., 1994—, contbr. Boston Globe, Great Speeches in History. Susan B. Anthony List, Alexandria, 1997—. Mem. Alpha Phi Women's Found. Avocations: gardening, travel, oil painting. Office: Feminists for Life of Am 733 15th St NW Ste 1100 Washington DC 20005-2112

FOSTER, SONJA MARGUERITE, musician, educator; d. Lyle P. and Ruth D. Foster; m. Frank Stephen Allen, Apr. 29, 1989. BMus in Violin Performance, Juilliard Sch., 1972. First violin Grant Pk. Symphony, Chgo., 1970—77; artist, tchr. Trinity Coll., Deerfield, Ill., 1972—78; violin faculty Wheaton (Ill.) Coll., 1975—83; instr. violin Studio for Gifted, Norcross, Ga., 1982—; artist, tchr. Emory U., Atlanta, 1985—92. Performer; tchr. master classes; presenter in field. Musician: (albums) Sacred Music for the Violin, 2003; author: Teaching Gifted Children. Mem. adv. bd. Gwinnett Philharm., Duluth, Ga., 1995—2001. Scholar Full scholar, Curtis Inst. Music, 1964—68, Meadowmount Sch. Music, 1965—68, The Juilliard Sch., 1968—72. Mem.: Atlanta Music Club, Am. String Tchrs. Assn., Music Tchrs. Nat. Assn. Republican. Achievements include research in stage fright and positive performing. Avocation: travel. Personal E-mail: sallen2000@comcast.net.

FOSTER, STEPHAN LYLE, pharmacist, educator; b. Aug. 16, 1952; PharmD, U. Tenn., Memphis, 1977; BS in Pharmacy, U. N.Mex., Albuquerque, 1976. Clin. pharmacist Indian Health Svc., 1977-90, dir. pharmacy tng., 1990-98; assoc. prof. U. Tenn. Coll. Pharmacy, Memphis, 1998—; liaison rep. adv. com. on immunization practice Ctr. for Disease Control and Prevention. Contbr. articles to profl. jours., chpt. to book. Served as capt. USPHS, to 1998. Named Pharmacist of Yr. Indian Health Svc., 1997, USPHS, 1998. Office: U Tenn Coll Pharmacy Dept Pharm Memphis TN 38163-0001

FOSTER, STEPHEN KENT, banker; b. St. Louis, Dec. 14, 1936; s. John William and Josephine Fladune (Bushman) F.; m. Rosanne Pleier, Sept. 13, 1958; children: John Andrew, Stephanie Mary. BBA, U. Wis., 1959, MBA (H.B. Earhart fellow), 1964. Asst. export mgr. Cargill, Inc., Portland, Oreg., 1959-61; with 1st Interstate Bank Oreg. (formerly 1st Nat. Bank Oreg.), Portland, 1964-81, sr. v.p. loan adminstrn., 1973-75, sr. v.p. br. and loan adminstrn., 1975-76, exec. v.p., 1976-81, First State Bank Oreg. (later Pacific Western Bank), Milwaukie, 1981-82; pres., chief operating officer, dir. Pacific Western Bank, Milwaukie, 1983-86; sr. v.p. Pacwest Bancorp, 1981-83, pres., 1983-86; pres., chief adminstrv. officer Key Bank of Oreg., 1986-89, also bd. dirs., mem. exec. com.; pvt. investor, 1990—. Bd. dirs., treas. Lake Oswego Corp.; gov.'s appointment to Oreg. State Banking Bd., 1985, chmn., 1986, mem., 1987-89. Bd. dirs. United Cerebral Palsy of N.W. Oreg., 1967-80; bd. dirs. Oreg. Council on Econ. Edn., 1970-80, Portland Opera Assn., 1970-74, United Way of Columbia-Willamette, 1973-75, Oreg. Ind. Coll. Found., 1983-91, vice chmn., 1985-91, mem. exec. com., 1985-91; bd. regents U. Portland, 1976-88, mem. fin. com., 1976-78, mem. exec. com., 1979-88, chmn. acad. affairs com., 1980-88, chmn. presdl. rev. com., 1981; mem. adv. coun. chair Entrepreneurship, 1998-2001; trustee St. Vincent's Hosp. Med. Found., 1986-90. Served with U.S. Army, 1958, 61-62. Recipient Service to Legal Edn. award Oreg. Bar Assn., 1971, Ednl. and Service award Bank Adminstrn. Inst., 1971 Mem. Portland C. of C., Oreg. Assn. Credit Mgmt. (Leadership Svc. award 1973), Am. Bankers Assn., Robert Morris Assocs., Am. Fin. Assn., Nat. Assn. Accts. (Ednl. and Svc. award 1971), Senior's Northwest Golf Assn., Arlington Club (bd. dirs. 1986-89, treas. 1987-88, 2d v.p. 1988-90), Univ. Club Portland (bd. dirs. 1986-95, chmn. libr. and reciprocal mems., sec. 1990-91, chmn. membership com. 1991-92, treas. 1992-93, v.p. 1993-94, pres. 1994-95), Waverley Country Club (long-range planning com. 1990-94), Astoria Golf and Country Club, Phi Beta Kappa, Phi Kappa Phi, Phi Eta Sigma, Beta Gamma Sigma, Sigma Chi.

FOSTER, STEPHEN WILLIAM, mental health nurse; b. San Francisco, Calif., Feb. 11, 1947; s. Martin David Foster and Edna Jane Berger. BA in Anthrop., Reed Coll., 1969; MA in Cultural Anthrop., U. Wash., 1970, Princeton U., 1974, PhD in Cultural Anthrop., 1977; MSN in Psychology, Yale U., 1983. RN Calif., 1983. Park ranger archeologist Mesa Verde (Colo.) Nat. Pk., 1968; instr. Cherry Lawn Sch., Darien, Conn., 1971—72; libr. tech. Oakland (Calif.) Pub. Libr., 1972—73; libr. tech. II Merritt Coll. Libr., Oakland, 1973; asst. instr. Dept. Anthrop. Princeton (N.J.) U., 1973—75; libr. asst. II Social Sci. Libr. U. Calif., Berkeley, 1977—79; mem. staff Yale-New Haven (Conn.) Hosp., 1980—83; lectr. in anthrop. Smith Coll., Northampton, Mass., 1980—83; vis. lectr. in anthrop. U. Calif., Berkeley, Calif., 1983—85; psychiat. nursing supr. San Francisco (Calif.) Gen. Hosp., 1984—. Cons. in field; lectr. in field. Contbr. articles to profl. jours. Fellow, Princeton U., 1973—77, NIMH, 1975—77, Kellog fellowship, Yale U., 1979—80, Am. Coun. Learned Socs., 1989—90; grantee, NSF, 1969—70; scholar, U. Calif., 1965, Richard Y. Townsend scholarship, Reed Coll., 1967—68. Mem.: Am. Anthrop. Assn., Sigma Theta Tau. Episcopalian. Avocations: travel, poetry, travel journals. Home: 4473 Montgomery St Oakland CA 94611 Office: Psychiatric Nursing Divsn SF Gen Hosp 1001 Potrero Ave San Francisco CA 94110

FOSTER, SUTTON, actress; b. Statesboro, Ga., Mar. 18, 1975; Postgrad., Carnegie Mellon U., Hunter Coll., N.Y.C. Actor: (Broadway musical) Grease, Annie, Scarlet Pimpernel, Les Misérables, Thoroughly Modern Millie (winner Tony award for Best Performance by a Leading Actress in a Musical, 2002). Office: Marquis Theatre 211 W 45th St New York NY 10036

FOSTER, TERESA E. choral director, piano teacher; b. Hardinsburg, Ky., Aug. 11, 1971; m. Michael S. Foster. B Music Edn., U. Louisville, 1993. Choral dir. Sacred Heart Acad., Louisville, Ky., 1997—. Louisville Youth Choir, Louisville, Ky., 2000—; pvt. voice tchr. Ursuline Sch. For The Performing Arts, Louisville, Ky., 1997—; chorus mem. Ky. Opera, Louisville, Ky., 1990—99; choral dir. Bullitt Ctrl. H.s., Shepherdsville, Ky., 1995—97, St. Patrick Sch., Louisville, Ky., 1993—95. Mem.: Nat. Cath. Educators Assn., Tri-M Internat. Music Honor Soc., Ky. Choral Dir.'s Assn., Am. Choral Dir.'s Assn., Ky. Music Educator's Assn., Music Educator's Nat. Conf., Delta Omicron (pres. 1994—95). Office: Sacred Heart Acad 3175 Lexington Rd Louisville KY 40206

FOSTER, VICTOR LYNN, translator; b. Oklahoma City, Jan. 17, 1959; s. William James and Barbara Jean (Langston) F. BA in French Studies, U. Ctrl. Okla., 1995; MA in French Lit., Okla. U., 1999; MA in French Translation, Kent

State U., 2000. Mgr. Hardees Food Sys., Oklahoma City, 1987-89; asst. Conseil Regional Auvergne, Clermont-Ferrand, France, 1996-97; grad asst. in French, Kent State U., 1999—2000; terminology project lang. svcs. U.S. Dept. State, Washington, 2002—03; translator JHPIEGO, 2003—. Translator Jean-Paul Pavlus, Clermont-Ferrand, 1996—97, E.G. Localisation, Brest, France, Euro Texte, Paris, Liquid Crystal Inst., Kent State, Art Internat., Paris; French tutor U. Okla., 1997—99; interpretor Bowne Global Solutions, 2003—; Trados terminology conversions, medieval translations JHPIEGO, 2003. Mem. Kappa Alpha Psi, Kappa Gamma Epsilon (pres. 1998-99, ways and means com. student senate 1998-99), Phi Sigma Iota. Baptist. Avocations: reading, writing, sports. Home and Office: 1957 Seminary Rd Silver Spring MD 20910 E-mail: lalicorne1@excite.com.

FOSTER, WALTER HERBERT, JR., real estate company executive; b. Belmont, Mass., Nov. 2, 1919; s. Walter Herbert and Gertrude (Sullivan) F.; m. Hazel Campbell, Aug. 7, 1942 (div. July 1979); children: Katherine D., Walter H. III, Stephen C., Banton T.; m. Nedra Ann Thompson, July 3, 1981; 1 child, Timothy John. Student, Harvard U., 1937-38; BS, U. Maine, 1947; grad. in real estate, Tri-State Inst., 1968-70. Cert. gen. appraiser, Maine. Owner, mgr. Foster Bros., Lyndeborough, N.H., 1947-56; ter. sales mgr. Beacon Milling Co., Oakland, Maine, 1956-64; v.p. Sherwood & Foster, Inc., Old Town, Maine, 1964-67; sales rep. Bangor (Maine) Real Estate, 1967-73; chief appraiser James W. Sewall Co., Old Town, 1970-73; mgr. J.F. Singleton Co., Bangor, 1973-80; pres. Coldwell Banker Am. Heritage, Bangor, 1980—. Dean Tri-State Inst., 1981; mem. Maine Real Estate Commn., 1987-93, chmn. 1991. Mem. Rep. Nat. Com., Washington, 1980; mem. assessment bd. appeals Old Town, Maine, Holden Assessment Bd. of Appeals; bd. dirs. Penobscot Theatre, 1987-92, treas., 1989, mem. Maine State Bd. Property Rev., 1998—. Capt. USAF, 1941-46, USAFR ret., 1966. Mem. Nat. Assn. Realtors (bd. dirs. 1980-81), Maine Assn. Realtors (life, bd. dirs. 1976-80, pres. 1980, Realtor of Yr. 1984), Bangor Bd. Realtors (bd. dirs. 1973-74, pres. 1976, Realtor of Yr. 1976, 84), Maine Real Estate Commn. (chmn. 1991-92), Maine State Bd. Property Tax Review, Commn. to Study Real Estate Appraiser Cert. and Licensing, Nat. Assn. Rev. Appraisers, Am. Assn. Cert. Appraisers, Res. Officers Assn., Appraisal Inst. (assoc.), Nat. Assn. Ind. Fee Appraisers (sr.), Harvard Club of Ea. Maine (treas.), Rotary (bd. dirs. local club), Am. Legion., Ret. Officers Assn., Mil. Officers Assn. Am. Episcopalian. Avocations: woodworking, gardening. Home: 68 Dole Hill Rd Holden ME 04429-9802 Office: Coldwell Banker Am Heritage 510 Broadway Bangor ME 04401-3468 E-mail: cbah@midmaine.com.

FOSTER, WALTON BROWN, political science educator; b. Rome, Ga., June 1, 1956; d. Samuel Edward and Orchid Lyons Brown; m. Benjamin Foster, Jr., Dec. 28, 1995; 1 child, Suliman Samuel BenAmee. BA, U. of Mich., 1977, MA, PhD, 1982. Asst. prof. U. of Ga., Athens, 1982—83; prof. Cen. Conn. State U., New Britain, Conn., 1984—. Faculty cons. Charter Oak State Coll., New Britain, Conn., 1985—. Author: (book) Democracy and Race, 1997; editor: (newsletter) AfricaUpdate. Mem.: Nat. Conf. of Black Polit. Scientists, Women in Internat. Security, Am. Polit. Sci. Assn., Delta Sigma Theta. Avocations: travel, walking, gardening, sewing. Home: 6 Croydon Dr Bloomfield CT 06002 Office: Cen Conn State U 1615 Stanley St New Britain CT 06050 Home Fax: 860-232-5505; Office Fax: 860-832-3013. Personal E-mail: orchidl@cs.com. E-mail: brownw@ccsu.edu.

FOSTER, WILLIAM ANTHONY, management consultant, educator; b. Washington, Nov. 26, 1929; s. Willard Hill and Evelyn Marie (Serrin) F.; m. Donna Roy Hayden, Feb. 5, 1955 (div. July 1985); children: Serrin M., Donna L., Shickel, Laura A. Valentine; m. Frances Christian Meacham, Dec. 6, 1995. BS in Bus. and Pub. Adminstrn., U. Md., 1956; MSPA, Nova Southeastern U., 1975, DPA, 1977. Registered profl. engr., Calif. Dir. indsl. engring. Washington region U.S. Postal Svc., 1969-71, mgr. indsl. engring. and plant maintenance Ea. Region, 1971-72, mgr. indsl. engring., 1972-80, nat. coord., 1980-83, program mgr. tng., 1983-86; pres., educator, trainer, cons. William A. Foster Assoc., Washington, 1986—. Educator, trainer, cons. U.S. Postal Svc., Washington, 1983-86, Embry-Riddle U., Daytona Beach, Fla., 1993, U. D.C., Washington, 1977-83, Southeastern U., 1980; dir., mgr. ops. U.S. Postal Svc., Washington, 1962-83. Author exec. tng. books; moderator TV show (Inaugural award 1991). Charter mem. Charleston Assn., Springfield, Va., 1968-84. Mem. ASTD (com. mem. 1986—), Am. Inst. Indsl. Engrs. (govt. liaison 1976-80, Nat. award for excellence 1969), Am. Soc Pub. Adminstrn. (cons. 1980-84), D.C. Coun. Engring. and Archtl. Socs. (chmn., PBS chair 1979-81, Outstanding Svc. award 1981, Bicentennial Engring. and Archtl. award 1976). Republican. Roman Catholic. Avocations: public speaking, american history, family, travel. Home: 1441 Northgate Sq Apt 12B Reston VA 20190-3754

FOSTER, WILLIAM EDWIN (BILL FOSTER), nonprofessional basketball coach; b. Ridley Park, Pa., Aug. 19, 1929; s. Howard M. and Viola Jane (Beaston) F.; m. Shirley Ann Junkin, June 17, 1957; children: Vicki R., Debra Jo, Julia Ann, Mary K. BS, Elizabethtown Coll., 1954; MEd, Temple U., 1957. Coach, tchr. Chichester (Pa.) High Sch., 1954-57, Abington (Pa.) High Sch., 1957-60; coach, instr. Bloomsburg (Pa.) State Coll., 1960-63; head basketball coach Rutgers U., New Brunswick, N.J., 1963-71, U. Utah, Salt Lake City, 1971-74; head basketball coach, asst. athletic dir. Duke U., Durham, N.C., 1974-80, U. S.C., Columbia, 1980-86; head basketball coach, interim athletic dir. Northwestern U., Evanston, Ill., 1986-93, athletic dir., 1993; assoc. commr. S.W. Conf., Dallas, 1993-96; cons. Com. of Big 12 Conf. for basketball, 1996-99; spl. asst. to the commr. Western Athletic Conf., 1999—. Chmn. of the bd. Naismith Meml. Basketball Hall of Fame, 1997-98, bd. trustees; pres. Nat. Sports Video Seminars. Served with USAF, 1951-52. Named Nat. Coach of Yr., Sporting News Playboy Mag., 1978, S.C. Coach of Yr., 1981, NIT Man of Yr., Met. Intercollegiate Basketball Assn., 2003, Nat. Invitation Tournament's Man of Yr., Met. Coaches Assn., 2003; named to Elizabethtown Coll. Sports Hall of Fame, Pa., Rutgers Basketball Hall of Fame, Delaware County (Pa.) Hall of Fame. Mem. Nat. Assn. Basketball Coaches (past pres., co-coach of yr. 1978), Met. Intercollegiate Basketball Assn. (elected 2003). Address: 20907 W Sandhill Dr Galveston TX 77554 Office: PO Box 5295 Galveston TX 77554-0295 E-mail: mfoster689@aol.com.

FOSTER, WILLIAM SILAS, JR., minister; b. Kansas City, Mo., Nov. 5, 1939; s. William Silas and Edna LaResta (Scott) F.; m. Susan Jean Mannle, June 5, 1983; children Robert Light, Beth Light Sierra, Stacey Light; children from previous marriage, Beth Ann, Amy Lynne. BA, Mo. Valley Coll., 1962; MDiv, McCormick Sem., 1966. Ordained to ministry Presbyn. Ch. (USA), 1966. Asst. min. 1st Presbyn. Ch., Edwardsville, Ill., 1966-68; min. St. Paul's Presbyn. Ch., St. Louis, 1968-71, Moro (Ill.) Presbyn. Ch., 1971-83, 1st Presbyn. Ch., North Kansas City, Mo., 1983-84, Worland, Wyo., 1985—. Commr. to Gen. Assembly Presbyn. Ch. (U.S.A), Omaha, Balt., Albuquerque, 1973, 91, 95; stated clk. Presbytery Wyo., Casper, 1990-00, Com. of the Office of Gen. Assembly; instr. calligraphy Synod Sch., 1982-83; pres. Presbyn. Alcohol Info. Network, 1982-83, Ill. Impact Bd., 1983. Resource person 1980 Youth Triennium, Bloomington, Ind., 1980; bd. dirs. Edwardsville Sch. Bd., 1976-83, Mental Bd. Washakie County, 1989—, pres., 1999. Recipient M. Keith Upson award U.S. Jaycees, 1974; named Outstanding New Mem., Ill. Jaycees, 1972, Outstanding Mem., 1973. Mem. Lions (2d v.p. 1989-91). Home: 1515 Yellowstone Ave Worland WY 82401-2206 Office: 1st Presbyn Ch PO Box 53 Worland WY 82401-0053 *In the 21st Century, we are called as Abraham to live on a wilderness frontier of life. This radically unique environment demands creative risks and personal ethical choices. Listening to one another's wilderness journeys, learning from each other and supporting others are the keys for genuine faith, hope and love in the future.*

FOSTER-WELLS, KAREN MARGARET, artist; b. Pasadena, Calif., Oct. 26, 1942; d. Ray Russell Foster and Margaret Victoria Ray; m. David Roycroft Rory Wells, Sept. 17, 1988; children: John McCarthy, Sabisha Friedberg. AA, Orange Coast Coll., Costa Mesa, Calif., 1962; student, U. Calif., Irvine, 1967-68, Laguna Beach Sch. Art/Design, Calif., 1965-67. Illustrator, 1963—. One-woman shows include Santa Barbara (Calif.) of Natural History, 1979, Morro Bay (Calif.) Mus. of Natural History, 1988, Great Western Bank, San Luis Obispo, Calif., 1989, Cayucos (Calif.) Art Assn., 1993, Chelsea Bookshop, Paso Robles, Calif., 1993, Paso Robles Art Assn. Gallery, 1993, Wild Horse Found., Santa Barbara, Summerwood Winery, 2002; group exhbns. include Waterside Gallery, Morro Bay, Calif., 1997, 98, Johnson Gallery and Framing Studio, San Luis Obispo, 1999, 2000, Coll. of Creative Studies, Santa Barbara, 2000, Santa Barbara Mus. Natural History, 2000, Carnegie Western Art Gallery, Paso robles, 2000-2001, San Luis Obispo Art Ctr., 2001, Cayucos Art Assn., 2001, Biennale Internazionale Dell'arte Contemporanea, Florence, Italy, 2003, Santa Clarita Quick Draw, 2003; artist (cover) The Path of Return, 2001, Monterey Mus. Art, 2002. Recipient Bronze medal Art of Calif. Discovery awards, 1993, 1st Pl. Calif. Mid-State Fair Art Show, 1994, 98, 1st Pl. and Coord. award Calif. Mid-State Fair Art Show, 2000, Best of Show Paso Robles Art Assn., 2000. Mem. The Oak Group, Calif. Art Club, San Luis Outdoor Painters Enterprise (co-founder), Am. Soc. Portrait Artists, Women Artists of the West. Avocations: horses, natural history. Office: Karen Foster Artist dot com PO Box 1114 Templeton CA 93465 E-mail: horseart@tcsn.net.

FOTA, FRANK GEORGE, artist; b. Northampton, Pa., Feb. 20, 1921; s. Frank Michael and Elizabeth Rose (Simko)F.; m. Christine June Ringwald, Oct. 18, 1947. Student, Chgo. Acad. of Fine Art, 1951-53. Artist Studio Maintained in Residence, S. Holland, Ill.; comml. artist, designer Triangle Outdoor Advt. Co., Chgo., 1956-61, Gen. Outdoor Advt. Co., Chgo., 1961-63; art dir. Triangle Outdoor Advt. Co., Chgo., 1963-83. Artist: (paintings) The Juniper Tree, 1971, Moab, Utah, 1974, Give Us This Day, Crete, Ill., 1972; exhibits include Wally Findlay Gallery, Chgo., 1953, 54, 55, Richard H. Love Gallery, Steger, Ill., Olympia Fields, Ill., Chgo., 1973, 74, 75, others. Mem., photographer Dolton (Ill.) Civic Assn., 1983-85 Mem.: Veteran of Foreign Wars, Dolton, Ill. (Trustee), Am. Legion, Riverdale, Ill. (Photog.). Roman Catholic. Avocations: photography, music. Home: 16748 Clyde Ave South Holland IL 60473-2611

FOTE, CHARLES T. computer company executive; V.p. ops. Farmington Trust; dir. spl. projects First Data Corp., 1975, pres., COO, 1998—. Office: First Data Corp Ste 1400 5660 New Northside Dr NW Atlanta GA 30328-5825

FOTI, JOANNE ERMINIA, painter, textile designer, educator; b. Bklyn., Feb. 9, 1954; d. Peter M. and Marian (Oppedisano) F. BFA, Pratt Inst., 1975; MA in Art Edn., Bklyn. Coll., 2001. Textile designer, colorist New Wave Fabrics Ltd., N.Y.C., 1978-82; textile colorist New Point Fabrics Ltd., N.Y.C., 1982-84; textile designer, colorist Merry Mary Fabrics, N.Y.C., 1984-86; print stylist dress divsn. Liz Claiborne Dresses, N.Y.C., 1986-89; print stylist, color advisor St. Gillian.Bichon, N.Y.C., 1989-90; textile stylist domestic and imported women's wear Hi Fashion Fabrics, N.Y.C., 1990-92; asst. to owner for domestic textiles Euro-Am. Textile Corp., N.Y.C., 1992-93; freelance textile designer, artist, N.Y.C., 1993—. Art educator NYC Pub. H.S., 1995—. Avocations: travel, reading, music. E-mail: jjf2954@aol.com.

FOTI, MARGARET, association executive, publisher, editor, lecturer; b. Phila., Dec. 15, 1944; d. Samuel A. and Margaret M. (DiBiase) F. BA, Temple U., 1975, MA in Comm., 1985, PhD in Comm., 1995; MD (hon.), U. Rome, 2003. Tech. editor U. Pa., Phila., 1962-64, asst. to bus adminstr., 1964-65; sr. editorial asst. Cancer Rsch. Jour., Phila., 1965-69, mng. editor, 1969—; CEO, Am. Assn. Cancer Rsch., Phila., 1982—. Adminstrn., pub. edn., devel., editorl. and pub. cons., lectr. in field. Contbr. articles to profl. jours. Pres. Nat. Coalition for Cancer Rsch., 1994-96. Recipient cert. of appreciation Am. Assn. Cancer Rsch., 1975, 85, 90, 99, Woman of Distinction award, 1999, Cino del Duca award, 2000, Ville de Paris award, 2000, award City of Trento, Italy, 2002, Solemn Encomium recognition U. Palermo, Italy, 2003. Mem.: AAAS, European Assn. Cancer Rsch., Coun. Engrs. and Sci. Soc. Execs., Coun. Biology Editors (pres. 1980—81), Soc. for Scholarly Publs. (pres. 1996—97), Internat. Fedn. Sci. Editors, European Assn. Sci. Editors, European Assn. Cancer Rsch. (disting.), Am. Assn. Cancer Rsch., Am. Soc. Assn. Execs., Japanese Cancer Assn. (hon.). Democrat. Roman Catholic. Home: 220 Locust St Apt 24A Philadelphia PA 19106-3932 Office: Am Assn Cancer Rsch 615 Chestnut St 17th Fl Philadelphia PA 19106-4404 E-mail: foti@aacr.org.

FOTI, VÉRONIQUE M. philosophy educator; b. Hungary; arrived in US, 1959; d. Lajos Fóti and Yolanda B. Stouder; 4 children. BA summa cum laude, Oglethorpe U.; MLS, Simmons Coll. Sch. Libr. Sci.; PhD in philosophy, Boston Coll. Asst. prof., philosophy U. Ky., Lexington, 1978—80, Coll. of Holy Cross, Worcester, Mass., 1980—81, New Sch. U., N.Y.C., 1981—85, Pa. State U., U. Park, 1985—92, assoc. prof., philosophy, 1992—. Author: Heidegger and the Poets; Poiesis, Sohia, Technê, 1992; editor: Merleau-Ponty: Difference, Materiality, Painting, 1996; author: Vision's Invisibles: Philosophical Explorations, 2003, (articles) various profl. jours. Recipient Fulbright lectureship, India, 1987; grantee Woodrow Wilson fellowship, 1962, Fulbright Summer grant, Costa Rica, 1996. Mem.: Internat. Assn. for Philosphy and Lit., Soc. for Existential Philosophy and Phenomenology, Am. Philos. Assn. Avocations: painting, graphic art, horticulture. Office: PA State U Dept of Philosophy 240 Sparks University Park PA 16802

FOTIADES, GEORGE L. pharmaceutical executive; BA in econ., Amherst Coll.; MBA, Northwestern U. Sr. mgmt. Procter & Gamble and Richardson-Vicks; pres. Bristol-Meyers Squibb's Consumer Products Group, Japan, Warner Welcome Consumer Healthcare, Warner Lambert Co.; group pres., Americas and Asia/Pacific R.P. Scherer, pres. and COO; group pres. Cardinal Health, 1998—, pres. and COO, pharm. techs. and svcs., 2000—, exec. v.p.; mem. bd. trustees ProLogis, 2001—. Office: R P Scherer Inc 645 Martinsville Rd Ste 200 Basking Ridge NJ 07920

FOTSCH, DAN ROBERT, elementary education educator; b. St. Louis, May 17, 1947; s. Robert Jarrel and Margaret Louise (Zimmermann) F.; m. Jacquelyn Sue Rotter, June 12, 1971; children: Kyla Michelle, Jeffrey Scott, Michael David. BS in Edn. cum laude, U. Mo., 1970; MS in Edn., Colo. State U., 1973. Cert. K-12 phys. edn. and health tchr. Mo., Colo. Tchr. phys. edn., coach North Callaway Schs., Auxvasse, Mo., 1970-71; grad. teaching asst., asst. track coach Colo. State U., Ft. Collins, 1971-73; tchr. elem. phys. edn., coach Poudre R-1 Sch. Dist., Ft. Collins, 1973—; tchr. on spl. assignment Elem. Phys. Edn. Resource, 1990; adminstrv. asst. Moore Sch., Ft. Collins, 1990—, acting prin., 1997, tchr. on spl. assignment dist. phys. edn. coord., 1998, k-12 coord. dist. phys. edn., 1998— Co-dir. Colo. State U. Handicapped Clinic, Ft. Collins, 1973-93; dir. Moore Elem. Lab. Sch., Ft. Collins, 1979—; dir. Colo. State U. Super Day Camp, 1979—; affiliate faculty mem. Colo. State U. Dept. Health and Exercise Sci., 1980-2000, Dept. Edn., 2000-02; presenter for conf. in field. Contbr. articles to profl. jours. State dir. Jump Rope for Heart Project, Denver, 1981. Recipient Scott Key Acad. award, Sigma Phi Epsilon, 1969, Honor Alumni award, Coll. of Profl. Studies of Colo. State U., 1983; grantee Colo. Heart Assn., 1985; recipient Coaching Excellence award Ft. Collins Soccer Club, 1991-92. Mem. NEA, AAHPERD (exec. bd. mem. coun. on phys. edn. for children 1983-86, reviewer Jour. Phys. Edn., Recreation and Dance 1984—, fitness chairperson, conv. planner 1986), ASCD, Poudre Edn. Assn., Colo. Edn. Assn., Colo. Assn. Health, Phys. Edn., Recreation and Dance (pres. 1979-82, Tchr. award 1977, Honor award 1985), Internat. Platform Assn., Ctrl. Dist. Alliance for Health, Phys. Edn., Recreation and Dance (elem. divsn. chairperson for phys. edn. 1989—), Phi Delta Kappa (found. rep. 1985), Phi Epsilon Kappa (v.p. 1969, pres. 1970). Republican. Avocations: marathons, triathlons, racketball, volleyball, swimming (Colo. State Swimming Championship Village Green Team, 1987, 89). Home: 2807 Blackstone Dr Fort Collins CO 80525-6190 Office: Moore Elem Sch 1905 Orchard Pl Fort Collins CO 80521-3210

FOTSCH, GEORGE BERNARD, III, chemical addiction counselor; b. Abbeville, La., May 9, 1945; s. George Bernard Fotsch Jr. and Norma Jeanne Fotsch; m. Evelyn Colleen Hunziker, Oct. 17, 1971 (div. Dec. 1988); children: Sandra, George, Seth, Evelyn, Troy; m. Jamie Linn Harper, June 21; 1 child, Candice Nicole. Student, U. Md., 1962—64, U. S.W. La., 1967—68, Am. Petroleum Inst., Long Beach, Calif., 1974—75. Lic. chem. dependency counselor TCADA, 1998. Mgr. Hollywood Diamond Exch., Long Beach, Calif., 1969; regional mgr. LeeRoy Barrys Jewelers, Riverside, Calif., 1970; ops. mgr. Armstrong Petroleum, Newport Beach, Calif., 1971—72; gen. mgr. Burmah Phillips Petroleum, Huntington Beach, Calif., 1973—83; counselor-in-tng. VA Chem. Dependency Treatment, Canandeiqua, NY, 1983—86; chem. dependency counselor Tex. Alcoholism Found., Houston, 1987—92; clin. dir. Cenikor Found., Inc., Deer Park, Tex., 1993—. Author: (book) Thee Book, 2002. Avocations: astronomy, cosmology, physics. Home: 10026 Antrium Ln La Porte TX 77571 Office: Cenikor Foundation Inc 4525 Glenwood Ave Deer Park TX 77536

FOTTLER, MYRON DAVID, health services educator; b. Boston, Sept. 5, 1939; s. Myron Dustin and Anna Eileen Fottler; m. Carol Ann Fottler, Aug. 11, 1972. BS, Northeastern U., 1962; MBA, Boston U., 1963; PhD, Columbia U., 1970. Asst. prof. SUNY, Buffalo, 1967—75; from assoc. prof. to prof. U. Ala., Tuscaloosa, 1976—83, prof., PhD program dir. Birmingham, 1983—99; prof., program dir. U. Ctrl. Fla., Orlando, 1999—. Cons. numerous legal firms and corps. Author 12 books; contbr. over 20 chpts. to books and over 100 articles to profl. jours. Recipient Hayhew award, Am. Coll. Health Care Execs., 1997, Outstanding Svc. award, Acad. Mgmt.-Healthcare Mgmt. Divsn., 1999, Faculty Pub. of Yr., Am. Acad. Med. Adminstrs., 2001. Episcopalian. Avocation: tennis. Office: Univ Ctrl Fla Coll Health and Pub Affairs 210A HPA2 Orlando FL 32816-0001 E-mail: fottler@mail.ucf.edu.

FOUCART VINCENTI, VALERIE, retired art educator; m. Stephen C. Vincenti; 1 child, Kayla. BS in Art Edn., Mansfield (Pa.) State U., 1975; MFA in Weaving, Marywood U., Scranton, Pa., 1993. Art tchr. Lycoming Valley Mid. and Roosevelt Mid. Schs., Williamsport, Pa., 1975—2003. Tchr. gifted arts program Pa. State U., Wilkes-Barre, Lehman Campus, 1990; presenter Pa. Art Edn. Assn. Art Conf., 2002. Editor The Lion newsletter St. Mark's Luth. Ch., Williamsport, 1985-88; editor, layout and design Roosevelt Roundup, 1997-2003. Playground arts instr. Williamsport Recreation Commn., summers 1980's; vol. ARC, Williamsport, 1980's; mem. ELCA Luth. Ch. Women; mem. planning com. PAEA State Conf. for 2002; sch. art exhbn. coord. Lycoming County Fair, 2000-03. Recipient 3rd pl. award painting and photography Bald Eagle Art League and Williamsport Recreation Commn., 1975-76, Nat. Program Stds. award Nat. Art Edn. Assn., 1994. Mem.: Williamsport Edn. Assn. (faculty rep.), Pa. State Edn. Assn., Pa. Art Edn. Assn. (com. state conf. 2000—02), Nat. Art Edn. Assn., Lycoming County Hist. Soc., Williamsport-Lycoming Arts Coun., Coalition Ind. Artists and Artisans, Handweavers Guild Am., Bald Eagle Art League, Susquehanna Valley Spinners and Weavers Guild, Ea. Star, Kappa Pi (Zeta Omicron chpt.). Democrat. Lutheran. Avocations: weaving, racquetball, travel, collecting art. Home: 801 Clearview Ave Pittsburgh PA 15205-3203

FOUCAULD, JEAN, cardiologist; b. San Juan, July 16, 1959; s. Jean and Josette Foucauld; m. Mirna Calvo, Jan. 29, 1983; children: Natalie, Patrick. BS in Biology, U. P.R., Mayaguez, 1978; MD, U. P.R., San Juan, 1982. Diplomate in internal medicine and cardiovascular disease Am. Bd. Internal Medicine. Intern Tripler Army Med. Ctr., Hawaii, 1982-83, resident, 1983-85; fellow Fitzsimons Army Med. Ctr., Colo., 1985-87; army staff cardiologist, 1987-92; cardiologist Texoma Cardiology, Denison, Tex., 1992-94, Cardiology Ptnrs. Palm Beach, Wellington, Fla., 1994—; dir. catheterization lab. Columbia Palms West Hosp., Loxahatchee, Fla., 1996—. Maj. U.S. Army, 1982-92. Decorated Meritorious Svc. medal, Army Achievement medal. Fellow Am. Coll. Cardiology. Roman Catholic. Avocations: long distance bicycling, tennis, skiing, reading. Office: Cardiology Ptnrs of the Palm Beaches 12953 Palms West Dr Ste 102 Loxahatchee FL 33470

FOUCHÉ, HELEN STROTHER, editorial design executive; b. Washington, Apr. 19, 1939; d. James Herschel and Elizabeth Ellen (Wright) Strother; m. Robert Michael Fouché, Oct. 20, 1962; children: James Michael, David Carroll, Stephen Charles. BA cum laude, Auburn U., 1960; student, Belles Artes, Managua, Nicaragua, 1964-65; student Intensive Lang. Tng., Fgn. Svc. Inst., 1961, 73; grad., Am. Transp. Inst., 1983. Asst. producer-dir. Internat. TV Svcs., U.S. Info. Agy., Washington, 1960-62; diplomatic svcs. with fgn. svc. husband U.S. Dept. of State, Europe, Africa, Cen./So. Am., 1963-81; art instr. for internat. children's classes La Paz, Bolivia, 1979; community liaison officer U.S. Embassy, La Paz, 1979-81; internat. group coord. Group Travel Unlimited, Alexandria, Va., 1983-84, mktg. creative/tech. writer, 1985-86; mng. editor Am. Leisure Industries, Lanham, Md., 1986-87; editor, cons. Washington Editl. Svcs., DC and Met. area, 1987-88, pres. Washington, Arlington, Va., 1988—2002. Founding bd. dirs. Fgn. Svc. Youth Found., Washington, 1989-91; cons. Overseas Briefing Ctr., Fgn. Svc. Inst., U.S. Dept. of State, Arlington, 1981-93; internat. tour mgr. Acad. Travel Abroad, Inc., 1990—; in mktg. sales Va. Divsn. of Tourism, 1994-97; media cons. designed slide shows, wrote scripts for non-profit causes. Contbg. editor, columnist: Diplomatic Digest, others; editor FS EYE for U.S. Dept. of State, 1991-94; mem. editorial bd. Fgn. Svc. Jour., 1989-92; executed murals, Crippled Children's Ward Managua (Nicaragua) Gen. Hosp., 1964, Montessori Sch., La. Paz, 1980; contbr. articles to profl. publs. Pres. Episcopal Ch. Women of St. Michael's, 1989-90, mem. vestry, 1990-94; mem. Altar Guild, 1982-99, lector, 1984-99; mem. Habitat for Humanity coms. St. Philip's Cathedral, Atlanta. Recipient Vol. of Yr. award, Tampa, Fla., 1970; named one of Outstanding Young Women of Am., 1973. Mem. AAUW, DAR, Assn. of Am. Fgn. Svc. Women (bd. mem., editl. com., newsletter editor), Nat. Press Club, Atlanta Press Club, Jamestown Soc. Democrat. Episcopalian. Avocations: art, theatre, travel, hiking. Home: 2460 Peachtree Rd NW Apt 1605 Atlanta GA 30305-4158

FOUCHI, DANA RAY, physician; b. New Orleans, Nov. 17, 1960; s. Frank E. Fouchi and Sheila G. (Fry) Hornbostel; m. Yvette Marie Thibodeaux, June 2, 1984 (div. Sept. 1994); children: Chantel Liana, Frank Dana (dec.); m. Jana Lynn Peno, July 31, 1997 (div. May 2000); 1 child, Joshua Ray; 1 stepchild, Zachary Scott Ledet; m. Mellea Theresa Magnuson, Dec. 29, 2000. BS in Biology, Loyola U., New Orleans, 1982; MD, La. State U., 1986. Diplomate Am. Bd. Family Practice. Resident in family practice La. State U., Bogalusa, 1986-89; physician Ochsner Clinic, Metairie, La., 1989-95, Kenner (La.) Regional Med. Ctr., 1995—, Jacob's Med. Ctr., Laplace, La., 1995-96; pvt. practice Kenner, 1996—; med. dir., owner River Region Hospice, 2000—. Mem. family practice rsch. com., patient edn. com. Ochsner Clin., Metairie, 1990-93. Mem. alumni bd. Loyola U., New Orleans, 1987-89, 92-95. Fellow Am. Acad. Family Practice; mem. Am. Med. Soc., La. State Med. Soc., Jefferson Parish Med. Soc., Aquarium of Ams. Avocations: exercise, nutrition. Home: 2504 Danny Park Metairie LA 70001-1557 Office: 613 Williams Blvd Kenner LA 70062-7635 E-mail: danarf@aol.com.

FOUDREE, BRUCE WILLIAM, lawyer; b. Des Moines, Mar. 27, 1947; s. Shie Wilbur and Dorothy Mable (Lynde) F.; m. Suzanne Joan Floss Reade, May 31, 1986; children: Andrew A., Grant R. BA, Drake U., 1969; student, U. Geneva, Switzerland, 1968, U. Vienna, Austria, 1968; JD, Drake U., 1972; LLM, U. Pa., 1975. Bar: Iowa 1972, U.S. Ct. Appeals (8th cir.) 1976, U.S. Supreme Ct. 1977, Ill. 1986. Asst. atty. gen. Iowa Dept. Justice, Des Moines, 1976-80; ins. commnr. Iowa Ins. Dept., Des Moines, 1980-86; of counsel Mitchell, Williams, Selig and Tucker, Little Rock, 1986-88; shareholder Keck, Mahin & Cate, Chgo., 1988-96; of counsel Lord, Bissell & Brook, Chgo., 1996—. Commr., chmn. Iowa Ins. Dept., 1980-86; commr. Iowa Health Data Commn., 1983-86, chmn. 1985. Assoc. editor Drake Law Rev., 1971-72; dir. Jour. Ins. Regulation, 1982-89. Mem. ABA (TIPS scope and correlation com. 1991-94, chmn. fin. svcs. com. 1990-91, professionalism com. 1994-96), Nat. Assn. Ins. Commrs. (chmn. 1984, pres. 1985), Ins. Regulatory Examiners Soc. Found. (bd. dirs. 1991—, chmn. 1999-2000), Iowa State Bar Assn., Union League Club of Chgo. (chmn. ins. group 1989-92), The Chicago Lighthouse (bd. dirs. 1995—, sec. 1998, chmn. 2002-). Avocations: travel, history, literature, music. Office: Lord Bissell & Brook 115 S La Salle St Fl 3600 Chicago IL 60603-3902 E-mail: bfoudree@lordbissell.com.

FOUDREE, CHARLES M. retired financial executive; BS in acctg., Truman State U., 1966. CPA Kans., Mo. Mem. audit staff Peat, Marwick, Mitchell, and Co., Kans. City, Kans., 1966-72; CFO, bd. dir. Harmon Industries, Inc., Blue Springs, Mo., 1972-99, ret., 1999. Bd. dir. OTR Express, Inc., Olathe, Kans., 1995—2001. Past chmn., bd. assoc. St. Mary's Hosp., Blue Springs; bd. dir. Harry S. Truman Libr. Inst.; treas., Truman State U. Found.; treas., trustee St. Paul Sch. Theology, Kansas City, Mo.; chmn. St. Mary's Hosp. Found., 2003; chmn. Truman State U. Found., 2003. Mem. AICPA; Mo. Soc. CPA; Fin. Exec. Inst. (bd. dir., past pres. Kansas City chpt., nat. bd. dir. 1995-98); Independence C. of C. (past dir., treas.); Rotary, Blue Key; Sigma Tau Gamma. Home: 4124 N E Pembroke Ln Lees Summit MO 64064-1622 E-mail: cfoudree@aol.com.

FOUDY, JULIA MAURINE, soccer player; b. San Diego, Jan. 23, 1971; m. Ian Sawyers, July 1995. BSW in Biology, Stanford U., 1993. Mem. U.S. Women's Nat. Soccer Team. Color commentator Men's World Cup, ESPN, 1998. Mem. Tyresco Football Club, Sweden, 1994. Recipient Gold medal, Centennial Olympic Games, 1996. Achievements include appeared on cover

Women's Soccer World mag., 1997; mem. championship team World Championships, Sweden, 1995; CONCACAF, Montreal, 1994. Office: c/o US Soccer Fedn 1801 S Prairie Ave # 1811 Chicago IL 60616-1319

FOUILLADE, JEAN-PAUL ERIC, management consultant; b. Neuilly-Sur-Seine, France, Aug. 7, 1950; came to US, 1989; s. Paul Henri and Andrèe Françoise Fouillade; m. Fabienne Patricia Ide, June 17, 1972 (div. June 1994); children: Jean-Sèbastien, Aurèlie, Lorraine; m. Katherine Ruth Hensel, Sept. 24, 1994 (div. Dec. 2001). MBA, Hautes Etudes Commerciales, HEC, Jouy-en-Josas, France, 1972. Asst. treas. Lesieur Group, Paris, 1972-74, UTA French Airlines, Paris, 1975-76, treas., 1977-80; dir. control Usinor Sacilor Group, Paris, 1981-89; sr. v.p. fin. and adminstrn. Francosteel Corp., NYC, 1990-96; pres. Whitridge Enterprises, Jersey City, 1997—2001. Prof. Inst. Formation Continue, Paris, 1978-79. Treas., UMP-USA, NYC, 1997—; dir. Summit (NJ) Child Care Ctr., 1996-99; trustee Com. French Speaking Soc., 2000-2003, French Am. Conservatory of Music, 2001-02. Mem.: Union pour un Mouvement Populaire. Union Pour La Democratie Francaise. Roman Catholic. Avocations: horseback riding, skiing, plane pilot. Home and Office: 69 Big Spring Rd Califon NJ 07830

FOULADVAND, HENGAMEH, artist; b. Tehran, Iran; naturalized U.S. citizen, 1974; d. Mansour and Mahin F.; m. Masoud B. Mansouri, Feb. 20, 1981; 1 child, Tia. BA, San Jose State U., 1976; M, Calif. State U., 1979. Exec. dir. Ctr. Iranian Modern Arts, 1998—. Art cons. T.H.E. Graphics & Design, 1990-96; graphic & prodn. cons. Metro Lables, 1994-96. Exhibited in solo and group shows including Columbia U., N.Y.C., 1989, L.I. U., 1989, 91, Strathmore Arts Ctr., Md., 1991, Port Washington Pub. Libr., 1991, Huntington Arts Coun., Hecksher Mus., 1993, 95, McArthur Airport Terminal Bldg., L.I., 1996-97, Columbia U., Hamilton Bldg., N.Y.C., 1997, Lindberg Gallery, N.Y.C., 1999, GORA Gallery, Montreal, 1999, La Maison Francaise, Columbia, 2000; represented in permanent collections Ency. Iranica Found., N.Y., Line & Tone Typographics, N.Y., numerous pvt. collections; mem. editl. bd.: Tavoos Art Quarterly, 1999--. Mem. N.Y. State Coun. Arts, N.Y. Found. Arts, Huntington Art League and Coun. Long Island. Home: 34 Lisa Dr Dix Hills NY 11746 E-mail: hengameht@earthlink.net.

FOULKE, EDWIN GERHART, JR., lawyer; b. Perkasie, Pa., Oct. 30, 1952; s. Edwin G. and Mary Claire (Keller) F. BA, N.C. State U., 1974; JD, Loyola U., New Orleans, 1978; LLM, Georgetown U., 1993. Bar: S.C. 1979, U.S. Dist. Ct. S.C. 1979, U.S. Ct. Appeals (4th cir.) 1979, Ga. 1986, U.S. Ct. Appeals (11th cir.) 1986, D.C. 1989, U.S. Ct. Appeals (D.C. cir.) 1989, U.S. Supreme Ct. 1990, N.C. 1997. Assoc. Thompson, Mann & Hutson, Greenville, S.C., 1978-83, Rainey, Britton, Gibbes & Clarkson, Greenville, 1983-85; ptnr. Constangy, Brooks & Smith, Columbia, S.C., 1985-90; chmn. Occupational Safety and Health Rev. Commn., Washington, 1990-95; ptnr. Jackson Lewis, Greenville, S.C., 1995—. Instr. St. Mary's Dominican Coll., New Orleans, 1977-78. Field rep. Reagan/Bush Campaign, Columbia, 1980, S.C. state coord., 1984; sec., treas. Employment Labor Law Sect., Columbia, 1981-82. Mem. ABA, S.C. Bar Assn., Ga. Bar Assn., Greenville County Bar Assn. (chmn. pub. rels. com. 1984-85), SAR, Rotary. Roman Catholic. Avocations: swimming, tennis, skiing, golf. Office: Jackson Lewis & Krupman 301 N Main St Ste 2100 Greenville SC 29601-2122

FOULKE, JUDITH DIANE, health physicist; b. Bucyrus, Ohio, Nov. 22, 1945; d. Lawrence Kern Foulke and Alberta Amelia (Foulke) Houpt; m. Mark Allen Elrod, July 17, 1981. BA, St. Mary of the Springs, 1967; MS, U. Mich., 1969; PhD, Purdue U., 1973. Health physicist NASA Goddard Space Flight Ctr., Greenbelt, Md., 1969-71, U.S. Atomic Energy Commn., Washington, 1973-77; radiobiologist U.S. Nuc. Regulatory Commn., Washington, 1977-87; health physicist U.S. Dept. Energy, Washington, 1987—. Mem. Spires Brass Band, Frederick, Md. Mem. AAAS, Am. Nuc. Soc., Health Physics Soc. Democrat. Roman Catholic. Home: 10 Sunnyview Ct Germantown MD 20876-4025

FOULKE, ROBERT DANA, English educator, travel writer; b. Mpls., Apr. 25, 1930; s. Robert William and Bertha Almeda (Peterson) F.; m. Patricia Ann Nelson, Dec. 29, 1953; children: David William, Carolyn Denise, Deborah Ann. AB, Princeton U., 1952; MA, U. Minn., 1957, PhD, 1961. Instr. English U. Minn., Mpls., 1956-61; asst. prof. English Trinity Coll., Hartford, Conn., 1961-66, assoc. prof. English, 1966-70; prof. English Skidmore Coll., Saratoga Springs, N.Y., 1970-92, chmn. dept. English, 1970-80, dir. NEH grant, 1981-83; scholar, writer, 1992—. Vis. prof. Sea Edn. Assn., Woods Hole, Mass., 1980, 83, mem. corp., 1990—; vis. prof. Williams-Mystic (Conn.) Program, 1982, Regents Coll., London, 1989; vis. assoc., life mem. Clare Hall, Cambridge (Eng.) U., 1976-77, 90-91; vis. fellow dept. English Princeton U., 1988. Co-editor, author: An Anatomy of Literature, 1972; co-author (with Patricia Foulke): Europe Under Canvas, 1980; co-editor: The Writer's Mind, 1983; co-author: Daytrips and Getaway Weekends in New Eng., 1983, Fielding's Motoring and Camping Europe, 1986, Daytrips and Getaway Weekends in the Mid-Atlantic States, 1986, Daytrips and Getaway Weekends in New Eng., 1988; script writer, host Sailing with Confidence, 1989; co-author: Daytrips and Getaway Weekends in the Mid-Atlantic States, 1989, Exploring Europe by Car, 1991, Daytrips and Getaway Weekends in New Eng., 1991, Fielding's The Great Sights of Europe, 1992, Daytrips and Getaway Weekends in the Mid-Atlantic States, 1993, Daytrips and Getaway Weekends in New Eng., 1994, Fielding's The Great Sights of Europe, 1994, A Guide to Colonial America, 1995, Daytrips and Getaway Weekends in the Mid-Atlantic States, 1996; author: The Sea Voyage Narrative, 1997; ; co-author: Daytrips and Getaway Weekends in New Eng., 1997, Romantic Weekends: New England, 1998, Daytrips and Getaway Weekends in New Eng., 1999, Daytrips and Getaway Weekends in the Mid-Atlantic States, 1999, 2001; author: 2d edit., 2002, The Sea Voyage Narrative, 2002, Daytrips and Getaway Weekends in Conn., RI, and Mass., 2002, Daytrips and Getaway Weekends in Vt., New Hampshire and Maine, 2002, Adventure Guide to the Champlain and Hudson River Valleys, 2003. Dir. The Lake George Club, Diamond Point, N.Y., 1977-82, commodore, 1981-82; elder First Presbyn. Ch., Glens Falls, N.Y., 1982—; trustee Glens Falls Hist. Assn., 1988-93; exec. com. Black Watch Coun., N.Y.C., 1993-96. Fulbright fellow U. London, 1959-60, Alexander O. Vietor fellow John Carter Brown Libr., Brown U., 1993. Mem.: MLA, Travel Journalists Guild, Coll. English Assn. (dir. 1981—84), N.Am. Snowsports Journalists Assn., Soc. Am. Travel Writers, N.Am. Soc. Oceanic History (exec. coun. 1995—2000), Am. Soc. Journalists and Authors, Travel Journalists Guild (second v.p. 2002—04), Soc. for Nautical Rsch., Melville Soc., Hakluyt Soc, Joseph Conrad Soc., Nat. Maritime Hist. Soc., Lake George Rotary Club (dir. 1984—86, 1998—2000). Presbyterian. Avocations: sailing, skiing, canoeing, heritage travel, cruises.

FOULKE, WILLIAM GREEN, retired banker; b. Whitemarsh, Pa., Nov. 20, 1912; s. Walter Longfellow and Helen (Pardee) F.; m. Louisa Lawrence Wood, Nov. 2, 1934; children: Louisa Lawrence Foulke Newlin, Walter Longfellow, William Green. AB, Princeton U., 1934. Asst. treas. Provident Trust Co., Phila., 1940-41, trust officer, 1945-50, v.p., 1950-57; sr. v.p. charge trust divsn. Provident Tradesmens Bank and Trust Co., Phila., 1957-60, exec. v.p., 1960-62, pres., 1962-64, Provident Nat. Bank, Phila., 1964-69, chmn. chief exec. officer, 1969-74; chmn., chief exec. officer Provident Nat. Corp., 1969-73, chmn., 1973-74; ret. Gen. chmn. United Campaign, 1975. Served to lt. comdr. USNR, 1941-45. Mem. Pa. Bankers Assn. (pres. 1970-71) Clubs: Racquet; Ivy (Princeton). Episcopalian. Home: 321 Evergreen Ave Philadelphia PA 19118

FOUNTAIN, ANDRE FERCHAUD, academic program director; b. Oklahoma City, Nov. 12, 1951; s. J. E. and Neaumatta Abilene (Edwards) F.; m. Linda K. Young. BS in Nursing, U. Okla., 1978. RN, Okla; cert. master hyrdotherapist, Kniepp Inst., Germany, massage therapist. Exec. dir. New Life Programs, Oklahoma City, 1981-87; dir. Praxis Coll. Health, Arts and Scis., Oklahoma City, 1988—. Speaker in field. Author: A Psychoprophylactic Workbook, 1981; co-author: Psychological Reports, 1977. Found. Caucus for Men in Nursing, Norman, 1976. Recipient 1st Pl. award Internat. Sci. Fair Balt., 1970; honored for Oklahoma City bombing vol. work, U.S. Dept. Justice. Mem. Internat. Childbirth Edn. Assn. (state coord. 1982-84), Am. Soc. Psychoprophylaxis in Obstetrics, Body Workers and Wellness Therapies Assn., Okla. Sports Massage Assn., Masons.

FOUNTAIN, CLARA GARRETT, archivist, librarian; b. Danville, Va., May 22, 1941; d. Albert Earle and Evelyn Hull (Steele) Garrett; 1 child, Marc. AA, Averett Coll., Danville, Va., 1962; BA, U. N.C., 1964, MLS, 1985. Libr. Danville/Pittsylvania County Schs., Danville, Va., 1966—84; archivist Dan River, Inc., Danville, 1981—85; ref. libr. Ferrum Coll., Va., 1986—88; ref. libr., archivist Averett Coll., Danville, 1989—2001, Averett U., Danville, 2001—. Author: (children's book) The Wreck of the Old 97, 1976, (history book) Danville: A Pictorial History, 1979, Danville, Va.: Postcard History, 2000. Mem.: Danville Hist. Soc., Va. Libr. Assn., Danville Mus. Fine Arts and History. Office: Averett University Blount Library 344 W Main St Danville VA 24541

FOUNTAIN, ELLEN ALLGAIER, artist, educator; b. Lewiston, Idaho, Dec. 5, 1942; d. Bruce E. Allgaier and Carol Irving Rock; m. James Thomas Fountain, Aug. 30, 1968. BFA with honors, U. Ariz., 1974, MA, 1977. Owner, artist Fountain Studio, Tucson, 1974—; art tchr. Sahuarita (Ariz.) Sch. Dist., 1974-80; adj. faculty mem. art edn. dept. U. Ariz., Tucson, 1981-82; art instr. Tucson Art Inst., 1983-91; artist, instr. Artists-in-Edn. program Ariz. Commn. on Arts, Phoenix, 1988-93; art instr. The Drawing Studio, Tucson, 2002—. Awards juror various arts orgns. including Southwestern League Fine Arts, Pima County Fair, Pima C.C., Santa Cruz Valley Art League, 1984—. Featured artist mag. article Art about Art, Watercolor mag., 1990. Visual Artists fellow Tucson-Pima Arts Coun., 1989; executed murals in children's rm. Tucson-Pima Main Libr., 1992; exhibited at U. Ariz./Joseph Gross Gallery, Tucson, 1993; represented in permanent collection Tucson Mus. Art. Mem. Nat. Watercolor Soc. (signature, Juror's award 1988), Western Fedn. Watercolor Socs. (signature, del. 1985-86), Ariz. Watercolor Soc. (signature), Watercolor West (signature). Avocations: botany, sewing, reading, computers. Home: 4425 N Tombolo Tr Tucson AZ 85745 E-mail: elf@fountainstudio.com.

FOUNTAIN, JOANNA FRASER, library consultant, business owner; b. Huauchinango, Puebla, Mexico, May 2, 1945; d. Thomas E. and Iona F.; m. Raymond L. Schroeder, 1985; 1 child, Stacey H. Chambers. BA, Syracuse U., 1966; MLS, U. Tex., 1970; PhD, Tex. Woman's U., 1982. Libr. Emerson Elem. Sch., Miami, Fla., 1967-69; libr., dir. Oak Springs br. Austin (Tex.) Pub. Libr., 1970-72; bilingual rsch. libr., Edn. Svc. Ctr., Region 13, Austin, 1972-76, tng. specialist, 1976-78; editorial dir. Voluntad Pubs., Austin, 1978-79; assoc. dir. for collection devel. Tex. So. U. Libr., Houston, 1981-83; dir. libr. tech. svcs. Southwestern U., Georgetown, Tex., 1983-90; adj. faculty U. Tex., Austin, 1990—; owner, sole propr. Bibliotechnics, Georgetown, 1990—; tech. svcs. libr. Austin Ind. Sch. Dist., 1995-98. Adj. faculty Western Md. Coll. (name now McDaniel Coll.), Westminster, 1998—. Author: Headings for Children's Materials, 1993, Hey, Miss! You Got A Book For Me?, 1978, 81, Subject Headings for School and Public Libraries, 1996, 3rd edit., 2001; contbr.: Getting Libraries the Credit They Deserve, 2002; editor, compiler bibliography CARTEL, 1973-76, Guide to Title VII Bilingual Bicultural Education Programs, 1973-75. Recipient Grad. fellowship Tex. Woman's U., 1979-81, Higher Edn. Act grant U. Tex. at Austin, 1969-70; named Most Amazing Libr. Tex. Computer Edn. Assn., 2003. Mem. ALA, Tex. Libr. Assn., OnLine Audiovisual Catalogers, Tex. Libr. Connection: Cataloging Focus Group (onvener). Presbyterian. Avocations: reading, handicrafts. Home and Office: 117 Village Park Dr Georgetown TX 78628 Office Fax: 512-869-1341. E-mail: fountain@thegateway.net., fountain@gslis.utexas.edu.

FOUNTAIN, KAREN SCHUELER, physician; b. Aberdeen, S.D., Oct. 14, 1947; BA, No. State Coll., Aberdeen, S.D., 1968; MD, U. Md., Balt., 1972. Diplomate Nat. Bd. Med. Examiners, Am. Bd. Radiology in Therapeutic Radiology. Intern Md. Gen. Hosp., Balt., 1972-73, resident in radiation oncology, 1973-74; fellow in radiation oncology Mayo Clinic, Rochester, Minn., 1974-76, cons. in oncology, 1976-81; clin. asst. prof. Columbia U., N.Y.C., 1981-83, residency program dir. dept. radiation oncology, 1981-93, clin. assoc. prof., 1983—2001. Mem. med. bd. Presbyn. Hosp., N.Y.C., 1983-86; faculty coun. mem. Columbia U., 1982-89; del. N.Y. State Radiological Soc., N.Y.C., 1987—. Fellow Am. Coll. Radiology (councilor 1999—), N.Y. Acad. Medicine; mem. Am. Soc. Therapeutic Radiology and Oncology, Radiol. Soc. N.Am., Am. Radium Soc., Am. Soc. Clin. Oncology, Am. Assn. for Women Radiologists (bd. dirs. 1995-96), N.Y. Roentgen Soc. (sect. chmn. 1989-90), N.Y. State Radiol. Soc. (bd. dirs. 1996-2002). Office: Long Island Radiation Therapy 1129 Northern Blvd Manhasset NY 11030

FOUNTAIN, LINDA KATHLEEN, health science association executive; b. Fowler, Kans., Apr. 30, 1954; d. Ralph Edward and Ruth Evelyn (Cornelson) Young; m. Andre Fountain. BS in Nursing, Cen. State U., Edmond, Okla., 1976. RN, Okla. Staff nurse med./surg. and coronary care unit Presbyn. Hosp., Oklahoma City, 1976-79; mgr. nursing Hillcrest Osteo. Hosp., Oklahoma City, 1979-80; staff nurse, mgr. Oklahoma U. Teaching Hosp., Oklahoma City, 1981-82; pres. New Life Programs, Oklahoma City, 1981-88, Nursing Entrepreneurs, Ltd., Oklahoma City, 1988—; mgr. Internat. Health Supply, Oklahoma City, 1988—. Coord. lactation cons. program State of Okla., 1981-98, new life car seat rental program at various hosps., 1983-92, also speaker Success Co., Oklahoma City, 1984—; owner Rainbows Overhead Graphic Media, Oklahoma City, 1984-91; speaker in field. Founder Praxis Coll., Oklahoma City, 1988. Named Mentor of Yr., Okla. Metroplex Childbirth Network, Oklahoma City, 1984; honored for vol. work with families and rescue after Oklahoma City bombing, U.S. Dept. Justice, 1995. Mem. Am. Nurses Assn., Internat. Lactation Cons. Assn., Internat. Platform Assn., Bodyworkers and Wellness Therapies Assn. Avocations: gemology, travel.

FOUNTAIN, ROBERT ALLEN, organizational management executive; b. Toledo, Nov. 19, 1947; s. Ellis Allen Fountain and Florence Delores (Hay) Stump; m. Mary Ann Buckmaster, Mar. 7, 1975 (div.); children: Donna, Meredith; m. Clare Bradshaw, Dec. 5, 1993. AS, State Tech. Inst., 1987; BS summa cum laude, Tusculum Coll., 1989. Quality controller Burroughs Corp. (UNISYS), Holland, Ohio, 1969-73, field service rep., 1973-78, internat. traffic analyst and specialist, 1978-81; gen. traffic mgr. Buckman Labs. Inc., Memphis, 1981-85, mgr. transp. and credit adminstrn., 1985-90, spl. projects mgr., 1990—. Past master of Tipton # 226 Free & Accepted Masons (F&AM). Author computer programs. With USN, 1967-69, 1st lt., adjutant 105th Bn., Tenessee State Guard, 2002—. Recipient Cert. honor Internat. Trade Mart, 1983, Acad. Excellence award State Tech. Inst.; named Hon. Harbor Master of Port of New Orleans. Mem. State Tech. Inst. Alumni Assn. (v.p. 1988-89), Tenn. Grand Lodge of F&AM, Am. Legion, Phi Theta Kappa (v.p. 1986-87). Republican. Avocations: painting, custom woodworking. Home: 301 Yarbrough Rd Covington TN 38019-4566 Office: Buckman Labs Inc 1256 N Mclean Blvd Memphis TN 38108-1241

FOUNTAIN, ROBERT ROY, JR., farmer, industrial executive, naval officer; b. Norfolk, Va., Jan. 25, 1932; s. Robert Roy and Hilda (Burton) F.; m. Elizabeth Whitmarsh Bean, June 4, 1955; children: Robert, Dorothy, Sally, Edwin. Student, U. Rochester, 1950-51; BS Engring. with distinction, U.S. Naval Acad., 1955. Commd. ensign U.S. Navy, 1955, advanced through grades to rear adm., 1980; nuclear engr. serving in destroyers, cruisers, and nuclear submarines; comdg. officer U.S.S. Sea Devil, 1970-74; comdr. Submarine Devel. Squadron 12, New London, Conn., 1976-78; comdr. U.S. Naval Forces Marianas, comdr. U.S. Naval Base Guam comdr. in chief Pacific rep. Guam and Trust Ter. Pacific Islands, 1979-81; dep. chief Naval Sea Sys. Command, ASW and Undersea Warfare Sys., Navy Dept., Washington, 1981-85; ret., 1985; dir. Offshore Sys. Marine Sys. divsn. Honeywell, Seattle, 1986-88; v.p. Honeywell Advanced Marine Sys. Operation, Mpls., 1988, San Diego, 1989, Arlington, Va., 1990-91; dir. tech. plans & resources Alliant Techsystems Inc., Arlington, Va., 1991-92. Chmn. bd. dirs. Rappahannock C.C.; presdl. elector, 1996; chmn. Westmoreland County Rep. Com. Decorated Legion of Merit (3), Def. Superior Service medal, Meritorious Service medal (2), Navy Commendation medal. Mem.: SAR, Assn. Preservation Va. Antiquities, Va. Small Grains Assn., No. Neck Hist. Soc. (pres.), Naval Submarine League, Mil. Officers Assn., Naval Acad. Alumni Assn., Am. Legion. Home: Stillwater 4750 Zacata Rd Montross VA 22520-3510 E-mail: bfountain@3n.net.

FOUNTAIN, RONALD GLENN, management consultant, finance/marketing executive, management educator; b. Mason City, Wash., Feb. 12, 1939; s. Aldine Shirah and Ella Maude (Fordham) F.; m. Ethel Joan Hightower, Aug. 22, 1968; children: John Hightower, Dana Leigh. AS, Ga. Southwestern Coll., 1959; BS, Valdosta State U., 1965; MBA, Case Western Res. U., 1983, ExecDrMgmt, 1999. V.p. nat. accounts Ctrl. Bancshares, Birmingham, Ala., 1973-74; cash control mgr. White Consol., Cleve., 1974-76, asst. treas., 1976-79, treas., dir. investor rels., 1979-82, v.p., treas., 1982-83, v.p. fin., treas., 1983-86; pres. Dix & Eaton, 1986-88; v.p. fin., CFO M.A. Hanna Co., Cleve., 1988-93; mng. prin. The Commonwealth Group, Cleve., 1993-04; sr. exec. v.p. Roulston & Co., Cleve., 1994-96; adv. dir. InfoSource, Harris Co., 1995-98; ptnr. The Parkland Group, 1996—; pres., CEO United Truck Fin. & Mktg., 1998—2001; prof. mgmt. Walsh U., North Canton, Ohio, 2003—. Adj. faculty Weatherhead Sch. Mgmt., exec. dir. profl. fellow program, 2000-02; bd. dirs. Dise & Co., Delta Sys. Inc. Trustee Notre Dame Coll., Cleve., 1984-90, Laurel Sch., 1986-90, Pub. Radio Sta. WCPN, 1990-93, MetroHealth Sys., Ctr. Families and Children; chmn. N.E. Hospice Study Com., 1989-93; bd. dirs. Jr. Achievement Cleve., 1982, Nat. Adoption Exch., Phila., 1983, Cleve. Edn. Fund, 1983-87. Mem.: Planning Forum (pres. 1992—94), Nat. Investor Rels. Inst. (pres. 1978—79), Assn. Corp. Growth, Fin. Execs. Inst. (membership chmn. 1983—84), Alumni Assn. Weatherhead Sch. Mgmt. (pres. 1985—88), Country Club, Union Club, Rowfant Club. Home: 2908 Paxton Rd Cleveland OH 44120-1824

FOUQUET, ANNE (JUDY FUQUA), musician, music educator; b. Wurtland, Ky., Oct. 2, 1938; d. John Paul and Garnet May (Gibson) Hillman; m. Warren Russell Fuqua, Dec. 21, 1961 (div. Dec., 1992); children: Bryan David, Faith Fuqua-Purvis, Paul Carroll. BMus., Am. Conservatory, Chgo., 1962; MMus., No. Ill. U., 1967; MFA, U. Iowa, 1971, D in Musical Arts, 1997. Organist various churches and denominations, Ill., 1960—; profl. accompanist Wis., Ill., 1970—; piano instr. Beloit (Wis.) Coll., 1972—; instr. Rockford (Ill.) Coll. Acad., 1991—; ind. instr. Keyboard Studio, Rockford, Ill., 1971—; clarinet player Rockford (Ill.) Park Band, 1995—. Composer: (song cycle soprano) Spinner of the Seasons, 1987, (suite for flute and hapsichord) Issar Suite, 1992; author: (play) Miracle of Love, 1982; (novel) If It Hadn't Been for Joel, 1980; (memoirs) Daddy Was a Farmer, Mother Was a City Girl, 1999; concert artist duo-piano with Robin Wooten, 1999, 2001; solo harpsichord recitals, 2001, 02. Mentor Helping One Student To Succeed, Structured Reading, Kishwaukee Sch., Rockford, Ill., 1997-98, adult lit. tutor READ Chatanooga, 1999—; interim organist, choirmaster Trinity Luth. Ch., 2000, Northminster Presbyn. Ch., Chattanooga, summer 2001; organist St Thaddeus Episcopal Ch., 2003—; Suzuki piano instr. Tenn. Valley area, 1998--; active concert artist, harpsichord, and piano. Nominee Best Classical Pianist Rockford Area Music Industry, 1996. Mem. Am. Guild of Organists, Music Tchrs. Nat. Assn., Ill. Music Tchrs. Assn. (adjudicator 1994-97), Kishwaukee Valley Concert Band, Suzuki Assn. of the Americas, Midwest Hist. Keyboard Soc., Mendelsson Club (founder composer showcase concerts Rockford 1991-97, bd. dirs. 1993-97), Am. Fedn. of Musicians, Tenn. Music Tchrs. Assn. (adjudicator 1999-2000), Sierra Club. Avocations: hiking, langs. (German, French, Hebrew), cooking, gardening, astronomy. Office: Cadek Conservatory Music U Tenn Chattanooga 724 Oak St Chattanooga TN 37403-2406

FOURER, ROBERT HAROLD, industrial engineering educator, consultant; b. Phila., Sept. 2, 1950; s. Herbert S. and Priscilla (Silver) F. BS in Math., MIT, 1972; MS in Ops. Rsch., MS in Stats., Stanford U., 1979, PhD in Ops. Rsch., 1980. Rsch. analyst Nat. Bur. Econ. Rsch., Cambridge, Mass., 1974-77; asst. prof. dept. indsl. engring. and mgmt. scis. Northwestern U., Evanston, Ill., 1979-85, assoc. prof., 1985-93, dept. chair, 1989-95, prof., 1993—. Vis. mem. tech. staff AT&T Bell Labs., Murray Hill, N.J., 1985-86, 95-96; cons. AT&T, Exxon, Goldman Sachs & Co., Keebler Co., Kraft Foods, Sears Roebuck & Co. Co-author: AMPL: A Modeling Language for Mathematical Programming, 1993; assoc. editor Mgmt. Sci., 1983—, Ops. Rsch., 1986—; contbr. articles to profl. jours. Recipient Computer Sci. Tech. Sect. prize, Ops. Rsch. Soc. Am., 1993; NSF grantee; John Simon Guggenheim Meml. Found. fellow, 2002. Mem. Inst. Indsl. Engrs., Soc. Indsl. and Applied Math, Inst. Ops. Rsch. and Mgmt. Scis. (chair Computer Sci. Tech. sect., 1996-97), Math. Programming Soc. (mem.-at-large, coun. 1994-97). Achievements include AMPL modeling lang. Office: Northwestern Univ Dept Ind Eng and Mgmt Scis 2145 Sheridan Rd Evanston IL 60208-3119 E-mail: 4er@iems.northwestern.edu.

FOURKAS, JOHN T. chemistry educator; Prof. dept. chemistry Boston Coll., Chestnut Hill, Mass. Chemistry grantee Camille and Henry Dreyfus Found., 1994; Cottrell scholar, 1997, Camille Dreyfus Tchr.-scholar, 1999; Sloan Rsch. fellow, 1998; named Beckman Young Investigator, 1997. Office: Boston College Dept Chemistry Chestnut Hill MA 02467 E-mail: fourkas@bc.edu.

FOURNARIS, THEODORE JAMES, lawyer; b. Lancaster, Pa., Apr. 27, 1946; s. James S. and Stella (Petrakis) F.; m. Ana M. Cartaya, Dec. 30, 1979; children: Ana Nicole, Alexander. BA, Franklin and Marshall Coll., 1968; MA, Boston U., 1971; JD, U. Miami, 1973. Bar: Fla. 1974, U.S. Dist. Ct. (so. dist.) Fla. 1986. Staff atty. FPC, Washington, 1974; assoc. Friedman, Britton & Stettin, Miami, Fla., 1975-76; ptnr. Carey Dwyer Cole Selwood & Bernard, Miami, 1977-82; pvt. practice Fournaris & Sanet, P.A., Miami, 1982—. With U.S. Army Intelligence, 1968-71. Mem. ATLA, Am. Coll. Legal Medicine, Fla. Acad. Trial Lawyers. Avocations: boating, travel. Office: 145 Almeria Ave Coral Gables FL 33134-6008

FOURNELLE, RAYMOND ALBERT, engineering educator; b. St. Louis, Dec. 9, 1941; s. August Carl and Adella Emma (Fleer) F. BS in Metall. Engring., U. Mo., 1964, MS in Metall. Engring., 1968, PhD in Metall. Engring., 1971. Registered profl. engr., Wis. Rsch. engr. Shell Oil Co., Wood River, Ill., 1964-66; rsch. assoc. Northwestern U., Evanston, Ill., 1971-72; asst. prof. Marquette U., Milw., 1972-78, assoc. prof., 1978-86, prof., 1986—; interim chairperson Dept. of Mech. and Indsl. Engring., 1998—2001. Contbr. articles to profl. jours. 1st lt. U.S. Army, 1964-66, Fed. Republic Germany. Rsch. grantee NSF, 1975, 79, 86; Fulbright fellow U. Stuttgart (Germany), 1983-84, 90-91, Alexander von Humboldt fellow, 1985-88, Mac-Planck-Forschungspreis, 1994, ASM Internat. fellow, 1996. Mem. ASME, ASTM, AAUP, ASM Internat. (bd. rev. 1981—), Minerals, Metals and Materials Soc. (com. mem.), Am. Ceramic Soc., Am. Soc. Engring. Edn. Achievements include development of theories and models for various solid state reactions in metals and alloys, including discontinuous precipitation, coarsening, and dissolution, diffusion induced grain boundary and liquid film migration. Home: 1129 N Jackson St Apt 1207 Milwaukee WI 53202-3290 Office: Marquette U Dept Mech/Indsl Engring PO Box 1881 Milwaukee WI 53201-1881 E-mail: raymond.fournelle@marquette.edu.

FOURNIER, DONALD JOSEPH, JR., mechanical engineer, consultant, educator; b. Norwich, Conn., July 27, 1962; s. Donald Joseph Sr. and Juanita L. (Malone) F.; children: Catherine, Jacqueline, Evan. BSME, U. Fla., 1986, MSME, 1988. Registered profl. engr., Fla.; cert. fire and explosion investigator, XL tribometrist. Rsch. engr. Combustion Lab. U. Fla., Gainesville, 1985-88; mech. engr. Envireco, Gainesville, 1987-88; project engr. Acurex Environ., Jefferson, Ark., 1988-94; rsch. engr. and cons. Gould, Lewis & Proctor, Gainesville, 1992-98; project engr. Combustion Tec, Orlando, Fla., 1995-96; pres. Spectrum Design and Cons., Orlando and Hattiesburg, 1996—; asst. prof. U. So. Miss., Hattiesburg, 1998-2000; project mgr. Zook, Moore & Assocs., Orlando, 2000—02; assoc. Kinley-Horn and Assocs., 2002—. Bd. dirs. Internat. Process Tech. Alliance, 1999. Contbr. articles on topics related to combustion, incineration, accident reconstrn., tng. and engring. to profl. jours.; patentee in field. U. Fla. grad. scholar's fund fellow, 1986. Mem. ASTM, ASME, NSPE, Soc. Automotive Engrs., Nat. Acad. Forensic Engrs., Nat. Assn. Fire Investigators, Nat. Fire Protection Assn., Am. Soc. Safety Engrs., Fla. Engring. Soc., Internat. Code Coun., Tau Beta Pi, Pi Tau Sigma. Achievements include identification of metal behavior in hazardous waste incineration; invention of OXY-Plus, oxygen-based reformer; work as court qualified engineer. Office: Kimley-Horn and Assoc Inc 3660 Maguire Blvd Ste 200 Orlando FL 32803 Office Fax: 407-894-4791. E-mail: don.fournier@kimley-horn.com.

FOURNIER, JOSEPH ANDRE ALPHONSE, nurse, social worker, psychotherapist; b. Norwich, Conn., Jan. 11, 1942; s. Alphonse J. and Eva Marie (Duhaime) F.; children from previous marriage: Elizabeth A., Michael J., Michelle D.; m. Lorinda Bonnette, Dec. 29, 1990; 1 child, Eva M. AA, U. Md., 1977; BSN, Med. Coll. Ga., 1981; MSW, U. Ga., 1987. RN; cert. employee assistance profl.; cert. in marriage and family therapy; bd. cert. diplomate in clin. social work. Sr. staff nurse, psychiatry Med. Coll. Ga., Augusta, 1982-94, psychotherapist employee, faculty assistance program, 1988-2000; mgr. homeless vets. program VA Med. Ctr., Augusta, 1987-88; psychotherapist Family Counseling Ctr. of CSRA, 1992-98; asst. clin. prof. psychiatry and health

behavior Med. Coll. Ga., Augusta, 1988—; pvt. practice, 2001—. Founder Comfort House, Inc. Recipient 79th Point of Light award Pres. George Bush, 1990, Vol. Svc. award Augusta chpt. ARC, 1995. Mem. Employee Assistance Profl. Assn., Ga. Soc. Clin. Soc. Work. Home: 214 Taft Dr Evans GA 30809-3037 E-mail: jfournier@mcgalumni.com. *When having to choose between being respected and being liked, always pick respect.*

FOURNIER, WALTER FRANK, real estate executive; b. Northampton, Mass., Feb. 26, 1912; s. Frank Napoleon and Marie Ann F.; m. Ella Mae Karrey, May 16, 1938; children: Margaret Irene, Walter Karrey. BS in Mktg., Boston U., 1939; postgrad., Anchorage Community Coll., 1963-64, Alaska Pacific U., 1964-65. Coin sales supt. Coca Cola Co., Springfield, Mass., 1946-48; sales coord. for pre-fabricated homes Sears Roebuck & Co., Western Mass., 1948-49; wholesale sales rep. Carl Wiseman Steel and Aluminum Co., Great Falls, Mont., 1949-51; supt. City Electric Co., Anchorage, 1951-52; owner, adminstr. Acme Electric Co., Anchorage, 1953-64; appraiser Gebhart & Peterson, Anchorage, 1964-68; broker, owner Walter F. Fournier & Assocs., Anchorage, 1968—. Pres. Alaska Mortgage Cons., Anchorage, 1968-69; owner Alaska Venture Capital, 1981—. Pres. Fairview Community Council, Anchorage, 1980-81. Served with U.S. Army, 1928-31, with USN, 1944-45, PTO. Recipient Spl. Recognition award HUD, 1967. Mem. Review Mortgage Underwriters, Inst. Bus. Appraisers, Internat. Soc. Financiers, Soc. Exchange Counselors (rep. 1970), Alaska Creative Real Estate Assn. (pres. 1978, Gold Pan award 1988), Alaska Million Plus Soc. (pres. 1983). Lodges: KC. Roman Catholic. Avocations: weight lifting, flying, fishing.

FOURQUET, JOSE A. federal agency administrator; Grad., Georgetown U.; MBA, Columbia U. Ops. officer CIA, 1988—94; mem. Secret Svc., 1997—98; v.p. emerging debt market sales group, v.p. office career devel. Goldman, Sachs and Co., 1996—2001; U.S. exec. dir. Inter-Am Devel. Bank, Washington, 2001—. Office: Inter-Am Devel Bank 1300 New York Ave NW Washington DC 20577

FOUSE, ANNA BETH, education educator; b. Austin, Tex., Jan. 11, 1947; d. Wilfred Davis and Doris Faye (Thomas) Chrisner; m. William Douglas Fouse; children: Douglas Lee, Alan Dale, Michael Wade, Robert Lynn. BS, U. Tex., Austin, 1967; MEd, Tex. Woman's U., 1973, PhD, 1976; various postgrad., Tex., 1980-81, 85-89. Cert. elem. tchr., spl. edn. tchr., Tex. 1st grade tchr. Austin Ind. Sch. Dist., 1967-68, Pasadena Ind. Sch. Dist., 1968-69; 3rd grade tchr. Harlingen (Tex.) Ind. Sch. Dist., 1969-70; homebound tchr. Irving (Tex.) Ind. Sch. Dist., 1970-71, tchr. emotionally disturbed, 1971-73; spl. edn. dir. Paris (Tex.) Ind. Sch. Dist., 1975-85, Region VII ESC, Kilgore, Tex., 1985-91; instr. U. Tex., Tyler, 1990-91, asst. prof., 1991-96, assoc. prof., 1996-98; ednl. cons., autism specialist, 1995—; pres. Ark-La-Tex Shredding Co., Inc., 2000—. Consulting editor bd. Acad. Therapy Jour., Austin, 1988-89. Author: Creating a Win-Win/EP for Students with Autism, 1996, 2nd edit., 1999; co-author: (tech. asst. manual) Assessment Manual for Appraisal Personnel, 1987, Guidelines for Speech Pathologists, 1987, Accreditation for Special Educators, 1988, A Primer About Attention Deficit Disorder, 1993, A Treasure Chest of Behavioral Strategies for Individuals with Autism, 1997. Chair Paris Regional Habilitation Ctr. Adv. Bd., 1980-85, High Priority Infant Transitional Svcs. Adv. Bd., Longview, Tex., 1989-90; chair mental retardation/DD adv. bd. Sabine Valley Ctr., 1997-99, mem. hubam rights and behavior mgmt. com., 2002-03; profl. adv. bd. so. region Attention Deficit Disorders Assn., 1990—; mem. adv. bd. Lamar County Alcohol and Drug Ctr., Paris, 1984-86; active Citizens Planning and Adv. Com., Tex. Dept. Mental Health and Mental Retardation, 1999—; bd. dirs., treas. Real Jobs for Youth, Inc., 2003. Mem. Autism Soc. of Ams. (vice chmn. 2002-2003), Tex. Coun. for Exceptional Children (v.p., pres., pres.-elect, bd. dirs.), Tex. Coun. of Adminstrs. in Spl. Edn., Assn. for Children with Learning Disabilities, Tex. Ednl. Diagnosticians Assn., Internat. Coun. for Exceptional Children, Phi Delta Kappa (pres. chpt. 1324 1991-93). Avocations: ceramics, crocheting, reading. Home and Office: 517 E Fairmont St Longview TX 75601-3804 E-mail: bfouse@worldnet.att.net.

FOUSE, DAVID JESSE, architect; b. Little Rock, Ark., Dec. 14, 1960; s. Richard Paul and Alice Mae (Aguilera) F. BS in Meteorology, Tex. A&M U., 1983; BS in Computer Sci., U. Tex. at San Antonio, 1987; MS in Computer Sci., Tex. A&M U. at Commerce, 1992. Assoc. software engr. E-Sys. Greenville (Tex.) Divsn., 1988—90, software engr., 1990—92, sr. software engr., 1992—95, E-Sys. Garland (Tex.) Divsn., 1995—97; software engrng. specialist Lockheed Martin Vought Sys., Grand Prairie, Tex., 1997—98; lead application developer Wyndham Internat., Dallas, 1998—2002; chief architect do IT solutions, Arlington, Tex., 2002—. Asst. coach YMCA Youth Soccer, Greenville, 1994-95. Mem. KC. Roman Catholic. Avocations: running, weight tng, volley ball. Home and Office: 1508 Stoneleigh Ct # 2050 Arlington TX 76011-2762

FOUST, CHARLES WILLIAM, judge; b. Bethlehem, Pa., May 27, 1952; s. Alan Shivers and Helen Elizabeth (Aigler) F.; m. Melissa A. Cherney, July 31, 1982; children: Kyle Cherney, James Terrell. BA, U. Wis., 1974, JD, 1978. Bar: Wis. Bar, U.S. Dist. Ct. (we. dist.) Wis. 1978. Asst. dist. atty. Dane County Dist. Atty.'s Office, Madison, 1979-82; asst. pub. defender State Pub. Defender's Office, Milw., 1982-83; assoc. Smoler & Albert SC, Madison, 1983-88; dist. atty. Dane County, Madison, 1988-97; judge Dane County Circuit Ct., Madison, 1997—, presiding judge criminal divsn., 2001—. Mem. govs. adv. bd., Dane County adv. bd. Treatment Alternatives Program; chair coordinated commun. response task force on domestic violence Dane County Commn. on Sensitive Crimes; mem. Dane County Jail/Space Needs, Dane County Long Range Jud. Planning; mem. Dane County Jury Selection, Wis. Jud. Coun. Commn. on Criminal Procedure; mem. Wis. Working Group on Sentencing and Corrections. Mem. State Bar Wis., Dane County Bar Assn. (bd. dirs. criminal law sect. 1985-89, chmn. 1985-89), Wis. Dist. Attys. Assn. (exec. bd., 1st v.p., com. on DNA evidence, dir. state cts. criminal benchbook com. 2000—, chmn. 2002—). Home: 2105 Madison St Madison WI 53711-2131 Office: Dane County Circuit Ct Br 14 210 Martin Luther King Jr Blvd Madison WI 53703 E-mail: william.foust@wicourts.gov.

FOUST, LEANNE, voice educator, vocalist; d. Leon and Dyanne Foust; m. Paul Ragan, Nov. 29, 2003. BME in Vocal Music Edn., Ark. State U., Jonesboro, 1990; postgrad., U. Iowa, 1994—. Cert. tchr. vocal music grades K-12 Ark. Bd. Edn., 1990. Vocal music tchr. Forrest City (Ark.) Sch. Sys., 1990—92; pvt. voice instr. Forrest City, 1990—94; tchg. asst. voice U. Iowa, Iowa City, 1995—99; adj. voice instr. Kirkwood C.C., Cedar Rapids, Iowa, 1999—. Dir.: (musical theater prodn.) Into the Woods; singer (soloist): (oratorio) LAllegro by Handel, Messiah by Handel, (choral work) Magnificat by Bach; singer: (lady billows) (opera) Albert Herring; singer: (sister angelica) Sister Angelica by Puccini; singer: (marchellina) Marriage of Figaro by Mozart; singer: (monica) The Medium by Menotti; singer: (lucy) The Telephone by Menotti; singer: (the angel) (choral work) Laud to the Nativity by Respighi; singer: (soloist with the omaha chamber singers) (choir and orchestra) In the Beginning by Copland; singer: (soloist) (choral and orchestral) King David by Honnegger. ACT scholar, Ark. State U., 1986—90. Mem.: Sigma Alpha Iota - Iowa City Alumnae Chpt., Sigma Alpha Iota - Epsilon Gamma Chpt. (life; pres. 1988—90, Sword of Honor 1990, Honors Cert. 1990). Office: Kirkwood Community College Cedar Rapids IA Personal E-mail: singerflf@hotmail.com.

FOUST, ROBERT SCHMERTZ, senior policy advisor; b. New Holland, Pa., Jan. 20, 1941; s. Wilson Arbogast and Elizabeth (Schmertz) F. BA in Polit. Sci., Upsala Coll., 1964; MA in Internat. Rels., Lehigh U., 1971. Asst. dir. admissions Upsala Coll., East Orange, N.J., 1965-69; legis. asst. Office of Senator Claiborne Pell, Washington, 1970-89; cons. Indochinese Cmty. Ctr., Washington, 1990-91; sr. policy adv. Office of Senator Kent Conrad, Washington, 1991—. Panelist Nat. Edn. Assn. Safety Summit, L.A., 1995. Named Outstanding Young Men of Am., Jaycees, 1973; recipient U.S. Coast Guard commendation, U.S. Dept. Veterans Affairs commendation. Mem.: Asia Soc., The Army and Navy Club. Office: 530 Hart Senate Office Bldg Washington DC 20510-0001 E-mail: jurongsq@aol.com.

FOUT, LARRY ROY, physician; b. Piqua, Ohio, Feb. 15, 1930; s. Earl S. and Marilyn M. (Bright) F.; m. Jane Marie Collins, Jan. 29, 1949; children: Jill, Teresa. BS, Ohio No. U., 1955; MD, Ohio State U., 1959; MPH, Tulane U., 1969. Intern Grant Hosp., Columbus, Ohio, 1959-60; resident Tulane Univ., New Orleans, 1968-71, Naval Aerospace Med. Ctr., Pensacola, Fla., 1968-71; commd. capt. M.C., U.S. Navy, 1960, served in various locations, 1960-83; family practice physician Defiance (Ohio) Clinic, 1990—. Contbr. articles to med. jours. Fellow Am. Acad. Family Physicians, Am. Coll. Preventive Medicine, Aerospace Med. Assn.; mem. AMA, ACP, APHA, Am. Soc. Clin. Hypnosis. Roman Catholic. Avocations: tennis, golf, fishing. Office: Defiance Clinic 1400 E 2nd St Ste 2 Defiance OH 43512-2494

FOUT, MARY JANE, librarian, educator; b. East St. Louis, Oct. 26, 1937; d. William Pomeroy and Phebe Georgia (Anderson) Eaton; m. John Calvin Fout, Feb. 26, 1960 (div. May 1973); children: Justine Alyss, Elizabeth, John Eric. BA in German and History, U. Omaha, 1959, MA in History, 1963; M of Libr. and Info. Sci., U. Calif., Berkeley, 1977. Cert. tchr., Nebr., N.Y., Calif. Tchr. Indian Hills Jr. H.S., Omaha, 1959-60, Tech. Jr. High Sch., Omaha, 1962-64, Heidelberg Jr. H.S., Germany, 1964-65; archivist intern Social Welfare History Archives, U. Minn., Mpls., 1965-67; lectr. history U. Nebr., Omaha, 1967-68; interlibr. loan libr. Bard Coll., Annandale-on-Hudson, N.Y., 1971-73; career ctr./attendance clk. Armijo High Sch., Fairfield, Calif., 1974-76, career ctr./English Libr. libr., 1976-82, tchr. fgn. lang. and pub. svc., 1982-89, libr., 1989—. Summer youth employment tng. program counselor, summers 1980—. Contbg. author: Social Welfare History archives Collection, 1972. Mem. AAUW (past pres.), World Affairs Coun. No. Calif., Calif. Media Libr. Educators Assn. (charter), Am. Field Svc. (dist. rep., past pres. chpt., Pat Lawrence award 1990), Overseas Brats, Commonwealth Club, Alpha Xi Delta, Delta Kappa Gamma. Democrat. Avocations: reading murder mysteries, spectator sports, travel.

FOUTCH, MICHAEL JAMES, actor, dancer, lighting designer, producer; b. Dallas, Dec. 18, 1951; s. G.E. and Mary Muriel (Stanphill) F. BFA in Theatre, So. Meth. U., 1973. Cert. tchr. theatre and speech. Tech. dir. Eastfield Theatre, Dallas, 1973-77; dancer San Antonio Ballet, 1982, Dallas Concert Ballet, 1982-83; gen. ptnr. Stanphill Energy Partnership, Dallas, 1990-91; exec. dir. The Dallas Gilbert and Sullivan Soc., 1991-92. Lighting designer Dallas Repertory Theatre, 1975, Die Fledermaus, 1999; dancer TV Project, Shreveport, La., 1981; tchr. various ballet cos., Tex., La., 1983—; hist. dance study Early Dance Inst., Balt., 1988. Appeared in play The Mousetrap, 1976, ballets Giselle, 1980, Les Sylphides, 1982, The Nutcracker, 1983, 84, 92, 93, 94, 97, Cinderella, 1983, Swan Lake, 1983, Romeo and Juliet, 1984, dancer in operas Orfeo, 1986, Andrea Chenier, 1987, Iolanthe, 1989. Mem.: U.S. Inst. for Theatre Tech., Mensa. Avocations: tennis, music, movies. Office: Po Box 720951 Dallas TX 75372 E-mail: michaelfoutch@yahoo.com.

FOUTS, ELIZABETH BROWNE, psychologist, metals company executive; b. New Orleans, July 5, 1927; d. Donovan Clarence and Mathilde Elizabeth (Hanna) B.; m. James Fremont Fouts, June 19, 1948; children: Elizabeth, Donovan, Alan, James. BA, Tulane U., 1948; MS, N.E. La. U., 1973, postgrad., 1984. Cert. sch. psychologist, La.; cert. reality therapist, La. Instr. spl. edn., psychol. cons. N.E. La. U., Monroe, 1971-73; sch. psychologist Ouachita Parish Schs., Monroe, 1973-87; sec.-treas. Fremont Corp., Monroe, 1967—, Auric Metals Corp., Salt Lake City, 1975-99. Dir. La Fonda Hotel, Santa Fe, N.Mex., 1993—; pres. Sunbelt Reality Therapist, 1989-90. Exec. bd. Episc. Diocese Western La., 1986-87, 99-2002, commn. ministry, 1987-94; res. family resource ctr. N.E. La. U., 1993-94; bd. dirs. Assn. for Retarded Citizens, Monroe, 1982-88, treas., 1984, pres., 1987. Named Outstanding Sch. Psychologist, State of La., 1987. Mem. Nat. Assn. Sch. Psychologists, La. Sch. Psychologists Assn. (pres. 1978-79, Outstanding Woman Sch. Psychologist 1984, newsletter editor 1988-93). Avocations: biking, walking, swimming. Home: PO Box 7070 Monroe LA 71211-7070 Office: 4002 Bon Aire Dr Monroe LA 71203-3015

FOUTS, JAMES FREMONT, mining company executive; b. Port Arthur, Tex., June 3, 1918; s. Horace Arthur and Willie E. (Edwards) F.; m. Elizabeth Hanna Browne, June 19, 1948; children: Elizabeth, Donovan, Alan, James. BChemE, Tex. A&M U., 1940. Div. supt. Baroid divsn. N.L. Industries, U.S. Rocky Mountain area and Can., 1948-60; pres. Riley-Utah Co., Salt Lake City, 1960-67, Fremont Corp., Monroe, La., 1967—, Auric Metals Corp., Salt Lake City, 1972-2000. Bd. dirs. La Fonda Hotel, Santa Fe, High Plains Natural Gas Co., Canadian, Tex. Hon. asst. sec. of State of La. Served to lt. col. arty U.S. Army, 1942-46. Mem. Wyo. Geol. Assn. (v.p. 1958), Rocky Mountain Oil & Gas Assn. (bd. dirs. 1959), Res. Officers Assn. Wyo. (pres. 1948), Am. Assn. Petroleum Geologists, Internat. Geol. Assn., Mont. Geol. Assn., Ind. Petroleum Producers Assn. Clubs: Univ. Lodges: Elks. Republican. Episcopalian. Home: 4002 Bon Aire Dr Monroe LA 71203-3015 Office: Fremont Corp PO Box 7070 Monroe LA 71211-7070

FOWLER, ALAN BICKSLER, retired physicist; b. Denver, Oct. 15, 1928; s. Alan Bruce and Minnie Edna (Bicksler) F.; m. Kathleen Teresa Devlin, Sept. 4, 1950; children: Stephen B., Susan Fowler-Finn, Andrew A., Sarah A. BS, Rensselaer Poly. Inst., 1951, MS, 1952; PhD, Harvard U., 1958. Rsch. staff mem. Raytheon Mfg. Co., Rsch. Div., Waltham, Mass., 1953-56, IBM Rsch. Div., Yorktown Heights, N.Y., 1958-83; IBM fellow Yorktown Heights, N.Y., 1983-93; IBM fellow emeritus, 1993—. With U.S. Army, 1946-48, 1st lt. Signal Corps, 1952-53. Recipient John Price Wetherill medal Franklin Inst., 1981, Alexander von Humboldt Preistraeger, 1982, David Sarnoff medal IEEE, 1987, Buckley prize Am. Phys. Soc., 1988. Mem.: NAE, NAS, IEEE, Royal Soc. of London (fgn.), Am. Acad. Arts and Scis., Am. Phys. Soc. Office: IBM T J Watson Rsch Ctr PO Box 218 Yorktown Heights NY 10598-0218

FOWLER, BETTY JANMAE, dance company director, editor; b. Chgo., May 23, 1925; d. Harry and Mary (Jacques) Markin; 1 child, Sherry Mareth Connors. Student, Art Inst. Chgo., 1937-39, Stratton Bus. Coll., Chgo., 1942-43, Columbia U., 1945-47; BA, Ea. Wash. U., 1984. Cert. metabolic technician Internat. Health Inst. Mem. pub. rels. dept. Girl Scouts U.S.A., N.Y.C., 1961-63; adminstrv. asst. to editor-in-chief Scholastic Mags., N.Y.C., 1963-68; adminstrv. dir. Leonard Fowler Dancers, Fowler Sch. Classical Ballet, Inc., N.Y.C., 1959-78, tchr. ballet, 1959-61; pvt. practice Ecol. Lifestyle Advisor, 1980—. Instr. Spokane Falls Community Coll., 1978. Founder Safe Water Coalition Wash. State, 1988. Mem. Kiwanis (editor bulletin weekly publ., adminstrv. sec.) Avocations: travel, reading. Office: Safe Water Coalition Washington State 5615 W Lyons Ct Spokane WA 99208-3777

FOWLER, BRUCE ANDREW, toxicologist, researcher; b. Seattle, Dec. 28, 1945; s. Andrew and Dolores Yvonne F.; children from previous marriage: Glenn Andrew, Randall Bruce. BS in Fisheries, U. Wash., 1968; PhD in Pathology, U. Oreg., 1972. From staff fellow to head metal toxicology Nat. Inst. Environ. Health Scis., Research Triangle Park, NC, 1972—86, head metal toxicology, 1986—87; dir. toxicology program U. Md., 1987—2001; sr. rsch. advisor Agy. for Toxic Substances and Disease Registry, Atlanta, 2002—03, asst. dir. for sci., divsn. toxicology, 2003—. Prof. pathology U. Md. Med. Sch., 1987—2001, prof. epidemiology and toxicology, 2001—03, dir. lab. of cellular and molecular toxicology dept. of epidemiology and preventive medicine, 2001—03; dir. office collaborative studies on adaptive responses estuarine species U. Md., 1988—2001; Meyer Bodansky lectr. Dept. Pathology, U. Tex. Med. Br., Galveston; adj. assoc. prof. U. N.C.; temporary adv. WHO; work group mem. Internat. Agy. Rsch. Against Cancer; mem. Internat. Commn. Occupl. Health; mem., chmn. Sci. Com. on Toxicology of Metals; mem. Md. Gov.'s Coun. on Toxic Substances, 1988—93, chmn., 1990—93, Dahlem Workshop on Mechanisms of Cell Injury: Implications for Human Health, Berlin, 1985; mem. toxicology info. program com. on toxicology; chmn. com. on measuring lead in critical populations; mem. com. on women in sci. and engrng., com. on biologic markers in urologic toxicology NAS/NRC, 1989—93, com. on evaluation on viability of augmenting potable water supplies with reclaimed water, 1996—97, subcom. on arsenic in drinking water, 1997; co-chmn. N.Y. Acad. Scis. Conf. on Mechanisms of Chem.-Induced Porphyrinopathies, Rye, NY; Swedish Med. Rsch. Coun. vis. prof. Karolinska Inst., 1994—95; Colgate-Palmolive vis. prof. U. Wash., 1998—99; mem. Fulbright scholarship rev. com., Scandinavia, 1999—2001, chair, Scandinavia, 2000—01; mem. nat. metals assessment panel sci. adv. bd. U.S. EPA, 2002—; mem. expert panel on reproductive and devel. toxicity of ethylene glycol and propylene glycol Nat. Toxicology Program-Ctr. Evaluation of Risks to Human Reproduction, 2003—. Editor: Biological and Environmental Effects of Arsenic, 1983, Mechanisms of Cell Injury: Implications for Human Health; co-editor: Mechanisms of Chemical Induced Porphyrinopathies; editl. bd. Chemico-Biol. Interactions, 1980-85, Environ. Health Perspectives, 1981-97, Toxicology and Applied Pharmacology, 1985-96, Jour. Toxicology and Environ. Health, 1986-97, Internat. Archives of Environ. Health, 1986—, Renal Failure, 1988—, Internat. Jour. Occupl. and Environ. Health, 1994-96, Jour. Biochem. and Molecular Toxicology, 2000—; contbr. articles to profl. jours., chpts. to books. Rsch. fellow Japanese Soc. Promotion of Sci., 1990; Fulbright scholar Karolinska Inst., 1994. Fellow Acad. Toxicol. Scis.; mem. AAAS (recruitment and screening panel ct. apptd. sci. experts project 2000—), Am. Inst. Biol. Scis., Am. Soc. Pharmacology and Exptl. Therapeutics, Soc. Toxicology (councilor mechanisms of toxicity sect., pres. metals specialty sect. 1996, councilor nat. capitol area regional chpt. 1994-95, v.p. in-vitro specialty sect. 2001-02, pres. in-vitro specialty sect. 2003—), Am. Coll. Toxicology (councilor 1995-98), Soc. Occupl. and Environ. Health (councilor 1988, v.p. 1993), Fulbright Assn., N.Y. Acad. Sci., Internat. Commn. Occupl. Health (chmn. scientific com. toxicology of metals 1996-2003), Profl. Assn. Diving Instrs., Sigma Xi. Office: ATSDR MSE-29 1600 Clifton Rd NE Atlanta GA 30333 E-mail: drtox@earthlink.net., bxf9@cdc.gov.

FOWLER, CHARLES ALBERT, electronics engineer; b. Centralia, Ill., Dec. 17, 1920; s. Clarence J. and Bess (Maxwell) F.; m. Kathryn Elizabeth Grimes, Oct. 23, 1943; children: Patricia Ann Paul, Mary Catherine Leathem. BS in Engrng. Physics, U. Ill., 1942. Mem. staff radiation lab. MIT, 1942-45; head radar systems dept. Airborne Instruments Lab., Deer Park, N.Y., 1946-66; dep. dir. (tactical warfare) def. research and engrng. Dept. Def., 1966-70; v.p., mgr. equipment devel. labs. Raytheon Co., Sudbury, Mass., 1970-76; sr. v.p., gen. mgr. Bedford (Mass.) ops. Mitre Corp., 1976-85; pres C.A. Fowler Assocs., 1986—. Mem. sci. adv. com. Def. Intelligence Agy., 1971—2000, chmn. sci. adv. com., 1976—82; mem. Air Force Sci. Adv. Bd., 1971—77, Def. Sci. Bd., 1972—98, chmn., 1984—88, vice chmn., 1988—90. Contbr. articles in field. Mem. East Norwich Sch. Bd., 1955-61, East Norwich Library Bd., 1956-62. Fellow IEEE, AAAS, AIAA; mem. Nat. Acad. Engring. Office: 15 Woodberry Rd Sudbury MA 01776-2227 Office Fax: 978-443-7509.

FOWLER, CHARLES ALLISON EUGENE, retired architect, engineer; b. Halifax, N.S., Can., Jan. 24, 1921; s. Charles Allison and Mildred (Crosby) F.; m. Dorothy Christine Graham, Aug. 30, 1947; children: Graham Allison, Beverly Anne. BSc, Dalhousie U., 1942; B in Engring., McGill U., 1944; BArch., U. Man., 1948; DEng (hon.), Tech. U. of Nova Scotia, 1975. With C.A. Fowler, Bauld & Mitchell, Ltd. (and predecessor firms), Halifax, 1946-80, sr. ptnr., 1950-70, pres., 1970-80, chmn., 1980-81; pres. C.A. Fowler & Co., 1950-70, 81-95; ret., 1995. Prin. works include Miners Mus., Glace Bay, N.S., Dalhousie U. Fine Arts Ctr., 1970, univ. ctr. Acadia U., Acad. Ctr. at Mt. St. Vincent U., Halifax Law Cts., Canadian Martyrs Ch., Can. Permanent Bldg. Hfx., Halifax Metro Ctr., Stadacona Hosp., Victoria Gen. Hosp., Centre 200, Sydney, N.S. Past chmn. bd. dirs. N.S. Coll. Art and Design. With Can. Army, 1943-46. Fellow AIA (hon.), Royal Archtl. Inst. Can. (pres. 1965), Can. Soc. for Civil Engring.; mem. Engring. Inst. Can. (life). Mem. United Ch. Home: 2 Hall's Rd Halifax NS Canada B3P 1P3

FOWLER, CHUCK, former state legislator; b. Dec. 21, 1939; m. Debra Fowler; 2 children. Grad. H.S. Product mgr. 3M Co.; mem. Minn. State Senate, 2000—02, vice chair taxes com., mem. edn. com., mem. agr., gen. legislation and vets. affairs com., mem. higher edn. budget divsn. com., mem. income and sales tax budget divsn. com., state and local govt. ops. com. Home: 710 N State St Fairmont MN 56031

FOWLER, CONRAD MURPHREE, retired manufacturing company executive; b. Montevallo, Ala., Sept. 17, 1918; s. Luther J. and Elsie (Murphree) F.; m. Virginia Evelyn Mott, June 15, 1945; children: Conrad, Randolph. BS, U. Ala., 1941, JD, 1948. Bar: Ala. 1948. Practiced in, Columbiana, 1948-53; mem. firm Ellis and Fowler, 1948-53; dist. atty. 18th Jud. Circuit Ala., 1953-59; probate judge, chmn. Shelby County Commn. Shelby County Ct., Columbiana, 1959-77; v.p. pub. affairs West Point-Pepperell, Inc., 1977-89, ret., 1989. Mem. Presdl. Adv. Commn. on Intergovtl. Relations, 1970-77 Mem. Ala. Dem. Exec. Com., 1966-77; chmn. Ala. Constl. Commn., 1970-76; bd. dirs. Associated Industries Ala., 1979-87, Pub. Affairs Coun., 1979-89; v.p. Am. Lung Assn., 1980-82, pres., 1982-83; mem. coun. Nat. Mcpl. League, 1976-82; vice chmn. Pub. Affairs Coun., 1987-89; bd. dirs. Ga. Bus. Coun., 1987-89. Col. USMCR, 1941-78. Decorated Silver Star with gold star, Purple Heart (2); named to Ala. Acad. Honor, 1981; recipient William Crawford Gorgas award Ala. Med. Assn., 1985; Rotary Paul Harris fellow, 1997; Kiwanis George F. Hixson fellow, 1999. Mem.: West Ala. Ret. Officers Club (pres. 2000—01), Probate Judges Assn. Ala. (pres. 1968—69), Assn. County Commrs. Ala. (pres. 1970—71), Nat. Assn. Counties (pres. 1969—70), Murphree Geneal. Assn. (pres. 1990—91), U. Ala. Nat. Alumni Assn. (pres. 1969, Alumnus of Yr. 1992), Tuscaloosa Exch. Club. Home: 1605 Bellingrath Dr Tuscaloosa AL 35406-2020

FOWLER, DANIEL L.T. legal services executive; b. Portland, Maine, Mar. 19, 1972; BA in Polit. Sci., Trinity U., Sioux Falls, S.D.; Paralegal Cert., Blackstone Sch. Law, Dallas. Cert. consumer credit counselor; cert. housing counselor HUD. Paralegal Law Offices of Carl R. Trynor, Portland, Maine, 1995-96; case mgr. Consumer Credit Counseling Svcs., South Portland, Maine, 1996-98; collections mgr. Ocean Cmtys. FCU, Biddeford, Maine, 1998-2000; owner Danter Svcs., Old Orchard Beach, Maine, 2000—. Author: Fowler's Spending Ledger: A Daily Budgeting Tool. Mem. Maine Libr. Commn., Resp. Senatorial Com.; mem. South Portland Planing Bd.; vice chmn. Old Orchard Beach Commn., chmn.; vice chmn. Main State Cultural Affairs Coun.; dedimus justice; mem. adv. bd. S. Portland Libr.; chmn. Your Voice Your Vote PAC. Mem. Nat. Paralegal Assn., Am. Fgn. Svcs. Assn. (assoc.), World Affairs Coun. Maine, Lions Club (officer). Office: PO Box 237 Old Orchard Beach ME 04064

FOWLER, DAVID LUCAS, corporate lawyer; b. Heidelberg, Germany, Sept. 26, 1952; s. James Daniel and Nannie Romay (Lucas) F.; m. Cynthia Lou Smith, Aug. 19, 1989. BS, U.S. Mil. Acad., 1974; JD, Georgetown U., 1981. Bar: N.J. 1982, Calif. 1990, U.S. Ct. Fed. Claims 1990, U.S. Dist. Ct. (cen. dist.) Calif. 1990. 2d lt. U.S. Army, 1974, advanced through grades to maj., infantry platoon leader, 1975-76, asst. protocol officer, 1976-77, aide-de-campe U.S. comdr., 1977—78; minority augmentation recruit officer U.S. Mil. Acad., 1978; chief adminstrv. law sect. U.S. Army Tng. Ctr., Ft. Dix, N.J., 1983-86; command judge advocate U.S. Army Field Sta., Sinop, Turkey, 1985-86; govt. contracts trial atty. U.S. Army Legal Svcs. Agy., Falls Church, Va., 1986-89; resigned U.S. Army, 1989; corp. staff counsel Hughes Aircraft Co., L.A., 1989-94, sr. sgt. counsel Electro-Optical Sys. El Segundo, Calif., 1994-95, asst. gen. counsel Arlington, Va., 1996-97; v.p., dep. gen. counsel Raytheon Sys. Co., Arlington, 1998-99; v.p. legal Raytheon Washington Ops., 1999—; v.p., dep. gen. counsel Raytheon Co., Arlington, 2000—; v.p., gen. counsel, sec. Raytheon Internat. Inc., Arlington, 2000—. Mem. Army Sci. Bd., Bd. Contract Appeals Bar Assn. (bd. govs.). Avocations: reading, weightlifting, golf. Office: Raytheon Co 1100 Wilson Blvd Ste 2000 Arlington VA 22209-2297

FOWLER, DAVID THOMAS, lawyer; b. Flushing, N.Y., June 16, 1955; s. David Thomas Jr. and Ellen (McGrath) F.; m. Margaret Anne Conway, Apr. 8, 1979; children: Matthew, Elizabeth, Timothy, Jacqueline. BA cum laude, St. John's U., 1977, JD, 1980. Bar: N.Y. 1981, U.S. Dist. Ct. (ea. and so. dists.) N.Y. 1981. Law clk. Richard J. Finamore, Great Neck, N.Y., 1979-80, assoc., 1981-83, Newman, Schlau, N.Y.C., 1983-86, ptnr., 1986-88; assoc. McCabe & Cozzens, Mineola, N.Y., 1988-92, ptnr., 1992-97, McCabe, Collins, McGeough & Fowler, LLP, Mineola, 1998—. Trustee Floral Park (N.Y.) Bellerose Sch. Dist., 1997—, v.p., 2000—; mem. bd. dirs. Brehon Law Soc. Nassau County, 2002-; co-v.p. L.I. chpt. Adoptive Parents Com., Bellmore, N.Y., 1996-98; treas., bd. dirs. Floral Park Little League, 1993-99, treas., 1994-97; mgr. baseball 1991-94, 2000—, softball, 1999-2000, 03-; coord. T-Ball program 1993-98. Recipient Disting. Svc. award L.I. chpt. Adoptive Parents Com., 1996, Ken Kramer award Floral Park Little League, 1998. Mem. Brehon Law Soc. of Nassau County (bd. dirs. 2002—), Nassau-Suffolk Trial Lawyers Assn., Nassau Bar Assn., Southside Civic Assn., Floral Park Indians Athletic Club (coord. basketball divsn. 1993—, coord. soccer divsn. 1995-97, basketball coach 1992—, soccer coach 1994—). Avocations: golf, softball, reading, basketball, travel. Home: 43 Oak St Floral Park NY 11001-3409 Office: McCabe Collins McGeough Fowler LLP 114 Old Country Rd Mineola NY 11501-4400 E-mail: dfowler@mcmf4law@aol.com.

FOWLER, DAVID WAYNE, architectural engineering educator; b. Sabinal, Tex., Apr. 25, 1937; s. Otis Lindley and Sadie Gertrude (Cox) F.; m. Maxine Yvonne Thomson, Mar. 31, 1961; children: Teresa, Leah. BS in Archtl.

Engring., U. Tex., 1960; MS, U. Tex., Austin, 1962; PhD in Civil Engring., U. Colo., 1965. Design engr. W.C. Cotten (Cons. Engr.), Austin, Tex., 1961-62; asst. prof. archtl. engring. U. Tex., Austin, 1964-69, assoc. prof., 1969-75, prof., 1975—, Taylor prof., 1981—, dir. Ctr. Aggregates Rsch., 1992—, Joe J. King chair, 1998—. Vis. prof. Nihon U., Japan, 1981, Chulalongkorn U., Thailand, 2001; bd. dirs. Univ. Fed. Credit Union, 1976-84; pres. Internat. Congress on Polymers in Concrete, 1981-87, bd. dirs. Univ. Coop, 2000—. Editor procs. 2d Internat. Congress on Polymers in Concrete, 1978, 2001; contbr. articles to profl. jours. Recipient Teaching award Gen. Dynamics, 1975, Teaching award Amoco Found., 1978, Disting. Engring. Alumnus award U. Colo., 1993, Owen Nutt award ICPIC, 1995, Joe J. King Profl. Achievement award, 2000, Claude Hocott Rsch. award, 2002; named to Acad/ Disting. Tchrs., 2000; cited by Engring.-News Record, 1975, Concrete Repair, 1995; Ford Found. faculty devel. grantee, 1962-64. Fellow ASCE (pres. Austin br. 1976-77), Am. Concrete Inst. (Delmar L. Bloem award 1985, bd. dirs. 1993-96, Robert Philleo award 2003); mem. NAE, Concrete Rsch. Coun. (chmn. 1996-2002), Concrete Rsch. Found. (chmn. 2000-2001), Am. Soc. Engring. Edn. (chmn. archtl. engring. divsn. 1971-72), Tex. Soc. Profl. Engrs. (bd. dirs. Travis chpt. 1968), Russian Acad. Engring. (hon.), Tau Beta Pi, Chi Epsilon. Mem. Ch. of Christ. Home: 612 Brookhaven Trl Austin TX 78746-5455 Office: Univ Tex ECJ 5208 Archtl Engring Group Austin TX 78712 Personal E-mail: dwfowlerpe@austin.rr.com. Business E-Mail: dwf@mail.utexas.edu.

FOWLER, DONA SYLVIA B. trade union executive; b. Paducah, Ky. d. Charles Andrew Fowler and Helen Frances Sherrill; m. Howard Kaminsky, 1965 (div. 1967). BA in English, U. Calif., Berkeley; grad., Christ Ch., Oxford, 1992; postgrad., Emmanuel Coll., Cambridge, 1993. Copy editor ASHRAE, N.Y.C., 1963; contr. Columbia U., 1966; from asst. editor to assoc. editor, prodn. editor Scholastic Mags., N.Y.C., 1967-75; editor-in-chief Frontpage, local rep. Newspaper Guild N.Y., CWA, AFL-CIO, Can. Labor Conf., 1975—, chmn. local rep. guild, 1997—. Pres. Hoyt Hall. U. Calif. Alumni scholar, Genevieve McEnerney scholar, Students Coop. Assn. scholar. Mem. Internat. Labor Comm. Assn. (Best Headline award 1979, 1st award for unique performance 1986, 2d award for best feature 2001, 3d award for best front page 2002), Labor Press Coun. Met. N.Y. (award of merit for best news writing 1977, 80, best writing 1987, 1st award best writing, 1992, 1st award for best single article 1992, 1st award unique performance 1992, 3d award best writing 1994, 1st best feature writing 2001, 2d award best feature writing 2001, Mary Heaton VORSE award 2001, 1st award unique performance 2002, Comms. Workers of Am. 3d pl. gen. excellence 2000, 1st award best news writing 2002), Newspaper Guild N.Y. (chmn. scholastic unit 1967-75, chmn. rep. assembly, exec. com. 1971-75), Tower and Flame, Mask and Dagger, Thalia. Democrat. Avocations: study of medieval english history, non-smokers rights, animal rights activist, environmental issues, native americans' rights. Office: Newspaper Guild NY 1501 Broadway Ste 708 New York NY 10036-5501

FOWLER, DONALD RAYMOND, retired lawyer, educator; b. Raton, N.Mex., June 2, 1926; s. Homer F. and Grace B. (Honeyfield) F.; m. Anna M. Averyt, Feb. 6, 1960; children: Mark D., Kelly A. BA, U. N.Mex., 1950; JD, 1951; MA, Claremont Grad. Sch., 1979, PhD, 1983. Bar: N.Mex. 1951, Calif. 1964, U.S. Supreme Ct. 1980. Atty. AEC, Los Alamos and Albuquerque, 1951-61, chief counsel Nev. Ops., 1962-63; pvt. practice, Albuquerque, 1961-62; asst., then dep. staff counsel Calif. Inst. Tech., Pasadena, 1963-72, staff counsel, 1972-75, gen. counsel, 1975-90; lectr. exec. mgmt. program Claremont Grad. Sch., Calif., 1981-84. Contbr. articles to profl. publs. Served with USAAF, 1944-46. Recipient NASA Pub. Svc. award, 1981. Mem. Calif. State Bar Assn., Fed. Bar Assn., Nat. Assn. Coll. and Univ. Attys. (exec. bd. 1979-82, 84-90, chmn. publs. com. 1982-84, pres. 1987-88, chmn. nominations com. 1988-89, chmn. honors and awards com. 1989-90, Life Mem. award 1991, Disting. Svc. award 1992), Calif. Assn. for Rsch. in Astronomy (sec. 1985-90).

FOWLER, FLORA DAUN, retired lawyer; b. Washington, Aug. 11, 1923; d. Herman Hartwell and Flora Elizabeth (Adams) Sanford; m. Kenneth Leo Fowler, Aug. 22, 1941; children: Kenneth Jr., Michael, Kathleen, Daun, Jonathan, Colin, Kevin, James, Shawn, Maureen, Wendelyn, Liam, Tobias, Melanie. Student, Wilson Tchrs. Coll., 1940-41; AA, U. Md., 1973; JD, U. Balt., 1976. Bar: Fla. 1977, U.S. Dist. Ct. (mid. dist.) Fla. 1979, U.S. Ct. Appeals (5th and 11th cirs.) 1981. Staff atty. Cen. Fla. Legal Services Inc., Daytona Beach, 1978-80, mng. atty., 1980-81; pvt. practice, Daytona Beach, 1981-93; ret., 2001. *By the time she entered law school, she had 14 children (9 sons and 5 daughters) and she had "practiced" in proper person in county and circuit courts of Prince Georges County, Maryland and in the Maryland Court of Appeals, in the Court of D.C., and of Virginia, and on petition for Certiorari to the United States Supreme Court. Justice William O. Douglas wrote: "To Flora Daun Fowler, in the hope that she will succeed in her quest for justice". Now, at 80, she is writing a book about her colorful career.* Past editor Seabrook Acres Citizens' League Newsletter; columnist Bowie Express & Community Times; contbr. poems to New Voices in American Poetry, 1974. V.p. Seabrook (Md.) Acres Citizens League, 1970; past v.p. Prince Georges County Civic Fedn., Md.; past unit chmn. League of Women Voters, Prince Georges County; past pres., v.p., publicity chmn. Lanham-Bowie Dem. Club, Seabrook. Recipient Evening Star Trophy award Prince Georges County Civic Fedn., 1969. Mem. Fla. S. Ct. Hist. Soc. Democrat. Roman Catholic. Avocations: swimming, creative writing. cursillo. E-mail: daunfowler@msn.com.

FOWLER, FLOYD JACKSON, JR., researcher; b. Akron, Ohio, July 4, 1939; s. Floyd Jackson Fowler and Marion Vaughn Holoman; m. Julia Ann Chambliss, Nov. 19, 1977; m. Diane Davant West, Sept. 3, 1960 (div. June 1974); children: Alex J., Randolph W., Elizabeth D. BA, Wesleyan U., 1960; MA, U. Mich., 1962, PhD, 1966. Asst. dir. Cmty. Rsch. Project Combined Jewish Philanthropies, Boston, 1965—68; asst. dir. Survey Rsch. Program Joint Ctr. for Urban Studies MIT and Harvard U., Cambridge, Mass., 1968—71; sr. rsch. fellow Ctr. for Survey Rsch. U. Mass., Boston, 1971—. Pres. Found. for Informed Med. Decision Making, Boston, 2002—; rschr. Dartmouth Med. Sch., Hanover, NH, 1984—. Author: Improving Survey Questions, 1995, Survey Research Methods, 2002; co-author: Standardized Survey Interviewing, 1990; mem. editl. bd.: Pub. Opinion Quarterly, 2003—. Mem.: Am. Statis. Assn., Am. Assn. Pub. Opinion Rsch. Avocation: writing. Office: Center for Survey Research U Mass Boston 100 Morrissey Blvd Boston MA 02125

FOWLER, FREDERICK VICTOR, JR., import company executive; b. Newton, Mass., May 27, 1933; s. Frederick Victor and Priscilla (Coffin) F.; m. Nancy White, Apr. 18, 1959; children: Cynthia, Frederick III. BSBA, Boston U., 1955. Salesman Fred V. Fowler Co., Newton, 1958-69; v.p. UNA Corp., Boston, 1969-72; pres., CEO Fred V. Fowler Co., Inc., Newton, 1972—. Ptnr. J-L Crescent Co., Detroit, 1988—. Col. USAF, 1955-78. Mem. Soc. Mgr. Engrs., Am. Measuring Tools Mfrs. Assn. (pres.), Nat. Machine Tool Builders Assn., Nat. Bus. Aircraft Assn., Aircraft Owners and Pilots Assn., Air Force Assn., Res. Officers Assn., Rep. 500 Club, Boston U. Alumni Club (v.p. 1975-78). Episcopalian. Avocations: flying, golf, skiing, travel. Office: Fred V Fowler Co Inc 66 Rowe St Auburndale MA 02466-1530

FOWLER, GEORGE SELTON, JR., architect; b. Chgo, Jan. 20, 1920; s. George Selton and Mabel Helena (Overton) F.; m. Yvonne Fern Grammer, Nov. 25, 1945; 1 child, Kim Ellyn. Cert. in European geo-politics and advanced language study, Hamilton Coll. (Army Specialized Tng. Program), 1944; BS in Architecture, Ill. Inst. Tech., 1949, postgrad. City and Regional Planning, 1968. Cert. Elec. Assn. Ill., 1976; reg. arch., Ill., Ohio. Co-founder, pres. The Modern Arts Press, Chgo., 1946; instr. archtl. and related engring. subjects Am. Sch. and Tech. Soc., Chgo., 1948-65; urban planner Chgo. Land Clearance Commn., 1949-50; liaison architect Chgo. Housing Authority, 1950-68, chief design-tech. divsn., 1968-80, dir. dept. engring., 1980-84; prin. George S. Fowler Architect, Chgo., 1984-90. Treas., bd. dir. Chgo. Housing Authority Credit Union, 1963-65; architect, cmty. planner and cons. Interconco., 1965-66. Author: (textbook study guide) Reinforced Concrete Design, 1959. Patentee, subcom. chmn. Mayor's Adv. Commn. to Revise the Bldg. Code, 1986-91; founder, pres., EFCO Creative Concepts Rsch., 1988-2003. Served with Corp. of Engrs., US Army, 1942-46, group sgt. maj., 1944-46. Recipient citation for residential devel. Mayor Richard J. Daley, Chgo., 1960, Black Achievers of Industry Recognition award YMCA, Chgo., 1977; Kappa Alpha Psi grantee, 1936. Mem. Nat. Assn. Housing and Redevel. Ofcl., Internat. Platform Assn., Inventors Coun. Chgo. Home and Office: 8209 S Rhodes Ave Chicago IL 60619-5005

FOWLER, H(ORATIO) SEYMOUR, retired science educator; b. Detroit, Mar. 1, 1919; s. Horatio Seymour and Bessie Liona (Ladd) F.; m. Kathleen M. Marshall, Nov. 21, 1945 (dec.); 1 dau., Kathleen Marie Fowler Barto. BS, Cornell U., 1941, MS, 1946, PhD, 1951. Tchr. sci. McLean (N.Y.) Central Sch., 1946-47, Dryden (N.Y.) Freeville Central Sch., 1947-49; asst. prof. sci. edn. So. Oreg. Coll., Ashland, 1951-52; asst. prof. biology U. No. Iowa, Cedar Falls; also dir. Iowa Tchrs. Conservation Camp, 1952-57; prof. edn., dir. Pa. Conservation Lab. for Tchrs., Pa. State U., University Park, 1957-83, chmn. sci. edn. faculty, 1969-83, coordinator div. acad. curriculum and instrn., 1974-76, prof. nature and sci. edn. emeritus, 1983—; dir. Pa. Gov.'s Sch. for Scis., 1978-79. Sci. advisor Nat. Jr. Sci. and Humanities Symposium, Program U.S. Army Research Office, Acad. Applied Sci., 1979—. Author: Secondary School Science Teaching Practices, 1964, Las Ciencias en la Esquelas Secundarias, 1968, Fieldbook of Natural History, 1974; contbr. articles to profl. jours. Served with 9th inf. div. AUS, 1942-45, ETO. Fulbright lectr. Korea, 1968-69; recipient citation Pa. Dept. Edn., 1970, 83, Centre County (Pa.) Conservation award, 1973, Faculty Service award Nat. Univ. Continuing Edn. Assn., 1983, citation Pa. Ho. of Reps., 1983, Service award U.S. Army Office of Research, 1983; Paul Harris fellow Rotary Club, 1983 Fellow AAAS, Iowa Acad. Sci., Explorers Club; mem. Am. Nature Study Soc. (pres. 1967), Nat. Assn. Biology Tchrs. (v.p. 1956, dir. region II 1971-74, hon. mem. 1974), Nat. Assn. Rsch. in Sci. Teaching, Nat. Sci. Tchrs. Assn. (Disting. Svc. citation 1976), Pa. Sci. Tchrs. Assn. (dir. 1971—, v.p. 1975, pres. 1976, meritorious svc. to sci. teaching citation 1975), Korean Sci. Tchrs. Assn., Royal Asiatic Soc., Masons, Shriners, Rotary (1st v.p. 1981, pres. 1982, gov. dist. 735 1988-89), Elks, Sigma Xi, Phi Kappa Phi, Phi Delta Kappa (chpt. v.p. 1973, pres. 1974-75, Leadership award 1983), Beta Beta Beta. Clubs: Masons, Shriners. Home: 1342 W Park Hills Ave State College PA 16803-3273 Office: Pa State U Sci Edn Dept University Park PA 16802

FOWLER, HUGH CHARLES, charter school consultant & developer; b. Chgo., May 21, 1926; s. Frank Parker and Dorothy Valentine Hinckley F.; m. Shirley Sprague, July 7, 1949; children: Laurie Lynn, Hugh C. Jr. BS in Bus., U. Colo., 1948. V.p. Tool & Fowler, Inc., Denver, 1958-62, Campbell Mithun, Inc., Mpls., 1962-66; pres. Fowler & More, Inc., Denver, 1966-76; v.p. HMO Sys., Inc., Denver, 1976-81, Hillsdale (Mich.) Coll., 1981-85; pres. Wishy Washy, Inc., Denver, 1985-92, Classic Schs., Inc., Denver, 1992—. Mem. Colo. State Senate, 1968-80; regent-at-large U. Colo., 1982-89; commr. White House Pres. Scholars, Washington, 1980-92; dir., sec./treas. Colo. Monorail Authority, Idaho Springs, 1998—. Lt. USNR, 1943-58. Republican. Presbyterian.

FOWLER, J. EDWARD, lawyer; AB, Princeton U., 1953; LLB, Yale U., 1959. Bar: N.Y. 1960. Atty. Debevoise, Plimpton, Lyons & Gates, 1959-68; gen. counsel internat. divsn. Mobil Oil Corp., 1974-77, asst. gen. counsel, 1977-78, assoc. gen. counsel, 1979-83, gen. counsel mktg. and refining divsn., 1983-86; gen. counsel Mobil Corp., Fairfax, Va., 1986-95; sr. ptnr. Holland & Knight, Washington, D.C., 1995-98. Bd. editors Yale Law Jour., 1958-59. Trustee Shakespeare Theatre, 1993—2000; bd. dirs. Nat. Symphony Orch. Assn., 1991—, pres., 1995—98; bd. dirs. Adirondack Nature Conservancy, 1998—, chmn., 2001—; bd. dirs. Adirondack Coun., 1998—. Office: 2101 Connecticut Ave Washington DC 20008-1760

FOWLER, JOHN DALE, JR., biotechnology executive; b. Norfolk, Va., May 15, 1957; s. John Dale and Margaret (Kimmel) F.; m. Corey Keane Phillips, Aug. 2, 1980; children: John Dale III, Douglas Houghton, Grace Phillips. BA, U. Va., 1979, MBA, JD, 1986. Asst. v.p. Jefferson Nat. Bank, Charlottesville, Va., 1979-82; fin. analyst Marine Midland Bank, N.Y.C., 1983; assoc. law Hawkins, Delafield & Wood, N.Y.C., 1984; assoc. Merrill Lynch Capital Markets, N.Y.C., 1985; v.p. Salomon Bros. Inc., N.Y.C., 1986-92; mng. dir. Wheat First Butcher & Singer Capital Markets, Richmond, Va., 1992; mng. dir. Health Care Group Salomon Bros. Inc., N.Y.C., 1992—98; mng. dir. J.P. Morgan, 1998—2001; pres. Large Scale Biology, 2001—03; mng. ptnr. Baycrest Capital LLC, 2003—. Mem. N.Y. Bar Assn. Office: Dir Large Scale Biology, Dir Beverly Enterprises Inc (pub nursing Home) 123 Seventh Ave # 246 Brooklyn NY 11215 Fax: 718-965-0237.

FOWLER, JOHN M. financial services executive; b. Youngstown, Ohio, Apr. 12, 1949; s. William E. Jr and Jean L. (Moore) Fowler; m. Brooke McMurray, Oct. 1999; children: Evan, Ned 1 stepchild, Grey McMurray. BS, Yale U., 1971; JD, U. Pa., 1974. Bar: Pa 1974, US Dist Ct (ea dist) Pa 1974. Assoc. White and Williams, Phila., 1974-77; v.p., chief fin. officer Reading Co., Phila., 1977-81; gen. counsel U.S. Dept. Transp., Washington, 1981-83; exec. v.p., pres. Warner Amex Cable Comm., Inc., Blue Bell, Pa., 1983-86; pres., CEO Gulf Ins. Co., Dallas, 1986-94, chmn., 1991-94; exec. v.p., chief adminstrv. officer Primerica Co. (now Citigroup Inc.), N.Y.C., 1986-94; exec. v.p., CFO MoneyGram Payment Systems, Inc., 1996-98. Office: 115 E 69th Street New York NY 10021

FOWLER, JOHN WELLINGTON, lawyer; b. Waterbury, Conn., May 26, 1935; s. Donald Eugene and Elsie (Paige) F.; m. Judith Seymour, July 27, 1957; children— Stephen, Jeannine, Suzanne. A.B., Harvard U., 1957; J.D., U. Calif.-Berkeley, 1965. Bar: Calif. 1965, U.S. Dist. Ct. (no. dist.) Calif. Assoc. McCutchen, Doyle, Brown, and Enersen, San Francisco, 1965-72, ptnr. 1972—2000, mng. ptnr., San Jose, 1981—2000; ptnr. Bergeson Eliopoulos, LLP, San Jose, 2002—; lectr. Calif. Continuing Edn. of Bar, 1980-81, 84. Pres. Santa Clara Bar Found., San Jose, 1984, Moraga Park and Recreation Commn., Calif. 1972, Moraga Parks Found., 1974; pres. Moraga Community Assn., 1971; councilman, mayor Town of Moraga, 1977-81; bd. dirs. Silicon Valley Law Found., 1983-2001. Served to capt. USMC, 1957-62. Mem. ABA, Santa Clara County Bar Assn. Office: Bergeson Elipoulos LLP 55 Almaden Ste 400 San Jose CA 95113- Office Fax: 408-297-6000. E-mail: jfowler@be-law.com.

FOWLER, LINDA MCKEEVER, hospital administrator, management educator; b. Greensburg, Pa., Aug. 7, 1948; d. Clay and Florence Elizabeth (Smith) McKeever; m. Timothy L. Fowler, Sept. 13, 1969 (div. July 1985). Nursing diploma, Presbyn. U. Hosp., Pitts., 1969; BSN, U. Pitts., 1976, M in Nursing Adminstrn., 1980; D in Pub. Adminstrn., Nova U., 1985. Supr., head nurse Presbyn. Univ. Hosp., Pitts., 1969-76; mem. faculty Western Pa. Hosp. Sch. Nursing, Pitts., 1976-79; acute care coord. Mercy Hosp., Miami, 1980-81; asst. adminstr. nursing North Shore Med. Ctr., Miami, 1981-84, v.p. patient care, 1984-88, Golden Glades Regional Med. Ctr., Miami, 1988-89, Humana Hosp.-South Broward, Hollywood, Fla., 1989-91, assoc. exec. dir. nursing; v.p., chief nursing officer Columbia Regional Med. Ctr., Bayonet Point, 1991-96; COO, chief nursing officer Greenbrier Valley Med. Ctr., 1996-97; quality mgmt. coord. Greenbrier Valley Hospice, 1997-98; pvt. practice healthcare cons., 1998-99; chief nursing officer Marlboro Park Hosp., 1999—2002; pvt. practice healthcare cons., 2002—; chief clin. officer Intermedical Hosp. of S.C., 2003—. Mem. adj. faculty Barry U., Miami, 1984-97, Broward C.C., Ft. Lauderdale, 1984-85, Nova U., 1986-87; cons. Strategic Health Devel. Inc., Miami Shores, Fla., 1986-90, So. Coll., Cleveland, Tenn., 1995-96. Dept. HEW trainee, 1976, 79-80; bd. dirs. Pasco County Am. Cancer Soc., 1992-95. Mem. Am. Orgn. Nurse Execs. (legis. com. 1988-90), Fla. Orgn. Nurse Execs. (bd. dirs. 1986-88), S.C. Orgn. Nurse Execs., South Fla. Nurse Adminstrs. Assn. (sec. 1983-84, bd. dirs. 1984-86), U. Pitts. Alumni Assn., Presbyn. U. Alumni Assn., Portuguese Water Dog Club Am. (bd. dirs. 1988-89), Ft. Lauderdale Dog Club (bd. dirs. 1981-82, 83-85, v.p. 1982-83), Am. Kennel Club (dog judge), Moore County Kennel Club, Sigma Theta Tau. Lutheran. Office: Taylor at Marion Sts Columbia SC 29220

FOWLER, MARILYN S. ATLAS, social worker; b. Portsmouth, Ohio, Apr. 20, 1954; d. Morton G. Atlas and Annadine K. Jaffee; m. John R. Fowler, Sept. 24, 1978 (div. Sept. 18, 1996); children: Gretchen R., Michelle J. BA in Psychology, U. Kans., 1976; MSSW, U. Wis., 1978. Diplomate Am. Psychotherapy Assn.; lic. ind. social worker S.C., cert. bd. cert. diplomate in clin. social work. Bd. cert. hypnotherapist Assocs. in Psychol. Medicine, St. Louis, 1984—87; psychotherapist Psychiat. Coverage, Ltd., St. Louis, 1987—89, Family Psychiat. Assocs., Myrtle Beach, SC, 1989—94; pres., psychotherapist Fowler Counseling Inc. dba Grand Strand Counseling Ctr., Myrtle Beach, 1990—. Recipient Undergrad. Rsch. award, NIMH; scholar. Mem.: NASW (diplomate in clin. social work), Am. Assn. Profl. Hypnotherapists, Nat. Guild Hypnotist, Am. Psychotherapy Assn., Optimist Club, Phi Beta Kappa. Jewish. Avocations: dancing, camping, hiking, boating, swimming. Home: Unit 117D 424 D Garden Dr Myrtle Beach SC 29575 Office: 1700 A Oak St Myrtle Beach SC 29577

FOWLER, MARJORIE ELLEN REES, pathologist; b. Albuquerque, Apr. 18, 1943; d. Martin Loren and Evelyn Gertrude (Hicks) Rees; m. Peter James Fowler, June 4, 1966. BS, La. Poly. Inst., 1965; MD, La. State U., New Orleans, 1968. Pathology resident and intern Albany Med. Ctr. and VA Hosp., NY, 1968—70; gen. med. officer 36th Tactical Hosp., Bitburg, Germany, 1971—74; pathology resident Washington U., St. Louis City Hosp., 1975—78; pathologist, prof. pathology La. State U. Health Scis. Ctr., Shreveport, 1978—. Mem.: Am. Assn. Neuropathologists, Coll. Am. Pathologists, Am. Soc. Clin. Pathologists, U.S. and Can. Assn. Pathology. Office: LSU HSC PO Box 33931 1501 Kings Hwy Shreveport LA 71103

FOWLER, MARTI, fine arts consultant; b. St. Louis, Mar. 25, 1952; d. Chester Felix and Emily (Kohout) Czarcinski; m. Robert Lee Fowler, Mar. 26, 1988. BA, So. Ill. U., 1973, MA, 1981. Cert. tchr. English, speech and theatre, Mo. Tchr. asst. Hazelwood Sch. Dist., St. Louis, 1974-76; instr. Jefferson Coll., 1991-92, St. Louis C.C. at Meramec, St. Louis, 1990-98; tchr. Hazelwood East H.S., St. Louis, 1976-97; dept. chair fine arts Hazelwood East H.S. and Kirby Jr. H.S., 1997-99; cons. fine arts Hazelwood Sch. Dist., 1999—2003; owner, prodr. Interactive Ednl. Video LLC, 2003—. Co-playwright/lyricist: (musical theatre) Difficult Choices, 1988; dir. and choreographer numerous prodns., 1973—; co-producer: Practical Technical Theatre-Interactive Educational DVD Series, 2003-. Recipient Adminstr. of Yr. award, Mo. Thespians Ednl. Theatre Assn., 2001—02. Mem. Am. Alliance for Theatre in Edn. (Mo. state chmn. 1993-97, Dina Reese Evans award 1998), Theatre Edn. Assn. (Mo. state chmn. 1993-97, coord. Mo. State Thespian Conf. 1996, 99, Dina Rees Evans award for theatre in our schs. advocacy), Mo. State Thespian Bd. Dirs., Speech Theatre Assn. of Mo., Internat. Thespian Soc., Zeta Phi Eta (pres. 1972-73). Avocations: attending theatre, reading. Home: 15685 Silver Lake Ct Chesterfield MO 63017-5128 E-mail: marti@interactiveeducationalvideo.com.

FOWLER, MICHAEL ROSS, law and politics educator; b. Washington, Apr. 14, 1960; s. James Randlett and Margaret (Williamson) F.; m. Julie Marie Bunck, May 29, 1989. BA in History, Dartmouth Coll., 1982; MA in Fgn. Affairs, U. Va., 1985; JD, Harvard U., 1986. Bar: Mass. 1986, U.S. Dist. Ct. Mass. 1986, D.C. 1988, Md. 1990. Scholar-in-residence The White Burkett Miller Ctr. Pub. Affairs, Charlottesville, Va., 1986; assoc. Mintz, Levin, Cohn, Ferris, Glovsky & Popeo, Boston, 1986-90; vis. lectr. Tufts U., Medford, Mass., 1990; rsch. fellow Inst. for Study of World Politics, Washington, 1990-91; vis. lectr. U. Va., Charlottesville, 1991-92; Fulbright scholar U. Ryukyus, Okinawa, Japan, 1992-93; profl. lectr. Georgetown U., 1993-94. Ford Found. lectr. to Vietnam, Inst. for Internat. Rels. in Hanoi, 1995, 2002; vis. asst. prof. U. Louisville, 1996-99; vis. scholar U. Ryukyus, Okinawa, Japan, 1999-2000; PISA lectr. to Laos, Inst. of Fgn. Affairs in Vientiane, 2003; dir. Muhammad Ali Inst. Peacemaking and Conflict Resolution; assoc. prof. U. Louisville, 2000—. Author: Winston S. Churchill: Philosopher and Statesman, 1985, Thinking About Human Rights, 1987, Law, Power and the Sovereign State, 1995, With Justice For All?: The Nature of the American Legal System, 1998. White House intern Carter Adminstrn., Washington, 1979-80. Democrat. Episcopalian. Office: Ali Inst Brandeis Sch Law U Louisville Louisville KY 40292

FOWLER, NOBLE OWEN, physician, university administrator; b. Vicksburg, Miss., July 14, 1919; s. Noble Owen and Annie Lou (Robertson) F.; m. Charlotte Ruth Walters, June 13, 1942; children: Jo Ann, Michael Owen, Anne Stewart. Student, Memphis State U., 1936-38; MD, U. Tenn., 1941. Diplomate Am. Bd. Internal Medicine (examining bd. 1970-72, cardiovascular subspecialty examining bd. 1966-72, chmn. cardiovascular subspecialty bd. 1970-72). Intern Cin. Gen. Hosp., 1942-43, resident in internal medicine, 1945, 47-48, fellow in cardiology, 1948-52; resident in internal medicine Peter Bent Brigham Hosp., Boston, 1946; instr. U. Cin., 1950-51, asst. prof. medicine, 1951-52, assoc. prof., 1957-64, prof., 1964—, prof. pharmacology and cell biophysics, 1980-84, prof. emeritus, 1984—, assoc. dir. dept. medicine, 1970-79, dir. divsn. cardiology, 1970-86. Asst. prof. SUNY, 1952-54; chmn. cardiovascular research Emory U., 1954-57; mem. adv. com. on cardiovascular and renal drugs FDA, 1970-78, chmn., 1974-78; sci. adv. com. Nat. Inst. Aging, NIH, Balt., 1983-86. Author: Cardiac Diagnosis and Treatment, 3d edit., 1980, Myocardial Diseases, 1973, Cardiac Arrhythmias; Diagnosis and Treatment, 1977, Pericardium in Health and Disease, 1985, Diagnosis of Heart Disease, 1991, Diagnosis in Color: Physical Signs in Cardiology, 1998, Clinical Electrocardiographic Diagnosis, 2000. Capt. M.C., AUS, 1943-44. Recipient award for contbns. to cardiology Georgetown U., 1978; Nat. Heart and Lung Inst. grant, 1961-73. Fellow ACP, Am. Coll. Cardiology (Master Tchr. award 1974), Am. Heart Assn. Coun. on Clin. Cardiology; mem. Am. Clin. and Climatol. Assn., Am. Physiol. Soc., Cttrl. Soc. Clin. Rsch., Am. Fedn. Clin. Rsch., Assn. Univ. Cardiologists (founding mem., pres. 1976), Am. Heart Assn. (local chpt. trustee, exec. com., pres. 1979—, Samuel Kaplan Rsch. award 1994, Spl. Recognition award Laennec Soc. 1994), U. Tenn. Coll. Medicine (Disting. Alumnus award 1992), Sigma Xi, Alpha Omega Alpha, Phi Chi. Presbyterian. Home: Cincinnati, Ohio. *Dig deeply. Know more about one area than anyone else. Do things for other people. At the end of your career these will be more important than your research.* Died Mar. 8, 2003.

FOWLER, PAUL RAYMOND, physician, lawyer; b. Washington, Apr. 30, 1958; s. Charles Raymond and Dora E. (Burger) Fowler; m. Mary Jane Weber, Oct. 4, 1986; children: Christina D., Laura M., Joshua P. BS, U. Md., 1980, postgrad., 1980—81; DO, U. Des Moines, Des Moines, Iowa, 1985; JD with honors, Drake U., 1994. Bar: U.S. Supreme Ct., Fla. 1995, Ill. 1996, D.C. 1996, Ky. 1998; diplomate Am. Bd. Forensic Examiners, Am. Osteo. Bd. Family Practice, Am. Osteo. Bd. Preventive Medicine, cert. Am. Bd. Disability Analysts, diplomate Am. Bd. Family Practice. Intern Des Moines Gen. Hosp., 1985—86; resident Ea. Va. Grad. Sch. Medicine, Norfolk, 1986—88; pvt. practice medicine Norfolk, 1988—90; staff Iowa Meth. Med. Ctr., Des Moines, 1990—95, Mercy Med. Ctr., Des Moines, 1992—94; med. dir. Occupl. Health Svcs., Des Moines, 1990—95; chief physician Ford Motor Co., Hapeville, Ga., 1995—97; med. dir. Quorum Health Sys., Spartanburg, SC, 1997—2000; legal medicine officer to surgeon gen. U.S. Army, Washington, 2000—. Mem. mock trial team Med. Malpractice Rev. Bd., Commonwealth of Va., 1988—90, Drake U. Law Sch., 1992; assoc. clin. prof. U. Des Moines, 1990—; judge Nat. Mock Trial Coll. Comp., 1992; clin. prof. Pikevill Coll. Osteo. Medicine, 1997—; pvt. practice law, 1994—. Reviewer: Am. Forensic Examiner, 1997—, Fed. Practitioner; contbr. articles to profl. jours. Active Silver Spring Vol. Fire Dept., 1978—81; mem. bioethics com. Iowa Meth. Med. Ctr., Des Moines, 1992—95. Recipient Good Citizen award, Clifton Park Citizens Assn.; Health Policy Scholars fellow, Ctrs. for Medicare and Medicaid, 2003—. Fellow: Am. Coll. Legal Medicine, Am. Acad. Family Physicians; mem.: Am. Osteo. Coll. Preventive and Occupl. Medicine (gen. counsel, trustee, v.p.), Am. Osteo. Assn. (tech. task force, ho. dels.), Md. Acad. Family Physicians (bylaws com., chmn. resolutions com.), Am. Bd. Med. Specialties, D.C. Bar Assn., Ill. Bar Assn., Ky. Bar Assn., Fla. Bar Assn., Phi Sigma (pres. 1984—85). Avocations: tennis, running, philately. Home: 18313 Leedstown Way Olney MD 20832 Office: Walter Reed Army Med Ctr Rm 2-65 Delano Hall Washington DC 20307-5001 E-mail: prfowler@pol.net.

FOWLER, RAYMOND DALTON, psychologist, educator; b. Jasper, Ala., Dec. 22, 1950; s. Raymond Dalton and Willie (Sanders) F.; m. Nancy Allebach, Aug. 13, 1955 (dec.); children: Karen Sydney, Derek Tyson, Michael Allan; m. Sandra Mumford, May 5, 1984. Student, Vanderbilt U., 1948-50; BA, U. Ala., 1952, MA, 1953; PhD, Pa. State U., 1957. Diplomate in clin. psychology Am. Bd. Profl. Psychology; lic. psychologist, Ala. Rsch. asst. Psychoacoustics Lab., Pa. State U., University Park, 1953-54; fellow USPHS, 1954-56; asst. prof. psychology, asst. dir. Psychol. Clinic, U. Ala., Tuscaloosa, 1956-59, assoc. prof., dir. Psychol. Clinic Birmingham, 1959-65, prof., chmn. dept., 1965-83, prof. (on leave), 1983-86, prof. emeritus, 1986—; sr. cons. Psych. Sys. and Nat. Computer Sys., Balt. and Washington, 1983-86; prof. psychology, head dept. U. Tenn., Knoxville, 1986-89; exec. v.p., CEO APA, Washington, 1989—2002, exec. v.p., CEO emeritus, 2003. Participant White House Conf. on Health, 1965, Nat. Conf. on Criminal Justice Stds. and Goals, 1973; mem. nat. adv. com. on alcoholism HEW, 1970-72, chmn. com. on rsch., 1970; mem. task panel on manpower and pers. President's Commn. on Mental Health, 1977-78; mem. Ala. Gov.'s Adv. Com. on Alcoholism and Drug Abuse, 1973-82; vice chmn. program com. N.Am. Congress on Alcohol and Drug Addiction, 1974; mem. sci. adv. com. Nat. Coun. on Alcoholism, 1974-78; mem. rsch. tng. rev. com. Nat. Inst. Alcohol Abuse and Alcoholism, 1975-78; dir. Ala. Prison Classification Project, 1976-77; chmn. So. Sch. Alcohol Studies, 1960-62; cons. Ala.

Commn. on Alcoholism, 1958-70, VA, 1959-65, Estate of Howard R. Hughes, 1976-84; prin. cons. Roche Psychiat. Svc. Inst., Nutley, N.J., 1966-77, Med. Computer Svc., Basel, Switzerland, 1968-76, Med. Computer Svc., Hans Huber Verlag, Berne, Switzerland, 1976-89; cons. to adminstr. Law Enforcement Assistance Adminstrn., U.S. Dept. Justice, Washington, 1971-73; program cons. div. alcoholism Ala. Dept. Mental Health, 1973-75; sr. cons. Nat. Computer Sys., Mpls., 1983-89 Contbg. author: Assessment for Decision, 1987, Handbook of Psychological Assessment, 1990; editor Am. Psychologist, 1989-2002; contbr. articles and revs. to profl. jours. Vice pres. Ala. Coun. on Human Rels., 1965-68, Rehab. Rsch. Found., 1965-80, alumni fellow Pa. State U., 1988—; bd. dirs. Rosalynn Carter Inst. for Human Devel., 1988-98. Named Disting. Practitioner, Nat. Acad. Practice, 1986; recipient significant Minn. Multiphasic Personality Inventory contbn. award U. Minn., 1988; grantee Ala. Commn. on Alcoholism, 1962-63, 64-68, NIMH, 1963-64, Roche Psychiat. Svc. Inst., 1967-76, Ala. Dept. Mental Health, 1969-70, U.S. Dept. Justice, 1971-82, Ala. Bd. Corrections, 1972-73, Ala. Law Enforcement Planning Agy., 1972-74, Nat. Inst. Alcohol Abuse and Alcoholism, 1973-83. Fellow APA (pres. div. 13, 1978-79, coun. reps. 1965-68, 70-73, 75-78, bd. dirs. 1979—, treas. 1983-87, pres.-elect 1987-88, pres. 1988-89, presdl. citation 1990), Soc. for Personalaity Assessment; mem. AAUP (pres. U. Ala. chpt. 1969-70), Southeastern Psychol. Assn. (pres. 1971-72, dir. continuing edn. 1973-89, dist. speaker 1982, 87), Ala. Psychol. Assn (pres. 1962, award for outstanding contbns. 1979), Alcohol and Drug Problems Assn. N.Am. (program chmn. 1974-76, bd. dirs. 1975-77), Internat. Coun. Psychologists, Sigma Xi (life), Psi Chi (nat. v.p. 1980-84, disting. speaker 1977, 88), Omicron Delta Kappa, Phi Kappa Phi. Democrat. Avocations: running, gardening, cooking. Home: 4020 Linnean Ave NW Washington DC 20008-3805 Office: Am Psychological Assoc 750 1st St NE Washington DC 20002-4241

FOWLER, ROBERT ARCHIBALD, infosystems company executive; b. Lewistown, Pa., May 29, 1931; s. Harry K. Fowler and Margaret (Elder) Mann; m. Gail Brewer; children: R. Wendell, Ann, Allen. BS in Econs., Franklin and Marshall Coll., 1953; MBA, Cornell U., 1958. Auditor Gen. Motors Corp., Rochester, N.Y., 1953-54; exec. trainee Mfr.'s Hanover Bank, N.Y.C., 1958-60; credit rep. Cen. Trust Corp., Rochester, 1960-61; mktg. exec. Voplex Corp., Rochester, 1961-70; chmn. 5 W Info. Services, Rochester, 1970—. Treas. Clover Investment Group, Rochester, 1960—. Author: Careerism, 1970, Buyerism, 1971, Creative Winemaking, 1973; contbr. articles to profl. jours. Served with U.S. Army, 1954-56. Mem. Am. Legion, Midtown Tennis Club, Counterpointe Golf Club. Republican. Presbyterian. Avocation: tennis. Office: 5W Info Svcs Inc Ste 107B 2509 Browncroft Blvd Rochester NY 14625-1522

FOWLER, ROBERT ASA, diplomat, consultant, business director; b. Sewickley, Pa., Aug. 5, 1928; s. William Henry and Violet Lee (Baker) F.; m. Monica Hedén; children: William Henry, Thomas Grasselli, Robert Saxton, Mary Antonia. BA, Princeton U., 1950; MBA, Harvard U., 1955. With Conoco, Inc., 1955-85; comml. mgr. Conch Methane Services Ltd., U.K., 1960-65; gen. mgr. adminstrv. and ops. Conoco Ltd. (U.K.), London, 1965-68; mktg. devel. mgr. Conoco Inc. (U.S.A.), Houston, 1968-73, area mgr., 1973-78; chmn., mng. dir. Conoco Ltd., U.K., 1978-81; v.p. internat. mktg. Conoco Inc. (U.S.A.), Houston, 1981-85; owner, prin. cons. Fowler Internat., 1986—; counsul gen. Sweden, 1989-98. Served to lt. USNR, 1950-53, Korea. Mem. Am. Petroleum Inst. Clubs: Knickerbocker (N.Y.C.), River (N.Y.C.); Allegheny Country (Sewickley, Pa.); Chagrin Valley Hunt (Gates Mills, Ohio); Hurlingham (London). Republican. Episcopalian.

FOWLER, ROBERT RAMSAY, former Canadian government official; b. Ottawa, Ont., Can., Aug. 18, 1944; s. Robert MacLaren and Sheila Gordon (Ramsay) F.; m. Mary Stoker, June 13, 1981; children: Linton, Ruth, Antonia, Justine. BA, Queen's U., Kingston, Ont., 1968. Joined Fed. Pub. Svc. Can. Internat. Develop. Agy., Ottawa, 1968-69, dept. external affairs, 1969-71; 2nd sec. Can. Embassy, Paris, 1971-74; with comml. policy divsn. external affairs, 1974-76; 1st sec., counsellor Can. Permanent Mission to UN, N.Y.C., 1976-78; exec. asst. to under-sec. state, external affairs Can. Ottawa, 1978-80; asst.ssec. to cabinet, fgn. and def. policy Privy Coun. Office, Ottawa, 1980-86; asst. dep. min. (policy) Dept. Nat. Def., Ottawa, 1986-89, dep. min., 1989-95; amb. and permanent rep. UN Permanent Mission of Can. to UN, N.Y.C., 1995—. Avocation: photography. Office: Perm Mission of Canada to UN 885 2nd Ave Fl 14 New York NY 10017-2201

FOWLER, STEPHEN EUGENE, retired military officer, human resources executive; b. Pilot Point, Tex., Dec. 10, 1940; s. Stephen Lafette and Virginia (Whitten) F.; m. Patricia Ann Chichilla, July 16, 1966 (div. May 1982); children: Shannon Jean Imran, Brittany Michelle Inmon; m. Cristine Ann Buttafoco, May 25, 1985; 1 child, Beth Ann Skamser. BA, U. North Tex., 1966; MA, Ball State U., 1974. Commd. 2d lt. USAF, 1966, advanced through grades to lt. col., 1982; chief airman support assignment Hdqrs. USAF Europe, Ramstein AB, Fed. Republic of Germany, 1973-76; chief, sec. police, intelligence and OSI Air Force Mil. Personnel Ctr., Randolph AFB, Tex., 1976-79, chief Air Force Classification and Control Sect., 1979-81; comdr. 3537th Recruiting Squadron, Sumter, S.C., 1981-84; chief airman assignments Hdqrs. Strategic Air Command, Offutt AFB, Nebr., 1984-86; chief inspections and inquiries 55th Wing, Offutt AFB, Nebr., 1986-92; mgr. field and logistics hr. and team mem. rels. Pamida, Inc., Omaha, 1994—2001. Mem. Omaha Sister City Assn.; vol. tchr. non-profit agy.; mem. pvt. industry task force State of Nebr. Decorated Republic of Vietnam Cross of Gallantry; named Admiral (mythical) Nebr. Navy, Gov. Orr, State of Nebr. Mem. Pi Sigma Alpha. Republican.

FOWLER, STEVEN LANE, compliance officer; s. Robert Lee Fowler and Verna Elizabeth Lane; m. Karen J. D., Nov. 25, 1989; children: Jacob Steven, Brian Lane. BA in Bus. Admin., Fla. Atlantic U, 1986, MPA, 2001. Acct. Hamilton, Rives & Mayer, PA, CPAs, Tequesta, Fla., 1987—88; CPA Goldberg & Dorra, PA, CPAs, West Palm Beach, Fla., 1988—90, Pvt. Practice, West Palm Beach, 1990—93; acct. Jupiter (Fla.) Med. Ctr., 1993—95; sr. acct. City of West Palm Beach (Fla.), 1995—2001; compliance officer Health Care Dist. of Palm Beach Cmty., 2001—. Mem.: The Am. Soc. for Pub. Admin., Health Care Complian Assn. (assoc.), The Acad. of Pol. Sci., The Am. Acad. of Pol. and Social Sci. Office: Health Care Dist of Palm Beach County 324 Datura St No 401 West Palm Beach FL 33401

FOWLER, SUSAN MICHELE, real estate broker, entrepreneur; b. East Liverpool, Ohio, Jan. 6, 1952; d. George Robert and Mary Helen (Gilliland) F.; m. Paul Joseph Cusumano, Nov. 5, 1988. BA, West Liberty Coll., 1973; MEd, Kent State U., 1995. Lic. real estate broker, Ohio. Sales rep. Tropic-Cal, L.A., 1974-76; project mgr. R&B Enterprises, L.A., 1977-80; regional leasing mgr. First Union Mgmt., Inc., Cleve., 1981-82; comml. real estate broker Adler, Galvin, Rogers, Inc., Cleve., 1983-86, Coldwell Banker Comml. Real Estate, Cleve., 1986-90; pres. Comml. Real Estate Co., Cleve., 1990—; owner Susan M. Fowler Comml. Real Estate Co., Chagrin Falls, Ohio, 1990—, Empower Yourself Seminars, Chagrin Falls, 1992—; v.p., dir. offices First Union Real Estate Investment Trust, Cleve., Susan M. Fowler Comm. Real Estate Svcs., Inc., Chgo., 2000—, Susan M. Fowler Comml. Real Estate Svcs., Inc., Barrington, Ill., 2000—. Pres. Christopher Real Estate Investment, Cleve., 1989—, Christopher Mgmt. Co., Cleve., 1989—; founder, speaker Empower Yourself Seminars, 1992. Trustee, pres. West Side Community Mental Health Ctr., Cleve., 1985—; trustee, v.p. Child Conservation Coun., Cleve., 1988—; trustee Big Bros. and Big Sisters Greater Cleve., 1989, Visions for Youth, 1991; mem. Cleve. Mus. Art, Geauga County Humane Soc., Fairmount Arts Centre. Mem. Comml. Real Estate Women, Cleve. Area Bd. Realtors (speakers bur.), Nat. Assn. Realtors, Ohio Assn. Realtors, Cleve. Mus. Art, Pine Lake Trout Club. Home: 1014 Oakland Dr Barrington IL 60010-6307

FOWLER, THOMAS KENNETH, physicist; b. Thomaston, Ga., Mar. 27, 1931; s. Albert Grady and Susie (Glynn) F.; m. Carol Ellen Winter, Aug. 18, 1956; children: Kenneth, John, Ellen. BS in Engring, Vanderbilt U., 1953, MS in Physics, 1955; PhD in Physics, U. Wis., 1957. Staff physicist Oak Ridge Nat. Lab., 1957-65, group leader plasma theory, 1961-65; staff physicist Gen. Atomic Co., San Diego, 1965-67, head plasma physics divsn., 1967; group leader plasma theory Lawrence Livermore Lab., Livermore, Calif., 1967-69, div. leader, 1969-70, assoc. dir. magnetic fusion, 1970-87; prof., chmn. dept. nuclear engring. U. Calif., Berkeley, 1988-94, prof. emeritus, 1995—. Calif. Coun. Sci. Tech. fellow, 1997—. Fellow Am. Phys. Soc. (chmn. plasma physics div. 1970); mem. Nat. Acad. Scis., Sigma Xi, Sigma Nu. Home: 221 Grover Ln Walnut Creek CA 94596-6310 Office: U Calif 4167 Etcheverry Hall Berkeley CA 94720-1731 Business E-Mail: fowler@nuc.berkeley.edu.

FOWLER, TILLIE KIDD, lawyer; b. Milledgeville, Ga., Dec. 23, 1942; d. Culver and Katherine Kidd; m. L. Buck Fowler, 1968; children: Tillie, Elizabeth. BA in Polit. Sci., Emory U., 1964, JD, 1967. Legis. asst. Rep. Robert G. Stephens, 1967—70; counsel White House Office of Consumer Affairs, 1970—71; mem. 103d-106th Congresses from 4th Fla. dist., 1993—2001, mem. armed svcs. com., transp. and infrastructure com.; majority dep. whip; chmn. transp. subcom. on oversight, investigation & mgmt.; atty. Holland & Knight, Washington, 2001—; chmn., Def. Policy Bd. U.S. Dept. Def., Washington, 2003—. Vice chair Ho. Rep. Conf. Pres. Jr. League, Jacksonville, Fla., 1982—83; chmn. Fla. Humanities Coun., 1989—91; pres. Jacksonville City Coun., 1989—90, mem., 1985—91; mem. bd. visitors U.S. Naval Acad., 1995—; chmn. ho. page bd., 1996—; mem. Chief of Naval Ops. Executive Bd., 2003—. Republican. Office: Holland & Knight 2099 Pennsylvania Ave NW Ste 100 Washington DC 20006*

FOWLER, VANCE GARRISON, JR., internist, educator; b. Asheville, N.C., Dec. 27, 1965; s. Vance Garrison Fowler Sr. and Della Mae Fowler; m. Amy Bingham, June 4, 1994; children: Madeline Suzanne, Vance Garrison Fowler III, Lily Elizabeth. AB in English and Zoology, Duke U., 1988, MHS, 1999; MD, U. N.C., 1993. Diplomate Am. Bd. Internal Medicine, Infectious Diseases, cert. Clin. Tropical Medicine and Travelers Health, lic. N.C., 1995. Rsch. assoc. Nat. Inst. Med. Rsch., Amani, Tanzania, 1990—91; resident internal medicine, fellow infectious diseases Duke Med. Ctr., Durham, NC, 1993—99, assoc. dept. medicine, 1999—2000, asst. prof. infectious diseases, 2000—. Contbr. . Recipient Young Investigator award, Merck/Am. Soc. Microbiology, 2001; grantee in field. Mem.: ACP, Am. Fedn. Med. Rsch. (Jr. Physician Investigator award 2001), Am. Soc. Tropical Medicine and Hygiene, Infectious Diseases Soc. Am., N.C. Infectious Diseases Soc. (assoc.), N.C. Med. Soc. (assoc.), Alpha Omega Alpha. Office: Duke Med Ctr Dept Medicine PO Box 3281 Durham NC 27710

FOWLER, VIRGINIA C. literature educator; b. Lexington, Ky., Mar. 29, 1948; d. Bill M. Fowler and Betty Wills Jacoby. BA in English, U. Ky., 1969; MA in English, U. Pitts., 1971, PhD in English, 1976. From asst. prof. English to prof. Va. Poly. Inst. and State U., Blacksburg, Va., 1977—96, Va. Poly. Inst., 1996—. Author: Henry James's American Girl, 1984, Nikki Giovanni, 1992, Gloria Nayler: In Search of Sanctuary, 1996. Fellow, Woodrow Wilson Found., 1969—70; grantee, NEH, 1990. Mem.: Phi Beta Kappa. Avocations: tennis, travel, book collecting. Home: 1000 Flint Drive Christiansburg VA 24073 Office: Dept English Virginia Tech Shanks Hall Blacksburg VA 24061-0112 E-mail: vfowler@vt.edu.

FOWLER, VIVIAN DELORES, insurance company executive; b. Knoxville, Tenn., Sept. 26, 1946; d. Rance James Pierce and Margaret Willadene (Crowe) Compton; m. James Hubert Fowler, May 12, 1979. Student, U. Tenn., Knoxville. CPCU. Clk. The Travelers Ins. Co., Knoxville, 1967-84, adminstv. staff, 1984, comml. mktg. asst., 1984-86, comml. account analyst Nashville, 1986-89, sr. account analyst, 1989-90, account mgr., 1990-93, regional asst. mgr. small bus. unit coml. lines Atlanta, 1993—; regional underwriting mgr. select accounts mktg. Travelers/Aetna Ins. Co. (name changed to Travelers Property and Casulty Co.), Atlanta, 1996. Lay witness speaker, United Meth. Ch., Knoxville 1979-82; charter mem. St. Thomas Hosp. Found. Soc., 1990; mem. Arthritis Found., 1991. Mem. NAFE, Soc. CPCU, Soc. Cert. Ins. Counselors (cert. 1987), Nat. Assn. of Ins. Women (cert. Profl. Ins. Woman 1975), Internat. Platform Assn., Ins. Professionals of Atlanta, 1998. Republican. United Methodist. Home: 604 Ashley Forest Dr Alpharetta GA 30022-6133 Office: Travelers Property and Casulty Co 4400 Northpoint Pkwy Alpharetta GA 30022-2429 E-mail: Vivian_Fowler@travelers.com.

FOWLER, WALTON BERRY, franchise developer, educator; b. Tulsa, Dec. 4, 1946; s. Walton Rector Fowler and Martha Jean (Berry) Oliver; m. Deborah Martz, Oct. 1, 1972 (div. Feb. 1985); 1 child, Cullen Brian; m. Anne Sadler, Sept. 23, 1985; children: Nicole Anne, William Dean, Catherine Elizabeth. BA, Chapman Coll., 1972; teaching cert., Calif. State U., Fullerton, 1973. Mgr. Al Mayton Prodns., Universal City, Calif., 1968-72; dept. chmn., tchr. Anaheim (Calif.) High Sch. Dist., 1973-78; founder, chmn. Sylvan Learning Corp., Montgomery, Ala., 1979-88; v.p., treas. Vincent, Hanna, Fowler Investments, Bellevue, Wash., 1987-92; chmn. The Little Gym Internat. Inc., Kirkland, Wash., 1992-94; founder, pres. Krypton Inst., Spokane, Wash., 1995-97; pres. W. Berry Fowler & Assocs., 1997—. Dept. chmn., tchr. Anaheim (Calif.) High Sch. Dist., 1968-72; bd. dirs. The Wilcox Group, Mercer Island; lectr. Nat. Honor Soc. Mem. Com. for Tchr. Tng. Chapman Coll., Orange, Calif., 1973, planning com. Boy Scouts Am., Mercer Island; founder, chmn. A Thousand Points of Knowledge Learning Ctrs. Mem. NEA, Internat. Franchise Assn., Venture Founders Assn. Republican. Avocations: boating, traveling, reading, art. Office: A Thousand Points of Knowledge Inc 3016 S Grand Blvd Fl 3 Spokane WA 99203

FOWLER, WAYNE LEWIS, SR., internist; b. Topeka, Kans., Jan. 5, 1923; s. Morrill George and Grace Anna (Carlson) F.; m. Violet June Ransom, Sept. 4, 1948; children: Wayne Jr., Deborah. BS, Washburn U., 1945; MD, U. Ind., 1947. Diplomate Am. Bd. Internal Medicine. Intern Kansas City (Mo.) Gen. Hosp., 1947-48, resident internal medicine, 1948-51; internist Galvin-Haughey Clinic, Concordia, Kans., 1953-95, NCK Med. Clinic, Concordia, Kans., 1995—. Past pres. med. staff St. Joseph Hosp., Concordia Kans. Capt. US Air Force, 1951-53, Fellow Am. Coll. Physicians (Laureate award Kans. chpt. 1994), Am. Coll. Chest Physicians; mem. AMA, Cl. County Med. Soc., Kans. Med. Soc., Am. Soc. Internal Medicine, Concordia Elks, Concordia Moose, Topeka Masonic Lodge # 17, Scottish Rite Bodies Topeka, ISIS Shrine alina. Republican. Episcopalian. Avocation: amateur radio. Home: 332 W 8th St Concordia KS 66901-3406 Office: NCK Med Inc 1010 3rd Ave Concordia KS 66901-4003

FOWLER, WILLIAM A. accounting firm executive; BA, MBA, U. Wash. CFO Deloitte Touche Tohmatsu, N.Y.C., 1995—. Office: Deloitte Touche Tohmatsu 1633 Broadway New York NY 10019

FOWLER, WYCHE, JR., ambassador; b. Atlanta, Oct. 6, 1940; s. William Wyche and Emelyn (Barbre) F.; 1 dau., Katherine Wyche. BA, Davidson Coll., 1962; JD, Emory U., 1969. Bar: Ga. 1970. Chief asst. to Congressman Charles Weltner, 1965; mem. Atlanta Bd. Aldermen, 1969-73; pres. Atlanta City Council, 1973-77; mem. 95th-99th Congresses from 5th Ga. Dist., 1977-87; U.S. Senator from Ga., 1987-92; with Powell, Goldstein, Frazer & Murphy, Washington & Atlanta, 1993-95; pvt. practice law, 1996; U.S. amb., 1996—. Served in U.S. Army. Recipient Myrtle Wreath award, 1972, Congl. sunbelt coun. ann. award, 1981, Ga. Citizens Coalition on Hunger award, 1982; named Outstanding Young Man Atlanta Jaycees, 1972, Outstanding Young Man Ga. Jaycees, 1973 Mem. ABA, State Bar Ga., Phi Delta Theta. Democrat. Office: US Embassy Unit 61307 Apo AE 09803-1307

FOWLES, GEORGE RICHARD, physicist, educator; b. Glenwood Springs, Colo., Apr. 2, 1928; s. Howard Payne and Phyllis Kathleen (Gibson) F.; m. Dorothy Ellen Evans, Oct. 8, 1954 (dec. Dec. 1987); children: John Reed Maxon, Louise, Kathleen, Jefferson; m. Colleen Elizabeth Murphy, Sept. 17, 1988; stepchildren: Karla Sanger, Joseph Sanger, Kristina Sanger. BS, Stanford U., 1952, MS, 1954, PhD, 1962. Geophysicist Phelps Dodge Corp., Douglas, Ariz., 1954-55; physicist SRI Internat., Menlo Park, Calif., 1955-62, group leader, 1962-66; assoc. prof. Wash. State U., Pullman, 1966-73, prof. physics, 1973-95, prof. emeritus physics, 1995—, chmn. dept., 1984-90. Cons. Nat. Materials Adv. Bd., Washington, 1970, 77-78; cons. numerous govt. labs., Washington, 1968—; vis. prof. Australian Nat. U., Canberra, 1983. Contbr. 50 sci. articles to physics jours. Served with USN, 1946-48. Fulbright rsch. fellow Nat. Edn. Found., U. Auckland, New Zealand, 1975. Fellow Am. Phys. Soc. Avocation: guitar making. Home: PO Box 327 Eastsound WA 98245-0327 E-mail: rfowles@rockisland.com.

FOWLES, JOHN, author; b. Essex, Eng., Mar. 31, 1926; s. Robert and Gladys (Richards) F.; m. Elizabeth Whitton, Apr. 2, 1954 (dec. 1990); m. Sarah Smith, Sept. 3, 1998. Honours degree in French, Oxford U., 1950; D.Litt., Exeter U., 1983; LittD, U. East Anglia, 1997. Author: The Collector, 1963, The Aristos, 1964, The Magus, 1966, The French Lieutenant's Woman, 1969, Poems, 1973, The Ebony Tower, 1974, Shipwreck, 1977, Daniel Martin, 1977, Islands, 1978, The Tree, 1979, Mantissa, 1982, A Maggot, 1985, Wormholes, 1998, John Fowles, Journals, Vol. 1, 2003, Vol. II, 2004. Hon. fellow New Coll., Oxford, 1997. Office: 29 Fernshaw Rd London SW10 0TG England E-mail: anthonysheil@gillonaitkenassocs.ltd.

FOWLKES, NANCY LANETTA PINKARD, social worker; d. Amos Malone and Nettie (Barnett) Pinkard; m. Vester Guy Fowlkes, June 4, 1955 (dec. 1965); 1 child, Wendy Denise. BA, Bennett Coll., 1946; MA, Syracuse U., 1952; MSW, Smith Coll., 1963; MPA, Pace U., 1982. Dir. publicity Bennett Coll., Greensboro, N.C., 1946-47, 49-50; asst. editor Va. Edn. Bull. ofcl. organ Va. State Tchrs. Assn., Richmond, 1950-52; asst. office mgr. Cmty. Svc. Soc., N.Y.C., 1952-55; social caseworker, asst. supr. Dept. Social Svcs. Westchester County, White Plains, N.Y., 1959-67, supr. adoption svcs., 1967-77, supr. adoption and foster care, 1977-89. Mem. adv. bd. White Plains Adult Edn. Sch. First v.p. Eastview Jr. H.S., 1970-71; area chmn. White Plains Cmty. Chest, 1964; sec. Mt. Vernon Concert Group, 1952-54; fund raising co-chmn. Urban League Guild of Westchester, 1967; pres. White Plains Interfaith Coun., 1972-74; pres. northeastern jurisdiction United Meth. Ch., 1988-92; chmn. adminstrv. bd. Meth. Ch., 1970-72, 82-83, vice chmn., 1978 80, vice chmn. trustees, 1973-77, treas., 1978-83; lay spkr., v.p. Met. dist. United Meth. Women, 1977-79, exec. bd. N.Y. conf.; N.Y. conf. rep. Upper Atlantic Regional Sch., 1981-83, mem. nominating com., 1982-83, trustee N.Y. conf., 1982-88, pres. N.Y. conf., 1983-87; bd. dirs. Global Ministries United Meth. Ch., 1988-96, women's divsn., 1988-96, v.p., chair sect. finance women's divsn., 1992-96, supt., 1997—, chair program divsn. N.Y. conf., 1989-93; v.p. superintendency commn. Met. North Dist., 1997—; chair Episcopal residence N.Y. Conf. Episcopacy Com., 1997—; mem. N.Y. Conf. Bd. Ordained Ministry, 2000—; chmn. Dist. Coun. on Ministry, 2002-; bd. dirs. Family Svc. Westchester, Bethel Meth. Home, Ossining, N.Y., White Plains YWCA, 1985-93, Scarritt Bennett Ctr., Nashville, 1990-2000, Gum Moon Women's Residence, San Francisco, 1992-96, White Plains-Greenburg NAACP, 1993-98. Mem. NASW, Acad. Cert. Social Workers, Jack and Jill of Am. Inc. (chpt. pres. 1954-56, regional sec.-treas. 1967-71), Nat. Bus. and Profl. Women's Club (chpt. sec. 1954-56), Internat. Platform Assn., Theta Sigma Phi (sec.-treas.), Zeta Nu Omega, Alpha Kappa Alpha (pres. 1960-64, treas. 1975-78), Regency Bridge Club (pres. 1963-65). Home: 107 Valley Rd White Plains NY 10604-2316

FOX, ALISSA BENIMOFF, dermatologist; b. Cin., Sept. 20, 1954; d. Murray and Norma (Woldman) Benimoff; m. James A. Fox, May 29, 1977; children: Jonathan, Alexandra. AB, Smith Coll., Northampton, Mass., 1976; MD, NYU, N.Y.C., 1980. Diplomate Am. Bd. Dermatology. Med. intern Montefiore Hosp. Medicine, Bronx, N.Y., 1980-81; resident in dermatology N.Y. Hosp., Cornell U. Med. Ctr., N.Y.C., 1981-84; ptnr. Fox Skin & Allergy Assocs., Somerville, N.J., 1984—. Mem. active staff Somerset Med. Ctr., Somerville, N.J., 1984—; mem. courtesy staff Hunterdon Med. Ctr., Flemington, N.J., 1984—. Recipient Vol. Leadership award Am. Cancer Soc., 1989, Physicians Recognition award AMA, 2000. Fellow Am. Acad. Dermatology, Med. Soc. N.J. Office: 3461 US Hwy 22 Somerville NJ 08876-

FOX, ALLAN B. literature educator; b. Phila., Aug. 28, 1939; s. Isadore and Ethel Ann Fox; children: Ilana Michelle, Laura Suzanne. BA in English, Temple U., 1961, MA in English, 1963; PhD in English Lit., U. Chgo., 1969. Cert. automated info. mgmt. cons., magnum code software, hardware. Instr. English Kent (Ohio) State U., 1963—65; tchg. fellow U. Chgo., 1968—69; asst. prof. English U. Cin., 1969—75; marking sys. cons. UARCO, Inc., Great Lakes Region, 1981—84, sr. product mgr. Barrington, Ill., 1984—91, NCR, Inc., Miamisberg, Ohio, 1991—92; mgr. marking sys. Premier Print, Chgo., 1993—; pres. Hrothgar Enterprises, LLC, Dayton, Ohio, 1999—; asst. prof. English Wilberforce (Ohio) U., 2001—. Adj. instr. English U. Cin., 1977—83, William Rainey Harper C.C., Palatine, Ill., 1984—90. Contbr. articles to profl. jours. Mem. Simon Wiesuthal Found., L.A., Calif., 1996—; charter mem. So. Poverty Law Ctr., Montgomery, 2001—. Tchg. fellow, The New Collegiate Divsn., U. Chi., 1969, Taft faculty rsch. grant, U. Cin., 1974. Mem.: MLA, Nat. Coun. Tchrs. English, Wilberforce U. Faculty Assn. (tenure com. 2003). Achievements include patent for chair for use by adult on child. Avocations: theater, collecting political cartoons, basketball. Home: 3030 Shroyer Rd Kettering OH 45429

FOX, ALVIN NONE, bacteriology educator, researcher; b. London, Eng., Apr. 4, 1952; s. Emmanuel and Rebecca Fox; m. Karen Fleming, May 2, 1956; children: Amanda Fleming, Nyssa Fleming. PhD, Leeds (Eng.) U., 1976. Prof. U. of S.C., Columbia, 1980—. Editor: Analytical Microbiology; editor-in-chief: Jour. Microbiol. Methods. Recipient Postdoctoral fellowship, Arthritis and Rheumatism Coun., 1976. Achievements include patents for Automated Evaporator. Avocation: Tae Kwon Do. Home: 225 Olde Springs Columbia SC 29223 Office: U S C Sch Medicine Garners Ferry Rd Columbia SC 29223 Office Fax: 803-733-3192. E-mail: afox@med.sc.edu.

FOX, ARTHUR CHARLES, physician, educator; b. Newark, Sept. 16, 1926; s. Jacob and Mae (Bonda) F. Student, Harvard U., 1943-44; MD, N.Y. U., 1948. Intern, asst. resident and chief resident in medicine Bellevue Hosp., N.Y.C., 1948-52; from asst. to prof. N.Y. U. Sch. Medicine, N.Y.C., 1954—, chief cardiology sect., 1968—2001. Cons. Manhattan VA Hosp. Contbr. articles to profl. jours. Served with M.C. USAF, 1952-54. NIH fellow, 1954-56; grantee, 1956-80 Master ACP (gov. region 1981-86); fellow Am. Coll. Cardiology; mem. Am. Fedn. Clin. Research, N.Y. Heart Assn. (pres. 1987-89), N.Y. Cardiologic Soc. (pres. 1992-93), Alpha Omega Alpha, AAAS, Sigma Xi. Home: 330 E 33rd St Apt 20-L New York NY 10016-9466 Office: 550 1st Ave New York NY 10016-6402

FOX, ARTHUR JOSEPH, JR., editor; b. Bklyn., Sept. 19, 1923; s. Arthur Joseph and Mary Loretta (Foley) F.; m. Ann Marie McElroy, Sept. 7, 1946; children: Jane Ann, John Arthur; m. Lorraine Cecelia Hodge, Sept. 10, 1993. BS in Civil Engring, Manhattan Coll., 1947, DSc (hon.), 1982. Structural designer Sanderson & Porter, N.Y.C., 1947-48; asst. editor Engring. News-Record, McGraw-Hill Publs., N.Y.C., 1948-54, asso. editor, 1954-58, sr. editor, 1956-57, sr. staff editor, 1957-60, mng. editor, 1960-64, editor-in-chief, 1964-88; mng. dir. Constrn. Industry Presidents Forum, Potomac, Md., 1989-97; exec. dir. Constrn. Industry Round Table, 1998. Mem. N.Y.C. Environ. Control Bd., 1974-77. Served with AUS, 1943-45. Decorated Bronze Star; recipient award of merit Am. Cons. Engrs. Council, 1975, medal of profl. excellence, 1985; recipient Met. Civil Engr. of Year award, 1975, We Dig America award Nat. Utility Contractors Assn., 1987, Golden Beaver svc. award, 1988; recipient Silver Shovel award Am. Subcontractors Assn., 1975, hon. mem. 1987, Carroll H. Dunn award Constrn. Industry Inst., 2000; elected to Nat. Acad. of Constructon, 2001; named hon. mem. AIA, 1986. Fellow ASCE (pres. 1975-76); mem. Am. Acad. Environ. Engrs. (past trustee), Nat. Acad. Constrn., Engrs. Coun. for Profl. Devel. (dir. 1969-75), Nat. Constrn. Industry Coun. (exec. com. 1976-77, Saul Horowitz Career Achievement award 1987), N.Y. Bldg. Congress (bd. govs. 1969-73, 78-86), Engrs. Joint Coun. (dir. 1976-77, v.p. 1978-80), The Moles, Manhattan Coll. Alumni Soc. (past pres.), Chi Epsilon, Tau Beta Pi. Clubs: Congl. Country. Home and Office: 10108 Garden Way Potomac MD 20854-3966 E-mail: coinrt@aol.com.

FOX, ARTURO ANGEL, Spanish language educator; b. Hoguín, Cuba, Aug. 2, 1935; came to U.S., 1962, naturalized, 1972; s. Arturo Roberto and Dulce Maria (Macle) F.; m. Rosa del Carmen Portilla, Jan 17, 1959 (dec. June 1998); children: Franz, Alexandra. B. Letters and Scis., Friends Sch., Holguin, Cuba, 1952; LL.D., U. Havana, 1960; MA in Spanish, U. Minn., 1968, PhD, 1971. Bar: Cuba 1960. Pvt. practice law, Holguín, 1960-62; instr. Spanish Luther Coll., Decorah, Iowa, 1963-66; asst. prof. Spanish Dickinson Coll., Carlisle, Pa., 1966-72, assoc. prof., 1972-79, prof., 1979-98, chmn. dept. modern langs., 1972-74, chmn. depts. Spanish and Italian, 1978-79, chmn. dept. Spanish, 1981-84, 90-93. Coord. Latin Am. Studies program, 1968-77; dir. Colombia Semester program Ctrl. Pa. Consortium, 1977-78, Dickinson in Spain, Malaga, 1985-86, 88-90, 93-95; apptd. William W. Edel prof. humanities; honorary chair, 1992. Author: three Spanish textbooks, (novel) Anecdotario del Comandante, 1976; (lit. criticism) El Edipo en Unamuno, 2001; contbr. articles in field

to profl. publs. Ford grantee, 1969-70; Lilly and Mellon faculty devel. grantee, 1978, 79; recipient Christain R. and F. Lindback Found. Disting. Teaching award, 1981 Mem. Am. Assn. Tchrs. Spanish and Portuguese Office: Dickinson Coll Dept Spanish Carlisle PA 17013 E-mail: foxar@aol.com.

FOX, BARRY HOWARD, software engineer; b. Long Beach, N.Y., Dec. 18, 1957; s. Donald Irwin and Rosalind Audrey (Rubin) F.; m. Joan Renee Schindler, May 27, 1988; children: David Roy, Stephen Gregg. BS in Nuclear Engring., Rensselaer Poly. Inst., 1980; MS in Info. Sys., Shippensburg U., 1999. Prin. staff ORI, Inc., Alexandria, Va., 1984—85; sr. reliability engr. GPU Nuc. Corp., Middletown, Pa., 1985—94; sr. I.S. programmer/analyst AMP, Inc., Harrisburg, Pa., 1994—98; lead software engr. Arbitron Inc., Columbia, Md., 1998—. Cons. Fox Computer Consulting, Harrisburg, Pa., 1990-98. Author: (tech. paper) 17th Inter-RAM Conf., 1990, Inter-RAMQ Conf., 1992, ANS/ASME Nuclear Energy Conf., 1992. Lt. USN, 1980-84. Republican. Jewish. Home: 6358 Red Haven Rd Columbia MD 21045-5407 Office: Arbitron Inc 9705 Patuxent Woods Dr Columbia MD 21046-1572

FOX, BETH WHEELER, library director; b. Oklahoma City, May 4, 1945; d. Robert R. and Marjorie (Woodberry) Wheeler; m. Dennis Dean Fox, July 15, 1963; children: Rebecca, Julia, Bryce. BS in Libr. Sci./History cum laude, U. North Tex., 1967. Cataloger George Williams Coll., Downers Grove, Ill., 1967-68; br. libr. Libr., Ft. Benning, Ga., 1968-69; ref. libr. Palos Verdes (Calif.) Pub. Libr., 1969-72; libr. vol. Am. Luth. Sch. Libr., Burbank, Calif., 1979-81, Stevenson Elem. Sch. Libr., Burbank, 1981-82; libr. dir. Westbank Community Libr., Austin, Tex., 1983—. Mem. pub. libr. steering com. Tex. State Libr., 2002-03; presenter in field. Author: The Dynamic Community Library: Practical, Creative and Inexpensive Ideas of the Library Director, 1988, Behind the Scenes at the Dynamic Library: Simplifying Essential Operations, 1990. Bd. dirs. Westbank Community Bds. Recipient Hon. Svc. award Burbank Coun. PTA, 1981, Vol. of Yr. award, 1982. Mem. ALA (John Cotton Dana award 1986, 90), Tex. Libr. Assn. (co-founder small cmty. libr. round table 1986, program chmn. dist. III 1986, rep. state fin. rev. 1991, structure/orgn. coun. 1994, rsch. grant recipient 1987, pub. rels. com. 1995-98, scholarship com. 1995-98, Access Tex. com. 1996—, Cmty. Libr. of Yr. 1988, legis. com. 2000—, founder and chair dist. libr. discussion group 2000—, devel. pub. libr. task force2003, salary compensation task force 2003), Ctrl. Tex. Libr. Sys. (automatiion com. 1986), Network for Smaller Librs. (founder 1985), Tex. Mcpl. Libr. Dirs. Assn., Settlement Club (vol. coord. book nook), Rotary (scholarship com. 1996, 98), Rotary (tchr. excellence com. 1997, program com. 1997-2000), Phi Alpha Theta. Avocations: genealogy, gardening, home repair, stained glass, sailing. Home: 1606 Bay Hill Dr Austin TX 78746-6248

FOX, CAROL JEAN, librarian; b. LaSalle, Ill., May 9, 1942; d. Ralph Francis and Hazel Mabel Mindock;m. DeLon E. Fox, June 20, 1981; m. Curtis A. Wingerter, Feb. 20, 1965 (div. 1973); 1 child, Grechen Lynne Wingerter. BA, MacMurray Coll., 1964; MLS, U. R.I., 1968; postgrad., No. Ill. U., 1973-88, U. Ill., 1995—96. Libr. asst. Indpls. Pub. Libr., 1964-65; 6th grade tchr. Denby Park Day Sch., Norfolk, Va., 1965-66; children's librarian Newport (R.I.) Pub. Libr., 1966-69; sch. librarian Tiverton (R.I.) Pub. Schs., 1969-70; sch. libr. media specialist Rockford (Ill.) Pub. Schs., 1971-85; reading cons. Elgin (Ill.) Pub. Schs., 1986-88; sch. libr. media specialist Highland Park (Ill.) Sch. Dist. 108, 1988-89; youth svcs. cons. Ill. State Libr., Springfield, 1989-93; cons. No. Ill. Libr. System, Rockford, 1993—95; grant mgr., exec. dir. Sinn Valley Info. Network, 1995—96; libr. media specialist Mary Watts Elem. Sch., Naperville, Ill., 1996—2003, Montessori Magnet Sch., Rockford, Ill., 2003—. Adj. faculty Rockford (Ill.) Coll., 1976-88, Nat. Coll. Edn., Evanston, Ill., 1989; chair Rebecca Caudill Young Readers' Book Award Com. Co-author: Celebrate Literature, 1989; contbr. articles to profl. jours. Mem. ALA (mem. coun. 1992-4), ASCD, Ill. Sch. Libr. Media Assn. (bd. dirs., pres. 1995-96, Polestar award 1991), Am. Assn. Sch. Librs., Ill. Sch. Libr. Media Assn., Phi Delta Kappa.

FOX, CLAUDE EARL, former federal health official; b. Charleston, Miss., Nov. 8, 1946; s. Claude Earl Jr. and Shirley (Houston) F.; children: Stephanie Ryan, Victoria Crossley. BS with distinction, Miss. Coll., 1968; MD, U. Miss., 1972; MPH, U. N.C., 1975. Diplomate Am. Bd. Preventive Medicine, Am. Bd. Pub. Health; qualified Am. Bd. Pediatrics. Pediatric intern U. Miss. Med. Ctr., Jackson, 1972-73, pediatric resident, 1979-80, Johns Hopkins Hosp., Balt., 1978-79; with Miss. State Dept. Health, 1973-86; local health officer Charleston, 1973-74; dist. health officer Tupelo, Miss., 1975-78; chief Bur. Family Health Service Jackson, 1980-81; chief Bur. Personal Health Service, 1980-86; state health officer Ala. Dept. Pub. Health, Montgomery, from 1986; adminstr. health resources and svcs. administrn. Dept. HHS, Rockville, Md., 1997—2001; dir. Inst. for Urban Health, Johns Hopkins U., Balt., 2001—. Med. cons. N.C. Dept. Health, Chapel Hill, 1974-75, Rockwell Internat., Tupelo, 1976-78, Mo. Dept. Health, 1984; vis. tchr. maternal and child health U. Miss. Med. Ctr., 1980-86, mem. adv. council; vis. teaching staff Sch. Pub. Health and Sch. Medicine, U. Ala.; adv. group on prevention Sen. Com. Labor and Human Resources, Washington; mem. Ala. Statewide Health Coordinating Council; mem. Ala. State Child Abuse and Negelect Prevention Bd., Ala. Commn. on Aging, Ala. Youth Services Bd., Planning and Adv. Council for Devel. Disabilities, Pesticides Adv. Com., Ala. Bd. Examiners Nursing Home Adminstrs.; chmn. Ala. Task Force Prevention and Perinatal Health, Ala. Radiation Adv. Bd. Health; adv. com. Emergency Med. Services; past mem. work group to revise 1988 U.S. standard birth certificate Nat. Ctr. Health Stats., primary care work group Miss. Gov.'s Office; past chmn. infant mortality task force, adolescent pregnancy task force Gov.'s Council on Children and Youth; adj. assoc. prof. George Washington U., 1999—. Mem. Ala. Resource Devel. Com.; bd. dirs. Montgomery chpt., bd. dirs. Ala. div., med. adv. com. ARC.; mem. external adv. com. Sch. Pub. Health U. Ala. Birmingham; mem. Ala. State Bldg. Commn. Recipient Sidney Chipman award for Outstanding Achievement in Maternal and Child Health U. N.C., 1982; named Pub. Citizen of Yr. Nat. Assn. Social Workers, Montgomery unit, 1987, Ala. chpt. 1987, Disting. Alumnus award sch. pub. health U. N.C., 1999, Leadership award Washington Bus. Group on Health and Nat. Assn. Cmty. Health Ctrs., 1999. Mem. Nat. Assn. Maternal and Child Health and Crippled Children's Dirs. (past steering com., legis. com., data com., pres-elect), Med. Assn. State Ala, Montgomery County Med. Soc., Am. Pub. Health Assn. (past Miss. del. Governing Council, Young Profl. Yr. award Maternal and Child Health sect. 1984), Ala. Pub. Health Assn., Assn. State and Terr. Health Officials (past forms revision com.), Am. Coll. Ob-gyn (past com. revision natality terminology). Avocations: antique cars, antique clocks, music. Office: Inst for Urban Health Affairs Johns Hopkins U 111 Market Pl Ste 850 Baltimore MD 21202

FOX, CONNIE STEITZ, freelance writer, editor, graphic designer; b. Sanger, Calif., Oct. 25, 1946; d. Warren Chester and Viletta (Petersen) Steitz; m. Meredith George Fox, Sept. 27, 1969; children: Todd Christian Fox, Emily Kirsten Fox Samson. Student, Ariz. State U., 1964-66; Registered Dental Hygienist, U. Tex., Houston, 1969; cert. in tech. writing, desktop pub., Houston C.C., 1996; AAS in Tech. Comm. with high honors, Advanced Cert., 1999. Lic. dental hygienist, Tex., Ohio; lic. real estate sales, Tex. Dental hygienist Myers Thornton, DDS, Dallas, 1969-71, Rick Hammond DDS, Houston, 1980-83; owner, prin. Noteworthy Writing and Editing, Houston, 1987—. Copy editor, cons. Desktop Pub., 1990—; editor Tex. Monthly, Wall St. Jour., corp. websites, 1997— Brownie leader Troop 5286, Houston, 1983-86; 1st soprano adult choir Kingsland Bapt. Ch., Katy, Tex., 1983-89, Tallowood Bapt. Ch., Houston, 1991-95; pres. Chronic Fatigue and Immune Dysfunction Support Group, Houston, 1989-90; ptnr. St. Jude's Children's Rsch. Hosp., Memphis, 1998—; charter mem. Rep. Nat. Com. Profl. Digital Pubs. scholar, 1991. Mem. NAFE, Internat. Assn. Bus. Communicators, Phi Theta Kappa, Delta Delta Delta. Republican. Avocations: travel, photography, gardening, investing. Office: PO Box 840648 Houston TX 77284-0648

FOX, DANIEL MICHAEL, foundation executive, author; b. N.Y.C., Aug. 20, 1938; s. Alexander E. and Rose (Leitner) F.; m. Carol Anne Kemps, Sept. 8, 1963 (div. 1985); children: Aaron, Miriam, Joshua, Benjamin; m. Louise O. Vasvari, Dec. 26, 1988 (div. 2003). AB, Harvard U., 1959, AM, 1961, PhD, 1964. Instr. Harvard U., Cambridge, Mass., 1964-65; dir. field ops. Applachian Vols., Berea, Ky., 1965—66; assoc. dir. Commonwealth of Mass. Svc . Corps, 1965—67; asst. prof. Harvard U., Cambridge, Mass., 1967-72; prof., v.p. SUNY, Stony Brook, 1972-89. Assoc. dir. Nat. Ctr. for Health Svcs. Rsch., Rockville, Md., 1975-78; pres. Milbank Meml. Fund, N.Y.C., 1990—; cons. in field. Author: Engines of Culture, 1963, rev. edit., 1995, The Discovery of Abundance, 1967, electronic edit., 2002, Economists and Health Care, 1979, Health Policies, Health Politics, 1986, Photographing Medicine, 1988, AIDS: The Burdens of History, 1989, AIDS: The Making of a Chronic Disease, 1992, Power and Illness: The Failure and Future of American Health Policy, 1993, 95. Bd. dirs. Village Care N.Y. Inc., vice chmn., 1996—; bd. dirs. Employee Benefit Rsch. Inst., treas., 2003—; bd. dirs. ECRI, The Health Tech. Ctr., Am. for Better Care of the Dying, Global Enterprise for Water Tech., Health Quality Coun. Sask. Shaw traveling fellow Harvard U., 1959-60, Sheldon traveling fellow, 1962; also numerous grants. Mem.: NAS, Am. Pub. Health Assn., N.Y. Acad. Medicine, Am. Assn. for the History of Medicine, Nat. Acad. Social Ins., Am. Hist. Assn. (Beveridge prize 1965), Coun. on Fgn. Rels., Inst. Medicine of NAS, Harvard Club of N.Y. Jewish. Office: Milbank Meml Fund 645 Madison Ave Fl 15 New York NY 10022-1010 E-mail: dmfox@milbank.org.

FOX, DAVID ALAN, rheumatologist, immunologist; b. Montreal, July 5, 1953; s. Lester L. and Zelda L. (Rothbart) F.; m. Paula L. Bockenstedt, July 10, 1977; children: Sharon Elizabeth, Michelle Caroline, Jonathan William. BS, MIT, 1974; MD, Harvard U., 1978. Diplomate Am. Bd. Internal Medicine, Am. Bd. Rheumatology. Intern, then resident Brigham and Women's Hosp., Boston, 1978-81; fellow in rheumatology and immunology Harvard U. Med. Sch., Boston, 1981-85; asst. prof. U. Mich., Ann Arbor, 1985-90, assoc. prof., 1990-95, prof., 1995—, acting chief divsn. rheumatology, 1990-91, chief divsn., 1991—. Dir. U. Mich. Multipurpose Arthritis Ctr., Ann Arbor, 1990—2001, U. Mich. Rheumatic Disease Core Ctr., 2001—; trustee Arthritis Found., 1992—. Assoc. editor Jour. Clin. Investigation, 1997-2002; contbr. chpts. to books, articles to profl. jours. Mem.: Assn. Am. Physicians, Am. Soc. Clin. Investigation, Am. Assn. Immunologists, Am. Coll. Rheumatology. Achievements include discovery of T lymphocyte surface molecules and development of various monoclonal antibodies. Office: U MichMed Ctr Rackham Arthritis Rsch Unit 3918 Taubman Ctr Ann Arbor MI 48109

FOX, DAVID WAYNE, banker; b. Aurora, Ill., Aug. 29, 1931; s. Wayne Stauffer and Helen Katherine (Lynch) F.; m. Mary Ann Evans, Sept. 22, 1956; children: Susan E., David Wayne, Katherine A., Thomas E. BS in Fin., U. Notre Dame, 1953; MBA, U. Chgo., 1958. With No. Trust Co., Chgo., 1955-95, sr. v.p., 1974-78; exec. v.p. No. Trust Corp. and Co., Chgo., 1978-81, vice chmn., dir., 1981-87, pres., COO, 1987-89, chmn. bd., CEO, 1989-95. Bd. dirs. USG Corp., Chgo., Fed. Res. Bank Chgo.; chmn. Chgo. Stock Exch., 1996-2000. Chmn. bd. govs. Hinsdale (Ill.) Community House, 1983; trustee Adler Planetarium, Chgo., 1983—, Northwestern Meml. Hosp., Chgo., 1983—, Chgo. Symphony Orch., 1988—; bd. dirs. United Way Chgo., 1988-91, Lyric Opera Chgo., 1990—; mem. bus. adv. coun. U. Notre Dame, Inc., 1981-87, Kellogg Grad. Sch. Bus., Northwestern U., Evanston, Ill., 1988—; trustee De Paul U., Chgo., 1988—, mem. bus. adv. coun., 1982-91; mem. adv. coun. grad. sch. bus. U. Chgo., 1995— Mem. Marine Corps Res. Officers Assn., Chgo. Club, U. Club., Commonwealth Club, Econ. Club, Comml. Club, Mid-Day (Chgo.) Club, Hinsdale (Ill.) Golf Club, Casino Club, Sea Island Club. Republican. Roman Catholic. Avocations: tennis, skiing, golf, fishing. Office: 21 S Clark St Ste 2530 Chicago IL 60603-2092

FOX, DAWNE MARIE, safety scientist; b. West Lafayette, Ind., Aug. 3, 1948; d. Gerhard P. and Betty M. (Norris) F.; m. Gerald C. Newmeyer, Oct. 4, 1969 (div. 1981); children: Mimie, Jerry. Grad. magna cum laude, Lord Fairfax, Middletown, Va., 1979; grad., Casper (Wyo.) Coll., 1985; cert. in indsl. safety and health, Ga. Inst. Tech., 1998, cert. in hazardous material mgmt., cert. in environ. mgmt., cert. in constrn. safety and health, Ga. Inst. Tech., 1999. Cert. environ. trainer Nat. Environ. Tng. Assn.; EPA cert. instr. in asbestos abatement, supr., insp. and mgmt. planner, project designer tng. courses; approved instr. occupl. safety and health adminstrn., U.S. Dept. Labor, Nat. Tng. Inst.; cert. in indsl. safety and health; registered environ. mgr. Nat. Registry Environ. Profls.; cert. hazardous materials mgr. Inst. Hazardous Material Mgrs. Regional safety coord. Milchem Inc., Casper, 1979-83; safety dir. Energy Insulation Inc., Casper, 1983-85; safety mgr. Western States Constrn., Loveland, Colo., 1985-86; safety officer Govt. of D.C., 1987-89; dir. safety, health svcs. Denver and Rio Grande R.R., Denver, 1989-90; safety mgr. Browning-Ferris Inc., Hyattsville, 1990-91; sr. safety scientist Gen. Physics Corp., Columbia, Md., 1991—. Cons., Casper, 1983-85. Instr. ARC, Casper, 1981-85, Am. Heart Assn., Casper, 1982-85; spl. aide to Spl. Olympics, Casper, 1983-85. Mem. Nat. Safety Coun., Am. Soc. Safety Engrs. (v.p. 1982-83, pres. 1983-84, Safety Profl. award 1982), Assn. Am. Railroads Safety Coun. (past del.). Republican. Roman Catholic. Avocations: skiing, bowling. Home: 8706 Mission Rd Jessup MD 20794

FOX, DONALD LEE, mental health counselor, consultant; b. Seymour, Ind., Sept. 9, 1948; s. John L. and Thelma P. (Engel) F.; m. Patricia L. Sain, Aug. 26, 1978; children: Ashley M., Aimee E. BA, Ind. U., Indpls., 1978; MS, Ind. State U., 1979. Lic. clin. social worker, social worker, marriage and family therapist. Coord. mental health Cath. Social Svcs., Indpls., 1979—85; coord. psychiat. assessment Valley Vista Hosp., Greenwood, Ind., 1985—86; clin. dir. Fox Counseling, Speedway, Ind., 1986—. Lectr., cons. Butler U., Indpls., 1988—89; adj. prof. Ind. U./Purdue U., Indpls., 1980—, U. Indpls., 1990—2002; cons. Wayne Twp. Vol. Fire Dept., Indpls., 1984—, LaPorte (Ind.) Child Welfare Dept., 1988—2002. Pres., CEO Fire Stop of Ind.: A Program for Youth, Inc., 1987-92. Mem.: ACA, Ind. Mental Health Counselors Assn. (pres.-elect 1989—91, pres. 1991—92, Outstanding Svc. award 1989), Ind. Assn. Counseling and Devel. (conf. chmn. 1989), Am. Mental Health Counselors Assn. (nat. conf. com. 1990). Roman Catholic. Avocations: gardening, woodworking, financial planning, money management. Home: 730 Greenlee Dr Indianapolis IN 46234-2237 E-mail: dlfox@myexcite.com.

FOX, DONALD THOMAS, lawyer; b. Council Bluffs, Iowa, June 12, 1929; s. Donald and Genevieve (Tinley) F.; m. Ana Clemencia Tercero-Graham; children: Mark, Matthew, Genevieve, Melissa. AB magna cum laude, Harvard U., 1951; LLB, N.Y. U., 1956; Brevet de Traduction et de Terminologie Juridiques, U. Paris, 1957, Diplome de Droit Comparé, 1961. Bar: N.Y. 1957, U.S. Ct. Claims 1960, U.S. Dist. Ct. (so. and ea. dists.) N.Y. 1960, U.S. Ct. Appeals (2nd cir.) 1960, D.C. 1968, U.S. Tax Ct. 1973. Instr. Inst. Comparative Law, NYU, 1957-59; assoc. Davis, Polk, Wardwell, Sunderland & Kiendl, N.Y.C., 1958-67; ptnr. Fox Horan & Camerini, LLP and predecessor firms, N.Y.C., 1968—. Bd. dirs. Washington Sq. Legal Svcs., Inc., N.Y.C., 1974-85, Uniroyal Goodrich Tire Co., 1990-96, Michelin Licensing Svcs. Inc., Globalstar do Brazil, 1995-99; mem. adv. com. on history and theory Harvard U. Grad. Sch. Design, 1990—. Author: Conciliation of International Economic Disputes, 1964, Human Rights in Guatemala, 1979, Report on Contra Activity in Nicaragua, 1985, Violence in Colombia, 1989, Hungarian Constitutional Reform and the Rule of Law, 1993, Elections in Ethiopia, 1995, Elections in Nicaragua, 1996, 2000, Elections in Mexico, 1997, Lessons of the Colombian Constitutional Reform of 1991 (U.S. Inst. of Peace), 2002; editor: The Cambodian Incursion: Legal Issues, 1971; mem. panel advisors Jour. Internat. Law and Politics, 1968-99; contbr. articles to legal jours. Trustee Law Ctr. Found., N.Y.U., 1975-86, chmn. campaign fund,, 1980; mem. Am. Soc., 1975—; Coun. on Fgn. Rels., 1973—; Pres.'s assocs. Harvard U., 2000—. 1st lt. USAF, 1951-53. Named to Com. of Honor, Giulio Romano Exhbn., Mantova, Italy, 1989; Albert Gallatin fellow, 1978; Nat. scholar Harvard U., Root-Tilden scholar NYU, Fulbright scholar U. Paris. Fellow: Am. Bar Found. (life); mem.: The Century Assn. (chmn. wine com.), Humanitarian Found. for Nicaragua (exec. com. bd. dirs. 1991—96), NYU Alumni Fedn. (pres. 1983—85), NYU Law Alumni Assn. (pres. 1971—73), Assn. of Bar of City of N.Y. (chmn. com. lawyers role in search for peace 1969—71, chmn. com. profl. responsibility 1971—74, chmn. com. audit 1978—80, treas. 1982—84, chmn. fin. com. 1982—84), Am. Arbitration Assn. (panel arbitrators 1970—), Am. Assn. Internat. Commn. Jurists (exec. com., bd. dirs. 1970—, chmn. 1991—), Am. Law Inst. (sustaining life), Harvard Club of N.Y.C. Office: Fox Horan & Camerini LLP 825 3rd Ave New York NY 10022-7519 Fax: 212 269-2383. E-mail: dtfox@foxlex.com.

FOX, EDWARD A. business executive; b. N.Y.C., July 17, 1936; s. Herman and Ruth F.; divorced; children: Brian, Laura, Jacqueline. AB, Cornell U., 1958; MBA, NYU, 1975. Pres., CEO, Student Loan Mktg. Assn., Washington, 1973-90; dean Amos Tuck Sch. Dartmouth Coll., Hanover, N.H., 1990-94; chmn. SLM Corp., Reston, Va., 1997—. Bd. dirs. Delphi Fin. Group, Inc., Greenwich Capital Holdings, Inc. Trustee U. Maine sys.; vice chmn. bd. dirs. Am. Ballet Theater. Office: SLM Corp 11600 Sallie Mae Dr Reston VA 20190-4796

FOX, ELEANOR MAE COHEN, lawyer, educator, writer; b. Trenton, N.J., Jan. 18, 1936; d. Herman and Elizabeth (Stein) Cohen; children: Douglas Anthony, Margot Alison, Randall Matthew. BA, Vassar Coll., 1956; LLB, NYU, 1961. Bar: N.Y. 1961, U.S. Dist. Ct. N.Y. 1964, U.S. Supreme Ct. 1965. Ptnr. Simpson Thacher & Bartlett, 1970—76, of counsel, 1976—; prof. Law Sch. NYU, N.Y.C., 1976—, Walter J. Derenberg prof. trade regulation, 1999—. Lectr. on antitrust and internat. competition policy, globalization markets; mem. Pres. Carter's Nat. Commn. Rev. Antitrust Laws and Procedures, 1978-79; mem. adv. bd. Bur. Nat. Affairs Antitrust and Trade Regulation Reporter, 1977—; trustee NYU Law Ctr. Found., 1974-92; trustee Lawyers' Com. Civil Rights Under Law, 1988—; mem. Coun. Fgn. Rels., 1993—; mem. Pres. Clinton's internat. competition policy adv. com. to advise the U.S. Atty. Gen., 1997-2000. Author: (with Byron E. Fox) Corporate Acquisitions and Mergers, Vol. 1, 1968, Vol. 2, 1970, Vol. 3, 1973, Vol. 4, 1981, rev. edit., 2003; (novel) W.L., Esquire, 1977, (with Lawrence A. Sullivan) Antitrust—Cases and Materials, 1989, supplement, 1995, (with G. Bermann, R. Goebel, W. Davey) European Union Law, Cases and Materials, 2002, The Competition Law of the European Union--Cases and Materials, 2002; (with J. Fingleton, D. Neven, P. Seabright) Competition Policy and the Transformation of Central Europe, 1996; mem. bd. editors N.Y. Law Jour., 1976-99, Antitrust Bull., 1986—; mem. adv. bd. Rev. Indsl. Orgn., 1990-2001, EEC Merger Control Reporter, 1992—, Gaceta Juridica de la CE y de la Competencia, 1992-2001, World Competition: Law and Economics Review, 1999—, Inst. for Consumer Antitrust Studies, 2002--. Fellow Am. Bar Found., N.Y. Bar Found.; mem. ABA (chmn. merger com. antitrust sect. 1974-77, chmn. publs. com. 1977-78, chmn. Sherman Act com. 1978-79, mem. council antitrust sect. 1979-83, 90-94, vice chmn. antitrust sect. 1992-94, chair NAFTA Task Force, 1993-99), N.Y. State Bar Assn. (chmn. antitrust sect. 1978-79, mem. exec. com. antitrust sect. 1979-83), Fed. Bar Council (trustee 1974-76, v.p. 1976-78), Assn. of Bar of City of N.Y. (v.p. 1989-90, exec. com. 1977-81, chmn. trade regulation com. 1973-76, lawyer advt. com. 1976-77, chmn. com. on U.S. in a global economy, 1991-94), Am. Law Inst., Assn. Am. Law Schs. (chmn. sect. antitrust and econ. regulation 1981-83), NYU Law Alumni Assn. (bd. dirs. 1974-79, 87-91), Am. Fgn. Law Assn. (v.p. 1979-82, 98-2001).

FOX, FRANCIS HANDY, lawyer; b. Attleboro, Mass., May 28, 1933; s. Francis Joseph and Mary Frances (Brady) F.; m. Cynthia Ann Blundell, Dec. 27, 1959; children: Cynthia, Martin, Matthew, Kalarn. BS in Econs., Coll. Holy Cross, 1955; LLB, Harvard U., 1963. Bar: Mass. 1963, U.S. Ct. Appeals (1st cir.) 1963, U.S. Supreme Ct. 1977. Assoc. Bingham, Dana & Gould, Boston, 1963-70; ptnr. Bingham McCutchen LLP and predecessor firms, Boston, 1970—. Mem. adv. com. on civil rules Jud. Conf. of U.S., 1992-98. Capt. USNR, 1955-78. Fellow Am. Coll. Trial Lawyers. Home: 77 Cottage St Sharon MA 02067-2132 Office: Bingham McCutchen LLP 150 Federal St Boston MA 02110-1726 E-mail: francis.fox@bingham.com.

FOX, FRANCIS HENRY, retired veterinarian; b. Clifton Springs, N.Y., Mar. 11, 1923; s. Henry Sylvester and Alma (Lindner) F.; m. Mildred Genevieve Cullen, Aug. 6, 1946; children— Rosanna, Laurinda, Teresa, Henry. D.V.M., N.Y. State Veterinary Coll., 1945. Diplomate: Charter diplomate Am. Coll. Veterinary Internal Medicine. Research asst. N.Y. State Veterinary Coll.-Cornell U., 1945-46, mem. faculty, 1947-92, prof. veterinary medicine and obstetrics, 1953-92, chmn. dept. large animal medicine, obstetrics and surgery, 1972-77; instr. surgery Veterinary Coll., Ohio State U., 1946-47. Author articles in field. Mem. Nat. Acad. Practice, Am. Vet. Med. Assn. (exec. bd. dist. I 1966-81, chmn. 1973-74, 77-78), So. Tier (sec.-treas. 1957-62), N.Y. State veterinary med. assns., N.Y.State Assn. Professions, Am. Assn. Bovine Practitioners (pres. 1971-72), Sigma Xi, Alpha Psi, Phi Zeta, Phi Kappa Phi., Omega Tau Sigma. Home: 11 Muriel St Ithaca NY 14850-1835

FOX, FRANK G. school librarian, writer; b. Lake Charles, La., Oct. 16, 1956; s. Hubert Jackson Fox and Mary Margaret Hebert. BS in Fin., McNeese State U., 1980; MS in Econs., La. State U., 1982, MS in Libr. Sci., 1985. Cert. journeyman wireman. Br. libr. Westwego, Jefferson Parish Libr., Metairie, La., 1986—87; asst. dir. St. Charles Parish Libr., Luling, La., 1987—89; info. broker Frankenstein's Fax, Harvey, La., 1990—94; sch. libr. Plaquemines Parish Sch. Bd., Belle Chasse, La., 1994—98; regional libr. FDIC, Memphis, 1998—2000; evening reference libr. S.W. Tex. State U., San Marcos, 2000—. Author: (book) Funky Butt Blues, 1996, Bizarre New Orleans, 1997 (River Rd. award, 1998), 19 1/2 Revelations, 2002, Jean Lafitte and the Big Ol' Whale, 2003. Mem.: ALA, Internat. Brotherhood Elec. Workers, Assn. Ind. Info. Profls., Tex. Libr. Assn., Phi Kappa Phi. Democrat. Roman Catholic. Avocations: reading, writing, travel. Home: 109 Craddock Ave San Marcos TX 78666 Office: Tex State U Alkek Libr 601 University Dr San Marcos TX 78666 Office Fax: 512-245-3002. Personal E-mail: fgf01@yahoo.com. E-mail: ff10@txstate.edu.

FOX, GALEN W. state representative; b. Hilo, Feb. 24, 1943; m. Carol Fox; children: Derek, MeiMei. BA, U. of Redlands, 1965; MPA, Princeton U., 1967, PhD, 1978. Fgn. svc. officer U.S. Dept. of State, 1966—82; rsch. fellow East-West Ctr., 1982; exec. asst. Mayor of Honolulu, 1985—99; chief Hawaii Dept. of Bus., 1991—96; adminstr. Economy Dept. and Tourism, 1991—96; chief Hawaii Dept. of Econ. Devel., Bus. Devel. and Mktg. Divsn., 1991—99. Chair Sec. of State's Open Forum, 1978—79; sec. Am. Fgn. Svc. Assn., 1979—81; chair, vice chair Neighborhood Bd. #3, 1989—96; house rep. whip Hawaii State House of Reps., 2000—. Mem., treas. Oahu Pvt. Industry Coun., 1985—91; pres. Hawaii Cmty. Svcs. Coun., 1995—96; sec., treas. East-West Ctr. Internat. Alumni Exec. Com., 1995—2000; mem. Aloha United Way Allocations Com., 1996—; historian Hasaii Found. Pacific and Asian Affairs Coun.; exec. bd. Ch. of the Crossroads, 2001—. Mem.: Waikki Residents Assn., Waikki Improvement Assn. Republican. Mem.United Church Of Christ. Office: State Captial Rm 318 415 S Beretania St Honolulu HI 96813 Fax: 808-586-8524. E-mail: repfox@capitol.hawaii.gov.*

FOX, GEOFFREY EDMUND, writer, editor, translator; b. Chgo., Apr. 3, 1941; s. Oswald Irvin and Dorothy Mae (Knickerbocker) Fox; m. Sylvia Herrera, 1966 (div. 1975); m. Susana Amelia Torre, 1980; children: Alex, Joaquin. AB, Harvard U., 1963; PhD, Northwestern U., 1975. Cmty. developer ACCION en Venezuela, Caracas, 1963-64; rsch. supr. U. P.R., San Juan, 1966-67; instr. U. Ill., Chgo., 1970-75; asst. prof. various schs., Ill., Wis., Ohio, Minn., 1975-79; UN rep. World Fedn. Trade Unions, N.Y.C., Prague, Czech Republic, 1979-80; freelance writer, translator N.Y.C., 1980—; dir. comm. N.Y.C. Commn. Human Rights, 1994-95; coord. sch./coll. articulation Bronx Ednl. Alliance, 1998-99. Author: Welcome to my Contri, 1988, Hispanic Nation: Culture, Politics and the Constructing of Identity, 1996, The Land and People of Argentina, 1990, The Land and People of Venezuela, 1991. NEH fellow, 1977, 81, rsch. fellow NYU, 1983-84. Mem.: Authors Guild, Nat. Writers Union (ea. regional v.p. 2001—02). Avocations: guitar, sailing. Home and Office: 14 E 4th St Apt 812 New York NY 10012-1142

FOX, GEORGE EDWARD, molecular biology educator; b. Syracuse, N.Y., Dec. 17, 1945; s. Charles Dainer and Henrietta L. (Carpentier) F.; m. Carolyne Ann Tordiglione, Sept. 1, 1973; children: Brian Trevor, Kevin William. BSChemE, Syracuse U., 1967, PhD in Chem. Engring., 1974. Research assoc. U. Ill., Urbana, 1973-77; asst. prof. biochemistry U. Houston, 1977-82, assoc. prof., 1982-86, prof., 1986—. Editl. bd. mem.: Jour. Molecular Evolution, 1978—2000; contbr. chapters to books and articles to profl. jours. NASA grantee, 1977—; EPA grantee, 1994-2000; Welch Found. grantee, 2000—. Mem. Am. Soc. Microbiologists, AAAS, Am. Chem. Soc., Sigma Xi, Theta Tau. Avocations: bridge, chess. Office: U Houston Dept Biology & Biochem Houston TX 77204-5001 E-mail: fox@uh.edu.

FOX, GRETCHEN HOVEMEYER, freelance editor, genealogical consultant; b. Erie, Pa., Jan. 2, 1940; d. Ernst Henry and Marjory Etta (Hollister) Hovemeyer; m. Kenneth Roland Fox, Apr. 23, 1989. AB, Radcliffe Coll., 1961. Manuscript sec. Internat. Tax Program Harvard U. Law Sch., Cambridge, Mass., 1961-63, copy editor, 1963-65, editorial asst., 1965-66, publs. asst., 1966-76, editorial and pub. dir., 1976-89; freelance editor, cons. pub. and genealogy Cambridge, 1989—; database/rsch. asst. innovations program John

F. Kennedy Sch. of Govt., Harvard U., Cambridge, Mass., 1991-93, staff asst. innovations program, 1993—2002; ret., 2002—. Mem. New Eng. Hist. Geneal. Soc., Orange County Geneal. Soc. (pub. cons. 1983-91), Sullivan County (N.Y.) Hist. Soc., DAR (chpt. registrar, chpt. historian 1978-83).

FOX, HAMILTON PHILLIPS, III, lawyer; b. Salisbury, Md., Sept. 18, 1945; s. Hamilton Phillips and Evelyn Louise (Jefferson) F.; m. Mary Shannon Lafans, Aug. 31, 1968 (dissolved); children: Gretchen Robinson, Hamilton Duke, Caleb Savage; m. Barbara Daniels Robinson, Dec. 13, 1986. BA with honors, U. Va., 1967; LLB, Yale U., 1970. Bar: Maine 1971, D.C. 1972, U.S. Dist. Ct. Md., U.S. Ct. Appeals (1st, 9th and D.C. cirs.), U.S. Supreme Ct. Law clk. to judge U.S. Ct. Appeals (1st cir.), Portland, Maine, 1970-71; law clk. to Hon. Stanley Reed and Lewis F. Powell Jr. U.S. Supreme Ct., Washington, 1971-72; asst. U.S. atty. U.S. Atty.'s Office, Washington, 1972-73, 74-77; asst. spl. prosecuter Watergate Prosecution Force, Washington, 1973-74; dep. chief organized crime sect. U.S. Dept. Justice, Washington, 1977-80; sole practice Washington, 1980-84; ptnr. Dewey, Ballantine, Bushby, Palmer & Wood, Washington, 1984-90; now ptnr. Sutherland, Asbill & Brennan, Washington. Lectr. law U. Va., Charlottesville, 1980-82; assoc. dep. counsel com. on standards of official conduct U.S. Ho. of Reps., 1983-84. Home: 729 Massachusetts Ave NE Washington DC 20002-6007 Office: Sutherland Asbill Brennan 1275 Pennsylvania Ave NW Ste 1 Washington DC 20004-2415

FOX, HAROLD EDWARD, obstetrician, gynecologist, educator, researcher; b. East Orange, N.J., Feb. 19, 1945; s. Willis Edward and Elizabeth (Strathearn) F.; m. Rhea Keller, June 18, 1966; children: Harold Hamilton, Andrhea Alicia. BA, U. Rochester, 1967, MS, MD with honors, 1972. Diplomate Am. Bd. Ob-Gyn., Am. Bd. Maternal-Fetal Medicine. Intern, resident Strong Meml. Hosp., Rochester, N.Y., 1972-75; dir. Regional Perinatal Program, Rochester, N.Y., 1975-79; dir. obstetrics and maternal fetal medicine U. Rochester, 1977-79; dir. maternal fetal medicine Columbia U., N.Y.C., 1979-95, dir. obstetrics, 1985-88, vice-chmn. ob-gyn., 1988-91, chmn. protem dept. ob-gyn., 1991-95; Oscar I. and Mildred S. Dodek prof., chmn. ob-gyn. George Washington U., Washington, 1995-96, exec. dir. Ctr. Excellence for Women's Health, 1995-96; ob-gyn. in-chief Johns Hopkins Medicine, Balt., 1996—, Dr. Dorothy Edwards prof. ob-gyn., 1996—, chair women's health ctr. oversight com., 1997—, chmn., dir. ob-gyn. Trustee Johns Hopkins Med. Svc. Corp., Johns Hopkins Home Care Group, 1996—, Kemed Kreige Inst., 1996—; vice chair med. bd. Johns Hopkins Hosp., 1999-2002, chair med. bd., 2002—, physician, 1996—; mem. adv. bd. Johns Hopkins Medicine; dir. ob-gyn Johns Hopkins Medicine, 1996—, bd. govs. CPA; chmn. women and infant transmission study NIH, 1988-93; mem. pediatric com. AIDS clin. trials group, 1988-91; organizing mem. women's com.; mem. obstet. adv. com. N.Y.C. Dept. Health; bd. midwifery N.Y. State Edn. Dept., 1994-95; chmn. N.Y. Acad. Medicine Ob-gyn. sect., 1993-94; mem. Gov.'s Commn. on Infant Mortality, State Md., 1999—; co-chair innovations in patient care. Editor Pediatric AIDS, 1991-95, Practical Revs. in Ob-Gyn.; contbr. articles to profl. jours. Grantee NIH, 1988-95, USPHS, 1991-95, March of Dimes. Fellow Soc. Gynecologic Investigation, ACOG; mem. Internat. AIDS Soc., Am. Gynecol. and Obstet. Soc., Am. Inst. Ultrasound in Medicine, Perinatal Rsch. Soc., Washington Acad. Medicine, Washington Gynecol. Soc., N.Y. Obstet. Soc., Alpha Omega Alpha, Phi Beta Delta. Avocations: boating, art, fitness. Home: PO Box 142 Gibson Island MD 21056-0142 Office: Johns Hopkins Medicine Dept Gyn-Ob 600 N Wolfe St Rm 264 Baltimore MD 21287-0005 E-mail: hfox@jhmi.edu.

FOX, HUGH BERNARD, JR., writer, archaeologist; b. Chgo., Feb. 12, 1932; s. Hugh Bernard and Helen Marie Fox; m. Maria Bernadete Costa-Fox; children: Hugh B. III, Cecilia, Marcella, Margaret, Alexandra, Christopher, Nona W. BS in Humanities, Loyola U., Chgo., 1955, MA, 1956; PhD, U. Ill., 1958. Prof. Loyola U., L.A., 1958-68, Mich. State U., East Lansing, 1968-99, prof. emeritus, 1999—. Fulbright prof. U. Sonora, Hermosillo, Mexico, 1961, Inst. Pedagogico, Caracas, Venezuela, 1964-66, U. Santa Catarina, Florianopolis, Brazil. Author: Henry James, 1968, Charles Bukowski: A Critical and Bibliographical Study, 1969, The Gods of Cataclysm, 1976, Honeymoon/Mom, 1978, First Fire: Central and South American Indian Poetry, 1978, Leviathan, 1980, Lyn Lifshin: A Critical Study, 1985, The Mythological Foundations of the Epic Genre: The Solar Voyage as teh Hero's Journey, 1989, The Sacred Cave, 1992, Shaman, 1995, Stairway to the Sun, 1996, The Angel of Death, 2000, Me, 2000, Immortal Jaguar, 2002, Hugh Fox: Greatest Hits, 2003. John C. Brown Libr. fellow Brown U., Providence, 1968; grantee Orgn. Am. States, 1971, 86. Home and Office: 815 Seymour Ave Lansing MI 48906-5130 E-mail: hughfox@aol.com.

FOX, IRVING HARVEY, clinical researcher, medical products executive; b. Montreal, Que., Can., Dec. 7, 1943; came to U.S., 1976; s. Nathan and Phyllis (Maron) F.; m. Gloria Phyllis Godine, June 21, 1966; children: Caroline, Sharon, Joanna BSC, McGill U., Montreal, 1965, MD, CM, 1967; student in rsch. tng. program, Duke U. Med. Ctr., 1969-70. Diplomate Am. Bd. Internal Medicine; lic. physician, Mich., Mass. Rotating intern Royal Victoria Hosp., Montreal, 1967-68, jr. asst. resident in medicine, 1968-69; rsch fellow div. rheumatic and genetic diesase Duke U. Med. Ctr., Durham, N.C., 1969-71, sr. asst. resident in medicine, 1971-72; physician The Wellesley Hosp., 1972-76; assoc. dir. Clin. Rsch. Ctr. U. Mich. Hosp., 1976-77, acting program dir., 1977-78, program dir., 1978-90; interim div. chief in rheumatology U. Mich., 1986-88; v.p. med. affairs Biogen Inc., Cambridge, Mass., 1990-99; clin. prof. medicine Harvard Med. Sch., Boston, 1991—; assoc. in gen. medicine Mass. Gen. Hosp., Boston, 1990—2000; vis. attending physician Beth Israel Deaconess Med. Ctr., 2000—; med. advisor Millenium Pharms., Inc., Cambridge, Mass., 1999—; product devel. cons. to biotech. cos., 1999. Asst. prof. medicine U. Toronto, Can., 1972-76; assoc. prof. internal medicine U. Mich., 1976-78, prof., 1978-90, asst. prof. biol. chemistry, 1976-80, assoc. prof., 1980-84, prof., 1984-90; advisor Henry Ford Hosp. clin. rsch. unit com., 1977; mem. fellowship subcom. Arthritis Found., 1977-80, AIDS and Related Therapy Study Sect. NIH, 1990-91, Nat. Inst. Arthritis and Musculoskeletal and Skin Diseases Task Force NIH, 1991—; ad hoc mem. Metabolism Study Sect. NIH, 1977, 78, site visit team Gen. Clin. Rsch., 1978, 81; cons. Warner Lambert/Park Davis Rsch. Labs., 1979-83, 85, Proctor and Gamble Rsch. Labs., 1982, Lily Rsch. Labs., 1983, Kenyon and Kenyon, Patent Lawyers, 1983-84, Pfizer, Inc., 1987-88, Nat. Cancer Inst. Nutrition Rsch. Lab., 1988; mem. com. for med. student rsch. U. Mich., mem. biomed. rsch. coun., 1977-80, mem. athritis ctr. operating com., 1978-81, mem. molecular and cellular biology program com., 1983-85, postdoctoral rsch. tng. com., 1984, mem. v.p.'s budget priorities com., 1985-87, mem. exec. com. Sch. of Medicine, 1987-90; program dir. Gen. Clin. Rsch. Ctr., 1977-90; dir. core facilities, prin. investigator molecular subproject Multipurpose Arthritis Ctr., 1988—; active numerous other orgns. Author: (with others) Purine Metabolism in Man, 1974, Combined Immunodeficiency Disease and Adenosine Deaminase Deficiency: A Molecular Defect, 1975, Purine Metabolism in Man-II, 1977, Farmacologic Clinica e Terapia, 1978, Handbook of Experimental Pharmacology, 1978, Purine Metabolism in Man-III, 1980, Regulatory Function of Adenosine, 1983, 5th rev. edit. Nutrition and Gout, 1984, Purine Metabolism in Man IV, 1984, Physiology and Pathology of Electrolyte Metabolism, 1985, Metabolic Basis of Inherited Disease, 6th edit., 1986, Rheumatology and Immunology, 2nd edit., 1986, Primer on the Rheumatic Diseases, 1988, Textbook of Internal Medicine, 1st edit., 1989, Textbook of Rheumatology, 3rd edit., 1990, Purines in Cell Signaling, 1990; numerous others; contbr. articles to profl. jours. including Am. Jour. Med. Sci., Biochemistry, Molecular Pharmacology, Burns, Jour. Biol. Chemistry, New Eng. Jour. Medicine, Jour. Clin. Investigation, Am. Jour. Physiology, Clin. Chemistry, Archives Biochem. Biophys., Am. Jour. Medicine, Brain Rsch., Neurology, numerous others; mem. editorial bd. Jour. Rheumatology, 1974—, Clin. Rsch., 1978-81, Metabolism, 1979—, Jour. Lab. and Clin. Medicine, 1988-92. Fin. v.p. Temple Beth Emeth, Ann Arbor, Mich., 1979-81, pres., 1981-83; treas. Genesis Bd., St. Clare's Episcopal Ch. and Temple Beth Emeth, 1985-86, pres., 1986-87, sec., 1987-88; chmn. biotech. sect. Combined Jewish Philanthropies, 1996-98, chmn. MetroWest planning group, 1998-2000; assoc. chair rsch. and tech. adv. com. Beth Israel Med. Ctr., 1999--, bd. trustees, 2001--, fin. com. bd. trustees, 2002--; bd. trustees Combined Jewish Philanthropies, 2001--. Named Frederick Smith Meml. scholar, 1966-67, postdoctoral fellow Med. Rsch. Coun. Can., 1969-71; grantee So. Med. Assn., 1971-72 and numerous other grants. Fellow in Medicine Royal Coll. Physicians; mem. ACP (chmn. rheumatology subsect. 1986-88), Am. Soc. Biol. Chemists, Am. Fedn. Clin. Rsch. (sec.-treas. Midwest sect. 1979-82, program com. 1980, 83, chmn. communications com. 1982-84, chmn. pub. policy com. 1983-84, chmn. Midwest sect. 1983-84), Am. Rheumatism Assn. (chmn. com. publ. of arthritis and rheumatism 1984-86, chmn. sci. program 1987 nat. meeting, rsch. coun. 1986-89, chmn. subcom. to define rheumatologic tng. 1986-87), Am. Soc. Clin. Investigation (mem. nominating com. 1984, sec.-treas. 1986-89), Inst. of Medicine (com. on addressing career paths for clin. rsch. 1991-93), Can. Arthritis and Rheumatism Soc., Can. Biochem. Soc., Can. Rheumatism Assn., Can. Soc. for Clin. Investigation, Cen. Soc. Clin. Rsch., Royal Coll. Physicians and Surgeons Can., Alpha Omega Alpha. Jewish. Achievements include research in soluble 5'-nucleotidase: molecular basis for variation, regulation of dAdenosine and dGuanosine Kinases, structural basis for Adenosine Kinase function, PEG-superoxide dysmutase in trauma, clinical trials for hirulog, a thrombin inhibitor, and beta interferon. Office: Millenium Pharms Inc 75 Sydney St Cambridge MA 02139 Business E-Mail: fox@mpi.com. E-mail: irvfox@aol.com.

FOX, JACK JAY, chemist, educator; b. N.Y.C., Dec. 21, 1916; s. Samuel and Celia (Stern) F.; m. Ruth C. Inabu, June 13, 1939; children: Dolores M. Emspak, John Reed. AB, U. Colo., 1939, PhD, 1950. With Sloan-Kettering Inst. for Cancer Research, N.Y.C., 1952-88, mem. emeritus, 1988—; head Lab. Organic Chemistry, prof. biochemistry Cornell U. Grad. Sch. Med. Scis., N.Y.C., 1958—. Recipient Alfred P. Sloan award cancer rsch., 1956, C.S. Hudson award in carbohydrate chemistry Am. Chem. Soc., 1977, Pap award for sci. achievement, 1983, Norlin award U. Colo. Alumni Assn., 1984; NRC fellow, 1950-52; postdoctoral fellow Free U. Brussels, 1950-52; Damon Runyon Meml. Fund fellow, 1952-54. Mem. Am. Chem. Soc., Westchester Chem. Soc., Am. Soc. Biol. Chemists, Am. Assn. Cancer Rsch., Am. Soc. Antiviral Rsch., Sigma Xi. Achievements include research, numerous publs. on design, synthesis and structural elucidation of anticancer and antiviral agts., specific syntheses of compounds related to nucleic acid components, carbohydrate and heterocyclic chemistry. E-mail: jackfx252. Home: 110 S Henry St Apt 1511 Madison WI 53703-3168 Office: Meml Sloan-Kettering Cancer Ctr 1275 York Ave New York NY 10021-6094

FOX, JAMES, actor; b. London, May 19, 1939; s. Robin and Angela Muriel (Worthineton) F.; m. Mary Elizabeth Piper, Sep. 15, 1973; children: Thomas, Robin, Laurence, Lydia, Jack. Grad. high sch. Appeared in Mrs. Miniver, 1950, The Servant, 1963, Magnificient Men in Flying Machines, 1964, Thoroughly Modern Millie, 1966, The Chase, 1967, Performance, 1969, Passage to India, 1985, Russia House, 1989, Remains of the Day, 1994, Anna Karenina, 1996, Up at the Villa, 1999, The Golden Bowl, 1999, Sexy Beast, 2001, The Mystic Masseur, 2001, The Lost World, 2001. Avocation: russian language and culture. Home: c/o ICM Oxford House 76 Oxford St London England

FOX, JAMES ALLEN, allergist, immunologist, pediatrician; b. Oak Ridge, Tenn., Apr. 25, 1951; MD, Yale U., 1977. Diplomate Am. Bd. Allergy & Immunology, Am. Bd. Pediatrics. Intern Bronx Mcpl. Hosp., N.Y.C., 1977-78, resident in pediatrics, 1978-80; fellow in allergy & immunology Colulmbia-Presbyn. Med. Ctr., N.Y.C., 1980-82; pvt. pratice Somerville, Flemington, N.J. Mem. active staff Somerset Med. Ctr., Somerville; mem. courtesy staff Hunterdon Med. Ctr., Flemington, N.J.; clin. instr. U. Medicine and Dentistry of N.J.-RWJMS, 2000—. Fellow Am. Acad. Allergy Asthma & Immunology, Am. Coll. Allergy Asthma & Immunology; mem. AMA, N.J. Allergy Soc. Office: 3461 Hwy 22 Somerville NJ 08876-6021

FOX, JAMES EDWARD, JR., federal agency administrator; b. Columbus, Ohio, Dec. 1, 1948; s. James Edward and Alice Jane (Andrix) F.; m. Julianne Feller, Sept. 12, 1970; children— Abigail, Katharine, James Edward BA, Ohio State U., 1972; MA, George Washington U., 1976. Research asst. U.S. Congress, Washington, 1973-74, legis. asst., 1974-75; minority cons. com. on fgn. affairs U.S. Ho. of Reps., Washington, 1975-83; dep. asst. sec. Dept. State, Washington, 1983-84, prin. dep. asst. sec., 1985; spl. asst. to Pres. White House, Washington, 1985-86; asst. sec. legis. affairs Dept. of State, Washington, 1986—89; asst. adminr. bur. for legis. and public affairs USAID, Washington, 2001—. Republican. Office: USAID Bur for Legis and Public Affairs RRB 1300 Pennsylvania Ave NW Washington DC 20523 Office Fax: 202-216-3237.

FOX, JAMES HOPPES, retired lawyer; b. Jeffersonville, Ind., Mar. 25, 1948; s. Charles C. and Margery M. F.; m. Martha Leich, July 9, 1977; children: Charles M., Katherine E. BSEE, Purdue U., 1970, MSEE, 1971; JD, U. Chgo., 1978. Bar: N.J. 1978, U.S. Dist. Ct. N.J. 1978, U.S. Ct. Appeals (fed. cir.) 1982. Patent atty. AT&T Bell Labs, Murray Hill, N.J., 1978-83, Allentown, Pa., 1983—95; corp. counsel Lucent Technologies, Inc., 1996—2001; ret., 2001. Capt. USAF, 1971-75. Home: 4465 Farm Dr Allentown PA 18104-1937

FOX, JAMES R. telecommunications technician; b. N.Y.C., Dec. 24, 1947; s. Peter Joseph and Ann Loretta Fox; m. Jacqueline Frances Mohr; children: Tara Conner, Erin, Terri. Degree in liberal arts, Queensborough C.C., N.Y.C., 1976. Clk. A&P, Jackson Heights, NY, 1966—67, Equitable Life, N.Y.C., 1967; pipe insulator Keene Insulation, N.Y.C., 1971—74; sales rep. Howard Clothes, Ridgewood, NY, 1974, MW Houdl, Rye, NY, 1975—80; svc. technician AT&T, Forest Hills, NY, 1981—84, NYNEX, Laurelton, NY, 1984—95, Bell Atlantic, Jamaica, NY, 1995—2000, Verizon, St. Albans, NY, 2000—. Author: The Map of the Carpenter, 2000, Christmas Eve, 2001, Wisdom of Wishes, 2003. Served with USN, 1967—71. Roman Catholic. Avocations: writing, music, travel, sports. E-mail: teop122447@aol.com.

FOX, JANIE, environmental engineer; b. Oliver Springs, Tenn., Dec. 22, 1955; d. Douglas P. and Ina H. Scarbrough; children: Lorie, Joseph, Stephanie Grant, Sarah. Student, Roane State C.C., Harriman, Tenn., 1978—79. Cert. environ. technician, 1993. Sr. constrn. asst. Stone & Webster Constrn. Corp., Spring City, Tenn., 1997; tech. support technician Lockheed Martin Energy Systems, Oak Ridge, Tenn., 1998; subject matter expert/records mgr. Mfg. Scis. Corp., Oak Ridge, Tenn., 1998—99; records mgr. British Nuc. Fuels Ltd., Oak Ridge, Tenn.; engring. supr., document control Morrison Knudsen Corp., Oak Ridge, Tenn., 1990—94; asst. project mgr., records mgr. Foster Wheeler Environ. Corp., Oak Ridge, Tenn., 1999—; with Knight-Jacobs, Oak Ridge, 2002, Mesa Assocs., Oak Ridge, 2003—. Cons. CDI Tech. Svcs., Oak Ridge, 1998—. Author: A Hard Night's Day, 2002, Raised Right, 2003. Mem.: Assn. Records Mgrs. and Adminstrs. Avocations: writing, billiards. Home: 304 Florida Ave Oak Ridge TN 37830

FOX, JEAN, piano educator; b. Madison, Wis., Mar. 1, 1941; d. Robert Lewis and Virginia Leonie (Burnier) Meriwether; m. Virgil Grant Fox, Mar. 3, 1962; children: Linda, Frederick, Steven, Barbara. BA, Kans. State U., 1965. Pvt. piano tchr., Manhattan, Kans., 1963-66, Denver, 1966-74, Allentown, Pa., 1974—. Founder Cmty. Music Sch., Allentown, 1981, mem. faculty, 1981-88; spkr. del. Music Tchrs. Conv., Wichita, Kans., 1989, L.A., 1999, WI-00 Music Tchrs. State Conv.; lectr. workshop clinician on pvt. music tchg., Del., Md., Kans., Fla., N.Y., Pa., N.J., Oreg., Calgary, B.C.; sec. Advanced Speechmasters, 1992-93. Author: Performance with Pleasure, 1987 Piano Guild Notes; contbr. articles to profl. jours. Music del. People to People Program, S.E. Asia, 1989; v.p., bd. dirs. Pa. Sinfonia Orch., 1991-94. Named to Hall of Fame Am. Coll. Musicians, Austin, Tex., 1986. Mem. AAUW, Nat. Guild Piano Tchrs. (adjudicator 1980—), Nat. Music Tchrs. Assn. (chair ind. music tchr. com. Ea. divsn. 1985-90), Pa. Music Tchrs. Assn. (sec. 1987-89, 1st v.p. 1989-91, pres. 1991-93), Lehigh Valley Music Tchrs. Assn. (pres. 1987-89, treas. 1998—), Ind. Music Tchrs. (chair 1985-90), Lehigh Valley Music Tchrs. Assn. (treas. 1998—), Music Tchrs. Nat. Assn. (pres. Ea. divsn. 1994-96, v.p 1989-91, bd. dirs. 1996-98), Rotary. Avocations: gourmet cooking, reading. Home: 4102 Kilmer Ave Allentown PA 18104-3310

FOX, JEANNE MARIE, lawyer; b. Phila., May 30, 1952; d. Samuel Cooper and Palmira Caroline (Ungerbuehler) F.; m. Stephan DeMicco, Sept. 29, 1979. BA, Douglass Coll., Rutgers U., New Brunswick, 1975; JD, Rutgers Sch. of Law, Camden, 1979; completed Program for State and Local Govt. Execs., Harvard U., 1990. Letter carrier U.S. Post Office, Wildwood, 1971, Delran, 1973, Willingboro, 1976; intern U.S. Dept. of Environ. Protection, Edison, Phila., 1974, 77; law clerk Bd. of Pub. Utilities, Newark, N.J., 1978, N.J. Supr. Court, Camden, N.J., 1978, 79; policy dir. N.J. Democrat. State Com., Trenton, N.J., 1979-80; atty. N.J. Office of the Sec. of State, 1980-81; regulatory officer N.J. Bd. Pub. Utilities, Newark, 1981-85, dep. dir., 1985-87; dir. N.J. Bd. of Pub. Utilities, Newark, 1987-90, sr. advisor for policy and mgmt., 1990-91; chief of staff N.J. Dept. of Environ. Protection and Energy, Trenton, 1991-92; dep. commr. N.J. Dept. Environ. Protection and Energy, Trenton, 1992-93, commr., 1993-94, commr. Delaware River Basin Commn., 1991-94; regional adminstr. Region II, EPA, N.Y.C., 1994-2001. Vis. lectr. in pub. and internat. affairs Woodrow Wilson Sch., Princeton U., 2001; vis. disting. lectr. Bloustein Sch. Planning & Pub. Policy Rutgers U., 2001; pres. N.J. Bd. Pub. Utilities, Newark, 2002—. Mem. Commn. on Status of Women, Middlesex, 1985—94, chmn., 1985—89; bd. dirs. Douglass Coll. Assoc. Alumnae, 1986—2001; trustee Rutgers U., 1989—2001; mem. N.J. Commn. on Sex Discrimination in Statutes, 1989—94; bd. dirs. Del.-Raritan coun. Girl Scouts USA, co-chair devel. com., 2001—; del. Dem. Nat. Conf., 1992; pres. Middlesex County Women's Polit. Caucus, 1984—86; v.p. Nat. Women's Polit. Caucus, 1991—94, mem. steering and adminstrn. coms., 1989—94; chmn. Dem. Task Force Women's Polit. Caucus, NJ, 1991—94; co-chair edn. and tng. com. Women's Polit. Caucus of N.J., 2001—; pres. Women's Polit. Caucus N.J., 1988—91, bd. dirs., 2001—. Named Outstanding Young Woman N.J., N.J. Woman of Achievement, N.J. Women's Clubs and Douglass Coll., 1986, Jerseyan of Week, Star Ledger, 1986, Bus. and Profl. Woman of Yr., Bus. and Profl. Women, 1993, Environmentalist of the Yr., N.J. Environ. Lobby, 2001; recipient Alumni Meritorious Svc. award Rutgers U. Alumni Fedn., 1991, award Douglass Soc., 1994, Waterfront Visionary award N.Y. League Conservation Voters, 2000, Corwin award Douglass Coll., 2002; honored in Rutger U.'s Hall of Disting. Alumni, 1997. Mem. Nat. Women's Polit. Caucus (N.J. chpt. 2000) Barbara Boggs Sigmund award 2000), N.J. State Bar Assn., Rutgers Sch. of Law Alumni Assn., Rutgers Club. Democrat. Home: 227 New York Ave New Brunswick NJ 08901-1715 Office: NJ Bd Pub Utilities Two Gateway Ctr Newark NJ 07102

FOX, JEFFREY, journalist; b. N.Y.C., May 9, 1951; s. Hyman and Ida Fox; m. Hannah Etta Fogel, Mar. 24, 1979. BSE, SUNY, Stony Brook, 1972; MS, Harvard U., 1978—, Columbia U., 1990. Computer programmer Citibank, N.Am., N.Y.C., 1972-75; systems programmer Rapidata, Fairfield, N.J., 1975-77; project mgr. Monchik-Weber, N.Y.C., 1978-80; asst. v.p. Marsh & McLennan, Inc., N.Y.C., 1980-81; pres. Fox & Geller, Inc., Elmwood Park, N.J., 1981-88, J.F. Assocs., Teaneck, N.J., 1988—; ind. cons., 1988—. Featured speaker at industry trade shows; mem. exec. bd. advisors Softcon, 1985. Author: (software) Quickcode, 1982, Quickreport, 1984; asst. editor Consumer Reports, 1990—97, sr. editor, 1997—2002, sr. project editor, 2002—. N.Y. State Regents scholar, 1968. Mem.: Tau Beta Pi. Avocations: writing, cycling, gardening.

FOX, JEFFREY HARRISON, language educator; b. Chgo., July 8, 1953; s. Robert Emmanuel and Carol Ann Fox; m. Lauren Colette Cocquerelle, May 19, 1982; 1 child, Nina. BA, U. Chgo., 1979; MA, U. Provence, France, 1985, PhD, 1988. Prof. French Morningside Coll., Iowa, 1989, Auburn U., Montgomery, Ala., 1989—91; prof. French and Romance langs. Coll. DuPage, Glen Ellyn, Ill., 1991—. Scholar, reference Alliance Francaise, Chgo. suburbs. Mem.: Am. Assn. Tchrs. French. Office: Coll DuPage 425 Fawell Blvd Glen Ellyn IL 60137 Office Fax: 630-942-3711. E-mail: foxjef@cdnet.cod.edu.

FOX, JENNIFER JOY, artist, educator; b. Lancaster, Pa. d. Max III and Linda Jane Fox. AA in Visual Art and Photography, Harrisburg (Pa.) Area C.C., 1992; grad. cum laude, Towson (Md.) U., 2000. Asst. mgr. Md. Inst. Coll. Art, Balt., 1994-98; technician/photo lab. Balt., 1998; camp counselor Cmty. Arts/Towson U., 1998—2000; substitute tchr. Balt. County Sch., 2000—; long-term substitute tchr. Parkville Mid. Sch., 2001; tchr. Perryville H.S., 2001—. Vol. Pets on Wheels, 1996—98, SPCA of Md., 1996—2003, Lancaster County Hist. Soc., 1993—94; vol. student mentor, 2001—02; camp counselor Nature Camp, 2001—02; mem. Cecil County Arts Coun. Charlette W. Newcombe scholar, 1998, 99, Hope Tchrs. scholar, 1999-2000, German Soc. Md. grantee, 1999-2000, book technology grantee, 2002—. Mem. AAUW, NEA, Md. SPCA, Md. Art Edn. Assn., Harrisburg Area C.C. Alumni, Nat. Art Edn. Assn. Avocations: photography, dog walking, coaching tennis.

FOX, JOAN PHYLLIS, environmental engineer; b. Rockledge, Fla., July 16, 1945; d. John A. and Nonie L. (Knutson) Fox. BS in Physics with high honors, U. Fla., 1971; PhD in Civil/Environ. Engring., U. Calif., Bekeley, 1980. Registered profl. engr., Ariz., Fla., Calif., Ga., Wash., Am. Acad. Environ. Engrs., cert. air pollution control, registered environ. assessor, Calif. Engr. Bechtel, Inc., San Francisco, 1964—66, 1971—76; dir. program and prin. investigator Lawrence Berkeley Lab., 1977-81; prin. engr., pres. Environ. Mgmt., Berkeley, 1981—. Guest lectr. dept. conservation and resource studies U. Calif., Berkeley, 1980-84; expert witness in litigation involving air pollution, odor, nuisance, indsl. accidents, groundwater contamination, hazardous wastes, risk assessment and cooling systems. Contbr. articles to profl. pubs. Grantee Dept. Energy, 1976-81, EPA, 1976-81. Mem. AIChE, ASCE, NAS (past mem. com. surface mining and reclamation, mem. subcom. on QA/QC of irrigation-induced water quality problems 1986-90), Am. Chem. Soc., Am. Indsl. Hygiene Assn., Air and Waste Mgmt. Assn., Phi Beta Kappa, Sigma Pi Sigma. Achievements include design and development of methods to analyze air pollutants. E-mail: fox@aeroaquaterra.com.

FOX, JOHN, professional football coach; b. Virginia Beach, Va., Feb. 8, 1955; m. Robin Fox; children: Matthew, Mark, Cody, Halle. Student, Southwestern Coll., 1974—75; PhB, San Diego State; degree in sec. edn. tchg., 1977. Grad. asst. San Diego State, 1978; asst. coach U.S. Internat. U., 1979; sec. coach Boise State, 1980, Long Beach State, 1981, Utah, 1982, Kans., 1983, Iowa State, 1984, L.A. Express (USFL), 1985; defensive coord., sec. coach U. Pitts., 1986—88; sec. coach Pitts. Steelers, 1989—91; sec. coach San Diego Chargers, 1992—93; defensive coord. Oakland Raiders, 1994—95; cons. St. Louis Rams, 1996; defensive coord. N.Y. Giants, 1997—2001; head coach Carolina Panthers, 2002—. Named Asst. Coach of Yr., Pro Football Weekly. Office: Carolina Panthers 800 S Mint St Charlotte NC 28202

FOX, JOHN DAVID, educator, physicist; b. Huntington, W.Va., Dec. 8, 1929; s. David and Eleanor (Griffin) F.; children: Heidi Roberts Fox, Lise, Peter, Paul, Michelle Fox Lundy; m. Georgiana Fry Vines, Oct. 23, 1993. SB, MIT, 1951; Fulbright fellow, Rijksuniversiteit, Groningen, Netherlands, 1951-52; MS, U. Ill., 1954, PhD, 1960. Asst. physicist Brookhaven Nat. Lab., Upton, N.Y., 1956-59; asst. prof. physics Fla. State U., Tallahassee, 1959-63, asso. prof., 1963-65, prof., 1965-94, prof. emeritus, 1994—. Adj. prof. U. Tex., El Paso, 1996; guest scientist Max-Planck Inst. für Kernphysik, Heidelberg, Germany, 1968-69, Inst. für Kernphysik U. Köln, 1975; cons. physics divsn. Argonne Nat. Lab., 1982—; guest scientist Oak Ridge Nat. Lab., 1994—, program dir. nuclear physics NSF, 1990-92, 95-97; dir. Branchland Pipe & Supply Co., Huntington, W.Va., 1965-81; mem. MIT Ednl. Coun., 1981-90; cons. physics dept. U. Tenn., Knoxville, 1999—. Co-editor: Isobaric Spin in Nuclear Physics, 1966, Nuclear Analogue States, 1976; Contbr. articles to sci. jours. Mem. Leon County Dem. Com., 1970-74; mem. Dem. Nat. Com.; bd. dirs. LeMoyne Art Found., Tallahassee, 1971-73. NSF Grad. fellow, 1955-56; Sr. postdoctoral fellow, 1968-69; sr. U.S. scientist award Alexander von Humboldt-Stiftung, 1975 Fellow Am. Phys. Soc.; mem. AAAS, ACLU, Fedn. Am. Scientists, Sigma Xi.

FOX, JOHN BAYLEY, JR., university dean; b. Cambridge, Mass., Nov. 6, 1936; s. John Bayley and Eunice (Jameson) F.; m. Julia Garrett, July 22, 1967; children— Sarah Cleveland, Thomas Bayley AB, Harvard U., 1959; BA, Oxford U., Eng., 1961, MA, 1962. Assoc. div. internat. fellowships Commonwealth Fund of N.Y., N.Y.C., 1963-67; dir. Office Career Services Harvard U., Cambridge, 1967-71, spl. asst., asst. dean of faculty, 1971-76, dean Harvard Coll., 1976-85, adminstrv. dean Grad. Sch. Arts and Scis., 1985-91; sec. faculty arts and scis., sec. faculty coun., 1992—. Unitarian. Home: 125 Prince St West Newton MA 02465-2603 Office: Harvard U Faculty Arts and Scis University Hall 1 Cambridge MA 02138-5722 E-mail: John_Fox@harvard.edu.

FOX, JON D. former congressman; b. Phila., Pa., Apr. 22, 1947; s. William L. and Elainne (Brickman) F.; m. Judithann Wilbert, June 27, 1992. BA in Pub. Svc., Pa. State U., 1969; JD, Widener U., 1975. Asst. dist. atty. County of Montgomery, Pa., 1976-80, bd. commrs., 1991-94, Twp. of Abington, Pa., 1980-84; mem. Pa. Ho. of Reps., 1984-91, 104th-105th Congress from Pa. 13th dist., 1995-98; mem. banking and fin. svcs., internat. rels., vets. affairs com.; assoc. Jaffe, Friedman, Schuman, Sciolla, Nemeroff & Applebaum. Co-founder Montgomery County AIDS Task Force; active Montgomery County Legal Aid, Ea. Montgomery County Red Cross, Jewish Cmty. Rels. Coun., Aldersgate Youth Svc. Bur., Montgomery County Spinal Cord Assn., Am. Cancer Soc., Manor Coll., Willow Grove Sr. Citizens Ctr., Citizens' Com. for Environ.

Control, Friends of Abington Free Libr., Montgomery County Office on Aging and Adult Svcs. Sgt. USAF, 1969-75. Mem. VFW, Am. Legion, Optimist Club of Ea. Montgomery County, Elks, Masons, Kiwanis, B'nai B'rith. Republican. Jewish.

FOX, JONATHAN RANDALL, banker, real estate broker, insurance agent; b. Pueblo, Colo., June 2, 1958; s. Joseph Marlin and Maxine (Randall) F.; m. Shari L. Baublits; children: Sean Andrew, Ashleigh Diane, Emilie Anne. BS, U. Colo., 1980. Asst. cashier Fowler State Bank, Colo., 1980-82, asst. v.p., 1983-84, v.p., 1985-91, ptnr., 1980—, CEO, chmn., 1992—; also dir. Sec., treas. Ark. Valley Clearing House, Southeast Colo., 1983. Mem. governing bd. Pioneers Meml. Hosp. and Nursing Home, Rocky Ford, Colo., 1982-86; trustee Pioneers Meml. Hosp. Health Ins. Fund, Rocky Ford, 1983-86; bd. dirs. Ark. Valley Regional Med. Ctr., 1986-97, treas., 1988-90, 94-98, vice-chmn., 1990-93; treas. Mo. Day Assn., Fowler, Colo., 1983—; bd. dirs. Ark. Valley 4-H Found., Rocky Ford, 1984-88, Rosemount Mus., 1999—; adv. coun. Future Bus. Leaders Am., Fowler, 1983—, chmn., 1985—; active in Colo. Soc. SAR, Colo., 1983—; chmn. pub. rels. Fowler Cmty. Assn. Chs., 1982-84; pres. Kittredge Cmty. Bd. U. Colo., Boulder, 1977; mem. exec. coun. Boy Scouts Am., Fowler, 1991-92, treas. Rock Mountain Coun., 1993-95; mem. Coll. Music Found. bd. U. Colo., Boulder, 1996—. Mem. Fowler C. of C. (v.p. 1983-84, pres. 1985-86, bd. dirs. 1983-91, 98—, v.p. 1991, 2000), Am. Bankers Assn., Colo. Bankers Assn. (bd. dirs. 1988-91), Ind. Bankers Assn. Am., Bank Adminstrn. Inst., Nat. Assn. Realtors, Ark. Valley Bd. Realtors (G.R.I. award 1981), Colo. Hosp. Assn. (bd. dirs., panel trustees 1987-89). Republican. United Methodist. Home: 3502 County Road Kk 75 Fowler CO 81039-9714 Office: Fowler State Bank 201 S Main St Fowler CO 81039-1132

FOX, JOYCE NANESS, dermatologist; b. Miami, Aug. 22, 1946; d. Albert and Esther Naness; m. Warren S. Fox, June 1976; 1 child, Marla. BS, U. Fla., 1968; MD, U. Miami, 1972. Diplomate Am. Bd. Dermatology. Resident in dermatology U. So. Calif., L.A., 1976; dermatologist Cigna/Friendly Hills. Med. Group, L.A., 1976-96, Cedars-Sinai Med. Group, Beverly Hills, Calif., 1996—. Clin. prof. dermatology U. So. Calif.; asst. clin. prof. dermatology UCLA. Mem. Am. Acad. Dermatology, Pacific Dermatol. Assn., Soc. Pediat. Dermatologist, L.A. Metro. Dermatol. Soc. (past pres.), L.A. Acad. Medicine (past pres.). Office: 200 N Robertson Blvd Ste 205 Beverly Hills CA 90211 E-mail: foxj@csmns.org.

FOX, KARL AUGUST, economist, eco-behavioral scientist; b. Salt Lake City, July 14, 1917; s. Feramorz Young and Anna Teresa (Wilcken) F.; m. Sylvia Olive Cate, July 29, 1940; children: Karl Richard, Karen Frances Anne. BA, U. Utah, 1937, MA, 1938; PhD, U. Calif., 1954. Economist USDA, 1942-54; head divsn. statis. and hist. rsch. Bur. Agrl. Econs., 1951-54; economist Coun. Econ. Advisers, Washington, 1954-55; head dept. econs. and sociology Iowa State U., Ames, 1955-66, head dept. econs., 1966-72, disting. prof. scis. and humanities, 1968-87, prof. emeritus, 1987—. Vis. prof. Harvard, 1960-61, U. Calif., Santa Barbara, 1971-72, 78, vis. scholar, Berkeley, 1972-73; William Evans vis. prof. U. Otago, N.Z., 1981; Bd. dirs. Social Sci. Rsch. Coun., 1963-67, mem. com. econ. stability, 1963-66, chmn. com. areas for social and econ. statistics, 1964-67; mem. Com. Reg. Accounts, 1963-68 Author: Econometric Analysis for Public Policy, 1958, (with M. Ezekiel) Methods of Correlation and Regression Analysis, 1959, (with others) The Theory of Quantitative Economic Policy, 1966, rev. edit., 1973, Intermediate Economic Statistics, 1968, rev. edit, (with T.K. Kaul), 1980, (with J. K. Sengupta) Economic Analysis and Operations Research, 1969, (with W.C. Merrill) Introduction to Economic Statistics, 1970, Social Indicators and Social Theory, 1974, Social System Accounts, 1985, The Eco-Behavioral Approach To Surveys and Social Accounts for Rural Communities, 1990, repub., 1994, Demand Analysis, Econometrics and Policy Models, 1992, Urban-Regional Economics, Social System Accounts and Eco-Behavioral Science, 1994; author-editor: Economic Analysis for Educational Planning, 1972; co-editor: Readings in the Economics of Agriculture, 1969, Economic Models, Estimation and Risk Programming (essays in honor of Gerhard Tintner), 1969, Systems Economics, 1987; contbr. articles to profl. jours. Recipient superior service medal USDA, 1948, award for outstanding pub. research Am. Agrl. Econs. Assn., 1952, 54, 57, for outstanding doctoral dissertation, 1953 Fellow Econometric Soc., Am. Statis. Assn. (Census Research fellow 1980-81), Am. Agrl. Econs. Assn. (v.p. 1955-56, award for publ. of enduring quality 1977), AAAS; mem. Am. Econs. Assn. (research and publs. com. 1963-67), Regional Sci. Assn., Ops. Research Soc. Am., Am. Ednl. Research Assn., Phi Beta Kappa, Phi Kappa Phi. Home: 1801 20th St Apt J-31 Ames IA 50010-5166 Office: Iowa State U Econs Dept Ames IA 50011-0001 E-mail: fox328L@aol.com.

FOX, KATHY PINKSTAFF, lawyer; b. Indpls., Mar. 8, 1942; d. Kenneth Ellsworth and Mary Margaret (Spence) Pinkstaff; m. Richard T. Fox; children: Amy, Michael, John Saxton. BA, DePauw U., 1964; JD, Northwestern U., 1979. Bar: Ill. 1979, U.S. Dist. Ct. (no. dist.) Ill. 1979, U.S. Ct. Appeals (7th cir.) 1989, U.S. Dist. Ct. (cen. dist.) 1990, U.S. Ct. Appeals (5th cir.) 1993, U.S. Supreme Ct. 1996. Ptnr. Wildman, Harrold, Allen & Dixon, Chgo., 1979—. Mem. ABA, Phi Beta Kappa. Home: 661 Sheridan Rd Winnetka IL 60093-2323 Office: Wildman Harrold Allen & Dixon 225 W Wacker Dr Chicago IL 60606-1224 Business E-Mail: fox@wildmanharrold.com.

FOX, KELLY DIANE, financial adviser; b. Brockton, Mass., Sept. 9, 1959; d. James H. and Betty Jane (Calloway) F.; m. Alan David Goldberg, July 6, 1985; 1 child, Andrew Jason. BA, Allegheny Coll., 1980; postgrad. in Bus. Adminstrn., Suffolk U., 1983—84; student, Temple U., London, 1978, Syracuse U., 1979. Cert. fin. planner practitioner. Asst. mgr. Casual Male, Braintree, Mass., 1980, Hit or Miss, Braintree, 1981-82; merchandiser Foxmoor, West Bridgewater, Mass., 1982; distbr. Hill's Dept. Stores, Canton, Mass., 1982-85; asst. buyer BJ's Wholesale Club, Natick, Mass., 1985-92; advanced advisor team, personal fin. advisor Am. Express Fin. Advisors, 1993—. Am. Express Fin. Advisors Boston steering com., diversity chair 1995-96; mem. spkrs. bur. Women's Union, 1997-2001; contbr. ADVICE + program State Atty. Gen's. Office for Elder Affairs; guest lectr. MBA in a Day program Wheaton Coll.; mem. Mass. Dept. Edn. Gifted and Talented Adv. Coun.; founder Women's Resource Room, 1995—97; co-founder The Women's Connection, 2001—; founding bd. dirs. Women at Work Mus., 2003. Contbr. columns in newspapers. Treas., bd. dirs. Attleboro Area Coun. Children, 1993—; bd. dirs. Attleboro Area Parents Anonymous, 1996, 1996—98; cheerleading coach Avon High Sch., Mass., 1982—83; co-chair enrichment program Falls Elem. Sch., 1994—95, 1997—98; mem. John Woodcock Sch. Coun., 1993—94; vol. Foxborough Regional Charter Sch. SABIS. Methodist. Avocations: theater, travel, bell choir, art galleries. E-mail: Kelly.D.Fox@AEXP.com.

FOX, KEVIN CHRISTOPHER, marketing professional; b. Wichita, Kans., Nov. 8, 1963; s. Celestine Bud and Lucile Martha (Schmidt) F. AA, Butler County Community Coll., 1984; BFA, Wichita State U., 1987. Artist, designer Wichita Graphics, 1986; graphic designer KAKE TV Channel 10, 1987, Staats Decal, 1988; photographer, asst. Steven Ledell Photography, 1988-90; owner Studio 151, 1990-94; creative dir. Soft-tek Internat., 1994-96; sr. art dir. Am. Identity, 1996-98; corp. mktg. mgr. Burns & McDonnell, 1998—. Art dir. Game Day Sports Shop, Wichita, 1988-91; photographer Good Life Mag., Wichita, 1989-91; freelance graphic artist K. Christopher Designs, Wichita, 1987-96; photographer Editl. Portrait Printing, Inc., 1988, Eye Care Mag., 1989; cons. creative dir. PreGame Athletics, 1999—; webmaster Ruskin Heights Luth. Ch., 2000—. Editor: (photos) Natural Physique Mag., 1993; art dir./photographer Baseball Card/The Wichita State U., 1989-91; photographer Wichita Wranglers Baseball, 1992— (award Best Cover), Coleman Peak 1 Catalog, 1993, Wichita Wranglers SportsPrint (award Excellence/Poster); contbr. articles to profl. jours. Fin. sec. Belton Bd. Parks Dirs., 2002—03, pub. rels. dir., 2003; ch. coun. Ruskin Heights Luth. Ch.; adv. bd. Grace Early Edn. Ctr., Belton, 2000—01; bd. dirs. City of Belton Bd. of Parks, 2001—03; instr. ARC, Wichita, 1981—; vol. troop 613 Adult Girl Scouts U.S., 2001—02; head coach Valley Center (Kans.) Swim Club, 1986—87; Hearts head coach Grandview Belton Soccer Clubs, 2002—03. Recipient Award of Excellence, Advt. Fedn., 1990, Bronze Quill, Internat. Assn. Bus. Communicators, 1998, 2000—03, Blue Quill, 2001—02. Mem. Am. Inst. Graphic Artists (photographer Wichita chpt. 1992), Bus. Mktg. Assn. (bd. dirs. 2001—, Fountain award 2001, Chpt. Excellence award 2002). Democrat. Lutheran. Avocations: coaching, photography, website design, computers and technology. Home: 15900 Allen Ave Belton MO 64012-1514 E-mail: kfox@burnsmcd.com.

FOX, LINDA CHODOSH, Spanish language educator; b. Charlottesville, Va., May 20, 1943; d. Maurice Allen Chodosh and Miriam Yuter; m. William P. Fox, Aug. 20, 1967; children: Daniel Eric, Jeremy Seth. BA with honors, Douglass Coll., 1965; MA, Ind. U., 1967; PhD, U. Wis., 1974. Cert. secondary tchr., N.J. Lectr. Ind. U.-Purdue U., Fort Wayne, 1971-74, asst. prof., 1974-96, dir. women's studies, 1982-88, 95—, assoc. prof., 1996—. Sunday sch. tchr. The Temple, Fort Wayne, Ind. Named Tchr. of Yr. Ind.-Purdue Ft. Wayne Friends, 1996; recipient Zonta Summit award, 2000, Great Men and Women Who Made a Difference award IPFW, 2001. Mem. MLA, Am. Assn. of Tchrs. of Spanish and Portuguese, Ft. Wayne Women's Bur., Am. Coun. for Tchg. of Fgn. Langs., Nat. Women's Studies Assn., Feministas Unidas (newsletter editor 1980-95), Phi Beta Kappa. Avocations: piano, reading. Office: Ind U-Purdue U Fort Wayne 2101 E Coliseum Blvd Fort Wayne IN 46805-1445 E-mail: fox@ipfw.edu.

FOX, LLOYD ALLAN, insurance company executive; b. Bklyn., Sept. 20, 1945; s. Samuel Morris and Adele (Sheingold) F.; m. Lenore Judith Weinstock, Aug. 10, 1968; children: Jennifer Lynn, Elizabeth Susan. BS in Pharmacy, Long Island U., 1968; JD, U. Mich., 1974. Bar: Ga. 1974, D.C. 1979; lic. ins. agent, Ga. Mng. ptnr. Stokes, Shapiro, Fussell, Fox & Wedge, Atlanta, 1974-87; exec. v.p., gen. counsel Splty. Systems, Inc., Indpls., 1987-90; chmn., CEO Environ. Mgmt. Group Inc., Atlanta, 1987-90; pres. Am. Safety Ins. Svcs. Inc., Atlanta, 1990—2001, Am. Safety Casualty Ins. Co., 1993—2002, Am. Safety Ins. Group, Ltd., 1997—2002, Intersure Reinsurance Co., 1995—. Author: Employer's Guide to Employee Retirement Income Security Act, 1974, Businessman's Guide to Mergers and Acquisitions, 1977, Business Planning for the Closely-Held Company, 1980, Asbestos Management and Removal-Legal Considerations and Planning, 1985, Legal Considerations of Asbestos Management Plans, 1987. Pres. Chastain Park Civic Assn., Atlanta, 1976; bd. dirs., v.p. Nat. Kidney Found., Atlanta, 1977-88; bd. dirs. Asbestos Abatement Coun. Assn. Wall and Ceiling Industries Internat., Washington, 1987-90, pres., 1989-90. Lt. USPHS, 1968-71. Recipient Pres.'s award Nat. Kidney Found. Ga., 1984. Mem.: D.C. Bar, State Bar Ga., Alpha Zeta Omega. Jewish.

FOX, MARY ANN WILLIAMS, librarian; b. Savannah, Ga., Jan. 16, 1939; d. Alton F. and Arthur (Colquitt) Williams; m. William Francis Fox, Dec. 26, 1960 (div. 1984); children: Katherine Frances, William Francis Jr. BA, U. Ga., 1960; MLS, Rutgers U., 1984. Libr. Metuchen (N.J.) Pub. Libr., 1983-85, Mable Smith Douglas Libr. Rutgers U., New Brunswick, N.J., 1984, Firestone Libr. Princeton (N.J.) U., 1985, The Hun Sch. of Princeton, 1985—. Bd. dirs. Ctrl. Jersey Regional Libr. Coop., 1997—, Region 5 Libr. Coop., N.J., 1985-92. Trustee East Brunswick (N.J.) Pub. Libr., 1979-92; bd. dirs. Ctrl. Jersey YWCA, New Brunswick, 1985-88, Ctrl. Atlantic Conf. United Ch. of Christ, 1985-88. Mem. ALA, N.J. Libr. Assn., N.J. Ind. Sch. Assn. (chair libr. sect. 1988—), Edn. Media Assn. N.J. (bd. dirs. 1987-92), Librs. of Middlesex (pres.). Democrat. Mem. United Ch. of Christ. Home: 10 Redcoat Dr East Brunswick NJ 08816-2759 Office: Hun Sch Princeton 176 Edgerstone Rd Princeton NJ 08540 E-mail: mafox@hun.k12.nj.us.

FOX, MARY FRANK, sociology educator and researcher; BA, U. Mich., 1967, MA, 1969, PhD, 1978. NSF Advance prof. sociology Sch. History, Tech. and Sci. Ga. Inst. Tech., Atlanta, co-dir. Ctr. for Study of Women, Sci. and Tech. Rsch. study panel NRC/Nat. Acad. Scis., Washington, 1995-99, cons. 1998-2000; adv. bd. on women in sci. and engring. Alfred Sloan Found., 1993-95; rsch. rev. panel NSF. Assoc. editor Sex Roles, 1992—, Gender and Society, 1986-90; mem. editl. bd. Social Studies Sci., 1996—; co-editor: Women, Gender and Technology book series. Recipient Feminist Lectr. 2000 award; NSF rsch. grantee, 1985-88, 91-95, 2000—, Betty Vetter Rsch. award Women in Engring. Programs, 2002. Mem. Sociologists for Women in Society (pres. 1995), Am. Sociol. Assn. (chair sex and gender sect. 1986-87, coun. sex and gender sect. 1993-96, coun. sci., knowledge and tech. sect. 1987-92, publs. com. 1989-92, sec.-treas. 1999—), Soc. for Social Studies of Sci. (chair ednl. bd. handbook of sci. and tech. studies 1990-95). Office: Ga Inst Tech 116 Dm Smith Bldg Atlanta GA 30332-0345 E-mail: mary.fox@hts.gatech.edu.

FOX, MATTHEW IGNATIUS, publishing company executive; b. NYC, Apr. 10, 1934; s. Matthew I. and Lucille V. (Reilly) F.; children: Cathleen, Matthew, Patricia. AB, Rutgers U., 1956. Field rep. Prentice-Hall, Inc., N.Y.C., 1958-60, editor engring., 1960-67, exec. editor, asst. v.p., 1967-71, exec. editor, 1981-83, editor-in-chief, 1983-85, pub., 1985—; pres. Reston Pub. Co., Va., 1971-81. Cons. in pub., 1987—; bd. dirs. Fairmont Press, Atlanta. Dep. mayor, mayor, Rivervale (NJ), 1964-67, commr., Bergen County, NJ, 1966-70; del. Fairfax County (Va.) Dem. Com., 1976-81; leader City of Cape May Dem. Party. Mem. Rutgers U. Alumni Assn., Cape May Cottagers and Beach Club, Corinthian Yacht Club. Democrat. Roman Catholic. Home: 1103 Illinois Ave Cape May NJ 08204-2608

FOX, MAURICE SANFORD, molecular biologist, educator; b. N.Y.C., Oct. 11, 1924; s. Albert and Ray F.; m. Sally Cherniavsky, Apr. 1, 1955; children: Jonathan, Gregory, Michael. BS in Meteorology, U. Chgo., 1944, MS in Chemistry, PhD, U. Chgo., 1951; Docteur Honoris causa, Université Paul Sabatier, Toulouse, France, 1994. Instr. U. Chgo., 1951-53; asst. Rockefeller Inst., 1953-55, asst. prof., 1955-58, assoc. prof., 1958-62, MIT, Cambridge, 1962-66, prof., 1966-79, Lester Wolfe prof. molecular biology, 1979-96, head dept. biology, 1985-89. Mem. Radiation Effects Rsch. Found., Hiroshima, 1997—2000. Mem. Internat. Bioethics Com. UN Ednl., Sci. and Cultural Orgn., 1997-2003. Served with USAAF, 1943-46. USPHS fellow, 1952-53; Nuffield Research fellow, 1957; Fogarty scholar, 1991. Fellow AAAS; mem. NAS, Am. Acad. Arts and Scis., Inst. Medicine. Office: MIT Dept Biology 77 Massachusetts Ave Cambridge MA 02139-4307

FOX, MICHAEL DAVID, retired art educator; b. Dec. 29, 1937; s. Donald F. and Ethel (Allen) Sullivan; m. Carol Ann Hampston, Nov. 5, 1967; 1 child, Kathryn Gabrielle. BS, SUNY, Buffalo, 1962, MS, 1969; cert. in sculpture, Bklyn. Mus. Sch., 1964. Tchr. art City Schs., Rochester, NY, 1962-63, 64-65; prof. art Morehead State U., Ky., 1965-67, SUNY, Oswego, 1967—2000; ret., 2000. Vis. artist univs. and art ctrs., United States, Canada; dir. Popular Image Gallery, Oswego, 1967—2003; spkr. in field; lectr. in field. Work featured on CBS-TV, 1976, 1978, 1980, also featured in N.Y. Times, Look, Evergreen Rev., Nat. Lampoon, Scanlon's Monthly, Cavalier, Sch. Arts, others, featured in texbooks Sculpture: Techniques, Form and Content, 1988, Represented in permanent collections, U.S., Can., Japan, Africa, Asia, Europe, S.Am.; reviewer textbooks. Recipient Outstanding Tchg. award, Morehead State U., 1967—2000, Chancellors award for excellence in tchg., State Univ. Coll., Oswego, NY, 1981, numerous awards for drawing, painting and sculpture, 1962—. Mem.: United Univ. Profs. (v.p., del). Home: 38 W End Ave Oswego NY 13126-1758

FOX, MICHAEL EDWARD, lawyer; b. Chgo., Apr. 14, 1938; s. Charles and Beatrice (Chazin) F.; children— William Bradley, Elizabeth Rachel Ohana; m. Karen A. Fox; stepchildren: Christopher S. Riback, Melissa J. Riback, L. Brandon Liss; B.S., U. Ill., 1959; J.D., Harvard U., 1962. Bar: Ill. 1962, U.S. Dist. Ct. (no. dist.) Ill. 1963, U.S. Supreme Ct. 1967. Assoc. firm Rusnak, Deutsch & Gilbert, Chgo., 1963-65; staff atty. Joint Com. on Internal Revenue Taxation, U.S. Congress, Washington, 1965-68; assoc. firm Seyfarth, Shaw, Fairweather & Geraldson, Chgo., 1968-72, ptnr., 1972-74; ptnr. firm Adams, Fox, Adelstein & Rosen, Chgo., 1974—89; ptnr. Jenner & Block, 1989-92; ptnr. Aronberg, Goldgehn, Davis & Garmisa, 1992-94; ptnr. Michael E. Fox & Assocs., 1994-95; ptnr. Fox, Swibel & Lewvin, 1995-99; ptnr. Fox, Hefter, Swibel, Levin & Carroll, 1999-, mgr. Icon LLC and Affiliates, 1999-. Contbr. articles to Jour. of Taxation. Bd. dirs., trustee Goodwill Industries of Chgo. and Cook County, 1973-83. Mem. Chgo. Bar Assn., Ill. Bar Assn., ABA. Home: 529 Voltz Rd Northbrook IL 60062-4709 Personal E-mail: MEFox15@comcast.net. Business E-Mail: MEFox@FHSLC.com.

FOX, MICHAEL F. controller; b. Fairfax, Va., Aug. 18, 1959; s. Doy Ray and Sheila Ann (Gold) F.; m. Angelina Marie, June 27, 1981; children: Christina M., Stephen A. BS in Acctg., U. Md., 1981. CPA, Md. Inst. CPA. Auditor Deloitte, Haskins & Sells, Washington, 1981-82, Snyder, Young & Co., Silver Spring, Md., 1982-85; CFO Business Bank, Vienna, Va., 1985-94; contr. Geneva Coll., Beaver Falls, Pa., 1994—. Mem. adv. coun. Sage Scholars. Elder Immanuel Bible Ch., 1991-93, treas., Beaver County Christian Sch., 2002. Mem. Nat. Assn. Coll. & U. Bus. Officers, Assn. Bus. Adminstrs. at Christian Colls. Office: Geneva Coll 3200 College Ave Beaver Falls PA 15010-3557 E-mail: mffox@geneva.edu.

FOX, MICHAEL VASS, Hebrew educator; b. Detroit, Dec. 9, 1940; s. Leonard W. and Mildred (Vass) F.; m. Jane Schulzinger, Sept. 4, 1961; children: Joshua, Ariel BA, U. Mich., 1962, MA, 1963; PhD, Hebrew U., Jerusalem, 1972. Ordained rabbi, 1968. Lectr. Haifa U., Israel, 1971-74, Hebrew U., Jerusalem, 1975-77; prof. Hebrew U. Wis., Madison, 1977—, chmn. dept., 1982-88, 92-99, Weinstein-Bascom prof. in Jewish studies, 1990—, Halls-Bascom prof., 1999—. Author: The Song of Songs and the Ancient Egyptian Love Songs, 1985, Shirey Dodim Mimitzrayim Ha'atiqa, 1985, Qohelet and his Contradictions, 1988, The Redaction of the Books of Esther, 1991, Character and Ideology in the Book of Esther, 1991, 2001, A Time to Tear Down and a Time to Build Up: A Rereading of Ecclesiastes, 1999; editor: Anchor Bible: Proverbs, vol. I, 2000; contbr. articles to profl. jours. Named Vilas assoc., U. Wis., 1988—90; recipient Wahrburg prize, Hebrew U., 1971—72, Kellett Mid-Career award, U. Wis., 1999; fellow, Brit. Friends of Hebrew U., Liverpool, 1974—75, NEH, 1992; Leverhulme fellow, U. Liverpool, Eng., 1974—75, Am. Coun. Learned Socs. fellow, 2001, Am. Acad. for Jewish Rsch. fellow. Mem. Soc. for Bibl. Lit. (editor SBL Dissertation Series 1994-99, editl. bd. Jour. Bibl. Lit. 1991-95; pres. midwest region 1998-2000), Nat. Assn. Profs. Hebrew (editor Hebrew Studies 1985-93, v.p. 2000—). Home: 2815 Chamberlain Ave Madison WI 53705-3607 Office: U Wis Dept Hebrew 1220 Linden Dr Rm 1338 Madison WI 53706-1525

FOX, MICHAEL WILSON, veterinarian, bioethicist, animal behaviorist; b. Bolton, Eng., Aug. 13, 1937; came to U.S., 1962; s. Geoffrey and Elizabeth (Wilson) F.; m. Deanna L. Krantz, May 1989; children by previous marriage: Michael Wilson, Camilla, Mara. B. in Vet. Medicine, Royal Vet. Coll., London, 1962; PhD, U. London, 1967, D.Sc., 1975. Postdoctoral fellow Jackson Lab., Bar Harbor, Maine, 1962-64; med. research assoc. State Research Hosp., Galesburg, Ill., 1964-67; assoc. prof. psychology Washington U., St. Louis, 1967-76; v.p. Humane Soc. U.S., Washington, 1986-98, sr. scholar bioethics, 1998—2002; chief cons./vet. India Project for Animals & Nature, 1996—. Author: syndicated newspaper column Ask Your Animal Doctor; author: Canine Behavior, 1965, Canine Pediatrics, 1966, Integrative Development of Brain and Behavior in the Dog, 1971, Behavior of Wolves, Dogs and Related Canids, 1971, Understanding Your Dog, 1972, Understanding your Cat, 1974, Concepts in Ethology: Animal and Human Behavior, 1974, Between Animal and Man: The Key to the Kingdom, 1976, The Dog, Domestication and Behavior, 1977, (juveniles) Wild Dogs Three, 1977, What Is Your Cat Saying?, 1978, The Wolf, 1973 (Christopher award), Vixie, The Story of a Fox, 1973, Sundance Coyote, 1974, Ramu and Chennai, 1975 (Sci. Tchrs. award); co-author: (juveniles) What is Your Dog Saying?, 1977, Dr. Fox's Fables, 1980, The Touchlings, 1981, Animals Have Rights Too, 1991, (adult) Understanding Your Pet, 1978, The Soul of the Wolf, 1980, One Earth One Mind, 1980, Returning to Eden: Animal Rights and Human Responsibility, 1980, How to be Your Pet's Best Friend, 1981, The Healing Touch, 1982, Love is a Happy Cat, 1982, Farm Animal Husbandry, Behavior and Veterinary Practice, 1983, The Whistling Hunters: Field Studies of the Asiatic Wild Dog (Cuon alpinus), 1984, The Animal Doctor's Answer Book, 1984, Laboratory Animal Care, Welfare and Experimental Variables, 1986, Agricide-The Hidden Crisis That Affects Us All, 1986, The New Animal Doctor's Answer Book, 1989, The New Eden, 1989, Superdog, 1990, Inhumane Society, The American Way of Animal Exploitation, 1990, You Can Save The Animals; 50 Things to Do Right Now, 1991, Supercat, 1991, Superpigs and Wondercorn: How the Brave New World of Biotechnology Will Affect Us All, 1992, The Boundless Circle: Caring for Creatures and Creation, 1996, Eating With Conscience: The Bioethics of Food, 1997, Beyond Evolution: The Genetically Altered Future of Plants, Animals, The Earth...and Humans, 1999, Bringing Life to Ethics: Global Bioethics for a Humane Society, 2001; editor: Abnormal Behavior in Animals, 1968, Readings in Ethology and Comparative Psychology, 1973, The Wild Canids, 1975, On the Fifth Day: Animal Rights and Human Ethics, 1978, Internat. Jour. for study of Animal Problems, Advances in Animal Welfare Sci. Mem.: AVMA, Brit. Vet. Assn. *My life was shaped in childhood by close contact with animals and nature. Empathy and concern for the well-being of non-human beings led to a veterinary degree and curiousity about their behavior and inner awareness to several years research. Most influential teacher: the wolf. My philosophy: reverence for all life; humankind as steward living in co-creative communion with nature and all.*

FOX, MITCHELL B. magazine publisher; married; 3 children. Degree, SUNY. Sr. v.p. sales and promotion Bergdorf Goodman; pub. Vanity Fair mag., N.Y.C., 1994—97, v.p., 1997—99; sr. v.p., corp. sales Conde Nast, 1999—2000, exec. v.p. sales and mktg., 2000—01; pres. The Golf Digest Cos., 2001—, CEO, 2001—. Office: Golf Digest 5520 Park Ave Trumbull CT 06611-3400*

FOX, MURIEL, retired public relations executive; b. Newark, Feb. 3, 1928; d. M. Morris and Anne L. (Rubenstein) F.; m. Shepard G. Aronson, July 1, 1955; children: Eric R., Lisa S. Student, Rollins Coll., 1944-46; BA summa cum laude, Barnard Coll., 1948. Art critic, bridal editor Miami (Fla.) News, 1946; reporter U.P.I., 1946-48; polit. speechwriter, publicist, 1949-50; from TV-radio writer to exec. v.p. Carl Byoir & Assos., N.Y.C., 1950-85; pres. subs. MediaCom Comm. Tng., 1975-85, By/Media Inc., 1981-85; sr. cons. Hill & Knowlton, Inc., 1986-90. Dir. Harleysville Ins. Co., Rorer Group Inc.; Co-chmn. Vice Presdl. Task Force on Women, 1968; mem. steering com. Women's Forum, 1974-79, pres., 1976-78; mem. Women's Econ. Adv. Com., N.Y.C., 1974-78; mem. nat. adv. com. Nat. Women's Polit. Caucus; nat. adv. bd. Women Today, Ethnic Woman Bd. dirs. N.Y. Diabetes Assn., 1956-66, Holy Land Conservation Fund, United Way of Tri-State, Internat. Rescue Com., 1977-84; v.p. Rockland Ctr. for the Arts, 1985—; pres. Hickory Hill Coop., Inc., 1995-99; chair bd. dirs. Vet. Feminists of Am., 1997—. Named one of 100 Top Corp. Women Bus. Week mag., 1976; recipient Matrix award Women in Communications, 1977, Bus. Leader of Year award ADA, 1979; Disting. Alumna award Barnard Coll., 1985, Eleanor Roosevelt Leadership award, 1985 Mem.: NOW (v.p. 1967—70, chmn. bd. 1971—73, chair nat. adv. com. 1973—74, bd. dirs. legal def. and edn. fund 1974—, v.p. fund 1977—78, pres. 1978—81, chair bd. 1981—92, hon. chair bd. 1993—, founder, Muriel Fox Comm. Leadership award 1991, Our Hero award 1995, Caroline Lexow Babcock award 1997), Am. Arbitration Assn. (bd. dirs. 1983—87), Am. Women in Radio and TV (bd. dirs. 1950—51, chair nat. publicity com. 1955—57, chair nat. pub. rels. com. 1957—59, Achievement award 1983), Vet. Feminists of Am. (chair bd. dirs. 2000—). Home and Office: 66 Hickory Hill Rd Tappan NY 10983-1804 E-mail: mfox66@optonline.net. *As a business executive, a founder and leader of the modern women's movement, and a fulfilled wife and mother, I hope I have helped to prove that women can enjoy success at many levels-professionally, politically and personally-without being forced to sacrifice one aspect of life for another. I also hope I've helped make such multifaceted success more attainable for other women in the present and future.*

FOX, PATRICIA SAIN, academic administrator; b. Indpls., Jan. 8, 1954; d. Thomas Troy and Faye Melba (Martinez) Sain; m. Donald Lee Fox, Aug. 26, 1978; children: Ashley Marie, Aimee Elizabeth. BS in Acctg., Ind. U., 1980; MBA, Butler U., 1985. Adminstrv. asst. Sch. Engring. and Tech. Ind. U.-Purdue U., Indpls., 1980-83, asst. to the dean Sch. Engring. and Tech., 1983-86, asst. dean Sch. Engring. and Tech., 1986—2002, assoc. dean, 2003—. Cons. Gene Glick Mgmt. Co., Indpls., 1986-87. Eucharistic min. St. Christopher Ch., Speedway, Ind., 1983. Mem. Am. Soc. for Engring. Edn. Roman Catholic. Avocation: walking. Office: Ind U-Purdue U Sch Engring & Tech 799 W Michigan St Indianapolis IN 46202-5195

FOX, PATRICK JOHN, sociology educator; b. Ramey AFB, P.R., Sept. 25, 1953; s. Leon James and Frances Valeria Fox; m. Sabrina Watson, July 30, 1978. BS in Social Sci., MA in Edn., Calif. Poly. State U., 1976; MSW in Social Welfare, U. Calif., Berkeley, 1978; MA in Sociology, U. Calif., San Diego, 1977; CPhil in Sociology, U. Calif., San Francisco, 1984, PhD in Sociology, 1988. Pub. adminstrn. analyst Inst. Health & Aging U. Calif. Sch. Nursing, San Francisco, 1985-87, sr. pub. adminstrn. analyst Inst. Health & Aging, 1987-89, prin. pub. adminstrn. analyst Inst. Health & Aging, 1989-90, from asst. prof. to assoc. prof. sociology in residence, 1990—, assoc. dir. for rsch./strat. planning Inst. Health & Aging, 1996-99, assoc. dir. Ctr. Healthy & Active Aging/Inst.

Health & Aging, 1999—, prof. sociology in residence dept. social/behavioral scis., 1999—, co-dir. Inst. Health & Aging, 1999—. Guest prof. Inst. for Population Studies, East China Normal U., Shanghai, 1997-2000; mem. Ctr. for Health and Cmty., U. Calif., San Francisco, 1996—; mini residency in geriatrics U. Calif. San Diego Med. Ctr., 1987; invited lectr. sociology grad. student rsch. forum U. Calif., San Francisco, 1983, interpretive methods colloquium U. Calif., Berkeley, 1984, health and med. apprenticeship program, 1985; reviewer books and jours. for Scott, Foresman & Co., 1989—; reviewer proposals for various panels and confs.; presenter in field. Reviewer: Social Science and Medicine, 1989—, The Gerontologist, 1989—, PharmacoEconomics, 1989—, Am. Jour. Preventive Medicine, 1989—, Am. Jour. Pub. Health, 1989—, Am. Jour. Managed Care, 1989—, Health Care for Women Internat., 1989—, Brain Research, 2002, Health Policy, 2002. Regents fellow U. Calif.-San Diego, 1981-82, Pew doctoral fellow U. Calif.-San Francisco, 1985-87; Laura Hawkins scholar U. Calif.-San Diego, 1981-82; Chancellor's Patent Fund grantee for grad. student rsch. U. Calif.-San Francisco, 1986. Mem. APHA, AAAS, Gerontol. Soc. Am., Am. Soc. on Aging, Assn. for Health Svcs. Rsch., Pi Gamma Mu. Avocations: music, swimming, film. Office: U Calif Ste 340 3333 California St San Francisco CA 94118

FOX, PATRICK JOSEPH, lawyer; b. Atlanta, May 30, 1950; s. Joseph M. and Betty J. (Garvey) F.; m. Martha Ann Adams, June 12, 1976; children: Meredith Ashley, Patrick Joseph Jr. AB, U. Ga., 1972, JD, 1975. Bar: U.S. Dist. Ct. (no. dist.) Ga. 1976, U.S. Ct. Appeals (11th cir.) 1981, U.S. Supreme Ct. 1979. Assoc. Thomas K. McWhorter, Jonesboro, Ga., 1975-78, Glaze McNally & Glaze, Jonesboro, 1978-80; ptnr. Glaze & McNally P.C., Jonesboro, 1980-86, McNally, Fox, Mahler, Cameron and Stephens, P.C. (formerly McNally, Fox, Mahler & Cameron, P.C.), Fayetteville, Ga., 1986—. Mem. Ga. Trial Lawyers Assn. (v.p. 1986—), Assn. Trial Lawyers Am., State Bar Assn. Ga., Clayton Bar Assn., Fayette County Bar Assn., Lawyers Club Atlanta, Atlanta Bar Assn. Home: 135 Stable Creek Rd Fayetteville GA 30215-7408 Office: McNally Fox Mahler & Cameron PC 100 Habersham Dr Fayetteville GA 30214-1381

FOX, PAUL T. lawyer; b. N.Y.C., Jan. 17, 1953; BA, Northwestern U., 1975, JD cum laude, 1978. Bar: Ill. 1978, U.S. Dist. Ct. (no. dist. trial bar) Ill. 1979, U.S. Ct. Appeals (7th cir.) 1979, U.S. Supreme Ct. 1986, U.S. Ct. Appeals (fed. cir.) 1987, Wis. 1989. Mng. shareholder Greenberg Traurig, Chgo. Faculty mem. Nat. Inst. for Trial Advocacy; adj. prof. Northwestern U. Sch. Law. Mem. ABA (mem. litigation sect.), State Bar Wis., Chgo. Bar Assn., Order of Coif. Office: Greenberg Traurig 77 W Wacker Drive Ste 2500 Chicago IL 60601

FOX, PAUL WALTER, lawyer; b. Temple, Tex., June 22, 1949; s. Robert Bryan and Geraldine (Davis) F.; m. Dana Hendricks, Mar. 15, 1975. A.B. cum laude, Harvard U., 1970; J.D., U. Tex., 1972. Bar: Tex. 1973, D.C. 1975, U.S. Ct. Appeals (D.C. cir.) 1975, U.S. Ct. Appeals (5th cir.) 1974, U.S. Ct. Appeals (10th cir.) 1984, U.S. Supreme Ct. 1976. Assoc. Ashton & Fox, Austin, Tex., 1973-75, Glendening & Schmid, Washington, 1975-77; ptnr. Bracewell & Patterson, Washington, 1977— . Mem. ABA, Fed. Energy Bar Assn., U. Tex. Law Sch. Alumni Assn. (dist. bd. dirs. 1981—). Democrat. Episcopalian. Clubs: Gibson Island, International, Harvard (Washington). Home: Stillwater Rd Gibson Island MD 21056 Office: Bracewell & Patterson 2000 K St NW Ste 500 Washington DC 20006-1872

FOX, PAULA (MRS. MARTIN GREENBERG), writer; b. N.Y.C., Apr. 22, 1923; d. Paul Hervey and Elsie (de Sola) F.; m. Richard Sigerson (div. 1954); children: Adam, Linda, Gabriel; m. Martin Greenberg, June 9, 1962. Student, Columbia U. Condr. writing Seminars U. Pa. Author: 22 children's books and 6 novels, including How Many Miles to Babylon, 1966, Portrait of Ivan, 1968, Blowfish Live in the Sea, 1970; (novels) Poor George, 1967, Desperate Characters, 1970, The Western Coast, 1972, The Slave Dancer, 1974 (John Newbery medal), The Widow's Children, 1976, The Little Swineherd and Other Tales, 1978, A Place Apart, 1983 (Am. Book award), A Servant's Tale, 1984, One-Eyed Cat, 1985 (Newbery honor book 1985), Maurice's Room, 1985, The Moonlight Man, 1986, The Stone-Faced Boy, 1987, The Village by the Sea, 1988, Lily and the Lost Boy, 1989, The God of Nightmares, 1990, Monkey Island, 1991, Amzat and His Brothers, 1993, Western Wind, 1993, The Eagle Kite, 1995, Radiance Descending, 1997, Borrowed Finery: A Memoir, 2000 (PEN/Martha Albrand award). Recipient Arts and Letters award Nat. Inst. Arts and Letters, 1972, Hans Christian Andersen medal, 1978, fiction citation Brandeis U., 1984, Empire State award for children's lit., 1994; Guggenheim fellow, 1972. Mem. Authors League, Am. Acad. Arts and Letters (recipient medal and cash award). Office: care Robert Lescher 47 E 19th St New York NY 10003-1323

FOX, RAYMOND GRAHAM, educational technologist; b. Portland, Oreg., May 31, 1923; s. George Raymond and Georgia Dorothy (Beckman) F.; B.S., Rensselaer Poly. Inst., 1943; m. Harriet Carolyn Minchin, Apr. 17, 1948; children: Susan, Christine, Ellen, Laura, John. Salesman IBM Corp., N.Y.C., 1946-48, br. mgr., 1949-56, systems mgr., 1957-65, edn. systems devel. mgr., 1965-76; chmn. bd. Learning Tech. Inst., Warrenton, 1975— . Mem. Va. Council for Deaf, 1978-84; chmn., 1980-83; mem. Sec. of Navy Adv. Bd. on Edn. and Tng., 1972-77; cons. for tech. Va. Legis. Adv. Com. on Handicapped, 1970; mem. Nat. Def. Exec. Reserve, 1970-83; mem. emeritus, 1983— . Served with USNR, 1943-46. Mem. Soc. Applied Learning Tech. (pres. 1972—), Nat. Security Indsl. Assn. (chmn. tng. group 1974-76). Anglican. Clubs: Army & Navy (Washington); Fauquier (Warrenton, pres. 1993-94); Columbia Country (Chevy Chase, Md.); Moorings (Vero Beach, Fla.). Patentee interactive multimedia instruction delivery sys. Home: PO Box 376 Warrenton VA 20188-0376 Office: 50 Culpeper St Warrenton VA 20186-3207

FOX, REEDER RODMAN, lawyer; b. Easton, Pa., Oct. 18, 1934; s. Louis Rodman and Mary Catherine (Cannon) F.; m. Marion Laffey, May 12, 1962; children: Rodman R., Drew D., Vanessa S. BA, Yale U., 1956; LLB, Harvard U., 1959. Bar: Pa. 1960, U.S. Dist. Ct. (ea. dist.) Pa. 1960, U.S. Ct. Appeals (3d cir.) 1960. Assoc. Duane, Morris & Heckscher, Phila., 1960-65, ptnr., 1965—. Served with Pa. N.G., 1959-60. Mem.: ABA, Internat. Assn. Def. Counsel, Phila. Bar Assn., Pa. Bar Assn. Republican. Office: Duane Morris & Heckscher Ste 4200 1 Liberty Pl Philadelphia PA 19103 E-mail: fox@duanemorris.com.

FOX, RENÉE CLAIRE, sociology educator; b. N.Y.C., Feb. 15, 1928; d. Paul Fred and Henrietta (Gold) F. AB summa cum laude, Smith Coll., 1949, LHD, 1975; PhD, Harvard U., 1954; MA (hon.), U. Pa., 1971, U. Oxford, 1996; ScD (hon.), Med. Coll. Pa., 1974, St. Joseph's Coll., Phila., 1978; D (hon.), Katholieke U., Leuven, 1978; LHD (hon.), La Salle U., Phila., 1988; DSc (hon.), Hahnemann U., 1991, U. Nottingham, UK, 2002. Rsch. asst. Bur. Applied Social Rsch., Columbia U., 1953-55, rsch. assoc., 1955-58; lectr. dept. sociology Barnard Coll., 1955-58, asst. prof., 1958-64, assoc. prof., 1964-66; lectr. sociology Harvard U., 1967-69; rsch. fellow Center Internat. Affairs, 1967-68, research assoc. program tech. and soc., 1968-71; prof. sociology, psychiatry and medicine U. Pa., Phila., 1969-98, Annenberg prof. social scis., 1978-98, chmn. dept. sociology, 1972-78, Annenberg prof. social scis. emerita, 1998—. Rsch. assoc. Refugee Studies Centre, Queen Elizabeth House, U. Oxford, 1998—; sci. advisor Centre de Recherches Sociologiques, Kinshasa, Zaïre, 1963-67; vis. prof. sociology U. Officielle du Congo, Lubumbashi, 1965; vis. prof. Sir George Williams U., Montreal, Que., Can., summer 1968; Phi Beta Kappa vis. scholar, 1973-75; dir. humanities seminar med. practitioners NEH, 1975-76; maitre de cours U. Liège, Belgium, 1976-77; vis. prof. Katholieke U., Leuven, Belgium, 1976-77; Wm. Allen Neilson prof. Smith Coll., Mass., 1980; dir. d'Etudes Associè, Ecole des Hautes Etudes en Sciences Sociales, Paris, summer 1989; George Eastman vis. prof. Oxford U., 1996-97; vis. scholar Tokyo Med. and Dental U., 2001; mem. bd. clin. scholars program Robert Wood Johnson Found., 1974-80; mem. Pres.'s Commn. on Study of Ethical Problems in Medicine, Biomed. and Behavioral Rsch., 1979-81; dir. human qualities of medicine program James Picker Found., 1980-83; Fae Golden Kass lectr. Harvard U. Sch. Medicine and Radcliffe Coll., 1983, Kate Hurd Mead lectr. Med. Coll. Pa./Coll. Physicians Phila., 1990, Lori Ann Roscetti Meml. lectr. Rush-Presbyn.-St. Luke's Med. Ctr., Chgo., 1990; vis. scholar Women's Ctr., U. Mo., Kansas City, 1990, vis. scholar Case Western Reserve Sch. of Med., 1992; opening address 13th Internat. Conf. on Social Scis. and Medicine, Hungary, 1994, vis. prof. U. Calif., San Francisco Sch. of Med., 1994; lectr. founds. of medicine Faculty of Medicine McGill U., Montreal, Can., 1995; Supernumerary fellow Balliol Coll. Oxford U., 1996-97; WHR Rivers disting. lectr. Dept. of Social Medicine, Harvard Med. Sch., 1998; assembly series lectr. Washington U., St. Louis, 1998; William J. Rashkind Meml. lectr, Am. Heart Assn., 1998, Salinger-Forlang lectr. U. Tex. Health Scis. Ctr. at San Antonio, 1999, Frances H. Schlitz lectr. U. Kans., Wichita, 2002; affiliated faculty Solemon Asch. Ctr. for Study of Ethmopolitical Conflict, U. Pa., 2001—. sr. fellow, Ctr. Bioethics, U. of Pa., 1999-. Author: Experiment Perilous, 1959, (with Willy DeCraemer) The Emerging Physician, 1968, (with Judith P. Swazey) The Courage to Fall, 1974, rev. edit. 1978, 2002, Essays in Medical Sociology, 1979, 2d edit., 1988, L'Incertitude Medicale, 1988, The Sociology of Medicine: A Participant Observer's View, 1989, (with Judith P. Swazey) Spare Parts: Organ Replacement in American Society, 1992, In the Belgian Château: The Spirit and Culture of European Society in an Age of Change, 1994, French language edit., 1997, Organ Transplantation: Meanings and Realities (edited with Stuart Youngner and Laurence O'Connell), 1996, (in Japanese) Looking Intimately at Bioethics: Fifty Years as a Medical Sociologist, 2003; assoc. editor: Am. Sociol. Rev, 1963-66, Social Sci. and Medicine; mem. editl. com.: Ann. Rev. Sociology, 1975-79; assoc. editor Jour. Health and Social Behavior, 1985-87, Perspectives in Biology and Medicine, 1996—; mem. editl. adv. bd. Tech. in Soc., Sci., 1982-83; mem. editl. bd. Bibliography of Bioethics, 1979—, Culture, Medicine and Psychiatry, 1980-86, Jour. of AMA, 1981-94, Am. Scholar, 1994-99, Current Revs. in Publs., 1994—, Am. Jour. Bioethics, 1999—; vice chair adv. bd. Am. Jour. Ethics and Medicine; contbr. articles to profl. jours.; A Festschrift published in his honor: Society and Medicine: Essays in Honor of Renée Fox, 2003. Bd. dirs. Medicine in Pub. Interest, 1979-94; mem. tech. bd. Milbank Meml. Fund, 1979-85; mem. overseers com. to visit univ. health svcs. Harvard Coll., 1979-86; trustee Russell Sage Found., 1981-87; vice chmn. bd. dirs. Acadia Inst., 1990-97; mem. adv. com. Sch. Nursing LaSalle U., 1998—; mem. external bd. Ctr. for Bioethics, Columbia U., mem. advancement com. King Baudouin Found. U.S. Inc., 1998—, mem., sec. bd. dirs. Acadia Inst., 2002—; mem. info. sci. adv. coun. Innovia Found., The Netherlands, 2002—; mem. external bd. Ctr. for Bioethics, Columbia U., 2002—; mem. Internat. and Sci. Adv. Coun., 2002—. Recipient E. Harris Harbison Gifted Teaching award Danforth Found., 1970, Radcliffe Grad. Soc. medal, 1977, Lindback Found. award for teaching U. Pa., 1989, Centennial medal Grad. Sch. Arts and Scis. Harvard U., 1993, Chevalier de l'Ordre de Leopold II (Belgium), 1995; Wilson Ctr., Smithsonian Instn. fellow, 1987-88, Guggenheim fellow, 1962, Sr. fellow Ctr. Bioethics U. Pa., 1999—; Fulbright Short-Term Sr. scholar to Australia, 1994; 1st W.H.R. Rivers Disting. lectr. Harvard Med. Sch., 1998. Fellow African Studies Assn., AAAS (dir. 1977-80, chmn. sect. K 1986-87), Am. Sociol. Assn. (council 1970-73, 79-81, v.p. 1980-81), Am. Acad. Arts and Scis. (co-chair Class III section I membership com., 1994-96), Inst. Medicine (Nat. Acad. Scis., council 1979-82), Inst. Soc., Ethics and Life Scis. (founder, gov.); mem. AAUP, AAUW, Assn. Am. Med. Colls., Social Sci. Research Council (v.p., dir.), Eastern Sociol. Soc. (pres. 1976-77, Merit award 1993), N.Y. Acad. Scis., Soc. Sci. Study Religion, Inst. Intercultural Studies, 1969-93, (asst. sec. 1969-78, sec. 1978-81, 89-92, v.p. 1987-89), Am. Bd. Med. Specialists, Coll. of Physicians of Phila. (coun. 1993-98), Phi Beta Kappa (senate 1982-87, Ralph Waldo Emerson book award com. 1998-2001). Home: The Wellington 135 S 19th St #1104 Philadelphia PA 19103-4912 E-mail: rcfox@ssc.upenn.edu.

FOX, RICHARD GABRIEL, anthropologist, educator; b. N.Y.C., Mar. 3, 1939; s. Joseph Fox and Elizabeth(Cetron) Swig; m. Judith Lynn Huff, Dec. 18, 1974; 1 child, Sarah. BA, Columbia U., 1960; MA, U. Mich., 1961, PhD, 1965. Asst. prof. Brandeis U., Waltham, Mass., 1965-68; assoc. prof. Duke U., Durham, N.C., 1968-74, prof. anthropology, 1974-93; prof. Washington U., St. Louis, 1993-99. Pres. Wenner-Gren Found. for Anthropological Rsch., 2000—; vis. scholar Sch. Am. Rsch., Santa Fe, 1987-88; mem. Inst. Advanced Study, Princeton, N.J., 1972-73. Author: Kin, Clan, Raja and Rule, 1972, Urban Anthropology, 1977, Lions of the Punjab, 1985, Gandhian Utopia, 1989. John Simon Guggenheim Found. fellow, N.Y.C., 1987-88; grantee NSF, NEH, NIH. Fellow Am. Anthropol. Assn. Office: Wenner-Gren Found 220 5th Ave Fl 16 New York NY 10001-7708 E-mail: rfox@wennergren.org.

FOX, ROBERT AUGUST, food company executive; b. Norristown, Pa., Apr. 24, 1937; s. August Emil and Elizabeth Martha (Deimling) Fox; m. Linda Lee Carnesale, Sept. 19, 1964; children: Lee Elizabeth, Christina Carolyn. BA with high honors, Colgate U., 1959; MBA cum laude, Harvard U., 1964. Unit sales mgr. Procter & Gamble Co., 1959—62; gen. sales mgr. T.J. Lipton Co., 1964—69; v.p. mktg. Can. Dry Corp., 1969—72; pres., CEO, dir. Can. Dry Internat., 1972—75; exec. v.p., dir. Hunt-Wesson Foods, Inc., 1975—78; pres., CEO, dir. R.J. Reynolds Tobacco Internat. S.A., 1978—80; chmn., CEO, dir. Del Monte Corp., San Francisco, 1980—85; vice chmn. Nabisco Brands, Inc., East Hanover, NJ, 1986—87; pres., COO Continental Can Co., Norwalk, Conn., 1988—90; chmn., CEO Clarke Hooper Am., Irvine, Calif., 1990—92, also bd. dirs.; pres. Revlon Internat., N.Y.C., 1992; pres., CEO Foster Farms, Livingston, Calif., 1993—. Bd. dirs. New Perspective Fund, Growth Fund Am., Income Fund Am., Am. Balanced Fund, New World Fund, Crompton Corp., Fundamental Investors; trustee Euro-Pacific Growth Fund. Trustee Colgate U. Mem.: San Francisco C. of C. (bd. dirs., pres. 1984), The Olympic Club, Pacific Union Club. Office: Foster Farms PO Box 457 Livingston CA 95334-0457

FOX, ROBERT WILLIAM, mechanical engineering educator; b. Montreal, Que., Can., July 1, 1934; s. Kenneth and Jessie (Glass) F.; m. Beryl Williams, Dec. 15, 1962; children— David, Lisa. BS in Mech. Engring, Rensselaer Poly. Inst., 1955; MS, U. Colo., 1957; PhD, Stanford U., 1961. Instr. mech. engring. U. Colo., Boulder, 1955-57; research asst. Stanford (Calif.) U., 1957-60; mem. faculty Purdue U., Lafayette, Ind., 1960-99, assoc. prof., 1963-66, prof., 1966-99, asst. head mech. engring., 1971-72, asst. dean engring. for instrn., 1972-76; acting head Purdue U. (Sch. Mech. Engring.), 1975-76, asso. head, 1976-98, chmn. univ. senate, 1971-72, prof. emeritus, 1999. Cons. Owens-Corning Fiberglass Co., Edn. Services Inc., Nelson Mfg. Co., Peoria, Ill., B. Offen Co., Chgo., Agard Co., Johns-Marsville Co., Richmond, Ind., Babcox & Wilcox, Alliance, Ohio. Named Standard Oil Outstanding Tchr. Purdue U., 1967; recipient Harry L. Solberg Outstanding Tchr. award, 1978, 83, Donald E. Marlowe awd., Am. Soc. for Engineering Education, 1992. Fellow ASME, Am. Soc. for Engring. Edn.; mem. Sigma Xi, Pi Tau Sigma, Tau beta Pi, Delta Tau Delta. Home: 3627 Chancellor Way Lafayette IN 47906-8809 Office: Purdue U Sch Mech Engring Lafayette IN 47907

FOX, RONALD ERNEST, psychologist; b. Conover, N.C., May 11, 1936; s. Fred Yount and Carolyn Victoria (Weeks) F.; m. Margaret Elizabeth Smith, Dec. 27, 1956; children: Kelley Victoria, Brett Anthony, Jonathan Eric. AB, U. N.C., 1958, MA, 1961, PhD, 1962. Diplomate: Am. Bd. Profl. Psychology. Asst. prof. dept. psychiatry and psychology U. N.C., 1963-68; asso. prof. dept. psychiatry and psychology Ohio State U., 1968-74, prof., 1974-77, coord. edn. and tng. dept. psychiatry, 1968-77, dir. Family Therapy Clinic, Med. Sch., 1970-77; dean Sch. Profl. Psychology, Wright State U., 1977-92; CEO Piedmont Care, Chapel Hill, N.C., 1992-95; sr. ptnr. Norton, Fox and Assocs., Inc., Chapel Hill, N.C., Cin., 1993-97; exec. dir. The Cons. Group divsn. HRC, 1997—; chair of bd. Assn. Advancement of Psychology, 2002—. Author: (with others) Patients View Their Psychotherapy, 1968, (with others) Abnormal Psychology, 1972, (with Norton) The Change Equation: Capitalizing on Diversity for Effective Organizational Change, 1997; contbr. articles to sci. jours. Fellow APA (pres. 1994); mem. Ohio Psychol. Assn., N.C. Psychol. Assn., Nat. Acads. Practice. Home: 309 Brookside Dr Chapel Hill NC 27516-2905 Office: 100 Europa Dr Ste 260 Chapel Hill NC 27517-2394 E-mail: drronfox@nc.rr.com.

FOX, RONALD FORREST, physics educator; b. Berkeley, Calif., Oct. 1, 1943; s. Sidney Walter and Raia (Joffe) F.; children: Daniel, Lara. BA, Reed Coll., 1964; PhD, Rockefeller U., 1969. Postdoctoral fellow Miller Inst., U. Calif., Berkeley, 1969-71; asst. prof. Ga. Inst. Tech., Atlanta, 1971-74, assoc. prof., 1974-79, prof., 1979—, Regents prof. physics, 1991—, asst. dir. Sch. Physics, 1982-84, assoc. dir. Sch. Physics, 1986-89, 97-99, acting chair, 1999-2000, chair, 2001—. Author: Biological Energy Transduction, 1982, Energy and the Evolution of Life, 1988; contbr. over 100 articles to sci. jour., over 20 chpt. to books. Recipient W. Roane Beard Outstanding Tchr. award Ga. Inst. Tech., 1992, Sigma Xi Sustained Rsch. award Ga. Inst. Tech., 1997; fellow Alfred P. Sloan Found., 1974-78, Guggenheim fellow, 1985; grantee NSF, 1973-2003. Fellow Am. Phys. Soc.; mem. NY Acad. Sci. Avocations: racquetball, jazz piano. Office: Ga Inst Tech Dept Physics Atlanta GA 30332-0430 E-mail: ron.fox@physics.gatech.edu.

FOX, RONNIE ILAINE, volunteer educator, densitometry technician; b. Rochester, NY, Aug. 11, 1943; d. Lloyd Zultan and Alice (Temkin) Purvin; m. Melvin Fox, Dec. 14, 1969; children: Shari Charna, Jason Issac, Michele Mara. Grad., Durham Bus. Coll., El Paso, Tex., 1962; BS in Edn., U. Tex., 1989. Pathology sec., asst. Kaiser Found. Hosp., Hollywood, Calif., 1964-68; substitute tchr. El Paso Pub. Sch., Tex., 1981-82; densitometry technician Beta Diagnostics, Inc., El Paso, Tex., 1983-94. Active El Paso Com., Texpac, Assn. Retarded Citizens; mem. adv. coun. Elder Abuse El Paso Region 945, Drive-A-Meal Coun., 1980-82; regional bd. dirs. United Synagogue Women's League, 1992-96; pres. SW branch Women's League for Conservative Judaism, 1998-2000. Mem. NAFE, AAUW, Nat. Coun. Jewish Women (pres. 1992-94), Orgn. Rehab. through Tng., U.Tex. El Paso Alumni Assn., B'nai B'rith Women, El Paso County Med. Soc. Aux. (pres. 1982-83), B'nai Zion Sisterhood (pres. 1987-89), Russian Resettlement in El Paso (chair acculturation 1991—), Hadassah, Alpha Epsilon Phi (alumni pres. 1974-89). Republican. Jewish. Avocations: golf, sewing, travel, reading, skiing. Home: 810 River Oaks Dr El Paso TX 79912-3420

FOX, SANDRA GAIL, insurance marketing executive; b. N.Y.C., Aug. 12, 1960; d. Joseph A. and Rhoda (Levine) Fried; m. David A. Fox, Sept. 21, 1986; children: Alexander, Peter. BA, Ind. U., 1982. Lic. Series 26, 7 and 63, NASD. Examiner nat. compliance Dean Witter, N.Y.C., 1983-84, from sales supr. active assets acct. to mktg. assoc., 1984-86; pvt. practice Hackensack, N.J., 1986-87; dir. alt. distbn. mktg. Mut. of N.Y., Teaneck, N.J., 1987-89, dir. spl. markets and annuities, 1989-94, asst. v.p. annuities mktg., 1994-97; product developer Prudential, Newark, 1997—, v.p. annuity product devel., 1998, 1998—. Mem. work life force com. Mut. N.Y., Teaneck, 1991-97. Vol. presch. activities YW-YMHA, Wayne, N.J., 1993-94; vol. Wayne PTA (fundraisers), 1996—; fundraiser United Jewish Fedn., Bergen and Passaic, N.J., 1992-96, Kidney Found., 1994; mem. annuity exam. rev. panel LOMA, 1998-2003, annuity programs steering com., 1999, 2002, expert reviewer for Annuity Principles and Products book. Griswald acad. scholar Ind. U., 1980, 81. Mem. Nat. Assn. Variable Annuities (edn. com. 1996—, publ. chmn. 1996), Phi Beta Kappa. Avocations: tennis, running, theater. Office: Prudential 3 Gateway Ctr 8th Fl 100 Mulberry St Newark NJ 07102

FOX, STUART IRA, physiologist; b. Bklyn., June 21, 1945; s. Sam and Bess F.; m. Ellen Diane Berley; 1 child, Laura Elizabeth. BA, UCLA, 1967; MA, Calif. State U., L.A., 1967; postgrad., U. Calif., Santa Barbara, 1969; PhD, U. So. Calif., 1978. Rsch. assoc. Children's Hosp., L.A., 1972; prof. physiology L.A. City Coll., 1972-85, Calif. State U., Northridge, 1979-84, Pierce Coll., 1986—. Cons. McGraw-Hill, 1976—. Author: Computer-Assisted Instruction in Human Physiology, 1979, Laboratory Guide to Human Physiology, 2nd edit., 1980, Textbook of Human Physiology, 1986, 7th edit., 2002, Human Anatomy and Physiology, 1986, Perspectives on Human Biology, 1991, Laboratory Manual for Anatomy and Physiology, 1986; : 5th edit., 1999; ; co-author: Biology, 5th edit., 1999, Synopsis of Anatomy and Physiology, 1997. Mem. AAAS, Am. Physiol. Soc., Am. Anatomy & Physiology Soc., Sigma Xi. Home: 5556 Forest Cove Ln Agoura Hills CA 91301-4047 Office: Pierce Coll 6201 Winnetka Ave Woodland Hills CA 91371-0001

FOX, SYLVAN, journalist, educator; b. Bklyn., June 2, 1928; s. Louis and Sophie (Shapiro) F.; m. Gloria R. Endleman, Sept. 8, 1948; 1 child, Erica. BA, Bklyn. Coll., 1951; MA, U. Calif., Berkeley, 1952. Reporter Little Falls (N.Y.) Evening Times, 1954, Schenectady (N.Y.) Union Star, 1954-55, Buffalo Evening News, 1955-59; successively rewriteman, asst. city editor, city editor N.Y. World Telegram and Sun, 1959-66; dep. police commr. for press relations City of N.Y., 1966-67; successively rewriteman, reporter, dep. met. editor, Saigon bur. chief N.Y. Times, N.Y.C., 1967-73; Nassau editor Newsday, L.I., N.Y., 1973-77, nat. editor, then asst. mng. editor nat. and fgn. news, 1977-79, editor editorial pages, 1979-88; travel columnist, 1994-95. Tchr. journalism NYU, 1965, L.I.U., 1967, Baylor U., Waco, 1985, 88; asst. prof. journalism NYU, 1989-90. Author: The Unanswered Questions About President Kennedy's Assassination, rev. edit., 1975. Recipient Pulitzer prize local reporting, 1963. Mem. Soc. of Silurians. Home: 401 E 65th St New York NY 10021-6943 E-mail: sylglo@aol.com.

FOX, THOMAS GEORGE, health science educator; b. N.Y.C., Sept. 15, 1942; s. Thomas Peter and Alice Cecilia (Ehler) F.; m. Mary Patricia Palmer, Aug. 29, 1980; children: Christopher Adam, Thomas Andrew, Stephen Baron. BA, Coll. N.J., 1964; MEd, U. Vt., 1966; PhD, U. Mich., 1972. Asst. to dean U. Mass., Amherst, 1966; dir. counseling and student svcs. U. Mich., Ann Arbor, 1966-68, sr. adminstrv. asst. Med. Ctr., 1968-69, adminstrv. assoc., 1969-71; asst. dean Robert Wood Johnson Med. Sch., Piscataway, N.J., 1972-77, assoc. dean, 1977-83; sr. v.p. Robert Wood Johnson U. Hosp., New Brunswick, N.J., 1983-86; exec. v.p. U. Health System of N.J., New Brunswick, 1986-90; prof., v.p. devel. and univ. rels. Oreg. Health Scis. U., Portland, 1990-94; CEO Univ. Found., 1990-94; pres., CEO, Liberty Sci. Ctr., Jersey City, 1994-96; CEO, Operation Smile, Norfolk, Va., 1996-2000; sr. v.p. Advancement and Sponsored Programs, Wheeling (W.Va.) Jesuit U., 2000—. Asst. prof. U. Medicine and Dentistry N.J., 1973-79, assoc. prof., 1979-83, clin. assoc. prof., 1983-90. Contbr. articles to profl. jours. Trustee Francis E. Parker Meml. Home, 1981-90, 96—. Fellow: Acad. Medicine N.J.; mem.: Jesuit Advancment Assn. (exec. com.), Coun. for Advancement and Support of Edn. (nstl.lead), Am. Coll. Healthcare Execs. (diplomate). Home: 11 Barrington Dr Wheeling WV 26003-6683 Office: Wheeling Jesuit Univ 316 Washington Ave Wheeling WV 26003-6295 E-mail: tfox@wju.edu.

FOX, VICENTE (VICENTE FOX QUESADA), President of Mexico; b. Mexico City, July 2, 1942; s. Jose and Mercedes (Quesada) Fox; children: Ana Cristina, Vicente, Paulina, Rodrigo; m. Marta Sahagun Jiménez, July 2, 2001. Degree in bus. adminstrn., U. Iberoamericana, Mexico City, 1964; postgrad. Sch. Bus., Harvard U., 1974. Route supr. Coca Cola Export Co., Mexico, 1964-65, various mktg. positions, 1965-70, mktg. dir., 1970-75, pres., 1975-79, Grupo Fox, Lean, Mexico, 1980—; fed. congressman, 1988—91; gov. State of Guanajuato, 1995—99; pres. Republic of Mexico, 2000—. Pres. Patronato U. Iberoamericana, Patronato Casa Cuna Purigo Daniel A.C. Contbr. articles to profl. jours. Named Civic Man of Yr. Alianza Civica, 1991. Partido Accion Nacional. Roman Catholic. Avocations: sports, horses, reading, cultural activities. Office: Office of the President Puerti Col San Miguel 11850 Mexico City Mexico

FOX, WAYNE C. brokerage house executive, corporate financial executive; BA, U. Waterloo, 1971; MBA, McMaster U., 1973. With Can. Imperial Bank Commerce, head of world markets global capital markets activities, vice chmn. treasury and balance sheet mgmt., 1999—; chmn. Toronto Stock Exch., 2001—. Dir. Can. Imperial Bank Commerce ESC Advisors LLC, Can. Imperial Bank Commerce Investments Ltd., Can. Imperial Bank Commerce Mellon Global Securities Svcs. Co., Can. Imperial Bank Commerce Mellon Trust Co., Can. Imperial Bank Commerce Mortgages Inc., Can. Imperial Bank Commerce Offshore Banking Svcs. Corp., Barbados and Can. Imperial Bank Commerce Offshore Svcs. Inc., Can. Imperial Bank Commerce World Markets Inc. Bd. govs. McMaster U.; gov. emeritus Appleby Coll.; bd. dirs. and chmn. Canada-Helps org Inc. Office: Toronto Stock Exch PO Box 450 3rd fl 130 King St W Toronto ON Canada M5X-1J2*

FOX-CLARKSON, ANNE C. computer company executive; 1 child. BS in Edn., Bucknell U., 1967; MS in Reading, Syracuse U., 1973, PhD in Tchr. Edn., 1975. Cert. elem. tchr., adminstr., Idaho. Postdoctroal work in edn. adminstrn. U. Idaho; tchr. elem.; prin., supt. pub. schs., 1978-84; assoc. prof. ednl. adminstrn. Gonzaga U., 1987-94; supt. pub. instrn. State of Idaho, 1995-98; v.p. ednl. markets Shop2gether.com, 2000; pres. Human Resources Dynamics, Inc., Boise, 2001—. Mem. State Bd. Edn., State Land Bd., State Libr. Bd., State Endowment Fund, State Investment Bd.; pres., co-founder Children's Village Homes for Abused Children; grant writer, mgmt. cons.; spkr. in field. Former pres. Idaho State Elem. Prin. Assn., Wash. State Univ. Profl. Adminstr. Assn.

FOXEN, RICHARD WILLIAM, manufacturing company executive; b. N.Y.C., Nov. 12, 1927; s. William alyisus and Mae Dorothea (Scully) F.; m. Hilda Duran-Ballen, Feb. 11, 1956; children: Richard, Theresa, Thomas, Patricia, Anthony. B.M.E., Bklyn. Poly. Inst., 1950. V.p. corp. staffs Westinghouse Air Brake Co., Pitts., 1961-69; pres. European indsl. group Am. Std., Brussels, 1969-73; v.p. Europe bus. divsn. GE, Brussels, 1973-78; sr. v.p.

Rockwell Internat., 1978-88. Adj. prof. bus. adminstrn. Carnegie Mellon U., U. Pitts.; chmn. Mercy Health Sys., Inc., Pitts.; bd. dirs. Cordis Corp. Bd. trustees N.Y. Poly. U.; bd. dirs. Mannesmann U.S. Adv. Conflict Resolution Ctr. Internat.; chmn. Mendelssohn Choir Pitts., Pressley-Ridge Schs., We. Pa. Family Ctr., Pitts. With U.S. Army, 1946-48. Mem. Pitts. Athletic Assn., Duquesne, Pitts. Athletic, Seabrook Is., Tau Beta Pi, Pi Tau Sigma. Roman Catholic. Home: 1292 Puritan Ave Birmingham MI 48009-4815

FOX-FREUND, BARBARA SUSAN, real estate company executive; b. Rocky Mount, N.C., Jan. 17, 1949; d. Albert Richard and Anita (Levinson) Fox; m. James Coleman Freund, Jan. 12, 1985. Student, Centenary Coll., 1968, Boston U., 1970. Real estate broker Whitbread-Nolan, Inc., N.Y.C., 1972-80; v.p. Stribling and Assocs., Ltd., N.Y.C., 1980-82; exec. v.p. Cross and Brown Residentials, Inc., N.Y.C., 1982-88; pres. Fox Residential Group, Inc., N.Y.C., 1988—. Bd. dirs. Riverside Symphony, N.Y.C., 1989-99, WOOF Animal Rescue, 2003—; bd. dirs., pres. 55 W. 73d St. Corp., N.Y.C., 1986-97; chmn. bd. Stray from the Heart, 2000-03. Mem. Real Estate Bd. N.Y. (chmn. residential com. 1986-89, ethics com. 1989-92, bd. dirs. brokerage com. 1988-92, tchr. 1986—, chmn. inter-firm rels. com. 1991-93, bd. dirs. residential divsn. 1994-, bd. govs. 1994-99, chmn. interfirm forum 1995-99, residential ethics com. 1995-2002, co-chmn.; chmn. bd. dirs. brokerage com., 1999—. Republican. Jewish. Avocations: sculpture, tennis, skiing. Home: 55 W 73rd St New York NY 10023-3136 Office: Fox Residential Group Inc 1015 Madison Ave New York NY 10021-0261 E-mail: bfox@foxresidential.com.

FOX-GENOVESE, ELIZABETH ANN TERESA, humanities educator, educator; b. Boston, May 28, 1941; d. Edward Whiting and Elizabeth Mary (Simon) Fox; m. Eugene Dominick Genovese, 1969. BA, Bryn Mawr Coll., 1963; MA, Harvard U., 1966, PhD, 1974; LittD (hon.), Millsaps Coll., 1992. Teaching fellow Harvard U., Cambridge, Mass., 1965-66, 1967-69; asst. prof. U. Rochester, N.Y., 1973-76, assoc. prof., 1976-80; prof. SUNY, Binghamton, 1980-86, Emory U., Atlanta, 1986—, Eleonore Raoul prof. of humanities, 1988—. Adj. prof. Auburn (Ala.) U., 1987; Eudora Welty prof. Millsaps Coll., 1990. Author: Origins of Physiocracy, 1976, (with others) Fruits of Merchant Capital, 1983, Within the Plantation Household, 1988, Feminism Without Illusions, 1991, Feminism Is Not the Story of My Life: How the Elite Women's Movement Has Lost Touch with the Real Concerns of Women, 1996, Women and the Future of the Family, 2000, co-editor: Reconstructing History: The Emergence of a New Historical Society, 1999; mem. editl. adv. bd. First Things; mem. editl. bd. Books and Culture; editor Jour. Hist. Soc., 1999—; contbr. numerous articles to profl. jours. Mem. acad. adv. bd. Inst. for Am. Values, 1994—; adv. bd. Campaign for the Am. Family, 1995—, Ind. Women's Forum, 1993—. Mem. LWV, MLA, Soc. Am. Historians, The Hist. Soc. (mem. exec. com.), So. Hist. Assn. (life), So. Assn. for Women Historians (life), Am. Comparative Lit. Assn. (adv. bd. 1991-95), Orgn. Am. Historians (life, proglram com. 1991), Am. Studies Assn. (program com. 1987), Soc. for Study So. Lit. (exec. coun. 1990-93), South Atlantic MLA (chair women's studies network 1989-90), Social Sci. Hist. Assn. (exec. coun. 1986-88), Am. Hist. Assn., Am. Polit. Sci. Assn., Assn. of Lit. Scholars and Critics, Am. Acad. Liberal Edn. (bd. dirs.), Nat. Coun. on Hist. Standards (steering commn.), Hist. Soc. (mem. exec. com.), Atlanta Hist. Assn. (acad. adv. com.), Am. Antiquarian Soc., Nat. Alumni Forum (adv. bd.), Cosmos Club, Harvard Club of Boston. Roman Catholic. Avocations: family, films, fashion, reading, major league baseball. Home: 1487 Sheridan Walk NE Atlanta GA 30324-3253 Office: Emory U Dept History Atlanta GA 30322-0001

FOXHOVEN, JERRY RAY, lawyer; b. Yankton, S.D., July 24, 1952; s. Elmer William and Ida Elizabeth (Lubbers) F.; m. Julie Ann Greco, Apr. 6, 1985; children: Anthony Michael, Peter Joseph. BS summa cum laude, Morningside Coll., 1974; JD, Drake U., 1977. Bar: Iowa 1977, U.S. Dist. Ct. (so. and no. dists.) Iowa 1977, U.S. Ct. Appeals (8th cir.) 1977, U.S. Supreme Ct. 1981, Nebr. 1985, U.S. Dist. Ct. Nebr. 1985, Wis. 1986. Assoc. Critelli & Pille, Des Moines, 1977-79, ptnr., 1979-82, Foxhoven & McCann, Des Moines, 1982-88, Peddicord, Wharton, Thune, Foxhoven & Spencer, P.C., 1988-91; pvt. practice, 1991-2000; adminstr. Child Advocacy Bd., Des Moines, 2000—; sr. fellow Ctr. Adoption Rsch. U. Mass., 2002—. Instr. criminaljustice dept. Des Moines Area Community Coll., Ankeny, Iowa, 197 8-81, Am. Inst. Banking, 1982-85. Mem. steering con. Culver for U.S. Senate, Des Moines, 1980; chmn. Iowa State Foster Care Rev. Bd., 1986-99; bd. dirs., nat. pres. Nat. Assn. Foster Care Reviewers, 1988-01; mem. parish coun. Sacred Heart Roman Cath. Ch., West Des Moines, 1982. Lodge: Masons (master 1990). Democrat. Home: 1608 NW 101st St Clive IA 50325-6716 Office: Lucas Bldg 321 E 12th St 4th Fl Des Moines IA 50319-0083 E-mail: jfoxhoven@dia.state.ia.us.

FOXLIN, ERIC MICHAEL, entrepreneur, researcher; b. Pitts., May 28, 1965; s. Franklin and Carlilyn Zeitlin Fuchs; m. Susan Chu Lin, Sept. 6, 1992; 1 child, Kayla Rei. BA in Physics, Harvard U., 1987; MS in Elec. Engring. and Computer Sci., MIT, 1993, PhD candidate in Elec. Engring. and Computer Sci., 1996. Fgn. expert Nanjing U., China, 1987—88; rsch. asst. Mass. Gen. Hosp., Boston, 1988—90; founder, chief tech. officer, and v.p. rsch. and devel. InterSense Inc., Burlington, Mass., 1996—. Chmn., dir. InterSense Inc., Burlington, Mass., 1996—; program com. mem. Internat. Symposium on Mixed and Augmented Reality, 1998—; dir. Ocean State Tech. Corp., Providence, 2003—. Contbr. book; author: (book chpt.) Motion Tracking chapter in Handbook of Virtual Environments; reviewer IEEE, ACM and MIT Press Jours. and Confs.; author: (15 tech. articles) various Conf. Procs. and Periodicals. Recipient $10K award, MIT Bus. Plan Competition, 1996, Innovation award, Computer Graphics World, 1999, Engring. Innovation award, Frost & Sullivan, 2000; fellow Fellowship, Link Found., 1994—95; grantee Student-initiated Rsch. Grant, Rowland Found., 1986. Mem.: Inst. of Nav., IEEE. Achievements include patents for Miniature gyroscopic orientation tracker with automatic drift correction; Scalable motion tracking sys. using constellation of wireless ultrasonic transponders; Improved ultrasonic ranging methods in air; Differential inertial sys. for tracking pilot's head relative to moving vehicle; patents pending for Self-Referenced Tracking System For Wearable Computers; Generalized Sensor Fusion Architecture; Circular barcode and machine vision detection system. Avocations: bluegrass guitar, travel, chinese language. Home: 285 Highland Ave Arlington MA 02476 Office: InterSense Inc 1 North Ave Burlington MA 01803

FOXMAN, ABRAHAM HENRY, advocacy organization administrator; b. Poland; came to U.S., 1950; s. Helen and Joseph F. BA in Polit. Sci., CCNY, 1962; postgrad., Jewish Theol. Sem., 1958-60, New Sch. Social Rsch., 1963-64; JD, NYU, 1965; LLD (hon.), Fla. Internat. U., 1992. Asst. dir. law dept. Anti-Defamation League of B'nai B'rith, N.Y.C., 1965-68, dir. Mid. Ea. affairs, 1968-73, nat. leadership dir., 1973-79, assoc. nat. dir., 1979-87, nat. dir., 1987—. Mem. Pres.'s U.S. Holocaust Meml. Coun., N.Y.C. Holocaust Meml. Commn. (adv. coun.), Am. Gathering, Jewish Holocaust Survivors. Office: Anti-Defamation League 823 United Nations Plz New York NY 10017-3518

FOXMAN, BRUCE MAYER, chemist, educator; b. Youngstown, Ohio, Mar. 12, 1942; s. Jerome Jay and Phyllis E. (Altshuler) Foxman; m. Carole J. Wittkopf, Sept. 14, 1968; children: Gregory Michael, Andrew Craig. BS with distinction, Iowa State U., 1964; PhD in Inorganic Chemistry, MIT, 1968. Rsch. fellow Australian Nat. U., Canberra, 1968-72; asst. prof. Brandeis U., Waltham, Mass., 1972-78, assoc. prof., 1978-85, prof., 1985—. Vis. prof. Thomas J. Watson Rsch. Ctr., IBM, Yorktown Heights, NY, 1975, Max-Planck-Inst. fuer Polymerforschung, Mainz, Germany, 1995—96; hon. prof. U. Birmingham, England, 2001; invited prof. U. Louis Pasteur, Strasbourg, France, 2002; cons. Polaroid Corp. Mem.: Coll. Bd. Advanced Placement Exam. Com. (chair chemistry 1993—96), Royal Soc. Chemistry, Materials Rsch. Soc., Am. Crystallographic Assn., Am. Chem. Soc., Sigma Xi, Lambda Upsilon, Phi Kappa Phi. Home: 74 N Hill Ave Needham MA 02492-1223 Office: Brandeis Univ Dept Chemistry Waltham MA 02454-9110 Business E-Mail: foxman1@brandeis.edu.

FOXWELL, ELIZABETH MARIE, editor, writer; b. Somerville, N.J., Aug. 30, 1963; d. James Adolph and Rita Ann (Drohan) F. BS in Journalism, U. Md., 1985; MA in Liberal Studies with distinction, Georgetown U., 1990. Coord. publs. internat. student exch. program Georgetown U., Washington, 1987-91; editor Am. Assn. Colls. for Tchr. Edn., Washington, 1992-97, dir. publs. and mktg., 1994-97; publs. mgr. Soc. for Am. Archaeology, 1998-2000; pubs. dir. section internat. law and practice Am. Bar Assn., 2000—02; mng. editor Heldref Pubs., 2001—. Bd. dirs. Malice Domestic, Bethesda, Md., publicity liaison, 1988-94, vice-chair, 1993-95, chair, 1995-97, Mystery Writers of Am., bd. dirs. 2003—; presenter Vera Brittain Centenary Conf., 1993, Popular Culture Assn. Conf., 1995-96. Editor: The Usual Suspects, 1992—95, The 3rd Degree, 2003; contbg. editor: MysteryScene, 2000—; co-editor: (anthologies) Malice Domestic 5, 1996, Malice Domestic 6, 1997; editor: Malice Domestic 7, 1998, Malice Domestic 8, 1999, Malice Domestic 9, 2000, Malice Domestic 10, 2001; co-editor: Murder, They Wrote I, 1997, Murder, They Wrote II, 1998, More Murder, They Wrote, 1999; editor (in-chief): The Armchair Detective, 1997—98; contbr. (short stories) Crime Through Time II, 1998, Cat Crimes Through Time, 1999; author: Crime Through Time III, Crafty Cat Crimes, 2000; contr. (short stories) Blood on Their Hands, 2003; contbr. articles to profl. jours. Recipient 2d prize in play contest N.J. Ctr. for the Performing Arts, 1981, honorable mention in writing contest Interlochen Arts Acad., 1981, 1st prize Cape Fear (N.C.) Crime Festival Short Story Contest, 2003. Mem.: Sisters in Crime, Mystery Writers Am. Home: 1568 Mt Eagle Pl Alexandria VA 22302-2120

FOXWORTH, JO, advertising agency executive; b. Tylertown, Miss. Grad. in Journalism, U. Mo. Exec. McCann-Erickson, Interpub. Group of Cos.; owner Jo Foxworth Inc., N.Y.C., 1968—; co-owner Foxworth-Gold, Inc. Author: Boss Lady, 1979, Wising Up, 1981, Boss Lady's Arrival and Survival Plan, 1986, The Bordello Cookbook, 1997, Murder Under Wraps, 2002. Named to AAF Hall of Fame, 1997. Office: 740 Broadway New York NY 10003-9518

FOXWORTH, JOHNNIE HUNTER, state agency administrator; b. Anderson, S.C., Feb. 13, 1921; d. John Ira and Bessie (Hatton) Hunter; m. Marvin Ardell, Sept. 21, 1941. Attended colleges, univ., Atlanta, Bridgeport, Conn. Cashier examiner, office supr. Motor Vehicle Dept., State Conn., Bridgeport, 1957—72; br. office mgr. various locations in state, 1972—77; br. office dist. supr. Wethersfield, Conn., 1977—81; asst. dir., 1981—85; cons., tng. instr., 1985—88. Writer: manual in field. Mem. Commrs. Affirmative Action Com., 1987. Recipient Profl. Achievement award, Bridgeport chpt. Nata. Bus. and Profl. Women, 1972, (2) Disting. Managerial Svc. award, State of Conn., Wethersfield, 1982, Woman of Yr. award, Nat. Coun. Negro Woman, Bridgeport, 1972. Mem.: The Links, Inc. (Waterbury) (pres. 1980—85), Les Treize (Bridgeport) (pres. 1966—68). Home: 496A Heritage Vlg Southbury CT 06488-1525

FOY, ALEXIS, professional athletics coach; BS, Calif. State U., Northridge, 1991. Adj. prof. Calif. State U., Northridge, 2000—; profl. voiceover artist. Author: The Internationalization Of Adult Skating, Coaching: Adults vs. Kids; contbr. articles to newsletters;, author poetry. Mem.: U.S. Figure Skating Assn. (assoc.; regional announcer 2001, pacific coast sectional vice-chair 2002—, equal representation com. - adult com. rep. 2002—, Silver medalist 1998, two-time nat. Silver medalist 1996), Profl. Skaters' Assn. (assoc.). Personal E-mail: frozen_pond@hotmail.com.

FOY, BETSY D. counseling administrator, educator; b. Milw., Apr. 5, 1953; d. Homer Charles Foy and Dorothy Louise Rohlfing; m. Mark T. Cockson, Sept. 2, 1978; children: Emily L. Cockson, Luke T. Cockson, Dylan J. Cockson. BA, St. Louis U., 1975; M in Health Sci., Wash. U., St. Louis, 1996. Cert. Health Edn. Specialist Nat. Commn. for Health Edn. Credentialing, 1997; Qualified Profl. Mo. Dept. of Mental Health/Divsn. of Alcohol and Drug Abuse, 2001. Supr. social svc. worker Mo. Dept. of Social Svcs., St. Louis, 1975—90; child care specialist Mo. Dept. of Health, St. Louis, 1990—97; asst. dir. Wash. U. Student Health & Counseling Ctr., St. Louis, 1997—. Bd. trustee Mo. Soc. for Pub. Health Edn., St. Louis, 1998—2000; founder, chair St. Louis Higher Edn. Health & Wellness Collaborative. Author: (several articles) Jour. of Am. Coll. Health, (article) Health Promotion Practice Jour., Health Edn. and Behavior Jour.; cons. editor Jour. Am. Coll. Health, 2002—03. Parents adv. bd. Voluntary Interdistrict Coordinating Coun., St. Louis, 1995—99; fundraising Wash. U. Arts & Scis. Alumni Assn., St. Louis, 1998—2003; leader Girl Scouts of Am., St. Louis, 1992—94. Alcohol Prevention Grant, NCAA- NCAA, 2002—. Mem.: Soc. for Pub. Health Edn., Am. Coll. Health Assn. (alcohol & drug task force 1999—2003), Toastmasters Internat., Alpha Sigma Nu, Nat. Honor Soc. Achievements include development of WU Walks-Campus Walking Club; Health & Wellness Collaborative among St. Louis Insts. of Higher Edn. Avocations: walking, letter writing. Home: 7418 Hoover Saint Louis MO 63117 Office: Washington U Campus Box 1201 One Brookings Dr Saint Louis MO 63130 Personal E-mail: betsy_foy@wustl.edu.

FOY, CHARLES DALEY, retired soil scientist; b. Buena Vista, Ky., Aug. 19, 1923; s. Charles Clinton and Zylphia Gertrude (Binkley) F.; m. Doris Blanche Hornbaker, June 4, 1950; 1 child, David Alden. BS in Agriculture, U. Tenn., 1949; MS in Soil Sci., Purdue U., 1953, PhD in Soil Fertility, 1955. Tchr. Vets. Inst. on Farm Tng. Program, Connersville, Ind., 1949-51; rsch. fellow Purdue U., West Lafayette, Ind., 1951-55, asst. prof. agronomy, 1955-57; rsch. soil scientist, dept. agronomy USDA U. Ark., Fayetteville, 1957-61; rsch. soil scientist, climate stress lab. USDA Agrl. Rsch. Sta., Beltsville, Md., 1961-95; collaborator, 1995—. Cons. and lectr. in U.S. and abroad. Contbr. articles to profl. jours. With U.S. Army, 1943-46, PTO. Recipient Environ. Quality award Am. Soc. Hort. Sci., 1974, Cert. of Recognition for outstanding contbn. Orgn. Com. of IV Internat. Symposium on Plant-Soil Interactions at Low pH and Nat. Maize and Sorghum Rsch. Ctr., Belo Horizonte, Brazil, 1996; Purdue U. grad. rsch. fellow, 1953-55. Fellow Am. Soc. Agronomy, Soil Sci. Soc. Am., Crop Sci. Soc. Am.

FOY, EDWARD JOSEPH, sociologist, educator, social worker; b. Passaic, N.J., Oct. 22, 1931; s. William and Alice Ellen Foy. MSS, Fordham U., 1958; PhD, St. John's U., 1965; MPH, Harvard U., 1975. Cert. social worker N.Y. State Edn. Dept. Edn. specialist U.S. Army Hdqs., Antilles, San Juan, PR, 1953—56; assoc. study dir. N.Y.C. Dept. Correction, 1963—65; rsch. assoc. Child Welfare League Am., N.Y.C., 1965—67; dir. rsch. N.Y. Office Probation, 1967—68; sr. ptnr. Foy, Falcier Assocs., 1968—73; dir. rsch. ICIS/The Door, N.Y.C., 1975—77; asst. prof. U. Miami, Fla., 1976—78; pvt. practice clin. social work, N.Y.C., 1978—94; semi-ret., 1996—. Dir. rsch. Renaissance House, Newark, 1994—96; dir. Counseling Ctr. U.S. Army, Pusan, Republic of Korea, 1987—88; condr. insvc. tng. Contbr. articles to profl. jours. Grant writer Meml. Sloan-Kettering Cancer Ctr., N.Y.C., 1980—81. Fellow, NIMH, Harvard U., 1974. Avocations: photography, writing.

FOY, HERBERT MILES, III, lawyer, educator; b. Statesville, N.C., Mar. 22, 1945; s. Herbert Miles Jr. and Perci Aileen (Lazenby) F.; m. Eleanor Jane Meschan, June 27, 1970; children: Anna Meschan, Sarah Aileen. AB, U. N.C., 1967; MA, Harvard U., 1968; JD, U. Va., 1972. Bar: N.C. 1973, U.S. Dist. Ct. (mid. and we. dists.) N.C., 1973, U.S. Ct. Appeals (4th cir.), 1975, U.S. Supreme Ct., 2002. Jud. clk. U.S. Ct. Appeals (5th cir.), Atlanta, 1972-73; assoc. Smith, Moore, Smith, Schell & Hunter, Greensboro, N.C., 1973-77, 81-83, ptnr., 1983-84; sr. atty. advisor office legal counsel U.S. Dept. Justice, Washington, 1977-81; assoc. prof. Sch. Law Wake Forest U., Winston-Salem, N.C., 1984-87, prof., 1987—, assoc. dean acad. affairs, 1990-95, Law Sch., Wake Forest U., Winston-Salem, 2000—. Contbr. articles to legal jours. Morehead scholar, 1963; Woodrow Wilson fellow, 1968. Mem. ABA, N.C. Bar Assn., N.C. State Bar Assn., Fosythe County Bar Assn., Order of Coif, Phi Beta Kappa. Democrat. Methodist. Avocations: banjo playing, gardening, athletics, poetry. Home: 2328 Oak Ridge Rd Oak Ridge NC 27310-9701 Office: Wake Forest U Sch Law PO Box 7206U Winston Salem NC 27109-7206

FOY, MARTIN THOMAS, JR., pharmacist; b. N.Y.C., Feb. 14; m. Suzanne Foy; 3 children. BS in Pharmacy, Long Island U., 1986. Registered pharmacist, N.J., Fla.; registered natropath, D.C.; diplomate homeopathic pharmacy. Pharmacist Liss Pharmacy, Summit, N.J., 1986-87, pharmacist/co-owner Madison, N.J., 1987-97; pres. Liss Home Care, Summit, 1993-97; pharmacy owner Bottle Hill Pharmacy, Madison, 1997—. Bd. dirs. James Jersey Assn. Med. Equipment Svcs., 1995-2000. Bd. dirs. Madison Area YMCA, 1999—, Grace Counseling Ctr., 1999—. Mem. Madison C. of C., Rotary (treas. Madison 1994-96, pres. 1997-98, Pres. award 1995, 99, Paul Harris fellow 1996). Office: Bottle Hill Pharmacy 42 Main St Madison NJ 07940-1814

FOY, ROBERT W(ILLARD), utilities executive; b. San Francisco, Sept. 18, 1936; BS with honors in Bus. and Indsl. Mgmt., San Jose State U., 1959. Mgmt. trainee, purchasing agt. Continental Group Inc. (formerly Continental Can Co.), Stockton, Calif., 1962-64; with Pacific Storage Co., Stockton, 1964-96, pres., CEO, 1977-96; chmn. bd. dirs. Calif. Water Svc. Co., San Jose, 1996—. Bd. dirs. Pacific Storage Co.; mem. bd. agts. com. Bekins Van Line Co. Mem. selection com. Mil. Acad. 14th Congl. Dist.; vol. adv. com. State of Calif. Atty. Gen. Office, San Joaquin County Grand Jury, Calif.; bd. dirs. Boy's Club, San Joaquin County Better Bus. Bur., Calif., San Joaquin County Mental Health Assn., Calif.; chmn. Stockton parole adv. com. State of Calif.; pres. United Way, San Joaquin Employer's Coun.; co-chmn. Make Brighter Tomorrows campaign A Safe Pl. for Battered Women; hon. chmn. San Joaquin/Calaveras unit Am. Cancer Soc.; active San Jose State U. Spartan Found.; chmn. bd. commrs. Stockton Port Dist.; chmn. Congressman Norman D. Shumway campaign, 1978—90; pres. St. John's Episcopal Ch.; chmn. bd. trustees St. Joseph's Med. Ctr.; bd. advisors Coll. Internat. Bus., San Jose State U.; chmn. presdl. task force U. Pacific. Capt. inf. USAR. Recipient disting. Alumnus award, Sch. Bus. San Jose State U., 1981, Conservative of Yr. award, Norman D. Shumway-Lincoln Club Ctrl. Calif., 1987. Mem.: Nat. Moving and Storage Assn. (chmn. bd. dirs.), Calif. Moving and Storage Assn. (pres., sec.-treas., v.p.), Am. Soc. Pub. Adminstrn. (mem. com. rels. bus., industry), Nat. Def. Transp. Assn., Central Valley Purchasing Agts. Assn. (chmn.), San Jose State U. Alumni Assn., Greater Stockton C. of C. (bd. dirs., pres.), San Jose State U. Quarterback Club, Yosemite Club, West Lane Tennis Club. Republican. Avocations: backpacking, reading, wine collecting, san jose state intercollegiate athletics. Address: 933 W Monterey Ave Stockton CA 95204-3028 Office: Calif Water Svc Co 1720 N 1st St San Jose CA 95112-4598

FOY, THOMAS PAUL, lawyer, retired state legislator, retired banker; b. Silver City, N.Mex., Oct. 19, 1914; s. Thomas J. and Mary V. Foy; m. Joan Carney, Nov. 17, 1948 (dec. June 1994); children: Celia, Thomas Paul Jr. (dec.), Muffet (Mary Ann), J. Carney, James B. BS in Commerce, Notre Dame U., 1938, JD, 1939. Bar: N.Mex. 1946. Dist. atty. N.Mex. 6th Jud. Dist., Silver City, 1949-57; atty. Village of Bayard, N.Mex., 1954-68, Village of Ctrl., N.Mex., 1960-70; v.p., counsel, bd. dirs. Sunwest Bank, Silver City, 1946-84, chmn. bd. dirs., 1969-84, chmn. emeritus, 1984-97; state rep. Dist. 39 State of N.Mex., Grant-Hidalgo, 1971-98; chmn. jud. com. N.Mex. State Legis., Santa Fe, 1984-98; pres. Foy & Vesely and Foy, Foy & Castillo, Silver City, 1946-99, Foy Law Firm PC, 1999—. 1st lt. U.S. Army, 1941-46; prisoner of war, PTO, 1942-45. Decorated Bronze Star, Purple Heart, Asiatic-Pacific Ribbon with 3 oak leaf clusters; recipient Citizen of Yr. award Silver City-Grant County C. of C., 1965, Dedication to Advancement award Trial Lawyers Assn., 1993, N.Mex. Disting. Svc. medal, 1994. Mem. ABA, N.Mex. Bar Assn. (bar commr. 1967-85, v.p. N.Mex. bar commn. 1978-79, Disting. Svc. of Laws award 1987), Am. Judicature Soc., Bataan Vets. Orgn. (state comdr. 1965-66, 98-99), KC (Grand Knight 1936-37), VFW (state comdr. 1959-60), Lions (dist. gov. 1956-57), Elks. Democrat. Roman Catholic. Avocations: football, baseball, travel, conventions. Office: The Foy Law Firm PC 210 W Broadway St Silver City NM 88061-5353

FOY, WADE HAMPTON, research scientist; b. Richmond, Va., Jan. 26, 1925; s. Wade Hampton and Eliza Belle (Wilkinson) Foy; m. Raymonde van Laar, May 19, 1952; children: Virginia E. Foy Streeter, Wade Charles. BS, U.S. Naval Acad., 1946; BEE, N.C. State Coll., 1951; MSEE, MIT, 1955; D in Engring., Johns Hopkins U., 1962. Registered profl. engr., Calif. Sect. head math. Martin Co., Balt., 1956—62; engr. Stanford Rsch. Inst., Menlo Park, Calif., 1962—68; prin. scientist SRI Internat., Menlo Park, Calif., 1968—91. Lectr. Drexel Inst. Tech., Balt., 1957—61; adj. lectr. Santa Clara (Calif.) U., 1963—2001. Contbr. articles to profl. jours. Ensign USN, 1946—48, lt. USNR, 1951—53. Mem.: IEEE, U.S. Naval Inst. Republican. Avocations: research, tennis, ship models. Home: 131 Callecita Los Gatos CA 95032

FOYE, LAURANCE VINCENT, physician, hospital administrator; b. Seattle, Nov. 26, 1925; s. Laurance Vincent and Sara Pauline (Given) F.; m. Laura Marian Love, June 22, 1951; children: Patricia Marian, Michael Laurance. AB, U. Calif., Berkeley, 1949; MD, U. Calif., San Francisco, 1952. Diplomate: Am. Bd. Internal Medicine. Intern San Francisco Gen. Hosp., 1952-53; resident in medicine VA Hosp., San Francisco, 1953-55, 56-57, Stanford U. Hosp., San Francisco, 1955-56; asst. chief med. service VA Hosp., San Francisco, 1958-66; chief clin. investigations br. Nat. Cancer Inst., Bethesda, Md., 1966-70; dir. edn. service VA, Washington, 1970-74; dep. chief med. dir., 1974-78; dir. VA Med. Center, San Francisco, 1978-86; assoc. clin. prof. medicine U. Calif. Sch. Medicine, San Francisco, 1979-86. Mem. adv. council Nat. Heart and Lung Inst., 1971-73 Contbr. articles on cancer research to profl. jours. Mem. governing bd. West Bay Health Systems Agy., 1978-82; mem. Fed. Exec. Bd., San Francisco, 1978-86. Served with U.S. Army, 1944-46. Recipient Exceptional Service award VA, 1978, Disting. Career award, VA, 1986. Fellow ACP; mem. Phi Beta Kappa, Sigma Xi, Alpha Omega Alpha. Address: 125 Cambon Dr Apt 10-h San Francisco CA 94132-2512

FOYE, THOMAS HAROLD, lawyer; b. Rapid City, S.D., Nov. 23, 1930; s. Harold Herbert and Jean Winifred (McCormick) F.; m. Laurene Fowler, Aug. 7, 1972; children: David Snyder, Stewart Snyder BS in Commerce, Creighton U., 1952; LLB, Georgetown U., 1955. Bar: S.D. 1955, D.C. 1955, U.S. Supreme Ct. 1968. Trial atty. tax div. U.S. Dept. Justice, Washington, 1955-58; assoc. Bangs, McCullen, Butler, Foye & Simmons, predecessor firms, Rapid City, 1958-60, ptnr., 1960—. Lectr. in field Fellow Am. Coll. Trust and Estate Counsel, Am. Bar Found.; mem. ABA, State Bar S.D. (pres. 1982-83), Pennington County Bar Assn. (pres. 1962), Am. Coll. Real Estate Lawyers, Internat. Acad. Estate and Trust Law., Am. Coll. Tax Counsel. Clubs: Arrowhead Country (Rapid City). Democrat. Roman Catholic. Avocations: snow skiing, water skiing, hiking. Office: Bangs McCullen Butler Foye & Simmons PO Box 2670 Rapid City SD 57709-2670

FOYT, LARRY, race car driver; Race car driver ASA ACDelco Challenge Series, Busch Series. Office: c/o AJ Foyt Racing 128 Commercial Dr Mooresville NC 28115

FOZZATI, ALDO, investment banker; b. Italy, Mar. 10, 1950; arrived in U.S., 1978; s. Danilo and Piera (Bretto) F.; m. Ana Maria Ruiz, June 7, 1977; children: Giacomo, Hugo, Daniel. PhD in Aero. Engring., Poly. U. of Turin, Italy, 1975. Registered profl. engr., Europe, U.S. and Can. Project mgr. Fiat Aerospace, Turin, 1975-78; U.S. rep. Fiat Corp., N.Y.C. and Detroit, 1978-82; ind. internat. bus. cons. Los Angeles, Paris and N.Y.C., 1982-84; program dir. GM, Detroit, 1984-87; dir. new bus. devel. GM Europe, Zurich, Switzerland, 1987-91, purchasing exec. dir. Rüsselsheim, Germany, 1991-92; v.p., gen. mgr. Kelsey-Hayes Europe, Wiesbaden, Germany, 1992-94, Delco Remy Internat. Europe, Frankfurt, Germany, 1995-98; mem. adv. bd. Citicorp Venture Capital, N.Y.C., 1998—. Founder Fozzati & Co., Swan Wealth Mgmt., Boulders Capital, Frankfurt (Germany) Internat. Sch., Sonic Telecom, Chantilly, Va., RAC, Moscow; mem. global adv. coun. Thunderbird Am. Mgmt. Sch., Phoenix; sr. advisor Parthenon, Boston; mem. adv. bd. Artoc Group, Cairo. Mem. Soc. Automotive Engrs., Am. Security Coun. Democrat. Roman Catholic. Avocations: skiing, tennis, golf. Home: 250 Marlborough Dr Bloomfield Hills MI 48302-0644 Office: Fozzati & Compagnie Frankfurter St 92 Frankfurt Germany E-mail: afozzati@aol.com.

FRACKMAN, NOEL, art critic; b. N.Y.C., May 27, 1930; d. Walter David and Celeste (Barman) Stern; m. Richard Benoit Frackman, July 2, 1950; 1 child, Noel Dru Pyne. Student Mt. Holyoke Coll., 1948-50; BA, Sarah Lawrence Coll., 1952, MA, 1953; postgrad. Columbia U., 1964-67; MA, Inst. Fine Arts, NYU, 1976, PhD, 1987. Art critic Scarsdale Inquirer (N.Y.), 1962-67, Patent Trader, Mt. Kisco, N.Y., 1962-71; assoc. Arts Mag., N.Y.C., 1968-92; lectr. Aldrich Mus. Contemporary Art, Ridgefield, Conn., 1967-75, Gallery Passport Ltd., N.Y.C., 1968-96; contractual lectr. Met. Mus. Art, N.Y.C., 1994-95; curator of edn. Storm King Art Ctr., Mountainville, N.Y., 1973-75; instr. continuing edn. divsn. SUNY, Purchase, 1988-2002; adj. assoc. prof. humanities, 1997—; bd. dirs. Friends of the Neuberger Mus. Art, Purchase (N.Y.) Coll., SUNY, 1994—. Author (catalogue) John Storrs, Whitney Mus. of Am. Art, 1986; contbr. articles and/or revs. to various mags. including: Arts Mag.,

Harper's Bazaar, Feminist Art Jour., Art Voices. Sarah Williston scholar, 1948-50; recipient 1st prize, coll. publs. contest Mademoiselle mag., 1961. Mem. Internat. Assn. Art Critics, Art Table Inc., Coll. Art Assn. Home: Scarsdale, NY. Died Jan. 2, 2002.

FRACKMAN, RUSSELL JAY, lawyer; b. N.Y.C., July 3, 1946, s. Sam and Doris (Wasserberg) F.; m. Myrna D. Morganstern, Aug. 3, 1980; children: Steven Howard, Abigail Zoe. BA in History, Northwestern U., 1967; JD cum laude, Columbia U., 1970. Bar: Calif. 1971, U.S. Dist. Ct. (ctrl., ea. and no. dists.) Calif., U.S. Ct. Appeals (2d and 9th cirs.), U.S. Supreme Ct. Assoc. Mitchell, Silberberg & Knupp, L.A., 1970-76, ptnr., 1976—, chmn. litigation dept., 1994-96. Lectr. on intellectual property and entertainment law various instns. including Practising Law Inst., L.A. Copyright Soc., Beverly Hills Bar Assn., U. So. Calif. Sch. Law, Am. Film Mktg. Assn., Calif. Copyright Conf. Bd. editors Columbia Law Rev., 1969-70; contbr. articles and revs. to legal jours. Co-chmn. internat. leadership devel. forum CARE, 1990; bd. trustees CARE Found., 1991—, Twitty, Milsap, Sterban Found., 1988-92. Mem. ABA (chmn. copyright subcom. litigation sect. 1990-93, lectr. various confs.), Am. Film Mktg. Assn. (mem. arbitration tribunal). Democrat. Jewish. Office: Mitchell Silberberg & Knupp 11377 W Olympic Blvd Los Angeles CA 90064-1625

FRADE, PETER DANIEL, chemist, educator, administrator; b. Highland Park, Mich., Sept. 3, 1946; s. Peter Nunes and Dorathea Grace (Gehrke) F.; m. Karen L. Kovich, Mar. 14, 1992. BS in Chemistry, Wayne State U., 1968, MS, 1971, PhD, 1978. Chemist Henry Ford Hosp., Detroit, 1968-75, analytical chemist, toxicologist dept. pathology, divsn. pharmacology and toxicology, 1975-86, sr. clin. lab. scientist dept. pathology divsn. clin. chemistry and pharmacology, 1987-96; assoc. prof. Eugene Applebaum Coll. of Pharmacy and Allied Health Sci. Wayne State U., Detroit, 1996—, interim chair dept. mortuary sci., 2000—03, chair, dept. Mortuary Sci., 2003—. Rsch. assoc. in chemistry Wayne State U., Detroit, 1978—79; vis. scholar U. Mich., Ann Arbor, 1980—90; vis. scientist dept. hypertension rsch. Henry Ford Hosp., Detroit, 1986—88; adj. prof. Eugene Applebaum Coll. of Pharmacy and Health Scis. Wayne State U., 1991—96; dir. Anatomic Pathologists' Assts. Program. Contbr. sci. articles to profl. jours.; peer reviewer for profl. jours., 1988—. Mem. Rep. Presdl. Task Force, 1984-88; organist St. John's Episcopal Ch., Royal Oak, Mich., 1995-97. Recipient David F. Boltz Meml. award, Wayne State U., 1977, Teaching Excellence award. Fellow Am. Inst. Chemists, Nat. Acad. Clin. Biochemistry, Assn. Clin. Scientists; mem. Am. Coll. Forensic Examiners, Am. Chem. Soc., Am. Soc. Forensic Odontology, Am. Assn. Clin. Chemistry, Am. Guild Organists, Assn. Analytical Chemists, Mich. Inst. Chemists (treas. 1994—), N.Y. Acad. Scis., Am. Coll. Toxicology, Royal Soc. Chemistry (London), Titanic Hist. Soc., Virgil Fox Sox., Sigma Xi, Phi Lambda Upsilon, Alpha Chi Sigma. Episcopalian. Home: 20200 Orleans St Detroit MI 48203-1356 Office: Wayne State U 5439 Woodward Ave Detroit MI 48202-4009

FRADIS, ANATOLY ADOLF, film producer; b. Odessa, USSR, Sept. 26, 1948; came to U.S., 1980; s. Adolf Fradis; m. Marlene Gerdts, Dec. 17, 1983 (div. Dec. 1993); children: Olga, Alexander Nicholas, Andrew Robert; m. Lyudmila Fradis, June 26, 1999. Film dir. Mosflim Studios, Moscow, 1970-80, pres. Alfa-Film Enterprises, L.A., 1980—. Film commr. Russian Film Commn., L.A., 1991—. Prodr. films: Haunted Symphony, 1993, Beyond Forgiveness, 1994, Burial of the Rats, 1995, Marquis DeSade, 1996, Business for Pleasure, 1996, Termination Man, 1996, Red Shoe Diaries, 1998, Masked and Anonymous, 2002, others. Mem. Union of Russian Filmmakers (hon.). Republican. Jewish. Avocation: boxing. Office: Alfa-Film Enterprises Inc Ste 1138 264 S La Cienega Blvd Beverly Hills CA 90211-2832 E-mail: sidarfov@earthlink.net.

FRADKIN, DAVID MILTON, physicist, educator; b. Los Angeles, Apr. 20, 1931; s. Aaron and Annie (Gordon) F.; m. Dorothea Edna Fairweather, Nov. 25, 1959; children: Lee, Mark, Steven. BS, U. Calif., Berkeley, 1954; PhD, Iowa State U., 1963. Exploitation engr. Shell Oil Co., Los Angeles, 1954-56; research assoc. Iowa State U. and Ames Lab., Ames, Iowa, 1963-64; NATO postdoctoral fellow U. Rome, 1964-65; asst. prof. physics Wayne State U., Detroit, 1965-69, assoc. prof., 1969-75, prof., 1975-94, chmn. dept. physics, 1981-91; prof. emeritus, 1994—. Del. Argonne (Ill.) Univs. Assn., 1981-83; vis. fellow U. Durham, Eng., 1991-92. Contbr. articles to profl. jours. Vice chmn. adv. bd. Detroit pub. schs., 1972-73; trustee Detroit Sci. Ctr., 1986-94. Recipient award Probus Club, 1973; sr. postdoctoral fellow U. Edinburgh, Scotland, 1977-78. Mem. Am. Phys. Soc., Sigma Xi. Avocations: tennis, fishing, golf, sailing.

FRADLEY, FREDERICK MACDONELL, retired architect; b. Bronxville, N.Y., July 31, 1924; s. Justis Frederick and Helen Josephine (Macdonell) F.; m. Dorothy Davis Richard, Aug. 7, 1948; children: Stephen Davis, Wendy Fradley Monroe. BS, Brown U., 1948; M.F.A. (Lowell M. Palmer fellow), Princeton, 1954. Office engr. Turner Constrn. Co., Phila., 1948-51; project architect Vincent G. Kling, Phila., 1954-61; partner Bower & Fradley Architects, Phila., 1961-78. Important works with Bower in Phila. area include 1500 Walnut St. Office Bldg., Internat. House Student Ctr., Wharton Grad. Ctr. (Vance Hall), Gallery at Market East, 1234 Market St. Office Bldg., Yarway Corp. Hdqs., SKF Industries Hdqrs., in Balt. the W.R. Grace Bldg. Served with USAAF, 1942-46, PTO. Mem. Phi Delta Theta. Home: 5000 4A Enighed # 332 Saint John VI 00830 Home (Summer): 20 McFarland Shore Rd New Harbor ME 04554-4827

FRAEDRICH, ROYAL LOUIS, magazine editor, publisher; b. Weyauwega, Wis, Apr. 23, 1931; s. Clarence Otto and Libbie Clara (Trojan) F.; m. Phyllis Bohren, June 26, 1955; children— Lynn, Craig, Ann, Sarah, Paul. BS, U. Wis., 1955. With Doane Agrl. Svc., St. Louis, 1955-57; info. specialist Mich. State U., East Lansing, Mich., 1957-59; mng. editor Agrl. Pubs., Inc., Milw., 1959-64; editor Big Farmer mag., Milw., 1964-69, Frankfort, Ill., 1969-73, Farm Futures mag., Milw., 1973-81, pub., 1981-85; exec. v.p. Top Farmers Am. Assn., Milw., 1973-81; pub. print services AgriData Resources, Inc., 1981-85, v.p. editorial and adminstrn., 1986-89, v.p., sr. editorial dir., 1990-92; sr. editorial dir. ARI Network Svcs. Inc., 1992-94; sr. editor AgEd Network Stewart-Peterson Group, West Bend, Wis., 1994-96, cons. editor, 1996—. V.p., dir. Big Farmer Inc., 1969-73; v.p. Market Communications Inc., Milw., 1973-78 Editor: Grace History, 2002—. Vice pres. Grace Lutheran Ch., Menomonee Falls, Wis., 1963, mem. stewardship com., 1965-67, sec. bd. elders, 1974-77, mem. bd. elders, 1987-89, editor Grace History Committee, 2002. Mem. Am. Agrl. Editors Assn. Home: N95w16529 Richmond Dr Menomonee Falls WI 53051-1452 Office: 137 S Main St West Bend WI 53095-3321

FRAENKEL, DAN, oil industry executive, researcher; b. Petah Tiqwa, Israel, Apr. 1, 1946; s. Shulamit and Meir Oscar Max Fraenkel; m. Rachel Khodadadi, Aug. 13, 1980; children: Ronit, Limor, Eran Meir. BS, Technion, Israel Inst. Tech., 1968, DS, 1973; BA in Theater, Tel Aviv U., 1977. Scientist Weizmann Inst. Sci., Rehovot, Israel, 1974—77, scientist, cons., 1980—88; rsch. asst. U. Pitts., 1988—89, asst. prof., 1989—90; rsch. assoc. Engelhard Corp., Iselin, NJ, 1990—95; sr. rsch. scientist Matheson Tri-Gas, Longmont, Colo., 1996—2001; rsch. assoc. ConocoPhillips, Ponca City, Okla., 2001—. Cons. Matheson Tri-Gas, 2002—. Contbr. more than 30 articles to profl. publs. Fellow, U. Del., Newark, 1977—79. Mem.: Am. Chem. Soc. Achievements include 10 U.S. Patents on catalysts and gas purifiers; patents in field. Avocations: travel, hiking, violin, theater, soccer. Office: ConocoPhillips 1000 South Pine St Ponca City OK 74601 Office Fax: 580-767-3321. E-mail: dan.fraenkel@conocophillips.com.

FRAENKEL, GEORGE KESSLER, chemistry educator; b. Deal, N.J., July 27, 1921; s. Osmond Kessler and Helene (Esberg) F.; m. Johanna-Maria Herzog, June 30, 1951 (div. Aug. 1965); m. Elizabeth R. Rosen, Nov. 11, 1967 (div. Jan. 1990); m. Eva S. Cantwell, Feb. 3, 1990. BA, Harvard U., 1942; PhD, Cornell U., 1949. Research group leader National Def. Research Com., 1943-46; instr. chemistry Columbia U., N.Y.C., 1949-53, asst. prof., 1953-57, assoc. prof., 1957-61, prof., 1961-91, Eugene Higgins prof. Grad. Sch. Arts and Scis., 1986-91, prof. emeritus, 1992—, chmn. dept. chemistry, 1966-68, dean grad. sch. arts and scis., 1968-83, dean emeritus, 1983—, v.p. spl. projects, 1983-86. Mem. postdoctoral fellowship com. Nat. Acad. Sci.-NSF, 1964-65; chmn. Gordon Research Conf. Magnetic Resonance, 1967; mem. Arts Coll. adv. council Cornell U., 1964-74; mem., bd. dirs. Atran Found., N.Y.C., 1968—, com. on budget and fin., 1986—; treas. Atran Found., 1988—. Assoc. editor: Jour. Chem. Physics, 1962-64; Mem. adv. editorial bd.: Chemical Physics Letters, 1966-71; editorial bd.: Jour. Magnetic Resonance, 1969-70. Trustee Columbia U. Press, 1968-71, Walden Sch., N.Y.C., 1964-66. Recipient Army-Navy certificate of appreciation, 1948; Harold C. Urey award Phi Lambda Upsilon, 1972; decorated officer Ordre des Palmes Académiques. Fellow AAAS, Am. Phys. Soc., Am. Chem. Soc., Internat. Electron Spin Resonance Soc.; mem. Assn. Grad. Schs. (exec. com. 1976-80, v.p. 1977 78, pres. 1978-79, chmn. com. policies on grad. edn. 1969-71), Phi Beta Kappa, Sigma Xi, Phi Kappa Phi. Achievements include research in field of electron spin resonance with particular emphasis on the electron spin resonance of organic free radicals. Home: 520 W 114th St Apt 82 New York NY 10025-7852

FRAGA, MIKE A. history educator, accountant; s. Ramon Miguel Fraga and Mary Morales Armendariz. BA in History, Stanford U., 1978; MA in History, UCLA, 1980, postgrad. in history PhD program, 1981—84. Instr. Valley Torah Yeshiva, North Hollywood, Calif., 1986—88; vis. instr. Loyola Marymount U., Los Angeles, Calif., 1988—89; vis. instr./fellow Oberlin Coll., Oberlin, Ohio, 1989—90; instr./asst. dir. No. Ill. U., DeKalb, 1990—92; instr. Ill. Math and Sci. Acad., Aurora, 1992—94, El Paso C.C., Tex., 1995—. Cons. Tohono O'odham Nation, Sells, Ariz., 1987—89. Prodr.: (documentary radio series) Preservation and Revival of Am. Indian Arts, 1980—81; contbr. articles to profl. jours. Mem.: Nat. Assn. for Chicano/Chicana Studies (assoc.), Am. Hist. Assn. (assoc.), Orgn. of Am. Historians (assoc.).

FRAGALA, GUY ANDREW, safety engineer, educator; b. Lawrence, Mass., Sept. 28, 1947; s. Andrew F. and Margaret (Hyder) F.; m. Susan Fucarile, Sept. 9, 1972; children: Matt, Maren, Michael. BS, U. N.H., 1969; MS, U. Mass., 1971, MEd, 1974, PhD, 1982. Loss prevention rep. Comml. Union Assurance Co., Boston, 1972-74; mem. corp. risk mgmt. and safety staff E.I. DuPont de Nemours & Co., Inc., Wilmington, Del., 1974-76; instr. U. Wis.-Stout, Menomonie, 1976-77; campus safety and fire prevention engr. U. Mass., Amherst, 1977-78; dir. risk mgmt. and safety assurance, asst. prof. U. Mass. Med. Ctr., Worcester, 1978—. Adj. faculty Inst. Safety and Systems Mgmt., U. So. Calif., Eastern region, 1982—; adj. faculty dept. indsl. engring. and ops. rsch. U. Mass., Amherst, 1983—; adj. faculty dept. mgmt. Worcester Poly. Inst., 1986—; cons., lectr. in field. Contbr. indsl. safety articles in field to profl. publs. Mem. City of Worcester Loaned Exec. Coun., 1979-80. Mem. Am. Soc. Safety Engrs., Am. Soc. Hosp. Risk Mgmt. (dir. 1984—), Nat. Fire Protection Assn., Nat. Safety Coun. (mem. exec. com. health care sect. 1981—). Home: 9 Coram Farm Rd Northborough MA 01532-1301 Office: 55 Lake Ave N Worcester MA 01655 0002

FRAGEN, ROBERT JOSEPH, physician, anesthesiologist; b. Whiting, Ind., Jan. 18, 1935; s. Nathan and Ruth (Seitzick) F.; m. Joan Maureen Arenson, June 13, 1957; children: Daniel Scott, Kathleen Susan, Michael Philip, Patricia Beth. AB, Ind. U., 1956; MD, Ind. U., Indpls., 1959. Diplomate Am. Bd. Anesthesiology. Dir. dept. anesthesia Ravenswood Hosp., Chgo., 1964-74; staff anesthesiologist Northwestern U., Chgo., 1974—. Contbr. articles to profl. jours. Served to lt. USN, 1962-64. Mem. Am. Soc. Anesthesiologists, Internat. Anesthesia Rsch. Soc., Ill. Soc. Anesthesiologists, Chgo. Soc. Anesthesiologists. Jewish. Avocations: bicycling, stamp collecting. Home: 1230 Lindenwood Dr Winnetka IL 60093-3724 Office: U Med Sch Dept Anesthesia 251 E Huron St Chicago IL 60611-2908 E-mail: rfragen@yahoo.com.

FRAGER, ALBERT S. retired retail food company executive; b. Boston, Dec. 29, 1922; s. Oscar and Anna (Polterak) F.; m. Marion Nathan, June 15, 1950; children: Owen R., Bonnie L. Frager Franks, Laurie J. Burton, Sherri Frager Goodstein. Student, Amos Tuck Sch. Bus., Dartmouth Coll., 1943; BS in Bus. Adminstrn, Northeastern U., 1944. Internal revenue agt. IRS, 1945-56; v.p., controller Stop & Shop, Inc., Boston, 1956-67, treas., 1967-86, fin. v.p., 1969-79, sr. v.p., 1979-86. Past trustee South Palm Beach County Jewish Fedn.; bd. dirs. Donna Klein Jewish Acad.; mem. corp., past bd. overseers Northeastern U.; past pres. Jewish temple. With USNR, 1943-44. Mem. AICPA, Mass. Soc. CPAs. Home: 4740 S Ocean Blvd Apt 911 Highland Beach FL 33487-5354

FRAGNER, MATTHEW CHARLES, lawyer; b. N.Y.C., Jan. 12, 1954; s. Berwyn N. and Marcia R. (Salkind) F.; m. Mariann Donahue, June 19, 1983; children: Rachel Jade, Jaron Roark, Bailyn Natalie, Talia Colby. BA, Yale U., 1975; JD, U. Calif., Berkeley, 1978. Bar: Calif. 1978, U.S. Tax Ct. 1979, U.S. Ct. Appeals (9th crct.) 1979. Atty. Thomas Shafran & Wasser, L.A., 1978-83; ptnr. Shafran & Fragner, L.A., 1984-87, Lane & Edson, L.A., 1987-88, Mayer Brown & Platt, L.A., 1989-92, Sonnenschein Nath & Rosenthal, L.A., 1992-2000; pres. Somnolence, Inc., L.A., 1989—; gen. cousel, dir. investments Citadel Capital Mgmt. Corp., 2000—02; founder, chmn. Tools to Talent Non Profit Corp., 2001—02; ptnr. Liner Yankelevitz Sunshine & Regenstreif, Santa Monica, Calif., 2002. Lectr. U. So. Calif., 1994—99. Active Berkeley (Calif.) Law Found., 1978-83. Mem. Los Angeles County Bar Assn. (chair comml. devel. and leasing subsect.). Office: 1100 Glendon Ave 14th Fl Los Angeles CA 90024 E-mail: mfragner@linerlaw.com.

FRAGO-ZITO, IVY MARIE, accountant; b. Hartford, Conn., Mar. 12, 1956; d. Frank Charles and Irene Lena (Koloski) F.; m. Paul Charles Zito, May 18, 1979. BS in Acctg., U. Hartford, 1978. CPA, Conn. Sr. acct. Ernst & Young, Hartford, 1978-81; supr. Cohen, Rosenfeld & Lieberman CPAs, Hartford, 1981-84; acctg. mgr. Dutch Point Credit Union, Wethersfield, Conn., 1984-85; supr. Cole, Frago, Cusick & Chestler CPAs, Wethersfield, 1985-88; pvt. practice Marlborough, Conn., 1988-96; v.p. fin., CFO QSA Optical Co., Inc., South Windsor, Conn., 1996—2001; CFO, Encore Optics LLC, South Windsor, 2003—. Mem. AICPA, Conn. Soc. CPAs, Am. Soc. Women Accts. (nat. pres. 1995-96). Democrat. Roman Catholic. Avocations: gardening, reading, dancing, exercising.

FRAGUELA, JAMES, publishing executive; b. Bklyn. s. G. and Sophie (Vidal) F.; m. Susan Baron, Aug. 15, 1988; 1 child, Kate. BA in Bus. Adminstrn., Curry Coll. Sales rep. Woman's Day Mag., 1973-75; account mgr. Family Cir. Inc., 1975-81, assoc. Eastern mgr., 1981-82, Eastern advt. mgr., 1982-84, v.p., advt. dir., 1984-87; pub. Lear Pub., Inc., 1988-91; v.p., mktg. dir. Electronic Mktg. and Retail Comm., 1992-95; sr. v.p., pub. Globe Comm. Corp., N.Y.C., 1995-99; pub. Hachette Filipacchi Mags., N.Y.C., 2000—. Avocations: motorcycling, jogging, tennis. Home: 300 E 74th St New York NY 10021-3712

FRAGUELA, RAFAEL J. assemblyman; b. June 7, 1955; BA in Social Studies, Montclair State Coll.; MA in secondary edn., adminstrn. supervision, Seton Hall U. Pres. Union City Bd. of Edn., NJ, 1988—92; commr. Hudson County Bd. of Taxation, NJ, 1990—93, Union City Bd. of Commrs., NJ, 1992—; assemblyman N.J. Gen. Assembly, NJ, 2002—. Republican. Office: 4808 Bergenline Ave Union City NJ 07087 Fax: 201-863-6329. E-mail: AsmFraguela@njleg.org.*

FRAHER, ELAINE ADEL, retired music educator; b. Eau Claire, Wis., Sept. 28, 1926; d. Joseph Francis and Alice Lorraine (Lundy) F. BA, Mt. Mary Coll., 1955; MA, MacPhail Conservatory of Music, 1964. Tchr. music St. Mary's H.S., New England, N.D., 1955-57, St. Michael (Minn.) H.S., 1957-59, St. Agnes H.S., St. Paul, 1959-66, Good Counsel Acad., Mankato, Minn., 1966-72, Grace H.S., Fridley, Minn., 1972-76; dir. music, organist Sacred Heart Ch., St. Paul, 1976-83, Assumption Ch., Richfield, Minn., 1987-90, St. Gabriel Ch., Chgo., 1990-94; tchr. piano, organist K and S Conservatory, Woodbury, Minn., 1994—2003. Sec. archdiocesan Worship Bd., St. paul, 1979-83. Mem. Am. Guild of Organists, St. Paul Piano Tchrs. assn., Minn. Music Tchrs. Assn. (life), Common Cause. Roman Catholic. Avocations: cooking, reading. Office: K and S Conservatory Music 1976 Woodale Woodbury MN 55125 Home: 8262 Hudson Blvd N Saint Paul MN 55128-7038

FRAHM, SHEILA, association executive, former government official, academic administrator; b. Colby, Kans., Mar. 22, 1945; m. Kenneth Frahm; children: Amy, Pam, Chrissie. BS, Ft. Hays State U., 1967. Mem. bd. edn. State of Kans., 1985-88; mem. Kans. Senate, Topeka, 1988-94, senate majority leader, 1993-94; lt. gov. State of Kans., 1995-96; mem. from Kans., U.S. Senate, Washington, 1996; exec. dir. Kans. Assn. C.C. Trustees, Topeka, 1996—. Mem. AAUW (Outstanding Br. Mem. 1985), Thomas County Day Care Assn., Shakespeare Fedn. Women's Clubs, Farm Bur., Kans. Corn Growers, Kans. Livestock Assn., Rotary (Paul Harris fellow 1988). Republican. Home: 410 N Grant Colby KS 67701-2036 Office: 700 SW Jackson St Ste 401 Topeka KS 66603-3757 E-mail: sfrahm@colbyweb.com.

FRAIDIN, STEPHEN, lawyer; b. Boston, July 29, 1939; s. Morris and Freda (Rozeff) F.; m. Lori Kramer, Oct. 27, 2001; children from previous marriage: Matthew, Sam, Sarah AB, Tufts U., 1961; JD, Yale U., 1964. Bar: NY 1965. Ptnr. Fried, Frank, Harris, Shriver & Jacobson, N.Y.C., 1964—2003, Kirkland & Ellis, NYC, 2003—. Vis. lectr. Yale U. Law Sch., 1988—, mem. exec. com.; bd. dirs. Children's Scholarship Fund. Contbr. numerous articles to profl. jours. Past chmn. UJA-Fedn., NY Lawyers Divsn. Recipient Judge Joseph M. Proskauer award, 2002. Mem.: ABA, Assn. of Bar of City of NY.

FRAIMAN, NELSON, educator; b. Montevideo, Uruguay, Nov. 26, 1946; arrived in U.S., 1963; s. Aron Fraiman and Carlota Lydia Maus; m. Katharine A. Morgan. BS, Columbia U., 1968, MS, 1969, MBA, 1971, PhD, 1977. Asst. prof. Rutgers U., Newark, 1973—76; chief tech. officer Internat. Paper, Hawthorne, NY, 1977—95; prof. Columbia U., N.Y.C., 1995—. Contbr. chapters to books, articles to profl. jours. Fellow, Orgn. Am. States; grantee, NSF. Home: PO Box 20 Chappaqua NY 10514-0020 Office: Columbia Univ 405A Uris Hill New York NY 10027

FRAITAG, LEONARD ALAN, product development engineer; b. N.Y.C., Dec. 23, 1961; s. David and Lucille Reneé (Jay) F.; m. Beth Fraitag; children: Shoshana Elizabeth, Aaron Joseph. BSME, San Diego State U., 1987; AA, Grossmont Coll., 1983. Design engr. Restaurant Concepts, San Diego, 1987; mech. engr. Vantage Assocs., Inc., San Diego, 1988-89; design engr. Mainstream Engring. Co., Inc., San Diego, 1989; project engr. Pilkington Barnes Hind, San Diego, 1989-96, Advanced Structures, Inc., Escondido, 1996-99; product devel. engr. Sybron Dental Spltys., Ormco/ACO, San Diego, 1999-2001; engring. mgr. Display Rsch. Labs., San Diego, 2001—03; product/tooling/machine devel. cons. Fraitag Engring. Co., San Diego, 2003—. Inventor safe product moving device for contact lens. Mem. Shriners (Al Bahr shrine), Masons (past master), Pi Tau Sigma. Avocations: computers, sports, camping, skiing, scuba diving. Office: Fraitag Engring San Diego CA 92120

FRAKER, DOUGLAS L. oncologist, endocrinologist, surgeon, educator; b. Waverly, Iowa, Dec. 15, 1956; s. Chester L. and Oma B. (Hulderson) Fraker; m. Mary Louise D'Andrea, Oct. 1, 1983; children: Matthew, Kristen, Luke. BA in Molecular Biology, U. Wis., 1979; MD, Harvard U., 1983. Diplomate Am. Bd. Surgery. Sr. investigator, surgery br. Nat. Cancer Inst., Bethesda, Md., 1991-95, head metabolism sect., surgery br., 1992-95; vice chmn. clin. affair, dir. gen. surgery, chief divsn. surg. oncology, Jonathon Rhoads prof. surgery U. Pa., Phila., 1995—. Sci. adv. bd. Direct Therapeutics, Rye, NY, 1996—97, Boston Sci., 2002—; cons. Codman Internat., 1998—. Co-editor: J. Clin. Oncology, 1995—97, assoc. editor: Annals Surg. Oncology; contbr. articles to profl. jours. Fellow: ACS (mem. exec. oncology group); mem.: Soc. Surg. Oncology (mem. exec. com.), Soc. Univ. Surgeons, Phi Beta Kappa. Office: U Pa Dept Surgery 3400 Spruce St Philadelphia PA 19104-4206

FRAKES, JAMES TERRY, physician, gastroenterologist, educator; b. Burlington, Iowa, Feb. 22, 1946; s. Harold Decatur amd Marjorie Marie (Kinnison) F.; m. Nancy Jean French, June 15, 1968; children: Sarah Jane Frakes, David Harold Frakes. BS, U. Ill., Urbana, 1968, MS, 1972; MD, U. Ill., Chgo., 1976. Diplomate Am. Bd. Internal Medicine and Gastroenterology, Nat. Bd. Med. Examiners; lic. Ill. Staff engr. Westinghouse Astronuc. Lab., Pitts., 1968-69; staff scientist Los Alamos (NMex.) Sci. Lab., 1970-71; intern, resident in internal medicine U. Mo. Med. Ctr., Columbia, 1976-78; fellow in gastroenterology U. N. Carolina Sch. Medicine, Chapel Hill, 1978-80; physician, gastroenterologist Rockford (Ill.) GE Assoc., Ltd., 1980—. Clin. prof. medicine U. Ill. Coll. Medicine, Rockford, 1981—; dir. digestive disease unit Saint Anthony Med. Ctr., Rockford, 1983—; course dir. AGA/ASGE, 1991—; med. lectr., 1987—. Bd. dirs. U. Ill. Alumni Assn., 1991-96; mem. U. Ill. Found., Urbana, 1991—, mem. pres.'s coun., 1994—. Recipient Faculty Disting. Tchg. award U. Ill. Coll. Medicine, Rockford, 1990, Faculty Disting. Svc. award, 1997, Disting. Alumnus award, 1999. Fellow ACP, Am. Coll. Gastroenterology; mem. AMA, Am. Gastroenterol. Assn. (numerous coms.) Am. Soc. Gastroinestinal Endoscopy (treas. 1995-98, pres.-elect 1998-99, pres. 1999-00), World Orgn. of Gastroenterology (dep. treas. 2002—). Republican. Avocations: gardening, wine collecting, college sports. Office: Rockford Gastroenterology Assocs Ltd 401 Roxbury Rd Rockford IL 61107-5078

FRAKES, RODNEY VANCE, plant geneticist, educator; b. Ontario, Oreg., July 20, 1930; s. Wylie and Pearl (Richardson) F.; m. Ruby L. Morey, Nov. 27, 1952; children: Laura Ann, Cody Joe. BS, Oreg. State U., 1956, MS, 1957; PhD, Purdue U., 1960. Instr. dept. agronomy Purdue U., West Lafayette, Ind., 1959-60; asst. prof. dept. crop sci. Oreg. State U., Corvallis, 1960-64, assoc. prof., 1964-69, prof., 1969—, assoc. dean research, 1981-88, emeritus dean of rsch., prof. emeritus crop sci., 1989—. Author numerous papers and abstracts; contbr. to books in field Served with USCG, 1950-53 Named Man of Yr., Pacific Seedsmen's Assn., 1972; recipient Elizabeth P. Ritchie Disting. Prof. award Oreg. State U., 1980. Fellow Am. Soc. Agronomy, Crop Sci. Soc. Am.; mem. AAAS, Soc. Research Adminstrs., Nat. Council Univ. Research Adminstrs., Western Soc. Crop Sci. (pres. 1978), Model A Ford Club of Am., Model T Ford Club of Am., Rotary. Avocations: antique autos, Am. history, amateur radio. Home: 2625 NW Linnan Cir Corvallis OR 97330-1221 Office: Oreg State U Rsch Office Corvallis OR 97331

FRALEY, F. RONALD, lawyer; b. Steubenville, Ohio, Dec. 16, 1931; s. Floyd Emerson and Anna Margaret Fraley; m. Nancy Naylor, June 6, 1958; children: Ronald, Douglas, Gregory, Mitchell, Anne Marie. BA, Kenyon Coll., Gambier, Ohio, 1953; JD, U. Mich., 1958. Bar: Fla. 1958. Ptnr. Shackleford Farrior Stallings & Evans, Tampa, Fla., 1958-91; founder, ptnr. Fraley & Fraley, Tampa, 1991—. Sgt. USMC, 1953-55. Fellow Am. Coll. Trial Lawyers; mem. ATLA, Fla. Bar Assn., Acad. of Fla. Trial Lawyers, Univ. Club, Palma Ceia Golf and Country Club (bd. dirs. 1985), Commerce Club (pres. 1979). Avocations: golf, reading. Home: 1914 S Wykagyl St Tampa FL 33629 Office: Fraley and Fraley 501 E Kennedy Blvd #1200 Tampa FL 33602

FRALINGER, JACK BRUCE, surgeon; b. Balt., Dec. 7, 1967; s. Jack Martin and Audrey Ann Fralinger; m. Ona Lynn Streitberger, Aug. 14, 1999; children: Jackson William children: Bethany Cohnheim, Emma Cohnheim, Dandro George. BS in Zoology, BA in History, U. Nev., 1992; MD, U. Minn., 1996. Resident in surgery Swedish Med. Ctr., Seattle, 1996—99; physician Indian Health Svc., Neah Bay, Wash., 2001, N.E. Wash. Med. Group, Colville, Wash., 2001; resident in surgery Waterbury Surg. Residency, Conn., 2001—. Mem.: ACS, AMA, Assn. Am. Indian Physicians. Avocations: travel, cooking, hiking, hunting.

FRAME, JOHN FAYETTE, sculptor; b. Colton, Calif., Nov. 27, 1950; s. Rudolph Randolph and Mildred Louise (Jones) F.; m. Laura Lynn Dierker, Sept. 3, 1977; children: Katherine, Ashley, Lilian. BA in English, San Diego State U., 1975; MFA in Art, Claremont Grad. Sch., 1980. One person shows include Francine Seders Gallery, Seattle, 1981, Jan Turner Gallery, L.A., 1982, 84, 87, 90, 93, 96, Mattingly Baker Gallery, Dallas, 1982, Installation Gallery, San Diego, 1983, L.A. County Mus. Art, 1992; exhibited in group shows L.A. Mcpl. Art Gallery, 1981, 86, 87, The Fountain Gallery, Portland, Oreg., 1982, Triton Mus., Santa Clara, Calif., 1984, Montgomery Art Gallery, Claremont, 1984, Galerie Hartje, Berlin, 1985, San Diego State U., 1987, Artspace Gallery, L.A., 1988, Nakazawa Gallery, Tokyo, 1989, U. Hawaii, Honolulu, 1990, Sezon Mus. Art, Tokyo, 1991, Susan Cummins Gallery, Mill Valley, Calif., 1992, 93, Koplin Gallery, L.A., 1993, Dorothy Goldeen Gallery, Santa Monica, 1993, Lew Allen Gallery, Santa Fe, 1993, Tawain Mus. Art, Taichung, 1994, Louis Newman Gallery, Beverly Hills, Calif., 1994, Armory Ctr. for Arts, Pasadena, Calif., 1994, Laband Art Gallery, Loyola Marymount U., L.A., 1994, Garth Clark Gallery, L.A., 1994, Palm Springs Desert Mus., 1995, Cheney Cowles Mus., Spokane, Wash., 1995, Las Vegas Inst. Contemporary Art, 1995; works included in publs. including Artweek, L.A. Weekly, L.A. Times, Images and Issues, World Art Trends 1983-84, L.A. Herald Examiner, Daily News, Reader,

Sculpture, Visions, Connections, Angeles Mag., San Francisco Chronicle. Recipient Young Talent award L.A. County Mus., 1985; individual artist fellow Nat. Endowment for Arts, 1984, 86, J. Paul Getty Mus., 1995. Home: PO Box 3070 Wrightwood CA 92397

FRAME, KATHLEEN S. non-profit education association administrator; b. Olean, N.Y., June 13, 1946; d. Anthony Wallace and Thelma Genieve (Crowley) Spehar; m. Charles L. Frame, Dec. 16, 1967; children: Kelly Marie Frame Winslow, Richard Alan Frame. BS in Biol. Edn., Slippery Rock U., 1968; MS in Interdisciplinary Sci.-Biology, Johns Hopkins U., 1997. Lic. tchr., Va. Sci. tchr. Biglerville (Pa.) H.S., 1968; royalties clk., asst. editor Leisure Press, West Point, N.Y., 1978-79; elem. sch. tchr. English and reading Our Lady of Lourdes Sch., Melbourne, Fla., 1979-80; tchr. biology and math. sci. Melbourne Ctrl. Cath. H.S., 1981-83; tchr. chemistry Bishop O'Connell H.S., Arlington, Va., 1983-85, asst. dept. chair, tchr. sci. and biology, 1985-89, dept. chair, 1985—92, tchr. sci. and biology, 1989-92; rsch. asst. Nat. Assn. Biology Tchrs., Reston, Va., 1992-94, dep. dir. edn., 1995-96, dir. edn., 1995—2001; dir. edn. programs Biotech. Inst., Arlington, 2001—. Dir. Intel Talent Search Va., 1990—. Editor: Working with DNA in Pre-college Classrooms, 1993, Biology 'On a Shoe-string', 1995, Neuroscience Activities for Classroom, 1996, Student Research Activities, 1999, Shoestring Biotech Activities, 1999—2002. Nat. Audubon Soc. tchr. scholar, 1991; recipient High Quality Biotech. award NSF, 1995—. Mem. AAAS, Nat. Assn. Sci. Tchrs., Nat. Assn. Biology Tchrs., Va. Assn. Biology Tchrs. (pres. 1994—), Delta Kappa Gamma (pres. Alpha Delta chpt. 1996—). Avocations: gardening, skiing, family. Home: 13112 Nestlewood Ct Oak Hill VA 20171-3904 Office: Biotech Inst 1840 Wilson Blvd # 202 Arlington VA 22201

FRAME, LAWRENCE MILVEN, JR., inventor; b. Adrian, Mich., Apr. 13, 1951; s. Lawrence M. Sr. and Margret L. Frame. Student, Art Instrns. Sch., Cin., North Light Sch. Gen. laborer USAF; owner Frame & Co.flabs, Arts. Patentee; songwriter; author: 100% Service Connected and Social Security Disability, Golden Book of Short Stories, Part VI; art exhibited in show at Scioto Paint Valley Mental Health Ctr., 1993. With USAF, 1971-75. Recipient several art and writing awards. Mem. Am. Legion, Disabled Am. Vets. Avocations: art, writing, electrophysics. Address: Frame & Co Labs Arts PO Box 266 Napoleon OH 43545-0266

FRAME, NANCY DAVIS, lawyer; b. Brookings, S.D., Dec. 13, 1944; m. J. Davidson Frame, Mar. 28, 1970 (div. Oct. 1994); 1 child, Katherine Adele; m. Kelly C. Kammerer, Oct. 2, 1999. BS, S.D. State U., 1966; MA, Georgetown U., 1968, JD, 1976. Bar: D.C. 1976. Atty., advisor AID, Washington, 1976-81, asst. gen. counsel, 1981-86; dep. dir. Trade and Devel. Agy., Washington, 1986-99. Bd. dirs. Daktronics, Inc. Recipient Superior Honor award AID, 1984, Presdl. Meritorious Rank award, 1993, Disting. Alumnus award S.D. State U., 1998, Presdl. Disting. Rank award, 1998; Fulbright fellow, 1966, NDEA fellow, 1967. Home: Psc 116 Box Oecd Apo AE 09777-5000 also: 11 bis Boulevard Jules Sandeau 75016 Paris France E-mail: ndframe@hotmail.com.

FRAME, TED RONALD, lawyer; b. Milw., June 27, 1929; s. Morris and Jean (Lee) F.; m. Lois Elaine Pilgrim, Aug. 15, 1954; children: Kent, Lori, Nancy, Owen. Student, UCLA, 1946-49; AB, Stanford U., 1950; LLB, 1952. Bar: Calif. 1953. Gen. agri-bus. practice, Coalinga, Calif., 1953—; sr. pntr. Frame & Matsumoto and predecessor, Coalinga, 1965—. Trustee Baker Mus.; dir. West Hills Coll. Found. Mem. ABA, Calif. Bar Assn., Fresno County Bar Assn., Kings Co. Bar Assn., Am. Agrl. Law Assn., Coalinga C. of C. (past pres.), Masons, Shriners, Elks. Avocations: bicycling, hiking. Home: 1222 Nevada St Coalinga CA 93210-1239 Office: 201 Washington St Coalinga CA 93210-0895 E-mail: lawfirm@lightspeed.net.

FRAMIL, ARMANDO RAMON, business developer; b. Aug. 12, 1948; came to U.S., 1960, naturalized, 1976; s. Armando and Maria Araceli (Fernandez) F.; m. Maria Del Carmen Rodriguez, May 12, 1977 (div. 2002); children: Carolynne, Carmen Victoria BA, Fla. Atlantic U., 1972; MEd, U. Miami, 1977. Counselor Office Youth Svcs. Fla. State Dept. Health and Rehab. Svcs., 1973-77; supr. City of Miami Police Dept., 1977-79, spl. projects mgr., 1979-80; sr. bus. developer internat. sect. City of Miami Dept. Trade and Commerce Devel., 1980-82; profl. rep. Merck, Sharp & Dohme divsn. Merck & Co., Inc., West Point, Pa., 1982-92, exec. rep., 1990-92, sr. hosp. rep., 1984—. Mgr. dist. sales Astra U.S.A. Inc., Westborough, Mass., 1992-95; sr. regional mktg. mgr. Simon & Schuster Tech. Group (a Viacom Co.), San Diego, 1995-98; pres., founder, dir. sales and mktg. A+ Techs. Corp., Miami; exec. clin. specialist Neuro Health Divsn., Glaxo-Smithkline, Inc., 2000—. Assoc. inventor, patentee oscillating cutting mechanisms. Bd. dirs. Dade County Youth Adv. Bd., 1979-84; mem. Dade County Latin Substance Abuse Task Force, 1976, Drug Abuse Trust Fund, 1977-78; chmn., founder Coral Way Crime Prevention Subcouncil, 1988-91; vice-chmn. Miami Police Dept. Crime Prevention Coun., 1988-89, chmn., 1989-90; pres., founder Miami Rds. Neighborhood Civic Assn., 1986-2002; mem. Dade County Dem. Exec. Com., 1989-92; trustee Greater Miami C. of C., 1997, mem., 1999; trustee Miami-Dade One Comty. One Goal Edn. Com., 1997-2000, English Ctr. Edn. Excellence Coun., 1997-99; active Dade County Pub. Schs. Multilingual Task Force, 1997, Dade County One Comty. One Goal Edn. Com., 1997—. With USCG Aux., 1996—. Mem. Merck, Sharp & Dohme V.P.'s Club, Mary Brickell's Garden Club (founder, treas. 1990), Invest Learning Summit Club (100% Club 1997). Home: 260 Woodcrest Rd Key Biscayne FL 33149-1320 Office: Glaxo Smith Kline Inc Neuro Health Divsn Research Triangle Park NC 27709

FRAMME, LAWRENCE HENRY, III, political organization administrator, lawyer; b. Louisville, Oct. 8, 1949; s. Lawrence Henry and Margaret Gertrude (Hayes) F.; m. Frances Claire Schwacke, Dec. 27, 1969; children: Jessica Marie, Lawrence Henry IV, Benjamin Hayes. BA, Centre Coll., 1971; JD cum laude, Washington and Lee U., 1974. Bar: Va. 1974, U.S. Dist. Ct. Va., 1974, U.S. Ct. Appeals (4th cir.) 1974. Assoc. McGuire, Woods & Battle, Richmond, Va., 1974-81, Lacy & Baliles, Richmond, 1981-82; mem. firm, dir. Mezzullo, McCandlish & Framme, Richmond, 1982-90; sec. econ. devel. (gov's. cabinet) Commonwealth of Va., 1990-92; chmn. Virginians for Progress Found., 1992; v.p. LeClair, Ryan, Joynes, Epps & Framme, Richmond, 1992-95; prin. Framme Law Firm, 1995—; co-chmn. gov's. adv. coun. Workforce 2000, 1990-91. Chmn. Dem. Party Va., 1986-90, 2001-. Va. State Bd. Cmty. Colls., mem. 1987-90, chmn. 1989-90; bd. visitors Va. Commonwealth U., 1992-96; mem. bd. dirs. Downtown YMCA, 1986-95, chmn. 1992-94; bd. dirs., sec. Va. Biotech. Rsch. Park Authority, 1991-92, 93-95, 2002-, Va. Biotech. Rsch. Park Corp., 1994-2002, Leadership Metro Richmond, 1991-94; bd. dirs., legal advisor Richmond Urban League, 1985-86; mem. bd. dirs. Metro Richmond YMCA, 1995-2000. Recipient Legal award Housing Opportunities Made Equal, Richmond, 1983; named Alumni of Yr., Leadership Metro Richmond, 1990. Mem. ABA, VSB, Va. Bar Assn., Richmond Bar Assn., Omicron Delta Kappa. Roman Catholic. Office: Framme Law Firm PC One Capital Square 830 E Main St 19th Fl Richmond VA 23219-3539 Home: 2420 Hanover Ave Richmond VA 23220 Business E-Mail: lframme@frammelaw.com.

FRAMPTON, PAUL HOWARD, physics researcher, educator; b. Kidderminster, Eng., Oct. 31, 1943; came to U.S., 1968; naturalized citizen, 1989; s. Harold Albert and Grace Elizabeth (Howard) Frampton; m. Anne-Marie Frampton, 1993. BA, U. Oxford, Eng., 1965, MA, DPhil, U. Oxford, Eng., 1968, DSc, 1984. Rsch. assoc. U. Chgo., 1968-70; fellow CERN, Geneva, 1970-72; vis. prof. Bielefeld (Germany) U., 1972, 99, Syracuse U., 1972-75; vis. assoc. prof. UCLA, 1975-77; vis. scholar Harvard U., Cambridge, Mass., 1978-81; from asst. prof. physics to prof. U. N.C., Chapel Hill, 1981-96; disting. prof. physics The Louis D. Rubin Jr., 1996—. Vis. prof. U. Tex., fall 1983, Boston U., 1986-87, U. d'Aix-Marseille, 1993, CERN, 1996, 98, 2000, 2003; chmn. steering com. Workshops on Grand Unification, 1980-89; chmn. organizing com. 1st workshop U. N.H., 1980, 3d workshop, U. N.C., 1982, 10th and last workshop U. N.C., 1989; symposium chair 8th Internat. Symposium on Particles, Strings and Cosmology, U. N.C., 2001. Author: Dual Resonance Models, 1974, Dual Resonance Models and Superstrings, 1986, Gauge Field Theories, 1986, 2d edit., 2000; editor books in field; contbr. more than 300 articles to profl. jours., also chpts. to books. Gov.'s project dir. for supercollider in N.C., 1987. Fellow AAAS, Am. Phys. Soc., Brit. Inst. Physics. Achievements include research in high-energy theoretical physics including particle phenomenology, string theory and theoretical cosmology. Home: 101 Cedar Ridge Way Durham NC 27705-1980 Office: U NC Dept Physics And Astromomy Chapel Hill NC 27599-0001 E-mail: frampton@physics.unc.edu.

FRAN, GRANDMA See BROWN, FRANCES LOUISE

FRANCAVILLA, DONNA T. journalist; b. Camden, N.J., Dec. 4, 1960; d. Lelio and Aurora (DeVuono) Ciccotelli; m. Thomas Louis Francavilla, May 29, 1957; children: Michael, Lisa, Jessica, Gregory. BS, Emerson Coll., Boston, 1985. Talk show prodr. WWDB-FM Talkradio, Phila., 1980-81; desk asst., prodn. asst. KYW Newsradio 1060 AM, Phila., 1981-82; talk show prodr. WRKO-AM, Boston, 1982-85; news anchor radio network Internat. Media News, Washington, 1986-88; program dir., news dir. Westinghouse WPGC AM & FM, Washington, 1988-90; traffic reporter Metro Traffic Control, Phila., 1990-92; news anchor, all news radio WINZ-AM, Miami, 1993-94; news reporter NBC, WVTM-TV, Birmingham, Ala., 1996—99; radio corr. CBS Radio News, 1999—; freelance reporter/anchor Radio Ala., Alabaster; contbr. Westwood One's Am. in the Morning Program, 1999—; freelancer reporter, fill-in anchor Radio Ala., Alabaster, 2002—; freelance reporter Agy. France Aesse, Washington, 2000—, CBS News Path, 2003—, Am. Urban Radio Networks, 2003—, Voice of Am. Owner Frankly Speaking Comm., LLC; participant RIAS German Journalist Exch. Program, 1999; freelance writer Birmingham Mag., 1999; news reporter APTV Ala. Pub. TV, Montgomery, 1999. Freelance wire svc. reporter Agy. French Press, 2000—. V.p. Greystone Ladies Club, Birmingham, 1995 Mem. Jefferson County Med. Alliance; public rels. dir., Jefferson County Med. Alliance. Roman Catholic. Avocations: exercising, dancing, skiing, cooking, writing. Home: 5079 Greystone Way Birmingham AL 35242-6456 E-mail: newsmom@hotmail.com.

FRANCE, BELINDA TAKACH, lawyer, business owner; b. Jacksonville, Fla., June 10, 1964; d. Bruce Albert and Bertha Loretta (Hawkins) Takach; m. Alden Whitney France, July 27, 1985. BS, U. Tampa, Fla., 1985; JD, Stetson U., 1987; LLM in Taxation, U. Fla., 1989. Bar: Fla. 1989, U.S. Dist. Ct. (mid. dist.) Fla. 1989, U.S. Ct. Claims 1989, U.S. Tax Ct. 1989, U.S. Ct. Appeals (11th cir.) 1989, U.S. Ct. Appeals (Fed. cir.) 1990. Tax preparer H&R Block, Tampa, 1983-84; acct. Robert Osborne & Assocs., Tampa, 1984-85; assoc. Thomas C. Little, P.A., Clearwater, Fla., 1987-88; co-counsel Bruce R. Young, P.A., Clearwater, 1988; prin. Belinda Takach France, P.A., Tallahassee, Fla., 1988—. Prof. Ft. Lauderdale Coll., Tallahassee, 1989; adj. instr. Tallahassee C.C., 1991—; vice chmn. bd. dirs. Someplace Else, Tallahassee; owner Catalyst Seminars; expert witness in taxation and pension matters. Mem. Tallahassee Rep. Women, 1989-90. Named Best Atty. Tallahassee mag., 2000. Mem. ABA (com. domestic rels. tax problems, com. attys. in small law firms), Fla. Bar Assn., Tallahassee Bar Assn., Tallahassee Women Lawyers Assn., Tallahassee C. of C. Office: 703 E Tennessee St Tallahassee FL 32308-4984 E-mail: btf@francelawfirm.com.

FRANCE, DOROTHY DANIEL, minister; b. Danieltown, Va, Nov. 23, 1926; d. Arthur R. and Susan G. (Waller) Daniel; m. Carl G. France, Aug. 6, 1946 (dec. Nov. 1997); 1 child, Dorothy Gail France Frankle. BA, Bethany Coll., 1950; post grad., William and Mary Coll., 1964, Va. Commonwealth U., 1966. Dir. Army Dir. Svc., Camp Pickett, Va., 1944-46; tchr. Nottoway County Pub. Sch., Crewe, Va., 1950-55, Henrico Pub. Sch., Richmond, Va., 1961-63, Petersburg Pub. Sch., Va., 1964-68; dir. Cmty. Devel., New River Cmty Action, Radford, Va., 1969-73; min. Petunia Christian Ch., Wytheville, Va., 1969-72, Galilee Christian Ch., Wytheville, 1973-75; assoc. dir. CROP/Ch. World Svc., Va., NC, 1975-76; dir. CROP/Ch. World Svc. for Va., Richmond, 1977-80; dir. resource devel. Va. Inst. of Pastoral Care, Richmond, 1980-81; min. Prospect Christian Ch., Dinwiddie, Va., 1982-87; dir. Refugee Resettlement CWS/EMM, Va. Coun. of Ch., Richmond, 1981-91. Cons. on Am. corp. involvement in South Africa Christian Ch., Indpls., 1971. Author: Special Days of the Church Year, 1969, Newness of Life, 1970, Partners in Prayer, 1986, Welcome to the United States An Orientation Guide for Refuges, 1988, Blessed Assurance, 1999, (with Jason and David Frankle) You Might Be a Football Fan If....Simplified Game Notes for Would Be Fans, 2000; (with Jason and David Frankle, 2003); author/editor: At Christ's Table, 1997; author: (with others) Go Quickly and Tell, 1973; editl. com. Toward Better Grouping in Reading, 1968. Recipient Valiant Woman award Ch. Women United. Mem. AAUW, Va. Coalition on Nutrition, Delta Kappa Gamma (chair personal growth and devel. com. 1968). Avocations: writing, travel. Home and Office: DDF Enterprises 2968 Silver Maple Dr Fairlawn OH 44333-3295 E-mail: ddfenprise@aol.com.

FRANCE, JOSEPH DAVID, securities analyst; b. Smithville, Mo., July 24, 1953; s. Raymond Hughes and Bonnie Lee (Cavin) F; 1 child, Lucille Terrell. BS in Pharmacy, U. Kans., 1977, MBA, 1980. Chartered fin. analyst. Staff pharmacist U. Kans. Med. Ctr., Kansas City, 1977-80; securities analyst First Nat. Bank Chgo., 1980-82, Smith Barney, Harris Upham & Co., Inc., N.Y.C., 1982-86, mng. dir., 1986-93; 1st v.p. Merrill Lynch, N.Y.C., 1993-95; sr. v.p. Dillon, Read & Co., 1995-96; dir. CS First Boston, N.Y.C., 1996—2003; mng. dir. Banc Am. Securities, 2003—. Mem. Am. Soc. Health-Sys. Pharmacists, N.Y. Soc. Securities Analysts, Assn. for Investment Mgmt. and Rsch., Am. Math. Soc. Democrat. Jewish. Avocations: reading, computers, writing. Office: Banc America 9 West 57th St 28th Floor New York NY 10019 E-mail: joseph.d.france@bofasecurities.com.

FRANCE, MARY PEARRE, rehabilitation nurse, consultant; b. Balt., Nov. 5, 1948; d. Oliver Jackson and Rosalie (Bowie) Pearre; m. Lawrence Joseph France, June 27, 1970; children: Lawrence Jackson, Mathew Todd. BSN, Georgetown U., 1970; MA in Rehab., Towson State U., 1987. RN, Md.; CRRN. Orthopedic nurse U. Md. Hosp., Balt., 1970-74; rehab. cons. Vocat. Placement Svcs. Inc., Richmond, Va., 1980-83; med. coord. Self-Insured Co., Inc., Towson, 1983-88; pres., CEO Recover, Inc., Arnold, Md., 1988-96. Bd. dirs. Vols. for Med. Engring., Balt., 1988—93; sr. v.p. The Guilford Grup, Balt., 1991—2001, Md. Ctr. for Pain Mgmt., 1991—93. Mem. Am. Assn. Rehab. Nurses, Nat. Rehab. Assn., Md. Ins. Rehab. Coords. (charter sec. 1987); vol. Meals on Wheels, 2002-. Avocations: sailing, scuba, reading. Home and Office: 112 Spot Club Rd Arnold MD 21012-1002 E-mail: lfrance@bellatlantic.net.

FRANCE, NEWELL EDWIN, former hospital administrator, consultant; b. Massillon, Ohio, Sept. 30, 1927; s. Lawrence Joel and Marcella Ruth (Nelson) F.; m. Eve Elisabeth Voluter, 1953; children: Philip J., Corinne E., Anne-Claire I., Stephen C., Louise A. BS, Northwestern U., 1953, MS in Hosp. Adminstrn, 1955. Adminstrv. resident Herrick Meml. Hosp., Berkeley, Calif., 1954-55; evening supt. Chgo. Wesley Meml. Hosp., 1955-56; asst. adminstr. St. Lukes Episcopal and Tex. Children's hosps., Houston, 1956-58, assoc. adminstr., 1958-64, adminstr., 1964-73, exec. dir., 1973-83; pres. emeritus Tampa Gen. Hosp., Fla., 1983-91, 91—; pres. Patrick Philbin & Assocs., Austin, 1993—; cons. Hok Architecture, 1995—. Assoc. adminstr. Tex. Heart Inst., Houston, 1958-64, adminstr., 1964-73, exec. dir., 1973-83; cons. adv. council HEW and NIH; staff cons. AID, 1969— ; cons. program projects rev. com. Nat. Inst. Neurol. and Communicative Disorders and Stroke; mem. com. pediatrics NRC-Nat. Acad. Scis., 1975— ; chmn. Greater Houston Hosp. Coun., Children's Hosps. Execs. Council, 1972-73; dir. Child Care Center, Tex. Med. Ctr., 1967—; adj. assoc. prof. Sch. Architecture, Rice U.; prof. health scis. Tex. Women's U. Bd. dirs. Met. Houston chpt. Nat. Found. March of Dimes, First City Bank Med. Center; trustee Pin Oaks Charity Horse Show Assn., Houston Bot. Soc.; mem. exec. bd. South Main Center Assn., Inc.; active Houston/Baku Sister City Assn. Served with USNR, 1946-48, 51-52. Fellow Am. Coll. Hosp. Adminstrs.; mem. Am. Hosp. Assn., Tex. Hosp. Assn. (chmn. coun. hosp. auxs. 1969-73, trustee 1972—, adviser, chmn. coun. on profl. svc. 1976—), Houston Area Hosp. Assn. (pres. 1968-69), Nat. Assn. Childrens Hosps. and Related Instns. (pres. 1969-70, conf. chmn. 1969, trustee 1971—, chmn. coun. past pres.'s 1973-74), Am. Assn. Hosp. Planning, Statutory Teaching Hosps. Coun. (Fla.) (chmn. 1988-91). Clubs: Rotary Internat; Doctors (Houston). Methodist. Home: 6609 Coolglen Dr Dallas TX 75248-2902

FRANCE, OLIN KENNETH, JR., psychologist; b. Miami Beach, Fla., Feb. 22, 1949; s. Olin Kenneth and Eva (Center) F.; m. Mary Duncan, Aug. 16, 1969; 1 child, Micah Duncan. BA, Wake Forest U., 1971; MS, Fla. State U., 1973, PhD, 1975. Lic. psychologist, Pa.; registrant Nat. Register of Health Svc. Providers in Psychology. Asst. prof. Francis Marion Coll., Florence, S.C., 1975-78; prof. Shippensburg (Pa.) U., 1978—; ind. practice of psychology S.C., Pa., 1975—. Coord. Pa. Summer Acad., 1999—, Ann. Conf. Advancement Coll. Tchg. and Learning, Pa. State Sys. Higher Edn., 2001—. Author: Crisis Intervention, 1982, 4th edit., 2002, Body Conditioning, 1985, The Hospital Patient, 1987, Basic Psychological Skills, 1993, Supportive Interviewing, 1995. Recipient Salute to Teaching, Shippensburg U. and the Pa. State Sys. of Higher Edn., 1990, Excellence Tchg. award Pa. Soc. Tchg. Scholars, 1999; named Vol. of Yr. New Hope Online, 2001. Mem. APA, Pa. Psychol. Assn., Am. Assn. Suicidology, Phi Delta Kappa. Office: Shippensburg U Psychology Dept 1871 Old Main Dr Shippensburg PA 17257-2299

FRANCE, WILLIAM CLIFTON, JR., professional sports team executive; b. Washington, 1933; s. William France Sr.; m. Betty Jane Zachary; children: Lesa Kennedy, Brian. Student, U. Fla. Pres. NASCAR, Daytona Beach, Fla., 1972—2000; dir., CEO Internat. Speedway Corp., Daytona Beach, Fla., 1972—; chmn. bd. NASCAR, Daytona Beach, Fla., 2000—. Dir. Nat. Motorsports Coun. of ACCUS. With USN. Office: NASCAR/ISC 1801 W Internat Speedway Blvd Daytona Beach FL 32114

FRANCE-LITCHFIELD, RUTH A. reading and early literacy specialist; b. Cleve., Mar. 17, 1945; d. Elizabeth Ann (Way) France; children: Katherine Ann, C. Robert. AA, Christian Coll., Columbus, Mo., 1965; BS in Elem. Edn. and French, U. Mo., 1969; MEd in Reading, U. Hawaii, 1974; cert. advanced grad. study, Boston U., 1995. Cert. advanced grad. study, consulting tchr. of reading, French K-9, Mass., K-12 reading tchr.; trained and cert. Orton Gillingham. Tchr. Severence Millikin Sch., Cleveland Heights, Ohio, 19699; elem. tchr. Claude O. Markoe Sch., Fredericsted, St. Croix, V.I., 1969-70; tchr. Ecole Active Bilingue, Paris, 1970-71; elem. tchr. Punahou Sch., Honolulu, 1971-74; nat. cons., asst. editor, editor, asst. to mng. editor The Economy Co.-McGraw Hill Divsn., Oklahoma City, 1974-81; pvt. cons., tutor U.S. Army, West Germany, 1981-84; tchr., substitute Community Nursery Sch., Lexington, Mass., 1985-89; substitute tchr. Lexington (Mass.) Pub. Schs., 1989-91; instrnl. aide Bridge Elem. Sch., Lexington, 1991-92, reading recovery trainee, 1992-93; reading recovery tchr. Davis Elem. Sch., Bedford, Mass., 1994, Bridge Elem. Sch., Lexington, 1992—; rsch. asst. Harvard U. Sch. Edn., 1993—; pvt. tutor, 1995—; reading/early literacy specialist, 1997—. Workshop presenter in field. Contbr. articles to profl. publs. Mem. ASCD, Internat. Reading Assn. (local bd. dirs., pres. 1998-99),. Nat. Reading Assn., Mass. Reading Assn., Ohio Reading Assn., New Eng. Reading Assn., Mass. Assn. Bilingual Edn., Reading Recovery Coun. of N.Am., Phi Delta Kappa, Pi Lambda Theta, Delta Kappa Gamma. Avocations: reading, swimming, knitting, cooking/baking, sewing, crafts. Home: 6 Conestoga Rd Lexington MA 02421-6427 Office: 55 Middleby Rd Lexington MA 02421-6920 E-mail: ruthkb3@hotmail.com., rfrance@sch.ci.lexington.ma.us.

FRANCES, KATRINA See VAN ALLEN, KATRINA

FRANCESCHI, ERNEST JOSEPH, JR., lawyer; b. L.A., Feb. 1, 1957; s. Ernest Joseph and Doris Cecilia (Beluche) F. BS, U. So. Calif., 1978; JD, Southwestern U., L.A., 1980. Bar: Calif. 1984, U.S. Dist. Ct. (cen. dist.) Calif. 1984, U.S. Dist. Ct. (ea. dist.) Calif. 1986, U.S. Dist. Ct. (no. and so. dists.) Calif. 1987, U.S. Ct. Appeals (9th cir.) 1984, U.S. Supreme Ct. 1989. Pvt. practice law, L.A., 1984—; judge pro tem L.A. Superior Ct., 1999—. Mem. Assn. Trial Lawyers Am., Calif. Trial Lawyers Assn., L.A. Trial Lawyers Assn., Trial Lawyers for Pub. Justice, Fed. Bar Assn. Office: 445 S Figueroa St Ste 2600 Los Angeles CA 90071-1630

FRANCESCHI, RENNY THEODORE, medical educator, dean; b. Burbank, Calif., Nov. 27, 1949; s. Renzo Italo and Ida D'Angelo Franceschi; m. Mary Leon Franceschi, Apr. 5, 1986; children: Amelia Laura, Julia O'Rorke. BA, U. Vt., 1971; PhD, Purdue U., 1978. Postdoctoral fellow U. Wis., Madison, 1978—80; asst. prof. biochemistry Harvard U. Sch. Pub. Health, Boston, 1980—89; assoc. prof. biochemistry U. Tex. Dental Br., Houston, 1989—92; assoc. prof. dentistry U. Mich. Sch. Dentistry, Ann Arbor, 1993—98; assoc. prof. biochemistry U. Mich. Sch. Medicine, Ann Arbor, 1993—2002; prof. dentistry and biochemistry U. Mich. Sch. Dentistry, Ann Arbor, 2002—, assoc. dean for rsch., 2002. Cons. NIH, Bethesda, Md., 1990—. Contbr. articles to profl. jours. Grantee, NIH, 1982—; Predoctoral fellow, 1975—78, Postdoctoral fellow, 1978—80. Mem.: Internat. Assn. for Dental Rsch. (mineralized tissues group pres. 2002—03), Am. Soc. for Bone and Mineral Rsch., Am. Soc. for Biochemistry and Molecular Biology, Omega Kappa Upsilon (hon.). Democrat. Roman Catholic. Achievements include research in basic mechanisms of skeletal development and regeneration; gene therapy approaches for skeletal regeneration. Avocations: skiing, ice hockey, sailing, hiking. Office: Univ Mich Sch Dentistry 1011 N University Ann Arbor MI 48109-1078 Office Fax: 734-763-5503. Personal E-mail: rennyf@umich.edu. E-mail: rennyf@umich.edu.

FRANCFORT, ALFRED JOHN, JR., educator; b. Washington, 1939; m. Elisabeth A. Dey. BS, Monmouth Coll., 1964; MA, U. Pitts., 1969, PhD, 1972. Instr. econs. Chatham Coll., Pitts., 1970-72; teaching fellow U. Pitts., 1966-70, asst. prof. econs., 1972-77, assoc. prof., 1977-83; prof. fin. James Madison U., Harrisonburg, Va., 1983—, head fin. and bus. law dept., 1997—. Cons. on electric utility rate cases and regulation, 1977—; lectr. corp. mgmt. tng. programs, 1973—; mem. U. Pitts. Steering Com. on Regional Econ. Devel., 1973-75. Mem. editorial bd. Jour. Econ. Lit., 1970-83; contbr. articles to profl. jours. MIT scholar, 1974; fellow Univ. Chgo., 1977; faculty fellow U.S. Gen. Acctg. office, Washington, 1979-80; Fulbright Sr. scholar, 1987. Mem. Am. Fin. Assn., Ea. Fin. Assn., Fin. Mgmt. Assn., So. Fin. Assn. Office: James Madison U Dept Fin & Bus Law Msc 0203 Harrisonburg VA 22807-0001

FRANCH, HAROLD AUGUST, nephrologist, researcher; b. Atlanta, July 5, 1961; s. Robert H. and Haroldina L. Franch; m. Victoria Harrington, July 5, 1983; children: Carolina Anne, Michael Harrington, James August. BA, Harvard U., 1983; MD, U. of Pa., 1988. Diplomate Am. Bd. of Internal Medicine, 1991, cert. in nephrology and hypertension Am. Bd. of Internal Medicine, 1994. Resident in internal medicine U. Tex. Southwestern, Dallas, 1988—91, fellow in neurology, 1991—95; asst. prof. of medicine Sch. of Medicine Emory U., Atlanta, 1995—; staff physician Atlanta Vets. Affairs Med. Ctr., Atlanta, 1996. Pres. Nat. Kidney Found. of Ga., Atlanta, 2002—. Office: Emory University School of Medicine WMRB 338 1639 Pierce Drive Atlanta GA 30322

FRANCH, RICHARD THOMAS, lawyer; b. Melrose Park, Ill., Sept. 23, 1942; s. Robert and Julia (Martino) F.; m. Patricia Staufenberg, Apr. 18, 1971 (dec. Apr. 1994); children: Richard T. Jr., Katherine J.; m. Susan L. Rice, Sept. 1, 1995. BA cum laude, U. Notre Dame, 1964; JD, U. Chgo., 1967. Bar: Ill. 1967, U.S. Dist. Ct. (no. dist.) Ill. 1967, U.S. Supreme Ct. 1980, U.S. Ct. Appeals (2d cir.) 1984, U.S. Ct. Appeals (3d cir.) 1981, U.S. Ct. Appeals (6th cir.) 1991, U.S. Ct. Appeals (7th cir.) 1971, U.S. Ct. Appeals (8th cir.) 1981, U.S. Ct. Appeals (9th cir.) 1997, U.S. Dist. Ct. (no. dist.) Wis. 1989, U.S. Tax Ct. 1994. Assoc. Jenner & Block, Chgo., 1967-68, 70-74, ptnr., 1975—. Former mem. Ill. Supreme Ct. Rules Com. Served to capt. U.S. Army, 1968-70 Decorated Bronze star, Army Commendation medal. Fellow Am. Coll. Trial Lawyers; mem. Am. Law Inst. Office: Jenner & Block Ste 4600 One IBM Plz Chicago IL 60611 E-mail: dickfranch@aol.com., rfranch@jenner.com.

FRANCHINI, GENE EDWARD, state supreme court justice; b. Albuquerque, May 19, 1935; s. Mario and Lena (Vaio) F.; m. Glynn Hatchell, Mar. 22, 1969; children: Pamela, Lori (dec.), Gina, Joseph James, Nancy. BBA, Loyola U., 1955; degree in adminstrn., U. N.Mex., 1957; JD, Georgetown U., 1960; LLM, U. Va., 1995. Bar: N.Mex. 1960, U.S. Dist. Ct. N.Mex. 1961, U.S. Ct. Appeals (10th cir.) 1970, U.S. Supreme Ct. 1973. Ptnr. Matteucci, Gutierrez & Franchini, Albuquerque, 1960-70, Matteucci, Franchini & Calkins, Albuquerque, 1970-75; judge State of N.Mex. 2d Jud. Dist., Albuquerque, 1975-81; atty.-at-large Franchini, Wagner, Oliver, Franchini & Curtis, Albuquerque, 1982-90; chief justice N.Mex. Supreme Ct., Santa Fe, 1990-99, justice, 1999—2003. V.p. bd. dirs. Conf. Chief Justices, 1997-98. Chmn. Albuquerque Pers. Bd., 1972, Albuquerque Labor Rels. Bd., 1972, Albuquerque Interim Bd. Ethics, 1972. Capt. USAF, 1960-66. Recipient Highest award Albuquerque Human Rights Bd., 1999. Mem. Am. Bd. Trial Advocates, N.Mex. Trial Lawyers (pres. 1967-68), N.Mex. Bar Assn. (bd. dirs. 1976-78), Albuquerque

Bar Assn. (bd. dirs. 1976-78, Outstanding Judge award 1997). Democrat. Roman Catholic. Avocations: fishing, hunting, golf, mushroom hunting. Home: 4901 Laurene Ct NW Albuquerque NM 87120-1026*

FRANCHINI, ROXANNE, bank executive; b. N.Y.C., Mar. 20, 1951; d. Tullio and Jean (Brady) Franchini. Student, Emerson Coll., Ricker Coll., New Sch. Social Rsch. With Princess Marcella Borghese divsn. Revlon, N.Y.C., 1972-73, TWA Airlines, 1973-74; asst. to pres. N.Y. Shipping Assn., N.Y.C., 1974-79; benefits mgr. Kidde, Inc., N.Y.C., 1979-83; 2d v.p. pension trust fin. svcs. Chase Manhattan Bank, N.A., N.Y.C., 1983-85, v.p. mgr. global securities, 1985-89; v.p., sales dir. global custody worldwide securities svcs. Citibank, N.Y.C., 1989-91; v.p. Mellon Bank, Pitts., 1991—2001; 1st v.p. Mellon Fin. Corp., Pitts., 2002—. Chair fin. local fund raising campaigns. Mem.: So. Assn. Coll. and Univ. Bus. Offices, Ea. Assn. Coll. and Univ. Bus. Offices, Nat. Assn. Coll. and Univ. Bus. Offices. Home: 1415 Ocean Shore Blvd Ormond Beach FL 32176-3673

FRANCIOSA, ANTHONY (ANTHONY PAPALEO), actor; b. N.Y.C., Oct. 28, 1928; s. Anthony and Jean (Franciosa) Papaleo; m. Rita Thiel, 1970; children: Christopher, Marco, Nina. Ed. high sch., N.Y.C.; studied drama with Joseph Geiger; scholarship Dramatic Workshop, New Sch. Social Rsch.; studied Actor's Studio. Worked with drama groups including Off Broadway, Inc., N.Y. Repertory Theatre; internat. tour Grand Hotel, 1990-91, Love Letters, 1992, 93, 94, 95; appeared in Broadway prodns. End as a Man, 1953, Wedding Breakfast, 1954-55, A Hatful of Rain, 1955 (Tony award nomination 1956, Acad. award nomination 1957); motion pictures include A Face in the Crowd, 1957, This Could Be the Night, 1957, Long Hot Summer, 1958, Naked Maja, 1959, Career, 1960 (Golden Globe award for best motion picture actor), Story on Page One, 1960, Go Naked in the World, 1960, Senilita, 1961, Period of Adjustment, 1962, Assault on a Queen, 1966, A Man Could Get Killed, 1966, The Swinger, 1966, Fathom, 1967, A Man Called Gannon, 1968, The Sweet Ride, 1968, In Enemy Country, 1968, Across 110th Street, 1972, Ghost in the Noonday Sun, 1973, The Drowning Pool, 1975, Firepower, 1979, The World is Full of Married Men, 1979, Death Wish II, 1982, Soot gli occhi dell'Assassino, 1982, Tenebrae, 1983, Avitami ai Sognare, 1984, La Cicala, 1985, Death House, 1988, La Morte e di Mona, 1990, Backstreet Dreams, 1990, Double Threat, 1992, City Hall, 1995; TV mini-series: Aspen, 1974, Wheels, 1975; movies for TV: Fame Is the Name of the Game, 1970, Earth II, 1971, The Deadly Hunt, 1974, Hide and Go Seek, 1975, The Catcher, 1976, This Is the Week That Was, 1977, Sideshow, 1979, The Black Widow, 1980, Matt Helm, 1982, Till Death Do Us Part, 1983, Stagecoach, 1987, Ghost Writer, 1990; star TV series Valentine's Day, 1964-65, The Name of the Game, 1968-72, Search, 1972-73, Matt Helm, 1975-76, Finder of Lost Loves, 1984-85; narrator for A Lincoln Portrait with St. Louis Symphony Orch., 1971, conducted by Andre Previn. Recipient Count Volpe Di Misurata cup Venice Film Festival for Hatful of Rain, 1958, Daniel Blum's Theatre World award for best leading actor in Hatful of Rain, 1955, Critics Outer Circle award, 1956, Goledn Globe award for best motion picture actor in drama for film Career, World Foreign Press, 1960.

FRANCIOSA, JOSEPH ANTHONY, health care consultant; b. Easton, Pa., Apr. 24, 1936; s. Joseph and Letitia Beatrice (Cascioli) F.; m. Antonietta Battistoni, Feb. 8, 1964 (div. 1972); m. Barbara Ann Neilan, Aug. 3, 1973 (div. 1989); 1 child, Christopher David; m. Robin L McGaw, Oct. 4, 1999. BA, U. Pa., 1958; MD, U. Rome, 1963. Diplomate Am. Bd. Internal Medicine; lic. in Pa., Md., Ark. Intern USPHS Hosp., S.I., N.Y., 1964-65; resident Washington Hosp. Ctr., 1967-69; cardiology fellow VA Hosp.-Georgetown U., Washington, 1969-71; chief ICU Va. Hosp., Washington, 1971-73; asst. prof. medicine Georgetown U. Med. Sch., 1971-73, assoc. dir. cardiovascular tng. program, 1974-75; dir. CCU Va. Hosp., Mpls., 1974-76; asst. prof. medicine U. Minn., Mpls., 1977-79; chief cardiology VA Hosp., Phila., 1979-82; assoc. prof. U. Pa., Phila., 1979-82. Adj. prof. 1987-98; adj. prof. medicine Mt. Sinai Med. Sch., N.Y.C., 1989—, Cornell U. Coll. Med., N.Y.C., 1999—; dir. cardiology div. U. Ark., Little Rock, 1982-86; prof., 1982-86; dir. cardio-renal drugs ICI Americas Inc., Wilmington, Del., 1986-88; v.p. R&D Zambon Corp., East Rutherford, N.J., 1988-90; exec. dir. med. affairs Ciba-Geigy Pharm., Summit, N.J., 1990-91; exec. dir. med. svcs. Ciba-Geigy, 1992-95; health care/pharm. cons., N.Y.C., 1995—. Contbr. numerous articles to med. jours. Mem. med. rsch. com. Am. Heart Assn., Mpls., 1976-79, Phila., 1981-82. Lt. comdr. USPHS, 1965-67. VA grantee, 1974-84, U. Ark. grantee, 1982-83. Fellow ACP, Am. Coll. Cardiology, Am. Coll. Chest Physicians (chmn. hypertension com. 1981-83, gov. Ark. 1984-86), Am. Heart Assn. (circulation coun. 1978—, coun. high blood pressure rsch. 1982—, clin. cardiology coun. 1984, bd. dirs. N.J. affiliate 1994-98); mem. Am. Soc. Clin. Pharmacology and Therapeutics (vice chmn. cardiopulmonary com. 1981-89), Assn. Univ. Cardiologists, Am. Acad. of Pharm. Physicians (charter mem. v.p. publs. com. 2002—), Heart Failure Soc. Am. Avocations: computers, gardening, physical fitness. E-mail: jfrancios@cs.com.

FRANCIS, CHARLES GORDON, business executive, writer; b. Murdo, S.D., July 31, 1924; s. John Russell and Constance Abby (Bottum) F.; m. Barbara Klipper Francis, June 15, 1949; children: Abby Constance, Paul Erwin. BA, UCLA, 1949. Reporter United Press, L.A., 1949-50; mem. pub. rels. staff Santa Barbara (Calif.) Coll., 1950-53, UCLA, 1953-57; comms. exec. IBM Corp., L.A., 1957-61, Armonk, N.Y., 1961-88; founder, owner IdeaBank, Inc., Rye, N.Y., 1988—. Contbr. articles to profl. publs. Pres. PTA, Chappaqua, N.Y., 1969. Staff sgt. U.S. Army, 1943-46. Mem. Assn. Nat. Advertisers (dir. 1982-88), Internat. Advt. Assn. (dir. 1982-88). Office: IdeaBank Inc 5025 Theall Rd Rye NY 10580 E-mail: francis@idea-bank.com.

FRANCIS, CHARLES K. medical educator; b. Newark, May 24, 1939; BA, Dartmouth Coll., 1961; MD, Jefferson Med. Coll., 1965. Med. intern Phila. Gen. Hosp., 1965—66; med. resident Boston City Hosp., Tufts U., 1969—70; clin. fellow cardiology Tufts Circulation Lab., 1970—71; clin. and rsch. fellow cardiology Mass. Gen. Hosp., 1971—72, sr. med. resident, 1972-73; chief cardiac catheterization lab. divsn. cardiology Martin Luther King Jr. Gen. Hosp., L.A., 1973—74, chief cardiology divsn., 1974—77; dir. cardiology divsn. Mt. Sinai Hosp., Hartford, Conn., 1977—80; assoc. dir. hypertension svc., assoc. prof. medicine, dir. cardiac catheterization lab. Yale Med. Sch., Hartford, Conn., 1980-87; dir. dept. medicine Harlem Hosp. Ctr., N.Y.C., 1987—98; prof. clin. medicine Columbia U. Coll. Physicians and Surgeons, 1987—98; pres. Charles R. Drew U. Med. and Sci., 1998—. Clin. instr. medicine Sch. Medicine Tufts U., 1970—71; tchg. fellow Harvard Med. Sch., 1971—72, clin. fellow, 1972—73; asst. prof. medicine Charles R. Drew Postgrad. Med. Sch. & Sch. Medicine U. Calif., 1973—75; asst. prof. medicine, dir. Burgdorf Hypertension Clin., Med. Sch. U. Conn., 1977—80; mem. cardiac adv. com. Nat. Heart, Lung & Blood Inst., NIH, 1977—79; asst. prof. medicine Sch. Medicine Yale U., 1980—81, assoc. prof., 1981—87. Fellow: ACP, Am. Coll. Cardiology; mem.: Assn. Black Cardiologists (chmn. bd. 1994—), Am. Heart Assn., Am. Fedn. Clin. Rsch., Inst. Medicine-NAS. Address: Charles Drew U of Med & Sci 1621 E 120th St Los Angeles CA 90059-3025

FRANCIS, CHARLES MACKENZIE, wildlife biologist; b. Pretoria, South Africa, Dec. 1, 1958; BSc in Fisheries and Wildlife Biology with honors and distinction, U. Guelph, 1980; MSc in Biology, Queen's Univ., Kingston, 1987, PhD in Biology, 1990. Computer programmer, sys. mgr. U. Wollongong, Australia, 1981; CUSO vol. ornithologist wildlife sect. Sabah Forest Dept., Malaysia, 1981-84; computer programmer Can. Wildlife Svc., 1986; Natural Scis. & Engring. Rsch. Coun. postdoctoral fellow Duke U., Durham, N.C., 1990-92; wildlife biologist Can. Wildlife Svc. and U.S. Nat. Biol. Surveys, 1993-95; sr. sci. Bird Studies Can., Port Rowan, Canada, 1995—2002; chief, migratory birds population divsn. Nat. Wildlife Rsch. Ctr., Ottawa, Canada, 2002—. Adj. prof. biol. dept. Queen's U., 1995—; adj. prof. geography dept. U. Western Ont., 1996-98; rsch. assoc. Wildlife Conservation Soc., 1991—, zool. dept. U. Malaya, 1991-96, Royal Ont. Mus., 1997—; tchg. asst. Queen's U., 1985, 88, 89, 90, Guelph U., 1978, 79. Author: A Pocket Guide to the Birds of Borneo, 1985, A Pocket Checklist of the Birds of Sabah, 1986, A Photographic Guide to Mammals of South East Asia, 2001; co-author: A Field Guide to the Mammals of Borneo, 1986; contbr. articles to profl. jours. Urlla Carmichael scholar, 1989, Alma Mater scholar, 1979, Audubon Wildlife scholar, 1980, Can. Nat. Sportsman's Fund scholar, 1979, Natural Scis. & Engring. Rsch. Coun. scholar, 1985-88; grantee Natural Scis. & Engring. Rsch. Coun., 2000—, Wildlife Conservation Soc., 1991—, AOU Travel award, 1994, AOU Marcie Brady Tucker Travel award, 1990; Can. Wildlife Svc. Rsch. grantee, 1989, Am. Mus. Nat. History Chapman Fund grantee, 1986, 87, 89, Queen's Sch. Grad. Studies and Rsch. Travel grantee, 1985, 87, 88, 89. Mem. Wildlife Soc., Am. Ornithologists' Union, Brit. Ornithologists' Union, Assn. Tropical Biologists, Royal Australian Ornithologists' Union, Cooper Ornithol. Soc., Assn. Field Ornithologists, Oriental Bird Club, Can. Soc. Ornithologists, Am. Soc. Mammalogists. Office: Nat Wildlife Rsch Ctr Can Wildlife Svc Ottawa ON Canada

FRANCIS, EDWARD D. architect; b. Cleve., Aug. 15, 1934; s. Michael and Anna (Buchinsky) F.; m. Betty-Lee Seydler, Aug. 25, 1956 (div. 1982); children— Tameron, Theron; m. Lynne Marie Merrill, Sept. 6, 1984. B.Arch, Miami U., 1957. Draftsman, designer David Maxfield, Oxford, Ohio, 1953-59; draftsman Austin Co., Cleve., summers 1954, 56; designer Meathe, Kessler & Assoc., Grosse Pointe, Mich., 1959-68; prin. William Kessler & Assoc., Detroit, 1968—, pres., 1985-95, Kessler Assoc. Inc., 1995-99; CEO Kessler/Francis/Cardoza Architects, 1999—. Mem. archtl. adv. com. Ferris State U., Big Rapids, Mich. Chmn. Franklin Village Hist. Commn., Mich., 1971-79; pres. Friends of Capitol, Lansing, 1984-85, State Hist. Preservation Rev. Bd., 1984-94. Fellow AIA (Gold medal Detroit and Mich. chpts.); mem. Frank Lloyd Wright Found., Frank Lloyd Wright Preservation Trust, Nat. Trust for Hist. Preservation, Mich. Hist. Preservation Network (Lifetime Achievement award 2001), Gabriel Richard Hist. Soc. (bd. dirs.). Office: Kessler/Francis/Cardoza 300 River Pl Ste 1650 Detroit MI 48207 E-mail: kessler@ameritech.net.

FRANCIS, ELIZABETH ROMINE, secondary school educator, theater director; b. Clarksburg, WVa., Sept. 10, 1920; d. John Ransel and Virginia Snider Romine; m. Jack Stanley Francis, Feb. 13, 1943; children: Michael Stanley, John Maurice. BM, WVa. U., 1942, MM, 1963, JD; grad. drama, Ohio U., 1980. Tchr. Elem. Sch., Clarksburg, W.Va., 1942—43, Jr. H.S., Clarksburg, W.Va., 1943—44, Sr. H.S., Clarksburg, W.Va., 1943—45, New Martinville, W.Va., 1960—93; tchr. adult edn. WVa. U. Ext., New Martinville, 1960—70; Fred Waring workshop staff mem. Waring Enterprises, Delaware Water Gap, 1988—90; dir. theater activities Park & Recreation, New Martinville, W.Va., 1993—2001. Chmn. theater divsn. Parks and Recreation, New Martinsville, W.Va., 1993—2001. Prodr., dir. : (musical theater) Cmty. Theater, 1993—2001. Recipient Acad. Excellence award, State of WVa., 1985. Republican. Methodist. Avocations: golf, bridge. Office: New Martinsville Parks and Recreation 191 Main St New Martinsville WV 26155 Personal E-mail: eliza@ovis.net.

FRANCIS, HERBERT EDWARD, JR., writer; b. Bristol, R.I., Jan. 11, 1924; s. Herbert Edward Francis and Evelyn Estelle Verity; 1 adopted child, Carlos Roberto. BA, U. Wis., 1948; MA, Brown U., Providence, 1950; DHL (hon.), U. Ala., 1989. Instr. Pa. State U., 1950—52, U. Tenn., Knoxville, 1954—56, DeKalb State U., Ill., 1956—58; asst. prof. English Emory U., Atlanta, 1958—66; prof. English U. Ala., Huntsville, 1966—88. Adv. bd. The Literary Rev., Teaneck, NJ, Manoa, Honolulu; founding editor Poem, Huntsville; poetry editor This Issue, Atlanta; contbg. editor Thunder Mountain Rev., Birmingham. Author: Cinco milias hasta diciembre y Como los peces, comolos pájaros, 1966, Toda la gente que nunca tuve, 1966, The Itinerary of Beggars, 1973 (Iowa Sch. of Letters award for short fiction, 1973), Had, 1973, Naming things, 1980 (Ill. Fiction Series award, 1980), A Disturbance of Gulls, 1983, The Sudden Trees, 1999, Goya, Are You With Me Now?, 1999, The Invisible Country, 2003, over 200 stories in lit. mags.; translator: numerous short fiction from Spanish. Founding mem. Old Town Hist. Dist., Huntsville, Huntsville Literary Assn., 1967. With USAAF, 1942—45, ETO. Recipient Fulbright awardee, 1964—65, Fulbright Tchg. award, 1964—67; grantee Tchg. grantee, U. Ala., 1970. Avocations: acting, swimming. Home: 508 Clinton St E Huntsville AL 35801

FRANCIS, JAMES CLARK, IV, judge; b. Tulsa, Okla., Oct. 3, 1952; s. James C. and F. Ruth Francis; m. Elizabeth Bradford, Aug. 19, 1978; children: Nathaniel, Jeremy. BA, Yale Coll., 1974, JD, 1978; M of Pub. Policy, Harvard U., 1978. Bar: N.Y. 1979, U.S. Dist. Ct. (so. dist.) N.Y. 1979, U.S. Dist. Ct. (ea. dist.) N.Y. 1980, U.S. Ct. Appeals (2nd cir.) 1980. Law clk. Hon. Robert L. Carter, N.Y.C., 1978-79; staff atty. Legal Aid Soc., N.Y.C., 1979-85; U.S. Magistrate judge U.S. Dist. Ct. (so. dist.) N.Y., N.Y.C., 1985-98, chief U.S. Magistrate judge, 1998—2000. Adj. prof. Fordham Law Sch., 2003. Author: (chpts.) Moore's Federal Practice, 1997; curator exhibit Discreet Persons Learned in Law, 1995, Thou Shald Not Ration Justice, 2001. Mem. profl. adv. bd. Epilepsy Inst., N.Y.C.; bd. dirs. Port Washington (N.Y.) Soccer Club. Mem. N.Y. State Bar Assn. (jud. com. 1989—), Assn. Bar of City of N.Y. (fed. cts. com. 1995-98). Democrat. Avocations: travel, scuba, sports, coaching soccer. Office: US Court 500 Pearl St New York NY 10007-1316

FRANCIS, JAMES DELBERT, oil company executive; b. Orange, N.J., Jan. 8, 1947; s. Delbert Matthew and Margaret Janet F.; m. Shirley Ann Waters; children: Elizabeth M., John A., David S., Virginia a., Grace A., J. Thornley. BS in Commerce, U. Va., 1970; JD, U. Fla., 1973. Bar: Fla. 1973. Ptnr. Smith and Hulsey, Jacksonville, Fla., 1973-82; exec. v.p. Charter Oil Co., Fla., 1982-83, pres., 1983-86; chmn., CEO Ray Distbg. Co., 1987—; ptnr. First Coast Energy, LLP, 1997—. Bd. dirs. Petro Distbg., Inc. Bd. dirs., chmn. Children's Home Soc., Jacksonville, 1976—; elder St. Johns Presbyn. Ch., 1985—; pres. CHS Found., Inc., 2000—; trustee Riverside Presbyn. Day Sch., 2001-2002; bd. dirs. Seamark Ranch. Mem. ABA, Fla. Bar, Jacksonville Bar Assn., Fla. Yacht Club, River Club (Jacksonville), Timuquana Country Club. Republican. Home: 4284 Mcgirts Blvd Jacksonville FL 32210-4368 Address: First Coast Energy LLP 7014 A C Skinner Pkwy Ste 290 Jacksonville FL 32256-6940

FRANCIS, MARION DAVID, consulting chemist; b. Campbell River, B.C., Can., May 9, 1923; came to U.S., 1949; s. George Henry and Marian (Flanagan) F.; m. Emily Liane Williams, Aug. 27, 1949 (dec. 1995); children: William Randall, Patricia Ann; m. Jacqueline S. Lohman, June 14, 1997. BA, U. B.C., Vancouver, 1946, MA, 1949; PhD, U. Iowa, 1953. Instr. U. B.C., Vancouver, Can., 1946-49; chemist Can. Fishing Co., Vancouver, Can., 1946; research asst. U. Iowa, Iowa City, 1949-51; research chemist Procter & Gamble Co., Cin., 1952-76, sr. scientist, 1976-85, Norwich Eaton Pharms., Inc., Norwich, N.Y., 1985-89; rsch. fellow Victor Mills Soc., Cin., 1990-93; cons. Cin., 1993—. Chmn. Gordon Rsch. Conf., N.H., 1968, 79, session chmn., 1985; panel mem. Internat. Conf. on Crystal Deposition and Dissolution in Tissues, Evion, France, 1985; session chmn. workshop, Sienna, Italy, 1992; co-chmn. Bisphosphonate Therapies for Osteoporosis: Today and Tomorrow Symposium, Davos, Switzerland, 1996, chmn. Internat. Conf. on Phosphorus Chemistry, Cin., 1998, others; session chmn. Internat. Congress on Arts and Comms., Lisbon, Portugal, 1999, Washington, 2000, Cambridge, Eng., 2001, Vancouver, B.C., 2002; spkr. and lectr. in field. Contbr. articles to sci. jours.; patentee in field. Dist. chmn. Cin. United Appeal, 1956-60. Recipient Profl. Accomplishment award Tech. and Sci. Socs. Cin., 1979, Tech. Innovation award Victor Mills Soc., 1990, Perkin medal Soc. of Chem. Industry, 1996, Disting. Alumnus Achievement award U. Iowa Carver Coll. Medicine, 2003; U.S. Pub. Health predoctoral fellow, 1951-52. Fellow AAAS, Am. Inst. Chemists, Am. Soc. Bone and Mineral Rsch., Am. Chem. Soc. (program chmn. cen. regional meeting 1983, invited symposium spkr. nat. meeting 1987, 92, invited awards symposium spkr. 1994, Cin. Chemist of Yr. award 1977, Nat. Indsl. Chemist award 1994, Morley medal 1996, Heros of Chemistry award 2000), Am. Coll. Rheumatologists, Dance Club (pres. 1972-73), Wyo. (Ohio) Sunday Supper Club (pres. 1998-99). Republican. Roman Catholic. Home and Office: 23 Diplomat Dr Cincinnati OH 45215-2074 E-mail: dinbug4me@compuserve.com.

FRANCIS, MARY FRANCES VAN DYKE, real estate executive, editor; b. Sedalia, Mo., Nov. 17, 1925; d. Frank B. and Mary Irene (Sims) Van Dyke; m. Harold E. Francis, Apr. 23, 1944 (div. 1980); children: David Eugene, Lois Irene Valero, Roland Wayne, Eric Brian, Student, Ctrl.Mo. State Coll. Tchr. grade sch. Pettis County, Mo., 1943-44; timekeeper Montgomery Ward & Co., Kansas City, Mo., 1944-45; instr. new operators Southwestern Bell Telephone Co., Independence, Mo., 1945-47; real estate salesman Russell Realtors, Independence, 1958-66; owner Mary Francis, Realtor, Independence, 1967—. Exec. sec., editor Eastern Jackson County Bd. Realtors, 1962-68; exec. asst., pub. relations dir., editor Kansas City Realtor, 1968-71; marketing asst. South Central region Chgo. Title Ins. Co., Kansas City, 1971-75; pres. Maranco, Inc., real estate, 1975— ; v.p. Raintree Lake Realty, 1980-83. Contbr. articles to realty publs. Cub Scout den mother coun. Boy Scouts Am. Recipient Outstanding Svc. award Eastern Jackson County Bd. Realtors, 1964, Salesmanship award, 1965, CPW Real Estate Exch. award, Expo, 1983. Mem. Nat. Assn. Real Estate Bds. (charter pres. Greater Kansas City chpt., gov., pres. Mo. Women's Coun.), Mo. Real Estate Assn. (mem. Spkrs. Bur.), Soroptimist (past pres.). Address: PO Box 1158 Independence MO 64051-0658

FRANCIS, MICHAEL JACKSON, educational administrator; b. Oberlin, Kans., Mar. 24, 1938; s. Lowell Alexander and Helen Dannefer Francis; m. Patricia Ann McKevitt, Jan. 27, 1983; children: Catherine, Lowell, Eric. PhD, U. Va., 1963. Instr. govt. Tex. A&M U., College Station, 1963-65; asst. prof. polit. sci. Calif. State Coll., Fullerton, 1965-66; prof. govt. U. Notre Dame, Ind., 1966—, asst. provost internat. studies, 1997—. Vis. scholar U. Mich., Ann Arbor, 1976-77. Author: Limits of Hegemony, 1977. Mem. Am. Polit. Sci. Assn., L.Am. Studies Assn., Internat. Studies Assn. Avocations: travel, golf. Home: 70260 Sun Rise Dr Edwardsburg MI 49112 Office: U Notre Dame 319 Hesburgh Ctr Notre Dame IN 46556 E-mail: Michael.J.Francis1@nd.edu.

FRANCIS, PETER T. gas industry executive, oil industry executive; b. 1952; BA, Middlebury Coll.; MBA, Stanford U., 1987. Bd. dirs. JM Huber Corp., Edison, NJ, 1985—87, 1990—93, chmn. bd., 1993, pres., CEO; pres. AMS Subs. Corp., Seattle, 1988— ; chmn., CEO, pres. Cascade Cabinet Corp., Woodinville, Wash., 1990—. Office: J M Huber Corporation 333 Thornall St Edison NJ 08837-2220*

FRANCIS, PHILIP HAMILTON, management consultant; b. San Diego, Apr. 13, 1938; s. William Samuel and Ruth Kathryn (Allison) F.; m. Regina Elizabeth Kirk, June 10, 1961 (div. May 1971); m. Diana Maria Villarreal, July 15, 1972; children: Philip Scott, Edward Philip, Mary Allison, Kenneth Joseph. BSME, Calif. Poly. State U., 1959; MSME, U. Iowa, 1960, PhD in Engring. Mechanics, 1965; MBA in Mgmt., St. Mary's U., San Antonio, 1972. Registered profl. engr., Tex. With Douglas Aircraft Co., Santa Monica, Calif., 1960-62, S.W. Rsch. Inst., San Antonio, 1965-79; prof., chmn. dept. mech. and aerospace engring. Ill. Inst. Tech., Chgo., 1979-84; with Indsl. Tech. Inst., Ann Arbor, Mich., 1984-86; dir. advanced mfg. tech. Motorola Inc., Schaumburg, Ill., 1986-88; corp. v.p. Square D Co. (Schneider-N.Am.), Palatine, Ill., 1988-94; client ptnr. AT&T Solutions, AT&T, Chgo., 1995-96; mng. ptnr. Mascon Global, Ltd., Schaumburg, Ill., 1996—2002; pres. Group Francis, LLC, Georgetown, Tex., 2001—. Adj. prof. engring. Northwestern U., 2003—. Mem. various indsl. and acad. adv. bds. Recipient Gustas Larson award ASME and Pi Tau Sigma, 1978 Fellow ASME; mem. Soc. Mfg. Engrs., Sigma Xi, Tau Beta Pi, Pi Tau Sigma. Roman Catholic. Avocation: writing. E-mail: phil@groupfrancis.com.

FRANCIS, RELL GARDNER, artist, photographer, writer; b. Lake Shore, Utah, Jan. 27, 1928; s. S. Evan and Barbara (Ferguson) F.; m. Janet Oaks Francis, July 18, 1958; children: Sean Francis, Lewis Francis, Dana Francis Lepore. BA, Brigham Young U., 1954, MA, 1963; postgrad., Ill. Sch. Design, Chgo., summer 1957, Ohio State U., summer 1968, U. Utah, 1968-69. Cert. tchr. Monument designer A.H. Child & Son Monuments, Springville, Utah, 1945-54; art and English tchr. Nebo Sch. Dist., Springville, 1954-74; home study art instr. Brigham Young U., Provo, Utah, 1964-70; photo tchr. European Art Acad., Paris, summer 1966; dir. art mus. Springville Mus. Art, 1976; dir. City Spirit art Nat. Endowment for Arts, Springville City, Utah, 1974-75; owner Photo Gallery, Heritage Prints Photography, Provo, 1977-90. Cons. photography Clio, Inc., N.Y.C., 2001, PBS (Judy Crichton) Am. 1900, Boston, N.Y.C., 1996-97; lectr. Cyrus E. Dallin at Rockwell Mus. Exhibit, Corning, N.Y., 1995; cons. Cyrus E. Dallin Art Mus., Arlington, Mass., 2000; photography advisor CLIO, Inc., N.Y.C., 2000-01; vol. docent, guest exhibitor Utah photos SLC Cultural Olympiad, 2002. Author: Cyrus E. Dallin, 1976, The Utah Photographs of George Edward Anderson, 1979; film prodr.: Stoneman Sheepherder, 1969, Que Bonita, 1972; contbr. articles to profl. jours.; one-person show at Provo Utilities Gallery, Provo, 1969; exhibited in group shows at Springville Mus. Art, 1982, 88, LDS Ch. Mus. Art and History, Salt Lake City, 1985, Amon Carter Mus., Ft. Worth, 1979, Brigham Young U. and Springville Mus. Art, 1974, Segnali de Fumo, Italy, 1994; retrospective exhibit of Mex. photographs and paintings, Springville Mus. Art, 1999, Peteetneet Acad. Art, Payson, Utah, 2003. Trustee Springville Mus. Art, 1958-74; environ. activist Audubon Soc., Provo, 1995—; hon. vol. mentor Slate Canyon Youth Ctr. Program, Provo, 2000. Recipient Best of Show, photography Utah State Fair, 1966, 67, Meritorious Svc. award in photography Brigham Young U., Provo, 1974, Morris Rosenblatt award Utah Hist. Quar., Salt Lake City, 1976. Mem. Utah Hist. Soc., Springville Hist. Soc. (trustee 1975-2001, 2003). Mem. Lds Ch. Avocation: writing poetry. Home: 750 E Chase Ln Springville UT 84663-2053

FRANCIS, ROBERT, professional hockey coach; m. Deborah Francis; children: Kelley, Kristine, Ryan. Student, U. N.H. Hockey player Detroit Red Wings, 1980-86; player/asst. coach Salt Lake Golden Eagles, 1986-87, asst. coach, 1987-88, head coach, 1989-93, Calgary Flames, 1993-94, Bruins AHL affiliate in Providence; asst. coach Boston Bruins, 1997-99; head coach Phoenix Coyotes, 1999-. Office: Phoenix Coyotes Cellular One Ice Den 9375 E Bell Rd Scottsdale AZ 85260-1500

FRANCIS, RON, professional hockey player; b. Sault Ste Marie, Ont., Can., Mar. 1, 1963; Center Pitts. Penguins, 1991-98, Carolina Hurricanes, 1998—. Office: c/o Carolina Hurricanes KTR Hockey Ltd Partnership 5000 Aerial Center Pkwy Ste 100 Morrisville NC 27560-8418

FRANCIS, SAMUEL TODD, columnist; b. Chattanooga, Apr. 29, 1947; s. Todd Ware and Julia (Ford) F. BA, Johns Hopkins U., 1969; MA, U. N.C., 1971, PhD, 1979. Policy analyst Heritage found., Washington, 1977-81; legis. asst. U.S. Senator John P. East, Washington, 1981-86; editorial writer Washington Times, 1986-87, dep. editorial page editor, 1987-91, acting editorial page editor, 1991, columnist, 1991-95; pres. Ctr. for Nat. Rsch., Alexandria, Va., 1995—. Author: Soviet Strategy of Terror, 1981, Power and History: The Political Thought of James Burnham, 1984, rev. edit., 1999, Beautiful Losers: Essays on the Failure of American Conservatism, 1994, Revolution from the Middle, 1997, America Extinguished, 2002; contbg. editor Chronicles: A Mag. of Am. Culture, Rockford, Ill., 1987-2003, polit. edit.r, 2003—; editor-in-chief Citizen's Informer; assoc editor Occidental Quarterly, 2001. Nat. bd. dirs. Coun. of Conservative Citizens, 1995—. Recipient Disting. Editorial Writing award Am. Soc. Newspaper Editors, 1988, 89. Mem. The Phila. Soc. (bd. dirs. 1989-93), The John Randolph Club (bd. dirs.), Phi Kappa Psi. Office: PO Box 19627 Alexandria VA 22320-0627

FRANCIS, TIMOTHY DUANE, chiropractor; b. Chgo., Mar. 1, 1956; s. Joseph Duane and Barbara Jane (Sigwalt) F. Student, U. Nev., 1974-80, We. Nev. C.C., 1978; BS, L.A. Coll. Chiropractic, 1982, Dr. of Chiropractic magna cum laude, 1984; postgrad., Clark County C.C., 1986—; MS in Bio/Nutrition, U. Bridgeport, 1990. Diplomate Internat. Coll. Applied Kinesiology, Am. Acad. Pain Mgmt., Am. Naturopathic Med. Bd.; cert. kinesiologist, applied kinesiology tchr.; lic. chiropractor, Calif., Nev. Instr. dept. recreation and phys. edn. U. Nev., Reno, 1976-80; from tchng. asst. to lead instr. dept. principles & practice L.A. Coll. Chiropractic, 1983-85; pvt. practice Las Vegas, 1985—. Asst. instr. Internat. Coll. Applied Kinesiology, 1990, chmn. exam review com., 1993, chmn. syllabus review com., 1994; adj. faculty The Union Inst. Coll. of Undergrad. Studies, 1993; joint study participant Nat. Olympic Tng. Ctr., Beijing, China, 1990. Mem. edit. rev. bd. Alternative Medicine Rev., 1996; contbr. articles to profl. jours. including Internat. Coll. Applied Kinesiology. Charles F. Cutts scholar, 1980. Fellow Internat. Acad. Clin. Acupuncture, British Inst. Homeopathy (homeopathy diploma 1993); mem. Am. Chiropractic Assn. (couns. on sports injuries, nutrition, roentgenology, technic, and mental health), Nev. State Chiropractic Assn., Nat. Strength and Conditioning Assn., Gonsted Clin. Studies Soc., Found. for Chiropractic Edn. and Rsch., Internat. Chiropractors Assn., Internat. Coll. Applied Kinesiology, Internat. Fedn. Practitioners Natural Therapeutics, Nat. Inst. Chiropractic Rsch., Nat. Strength and Conditioning Assn., Am. Naturopathic Med. Assn., Nat. Acad. Rsch. Biochemists, Phi Beta Kappa, Phi Kappa Phi (v.p. 1979-80, Scholar of the Yr. award, 1980), Delta Sigma. Republican. Catholic. Avocations: Karate, weight-lifting. Home: 2620 Regatta Dr # 102Ste 100 Las Vegas NV 89128

FRANCIS, WALTON JOSEPH, economist; b. Washington, July 19, 1942; s. Robert Joseph and Margaret Karen (Bittner) F.; m. Frances Leiko Enseki, June 9, 1969 (div. May 1988); children: Margaret Misao, Elizabeth Hanako; m. Sarah Willis Wilcox, Sept. 9, 1989. BA with highest distinction, Ind. U., 1963; MA,

Yale U., 1964; MPA, Harvard U., 1971, M in Pub. Policy, 1972. Budget examiner Office Mgmt. and Budget, Washington, 1964-70; dir. policy analysis Office of Sec. HHS, Washington, 1972-97; economist, cons., 1997—. Author: CHECKBOOK'S Guide to Health Insurance Plans for Federal Employees, ann. edit., 1979—. Woodrow Wilson fellow, 1964. Mem. Phi Beta Kappa. Home and Office: 5700 Robeys Meadow Ln Fairfax VA 22030-5833 E-mail: waltonjf@aol.com.

FRANCISCHINE, JANICE MARIE, pediatrics nurse; b. Bronx, N.Y., Sept. 14, 1966; d. Ronald James and Veronica Louise (Gorga) F. BSN, Molloy Coll., 1988; MS, SUNY, Stony Brook, 1994. Cert. BLS instr., ACLS instr., PALS instr., trauma nursing care course, Am. Heart Assn., pediat. nurse practioner, orthopaedic nursing. Staff nurse adult medicine oncology L.I. Jewish Med. Ctr., New Hyde Park, N.Y., 1988-90, staff nurse adult ICU, 1990, staff nurse pediatric emergency rm., 1990—, mem. scheduling com., 1992, asst. nursing care coord. pediatric emergency rm., 1992-95; PNP Office of Dr. Louis O. Pupo, MD, Bronx, N.Y., 1994-97; pediatric nurse practitioner in pediatric orthopedics L.I. Jewish Med. Ctr., New Hyde Park, N.Y., 1997-2000, nurse eductor, emergency dept., 2000—; prof. nursing Molloy Coll., 2002—. Trainer BLS instr., Hazmat awareness, Hazmat oper. level, Critical incident support mgmt. Author: The Nurse Practioner, 1999. Mem. NAPNAP (pres. L.I. chpt.), Emergency Nursing Assn., Nat. Assn. PNPs, L.I. Assn. Nurse Practitioners (pres. 2001), Nat. Assn. Orthopedic Nursing (pres. 1999—), L.I. Spine Club, Sigma Theta Tau. Roman Catholic. Home: 5 Birchwood Ct Apt 4N Mineola NY 11501 Office: LI Jewish Med Ctr Lakeville Rd New Hyde Park NY 11040

FRANCISCO, DEBORAH ANTOSH, educational administrative professional; b. Wilkes-Barre, Pa, Mar. 8, 1952; d. Albert and Marie Iris (Stuka) Antosh; m. John Thomas McCauley, Sept. 11, 1970 (div. Sept. 1983); 1 child, John-Austen; m. John Patrick Francisco, July 28, 1988; 1 child, Theresa. BA, Cedar Crest Coll., Allentown, Pa., 1984; EdM in Ednl. Adminstrn., Rutgers U., 2003. Cert. elem. tchr., Pa.; cert. elem. and nursery sch. tchr., N.J. Elem. tchr. Allentown Sch. Dist., 1984-88; tchr. basic skills Perth Amboy Sch. Dist., NJ, 1988-89, elem. tchr., 1989—90; tchr. St. Matthias, Somerset, NJ, 1993—96; order processor divsn. housing and confs. Rutgers U., 1997—99, asst. mgr. adminstrn. Coll. Ave. campus, 1999—. Democrat. Roman Catholic. Home: 14 Canadian Woods Rd Marlboro NJ 07746-1672

FRANCISCO, WAYNE, automotive executive; b. June 14, 1943; s. George Lewis and Helen M. (Markland) F.; m. Susan Francisco; children: Diana Lynn, W. Michael. Student, Ohio State U., 1962-63; BS in Mktg. and Acctg., U. Cin., 1967. Unit sales mgr. Procter & Gamble, Cin., 1967-69; mktg. mgr. Nat. Mktg. Inc., Cin., 1969-70; pres. Retail Petroleum Marketers, Inc., Cin., 1970-72, chmn. bd., CEO Phoenix, 1972-85, DMC Industries, Inc., 1985-99. Pres., CEO Cassia Petroleum Corp., Vancouver, B.C., Can., 1980-84; bd. dirs. P.F.K. Enterprises, F.I.C. Inc., Internat. Investment and Fin. Enterprises, Inc., Alpha Realty, Inc. Class agt. 62G Culver Mil. Acad., 1958-62. Mem. Culver Legion, bd. trustees, 1990—; mem. Phoenix Bd. Appeals, 1978-80; v.p. Cuernavaca Homeowners Assn., 1982, pres., 1983-86. Recipient Image Maker award Shell Oil Co., 1979, Top Performer award Phoenix dist. Shell Oil Co., 1979, 80. Mem. Petroleum Retailers Ariz. (pres. 1977-79), Nat. Congress Petroleum Retailers (adv. bd.), Automotive Svc. Excellence (cert.), Studebaker Drivers Club (zone coord. Pacific S.W. 1983, nat. v.p. 1986, 87, 88, nat. pres. 1989-90, Grand Canyon chpt. pres. 1986), Avanti Owners Assn. (nat. bd. dirs. 1975-96, internat. pres. 1986-89), Eugene C. Eppley Club, Optimists (bd. dirs. Paradise Valley club 1984, sec.-treas. 1984). Republican. Fax: 820-948-4535.

FRANCK, ARDATH AMOND, psychologist; b. Wehrum, Pa., May 5, 1925; d. Arthur and Helen Lucille (Sharp) Amond; m. Frederick M. Franck, Mar. 18, 1945; children: Sheldon, Candace. B.S. in Edn., Kent State U., 1946, M.A., 1947; Ph.D., Western Res. U., 1956. Cert. high sch. tchr., elem. supr., sch. psychologist, speech and hearing therapist. Instr., Western Res. U., Cleve., summer 1953, U. Akron, 1947-50; sch. psychologist Summit County Schs., Ohio, 1950-60; cons. psychologist Wadsworth Pub. Schs., Ohio, 1946-86; dir. Akron Speech & Reading Ctr., Ohio, 1950—; pres. Twirling Unlimited; cons., dir. Hobbitts Pre-Sch., 1973-88. Author: Your Child Learns, 1976. Pres. Twirling Unltd., 1982—. Mem. Am. Speech and Hearing Assn., Internat. Reading Assn., Ohio Psychol. Assn., Mensa, Soroptomist (Akron). Home: 631 Ghent Rd Akron OH 44333-2629 Office: Akron Speech & Reading Ctr 700 Ghent Rd Akron OH 44333-2698

FRANCK, FREDERICK SIGFRED, artist, author, dental surgeon; b. Maastricht, The Netherlands, Apr. 12, 1909; came to U.S., 1939, naturalized, 1945; s. Daniel and Helen (Foyer) F.; m. Claske Berndes Franck, July 15, 1960; 1 son, Lukas van Witsen Franck. Student, U. Amsterdam, 1926-31; Chirurgien Dentiste, Antwerp Dental Sch., 1935; LDS, Royal Coll. Surgeons, Edinburgh, Scotland, 1937; DMD, U. Pitts., 1942, DFA (hon.), 1963; ArtsD (hon.), Mt. St. Mary Coll., 1994. Practice dentistry, London, 1937-39; resident oral surgery U. Pitts., 1942-44; anaesthetist Elizabeth Steel Magee Hosp.; staff Children's Hosp., Pitts., 1942-44; service cons. Netherlands East Indies govt., 1944-46; dentist N.Y.C., 1946-66; vis. staff Albert Schweitzer Hosp., 1958-60. Chief mission Med. Internat. Coop., 1958; research fellow Nanzan U., Nagoya, 1981 Author: Open Wide, Please, 1957, Au Pays de Soleil, 1958, Days with Albert Schweitzer, A Lambarene Landscape, 1959, reissued 1992, (juvenile) My Friend in Africa, 1960, reissued 1995, African Sketchbook, 1961, My Eye is in Love, 1963 (Art Am. 50th Anniversary spl. citation 1963), Au Fil de L'Eau, 1964, Outsider in the Vatican, 1965, Met Het Oog Op Het Vatikaan, 1965, Au Pays Du Soleil, 1965, I Love Life, 1967, Exploding Church, 1968, Open Boek, 1967, Au Fil De L'Eau, 1968, Croquis Parisiens, 1969, Tutte le Strade portano a Roma, 1969, Le Paris de Simenon, 1969, Simenon's Paris, 1970, Tussen Broek en Brooklyn, 1971, The Zen of Seeing, 1973, Pilgrimage to Now/Here, 1973, (play) Inquest on a Crucifixion, 1975, An Encounter with Oomoto, 1975, The Book of Angelus Silesius, 1976, Zen and Zen Classics, 1977, EveryOne, The Timeless Myth of Everyman Reborn, 1978, The Awakened Eye, 1979, Art as a Way, A Return to the Spiritual Roots, 1981, The Buddha Eye, An Anthology of the Kyoto School, 1982, The Supreme Koan, Confessions of a Journey Inward, 1982, Messenger of the Heart, The Book of Angelus Silesius, 1982, De Zen van het Zien, 1983, 92, Echoes from the Bottomless Well, 1985, De Droomzolder--Oog in Oog met Venetie, 1985, Life Drawing Life, 1989, Little Compendium on that Which Matters, 1989, reissued 1993, To Be Human Against All Odds, 1991, reissued 1996, Zen Seeing, Zen Drawing: Meditation in Action, 1993, Fingers Pointing Toward the Sacred, 1994, The Tao of the Cross, 1996; co-author What Does It Mean to be Human?, 1998, 2000, Beyond Hiroshima, 1999, Watching the Vatican, 2000, Pacem In Terris A Love Story, 2000, Moments of Seeing, 2000, Seeing Venice: An Eye in Love, 2002, A Passion for Seeing, 2003; contbg. editor Parabola Quar.; rsch. editor Nanzan Monograph Series; contbr. articles, drawings to various mags. and periodicals; one-man shows include Contemporary Arts Gallery, Lilienfield Galleries, Passedoit Gallery, Albert Landry Gallery, (all N.Y.C.), 1959-60, Saginaw (Mich.) Mus., Doll & Richards Gallery, Boston, Ringling Mus. Art, M.H. De Young Mus., San Francisco, Waddell Gallery, Far Gallery, both N.Y.C., Foster-White Gallery, Seattle, 1976, U. Puget Sound Gallery, Seattle, 1977, Thorpe Intermedia Gallery, N.Y.C., 1977, The InterFaith Ctr., N.Y.C., 2000, others; shows in Paris, Amsterdam, Geneva, London, Rotterdam, Brussels, Rome, Tokyo, Kyoto, 1971, U. Maine, 1970-72, Melbourne, Australia, 1972, Interchurch Ctr. Gallery, 1972, Greater Middletown Arts Coun., 1973, Far Gallery, 1973, Singer Meml. Mus., The Netherlands, 1986, Pa. State U., 1989, Cathedral of St. John the Divine, N.Y.C., 1993, Albert Schweitzer Ctr., Great Barrington, Mass., 1993, Quinnipiac Coll., Hamden, Conn., 1994, Amber Gallery, Leiden, The Netherlands, 1994, Van Rijn Gallery, Maastricht, The Netherlands, 1994, Oude Kerk, Amsterdam, The Netherlands, 1994, Paul Mellon Arts Ctr. Choate Rosemary Hall, Wallingford, Conn., 1996; touring exhbn. Drawings of Lambarene, Albert Schweitzer's Hospital in Action, 1995, 96, 97, 98, Cathedral of St. John the Divine, N.Y.C., Newark, 1996, Weimar Gallery, Germany, 1999, Vanderbilt Gallery U. Tenn.; group shows include Met. Mus., Whitney Mus., Corcoran Biennale, Indpls. Mus., Mpls. Mus., Nanzan U. Mus., Nagoya, Japan, 1981; represented in permanent collections including M.H. De Young Mus., Fogg Art Mus., San Francisco Mus. U. Ill., Mus. Modern Art, The Vatican, Witherspoon Gallery, Raleigh, N.C., Tokyo Nat. Mus., Nat. Collection Fine Arts, Washington, Santa Barbara Mus., Amsterdam, Eindhoven, Maastricht, N.Y. Pub. Libr., Seattle Mus., Dartmouth Coll., Cornell U., Aschenbach Found., Ga. Mus., Whitney Mus., N.Y.U., State Capitol Mus., Wash., Fordham U. Lowenstein Gallery, Roanoke Mus. Fine Arts, Cathedral of St. John the Divine, N.Y.C., U. Nymegen, The Netherlands, U. Pa., Kans. State U., New Harmony, Ind., Cath. Ctr., Stedelijk Mus., Bonnefanten Mus., Musées Nationaux Français, Nanzan U., Santa Barbara Mus., others; traveling exhbn. to 12 univs. and colls., 1970-72, to The Netherlands and Belgium, 1991, 92; drawing exhbn. Amber Gallery, Leiden, Holland, 1999; built Pacem in Terris Trans-religious Sanctuary, Warwick, N.Y., 1966; steel sculptures commd. Genesis Farm, N.J., 1990, Omega Inst., N.Y., 1991, Pa. State U., 1991, Ch. of Saviour, Washington, 1991, Wainwright House, Rye, N.Y., 1991, Fondacion Elpis, Buenos Aires, 1991, Cath. St. John the Divine, N.Y.C., Bucknell U., Peace Garden, Harrisburg, Pa., Hengelo, The Netherlands, 1993, Sarajevo, 1994, Belgium, 1995, New Cmty. Corp., Newark, 1995, Choate Rosemary Hall, Wallingford, Conn., 1995, Santa Cruz, Calif., 1995, Ittoen Found., Kyoto, Japan, 1997, Assisi, Italy, Dandelion Trust, England, Bosnia, Sarajevo. Bd. dirs. St. Francis Assisi, Italy, 1999, Mount Saviour, Elmira, NY, 2001, Gannon U., Erie, Pa., 2001, Pitts., 2002. Recipient award of Excellence, Chapmen U. and Albert Schweitzer Inst., 1995, purchase prize, U. Ill., Am. Inst. Arts Letters, Living Arts Found., 1st prize Garnegie Inst., prize, Musees Nationaux Francais, medal for drawings, Pope John XXIII, 1963, Revered Citizen award, Orange County, N.Y., 2000, Ruth Bayley Peace award, PeaceLinks, 2000, Disting Citizen award, Warwick, N.Y., 2000, Ut Diligatis Invicem award, Gannon U., 2001, World Citizen award, Nuclear Age Peace Found., Santa Barbara, Calif., 2001, Spirituality and Health award, 2001. Fellow Internat. Inst. Arts and Letters, Soc. for Arts, Religion and Contemporary Culture (dir.), Knighthood Order of Orange Nassau; mem. Artists Equity Assn. (hon. dir. N.Y.), P.E.N. Home: Pacem in Terris 96 Covered Bridge Rd Warwick NY 10990-2854 *I discovered that to defy the general trend towards specialization as a writer, painter, draughtsman, playwright, sculptor, does not mean "to spread oneself thin", is only seemingly a multiple commitment, and is in my case a single-minded obedience to what my very nature bids me to express in any medium I can handle.*

FRANCK, THOMAS MARTIN, law educator; b. Berlin, July 14, 1931; naturalized, 1977; s. Hugo and Ilse (Rosenthal) F. BA, U. B.C., 1952, LLB, 1953, LLD (hon.), 1995; LLM, Harvard U., 1954, SJD, 1956; DHL (hon.), Monterey Inst. Internat. Studies, 2003. Asst. prof. law U. Nebr., 1954-56; from assoc. prof. to prof. law NYU, 1960—2002, prof. law emeritus, 2002—, dir. Ctr. Internat. Studies, 1965—2002; judge ad hoc Internat. Ct. Justice, 2001—02. Acting dir. internat. law Carnegie Endowment Internat. Peace, 1973-75, dir., 1975-79; vis. prof. Stanford U., 1963, U. East Africa, 1964, 65, York U. Osgoode Hall Law Sch., 1972-73, 74-76; dir. rsch. UN Inst. Tng. and Rsch., 1980-82; cons. U.S. AID Dept. State, 1970-72, 85; constl. adviser govts. Tanganyika, 1963, Zanzibar, 1963, 64, Mauritius, 1965; mem. Sierra Leone Govt. Commn. Legal Edn., 1964, Nat. Liberal Adv. Coun. Can., 1952-53; lectr. Woodrow Wilson Sch., Princeton U., 1979, Hague Acad. Internat. Law, 1993; vis. fellow Trinity Coll., Cambridge, Eng., 1996-97. Author: Race and Nationalism, 1960, The United Nations in the Congo, 1963, East African Unity Through Law, 1965, Comparative Constitutional Process, 1968, The Structure of Impartiality, 1968, Why Federations Fail, 1968, A Free Trade Association, 1968, Word Politics, 1971, Secrecy and Foreign Policy, 1973, Resignation in Protest, 1975, Control of Sea Resources by Semi-Autonomous States, 1978, Foreign Policy by Congress, 1979, The Tethered Presidency, 1981, Human Rights in Third World Perspective, 1982, Nation Against Nation: What Happened to the U.N. Dream and What the U.S. Can Do About It, 1985, Judging the World Court, 1986, Foreign Relations and National Security Law, 1987, The Power of Legitimacy Among Nations, 1990, Political Questions/Judicial Answers, 1992, Fairness in the International Legal and Institutional System, 1993, Fairness In International Law and Institutions, 1995, The Empowered Self: Law and Society in the Age of Individualism, 1999, Recourse to Force: State Action Against Threats and Armed Attacks, 2002; co-author: U.S. Foreign Relations Law, vols. I-III, 1980-81, vols. IV & V, 1984, Foreign Relations and National Security Law, 2d edit., 1993; editor-in-chief Am. Jour. Internat. Law, 1984-93; editor: Delegating State Powers: The Effect of Treaty Regimes on Democracy and Sovereignty, 2000; co-editor: Internat. Law Decisions in Nat. Cts., 1996. Lt. Can. Army, 1953. Guggenheim fellow, 1973-74, 82-83 Mem. Inst. de Droit Internat., State Dept. Adv. Com. on Internat. Law, Can. Coun. Internat. Law, African Law Assn., Assn. Am. Law Schs., Am. Soc. Internat. Law (pres. 1998-2000), Am. Acad. Arts and Scis., Internat. Law Assn. (v.p. U.S. br.), Coun. on Fgn. Rels. Home: 15 Charlton St New York NY 10014-4910

FRANCK, WALTER ALFRED, rheumatologist, medical administrator, educator; b. Shanghai, Sept. 2, 1941; s. August Albert and Hilda Sylvia (Vandamme) F.; m. Linda Ashley Callanen, June 6, 1964; children: Christopher, Patrick, Kevin, Natalee. BA, Yale U., 1960; MD, Columbia U., 1964. Intern U. Mich., Ann Arbor, 1964-65, resident in medicine, 1965-68; fellow in rheumatology Harvard U./Mass. Gen. Hosp., Boston, 1971-73; attending physician in medicine and rheumatology Mary Imogene Bassett Hosp., Cooperstown, N.Y., 1973—, chief of medicine, 1980—; prof. clin. medicine Columbia U., N.Y.C., 1981—, assoc. dean Bassett Healthcare-Coll. Physicians and Surgeons, 1998—. Adj. prof. clin. medicine Rochester (N.Y.) Sch. Medicine, Albany (N.Y.) Sch. Medicine, Dartmouth Sch. Medicine, Hanover, N.Y., SUNY, Syracuse. Contbr. numerous articles to profl. publs. Trustee, mem. fin. com. St. Mary's Ch., Cooperstown, 1991—. Maj. U.S. Army, 1968-71. Fellow ACP, Am. Coll. Rheumatology. Roman Catholic. Avocations: philately, gardening, fishing, hiking. Home: 6 Lakeview Dr S Cooperstown NY 13326-3003 Office: Bassett Hosp 1 Atwell Rd Cooperstown NY 13326-1394

FRANCKE, GLORIA NIEMEYER, pharmacist, editor, publisher; b. Dillsboro, Ind., Apr. 28, 1922; d. Albert B. and Fannie K. (Libbert) Niemeyer; m. Donald Eugene Francke, Apr. 15, 1956. BS in Pharmacy, Purdue U., 1942; PharmD (hon.), 1988—; PharmD, U. Cin., 1971; postgrad., U. Mich., 1945. Pharmacist Dillsboro Drug Store, 1943-44; instr. Sch. Pharmacy Purdue U., Lafayette, Ind., 1943; asst. to chief pharmacist U. Mich. Hosp., Ann Arbor, 1944-46; assoc. editor Am. Jour. Hosp. Pharmacy, Washington, 1944-64; asst. dir. divsn. hosp. pharmacy Am. Pharm. Assn., Washington, 1946-56; exec. sec. Am. Soc. Hosp. Pharmacists, Ann Arbor, 1949-60, acting dir. dept. comm. Washington, 1963-64; drug lit. specialist Nat. Libr. Medicine, Bethesda, Md., 1965-67; clin. pharmacy tchg. coord. VA Hosp., Cin., 1967-71; asst. clin. prof. clin. pharmacy Coll. Pharmacy U. Cin., 1967-71; chief program evaluation br. Alcohol & Drug Dependence Svc. VA Ctrl. Office, Washington, 1971-75; dir. Pharmacy Intelligence Ctr. Am. Pharm. Assn., Washington, 1975-85. Mem. Roche Hosp. Pharmacy Adv. Bd., 1971-74; judge for ann. Lunsford Richardson Pharmacy awards, 1963, 64; mem. com. stds. for drug abuse treatment and rehab. programs Joint Commn. Accreditation of Hosps., 1974-75. Author: (with D.E. Francke, C.J. Latiolais and N.F.H. Ho) Mirror to Hospital Pharmacy, 1964; contbr. articles to profl. jours. Bd. dirs., mem. found., co-chair women's bd. Ingleside Presbyn. Retirement Cmty., Washington., 1999—. Recipient Harvey A.K. Whitney award Mich. Soc. Hosp. Pharmacists, 1953, Disting. Alumnus award Purdue U. Sch. Pharmacy, 1985, Remington Honor medal, 1987, Career Achievement award Profl. Frat. Assn., 1991, Fedn. Internat. Pharm. Lifetime Achievement in the Practice of Pharmacy award, 1996; also various commendations. Mem. Internat. Pharm. Fedn., Am. Inst. History of Pharmacy (exec. sec. 1968-78), Tex. Soc. Hosp. Pharmacists (hon.), Am. Pharm. Assn. (hon. chmn. 1986, Gloria Niemeyer Francke Leadership Mentor award named in her honor 1995), Am. Soc. Hosp. Pharmacists (Donald E. Francke medal 1995), Kappa Epsilon, Rho Chi. Presbyterian. Home and Office: Apt 441B 4000 Cathedral Ave NW Washington DC 20016-5289 E-mail: glor238@aol.com.

FRANCKE, LINDA BIRD, journalist; b. N.Y.C., Mar. 14, 1939; d. Samuel Curtis and Janet (King) Bird; m. G.D. Mackenzie, Jan. 12, 1961; 1 son, Andrew Mackenzie; m. Albert Francke III, Oct. 7, 1967; 2 daughters: Caitlin, Tapp. Student, Bradford Jr. Coll., 1958, New Sch. for Social Rsch., 1963—65. Copywriter Young & Rubicam, Inc., N.Y.C., 1960-63, Ogilvy & Mather, Inc., N.Y.C., 1965-67; contbg. editor N.Y. Mag., N.Y.C., 1968-72, 80—; gen. editor Newsweek Mag., N.Y.C., 1972-77; columnist N.Y. Times, 1977—; TV news commentator Spl. Edit., 1978-79. Dir. New Directions; juror Am. Book Awards, 1981; Co-chmn. Writer's Resource Center, Southampton, N.Y. Contbr. (works to anthologies including) The N.Y. Spy, 1967, The Power Game, 1970, Running Against the Machine, 1969, Women: A Book for Men, 1979, Hers: Through Women's Eyes, 1985, America Firsthand, Vol. II: From Reconstruction to the Present, 1994; author: The Ambivalence of Abortion, 1978, Growing Up Divorced, 1983, Ground Zero: The Gender Wars in the Military, 1997; collaborator: First Lady from Plains, 1984, Ferraro: My Story, 1985, A Woman of Egypt, 1987, Daughter of Destiny, 1989, Signature Life, 1998, Life So Far, 2000, On Faith, 2002. Mem. Women's Commn. for Refugee Women and Children, Internat. Rescue Com. Inc.; chmn. East End Choice; candidate N.Y. State Assembly, 2d Dist., 1990; del. to Dem. Nat. Conv., 1992; bd. dirs. Bridgehampton Child Care & Recreational Ctr., Inc., The Retreat. Recipient award Cannes Film Festival, 1969, Nat. Clarion award, 1994; finalist Helen Bernstein Book award Excellence in Journalism, 1998. Mem. Authors Guild, Women's Media Group N.Y.C., Eastville Hist. Soc., Women Mil. Aviators, Inc.

FRANCKE, UTA, medical geneticist, genetics researcher, educator; b. Wiesbaden, Germany, Sept. 9, 1942; arrived in U.S., 1969; d. Kurt and Gertrud Muller; m. Bertold Richard Francke, May 27, 1967 (div. 1982); m. Heinz Furthmayr, July 27, 1986. MD, U. Munich, Fed. Republic Germany, 1967; MS, Yale U., 1985. Diplomate Am. Bd. Pediatrics, Am. Bd. Med. Genetics (bd. dirs. 1981-84). Asst. prof. U. Calif., San Diego, 1973—78; assoc. prof. Yale U., New Haven, 1978—85, prof., 1985—88; prof. genetics Stanford (Calif.) U., 1989—2000. Investigator Howard Hughes Med. Inst., Stanford, 1989—, mem. sci. rev. bd., Bethesda, Md., 1986—88; mem. mammalian genetics study sect. NIH, Bethesda, 1990—94. Profl. advisor March of Dimes Birth Defects Found., White Plains, NY, 1990, Marfan Assn., Port Washington, NY, 1991. Mem.: Am. Soc. Human Genetics (pres. 1999, bd. dirs. Rockville, Md. chpt. 1981—84), Soc. for Inherited Metabolic Disorders, Soc. for Pediatric Rsch., Human Genome Orgn., Inst. Medicine of NAS (assoc.). Avocation: piloting. Office: Stanford U Med Sch Beckman Ctr Stanford CA 94305-5323 E-mail: francke@cmgm.stanford.edu.

FRANCL, MICHELLE, chemist, educator; b. New Orleans, La., Apr. 12, 1958; d. Eugene James and Lois Cullen Miller; m. Victor Jose Donnay, Sept. 5, 1992; children: Michael Donnay, Christopher Donnay; m. Thomas John Francl, Aug. 16, 1981 (dec. Apr. 16, 1987). BA, U. Calif., Irvine, 1979, PhD, 1983. Prof. Bryn Mawr Coll., Pa., 1986—. Mem.: Am. Chem. Soc. (councilor 1999—, chair sucession 2003—). Office: Bryn Mawr Coll 101 N Merion Ave Bryn Mawr PA 19010 Office Fax: 610-526-5086. E-mail: mfrancl@brynmawr.edu.

FRANCO, ADOLFO ALBERTO, federal agency administrator, lawyer; b. Cardenas, Matazanas, Cuba, Jan. 23, 1956; came to U.S., 1961; s. Adolfo M. and Miriam (Mesa) F. BA in History, U. No. Iowa, 1978, MA in History, 1980; JD cum laude, Creighton U., 1983. Bar: D.C. 1984, Mo. 1983. Atty. Shughart, Thomson & Kilroy, Kansas City, Mo., 1983-84, Cole & Corelte, P.A., Washington, 1984-85; dep. gen. counsel Inter-Am. Found., Arlington, Va., 1985-93, gen. counsel, 1993—; asst. adminr. bur. for latin america and caribbean USAID, Washington, 2002—. Office: USAID Bur for Latin America and Caribbean RRB 1300 Pennsylvania Ave NW Washington DC 20523-5900 Office Fax: 202-216-3012.

FRANCO, ANNEMARIE WOLETZ, editor; b. Somerville, N.J., Sept. 18, 1933; d. Frederick Franz and Bertha (Laugginger) Woletz; m. Frederick Nicholas Franco, June 11, 1977 (dec. Feb. 1998). Student, Wood Coll. of Bus. Editorial asst. Internat. Musician, then assoc. editor, 1965-88, ret., 1988. Republican. Presbyterian. Avocations: writing, music, cooking, travel. Home: 166 Wellstone Dr Palm Coast FL 32164-4111

FRANCO, ANTHONY M. public relations executive; b. Detroit, July 7, 1933; s. John Richard and Evelyn Louise F.; m. Melissa R. Rohde, Aug. 27, 1983; children: Catherine, Suzanne, Anne, Anthony, Patricia, Michael, David, Meredith, Christopher. Student, U.S. Naval Acad., 1955-57; BS, Wayne State U., 1958. Dir. pub. rels. Dawson-Murray Advt., Detroit, 1958-60, Fred M. Randall Co., Detroit, 1960-62, Denman & Baker Advt., Detroit, 1962-64; founder, chmn. Anthony M. Franco, Inc., Detroit, 1964-95; editl. dir. WJBK-TV (Fox), 1994-97. Bd. dirs. Ziebart Internat., Cmty. Found. Collier County, Fla., The Cmty. Sch. Naples, Fla.; adj. prof. grad. sch. Walsh Coll., Mich.; cons. Broad, Vogt and Conant; cons. Stone, August, Medrich Co. Past trustee Marygrove Coll., Detroit; trustee U. Detroit, Cmty. Sch. Naples (Fla.), Cmty. Found. Collier County (Fla.); corp. bd. dirs. Boys Clubs Met. Detroit, 1972-87; emcee Celebrity Night fundraising dinner, St. Joseph Mercy-Oakland Hosp.; pres. Met. Detroit coun. Boy Scouts Am., 1985; chmn. Channel 56, 1988-90; bd. dirs. Mich. Libr. Found., 1988-95, Mich. Hist. Found.; bd. dirs. Alma (Mich.) Coll. Comms. Ctr. at St. Joseph Mercy-Oakland Hosp. named in his honor; named one of 100 superstars in pub. rels. Pub. Rels. Quarterly, 1990. Mem. Internat. Pub. Rels. Group of Cos. (v.p., dir.), Pub. Rels. Soc. Am. (pres. 1986, dir. Detroit chpt., pres. 1974, chmn. east ctrl. dist.), Mich. C. of C., Greater Detroit C. of C. (vice-chmn. exec. com., chmn. 1990-91), U.S. Naval Acad. Alumni Assn., Bloomfield Open Hunt Club (pres. bd. dirs.), Royal Poinciana Golf Club, Bloomfield Hills Country Club, McAuley Club. Presbyterian. Home: 6621 George Washington Way Naples FL 34108-8222 E-mail: tony2k@hotmail.com.

FRANCO, CAROLE ANN, international consultant; b. Hartford, Conn., Dec. 21, 1948; d. Nicholas Lawrence and Mary Elizabeth (LaRosa) F. BA in Spanish, Duke U., 1970; grad. cert. in edn., Trinity Coll., Hartford, 1971; postgrad. in French, Sorbonne, Paris, 1980; M Internat. Rels., Cambridge (Eng.) U., 1981. Tchr. West Hartford (Conn.) Pub. Schs., 1970-76; researcher on biography of Sumner Welles Washington, 1976-77; adminstr. Ctr. for Strategic and Internat. Studies, Washington, 1978-79; broker, mgr. Parks Capital Mgmt., N.Y.C., 1981-83; assoc., cons. Burgess Mgmt. Assocs., N.Y.C., 1984-88; producer, owner Kingdom Prodns., New Paltz, N.Y., 1988-93; internat. cons. Strategic Ptnrs. Internat., New Paltz, 1993-96, 99—, Lady Mayoress of City of Westminster, London, 1996-97. Mem. Duke U. Alumni Assn. N.Y., Cambridge U. Alumni Assn. N.Y. (founder, bd. dirs. 1987—), United Oxford-Cambridge U. Club (London), Pilgrims. Republican. Roman Catholic. Home: 79 Two Stone Dr Wethersfield CT 06109-4167 E-mail: cfr7217964@aol.com.

FRANCO, CHARLES, language educator; b. Italy, Dec. 9, 1941; arrived in U.S., 1971; m. Nina Franco; children: Marco, Flavia. PhD, Rutgers U., 1977. Chmn. Dept. European Langs. Stony Brook (N.Y.) U., 1998—. Author: La Beatrice di Dante, 1981, Arte e Poesia net RCD-Barbaino, 1982; editor: Dante, Summa Medievalis, 1995. Office: European Lang Dept SUNY at Stony Brook 100 Nicolls Rd Stony Brook NY 11794-0002

FRANCO, ELAINE ADELE, librarian; b. N.Y.C., Jan. 24, 1948; d. Alexander and Sarah Eleanor (Johnson) Franco; m. James Paul Webster, Dec. 29, 1982 (dec. Sept. 1993). BA magna cum laude, Hope Coll., Holland, Mich., 1969; MLS, U. Mich., 1975, MA, 1976. Cataloger U. Nebr.-Lincoln Librs., 1977-81, prin. cataloger, 1981-90, Shields Libr., U. Calif., Davis, 1990—. Bibliographer: MLA International Bibliography, 1979—, First Printings of American Authors, 1977-79; editor conf. procs. Recipient Disting. Svc award Nebr. Libr. Assn. Coll. and Univ. Sect. 1984. Mem. MLA, ALA (councilor-at-large 1987-91), Calif. Libr. Assn. (pres. access, collections and tech. svcs. sect. 1998-99), Calif. Acad. and Rsch. Librs., Beta Phi Mu. Office: U Calif Shields Libr 100 NW Quad Davis CA 95616-5292 E-mail: eafranco@ucdavis.edu.

FRANCO, JAMES, actor; Actor, 1993—. Actor: (TV series) Freaks and Geeks, 1999; (films) Never Been Kissed, 1999, Whatever It Takes, 2000, At Any Cost, 2000, If Tomorrow Comes, 2000, Some Body, 2001, James Dean, 2001, Mean People Suck, 2001, Blind Spot, 2001, Spider-Man, 2002, Deuces Wild, 2002, City by the Sea, 2002, Sonny, 2002. Office: Miles Levy-James/Levy/Jacobson Mgmt 3500 W Olive Ave Ste 920 Burbank CA 91505

FRANCO, OMAR, governmental relations administrator; b. Miami, Fla., Oct. 11, 1965; s. Israel and Gloria (Santamaria) F.; m. Adria Elena Franco, Aug. 16, 1997; children: Alyssa Nicole and Andrew Joseph (twins). AA, Miami-Dade C.C., 1985; BA in English and Bus., Fla. State U., 1988; postgrad., Fla. Internat. U., 2002—. Registered legis. lobbyist, Notary Pub. Dist. legis. asst. Rep. Art Simon, Miami, 1993-94; campaign mgr. Annie Betancourt Re-election Campaign, Miami, 1996; dist. legis. asst. Rep. Annie Betancourt, Miami, 1994-96; dist. sr. legis. asst. Sen. Mario Diaz-Balart, Miami, 1996-98; field office dir. Fla. Med. Assn., Tallahassee, 1998-99; dir. govt. rels. Sch. Medicine, U. Miami, 1999—2001, asst. v.p. govtl. rels., 2001—03; chief of staff Congressman Mario Diaz-Balart, 2003—. Pub. policy and advocacy com. U. Miami Mailman Ctr., 2000—02; mem. Miami-Dade Alliance for Aging, 2003. Mem. Leadership Miami; mem. Hispanic Leadership Tng. Program Cuban Am. Nat. Coun., 1996; mem. bd. dirs. Kendall Fedn. Homeowner's Assn., Miami, 1996—2000; v.p. Kendall Lakes Master Condominium Assn., Miami, 1998—2001; mem. steer-

ing com. Nat. Multiple Sclerosis Soc., Miami, 1998—99. Recipient Leadership award Nat. Multiple Sclerosis Soc., 1997. Mem. Am. Polit. Sci. Assn., Acad. Polit. Sci., Fla. Polit. Sci. Assn., Pi Sigma Alpha, Delta Sigma Pi, Sigma Phi Epsilon. Home: 12823 Dogwood Hills Lane Fairfax VA 22033 Office: 313 Cannon Bldg Washington DC 20515 E mail: Omar.Franco@mail.house.gov.

FRANCO, RAMON ARTURO, medical educator; b. N.Y.C., N.Y., Mar. 31, 1970; s. Ramon Arturo and Milagros Franco; children: Isabella Marie, Sarah Elizabeth Morangello. BA, Lehigh U., 1991; MD, Pa. Sch. Medicine, 1995. Cert. otolaryngology - head and Neck surgery Am. Bd. Otolaryngology, 2001, laryngology - care of the profl. voice Harvard Med. Sch., 2001. Gen. surgery intern, 1996; otolaryngology - head and neck surgery resident, 2000; clin. asst. instr. Harvard Med. Sch., Boston, 2000—. Contbr. articles to profl. jours. Recipient Philanthropy award of Recognition, SE Neighborhood Ctr., 1991, Poster Day Presentation award, NIH, 1991, 1992, First Pl. - Basic Sci. Rsch. award, Am. Rhinologic Soc., 1995. Fellow: Am. Acad. Otolaryngology - Head and Neck Surgery (Outcomes Rsch. grant 1997). Achievements include research in application of 585nm Pulsed Dye Laser in the treatment of laryngeal pathology; first to use of aminolevulinic acid in the treatment of laryngeal pre-malignant leions; design of operating microscope adapter for the Olympus C-series digital camera for medical photography. Avocations: musical composition, digital and black & white photography, bicycling. Office: Harvard Med Sch-Mass Eye & Ear Infirmary 243 Charles St Boston MA 02114 Office Fax: 617-573-3626. E-mail: ramon_franco@meei.harvard.edu.

FRANCO, ROBERT, economist; b. Cairo, Aug. 11, 1941; came to U.S., 1960; s. Edgard and Speranza Franco; m. Martine Pastor, June 9, 1978; children: Erik, Arnaud. BA, U. Calif., 1963, PhD, 1970; MA, San Diego State U., 1965. Economist Transp. Inst., Washington, 1970-72; mgr. CACI, Arlington, Va., 1972-74; asst. divsn. chief IMF, Washington, 1974-94, resident rep. Senegal, 1984-87; sr. country economist World Bank, Washington, 1994-96; resident rep. IMF, Harare, Zimbabwe, 1996-2000, Burkina Faso, 2001—. Cons. OECD, Paris, 1970-74; prof. U. Md., College Park, 1970-80. Mem. Am. Econ. Assn., AAUP, Omicron Delta Epsilon. Avocations: tennis, music, fishing, boating. Home: PO Box 9457 Ouagadougou Burkina Faso Office: IMF C 200 700 19th St NW # C-200 Washington DC 20431-0001 E-mail: rfranco@imf.org.

FRANCO, VICTOR, theoretical physics educator; b. N.Y.C., Dec. 15, 1937; s. Isaac and Regina (Ferezy) F.; m. Jieying Zong, Sept. 12, 1983; children: Zachary M., Anna L., Eugene R. BS, NYU, 1958; MA, Harvard U., 1959, PhD, 1964 Research assoc. MIT, Cambridge, 1963-65, Los Alamos Sci. Lab., 1965-67, Lawrence Radiation Lab., Berkeley, Calif., 1967-69; assoc. prof. Bklyn. Coll., 1969-72, prof., 1973—. Guest sci. Internat. Centre for Theoretical Physics, Trieste, 1970, 75; vis. staff mem. Los Alamos Nat. Lab., 1969-75; vis. physicist Lawrence Berkeley Lab., 1974; fgn. collaborator Centre d'Etudes Nucleaires, Saclay, France, 1975-76, 86; vis. sci. U. Trondheim, Norway, 1980, U. Alta., Can., 1982, U. Karlsruhe, Germany, 1985; vis. scholar U. Wash., Seattle, 1980; sr. rsch. assoc. Harvard U. Cambridge, 1983-84; NAS exch. scholar Inst. High Energy Physics, Beijing, China, 1984; guest prof. New Sch. Social Rsch., N.Y.C., 1988, 89; cons. in the field 1973—. Contbr. numerous articles to sci. jours. Recipient various fellowships and research grants Fellow Am. Phys. Soc.; mem. Sigma Xi Office: Brooklyn College Physics Dept Brooklyn NY 11210 E-mail: vfranco@eudoramail.com.

FRANCOEUR, RICHARD BENOIT, social worker, educator; b. Salem, Mass., July 30, 1962; BS, Cornell U., 1984; MS, Mich. State U., 1987; MSW, U.Pitts., 1992; PhD, U. Pitts., 1998. Econ. analyst Hosp. Assn. N.Y., Albany, 1988—89; med. social worker VA Pitts. Healthcare Sys., 1991—98; asst. prof. Columbia U., N.Y.C., 1998—. Instr. U. Pitts., 1994; rsch. curriculum chair Columbia U., N.Y.C., 2001—; rsch. cons. Harlem Palliative Care Network, N.Y.C., 2001—. Contbr. articles to profl. jours.; mem. editl. bd.: Jour. Psychosocial Oncology. Grantee, NIMH, Bethesda, Md., 2002—, Project on Death in Am./Open Soc. Inst., Soros Found., N.Y.C., 2002—. Mem.: Gerontol. Soc. Am., Assn. Oncology Social Workers. Office: Columbia Univ Sch Social Work 622 W 113th St New York NY 10025

FRANCO GOMEZ, MARIA ANGELES, language educator; arrived in U.S., 1980; d. Salvador Franco-Correa and Angela Patino-Franco; m. Javier Gómez-Calderón, Apr. 10, 1976; children: Javier Gómez-Calderón, Angie Gómez-Calderón, Lili Gómez-Calderón. Bachelor's in Math., Normal Superior Nueva Galicia, Guadalajara, Mex., 1975—86; MA, U. Pitts., 1991, doctoral candidate. Instr. Spanish Pa. State U., Upper Burrell, 1995—, U. Pitts., 1998—. Co-author: Symbolic Logic, 1978. Office: Pa State U 3550 Seventh Street Rd Upper Burrell PA 15068

FRANCOIS, FRANCIS BERNARD, retired association executive, lawyer, transportation consultant; b. Barnum, Iowa, Jan. 21, 1934; s. Rudolph John and Irene Frances (McDonough) F.; m. Eileen M. Schmelzer, Feb. 6, 1960; children: Joseph, Marie, Michael, Monica, Susan. BS, Iowa State U.; LL.B., George Washington U. Bar: Md. 1960, U.S. Patent and Trademark Office. Chief judge Orphan's Ct. Prince George's County, Upper Marlboro, Md., 1962-66; commr. Prince George's County, Upper Marlboro, Md., 1966-71, councilman, 1971-80; exec. dir. Am. Assn. State Hwy. and Transp. Ofcls., Washington, 1980-99; retired; chmn. Md. Transp. Commn., 2002—. Adv. com. Ctr. Transp. Studies, MIT, 1983-99; mem. adv. panel White House Intergovtl. Sci. and Engring. Tech., 1976-80; mem. Washington Suburban Transit Commn., 1978-80, chmn., 1979; dir. Washington Met. Area Transit Authority, 1978-80; exec. com. Transp. Rsch. Bd., 1980-99, Strategic Hwy. Rsch. Program, 1986-92; mem. permanent internat. commn. Permanent Internat. Assn. Rd. Congresses, 1990-99; bd. dirs. Internat. Rd. Fedn., 1991-99, Nat. Ctr. for Asphalt Tech., 1991-99, Intelligent Transp. Soc. Am., 1991—, chmn., 1992-93; chmn. Md. Transportation Commn., 2002—; lectr. in field. Contbr. articles to profl. jours. Mem. adv. coun. Nat. Cmty. Energy Mgmt. Ctr., 1981-82; mem. local govt. energy policy adv. com. Dept. of Energy, 1979-80; vice chmn. Md. Potomac Water Authority, 1970-80; air quality control adv. coun. State of Md., 1975-80; chmn. Water Resources Planning Bd., 1975-77; mem. Gov.'s Interstate Water Quality Planning Com., 1973-74; v.p. Md. Com. for Fair Representation, 1962; counselor Washington Career Inst., 1963; bd. dirs. Bowie Jaycees, Bowie Fine Arts Soc., Bowie YMCA; trustee Md. Easter Seal Soc., Prince George's United Way, Md. Soc. Crippled Children and Adults. Recipient Cmty. Svc. award Nat. Capital chpt. ASCE, 1980, Cmty. Svc. award Bowie Jaycees, 1980, Cmty. Svc. award Cedar Heights Civic Assn., 1978, Profl. Achievement on Engring. award Iowa State U., 1984, W.N. Carey Jr. Disting. Svc. award Transp. Rsch. Bd., 1990; named Washingtonian of Yr. Washingtonian Mag., 1973; Theodore M. Matson Meml. award, Am. Assn. State Hwy. and Transp. Ofcls., Am. Rd. and Transp. Builders Assn., Fed. Hwy. Adminstrn., Am. Hwy. Users Alliance, Inst. Transp. Engrs., Matson Meml. Assocs., and Transp. Rsch. Bd., 1993; Pioneer award Conf. Minority Transp. Ofcls., 1995, Chi Epsilon, Nat. Civil Engring Honor Soc., 1995. Mem. Nat. Assn. Counties (pres. 1979-80), Nat. Assn. Regional Coun. (pres. 1972-73), Washington Met. Coun. Govts. (dir. 1966-80, pres. 1971), Cmty. Assns. Inst. (dir. 1975-80, pres. 1979-80), K.C., Chi Epsilon Democrat. Roman Catholic. Home and Office: 12421 Seabury Ln Bowie MD 20715-3113

FRANCOIS, WILLIAM ARMAND, lawyer; b. Chgo., May 31, 1942; s. George Albert and Evelyn Marie (Smith) F.; m. Barbara Ann Sala, Aug. 21, 1965; children: Nicole Suzanne, Robert William. BA, DePaul U., 1964, JD, 1967. Bar: Ill. 1967. Pvt. practice, Lyons, Ill., 1967-68; with Am. Nat. Can Group, Inc., Chgo., 1970, sec., 1974, v.p., 1978, sr. v.p., gen. counsel, sec., 1999-2000; dep. gen. counsel N.Am. Pechiney Group, 1996-99; pvt. practice Lake Forest, Ill., 2000—. Served to capt. U.S. Army, 1968—70. Mem. ABA, Ill. Bar Assn., Chgo. Bar Assn., Am. Soc. Corp. Secs., Am. Corp. Counsel Assn. Office: 642 Balmoral Ct Lake Forest IL 60045-4842 E-mail: chgowaf@aol.com.

FRANCONA, TERRY JON, professional baseball manager; b. Aberdeen, S.D., Apr. 22, 1959; s. Tito F.; m. Jacque Lang, Jan. 9, 1982; children: Nick, Alyssa, Leah, Jamie. Student, U. Ariz. First baseman/outfielder maj. league baseball Montreal Expos, 1980, Chgo. Cubs, Cin. Reds, Cleve. Indians, Milw. Brewers; hitting instr. Sarasota, Gulf Coast Rookie League Chgo. White Sox orgn., 1991; mgr. S. Bend, 1992; coach Grand Canyon, Ariz. Fall League, 1992; mgr. Birmingham AA, 1993-95, Dominican Winter League, 1995-96, Phila. Phillies, Phila., 1996—. Recipient So. League Title, 1993, Minor League Mgr. of Yr., So. League, 1993, Minor League Mgr. of Yr., Baseball Am., 1993; named Top Managerial Prospect among minor league mgrs. Baseball Am., 1994. Avocation: golf. Office: The Phillies PO Box 7575 Philadelphia PA 19101-7575 Fax: (215) 389-3050.

FRANCO-SAENZ, ROBERTO, physician; b. Bogota, Colombia, July 13, 1937; s. Miguel Antonio Franco and Leonor Saenz; m. Carmen Ditore, Sept. 23, 1992; m. Kathleen Netzley, Sept. 7, 1973 (div.); children: Mario Franco, Roberto Anthony Franco, John Carlos Franco. MD, Univ. Nat. de Colombia, Bogota, 1962; BS, Inst. Nicolas Esguerra, 1955. American Board of Internal Medicine, Internal Medicine Am. Bd. of Internal Medicine, 1970, American Board of Internal Medicine, Endocrinology & Metabolism Am. Bd. of Internal Medicine, 1975. Asst. prof. of medicine Universidad de Colombia, Bogota, Colombia, 1969—71, Med. Coll. of Ohio, Toledo, Ohio, 1971—75, acting chief, divsn. of endocrinology & metabolism, 1973—75, assoc. prof. of medicine, 1975—79, prof. of medicine, 1979—, chief, divsn. of endocrinology & metabolism, 1981—. Author: (90 journal articles) various journals including Annals of Internal Medicine; Jour. of Clin.l Endocrinology and Metabolism; Jour. of Clinical Investigation; Endocrinology; Hypertension;; contbr. textbook; author (chapter author): (textbook) Handbook of Cancer Chemotherapy, 1st edit. 1982, 2nd edit. 1986, 3rd edit. 1991 and 4th edit. 1995; author: (co-author) The Adrenal Gland. Recipient Laureate of ACP, Ohio Chpt., 1993, Golden Apple for Tchg. excellence, Med. Coll. of Ohio, 1974, 1975, 1976, 1978; grantee numerous, Am. Heart Assn.; Nat. Inst. of Health; Kidney Found.; Merck, 1986 to present. Fellow: Am. Heart Assn., Coun. for High Blood Pressure Rsch., ACP; mem.: Endocrine Soc.; Am. Fedn. for Clin. Rsch.; Ctrl. Soc. for Clin. Rsch., Alpha Omega Alpha; Am. Soc. for Hypertension; Internat. Soc. of Hypertension. Office: Med Coll of Ohio 3120 Glendale Toledo OH 43614 Office Fax: 419-383-6244. E-mail: rfrancosaenz@mco.edu.

FRANCUCH, PAUL CHARLES, broadcast journalist; b. Highland Park, Mich., June 26, 1950; s. Charles and Anna (Protasevich) F. BA, Wayne State U., 1972; MA, U. Mich., 1973. From midwest corr. to London bur. chief Voice of Am., Chgo., 1980—96, London bur. chief, 1996—99; sci. engring. editor U. Ill., Chgo., 2001—. Mem. Phi Beta Kappa. Avocations: cycling, photography, amateur astronomy. Office: 601 S Morgan St MC 288 Chicago IL 60607-7113

FRANCZEK, JAMES CLEMENT, JR., lawyer; b. Hammond, Ind., Nov. 11, 1946; s. James Casmir and Eleanor M. (Shillens) Franczek; m. Deborah Chase, Aug. 28, 1971. BS magna cum laude, U. Notre Dame, 1968; JD, U. Chgo., 1971. Bar: Ill. 1971, U.S. Dist. Ct. (no. dist.) Ill. 1978, U.S. Ct. Appeals (6th cir.), U.S. Ct. Appeals (7th cir.), U.S. Supreme Ct. 1971. Assoc. Anthony Scarianao & Assocs., Chgo. Heights, Ill., 1971—74, Vedder, Price, Kaufman & Kammholz, Chgo., 1974—77, ptnr., 1977—. Lectr. in field; past instr. U. Chgo. Bus. Sch., Northwestern U. Bus. Sch., Northeastern Il. U., Chgo. State U., Loyola U. Sch. Indsl. Rels. Contbr. articles to legal jours. Mem.: ABA (com. on state and local govt.), Chgo. Bar Assn. (chmn. labor and employment law com. 1981—82), Coun. Sch. Attys., Ill. State Bar Assn., Ill. Assn. Commerce and Industry, Chgo. Assn. Commerce and Industry (co-chmn. com. on pub. sector labor law), U. of Chgo. Club. Office: Vedder Price Kaufman & Kammholz 222 N La Salle St Ste 2600 Chicago IL 60601-1100

FRANDINA, PHILIP FRANK, civil engineer, consultant; b. Buffalo, N.Y., June 4, 1928; s. Francesco Filippo and Rose (Gugino) F.; m. Josephine Falsone, Apr, 15, 1950 (widowed Apr. 1983); children: Frank Philip, Joseph S., Rosanne; m. Mary Lou Klice, May 3, 1986. BS in Civil Engring., SUNY, 1964. Cert. prof. engr., surveyor. Asst. engr. Erie County, Buffalo, N.Y., 1958-60, hwy. maint. engr., 1960-64, sr. civil engr., 1964-72, chief engr., 1972-81, supt. of hwys., 1981-82, commr. pub. works, 1982-88; cons. pvt. practice, Buffalo, N.Y., 1988—. Bd. mem. Erie C.C. Adv. Bd., Buffalo, N.Y., 1975—; arbitrator Am. Arbitrator Assn., 1985—; chmn. Transp. Adv. Bd., Buffalo, N.Y., 1988—; bd. mem. N.Y. State Hazardous Waste Citing Bd., Albany, N.Y., 1992—. Sec., treas. Erie County Credit Union, Buffalo, N.Y., 1974-81; founder, mgr., N. Buffalo Rockets, Buffalo, N.Y., 1976-80; chmn. Blessed Sacrament Parish Adminstr. Commn., Buffalo, N.Y., 1978-80. Recipient Engr. of Yr. award N.Y. State Soc. Profl. Engrs., 1987, Buffalo, Meritorious Svc. awarrd, 1995; named One of Top 10 Pub. Works Ofcls. in U.S., Am. Pub. Works Assn., 1988; recipient resolution of commendation Erie County Legislature, 1987, Nina award Nat. Columbus Day Commn., Buffalo, 1989, Engr. of Yr. award, U. Buffalo Engring. Alumni Assn., 2001. Fellow ASCE; mem. Assn. for Bridge Constrn. and Design (founder Western N.Y. chpt.), Am. Acad. Forensic Sci., Triple Nine Soc. (ombudsman). Republican. Roman Catholic. Achievements include design and construction of the new Erie County Correctional Facility and the Erie County Holding Ctr.; development of energy saving concepts in Erie County Bldgs. with significant cost savings. Home: 270 Lincoln Pkwy Buffalo NY 14216-3126 Office: 289 Delaware Ave Buffalo NY 14202 E-mail: p.frandina@att.net.

FRANEY, BILLIE NOLAN, political activist; b. Eveleth, Minn., Sept. 17, 1930; d. Mark and Ann Murray Nolan; m. Neil Joseph Franey; children: Kathleen, Timothy, Nora, Colin, Patrick. Student, Carleton Coll., 1948-49, U. Minn., 1949-50; BA, Coll. St. Scholastica, 1952. Social worker Cath. Welfare, Mpls., 1952-53. Contbr. articles to profl. jours. Chair Indian Affairs, Minn. Mrs. Jaycees, 1962; mem. Charter Commn., White Bear Lake, Minn., 1962-65; pres. White Bear Lake LWV, 1965-67; lobbyist Common Cause of Minn., 1979, Minn. LWV, 1980, AAUW, 1987-89; mem. met. futures task force Met. Coun., 1988-89; co-chair Women Come to The Capitol, Minn. Women's Consortium. Named Outstanding Young Women of Am., 1966; revipient Sister Ann Edward Scholar award The Coll. of St. Scholostica, 1992. Mem. AAUW (pres. 1992-94, St. Paul program v.p. 1990-92, legis. pub. policy chair 1987-89, Minn. chpt. legis. pub. policy v.p. 1987-89, scholarship named for as a gift from St. Paul AAUW 1989, Women as Agts. of Change award 1991, chair St. Paul scholarship trust 2001—), Coun. Met. Area LWV (chair 1981-83, program and study chair 1979-81, bd. mem. 1978-79). Avocations: reading, biking, cross-country skiing, gardening. Home: 1323 Hedman Way Saint Paul MN 55110-3360

FRANGOPOULOS, ZISSIMOS A. banker; b. Athens, Greece, Dec. 16, 1944; s. John and Thalia (Landi) F.; m. Ruth Snowdon Hoopes, Nov. 21, 1981. BA, Yale U., 1967; MBA, Columbia U., 1969. Lending officer Chem. Bank, N.Y.C., 1969-74, v.p. energy group London, 1974-79, sr. v.p. merchant banking N.Y.C., London, 1979-84; mng. dir., chief exec. officer Chem. Bank Internat. Ltd., London, 1981-84; sr. v.p., dir. for corp. fin. Chem. Banking Corp., N.Y.C., 1984-90, treas., 1990-92; sr. v.p., treas. Chem. Bank, N.Y.C., 1992-94; mng. dir. Chase Securities, Inc., N.Y.C., 1994-99; dir., treas. Cancer Care Connection, Inc., Newark, Del., 2000—01; exec. v.p., CFO, Christiana Bank & Trust Co., Wilmington, Del., 2001—02, pres., CEO, 2002—. Bd. dirs. Christiana Bank & Trust Co., Wilmington, Del. Home: 403 Spring Mill Rd Chadds Ford PA 19317 Office: PO Box 620 Mendenhall PA 19357

FRANK, ALAN I W, manufacturing company executive; b. Pitts., Mar. 6, 1932; s. Robert and Cecelia F.; children: Darcy Frank Kotun, Kimberly Frank Shaw. AB cum laude, Harvard U., 1954; LLB, Columbia U., 1960. Bar: N.Y., 1961, Pa., 1982. Pres. Nat. Petroleum Corp., 1954-69; pres., chmn. bd. AIWF Corp., 1962—. Pres. & bd. dirs. numerous corps.; gen. chmn. $200 million campaign Pitts. area, Columbia U., N.Y.C., 1968-70, mem. nat. devel. bd., 1974—; mem. Rensselaer coun. Rensselaer Poly. Inst., 1974-83; mem., chmn. various coms. Harvard Coll., 1961—; trustee Pitts. History and Landmarks Found., 1996—. Patentee in field. Served with Counter Intelligence Corps, Spl. Agt. U.S. Army, 1955-57. Mem. N.Y. Bar, Pa. Bar, Mid Ocean Club (Bermuda). Address: 96 E Woodland Rd Pittsburgh PA 15232-2861

FRANK, AMÉLIE LORRAINE, marketing professional; b. L.A., Feb. 5, 1960; d. Lawrence Bruce and Phébé Exilda (Brodeur) Frank. BA in English, Creative Writing, U. Calif., Irvine, 1981. Letters editor Petersen Pub., West Hollywood, Calif., 1983-85; owner, writer Mysterious Affairs, Hollywood, 1984-88; script svcs. supr. Universal City (Calif.) Studios, 1985-86; mkt. rschr. Universal Pictures Mktg., Universal City, 1986-94; owner, pub. Sacred Beverage Press, Venice, Calif., 1994—; rsch. coord. Buena Vista Pictures Mktg., Burbank, Calif., 1994—. Host poetry readings Hot Ho. Cafe, North Hollywood, 1996—99, Exile Books & Music, 1999—2000; co-dir. Valley Contemporary Poets, 1999—2002; host Killer Poetry, 2000—01; co-webmaster Billybobapalooza Ofcl. Billy Bob Thornton website. Author: (poems) A Resilient Heart and Other Visceral Comforts, 1992, Flame and Loss of Breath, 1996, Doing Time on Planet Billy Bob, 2000; co-author: Drink Me, 1997, Bird Interpretations, 1998; editor: (book) God the Motion Picture, 1994; co-editor: Blue Satellite Jour., 1994—2000; performer spoken word (albums) The Essential Girl, 2001, Retro Hell music reviewer Ind. Revs. Site. Facilitator buddy program AIDS Project, L.A., Hollywood, 1988—92; trustee Beyond Baroque, 1999—, artist, cmty. advisor coun., 1998—99; mem. med. staff Disney Disaster Preparedness, Burbank, 1994—. Named L.A. Newer Poet, Beyond Baroque in conjunction with L.A. Poetry Festival, 1999; recipient award for favorite new poetry book, Readership, NEXT Mag., 1996. Mem.: NOW, Poetry Soc. Am., Office Profl. Employees Internat. Union (newsletter editor 1991—94), PETA. Green Party. Avocations: reading, choral music, travel, films, working with animals. Office: The Sacred Beverage Press PO Box 10312 Burbank CA 91510-0312 E-mail: poetamelie@aol.com.

FRANK, ANTHONY MELCHIOR, federal official, former financial executive; b. Berlin, May 21, 1931; came to U.S., 1937, naturalized, 1943; s. Lothar and Elisabeth (Roth) F.; m. Gay Palmer, Oct. 16, 1954; children: Tracy, Randall BA, Dartmouth Coll., 1953, MBA, 1954; postgrad. in fin., U. Vienna, 1956. Asst. to pres., bond portfolio mgr. Glendale (Calif.) Fed. Savs. Assn., 1958-61; v.p., treas. Far West Fin. Corp., Los Angeles, 1962; adminstrv. v.p., v.p. savs. First Charter Fin. Corp., Beverly Hills, Calif., 1962-66; pres. State Mut. Savs. and Loan Assn., Los Angeles, 1966-68, Titan Group, Inc., N.Y.C. and Los Angeles, 1968-70, INA Properties, Inc., 1970-71, Citizens Savs. & Loan, San Francisco, 1971-73, vice chmn., chief exec. officer, 1973-74; chmn. bd., pres., chief exec. officer FN Fin. Corp., 1974-88; postmaster gen. U.S. Postal Svc., 1988-92; founding chmn. Belvedere Capital Ptnrs., San Francisco. Also pres., vice chmn., industry dir. Fed. Home Loan Bank San Francisco, 1972-77; trustee, treas. Blue Shield of Calif., from 1976-88; bd. dirs. Temple Inland, Schwab, Bedford Property Investors Inc., Crescent Real Estate Equities. Chmn., bd. dirs. Calif. Housing Fin. Agy., Sacramento, 1978-86; trustee Am. Conservatory Theater; chmn. bd. visitors Sch. Architecture and Planning UCLA, 1971-86; bd. overseers Tuck Sch.; del. Calif. Dem. Conv., 1968. Served with AUS, 1954-56 Mem. SAG, Chief Execs. Orgn., World Bus. Forum, Dartmouth Club No. Calif., Bohemian Club. Democrat. Office: Belvedere Capital Ptnrs One Maritime Plz Ste 825 San Francisco CA 94111-6114

FRANK, ARTHUR LEONARD, physician, educator; b. Sacramento, June 9, 1947; s. Arthur and Senta (Levite) F.; m. Joanne Batzinger, May 30, 1976; children: Matthew Joshua, Rebecca Ruth, Aaron Daniel. BA, SUNY, Buffalo, 1968; MD, Mount Sinai Sch. Medicine, 1972; PhD, CUNY, 1977. Bd. cert. internal medicine and occupl. medicine. From instr. to assoc. prof. Mount Sinai Sch. Medicine, N.Y.C., 1977-83; prof., chmn. dept. preventive medicine and environ. health U. Ky. Coll. Medicine, Lexington, 1983-94; v.p. med. edn., prof. U. Tex. Health Ctr., Tyler, 1994—2002; prof. pub. health Drexel U., Phila., 2002—. Lt. comdr. USPHS, 1973-75. Fellowship Collegium Ramazzini, Carpi, Italy, 1984. Fellow Am. Coll. Preventive Medicine, Am. Coll. Occupl. and Environ. Medicine; mem. Soc. Occupl. and Environ. Health, Assn. Tchrs. Preventive Medicine (Educator of Yr. award). Office: Drexel Univ Sch of Public Health 245 N 15th St MS660 Philadelphia PA 19102

FRANK, BARBARA BALIS, gastroenterologist, educator; b. Reading, Pa., Jan. 11, 1937; d. Irvin and Ruth Helen (Knoblauch) B.; m. Leonard Arnold Frank, Aug. 17, 1958; children: Michael Scott, Bradford Allan. BA magna cum laude, Smith Coll., 1958; MD, U. Pa., 1962. Diplomate Am. Bd. Internal Medicine and Gastroenterology. Intern, fellow gastroenterology Hosp. U. Pa., Phila., 1962-63, 63-64; instr. internal medicine, 1966-69; resident internal medicine Bryn Mawr Hosp., Pa., 1964-66; clin. asst. prof. medicine Hahnemann U., Phila., 1973-75; clin. assoc. prof., 1975-85; clin. prof., 1985—; dir. divsn. gastroenterology Crozer-Chester med. Ctr., Chester, Pa., 1968-89; attending gastroenterologist, 1989-94. Cons. Sacred Heart Hosp., chester, 1974-94; mem. sci.adv. com. Nat. Found. Ileitis and Colitis, Phila., 1980—; mem. gastroenterology-urology devices panel FDA, 1988-90, chmn., 1990-92, cons., 1993-94, mem. gastroenterology drug adv. com., 1996-99; mem. Physician Payment Rev. Commn., Consensus Panel for Evaln. and Mgmt. Svcs., 1990; rep. for gastroenterology carrier adv. com. Pa. Medicare; v.p. N.Am. Congresso Panamericano de Endoscopia, 1993-95, 99—. Assoc. editor MKSAP in gastroenterology and hepatology 2; contbr. articles to profl. jours. Recipient History of Medicine prize U. Pa. Sch. Medicine, 1962, Legion of Honor award Chapel of Four Chaplains, Phila., 1978; rsch. grantee U. Pa., 1961-62. Fellow ACP, Coll. Physicians Phila., Am. Coll. Gastroenterology (ad hoc com. on women in gastroenterology 1989—, gov. ea. Pa. 1992-96, 2003—, regional councillor, bd. govs. 1994-96, chmn. com. for ICD-9-CM revision 1986-89, mem. govt. rels. com. 1987-88, sci. exhibits com. 1985-86, ann. sic. selection com. 1984-85, 90-91, nominating com. 1988-89, ednl. affairs com. 1992-2001); mem. Am. Soc. Gastrointestinal Endoscopy (councillor, governing bd. dirs. 1986-90, 92-94, pres. 1991-92), AMA, Am. Gastroenterol. Assn. (patient care com. 1986-88, tng. adn edn. com. 1989-90, abstract selection com. 199, nominating com. 1986-87, program evaln. com. 1981-85, mem. pub. policy com. 1992-93, mem. clin. svcs. task force 1994-95, chmn. nominating com. 1995-96, others) Am. Assn. Study Liver Disease, Am. Liver Found., Internat. Assn. for Study of the Liver, Pa. Med. Soc., Phila. GI Tng. Group (pres. 1987-93), Phila. Gastrointestinal Rsch. Forum, Delaware County Med. Soc., Delaware Valley Soc. Gastrointestinal Endoscopy (pres. 1984-86, councillor, governing bd. dirs. 1986-88), Pa. Soc. Gastroenterology councillor for Phila. 1982-84, 87-91, 2001—, governing bd. dirs.), Israel Med. Assn., Alpha Omega Alpha, Sigma Xi, Alpha Phi, Kappa Psi, Phi Beta Kappa Del. Valley (gov. coun. 1991-93, 98— v.p. 1993-95, pres. 1995-97, 98—). Democrat. Jewish. Avocations: sketching, dancing. Office: Fl 5 MS 913 219 N Broad St Philadelphia PA 19107

FRANK, BARNEY, congressman; b. Bayonne, N.J., Mar. 31, 1940; s. Samuel and Elsie (Golush) F. AB, Harvard U., 1962, JD, 1977. Exec. asst. to mayor City of Boston, 1968-71; adminstrv. asst. to U.S. congressman, 1971-72; mem. Mass. Ho. of Reps., 1972-80, 97th-108th Congresses from 4th Dist. Mass., 1981—; mem. banking and fin. svcs. com., mem. judiciary com., homeland sec. com. Teaching fellow govt. Harvard U., 1963-67, asst. to dir. Inst. Politics John F. Kennedy Sch. Govt., 1966-67, fellow Inst. Politics, 1971. Democrat. Office: US Ho of Reps 2252 Rayburn HOB Washington DC 20515-0001*

FRANK, BEN WILLIAM, lawyer, administrator; b. Lampasas, Tex., Oct. 23, 1929; s. Hugo C. and Nadine G. (Machen) F.; m. Maymie A. Bowles, July 30, 1961 (dec. June 1994); children: Carl, Rick; m. Eleanor B. Bodenhamer, July 5, 1997. BA, U. Tex., 1956; LLB, Ark. U., 1964, JD, 1979. Bar: Ark. 1964. Claims mgr. CNA, Little Rock, 1958-64, Comml. Union, Little Rock, 1964-79; adminstr. Ark. Workers Compensation Commn., Little Rock, 1979-98. City judge, city atty. Traskwood, Ark., 1971-92; commr. Ark. Worker's Compensation Commn., Little Rock. Staff Sgt. USAF, 1948-54. Mem. Ark. Adjuster Assn. (pres. 1978), Claim Mgrs. Coun. (chmn. 1970), Ins. Arbitration Commn. (chmn. 1972), Ark. Spl. Arbitration Commn. (chmn. 1972-79), Little Rock Power Squadron. Republican. Lutheran. Avocation: boating. Home: 25 Shannon Dr Little Rock AR 72207-5144

FRANK, CHARLES RAPHAEL, JR., financial advisor; b. Pitts, May 15, 1937; s. Charles Raphael and Lucille (Briscoe) M.; m. Susan Patricia Backman, Mar. 9, 1963 (div. June 1976); children: Elizabeth Grace, Stephen Raphael; m. Eleanor Sebastian, July 19, 1976; children: Paul Sebastian, Philip Sebastian; stepchildren: Joyce Oxman, Alan Oxman. BS in Math., Rensselaer Poly. Inst., 1959; MA in Econs., Princeton U., 1961, PhD in Econs., 1963. Sr. rsch. fellow East African Inst. Social Rsch. Makerere U. Coll., Kampala, Uganda, 1963-65; asst. prof. econ. Yale U., New Haven, 1965-67; assoc. prof. econ. and internat. affairs Princeton U., NJ, 1967-70, prof., 1970-74; assoc. dir. rsch. program econ. devel. Woodrow Wilson Sch., 1967-70, dir., 1970-74; sr. fellow Brookings Inst., 1972-74; mem. policy planning staff US Dept. State, 1974-77, dep. asst. sec. state for econ. and social affairs, 1977-78; v.p. Salomon Bros. Inc., 1978-87; pres. Frank & Co. Inc., 1987-88; v.p. project fin. GE Capital Corp., Stamford, Conn., 1988-97; 1st v.p. European Bank for Reconstruction and Devel., London, 1997-2001. Bd. dirs. Ctrl. and Eastern European Media Enterprises, Romanian Am. Enterprise Fund, 2003- and Banease Investments; ops. rsch. analyst US Steel, summers 1960, 61; cons. Govt. Uganda, 1964, UN Econ. Commn. for Asia and Far East, 1969, IBRD, 1969-72, Korea Devel. Inst., 1973-74, Mathematica, 1967-68, Nat. Conf. Bd., 1969-70, Nat. Bur. Econ. Rsch., 1970 75, Brookings Instn., 1969; mem. rsch. adv. com. AID, 1971-75, cons., Washington, 1966-68, Korea, 1971-73. Author: Prodn. Theory and

Indivisible Commodities, 1969, The Sugar Industry in East Africa, 1965, (with Brian Van Arkadie) Econ. Accounting and Develop. Planning, 2d edit., 1969, Debt and the Terms of Aid, 1970, Stats. and Econometrics, 1971, Am. Jobs and Trade with the Develop. Countries, 1973, Fgn. Exchange Regimes and Econ. Develop., The Case of South Korea, 1975, Fgn. Trade and Domestic Adjustment, 1976, Income Distribution and Econ. Growth in the Less Developed Countries, 1977. Mem. Coun. Fgn. Rels.

FRANK, DANA HUNT, internist, educator; b. N.Y.C, Feb. 22, 1951; s. Hiram H. and Clemence (Eskanazi) Frank; m. Wendy S. Williams, May 7, 1977; children: Leah Susan, Andrew William. BA in Psychology, Brown U., 1973; MD with distinction, George Washington U., 1978. Diplomate Am. Bd. Internal Medicine, Nat. Bd. Med. Examiners. Intern, resident in medicine Johns Hopkins Hosp., Balt., 1978-81; physician Speed Headache Assocs., Balt., 1981-83; internist Watson Clin., Lakeland, Fla., 1983; physician Park Med. Assocs., Lutherville, Md., 1983—, pres., 1996—; asst. prof. Johns Hopkins Sch. Med., Balt. Chmn. bd. Johns Hopkins Physicians Group, Balt., 1994-96; pres. Flagship Health, Balt., 1996-99, Flagship Health, Pa., 1996-99, Physicians Quality Care, 1997-99. Contbr. articles to profl. jours. including Clin. Rsch., Med. Care, others. Fellow ACP; mem. Am. Assn. for Study Headaches (pres. 1992-94), Am. Soc. Internal Medicine, Md. Soc. Internal Medicine, Alpha Omega Alpha. Avocations: banjo-bluegrass music, hiking, traveling. Office: Park Med Assocs 10755 Falls Rd Ste 200 Lutherville MD 21093-4520 E-mail: dfrank@jhmi.edu.

FRANK, DAVID ANTHONY, educator; b. Topeka, Kans., Mar. 23, 1955; s. Arthur Martin and Rosemary Boles Frank; m. Marjorie Machie Enseki, July 3, 1988; children: Michael, Justin. BA, Western Wash. U., 1978, MA, 1979; PhD, U. Oreg., 1983. Grad. tchg. fellow Western Wash. U., Bellingham, 1978-79, U. Oreg., Eugene, 1979-81, instr., 1981-82, asst. prof., 1982-88, assoc. prof. in rhetorical studies, 1988—2003, prof., 2003—, dir. Honors coll., 2000—03. Cons. U.S. Forest Svc., Eugene, 1993—; expert witness in field, 1994; speech cons. Oreg. Sec. of State, Salem, 1998—; trajectories of Israeli-Palestinean Symbol Use. Author: Debating Values, 1993, Creative Speaking, 1991, Lincoln Douglas Debate, 1995; contbr. articles to profl. jours. Chair Savage com. on Peace U. Oreg., 1997—; chmn. bd. dirs. Koinia Ctr., Eugene, 1991-94. Recipient Prof. of Month award Mortar Bd., 1988, 90, Disting. Svc. award N.W. Forensics Conf., 1998; Blue Key Hon. Inductee, 1999. Democrat. Congregationalist. Office: U Oreg Honors Coll Eugene OR 97403 E-mail: dfrank@oregon.uoregon.edu.

FRANK, DAVID LEWIS, lawyer; b. N.Y.C., Nov. 18, 1963; s. Harvey and Judith Lewis Frank; m. Sharon Rae Olliges, Dec. 9, 1990; children: Rebecca Lynne, Daniel Lewis. BA summa cum laude, U. Pa., Phila., 1985; JD cum laude, Harvard U., 1988. Bar: Pa. 1988, U.S. Ct. Appeals (3d cir.) 1990, U.S. Dist. Ct. (ea. dist.) Pa. 1989. Atty. Duane, Morris & Heckscher, Phila., 1988-95; profl. staff Com. on Edn. and the Workforce U.S. Ho. of Reps., Washington, 1995-2001; legal counsel U.S. Equal Employment Opportunity Commn., Washington, 2001—. Elected Rep. committeeman Rep. City Com. of Phila., 1992-95. Republican. Jewish. Avocations: sports, traveling. Office: US Equal Employment Opportunity Commn Rm 6002 1801 L St Washington DC 20507 Fax: (202) 663-4639. E-mail: david.frank@eeoc.gov.

FRANK, DENNIS, psychotherapist, educator; b. Cherry Point, N.C., Apr. 17, 1954; s. Charlotte Dotzauer and Robert Frank; children: Maximillian, Alexander. MS, U. Wis., Milw., 1997. Psychotherapist Ravenswood Clinic, Inc., Milw., 1997—2002; area supr. ATTIC Correctional Svcs. Inc., Milw., 1999—2001, also bd. dirs.; psychotherapist St. Mary's Hosp., 2001—; ad hoc prof. Concordia U. Grad Sch. Instr. Upper Iowa U., 2002—. Com. mem. The Benedict Ctr., Milw., 2000. Specialist Army, Germany, 1971-74. Mem. ACA, Am. Correctional Assn., Internat. Assn. of Addictions and Offender Counselors, Internat. Cmty. Corrections Assn. Office: Columbia St Mary's 2350 N Lake Dr Milwaukee WI 53211

FRANK, DIETER, retired chemicals executive; b. Erfurt, Thuringia, Germany, May 21, 1930; came to U.S., 1975; s. Karl Hermann and Luise (Metz) F.; m. Edith Anna Laufer, July 19, 1957; children: Martin, Susanne, Beate. DEng, Tech. U., Berlin, 1963. Rsch. chemist Glanzstoff A.G., Obernburg, Federal Republic of Germany, 1965-69, sect. head, 1969-71; assoc. dir. AKZO Corp. Rsch., Obernburg, Federal Republic of Germany, 1971-75; dir. rsch. ARMAK (AKZO), Chgo., 1975-76; v.p. rsch. AKZO Chems., Chgo., 1976-90, ret., 1990; tech. cons., 1991—96. Mem. indsl. adv. bd. U. Fla., Gainsville, 1987-90. Contbr. to Ullman Ency., 1985, 90, also articles on organic chemistry; patentee chemicals. County vice chmn. Social Dem. Party of Germany, Obernburg, 1968; pres. Soccer Club, Elsenfeld, Federal Republic of Germany, 1974, 75; chmn. bd. dirs. Fine Arts Found. Schleusingen, 2000-03. Recipient G.E. Meade award, Sugar Industry Technologists, 1986. Mem. AAAS, Indsl. Rsch. Inst. (rep. 1979-90, bd. editors 1981-83). Avocations: woodworking, jazz player. Home and Office: An der Hauptstr 93 98553 Schleusingen-Gethles Germany E-mail: dfrankgeth@aol.com.

FRANK, EDGAR GERALD, retired financial executive; b. Cin., May 15, 1931; s. Carl F. and Marcella M. F.; m. Joy Hueber, Oct. 30, 1954; children: Thomas, Phillip, Angela, Walter. BBA, U. Cin., 1955. Acct. Wm. S. Merrell Co., Cin., 1960-61; asst. sec. Emery Industries, Cin., 1961-66; fin. v.p. Samuel Moore & Co., Aurora, Ohio, 1966-79; v.p. fin. Telex Corp., Tulsa, 1979-88, ret., 1988. Served with USN, 1955-58. Mem. AICPA, Fin. Execs. Inst.

FRANK, EDMUND PAUL, JR., accountant; b. Norman, Okla., Jan. 8, 1952; s. Edmund P. and Esther G. Frank; m. Margaret A. Hintze, July 10, 1976; children: Daniel, Keith, Philip, Amanda. BBA, U. Tex., 1974. Field auditor I, Tex. Edn. Agy., Austin, 1974-77, auditor II, 1977-79, acct. III-reports analyst, 1979-81, acct. IV, 1981-83, chief acct. I/acct. VI, 1983—2003; acct. VII Tex. Dept. Housing and Cmty. Affairs, 2003—. Mem. situational leadership program USDA, Dallas, 1983-84; mem. 1st level mgmt. program of gov. State of Tex., Austin, 1984; contbg. cons. Tex. Comptr. Pub. Accounts, Austin, 1991-92, gen. ledger leader in devel. integrated statewide adminstrv. sys., 1994-98; host Tex. Edn. Assn. Mid-Winter Conf., 1975-77, 96-98. Author: Field Auditor's Manual, 1977. Precinct election chmn. various sch. dist., county, utility dist., Austin, 1974-85, 99-2000; treas. Our Savior Luth. Ch., Austin, 1977-80, chmn. youth bd., 1993-2000, mem. constn. revision com., 1998-2000, congl. pres., 2001-02. Mem.: Delta Sigma Pi.

FRANK, EDWARD DAVID, II, history educator; b. Boston, June 7, 1951; s. Howard Alvin and Sally (Bernkopf) F.; m. Susan Gibson Lea, Dec. 13, 1997; children: William Howard Day, Edward Morgan Day; 1 stepchild: Eleanor Talbot West. JD, NYU, 1976; BA in History, Yale U., 1973; MA in Internat. Rels., U. Pa., 1984. Assoc. Sherman & Sterling, N.Y.C., 1976-79, Sullivan & Worcester, Boston, 1979-81; chief counsel Bur. Profl. and Occupl. Affairs Commonwealth of Pa., Harrisburg, 1982-83; internat. polit. risk cons. Bus. Environment Risk Info., Washington, 1985-86; history tchr. The Agnes Irwin Sch., Rosemont, Pa., 1985-97, chair history, 1997—, pres. Cum Laude Soc., 1991—. Spl. asst. to pres. Barnes Found., Merion, Penn., 1989-90. Bd. dirs. Phila. Area Multicultural Resource Ctr., Bryn Mawr, Pa., 1990—; chair 25th Reunion of Yale Class of 1973, New Haven, Conn., 1993-98; trustee Agnes Irwin Sch., Rosemont, 1992-95, Lincoln U., 1985-91. Mem. Assn. Yale U. Alumni (bd. govs. 1972-73, sec. Class of 73, 1972-78). Home: 843 Parkes Run Ln Villanova PA 19085 Office: Agnes Irwin Sch Ithan Ave & Conestoga Rd Bryn Mawr PA 19010 E-mail: WigsFrank@aol.com.

FRANK, ELIZABETH, English literature, author; b. L.A., Sept. 14, 1945; d. Melvin G. and Anne R. Frank; 1 child, Anne Louise Buchwald. Student, Bennington Coll.; BA, MA, PhD, U. Calif., Berkeley. Prof. modern langs. and lit. Bard Coll., Annandale-on-Hudson, NY, 1982—. Author: Jackson Pollock, 1983, Louise Bogan: A Portrait, 1985 (Pulitzer prize for biography, 86), Esteban Vicente, 1995. Office: Joy Harris Lit Agy 156 5th Ave Ste 617 New York NY 10010-7002 also: Bard Coll Dept Lang & Lit Annandale On Hudson NY 12504

FRANK, ELIZABETH AHLS (BETSY FRANK), art educator, artist; b. Cin., Sept. 27, 1942; d. Edward Henry and Constance Patricia (Barnett) Ahls; m. James Russell Frank, Aug. 10, 1963; children: Richard Scott, Robert Edward. Student, Hiram (Ohio) Coll., 1960-63; BA, U. Denver, 1964; MA, U. South Fla., 1988. Cert. profl. educator, Fla. Remedial reading tchr. Willoughby-Eastlake (Ohio) Schs., 1971-72; elem. tchr., grade level chmn. Lee County Pub. Schs., Ft. Myers, Fla., 1972-79, tchr. art, 1979—, mem. arts coun., long range and model schs. planning coms., 1997-98. Contbg. author Davis Art Edn. Publs., Worcester, Mass. Vol. Mann Performing Arts Hall, Fort Myers, 1986-98, Harborside Convention Ctr., 1991-95; sec. Colonial Acres Homeowners Assn., North Fort Myers, Fla., 1994-99. Named Golden Apple Tchr. of Distinction, Lee County Schs. Found., 1991—2002; recipient, Seminar Fla. Humanites Coun., 2000. Mem.: NEA, Edison African Violet Soc. (1st v.p. 1997—2000), Tchrs. Assn. Lee County (rep. bd. 1972—99, mem. exec. bd. 1990—91, M.M. Bethune Humanities award 1992), Fla. Edn. Assn., Lee Art Edn. Assn. (pres. 1991—92, founder, Art Educator of Yr. 1991—92), Calusa Nature Ctr., Southwest Fla. Rose Soc., Fla. Art Edn. Assn. (workshop presenter), Nat. Art Edn. Assn., Audubon of S.W. Fla.. (recording sec. 2002—03, Educator of Yr. 1998), Delta Kappa Gamma (v.p. 1986—88, pres. 1988—90, sec. 1996—98, state chmn. arts and crafts com. 1997—99, sec. 2001—03, state mem. world fellowship com., Fla. scholar 1988), Phi Delta Kappa, Phi Kappa Phi. Democrat. Avocations: gardening, camping, boating, arts and crafts, birdwatching. Home: 4583 S Sawgrass Cir Homosassa FL 34446-3602 Office: North Ft Myers Acad Arts 1858 Suncoast Ln Fort Myers FL 33917-1898 E-mail: jrfrank@mindspring.com.

FRANK, ELLEN, medical educator, psychiatrist, psychologist, researcher; Grad., Vassar Coll., 1966; M in Eng., Carnegie Mellon U., 1967; PhD in Psychol., U. Pitts., 1979. Prof. psychiatry, psychology U. Pitts., 1979—. Mem. task force on DSM-IV Am. Psychiat. Assn.; chair psychopharmacologic drugs avd. panel FDA; mem. MacArthur Found. Rsch. Network on Psychopathology and Devel.; chair task force on continuing edn. Am. Coll. Neuropsychopharmacology. Grantee Nat. Inst. Mental Health. Fellow: Am. Psychiatric Assn. (hon.); mem.: Inst. Medicine. Office: Bellefield Twrs 8th Fl Pittsburgh PA 15213

FRANK, FREDERICK, investment banker; b. Salt Lake City, May 31, 1932; s. Simon and Suzanne (Seller) F.; m. Mary Ann Nahum (div. 1979); children: Jonny Ann, Laura Kim, Frederick S.; m. Mary Catherine Tanner. BA, Yale U., 1954; MBA, Stanford U., 1958. Chartered fin. analyst. Mng. dir. Smith Barney & Co., N.Y.C., 1958-69, Lehman Bros., N.Y.C., 1969-85, sr. mng. dir., 1985-95, vice chmn., 1995—. Bd. dirs. Pharm. Product Devel., Wilmington, NC, AXS, Berkeley, Calif., Diagnostic Products, L.A., Landec Corp., Bus. Engine Inc.; chmn. bd. dirs. Physiome Scis. Trustee Irvington Inst. of Immunological Rsch.; with Nat. Genetics Found., N.Y.C., 1985—; bd. dirs. Salk Inst., La Jolla, Calif.; trustee Hotchkiss Sch., Lakeville, Conn.; adv. dir. Yale U. Sch. Mgmt. With U.S. Army, 1954—56. Mem. Chartered Fin. Analysts, N.Y. Soc. Security Analysts. Avocations: skiing, tennis, running. Home: 109 E 91st St New York NY 10128-1601 Office: Lehman Bros 745 7th Ave New York NY 10019-0001 E-mail: ffrank@lehman.com.

FRANK, FREDERICK NEWMAN, lawyer; b. Pitts., Jan. 10, 1947; s. Abraham C. and Nancy (Newman) F. BA, U. Pitts., 1967, JD, 1970. Bar: Pa. 1970, U.S. Dist. Ct. (we. dist.) Pa. 1970, U.S. Ct. Appeals (3d cir.) 1972. Law clk. Pa. Ct. of Common Pleas, Pitts., 1970-71; asst. atty. gen. Pa. Dept. of Justice, 1971-73; ptnr. Raphael-Sheinberg & Barmen, 1973-79, Baskin, Flaherty, Elliott & Mannino, P.C., Pitts., 1979— ; solicitor Allegheny County Treas., 1974-94. Contbr. articles to law revs. Chmn. Urban Affairs Found., Pitts., 1976-79; treas. Allegheny County Democratic Com., 1980— ; bd. dirs. United Jewish Fedn. Recipient Stark Young Leadership award 1976, Levinson Human Relations award, 1984 (both United Jewish Fedn.). Mem. Pa. Bar Assn. (council family law sect. 1985—, editor newsletter, 1975-77), Allegheny County Bar Assn. (sec. family law sect. 1987—, vice chmn. council young lawyers div. 1978-79). Democrat. Jewish. Clubs: Concordia, Pitts. Athletic Assn. Office: Gulf Towers Fl 34 Pittsburgh PA 15219

FRANK, GELYA, anthropologist, educator; b. N.Y.C., Dec. 12, 1948; d. Charles Samuel and Betty Sarah (Gordon) Frank; life ptnr. Marita Giovanni; 1 child, Rebecca S'manga. BA in Anthropology summa cum laude, UCLA, 1973, MA in Anthropology, 1975, PhD in Anthropology, 1981. Asst. prof. dept. occupl. therapy and anthropology U. So. Calif., L.A., 1982—88, assoc. prof. dept. occupl. sci., occupl. therapy and anthropology, 1988—2001, prof., 2001—. Hist. cons. Tule River Tribal Coun., Porterville, Calif., 1972—; vis. prof. dept. sociology and social anthropology The Hebrew U. of Jerusalem, 1986—87. Author: Venus on Wheels: Two Decades of Dialogue on Disability, Biography and Being Female in America (Eileen Basker Meml. prize Soc. Med. Anthropology, 2000, Faculty Recognition award Phi Kappa Phi, 2001); co-author: Lives: An Anthropological Approach to Biography. Named Grad. Woman of Yr., Assn. of Acad. Women, UCLA, 1981; fellow, Pacific Ctr. Health Policy and Ethics, 1999, NEH, 2002—03; grantee, U. So. Calif. Faculty Rsch. and Innovation Fund, 1986, U. So. Calif. Neighborhood Outreach, 1998—2000, Tulare County Hist. Soc., 2002—03, NEH Resident Scholar Program, Sch. Am. Rsch., 2002—03. Mem.: Am. Anthrop. Assn. (pres. Soc. Humanistic Anthropology 1986—88), Phi Beta Kappa, Phi Kappa Phi (hon.). Jewish. Office: U So Calif Dept Occupl Sci & Therapy 1540 Alcazar St CHP 133 Los Angeles CA 90089-9003 E-mail: gfrank@usc.edu.

FRANK, GEORGE ANDREW, lawyer; b. Budapest, Hungary, Apr. 6, 1938; came to U.S., 1957; s. Alex and Ilona (Weiss) F.; m. Carole Shames, Feb. 14, 1979; children: Cheryl, Charles. BS, Colo. State U., 1960; PhD in Organic Chemistry, MIT, 1965; JD, Temple U., 1977. Bar: Pa. 1977, U.S. Dist. Ct. (ea. dist.) Pa. 1977, D.C. 1980, U.S. Ct. Appeals (fed. cir.) 1982, U.S. Supreme Ct. 1984. Sr. chemist Rohm & Haas Co., Phila., 1965-69; lab. head Borden Chem., Phila., 1969-73; sr. scientist Thiokol Corp., Trenton, N.J., 1973-74; counsel Du Pont Corp., Wilmington, Del., 1974-85, sr. counsel, 1986-92, corp. counsel, 1992-2001, intellectual property law group leader, 2000-2001; of counsel, chair licensing and tech. transfer practice group Drinker Biddle & Reath LLP, Philadelphia, 2001—. External adv. com. Colo. State U. Coll. Natural Scis., 1996—; mem. intellectual property adv. com. Pa. Bar Inst., 2002-. Contbr. articles to profl. jours; patentee in field. Recipient Merck award Merck & Co., 1960; Sun Oil Co. grantee, 1964; fellow NIH. Mem. ABA (chair divsn. biotech. 1993-94, coun. 1994-98, chair chem. practice com. 1998-2000, chair divsn. biotech. and chem. practice 2000-02, chair divsn. profl. practice and sect. rels. 2002—), Phila. Patent Lawyers Assn. (chair bioscis. com. 1983-87, bd. govs. 1987-92, pres. 1992-93), Am. Intellectual Property Law Assn. (chair task force 1986), Benjamin Franklin Am. Inn of Cts. (v.p. 1996-97, pres. 1997-98). Republican. Avocations: tennis, squash, travel, books, opera. Home: 520 Lindy Ln Bala Cynwyd PA 19004-1331 Office: Drinker Biddle & Reath LLP 1 Logan Square 18th & Cherry St Philadelphia PA 19103 E-mail: frankga@dbr.com.

FRANK, GERALD WENDEL, civic leader, journalist; b. Portland, Oreg., Sept. 21, 1923; s. Aaron Frank and Ruth (Rosenfeld) F. Student, Stanford U., 1941-43, Loyola U., L.A., 1946-47; BA with honors, Cambridge U., 1948, MA, 1953; D Bus. Adminstrn. (hon.), Greenville (Ill.) Coll., 1971; LLD (hon.), Pacific U., 1983. Mgr. Meier & Frank Co., Salem, Oreg., 1955-65; v.p. Meier & Frank Co., Ltd., 1948-65; also bd. dirs.; pres. Gerry's Frankly Speaking, Salem, Oreg., 1996—; co-owner Gerry Frank's Konditorei, Inc., Salem, Oreg., 1982—. Bd. dirs. World Masters Games 1998, Inc. Author: Where to Find It, Buy It, Eat It in New York, 13 edits., 1980—, Joan and Gerry's Little Black Book of Shopping Secrets, 1991, Frank's Friday Surprise, 1995; sr. corres. Northwest Reports, 1992-96; commentator/reporter Morning news shows KPTV, Portland, 1993-2001, KATU, AM Northwest TV personality, 2002—. Active Found. Infantile Paralysis, Arthritis and Rheumatism Found., Nat. Coun., Boy Scouts Am., Travelers Aid Soc., Nat. Mcpl. League, Nat. Retail Merchants Assn., Am. Heart Soc., Am. Legion, Portland C. of C., Salem Area C. of C.; active Sunshine divsn. Portland Police Res.; active Portland Area Coun., Cascade Area Coun., Cascade Area Pacific Coun., Portland Rose Festival Assn., Jr. Achievement, Salem Pub. Libr. Found., Portland United Fund, Marion-Polk Counties United Good Neighbors, Salem Gen. Hosp., Citizens' Conf. for Govtl. Coop., Gov.'s Econ. Devel. Commn., Oreg. Retail Distbrs. Inst., Orge. Rsch. Assn., Salem 4-H Club, Willamette River Days, Salem YWCA; bd. trustees League of Women Voters; active Grad. Inst. Sci. and Tech., Portland Met. Futures Unltd., Inc., Oreg. Coast Aquarium, 1990—, Oreg. Symphony Soc.; chair Oreg. State Police Found., 2002—; gen. chmn. Mark O. Hatfield for U.S. Sen., 1966, 1972, 1978, 1984, 1990; mem. mgmt. com. U.S. Senate, 1978; chief of staff Sen. Mark O. Hatfield, 1973—92; mem. Culver Commn. on Reorgn. U.S. Senate, 1975—76; trustee Lorene Sails Higgins Charitable Trust, 1993—2000; mem. exec. com. U.S. Com. for UNICEF, 1990—99, Salvation Army; bd. trustees Willamette U.; active Marion-Salem Bldg. Study Com.; mem. exec. com. Oreg. High Desert Mus., Salem Art Assn., Parry Ctr. Children, St. Vincent Hosp. and Med. Ctr., Oreg. Health Scis. U., OMSI, chair, dir., 1996—97; active AAA of Oreg., Oreg. Garden Found.; mem. Oreg. State Bar Ho. Dels.; active Miss Oreg. Scholarship Program; chmn. Oreg. Tourism Commn., 1996—2001, Oreg. Ind. Coll. Found., 2000. Recipient numerous awards including Silver Beaver Boy Scouts Am., 1963, Reginald H. Vincent trophy United Good Neighbor of Yr., 1980, Brotherhood Nat. Conf. Christians and Jews, Portland, 1984, Glenn Jackson leadership Willamette U., 1984; named Oreg. Premier Citizen, 2000; Tom Lawson McCall fellow Pacific U., 1987. Mem. Am. Legion, Elks, Rotary (Paul Harris fellow 1986). Avocations: travel, gourmet dining. Home: 3250 Crestview Dr S Salem OR 97302-5959 Office: Gerry's Frankly Speaking Inc 2601 25th St SE Ste 500 Salem OR 97302-1287 also: PO Box 2225 Salem OR 97308-2225 E-mail: gerry@teleport.com.

FRANK, HARVEY, lawyer, author; b. N.Y.C., Aug. 24, 1930; s. Leon and Hannah (Lehr) F.; m. Judith Ellen Lewis, Nov. 29, 1959; 1 child, David . AB, NYU, 1951, LLM, 1961; JD, Harvard U., 1954. Bar: N.Y. 1954, Md. 1981, Ohio 1982. Ptnr. Hays Feuer Porter & Spanier, N.Y.C., 1963-69, Burns, Summit, Rovins & Feldesman, N.Y.C., 1970-74; prof. law Coll. William and Mary, Williamsburg, Va., 1974-80; adj. prof. Johns Hopkins U., Balt., 1981; ptnr. Benesch Friedlander, Coplan & Aronoff, Cleve., 1982-93; pvt. practice Law Offices Harvey Frank, Phila., 1993—. Sec. Banner Aerospace, 1990-93. Author: The ERC Closely Held Corporation Guide, 1981, 2d edit., 1984; contbr. articles to law jours. Mem. ABA, Am. Law Inst. Home and Office: Law Offices of Harvey Frank 1215A Waverly Walk Philadelphia PA 19147

FRANK, HOWARD, systems company executive, dean, educator; b. N.Y.C., June 4, 1941; s. Herman and Tina (Sander) F.; m. Jane Steinberg, Apr. 23, 1965; children: David, Laura, Erica. BSEE, U. Miami, 1962; MS, Northwesten U., 1964; PhD, Northwestern U., 1965. Asst. prof. U. Calif.-Berkeley, 1965-68, assoc. prof., 1969; exec. v.p. Network Analysis Corp., Glen Cove, N.Y., 1969, pres., 1970-81, Contel Info. Systems Inc., Great Neck, NY, 1982-85, Howard Frank Assocs., 1985—; chmn. Network Mgmt., Inc., 1987—91; dir. Def. Adv. Rsch. Project Agy.'s Info. Tech. Office; pres., CEO Contel Info. Sys. (sub. Contel Corp.); pres., CEO, founder Network Analysis Corp.; prof. mgmt. scis. Smith Sch., 1997—; dean Robert H. Smith Sch. Bus. U. Md., 1997—. Bd. dirs. Contel Corp.; vis. cons. Exec. Office Pres. U.S., 1968; founder, chmn., CEO Network Mgmt. Inc., Fairfax, Va., 1986-91; spkr. bus. and profl. meetings; adj. prof. decision scis. Wharton Sch.; assoc. prof. electrical engring. and computer scis. U. (Berkeley) California. Author: Communications, Transmission and Transportation Networks, 1971; contbr. over 190 articles and chpts. in books on tech. and mgmt. of tech.; mem. 7 editl. bds. NASA fellow, 1963-65; Gen. Motors fellow, 1958-62 Fellow IEEE (Leonard G. Abraham 1969, Eric Sumner award 1999), SEI Ctr. Advanced Studies in Mgmt. (sr. fellow, mem. bd. dirs.); mem. AAAS, AACSB, Mid-Atlantic Assn. Colls. and Bus. Adminstrn. (pres), Ops. Research Soc., Ams. Internat. Acad. Mgmt. (vice chancellor), Carnegie Mellon's Heinz Sch. (mem. adv. bd.), Global Tech. and Mgmt. Consortium (mem. exec. com.), Macklin Inst. Mont. Coll. (bd. dirs.), Nat. Inst. Stds. and Tech.'s Advanced Tech. Program (fed. adv. com.), Nat. Acad. Engring., N.Y. Acad. Scis. Office: Robert H Smith Sch Bus U Md 2410 Van Munching Hall College Park MD 20742-1815

FRANK, IRWIN NORMAN, urologist, educator; b. Rochester, N.Y., Mar. 24, 1927; s. Harry and Bess (Smalline) F.; m. Marilyn Ellowitch, June 13, 1954; children— Gary, Steven, Lawrence BA, U. Rochester, 1950, MD, 1954. Diplomate Am. Bd. Urology. Intern Strong Meml Hosp., Rochester, 1954-55, asst. resident, 1955-58, Nat. Cancer Inst. trainee, 1957-59, chief resident urology, 1958—59, med. dir., 1985-95; asst. prof. urology U. Rochester, 1959-67, assoc. prof., 1967-74, prof., 1974-97, acting chmn. dept. urology, 1967-69, sr. assoc. dean Sch. Medicine and Dentistry, 1985-95, prof. emeritus, 1997—. Contbr. chpts., numerous articles to profl. publs. Med. adv. bd. Kidney Found. Upstate N.Y., Rochester. Served with USN, 1944-46; PTO Am. Cancer Soc. fellow 1951 Fellow ACS, Am. Acad. Pediatrics; mem. Am. Urol. Assn. (bd. dirs. 1987-95, pres. elect 1999-2000, pres. 2000-01), Am. Urol. Assn. N.E. (pres. 1983-84), N.Y. State Urol. Soc. (pres.), Irondequoit Country Club, Joint Commn. on Accreditation of Healthcare Orgns. (commrs. 1995-2002, exec. com. 1997-2002, sec. 2001-02). Home: 7 Callahan Ct Pittsford NY 14534 Office: U Rochester Med Sch 601 Elmwood Ave Rochester NY 14642-0001 E-mail: infrank@aol.com.

FRANK, ISAIAH, economist, educator; b. N.Y.C., Nov. 7, 1917; s. Henry and Rose (Isserles) F.; m. Ruth Hershfield, Mar. 23, 1941; children: Robert E., Kenneth D. B in Social Sci., CCNY, 1936; MA in Econs., Columbia U., 1938, PhD in Econs., 1960. Rsch. assoc. in econs. Columbia U. Council for Research in Social Scis., 1936-39; tchg. fellow, instr. econs. Amherst Coll., 1939-41; Carnegie fellow Nat. Bur. Econ. Rsch., 1941-42; cons. WPB, 1942; sr. economist OSS, 1942-44; various positions U.S. Dept. State, 1945-63; dir. Office Internat. Trade, 1957-59, Office Internat. Financial and Devel. Affairs, 1961-62, dep. asst. sec. for econ. affairs, 1962-63; William L. Clayton prof. internat. econs. Sch. Advanced Internat. Studies, Johns Hopkins U., 1963—. Mem. Industry-Govt. Iron and Steel Mission to Europe, 1947; adviser U.S. del. Econ. Commn. for Europe, 1948; dep. dir. fgn. resources div. Pres.'s Materials Policy Commn., 1951-52; head U.S. del. Conf. on Dollar Liberalization, OEEC, Paris, 1955-56; chmn. U.S. del. GATT, Geneva, 1958; alt. U.S. rep. Fourth Meeting Devel. Assistance Group, London, 1961; chmn. U.S. del. to prep. com. UN Conf. Trade and Devel., Geneva, 1963— ; U.S. rep. Spl. Trade Conf. OAS, Alta Gracia, Argentina, 1964; exec. dir. Pres.'s Commn. on Internat. Trade and Investment Policy, 1970-71; adv. com. UN Trade and Devel. Bd.; dir. internat. econ. studies Com. Econ. Devel.; mem. adv. council Inst. for Latin Am. Integration; mem. adv. com. Inst. Internat. Econs.; cons. World Bank; chmn. adv. com. on internat. investment State Dept.; mem. svcs. policy adv. com. U.S. Trade Rep.; mem. adv. com. on internat. econ. policy U.S. Dept. State. Author: The European Common Market: An Analysis of Commercial Policy, 1960, Foreign Enterprise in Developing Countries, 1980, Finance and Third-World Economic Growth, 1988, Breaking New Ground in U.S. Trade Policy, 1991, U.S. Trade Policy Beyond the Uruguay Round, 1994, U.S. Economic Policy Toward the Asia-Pacific Region, 1997; co-author, editor: The Japanese Economy in International Perspective, 1975; contbr. articles to profl. publs. 1st lt. AUS, 1944-45. Recipient Rockefeller Pub. Svc. award, 1959-60 Mem. Coun. Fgn. Rels., Am. Econ. Assn., Cosmos Club, Phi Beta Kappa. Home: 3102 Hawthorne St NW Washington DC 20008-3539 Office: Johns Hopkins U 1740 Massachusetts Ave NW Washington DC 20036-1903

FRANK, JACOB, lawyer; b. Albany, Apr. 4, 1936; s. Isidore and Sara F.; m. Yoelith Frank, Aug. 26, 1936; children: Eytan, Michael, Adam, Orly. BEE, Rensselaer Poly. Inst., 1957; LLB, Am. U., 1963; postgrad., George Washington U. Coll. Law, 1964-67, NYU Law Sch., 1969-73. Bar: D.C. 1963, Mass. 1979, Va. 2001, U.S. Patent Office. Of counsel Alliance Law Group, Tysons Corner, Va., 2000—. Home: 17040 Thousand Oaks Dr Haymarket VA 20169 E-mail: JYFRANK8@aol.com.

FRANK, JAMES AARON, magazine editor, author; b. Englewood, N.J., Apr. 13, 1954; s. Reuven and Bernice (Kaplow) F.; m. Belle Gross, Aug, 14, 1977; children: William Moses, Rebecca Ann. BA, Kenyon Coll., 1976. From editorial asst. to assoc. editor Diversion Mag., N.Y.C., 1976-79; sr. editor US Air Mag., N.Y.C., 1979-82; editor Amtrak Express Mag., N.Y.C., 1982-84; exec. editor Golf Mag., N.Y.C., 1984—, now editor; v.p. Golf Mag. Properties. Author: The Golfer's Companion, 1993, Golf Secrets, 1994, Precision Putting, 1998; editor: Golf Magazine's Private Lessons, 1990; co-author, co-editor: Golf in America: The First 100 Years, 1988; co-author: PGA Championship 1916-84, 1984, The Golf Magazine Complete Book of Golf Instruction, 1997, Dave Pelz's Short Game Bible, 1999, Dave Pelz's Putting Bible, 2000. Avocation: golf. Office: Golf Magazine Time4Media 2 Park Ave New York NY 10016-5604

FRANK, JAMES S. automotive executive; b. Chgo., 1942; BS, Dartmouth Coll.; MBA, Stanford U. With ZF, Inc., 1965, Wheels, Inc., Des Plaines, Ill., 1965; pres. Four Wheels, Inc., Des Plaines, Ill., 1965; pres., CEO Frank Consol. Enterprises, Des Plaines, Ill., 1967—, Wheels (subs. Frank Consol. Enterprises), Des Plaines, Ill., 1974—. Pres. Michael Reese Med. Rsch. Inst. Coun. Jr. Bd.; bd. trustees U. Chgo. Hosps., U. Chgo.; bd. overseers Thayer Engring.

Sch. Dartmouth Coll. Mem.: Am. Automobile Leasing Assn. (past pres. and chair, bd. dirs., chair fed. gtax and legis. com., past chair industry com.). Office: Frank Consol Enterprises 666 Garland Pl Des Plaines IL 60016-4725*

FRANK, JEREMY D. computer scientist; b. Washington, Aug. 1, 1968; s. Steven B. and Katrin E. F.; m. Amy Lynn Schmieder, July 9, 2000. BA, Pomona Coll., 1990; PhD, U. Calif., Davis, 1997. Computer scientist Caelum Rsch. Corp., 1997—2001, QSS Group Inc., 2000—01, NASA Ames Rsch. Ctr., 2001—. Mem. Am. Assn. Artificial Intelligence, Am. Math. Soc. Avocations: cooking, literature, games of strategy. Home: 664 Vinemaple Ave Sunnyvale CA 94086-8455 E-mail: frank@ptolemy.arc.nasa.gov.

FRANK, JOANN, photographer; b. Phila., Apr. 11, 1947; d. Herbert and Irene Frank. BFA, Moore Coll. Art, Phila., 1968. Photographer (book) 3 Dozen, 1977; one-woman shows include The Halsted 831 Gallery, Birmingham, Mich., 1974, Enjay Gallery of Photography, Boston, 1975, The Witkin Gallery, N.Y.C., 1979, Drew U., Madison, N.J., 1990, exhibited in group shows at U. Kans. Mus. Art, Lawrence, 1974, San Francisco Mus. Modern Art, 1975, Addison Gallery of Am. Art, Andover, Mass., 1975, Balt. Mus. Art, 1977, L.A. Inst. Contemporary Art, 1978, exhibited in group shows, Phila., 1983, exhibited in group shows, IBM Gallery, 1984, Print Club of Phila., 1986, Zabriskie Gallery, N.Y.C., 1989, Drew U., Madison, 1993, Witkin Gallery, 1995, numerous others, Represented in permanent collections Met. Mus. Art, N.Y.C., Bibliotheque Nationale, Paris, San Francisco Mus. Modern Art, Sheldon Meml. Art Gallery, U. Nebr., Lincoln, Australian Nat. Gallery, Canberra, Inst. Photography, Tokyo, New Orleans Mus. Art, U. Kans. Mus. Art, Centro Cultural/Arte Contemporaneo, Mexico City, Estado da Cultura, Lisbon, Portugal, numerous others; photography in numerous pubs.

FRANK, JOHN LEROY, lawyer, government executive, educator; b. Eau Claire, Wis., Mar. 13, 1952; s. George LeRoy and Frances Elaine (Torgerson) F. BS summa cum laude, U. Wis., Eau Claire, 1974; JD cum laude, U. Wis., Madison, 1977. Bar: Wis. 1977, U.S. Dist. Ct. (we. dist.) Wis. 1977, U.S. Supreme Ct. 1982. Instr. law U. Wis., Madison, 1976-77; assoc. Garvey, Anderson, Kelly & Ryberg, S.C., Eau Claire, 1977-81; legis dir., counsel Congressman Steve Gunderson, Washington, 1981-85, chief of staff, counsel, 1985-89; staff coord. 92 Group, Washington, 1987-89; instr. Chippewa Valley Tech. Coll., 1989-93, 97—, chair dept. behavioral sci. & civic effectiveness, 2003—, pvt. practice, 1990-93, 97—; counsel, minority cons. House Subcommittee on Livestock, Washington, Wis., 1993-95; counsel Congressman Steve Gunderson, Washington, 1993-97; dep. minority counsel House Com. on Agr., Washington, 1993-95, dep. chief counsel, 1995-97; commr. W. Ctrl. Wis. Regional Planning Commn., Eau Claire, 1998—; vis. prof. U. of Wis. - Eau Claire, Wis., 2002—03. Pol. analyst, commentator WEAU-TV, Eau Claire, Wis., 1998—; mem. Bush-Cheney Transition Adv. Com., 2001; dir. paralegal program Chippewa Valley Tech. Coll., 1992-93, 97-2001, 03—. Mem.: FBA, ABA, Assn. Career and Tech. Edn. (legis. com. 2003—, Region III award of merit 2003), Wis. Bar Assn., U. Wis. Alumni Assn. (outstanding sr. arts & scis. 1974, Disting. Achievement award 2001), The Presto Found. (v.p. 1992—93, bd. dirs. 1992—93, 2000—, v.p. 2000—), Wis. Assn. for Career and Tech. Edn. (legis. com. chair 2000—01, bd. dirs. 2000—, chmn. strategic planning com. 2001—02, pres. 2002—03), Phi Gamma Delta (Durrance award 1978), Phi Delta Phi. Republican. Lutheran. Address: 2113 Meadow Ln Eau Claire WI 54701-7965

FRANK, JOHN V. foundation executive; b. Cleve., Oct. 14, 1936; s. Paul A. and Frances (Halbert) F. Student, Babson Coll., 1956-57; BBA, U. Miami-Fla., 1960. Mgmt. trainee Nat. City Bank, Cleve., 1960-62; investment analyst First Nat. Bank, Akron, 1962-70, asst. trust officer, 1970-73, trust officer, 1973-80, v.p., trust officer, 1980-81; pres. Summit Capital Mgmt. Co., Akron, 1982-99. Treas. Fairlawn Heights Assn., Inc., Akron, 1971-02; pres. Ohio Ballet, 1973-74; trustee Howland Meml. Fund, Akron, 1974—; pres., trustee Burton D. Morgan Found., Akron, 1976—; councilman City of Akron, 1978-98; trustee Akron Art Mus., 1976-83, pres. 1979-81; trustee Akron City Hosp. Found., 1980-83, 92, Summa Health Systems Found., 1992—, treas./chmn., 2003—, The Rectory Sch., 1999—, chair exec. com., 2001—; mem. Coun. on Founds. Com. on Legis. and Regulations, 1990-94; nat. steering com. Coll. Wooster, 1992-96; mem. Akron Charter Rev. Commn., 1980, vice chmn., 1990, mem. 2000; mem. fin. and fiscal policy investment subcom. U. Akron, 1996-99; mem. 50th anniversary com. UN Grace Cathedral Ch., San Francisco, 1993-95, St. Paul's Episc. Ch.; bd. overseers Blossom Music Ctr., 1996-99; trustee Akron Rural Cemetery, 1994—, v.p. 1997—, pres., trustee Akron Civil War Meml. Soc., 1996—; mem. Akron Emergency Med. Adv. Bd., 1986—; mem. nat. coun. Norman Rockwell Mus., 2002—, trustee Our Lady of Elms Sch., 2002[0097] . 1st lt. USAR, 1963-69. Mem. Cleve. Soc. Security Analysts, Portage Country Club, Hillsboro Club (Hillsboro Beach, Fla.). Republican. Episcopalian. Avocation: art collecting. Office: Burton D Morgan Found PO Box 1500 Akron OH 44309-1500

FRANK, JOSEPH ELIHU, lawyer; b. Burlington, Vt., Jan. 28, 1934; s. Max and Sara Ruth (Bramson) F.; m. Catherine Hartman Layne, Aug. 28, 1971; chldren: Sara Rebecca, Cheryl Elizabeth. AB, Harvard U., 1956, JD, 1959. Bar: Vt. 1960, U.S. Dist. Ct. Vt. 1960, U.S. Ct. Appeals (2d cir.) 1961. U.S. Supreme Ct. 1965. Law clk. to judge U.S. Dist. Ct. Vt., 1960; asst. U.S. atty. Dist. of Vt., 1961; sole practice Burlington, 1961-68; mem. Paul, Frank & Collins P.C., Burlington, 1968-96, of counsel, 1996—. Spl. counsel to Vt. Hwy. Bd., 1962-75, to Pub. Service Bd., 1965-69; chmn. adv. com. civil rules Vt. Supreme Ct., 1983-89. Alderman, City of Burlington, 1971-73; trustee Med. Ctr. Hosp. of Vt., Burlington, 1977-86. Mem. ABA, Vt. Bar Assn. (pres. 1983-84), Chittenden County Bar Assn., Am. Judicature Soc. Home: 8 Bay Crest Dr South Burlington VT 05403-7713 Office: Paul Frank & Collins PC 1 Church St Burlington VT 05402-1307 E-mail: w1sov@earthlink.net.

FRANK, JULIE ANN, lawyer; b. Omaha, Aug. 5, 1953; d. Morton Stanley Frank and Elaine Edith (Meyerson) Potts; m. Howard Nathan Kaplan, Oct. 26, 1985; 1 child, Martin Kaplan. BA in Psychology, U. Tex., 1974; JD, Creighton U., 1979. Bar: Nebr. 1979, Tex. 1980. Clk. to Justice Nebr. Supreme Ct., Lincoln, 1979-80; assoc. Qualley, Larson & Jones, Omaha, 1980-81; sole practice Omaha, 1981-83; pntr. Pollak, Frank & Hicks, Omaha, 1983-90; ptnr. Frank & Gryva, Omaha, 1990—. Instr. Met. Community Coll., Omaha, 1982-84, Buena Vista Coll., Omaha, 1982-84, U. Nebr., 1983. Bd. dirs. Nebr. Civil Liberties Union, 1981-85, Omaha Jewish Family Svcs., 1989-97; sec. bd. Jewish Family Svcs., 1991-92, v.p., 1992-93, pres., 1993-96; adminstrv. coord. Douglas County Dems., 1982; del. Douglas County Conv., 1984, 86; mem. cen. com. Nebr. Dem. Com., 1984-86; mem. Nat. Coun. Jewish Women, Omaha; mem. community rels. com. Anti-defamation League, 1987-90, bd. dirs., 1992-94; chmn. Nebr. Women's Polit. Caucus; bd. dirs. Assn. of Jewish Family and Children's Agencies, 1996-2002—. Mem. ABA, Nebr. State Bar Assn. (co-chairperson Women and Law sect. 1987-88, bd. dirs. 1987-89), Omaha Bar Assn. (lawyers referral com., particpant in law day "Meet a Lawyer" program, 1986-88, 97). Home: 661 N 57th St Omaha NE 68132-2031 Office: Frank & Gryva 1823 Harney St Ste 201 Omaha NE 68102-1913 E-mail: jfrank1@cox.net.

FRANK, KERRY DEAN, psychology educator, consultant; b. Eunice, La., June 30, 1950; s. Letell and Wirvely Frank; m. Jan Louise Hintz, Aug. 9, 1998. BS, McNeese State U., 1972; MEd, U. Southwestern La., 1977; PhD, U. Minn., 1992. Cert. tchr., La., Minn.; cert. counselor and adminstr., La. Tchr. Maplewood (La.) Jr. H.S., 1972-73, Acadiana H.S., Lafayette, La., 1973-81; lectr., rsch. assoc. U. Minn., Mpls., 1981-89, tchr. asst. in stats. Humphrey Inst. Pub. Affairs, 1985-88; instr. psychology U. St. Thomas, St. Paul, 1989-92, asst. prof., 1992-2000, assoc. prof., 2000—. Counselor, advisor Black Learning Resource Ctr., U. Minn., 1987-88; cons. Mpls.-St. Paul Pub. Schs., 1989—; discussant Julian Parker Lecture Series, St. Paul, 1999—; reviewer Jour. Critical Inquiry, 1999—; presenter Internat. Soc. for Justice Rsch., Israel, 2000. Contbr. articles to profl. jours., including Procs. Nat. Assn. for Multicultural Edn. Cons., advisor gang resistance edn. and tng., St. Paul, 1993-95, Ramsey County Juvenile Ctr., St. Paul, 1998—; vol. Ctr. for Victims of Torture, St. Paul, 2000—. Mem. APA, NAACP, Am. Ednl. Rsch. Assn., Soc. for Psychol. Study Social Issues, Nat. Assn. for Multicultural Edn., Kappa Alpha Psi. Avocations: jogging, reading, playing chess, playing horns, travel. Home: 650 Grove Ave Saint Paul MN 55126 Office: U St Thomas 1000 LaSalle Ave Minneapolis MN 55403-2009 E-mail: kdfrank@stthomas.edu.

FRANK, LAURA JEAN, computer scientist; b. New Rochelle, N.Y., May 21, 1945; d. James Florian and Erma (Guttag) F. BA, U. Vt., 1967; MBA, Iona Coll., New Rochelle, 1971; postgrad., China Inst., N.Y.C., Polytechnic Inst., White Plains, N.Y.; Assoc. Masters, George Washington U., 2001. Cert. project mgmt. profl. Project Mgmt. Inst., 2002, Project Mgmt. Inst. With Equitable Life Assurance Soc., N.Y.C., 1967-79, project leader, 1978-79; sr. planning specialist PHH Relocation, Wilton, Conn., 1979-80, project mgr., 1980-83, sys. mgr., 1983-88, mgr. office tech., 1988-91; founding prof. Homequity U., Wilton, Conn., 1985-91; sys. cons. LJF Assocs., Stamford, Conn., 1991-95; sys. mgr. Fiberlux, Purchase, NY, 1994-98; pjt mgr. Synapse Group, Stamford, 1998—. Bd. dirs. Tri-State Trainers. Editor and bd. dirs.: newspaper Stamford First Nighter; contbr. articles to profl. jours. Mem. Stamford Hist. Soc., Women in Mgmt., Friends of Stamford Symphony, Literacy Vols. of Am. Office: 4 High Ridge Park Stamford CT 06905-1325 E-mail: lfrank@synapsemail.com.

FRANK, LAWRENCE JAMES, library director; b. Detroit, Oct. 9, 1943; s. George A. and Marjorie J. (McConkey) Frank; m. Bonnie L. Bonsky; children: Alyssa Ann, Nathan D. BA with honors, Western Mich. U., 1976, MA magna cum laude, 1977; AMLS, U. Mich., 1979; cert. pub. adm. advanced mgmt. program, Miami U., Oxford, Ohio, 1983; cert. edn., U. Wis., 1996. Exec. dir. Amos Meml. Pub. Libr., Sidney, 1981—85; dir. Boyd County Pub. Libr., Ashland, Ky., 1986—95, St. Clair County Libr., Port Huron, Mich., 1995—99, Onondaga County Pub. Libr., Syracuse, NY, 1999—2001, Hinsdale Pub. Libr., Ill., 2001—03, Knox County Libr., Knoxville, Tenn., 2003—. Cons./tchr., missionary The Lang. Inst., Japan Luth. Ch., Tokyo and Niigata, Japan, 1968—71; cons. in libr. design and orgn. Port Huron, 1996—98. Contbr. articles to profl. jours.; author numerous poems, (mystery novel) Arius Project, 2003. Bd. dirs. Ky. Coun. on Econ Edn., Ashland, 1986-95; chronic disease steering com., U. Cin. Children's Hosp., Ashland, 1987-90; active Main St. Port Huron, 1996-98. Named Boss of Yr., Jaycees, Ashland; U. Mich. scholar, Ann Arbor, 1978-79. Mem.: PLA, ACLU (ctrl. N.Y. chpt.), ALA, ASPA. Avocations: wine, writing, drawing, hiking, environmental design.

FRANK, LEONA, artist; b. Kew Gardens, N.Y., Nov. 23, 1946; d. Edward Elliot and Sylvia Lois (Moskowitz) Kliegman; m. Richard Frank, June 15, 1968; children: Hillary Dena, Joshua Eric. BA in Art cum laude, Queens Coll., 1968. Calligrapher, 1970—; fine art painter, 1989—. One-person shows include Slater Meml. Mus., Norwich, Conn., 1992, Ctr. for Fin. Studies, Fairfield U., 1993, Design Ctr., Boston, 1994, Westport Arts Ctr., 1994, Picture This Gallery, Westport, 1996, Mitchells Window Exhbn., Westport, 1999; exhibited in group shows Castle Gallery, Coll. New Rochelle, N.Y., 1993, Nan Miller Gallery, Rochester, N.Y., 1994, Met Life Windows Exhbn., N.Y.C., 1994, New Art Ann. Stamford Mus., 2000, Art of Northeast Silvermine Arts Ctr., NEw Canaan, Conn., 2000, The Conn. Vision Mattatuck Mus., Waterbury, Conn., 2002; represented in pub. and corp. collections Hale & Dorr, Boston, Linsco Pvt. Ledger, Boston; permament collection Westport Schs.; works featured in publs. including Woman's Day Mag., Conn. Artists' Calendar, The William & Mary Rev., Conn. Mag. Recipient Best in Show awards Ridgefield Guild of Artists, 1990, Conn. Artists' Exhbn.-Slater Meml. Mus., 1991. Mem. Conn. Women Artists, New Haven Paint & Clay Club (Ann. Juried Exhbn. Eder Found. award 2003).

FRANK, LEONARD ARNOLD, physician; b. Phila., Nov. 28, 1935; s. Charles and Rose F.; m. Barbara Balis, Aug. 17, 1958; children: Michael, Brad. BS, Franklin & Marshall Coll., 1957; MD, Hahnemann U., 1961. Intern Phila. Gen. Hosp., 1961-62; resident Bryn Mawr (Pa.) Hosp., 1964-65, Jefferson Med. Coll., Phila., 1965-68; co-chmn. urology Sacred Heart Hosp., Norristown, Pa., 1980-85, Montgomery Hosp., Norristown, Pa., 1980-85; chmn. urology Sacred Heart Hosp., 1985-93; clin. asst. prof. Jefferson Med. Coll., 1996—. Pres. med. staff Sacred Heart Hosp., 1982—84. Lt. USN, 1962—64. Rsch. grantee Hahnemann Med. Coll., 1960. Mem. AMA, Am. Urologic Assn., Pa. Med. Soc., Urologic Assn. Pa. (pres. 1988-89), Montgomery County Med. Soc., Phila. Urologic Soc. (pres. 1980-81). Avocations: gardening, hiking, skiing, sculpture. Office: Jefferson Med Coll 1025 Walnut St Philadelphia PA 19107-5001

FRANK, LILLIAN GORMAN, human resources executive, psychologist, management consultant; b. N.Y.C., July 4, 1953; d. Helmuth H. and Ida (Malitsch) Degen; m. Stephen F. Frank, Feb. 10, 2001. BA in Psychology, Lehman Coll., CUNY, 1975; MA in Indsl. Psychology, Case Western Res. U., 1978, PhD in indsl. Psychology, 1979; MBA in Corp. Fin., U. So. Calif., 1986. Econ. benefits asst. Girl Scouts U.S.A., N.Y.C., 1971—75; psychologist Pers. Rsch. Svcs., Cleve., 1975—79; cons. psychologist Pers. Rsch. & Devel. Corp., Cleve., 1977—78; mgr. pers. rsch. 1st Interstate Bank, L.A., 1979—82, v.p., mgr. human resource planning and devel., 1982—85; v.p., mgr. human resource planning and exec. devel. 1st Interstate Bancorp, L.A., 1985—86; exec. v.p., human resources dir. First Interstate Bank of Calif., 1986—90; exec. v.p. human resources First Interstate Bancorp, 1990—96; sr. v.p. human resources Edison Internat., Rosemead, Calif., 1996—2000; prin. Frank Insights, L.A., 2000—. Trustee Autry Mus. Western Heritage, 2001—; bd. dirs. INROADS/So. Calif., 1986—, YMCA of Met. L.A., 2002—. Mem. APA, Soc. for Psychologists in Mgmt. (bd. dirs. 1993-97), Orgn. for Women Execs., Soc. for Human Resources Mgmt. Home and Office: 207 N Glenroy Ave Los Angeles CA 90049-2417 E-mail: lillian@frankinsights.com.

FRANK, LLOYD, lawyer, retired chemical company executive; b. N.Y.C., Aug. 9, 1925; s. Herman and Selma (Lowenstein) F.; m. Beatrice Silverstein, Dec. 26, 1954; children: Margaret Lois, Frederick. BA, Oberlin Coll., 1947; JD, Cornell U., 1950. Bar: N.Y. 1950, U.S. Supreme Ct. 1973. Lawyer, N.Y.C., 1950—64; sec., dir. Grow Group, Inc., N.Y.C., 1964-95; sr. ptnr., exec. com., chmn. corp. dept. Parker Chapin LLP, N.Y.C., 1985—2003; sr. ptnr. Jenkens Gilchrist Parker Chapin, LLP, N.Y.C., 2000—. Bd. dirs. Volt Info. Scis. Inc., (NYSE) N.Y.C., Madison Industries, Inc., N.Y.C., Dryclean, USA, Inc., Miami, Fla., AMEX, Pub. Art Fund, Inc., N.Y.C., Park Electrochem. Corp., (NYSE) Lake Success, N.Y., Internat. Longevity Ctr. U.S.A. Ltd., N.Y.C., Kulite Semicondr., Inc., Leonia, N.J.; sec. Esquire Radio & Electronics, Inc., Bklyn.; lectr. Am. Mgmt. Assn., 1967-77, Probe Internat., Inc., 1975-77, Corp. Seminars, Inc., 1968-71. Mem. ABA (com. negotiated acquisitions), Assn. Bar City of N.Y. (com. on internat. environ. law com. on product liability, com. on lawyers in transition, com. on securities law), N.Y. County Lawyers Assn. (com. on corp. law depts.), Home: 25 Central Park W Apt 17Q New York NY 10023-7211 Office: Jenkens & Gilchrist Parker Chapin LLP Chrysler Bldg 405 Lexington Ave New York NY 10174-0002 E-mail: lfrank@jenkens.com.

FRANK, MARJORIE SLAVICK, educational curriculum specialist, composer; b. Milw., July 8, 1948; d. Monroe S. and Betty S. (Mintz) Slavick; children: Adam Robert, Benjamin Steven. BS, U. Wis., 1972; MS, Georgetown U., 1974. Cert. tchr., Wis. Dir. devel. Inst. Modern Lang., Silver Spring, Md., 1974-76; freelance writer edn. materials Bklyn., 1976-81; pres. M&H Ideas, Inc., Bklyn., 1981—. Author: (children's book) Map Adventures, 1992, (children's sci. program) Harcourt Science, 2002, (ednl. software), Sports Media, 1999, (CD) Science Songs, 2001, Performing Arts, 2002; contbr. articles to profl. jours. Overnight host Bklyn. Heights Synagogue Shelter, 1992—. Mem. NSTA, TESOL, Nat. Coun. Tchrs. English, Internat. Reading Assn., Linguistic Soc. Am. Office: M&H Ideas Inc 18 Verandah Pl Brooklyn NY 11201-6106

FRANK, MARKUS HERMANN, physician, researcher; b. Kirchheim, Germany, May 14, 1965; s. Hermann Joseph and Theresia Walburga (Wanner) F.; m. Natasha Yuri Melnik, Dec. 5, 1995; children: Maximilian, Alexander, Andreas. AB magna cum laude, Harvard U., 1989; MD magna cum laude, U. Heidelberg, 1992. Diplomate Am. Bd. Internal Medicine. Instr. anatomy U. Heidelberg, Germany, 1987-88; resident in internal medicine U. Munich, 1993-94, Albert Einstein Coll. of Medicine, N.Y.C., 1994-97; clin. fellow in medicine Harvard U. Sch. Medicine, Boston, 1997-98, rsch. fellow in medicine, 1998-2001, instr. medicine, 2001—; assoc. physician Brigham and Women's Hosp., Harvard Med. Sch., Boston, 2001—. Staff physician West Roxbury VA Med. Ctr., Boston, 1998—; instr. medicine Harvard U. Sch. Medicine, Boston, 2001—. Co-author: Transplantation 1999: Progress on the Cusp of the Millennium, 1999; contbr. articles to sci. and profl. jours. Vol. Rural Area Med. Aid Soc., Bangkok, 1989. Recipient Theodore I. Steinman Clin. Rsch. award, Nat. Kidney Found., Mass., R.I., N.H., Vt., 2001. Mem. AMA, ACP, Am. Soc. Transplantation (com. faculty grantee 2001—), United World Colls. Network, Mass. Med. Soc. (com. on young physicians 2001—), Harvard Club of Boston. Recipient Theodore Steinman award in clin. rsch. Nat. Kidney Found., 2001. Avocations: violin, opera, literature, sailing. Home: 9 Brewer St Cambridge MA 02138 Office: Harvard U Sch Medicine Lab Immunogens/Transp B&W Women Hosp 75 Francis St Boston MA 02115 E-mail: mfrank@rics.bwh.harvard.edu.

FRANK, MARSHALL, protective services official, writer; b. N.Y.C., Apr. 28, 1939; s. Arthur Frank and Vivien Peterson; m. Suzanne Elizabeth Parisien, June 14, 1989; children: Annette, Bennett, Russell, Lysa, Jennifer. BS, Fla. Internat. U., 1977. Police capt. Metro Dade Police Dept., Miami, Fla., 1960—90; security mgr. Wackenaut Corp., Miami, 1990—94. Author: (novels) Beyond the Call, 2000, Dire Straits: A Miami Novel, 2001, (anthology) Frankly Speaking, 2002. Avocation: violin.

FRANK, MARTIN, physiology educator, health scientist, association executive; b. Chgo., Oct. 22, 1947; s. Edward D. and Ann (Horwitz) F.; m. Cheryl Lynn Motel, Aug. 19, 1970; children: Beth Susan, Eric Lawrence. AB (Evans scholar), U. Ill., 1969, MS, 1971, PhD, 1973. USPHS predoctoral research trainee U. Ill., 1971-73; research assoc. Mich. Cancer Found., Detroit, 1973-74; dept. pharmacology Mich. State U., 1974-75; assoc. prof. physiology George Washington U., 1980—. Exec. sec. physiology study sect. divsn. rsch. grants NIH, Bethesda, Md., 1978—85; exec. dir. Am. Physiol. Soc., Bethesda, 1985—; pres., treas., bd. dirs. Commn. on Profls. in Sci. and Tech., 1986—2000; mem. internat. adv. panel Galileo Found., 1990—93; mem. life scis. subcom. NASA Space Sci. and Applications Adv. Com., 1991—94. Editor Physiologist, 1985—; contbr. articles to profl. jours. Vice pres., bd. dirs. Bennington Community Assn., Gaithersburg, Md., 1976-78, 80-81, mem. Gaithersburg City Planning Commn., 1982-85. Recipient Disting. Alumni award dept. molecular and integrative physiology U. Ill., Urbana, 2001; Nations' Capitol Affiliate Am. Heart Assn. grantee-in-aid, 1975-78; NIH grantee; NSF grantee. Mem. AAAS, Am. Physiol. Soc., Am. Soc. Assn. Execs., Coalition Engrng Scientific Soc. Execs. Office: Am Physiol Soc 9650 Rockville Pike Bethesda MD 20814-3998 E-mail: mfrank@the-aps.org.

FRANK, MARY LOU, retired elementary education educator; b. Cleve., May 18, 1915; d. William Henry and Martha Ann (Brown) Parsons; m. Russell Edward Frank, May 18, 1935; children: Richard Edward, James Russell. BS in Edn., Cleve. State U., 1960; MS in Edn., U. Akron, Ohio, 1967, Miami U., Oxford, Ohio, 1934-35; student, Baldwin-Wallace Coll., 1933-34. Cert. tchr., Ohio. Substitute tchr. Cleve. Pub. Schs., 1963; tchr. elem. Brecksville (Ohio) City Sch. Dist., 1953-71, Lee County Bd. of Edn., Ft. Myers, Fla., 1971-74, ret., 1974. Mem. ambassadors to China from Fla., Children's Palaces Homes Hosps., 1980. Martha Holden Jennings Found. scholar, 1963-64, grantee, 1965. Mem. U.S. Power Squadron Aux. (pilot), Collier Reading Coun., Delta Kappa Gamma. Avocations: boating, travel, oil painting. Home: 61 Impala Ct # 23 Fort Myers FL 33912-6338

FRANK, MARY LOU BRYANT, psychologist, educator; b. Denver, Nov. 27, 1952; d. W. D. and Blanche (Dean) Bryant; m. Kenneth Kerry Frank, Sept. 9, 1973; children: Kari Lou, Kendra Leah. BA, Colo. State U., 1974, MEd, 1983, MS, 1986, PhD, 1989. Tchr. Cherry Creek Schs., Littleton, Colo., 1974—80; grad. dir. career devel. Colo. State U., Ft. Collins, 1980—86; intern U. Del., Newark, 1987—88; psychologist Ariz. State U., Tempe, 1988—93; assoc., lead prof. psychology Clinch Valley Coll. U. Va., Wise, 1992—96, asst. acad. dean, 1993—95; head psychology dept., prof. North Ga. Coll. and State U., Dahlonega, 1996—2001; dean undergrad. and univ. studies, prof. psychology Kennesaw State U., 2001—. Chmn. bd. regents adv. com. Psychology, 2000—01; instr. Colo. State U., Ft. Collins, 1981—82, counselor, 1984—85, Ft. Collins, 1986—87; psychologist Ariz. State U., Tempe, 1989—92; assoc. prof. psychology Clinch Valley Coll. U. Va., 1992—96; spkr. in field. Author: (program manual) Career Development, 1986; contbr. book chpts. on eating disorders and existential psychotherapy, 1996, 1998, 1999, 2002; reviewer: Buros Mental Measurements Yearbook. Bd. dirs. Ct. Apptd. Spl. Advocates, 2000—. Enotah Legis. Dist., Helping Teens Succeed, 2003; Youth Adv. Coun. Lumpkin County, 2000—. Mem.: AACSU, AAUP, AAHE, ACES, APA, Ga. ACE Network (mem. exec. com. 2001—), Ga. Assn. Women Higher Edn. (pres. 2001—), Southeastern Psychol. Assn. (chair undergrad. rsch. 1996—2000), AACD, Odeka, Phi Beta Kappa, Psi Chi (Ga. Woman of the Yr. com. 1999—2003, vice chair 2003—, documentary project), Pi Kappa Delta, Phi Kappa Phi (vice chair 2002, chair elect local chpt. 2003—, Internat. Womans Day program com. 2003, planning com. so. women in pub. svc. conf. 2003—, Promotion of Excellence grantee 2002—03). Avocations: music, hiking, reading. Office: Kennesaw State U Off Dean Undergrad & Univ Studies 1000 Chastain Rd - Kennesaw Hall 4443 Kennesaw GA 30144-5591 E-mail: mlfrank@kennesaw.edu.

FRANK, MICHAEL VICTOR, risk assessment engineer; b. N.Y.C., Sept. 22, 1947; s. David and Bernice (Abrams) F.; m. Jane Griminger, Dec. 21, 1969; children: Jeffrey, Heidi, Heather. BS, UCLA, 1969; MS, Carnegie-Mellon U., 1972; PhD, UCLA, 1978. Registered profl. engr., Calif.; cert. profl. cons. to mgmt., cert. hazard and operability study leader. Engr. Westinghouse Electric Corp., Pitts., 1970-72, Southern Calif. Edison, Los Angeles, 1972-74; lectr. U. Calif., Santa Barbara, 1976-77; task leader General Atomics, San Diego, 1977-81; sr. exec. engr. NUS Corp., San Diego, 1981-85; with Mgmt. Analysis Co., San Diego, 1985-86; sr. cons. PLG, Newport Beach, Calif., 1986-89; pres. Safety Factor Assocs., Inc., Encinitas, Calif., 1989—. Tech. dir. risk and reliability studies of NASA facilties, space and launch vehicles, internat. space sta., stratospheric obs. for infrared astronomy, space nuclear power systems and terrestrial nuclear facilities worldwide; risk assessment cons. to U.S. Interagy. Nuclear Safety Rev. Panel, NASA hdqrs., NASA Ames Rsch. Ctr., Nat. Space Devel. Agy. of Japan; lectr. on risk assessment at NASA ctrs.; probabilistic risk assessment cons. to U.S. nuclear regulatory commn., ctr. for nuclear waste regulatory analysis and utility co., qualified forensic cons. in product defects and hazards, fires and explosions, safety and reliability; engrng. risk mgmt. cons. European Space Agy.; mem. tech. program com. probabilistic safety assessment and mgmt. confs. Contbr. more than 80 articles to Reliability Engrng. and System Safety, Risk Analysis, Nuclear Engrng. and Design, ASME, European Safety and Reliability Soc., others. Mem. IEEE (past pres. San Diego chpt. Reliability Soc.), Soc. for Risk Analysis, Nat. Bur. Cert. Cons. Avocations: family activities, running, skiing, hiking. Office: Ste 16 1410 Vanessa Cir Encinitas CA 92024-2440 E-mail: riskexpert@ieee.org.

FRANK, PAULA FELDMAN, business executive; b. Tulsa; d. Maurice M. and Sarah (Bergman) Feldman; m. Gordon D. Frank, Dec. 15, 1955; children: Cynthia Jan, Margaret Jill. B.S., Northwestern U., 1954. Directed, wrote and appeared in TV films for Nat. Safety Coun., Chgo., 1954-55; appeared in TV commls., 1955-56; asst. prodn. mgr. Kling Films, Chgo., 1956; pres. Gaston Ave. Optical Inc., ret. 1990; Dallas. Social chmn. Baylor Hosp. Vol. Corp., Dallas, 1962—; asst. dir. Des Plaines (Ill.) Theater Guild, 1956-57, Pearl Chappell Playhouse, Dallas, 1962-63, Dallas Theater Center, 1964. Mem. Hockaday Alumni Assn., Tau Gamma Epsilon, Phi Beta, Sigma Delta Tau. Home: 7123 Currin Dr Dallas TX 75230-3645

FRANK, RICHARD ASHER, lawyer, health products executive; b. Omaha, Nov. 4, 1936; s. Alexander David and Sarah R. (Katz) F.; m. Susan Marie Kling; children: Brian, Hilary, Alexander, Nicholas. AB, Harvard U., 1958, JD, 1962. Bar: D.C. 1962, U.S. Supreme Ct. Asst. legal advisor U.S. State Dept., Washington, 1962-69; dir. Ctr. Law and Social Policy, Washington, 1970-77; adminstr. NOAA, Washington, 1977-81; ptnr. Wald, Harkrader, Ross, Washington, 1981-87; pres. Population Svcs. Internat., Washington, 1987—. Adj. prof. Georgetown Law Sch., 1988—. Editor: The Constitution and the Conduct of Foreign Policy, 1976; contbr. articles to profl. jours. 1st lt. U.S. Army, 1959—66. Mem.: Coun. Fgn. Rels. Avocations: sailing, tennis. Home: 3405 Lowell St NW Washington DC 20016-5024 Office: Population Svcs Internat 1120 19th St NW Washington DC 20036-3605 E-mail: rfrank@psiwash.org.

FRANK, RICHARD G. health educator; b. Boston, Apr. 27, 1952; BA in Econs., Bard Coll., 1974; PhD in Econs., Boston U., 1982. Prof. dept. health econs. Harvard Med. Sch., Boston, 1994-99, Margaret T. Morris prof. health econs., 1999—. Rsch. assoc. Nat. Bur. Econ. Rsch., Cambridge, Mass. and N.Y.C., 1987—. Office: Harvard Med Sch Dept Health Care Policy 180 Longwood Ave Boston MA 02115-5821

FRANK, RICHARD SANFORD, retired magazine editor; b. Paterson, N.J., July 28, 1931; s. David and Shirley (Dwoskin) F.; m. Margaret Schwartz, June 30, 1957 (dec. Apr. 2001); children: Daniel, Peter. BA, Syracuse U., 1953; MA, U. Chgo., 1956. Reporter Balt. Evening Sun, 1957-64, Phila. Bull., 1965-71; asst. to mayor City of Balt., 1964-65; reporter Nat. Jour., Washington, 1971-72, editor, 1972-76, editor-in-chief, 1976-97. Served with U.S. Army, 1953-55. Mem. Am. Soc. Mag. Editors Home: 5111 Wessling Ln Bethesda MD 20814-1232 E-mail: richard.s.frank@verizon.net.

FRANK, ROBERT ALLEN, advertising executive; b. Albany, N.Y., Sept. 26, 1932; s. Edward and Marian (Kostelanetz) F.; m. Cynthia Tull, Aug., 1984; children: David, Chelsea, Alison. BA, Colby Coll., 1954; MBA, Amos Tuck Sch. Bus. Adminstrn., Dartmouth Coll., 1958. Cost control adminstr. ABC-TV, N.Y.C., 1958-59; corp. auditor CBS, Inc., N.Y.C., 1959-60, TV sales svc. account exec., 1961, account exec. radio network sales, 1962-69; exec. v.p., co-founder SFM Media Corp., N.Y.C., 1969—, pres. Media Svc. div., 1981; pres., CEO, SFM Media LLC, N.Y.C., 1998-2000; vice-chmn. Media Planning Group USA, N.Y.C., 2001—02; cons., 2003—. Radio-TV cons. Nat. Kidney Fund., 1974; active radio TV for various polit. campaigns including Robert Kennedy for Senator, 1964, Richard Nixon for Pres., 1972, Ford for Pres., 1976, Bush for Pres., 1980, Reagan for Pres., 1980, Du Pont for Pres., 1988; mem. Leadership Coun. Nat Rep. Congl. Com., Rep. Nat. Com., Pres.' Club, 1984-88, Rep. Nat. Senatorial Com. Inner Circle, 1985-88, Citizens for Rep. Pres. Com., 1984-88; trustee Nat. Child Labor Com., 1984-96, vice chmn., 1994-96; trustee Myasthenia Gravis Found., 1984-93. Served to capt. USAF, 1954-56. Mem. Internat. Radio-TV Soc., Amos Tuck Alumni Assn. N.Y. (pres. 1976-77, dir. 1979), Dartmouth Club (N.Y.C.), Pi Gamma Mu. Home: 35 Lounsbury Rd Ridgefield CT 06877-4710 Office: Conn Mktg One Grumman Hill Rd Wilton CT 06897

FRANK, ROBERT EDWIN, artist; b. Oct. 29, 1931; BA, U. Cin., 1956. Comml. artist, Ohio, 1951-90; landscape painter, 1990—. Address: 128 Bob o Link Cir Daytona Beach FL 32114 E-mail: rainbowsend@webtv.net.

FRANK, ROBERTA, English language educator; b. N.Y.C., Nov. 9, 1941; d. Norman Berton and Doris (Birnbaum) F.; m. Walter André Goffart, Dec. 31, 1977. BA, NYU, 1962; MA, Harvard U., 1964, PhD, 1968. Asst. prof. U. Toronto, 1968-73, assoc. prof., 1973-78, prof. English, 1978-2000, Univ. prof., 1995-2000, dir. grad studies dept. English, 1980-85, dir. Ctr. for Medieval Studies, 1994-99; Douglas Tracy Smith prof. English Yale U., 2000—. Mem. bus. bd. U. Toronto Press. Author: Old Norse Court Poetry, 1978, also articles; co-editor: Computers and Old English Concordances, 1970, A Plan for the Dictionary of Old English, 1973; gen. editor: Toronto Old English Series, 1976-2003; publs. of Dictionary of Old English, 1984-2003. Recipient Guggenheim award, 1985, Bowdoin prize in humanities Harvard U., 1968. Fellow Medieval Acad. Am. (councillor 1981-84, Elliott prize 1972), Royal Soc. Can.; mem. MLA (mem. Old English exec. com. 1974-78, 95-99), Internat. Soc. Anglo-Saxonists (pres. 1985-87). Home: 171 Lowther Ave Toronto ON Canada M5R 1E6 Office: Yale U Dept English New Haven CT 06520-8302 E-mail: rfrank@chass.utoronto.ca, roberta.frank@yale.edu.

FRANK, RONALD EDWARD, marketing educator; b. Chgo., Sept. 15, 1933; s. Raymond and Ethel (Lundquist) F.; m. Iris Donner, June 18, 1958; children: Linda, Lauren, Kimberly. BSBA, Northwestern U., 1955, MBA, 1957; PhD, U. Chgo., 1960. Instr. bus. statistics Northwestern U., Evanston, Ill., 1956-57; asst. prof. bus. adminstrn. Harvard U., Boston, 1960-63, Stanford U., 1963-65; assoc. prof. mktg. Wharton Sch., U. Pa., 1965-68, prof., 1968-84, chmn. dept. mktg., 1971-74, vice dean, dir. rsch. and PhD programs, 1974-76, assoc. dean, 1981-83; dean, prof. mktg. Krannert Grad. Sch. Mgmt., Purdue U., 1984-89; dean, Asa Griggs Candler prof. mktg. Goizueta Bus. Sch. Emory U., Atlanta, 1989-98, dean, Asa Griggs Candler prof. mktg. emeritus, 1998-99; mktg. cons., 1999—; pres. Singapore Mgmt. U., 2001—. Bd. dirs. Lafayette (Ind.) Life Ins. Co., The MAC Group, Home Hosp., Lafayette; cornerstone rsch. cons. to industry; mem. strategic issues com. Am. Assembly Collegiate Schs. of Bus., 1988-92, bd. dirs., 1992-96, chmn. audit com., 1993-94, mem. strategic planning and ops. com., 1994-95; chmn. Orgn. for the Future Task Force, 1996-97; trustee Singapore Mgmt. U., 2000-01. Author: (with Massy and Kuehn) Quantitative Techniques in Marketing Analysis, 1962, (with Matthews, Buzzell and Levitt) Marketing: an Introductory Analysis, 1964, (with William Massy) Computer Programs for the Analysis of Consumer Panel Data, 1964, An Econometric Approach to a Marketing Decision Model, 1971, (with Paul Green) Manager's Guide to Marketing Research, 1967, Quantative Methods in Marketing, 1967, (with Massy and Lodahl) Purchasing Behavior and Personal Attributes, 1968, (with Massy and Wind) Market Segmentation, 1972, (with Marshall Greenberg) Audience Segmentation Analysis for Public Television Program Development, Evaluation and Promotion, 1976, The Public's Use of Television, 1980, Audiences for Public Television, 1982. Bd. dirs., fin. com. Home Hosp. of Lafayette, 1985-89; bd. dirs. The Washington Campus, 1984-89, 95-98. Recipient pub. TV rsch. grants John and Mary R. Markle Found., 1975-82. Mem. Am. Mktg. Assn. (dir. 1968-70, v.p. mktg. edn. 1972-73), Inst. Mgmt. Sci., Assn. Consumer Rsch. Office: Singapore Mgmt Univ 469 Bukit Timah Rd Oei Tion Singapore 259756 Singapore Home: 1609 Wind Song Ln Aurora IL 60504-5561 E-mail: ref@bus.emory.edu.

FRANK, RONALD WILLIAM, lawyer, financier; b. Greensburg, Pa., Mar. 11, 1947; s. William John and Louise (Mautino) F.; m. Marsha Ann Kolesar, Aug. 30, 1969. BSChemE, Carnegie Mellon U., 1969; JD, Duke U., 1972. Bar: Pa. 1972. Ptnr. Buchanan Ingersoll P.C., Pitts., 1972-93, Babst, Calland, Clements & Zomnir, P.C., Pitts., 1993-99, Reed Smith LLP, Pitts., 2000—. Sec. Akers Nat. Roll Co. Contbr. articles to profl. jours. Chmn. nat. fund raising com., Carnegie-Mellon U., Pitts., 1983-88, bd. advisors Sch. Engring. and Sci., Carnegie Mellon U.; mem. bd. visitors sch. law Duke U., Durham, N.C. Mem. ABA, Pa. Bar Assn. (chmn. Internat. and Comparative law sect. 1992—), Allegheny County Bar Assn., Internat. Bar Assn., Duquesne Club, Shannopin Country Club. Avocations: golf, skiing, computers, amateur radio. Home: 1675 Gloucester Ct Sewickley PA 15143-8518 Office: Reed Smith 435 6th Ave Pittsburgh PA 15219-1886 E-mail: rfrank@reedsmith.com.

FRANK, RUBY MERINDA, employment agency executive; b. McClusky, N.D., June 28, 1920; d. John J. and Olise (Stromme) Hanson; m. Robert G. Frank, Jan. 14, 1944 (dec. 1973); children: Gary, Craig. Student, Coll. Mankato, Minn., Aurora (Ill.) U. Home: 199 Hunt Club Dr Saint Charles IL 60174-2393 Office: Arcada Theater Bldg 12 S 1st Ave Saint Charles IL 60174-1957

FRANK, SARAH MYERS, lawyer; b. Indpls., Jan. 19, 1937; s. Dewey Everett and Minnie Estelle (Mitchell) M.; m. Ronald Marsh, Aug. 25, 1956; children: James, John, Janet. Student Principia Coll., Elsah, Ill., 1954-56; BS with Distinction, Purdue U., 1958; JD, Ind. U., 1977. Bar: Ind. 1977, U.S. Dist. Ct. (so. dist.) Ind. 1977, U.S. Ct. Appeals (7th cir.) 1984. Tchr. Colfax High Sch. (Ind.), 1958-59, Washington Twp. Schs., Indpls., 1973-74; sr. law clk. Ind. Supreme Ct., Indpls., 1977-85; staff atty. Hyatt Legal Svcs., Indpls., 1985-86, UAW Legal Svcs. Plan, Indpls., 1986-92; pvt. practice, 1992—. V.p. bd. dirs. Camp Fire, Inc., Indpls., 1983-85; bd. dirs. Dela. Trails Sch., Indpls., 1967-69, Ind. State Mus. Soc., 1992—. Mem. Ind. Bar Assn., Indpls. Bar Assn. (co-chmn. spl. projects women's div., family law sect., probate law sect.), AAUW (bd. dirs. 1981-82). Republican. Club: Principia (pres. 1983-84). Office: UAW-Ford Legal Svcs Plan 320 N Meridian St Ste 628 Indianapolis IN 46204-1725

FRANK, STANLEY DONALD, publishing company executive; b. N.Y.C., June 30, 1932; s. Arthur and Jessie (Schwartz) F.; m. Sheila Rose, Dec. 25, 1958; children: Bradley Scott, Tracy Lynne. BS, CCNY, 1953, MS, 1956; EdD, Columbia U., 1961. Counselor N.Y.C. Pub. Schs., 1955-61; dir. pupil pers. svcs. San Diego County Dept. Edn., 1959-61; dir. mktg. Sci. Rsch. Assocs. subs. IBM, Chgo., 1961-68, v.p. mktg. and ops., 1968-73; pres. Holt, Rinehart & Winston, Inc. subs. CBS, N.Y.C., 1974-77, CBS Ednl. Pub. Div., 1975-78; exec. v.p., chief oper. officer CBS Pub. Group, 1978-80, pres., 1980-84, Britannica Learning Corp., Chgo., 1985-90; exec. v.p. Ency. Britannica, Inc., 1985-93; pres. Comptons Multi Media Pub. Group, Inc., Chgo., 1991—; chmn. bd. dirs. Am. Learning Corp., 1985—; pres., CEO Ctr. for the Assessment of Human Potenial Inc., Boca Raton, Fla., 1994—; mng. ptnr. New Media Ventures, Boca Raton, 1995; pres. New Media Ptnrs., Inc., 1999—; chmn. Restorigen, Inc., 2001—. Bd. dirs. Childcraft Ednl. Corp., Designware, Inc.; cons. Morgan Stanley Capital Markets, 1996—; dir. Golbal Learning Systems.com, 2000—. Mem. Bd. Edn. Dist. 67, Niles, Ill., 1972-73; mem. council Rockefeller U. Served with AUS, 1953-55. Andrew Wellington Cordier fellow Columbia U. Sch. Internat. Affairs. Mem. Am. Psychol. Assn., Phi Delta Kappa.

FRANK, STEPHEN IRA, political science educator; b. Seattle, Oct. 14, 1942; s. Nancy Ann (Schwartz) Frank; m. Barbara Ann Covey; 1 child, Thomas Aaron. BS in Edn., History and Polit. Sci., Ctrl. Mich. U., 1966, MA in Polit. Sci., 1969; PhD in Polit. Sci., Wash. State U., Pullman, 1976. Tchr. social sci. Clarkston HS, Mich., 1967-69; instr. in polit. sci. Gogebec Cmty. Coll., Ironwood, Mich., 1967-69, Lamar U., Beaumont, Tex., 1975-76; prof. polit. sci. N.E. La. U., Monroe, La., 1976-78, St. Cloud State U., Minn., 1978—, chair dept. polit. sci., 2001—03. Co-dir., founder St. Cloud State U. Survey. Author: We Shocked the World: A Case Study of Jesse Ventura's Election As Governor of Minnesota, 1999, 2d edit., 2001; contbr. articles to profl. jour., and chapters to books. Mem. Am. Polit. Sci. Assn., Minn. Polit. Sci. Assn. (bd. dir., treas.), Am. Assn. Pub. Opinion, Nat. Assn. Prelaw Advisors, Midwest Prelaw Advisors Assn. (bd. dir. 1999-2002), St. Cloud State U. Faculty Assn. (pres. 1993-94), Phi Kappa Delta. Avocations: gardening, walking, reading. Office: St Cloud State U Dept Polit Sci 319 Brown Hall Saint Cloud MN 56301-4444

FRANK, STEVEN NEIL, chemist; b. Red Oak, Iowa, Feb. 15, 1947; s. Robert Joseph and Joyce (Erickson) F.; m. Carol Bert Femmer, Jan. 4, 1975. BS, Colo. State U., 1969; PhD, Calif. Inst. Tech., 1974. Sr. mem. tech. staff, solar energy project Tex. Instruments, Dallas, mgr. fuel cell devel., 1980-83, mgr. charge coupled imagers, 1983-86, mgr. wafer fabrication, focal plane array, 1986-88, mfg. mgr., focal plane array, 1988-90, mgr. focal plane array assembly and testing, 1990-91, mgr. uncooled IR imaging, 1990-99; chief engr. Raytheon Comml. Infared, Dallas, 1999—2002, chief tech. officer, 2002—. Author: (with others) Laboratory Techniques in Electro-Analytical Chem, 1996; referee Jour. Applied Physics, 1977—, Jour. Phys. Chemistry, 1977—; contbr. articles to profl. jours. Robert A. Welch fellow U. Tex., 1974-77. Mem. AAAS, Am. Chem. Soc., Electrochem. Soc. Achievements include 20 patents and numerous papers and presentations. Home: 471 Hackberry Dr Mc Kinney TX 75069-1569 Office: Raytheon Co MS 37 PO Box 660246 Dallas TX 75266-0246

FRANK, STUART, cardiologist; b. N.Y.C., Dec. 25, 1934; s. Henry and Kitty (Sternberg) F.; m. Nanchen O'Brien, Aug. 1976 (div. Feb. 1980); children: Rachel Arthur, Sebastian Noah; m. Amber Barnhart, June 22, 1992; children: Amelia Elizabeth, Abigail Kitty, Jessica Cole. BS in Chemistry, MIT, 1956; MD, NYU, 1960. Diplomate Am. Bd. Internal Medicine, Am. Bd. Cardiovascular Disease. Intern and resident in internal medicine Yale U. New Haven Hosp., 1960-64; postdoctoral fellow Inst. Cardiology, London, 1964-65, Nat. Heart Inst., Bethesda, Md., 1965-67; chief cardiology Kaiser Permanente Med. Ctr., San Francisco, 1967-77; assoc. prof. dept. medicine So. Ill. U., Springfield, 1977-86, chief div. cardiology, 1977-90, asst. chmn. dept. medicine, 1981-88, prof. dept. medicine, 1986—, dean of students, 1990-95. Author: The People's Handbook of Medical Care, 1972; contbr. numerous articles to profl. jours. Recipient Nellie Westerman prize Am. Fedn. Clin. Research, 1986. Fellow ACP, Am. Coll. Cardiology, Am. Coll. Chest Physicians, Am. Heart Assn. (council clin. cardiology), Laennec Soc. Office: So Ill Univ Medicine Dept Cardiology PO Box 19636 Springfield IL 62794-9636

FRANK, THEODORE DAVID, lawyer; b. Bklyn., Apr. 1, 1941; s. Paul and Bessie Frank; m. Louise Quinby Gorrell, Oct. 19, 1969; children: Carolyn Quinby Judge, Rachel Jackson. BS in Math., Rensselaer Polytech. Inst., 1963; LLB, U. Tex., 1966; LLM, Harvard U., 1969. Bar: Tex. 1966, D.C. 1969, U.S. Ct. Appeals (1st cir. and 2d cir.) 1977, U.S. Ct. Appeals (5th and 9th cir.) 1980, U.S. Ct. Appeals (3rd cir. and 11th cir.) 1981, U.S. Ct. Appeals (D.C. cir.) 1970, U.S. Supreme Ct. 1978. Law clk. to Hon. Walter P. Gewin U.S. Cir. Ct., 5th cir., Tuscaloosa, Ala., 1966-67; faculty asst. for Ames Competition Harvard Law Sch., Cambridge, Mass., 1967-69; assoc. Arent, Fox, Kintner, Plotkin & Kahn, Washington, 1969-75, ptnr., 1976-97, Arnold & Porter, Washington, 1997—. Mem. hearing com. bd. profl. responsibility D.C. Bar, 1997-2003; co-chair Nat. Telecomms. Moot Ct. Com., 1999-2001; co-chair profl. responsiblity com. Fed. Comm. Bar Assn., 2001-03. Chmn. zoning and tax coms. Springfield Civic Assn., Bethesda, Md., 1989—98. Mem. ABA, Fed. Comm. Bar Assn. (exec. com. 1996-98). Jewish. Avocations: woodworking, bike riding. Office: Arnold & Porter 555 12th St NW Washington DC 20004-1206 E-mail: theodore_frank@aporter.com.

FRANK, THOMAS, design, construction and management executive; b. Salt Lake City, Nov. 23, 1937; s. Simon and Suzanne (Seller) F. BFA, U. Utah, 1963. Lic. contractor Utah. Owner Thomas Frank Designers & Specifiers, Salt Lake City, 1962—; owner, pres. OmmiComputer West, Salt Lake City. Bd. dirs. Inter Active Learning Systems; cons. in field; instr. design, textiles and drafting LDS Jr. Coll., Salt Lake City, 1963-86; lectr. on interior design for jr. and high schs. Bus. & Industry Coop. Edn. Program; profl. adviser interior design curriculum devel. program U. Utah; mem. inter-profl. adv. coun. Utah State Bldg. Bd.; lectr., presenter seminars in field. Contbr. articles to profl. publs. Exec. v.p. Salt Lake Art Ctr., 1977-80; spl. advisor Children's Ctr.; co-chmn. spl. events Utah divsn. Am. Cancer Soc., 1978. Recipient awards U. Utah, 1962, Utah Designers Craftsman Guild, 1962, State Fair Fine Arts, 1962, Recognition award Gov. Mrs. Scott Matheson, 1980, Honor award Utah Soc. AIA, 1980. Fellow Am. Soc. Interior Designers; mem. N.Am. Autocadd Users Group, Nat. Kitchen and Bath Assn. (pres. mountain states chpt. west 1991-92), Am. Soc. Interior Designers (nat. long-range planning com. 1985-87, nat. comms. area coord. 1985, nat. membership devel. com. 1986-87, nat. regional dir. 1991-92, nat. edn. com. 1981, nat. chmn. energy conservation 1980-82, nat. chpt. pres.' orientation task force 1980, nat. bd. dirs. 1977-82, chmn. regional indsl. rels. 1977-78, numerous other offices, numerous awards), AID (sec. Utah 1969-71, bd. govs. 1970-74, Utah pres. 1973-75), Nat. Coun. Interior Design Quantification. Avocations: tennis, skiing, art collecting. Home: 2360 Oakhill Dr Salt Lake City UT 84121-1520 Office: Thomas Frank Designers 3369 Highland Dr Salt Lake City UT 84106-3356 E-mail: answerman.TF@excite.com., ocwest@excite.com.

FRANK, WILLIAM FIELDING, computer systems design executive, consultant; b. N.Y.C., Oct. 27, 1944; s. Karl Frederick and Margaret Ruth (Denisson) F.; m. Linda Carol Hainfield, Dec. 20, 1965 (div. 1972); children: Aaron, Tobin. BA, Middlebury Coll., 1966; MA, U. Chgo., 1969; PhD, U. Pa., 1976. Assoc. prof. Oreg. State U., Corvallis, 1969-79; mem. tech. staff Bell Labs., Whippany, N.J., 1979-81; pres. Enterprise Engring. Assts. Inc., Warren, Vt., 1982-99; founder, chief scientist Cmty. Integration Tech., Manchester by the Sea, Mass., 1999—. Assoc. prof. MIT, Cambridge, 1981-85; cons. Citibank, 1982—, AT&T, 1984, N.Y. Times, 1985, Bank of Am., 1985, State of Calif., 1986—, Digital Equipment Corp., 1987-89, Soviet Ministry of Trade, 1990, Bankers Trust, 1991, Fidelity Investments, 1993—, Reuters, 1996, Ameritech, 1996, NEC, 1998—, U.S. chief delegate Internat. Stnds. Orgn., 1999—; tech. adv. bd. LIMITrader, 2000—, Bank of N.Y., 2000—. Contbr. articles to profl. jours. Rsch. grantee NSF, 1971, 77, NEH, 1976, 81. Mem. Assn. for Computing Machinery, Computer Soc. IEEE. Republican. Congregationalist. Achievements include pioneering of object-oriented enterprise modelling, client role modelling and research in business rule driven software design. Office: FSA Ste 341 2 Portland Fish Pier Portland ME 04101

FRANKE, BRENT DOUGLAS, real estate/insurance executive; b. Milw., Feb. 13, 1949; s. Herbert Carl and Margaret A. (Custer) F. Assoc. Equitable/Stefaniak Realty, Brookfield, Wis., 1985-89, Prudential Life Ins. Co., 1989-90; agt. Nat. Guardian Life Ins. Co., Menomonee Falls, Wis., 1987-89. Owner Poplar Creek Enterprises Inc., 1989—, Opus IV Ltd., Brookfield, 1989— (formerly Poplar Creek Ltd.); State of Wis. regional mgr. Builder Profile Mag., 1991-94; illustrated parts list writer Briggs and Stratton Corp., Wauwatosa, Wis., 1994—. With USNR, 1970-76. Mem. Grad. Realtors Inst. Avocations: skiing, photography, art, reading, computers. Home and Office: 2126 N Wauwatosa Ave Wauwatosa WI 53213-1731

FRANKE, JACK EMIL, foreign language educator; b. Pine Bluff, Ark., July 8, 1965; s. Ernest Rudolph and Charlotte (Harris) F.; m. Lyudmila Veniaminovna Vagun, Aug. 30, 1996; 1 child, Maria. BA, U. Tex., 1987; MA, Monterey Inst. Internat. Studies, 1992; PhD, St. Petersburg (Russia) State U., 1995. Interpreter/at-sea rep. Marine Resource Corp., Seattle, 1988-90; tng. specialist-Russian Def. Lang. Inst., Monterey, Calif., 1990-94, prof. Russian, 2001—; computer-aided lang. instrn. dir. Dept. Fgn. Langs. George C. Marshall Ctr., Garmisch-Partenkirchen, Germany, 1994-97. Pres. Ganbaru Yudanshakai, Monterey, Monterey, 1997—2001; chmn. acad. adv. coun. Def. Lang. Inst., 2002—. Co-author: Russian Topical Reader, 1992; (CD-ROM) Basic Military Language Course-Russian, 1993, The Big Red Book of Russian Verbs, 2003. Pres. acad. adv. coun. Def. Lang. Inst. Fgn. Lang. Ctr., 2002—. With U.S. Army, 1983—85. Mem. DAV, Am. Legion, U.S. Judo Fedn., Computer-Aided Lang. Instrn. Consortium, Am. Coun. on Tchg. Fgn. Langs., Phi Sigma Iota. Republican. Russian Orthodox. Avocations: Judo, racquetball, travel. Home: 370 Clay St Apt 13 Monterey CA 93940-2254 Office: Def Lang Inst PO Box 5818 Monterey CA 93944-0818 Fax: (831) 373-2782. E-mail: drfranke@yahoo.com.

FRANKE, JOHN CHARLES, retired human resources executive; b. Rochester, Minn., June 21, 1937; s. John Paul and Sophie (Thorson) F.; m. Marlys Jean Nordin Jones, Jun 4, 1960 (div. Dec. 1978); children: John Richard, Gregory Wayne; m. Lois Ann Monnin, Dec. 22, 1979; step child, Timothy Jones. BBA, U. Minn., Mpls., 1959, MA in Indsl. Rels., 1968. Life cert. sr. profl. in human resources. Rsch. asst. U. Minn. Indsl. Rels. Ctr., Mpls., 1960-61; group pers. dir. Mead Johnson & Co., Evansville, Ind., 1961-69; dir. pers. Charles F. Kettering Found., Dayton, Ohio, 1969-72; v.p. pers. Assoc. Mortgage Cos., Inc., Washington, 1972-74; founder, prin. Johns Assocs., Inc., Fairfax, Va., 1974-77; div. dir. human rels. TRW Motor Div., Dayton, 1977-82; dir. human resources Miami Valley Pub. Co., Dayton, 1983-84; dir. pers. Sverdrup Tech., Inc., 1984-85; v.p., dir. human resources Sverdrup Corp., St. Louis, 1986-93; dir. human resources, svc. contracts divsn. Calspan Corp., Tullahoma, Tenn., 1993-96. Adj. prof. Wright State U., Dayton, 1982-83, vis. asst. prof., 1983-84; cons., adj. prof. U. Evansville, Ind., 1964-67; conf. speaker Profl. Svcs. Mgmt. Assn., Washington, 1986; seminar speaker Profl. Women in Architecture/Engring., Phoenix, 1988. Bd. dirs. Fairfax (Va.) Little League, 1975-76; v.p. exec. com. Fairfax Police Youth Club, Inc., 1974-77; bd. dirs. Inroads of St. Louis, Inc., 1988-93; mem. Tullahoma Regional Planning Commn. and Bd. Zoning Appeals, 1994-96. Named Disting. Alumnus, Tech. H.S., 2001. Mem. Soc. Human Resource Mgmt., Am. Mgmt. Assn., Human Resource Mgmt. Assn. Greater St. Louis (bd. dirs. 1990-93), Highland Rim Human Resource Mgmt. Assn. (treas. exec. com. 1985, pres. 1994, chair exec. com. 1994, exec. com. 1995), Tenn. State Coun., Soc. Human Resource Mgmt. (sec.-treas. 1995), St. Louis Area Health Care Buyers Coalition (adv. bd. 1992), Franklin/Coffee County Health Care Coalition (v.p. 1985), Imperial Lakes Condominium Assn. (sec./treas. 2000, v.p. 2001, pres. 2002), Master Alumni Rotary, Lakewood Country Club. Republican. Avocations: photography, classic films, music, genealogy.

FRANKE, KATHLEEN ELEANOR, medical social worker; b. Columbus, Ohio, Nov. 24, 1943; d. Henry Clinton Ludeman and Mary Kathleen (Snively) Dowell; m. Gordon Lester Franke, June 25, 1967; children: Gordon Christopher, Elizabeth Kathleen. BA, Beloit Coll., 1965; postgrad., U. Ill., 1965-66; MA in Social Work, U. Chgo., 1968. LCSW La. Social worker Ill. Dept. Children & Family Svcs., Chgo., 1966-70; sch. social worker Rockford (Ill.) Pub. Schs., 1970-73; clin. social worker Forest Glen Adolescent Treatment Ctr., Pineville, La., 1973-74; sch. social worker DeKalb (Ill.) Cmty. Unit Schs., 1974-77; med. social worker Bogalusa (La.) Cmty. Med. Ctr., 1977-80, St. Tammany Parish Renal Ctr., Slidell, La., 1980-85, Highland Pk. Hosp., Covington, La., 1979-86, Capitol Hospice, Ponchatoula, La., 1986-90. Bio-Med. Applications/Artificial Kidney Ctrs., Hammond, La., 1986—96, Fresenius Med. Care Artificial Kidney Ctrs., Mandeville, La., 1996—2001, R and R Home Care, Mandeville, 2001—. Panel moderator ann. meeting Nat. Assn. Patients on Hemodialysis & Transplant; program chairperson Am. Assn. Kidney Patients Seminar for Patients, New Orleans, 1991. Legis. chairperson Woodlake Elem. P.T.A., Mandeville, La., 1987-88. Named Social Worker of Yr. New Orleans chpt. Nat. Assn. Patients on Hemodialysis and Transplant. Mem. La. Coun. Nephrology, Social Workers of the Nat. Kidney Found. (legis. liason 1983-84, membership chair 1984, v.p. 1983-84, sec. 1986-87), Am. Assn. Kidney Patients (bd. mem. New Orleans chpt. 1985-98), Nat. Kidney Found. of La. (patient svcs. com. mem. 1982-83), New Orleans Kidney Patient Assn. (bd. dirs. 1998-2001). Avocations: reading, yoga, travel. Home: 1404 Soult St Mandeville LA 70448-4218 Office: R and R Home Care Inc 1114 Bayou Dr Mandeville LA 70448-4218

FRANKE, RICHARD JAMES, arts advocate, former investment banker; b. Springfield, Ill., June 23, 1931; s. William George and Frances Marie (Brennan) F. BA, Yale U., 1953; MBA, Harvard U., 1957. With John Nuveen & Co., Chgo., 1957-96, v.p., 1965-69, exec. v.p., 1969-74, chief adminstrv. officer, 1970-74, pres., 1974-89, CEO, 1974-96, chmn., 1988-96, also dir., chmn., CEO emeritus, 1996—. Vice chmn. Yale Corp., 1987-94, chmn., 1994—. Chmn. investment com. Yale U.; mem. Pres.'s Com. on the Arts and Humanities; trustee Chgo. Symphony Orch.; trustee U. Chgo.; bd. dirs. Lyric Opera, Newberry Libr. 1st lt. U.S. Army, 1953-55. Office: 400 N Michigan Ave Ste 300 Chicago IL 60611-4130

FRANKE, WAYNE THOMAS, retired government affairs director, consultant; b. San Angelo, Tex., June 23, 1950; s. Bernard Raymond and Henrietta Elizabeth (Kozelsky) F.; m. Regina Gale Frantze; 1 child, Mauri Jane. BBA in Gen. Bus., Angelo State U., 1972. Adminstrv. clk. Gen. Telephone Co. of the S.W., San Angelo, 1968-72, comm. cons. Irving, Tex., 1972-75, asst. govt. affairs mgr. San Angelo, 1975-78, govt. affairs mgr. Austin, Tex., 1976-86, govt. affairs dir., 1986-98; owner MJWT Cons., Austin, 1998—; co-owner Cemaur Benefits, LLC; ptnr. Bus. Ptnrs. Ltd., Austin, BGWT, LLC. Mem. legis. affairs com. Tex. Indsl. Devel. Coun., College Station, 1977—84, chmn., Austin, 1981—83, mem. energy and awards coms., 1978—79; bd. dirs. Molecular Solutions, Inc.; mem. U.S. Spkr. Jim Wright's Diplomatic Mission to Moscow, 1987. Fundraiser Boy Scouts Am., Austin, 1987-88, Austin Performing Arts Ctr., 1998-2000; loaned exec. Tarrant County United Way, 1973-74; issues mgmt. adv. coun. North Tex. Commn., Dallas, 1985-87; program chmn. John Ben Shepperd Leadership Forum, Odessa, Tex., 1986, chmn., Austin, 1987, John Ben Shepperd Alumni Forum, 1988; mem. John Ben Shepperd Governing Bd., 1990-91, chmn. fin., 1990-91, fin. com. 1990-92, adv. bd., 1991-93, vice-chmn. John Ben Shepperd Found., 1997-98, chmn., 1998-99, bd. dirs., 1997-2001; corp. co-chmn. drive United Cerebral Palsy Assn., Austin area, 1990-96; mem. Hays Country Oaks Archtl. Control & Protection Com., 1993-96; steering com., fundraising Travis County Assn. Retarded Citizens; trustee West Tex. Boy's Ranch Found., 1995—, treas. exec. com., 1999-2001, chmn. 2001-02; chmn. Tex. Statehood Sesquicentennial Program, 1996; bd. dirs. Angelo State U. Ex-Students Assn., 1999—; mem. task force schs. and coms. offering positive explanations, Hays ISD, 2003—. Recipient External Team Excellence award GTE, 1992-93, Strive for Excellence award, 1992; named Lobbyist of the Year for GTE Corp., 1987, 91, 1989 Disting. Alumnus, Angelo State U.; Wayne Franke Day proclaimed by San Angelo, Tex. City Council Oct. 14, 1989, one of ten Rising Stars of Tex., Tex. Bus. mag., 1988. Mem.: KC (reporter 2003—), Lewisville/San Angelo C. of C. (amb. 1974—77, Amb. of Yr. 1975, 1976), Bus. Ins. Consumers Assn. (exec. com. 1990—95), West Tex. C. of C. (state affairs com., legis. adv. coun.), Homeowners Assn., Tex. Self-Ins. Assn. (co-chair legis. com. 1993), Tex. Taxpayers and Rsch. Assn. (state affairs com. 1985—97), Tex. Assn. Bus. and C. of C. (chmn. state affairs com. 1977—79, bd. dirs. Austin chpt. 1985—88, vice chmn. 1987, statewide state affairs com.), St. Paul's Cath. Ch. Men's Club (vision com. 2001—02), Optimists (sec. Irving chpt. 1973-74, v.p. youth work, 1974-75, pres., 1975, bd. dirs. San Angelo chpt. 1977, lt. gov. North Tex. dist., 1978-79). Roman Catholic. Avocations: golf, rock work, fishing, tree trimming, camping.

FRANKE, WILLIAM AUGUSTUS, corporate executive; b. Bryan, Tex., Apr. 15, 1937; s. Louis John and Frances (Hanna) F.; m. Carolyn Diane Franke; children: Catherine Anne, Paige Estelle, Brian Hanna, David Parker, Rebecca. BA, Stanford U., 1959, LLB, 1961. Bar: Wash. 1961. With MacGillivray, Jones, Clark & Schiffner, Spokane, 1962-69; ptnr. S.W. Forest Industries, Phoenix, 1970-86; CEO, S.W. Forest Industries (merged with Stone Container Corp.), Phoenix, 1978—87; pres., owner Franke & Co., Inc., Phoenix, 1987—; chmn., CEO Am. West Holdings Corp., Phoenix, 1994—2001; mng. ptnr. Newbridge L.Am., LLP, 1996—, Indigo Ptnrs. LLC, 2001—. Chmn. bd., CEO Am. West Airlines, Inc., Phoenix, 1994—2001; bd. dirs. Phelps Dodge Corp., ON Semiconductor, Inc.; mng. ptnr. Newbridge Latin Am. LLP; pres., CEO Indigo Ptnrs. LLC. Served to capt. U.S. Army, 1961-62. Mem. ABA, Wash. Bar Assn., Chief Execs. Orgn. Clubs: Paradise Valley Country, Desert Mountain Country. Episcopalian. Office: 2525 E Camelback Rd Ste 800 Phoenix AZ 85016-4230

FRANKEL, ALBERT J. registrar; b. Wilmington, Del., Nov. 24, 1957; s. Albert and Dorothy B. Frankel; m. Lisa Anne Gibson, Dec. 27, 1986; 1 child, Bethany. BA, U. Del., Newark, 1982; MS, Wilmington Coll., Newcastle, 2002. Camp counselor, dir. YMCA, Newark, Del., 1971—81; mgr. Tideline Gallery, Rehoboth Beach, Del., 1982 86; transp. mgr. U. Del., Newark, 1980—87, asst. registrar, 1987—96; registrar Wilmington Coll., New Castle, Del., 1996—2001, U. New Eng., Biddeford, Maine, 2003—. Driver U.S. Vice Presdl. Motorcade. Designer (graphics) UD Transit Design and Logo. Bd. dirs. U. Del. Nat. Youth Sports Program, Newark, 1990—91; v.p. Fox Hunter Crossing Svc. Corp., Middletown, Del., 2001—02, pres., 2003—. Mem.: Middle States Assn. Coll. Registrars and Admissions, Am. Assn. Coll. Registrars and Admissions, Delaware Valley Registrars Assn. Avocations: softball, camping, surfing, Fine Arts, photography.

FRANKEL, ALICE KROSS, physician, director; b. N.Y.C., Feb. 3, 1929; d. Isidor and Anna (Moscowitz) Kross; m. Julian B. Schorr, May 14, 1951 (div. 1963); children: David, Ellen; m. Marvin E. Frankel, Aug. 22, 1965; 1 stepchild, Eleanor Frankel Perlman; 1 child, Mara. BA, Oberlin (Ohio) Coll., 1949; MD, Columbia U., 1953. Pvt. practice, N.Y.C., 1956-66, 85—, Larchmont, N.Y., 1966-85; assoc. clin. prof. psychiatry Med. Coll. Cornell U., N.Y.C., 1970-90; dir. Child Devel. Ctr. Jewish Bd. Family & Children's Svcs., N.Y.C., 1984—; supervising and tng. psychoanalyst Psychoanalytic Ctr. Tng. & Rsch. Columbia U., N.Y.C., 1984—. Mem. Am. Psychiat. Assn., Am. Psychoanalytic Assn., Am. Acad. Child and Adolescent Psychiatry, Assn. for Child and Adolescent Analysis, N.Y. County Med. Soc., N.Y. State Med. Soc. Democrat. Jewish. Office: Jewish Bd Family Childrens Svcs Child Devel Ctr 120 W 57th St New York NY 10019-3320

FRANKEL, BARBARA BROWN, cultural anthropologist; b. Phila., Dec. 24, 1928; d. Paul and Sarah (Magil) Brown; m. Herbert L. Frankel, Feb. 27, 1949 (dec. Sept. 1976); children: Claire R. Sholes, Joan L. Frankel, David S. Frankel; m. Donald T. Campbell, Mar. 19, 1983 (dec. May 1996). PhB, U. Chgo., 1947; BA, Goddard Coll., 1966; MA in Anthropology, Temple U., 1970; PhD, Princeton (N.J.) U., 1974. Asst. prof. Lehigh U., Bethlehem, Pa., 1973-77, assoc. prof., 1977-85, assoc. dean arts and sci., 1981-83, prof. anthropology, 1985-93, prof. emerita, 1994—; rsch. assoc. prof. Boston U., 1980-81. Author: Childbirth in the Ghetto, 1977, Transforming Identities, 1989; contbr. articles to profl. jours. Bd. dirs. Pinebrook Svcs. for Children and Youth, Whitehall, Pa., 1987-93. Grad. fellowship for Women Danforth Found., Princeton U., 1969-73; predoctoral fellowship AAUW, 1971-72; rsch. grant Mellon Faculty Devel. Grant, Boston U., 1980-81, Provost's Rsch. award Lehigh U., 1987. Fellow Am. Anthrop. Assn. (ethics commn. 1994-97), Soc. for Applied Anthropology (chmn. ethics com. 1986-88); mem. AAAS, Phila. Anthrop. Soc. (pres. 1988), LWV (bd. dirs. Bethlehem area 1993—, chmn. study com. 1994-97, pres. 1997-99, program chair 1999-2001), Phi Beta Kappa (pres. Beta chpt. 1989-90). Democrat. Agnostic Jewish. Achievements include rsch. on utopian/therapeutic communities, urban society, epistemology of anthropology. Home: 637 N New St Bethlehem PA 18018-3915 Office: Lehigh U Sociology and Anthropology 681 Taylor St Bethlehem PA 18015-3107 E-mail: bf02@lehigh.edu.

FRANKEL, BERNARD, advertising executive; b. 1929; B in Mktg., U. Buffalo, 1951. Sales rep. Rugby Knitting Mi, Chgo., 1951-54; midwest rep. E.O. Hirsch & Assocs., Chgo., 1954-57; dir. sales promotion Kling Studios, Chgo., 1957-59; account exec., account supr., v.p. Knipschild Robinson, Inc. (now William A. Robinson and Co.), 1959-62; CEO Frankel & Co., Chgo., 1962—2002, also chmn. bd. dirs., 1962—2002, chmn. emeritus, 2002—. Media rep., advt. sales mgr., advertising and promotion mgr. Concrete Pub. Co., Chgo., 1955-57. Office: Frankel & Co 111 E Wacker Dr Chicago IL 60601-3713

FRANKEL, CHARLES JAMES, III, banker; b. Charlottesville, Va., Feb. 14, 1944; s. Charles James II and Gladys (Birmingham) F.; m. Dawn Marie Hornung, Oct. 23, 1964; 1 child, Kimberly Mavourneen. Student, U. Va., 1961-65; BS, Fla. Atlantic U., 1966, MEd, 1967. Asst. v.p. Wachovia Bank & Trust Co., Winston-Salem, N.C., 1967-74; exec. v.p. Sun Bank/So. Fla., Nat. Assn., Ft. Lauderdale, 1974-85; pres. Pan Am. Bank of Broward, Ft. Lauderdale, 1985-86; sr. v.p. and dir. private banking, ea. U.S. and internat. Nations Bank, Ft. Lauderdale, 1989-91; with Fla. pvt. banking, 1986-88, 92-93; mng. dir., bd. dirs. U.S. Trust Co. Fla., Boca Raton, Fla., 1993—. Private lending com. Robert Morris Assocs., Phila., 1990-93; speaker various profl. confs. Pres. Greater Ft. Lauderdale Touchdown Club, 1981; chmn. Blockbuster Bowl, Ft. Lauderdale, 1992; bd. dirs. Ft. Lauderdale Beach Redevel. Bd., 1991, Greater Ft. Lauderdale C. of C. Found., 1992, Ft. Lauderdale Parks and Recreation Bd., 1992-96, bd. dirs. Fla. Atlantic U. Found., 1997—; bd. dirs. Gulf Stream (Fla.) Civic Assn., 2001—; mem. Va. Student Aid Found., U. of Va. Nat. Campaign Com., nat. leadership gifts coun. 1996-2000; lay eucharistic minister All Saints Episcopal Ch., 1994-98; chalice bearer and lector St. Paul's Episcopal Ch., 1998-2001; mem., lector Bethesda-by-the Sea Episcopal Ch.; bd. dirs., chmn. investment com. Bethesda Meml. Hosp. Found., 2000-2003, investment com., 2003—; mem. archtl. rev. bd. Town of Gulf Stream, 1999—, dir. Golden Bell Found. Recipient Disting. Am. award Nat. Football Found., Brian Piccolo chpt., 1991; named Cystic Fibrosis Leading Man of Palm Beach County, 2002. Mem. Am. Bankers Assn. (pvt. banking exec. com. 1991-92), Jr. Achievement (bd. advisors 1988-91), Lauderdale Yacht Club (bd. govs. 1984-88), Tower Club (bd. dirs. 1985-93), Boca Raton C. of C. (bd. dirs. 1997—, treas. 2000-01, vice chmn. 2002—, chair-elect 2003—), Lago Mar Beach Club, Boca Raton Hist. Soc. (bd. dirs. 1995-2001, bd. advisors 2001—), Scuttlebutt Club, Sunshine Football Classic (trustee, exec. com., 1992-2001), Gulf Stream Bath and Tennis Club (bd. govs., pres.), Hundred Club of Palm Beach County. Episcopalian. Avocations: tennis, arts. Office: 280 E Palmetto Park Rd Boca Raton FL 33432 E-mail: cfrankel@ustrust.com.

FRANKEL, EMIL H. transporation policy secretary; BA, Wesleyan Univ., 1961; LLB, Harvard Univ. Law Sch., 1965. Commr. Conn. Dept. of Transp., Conn., 1991—95; Of Counsel Day, Berry & Howard, LLP, Harford, Conn., 1995—2001; trustee Wesleyan Univ., 1981—97; mgmt. fellow Yale Sch. of Mgmt., 1995—2001; sr. fellow Yale Sch. of Forestry and Environ. Studies, 1995—2001; adj. prof. of transp. policy Univ. of Conn., Conn., 2000; asst. Sec. for Transp. Policy US Dept. of Transp., 2002. Achievements include the Senate has confirmed Emil H. Frankel as Asst. Sec. of Transp. for Transp. Policy. Mr. Frankel formerly served in this position as a Recess Appointee. Office: Dept of Transp 400 Seventh St SW Rm 10228 Washington DC 20590

FRANKEL, ERNST GABRIEL, shipping and aviation business executive, educator; b. Beuthen, Germany, Oct. 17, 1923; came to U.S., 1959, naturalized, 1964. s. Siegfried Samuel and Martha (Blumenthal) F.; m. Inna Kordonsky, Sept. 9, 1990; 1 child, Michael. BS, London U., 1948; MS in Marine-Mech. Engring., MIT, 1960; MBA, Boston U., 1979, D of Bus. Adminstrn., 1986; PhD in Econs., U. Wales, 1985. Chief engr. ZimNav Co., Haifa, Israel, 1950-59; asst. prof. MIT, Cambridge, Mass., 1960-64, assoc. prof., 1964-65, mem. faculty, 1970—, prof. marine systems, 1970—, prof. mgmt. Sloan Sch., 1993—; chief divsn. operation analysis maritime adminstrn. Dept. of Commerce, 1965-66; tech. dir. Litton Industries, Beverly Hills, Calif., 1966-70. Pres. E.G. Frankel, Inc., Boston, 1969—; port, shipping and aviation advisor World Bank, 1983-86; sr. advisor on ports to sec. gen. Internat. Maritime Orgn., 1987-98; chmn. Am. Pres. Lines, Inc., 1997-2000; bd. dirs. Am. Eagle Tankers, Am. Pres. Lines Inc., APL Inc., Panama Canal Auth.; adv. Maritime Port Auth. of Singapore, 1997-02. Author: Ocean Transportation, 1973, Regulation and Policies of American Shipping, 1982, Management and Operations of American Shipping, 1982, Systems Reliability and Risk Analysis, 1984, Port Planning and Development, 1986, The World Shipping Industry-Economic Transition, 1987, Project Management, 1989, Management of Technological Change, 1989, In Pursuit of Technological Excellence, 1993, Ocean Environmental Management, 1994, America's Institutional Dilemma, 1998. Served with Royal Navy, 1942-45. Recipient Gold medal Brit. Govt., 1956. Mem. Am. Soc. Civil Engrs., Soc. Naval Architects and Marine Engrs., Ops. Rsch. Am., The Inst. of Man Scis., Soc. Internat. Devel., Royal Inst. Naval Architects, Inst. Marine Engrs., Internat. Assn. Maritime Economists (pres. 2003—). Home: 283 Buckminster Rd Brookline MA 02445-5841 E-mail: efrankel@mit.edu.

FRANKEL, FRANCINE RUTH, political science educator; b. N.Y.C., Aug. 31, 1935; d. William and Dora (Tuchschneider) Goldberg; m. Douglas Vernon Verney, Nov. 28, 1975; stepchildren: Andrew, Jonathan. BA, CCNY, 1956; MA, Johns Hopkins U., 1958; PhD, U. Chgo., 1965. Asst. prof. U. Pa., Phila., 1965-70, assoc. prof., 1970-79, prof., 1979—, prof. South Asian studies, 1978—, chmn. grad. program polit. sci., 1980-83, founding dir. Ctr. Advanced Study of India, 1992—. Vis. fellow Ctr. of Internat. Studies, Princeton (N.J.) U., 1969-73; resident scholar Bellagio Study and Conf. Ctr., 1975; vis. mem. Inst. Advanced Study, 1976; mem.-at-large Commn. Internat. Rels., Nat. Acad. Scis., 1973-79; mem. del. South Asian specialists to China, 1986; founding mem., mem. governing coun. U. Pa. Inst. for Advanced Study of India, New Delhi, 1995—. Author: India's Political Economy, 1947-77, The Gradual Revolution, 1978, Chinese edit., 1990, India's Green Revolution, 1971; editor, contbr. Dominance and State Power in Modern India, Decline of a Social Order, 2 vols., 1989-90, Bridging the Non-Proliferation Gap: India and the United States, 1995, Transforming India, Social and Political Dynamics of Democracy, 2000; contbr. articles on India's polit. economy to profl. jours. Grantee Am. Inst. Indian Studies, 1979-80, Smithsonian Instn., 1983-86, Social Sci. Rsch. Coun., 1989-91; Woodrow Wilson fellow, 1997-98. Mem. Am. Polit. Sci. Assn., Assn. Asian Studies, Coun. Fgn. Rels. Home: 104 Pine St Philadelphia PA 19106-4312 Office: Ctr Advanced Study of India 3833 Chestnut St Philadelphia PA 19104 E-mail: ffrankel@sas.upenn.edu.

FRANKEL, GENE, theater director, writer, producer, educator; b. N.Y.C., Dec. 23, 1923; s. Barnet and Anna (Talerman) F.; m. Pat Ruth Carter, May 1, 1963; children: Laura Ann, Ethan-Eugene. BA, NYU, 1943. Artistic dir. Gene Frankel Theatre, N.Y.C., 1963—; exec. dir. Gen. Frankel Theatre, N.Y.C., 1973—; founding dir. Berkshire Theatre Festival, Stockbridge, Mass., 1965-66. Vis. Arena Stage, Washington, 1969-71; cultural exchange dir. U.S. Dept. State, Belgrade, Yugoslavia, 1968-69; dir. Hartman Theatres, Stamford, Conn., 1976-79; vis. prof. Boston U., 1967-69, Queens Coll., N.Y.C., 1969-71, Columbia U., N.Y.C., 1972-73; cons. dir. Nat. Shakespeare Co., N.Y.C., 1966—; dir. various regional theaters, 1969-80 Dir.: Broadway, 1969 (Burns Mantle 1969, Best Play award), Emperor Jones, European tour, 1970, Oh Dad, Poor Dad, Belgrade, Yugoslavia, 1969, Lost in the Stars, Broadway, 1971, The Night That Made American Famous, 1975, Cry of Players, 1967, The Blacks, Off-Broadway, 1961 (Obie award 1963), also European tour, Brecht on Brecht, Off-Broadway, 1965, To Be Young Gifted and Black, Off-Broadway, 1970, Enemy of the People, Off-Broadway, 1969, Indians, On Broadway, 1979, Pueblo, 1981, 27 Wagons Full of Cotton, 1985, Talk To Me Like the Rain, 1985, War Play, 1986, The Marriage, 1986, Private Wars, 1987, Sister Aimee, 1987, The Dutchman, 1988, Carreno, 1989—; author, dir. The Actor Then Ma, 1979; co-author, dir.: (play/concert) Carreno, 1990, See Moscow and Die, 1991, (play) Hallowed Ground The Private Thoughts of Abraham Lincoln, 1997; author: So This is the Wicked Stage, 1993, Notes on Othello, 1998, What's Absurd About the Theatre of the Absurd?, 1998, People do Not Want to Suffer, Only Actors Do, 1999; taught and directed numerous actors and actresses including Anne Bancroft, Maya Angelou, Morgan Freeman, Vincent Gardenia, Frank Langella, Fred Gwynne, Louis Gosset, Jr., Walter Matthau, Rod Steiger, Beau Bridges, James Earl Jones, Loretta Swit, Judd Hirsh, Stacy Keach, Lee Marvin, Raul Julia, others. With U.S. Army Air Force, World War II. Recipient Lola D'Annunzio award, 1958; recipient Obie award for Volpone, Village Voice, 1958, Obie award for Machinal Village Voice, 1963, Vernon Rice award for Machinal, Drama Desk-N.Y. Post, 1963; Ford Found. fellow, 1969-71. Mem. SAG, Soc. Choreographers and Dirs., Actors Equity Assn. Office: 4 Washington Square Vlg New York NY 10012-1936 also: Gene Frankel Theatre 24 Bond St New York NY 10012-2424 E-mail: genefrankel@genefrankel.com. *"To acquire knowledge and insight, one must learn from others. In so doing, it can happen that a pygmy standing on the shoulders of a giant may see further than the giant. So learn-learn-learn-then teach so that you can learn some more".*

FRANKEL, JAMES BURTON, retired lawyer; b. Chgo., Feb. 25, 1924; s. Louis and Thelma (Cohn) F.; m. Louise Untermyer, Jan. 22, 1956; children: Nina, Sara, Simon. Student, U. Chgo., 1940-42; BS, U.S. Naval Acad., 1945; LLB, Yale U., 1952; MPA, Harvard U., 1990. Bar: Calif. 1953. Mem. Steinhart, Goldberg, Feigenbaum & Ladar, San Francisco, 1954-72; of counsel Cooper, White & Cooper, San Francisco, 1972-97; ret., 2000. Sr. fellow, lectr. in law Yale U., 1971—72; lectr. Stanford U. Law Sch., 1973—75; vis. prof. U. Calif. Law Sch., 1975—76, lectr., 1992—2000, U. San Francisco Law Sch., 1994—2000; adj. asst. prof. Hastings Coll. Law, 1996—2000. Pres. Coun. Civic Unity of San Francisco Bay Area, 1964-66; chmn. San Francisco Citizens Charter Revision Com., 1968-70; mem. San Francisco Pub. Schs. Commn., 1975-76; trustee Natural Resources Def. Coun., 1972-77, 79-92, staff atty., 1977-79, hon. trustee, 1992—; chmn. San Francisco Citizens Energy Policy Adv. Com., 1981-82. Mem. ABA, Calif. Bar Assn.

FRANKEL, JEFFREY, neurologist; b. Washington, N.J., Sept. 1, 1941; s. Leon and Libby (Kor) F.; m. Trina Gail Newstein, June 21, 1964; children: Laura Frankel Harper, Katherine Frankel Azaro. Student, U. Pa., 1959-62; MD, U. Chgo., 1966. Diplomate Am. Bd. Psychiatry and Neurology. Intern Mt. Sinai Hosp., N.Y.C., 1966-67; resident in neurology Alfert Einstein Coll. Medicine Affiliated Hosps., N.Y.C., 1967-70; pvt. practice, East Orange, NJ, 1972—75, Livingston, NJ, 1975—2000. Chmn. profl. adv. com., trustee No. N.J. chpt. Nat. Multiple Sclerosis Soc., 1982-94, mem. profl. adv. com. Greater North Jersey chpt., 1996— Chmn. neurology sect. Acad. Medicine N.J., 1984-94. Asst. surgeon USPHS, 1970-72. Fellow Am. Acad. Neurology. Jewish. Avocation: ballroom dancing.

FRANKEL, JENNIE LOUISE, writer, composer, playwright, publisher; b. Chgo., Aug. 7, 1949; Student, Roosevelt U., 1968, U. Hawaii, 1969-71, Golden West Law Sch., 1976. Fashion model, singer/actor in TV commls., 1967—81, 1979—81; performer Comedy Store and the Improvisation, L.A., 1977—79. Co-author: You'll Never Make Love in this Town Again, 1996 (N.Y. Times Bestseller), Unfinished Lives, 1996, Tales From the Casting Couch, 1996; author; (Detective Sabrina Fortune crime novels) Sex with the Proper Killer, 2003, Natural Blonde Killer, 2003; editor-in-chief Page Turner Pub.; composer network TV theme songs, 1998-99, Youth at the Greek, 1999, Heartwalk L.A. Theme; columnist. Active USO Vietnam Tour, 1968; bd. govs. Hollywood Scriptwriting Inst.; judge Cable Ace Awards, 1987—96. Mem. Acad. TV Arts & Scis. (blue ribbon panel judge), L.A. Women in Music (bd. dirs. 1991-92), Circumnavigators Club. Avocation: comedy. Office: PO Box 346 Sedona AZ 86339-0346

FRANKEL, JUDITH JENNIFER MARIASHA, clinical psychologist, consultant; b. Bklyn., May 25, 1947; m. Anthony R. D'Augelli, Sept. 1, 1968 (div. 1985); children: Jennifer Hadley Frankel, Rebekah Lindsey Frankel. BA, New Coll. at Hofstra U., 1968; MA, U. Conn., 1971, PhD, 1972. Lic. psychologist, Pa. Rsch. psychologist Family Consultation Ctr., Roslyn, N.Y., 1968, Conn. State Dept. Mental Health, Hartford, 1969-71; staff intern VA Hosp., West Haven, Conn., 1971—72; asst./assoc. prof., dir. program devel. and evaluation Pa. State U., University Park, 1972—81, spl. admissions asst. Schreyer Honors Coll. State Coll., 1998, pvt. practice psychology, clin. and consulting psychology, clin. health psychology, and exec. coaching State College, 1976—. Psychol. cons. PYRAMID Orgn., Walnut Creek, Calif., 1975-78, N.Y. Dept. Mental Health, 1976, Nat. Inst. Alcohol Abuse Prevention, Nat. Inst. Drug Abuse Prevention, Nat. Youth Alternatives Program, 1975-79, Meadows Psychiatric Ctr. Women's Program, 1993-95; v.p. Mental Health Profls., State College, 1978-80, pres., 1980-82; exec. bd. Ctrl. Pa. Psychol. Assn., 1989-90. Author: Decisions Are Possible, 1975, Communication and Parenting Skills, 1976, Helping Others, 1980; contbr. articles to profl. jours. Campaign cons. Stein for Rep., 1982, Wachob for Congress, 1984; chair cmty. action Congregation Brit Shalom, State College, 1985-87, coord. ednl. liaison, 1985-87; v.p. Jewish Cmty. Coun. Women, 1988-90, pres., 1990-93, bd. dirs. Congregation Brit. Shalom, 1985-87, 90-93; v.p. Hadassah, 1995-2001. USPHS fellow, U. Conn., 1969-71. Mem.: APA (clin. psychology, psychology of women, ind. practice, health psychology, internat. psychology and counseling psychology divsns.), Ctrl. Pa. Psychol. Assn. (exec. bd. 1989—90), Ea. Psychol. Assn., Pa. Psychol. Assn., Hadassah (v.p. programming 1995—98, v.p. fundraising 1998—2000, v.p. ednl. programming 2000—02), Jewish Cmty. Coun. Women (bd. dirs. 1990—94, pres. 1991—94), Jewish Cmty. Ctr. (bd. dirs., cmty. action chair 1985—87), Phi Kappa Phi, Phi Beta Kappa. Democrat. Jewish. Avocations: art, music, film, literature, gardening.

FRANKEL, JUDITH LEIBHOLZ, bank executive; b. Phila., Oct. 18, 1961; d. Stephen Wolfgang and Ann Ester (Greenberg) Liebholz; m. Oliver Lincoln Frankel, Oct. 6, 1990; 1 child, Miles Richard. BA in Econs., Trinity Coll., 1983; M of Internat. Mgmt., Am. Grad. Sch. Internat. Mgmt., 1985. With customer svc. Merrill Lynch, N.Y.C., 1983-84; pres. Kinko's Word Processing, Phoenix, 1984-85; head of ops. Analytics Inc., Dayton, Ohio, 1985; credit analyst, loan officer Nationsbank Tex., Dallas, 1985-87; syndicate mgr. Banque Indosuez, N.Y.C., 1987-90; v.p., syndicate mgr. The Indsl. Bank of Japan, N.Y.C., 1990—. Bd. dirs. Analytics Inc., Phila., 1989-91; career advisor Am. Grad. Sch. Internat. Mgmt., 1988-91. Bd. dirs., big sister Jewish Bd. Child and Family Svcs. Big Bros/Big Sisters, N.Y.C., 1987-91. Avocations: reading, painting, skiing, tennis. Office: The Indsl Bank of Japan 245 Park Ave New York NY 10167-0002

FRANKEL, KENNETH MARK, thoracic surgeon; b. Bklyn., July 29, 1940; s. Clarence Bernard and Ruth (Rutes) F.; m. Felice Cala Oringel, Dec. 10, 1967; children: Matthew David, Michael Jacob. BA, Cornell U., 1961; MD, SUNY, Bkyln., 1965. Diplomate Am. Bd. Surgery, Am. Bd. Thoracic Surgery. Intern in surgery Yale New Haven Hosp., 1965-66; resident in surgery Kings County-SUNY Med. Ctr., Bklyn., 1966-67, 69-71, chief resident in gen. surgery, 1971-72, resident in thoracic surgery, 1972-73, chief resident thoracic and cardiovascular surgery, 1973-74; attending thoracic surgeon Mercy Hosp., Springfield, Mass., 1974—, Holyoke (Mass.) Hosp., 1974—; pvt. practice medicine specializing in thoracic surgery Springfield, 1974—; chief thoracic surgery Baystate Med. Ctr., Springfield, 1977—; clin. prof. cardiothoracic surgery Tufts U. Sch. Medicine, 1978—. Cons. Shriners Hosp. for Children, Mary Lane Hosp., Ware, Mass., 1997—; bd. dirs. Pioneer Health Care Inc., 1997—, sec. of bd., 1998-2001, v.p. of bd., 2001—. Contbr. articles to profl. jours. Corporator Springfield (Mass.) Symphony Orch.; rep. to Blue Cross/Blue Shield Regional Health Care Improvement Coun., 1995-98. Capt. U.S. Army, 1967-69. Decorated Bronze Star, Gallantry Cross (Republic of Vietnam). Fellow ACS, Am. Coll. Chest Physicians; mem. AMA, ACLU, Soc. Thoracic Surgeons, Am. Thoracic Soc., New Eng. Cancer Soc., Springfield Acad. Medicine (past pres.), Mass. Med. Soc. (councilor 1981-83), Hampden Dist. Med. Soc. (exec. com. 1990-96), Physicians for Social Responsibility, Maimonides Med. Club (past pres.), AMnesty Internat., Internat. Physicians for Prevention Nuc. War, Union Concerned Scientists, Cornell Club Wester Mass., Porsche Club Am. Democrat. Jewish. Home: 202 Ellington Rd Longmeadow MA 01106-1510 Office: Baystate Med Ctr Office Bldg 2 Medical Center Dr Ste 304 Springfield MA 01107-1271

FRANKEL, MARTIN RICHARD, statistician, educator, consultant; b. Washington, June 16, 1943; s. Lester R. and Vera B. Frankel; m. Jean L. Kaiser, Mar. 24, 1970; children: Jennifer, Margaux. AB, U. N.C., 1965; MA, U. Mich., 1967, PhD, 1971. Asst. prof. stats. U. Chgo., 1971-73, assoc. prof., 1974-76; prof. stats. and computer info. systems Baruch Coll., CUNY, 1977—, assoc. chair, 1995—; tech. dir. Nat. Opinion Research Ctr., U. Chgo., 1972-96; sr. statis. scientist Abt Assocs., Cambridge, Mass., 1996—; chnm. Quality Research Council, Advtg. Research Found., 1988—; cons. statis. methods and quality control, 1965—; mem. panel on occupational and health stats., com. on nat. stats. Nat. Rsch. Coun., NAS, 1985-87; pres. Market Rsch. Coun., 1995—. Author: Inference from Survey Samples: An Empirical Investigation, 1971; (co-author) SEPP: Sampling Error Program Package, 1972, Total Survey Error: Applications to Improve Health Surveys, 1979; also articles; mem. editorial bd. Pub. Opinion Quar., Ency. Statis. Scis., Sociol. Research and Methods. Fellow Am. Statis. Assn. (chmn. census adv. com. 1981, chmn. sect. survey research methods 1975-76, editorial bd. jour.), Royal Statis. Soc., Internat. Statis. Inst.; mem. Am. Assn. Pub. Opinion Research (chmn. standards com.), Market Rsch. Coun. (pres. 1995-96). Home: 14 Patricia Ln Cos Cob CT 06807-1734 Office: Baruch Coll 17 Lexington Ave New York NY 10010-5518 E-mail: martin_frankel@baruch.cuny.edu.

FRANKEL, MAX, retired journalist; b. Gera, Germany, Apr. 3, 1930; came to U.S., 1940, naturalized, 1948; s. Jacob A. and Mary (Katz) F.; m. Tobia Brown, June 19, 1956 (dec. Mar. 1987); children: David M., Margot S., Jonathan M.; m. Joyce Purnick, Dec. 11, 1988. AB, Columbia, 1952, MA in Polit. Sci, 1953. Mem. staff N.Y. Times, N.Y.C., 1952-94, chief Washington corr., 1968-73, Sunday editor, 1973-76, editl. pages editor, 1977-86, exec. editor, 1986-94; ret., 1995. Columnist N.Y. Times mag., 1995-2000. Served with AUS, 1953-55. Recipient Pulitzer prize for internat. reporting, 1973 Office: 15 West 67 St New York NY 10023-6226

FRANKEL, TERRIE MAXINE, writer, composer, playwright, publisher, producer; b. Chgo., Aug. 7, 1949; d. David Frankel and Jewell Hennigan. Student, Roosevelt U., 1968, U. Hawaii, 1971, U. Hong Kong, 1979-80. Entertainer USO, Viet Nam, 1968; performer Comedy Store, Improvisation, others, 1969-79; pres. Page Turner Pub., Scottsdale, Ariz. Fashion model, 1967—81. Co-author: You'll Never Make Love in this Town Again, 1996 (N.Y. Times Best Seller List), Unfinished Lives, 1996, (Det. Sabrina Fortune crime novels) Sex With the Proper Killer, 2003, Natural Blonde Killer, 2003; author, editor: Tales from the Casting Couch, 1996, theme song Youth at the Greek, 1998-99,Heartwlk L.A. Theme, 1999; columnist Fabulous Boomer Babes, 1999, sr. editor: The Industry Mag., 2000; model tv commercials, 1971-81. Judge, comedy Cable Ace Award, 1988—96. Mem. Producers Guild of Am. (bd. dirs., sr. editor POV mag. 1990-2001), Hollywood Script Writing Inst. (bd. govs.), Authors Guild, Circumnavigators Club. Avocation: speaking Cantonese and Mandarin Chinese. Home: PO Box 346 Sedona AZ 86339-0346

FRANKEN, DARRELL, counselor, writer, publisher; b. Oskaloosa, Iowa, Oct. 28, 1930; s. Henry E. and Harriet J. (Dykshorn) F.; m. Marilyn (Tanis); children: Kent, Julie, Todd. BA, Ctrl. U. Iowa, 1952; MDiv, Western Theol. Sem., Holland, Mich., 1955; MA, U. Chgo., 1963; PhD, La Salle U., 1995. Pastor New Life Reformed Ch. (formerly Everglades Reformed Ch.), Grand Rapids, Mich.; missionary Bahrain Arabian Gulf; counselor Christian Counseling Svc., Holland, Mich. Author: Health Through Stress Reduction, 1985, Psychological First Aid Kit, 1992, Character Education Psychology: Optimum Psycho-Social Lifeskills, 1996-2000, 13 Core Values, 1995, Optimum Christian Lifeskills, Lifeskills 101: Higher Core Values Winners Live By, Lifeskills 202: Skills for Optimum Personal Relations, Lifeskills 303: Optimum Lifeskills for Stress Management, founder of Lifeskills Trng. Ctrs. Inc.; creator various computer software programs for personality testing. Fellow Am. Assn. Pastoral Counselors, Mich. Lic. Marriage and Family Counselors. Avocation: photography. Home: PO Box 2397 930 S Shore Dr Holland MI 49423-4539 E-mail: dfranken@lifeskillstraining.org.

FRANKEN, JOY R. exercise physiologist; b. Edmond, Wash., Aug. 27, 1974; d. Victor C. and Nancy K. Schkade. Student, St. Philip's Coll., 1993; grad. in Health and Exercise Sci., Oral Roberts U., 1997. Cert. tchr. physical and health edn., AHA basic life support level C, cert. Arrhythmia. Exercise physiologist, med. asst. Cadiology Tulsa, Okla., 1997—2000; health and fitness tchr. Monroe Mid. Sch., Tulsa, 2000—03, coach mid. sch. cheerleading and high sch. soccer, 2000—01. Vol. exercise physiologist Am. Heart Assn., Tulsa, 1997—2000; soccer coach Lincoln Christian Sch., 1998—99. Republican. Christian. Avocations: coaching and playing soccer, fitness and exercise, football, babysitting. Home: 6616 S Zunis Ave Unit 205 Tulsa OK 74136 Office: Monroe Middle Sch 2010 E 48th St N Tulsa OK 74130 E-mail: jneknarf@aol.com.

FRANKENA, KARL ROELOFS, lawyer; b. Ann Arbor, Mich., June 9, 1939; s. William K. and Sadie R. Frankena; m. Gloria D. Sauer, June 4, 1966; children: Jason T., Lara K. Student, Internat. Sch. Geneva, U. Wash., U. Grenoble; BA with honors, U. Mich., 1961, JD, 1964. Bar: Mich. 1964. Law clk. Mich. Ct. Appeals, Lansing, 1965-66; assoc. Conlin, Kenney & Green, Ann Arbor, 1966-68; ptnr. Conlin, McKenney & Philbrick, Ann Arbor, 1968—. Chmn. Ann Arbor Twp. Planning Commn., 1978—83; dir. Washtenaw Land Trust, Ann Arbor, 1978—. Mem. ABA, Washtenaw County Bar Assn., Mich. Bar Assn. (coun. mem. young lawyers sect. 1966-70). Avocations: travelling, skiing. Home: 3632 Creekside Dr Ann Arbor MI 48105-9308 Office: Conlin McKenney & Philbrick 350 S Main St Ste 400 Ann Arbor MI 48104-2131

FRANKENBERGER, BERTRAM, JR., investor, consultant; b. New Haven, Jan. 24, 1933; s. Bertram and Thelma (Wisan) F.; m. Marjorie Green, Dec. 20, 1953 (dec. June 1997); children: Linda Frankenberger Reason, Wendy Frankenberger Goldstein; m. Harriet Feldman Newman, July 26, 1998. BS cum laude, U. Conn., 1954. CPA, Conn. Auditor Haskins & Sells, New Haven, 1956-61; ptnr. Weinstein & Timm CPAs, New Haven, 1961-70, Deloitte Haskins & Sells, New Haven, 1970-76; U.S. ptnr in charge mergers and acquisitions exec. office N.Y.C., 1976-85; dir. Sheffield Mgmt. Co., N.Y.C., 1985-99, Sheffield Investments, Inc., N.Y.C., 1985-96, Lafayette Am. Bank &

Trust, Hamden, 1985-96. Treas. Human Rels. Area Files, New Haven, 1963-70, 86—, assoc. sec., 1985—; cons., New Haven, 1985-94, Boynton Beach, Fla., 1994—; chmn. bd. Chargar Corp., Hamden, Conn., 1980—, Graham-Worldtek Travel, New Haven, 1985-2001; lectr. in field. Contbr. articles to profl. publs., chpt. to book. Pres., dir. Camp Laurelwood, Madison, Conn., 1970-72; pres., trustee Congregation Mishkan Israel, Hamden, Conn., 1974-76; bd. trustees Union Am. Hebrew Congregations, N.Y.C., 1976-84; treas. Religion in Am. Life, N.Y.C., 1983-89, dir., 1983-94. Capt. USAF, 1954-56. Recipient Pres.'s award New Haven Jaycees, 1960; Pres.'s award Camp Laurelwood, 1969. Mem. AICPA, Conn. Soc. CPAs, Assn. Corp. Growth, Hunters Run Golf and Racquet Club (Boynton Beach), Okemo Valley Golf Club. Avocations: skiing, golf, tennis, stamp collecting.

FRANKENBERGER, JANE ROSSING, agricultural engineer; b. Northfield, Minn., Jan. 18, 1958; d. Thomas D. and Dorothy A. (Rosen) R.; m. James Rossing Frankenberger, July 22, 1995. BA in Physics and Religion, St. Olaf Coll., Northfield, 1979; MS in Agrl. Engring., U. Minn., St. Paul, 1984; PhD in Agrl. and Biol. Engring., Cornell U., 1996. Physics and math. tchr. Mennonite Ctrl. Com., Zaire, 1979-82; agrl. devel. specialist Evang. Luth. Chs. in Am., Senegal, 1985-90; asst. prof. Purdue U., 1996-00, assoc. prof., 2001—. Claire Boothe Luce fellow Luce Found.-Cornell U., 1990. Mem. Phi Beta Kappa, Gamma Sigma Delta, Phi Kappa Phi, Alpha Epsilon. Home: 2640 Newman Rd West Lafayette IN 47906-4530 Office: Purdue U Agrl and Biol Engring 225 S University St West Lafayette IN 47907 E-mail: frankenb@purdue.edu.

FRANKENHEIM, SAMUEL, retired lawyer; b. N.Y.C., Dec. 20, 1932; s. Samuel and Mary Emma (Ward) F.; m. Nina Barbara Mennerich, Sept. 2, 1960; children: Robert Mennerich, John Frederick. BA, Cornell U., 1954, LLB, 1959. Bar: N.Y. 1959, Mass. 1976. Law clk. N.Y. Ct. Appeals, 1959-61; assoc. Shearman & Sterling, attys., N.Y.C., 1961-68, ptnr., 1968-69; sr. v.p., dir. Damon Corp., Needham Heights, Mass., 1969-78; sr. v.p., gen. counsel mem. Office of Chmn. Gen. Cinema Corp., Chestnut Hill, Mass., 1979-92; counsel Ropes & Gray, Boston, 1992-2000. Mem. corp. Ptnrs. Healthcare Sys., Inc., 1999—. Bd. govs. Newall Health Care Sys., 1983—93; trustee Wang Ctr. for Performing Arts, Boston, 1987—97, Huntington Theatre Co., Boston, 1993—2002, overseer, 2002—; chmn. bd. Internat. Alliance of First Night Celebrations, 1994—99, treas., 1999—2000; overseer Newton-Wellesley Hosp., Newton, Mass., 1973—85, pres., 1980—82; overseer Wang Ctr. for Performing Arts, Boston, 1985—87; assoc. First Night, Inc., 1988, chmn. bd., 1991—93. 1st lt. USAF, 1955—57. Mem. ABA. Home: 115 Shornecliffe Rd Newton MA 02458-2420

FRANKENTHAL, DANIELLE, painter, sculptor; b. N.Y.C., Apr. 29, 1947; d. Leon and Eugenia (Tchudnovski) Frankenthal; m. David Joseph Ruzich, May 10, 1991. BA in Philosophy, Brandeis U., 1969. (exhibitions) Gallery 23 Garden St., Cambridge, Mass., Galeria del Patronata de Bellas Artes, Guatemala City, Guatemala, Green County Coun. on the Arts, Catskill, N.Y., Retrospective Gallery, San Diego, Lawrence Price Gallery, N.Y.C., Reza Namazi Real Estate Corp., Full House Gallery, Hoboken, N.J., La Galeria Panajachel, Guatemala, 2002, Brodsky Gallery of Ets, Princeton, N.J., 2002, (group exhbns.) Novelle Gallery, Northampton, Mass., Bergen (N.J.) Mus. Art and Sci., Helo Gallery, N.Y.C., City Without Walls, Newark, Seton Hall U. Sch. Law, B. Beamsderfer Galley, Highland Park, N.J.; Exhibited in group shows at Palmer Mus., Springfield, N.J., 2003; (group shows) Exhibit:A Gallery, N.Y.C., 2003, works in pvt. collections; Exhibited in group shows at Monmouth Mus., Lingraf, N.J., 2003, Palmer Mus., Springfield, N.J., 2003, Installation, Reseve Natural Atitlon, Panagachel, Guatemala, 2003. Vol. Compassionate Care Hosp., Clifton, N.J., 1997-98; bd. dirs. Friendly Visitors Inc., Riker's Island, N.Y.C., 1999—. Office: 300 Observer Hwy 4th Flr Hoboken NJ 07030-2412 E-mail: Tzanqui@optonline.net.

FRANKER, STEPHEN GRANT, investment executive; b. Spencer, Iowa, July 29, 1949; s. Oscar Grant and Betty Jean (Greenwaldt) F.; m. Dianne Alice Russell, Aug. 23, 1970; children: Derek, Leah. BA, U. No. Iowa, 1971. CPA, Iowa. Staff acct. McGladrey, Hansen, Dunn & Co., CPA's, Mason City, Iowa, 1971-75; audit supr. Clinton, Iowa, 1975-76; contr. 1st Fed. Savs. & Loan Assn., Spirit Lake, Iowa, 1976-82, pres., 1982-83; v.p. NW Fed. Savs. Bank, Spencer, 1983-90; investment exec. US Bancorp Piper Jaffray, Storm Lake, Iowa, 1990—. Republican. Lutheran. Avocations: reading, running, bicycling. Home: 503 9th St Spirit Lake IA 51360-1701 Office: US Bancorp Piper Jaffray Inc 304 E 5th St Storm Lake IA 50588-1008

FRANKFORTER, WELDON DELOSS, retired museum administrator; b. Tobias, Nebr., May 1, 1920; s. Archie and Mary Ann (Schroder) F.; m. Laura Glea Nicholas, Sept. 12, 1943; children: Mary Glea, Nicholas Dean, Gary Don, Matthew Jason, Lori Ann. BSc, U. Nebr., 1944, MSc, 1949. Student asst., assoc. curator U. Nebr. State Mus., Lincoln, 1941-50; dir. Sanford Mus. and Planetarium, Cherokee, Iowa, 1951-62; asst. dir. Grand Rapids Pub. Mus., Mich., 1962-64, dir., 1965-88. Mem. faculty Williamsburg Seminar, Va., 1971-73; mem. adv. council Nat. Mus. Act, Washington, 1971-76, Mich. Hist. Preservation Act, 1971-78; advisor for Mich. Nat. Trust Hist. Preservation, 1972-78, regional v.p., 1975-76; mem. Kent County Council for Historic Preservation, 1972—, pres., 1973-74; mem. extension inst. Mich. State U., East Lansing, 1973-75 Contbr. articles to profl. jours. Active Family Svc. Assn., Grand Rapids, 1967-73, West Mich. Environ. Action Coun., Grand Rapids, 1967—, Mich. Sesquicentennial Found., 1983-87; mem. Western Mich. World Affairs Coun., 1973—, pres., 1980-83; city liaison Grand Rapids Hist. Commn., 1974-88; bd. dirs. Hispanic Ctr. Western Mich., 1988-91; bd. govs. Aquinas Emeritus Coll., 1991-97, chmn., 1993-95; bd. dirs. West Mich. Interactive Sci. Ctr., 1990—. Fellow Geol. Soc. Am.; mem. Am. Assn. Mus. (exec. bd. 1973-75, v.p. 1977-80, mem. mus. accreditation com. 1970), Midwest Mus. Conf. (pres. 1966-67), Mich. Archaeol. Soc. (pres. 1968-69), Nebr. State Hist. Soc., Hist. Soc. Mich., Soc. Vertebrate Paleontology, Nebr. Acad. Scis., Mich. Acad. Scis., Arts and Letters, Iowa Acad. Scis., Iowa Archaeol. Soc., Mich. Mus. Assn., Nebr. State Genealogical Soc., Grand Rapids Hist. Soc. (v.p. 1993-94), Grand Forum (bd. dirs. 1995—), Edelweiss Club Grand Rapids (v.p. 1991-93), Torch Club (v.p. 1993-94, pres. 1994-95), Collectors Club Grand Rapids (pres. 2000-02), Rotary, Sigma Xi. Episcopalian. Avocations: travel; photography; landscape gardening; building log cabins; art. Home: 4856 Fuller Ave SE Grand Rapids MI 49508-4738

FRANKHOUSER, HOMER SHELDON, JR., engineering and construction company executive; b. Reading, Pa., Sept. 6, 1927; s. Homer Sheldon Sr. and Helen May (Geisewite) F.; m. Betty Carpenter, Sept. 2, 1972; children: Karl, Lorelei, Kurt, Michelle, Brandt. BCE, Lehigh U., 1952. Engr., then supt. Dravo Corp., Pitts., 1954-69; v.p. Dravo Ocean Structures, New Orleans, 1969-72; sr. project mgr. Brown & Root Inc., Houston, 1972-74, v.p., 1977-85, Brown & Root (U.K.) Ltd., London, 1974-77, dep. chmn., COO, 1980-89; sr. v.p. Brown & Root Inc., Houston, 1985-92; pres. Frankhouser & Assocs. Inc., Houston, 1992—, Internat. Indsl. Devel. Corp., 1997—, PetroAm. Corp., 1997—; chmn. Pulse Radar, Inc., 1997—. Chmn. bd. Brown & Root Norge A.S., Oslo. 1st lt. U.S. Army, 1952-54, Korea. Mem. ASCE (life), Oil Industries Club (London), Inst. Dirs. (London), Masons. Republican. Avocation: oil painting. Home: 9095 Briar Forest Dr Houston TX 77024-7221 Office: Frankhouser & Assocs Inc 3535 Briarpark Dr Ste 207 Houston TX 77042-5234 E-mail: hfrankhous@aol.com.

FRANKISH, BRIAN EDWARD, film producer, director; b. Columbus, Ohio, July 28, 1943; s. John (Jack) Fletcher Frankish and Barbara Aileen (Tondro) Gray; m. Tannis Rae Benedict, Oct. 13, 1985; children: Merlin L. Reed III, Michelle Lynn Reed. AA, Chaffey Coll., 1964; BA, San Francisco State U., 1967. Freelance producer, L.A.; prin. Frankish-Benedict Entertainment, L.A. Prodr. (film) Vice Squad, 1981, (TV series) Max Headroom, 1987; assoc. prodr.: (films) Elephant Parts, 1981, Strange Brew, 1982, The Boy Who Could Fly, 1985, In the Mood, 1986, Stuart Little, 1999; exec. prodr., unit prodn. mgr. (film) Field of Dreams, 1989, Flight of the Intruder, 1990, American Me, 1991, Life As A House, 2001; prodr. visual effects for film Turbulence, 1996; prodr., dir. (theatrical play) Timing is Everything, 1991; 1st asst. dir.: (TV shows) Big Shamus, 1979, Skag, 1979, Why Me?, 1983, Making Out, 1984, Berrengers, 1984, (films) Strange Brew, 1982, Uncle Joe Shannon, 1978, Savage Harvest, 1980, Dead and Buried, 1980, Spring Break, 1982, Brainstorm, 1982-83, The Last Starfighter, 1983, The New Kids, 1983, Aloha Summer, 1984, The Best of Times, 1985, Odd Jobs, 1985, The Fugitive, 1993, Demolition Man, 1993, Roswell, 1994; unit prodn. mgr. Second Serve, 1986, The Net, 1995, Stuart Little, 1999; distbr.'s rep. and completion bond rep. Made in Heaven, 1986; prodn. mgr.: The Net, 1995; other prodn. credits include: Play it Again, Sam, 1971, Everything You Always Wanted to Know About Sex..., 1972, Time to Run, 1972, Haunts, 1975, Mahogany (Montage), 1975, King Kong, 1976, The Betsy, 1977. Mem. Dirs. Guild Am., Calif. Yacht Club.

FRANK-KAMENETSKII, MAXIM D. biomedical engineer; b. Nizhniy Novgorod, Russia, Aug. 7, 1941; came to U.S., 1993; s. David A. and Elena E. (Fridman) F.; m. Alla D. Voskoboinik, Jan. 7, 1961 (dec. 1985); 1 child, Michael. MS, Moscow Phys. & Tech. Inst., 1964, PhD, 1967; DSc, Inst. Chem. Physics Moscow, 1972. Jr. scientist Kurchatov Inst. Atomic Engery, Moscow, 1967-72, sr. scientist, 1972-78; head lab. Inst. Molecular Genetics, Moscow, 1979-89, head. dept., 1989-93; prof. Boston U., 1993—. Disting. vis.prof. U. Ala., Birmingham, 1989, Ohio State U., Columbus, 1991-92. Author: Unraveling DNA, 1993, 97. Avocation: tennis. Office: Boston U Dept Advanced Biotechnology 36 Cummington St Boston MA 02215-2427 E-mail: mfk@bu.edu.

FRANKL, JEANNE SILVER, association executive, lawyer; m. Kenneth R. Frankl; 1 dau., Kathryn. AB in Lit. summa cum laude, Brown U., 1952; LLB, Yale U., 1955. Bar: Conn. 1955, N.Y. 1956. Law sec. to Hon. Edmund L. Palmieri, 1955-56; atty. Port of N.Y. Authority, 1956-60; assoc. Rosenman Colin Kaye Petschek Freund & Emil, N.Y.C., 1960-67; chief of program plannnig Office of Edn. Liaison City Human Resources Adminstrn., 1967-69; spl. asst. to dep. admistr. N.Y.C. Human Resources Adminstrn., 1969-70; asst. dir. Community Sch. System Project N.Y. Lawyers Com. for Civil Rights under Law, 1970, dir., 1970-73; counsel, law project dir. Pub. Edn. Assn., N.Y.C., 1973-80, exec. dir., 1980-93. Lectr. Rutgers U. Law Sch. Edn. Law Seminar, 1972-73. Mem. Phi Beta Kappa. Home and Office: PO Box 955 67 Old Montauk Hwy Amagansett NY 11930 E-mail: jsfrankl@optonline.net.

FRANKL, KENNETH RICHARD, retired lawyer; b. N.Y.C., May 23, 1924; s. Hugo Joseph and Sydney (Miller) F.; m. Jeanne Ritchie Silver, Aug. 6, 1972; 1 child, Kathryn; 1 son by previous marriage, Keith E. AB cum laude, Harvard U., 1945, LLB, 1950. Bar: N.Y. 1951, U.S. Ct. Appeals (2d cir.) 1956. Asst. dist. atty. N.Y. County, 1951-56; assoc. firm Liebman Eulau & Robinson, N.Y.C., 1959-60; asst. gen. atty. CBS, 1960-69; gen. counsel, asst. sec. Bishop Industries, Inc., 1969-70; v.p., gen. counsel, sec. RKO Gen., Inc. and Subs., 1970-84, cons.; ptnr. Law Offices of Ronald Kahn, N.Y.C., 1986; v.p. Charles H. Greenthal Comml. Co., N.Y.C., 1989-91. Dir. staff Spl. Com. to Study Defender Sys. of N.Y.C. Assn. of the Bar, 1957-58. Co-author: (report) Equal Justice for the Accused, 1959. Mem. Amagansett Citizen Adv. Com., East Hampton Jewish Ctr. Served Signal Corps U.S. Army, 1943—46, PTO. Decorated Okinawa Battle Star and Army Unit Commendation medal. Mem.: Harvard Club N.Y. Home: PO Box 955 67 Old Montauk Hwy Amagansett NY 11930

FRANKL, RAZELLE, management educator; BA in English, Temple U., 1955; MA in Polit. Sci., Bryn Mawr Coll., 1966; MBA in Organizational Devel., Drexel U., 1973; PhD, Bryn Mawr Coll., 1984. Chair codes and ordinance com. Exec Com. Neighborhood Improvement Program, Lower Merion Twp., 1967-68; pres. LWV Lower Merion Twp., 1967-68; v.p. for organizational affairs LWV, Springfield, Mass., 1968-70; chair environ. quality com. LWV Radnor Twp., 1970-71; instr. applied behavioral sci. Drexel U. Sch. Bus., 1972-73; planner office of mental health/mental retardation Dept. Pub. Health, City of Phila., 1971-73, planner office of health planning, 1971-73; coord. for health programs Phila. '76 Inc. (Official Bicentennial Corp.), 1972-74; adj. faculty dept. mgmt. adminstrv. studies divsn. Coll. Bus. Rowan U. (formerly Glassboro State Coll., Rowan Coll.), 1974-77, 81-82; asst. prof. Glassboro (N.J.) State Coll., 1982-88, assoc. prof. dept. mgmt., 1988-95, prof., 1995—2002, prof. emerita, 2002—. Author: Televangelism: The Marketing of Popular Religion, 1987, Popular Religion and the Imperatives of Television: A Study of the Electric Church, 1984; author: (with others) Religious Television: Controversies and Conclusions, 1990, Teleministries as Family Businesses, 1990, New Christian Politics, 1984, Culture Media and Religious Right, 1997, The Encyclopedia of Religion and Society, 1997; contbr. (book chpt.) Transformation of Televangelism: Repackaging of Christian Family Values, 1997, articles to profl. jours. Dir. nat. bd. Allegheny U. Health Scis., chair spring program; chair, bd. dirs. Anti-Violence Partnership of Phila.; founder, chair Friends of Rowan U. Libr., 1995—. Rsch. grantee Rowan Coll. N.J. (formerly Glassboro State Coll.), 1986-87, 90, 91, 93-94, 94-95, All-Coll. Rsch. grantee, 1987-88. Mem. Am. Acad. Mgmt. (chair membership com. div. mgmt. edn. and devel., chair media rels. com., div. women in mgmt.), Soc. for Human Resource Mgmt., Am. Sociol. Assn., Ea. Sociol. Soc., Assn. for Sociology Religion, Religious Rsch. Assn., Soc. for Sci. Study Religion (chair womens caucus), Internat. Sociol. Assn. Home: 536 Moreno Rd Wynnewood PA 19096-1121 E-mail: frankl@rowan.edu.

FRANKL, SPENCER NELSON, dentist, university dean; b. Phila., Nov. 19, 1933; s. Louis and Vera F.; m. Rhoda Lee, June 12, 1955; children: Elizabeth Ann, Catherine Susan. D.D.S., Temple U., 1958; postgrad., Children's Hosp. D.C., 1958-59; MS, Tufts U., 1961. Asst. prof. dentistry Tufts U., 1961-64; asso. prof. Boston U., 1964-67, prof., 1967—, chmn. dept. dentistry, 1964-67, asst. dean, 1970-73, asso. dean, 1973—; dean Boston Univ. Sch. of Dental Medicine, 1977—; dep. dir. Boston U. Med. Ctr., 1980—. Chief pedodontics Boston U. Med. Center U. Hosp., 1964; head pediatric dentistry Beth Israel Hosp., 1964; chief dental service Joseph P. Kennedy Jr. Meml. Hosp., Brighton, Mass., 1968— Contbr. articles to profl. jours. Fellow Am. Coll. Dentists, Internat. Coll. Dentists, Am. Acad. Pediatric Dentistry; mem. APHA, ADA, Am. Soc. Dentistry for Children, Mass. Soc. Dentistry for Children (past pres.), Internat. Assn. for Dental Rsch., Am. Bd. Pedodontics (examiner). Office: 100 E Newton St Boston MA 02118-2308

FRANKL, WILLIAM STEWART, cardiologist, educator; b. Phila., July 15, 1928; s. Louis and Vera (Simkin) F.; m. Razelle Sherr, June 17, 1951; children: Victor S. (dec.), Brian A. BA in Biology, Temple U., 1951, MD, 1955, MS in Medicine, 1961. Diplomate Am. Bd. Internal Medicine, Am. Bd. Cardiovasc. Disease. Intern Buffalo Gen. Hosp., 1955-56; resident in medicine Temple U., Phila., 1956-57, 59-61; faculty Temple U. Sch. Medicine, 1962-68, dir. EKG sect. dept. cardiology, 1966-68, dir. cardiac care unit, 1967-68; prof. medicine, dir. divsn. cardiology Med. Coll. Pa., Phila., 1970-79; prof. medicine, assoc. dir. cardiology divsn. Thomas Jefferson U., Phila., 1979-84; physician-in-chief Springfield (Mass.) Hosp., 1968-70; prof. medicine, co-dir. William Likoff Cardiovascular Inst. Hahnemann U., Phila., 1984-86, dir. William Likoff Cardiovascular Inst., dir. div. cardiology, 1986-92, Thomas J. Vischer Prof. medicine, chmn. dept. medicine, 1987-92; prof. medicine, dir. cardiovascular regional programs Allegheny U. of the Health Scis., 1992-98; dir. cardiovascular regional programs Allegheny U. Hosps., 1992-98; v.p. cardiovascular program devel. Allegheny U. Hosps. System, 1995-98; prof. medicine cardiology divsn. dept. medicine Temple U. Sch. Medicine, 1998-2000. Cons. cardiology Phila. Va Hosp., 1970-79; Fogarty Sr. Internat. fellow Cardiothoracic Inst., U. London, 1978-79; pres. Pa. affiliate Am. Heart Assn., 1985-86; clin. prof. of medicine, Temple U. Sch. of Medicine, 2000—. Contbr. articles to profl. jours. Capt. (M.C.), U.S. Army, 1957-59. Cardiovascular Rsch. fellow U. Pa., Phila., 1961-62; recipient Golden Apple award Temple U. Sch. Medicine, 1967; award Med. Coll. Pa., 1972; Lindback award for disting. teaching, 1975. Fellow ACP, Am. Coll. Cardiology (gov. Ea. Pa. 1986-89), Phila. Coll. Physicians, Am. Coll. Clin. Pharmacology (regent 1980-85, 93-98), Coun. Clin. Cardiology of Am. Heart Assn. (coun. on arteriosclerosis); mem. AAUP, AAAS, N.Y. Acad. Scis., Am. Fedn. Clin. Rsch., Assn. Am. Med. Colls., Am. Heart Assn. (bd. govs. S.E. Pa. chpt. 1972-84, pres. 1976, Pa. affiliate pres. 1984-85), Am. Soc. Clin. Pharmacology and Exptl. Therapeutics, Phila. County Med. Soc. (pres. 1993-94, 1st dist. trustee to Pa. Med. Soc. bd. trustees 1998-2001). Home and Office: 536 Moreno Rd Wynnewood PA 19096-1121 E-mail: wfrankl@earthlink.net. *The essence of humanity and being human is caring. When one cares, life takes on a new dimension and provides one the ability to transcend the thin veneer which separates human and animal.*

FRANKLIN, ARETHA, singer; b. Memphis, 1942; d. Clarence L. and Barbara (Siggers) Franklin; m. Ted White (div.); m. Glynn Turman, Apr. 11, 1978. First record at age 12, rec. artist with Columbia Records, N.Y.C., 1961, then with Atlantic records, now with Arista Records; singer: (albums) Aretha, 1961, Electrifying, Tender Moving and Swinging, 1962, Laughing on the Outside, 1963, Unforgettable, Songs of Faith, Running Out of Fools, 1964, Yeah, 1965, Soul Sister, 1966, Queen of Soul, Take It Like You Give It, Lee Cross, Greatest Hits, I Never Loved a Man, Once in a Lifetime, Aretha Arrives, 1967, Lady Soul, Greatest Hits, Vol. 2, Best of Aretha Franklin, Live at Paris Olympia, Aretha Now, 1968, Soul 69, Today I Sing the Blues, Soft and Beautiful, Aretha Gold's, Satisfaction, I Say a Little Prayer, 1969, This Girl's in Love with You, Spirit in the Dark, Don't Play that Song, 1970, Live at the Fillmore West, Young Gifted and Black, Aretha's Greatest Hits, 1971, Amazing Grace, 1972, Hey Hey Now, Firest 12 Sides, 1973, Let Me Into Your Life, 1974, With Every Thing I Feel in Me, You, 1975, Sparkle, Ten Years of Gold, 1976, Sweet Passion, 1977, Almighty Fire, Star Collection, 1978, La Diva, 1979, Aretha, 1980, Who's Zoomin' Who, 1985, One Lord, One Faith, One Baptism, 1987, Aretha Sings the Blues, 1965, 85, Lady Soul, 1988, Through the Storm, 1989, What You See is What You Sweat, 1991, Jazz to Soul, 1992, Aretha After Hours, Chain of Fools, 1993, Unforgettable: A Tribute to Dinah Washington, 1995, Love Songs, 1997, The Delta Meets Detroit, A Rose Is Still A Rose, 1998, Amazing Grace, 1999; actress Blues Brothers, 1980, (films) Shindig! Presents Soul, Shindig! Presents Groovy Gals, 1991, History of Rock 'N' Roll, 1995, Blues Brothers 2000, 1998, (TV films) Bob Hope on Campus, 1975, Aretha Franklin: The Queen of Soul, 1988, (TV miniseries) Motown 40: The Music Is Forever, 1998; performer (Showtime prodn.): Aretha, 1986; performer: (concert tours) in U.S. and Europe. Named Top Female Vocalist, 1967, Number One Female Singer 16th Internat., Jazz Critics Poll, 1968; named to Hollywood Walk of Fame, 1979, Rock and Roll Hall of Fame, 1987; recipient Grammy award for best female rhythm and blues vocal, 1967—74, 1981, 1985, 1987, for best rhythm and blues rec., 1988, for best soul gospel performance, 1972, for best rhythm and blues duo vocal (with George Michael), 1987, Am. Music award, 1984, Kennedy Center Honor, 1994, 1994. Office: care Arista Records c/o Gwen Quinn 6 W 57th St New York NY 10019-3901

FRANKLIN, BARRY ALLAN, health facility administrator, physiologist; b. Cleve., May 23, 1948; s. Norman Paul and Lottie (Medow) f.; m. Linda Alice Dreyfuss, June 5, 1971; children: Michael, Laura. BS, Kent State U., 1970; MS in Applied Physiology, U. Mich., 1971; PhD in Physiology, Pa. State U., 1976. Coord. cardiac evaluation and reconditioning Millard Fillmore Hosp., Buffalo, 1976-77; asst. prof. medicine, exercise physiologist Case Western Res. U., Cleve., 1977-78; program dir. cardiovascular fitness and rehab. Sinai Hosp., Detroit, 1979-85; prof. biology Mercy Coll., Detroit, 1979-84; asst. prof. physiology Wayne State U., Detroit, 1979-81, assoc. prof. physiology, 1986-94, prof. physiology, 1994—; dir. cardiac rehab. and exercise labs. William Beaumont Hosp., Royal Oak, Mich., 1985—; clin. prof. exercise sci. Oakland U., Rochester, Mich., 1992—; prof. family medicine U. Mich., Ann Arbor, 1998—. Cert. exercise specialist Am. Coll. Sports Medicine, 1976 (faculty examiner exercise specialist workshops, 1978-94, fellow 1982, dir. exercise specialist workshop and cert. 1982—, chmn. program dir. subcom. 1984-86, exercise specialist subcom. 1980-84, cert. program dir. 1980, chmn. 1982-84, sci. exhibits subcom. 1984, pres.-elect Midwest Regional Chpt. 1986-87, pres. 1988, adminstrv. coun. bd. trustees 1986-87, area rep. cardiopulmonary rehab. ann. meeting 1990-91, 94-96, profl. edn. com. 1989-95, v.p. 1993-95, program com. 1993-95, budget fin. com., 1994-97, chair ad hoc liason com. 1994-97); mem. exercise com. Am. Heart Assn. Mich.; mem. med. adv. bd. Nat. Alliance Cardiovasc. Technologists, 1984-86; vis. prof. U. Ill. Coll. Medicine, 1982; vis. scholar Western Mich. U., Kalamazoo, 1984; bd. trustees, v.p. Am. Assn. Cardiovasc. Pulmonary Rehab., 1985-87 (chmn. sci. sessions 1986, abstract reviewer 1986—, pres.-elect 1986-87, pres. 1987-88, program chmn. 1987, chmn. reimbursement com. 1989-91, mem. at large 1989-91, award excellence 1992); sci. adv. bd. Rockport Walking Inst., 1985-91; chmn. exercise cardiac rehab. com. Am. Heart Assn. Mich., 1986-91 (bd. trustees 1989-95, chmn. program com. 1992-93, pres.-elect 1993-94, pres. 1994-95); projects com. Rsch. Inst. William Beaumont Hosp., 1989—; mem. couns. clin. cardiology Am. Heart Assn., 1992—; sci. adv. bd. Life Fitness, 1993; mem. Gov's. Coun. Phys. Fitness, Health Sports, 1994—; invited participant NIH consensus Devel. Conf. Phys. Activity Cardiovasc. Health, 1995; sci. adv. bd. Duke U. Med. Ctr., 1997—. Author, editor over 300 articles to sci. books, jours. including Am. Jour. Health Promotion, Am. Jour. Cardiology, Jour. Cardiopulmonary Rehab. (rev. bd. 1983—, editor-in-chief 1991-95, cons. editor 1996—), Cardiopulmonary Phys. Therapy Journal, Heartline, The Physician and Sportsmedicine, The Exercise Standards and Malpractice Reporter, Medicine and Sci. in Sports and Exercise, Jour. Cardiovasc. Nursing, others; mem. editl. bd. Am. Jour. Cardiology, 1994—, The Physician and Sportsmedicine, 1987—; editor-in-chief Am. Jour. Medicine and Sports, 2001—; columnist The Detroit Free Press, 1998—; Med. adv. bd. mem. Jewish Cmty. Ctr. Met. Detroit, 1979-85, Young Men's Christian Assn. Met. Detroit, 1983-92; host dir. Nat. Multiple Sclerosis Soc., William Beaumont Hosp., 1991-93; bd. trustees Am. Heart Assn., Mich. Affiliate, 1989-98; adj. faculty Wayne State U. Sch. Medicine, U. Mich., Oakland U. Recipient George Altman award outstanding grad. sr., Kent State U., 1970, BEACON Wellness award Blue Care Network Southeastern Mich., 1991, Media award San Diego County Med. Soc., 1995, Disting. Svc. award Am. Assn. Cardiovasc. Pulmonary Rehab., Middleton, Wis., 1996, Horace Elgin Dodge Award Am. Heart Assn. Mich., 1998, Glen V. Swengros Meml. award Nat. Assn. for Health and Fitness, 2002; Rackham Grad. Sch. fellow, U. Mich., 1970-71. Fellow: Am. Assn. Cardiovasc. Pulmonary Rehab., Am. Coll. Sports Medicine (pres. 1999—2000, Citation award 2002); mem.: Am. Heart Assn. (F. Dewey Dodrill award for excellence 2003), Am. Coll. Sports Medicine Found. (pres. 2001—02). Jewish. Avocations: distance walking, travel, writing, golf. Home: 2853 Baltane Rd West Bloomfield MI 48323-3101 Office: Beaumont Health Ctr Cardiac Rehab 4949 Coolidge Hwy Royal Oak MI 48073- E-mail: bfranklin@beaumont.edu.

FRANKLIN, BENJAMIN A. editor, reporter; b. N.Y.C., Nov. 12, 1927; s. Benjamin A. and Zilpha C. Franklin; m. Jane Burrage, June 10, 1950; children: Abigail, Elizabeth, Clare. BA, U. Pa., 1948; MS in Journalism, Columbia U., 1950. Reporter Evening Star, Washington, 1948—50, ABC Radio News, Washington, 1953—59, N.Y. Times, Washington, 1959—91, Nucleonics Week, Washington, 1991—93; editor Washington Spectator, 1993—. Lt. (j.g.) USCG, 1950—53, N. Atlantic. Recipient Weatherford award, Berea Coll., Ky., 1970, Disting. Svc. award, Soc. Profl. Journalists, 1973, Honors award, Environ. Policy Inst., Washington, 1974. Mem.: Washington Nat. Press Club. Democrat. Episcopalian. Home and Office: PO Box 90 11404 Rokeby Ave Garrett Park MD 20896

FRANKLIN, BENJAMIN BARNUM, dinner club executive; b. Topeka, Nov. 7, 1944; s. Charles Benjamin and Margaret Lavona (Barnum) F. BA in Speech, U. Colo., 1967. With Associated Clubs, Inc., Topeka, 1967—, v.p., 1972-83, pres., 1983—. Editor (newsletter): The Dinner Gong; contbr. articles to profl. jours. Chmn. steering com. Capper Found. for Crippled Children, Topeka, trustee, 1994—2001, John Austin Cheley Found., 1995—, bd. dirs., 1995—2003. Named honoree, Benjamin Barnum Franklin Day, Lima, Ohio, 1983. Mem. Internat. Platform Assn. (gov. 1975-2000), Topeka Sales and Mktg. Execs. (bd. dirs. 1985—), Explorers Club, Am. Alpine Club, Knife and Fork Club (internat. v.p. 1991), Internat. Knife and Fork Club (pres. 1994—), Topeka Knife and Fork Club, Met. Dinner Club (pres. 1983—), Exec. Dinner Club (pres. 1983, lectr. 1969-76), Rotary (bd. dirs. 1975-78, Paul Harris fellow), Sigma Phi Epsilon. Republican. Presbyterian. Office: PO Box 4585 Topeka KS 66604-0585

FRANKLIN, BILLY JOE, international higher education specialist; b. Honey Grove, Texas, Jan. 30, 1940; s. John Asia and Annie Mae (Castle) F.; m. Sonya Kay Erwin, June 1, 1958; children: Terry Daylon, Shari Dea. BA, U. Tex., 1965, MA, 1967, PhD, 1969. Asst. prof. sociology U. Iowa, Iowa City, 1969-71; chmn. Western Carolina U., Cullowhee, NC, 1971-72, Wright State U., Dayton, Ohio, 1973-75; dean SW Tex. State U., San Marcos, Tex., 1975-77; v.p. acad. affairs Stephen F. Austin State U., Nacogdoches, Tex., 1977-81; pres. Tex. A&I U., Kingsville, Tex., 1981-85, Lamar U., Beaumont, Tex., 1985-91; exec. v.p. Tex. Internat. Edn. Consortium, Austin, 1991-96, pres., 1996-2000. Adj. prof. U. Tex., Austin, 2000—; mem. nat. agrl. rsch. com. USDA, 1982-85; policies and purposes com. Am. Assn. State Colls. and Univs., 1985-91, nominating com., 1986-88, mem. exec. com. bd. dir., 1990-91; pres. Assn. Tex. Colls. and Univs., 1985-86, Tex. Acad. Sci., 1986-87; commr. commn. on coll. So. Assoc. Coll. and Sch., 1985-90, chmn., 1987-90, pres.-elect, 1990-91; chmn. Coun. Pub. Univ. Pres. and Chancellors, 1988-91; bd. dir. Tex. Ptnr. of Am., Scheriner U. Co-editor: Research Methods: Issues and Insights, 1971, Social Psychology and Everyday Life, 1973; contbr. articles to profl. jour. Mem. sr. adv. bd. Tex.

Lyceum, Inc., 1982-88; bd. dir. United Way of Coastal Bend, 1981-84, United Way of Beaumont, Tex., Tex. Ptnr. of . Energy Mus., 1987, pres., 1987-90; mem. exec. com. Muscular Dystrophy Assoc., 1985-91. Presbyterian. Fellow Tex. Acad. Sci.; mem. Am. Sociol. Assn., Kingsville C. of C. (bd. dir. 1981-83, pres. 1984), Beaumont C. of C. (bd. dir. 1986-91, chmn. 1988-89), East Tex. C. of C. (bd. dir. 1985-87), East Tex. Venture Capital Group (bd. dir. 1985-87), Schreiner Univ. (bd. trustees, 2003-). E-mail: billf@gvtc.com.

FRANKLIN, BLAKE TIMOTHY, lawyer; b. San Mateo, Calif., Sept. 28, 1942; s. Harvey James and Marie Agnes (Leane) F. AB, Dartmouth Coll., 1963; JD, Harvard U., 1966. Bar: Calif. 1966, D.C. 1969, U.S. Supreme Ct. 1970, N.Y. 1976. AID contractor Peace Corps; vis. prof. comml. law U. Costa Rica, San Jose, 1966-68; assoc. Coudert Bros., Washington, 1969-74, ptnr. N.Y.C., 1975-83, Gibson Dunn & Crutcher, N.Y.C., 1983—. Bd. dirs. Union Theol. Sem., N.Y., Nat. Law Ctr. for Inter-Am. Free Trade, Tucson, Bolivian-Am. C. of C. Chancellor of vestry St. Michael's Ch., N.Y.C., 1987-93; trustee Aids Svc. Found. of Orange County, Calif., 1994-97; St. Hilda's and St. Hugh's Sch., N.Y.C., 1988-92; mem. bd. gov.'s USO, 1987-90. Mem. ABA, Inter-Am. Bar Assn., Am. Soc. Internat. Law, Assn. of Bar of City of N.Y. Episcopalian. Office: Gibson Dunn & Crutcher 200 Park Ave Fl 47 New York NY 10166-0193

FRANKLIN, BONNIE SELINSKY, retired federal agency administrator; b. Oakland, Calif., Mar. 17, 1944; d. Harold Joseph and Madge (Warden) Selinsky; m. Alfred Carl Franklin, Jan. 24, 1981; 1 child, Amy Beth. AB in Am. Studies, George Washington U., 1966, MBA in Acctg., 1977. Tax auditor IRS, Baileys Crossroads, Va., 1966-71, from program analyst to tax law specialist Washington, 1971-77, from program analyst appeals to chief procedures sect., 1979-82, tech. asst. to nat. chief appeals, 1985-2000, program mgr., 2000—01, regional analyst conf. Atlanta, 1977-79. Chair Arlingtonians for a Better County, Arlington, Va., 1994-97, archivist, 1999-2000; active Friends of the Libr., Arlington, 1996—. Recipient Albert Gallatin Devoted Svc. award, U.S. Treasury Dept. Mem. LWV (treas. Arlington Va. chpt. 1998-2001, pres. 2001—), AAUW. Democrat. Lutheran. Avocations: reading, travel.

FRANKLIN, BRUCE WALTER, lawyer; b. Ellendale, N.D., Feb. 26, 1936; s. Wallace Henry and Frances (Webb) F.; m. Kristy Ann Jones, Feb. 7, 1944; children: Kevin, Monica, Taylor. Student, U. Mich., 1954-56; LLB, Detroit Coll. Law, 1962. Bar: Mich. 1963. Sole practice, Troy, Mich., 1962-90; mng. ptnr. Franklin, Bigler, Berry & Johnston, P.C., Troy, Mich., 1991-98, Franklin & Davis, Troy, 1998—. Bd. dirs. First Union-Newnan Bank; pres., CEO Landward III Devel. Corp. (Arbor Springs Plantation). Past chmn. Mich. Young Reps., United Meth. Retirement Cmtys.; bd. dirs. Peachtree Hosp., Wesley Woods. Served with U.S. Army. Office: Landward III 250 Arbor Springs Plantation Dr Newnan GA 30265 E-mail: BFranklin@numail.org.

FRANKLIN, CHARLES E. manufacturing executive; b. Birmingham, Ala., July 17, 1938; BS in Mech. Engring, Ga. Inst. Tech., 1961; MS in Aeromech. Engring., Air Force Inst. Tech., 1967. Ret. as lt. gen. USAF, 1996; v.p. Lockheed Martin, 1998—2002; sr. exec. Raytheon Co., Tewksbury, Mass., 1998—.

FRANKLIN, CHARLES SCOTHERN, lawyer; b. Knoxville, Tenn., Dec. 12, 1937; s. Samuel Leroy and Mildred (Gibson) F.; m. Lynn Kerr; children: Jill Parvin, Melissa Ann, Samuel Arthur. BS, U. Tenn., 1958, MS, 1960; LL.B., Vanderbilt U., 1966. Bar: Calif. 1967, Nev. 1971. Instr. econs. U. Tenn., Knoxville, 1960-61; Ford Found. fellow in econs. U. Calif., Berkeley, 1962; assoc. firm Kent Brookes & Anderson, San Francisco, 1966-70; gen. counsel, sec. Harrah's, Reno, 1970—79; pvt. practice Reno, 1980—85, Sacramento, 1985-94. Mem. Nev. State Bar, Calif. State Bar. Home: 2891 Greystone Cove N Atlanta GA 30341-5858

FRANKLIN, DAVID, small business owner, researcher; b. Brockton, Mass., Aug. 8, 1932; s. Ira Simpson and Edith Nancy Franklin; m. Loretta Jean Clement, Oct. 18, 1980; m. Lydia Englander, June 7, 1956 (div. May 9, 1969); children: Michael Simon, Joanne Eve, Joseph Aaron. BA in Physics, NYU, 1954—56. Project engr./project head US Naval Applied Sci. Lab., Bklyn., 1957—70, MIT/Draper Laboratories, Cambridge, 1971—73; pres. Rabbit Products Inc, Somerville, 1974—85; rsch. affiliate MIT/RLE, Cambridge, 1976—77; pres./ceo/dir. of rsch. Audiological Engring. Corp., Somerville, 1982—. Cons. Data Technologies Inc, Woburn, 1979—80. Grantee 28 Grants for Rsch. relating to Hearing Problems, NIH, 1982 through 2003. Achievements include 6 Patents relating to hearing issues; design and devel. of a line of tactile aids; design and devel. of a multiple modality Assistive Listening Device; Design and devel. of a new type of directional microphone (Excloid). Avocations: writing (physics), writing (humor), tennis, woodworking, fishing. Home: 9 Preston Rd Somerville MA 02143 Office: Audiological Engring Corporation 9 Preston Rd Somerville MA 02143 Office Fax: 617-666-5228. Personal E-mail: davidtact@erols.com. E-mail: davidf@tactaid.com.

FRANKLIN, DAVID PERDUE, vascular surgeon, educator; b. Decatur, Ga., Apr. 7, 1957; m. Pamela Sue Keffer, July 10, 1982; children: Molly Elizabeth, Hannah Blair, Lucas Solomon. BA, Emory U., 1979; MD, Wake Forest U., 1983. Diplomate Am. Bd. Surgery, Am. Bd. Vasc. Surgery. Resident in gen. surgery Dartmouth-Hitchcock, Hanover, N.H., 1983-88; fellow in vasc. surgery Mass. Gen. Hosp., Boston, 1988-89; dir. vasc. lab. Geisinger Clinic, Danville, Pa., 1991—, chief vasc. surgery, 1997—, program dir. fasc. fellowship, 1998—, vice chmn. surgery, 2002—. Clin. assoc. prof. surgery Thomas Jeffferson U. Elder Grove Presbyn. Ch., Danville, Pa., 1994—. Fellow ACS; mem. Soc. Vascular Surgery, Internat. Soc. Cardiovasc. Surgeons, Eastern Vasc. Soc., Perpheral Vasc. Surg. Soc. Office: Geisinger Clinic Sect Vascular Surgery Danville PA 17822-0001

FRANKLIN, DIANA JEANNE, chiropractor; b. Davenport, Iowa, Feb. 2, 1956; d. Donald Dewane and Sheila Kathleen Laws; m. Robert Todd Franklin, Nov. 19, 1983; 1 child, Robert Christopher. D. in Chiropractic, Palmer Coll Chiropractic, 1981. Diplomate Am. Bd. Nutrition, cert. naturopathic physician, clinical nutritionist, lic. nutrition counselor. Chiropractor Laws Chiropractic Clinic, Quincy, Ill., 1981-95; pvt. practice Quincy, 1995—. Mem. adv. bd. Inst. Nutritional Sci., San Diego, 1996-98. Bd. dirs. QUANADA, Quincy, 1996—; bd. dirs. Palm of My Hand, 2000. Mem. NAFE, Am. Bus. Women Assn., Am. Chiropractic Assn., Inst. Functional Medicine, Internat. and Am. Assn. Clin. Nutritionists, Ill. Chiropractic Soc. Avocations: reading, stained glass, remodeling old home, cycling. Office: 1210 N 24th St Quincy IL 62301-2233 E-mail: drdi@ksni.net.

FRANKLIN, EDWARD WARD, international investment consultant, lawyer, actor; b. N.Y.C., Sept. 23, 1926; s. Albert Ward and Edith (Meyers) F.; m. Joan Rice, Aug. 25, 1956; children— Caroline, Melissa, Edward Ward. AB magna cum laude, Harvard U., 1947, LLB, 1950. Bar: N.Y. 1951. Assoc. Cadwalader, Wickersham & Taft, N.Y.C., 1950-56; gen. counsel N.Y. Air Brake Co., 1956-67, v.p. internat. and legal, 1962-67; v.p., gen. counsel Gen. Signal Corp., N.Y.C., 1967-80, sec., 1969-80, sr. v.p., 1980-83, vice chmn., 1983-85, also dir., mem. exec. com. Chmn. bd. Hamworthy Hydraulics, Ltd., Poole, Eng.; dir. Holborn Internat. Portfolio Mgrs., Ptnrs. Fund, Inc., Pacus Ventures Ltd., Chase NBW Bank. Life gov., trustee N.Y. Presbyn. Hosp., Trinity Episcopal Schs. Corp.; chmn. bd. trustees Gracie Square Hosp., N.Y.C. Mem. AEA, SAG, AFTRA, Assn. Bar City of N.Y., The Players, Knickerbocker Club, Harvard Club (N.Y.C.), Misquamicut Club (Watch Hill, R.I.), Phi Beta Kappa. Home and Office: 1185 Park Ave New York NY 10128-1308

FRANKLIN, FREDERICK RUSSELL, retired legal association executive; b. Mar. 20, 1929; s. Ernest James and Frances (Price) F.; m. Barbara Ann Donovan, Jan. 26, 1952; children: Katherine Elizabeth, Frederick Russell. AB, Ind. U., 1951, JD with high distinction, 1956. Bar: Ind. 1956. Trial atty. criminal div. and ct. of claims sect. civil div. U.S. Dept. Justice, Washington, 1956-60; gen. counsel Ind. State Bar Assn., Indpls., 1960-67; dir. continuing legal edn. for Ind., adj. prof. law Ind. U., Indpls., 1965-68; staff dir. profl. standards ABA, Chgo., 1968-70, legal edn. and admissions to the bar, 1972-92, sr. lawyers divsn., 1985-93; ret., 1993. Exec. v.p. Nat. Attys. Title Assurance Fund, Inc., Indpls., 1970-72. Trustee Olympia Fields (Ill.) United Meth. Ch., 1980-84; treas. bd. dirs. Olympia Fields Pub. Libr., 1984-91; mem. Olympia Fields Pub. Safety Bd., 1983-92. Capt. USAF, 1951-53. Named to Honorable Order Ky. Cols., 1967, 74, Adm. Tex. Navy, 1967, Adm. Nebr. Navy, 1972, 74, Sagamore of Wabash, 1972. Fellow Ind. Bar Found. (life); mem. ABA (coun. sr. lawyers divsn. 1993—, mem. com. bar admissions 1993-97, 99—, vice chair affiliate outreach com. divsn. sr. lawyers 1995—, vice-chmn. membership com. sr. lawyers divsn. 1995—, vice-chmn. pub. com. 1995—, vice-historian 1995-96, historian 1996—, long range planning com. 1995-2002, vice-chmn. social security com. 1998-2002, vice-chmn. real estate com. 1999-2002), Ind. State Bar Assn. (sec.-treas. sr. lawyers sect. 1998-2002, coun. sr. lawyers sect. 1996-2002, editor sr. lawyers sect. newsletter 1996-98, coun. profl. legal edn. sect. 2000-2002, vice-chmn. articles and bylaws com. 1994—, legal edn. and bar admissions com. 1990-2002, chmn. articles and bylaws com. 1999-2002, ho. of dels. 1999-2002, coun., profl. edn. sect.), Fed. Bar Assn. (officer, found. bd. dirs. 1974—, historian 1979—, life fellow 1976—, treas. sr. lawyers divsn. 1993-95, sec. 1995-97, dep. chmn. 1997-98, chmn. 1998-99, nat. coun. 1961-93, 97-2002, nat. v.p 1967-69, chpt. pres. 1965-66, chmn. admission to practice and recert. com. 1980-82, bd. dirs. Chgo. chpt. 1984-93), Nat. Orgn. Bar Counsel (pres. 1967), Ind. U. Air Force ROTC Alumni Assn. (pres. 1997-98), Lakeview Hills Homeowners Assn. (pres. 1997-99), Kiwanis, Elks, Order of Coif, Am. Legion (life), Phi Delta Phi. Home: 712 Romans Ct Bloomington IN 47401-8676

FRANKLIN, G(EORGE) CHARLES, retired academic administrator; b. Normangee, Tex., Dec. 27, 1935; married; 3 children. BBA, Sam Houston State U., 1958, postgrad., 1958—. Chief acct., instr. acct. Sam Houston State U., Huntsville, Tex., 1959-62; asst. to dir. Commn. on Coord. Higher Edn. Fin. State of Ark., 1962-64; contr. Ark. State U., Jonesboro, 1964-65; v.p. for bus. affairs Midwestern U., Wichita Falls, Tex., 1965-69; bus. mgr. U. Tex., Austin, 1969-71, v.p. for fiscal affairs San Antonio, 1971-72, v.p. for adminstrn. and fin., Health Sci. Ctr. Houston, 1972-79, v.p. adminstrv. svcs. Austin, 1979-80, v.p. for bus. affairs, 1980-2000, sr. v.p., CFO, 2000—01; ret., 2001. 2d lt. U.S. Army, 1958-59. Mem. Nat. Assn. Coll. and Univ. Bus. Officers, So. Assn. Coll. and Univ. Bus. Officers, Tex. Assn. State Sr. Coll. and Univ. Bus. Officers (pres. 1988). Home: 6603 Cypress Pt N Austin TX 78746-7104 E-mail: g.c.franklin@austin.rr.com.

FRANKLIN, H. ALLEN, electric company executive; b. 1945; BEE, U. Ala., 1966. Various engring. positions Southern Co., Birmingham, Ala., 1970-79, exec. v.p., 1983—; asst. to exec. v.p. Ala. Power, 1979-81, sr. v.p., 1981-83; pres., CEO Georgia Power, 1999, So. Co., Peachtree, Ga., 2001—. Office: So Co Svcs Inc 800 Shades Creek Pkwy Birmingham AL 35209-4532 also: Southern Co 270 Peachtree St NW Atlanta GA 30303

FRANKLIN, H. BRUCE, language educator, writer; b. Bklyn., Feb. 28, 1934; s. Robert and Florence (Cohen) F.; m. Jane Morgan, Feb. 11, 1956; children: Karen, Gretchen, Robert Morgan. BA, Amherst Coll., 1955; PhD, Stanford U., 1961. Tugboat deckhand, mate Pa. R.R., Jersey City, 1955-56; asst. prof. English, assoc. prof. Stanford (Calif.) U., 1961-64, 65-72; asst. prof. English Johns Hopkins U., Balt., 1964-65; vis. prof. English Wesleyan U., Middletown, Conn., 1974-75; prof. English Rutgers U., Newark, N.J., 1975-87, John Cotton Dana prof. English, 1987—. Cons. Stanford Rsch. Inst., 1962-64, Sugarloaf Films, 1993; adv. bd. mem. Vietnam Generation, 1994—. Author: The Wake of the Gods: Melville's Mythology, 1963, rev. edit., 1983, Future Perfect: American Science Fiction of the 19th Century, 1966, 4th edit., 1995, Herman Melville's Mardi: And a Voyage Thither, 1964, The Scarlet Letter, Together With Main Street, Ethan Brand, and Hawthorne's Published Critical Writings, 1967, Herman Melville's the Confidence-Man: His Masquerade, 1967, Who Should Run the Universities, 1969, From the Movement: Toward Revolution, 1971, The Essential Stalin: Major Theoretical Writings, 1905-52, 1972, Back Where You Came From, 1975, The Victim as Criminal and Artist: Literature From the American Prison, 1978, Robert A. Heinlein: America as Science Fiction, 1980, American Prisoners and Ex-Prisoners: An Annotated Bibliography of Their Writings, 1798-1981, 1982, Countdown to Midnight, 1984, Vietnam and America: A Documented History, 1985, rev. edit., 1995, War Stars: The Superweapon and the American Imagination, 1988, M.I.A. or Mythmaking in America, 1992, The Vietnam War in American Stories, Songs, and Poems, 1996, Prison Writing in 20th Century America, 1998, Vietnam and Other American Fantasies, 2000; edit. bd. cons. Sci.-Fiction Studies, 1973—; contbr. articles to profl. jours. 1st lt. USAF, 1956-59. Fellow Am. Coun. Learned Societies, 1968-69, grantee, 1967; Stanford Wilson fellow, 1960-61, Rockefeller Found. Humanities fellow, 1975-76; grantee Nat. Endowment Humanities, 1982, William Joiner Ctr., 1987; recipient Alexander Cappon prize, 1978, Eaton award, 1981, Pilgrim award, 1983, Disting. Scholar award Internat. Assn. Fantastic in Arts, 1990, Pioneer award, 1991. Office: English Dept Rutgers Univ Newark NJ 07102 E-mail: hbf@andromeda.rutgers.edu.

FRANKLIN, JEANNE F. lawyer; b. N.Y.C., July 22, 1946; BA cum laude, Vassar Coll., 1968; JD, U. Va., 1971. Bar: Mich. 1971, U.S. Dist. Ct. Mich. (ea. dist.) 1975, U.S. Ct. Appeals (10th cir.) 1975, N.Mex. 1977, D.C. 1977, Va. 1981, U.S. Dist. Ct. Va. (ea. dist.) 1984. Sole practice, Alexandria, Va. Fellow: Am. Bar Found.; mem.: D.C. Bar (mem. health law sect.), Va. State Bar (mem. health law sect.), Am. Health Lawyers Assn., Alexandria Bar Assn., Va. Bar Assn. (mem. exec. com. 1997—, pres. 2000—01), ABA. Office: 604 Cameron St Alexandria VA 22314

FRANKLIN, JOEL NICHOLAS, mathematician, educator; b. Chgo., Apr. 4, 1930; m. Patricia Anne; 1 dau., Sarah Jane. BS, Stanford, 1950, PhD, 1953. Research asso. N.Y. U., 1953-55; asst. prof. math. U. Wash, 1955; mem. faculty Calif. Inst. Tech., 1957—, prof. applied sci., 1966-69, prof. applied math., 1969—. Author: Matrix Theory, 1968, Methods of Mathematical Economics, 1980, also articles. Mem. Am. Math. Soc., Soc. Indsl. and Applied Math., Phi Beta Kappa. Home: 1763 Alta Crest Dr Altadena CA 91001-2130 Office: Calif Inst Tech 217 50 Pasadena CA 91125-0001

FRANKLIN, JOHN HOPE, historian, educator, author; b. Rentiesville, Okla., Jan. 2, 1915; s. Buck Colbert and Mollie (Parker) Franklin; m. Aurelia E. Whittington, June 11, 1940; 1 child, John Whittington. AB, Fisk U., 1935; AM, Harvard, 1936, PhD, 1941; hon. degrees, Morgan State Coll., Va. State Coll., Lincoln (Pa.) U., Cambridge (Eng.) U., Drake U., Mich. State U., U. Ill. at Chgo., Carnegie-Mellon U., Columbia U., Columbia Coll., Chgo., Loyola U., Bklyn. Coll., Bard Coll., Boston Coll., Brown U., Tuskegee Inst., Grand Valley Coll., Marquette U., Lincoln Coll., Ill., Princeton, Hamline U., Fisk U., R.I. Coll., Dickinson Coll., Howard U., U. Md., U. Notre Dame, Tulsa U., Morehouse Coll., Miami U., Johnson C. Smith U., Lake Forest Coll., Tougaloo Coll., Union Coll., Northwestern U., Whittier Coll., U. Mass., U. Mich., Seattle U., U. Toledo, Yale U., L.I. U., Catholic U. Am., Tulane U., Temple U., Kalamazoo Coll., Washington U., St. Louis, Trinity Coll. (Conn.), Ariz. State U., SUNY, Albany, No. Mich. U., U. Utah, Coll. New Rochelle, George Washington U., Governors State U., Harvard U., U. Pa., Ripon Coll., Atlanta U., Wayne State U., U. N.C.-Chapel Hill, Dillard U., Manhattan Coll., Roosevelt U., N.C. Central U., Ind. State U., St. Olaf Coll., Emory U., U. Miami, U. Conn., U. N.C.-Charlotte, Brandeis U., Wake Forest U., Wilkes Coll., Queen's Coll., N.Y., Wilmington Coll., Hope Coll., Bryant Coll., SUNY-Binghamton, Indiana U., N.C. Weslyan U., N.C. State U., So. Meth. U., Berea Coll., Grad Ctr. CUNY, Suffolk U., Washington Coll., Eckerd Coll., Rutgers U., U. N.C., Greensboro, St. Augustine Coll., U. Okla., Oreg. State U., Winston-Salem State U., Queens Coll., Charlotte, N.C., Ill. State U., Bates Coll., Williams Coll., U. of the South, U. N.C.-Wilmington, Am. U.; hon. degree, Furman U., Georgetown U., Tufts U., Elizabeth City State U., Shaw U., San Francisco U., Washington and Lee U., Columbia U., Chgo., Lincoln Meml. U., Elmira Coll., Lane Coll., Bethune-Cookman Coll., Amherst Coll., U. Cin., Dartmouth Coll., U. Ky., Duke U., San Francisco State U., York Coll., Northeastern U., Occidental Coll., U. Akron, U. Vermont, Bennett Coll., San Diego U., Pa. State U., Tex. A&M U., Pomona Coll., U. San Diego, U. Vt., U. Akron, U. N.C., Pembroke. Prof. history St. Augustine's Coll., 1936—37, N.C. Coll. at Durham, 1943—47, Howard U., 1947—56; chmn. dept. history Bklyn. Coll., 1956—64; prof. Am. history U. Chgo., 1964—82, chmn. dept. history, 1967—70, John Matthews Manly Distinguished Service prof., 1969—82; James B. Duke prof. history Duke U., 1982—85; prof. legal history Duke U. Law Sch., 1985-92. Pitt. prof. Am. history and instns. Cambridge U., 1962—63; vis. prof. Harvard U., U. Wis., Cornell U., Salzburg Seminar, U. Hawaii, U. Claif.; chmn. bd. fgn. scholarships, 1966—69, Nat. Coun. on Humanities, 1976—79; trustee Nat. Humanities Ctr., 1980—91, chmn. adv. bd. to pres.'s initiative on race, 1997—98; Fulbright prof., Australia, 1960; lectr. in field; chmn. adv. bd. Nat. Pk. Svc. Author: Free Negro in North Carolina, 1943, From Slavery to Freedom: A History of African Americans, 2000, Militant South, 1956, Reconstruction After the Civil War, 1961, The Emancipation Proclamation, 1963, A Southern Odyssey, 1976, Racial Equality in America, 1976, George Washington Williams, A Biography, 1985, Race and History, 1990; co-author: Land of the Free, 1966, Illustrated History of Black Americans, 1970, The Color Line: Legacy for the 21st Century, 1993; co-author: (with Loren Schweninger) Runaway Slaves: Rebels on the Plantation, 1999; editor: Civil War Diary of James T. Ayers, 1947, A Fool's Errand by Albion Tourgee, 1961, Army Life in a Black Regiment by Thomas Higginson, 1962, Color and Race, 1968, Reminiscences of an Active Life by John R. Lynch, 1970; co-editor (with August Meier): Black Leaders in the Twentieth Century, 1982; co-editor: (with Abraham Eisenstadt) Harlan Davidson's American History Series; mem. editl. bd.: Am. Scholar, 1972—76, 1994—, My Life and An Era (with John W. Franklin), —. Trustee Chgo. Symphony, 1976—80, Fisk U., 1947—80; bd. dirs. Salzburg Seminar, Mus. Sci. and Industry, 1968—80, DuSable Mus., 1970—. Named to Okla. Hall of Fame, 1978, Okla. Historians Hall of Fame, 1996; recipient Cleanth Brooks medal, Fellowship So. Writers, 1989, Gold medal, Ency. Britannica, 1990, Caldwell medal, N.C. Coun. on Humanities, 1992, 1993, Charles Frankel medal, 1993, Spingarn medal, NAACP, 1995, Bruce Catton award, Soc. Am. Historians, 1994, award, Cosmos Club, 1994, Presdl. medal of Freedom, 1995, Peggy V. Helmerich Disting. Author award, 1997, Smithson Bicentennial medal, 1997, Lincoln prize, 2000, Harold Washington Lit. award, 2000, Gold medal award, Am. Acad. Arts and Letters, 2002, Disting. Author award, Bergen County, 2002, Arthur Schlesinger Lifetime History award, 2002; fellow Edward Austin fellow, 1937—39, Guggenheim fellow, 1950—51, 1973—74, Pres.'s fellow, Brown U., 1952—53, Ctr. for Advanced Study in Behavioral Sci., 1973—74, Sr. Mellon fellow. Fellow: Am. Acad. Arts and Scis.; mem.: AAUP, Am. Philos. Soc. (Jefferson medal 1993), Am. Studies Assn. (past pres.), Assn. for Study Negro Life and History, Orgn. Am. Historians (pres. 1974—75), So. Hist. Assn. (pres. 1970—71), Am. Hist. Assn. (pres. 1978—79), Phi Alpha Theta, Phi Beta Kappa (senate 1966—82, pres. 1973—76, Sidney Hook award 1994). Home: 208 Pineview Rd Durham NC 27707-2846

FRANKLIN, JOHN THOMAS IKEDA, English educator; b. Knoxville, Tenn., July 12, 1956; s. John Wesley and Yoshiko (Ikeda) F.; m. Elizabeth Anne Minerva, Aug. 11, 2001. BA in English and Econs., Rice U., 1978; MA in English, Miami U., Oxford, Ohio, 1986; PhD in English, U. Fla., 1994. Cert. educator, Tex. Tchr. English Jesse Jones H.S., Houston, 1978-84; TV prodr. Fredonia Hill TVM, Nacogdoches, Tex., 1991-94; prof. English Pitts. (Kans.) State U., 1995—, dir. writing ctr., 1997—. Chair grad. student forum South Atlantic MLA, Tampa, Fla., 1990; advisor Sigma Tau Delta, Pittsburg, 1995-99. Producer: (TV program) 21st Century Composition, 1991-94. Vol. Women's Shelter, Nacogdoches, 1992-93, St. John's Hospice, Joplin, Mo., 1996—. Recipient scholarship English Speaking Union, Houston, 1981, Herbert fellowship U. Fla., Gainesville, 1986. Mem. Midwest Writing Ctrs. Assn. (sec./archivist 1999-2000, treas. 2000-02), Nat. Coun. Tchrs. English, Kans. Assn. Tchrs. English (exec. bd. 1997—, editor Kans. English, 1999—). Avocations: travel, video prodn., correspondence, baseball. Office: Pittsburg State U 1701 S Broadway St Pittsburg KS 66762-7500 E-mail: jfrankli@pittstate.edu.

FRANKLIN, JON DANIEL, writer, journalist, educator; b. Enid, Okla., Jan. 12, 1942; s. Benjamin Max and Wilma Irene (Winburn) F.; m. Nancy Sue Creevan, Dec. 12, 1959 (div. 1976, dec. 1987); children: Teresa June, Catherine Cay; m. Lynn Irene Scheidhauer, May 20, 1988. BS with high honors, U. Md., 1970; LHD (hon.), U. Md., Balt. County, 1981, Coll. Notre Dame, Balt., 1982. With USN, 1959-67; reporter/editor Prince Georges (Md.) Post, 1967-70; sci. and feature writer Balt. Evening Sun, 1970-85; assoc. prof. U. Md. Coll. Journalism, 1985-88, prof., 1988-89; prof., chmn. dept. journalism Oreg. State U., Corvallis, 1989-91; prof. creative writing, dir. U. Oreg., Eugene, 1991-98; sci. writer, spl. assignments editor Raleigh News and Observer, Raleigh, N.C., 1998-2001; Philip Merrill prof. journalism U. Md., College Park, 2001—. Author: Shocktrauma, 1980, Not Quite a Miracle, 1983, Guinea Pig Doctors, 1984, Writing for Story, 1986, The Molecules of the Mind, 1987. pub.: *Bylines*, WriterL. Recipient James T. Grady medal Am. Chem. Soc., 1975, Pulitzer prize for feature writing, 1979, Pulitzer prize for explanatory journalism, 1985, Carringer award Nat. Mental Health Assn., 1984, Penney-Mo. Spl. award for health reporting, 1985; named to Newspaper Hall of Fame, Md.-Del.-D.C. Press Assn.,also Feature Writers Hall of Fame, 2002. Mem. Nat. Assn. Sci. Writers (bd. dirs.), Soc Profl. Journalists, Authors Guild.

FRANKLIN, JUDE ERIC, electronics executive; b. St. Marys, Pa., Aug. 3, 1943; s. William Nelson and Elizabeth (Kronenwetter) F.; m. Mary Frances Bizot, Sept. 17, 1966; children: Pamela Mary, Erik Jude. BEE, Cath. U., 1965, MEE, 1968, PhDEE, 1980. Program mgr. Chesapeake Instrument Corp. (now divsn. of GE), Shadyside, Md., 1966-75; v.p. MAR, Inc., Rockville, Md., 1975-81; mgr. Navy Artifical Intelligence Ctr. Naval Rsch. Lab., Washington, 1981-85; sr. v.p. tech. div. Planning Rsch. Corp., McLean, Va., 1985-87, sr. v.p., 1987-92, chief tech. officer and v.p., 1991—. Bd. dirs. Am. Univ., Washington Juvenile Diabetes Found. Contbr. to Artifical Intelligence Ency., 1987; also articles to profl. jours. V.p. Prince Mont Swim League; vol. U.S. Swimming Referee and Starter; PRC team leader Juvenile Diabetes Found., 1995. Recipient Meritorious Svc. award Armed Forces Communications and Electronics Assn., 1988, Fed. "100" award Fed. Computer News, 1992, Best Paper of Yr. award Signal Mag., 1995. Fellow AIAA (assoc.), Washington Acad. Sci.; mem. IEEE (sr., guest editor Expert Mag., 1989), Kettering Civic Fedn. (pres. 1971-72), Sigma Xi. Democrat. Roman Catholic. Home: 7616 Carteret Rd Bethesda MD 20817-2021 Office: Raytheon Commd/Control 6225 Brandon Ave Ste 230 Springfield VA 22150-2519 E-mail: jude_e_franklin@raytheon.com.

FRANKLIN, JULIAN HAROLD, political science educator; b. N.Y.C., Mar. 26, 1925; s. Jerome A. and Molly (Seidenstein) F.; m. Paula Angle, Feb. 23, 1928. BA summa cum laude, Queens Coll., 1946; MA, Columbia U., 1950, PhD, 1960. Instr. Columbia U., N.Y.C., 1951-59, assoc. prof., 1962-68, prof., 1968-96, prof. emeritus, 1997—; vis. asst. prof. New Sch. for Social Research, N.Y.C., 1959-60; asst. prof. Princeton (N.J.) U., 1960-62. Acting chmn. summer session Columbia U., 1962—, dir. grad. studies polit. theory, 1968—, dept. rep., 1971-72, 86—, dept. del. com. on instruction faculty polit. sci., 1971-73, 81-82, chmn., 1973-74, co-founder, adj. chmn. sem. on polit. and social thought; mem. adv. council dept. politcs. Princeton U., 1973-76. Author: Jean Bodin and the Sixteenth Century Revolution in the Methodology of Law and History, 1963, Constitutionalism and Resistance in the Sixteenth Century, 1969, Jean Bodin and the Rise of Absolutist Theory, 1973, rev. edit. (in French), 1993, John Locke and the Theory of Sovereignty, 1978; editor and translator: Jean Bodin on Sovereignty, 1992; editl. cons. in polit. theory Polity, 1977-79; mem. editl. bd. Polit. Theory; contbr. articles to profl. jours. Served with USAF, 1943-46. Queens Coll. scholar, 1946, Social Sci. Research Council fellow, 1950-51, William Bayard Cutting travelling fellow, 1950-51, NEH fellow, 1975-76, 89-90, Phi Beta Kappa fellow, 1990. Mem. Conf. for Study Polit. and Social Thought. Jewish. Office: Columbia U Dept Polit Sci 116th St And Broadway New York NY 10027

FRANKLIN, KENNETH RONALD, franchise company executive, consultant; b. N.Y.C., June 6, 1932; s. Lawrence and Gladys (Siegel) Franklin; m. Harriet Faye Lewis, Dec. 27, 1960; children: Gregg E., Erica G. BS, Syracuse U., 1953, MBA, 1954. Cert. mgmt. cons. Instr. Harpur Coll. Syracuse U., Vestal, N.Y., 1956-57; sales rep. IBM, Pitts., 1957-64; br. mgr. ABS, Pitts., 1964-66; v.p. franchising Arby's Inc., Youngstown, Ohio, 1966-70; pres. Franchise Devel. Inc., Pitts., 1970—. With Spl. Svcs., 1954-56, ETO. Mem. Inst. Mgmt. Cons., Pitts. Athletic Assn., Concorcia Club, Westmoreland C.C. Avocations: tennis, reading, traveling. Office: Franchise Devel Inc Hampshire Hall 4730 Centre Ave Pittsburgh PA 15213-1759

FRANKLIN, LYNNE, business communications consultant, writer; b. St. Paul, Minn., Aug. 24, 1957; d. Lyle John Franklin and Lois Ann (Cain) Kindseth; stepdau. Thomas John Kindseth; m. Lawrence Anton Pecorella, Sept. 2, 1989; 1 stepchild, Lauren. BA in Psychology and English, Coll. St. Catherine, 1979; MA, Hamline U., 1989. Residential treatment counselor St. Joseph's Home, Mpls., 1979-80; staff writer Comml. West Mag., Mpls., 1980-81; acct. exec. Edwin Neuger & Assocs., Mpls., 1981-83, Hill and Knowlton, Mpls.,

1983-84; mgr. pub. rels. Gelco Corp., Eden Prarie, Minn., 1984-86; dir. financial rels. Dunstan & Assocs., Mpls., 1986; cons. MC Assocs., Chgo., 1986-87; v.p. Fin. Rels. Bd., Chgo., 1987—; prin. Wordsmith, Glenview, Ill., 1993—. Trustee Lawrence Hall Youth Svcs.; v.p. Skokie Valley chot., Bus. Networking Internat., 2003; judge achievement awards Internat. Assn. of Bus. Communicators, Mpls., 1986, presenter fin. rels., 1990; judge achievement awards Publicity Club of Chgo., 1992-94; presenter annual report seminar Nat. Investor Rels. Inst., Chgo., 1992. Author: (novel) Second Sight, 1989. Tchr. Great Books Program, St. Paul, 1976-79, Minn. Literacy Coun., 1985-87. Recipient Ann. Report Excellence award, Fin. World Mag., 1991—98, award, MerComm-ARC Competition, 1992—2002, Nat. Assn. Investors Corp., 1994—2002, Equities Mag., 1999—2002. Office: Wordsmith 2019 Glenview Rd Glenview IL 60025-2849

FRANKLIN, MARC ADAM, law educator; b. Bklyn., Mar. 9, 1932; s. Louis A. and Rose (Rosenthal) Franklin; m. Ruth E. Korzenik, June 29, 1958 (dec. Dec. 2000); children: Jonathan, Alison. AB, Cornell U., 1953, LLB, 1956. Bar: N.Y. 1956. Assoc. Proskauer Rose Goetz & Mendelsohn, N.Y.C., 1956-57; law clk to Hon. Carroll C. Hincks, New Haven, 1957-58; prof. law Stanford U., Calif., 1962-76, Frederick I. Richman prof. law, 1976—2001, emeritus, 2001—; prof. law Columbia U., 1959-62; law clk to Earl Warren, U.S. Supreme Ct., Washington, 1958-59. Author: Biography of a Legal Dispute, 1968, Dynamics of American Law, 1968, Cases and Materials on Tort Law and Alternatives, 1971; co-author (with R.L. Rabin): Cases and Materials on Tort Law and Alternatives, 7th edit., 2001; author: Mass Media Law, 1977; co-author (with D.A. Anderson and F.H. Cate): Mass Media Law, 6th edit., 2000; author: The First Amendment and the Fourth Estate, 1977; co-author (with T.B. Carter and J.B. Wright): The First Amendment and the Fourth Estate, 8th edit., 2001; author: The First Amendment and the Fifth Estate, 1986; co-author (with T.B. Carter and J.B. Wright): The First Amendment and the Fifth Estate, 6th edit., 2003. Fellow Ctr. for Advanced Study in Behavioral Scis., 1968—69; scholar Fulbright, Victoria U., 1973. Home: 999 Green St # 2005 San Francisco CA 94133 Office: Stanford U Law Sch Nathan Abbott Way Stanford CA 94305

FRANKLIN, MARGERY BODANSKY, psychology educator, researcher; b. N.Y.C., Mar. 18, 1933; d. Oscar and Barbara (Biber) Bodansky; m. Raymond S. Franklin, Aug. 22, 1962; children— Kenneth, David AB, Swarthmore Coll., 1954; MA, Clark U., 1956, PhD, 1961. Instr. psychology Vassar Coll., Poughkeepskie, N.Y., 1960-62, asst. prof., 1962-64; research assoc. Bank St. Coll. Edn., N.Y.C., 1967-72; prof. Sarah Lawrence Coll., Bronxville, NY, 1965—2002. Co-editor: Developmental Processes: Heinz Werner's Selected Writings, 1978, Symbolic Functioning in Childhood, 1979, Child Language: A Reader, 1988, Development and the Arts: Critical Perspectives, 1994; contbr. articles to profl. jours., chpts. to books. Fellow Am. Psychol. Assn. (pres. psychology and arts divsn. 1990-91); mem. Soc. for Rsch. in Child Devel. Avocation: photography.

FRANKLIN, MARY ANN WHEELER, educator, higher education and management consultant; b. Boston; d. Arthur E. Wheeler Sr. and Madeline Ophelia (Hall) Wheeler-Brooks; m. Carl Matthew Franklin; 1 child, Evangeline Rachel Hall Franklin. BS, U. N.H., 1942; MEd, U. Buffalo, 1948; EdD, U. Md., 1982. Cert. tchr., N.Y., Ga. Instr. sci. edn. W.Va. State Coll., 1947; tchr. gen. sci. John Marshall Jr. High Sch., Bklyn., 1952-58, 59-60; assoc. prof. sci. Elizabeth City State Coll., 1960-67; asst. dean of the coll. Morgan State Coll., Balt., 1967-77; asst. dean Coll. Arts and Scis. Morgan State U., Balt., 1977-78, asst. v.p. acad. affairs, 1978-82; asst. prof. bus. Catonsville (Md.) Community Coll., 1982; asst. to dean evening and weekend coll. So. U. New Orleans, 1983-92. Cons. numerous locations including Herford County Tchrs., Murfreesboro, N.C., 1961, St. Catherine's Sch., Elizabeth City, N.C., 1962-64, St. Elizabeth Cath. Sch., Elizabeth City; cons., bd. dirs. Archbishop Keough H.S., Balt., 1970-80, Hampton (Va.) Inst., 1971, St. Paul Coll., 1972; presenter confs., seminars and workshops; spkr. in field. Editor Morgan State U. Acad. Affairs Newsletter, 1980-82; editor, pub. Morgan State U. Catalog, 1969-82, So. U. New Orleans Catalog, 1986-84, 89-92; author: The How and Why of Testing at Elizabeth City State College, 1962, Report on Princeton University Program for Physics Teachers in HBCU's, 1964, A Descriptive Report of Pre-College Study Booster Program, 1965, 66, Learning Summer Camp Code, National Library of Poetry, 1992, Interrogations of a Metropolis of the Day, Who Are We/Who We Are, 1994. Mem. com. higher edn. Citizens League, Balt., 1979-81; assoc. dir. youth camp NCCJ, 1974-75, bd. dirs., 1969-80; dir., originator Vestibule Program and Parents Workshop for New Citizens and Residents, SUNO Summer Learning Camp, 1984-95, Ctr. Women Against Crime Conf.; pres. Lake Willow Homeowners Assn., 1994-96. Fellow NSF, Harvard U., 1958-59, Carnegie-Ford-NSF, Princeton U., 1964; recipient Education award Am. Assn. of Coll. Tchrs. Edn., 1966. Mem. AAUW, Am. Mgmt. Assn., Nat. Coun. Negro Women, Am. Assn. Higher Edn., Am. Assn. Continuing Higher Edn., Nat. Assn. Trainers and Educators for Alcohol and Substance Abuse Counselors (bd. dirs.), La. Assn. Continuing Higher Edn., Md. Assn. Higher Edn., Urban League, Delta Sigma Theta, Phi Sigma, Pi Lambda Theta. Avocations: fine arts, portraits, pastels, listening to classical music and popular show tunes, swimming.

FRANKLIN, MICHAEL HAROLD, arbitrator, lawyer, consultant; b. Los Angeles, Dec. 25, 1923; m. Betty Chernow, 1989; children from previous marriage: Barbara, John, James, Robert. AB, UCLA, 1948; LL.B., U. So. Calif., 1951. Bar: Calif. 1951. Practiced in, Los Angeles, 1951-52; pvt. practice, 1951-52; atty. CBS, 1952-54, Paramount Pictures Corp., 1954-58; exec. dir. Writers Guild Am. West, Inc., 1958-78; nat. exec. dir. Dirs. Guild Am., Inc., 1978-88. Mem. Fed. Cable Adv. Commn. Served with C.E. AUS, 1942-46. Mem. Order of Coif.

FRANKLIN, MORTON JEROME, emergency physician; b. Boston, Dec. 25, 1927; s. Jacob and Rose Ann (Borax) F. BA, Harvard U., 1949, MD, 1954. Diplomate Am. Bd. Emergency Medicine. Many positions as emergency physician, various cities and states, 1955-2001. Lt. cmmdr. USN, 1955-57. Home: 20 Hammond Pond Pkwy Apt 11 Chestnut Hill MA 02467-2129

FRANKLIN, MURRAY JOSEPH, retired steel foundry executive; b. Orange, N.J., Apr. 1, 1922; s. Joseph Charles and Edna S. F.; m. Jane Modlin, Oct. 25, 1946; children: Gail Lee, Martha Ann. BA, Ohio Wesleyan U., 1943; MA (univ. fellow 1946-49), U. Mich., 1947, PhD, 1963. Assoc. prof. bus. U. Mich., 1963-65; with Hayes-Albion Corp., Jackson, Mich., 1968-70; v.p., gen. mgr. Westinghouse Airbrake divsn. Am. Standard Corp., Pitts., 1970-77; pres. transp. equipment divsn. Dresser Industries, Inc., DePew, N.Y., 1977-84. Adj. assoc. prof. SUNY, Buffalo, 1990-95; pres. Coll. Counseling Assocs., Orchard Park, N.Y., 1990-98. Bd. dirs. Better Bus. Bur. Chgo., 1966-67. With USMCR, 1943-46. Mem. Ry. Progress Inst. (exec. com., bd. govs.) Home: 20 Lancaster Ln Orchard Park NY 14127-2852 E-mail: mjfra@acsu.buffalo.edu.

FRANKLIN, PAUL DEANE, financial services executive, investor; b. Shreveport, La., Oct. 17, 1942; s. Paul Amerideth and Marjorie (Hyde) F.; m. Carol Fillmore Talley, Aug. 30, 1966 (div. July 1982); children: Kyle D., Sean R.; m. Barbara Joyce, Oct. 12, 1985. BS in Bus., La. Tech. U., 1964; MBA in Fin., La. State U., 1965. CFP. Pers. rep. Monsanto Co., El Dorado, Ark., 1966-68, supr. pers. Muscatine, Iowa, 1968-70, supt. pers. Stonington, Conn., 1970-71, Comml. Solvents Corp., Terre Haute, Ind., 1971-74; mgr. human resources Mobay Chem. Corp., Baytown, Tex., 1974-85; pres. Micro Energy Sys., Inc., Pitts., 1985-88; mgr. human resources Miles Inc. (name now Bayer Corp.), Charleston, S.C., 1988-95; dir. human resources Bayer Corp., Charleston, S.C., 1995-98; owner Franklin & Assocs. Inc., Charleston, 1998—, Franklin Funding, Inc., 1999—. Co-chmn. United Way, Baytown, Tex., 1983-84; coach Boys Club Am., Terre Haute, 1972-74; scoutmaster Boy Scouts Am., Baytown, 1975-76; bd. dirs. Pvt. Industry Coun., Charleston County, 1994-95, Goodwill Industries of Lower S.C., Inc., 1996-2002, Pvt. Industry Coun. Berkeley County, 1996-98, Trident Work Force Devel. Bd., 1998-99; bd. govs. Trident Area Consortium for Tech., 1994-98; mem. Trident United Way Supporting Older People Vision Coun., 2001—, Berkley-Charleston-Dorchester Regional Devel. Corp., 2001—. Mem.: Fin. Freedom Sr. Funding Corp. (advisory coun. 2003—), Rotary (sgt.-at-arms), Trident Indsl. Rels. Com., Nat. Reverse Mortgage Lenders Assn. (bd. dirs.), Fin. Planning Assn., Delta Sigma Pi (internat. mem.0, Beta Gamma Sigma (scholastic achievement award 1964). Republican. Avocations: travel, reading, physical fitness. Home: 648 Harbor Creek Pl Charleston SC 29412-3203 Office: 147 Wappoo Creek Dr Ste 105 Charleston SC 29412-2122 E-mail: paulf@quik.com.

FRANKLIN, PHYLLIS, professional association administrator; b. N.Y.C., Apr. 21, 1932; d. Matthew Pine and Helen Lutsky; m. Irwin Franklin, Apr. 21, 1958 (div. 1971); children: James, Jody. AB, Vassar Coll., 1954; MA, U. Miami, 1965, PhD, 1969; LHD (hon.), George Washington U., 1986. From asst. to assoc. prof. U. Miami, Coral Gables, 1969-80; spl. asst. to dean Coll. Arts & Scis. Duke U., Durham, N.C., 1980-81; dir. English programs MLA, N.Y.C., 1981-85, exec. dir., 1985—. Adj. prof. English programs NYU, 1987-88. Editor ADE Bull., 1981-85, Profession, 1985—. Fellowship, Danforth Found., 1966-68, Am. Council on Edn., 1980-81; stipend NEH, 1971. Mem. USSR Acad. Scis., Am. Coun. Learned Socs. (bd. dirs. 1987-89, commn. on humanities and social scis. 1987-88, chair conf. secs. 1987-90), Nat. Humanities Alliance (bd. dirs. 1986-88, v.p. 1990-91, pres. 1991-96), Nat. Fedn. Abstracting and Info. Svcs. (bd. dirs. 1994-96). Democrat. Jewish. Office: Modern Language Assn 26 Broadway New York NY 10004-1703

FRANKLIN, RANDY WAYNE, lawyer; b. Chgo., Mar. 28, 1945; s. Sidney Aaron and Hilda (Goldstein) Franklin Skora; m. Danette Penny Siegel, Dec. 21, 1974; children: Jennifer Rose, Jason Adam, Seth Peter. BS., Bradley U., 1967; JD, Massey U., 1971. Bar: Ga. 1972, Ill. 1973, Wis. 1987. Tchr. high sch., Chgo. Bd. Edn., 1968-70; asst. pub. defender Cook County, Chgo., 1973-79; assoc. McLennon, Nelson, Gabriele & Nudo, Park Ridge, Ill., 1979-81; ptnr. Gabriele & Franklin, Park Ridge, 1981— . Bd. dirs. Young Men's Jewish Council, Chgo., 1974-76, Main Family and Mental Health Ctr., Little Mexico Convent Holy Spirit, Mt. Prospect, Ill., 1980— ; advisor Northeastern Ill. U. Sch. of Bus. Mem. ABA, Ill. Bar Assn., Ga. Bar Assn., No. Suburban Bar Assn. (bd. of mgrs.), Nat. Assn. Criminal Def. Lawyers, Assn. Trial Lawyers Am. Home: 330 Landis Ln Deerfield IL 60015-3422 Office: Randy W Franklin & Assocs 1550 N Northwest Hwy Sute 308 Park Ridge IL 60068 also: 151 N Michigan Ave Suite 3314 Chicago IL 60601

FRANKLIN, RICHARD MARK, lawyer; b. Chgo., Dec. 13, 1947; s. Henry W. and Gertrude (Gross) F.; m. Marguerite June Wesle, Sept. 2, 1973; children: Justin Wesley, Elizabeth Cecilia, Catherine Helena, Caroline Lucinda. BA, U. Wis., 1970; postgrad., U. Freiburg, Fed. Republic Germany, 1968-69; JD, Columbia U., 1973. Bar: Ill. 1973, U.S. Dist. Ct. (no. dist.) Ill. 1973, U.S. Ct. Appeals (7th cir.) 1973. Assoc. Baker & McKenzie, Chgo., 1973-79, Frankfurt, Fed. Republic Germany, 1979-80, ptnr. Chgo., 1980—. Mem. ABA, Ill. Bar Assn., Chgo. Bar Assn. Mem. United Ch. Christ. Avocations: music, literature, theatre, outdoor activities. Home: 1161 Oakley Ave Winnetka IL 60093-1437 Office: Baker & McKenzie 1 Prudential Plz 130 E Randolph St Ste 3700 Chicago IL 60601-6342 E-mail: rmfwinn@aol.com., richard.m.franklin@bakenet.com.

FRANKLIN, ROBERT DRURY, oil company executive, lawyer; b. Mead, Okla., June 6, 1935; s. Sam Wesley and Frankie Marjorie (Gooding) F.; m. Barbara Jean Bellis, May 30, 1958 (div. 1973); children: Philip Foster, Elizabeth Jean. BS in Petroleum Engring., U. Okla., 1957; JD, So. Methodist U., 1964. Registered profl. engr., Tex. Petroleum engr. Mobil Oil Corp., Denver City, Tex., 1957-59; prodn. mgr. Bayview Oil Corp., Dallas, 1959-65; sec., dir. Siboney Corp., Dallas, 1965-70; pres., dir. Northland Oils Ltd., Dallas, 1970-89, Costa Resources, Inc., Dallas, 1972—; v.p., dir. Internat. Oil & Gas Corp., Dallas, 1979-84; with Tex. Legal Svcs. Ctr. Mem. Rep. Eagles, Washington. Mem. State Bar Tex., Ind. Petroleum Assn. Am., Soc. Petroleum Engrs., Am. Petroleum Inst., Energy Club of Dallas, Mensa, Willow Bend Polo Club, Midland Country Club. Presbyterian. Avocations: polo, tennis, skiing. Home: Costa Resources Inc 2293 Common St Apt 85 New Braunfels TX 78130-3184 Office: 815 Brazos St Ste 1100 Austin TX 78701

FRANKLIN, ROBERT MCFARLAND, book publisher; b. Memphis, Mar. 13, 1943; s. Robert Dumont and Mary McFarland (Wilson) F.; m. Cheryl Jane Rehrs, Jan. 18, 1975; children: Charles McRee, Nicholas Roberts, William Holliday. AB, Yale U., 1965. Cataloger Columbia U. Libr., N.Y.C., 1965-66; editor to exec. editor Scarecrow Press, Metuchen, N.J., 1969-79; pres., founder McFarland & Co., Inc., Publishers, Jefferson, N.C., 1979—. Pub. Jour. Info. Ethics, 1992—; contbr. articles to profl. jours. Dir., actor Ashe County Little Theatre, Jefferson, 1980—; libr. adv. bd. Appalachian State U., 1995—. With U.S. Army, 1966-68. Recipient Gov.'s Bus. award in arts and humanities, State of N.C., 1984, 87, 97, N.C. State Arts Coun. Outstanding Vol. award 1991. Mem. ALA (pub. com. 1984-88, coun. governing body 1988-2000, pay equity com. 1991-93, intellectual freedom com. 1994-96), Am. Soc. for Psychical Rsch. (dir. 1984-88). Avocations: chess, go, European languages and cultures, self taught or outsider art, acting, piano. Home: 338 Cut Laurel Gap Rd Creston NC 28615-9049 Office: McFarland & Co Inc Pubs Box 611 Jefferson NC 28640-0611 E-mail: rfranklin@mcfarlandpub.com.

FRANKLIN, ROBERT RICHARD, retired federal agency administrator, farmer; b. Middletown, Conn., Mar. 11, 1943; s. John Henry and Helen (Morris) F.; m. Anne Marie Henderson, Aug. 20, 1971; children: Charles Michael, Amy Louise. BS in Acctg., U. Conn., 1965; cert., Naval Postgrad. Sch., 1981. Cert. acquisition profl. Dept. Def.; cert. internal auditor Inst. Internal Auditors. Auditor Def. Supply Agy., Alameda, Calif., 1965-67, supervisory auditor Boston, 1967-75; dep. comptr. Def. Logistics Agy., Boston, 1975-88, dep. comdr. Hartford, Conn., 1988-98; ret., 1998; farmer, 1998—. Recipient Outstanding Young Man Am. award U.S. Jaycees, 1976. Mem. Def. Acquisition Corps, Conn. Fed. Exec. Assn. (chmn. 1992-93, sec.-treas. 1996-98), KC (3d deg.). Democrat. Avocations: fishing, gardening, genealogy, travel, birding. Home: 181 Pokorny Rd Higganum CT 06441-4418 E-mail: ARFranklin@aol.com.

FRANKLIN, ROBERT STAMBAUGH, lawyer; b. N.Y.C., Jan. 28, 1942; s. John Edward and Bernice (Stambaugh) F.; m. Eva Johanna D'Addario, July 22, 1967 (div. 1984); children— David, Kathryn; m. Patricia Lee Posner, Jan. 2, 1986. B.A., Harvard U., 1963, J.D., 1966; LL.M., NYU, 1973. Bar: N.Y. 1966, U.S. Tax Ct. 1982. Clk. N.Y. County Dist. Atty.'s Office, N.Y.C., 1964; assoc. Milbank, Tweed, Hadley & McCloy, N.Y.C., 1969-72, Debevoise, Plimpton, Lyons & Gates, N.Y.C., 1973-75; assoc. Coudert Bros., N.Y.C., 1975-78, ptnr., 1978— ; lectr. NYU Sch. Continuing Edn., 1981. Served to 1st. lt. U.S. Army, 1966-69. Mem. ABA, N.Y. State Bar Assn. Roman Catholic. Home: 392 South Ave New Canaan CT 06840-6313 Office: Coudert Bros 1114 Avenue Of The Americas Fl 4 New York NY 10036-7710

FRANKLIN, ROOSEVELT, minister; b. Chattanooga, Aug. 30, 1933; s. James R. and Cora Ann (Ponds) F.; m. Darnell Pinkston, Sept. 30, 1972; children: Sophia, Siemoran Dellazar. BS, Northeastern U., 1958; MA (hon.), Savannah State Coll., 1962; M. of Cybernetics, Grad. Sch. Wicca, St. Charles, Mo. Lic. metaphysician. Pastor Free For All Bapt. Ch., Greenwood, S.C., 1959-61; radio min. Spiritual Ch., Aiken, S.C., 1961-63; nat. lectr. United Coun. Spiritual Ch., Raleigh, N.C., 1963-66; min. Holy Trinity House of God, Macon, Ga., 1966—. Youth dir. Holy Trinity Ch., Macon, 1966-72, talent coord., 1966-73; dir. Spiritual Singers, 1966—; lectr. in field; world renown authority on witchcraft and transcendental meditation; expert in clairvoyance, spiritual meditation; supporter Macon County Little League Baseball; internat. tour Prosperity Way of Living Teachings. Editor: Prosperity Way of Living. Organizer voters registration, Macon, 1977; pub. relations vol. Nat. Dem. Party, Atlanta, 1984; bd. dirs. Retired Persons Assn., 1980—. Capt. U.S. Army, 1951-54, Korea. Named extrovert promoter Music Workshop, 1979; recipient Proclamation and Key to City, Roanoke, Va., 1977, Afro Am. Heritage award Afro Am. Heritage Mus., 1987, Golden Eagle award Macon Courier, 1988, Nat. Achievers award Nat. Black Secs. Assn., 1990, Ednl. award Ptnrs. Youth Club, 1991, Golden Eagle award 500 Black Men of Am. Club, 1992, Black Achievement award Nat. Negro Achievers Assn., 1993, Humanitarian award. Gov. of Ga., 1993, Nat. Rschrs. Occult award United Spiritual Coun. Chs., 1994, Hon. Citizens award, Tuskegee, Ala., 1994, Mahogany Triumph award Am. Black Affluent Assn. Am., 1995, Cert. Recognition City of Memphis, 1995, Concerned Citizens award People in Action Club, 1996, Good Samaritan award United Youth Fellowship Club, 1997, Model Citizen's award Office of the Gov. Ga., 1997, Registered Spiritual award, Registered Psychic award and Mystic award United Spiritual Coun. Assn., 1998, Self Awareness Lecture award, Howard U., 1998, Appreciation award for continuous contbns. UNCF, 1998, Commemorative award Ga. Farmer's Assn., 1998, Activist award Boys Clubs Am., 1998, Outstanding Activities award United Fraternities Am., 1998, Presdl. Acknowledgement, Nat. Assn. Disabled Persons, 1999, Dr. of Metaphysics award, Dr. of Biblical Counseling award and Dr. of Religion award, 1999, Outstanding Citizenship award, Pilot Club, 1999, Contemporary Spkr. award, Chgo., 2000, Lectr. of Yr. award Nat. Bible Soc., Silver Raven award, 2002, Ea. Mysteries award for excellence, 2002, Order of Nostradamus, Cert. Seminar of Appreciation, 2002, Spkr. of Yr. award Spiritism, 2002, others. Mem. NAACP (life), SCLC (life), Nat. Assn. Pastoral Counselors (career specialist advisor 2000, dir. conf. on prosperity), Ednl. Media Assn. (founder 2002, counseling tax force 2001, Pursuit of Excellence award 2002), Inner Circle Congl. Aides, C. of C., Ministers Alliance (v.p. 1966—, Citizens award 1979), Ga. Black Am. Pageant (coord. 1980—, Leadership award 1982), Direct Sellers League, Smooth Ashlar (dist. dep. 1970—), Rolls-Royce Club, Woodsmen of Am., Pioneer Club, Shriners (nat. amb.), Masons (33 deg., sovereign grand gen. inspector, Grand Orator 33 deg. Scottish Rite 2002), Optimists, Kiwanis, Civitan, Elks, Nat. Lodge (treas. 1987—), Potentate of the Rosicrucsians, Sertoma, Lions, VFW (life), DAV (life), Am. Legion (life). Democrat. Avocations: martial arts, billiards. Office: Holy Trinity House of God 280 Straight St Macon GA 31204-6100

FRANKLIN, SCOTT BRADLEY, accountant, lawyer; b. Milw., 1970; BBA in Acctg., U. Wis., 1992; JD, Marquette U., 1995. Bar: Wis. 1995, U.S. Dist. (ea. dist.) Wis. 1995, U.S. Tax Ct. Bar 1995; CPA, Wis. Intern Office U.S. Atty., Milw., 1993-94, Milwaukee County Circuit Ct., Milw., 1994; intern Office Dist. Counsel, IRS, Milw., 1994; tax mgr. Kohler and Franklin, CPA's, Milw., 1995—. Instr. Becker Conviser C.P.A. Rev. Course, Milw., 1996—; lectr. in field; media commentator; adj. prof. :Lakeland Coll. Online, 2001, 2002. Contbr. articles to profl. jours. Fellow Wis. Inst. CPA's (fed. taxation com. 1997—); mem. AICPA. Office: Kohler and Franklin CPA's 250 W Coventry Ct Ste 211 Milwaukee WI 53217-3966 E-mail: sbfcpa@execpc.com.

FRANKLIN, SHIRLEY CLARKE, mayor; b. Phila., May 10, 1945; d. Eugene Haywood Clarke and Ruth (Lyons) White; m. David McCoy Franklin, Feb. 5, 1972 (div. 1980); children: Kai Ayanna, Cabral Holsey, Kali Jamilla. BA, Howard U., 1968, LLD (hon.), 2002; MA, U. Pa., 1969. Contract compliance officer U.S. Dept. Labor, Washington, 1966-68; instr. social scis. Talledega (Ala.) Coll., 1969-71; from dir. to commr. Dept. Cultural Affairs, Atlanta, 1978-82; chief adminstrv. officer City of Atlanta, 1982-90, exec. officer for ops., 1990—2001; pvt. practice, 1997—; mayor, 2001—. Trustee Atlanta Symphony Orch., 1977-81, Atlanta Found., 1980—; mem. Ga. Council for the Arts, Atlanta, 1979-82, adv. bd. Ga. Women's Polit. Caucus, Atlanta, 1982-84; chmn. expansion arts panel Nat. Endowment for the Arts, Washington, 1980-82; bd. dirs. Nat. Urban Coalition, Washington, 1980-83; dep. campaign mgr. Young for Atlanta, 1981-82; sr. v.p. external rels. Atlanta Com. Olympic Games, 1991-97; majority ptnr. Urban Environ. Solutions, LLC, 1998-. Recipient Disting. Alumni award Nat. Assn. for Equal Opportunity Higher Edn., 1983, Leadership award Atlanta chpt. NAACP, 1987; named to Acad. Women Achievers YWCA Greater Atlanta, 1986. Mem. Nat. Forum Black Pub. Adminstrs. Clubs: Chautauqua Circle. Democrat. Avocations: gardening, traveling, politics, fine arts. Office: City Hall 55 Trinity Ave SW Atlanta GA 30303-3520*

FRANKLIN, STANLEY PHILLIP, computer scientist, cognitive scientist, mathematician, educator; b. Memphis, Aug. 14, 1931; s. Sam and Lily (Rosenblum) F.; m. Jeannie Stonebrook, Apr. 1, 1979; children— Lynn Ann, Michele Suzanne, Phillip Byron, Bruce Eric, Halli Eileen, Elena Simone, Sunny Patrice, Sam Elliot. BS, U. Memphis, 1959; MA, UCLA, 1962, PhD, 1963; NSF postdoctoral fellow, U. Wash., Seattle, 1963-64. Asst. prof. math. U. Fla., 1964-65; assoc. prof., then prof. Carnegie-Mellon U., 1965-72; prof. math., chmn. dept. math. scis. U. Memphis, 1972-84, prof. computer sci., 1984—, co-dir. Inst. for Intelligent Systems, 1987—, Dunarant prof. computer sci., 2000—. Vis. prof. Indian Inst. Tech., Kanpur, Technion, Haifa, Israel; vis. mem. Mathematische Centrum, Amsterdam, Netherlands; condr. workshops, cons. in field. Author research papers and books in field. Served with USMCR, 1951-53. Recipient Bd. Visitors Eminent Faculty award, 1997. Mem. Assn. for Computing Machinery, Am. Assn. for Artificial Intelligence, Cognitive Sci. Soc., Internat. Neural Network Soc., Sigma Xi, Pi Mu Epsilon. Home: 5736 Rich Rd Memphis TN 38120-2086 Office: U Memphis Dept Math Sci Memphis TN 38152-0001 E-mail: franklin@memphis.edu.

FRANKLIN, TIMOTHY A. editor-in-chief, editor; m. Alison Franklin; 2 children. BJ and Polit. Sci., Ind. U., 1982. Reporter county govt. to assoc. mng. editor Chgo. Tribune, 1982—97; v.p., editor Ind. Star, 2000, Orlando Sentinel, 2000—. Nominee Pulitzer prize, series state's child welfare sys., 1986; named One of the Nation's Most Influential Bus. Journalists, TJFR mag.; recipient Barney Kilgore award, Soc. Profl. Journalists. Mem.: Am. Soc. Newspaper Editors (mem. leadership com.), Fla. Soc. Newspaper Editors (co-chmn. orgn.'s pub. access com.). Office: Orlando Sentinel 633 N Orange Ave Orlando FL 32801*

FRANKLIN, WILLIAM GEORGE, manufacturing executive; b. Schenectady, N.Y., Sept. 14, 1921; s. Raymond Fred and Edna Laura (Faustmann) F.; m. Florence Smith, Mar. 27, 1948; William George, Cynthia Lee; m. Frances Engwall, Jan. 30, 1995 BS, MIT, 1943. Chem. engr. Exxon, Elizabeth, N.J., 1943-48; v.p. David Smith Steel Co., Bklyn., 1948-69; pres. Hillside Spinning & Stamping, Union, N.J., 1969—. Pres. Hillside Metal Ware Co., Union, 1969—, Aero Metal Products Co., Union, 1981—. Chmn. Gov.'s Debt Collection, Trenton, N.J., 1982-83; pres. Union County Econ. Devel., Union, 1985-86; dir. YMCA, Scotch Plains, N.J., 1972-81; mem. Summit Rep. Com. Mem. Nat. Housewares Assn., Nat. Assn. Food Equipment, Mfrs. Assn., Baltusrol Golf Club, Wyndemere Country Club. Republican. Presbyterian. Avocations: golf, model railroading, snow skiing, charities. Office: Hillside Spinning & Stamping Co 1060 Commerce Ave Union NJ 07083-5026

FRANKLIN, WILLIAM JAY, lawyer; b. Logansport, Ind., Mar. 1, 1945; s. Frederick Arthur and Ferne (Friskney) F.; m. Kathleen Killette, Feb. 5, 1988; 1 child, James Frederick. BSME with highest distinction, Purdue U., 1968, MS in Computer Sci., 1970; JD, Georgetown U., 1977. Bar: D.C. 1977, U.S. Dist. Ct. D.C. 1978, U.S. Ct. Appeals (D.C. cir.) 1977, U.S. Supreme Ct. 1981. Computer specialist antitrust div. U.S. Dept. Justice, Washington, 1976-77; assoc. Lowenstein, Newman Reis & Axelrad, Washington, 1977-80, Becker, Gurman, Lukas, Meyers & O'Brien, Washington, 1980-82; prin. Mahn, Franklin & Goldenberg, P.C., Washington, 1982-85; ptnr. Bell, Boyd & Lloyd, Washington, 1985-87, Pepper & Corazzini, Washington, 1988—. Guest lectr. Brookings Instn., Washington, 1982. Author monthly column: Legal Briefs, 1984—. Mem. ABA, Fed. Communications Bar Assn., Tau Beta Pi. Home: 6300 Stratford Rd Bethesda MD 20815-5321

FRANKO, BERNARD VINCENT, pharmacologist, educator; b. West Brownsville, Pa., June 9, 1922; m. Marie Burke, June 25, 1946; 9 children BS in Pharmacy, W.Va. U., 1954, MS in Pharmacology, 1955; PhD in Pharmacology, Med. Coll. Va., 1958. With A.H. Robins Co., Richmond, Va., 1958—, assoc. dir. pharmacology, 1968-71, 73-77, dir. pharmacologic research, 1971-73, monitor, dir. good lab. practices dept., 1978-81, mgr. research coordination and tng. sect., 1981-90, ret., 1990; asst. prof., adj. asst. prof. pharmacology Med. Coll. Va., Richmond, 1961—. Contbr. numerous articles to profl. jours. Fellow AAAS; mem. Am. Soc. Pharmacology and Exptl. Therapeutics, Soc. Exptl. Biology and Medicine. Home: 4012 Patterson Ave Richmond VA 23221-1913

FRANKS, ALLEN P. research institute executive, educator; b. Cleve., Nov. 12, 1936; s. Stanley Arthur and Helen Dorothy (Kulwicki) F.; m. Cary Bajko, Feb. 2, 1963; children: Mathew, Sara. BS, U. Miami, 1959; LLB, Case Western Res. U., 1963, JD, 1968. Cert. chem. engr. Patent atty. B.F. Goodrich Co., Akron, Ohio, 1963-65; chemist, mgr. paint testing lab. PPG Industries, Barberton, Ohio, 1965-66; tech. dir., lab. mgr. Reichhold Chems., Inc., Cuyahoga Falls, Ohio, 1966-76; instr. Inst. Astral Studies, Inc., Akron, 1974-80, pres., 1977-80; mgr. tech. sales Sovereign Chem. Co., Cuyahoga Falls, 1980-86; pres. I.A.S. Inc., 1986-94; sec.-treas. rsch. divsn. IAA, 1990-95, pres., 1995—; CEO Cary Franks Inc., 1995—. Lectr. astrology, biorhythms, tennis Akron U., 1974-79, Kent (Ohio) State U., 1973-77. Contbr. articles to profl. jours. Bd. dirs.

Persephone Found., Bath, Ohio, 1974-80, chmn., 1981-86; instr. tennis YWCA, Goodyear Racquet Club. With USCGR, 1954-62. Fellow Am. Inst. Chemists; mem. AAAS, N.Y. Acad. Scis., Ohio Inst. Chemists (treas. 1976-84, pres. 1984-90), Am. Chem. Soc., Akron Rubber Group, N.E. Ohio Rubber Group, Theosophical Soc. South Fla. (treas. 1996-99), Mensa, Intertel, Crystal Lake Country Club, Am. Legion, Fraternal Order Police, Univ. Club, Goodyear Racquet Club, Phi Delta Phi. Home: 1887 NW 70th Ln Margate FL 33063-2487 E-mail: A8531A@cs.com.

FRANKS, CANDACE ANN, bank executive; b. Memphis, Nov. 18, 1952; d. James William and Barbara Elizabeth Webb; m. Roger Allen Franks, July 23, 1977; 1 child, Ava Elizabeth. BA, Ark. State U., 1974, MA, 1976; JD, U. Ark., 1979. Bar: Ark. 1979. Gen. counsel Ark. State Bank Dept., Little Rock, 1980-95, dep. bank commr., 1995—. Mem. Gov.'s Task Force to Revise Banking Code, Legis. Task Force to Study NAFTA, 1995, Gov.'s Task Force on Interstate Banking, 1997—; mem. legis. com. Conf. State Bank Suprs., Washington, 1997—. Named one of Top 10 Women in Ark., Ark. Bus. Mag., 1996, 97, 98. Mem. Ark. Bar Assn., Pulaski County Bar Assn., Conf. State Bank Suprs. Office: Ark State Bank Dept Sedgwick Ctr 400 Hardin Rd Ste 100 Little Rock AR 72211-2613 E-mail: cfranks@banking.state.ar.us.

FRANKS, CHARLES LESLIE, investments executive; b. Columbus, Miss., Jan. 21, 1934; s. Leslie J. and Almeda (Morris) F.; m. Cecile Alice Cronovich, Feb. 7, 1959; children— Carolyn Anne, Charles Christopher. BS summa cum laude, Miss. State U., 1956. Cert. internal auditor; C.P.A.; chartered bank auditor. Acct. Arthur Andersen & Co., Houston, 1959-61; mgr. internal audit dept. Bank of S.W., Houston, 1961-71; gen. auditor Southwest Bancshares, Inc., 1972-79; v.p., auditor Merc. Nat. Bank, Dallas, 1979-82, sr. v.p., auditor, 1982-86; sr. v.p., dir., internal auditor Bright Banc, Dallas, 1986-89, sr. v.p., chief fin. officer, 1989-90; pvt. practice investments, 1991—. Instr., speaker various Bank Adminstrn. Inst. seminars, meetings and convs. Served to capt. USAF, 1956-59. Mem. Tex. Soc. C.P.A.s (sec. Houston chpt. 1971-72), Bank Adminstrn. Inst. (v.p. Gulf Coast chpt. 1971-72, pres. 1973-74, dir. 1974-75, state dir. 1975-77, dir. Dallas chpt. 1980-84), Am. Inst. Banking, Inst. Internal Auditors (gov. 1973-78, pres. Houston chpt. 1974-75), Houston C. of C., Arnold Air Soc., Phi Eta Sigma, Chi Lambda Rho, Phi Kappa Phi, Alpha Kappa Psi. Roman Catholic. Home: 206 Brocket St Stafford TX 77477-4708

FRANKS, HERBERT HOOVER, lawyer; b. Joliet, Ill., Jan. 25, 1934; s. Carol and Lottie (Dermer) F.; m. Eileen Pepper, June 22, 1957; children: David, Jack, Eli. BS, Roosevelt U., 1954; postgrad., Am. U., 1960. Bar: Ill. 1961, U.S. Dist. Ct. (no. dist.) Ill. 1961, U.S. Supreme Ct. 1967. Ptnr. Franks, Gerkin & McKenna, 1985—. Mem. exec. com. 1st Nat. Bank, Marengo, Ill., 1976—; commr. Ill. Cts. Commn., 2003—. Bus. editor Am. U. Law Rev., 1959, 60. State pres. Young Dems. of Ill., 1970-72; trustee Hebrew Theol. Coll., Skokie, Ill., 1974—; trustee, sec. Forest Inst. Profl. Psychology, Springfield, Mo., 1979-91; chmn. Forest Hosp., Des Plaines, 1980-88. With U.S. Army, 1956-58. Mem.: Ill. Trial Lawyers (mng. bd. 1975—92, treas. 1985—87), Ill. State Bar Assn. (state pres. 2000—01), Shriners, Masons (33 deg.), Sigma Nu Phi (pres. 1980—82). Home: 19324 E Grant Hwy Marengo IL 60152-9438 Office: Franks Gerkin & McKenna 19333 E Grant Hwy Marengo IL 60152-8234 E-mail: franklaw@mc.net.

FRANKS, HERSCHEL PICKENS, judge; b. Savannah, Tenn., May 28, 1930; s. Herschel R. and Vada (Pickens) F.; m. Judy Black; 1 child, Ramona. Student U. Tenn.-Martin, U. Md.; JD, U. Tenn.-Knoxville; grad. Nat. Jud. Coll. of U. Nev. Bar: Tenn. 1959, U.S. Supreme Ct. 1968. Claims atty. U.S. Fidelity & Guaranty Co., Knoxville, 1958; ptnr. Harris, Moon, Meacham & Franks, Chattanooga, 1959-70; chancellor 3d Chancery div. of Hamilton County, 1970-78; judge Tenn. Ct. Appeals, Chattanooga, 1978—; spl. justice Tenn. Supreme Ct., 1979, 86, 87; presiding judge Hamilton County Trial Cts., 1977-78; spl. judge Tenn. Ct. of Criminal Appeals, 1990-92; mem. commn. to study appellate cts., 1990-92. Served with USNG, 1949-50, USAF, 1950-54. Mem. ABA (award of merit), Tenn. Bar Assn. (award of merit 1968-69), Tenn. Bar Found., Chattanooga Bar Found., Chattanooga Bar Assn. (pres. 1968-69, Founds. of Freedom award 1986), Am. Judicature Soc., Inst. Jud. Adminstrn., Optimists (pres. 1965-66), Community Service award 1971), Mountain City Club, City Farmers Club, Phi Alpha Delta. Mem. United Ch. of Christ. Address: 540 Mccallie Ave Ste 562 Chattanooga TN 37402-2039

FRANKS, JACK DARROW, lawyer; b. Belvidere, Ill., Oct. 2, 1963; s. Herbert Hoover and Eileen Rosalyn (Pepper) F. Student, London Sch.Econs., 1984; BA cum laude, U. Wis., Madison, 1985; JD cum laude, Am. U., 1989. Bar: Ill. 1989, U.S. Dist. Ct. (no. dist.) Ill. 1989, U.S. Dist. Ct. D.C. 1990. Assoc. Wildman, Harrold, Allen and Dixon, Chgo., 1989—. Bd. dirs. The Bricton Group, Northbrook, Ill., Al Gelato Ice Cream, Franklin Park, Ill. Editor Adminstrv. Law Jour., 1988-89. Vol., Chgo. Multiple Sclerosis Assn., 1989. Mem. ABA, Ill. State Bar Assn., Chgo. Bar Assn., Ill. Trial Lawyers Assn., Chgo. Coun. Fgn. Rels., Brazilian Am. Cultural Com. Democrat. Jewish. Avocations: portuguese and spanish studies, travel, fishing. Home: 19324 E Grant Hwy Marengo IL 60152-9438 Office: Wildman Harrold Allen Dixon 225 W Wacker Dr Chicago IL 60606-1224*

FRANKS, JON MICHAEL, lawyer, mediator; b. Marshall, Tex., Sept. 26, 1941; s. Francis William and Clara Bell (Caldwell) F.; m. Sue Powers, May 23, 1987; children: Brian Alan, Michael Shawn. BA, Southwestern U., 1963; LLB, U. Tex., 1966. Bar. Tex. 1966, U.S. Dist. Ct. (no. dist.) Tex.; cert. family lawyer, Tex. Bd. of Legal Specialization. Lawyer Pettigrew and Buckley, Grand Prairie, Tex., 1966-67; pvt. practice Irving, Tex., 1967-68, 71-79, 88—; ptnr. Franks and Vice, Irving, 1968-71, Franks and Luce, Irving, 1979-88. Mem. child support and visitation guidelines com. Tex. Supreme Ct., Austin, 1989; mem. Southlake Ct. of Records Com., 1990—. Commr. Irving Planning and Zoning Bd., 1971-74; judge Mcpl. Ct., Irving, 1974-78, Southlake, Tex., 1978-88, Southlake City Coun., 1992—. Fellow Am. Acad. Matrimonial Lawyers; mem. ABA (family law sect.), Tex. Acad. Family Law Specialists (bd. dirs. 1988-90), North Tex. Assn. Family Law Specialists (pres. 1985-87), Tex. Bar Assn. (family law sect.), Dallas Bar Assn. (pres. family law sect. 1989), Tarrant County Family Law Assn., Am. Acad. Atty.-Mediators. Republican. Methodist. Avocations: gun collector, competition shooting, bicycling, tennis. Office: 128 E Texas St Grapevine TX 76051-5307

FRANKS, LEWIS E. electrical and computer engineering educator, researcher; b. San Mateo, Calif., Nov. 8, 1931; s. Lloyd C. and Leora (Embree) F.; m. Mary B. Harris, June 21, 1954; children: Janet K., Jill M., Daniel J. BSEE, Oreg. State U., 1952; MSEE, Stanford U., 1953, PhD, 1957. Mem. tech. staff Bell Telephone Labs., Murray Hill, N.J., 1958-62, supr. North Andover, Mass., 1962-69; assoc. prof. U. Mass., Amherst, 1969-71, prof., 1971-96, chmn. dept elec. and computer engring., 1975-78, acting head dept. elec. and computer engring., 1991-93, prof. emeritus, 1996—. Author: Signal Theory, 1969; editor: Data Communication, 1974; contbr. over 60 articles to profl. jours. Hewlett Packard fellow, Stanford U., 1952. Fellow IEEE; mem. NSF (program dir. networking and communications rsch., 1988-90). Office: Univ of Mass Dept of Elec & Computer Engring Amherst MA 01003 E-mail: franks@ecs.umass.edu.

FRANKS, LUCINDA LAURA, journalist; b. Chgo., July 16, 1946; d. Thomas Edward and Lorraine Lois (Leavitt) F.; m. Robert M. Morgenthau, Nov. 1977; children: Joshua Franks Morgenthau, Amy Elinor Morgenthau. BA, Vassar Coll., 1968. Journalist specializing youth affairs, civil strife in No. Ireland UPI, London, 1968-73, N.Y. Times, N.Y.C., 1974-77; freelance writer N.Y. Times Mag., N.Y. Times Book Rev., Talk Mag., The Atlantic, The New Yorker, N.Y. mag., The Nation. Vis. prof. Vassar Coll., 1977-82; Ferris prof. journalism Princeton U., 1983 Author: Waiting Out A War: The Exile of Private John Picciano, 1974, Wild Apples, 1991. Recipient Pulitizer prize for nat. reporting, 1971, N.Y. Newspaper Writers Assn. award, 1971, Nat. Headliners award Soc. Silurians journalism award, 1976, EDI award for print journalism Easter Seals, 1999. Mem. Am. PEN Club (membership bd.), Author's League, Coun. on Fgn. Rels., Writers Rm. Inc. (past pres.). Address: 64 E 86th St New York NY 10028-1016

FRANKS, PETER JOHN, educational administrator; b. Lexington, Mass., Feb. 25, 1948; s. Charles Henry and Evelyn Rebecca (Anderson) F.; m. Jane Karen Campbell, Sept. 9, 1972; children: Andrew C., Meredith C. BA, Northeastern U., 1971, MEd, 1974. Adminstrv. asst. to dir. suburban campus Northeastern U., Boston, 1971-72, asst. to dean of students, 1972-77, asst. dean of students, 1977-84; v.p. Nat. Commn. for Coop. Edn., Boston, 1984-95; CEO World Assn. for Coop. Edn., Boston, 1995—. Mem. site-based mgmt. coun. Lexington (Mass.) Sch. Sys., 1990-94; chmn. edn. com. Hancock Ch., 1989-94, endowment com., 1995-2000, co-chair 1998-2000; bd. trustees Charles I. Travelli Fund. Named one of Outstanding Young Men of Am., U.S. Jaycees, 1979. Mem. New Eng. Assn. Field Experience, World Assn. for Coop. Edn., Coop. Edn. and Internship Assn., Employment Mgmt. Assn. Found. (bd. dirs. 1995—, sec.-treas. 1997-98, pres., 1998-2000), Soc. for Human Resource Mgmt., Internat. Scholars Soc., Kappa Delta Pi, Phi Beta Delta. Home: 7 Dexter Rd Lexington MA 02420-3303 Office: World Assn for Coop Edn Ste 384 CP 360 Huntington Ave Boston MA 02115-5005

FRANKS, ROBERT D. (BOB FRANKS), former congressman; b. Hackensack, N.J., Sept. 21, 1951; s. Norman A. and June Evans F. BA, Depauw U., 1973; JD, So. Methodist U., 1976. Exec. dir. People for Bateman, 1977; cons. Jim Courter for Congress Com., 1978; v.p. Med Data Inc., 1978-80; co-owner County News, 1980-83; cons. Tom Kean for Gov. Com., 1981; mem. N.J. State Assembly from 22nd Dist., Trenton, 1979-93, 103d-106th Congresses from 7th N.J. Dist., 1993-2001; mem. budget com., mem. transp. and infrastructure com.; pres. Healthcare Institute of N.J. Bd. dirs. Intrenet.; mgmt. cons. in field; founder CREO; mem. Econ. Steering Com., 1980, Com. on Energy and Nat. Resources, 1981-83, Com. on State Govt., Civil Svc., Elections, Pensions and Vet. Affairs, 1981-85, N.J. State Pension Study Commn., 1982, Com. Revenue, Finance and Appropriations, 1984-93, State and Local Expenditure and Revenue Policy Commn., 1985-93, Waste Mgmt. Planning and Recycling Com., 1990-91; chmn. Task Force to Reform Congress Redistricting Process, 1982, N.J. Coalition for Regulatory Efficiency, 1985-93, Republican Policy Com., 1990-91, N.J. State Rep. Party, 1988-93; campaign mgr. Congressman Jim Courter, 1982, Congressman Dean Gallo, 1984; assembly liaison Rep. Majority, 1985. Bd. mgrs. Children's Specialized Hosp., Mountainside, N.J., 1980; mem. long range planning com. Overlook Hosp., Summit, N.J., 1982; mem. domestic task force Hands Across Am., 1986; mem. N.J. Jaycees. Named Legislator of Yr. Nat. Rep. Legislators Assn., 1986. Republican. Office: 391 George St New Brunswick NJ 08901

FRANKS, RONALD DWYER, university dean, psychiatrist, educator; b. Balt., Jan. 15, 1946; s. Wylie and H. Jeanette (Dwyer) F.; m. Vicky Ruth Vicklund; children: Aaron Matthew, Alexis Linda. Student, Albion Coll., 1964-67; MD with distinction, U. Mich., 1971. Intern Virginia Mason Hosp., Seattle, 1971-72; resident in psychiatry U. Colo. Med. Ctr., Denver, 1972-76; instr. psychiatry U. Colo. Sch. Medicine, Denver, 1976-77, asst. prof. psychiatry, 1977-83, assoc. prof., 1983-88, asst. dean student affairs, 1982-84, asst. dean student and curricular affairs, dir. inpatient svcs. dept. psychiatry, 1986-88; dean, prof. psychiatry U. Minn. Sch. Medicine, Duluth, 1988-97; dean, prof. psychiatry and behavioral scis. East Tenn. State U. Coll. Medicine, Johnson City, 1997—. Contbr. numerous articles to profl. jours. Mem. AMA, So. Med. Assn., Tenn. Med. Assn., Am. Psychiat. Assn., Alpha Omega Alpha. Home: 3007 Moss Creek Dr Johnson City TN 37604-2203 Office: East Tenn State U James H Quillen Coll Med PO Box 70694 Johnson City TN 37614-1710

FRANKS, SONDRA LOU, music educator, organist; b. Portland, Ind., Mar. 23, 1945; d. Alva B. and Ruth E. Cheesman; m. Richard Lee Franks, Oct. 26, 1963; children: Terri Lyn, Christopher Allen. MusB magna cum laude, Ind. U., 1979. Organist First United Meth. Ch., Auburn, Ind., 1972-99, music dir., 1979-86, 92-97; piano tchr. Frankly Music, Auburn, 1972-99; music dir., condr. DeKalb Oratorio Chorus, Auburn, 1984-98; organist St. Mark's United Meth. Ch., Tucson, 1999—; profl. accompanist, 1979—. Accompanist Fort Wayne (Ind.) Children's Choir, 1982—94, Hoosier Chorale, Auburn, 1992—98. Past pres., v.p. DeKalb Cmty. Concerts, Auburn, 1993—99. Mem.: Tucson Music Tchrs. Assn. (treas.), Nat. Pedagogy Conf., Ariz. Music Tchrs. Assn., Nat. Music Tchrs. Assn., Sigma Alpha Iota. Methodist. Home and Office: 8501 N Breezewood Pl Tucson AZ 85704-0906 E-mail: sondralf@cs.com.

FRANKS, TOMMY RAY, retired army officer; b. Wynnewood, Okla., June 17, 1945; m. Cathryn Carley, Mar. 22, 1969; 1 child, Jacqueline Franks Matlock. BSBA, U. Tex., Arlington, 1971; MS in Pub. Adminstrn., Shippensburg U. Pa., 1985; grad., Armed Forces Staff Coll., U.S. Army War Coll. Commd. 2d lt. U.S. Army, 1967, advanced through grades to gen., 2000; comdr. 2d bn. 78th F.A. 1st Armored Divsn., Germany, 1981-84; dep. asst. chief staff G3 III Corps, Ft. Hood, Tex., 1985-86; comdr. div. arty. 1st Cav. Div., 1987-88, chief staff, 1988-89, asst. divsn. comdr. Operation Desert Shield-Storm, 1990-91; asst. comdt. U.S. Army F.A. Sch., Ft. Sill, Okla., 1991-92; dir. La. Maneuvers Task Force, Office Chief of Staff U.S. Army, Ft. Monroe, Va., 1992—94; asst. chief staff C3/J3/G3 UN and combined forces command U.S. Forces Korea, 8th U.S. Army, 1994—95; commdr. second infantry divsn., 1995-97; comdr. 3rd United States Army, 1997-2000; U.S. comdr.-in-chief Central Command, MacDill AFB, Fla., 2000—03; with Operation Enduring Freedom Afghanistan, 2001—02; with Operation Iraqi Freedom, 2003. Decorated Def. Disting. Svc. Medal, Disting. Svc. Medal with one oak leaf cluster, Legion of Merit with 3 oak leaf clusters, Bronze Star medal with V device and 4 oak leaf clusters, Purple Heart with 2 oak leaf clusters.

FRANKS, TRENT, congressman; b. Uravan, Colo., June 19, 1957; m. Josephine Franks. Student, Ottawa U. Mem. Ariz. Ho. Reps., 1985—87, vice-chmn. commerce com., chmn. sub-com. on child protection and family preservation, mem. human resources com., mem. agr. com., mem. judiciary com.; head Ariz. Govs. Office for Children, 1987; exec. dir. Ariz. Family Rsch. Inst.; pres. Strategic Consulting and Liberty Petroleum Corp.; congressman 2nd Dist. Ariz. U.S. Ho. Reps., 2003—. Pres. Children's Hope Scholarship Assn.; active North Phoenix Bapt. Ch. Republican. Office: 1237 Longworth House Office Bldg Washington DC 20515-0302 also: Ste 200 7121 W Bell Rd Glendale AZ 85308*

FRANKS, WILLIAM J. judge; b. Uniontown, Pa., Jan. 6, 1932; m. Lena Franks; 1 child, Regina. BA in Pre-law, U. Pitts., 1953, LLB, 1956, JD, 1968; postgrad., U. Ga., 1958. Bar: Pa. 1956, U.S. Dist. Ct. (we. dist.) Pa. 1961. Pvt. practice, Uniontown, 1956-77; asst. dist. atty. Fayette County, Uniontown, 1960-69; judge Ct. Common Pleas Fayette County, Uniontown, 1978-96, pres., judge, 1996—2002, sr. judge, 2003—. Instr. bus. law U. Ga., 1958; instr. Am. Inst. Banking, 1960-65; solicitor Fayette County Contr., 1970; counsel Fayette County Child Welfare Svcs., Fayette County Cmty. Action Agy. With JAGC, U.S. Army, 1957-59. Mem. ABA, ATLA, Am. Judges Assn., Am. Arbitration Assn., Pa. Bar Assn., Fayette County Bar Assn., AMVETS, Cath. War Vets., Sons of Italy, KC (4th degree), Phi Beta Kappa, Phi Alpha Delta. Roman Catholic. Office: Fayette County Ct Common Pleas 61 E Main St Uniontown PA 15401-3514

FRANKS, WILLIAM WOOLERY, lawyer; b. Bryn Mawr, Pa., Dec. 18, 1947; s. Ernest H. and Eleanore W. (Woolery) F.; m. Cat Austin, May 3, 1980; children: Sebastian, Nikolas, Robin. BS in Psychology, Colo. State U., 1970; MEd, Plymouth State Coll., 1974; JD, Franklin Pierce Law Ctr., 1978. Bar: N.H. 1978, U.S. Dist. Ct. N.H. 1978, U.S. Supreme Ct. 1986, U.S. Ct. Appeals (1st cir.) 1981, U.S. Virgin Islands 1997. Assoc. Falardeau, & Mahan, Tilton, N.H., 1978-80; ptnr. Falardeau, Mahan & Franks, Tilton, 1980-83, Falardeau & Franks, Tilton, 1983-86; pres., shareholder Franks & Shepherd PA, Tilton, 1987-95, William W. Franks, PA, Tilton, 1995-97; mng. atty., litigation dir. Legal Svcs. V.I., St. Croix, 1998—. Adv. bd. First Deposit Nat. Banks, Tilton, 1986-98; investigator 1st Security Svcs. Corp., Boston, 1975-78. Dem. nominee for N.H. Ho. Reps., 1994; incorporator Spaulding Youth Ctr., Northfield, N.H., cottage tchr., trainer, 1970-75; vice chair Town of Sanbornton, N.H. Zoning Bd., 1994-96 Office: Christiansted 3017 Estate Orange Grv Christiansted VI 00820-4329 E-mail: lsvistxma@vipowernet.net.

FRANKSON-KENDRICK, SARAH JANE, publisher; b. Bradford, Pa., Sept. 24, 1949; d. Sophronus Ahimus and Elizabeth Jane (Sears) McCutcheon; m. James Michael Kendrick, Jr., May 22, 1982. Customer svc. rep. Laros Printing/Osceola Graphics, Bethlehem, Pa., 1972-73; assoc. editor Babcox Publs., Akron, Ohio, 1973-74, Bill Comms., Akron, Ohio, 1974-75, sr. editor, 1975-77, editor-in-chief, 1977-81; assoc. pub. Chilton Co./ABC Pub., Chgo., 1981-83, pub., 1983-89, group pub. Radnor, Pa., 1989 93; group v.p. Chilton Bus. Info. (formerly Chilton Co.), Radnor, Pa., 1993-98; divsn. v.p. Primedia Intertec, Chgo., 1999—2001. Exec. MBA prof. Northwood U., mem. adv. coun. Mem. oper. com. Primedia Intertec. Recipient Automotive Replacement Edn. award Northwood Inst., 1983, award for young leadership and excellence Automotive Hall of Fame, 1984; bd. dirs. Automotive Hall of Fame. Mem. Automotive Found. for Aftermarket (trustee), Automotive Parts and Accessories Assn. (bd. dirs., exec. com., sec., treas., strategic planning com., edn. com., Disting Svc. award 1993), Automotive Svc. Industry Assn. (bd. dirs. automotive divsn. com.), Automotive Svc. Assn. Mgmt. Inst. (trustee, exec. com.), Palm Beach (Fla.) Polo and Country Club, Winged Foot Golf Club (Mamaroneck, N.Y.). Republican.

FRANO, ANDREW JOSEPH, lawyer, civil engineer; b. Chgo., July 14, 1953; s. Joseph Neil Frano and Lorraine Rose (Jeczalik) Patchett-Keller; children: Alaina Marie, Jacqueline Elyse. BSCE, Bradley U., 1975, MSCE, 1976; JD, Chgo.-Kent Coll. Law, Ill. Inst. Tech., 1982. Registered profl. engr., Ill., Ind., Nebr., Wis., Minn., lic. gen. engring. constrn. contractor, Fla., Utah; bar: Ill. 1982, Nebr. 1986, U.S. Dist. Ct. (no. dist.) Ill. 1982, U.S. Dist. Ct. Nebr. 1992, Ariz. 1993, Tex. 1997. Soils lab. instr. and residence hall dir. Bradley U., Peoria, Ill., 1975-76; draftsman, engr. in tng. Harza Engring. Co., Chgo., 1973—76, civil engr., 1976—85; pvt. practice Chgo., 1982-85; pres. GEC Engring. Co. Inc., Chgo., 1985—86; corp. constrn. atty. Peter Kiewit Sons Inc., Omaha, 1986-92; asst. gen. counsel Harza Engring. Co., Chgo., 1992-95; owner The Law and Engring. Office of Andrew J. Frano, 1996—. Adj. asst. prof. dept. civil and architectural engring. Ill. Inst. Tech., Chgo., 1993—98; corp. atty., civil engr. T.J. Lambrecht Constrn., Inc., Joliet, Ill., 1996—98; prin. engr. Mirza-RSV Engring., Inc., Chgo. and Schaumburg, 1998—2000, Bloom Consultants, LLC, Schaumburg, 2001—. Chmn. San. Improvement Dist. 111, Sarpy County, Nebr., 1987-92; vol. atty. Chgo. Vol. Legal Svcs., 1983-85; bd. dirs., treas. Trails Assn. Inc., Roselle, Ill., 1983-86. Mem. ASCE, Tau Beta Pi, Chi Epsilon. Home: 2 N Dee Rd Unit 107 Park Ridge IL 60068-2871 Office: Bloom Consultants LLC 1870 N Roselle Rd Ste 101 Schaumburg IL 60195-3100 Fax: 847-843-3047.

FRANTISKA JR. JOSEPH JOHN, systems engineer, educator; b. Westfield, Mass., July 22, 1957; s. Joseph John and Madeline Francis Frantiska. BA in Math./Gen. Sci., Westfield State Coll., 1975—79; Cert. in Software Engring., Northeastern U., 1983—86; MS in Computer Sci., Fitchburg State Coll., 1985—89; Cert. in Artificial Intelligence, Northeastern U., 1987—90; BS in Bus. Adminstrn., Fitchburg State Coll., 1988—92; EdD, U. of Mass., 1992—2001; MBA, Western New Eng. Coll., 1993—97. EMT Mass., 1982, CPR Instructor Am. Heart Assn., 1996; Comml. Pilot Lic. FAA, 1979. Mem. of the tech. staff MITRE Corp., Bedford, 1981—84, Calspan Corp., Lexington, 1984—85; software engr. Raytheon Co., Bedford, 1985—88; sys. engr. G.T.E., Needham, 1988—93, MITRE Corp., Bedford, 1993—95; database developer U. of Mass., 1995—97; course developer Progress Software, Bedford, 1997—99; sys. engr. / tech. writer Raytheon Co., 1999—. Faculty cons. Ednl. Testing Svc., Princeton, NJ, 1994; textbook reviewer Jones and Bartlett, Sudbury, 2001—02; industry faculty mem. Northeastern U., Dedham, Mass., 1987—89, 1993, vis. lectr. Fitchburg State Coll., Mass., 1990—. Mem.: IEEE, NEA (assoc.), ISTE (assoc.), Conn. Aviation Hist. Assn. (assoc.). Avocations: flying, sailing, golf, aviation history, emergency medical technology.

FRANTZ, ANDREW GIBSON, endocrinologist, educator, dean; b. N.Y.C., May 22, 1930; s. Angus Macdonald and Virginia (Kneeland) F. AB magna cum laude, Harvard U., 1951; MD, Columbia U., 1955. Intern Presbyn. Hosp., N.Y.C., 1955-56, resident in medicine, 1956-58; fellow in endocrinology Columbia U., N.Y.C., 1958-60, asst. prof. medicine, 1966-68, assoc. prof., 1968-73, prof., 1973—, chief divsn. endocrinology, 1971-87; chmn. admissions com., assoc. dean for admissions Columbia U. (Coll. Physicians and Surgeons), 1981—. Assoc. in medicine Harvard U., 1962-66; asst. in medicine Mass. Gen. Hosp., Boston, 1962-66; mem. staff Presbyn. Hosp., N.Y.C.; mem. med. adv. bd. Nat. Pituitary Agy., 1970-73; established investigator Am. Heart Assn., 1968-73 Contbr. articles on prolactin and other pituitary hormones and functions to med. and sci. jours.; mem. editorial bd.: Jour. Clin. Endocrinology and Metabolism, 1971-76; assoc. editor: Metabolism, 1969— . Served to lt. comdr. USNR, 1960-62. Recipient Silver Medal Coll. Physicians and Surgeons, Columbia U., 1981, Alumni Fedn. medal Columbia U., 1984, Disting. Tchr. award, Coll. Physicians and Surgeons, Columbia U., 1989. Mem. AAAS, Endocrine Soc., Assn. Am. Physicians, Am. Soc. Clin. Investigation, Internat. Soc. for Neuroendocrinology, Harvey Soc., Practitioners Soc. (pres. 1993-2000), Charaka Club, Am. Fedn. Med. Rsch., N.Y. Acad. Scis., N.Y. Acad. Medicine, Union Club, Century Assn. (N.Y.C.), P and S Alumni Assn. (pres. 1991-93), Alpha Omega Alpha. Episcopalian. Home: 1185 Park Ave New York NY 10128-1308 Office: 630 W 168th St New York NY 10032-3702

FRANTZ, CHARLES FREDERICK, music educator; b. Lancaster, Pa., Feb. 27, 1951; s. Charles Weller Frantz and Eleanor Emma Brower. BA, Temple U., 1981, MA, 1987; PhD, Rutgers U., 1997. Pvt. sch. cert. Pa. Music dir. The Conservatory Music, Lawrenceville, NJ, 1972—; prof. piano Temple U., Phila., 1987—96; prof. music theory Coll. NJ., Ewing, 1996—2000; prof. music theory, history Westminster Choir Coll., Rider U., Princeton, NJ, 2000—. Lectr., performer in field N.Y., NJ., Pa., Mass. Contbr. articles to profl. jours. Mem.: Soc. Music Theory (licentiate), Am. Musicological Soc. (licentiate). Lutheran. Avocations: hiking, astronomy, geology, reading. Office: The Conservatory of Music 1601 Lawrenceville Rd Lawrenceville NJ 08648 E-mail: cffrantz@worldnet.att.net.

FRANTZ, DEAN LESLIE, psychotherapist; b. Beatrice, Nebr., Mar. 27, 1919; s. Oscar C. and Flora Mae (Gish) F.; m. Marie Flory, Aug. 31, 1940; children: Marilyn, Shirley, Paul. BA, Manchester (Ind.) Coll., 1942; MDiv, Bethany Theol. Sem., Oak Brook, Ill., 1945; diploma, C.G. Jung Inst. Zurich, 1977. Assoc. prof. Bethany Theol. Sem., 1957-64; dir. ch. rels. Manchester Coll., North Manchester, Ind., 1964-72; pvt. practice Ft. Wayne, Ind., 1977—. Author: Meaning for Modern Man in the Paintings of Peter Birkhauser, 1977; editor: Barbara Hannah: The Cat, Dog, and Horse Lectures, and the Beyond, 1992, Barbara Hannah: The Inner Journey, 1999. Mem. Internat. Assn. Analytical Psychology, Assn. Grad Analytical Psychologists. Home: Apt 24C 3143 Golden Years Homestead Dr 24C New Haven IN 46774-3002

FRANTZ, PHARES ALBERT, architect; b. New Orleans, Nov. 1, 1923; s. Roy Florestan and Marie Lucile (O'Kelley) F.; m. Elinor Mae(McCloskey), Feb. 20, 1954; children: Ninette Marie, Colleen Marie, Melinda Marie. BArch, Tulane U., La., 1950. Registered arch., La., Miss., Tenn. Draftsman Richard Koch Arch., New Orleans, 1950-52, arch., 1952-55; assoc. Richard Koch & Samuel Wilson Jr. Archs., New Orleans, 1955-72; ptnr. Koch and Wilson, Archs., P.C., New Orleans, 1986-96. Mem. Citizens Adv. com. Studying Revisions to City Zoning Ordinance, 1969; bd. dirs. Incarnate Word Parish Sch. Bd., 1971-80, pres., 1977-80; bd. dirs. France Amerique, 1981; pres. La. Polit. Com. Design Profls., 1984. Decorated Order of St. Louis Archdiocese of New Orleans. Mem. AIA (mem. hist. resources com. 1975-83, mem. New Orleans chpt. 1950—, pres. 1969, dir. 1970-71, state preservation coord. 1982), La. Inst. Bldg. Scis. (dir. 1980), La. Archs. Assn. (pres. 1980), Constrn. Specifications Inst. (pres. New Orleans chpt. 1960), Friends of Cabildo, La. Landmarks Soc., Sons of the Revolution, Nat. Trust, Mag. St., Round Table Club (v.p. 1992-93, pres. 1994-95), Delta Tau Delta. Republican. Roman Catholic. Home: 7525 Pearl St New Orleans LA 70118-3835

FRANTZ, RAY WILLIAM, JR., retired librarian; b. Princeton, Ky., Aug. 17, 1923; s. Ray William and Marjorie (Kevil) F.; m. Doris Methvin, Aug. 26, 1951; children: Katherine Kevil, Paul William. AB, U. Nebr., 1948; MLS, U. Ill., 1949, MA, 1951, PhD in English, 1955. Dir. libr. U. Richmond, Va., 1955-60; asst. dir. Ohio State U. Libr., Columbus, 1960-62; dir. libraries U. Wyo. Libr., 1962-67; libr. U. Va. Libr., Charlottesville, 1967-93. Chmn. bd. dirs. Southeastern Libr. Network, 1975-76; vice chmn., bd. dirs. 18th Century Short-Title Catalogue, N.Am., 1985—. With. inf. AUS, 1943-46. Mem. ALA, Assn. Rsch. Libro. (pres. 1977-78), Assn. Southeastern Rsch. Librs. (chmn. 1975—), Bibliog. Soc. Am., Bibliog. Soc. U. Va. (sec.-treas. 1967—). Home: 540 Worthington Dr Charlottesville VA 22903-4651

FRANTZ, THOMAS RICHARD, lawyer; b. Waynesboro, Pa., Sept. 10, 1947; s. John Richard and Janet (Donnelly) F.; m. Dianne Boffa June 22, 1985; children: Thomas Richard, Lindsey Amore, Elissa Noel. BA, College William and Mary, 1970, JD, 1973, LLM, 1981. Bar: Va., U.S. Dist. Ct. (ea. dist.) Va. 1974,

U.S. Ct. Appeals (4th cir.) 1974, U.S. Supreme Ct. 1978. Supr. tax dept. Peat Marwick, Mitchell & Co., 1973-74; officer, dir. Williams Mullen, Virginia Beach, Va., 1974—. Adj. prof. law Coll. William and Mary, 1981-82, trustee tax conf. 1984—; planning com. Old Dominion U. Tax Conf., 1977-81, chmn., 1981. Contbr. articles to profl. jours. King Neptune XXIII, Virginia Beach Neptune Festival, 1996; mem. exec. com. Va. Marine Sci. Mus., 1980—, pres., 2000-02, chmn., 2002--; bd. dirs. Cape Henry Collegiate Sch., 1986-98, chmn., 1991-92; bd. dirs. Virginia Beach Found., 1987—, chmn., 1995-97; bd. dirs. Virginia Beach Vision, 1993—, pres., 2002--; bd. dirs. Hampton Roads Partnership, 1997—. Capt. USAR, 1972-79. Mem. AICPA, ABA (tax, bus. and health law sects.), Am. Coll. Tax Counsel, Am. Coll. Trusts and Estates Counsel, Best Lawyers in Am. (tax, trusts and estates, corp. law), Am. Assn. Attys.-CPAs, Va. Bar Assn., Va. State Bar, Virginia Beach Bar Assn., Princess Anne Country Club, Cavalier Yacht and Country Club. Mem. Galilee Episcopal Ch. Home: Ste 1700 222 Central Park Ave Virginia Beach VA 23462-3035 E-mail: frantzfam@aol.com., tfrantz@williamsmullen.com.

FRANTZE, DAVID WAYNE, lawyer; b. Kansas City, Mo., Jan. 28, 1955; s. James W. and Margaret M. (Pursley) Frantze; m. Geri L. Sexton, July 28, 1979; children: Kevin, Lisa, Christopher, Timothy. BA, Avila U., 1976; JD, U. Mo., Kansas City, 1981. Ptnr. Stinson Morrison Hecker LLP, Kansas City, 2002—. Trustee Mid-Am. chpt. Leukemia and Lymphoma Soc., 1992—, chpt. pres., 1998—2000, nat. trustee, 2001—, mem. exec. com., 2003—; trustee Victor and Caroline Schutte Found., 2000—, U. Mo.-Kansas City Law Found., 1996—; exec. com. U. Mo.-Kansas City Law Found., 2000-, sec., 2001-; treas. U. Mo.-Kansas City Law Found., 2000-, sec., 2001-02; mem. Civic Coun. Kansas City, 1995—, urban core com., 1996—, bd. dirs., 2001—; sec. U. Mo-Kansas City Law Found., 2001, treas., 2002—; bd. dirs. Kansas City Spirit, Inc., 1986—88, pres., 1988, adv. coun., 1989—; bd. dirs. Kansas City Neighborhood Alliance, 1987—, chmn., 1994—96; mem. Greater Downtown Devel. Authority, 2002—; bd. counselors Avila U., 1989—2002, bd. trustees, 2002—. Mem.: ABA, Am. Coll. Real Estate Lawyers, Lawyers Assn. Kansas City, Kansas City Met. Bar Assn. (chmn. real estate law com. 1992), Mo. Bar Assn. Roman Catholic. Home: 11812 Central St Kansas City MO 64114-5536 Office: Stinson Morrison Hecker LLP 1201 Walnut St Ste 2600 Kansas City MO 64106-2150 E-mail: dfrantze@stinson.com.

FRANTZEN, HENRY ARTHUR, retired investment company executive; b. Orange, N.J., Nov. 28, 1942; s. Henry and Natalie (Johnson) F.; m. Julie Louise Haverty, Aug. 14, 1965; children— John Blair, Jill Marie, Eric Patrick Student, Hamline U., 1960-62; BSBA, U. N.D., 1964. Sr. securities analyst Chem. Bank, 1968-71; adminstrv. asst. Coll. Retirement Equities Fund, 1971, asst. investment officer, 1972, investment officer, 1973, asst. v.p., 1974-76, 2d v.p., 1976, v.p., investment mgr., mem. investment com., 1976; sr. v.p., investment mgr. Tchrs. Ins. and Annuity of Am., N.Y.C., 1980-87, Coll. Retirement Equities Fund, N.Y.C., 1980-87; dir. SBC Portfolio Mgmt. Internat. Inc., Amsterdam, 1987-89; chmn., chief investment officer Yamaichi Capital Mgmt. Corp., 1987-89; pres. Yamaichi Funds Inc., 1987-89, chmn., 1988-89; exec. v.p., dir. equities Oppenheimer Mgmt. Corp., N.Y.C., 1989-91; CIO, exec. v.p. Federated Global Investment Mgmt., N.Y.C., 1995—2002. Mgr. Brown Bros Harriman & Co., 1992-95, Brown Bros. Harriman & Co. Investment Mgmt. Ltd., London, 1992-95; exec. v.p. Federated Global Investment Mgmt. Corp., 1995-2002; exec. v.p. Federated Investment Mgmt. Corp., 1995-2002; v.p. Federated Investors, 1995; chief investment officer Global Equities and Fixed Income. Served to lt. USNR, 1964-68 Fellow Fin. Analysts Fedn.; mem. N.Y. Soc. Security Analysts, Econs. Club (N.Y.C.), Sigma Nu, Alpha Kappa Psi. Republican. Avocations: sailing; golfing; tennis; body surfing. Home: 669 Gulf Shore Blvd N Naples FL 34102

FRANTZICH, STEPHEN EDWARD, political science educator; b. Mpls., Mar. 4, 1944; s. Wensell S. and Winfred (Vettel) Frantzich; m. Jane Fouts, July 21, 1968; children: Mark, Matthew, Andrew. BA, Hamline U., St. Paul, 1966; PhD, U. Minn., 1970. Asst. prof. Denison U., Granville, Ohio, 1971—73, Hamilton Coll., Clinton, NY, 1973—77; prof. U.S. Naval Acad., Annapolis, Md., 1977—. Cons. Office of Tech. Assessment, Washington. Author: Presidential Popularity, 1979, Computers in Congress, 1982, Write Your Congressman, 1985, The C-Span Revolution, 1996, Citizen Democracy, 1999, Cyberage Politics 101, 2001. Chmn. Annapolis YMCA, 1982—. Nat. Def. Edn. Act grantee, 1966—70, Ford Found. grantee, 1969—70, Sr. Fulbright scholar, 1989, 2002. Mem.: Am. Polit. Sci. Assn. Methodist. Home: 2536 Davidsonville Rd Gambrills MD 21054-2110 Office: US Naval Acad Dept Polit Sci Annapolis MD 21402 E-mail: frantzic@usna.edu.

FRANTZIS, THEODOSIOS GEORGE, periodontist; b. Tampa, Fla., Oct. 13, 1941; s. George Theodosios and Zula (Pappas) F.; m. Carol Elaine Timm, Dec. 12, 1971; children: Franklyn Timothy, Hariklia Maria, Georganna Eleni. Student, U. Fla., 1959-60, Fla. state U., 1960-62; DDS, Emory U., 1966; MS in Dentistry, Mayo Grad Sch./U. Minn., 1971. Diplomate Am. Bd. Periodontology, lic. healthcare risk mgr. State Fla. Agy. for Health Care Adminstrn. Pvt. practice, Clearwater, Fla., 1971-78; asst. prof. periodontics Med. Coll. Va., Va. Commonwealth U., Richmond, 1978-80; pvt. practice Tampa, Fla., 1986—. Pres., CEO Mermaid Gifts, Inc., Tarpon Springs, 1985—; clin. asst. prof. U. N.C. Chapel Hill, 1985-86, U. Tex. Dental Br., Houston, 1981-82, U. Tex. Dental Br., San Antonio, 82-84; founding chmn. Leadership Pinellas, 1977, Dental Forum Clearwater, 1972-73; chmn. City of Tarpon Springs, Firefighters Pension Bd., 1989; apptd. mem. City of Tarpon Springs Health Facilities Authority Bd., 1995. Author: Recognizing and Describing Gingival Changes in Chronic Inflammatory Periodontal Disease, 1979, Setting Up a Speaker's Bureau, 1977; co-editor: Strangers at Ithaca: Story of the Spongers of Tarpon Springs, 2001; contbr. articles to sci. publs. Mem. Sunday sch. tchg. staff St. Nicholas Greek Orthodox Cathedral, Tarpon Springs, 1995. Capt. U.S. Army, 1966-68, lt. col. USAF, 1980-85, 91, Persian Gulf War, USAFR, 1985-98, ret. Mayo Found. fellow, Mayo Clinic, 1968-71, Diabetes Vascular Rsch., 1968-70; A.D. Williams Rsch. grantee Med. Coll. Va., 1978-80. Mem. ADA, Am. Acad. Periodontology (continuing edn. com. 1981-82, pub. rels. com. 1982-85, constn. by-laws com. 1983-84, Rsch. award 1970), Fla. Dental Assn. (chmn. speakers bur. 1975-76), Fla. Soc. Periodontists (chmn. pub. rels. com. 1975-76), Fla. Soc. Healthcare Risk Mgmt., Fla. Hosp. Assn., West Coast Dental Assn. (chmn., founder speaker's bur. 1975-76, chmn. Ho. of Dels. 1976-77, chmn. coun. on publs. and pub. info. 1977), Mayo Grad. Sch. Medicine Alumni Assn., Dental Forum Milw. (hon. life), Richmond Dental Soc. (chmn. speaker's bur. 1979-80), Gulf Coast Dental Study Club (Pinellas/Pasco chpt.), West Pasco Dental Implant Study Club, Toastmasters (Speaker Yr. 1973, Toastmaster Yr. 1974), Alpha Epsilon Delta, Psi Omega. Republican. Greek Orthodox. Avocations: photography, bass fishing, jogging, walking, deep-sea fishing. Home: 1005 Rosetree Ln Tarpon Springs FL 34689-2854 Office: Ste C-East 4326 Park Blvd Pinellas Park FL 33781-3555

FRANTZVE, JERRI LYN, psychologist, educator, consultant; b. Huntington Beach, Calif., Sept. 9, 1942; d. Rolland and Marjorie Weiland. Student, Purdue U., 1964-68; BA in Psychology and History, Marian Coll., 1969; MS in Organizational Psychology, George Williams Coll., 1976; PhD in Indsl. and Organizational Psychology, U. Ga., 1979. Sr. mktg. rsch. analyst Quaker Oats Co., Barrington, Ill., 1971-75; asst. prof. sch. of mgmt. SUNY, Binghamton, 1979-83; dir. employee rels. Conoco/DuPont, Ponca City, 1983-88; cons. psychologist Mass., 1988-89; assoc. prof. psychology Radford (Va.) U., 1989-94; mgmt. cons. J.L. Frantzve & Assocs., Bklyn., 1994—; divsn. head human svcs. Coll. New Rochelle, 1994-99; affiliate prof. Milano Grad. Sch. of Mgmt. New Sch. U., N.Y.C., 1999—. Instrn. cons. USAF, Rome, N.Y., 1979-83; dir. Israel Overseas Rsch. Program, Ginozar, Israel, 1982, Japanese Overseas Rsch. Program, Tokyo, 1983; coord. rsch. Ctr. for Gender Studies, Radford U., 1989-99; adj. prof. dept. psychology Bklyn. Coll., 2000—. Author: Behaving in Organizations: Tales from the Trenches, 1983, Guide to Behavior in Organizations, 1983; contbr. articles to profl. jours. Bd. dirs. Broome County Alcoholism Clinic, Binghamton, N.Y., 1980-83, bd. dirs. Broome County Mental Health Clinic, Binghamton, 1981-83; del. Dem. Caucus, Okla., 1985. Mem. APA (com. on women in psychology 1986-88), AAUW, Acad. Mgmt., Internat. Pers. Mgmt. Assn., Assn. for Women in Psychology. Avocations: ceramics, jazz, murder mysteries. Home and Office: 1804 Glenwood Rd Brooklyn NY 11230-1816 E-mail: drj4647@aol.com.

FRANZ, DANIEL THOMAS, financial planner; b. Dayton, Ohio, Jan. 30, 1949; s. Albin Benedict and Monica Elizabeth (Moeller) F.; m. Sally Ann Stickley, Oct. 11, 1968; children: Amanda Marie, Stephanie Ann. BS, Charleston So. U., 1971, postgrad., 1975, S.C. State U., 1974. Cert. fin. aid adminstr., fin. planner. Coach, admissions officer Bapt. Coll., Charleston (S.C.) So. U., 1971-72; dir. fin. aid Bapt. Coll., Charleston, S.C., 1972-76; pvt. practice fin. planning Greenville, Ohio, 1977—. Cons. S.C. Bapt. Conv., Columbia, 1974-76, U.S. Office Edn., Atlanta, 1974-76, Corning Glass Works, Greenville, 1984—, Franklin-Monroe High Sch., Pitsburg, Ohio, 1985—, United Telephone Co., Bellefontaine, Ohio, 1986—. Bd. dirs. Darke County Supts. Roundtable, Greenville, 1983—, Darke County Widows Assn., 1984-86; mem., chmn. bd. dirs. S.C. Com. Higher Edn., Columbia, 1974-76, Darke County Mental Health Clinic, 1984-90; bd. dirs. Coun. on Rural Svcs. Programs, 1991—; chmn. bd. dirs. Ch. of the Transfiguration Cath. Ch., West Milton, Ohio, 1978-82. Mem. Inst. Cert. Fin. Planners, Internat. Assn. Fin. Planners, Nat. Assn. Life Underwriters, Miami Valley Assn. Life Underwriters, S.C. Assn. Student Fin. Aid Adminstrs. (bd. dirs. 1971—), Darke County C. of C. (bd. dirs. 1993—), Lions. Republican. Avocation: sports. Office: Fin Achievement Svcs PO Box 657 5116 Childrens Hm Bradford Rd Greenville OH 45331-9327

FRANZ, DARREN M. writer; b. Jamaica, NY, Nov. 20, 1966; s. James Robert Franz and Anna Katharine Fischer; m. Barbara Ann Secrist, Sept. 2, 1990; 1 child, Robert Matthew. Grad., Richmond Hill (NY) H.S., 1984. Guest author I-Con Convention, Stonybrook, NY. Author: Jack Frost, 2000; contbr. short story to lit. publ. Cpl. U.S. Army, 1988, 84. Recipient Best Short Story award, Writer's Forum, 2000. Mem.: Horror Writer's Assn. Avocations: reading, hobby kits, pool, hiking. Home: 733 Stowe Ave Baldwin NY 11510 E-mail: darfranz@earthlink.net.

FRANZ, DAVID ARTHUR, library director; b. Albany, N.Y., June 10, 1943; s. Norman Joseph and Mary Frances (Loux) F.; m. Clara Rose (Plumeri), Nov. 23, 1973; 1 child, Thomas. BA, SUNY, Albany, 1965, MA, 1966, MLS, 1974; PhD, U. N.Mex., 1973. Cert. pub. libr., secondary social studies tchr., N.Y. Reference libr. Vestal (N.Y.) Pub. Libr., 1974-86, dir. Ogdensburg (N.Y.) Pub. Libr., 1986—. Chmn. Lib. Comm. St. Lawrence County, 1997. 1st lt. U.S. Army, 1966-68. Mem. ALA, N.Y. Libr. Assn., North Country Pub. Libr. Dirs. Orgn. (pres. 1991-92, sec. 1993). Republican. Roman Catholic. Avocations: collecting rocks, minerals and stamps, coin shooting. Home: 815 Knox St Ogdensburg NY 13669-2725 Office: Ogdensburg Pub Libr 312 Washington St Ogdensburg NY 13669-1518 E-mail: franz@northnet.org.

FRANZ, DENNIS, actor; b. Maywood, IL, Oct. 28, 1944; Stage appearances include: Bleacher Bums, 1978, Brothers, 1983; films include: The Fury, 1978, Remember My Name, 1978, Stony Island, 1978, A Wedding, 1978, A Perfect Couple, 1979, Dressed to Kill, 1980, Popeye, 1980, Blow Out, 1981, Psycho II, 1983, Body Double, 1984, A Fine Mess, 1986, The Package, 1989, Die-Hard 2, 1990, The Player, 1992, American Buffalo, 1996, City of Angels, 1998; TV appearances include: (series) Chicago Story, 1982, Hill Street Blues, (as "Bad Sal" Benedetto) 1982-83 (as Lieutenant Norman Buntz) 1987-88, Bay City Blues, 1983, Beverly Hills Buntz, 1987-88, Nasty Boys, 1990, NYPD Blue, 1993— (Emmy award 1994) (movies) Deadly Messages, 1985, Kiss Shot, 1989, Moment of Truth: Caught in the Crossfire, 1994, Texas Justice, 1995, Buddy Fatso, 1998. Recipient Emmy awards, 1996, 97, 99, SAG awards, 1995, 97, Golden Globes, 1995, Q awards, 1994, 96-99, Star on Walk of Fame, 1999. Office: Paradigm Talent Agency 10100 Santa Monica Blvd Fl 25 Los Angeles CA 90067-4003*

FRANZ, ELDON HENRY, environmental scientist, educator, ecologist; b. Omaha, Dec. 22, 1943; s. Henry Alfred and Virginia Grace Franz; m. Kristi Rennebohm, June 17, 1967; children: Wendy Elizabeth Franz Torrance, Benjamin Robert Franz-Knight, Matthew Zachary. AB, Grinnell (Iowa) Coll., 1966; MS, PhD, U. Ill., 1971. Instr. U. Ill., Champaign-Urbana, 1968—70; asst. prof. U. Ga., Athens, 1971—77; assoc. prof. Wash. State U., Pullman, 1977—. Assoc. editor: NW Sci., 1993—; contbr. articles to profl. jours., chapters to books. Charles Bullard fellow, Harvard U., 1996—97. Mem.: Ecol. Soc. Am. (chair edn. com., vice chair applied ecology sect. 1980—83). Office: Wash State Univ PO Box 644430 Pullman WA 99164-4430 E-mail: franz@wsu.edu.

FRANZ, ELIZABETH, actress; b. Akron, Ohio, June 18, 1941; Actress with Broadway credits in: Death of a Salesman, The Cripple of Inishmaan, Brighton Beach Memoirs (Tony and Drama Desk nominations), Broadway Bound, Uncle Vanya, Getting Married, The Cemetery Club, The Octette Bridge Club, The Cherry Orchard, Mornings at Seven, 2002; off-Broadway credits include: Sister Mary Ignatius (Obie award, Drama Desk nomination), Minutes from the Blue Route, The Comedy of Errors; regional credits include: Eleanor of Aquataine in The Lion in Winter (Cleve.), Amanda in The Glass Menagerie, Dividing the Estate (Great Lakes), A View From the Bridge, Woman in Mind (Berkshire Theatre Festival), Dolly in The Matchmaker, Agnes of God, Hamlet, Buried Child, The Wicked Witch in The Wizard of Oz, Miss Haversham in Great Expectations; appeared in numerous TV series and movies including: Roseanne, Sister, A Town's Revenge (Emmy nomination), Notes for My Daughter, Nothing Personal, Shameful Secrets, Face of a Stranger, Dottie, The Rise and Rise of Daniel Rocket, Love and Other Sorrows, A Girl Thing, Death of a Salesman (Emmy nomination, 2000), Gilmore Girls, 2001, Judging Amy, 2001; film credits include: Sabrina, 1995, The Substance of Fire, 1996, The Pallbearer, 1996, Thinner, 1996, Twisted, 1997, Jacknife, 1989, Secret of My Success, 1987, School Ties, 1992 Winner 1999 Tony award for featured actress in Death of a Salesman, also Drama Desk award, Outer Critics Circle award. Office: c/o Michael Slessinger Assocs 8730 W Sunset Blvd Ste 220 Los Angeles CA 90069-2275

FRANZ, FRANK ANDREW, university president, physics educator; b. Phila., Sept. 16, 1937; s. Russell Ernest and Edna (Keller) F.; m. Judy Rosenbaum, July 11, 1959; 1 child, Eric Douglas. BS in Physics, Lafayette Coll., 1959; MS in Physics, U. Ill., 1961, PhD in Physics, 1964. Research assoc. U. Ill., Urbana, 1964-65; asst. prof. physics Ind. U., Bloomington, 1967-70, assoc. prof., 1970-74, prof., 1974-85, assoc. dean Coll. Arts and Scis., 1974-77, dean faculties, 1977-82; prof. physics, provost, v.p. academic affairs and research W.Va. U., Morgantown, 1985-91; prof. physics, pres. U. Ala., Huntsville, 1991—. Guest scientist Swiss Fed. Inst. Tech., Zurich, 1965-67, U. Munich, 1978. Contbr. articles to profl. jours. NSF fellow, 1965-67, Alfred P. Sloan fellow, 1968-70. Fellow Am. Phys. Soc.; mem. AAAS, AAUP (pres. Bloomington, Ind. chpt. 1972-73), Am. Assn. Physics Tchrs., Sigma Xi. Avocation: tennis. Office: U Ala in Huntsville Office of the President Huntsville AL 35899-0001

FRANZ, JENNIFER DANTON, public opinion and marketing researcher; b. Oakland, Calif., Oct. 31, 1949; d. Joseph Periam and Lois (King) Danton; m. William Edwin Behnk, July 30, 1978. BA, Antioch Coll. West, 1973; MA, Stanford U., 1974; PhD, U. Calif., Berkeley, 1991. Cert. Community Coll. Student Personnel Worker, Calif., Community Coll. Supr., Calif. Cons. Alum Rock Union Elem. Sch. Dist., San Jose, Calif., 1973-75; rsch. asst. Far West Lab. for Ednl. Rsch. and Devel., San Francisco, 1974-75; project dir. Hartnell Coll., Salinas, Calif., 1975-77; project dir. Chancellor's Office Calif. Community Colls., Sacramento, 1978-80; pres., owner J.D. Franz Rsch., Sacramento, 1981—. Topic expert Nat. Mktg. Summit, 1995; adj. asst. prof. Golden Gate U., 1982—; instr. mktg. cert. program U. Calif. at Davis Extension, 1990—; lectr. Calif. State U., Sacramento, 1995—; instr. U. Calif.-Berkeley Ext., 1997—. Contbr. numerous articles to profl. jours. Mem. small bus. adv. com. Calif. Senate, Sacramento, 1986-92; bd. dirs. Jr. Achievement Sacramento, 1989-91, Episc. Cmty. Svcs. Sacramento, 1991-92; bd. dirs. Sacramento (Calif.) Philharmonic Orch., 2002—, v.p., 2003—. Recipient various rsch., svc. awards. Mem. Am. Mktg. Assn., Am. Assn. Pub. Opinion Rsch. (bd. dirs. Pacific Coast chpt., 2002—, sec., 2003—), Am. Ednl. Rsch. Assn. (editor 1984-86, mem. div. H evaluation steering com. 1984-85, polit. edn. spl. interest group, survey rsch. spl. interest group, judge div. H awards competition 1984, program reviewer 1982—), Mktg. Rsch. Assn., Sacramento Met. C. of C. (bd. dirs. 1990-93, state govt. affairs, local govt. affairs, pub. rels. coms. 1985—), Sacramento Valley Mktg. Assn. (bd. dirs. 1987-94, pres. 1993-94). Democrat. Episcopalian. Avocations: playing piano, swimming, reading, playing organ, tennis. Address: JD Franz Rsch 550 Bercut Dr Ste H Sacramento CA 95815 E-mail: jdfranz@jdfranz.com., jdfranz@earthlink.net.

FRANZ, JOHN E. bio-organic chemist, researcher; b. Springfield, Ill., Dec. 21, 1929; m. Elinor Theilken, Aug. 18, 1951; children: Judith, Mary, John, Gary. BS, U. Ill., 1951; PhD, U. Minn., 1955. Sr. research chemist Monsanto Agrl. Co., St. Louis, 1955—60, research group leader, 1960—63, fellow, 1963—75, sr. fellow, 1975—80, disting. fellow, 1980—90; ret., 1991. Co-author: Glyphosate: A Unique Global Herbicide, 1997; inventor roundup herbicide, holder 840 U.S. and fgn. patents; contbr. Recipient Indsl. Rsch. Mag. award, 1977, Indsl. Rsch. Inst. Achievement award, Washington, 1985, J.F. Queeny award, Monsanto Co., 1981, Inventor of Yr. award, St. Louis Bar Assn., 1986, The Nat. Medal of Tech., Washington, 1987, Outstanding Achievement award, U. Minn., 1988, The Mo. award, Gov. of Mo., 1988. Mem.: Am. Chem. Soc. (Carother's award Del. sect. 1989, Perkin medal Am. sect. 1990).

FRANZ, JUDY R. physics educator; BA in Physics, Cornell U., 1959; MS in Physics, U. Ill., 1961, PhD in Physics, 1965. Rsch. physicist IBM Rsch. Lab., Zurich, Switzerland, 1965-67; asst. prof. dept. physics Ind. U., 1968-74, assoc. prof., 1974-79, prof., 1979-87; prof. dept. physics W.Va. U., 1987-91, U. Ala. Huntsville, 1991—; exec. officer Am. Phys. Soc., 1994—. Vis. prof. Tech. U. Munich, 1978-79, Cornell U., 1985-86, 88, 90; assoc. dean coll. arts and scis. Ind. U., 1980-82; mem. coun. on materials sci. Dept. of Energy, 1997-2002; mem. rev. com. for materials sci and tech. divsn. Los Alamos Nat. Lab., 1999-2002; sec. gen. Internat. Union Pure & Applied Physics, 2002—, assoc. sec. gen., 1999-2002. Mem. editorial bd. Am. Jour. Physics, 1985-88; contbr. numerous articles to profl. jours. Mem. divsn. materials rsch. adv. com. NSF, 1986-89, mem. divsn. undergrad. edn. adv. com., 1991-93. Humboldt rsch. fellow Munich, 1978-79; recipient Distinguished Service Citation awd., Am. Assn. of Physics Teachers, 1993, Disting. Alumni award Coll. Eng., U. Ill., Urbana-Champaign, 1997. Fellow AAAS (coun. 1995-98), Am. Phys. Soc. (various coms. and offices, chair exec. com. divsn. condensed matter physics 1993-94); mem. Am. Assn. Physics Tchrs. (pres. 1990-91), Assn. Women in Sci., Am. Inst. Physics (various coms., gov. bd. 1994—, exec. com. 1996-00), Coun. Sci. Soc. Pres. (exec. bd. 1990), Phi Beta Kappa, Sigma Xi (pres. local chpt. 1981-82). Avocations: tennis, reading. E-mail: franz@aps.org.

FRANZ, LAURENCE W(ERNER), economics educator, college official; b. Buffalo, June 27, 1939; s. A. Lawrence and Alma Elizabeth (Werner) F.; m. Eileen Frances Vanderburgh, Dec. 28, 1963; children: Laura Frances, Marcus Vanderburgh. BS, SUNY, Buffalo, 1961, MA, PhD, 1968. Asst. prof. econs. and fin. Canisius Coll., Buffalo, 1965-69, assoc. prof., 1969—, chmn. dept., 1974-77, v.p., treas., 1978—. Mem. investment com. Healthnow N.Y., Inc., Cmty. Found. for Greater Buffalo. Mem.: Fin. Mgmt. Assn., Ea. Assn. Coll. and Univ. Bus. Officers, Assn. Jesuit Coll. and Univ. Bus. Officers, Fin. Execs. Inst. Avocations: boating, fishing. Home: 6776 Lake Shore Rd Derby NY 14047-9739 Office: Canisius Coll 2001 Main St Buffalo NY 14208-1035 E-mail: franz@canisius.edu.

FRANZ, MARION J. dietician, consultant; b. Mountain Lake, Minn., May 30, 1933; d. Leando M and Margaret E Jungas; m. Peter H. Franz, Sept. 3, 1956; children: Timothy James, Thomas Gregory, Laura Kay, Lynn Ellen. MS, U. of Minn., 1974—76; BS, Bethel Coll., 1951—55. Cert. Diabetes Educator Nat. Cert. Bd. for Diabetes Educators, 1986, registered Dietitian Commn. on Dietetic Registration, 1956. Rsch. dietitian U. of Minn. Hospitals, 1956—59; clin. dietitian Fairview-Southdale Hosp., Mpls., 1971—73; dir. of nutrition and profl. edn. Internat. Diabetes Ctr., Mpls., 1976—99; nutrition/health cons. Nutrition Concepts by Franz, Inc., Mpls., 2000—. Bd. mem. Am. Diabetes Assn., Alexandria, Va., 1986—91. Contbr. articles to profl. jours., chapters to books. Recipient Dr. Charles H. Best medal for Disting. Svc. in the Cause of Diabetes, Am. Diabetes Assn., 2001. Mem.: Am. Assn. of Diabetes Educators, Am. Diabetes Assn. Profl. Sect., Am. Dietetic Assn. Home and Office: Nutrition Concepts by Franz Inc 6635 Limerick Dr Minneapolis MN 55439 Office Fax: 952-941-6734. E-mail: marionfranz@aol.com.

FRANZ, WILLIAM MANSUR, lawyer; b. Dayton, Ohio, Dec. 3, 1930; s. Robert and Muriel (Bisbee) F.; m. Jane Speers, May 26, 1962; children: David, Julie, Elizabeth, Susan. BA in Russian Studies, Syracuse U., 1953; LLB, Chgo.-Kent Coll. Law, 1959. Bar: Ill. 1959, U.S. Dist. Ct. (no. dist.) Ill. 1959. Assoc. Righeimer & Righeimer, Chgo., 1959, Corcoran & Corcoran, Evanston, Ill., 1959-61; ptnr. Franz & Franz, Crystal Lake, Ill., 1961-73, Franz, Naughton & Leahy, Crystal Lake, 1974-87, Franz & Kerrick, Crystal Lake, 1987-99, William Franz & Assocs., Crystal Lake, 1999—2003, Hinshaw & Culbertson, Crystal Lake, 2003—. Served to 1st lt. USAF, 1951-53. Mem. Ill. Bar Assn., McHenry County Bar Assn. Clubs: Crystal Lake Country. Lodges: Lions. Home: 623 Leonard Pky Crystal Lake IL 60014-5209 Office: Hinshaw & Culbertson 453 Coventry Green Crystal Lake IL 60014-7504 E-mail: wfranz@hinshawlaw.com.

FRANZE, ANTHONY JAMES, pharmacist, lawyer; b. Albany, N.Y., Sept. 22, 1941; s. Vincent J. and Susie Franze; m. Kaoru Marie Nakamura, July 15, 1940; children: Vincent, Francis. BS in Pharmacy, St. John's Coll., 1963, JD, 1966. Bar: N.Y. 1966, U.S. Ct. Appeals (D.C. cir.) 1971, U.S. Patent Ct 1971; lic. pharmacist. Patent counsel Norwich (N.Y.) Eaton Pharms., 1970-84; assoc. city ct. judge City of Norwich, 1981-84; assoc. trademark and copyright coun. Bristol-Myers Squibb Co., N.Y.C., 1984-2000; ret., 2000. Mem. Emergency Svcs. Commn., Norwich, 1982-84; arbitrator N.Y.C. Small Claims Ct., N.Y.C., 1991—. Pres. PTO, Norwich, 1980-82; com. mem. Boy Scouts Troop 43, Princeton, N.Y., 1986-92. Col. U.S. Army, 1966-93 (active duty 1966-70). Mem. ABA, Am. Pharm. Assn., Am. Intellectual Property Assn., N.Y. State Bar Assn., Internat. Trademark Assn. Home: 387 Gallup Rd Princeton NJ 08540-7315

FRANZEL, BRENT STEVEN, lawyer; b. St. Louis, June 29, 1961; s. Richard and Lorraine Franzel; m. Ellen B. Brown. BJ, U. Mo., 1983; JD, Duke U., 1986. Bar: D.C. 1988, Mo. 1988. Legis. counsel Office of Senator Kit Bond, Washington, 1986-94; staff dir. Senate Banking Subcom. on Internat. Fin., Washington, 1995-96; ptnr. Tighe, Patton & Babbin, Washington, 1996—. Sr. advisor US-Asean Bus. Coun., Washington, 1996—. Office: Tighe Patton Armstrong Teasdale # 300 1747 Pennsylvania Ave NW Washington DC 20006-4688

FRANZEN, BYRON T. (JOHN FRANZEN), media specialist; b. Britton, SD, Apr. 16, 1946; s. Harold G. and Marian E. (Swenson) F. BA in English and Philosophy, Concordia Coll., 1968; MA in English, McGill U., Montreal, Que., Can., 1971. Press sec. McGovern for Pres. Campaign, N.H., Ill. Oreg., N.Y., 1971-72; pub. rels. and press. sec. various orgns., Washington, Ala., N.Y., 1973-74; lesig. aide Hon. Michael Harrington U.S. Ho. Reps., Washington, 1975-76; mgr. Panetta for Congress Campaign, Calif., 1976; chief staff Hon. Leon Panetta U.S. Ho. Reps., Washington, 1977-78; pres., prin. Franzen & Co., Washington, 1979—. Lectr. U.S. Info. Agy., various countries, 1988—. Designer Harriman Comm. Ctr., Nat. Dem. Hdqs., Washington, 1982-85; works represented in permanent collection Smithsonian Mus. Am. History. Founding chmn. R.A. Overbeck Capitol Hill History Project. Recipient Excellence award Internat. TV Assn., 1985, Silver award Houston Internat. Film Festival, 1987, Gold award, 1988, Nat. Telly award, 1987, 93, 98, 99, Nat. Silver Microphone award, 1987, 94, 97, 2001, Addy award, 1987, Vision award, 1992, 95, 2000. Mem. Am. Assn. Polit. Cons. (bd. dirs. 1991—, Pollie award 1986, 88, 94, 2000). Avocations: architectural design, art, antiques, community history. Office: Franzen & Co 610 C St NE Washington DC 20002-6002

FRANZEN, JANICE MARGUERITE GOSNELL, magazine editor; b. LaCrosse, Wis. d. Wray Towson and Anna Heldena (Renstrom) Gosnell; m. Ralph Oscar Franzen, Feb. 15, 1964. BS cum laude, Wis. State U., LaCrosse, 1943; MRE, No. Bapt. Theol. Sem., 1947. Tchr. history and social sci. Galesville (Wis.) High Sch., 1943-45; registrar Christian Writers Inst., Chgo., 1947-49, dir., 1950-63, dir. studies, 1964-86; fiction editor Christian Life Mag., Wheaton, Ill., 1950-63, woman's editor, 1964-72, exec. editor, 1972-86; mem. editorial bd. Creation House, Wheaton, 1972-86. Speaker writers confs. Author: Christian Writers Handbook, 1960, 61, The Adventure of Interviewing, 1989; editor: Christian Author, 1949-54, Christian Writer and Editor, 1955-63; compiler, contbr.: The Successful Writers and Editors Guidebook, 1977; contbr. articles to various mags. Sec., bd. dirs. Christian Life Missions, Lake Mary, Fla., 1971-95; bd. dirs. Ralph O. Franzen Charitable Found., 1990—, Wesley Luehring Found., 2000—. Home: 140 Windsor Park Dr Apt E201 Carol Stream IL 60188-5314

FRANZEN, RICHARD, writer; b. Chgo., Nov. 11, 1946; s. Leona Elizabeth Franzen and Norman Harry Franzen; life ptnr. Cyndi Kathleen Sepulveda; m. Judith Ann Loos (div. Nov. 15, 1985); children: Richard Jr., Carrie, Shelley. BS, Mont. State U., 1972; MA, Governor's State U., 1977. Author: (novels) Implant, 1988, Second Death in Purgatory, 1997, Sea Dancers, 2001; columnist: Journalism, 1988; author: (short stories) The Sleep Killer, 1985, Everything You Wanted and Nothing More, 1987, A Modern Vampire, 1989, Wishes, 1993, The Asshole Bureau, 1998, A Murderer for the Masses, 1998, Collage Man, 1999, Blast Day, Passage, 2000; columnist: Drama Critic, 1987; dir.: (short animation) Mourning and Evening, 2002, (film short) The Pine Box, 2001, (animation short) Split Decision, 2001, (animation) The Cost of Living, 2001, (animation short) Life with Cyndi, 2002, The Head Family, 2002, A half a thumb up, 2002, Ziz, 2002, (animation) An Almost Perfect Marriage, 2002, Fatulence, 2002. Recipient First Pl., Profl. Black and White Photo award, Luminous Photographic Papers, 1995. E-mail: rich_franzen@hotmail.com.

FRANZEN, ULRICH J. architect; b. Rhineland, Germany, Jan. 15, 1921; s. Erik and Elizabeth (Hellersberg) F.; m. Joan Cummings, May, 1942 (div. 1962); children— Peter, David, April; m. Josephine Laura Hughes, Sept. 2, 1980 BFA, Williams Coll., 1942, LHD (hon.), 1972; MArch, Harvard U., 1949. Designer I.M. Pei & Ptnrs., N.Y.C., 1950-55; head Ulrich Franzen & Assocs., N.Y.C., 1955—. Vis. critic, prof. Washington U., St. Louis, 1960-61, Yale U., New Haven, 1962-69, 79, 80, 81, Harvard U., Cambridge, Mass., 1961, Columbia U., N.Y.C., 1983, 84; chmn. Archtl. Bd. Rev., Rye, N.Y., 1960-62; mem. Cin. Archtl. Bd. Rev., 1964-66 Prin. works include Alley Theatre, 1968 (AIA honor 1970), Agronomy Bldg., 1970 (AIA honor 1971), Christensen Hall, 1970 (AIA honor 1972), Harlem Sch. of Arts, 1982, Hunter Coll. N.Y.C., 1983, Philip Morris World Hdqrs., 1984, Whitney Mus. Br., 1984, Champion Internat. World Hdqrs. with Whitney Mus. Br., 1985. With U.S. Army, 1943-45. Decorated Bronze Star, Croix de Guerre Avec Palme, Belgium; recipient Bruner prize Inst. Arts and Letters, N.Y.C. Fellow AIA (Thomas Jefferson award); mem. AIA (gold medal N.Y. chpt.), Archtl. League N.Y. (pres. 1968-70, bd. dirs. 1962—), N.Y.C. Landmarks Preservation Commn. (commr. 1992-96), Century Assn. Home: 27 Lamy Dr Santa Fe NM 87506-6907 Office: Ulrich Franzen Architect 530E 76th St Unit 29D New York NY 10021-3561

FRANZETTI, LILLIAN ANGELINA, former automobile dealership owner; b. N.Y.C., Nov. 24, 1925; d. Anthony and Jenny (De Santis) Spilotro; m. Louis Mario Franzetti, Apr. 27, 1946 (dec. Oct. 1986); 1 child, Paul. Clk. typist U.S. Guarantee Ins. Co., N.Y.C., 1943-44, payroll asst. mgr., 1944-46; clk. typist N.J. Div. of Motor Vehicles, Westwood, 1950-54; office mgr. Lakeview Motors, Inc., Woodcliff Lake, N.J., 1954-58, mgr., owner Westwood, 1958-93. Sec. Tri-State Jeep, Eagle Adv. Assn., Tappan, N.Y., 1978-93. Recipient Bus. Mgmt. award, Am. Motors Corp., 1978. Republican. Roman Catholic.

FRANZKE, RICHARD ALBERT, lawyer; b. Lewistown, Mont., Mar. 7, 1935; s. Arthur A. and Senta (Clark) F.; divorced; children: Mark, Jean, Robert. BA in Polit. Sci., Willamette U., 1958, JD with honors, 1960. Bar: Oreg. 1960, U.S. Dist. Ct. Oreg., 1960, U.S. Supreme Ct., 1961. Ptnr. Stoel, Rives, Portland, 1960—. Bd. dirs., chmn. various coms. Assn. Gen. Contractors Am., Portland, 1972-79; mem. com. on legis. affairs Assn. Builders & Contractors, Portland, 1980—. Author: A Study of the Construct by Contract Issue, 1979. Mem. Gov.'s Task Force on Reform of Worker's Compensation, Salem, Oreg., 1980-81; atty. gen.'s com. on Pub. Contracting. Recipient SIR award Assn. Gen. Contractors, 1979, Nat. Winner Outstanding Oral Argument award U.S. Moot Ct., 1959. Mem. ABA (sect. pub. contract law), Oreg. Bar (law sch. liaison, com. on practice and procedure specialization), Multnomah County Bar Assn. Republican. Avocations: antique autos, antique furniture, boating. Home: 14980 SW 133rd Ave Tigard OR 97224-1646 Office: Stoel Rives 900 SW 5th Ave Ste 2300 Portland OR 97204-1229 E-mail: rafranzke@stoel.com.

FRANZMANN, ALBERT WILHELM, wildlife veterinarian, consultant; b. Hamilton, Ohio, July 19, 1930; s. Wilhelm Heinreich and Louise Marie (Schlichter) F.; m. Donna Marie Grueser, Dec. 13, 1953; children: Karl Wilhelm, Louise Ann. DVM, Ohio State U., 1954; PhD, U. Idaho, 1971. Diplomate Am. Coll. Zool. Medicine (hon.). Veterinarian Tiffin (Ohio) Animal Hosp., 1956-59; gen. practice vet. medicine Hamilton, 1959-68; NDEA rsch. fellow U. Idaho, Moscow, 1968-71; wildlife cons. F-2 Wildlife Cons., Moscow, 1971-72; dir. Kenai Moose Rsch. Ctr. Alaska Dept. Fish and Game, Soldotna, 1972-87; cons. AWF Profl. Svcs. Affil. assoc. prof., U. Alaska, Fairbanks, 1972-87; bd. dirs. Internat. Wildlife Vet. Svc. Inc., Laramie, Wyo., Hamilton Tool co., Bd. of Game State of Alaska, Alaska Outdoor Coun., Challenger Learning Ctr. Alaska, N. Am. Moose Found. Contbr. over 100 articles to profl. jours., 15 chpts. to books. Bd. dirs. N.Am. Moose Found. Capt. USAF, 1954-56. Named Disting. Moose Biologist, N.Am. Moose Conf., Prince George, B.C., Can.,1983; recipient Disting. Alumnus award Ohio State U. Coll. Vet. Medicine, Lifetime Conservation award Kenai Penisula chpt. Safari Club Internat., 2001. Mem. AVMA, Am. Assn. Wildlife Veterinarians (pres. 1979-81), Wildlife Disease Assn. (council 1980-81, Emeritus award 1996), Am. Assn. Zoo Veterinarians, Am. Coll. Zool. Medicine (hon. diplomate), The Wildlife Soc. (cert. wildlife biologist, Einarsen award N.W. sect.), Phi Zeta, Xi Sigma Pi. Lodges: Elks. Republican. Avocations: photography, hunting, fishing, travel, exploration. Home and Office: PO Box 666 Soldotna AK 99669-0666 *The anxioms that were important in my life were: prepare myself, follow my instincts, and don't fear failure.*

FRANZONI, DELAINA DAY, special education educator, department chairman; b. Roswell, N.Mex., Jan. 4, 1961; d. Robert H. Day and Elaine French, Billy C. French (Stepfather); 1 child, Darin. BE, MEd, N.Mex State U. Cert. elem. edn. K-8, spl. edn. K-12, sch. adminstrn. Spl. edn. tchr. Valley View Elem., RISD, Roswell, N.Mex., 1983—92, Adolescent Day Treatment Ctr., RISD, Roswell, N.Mex., 1992—93, Roswell H.S., RISD, Roswell, N.Mex., 1993—99, spl. edn. dept. chair, 1999—. Instr. Positive Parenting, Roswell, 1990—90; tutor Roswell Assurance Home, Roswell, N.Mex., 1992—94; sponsor Conflict Mediation, Roswell H.S., Roswell, N.Mex., 1996—99. Mem.: Delta Kappa Gamma (Alpha Theta chpt.). Episcopalian. Avocations: choir, racquetball, needlepoint. Home: 1609 S Washington Roswell NM 88203

FRAPPIA, LINDA ANN, management executive; b. St. Paul, May 14, 1946; d. Orville Keith Ferguson and Marilyn Ardis (Morris) Bidwell; 1 child, Jennifer Frappia Barrett. Grad. high sch., Seattle. Cert. claims adminstr. Claims rep. Fireman's Fund Ins., L.A., 1965-68; adminstrv. asst. to v.p. Employee Benefits Ins., Santa Ana, Calif., 1969-72; claims specialist Indsl. Indemnity Ins., Orange, Calif., 1972-83; claims supr. CNA Ins., Brea, Calif., 1983-85; claims mgr. EBI Ins. Svcs., Tustin, Calif., 1985; v.p. United Med. Specialists, Santa Ana, Calif., 1985-91; chief exec. officer United Ind. Specialists, Santa Ana, 1990—; chief executive officer United Chiropractic Specialists, Santa Ana, 1987—. Instr. Ins. Edn. Assn., Brea, 1988—; speaker Western Ins. Info. Svc., Orange, 1976-83. Mem. Calif. Mfrs. Assn., Pub. Agencies Risk Mgmt. Assn., Calif. Self-Insured Assn., Toastmasters Internat. (v.p. Orange chpt. 1978). Republican. Avocations: sailing, reading, traveling.

FRARY, CHARLES O., III, (CHUCK FRARY), venture capitalist; b. Chgo., Mar. 9, 1931; s. Charles Ossian Frary Jr. and Violet Brunner; m. Doris Lorraine Money, Apr. 18, 1953 (div. July 15, 1979); children: Charles, Lori, Lisa; m. Joyce Ellen McCulley, Apr. 23, 1983; children: Ashley, Kelley. Student, U. Miami, 1950, student, 1953, U. Calif., 1951—52. Cert. internat. financier. Buyer, merchandise mgr. Rich's, Burdines, H&S Pogue, Atlanta, Miami, Cin., 1954—62; founder, pres. Chuck Frary Interiors, Inc., Evansville, Ind., 1962—92; founder, chmn. Concept Devel. Assoc., Evansville, 1986—2002; founder, pres. Dealmaker Capital Corp., Evansville, 1993—2002. Editor: (newspaper) Clark Field News, 1951—54; columnist: Evansville Courier & Press, 1980; contbr. articles to newspapers;, author poetry. Chmn. tourism C. of C., Henderson, Ky., 1969; chmn. fundraising Am. Heart Assn., Evansville, 1971—73; pres. Evansville Civic Theatre, 1971—74; founder Riverview Art Gallery/Supper Club/Dinner Theatre. Tech. sgt. USAF, 1950—54. Named Ky. Col., Commonwealth Ky., 1970. Mem.: Internat. Soc. Financiers (bd. advisors 1994—2003, dir. policy 1995—2002, chmn. stds./ethics 1995—2003), Evansville C. of C., Downtown Evansville Inc, Better Bus. Bur., Arts and Edn. Coun., Venture Club Ind., Petroleum Club. Republican. Methodist. Avocation: golf. Home: PO Box 15245 Evansville IN 47716 Office: Concept Devel Assocs Inc PO Box 15245 Evansville IN 47716

FRASCELLA, DANIEL WILLIAM, JR., scientist; b. New Brunswick, N.J., July 6, 1934; s. Daniel William Sr. and Jenny (Revere) F.; m. Mary Patricia Fitzpatrick, Sept. 2, 1956; children: Daniel III, Nancy, Thomas. BS in Pharmacy magna cum laude, Rutgers U., 1960, MS in Physiology, 1962, PhD in Physiology and Biochem., 1968. Jr. pharmacologist Carter-Wallace Pharm. Cranbury, N.J., 1960-61; rsch. assoc. U. Pa., Phila., 1962-63; rsch. fellow Rutgers U., New Brunswick, 1963-65, asst. prof., 1965-68; rsch. fellow Merck Inst. Med. Rsch., Rahway, N.J., 1968-69; asst. prof. St. John's U., Jamaica, N.Y., 1970-74; assoc. dir. Hoechst-Roussel Pharm., Somerville, N.J., 1974—. Vis. assoc. prof. City U. S.I., N.Y., 1972-74; diabetes cons. Hoechst-Roussel, 1974-96, CME program devel., 1974-82; ind. med. mktg. cons. on diabetes, competitive intelligence; pres. Diabetologics, 1996—, cons. Aon Cons., 2002-. Author: (with others) Secondary Diabetes, 1980. With USN, 1952-55. Recipient H.A.B. Dunning award Am. Pharm. Assn., 1986, Edn. award Calif. Pharm. Assn., 1985. Fellow Royal Soc. of Medicine; mem. AAAS, Am. Diabetes Assn. (profl.), Am. Coll. Clin. Pharmacology, N.Y. Acad. Sci., Sigma Xi. Republican. Roman Catholic. Avocations: early american antiques, books and paper americana, collecting stamps. Home: 1006 Stanton Lebanon Rd Lebanon NJ 08833-3109 Office: Diabetologics 1066 Stanton-LeBanon Rd Lebanon NJ 08833 E-mail: dfrascella@worldnet.att.net.

FRASE, LARRY LYNN, medical oncologist; b. Austin, Tex., June 18, 1957; s. Leland Leo and Mary Dawn (Courtney) F.; m. Debra Lynn Kimble, May 26, 1979; children: Scott, Laura, Kevin. BS summa cum laude, Baylor U., 1979; MD, U. Tex. Southwestern, 1983. Diplomate in internal medicine and med. oncology Am. Bd. Internal Medicine. Chief med. resident, asst. instr. internal medicine U. Tex. Southwestern Med. Sch., Dallas, 1986-87; internist, v.p. Internal Medicine Assn. Longview, Tex., 1988-95; physician Tex. Oncology, P.A., 1997—. Chief of medicine Good Shepherd Med. Ctr., Longview, 1990—92, pres. med. staff, 1993—94. Contbr. articles to med. jours. Pres. Am. Heart Assn., Longview, 1992-93. Student rsch. fellow Am. Gastroenterol. Assn., 1981. Mem. ACP, Tex. Acad. Internal Medicine (bd. dirs. 1999—), Tex. Med. Assn., Am. Soc. Clin. Oncology, Am. Soc. Hematology, Phi Beta Kappa, Alpha Omega Alpha. Republican. Methodist. Avocations: tennis, computers, wine tasting. Home: 104 Deer Run Trail Longview TX 75605 Office: Longview Cancer Ctr 1300 N 4th St Longview TX 75601-5500 E-mail: larry.frase@usoncology.com.

FRASE, LAWRENCE THOMAS, psychologist, science administrator; b. Oak Park, Ill., May 10, 1935; s. Lawrence Michael and Elizabeth Grace (Stybr) F.; m. Concetta Ann Rascati; children: David, Scott. AB, U. Miami, 1959; MS, U. Ill., 1962, PhD, 1965. Asst. prof. U. Mass., Amherst, 1965-68; rschr. Bell Labs, Murray Hill, N.J., 1968-89; head basic skills Nat. Inst. Edn., Washington, 1976-78; exec. dir. rsch. Edn. Testing Svc., Princeton, N.J., 1990-99; rsch. prof. George Mason U., Fairfax, Va., 2000—. Mem. editl. bds. of numerous jours.; author software. Fellow APA, AAAS, Am. Psychol. Soc. Avocation: sailing. Home: 6 Nicole Rd Branford CT 06405-6250 E-mail: lfrase@comcast.net.

FRASER, AILANA MARGARET, mathematician, educator; b. Toronto, Ontario, Canada, Aug. 31, 1971; d. Judith P. and Donald A. S. Fraser. BS, U. of Toronto, 1993; PhD, Stanford U., 1998. Courant instr. NYU, 1998—99; tamarkin asst. prof. Brown U., Providence, 1999—2002; asst. prof. U. of BC, Vancouver, Canada, 2002— . Author: (rsch. article) Annals of Math., Am. Jour. of Math. Recipient U. Faculty award, Natural Scis. and Engring. Rsch. Coun., 2002—; Rsch. Grant in Geometric Analysis, NSF, 1999—2002, Discovery Grant, Natural Scis. and Engring. Rsch. Coun., 2002—. Mem.: Am. Math. Soc. Avocation: windsurfing.

FRASER, CATHERINE ANNE, Canadian chief justice; b. Campbellton, N.B., Can., Aug. 4, 1947; d. Antoine Albert and Anne (Slevinski) Elias; m. Richard C. Fraser, Aug. 17, 1968; children: Andrea, Jonathan. BA, U. Alta., Can., 1969, LLB, 1970; ML, U. London, 1972. Assoc., ptnr. Lucas, Bishop & Fraser, Edmonton, Alta., 1972-89; justice Ct. Queen's Bench Alta., Edmonton, 1989-91, Ct. Appeal Alta., Edmonton, 1991-92, chief justice Alta. and NW Ter., 1992—, chief justice Nunavut, 1999—. Dir. Can. Inst. Adminstrn. Justice, 1991-95. Recipient Tribute to Women award YWCA, 1987. Mem. Can. Bar Assn. Office: Ct Appeal Alta Law Courts Bldg Edmonton AB Canada T5J OR2

FRASER, DAVID WILLIAM, epidemiologist; b. Abington, Pa., May 10, 1944; s. Grant Clippinger and Ella Finlaw (Ayars) F.; m. Barbara Josephine Gaines, June 25, 1966; children: Evan Grant, Leigh Robertson. BA, Haverford (Pa.) Coll., 1965, D.Sc. (hon.), 1991; MD, Harvard U., 1969; Sc.D. (hon.), Moravian Coll., 1987. Diplomate Am. Bd. Internal Medicine. Intern in internal medicine U. Pa. Hosp., Phila., 1969-70, resident, 1970-71, chief resident in internal medicine, 1973-74, fellow in infectious diseases, 1974-75; commd. officer USPHS, 1971-73, 75-82; chief spl. pathogens br., bacterial diseases divsn. Bur. Epidemiology, Center Disease Control, USPHS, Atlanta, 1975-80, med. epidemiologist, asst. dir. bacterial diseases divsn., 1981-82; pres. Swarthmore (Pa.) Coll., 1982-91; head dept. social welfare Secretariat of His Highness Aga Khan, Gouvieux, France, 1991-95; cons. in internat. health and edn., 1996, 2000—; exec. dir. INCLEN, Inc., 1996-2000; rsch. assoc. Asian sect. U. Pa. Mus. Archaeology and Anthropology, 1999—. Adj. prof. medicine U. Pa. Sch. Medicine, 1983-91, adj. prof. epidemiology, 1997—. Author: A Guide to Weft Twining and Related Structures with Interacting Wefts, 1989; editl. bd. Annals of Internal Medicine, 1991-94; contbr. articles to profl. med. and textile jours. Bd. mgrs. Haverford Coll., 1980-83; bd. advisors Educators for Social Responsibility, 1986-91; chmn. bd. Consortium on Financing Higher Edn., 1986-87; trustee The Textile Mus., Washington, 1986—, v.p., 1990-91, 96, pres., 1997—; bd. dirs. Albert G. Oliver Found., 1985-91; sci. adv. bd. Ctr. for Infectious Diseases, 1989-91; mem. immunization practices adv. com. Ctrs. for Disease Control, 1988-92; mem. com. to visit med. sch. and sch. dental medicine Harvard U., 1988-94; costume and textile com. Phila. Mus. Art, 1988-91. Recipient Meritorious Svc. medal USPHS, 1978, John Scott award, 1986; Clementine Cope fellow Haverford Coll., 1965, Daland fellow Am. Philos. Soc., 1974 Fellow ACP (Richard and Hinda Rosenthal Found. award 1979), Infectious Diseases Soc. Am., Am. Coll. Epidemiology; mem. Am. Epidemiol. Soc., Aesculapian Club, Founders Club (Haverford Coll.) Home and Office: 907 N Pennsylvania Ave Yardley PA 19067-2023

FRASER, DONALD C. engineering executive, educator; b. N.Y.C., Apr. 20, 1941; s. Donald Fraser and Anna Thurston; children: Lynn, Eric. S.B., MIT, Cambridge, 1962, MS, 1963, Sc.D., 1967. Tech. staff MIT Instrumentation Lab., Cambridge, Mass., 1967-69; divsn. leader C.S. Draper Lab., Inc., Cambridge, 1969-81, v.p. tech. ops., 1981-88, exec. v.p., 1988-90; dep. dir. operational test and evaluation Office Sec. Def., Washington, 1990-91; prin. deputy under sec. def. for acquisition Office Sec. of Def., Washington, 1991-93; vis. prof. Stanford U., Calif., 1970-71; lectr. MIT Aero/Astro Dept., Cambridge, 1972-91; founder, dir. Ctr. Photonics prof. engring. and physics Boston U., 1993—. Active Air Force Studies Bd. Com. Advanced Avionics, 1979-83; chmn. Air Force Studies Bd. Com. Fault Isolation, 1982-85; active USAF Aero Systems Divsn. Adv. Group, 1984-90; mem. NASA Adv. Coun. Space Systems and Tech. Adv. Com., 1982-91, U.S. Army Sci. Bd., 1987-90, NRC Aeronautics and Space Engring. Bd., 1995-2001; mem. adv. coun. NASA, 2002—; bd. dirs. DRS Techs., Aurora Flight Scis., Photo Search, PhotoDetection Sys., Improvica, Solx, Ctr. for Tech. Commercialization. Assoc. editor AIAA Jour. Spacecraft and Rockets, 1970-72, editor-in-chief, 1974-78; founder, editor-in-chief AIAA Jour. Guidance, Control and Dynamics, 1977-91. Recipient Def. Disting. Svc. medal. Fellow AAAS, AIAA (bd. dirs. New Eng. sect. 1973-75, publs. com. 1973-74); mem. NAE, Tau Beta Pi, Sigma Xi, Sigma Gamma Tau. Avocations: flying, hiking, skiing, bicycling.

FRASER, DONALD MACKAY, former mayor, former congressman, educator; b. Mpls., Feb. 20, 1924; s. Everett and Lois (MacKay) F.; m. Arvonne Skelton, June 30, 1950; children: Thomas Skelton, Mary MacKay, John DuFrene, Lois MacKay (dec.), Anne T. (dec.), Jean Skelton. BA cum laude, U. Minn., 1944, LLB, 1948. Bar: Minn. 1948. Ptnr. Lindquist, Fraser & Magnuson (and predecessors), 1948-62; mem. Minn. State senator, 1954-62; sec. Senate Liberal Caucus, 1955-62; mem. 88th-95th Congresses from 5th Dist. Minn., mem. fgn. affairs com., chmn. subcom. on internat. orgn., mem. budget com.; mayor City of Mpls., 1980-93; mem. study and rev. com. Dem. Caucus; mem. Commn. on Role and Future Presdl. Primaries, 1976; adj. prof. law and pub. affairs U. Minn., Mpls. Vice chmn., dir. Mpls. Citizens Com. on Pub. Edn., 1950-54; Sec. Minn. del. Democratic Nat. Conv., 1960; chmn. Minn. Citizens for Kennedy, 1960; mem. platform com. Dem. Nat. Conv., 1964, mem. rules com., 1972, 76; vice chmn. Com. Dem. Selection Presdl. Nominees, 1968; chmn. Democratic Study Group Congress, 1969-71, Commn. on Party Structure and Del. Selection Dem. Party, 1971-72; 1st Am. co-chmn. Anglo-Am. Parliamentary Conf. on Africa, 1964; mem. U.S. del. 7th spl. session and 30th session UN Gen. Assembly, 1975; Congl. adviser to U.S. del. to UN Conf. on Disarmament, 1967-73, to U.S. del. to 3d Law of Sea Conf., 1972, to UN Commn. on Human Rights, 1974; cons. on families HUD, 1994. Chair health com. U.S. Conf. Mayors; bd. dirs. Mpls. United Way, 1986-93, Twin Cities Rise!, 1994—, Connect/U.S.-Russia, 1994—, Greater Mpls. Coun. Chs., 2000—; co-chair Ctr. for Internat. Policy, 1976-94, Early Care and Edn. Fin. Commn., 1999—; co-founder, pres. Dem. Farmer-Labor Edn. Found.; initiated numerous youth programs such as Transitional Work Internship Program, Youth Work Internship Program, Neighborhood Early Learning Ctrs., Youth Coordinating Bd., Youth Trust. Lt. (J.G.) USNR, 1944-46. Recipient 1st Minn. Internat. Human Rights award, 1985, Disting. Svc. award Mpls. United Way, 1992; fellow Kennedy Sch., spring 1994. Mem. Mpls. Fgn. Policy Assn. (pres. 1952-53), Citizens League Greater Mpls. (sec. 1951-54), Minn. Bar Assn., Hennepin County Bar Assn., Ams. for Dem. Action (nat. chmn. 1973-76), Dem. Conf. (nat. chmn. 1976-78), U. Minn. Law Alumni Assn. (dir. 1958-61), Univ. Dist. Improvement Assn. (pres. 1950-52), Nat. League of Cities (2d v.p. 1991, 1st v.p. 1992, pres. 1993), Minn. Advocates for Human Rights (co-founder, bd. dirs. 1983-92, 2000—), League of Minn. Cities (bd. dirs. 1991-93).—. Democrat.

FRASER, FREDERICK EWART, art educator; b. Dec. 10, 1939; m. Mary Louise Washburn Fraser, Aug. 8, 1965; children: Carol Louise, Paul Frederick. AA, Boise Jr. Coll., 1960; BS in Edn., U. Idaho, 1967; MS, U. Oreg., 1970. Elem. tchr. Emmett (Idaho) Pub. Schs., 1961-62, Nampa (Idaho) Pub. Schs., 1962-66, Boise (Idaho) Pub. Schs., 1967-69; elem. art tchr. Eugene (Oreg.) Pub. Schs., 1969-70; elem. art specialist Richland (Wash.) Pub. Schs., 1970-98, chmn. art dept., 1983-84; prof. painter and photographer, 1999—. Adj. prof. Ea. Wash. State U., Cheney, 1980-83; adj. instr. art Columbia Basin Coll., Pasco, Wash., 1999-2002; workshop presenter Wash. Art Edn. Assn., 2000; pvt. art instr., 2000-; guest lectr. Wash. State U., Tri-Cities. Prin. works include 2-D sculpture American Me, 1994; prints and paintings in numerous pvt. collections. Campaign worker Richland Dem. Com., 1972. Grantee Ednl. Dist. Svc. No. 123, Pasco, 1978, computer graphics in elem. art grantee Richland Pub. Schs., 1991. Mem. NEA, Nat. Art Edn. Assn. (workshop presenter 1997), Wash. Art Edn. Assn. (chmn. Pasco 1972, state elem. art educator of yr. award 1995), Columbia Basin Model A Ford Club, Three Rivers Model T Ford Club. Methodist. Avocations: art, photography, antique auto restorer.

FRASER, GALE WILLIAM, II, civil engineer; b. Chgo., Sept. 14, 1954; s. Gale William and Marilyn (Peeken) F.; m. Brenda Jean Trom, Sept. 6, 1974; children: Gale William III, James, Michael. BSCE, N.D. State U., 1977. Registered profl. engr., N.D., Minn., Nev. Staff engr. Houston Engring., Inc., Fargo, N.D., 1977-86; planning engr. City of Las Vegas, Nev., 1986-88; asst. gen. mgr. Clark County Regional Flood Control Dist., Las Vegas, 1988-93, gen. mgr., 1993—. Vice chmn. all hazards mitigation adv. com. State of Nev., Carson City, 1999—. Mem. NSPE (Young Engr. of Yr., So. Nev. chpt. 1990), ASCE, Am. Pub. Works Assn., Nat. Assn. Flood and Stormwater Agys. (co-chair flood control com. 1998—). Lutheran. Avocations: baseball, skiing, camping. Office: Clark County Reg Flood Control Dist 600 S Grand Central Pkwy Las Vegas NV 89106-4511 Fax: 702-455-3870. E-mail: galerfc@co.clark.nv.us., GFraser@ccrfcd.org.

FRASER, JOHN WAYNE, insurance executive, consultant, underwriter; b. Ashland, Ala., Jan. 19, 1944; s. Elliott Nathaniel and Maurice Jennette (Glenn) F.; m. Diana Louise Renn, Jan. 20, 1963; children: Christine Celeste, Sean Elliott. AA in Bus. Adminstrn., St. Petersburg Jr. Coll., 1969; BA with honors, U. South Fla., 1974. Dir. mfg. svcs. Milton Roy Co., St. Petersburg, Fla., 1965-74; sales rep. Fla. Forms Co., Tampa, 1975-76, Graphic Bus. Systems, St. Petersburg, 1976-79; dist. mgr. Blue Cross/Blue Shield Fla., St. Petersburg, 1979-86; sr. v.p. Wittner Cos., 1986-98; pres. Advocate Cons., Inc., Clearwater, Fla., 1998—2003; v.p. Wallace, Welch and Willingham, Inc., 2003—. Mem. editl. bd., monthly contbr. COBRA Advisory, 1997-02. Former mem. Internat. Found. Employee Benefit Welfare Plans; pres. Benefit One of Am., Inc., 1997-98. With U.S. Army, 1962. Mem. Fla. West Coast Employee Benefit Coun. (bd. dirs. 1994—, pres. 2002-03), Nat. Assn. Health Underwriters (trustee West Coast chpt. 1988-98, pres. 1992-93, Tampa Bay Pension Coun. 1999—), Fla. Assn. Health Underwriters (bd. dirs. 1992-93, 1st v.p. 1993-94, pres. 1994-95), Cen. Pinellas Jaycees (treas. 1975, v.p. 1976), Suncoast Investors Club (pres. 1996-), U. South Fla. Alumni Assn. Unitarian-Universalist. Avocations: photography, golf. Office: 300 First Ave So Saint Petersburg FL 33701 E-mail: jfraser2@tampabay.rr.com.

FRASER, MALCOLM CAVANAGH, mayor; b. Englewood, N.J., Nov. 26, 1929; s. Stanley and Helen L. (Cavanagh) F.; m. Joan Marie Iversen, May 1, 1954; children: Gordon, David, Stephen, Janice, Bruce, Andrew. Mech. Engr., Stevens Inst. of Technology, Hoboken, N.J., 1951, Alexander Hamilton Inst., N.Y.C., 1958. Mktg. engr. Ingersoll-Rand Co., N.Y.C., 1951-60, internat. coord., 1960-66, mktg. mgr., sml. process compressors Painted Post, N.Y., 1967-72, mgr. govt. opers., 1972-75, gen. mgr. European opers. Rijswijk, Netherlands, 1975-80, gen. mgr. for oil industry Houston, 1980-82; internat. mgr. IR Compression Svcs., Houston, 1983-86; gas engine product mgr. Dresser-Rand Co., Painted Post, 1986-90; mayor Borough of Cape May Point, N.J., 1992—. Author: (book) The Charmed Circle, 1986. Pres. YMCA Men's Svc. Club, Westfield, N.J., 1967; residential co-chair United Fund, Westfield, 1967; treas. troop com. Boy Scouts Am., Corning, N.Y., 1968-72; ch. vestryman, Corning, 1971-74; bd. dirs. YMCA, Corning, 1967-75, pres. 1970-73; mem. Am. Sch. Bd. The Hague, Netherlands, 1978-80; bd. dirs. Taxpayers Assn., Cape May Point, 1988-92, pres. 1990-92; trustee Hist. St. Peters-by-theSea Ch., Cape May Point, 1990—, others. Cpl. U.S. Army, 1954-56. Recipient Excellence in Cmty. Svc. award DAR, Cape May County, 1997, Outstanding Leadership award N.J. Mayor's Assn., Dunellen, 1998, Lifetime Achievement award Cape May Point Taxpayers Assn., 2001, award est. in his name N.J. Rural Water Assn., Tuckerton, N.J., 1999. Mem. ASME, N.J. Rural Water Assn. (pres. 1995-98, bd. dirs. 1994-2000), N.J. State League of Municipalities (bd. dirs. 1995—), Cape May County League of Municipalities (v.p., pres. 1996-98), N.J. Conf. Mayors (bd. dirs. 2001—). Episcopalian. Avocations: baseball, history. Home: PO Box 323 Cape May Point NJ 08212-0323 Office: Borough of Cape May Point PO Box 490 215 Lighthouse Ave Cape May Point NJ 08212

FRASER, PAMELA, artist; b. Smyrna, Tenn., 1965; BFA, Sch. Visual Arts, N.Y.C., 1988; MFA, UCLA, 1992. One-woman shows include Casey Kaplan, N.Y.C., 1998, 2000, exhibited in group shows at Lotus Motel, Inglewood, Calif., 1995, White Columns, N.Y.C., 1996, Exit Art, 1999, Elga Wimmer Gallery, 1999, Pudewil, Berlin, 2000, Wurtembergischer, Stuttgart, 2000, Dundee Ctr. of Contemporary Art, Scotland, 2000, others. Recipient Louis Comfort Tiffany award, 1997; Skowhegan Sch. Painting and Sculpture fellow, 1988. Office: care Casey Kaplan Gallery 416 W 14th St New York NY 10014-1031 Fax: 212-645-7335..

FRASER, ROBERT BURCHMORE, lawyer; b. Newton, Mass., Aug. 13, 1928; s. Alfred Alexander and Helen Louise (Comiskey) F.; m. Mary-Ann Jackson, Sept. 7, 1963; children: Melanie, Jennifer Amy, Matthew John. AB, Harvard U., 1949, LLB, 1952, LLM, 1955. Bar: Mass. Assoc. Goodwin Procter LLP, Boston, 1955-63, ptnr., 1964-97, chmn., 1984-97. Spl. advisor to Mayor of Boston and Boston Police Commr., 1997-2000; bd. dirs. Investors Fin. Svcs. and Investors Bank and Trust Co., 1996—. Mem. Mass. Gov.'s Jud. Nominating Commn., 1979-82; mem. adv. com. Mass. Commr. Revenue, 1979-82; chmn. adv. com. Mass. Housing Fin. Agy, 1979-83; chmn. Boston Pub. Health Commn., 1996-97; chmn. Vol. Lawyers for Arts of Mass., 1990-97; bd. dirs. Greater Boston YMCA, 1981-87, Greater Boston Arts Fund, 1987—, Boston Pvt. Industry Coun., 1988-99, Citywide Ednl. Coalition, 1988-2000, Boston Against Drugs, 1988-93, chmn. 1990-93, Boston Ptnrs. in Edn., 1989-99, Am. Student Assistance Corp., 1989-97, Greater Boston C. of C., 1993—, Jobs for Mass., 1993-98, Boston Pub. Libr. Found., 1992-2000, Boston Mgmt. Consortium, 1994-2001, NCCJ, 1994-2002, chmn. 1997-99, Mass. Bus. Alliance Edn., 1995—, Ctr. for Collaborative Edn., 1998-99, The Med. Found., 1995-99, MassInc., 1996—; trustee New Eng. Conservatory Music, 1987-2001, Boston Plan for Excellence in Pub. Schs., 1987-99, chmn., 1992-95, Boston Adult

Literacy Fund, 1989-96; trustee Lesley Coll., 1992-96; overseer Boston Lyric Opera, 1994-99; chmn. Boston Music Edn. Collaborative, 1999-2001; chmn. Arts & Bus. Coun. Greater Boston, 2000—. Mem. ABA, Mass. Bar Assn., Boston Bar Assn., Harvard Mus. Assn. Harvard Club (Boston.). Home: 90 Allandale St Jamaica Plain MA 02130-3442 Office: Goodwin Procter Exchange Pl Boston MA 02109-2803 Personal E-mail: fraserrb@comcast.net.

FRASER, RUSSELL ALFRED, author, educator; b. Elizabeth, N.J., May 31, 1927; s. Roger John and Mary Louise (Narden) F.; m. Eleanor Jane Phillips, May 31, 1947 (div. 1979); children— Karen Mildred, Alexander Varennes; m. Mary Nelva Zwiep, July 5, 1980. AB, Dartmouth Coll., 1947; MA, Harvard U., 1949, PhD, 1950. Instr. English UCLA, 1950; postgrad. study, Eng., 1951-52; instr., then asst. prof. English Duke U., 1952-56; asst. prof., then assoc. prof. English Princeton U., 1956-65, assoc. dean Grad. Sch., 1962-65; prof., chmn. English Vanderbilt U., Nashville, 1965-68; prof. English U. Mich., Ann Arbor, 1968—, chmn. dept., 1968-73, Austin Warren prof., 1983-95, prof. emeritus, 1995—. Resident Inst. for Advanced Study, Princeton U., 1976 Author: Shakespeare's Poetics, 1962, The War Against Poetry, 1970, An Essential Shakespeare, 1972, The Dark Ages and the Age of Gold, 1973, The Language of Adam, 1977, A Mingled Yarn The Life of R.P. Blackmur, 1982, The Three Romes, 1985, Young Shakespeare, 1988, Shakespeare, The Later Years, 1992, Singing Masters Poets In English 1500 To The Present, 1999; editor: The Court of Venus, 1955, The Court of Virtue, 1961, King Lear, 1963, Oscar Wilde, 1969, (with others) Drama of the English Renaissance, 2 vols, 1976; All's Well That Ends Well, 1985 Served with USNR, 1944-46. Grantee Am. Council Learned Socs., 1951-52, 60, 68; Grantee Am. Philos. Soc., 1951-52, 60, 68; Grantee Dartmouth, 1951-52; jr. fellow Council Humanities, Princeton, 1960; NSF grantee, 1964-67; Guggenheim fellow Rome, 1973-74; Rockefeller resident scholar Bellagio, 1975; sr. Fulbright-Hays scholar, 1975; Nat. Endowment Humanities fellow, 1978-79 Mem. Caledonian Soc. of Hawaii, Harvard Club of Mich.,Navy League. E-mail: rafraser@umich.edu.

FRASER, WILLIAM NEIL, government official, retired; b. Vancouver, B.C., Can., May 25, 1932; s. James Herbert and Katherine Baikie (Grieve) F.; m. Marie Helm, Dec. 19, 1986; children by previous marriage: Gordon, Alan, Katherine, Ian. Student, Banff Sch. Advanced Mgmt., 1967. Product mgr. Masonry, Deeks-McBride Ltd., Vancouver, 1952-68; gen. mgr. Masonry Contractors Assn. B.C., Vancouver, 1968-71; exec. dir. Can. Masonry Contractors Assn., Toronto, 1971-87; mem. Ont. Labour Rels. Bd., 1988-98, ret., 1999. With Can. Navy Res., 1953-57. Mem.: Royal Can. Mil. Inst., Inst. Assn. Execs. (past pres. Toronto chpt.), Capt. Olde 78th Fraser Highlanders, Grant of Arms Can. Heraldic Authority, Heraldry Soc. of Scotland, Scottish Studies Found. (patron, gov.), Clan Fraser Soc. Can. (chmn.), St. Andrew's Soc. of Toronto, Heraldry Soc. Can., Monarchist League of Can., Clans and Scottish Socs. of Can. (past pres.), Vancouver Golf Club. Home: 71 Charles St E Apt 1101 Toronto ON Canada M4Y 2T3 E-mail: neil.fraser@clanfraser.ca.

FRASIER, RALPH KENNEDY, lawyer, banker; b. Winston-Salem, N.C., Sept. 16, 1938; s. LeRoy Benjamin and Kathryn O. (Kennedy) F.; m. Jeannine Quick, Aug. 1981; children: Karen D. Frasier Alston, Gail S. Frasier Cox, Ralph Kennedy Jr., Keith Lowery, Marie Kennedy, Rochelle Doar. BS, N.C. Cen. U., Durham, 1963, JD, 1965. Bar: N.C. 1965, Ohio 1976. With Wachovia Bank and Trust Co., N.A., Winston-Salem, N.C., 1965-70, v.p., counsel, 1969-70; asst. counsel, v.p. parent co. Wachovia Corp., 1970-75; v.p., gen. counsel Huntington Nat. Bank, Columbus, Ohio, 1975-76, sr. v.p., 1976-83, sec., 1981-98, exec. v.p., 1983-98, cashier, 1983-98. V.p. Huntington Bancshares Inc., 1976-86, gen. counsel, 1976-98, sec., 1981-98; sec., dir. Huntington Mortgage Co., Huntington State Bank, Huntington Leasing Co., Huntington Bancshares Fin. Corp., Huntington Investment Mgmt. Co., Huntington Nat. Life Ins. Co., Huntington Co., 1976-88; v.p., asst. sec. Huntington Bank N.E. Ohio, 1982-84; asst. sec. Huntington Bancshares Ky., 1985-97; sec. Huntington Trust Co., N.A., 1987-97, Huntington Bancshares Ind., Inc., 1986-97, Huntington Fin. Services Co., 1987-98; dir. The Huntington Nat. Bank, Columbus, Ohio, 1998—; of counsel Porter Wright Morris & Arthur LLP, Columbus, 1998—; trustee OCLC Online Computer Libr. Ctr., Inc., Dublin, Ohio, 1999—, mem. fin. com., 2000—, mem. audit com., 2000—, chair 2002—, exec. com., 2002—, pers. and compensation com., 2002-03; dir. ADATOM.COM, Inc., Milpitas, Calif., 1999-2001, mem. compensation com., 1999-2001, chair audit com., 1999-2001. Bd. dirs. Family Svcs. Winston-Salem, 1966-74, sec., 1966-71, 74, v.p., 1974; chmn. Winston-Salem Transit Authority, 1974-75; bd. dirs. Rsch. for Advancement of Personalities, 1968-71, Winston-Salem Citizens for Fair Housing, 1970-74, N.C. United Community Svcs., 1970-74; treas. Forsyth County (N.C.) Citizens Com. Adequate Justice Bldg., 1968; trustee Appalachian State U., Boone, N.C., 1973-83, endowment fund, 1973-83, Columbus Drug Edn. and Prevention Fund, Inc., 1989-92; trustee, vice chmn. employment and Edn. Commn. Franklin County, 1982-85; mem. Winston-Salem Forsyth County Sch. Bd. Adv. Coun., 1973-74, Atty. Gen's Ohio Task Force Minorities in Bus., 1977-78; bd. dirs. Inroads Columbus, Inc., 1986-95, Greater Columbus Arts Coun., 1986-94, Columbus Urban League Inc., 1987-94, vice chmn., 1990-94; trustee Riverside Meth. Hosp. Found., 1989-90, Grant Med. Ctr., 1990-95, Grant/Riverside Meth. Hosps., 1995-97; trustee Ohio Health Corp., 1997—, treas., chair Fin./Audit Com., 2001—, exec. com., 2002—; dir. Cmty. Mutual Ins. Co., 1989-92, mem. audit com., 1989-92; trustee N.C. Ctrl. U., Durham, N.C., 1993-2001, vice-chmn., 1993-94, chmn. 1995, chair ednl. planning and acad. affairs com., 1995-98, audit, devel. and personnel coms., 1998-2001, chair audit com., 1999-2001; mem. Ohio Bd. Regents, 1987-96, vice-chmn., 1993-95, chmn., 1995-96; trustee Nat. Jud. Coll., Reno, Nevada, 1996-2002, fin. and audit com., 1997-2002 treas., chair, 1999-2002, Columbus Bar Found., 1998— (fellows com. 1998—, grants com., 1998—); AEFC Pension Adminstrn. Com. defined benefit plan of the ABA, Am. Bar Endowment, Am. Bar Found., and Nat. Jud. Coll., Chgo, Ill., 1998-2002. With AUS, 1958-64. Fellow Ohio Bar Found. (life); mem. ABA, Nat. Bar Assn., Ohio Bar Assn., Columbus Bar Assn. Office: Porter Wright Morris & Arthur LLP 41 S High St Ste 3100 Columbus OH 43215-6194 E-mail: rfrasier@porterwright.com., rfrasier@columbus.rr.com.

FRASK, ROBIN ANN KOSTANESKY, secondary school educator; b. Hazleton, Pa., Apr. 27, 1971; d. John F. and Karen A. (Brandmier) Kostanesky; m. Randy Michael Frask, July 2, 1999; children: Gabrielle, Anthony. BS in Edn., Mansfield U., 1993; MEd, Wilkes U., 1999. Substitute tchr. Weatherly (Pa.) Area Sch. Dist., 1994-96, Hazleton (Pa.) Area Sch. Dist., 1994-96, sci. tchr., 1996—. Mem. NEA, Pa. State Edn. Assn. Home: 345 Shingle Mill Dr Drums PA 18222-1216 E-mail: robinfrask@yahoo.com., fraskr@hasd.k12.pa.us.

FRASSANITO, WILLIAM ALLEN, historian, consultant, writer; b. N.Y.C., Sept. 28, 1946; s. Americo Anthony and Edythe (Totten) F. BA, Gettysburg Coll., 1968; MA, SUNY, Oneonta, 1969. Lic. battlefield guide Gettysburg (Pa.) Nat. Mil. Park, 1966-68; apprentice jeweler Frassanito Bros. Jewelers, Huntington, N.Y., 1972-75; self-employed historian Gettysburg, 1975—. Cons. Nat. Hist. Soc., 1981-86, Time-Life Books, 1983-87, Greystone Comms., North Hollywood, Calif., 1993-2000; adviser Gettysburg Hist. Archtl. Rev. Bd., 1985-88; mem. Gettysburg Borough Planning Commn., 1988-93; participant in testimony Congl. hearing on Nat. Park Svc., Washington, 1994. Author: Gettysburg: A Journey in Time, 1975 (award Photographic Hist. Soc. N.Y. 1976), Antietam, 1978 (Founders award Mus. Confederacy 1979), Grant and Lee, 1983, The Gettysburg Bicentennial Album, 1987, Early Photography at Gettysburg, 1995, Gettysburg: Then & Now, 1996, The Gettysburg Then & Now Companion, 1997. 1st lt. U.S. Army, 1969-71, Vietnam. Decorated Bronze Star; recipient Disting. Alumni award Gettysburg Coll., 1984. Mem. Gettysburg Battlefield Preservation Assn. (Lincoln award 1997, treas., v.p. 1982-02, bd. dirs.) Adams County Hist. Soc. (bd. dirs. 1987-2000). Office: 333 Baltimore St Gettysburg PA 17325

FRASSINELLI, GUIDO JOSEPH, retired aerospace engineer; b. Summit Hill, Pa., Dec. 4, 1927; s. Joseph and Maria (Grosso) F.; m. Antoinette Pauline Clemente, Sept. 26, 1953; children: Lisa, Erica, Laura, Joanne, Mark. BS, MS, MIT, 1949; MBA, Harvard U., 1956. Treas. AviDyne Rsch., Inc., Burlington, Mass., 1958-64; asst. gen. mgr. Kaman AviDyne divsn. Kaman Scis., Burlington, 1964-66; asst. dir. strategic planning N. Am. ACFT OPNS, Rockwell Internat., L.A., 1966-71; from mgr. program planning to project mgr. advanced programs Rockwell Space Sys. Divsn., Downey, Calif., 1970-94; ret. Rockwell Space Systems Div., Downey, 1994. Mem. Town Hall of Calif., L.A., 1970—; treas. Ecology Devel. and Implementation Commitment Team Found., Huntington Beach, Calif., 1971-75; founding com. mem. St. John Fisher Parish Coun., Rancho Palos Verdes, Calif., 1978-85. Recipient Tech. Utilization award, NASA, 1971, Astronaut Personal Achievement award, 1985. Fellow AIAA (assoc.; tech. com. on econs. 1983-87, exec. com. L.A. sect. 1987-91, 94-98), Inst. for Advancement of Engrng.; mem. Sigma Xi, Tau Beta Pi. Roman Catholic. Achievements include determination of aircraft damage limits and atomic-weapon-delivery capabilities of aircraft; development of cost models to account for advances in engineering state of art, of cost prioritization techniques for space shuttle improvements, of software to produce business plans. Home: 29521 Quailwood Dr Rancho Palos Verdes CA 90275

FRATANTONI, JOSEPH CHARLES, medical researcher, hematologist, biotechnology executive; b. Bklyn., May 14, 1938; s. Joseph Edward and Providence Adeline (Bellante) F.; m. Pauline F. Jones, Jan. 30, 1965; children: David, Michael, Joan. BS in Chemistry egregia cum laude, Fordham Coll., 1959; MA in Chemistry, Harvard U., 1961; MD, Cornell U., 1965. Diplomate Am. Bd. Internal Medicine. Rsch. assoc. Sloan-Kettering Inst., N.Y.C., 1960-61; fellow dept. pharmacology Cornell U., 1961-64; intern, resident in medicine Cornell-N.Y. Hosp., 1965-67; staff assoc. Nat. Inst. Arthritis and Metabolic Diseases NIH, 1967-69; resident in medicine Cornell-N.Y. Hosp., 1969-70, fellow in hematology dept. medicine, 1970-71; instr. in medicine Cornell U., 1970-71; asst. prof. medicine, dir. Coagulation Lab. Georgetown U., 1971-72, from clin. asst. to assoc. prof. medicine and pharmacology, 1972-85; sr. staff physician hematology svc. Clin. Ctr. NIH, 1972-74; thrombosis program dir. Nat. Heart, Lung and Blood Inst., 1974-75, chief blood diseases br., 1975-77, chief blood resources br., 1977-78; chief lab. of cellular hematology Ctr. for Biologics Evaluation and Rsch., FDA, 1978-92; from assoc. prof. to clin. prof. medicine Uniformed Svcs. U., 1976-96; dir. divsn. hematology FDA, 1992-96; v.p. biologics C.L. McIntosh and Assocs., Rockville, Md., 1996-99; v.p. med. affairs, clin. devel. Max Cyte Inc., Rockville, Md., 1999—. Presenter in field. Patentee in non-invasive optical assessment of platelet viability, measurement of platelet aggregation using a microplate reader; contbr. over 100 articles to profl. jours. Served to capt. USPHS, 1967-96, ret. Recipient Spl. Citation, FDA Commr., 1988, Citation, USPHS, 1989, Meritorious Svc. medal USPHS, 1991. Fellow ACP; mem. Internat. Soc. Cellular Therapy, Am. Soc. Hematology, Am. Assn. Blood Banks (Disting. Svc. award 1998), Sigma Xi, Alpha Omega Alpha. Achievements include rsch. in hemostasis, platelet function and blood substitutes. Home: 9412 Overlea Dr Rockville MD 20850-3736 Office: MaxCyte Inc 9640 Medical Ctr Dr Rockville MD 20850

FRATESCHI, LAWRENCE JAN, economist, statistician, educator; b. Chgo., Oct. 7, 1952; s. Lawrence and Olga (Los) F. BS in Math. and Psychology, U. Ill., Chgo., 1975, MA in Econs., 1979, MS Pub. Health in Biostats. and Epidemiology, 1990, PhD in Econs., 1992. Teaching asst. dept. math, lectr. dept. info. and decision scis. U. Ill., Chgo., 1978-80, rsch. assoc. epidemiology and biostatistics Sch. Pub. Health, 1989-90; statistician Argonne (Ill.) Nat. Labs., 1980-81; asst. prof. econs. and stats. Coll. of DuPage, Glen Ellyn, Ill., 1981-86, assoc. prof., 1986-90, prof. econs., stats., 1990—; rsch. prof. epidemiology and biostats. Sch. Pub. Health U. Ill., Chgo., Ill., 1993—. Contbr. articles to profl. publs. Mem. Am. Econ. Assn., Am. Statis. Assn., Am. Pub. Health Assn., Soc. Epidemiologic Rsch., Midwest Econs. Assn., Ill. Econs. Assn., Ill. Pub. Health Assn., Phi Eta Sigma, Phi Kappa Phi, Delta Omega. Office: Coll of DuPage 425 22nd St Glen Ellyn IL 60137-6784 E-mail: fratesch@cdnet.cod.edu.

FRATT, DOROTHY, artist; b. Washington, Aug. 10, 1923; d. Hugh and Martha (Holt) Miller; m. Nicholas Diller Fratt, Sept. 4, 1943 (div. 1965); children: Nicholas, Hugh, Gregory, Peter; m. Curtis Calvin Cooper, Nov. 3, 1972. Studied with Nicolai Cikovsky, 1940; student, Mt. Vernon Coll., 1940-42, Am. U., 1942-43, Phillips Collection Art Sch., 1942-43; studied with Karl Knaths, 1943. Mem. commissioning panel for NEA grant, Scottsdale, Ariz., 1971; mem. adv. bd. U. Art Mus. Ariz. State U., Tempe, 1989-95. Exhibited at UN Club Gallery, 1948, Desert Art Gallery, Scottsdale, Ariz., 1959, Tucson Art Ctr., 1964, Phoenix Art Mus., 1964, 75, Riva Yares Gallery, Scottsdale, 1965, 82, 89, 94, 95, 2000, Calif. Legion Honor, San Francisco, 1965, Mickelson Gallery, Washington, 1967, State-Wide Touring Exhibit, 1974, Scottsdale Ctr. for Arts, 1980, Carson-Sapiro Gallery, Denver, 1981, Thomas Beabor Gallery, La Jolla, Calif., 1985, U. Ariz. Gallery, Tucson, 1986; represented in pub. collections at Phoenix Art Mus., Tucson Mus., Ariz. State Mus., Tempe, Mus. Fine Arts, Santa Fe, Mus. No. Ariz., Flagstaff; represented in various corp. collections; contbr. to Archives of Am. Art, 1996. Mem. Fine Arts Commn., Phoenix, 1965-71; mem. Sotheby Symposium Quality in Art, N.Y.C., 1990. Recipient Gov.'s Art award, 2000. Home: 6010 E Cholla Ln Scottsdale AZ 85253-6902 Office: Riva Yares Gallery 3625 Bishop Ln Scottsdale AZ 85251 also: 123 Grant Ave Santa Fe NM 87501

FRATTI, MARIO, playwright, educator; b. L'Aquila, Italy, July 5, 1927; came to U.S., 1963, naturalized, 1974; s. Leone and Palmira (Silvi) F.; children: Mirko, Barbara, Valentina. PhD, Ca Foscari U., 1951. Tchr., 1964-65; mem. faculty Columbia U., 1965-66; mem. Adelphi Coll., 1964-65; mem. faculty Hofstra U., 1973-74; prof. lit. New Sch. Hunter Coll., N.Y.C., 1967—. Drama critic Drama critic: Paese, 1963—, Progresso, 1963—, Ridotto, 1963—, Ora Zero, 1963—; playwright: Cage-Suicide, 1964, Academy-Return, 1967, Mafia, 1971, Races, 1972, Bridge, 1971, Eleven Plays in Spanish, 1977, Refrigerators, 1977; author: Eleonora Duse-Victim, 1981, Nine, 1982 (Tony), Biography of Fratti, 1982, A.I.D.S., 1987, V.C.R., 1988, (mus.) Encounter, 1989, Family, 1990, Friends, 1991, Lovers, 1992, Leningrad Euthanasia, 1993, Holy Father, 1994, Sister, 1995, Sacrifices, 1996, Jurors, 1997, also 8 plays in Russian, 1997, 4 plays in Japanese, 1997, 7 minidramas in Spanish, 1998, 4 plays in Spanish, 1999, Candida and Her Friends, 2000, Erotic Adventures in Venice, 2002. Served to lt. Italian Army, 1951-53. Recipient awards for plays and musicals Mem. Drama Desk, Am. Theatre Critics, Outer Critics Circle (v.p.) Democrat. Home: 145 W 55th St Apt 15D New York NY 10019-5355

FRATZSCHER, OLIVER, economist; b. Bonn, Germany, June 30, 1966; s. Guenther and Marion Fratzscher; m. Jianping Zhou; 1 child, Anne-Sophie. PhD, Harvard U., 1994; MSc, U. Montreal, Can., 1990; BSc, U. Karlsruhe, Germany, 1989. Chief economist ABN Amro Bank, London, 1997—99; chief economist (EMA) Deutsche Bank, London, 1996—97; economist International Monetary Fund, Washington, 1994—96; rsch. fellow Brookings Instn., Washington, 1993—94; advisor Coun. Mins., Warsaw, 1992—93. German Nat. Sci. Found. fellow Harvard U. Ctr. for European Studies, 1988—94. Mem. Washington Symphony Orch., 1994—96. Fellow, Konrad-Adenauer-Found., 1988—94. Home: 5121 Warren Pl NW Washington DC 20016 Office: The World Bank 1818 H St NW Washington DC 20433 Home Fax: 202-614-1041; Office Fax: 202-614-1041. Personal E-mail: ofratzscher@worldbank.org. Business E-Mail: ofratzscher@worldbank.org.

FRAUENHOFFER, ROSE MARIE, visual artist, cosmetologist; b. Evanston, Ill., July 24, 1926; d. Edward John and Rose Louise (Pantle) Kossow; m. Harold Voight Frauenhoffer, Oct. 14, 1950. Lic. cosmetologist, Ill. Mgr., buyer Del-Mar, Evanston, 1948-52; asst. mgr., buyer House of Harold Salon, Evanston, 1952-2000; mgr. buyer House of Harold Gifts, Evanston, 1952—; mgr. House of Harold Gallery, Evanston, 1952-2000; asst. mgr., designer House of Harold Engraving, Evanston, 1952-2000; artist, designer House of Harold Studio, Evanston, 1999-2000; artist, dir. Peinture de la Monde Studio, Gallery divsn. House of Harold, Evanston, 2000—. Exhibited works in solo shows at Aurelia Gallery, Evanston, Garland Bldg. Gallery, Chgo., Bank of Lincolnwood, Levy Ctr. La-Petite Gallery, Loft Gallery, Skokie, Ill.; group shows at Loft Gallery, John G. Blank Ctr. for Arts, Michigan City, Ind., Margaret Harwell Art Mus., Poplar Bluffs, Mo., Wilmette (Ill.) Pub. Libr., others; exhibited in nat. and internat. art shows. Alumnus, vol. Evanston Citizens Police Acad., 1997—; co-chair Skokie Centennial Art and Craft Fair, 1988. Recipient awards for art. Mem. Skokie Art Guild (v.p. 1980-81, pres. 1981-82), Midwest Watercolor Soc., Nat. Mus. Women in the Arts, Ill. Arts Coun., Evanston Arts Coun. Avocations: gardening, photography, sewing.

FRAUMENI, JOSEPH FRANCIS, JR., scientific researcher, medical educator, physician, military officer; b. Boston, Apr. 1, 1933; s. Joseph Francis and Pauline (Malta) Fraumeni; m. Patricia Welch D'Arcy, Apr. 23, 1977. AB, Harvard U., 1954; MD, Duke, 1958; ScM, Harvard U., 1965. Diplomate Am. Bd. Internal Medicine. Commd. lt. USPHS, 1962, advanced through grades to rear admiral (asst. surgeon gen.), 1997; med. intern, resident Johns Hopkins Hosp., Balt., 1958-60; med. resident, chief resident Meml. Sloan-Kettering Cancer Ctr., N.Y.C., 1960-62; staff assoc. Nat. Cancer Inst., Bethesda, Md., 1962-65, assoc. chief, 1966-75, chief environ. epidemiology br., 1975-82, dir. epidemiology & biostats. program, 1979-95, dir. epidemiology & genetics divsn., 1995—. Attending physician Clin. Ctr. NIH, Bethesda, Md., 1966—; adj. prof. epidemiology Uniformed Svcs. U., Bethesda, 1985—, Harvard U. Sch. Pub. Health, Boston, 1993—, George Washington U. Med. Ctr., 1997—. Mem. editl. bd.: more than a dozen med. and sci. jours.; contbr. chpts. to books, 750 articles to profl. jours. Recipient Disting. Svc. medal, USPHS, 1983, Gorgas medal, Assn. Mil. Surgeons U.S., 1989, W.W. Sutow award, U. Tex. M.D. Anderson Cancer Ctr., 1992, Disting. Alumnus award, Duke U. Med. Ctr., 1992, Alumni Award of Merit, Harvard Sch. Pub. Health, 1993, Wick Williams Meml. award, Fox Chase Cancer Ctr., 1993, Dir.'s award, NIH, 1994, Charles Mott prize, GM Cancer Rsch. Found., 1995, John Snow award, APHA, 1995, Selikoff award, Ramazinni Inst., 1996, Robert S. Gordon award, NIH, 1996, Dr. Nathan Davis award, AMA, 2002, Alton Ochsner award relating smoking and health, Am. Coll. Chest Physicians, 2002. Fellow: ACP (James D. Bruce Meml. award 1997), AAAS, Am. Coll. Preventive Medicine, Am. Coll. Epidemiology (bd. dirs. 1985—89, Abraham Lilienfeld award 1993, hon. fellow 1998); mem.: NAS, Assn. Am. Physicians, Am. Assn. Cancer Rsch. (bd. dirs. 1983—87, Am. Cancer Soc. award rsch. excellence epidemiology, prevention 1993), Am. Soc. Preventive Oncology (pres. 1981—83, Disting. Achievement award 1993), Inst. Medicine. Office: Nat Cancer Inst EPS/8070 Div Cancer Epidemology & Genetics Executive Plz S Rm 8070 Bethesda MD 20892-7242

FRAUNFELDER, FREDERICK THEODORE, ophthalmologist, educator; b. Pasadena, Calif., Aug. 16, 1934; s. Reinhart and Freida Fraunfelder; m. Yvonne Marie Halliday, June 21, 1959; children— Yvette Marie, Helene, Nina, Frederick, Nicholas. BS, U. Oreg., 1956, MD, 1960, postgrad. (NIH postdoctoral fellow), 1962. Diplomate Am. Bd. Ophthalmology (bd. dirs. 1982-90). Intern U. Chgo., 1961; resident U. Oreg. Med. Sch., 1964-66; NIH postdoctoral fellow Wilmer Eye Inst., Johns Hopkins U., 1967; chmn. dept. ophthalmology U. Ark. Health Scis. Ctr., 78-98, prof., 1978—; prof., chmn. dept. ophthalmology Oreg. Health Scis. U. Dir. Casey Eye Inst., 1992-98, Nat. Registry Drug-Induced Ocular Side Effects, 1976—; vis. prof. ophthalmology Moorfields Eye Hosp., London, 1974. Author: Drug-Induced Ocular Side Effects and Drug Interactions, 1976, 5th edit., 2001, Current Ocular Therapy, 1985, 5th edit., 2001, Recent Advances in Ophthalmology, 8th edit., 1985; assoc. editor: Jour. Toxicology: Cutaneous and Ocular, 1984-2002; mem. editl. bd. Am. Jour. Ophthalmology, 1982-92, Ophthalmic Forum 1983-90, Ophthalmology, 1984-89; contbr. over 200 articles on lens and eye toxicity rsch. to med. jours. Served with U.S. Army, 1962-64. FDA grantee, 1976-86; Nat. Eye Inst. grantee, 1970-87. Mem. AMA, ACS, Am. Acad. Ophthaolmology, Assn. Univ. Profs. in Ophthalmology (pres. 1976), Am. Ophthalmol. Soc., Am. Coll. Cryosurgery (pres. 1977), Assn. Research in Ophthalmology. Clubs: Lions, Elks. Lutheran. Home: 13 Cellini Ct Lake Oswego OR 97035-1307 Office: Casey Eye Inst 3375 SW Terwilliger Blvd Portland OR 97201-4197

FRAUTSCHI, STEVEN CLARK, physicist, educator; b. Madison, Wis., Dec. 6, 1933; s. Lowell Emil and Grace (Clark) F.; m. Mie Okamura, Feb. 16, 1967; children: Laura, Jennifer. BA, Harvard U., 1954; PhD, Stanford U., 1958. Research fellow Kyoto U., Japan, 1958-59, U. Calif.-Berkeley, 1959-61; mem. faculty Cornell U., 1961-62, Calif. Inst. Tech., Pasadena, 1962—, prof. theoretical physics, 1966—, exec. officer physics, 1988-97, master student houses, 1997—2002. Vis. prof. U. Paris, Orsay, 1977-78 Author: Regge Poles and S-Matrix Theory, 1963, The Mechanical Universe, 1986. Guggenheim fellow, 1971-72 Mem. Am. Phys. Soc. Achievements include research and publications on Regge poles, bootstrap theory, cosmology. Home: 1561 Crest Dr Altadena CA 91001-1838 Office: 1201 E California Blvd Pasadena CA 91125-0001

FRAUTSCHI, TIMOTHY CLARK, lawyer; b. Madison, Wis., Apr. 8, 1937; s. Lowell E. and Grace C. (Clark) F.; m. Pamela H. Hendricks, June 23, 1964; children: Schuyler, Jason; m. Susan B. Brumm, June 13, 1981; 1 child, Jacob. BA, U. Wis., 1959; LL.B., London Sch. Econs., U. Wis., 1963. Bar: Wis. 1963, U.S. Ct. Claims 1976, U.S. Tax Ct., 1976. Assoc. firm Foley & Lardner, Milw., 1963-70, ptnr., 1970—. Editor Wis. Law Rev. Co-founder Milw. Forum; pres. Lakeside Cmty. Coun., Present Music, Inc., 1991—98, Skylight Comic Opera, Ltd., 1980—85, Next Act Theatre, 2001—; bd. dirs. Am. Players Theater, Milw., Repertory Theater, Northcott Neighborhood House, United performing Arts Fund, Inc., Milw., Children's Svc. Soc., Wis. Theatre Tesseract; pres. Next Act Theatre, 1986—89, Watertower Landmark Trust, 1986—89; v.p. Frank Lloyd Wright Wis. Conservancy, 2001—; bd. dirs. St. Mary's Milw. Hosp. Found. Mem. Milw. Jr. Bar Assn. (pres. 1969-70), Milw. Bar Assn. (dir. 1971-74), Order of Coif, Phi Beta Kappa (pres. Milw. chpt. 1968-70), Phi Kappa Phi, Phi Eta Sigma Office: Foley & Lardner US Bank Ctr 777 E Wisconsin Ave Ste 3800 Milwaukee WI 53202-5367

FRAWLEY, MICHAEL KEITH, lawyer; b. Reading, Pa., Aug. 2, 1959; s. George Michael and Jolene Mercedes F.; m. Linda Ann Hewitt, Nov. 20, 1999. BA in Econs., U. Notre Dame, 1982; JD, U. of the Pacific, 1987. Bar: Calif. 1987. Prosecutor Ventura (Calif.) County Dist. Atty., 1987-92, supr., 1992-93, sr. deputy dist. atty., 1993-98, chief deputy dist. atty., 1998—. Bd. dirs. Habitat for Humanity, Ventura, 1995, 96, 97, Vols. in Parole, 2001—; lit. tchr. Project Literacy, Ventura, 1991; vol. Alameda County Big Bros./Big Sisters, 1983. Mem. Calif. Bar Assn., Ventura County Bar Assn. (jud. evaluations com. 2002—), Omicron Delta Epsilon. Avocations: tennis, swimming, hiking, reading, travel. E-mail: mike.frawley@mail.co.ventura.ca.us.

FRAWLEY, THOMAS FRANCIS, retired physician; b. Rochester, N.Y., June 27, 1919; s. Thomas J. and Mary (Leddy) F.; m. Marigrace Cecelia Gould, Feb. 23, 1946; children: Thomas Joseph II, Colleen, Brian (dec.). AB, U. Rochester, 1941; MD, U. Buffalo, 1944. Diplomate Am. Bd. Internal Medicine, Am. Bd. Endocrinology and Metabolism. Intern St. Mary's Hosp., Rochester, 1944-45; resident Buffalo Gen. Hosp., 1945-48; research fellow Harvard Med. Sch., 1948-52; resident Peter Bent Brigham Hosp., Boston, 1948-52; chief endocrinology and metabolism Albany (N.Y.) Med. Sch., 1952-58, assoc. prof. medicine, 1952-58, prof. medicine, 1960-63; research assoc. NIH, 1958-60; prof. medicine St. Louis U. Sch. Medicine, 1963—77, chmn. dept. internal medicine, 1963-73, chmn. emeritus, 1977—; chmn. Office of Grad. Med. Edn., St. John's Mercy Med. Center, St. Louis, 1981-95; physician-in-chief St. Louis U. Hosp., 1963-73. Mem. drug efficacy study panel Nat. Acad. Scis., 1966-69; med. adv. com. Cath. Hosp. Assn., 1966-69; mem. sci. rev. com. NIH, 1970-74; commr. Joint Commn. Accreditation of Hosps., 1976—, mem. resident rev. com. Int. Medicine, 1980-82, 89-93. Author books in field.; contbr. articles to profl. jours. Served to lt., M.C. AUS, 1946-47; surgeon USPHS, 1958-60. Recipient Disting. Alumni award U. Buffalo Sch. Medicine, 1989, Health Care Ministry award Archdiocese St. Louis, 2002. Fellow ACP (gov. Mo. 1971-75, regent 1976—, pres. 1981, master 1982, Laureate award 1986, Stengel award 1993), Royal Coll. Physicians Ireland, Royal Soc. Medicine London; mem. Assn. Am. Physicians, Am. Fedn. Clin. Rsch., Endocrine Soc., Ctrl. Soc. Clin. Rsch., So. Soc. Clin. Investigation, Am. Thyroid Assn., Am. Diabetes Assn. (profl. edn. com. 1983), Am. Clin. and Climatol. Assn., St. Louis Med. Soc. (Schlueter award 1994, St. Louis Health award 2002), Sigma Xi, Alpha Omega Alpha. Home: 14003 Baywood Villages Dr Chesterfield MO 63017-3450

FRAWLEY BAGLEY, ELIZABETH, government advisor, ambassador; b. Elmira, N.Y., July 13, 1952; m. Smith Bagley; 2 children. BA in French and Spanish cum laude, Regis Coll., 1974; JD in Internat. Law, Georgetown U., 1987. Staff Office Congl. Rels. Dept. State, spl. asst. to Amb. Sol Linowitz, congl. liaison Conf. on Security and Cooperation in Europe, amb. to Portugal, 1993-97, former amb. to Portugal, 1997—. Adj. prof. law Georgetown U. Washington. Home: 1539 29th St NW Washington DC 20007-3061

FRAWLEY-O'DEA, MARY GAIL, clinical psychologist, psychoanalyst educator; b. Lowell, Mass. d. John Edward and Mary Gail (Quinn) Frawley; m. Dennis Michael O'Dea, Jan. 1, 1996; 1 stepson, Daniel Patrick; children: Igor Ibradzic, Mollie Gilmore Chun O'Dea, Sally Kivlan Ying O'Dea, Sally Kivlan Ying O'Dea. BA, St. Mary's Coll., Notre Dame, Ind., 1972; MBA, So. Meth U., 1975; PhD, Adelphi U., 1988, postdoctoral diploma in psychoanalysis 1996. Psychologist II Pomona (N.Y.) Mental Health Clinic, 1987-91; asst. clin prof. Adelphi U., Derner Inst., Garden City, NY, 1989—91; pvt. practice clin psychologist/psychoanalyst Nyack, NY, 1990—2000, New City, NY, 2000—Faculty supr. Minn. Inst. Contemporary Psychoanalysis, Mpls.-St. Paul 1996—; continuing edn. faculty N.Y. Psychol. Assn. for Psycholanalysis

1998—; supr. and faculty Nat. Tng. Program for psychoanalysis, N.Y., 2000—; co-dir. Manhattan Inst. Psychoanalysis, 2001—; exec. dir. Manhattan Inst. Psychoanalysis Trauma Treatment Ctr., 2001—; mem. faculty supervisory tng. program Nat. Inst. for Psychotherapies, NY, 2002— ; mem. adv. bd. Nat. Orgn. for Male Sexual Victims, 2002—. Co-author: treating the Adult Survivor of Childhood Sexual Abuse, 1994, The Supervisory Relationship, 2000; mem. adv. bd. Jour. Nat. Inst. Psychotherapies, 2003—; contbr. chpts. to books, articles to profl. jours. Mem.: APA (mem. pub. com. div. psychoanalysis 2001—), Manhattan Inst. Psychoanalytic Soc., N.Y. State Psychol. Assoc., Westchester Soc. Psychoanalysis and Psychotherapy. Avocations: hiking, cooking, theater, symphony, reading. Home and Office: 5 Opal Ct New City NY 10956 E-mail: mgfod@aol.com.

FRAY, LIONEL LOUIS, management consultant; b. Paris, Jan. 17, 1935; came to U.S., 1942; s. Maurice and Esther Fray; m. Joanne Caroline Liberman, June 30, 1963; children: Sharon June, Elizabeth Ann. BS, MIT, 1957, MS, 1958; MBA, Harvard U., 1962. Co-founder U.S. Sonics, Inc., Cambridge, Mass., 1957-58; with Mitre Corp., Bedford, Mass., 1958-60, Mgmt. Systems Corp., 1962-64; v.p. Harbridge House, Boston, 1964-73, TBS Capital Corp., Lexington, Mass., 1973-86, Temple, Barker & Sloane, Lexington, Mass., 1973-86; pres. Lionel L. Fray Assocs., Inc., Lexington, Mass., 1986—. Bd. dirs., pres., CFO Am. Technion Soc., AOA Geophysics, Inc., AOA Geomarine Ops. LLC, 2002—; co-founder, bd. dirs., Technion Inst. of Mgmt. Author: Handbook of Strategic Management, 1985, How to Develop the Strategic Plan, 1987; contbr. articles to profl. jours. Mem. Strategic Leadership Forum, Inst. Mgmt. Cons. Clubs: Harvard. Avocations: tennis, skiing, jazz violin, flying. Home: 2361A Massachusetts Ave Lexington MA 02421-6733 Office: Lionel L Fray Assoc Inc 1620 Mass Ave Lexington MA 02420-3831 E-mail: lionel_fray@agoem.com.

FRAZEE, RONALD LEROY, lawyer; b. Billings, Mont., Nov. 19, 1946; s. Chester M. and Dorothy L. (Balock) F. BS, Ea. Mont. U., 1969; MBA, U.S. Internat. U., 1976; JD, U. Mont., 1977; LLM in Taxation, Boston U., 1978. Bar: Mont. 1977, U.S. Tax Ct. 1978, Tex. 1985, U.S. Dist. Ct. Mont. 1977, U.S. Dist. Ct. (no. dist.) Tex. 1985. Assoc. Crowley, Haughey, Hanson, Toole & Dietrich, Billings, 1978-81; sr. tax counsel Hunt Oil Co., Dallas, 1981-89; gen. counsel Mayfair Petroleum, Inc., Dallas, 1990—. Lt. USN, 1969-74. Decorated Air medal. Mem. ABA, Tex. Bar Assn., Dallas Bar Assn. Avocation: flying. Home: 4440 Rushing Rd Dallas TX 75287-2957 Office: Mayfair Petroleum Inc 4440 Rushing Rd Dallas TX 75287-2957

FRAZEN, MITCHELL HALE, lawyer; b. Great Lakes, Ill., Sept. 19, 1955; s. Sidney Joseph and Norma Ileane (Solomon) F.; m. Mary Elizabeth Huelsbusch, Sept. 14, 1974; children: Daniel Joseph, Christina Elizabeth. BA, U. Ill., 1977; JD, U. Mich., 1980. Bar: Ill. 1980, U.S. Dist. Ct. (no. dist.) Ill. 1980, U.S. Ct. Appeals (7th cir.) 1987, U.S. Dist. Ct. (ea. dist.) Wis. 1994, U.S. Ct. Appeals (8th cir.) 1995, U.S. Dist. Ct. (ea. dist.) Mich. 1995. Assoc. Phelan, Pope & John, Ltd., Chgo., 1980-87; shareholder Burditt & Radzius, Chartered, Chgo., 1987-98, dir., 1989-98; ptnr. Litchfield Cavo, Chgo., 1998—. Arbitrator, chairperson mandatory ct.-annexed arbitration program Cook County Cir. Ct., Chgo., 1990—, mediator vol. mediation program, 1992—. Bd. govs. Chgo. Coun. Lawyers, 1992-95; chair State Ct. Practices Com., 1995—. Mem. ABA, Chgo. Bar Assn., Phi Beta Kappa, Order of Coif. Democrat. Lutheran. Home: 617 W Ruhl Rd Palatine IL 60074 Office: Litchfield Cavo 303 W Madison St Ste 300 Chicago IL 60606-3309 E-mail: frazen@litchfieldcavo.com.

FRAZER, DAVID HUGH, JR., allergist; b. Montgomery, Ala., Mar. 31, 1937; s. David H. and Sue Ray (Durrett) F.; m. Johnnie Bowie Swetenburg, July 5, 1941; children: David Hugh III, Bowie Swetenburg Frazer Campbell, Wills Findley. BS, Tulane U., 1958, MD, 1961. Private practice, Atlanta, 1966-67, Montgomery, 1967—. Bd. dirs. S. Ala. State Fair, Montgomery, Brantwood Children's Home, Montgomery Metro YMCA Bd. With USAF, 1962-64. Fellow Am. Coll. Allergy and Immunology; mem. Am. Acad. Allergy and Immunology, Montgomery Kiwanis Club. Republican. Presbyterian. Office: 1420 Narrow Lane Pky Montgomery AL 36111-2654

FRAZER, JANET LYNN, historian, educator; b. Long Beach, Calif., June 1, 1945; d. Richard Henry Benish and R. L. Slay; m. Evan Wayne Frazer; children: John Rufus, Leah Ann, Susanna Jane. BA, Stanford (Calif.) U., 1967; MA Tchg. in History, U. Chgo., 1969. Tchg. intern Kenwood HS, Chgo., 1968—69; tchr. Radnor Jr. HS, Wayne, Pa., 1969—71, Internat. Sch. Kuala Lumpur, Malaysia, 1971—72, Abington Friends Sch., Jenkintown, Pa., 1989—; tchr., chmn. history dept. Springfield HS, Oreland, Pa., 1973—76. Mem. working group Friends Sch., Phila., 1993—2002; mem. Haverford (Pa.) Coll. Corp., 2000—. Mem. archives com. Merion (Pa.) Friends Mtg., 2000—. Recipient Piers award, Yale U., 2003; grantee, Fulbright Meml. Fund, 2000, NEH, 2001. Mem.: Quaker Hist. Soc., Am. Hist. Assn., World Hist. Assn. Democrat. Mem. Soc. Of Friends. Office: Abington Friends School 575 Washington Lane Jenkintown PA 19046

FRAZER, JOHN HOWARD, tennis association executive; b. Cin., June 3, 1924; s. H. Howard and Amelia (Spieth) F.; m. Joann Elizabeth McEvoy, Nov. 3, 1956; children: John Howard Jr., Victoria F. Fuller. BA, U. Cin., 1948, JD, 1950. Bar: Ohio 1950. V.p. H. Howard Frazer Co., Cin., 1950-62, pres., 1962-76; treas., dir. Cin. Transit Co., 1957-73; dir. Am. Controlled Industries, Cin., 1973-86, pres., 1974-75, exec. v.p., 1975-86; dir. Vulcan Corp., Cin., 1960-91, pres., 1975-88; sec., dir. Valley Industries, 1973-86, Colorpac, Inc., 1973-86. Chmn. U.S. Open Tennis Championships, 1993-94. Chmn. men's com. Cin. Symphony Orch., 1971-73; pres. Cincinnatus Assn., 1969-70; chmn. Western Tennis Championships, Cin., 1970-73; bd. dirs. Internat. Tennis Hall of Fame, 1979-2002, hon. dir., 2002—, exec. com. 1985-2002, chmn. internat. coun. 1996—. Served with USAAF, 1942-45. Recipient Highest Effort award, Sigma Alpha Epsilon, 1995, Chmn.'s award, Internat. Tennis Hall of Fame, 2000, induction into USTA/Midwest Tennis Hall of Fame, 2001, Golden Achievement award, Tennis Hall of Fame, 2003. Mem. USTA (mem. exec. com. 1975—, chmn. sanction and schedule com. 1973-86, bd. dirs. 1986-96, v.p. 1986-88, sec. 1988-90, 1st v.p. 1990-92, pres. 1993-94, chmn. nat. men's ranking com. 1971-73, long-range planning com. 1981-87, internat. com. 1999—, hon. chair 2003—), Internat. Tennis Fedn. (del. 1991-96, mem. com. mgmt. 1993-97, v.p. 1995-97, hon. life counsellor 1997—, mem. vets. com. 1996-99, chmn. vets. com. 1996-97, mem. constl. com. 1997-2003, mem. PILA com. 2000--, Svc. to the Game award 1998), Am. Footwear Industries Assn. (dir.), Rubber Mfrs. Assn. (dir.), Shoe Last Mfrs. Assn. (pres. 1978-79), Univ. Club, Cin. C.C., Cin. Tennis Club, Quail Creek C.C., (Naples), Bay Colony Club (Naples), River Club (N.Y.C.), All-Eng. Lawn Tennis Club (Wimbledon), Royal Poinciana Golf Club (Naples). Home: 8171 Bay Colony Dr Apt 1701 Naples FL 34108-7566 E-mail: joandbumpyfrazer@worldnet.att.net.

FRAZER, JOHN PAUL, surgeon; b. Rochester, N.Y., Sept. 14, 1914; s. Edward and Annie Margaret (Burdick) F.; m. Doris V. Larsen, Sept. 23, 1950; children: Karin Ann, Gail Sherry. MD, U. Rochester, 1939. Intern in pathology Cornell U. Med. Center - N.Y. Hosp., 1939-40; intern in surgery L.I. Coll. Hosp., 1940-41; resident ENT in ear, nose and throat Yale-New Haven Hosp., 1941-44, instr., 1945-48; practice medicine specializing in ear, nose and throat Honolulu, 1948-63; prof. surgery, chmn. dept. ENT surgery U. Rochester Sch. Medicine and Dentistry, 1963-81, prof., 1981-93, prof. emeritus, 1993—. Cons. to surgeon gen. Tripler Hosp., 1950-63, Tb and leprosy Sanitoria, Hawaii, 1949-63. Mem. ACS, Am. Laryngol. Assn., Am. Bronchoesophagological Assn., Am. Laryngol-Rhinol-Otol. Soc. Address: 329 Orchard Park Blvd Rochester NY 14609-3314

FRAZER, NIMROD THOMPSON, financial services company executive; b. Montgomery, Ala., Dec. 10, 1929; BA, Huntingdon Coll., 1954; MBA, Harvard U., 1956; LHD (hon.), Huntingdon Coll., 2000. Securities salesman Sterne Agee & Leach, Montgomery, 1956-57; adminstr. State of Ala., Montgomery, 1957-60; from salesman to exec. v.p. Thornton, Farish & Gauntt, Montgomery, 1961-75; chmn. The Frazer Lanier Co., Montgomery, 1976-96; chmmn, CEO The Enstar Group, Montgomery, 1990—. 1st lt. U.S. Army, 1950-53. Decorated Silver Star, U.S. and Korean Presdl. unit citations. Home: 663 Cloverdale Rd Montgomery AL 36106-1805 Office: Enstar Group Inc 401 Madison Ave Montgomery AL 36104-3629 E-mail: ntfrazer@enstargroup.com.

FRAZER, ROBERT LEE, landscape architect; BS in Landscape Architecture, Tex. A&M U., 1948; MS in Agriculture, East Tex. State U., 1951. Registered landscape architect, Tex. Landscape architect, instr. vocat. horticulture San Antonio Sch. Dist., 1948-49; landscape architect, instr., head campus maintenance East Tex. State U., Commerce, 1949-54; dir. parks and recreation City of San Antonio, 1955-73; univ. landscape architect, prof. landscape architecture Tex. Tech. U., Lubbock, 1973-74; v.p., prin., dir. landscape architecture Groves Fernandez Frazer & Assocs., Inc., San Antonio, 1974-83, Fernandez Frazer White & Assocs., Inc., San Antonio, 1984-92, v.p. emeritus, 1992—. Adj. prof. U. Tex., Arlington, 1993. Contbr. articles to profl. jours. Recipient Robert H. Hugman award for devel. San Antonio River Walk, 1987, Disting. Svc. award San Antonio Conservation Soc., 1973. Fellow Am. Soc. Landscape Architects (Terry Hershey award for Excellence in Field of Recreation Parks or Tourism), Am. Inst. Park Execs., Am. Acad. for Park and Recreation Adminstrn., Tex. Recreation and Park Soc.; mem. S.W. Park and Recreation Tng. Inst. (past pres., co-organizer), Tex. Mcpl. Park and Recreation Assn. (past pres., organizer), Tex. Turfgrass Assn. (past pres., co-organizer), Nat. River Parks and Waterfront Assn. (past bd. dirs.), Nat. Recreation Assn. (past mem. nat. adv. com.). Office: Fernandez Frazer White & Assoc 11824 Radium St San Antonio TX 78216-2711 E-mail: ffw@ffwinc.com.

FRAZER, STUART HARRISON, III, cotton merchant; b. Montgomery, Ala., Feb. 13, 1948; s. Stuart Harrison Jr. and Myrta Frances (Garrett) F.; m. Linda Gail Patterson, Nov. 21, 1971 (div. 1983); 1 child, Heather Allison; m. Mary Prue Coleman, Oct. 28, 1983; children: Laura Goldman, Meredith Jane. Student, Huntingdon Coll., Montgomery, 1966-68, Auburn (Ala.) U., 1970-73. V.p. Weil Bros. Cotton Inc., Montgomery, 1970-88; sr. v.p. Rollins Cotton Co., Montgomery, 1988-92, pres., 1992-94, Prodn. Mktg., Montgomery, 1994—. Mem. USDA adv. com. con Cotton Clasing, Washington, 1988—; bd. dirs. N.Y. Cotton Exch., Cotton Coun. Internat., Nat. Cotton Coun.; mem. agrl. adv. com. to Commodity Futures Trading Commn., Washington. Mem. YMCA Boys Work Com., pres. 1986-87. With U.S. Army, 1968-69. Mem. Am. Cotton Shippers Assn. (dir., 1st v.p. 1992, 2nd v.p. 1991, pres. 1993), Nat. Cotton Coun., Atlantic Cotton Assn. (pres. 1981-82), Montgomery Cotton Exch. (pres. 1976—), Montgomery Country Club. Episcopalian. Home: 2517 Darrington Rd Montgomery AL 36111-1527 Office: Prodn Mktg PO Box 210309 Montgomery AL 36121-0309

FRAZER, SUSAN HUME, independent scholar and consultant; b. Hinton, W.Va., Jan. 3, 1949; d. Dennis Ray and Wanda Marrs Hume; m. John Walker Frazer Jr., Oct. 6, 1989; children: Andrew Reno Collier II., Amy Marie Wilson Collier. BA Psychology, Chapman U., 1972; MS Interior Environments, U. Wis., 1992; PhD Art History, Va. Commonwealth U., 2001. V.p., dir. mktg. Signature Cmtys., Alexandria, Va., 1984—88; v.p. mktg. Miller and Smith, McLean, 1988—90; ind. scholar/cons. Am. Architecture and Decorative Arts, Richmond, 1998—. Contbr. articles to profl. jours. Mem.: Soc. Archtl. Historians, Sigma Sigma Sigma (past pres.), Kappa Omicron Nu (hon.), Delta Omicron (hon.) Presbyterian. Avocations: piano, tatter, baking, antiques. Home and Office: 2023 Hanover Ave Richmond VA 23220 Fax: 804-562-7186. E-mail: hume-frazer@erols.com.

FRAZER, VERNON, writer, musician; b. Middletown, Conn., Oct. 2, 1945; BA, U. Conn., 1968. Author: (poetry) A Slick Set of Wheels, 1987, Demon Dance, 1995, Sing Me One Song of Evolution, 1998, Free Fall, 1999, Demolition Fedora, 2000, Improvisations (I-XXIV), 2000, Improvisations (XXV-L), 2002; (fiction) Stay Tuned to This Channel, 1999, Relic's Reunions, 2000; Commercial Fiction, 2002; author, composer, bassist (recs.) Sex Queen of the Berlin Turnpike, 1988, SLAM!, 1991, Song of Baobab, 1997; guest artist (CD anthology) The Jazz Voice, Thomas Chapin-Alive; contbr. articles to Coda Mag., Jazz Hot, Cadence Mag., Hartford Advocate, Hartford Courant, others; contbr. fiction to Plain Brown Wrapper, Muse Apprentice Guild, First Intensity, others; contbr. poetry to Sidereality Rev., Lost and Found Times, Tunxis Poetry Rev., Tempus Fugit, others; appeared in numerous poetry-music performances, including St. Mark's Poetry Project. Bd. dirs. Conn. Jazz Confedn., Newington, 1990. Evelyn Preston Meml. Fund performance grantee, 1989, 90, 92, Middletown Commn. on Arts performance grantee, 1990, Adam Ward Seligman Fund grantee, 2000. Home: 568 Brittany L Delray Beach FL 33446 Home (Summer): 132 Woodscrest Dr East Hartford CT 06118 E-mail: vernonfrazer2002@yahoo.com.

FRAZER, WILLIAM JOHNSON, JR., economics educator; b. Greenville, Ala., Oct. 15, 1924; s. William Johnson Frazer and Margaret Thompson Winkler; m. Mary Ann Burford, Nov. 12, 1949 (div. 1982); children: William J. Frazer III. BA, Huntington Coll., 1950; postgrad., U. Tex., 1950-51; MA, Columbia U., 1953, PhD, 1968. Instr. of econs. Pratt Inst., Bklyn., 1953-54, Rensselaer Poly. Inst., 1954-56; economist Fed. Res. Bank of N.Y., 1956-57; sr. economist Fed. Res. Bank of Chgo., 1966-67; asst. prof. U. Fla., Gainesville, 1957-64, assoc. prof., 1964-68, prof., 1968—. Faculty fellow Harvard U., 1959-60, U. Pa., 1964-65; mem. faculty Fla. State U. program, London, 1989-90, 92; prof. London Sch. Econs., 1994. Author: (with William Yohe) The Analytics and Institutions of Money and Banking, 1956, The Demand for Money, 1967, Crisis in Economic Theory, 1973, Power and Ideas: Milton Friedman and the Big U-Turn Vol. I, The Background, and Vol. II, The U-Turn, 1988, The Legacy of Keynes and Friedman, 1994, The Central Banks, 1994, (with John Guthrie) The Florida Land Boom: Money, Speculation, and the Banks, 1995, The Friedman System: Economic Analysis of Time Series, 1997, Central Banking, Crises, and Global Economy, 2000, Business Conditions, Logging, and Sharecropping: A South Alabama Trade Area with European and Birmingham Connections, 2002; contbr. articles to profl. jours. and encyclopedias. Monetary and fin. advisor City of Gainesville, 1980—, chmn. pension rev. com., 1981-82. With USN, 1943-46. Republican. Methodist. Home: 2920 NW 16th Ave Gainesville FL 32605-3733

FRAZIER, AMY, professional tennis player; b. St. Louis, Mo., Sept. 19, 1972; Prof. tennis player USTA, 1990—. Mem. 1995 U.S. Fed. Cup Team. Named World Team Tennis MVP, 1994; winner Futures/Kona II, Hawaii 1987, Wichita, 1989, Okla. City, 1990, European Open, 1992, L.A., 1994, ITF/Mahwah, 1998, Japan Open, 1995, 99, among others; ranked 4th USTA, ranked 25th, 1998, ranked 66th, 1999. Office: USTA 70 W Red Oak Ln White Plains NY 10604-3602

FRAZIER, ANTHONY VINCENT EARL, addictions, small business, and technology specialist; b. Chgo., May 16, 1951; s. Sidney S. and RoxieMaria (McNutt) F.; m. Ruth Mary Fairfax, Jan. 12, 1970; children: Annika S. Frazier Muhammad, Darrius R. BA, Chgo. State U., 1977; Cert., Congrl. Rsch. Svc. Libr. of Congress, 1990; Cert. internat. trade exec. prog., U. Ill., Ill. World Trade Ctr., 1991; Cert. internat. trade prog., DePaul U., 1991; Cert. of Completion, Dartmouth Coll., 1992; MA, Govs. State U., 1993; Cert. law prog. cmty. developers and social workers, John Marshall Law Sch., 1996, Cert. of Completion, MIT, 1997. Cert. CPR specialist ARC, cert. profl. educator, Ill, Cert. of Completion, Mental Health: Alcoholism and Substance Abuse Counseling, Harold Washington Coll., Chgo., Ill., 2002. Exec. dir. South Shore Caucus Legis. and Cmty. Action, Chgo., 1979-81; grad. tchr. Govs. State U., Park Forest, Ill., 1982; adj. cmty. prof., grad. tchg. asst. Roosevelt U., Chgo., 1982; adminstrv. asst. Hon. Timothy C. Evans, Chief Judge, Cir. Ct. Cook COunty, former 4th Ward Alderman and Committeeman, Chgo., 1982-83; staff asst., legis. aide U.S. Senator Alan J. Dixon (Democrat-Ill.), Washington, 1983-86; fed. grants, contracts mgr. U.S. Rep. Charles A. Hayes (Democrat-Ill.), Chgo., 1987-92; congressional liason First Congressional District of Ill housing and small business task forces, 1987—92; social security ins. specialist, mem. Spkr.'s and Cmty. Outreach Bur. Social Security Adminstrn., Chgo., 1993—; vol. mgmt. cons., trainer AVEF Vol. Mgmt. Cons. and Trainer, Chgo., 1992—; aging specialist and mem. Ill. Coun. on Aging, Gubernatorial Reappointment by the Honorable George H. Ryan State of Ill., 2000—. Chmn. econ. devel. subcom. Cmty. Devel. Adv. Com., Richard M. Daley, Mayor, City of Chgo., 1987-93; mgmt. cons., trainer Minority Bus. Resource Adv. Com., NASA, Washington, 1992-96 (mem., chmn. technology-transfer rsch. and devel. and physically-disabled applications subcom., 1992-96); parlimentarian Black affirs adv. com. Soc. Security Adminstrn., 1993-1994; spkr. in field. Co-author: The Changing Economic Standing of Minorities in the Chicago Metropolitan Area, 1992, Chgo. Housing Authority Memorandum of Accord Legal Agreement, 1985-1986; Contbr. articles to profl. jours; television documentary, Second Summit for Fair Housing, 1987. Mem. affirmitive action com. Dem. Party Ill., Dem. Nat. Conv., 1992; vol. fundaiser, spkr. Combined Fed. Campaign, 1996, CARE, (ctrl. region), 1996—, Chgo. Fed. Exec. Bd., 1996, Internat. Svc. Agencies, 1999—; pres. Sunshine Club, Chgo., 1999—, Chgo. East Field Office, Social Security Adminstrn., 1999-2000. Recipient Certificate of Jury Svc. State of Ill., Circuit Court of Cook County, 1997, Meritorious Citation Combined Fed. Campaign Chgo. Fed. Exec. Bd., 1996, Small Business Advocacy award Grant Thornton, Inc., 1989, Homeless Network and Provider award Bur. of the Census U.S. Dept. of Commerce, 1989, Outstanding Achievement award for Vol. Svc. Soft Sheen Products, 1987, Cert. Appreciation Spl. Recognition for Outstanding Pub. Svc. U.S. Rep. Charles A. Hayes, 1993, NASA Minority Bus. Adv. Com., 1997, Pub. Employees Roundtable Pres.'s Intragenecy Coun. on Adminstrv. Mgmt., 2000; Named Perfect Resource Person Dearborn Homes Resident Mgmt. Corp. Chgo. Housing Authority, 1988, one of Outstanding Young Men of Am., 1990; Ill. Gen. Assembly scholar, Springfield, Ill., 1970; mem. nom. com. Outstanding Young Women of Am. award, 1997. Mem. Am. Fedn. Govt. Employees, Nat. Acad. Recording Arts and Scis., Latin Recording Acad., Hyde Park Coop. Soc., Lakefront Properties Housing Task Force, Acad. Country Music. Democrat. Baptist. Avocations: music, outdoorsman, writing, volunteering, spiritual consultant. Home and Office: AVEF Vol Mgmt Cons and Trainers 5521 S Everett Ave Ste B Chicago IL 60637-1956 E-mail: avefraz@aol.com.

FRAZIER, CHET JUNE, advertising agency executive; b. Waldron, Ark., May 17, 1924; s. R.C. and Alice (Terry) F.; m. Lucille Whetzel, Nov. 17, 1942; children: John, Lynette, Terry, Luanna. BS, Okla. State U., 1949, MS, 1950. Editor Okla. News Service, Stillwater, 1949-50; product sales mgr. Ralston Purina Co., St. Louis, 1951-58, advt. mgr., 1958-63; v.p. Bozell & Jacobs Internat., Inc., N.Y.C., 1964-68, sr. v.p., 1968-71, exec. v.p., 1971-76, pres., 1976-89, Bozell & Jacobs Internat., Inc. (Agrl. Div.), 1978-89, also dir., 1972-89; ret., 1989; pvt. practice agrl. mktg. cons., 1989—. Chmn. bd. Henke Machine, Inc., 1972—; bd. dirs. Fed. Land Bank Adminstrn. of Midlands, 1989. Contbr. articles on agrl. advt. to profl. jours. Served with U.S. Army, 1943-46, PTO. Named Advt. Man of Year Advt. Fedn. Am., 1968 Mem. Nat. Agrl. Advt. and Mktg. Assn. (pres. 1967-68, dir. 1967-70), U.S. Feed Grains Council (bd. dirs., chmn. pub. relations com.), Am. Feed Mfg. Assn., Agrl. Council Am. (bd. dirs.), Farm Equipment Mfg. Assn., Agrl. Pubs. Assn. Clubs: Kiwanis. Methodist. Home: 9770 Westchester Dr Omaha NE 68114-3875 *My business philosophy has always been one of honesty, integrity, hard work and respect for the rights of those with whom I work.*

FRAZIER, DOUGLAS BYRON, health care consultant; b. Danville, Va., Jan. 18, 1957; s. Calvin Luther and Frances Ann (Benbow) F.; m. Linda Camille Kane, Apr. 25, 1981; 1 child, John Byron. BS in Fin. with honors, U. Fla., 1979. Ops. analyst Whittaker Gen. Med., Miami, Fla., 1980, div. mgr., 1980-85; health care cons. Abbott Labs., Abbott Park, Ill., 1985-86, sr. health care cons., 1986-92; dir. cons. svcs. Abbott Labs, Abbott Park, Ill., 1992-93, dir. cons. and supply channel svcs., 1993-2000, dir., cons. supply channel and e commerce svcs., 2000—. Mem. Chgo. Coun. Fgn. Rels., Citizens Against Govt. Waste, Abbott Labs. Better Govt. Fund. Republican. Avocations: golf, tennis. Office: Abbott Labs Bldg Apt 6B Abbott Park IL 60064

FRAZIER, DUEWA M. literature educator, writer; b. Bklyn., Aug. 1, 1974; d. Eric and Sylvia J. Wilson Frazier. Degree in English, Hampton U., 1996. Copy editor The Challenge Group, Bklyn., 2000; book publicist Ruder Finn, N.Y.C., 2000—01; pub., cons. Lit Noire Pub., Bklyn., 2002—; instr. drama and poetry Rsch. Found. of CUNY, Bklyn., 2002—03; educator English, lang. arts Francis Scott Key Mid. Sch., Bklyn., 2003—. Cons. Lit Noire Pub., N.Y.C., 2002—. Author: (poetry volume) Shedding Light From My Journeys; actor, writer (documentary) Knives In My Throat, prodr., host (peformance event) Word Canvas. Participant Stop the Violence Campaign, Bklyn., 2000. Mem.: Nat. Assn. Black Journalists (assoc.; St. Louis, sec. 1997). Avocations: poetry, modern dance, African dance, performing, travel.

FRAZIER, HENRY BOWEN, III, retired judge, government official, lawyer; b. Bluefield, W.Va., Aug. 9, 1934; s. Henry Bowen and Margaret Beale (West) F.; m. Joan McIntosh, Dec. 30, 1959. BA with honors, U. Va., 1956; JD with honors, George Washington U., 1967; LLM in Labor Law, Georgetown U., 1969, MLT, 1985. Bar: Va. 1967, D.C. 1980, U.S. Supreme Ct. Pers. adminstr. Army Dept. Washington, 1959-63, spl. projects officer, 1963-67; dep. for civilian pers. policy and civil rights Office Sec. Army, 1967-70; chief program divsn. Fed. Labor Rels. Coun., Exec. Office Pres., 1970-71, dep. exec. dir., 1971-72, exec. dir., 1973-78; mem. Fed. Labor Rels. Authority, Washington, 1979-87, acting chmn., 1984-85; adminstrv. law judge EPA, Washington, 1987-89, chief adminstrv. law judge, 1990-94. Chmn. Employee Relations Commn., U.S. Fgn. Service, 1979-81; acting chmn. Fgn. Service Labor Relations Bd., 1984-85 With USAF, 1961-62. Mem. SAR, Fed. Adminstrv. Law Judges Conf., Jefferson Soc., U. Va. Alumni Assn. (nat. v.p. 1984-85, nat. pres. 1985-86, bd. mgrs. 1980-87), Va. Student Aid Found. (trustee 1990-97, v.p. 1995, pres. 1996), U. Va. Athletic Adv. Coun., Raven Soc., Order of Coif, Colonnade Club (bd. govs. 1997-2000), Glenmore Country Club, Duck Woods Country Club, Phi Beta Kappa, Omicron Delta Kappa, Phi Kappa Psi.

FRAZIER, JO FRANCES, religious organization administrator; b. Tulsa, Okla., Dec. 20, 1928; d. Joseph and Eva Mae Fulcher; m. Chester Jerome Frazier, July 19, 1950; children: David, Linda Frazier Parizo, Susan Frazier Kelly. Student, Duke U., 1946—49; BA, Tulsa U., 1950. Publicity chmn. Ventura (Calif.) County Mental Health Adv. Bd., 1978—81; adv. bd. mem. Charter Hosp. Bd. Trustees, Bakersfield, Calif., 1983—85, Desert Counseling Ctr., Bakersfield, 1983—85; founder, dir. Saints Alive Ministry, Bakersfield, 1995—. Lectr./spkr. in field. Prodr.: (films) Any One of Us, 1980, (video) Saints Alive Ministry, 1999; author: Second Chance, 1987, Saints for Today's Youth, Books 1, 2 and 3, 1995—2002, children's books on Catholic saints. Mem.: Audobon Soc., Nature Conservancy, World Wildlife Fund, Italian Cath. Fedn. (sec. 1984—86). Avocations: swimming, reading. Home and Office: Saints Alive Ministry 4707 Mount Hood Dr Bakersfield CA 93309

FRAZIER, KENNETH C. pharmaceutical executive; BA in Polit. Sci., Pa. State U., 1975; JD, Harvard U., 1978. Bar: Pa. 1978, U.S. Dist. Ct. (ea. dist.) Pa. 1978, U.S. Supreme Ct. 2002. Ptnr. dept. litigation Drinker Biddle & Reath, 1978—92; v.p., gen. counsel, sec. Astra Merck, 1992—94; v.p. pub. affairs Merck & Co., Inc., 1994—96, v.p. pub. affairs, asst. gen. counsel, 1997—98, v.p., dep. gen. counsel, 1999, sr. v.p., gen. counsel, 1999—. Bd. dirs. Cornerstone Christian Acad., Legal Svcs. N.J.; chmn. Ethics Resource Ctr.; mem. adv. bd. Law and Econ. Ctr., U. Pa.; mem. adv. bd. Health Law and Policy Ctr., Seton Hall U.; mem. adv. bd. Rand Inst. for Civil Justice, CorporatePro-Bono.Org; mem. Corp. Exec. Bd.'s Gen. Counsel Roundtable; mem. CLO Roundtable-U.S., Coun. on Fgn. Rels. Mem.: ABA, Am. Law Inst., Pa. Bar Assn. Office: Merck and Co Inc One Merck Dr Whitehouse Station NJ 08889-0100

FRAZIER, LEROY See DYYON, MARIO

FRAZIER, LOIS E. business and economics educator; b. Spray, N.C., June 20, 1920; d. Joseph Robert and Viola Edith (Hodges) F. Diploma, Brevard Coll., 1940; BS, U. N.C., Greensboro, 1942, MS, 1948; EdD, Ind. U., 1961. Tchr. bus. Leaksville (N.C.) H.S., 1942-44; head dept. bus. Brevard (N.C.) Coll., 1944-46, 47-52; assoc. prof. Flora Macdonald Coll., Red Springs, N.C., 1953-54; head dept. bus. and econs. Meredith Coll., Raleigh, N.C., 1954-85, dir. MBA program, 1983-90, Wainwright prof. bus., 1990-91, Wainwright prof. emeritus, 1991—. Vis. instr. U. N.C., Greensboro, 1946-47, 52-53; vis. prof. U. Tenn., Knoxville, 1966, 67; edit. cons. MPC Pub. Co., Bronx, N.Y., 1975-85; speaker in field. Author: History of N.C. Business Education Assn., 1984; co-author: Guide to Transcription, 1978; editor, cons.: Office Procedures, 1980: contbr. articles to profl. jours. Mem. Dem. Women of Wake County, sec., 1991—93, asst. chaplain, 1997—99, mem. nominating com., 1999—2000; mem. task force Gov.'s White House Conf. on Aging, 1980; bd. dirs. Edmonton St. Meth. Ch., 1968—71, 1976—81, 1986—91, 1996—98, lay shepherd leader, 1995—, mem. scholarship com., 1999—2000; bd. dirs. Friends of Campbell Libr., Meredith Coll., 1997—2000; Lottie, Lois and Virginia Frazier scholarship established Brevard Coll., NC, 2002. Fellow Case Western Res. U., 1969; named to Acad. of Women Wake County YWCA, 1985. Mem. AAUW (hon. life, pres. Raleigh br. 1993-94, bd. dirs. state assn. 1993-94), Nat. Bus. Edn. Assn. (bd. dirs. 1972, 76-79), So. Bus. Edn. Assn. (pres. 1972, Outstanding Leadership award 1980),

N.C. Coun. Econ. Edn. (bd. dirs. 1972—), N.C. Bus. Edn. Assn. (hon., bd. dirs. 1980-82, historian 1983-84, Mem. of Yr. award 1975), Assn. for Bus. Comm., Nat. Fedn. of Bus. and Profl. Women's Clubs (treas. 1961-63), N.C. Fedn. Bus. and Profl. Women's Clubs (pres. 1956-58), Alumni Assn. U. N.C. Greensboro (v.p. 1975-77, trustee 1967-69, Alumni Disting. Svc. award 1996), Alumni Assn. Brevard Coll. (pres. 1989-91, Hall of Fame 1988), Raleigh Bus. and Profl. Women's Club (pres. 1965-66), Adminstrv. Mgmt. Soc. (pres. 1978-79, bd. dirs. 1972-82, 90-92, mem. nat. com. 1974-75, Diamond award 1986), Pilot Club (Woman of Yr. 1979), Delta Pi Epsilon (chpt. pres. 1953, mem. nat. com. 1972-76), Delta Kappa Gamma (treas. Gamma Eta chpt. 1980-82), Pi Lambda Theta. Methodist. Avocations: travel, reading.

FRAZIER, MARIE DUNN, speech educator, public relations and human resources specialist; b. Milton, Mass., Oct. 26, 1932; d. Lawrence Daniel and Margaret Ethel (Henry) D.; m. M. Timothy Sullivan, Apr. 17, 1960 (div. 1974); 1 child, M. Timothy Dunn Sullivan; m. John Robinson Frazier, Aug. 28, 1975. BA, Emerson Coll., 1954, MA, 1958. Cert. tchr., Mass. Mng. theater dir. Peabody Playhouse, Boston, 1955-60; dir. alumni rels. Emerson Coll., Boston, 1971-73; dir. activities, personal devel. faculty Katharine Gibbs, Boston, 1974-78; dir. rsch. and devel. Aquinas Coll., Milton, Mass., 1981-82; dir. cmty. rels. Bryman Sch., Brookline, Mass., 1981-84; resource developer Quincy (Mass.) Cmty. Action, 1987-89; adjunct faculty, lead program Eastern Nazarene Coll., Quincy, Mass., 1993-98. Adv. bd. Ctr. Lifelong Learning, Curry Coll., Milton, 1977; tng. in speech comm. for Digital Corp., Am. Sci. and Engring. Co., Gen. Time and Security Corp., Children's Hosp., Milton Savs. Bank; mem. speech comm. faculty Garland Jr. Coll., Boston, 1967-70, Aquinas Coll., Newton, Mass., 1991. Developed (seminar) Reflections on Tea, 1993. Bd. dirs. ACCLAIM Arts Group, Milton, 1989, D.W. Dunn Co., Jamaica Plain, Mass., 1962-65, Milton Hist. Soc., 1990-92, Coastlin Coun. for Children, 1987; mem. bd. Mayor's Commn. for Women, Quincy, 1988-2003; ambassador South Shore C. of C., Quincy, 1990—. Mem. AAUP, Zeta Phi Eta. Home: 25 Whitelawn Ave Milton MA 02186-3514

FRAZIER, MARY ANN, artist; b. Tulsa, Okla., Sept. 11, 1937; d. Dolphus Leonard and Elouise (Reedy) Cagle; m. Robert E. Frazier, May 14, 1954 (div. Mar. 1971); children: Robert E. Frazier, Jr. (dec.), Robbyne Elisa. Student, Tulsa C.C., 1990-92; studied with numerous artists, including, David Leffel, Ben Konis, Doug Dawson, William Herring, Mary Russell, Del Gish, others. Oil portrait David Moss, David L. Moss Correctional Ctr., Tulsa; permanent collections of portrait and other paintings in pub. and pvt. collections throughout the U.S. Home: 3338 E 27th Pl Tulsa OK 74114-5910

FRAZIER, PAUL IGNATIUS, marketing professional; b. Mt. Vernon, N.Y., June 22, 1962; s. George James and Dolores Fox F.; m. Eileen Sophie Morris, Apr. 15, 1994 (div. Nov. 1998); m. Dorian Hughes, Dec. 4, 1999; 1 child, Justin James. BS in Econs., Strayer U., 1999. Specialist Merrill Lynch Mortgage Capital, N.Y.C., 1988-91; mktg. mgr. Reuters Am., Inc., N.Y.C., 1992-97; v.p. mktg. & bus. devel. Applix, Inc., Westboro, Mass., 1998-99; chief tech. officer Spatial Techs. Industry Assocs., Washington, 1998-2000; v.p. mktg. Infovista Corp., Columbia, Mo., 2000—. Dir. tech. com. GWB Network, Washington, 1999-2000. Inventor in field. Mem. Rep. Nat. Com., Washington, 1990—. Mem. SAR. Roman Catholic. Home: 6919 Espey Ln Mc Lean VA 22101 Office: Infovista Corp 12950 Worldgate Dr 4th Fl Herndon VA 20170 E-mail: paul@intervaluary.com.

FRAZIER, THOMAS C. protective services official; married; 3 children. BA in Social Scis., MS in Adminstrn. of Criminal Justice, San Jose State U. Mem. San Jose (Calif.) Police Dept., 1967-94, dep. chief bur. field ops.; commr. Balt. Police Dept., 1994-99; nat. dir., 1999—. Trustee Milton S. Eisenhower Found.; v.p. exploring Balt. Area coun. Boy Scouts Am.; mem. Empower Balt. Mgmt. Corp.; co-chair Gov.'s Coun. on Criminal and Juvenile Crime; active Md. Spl. Olympics, Project RAISE, Hist. East Balt. Cmty. Action Coalition, Inc., Downtown Partnership Pub. Safety Coalition; mem. Mayor's Adv. Commn. on Tourism, Entertainment and Culture. Decorated Bronze Star, Air medal. Mem. Internat. Assn. Chiefs of Police, Police Exec. Rsch. Forum, Major Cities Chiefs, Md. Chiefs of Police Assn., Fraternal Order of Police.

FRAZIER, WALTER RONALD, real estate investment company executive; b. Mar. 3, 1939; s. Walter and Gracie Neydene (Bowers) F.; m. Bertina Jan Simpson, May 10, 1963; children: Ronald Blake, Stephen Bertram. BSCE, BS in Archtl. Constrn., Tex. A&M U., 1962. Tech. dir. Marble Inst., Washington, 1965-68; dir. mktg. Yeonas Co., Vienna, Va., 1969-72; pres. McCarthy Co., Anaheim, Calif., 1972-76; chmn. Equity Programs Investment Corp., Falls Church, Va., 1980-85; pres., dir. Cmty. Constrn. Co., Falls Church, 1982-85; pres. Palestrina Corp., Falls Church, 1987-99; prin. The Williamson Group, 1999—. Bd. dirs. Annandale Jaycees, 1967-69, Annandale Nat. Little League, 1983-85. 1st lt. U.S. Army, 1963-65. Named as one of Outstanding Young Men of Am., U.S. Jaycees, 1973. Mem. Nat. Assn. Home Builders (bd. dirs. 1991-96), No. Va. Bldg. Industry Assn. (1st v.p., bd. dirs. 1991-95, pres. 1994), Prince William County C. of C. (pres. bd. dirs. 1989-92). Republican. Methodist. Avocations: golf, boating. Home: 4203 Elizabeth Ln Annandale VA 22003-3668 Office: The Williamson Group 1700 Rockville Pike Ste 440 Rockville MD 20852

FRAZIER, WILLIAM EDWARD, materials engineer; b. Phila., July 6, 1954; s. William Edward Frazier, Mildred Frazier; m. Janet Brownstein; children: Laura, William. BS in Materials Engring., Drexel U., 1981, MS in Materials Engring., 1984, PhD in Materials Engring., 1987; Sr. Exec. Mgmt. Devel., Naval Aviation Exec. Inst., Patuxent River, MD, 1998; Advanced Sys. Mgmt., Def. Sys. Mgmt. Coll., Fort Belvoire, VA, 1998. EIT Pa. Materials engr. Naval Air Devel. Ctr., Warminster, Pa., 1981—95; metals, ceramics and nondestructive inspection competency mgr. Naval Air Sys. Command, Patuxent River, 1995—. Reviewer Jour. Advanced Material. Editor: Low Density, High Temperature P/M Alloys, 1991, Computational & Numerical Techniques in Powder Metallurgy, 1993, Powder Processing Education for the Year 2000, 1994, In situ Reaction for Synthesis of Composites, Ceramics, and Intermetallics, 1995, Light Weight Alloys for Aerospace Applications IV, 1997, Light Weight Alloys for Aerospace Application IIV, 2001; contbr. articles to profl. jours. Recipient Outstanding Sci. and Engring. award, Naval Air Warfare Ctr., 1992, Commanding Officer and Exec. Dir. Sci. Achievement award, 1994; fellow, Naval Air Sys. Command, 2002. Fellow: ASM Internat. (mem. AeroMat com.); mem.: TMS. Achievements include patents for Metal Matrix Composite Material with Reinforcing Polymer Fibers/Films Produced In-situ During Processing; Elevated Temperature Aluminum-Titanium Alloy By Powder Metallurgy Process; invention of Reactive Phase, Hot Isostatic Pressing of Intermetallic Alloys and Intermetallic Matrix Composites. Office: Naval Air Sys Command 48066 Shaw Rd Patuxent River MD Office Fax: 301-342-8062. Business E-Mail: frazierwe@navair.navy.mil.

FRAZIN, RHONA SONDRA, non-profit executive; b. Chgo., Feb. 4, 1949; d. Herman C. and Harriet (Pozner) Berkowitz; m. Julian J. Frazin, Oct. 6, 1990. BS in Comm., U. Ill., 1970; postgrad., DePaul U., Chgo., 1971-72. Pub. info. coord. Ill. Arts Coun., Chgo., 1970-71; pub. rels. dir. Goodman Theatre, Chgo., 1971-76; asst. dir. The Nature Conservancy, Chgo., 1976-80; prin. Rhona Schultz & Assocs., Chgo., 1977-80; dir. devel./alumni The John Marshall Law Sch., Chgo., 1980-86; exec. v.p. Met. Family Svcs., Chgo., 1986—. Comm. cons. Rhona Schultz & Assocs., 1977-80; devel. cons. Internat. Theater Festival of Chgo., 1986. Contbr. articles to profl. jours.; collaborator gridiron rev. Chgo. Bar Assn. Christmas Spirits, 1989-2000. Mem. com. justice for youth Chgo. Bar Assn., 1989-93; mem. Chgo. coun. of Planned Giving; mem. friends com., pub. chair Jesse Owens Found., 1993-97; founding dir. A Sporting Chance Found., mem. exec. com., 1995-2001. Recipient Bronze Tablet award U. Ill., 1970. Mem. Nat. Soc. Fundraising Execs., U. Ill. Chgo. Scholarship Assn. Avocations: writing satire, tennis, hiking. Home: 1560 N Sandburg Ter Chicago IL 60610-1351 Office: Metropolitan Family Svcs 14 E Jackson Blvd Ste 1400 Chicago IL 60604-2298 E-mail: jjfrazin@mindspring.com., frazinr@metrofamily.org.

FRAZZETTA, THOMAS HENRY, evolutionary biologist, functional morphologist, educator; b. Rochester, N.Y., May 13, 1934; s. Joseph H. and Louise V. (Cross) F. BS, Cornell U., 1957; PhD, U. Wash., 1964. Instr. in zoology U. Wash., Seattle, 1963-64; assoc. in herpetology Harvard U., Cambridge, Mass., 1964-65; asst. prof. U. Ill., Urbana, 1965-71, assoc. prof., 1971-76, prof. dept. ecology, ethology, evolution, 1976—. Author: Complex Adaptations in Evolving Populations, 1975; contbr. articles to jours. Active ACLU, World Wildlife Fedn., Planned Parenthood Fedn. Am., Zero Population Growth, Amnesty Internat. NIH postdoctoral fellow, 1964; NSF research grantee, 1969, 77, 86. Mem. AAAS, Am. Soc. Naturalists, Soc. Study of Evolution, Am. Soc. Ichthyologists and Herpetologists, Am. Elasmobranch Soc., Soc. for Integrative and Comparative Biology. Democrat. Office: Univ Ill Dept Animal Biology 515 Morrill Hall Urbana IL 61801 E-mail: tomfrazz@life.uiuc.edu.

FREAR, JON S. pet services company executive; b. Salt Lake City, July 23, 1973; s. Joseph W. and Linda Joyce Frear; m. Angela Marie Blair, Jan. 25, 1996; children: Joshua, Brielle. Owner Rocky Mountain Kennels, Sandy, Utah, 1991-94; pres., CEO, Rocky Mountain Kennel Club Co., Salt Lake City, 1993—, Internat. League Pet Svcs., Salt Lake City, 1993—. Pres. Apollo Group, Salt Lake City, 1998—. Author: (children's book) The Life of a Young Inventor, Book 1, 1996, The S.P.I.C.E. Book, 1999. Mem. Lds Ch. Avocations: writing, cooking, camping, hiking.

FREAR, LORRIE, graphic designer, educator; b. Rochester, N.Y., July 23, 1955; d. Charles Richard and Muriel Jean F; m. John Paul Dodd, Feb. 29, 1992. BFA, Rochester Inst. Tech., 1978, MFA, 1981. Graphic designer Gannett (newspapers), Rochester, N.Y., 1981-82, Robert Meyer Design, Rochester, N.Y., 1981-82, Gregory Fossella Assocs., Boston, 1982-84, McKesson Corp., San Francisco, 1984-88, Landor Assocs., 1985, Great Ideas Advtsg., Buffalo, 1988-99, Lorrie Frear Design, Canandaigua, N.Y., 1990—; lectr. graphic design Rochester Inst. Tech., 1990—. Art dir. Nat. Ctr. Missing & Exploited Children, Rochester, 1998; water safety instr., 1973-93; IDEA cert. fitness instr., 1987-93. Mem. Lake County Garden Club (art dir. 1999—), Genesee Valley Calligraphy Guild, Phi Kappa Phi. Independent. Baptist. Avocations: calligraphy, fitness, movies, gardening, piano. Home: 5434 Lower Egypt Rd Canandaigua NY 14424-8850 Office: RIT Sch Design Coll Imaging Arts & Scis 73 Memorial Dr Rochester NY 14623 E-mail: lxfcad@rit.edu.

FREAS, GEORGE WILSON, II, computer consultant; b. Franklin, Ky., Oct. 27, 1955; s. George Wilson and Audrey Carolyn Freas; m. Cynthia Anne Fleming, Feb. 19, 1984 (div. Oct. 1990); 1 child, Alexander Morange. BS in Computer Sci., Western Ky. U., 1979; MS in Computer Sci., U. Ala., Huntsville, 1994. Pres. Synergistic Cons., Inc., Huntsville, 1991—; software cons. Bell South Telecom., Birmingham, Ala., 1995-98; software cons. Boeing Internat. Space Sta. Marshall Space Flight Ctr., Ala., 1999—. Adj. prof. Am. Coll. Computer and Info. Scis., Birmingham, Ala., 1997—; guitarist Joyful Creations, 1999—. Author: Canny Canon, 1990; author: (software) GEN7 Desktop, 1993, LALL-LL(1), 1992. Home: PO Box 2885 Huntsville AL 35804-2885 Office: Synergistic Consultants Inc PO Box 18888 Huntsville AL 35804-8888 E-mail: marquis@gen7.net.

FREASIER, AILEEN W. special education educator; b. Edcouch, Tex., Nov. 12, 1924; d. James Ross and Ethel Inez (Riley) Wade; m. Ben F. Freasier, Mar. 9, 1944 (dec.); children: Ben. C., Doretha J. Christoph, Barbara F. McNally Protzman, Raymond E. (dec.), John F. BS HE, Tex. A and I Coll., 1944; MEd, La. Tech. U., 1966; postgrad. 90 hours, La. Tech. U. Tchr. Margaret Roane Day Care Ctr., Ruston, La., 1965-71; tchr. spl. edn. Lincoln Parish Schs., Ruston, 1971-81; individualized edn. program facilitator La. Tng. Inst. Monroe Spl. Sch. Dist. # 1, 1981-89; ednl. diagnostician LTI Monroe (La.) SSD # 1, 1985-95. R.S.V.P. vol. tutor, Lincoln Parish Detention Ctr., 1995—; citizen amb. People Conf. on Edn., Beijing, 1992, South Africa, 1995; presenter in field. Mem. editl. bd.: Jour. Correctional Edn., 1983—95, editor learning tech. sect.:, 1991—95; contbr. articles. Treas. Ruston Mayor's Commn. on Women, 1996—. Named Spl. Sch. Dist. #1 Tchr. of Yr., 1988; recipient J.E. Wallace Wallin Educator of Handicapped award La. Fedn. CEC, 1994, Meritorious Svc. award La. Dept. Pub. Safety and Corrections, 1995, Pres.'s award La. CEC-Tech. and Media, 1997. Mem. AAUW (pres. Ruston br. 1995—, state co-chair diversity task force 1993-94, state chmn. diversity com. 1994-2002, state treas. 2001-03, La. Named Gift honoree AAUW Edn. Found. 1994), CEC-Tech. and Media (treas. La. divsn. 1993-96, 2001—, Pres.'s award 1997), Internat. Correctional Edn. Assn. (spl. edn. spl. interest group, newsletter editor 1991-94, chmn. 1994-96, editl. bd. CEA Yearbook of Correctional Edn. 1998—), Nat. Soc. DAR (Long Leaf Pine chpt., regent 1997-99, constitution week chmn. 2000—), Lincoln Parish Ret. Tchrs. Assn. (yearbook editor 1996—, pres. 1998-2000), Phi Delta Kappa (past pres. chpt. 1994-96, newsletter editor 1989-93, 97-98, treas. 2002—), Kappa Kappa Iota (state pres. 1991-92, nat. scholarship com. 1995-97, nat. tech. com. 1997-99, chmn. nat. tech. com. 1999-2000, nat. profl. devel. com. 2001-03, chmn. Eta State Scholarship Com., 2002-03, chmn. bylaws com. 2003—, v.p. 2003—, chmn. Eta State Loretta Doerr award 1995, Epsilon conclave pres. 1985-87, 99-2000). Home: PO Box 1595 Ruston LA 71273-1595 E-mail: aileenwf@bayou.com.

FRECH, HARRY EDWARD, III, economics educator, consultant; b. St. Louis, Nov. 11, 1946; s. Harry Edward Jr. and Margaret Byrne (O'Reilly) F.; m. Carol Ann Vouga, June 8, 1968 (div. Aug. 1980); children: Jon Clayton, Justin Tyler; m. Elizabeth Chen, Apr. 9, 1983; 1 child, Michael Anthony. BS in Indsl. Engring., U. Mo., 1968; MA in Econs., UCLA, 1970, PhD in Econs., 1974. Economist HEW, Rockville, Md., 1970-72; asst. prof. econs. U. Calif., Santa Barbara, 1973-77, assoc. prof. econs., 1977-81, prof., 1981—, chmn. dept., 1993-94. Vis. asst. prof. econs. Harvard U., Cambridge, Mass., 1976-77; vis. prof. U. Chgo., 1982; econs. cons. FTC, Washington, 1977—, HHS, Washington, 1973-78, CNA Corp., 2000-02; expert witness U.S. Dept. Justice, Washington, 1984; adj. scholar Am. Enterprise Inst. Pub. Policy Rsch.; adj. prof. Scis. Po Paris.; vis. prof. Curtin U., Perth, Australia, 2001. Author: Competition and Monopoly in Medical Care, 1996; co-author: Public Insurance in Private Medical Markets, 1978, Taxing Energy: Oil Severance Taxation and The Economy, 1990, The Productivity of Healthcare and Pharmaceuticals: An International Comparison, 1999; assoc. editor Econ. Inquiry, 1975-78; editor: Health Care in America: The Political Economy of Hospitals and Health Insurance, 1988, Regulating Doctor's Fees, 1991; co-editor Health Economics Worldwide, 1992; N.Am. editor Internat. Jour. Econs. of Bus., 1992—; mem. editl. bd. Am. Econ. Rev., 1980-82, Econ. Inquiry, 1991-96, Regulation, 1999—, Internat. Jour. Health Care Fin. and Econ., 2000—; series editor Health Econs. and Pub. Policy; contbr. articles to profl. jours. Bd. dirs. Christ Luth. Ch., Goleta, Calif., 1978; co-organizer 2d World Congress on Health Econs., Zurich, Switzerland, 1990. Research grantee HEW, 1976, Found. for Research in Econs. and Edn., 1974, Scis. Po Paris, 1996-98. Mem. Am. Econ. Assn., So. Econ. Assn., Western Econ. Assn.. Republican. Avocations: skiing, sports car racing, sailing, reading. Home: 438 Pitzer Ct Goleta CA 93117-4013 E-mail: frech@econ.ucsb.edu.

FRÉCHET, JEAN MARIE JOSEPH, chemistry educator; b. Chalon, France, Aug. 18, 1944; came to U.S., 1967; children: Jacques Christopher, Marc Alexander. MSc, SUNY, Syracuse, 1969, PhD, 1971, Syracuse U., 1971; Doctorate (hon.), U. Lyon, 2002. Asst. prof. chemistry U. of Ottawa, Can., 1973-78, assoc. prof. chemistry, 1978-82, prof. chemistry, 1982-87; IBM prof. chemistry Cornell U., Ithaca, N.Y., 1987-95, P.J. Debye chair chemistry, 1996—98; prof. chemistry U. Calif., Berkeley, 1996—; head materials chemistry Lawrence Berkeley Nat. Lab., 1999—. Vis. scientist IBM Rsch. Lab., San Jose, Calif., 1979, 83; vice dean grad. studies and rsch. U. Ottawa, 1983-87; cons. Xerox Corp., 1979-88, Allied Signal Corp., Morristown, 1986-93, Exxon Corp., Linden, NJ, 1988—, E.I. duPont de Nemours, Wilmington, 1990-93, Loctite, 1993—, Pharmacia, 1993-95, Miles, 1994, Bayer, 1996—, Symyx, 1996—, Rhone Poulenc, 1994-99, Pharmacopeia, 1995-2001, Kodak, 1997—, Xenoport, 2000—, 3M Corp., 1999-2002; bd. dirs. Ont. Ctr. for Materials Rsch., Toronto Contbr. numerous articles to profl. jours.; patentee in field. Recipient Internat. Union Pure and Applied Chemistry award, 1983, Polymer Soc. Japan, 1986, A.K. Doolittle award, 1986, Coop. Rsch. award Am. Chem. Soc., 1994, Applied Polymer Chem. award Am. Chem. Soc., 1996, 2000, Kosar Meml. award Soc. Imaging Sci. Tech., 1999, Salute to Excellence award Am. Chem. Soc., 2001; A.C. Cope scholar Am. Chem. Soc., 2001; numerous rsch. grants. Fellow AAAS; mem. Nat. Acad. Scis., Nat. Acad. of Engring., Am. Acad. of Arts and Scis. Avocation: oenophile. Office: U Calif 718 Latimer Hl Berkeley CA 94720-1460

FRÉCHETTE, LOUISE, international organization official; Mem. General Assembly, Canada, 1972; second sec. Canadian Embassy, Athens, 1972—75; with European Affairs Div., Dept. of External Affairs, 1975—77; first sec. Canadian Mission to the UN, Geneva, 1978—82; deputy dir. Trade Policy Div., Dept. of External Affairs, 1982—83; dir. European Summit Div., 1983—85; amb. to Argentina and Uruguay Govt. of Can., 1985; asst. dep. min. for L.Am. and Caribbean Ministry of Fgn. Affairs, 1988, asst. dep. min. for internat. econ. and trade policy, 1991-92; amb. to UN, 1992-94; assoc. dep. min. Can. Dept. Fin., 1994-95, Can. Dept. of Fin., 1995; dep. minister def. Govt. of Can., 1995-98; dep. sec. gen. UN, 1998—.

FRECHETTE, PETER LOREN, dental products executive; b. Janesville, Wis., Aug. 15, 1937; s. Francis Michael and Gladys Jean F.; m. Patricia Jean O'Brien, June 24, 1961; children: Kathleen and Kristen (twins). BS in Econs., U. Wis., 1960; MBA, Northwestern U., 1980. Pres. Sci. Products, McGaw Park, Ill., 1975-82; pres., CEO Patterson Dental Co., Mpls., 1982—. Served with U.S. Army, 1961-63. Mem. Am. Dental Trade Assn. Office: Patterson Dental Co 1031 Mendota Heights Rd Mendota Heights MN 55120-1401

FRECKLETON, JON EDWARD, engineering educator, consultant, retired military officer; b. Rochester, N.Y., Feb. 23, 1939; s. William Howard and Kathryne Ann (Staud) F.; m. Terence Quirke Washburn, Mar. 15, 1966 (div. Mar. 1975); children: Melinda Leigh (DVM), Jon Karl. BSME, U. Rochester, 1961; MS in Edn., Nazareth Coll., Rochester, 1986. Profl. engr., N.Y. Engr. Eastman Kodak, Rochester, 1961-67; tree farmer Rochester, 1963—; ins. agt. W. Howard Freckleton Agy., Rochester, 1967-69; engr. N.Y. Dept. Transp., Rochester, 1969; mgr. Xerox Corp., Rochester, 1969-84; tchr. McQuaid Jesuit High Sch., Rochester, 1984-85; engring. cons. Rochester, 1984—; assoc. prof. emeritus Coll. Engring. Rochester Inst. Tech., 1985-98. Vis. assoc. prof. CAST RIT, 1998—; cons. RIT Rsch. Corp., Rochester, 1987—; workshop leader Boothroyd Dewhurst Inc., Wakefield, R.I., 1985—; workshop presenter RIT Profl. Tng. & Devel., Rochester, 1989—; com. mem. Ctr. for Integrated Mfg., Rochester, 1990-96. Editor graphics text; co-author software program; contbr. articles to profl. jours. Mem. region fish and wildlife mgmt. bd. N.Y. State Dept. Environ. Conservation, Avon, 1991-99; mem. Penfield (N.Y.) Planning Bd., 1987-89; treas. N.E. Penfield Fire Dist., 1990-97, commr., 1998—, chmn., 1999—; mem. treas. Webster Vol. Fire Dept., N.Y., 1979-83, bd. dirs., 1998-2002; committeeman Rep. Town & Country Com., Penfield & Monroe City, 1972—. With USAF, 1961-89, lt. col. USAFR ret. Named Fireman of Yr. Webster Fairport Elks, 1986; recipient N.Y. State Conspicuous Svc. Cross, 1994; Mosey fellow U. Western Australia, Perth, 1989. Mem. NSPE, N.Y. State Soc. Profl. Engrs. (life), Monroe County Soc. Profl. Engrs. (bd. dirs. 1995-97), Am. Soc. Engring. Edn., N.Y. State Forest Owners, N.Y. State Christmas Tree Growers, Adirondack Mountain Club (treas. Genesee chpt. 1991-93), Tau Beta Pi. Republican. Roman Catholic. Avocations: mountain climbing, photography, woodworking, travel, gardening. Home: 1651 Harris Rd Penfield NY 14526-1815 Office: Rochester Inst Tech 1 Lomb Memorial Dr Rochester NY 14623-5603

FRED, ROGERS MURRAY, III, veterinary oncologist; b. Leesburg, Va., July 22, 1955; s. Rogers Murray Jr. and Barbara Ann (Stewart) F.; m. Kimberly Edna Shepherd, Oct. 15, 1989; 1 child, Asa Hugh Shepherd. BS, Washington and Lee U., 1977; postgrad., U. Ga., 1979-81; DVM, Va. Poly. Inst., 1985. Staff veterinarian Abbey Animal Hosp., Balt., 1986-89; resident in vet. oncology U. Pa., Phila., 1989-91; clin. oncologist Red Bank (N.J.) Vet. Hosp. & Referral Svc., 1991—. Lectr. in field. Co-author: Connective Tissues in Health & Disease, 1980, Global Leukocyte Tumor in ats: 6 Cases, 1993, Liposome-Encapsulated Doxonubicin (Doxil) and Doxorubicin in the Treatment of Vaccine-Associated Sarcoma in Cats, 2002. Bd. dirs. Ebenezer Chs. and Cemetery Co., Bloomfield, Va., 1986—, Monmouth Hills (N.J.), Inc. Mem. SCV (camp comdr. 1988-90), Am. Vet. Med. Assn., Vet. Cancer Soc., N.J. Vet. Med. Assn., Civil War Preservation Trust, Phi Kappa Phi, Phi Zeta. Republican. Episcopalian. Avocations: reading, walking, battlefield touring, bird watching. Home: 15 Monmouth Hills Highlands NJ 07732 Office: Red Bank Vet Hosp 210 Newman Springs Rd Red Bank NJ 07701-1465

FREDERICI, C. CARLETON, lawyer; b. Jan. 17, 1938; s. Cecil Carleton and Lois Alida (Selzer) F.; m. Virginia A. Gregori, Oct. 14, 1961 (div.); m. Susan A. Low, Oct. 1, 1983; children: Gloria M., Carleton J., Charles W., Seth L. Student, Iowa State U., 1956; BA, U. Iowa, 1960, JD with high distinction, 1965. Bar: Iowa 1965, N.Y. 1966, U.S. Dist. Ct. (no. dist.) Iowa 1968, U.S. Dist. Ct. (so. dist.) Iowa 1969, U.S. Supreme Ct. 1970, U.S. Ct. Appeals (8th cir.) 1970, U.S. Ct. Appeals (3d cir.) 1973. Assoc. Willkie, Farr & Gallagher, N.Y.C., 1965-68, Shull, Marshall & Marks, Sioux City, Iowa, 1968-69, Davis, Brown, Koehn, Shors & Roberts, P.C., Des Moines, 1969-71, jr. ptnr., 1971-73, sr. ptnr., 1973-90, shareholder, 1990-95, counsel, 1996—. Spkr. Supreme Ct. Day, Law Sch. Drake U., 1973. Contbr. articles to legal publs. Vestryman St. Luke's Ch., bd. dirs., 1976-78, 82-85; mem. Polk County Rep. Cen. Com., 1969-71. 1st lt. U.S. Army, 1961-62. Mem. ABA (chmn. 8th cir. commn. on class actions and derivative suits), Iowa Bar Assn. (chmn. prison reform com., adv. mem. fed. practice commn., litigation sect. bench and bar com.), Polk County Bar Assn. (bench and bar com.), Assn. Bar City of N.Y., Am. Judicature Soc. (bd. dirs. Iowa 1990-96), Order of Coif, Wakonda Club. Office: Davis Brown Koehn Shors & Roberts PC 666 Walnut St Ste 2500 Des Moines IA 50309-3904 E-mail: ccf@lawiowa.com.

FREDERICK, ALBERT R., JR., ophthalmologist, surgeon; b. St. Petersburg, Fla., May 17, 1935; s. Albert R. Frederick; m. Suzanne Margareta Westerberg, May 3, 1969. SB, U. Fla., 1957; MD, Harvard U., 1961. Diplomate Am. Bd. Ophthalmology. Intern Boston City Hosp. II & IV Med. Svcs., 1961; resident then fellow Mass. Eye & Ear Infirmary, Boston; ophthalmic surgeon Ophthalmic Consultants Boston. Capt. USAF, 1966—68. Mem.: Boston Harvard Club. Avocations: photography, hunting, beekeeping, scuba diving, coin collecting. Office: Ophthalmic Consultants B oston Ste 600 50 Staniford St Boston MA 02114

FREDERICK, DOLLIVER H. merchant banker; b. Edmonton, Alta, Can., Apr. 2, 1944; m: Joan B. Dickau. Student, Alta Coll., U. Alta; No. Alta Inst. Tech.., 1965. With Imperial Oil Ltd., Edmonton, 1965-72; sr. analyst mktg. Toronto, Ont., Can., 1972-73; corp. devel. mgr. Hees Internat. (formerly Bovis Corp. Ltd.), 1973-75, copr. v.p., 1975-79; pres., chief operating officer Gen. Supply Co. Can. (1973) Ltd., 1975-79, Equipment Fed. Que. Ltd., 1975-79; pres. CEO, dir. CanWest Investment Corp., Toronto, Ont., 1979-81; chmn. exec. com., dir. Na-Churs Plant Food Co., Marion, Ohio, 1979-81, Macleod-Stedman, Inc., Winnipeg and Toronto, 1980-81; chmn., pres. CEO, dir. Cochran-Dunlop Lt., 1982-87, Frederick Capital Corp. (Can.) Inc., 1981—; pres., CEO, dir. Comterm Inc., 1989-90, Electrohome Ltd., 1985-87. Bd. dirs. So. Counties Oil Co., Cardlock Fuels System, PNEC Corp., Fleet Fuels. Mem. Can. Coun. Christians and Jews, dir. the Nat. Conf., 1997—. Mem. Engineers Club of Toronto, Assn. Corp. Growth, World Pres.'s Orgn., CChief Executive Org., Nat., Can. Club N.Y., Pacific Club. Republican. Office: Frederick Capital Corp 5000 Birch St Ste 3000 Newport Beach CA 92660-2140 E-mail: dhfrederick@frederickcapital.com.

FREDERICK, EDWARD CHARLES, university official; b. Mankato, Minn., Nov. 17, 1930; s. William H. and Wanda (MacNamara) F.; m. Shirley Lunkenheimer, Aug. 16, 1951; children: Bonita Frederick Treangen (dec.), Diane Frederick Fox, Donald, Kenneth, Karen Frederick Swenson. BS in Agrl. Edn, U. Minn., 1954, MS in Dairy Husbandry, 1955, PhD in Anatomy and Physiology, 1957. Animal scientist, instr. N.W. Sch. and Expt. Sta. U. Minn., Crookston, 1958-64, supt. So. Sch. and Expt. Sta. Waseca, 1964-69, provost Tech. Coll., 1969-85, chancellor Tech. Coll., 1985-90; sr. fellow Hubert H. Humphrey Inst. Pub. Affairs, 1990-91, U. Minn. Coll. of Agr., Food and Environ. Sci., 1991—. Mem. Tech. Agrl. Edn. Study Team to Morocco, 1977. Contbr. articles on dairy physiology, mgmt., agrl. edn. and adminstrn. to tech. jours. and popular publs. Bd. dirs. Bob Hodgson Student Loan Fund, 1971-90, Minn. Agrl. Interpretive Ctr., 1978—, chair, 1994—; bd. dirs. Minn. Agri-Growth Coun., 1980—, pres. 1992—; bd. dirs. Southeastern Minn. Initiative Fund, 1986-92, v.p., 1991-92; bd. dirs. Waseca area United Way, 1988-94, pres. 1992; bd. dirs. Minn. Agriculture in the Classroom, 1993-99, pres., 1995-96. Recipient Alumni award 4-H, 1972, Good Neighbor award, WCCO, 1990, Ed Frederick Day award State of Minn., 1990, Award of Merit Gamma Sigma Delta, 1994, Waseca Cmty. Svc. Above Self award, 2002, Minn. Rural Ptnrs. Lifetime Leadership award, 2002, So. Minn. Initiative Found. Ground Breaker award, 2002. Mem. Am. Dairy Assn., Am. Soc. Animal Prodn., AAAS, Nat Assn. Colls. and Tchrs. Agr. (pres. 1976-77), Am. Assn. Community and Jr

Colls. (pres. Council of Two Yr. Colls. of Four Yr. Instns. 1988-90), Minn. FFA Alumni Assn. (pres. 1998-00), South Central Edn. Assn. (Disting. Service award 1971), Waseca Area C. of C. (dir. 1979), Phi Kappa Phi. Clubs: Foresters. Lodges: Rotary (gov. dist. 596 1982-83); K.C. Roman Catholic. Home: 39031 State Highway 13 Waseca MN 56093-4212 Office: U Minn Coll Agrl Food and Env Sci Waseca MN 56093 E-mail: frede010@umn.edu.

FREDERICK, ELIZABETH ELEANOR TATUM, watercolor artist, retired educator; b. Clovis, N.Mex., Dec. 22, 1915; d. John Hardy Tatum and Bessie Elizabeth Weathers Tatum; m. George Achias Frederick, June 7, 1937 (dec. Apr. 1991); children: Ronald W., George Douglas, Barbara Elizabeth Frederick Ewing, John Lawrence. BS in Edn., U. N.Mex., 1937, MS, 1943; postgrad., Highland U., Las Vegas, N.Mex., 1944, Ea. N.Mex. U., 1944, 45. Tchr. Ctrl. H.S., Kirtland, N.Mex., 1936-37, Bellview (N.Mex.) H.S., 1940-42, Hot Springs (N.Mex.) Jr. H.S., 1943-45, 1951-53, Hot Springs (N.Mex.) H.S., 1954; ret., 1967. Exhibitions include Sierra Art Soc., N.Mex., Willamette Oaks Retirement Ctr., Eugene, Oreg., 1995, El Paso Mus. Art, N.Mex. Art League, N.Mex. Watercolor Soc., Albuquerque. Represented in permanent collections. Mem. Nat. League Am. Pen Women (pres. Rio Grande br. 1975-76), Sierra Art Soc. (pres. 1974-75, funding and program chmn. 1975-89), N.Mex. Watercolor Soc., Black Range Artists (sec.-treas. 1978-79). Republican. Avocations: sweepstakes, worldwide travel.

FREDERICK, GEORGE FRANCIS, retired manufacturing executive; b. Cleve., Jan. 24, 1937; s. George Henry and Margaret Mary (Gibson) F.; m. Mary Jane Masielli, Oct. 20, 1956; children: Denise Marie, George Charles, Donna Marie, Karl Stephen. Assoc. in Machine Design, Cleve. Engring. Inst., 1957; BS, SUNY, Albany, 1977. Cert. mfg. engr. Supr. mfg. engring. Sq. D Co., Cleve., 1956-66; supr. stds. engring. TRW, Cleve., 1966-69; mgr. engring. Rossgear divsn. TRW, Ind. and Tenn., 1969-80; ops. mgr. Control Concepts divsn. TRW, Newton, Pa., 1980-82; gen. mgr. Falcon Products, Greeneville, Tenn., 1982-84; sr. v.p. ops. Lockley Mfg. Group divsn. of Entwistle Co., Hudson, Mass., 1984-92, pres., 1992-95; exec. v.p., gen. mgr., dir. Advanced Tech. and Rsch. Corp., Burtonsville, Md., 1996-99; project mgr. John Deere & Co., Greeneville, 1999—2002; with Frederick & Assocs., 2002—. Bd. dirs. Jameson Health Care System, Lawrence County Econ. Devel. Corp. Co-chmn. New Castle Area Labor Mgmt. Com., 1987-95; dist. chmn. Boy Scouts Am., Greeneville, 1982-83, 1987-88; bd. dirs. United Way, 1981. Mem. KC, Inst. Indsl. Engrs. (sr. mem. exec. bd. 1972-74), The Mfrs. Assn., Lions. Republican. Roman Catholic. Avocations: golf, reading, computers. Home and Office: 255 Par Ln Greeneville TN 37743-2282 E-mail: gfrederick4@juno.com.

FREDERICK, NANCY ACKERMAN, real estate broker; b. Cleve., Apr. 1, 1942; d. William Houston Ackerman and Margaret Post; m. Nicholas Frederick, June 26, 1965; children: Jacqueline, Barbara Hinckley, Nicholas. BS in Elem. Edn., Taylor U., 1964; postgrad., Glassboro State U. Lic. real estate salesperson, N.J., real estate broker. Tchr. Kingston Elem. Sch., Cherry Hill, N.J., 1964-68; real estate salesperson Sterling Assocs., Somerdale, N.J., 1974-75, Bob Pritchett & Co., Cherry Hill, 1975-79, office mgr. Merchantville, N.J., 1980-81, Cherry Hill, 1981-82; sales rep., broker Prudential Fox & Roach Realtors, Cherry Hill, 1982—. Mem. social planning com., fellow Camden County Bd. Realtors, Cherry Hill, 1974-75; site mgr. Home Equity Relocation Co., Danbury, Conn., 1983-96. Bldg. rep. Cherry Hill Edn. Assn., 1965-68; vol. officer Camden County Probation Dept., 1970-72; tchr. Sunday sch. Bethel Bapt. Ch., Cherry Hill, 1967-77, University Bapt. Ch., Sarasota, Fla., 1999-2002; sec. bd. trustees Ocean Colony Condominium, Ocean City, N.J., 1988-89, mem. 5-yr. planning bd.; chmn. memberships Home and Sch. Assn., Cherry Hill, 1983; mem. Barclay Farm Civic Assn., Cherry Hill, 1985-96. Fellow N.J. Assn. Realtors (Million Dollar Sales awards 1983-94); mem. AAUW, NAFE, Barclay Farm Swim Club. Republican. Avocations: gardening, swimming, walking, bicycling, traveling. Home: 6712 Spring Moss Pl Bradenton FL 34202-2236

FREDERICK, NORMAN L., JR., electrical engineer; b. Hopkinsville, Ky., Feb. 7, 1965; s. Norman L. and Nancy A. (Bass) F. ASES, Hudson Valley C.C., 1985; BSEE, Union Coll., Schenectady, 1987; MSEE, Syracuse U., 1990. Comm. engr. GE, Schenectady, 1986; systems engr. Rome Air Force devel. ctr. MITRE, Griffiss AFB, Rome, N.Y., 1987-89; researcher, teaching asst. Syracuse (N.Y.) U., 1989-90; R&D elec. engr. HP EESOF divsn. Hewlett Packard, Westlake Village, Calif., 1991-98; sr. RF engr. Qualcomm, Inc., San Diego, 1998—. Mem. IEEE, Tau Beta Pi, Eta Kappa Nu, Sigma Xi. Achievements include research on one to three phase converter circuits, near fields for phased array antennas; development of T-Matrix method for relation of current distribution to near field, communication systems and RF-microwave circuit simulators, RX,TX design for cellular phones and RFIC Inductor modeling. Office: Qualcomm Inc 5775 Morehouse Dr San Diego CA 92121-1714 E-mail: normanf@qualcomm.com.

FREDERICK, PAUL G. financial services systems company executive; Assoc. ptnr. Andersen Cons.; CEO AIT (USA) Inc., Meriden, Conn., 1995—. Office: AIT (USA) Inc 639 Research Pkwy Ste 100 Meriden CT 06450

FREDERICK, RANDALL DAVIS, political organization administrator, state legislator; m. Cindy Abraham; 3 children. Student, S.D. State U., 1974-76. Mem. S.D. Ho. of Reps., 1989-92, mem. appropriations com., 1992-93, mem. taxation and transp. coms., 1992—, chmn. appropriations com., 1994—, co-chmn. joint appropriations com., 1994—; senator S.D. State Senate, 1993—, co-chair appropriations com., 1993—; chmn. S.D. Republican Party, 2003—. Farmer, Hayti, S.D., 1976—. Home: RR 1 Box 106 Hayti SD 57241-9629 Office: SD Republican State Ctrl Com PO Box 1099 401 E Sioux Ave Pierre SD 57501*

FREDERICK, RICHARD JOHN, education educator; b. Lowell, Mass., Jan. 11, 1950; s. Richard Dix and Emma Frederick; m. Phyllis Kay Wallace, July 2, 1976; children: Candace Lynn, Lisa Marie. AAS, U. of Ky. C.C. Sys., 1978—80; BBA, Austin Peay State U., 1980—82; MBA, U. of Memphis, 1999—2000. Lic. State of Tenn., 1987. Prodn. ops. mgr. Cress Mfg., Hopkinsville, 1974—78; retail 41 North Liquor, Hopkinsville, 1978—82; mgmt. Credit Thrift of Am., Hopkinsville, Ky., 1982—85, Prudential Ins. Co., Memphis, Tenn., 1987—2000; instr. of mgmt. Rust Coll., Holly Springs, Miss., 2000—. Sports writer: golf stories for local paper. Deacon Ross Rd. Ch. of Christ, Memphis, Tenn., 1991—2003. With USN, 1970—74. Recipient Mem. Million Dollar Round Table, Life Underwriters, 1989 and 1990, Agt. of the Yr., 1989, Alpha Beta Gamma, Nat. Bus. Honor Soc., 1980, Omicron Delta Epsilon, Honor Soc. of Economics, 1981. Republican. Avocations: golf, photography, basketball. Home: 7480 Hedgington Dr Memphis, TN 38125 Office: Rust Coll 150 Rust Ave Holly Springs, MS 38635 Personal E-mail: rjfred1054@aol.com. E-mail: rfrederick@rustcollege.edu.

FREDERICK, ROBERT ALLEN, history educator; b. Mishawaka, Ind., Feb. 3, 1928; s. Ralph Leon and Garnet Laree (Bowles) F.; m. Mary Billington Swartz, Nov. 23, 1950 (div. Sept. 1967); children: Julia Christian, John Billington, Peter Carey; m. Saradell Carolyn Ard, Sept. 9, 1969 (div. April 1983). BA, Hanover Coll., 1950; MS in Edn., Ind. U., 1951, PhD in History, 1960. Assoc. dean students Tex. Technol. Coll., Lubbock, 1951-53; instr. history U.S. Naval Acad. Prep Sch., 1953-56; grad. asst. history Ind. U., Bloomington, 1956-58, fellow dept. history, 1958-60; assoc. prof. history Alaska Meth. U., Anchorage, 1960-66, prof. history, chmn. dept., 1966-73; exec. dir. Alaska Hist. Commn., Anchorage, 1973-80; ind. rschr./writer Alaska Hist. Soc., Anchorage, 1980-85; editor Ind. German Heritage Soc., Indpls., 1986-88; Richard Lieber rschr. Brown County Hist. Soc., Nashville, Ind., 1988-93. Dir. Alaska humanities task force NEH, 1972-73. Editor/contbr. Frontier Alaska: Historical Opportunity, 1968, Writing Alaska's History: A Guide to Research, 1974; contbr., hist. photo editor Anchorage: Star of the North, 1982; author: Alaska's Quest for Statehood: 1867-1959, 1985, Passage to Community: Creating the State-Based Alaska Humanities Forum, 1973; editor: newsletter Ind. German Heritage Soc., 1986-89. Pres. Cook Inlet Hist. Soc., Anchorage, bd. dirs., 1963-66; pres. Alaska Hist. Soc., 1968-69, bd. dirs., 1967-74; mem. nat. archives adv. bd. Nat. Archives and Records Svcs., Regions IX and X, 1974-77; chmn. Nat. Trust for Hist. Preservation, 1975-77, bd. advisors, 1969-78, advisor emeritus, 1979—; dir. A Pioneer Family in Alaska (film) U. Alaska Found., Homer, 1982. Lt. USNR, 1953-56. Ind. Heritage Rsch. grantee Ind. Humanities Coun., 1987-91. Mem. Historic Landmarks Found. Ind., Sigma Chi (life). Democrat. Avocations: hiking in wilderness, visiting natural and historical sites. Home: 1950 S Dayton St #220N Denver CO 80247-3454

FREDERICK, ROBERT MELVIN, retired farm organization executive; b. Wadsworth, Ohio, Feb. 1, 1923; s. Llewellyn Rorthrock and Golda May (Joycox) F.; m. Rosemary Rothgary, Feb. 14, 1955; children: Pamela Sue, Mark Llewllyn. BA, Ohio State U., 1948. Horticulturist family farm, Wadsworth, 1948-56; ext. horticulturist Purdue U., Vincennes, Ind., 1957-59; exec. sec. Am. Vegetable Growers Assn., Washington, 1959-61; gen. mgr. Fla. Flower Assn., Ft. Myers, 1961-63, Fla. Growers Coop., Ft. Myers, 1963-66; pres. Ruke Transport, Ft. Myers, 1966-67; sales mgr. Green Thumb Products, Toledo, 1967-68; legis. dir. Nat. Grange, Washington, 1968-96, dir. adminstrn., 1996—. Mem. agr. policies adv. com. USDA/U.S. Trade Rep., Washington, 1970-80, mem. fruit and vegetable com., 1970-84; mem. agr. census adv. com. Dept. Commerce, Washington, 1971-85. Mem. Medina County (Ohio) Rep. Com., 1956. Sgt. USMCR, 1942-45, PTO. Recipient Alumni Disting. Svc. award Ohio State U., 1995, Agr. Frat. Centennial hon. Alpha Zeta, 1997. Mem. Nat. Planning Assn. (food and agr. com.), Nat. Grange (7th degree, past master, ec., exec. com. Potomac chpt.). Avocation: gardening.

FREDERICK, SHERMAN, publishing executive; Pub. Las Vegas (Nev.) Rev.-Jour.; pres. Stephens Media Group (formerly Donrey Media Group). Office: Las Vegas Rev-Journal PO Box 70 1111 W Bonanza Rd Las Vegas NV 89125*

FREDERICK, SUSAN LOUISE, preschool educator; b. Somers Point, N.J., May 2, 1964; d. Ingeborg Louise (Böhmer) Kimbark; m. R. Scott Frederick, Oct. 6, 1984; 1 child, Taylor Scott. BS in Edn. with honors, Millersville (Pa.) U., 1993; postgrad., Millersville U., 2002—. Cert. elem. and early childhood tchr. Graphic artist Datcon Instrument Co., East Petersburg, Pa., 1984-86; day care provider Small Steps Early Learning Ctr., Lancaster, Pa., 1986-89; substitute elem. tchr. Lancaster County Sch. Dists., 1993-94; elem. co-op tchr. Manheim Twp. Parent's Co-op, Lancaster, 1993; day care provider Small Frey's Children's Ctr., Manheim, Pa., 1991-96; pre-kindergarten, presch. tchr. St. Peter's Presch., Lancaster, 1993—; elem. co-op. tchr. Manheim Twp. Parent's Co-op., Lancaster, 1995, 1997—2000, supr. student tchr., 2003. Mem. bd. Christian edn. St. Paul's United Ch. of Christ, Manheim, Pa., 1985-87, co-dir. vacation bible sch., 1987; mem. Manheim Area Jaycees, 1988-89; v.p. Stiegel Elem. Sch. P.T.O., 2001-2002, pres., 2003-; sponsor Youth Encouragement program St. Paul's U.C.C., Manheim, Pa., 2001—. Mem. ASCD, Phi Kappa Phi. Avocations: crafts, reading, gardening, decorating, indoor soccer. Home: 125 E Ferdinand St Manheim PA 17545-1605

FREDERICK, WILLIAM GEORGE DEMOTT, defense company executive, consultant; b. Toledo, Ohio, June 23, 1936; s. Rolland Leslie Frederick and Ruth Matilda (Collins) Gates; m. Nancy Lee Spalding, June 14, 1958 (div. July 14, 1981); m. Geralyn Goldman Middleton, Aug. 14, 1981; children: William George DeMott, Rebecca Ann Rudich, Frank Gibson Goldman. BS in Engring. Physics, U. Toledo, 1954—58; MS in Physics, U. Dayton, Ohio, 1965—68; PhD in Materials Sci., U. Cin., 1969—73; MS in Mgmt., MIT, Cambridge, Mass., 1979—80. Physicist Air Force Materials Lab., Dayton, Ohio, 1958—83; staff specialist, early warning, air def., and attack assessment Office of Sec. of Def., Washington, 1983—84; dir., sensor tech. Strategic Def. Initiative Orgn., Washington, 1984—92; asst. dep. for tech. Ballistic Missile Def. Orgn., Washington, 1992—99, chief scientist, 1999—2000, dep. for spl. projects, 2000—01; corp. v.p. Photon Rsch. Assocs., Inc., Arlington, Va., 2001—. Editor: (handbook) Strategic Defense Initiative Launch Phenomenology, 1994; contbr. articles to profl. jours. Recipient Arthur S. Flemming Award, Downtown Jaycees, Wash., DC, 1976, Levinstein Award, Detector Speciality Group, Infrared Info. Symposium, 1989, Jerry L. Beard Award, Targets, Backgrounds, and Discrimination Group, IRIS, 1995, John A. Jamieson Meml. Award, Sensors, Enviroments and Algorithms, Mil. Sensing Symposium, 2001; fellow, Mil. Sensing Symposium, 2001. Mem.: AIAA (Strategic Def. Lifetime Achievement Award 1995), AAAS, Am. Phys. Soc. Avocation: travel. Home: 11511 Stonewood Ln North Bethesda MD 20852-4309 Office: Photon Rsch Assocs Inc 1911 N Fort Myer Dr Ste 408 Arlington VA 22209 Home Fax: 301-468-2966; Office Fax: 703-243-6619. Personal E-mail: wgdf@aol.com. E-mail: wfrederick@photon.com.

FREDERICKS, DAVID MICHAEL, merchant banker, venture capitalist; b. Balt., Sept. 17, 1950; s. John Leonard and Emily F.; children: Marcy Lee, Ian Michael. BS in Mgmt., Indiana U. of Pa., 1972. CPA, N.Y. Owner, ptnr. K&F Constrn., L.I., N.Y., 1967-69, ICW Ltd., L.I., N.Y., 1969-71; staff acct. Price Waterhouse & Co., L.I., N.Y., 1972-75; ptnr. Touche Ross & Co., N.Y.C., 1975-84; mng. dir. Fredericks Michael & Co. Inc., N.Y.C., 1985—; non-exec. chmn. bd. dirs. Fredericks Michael & Co. Ltd., London, 2001—. Chmn. FM Ventures, Inc., 1989—. Contbr. in field. Mem. Concerned Citizens of Montauk (N.Y.), 1976—, bus. adv. coun. Ind. U. of Pa., 1996—; bd. dirs. N.Y. Gilbert & Sullivan Players, N.Y.C., 1982-86. Named Eberly Entrepreneur of Yr. Achievements in Finance, 1997. Mem. AICPA, N.Y. State Soc. CPAs, N.Y. Athletic (N.Y.C.) Club, Union (N.Y.C.) Club. Roman Catholic. Home: Dogwood St PO Box 520 Montauk NY 11954-0501 Office: 2 Wall St New York NY 10005-2001 E-mail: fredericks@fm-co.com.

FREDERICKS, JEANNE MARIA JUDSON, literary agent; b. Mineola, N.Y., Apr. 19, 1950; d. Howard William and Christina Hannah Judson; m. Wesley Charles Fredericks, Jr., May 19, 1973; children: Carolyn Anne, Wesley Charles III. BA, Mt. Holyoke Coll., 1972; MBA, NYU, 1979; publ. procedures course, Radcliffe Coll. Asst. to editl. dir., subs. rights dir. Basic Books, N.Y.C., 1972-74; asst. mng. editor Macmillan Publ. Co., N.Y.C., 1974-76, mng. editor, 1976-78, acquisitions editor, 1978-80; editl. dir. Ziff-Davis Books, N.Y.C., 1980-81; literary agent Susan P. Urstadt, Inc., New Canaan, Conn., 1990-96, acting dir., 1996-97; pres. Jeanne Fredericks Literary Agy., Inc., New Canaan, 1997—. Spkr. in field. Co-chair, co-founder Mothers' Group Congl. Ch., Wilton, Conn., 1984-87; bd. dirs. New Canaan H.S. Crew, 1999—2002, co-pres., 2002-03; trustee New Canaan Congregational Ch., 2001—. Mem. Assn. Authors' Reps., Authors Guild, Inc., Phi Beta Kappa. Republican. Congregationalist. Avocations: crew, tennis, gardening, reading. Office: Jeanne Fredericks Literary Agy Inc 221 Benedict Hill Rd New Canaan CT 06840-2913

FREDERICKS, JOAN DELANOY, retired health science administrator; b. Dobbs Ferry, N.Y., Feb. 27, 1928; d. Robert Bert and Amelia (DeLanoy) F.; m. Stanley Whetstone, Mar. 20, 1993. BA, Skidmore Coll., Saratoga Springs, N.Y., 1949; MA, Syracuse U., 1954. Rsch. asst. C.F. Kettering Found., Yellow Springs, Ohio, 1949-50; rsch. tech. SUNY Upstate, Syracuse, 1950—54, Duke U. Med. Sch., Durham, N.C., 1954-58, NIH, Bethesda, Md., 1958-88; ret., 1988. Chemist Nat. Inst. Arthritis and Metabolic Diseases, NIH, Bethesda, 1958-63, scientific grant asst. Nat. Inst. Heart, Lung and Blood Diseases, Bethesda, 1963-70, asst., program dir. Nat. Inst. Arthritis Metabolism and Digestive Diseases, 1970-81, exec. sec. divsn. Rsch. Grants, 1981-88; cons. in field. Mem. Summer Sq. Condominium Assn., NIH Alumni Assn. (bd. dirs.). Avocations: painting with watercolors, travel, elderhostels, hiking, water aerobics, playing violin.

FREDERICKS, LILLIAN ELIZABETH, anesthesiologist; b. Vienna, Jan. 23, 1914; MD, Med. Coll. Pa., 1941. Diplomate Am. Bd. Anesthesiology. Intern Montgomery Hosp., Norristown, Pa., 1941-42; resident anesthesiology Women's Med. Coll. Hosp., Phila., 1949-50, Hahnemann Hosp., Phila., 1950-51, anesthesiologist Albert Einstein Med. Ctr., Phila., 1952-72, U. Pa. Hosp., Phila., 1972-80. Fellow Soc. Clin. and Exptl. Hypnosis, Am. Soc. Clin. Hypnosis, Internat. Soc. Clin. Hypnosis; mem. Am. Bd. Med. Hypnosis (cert.), Am. Med. Women's Assn. Home and Office: 3360 S Ocean Blvd Apt 3hs Palm Beach FL 33480-5668 E-mail: lillianf@bellsouth.net.

FREDERICKS, PATRICIA ANN, real estate executive; b. Durand, Mich., June 5, 1941; d. Willis Edward and Dorothy (Plowman) Sexton; m. Ward Arthur Fredericks, June 12, 1960; children: Corrine Ellen, Lorraine Lee, Ward Arthur II. BA, Mich. State U., 1962; cert. mediator, U. Calif., 1999. Cert. Grad. Real Estate Inst., residential broker, residential salesperson; cert. real estate broker. Assoc. Stand Brough, Des Moines, 1976-80; broker Denton, Tucson, 1980-83; broker-trainer Coldwell Banker, Westlake Village, Calif., 1984-90; broker, br. mgr. Brown, Newbury Park, Calif., 1990-94; dir. tng. Brown Real Estate, Westlake Village, Calif., 1994-95; gen. mgr., dir. mktg. Coldwell Banker Town & Country Real Estate, Newbury Park, Calif., 1994—; dir. mktg. Coldwell Banker Town and Country, 1995—. Bd. sec. Mixtec Corp., Thousand Oaks, Calif., 1984—; pres. Mixtec Real Estate Tng. Contbr. articles to profl. jours. Pres. Inner Wheel, Thousand Oaks, 1991, 96-97; bd. dirs. Community Leaders Club, Thousand Oaks, 1991, Conejo Future Found., Thousand Oaks, 1989-92, Wellness Community Ventura Valley, 1994—. Mem. ABA, Calif. Assn. Realtors (dir. 1988-95 regional chair 1995, vice-chair expn. 1997, chair Calif. Expo 1998), Calif. Assn. Edn. (com. chair 2003), Conejo Valley Assn. Realtors (sec., v.p., pres.-elect 1989-92, pres. 1993, Realtor of Yr. 1991), Calif. Desert Assn. Realtors (bd. dirs. 2003—), Pres.'s Club Mich. State U., Com. 100, Cmty. Concerts Assn., Alliance for the Arts, Conejo Valley Symphony Guild, Wellness Cmty., Indian Wells Country Club, North Ranch Country Club, Sherwood Country Club, Aviation Country Club Calif. E-mail: classybker@aol.com.

FREDERICKS, ROBERT JOSEPH, language company executive; b. N.Y.C., Dec. 26, 1934; s. Harold D. and Mary E. (McCarthy) F.; m. Jeanette C. Kubin, July 7, 1984. BS in Chemistry, Villanova U., 1957; MS in Chemistry, St. Joseph's Coll., Phila., 1959; PhD in Chemistry, Lehigh U., 1965. Rsch. chemist GAF Corp., Easton, Pa., 1960-67; rsch. supr. Allied Chem. Corp., Morristown, N.J., 1968-72; mgr. analytical chemistry Ethicon, Inc., Somerville, N.J., 1972-74, dir. rsch. svcs., 1974-76, assoc. dir. rsch., 1976-78; v.p. R&D, bd. dirs. Surgikos, Piscataway, NJ, 1978-79, Johnson & Johnson Dental Products Co., East Windsor, NJ, 1980-81; sr. v.p., gen. mgr., COO Biosci. Med. Products, Somerville, NJ, 1982-85; pres. Allen Transl. Svc., Morristown, N.J., 1985—. Author: X-Ray Diffraction for the Industrial Chemist, 1971; contbr. articles to profl. jours. Pres. Morris County Hist. Soc., Morristown, 1982—86, trustee, 1975—93; pres. Washington Assn. N.J., Morristown, 1988—92, 1993—99, trustee, 1983—2002, Craftsman Farms Found., 1994; mem. adv. bd. New Philharm., NJ, 1992—99, trustee, 1994—98, 1st v.p., 1995—98; hon. historian Twp. of Morris, 1992—. Lt (j.g.) USN, 1958—60. Recipient Achievement award Washington Assn., 2000. Mem.: AAAS, N.Y. Acad. Scis., Am. Chem. Soc., Am. Assn. Sovereign Mil. Order of Malta (N.J. state chmn. 2003—, chmn. Lourdes 2003 pilgrimage, N.J. Hospitaller), Rotary (bd. dirs. 1992—93), Morristown Club (bd. govs. 1996—, v.p. 1998, pres. 1999—2002), Morristown Field Club, Sigma Xi, Delta Epsilon Sigma. Republican. Roman Catholic. Avocations: tennis, gardening. Home: 16 Butterworth Dr Morristown NJ 07960-2625

FREDERICKS, SHARON KAY, nurse's aide; b. Grand Rapids, Mich., July 12, 1942; d. Leroy and Edith Luella (Crawford) F. Cert. in Interior Decorating, LaSalle U., 1975; AAS, Community Svc. Asst., Kalamazoo Valley Coll., 1982; assoc. paralegal studies, Internat. Corr. Schs., Scranton, Pa., 1993; AAS in Bus. Mgmt., Davenport Coll., 1994, BBA in Bus. Adminstrn., 1997. Cashier Goodwill Industries, Battle Creek, Mich., 1963; dishwasher Woolworths, Kalamazoo, 1963; nurses aide Mary L. Bocher, Kalamazoo, 1964-69, Sisters St. Joseph, Nazareth, Mich., 1976-98; kitchen aide Saga Foods, Kalamazoo Valley C.C., 1981-82, Saga Foods, Nazareth Coll., 1983-84; ind. sales rep. Avon, 2000—01. Vol. Portage Ctrl. Jr. and Sr. High Sch., 1961-62, Bronson Meth. Hosp., Kalamazoo, 1961-62, nurse aide ARC, 1964-69, Bloodmobiles Bronson Meth. Hosp., 1970-75, Borgess Med. Ctr., 1977, Kalamazoo (Mich.) Juvenile Ct., 1980-86; sec.-treas. 3d Order St. Francis Secular, 1976-79, pres., dir. pres. pub. rels. and bulls., 1979-81, participant neighborhood watch Vine Neighborhood, Kalamazoo, 1985-88; vol. Cath. Family Svcs., 1991—; vol. adminstrv. aide, Kalamazoo, 1991—; vol. monitor Kalamazoo Women's Festival, 1991, 92; mem. grounds com. New Horizon Village, 1998, neighborhood watch com., 1999; chair pet com. New Horizon Village, Kalamazoo; active Mich. Campaign for Quality Care, 2002—; amb. AARP, Mich., 2002-03; public rels. AARP, Kalamazoo chpt., 2003—. Thomas F. Reed Jr. scholar Davenport Coll., 1993; recipient John Edgar Hoover gold medal, 1991; named Vol. of Month, Kalamazoo Regional Psychiat. Hosp., July 1976; named Vol. of Week, Cath. Family Svcs., Sept. 13, 1993, Oct. 1995. Mem.: AARP (Mich. amb. vol. 2001—03, pub. rels. vol. A.A. chpt. 1020 Kalamazoo br.), Davenport U. Alumni Assn. Roman Catholic. Avocations: photography, textile painting, helping people, reading, learning wildlife, environmental policies, pet policies, governmental policies. Home: 2310 Inverness Ln Apt 204 Kalamazoo MI 49048-1459 *Read, keep learning, love your fellow man, look for the good in every person. Reach for the stars, be prepared. Life isn't always easy, it can be a roller-coaster, it can be interesting too.*

FREDERICKS, WARD ARTHUR, venture capitalist, food industry consultant; b. Tarrytown, N.Y., Dec. 24, 1939; s. Arthur George and Evelyn (Smith) F.; m. Patricia A. Sexton, June 12, 1960; children: Corrine E., Lorrine L., Ward A. BS cum laude, Mich. State U., 1962, MBA, 1963, PhD. Assoc. dir. Technics Group, Grand Rapids, Mich., 1964-68; gen. mgr. logistics systems Massey-Ferguson, Inc., Toronto, Ont., Can., 1968-69, v.p. mgmt. svcs., comptr., 1969-73, sr. v.p. fin., dir. fin. Americas, 1975—; comptr. Massey-Ferguson Ltd., Toronto, Ont., Can., 1973-75; prin. W.B. Saunders & Co., Washington, 1962—64; sr. v.p. mktg. Massey.Ferguson, Inc., 1975-78, also pres., gen. mgr. tractor divsn., 1978-80; gen. mgr. Rockwell Graphic Sys., 1980-82; pres. Goss Co.; v.p. ops. Rockwell Internat., Pitts., 1980-84; v.p. Fed. MOG, 1983-84; chmn. MIXTEC Group LLC, 1998—2002; also dir., chmn.; prin. Venture Assocs., 1993—. Dir. Polyfet RF, Inc., Venture Assocs., Badger Horthland, Inc., MST, Inc., Calif., Tech-Mark Group, Inc., Spectra Tech., Inc., Mixtec Group-Venture Capital, Inc., Unicorn Corp., Mixtec Food Group Calif., Mixtec Signal Tech., Harry Ferguson, Inc., M.F. Credit Corp., M.F. Credit Co. Can Ltd.; chmn. ProduceCareers.com., 2000-2002.; mem. bd. councillors Calif. State U., 2002. Author: (with Edward Smykay) Physical Distribution Management, 1974; author: Management Vision, 1988, Competitive Advantage in Technology Organizations, 1986, Competitive Advantage in Technology Firms, 1996; contbr. articles to profl. jours. Bd. dirs., mem. exec. com. Des Moines Symphony, 1975-79; pres. Conejo Symphony, 1988-90; pres. Westlake Village Cultural Found., 1991; mem. exec. com. Alliance for Arts; pres. Conejo Valley Indsl. Assn., 1990, 93; mem. Constn. Bicentennial Com., 1987-88, Ventura County Airport Commn., 1995-99, La Quinta Arts Found.; mem. World Affairs Coun. of the Desert, pres., 2002--; bd. dirs. Ventura County Bus. Incubator, 1996-99, Cochella Valley Cmty. Concerts Assn., 1992-95; pres. Indian Wells Desert Symphony, 2002; v.p. Com. Leaders Club, 1988, pres., 1989-90, pres. Westlake Cultural Found., 1991; vice chair Alliance for the Arts; bd. regents Calif. Luth. U., 1990-99, chmn. acad. affairs, 1993-99, exec. com., 1992-99, chmn. acad. affairs, 1992-99, vice chmn., 1997-98; pres. Aviation C.C. of Calif., 2001; pres. coun. McCallen Theater, Palm Desert; mem. Pres.'s circle Coll. of the Desert, Palm Desert; pres. World Affairs Coun. of the Desert, 2002--; mem. Rep. Ctrl. Com., State of Calif., 1993-98; bd. dirs. Indian Wells Desert Symphony, 2001-02; pres. World Affairs Coun. of the Desert, 2001—; bd. dirs. Coll. Desert of Found., 2003—; pres. Fredericks Found., 2002—; chmn. Westlake Village C. of C., 1990. Fellow Am. Transp. Assn.; mem. AAAS, IEEE, SAR, Am. Mktg. Assn., Nat. Coun. Phys. Distbn. Mgmt. (exec. com. 1974), Produce Mktg. Assn., United Fresh Fruit and Vegetable Assn., Internat. Fresh-Cut Produce Assn., Soc. Automotive Engrs., U.S. Strategic Inst., Tech. Execs. Forum (Tech. Corridor 100 award 1989), Internat. Food Mfg. Assn., Produce Mktg. Assn., Toronto Bd. Trade, Westlake Village C. of C. (chmn. 1990), Old Crows, Assn. Advanced Tech. Edn., Air Force Assn., Aerospace Soc., Exptl. Aircraft Assn., Mil. Order World Wars, Conf. Air Force (Col.), Westlake Village C. of C. (chmn. bd. 1990-91), Cmty. Leaders Club, Pres.'s Club Mich. State U., Pres.'s Circle/Coll. of the Desert, English-Spkg. Union, Friends of Parliament, Indian Wells Country Club, Sherwood Country Club, St. Georges Club (U.K.), Aviation Country Club of Calif. (v.p. 1999, pres. 2000), Rotary (dir. 2003—), Flying Rotarians, World Affairs Coun., Beta Gamma Sigma. Lutheran. Home: 75375 Painted Desert Dr Indian Wells CA 92210 Office: 709 E Colorado Blvd Pasadena CA 91101

FREDERICKS, WENDY ANN, graphic designer; b. Queens, N.Y., Oct. 27, 1955; d. Robert John and Margaret Ellen (Wright) Politica; children: Dawn, Kurt. BFA in Graphic Design cum laude, SUNY, Buffalo, 1978. Freelance book designer and promoter, 1980-86; book promotions and cover designer Thieme Med. Pubs., N.Y.C., 1986-88; sr. designer Caliber Design, Long Island City, N.Y., 1988-91, HarperCollins Pubs., N.Y.C., 1992-93, design mgr., 1993-96, Pearson Longman, N.Y.C., 1996—. Brownie and jr. scout leader Girl Scouts U.S., Valley Stream, N.Y., 1990-93. Regents scholar, 1973; recipient 1st Place series design Bookbinders Guild, 1998, Merit award for book design Book-

binders Guild, 2000. Mem. Unity Ch. of Christianity. Home: 7 Hunter Ave Valley Stream NY 11580-3027 Office: Pearson Longman Ste 1700 1185 Avenue Of The Americas 26th Fl New York NY 10036-2601

FREDERICKS, WESLEY CHARLES, JR., lawyer; b. N.Y.C., Mar. 31, 1948; s. Wesley Charles and Dionysia W. (Bitsanis) F.; m. Jeanne Maria Judson, May 19, 1973; children: Carolyn Anne, Wesley Charles III. BA, Johns Hopkins U., 1970; JD, Columbia U., 1973. Bar: N.Y. 1974, Conn. 1976, U.S. Supreme Ct. 1979. Assoc. Shearman & Sterling, N.Y.C., 1973-83; chmn. bd. Lotus Performance Cars, L.P., Norwood, N.J., 1983-87; group exec. cons. Group Lotus PLC, 1987; automotive industry cons., 1988-90; pres., CEO Mfrs. Products Co., 1990-94; counsel Gersten, Savage, Kaplowitz & Fredericks, LLP, N.Y.C., 1994, ptnr., 1995-98, Dorsey & Whitney LLP, N.Y.C., 1998—, co-head Worldwide Corp. Dept., 2003—. Mem. Johns Hopkins U. Alumni Schs. Com. With USMC, 1968-69. Mem. ABA (vice-chmn. bus. law sect. com. on internat. bus. law, 2002—, co-chmn. subcom. multinat. mergers and acquisitions 1996—, mem. com. on negotiated acquisitions 1997—), Mashomack Fish and Game Preserve, Campfire Am. Club (N.Y.), Weston Gun Club (Conn.), Columbia Club of New York, Sigma Phi Epsilon. Republican. Congregationalist. Home: 221 Benedict Hill Rd New Canaan CT 06840-2913 Office: Dorsey & Whitney LLP 250 Park Ave New York NY 10177-0001

FREDERICKS, WILLIAM CURTIS, lawyer; b. Washington, July 3, 1961; s. J. Wayne and Anne Curtis Fredericks; m. Ivy Lindstrom, Jan. 21, 1995; children: Charlotte Lindstrom, Thomas Curtis. BA in Polit. Sci. with high honors, Swarthmore Coll., 1983; MLitt in Internat. Rels., Oxford (Eng.) U., 1988; JD, Columbia U., 1988. Bar: N.Y. 1990, U.S. Dist. Ct. (so. and ea. dists.) N.Y. 1990, U.S. Ct. Appeals (2d cir.) 1991, U.S. Ct. Appeals (10th cir.) 1997, U.S. Ct. Appeals (6th cir.) 1998, U.S. Dist. Ct. Colo. 1998, U.S. Ct. Appeals (3d cir.) 2001. Law clk. hon. Robert S. Gawthrop U.S. Dist. Ct. Pa., Phila., 1988-89; assoc. Simpson Thacher & Bartlett, N.Y.C., 1989-93, Willkie Farr & Gallagher, N.Y.C., 1993-97, Milberg Weiss Bershad Hynes & Lerach LLP, N.Y.C., 1997-98, ptnr., 1999—. Articles editor Columbia Jour. Transnational Law, 1987-88. V.p. Swarthmore Coll. Alumni Assn., 1988-90. Mem. Assn. of the Bar of the City of N.Y. (chair com. on mil. affairs and justice 1997-99). Democrat. Office: Milberg Weiss Bershad Hynes & Lerach LLP One Pennsylvania Plaza New York NY 10119-0165

FREDERICKS, WILLIAM JOHN, chemistry educator; b. San Diego, Sept. 18, 1924; s. William and Jenney (Cunnion) F.; m. Lola M. Schneider, Sept. 20, 1942. BS, San Diego State Coll., 1951; PhD, Oreg. State U., 1955. Technician, planner USN, San Diego, 1942-46; electronics technician Waldorf Appliance Co., San Diego, 1946-47; jr. civil engr. Calif. Div. Architecture, San Diego, 1947-51; phys. chemist, solid state mgr. Stanford Research Inst., Menlo Park, Calif., 1956-62; prof. chemistry Oreg. State U., Corvallis, 1962-87, prof. chemistry emeritus, 1988—. Rsch. prof. chemistry and materials sci. U. Ala., Huntsville, 1988-94, ret.; vis. acad. Atomic Research Establishment, Harwell, Eng., 1973-74; sr. vis. fellow U. Western Ont. Ctr. Chem. Physics, 1982; cons. in field; faculty advisor Oreg. State U. Flying Club. Contbr. articles to profl. jours. Chmn. Corvallis Airport Commn., 1979-83. Fulbright fellow 1955-56. Mem. AAAS. Am. Assn. Crystal Growth (mem. exec. bd. West Sect. 1976-86), Am. Chem. Soc. (sect. chmn.), Am. Phys. Soc., Materials Research Soc. Democrat. Avocations: flying, fishing, bonzai, golfing. Office: 11443 SW 82nd Court Rd Ocala FL 34481-3566

FREDERICKSEN, DICK HARTMAN, retired computer programmer; b. Great Falls, Mont., Jan. 16, 1931; s. Frederick Hartman and Helen Dickinson Fredericksen; m. Ann Bancroft, July 30, 1960 (div. Oct. 1990); children: Diane, Judith, Alice, Victor. AB, U. Chgo., 1951, postgrad., 1951-60, MS, 1968. Systems engr. IBM Corp., Chgo., 1960-64, programmer Poughkeepsie, 1965-66, programmer T.J. Watson Rsch. Ctr. Yorktown Heights, N.Y., 1969-90; part-time programmer Nat. Optical Astronomy Observatories, Tucson, 1990-92, ret., 1992. Nat. chmn. Young Peoples Socialist League, 1951-53; mem. L5 Soc./Nat. Space Soc., N.Y., Ariz., 1976—. Mem. Sonoran Arthropod Studies Inst., Tucson Space Soc. (v.p. 2000, sec.-treas. 2001--), Tucson Computer Soc. Avocations: web publishing, hiking, motorcycling, wildlife photography, commentary. Home: 7351 E Speedway Blvd Apt 11G Tucson AZ 85710-1513 E-mail: dhfred@ultrasw.com., dhfred@mindspring.com.

FREDERICKSON, ARMAN FREDERICK, minerals and petroleum company executive; b. Glenboro, Man., Can., May 5, 1918; came to U.S., 1923, naturalized, 1940; s. Albert F. and Ethel M. (Wilton) F.; m. Mary Maxine Stubblefield, Sept. 23, 1943; children: Mary Christene, Clover Diane, Penny Kathlene, Kimberly Mei, Sigrid, Janice BS in Mining Engring, U. Wash., 1940; MS in Metall. Engring, Mont. Sch. Mines, 1942; Sc.D. in Geology, Mass. Inst. Tech., 1947. Registered profl. engr., Tex., Colo., Nev., Mo.; cert. petroleum geologist. Mining engr., chief geologist Cornucopia Gold Mines, Oreg., 1939-40; instr. mineral dressing Mont. Sch. Mines, 1941-42; research asst. Mass. Inst. Tech., 1942-43; prof. geology and geol. engring. Washington U., St. Louis, 1947-56; organizer, supr. geol. research Standard (Amoco) Oil and Gas Co., Tulsa, 1955-60; prof. geology, chmn. dept. earth and planetary sci., dir. oceanography U. Pitts., 1960-65; sr. v.p., dir. research, mgr. petroleum prospecting and mineral programs in U.S., Middle East, Africa, Latin Am., 1965-71; pres., chief engr. Sorbotec, Inc., Houston, 1971-74; pres. Global Survey, 1972—. V.p. Samoco (Panama) Challenger Desert Oil Corp., 1977-81; cons. in mining and petroleum exploration, 1971—; v.p. SAMOCO, Del., 1977-81; v.p. ops. CHADOIL, 1978-81, Crown Gems, Inc., Thailand; pres. Global-Thai Exploration Corp., Thailand; organizer, past chmn. clay minerals com. Nat. Acad. Sci.-NRC; organizer, econ. analyst land and real estate projects, Calif.; negotiator oil, gemstone and mining programs, U.S., Africa, Thailand, Middle and Far East, Latin Am., exploration specialist. Author tech. papers in field, hist. novels; patentee fertilizer, oil and water pollution processes and products. Served with USNR, 1943-45. Fulbright prof. Norway, 1955. Fellow Geol. Soc. Am., Mineral Soc. Am.; mem. Am. Inst. Mining, Metall. and Petroleum Engrs., Am. Assn. Petroleum Geologists, Soc. Econ. Geologists, Geochem. Soc. Am., Underwater Soc. Am. Republican. Lutheran. numerous clubs. Home: 97 Mission Dr Petaluma CA 94952-5228

FREDERICKSON, CHRISTOPHER JOHN, neuroscientist; b. Norman, Okla., Aug. 1, 1945; s. John Henry and Joan Munson Frederickson; m. Cathleen Jean McCartney, Apr. 30, 1995; 1 child, Isabel. AB magna cum laude, Harvard Coll., 1968; PhD, U. Chgo., 1972. Asst. prof. neurosci. Carnegie Mellon, Pitts., 1972-75, U. Tex. Dallas, Richardson, 1975-78, assoc. prof. neurosci., 1978-85, full prof. neurosci., 1985-99; CEO NeuroBio Tex, Little Elm, Tex., 1999—. Dir. biotech. MicroFab Tech., Inc., Plano, Tex., 1996—99, U. Tex. Med. Br., Galveston, 1999—2000; mem. adv. bd. Tex. A&M Biomed. Engring., College Station, 1998—99; inaugural chair NIH Zinc in Health/Zinc in the Brain/Metals in Medicine, 2002; spkr. in field. Editor: Zinc Neurobiology, 1985; contbr. articles to profl. jours.; patentee in field. Bd. mem. YMCA, Richardson, 1995. Small Bus. Innovation and Rsch. grantee NIH, Washington, 1998. Mem. Soc. for Neurosci., Soc. Photo-Optical Instrumentation Engrs., Am. Chemosensory Soc. Avocation: sailing. Office: NeuroBioTex 101 Christopher Columbus 14th Stus 14 Galveston TX 77550 E-mail: chris@neurobiotex.com.

FREDERICKSON, GREG NORMAN, computer science educator; b. Balt., May 20, 1947; s. Howard Norman and Margaret Finger Frederickson; m. Susanne Edda Hambrusch, Feb. 17, 1984; children: Nora, Paul. AB in Econs., Harvard U., 1969; MS in Computer Sci., U. Md., 1976, PhD in Computer Sci., 1977. Tchr. Balt. City Pub. Schs., 1969-72; tchg. asst. U. Md., College Park, 1973-77; asst. prof. Pa. State U., University Park, 1977-82; assoc. prof. Purdue U., West Lafayette, Ind., 1982-86, prof., 1986—. Author: Dissections: Plane and Fancy, 1997, Hinged Dissections: Swinging and Twisting, 2002; mem. edit. bd. Algorithmica, 1992—. Recipient Single Investigator award NSF, 1979-2002. Mem. Assn. for Computing, Soc. for Indsl. and Applied Maths. (editl. bd. Jour. on Computing 1983-98). Office: Purdue U Dept Computer Sci West Lafayette IN 47907

FREDERICKSON, HORACE GEORGE, former college president, public administration educator; b. Twin Falls, Idaho, July 17, 1937; s. John C. and Zelpha (Richins) F.; m. Mary Williams, Mar. 14, 1958; children— Thomas, Christian, Lynne, David. BA, Brigham Young U., 1959; M.P.A., UCLA, 1961; PhD, U. So. Calif., 1967; LL.D. (hon.), Dongguk U., Korea. Intern Los Angeles County, 1960; research asst. Bur. Govtl. Research, U. Calif., Los Angeles, 1960-61; lectr. pub. adminstrn. U. So. Calif., 1962-64; lectr. govt. and politics U. Md., 1964-66; asst. prof. polit. sci. Maxwell Sch., Syracuse U., 1967-71; assoc. dir. Met. Studies Program, 1970-72, assoc. prof. polit. sci., 1971-72; fellow in higher edn. fin. adminstrn. U. N.C. System, 1972; chmn. Grad. Program, Sch. Pub. and Environ. Affairs, Ind. U., 1972-74, assoc. dean for policy and adminstrv. studies, 1973-74; dean Coll. Pub. and Community Services, prof. regional and community affairs U. Mo., Columbia, 1974-76; pres. Eastern Wash. U., Cheney, 1976-87; Edwin O. Stene Disting. prof. pub. adminstrn. U. Kans., Lawrence, 1987—. Author: New Public Administration, 1980, The Spirit of Public Administration, 1997; editor: Ethics and Public Administration, 1993, Public Policy and the Two States of Kansas, 1994, Ideal and Practice in Council-Manager Government, 2nd edit., 1994; editor in chief Jour. Pub. Adminstrn. Rsch. and Theory, 1991—. Haynes Found. fellow U. So. Calif., 1963-64 Mem. Am. Soc. Pub. Adminstrn. (pres.), Nat. Acad. Pub. Adminstrn. Home: 3420 Doral Ct Lawrence KS 66047-2131 Office: U Kans 1541 Lilac Ln #318 Lawrence KS 66044-3177

FREDERICKSON, JON JULIUS, social worker; b. Mason City, Iowa, May 31, 1952; d. Laurence F. and Florine E. (luther) F.; m. Kathleen S. Golding, Dec. 10, 1953. MSW, Catholic U., 1982. ACSW; lic. clin. social worker, D.C. Supr. D.C. Inst. Mental Health, Washington, 1983-95; supr. Ctr. Psychol. and Learning Svcs. Am. U., Washington, 1986-90. Pvt. practice, Washington, 1983—; mem. faculty Washington Sch. Psychiatry, 1988—. Author: Sociological Study of the Free-lance Classical Musician, 1991, Psychodynamic Psychotherapy: Learning To Listen from Multiple Perspectives, 1999; contbr. articles to profl. jours. Home: 1844 47th Pl NW Washington DC 20007-1909 Office: Apt 400 3000 Connecticut Ave NW Washington DC 20008-2509

FREDERIKSE, YOLANDA ROSSI, painter, printmaker, art educator; b. Beverly, Mass., May 27, 1927; d. Louis and Louise Gaetana (Di Palma) Rossi; m. Hans Pieter Frederikse, July 6, 1952; children: Julie Alida, Peter Hans, Thomas Anthony. BFA, Mass. Coll. Art, Boston, 1949; BFA in Art Edn., U. Ill., 1950; MA, Am. U., 1961. Art instr. Purdue U., West Lafayette, Ind., 1950-52, Marjorie Webster Jr. Coll., Washington, 1965-70; chair fine arts dept. Immaculata Coll. Washington, 1970-78. Asst. dir. Town Ctr. Gallery, 1978-89; watercolor workshop instr. 1980—. Illustrator, contbr. text: Monotype—Mediums and Methods, 1991, Creative Watercolor Guide and Showcase, 1995, Best of Watercolor Painting with Light, 1997, The Collected Best of Watercolor, 2002; contbr. (mags.) Watercolor 91, Watercolor Magic. Lectr./demonstrator Gaithersburg (Md.) Fine Arts Soc., 1995, Fairfax (Va.) Art Soc., 1989, 94, Howard County Art Assn., Ellicott City, Md., 1993, 97. NEH fellow, 1975; prints selected for reprodn. Alexandria (Va.) Bicentennial Commn., 1975. Mem. Nat. Watercolor Soc. (signature mem.), Nat. League Am. PEN Women (pres. Md. chpt. 1989-91, lectr./demonstrator 1995), So. Watercolor Soc. (signature mem.), Potomac Valley Watercolorists (pres. 1989-91), Montgomery County Art Assn. (pres. 1985-87, lectr./demonstrator 1992). Home: 9625 Dewmar Ln Kensington MD 20895-3635

FREDERIKSEN, MARILYNN C. physician; b. Chgo., Sept. 12, 1949; d. Paul H. and Susanne (Ostergren) Conners; m. James W. Frederiksen, July 11, 1971; children: John K., Paul S., Britt L. BA, Cornell Coll., 1970; MD, Boston U., 1974; grad. Exec. Leadership in Acad. Medicine, Allegheny U. Health Scis., 1998. Diplomate Am. Bd. Ob-Gyn., Am. Bd. Maternal-Fetal Medicine, Am. Bd. Clin. Pharmacology. Pediat. intern U. Md. Hosp., 1974-75, resident in pediat., 1975-76; resident in ob-gyn. Boston Hosp. for women, 1976-79; fellow in maternal fetal medicine Northwestern U., 1979-81, fellow clin. pharmacology, 1981-83, instr. ob-gyn., 1981-83, asst. prof. ob-gyn., assoc. clin. pharmacology, 1983-91, assoc. prof. ob-gyn., 1991—, sect. chief gen. ob-gyn., 1993—2001. Mem. gen. faculty com. Northwestern U., Chgo., 1994—97, mem. ob-gyn. adv. panel, 1985—2000, chair ob-gyn. adv. panel, 2000—; mem. U.S. Pharm. Com. Revision, Rockville, Md., 1986—; del. U.S. Pharm. conv. Northwestern U. Med. Sch., 1990, 95, 2000; mem. gen. clinic rsch. ctr. com. NIH, 1989—93, chairperson, 1992—93; mem. Task Force Writing Group on Asthma in Pregnancy, Nat. Heart, Lung and Blood Inst., 1991—92; examiner Am. Bd. Ob-Gyn., 1997—; mem. Task Force Working Group, Nat. Bd. Med. Examiners, 1997—98, mem. acute care com., 1999—2001. Mem. editorial bd. Clin. Pharmacology & Therapeutics, 1993; contbr. numerous articles to profl. jours. Bd. dirs. Cornell Coll. Alumni Assn., Mt. Vernon, Iowa, 1986—90, PRCH, 1997—, Planned Parenthood of Chgo. Area, 1999—, Northwestern Med. Faculty Found., 1995—98. Recipient Pharm. Mfrs. Assn. Found. Faculty Devel. award, 1984-86, Civil Liberties award ACLU, 1991. Fellow Am. Coll. Ob-Gyn.; mem. Soc. Maternal Fetal Medicine, Ctrl. Assn. Obstetricians and Gynecologists (bd. dirs. 1997-99), Am. Soc. Clin. Pharmacology and Therapeutics (bd. dirs. 1994-97), Chgo. Gynecologic Soc. (treas. 1994-97), Phi Beta Kappa. Episcopalian. Avocations: gardening, needlework. Office: Northwestern Perinatal Assocs Stte 1230 680 N Lake Shore Dr Chicago IL 60611 E-mail: mcf810@northwestern.edu.

FREDETTE, DIANE KAUFMAN, architect; b. Middletown, Ohio, Apr. 13, 1956; d. John Michael and Betty (Reddington) Kaufman; m Russell John Fredette, June 10, 1978. Student, Oxford U., Eng., 1975; BS in Architecture, Ohio State U., 1978, MArch, 1993; MS in Advanced Arctl. Design, Columbia U., 1994. Registered architect, Ohio, N.Y.; cert. Nat. Council Archtl. Registration Bd. Architect Prindle & Patrick, Columbus, Ohio, 1978-79; project co-ordinator Karlsberger & Assoc., Inc., Columbus, 1979-85; project mgr., assoc. Bohm-NBBJ, Inc., Columbus, 1985-92; pvt. practice, 1994—99; architect Perkins Eastman Architects, N.Y.C., 1999—2002; pvt. practice N.Y.C., 2002—. Adj. faculty Kent (Ohio) State U., 1995-97, Ohio State U., 1999. Mem. hist. dist. com. Upper Arlington Hist. Soc., Columbus. Mem. AIA. Avocations: hist. renovation, travel. Home: 99 John St Apt 2006 New York NY 10038-2932

FREDIANI, DIANE MARIE, graphic designer, interior designer; b. Bklyn., June 20, 1963; d. Albert Michael and Mary (Piantino) F. BFA in Graphic Design, Centenary Coll., 1985, teaching cert., 1991. Cert. graphic designer. Cashier, dept. supr. Reynolds, Hackettstown, N.J., 1982-85, window displays and promotions staff, 1985-86; clerical asst. AT&T, Basking Ridge, N.J., 1986-87, typesetter, bd. artist Parsippany, N.J., 1988-89, project mgr. interior design Basking Ridge, 1989-99, supplier diversity specialist supplier mgmt. divsn., 1999—. Graphic designer St. Mary's Sch., Hackettstown, 1985—; nominee for White House Fellowship Com., 1994. Mem. Centenary Alumni Assn. (forensic judge oral speaking competitions 1993—), N.J. Supplier Diversity Devel. Coun., N.Y./N.J. Minority Purchasing Coun. (sec. 1999—). Roman Catholic. Avocations: photography, painting, reading, going to sporting events. Home: 203 Hudson Ct Hackettstown NJ 07840-1690 Office: AT&T 295 N Maple Ave Basking Ridge NJ 07920-1025

FREDMAN, HOWARD S. lawyer; b. St. Louis, Feb. 1, 1944; s. Manuel and Sydine Fredman; children: Jocelyn Bly, Amber Alexandra, Cameron Penn. BA, Princeton U., 1966; JD, Columbia U., 1969. Bar: Calif. 1970, U.S. Dist. Ct. (no. dist.) Calif. 1970, U.S. Ct. Appeals (9th cir.) 1970, U.S. Dist. Ct. (so. dist.) Calif. 1974, U.S. Dist. Ct. (ctrl. dist.) Calif. 1975, U.S. Dist. Ct. (ea. dist.) Calif. 1996, U.S. Dist. Ct. Colo. 2000. Law clk. to Hon. Milton Pollack U.S. Dist. Ct. (so. dist.) N.Y., N.Y.C., 1969-70; assoc. McCutchen, Doyle, Brown & Enersen, San Francisco, 1970-75; counsel, sr. atty., atty. legal divsn. Atlantic Richfield Co., L.A., 1975-87; assoc. Frandzel & Share, L.A., 1987-90, ptnr., 1990—99; pvt. practice L.A., 1999—2002; ptnr. Fredman/Lieberman LLP, L.A., 2002—. Mem. faculty Practicing Law Inst., 1982, 86-88; lectr., spkr. in field. Mem. editl. adv. bd. Calif. Causes of Action, 1998. Mem. com. to nominate alumni trustees Princeton Alumni Coun., 1998—2001, treas., exec. com., 2001—03, mem. strategic planning com., 1997—98; chair alumni schs. com. L.A. area Princeton, 1992—94. Recipient cert. of recognition, U.S. Dist. Ct. (ctrl. dist.) Calif., 2002. Mem. ABA, Assn. Bus. Trial Lawyers, Fed. Bar Assn., L.A. County Bar Assn. (chmn. antitrust sect. 1986-87, exec. com. antitrust sect. 1982—, nominating com. 1986-87, del. state bar conf. dels. 1987, 88), Princeton Club So. Calif. (pres. 1994-96). Democrat. Jewish. Office: Fredman/Lieberman LLP 1875 Century Park E Ste 2200 Los Angeles CA 90067-2523 E-mail: hsflawyer@aol.com.

FREDMAN, MIMI UNGAR COPPERSMITH, advertising and publishing executive; b. Wilkes-Barre, Pa., June 11, 1933; m. Samuel G. Fredman; children: Carol L. Barash, Nan R. Barash. BA in Journalism with honors, Pa. State U., 1953, postgrad., 1953-55. Instr. speech Pa. State U., 1953-55, 61; ptnr. Barash Advt., 1959-60, Morgan Signs, Inc., 1960-75; CEO The Barash Group, 1975-2000, chair, 2000—. Guest lectr. speech, journalism, mktg. Pa. State U., 1965—, instr. mktg., 1974-75, 78; mem. adv. coun. of subcom. small bus. Bus. and Commerce Com. of Pa. Ho. of Reps., 1981-84; pub. Town & Gown Mag., Penn State Footbal & Basketball Annuals; bd. dirs. Reliance Bank, White Plains, N.Y., Village Auction.com, Pa. Pa. State Hershey Med. Ctr., Centre County Youth Svc. Bur., Ctrl. Pa. Festival of the Arts. Bd. govs. Pa. Free Enterprise Week, 1981-84; mem. leadership coun. Ctr. for Performing Arts, SUNY, Purchase, 1994-99; bd. advisors Palmer Mus. of Art, 1994—, pres., 1999—2001; bd. dirs. State College Area C. of C., 1974-79, Pa. Chamber Bus. and Industry, 1975-92, Altoona Area C. of C., 1977, Capital Blue Cross, 1978-85, Pa. Women's Campaign Fund, 1982-84, Pa. Humanities Coun., 1984-88, Pa. Ctr. Stage, 1987-90, Allegheny Highlands Regional Theatre, 1988-99, Ctrl. Pa. Festival of Arts, 1995-2000, pres., 1997-99; co-chmn. Centre County Cancer Crusade, 1975-77; chmn. spl. gifts Cambria County Cancer Crusade, 1979; pres. Renaissance Scholarship Fund Bd., Pa. State U., 1980-87; vice-chmn., bd. govs. Centre County Cmty. Found., 1981-89, chmn., 1986-89; alumni mem. bd. trustees Pa. State U., 1975-97, pres. bd., 1991-93, emeritus, 1997—; mem. Friends of Palmer Mus. of Art, Pa. State U., State College Air Pollution Commn., 1969-75; founding dir., mem. Back the Lions. Recipient Outstanding Svc. award United Fund, College area, 1968-69, Kiwanis Club award for Cmty. Svc., 1976, spl. awards Centre County and Pa. divsn. Am. Cancer Soc., 1976, Award for Disting. Svc. to State Govt., Nat. Gov.'s Assn., 1981, 50 Best Women in Bus. award Dept. Commerce and Gov.'s Commn. for Women with Bus. Jour. Pa., 1996; named Pa. Small Businessperson of Yr., Small Bus. Adminstrn., 1981, Disting. Pennsylvanian, Phila. C. of C., 1981, Disting. Daughter of Pa. 1990, Entrepreneur of Yr. in Media in Ctrl. Pa., 1996; honoree Pa. State Renaissance Scholarship Fund, 1990, Pa. State Hillel Found. Dinner, 1993; Alumni fellow Pa. State U., 1997, Disting. Alumnus, 1998. Mem. AAUW, LWV, Women in Comms., Outdoor Advt., Inc., Pa. Outdoor Advt. Assn., Outdoor Advt. Assn. Am., Eight-sheet Outdoor Advt. Assn., Specialties Advt. Assn., Inc., Parmi Nous (hon.), Nittany Lion Club, Delta Sigma Rho, Omicron Delta Kappa, Theta Sigma Phi. E-mail: mimi@barashgroup.com.

FREDMAN, SUSAN MIRIAM, interior designer; b. Chgo, Nov. 14, 1950; d. David Wolfe Fredman and Selma (Lobelson) Florio; m. Martin Donald Zitlin, Jan. 28, 1984 (div. 1988); 1 child, Amanda Beth. BS, Ill. State U., 1973. Owner, pres. Susan Fredman & Assoc., Ltd, cmty. svc. class @ Harrington Instit. of Interior Design, 2002. Commr. Appearance Rev. Commn., Highland Park, 1989—; mem. Color Mktg. Group, 1990—. Contbr. to numerous local publ. V.p. ways and means Ravinia Nursery Sch., Highland Park, 1988—. Mem. Internat. Soc. Interior Designers (bd. dir. Ill. chpt. 1984-86), Color Mktg. Group. Avocation: painting. Office: Interior Accents Ltd 425 N Avenl Rd #6B Novubrook IL 60062

FREDMANN, MARTIN, ballet artistic director, educator, choreographer; b. Balt., Feb. 3, 1943; s. Martin Joseph and Hilda Adele (Miller) Fredmann; m. Kaleriyam Fedicheva Fredmann (div. Jan. 2, 1973); m. Patricia Renzetti, June 12, 1980. Student, Nat. Ballet Sch., Washington, 1962-64, Vaganova Sch., Leningrad, 1972. Prin. dancer The Md. Ballet, Balt., 1961-64; dancer The Pa. Ballet, Phila., 1964-65, Ballet of the Met. Opera Co., N.Y.C., 1965-66; prin. dancer Dortmund (Fed. Republic Germany) Ballet, 1973-75, Scapino Ballet, Amsterdam, Holland, 1975-76; tchr. German Opera Ballet, West Berlin, Fed. Republic Germany, 1979, Netherlands Dance Theater, 1979, Royal Swedish Ballet, 1980, San Francisco Ballet, 1981; tchr., coach Australian Ballet, 1982; tchr. Tokyo City Ballet, Hong Kong Ballet, 1985, 86, 87, London Festival Ballet, 1981-83; dir. ballet Teatro Comunale, Florence, Italy, 1984-85; artistic dir. Tampa (Fla.) Ballet, 1984-90; artistic dir. in alliance with The Tampa Ballet Colo. Ballet, Denver, 1987-90, artistic dir., 1987—. Tchr. German Opera Ballet, 1982, Ballet Rambert, London, 1983, Bat Dor summer course, Israel, 1983, Cullberg Ballet, Sweden, 1983, Hong Kong Acad. For Performing Arts, 1985—89, 1991, Tokyo City Ballet, 1985—90, Ballet West, 1990, Nat. Ballet Korea, 1991, Dance Divsn. Tsoying High Sch., Kaohsiung, Taiwan, 1992; guest lectr., tchr. Cen. Ballet China, Beijing Dancing Acad., P.L.A. Arts Coll., Beijing, 1990; tchr. Legat Sch., 1978, examiner, 80; tchr. Eglevsky Sch., N.Y.C., 1980; asst. dir. ballet master Niavaron Cultural ctr., Tehran, Iran, 1978; tchr. Ballet Arts Sch. Carnegie Hall, N.Y.C., 1979—81; choreographer Estonia Nat. Theatre, Russia, 1991; dir. Marin Ballet., Calif., 1981. Choreographer Romeo and Juliet, 1983, Sachertorte, 1984, A Little Love, 1984, Ricordanza, 1986, Cinderella, 1986, Coppelia, 1987, The Nutcracker, 1987, Beauty and the Beast, 1988, Masquerade Suite, 1989, Silent Woods, 1989, The Last Songs, 1991, Centenial Suite, 1994. Recipient Recipient Mayor's award, Denver, 1996, Dance Mag. award, 1999, Bonfils-Stanton Found. award, 2000. Mem.: Nat. Assn. Regional Ballet., Fla. State Dance Assn, Am. Guild Mus. Artists. Avocations: cooking, cook book collecting, travel, opera. Home: 836 E 17th Ave Apt 3A Denver CO 80218-1449 Office: Colo Ballet 1278 Lincoln St Denver CO 80203-2114

FRED-MENSAH, BEN KWAME, international development educator, consultant; b. Accra, Ghana, Oct. 8, 1953; s. Frederick Kofi Mensah Gbotsyo and Rosina Adzoyo Atitoe; m. Josephine Afi Dzoku, May 22, 1963; children: Selorm, Akorfa. MPhil, Cambridge (Eng.) U.; PhD, Johns Hopkins U., 1999. Tchr., supt. Ghana Edn. Svc., 1973-86; cons. World Bank, Washington, 1991-96; asst. prof. govt. Hamilton Coll., Clinton, N.Y., 1998-2000, hon. vis. scholar Arthur Levitt Pub. Affairs Ctr., 2001—; dir. African Ctr. for Innovative Literacy and Learning, Washington, 2001—. Postdoctoral fellow, Brown U., Providence, 1996-98. Numerous publs. in field. Recipient numerous awards; Rockefeller Found. fellow, 1994. Mem. Fellow Cambridge Commonwealth Soc. at Cambridge in U.K. (life). Presbyterian. Avocation: observing nature.

FREDRICHS, ANNE MARIE JOHNSON, pediatric nurse practitioner; b. Omaha, Nebr., Mar. 19, 1952; d. Richard Nicholas and Helen Harvey Johnson; divorced; 1 child, Alexandra Nicole. BSN, U. Nebr., 1995, MSN, 1999. RN, CPNP. Staff nurse Boystown Nat. Rsch. Hosp., Omaha, 1996-98; rsch. nurse U. Nebr. Med. Ctr. Mobile Nursing unit, Omaha, 1999-2000; rsch. nurse coord. Nebr. Found. Spinal Rsch., Nebr. Spine Ctr., 1999—2001; faculty instr. U. Nebr. Med. Coll. Nursing, 2001—02; clin. rsch. coord. dept. internal medicine U. Nebr. Med. Ctr., 2002—. Scholarship U. Nebr., 1994, Nu chpt. Phi Delta Gamma, 1998. Mem. Nebr. Nurse Practitioners, Nat. Assn. of Pediatric Nurse Assocs.-Practitioners, Soc. of Pediatric Nurses, Midwest Nursing Rsch. Soc., U. Nebr. Nursing Alumni Assn., Sigma Theta Tau (scholarship 1998). Republican. Roman Catholic. Avocations: community volunteer, gourmet cooking, gardening, dance. E-mail: amjf@tconl.com.

FREDRICK, DAVID WALTER, academic administrator; b. Oelwein, Iowa, May 12, 1944; s. Walter Junior and Jean Louise (Carran) Fredrick; m. Merry Lou Bunger, Feb. 17, 1948; children: Erika Fredrick Stein, Adrian, Andre. BA, Wartburg Coll., 1965; MA, Clark U., 1970. Mktg. svcs. mgr. Koehring Comp., Waverly, Iowa, 1966-69; U.S. diplomatic svc. U.S. Agy. Internat. Devel., Washington, 1969-86, 90-96; dir. Morocco Peace Corps, 1986-90; internat. admissions Wartburg Coll., Waverly, 1996—. Com. for Europe, Mid. East and Africa Coun. Internat. Schs. Contbr. articles to profl. jours. V.p. Promote Internat. Edn. in Iowa; councilman City of Waverly, 1967—69; bd. dirs. Self Help Found., Waverly, 1996—. Recipient Disting. Svc. award U.S. Agy. for Internat. Devel., 1996, Meritorious Svc. award, 1993. Mem. Am. Fgn. Svc. Assn., Rotary. Lutheran. Avocations: fishing, hiking, travel, tennis. Home: 1105 Gateway Blvd Waverly IA 50677-1462 E-mail: david.fredrick@wartburg.edu.

FREDRICK, LAURENCE WILLIAM, astronomer, educator; b. Stroudsburg, Pa., Aug. 27, 1927; s. Ishmeal T. and Grace (Slider) F.; m. Frances I. Schwenk, Feb. 5, 1949; children— Laura Grace, Theodore David, Rebecca Lyn BA, Swarthmore Coll., 1952, MA, 1954; PhD, U. Pa., 1959. Research asst. Sproul Obs., Swarthmore, Pa., 1952-56; research assoc. Flower and Cook Obs., Malvern, Pa., 1957-59; astronomer Lowell Obs., Flagstaff, Ariz., 1959-63; mem. faculty U. Va., Charlottesville, 1963-95, prof. astronomy, 1965-95, rsch. prof., 1995—; prof. U. Vienna, Austria, 1972-73. Cons. in field; Fulbright-Hays exch. lectr., Austria, 1972-73; assoc. astronomer European So. Obs., Munich, Fed. Republic Germany, 1982-83; vis. fellow Australian Nat. U., Canberra, 1991-92. Co-author: Astronomy, 10th edit., 1976, Descriptive Astronomy, 1978, An Introduction to Astronomy, 9th edit., 1980 Served with USN, 1945-48 Named Alumnus of Yr., Milton Hershey Sch., 1961 Mem. Am. Astron. Soc. (sec. 1969-80), Internat. Astron. Union (sec. U.S. nat. com. 1970-80), Am. Inst.

Physics (bd. govs. 1969-79), Univs. for Space Research Assn. (trustee), Royal Astron. Soc., Soc. Sci. Exploration (sec. 1981—), Sigma Xi Home: 2602 Bennington Rd Charlottesville VA 22901-2211

FREDRICK, SUSAN WALKER, tax company manager; b. Painesville, Ohio, Nov. 17, 1948; d. Floyd Clayton and Margaret (Merkel) Walker; m. Stephan Douglas Fredrick, Oct. 20, 1973. BS, Mt. Union Coll., Alliance, Ohio, 1970; MS, U. Conn., 1973. Research asst. Boyce Thompson Inst., Yonkers, NY, 1971-74; dir. quality control Lawley, Matusky, Skelly, Tappan, NY, 1974-75; field supr. Ecological Analysts, Middletown, NY, 1975-76; scientist Pandullo Quirk Assocs., Wayne, NJ, 1976-78; editor Biosis. Info. Service, Phila., 1978-80; tax preparer H&R Block, Inc., King of Prussia, Pa., 1978-80, dist. mgr. Malvern, Pa., 1980—2002, franchise dist. mgr. Easton, Md., 2002—; dist. man. Franchise, 2002; tax preparer HRB, Maluern, Pa., 1978—80, dist. mgr. King of Prussia, Pa., 1980—92, Westchester, Pa., 1992—2002. Guest lectr. Temple U., 1981-86. Mem. Nat. Assn. Enrolled Agts., Pa. Soc. Enrolled Agts., Nat. Assn. Underwater Instrs. (active instr.), Keystone Divers Club (West Chester, Pa.). Avocations: scuba diving, hiking, swimming. Office: 8719 Brooks Ln Unit 1 Easton MD

FREDRICKSON, GEORGE MARSH, history educator; b. Bristol, Conn., July 16, 1934; s. George Fredrickson and Gertrude (Marsh) F.; m. Helene Osouf, Oct. 16, 1956; children: Anne, Laurel, Thomas, Caroline. AB, Harvard U., 1956, PhD, 1964. Instr. history Harvard U., Cambridge, Mass., 1963-66; assoc. prof. history Northwestern U., Evanston, Ill., 1966-71, prof., 1971-84, William Smith Mason prof. Am. history, 1979-84; Edgar E. Robinson prof. U.S. history Stanford U., Calif., 1984—2002, prof. emeritus, 2002—. Fulbright prof. Moscow U., 1983, Harmsworth prof. Am. history Oxford U., 1988-89. Author: The Inner Civil War, 1965, 2d edit., 1993, The Black Image in the White Mind, 1971, 2d edit., 1987 (Anisfield-Wolf award 1972), White Supremacy, 1981 (Ralph Waldo Emerson award 1981, Merle Curti award, 1982, Pulitzer prize finalist 1982), The Arrogance of Race, 1988, Black Liberation, 1995, The Comparative Imagination, 1997, Racism: A Short History, 2002; co-author: America: Past and Present, 6th edit., 2002; editor: A Nation Divided, 1975. Served to lt. USN, 1957-60. Guggenheim fellow, 1967-68; NEH fellow, 1973-74; Ctr. for Advanced Studies in Behavioral Scis. fellow, 1977-78; NEH fellow, 1985-86; Ford sr. fellow DuBois Inst., Harvard U., 1993. Fellow Soc. Am. Historians, Am. Antiquarian Soc., Am. Acad. Arts and Scis.; mem. Am. Hist. Assn., Orgn. Am. Historians (pres. 1997-98), So. Hist. Assn. Home: 741 Esplanada Way Palo Alto CA 94305-1013 Office: Stanford Univ Dept History Stanford CA 94305 E-mail: fredrick@stanford.edu.

FREDRICKSON, KAREN LORAINE, librarian; b. Kansas City, Mo., Sept. 27, 1952; d. Kenneth Eugene Kruse and Loraine Lulu (Neugebauer) Morse; m. Timothy Dean Cox, Sept. 1, 1973 (dec. Sept. 1984); m. David Dean Fredrickson, June 10, 1989; children: Jennifer, Rachel. BS, Cen. Mo. State U., 1974, MS, 1979. Cert. tchr. Kans., Mo. Tchr./libr. Lone Jack (Mo.) Schs., 1974-76; tchr. Clarksville-Montgomery County Schs., Tenn., 1977; tchr./libr. St John's Luth. Sch., Indpls., 1978-82; libr. media specialist Lawrence (Kans.) Public Schs., 1985—. Mem. Lawrence In-Svc. Coun., 1986-88. Recipient Kans. Ednl. Excellence Program award Southwestern Bell, Lawrence, 1991. Mem. ALA, Am. Assn. Sch. Libr., Kans. Assn. Sch. Libr. Luth. Avocations: sewing, crocheting. Office: Langston Hughes Sch 1101 George Williams Way Lawrence KS 66049 E-mail: klfredri@usd497.org.

FREDRICKSON, L(AWRENCE) THOMAS, composer; b. Kane, Pa., Sept. 5, 1928; s. Eric Lawrence Fredrickson and Esther Linnea (Skoog) Bussell; m. Betty Jean Blessing, July 30, 1950; children: Lawrence Alan, Linda Kay, Gail Diane. MusB, Ohio Wesleyan U., 1950; MusM, U. Ill., Urbana, 1952, MusD, 1960. Jazz musician, Ill., 1952—; composer, arranger, 1952—; instr. music U. Ill., Urbana/Champaign, 1952-60, asst. prof., 1960-63, assoc. prof., 1963-67, prof., 1967-93, prof. emeritus, 1993, dir. Sch. of Music, 1970-74. Composer: Brass Quintet, Impressions, Deja Vu, Music for the Double Bass Alone; commns. include works for orch., band, chamber music, solo works; performer double bass in chamber music and jazz groups, symphony orchs. Mem. ASCAP, Am. Fedn. of Musicians. Home: 1814 Robert Dr Champaign IL 61821-6031

FREDRICKSON, ROBERT ALAN, lawyer; b. Rockford, Ill., June 1, 1945; s. Robert D. and M. Maxine (Klenner) F.; m. Carol A. Janicki; children: Kristen D., Karen J., Robert S. BBA with honors, U. Wis.-Madison, 1967, JD with honors, 1971. Bar: Wis. 1971, Ill. 1971, U.S. Dist. Ct. (we. dist.) Wis. 1971, U.S. Dist. Ct. (no. dist.) Ill. 1971, U.S. Supreme Ct. 1983. Assoc. Reno, Zahm, Folgate, Lindberg & Powell, Rockford, 1971-74, ptnr., 1974–. Mem. ABA, Am. Arbitration Assn., State Bar Wis., Assn. Trial Lawyers Am., Ill. Trial Lawyers Assn., Winnebago County Bar Assn., Rotary. Congregationalist. Avocations: fishing, outdoor activities, house construction, skiing, horseback riding. Home: 4106 Eaton Dr Rockford IL 61114-6123 Office: Reno Zahm Folgate Lindberg & Powell 1415 E State St Ste 905 Rockford IL 61104-2333 E-mail: RA7@renozahm.com.

FREDRICKSON, SCOTT ALFRED, instructional technology educator, consultant; b. San Mateo, Calif., Nov. 4, 1950; s. Raymond Anton William and Lois Elaine (Austin) F.; m. Lynn Ann Traylor, June 17, 1973; children: Lance Raymond, Jeffrey Ryan. BS in Criminal Justice, U. Nebr., Omaha, 1976; MED, Tex. Tech U., 1983, PhD, 1989. With identification divsn. FBI, Washington, 1970; aircraft mechanic USAF, 1970-74; dep. sheriff Lubbock (Tex.) Sheriff's Dept., 1979-82; tchr. Lubbock Ind. Sch. Dist., 1981-89; asst. prof. U. Alaska SE, Sitka, 1989-92; prof. U. Nebr., Kearney, 1992—. Presenter in field. Author: Teaching Incarcerated Youths Using MicroComputer Distance Education Technology, 1989, Alaskan High Schools Graduates: A Study of the 1986-1989 Graduates, 1990, Contemporary Issues in Education, 1993, Going The Distance in Central Nebraska: A Distance Education Needs Assessment, 1994, Distance Education: Technologies and Teaching Strategies for University Faculty, 1995; contbr. articles to profl. jours. Sgt. USAF, 1970-74, lt. U.S. Army, 1976-79. Mem. Phi Delta Kappa (v.p. Sitka chpt. 1989-92). Republican. Lutheran. Avocations: scuba diving, chess, reading. Office: U Nebr Kearney Coll Edn Kearney NE 68849-0001

FREDRICKSON, SHARON WONG, accountant, controller; b. Cleve., Nov. 24, 1956; d. Jack Don and Fung Suey Wong; m. Brant M. Fredrickson, Mar. 19, 1988; children: Eric Brant, Saul Wong. BS in Acctg. summa cum laude, Case Western Res. U., 1978, MBA, 1987. CPA, Ohio. Acct. Price Waterhouse, Cleve., 1978-81, sr. acct., 1981-84; acctg. rsch. and planning analyst BP Am., Inc. (formerly Standard Oil Co.), Cleve., 1984-85, sr. fin. analyst rsch. and devel. acctg., 1985-88, bus. analyst, regional ctr. fin. reporting, 1989-93; fin. reporting analyst BP Oil Co., 1994-96; project mgr. control svcs. Key Svcs. Corp. subs. Key Corp., Cleve., 1996-97; acct. Glazer & Co., Pepper Pike, Ohio, 1997-99; contr. Mentor Harbor Yachting Club, Mentor, Ohio, 2000-01. Bus. advisor Inroads Cleve., Inc., 1982-84. Mem. AICPA, Am. Woman's Soc. CPAs (Northeastern Ohio affiliate pres. 1985-86, v.p. 1984-85, sec. 1983-84), Ohio Soc. CPAs (state bd. dirs. 1985-86, 88-89, sec. Cleve. chpt. 1987-88, chpt. bd. dirs. 1986-87), Young Profls. Cleve. (trustee 1984-85). Avocations: travel, exercise, reading.

FREDRIK, BURRY, theatrical producer, director; b. NYC, Aug. 9, 1925; d. Fredric Kreuger and Erna Anita (Burry) Gerber; m. Gerard E. Meunier, Dec. 27, 1945 (div. 1949). Grad., Sarah Lawrence Coll., 1947. Ind. theatrical dir., producer, U.S. and abroad, 1955—; lit. mgr., dir. Boston Post Road Stage Co., 1988-92; artistic dir. Fairfield County Stage Co. (formerly Boston Post Road Stage), 1992-93. Prodr.: (Broadway plays) Too Good to be True, 1964—65 (nominated Tony award, 1965), Travesties, 1976 (Tony award, 1976), An Almost Perfect Person, 1977, The Night of the Tribades, 1978, To Grandmother's House We Go, 1981, The Royal Family, 1975—76 (Drama Desk award, 1976), (off-Broadway plays) Thieves Carnival, 1955 (Spl. Tony award, 1955), Exiles, 1956 (OBIE award, 1956), Buried Child (Pulitzer prize, 1980); dir.: (nat. tours) Misalliance, 1953, Milk and Honey, 1963, Dark at the Top of the Stairs, 1958, Dear Love, 1971, To Grandmother's House We Go, 1982, (off-Broadway prodns.) The Decameron, 1961, Catholic School Girls, 1981, (Broadway prodn.) Wild and Wonderful, 1972; prodr.: (off-Broadway) Pretzels, 1974; dir.: (plays, Sad Hotel) White Barn Theatre, 2001—; (plays, Swansong), 2002—. Chmn. Weston Commn. Arts, 1997—2000; mem. fin. commn., trustee Long Wharf Theatre, New Haven, 1998—. Recipient Disting. Adv. Arts award, State of Conn. Commn. Arts, 2001. Home and Office: 51 Hillside Rd N Weston CT 06883-1513 Fax: 203-222-9478.

FREDRIKSEN, MARYELLEN, physician assistant; b. New Brunswick, N.J., Oct. 21, 1963; d. Joseph Saverio and Naomi Yolanda (Alvarado) Iacovacci; m. Olaf Rune Fredriksen, May 13, 1990 (div. 1996). BA in Chemistry, Boston U., 1986; BS in Health Science, CUNY/Columbia U., 1996; M Physican Asst. Studies, U. Nebr., 1999. Reg. physician assistant, N.Y.; cert. in basic life support, advanced cardiac life support, neonatal advanced life support, pediatric advanced life support, advanced trauma life support; cert. HIV/AIDS counselor. Biochem. rsch. tech. Boston U., 1984-86; biochem. rsch. tech. Sch. Medicine Harvard U., Boston, 1986-87; rsch. tech. Cold Spring Harbor (N.Y.) Lab., 1987-90, buyer, 1990-94; physician asst., house staff officer dept. surgery and medicine Samaritan Med. Ctr., Watertown, N.Y., 1997-2000, mem. staff emergency dept., 2000—. House staff officer Benedictine Hosp., Kingston, N.Y., 2000-2001; mem. staff emer. dept. EJ Noble Hosp., Alexandria Bay, N.Y., 2001-. With Students Teaching AIDS to Students, 1995-96; vol. physician asst. student N.Y.C. Marathon, 1995, 96; participant Teddy Bear Clin., 1997; organizer Hurricane Georges Relief for St. Kitts, 1998, Women's Jour. Club, 1999—. N.Y. State Soc. Physician Assts. scholar, 1996. Fellow Am. Acad. Physician Assts. (treas. Student Soc. Student Acad. 1994-96); mem. N.Y. State Soc. Physician Assts. (cert., student treas. local chpt. 1994-96, rep. Project Access program 1995-96). Democrat. Avocations: archery, skiing. Home: 719 Washington St Watertown NY 13601-3902 Office: Samaritan Med Ctr 830 Washington St Watertown NY 13601-4099

FREE, ANN COTTRELL, writer; b. June 4, 1916; d. Emmett Drewry and Emily (Blake) Cottrell; m. James Stillman Free, Feb. 24, 1950; 1 child, Elissa. Grad., Collegiate Sch. for Girls, Richmond, 1934; student Richmond divsn., Coll. William and Mary (now Va. Commonwealth U.), 1934-36; AB, Barnard Coll. Columbia U., 1938. Reporter Richmond Times Dispatch, 1938-40; Washington corr. Newsweek, 1940-41, Chgo. Sun, 1941-43, N.Y. Herald Tribune, 1943-46; pub. info. dir., China corr. UN Relief Rehab. Adminstrn., China Mission, Shanghai, 1946-47; corr. Mid. and Near East and Europe, 1947-48; writer-photographer Marshall Plan, Washington/Western Europe, 1949-50; Washington corr. N.Am. Newspaper Alliance, 1955—85; former Washington editor EnviroSouth Quar., 1977-82; freelance writer. Pres. Flying Fox Press. Author: (book) Forever the Wild Mare, 1963, Animals, Nature and Albert Schweitzer, 1982, No Room, Save in the Heart, 1987, Since Silent Spring: Our Debt to Albert Schweitzer and Rachel Carson, 1992; contbr. oral history. Hon. founding mem. Friends of the Rachel Carson nat. Wildlife Refuge; chmn. Mrs. Roosevelt's Press Conf. Assn., 1943; cons. expert Rachel Carson Coun.; v.p. Vieques (P.R.) Humane Soc.; past coord. Albert Schweitzer Summer Fellows Program; past bd. dirs. Albert Schweitzer Fellowship; pres. Albert Schweitzer Coun. Animals and Environment; trustee Albert Schweitzer Animal Welfare Fund. Named to Va. Comms. Hall of Fame, 1996; recipient Dodd Mead-Boy's Life Writing award, 1963, Albert Schweitzer medal, Animal Welfare Inst., 1963, Jr. Book award cert., Boys Club Am., 1964, Humanitarian of the Yr. award, Washington Animal Rescue League, 1971, Montgomery County Humane Soc., 1971, Washington Humane Soc., 1983, News Writing award, Dog Writers Assn., 1975, 1978, Rachel Carson Legacy award, 1987, Disting. Alumni award, Collegiate Schs., 1992, Cert. Appreciation for role in establishing Rachel Carson Nat. Wildlife Refuge, Dept. Interior Fish and Wildlife Svc., 1995, Lifetime Svc. award, Washington Animal Rescue League, 1997. Mem.: Am. News Women's Club, Nat. Press Club, Soc. Woman Geographers. Home: 4700 Jamestown Rd Bethesda MD 20816-2913 also: 56 Bell's Ln Lantz Mill Edinburg VA 22824 E-mail: anncottrellfree@aol.com.

FREE, E. LEBRON, lawyer, mediator; b. Cleveland, Tenn., Jan. 27, 1940; s. James D. and Mary Kathleen (Hunt) F.; children: Jason LeBron, Ryan Edward. BA, Berea Coll., 1963; MTh, So. Meth. U., 1966; JD, Okla. City U., 1974. Bar: Ga. 1974, Fla. 1975, U.S. Dist. Ct. (mid. dist.) Fla. 1975, U.S. Supreme Ct. 1975; cert. cir. civil and family law mediator. Litigation atty. Jim Walter Corp., Tampa, Fla., 1975-79; prin. E. Lebron Free, P.A., Clearwater, Fla., 1980– . Editor Res. IPSA Loquitur, 1996—. Bd. dirs. Ye Mystice Krewe of Neptune, Pinellas County, Fla., 1980-90, capt., 1984; bd. dirs. Hospice of the Fla. Suncoast, 1981-91; chmn., 1984; mem. Met. Planning Orgn., Pinellas County, 1984, Zoning Bd., Clearwater, 1984; bd. dirs. Family Svc. Ctrs., 1993—. Mem. ABA, ATLA, Canakaris Inns of Ct. (bd. dirs. 1997—), Fla. Bar Assn. (family law sect., chmn. fee arbitration com. 1991), Fla. Acad. Trial Lawyers, Clearwater Bar Assn., Rotary (Paul Harris fellow 1992), Masons. Avocation: sailing. Office: 3005 State Rd 590 Ste 206 Clearwater FL 33759-2539 Fax: 727-726-4677.

FREE, HELEN MAE, chemist, consultant; b. Pitts., Feb. 20, 1923; d. James Summerville and Daisy (Piper) Murray; m. Alfred H. Free, Oct. 18, 1947; children: Eric, Penny, Kurt, Jake, Bonnie, Nina. BA in Chemistry, Coll. of Wooster, Ohio, 1944, DSc (hon.), 1992; MA in Clin. Lab. Mgmt., Ctrl. Mich. U., 1978, DSc (hon.), 1993. Cert. clin. chemist Nat. Registry Cert. Chemists. Chemist Miles Labs., Elkhart, Ind., 1944—78, dir. mktg. svcs. rsch. products divsn., 1978-82; chemist, mgr., cons. diagnostics divsn. Bayer Corp., Elkhart, 1982—. Mem. adj. faculty Ind. U., South Bend, 1975—96. Author (with others): (book) Urodynamics and Urinalysis in Clinical Laboratory Practice, 1972, 1976; contbr. articles to encys. and profl. jours. Bd. dirs. Nat. Inventors Hall of Fame Found.; women's chmn. Centennial of Elkhart, 1958; mem. adv. bd. Intellectual Property Sch. Law, Akron U.; indsl. adv. bd. chemistry/chem. engring. Tri-State U., Angola, Ind. Named Woman of Yr., YWCA, 1993, Kilby Found. laureate, 1996; named to Hall of Excellence, Ohio Found. Ind. Colls., 1992, Nat. Inventors Hall of Fame, 2000, Engring. and Sci. Hall of Fame, 1996; recipient Disting. Alumni award, Coll. of Wooster, 1980, award, Medi Econ Press, 1986, Nat. Leadership award, Lab. Pub. Svc., 1994. Fellow: AAAS, Royal Soc. Chemistry, Am. Inst. Chemists (co-recipient Chgo. award 1967); mem.: Nat. Com. Clin. Lab. Stds. (bd. dirs.), Am. Soc. Clin. Lab. Sci. (chmn. assembly, Achievement award 1976), Soc. Chem. Industry (hon.), Assn. Clin. Scientists (diploma of honor 1992), Am. Assn. Clin. Chemistry (coun., bd. dirs., nominating com. and pub. rels. com., nat. membership com., coord. profl. affairs, pres.), Am. Chem. Soc. (pres. 1993, bd. dirs., chmn. Chemistry Week task force, bd. com. pub. affairs and pub. rels., chmn. women chemists com., internat. activities com., grants and awards com., prof. and mem. rels. com., nominating com., coun. policy pub. affairs and budget, councilor, Garvan medal 1980, Svc. award local chpt. 1981, co-recipient Mosher award 1983, 1st recipient Helen M. Free Pub. Outreach award 1995, Helen M. Free award named in her honor 1995), Altrusa (pres. 1982—83, bd. dirs.), Sigma Delta Epsilon (hon.), Iota Sigma Pi (hon.). Presbyterian. Achievements include patents in field. Home: 3752 E Jackson Blvd Elkhart IN 46516-5205 Office: Bayer Corp Diagnostics Divsn 1884 Miles Ave Elkhart IN 46514-2291 E-mail: Hmfree23@aol.com., helen.free.b@bayer.com.

FREE, MARY MOORE, biological and medical anthropologist; b. Paris, Tex., Mar. 6, 1933; d. Dudley Crawford and Margie Lou (Moore) Hubbard; m. Dwight Allen Free Jr., June 26, 1954 (dec.); children: Hardy (dec.), Dudley (dec.), Margery, Caroline. Student, Ward-Belmont Coll., 1951; BS, So. Meth. U., 1954, MLA, 1981, MA, 1987, PhD, 1989. Instr. So. Meth. U., Dallas, 1982-89, prof. continuing edn., 1989-90; prof. So. Meth. U., Dedman Coll., Dallas, 1990—; adj. asst. prof. dept. anthropology So. Meth. U., Dallas, 1990—. Prof. Richland C.C., Dallas, 1986; house anthropologist Baylor U. Med. Ctr., mem. adv. bd. Inst. for Study of Earth and Man, 1995, preceptor clin. edn. affiliation, 1990—, chair Class 1954 sustentation drive, organ/tissue transplantation task force, 1997; cardiothoracic transplantation team Baylor U. Med. Ctr., S.W. transplantation team Baylor U. Med. Ctr./U. Tex. Southwestern Med. Sch., 1990— (cardiothoracic transplantation award for excellence in svc., 1998); adv. bd. geriatrics Vis. Nurse Assn., Dallas, 1984-91; presenter in field anthropology, medicine, women's issues; bd. Dedman Coll. SMU Excellence in Sci. Lecture Series, Dallas Soc. SMU, Collegium de Vinci, SMU; contbr. AMA/JAMA protocol on authorship; spokesperson, adv. bd. Lisa Landry Childress Found. for Organ Donation Awareness. Author: The Private World of the Hermitage: Lifestyles of the Rich and Old in an Elite Retirement Home, 1995; contbr. numerous chpts. in sci. books, ednl. TV, and articles to Anthropology Newsletter, Am. Anthropologist, Am. Jour. Cardiology, Cahiers de Sociologie Economique et Culturelle-Ethnopsycholie, Jour. Heart Failure, Jour. Internat. Soc. Dermatology, Jour. Leadership Ctr., Baylor Health Care System, Jour. Lisa Landry Childrens Found., ; mem. editl. bd. Baylor U. Med. Ctr. Procs.; editor/contbr. Jour. Kimberly H. Courtwright and Joseph W. Summers Inst. of Metabolic Disease, BUMC, 1998; contbr. numerous articles to profl. jours. Bd. dirs. New Hearts and Lungs, Baylor Med. Ctr., 1994—, Lisa Landry Childress Found. for Organ Donor Awareness, Victims Outreach, 1997—, Isis Soc. and internat. issues com. Baylor U. Med. Ctr.; active various svc. and social orgns. Named one of Notable Women of Tex., 1984; recipient Outstanding Svc. Cardiothoracic Transplantation award Baylor U. Med. Ctr., 1998; provide Dr. Mary Moore Free Endowment for grad. study fieldwork in anthropology So. Meth. U. Fellow Am. Anthrop. Assn., Inst. for Study of Earth and Man; mem. AAAS, Internat. Soc. Heart Failure (sci. adv. bd.), Internat. Acad. Cardiology Inc. (internat. sci. adv. bd.), Internat. Congress Heart Disease (internat. sci. adv. bd.), Internat. Soc. Heart Disease (sci. adv. bd.), Soc. Heart Edn. (sci. adv. bd.), Dallas Women's Club, Dallas Petroleum Club, Brook Hollow Golf Club, Pi Beta Phi. Methodist. Achievements include development of position of house anthropologist in non-academic medical center, community medicine program; cross-cultural research on old age, women and cardiology. Home: 4356 Edmondson Ave Dallas TX 75205-2602 Office: Baylor U Med Ctr 3500 Gaston Ave Dallas TX 75246-2096

FREE, ROBERT ALAN, lawyer; b. San Diego, July 29, 1946; s. Albert Joe and Nelly Fay (Cox) F.; m. Carolyn Corker, Apr. 21, 1970; children: Brian, Tyler, Jay. BA, U. Calif., Berkeley, 1969; MA, Stanford U., 1970; JD, U. Wash., 1975. Bar: Wash. 1975, U.S. Dist. Ct. (we. dist.) Wash. 1975, U.S. Ct. Appeals (9th cir.) 1983, U.S. Dist. Ct. Hawaii, 1993, U.S. Supreme Ct. 1996. Of counsel Damon Key Bocken Leong & Kupchak, Honolulu, 1991-93; ptnr. MacDonald, Hoague & Bayless, Seattle, 1975-91, 93—. Co-author: Visa Processing Guide; contbr. articles to law jours. Mem. legal com. ACLU, Seattle, 1975-98; pres. Wash. Citizens for Abortion Reform, Seattle, 1978; bd. dirs. Planned Parenthood Seattle-King County, 1988-91; mem. adv. com. Compassion in Dying, Seattle, 1997—; bd. dirs. Seattle Habitat for Humanity, 2000—. Mem. Am. Immigration Lawyers Assn. (pres. Wash. chpt. 1985-86, nat. bd. dirs. 1988-91), King County Bar Assn. Office: MacDonald Hoague & Bayless 705 2nd Ave Ste 1500 Seattle WA 98104-1745

FREEARK, ROBERT JAMES, surgeon, educator, administrator; b. Chgo., May 14, 1927; s. Ray H. and Lizette (Stauffer) F.; m. Ruth Nelson, June 24, 1950; children: Kris, Kim. BS, Northwestern U., 1949, MD magna cum laude, 1952; grad., Oak Ridge Inst. Nuclear Studies, 1953. Diplomate Am. Bd. Surgery (dir. 1980-86), Nat. Bd. Med. Examiners. Rotating intern, then resident in gen. surgery Cook County Hosp., Chgo., 1952-58, dir. surgery, 1958-68, attending physician, 1960-70, hosp. dir., 1968-70; research fellow Jerome D. Solomon Found. Chgo., 1953-54; mem. faculty Northwestern U. Med. Sch., 1960-70, prof. surgery, 1968-70; prof. surgery, chmn. dept. Loyola U.-Stritch Sch. Medicine, Maywood, Ill., 1970-95. Surgeon-in-chief Loyola U.-Foster G. McGaw Hosp., 1970-95, prof. emeritus, 1995—; asst. to pres. Loyola U. Health Sys., 1995-2002. Served with USMCR, 1945-46. Recipient Outstanding Clin. Prof. award Stritch Sch. Medicine, 1973, Alumni medal Northwestern U., 1980, Stritch medal Loyola U., 1981; named to Navy Pier Hall of Fame, Alumni Assn./U. Ill., Chgo, 1991. Fellow ACS (Surgeons award Nat. Safety Council 1987); mem. Am. Assn. Surgery Trauma (pres. 1982), Am. Surg. Assn. (v.p. 1995), AMA, Am. Trauma Soc. (pres. 1982), Central Surg. Assn. (pres. 1980-81), Soc. Internat. de Chirurgie, Soc. Surgery Alimentary Tract, Soc. Surg. Chmn., Soc. U. Surgeons, Western Surg. Assn., Ill. Surg. Soc. (pres. 1983-84), Ill. Med. Soc., Midwest Surg. Soc. (pres. 1970), Chgo. Med. Soc., Inst. Medicine Chgo., Chgo. Surg. Soc. (pres. 1984), Alpha Omega Alpha, Omega Beta Pi. Congregationalist. Office: 2160 S 1st Ave Maywood IL 60153-3304

FREEBERG, EDWARD RONALD, lawyer; b. Omaha, Nov. 26, 1943; s. Edward Frederic and Janice Ellen (Miller) F.; m. Norena Marie Anderson, Aug. 23, 1969; children: Edward Miller, Gregory Trent. BS, U. Nebr., 1970; JD, Creighton U., 1973. Bar: Nebr. 1973, Mich. 1977, U.S. Dist. Ct. Nebr. 1973, U.S. Ct. Appeals (8th cir.) 1974, U.S. Dist. Ct. (we. dist.) Mich. 1980, U.S. Dist. Ct. (ea. dist.) Mich. 1984, U.S. Ct. Appeals (6th cir.) 1985. Labor counsel Midwest Employers Council, Omaha, 1973-76; corp. labor relations atty. Whirlpool Corp., Benton Harbor, Mich., 1976-80; ptnr. Gemrich Moser, Dombrowski, Bowser and Fette, Kalamazoo, 1980-88; ptnr. Durant, Freeberg, Schanz & Connelly, Kalamazoo, 1988—. Contbr. chpts. to legal publs. Mem. ABA (equal employment opportunity law com. 1977—), Internat. Found. Employee Benefit Plans. Republican. Lutheran. Home: 7689 N 14th St Kalamazoo MI 49009-6391 Office: Durant Freeberg Schanz & Connelly 5955 W Main St Kalamazoo MI 49009-8700

FREEBORN, MICHAEL D. lawyer; b. Mpls., June 30, 1946; s. Andrew W. and Verena M. (Keller) F.; m. Nancie L. Siebel, Oct. 19, 1947; children: Christopher A., Nathan M., Joel C., Paul K. BS, USAF Acad., 1968; MBA, U. Chgo., 1975; JD, Ind. U., 1972. Bar: Ill. 1972, Ind. 1972. Assoc., ptnr. Rooks, Pitts & Poust, Chgo., 1972-83; ptnr. Freeborn & Peters, Chgo., 1983—. Writer, lectr. in field. Assoc. editor Ind. Law Rev., 1970-71. Vice chmn. Voices for Ill. Children, 1993—; bd. dirs. Constnl. Rights Found. Chgo., 1996—, Chgo. Youth Ctrs., 1998—; chmn. citizens adv. coun. Ill. Coastal Zone Mgmt. Program, Chgo., 1979. Capt. USAF, 1968-72. Recipient Founders Day award Ind. U. Law Sch., 1972. Mem. Ill. Bar Assn., Ind. Bar Assn., Union League, Legal (Chgo.). Lutheran. Office: Freeborn & Peters 311 S Wacker Dr Ste 3000 Chicago IL 60606-6679

FREEBURG, RICHARD GORMAN, financial derivatives company executive; b. Princeton, Ill., July 2, 1938; s. Eugene Victor and Mary Catherine (Albrecht) F.; m. Cheryl Rue, Mar. 16, 1957; children: Wesley Eugene, Michael James, Margaret Denise. BS in Fin., Ariz. State U., 1961. Account exec. Merrill Lynch & Co., San Diego, 1962-67, trade devel. mgr. N.Y.C., 1967-72, nat. mktg. mgr. futures divsn., 1972-75, regional office mgr., 1976-81; pres. Merrill Lynch Futures, N.Y.C., 1981-85; ind. cons. N.Y.C., 1985-88; mng. dir. Chase Futures Mgmt., Inc., N.Y.C., 1988-95; pres., CEO Derivatives Cons. Group, Inc., 1995—. Bd. govs. N.Y. Coffee & Sugar Exch., 1973-79, Chgo. Mercantile Exch., 1984-85. Founder Bowling Green Improvement Assn., 1982—85; bd. dirs. Ethan Allen Inst., 1997—2002, chmn., 2000—; trustee Mahaffey Theater Found., 2002—; chmn. Vt. State Rep. Fin. Com., 1997—2000, Windsor County GOP Fin. Com., 1996—2000. Recipient Fin. award Wall St. Jour., 1961; Ariz. Bankers Fin. scholar Ariz. Bankers Assn., 1960. Mem. Futures Industry Assn., Internat. Winston Churchill Soc. Episcopalian. Avocations: winston churchill book collector, gardening, birdwatching. Office: 200 4th Ave S # 328 Saint Petersburg FL 33701 E-mail: rfreebur@tampabay.rr.com.

FREEBY, STEPHEN JOHN, JR., music educator; b. Miami, Fla., Jan. 3, 1973; s. Stephen John Freeby, Sr. and Judy Freeby. MusB in Edn., Fla. State U., 1997. Cert. tchr. Fla. Dir. of bands Lafayette HS, Mayo, Fla., 1998—2001; asst. dir. of bands Bradford HS, Starke, Fla., 2001—; dir. of bands Newberry HS, 2002—03. Musician: (performance in a musical) Annie, 2001, Music Man, 2002. Band dir. Lafayette H.S. Band, Mayo. Mem.: Internat. Trombone Assn., Music Educators Nat. Conf., Fla. Bandmasters Assn. Conservative. Avocations: racquetball, rollerblading, hydrosliding. Home: 1543 SW Caroline Ct Lake City FL 32025 Personal E-mail: letesteb@bellsouth.net.

FREED, ARTHUR, civil engineer; b. Dec. 11, 1930; s. Harry and Mollie (Feinberg) Freed; m. Judith Lois Kaplan, July 31, 1960; children: Lisa Anne, Andrew Scott. *Arthur Freed's professional life has been both mirrored and supported by his family. Wife Judy, BA Queens College 1958, Ed.M. Harvard University Graduate School of Education 1959, taught elementary school for 6 years. She followed this with raising two exceptional children, and an active volunteer role in both the local school system and currently with the American Cancer Society. Daughter Lisa, BCE Union College 1986, M.L.A. Harvard University Graduate School of Design 1989, worked for an architectural firm in Cambridge Ma. And then spent 7 years as an engineer on the Big Dig project downtown Boston. She currently implements major outreach programs designed to motivate Boston area high school students to consider engineering careers. She has a son, Robert 5. Son Andrew, B.A. Harvard College 1990, M.P.P. Harvard University Kennedy School of Government 1994, has managed political campaigns for a congressman, and the former Governor of Maine. He is currently an executive with a Management Corporation. He and his wife Catherine have three children, Rachel 5, Lauren 3, Daniel 1.* Registered profl. engr., NY. Jr. civil engr. Westchester County (NY) Dept. Pub. Works, 1953—58, asst. civil engr., 1958—60, sr. civil engr., 1960—62, traffic engr., 1962—79, dir.

traffic engring. and hwy. safety, 1979—86, 1986—87, dep. commr. pub. works, chief of ops., 1987—91, exec. dir. Traffic Safety Bd., 1971—91; ret., 1991. Vis. lectr. U.S. Mil. Acad., West Point, NY; instr. FBI Command Sch.; lectr. in field. *Throughout his professional life, Arthur Freed, P.E., F.NSPE has introduced a series of innovative engineering programs and projects. Working for Westchester County, NY for over 42 years, before retiring in 1991, he became the first traffic engineer employed by any County in the State. He brought the first reflectorized pavement markings and guide signs to the County, and the first County-operates computerized traffic control system in the State. His efforts in the late 1950's brought about the development of new median barriers and guide rails. In 1990 he created a Public/Private Communications Center that has led to widespread multimedia dissemination of real time transportation information. His efforts were not confined to highways alone. In later years as Chief of Operations he was responsible for all County roads, parkways, bridges and buildings, these included a 23-story courthouse, Penitentiary, Hospital, Power plants and Office buildings. Mr. Freed created the County Emergency Medical Council, as well as a Teddy Bear Program that provided donated bears to police cars, ambulances, emergency vehicles and hospitals, for children involves in traumas. Over 22,000 bears were distributed. After retirement, Mr. Freed volunteered his time as a lecturer at West Point, a member of many civic organizations and a fundraiser for both 9/11 Police and Fire Widows and Children, and the New York City Police Museum. He remains active in all of these areas.* Contbr. articles to profl. jours.; exhibited at NYC museums. Mem. NY State traffic engring. adv. com. to Dept. Motor Vehicles, 1959—68, Nat. Adv. Com. on Uniform Traffic Control Devices, 1972—79; chmn. Nat. Assn. Counties Del.; rep. Pres.' Com. on Traffic Safety; mem. Hwy. Rsch. Bd. Commn. on Motor Vehicle and Traffic Law, 1965—76; v.p. NY State Assn. Traffic Safety Bds., 1972—79, pres., 1979—81; mem. tech. transfer adv. com. Cornell U., Westchester C.C., 1971—91; mem. adv. bd. on tech. transfer Cornell U.; instr. NY State Police Acad.; mem. Gov.'s Youth Safety Com., Gov.'s Task Force on Alcohol and Hwy. Safety.; mem. traffic engring. adv. com. NY State Dept. Transp., 1978—; fundraiser N.Y. C. Police Mus.; bd. dirs. White Plains Beautification Found. With U.S. Army, 1953—55. Recipient award of merit, State Traffic Safety Coun., 1964, Engr. of Yr. award, Internat. Inst. Transp., 1978, award for pub. svc., Nat. Hwy. Traffic Safety Adminstrn., 1985. Fellow: NSPE (hon.; pres.-coll. guidance com.); mem.: NAS, ASCE, Nat. Assn. County Info. Officers (award of excellence 1981), Nat. Hwy. Traffic Safety Adminstrn., Nat. Assn. Counties (chmn. traffic adv. com., County achievement award 1977, 1981, 1985, 1987, 1989), Physicians for Auto Safety, Am. Rd. and Transp. Builders Assn., Am. Pub. Works Assn., Hwy. Users Fedn., Greater NY Safety Coun., NY State Safety Coun., NY Soc. Profl. Engrs. (chmn. guidance com. Westchester county, state scholastic coord., Outstanding Engr. in Cmty. Svc. award 1982, Outstanding Engr. in Svc. to Profession award 1984, Engr. Yr. 1988), Inst. Transp. Engrs. (pres. NY-NJ 1965—66, chmn. student activities). Home: 6 Patricia Ln White Plains NY 10605-4009

FREED, CHARLES, engineering consultant, researcher; b. Budapest, Hungary, Mar. 21, 1926; came to U.S., 1949; s. Erno and Ernestine (Duschnitz) F.; m. Florence Joan Wallach, Apr. 16, 1956; children: Lisa Ernestine, Josie Anne. BEE, NYU, 1952; SM, MIT, 1954, EE, 1958. Registered profl. engr., Mass. Rsch. asst. MIT, Cambridge, Mass., 1952-55, mem. staff, 1955-58; sr. engr., dept. head Raytheon, Waltham, Mass., 1958-62; mem. staff Lincoln Lab., Lexington, Mass., 1962-78, sr. staff mem., 1978-94. Lectr. dept. elec. engring. and computer sci. MIT, Cambridge, 1969-99. Contbr. over 60 articles to profl. jours. Fellow IEEE, Mil. Sensing Symposia; mem. Tau Beta Pi, Eta Kappa Nu, Sigma Xi. Achievements include patent in field. Home: 16 Browning Ln Lincoln MA 01773-3911 Office: MIT Lincoln Lab 244 Wood St Lexington MA 02421-6426

FREED, DANIEL JOSEF, law educator; b. New York, May 12, 1927; s. Jules L. and Sara (Lobel) F.; m. Judith Darrow, June 30, 1967; children: Peter Jacob, Emily Sara;children from previous marriage: Jonathan Michael, Amy. BS, Yale U., 1948, LLB, 1951; LLD (hon.), New England Coll., 1994. Bar: N.Y. 1952, D.C. 1953, U.S. Supreme Ct. 1955. Atty.-investigator, preparedness subcom., com. on armed svcs., U.S. Senate, Washington, 1951-52; assoc. Ford, Bergson, Adams & Borkland, Washington, 1952-59; sr. trial atty. antitrust divsn. U.S. Dept. Justice, Washington, 1959-64, assoc. dir. office of criminal justice, 1964-66, acting dir., 1966-68, dir., 1968-69; prof. law and its adminstrn. Yale U., New Haven, 1969-75, clin. prof., 1975-94, clin. prof. emeritus, profl. lectr. in law, 1994—. Dir. clin. program law Yale U., 1969-72, dir. Daniel and Florence Guggenheim program in criminal justice, 1972-87, dir. criminal sentencing program, 1988-96. Co-author: (with Wald) Bail in the United States: 1964, publ.1964; editor (periodical) Fed. Sentencing Reporter, 1988—; contbr. articles to profl. jours. Trustee Vera Inst. Justice, NY, 1970—, Boston Grad. Sch. of Psychoanalysis, 2001—; pres. Yale Law Sch. Assn. Washington, 1968. With USN, 1945—46. Recipient Glenn R. Winters award Am. Judges Assn., 1992. Democrat. Jewish. Avocations: metal sculpture, swimming. Home: 53 Freed Rd Guilford VT 05301 Office: Yale Law Sch 127 Wall St PO Box 208215 New Haven CT 06520-8215 E-mail: daniel.freed@yale.edu.

FREED, DAVID CLARK, artist; b. Toledo, May 23, 1936; s. J. Clark and Thelma F.; m. Mary Lichtenwald, Sept. 3, 1962; children— Aaron, Michael. BFA, Miami U., Oxford, Ohio, 1958; MFA, U. Iowa, 1962; postgrad., Royal Coll. Art, 1963-64. Instr. art Toledo Mus., 1964-66; prof. printmaking Va. Commonwealth U., Richmond, 1966—; instr. Central Sch. Art, London, 1969. One-man shows include Franz Bader Gallery, Washington, 1967, 70-71, 73, 76, 79, 82, Va. Mus. Fine Arts, 1977, Am. Cultural Ctr., Belgrade, 1982, Il Bisonte, Florence, Italy, 1989; retrospective exhbn. Anderson Gallery at Va. Commonwealth U., 2001; exhibited in group shows at World Print Show, San Francisco Mus. Modern Art, 35 Artists of the S.E., High Mus., Atlanta Art of Poetry, Nat. Coll. Fine Arts; represented in permanet collections Corcoran Gallery Washington, Mus. Modern Art, N.Y.C., Nat. Mus. Am. Art, Washington, Chgo. Art Inst., Victoria and Albert Mus., govt. collections of U.K., Yale U., U. of Va., N.Y. Pub. Libr.; artist books include (with Steven Lautermilch) What Light Guides This Hand—Poems by Izumi Shikibu; (with Charles Wright) 6 Poems, 1964, Yard Journal, 1985; (with Larry Levis) Elegy with a Thimbleful of Water, 1995; (with Philip Levine) An Ordinary Morning, 1995. Fulbright grant, 1963-64; Va. Mus. fellow, 1983-84, Nattie Marie Jones fellow creative work, 1983, Theresa Pollak award Home: 1825 W Grace St Richmond VA 23220-2104 Studio: 308 S Laurel St Richmond VA 23220-6231 E-mail: commenius@vcu.org.

FREED, DEBOW, college president; b. Hendersonville, Tenn., Aug. 26, 1925; s. John Walter and Ella Lee (DeBow) F.; m. Catherine Carol Moore, Sept. 10, 1949; 1 child, Debow II. BS, U.S. Mil. Acad., 1946; grad., U.S. Inf. Sch., 1953, U.S. Army Command and Gen. Staff Coll., 1959; MS, U. Kans., 1961; PhD, U. N.Mex., 1966; grad., U.S. Air War Coll., 1966; LLD, Monmouth (Ill.) Coll., 1987; DLitt (hon.), Ohio No. U., 1999. Comdg. officer U.S. Army, 1946; comdr. 35th Inf. Japan, 1947-48; asst. to cmdr. 17th Airborne Div., 1948-49; comdr. 26th Inf., Federal Republic of Germany, 1949-51; asst. to chief U.S. Mission, Iran, and chief Middle Ea. Affairs, 1951-53; instr. The Inf. Sch., 1953-56; comdr. 32d Inf., Korea, 1956-57; instr. Command and Gen. Staff Coll., 1957-58; chief nuclear br. U.S. Atomic Energy Agy., 1961-65; chief plans divsn. US Army, Vietnam, 1966-67; prof. physics dept. U.S. Mil. Acad., 1967-69, ret., 1969; dean Mt. Union Coll., 1969-74; pres. Monmouth Coll., 1974-79, Ohio No. U., Ada, 1979—99, pres. emeritus, 1999—; pres. U. Findlay, 2003—. Chmn. Assoc. Colls. of Midwest, 1977-79, others. Author: Using Nuclear Capabilities, 1959, Pulsed Neutron Techniques, 1965; contbr. articles, revs. to profl. publs.; editor: Atomic Development Report, 1962-64. Bd. dirs. Presbyn. Coll. Union, 1974-79; trustee Ctr. Sci. and Industry, 1982—, Toledo Symphony, 1994—, Blanchard Valley Health Assn., 1999—, Blanchard Valley Health Found., 2000—; chmn., bd. trustees, COSI Endowment Found., 2001; v.p., dir. Buckeye coun. Boy Scouts Am., 1972-74, dir. Prairie coun., 1974-78. Decorated Bronze Star, (2) Legion of Merit, Legion of Honor Iran, Army Commendation medal, Air medal, Joint Svcs. Commendation medal, others; recipient various civic awards; Associated Western Univs. fellow, 1963-65; AEC fellow, 1963-65; Fgn. Policy Rsch. Inst. fellow, 1966; named Ohio Commodore, 1990. Mem. Assn. Meth. Colls. and Univs. (bd. dirs. 1979-99), Ohio Coll. Assn. (bd. dirs. 1980-84, 85-88, pres. 89-90), Ohio Found. Independent Colls. (bd. dirs. 1979-99), Am. Assn. Pres. of Colls. and Univs. (bd. dirs. 1988-99, treas. 1997-98, v.p. 1998-99), Ohio Commodores, Sixma Xi, Phi Kappa Phi, Phi Eta Sigma, Delta Theta Phi, Omicron Delta Kappa. Home: 205 W Lima Ave Ada OH 45810-1635 Office: Ohio No U Office of Pres Emeritus Ada OH 45810 E-mail: d-freed@onu.edu.

FREED, DONALD CALLEN, vocal and choral musician, educator; b. Holdrege, Nebr., Aug. 19, 1952; s. Donald William and Mary Louise (Callen) F. BM, Nebr. Wesleyan U., 1974; MM, U. Nebr., 1978, PhD, 1991. Instr. music Peru (Nebr.) State Coll., 1983-87; vis. prof. music U. Nebr., Lincoln, 1992-93, Hastings (Nebr.) Coll., 1993—. Composer/arranger choral music, including What a Friend We Have in Jesus, A Place for You, Away in a Manger, The Snow Lay on the Ground, Look on This Beautiful World, I'll Tell You How the Sun Rose; contbr. articles to profl. jours. Adjudicator music contests Nebr. Sch. Activities Assn., 1984—; program writer Nebr. Chamber Orch., 1987-88; instr. Malone Cmty. Ctr., Lincoln, 1987-90. Peru State Coll. travel grantee, 1986; musical pieces commd.; grantee Lilly Found., 2003. Mem.: ASCAP (composition award 2001, 2002, 2003), Coll. Music Soc., Am. Guild of Organists, Am. Choral Dirs. Assn., Nat. Assn. Tchrs. Singing (bd. dirs., auditions chmn. West Ctrl. region 1996—99), Kappa Delta Pi. Avocations: writing, composition, bicycling, train travel, theatre. Home: 2660 Ryons St Lincoln NE 68502-4028 Office: Hastings Coll 46 Fuhr Hall 800 Turner Ave Hastings NE 68901-96 E-mail: dcfreed@inebraska.com., dfreed@hastings.edu.

FREED, ERIC COREY, architect; b. Phila., Aug. 7, 1970; s. Edmond Lee and Phyllis Claire (Taylor) Freed. BArch, Temple U., Phila., 1994. Project mgr. Boniface & Assocs., Santa Fe, 1995—97; principal Organic Architect, San Francisco, 1997—. Com. mem. Friends of Kebyar, San Francisco, 1999—; bd. dirs. ADPSR, Berkeley, Calif., 2001—; mem. U.S. Green Bldg. Coun., 2002; chair, arch. San Francisco Design Mus., 2002—; prof. Acad. Art., San Francisco, 2003—. Mem. San Francisco C. of C., 2001. Mem.: AIA (mem. com. on environment 2000—). Avocations: sculpting, singing, geometry. Home: 2082 Bush St San Francisco CA 94115

FREED, EVAN PHILLIP, lawyer; b. L.A., Sept. 11, 1946; s. Joseph Yale and Miriam Freed. BA, Calif. State U., L.A., 1970; JD, U. West L.A., 1978. Bar: Calif. 1979. Dep. pub. defender L.A. County Pub. Defender, 1982-87; criminal def. atty. Alt. Def. Counsel, L.A., 1987-95; criminal prosecutor City Atty., L.A., 1995-97; pvt. practice law Redondo Beach, Calif., 1997—. Mem. Calif. Pub. Defenders Assn., L.A. County Bar, Masons. Republican. Jewish. Avocation: computer internet. Fax: 310-943-3111. E-mail: law@epfz.com.

FREED, JACK HERSCHEL, chemist, educator; b. N.Y.C., Apr. 19, 1938; s. Nathan and Pauline (Wolodarsky) F.; m. H. Renée Strauch, Mar. 25, 1961; children: Denise Elaine, Nadine Debra. BE, Yale U., 1958; MS, Columbia U., 1959, PhD, 1962. NSF fellow Cambridge U., 1962-63; asst. prof. chemistry Cornell U., 1963-67, asso. prof., 1967-73, prof., 1973—. Vis. prof. Tokyo U., 1969, Weizmann Inst. Sci., 1970, Aarhus U., 1974, U. Geneva, 1977, Delft U. of Tech., 1978, École Normale Supérieure, Paris, 1984—85, Hebrew U., Jerusalem, 1990, U. Padua, Italy, 1991, Yamagata U., 1998; fellow Inst. for Advanced Study, Hebrew U.; dir. Nat. Biomed. Ctr. for Advanced Electron Spin Resonance Techs., 2001—. Mem. edit. bd. Jour. Chem. Physics, 1976-78, Jour. Phys. Chemistry, 1979-83, Chem. Phys. Letters, 1988-90, Applied Magnetic Resonance, 1990—, Magnetic Resonance Rev., 1993—; contbr. numerous articles to profl. jours. Recipient Buck-Whitney award Ea. N.Y. sect. Am. Chem. Soc., 1981, Gold medal award Internat. Electron Spin Resonance Soc., 1994, Irving Langmuir prize in chem. physics Am. Phys. Soc., 1997, Internat. Zavoisky award Zavoisky Inst. of Russian Acad. Scis., 1998; named Ramsay Meml. fellow, 1962-63, A.P. Sloan Found. fellow, 1966-68, sr. Weizmann fellow, 1970, Guggenheim fellow, 1984-85, Bruker lectr. Chem. Soc. U.K., 1990, MacDowell lectr. in chemical physics, U.B.C., 1997. Fellow Am. Phys. Soc., Am. Acad. Arts and Scis., 1997; mem. Nat. Magnetic Resonance Soc. India (hon.). Jewish. Home: 108 Homestead Cir Ithaca NY 14850-6214 Office: Cornell U Dept Chemistry Baker Lab Ithaca NY 14853-1301 E-mail: jhf@ccmr.cornell.edu.

FREED, JAMES INGO, architect; b. Essen, Germany, July 23, 1930; arrived in U.S., 1939, naturalized, 1948; s. Michael and Dora Freed; m. Hermine Gerberg, May 28, 1967; 1 child, Dara Michaella. BArch, Ill. Inst. Tech., 1953. Registered N.Y., D.C., Ill., Ohio, Nebr., Mo., Wis., Calif., Tex., Ark., Ariz., Minn., Colo., Va., N.J., Conn. Practice architecture Danforth & Speyer, Chgo., 1951—52, Michael Reese Planning Assn., Chgo., 1952—53; designer Office Mies Van der Rohe, N.Y.C., 1955—56, I.M. Pei & Ptnrs., N.Y.C., 1956—79, ptnr., 1980—89, Pei Cobb Freed & Ptnrs., N.Y.C., 1989—; prof. architecture, dean Coll. Architecture, Planning and Design Ill. Inst. Tech., 1975—78. Adj. prof. architecture Columbia U., 1984; Eero Sarrinen prof. archtl. design Yale U., 1985; adj. instr. design Cooper Union, 1959, 1965—69; vis. critic Cornell U., 1962, 67, R.I. Sch. Design Dept. Architecture, 1983; critic, jury mem. various univs.; lectr. in field; mem. steering com. coun. on tall bldgs. and urban habitat, 1982—. Exhibitions include Gray Gallery, Chgo., 1976, Walter Kelly Gallery, 1977, Graham Found., 1978, Walker Art Ctr., Mpls., 1978—79, The New Sch., N.Y.C., 1982, U. Calif., Berkeley, 1982, Whitney Mus., N.Y.C., 1984, San Francisco Mus. Modern Art, 1985, Cleve. Ctr. for Contemporary Art, 1985, NAD, 1987, Am. Acad. and Inst. Arts and Letters, 1987, Ill. Inst. Tech. Exhbn., Chgo., 1988, N.Y. Architects, 1987—88, Chgo. Antheneum, 1993—94, Century Assn., N.Y.C., 1994, prin. works include Kips Bay Plz. Apts., 1962 (City Club N.Y. Albert S. Bard award, 1965), NYU Towers, 1969 (Concrete Industry Bd. award, 1966, AIA Honor award, 1967, City Club N.Y. Albert S. Bard award, 1967), Univ. Plz. (AIA Honor award, 1967), 88 Pine St., N.Y.C., 1973 (R.S. Reynolds Meml. award, 1974, AIA Honor award, 1975), FAA Air Traffic Control Towers, various cities, 1965—72, Nat. Bank Commerce, Lincoln, Nebr., 1976 (Concrete Reinforcing Steel Inst. award, 1977), West Loop Plz., Houston, 1980, Gem City Savs. and Home Savs., Dayton, Ohio, 1981, Warwick Post Oak, Houston, 1982, Jacob K. Javits Conv. Ctr., N.Y.C., 1986, 1988 (AIA Honor award, 1988, Concrete Industry Bd. award of merit, 1988), Potomac Tower, Rosslyn, Va., 1990, First Bank Pl., Mpls., 1992, 1299 Pennsylvania Ave., Washington, 1993, U.S. Holocaust Meml. Mus., 1993 (AIA Honor award, 1994), LA Convention Ctr., 1993 (Art/LA Internat. Arts award for architecture, 1993), San Francisco Main Libr., 1996, The Washington House, numerous others. Archtl. commr. Art Commn. of N.Y.C., 1983—; bd. dirs. Creative Time, N.Y.C., 1975—78, Bright New City, Chgo., 1976—78, Art in Pub. Places, Chgo., 1976—78, 1980—; mem. N.Y. Mcpl. Arts Soc., 1983—, Syracuse U. Adv. Com., 1983—, Archtl. Commn. U. Seattle, 1983—; bd. dirs. Regional Plan Assn., NY, 1985—88, 1985—88, 1985—88. C.E. U.S. Army, 1953—55. Recipient R.S. Reynolds Meml. award, 1975, Men of Industry award, Concrete Industry Bd. Inc., 1987, Arnold W. Brunner Meml. Prize in Architecture, 1987, Nat. Arts medal, NEA, 1995. Fellow: AIA (chmn. nat. com. on design 1974, nat. com. on design 1972—77, vice chmn. design com. 1974, Chgo. Architecture award 1985, medal of honor N.Y. chpt. 1987, 1st ann. Thomas Jefferson award 1993); mem.: NEA (tilted arc adv. panel 1987), Am. Acad. Arts and Letters (Presdl. Design award 1997), N.Y. Mcpl. Arts Soc., N.Y. Soc. Architects, Archtl League N.Y., Nat. Acad. Design (assoc.). Office: Pei Cobb Freed & Ptnrs 600 Madison Ave New York NY 10022-1615

FREED, KARL FREDERICK, chemistry educator; b. Bklyn., Sept. 25, 1942; s. Nathan and Pauline Freed; m. Gina P. Goldstein, June 14, 1964; children: Nicole Yvette, Michele Suzanne. BS, Columbia U., 1963; A.M., Harvard U., 1965, PhD, 1967. NATO postdoctoral fellow U. Manchester (Eng.), 1967-68; asst. prof. U. Chgo., 1968-73, assoc. prof., 1973-76, prof. chemistry, 1976—, dir. James Frank Inst., 1983-86. Bd. dirs. Telluride Summer Rsch. Ctr., 2003—. Author: Renormalization Group Theory of Macromolecules, 1987; editl. bd. Jour. Statis. Physics, 1976-78, Advances in Chem. Physics, 1985—, Computational Theoretical Polymer Sci., 1996—; adv. editor Chem. Physics, 1979-92, Chem. Revs., 1981-83, Internat. Jour. Quantum Chemistry, 1995-99; assoc. editor Jour. Chem. Physics, 1982-84; contbr. articles to profl. jours. Recipient Marlow medal Faraday div. Chem. Soc. London, 1973; recipient Pure Chemistry award Am. Chem. Soc., 1976; fellow Sloan Found., 1969-71; Guggenheim fellow, 1972-73; fellow Dreyfus Found., 1972-77 Fellow: Am. Phys. Soc.; mem.: Am. Chem. Soc., Royal Soc. Chemistry. Office: U Chgo 5640 S Ellis Ave Chicago IL 60637-1433 E-mail: k-freed@uchicago.edu.

FREED, KENNETH ALAN, lawyer; b. Buffalo, Apr. 28, 1957; s. Sherwood E. and Renee (Liebesman) F.; m. Odette Ashley Freed; children: David Benjamin, Daniel Lawrence, Lauren Allyssa. BA in Econs. magna cum laude, Boston U., 1979; JD, U. Chgo., 1982. Bar: Calif. 1982, U.S. Dist. Ct. (no. dist.) Calif., 1982. Prin., shareholder Feldman, Waldman & Kline, San Francisco, 1982-95; sr. v.p., gen. counsel Sydran Svcs., LLC, San Ramon, Calif., 1995—. Mem. ABA, Calif. Bar Assn. Office: 3000 Executive Pkwy Ste 515 San Ramon CA 94583-4254 E-mail: kfreed@sydran.com.

FREED, MELVYN NORRIS, retired higher education administrator and educator, writer; b. Kansas City, Mo., Apr. 30, 1937; s. Carl and Betty (Wachtel) F.; m. Janet Lea Triplitt, Dec. 26, 1971; children: David A., Edward L. BA in Econs. with distinction, U. Mo., Kansas City, 1959; MS in Edn., So. Ill. U., Carbondale, 1962, PhD in Higher Edn., 1965. Dir. instl. rsch. Ark. State U., Jonesboro, 1965-72, v.p. for adminstrn., 1972-76, Govs. State U., University Pk., Ill., 1977-82, univ. prof., rsch. assoc., 1982-87; writer, 1987—. Co-founder, past dir. measurement and rsch. So. Ctrl. Region Edn. Lab., Little Rock; past evaluator rsch. grants U.S. Office of Edn., Washington; mem. Evans Scholars Found., 2002—; co-founder U.S. River Acad. (chartered by Congress) in the late 1960s. Co-author: The Educator's Desk Reference, 1989 (1 of 30 Best Reference Books 1989, Best Single Vol. Reference Book in Edn. 1989), 2d edit., 2002, Business Information Desk Reference, 1991, Patient's Desk Reference, 1994, others; contbr. articles to profl. jours.; editor: Handbook of Statistical Procedures and Their Computer Applications, 1991; tool inventor. Village trustee, Hazel Crest, Ill., 1997—; plan commr., 1988—97; adminstrv. asst. Congressman William Alexander, Washington, 1969; v.p., bd. dirs. Calumet Coun. Boy Scouts Am., Munster, Ind., 1978—95, 2001—; bd. dirs. Bremen H.S. Dist. 228 Ednl. Found., 1998—, pres., 2002—. Recipient U.S. Congl. citation, Washington, 1971, Silver Beaver award Boy Scouts Am., 1976, Disting. Svcs. award Ark. State U., 1975, Nat. Endowment award, James E. West fellow Calumet Coun. Boy Scouts Am., 2002, Daniel Carter Beard Masonic Scouter award Boy Scouts Am., 2003. Mem. Masonic Lodge (past master), Scottish Rite of Freemasonry (named Knight Comdr. of the Ct. of Hon. 1979), Par Club (sus. life mem.), Alpha Epsilon Pi (life), Phi Kappa Phi, Omicron Delta Kappa. Home: 17023 Magnolia Dr Hazel Crest IL 60429-1020

FREED, STANLEY ARTHUR, retired museum curator; b. Springfield, Ohio, Apr. 18, 1927; m. Ruth Shelley, Sept. 12, 1955. Ph.B., U. Chgo., 1949; BA, U. Calif. at Berkeley, 1951, PhD, 1957. Vis. asst. prof. anthropology U. N.C., 1959-60; mem. staff Am. Mus. Natural History, N.Y.C., 1960—, curator, chmn. dept. anthropology, 1969-76, curator, 1976-2000, retired, 2000. Adj. prof. Columbia U., 1992—; research fellow Am. Inst. Indian Studies, 1977-78 Served with AUS, 1945-46. Postdoctoral fellow Social Sci. Research Council, 1957; Postdoctoral fellow NSF, 1958 Mem. N.Y. Acad. Scis. (chmn. anthropology sect. 1974-75) Office: Am Mus Natural History Central Park W & 79th St New York NY 10024 E-mail: sfreed@amnh.org.

FREED, THOMAS ALEXANDER, retired radiologist; b. Cleve., Sept. 27, 1935; s. Alexander Norbert and Catherine Evelyn (Balogh) F.; m. Sally Joanna Catherine Twist, Aug. 8, 1963; children: Eric, Andrew. AB, Harvard U., 1957; MD, Case Western Res. U., 1961. Diplomate Am. Coll. Radiology. Resident Stanford (Calif.) U., 1962-66; asst. prof. radiology Med. Coll. Va., Richmond, 1966-67; sr. surgeon NIH, Bethesda, Md., 1967-69; radiologist Marin Gen. Hosp., Greenbrae, Calif., 1969-2000, ret., 2000. Asst. prof. radiology Stanford U., 1969—; pres. Marin Radiology, Larkspur, Calif. 1982—. Contbr. articles to profl. jours. Served with USPHS, 1967-69. Mem. Am. Coll. Radiology, Radiol. Soc. N.Am., Western Angiography Soc., Marin Tennis Club (San Rafael, Calif.), Meadow Club. Avocations: reading, walking, golf. Home: 14 Tamal Vista Ln Kentfield CA 94904 E-mail: tafreed@pacbell.net.

FREED, WALTER EVERETT, petroleum company executive, state representative; b. Providence, R.I., Aug. 13, 1951; s. Richard Anthony and Alice Marie (Livesey) F.; m. Margery Anne Tyler, Oct. 19, 1974; children: Jonathan, Meghan, Meredith. BA, Dartmouth Coll., 1974. V.p. Johnson's Fuel Svc. Inc., Manchester, Vt., 1979-85; pres. Apollo Industries, Inc. (formerly Johnson's Fuel Svc., Inc.), Manchester, Vt., 1985—; state rep. dist. 15 Vt.; spkr. of the House, 2001—. Elected chair, freshman Rep. caucus, 1993. State chmn. Vt. Rep. Party, Montpelier, 1988-91; state rep. Vt. Gen. Assembly, 1992, 94, 96, house minority whip, 1995, house minority leader, 1997; bd. dirs. Vermont Chamber of Commerce, Southern Vermont Art Center, Long Trail Sch., Manchester Little League. Former chair, Dorset sch. bd.; former dir., Bennington-Rutland Supervisory Union. Former Rep. Nat. Conv. Del. 1992, 1996, 2000. Mem. Mcpl. Corp. Com. 1993-1994, local govt. & Rules Com., 1995-1996, Fish, Wildlife, and Water Resources Com., Rules & Joint Com. 1997-1998, local govt., Rules, and Joint Rules Com., 1999-2000. Avocations: sailing, flying, skiing, tennis. Office: Apollo Industries Inc 105 N End Dr North Clarendon VT 05759-9762 also: Office of the Speaker of the House Vermont State House Montpelier VT 05633-5201

FREEDBERG, A. STONE, physician; b. Salem, Mass., May 30, 1908; s. Hyman and Rachel Leah (Freedberg) F.; m. Beatrice Gordon, Aug. 29, 1935; children: Richard Gordon, Leonard Earl. AB, Harvard U., 1929; MD, U. Chgo. (Rush), 1935. Diplomate: Am. Bd. Internal Medicine (cardiology). Intern Mt. Sinai Hosp., Chgo., 1934-35, Mass. Meml. Hosp., Boston, summer 1935; resident Cook County Hosp., Chgo., 1935-36; house officer pathology R.I. Hosp., 1936-37; practice medicine, specializing in internal medicine Boston, 1946—. Asst. in medicine Beth Israel Hosp., 1938-40, jr. vis. physician, 1940-46, assoc. in med. research, 1940-50, assoc. vis. physician, 1946-48, vis. physician, 1949-63, assoc. dir. med. research, 1950-63, sr. Ziskind fellow, 1956, physician, 1964-84, acting physician-in-chief dept. medicine, 1973, dir. cardiology unit, 1964-69, bd. consultation, 1984-87, hon. bd. consultation, 1988—; research fellow medicine Med. Sch., Harvard U., 1941-42, asst. in medicine, 1942-46, instr. medicine, 1946-47, assoc. in medicine, 1947-50, asst. prof., 1950-57, assoc. prof., 1958-69, prof., 1969-74, prof. emeritus, 1974—, adminstrv. bd. faculty medicine, 1958-62; physician Harvard U. Health Svcs., 1974—; cons., com. mem. med. div. Oak Ridge Inst. Nuclear Studies, 1955-56; spl. cons. metabolism study sect. USPHS, 1956-60; mem. sr. cons. staff Nuclear Medicine Inst., 1966-67 Mem. editorial bd.: Circulation, 1956-60, 62-67; contbr. articles profl. jours. Guggenheim fellow Oxford U., 1967-68 Fellow Am. Heart Assn. (bd. dirs.; mem. council clin. cardiology); mem. Mass. Heart Assn. (dir., past pres., com. chmn.), Am. Thyroid Assn. (v.p.), Mass., Charles River Dist. med. socs., Am. Soc. Clin. Investigation, Am. Physiol. Soc., Assn. Am. Physicians, New Eng. Cardiovascular Soc. (pres. 1971-72), Assn. Profs. Medicine. Home: 111 Perkins St Boston MA 02130-4313 Office: 275 Longwood Ave Boston MA 02115-5704 E-mail: gordonbea@comcast.net.

FREEDBERG, DAVID ADRIAN, art educator, historian; b. Capetown, South Africa, June 1, 1948; s. William and Eleonore (Kupfer) F.; children: Hannah, William. BA, Yale U., 1969; DPhil, Oxford U., 1973. Lectr. art Westfield Coll., U. London, 1973-76, Courtauld Inst. Art, U. London, 1976-84; prof. Barnard Coll., Columbia U., N.Y.C., 1984-86, Columbia U., 1986—, dir. Italian Acad. Advanced Studies in Am., 2000—. Slade prof. fine art U. Oxford, 1983-84; dir. Print Quar., London, 1983—; Andrew W. Mellon prof. Nat. Gallery Art, 1996-98. Author: Dutch Landscape Prints of the Seventeenth Century, 1980, Rubens: The Life of Christ After the Passion, 1984, Iconoclasts and Their Motives, 1985, Iconoclasm and Painting in the Revolt of the Netherlands, 1566-1609, 1988, The Prints of Pieter Bruegel the Elder, 1989, The Power of Images: Studies in the History and Theory of Response, 1989, Joseph Kosuth the Play of the Unmentionable, 1992, Peter Paul Rubens: Paintings and Oil Sketches, 1995, The Eye of the Lynx: Galileo, His Friends, and the Beginnings of Modern Natural History, 2002; author: (with E. Baldini) The Paper Museum of Cassiano dal Pazzo: Citrus Fruit, 1997; author: (with A. Scott) The Paper Museum of Cassiano dal Pazzo: Fossil Woods, 2000. Mem. Am. Acad. Arts and Scis., Am. Philos. Soc. Office: Columbia University Schermerhorn Hall New York NY 10027

FREEDBERG, IRWIN MARK, dermatologist; b. Boston, July 4, 1931; s. Arthur Harris and Sayde Ruth (Bixby) F.; m. Irene Sybil Lisman, July 4, 1954; children— Marjorie, Kenneth, Deborah. Student, Dartmouth Coll., 1949-52; MD, Harvard U., 1956. Intern Beth Israel Hosp., Boston, 1956-57, resident in internal medicine, 1957-59; resident in dermatology Mass. Gen. Hosp., Boston, 1959-62; instr. to prof. dermatology Harvard U. Med. Sch., Boston, 1962-77; prof., chmn. dept. dermatology Johns Hopkins Sch. Medicine, Balt., 1977-81; George Miller McKee prof. and chmn. dept. dermatology NYU Sch. Medicine, N.Y.C., 1981—. Adv. council Nat. Inst. Arthritis, Diabetes and Digestive and Kidney Diseases, 1984-86, musculoskeletal and skin diseases, 1986-87. Contbr. articles in field to profl. jours.; editor: Jour. Investigative Dermatology, 1972-77 Guggenheim fellow, 1969-70; NIH grantee, 1962— ; Am Cancer Soc., Am Contract Bridge League faculty research asso., 1965-70 Fellow AAAS; mem. Inst. Medicine of Nat., Acad. Sci.; mem. Coun. Biologic Editors, Am. Soc. Biol Chemistry, Am. Soc. Clin. Investigation, Soc. Investigative Dermatology (pres. 1981-82), Harvey Soc., Am. Fedn. Clin. Rsch., Assn. Am. Physicians, Assn

Profs. Dermatology (pres. 1986-88), Am. Dermatologic Assn. (treas. 1987-92, dir. 1992-97, pres. 1997-98), Am. Soc. Cell Biology, Am. Bd. Dermatology (dir. 1984-94, v.p. 1992, pres. 1993), Am. Med. Assn. (Ho. of Dels. 1990—), N.Y. Acad. Medicine (sect. on dermatology 1986-87, chmn. 1987-88), Am. Acad. Dermatology (dir. 1991-96), French Dermatology Soc. (hon.), Korean Dermatology Soc. (hon.). Home: 333 E 68th St New York NY 10021-5693 Office: 562 1st Ave New York NY 10016-6402 E-mail: irwin.freedberg@med.nyu.edu.

FREEDENBERG, DEBRA, physician, geneticist; b. N.Y.C., May 4, 1955; d. Martin and Shirley Freedenberg. PhD, MPhil, Mt. Sinai Sch. Medicine, 1979; MD, SUNY, Buffalo, 1982. Diplomate Am. Coll. Med. Genetics, Am. Acad. Pediat. Intern, residency Yale New Haven Hosp., 1982—83, resident, 1983—85; med. sch. faculty U. Tex. Southwestern, Dallas, 1989—92, Tex. A&M, Temple, 1993—95, U. Iowa, Iowa City, 1995—96; med. dir. Genetics Inst. Austin, Tex., 1997—. Contbr. articles to profl. jours. Fellow Am. Coll. Med. Genetics (founder); mem. Am. Acad. Pediat., Am. Soc. Human Genetics. Office: Genetics Inst Austin 900 E 30th St Ste 220 Austin TX 78705-3323 E-mail: dfreedenberg@geneticsinstituteofaustin.com.

FREEDLAND, JACOB BERKE, dentist, endodontist; b. Wilmington, N.C., Mar. 19, 1913; s. Morris and Molly (Burke) F.; m. Charlotte Soble, Sept. 7, 1939; children: Martin B., Leslie Ann Freedland Locke. Student, U. N.C.; DDS, Emory U., 1936; D of Pub. Svc. (hon.), U. N.C., Charlotte, 1990. Diplomate Am. Bd. Endodontists. Pvt. practice dentistry, Charlotte, N.C., 1938—; ret., 1987. Adj. prof. U. N.C., Chapel Hill, 1963—; vis. lectr. Columbia, Pa., N.Y., 1970—; cons. lectr. U.S. Army Dental Corps, Walter Reed, 1964-86, USN Dental Corps, Nat. Naval Ctr., 1964-78, Area Health Edn. Ctrs., Charlotte; cons. dept. oral medicine Carolinas Med. Ctr., Charlotte, scientist-in-residence; dir. dental programs Charlotte Area Health Edn. Ctr., Carolinas Med. Ctr., Charlotte; dir. program devel. AHEC, 1990. Contbr. articles to profl. jours. Bd. dirs. Charlotte Symphony, Mecklenburg Red Cross, Mecklenburg County Blood Bank; bd. visitors U. N.C., 1985-89. Maj. Dental Corps U.S. Army, 1941-45, ETO. Recipient Charlotte Dental Soc. award, 1965, Disting. Alumnus award U. N.C., 1979, Edgar D. Collidge award, L.A., 1980, Disting. Practitioner award Nat. Acad. Dentistry, 1987, Thomas P. Hinman Disting. Svc. award, 1988, Louis Grossman Internat. award Soc. Francaise d'Endodontie, New Orleans, 1989, Achievement award Am. Fund Dental Health, Chgo., 1990, Disting. Svc. scroll N.C. Dental Soc., 1990, Distg. Philanthropist award Am. Rsch. and Endowment Found., Chgo., 1993; Jacob B. Freedland D.D.S. Conf. Rm. Spl. Care Dental Ctr., Huntersville Oaks Nursing Home named in his honor, 1990; Jacob B. Freedland Chair endowed in his honor U. N.C. Sch. Dentistry, Doctor of Pub. Svc. award U. N.C., 1990; Freedland Scholarship in endodontics established U. N.C. Sch. Dentistry, 1993. Fellow Am. Coll. Dentists, Internat. Coll. of Dentists, Am. Assn. Endodontists (1st Disting. Philathropist award Rsch. Edn. Found. 1993), Acad. Dentistry Internat. (named Internat. Dentist of Yr., 1994); mem. ADA (cons., commn. on accreditation, coun. on dental edn. 1964-86, del. to internat. profl. orgns. 1982, 86, 87, Presdl. citation 1988), Am. Assn. Endodontists (pres. 1964-65), N.C. Dental Soc. (pres. 2nd dist. 1964-65), Am. Inst. Oral Scis. (pres. 1965-67), Am. Assn. Hosp. Dentists, Am. Fund Dental Health (trustee, adviser), Dental Found. N.C. (pres. 1975, bd. dirs.), Nat. Inst. Dental and Craniofacial Rsch. Found. (bd. dirs. 1998—, mem. exec. com. Friends chpt. 1999-2000). Jewish. Avocations: travel, history, anthropology, archaeology, education. Home: 2633 Richardson Dr Charlotte NC 28211-3355 Office: Carolinas Med Ctr 202 Med Edn Bldg PO Box 32861 Charlotte NC 28232-2861

FREEDLAND, RICHARD ALLAN, retired biologist, educator; b. Pitts., May 9, 1931; s. Milton and Gertrude (Davis) F.; m. Beverly Jane Pachefsky, June 22, 1958; children: Howard M., Judith L., Stephen J. BS, U. Pitts., 1953; MS, U. Ill., 1955; PhD, U. Wis., 1958. Research assoc. U. Wis., Madison, 1958-60; lectr. U. Calif., Davis, 1960-61, asst. prof., 1961-65, assoc. prof., 1965-69, prof. physiol. chemistry, 1969-74, prof., chmn. physiol. scis., 1974-93. Wellcome vis. prof. U. Ga., Athens, 1990-91. Author: A Biochemical Approach to Nutrition, 1977, Biochemistry: A Short Course, 1997; mem. edil. bd. Archives Biochemistry and Biophysics, 1978-2001, Jour. Biol. Chemistry, 1985-91, Fedn. Am. Socs. for Exptl. Biology Jour., 1991-94; assoc. editor Jour. of Nutrition, 1984-88, editor, 1988-89. Fulbright scholar, Australia, 1987-88. Fellow AAAS, Am. Soc. Nutrition Sci.; mem. Am. Soc. Biol. Chemists. Office: U Calif Dept Molecular BioSci Davis CA 95616 E-mail: rafreedland@ucdavis.edu.

FREEDMAN, AARON DAVID, medical educator, former university dean; b. Albany, N.Y., Jan. 4, 1922; s. Jacob Abraham and Pauline Rebecca (Hoffman) F.; m. Alice Maurer, Sept. 10, 1948; children: Abigail, Jonathan, Jeremy. AB, Cornell U., 1942; MD, Albany Med. Coll., 1945; PhD, Columbia U., 1958; MA, U. Pa., 1972. Diplomate Am. Bd. Internal Medicine. Asst. prof. medicine and biochemistry Columbia U., N.Y.C., 1958-65; clin. prof. U. Kans., Kansas City, 1965-69, chmn. dept. medicine Menorah Med. Ctr., 1965-69; prof., assoc. dean U. Pa., Phila., 1969-75, exec. dir. Grad. Hosp., 1972-75; prof. medicine Med. Sch. CUNY, 1975—, acting dean, 1978-79, dep. dean acad. affairs, 1990-92. Examiner N.Y. State Bd. Med. Examiners, Albany, 1962-65; cons. Touro Coll., N.Y.C., 1980; career investigator N.Y. Pub. Health Rsch. Coun., 1963-65; dir. Danciger Med. Inst., Kansas City, Mo., 1966-69. Mem. Ardsley (N.Y.) Bd. of Edn., 1962-65. Libman Fund fellow, 1951-54, USPHS fellow, 1958-60. Mem. Am. Soc. for Cell Biology, Am. Soc. Biochemistry and Molecular Biology. Jewish. Office: CUNY Med Sch 135th St & Convent Ave New York NY 10031 E-mail: adf53@columbia.edu.

FREEDMAN, ALBERT Z. publishing company executive; b. Taunton, Mass. s. Frank and Bessie (Kanaber) F.; m. Esther Hilda Katz, Sept. 23, 1954 (dec.); children: Mara (dec.), Lisa, Tani, Derek; m. Nancy Lee Dworman, Aug. 17, 1984. Student, Boston U., 1945-46; BA, U. So. Calif., 1948; postgrad., Inst. Hautes Etudes Cinématagraphiques, Paris, 1949-50; PhD, Inst. for Advanced Study Human Sexuality, San Francisco, 1981. Radio writer, Los Angeles, N.Y.C., 1950-52; TV writer, producer WOR-TV, N.Y.C., 1952, NBC, CBS, 1952-58; playwright Mex., 1959-60; with KTLA, ABC-TV, L.A., 1961-64; free lance writer London, 1964-66; editor Forum, Jour. Human Rels., London, 1967-75, co-pub. N.Y.C., 1975-82; mng. dir. Penthouse Publs., London, 1970-75; v.p. Penthouse Internat., 1982—. Prof. Inst. for Advanced Study of Sexology. Mem. editl. bd. Alternative Medicine Publ. Mem. Am. Bd. Sexology (diplomate, bd. dirs.), Soc. Sci. Study of Sex. Home: 11 Laderman Ln Greenbrae CA 94904-2482 Office: Gen Media Inc 11 Penn Plz New York NY 10001-2006 E-mail: azurof@attbi.com.

FREEDMAN, ALFRED MORDECAI, psychiatrist, educator; b. Albany, N.Y., Jan. 7, 1917; s. Jacob Abraham and Pauline Rebecca (Hoffman) F.; m. Marcia Irene Kohl, Mar. 24, 1943; children: Paul Harris, Daniel Sholom. AB, Cornell U., 1937; MD, U. Minn., 1941. Diplomate Am. Bd. Psychiatry and Neurology. Intern Harlem Hosp., N.Y.C., 1941-42; resident and fellow Bellevue Hosp., N.Y.C., 1948-51, sr. psychiatrist, 1951-54; asst. pediatrician Babies Hosp.-Columbia, N.Y.C., 1953-60; assoc. prof. psychiatry SUNY Downstate Med. Sch., Bklyn., 1955-60; prof., chmn. psychiatry N.Y. Med. Coll., Valhalla, 1960-89, prof. psychiatry emeritus, 1989—. Vis. prof. Harvard Med. Sch., Boston, 1988-93; hon. prof. Hunan Med. U., China, 1993; dir. psychiatry Westchester Med. Ctr., Valhalla, 1979-89; cons. WHO, Geneva, 1984, 89—; Roche vis. prof., Australia and New Zealand, 1988; S.Y. Mak vis. prof. U. Hong Kong, 1989; mem. awards jury Anna Monika Stiftung, Dortmund, Germany, 1983-94; mem. Internat. Com. Prevention and Treatment of Depression, 1983-96; sec.-treas. Ctr. for Comprehensive Health Practice Svc., N.Y.C., 1990—adv. com. Memory Ctrs., Internat., 1997—. Sr. editor: (textbook) Comprehensive Psychiatry, 1967-80; sr. editor: Issues in Psychiatric Classification, 1986; editor-in-chief Polit. Psychology, 1981-90, Integrative Psychiatry, 1981-97, Highlights of Modern Psychiatry, 2000; contbr. articles to profl. jours. Mem. N.Y. State Commn. to Evaluate Drug Laws, Albany, 1970-73; founding trustee Ctr. for Urban Edn., N.Y.C., 1965-70; dir. Upper Park Ave. Boys Club of Am., N.Y.C., 1970-80; NGO rep. UN for World Psychiat. Assn., 1985-90, NGO rep. UN for World Assn. Psychosocial Rehab., 1990—; trustee N.Y. Acad. Medicine; trustee Internat. Found. for Human Scis., Paris, 1987-97. Recipient Henry Wismer Miller award Manhattan Soc. Mental Health, 1964, Terence Cardinal Cooke medal N.Y. Med. Coll., 1985, Lapinlahti medal U. Helsinki, 1990, Wyeth Ayerst award World Psychiat. Assn., Athens, 1989, A.M. Freedman Ann. award Internat. Soc. for Polit. Psychology, 1990, Presdl. commendation for contbns. to Am. Psychiat. Assn., 1999, Tom Levin award for cmty. svc. Am. Assn. for Psychosocial Rehab., 1999. Fellow Am. Psychiat. Assn. (disting., pres. 1971-72, ethics appeals bd. 1993-99, Rush medal 1974, ann. award, Spl. Presdl. commendation 1999), Am. Psychopathol. Assn. (pres. 1971-72, Hamilton medal 1972), Am. Coll. Neuropsychopharmacology (pres. 1972-73), Am. Orthopsychiat. Assn. (dir. 1962-64), Acad. Medicine et Psychiatricae Found. (founding fellow, pres. 1990—); mem. N.Y. Psychiat. Soc. (pres. 1986-87), Nat. Com. on Confidentiality of Health Records (pres. 1976-95), Internat. Found. Mental Health and Neuroscis. (U.S. dir., v.p. 1996—), Assn. Advancement of Philosophy and Psychiatry (founding exec. com. 1989—), Inst. Victims of Trauma (trustee 1992). Avocations: music, travel, gardening, sailing. Home and Office: 1148 Fifth Ave New York NY 10128-0807 E-mail: alfredm@pipeline.com.

FREEDMAN, CARL HOWARD, education educator; BA with highest honors, U. N.C., 1973; BA in English, Oxford U., 1975, PhD in English, 1983. Andrew W. Mellon post doctoral fellow Ctr. for the Humanities, Wesleyan U., 1983—84; asst. prof. English La. State U., 1984—89, assoc. prof. English, 1989—2001, prof. English, 2001—. Dir. grad. humanities program La. State U., 1989—90. Author: (book) The Incomplete Projects, 2002, Critical Theory and Science Fiction, 2000 (named outstanding academic book by Choice, 2000), George Orwell: A Study in Ideology and Literary Form, 1988; contbr. articles to profl. jours.; mem. editl. bd. Extrapolation, 2000—, manuscript referee Rethinking Marxism, 1988—, editl. cons. Science Fiction Studies, 1987—, editl. assoc. Social Text, 1983—92. Manship Summer Rsch. grant, La. State U., 2003, Regents Rsch. grant, 2002, grant, 1994, 1992, 1989, 1989, 1985, 1984. Office: Dept English La State U Baton Rouge LA 70803

FREEDMAN, CHARLES, bank executive; b. Toronto, Ont., Can., Sept. 1, 1941; s. Nathan and Freda (Glicksman) F.; m. Aviva Kravetz, Aug. 21, 1966; children: Barry, Daniel. BComm., U. Toronto, 1963; BA (hon.), Oxford (Eng.) U., 1965; PhD, MIT, 1970. Asst. prof. U. Minn., Mpls., 1969-74; rsch. advisor Bank of Can., Ottawa, 1974-78, dep. chief, 1978-79, chief, 1979-84, advisor to gov., 1984-88, dep. gov., 1988—. Author: Foreign Currency Business of Canadian Banks, 1974; contbr. 80 articles to profl. jours., conf. volumes. Gov.'s Gen. medal U. Toronto, 1963; Can. Coun. fellow, 1968. Mem. Am. Econs. Assn., Can. Econs. Assn. Jewish. Avocations: reading, traveling, cross-country skiing. Office: Bank of Can 234 Wellington St Ottawa ON Canada K1A 0G9 Fax: 613-782-7922. E-mail: cfreedman@bank-banque-canada.ca.

FREEDMAN, DAVID AMIEL, statistics educator, consultant; b. Montreal, Que., Can., Mar. 5, 1938; came to U.S., 1958; s. Abraham and Goldie (Yelin) F.; children: Deborah, Joshua. B.Sc., McGill U., Montreal, 1958; MA, Princeton U., 1959, PhD, 1960. Prof. stats. U. Calif.-Berkeley, 1961—, Miller prof., 1991, chmn. dept. stats., 1981-86. Cons. Bank of Can., Ottawa, 1971-72, WHO, 1973, Carnegie Commn., 1976, Dept. Energy, 1978-87, Bur. Census, 1983, 98, Dept. Justice, 1984, 89-92, 96, 2002, Brobeck, Phleger & Harrison, 1985-89, Skadden Arps, 1986, 2002, County of Los Angeles, 1989, Fed. Jud. Ctr., 1993. Author: Markov Chains, 1971, Brownian Motion and Diffusion, 1971, Approximating Countable Markov Chains, 1972, Mathematical Methods in Statistics, 1977, Statistics, 1978, 3d edit., 1997; contbr. numerous articles to profl. publs. Recipient John J. Carty award for Advancement of Sci., NAS, 2003; fellow, Can. Coun., 1960, Sloan Found., 1964. Mem. Am. Acad. Scis., Nat. Acad. Scis. Home: 901 Alvarado Rd Berkeley CA 94705-1551 Office: U Calif-Berkeley Dept Stats Berkeley CA 94720-3860

FREEDMAN, DAVID NOEL, religious studies educator; b. NYC, May 12, 1922; s. David and Beatrice (Goodman) F.; m. Cornelia Anne Pryor, May 16, 1944; children: Meredith Anne, Nadezhda, David Micaiah, Jonathan Pryor. Student, CCNY, 1935-38; AB, UCLA, 1939; BTh, Princeton Theol. Sem., 1944; PhD, Johns Hopkins U., 1948; LittD, U. Pacific, 1973; ScD, Davis and Elkins Coll., 1974. Ordained to ministry Presbyn. Ch., 1944; supply pastor in Acme and Deming, Wash., 1944-45; tchg. fellow, then asst. instr. Johns Hopkins U., 1946-48; asst. prof., then prof. Hebrew and Old Testament lit. Western Theol. Sem., Pitts., 1948-60; prof. Pitts. Theol. Sem., 1960-61, James A. Kelso prof., 1961-64; prof. Old Testament San Francisco Theol. Sem., 1964-70, Gray prof. Hebrew exegesis, 1970-71, dean of faculty, 1966-70, acting dean of sem., 1970-71; prof. Old Testament Grad. Theol. Union, Berkeley, Calif., 1964-71; prof. dept. Nr. Ea. studies U. Mich., Ann Arbor, 1971-92, Thurnau prof. Bibl. studies, 1984-92, dir. program on studies in religion, 1971-91; prof., endowed chair in Hebrew Bibl. studies U. Calif., San Diego, 1987—, dir. religious studies program, 1989-97. Danforth vis. prof. Internat. Christian U., Tokyo, 1967; vis. prof. Hebrew U., Jerusalem, 1977, Macquarie U., N.S.W., Australia, 1980, U. Queensland (Australia), 1982, 84, U. Calif., San Diego, 1985-87; Green vis. prof. Tex. Christian U., Ft. Worth, 1981; dir. Albright Inst. Archeol. Rsch., 1969-70, dir., 1976-77; lectr. in field. Author: The Published Works of W.F. Albright, 1975, Pottery, Poetry and Prophecy, 1980, The Unity of the Hebrew Bible, 1991 (paperback edit., 1993), Divine Commitment and Human Obligation, 1997, Psalm 119, 1999, The Nine Commandments, 2000; co-author: (with J.D. Smart) God Has Spoken, 1949, (with F.M. Cross, Jr.) Early Hebrew Orthography, 1952, (with John M. Allegro) The People of the Dead Sea Scrolls, 1958, (with R.M. Grant) The Secret Sayings of Jesus, 1960, (with F.M. Cross, Jr.) Ancient Yahwistic Poetry, 1964, rev. edit., 1975, 97, (with M. Dothan) Ashdod I, 1967, (with L.G. Running) William F. Albright: Twentieth Century Genius, 1975, 2d edit., 1991, (with B. Mazar, G. Cornfeld) The Mountain of the Lord, 1975, (with W. Phillips) An Explorer's Life of Jesus, 1975, (with G. Cornfeld) Archaeology of the Bible: Book by Book, 1976, (with K.A. Mathews) The Paleo-Hebrew Leviticus Scroll, 1985, The Unity of the Hebrew Bible, 1991, (with D. Forbes and F. Andersen) Studies in Hebrew and Aramaic Orthography, 1992, (with Sara Mandell) The Relationship between Herodotus' History and Primary History, 1993; co-author, editor: (with F. Andersen) Anchor Bible Series Hosea, 1980, Anchor Bible Series Amos, 1989, Micah, 2000; editor: (with G.E. Wright) The Biblical Archaeologist, Reader I, 1961, (with E.F. Campbell, Jr.) The Biblical Archaeologist, Reader 2, 1964, Reader 3, 1970, Reader 4, 1983, (with W.F. Albright) The Anchor Bible, 1964—, including, Genesis, 1964, James, Peter and Jude, 1964, Jeremiah, 1965, Job, 1965, 2d edit., 1973, Proverbs and Ecclesiastes, 1965, I Chronicles, II Chronicles, Ezra-Nehemiah, 1965, Psalms I, 1966, John I, 1966, Acts of the Apostles, 1967, II Isaiah, 1968, Psalms II, 1968, John II, 1970, Psalms III, 1970, Esther, 1971, Matthew, 1971, Lamentations, 1972, 2d edit., 1992, To the Hebrews, 1972, Ephesians 1-3, 4-6, 1974, I and II Esdras, 1974, Judges, 1975, Revelation, 1975, Ruth, 1975, I Maccabees, 1976, I Corinthians, 1976, Additions, 1977, Song of Songs, 1977, Daniel, 1978, Wisdom of Solomon, 1979, I Samuel, 1980, Hosea, 1980, Luke I, 1981, Joshua, 1982, Epistles of John, 1983, II Maccabees, 1983, II Samuel, 1984, II Corinthians, 1984, Luke II, 1985, Judith, 1985, Mark, 1986, Haggai-Zechariah 1-8, 1987, Ecclesiasticus, 1987, 2 Kings, 1988, Amos, 1989, Titus, 1990, Jonah, 1990, Leviticus I, 1991, Deuteronomy I, 1991, Numbers 1-20, 1993, Romans, 1993, Jude and 2 Peter, 1993, Zechariah 9-14, 1993, Zephaniah, 1994, Colossians, 1995, Joel, 1995, James, 1995, Obadiah, 1996, Tobit, 1996, Ecclesiastes, 1997, Ezekiel 21-37, 1997, Galatians, 1997, Malachi, 1998, Acts of the Apostles, 1998, Exodus 1-18, 1999, Jeremiah 1-20, 1999, Mark 1-8, 2000, Numbers 21-36, 2000, 1 Peter, 2001, Isaiah 1-39, 2000, Thessalonians 1&2, 2000, Leviticus 17-22, 2000, Proverbs 1-9, 2000, Micah, 2000, Philemon, 2000, Timothy 1&2, 2001, Hebrews, 2001, Leviticus 23-27, 2001, Habakkuk, 2001, 1 Kings, 2001, Isaiah 40-55, 2002, Isaiah 56-66, 2003; editor Anchor Bible Ref. Libr., Jesus Within Judaism, 1988, Archaeology of the Land of the Bible, 1990, The Tree of Life, 1990, A Marginal Jew Vol. 1, 1991, The Pentateuch, 1991, The Rise of Jewish Nationalism, 1992, History and Prophecy, 1993, Jesus and the Dead Sea Scrolls, 1993, The Birth of the Messiah, 1993, The Death of the Messiah, 2 vols., 1994, Introduction to Rabbinical Literature, 1994, A Marginal Jew, vol. 2, 1994, vol. 3, 2001, The Scepter and the Star, 1995, The Gnostic Scriptures, 1995, Reclaiming The Dead Sea Scrolls, 1995, An Introduction to the New Testament, 1997, Education in Ancient Israel, 1998, Warrior, Dancer, Seductress, Queen, 1998, A History of the Synoptic Problem, 1999, Archaeology of the Land of the Bible, vol. 2, 2001, A Marginal Jew, vol. 3, 2001, Peoples of an Almighty God, 2002, Introduction to the Gospel of John, 2003; editor: Eerdmans Critical Commentary, 1 and 2 Timothy, 1999, Biblical Resource Series, The Parables of Jesus, 2000, The Rivers of Paradise, 2000, Bibleim its World Series: David's Secret Demons, 2001, Music in Ancient Israel/Palestine, 2002, Injustice Made Legal: Deuteronomic Law and the Plight of Widows, Strangers, and Orphans in Ancient Israel, 2002, The Psalms, 2003, Piety and Politics, 2003; (with J. Greenfield) New Directions in Biblical Archaeology, 1969; (with J.A. Baird) The Computer Bible, 1971, A Critical Concordance to the Synoptic Gospels, 1971, An Analytic Linguistic Concordance to the Book of Isaiah, 1971, I, II, III John: Forward and Reverse Concordance and Index, 1971, A Critical Concordance to Hosea, Amos, Micah, 1972, A Critical Concordance of Haggai, Zechariah, Malachi, 1973, A Critical Concordance to the Gospel of John, 1974, A Synoptic Concordance of Aramaic Inscriptions, 1975, A Linguistic Concordance of Ruth and Jonah, 1976, A Linguistic Concordance of Jeremiah, 1978, Syntactical and Critical Concordance of Jeremiah, 1978, Synoptic Abstract, 1978, I and II Corinthians, 1979, Zechariah, 1979, Galatians, 1980, Ephesians, 1981, Philippians, 1982, Colossians, 1983, Pastoral Epistles, 1984, 1 & 2 Thessalaians, 1985, Density Plots in Ezekiel, 1986, Exodus, 1987, Hebrews, 1988, Ruth, 1989, James, 1991, 1 & 2 Peter, 1991, 1, 2 & 3 John and Jude, 1991, Psalms, Job and Proverbs, 1992, Apocalypse, 1993, The Pentateuch, 1995, Aramaic Inscriptions, 1975, (with T. Kachel) Religion and the Academic Scene, 1975, Am. Schs. Oriental Research publs; co-editor: Scrolls from Qumran Cave I, 1972, Jesus: The Four Gospels, 1973, Palestine in Transition, 1983, The Bible and its Traditions, 1983, Pomegranates and Golden Bells, 1995; Reader's Digest editor: Atlas of the Bible, 1981, Family Guide to the Bible, 1984, Mysteries of the Bible, 1988, Who's Who in the Bible, 1994, The Bible Through the Ages, 1996, Complete Guide to the Bible, 1998; The Leningrad Codex, 1998, Untold Stories: The Bible and Ugaritic Studies in the Twentieth Century, 2001; assoc. editor Jour. Bible Lit., 1952-54, editor, 1955-59; cons. editor Interpreter's Dictionary of the Bible, 1957-60, Theologisches Wörterbuch des Alten Testaments, 1970—, English Translation Theological Dictionary of the Old Testament, 1975—; editor in chief The Anchor Bible Dictionary, 6 vols., 1992, Eerdmans Dictionary of the Bible, 2000; co-editor (with W.H. Propp and Baruch Halpern) The Hebrew Bible and Its Interpreters, 1990; contbr. articles to profl. jours. Recipient prize in New Testament exegesis Princeton Theol. Sem., 1943, Carey-Thomas award for Anchor Bible, 1965, Layman's Nat. Bible Com. award, 1978, 3 awards for Anchor Bible Bibl. Archaeol. Soc., 1993; William H. Green fellow in Old Testament, 1944, William S. Rayner fellow Johns Hopkins U., 1946, 47, Guggenheim fellow, 1959, Am. Assn. Theol. Schs. fellow, 1963; Am. Coun. Learned Socs. grantee-in-aid, 1967, 76; named Disting. Faculty lectr. U. Calif., San Diego, 2002. Fellow U. Mich. Soc. Fellows (sr., chmn. 1980-82); mem. Soc. Bibl. Lit. (pres. 1975-76), Am. Oriental Soc., Am. Schs. Oriental Rsch. (v.p. 1970-82, editor bull. 1974-78, editor Bibl. Archeologist 1976-82, dir. publs. 1974-82), Archaeol. Inst. Am., Am. Acad. Religion, Bibl. Colloquium (sec.-treas. 1960-90), Bibl. Colloquium West (sec., treas. 2000—). Presbyterian. Office: U Calif San Diego Dept History 0104 9500 Gilman Dr La Jolla CA 92093-0104 E-mail: dnfreedman@ucsd.edu.

FREEDMAN, DEBORAH COLETTE, playwright, actor; d. Robert Owen and Sharon Center Freedman. BA, Haverford Coll., 1990; MA, Colgate U., 1992. Author: (plays) First to the Egg, 2002, Shoshanah's Shabat, 2003, Finding Fred Mertz, 2003. Address: 1527 N Orange Grove AVe Los Angeles CA 90046 E-mail: zafteeg@earthlink.net.

FREEDMAN, ERIC, journalist, educator, writer; b. Brookline, Mass., Nov. 6, 1949; s. Morris and Charlotte (Nadler) Freedman; m. Mary Ann Sipher, May 24, 1974; children: Ian Sipher, Cara Sipher. BA, Cornell U., 1971; JD, NYU, 1975. Bar: N.Y. 1976, Mich. 1985. Congl. aide U.S. Rep. Charles Rangel, Washington and N.Y.C., 1971—76; reporter Knickerbocker News, Albany, NY, 1976—84, Detroit News, Lansing, Mich., 1984—95. Asst. prof. journalism Mich. State U., 1996—; Fulbright sr. lectr. Uzbekistan, 2002. Author: Pioneering Michigan, 1992, On the Water, Michigan, 1992, Michigan Free, 1993, Great Lakes, Great National Forests, 1995, How to Transfer to the College of Your Choice, 2002; co-author: What to Study, 1997; contbr. Recipient Merit citation, Am. Judicature Soc., Journalism awards, AP, Pulitzer Prize for beat reporting, 1994. Mem.: N.Y. State Bar Assn. (Journalism awards), State Bar Mich., Investigative Reporters and Editors (Journalism award), Am. Soc. Writers on Legal Subjects. Avocations: travel, writing. Home and Office: 2698 Linden Dr East Lansing MI 48823-3814 E-mail: freedma5@msu.edu.

FREEDMAN, FRANK HARLAN, federal judge; b. Springfield, Mass., Dec. 15, 1924; s. Alvin Samuel and Ida Hilda (Rosenberg) F.; m. Eleanor Labinger, July 26, 1953; children: Joan Robin Goodman, Wendy Beth Greedman Mackler, Barry Alan. LL.B., Boston U., 1949, LL.M., 1950; PhD (hon.), Western New Eng. Coll., Springfield, 1970. Pvt. practice law, 1950-68; mayor City of Springfield, 1968-72; judge U.S. Dist. Ct. Mass., Springfield, 1972-86, chief judge, 1986-92; now sr. judge, 1992—. Chmn. fund raising drs. Muscular Dystrophy, Leukemia Soc.; mem. Susan Auchter Kidney Fund Raising Com.; mem. Springfield City Council, 1960-67, pres., 1962; del. Republican Nat. Conv., 1964, 68; mem. Springfield Rep. Com., 1959-72. Served with USNR, 1943-46. Greenaway Drive Elem. Sch. rededicated as Frank H. Freedman Sch., 1974; recipient Silver Shingle award for disting. service Boston U., 1984. Mem. Hampden County (Mass.) Bar Assn., Lewis Marshall Club on Jurisprudence (pres.) Jewish. Office: US Dist Ct 1550 Main St Rm 525 Springfield MA 01103-1428

FREEDMAN, GERALD M. lawyer; b. Hampton, Va., July 26, 1943; s. Henry and Arlene L.; m. Kristin King; 1 child, Eliza King. BA, Columbia U., 1964, JD, 1967. Bar: N.Y. 1968, U.S. Dist. Ct. (so. and ea. dists.) N.Y. 1970, U.S. Ct. Appeals (2d cir.) 1976. Adminstr. Columbia U., N.Y.C., 1967-69; assoc. Kelley, Drye & Warren, N.Y.C., 1969-71, Trubin Sillcocks Edelman & Knapp, N.Y.C., 1971-76, ptnr., 1976-84, Morgan, Lewis & Bockius, N.Y.C., 1984—. Contbr. articles to profl. jours. Ptnr., N.Y.C. Partnership, 2001—. Mem. ABA, Assn. of Bar of City of N.Y., Am. Bankruptcy Inst., Univ. Club. Office: Morgan Lewis & Bockius 101 Park Ave Fl 44 New York NY 10178-0060 E-mail: gfreedman@morganlewis.com.

FREEDMAN, GERALD STANLEY, radiologist, healthcare administrator, educator; b. Bklyn., May 28, 1936; s. Martin and Adele (Goodman) F.; m. Karen Johnson, May. 13, 1972; children: David, Julia, Sarah. BME, Cornell U., 1959; MD, Columbia U., 1964; MPH, Yale U., 2000. Resident in gen. radiology Columbia-Presbyn. Hosp., N.Y.C., 1965-68; mem. faculty Sch. Medicine Yale U., New Haven, 1968—2002, assoc. clin. prof. radiology, 1978—; dir. nuclear med. program, dir. radiology Temple Med. Ctr., New Haven, 1978-95; pres. Radiol. Cons. P.C., 1977-87; dir. radiology Yale Health Svcs., New Haven, 1991; with Yale-New Haven Ambulatory Plan, 1994-98; pres. Freedman Nuc. Medicine, 1978-97, attending physician VA Hosp.; dir. tng. program Yale Nuclear Medicine, 1999—. Adj. prof. radiology Vanderbilt U., 1978-2000; mem. Conn. Computerized Tomography Task Force, 1978; indsl. cons.; mem. med. adv. bd. Blue Cross/Blue Shield, 1978-85. Editor: Tomographic Imaging in Nuclear Medicine, 1973, Management Concepts in Nuclear Medicine, 1977; contbr. numerous articles to profl. jours., chpts. to books; patentee in field. Fellow Timothy Dwight Coll. Yale U. Fellow Am. Coll. Radiology; mem. Radiol. Soc. N.Am., Am. Coll. Nuc. Physicians, Soc. Nuc. Medicine (trustee, fin. chmn. 1980, co-chairperson sci. program). Home: 104 Riverview Ave Branford CT 06405-4719 Office: 60 Temple St New Haven CT 06510-2716 Fax: (203) 688-8326). E-mail: Gerald.Freedman@yale.edu.

FREEDMAN, GREGG, real estate appraisal company executive; b. Burbank, Calif., Feb. 1957; s. Morton Ira and Charlotte Freedman; m. Laura Jean Anderson, May 20, 1989; 1 child, Hillary Anne. Student, U. So. Calif., Calif. State U., L.A. Cert. gen. real estate appraiser Calif., Am. Soc. Appraisers, ASA Sr.-Real Property/Urban. Appraiser, mgr. Freedman and Freedman Cons., Monrovia, Calif., 1984-88; pres. Gregg Freedman and Assocs., Inc., Arcadia, Calif., 1988—. Past chmn., bd. dirs. Pacific Commerce Credit Union. Former commr. City of Duarte Econ. Devel. Coun.; bd. dirs. Meth. Hosp. Arcadia Found.; past bd. dirs. Pasadena Conservatory Music. Fellow Coll. Real Estate Appraisers; mem. U. So. Calif. Alumni Assn., Appraisal Inst. (assoc. mem.), Nat. Assn. Ind. Fee Appraisers (cert.). Home: 195 S Canon Ave Sierra Madre CA 91024-2601 Office: G Freedman & Assocs 124 N 1st Ave Arcadia CA 91006-3202 E-mail: GF@gfassociates.com.

FREEDMAN, HARRY, composer; b. Lodz, Poland, Apr. 5, 1922; came to Can., 1925; s. Max and Rose (Nelken) F.; m. Mary Louise Morrison, Sept. 15, 1951; children: Karen Liese, Cynthia Jane, Lori Ann. Student, Winnipeg Sch. Art, 1936-40, Royal Conservatory Music, 1945-50. Musician Toronto Symphony, 1946-70; dir. Canadian Music Centre. Composer: Tableau, 1952, Images, 1958, Tokaido: chorus and wind quintet, 1964, (orch.) Tangents, 1967, Tapestry, 1973, A Dance on the Earth, 1988, Town, 1981, Concerto for Orch, 1982, Third Symphony, 1983, (ballets) Rose Latulippe, 1966, Romeo and Juliet, 1973, Oiseaux Exotiques, 1984, (soprano and flute) Toccata, 1968, Debussy orchestration Piano Preludes, 1971, (childrens choir) Keewaydin, 1971,

Rhymes from the Nursery, 1986, Aqsaqniq, 2001, (violin and piano) Encounter, 1974, (clarinet) Lines, 1974, (narrator and chamber ensemble) The Explainer, 1976, (saxophone and orch.) Celebration, 1977, (choir) Green...Blue...White, 1978, Voices, 1999, Valleys, 2002, (Operas) Abracadabra, 1979, (chorus and orch.) Nocturne 3, 1980, (brass quintet and orch.) Royal Flush, 1980, (clarinet and string quartet) Chalumeau, 1981, (narrator and orch.) A Garland for Terry, 1985, (string orch.) Contrasts, The Web and the Wind, 1986, (music theater) Fragments of Alice, 1987, (concerto for percussion ensemble and orch.) Touchings, 1989, (marimba solo) Bones, 1989, (piano and choir) Songs from Shakespeare, 1990, (soprano and string quartet) Spirit Song, 1990, (22 solo strings) Indigo, 1994, (flute, viola and harp) Touchpoints, 1994, (soprano and lute) Bright Angels, 1995, (saxophone quartet) Saxtet, 1995, (bass clarinet and cello) Higher, 1996, (orchestra and 4 choirs) Borealis, 1997, (harp solo) Dances, 1997, (viola and orch.) Marigold, 1999, (16 solo strings) Graphic 9: for Harry Somers, 2000, (string quartet) Graphic 8, 2000, Phoenix, 2003, (symphonic) Duke, 2001, (flute) Romp and Reverie, 2002, (scores) Stratford Shakespeare Festival, films, stage, TV, (soprano and piano) Spanish Skies, 2003; host : Music on a Sunday Afternoon, 1987. Served with RCAF, 1942-45. Decorated officer Order of Can.; Can. Coun. sr. arts grantee, 1960, 63, 73-74, 81, 97-98; recipient Can. film awards, 1970, Composer of Yr. award Can. Music Coun., 1979, Lynch-Staunton award Can. Coun., 1998; Tanglewood scholar, 1949, Royal Conservatory scholar, 1950. Mem. Canadian League Composers (founding mem., pres. 1975-78) Address: 616 Avenue Rd Ste 503 Toronto ON Canada M4V 2K8

FREEDMAN, HELEN E. justice; b. N.Y.C., Dec. 15, 1942; d. David Simeon and Frances (Fisher) Edelstein; m. Henry A. Freedman, June 7, 1964; children: Katherine Eleanor, Elizabeth Sarah. BA, Smith Coll., 1963; JD, NYU, 1967. Bar: N.Y. 1970, U.S. Dist. Ct. (so. and ea. dists.), U.S. Supreme Ct. 1979. Staff atty. office of gen. counsel Am. Arbitration Assn., N.Y.C., 1967-69; assoc. Hubbel, Cohen & Stiefel, N.Y.C., 1970-71, Shaw, Bernstein, Scheuer, Boyden & Sarnoff, N.Y.C., 1971-74; law sec. Civil Ct., N.Y.C., 1974-76; sr. atty. housing litigation bur. N.Y.C. Dept. Housing Preservation and Devel., 1976; supervising atty. Dist. Coun. 37 Legal Svcs. Plan, N.Y.C., 1976-78; judge Civil Ct., N.Y.C., 1979-88; acting justice Supreme Ct., N.Y.C., 1984-88, justice, 1989-95; apptd. to appellate term 1st dept. NY Supreme Ct., N.Y.C., 1995-99, apptd. to comml. divsn., 2000—, pres. judge mass tort litigation panel, 2002—. Co-chair State Judges Mass Tort Litigation Com.; mem. pattern jury instrns. com., Supreme Ct. Justices; adj. prof. N.Y. Law Sch., 1999, 2000, 03; lectr. in field. Author: New York Objections, 1999, rev. edits., 2000, 01, 02; contbr. articles to profl. jours. Recipent Disting. Alumna award Smith Coll., 2000. Fellow Am. Bar Found., N.Y. State Bar Found.; mem. ABA (chair small claims ct. com. 1986-89, bioethics com. nat. conf. spl. ct. judges, N.Y. State Ct. del. to ann. meetings, nat. conf. spl. ct. judges, 1987, 88, Spl. Cts. Conf. award 1987, 88, 93, Jud. Excellence award 1998), Nat. Assn. Women Judges, N.Y. State Bar Assn. (del.), N.Y. Fed. State Jud. Coun., N.Y. Women's Bar Assn., N.Y. State Assn. Women Judges (pres. 1995-97), Assn. of Bar of City of N.Y. (mem. various coms., chair com. med. malpractice, v.p. 1994-95), Judges and Lawyers Breast Cancer Alert (pres.). Home: 150 W 96th St New York NY 10025-6469 Office: NY Supreme Ct 60 Centre New York NY 10007-1488

FREEDMAN, HOWARD JOEL, lawyer; b. Cleve., Jan. 30, 1945; s. Samuel Brooks and Marian (Kirschner) Freedman; m. Terry Jay Greene, Dec. 22, 1966 (div.); children: Randall Greene, Jonathan Jay; m. Rita Bialosky, June 20, 1981. BA, Tulane U., 1967; JD, Case-Western Res. U., 1970. Bar: Ohio 1970. Assoc. Benesch, Friedlander, Coplan & Aronoff and predecessor firms, Cleve., 1970-75; founding ptnr. Friedman, Freedman & Kurland and predecessor firms, Cleve., 1975-85, Goodman Weiss Miller and predecessor firms, Cleve., 1986-88, of counsel, 1988-95; founding partner Weiss & Freedman LLP, Chagrin Falls, Ohio, 1997—. Trustee, pres. Spaces, 1993—; nat. bd. dirs. Facing History and Ourselves, 2002—. Mem.: ABA, Ohio-Israel C. of C. (trustee, sec. 1996—), Cleve. Film Soc. (trustee 1995—), Bar Assn. Greater Cleve., Ohio Bar Assn. Home: 2951 Montgomery Rd Shaker Heights OH 44122-2828 Office: 35 River St Chagrin Falls OH 44022-3031 E-mail: hjf@weissfreedman.com.

FREEDMAN, HOWARD MARTIN, financial planner; b. Bronx, N.Y., Mar. 5, 1953; s. Ralph and Jean (Hoffman) F.; m. Ann Beth Roberts, Aug. 20, 1978; children: Richard, Andrew, Tania. BA, Bradley U., Peoria, Ill., 1974; MBA in Fin. Mgmt., Pace U., 1977; postgrad., NYU, 1978. Registered investment advisor. Fin. planner personal fin. planning div. E.F. Hutton Group, N.Y.C., 1978-83, account supr. Providence, 1983-86; sr. fin. advisor E.F. Hutton Group-Shearson Lehman Hutton, Stamford, Conn., 1987-89; prin. Freedman Planning & Mgmt., Norwalk, Conn., 1989—. Advisor planned giving com. Pace U., N.Y.C., 1983-86. Advisor gifting program, fin. com., budget com. Temple Shalom, Norwalk. Republican. Avocations: photography, travel. Office: 304 Main Ave Ste 412 Norwalk CT 06851

FREEDMAN, IRVING MELVIN, lawyer; b. Aug. 18, 1928; s. Max and Celia (Cooperstock) F.; m. Daryl Nadine Siegel, July 6, 1952; children: Debbie, Wendy. BSEE, Northeastern U., 1954; JD with hons., George Washington U., D.C., 1958. Bar: U.S. Patent and Trademark Office 1957, Mass. 1958, D.C. 1962, U.S. Ct. Appeals (fed. cir.) 1962, U.S. Supreme Ct. 1964, N.C. 1988. Engring. trainee GE, Lynn, Mass., 1953-55; patent atty. trainee GE Patent Operation, Washington, 1955-56; patent atty GE Instruments, Lynn, Mass., 1958-62; patent counsel GE Elec. Aerospace, Utica, N.Y., 1962-81, GE Semiconductor, Rsch. Triangle, N.C., 1981-84; intellectual property counsel GE Indsl. Electronics, Charlottesville, Va., 1984-88; intellectual property lawyer pvt. practice, Chapel Hill, N.C., 1988—. Consultant, patent prosecution GE Med. Florence, S.C., 1992—; expert witness, cons., various law firms, N.C., 1996—. With USCG, 1946-49. Mem. Am. Intellectual Property Law Assn. (life), Carolina Intellectual Property Law Assn., Licensing Execs. Soc. (various coms. 1964—). Avocations: travel, continuing education. Home and Office: 33 Wedgewood Rd Chapel Hill NC 27514-9025

FREEDMAN, JAMES OLIVER, former university president, lawyer; b. Manchester, N.H., Sept. 21, 1935; s. Louis A. and Sophie (Gottesman) Freedman, Louis A. and Sophie (Gottesman) Freedman. AB, Harvard U., 1957; LLB, Yale U., 1962; LLD (hon.), Cornell Coll., 1982; LLD (hon.), So. Meth U., 1988; LLD (hon.), Mt. Holyoke Coll., 1988, Vt. Law Sch., 1992, U. N.H., 1992; LHD (hon.), St. Ambrose U., 1984, Colby-Sawyer Coll., 1995, Dartmouth Coll., 1998, Hebrew Union Coll., 1998, Brown U., 1999, Whitman Coll., 1999; LHD (hon.), U. Rochester, 2002. Bar: N.H. 1962, Pa. 1971, Iowa 1982. Prof. law U. Pa., 1964—82, assoc. provost, 1978, dean, 1979—82, also univ. ombudsman, 1973—76; pres., disting. prof. law and polit. sci. U. Iowa, 1982—87; pres. Dartmouth Coll., Hanover, 1987—98, Am. Acad. Arts and Scis., 2000—01; Henry N. Rapaport lectr. Jewish Theol. Sem., 2001. 8th ann. Roy R. Ray lectr. So. Meth. U. Sch. Law, 1985; Tyrell Williams lectr. Washington U. Sch. Law, 1984; Francis Greenwood Peabody lectr. MIT, 1999; W.E.B. du Bois lectr. U. Md.-Balt. County, 1999; bd. dirs. Houghton Mifflin Co., 1991—2001; Howard R. Bowen lectr. Claremont Grad. U., 1997; Simon H. Rifkind lectr. CCNY, 2000. Author: Crisis and Legitimacy: The Administrative Process and American Government, 1978, Idealism and Liberal Education, 1996; contbr. Bd. govs. Am. Jewish Com., 1999—; mem. Phila. Bd. Ethics, 1981—82; chmn. Pa. Legis. Reapportionment Commn., 1981, Iowa Gov.'s Task Force on Fgn. Lang. Studies and Internat. Edn., 1982—83; trustee Jewish Pub. Soc., 1979—88, Brandeis U., 2000—, Hebrew Union Coll., 2001—; bd. dirs. Am. Coun. on Edn.; bd. dirs. Jacob K. Javits fellows program U.S. Dept. Edn., 1993—97; bd. dirs. Salzburg Seminar Am. Studies, 1988—92, 1994—97. Recipient Am. Book award, 1990, William O. Douglas First Amendment award, Anti-Defamation League, 1991, Gilda Radner award, Wellness Cmty. Greater Boston, Frederic W. Ness award, Assn. Am. Coll. and Univ., 1997; fellow, NEH, 1976—77; scholar Pa. chpt., Order of Coif, 1981, vis., Phi Beta Kappa, 1999—2000. Mem.: Am. Phil. Soc., Am. Acad. Arts & Scis., Am. Law Inst., Clare Hall Cambridge U. (life). Office: Dartmouth Coll 236 Baker Libr Hanover NH 03755-3529*

FREEDMAN, JANET WHITTLE, retired academic administrator, writer; b. Balt., Oct. 23, 1945; d. Howard Marvin Whittle and Margaret Ethel Nash; m. Irving Freedman, Dec. 14, 1970; children: Jason Matthew, Jeannette Elizabeth. BFA, The Md. Inst., Balt., 1970; M.Liberal Arts, Johns Hopkins U., Balt., 1999. With Johns Hopkins U., Balt. Co-chair alumni adv. bd. Master of Liberal Arts Program, Johns Hopkins U., Balt., 2002—03. Author: (memoir and history) Kent Island:The Land That Once Was Eden. Mem.: Phi Delta Gamma (v.p.). Avocation: oil painting. Home: 1920 Greenhaven Dr Baltimore MD 21209 Personal E-mail: jfreed@baltimorefirst.com.

FREEDMAN, JAY WEIL, lawyer; b. Washington, May 19, 1942; s. Walter and Maxine (Weil) F.; m. Linda Newman, Aug. 7, 1966; children: Courteney, Spencer. BA, Williams Coll., 1964; JD, Yale U., 1967. Bar: D.C. 1968, U.S. Supreme Ct. 1973. Atty. office of gen. counsel FCC, 1967-68; assoc. Freedman, Levy, Kroll & Simonds, Washington, 1968-72, ptnr., 1972-2001, Foley & Lardner (formerly Freedman, Levy, Kroll & Simonds), Washington, 2001—. Pres. Am. Jewish Com., Washington, 1987—89; bd. dirs. Smithsonian Instn. Librs., 2001—, Georgetown Partnership, 2002—, Heifitz Internat. Music Inst., 2003—; pres. Washington Hebrew Congregation, 1982—84. Mem. ABA, D.C. Bar Assn., Woodmont Country Club (pres. 1997-99), Yale Law Sch. Alumni Assn. (exec. com. 1999—, sec. 2003—), Econ. Club, Phi Delta Phi; bd. dirs. Heifetz Internat. Music Inst., 2002-; bd. trustees The Kreeger Mus., 2002-. Office: Foley & Lardner 3000 K Street NW Ste 500 Washington DC 20007 E-mail: jfreedman@foleylaw.com.

FREEDMAN, JONATHAN BORWICK, journalist, writer, lecturer, educator; b. Rochester, N.Y., Apr. 11, 1950; s. Marshall Arthur and Betty (Borwick) F.; children: Madigan, Nicholas; m. Isabelle Rooney, 1999; children: Genevieve, Lincoln. AB in Lit. cum laude, Columbia Coll., N.Y.C., 1972. Reporter AP of Brazil, Sao Paulo and Rio de Janeiro, 1974-75; editorial writer The Tribune, San Diego, 1981-90; syndicated columnist Copley News Service, San Diego, 1987-89; free-lance opinion writer L.A. Times, 1990—; free-lance editorial writer N.Y. Times, 1990-91; dir. Hope Lit. Project, 1998—. Dist. vis. lectr. and adj. faculty San Diego State U., 1990—; mem. U.S.-Japan Journalists Exch. Program, Internat. Press Inst., 1985. Author, illustrator: The Man Who'd Bounce the World, 1979; author: The Editorials and Essays of Jonathan Freedman, 1988, Wall of Fame, 2000; contbg. author: Best Newspaper Writing, From Contemporary Culture, 1991, (nonfiction) From Cradle to Grave: The Human Face of Poverty in America, 1993; freelance columnist, 1979-81; dir. (TV documentary) Pedaling Hope, 1998; contbr. articles to N.Y. Times, Chgo. Tribune, San Francisco Examiner, Oakland Tribune, others. Moderator PBS, San Diego, 1988; bd. dirs. Schs. of the Future Commn., San Diego, 1987. Recipient Copley Ring of Truth award, 1983, Sigma Delta Chi award, 1983, San Diego Press Club award, 1984, Spl. citation Columbia Grad. Sch. Journalism, 1985, Disting. Writing award Am. Soc. Newspaper Editors, 1986, Pulitzer prize in Disting. Editorial Writing, 1987; Cornell Woolrich Writing fellow Columbia U., 1972, Eugene C. Pullian Editorial Writing fellow Sigma Delta Chi Found., 1986, Media fellow Hoover Instn., Stanford, Calif., 1991, Kaiser Media fellow, 1995, Peacemaker award San Diego Mediation Ctr., 1999, one of 45 Am. Heroes, Esquire mag., 1998. Mem. Soc. Profl. Journalists (Disting. Svc. award 1985, Casey medal for meritorious journalism 1994), Nat. Conf. Editl. Writers, Authors Guild, Phi Beta Kappa. Jewish. Avocations: skiing, tai chi. Office: 755 Genter St La Jolla CA 92037-5459

FREEDMAN, JOSEPH, sanitary and public health engineering consultant; b. Brighton, Mass., Oct. 16, 1923; s. Edwin and Fanny (Wine) Freedman; m. Emily Ann Feltman, Nov. 4, 1959 (dec. Oct. 5, 2002); 1 child, Susan Alexandra Freedman Noa. BS in Pub. Health Engring., Ga. Tech., 1943; MS in Sanitary Engring., U. N.C., 1945; SM in Sanitary Engring., Harvard U., 1955; cert. in groundwater devel., U. Minn., 1959. Registered profl. engr., Mass. Sanitary engr. Holmes & Narver, Architect Engrs., Okinawa, Japan, 1946-48; chief sanitary engr. R & U div. Mariannas Bonins Command, Dept. of the Army, Guam, 1948-50; engr. Charles T. Main, Consulting Engrs., Boston, 1951-54; sanitary engr. Pan Am. Health Orgn., Honduras, 1955-61; advisor Govt. of Honduras, Tegucigalpa, 1955-61; chief sanitary engr., advisor to govts. U.S AID, La Paz, Bolivia and Asuncion, Paraguay, 1961-63; chief sanitary engr. Inter-Am. Devel. Bank, Washington, 1963-73; sr. sanitary engr. Latin Am. Caribbean region World Bank, Washington, 1973-79; water/waste advisor Ctrl. Office World Bank, Washington, 1979-86. Cons. various water supply, sewage and pollution control and tourist projects World Bank, OAS, VITA, 1989—; cons. on devel. North Coast and Bay Islands, Honduras Govt./OAS, 1986-87; cons. Arthur Young Assocs., Reorgn. and Decentralization Nat. Water and Sewer Authority, Honduras, 1987; World Bank rep. on bd. dirs. Internat. Ref. Ctr. for Cmty. Water Supply and Sanitation, The Hague, Netherlands, 1983-85. Author: Plan for the Development of the Hydraulic Resources of Honduras, 1953; asst. contbr. report Unified Devel. of the Hydraulic Resources of the Jordan River Valley, 1951-52; co-author: National Health Plan and Training Center for Government of Honduras, 1956-57, Development of National and Local Institutions for Planning, Building, Maintaining and Financing Urban and Rural Water and Sewer Programs. Buenos Aires Convention fellow, 1953. Fellow ASCE; mem. Inter-Am. Soc. Sanitary Engrs. (charter mem.), World Bank 1818 Soc., Sigma Xi, Phi Eta Sigma, Phi Kappa Phi. Avocation: genealogy. Home: 6504 Elgin Ln Bethesda MD 20817-5442 E-mail: josephandemily@mindspring.com.

FREEDMAN, LOUIS MARTIN, dentist; b. Newark, Mar. 19, 1947; s. Morris and Sylvia (Swimmer) F.; m. Elizabeth Norine Palmer, June 17, 1978; children: Steven, Julie, Brian. Student, Emory U., 1963-66, DDS, 1970. Gen. dentist Freedman, Freedman & Weitman DDS, P.C., Atlanta, 1970—; clin. instr. Emory U. Dental Sch., Atlanta, 1970-77. Team dentist Atlanta Hawks Basketball Team, 1971—, Atlanta Flames Hockey Team, 1979-80, Atlanta Knights Hockey Team, 1992-96, Atlanta Fire Ants Roller Hockey Team, 1994-96. Mem. Exch. Club, Atlanta, 1970-73; mgr. Sandy Springs Youth Sports Little League Baseball, 1979-96; head coach Sandy Springs United Meth. Ch. basketball program, 1991-96. Mem. Acad. Osseointegration, Alpha Epsilon Delta, Omicron Kappa Upsilon. Jewish. Avocations: softball, little league managing, gardening, snow skiing, water skiing, swimming. Office: Freedman Freedman & Weitman 3111 Piedmont Rd NE Atlanta GA 30305-2507

FREEDMAN, MARC ALLAN, investment advisory executive; b. Buffalo, Sept. 8, 1958; s. Gerald Kenneth and Marlene (Celniker) Freedman; m. Sheryl Renee Lechtner, May 23, 1982; children: Hallie Michelle, Max Aaron. Student, Rochester Inst. Tech., 1976-78, George Washington U., 1978-80. Cert. investment mgmt. analyst; cert. investment mgmt. cons. Account exec. Clayton Brokerage of St. Louis, Inc., McLean, Va., 1982-83, Smith Barney Harris Upham & Co., Rockville, Md., 1983, E.F. Hutton & Co., Inc., Alexandria, Va., 1983-86; v.p. investments Gruntal & Co., Inc., Washington, 1986-91, Prudential Securities, Inc., Washington, 1991-93; pres., mng. ptnr. TriCapital Advisors Inc., North Bethesda, Md., 1993—. Pres. Washingtonian Towns Homeowners Assn., Gaithersburg, Md., 1984-91; treas. Congregation B'nai Tzedekk, Potomac, Md., 1989-91, v.p. fin., 1991-93, bd. trustees, 2001—, pres. Brotherhood, 1995-97. Republican. Jewish. Avocations: golf, skiing, reading, landscape design, racquetball. Office: TriCapital Advisors Inc 11140 Rockville Pike Ste 600 Rockville MD 20852-3117

FREEDMAN, MARYANN SACCOMANDO, lawyer; b. Buffalo, N.Y., Sept. 12, 1934; d. James Vincent Saccomando and Rosaria Rizzo; m. Robert P. Freedman, Apr. 9, 1961; children: Brenda M., Donald V. JD, U. Buffalo, 1958. Bar: N.Y., 1959; U.S. Dist. Ct. (we. dist.) N.Y., 1959; U.S. Bankruptcy Ct., 1959. U.S. Supreme Ct., 1963. Law clk. Saperston, McNaughton & Saperston, 1957-59, assoc., 1959-61; ptnr. Freedman & Freedman, 1961-75, 93-95; confidential legal rsch. asst. Buffalo City Ct., 1972-75; asst. atty. gen. N.Y. State Dept. of Law, 1975-77; law clk., matrimonial referee, hearing referee N.Y. State Supreme Ct., 1977-90, 80-90; spl. counsel Lavin & Kleiman, 1991-95; of counsel Cohen & Lombardo, P.C., 1995—. Hearing referee Jud. Conduct Commn., 1998—; founder and panel mem. Alliance for Dispute Resolution, 1997—; arbitrator, mediator U.S. Arbitration and Mediation of Upstate N.Y., 1992-94, arbitrator Am. Arbitration Assn., 1985—; lectr. Buffalo & Erie Co. Police Acad., 1975-86, Erie Co. Emergency Med. Tech. Tng. Program, 1975-83; asst. prof. paralegal studies Erie C.C., 1975-76; guest lectr. SUNY Coll., Buffalo, others. Contbr. articles to profl. jours. and publs. Mem. numerous civic orgns. including steering com. Women's Pavilion Pan Am 2001, 1999—, Italian-Am. Women of We. N.Y., 1994—, Temple Beth Zion Sisterhood, Buffalo Geol. Soc., others. Named Western N.Y. Women's Hall of Fame, 2001; recipient Outstanding Italian Am. Woman award, Ann. of Italian Am. Women, Western N.Y., 1989, Woman of Yr award, Buffalo Philharmonic Orchestra, 1993. Mem.: ABA (ho. of dels. 1986—), Legal Svcs. for the Elderly (dir. 1978—85, others), Legal Aid Bur. (bd. dirs. 1980—81), Vol. Lawyers Project (adv. coun. 1982—86), Assn. Women Lawyers, Mid-Atlantic Conf. of State Bar Pres., N.Y. State Bar Jour. (bd. editors 1983—97), Pre-Trial Svcs., Inc. (pres. 1981), Erie County Aid to Indigent Prisoners Soc., Inc. (pres. 1981—82), Erie County Bar Found. (bd. dirs. 1974—77, treas. 1962—63, others), Erie County Bar Assn. (pres. 1981—82, v.p. 1980—81, others), N.Y. State Bar Found. (pres. 1997—2000, v.p. 1994—97, bd. dirs. 1982—, others), N.Y. State Bar Assn. (pres. 1987—88, pres.-elect/chair ho. of dels. 1986—87, sec. 1984—86, exec. com. 1982—89, Ruth G. Schapior award 1994, others). Avocations: rocks, music, gardening, reading. Office: Cohen & Lombardo PC 343 Elmwood Ave Buffalo NY 14222-2203

FREEDMAN, (MOSES) MAURICE, historian, researcher; b. Winnipeg, Man., Can., July 26, 1918; arrived in U.S., 1952; s. Sholom and Rose Rachel Freedman; m. Mollie Cecille Springer, Aug. 10, 1945. B in Commerce, Carleton U., Ottawa, Can., 1949. Sec. R.J. Jewell Ins., Sioux Lookout, 1938—40; clk. grade 1 to 3 civil servant Ctrl. Registry, Ottawa, 1940—42; founder, pres. Bridgepoint Playing Card Co., Phila., N.Y.C., 1952—72. Rschr. Declaration of Independence, 1970—2003; mem. Coll. of Arms, London. Editor: Pensions and Insurance Pamphlet, 1945, author poetry and articles. Leader YMCA Boys Stamp Club, Ottawa, Canada. Lt. Royal Can. Navy, 1942—52. Mem.: AAAS, N.Y. Acad. Sci., Mendelssohn Glee Club, Princeton Club. Office: PO Box 128 Grand Central New York NY 10163

FREEDMAN, MERVIN BURTON, psychologist, educator; b. N.Y.C., Mar. 6, 1920; s. Eli and Rose (Weithorn) F.; m. Marjorie Ellingson, Feb. 16, 1952; children: Eric, Kristin, Rolf, Anne Marie. BS, Coll. City N.Y., 1940; PhD, U. Calif. at Berkeley, 1950. Lectr. dept. psychology U. Calif. at Berkeley, 1950-53; research asso. Mellon Found. for Advancement Edn., Vassar Coll., 1953-58; dir. Mellon Found., 1958-60; research assoc. Inst. for Study Human Problems Stanford U., 1962-63, asst. dean undergrad. edn. Stanford U., 1963-65; chmn. dept. psychology San Francisco State U., 1965-68, prof. psychology, 1968—; dean grad. sch. Wright Inst., Berkeley, 1969-79. Sr. Fulbright research scholar U. Oslo, 1961-62; fellow Center for Advanced Study Behavioral Sci., 1960-61 Author: The College Experience, 1967; (with others) Search for Relevance, 1969, Academic Culture and Faculty Development, 1978, Human Development in Social Settings, 1983, Personality and Social Change, 1986, Americans and the Irrational, 1990, A Traveller in Inner Landscapes, 1990, Closing Time, 1999; assoc. editor: Polit. Psychology. Vice pres. San Francisco Am.-Scandinavian Found. Served with AUS, 1941-45. Decorated Bronze Star. Fellow Am. Psychol. Assn., Am. Psychol. Soc.; mem. Western Psychol. Assn., Internat. Soc. Polit. Psychology. Home: 866 Spruce St Berkeley CA 94707-2043

FREEDMAN, MICHAEL LEONARD, geriatrician, educator; b. Newark, Dec. 12, 1937; s. David Hyman and Alice Ella (Zwain) F.; m. Cora Ruth Singer, June 24, 1962; children: Lawrence Andrew, Deborah Lynn. AB with honors, Colgate U., 1959; MD cum laude, Tufts U., 1963. Diplomate Am. Bd. Internal Medicine, Am. Bd. Hematology, Am. Bd. Geriatric Medicine. Intern, then resident NYU/Bellevue Med. Ctrs., 1963-65, 68-69; rsch. assoc. lab physiology to staff investigator Nat. Cancer Inst., NIH, Bethesda, Md., 1965-68; asst. prof. NYU Med. Ctr., 1969-74, assoc. prof., 1974-77, prof., 1977—, firm chief, dir. geriatrics, 1979—; Diane and Arthur Belfer prof. geriatric medicine NYU, 1987—. Cons. CBS Inc., Bristol Meyers Corp., Kimberly-Clark Corp., Pfizer Corp., Nutrasweet Corp., Citicorp. Editor: Hematology in the Elderly, 1985; contbr. over 185 articles to profl. jours. Lt. comdr. USPHS, 1965-68. NIH rsch. grantee, 1969—; recipient Wholeness of Life award Hosp. Chaplaincy, 1988; named one of the Heroes of Bellevue, 1987. Fellow ACP, Am. Geriatrics Soc. (com. chmn. 1985—), Am. Soc. Hematology, Gerontol. Soc. Am. (com. chmn. 1984—); mem. Am. Soc. Clin. Investigation, Am. Soc. Hematology, AAAS, Am. Fed. Aging Rsch. (founder, mem. nat. adv. coun.), Alpha Omega Alpha. Democrat. Jewish. Avocations: photography, travel, tennis. Office: NYU Med Ctr 550 1st Ave New York NY 10016-6402 E-mail: freedman01@med.nyu.edu.

FREEDMAN, MOLLIE CECILLE, researcher; b. Toronto, Ont., Can., Mar. 28, 1915; arrived in U.S., 1952; d. Harry and Kate (Lawfer) Springer; m. Moses Maurice Freedman, Aug. 10, 1945. Student, Glebe Collegiate, Ottawa, Ont.; M in Graphoanalyst, Internat. Graphoanalysis Soc.; cert. in investigation and fingerprinting, Inst. Applied Sci. Nurse, sec. Dr. Louis Kazdan, Toronto, 1931—45; chmn. home play com. Citizens Com. on Children, Ottawa, 1950—52; freelance handwriting analyst and document examiner N.Y.C., NY, 1965—95. Sales mgr. Bridgepoint Playing Card Co., Phila., N.Y., Toronto, 1952—74; ptnr. Sun & Tranquility Calendar, 1959—2002; ptnr. rsch. Declaration of Ind., 1975—2002; lectr. handwriting analysis, N.Y.C., 1965—95; featured guest TV and radio stas.; tchr. Cooper Union Coll. Composer: Big Ben Franklin/Independence, 1962—65, Love Trees for Children of World, 1964; contbr. articles. Mem.: Internat. Platform Soc., Inst. Applied Sci., Internat. Acad. Criminology, Internat. Graphanalysis Soc. (pres. N.Y.C. chpt. 1974, Cooperator of Yr.). Address: PO Box 128 Grand Central NY 10163

FREEDMAN, MONROE HENRY, lawyer, educator, columnist; b. Mt. Vernon, N.Y., Apr. 10, 1928; s. Chauncey and Dorothea (Kornblum) F.; m. Audrey Willock, Sept. 24, 1950 (dec. 1998); children: Alice Freedman Korngold, Sarah Freedman Izquierdo, Caleb (dec. 1998), Judah. AB cum laude, Harvard U., 1951, LLB, 1954, LLM, 1956. Bar: Mass. 1954, Pa. 1957, D.C. 1960, U.S. Dist. Ct. (ea. dist. N.Y.), U.S. Ct. Appeals (D.C. cir.) 1960, U.S. Supreme Ct. 1960, U.S. Ct. Appeals (2d cir.) 1968, N.Y. 1978, U.S. Ct. Appeals (9th cir.) 1982, U.S. Ct. Appeals (11th cir.) 1986, U.S. Ct. Appeals (Fed. cir.) 1987. Assoc. Wolf, Block, Schorr & Solis-Cohen, Phila., 1956-58; ptnr. Freedman & Temple, Washington, 1969-73; dir. Stern Community Law Firm, Washington, 1970-71; prof. law George Washington U., 1958-73; dean Hofstra Law Sch., Hempstead, N.Y., 1973-77, prof. law, 1973—, Howard Lichtenstein Disting. prof. legal ethics, 1989—2003; Drinko-Baker & Hostetler chair in law Cleve. State U., 1992; CFO Olive Tree Mktg. Internat., 1998—. Faculty asst. Harvard U. Law Sch., 1954-56, instr. trial advocacy and legal ethics, 1978—; lectr. on lawyers' ethics; exec. dir. U.S. Holocaust Meml. Coun., 1980-82, gen. counsel, 1982-83, sr. adviser to chmn., 1982-87; cons. U.S. Commn. on Civil Rights, 1960-64, Neighborhood Legal Services Program, 1970; legis. cons. to Senator John L. McClellan, 1959; spl. com. on courtroom conduct N.Y.C. Bar Assn., 1972; exec. dir. Criminal Trial Inst., 1965-66; expert witness on legal ethics state and fed. ct. proceedings, U.S. Senate and House Coms., U.S. Dept. Justice, FDIC; spl. investigator Rochester Inst. Tech., 1991; reporter Am. Lawyer's Code of Conduct, 1979-81; mem. Arbitration panel U.S. Dist. Ct. (ea. dist.) N.Y., 1986—; Inaugural Wickwire lectr. Dalhousie Law Sch., N.S., 1992; lectr. S.C. Bar Found., 1993, numerous profl. confs; adv. subgroup on ethics U.S. Dist. Ct. (ea. dist.) N.Y., 1994-96. Author: Contracts, 1973, Lawyers' Ethics in an Adversary System, 1975 (ABA gavel award, cert. of merit 1976), Teacher's Manual Contracts, 1978, American Lawyer's Code of Conduct, 1981, Understanding Lawyers' Ethics, 1990, (with Abbe Smith) 2d edit., 2002, Group Defamation and Freedom of Speech—The Relationship Between Language and Violence, 1995; co-editor; columnist Cases and Controversies, Am. Lawyer Media, 1990-96, (with Supreme Ct. Justice Ruth Bader Ginsburg) Freedom, Life, & Death: Materials on Comparative Constitutional Law, 1997; mem. panel acad. contbrs. Black's Law Dictionary, 2002-2003; television appearances include Donohue, CNN Money Line, CBS 60 Minutes, CNN Late Edition, Court TV, and others; contbr. articles to profl. jours. Recipient Martin Luther King Jr. Humanitarian award, 1987, The Lehman-LaGuardia Award for Civic Achievement, 1996. Fellow Am. Bar Found. (life); mem. ABA (ethics adv. to chair criminal justice sect. 1993-95, Michael Franck award 1998), ACLU (nat. bd. dirs. 1970-80, nat. adv. coun. 1980—, spl. litigation counsel 1971-73), Am. Law Inst. (consultative group on the law governing lawyers, 1990-99, consultative group on Uniform Comml. Code art. 2 1990-2002), Soc. Am. Law Tchrs. (mem. governing bd. 1974-79, exec. com. 1976-79, chmn. com. on profl. responsibility 1974-79, 87-90), ABA (vice chmn. ethical considerations com. criminal justice sect. 1989-90, ethics advisor to chmn. criminal justice sect., 1993-96), N.Y. State Bar Assn. (com. on legal edn. and admission to bar 1988-92, criminal justice sect. com. on profl. responsibility, 1990-92, award for Dedication to Scholarship and pub. svc. 1997), Assn. Bar City N.Y. (com. on profl. responsibility 1987-90, com. on profl. and jud. ethics 1991-92), Fed. Bar Assn. (chmn. com. on profl. disciplinary standards and procedures 1970-71), Am. Soc. Writers on Legal Subjects (mem. com. on constitution and bylaws 1999—), Am. Bd. Criminal Lawyers (hon. 2003-), Am. Jewish Congress (nat. governing coun. 1984-86), Am. Arbitration Assn. (arbitrator, nat. panel arbitra-

tors 1964—, cert. svc. award 1986), Nat. Network on Right to Counsel (exec. bd., exec. com. 1986-90), Nat. Prison Project (steering com. 1970-90), Nat. Assn. Criminal Def. Lawyers (vice chmn. ethics adv. com. 1991-93, co-chmn., 1994). Democrat. Jewish.

FREEDMAN, MORRIS, English language educator; b. N.Y.C., Oct. 6, 1920; s. Boris and Anna (Katz) F.; m. Charlotte Kopelman, Apr. 22, 1945 (div. 1974, dec. 1979); children: Paul, Iris; m. Roxanne Elise Charleston, May 1, 1981. BA, CCNY, 1941; MA, Columbia U., 1950, PhD, 1953. Instr. CCNY, N.Y.C., 1947-53; assoc. editor Commentary Mag., N.Y.C., 1953-55; asst. prof., prof. English U. N.Mex., Albuquerque, 1955-66; prof. English U. Md., College Park, 1965-91, chmn. dept., 1967-72, prof. emeritus, 1991—. Author: Confessions of Conformist, 1961, Chaos in Our Colleges, 1963, Compact English Handbook, 1965, Moral Impulse: Modern Drama, 1967, Tragedy: Texts and Commentary, 1969, American Drama in Social Context, 1971. With USAF, 1943—45. Home: 4007 Clagett Rd Hyattsville MD 20782-1133 E-mail: mf18@umail.umd.edu.

FREEDMAN, PAMELA GOTTESMAN, gastroenterologist; b. Bklyn., June 27, 1952; d. Elihu and Muriel G.; m. Herbert T. Freedman, Jan. 6, 1974; children: Adam, Joshua. BA magna cum laude, U. Pa., 1973, MA, 1975; MD, Albert Einstein Coll. Medicine, 1980. Diplomate Am. Bd. Internal Medicine, Am. Bd. Gastroenterology. Intern Montefiore Hosp., Bronx, 1980-81, resident, 1981-83; fellow in gastroenterology Bellevue Hosp.-NYU, 1983-85; pvt. practice gastroenterologist Randolph, N.J., 1986-95; gastroenterologist Gastro Assocs of North Jersey, Dover, N.J., 1995—. Contbr. articles to Am. Jour. Gastroenterology. Mem. sci. fair com. Chester (N.Y.) Pub. Sch., 1996—. Fellow Am. Coll. Gastroenterology; mem. AMA, Am. Med. Women's Assn., Med. Soc. N.J., N.J. Gastroenterol. Soc., Alpha Omega Alpha, Phi Beta Kappa. Avocations: tennis, piano, dance, reading. Office: Gastroent Assoc North Jers 361 W Blackwell St Dover NJ 07801-2519

FREEDMAN, PAUL HARRIS, historian, educator; b. N.Y.C., Sept. 15, 1949; s. Alfred M. and Marcia (Kohl) F.; m. Bonnie Roe, Aug. 15, 1982. BA, U. Calif., Santa Cruz, 1971; PhD, U. Calif., Berkeley, 1978. Asst. prof. to prof. history Vanderbilt U., Nashville, 1979-97; prof. history Yale U., New Haven, 1997—. Author: The Diocese of Vic, 1983, The Origins of Peasant Servitude in Medieval Catalonia, 1992 (Premio del Rey prize 1992), Images of the Medieval Peasant, 1999, (Kayden prize 2000, Gründler prize 2001, Haskins prize, 2002). Fellow Medieval Acad. Am., Inst. Catalan Studies (corr.). Office: Yale U Dept History P O Box 208324 New Haven CT 06520

FREEDMAN, PHILIP, physician, educator; b. London, June 25, 1926; came to U.S., 1963, naturalized, 1970; s. Myer and Mildred (Frankel) F.; m. Jean Kennis Cunningham, Dec. 21, 1954; children: Simon John, Marion Rose, Mark Alexander, Paul Daniel, Adam James. MB, BS with honors, Univ. Coll. Hosp. Med. Sch., London, 1948, MD, 1951. House surgeon Univ. Coll. Hosp., 1948, med. registrar, 1953-56, rsch. asst. professorial med. unit, 1956-57, Bilton Pollard fellow, 1957-59; sr. house physician Chase Farm Hosp., 1949; 1st asst. physician St. George's Hosp., London, 1959-60; cons. Woolwich Hosp. Group, London, Redhill Hosp. Group, Surrey, Eng., 1960-63; chief Chgo. Med. Sch. Divsn., Dept. Medicine Cook County Hosp., 1963-66; prof., chmn. dept. medicine Chgo. Med. Sch., 1967-74; dir. renal unit Cook County Hosp., Chgo., 1963-66; chmn. dept. medicine Mt. Sinai Hosp. Med. Ctr., Chgo., 1966-79; prof., sr. attending physician Rush Med. Coll., Rush-Presbyn.-St. Luke's Med. Ctr., Chgo., 1975-96; clin. prof. medicine U. Ill. Coll. Medicine, Urbana-Champaign, 1999—. Contbr. articles to profl. jours. With M.C. Brit. Army, 1951-53. Fellow ACP, Royal Coll. Physicians; mem. Ctrl. Soc. Clin. Investigation, Med. Rsch. Soc. London, Alpha Omega Alpha (faculty mem.). Home: 2304 Sandpoint Champaign IL 61822-9297 E-mail: philip0005@aol.com.

FREEDMAN, ROBERT LOUIS, lawyer; b. Phila., Apr. 8, 1940; s. Abraham L. and Jane G. (Sunstein) F.; m. Diane Stoller, July 25, 1965; children: Elizabeth, Paul, Jonathan AB, Harvard U., 1962; MA in Econs., Columbia U., 1963, LLB, 1966. Bar: Pa. 1967. Law clk., 1966-68; assoc. Dechert Price & Rhoads, Phila., 1968-75, ptnr., 1975—; lectr. in law Temple U. Law Sch., 1969-74. Adj. prof. U. Pa. Law Sch., 1997—2001. Adv. com. on decedents' estates Pa. Joint State Govt. Commn.; trustee Fgn. Policy Rsch. Inst. Mem. Am. Law Inst., Am. Coll. Trust and Estate Counsel, Phila. Bar Assn. (chmn. sect. on probate and trust law 1983) Clubs: Germantown Cricket. Jewish. Office: Dechert LLP 4000 Bell Atlantic Tower 1717 Arch St Philadelphia PA 19103-2793 E-mail: robert.freedman@dechert.com.

FREEDMAN, RONALD, sociology educator; b. Winnipeg, Man., Can., Aug. 8, 1917; came to U.S., 1924, naturalized, 1930. s. Isador and Ada (Greenstone) F.; m. Deborah Gail Selin, May 4, 1941 (dec. 2000); children: Joseph Selin, Jane Ilene (dec.). BA, U. Mich., 1939, MA, 1940; PhD, U. Chgo., 1947. Mem. faculty U. Mich., Ann Arbor, 1946—, prof. sociology, 1954—, Roderick D. McKenzie prof. sociology, 1979-87, now Roderick D. McKenzie disting. prof. emeritus; rsch. assoc. Survey Rsch. Ctr., 1954-70; dir. Population Studies Ctr., 1962-71. Co-dir. Taiwan Population Studies Ctr., 1962-64; cons. to Taiwan govt., 1962-88; mem. tech. adv. com. 1970 Census of Population, 1965, Pres.'s Adv. Com. on Population and Family Planning. Author: The Sociology of Human Fertility, 1960, (with others) Family Planning, Sterility and Population Growth, 1959, Principles of Sociology, 1952, Family Planning in Taiwan, 1969; also articles and monographs. With USAAF, 1942-45. Recipient award excellence on teaching U. Mich. Class of, 1952, Disting. Faculty Svc. award U. Mich., 1970, Taeuber award, 1981; Guggenheim fellow, 1957-58; Fulbright fellow, 1957-58; fellow Center for Advanced Study in Behavioral Scis., 1970; Lady Davis fellow and Einstein fellow Hebrew U., 1987 Fellow Am. Acad. Arts and Scis., U.S. Nat. Acad. Sci., Am. Statis. Assn.; mem. NAS, Population Assn. Am. (pres. 1964-65), Internat. Union Study Population (v.p. 1966-67), Am. Sociol. Assn., Sociol. Rsch. Assn., Phi Beta Kappa. Home: # 510 1200 Earhart Rd Ann Arbor MI 48105-2768

FREEDMAN, RUSSELL BRUCE, author; b. San Francisco, Oct. 11, 1929; s. Louis Nathan and Irene (Gordon) F. BA, U. Calif., Berkeley, 1951. Newsman AP, San Francisco, 1953-56; with dept. TV publicity J. Walter Thompson Co., N.Y.C., 1956-60; faculty New Sch. for Social Rsch., N.Y.C., 1969-86. Author: Teenagers Who Made History, 1961, Jules Verne: Portrait of a Prophet, 1963, 2000 Years of Space Travel, 1965, Thomas Alva Edison, 1966, Scouting with Baden-Powell, 1967, Animal Architects, 1971, The First Days of Life, 1974, Growing Up Wild, 1975, Animal Fathers, 1976, Animal Games, 1976, Hanging On: How Animals Carry Their Young, 1978, Getting Born, 1978, Tooth and Claw, 1980, They Lived with the Dinosaurs, 1980, Immigrant Kids, 1980, When Winter Comes, 1981, Farm Babies, 1981, Animal Superstars, 1982, Killer Fish, 1982, Killer Snakes, 1982, Can Bears Predict Earthquakes? Unsolved Mysteries of Animal Behavior, 1982, Dinosaurs and Their Young, 1983, Children of the Wild West, 1983 (Western Heritage Wrangler award, Outstanding Western Juvenile Book award 1984), Rattlesnakes, 1984, Cowboys of the Wild West, 1985, Sharks, 1985, Holiday House: The First Fifty Years, 1985, Indian Chiefs, 1987, Abraham Lincoln: A Photobiography, 1987 (John Newbery medal 1988, Jefferson Cup award 1988), Buffalo Hunt, 1988, Franklin Delano Roosevelt, 1990 (Orbis Pictus award 1991, Jefferson Cup award 1991), The Wright Brothers: How They Invented the Airplane, 1991 (Newbery Honor Book 1992, Jefferson cup award 1992, Golden Kite award 1991), An Indian Winter, 1992 (Western Heritage Wrangler award 1993), Eleanor Roosevelt: A Life of Discovery, 1993 (Newbery Honor Book 1994, Golden Kite award 1993, Boston Globe Horn Book award 1993), Kids at Work, 1994 (Golden Kite award 1994, Jane Addams Book award 1995), The Life and Death of Crazy Horse, 1996 (Spur award Best Western Juvenile Non-fiction 1996), Out of Darkness: The Story of Louis Braille, 1997, Martha Graham: A Dancer's Life, 1998 (Golden Kite award 1998), Babe Didrikson Zaharias: The Making of a Champion, 1999, Give Me Liberty! The Story of the Declaration of Independence, 2000, In the Days of the Vaqueros: America's First True Cowboys, 2001 (Spur award Best Western Juvenile non-fiction, 2002), Confucius: The Golden Rule, 2002, In Defense of Liberty: The Story of America's Bill of Rights, 2003; co-author: (with James E. Morris) How Animals Learn, 1969, Animal Instincts, 1970, The Brains of Animals and Man, 1972. With M.I., U.S. Army, 1951-53; Korea. Mem. PEN, Author's Guild.

FREEDMAN, SAMUEL ORKIN, university official; b. Montreal, Que., Can., May 8, 1928; s. Abraham Orkin and Elvira (Gottheil) F.; m. Norah Lee Maizel, Aug. 28, 1955; children: David Orkin, Daniel Ari, Abraham Edward, Elizabeth Vera. B.Sc., McGill U., Montreal, 1949, MD, C.M., 1953, D.Sc. (hon.), 1992. Intern Jewish Gen. Hosp., Montreal, 1953-54; resident in internal medicine and allergy Montreal Gen. Hosp., also Roosevelt Hosp., N.Y.C., 1954-59; mem. faculty McGill U. Med. Faculty, 1959—, prof. medicine, 1968-2000, prof. medicine emeritus, 2000—, dean, 1977-81, vice-prin. (acad.), 1981-91; sr. advisor Jewish Gen. Hosp., Montreal, 2000—. Vis. prof. U. London, Eng., 1973-74; dir. divsn. clin. immunology and allergy Montreal Gen. Hosp., 1967-77; bd. dirs. Nat. Cancer Inst. Can., 1979—; chmn. com. immunology and transplanatation Med. Rsch. Coun. Can., 1968-73, mem. program grants com., 1975-78. Editor: Clinical Immunology, 2d edit, 1976. Decorated Order of Can.; recipient Queen's Silver Jubilee medal, 1977; Gairdner Internat. award for outstanding med. rsch., 1978, Commemorative medal for the 125th Anniversary of the Confedn. of Can., 1992, prix Armand Frappier, 1998, prix de Que., 1998, Queen's Golden Jubilee medal, 2002. Fellow Royal Soc. Can., Royal Coll. Physicians and Surgeons Can., ACP, Am. Acad. Allergy; Mem. Internat. Assn. Allergology and Clin. Immunology (v.p. 1982-88); mem. Am. Soc. Clin. Investigation, Am. Assn. Immunology, Am. Thoracic Soc., Canadian Soc. Clin. Investigation. Clubs: Univ. (Montreal). Jewish. Achievements include co-discoverer of the CEA test for cancer, 1969. Home: 658 Murray Hill Ave Montreal QC Canada H3Y 2W6 Office: Jewish Gen Hosp 3755 Cote Ste Catherine Rd Montreal QC Canada H3T 1E2 E-mail: freedman@videotron.ca., sfreedma@ldi.jgh.mcgill.ca.

FREEDMAN, SANDRA WARSHAW, former mayor; b. Newark, Sept. 21, 1943; m. Michael J. Freedman; 3 children. BA in Govt., U. Miami, 1965. Mem. Tampa (Fla.) City Coun., 1974—, chmn., 1983-86; mayor City of Tampa, 1986-95. Author: Specialties of the House (Recipes for People on the Go!), 2002. Bd. dirs. Jewish Cmty. Ctr., Boys and Girls Clubs Greater Tampa, Hillsborough Coalition for Health, Tampa Cmty. Concert Assn., Hillsborough Edn. Found., Judeo Christian Clinic, NCCJ, Human Rights Task Force; mem. sports adv. bd. Hillsborough Community Coll., 1975-76; sec. Downtown Devel. Authority, 1977-78; bd. dirs., v.p. Fla. Gulf Coast Symphony, 1979-80; vice chmn. Met. Planning Orgn., 1981-82; corp. mem. Neighborhood Housing Service; bd. fellows U. Tampa; mem. steering com. Hillsborough County Council of Govt.'s Constituency for Children; mem. exec. bd. Tampa/Hillsborough Young Adult Forum; chmn. bd. trustees Berkeley Prep. Sch.; trustee Tampa Bay Performing Arts Ctr., Inc., Tampa Mus.; mem. ethics com. Meml. Hosp.; mem. Tampa Preservation, Inc., Tampa/Hillsborough County Youth Council, Davis Islands Civic Assn., Tampa Hist. Soc., Met. Ministries Adv. Bd., Rodeph Sholom Synagogue, Sword of Hope Guild of Am. Cancer Soc., Friends of Arts. Recipient Spessar L. Holland Meml. award Tampa Bay Com. for Good Govt., 1975-76, Human Rights award City of Tampa, 1980, award Soroptimist Internat. Tampa, 1981, Status of Women award Zonta of Tampa II, 1986, Woman of Achievement award Bus. & Profl. Women, Jewish Nat. Fund Tree of Life award, Disting. Citizen award U. South Fla., 1995, Nat. Conf. of Christian and Jews Humanitarian award, 1995; named to Fla. Home Builders Hall of Fame. Mem. Hillsborough County Bar Aux., Greater Tampa C. of C., C. of C. Com. of 100 (exec. com.), Fla. League of Cities (bd. dirs.), Tampa Urban League, Nat. Council Jewish Women, U. Miami Alumni Assn., Athena Soc., Hadassah. Office: 3435 Bayshore Blvd Apt 700 Tampa FL 33629-8827

FREEDMAN, STANLEY MARVIN, manufacturing company executive; b. Frederick, Md., Aug. 26, 1923; s. Jacob Menaham and Ethel (Freiman) F.; m. Lynn Maureen Katchen, Apr. 24, 1957 (dec.); children: Rita, Lynn, Michael, Richard, Jon, Jack; m. Lottie Carnell, Dec. 31, 1994 (div.). Student, Georgetown U., 1944; AB in English, High Point Coll., 1946. Owner, operator retail bus., Bound Brook, N.J., 1949-63; dir. mktg. Franklin State Bank, Somerset, N.J., 1963-65; program dir. mktg. div. Am. Mgmt. Assn. N.Y.C., 1965-67; exec. dir. Internat. Bus. Forms Industries, Washington, 1967-69; dir. communications, dir. office machines group Bus. Equipment Mfrs. Assn., Washington, 1969-72; div. pres. Litton Industries, Hampton, Va., 1972-74, group v.p., paper, printing and forms group Virginia Beach, Va., 1974-86. Cons. bus. planning and devel; univ. lectr., 1986-91; dir. Somerset County Savs. & Loan; exec. in residence U. Wis. Grad. Sch. Bus., 1973; entrepreneur in residence U. of the Pacific, Stockton, Calif., 1996. Mem. Bound Brook Bd. Edn., 1955-63; trustee Raritan Valley Hosp., Somerset, N.J., 1960-62; chmn. Urban Devel., Bound Brook, N.J., 1963; mem. def. conversion team AID, Warsaw, Poland, 1995-96. Served with U.S. Army, 1943-46, PTO. Mem. Am. Transfer Print Assn. (conf. bd.), Am. Mgmt. Assn. Home and Office: 6826 E Nightingale Star Cir Scottsdale AZ 85262 E-mail: stanlmrjj@msn.net.

FREEDMAN, WALTER, lawyer; b. St. Louis, Oct. 30, 1914; s. Sam and Sophie (Gordon) F.; m. Maxine Weil, June 23, 1940; children— Jay W., Sandra Freedman Sabel. AB, JD, Washington U., 1937; LLM, Harvard, 1938. Bar: Mo., Ill., D.C. Atty. SEC, Washington, 1938-40, U.S. Dept. Interior, Washington, 1940-42; chief counsel Office Export Control, Foreign Econ. Adminstrn., 1942-44, dir., 1944-45; ptnr. Freedman, Levy, Kroll & Simonds (and predecessor firm), Washington, 1946-2001, Foley & Lardner, Washington, from 2001. Fairchild fellow Harvard U. Law Sch., 1937-38 Editor-in-chief: Washington U. Law Quarterly, 1936-37; Contbr. articles to profl. jours. Decorated chevalier de l'Order de la Couronne (Belgium); recipient Disting. Alumni award Washington U. Sch. Law, 1995. Mem. Am. Law Inst., ABA, Fed. Bar Assn., D.C. Bar Assn., Woodmont Country Club (bd. mgrs.), Cosmos Club, Phi Beta Kappa, Omicron Delta Kappa, Phi Sigma Alpha. Jewish (trustee temple). Home: Washington, DC. Died July 4, 2002.

FREEDMAN, WILLIAM MARK, lawyer, educator; b. Washington, Dec. 8, 1946; s. Henry E. and Dorothy (Markowitz) F.; m. Harriet Arnold, Mar. 9, 1980; children: Alex, Emily. BA, Carleton Coll., 1968; JD, Harvard U., 1973. Bar: Ohio 1973, U.S. Dist. Ct. (so. dist.) Ohio 1973, U.S. Tax Ct. 1974. Assoc. Dinsmore & Shohl, Cin., 1973-80, ptnr., 1980—. Adj. prof. grad. dept. health svcs. adminstrn. Xavier U., Cin. Contbr. articles to profl. jours. Trustee Jewish Fedn. Cin., 1983-94, Yavneh Day Sch., Cin., 1988—, Norther Hills Synagogue, 1988-2001, Cin. Symphony Orch., 1990-94; v.p. No. Hills Synagogue, Cin., 1992-94, pres., 1994-96; chair Jewish Fedn. Cin. Endoment Fund Profl. Advisers Roundtable. With U.S. Army, 1968-70. Mem. ABA, Ohio State Bar Assn., Cin. Bar Assn., Am. Health Lawyers Assn., Soc. Ohio Hosp. Attys. Home: 10405 Stablehand Dr Cincinnati OH 45242-4652 Office: Dinsmore & Shohl LLP 1900 Chemed Ctr 255 E 5th St Cincinnati OH 45202-4700 Fax: 513-977-8141. E-mail: bill.freedman@dinslaw.com.

FREEHLING, ALLEN ISAAC, rabbi; b. Chgo., Jan. 8, 1932; s. Jerome Edward and Marion Ruth (Wilson) F.; m. Lori Golden; children: Shira Susman, David Matthew, Jonathan Andrew. Student, U. Ala., 1949-51; AB, U. Miami, Fla., 1953; B of Hebrew Letters, Hebrew Union Coll., 1965, MA, 1967; PhD, Kensington U., 1977; DD (hon.), Hebrew Union Coll., 1992. Ordained rabbi, 1967. Asst. to pres. Stylaneze, Inc., 1953-54, Univ. Miami, 1954-56; exec. dir. Temple Israel, Miami, 1956-57; asst. to pres. Stevens Markets, Inc., 1957-59; acct. exec. Hank Meyer Assocs., 1959-60; exec. dir. Temple Emanu-El, Miami Beach, Fla., 1960 62; assoc. rabbi The Temple, Toledo, 1967-72; sr. rabbi Univ. Synagogue, L.A., 1972—2002, rabbi emeritus, 2002—; exec. dir. City L.A. Commn. on Human Rels., 2002—. Adj. prof. Loyola-Marymount U., St. Mary's Coll.; v.p. Westside Ecumenical Coun., 1979-81; v.p. Bd. Rabbis of So. Calif., 1981-85, pres., 1985-87; mem. com. on rabbinic growth Cen. Conf. Am. Rabbis; chair Regional Synagogue Coun., 1984-86; bd. dirs., mem. several coms. and commns. Jewish Fedn. Coun.; cons. social actions Union of Am. Hebrew Congregations, mem. nat. and Pacific S.W. region coms. on AIDS; mem. Rabbinic Cabinet, United Jewish Appeal; bd. dirs. Israel Bonds Orgn., Nat. Jewish Fund; bd. govs. Synagogue Coun. Am.; bd, dirs., newsletter editor Am. Jewish Com. Guest columnist L.A. Herald Examiner (Silver Angel award Religion in Media, 1987, 88); guest religion progs. Sta. KCBS, KABC; radio/TV host Nat. Conf. Christians and Jews. Chaplain L.A. Police Dept., 1974-86; bd. dirs., mem. exec. com., chair com. on pub. policy, chair govt. affairs com. AIDS Project L.A.; founding chair, exec. com. chmn. AIDS Interfaith Coun. So. Calif.; adv. bd. L.A. AIDS Hospice Com., Westside Children's Mus., Interreligious Info. Ctr.; apptd. mem., founding chair L.A. County Commn. on AIDS, 1987-89, chair svcs. com., 1989-91, L.A. County Commn. on Mental Health, 1992-95; AIDS-related grants proposal rev. com. Robert Wood Johnson Found., AIDS Task Force of United Way; com. on ethics, medicine and humanity Santa Monica Hosp., L.A. County Commn. on Pub. Social Svcs., 1984-86, Gate Ways Hosp. bd dirs., 1992-95, Jewish Big Bros., 1994—; City of L.A. Task Force on Diversity of Families, Commn. to Draft Ethics Code for L.A. City Govt.; mem. L.A. County Commn. on Juvenile Delinquency and Adult Crime, 1991—; bd. dirs. Jewish Homes for Aging of Greater L.A., NCCJ, 1989, exec. com., 2000—; bd. dirs. Health of the Bay; chmn. com. on fed. legislation commn. on law and legislation L.A. Jewish Cmty. Rels. Com., trustee; chair Ctrl. Conf. Am. Rabbi's/Union Am. Hebrew Congregations com. on HIV AIDS, Progressive Religious Alliance, City of L.A. 1998; vol. festival adv. com. Internat. Conf. on Allocation of Health Resources, Washington, 1997, Vienna, 1999, Cairo, 2000; exec. com., treas., bd. dirs. Heal the Bay; adv. com. Disability Rights Advocates; hon. bd. dirs. Jewish Fedn. Western Region Bd. Recipient Bishop Daniel Corrigan commendation Episcopal Diocese, 1987, Humanitarian award NCCJ, 1988, Social Responsibility award L.A. Urban League, 1988, Nat. Friendship award Parents and Friends of Lesbians and Gays, 1989, AIDS Hospice Found. Gene La Pietra Leadership award, 1989, Cath. Archdiocese's Serra Tribute award, 1989, Univ. Synagogue's Avodah award for Cmty. Svc., 1990, Am. Jewish Congress Tzedek award for Cmty. Leadership and Svc., 1990, Crystal Achievement award AIDS Project L.A., 1996, Planned Parenthood Disting. Svc. award, 1996, Cmty. Leadership award Beeth Chayim Chadashim Congregation. Mem. Am. Jewish Congress (pres. 1977-80, 82-84), Ams. for Dem. Action, Internat. Assn. Physicians in AIDS Care (chmn. bd. dirs.), AIDS Nat. Interfaith Network (bd. dirs.), Jr. C. of C. (chair internat. rels. com.), Sigma Alpha Mu, Omnicron Delta Kappa, Phi Mu Alpha. Jewish. Office: Human Rels Commn City of LA 200 N SPring St #1625 Los Angeles CA 90012 E-mail: rabbiallenf@mailbox.lacity.org.

FREEHLING, DANIEL JOSEPH, law educator, law library director; b. Montgomery, Ala., Nov. 13, 1950; s. Saul Irving and Grace (Lieberman) L. BS, Huntingdon Coll., 1972; JD, U. Ala., 1975, MLS, 1977. Ref. libr., asst. to assoc. dean U. Ala. Sch. Law, Tuscaloosa, 1975-77; assoc. law libr. U. Md., Balt., 1977-79, Cornell U., Ithaca, N.Y., 1979-82; law libr. dir., assoc. prof. U. Maine, Portland, 1982-86; law libr. dir., assoc. prof. law Boston U., 1986-92, prof., 1992—, assoc. dean for adminstrn., 1993-97, assoc. dean for info. svcs., 1999—. Mem. steering com., law program com. Rsch. Librs. Group, 1989-91; treas. New Eng. Law Libr. Consortium, 1989 91; vice chair, chair-elect sect. on law librs. Assn. Am. Law Schs., 1990-91, chair, 1992. Mem.: ABA (accreditation com. 1995—2001, coun. sect. legal edn. and bar admission 2002—), Am. Assn. Law Librs. (chair acad. law librs. spl. interest sect. 1981—82, edn. com. 1982—83, membership com. 1983—84, program chair 1987—88, local arrangements co-chair 1992—93, chair mentoring and retention com. 1995—96). Home: 106 Washington St Topsfield MA 01983 Office: Boston U Law Sch Pappas Law Libr 765 Commonwealth Ave Boston MA 02215-1401

FREEHLING, HAROLD GEORGE, JR., respiratory therapist, consultant; b. Benton Harbor, Mich., Nov. 20, 1947; s. Harold George and Wilma Louise (Backus) F.; m. Janet Louise Peppel, June 10, 1971; children: Wendy Brooke, Joel Zachary, Bret Jeromy, Melissa Bethann. AS, Lake Mich. Coll., 1972; Diploma in Respiratory Therapy, U. Chgo., 1977; B in Liberal Studies, Bowling Green State U., 1978; MA in Health Care Adminstrn., Cen. Mich. U., 1987. Dir. respiratory care Providence Hosp., Sandusky, Ohio, 1974-84; v.p. support svcs. O.E. Meyer Co., Sandusky, 1984—, bd. dirs., 1989-93, 2000—. Clin. evaluator Calif. Coll. of Helath Sci., Nature City, 1981—; chmn. Firelands Coll. Respiratory Care Adv., Huron, Ohio, 1984—; cons. Ohio Bd. Regents, Columbus, 1986. Pres. Erie County Cancer Svcs., 1990, 94. With USN, 1967-70, Vietnam. Recipient Ed Ruff Community Svc. award, Am. Lung Assn., South Shore, Milan, Ohio, 1987, Disting. Alumnus/Alumna award Bowling Green State U. Firelands Coll., 1993. Mem. Am. Assn. Respiratory Care (cert. tech., registered respiratory therapist), Ohio Soc. Respiratory Care (sec. 1986), Ohio Thoracic Soc., Ohio Assn. Med. Equipment Svcs. (sec. 1991-92, treas. 1992-93, v.p. 1994-96, pres. 1996-99), Erie County Health Planning Assn. Avocation: golf. Home: 154 Fairway Cir Norwalk OH 44857-1970 Office: O E Meyer Co PO Box 479 Sandusky OH 44871-0479

FREEHLING, PAUL EDWARD, lawyer; b. Chgo., June 10, 1938; s. Norman and Edna (Wilhartz) F.; m. Susan Seder, June 27, 1961; children: Daniel, Joel. AB, Harvard U., 1959, LLB, 1962. Bar: Ill. 1962, U.S. Dist. Ct. (no. dist.) Ill. 1962, U.S. Ct. Appeals (7th cir.) 1973, U.S. Ct. Appeals (6th cir.) 1980, U.S. Ct. Appeals (D.C. cir.) 1983, U.S. Supreme Ct. 1974. Law clk. to judge U.S. Dist. Ct. No. Dist. Ill., Chgo., 1962-64; assoc. Pope, Ballard, Shepard & Fowle, Chgo., 1964-70, ptnr., 1970-82, dir., mem., 1982-93; ptnr.l D'Ancona & Pflaum, Chgo., 1994—. Fellow: Am. Coll. Trial Lawyers; mem.: 7th Cir. Bar Assn., Chgo. Coun. Lawyers, Chgo. Bar Assn., Ill. Bar Assn., Am. Judicature Soc., Fed. Bar Assn., Am. Law Inst. (appointee, roster of disting. neutrals CPR Inst. for Dispute Resolutio), Std. Club (Chgo.), Northmoor Country Club (Highland Park, Ill.). Jewish. Office: D'Ancona & Pflaum LLC 111 E Wacker Dr Ste 2800 Chicago IL 60601-4209 E-mail: pFreehli@dancona.com.

FREEHLING, STANLEY MAXWELL, investment banker; b. Chgo., July 2, 1924; s. Julius and Juliette (Stricker) F.; m. Joan Steif, Jan. 26, 1947; children: Elizabeth, Robert Stanley, Margaret J. Student, U. Chgo., 1942-43, Ind. U., 1943-44, U. Stockholm, Sweden, 1946-47. With 1st Nat. Bank Chgo., 1947—52; ptnr. Freehling Bros., Chgo., 1948—, Freehling & Co., Chgo., 1960—87; spl. ltd. ptnr. Cowen & Co., 1987—2000; v.p. Lehman Bros., 2000—. Mem. Ill. Pub. Employees Pension Laws Commn., 1962-66; chmn. Ravinia Festival Assn., 1967-71; pres. men's coun. Art Inst. Chgo., 1962-65, trustee, 1970—, now life trustee; trustee Glenwood (Ill.) Sch. for Boys, 1967-80, Lake Forest Coll., 1972-83, Shedd Aquarium, U. Chgo., 1983—, Cradle Soc.; hon. mem. The Court Theatre; chmn. bd. Ill. Arts Coun., 1971-72; bd. dirs. Northwestern Meml. Hosp., Chgo., Chgo. Pub. Libr. Found.; hon. chmn. bd. Goodman Theatre; chmn. Pub. Arts Adv. Com., 1978-90; mem. Pres.'s Com. on Arts and Humanities, Washington, 1984-88; bd. govs. Smart Mus. Art. Mem. Northwestern U. Assocs., Arts Club, Bond Club, Commercial Club (Chgo.), Lake Shore Country Club (Glencoe, Ill.), Old Elm Country Club (Highland Park, Ill.), Mid-Day. Clubs: Arts, Bond, Commercial (Chgo.); Lake Shore Country (Glencoe, Ill.); Mid-Day. Home: 121 Belle Ave Highland Park IL 60035-2503 Office: 190 S La Salle St Chicago IL 60603-3410

FREEL, EDWARD J. former state official; b. Elizabeth, N.J., June 18, 1947; m. Maureen Freel. BA, Gannon Coll.; MA, MEd, U. Del. Dep. dir. Office Econ. Opportunity; spl. asst. to asst. dir. Fed. Cmty. Svc. Adminstr.; dir. Fed. Low Income Energy Asst. Program; sr. advisor, asst. to Congressman Thomas R. Carper; posit. dir. Carper for Gov. Campaign; chief of staff to Gov.; sec. of state State of Del., 1994—2001; policy scientist & instr. Institute for Public Adminstrn., Univ. of Delaware, 2001—. Bd. mem., treas. Bayard House. Mem.: Del. Hist. Soc. (trustee). Democrat. Home: 4633 Talley Hill Ln Wilmington DE 19803-4815 Office: University of Delaware 179 Graham Hall Newark DE 19716-7380*

FREELAND, AARON LEONARD, painter, printmaker; s. Harold and Gail Redhouse Freeland. Student, Inst. Am. Indian Arts, 1973—76. Exhibitions include Long Beach (Calif.) Mus. Art, Marilyn Pink Master Prints and Drawings, L.A., San Francisco State U., Gallery Piazza, Sausalito, Calif., Santa Monica (Calif.) Pub. Libr., Santa Fe Indian Market, 1988—2002, Inst. Am. Indian Arts Mus., Santa Fe, Gallery Graphic Arts, N.Y.C., Lincoln Ctr. for Performing Arts, Wheelwright Mus. Am. Indian, Santa Fe, 2002. E-mail: FRYBREAD_OO@hotmail.com.

FREELAND, ALAN EDWARD, orthopedic surgery educator, physician; b. Youngstown, Ohio, July 30, 1939; s. Harold Edward and Esther Amelia (Hanley) F.; m. Janis Ann Foerschl, Oct. 11, 1969; children: Matthew, Jennifer, Rebecca, Michael. BA, Johns Hopkins U., 1961; MD, George Washington U., 1965. Cert. hand surgery Am. Bd. Orthopaedic Surgery. Intern Church Home and Hosp., Balt., 1965-66; resident Johns Hopkins Hosp., Balt., 1967-70, Letterman Army Med. Ctr., San Francisco, 1973-75; prof. dept. orthopaedic surgery U. Miss. Med. Ctr., Jackson, 1978—, dir. hand surgery fellowship program, 1991—, chief of staff, 1986-87, also bd. dirs. Rowland Med. Libr., 1996-98. Chief surgery Miss. Meth. Rehab. Ctr., Jackson, 1991-93, pres. elect med. staff, 1994, pres. med. staff, bd. dirs., 1995-97. Author: Stable Internal Fixation of the Hand and Wrist, 1986, The First Twenty-Five Years: History of the American Association for Hand Surgery, 1996, Hand Fractures: Repair, Reconstruction and Rehabilitation, 2000; mem. editl. bd. Orthopedics, Slack, Inc., 1986—, Jour. Orthop. Trauma, 1993—2002, Year Book of Hand Surgery, 1997, Trauma Update, Orthop., 1989- ; sect. editor, sr. editor hand surgery: Jour. Orthop. Trauma, 1997—2002; bd. editors Microsurgery, 2001—, sect.

editor Trauma Update, Orthop., 1989—, Hand Surgery, 1997—2002. Mem. Fire Protection Dist., Brandon, Miss., 1990-93; bd. dirs. Miss. Sports Hall of Fame, 2002—. Lt. col. U.S. Army, 1971-78. Fellow: Am Acad. Orthopaedic Surgeons; mem.: S.E. Hand Club (sec.-treas. 1998—2000, v.p. 2001, pres.-elect 2002, pres. 2003), Miss. State Orthopaedic Assn. (pres. Jackson chpt. 1985, pres. 1986), Internat. Fedn. Socs. for Surgery of Hand (chmn. bone and joint com. 1992—), Am. Assn. Hand Surgeons (parliamentarian 1994, exec. com., bd. dirs. 1994—, historian 1995, treas. 1996—98, historian 1999, v.p. 2000, pres.-elect 2001, pres. 2002), Am. Soc. Surgery of Hand (governing coun. 1989—92), Am. Orthopaedic Assn. Home: 303 Swallow Dr Brandon MS 39047-6454 Office: 2500 N State St Jackson MS 39216-4500

FREELAND, CHARLES, lawyer, accountant; b. Balt., July 18, 1940; s. Benjamin and Beatrice (Polakoff) F.; m. Beverly Klaff, July 15, 1965; children— Stephen Jason, Jennifer Jill, Gwen Nicole, Kimberly Suzanne. B.S., U. Md., 1962, LL.B., 1965; diploma U.S. Naval Justice Sch., 1966. Bar: Md. 1965, U.S. Dist. Ct. Md. 1965, U.S. Tax Ct. 1966, U.S. Ct. Mil. Apls. 1966, U.S. Ct. Claims 1968, U.S. Supreme Ct. 1969, U.S. Ct. Appeals (4th cir.) 1974. Fin. v.p. Collins Electronics Mfg. Co.; dir. fin. planning Cellu-Craft, Inc., Stevensville, Md., 1963-65; controller Braun-Crystal Mfg. Co., Inc., Middle Village, N.Y., 1969-70, BCN Design Products, Inc., Bayshore, N.Y., 1969-70; asst. city solicitor City of Balt., 1972-82; pvt. practice law and acctg., Balt., 1971-93; ptnr. Kaplan, Freeland & Schwartz, Balt., 1982-86; pres. Charles Freeland, PC, 1986—. Served to lt. USNR, 1965-68. Mem. Am. Judicature Soc., Am. Assn. Attys.-CPA's, ABA, Md. Bar Assn., Balt. County Bar Assn., Am. Assn. CPA's, Md. Assn. CPA's, Am. Arbitration Assn. (nat. panel 1970—). Democrat. Jewish. Club: Woodholme Country. Home: PO Box 422 4 Timothys Green Ct Brooklandville MD 21022 Office: 1300 York Rd Ste 180 Lutherville MD 21093-6806

FREELAND, DARRYL CREIGHTON, psychologist, educator; b. Omaha, Feb. 22, 1939; s. Elverson Lafayette and Lauretta Joyce (Coffelt) F.; m. Tina Anne Richmond, July 21, 1979; children: Adam Daniel, Noah Nathan, Sarah Gilson. BS, U. Nebr., 1961; STB, Fuller Theol. Sem., 1965; MA, Calif. State U., Fullerton, 1966; PhD, U. So. Calif., 1972. Lic. psychologist, Calif. Tchr. elem. schs., Calif., 1961-66; instr. Glendale C.C., Calif., 1966-67, Citrus C.C., Glendora, Calif., 1967-79; pvt. practice psychology Laguna Niguel, Calif., 1969—. Field faculty, vis. prof. Calif. State U., L.A., Calif., 1970, San Marino Cmty. Presbyn. Ch., 1972, Calif. Sch. Profl. Psychology, L.A., 1972—73, U. Calif., Riverside, 1973, Humanistic Psychology Inst., San Francisco, 1976—79, U. Humanistic Studies, San Diego, 1983; tenured assoc. prof. psychology and family U.S. Internat. U., 1986—; dir. MFT Tng. Univ. Ctr., Orange County, 1998—2001; asst. dir. clin. psychology tng. Marital and Family Therapy Tng. Alliant Internat. U. Calif. Sch Profl. Psychology, 2001—, assoc. prof. marital and family therapy, coord. clin. tng.; pvt. post-secondary com. for qualitative rev. and assessment of licensure Calif. Dept. Edn., 1989—97. Finisher Newport Beach-Irvine Marathon, 1981, San Francisco Marathon, 1982, Long Beach Marathon, 1988. Office: 30131 Town Center Dr Ste 298 Laguna Niguel CA 92677-2086 E-mail: dfreeland@usiu.edu.

FREELAND, MARK SYDNES, economist; b. Des Moines, Mar. 5, 1943; s. Kermit Thomas and Flora Margaret (Sydnes) F. BS, Iowa State U., 1966; MA, U. Wis., 1968, PhD, 1972. Economist Social Security Adminstrn., Washington, 1971-79, Health Care Financing Adminstrn., Washington, 1980-84, chief economist Office of Actuary Balt., 1987-90, dir. div. statis. analysis, 1990, dir. div. health cost analysis, 1990—98; dep. dir. Office of Actuary Nat. Health Stats. Group, 1999—; vis. rsch. economist U. Calif., San Francisco, 1985-86. Cons. Nat. Inst. for Alcohol Abuse and Alcoholism, Rockville, Md. 1984, Inst. for the Future, Menlo Park, Calif., 1988, Assn. for Retired Persons, Washington, 1988. Contbr. articles to profl. jours. Health Policy fellow Pew Meml. Trust, 1985. Mem. Am. Econ. Assn., Health Svcs. Research Assn., Am. Statis. Assn., Soc. of Govt. Economists, Nat. Economists Club. Presbyterian. Avocations: hiking, travel, wine, ethnic restaurants. Home: Apt 709 250 S President St Baltimore MD 21202-4439 Office: Ctrs for Medicare and Medicaid Svcs 7500 Security Blvd Rm MS N3-02-02 Baltimore MD 21244-1850 E-mail: mfreeland5@aol.com.

FREELAND, RICHARD MIDDLETON, academic affairs administrator, historian; b. Orange, N.J., May 13, 1941; s. Harry Middleton and Margaret Lyons (Child) F. BA in Am. Studies, Amherst Coll., 1963; PhD in Am. Civilization, U. Pa., 1968; DHL (hon.), Amherst Coll., 1998, Am. Coll. Greece, 2000. Asst. to pres. U. Mass., 1970, asst. to chancellor, 1971-72, dir. Office of Ednl. Planning, asst. prof., 1972-74, dean Coll. Profl. Studies, 1974-79, assoc. prof., 1974-92, dean Coll. of Arts and Scis., 1982-92, prof. history, 1992; prof. history Grad. Sch. & Univ. Ctr. CUNY, 1992-96; vice chancellor for acad. affairs, pres. CUNY Rsch. Found., 1992-96; pres., prof. history Northeastern U., Boston, 1996—. Proposal reviewer NEH, Divsn. Rsch., 1989, Divsn. Edn. Programs, 1985, R.I. Bd. Higher Edn., 1987, Fund for the Improvement of Post Secondary Edn., 1988, Rockefeller Found., 1985, Am. Univ., 1988, 89, 90; cons. Am. Coun. Edn., 1994, U.S. Dept. Edn., 1989-90, 92; dir. Mass. Bus. Roundtable, Citizens Bank Mass., The Boston Globe, Boston Plan for Excellence, Assn. Ind. Colls. and Univs. Mass. Author: The Truman Doctrine and the Origins of McCarthyism, 1972, Academia's Golden Age, 1992; reader, reviewer numerous profl. jours. Recipient Rsch. grants Ford Found., 1979-80, NEH, 1980-81, Rockefeller Found., 1988. Office: Northeastern U 110 Churchill Hall 380 Huntington Ave Boston MA 02115-5000 E-mail: r.freeland@neu.edu.

FREELAND, ROBERT FREDERICK, retired librarian; b. Flint, Mich., Dec. 20, 1919; s. Ralph V. and Susan Barbara (Goetz) F.; m. June Voshel, June 18, 1948; children: Susan Beth Visser, Kent Richard. BS, Eastern Mich. U., 1942; postgrad., Washington & Lee U., 1945; MS, U. So. Calif., 1948, postgrad., 1949, U. Mich., 1950-52, Calif. State U., 1956-58, UCLA, 1960; LittD (hon.), Linda Vista Bible Coll., 1973. Music supr. Consol. Schs. Warren, Mich., 1946-47; music dir. Carson City (Mich.) Pub. Schs., 1948-49; librarian, audio-visual coord. Ford Found., Edison Inst., Greenfield Village, Dearborn, Mich., 1950-52, Helix High Sch. Library, 1952-77; librarian, prof. library sci. Linda Vista Bible Coll., 1976—; reference libr. San Diego Pub. Libr. System, 1967-97. Cons. edn., libr. and multimedia. Editor book and audio-visual aids review, Sch. Musician, Dir. and Teacher, 1950-75. Former deacon and elder Christian Reform Ch., libr., 1969-72, Classis archivist, 1991—; pub. affairs officer, sr. program officer, moral leadership officer Sq. 57 GP III, Calif. wing CAP. With USAAF, 1942-46. Named Scholar Freedoms Found., Valley Forge, Pa., 1976-80. Mem. NEA (life), ALA, Nat. Music Camp, Calif. Tchrs. Assn., Music Libr. Assn. So. Calif. (adviser exec. bd.), Calif. Libr. Assn. (pres. Palomar chpt. 1972-73), Sch. Libr. Assn. Calif. (treas. 1956-73), Calif. Media and Libr. Educators (charter mem.), Am. Legion (Americanism chmn. 22d dist. San Diego County, chmn. oratorical contest com. La Mesa post), Ret. Officers Assn., San Diego Aero Space Mus., San Diego Mus. Art, Alumnia Assn. Ea. Mich. U., La Mesa Hist. Soc. (bd. dirs. 2003—). Home: 4800 Williamsburg Ln Apt 223 La Mesa CA 91941-4651 E-mail: 112527.676@compuserve.com.

FREELEY, JAMES, labor union administrator; b. N.Y.C. Bachelors Degree, CCNY, 1979; Masters Degree, New Sch. for Social Rsch., 1985. Arbitration adv. Local 300 NPMHU, N.Y.C., 1991—, br. pres., 1996—2002. Mem. editl. staff: newspaper Local 300 Mail Hancken News, 1994; contbr. articles to profl. jours. Mem. N.Y. state com. Labor Party, 1996—2002, del. founding conv., 1996. Airman 1st class USAF, 1955—59. Avocations: fitness, history, social justice issues. Home: 6753 223rd Pl Oakland Gardens NY 11364-2639

FREELING, MICHAEL RICHARD, genetics educator, researcher; b. Ft. Wayne, ind., Jan. 14, 1945; s. Charles Theodore and Patricia Elizabeth Freeling; m. Catherine Briedwell, June 25, 1967 (div. Apr. 1998); children: Nathan, Marcus; m. Melissa Stevens Quilter, July 23, 2000; stepchildren: Alexander, Kathleen. BA, U. Oreg., 1967; PhD, Ind. U., 1973. Asst. prof. U. Calif., Berkeley, 1973-78, assoc. prof., 1978-83, prof. genetics, 1983—. Guggenheim Found. fellow, 1980-81; grantee NIH, NSF, U.S. Dept. Energy, others, 1974—. Mem. NAS. Democrat. Avocations: Judo, gardening. Office: U Calif Dept Plant & Microbial Biol Berkeley CA 94720 E-mail: freeling@nature.berkeley.edu.

FREELON, PHILIP G. architectural firm executive; b. Phila. B in Environ. Design (hons.), N.C. State U.; M in Arch., MIT. Sr. designer, project mgr., v.p. architecture O'Brien/Atkins Assocs., NC, 1982—90; founder, pres. Freelon Group, Inc., NC, 1990—. Adj. prof. Coll. of Design, N.C. State U.; lectr. Harvard U., Howard U., N.C. State U., Hampton U., Calif. Coll. of Arts and Crafts. Recipient 1st prize and design contract, PPG Furniture Design Competition; fellow, Am. Inst. of Architecture, 2003. Mem.: Nat. Orgn. of Minority Archs. (founding mem. N.C. chpt.). Office: The Freelon Group Archs PO Box 12876 Research Triangle Park NC 27709 also: The Freelon Group Archs PO Box 11735 Charlotte NC 28220 Fax: 919-941-0046; Office Fax: 704-334-7988.*

FREELS, JESSE SAUNDERS, JR., lawyer; b. Sherman, Tex., Feb. 8, 1943; s. Jesse Saunders Sr. and Margaret (Stout) F.; m. Valerie Wood, Jan. 16, 1971; children: J.S. "Trey" III, John Andrew. BA, BS, Howard Payne U., 1965; JD, St. Mary's U., San Antonio, 1969. Bar: Tex. 1969, U.S. Dist. Ct. (ea. and we. dists.) Tex. 1971. Asst. county atty. Grayson County, Sherman, 1969-71; ptnr. Doss, Thompson & Freels, Denison, Tex., 1971-78; judge Grayson County, Sherman, 1978-83; pres. Freels & Johnston, P.C., Sherman, 1983-2000; sole practice, 2000—. Bd. dirs. Am. Bank of Tex., Sherman, 1975—, Tex. Ctr. for the Judiciary, Austin, 1979-83. Mem. Tex. Bar Assn., Grayson County Bar Assn., Tex. Bar Found. (life), Masons (past master Lodge 403, Denison). Home: 109 Spring Valley Dr Denison TX 75020-3724 Office: 114 S Crockett St Sherman TX 75090-5906

FREEMAN, ALGEANIA WARREN, academic administrator; b. Benson, N.C. m. Ernest Freeman; 1 child, Ernest III. BS in English, Fayetteville State U., 1970; MS in Speech Pathology and Audiology, So. Ill. U., 1972; PhD in Speech Comm., Ohio State U., 1977; postgrad., Harvard U., 1993, postgrad., 1998. Ordained min. African Meth. Episcopal Zion Ch. Instr. Norfolk State U., 1973, acting v.p. advancement, prof.; with Morgan State U., East Tenn. State U., Orange Coast Coll., N.C. A&T State U.; v.p. advancement and program devel. So. Calif. Coll.; prof. speech comm. Norfolk U.; pres. Livingstone Coll., Salisbury, NC. Internat. cons. W.K. Kellogg Found. in So. Africa; mem. Va. Task Force on Sci. and Tech., Va. Bd. Examiners for Audiology and Speech Pathology. Bd. dirs. Calif. Assn. Instrnl. Adminstrs., Found. for the Carolinas, Kids Voting of Va., Montebello Rehab. Hosp./U. Md. Hosp. Sys., Md. Easter Seals, Friends of the Norfolk Juvenile Ct., Girl Scouts Ea. Tenn.; pres. Nat. Soc. Allied Health; exec. dir. Nat. Black Assn. for Speech, Lang. and Hearing. Fellow, U.S. Pentagon in the Army Ctr. Mil. History, Washington, 1999—2000. Fellow: Am. Soc. Allied Health. Office: Livingstone Coll 701 W Monroe St Salisbury NC 28144

FREEMAN, ANTOINETTE ROSEFELDT, lawyer; b. Atlantic City, Oct. 7, 1937; d. Bernard Paul and Fannie (Levin) Rosefeldt; m. Alan Richard Freeman, June 22, 1958 (div. Apr. 1979); children: Barry David, Robin Lisa. BA, Rutgers U., 1972; JD, Ind. U., 1975; LLM, Temple U., 1979. Bar: Pa. 1975, Wash. 1992, U.S. Dist. Ct. (ea. dist.) Pa. 1976, U.S. Ct. Appeals (3d cir.) 1982. Substitute tchr. Washington Twp. Sch. Dist., Indpls., 1972; dep. prosecutor intern Marion County Prosecutor, Indpls., 1974-75; asst. dist. atty. City of Phila., 1975-76; mgr. EEO Wyeth Labs., Radnor, Pa., 1976-80, SmithKline & French Labs., Phila., 1980-82; sr. counsel SmithKline Beecham Corp., Phila., 1982-91; assoc. gen. counsel Amgen Inc. (formerly Immunex Corp.), 1991—; arbitrator Am. Arbitration Assn., 1976—. Counsel Regional Interests Developing Efficient Transp., 1983-85; adv. bd. Family Svc. Phila., 1980-81, Greater Phila. C. of C., 1983; pres. Croskey Ct. Condominium Assn., 1983-87; bd. dirs. Logan Sq. Neighborhood Assn., 1983-91, pres., 1985-87; v.p., sec. Friends of Logan Sq. Found., 1985-91; counsel Hapoel Games USA; chairperson Ctr. City Coalition for Quality of Life; atty. Vol. Lawyers for the Arts, Phila., 1985-91; bd. dirs. Sr. Employment and Ednl. Svc., BathHouse Theater, 1991-99, v.p. 1994-96; bd. dirs. Bellini preview group Seattle Opera Guild, 1994-96 ; mem. Assoc. Corp. Coun. for Arts., 1992-93; mem. adv. bd. regulatory affairs cert. program U. Wash.; bd. dirs. Music of Remberance, 2002—. Bd. dirs. Music of Remembrance, 2002—. Mem. ABA, Pa. Bar Assn., Phila. Bar Assn., Wash. State Bar Assn., Merit Employers Coun. (1st v.p. 1978-79), Phila. Women's Network, Phila. Lawyers Club, Phila. King County Med. Soc./King County Bar Assn. (med.-legal com.). Democrat. Jewish. Office: Amgen Inc 51 University St Seattle WA 98101-2936

FREEMAN, ARTHUR, veterinarian, retired association administrator; b. Youngstown, Ohio, Jan. 12, 1925; Student, Stanford U., 1949-50; D.V.M., Ohio State U., 1955. Pvt. practice Bellingham (Wa.) Vet. Hosp., 1955-56; dir. profl. rels. Jensen Salsbery Labs., Kansas City, Mo., 1956-59; editor Am. Vet. Med. Assn., Chgo., 1959-72, asst. exec. v.p. Schaumburg, Ill., 1977-84, editor-in-chief, 1972-84, exec. v.p., 1985-89. Dir. Coun. of Sci. Editors, Chgo., 1982-85, pres., 1985-86; adj. asst. prof. vet. med. Purdue U., 1997-2000. Contbr. articles to profl. publs. Mem. Indpls. Mus. Art, Indpls. Symphony Orch. 1st lt. USAF, 1942-60. Recipient Disting. Alumnus award Ohio State U., 1976, Ind. Vet. of the Yr. award, 1995. Mem. AVMA, Am. Assn. Ret. Vets. (exec. dir. 1996—, editor), Ohio Vet. Med. Assn. (Meritorious Svc. award 1989), Ind. State Vet. Med. Assn. (hon.), Ill. Vet. Med. Assn. (hon.), Mich. Vet. Med. Assn. (hon.), Indpls. Exec. Svc. Corps (Frederic M. Hadley Svc. award 1995), Ind. Hist. Soc., Indpls. Aero. Club. E-mail: freemanart@webtv.net.

FREEMAN, ARTHUR MERRIMON, III, psychiatry educator, dean; b. Birmingham, Ala., Oct. 10, 1942; s. Arthur Merrimon II and Katherine (Lide) F.; m. Linda Poynter; children: Arthur M. IV, Katherin Leigh, Edward Todd. AB in Philosophy, Harvard U., 1963; MD, Vanderbilt U., 1967. Diplomate Am. Bd. Psychiatry and Neurology; lic. psychiatrist, Ala., N.C., La. Asst. prof. dept. psychiatry and behavioral scis. Stanford (Calif.) U., 1974-77; prof., vice chmn. dept. psychiatry U. Ala., Birmingham, 1977-90; med. dir. Appalachian Hall Hosp., Asheville, N.C., 1990-91; prof., chmn. dept. psychiatry La. State U. Med. Ctr., Shreveport, 1991—2003, dean, 1993-96. Regional med. dir. divsn. mental health La. Dept. Health and Hosps., 1992-94. Author: Psychiatry for the Primary Care Physician, 1979. Bd. dirs. Vols. of Am., Shreveport, 1993-96, Shreveport Symphony, C. of C., 1993-96. Lt. comdr. M.C., USN, 1972-74. Nat. Merit scholar Harvard U., 1959-63; Biochemistry fellow Karolinska Inst., Stockholm, 1965, fellow in hepatic disease Royal Free Hosp., London, 1966, Disting. Paul Harris fellow Rotary Club. Fellow APA, Am. Coll. Psychiatrists (Laughlin fellow 1971), Acad. Psychosomatic Medicine, So. Psychiat. Assn.; mem. Am. Assn. Chmn. of Depts. of Psychiatry, Biomed. Rsch. Found. N.W. La. (bd. dirs. 1993-96), La. Psychiatry Med. Assn. (pres.-elect), Royal Coll. Psychiatrists, Collegium Internationale Neuropsychopharmacologia. Home: 5929 E Ridge Dr Shreveport LA 71106-2423 Office: La State U Med Ctr Dept of Psychiatry 1501 Kings Hwy Shreveport LA 71103-4228

FREEMAN, BOB A. retired microbiology educator, retired dean; b. Eastland, Tex., May 7, 1926; s. Oswald Ledbetter and Osielee (Wilcox) F.; m. Rosemary David, June 4, 1960; children: Susan A., Robert D., Katherine E., Andrew W. BA, U. Tex., 1949, MA, 1950, PhD, 1954. Instr. biology Tex. A & M U., College Station, 1950-51; rsch. scientist I U. Tex., Austin, 1951-54; instr., asst. prof. U. Chgo., 1954-64; assoc. prof. U. Tenn., Memphis, 1964-66, prof., 1966-88, chmn. microbiology dept., 1970-83, vice chancellor, 1982-88, Disting. Svc. prof., 1988-96, interim dean Coll. Grad. Health Scis., 1993-96, dean, prof. emeritus, 1997—. Cons. WHO, Calcutta, India, 1968. Author: Burrows Textbook of Microbiology, 21st edit., 1979, 22d edit., 1984; mem. edit. bd. Jour. Dental Edn., 1980-83, U. Tenn. Press., 1983-2001; contbr. articles to profl. jours. Bd. dirs. Memphis Heart Gala, 1984-90. With USN, 1944-46, PTO. Grantee U.S. Army Rsch. and Devel. Command, USPHS, U.S. Dept. Agr. Mem. AAAS, Am. Soc. for Microbiology (br. councillor 1969-71), Imhotep Soc. (Memphis), Sigma Xi (chpt. pres. 1974-75). Republican. Methodist. Avocations: woodworking, outdoor activities. Home: 1319 E Crestwood Dr Memphis TN 38119-5000

FREEMAN, BRUCE GEORGE, fundraising consultant; b. Perth Amboy, N.J., Feb. 17, 1929; s. Benjamin George and Beatrice (Wright) F.; children: David B., Judith Ann, Mark D.; m. Marjorie V. Kler, Dec. 1983. BA, Rutgers U., 1952; MDiv, New Brunswick Theol. Sem., 1955; postgrad., Albany Med. Ctr., 1955-58, Andover Newton Theol. Ctr., 1955-58. Min. Presbyn. Ch., various locations, N.Y., 1955-64; asst. to pres. Buena Vista Coll., Storm Lake, Iowa, 1964-66; area dir. United Presbyn. Ch. U.S.A., 1966-67; campaign mgr. Marts & Lundy, N.Y.C., 1967-75, also bd. dirs., v.p., 1975-80, treas., 1980-82, founder electron. screening div. Lyndhurst, N.J., 1984, pres., 1982-91, chmn., CEO, 1991-94, ret., 1994; CEO B.G.F. Assocs., 1994—. Inventor Electric Screening. Trustee East Jersey Olde Towne, Inc., Piscataway, 1980—, Wilson Coll. Chambersburg, Pa., 1992-2000; trustee Makassed Found. Am., Rutgers U., 1994—; bd. dirs. Nat. Orgn. on Disability, Washington, 1990. Mem. Nassau Club (bd. dirs.), Raritan Valley Country Club. Republican. Avocations: sports, art. Home: 6 Mimosa Ct Princeton NJ 08540-9423

FREEMAN, CAROLE COOK, education educator; b. Hanover, N.H., Oct. 14, 1949; d. Sidney Leighton and Ruth Mary (Tyler) Cook; m. Michael Stuart Freeman, July 5, 1974; children: Alice Pearl, Josie Eleanor. BS in Edn., U. Vt., 1971; MEd, U. Ill., 1974; PhD, U. Pa., 1991. Elem. sch. tchr. Middlebury, Winooski, and Norwich schs., Vt., 1971-78; intern advisor Upper Valley Tchr. Tng., Hanover, N.H., 1978-80; asst./acting coord. svcs. for learning disabled students Coll. of Wooster, Ohio, 1982-85; 4th grade tchr. Friends Select Sch., Phila., 1986-87; supr. student tchrs. U. pa., Phila., 1987-88, 90-91, coord. field experiences, 1988-89; asst. prof. edn. LaSalle U., Phila., 1991-97, assoc. prof., chmn. dept. edn., 1997-2000; prin. Waits River Valley Sch., East Corinth, Vt., 2000—. Cons. Ctr. for Schs. Stucy Coun., Grad. Sch. Edn. U. Pa., Phila., 1988-2000. Co-author: Pets and Me: A Thematic Learning Experience Built on the Relationship Between People and Animals, 1991; author: A Literate Community: Common Threads and Unique Patterns in Teaching and Learning, 1995. Cmty. Svc. Rsch. grantee Pa. Campus Compact, 1994, Am. Counts grantee NSF, 1999. Mem. ASCD, Nat. Assn. for Edn. of Young Children, Nat. Acad. Early Childhood Programs (validator), Nat. Coun. Tchrs. English, Am. Ednl. Rsch. Assn., Assn. Childhood Edn. Internat., Phi Delta Kappa. Home: PO Box 192 East Corinth VT 05040-0192 Office: Waits River Valley Sch 6 Waits River Valley Rd East Corinth VT 05040 E-mail: cfreeman@wrvs.us.

FREEMAN, CAROLYN RUTH, radiation oncologist; b. Kettering, Eng., Jan. 2, 1950; emigrated to Can., 1974, naturalized, 78; d. Ivor Thomas and Winifred Mary (Scotney) F.; m. J.C. Negrete, July 25, 1981. Student, King's Coll. London U., 1967-69; MB, BS, Westminster Med. Sch. London U., 1972. Prof., chmn. dept. radiation oncology, faculty medicine McGill U., Montreal, 1979—; radiation oncologist-in-chief McGill U. Hosps., Montreal, 1979—. Contbr. articles to med. publs. Fellow Royal Coll. Physicians (Can.); mem. Can. Assn. Radiol. Oncologists (pres. 1991-93), Am. Soc. Therapeutic Radiology and Oncology. Home: 4270 deMaisonneuve W Montreal QC Canada H3Z 1K6 Office: 1650 Cedar Ave Montreal QC Canada H3G 1A4 E-mail: carolyn.freeman@muhc.mcgill.ca.

FREEMAN, CHARLES E. state supreme court justice; b. Richmond, Va., Dec. 12, 1933; m. Marylee Voelker; 1 child, Kevin. BA in Liberal Arts, Va. Union U., 1954; JD, John Marshall Law Sch., 1962, LLD (hon.), 1992. Bar: Ill. 1962. Pvt. practice, 1962—76; pvt. practice, Cook County, Chgo., 1962—76, asst. state's atty., 1964; asst. atty. Bd. Election Commrs., Chgo., 1964—65; mem. Ill. Indsl. Commn., Chgo., 1965—73, Ill. Commerce Commn., Chgo., 1973—76; judge law and chancery divsns. Cook County Cir. Ct., Chgo., 1976—86; judge Appellate Ct. Ill., 1986—90; justice Ill. Supreme Ct., 1990—, chief justice, 1997—2000. Recipient Cert. Achievement, Internat. Christian Fellowship Missions, Earl B. Dickerson award, Chgo. Bar Assn., Merit award, Habilitative Sys., Statesmanship award, Monarch Awards Found. of Alpha Kappa Alpha, Freedom award, John Marshall Law Sch. Mem.: ABA (task force opportunities minorities in jud. adminstrn. divsn., coms. opportunities minorities in profession, cert. Recognition), DuPage County Bar Assn., Cook County Bar Assn. (Kenneth E. Wilson award, Cert. Merit, Ida Platt award, Presdl. award, Jud. award), Ill. Judges' Assn., Ill. Jud. Coun. (Kenneth Wilson Meml. award, Meritorious Svc. award), Ill. State Bar Assn., Am. Judicature Soc., Am. Judges' Assn. Achievements include being first African-American to swear in a Mayor, City of Chicago, to serve on Illinois Supreme Court, 1990; being leader in case disposition by published opinion, 1988, 89.

FREEMAN, CHARLES E. writer, musician; b. Darwin, Ill., June 11, 1942; s. Andrew Jackson and Evelyn Veleine Freeman; m. Janet Leigh Tryon, Apr. 10, 1976 (div. July 5, 1988); children: Scott Eric, Derek Charles; m. Dorothy Marie Babcock, Apr. 3, 1993. At, Inst. for Children's Writing. Author: (book) The Promised One, 2001. Ssgt. USAF, 1959—75. Republican. Baptist. Avocations: mountain dulcimer, mandolin. Home: 906 Pine Marshall IL 62441

FREEMAN, CHAS. W., JR., government official, ambassador, writer; b. Washington, Mar. 2, 1943; divorced; 3 children; m. Margaret Van Wagenen Carpenter, 1993. BA, Yale U.; JD, Harvard U. Joined Fgn. Svc., 1965, assigned to India and Taiwan; Am. interpreter for Pres. Nixon, People's Republic China, 1972; vis. fellow East Asian Legal Rsch. Ctr., Harvard U., 1974-75; dep. dir. for Taiwan affairs, dir. pub. programs, dir. plans and mgmt. U.S. Dept. State, Washington, 1975-78; dir. program coord. and devel. USIA, Washington, 1978, acting U.S. coord. for refugee affairs; dir. China affairs U.S. Dept. State, 1979; dep. chief of mission Am. Embassy, Beijing, 1981, Bangkok, 1984; prin. dep. asst. sec. state for African affairs U.S. Dept. State, Washington, 1986; amb. to Saudi Arabia, Riyadh, 1989-92; asst. sec. def. The Pentagon, Washington, 1993-94; dist. fellow U.S. Inst. of Peace, Washington, 1994-95; chmn. bd. Projects Internat. Inc., Washington, 1995—. Co-chmn. U. S. China Policy Found., 1996—; vice-chmn. Atlantic Coun., 1997; pres. Middle East Policy Coun.; bd. dirs. Inst. for Def. Analyses, World Affair Coun., Washington, Assn. for Diplomatic Studies and Tng., Acad. Am. Diplomacy; bd. visitors Dept. Def. Regional Ctrs., 1998—2001; mem. U.S. Nat. Security Study Group, 1999—2001; bd. dirs. Pacific Pension Inst. Author: The Diplomat's Dictionary, 1994, revised edit., 1997; Arts of Power, 1997. Recipient Sec. Def. Meritorious Civilian Svc. award, 1991, Disting. Pub. Svc. awards, 1993-94, Sec. State Disting. Honor, 1991, Dir. Ctrl. Intelligence Shield Medallion award, 1991, First Class Order of Abd Al-Aziz award Saudi Arabian Govt., 1992. Mem.: Am. Acad. Diplomacy (bd. dirs.), Met. Club. Office: Projects Internat Inc 1800 K St NW Ste 1018 Washington DC 20006-2202 also: Mid East Policy Coun 1730 M St NW Ste 512 Washington DC 20036-4516 Home: 2500 Massachusetts Ave NW Washington DC 20008-2821 Business E-Mail: cfreeman@projectsinternational.com.

FREEMAN, CHESTER WILLIE, small business owner; b. Cullman, Ala., June 3, 1922; s. Willis Jessie and Sarah Ethel (Ponder) F.; m. Hilda Wood, Mar. 10, 1946; children: Carolyn, Phillip. Student, West Ga. Coll., 1974. Pres. Chester W. Freeman Enterprises, Cullman. Bd. advisors Wallace State Coll., Hanceville, Ala., 1962-93; pres. Cullman Lions Club, 1959-60; vice chmn. Cullman Reg. Med. Ctr., 1979—; chmn. Cullman Parks and Recreation, 1970-97; pres. City of Cullman Parks Found., 1988-97. With U.S. Army, 1942-45. Mem. Nat. Recreation and Park Assn. (life trustee, pres.), N.Am. Fedn. Fairs (pres. 1987), Cullman Area C. of C. (pres. 1991), Ala. Sight Assn. (pres.), Cullman County Fair Assn. (pres. 1962), Assn. Ala. Fairs (pres. 1975). Methodist. Avocations: travel, music, reading, hiking. Home: 1827 Edgewood Dr NW Cullman AL 35055-5721 Office: PO Box 543 Cullman AL 35056-0543

FREEMAN, CLARENCE CALVIN, financial executive; b. Lancaster, Pa., July 2, 1923; s. Clarence Calvin and Margaret (Hollinger) F.; m. B. Virginia Miller, Aug. 26, 1944; children: Margaret Ann, Elizabeth Ann, Martha Suzanne. AB cum laude, Franklin and Marshall Coll., 1951. Asst. bookkeeper Battery & Brake Service Co., Lancaster, 1941-42; supr. inventory records and receiving Armstrong Cork Co., Lancaster, 1946-48; accountant Internat. Latex Corp., Dover, Del., 1951-52, Ebasco Services, Inc., Holtwood, Pa., 1952-53; office mgr., accountant A.O. Smith Corp., Leola, Pa., 1953-54; office mgr., plant accountant Sybron-Permutit divsn. Lancaster, 1954-57; divsn. controller BCA divsn. Fed. Mogul Corp., Lancaster, 1957-64, controller Southfield, Mich., 1964-74; v.p., controller Addressograph-Multigraph Corp., Cleve., 1974-78; adminstrv. v.p., controller Irvin Industries, Stamford, Conn., 1978-79; v.p. fin. Technical Tape Inc., New Rochelle, N.Y., 1979-80; v.p. fin., treas., dir. K-D Mfg. Co., Lancaster, 1980-83; CFO C-F Manbeck, Inc., 1984-86; exec. v.p. Sensenich Corp., Lancaster, 1986-90, also bd. dirs.; sr. v.p. fin., CFO Sensenich Propeller Co., Lancaster, 1991-94; ret. Owner acctg. svc., 1953-64, Dairy Queen, 1956-60; lectr. Franklin and Marshall Coll., 1957-58, adj. faculty, 1983-89; lectr. Wayne State Grad. Sch., 1966-67; guest speaker Nat. Assn. Accts. Mem. Oakland County Planning Commn., 1967-68; adviser Jr. Achievement, 1957-58. Served with AUS, 1943-46, PTO. Mem. Nat. Assn. Accountants, Fin. Execs. Inst., Phi Beta Kappa (v.p. Detroit), Pi Gamma Mu. Republican. Presbyterian (elder, deacon). Club: Conestoga Country. Lodges: Masons, Kiwanis, Elks. Home: Apt H2 1117 Wheatland Ave Lancaster PA 17603-2462 *To succeed in life, it is important to have faith and confidence in*

one's own capability but to rely on this alone is disastrous; a faith and belief in a supreme being (God) more powerful than any human being is necessary not only to sustain us in times of our own failure, but each and every day as we face life's challenges.

FREEMAN, CORINNE, financial services, former mayor; b. N.Y.C., Nov. 9, 1926; d. Bernard J. Hirschfeld and Sidonie (Daxe) Lichtenstein; m. Michael S. Freeman, Mar. 14, 1948; children: Michael L., Stephan J., Adelphi Coll. Sch. Nursing, 1944-47. RN, N.Y., Mass. Nurse numerous hosps. in N.Y. and Mass., 1948-64; mayor, 1977-85; mem. Pinellas County Sch. Bd., St. Petersburg, Fla., 1989-98, chmn., 1996-98; bd. trustees Palms of Pasadena Hosp., St. Petersburg, 1998—. Fin. advisor Prudential Securities; bd. dirs. Creativity in Child Care. Chmn. Social Svc. Allocations Com., St. Petersburg, 1972-76, City Budget Rev. Com., 1973-76, Youth Svc. System, Pinellas County, 1975-76, West Coast Regional Water Supply Authority; past mem. community redevel. com. U.S. Conf. of Mayors; past pres. Fla. League Cities; past mem. Pinellas County Mayors Coun.; past mem. Nat. League of Cities Revenue and Fin. Task Force; pres. LWV, St. Petersburg, 1970-72, 75-76; trustee Fire Pension Bd., St. Petersburg, 1989-92, Bayfront Med. Ctr., Palms of Pasadena Hosp., 1999—; adv. com. Jr. League St. Petersburg, 1990-92. Recipient Disting. Alumni award Adelphi U. Mem. Fla. Nursing Assn. Republican. Home: 2101 Pelham Rd N Saint Petersburg FL 33710-3659 Office: 5858 Central Ave Saint Petersburg FL 33707-1728 E-mail: corinne_freeman@prusec.com.

FREEMAN, CORWIN STUART, JR., financial planner, investment advisor, consultant; b. Elmhurst, Ill., July 31, 1947; AA in Edn., Waubonsee C.C., Sugar Grove, Ill., 1971. LUTCF; cert. estate counselor; registered investment advisor; cert. sr. advisor. Pres. Valley Estate Planners Ltd., Elgin, Ill., 1980—. Chmn. Leaders Coun. Can. Life Assurance Co., 1988; mem. agts. coun. Delta Life and Annuity Co., 1993-95. Bd. dirs. McCauley Manor. With USMC, 1965-68, Vietnam. Named to Million Dollar Round Table, 1982-2001, life and qualifying mem., 2001, Ct. of Table Status, 1988, 2001, honor roll, 2001. Fellow Life Underwriter Tng. Coun.; mem. Nat. Tax Sheltered Annuity Assn. (charter mem. 1991-99), Elgin Area Life Underwriters (past pres. 1987-88), Ill. Life Underwriters Assn. (bd. dirs. 1991-93, region III v.p.). Home and Office: Valley Estate Planners Ltd 14n555 Tyrrell Rd Elgin IL 60123-7846 also: 150 Terrane Rdg Peachtree City GA 30269-4014 E-mail: CFreeman@valleyestateplanners.com.

FREEMAN, DAVID FORGAN, retired foundation executive; b. Chgo., June 25, 1918; s. Halstead Gurnee and Marion Kerr (Forgan) Freeman; m. Hazel Simms Farr, Sept. 5, 1947 (dec. Dec. 2001); children: David Forgan, Sims, Marion, John, Francis. AB, Princeton U., 1940; LLB, Yale U., 1947. Bar: N.Y. 1948. Atty. Debevoise, Plimpton & McLean, N.Y.C., 1947-50; exec. assoc. Ford Found., 1950-52; sec. Fund for the Republic, N.Y.C., 1952-54, v.p., 1954-57; assoc. Rockefeller Bros. Fund, N.Y.C., 1957-67; pres. Council on Founds., N.Y.C., 1968-78; exec. dir., treas. Scherman Found., N.Y.C., 1979-93; pres. So. Edn. Found., Atlanta, 1965-79; bd. dirs. Fund for N.J., 1980-87; exec. sec. major awards program Gulf & Western Found., 1981-86. Author: The Handbook on Private Foundations, 1981, rev. edit., 1991. Mem. Rumson Bd. Edn., N.J., 1952-55; mem. Monmouth County Mental Health Bd., N.J., 1985-90, mem. com. on religion and race Presbyn. Ch., 1958-61. With USNR, 1940-45. Decorated Legion of Merit. Home: 6 Clay Ct Locust NJ 07760-2307

FREEMAN, DAVID JOHN, lawyer; b. N.Y.C., Aug. 9, 1948; s. John L. and Josephine F. (Wilding) F.; m. Ellen Gogolick, Dec. 29, 1974; children: Matthew, Julie. BA, Harvard U., 1970; JD, 1975. Bar: Mass. 1975, D.C. 1977, N.Y. 1982, U.S. Dist. Ct. D.C. 1981, N.Y. 1982, U.S. Dist. Ct. D.C. 1981, U.S. Dist. Ct. (so. and ea. dists.) N.Y. 1982, U.S. Ct. Appeals (D.C. cir.) 1979, U.S. Ct. Appeals (2nd cir.) 1982, U.S. Supreme Ct. 1988. Spl. asst. to U.S. Senator Frank E. Moss, 1970-72; trial atty. FTC, Washington, 1975-77; assoc. Ginsburg, Feldman & Bress, Washington, 1977-81, Holtzmann, Wise & Shepard, N.Y.C., 1981-84; ptnr., 1984-94; ptnr., chmn. environ. dept. Battle Fowler, 1994-2000; ptnr., head N.Y. environ. practice group Paul, Hastings, Janofsky & Walker, N.Y.C., 2000—. Spl. legal counsel N.Am. Environ. Affairs, UN Environ. Programme; co-chair emeritus ISO 14000 Legal Issues Forum, U.S. Tech. Com. to TC-207, Internat. Com. Standardization. Editor-in-chief: Jour. Environ Law Practice (West), 1998-2000. Mem. ABA (environment, energy and resources sect.), Assn. Bar City of N.Y., Harvard Law Sch. Assn., N.Y. State Bar Assn. (environ. law sect., co-chair hazardous waste/site remediation com., co-chair task force on superfund reform). Office: Paul Hastings Janofsky & Walker LLP 75 E 55th St New York NY 10022-3205 E-mail: davidfreeman@paulhastings.com.

FREEMAN, DAVID RALPH, lawyer; b. Kansas City, Mo., Mar. 10, 1934; m. Marilyn Williams. BA in History, BJ, U. Mo., 1957, JD, 1965. Bar: Mo., U.S. Dist. Ct. (ea. and we. dists.), U.S. Ct. Appeals (7th and 8th cirs.), U.S. Dist. Ct. (so. dist.) Ill. Atty. Freeman & Williamson, Independence, Mo., 1965-68; prosecuting atty. State of Mo., Jackson County, 1967-72; atty. Sheridan, Sanders, Carr & White, Kansas City, 1970-72; fed. pub. defender Adminstrv. Office of U.S. Cts., Kansas City, 1973-79; dir. dept. social svcs. State of Mo., Jefferson City, 1979-81; atty. F. Joe DeLong III, Jefferson City, 1981-82; fed. pub. defender Adminstrv. Office U.S. Cts., St. Louis, 1982-95; ret., 1995; pvt. practice, 1995—. Fed. pub. defender, Mo., 1982—95, SD, 1982—95, Ill., 1982—95. Lt. Col. USMCR, 1957-61. Recipient Lon O. Hocker Meml. Trial Lawyer award Mo. Bar Found., 1969. Office: PO Box 975 Collinsville IL 62234-0975

FREEMAN, DEBORAH LYNN, lawyer; b. Santa Monica, Calif., Jan. 12, 1955; d. T.L. Gordon and Patricia I. (von Walden) F. BA in History with distinction, Stanford U., 1976; JD with honors, U. Denver, 1982. Bar: Colo. 1982. Ptnr. Saunders, Snyder, Ross & Dickson P.C., Denver, 1982—94, Trout, Witwer & Freeman, P.C., Denver, 1996—. Mem. ABA, Colo. Bar Assn. (chmn. environ. law sect. 1989-90), Denver Bar Assn. (sec. young lawyers div. 1985-86). Office: Trout, Witwer & Freeman PC 1120 Lincoln St Ste 1600 Denver CO 80203-2141 E-mail: dfreeman@troutlaw.com.

FREEMAN, DENISE, podiatrist, educator; b. New Haven, Conn., Apr. 25, 1952; DPM, Temple U., 1980; MS in Edn., Drake U., 2002. Diplomate Am. Bd. Podiatric Orthopedics and Primary Podiatric Medicine 1989. Assoc. prof. podiatric medicine Des Moines U., Des Moines, 1996—. Grantee rsch., Iowa Osteo. Edn. Assn., 1998—. Fellow: Am. Coll. Foot Orthopedists. Office: Des Moines U 3200 Grand Ave Des Moines IA E-mail: denise.freeman@dmu.edu.

FREEMAN, DONALD WILFORD, real estate developer, horse breeder; b. Brooksville, Fla., Sept. 25, 1929; s. Fred Maxwell and Dovie (Keef) F.; m. Ruby Jane Lewis, Feb. 25, 1956; children: Clifton Lewis, Susan Anne. BS, JD, U. Ala., 1953; LLM, NYU, 1957. CPA Ga. Acct. Ernst & Ernst, Atlanta, 1953-55; tax atty. Office Chief Counsel, U.S. Treasury Dept., N.Y.C., 1955-57, West Point Mfg. Co. (Ga.), 1957-58; treas. Ryder System, Inc., Miami, Fla., 1958-61; v.p., dir. Henderson's Portion Pak, Inc., 1961-63; pres. Biscayne Capital Corp., Miami, 1964-66; sr. assoc. Lazard Freres & Co., N.Y.C., 1967-69; pres. James A. Ryder Corp., Miami, 1969-78; owner Kiyara Arabians, 1978—. With AUS, 1946-48, PTO. Mem.: Fla. Inst. CPAs, Beta Gamma Sigma, Phi Kappa Sigma. Episcopalian. Home: 1570 S 42nd Cir 102 Vero Beach FL 32967

FREEMAN, DONNA COOK, small business owner; b. Waldron, Ark., Apr. 18, 1937; d. Oliver Raymond and Lura Edna (Doyel) Cook; m. Clarence Lee Freeman, Jan. 21, 1954; children: Scott, Kevin, Steven, Melissa, Melinda. Staff dept. aquaculture U. Calif. Bodega Marine Lab., 1976—77; real estate assoc., 1978—82; co-owner fishing vessel Noyo Belle, 1981—84; ptnr. Freeman's Union 76 Svc., Bodega Bay, 1983—93; owner, designer Compass Rose Gardens, 1986—. Vice chmn. Shoreline Trust Ednl. Program Svcs., 1981—85; founding chmn. Bodega Bay Fisherman's Festival, 1973—74, 1983; chmn. Spud Point Adv. Bd., 1985—; grand juror Sonoma County, Calif., 1983—84; hon. dir. Sonoma County Fair, 1995—; dir. Bodega Bay Fire Protection Dist., 1987—; alt. mem. Dem. Ctrl. Com., 1982; mgr. polit. campaign, 1984; bd. dirs. Bodega Bay Area Rescue, 1973—74; mem. local bd. SSS, 1982—; bd. dirs. Sonoma County Fair, 1985—95, Coastal Fisheries Found., 1986—; mem. regional adv. bd. Sonoma County Libr. Commn., 2002—. Mem.: Bodega Bay Cmty. Assn., Bodega Bay C. of C. (pres. 1979—81, bd. dirs. 1982—86), Bodega Bay Fisherman's Auz., Bodega Bay Grange. Home: 1409 Hwy 1 N Bodega Bay CA 94923-9716 E-mail: donna@compassrosegardens.com.

FREEMAN, DORIS BRANCH, retired marketing professional; b. Jackson, Tenn., Mar. 25, 1925; d. Felix Matthew and Mattie Belle (Weakes) Branch; m. James Herman Freeman, Nov. 21, 1942 (div. 1963); children: Patricia Freeman Little, Cynthia Freeman Haynie, James Vaughn, Constance Maurine. Student, U. Ga., 1982-83. Star Cousin Tuny Show WBBJ-TV, Jackson, 1955-67; account exec. WDXI-AM, Jackson, 1948-75; sales mgr. WJAK-AM, Jackson, 1975-80; pres., owner Cousin Tuny Mkrt. and Pub. Rels. Enterprises, Jackson, 1957-85; mktg. dir. Old Hickory Mall, Jackson, 1967-80, mgr., mkgt. dir., 1980-85; dir. mktg. and pub. rels. Jackson-Madison County Gen. Hosp., 1985-93; ret., 1993; entertainer, speaker Cousin Tuny Enterprises, Jackson, 1948—. Creator pediatric wing concept Little Gen.'s Palace, Jackson, 1989. Has emceed over 50 telethons, currently emcees 2 each year. Bd. dirs. Madison County Cancer Assn., 1966-76, Western Tenn. Cerebral Palsy Ctr., 1965—; spl. dep. sheriff Madison County, Jackson, 1968-90; hon. lifetime bd. dirs. Miss Tenn. Pageant, 1976—; mem. Jackson Clean Community Commn., 1984, Gov.'s Com. to Hire Disabled, 1989-91; adv. coun. Jackson State Community Coll., 1982-92; mem. Drug Free Madison County Com., 1989; mem. Pres. Bush's Thousand Points of Light, 1989; lifetime bd. mem. West Tenn. Cerebral Palsy Ctr., Carl Perkins Exch. Club Prevention of Child Abuse Ctr., 1996. Recipient Disting. Svc. award Am. Cancer Soc., 1968; named Jackson Woman of Yr., Altrusa Club, 1962, Hon. D Aerospaceology, USAF System Command, 1968, Hon. Col. Tenn. Nat. Guard, 1958, Point of Light, Pres. George Bush, 1989, Woman of Distinction, Girls Scouts Am. Mem. Am. Heart Assn. (lifetime), Am. Women in Radio and TV (Golden Mike award 1967), Crimestoppers (bd. dirs.), Elks (Disting. Citizenship award 1989), Rotary (Paul Harris fellow 1997). Democrat. Methodist. Home: 218 Fairmont St Jackson TN 38301-4118

FREEMAN, ELAINE LAVALLE, sculptor; b. Boston, May 22, 1929; d. John and Ellen (Tufts) Lavalle; m. Felix Joachim Freeman, Jr., June 16, 1951 (div. 1974); children: John Lavalle, William Baker, Ellen Candler. Student, NAD, 1973, Art Students League, N.Y.C., 1947-49, 70-73; BA, Fordham U., 1986. Profl. sculptor, N.Y.C. and Southampton, N.Y., 1973—; instr. Sculpture Ctr. Sch., N.Y.C., 1977-81; vol. gallery asst. Sculpture Ctr., N.Y.C., 1979-2000. Exec. com., sec., bd. trustees Sculpture Ctr., N.Y.C., 1985-2000. One-woman shows include Wheeler Gallery, Providence, 1979, Sculpture Ctr., N.Y.C., 1977, Southampton Gallery, N.Y.C., 1975; exhibited in group shows at Nat. Acad., Audubon Artists, Allied Artists, Parrish Mus., Nat. Arts Club, Am. Standard Corp. Gallery, Sculpture Ctr. Gallery, Huntington Twp. Art League, East Edn Arts Coun., others, 1973—; permanent collection include Martha Graham Sch. Contemporary Dance, Health Mgmt. Resources, N.Y., Southampton Hosp. Bd. dirs. Southampton Fresh Air Home for Crippled Children, 1980-86, sec., 1981-83, treas. 1980. Recipient Judges award Parrish Art Mus., Southampton, 1974, Am. Carving Sch. award Allied Artists, N.Y.C., 1977. Mem. Catharine Lorillard Wolfe Art Club (bd. dirs. 1997—, v.p. sculpture 1998-2001, 1st v.p. 2001—, 1st prize sculpture 1994, Anna Hyatt Huntington award 1983), Southampton Bathing Corp., Colony Club, Meadow Club. Democrat. Episcopalian. Avocations: travel, tennis, watercolor painting. Home: 132 Post Ln Southampton NY 11968-4919

FREEMAN, ERNEST ROBERT, engineering executive; b. Bklyn., Oct. 3, 1933; s. Nathan and Rose (Beginsky) F.; m. June Gladys Moser, June 6, 1954; children— Jesse David, Miriam Lisa, Sarah Ellen, Beth Bayla BSE.E., U. Miami, Coral Gables, Fla., 1955; M.E.A., George Washington U., 1966; Sc.D. (hon.), London Inst., 1977. Registered profl. engr., Md., NJ. Mem. tech. staff Bell Telephone Labs., Whippany, N.J., 1959-61; mgr. engring. dept. IIT Research Inst., Annapolis, Md., 1961-68; dir. engring. dept. Vertex Corp., Kensington, Md., 1968-69; pres., chief exec. officer SFA Inc., Landover, Md., 1969-91, exec. advisor, 1991-98, pres., chmn., CEO Largo, Md., 1998—. Lectr. Am U. Ctr. for Tech. and Adminstrn.; dir. Data Range Ltd., High Wycombe, England; mem. engring. adv. bd. U. DC, Washington. Author: (with others) Electromagnetic Compatibility Design Guide, 1981; Interference Suppression Techniques for Antennas and Transmitters, 1982; contbg. editor Attorney's Guide to Engring., 1986; editor-in-chief IEEE NCAC Scanner, 1997-98. Trustee People to People Internat. Served with USAF, 1956—59. Recipient Bausch & Lomb award, 1951, Electro '76 Best Session award. Fellow IEEE (life), Washington Acad. Sci. (life); mem. Assn. Fed. Comm. Cons. Engrs. (life mem.), Spectrum Planning Adv. Coun. (dept. commerce), Dept. Justice (peer rev. panel), Mensa. Trustee, People Internat.mem. adv. bd. U. of D.C. Avocations: scuba, flying, sailing. Home: 5357 Strathmore Ave Kensington MD 20895-1160 Office: SFA Inc 9315 Largo Dr W Ste 200 Upper Marlboro MD 20774-4755 E-mail: erfreeman@earthlink.net., efreeman@sfa.com.

FREEMAN, FLORENCE ELEANOR, lawyer; b. Cambridge, Mass., Feb. 25, 1921; s. Elbern and Olive Blanche (Rice) F.; AB, Wellesley Coll., 1942; JD, U. Pa., 1945. Bar: Del. 1947, U.S. Dist. Ct. Del. 1948, U.S. Ct. Appeals (3d cir.) 1950, Mass. 1954, U.S. Dist. Ct. Mass. 1960. Assoc., Lynch & Hermann, Wilmington, Del., 1946-53; sole practice, Weston, Mass., 1954-69; ptnr. Freeman & Conceison, Weston, 1970-83, Freeman & White, Weston, 1984— ; town counsel Town of Weston, 1968-86, spl. counsel, 1986-89. Author: (play) Portrait of a Prince, 1965. Pres. Weston LWV, 1960-62, Weston Drama Workshop, 1963-71; mem. bd. selectmen Town of Weston, 1964-68; sec., trustee So. New Eng. Conf. United Meth. Ch., Boston, 1971-74, chancellor, 1976-86 ; bd. visitors Boston U. Sch. Theology, 1978—; chmn. bd. advisors Anna Howard Shaw Ctr., 1988—; mem. council fin. and adminstrn. United Meth. Ch., Chgo., 1980-88, alt. jud. council, 1980-88, chmn. legal responsibilities com. 1980-88. Mem. ABA, Bar Assn. Club: Footlight (Boston) (pres. 1962-64); Wellesley Coll., Eastern Point Yacht. Office: Freeman & White 483 Boston Post Rd Weston MA 02493-1553

FREEMAN, FRED WESLEY, forester, educator; b. Logan, Ohio, Aug. 27, 1924; s. Harry and Ora May (Hicks) Freeman; m. Laura Alice Furgason, Oct. 17, 1986; children: Fred II, Cynthia Kogut, Carol Flegler; m. Jeanne Elizabeth Harbourt, July 12, 1946 (div. Nov. 30, 1973); stepchildren: Cheryl Vincent, Terry Furgason. BS, Mich. State U., 1949, MS, 1951, PhD, 1963. Registered forester Ohio, Mich. Soil scientist Bur. Reclamation, Bismarck, ND, 1950—51; forest ranger Ohio Divsn. Forestry, Rockbridge, 1951—53, forester Athens, 1953—55; horticulturist Hidden Lake Gardens Mich. State U., Tipton, 1955—61, dir. and asst. prof. Hidden Lake Gardens, 1961—68, dir. and assoc. prof. Hidden Lake Gardens, 1968—86, assoc. prof. emeritus E. Lansing. Trustee Mich. Horticulture Soc., Mich., 1967—71; dir. Am. Assn. Bot. Gardens and Arboretums, 1968—71; mem. Gov.'s Commn. Sch. Reorganization - Lenawee County, Mich., 1970. Editor: (jour.) Am. Assn. Bot. Gardens and Arboretums, 1965; contbr. articles to numerous mag. and newspaper articles. Treas. Tecumseh Sch. Bd., Mich., 1964—74. Sgt. airborne U.S. Army, 1943—46, S. Pacific. Fellow in horticulture, English Speaking Union, Brit. Isles & W. Europe, 1963, Complimentary fellow, Royal Horticulture Soc., London, 1976. Mem.: Am. Legion. Democrat. Avocations: reading, gardening, hunting, fishing, politics. Home: 278 North Ridge Rd Brooklyn MI 49230

FREEMAN, GARY EUGENE, civil engineer, researcher; b. Jerome, Idaho, Nov. 19, 1952; s. Junius Eugene and Stella Ida F.; m. Denise Heiner, Aug. 6, 1982; children: Daniel, Joshua, Desiree, Krista. AA, Coll. So. Idaho, Twin Falls, 1973; BS, Utah State U., 1978, MS, 1983; PhD, Tex. A&M U., 1992; JD, Brigham Young U., 2000. Registered profl. engr., Miss., Pa., Utah, Idaho, Ariz.;bar: Ariz., 2000. Rsch. assoc. U. Idaho, Kimberly, 1980-81; agrl. engr. Africare, Inc., Dire, Mali, 1986-87; rschr., tchg. asst. Utah State U., Logan, 1988-89; contract student U.S. Army Waterways Experiment Sta., Vicksburg, Miss., 1989-91, rsch. hydraulic engr., 1991-97; pres. River Rsch. Design, Gilbert, Ariz., 1997—; dir. Water Resources Engr., WEST, Cons., Inc. Cons. engr. Africare, Inc., Burkina Faso, West Africa, 1988, Egypt, 1991; interagency floodplain mgmt. rev. com. White House, 1993-94, scientific assessment strategy team, 1993-95. Contbr. articles to Water Internat., SAST Workshop; co-editor Selected Studies on Mississippi River Flood, 1997. Recipient Letter Appreciation, V.P. Al Gore, 1994, Civilian Svc. medal U.S. Army, 1994; Mills fellow Tex. A&M U., 1989-90. Mem. ABA, ASCE, U.S. Com. on Irrigation and Drainage, Sigma Xi. Republican. Avocations: water skiing, motorcycling, scuba diving. Office: 960 W Elliot Rd St Tempe AZ 85284

FREEMAN, GEORGE CLEMON, JR., lawyer; b. Birmingham, Ala., Jan. 3, 1929; s. George Clemon and Annie Laura (Gill) F.; m. Anne Colston Hobson, Dec. 6, 1958; children: Anne Colston McEvoy, George Clemon III, Joseph Reid Anderson. BA magna cum laude, Vanderbilt U., 1950; LLB, Yale U., 1956. Bar: Ala. 1956, Va. 1958, D.C. 1974. Law clk. to Justice Hugo L. Black U.S. Supreme Ct., 1956; assoc. Hunton & Williams, Richmond, Va., 1957-63, ptnr., 1963-95, sr. counsel, 1995—. Contbr. articles to profl. jours. Pres. Va. chpt. Nature Conservancy, 1962—63; counsel Va. Outdoors Recreation Study Com. Va. Legis., 1963—65; mem. sect. 301 Superfund Act Study Group Congl. Adv. Com., 1981—82; mem. Falls James Com., 1973—89; chmn. adv. coun. Energy Policy Studies Ctr. U. Va., 1981—85; chmn. legal adv. com. to Va. Commn. on Transp. in the 21st Century, 1986—87; mem. Va. Gov.'s Commn. to Study Historic Preservation, 1987—88, Va. Coun. on the Environment, 1989—91; chmn. Va. Bd. Hist. Resources, 1989—91; mem. The Atlantic Coun., 1986—95; bd. dirs. Nat. Mus. Am. History, 1997—2002; chmn. Richmond City Dem. Com., 1969—71. Lt (j.g.) USN, 1951—54. Ctr. for Pub. Resources fellow, 1990—. Fellow Am. Bar Found. (Va. state chmn. 1986-90); mem. ABA (chmn. standing com. on facilities of Law Libr. of Congress 1967-73, coordinating group on regulatory reform 1981-85, nominating com. 1984-87, chmn. civil justice coordinating com. 1990-92, sect. bus. law, sect. coun. 1976-79, chmn. ad hoc com. on Fed. Criminal Code 1979-81, chmn. program com. 1981-82, chmn. ad hoc com. on tort law reform 1986-87, sect. del. to ho. of dels. 1983-87, sec. 1987-88, vice-chmn. and ed. The Business Lawyer 1988-89, chmn.-elect 1989-90, chmn. 1990-91), Richmond Bar Assn., Va. Bar Assn., Am. Law Inst. (coun. 1980—, advisor to coun. on project on compensation and liability for product and process injuries 1986-91, advisor restatement of law, THRD, torts apportionment 1993-97, advisor restatement law THRD torts gen. prins. 1997—), Am. Judicature Soc., Country Club of Va., Knickerbocker Club, Met. Club, Phi Beta Kappa, Phi Delta Phi, Omicron Delta Kappa, Alpha Tau Omega. Democrat. Episcopalian. Avocation: gardening. Office: Hunton & Williams 951 E Byrd St Richmond VA 23219-0005 E-mail: gfreeman@hunton.com.

FREEMAN, GILL SHERRYL, judge; b. N.Y.C., June 24, 1949; d. Norman and Arlene (Vigdor) Jacovitz. Student, U. Wis., 1966-68; BS in Edn. cum laude, Temple U., 1970; MEd, U. Miami, Fla., 1973, JD cum laude, 1977. Bar: Fla. 1977, U.S. Dist. Ct. (so. dist.) Fla. 1977, U.S. Dist. Ct. (mid. dist.) Fla. 1984, U.S. Ct. Appeals (5th cir.) 1977. Tchr. Dade County Pub. Schs., Miami, 1970-76; assoc. Walton, Lantaff, Schroeder & Carson, Miami, 1977-82, Ruden, McClosky, Smith, Schuster & Russell, Miami, 1982—, ptnr., 1983-97; apptd. cir. ct. judge Dade County Fla., 1997—. Vice chair Fla. Supreme Ct. Gender Bias Commn., 1987—90; chair Fla. Supreme Ct. Gender Bias Study Implementation Commn., 1991—94; mem. Supreme Ct. Commn. Fairness, 1997, chair, 1999—; chmn. bd. disr. Journey Inst., 1997—2001. Trustee Dade County Law Libr., 1996—, chair, 2001—; bd. dirs. Family Counseling Svcs. of Greater Mami, 1995—, Spectrum Programs, 1993—, chair, 1996—98. Master: Family Law Inns Ct.; mem.: Cuban Am. Bar Assn., Fla. Assn. Women Lawyers (pres. 1984—85), Fla. Bar Assn. Avocations: alpine skiing, travel, racquetball. Office: 73 W Flagler St Rm 303 Miami FL 33130

FREEMAN, GLENN, political organization worker, retired noncommissioned military officer; b. Fayetteville, NC, July 6, 1935; Student, Met. C.C., 1986—87. Enlisted USAF, 1955, advanced through grades to Chief Master Sgt., 1985, ret., 1985. Author: Good Racism-Bad Racism, 1999. Appt. to U.S. Commn. on Civil Rights, 2000—04; pres. Omaha chpt. Freedoms Found. at Valley Forge; appt. commr. State Equal Opportunity Commn., 1989; dir. Douglas County Atty.'s Victim-Witness Program; hosp. svc. coord. Disabled Am. Vets., 1991—97; sr. aide US Sen. Chuck Hagel; asst. chmn. Douglas County Rep. Party, Nebr. Rep. Party; chmn. outreach com. Nebr. Rep. Party. Decorated Bronze Star, two meritorious Svc. medals, four Air Force commendation medals.

FREEMAN, HAROLD PAUL, oncologist, educator; b. Washington, Mar. 2, 1933; s. Clyde and Lucille Freeman; m. Arti Artholian Palmer, 1957; children: Harold P. Jr., Neale P. AB in Biology, Cath. U. Am., 1954; MD, Howard U., 1958; DSc (hon.), Albany Med. Sch., 1989, Niagara U., 1989; DS (hon.), Adelphi U., 1989, Cath. U., 1990. Diplomate Am. Bd. Surgery; lic. oncologist, N.Y., Md. Rotating intern Howard U. Hosp., Washington, 1958-59, resident in gen. surgery, 1959-62, chief resident in surgery, 1963-64; resident in surgery Meml. Sloan Kettering Hosp., N.Y.C., 1962-63, sr. resident, 1964-67; fellow in surgery Cornell U. Med. Ctr., N.Y.C., 1965-66; asst. in surgery Columbia U., 1967-70, instr. surgery, 1970-73, asst. clin. prof., 1973-74, assoc. prof. clin. surgery, 1974—, prof., 1989—; chair President's Cancer Panel, Bethesda. Asst. attending surgeon N.Y. Infirmary, N.Y.C., 1969-82, St. Luke's/Roosevelt Med. Ctr., N.Y.C., 1983—, Harlem Hosp. Ctr., N.Y.C., 1967-73, chmn. cancer com., 1968-73, attending surgeon, dir. surgery, 1974—; adj. attending surgeon Bklyn. Jewish Hosp., 1970-74, Meml. Sloan Kettering Hosp., 1981—; assoc. attending surgeon Presbyn. Hosp., N.Y.C., 1974—; attending surgeons Columbia Presbyn., 1998. Contbr. articles to profl. jours.; presentations in field. Nat. pres. Am. Cancer Soc., 1988-89, chmn. nat. adv. com. on cancer in the socio-economically disadvantaged, 1987-88, chmn. med. and sci. exec. com., 1986-87, chmn. med. and sci. com., 1985-86, chmn. nat. adv. com. on cancer in minorities, 1984-87, pres. Harlem unit, 1983-88, med. dir.-at-large bd. dirs.. 1977—, bd. dirs. N.Y.C. div., 1977—; mem. Columbia U. Comprehensive Cancer Ctr., 1987—; bd. trustees Howard U., 1994—; chmn. Pres. Cancer Panel, 1991—. Recipient Howard U. Women's Club award, 1977, Profl. award Nat. Assn. Negro Bus. and Profl. Women's Club, 1987, Disting. Lectr. award Manhattan Cen. Med. Soc., 1988, Disting. Community Svc. award Mut. of Am., 1989, Lasker Pub. Svc. award, 2000. Fellow N.Y. Acad. Medicine, Am. Surgical Assn.; mem. ACS (exec. com. 1989—, gov. 1988—, com. on cancer, 1981—, sr. mem. commn. on cancer 1987—, chmn. pres. cancer panel 1991—), NIH (breast cancer task force 1979-84), Nat. Cancer Inst. (subcom. on cancer detection rsch. and applications 1987 -90), Soc. Surg. Oncology (exec. coun. 1987—), Nat. Med. Assn. (chmn. surg. sect. 1984-86), Inst. Medicine Nat. Acad. Sci. (elected 1997), Internat. Soc. Surgeons, N.Y. Acad. Scis., Am. Surg. Assn., Inst. of Medicine Nat. Acad. of Sci., County Med. Soc. N.Y., Alpha Omega Alpha. Office: Harlem Hosp Ctr 135th & Lenox Ave New York NY 10037 also: North Gen Hosp 1879 Madison Ave Fl 5 New York NY 10035-2709

FREEMAN, HARRY LOUIS, investment executive; b. Omaha, Mar. 1, 1932; s. Joseph H. and Celia (Rivonne) F.; m. Lucile Carpenter, Dec. 26, 1965; children: Bennett, Lansing, Rachel, Alexandra. AB, U. Mich., 1953; JD, Harvard U., 1956. Bar: Nebr. 1956, Calif. 1957, U.S. Supreme Ct. 1967, D.C. 1968. Clk. U.S. Ct. Appeals, 9th Cir., 1956-57; mem. Janin, Morgan, Brenner & Freeman, San Francisco, 1957-66; dir. ins. divsn. AID, Dept. State, Washington, 1966-69; v.p. corp. planning OPIC, Washington, 1969-71, v.p. fin., 1974-75; mgr. comml. projects, mgr. project fin. group Bechtel Corp., San Francisco, 1972-74; v.p. Am. Express Co., Washington, 1975-77, sr. v.p. N.Y.C., 1977-79, sr. v.p., office of chmn., 1979-83, exec. v.p., 1984-89; pres. The Freeman Co., Washington, 1989—. Adj. prof. internat. law U. Calif., Berkeley, 1974, Georgetown U., 1975-76; prin. Ctr. for Excellence in Govt.; trustee U.S. Council for Internat. Bus. Contbr. articles to profl. jours. Trustee World Affairs Council No. Calif., 1960-66, Overseas Devel. Coun., Ctr. Excellence in Govt.; bd. dirs. Calif. Clinic for Psychotherapy, San Francisco, 1964-66, Fund for Multinat. Edn., 1984—; trustee Com. Econ. Devel., 1983—. Recipient Disting. Service award AID, 1969, Disting. Service award OPIC, 1971. Mem. ABA, Calif. Bar Assn., Nebr. Bar Assn., Washington Bar Assn., Coun. on Fgn. Rels., Harvard Club (N.Y.C.), Coalition Svc. Industry (sr. advisor), Mark Twain Inst. (chair). Democrat. Jewish. Home: 4708 Dorset Ave Chevy Chase MD 20815-5446

FREEMAN, HARRY LYNWOOD, retired accountant; b. L.A., May 5, 1920; s. Edward Church and Mildred Eaton (Noyes) F.; m. Ruth Turner, Feb. 14, 1941; children: Tracy Ruth (Mrs. Richard W. Flatow), Martin Harry. BS, UCLA, 1942. CPA, Calif. With Price Waterhouse & Co., CPAs, 1942-56, ptnr., 1956-73, ptnr.-in-charge Middle Americas firm, 1973-80. Chmn. auditing com. Am. Brit. Cowdray Hosp., 1962-68; bd. dirs., treas. YMCA of Mexico, 1967-73; bd. dirs. Inst. Mexicano-Norteamericano de Relaciones Culturales, 1961-69, Eastridge Homeowners Assn., 2000—; trustee, v.p. Fallbrook Hosp. Found., 1987-90, pres., 1990-92; bd. dirs. Fallbrook Hosp. Dist., 1994-98, v.p., 1996-98. With AUS, 1944-46. Mem. AICPA, Calif. Soc. CPAs, Am. C. of C. Mex. (past pres.), Assn. Am. C. of C. in Latin Am. (past pres.), Aero Club of So. Calif., Book Club Calif. Home: 1002 Ridge Heights Dr Fallbrook CA 92028-3671

FREEMAN, HERBERT, computer engineering educator; b. Frankfurt, Germany, Dec. 13, 1925; came to U.S., 1938; s. Leo and Johanna (Friedmann) F.; m. Joan Sleppin, Nov. 25, 1955; children: Nancy, Susan, Robert. BSEE, Union Coll., 1946; MSEE, Columbia U., 1948, DEngSc, 1956. Registered profl. engr.,

N.Y. Project engr. Sperry Gyroscope Co., Great Neck, N.Y., 1948-53, section head, 1953-57, dept. head, 1957-60; assoc. prof. computer engring. NYU, 1960-64, prof., chmn., 1965-75; prof. Rensselaer Poly. Inst., Troy, N.Y., 1975-85; dir. Ctr. for. Computer Aids for Indsl. Productivity Rutgers U., New Brunswick, N.J., 1985-90. Dir. Nat. Ctr. Geographic Info. and Analysis, 1988-93. Author: Discrete-Time Systems, 1965; co-editor: Map Data Processing, 1980, Software Engineering, 1981; editor: Introduction to Computer Graphics, 1981, Machine Vision for Three-Dimensional Scenes, 1990. NSF postdoctoral fellow, 1966, Guggenheim fellow, 1972; recipient Medaglia Teresiana award U. Pavia, Italy, 1996. Fellow IEEE (Computer Pioneer award 1999), Internat. Assn. for Pattern Recognition (treas. 1982-88, pres. 1978-80, K.S. Fu award 1994); mem. Computer Soc. of IEEE (chmn. Pattern Analysis and Machine Intelligence sect. 1976-78), Internat. Fedn. Info. Processing (program chmn. 1974, Silver Core award 1974), Assn. Computing Machinery, Pattern Recognition Soc. Avocations: stamp collecting, swimming. Office: Rutgers U Elec & Computer Engring 94 Brett Rd Piscataway NJ 08854-8058

FREEMAN, J. P. LADYHAWK, vicar, underwater exploration, security and transportation executive, educator, fashion model, legislative advocate; b. Berkley, Calif., Feb. 21, 1951; d. Gilbert Richard Freeman (dec.) and P.M. (Ann) Raistrick; children: Jennifer Patricia (dec.), Schne F. (dec.). BA in English, Davis & Elkins Coll., W.Va., 1973; grad., USAF Air Weapons Controller Sch., Tyndall AFB, Fla., 1973, USAF Air Command and Staff Coll., 1982, U.S. Marine Corps Command and Staff Coll., 1982, Dept. Def. Computer Inst., 1984; M in Aviation M in Aviation Mgmt., postgrad., Embry-Riddle Aeronautical U., Daytona Beach, Fla., 1986; grad., USAF Air War Coll., Montgomery, Ala., 1988. Cert. EMT; ordained vicar United Ch., 2002. Mem. 56th spl. ops. rescue for Southeast Asia NKP Royal Thai Air Force Base, 1974, 75; chief wing radar standardization/evaluation RAF Alconbury, England, 1980-83; commdr. joint U.S. forces Operation Raleigh, 1986; support chief of staff Hdqs. NORAD, Colorado Springs, Colo., 1987-89; dep. base commdr. NATO Hdqs. Allied Forces No. Europe, Norway, 1989-91; chief airport mgmt. divsn. Whiteman AFB, Knob Noster, Mo., 1991-93; dir. spl. projects USAF Acad. Regional Hosp., Colorado Springs, 1993-94; systems performance specialist Colo. Sport & Spine Rehab., Colorado Springs, 1994-95; dir. FLEET Internat. Explorations and Svcs. Co., Colorado Springs, 1995-97; fashion model, 1996—2001; vicar, 2002—. Spl. adv. for anti and counter terrorist security design for 1994 Internat. Olympic Games, Oslo, Norway, 1989-91; designer Automated Provider Credentialing System USAF Acad. Regional Hosp., USAF Acad., Colo., 1993-94; spl. adv. comms. NATO German High Commd., 1977-80; paralyzed Vet. of Am., sr. legist. advocate. U.S. Congress for Colo., Mont. Ut. and Wyo., 2002-; experience in 37 countries. Poet, poems included in numerous anthologies. Mem. bd. dirs. Johnson County (Mo.) United Way, 1991-93; surgery life support specialist ARC, USAF Acad. Regional Hosp., 1993-95; mem. nat. scholarship com. Red River Valley Fighter Pilots Assn., 1993—; hosp. vol., med. technician, provider credentialing system designer, oral surgery life support system specialist. Recipient 53 awards and decorations including Defense Meritorious svc. medal with 1 oak leaf cluster, Meritorious Svc. medal with 2 oak leaf clusters, Joint Svc. Commendation medal with 1 oak leaf cluster, air force commendation medal, Armed Forces Expeditionary medal with 2 bronze stars, 2 Humanitarian Svc. medals, 2 Kuwait Liberation medals, 2 Southwest Asia medals; named Adminstrsn. Officer of Yr. USAF, 1986; named one of the six top Support Officers USAF, 1986-87; 1st woman named dir. Fleet Internat. Mem. VFW, DAV, Am. Legion, Air Force Assn., Soc. of Profl. Journalists, Assn. of Old Crows, Lambda Lambda Lambda, Alpha Phi Omega, Iota Beta Sigma. Mem. United Anglican Ch. Avocations: writing, skiing, horseback riding, oil painting, music. Home: 4861 Chaparral Rd Colorado Springs CO 80917-1413 Office: FLEET Internat Explorations & Svcs Co PO Box 14192 Colorado Springs CO 80914-0192

FREEMAN, JAMES BEAUMONT, philosophy educator; b. Paterson, N.J., Mar. 27, 1947; s. Theodore Roosevelt and Marion Elizabeth (Evans) F. BA, Drew U., 1968; AM, Ind. U., 1971, PhD, 1973. Lectr. Ind. U., Bloomington, 1973-74, Butler U., Indpls., 1974, Bloomfield (N.J.) Coll., 1974-75; rsch. assoc. U. Victoria, B.C., Can., 1975-78; asst. prof. philosophy Hunter Coll., CUNY, 1978-84, assoc. prof., 1985-92, prof., 1993—, chmn. dept., 1992-98. Author: Thinking Logically: Basic Concepts for Reasoning, 1993, Dialectics and the Macrostructure of Arguments: A Theory of Argument Structure, 1991; contbr. articles to jours. in field; mem. editl. bd. Argumentation. Mem. Am. Philos. Assn., Soc. Christian Philosophers, Assn. for Informal Logic/Critical Thinking. Home: 478 Park Ave Paterson NJ 07504-1806 Office: Hunter Coll CUNY 695 Park Ave New York NY 10021-5024 E-mail: jfreeman@hunter.cuny.edu.

FREEMAN, JAMES DOUGLAS, music educator; b. Rochester, N.Y., July 4, 1939; s. Henry Schofield and Florence Knope Freeman; m. Dorothy Ellen Kidney, Sept. 29, 1964; children: Timothy James, Theodore John. BA, Harvard U., 1961, MA, 1964, PhD, 1978; postgrad., Acad. für Musik, Vienna, 1961—62. Underhill prof. music Swarthmore (Pa.) Coll., 1966—; artistic dir. Orch. 2001, Phila., 1988—. Contbr. articles to profl. jours. Fellow, NEA, 1978; Paine Travelling fellow, Harvard U., 1961—62, Fulbright fellow, Moscow, 1991. Avocations: hiking, running, tennis. Home: 206 Martroy Ln Wallingford PA 19086 Office: Swarthmore Coll Ste 2 500 College Ave Swarthmore PA 19081-1390

FREEMAN, JAMES MICHAEL, musician, vocalist; b. Pittsburgh, Pa., Aug. 28, 1955; s. Alfred and Laura Bell Freeman. Ride operator RCS Amusement, Tempee, Ariz., 1994—96; gen. contractor Self Employed, Long Beach, 1990—94; singer Consol. Energy Band, Pittsburgh, 1973—76; lead singer The Marcels, Pittsburgh, 1979—84; warehouse worker Robinson's May Co., Westminster, 1997; janitor 24-Hour Fitness, Irvine, 1999; gen. contractor Dan Mathis Contracting, Westminster, 2000. Author: (children's book) Willow Brook Pond. Driver Seniors & Disabled, Santa Ana, Calif., 2002; benefit shows Live Performances, Orange County, Calif., 1990—2002. Mem.: S.A.G. Avocations: fishing, playing video games. Home: 3337 S Bristol #48 Santa Ana CA 92704

FREEMAN, JEANNE MARIE, music educator, writer; b. Winchester, Mass, Sept. 11, 1948; d. Thomas Harold and Edith Georgiana Freeman; 1 child, Leigh Anne. BS in Ed., Salem State Coll., Mass., 1970; MA in Ed., Cambridge Coll., Cambridge, Mass, 2000. Music tchr. City of Woburn, Woburn, Mass., 1970—72, classroom tchr., 1972—, asst. prin., 2000—. Sch. coun. mem. Clapp Elem. sch., Woburn, Mass., 2000—. Author: (book) Katie's Pond, 2001. Local Cultural Coun. Sec. Reading Cultural Coun., Reading, Mass., 1993—99; bd. mem. Creative Arts, Reading, Mass., 2002—. Mem.: Woburn's Writer's Group. Achievements include development of developed land mgmt. plan for town forest in Danvers, Mass. Avocation: travel. Home: 16 Grant St Reading MA 01867 Office: Woburn Sch Dept Clapp Sch 40 Hudson St Woburn MA 01801

FREEMAN, JO, writer, political consultant, lawyer; b. Atlanta, Aug. 26, 1945; d. William Maxwell and Helen Mitchell Freeman. AB, U. Calif., Berkeley, 1965; PhD, U. Chgo., 1973; JD, NYU, 1982. Rsch. dir., fieldworker SCLC, Ala./Miss., 1965-66; asst. prof. polit. sci. SUNY, 1973-77; legal asst. U.S. Dist. Ct. (ea. dist.) N.Y., 1982-83; assoc. polit. dir. Cranston for Pres. campaign, Washington, 1983-84; asst. dist. atty. Kings County, N.Y., 1985-86; assoc. counsel Office of Spkr., N.Y. State Assembly, Albany, 1987-89; pvt. practice N.Y., 1989-2001. Cons. in field. Author: The Politics of Women's Liberation, 1975 (Am. Polit. Sci. Assn. award 1975), A Room At A Time: How Women Entered Party Politics, 2000, At Berkeley in the Sixties, 2003; editor: Women: A Feminist Perspective, 1975, 79, 84, 89, 95, Social Movements of the Sixties and Seventies, 1983, Waves of Protest: Social Movements Since the Sixties, 1999; co-editor: Victoria Johnson; mem. editl. bd. Women in Politics, 1980-2001; columnist seniorwomen.com. Brookings fellow U.S. Dept. Labor, 1977-78, fellow Nat. Inst. Mental Health, 1968-73, Root-Tilden fellow NYU Sch. Law, 1979-82. Mem. NOW (chpt. treas. 1978-79, Susan B. Anthony award N.Y.C. chpt. 2000), Am. Polit. Sci. Assn. (congl. fellow 1978-79), Women's Caucus for Polit. Sci. (treas. 1978-79, Mary Lepper award 1993), Nat. Women's Polit. Caucus, Nat. Writer's Union, Authors Guild. Democrat. Avocation: photography. Home: 410 E 8th St Brooklyn NY 11218 Office: 1738-B Riggs Pl NW Washington DC 20009 E-mail: jfrbc@hotmail.com.

FREEMAN, JOANNE BARRIE, history educator; b. N.Y.C., Apr. 27, 1962; d. Allan Edward and Barbara Odette Freeman. BA, Pomona Coll., Claremont, Calif., 1984; MA, U. Va., Charlottesville, 1993; PhD, 1998. Prodn. asst. Rapp & Collins, N.Y.C., 1986; supr. edn. South Street Seaport Mus., N.Y.C., 1987-88; curator, coord. exhibits Libr. Congress, Washington, D.C., 1989-90, assoc. coord. Am. Memory, 1990-92; instr. dept. history U. Va., 1995; asst. prof. history Yale U., New Haven, 1997—2002, prof. history, 2002—. Mem. adv. coun. Gilder-Lehrman Ctr. Study of Slavery, Resistance and Abolition, Yale U.; mem. adv. coun. Internat. Ctr. Jefferson Studies, Charlottesville, Va.; coord. numerous hist. exhbns.; presenter, cons. in field. Author: Affairs of Honor: National Politics in the New Republic, 2001 (Best Book prize Soc. Historians of the Early Am. Republic, 2002); editor: Alexander Hamilton: Writings, 2001; guest (numerous TV appearances including) The Duel (PBS), 2000, This Week in History, 2001, Founding Brothers, 2002; contbr. articles to profl. jours. Corcoran fellow U. Va., 1992; State of Va. fellow, 1993, Soc. Cincinnati fellow, 1994, Mass. Hist. Soc. fellow, 1995, Thomas Jefferson Meml. Found. fellow, 1995, Intercoll. Studies Inst. fellow, 1996, Yale U. fellow, 2000, Am. Hist. Assn. and Libr. Congress fellow, 2000—, Dirksen Congl. Rsch. Ctr. fellow, 2003. Mem.: AAUW, Am. Antiquarian Soc., Omohundro Inst. Early Am. History and Culture, Soc. Historians of Early Am. Republic (program planning com. 1997—98), Orgn. Am. Historians (Disting. lectr. 2002—), Am. Hist. Assn., Phi Beta Kappa. Office: Yale U Dept History PO Box 208324 New Haven CT 06520 E-mail: joanne.freeman@yale.edu.

FREEMAN, JOHN CLINTON, meteorologist, oceanographer; b. Houston, Aug. 7, 1920; s. John Clinton and Ann (Dotson) Freeman; m. Marjorie Schaefer, June 14, 1947; children: John C. III, Walter H., Jill F. Hasling, Cathryn F. Disch, Helen, Paul D. BA, Rice U., 1941; MS, Calif. Inst. Tech., 1942; postgrad., Brown U., 1946—48; PhD, U. Chgo., 1952. Commd. 2d lt. USAF, 1941, advanced through grades to lt. col., 1970; weather officer U.S. Army, 1941-46; math. rschr. grad. divsn. applied math. Brown U., Providence, 1946-48; rschr. in meteorology U.S. Weather Bur., Washington, 1948-49, Inst. Advanced Study, Princeton, NJ, 1949-50, U. Chgo., 1950-52; rschr. in meteorology and oceanography, prof. Tex. A&M, College Station, 1952-55; meteorology and oceanography rschr. Gulf Cons.-NESCO, Houston, 1955-66; prof., chmn. and dir. rsch. Inst. Storm Rsch.-U. St. Thomas, Houston, 1957-88; dir. rsch. Weather Rsch. Ctr., Houston, 1988—, past pres. Convenor, chmn. Internat. Conf. Coastal Engring, Houston, 1984; presenter in field. Contbr. chapters to books. Fellow: Am. Meterology Soc. (chmn. com applied meteorology 1975—76, Meisinger award 1950, Spl. award Tex. Tornado Radar Network 1961, award for outstanding contbn. advancement of applied meteorology 2003); mem.: Marine Tech. Soc. (local chmn. 1970), Am. Geophys. Union. Democrat. Ch. Of Christ. Achievements include co-discovery of orbital effect on the sun and the earth forming the link between the disturbances on the sun and disturbances in the earth's atmosphere. Avocation: dog training. Office: Weather Rsch Ctr 3227 Audley St Houston TX 77098-1901 Business E-Mail: jfreeman9@houston.rr.com.

FREEMAN, JOHN MARK, pediatric neurologist; b. Bklyn., Jan. 11, 1933; s. Leon Lucas and Florence (Kann) F.; m. Elaine Kaplan, Aug. 26, 1956; children: Andrew David, Jennifer Beth, Joshua Leon. BA, Amherst Coll., 1954; MD, Johns Hopkins U., 1958. Intern Harriet Lane Home, Johns Hopkins U., Balt., 1958-59, resident in pediatrics, 1959-61; fellow in neurology Columbia Presbyn. Hosp., N.Y.C., 1961-64; asst. prof. pediatrics and neurology Stanford (Calif.) U., 1966-69; asso. prof. neurology and pediatrics Johns Hopkins U., Balt., 1969-82, prof., 1982—, Lederer prof. pediatric epilepsy, 1991—2003; dir. pediatric neurology Johns Hopkins, Balt., 1969-90; dir. pediatric epilepsy ctr. Johns Hopkins U., Balt., 1973—2002, dir. birth defects treatment center, 1969-90. Pres. Epilepsy Assn. Md., 1977-82; mem. profl. adv. bd. Epilepsy Found. Am., 1975-82, sec., 1977, v.p., 1982—, hon. life dir., 1991—. Contbr. articles to profl. jours. Served with AUS, 1964-66. Named Physician of Yr., Gov.'s Com. on Employment Handicapped, 1979, Health Care Profl. of Yr., Gov.'s Com. on Employment of Persons with Disabilities, 1990; recipient Cmty. Leadership award, Epilepsy Assn. Md., 1991. Fellow: Am. Acad. Pediats. (chmn. neurology sect. 1978—80), Am. Acad. Neurology; mem.: Am. Neurol. Assn., Am. Epilepsy Soc. (Lennox award 1993, Penry award 2001), Am. Fedn. Clin. Rsch., Am. Pediat. Soc., Child Neurology Soc. (exec. com. 1979—81), Profs. of Child Neurology (pres. 1980—82). Home: 1026 Rolandvue Ave Baltimore MD 21204-6815 Office: John Hopkins Med Inst 600 N Wolfe St 2-147 Meyer Baltimore MD 21287-0005

FREEMAN, KENNETH W. laboratory executive; BS, Bucknell U.; MBA, Harvard U. Various acctg., control, fin. positions Corning (N.Y.), Inc., 1972; corp. controller, 1985—87; gen. mgr. Sci. Products divsn., 1989—90; pres. Corning Asahi Video Products Co., 1990—93; exec. v.p. Corning Inc.; pres., CEO Corning Clin. Labs. Corning Life Scis. Inc. subs. of Corning Inc., 1995—97; chmn., CEO Quest Diagnostics, Inc. (formerly Corning Clin. Labs.), Teterboro, NJ, 1995—. Office: Quest Diagnostics 1 Malcolm Ave Teterboro NJ 07608

FREEMAN, KEVIN DAVID, portfolio management executive, entrepreneur; b. Tulsa, Aug. 17, 1961; s. Kerry Landon and Evelyn Sue (Courtney) F.; m. Marnie Renee Westfall, Jan. 29, 1999; children: Madysen Morgan, Kieren Trois. BSBA and Econs., U. Tulsa, 1983. CFA. Pres., sr. editor, sr. market strategist DBA, The Personal Capitalist, Tulsa, 1981-91; mng. dir. Templeton Portfolio Adv., Carmel, Calif., 1991-2000; co-founder, chmn. Separate Account Solutions, 2000—. Cons. Templeton Galbraith & Hansberger, Nassau, The Bahamas, 1990; bd. dirs. Carmel Creamery, Inc. Author: (booklet) A Common Sense Guide to Investment Profits, 1990; co-author: Investing in Separate Accounts, 2002; author, editor (newsletter) The Personal Capitalist, 1985-91. Chmn., founder Adam Smith Found., Tulsa, 1989-92; pub. policy expert-econs. The Heritage Found., Washington, 1991-92; assoc. Hillsdale (Mich.) Coll., 1996—; bd. govs. Coun. for Nat. Policy, 1998—. Recipient Double Ruby award Nat. Forensic League, 1979. Mem. Assn. Investment Mgmt. and Rsch., Internat. Soc. Fin. Analysts, Pres. Club Hillsdale Coll. Republican. Baptist. Avocations: golf, scuba diving, horseback riding, entrepreneur. E-mail: k@separateaccounts.com.

FREEMAN, LEE ALLEN, JR., lawyer; b. Chgo., July 31, 1940; s. Lee Allen and Brena (Dietz) F.; m. Glynna Gene Weger, June 8, 1968; children: Crispin McDougal, Clark Dietz, Cassidy Bree. AB magna cum laude, Harvard U., 1962, JD magna cum laude, 1965. Bar: Ill. 1966, D.C. 1966, Mont. 1986, U.S. Supreme Ct. 1969. Practiced in, Washington, 1965-68, Chgo., 1968—; law clk. to Justice Tom C. Clark, Washington, 1965-66; asst. U.S. atty., 1966-68; v.p. Freeman, Freeman & Salzman, P.C., 1970—; spl. asst. atty. gen. Ill., 1969-82, 1973-79; spl. dep. atty. gen., 1971-82; spl. asst. corp. counsel, 1971-76. Pres. Chgo. Lyric Opera Guild; pres. Fine Arts Music Found.; dir. Chgo. Lyric Opera, 1995—; mem. Middlebury Coll. Arts Coun. Named Outstanding Young Citizen Chgo. Jaycees, 1976 Fellow: ABA Found.; mem.: ABA (coun. mem. antitrust sect. 1985—87), Am. Coll. Trial Lawyers, Chgo. Inn of Ct., Std. Club. Home: 232 E Walton St Chicago IL 60611-1507 also: 22 Bright Ln Wilsall MT 59086-9432 Office: 401 N Michigan Ave Chicago IL 60611-4255 E-mail: lfreemanjr@ffspc.com.

FREEMAN, LEONARD MURRAY, radiologist, nuclear medicine physician, educator; b. N.Y.C., Apr. 20, 1937; s. Joseph and Tillie (Krutman) F.; m. Marlene Carolyn Held, Apr. 28, 1967; children: Eric Lawrence, David Robert, Joy Esther. BA, N.Y. U., 1957; MD, Chgo. Med. Sch., 1961. Diplomate: Am. Bd. Radiology, Am. Bd. Nuclear Medicine. Intern Beth Israel Hosp. and Med. Center, N.Y.C., 1961-62; resident in radiology Bronx Municipal Hosp. Center, 1962-65; mem. staff Albert Einstein Coll. Medicine, N.Y.C., 1965—; co-dir. div. nuclear medicine Jacobi Med. Ctr., N.Y.C., 1965-83; dir. nuclear medicine Montefiore Med. Center, N.Y.C., 1976—, attending radiologist, 1977—; cons. nuclear medicine USPHS Hosp., S.I., N.Y., 1967-82, St. Barnabas Hosp., Bronx, 1967—, Beth Israel Hosp. and Med. Center, 1974—, Maimonides Hosp. and Med. Center, 1974-99, Bklyn. VA Hosp., 1984—; asst. instr. radiology Albert Einstein Coll. Medicine, Bronx, 1964-65, instr., 1965-67, asst. prof., 1967-72, assoc. prof., 1972-77, prof., 1977—, prof. nuclear medicine, 1983—, vice chmn. dept. nuclear medicine, 1987—. Mem. adv. com. nuclear medicine program Brookhaven Nat. Labs., Upton, N.Y., 1972-82; examiner nuclear medicine Am. Bd. Radiology. Author: Clinical Scintillation Scanning, 1969, Clinical Scintillation Imaging, 1975, Freeman and Johnson's Clinical Radionuclide Imaging, 1984; co-editor Seminars in Nuclear Medicine, 1970—, Physicians Desk Reference for Radiology and Nuclear Medicine, 1971-80; reviewer Jour. Nuclear Medicine, 1972—; editor Nuclear Medicine Ann., 1980—, Current Concepts in Diagnostic Nuclear Medicine, 1983-87, Advances in Functional Neuroimaging, 1988-90; mem. editl. bd. European Jour. Nuclear Medicine, 1979—, Jour. Nuclear Medicine and Allied Scis., 1982-96, Nuclear Medicine Communications, 1986-2002, Quar. Jour. Nuclear Medicine, 1996—; contbr. numerous articles to jours., also book chpts. Fellow Am. Coll. Radiology, Am. Coll. Nuclear Physicians, N.Y. Acad. Medicine (chmn. sect. nuc. medicine 2000-02); mem. Soc. Nuclear Medicine (gov. local chpt. 1973—, nat. trustee 1973-77, nat. v.p. 1977-78, nat. pres. 1979-80, chmn. pub. rels. com. 1981-91, chmn. correlative imaging coun. 1982-84, chmn. awards com. 1983-86, Disting. Edn. award 1993, Berson-Yallow award Greater N.Y. chpt. 1997), Radiol. Soc. N.Am., Soc. Gastrointestinal Radiologists, N.Y. State Med. Soc., New York County Med. Soc., Pan Am. Med. Assn. (hon. life), European Assn. Nuclear Medicine, L.I. Soc. Nuclear Med. Technologists (hon. life), Alpha Omega Alpha (hon.). Home: 50 Sutton Pl S New York NY 10022-4167 Office: 111 E 210th St Bronx NY 10467-2401 E-mail: lfreeman@montefiore.org.

FREEMAN, LESLIE GORDON, anthropologist, educator; b. Warsaw, N.Y., Sept. 9, 1935; s. Leslie Gordon and Theresa Rosalie (Stanbro) F.; m. Susan Tax, Mar. 20, 1964; 1 child, Sarah Elisabeth. AB, U. Chgo., 1954, AM, 1961, PhD, 1964. Asst. prof. anthropology Tulane U., 1964-65; asst. prof. U. Chgo., 1965-70, assoc. prof., 1970-76, prof., 1976-2000, prof. emeritus, 2000—; pres. Inst. Prehistoric Investigations, Chgo., 1983—2001. Rsch. assoc. Mont. State U., Bozeman, 1992—. Author (with J. Gonzalez): Cueva Morin, 2 vols., 1971, 1973, Vida y Muerte en Cueva Morin, 1978, Le Paleolithique Inferieur et Moyen en Espagne, 1998, La Grotte d'Altamira, 2001; editor: Views of the Past, 1978; editor: (with Sol Tax) Horizons of Anthropology, 1976; editor: (with others) Altamira Revisited, 1987, Beato de Liebana, 1995, Estudio del Manuscrito del Apocalipsis de San Juan, Beato de Liebana de San Miguel de Escalada, 2000. Corporator Internat. Inst. Spain. With U.S. Army, 1957-59. Recipient Silver Plaque Provincial Deputation of Santander, Spain, 1973 Fellow AAAS, Am. Anthropol. Assn., Royal Anthropol. Inst.; mem. Reial Academia Catalana de Belles Arts de Sant Jordi Barcelona (corr.), Reial Academia Catalana de Bones Lletres Barcelona (corr.), Chgo. Acad. Scis. (trustee, 2d v.p. 1981-83). Office: U Chgo Dept Anthropology Haskell Hall M-306 Chicago IL 60637 Home: PO Box 369 Whitehall MT 59759

FREEMAN, LEWIS BERNARD, forensic accountant, lawyer; b. Cortland, N.Y., May 4, 1949; s. Lawrence Freeman and Doris (Katzmen) Gold.; m. Eddi Ann R. Freeman, Nov. 26, 1976; children: Jaron, Abigail. BBA, U. Miami, Coral Gables, 1971; JD, 1974. Bar: Fla. Pres. Freeman & Ptnrs., Miami, 1992—; CPA Freeman, Dawson & Rosenbaum, CPAs, Miami, 1992—. Pres. Epilepsy Found. Fla., 1990-94; bd. mem. U. Miami Law Sch. Alumni, Coral Gables, 1990-98, Miami Children's Mus., 1994-97; com. Fla. Bar on CPA's, Talahassee, 1997. Named Humanitarian of Yr. EPIL Found. of Fla., Miami, 1996, Outstanding Alumnus of Yr., U. Miami, 1994, Outstanding Spkr. of Yr. Fla. Inst. CPAs, Tallahassee, 1982. Democrat. Jewish. Office: Lewis B Freeman & Ptnrs 2675 S Bayshore Dr Coconut Grove FL 33133-5232

FREEMAN, LINDA MARIE, consultant and technical writing company executive; b. Kansas City, Mo., Aug. 28, 1949; d. Harry William and Hulda Marie Peterson; m. Roger Donald Freeman, June 19, 1971; children: Christopher, Angela. BA, Macalester Coll., 1971. Exec. sec. Gen. Mills, Mpls., 1971-72; ind. cons. Mary Kay Cosmetics, St. Paul, Duluth, Minn., 1975-80; owner, founder Iron Range Computer Svcs., Hibbing, Minn., 1980-94; systems analyst Jasper Engring., Hibbing, 1982-83; instr. computer sci. Hibbing Tech. Coll., 1988-89; owner, founder M.P. Resources, Hibbing, 1994—; Caring Ministries coord. Wesley United Meth. Ch., Hibbing, 1999—2001; exec. dir. Range Helping Hands, Inc., 2002—. Chmn. Hibbing Park Bd., 1980-82, adv. bd. Hibbing Tech. Coll., 1989-91. Author: poetry, 1989-94; editor, writer (newsletters) Seasoned Saints Newsletter, 1994-99, Towards More Productivity, 1994. Del. to regional and state convs. Rep. Orgn., Minn., 1980-96; bd. dirs. Salolampi Found.; vol. Dir. of Ministries, Seasoned Saints Ministry. Recipient Pres. award Hibbing C. of C, 1984, Speech Contest award, Outstanding Toastmaster award Toastmasters Hibbing, 1986. Avocations: skiing, boating, fishing, hiking, mountain biking. Office: Range Helping Hands Inc Hibbing MN 55746

FREEMAN, LINTON CLARKE, sociology educator; b. Chgo., July 4, 1927; s. Willis and Kathryn Clarke (Kieffer) F.; m. Sue Carole Feinberg, Aug. 2, 1958; children: Stacey Elizabeth Vanhanswyk, Michael Andrew. BA, Roosevelt U., Chgo., 1952; MA, U. Hawaii, 1953; PhD, Northwestern U., 1956. Asst. prof., then assoc. prof. sociology Syracuse (N.Y.) U., 1956-67; prof. sociology and computer sci. U. Pitts., 1967-69; prof. sociology and info. sci. U. Hawaii, 1969-72; Lucy G. Moses distinguished prof. sociology Lehigh U., Bethlehem, Pa., 1973-79; prof. Sch. Social Scis., U. Calif., Irvine, 1979—, dean, 1979-82; Killam sr. lectr. sociology and anthropology Dalhousie U., Halifax, N.S., Can., 1972; directeur d'Etudes Associé Maison des Sciences de l'Homme, Paris, 1991. Ward supr. Onondaga County (N.Y.) Bd. Suprs., 1966-68 Author: Elementary Applied Statistics, 1965, Patterns of Local Community Leadership, 1968; co-author: Residential Segregation Patterns, 1970; editor: Social Networks; contbr. to profl. jours. Served with USNR, 1944-46. Home: 2705 Temple Hills Dr Laguna Beach CA 92651-2037 Office: U Calif Sch Social Scis Irvine CA 92697-1500 E-mail: lin@aris.ss.uci.edu.

FREEMAN, LOUIS S. lawyer; b. Cin., Apr. 21, 1940; s. Emanuel and Sadye (Harris) F.; m. Diane Ruth Edson, Jan. 28, 1967; children: Matthew E., James H., Jill E. BBA, U. Cin., 1963; JD, Harvard U., 1966; LLM in Taxation, NYU, 1972. Bar: Ohio 1966, N.Y. 1968, Ill. 1975. CPA. Mem. staff Coopers & Lybrand, N.Y.C., 1966-68; assoc. Mudge, Rose, Guthrie & Alexander, N.Y.C., 1968-74, Sonnenschein Nath & Rosenthal, Chgo., 1974-76, ptnr., 1976-97, Skadden, Arps, Slate, Meagher & Flom, Chgo., 1997—. Adj. prof. of taxation Ill. Inst. Tech., Chgo.-Kent Coll. of Law Grads. Program in Taxation, 1985-89 Mem. bds. of contbg. editors Jour. Corp. Taxation, Jour. Real Estate Taxation, Jour. Taxation of Investments; bd. advisors the M&A Tax Report, Jour. Corp. Taxation; also author articles. Fellow Am. Coll. Tax Counsel; mem. ABA (tax sect. com. on corp. tax), Chgo. Bar Assn., (chmn. exec. com. of fed. tax com. 1986-87), N.Y. Sate Bar Assn. (tax sect. exec. com. 1990-92), Am. Law Inst. (tax adv. group subchpt. C. Fed. Income Tax Project), Met. Club of Chgo. Office: Skadden Arps Slate Meagher & Flom 333 W Wacker Dr Chicago IL 60606-1220 E-mail: LFreeman@skadden.com.

FREEMAN, MARJORIE KLER, interior designer; b. Phila., June 30, 1929; d. Joseph H. and Elizabeth VanHoesen (Vaughan) Kler; m. John Martin Hale, Dec. 26, 1953 (div. 1974); children: John Marshall, David Maclain; m. Bruce George Freeman, Dec. 17, 1983. Cert. in interior design, Pratt Inst., 1951, BFA, 1952; MA, U. Mich., 1954. Dir. design studio Handicraft Furniture Co., Ann Arbor, Mich., 1953-63; design cons. dorms U. Mich., Ann Arbor, 1955-62; design cons. U. Del., Newark, 1963-67; bldg. and maint. designer and studio mgr. Vallery Miller Interiors, Woodland Hills, Calif., 1969-74; pres. Marjorie Kler Interiors Inc., Princeton, N.J., 1980—. Design cons. East Jersey Olde Towne, Inc., Piscataway, 1974. Author/editor cookbooks: Educated Palate, 1969, Grand Slam, 1990, Indian Queen Tavern, 1991. Pres. Bucceleuch Mansion Found., New Brunswick, 1983—; past pres., v.p. East Jersey Olde Towne, Inc., 1983—90, 1991—, treas., 1992—; pres. Rantan-Millstore Heritage Alliance; bd. dirs. Rec. for the Blind and Delexica, NJ. Mem. DAR (rec. sec., Jersey Blue chpt.), Penn Hall Alumnae Assn. (pres., bd. dirs. 1989—), Trowel Club New Brunswick (pres. 1993, 99—), Daus. of Cin., Soc. Daus of Holland Dames. Republican. Presbyterian. Avocations: bridge, flower arranging. Home and Office: 6 Mimosa Ct Princeton NJ 08540-9423 Fax: 732-324-2103.

FREEMAN, MARJORIE SCHAEFER, mathematician, educator; b. Chevy Chase, Md., Sept. 23, 1924; d. Herbert Stanley and Helen (Hummer) Schaefer; m. John C. Freeman, June 14, 1947; children: John C. III, Walter H., Jill F. Hasling, Cathryn F. Disch, Helen, Paul D. AB, Randolph-Macon Womans Coll., 1946; MS, Brown U, 1949; postgrad., U. Houston, 1973-75. Computer asst. Inst. for Advanced Study, Princeton, NJ, 1949-50; rsch. asst. Tex. A&M Rsch. Found., College Station, 1954-55; instr. Tex. A&M U., College Station, 1955; cons. Gulf Cons., Houston, 1955-56; instr. South Tex. Jr. Coll., Houston, 1961-74; asst. prof. U. Houston-Downtown, 1974-90, asst. prof. emeritus, 1990—. Sys. analyst, programmer TERA, Inc., Houston, 1985; cons. Inst. Storm Rsch., Houston, 1979—86; adv. bd. Weather Rsch. Ctr., Houston, 1987—. Mem.: Math. Assn. Am., S.W. Tracking Assn., Alamo Area Chesapeake

Bay Retriever Club, Am. Chesapeake Club, S. Tex. Obedience Club. Avocations: dog training, camping, crafts. Home: 4404 Mount Vernon St Houston TX 77006-5814 E-mail: jfreeman9@houston.rr.com.

FREEMAN, MARY ANNA, librarian; b. July 24, 1943; d. Wylie Lee and Thelma Anna (Elam) Johnson; m. Charles Edward Freeman, Jr., Aug. 26, 1963; children: Charles Edward III, Juliana Elizabeth, Mark Adrian, Lee Agustin. BS, Abilene Christian U., 1963; MLS, Tex. Woman's U., 1981. Tchr. 4th grade Las Cruces (N.Mex.) Pub. Sch., 1063-64, tchr. 2d grade, 1964-67; head audiovisual dept. El Paso (Tex.) Pub. Libr., 1972; head libr. Guillen Jr. H.S., El Paso, 1974-95; asst. libr. Andress H.S., El Paso, 1995-96, head libr., 1996—2003. Treas. Guillen PTA, El Paso, 1983-85, 86-89; mem. partnership in edn. liaison, 1986-90; Westside police area rep. El Paso Police Dept., 1997-2000; mem. Andress Campus Improvement Team, 2000-03. Mem. ALA, Tex. Libr. Assn. Office: Andress HS 5400 Sun Valley Dr El Paso TX 79924-3418

FREEMAN, MARYANN, poet, songwriter; b. Bklyn., Aug. 7, 1950; d. Henry and Albertha Elizabeth (Rivers) Fields; m. Daniel Freeman, Sept. 2, 1972; children: Daniel, Yolanda, Tonya, Danny, Jarrel, Jermaine. Student, Barbizon Sch. Modeling, 1976, Lincoln Sch. Nursing, 1977; diploma, Crown Bus. Inst., 1982. Poet, songwriter N.C.A. Recording Col, Coltrain Record Co., Nashville, 1990; prin., owner Empire Gen. Contracting. Contbr. poems to various anthologies. Recipient Outstanding Achievement in Poetry award Nat. Libr. Poetry, 1993. Mem. Smithsonian Instn., Internat. Soc. Poets (charter). Home: 218 Princeton St Hempstead NY 11550-2725 E-mail: freemanmaryann@aol.com.

FREEMAN, MAYNARD LLOYD, nuclear medicine physician, researcher; b. Chgo., June 19, 1950; s. Leonard Lawrence and Jerry Freeman; m. Carol Ilene Fox-Freeman, June 19, 1978; 1 child, Leland. MD, Rush Med. Coll., 1975. Diplomate Am. Bd. Nuc. Medicine. Editor: Am. Jour. Physiologic Imaging, 1985.

FREEMAN, MEREDITH NORWIN, former college president, education educator; b. Elvins, Mo., June 1, 1920; s. William J. and Zelpha (McGuire) F.; m. Helen Lorene Larkin, Aug. 3, 1941 (dec. Nov. 1970); children: James Michael, Judith Ann; m. Joyce Mary Liebsch, Oct. 23, 1971; stepchildren: Mary Ann, Dawn Joy. BS, Southeast Mo. State Coll., Cape Girardeau, 1949; MEd, U. Mo., 1951, EdD, 1955. Rural sch. tchr., St. Francis County, Mo., 1940-41; elementary tchr., also prin. New Haven, Mo., 1941-42, 46-50; high sch. sci. tchr., prin., 1947-50; supt. schs., 1951-52, New Haven, Mo., 1952-54; tchr. chemistry and physics Hickman High Sch., Columbia, Mo., 1954-55; assoc. prof. edn. Fort Hays State Coll., Kans., 1955-57; dir. spl. services, prof. edn. Mankato (Minn.) State U., 1957-64, asst. acad. dean, 1964-66, academic dean, 1966-67; pres. Black Hills State U., Spearfish, S.D., 1967-76, Concord Coll., Athens, W.Va., 1976-85; regents prof. edn. W.Va. Coll. Grad. Studies, Institute, 1985-90, ret., 1990. Mem. exec. com. Minn. Assn. Colls., 1964-67; sec. S.D. Council Coll. and Univ. Pres.'s, 1967-68, chmn., 1969-70, 74-75; mem. S.D. Indian Scholarships Com., 1967-76; pres. emeritus Black Hills State Coll., 1976, Concord Coll., 1985. Mem. exec. com. Black Hills Area Council Boy Scouts Am., 1966-76; mem. S.D. Gov.'s Scholarship Com., 1970-76, mem. exec. com. W.Va. Assn. Coll. Pres.'s; mem. W.Va. Adv. Council on Profl. Personnel, 1976-82; bd. dirs. Appalachia Regional Lab., 1981-85, Princeton Community Hosp. Served to sgt. U.S. Army, 1942-46, ETO. Mem. NEA, Am. Assn. Sch. Adminstrs., Am. Assn. State Colls. and Univs. (S.D. rep. 1971-75, W.Va. rep. 1981-83), Princeton C. of C. (dir.), Phi Delta Kappa (past faculty sponsor Epsilon Iota chpt.), Sigma Tau Gamma. Lodges: Masons, Rotary. Republican. Methodist. Avocations: painting, wood sculpture, hunting, fishing, traveling.

FREEMAN, MILTON MALCOLM ROLAND, anthropology educator; b. London, Apr. 23, 1934; came to Can., 1958; s. Louis and Fay (Bomberg) F.; m. Mini Christina Aodla; children: Graham, Elaine, Malcolm. BS, Reading U., Eng., 1958; postgrad., U. Coll., London, 1962-64; PhD, McGill U., 1965. Research scientist No. Affairs Dept., Ottawa, Ont., Can., 1965-67; asst. prof. Meml. U., St. John's, Nfld., Can., 1967-71, assoc. prof., 1971-72; dir. Inuit Land Use Study, Hamilton, Ont., 1973-75; prof. anthropology McMaster U., Hamilton, 1976-81; Henry Marshall Tory prof. U. Alta., Edmonton, Canada, 1982-99, prof. emeritus, 1999—, adj. prof. East Asian studies, 1993—99. Adj. prof. environ. studies U. Waterloo, Ont., 1977-81; sr. sci. advisor Indian and No. Affairs, Ottawa, 1979-81; sr. rsch. scholar Can. Circumpolar Inst., U. Alta., 1990—; McLean prof. Trent U., Peterborough, Can., 1995; chmn. UNESCO-MAB No. Sci. Network, 1983-88. Author: People Pollution, 1974, Cultural Anthropology of Whaling, 1989, Recovering Rights, 1992, Inuit, Whaling, and Sustainability, 1998; editor: Inuit Land Use and Occupancy Report, 1976, Procs. Internat. Symposium on Renewable Resources and the Economy of the North, 1981, Japanese Small-type Coastal Whaling, 1988, Endangered Peoples of the Arctic, 2000; co-editor: Adaptive Management of Marine Resources in the Pacific, 1991, Elephants and Whales: Resources for Whom?, 1994. Bd. dirs. Sci. Inst. N.W.T., 1985-87; chmn. adv. bd. Can. Circumpolar Inst., 1990-2001; chmn. Man-Environ. Commn., Internat. Union Anthrop. and Ethnol. Scis., 1977-82. Fellow: Soc. Applied Anthropology Can. (pres. 1984—85), Soc. Applied Anthropology, Arctic Inst. N.Am., Am. Anthropol. Assn. Home: 103-10520 80th Ave Edmonton AB Canada T6E 1V3 Office: U Alta Can Circumpolar Inst Edmonton AB Canada T6G 0H1 E-mail: milton.freeman@ualberta.ca.

FREEMAN, MORGAN, actor; b. Memphis, 1937; s. Grafton Curtis and Mayme Edna (Revere) F.; m. Jeanette Adair Bradshaw, Oct. 22, 1967 (div. 1979); m. Myrna Colley-Lee, June 16, 1984; children: Alphonse, Saifoulaye, Deena, Morgana. Student, L.A. City Coll. Actor: (stage prodns.) Niggerlover (debut), 1967, Hello Dolly (Broadway), 1967, Jungle of Cities, 1969, The Recruiting Officer, 1969, Scuba-Duba, 1969, Purlie (ANTA Theatre, N.Y.C.), 1970, Black Visions, 1972, Sisyphus and the Blue-Eyed Cyclops, 1975, Cockfight, 1977, Mighty Gents, 1978 (Clarence Derwent award, Drama Desk award, Tony award nomination), White Pelicans, 1978, Coriolanus, also Julius (N.Y. Shakespeare Festival), 1979, Mother Courage and Her Children, 1980, Othello, also All's Well That Ends Well (both Dallas Shakespeare Festival), 1982, Buck, 1983, Medea and the Doll, 1984, The Gospel at Colonus (Obie awards), Driving Miss Daisy, 1987, (feature films) Who Says I Can't Ride a Rainbow, 1971, Brubaker, 1980, Eyewitness, 1980, Harry and Son, 1983, Teachers, 1984, Street Smart, 1987 (Acad. award nomination), Clean and Sober, 1988, Lean On Me, 1989, Johnny Handsome, 1989, Driving Miss Daisy (Golden Globe award, Acad. award nomination), 1989, Glory, 1989, The Bonfire of the Vanities, 1990, Robin Hood, 1991, Unforgiven, 1992, The Shawshank Redemption, 1994, Outbreak, 1995, Seven, 1995, Chain Reaction, 1996, Moll Flanders, 1996, Deep Impact 1997, Kiss The Girls, 1997, The Long Way Home, 1996, Hard Rain, 1998, Water Damage, 1999, Under Suspicion, 1999, Mutiny, 1999, Nurse Betty, 2000, Along Came a Spider, 2001, High Crimes, 2002, The Sum of All Fears, 2002, Levity, 2003, Dreamcatcher, 2003, Bruce Almighty, 2003; dir. Bopha!, 1993; regular cast (TV show) The Electric Company; TV films include: Hollow Image, 1979, Attica, 1980, The Marva Collins Story, 1981, The Atlanta Child Murders, 1985, Resting Place, 1986, Flight for Life, 1987, Clinton and Nadine (Showtime TV), 1988. With USAF, 1955-59. Office: William Morris Agency 2472 Broadway #227 New York NY 10025-7449*

FREEMAN, MYRA JESSIE, retired farm owner, writer; b. Lake Charles, La., Aug. 19, 1939; d. William Lester and Mary Louise (Martin) Freeman; m. Billy Lee Tubb, 1958 (div.); 1 child, Victoria Leigh Tubb; m. Frank B. Watts, Dec. 22, 1978 (div. 1992). Officer Sufficient Data Computer Software Svcs. Co., Greenville, SC, 1985-92; owner, operator Animal Crackers Llamas, Anderson, SC, 1985-92, Toccoa, Ga., 1992—; retired. Author: Heat Stress in Llamas, 1988, rev. edit., 1994, First Air for Barn, 1988; regular columnist Llama Banner; contbr. numerous articles to profl. jours. Mem. Sunshine States Llama Assn. (pres. 1987-92), Llama Assn. N.Am., Internat. Llama Assn. (Pushmi-Pullyu awards), Greater Appalachian Llama Assn. Avocations: travel, social work. Home: 2417 Emerald Lake Dr Sun City Center FL 33573-3802

FREEMAN, MYRNA FAYE, county schools official; b. Danville, Ill., Oct. 30, 1939; d. Thomas Gene and Dorothy Olive (Chodera) F.; m. Lonnie Lee Choate, Aug. 16, 1959 (div. 1987); children: Leslie Rene, Gregory Lonn. BA in Pub. Adminstrn., San Diego State U., 1977, MA in Edn. Adminstrn., 1987. Employee benefits mgr. City of San Diego, 1974-84; dir. San Diego County Office Edn., San Diego, 1984—. Instr. Sch. Bus. Mgrs. Acad., Assn. Calif. Sch. Adminstrs., 1985—, Ins. Edn. Assn., Cert. Employee Benefits Specialist course, 1991—. Author: Adm. Impact of Implement Leg. 1987; Author: Article Risk Mgmt.-Emp. Benefits 1985, Risk Mgmt.-Workers' Comp. 1986, Risk Mgmt.-Loss Control 1986. Mem. Kaiser Consumer Coun., 1977-84, pres., 1979-80; bd. dirs. S.D. County Affirmative Action Adv. Bd., 1985; mem. adv. com. Vista Health Plan Pub. Policy, 1994—; adv. coun. Kaiser On-the-Job, 1994—. Recipient Appreciation award COMBO-Cultural Arts of San Diego 1977. Mem. Risk Ins. Mgmt. Soc. (pres. San Diego chpt. 1988), Calif. Assn. Sch. Bus. Ofcls. (chmn. risk mgmt. R&D comm. 1987-88), San Diego Group Ins. Claims Coun. (pres. 1987), S.D. Employers Health Cost Coalition (vice-chmn. 1987), Calif. Women in Govt. (bd. dirs. 1983-84), Calif. Assn. of Joint Powers Authority, Pub. Agys. Risk Mgmt. Assn., Pub. Risk Ins. Mgmt. Assn., Internat. Found. Employee Benefits Plans, San Diego Workers' Compensation Forum, Sigma Kappa, Phi Kappa Phi, Internat. Platform Assn Republican. Methodist. Home: 1545 Northrim Ct # 272 San Diego CA 92111-7341 Office: San Diego County Office Edn 6401 Linda Vista Rd Rm 505 San Diego CA 92111-7319 Fax: 858-569-5086. E-mail: ffreeman@sdcoc.k12.ca.us.

FREEMAN, NEAL BLACKWELL, communications corporation executive; b. N.Y.C., July 5, 1940; s. Malcolm T. and Virginia (Neal) F.; m. Jane Louise Metze, Mar. 19, 1966; children: Malcolm Trowbridge II, James Bragdon, Kathryn R. BA magna cum laude, Yale U., 1962. Asst. to pres. Washington Star Syndicate, 1965-66; assoc. producer TV show Firing Line, 1966-67; exec. editor King Features Syndicate, N.Y.C., 1968-73; v.p., editor King Features div. Hearst Corp., 1973-76; pres. Jefferson Communications, Inc., 1976-86; chmn. bd., chief exec. officer Blackwell Corp., 1982—; dir. Intelsat, Ltd. Exec. prodr. Pub. TV; bd. dirs. Comsat Corp., BTG, Inc., Nat. Rev., Denver Nuggets Profl. Basketball Club, Colo. Avalanche Profl. Hockey Club, GRC Internat.; bd. visitors Inst. on Polit. Journ alism, Georgetown U.; chmn. Washington Selection Panel Pres.'s Commn. on White House Fellows, 1998-2002, Found. Mgmt. Inst., 2000—; chmn. of agts. Yale Alumni Fund; bd. dirs. Corp. for Pub. Broadcasting, 1972-75; bd. dirs., vice-chmn. Ethics and Pub. Policy Ctr. Bd. dirs. Wolf Trap Found., 1984-90. Mem. Colony Found., Cosmos Club (Washington), Yale Club (N.Y.C.), York Country Club (Maine), Nat. Press Club, Sigma Delta Chi. Office: The Blackwell Corp PO Box 2169 Vienna VA 22183-2169

FREEMAN, NEIL, accounting and computer consulting firm executive; b. Reading, Pa., Dec. 27, 1948; s. Leroy Harold and Audrey Todd (Dornhecker) F.; m. Pamela Hong, May 30, 2000. BS, Albright Coll., 1979; MS, Kennedy-Western U., 1987, PhD, 1988. Cert. systems profl., data processing specialist, info. system security profl. Acct. Jack W. Long & Co., Mt. Penn, Pa., 1977-78; comptroller G.P.C., Inc., Bowmansville, Pa., 1978-79; owner Neil Freeman Cons., Bowmansville, 1980-81; program mgr., systems cons. Application Systems, Honolulu, 1981-82; instr. Chaminade U., Honolulu, 1983-96; owner Neil Freeman Cons., Kaneohe, Hawaii, 1982-96, Grand Junction, Colo., 1996—. Instr. Mesa State Coll., Grand Junction, 1997—. Author: (computer software) NFC Property Management, 1984, NFC Mailing List, 1984; (book) Learning Dibol, 1984. Served with USN, 1966-68, Vietnam. Mem. Nat. Assn. Accts., Am. Inst. Cert. Computer Profls., Assn. Systems Mgmt. Office: 1620 Canon Ave Grand Junction CO 81503

FREEMAN, PATRICIA ELIZABETH, library and education specialist; b. El Dorado, Ark., Nov. 30, 1924; d. Herbert A. and M. Elizabeth (Pryor) Harper; m. Jack Freeman, June 15, 1949; 3 children. BA, Centenary Coll., 1943; postgrad., Fine Arts Ctr., 1942-46, Art Students League, 1944-45; BSLS, La. State U., 1946; postgrad., Calif. State U., 1959-61, U. N.Mex., 1964-74; EdS, Peabody Coll., Vanderbilt U., 1975. Libr. U. Calif., Berkeley, 1946-47; libr. Albuquerque Pub. Schs., 1964-67, ind. sch. libr. media ctr. cons., 1967—. Painter lithographer; one-person show La. State Exhibit Bldg., 1948; author: Pathfinder: An Operational Guide for the School Librarian, 1975, Southeast Heights Neighborhoods of Albuquerque, 1993; compiler, editor: Elizabeth Pryor Harper's Twenty-One Southern Families, 1985; editor: SEHNA Gazette, 1988-93, N.Mex. AAUW, 1999—. Mem. task force Goals for Dallas-Environ., 1977-82; pres. Friends of Sch. Librs., Dallas, 1979-83; v.p., editor Southeast Heights Neighborhood Assn., 1988-93. With USAF, 1948-49. Honoree AAUW Edn. Found., 1979, 96; vol. award for outstanding service Dallas Ind. Sch. Dist., 1978; AAUW Pub. Service grantee 1980. Mem. ALA, AAUW (dir. Dallas 1976-82, Albuquerque 1983-85, 2003-, N.Mex. 1999—), LWV (sec. Dallas 1982-83, editor Albuquerque 1984-88), Nat. Trust Historic Preservation, Friends for the Pub. Libr., Colorado Springs Fine Arts Ctr., N.Mex. Symphony Guild, Alpha Xi Delta. Home: 612 Ridgecrest Dr SE Albuquerque NM 87108-3365

FREEMAN, PAULA S. social worker; b. Cullman, Ala., Nov. 9, 1969; d. Leon Douglas and Mary Sue Freeman. Student, Wallace State Coll.; BSW, Jacksonville State U., 1992; MSW, Ala. A&M U., 1997. Lic. social worker, Ala. Svc. social worker Dept. Human Resources, Anniston, Ala., 1992-96; clin. social worker intern Family Svcs. Ctr., Huntsville, Ala., 1996-97; family svc. worker Three Springs, Inc., Trenton, Ala., 1997-99; project dir. Auburn (Ala.) U., 1999—2002; trainer State Dept. Human Resources, 2002—. Vol. Hospice Caring House, Huntsville, 2001-, Children's Hosp., Birmingham, 1993—, Mt. Olive Ch. Food Bank, 1999, Habitat for Humanity, Anniston, 1995-96, USA Weekend's Make a Difference Day, Anniston, 1995. Named Foster Care Worker of Yr., Dept. Human Resources, 1995, Hon. Recognition award USA Weekend, 1995. Mem. NASW. Methodist. Avocations: exercise, travel, piano, family, running. Home: 3907 Harwood Ave SW Apt E28 Huntsville AL 35805-4463 Office: Madison County DHR 2206 Oakwood Ave Huntsville AL 35801

FREEMAN, PETER SUNDERLIN, textile executive; b. Bklyn., Apr. 23, 1944; s. Graydon Lavern and Ruth Crosby (Sunderlin) F.; m. Linda Raissa Blanco, Sept. 23, 1972; 1 child, Victoria Blanco. BS, Cornell U., 1966; MBA in Fin., Syracuse U., 1969; cert. acctg., NYU, 1979. CPA, Colo. New bus. devel. and product mgr. CBS Pub. Group, N.Y.C., 1970-73; sr. fin. analyst W.R. Grace Retail and Textiles, N.Y.C., 1973-75; dir. fin. analysis and reporting Grace Textiles, N.Y.C., 1975-79, divsn. controller, 1979—81; v.p. fin. Toyobo subs. Rosewood Fabrics, N.Y.C., 1981-85; v.p. fin. and adminstrn. Vitreous Internat. Trading Co., Inc., Great Neck, N.Y., 1986; corp. controller Liberty Fabrics, Inc., N.Y.C., 1986-92; cons. N.Y.C., 1993-95; v.p., fin. sec. Charles Samelson, Inc., N.,Y.C., 1995—. Served with U.S. Army, 1968-70, Vietnam. Mem. AICPA, Colo. Soc. CPA's, Cornell U. Lambda Alumni (pres. 1985-89, bd. dirs. 1982-96), Am. Life Fedn. (bd. dirs. 1997—, sec-treas. 2000—). Presbyterian. Avocations: sports, gardening. Home: 280 1st Ave Apt 5B New York NY 10009-1836 Office: Charles Samelson Inc 102 Madison Ave New York NY 10016-7417

FREEMAN, RALPH CARTER, investment banker, management consultant; b. La Grange, Ga., s. Ralph Carter and Alice (Cordell) F.; m. Carole Stephens, July 31, 1957 (div. 1977); children: Carter III, Allyson, Stephens, LeAnna; m. Nancy Lynn Brown, Apr. 8, 1977. BBA, Emory U., 1959. CPA, Mont.; cert. mgmt. cons.; real estate broker, Calif. From mem. staff to ptnr. Pannell Kerr Forster, Atlanta, Honolulu, 1959-72; mgmt. cons. Touche Ross & Co., Honolulu, Am. Samoa, Asia, South Pacific, 1972-75; pres. FP Industries, Inc., Hawaii, Mont., Ga., 1975-85, Janas Consulting, Huntsville, Ala., 1986-90; chmn. Janas Assocs. Investment Bankers and Mgmt. Cons., Pasadena, Calif., 1995—, Janas Assocs. Investment Bankers, Orange County, San Diego, Houston, 1999—. Founder Peoples Bank, LaGrange, Ga., 1966; founding investor Bank of Newnan, Ga., 1988, Profl. Bus. Bank, Pasadena, Calif., 2001—. Contbr. articles to profl. jours. and nat. trade mags. Mem. Inst. Mgmt. Cons. (cert., bd. dirs., treas. 1999-2000), Cash Flow Assn., All Cities Resource Group, Turnaround Mgmt. Assn., Sigma Alpha Epsilon. Avocations: fishing, tennis, camping. E-mail: rcf@janascorp.com.

FREEMAN, RICHARD DEAN, new business start-up service company executive; b. Rushville, Ind., Nov. 27, 1928; s. Verne Crawford and Mary Phyllis (Dean) F.; m. Mary Jane Barkman, Aug. 21, 1950; children: Debra Dean, Phyllis Lynn, Richard Paul, Tom Crawford. BS in Aero. Engring., BS in Naval Sci. and Tactics, Purdue U., 1950, MS in Indsl. Mgmt., 1954. Supr. indsl. engring. Gen. Motors Corp., Warren, Ohio, 1954-58; prodn. mgr. Ramo Wooldridge div. TRW Corp., Denver, 1958-62; mgr. missile programs Hughes Aircraft Co., Los Angeles, 1962-68; v.p. E Systems Inc., Dallas, 1968-72, Rockwell Internat. Co., Los Angeles, 1972-74; pres. Internat. Pacific Co., Newport Beach, Calif., 1974—. Sr. lectr. West Coast U., L.A., 1974-78; sec. proteus Corp., Newport Beach, 1978-80; chmn. Tech. Assocs. Corp., Newport Beach, 1984-85; chief exec. officer Equicenters, Inc., Irvine, 1988—. Author: Economation Approaches, 1958, Equator, 1984 (also film); prod. documentary film Zeros of the Pacific, 1979. Cubmaster, scoutmaster, dist. chmn. Boy Scouts Am., various locations, 1966-76; mem. librs. devel. adv. com. Purdue U., 1992; mem. restoration adv. bd. Marine Corps Air Sta., Tustin, 1994; pres. bd. trustees, elder Presbyn. Ch. Capt. USMC, 1946-58, Korea. Named Man of Yr., Sigma Alpha Tau, West Lafayette, Ind., 1971; recipient Disting. Engring. Alumnus award Purdue U., 1973, Outstanding Aerospace Engr. award Purdue U. Sch. Aeronautics and Astronautics, 1999. Mem. Am. Inst. Indsl. Engrs., Purdue U. Alumni Assn., Nat. Eagle Scout Assn. (pres. 1998), Exch. Club of Newport Harbor (pres. 1998-99), CA/NV Dist. Exch. Club (pres. 2001-2002, award 2002), Kappa Sigma (inducted into Hall of Fame 1997). Lodges: Masons (consistory 32 degree v.p.). Republican. Avocation: exploration for amelia earhart's missing aircraft. Home: 3910 Topside Ln Corona Del Mar CA 92625-1628 E-mail: interpac2000@yahoo.com.

FREEMAN, RICHARD LYONS, lawyer; b. Chgo., Oct. 29, 1932; s. Reuben L. and Bernice (Green) F.; m. Mary Leopold, May 2, 1959; children: Thomas R., Richard Lyons. AB cum laude, Harvard U., 1954; LLB, Yale U., 1957. Bar: Ill. 1958. Assoc. Friedman, Zoline & Rosenfield, Chgo., 1958-60; investment analyst Robert J. Levy & Co., Chgo., 1960-62; assoc. Schwartz & Freeman, Chgo., 1962-68, ptnr., 1968-91, of counsel, 1991—2001, Michael Best & Friedrich L.L.C., Chgo., 2001—. Bd. dirs. Chgo. Hearing Soc., pres., 1972-74. Served with Air N.G., 1957-63. Fellow Am. Coll. Trust and Estate Counsel; mem. ABA, Chgo. Bar Assn., Ill. Bar Assn., Lake Shore Country Club (Glencoe, Ill.). Office: Suite 1900 401 N Michigan Ave Chicago IL 60611-4274 E-mail: rundick@aol.com.

FREEMAN, RICHARD MERRELL, lawyer, corporate director; b. Crawfordsville, Ind., July 2, 1921; s. F. Rider and Ruth (Merrell) F.; m. Joanne Spears, Nov. 26, 1943; children: Randy, Mark, Candy, Marcia. AB, Wabash (Ind.) Coll., 1943; LLB, Columbia U., 1948. Bar: Tenn. 1948, Ill. 1957. Atty. TVA, Knoxville, 1948-57, dir., 1978-86; partner firm Belnap, Spencer, Hardy & Freeman, Chgo., 1957-67; v.p. law Chgo. & Northwestern Transp. Co., Chgo., 1967-78, also dir., voting trustee. Exec. com. Fla. West Coast Symphony; bd. dirs. TVA, 1978-86. With USNR, 1943-46. Mem.: Phi Beta Kappa. Democrat. Mem. Community Ch. Home: 775 Longboat Club Rd #303 Longboat Key FL 34228

FREEMAN, ROBERT SCHOFIELD, musicologist, educator, pianist; b. Rochester, N.Y., Aug. 26, 1935; s. Henry Schofield and Florence Margaret (Knope) F.; m. Carol Jean Morgan, Dec. 10, 1976; children: John Frederick, Elizabeth Poon, Scott Alan Henry. AB summa cum laude, Harvard U., 1957, MFA, Princeton U., 1960, PhD, 1967; MusD (hon.), Hamilton Coll., 1988. instr., asst. prof. Princeton U., 1963-68; asst. prof., assoc. prof. MIT, 1968-73; dir., prof. musicology Eastman Sch. Music, U. Rochester, 1972-96; pres. New England Conservatory, Boston, 1996-99; dean, Effie Marie Cain regents chair in fine arts Coll. Fine Arts U. Tex., Austin, 1999—. Chmn. nat. adv. bd. Ctr. for Black Music Research, Chgo., 1985-90; cons. for various Am. U.; vis. assoc. prof. Harvard U., 1972. Author: Opera Without Drama, 1981; contbr. articles to profl. jours. Trustee Conductors' Guild, China. Found. for Edn. and Culture. Harvard Sheldon fellow, 1958, Woodrow Wilson Found. fellow, 1959, Martha Baird Rockefeller Fund fellow, 1963, Fulbright fellow, 1960-62; recipient Civic medal Rochester C. of C., 1982. Mem. Am. Musicol. Soc. (chair New Eng. chpt. 1970-72, coun. mem. 1973-76), Coll. Music Soc. (coun. mem. 1973-76), Neue Bach Gesellschaft (chmn. 1977-82), Nat. Assn. Schs. Music (grad. commn. 1981-85), Harvard Music Assn., Headliner's Club of Austin, Princeton Club of N.Y., U. Tex. Club. Avocations: baseball, reading, animal welfare. Office: Coll Fine Arts U Tex at Austin Austin TX 78712 E-mail: RF3519@aol.com.

FREEMAN, ROSE BRODEUR, retired nursing educator; b. Penacook, N.H., Feb. 24, 1918; d. Felix and Patronyne Antoinette (Lavoie) Brodeur; m. James Francis Freeman, Nov. 26, 1942 (dec. 1990). RN, Sacred Heart Hosp., Manchester, N.H., 1938; BSN summa cum laude, St. Anselm Coll., Manchester, N.H., 1963; MS, Boston U., 1965. Pvt. duty/gen. hosp. duty/maternity/supr. nurse various hosps., N.H./Conn., 1938-46; office nurse gen. practitioners and pediatricians, Concord/Penacook, N.H., 1946-60; gen. and psychiatric hosp. nurse, part-time Concord Hosp., 1961-64; mem. faculty St. Anselm Coll., 1965-85, prof. nursing emeritus, 1985—. Pres. N.H. Nurses Assn., Concord, 1967-69, pres. Dist. 7, 1950; past bd. mem. other state and dist. nurses assns. Vol. Soc. Protection N.H. Forests, Concord, 1988—, Income Tax Assistance/Tax Counseling Elderly, 1986-2000, N.H. Hist. Soc., 2000—, income tax asst. IRS, Washington, 1986-2000; with ARC, 1954—, N.H. Hist. Soc., 1990—, Penacook, N.H. Hist. Soc., 1998—; pres. VFW Aux., Penacook, 1950. Project grantee St. Anselm Coll.-USPHS, 1972-77. Mem. Am. Assn. Ret. Persons (vol. income tax asst. 1986-2000), Am.-Can. Geneal. Soc. (charter), Assn. Canado-Ams., Women's Club of Penacook, Parish Group of Penacook, Sigma Theta Tau. Roman Catholic. Avocations: genealogy, gardening, herbs, senior center activities, swimming. Home: 19 Abbott Rd Concord NH 03303-1925

FREEMAN, RUSSELL FULLER, ambassador; b. Fargo, N.D., Oct. 25, 1939; married; 2 children. AB, Grinnell Coll., 1961; JD, Northwestern Univ., 1964. Former sr. law ptnr., pres. and dir. Nilles, Hansen & Davies, Ltd., Fargo, ND; U.S. amb. to Belize, 2001—. Bd. dirs. Children's Village Family Svcs., Fargo. Capt. JAG corp U.S. Army. Mem.: Cass County Bar Assn. (N.D.), N.D. State Bar Assn. Office: DOS Amb 3050 Belize Pl Washington DC 20521*

FREEMAN, SHAREE M. federal agency administrator; b. N.Y. BA, St. Lawrence U.; JD, Georgetown U. Law clk. Norma Holloway Johnson U.S. Dist. Ct. D.C., Washington; asst. dist. atty. Phila., 1982—84; with Solicitor's Office U.S. Dept. Interior, 1984—97, acting asst. solicitor Gen. Indian Legal Activities, atty. advisor; counsel U.S. Ho. of Reps. Internat. Rels. Com., 1997—2001; dir. cmty. oriented policing svcs. U.S. Dept. Justice, Washington, 2001—. Office: US Dept Justice Cmty Oriented Policing Svcs 1100 Vermont Ave NW Washington DC 20005-3505

FREEMAN, SHARON ELIZABETH, psychiatric nurse practitioner; b. Toledo, Sept. 26, 1955; d. Constantine Vincent Morgillo and Mary Elizabeth Dubry; m. David A. Cole, Feb. 18, 1984 (div. Oct. 18, 1993); 1 child, Heather Cole; m. Arthur Freeman, Apr. 29, 1997; children: April Stark, Laura Stone, Rebecca, Aaron, Andrew. BSN, Purdue U., 1991; MA Psychology, Adler Sch. Profl. Psychology, 1993; MSN, postgrad., U. Pa., 2000—; PhD, Canterbury U., 2002. Cert. advanced practice RN-CNS, addictions counselor. Program dir. Charter Med. Corp., Ft. Wayne, Ind., 1988—94; psychiat. nurse clinician John M. Rathburn, MD, PC, Ft. Wayne, 1994—97; assoc. faculty Purdue U., Ft. Wayne, 1995—97; corp. nurse recruiter U. Pa. Health Sys., Phila., 1997—99; clin. program dir. U. Pa. Presbyn. Med. Ctr., Phila., 1999—; invited faculty U. Pa. Sch. Medicine, Phila., 2001. Pres. Adler Assn., Ft. Wayne, 1992—94; assoc. faculty Adler Sch. Profl. Psychiatry, Ft. Wayne, 1992—94. Peer reviewer: AACN-Clin. Issues Jour., 2000—. Mem.: Ind. Assn. Alcohol/Drug Counselors (bd. dirs. 1993—97), Pa. Assn. Alcohol/Drug Abuse Counselors (pres. 2000—), Nat. Assn. Alcohol/Drug Abuse Counselors (bd. dirs., state rep. 2000—), Am. Psychiat. Nurses Assn., Sigma Theta Tau. Roman Catholic. Home: 7914 Ivy Ln Elkins Park PA 19027 Office: U Pa Presbyn Med Ctr 39th and Market St Wright 4th Fl Philadelphia PA 19104 Personal E-mail: MorgilloFreeman@aol.com. Business E-Mail: freemans@uphs.upenn.edu.

FREEMAN, SHERRY, education educator; b. Jackson, Tenn., Feb. 4, 1964; d. Larry Wayne and Betty Bolton Patterson; m. James Kent Freeman, Mar. 28, 1987; children: James Patterson, Frances Jean. BS in Edn., Union U., 1986, EdS, 2001; MEd, Mid. Ten. State U., 1991. Tchr. Rutherford County Schs., Tenn., 1988—93, Jackson County Schs., Jackson, 1993—99; asst. prof. edn. Lambuth U., Jackson, 1999—. Mem. libr. rev. bd. Jackson County Schs., 2002—; instr. Reading Excellence Act Grant, Memphis, 2002—. Treas. PTA, Jackson, 2000—02. Mem.: Tenn. Assn. Colls. Tchr. Edn. (West Tenn rep. 2002—), Internat. Reading Assn., ASCD. Baptist. Avocation: reading. Home: 401 Roland Ave Jackson TN 38301 Office: Lambuth U 705 Lambuth Blvd Jackson TN 38301 Fax: 731-425-3492. E-mail: freeman@lambuth.edu.

FREEMAN, SIDNEY LEE, minister, educator; b. Madison, Wis., Jan. 23, 1927; s. Jack and Gertrude (Kaifetz) F.; m. Evelyn Marie Gronberg, Feb. 3, 1950 (div. 1965); children: Lynn Claire, David Eugene, Michael John; m. Gaynell Bradley, Apr. 28, 1967. BS, U. Wis., 1947; MA, Bowling Green State U., 1949; PhD, Cornell U., 1951. Ordained to ministry Unitarian Universalist Assn., 1957. Min. Unitarian Ch. Charlotte, N.C., 1957-89, min. emeritus, 1989—. Instr. communication arts Cen. Piedmont Community Coll, Charlotte, part-time 1987—; chaplain Cedar Spring Hosp., Pineville, N.C., part-time 1989-98; pres. So. Unitarian Coun., Atlanta, 1953, Thomas Jefferson Unitarian Dist., Charlotte, 1963-64; lectr. Albert Schweitzer Coll., Churwalden, Switzerland, summer 1959, Starr King Sch. for Ministry, Berkeley, Calif., summer 1965. Pres. Charlotte Mental Health Assn., 1978-80; chair consulting bd. Cedar Spring Hosp., Pineville, N.C., 1993-98. Recipient Disting. Svc. award Charlotte Mental Health Assn., 1983. Mem. Unitarian Universalist Mins. Assn. (past sec.), Charlotte Area Clergy Assn. (past com.). Home: 4500 Rockford Ct Charlotte NC 28209-2924 *I try to live by the truth that sets us free, the hope that never dies, and the love that casts out fear.*

FREEMAN, SUSAN TAX, anthropologist, educator, culinary historian; b. Chgo., May 24, 1938; d. Sol and Gertrude Tax.; m. Leslie G. Freeman, Jr., Mar. 20, 1964; 1 dau., Sarah Elisabeth. BA, U. Chgo., 1958; MA, Harvard U., 1959, PhD, 1965. Asst. prof. anthropology U. Ill., Chgo., 1965-70, assoc. prof., 1970-78, prof., 1978—, prof. emerita, 1999—, chmn., 1979-82. Rsch. assoc. dept. sociology and anthropology Mont. State U., Bozeman, 1992—; panelist NEH, Council for Internat. Exchange of Scholars; mem. anthropology screening com. Fulbright-Hays Research Awards, 1975-78; mem. ad hoc com. on research in Spain Spain-U.S.A. Friendship Agreement, various yrs., 1977-84; field researcher Mex., 1959, Spain, 1962—, Japan, 1983; instr. Radcliffe Coll. Seminars on Food in History and Culture, 1998. Author: Neighbors: The Social Contract in a Castilian Hamlet, 1970, The Pasiegos-Spaniards in No Man's Land, 1979; assoc. editor: Am. Anthropologist, 1971-73, Am. Ethnologist, 1974-76; edit. bd. Gastronomica, 2000—. Fellow Inst. for the Humanities, U. Ill. Chgo., 1987-88; Wenner-Gren Found. for Anthrop. Research grantee, 1966-83; NIMH grantee, 1967, 68-71; NEH fellowships, 1978-79, 89-90. Fellow Am. Anthrop. Assn. (nominating com. 1981-82, Centennial Adv. Commn. 1999-2002), Royal Anthrop. Inst. Gt. Britain and Ireland; mem. Soc. for Anthropology of Europe (exec. com. 1987-88), Soc. Spanish and Portuguese Hist. Studies (exec. com. 1990-92), Coun. European Studies (steering com. 1980-83), Internat. Inst. Spain (corporator, bd. dirs. 1982-87, 2000-2003), Centro Estudios Sorianos (hon.), Assn. Anthropologia Castilla y Leon (hon.). Home: PO Box 369 Whitehall MT 59759 Office: U Ill Dept Anthro M/C 027 1007 W Harrison St Chicago IL 60607-7135

FREEMAN, THEODORE MONROE, physician; b. Orlando, Fla., Jan. 3, 1955; s. Fred Monroe and Mary Ann (Ridgeway) F.; m. Karen Bonaccorso, Aug. 11, 1978; children: Kathryn Maria, Michelle Terese, Jeannine Nicole, Jason Monroe. BS in Chemistry, Duke U., 1977; MD, U. So. Fla., 1980. Diplomate Am. Bd. Internal Medicine, Am. Bd. Allergy and Immunology. Intern Jacksonville (Fla.) U. Hosp., 1980-81; commd. capt. USAF, 1981, advanced through grades to col., resident internal medicine Keesler AFB, 1981-83, staff physician Dyess AFB Abilene, Tex., 1983-84, fellow allergy and immunology Wilford Hall Med. Ctr. Lakeland AFB San Antonio, 1984-86, fellow diagnostic lab. immunology Mass. Gen. Hosp. Boston, 1986-87, staff allergist and immunology Wilford Hall Med. Ctr., 1987-89, chmn. dept. allergy and immunology, program dir., 1989—. Med. dir. transplants Wilford Hall Med. Ctr., 1989-2002. Contbr. articles to profl. jours. Fellow Am. Coll. Physicians, Am. Coll. Allergy and Immunology, Am. Acad. Allergy and Immunology; mem. AMA, Soc. Air Force Physicians. Roman Catholic. Office: MMIA Wilford Hall Med Ctr 2200 Bergquist Dr Ste 1 San Antonio TX 78236-5322 E-mail: tfree95900@aol.com.

FREEMAN, THOMAS BENEDICT, neurosurgery educator; s. Harvey Seldon and Virginia F.; m. Susan Swartzman, Aug. 12, 1979; children: Daniel H., Andrew B., Jonathan S. SB, MIT, 1977; MD, Johns Hopkins U., 1981. Intern dept. surgery Columbia-Presbyn. Med. Ctr., N.Y.C., 1981-82; resident, chief resident dept. neurosurgery NYU Med. Ctr., N.Y.C., 1982-88, teaching asst., 1987-88; hon. registrar dept. neurology Nat. Hosp. at Queens Square, London, 1983; asst. prof. neurosurgery and pharmacology and exptl. therapeutics U. South Fla. Coll. Medicine, Tampa, 1988-95, assoc. prof. neurosurgery and pharmacology and exptl. therapeutics, 1995—99, prof. neurosurgery and pharmacology and exptl. therapeutics, 1999—. Attending physician Tampa Gen. Hosp., 1988—, H. Lee Moffitt Cancer Ctr., Tampa, 1988—, James A. Haley VA Hosp., Tampa, 1988—; med. dir. Ctr. Aging and Brain Repair, U. South Fla., 2000—, Saneron-CCEL Therapeutics, 2000—; pres., founding scientist Ciracell Corp., 2002; advisor FDA, Titan Pharms., Image-Guided Neurologics. Mem.: AAAS, Soc. Neurosci., Congress Neurol. Surgeons, Am. Soc. Neural Transplantation and Repair (pres. 2003—), Am. Assn. Neurol. Surgeons. Achievements include research in neural grafting for treatment of Parkinson's disease and Huntington's disease; characterization of factors influencing neural graft and survival; transplantation of striatal neurons in animal models and patients with Huntington's disease; proliferation of adult human cells in vitro for therapeutic purposes, including pancreas, neural, heart and liver cells. Office: U South Fla Div Neurosurgery 4 Columbia Dr Ste 730 Tampa FL 33606-3568

FREEMAN, TODD IRA, lawyer; b. Mpls., Nov. 24, 1953; s. Earl Stanley and Gretta Lois (Rudick) F.; m. Judy Lynn Sigel, June 15, 1975; children: Jennifer, Katie, Zachary. BS in Mktg., U. Colo., 1974; JD, U. Minn., 1978. Bar: Minn. 1978, U.S. Dist. Ct. Minn. 1978, U.S. Tax Ct. 1980; CPA, Minn. Acct. Coopers & Lybrand, Mpls., 1978-80; shareholder Larkin, Hoffman, Daly & Lindgren, Mpls., 1980—, treas., 1990—, also bd. dirs., 1990-93. Pres. The Group Inc. Mem. ABA (tax sect., past chmn. personal svc. orgns.), Minn. Soc. CPAs, Minn. State Bar Assn., Hennepin County Bar Assn. Avocations: tennis, golf. Office: Larkin Hoffman Daly & Lindgren 7900 Xerxes Ave S Ste 1500 Minneapolis MN 55431-1128

FREEMAN, TOM M. lawyer; b. Wauwatosa, Wis., Oct. 5, 1952; s. Max and Betty J. (Zimmerman) F.; m. Judith Casper, June 23, 1974; children: Sarah Carolyn, Benjamin Robert. BA with honors, U. Wis., 1974; JD cum laude, Harvard U., 1977. Bar: Wis. 1977, Ill. 1978, Calif. 1980, U.S. Dist. Ct. (we. dist.) Wis. 1977, U.S. Ct. Appeals (7th cir.) 1978, U.S. Dist. Ct. (no. dist.) Calif. 1980, U.S. Ct. Appeals (9th cir.) 1982. Law clk. Wis. Supreme Ct., Madison, 1977-78; staff atty. U.S. Ct. Appeals (7th cir.), Chgo., 1978-80; assoc. Brobeck, Phleger, Harrison, LLP, San Francisco, 1980-85, ptnr., 1985—2003, Morgan, Lewis & Bockius LLP, 2003—. Democrat. Jewish. Office: Morgan Lewis & Bockius LLP Spear St Tower 1 Market San Francisco CA 94105 E-mail: tfreeman@morganlewis.com.

FREEMAN, WENDELL LEE, minister; b. Indpls., Ind., Aug. 23, 1936; s. Paul Benton and Mildred Lucille Freeman; m. Ruby Berdene Rowe, Aug. 30, 1986; m. Ruth Ann Custer, Aug. 3, 1958 (dec. June 12, 1985); children: Beth Elaine, Amy Carole, Wendy Ann. AB in Bible, Cin. Bible Sem., Cincinnati, OH, 1958, MA in Theology, 1973. Ordained to ministry Ch. of Brethren. Min. Wrays Christian Ch., Medora, Ind., 1958—61, Driftwood Christian Ch., Vallonia, 1958—61; missionary Ctrl. African Mission, Gwelo, Rhodesia, South Africa, 1962—70; min. Winchester Ch. of Christ, 1971—73, Ho. Ch., Dayton, 1974—76; dir. Melting Pot Christian Coffee Ho., Johnson City, 1980—86; min. Ch. of the Brethren, 1986—. Educator Men's Bible Study Group, Jonesborough, Tenn. Avocations: Scrabble, puzzles, trains. Home: 117 Dawn Dr Johnson City TN 37615-3852

FREEMAN-WILSON, KAREN, former attorney general, prosecutor, educational association administrator; m. Carmen Wilson; 1 child, Jordan;3 stepchildren. BA cum laude, Harvard Coll., 1982, JD, 1985. Pub. defender Lake County; ptnr. Freeman-Wilson and Lewis; dir. Ind. Office Drug Control Policy; atty. gen., chief legal officer State of Ind., judge drug ct.; pub. defender, exec. dir. Ind. Civil Rights Commn.; dep. prosecutor Lake County, 1985—88; exec. dir. Ind. Civil Rights commn., 1989—92; judge Gary City Ct., 1994—2000; atty. gen. State Ind., Indpls., 2000—01; exec. dir. Nat. Drug Ct. Inst., 2002—; CEO Nat. Assn. Drug Ct. Profls., 2002—. Instr. Valparaiso U. Law Sch., Ind. U. Sch. Law; bd. dirs. Conf. for Legal Edn. and Opportunity, Ind. Supreme Ct. Trainer rape awareness Gary Commn. for Women; active Harbor House; bd. dirs. Rainbow Shelter. Democrat. Address: 4900 Seminary Rd Ste 320 Alexandria VA 22311 Business E-Mail: kfwilson@nadcp.org.

FREEMARK, MICHAEL SCOTT, pediatric endocrinologist and educator; b. Phila., Dec. 10, 1950; s. Morton and Molly (Blumberg) F.; m. Anne R. Slifkin, May 8, 1979; children: Samara, Yonah. BA magna cum laude, Brandeis U., 1972; postgrad., Temple U., 1972-74; MD, Duke U., 1976. Diplomate Am. Bd. Pediatrics, subspecialty bds. pediatric endocrinology, Nat. Bd. Med. Examiners; lic. physician, N.C. From resident pediatrics to prof. Duke U. Med. Ctr., Durham, NC, 1976—2003, prof. pediats., 2003—, chief pediatric endocrine divsn., 1991—. Med. dir. Pediatric Clinics, Harnett and Hoke Counties, N.C., 1979-80; ad hoc reviewer human embryology and devel. study sect. NIH, 1989, 90; dir. weekly endocrine and pediatric fellows rsch. seminars; lectr. in field. Mem. editl. bd.: Jour. Clin. Endocrinology and Metabolism, 1990—93, 2000—, Endocrinology, 1998—; contbr. Bd. dirs. Durham Nursery Sch. Assn., 1983-88; chmn. People's Alliance Subcom. on Pub. Edn.; mem. Durham County Commn. Merger Issues Task Force, 1988-89; tchr. Triangle Children's Shule, Chapel Hill, N.C., Durham Co. Comm. Child Protection Team, 1994-96. Recipient NIH-Nat. Rsch. Svc. award, 1982-85, NIH Clin. Investigator award, 1985-88, Rsch. award March of Dimes, 1988-92, NIH Rsch. Career Devel. award, 1990—; March of Dimes-Basil O'Connor Starter grantee, 1985-87, Trent Found. grantee, 1984-85, NIH grantee, 1988—; USEPA fellow, 1972, USPHS fellow, 1974, 75, Fogarty fellow, Paris, 1993. Mem. Am. Fedn. Clin. Rsch., N.C. Med. Assn., Am. Acad. Pediatrics, Endocrine Soc., Lawson-Wilkins Pediatric Endocrine Soc. (chair program com. 1991-94, chair drug and therapeutics com. 1999—), Soc. for Pediatric Rsch. (coun. endocrinology, metabolism and nephrology 1991-94). Home: 1309 Oakland Ave Durham NC 27705-3243 Office: Duke Univ Med Ctr PO Box 3080 Durham NC 27710-0001

FREER, COBURN, English language educator; b. New Orleans, Nov. 5, 1939; s. Wilbert Coburn and Lillian Jackson (Hicks) F.; m. Ramona Jean Salminen; children: Meagan, Elinor. BA, Lewis and Clark Coll., 1960; PhD, U. Washington, 1967. Instr. U. Ariz., Tucson, 1965-67; asst. prof to prof. U. Mont., Missoula, 1967-80; head dept. U. Ga., Athens, 1980-92, prof., 1980—. Author: Music for a King, 1972, The Poetics of Jacobean Drama, 1981; contbr. articles to profl. jours. Recipient Sr. Fulbright-Hays lectureship U. Oulu, Finland, 1971-72, NEH fellowship, London, 1974-75. Mem. MLA, Internat. Assn. Univ. Profs. English, Milton Soc., South Atlantic MLA, Southeast Renaissance Conf. Home: 400 Saint George Dr Athens GA 30606-3940 Office: Univ Ga Dept English Athens GA 30602

FREER, ROBERT ELLIOTT, JR., lawyer; b. Washington, Jan. 19, 1941; s. Robert E. and Alice (Barry) F.; m. Roberta Stapleton Renchard, Dec. 31, 1972; children: Kimberly Dunlap, R. Elliott III, Ashleigh Hamilton, Daniel Renchard. AB, Princeton U., 1963; JD, U. Va., 1966. Bar: Va. 1966, D.C. 1968, U.S. Supreme Ct. 1973. Trial atty. FTC, 1966-69, atty. advisor to chmn., asst. to gen. counsel, 1970-71; exec. asst. to gen. counsel U.S. Dept. Transp., Washington, 1971-74; Washington counsel Kimberly Clark Corp., 1974-83; staff v.p., 1975-80; corp. v.p., 1980-84; gen. counsel, 1983-84; pvt. practice Washington, 1984-2000; ret., 2001; founder Free Enterprise Found., 2002—. Mem. President's Commn. on White House Fellowships, 1985-93; pub. mem. Adminstrv. Conf. U.S., 1981-86; capt. land team President's Pvt. Sector Survey on Cost Control in Fedn. Govt., 1982-83; sec., gen. counsel U.S.-Cuba Bus. Coun., 1994-2000. Contbg. author, editor: Finding Our Roots/Facing Our Future: America in the 21st Century, 1997; contbr. articles to profl. jours. Founder, chmn. bd. trustees Washington Episc. Sch., 1986-94, chmn. emeritus, 1994—; chmn. bd. visitors Regent U. Sch. Law, 1995—; trustee Corcoran Gallery Art, 1986-93, asst. sec., chmn. bylaws com., 1990, sec., 1991; bd. trustees, pres. and CEO Free Enterprise Found., 2002—; chmn. Lawyers for the Republic, 1988—; asst. gen. counsel Rep. Nat. Conv., 1988, 92, 96; mem. Parents coun. Coll. Charleston, 1997, chmn., 2000-02. Mem. Rep. Nat. Lawyers Assn. (bd. govs. 1985-2000, gen. counsel 1985-89, vice chmn. 1988-89), Washington Met. Area Corp. Counsel Assn. (founder, pres. 1980-81, bd. dirs. 1980-84). Home: PO Box 59604 Potomac MD 20859-9604 Office: Free Enterprise Found PO Box 21569 Charleston SC 29413

FREERKSEN, GREGORY NATHAN, lawyer; b. Washington, Iowa, June 4, 1951; s. Floyd and Betty Jo (Frederick) F.; m. Patricia A. Menges, Mar. 21, 1981; children: Suzanna, Andrea, Paul, Timothy. B.S., No. Ill. U., 1973; J.D., DePaul U., 1976. Bar: Ill. 1976, U.S. Dist. Ct. (no. dist.) Ill. 1976, U.S. Supreme Ct. 1980, U.S. Ct. Appeals (D.C. cir.) 1983. Ptnr. Witwer, Burlage, Poltrock & Giampietro, 1988—; arbitrator in court annexed arbitration proceedings 18th Jud. Cir. and Cook County Cir. Cts. Author: (annotated bibliography) Children in the Legal Literature, 1976; Non-Salary Provisions in Negotiated Teacher Agreements, 1975. Editor Ill. law issue DePaul U. Law Rev., 1975-76. Mem. ABA, Ill. State Bar Assn., Chgo. Bar Assn., Appellate Lawyers Assn., DuPage Bar Assn. Democrat. Home: 645 Hill Ave Glen Ellyn IL 60137-5077 Office: Witwer Burlage Poltrock & Giampietro 125 S Wacker Dr Ste 2700 Chicago IL 60606-4401

FREESE, ANDREW, neurosurgeon, educator, scientist; b. Boston, July 4, 1959; s. Ernst and Elisabeth (Bautz) F.; m. Marcia Geary, June 14, 1986; children: John Alexander, Elisabeth Marguerite, Ernst Timothy, Matthew Andrew. BA, Harvard U., 1981; MD, Harvard U., Boston, 1990; PhD, MIT, 1990. Lic. physican, Pa.; trauma cert. Rsch. assoc. NIH, Bethesda, Md., 1982-83; surg. intern U. Pa., Phila., 1990-91, neurosurgery resident, 1991-97, dir. Lab. Molecular Neurosurgery Grad. Hosp., 1994-97, mem. Inst. Human Gene Therapy, 1994—; assoc. prof. neurosurgery, dir. neurosurgery rsch. Thomas Jefferson U., Phila., 1997—, vice chmn. neurosurgery, 2000—, assoc. dir CNS Gene Therapy Ctr., 1998—. Vis. scientist Wistar Inst., Phila., 1994-95; pres. Neurel, Inc., Boston, 1987-88, sci. dir., 1988-90; cons. Polykinetix, Inc., N.Y.C., 1993; exec. dir. Parkinson's Disease Gene Therapy Consortium. Editor: Biotechnology Processing, 1988, Neurological Disorders: Novel Experimental and Therapeutic Approaches, 1992; editor spl. issue Exptl. Neurology, 1997; contbr. articles to profl. jours. Fellow Sigma Xi; mem. AMA, Internat. Brain Rsch. Orgn., Soc. Neurosci., Congress Neurol. Surgeons, Controlled Release Soc. Achievements include patents for controlling the release of drugs using drug delivery system for neurological disorders; one of the first viral vector systems to deliver genes into neurons; the demonstration of the precursor effect on brain kynurenines; gene therapy for Parkinson's disease, epilepsy, pituitary adenomas, neurogenetic disorders, and stroke. Home: 101 Buck Ln Haverford PA 19041-1104 Office: Thomas Jefferson U Dept Neurosurgery Ste 8330 111 South 11th St Philadelphia PA 19107-4316 also: Thomas Jefferson U Neurosurgery Rsch Labs Ste Ste 511 1025 Walnut St Philadelphia PA 19107-5001

FREESE, BARBARA TAPP, nursing educator; b. Kansas City, Mo., Oct. 1, 1944; d. Ernest M. and Marjorie (McIntosh) Tapp; m. Hal Freese, Feb. 3, 1968; 1 child, Tiffany Jo. BSN, U. Mo., 1967; MSN, Clemson U., 1980; EdD, U. Ga., 1989. Nursing faculty Lander U., Greenwood, 1975—, dean sch. nursing, 1989-2000. Contbr. articles to profl. jours. Trustee Neuman Sys. Model Group. Fellow Royal Coll. Nursing, Australia; mem. ANA, Nat. League for Nursing, Mensa, Sigma Theta Tau., Kappa Delta Pi.

FREESE, KATHERINE, physicist, educator; b. Freiburg, Germany, Feb. 8, 1957; came to U.S., 1957; d. Ernst and Elisabeth Gertrude Maria (Bautz) F.; 1 child, Douglas Quincy Adams. BA, Princeton U., 1977; MA, Columbia U., 1981; PhD, U. Chgo., 1984. Postdoctoral fellow Harvard/Smithsonian Ctr. for Astrophysics, Cambridge, Mass., 1984-85, Inst. for Theoretical Physics, Santa Barbara, Calif., 1985-87, U. Calif., Berkeley, 1987-88; asst. prof. physics MIT, Cambridge, 1988-91; prof. physics U. Mich., Ann Arbor, 1991—. Gen. mem. Aspen Ctr. for Physics, 1991—; bd. dirs. Inst. for Theoretical Physics. Contbr. articles to profl. jours. William Rainey Harper fellow U. Chgo, 1982; Sloan Found. fellow, 1989; Presdl. Young Investigator NSF, 1990, rsch. grantee, 1991, 94; Presdl. fellow U. Calif., 1987. Mem. Am. Phys. Soc., Assn. for Women in Sci. Democrat. Avocations: water polo, swimming, skiing, tennis. Office: U Mich Dept Physics Ann Arbor MI 48109

FREESE, MELANIE LOUISE, librarian, professor, assistant dean; b. Mineola, N.Y., May 12, 1945; d. Walter Christian and Agnes Elizabeth (Jensen) F. BS in Elem. Edn., Hofstra U., 1967, MA in Elem. Edn., 1969; MLS, L.I. U., 1977. Cert. tchr., N.Y. Bibliographic searcher acquisitions dept. Adelphi U. Swirbul Libr., Garden City, N.Y., 1973-79, res. desk libr., 1979-83; catalog libr., assoc. prof. Hofstra U. Axinn Libr., Hempstead, N.Y., 1984—, asst. dean, chair libr. tech. svcs., 1998—2000, sr. cataloger, 2000—. Ch. librarian St. Peters Evang. Luth. Ch., Baldwin, N.Y., 1977—. Founder libr. Salvation Army Wayside Home and Sch. for Girls, Valley Stream, N.Y., 1993. Mem. ALA, Nassau County Libr. Assn. (corr. sec. acad. and spl. librs. divsn. 1986-88, v.p., pres.-elect 1989-90, pres. 1991), Bus. and Profl. Women's Club (pres. Nassau County chpt. 1990-92, 95-97, Woman of Yr. 1994). Republican. Avocations: needlework, knitting, crocheting. Office: Hofstra U Axinn Library 1000 Fulton Ave Hempstead NY 11550-1030

FREESE, RAYMOND WILLIAM, mathematics educator; b. Foristell, Mo., Dec. 17, 1934; s. Herman E. and Lydia D. (Giessmann) F.; m. Celia Ann Staubach, Aug. 10, 1957; children: Carl, William, Timothy. BS in Agrl., U. Mo., 1956, BS in Edn., MA in Math., U. Mo., 1958, PhD in Math., 1961. Asst. prof. math. St. Louis U., 1961-64, assoc. prof. math., 1964-67, prof. math., 1967-83, prof. math., chmn. dept., 1971-83, prof. math. and computer sci., chmn. dept., 1983-86, prof. math. and computer sci., 1983—, prof. edn., 1989—, acting dept. chair, 1999-2000. Contbr. articles to profl. jours. Mem. Francis Howell Sch. Dist. Bd. Edn., St. Charles, Mo., 1967-69. Mem. Mo. Sch. Bd. Assn. (exec. com. 1968-70), Math. Assn. Am. (Mo. sect. chmn. 1964-65, Mo. sect. gov. 1973-76), Am. Math. Soc., Math. Educators of Greater St. Louis, Nat. Coun. Tchrs. of Math., Sigma Xi. Mem. United Ch. of Christ. Avocations: ham radio, sci. fiction. Office: St Louis U Dept Math/Computer Sci 221 N Grand Blvd Saint Louis MO 63103-2006 E-mail: freeserw@slu.edu.

FREESE, RICHARD BRADLEY, health care executive; b. Detroit, July 6, 1950; s. Claude Bradley and Winifred (Hollyer) Freese; m. Ruth C. Miller, Feb. 14, 1980 (div. Dec. 1998); children: Michael Bradley, Molly Ruth; m. Sara L. Wennen, Aug. 2002. BS, U. Mich., 1972, MD, 1976. Diplomate Am. Bd. Internal Medicine. Resident internal medicine Hennepin County Med. Ctr., Mpls., 1976—80, chief resident internal medicine, 1979—80; practicing physician internal medicine Moses Lake (Wash.) Clin. Br., Wenatchee Valley Clinic, 1980—90, Park Nicollet Clinic, St. Louis Park, Minn., 1990, chmn. dept. medicine, 1993—96; sr. v.p. Park Nicollet Hlth. Svcs., St. Louis Park, Minn., 1996—. Mem. ACP. Avocation: fishing. Office: Park Nicollet Clinic Health Sys Minn 3800 Park Nicollet Blvd Minneapolis MN 55416-2505 E-mail: [illegible]@parknicollet.com.

FREEZE, JAMES DONALD, administrator, clergyman; b. Balt., Sept. 15, 1932; s. Frank Leo and Helen Angela (Sweeney) F. AB, Boston Coll., 1956, MA, 1957; S.T.L., U. Innsbruck, Austria, 1964. Joined S.J., Roman Catholic Ch., 1950, ordained priest, 1963; mem. faculty dept. philosophy Wheeling (W.Va.) Coll., 1965-70, chmn. dept., 1967-70; asst. dean Coll. Arts and Scis., Georgetown U., Washington, 1971-74, asst. v.p. for acad. affairs, 1974-79, exec. v.p., provost, 1979-91; dir. Loyola Retreat House, Faulkner, Md., 1992-97; v.p., treas. Corp. Roman Cath. Clergyman, Balt., 1997—2002. Trustee Georgetown Prep. Sch., Rockville, Md., 1975-79, chmn. bd., 1978-79; trustee Loyola Coll., Balt., 1982-88, U. Detroit, 1983-90, Fairfield U., 1990-96, Manresa Retreat House, Staten Island, N.Y., 1997-98. Home and Office: Manresa Hall 261 City Ave Merion Station PA 19068-1836

FREGOSI, JAMES LOUIS, professional baseball team manager; b. San Francisco, Apr. 4, 1942; m. Joni Fregosi; children: Jim Jr., Jennifer, Nicole, Robbie. Student, Menlo Coll. Profl. baseball player Angels, Calif., 1961-71, N.Y. Mets, 1972-73, Tex. Rangers, 1973-77, Pitts. Pirates, 1977-78; mgr. Calif. Angels, 1978-81, Louisville Redbirds, 1983-86, Chgo. White Sox, 1986-88; spl. assignment scout, coach Phila. Phillies, 1989-90, minor league pitching instr., spl. assignment scout, 1990, mgr., 1991-97; spl. asst. to gen. mgr. San Francisco Giants, 1997-98; mgr. Toronto (Ont.) Blue Jays, 1999—. Named to All-Star team, 1964, 66-70; recipient Gold Glove award, 1967. Office: Toronto Blue Jays 1 Blue Jays Way Ste 3200 Toronto ON Canada M5V 1J1

FREGULIA, JEANETTE MARIE, county official; b. Oakland, Calif., Dec. 18, 1963; d. Donald Bernard and Deanna Marie Fregulia; 1 child, Carmen. BA, U. Pacific, 1985; MA, U. London, 1987; postgrad., U. Nev., Reno, 2001—. Coord. Internat. Living Learning Ctr., Miami U., Oxford, Ohio, 1988-90; instr. polit. sci. Hartnell Coll., Salinas, Calif., 1990-94, Gavilan Coll., Gilroy, Calif., 1994-95; co-dir. AmeriCorps acad. mentor program Feather River Coll., Quincy, Calif., 1997-99; coord. grad. follow up study Plumas County Office Edn., Quincy, Calif., 1997—, dir. vol. program, 1999—2001; grad. asst. dept. history U. Nev., Reno, 2001—. Disting. tchg. asst. Western Traditions Program U. Nev., Reno, 2002—03; cons. Williams (Calif.) H.S., 1998; participant Calif. Gt. Tchrs. Seminar, 1993. Vol. Monterey County Dem. Com., Salinas, 1991-94; parent vol. Pioneer Elem. Sch., Quincy, 1996-2001; tchr. religious edn. St. John's Cath. Ch., Quincy, 1998-99; treas. Quincy Swim Team, 2000-01; coach Johnsville Jr. Ski Team, 2003—. Mem.: Rotary (dist. youth exch. com. 1997—). Democrat. Avocations: travel, skiing, reading, tennis, cooking. Home: 865 Manzanita Ln Reno NV 89509 Business E-Mail: fregulia@unr.edu. E-mail: jmfregulia@sbglobal.net.

FREI, EMIL, III, physician, medical researcher, medical educator; b. St. Louis, 1924; m. Elizabeth Smith (dec. Apr. 1986); children: Mary, Emil, Alice, Nancy, Judy; m. Adoria Smetana Brock, May 1987; stepchildren: Stephen, Francis, Peter, Vincent, John. MD, Yale U., 1948. Diplomate Am. Bd. Internal Medicine, Am. Bd. Med. Oncology. Intern St. Louis U. Hosp., 1948—49; resident in pathology Barnes Hosp., St. Louis, 1952—53; resident in internal medicine St. Louis U., 1953—54, VA Hosp., St. Louis, 1954—55; chief gen. medicine br. Nat. Cancer Inst., Bethesda, Md., 1955—65; head devel. therapeutics, assoc. dir. M.D. Anderson Hosp. and Tumor Inst., Houston, 1965—72; dir., physician-in-chief Children's Cancer Research Found. (now Dana-Farber Cancer Inst.), Boston, 1972—91; physician-in-chief emeritus Dana-Farber Cancer Inst., 1991—; prof. medicine Med. Sch. Harvard U., Boston, 1972—, Richard and Susan Smith prof. medicine, 1985, Richard and Susan Smith disting. prof. medicine, 1994—; nat. cons. in internal medicine-oncology USAF, 1968—72; mem. Eleanor Roosevelt internat. cancer fellowships com. Internat. Union Against Cancer, 1968—72; chmn. anti-neoplastic disease drug panel, drug efficacy study NAS, 1968—72; nat. cons. in internal medicine-oncology USAF. Mem. bd. sci. counselors Nat. Cancer Inst., 1986—90, mem. Presdl. Commn. for New Drugs for Cancer and AIDS, 1988—90; chmn. antitumor drug panel NAS, 1996. Lt. M.C. USNR, 1950—52. Recipient Lasker award, 1972, Lila W. Gruber award, 1979, Kettering prize, GM, 1983, Hamao Umezawa award, 1985, Armand Hammer Cancer Rsch. award, 1989, Disting. Alumnus award, NIH, 1990, Emil Frei III professorship in medicine, 1992, Morse award, 1996, Sidney Farber medal for contbns. to cancer rsch., 1998, 50th Anniversary Commemorative award, Leukemia Soc. Am., 1999, La Medaille de la Ville de Paris, 2000, Claude Jacquillat award, 2002. Fellow: ACP, Am. Acad. Arts and Scis.; mem.: AMA, Icon of Oncology (mem. 2003), Nat. Acad. Medicine, Inst. of Medicine, Assn. Am. Physicians, Am. Soc. Clin. Investigation, Am. Soc. Hematology, Am. Cancer Soc. (ann. Nat. award 1981), Am. Soc. Clin. Oncology (pres. 1968—69, Disting. Scientist award 1992), Am. Assn. for Cancer Rsch. (past pres.). Office: Dana Farber Cancer Inst D-1618 44 Binney St Boston MA 02115-6084

FREIBERG, RICHARD ALBERT, orthopaedic surgeon; b. Feb. 12, 1932; s. Joseph Albert and Louise R. (Rothenberg) F.; m. Adrianne Wilson, Apr. 2, 1994; children: Andrew, James, Robert. AB, Harvard U., 1953, MD, 1957. Diplomate Am. Bd. Orthopaedic Surgery. Practice orthopaedic surgery Orthopaedic Offices, Inc., Cin., 1962-98; clin. prof. U. Cin. Coll. Medicine, 1968—. Dir. othopaedic svc. Cin. VA Med. Ctr. Contbr. articles to profl. jours., papers in field. Bd. trustees Jewish Hosp. Cin., 1991—. Mem. Am. Acad. Orthopaedic Surgeons, Arthritis Found. (bd. govs. Cin. chpt.), Clin. Orthopaedic Soc. Home: 779 Windings Ln Cincinnati OH 45220-1087

FREIBERG, ROBERT JERRY, laser physicist, engineer, technology administrator, consultant; b. Chgo., Mar. 26, 1939; s. Jerry and Mildred (Lukes) F.; m. Deanna Corrine Qualls, July 8, 1968; children: Joseph, Sean, Jamison. BS in Physics, Rensselaer Poly. Inst., 1961; MS in Physics, U. Ill., 1963, PhD, 1966. Postgrad. rsch. assoc. U. Ill., Urbana, 1966-67; rsch. scientist Hughes Rsch. Labs., Malibu, Calif., 1967-69; group mgr. United Tech. Rsch. Labs., East Hartford, Conn., 1969-75; gen. mgr. United Tech. Optical Sys., West Palm Beach, Fla., 1975-79; bus. mgr. optics TRW, Redondo Beach, Calif., 1979-83; program dir. Baxter Healthcare, Inc., Irvine, Calif., 1983-86; dir. engring. and mfg. ops. Pfizer Laser Sys., Irvine, 1986-92; dir. engring. Lumonics, Inc.,

Camarillo, Calif., 1992-94; sr. v.p. engring. and program mgmt. View Engring., Inc., Simi Valley, Calif., 1994-97; v.p. engring. Indsl. Electronic Engrs. Inc., Van Nuys, Calif., 1997-2000; v.p. engr. Knowledge Universe, Inc., Los Gatos, Calif., 2000—02. Gen. ptnr., sr. tech. cons. Internat. Mktg. and Cons. Assocs., Kalispell, Mont., 1991—; chmn. tech. adv. bd. Premier Laser Sys., Irvine, 1992-99; bd. dirs. SurgiLight, Orlando, Fla.; presenter in field. Contbr. numerous articles to Procs. IEEE, Laser Focus, Applied Optics, IEEE Jour. Quantum Electronics, Jour. Applied Physics, Phys. Rev., Applied Physics Letters, Bull. Am. Phys. Soc. Asst. scoutmaster Boy Scouts Am., Mission Viejo, Calif., 1989-92, varsity scoutmaster, Newbury Park, Calif., 1994-96. Fellow NSF, 1962-66. Fellow Internat. Soc. for Optical Engring. (mem. membership com. 1994-99, chmn. 1994-96); mem. IEEE, Am. Electronics Assn., Optical Soc. Am., Am. Soc. for Laser Surgery and Medicine, Nat. Ctr. Mfg. Scis. (Strategic Initiative Group com. 1995-97), Soc. Info. Displays, Sigma Xi. Achievements include numerous patents for surgical lasers, endoscopic instrumentation, medical catheters, novel optical resonators, laser devices, and diagnostic instruments. Home: 112 River View Dr Kalispell MT 59901 E-mail: rjeagle@in-tch.com.

FREIBERGER, KATHERINE GUION, composer, retired piano educator; b. Mineral Wells, Tex., May 2, 1927; d. Waldo Burton and Kate Francis (Guion) Lasater; m. John Jacob Freiberger, July 22, 1950. AA, HocKaday Jr. Coll., Dallas, 1946; BA, U. Tex., 1949; MusB, So. Meth. U., 1966. Tchr. Dallas Ind. Schs., 1949-50; pvt. practice piano tchr. Dallas, 1961-85. Composer piano solos and duets, chamber, choral and incidental music. Mem. Dallas Civic Chorus, 1962-69, 72-76, chorus Dallas Civic Opera, 1959; alto soloist Preston Hollow Presbyn. Ch., Dallas, 1956-63; alto soloist, dir. youth choir Churchill Way Presbyn. Ch., Dallas, 1963-70; sole trustee David W. Guion Edn. and Religious Trusts I and II, Dallas, 1978-91; bd. dirs. Dallas Music Tchrs. Assn., 1979-91, Voices of Change, Dallas, 1980s, Dallas Civic Music, 1970s-80s, Durango/Purgatory Music in the Mts., Colo., 1990—. The Dallas Opera, 1989-97;artist in residence com. Ft. Lewis Coll., Durango, Co., 1998—.) Recipient; Elizabeth Mathias Award, Prof. Achievement, 2001. Mem. Musical Arts Club, Mu Phi Epsilon Alumni (First prize for composition 1989, Elizabeth Mathias award 2001). Home: 3825 Hawthorne Ave Dallas TX 75219-2212

FREIBERGER, WALTER FREDERICK, mathematics educator, actuarial science consultant, educator; b. Vienna, Feb. 20, 1924; came to U.S., 1955, naturalized, 1962. s. Felix and Irene (Tagany) F.; m. Christine Mildred Holmberg, Oct. 6, 1956; children: Christopher Allan, Andrew James, Nils H. BA, U. Melbourne, 1947, MA, 1949; PhD, U. Cambridge, Eng., 1953. Rsch. officer Aero. Rsch. Lab. Australian Dept. Supply, 1947-49, sr. sci. rsch. officer, 1953-55; tutor U. Melbourne, 1947-49, 53-55; asst. prof. divsn. applied math. Brown U., 1956-58, assoc. prof., 1958-64, prof., 1964—2002; prof. applied math., prof. cmty. health Brown U. Med. Sch., 1994—2002; prof. emeritus applied math. Brown U., 2002—, dir. Computing Center, 1963-69, dir. Ctr. for Computer and Info. Scis., 1969-76, chmn. divsn. applied math., 1976-82, chmn. grad. com., 1985-88, assoc. chmn. divsn. applied math., 1988 91, chmn. univ. ctr. for statis. sci., 1991—2002; joint appointment Brown U. Med. Sch., 1994—2002. Fmr. lectr., cons. program in applied actuarial sci. Bryant Coll.; joint appointment as prof. cmty. health Sch. Medicine Brown U., 1994-2002; mem. fellowship selection panel NSF, Fulbright fellowship selection panel; mem. Rep. Nat. Com. Author: (with U. Grenander) A Short Course in Computational Probability and Statistics, 1971; editor: The International Dictionary of Applied Mathematics, 1960, (with others) Applications of Digital Computers, 1963, Advances in Computers, Volume 10, 1970, Statistical Computer Performance Evaluation, 1972; mng. editor: Quarterly of Applied Mathematics, 1965—; Contbr. numerous articles to profl. jours. Served with Australian Army, 1943-45. Fulbright fellow, 1955-56; Guggenheim fellow, 1962-63; grantee NSF Office Naval Rsch. NIH. Mem. Am. Math. Soc. (assoc. editor Math. Reviews 1957-62), Soc. for Indsl. and Applied Math., Am. Statis. Assn., Inst. Math. Stats., Assn. Computing Machinery, Bristol Yacht Club, Univ. Club. Republican. Episcopalian. Home: 24 Alumni Ave Providence RI 02906-2310 Office: Box F Brown U 182 George St Providence RI 02912-9056 E-mail: Walter_Freiberger@Brown.edu.

FREIDBERG, STEPHEN ROY, neurosurgeon; b. Bklyn., Oct. 16, 1934; s. Leslie Max and Bess Bernblum; m. Helen Deorsay, May 1, 1964; children: Michael, Jonathan. AB, U. Pa., Phila., 1956; MD, Albert Einstein Coll., 1960. Intern U. Okla. Hosp., 1960-61; resident King's County Hosp., Bklyn., 1964-68; fellow Nat. Hosp. Queen's Sq., London, 1965; staff physician Lahey Clinic Med. Ctr., Burlington, Mass., 1969—, chmn. divsn. surgery, 1995. Chmn. dept. neurosurgery Lahey Clinic Med. Ctr., Burlington, 1984, bd. govs., 1978. Contbr. articles to profl. jours. Capt. U.S. Army, 1962-64. Mem. Am. Assn. Neurol. Surgeons, Congress Neurol. Surgeons, New Eng. Neurosurg. Soc. (pres. 1981-83), Mass. Med. Soc. Jewish. Avocations: hiking, skiing. Office: Lahey Clinic Med Ctr 41 Mall Rd Burlington MA 01805-0002

FREIDELL, HUGH VERNON, internist, nephrologist; b. Santa Barbara, Calif., June 21, 1923; s. Hugh Fredrick and Selina Maria (Saari) F.; m. Anna Mae Davis, Apr. 6, 1952; children: Kathy Ann Freidell Day, Susan Lee Freidell Mosby, Sharon Maria Freidell Paratte, Debra Mary Freidell Babai. MD, Baylor U., 1948. Diplomate in internal medicine and nephrology Am. Bd. Internal Medicine; diplomate Am. Bd. Forensic Examiners. Intern Highland-Alameda Hosp., Oakland, Calif., 1948-49; resident Santa Barbara (Calif.) Cottage-County Hosp., 1949-50, Univ. Hosp. of Nebr., Omaha, 1950-52; fellow artificial unit Cleve. Clinic, 1958; practiced medicine/nephrology Santa Barbara, 1954—97. Chmn. dept. internal medicine Santa Barbara Cottage Hosp., 1961-62, 87-88, med. dir. acute renal unit, 1959-85; co-med. dir. Santa Barbara Cmty. Dialysis Ctr., 1975-91. With U.S. Army, 1943-46, capt. M.C., USAF, 1952-54. Fellow ACP; mem. Calif. Med. Assn., Santa Barbara County Med. Soc. (pres. 1971), Aquatic Med. Soc., Am. Soc. Nephrology, Masons, Shriners. Republican. Presbyterian. Avocations: scuba diving, flying, horseback riding, fishing, water sports. Home: 1101-B Senda Verde Santa Barbara CA 93105

FREIDENBERGS, INGRID, psychologist; b. Latvia, Aug. 6, 1944; came to U.S, 1951; d. Olgerts and Marta (Purvins) F.; m. Jack Feder, June 21, 1980; 1 child, Paul. BA, CCNY, 1966, MS, 1970; MA, L.I. U., 1973, PhD, 1975; cert. in psychoanalysis, NYU, 1983. Lic. psychologist, N.Y. Sch. psychologist Bur. of Guidance N.Y.C. Bd. Edn., 1971-73; intern in clin. psychology Bellevue Psychiat. Hosp., N.Y.C., 1973-74; with Inst. Rehab. Medicine NYU, N.Y.C., 1974—, dir. psychology intern program Inst. Rehab. Medicine, 1983-85, dir. psychol. svcs. Cancer Rehab. Svc., 1979—. Adj. asst. prof. dept. counselor edn. NYU, 1978-82, clin. instr. dept. psychiatry NYU Med. Ctr., 1981—; presenter in field. Contbr. numerous articles to profl. jours. Mem. med. adv. bd. Skin Cancer Found. NSF fellow Yeshiva U., 1966, L.I. U. fellow, 1971-72. Mem. Am. Psychol. Assn., N.Y. State Psychol. Assn., Psychoanalytic Soc. of NYU, Assn. for the Advancement of Psychology. Avocation: art. Office: 31 W 10th St New York NY 10011-8942

FREIDHEIM, CYRUS F., JR., management consultant; b. Chgo., June 14, 1935; s. Cyrus F. and Eleanor Freidheim; m. Marguerite VandenBosch; children: Marguerite Lynn, Stephen Cyrus, Scott. BSChE, U. Notre Dame, 1957; MS in Indsl. Adminstrn., Carnegie Mellon U., 1963; Dr of Internat. Laws (hon.), Am. Grad. Sch. Internat. Mgmt., 1999. Plant mgr. Union Carbide Corp., Whiting, Ind., 1961; cons. Price Waterhouse, Chgo., 1962; fin. analyst Ford Motor Co., Dearborn, Mich., 1963-66; vice chmn. Booz, Allen & Hamilton, Chgo., 1966—2002; chmn., CEO Chiquita Brands Internat., Inc., 2002—. Bd. dirs. Household Internat. Inc. Author: The Trillion Dollar Enterprise, 1998. Trustee Thunderbird, The Am. Grad. Sch. Internat. Mgmt.; dir. Chgo. Coun. Fgn. Rels.; trustee Rush-Presbyn.-St. Luke's Med. Ctr., 1981—; assoc. Northwestern U., 1981—; life trustee Chgo. Symphony Orch.; vice chmn. bd. overseers Rush U., bd. dirs.; trustee Brookings Instn., 1998—. With USN, 1957-61. Mem. Coun. Fgn. Rels., U.S. Japan Bus. Coun., Am.-China Soc. (bd. dirs.), Chgo. Club, Econ. Club, Comml. Club (Chgo.), Stanwich Club (Greenwich, Conn.), Old Elm club, Lost Tree Club (North Palm Beach). Office: Chiquita Ctr 250 E Fifth St Cincinnati OH 45202 E-mail: cfreidheim@chiquita.com.

FREIDHEIM, STEPHEN C. investment company executive; b. Detroit, July 8, 1964; s. Cyrus Foster Freidheim and Marguerite Vanden Bosche. BA in Econs., Yale U., 1986. V.p. Kidder, Peabody & Co., N.Y.C., 1986-90; sr. v.p. Nomura Securities, N.Y.C., 1990-93; ptnr., mng. dir. Bankers Trust Co., N.Y.C., 1993-99; co-sr. mng. mem. Och ziff Freidheim, N.Y.C., 1999—. Bd. dirs. Intira Corp. Mem. Coun. Fgn. Rels., Yale Alumni Assn., Yale Club, N.Y. Athletic Assn. Avocations: 17th century swords, marathons. Office: Och Ziff Freidheim 9 W 57th St New York NY 10019

FREIDLIN, MARK IOSIF, mathematician, educator; b. Moscow, Jan. 21, 1938; arrived in US, 1987; s. Iosif M. and Soshe M. Freidlin; m. Valeria Kreizman, Mar. 23, 1963; children: Boris, Julie. MSc, Moscow U., 1959, PhD, 1962, DSc, 1970. Prof. Moscow U., 1962—79, U. Md., College Park, 1987—2000, disting. univ. prof., 2000—. Author (with A.D. Wentzell): Random Perfurbations of Dynamical Systems, 1984, 1998; author: Functional Integration and Differential Equations, 1985, Random Pertubations of Hamiltonian Systems, 1994, Markov Proceses and Differential Equations, 1996. Office: Dept Math Univ Md College Park MD 20742

FREIDLINE, CHARLES, science educator; b. San Francisco, Calif., Oct. 5, 1937; s. Lawrence Logan and Catherine Mae Freidline; m. Bethel Evelyn Freidline, Aug. 6, 1960; 1 child, Jonathan Lewis. BS chemistry, Westmont Coll., Santa Barbara, Ca, 1960; MS chemistry, U. Minn., 1963, PhD chemistry, 1966. Assoc. prof. of chemistry Ctrl. Meth. Coll., Fayette, Mo., 1965—82; prof. of chemistry Union Coll., Lincoln, Nebr., 1983—. The lab. insp. EPA, Kansas city, Kans., 1980—95. Author: (book of poetry) Amat Poetry, 1982. Ch. leadership SDA Ch., Columbia, Mo., 1970. Recipient Zapara Award, Union Coll., Lincoln, Ne, 1990. Mem.: Am. Chem. Soc. (assoc.). Sda. Avocations: music, singing & composing. Home: 5236 Prescott Ave Lincoln NE 68506 Fax: 402-486-2895. Personal E-mail: chfreidl@ucollege.edu.

FREIFELD, GERALD SHERMAN, neurosurgeon; b. N.Y.C., May 12, 1935; s. Isadore and Bessie (Dende) F.; m. Roberta Ellen Donde, Dec. 15, 1963; children: Brett, Mitchell, Andrea. BS, CCNY, 1956; MD, U. Lausanne, Switzerland, 1962. Diplomate Am. Bd. Neuro-Surgery. Intern Brookdale Med. Hosp.; resident in gen. surgery, neurology and neurol. surgery Kingsbridge VA Hosp./N.Y. Neurol. Inst.; pvt. practice Regional Neurol. Surg. Group, P.C., Middletown, N.Y., 1969—, pres., 1969—. Fellow ACS, Internat. Coll. Surgeons; mem. Am. Assn. Neurol. Surgeons, Congress Neurol. Surgeons, N.Y. State Neurosurg. Soc. Jewish. Avocations: golf, tennis, walking. Office: Reg Neurol Surg Group Plc 12 Grove St Middletown NY 10940-4806

FREIHEIT, CLAYTON FREDRIC, zoo director; b. Buffalo, Jan. 29, 1938; s. Clayton John and Ruth (Miller) F. Student, U. Buffalo, 1960; DHL (hon.), U. Denver, 1996. Caretaker Living Mus., Buffalo Mus. Sci., 1955-60; curator Buffalo Zool. Gardens, 1960-70; dir. Denver Zool. Gardens, 1970—. Contbr. articles to profl. jours. Named Outstanding Citizen, Buffalo Evening News, 1967 Mem. Internat. Union Dirs. Zool. Gardens, Am. Assn. Zool. Pks. and Aquariums (pres. 1967-68 Outstanding Svc. award). Home: 3855 S Monaco Pky Denver CO 80237-1271 Office: Denver Zool Gardens City Park Denver CO 80205

FREIJE, PHILIP CHARLES, lawyer; b. Princeton, N.J., July 27, 1944; s. Brahim K. and Evelyn M. (Haddad) F.; m. Karen Mae Janovic, Oct. 18, 1969; children: Michael P., James C., Christine L. BA, U. Conn., 1966, JD, 1969; LLM, George Washington U., 1972. Bar: Conn. 1970, D.C. 1970, U.S. Supreme Ct. 1973. Assoc. Conway, Londregan, Leuba & McNamara, New London, Conn., 1969; atty.-advisor Office of Fgn. Direct Investment, U.S. Dept. Commerce, Washington, 1970-73, asst. dir. litigation, 1974; legal advisor Social & Econ. Statistics Adminstrn., U.S. Dept. Commerce, Washington, 1974-75; dep. asst. gen. counsel adminstrn./econ. affairs Office of Gen. Counsel, U.S. Dept. Commerce, Washington, 1975-81, dep. asst. gen. counsel econ. affairs/regulation, 1981-85, dep. chief counsel for econ. affairs, 1985-92, chief counsel for econ. affairs, 1992-98; bureau coun. U.S. Census Bureau U.S. Dept. Commerce, 1998—. Dir. Lake Barcroft Community Assn., Falls Church, Va., 1980-82. Mem. ABA, Fed. Bar Assn., Conn. Bar Assn., D.C. Bar Assn., Am. Judicature Soc. Home: 6212 Beachway Dr Falls Church VA 22041-1423 Office: US Dept Commerce 14th & Constitution Ave NW Washington DC 20230-0001

FREILICH, IRVIN MAYER, lawyer; b. Ulm, Germany, Mar. 3, 1949; arrived in U.S., 1949; s. Charles J. and Sylvia (Schaengold) F.; m. Judith Ellen Pines, June 20, 1971; children: Jared P., Emily R. BA, U. Cin., 1971; JD, Georgetown U., 1974. Bar: N.Y. 1975, N.J. 1977, U.S. Dist. Ct. (so. and ea. dist.) N.Y. 1975, U.S. Dist. Ct. (no. dist.) N.Y. 1985, U.S. Dist. Ct. N.J. 1975, U.S. Ct. Appeals (3d cir.) 1983, U.S. Ct. Appeals (2d cir.) 1975, U.S. Ct. Appeals (D.C. cir.) 1996, U.S. Supreme Ct. 1987. Assoc. Kaye, Scholer, Fierman, Hayes & Handler, N.Y.C., 1974-77; from assoc. to ptnr. Hannoch Weisman, Roseland, N.J., 1977-90, 94-99; ptnr. Edwards & Angell, Newark, 1990-94, Robertson, Freilich, Bruno & Cohen, LLC, Newark, 1999—. Office: Robertson Freilich Bruno & Cohen LLC One Riverfront Plz Newark NJ 07102 E-mail: ifreilich@rfbclaw.com.

FREILICH, JOAN SHERMAN, utilities executive; b. Albany, N.Y., Nov. 3, 1941; d. Julius and Bess (Bergner) Sherman; m. Sanford J. Freilich, Jan. 24, 1965. AB in French magna cum laude, Barnard Coll., 1963; MA in French, Columbia U., 1964, PhD in French, 1971, MBA in Fin., 1980. Instr. CCNY, Columbia U., N.Y.C., 1965-75; tchr. Walden Sch., N.Y.C., 1970-74; asst. to dean Coll. of New Rochelle, N.Y., 1974-75, dir. admissions, 1975-78; sr. acct. Consol. Edison Co. N.Y., N.Y.C., 1978-81, mgr. acctg. rsch., 1981-82, contr. power generation, 1982-86, gen. mgr. power generation, 1986-89, exec. asst. to pres., 1989, asst. v.p. corp. planning, 1989-90, v.p. corp. planning, 1990-92, v.p., contr., chief acctg. officer, 1992-96, sr. v.p., CFO, 1996-98, exec. v.p., CFO, 1998—; also bd. dirs. Consol. Edison, Inc and Consol. Edison of N.Y., Inc., N.Y.C. Author: Paul Claudel's "Le Soulier de satin": A Stylistic, Structuralist and Psychoanalytic Interpretation, 1973; assoc. editor Claudel Studies, 1973-78; contbr. articles to profl. jours. Trustee Citizens Budget Commn., Coll. New Rochelle; mem. pres. adv. coun. Cooper Union. Publ. grantee Humanities Rsch. Coun. Can., 1972; Pres.'s fellow Columbia U., 1964, Henry Todd fellow, 1967, recipient scholarship N.Y. State Bd. Regents, 1959, Nat. Merit Found., 1959, Columbia U., 1965. Mem.: N.Y. State Women in Comms. and Energy, YWCA Acad. of Women Achievers, Phi Beta Kappa, Beta Gamma Sigma. Office: Consolidated Edison Co NY 4 Irving Pl New York NY 10003-3598

FREILICH, MORRIS, anthropologist, educator; b. Warsaw, July 26, 1928; s. Harry Aaron and Sura Charna (Kashket) F.; m. Natalie Asch, June 20, 1954 (div. July 1978); children: Harry, Steven; m. Mirjana Lakich, June 28, 1981; 1 child, Michael Neal. BA in Econs., Bklyn. Coll., 1951; PhD in Anthropology, Columbia U., 1960. Instr. U. Akron, Ohio, 1959-61; asst. prof. No. Ill. U., DeKalb, 1961-63; assoc. prof. Washington U., St. Louis, 1963-66, Northeastern U., Boston, 1966-74, prof. anthopology, 1974-98; vis. prof. Framingham State Coll., Boston, 2001—02. Editor, contbr. to books: Marginal Natives: Anthropologists at Work, 1970, The Meaning of Culture, 1972, The Relevance of Culture, 1989; sr. editor, contbr.: Deviance: Anthropological Perspectives, 1991. Cpl. U.S. Army, 1953-55. Fellow Am. Anthropol. Assn. Jewish. Avocations: chess, racquetball.

FREILICH, ROBERT H. lawyer, law educator, legal consultant; b. N.Y.C., Mar. 10, 1936; s. Julius and Evelyn R. (Ravitt) F.; m. Carole S. Traktman, Dec. 25, 1958; children— Amy Elizabeth, Bradley Lawrence. A.B., U. Chgo., 1954; LL.B., Yale U., 1957; M.I.A., Columbia U., 1958, LL.M., 1969, J.S.D., 1974. Bar: N.Y. 1958, Mo. 1968, Calif. 1989; U.S. Ct. Appeals (2d cir.) 1958, U.S. Ct. Appeals (4th cir.) 1974, U.S. Ct. Appeals (8th cir.) 1968, U.S. Ct. Appeals (9th cir.) 1976, U.S. Supreme Ct. 1960. prof. law in urban affairs Sch. Law, U. Mo., Kansas City, 1968— ; ptnr. Freilich, Leitner & Carlisle, P.C., Kansas City, 1972—; ptnr. Freilich, Kaufman, Fox & Sohagi, L.A., Calif.; cons. mcpl. law zoning, litigation and real estate devel.; vis. prof. Sch. Law, London Sch. Econs. and Reading U., 1974, Harvard U. Law Sch. 1984-85. Author: Cases and Materials on Land Use, 1993, Model Subdivision Regulations, 1993; Urban Growth Management Systems, 1978; The Land Use Awakening, 1982; The Sword and The Shield, 1983 . Dir. Mcpl. Legal Studies Ctr., Southwestern Legal Found., Rocky Mountain Land Use Inst. Mem. ABA (mem. council of sect. urban, state and local govt., editor Urban Lawyer jour.), Am. Planning Assn. (chair-elect, planning and law div.), Am. Coll. Real Estate Lawyers, Assn. Am. Law Schs. (chmn. sect. local govt. law). Home: 400 W 49th Ter Apt 2048 Kansas City MO 64112-2532 Office: Freilich, Leitner & Carlisle 1150 One Main Plaza 4435 Main Street Kansas City MO 64111-7727

FREILICHER, JANE, artist; b. N.Y.C., Nov. 29, 1924; d. Martin and Bertha (Niederhoffer); m. Joseph Hazan, Feb. 17, 1957; 1 dau., Elizabeth. AB, Bklyn. Coll., 1947; postgrad., Hans Hoffman Sch. Fine Arts, 1947; MA, Columbia U., 1948. Vis. lectr., critic art schs., colls. One-woman shows include Tibor de Nagy, 1952-68, 98, 2000, 2002, John Bernard Myers Gallery, 1971, Fischbach Gallery, 1975, 77, 79-80, 83, 85, 88, 90, 92, 95, Utah Mus. Fine Arts, 1979, Lafayette Coll., 1981, Kansas City Art Inst., 1983, David Heath Gallery, Atlanta, 1990, Reynolds Gallery, Richmond, Va., 1993, Nat. Acad., 2002; group exhbns. include Met. Mus. Art, 1979-80, Denver Art Mus., 1979, Pa. Acad., 1981, Am. Acad. and Inst. of Arts and Letters, 1981, 84-85, Bklyn. Mus. 1984, Yale U., 1986, Tibor de Nagy Gallery, 1992, Whitney Mus., 1955, 72, 95, Whitney Mus., Stamford, Conn., 1999, Artists Eye NAD, 2002, Women of Acad. NAD, 2003; curator Nat. Acad., 2002; represented in permanent collections Met. Mus. Art, Hirschorn Mus., Bklyn. Mus., NYU, Rose Art Mus., Whitney Mus., Cleve. Mus. Art, San Francisco Mus. Art, others; travelling retrospective in Currier Gallery Art, Parrish Mus., Contemporary Arts Mus., McNay Mus., 1986-87; illustrator Turandot and Other Poems, 1953, Paris Review, 1965, Descriptions of a Masque, 1998. Recipient Eloise Spaeth award Guild Hall Mus., East Hampton, N.Y., 1991, Lifetime Achievement award Guild Hall Mus., 1996; AAUW fellow, 1974; Nat. Endowment Arts grantee, 1976; Benjamin West Clinedinst Meml. medal Artists' Fellowship, 1997. Mem. NAD (academician) (Saltus Gold medal 1987, Benjamin Altman landscape prize 1995, Edwin Palmer prize 2003), Am. Acad. Arts and Letters.

FREILICHER, MORTON, lawyer, educator; b. NYC, June 23, 1931; s. Morris and Gertrude D. (Pedowitz) F.; m. Yseult A. Snepvangers, Dec. 3, 1972. BA, Columbia Coll., N.Y.C., 1953, JD, 1956. Bar: N.Y. 1957. Assoc. Hartman & Craven, NYC, 1956-60, Phillips, Nizer LLP, NYC, 1960-67, ptnr., 1967-94, counsel, 1995—. Adj. prof. law Sch. Fordham U., N.Y.C., 1982-92. Author: Estate Planning Handbook, 1970; editor-in-chief Jour. of Estate and Tax Planning for the Elderly and Disabled, 1986-91. Chmn. trusts and estates lawyers divsn. UJA Fedn., 1985; dir. The Edouard Found., 1996—. Harlan Fiske Stone scholar Columbia Law Sch., 1956. Fellow Am. Coll. Trusts and Estates Counsel; mem. ABA, N.Y. State Bar Assn., N.Y.C. Bar Assn. Democrat. Jewish. Avocations: hiking, exercise, reading. Home: 200 E 57th St New York NY 10022 Office: Phillips Nizer et al 666 5th Ave New York NY 10103-0001

FREIMAN, ALVIN HENRY, cardiologist, educator; b. N.Y.C., Jan. 26, 1927; s. Maurice and Beatrice (Freeman) Freiman; m. Nadine Roehr, June 12, 1959; children: Audrey L., Gail L., Marshall A. BA, N.Y. U., 1947, MD, 1953; MS, U. Ill., 1949. Diplomate Am. Bd. Internal Medicine. Intern Montefiore Hosp., N.Y.C., 1953—54; resident in medicine and cardiology Beth Israel Hosp., Boston, 1954—56; fellow in cardiology Meml. Hosp., N.Y.C., 1956—58; individual practive medicine specializing in internal medicine and cardiology N.Y.C., 1954—. Attending staff cardiology Meml. Sloan-Kettering Cancer Ctr., N.Y.C., 1971—, dir. clin. info. ctr., 1974—; attending physician Sloan-Kettering Inst., N.Y.C., 1995; prof. medicine Cornell U. Med. Coll., N.Y.C., 1995—. Contbr. articles. With USNR, 1945—46. Mem.: AAAS, Internat. Coll. Angiology, N.Y. Acad. Scis., Am. Heart Assn., Am. Coll. Angiology, Am. Coll. Chest Physicians, Am. Coll. Cardiology, A.C.P., Nat. Cancer Inst., Sigma Xi, Alpha Omega Alpha. Home: 74 Homestead Rd Tenafly NJ 07670 1109 Office: 178 E End Ave New York NY 10128-7762

FREIMAN, DAVID GALLAND, pathologist, educator; b. N.Y.C., July 1, 1911; s. Leopold and Dorothy (Galland) F.; m. Ruth Schein, Sept. 2, 1949; children: Nancy, Leonard. AB, CCNY, 1930; MD, L.I. Coll. Medicine (now Downstate Med. Center SUNY), 1935; AM (hon), Harvard U., 1962. Intern, house physician Jewish Hosp. of Bklyn., 1935-36; intern Kingston Ave. Hosp. (for Contagious Disease), Bklyn., 1938; intern, resident pathology Montefiore Hosp., 1938-43; asst. pathologist Mass. Gen. Hosp., 1944-50; attending pathologist Cin. Gen. Hosp., Drake Meml. Hosp., 1952-56; pathologist-in-chief, dir. labs. Beth Israel Hosp., Boston, 1956-79, emeritus, 1979—, spl. asst. to pres., 1979—; cons. pathologist VA, Hosps., Cin., Ft. Thomas, Ky., 1954-56, Boston, 1962-85; instr. pathology Med. Sch. Tufts U., 1947-48, Harvard U. Med. Sch., 1949-50, clin. prof. pathology, 1956-62, prof., 1962-84, Mallinckrodt prof. pathology, 1969-79, emeritus, 1984—; prof. anatomy, interim chmn. dept. anatomy U. Mass. Coll. Medicine, 1985-87; asst. prof. pathology Coll. Medicine, U. Cin., 1950-52; assoc. prof. U. Cin. Coll. Medicine, 1952-56; lectr. pathology Simmons, 1962-78. Cons. pathology Cambridge Hosp., 1968-85, Uniformed Services U. Health Scis., 1974-75, Children's Hosp. Med. Center, Boston, 1977-90; mem. joint faculty Harvard-MIT, 1975-79 Mem. editorial bd. Am. Jour. Pathology, 1961-82, Circulation, 1962-67, Human Pathology, 1969-93, assoc. editor, 1979-91; mem. editorial adv. com. Atlas of Tumor Pathology, 1966-87; contbr. articles to profl. jours. Recipient Stratford prize CCNY, 1931, Alumni prize L.I. Coll. Medicine, 1935; Kirstein fellow in med. edn. Harvard U., 1971-72 Mem.: AAAS, Internat. Soc. for Haemostasis and Thrombosis, New Eng. Soc. Pathologists, Mass. Med. Soc., Am. Soc. Clin. Pathologists, Histochem. Soc., Internat. Acad. Pathology, Am. Soc. for Investigative Pathology, Alpha Omega Alpha, Sigma Xi, Phi Beta Kappa. Home: 182 Homer St Newton MA 02459-1518 Office: Beth Israel Deaconess Med Ctr 330 Brookline Ave Boston MA 02215-5400 E-mail: dfreiman@caregroup.harvard.edu.

FREIMARK, JEFFREY PHILIP, corporate financial executive; b. Bklyn., Mar. 11, 1955; s. Benjamin and Fay (Lefton) F.; m. Hollis Joan Hauser, Aug. 27, 1978; children: Samara, Brandon. BS, U. So. Fla., 1976; MBA, NYU, 1980; JD, N.Y. Law Sch., 1984. Bar: N.J. 1985; CPA, N.J., Fla. Sr. staff acct. Abraham and Straus, Bklyn., 1976-78; internal audit dir. Stern's Dept. Store, Paramus, N.J., 1978-79; dir. acctg. Kings Super Markets, West Caldwell, N.J., 1979-82, controller, 1982-83, controller, sec., 1983-84, v.p. fin., 1985-86; sr. v.p. fin. and adminstrn., chief fin. officer, treas., dir. PXC & M Holdings Inc./Pueblo Xtra Internat. (formerly Pueblo Internat. Inc.), Pompano Beach, Fla., 1986-91, exec. v.p., chief fin. officer, sec., 1992-97; exec. v.p., CFO, sec., dir. Pueblo Xtra Internat., Inc., Pompano Beach, Fla., 1993-97, PXC&M, Inc., Pompano Beach, 1993-97; exec. v.p., CFO, chief adminstv. officer, treas., dir. The Grand Union Co., 1997—2000, pres., CEO, CFO, 2000—01; sr. exec. v.p., CFO OfficeMax, Inc., 2001—; exec. v.p., CFO, CIO Beverly Enterprises, Inc., Fort Smith, Ariz., 2002—. Vol. dir. NYU Grad. Sch. Bus. Mgmt. Decision Lab., 1980-81. Mem. ABA, N.J. Bar Assn., Am. Inst. CPA's, Fla. Soc. CPA's, N.J. Soc. CPA's, Assn. MBA Execs., Fin. Execs. Inst. Republican. Jewish. Avocations: reading, tennis, golf.

FREIMARK, ROBERT (BOB FREIMARK), artist; b. Doster, Mich., Jan. 27, 1922; s. Alvin O. and Nora (Shinaver) F.; m. Mary Carvin (dec.); 1 son, Matisse Jon; m. Lillian Tihlarik; 1 child, Christine Gay. B.E., U. Toledo, 1950; M.F.A., Cranbrook Acad. Art, 1951. Prof. art emeritus San Jose State U., 1964-86; W.I.C.H.E. prof. Soledad State Prison, 1967. Established artist in residence program Yosemite Nat. Park,1984-85, Fire Clay and Tile, Aromas, Calif., 1998; artist in residence Museo Regla, Cuba, 2000, Ferencsik Janos Zeneskola, L. Balaton, Hungary, 2002; panelist SECOLAS S.E. conf. Latin Am. Studies, Vera Cruz, Mex. Guest artist Harvard U., 1972-73; first Am. to make tapestries in Art Protis technique at Atelier Vlnena, Brno, Czechoslovakia.; contbr. to profl. publs.; Numerous solo shows including, Minn. Inst. Arts, Toledo Mus. Art, Salpeter Gallery, Morris Gallery, N.Y.C., Des Moines Art Center, Santa Barbara Mus., Moravska Mus., Czechoslovakia, Brunel U., London, Amerika Haus, Munich, Stuttgart, Regensburg, Joslyn Ctr. for Arts, Torrance, Calif, Stanford U., San Jose (Calif.) Mus. Art, Triton Mus., Santa Clara, Calif., Guatemalteco, Guatemala City, Dum Umeni Brno, CSFR, Strahov Closter, Prague, 1990, Walter Bischoff Gallery, Stuttgart, 1990, Kunstler aus den USA, Kunsthaus Ostbayern and Amerika Haus, Stuttgart, 1991, Max Planck Inst., Munich, The Gag Theatre, Prague, 1992, Haus Wiegand, Munich, 1993, San Jose State U., 1994, Viva!, Tokyo, 1994, Gallery Q, Sacramento, 1997, Parish Gallery, Wash. D.C., 1997, 2002, Barton Gallery, Sacramento, Calif., 1997, 2002; Galeria Galiano Havana, 1998, Galerie Weber, Viechtach, Germany, 1998, Point Gall., Brno, Czech Rep., 1998, Galerie Divadlo, Uherske Hradiste, C.R., 1998, Marco Polo Galleries, Carmel, Calif., 2001, Colton Hall Mus., Monterey, Calif., 2002; exhibited in group shows, Art Inst. Chgo., 1952, Pa. Acad. Fine Arts, 1953 (Lambert Fund prize), Detroit Inst. Arts, 1956, Mich. State U., 1956, N.A.D., 1956, Boston Print Symposium, 1997, Internat. Print Exhibition Portland (Oreg.) Art Mus., 1997, Honolulu Acad. Art, 1998, Internat. Graphic Triennial, Krakow, Poland, 1998, Internat. Small Engraving Salon, Florean Mus., Romania, Art Expo, N.Y.C., 2000, Internat. Woodprint Assn., Kyoto, Japan, 1999, Bklyn. Mus., Mus. Modern Art, Michael Stone Collection, D.C., Contempo Collection, Tokyo, Havana Bienale, 2000, others, L.A.,

Boston, San Francisco, Omaha, Oklahoma City, Des Moines, Dallas, Phoenix, San Jose, Havana, Tokyo, Manila, Rio de Janeiro, Mexico City, Sao Paulo, Brasilia, Buenos Aires, Prague, exhbn. 50 States toured, European Mus., 1970-71, represented in collections, Pa. Acad. Fine Art, Boston Mus. Fine Arts, Fogg Mus., Butler Inst. Am. Art, Ford Motor Co., South Bend Art Assn., Joslyn Art Mus., Seattle Art Mus., Ga. Mus., Huntington Gallery, Des Moines Art Center, Smithsonian Instn., Libr. Congress, L.A. County Art Inst., Brit. Mus., Nat. Gallery, Prague, Birmingham (Eng.) Mus., Moravske Mus., Brno, Czechoslovakia, Bibliotheque Nationale, Paris, Harn Mus., Gainsville, Fla., Portland Mus. Art (complete prints), Nat. Mus., Washington, Natl. Mus. of Cuba, La Habana, Nat. Mus. Costa Rica, San Jose, Nat. Mus. Egypt, Cairo, Mus. de Arte Contemporaneo, Bahia Blanca, Mus. Genaro Perez, Cordoba, Mus. de Bellas Artes, Cordoba, Argentina, Mus. Guayasamin, Quito, Ecuador, Mus. Nacional, Panama City, Panama, others; numerous tapestries in pub. and pvt. collections, created tapestry representing U.S. for Olympic Games, Moscow, 1980; prodr. film El Dia Tarasco, 1982; prodr. video documentary: Arte Cubano (Contemporary Art and Culture in Cuba, 1999, 2000, Los Desaparecidos--The Disappeared Ones, 2003; guest artist Joslyn Meml. Mus., 1961, instr. painting and drawing, Ohio U., 1955-59, artist in residence, Des Moines Art Center, 1959-63, dir., Crystal Lake Art Center, Frankfort, Mich., (1955-57), guest lectr., one man show, Columbia U., 1963, solo exhibit, Northamerican Cultural Inst., Mexico City, 1963; guest artist Riverside Art Center, 1964, Agora Vienna, Austria, 1994, Museo Guayasamin, Quito, Ecuador, 2002; curated exhibit Stuttgart, 1993; founder Bob & Lil Freimark Collection Portland Art Mus.; artist in residence Museo Regla, Cuba, 2002, Lake Balaton, Hungary, 2002; Am. corollary to Dakar Bienale, 5 works, Senegal, 2002; contbr. to craft and fibre publs. Served with USNR, 1939-46. Recipient 2d award for oil Northwest Territorial exhibit, 1954, Roulet medal Toledo Mus. Art, 1957, 1st award Print Exhbn., 1958, purchase award Midwest Biennial and Northwest Printmakers, Jurors award Berkeley Art Ctr, 1996; Calif. State Coll. Sys. spl. creative leave edit. serigraphs; elected to New Talent in U.S.A., 1957; Ohio U. rsch. grantee, 1958-59, Ford Found. grantee, 1965; Western Interstate Commn. for Higher Edn. grantee, 1967, San Jose State Coll. Found. grantee, 1966, 67, 68, 69, 70, 71, 85; designated ofcl. U.S. Bicentennial Exhbn. Amerika Hausen, Fed. Republic Germany, 1976; donated Bob & Lil Freimark Collection, Mexican Arts & Crafts, Gavilan Coll., Gilroy, Calif., 1996; represented by Parish Gallery, Washington, Triad Gallery, Seal Rock, Oreg., Haus Wiegand, Munich, Art Foundry Gallery, Sacramento, Greg Barlon Gallery, Sacramento, Hart Gallery, Chgo., Palm Desert and Carmel, Calif.. Achievements include being subject of TV interview, 1993. Home: 539A Dougherty Ave Morgan Hill CA 95037-9241 Office: Grass Valley Studios Morgan Hill CA 95037 E-mail: bfreimar@pacbell.net.

FREIMUTH, MARC WILLIAM, lawyer; b. Duluth, Minn., Sept. 23, 1946; s. Edgar and Marcia (Zuckerman) F.; m. Sharon Rae Sager, Feb. 7, 1946 (dec.); children: Ladeene Asher, Kyle Gregory, Joel Todd. BA, U. Minn., 1968, JD magna cum laude, 1971. Bar: Ohio 1971. Atty. Squire, Sanders, Dempsey, Cleve., 1971-78; sr. v.p., gen. counsel, sec. Ohio Savs. Fin. Corp., Cleve., 1978—. Sec. Superior Flux & Mfg. Co., Cleve., 1979-89, Solid Sound Inc., Chgo., 1982-92; dir. Sayer Corp., 1989-95. Trustee Bur. Jewish Edn., Cleve., 1980-90, Jewish Cmty. Fed., Cleve., 1986-91, 2000—, Cleve. Opera, 2003—; pres., trustee The Agnon Sch., Cleve., 1984—; trustee, v.p. Park Synagogue, 1984-94; assoc. v.p. United Way, Cleve., 1986-89; with Leadership Cleve., 1985; trustee, pres. Jewish Cmty. Ctr., Cleve., 1995—, Maccabi U.S.A., 2003—. Mem. ABA, Ohio State Bar Assn., Greater Cleve. Bar Assn. Avocations: golf, tennis, softball. Office: Ohio Savs Fin Corp 1801 E 9th St Cleveland OH 44114-3103

FREIRE, GLORIA MEDONIS, social worker; b. Pitts., Apr. 19, 1929; d. Vincent X. and Anastasia T. (Puida) Medonis; m. Luis Francis Freire, Aug. 30, 1958; children: Michael, Charles. BA in Polit. Sci. & Econs., Carlow Coll., 1950; MSSA, Case-Western Res. U., 1955; MPA, Cleve. State U., 1986; PhD, Union Inst., 1995. Teen-age dir. Merrick House, Cleve., 1955-62; group psychotherapist Cleve. Psychiat. Inst., 1966-73; lectr. sch. applied social scis. Case-Western Res. U., Cleve., 1973-75; cluster dir. Golden Age Ctrs., Cleve., 1975-76; specialist Cmty. Guidance & Human Svcs., Cleve., 1976, staff tng. & devel. coord., 1977, dir. consultation & edn., 1978-84; coord. psychiat. emergency svcs. systems Lake County Mental Health Bd., Ohio, 1984-86; adminstr. Hispanic office Cath. Social Svcs., Cleve., 1986-97; asst. prof. social work Cleve. State U., 1997—. Editor SASS mag., Case Western Res. U. Alumni, 1973-79. Chmn. steering com. East Cmty. Task Force on Desegregation; chmn. subcoun. of Ohio Cmty. Mental Health Ctrs. Consultations & Edn.; chmn. consultation & Edn. Coun. Cleve.; coord. Christian Formation cmty. of St. Malachi, 1975-77, coord. liturgy commn., 1978-80, coord. social concerns com., 1982-84; mem. Diocesan Commn. on Cath. Cmty. Action, 1982-88, vice chmn., 1986-87; mem. Urban League Edn. Adv. and Task Force on Minium Competency, 1978-80; trustee Cuyahoga County Pub. Libr., 2003—. Recipient Disting. Leadership award, Alumnae Assn. Carlow Coll., 1982. Mem. AAUW, NASW (task force on desegregation 1974-83, co-chmn. 1981-83, coord. polit. action com. 1977, dir. Cleve. chpt., 1975-77, sec.-treas. Ohio coun. chpts., 1975-76, steering com. Cleve. chpt. 1987-89), Acad. Cert. Social workers, Am. Soc. Pub. Adminstrn. (trustee Cleve. chpt. 1987-92, 98—), Am. soc. Profl. & Exec. Women, Nat. and Cuyahoga County Women's Polit. Caucus (exec. bd.), Am. Group Psychotherapy Assn., Am. Planning Assn., Coun. Social Work Edn., Union Inst. Learner Coun. Advocacy and Adv. Task Force (alt. chmn. 1991-92), Tri-State Group Psychotherapy Soc., Nat. Network Social Work Mgrs., Nat. Image Hispanic Profls. (trustee 1991-92, pres. N.E. Ohio chpt. 1992-94), Julia Burgos Ctr. (bd. dirs. 1998-99), Japan Soc. Cleve. (bd. dirs. 1996-98, exec. com. 1997-98), Japanese Am. Citizens League, Esperanza/Hispanic Edn. (mem. adv. bd. 1998-99, exec. bd. 1999—). Democrat. Roman Catholic. Home: 5001 Tuxedo Ave Cleveland OH 44134-1007 Office: Cleve State U Dept Social Work 2300 Chester Ave Cleveland OH 44114 E-mail: g.freire@csuohio.edu.

FREIRE, JOSE A. physicist, writer; b. Cienfuegos, Cuba, Apr. 18, 1925; arrived in U.S., 1968; s. Jose M. Freire and Maria C. Valle; m. Maria C. Paula Freire, Dec. 16, 1950; children: Maria C., Jose L., Jose A. BS, Mercy Coll.; D in Physics and Chemistry, Havana (Cuba) U. Mem.: Am. Assn. Physics Tchrs., Am. Legion (supporter). Republican. Roman Catholic. Home: 2356 SW 140 Pl Miami FL 33175

FREIREICH, EMIL J, hematologist, educator; b. Chgo., Mar. 16, 1927; s. David and Mary (Klein) F.; m. Haroldine Lee Cunningham, Mar. 13, 1953; children: Debra Ann, David Alan, Lindsay Gail, Thomas Jon. BS, U. Ill., 1947, MD with honors, 1949, D.Sc. (hon.), 1982. Diplomate Am. Bd. Internal Medicine. Intern Cook County (Ill.) Hosp., Chgo., 1949-50; resident in internal medicine Presbyn. Hosp., Chgo., 1950-53; rsch. assoc. in hematology Mass. Meml. Hosp., Boston, 1953-55; sr. investigator, head Leukemia Svc. USPHS, Nat. Cancer Inst., Bethesda, Md., 1955-65; prof. medicine U. Tex. System Cancer Ctr., Houston, 1965—, chief rsch. in hematology, 1965-85, head dept. devel. therapeutics, 1972-83, chmn. dept. hematology, 1983-85, dir. Adult Leukemia Rsch. Program, 1985—; prof. medicine U. Tex. Health Sci. Ctr. (Sch. Medicine), 1973—, chief divsn. oncology, 1973-81; mem. faculty Grad. Sch. Med., Health Scis. Ctr., 1965—. Mem. rev. com. drug. devel. div. cancer treatment NIH, 1975-80, Ruth Harriet Ainsworth chair in devel. therapeutics, 1980— Assoc. editor Cancer, 1976—, Cancer Research, 1977-86; mem. editorial bd. Oncology News, 1975-90, Cancer Treatment Reports, 1976-80, Leukemia Research, 1976-87, Med. and Pediatric Oncology, 1974—, Leukemia 1987—; contbr. numerous articles on research in hematology and oncology to profl. jours. Recipient Albert Lasker Med. rsch. award, 1972, Charles F. Kettering prize Gen. Motors Cancer Rsch. Found., 1983, Outstanding Investigator award Nat. Cancer Inst., NIH, 1985-92, Alumnus award NIH, 1990; named Alumnus of Yr., U. Ill. Alumni Assn., 1974, Alumni Achievement award, 2000. Fellow ACP, AAAS; mem. Internat. Soc. Hematology, Am. Soc. Hematology, Am. Fedn. Clin. Research, Am. Soc. Clin. Pharmacology and Therapeutics, Am. Soc. Clin. Oncology (David A. Karnofsky award 1976, pres. 1980-81), Am. Soc. Clin. Investigators, Am. Assn. Cancer Research, Leukemia Soc. Am. (pres. Gulf Coast chpt. 1968-70, trustee 1968-70, Robert Roesler DeVilliers award 1979, grant rev. subcom. 1986-89), Tex. Med. Assn., AMA (editorial bd. jour. 1973-83), Assn. Am. Physicians, Alpha Omega Alpha. Achievements include research in therapy of human acute leukemia and leukocyte physiology. Home: 810 Monte Cello St Houston TX 77024-4515 Office: M D Anderson Cancer Ctr 1515 Holcombe Blvd Houston TX 77030-4009 E-mail: efreirei@mdanderson.org. *The search for eternal physical and mental health has been at the forefront of man's striving to understand and to control his destiny. The opportunity to investigate, to discover and to apply new remedies for major human illness is a rare privilege, one of man's highest callings.*

FREIS, EDWARD DAVID, physician, medical researcher; b. Chgo., May 13, 1912; 3 children. BS, U. Ariz., 1936; MD, Columbia, 1940. Intern, house physician Mass. Meml. Hosp., Boston, 1940-41; sr. intern, house physician Boston City Hosp., 1941-42; asst. resident Evans Meml. Hosp., 1946-47, resident fellow cardiovascular disease, 1947-49; adj. clin. prof. Georgetown U. Sch. Medicine, 1949-57, assoc. prof., 1957-63, prof., 1963—; sr. med. investigator VA Med. Ctr., Washington, 1959-87, asst. chief medicine, 1949-54, chief, 1954-59; instr. Boston U., 1947-49. Served with M.C. USAAF, 1942-45. Recipient Albert Lasker Med. Research award, 1971, Ciba award in hypertension, 1981, E. Fries award Nat. Conf. High Blood Pressure Coun., 1985, Spl. Achievement award Am. Soc. Hypertension, 1990. Office: VA Med Ctr 50 Irving St NW Washington DC 20422-0001

FREISHTAT, ROBERT J. pediatrician, researcher; s. David D. and Rochelle E. Freishtat; m. Jamie A. Abramowitz, June 8, 1971; children: Nathaniel H., Maxwell H. MD, U. Md., 1997. Cert. bd. cert. pediats. Am. Bd. of Pediat. Fellow Children's Nat. Med. Ctr., Washington, 2000—. Office: Children's Nat Med Ctr 111 Michigan Ave NW Washington DC 20010 Office Fax: 202-884-3573. E-mail: rfreisht@cnmc.org.

FREITAG, CAROL WILMA, state official, political scientist; b. Ada, Okla., July 21, 1939; d. Lowell William and Lois Marie (Robertson) Petersen; m. Henry Wesley Freitag, Dec. 20, 1961 (dec. Nov. 1985); children: Bonita, Henry. Diploma in Dental Hygiene, Northwestern U., 1959; BA, Purdue U., Hammond, Ind., 1988. Registered dental hygienist, Ill. Pvt. practice dental hygiene Henry W. Freitag, D.D.S., Homewood, Ill., 1959-85; mem. group practice Chgo., 1970; faculty, interim dir. dental hygiene Prairie State Coll., Chgo. Heights, Ill., 1971-72; pvt. practice James J. Kreuz, D.D.S., Homewood, 1983-90. Contbr. articles to profl. jour. Chair US Constn. Bicentennial Commn., Village of Matteson, Ill., 1986-89; pres. Matteson Hist. Soc., 1987-89, panel spkr. South Suburban Heritage Assn., Homewood, 1990. Calumet rep. Bicentennial Com. Purdue U., 1988; vis. com. Northwestern Dental Sch., 1997-98; mem. centennial celebration com. Bloom Twp. HS, 2000; mem. Hist. Columbia Found. 2003—. Recipient Key to City, Village of Matteson, 1990, Svc. award Northwestern U., 1980, Good Neighbor award Village of Matteson, 1989, Outstanding Alumni 1950's Decade award Bloom Twp. H.S., 2000. Mem. Am. Dental Hygienists' Assn. (chair Ann. Session Program 1975), Ill. Dental Hygienists Assn. (pres. 1968-69, bd. dirs., Merit award 1979), G.V. Black Soc. (leader, pres. 1997-2001), Evelyn E. Maas Soc. (pres. 1989-90, bd. dirs., Merit award 1993), Northwestern Dental Sch. Alumni Assn. (bd. dirs. 1969-2001, pres. 1977-78, v.p. 1976-77, 90-93), Acad. Polit. Sci., Sigma Phi Alpha, Alpha Chi. Avocation: travel. Home: 117 Oak Trace Ct Chapin SC 29036

FREITAG, HARLOW, retired computer scientist and corporate executive; b. Bklyn., Apr. 17, 1936; s. Abraham and Eva (Levine) F.; 1 son, Adam. BS with honors, NYU, 1955; MS, Yale U., 1958, PhD, 1959. Research staff mem. IBM, Yorktown Heights, N.Y., 1961-70, asst. dir. computer sci., 1970-77, White Plains, N.Y., 1977-80, staff v.p., group exec., 1980-82, editor Jour. Rsch. and Devel., 1982-85; dep. dir. Supercomputing Rsch. Ctr., Bowie, Md., 1986-91; tech. staff Inst. for Def. Analysis, Alexandria, Va., 1991-94; ret., 1994. Recipient Outstanding Innovation award IBM, 1966; recipient Francis Mills Turner award Electrochem. Soc., 1959 Fellow IEEE (editor procs. of IEEE 1979-82, Centennial medal 1984), Yale Sci. and Engring. Assn. (exec. v.p. 1981-83, pres. 1983-85). E-mail: freitag@bellatlantic.net.

FREITAG, WOLFGANG MARTIN, librarian, educator; b. Berlin, Oct. 27, 1924; came to U.S. 1955, naturalized, 1961; s. Georg and Anne Marie (Friess) F.; m. Doris Christiane Pfeil, Oct. 25, 1952; children— Thomas Martin, Tilman George Dr. Phil., U. Freiburg, W. Ger., 1950; postgrad., Harvard U., 1951-52; MS in Library Sci., Simmons Coll., Boston, 1956. Reference libr., program dir. U.S. Info. Ctr., Frankfurt, Germany, 1950-53; editor Droemer-Knaur Publ., Munich, 1953-55; cataloger Harvard Coll. Library, Cambridge, Mass., 1955-60; head librarian Gordon McKay Library, Harvard U., 1960-62; chief undergrad. library planning Stanford U., Calif., 1962-64; librarian Fine Arts Library Fogg Art Mus., Harvard U., 1964-91, sr. lectr. bibliography and art historiography, 1967-91; lectr. libr. sci. Simmons Coll., Boston, Mass., 1991-92. Libr. cons. J.P. Getty Trust, L.A., 1982-83, U. Pitts, 1983, The Frick Collection, N.Y. 1984, Inst. Fine Arts, NYU, 1987; mem. vis. com. Met. Mus. Art, 1972-92; bd. vis. Sch. Info. Studies, Syracuse U., 1981-85, SUNY, Stony Brook, 1986, NYU Inst. Fine Arts, 1987. Editor: Artist Resource Manuals, Art Books: Monographs on Artists, 1985, 2d edit., 1997; cons. to pubs.; contbr. articles to profl. jours. Fulbright fellow, 1951, 68, Council Library Resources fellow, 1975. Mem. Art Libraries Soc. N.Am. (pres. 1980), Coll. Art Assn., Internat. Fedn. Library Assns. (exec. com. art librs. sect. 1985-93), Goethe Soc. New Eng., Boston Soc. Printers. Avocation: autograph collecting. Home: 43 Fair Oaks Dr Lexington MA 02421-6931

FREITAS, ANTOINETTE JUNI, insurance company executive; b. Kansas City, Mo., Feb. 14, 1944; d. ANthony P. and Mariam L. Freitas; m. Stephen R. Krajcar, July 4, 1980. BA, Calif. State U., Long Beach, 1966; MA, U. So. Calif., 1974. CLU; ChFC. Counselor U. So. Calif., 1967-70, assoc. dir. fin. aid, 1970-75; sales agt. Equitable Life Assurance Co., 1975-79, dist. mgr., 1979-84; pres. Group Mktg. Svcs., Inc.; field dir. Northwestern Mut. Life, San Francisco, 1984-86; pres. Penisula Fin. Group, Inc., 1986—; mktg. mgr. Home Life, H.L. Fin. Group, San Jose, Calif., 1986—. Registered rep. Carrilon, Investments, Securities, 1987-91. Author: A Study in Changing Youth Values, 1974. Bd. dirs. San Francisco Zoo1. Soc., 1996—. Recipient various sales and mgmt. awards; mem. Million Dollar Round Table. Mem. AAUW, Nat. Assn. Life Underwriters, Women LIfe Underwriters Conf., U. So. Calif. Alumni Assn. Republican. Episcopalian. Office: Peninsula Fin Group Inc 2995 Woodside Rd Ste 400 Woodside CA 94062-2448

FREITAS, DAVID PRINCE, lawyer; b. San Francisco, Oct. 21, 1940; s. Walter Francis and Marno Catherine (Prince) F.; m. Alice Urrutia, June 24, 1961 (div. 1972); children: Diane Phillips, Nancy Freitas, Megan Neale; m. Patricia Garbarino, June 20, 1996. BS, U. San Francisco, 1964; JD, San Francisco Law Sch., 1968. Bar: Calif. 1969. Atty. Freitas Law Firm, San Rafael, Calif., 1969-96, Ragghianti, Freitas, Montobbio & Wallace LLP, San Rafael, 1996—. Bd. dirs. St. Vincent's Sch.; lectr. in field; judge pro tempore San Francisco and Marin Counties; spl. master Superior Cts. of Marin and Sonoma. Contbr. articles to profl. jours. Bd. dirs. Guide Dogs for the Blind, San Rafal, 1994-95, Marin Agrl. Land Trust, 1991-92, Marin County Humane Soc., 1967-71. Fellow Am. Coll. Trial Lawyers, Internat. Acad. Trial Lawyers, Internat. Soc. Barristers; mem. Internat. Assn. Def. Counsel, Am. Bd. Trial Adv. (San Francisco chpt., pres. 1993, nat. bd. dirs. 1992—, exec. com. 1990—), Nat. Bd. Trial Adv. (diplomate), Assn. Def. Counsel N.C. (pres. 1985, bd. dirs. 1977-86), Calif. State Bar Assn. (adminstrn. justice com. 1982, jury instrns. com. 1977), Calif. Def. Counsel (bd. dirs. 1984), Marin County Bar Assn. (secr. 1987, treas. 1984), Def. Rsch. Inst. (Nat. Execptional Performance award 1985), Cal-ABOTA (bd. chair 1995), Edward J. McFetridge Am. Inn Ct. (pres. 1993, exec. com. 1990—), San Rafal C. of C. (bd. dirs. 1995—). Home: 19 Palm Ave San Rafael CA 94901-2221 Office: Ragghianti Freitas Montobbio Wallace LLP 874 4th St San Rafael CA 94901-3246

FREIZER, LOUIS A. radio news producer; b. N.Y.C., Oct. 10, 1931; s. Morris and Celia (Lassersohn) F.; m. Michèle Suzanne Orban, July 6, 1968; children: Sabine, Eric. BS, U. Wis., 1953; postgrad., U. Heidelberg, Germany, 1956; MA, Columbia U., 1964, postgrad., 1966—. Corr. UPI, Madison, Wis., 1953-54; desk asst. CBS News, N.Y.C., 1956-59, newswriter, 1959-60, Sta. WCBS, N.Y.C., 1960-62, news editor, 1963-68, sr. news prodr., 1968-73, sr. exec. news prodr., 1973—. Adj. prof. comm. Fordham U.; lectr., cons. journalism and internat. rels. Prodr.: (pub. affairs series) Let's Find Out, 1966, International Briefing series, 1968-72. Served to 1st lt. U.S. Army, 1954-56; capt. USAR. Recipient Am. Legion medal; Radio Journalism award AMA, Radio Journalism award Nat. Headliners Club, Radio Journalism Nat. award for Outstanding Newscast UPI, 1st place award for Best Regularly Scheduled Local News Program N.Y. State AP Broadcasters Assn., spl. mention for Best One Day News Effort N.Y. State AP Broadcasters Assn., Bene Merenti medal Fordham U.; winner German Study Program for U.S. Journalists sponsored by Radio in the Am. Sect. of Berlin Commn. and the Radio and TV News Dirs. Found.; fellow CBS News Found. Mem. Am. Polit. Sci. Assn., Acad. Polit. Sci., Am. Acad. Polit. and Social Scis., Radio-TV News Dirs. Assn., Broadcast Pioneers, Sigma Delta Chi. Home: 1619 3rd Ave New York NY 10128-3459 Office: Sta WCBS 51 W 52nd St New York NY 10019-6119

FRELICK, ROBERT WESTCOTT, physician, consultant; b. Potsdam, N.Y., Feb. 27, 1920; s. H. Victor and Ruth (Scott) F.; m. Jane Hayden, Jan. 22, 1944; children: Susan, Alcy, Sally, William, Scott. AB, Union Coll., 1941; MD, Yale, 1944. Diplomate Am. Bd. Internal Medicine, Am. Bd. Medical Onocology, Am. Bd. Nuclear Medicine. Intern New Haven Hosp., 1944-45; resident Meml. Hosp., Wilmington, Del., 1947-49, Meml. Hosp. Ctr., N.Y.C., 1949-50; pvt. practice Wilmington, Del., 1950-82; program dir. Nat. Cancer Inst., Bethesda, Md., 1982-87; cons. Del. Divsn. Pub. Health, Wilmington, 1987-96; med. dir. South Jersey Cancer Ctr., 1995-97, cons., 1998—. Chief medicine Wilmington Med. Ctr., Del., 1965-72. Contbr. to profl. jours. Bd. CARE coun. of bd. alumni, N.Y.C. then Atlanta, 1980-97; pres. Assn. Cmty. Cancer Ctrs., Rockville, Md., 1979-80. Capt. (Med. Svc. Corps.) U.S. Army, 1944-47. Recipient Disting. Svc. award Del. Med. Soc., 1977, Outstanding Svc. to Cmty. award Assn. Cmty. Cancer Ctrs., 1987, St. George's medal Am. Cancer Soc., 1990. Fellow ACP (laureate, gov.); mem. AMA, ACS (surveyor hosp. cancer programs 1988-97), Med. Soc. Del. (chair com. ethics, pres. 1980-81), Soc. Surg. Oncology, Am. Soc. Internal Medicine, Am. Soc. Clin. Oncology, Am. Pub. Health Assn., Am. Sch. Health Assns. Home: 1018 Overbrook Rd Wilmington DE 19807-2236 E-mail: rfrelick@dca.net.

FRELINGHUYSEN, RODNEY P. congressman; b. Apr. 29, 1946; m. Virginia Frelinghuysen; children: Louisine, Sarah. State and fed. aid coord., adminstrv. asst. Morris County, 1972; mem. Morris County Bd. of Chosen Freeholders, 1974-83, dir., 1980, mem. welfare and mental health bds., human svcs. and pvt. industry couns., mem. freeholder fin. com.; mem. N.J. Gen. Assembly, 1983-94, chmn. assembly appropriations com., 1988-89, 92-94; mem. U.S. Congress from 11th N.J. Dist., 1995—; mem. appropriations com. With 93d Engr. Bn. U.S. Army, 1969-71, Vietnam. Named Legis. of Yr. N.J. Assn. of Mental Health Agencies, Legis. of Yr. N.J. Assn. of Retarded Citizens. Mem. Am. Legion, VFW (Legis. of Yr.). Republican. Office: US House Reps 2442 Rayburn Ho Office Bldg Washington DC 20515-3011*

FRELOW, ROBERT DEAN, retired school system administrator, writer; b. Seminole, Okla., Aug. 1, 1932; s. Jasper Wallace and Florine (Hamilton) Frelow; m. Maxine Camille Gibbs Badgett, Dec. 25, 1952 (div. May 1983); m. Rena Hersh, Sept. 8, 1983; children: Robert Jr., Frederick, Michael. BA, San Francisco State U., 1954, MA, 1960; PhD, U. Calif., Berkeley, 1970. Cert. tchr. Calif., N.Y., adminstr. Calif., N.Y. Tchr. Oakland Unified Schs., Calif., 1960—66, Berkeley Unified Schs., Calif., 1966—67, asst. to supt., 1967—70; asst. supt. Greenburgh Schs., Hartsdale, NY, 1970—75, supt. schs., 1975—90. Adj. prof. Columbia U., N.Y.C., 1970—73, Pace U., N.Y.C., 1974—90; coord. sch. desegregation Berkeley Schs., 1967—70; cons. sch. desegregation, 1966—90; cons. Wise Svcs., White Plains, NY, 1990—. Author: The Berkeley Plan for Desegregation, 1968; co-author (editor): I Am a Blade of Grass.., 1989; author: (novels) Blood Runs Deep, 2002; contbr. Bd. dirs. Westchester Arts Coun., White Plains, NY, 1990, Westchester Cable Commn., White PlainsWhite Plains, 1990, Calif. Synod, Presbyn. Ch., 1966, Hartsdale Kiwanis, 2003. Capt. USAF, 1954—64. Recipient Citizen of the Yr. award, Kappa Alpha Psi, 1978, 1984, Exec. Leadership award, Bus. Careers Club, Hartsdale, 1991, Dedication, Dr. Robert D. Frelow Cultural Ctr., Hartsdale, 1991; grantee Urban Studies grantee, U. Calif.-Berkeley, 1969. Fellow: Rotary of Am. (bd. dirs., Paul Harris award 1991); mem.: U. Calif. Alumni Assn. Democrat. Presbyterian. Avocations: writing, reading, travel, photography, theater. Home: 17 Tara Dr Pomona NY 10970

FREMON, RICHARD C. retired infosystems specialist; b. St. Louis, May 28, 1918; s. Richard Horatio and Hazel Pauline (Rhea) F.; m. Virginia Isabelle Moore, Sept. 7, 1940; children: Carolyn E. Fremon Maycher, Richard L., James N., Nancy I. Brown. AB, Columbia U., 1939, BEE, 1940, MEE, 1944. With personnel Bell Telephones, N.Y.C., 1941-54; dir. salary adminstrn. Murray Hill, N.J., 1954-73; dir. adminstrv. systems, 1973-81; dir. computer ctr. Centenary Coll., Hackettstown, N.J., 1981-89. Contbr. chpt. to book in field. Trustee Sea Cliff Sch. Bd., N.Y., 1950-52; past chmn. Engring. Manpower Commn., N.Y.C., 1965. Mem. Inst. Indsl. Engrs. (sr.), Panther Valley Club. Democrat. Presbyterian. Home: 32 Barn Owl Dr Hackettstown NJ 07840-3205 E-mail: RCFremon@cs.com.

FREMONT, RONALD H., II, academic administrator, consultant; b. LA, June 22, 1959; s. Patricia C. Greene; m. Billi Jo Reed, Apr. 11, 1992; children: Andrew Richard, Trent Patrick. EdD, U. of La Verne, Calif., 2002. Asst. dir. athletics Cal Poly Pomona, Calif., 1988—99, assoc. v.p. for Univ. rels., 1999—. Office: Cal Poly Pomona 3801 W Temple Ave Pomona CA 91768 Office Fax: 909-869-3343. E-mail: rfremont@csupomona.edu.

FREMONT-SMITH, MARION R. lawyer; b. Boston, Oct. 29, 1926; d. Max and Frances (Davis) Ritvo; m. Joseph Miller, Sept. 12, 1948 (div.); children: Beth Miller Johnsey, Keith Lane Miller, E. Bradley Miller; m. Paul Fremont-Smith, July 6, 1961 (dec. July 2000). BA with high honors, Wellesley (Mass.) Coll., 1948; LLB cum laude, Boston U., 1951. Bar: Mass. 1951, U.S. Supreme Ct. 1979. Instr. dept. polit. sci. Wellesley Coll., 1958=59; asst. atty. gen. Commonwealth Mass., Boston, 1961-62; project dir. Russell Sage Found., Boston, 1963-65; assoc. Choate, Hall & Stewart, Boston, 1964-71, ptnr., 1971-96, sr. counsel, 1997—. Sr. rsch. fellow Hauses Ctr. for Nonprofit Orgns., Harvard U., 1998—; dir. Fed. Tax Inst. New Eng., Mount Auburn Cemetery, Aid to Artisans. Author: Foundations and Government: State and Federal Law and Supervision, 1965, Philanthropy and the Business Corporation, 1972; contbr. articles to profl. jours. Past dir. Ind. Sector, Washington; hon. trustee Carnegie Endowment for Internat. Peace, Washington; trustee Mass. Environ. Trust, Friends of Mt. Auburn Cementary. Fellow Am. Acad. Arts and Scis., Am. Bar Found., Am. Coll. Tax Counsel, Internat. Acad. Estate and Trust Law; mem. ABA (past chmn. com. on exempt orgns. tax sect.), Am. Law Inst. Office: Exchange Pl 53 State St Boston MA 02109-2804

FREMUND, ZDENEK ANTHONY, manufacturing company executive; b. Prague, Czech Republic, Oct. 6, 1946; came to U.S., 1969; s. Karl and Francis (Davidek) F.; div.; children: Brian David, Michelle Jean. Elec. Engring. degree, Czech Inst. Tech., 1969; BSME, Newark Coll. Engring., 1976. Profl. engr., N.J. Design engr. Computer Tech. Corp., Prague, 1965-68; machinist R.G. Laurence Co., Inc., Tenafly, N.Y., 1969-71, designer, 1971-74, prodn. mgr., 1974-79, v.p. mfg., chief engr., 1979-81; v.p. ops. Kleiner Metal Specialties, Inc., South Plainfield, N.J., 1981-86, pres., 1986-89; pres. & CEO Sava Industries, Inc., Riverdale, N.J., 1989—. Ptnr. Jordan Mfg. LLC, Lafayette, N.J., 1995—, DécorCable Innovations, LLC, Chgo., 1996—, Metaport Mfg. LLC, Dover, N.J., 2000—, Am. Lifting, LLC, Waukesha, Wis., 2002-. Mem. ASME, Wire Assn. Internat. Republican. Roman Catholic. Avocation: racquetball. Home: 24 Shadow Ridge Rd Wayne NJ 07470-4967 Office: Sava Industries Inc PO Box 30 4 N Corporate Dr Riverdale NJ 07457-1719

FRENCH, ANTHONY PHILIP, physicist, educator; b. Brighton, Eng., Nov. 19, 1920; came to U.S., 1955; s. Sydney James and Elizabeth Margaret (Hart) French; m. Naomi Mary Livesay, Oct. 6, 1945 (dec. 2001); m. Dorothy Ada Jensen, Apr. 30, 2002; children: Martin Charles, Gillian Ruth. BA with honors, Cambridge (Eng.) U., 1942, MA, 1946, PhD, 1948; ScD (hon.), Allegheny Coll., 1989. Mem. atomic bomb projects Tube Alloys and Manhattan Project, 1942-46; scientific officer Atomic Energy Rsch., 1946—48; demonstrator, lectr. physics Cambridge U., 1948-55; fellow Pembroke Coll., 1950-55; prof. physics U. S.C., 1955-63, chmn. dept., 1956-62; vis. prof. MIT, 1962-64, prof., 1964-91, prof. emeritus, 1991—; vis. fellow Pembroke Coll., Cambridge, 1975. Sci. officer Atomic Energy Rsch. Establishment, U.K., 1946-48; chmn. Internat. Commn. on Physics Edn., 1975-81. Author: Principles of Modern Physics, 1958, Special Relativity, 1968, Newtonian Mechanics, 1971, Vibrations and Waves, 1971, (with Edwin F. Taylor) Introduction to Quantum Physics, 1978, (with M.G. Ebison) Introduction to Classical Mechanics, 1986; editor: Einstein: A Centenary Volume, 1979, Physics in a Technological World, 1988; co-editor: Niels Bohr: A Centenary Volume, 1985, Physics History from AAPT Jours. II, 1995; contbr. articles to profl. jours. Recipient Univ. medal Charles U., Prague,

1980, Bragg medal Inst. Physics, U.K., 1988, Oersted medal Am. Assn. Physics Tchrs., 1989. Fellow Am. Phys. Soc.; mem. Am. Assn. Physics Tchrs. (pres. 1985-86, Oersted medal 1989, Melba Newell Phillips award 1993), Sigma Xi, Sigma Pi Sigma. Office: Mass Inst Tech Rm 6-101 Cambridge MA 02139

FRENCH, CHRISTY TILLERY, small business owner; b. Knoxville, Tenn., Sept. 2, 1952; d. Raymond Earl Tillery and Mildred Irene Clark; m. Gary Steven French, Sept. 23, 1972; children: Jonathan Steven, Cynthia Meghann. BA, U Tenn., 1975. Office mgr./legal asst. Jenkins and Jenkins, Knoxville, Tenn., 1974—89; owner Letter Perfect, Knoxville, 1989—2003, S.E. Cartage, Knoxville, 1995—98, C&S Forklift, Knoxville, 1998—, Indsl. Tire Svc., Knoxville, 2001—; author Pvt. Practice, Powell, Tenn., 2001—. Book reviewer Knoxville (Tenn.) News Sentinel, 2002—; editor/interviewer Intriguing Authors, internet, 2002—; chair.,pub. author Smoky Mountains Romance, Knoxville, 2002—. Author: (novels) Chasing Horses, 2001, Wayne's Dead, 2002, Chasing Demons, 2003. Recipient Book of the Month, SIsterNEws Book Club, 2001. Mem.: Sisters in Crime Knoxville Writers Guild, Mystery Writers of Am., Romance Writers of Am. Avocations: writing, gardening, boating, horseback riding, reading. Office: C&S Forklift Inc 1715 Linden Ave Knoxville TN 37915

FRENCH, CLARENCE LEVI, JR., retired shipbuilding company executive; b. New Haven, Oct. 13, 1925; s. Clarence L. Sr. and Eleanor (Curry) F.; m. Jean Sprague, June 29, 1946; children: Craig Thomas, Brian Keith, Alan Scott. BS in Naval Sci., Tufts U., 1945, BSME, 1947; ScD (hon.), Webb Inst., 1992. Registered profl. engr., Calif. Foundry engr. Bethlehem Steel Corp., 1947-56; staff engr., asst. supt. Kaiser Steel Corp., 1956-64; supervisory engr. Bechtel Corp., 1964-67; with Nat. Steel & Shipbldg. Co., San Diego, 1967-86, exec. v.p., gen. mgr., to 1977, pres., chief operating officer, 1977-84, chmn., chief exec. officer, 1984-86, outside dir., 1989-98. Past mem. maritime transp. rsch. bd. NRC. Bd. dirs. United Way, San Diego, YMCA, San Diego; past chmn., bd. dirs. Pres. Roundtable; chmn. emeritus bd. trustees Webb Inst. Lt. USN, 1943-53. Fellow Soc. Naval Architects and Marine Engrs. (hon., past pres.), Shipbuilders Council Am. (past chmn. exec. com.), ASTM, Am. Bur. Shipping; mem. Am. Soc. Naval Engrs., U.S. Naval Inst., Navy League U.S., Propeller Club U.S.

FRENCH, COLIN VAL, lawyer; b. Phila., July 20, 1957; s. Calvin Valdean and Ella LaVon (Crum) F.; m. Amanda Mitchell, June 16, 1984. BS magna cum laude, Graceland Coll., 1979; JD, Drake U., 1982; LLM in Tax, So. Meth. U., 1983. Bar: Iowa 1982, Tex. 1983. Nat. dir. endowment Boy Scouts Am., Irving, Tex., 1984-86; atty. So. Meth. U., Dallas, 1986-88, Boy Scouts Am. Nat. Office, Irving, Tex., 1988—. Mem. Legal Ethics and Sports Law Coms., Dallas, 1985—; bd. dirs. Charitable Accord, 1997—, Nat. Boy Scouts Found., 1998—; chmn., bd. dirs. Hillcrest Acad., 1997-99, now emeritus. Editor newspaper The Gavel, 1981-82, newsletter Finance Update, 1985-86, Tax and Issues Newsletter, 1998—; writer, dir. Nat. Endowment Teleconfs., 1995, 96, 99. Mem. ABA, Dallas Bar Assn. (entertainment law com., 1986—), Rotary (trustee Dallas found.). Republican. Mem. Community of Christ Church. Avocations: music writing and performance, golf, tennis. Home: 6215 Meadow Rd Dallas TX 75230-5138 Office: 1325 W Walnut Hill Ln Irving TX 75038-3008 E-mail: french6215@aol.com., cfrench@netbsa.org.

FRENCH, DANIEL J. former prosecutor; JD, Syracuse U. Law clk. to Judge Rosemary Pooler U.S. 2d Cir.; aide to U.S. Senator Daniel Patrick Moynihan; atty. U.S. Dept. Justice (no. dist.) N.Y., 1999—2001. Democrat.

FRENCH, DORRIS TOWERS BRYAN, volunteer; b. Kissimmee, Fla., May 15, 1926; m. Lawrence Cornwell French, Sept. 7, 1947; children: Layne Bryan, Leyland Bradley. Student, Art Inst., Costa Rica, 1940-42; BFA, Tulane U., 1946; student, U. Mex., 1943-44. Fabric designer Wembley Co., 1945-46; designer silver and jewelry New Orleans, 1945-47; head art dept. pvt. sch., 1947. Columnist From the Mayor's Desk; editor pub. Paw Prints, 1981-93. Founder, v.p. Peoples Animal Welfare Soc., 1977-96; past art dir., coord. internat. gladiola show Garden Club, Binghamton. Mem. AAUW, Zeta Tau Alpha. Avocations: animal welfare, writing, art. Home: 3510 Aransas St Corpus Christi TX 78411-1302

FRENCH, DOUGLAS DEWITT, medical facility administrator; b. Augusta, Ga., Jan. 14, 1954; married BS, Trevecca Nazarene Coll., 1976; M Health Adminstrn., Xavier U., 1979. Adminstrv. resident St. Thomas Hosp., Nashville, 1978-79, dir. ambulatory svcs. and planning, 1979, dir. mgmt. svcs., 1980, adminstrv. asst., 1980-82, asst. adminstr., 1982-85, v.p., 1985-86; exec. v.p., COO St. Mary's Med. Ctr., Evansville, Ind., 1986-89, pres., CEO, 1979-94; CEO St. Vincent's Hosp., Indpls., 1994; pres., CEO Ctrl. Ind. Health Sys., 1998; exec. v.p., COO Daughters of Charity Nat. Health Sys., 1998—99; COO Ascension Health, 1999—2001, pres., 1999—, CEO, 2001—. Active various cmty. ofgns. Fellow Am. Coll. Health Care Execs. Office: Ascension Health Inc 4600 Edmundson Rd Saint Louis MO 63134-3806

FRENCH, ELIZABETH IRENE, biology educator, violinist; b. Knoxville, Tenn., Sept. 20, 1938; d. Junius Butler and Irene Rankin (Johnston) F. MusB, U. Tenn., 1959, MS, 1962; PhD, U. Miss., 1973. Tchr. music Kingsport (Tenn.) Symphony Assn., 1962-64, Birmingham (Ala.) Schs., 1964-66; NASA trainee in biology U. Miss., Oxford, 1969-73; asst. prof. Mobile (Ala.) Coll. (name now U. Mobile), 1973-83, assoc. prof., 1983-94, prof., 1994—. Orch. contractor Am. Fedn. Musicians, 1983—; 1st violin Kingsport Symphony Orch., 1962-64, Birmingham Symphony Orch., 1964-66, Knoxville Symphony Orch., 1955-62, 66-68, Memphis Symphony Orch., 1970-73, Mobile Symphony Orch., 1974—, Pensacola Symphony Orch., Gulf Coast Symphony Orch. Violin recitalist Ala. Artists Series, 1978-81, Mobile Symphony Chamber Series, 2002. Mem. project Choctaw Nat. Wildlife Refuge, 1997-98; Mobile Symphony Chamber series, 2002. Named Career Woman of Yr., Gayfer's, Inc., 1985. Mem. Assn. Southeastern Biologists, Human Anatomy and Physiology Soc. (nat. com. to construct standardized test on anatomy and physiology), Wilderness Soc., Ala. Acad. Scis. (presenter 1996), Ala. Ornithol. Soc., Mobile Bay Audubon Soc. (bd. dirs. 1997—), Am. Fedn. Musicians, Ala. Fedn. Music Clubs (chmn. composition contest 1986-90, historian 1991-94), Schumann Music Club (pres. 1977-79, 85-87, 94-97, 2000—). Republican. Roman Catholic. Avocations: camping, photography, birdwatching. Home: 36 Ridgeview Dr Chickasaw AL 36611-1317 Office: U Mobile PO Box 13220 Mobile AL 36663-0220

FRENCH, HAROLD STANLEY, food company executive; b. Bklyn., Oct. 2, 1921; s. Morris and Fay (Kaufman) F.; m. Claire E. Weingart, Oct. 3, 1943 (dec. Mar. 1983); children: Madelaine Diane, Janet Gail. BA, L.I. U., 1942; postgrad., NYU, 1950, Columbia U., 1960, New Sch. U., 1970-71; PhD in Philosophy, Am. Coll., 1998. Asst. buyer R.H. Macy Co., N.Y.C., 1949-52; group mgr. Abraham & Straus Co., Hempstead, N.Y., 1952-54; mdse. mgr. Popular Club Plan, Passaic, N.J., 1954-60, Nat. Silver Co., N.Y.C., 1964-69; mktg. dir. Waverly Products Co., Phila., 1970-74; pres. Pet Food Industries, Inc., N.Y.C., 1974—, Harold French & Co., Inc., N.Y.C., 1974—, African Fruit Co. Inc., 1993—, Harold French Engring. Corp., 1993 . Pres. King Agro-Indsl. Corp., 1986, Globe King Agro-Indsl. Co. Ltd., Nigeria, 1988—; trade agt to Nigerian Govt., 1992—, also builder workers' housing, supplier of housing materials; founder, pres. The People Speak mag., 1995; founder, pres., pub. New Century Pub. Co. Inc., 1998. Author: Dating and Mating for Women Over 50, Over 60, Over 70, 1999, You Can be a Hero, For Men Over 50, Over 60, Over 70, 1999. Chmn., pres. The Nigeria Fund, Inc., 1989—; contbg. patron N.Y. Met. Opera, N.Y.C. Ballet; home builder for Nigerian Govt. Workers. With mil. intelligence, U.S. Army, 1943-45. Decorated Bronze Star. Home: 56 Rambling Brook Rd Chappaqua NY 10514-3730

FRENCH, HENRY PIERSON, JR., historian, educator; b. Rochester, N.Y., Nov. 21, 1934; s. Henry Pierson and Genevieve Lynn (Johnson) F.; m. Beverly Anne Bauernschmidt, Aug. 22, 1959; children: Henry Pierson III, Donna Lynn (dec.), William Dean, Susan Gayle, John Douglas. AB, U. Del., 1960; MA, U. Rochester, 1961, MA in Edn., 1962, EdD, 1968. Tchr. Pittsford (N.Y.) Ctrl. H.S., 1962-66; field svc. assoc. U. Rochester, N.Y., 1962-66, assoc. lectr., 1967-68, vis. asst. prof. Coll. Edn. and East Asian Ctr., 1968-69, asst. prof. edn., 1969-70, assoc. prof. Ctr. Spl. Degree Programs, 1970-72, lectr. East Asian studies, 1972-74, sr. lectr., 1974-95. Adj. asst. prof. history SUNY-Monroe C.C., 1964-67, asst. prof. history, 1967-70, assoc. prof., 1970-74, prof., 1974—, chmn. dept. history and polit. sci., 1979-85, chmn. tenure, promotion com., 1985—, sabbatical leave, 1986, chair history and polit. sci. cluster in dept. anthropology, history, polit. sci. and sociology, 2001--, coord. history and polit. sci. in dept. anthropology/history/polit. sci., sociology, 2001--; moderator, host Disciplines Within the Social Scis. series, 1968; moderator, permanent panelist Fgn. Policy Assn. and Rochester Assn. for UN Great Decisions, 1973, 77, 78 series Channel 21 Ednl. TV, Rochester; cons., panelist Great Decisions TV series, 1982, 84; vis. prof. history, 1988-89; prof. Canisius Coll., 1968, 69, 71, 73, 89, Dunlop Tire Corp. Japan Inst. faculty, 1989, Rochester Inst. Tech., 1969-70, spring 1977, 98, SUNY, Brockport, 1971; adj. mentor SUNY-Empire State Coll., 1976, 88, 89, spring/fall 1997; bd. dirs. polit. insts. Robert A. Taft Inst. Govt., 1962-65; co-dir., adminstr. NDEA insts., 1965-69; bd. dirs. Rochester Assn. UN, 1972-83, 85-91, chmn. policy com., 1972-74, v.p., 1975-77, pres., 1977-78, chmn. bd., 1978-79, chmn. nominating com., 1983-84; panelist 10th conf. Internat. Assn. Historians of Asia, 1986, 12th conf., 1991, 13th conf., chair, 1994, 14th conf., Bangkok, Thailand, 1996; presenter Gannett News Svc., Rochester, N.Y., 1994; contbr. CNN.com/china article on People's Rep. of China and Dynastieism, 1999. Contbr. articles to profl. jours. Vestryman St. Thomas Episcopal Ch., Rochester, 1965-68, Christ Episc. Ch., Pittsford, 1976-79, jr. warden, 1979-80, sr. warden, 1980-81, chmn. rector selection com., 1982; del. to diocesan Conv., 1989-91, 94-97; 1st provisional lay dep. 1991; lay dep., 1994, 97; mem. commn. on Ordained Ministry, Episc. Diocese of Rochester, 1987-94, chmn., 1992-94; advisor Shanghai-Rochester Bishops' Visitation in U.S. and China, 1989-90, co-leader lay delegation to Shanghai and China Christian Couns., China, 1992, 94, 97; coord. visit of Bishop Shen Yifan and Hong Luming to Rochester, Nov. 1-8, 1993; presenter Symposium on Protestant Christianity in Modern China and East Asia, Chongging and Nanjing, 1994; trustee Reynolds Libr. Bd., 1991—, Mendon Pub. Libr., 1996-97, Rochester Pub. Libr., 1992-2003, v.p., 1996-98, pres., 1998-2000; trustee Friends of Rochester Pub. Libr., 1983-2003, v.p., 1986-88, pres., 1988-91; trustee Rochester Regional Libr. Coun., 1998—; chmn., presenter Rochester Lit. award to James Baldwin, 1986; mem. Edn. Adv. Bd., 1988—, Preferred Care HMO, 1988—; mem. N.Y. State Citizens' Com. for the Bicentennial of the French Revolution, 1988-90. Programs and Comparative Studies grantee, 1970; recipient SUNY Chancellor's medal for philanthropy for estab. endowed chair Henry Pierson French Sr. chair in bus. adminstrn./econs. at Monroe C.C. Rochester, 1999, establish scholarship fund in polit. sci. in the name of Henry Pierson French, III at Monroe C.C. Rochester, 2002. Mem. Assn. Asian Studies, Mid. Atlantic and New Eng. Conf. for Can. Studies, Torch (bd. dirs. Rochester chpt. 1973-76, 97—, pres. 1974-75, Silver Torch award Internat. Assn. 2001), Brighton Schs. Alumni Assn. (co-chair 1998—), Univ. Club (v.p. 1975-76, sec. 1988-90, pres.-elect 1991-92, pres. 1992-93), Genesee Valley Club, Twenty Club, Delta Tau Delta. Episcopalian. Home: 78 Smith Rd Pittsford NY 14534-9727 also: SUNY-Monroe C C Rochester NY 14623 E-mail: hfrench@monroecc.edu.

FRENCH, JACQUELINE A. neurologist, educator; AB in Human Biology, Brown U., 1977, MD, 1982. Diplomate Am. Bd. Psychiatry and Neurology, Am. Bd. Clin. Neurophysiology. Intern Mt. Sinai Hosp., N.Y.C., 1982-83, resident in neurology, 1983-86; fellow in EGG/epilepsy Mt. Sinai Hosp.-Bronx VAMC, N.Y.C., 1986-88; fellow in epilepsy surgery VAMC-Yale U., New Haven, 1988-89; asst. prof. neurology U. Pa., Phila., 1989-97, assoc. prof. neurology, 1997—2001, prof. neurology, 2001—, co-dir. Penn Epilepsy Ctr., 2002—, attending physician Grad. Hosp., 1989-95. Ad hoc reviewer Annals of Neurology, Epilepsia, Neurology, Jour. Neurol. Scis., Epilepsy Rsch.; bd. dirs. Nat. EpiFellows Found.; bd. examiners Am. Bd. Clin. Neurophysiology; cons. NIH Epilepsy Br.; sci. program abstract reviewer Am. Acad. Neurology, 1999; mem. performance and safety monitoring bd. epilepsy br. NIOH, 1999; mem. grant rev. panel FDA, 1999; spkr. numerous confs., symposia. Editor: Epilepsy Update; mem. editl. bd. Clin. Neuropharmacology, 1999; contbr. articles to profl. jours. Recipient numerous grants including Wallace Labs., 1989-92, Merrell Dow Pharms., 1990-92, Abbott Labs., 1990-92, Parke-Davis, 1993-94, Dainippon Pharms., 1993-95, R.W. Johnson, 1992-98. Mem. Am. Epilepsy Soc. (ad hoc indsl. rels. com. 1994—, CME com. 1994-97, steering com. on use of antiepileptic drugs 1994—, sci. program com. 1995, fin. com. 1996, chair subcom. for stds. and guidelines for AEC practice com. 1998—), Am. Coll. Clin. Pharmacology (sci. program com. 1996), Am. Acad. Neurology (quality stds. subcom. 1995—), Am. Soc. Exptl. Neurotherapeutics (program com. 1998), Sigma Xi. Office: U Pa Med Ctr Dept Neurology 3 W Gates 3400 Spruce St Philadelphia PA 19104-4206

FRENCH, JAMES EDWARD, surgeon; b. Wahoo, Nebr., Apr. 14, 1953; BS in Biology, Wesleyan U., 1975; MD, U. Nebr., 1978. Diplomate Am. Bd. Surgery. Resident in gen. surgery Wesley Med. Ctr., Wichita, Kans., 1978-83, staff surgeon, 1983—, St. Joseph Med. Ctr., Wichita, 1983—, St. Francis Med. Ctr., Wichita, 1991—. Fellow Am. Coll. Surgeons; mem. AMA, Kans. Med. Soc. Office: 1515 S Clifton Ave Ste 420 Wichita KS 67218-2954

FRENCH, JAMES THOMAS, real estate broker; b. Wedowee, Ala., May 22, 1926; s. Jimmie Francis and Glema Calhoun French; m. Laura Major French, June 12, 1947 (div. May 1969); children: Thomas William, Carol Leigh; m. Verona Long French, Nov. 28, 1970 (div. Dec. 1999); 1 child, Jennifer Reagan; m. Sally Avery French, June 23, 2000. Student, Mercer U., 1944-45; NS & T in civil engring., Ga. Tech. U., 1945-46, B in Indsl. Engring., 1947-49. Registered profl. engr., Ga.; lic. real estate agt./broker; cert. residential specialist, real estate brokerage mgr. Grad. Realtors Inst. Traffic engr. So. Bell Telephone and Telegraph, Atlanta, 1949-51; mfg. engr. Lockhead Aircraft, Marietta, Ga., 1951-54; gen. mgr., pres. Southeastern Engring. and Mfg. Co., Atlanta, 1954-64; operating supr. Richs, Inc., Atlanta, 1964-79; realtor Duncan Realty, Cumming, Ga., 1979-86; broker Coldwell Banker French Prop., Cumming, 1986—. Dir. DeKalb Resolutions Ctr., Tucker, Ga., 1976-79; vice chmn. DeKalb Manpower Planning Coun., Decatur, 1976-79; adv. coun. for vocat. edn. DeKalb C.C., Decatur, 1978-79; founding pres. Forsyth Area Multiple Listing Svc., 1987, pres., 1987, 88, dir., 1987-89. Contbr. articles to profl. jours. Originator, chmn. Cumming-Forsyth County Trade Fair, 1985, 86, Stone Mountain Trade Fair, 1974, 75; dir. Sawnee Cmty. Ctr., Cumming, 1984-97, v.p., 1986, 87, pres. 1988, chmn. bldg. com. 1990-91; sec. Forsyth County Devel. Authority, 1986—; pres. Cumming-Forsyth C. of C., 1986, dir., 1983-89, 92-94. Lt. USN, 1944-47. Named Most Outstanding Indsl. Engr. in S.E. Am. Inst. Indsl. Engrs., 1958. Mem. Rotary Club (Rotarian of Yr. 1978, Paul Harris fellow 1979, pres. 1979), Lake Lanier Assn. (bd. dirs.), Ga. Assn. of Realtors, Nat. Assn. Realtors, Real Estate Mktg. Inst., Forsyth Area Bd. Realtors (pres. 1985, 92, Realtor of Yr. 1981, 83, 85, 92, 99, Phoenix award 1989, Crystal award 1999), Kappa Sigma, Tau Beta Pi, Phi Kappa Phi, Omicron Delta Kappa, Chi Epsilon, Pi Delta Epsilon, Alpha Pi Mu (disting. svc. award 1988), Alpha Pi Mu (founder 1949, nat. exec. sec. 1950-60, nat. v.p. 1961-62, nat. pres. 1963-64). Baptist. Avocations: boating, fishing, photography, crafts. Office: Coldwell Banker French Properties 889 Buford Rd Cumming GA 30041-2715

FRENCH, JEFFREY STUART, architect; b. Arlington, Va., Sept. 18, 1954; s. Orville Sidney and Doris G. French; m. Anne Harvey Hollibaugh, Sept. 26, 1981; children: Courtney Allen, Kyle Stuart, Allison Calvert. BA, Princeton U., 1976; MArch, U. Va., 1978. Registered architect, Pa., N.J., Mich., S.C., Ga., Del., Va., Mo., Ind., N.C., Ky., Tenn. V. p., dir. R&D facilities, COO The Ballinger Co., Architects/Engrs., Phila., 1978—. Instr. U. Wis., Madison, 1986; lectr. in rsch. facility design; grant rev. panel NSF, 1990. Co-author NSF guidebook on planning acad. rsch. facilities. Mem. AIA (cert., coll. of fellows), Nat. Coun. of Archtl. Registration Bds., Soc. Coll. and Univ. Planning, N.Y. Acad. Scis., Internat. Soc. Pharm. and Med. Device Profls. Avocations: semi-professional baseball, golf, watercolor painting, violin. Office: Ballinger 833 Chestnut St Ste 1400 Philadelphia PA 19107 E-mail: jfrench@ballinger-ae.com.

FRENCH, JERE STUART, landscape architect; b. St. Louis, Jan. 18, 1929; s. Charles Lewis and Elizabeth Park (Smith) F.; m. Joan Marion Edwards, Jan. 16, 1953; children: Daniel, Susan, Cecily, Andrew. BA, Washington U., St. Louis, 1951; BS in Landscape Arch., Mich. State U., 1956; MA, Calif. State U., Fullerton, 1970. Registered landscape architect, Calif., 1958. Intelligence officer CIA, Washington, 1951-52; landscape architect F.B. Stresau, Ft. Lauderdale, Fla., 1956-57; prof. landscape arch. Calif. State Poly. U., Pomona, 1965, dean Coll. Environ. Design, 1979-83; prin. Boltz, French & Moore, Pomona, 1958-60, Environ. Planning Assocs., Pomona, 1960-63; pvt. practice landscape arch. Claremont, Calif., 1963-94. Author: The Public Park Movement in the Age of Industry, 1971, Urban Green, 1973, Urban Space, 1978, Urban Space Revised, 1983, The California Garden, 1993, End of Fall, 1996, You Probably Don't Remember Me, 2001; author: (with others) City Landscape, 1983. Mem. trees and parkways commn. City of Claremont, 1966-68, park commn., 1968-71, arch. commn., 1975-79. With USNR, 1952-53. Recipient Ann. Heritage prize W. Fla. Literary Fedn., 1999; named Disting. Alumnus Dept. Landscape Arch., Mich. State U., 2000. Fellow Am. Soc. Landscape Architects (Bradford Williams medal 1971); mem. Audubon Soc. (editor The Skimmer 1998—), Phi Kappa Phi, Phi Alpha Theta, Sigma Delta Pi, Sigma Lambda Alpha (Disting. mem. 1982). Democrat. Unitarian Universalist. Avocations: environmental causes, birding. Home and Office: 2738 Sunrunner Ln Gulf Breeze FL 32563-5509 E-mail: JereFrench@connectmailsvc.com.

FRENCH, JOHN, III, lawyer, director; b. Boston, July 12, 1932; s. John and Rhoda (Walker) F.; m. Leslie Ten Eyck, Jan. 11, 1957 (div. 1961); children: John B., Lawrence C.; m. Anne Hubbell, Jan. 9, 1965 (div. 1983); children: Daniel J., Susanna H.; m. Marina Kellen, Nov. 21, 1987. BA, Dartmouth Coll., 1955; JD, Harvard U., 1958. Bar: N.Y. 1959, D.C. 1988. Assoc. Milbank, Tweed, Hadley & McCloy, N.Y.C., 1961-68, Satterlee & Stephens, N.Y.C., 1968-73; asst. gen. counsel Continental Group, Inc., Stamford, Conn., 1973-81; v.p., gen. counsel, sec. Peabody Internat. Corp., Stamford, Conn., 1981-82; ptnr. Appleton, Rice & Perrin, N.Y.C., 1982-84, Beveridge and Diamond, N.Y.C., 1985-93, counsel, 1993-99; chmn. Tudor Assocs., LLC, N.Y.C., 1999—. Lectr. Practising Law Inst., 1979-83, Am. Law Inst., 1978; bd. dirs. Resorts Mgmt., Inc., Tudor Assocs., LLC, N.Y.C. Contbr. articles to profl. jours. Trustee Hudson River Found., YMCA-YWCA Camping Svcs. of Greater N.Y., Inc.; bd. dirs. Third St. Music Sch. Settlement House, Inc., N.Y.C., Internat. House, Inc., N.Y.C., Met. Opera Club, Young Concert Artists, Inc., 33 E. 70th St. Corp., Teatro alla Scala Found.; mem. Westchester County Planning Bd., 1974-85; mem. N.Y. State Environ. Bd., 1976-88. Capt. JAGC, USAF, 1958-61. Mem.: VFW, ABA, Am. Soc. Corp. Secs., Environ. Law Inst., Assn. of Bar of City of N.Y. (lectr.), N.Y. State Bar Assn. (lectr.), Mayflower Descs., Met. Opera Soc., Century Assn., Am. Legion, The Pilgrims, Knickerbocker Club, Harvard Club, River Club. Republican. Office: Tudor Assocs LLC 33 E 70th St New York NY 10021-4941 E-mail: tudor33@aol.com., tudorassoc@aol.com.

FRENCH, JOHN DWYER, lawyer; b. Berkeley, Calif., June 26, 1933; s. Horton Irving and Gertrude Margery (Ritzen) F.; m. Annette Richard, 1955; m. Berna Jo Mahling, 1986. BA summa cum laude, U. Minn., 1955; postgrad, Oxford U., Eng., 1955-56; LLB magna cum laude, Harvard U., 1960. Bar: D.C. 1960, Minn. 1963. Law clk. Justice Felix Frankfurter, U.S. Supreme Ct., 1960-61; legal asst. to commr. FTC, 1961-62; assoc. Ropes & Gray, Boston, 1962-63, Faegre & Benson, Mpls., 1963-66, ptnr., 1967-75, mng. ptnr., 1975-94, chmn. mgmt. com., 1989-94. Mem. adj. faculty Law Sch. U. Minn., 1965-70, mem. search com. for dean of Coll. of Liberal Arts, 1996; mem. exec. com. Lawyers Com. for Civil Rights Under Law, 1978—; co-chmn. U.S. Dist. Judge Nominating Commn., 1979; vice chmn. adv. com., mem. dir. search com., chmn. devel. office search com. Hubert Humphrey Inst., 1979-87. Contbr. numerous articles and revs. to legal jours. Chmn. or co-chmn. Minn. State Dem. Farm Labor Party Conv., 1970-90, 94, chmn. Mondale Vol. Com., 1972, treas., 1974; assoc. chmn. Minn. Dem.-Farmer-Labor Party, 1985-86; mem. Dem. Nat. Com., 1985-86; mem. Dem. Nat. Conv., 1976, 78, 80, 84, 88; trustee Twin Cities Public TV, Inc., 1980-86, mem. overseers com. to visit Harvard U, Law Sch., 1970 75, 77-82; chmn. Minn. steering com. Dukakis for Pres., 1987-88; mem. Sec. of State's Commn. on Electoral Reform, Minn., 1994; mem. Mayor's Commn. on Regulatory Reform, Mpls., 1995. With U.S. Army, 1955-56. Rotary Found. fellow, 1955-56. Mem. ABA (editorial bd. jour. 1976-79, commn. to study fed. trade 1969—), Minn. Bar Assn., Hennepin County Bar Assn., Jud. Coun. Minn., Lawyers Alliance for Nuclear Arms Control (nat. bd. dirs. 1982-84), U. Minn. Alumni Assn. (exec. com. 1985-87, v.p. 1989-91, pres. 1991-92, Vol. of Yr. award 1988), Phi Beta Kappa. Episcopalian. Office: Faegre & Benson 2200 Wells Fargo Ctr 90 S 7th St Ste 2200 Minneapolis MN 55402-3901

FRENCH, JOHN LAWRENCE, university educator, researcher; b. High Point, NC, Dec. 30, 1941; s. John Lawrence French, Alice Beauregard Diamond; m. Linda Ann Mundy; 1 child, Emily. Ph. D, Cornell University, Ithaca, New York, 1971—77; MS in Management, Massachusetts Institute of Technology, Cambridge, Mass., 1969—71; MA in American Studies, University of Maryland, College Park, MD, 1965—67; BA in English, Wesleyan University, Middletown, CT, 1960—65. Associate Professor of Management Virginia Polytechnic Institute and State University, Falls Church, VA, 1987—2002, University of Texas-Arlington, Arlington, TX, 1979—86; Assistant Professor of Management Northeastern University, Boston, 1978—79. Interim Director Northern Virginia Graduate Center, Falls Church, VA, 1991—93. Volunteer Peace Corps, Natal, Brazil, 1967—69; Member Historical Preservation Committee, Washington Grove, MD, 2000—02. Mem.: Industrial Relations Research Association, Latin American Studies Association, Academy of Management. Avocation: tennis, hiking, carpentry, travel. Home: 201 Brown Street Washington Grove MD 20880 Office: Virginia Tech 7054 Haycock Road Falls Church VA 22043

FRENCH, JOSEPH JORDAN, JR., lawyer; b. Shreveport, La., Jan. 3, 1931; s. Joseph Jordan and Minnie Graham (Tomlinson) F.; m. Carol Jean Wesner, Dec. 22, 1954; children: Mary French Breckeen, Joseph Jordan III, Elizabeth French Pospick, Charles Robert. BS, Washington & Lee U., 1950; LLB, U. Tex., 1956. Bar: Tex. 1956, U.S. Dist. Ct. (no. dist.) Tex. 1956, U.S. Ct. Appeals (5th cir.), U.S. Tax Ct. Staff acct. W.O. Ligon & Co., Dallas, 1950-51; assoc. Thompson & Knight, Dallas, 1956-59; ptnr., shareholder Locke Purnell Rain Harrell, Dallas, 1959-93; prin. Joe French & Assocs., P.C., Dallas, 1993—. Sec. Trinity Industries, Inc., Dallas, 1969-97, Halter Marine Group Inc., 1996-97. 2nd lt. USAF, 1951-53. Home: 4440 Fairfax Ave Dallas TX 75205-3028 Office: Joe French & Assocs PC 5485 Beltline Rd Ste 150 Dallas TX 75254 E-mail: jfrench@joefrench.com.

FRENCH, JUDSON CULL, government official; b. Washington, Sept. 30, 1922; s. Morrison Brady and Ethel (Haviland) Cull French; m. Julia A. McAllister, Aug. 1, 1951; 1 child, Judson Cull. BS cum laude, Am. U., 1943; MS, Harvard U., 1949, postgrad. at bus. sch., 1968; postgrad., Johns Hopkins U., 1943-44, George Washington U., 1944-45, MIT, 1951. Instr. physics Johns Hopkins U., Balt., 1943-44, George Washington U., Washington, 1944-47; sec., dir. Home Title Ins. Co., Washington, 1956-71; with Nat. Bur. Standards (now Nat. Inst. Standards and Tech.), Commerce Dept., Washington, 1948—, asst. chief electron devices sect., 1964-68, chief electron devices sect., 1968-73, chief electronic tech. div., 1973-78, dir. Ctr. for Electronics and Elec. Engring., 1978-91; dir. Electronics and Elec. Engring. Lab., Nat. Inst. Standards and Tech., Gaithersburg, Md., 1991-99, dir. emeritus Electronics and Elec. Engring. Lab., 1999—. Guest rschr., 2000-; pvt. cons., 2000; mem. policy bd. Optoelectronic Computing Sys. Ctr. U. Colo., 1992—; bd. dirs. Nat. Electronics Mfg. Initiative, Inc., 1998-99; co-chmn. jt. mgmt. com. U.S.-Japan Jt. Optoelectronics Project, 1992-2002; founder NBS/NIST semicondr. metrology program, 1955. Contbr. articles to profl. jours. Recipient Silver medal for meritorious svc. Commerce Dept., 1964, Gold medal for exceptional svc., 1978, Edward Bennett Rosa award Nat. Bur. Standards, 1971, presdl. rank of Meritorious Exec., Sr. Exec. Svc., 1980, Disting. Exec., 1984, 93; Judson C. French award established in his honor Nat. Inst. Stds. and Tech., 1999. Fellow IEEE; mem. ASTM, Am. Phys. Soc., Nat. Acad. Engring., Sigma Pi Sigma, Pi Delta Epsilon, Alpha Kappa Pi. Office: Nat Inst Standards and Tech Metrology Bldg Rm B358 Electronics Electrical Engr Lab Gaithersburg MD 20899

FRENCH, KENNETH RONALD, finance educator; b. Franklin, N.H., Mar. 10, 1954; s. Vernon Cecil and Barbara Jean (Craig) F.; m. Vickie Anne Welch, Sept. 18, 1976; children: Robert Timothy, Laura Nancy, Elizabeth Anne. BSME, Lehigh U., 1975; MBA, U. Rochester, 1978, MS in Fin., 1981, PhD in Fin., 1983. Machine design engr. Eastman Kodak, Rochester, N.Y., 1975-77; rsch. fellow Found. for Rsch. in Econs. and Edn., UCLA, 1982-83; asst. prof. Grad. Sch. Bus., U. Chgo., 1983-85, assoc. prof., 1985-87, prof., 1987-89, Chgo. Mercantile Exch. prof., 1989-91, Leo Melamed prof., 1991-94; Edwin J. Beinecke prof. Yale Sch. Mgmt., New Haven, 1994-98, mng. dir. Intenat. Ctr. Fin., 1994-98; NTU prof. fin. Sloan Sch. Mgmt., MIT, Cambridge, Mass., 1998—. Rsch. assoc. Nat. Bur. Econ. Rsch., Cambridge, Mass., 1989—; dir. Ctr. for Rsch. in Security Prices, Chgo., 1990-94. Contbr. numerous articles to

profl. jours. Batterymarch Investment fellow, 1986; Sloan Found. grantee, 1989. Home: 85 Trescott Rd Etna NH 03750-4505 Office: MIT Sloan Sch Mgmt 50 Memorial Dr Cambridge MA 02142-1347

FRENCH, LAURENCE ARMAND, social science educator, psychology educator; b. Manchester, NH, Mar. 24, 1941; s. Gerald Everett and Juliette Teresa (Boucher) F.; m. Nancy Picthall, Feb. 13, 1971. BA cum laude, U. N.H., 1968, MA, 1970, PhD, 1975; postdoctorate, SUNY, Albany, 1978; PhD, U. Nebr., 1981; MA, Western N.M. U., 1994. Diplomate Am. Bd. Forensic Medicine, Am. Bd. Forensic Examiners, Am. Bd. Psychol. Specialties in Forensic Psychology & Neuropsychology, Am. Coll. Advanced Practice Psychologists; lic. psychologist, Ariz. Instr. U. So. Maine, Portland and Gorham, 1971-72; asst. prof. Western Carolina U., Cullowhee, N.C., 1972-77, U. Nebr., Lincoln, 1977-80; psychologist I N.H. Hosp., Concord, 1980-81; psychologist II Laconia (N.H.) State Sch., 1981-88; sr. psychologist N.H. Divsn. for Children & Youth Svcs., Concord, 1988-89; prof., chair dept. social scis. Western N.Mex. U., Silver City, 1989—2003, prof. emeritus of psychology, 2003—; rsch. assoc. justiceworks U. NH Inst. for Policy and Social Sci. Rsch., 2002—; prof., head dept. psychology Coll. Juvenile Justice and Psychology, Prairie View A&M U., 2003—. Profl. adv. bd. Internat. Coll. Prescribing Psychologists; cons. N.C. Dept. Mental Health, 1972—77, Cherokee (N.C.) Indian Mental Health Program, 1974—77, Nebr. Indian Commn., Lincoln, 1977—80; cons. alcohol program Lincoln Indian Ctr., 1977—80; adj. assoc. prof. U. So. Maine, 1980—84; faculty adviser Psi Chi Nat. Honor Soc. in psychology Western N.Mex. U., 1995—2003; mem. Psi Chi Rocky Mountain Regional Steering Com., 2001—02; faculty adviser Psi Chi Nat. Honor Soc. in psychology A&M U., 2003—. Author: The Selective Process of Criminal Justice, 1976; author: (with Richard Crowe) Wee Wish Tree: Special Qualla Cherokee Issue, 1976; author: (with Hornbuckle) Cherokee Perspective, 1981; author: (with Letman et al.) Contemporary Issues in Corrections, 1981; author: Indians and Criminal Justice, 1982, Psychocultural Change and the American Indian, 1987, The Winds of Injustice, 1994, Counseling American Indians, 1997, The Qualla Cherokee Surviving in Two Worlds, 1998, Addictions and Native Americans, 2000, Native American Justice, 2003; spl. issue editor Quar. Jour. Ideology, Vol. II, 1987, mem. editl. bd. Jour. Police and Criminal Psychology; contbr. articles to profl. jours. Commr. Pilsbury Lake Village Dist., Webster, N.H., 1995-00. With USMC, 1959-63, Badge of Honor, Republic of China, 1998. Recipient Hon. medal Rep. China, 1998, Nat. Int. Drug Abuse 1st Leadership in Rsch. award, 1999; Dissertation Yr. fellow U. N.H. 1971-72, Nebr. U. System grad. faculty fellow, 1978. Fellow: APA, Am. Coll. Forensic Examiners (diplomate), Soc. Psychol. Study Social Issues, Prescribing Psychologists Register (diplomate); mem.: VFW (life), N.Mex. Alcohol and Drug Abuse Counselors Assn. (Educator of Yr. 1997), Am. Soc. Criminology (life), Nat. Assn. Alcohol and Drug Abuse Counselors (clin. issue com. 1996—98, nat. chmn.), Internat. Coll. Prescribing Psychologists Inc. (profl. adv. bd.), Nat. Assn. Sch. Psychologists, 3d Marine Divsn. Assn. (life), Psi Chi (steering com. Rocky Mountain region 2001—, Regional Faculty Advisor award 2002—03), Phi Delta Kappa (treas. Rocky Mountain region 1990—91, pres. 1991—92). Office: Dept Psychology Prairie View A&M Univ Prairie View TX 77446 E-mail: Laurence_French@pvamu.edu., frogwnmue@yahoo.com.

FRENCH, LEURA PARKER, secondary educator; b. Owensville, Ind., June 4, 1926; d. Arthur William and Mildred Ruth Parker; m. Alvin L. French, July 14, 1947 (dec. Sept. 1996); children: Bruce A., Dwight L. BA cum laude, God's Bible Sch. and Coll., 1950; BS in Edn., Wesleyan U., Marion, Ind., 1952; MS in Edn., Butler U., 1962; postgrad., U. Calif., Davis, 1970-73. Tchr. Moorhead Jr. H.S., Indpls., 1957-58, Washington H.S., Indpls., 1962-63, Bella Vista H.S., Fair Oaks, Calif., 1963-65, Casa Roble H.S., Orangevale, Calif., 1967-84, Valley Oak H.S., Oakdale, Calif., 1987—. Study tours for WWII in Europe, China, Hong Kong, Bangkok, Singapore. Co-author booklet: Goals and Objectives for the San Juan Unified School District's Reading Program, 1972. Active Free Meth. Ch., Indpls., 1953-62, Orangevale, 1963-85, 89-96, Oakdale, 1985-89. Fellow Calif. Tchrs. Assn. Republican. Avocations: reading, research, writing, travel. Home: 1100 Roseville Pkwy #317 Roseville CA 95678-5351

FRENCH, LYLE ALBERT, surgeon; b. nr. Worthing, S.D., Mar. 26, 1915; s. Leslie V. and Bernice M. (McKinney) F.; m. Gene F. Richmond, Sept. 13, 1941; children— Frederick E., Eldridge T., Barbara Gene. Student, Macalester Coll., 1933—35; BS, U. Minn., 1936, MB, 1939, MD, 1940, MS, 1946, PhD, 1947. Diplomate: Am. Bd. Neurol. Surgery. Intern U. Hosp., Mpls., 1939-40; instr. neurosurgery U. Minn., St. Paul, 1947-49, asst. prof., 1949-52, assoc. prof., 1952-57, prof., 1957—, chmn. dept. neurol. surgery, 1960-72, v.p. health scis., 1970-82. Chief staff Univ. Hosps., Mpls., 1968-70; cons. neurosurgery Surgeon Gen. U.S. Army, 1962—; spl. cons. Central Office, VA, 1968-80. Chmn. editorial bd. Jour. Neurosurgery, 1973-75, Yearbook of Cancer; contbr. articles to profl. jours. in field. Adv. council Neurol. Diseases and Stroke NIH, 1971-75; mem. adv. bd. Nat. Paraplegia Found., Multiple Sclerosis Found. Served from lt. to maj. AUS, 1941-45. Recipient numerous awards. Mem. Am. Soc. Research in Stereoencephalotomy (v.p. 1968-70), Minn. Soc. Neurol. Scis. (pres. 1963), Neurosurg. Soc. Am. (pres. 1958), Minn. Soc. Neurology and Psychiatry (pres. 1962), Minn. Acad. Medicine (pres. 1973-74), Mpls. Acad. Medicine (pres. 1960), Am. Acad. Neurosurgery (pres. 1972-73), Am. Assn. Neurol. Surgery, Harvey Cushing Soc. (pres. 1973-74). Home: Casita 509 7501 Thompson Peak E Pkwy Scottsdale AZ 85255

FRENCH, MARILYN, writer, critic; b. N.Y.C., Nov. 21, 1929; d. E. Charles and Isabel (Hazz) Edwards; m. Robert M. French, Jr., June 4, 1950 (div. 1967); children: Jamie, Robert. BA, Hofstra Coll., 1951, MA, 1964; PhD, Harvard U., 1972. Secretarial, clerical worker, 1946-53; lectr. Hofstra Coll., 1964-68; asst. prof. Holy Cross Coll., Worcester, Mass., 1972-76; Mellon fellow Harvard U., 1976-77; writer, lectr., 1967—. Author: (criticism) The Book as World: James Joyce's Ulysses, 1976, Shakespeare's Division of Experience, 1981, (novels) The Women's Room, 1977, The Bleeding Heart, 1980, Her Mother's Daughter, 1987, Our Father: A Novel, 1994, My Summer with George, 1996, (nonfiction) Beyond Power: On Women, Men and Morals, 1986, The War Against Women, 1992, A Season in Hell, 1998, From Eve To Dawn: A History of Women, Vol. I, introductions to Edith Wharton's Summer and The House of Mirth, 1981. Mem. Virginia Woolf Soc., Phi Beta Kappa.*

FRENCH, MARY B. educator, editor, photographer, poet and former; b. Dallas, July 21, 1942; d. Harry Blake and Mary Virginia (Jones) F.; m. Richard Edelin Crouch, Feb. 6, 1965; children: John, Virginia. BA, Coll. William and Mary, 1965; MA, U. Va., 1966. Columnist, reporter Va. Gazette, Williamsburg, 1961-65; mng. editor William and Mary Rev., Williamsburg, 1963-64; asst. editor Microfilm Publ., U. Va., Charlottesville, 1966-67; lectr. Am. lit. and women in lit. U. Va., Falls Church, 1968-99. Instr. English, No. Va. C.C., Annandale, 1968-69; instr. English composition George Washington U., Washington, 1970; cons. in lit. humanities project Arlington County Libr., 1976 Author: The State Slate: A Guide to Legislative Procedures and Lawmakers, 1977; compiler: Women in Literature: A Bibliography, 1973; editor (with J.L. Anderson) Microfilm Edition of the Papers of R.M.T. Hunter, 1817-1887, 1966; editor Spokeswoman Mag., 1979-82, Washington Women's Rep. Newsletter, 1979-82; mng. editor Women's News Svc., 1979-82; assoc. editor Career Opportunities News, 1983—; mng. editor Army Mag., 1984-93, editor, 1993—; contbr. poetry to several anthologies. In chief Com. on Status of Women, Arlington, Va., 1976, steering com. Coalition on Optimum Growth, 1970-73. Mem. MLA, AAUW (chmn. women's studies, dir. Arlington br. 1974-76, assoc. editor Grad. Women mag. 1982, mng. editor publ. 1983), the Am. News Women's Club, the Acad. of Am. Poets, the Lyon Village Citizens Assoc., Hillsboro Cmty. Assn., English-Speaking Union, Edgar Jane Austen Soc., US Congress Periodical Press Corrs.'s Assn., Nat. Trust Hist. Preservation, Preservation Soc. Loudoun County, Old House Group Loudoun County, Soc. Profl. Journalists, Am. Soc. Mag. Editors, Va. Hist. Soc., Phot Comm. of the Nat. Press Club. Democrat. Episcopalian. Office: 2425 Wilson Blvd Arlington VA 22201-3326 Address: 14076 Mountain Rd Princeville VA 20132

FRENCH, MICHAEL FRANCIS, non-profit education agency administrator; b. La Crosse, Wis., July 25, 1948; s. Albert Frank Jr. and Kathryn Patricia (MacKoske) F.; m. Janet Alan Streeter Head, Nov. 26, 1991. BS in Edn., U. Wis., 1972. Cert. emergency med. technician. Tng. coord. emergency med. svcs. Wis. Dept. Health and Social Svcs., Madison, 1975-80, tng. dir. emergency med. svcs., 1980-84, chief emergency med. svcs., 1984-90; co-dir. Area Health Edn. Ctrs. office Kirksville (Mo.) Coll. Osteo. Medicine, 1990—, adj. instr. family medicine and cmty. health, 1990—. Emergency med. svcs. cons., Kirksville, 1984—; founding mem. Continuing Edn. Coordinating Bd. for Emergency Med. Svcs., Inc., Kirksville, 1992. Author: (tng. curriculum) EMS Instructor Training Course-U.S. Dept. Transportation, 1985; editor newsletter, editor-in-chief publs. Nat. Assn. Emergency Med. Technicians, 1983-91; author book chpts. V.p., pres. bd. dirs. Adair County Ret. Sr. Vol. Program, Kirksville, 1992-95; com. chair, bd. dirs. Mo. Rural Opportunities Coun., 2000—. Recipient Lunda Trauma award Am. Trauma Soc., 1982, Svc. awards Nat. Coun. State EMS Tng. Coords., 1982, 83, A. Roger Fox Founders award Nat. Assn. Emergency Med. Technicians, 1989, others. Mem. ASTM, ASCD, ASTD, APHA, Nat. Rural Health Assn. (rural health policy bd. 1998—, gov. affairs com. 2000—), Mo. Rural Health Assn. (bd. dirs. 1995-96, 99—, pres.-elect 1996-97, pres. 1997-99, exec. com. 1999—), Mo. PEW Health Professions Partnership (chair exec. com. 1994-95), Mo. Pub. Health Assn. (awards chair 1996), Wis. Emergency Med. Tech. Assn., Am. Coll. Healthcare Execs. (assoc.), Nat. Orgn. Area Health Edn. Ctr. Program Dirs. (nominations com. 1996), Mensa. Avocations: bicycling, reading, computer games. Office: KCOM AHEC Program 800 W Jefferson St Kirksville MO 63501-1443

FRENCH, RICHARD EDMUND, insurance company executive; b. Boise City, Okla., July 14, 1926; s. Joseph Oscar and Edna Mae (Harmon) F.; m. Betty Jeanne-Jacobs, Dec. 24, 1949; children: Janette Sue, J. Richard, John K. Student, U. Oreg. Underwriter Fireman's Fund, San Francisco, 1952-55; spl. agt. INA, Eugene, Oreg., 1955-60, San Jose, Calif., 1960-67, mgr. sales Ariz. Phoenix, 1967-70; pres. Ayres & French, Inc., Sedona, Ariz., 1970-88, sec.-treas., 1988—. Sec.-treas. Villa Share Ptnrs., Sedona, 1988-91; chmn. Pacer Panel, State of Ariz., 1981, Western region, 1982. Dir. Sedona Pub. Libr., 1978-86. With USN, 1945-49, PTO. Mem. Ind. Ins. Agts. Ariz. (pres. 1988-89, London Bridge award 1989, Chuck Trauble award 1990), Rotary (dir. 1983-86, outstanding svc. award 1982), Elks, Masons, Shriners. Republican. Avocations: travel, fishing, gardening. Office: Ayres & French Inc 1785 W 89th A # A Sedona AZ 86336 Home: 10106 W Campana Dr Sun City AZ 85351

FRENCH, RICHARD EDMUND, writer; b. Chgo., Dec. 12, 1929; s. Leonard Cortland and Ethel May French; m. Charlene Halbrook, May 14, 1952 (dec. June 6, 1988); children: Michael Alan, David; m. Doris Kaled, Oct. 2, 1988 (dec. Nov. 2002). BS in Bus. Mgmt., Ariz. State U., 1969. Lic. real estate agt., ins. and securities Ariz. Enlisted USAF, 1952, advanced through grades to lt. col., 1968, ret., 1974; agt. John Hancock Ins., Phoenix, 1975—78; owner Scottsdale (Ariz.) Silver Co., 1978—81; freelance writer various media, 1981—91. Author: Macedonian Gray, 2002, (articles) Ariz. Contractor's Jour. Decorated Silver Star, Disting. Flying Cross, 23 Air medals, Purple Heart, Vietnamese Cross of Gallantry with Palm. Mem.: Sabre Pilots Assn., Red River Fighter Pilots Assn., Eagles Lodge, Am. Legion. Home: 4217 Peachblossn Ln Las Vegas NV 89108

FRENCH, RODERICK STUART, university chancellor; b. LaGrande, Oreg., Apr. 5, 1931; s. Stuart Gautier and Laura A. (Richards) F.; m. Evelyn Fagg, 1955 (div. 1964); children: Roderick Stuart, Jr., Sarah Suzanne; m. Sally Stedman, May 8, 1965. AB, Kenyon Coll., 1954; MDiv, Episcopal Div. Sch., 1957; STM, Union Theol. Sem., 1965; PhD, George Washington U., 1971. Dir. youth dept. World Coun. Chs., Geneva, 1959-64; freelance writer Balt., Washington, 1964-67; spl. asst. office pub. affairs Peace Corps., Washington, 1967-68; assoc. dir. office exptl. programs George Washington U., Washington, 1969-78, dir., 1978-84, v.p. acad. affairs, 1984-95, dir. univ. seminars program, 1995-97; chancellor Am. U. of Sharjah, United Arab Emirates, 1998—2002, dir. Washington office, trustee, 2002—. Editor: What is Humanistic Education?, 1973, An Independent University in a Free Society, 1988; co-editor: The Public Humanities, 1984; gen. editor monograph series GW Washington Studies, 10 vols., 1974-82; contbr. articles to profl. jours. Chmn. D.C. Humanities Coun., 1979-81; v.p. Nat. Humanities Alliance, 1986-88, pres. 1988-92, exec. com., 1988-94; bd. dirs. Nat. Fed. State Humanities Councils, Washington, 1983-86, Potomac River Basin Consortium, Washington, 1981-85; bd. mgrs. Columbia Hist. Soc., Washington, 1980-84; trustee, 1st v.p. Ctr. for Advanced Study of the Americas, 1984-87, pres. 1987-88; trustee Nat. Cultural Alliance, 1990-92. Recipient Citation for Outstanding Contbn. to Cultural Life in Washington, Washington Rev., 1979, D.C. Pub. Humanities award, 1988; named Hon. Citizen, Winnipeg, Man., Can., 1961. Mem. Am. Soc. for Environ. History (v.p. 1977-81), Am. Soc. for 18th Century Studies, Am. Studies Assn., Cosmos Club, Golden Key, Phi Beta Kappa, Omicron Delta Kappa, Phi Beta Delta. Democrat. Home: 2801 New Mexico Ave NW Apt 1124 Washington DC 20007-3912 Office: Am Univ Sharjah Washington Office 3201 New Mexico Ave NW Washington DC 20016 E-mail: rfrench@american.edu.

FRENCH, STANLEY GEORGE, university dean, philosophy educator; b. Hamilton, Ont., Can., Sept. 24, 1933; s. Reginald George and Marie (Larson) F.; children: Shona, Sean, Lina, Ewan. BA, Carleton U., 1955; MA, U. Rochester, 1957; PhD, U. Va., 1959; spl. student, Oxford U., 1961, U. Nice, France, 1975-76, Royal Victoria Hosp., McGill U., Montreal, 1987-88. Assoc. prof. philosophy U. Western Ont., London, 1965-68; prof. philosophy Sir George Williams U., Montreal, Que., 1968, chmn. dept. philosophy, 1969-71; prof. philosophy, dean grad. studies Concordia U., Montreal, 1971-86, dir. humanities interdisciplinary doctoral program, 1992—97. Mem. joint com. on programs Council of Univs., 1972-75; chmn. Westmount Sch. Commn., 1972; pres. London Council for Adult Edn., 1965-66; chmn. Bd. Edn. City of London, 1968; bd. govs. Sir George Williams U., 1969-71; internat. vis. scholar The Hastings Ctr., 1992; vis. scholar U. B.C. Ctr. Rsch. Women's Studies and Gender Relations. Author: The North West Staging Route, 1957, Philosophers Look at Canadian Confederation, 1979, Interpersonal Violence, Health and Gender Politics, 1993, Violence Against Women: Philosophical Perspectives, 1998, also monographs; cons. editor: Humanities Research Coun. Can., 1970—; editorial adv.: Gnosis, 1977—; contbr. articles to profl. jours., chpts. to books. Served as officer RCAF, 1951-56. Can. Council grantee, 1962; Internat. vis. scholar The Hastings Ctr., 1992. Mem. Soc. for Philosophy and Pub. Affairs (exec. bd. dirs.), Montreal Conf. Polit. and Social Thought, Sociètè de Philosophie du Montreal, Sociètè de Philosophie du Quebec, Can. Philos. Assn., Am. Philos. Assn., Am. Soc. Polit. and Legal Philosophy, Mind Assn., Can. Assn. Grad. Schs. (sec.-treas. 1980-81), Can. Bioethics Soc. Home: Le Mas de Montfort 585 Newaygo Rd Wentworth North QC Canada J0T 1YO Office: Concordia U Dept Philosophy Montreal QC Canada H3G 1M8

FRENCH, WILLIAM HAROLD, retired newspaper editor; b. London, Ont., Can., Mar. 21, 1926; s. Harold Edward and Isabel (Brash) F.; m. Margaret Jean Rollo, June 23, 1951; children— Jane, Mark, Paul, Susan. BA, U. Western Ont., 1948; Nieman fellow, Harvard, 1954-55; DLitt (hon.), U. Western Ont., 1991. With The Globe and Mail, Toronto, Ont., Can., 1948-90, lit. editor, 1960-90; instr. journalism Ryerson Poly. Inst., 1955-88; asso. fellow York U., 1969-77; broadcaster Canadian Broadcasting Corp., 1964-90, ret., 1990. Cons. Can. Council, 1969— Author: A Most Unlikely Village, 1960. Recipient President's medal U. Western Ont., 1966; Nat. Newspaper award for critical writing, 1978, 79 Home: 78 N Hills Terr Don Mills ON Canada M3C 1M6

FRENK, JULIO JOSE, secretary of health for Mexico, health systems researcher, consultant; b. Mexico City, Mex., Dec. 20, 1953; s. Silvestre and Alicia (Mora) Frenk; m. Josefina Quezada (div. 1955); children: Esteban Frenk Quezada, Emilio Jose Frenk Quezada; m. Felicia Marie Knaul, Nov. 11, 1995; 1 child, Hannah Sofia Frenk Knaul. MD, Nat. U. Mex., 1979; MPH, U. Mich., Ann Arbor, 1981, MA, 1982, PhD, 1983. Asst. prof. Sch. Pub. Health U. Mich., Ann Arbor, 1982—84; founding dir. Ctr. for Publ. Health Rsch. Min. Health, Mexico, 1984—87; founding dir. gen. Nat. Inst. Pub. Health, Cuernavaca, Mexico, 1987—92; vis. prof. Ctr. for Population and Devel. Studies Harvard U., Cambridge, 1992—93; dir. Project of Health and Economy Mexican Health Found., Mexico, 1993—94; exec. v.p., dir. Mexican Health Found., Mexico, 1995—98; exec. dir. evidence info. policy World Health Orgn., Geneva, 1998—; sec. of health Govt. of Mexico, 2000—. Adj. prof. doctoral program Nat. Inst. Pub. Health, Cuernavaca, 1994—; part time adv. World Bank, Washington, 1995—96; regional editor for L.Am. and Caribbean Health Policy Jour., Leuven, Belgium, 1993—, mem., 1987—. Author 8 books, 1976, 1978, 1988, 1992, 1993, 1994; contbr. chapters to books; editor 7 books, 1985, 1990, 1991, 1995, 1997; contbr. articles to profl. jours. Mem. adv. group on reconstrn. of health svcs., Mexico City, 1985—86; mem. Adv. Scientific Coun. Sci. Mus. Nat. U. Mex., Mexico City, 1995—. Named Nat. Rschr., Nat. Rschrs. Sys., Mex., 1984—; recipient Cecilio A. Robelo award for scientific rsch., State Govt. Morelos, Mex., Cuernavaca, 1993. Mem.: APHA, Inst. Medicine NAS, Nat. Acad. Medicine. Avocations: classical music, opera, kaleidoscopes. Home: Jazmin 62 Col Tetelpan 01700 Mexico City Mexico Office: Chemin Champ Barbon 1 1290 Versoix Switzerland also: Lieja Num 7 Colonia Juarez-10 PISO 06696 Mexico*

FRENKEL, EUGENE PHILLIP, physician; b. Detroit, Aug. 27, 1929; s. David Eugene and Eva (Antin) F.; m. Rhoda Beth Smilay, Dec. 21, 1958; children: Lisa Michelle, Peter Alan. BS, Wayne State U., 1949; MD, U. Mich., 1953. Diplomate Am. Bd. Internal Medicine (hematology, med. oncology; bd. govs. 1980-87, chmn. subspecialty com. hematology 1980-85). Intern Wayne County Gen. Hosp., Eloise, Mich., 1953-54; resident in internal medicine Boston City Hosp., 1954-55; resident in internal medicine, then instr. U. Mich. Med. Center, 1957-62; mem. faculty U. Tex. Southwestern Med. Ctr., Dallas, 1962—, prof. internal medicine and radiology, 1969—, chief divsn. hematology-oncology, 1962-91, Patsy R. and Raymond D. Nasher Disting. chair in cancer rsch., 1990—, A. Kenneth Pye prof. in cancer rsch., 1994—; chief nuclear medicine, cons. hematology-oncology VA Med. Center, Dallas, 1962-80; Sydney and J.L. Huffines, Jr. disting. chair U. Tex. Southwestern Med. Ctr., 1998—. Cons. com. on evaluation rsch. hematology; nutrition Nat. Inst. Arthritis and Metabolic Diseases, 1979-82; active Am. Joint Commn. on Cancer, 1986-95; interim dir. divsn. hematology-oncology VA Med. Ctr., Dallas, 1995-97. Author numerous research papers in field. Served as officer M.C. USAF, 1955-57. Fellow ACP (coun. subsplty. socs. 1992—), Internat. Soc. Hematology; mem. Am. Soc. Hematology (treas. 1976-84), Am. Soc. Clin. Oncology (chmn. membership com. 1982-85), Am. Cancer Soc. (pres. Dallas unit 1970-71, dir. Tex. divsn. 1978—, sci. adv. com. on clin. investigations II-chemotherapy and hematology 1978-82, Emma Freeman prof., 1981-91, nat. clin. fellowship com. 1978-87, internat. rsch. grants com. 1988-90, sci. adv. coun. 1991-97), Assn. Am. Physicians, Am. Assn. Cancer Rsch., Am. Assn. Cancer Edn., Am. Soc. Biol. Chemists, Am. Soc. Clin. Investgation, So. Soc. Clin. Investigation, Am. Urol. Assn., Soc. Nuclear Medicine, Am. Fedn. Cli n. Rsch., Internat. Soc. Hematology (councillor 1992-97), Internat. Assn. Study Lung Cancer, Alpha Omega Alpha. Office: U Tex Southwestern Med Ctr Dallas TX 75390-8852

FRENKEL, HERBERT MILTON, lawyer, judge; b. N.Y.C., July 28, 1924; s. Herman and Renee (Roth) F.; m. Beverly Vivian Rosenberg, Apr. 2, 1967; 1 child, Charles Robert. LLB, N.Y. Law Sch., 1952; LLD (hon.), Philathea Coll., London, Ont., Can., 1969. Bar: N.Y. 1972, U.S. Dist. Ct. (so. and ea. dists.) N.Y. 1974. Investigator, tech. analyst writer EEOC, Newark 1972-74, dist. counsel, 1974-80, sr. trial atty., N.Y.C., 1979-81, administrv. judge, 1981-88, adminstrv. law judge, 1988—; ptnr. Telecommunications Rsch. Assocs., Scarsdale, N.Y. Contbr. in field. Served with M.C., U.S. Army, 1943-45, ETO. Lodge: Masons. Home: 205 E 78th St Apt 6H New York NY 10021-1232 Office: Social Security Adminstrv Office Hearings & Appeals 26 Federal Plz Ste 2909 New York NY 10278-0004

FRENKEL, RENATA, physician; b. Poland, 1939; came to U.S., 1960; MD, U. Vienna, 1968. Intern St. Lukes Hosp. Ctr., N.Y.C., 1971-72, resident, 1972-73, Roosevelt Hosp., N.Y.C., 1973-75; physician St. Lukes Roosevelt Hosp.-Lenox Hill Hosp. Fellow Am. Acad. Allergy & Immunology. Office: 30 W 60th St New York NY 10023-7902 E-mail: reniafrenkel@aol.com.

FRENKIEL, RICHARD HENRY, retired systems engineer, consultant; b. N.Y.C., Mar. 4, 1943; s. Lucjan and Stephanie (Komorowska) Frenkiel; m. Annamae Mary Rollason, Dec. 28, 1963; children: Scott Thomas, Kathleen Ann. BSME, Tufts U., 1963; MS in Engring. Mechanics, Rutgers U., 1965. Tech. staff Bell Labs., Holmdel, NJ, 1963—71, supr., 1973—77, dept. head, 1977—88, R & D dir., 1988—93, ret., 1993. Vis. prof. Rutgers U., dir. strategic planning WINLAB, 1994—. Com. mem. Manalapan Twp., NJ, 1995—99, dep. mayor, 1995, mayor, 1999. Named N.J. Inventor of Yr., 1995; recipient Achievement award, Indsl. Rsch. Inst., 1992, Nat. medal, Tech. U.S. Dept. of Commerce, 1994; fellow, Bell Labs., 1990. Fellow: IEEE (spkr. Outstanding Lecture Tour 1975—76, Alexander Graham Bell medal 1987); mem.: Nat. Acad. Engring. Republican. Achievements include design of first cellular telephone system in U.S; cordless telephone products; invention of Metroliner Radiotelephone System; cell splitting method; patents in field. Office: Rutgers WINLAB 73 Brett Rd Piscataway NJ 08854-8060

FRENZEL, FRANCES JOHNSON, registered nurse, educator, lecturer, poet, real estate broker; b. Bedford, Va., Feb. 2, 1911; d. J. James and Willie Calpernia (Markham) Johnson; m. Paul H. Frenzel, Dec. 21, 1933 (dec. 1990); children: Virginia Lee Frenzel Lawrence, Helen Marie Frenzel LaGourgue. RN, Wash. Adventist Hosp., Takoma Park, Md., 1932; BS, Columbia Union Coll., 1933; real estate license, Glendale (Calif.) C.C., 1968. Cert. real estate broker. RN supr. Glendale (Calif.) Adventist Med. Ctr., 1933-34; instr. various flower show schs., Nat. Coun. State Garden Clubs, U.S. & Mex., 1951-98; flower design instr. Edinburg (Tex.) Coll., 1953. Founder, chmn. World Flower Festival L.A. Garden Club and Greater L.A. Dist. Calif. Garden Clubs, Inc., 1962-98; lectr. in many states including Hawaii. Author: Arrangements on Parade, 1950; contbr. poems to books and nat. and state mags.; contbr. photographs of flower arrangements to profl. jours. Mem. City of Glendale Beautification adv. council, 1974—, L.A. County Med. Auxiliary Glendale, 1956—, pres., 1968—69; founder The Golden Garden Angel fund, 1998; election precinct officer L.A. County, Glendale, 1956—2000. Recipient numerous Garden Club awards, 1962—, Editor's Choice award, 1999, Lifetime Beautification Achievement award, City of Glendale and Com. for a Clean and Beautiful Glendale, 2001, various other awards from organizations and Los Angeles County; named Guardian Angel, Staff Golden Gardens Mag., 2001; grantee Proton Treatment Ctr., Loma Linda (Calif.) Med. Ctr. Mem.: Internat. Soc. Poetry, L.A. County Med. Assn. Alliance (pres. Dist. IV 1968—69), L.A. Garden Club (pres. 1960—62), Judges Coun. Orange County, Judges Coun. So. Calif. (chmn. 1978—80), Internat. Soc. Poets, Ikebana Internat. (L.A. chpt.), Greater L.A. Dist. Calif. Gardens Club (dir. 1962—64), Nat. Coun. State Garden Clubs Inc. (life), Calif. Garden Clubs Inc. (life; pub. rels. chmn. 1999—, founder golden gardens angel fund for bd. 1999—, bd. dirs., Woman of Yr. 2002). Avocations: flower arranging, gardening, gourmet cooking, interior decorating. Home: 31423 S Coast Hwy Laguna Beach CA 92651-6998

FRENZEL, JAMES CHARLES, lawyer; b. Ft. Monmouth, N.J., Dec. 12, 1945; s. Charles H. and Virginia L. Frenzel; m. Susan B. Frenzel, Sept. 29, 1979; 1 child, Charles J. BA in History, Duke U., 1967, JD, 1970. Bar: Ga., N.C., U.S. Supreme Ct., U.S. Ct. Appeals (4th, 6th and 11th cirs.). Assoc. Womble, Carlyle, Sandridge & Rice, Winston-Salem, N.C., 1970-77, ptnr., 1977-90, Smith, Gambrell & Russell, Atlanta, 1990-91, Greene, Buckley, Jones & McQueen, Atlanta, 1991-95; prin. James C. Frenzel, P.C., Atlanta, 1995—. Vis. prof. Wake Forest U. Sch. Law, Winston-Salem, 1985-87; dir. Southeastern Bankruptcy Law Inst., Atlanta, 1980-2003. Author: Problem Loans in N.C., 1985, Secured Lending in Georgia, 1992; editor: How to Start a Pro Bono Bankruptcy Program, 1996. Bd. dirs. Continuing Legal Edn. in Ga., Athens, 1993; speaker Ctrl. Eastern European Initiative-U.S. Aid, Romania, 1996. Mem. ABA (mem. bus. sect. ethics com. 1996-2003), Ga. Bar Assn. (chmn. bankruptcy sect. 1994-95), N.C. Bar Assn. (chmn. bankruptcy sect. 1989-90). Home: 8985 Huntcliff Trace Atlanta GA 30350-1733 Office: Atlanta Financial Ctr Ste 155 3343 Peachtree Rd NE Atlanta GA 30326-1429 Personal E-mail: sbfrenzel@attbi.com. Business E-mail: jcf-bklaw@mindspring.com.

FRERICHS, ERNEST SUNLEY, religious studies educator; b. S.I., New York, Apr. 30, 1925; s. Ernest V. and Eva (Sunley) F.; m. Sarah Hazel (Cutts), Aug. 20, 1949; children: John Allen (dec.), David Sunley, Elizabeth Ann. BA, Brown U., 1948; MA, Harvard U., 1949; STB, U. Mass., Boston, 1952, PhD, 1957; LHD (hon.), Hebrew Union Coll., 1992. Mem. faculty Brown U., Providence, 1953—, prof. religious studies, 1966-95, chmn. dept., 1964-70, asst. dean., 1958-59, dean grad. sch., 1976-82, program dir. in Judaic studies, 1982-95, prof. religious and Judaic studies emeritus, 1995—; exec. dir. Dorot Found., Providence, 1995—2003, pres., 2003—. Mem. Grad. and Profl. Sch. Fin. Aid Coun., 1978-82; mem. Grad. Record Exam. Bd., 1980-82; mem. com. on testing coun. Grad. Sch., 1980-82; mem. N.Am. com. Mellon Fellowship Program, 1982-92; chmn. coun. Grad. Studies in Religion, 1989-93. Mem. region I and II selection com. Woodrow Wilson Found., 1959-69; trustee Am. Sch. Oriental Rsch., 1976-82, 93—, v.p., 1993-96; trustee Hiatt Inst., Brandeis U., 1979-82; trustee Roger Williams Hosp., Providence, 1981-97; trustee

Palestine Endowment Fund Israel, Inc., 1999—; trustee Albright Inst. Archeol. Rsch., Jerusalem, 1974—, pres., 1976-82; bd. dir. Assn. Jewish Studies, 1990-98, Jewish Chautauqua Soc., 2002; with inf., AUS, 1943-46. Recipient Disting. Alumnus Award Boston U., 1994; Beebe fellow Boston U., 1952-53; Lilly postdoctoral fellow Heidelberg U., 1962-63. Mem. Soc. Bibl. Lit. (exec. com. New Eng. coun. 1977-82); Am. Acad. Religion (pres. New Eng. 1970-71); Phi Beta Kappa (sec. Brown U. chpt. 1964-68, pres. 1975-77). Home: 32 Vassar Ave Providence RI 02906-3420 Office: Dorot Found 439 Benefit St Providence RI 02903-2934

FRERICHS, JOY ROBERTA, elementary education educator; b. Sweetwater, Tenn., July 21, 1946; d. Elton F. and Lenis Abby (Edwards) F. AA, Hiwassee Jr. Coll., Madisonville, Tenn., 1966; BS, East Tenn. State U., 1968; MEd, West Ga. Coll., 1977. Tchr. Dug Gap, Dalton, Ga., 1966-75; lead lang. arts tchr. Valley Point Mid. Sch., Dalton, Ga., 1975-2000; tchr. New Hope Elem. Sch., Dalton, Ga., 2000—. Mem. Ga. state textbook adv. com., 1979-80. Author (tchg. ideas) English Counselor, 1986, Mailbox, 1993-98, 2000; reviewer children's jour., contbr. articles to profl. jour. Pres. Friends of the Libr., Dalton, 1994—; bd. dir. Assembly on the Lit. on Culture Appalachia, 2000—. Named Reading Tchr. of Yr., Cherokee Coun., Northwest Ga., 1986-87; NEH scholar, Ark., 1993, Tex., 1998, Fulbright Meml. Fund scholar, 1999. Mem. NEA (com. mem.), Nat. Coun. Tchrs. English (coord. Young Writers Program 1986), Internat. Reading Assn. (S.E. team leader Young Adult Choices, Young Adult Choices com. 2000-Teachers Choices Team leader, 2002-2004), Pilot Club (various offices including pres. 1986—, Ga. state parliamentarian 1988-89, lt. gov. 1991-93), Alpha Delta Kappa. Democrat. Methodist. Avocations: reading, serving community. Home: 4156-29A Hwy 225 N Chatsworth GA 30705 Office: 1175 New Hope Rd NW Dalton GA 30720-6338 E-mail: jfrerichs@whitfield.k2.ga.us.

FRESCH, MARIE BETH, court reporting company executive; b. Norwalk, Ohio, Jan. 16, 1957; d. Ralph Roy and Vonda Mae (Brunkhorst) Spiegel; m. James R. Fresch, Aug. 5, 1978; 1 child, Alexandra Jane. AS in Bus., Tiffin U., 1977; cert. in ct. reporting, Acad. Ct. Reporting, 1979. Registered profl. reporter, Ohio. Ofcl. reporter Seneca County Common Pleas Ct., Tiffin, Ohio, 1979-80; owner, operator Marie B. Fresch & Assocs., Norwalk, 1980—. Coach indoor and outdoor Soccer teams, 1994-99, summer softball teams, 1994—, girls volleyball coach, 1999-2002; leader Girl Scouts Am., 1995-2002, sch. organizer, team leader, 1997-2002, parade organizer, 1998-2002. Recipient Cert. of Merit, Nat. Ct. Reporters Assn., 1990; named Outstanding Leader, Girl Scout Coun., 1998, Outstanding Vol., 2000. Mem. Nat. Ct. Reporters Assn., Ohio Ct. Reporters Assn. (student promotions and pub. rels. coms. 1986-90, dist. rep. 1994-95, fundraising com. 1993-96), NOW (sec. Port Clinton chpt. 1984-86, treas. 1986-87, 91), Am. Legion Aux., Kappa Delta Kappa. Lodges: Order of Eastern Star (esther 1979-81). Democrat. Methodist. Avocations: swimming, biking, gardening, hiking. Home and Office: 47 Warren Dr Norwalk OH 44857-2447 E-mail: MBF1@AccNORWALK.com.

FRESE, EDWARD SCHEER, JR., information technology executive, consultant; b. N.Y.C., Oct. 17, 1941; s. Edward Scheer and Sylvana (Cerutti) F.; stepson Mary Margaret (Richardson) F.; m. Christine Ann Robinson, Oct. 27, 1979; 1 child, Edward Robinson. AB in Latin, Hamilton Coll., 1966; postgrad., NYU, 1970-72. Programmer trainee Mfr.'s Hanover Trust Co., N.Y.C., 1969-70, systems analyst, 1970-75, officer, 1975-81; project mgr. Macmillan, Inc., N.Y.C., 1981-84; dir. fin. systems Maxwell Macmillan Inc., N.Y.C., 1984-89, dir. corp. info. systems, 1989-90; prin. Bremen Assocs., Inc., N.Y.C., 1991-97; v.p. Year 2000 Cahners Bus. Info., 1997-98; v.p. Bremen Assocs., Inc., N.Y.C., 1998—. Mem. Soc. for Info. Mgmt., The Planning Forum. Clubs: Point O' Woods, University (N.Y.C.). Republican. Episcopalian. Avocations: writing, swimming, sailing, music. Home: 79 North Ave Westport CT 06880-2722 E-mail: bremenai@aol.com.

FRESH, LINDA LOU, government official; b. Ashland, Pa., June 29, 1957; d. Harold Foster and Norma Jean (Thomas) Geist; m. Bruce Alan Fresh, June 18, 1977; 1 child, Niccole Patricia. AA in Bus. Mgmt., U. Md., Okinawa, Japan, 1981; BS in Psychology, U. Md., Heidelberg, Germany, 1987; EdM in Counseling, Boston U., Heidelberg, 1994. Clinic liaison specialist U.S. Army, Augsburg, Germany, 1985, fin. counselor New Cumberland, Pa., 1989-92, Hanau, Germany, 1992-94; family support program specialist U.S. Army Res., Ft. Belvoir, Va., 1994-95; family life specialist USAF, Washington, 1995-96; family advocacy prevention and edn. specialist USN, Washington, 1996-99; EEO mgr., fed. women's program mgr., mgr. Upward Mobility program, EAP counselor FBI, Washington, 1999—, sexual harassment coord., 2000—. Mem. interagy. com. Fed. Women's Program, Washington, 1999; spl. asst. Fed. Women's Program to Federally Employed Women's Nat. Pres. and Bd. Mem. Mus. for Women in Arts, Women's Meml. With U.S. Army, 1975-78. Mem. AAUW, Women in Mil. Svc. for Am., Women's Army Corps Vets. Assn., Federally Employed Women (exec. v.p. N.W. D.C. chpt.), Women in Fed. Law Enforcement Inc., Toastmasters. Avocations: travel, movies, writing, reading, teaching. Home: 12993 Queen Chapel Rd Woodbridge VA 22193 Office: FBI 935 Pennsylvania Ave NW Washington DC 20535-0001

FRESHMAN, BRENDA LEE, psychologist, educator, psychologist, researcher; d. Samuel Krelitz and Ardyth Freshman. BS in Psychology, UCLA, 1985; MA in Applied Psychology, U. Santa Monica, 1993; PhD in Orgnl. Psychology, Calif. Sch. Profl. Psychology, 2000. Vis. asst. prof. UCLA, Westwood, 2000—; v.p., dir. orgnl. devel. Std. Multifamily Fund, L.P, L.A., 2002—; pres. Social Logistics, Santa Monica, Calif., 2002—. Dir. programs and rsch. Nature Trust of the Santa Monica Mountains, Malibu, Calif., 2001—. Composer (musician, producer): (cd) Infinity Road; contbr. articles to profl. jours. Chairperson Wetlands Recovery Project L.A. Task Force Edn. Com., 2001; bd. mem. Music Heals, Beverly Hills, Calif., 2001. Mem.: Orgnl. Behavior Tchg. Soc., Acad. Mgmt., Am. Soc. for Trainers and Developers- LA. Personal E-mail: info@sociallogistics.com.

FRESHWATER, MICHAEL FELIX, plastic surgeon, educator; b. N.Y.C., Feb. 4, 1948; s. Jack and Rhonda Freshwater. BS magna cum laude, Bklyn. Coll., 1968; MD, Yale U., 1972. Diplomate Nat. Bd. Med. Examiners, Am. Bd. Plastic Surgery. Asst. resident in surgery Yale New Haven Hosp., 1972-74; fellow in plastic surgery Med. Sch. Johns Hopkins U., Balt., 1974-77; resident, then chief resident in plastic surgery Jackson Meml. Hosp., 1977-78; Kleinert fellow hand and microsurgery Jewish Hosp., Louisville, 1979; pvt. practice medicine specializing in plastic/hand surgery Miami, Fla., 1979—; pres., dir. Miami Inst. Hand and Microsurgery, 1980—; dir. hand and microsurgery Cedars Med. Ctr., 1985—, chief surgery, 1988-90, bd. dirs., 1990-92. Vol. assoc. prof. plastic surgery U. Miami Sch. medicine, 1979—; vol. faculty mem. Barry U. Sch. Podiatric Medicine and Surgery, 1989—; vis. prof. Javeriana U., Bogota, 1983—85, Centro Medico de los Andes, 1983—86; cons. Fla. Children's Med. Svc., Tallahassee, 1979—, Fla. Elks Crippled Children Soc., Orlando, 1983—, Fla. Dept. Profl. Regulation, Tallahassee, 1984—95, League Against Cancer, 1983—, Scientists Inst. Pub. Info., 1985—, USCG, Miami Beach, 1992—. Contbr. chapters to books, articles to profl. jours.; mem. bd. reviewers: Plastic and Reconstructive Surgery, 1976—. Trustee Yale U. Med. Libr., New Haven, 1972—77, 2000—, D. R. Millard Found., 1987—; bd. dirs. V. and A. Gildred Found., 1980—86, Yale Sch. Medicine Fund, 1991—97, Campaign for Stuyvesant, 2003—; mem. nat. campaign com. Yale Sch. Medicine, 1993—97; mem. Fla. Bar Grievance Com., 1998—2001. Recipient Letter Commendation, Gov. Bob Graham, 1984; fellow Weinberger, NIH, 1974—76; scholar Jonas Salk, CUNY, 1968—72. Fellow: Internat. Coll. Surgeons; mem.: AMA (Physicians Recognition award 1976, 1979, 1982, 1985, 1988, 1990, 1993, 1996, 1999, 2001), Miami Assn. for Surgery of Hand (dir. 1991—), Am. Soc. Peripheral Nerve, Miami Soc. Plastic Surgeons (sec.-treas. 1987—88, v.p. 1988—89, pres. 1989—90), Royal Soc. Medicine, Internat. Soc. Reconstructive Microsurgery, Am. Soc. Reconstructive Microsurgery, Am. Burn Assn., Am. Assn. Hand Surgery, Assn. Yale Alumni in Medicine (bd. dirs. 1998—2000), Grove Isle Club (Miami), Yale Club (Miami, N.Y.), Phi Beta Kappa. Avocation: skiing. Office: 1 Datran Ctr Ste 502 Miami FL 33156-7814 E-mail: miamihandsurgery@bellsouth.net.

FRESTEDT, JOY LOUISE, science administrator; b. Oak Park, Ill., Jan. 31, 1959; d. James Albert Machnicki and Wanda Louise (McConnaughhay) Katzman; m. Robert LeVance Frestedt, Aug. 8, 1987; 1 child, Megan Marie. BA in Biology, Knox Coll., 1980; PhD in Pathobiology, U. Minn., 1996. Rsch. asst. Knox Coll., 1978-80; cytogeneticist Ill. Masonic Med. Ctr., Chgo., 1980-81; med. tech., asst. scientist, rsch. scientist, lab. dir. U. Minn., Mpls., 1981-89, 91-96; cancer rsch. scientist III, lab. dir. Roswell Park Cancer Inst., Buffalo, 1989-90; rsch. scientist, lab. dir. Mpls. Children's Med. Ctr., 1990-91; grad. fellow, safety expert, sr. scientist Sci. Mus. Minn., St. Paul, 1993—2001; rsch. scientist St. Jude Med. Inc., St. Paul, 1996-97. Adj. faculty Mpls. Cmty. Tech. Coll., 1996-99, North Hennepin C.C., 1997-98, Anoka Ramsey C.C., 1997-98, Rasmussen Bus. Coll., 1998-99, Medtronic/Mpls. Cmty. Tech. Coll., 1998, Normandale C.C., 1999; mgr. Busulfex Clin. Devel. Orphan Med., Inc., 1999-2000; med. info. scientist AstraZeneca Pharm., 2000—01; ops. mgr. clin. trials svc. Mayo Clinic, 2001-03; contract compliance auditor, 3M, 2002; mgr. regional clin. affairs Ortho Biotech Products, LP, 2002-. Co-author: Writing About Science, 1997, Considering Graduate School in the Sciences, 1999; referee, reviewer Jour. Women and Minorities in Sci. and Engring., contbr. articles to profl. jours. and books. Mem.: AAAS, Grad. Women in Sci. (pres. 1996—97, bd. dirs. 1999—2003, chair bd. dirs. 2002—03), Assn. Women in Sci., Sigma Xi. Avocations: softball, camping. Home: 1916 Scenic Point Ln SW Rochester MN 55902 E-mail: frest001@umn.edu.

FRESTON, THOMAS E. cable television programming executive; b. N.Y.C., Nov. 22, 1945; s. Thomas E. and Winifred (Geng) F.; m. Margaret Badali, Oct. 18, 1980; 1 child, Andrew. BA, St. Michaels Coll., 1967; MBA, NYU, 1969. Dir. mktg.- MTV MTV Networks, N.Y.C., 1980-81, dir. mktg.- The Movie Channel, 1982-83; v.p. mktg.-MTV MTV Networks Inc., N.Y.C., 1983-84, v.p. mktg., 1984-85, sr. v.p./gen. mgr. affiliate sales, mktg., 1985, sr. v.p./gen. mgr. MTV, VH-1, 1985-86, pres. entertainment, 1986-87, pres., CEO, 1987-89; chmn., CEO MTV Networks, N.Y.C., 1989—. Bd. dirs. Cable Advt. Bur., N.Y.C., 1987—, MTV Europe, London, 1986—, Rock 'n Roll Hall of Fame, N.Y.C., 1986—. Mem. Smithsonian com. Music in Am., 1987—. Mem. Cable TV Adminstrn. & Mktg. Assn., Nat. Acad. Cable Programming. Avocations: photography, travel, antique rugs.

FRETWELL, ELBERT K., JR., retired university chancellor, consultant; b. N.Y.C., Oct. 29, 1923; s. Elbert Kirtley and Jean (Hosford) F.; m. Dorrie Shearer, Aug. 25, 1951; children: Barbara Alice (Mrs. Peter Cooke), Margaret Jean (Mrs. John C. Cross), James Leonard, Katharine Louise (Mrs. Robert Saul). AB with distinction, Wesleyan U., Middletown, Conn., 1944, MA in Tchg., Harvard U., 1948; PhD, Columbia U., 1953; hon. doctorate, Tech. U. Wroclaw, Poland, 1976; LL.D. (hon.), Wesleyan U., 1981; D in Pub. Svc. (hon.), U. N.C., Charlotte, 1998. Stringer AP, 1942-44; staff writer ARC, 1944-45; vice consul Am. embassy, Prague, Czech Republic, 1945-47; tchr. Brookline (Mass.) Pub. Schs., 1948, Evanston (Ill.) Twp. High Sch. and Community Coll., 1948-50; adminstrv. sec. John Hay Fellowships, John Hay Whitney Found., 1951-53; asst. prof., asst. to dean Tchrs. Coll., Columbia U., 1953-56, assoc. prof., 1956; asst. commr. for higher edn. N.Y. State Dept. Edn., 1956-64; summer faculty U. Calif. at Berkeley, 1964; dean acad. devel. CUNY, N.Y.C., 1964-67; pres. SUNY Coll. at Buffalo, 1967-78; chancellor U. N.C., Charlotte, 1979-89, chancellor emeritus, 1989—; sr. assoc. MDC Inc., 1989-91; interim pres. U. Mass. System, 1991-92. Interim pres. U. North Fla., 1998; mem. commn. higher instns. Mid. States Assn. of Schs. and Colls., 1965-71, pres., chmn., 1973-74; trustee Carnegie Found. for Advancement Tchg., chmn., 1975-77; mem. Carnegie Coun. on Policy Studies in Higher Edn., 1973-79; bd. dirs. N.C. Transp. Mus. Found., 1996—; trustee Wesleyan U., 1967-70, Nichols Sch., Buffalo, 1969-78, Canisius Coll., 1969-76, Peace Coll., 1997-2003; exec. dir. com. on edn. N.Y. State Constl. Conv., 1967; mem. N.C. Med. Bd., 2001—. Decorated Order of Cultural Merit Poland; recipient Disting. Alumnus award Wesleyan U., 1974, Tchrs. Coll., Columbia U., 1983, Boy Scouts Am. Silver Beaver award. Mem. Am. Assn. State Colls. and Univs. (pres. 1978-79), Am. Assn. for Higher Edn. (pres. 1964-65), Am. Coun. Edn. (chmn. 1980-81), N.C. Assn. Colls. and Univs. (pres. 1985-86), Nat. Rlwy. Hist. Soc., Adirondack Mountain Club, Rotary (pres. Charlotte 1994-95). Home: 3738 Cypress Club Dr Apt D411 Charlotte NC 28210-2492 Office: U NC-Charlotte 9201 University City Blvd Charlotte NC 28223-0002

FREUD, NICHOLAS S. lawyer; b. N.Y.C., Feb. 6, 1942; s. Frederick and Fredericka (von Rothenburg) F.; m. Elsa Doskow, July 23, 1966; 1 child, Christopher. AB, Yale U., 1963, JD, 1966. Bar: N.Y. 1968, Calif. 1970, U.S. Tax Ct. 1973. Ptnr. Chickering & Gregory, San Francisco, 1978-85, Russin & Vecchi, San Francisco, 1986-93, Jeffer, Mangels, Butler & Marmaro, LLP, San Francisco, 1993—. Mem. joint adv. bd. Calif. Continuing Edn. of Bar, chair taxation subcom. 1987-87; mem. fgn. income adv. bd. Tax Management Internat. Jour., mem. bd. advs. The Jour. of Internat. Taxation; mem. adv. bd. NYU Inst. on Fed. Taxation; academician Internat. Acad. Estate and Tax Law; mem. tax commn., Union Internat. des Avocats. Author: (with Charles G. Stephenson and K. Bruce Friedman) International Estate Planning, rev. edit., 1997; contbr. articles to profl. jours. Fellow Am. Coll. of Tax Counsel; mem. ABA (tax sect. vice chair adminstrn. 2000-02, coun. dir. 1995-97, chair com. on U.S. activities of foreigners and tax treaties 1989-91, vice chair 1987-89, chair subcom. on tax treaties 1981-87), Calif. State Bar Assn. (taxation sect. exec. com. 1981-85, vice chair 1982-83, chair 1983-84, vice chair income tax com. 1981-82, chair 1982-83, vice chair personal income tax subcom. 1979-80, chair 1980-81, co-chair fgn. tax subcom. 1978-79, ert. specialist in taxation law), N.Y. State Bar Assn. (taxation sect., mem. com. on U.S. activities of fgn. taxpayers and fgn. activities of U.S. taxpayers), Bar Assn. of San Francisco, Bar Assn. of City of N.Y., San Francisco Tax Club (pres. 1988), San Francisco Internat. Tax Group. Office: Jeffer Mangels Butler & Marmaro LLP 5th Fl Two Embarcedero Ctr San Francisco CA 94111-3824 E-mail: nsf@jmbm.com.

FREUDENBERGER, HERMAN, retired economics educator; b. Eberbach, Germany, Apr. 14, 1922; came to U.S., 1934; s. Alfred and Frieda (Gruenebaum) F.; m. Paulette Ethel Gross, June 17, 1951; children— Joseph, Alfred Carl BS, Columbia U., 1950, MA, 1951, PhD, 1957. Instr. Bklyn. Coll., 1956-58, 59-60; lectr. Rutgers U., New Brunswick, N.J., 1958-59; asst. prof. U. Mont., Missoula, 1960-62; assoc. prof. Tulane U., New Orleans, 1962-66, prof. econs., 1966-92, prof. emeritus, 1992—. Author: The Industrialization of a Central European City, 1977, Lost Momentum, 2003, (with others) Von der Provinzstadt zur Industrieregion, 1975, A Redemptorist Missionary in Ireland 1851-1854, 1998; contbr. articles to profl. jours. Served U.S. Army, 1942—46, ETO. Home: 709 Ashlawn Dr New Orleans LA 70123-3809

FREUDENHEIM, MILTON B. journalist; b. New Rochelle, N.Y., Mar. 4, 1927; s. Milton Benjamin and Lenore Patricia (Kroh) F.; m. Elizabeth Ege, Mar. 7, 1952 (dec. Dec. 30, 1996); children: Jo Louise, Susan Patricia, John Milton Otto, Tom Henry; m. Grace Glueck, Oct. 20, 2000. AB, U. Mich., 1948. Reporter Louisville (Ky.) Courier-Jour., 1948-49; reporter Akron (Ohio) Beacon Jour., 1949-52, Washington corr., 1953-56; UN corr. Chgo. Daily News, 1956-66, nat. and fgn. editor, 1966-69, Paris corr., 1969-77; dir. public affairs for Region V HEW, Chgo., 1978-79; copy editor, writer N.Y. Times Week in Rev., 1979-87, bus. and health reporter, 1987—. Adv. U.S. del. UNESCO Gen. Conf., 1978; Pres. UN Corrs. Assn., 1966, Anglo-Am. Press Assn., Paris, 1975 Mem. Phi Beta Kappa, Sigma Delta Chi. Home: 91 Central Park W New York NY 10023-4600 Office: NY Times 229 W 43rd St New York NY 10036-3959

FREUDENTHAL, DAVID D. governor; b. Thermopolis, Wyo., Oct. 12, 1950; U.S. atty. for Wyo. U.S. Dept. Justice, Cheyenne, 1994—2001; gov. State of Wyo., Cheyenne, 2003—. Office: Office of the Governor State Capitol Bldg Rm 124 Cheyenne WY 82002*

FREUDENTHAL, ERNEST GUENTER, technology and business educator; b. Mannheim, Germany, July 22, 1920; came to the U.S., 1937; s. Leopold and Selma (Rosenthal) F.; m. Stephanie Karlsruher, Dec. 26, 1948; children: Pamela Hausman, Joan Fraifeld. BA in Econs., Vanderbilt U., 1948, MA in Econs., 1971. Employee Werthan Industries, Nashville, 1942-44, 46-48, middle mgmt. staff, 1948-69, v.p. mfg., 1969-71, sr. v.p., 1971-90. Adj. assoc. prof. bus., tech., pub. policy, indsl. mktg. Vanderbilt U., Nashville, 1971—. Co-editor: The Holocaust and other Genocide, 2002. Mem. Com. on Employment Projections of the Bus. Rsch. Adv. Coun., Washington, 1997—, Holocaust Edn. Colloquium, 1999—2000; Mem. Bus. Res. Adv. Coun. to the Bur. Labor Statis., Washington, 1981—; chmn. Metro Social Svcs. Commn., Nashville, 1989—2001; commr., treas. Tenn. Holocaust Commn., Inc., 1998—; pres. Jewish Cmty. Ctr., Nashville, 1965—67; trustee Tenn. Hist. Soc., 2000—. Staff sgt. U.S. Army, 1944—46, PTO. Recipient Sage award Coun. on Aging, Nashville, 1995. Mem. Jewish Fedn. Nashville (pres. 1974-76), The Temple (pres. 1986-88), Vanderbilt Inst. Pub. Policy Studies, Univ. Club, Phi Beta Kappa. Avocation: hiking. Home: 4406 Sunnybrook Dr Nashville TN 37205-3860 Office: PO Box 1518 Nashville TN 37202-1518

FREUDENTHAL, STEVEN FRANKLIN, lawyer, political organization chairman; b. Thermopolis, Wyo., June 8, 1949; s. Lewis Franklin and Lucille Iola (Love) F.; m. Janet Mae Mansfield, Aug. 30, 1969 (div. Sept. 1996); children: Lynn Marie, Kristen Lee; m. Barbara A. Crofts, Jan. 1, 1998; stepchildren: Shane C., Jeanne N. BA, Trinity Coll., Hartford, Conn., 1971; JD, Vanderbilt U., 1975. Bar: Wyo. 1975, U.S. Supreme Ct. 1981. Tax acct. Conn. Gen. Life Ins. Co., Hartford, Conn., 1971-72; asst. atty. gen. Wyo. Cheyenne, 1975-77; atty. gen. Wyo., 1981-82; state planning coordinator Office Gov. Wyo., Cheyenne, 1977-78; dep. under sec. Dept. Interior, Washington, 1978-79, exec. asst. to sec., 1979-80; ptnr Sherman & Howard, Cheyenne, Wyo., 1980-81; ptnr. Freudenthal, Salzburg & Bonds, Cheyenne, 1983—; mem. Wyo. Ho. Reps., 1987-91. Trustee United Med. Ctr., 1990-97, pres., 1993-96; bd. dirs. Cheyenne LEADS, 1990-93; chmn. Wyo. Dem. Party, 1999-2001. Office: 123 E 17th St Cheyenne WY 82003-0387 E-mail: steve@wyolaw.com.

FREUKES, PATRICIA E. pediatrics nurse, nursing supervisor; b. St. Louis, Oct. 13, 1954; d. Lawrence D. Sr. and Helen L. (Wooliver) F. Student, Jefferson Coll., 1973-74; RN, Luth. Med. Ctr. Sch. Nursing, 1977; student, Maryville Coll., 1977-78; BSN, St. Louis U., 1987. Staff nurse in orthopedics Luth. Hosp., St. Louis, 1977-79; staff nurse neurology/neurosurgery St. Louis Children's Hosp., 1979-88, adminstrv. supr., 1988—. Home: 3270 Bayshore Pkwy Arnold MO 63010-4034

FREUND, DEBORAH MIRIAM, transportation engineer; b. Bklyn., Apr. 9, 1957; d. Harry and Bertha (Fried) F.;m. Garey Douglas White, Feb. 22, 1981. BSCE, Washington U., 1979, MSc, 1982. Registered profl. engr., Tex. Grad. rsch. asst. Washington U., St. Louis, 1979-81; transp. planning engr. Mid-Am. Regional Coun., Kansas City, Mo., 1981-83; civil engr. Fed. Hwy. Adminstrn., Washington, 1983-85, rsch. hwy. engr., 1985-90, transp. specialist, 1990-92, sr. transp. specialist, 1992—99; sr. transportation specialist Fed. Motor Carrier Safety Admin., 2000—. Nat. tech. expert for vehicle rsch., 2001—; mem. com. operator and vehicle performance and simulation Transp. Rsch. Bd., Washington, 1993—96, mem. com. on vehicle user characteristics, 1997—, mem. com. on frt. econs. and regulation, 2000—, mem. com. on truck and bus safety, 2003—; presenter in field. Recipient award for meritorious achievement, Sec. of Transp., 1996; fellow, Coun. for Excellence in Govt., Washington, 1995—96. Mem. ASCE (sec. hwy. divsn. rsch. com. 1988-90), Soc. Automative Engrs. (co-chair total vehicle com. 1997—), Inst. Transp. Engrs., Sigma Xi (assoc.). Achievements include leadership in research on commercial motor vehicle driver safety; innovation in pavement infrastructure information systems. Office: Fed Motor Carrier Safety Adminstrn 400 7th St SW Washington DC 20590-0001 E-mail: deborah.freund@fmcsa.dot.gov

FREUND, EMMA FRANCES, medical technologist; b. 1922; d. Walter R. and Mabel W. (Loveland) Ervin; m. Frederic Reinert Freund, March 4, 1953; children: Frances, Daphne, Fern, Frederic. BS, Wilson Tchrs. Coll., Washington, 1944; MS in Biology, Cath. U., Washington, 1953; MEd in Adult Edn., Va. Commonwealth U., 1988. Tchr. math and sci. D.C. Sch. Sys., Washington, 1944-45; technician in parasitology lab. U.S. Dept. Agr., Beltsville, Md., 1945-48; histologic technician dept. pathology Georgetown U. Med. Sch., Washington, 1948-49; clin. lab. technician Kent and Queen Anne's County Gen. Hosp., Chestertown, Md., 1949-51; histotechnologist Med. Coll. Va. Hosp., Richmond, Va., 1951—. Cons. profl. meetings and workshops; exam. coun. Nat. Cert. Agy. Med. Lab. Pers. Co-author: (mini-course) Instrumentation in Cytology and Histology, 1985; editor Histo-Scope Newsletter. Asst. den leader Robert E. Lee coun. Boy Scouts Am., 1967-68, den leader, 1968-70. Mem. AAAS, NAFE, AAUW, APS, Am. Mgmt. Assn., Am. Soc. Clin. Lab. Sci. (rep. to sci. assenbly histology sect. 1977-78, chmn. 1983-85, 89-96), Va. Soc. Med. Tech. (Richmond chpt. corr. sec. 1977-78, bd. dirs. 1981-82, pres. 1984-85), Va. Soc. Histotech. (pres. 1994-96), Nat. Certification Agy. (clin. lab. specialist in histotech., clin. lab. supr. clin. lab. dir.), N.Y. Acad. Scis., Am. Assn. Clin. Chemistry (assoc.), Am. Soc. Clin. Pathologists (assoc.; cert. histology technician), Nat. Geog. Soc., Va. Govtl. Employees Assn., Nat. Soc. Histotech. (by-laws com. 1981—, C.E.U. com. 1981—, program com. regional meeting 1984, 85, 87, 97, 2000, chmn. regional meeting 1987, program chmn. state meeting 1998-99, Conv. scholarship award 1997, Clin. Chemists' Recognition award 1995, 98, 2002), Am. Mus. Natural History, Smithsonian Inst., Am. Mgmt. Assn., Am. Chem. Soc., Am. Soc. Quality, Clin. Lab. Mgmt. Assn., Van Slyke Soc., Soc. Human Resource Mgmt., Nat. Soc. Hist. Preservation, Math. Assn. Am., Sigma Xi, Phi Beta Rho, Kappa Delta Pi, Phi Lambda Theta. Home: 1315 Asbury Rd Richmond VA 23229-5305

FREUND, FRED A. retired lawyer; b. N.Y.C., June 18, 1928; s. Sidney J. and Cora (Strasser) F.; m. Rosalie Sampo, Nov. 18, 1975 (div. Apr. 1983); m. Patricia A. Gardner, Mar. 13, 1957 (div. Jan. 1967); children: Gregory G., K. Bailey AB, Columbia U., 1948, JD, 1949. Bar: N.Y. 1949, U.S. Supreme Ct. 1968. Law clk. to chief judge U.S. Dist. Ct. So. Dist. N.Y., N.Y.C., 1949-51; assoc. Kaye, Scholer, Fierman, Hays & Handler, N.Y.C., 1953-58, ptnr., 1959-93, ret., 1993. Served to 1st lt. USAF, 1951-53. Mem. ABA, Assn. Bar City N.Y., Phi Beta Kappa Home: 1085 Park Ave Apt 4C New York NY 10128-1179 *Balancing the quest for excellence with humility and humor.*

FREUND, FREDRIC S. real estate broker, property manager; b. Denver, Sept. 23, 1930; AB, Brown U., 1952. Sr. v.p. Hanford, Freund & Co., San Francisco, 1956—. Past adv. dir. Western Investment Real Estate Trust; bd. dirs. Berkeley Antibody Co.; instr. real estate mgmt. U. Calif. Ext.; guest lectr. Stanford U. Sch. Bus. Adminstrn. Commr. Calif. Senate Adv. Commn. on Cost Control in State Govt.; chair code adv. com. Bldg. Inspection Dept., San Francisco. Mem. Am. Soc. Real Estate Counselors (CRE, pres. no. Calif. 1987-88), San Francisco Assn. Realtors (pres. 1974-75, Realtor of Yr. 1975), Bldg. Owners & Mgrs. Assn. San Francisco, Realtors Nat. Mktg. Inst. (CCIM), Inst. Real Estate Mgmt. (CPM). Office: Hanford Freund & Co 47 Kearny St Ste 300 San Francisco CA 94108-5582 Home: 112 Alta St San Francisco CA 94133 Fax: 415-296-0725. E-mail: ffreund@hanfordfreund.com.

FREUND, GERHARD, medical educator; b. Frankfurt, Germany, Apr. 21, 1926; came to U.S., 1951; s. Adolf and Martha (Neuhaus) F.; m. Marion Healy, Sept. 24, 1955; children: Anne Freund Rubin, Michael S. MD, Goethe U., McGill U. Mem. Ctr. Neurobiol. Scis. U. Fla., Gainesville, 1967—; assoc. prof. medicine U. Fla. Coll. Medicine, Gainesville, 1970-75, prof. medicine, 1975—, prof. neurosci., 1976—, prof. emeritus, 2000—; chief endocrinology Va. Med. Ctr., Gainesville, 1970—. Dir. Alcohol Rsch. Ctr., Gainesville, 1982-87. Fellow Am. Coll. Physicians; mem. Soc. Neurosci., Soc. Biol. Psychiatry, Endocrine Soc., Rsch. Soc. Alcoholism (mem. exec. com. 1981-84). Home: 2031 NW 14th Ave Gainesville FL 32605-5208 Office: U Fla Coll Medicine Archer Rd Gainesville FL 32610-0277 E-mail: freundg@medicine.ufl.edu.

FREUND, HENRY PHILIP, physicist; b. N.Y.C., May 23, 1949; s. Andrew and Lena Katie (Levine) F.; m. Sandra Lee Cross, June 12, 1977; children: Lena Marion, Anna Jane. BS, Rensselaer Poly. Inst., 1971; PhD, U. Md., 1976. Postdoctoral rsch. assoc. Inst. Phys. Sci. and Tech. U. Md., College Park, 1976-77; vis. rsch. assoc. Univ. Fed. do Rio Grande do Sul, Porto Alegre, Brazil, 1977; resident rsch. assoc. Naval Rsch. Lab. Nat. Acad. Sci., Washington, 1977-79; rsch. physicist Sci. Applications Internat., Inc., McLean, Va., 1979—. Rsch. assoc. U. Md., 1982—; vis. scientist MIT, Cambridge, 1985—. Co-author: Principles of Free-Electron Lasers, 1992; contbr. articles to Scientific Am., Phys. Rev., Jour. Quantum Electronics, Phys. Fluids, IEEE Trans. Plasma Sci., Nuclear Instrumentation Methods Phys. Rsch., Phys. Rev. Letters, Math. Bioscis.; contbr. chpts. to books: Infrared and Millimeter Waves: Millimeter Components and Techniques, 1984, 1991 Yearbook of Encyclopedia of Phys. Sci. and Tech., Computer Applications in Plasma Sci. and Engring., 1991, Ency. Lasers and Optical Tech., 1991. Fellow Am. Phys. Soc.; mem. N.Y. Acad. Sci. Achievements include patent for free-electron lasers with tapered axial magnetic fields; analysis of effect of solenoidal magnetic field on the physics of free electron lasers, nonlinear analysis and numerical simulation of free electron lasers; research on development of technique for the back-calculation method of determining the spread of the virus (HIV) that causes AIDS. Office: Sci Application Internat 1710 Goodridge Dr Mc Lean VA 22102-3701

FREUND, JOHN RICHARD, former English educator; b. Chgo., Nov. 16, 1926; s. Charles Anton and Helen Mary Freund; m. Barbara Ann Krohn, Sept. 11, 1948; children: David Eric, Alaric James. BA, Miami U., Oxford, Ohio, 1949, MA, 1950; PhD, Ind. U., 1955. Asst. prof. English Western Mich. U., Kalamazoo, 1954-64; assoc. prof. English Grand Valley State Coll., Allendale, Mich., 1964-68; prof. English King's Coll., Wilkes-Barre, Pa., 1968-71, Ind. U. of Pa., Indiana, Pa., 1971-90, English prof. emeritus, 1990--. Supr. English Program for Disadvantaged Pre-Coll. Youth, Ind. Colls. Tng. Program, Kalamazoo, 1968; specialist, Adult Basic Edn. Tchr. Tng. Inst., Wilkes-Barre, 1971; cons. Consultant Cadre, Right to Read, State of Pa., 1977-78. Author: Broken Symmetries: A Study of Agency in Shakespeare's Plays, 1991; (with Arnold Nelson) Where Minds Meet edni. radio series, 1963; author/performer: The Nature of Perception closed-circuit TV program, 1964 (Ohio State Award); editor: Studies in the Humanities Jour., 1972-81. With USN, 1944-46, PTO. Mem. MLA, Assoc. Lit. Scholars and Critics. Democrat. Avocation: raising dogs and cats. Home: 8 Deborah Trl Fairfield PA 17320-8298 E-mail: jrfreund@blazenet.net.

FREUND, LAMBERT BEN, engineering educator, researcher, consultant; b. McHenry, Ill., Nov. 23, 1942; s. Bernard and Anita (Schaeffer) F.; m. Colleen Jean Hehl, Aug. 21, 1965; children: Jonathan Ben, Jeffrey Alan, Stephen Neil. BS, U. Ill., 1964, MS, 1965; PhD, Northwestern U., 1967. Postdoctoral fellow Brown U., Providence, 1967-69, asst. prof., 1969-73, assoc. prof., 1973-75, prof. engring., 1975—, Henry Ledyard Goddard prof., 1988—, chmn. div., 1979-83. Vis. prof. Stanford (Calif.) U., 1974-75, 95; cons. Aberdeen Proving Ground, U.S. Steel Corp.; vis. scholar Harvard U., 1983-84; mem.-at-large U.S. Nat. Com. for Theoretical and Applied Mechancis, NRC, 1985-97; mem. IUTAM Gen. Assembly, 1987—, treas., 1996—; Russell Severance Springer prof. U. Calif., Berkeley, 1995; cons. Advanced Rsch. Projects Agy. Def. Scis. Rsch. Coun.; disting. vis. scientist Jet Propulsion Lab NASA, 1994—. Author: Dynamic Fracture Mechanics, 1990; editor in chief: ASME Jour. Applied Mechanics, 1983-88, editor Cambridge monographs on Mechanics and Applied Mathematics, 1989—, Jour. Mechanics and Physics of Solids, 1992—; mem. editorial adv. bd. Acta Mechanica Sinica, 1990-2001; contbr. articles to tech. jours. NSF trainee, 1964-67; grantee NSF, Office Naval Rsch., Army Rsch. Office, Nat. Bur. Stads., Air Force Office Sci. Rsch., Dept. Energy; recipient Alumni Honor award Coll. Engring., U. Ill., 1996. Fellow ASME (Henry Hess award 1974, mem. applied mechanics divsn. exec. com. 1989-94, S.P. Timoshenko medal 2003), Am. Acad. Mechanics, Am. Acad. Arts and Scis., Soc. Engring. Sci. (William Prager medal 2000); mem. NAS, NAE, ASTM (George R. Irwin medal 1987). Home: 4 Connor Ln Barrington RI 02806-2750 Office: Brown U Dept Engngring Box D Providence RI 02912

FREUND, PEPSI, artist, art educator; b. N.Y.C., Oct. 17, 1938; d. Patrick and Mary (Walsh) Gibbons; m. Frank Freund, Oct. 8, 1960; children: Gerard, Theresa. Tchr. Venice Art League, Sarasota Arts Coun. Workshop presenter, tchr., Sarasota, Fla., Venice (Fla.) Art Ctr., Smithtown Art Coun., East End Arts Coun., Riverhead, N.Y.; series demonstrator Art in the Park, Sarasota, Fla. Works exhibited at Goodard Ctr. for Visual Arts, Ardmore, Okla., U. Gallery, U. S.W., Sewanee, Tenn., Mus. of the S.W., Midland, Tex., Richmond (Ind.) Art Mus., Owatonna (Minn.) Arts Ctr., Kimball Art Ctr., Park City, Utah, Palm Ave. GAllery, Sarasota, Fla., Soundview Art Gallery, Port Jefferson, N.Y.; illustrator (books) God's Tomatoes, Abuse, Offenses, Jezebel Spirit; her art work represented on posters and art work in Ireland and England. Civil activist Elmont (N.Y.) Community, 1983. Mem. Nat. Art League (sec. 1986-87), Malverne Artists (newsletter editor), Floral Park Art League (newsletter editor), Nat. Assn. Women Artists (rev. com. 1993-94), Aquarelle, 30 Artists (pres.). Avocations: reading, writing, swimming, evangelism. Home: 15 Penn Commons Yaphank NY 11980-2025 E-mail: Pepsi223@juno.com.

FREUND, PETER G.O. physicist, educator; b. Timisoara, Romania, Sept. 7, 1936; s. Joseph and Rose Freund; m. Lucy D. Macalpine, Aug. 1986; children: Pauline I., Caroline L. PhD in Physics, Vienna (Austria) U., 1960; DHC (hon.), West U. Timisoara, 1995. Rsch. assoc. U. Vienna, 1960—61; chef de travaux U. Geneva, 1961—62; rsch. assoc. U. Chgo., 1962—64; mem. Inst. Advanced Study, Princeton, NJ, 1964—65; asst. prof. physics U. Chgo., 1965—69, assoc. prof. physics, 1969—74, prof. physics, 1974—. Fellow: Am. Phys. Soc. Achievements include research in two-component duality, which led to string theory; higher-dimensional unification; theory of topological charges; solution of 11-dimensional supergravity which is basic in AdS/CFT correspondence; development of one of the most powerful procedures to study string theory. Avocation: writing short stories. Home: 720 S Dearborn St # 1301 Chicago IL 60605 Office: Enrico Fermi Inst U Chgo 5640 S Ellis Ave Chicago IL 60637

FREUND, PHILIP HERBERT, writer, educator; b. Vancouver, B.C., Canada, Feb. 5, 1909; s. Henry and Augusta (Robinson) Freund. BA, Cornell U., 1929, MA, 1932. Lectr. Inst. Film Techniques CCNY, N.Y.C., 1945—65; lectr. Hunter Coll., N.Y.C., 1946—78, Cornell U., N.Y.C., 1948; lectr. U. B.C., 1949—51; prof. Fordham U., N.Y.C., 1960—79, prof. emeritus, 1979—. Author: The Volcano God, The Zoltans, a Trilogy, The Dark Shore, The Evening Heron, Dreams of Youth, Easter Island, Searching; (plays) Prince Hamlet, Mario's Well, Black Velvet, Simon Simon, numerous short stories, criticisms, (nonfiction) The Art of Reading the Novel, 1965, Myths of Creation, 1963, 1964, rev. edit., 2003, Stage by Stage, 2003. Head scenario bd. rev. Signal Corp Photographic Ctr., N.Y.C., 1943—45; pres. Herbert Robinson Philanthropic Fund, 1960—. Fellow, Bur. New Plays, 1941. Mem.: Sigma Delta Chi. Home: 1025 5th Ave New York NY 10028

FREUND, RICHARD L. communications company executive, consultant, lawyer; b. N.Y.C., Jan. 30, 1921; s. Sidney J. and Cora (Strasser) F.; m. Esta Neiman, Apr. 16, 1950; children: Alice, Robert, Charles. BA, NYU, 1941; LLB, Columbia U., 1944. Bar: N.Y. 1944, U.S. Dist. Ct. (so. dist.) N.Y. 1944. Assoc. Lauterstein, Spiller, Bergerman & Dannett, N.Y.C., 1943-46; labor adminstr. Publix Shirt Corp., N.Y.C., 1946-47; atty. R.H. Macy & Co. Inc., N.Y.C., 1947-54; labor atty. NBC, N.Y.C., 1954-57; dir. labor relations ABC-Paramount Theatres Inc., N.Y.C., 1957-60; v.p. labor relations ABC, N.Y.C., 1960-72, corp. v.p. labor relations, 1972-86, Capital Cities/ABC Inc., N.Y.C., 1986-87, cons., 1987-91. Co-chmn. bd. trustee Am. Fedn. Musicians Pension Fund, N.Y.C., 1967-87; trustee AFTRA Health and Retirement Fund, N.Y.C., 1964-87, Nat. Assn. Broadcast Employees and Technicians Pension Fund, N.Y.C., 1964-87. Contbg. author: Susbidiary Rights and Residuals, 1968. Mem. Phi Beta Kappa. Jewish. Avocations: collecting antique silver and pewter, numismatics, golf. Home and Office: 90 Gerard Ave W Malverne NY 11565-1232

FREUND, ROLAND WILHELM, mathematician; b. Schweinfurt, Germany, Aug. 1, 1955; s. Wilhelm and Frieda F.; m. Susanne Ruehl, Oct. 31, 1979; children: Andreas Lance, Alexander Ray. Diploma in Math., U. Wuerzburg, Germany, 1982, PhD in Math., 1983, Habilitation in Math., 1991. Rsch. scientist NASA Ames Rsch. Ctr., Moffett Field, Calif., 1988-92; mem. tech. staff AT&T Bell Labs., Murray Hill, N.J., 1992-96, Bell Labs., Lucent Technologies, Murray Hill, 1996-99, Disting. mem. tech. staff, 1999—. Vis. rsch. assoc. Stanford U., Calif., 1985-86; part-time lectr. Rutgers U., New Brunswick, N.J., 1993; adj. asst. prof. Columbia U., N.Y.C., 1995; vis. lectr. Princeton U., N.J., 1996; mem. program com. Copper Mountain Conf., 1990—. Mem. editl. bd. SIAM Jour. Numerical Analysis, SIAm Jour. on Matrix Analysis, others; contbr. more than 115 articles to profl. publs.; patentee in field; author two software packages: QMRPACK, BL-QMR, 1993, 96. Recipient Best-Paper award Cad category, Design, Automation and Test in Europe Conf., Munich, 1999, SIAM activity group on linear algebra prize Soc. for Indsl. and Applied Math., Snowbird, Utah, 1994, Heinz-Maier-Leibnitz award German Sec. of Edn. and Sci., Muenster, Germany, 1989. Mem. Soc. Indsl. and Applied Math. Avocation: cycling. Office: Bell Labs 600 Mountain Ave Rm 2c-525 New Providence NJ 07974-0636 E-mail: freund@research.bell-labs.com.

FREUND, SAMUEL J. lawyer; b. Forenwald, Germany, Jan. 3, 1949; came to U.S., 1949; s. Abraham and Syma (Skop) F.;children: Alexandra, Stefanie. BSc in Acctg., Bklyn. Coll., 1971; JD, Bklyn. Law Sch., 1974; LLM in Taxation, NYU, 1980. Bar: N.Y. 1975, U.S. Dist. Ct. (so. and ea. dists.) N.Y. 1978, U.S. Tax Ct. 1981, Fla. 1981, N.J. 1988. Tax acct. Oppenheim, Appel and Dixon, N.Y.C., 1974-75, assoc., 1975; atty./advisor Bur. Hearing and Appeals, Dept. HEW, Johnstown, Pa., 1976-77; atty. Tax Dept. N.Y. State, N.Y.C., 1977-82; assoc. tax counsel CBS Inc., N.Y.C., 1982-84; sr. tax assoc. Am. Brands, Inc., N.Y.C., Friedman & Shaftan, P.C., 1986-89, Hugh Janow & Irwin Meyer, Pearl River, NY, 1990-96; pvt. practice Montclair, NJ, 1989-90, 96-97; v.p. taxation The Halpern Group, Springfield, NJ, 1998-99; of counsel Keenan Powers & Andrews, Hauppauge, NY, 2000—; adminstrv. law judge N.Y.C. Dept. Fin., 2001—. Mem.: ABA, Fla. Bar Assn. Avocations: computers, photography, music. E-mail: redbat@yahoo.com.

FREUND, WILLIAM CURT, economist, educator; b. Nuremberg, Ger., Sept. 4, 1926; came to U.S., 1937, naturalized, 1942; s. Hugo and Paula (Gruenstein) F.; m. Judith Irmgard Steinberger, Aug. 14, 1951; children: Hugo, Nancy, Sandra. BBA, CCNY, 1949; MS, Columbia U., 1950, PhD, 1954. Economist Prudential Ins. Co. Am., 1950-59; assoc. prof. fin. N.Y. U. Grad. Sch. Bus. Adminstrn., 1959-62; exec. dir., chief economist Prudential Ins. Co. Am., 1963-67; sr. v.p., chief economist N.Y. Stock Exchange, 1968-85; prof. econs. Grad. Sch. Bus. Pace U., 1972—, N.Y. Stock Exchange prof. econs., dir. Ctr. Study Equity Mkts., 1992—. Mem. econ. policy coun. to Gov. of N.J., 1969-90. Author: Investment Fundamentals, 5th edit, 1981, (with E. Epstein) People and Productivity, 1984; also articles. Named Disting. Alumnus Coll. City N.Y., 1974 Mem. Am. Econ. Assn., Am. Finance Assn., Nat. Assn. Bus. Economists. Office: Pace U Pace Plaza One Pace Plz New York NY 10038

FREVERT, JAMES WILMOT, financial planner, investment advisor; b. Richland Twp., Iowa, Dec. 19, 1922; s. Wesley Clarence and Grace Lotta (Maw) F.; m. Jean Emily Sunderlin, Feb. 12, 1949; children: Douglas James, Thomas Jeffrey, Kimberly Ann. BS in Gen. Engring., MIT, 1948. Prodn. mgr. Air Reduction Chem. Co., Calvert City, Ky., 1955-61; plant mgr. Air Products & Chems., West Palm Beach, Fla., 1961-62; pres. Young World HWD, Ft. Lauderdale, Fla., 1962-66; v.p. Shareholders Mgmt. Co., L.A., 1966-73, Thomson McKinnon Secs., North Palm Beach, Fla., 1973-89, Raymond James & Assoc., West Palm Beach, Fla., 1989-91. Founder, past pres. MIT Club Palm Beach County, dir., 1976—; ednl. council mem. 1977-81. Served to 1st lt. USAF, 1943-46. Mem. Palm Beach Pundits, Circumnavigators Club. Republican. Presbyterian. Home: 883 Country Club Dr North Palm Beach FL 33408

FREY, A. JOHN, JR., lawyer; b. Little Falls, Minn., Dec. 2, 1944; s. Arnold John and Mae A. (Monk) F.; m. Cheryl Ann McCoy, June 11, 1966; children—Deborah Lynn, Robert Christopher, Laura Kathleen. B.A. in Polit. Sci., U. Iowa, 1967, J.D. with distinction, 1969. Bar: Iowa 1969, U.S. Dist. Ct. (no. and so. dists.) Iowa 1973. Spl. agt. FBI, Washington, 1969-73; assoc. Jurgemeyer & Eddy, Clinton, Iowa, 1973-74; ptnr. Jurgemeyer & Frey, Clinton, 1974-75, Jurgemeyer, Frey & Haufe, Clinton, 1975— ; speaker Bridge-the-Gap Seminar, Des Moines, 1977; mem. faculty Clinton Community Coll., 1979-80. Bd. dirs. Eagle Point Nature Soc., Clinton, 1974-75, Clinton County Legal Aid, Inc., 1978-80, Clinton Y's Mens Club, 1978, Arch, Inc., Clinton, 1984, past pres. Clinton YMCA, 1984, Gateway United Way, Clinton, 1981-84; pres. Seton Sch. Bd. Edn., Clinton, 1982-84; councilman City of Clinton, 1984—. Recipient letters of commendation FBI, 1970-73. Mem. Clinton County Bar Assn. (pres. 1977-78), Iowa State Bar Assn., Assn. Trial Lawyers Am., Clinton C. of C. (past pres.) Republican. Roman Catholic. Lodge: K.C. (adv. 1979—). Home: 3221 Mckinley St Clinton IA 52732-1436 Office: Jurgemeyer Frey & Haufe 601 S 3rd St Clinton IA 52732-4313

FREY, ADAM LEWIS, performing company executive; b. Atlanta, June 1, 1956; s. William H. Frey and Brena Feldman. BA cum laude, Harvard U., 1978; MBA, U. Calif., Berkeley, 1983. Sr. asst. buyer Joseph Magnin Co., San Francisco, 1979-81; mdse. mgr. Sherman, Clay & Co., San Bruno, Calif., 1983-86, v.p. merchandising, 1986-90; adminstr. San Francisco Contemporary Music Players, 1991-94, exec. dir., 1994—. Bd. govs. C.G. Jung Inst. San Francisco, 1992-97, 2003—. Mem. Assn. Fundraising Profls., Devel. Execs. Roundtable. Avocations: piano, collecting and studying american popular song, world literature. Office: San Francisco Contemporary Music Players 44 Page St Ste 604A San Francisco CA 94102-5972

FREY, ANDREW LEWIS, lawyer; b. N.Y.C., Aug. 11, 1938; s. Daniel B. and Ruth J. Frey; children: Matthew S., Alexandra S. BA with high honors, Swarthmore Coll., 1959; LLB, Columbia U., 1962. Bar: N.Y. 1962, D.C. 1966, U.S. Supreme Ct. 1972. Law clk. to judge U.S. Ct. Appeals (D.C. cir.), 1963-64; spl. counsel to Gov. U.S. V.I., 1963-65; assoc. Koteen & Burt, Washington, 1965-70; ptnr. Dutton, Gwirtzman, Zumas, Wise & Frey, Washington, 1970-72; dep. solicitor gen. Office U.S. Solicitor Gen., Washington, 1972-86; ptnr. Mayer Brown Rowe & Maw, Washington, N.Y.C., 1986—. Notes editor Columbia Law Rev., 1961-62. Recipient John Marshall award Dept. Justice, 1975, Disting. Svc. award Atty. Gen., 1980, Presdl. award for Meritorious Svc., 1985. Mem. Am. Law Inst., Am. Acad. Appellate Lawyers, Phi Beta Kappa. Office: Mayer Brown Rowe & Maw 1675 Broadway Fl 19 New York NY 10019-5820 E-mail: afrey@mayerbrownrowe.com.

FREY, BOB HENRY, psychotherapist, sociologist, educator, poet, canon lawyer; b. Porterdale, Ga., Mar. 7, 1953; s. George Loyd Sr. and Betty Montine (Canup) F.; m. Deborah Ann Dunn Mar. 8, 1980. BA, Immanuel Coll., Peachtree City, Ga., 1976; MA, Immanuel Sem., Peachtree, 1977, DRE, 1980; EdD in Counseling and Adminstrn., Immanuel Sem., Atlanta, 1988; PhD in Sociology, Columbia Pacific U., 1985; MA in Counseling, Luther Rice Sem., 1992; PhD in Christian Counseling, Am. Bible Coll. and Seminary, 1998; postgrad., South Fla. Bible Coll. & Sem., 1996—; D Canon Jurisprudence, Romano-Byzantine Coll., Duluth, Minn., 1997; LLD (hon.), Christian Bible Coll., 1996; PhD in Psychology, All Am. U., 2003. Cert. med. psychotherapist, Am. Bd. Med. Psychotherapists and Psychodiagnosticians, bd. cert. disability analyst Am. Bd. Disability Analysts; cert. sociologist, cert. profl. sociol. practitioner, Am. Acad. Profl. Sociol. Practitioners and Nat. Assn. Forensic Counselors; lic. Mercian practitioner, Romano-Byzantine Synod Commn. on Religious Counseling and Healing. Dean Calvary Bapt. Bible Coll., Jonesboro, Ga., 1977-78; chief of police City of Hagan, Ga., 1986-87; caseworker prin. Toombs County Dept. Family and Children Svcs., Lyons, Ga., 1987; adj. faculty mentor Columbia Pacific U., San Rafael, Calif., 1987-89; adj. prof. Newport U., Newport Beach, Calif., 1989—; coord., mgr. Tidelands Community Mental Health, Mental Retardation and Substance Abuse Ctr., Savannah, Ga., 1990-91; psychotherapist, clin. dir. social and clin. svcs. Mel Blount Youth Home Ga., Vidalia, Ga., 1992—95; psychotherapist, clin. supr. Clayton Ctr. for Mental Health, Substance Abuse and Devel. Svcs., Riverdale, Ga., 1994—97, psychotherapist, auditor, monitor, 1997—2001; pres., CEO Christian-Frey Assn. Connection Elite Svcs., 2000—. Mentor adj. faculty Christian U. Kuaui, Hawaii, 1993-97; adj. faculty St. Martin's Coll. and Sem., Milw., 1995-2000; poet, Nat. Libr. Poetry, Owings Mills, Md.; canon lawyer, 1997-99. Author: A Biblical Perspective-The Writing of Divorcement, 1993, A Biblical Study Guide, 1993, The Frey Initiative on Accreditation-Discriminatory Practices Regional vs National, 1994, (pamphlets) The Bible, The Christian, Non-Christian and Nudism, 1982, The Frey Manifesto On Accreditation Issues, 1995, Christians Out-Of-Step With God, 1985; contbg. poet: Life, Not Fair, The Flight, The Old House Analogy, The Old Car Analogy. Lobbyist MADD, Atlanta, 1983; rsch. bd. advisors nat. divsn. Am. Biographical Inst., Raleigh, N.C., 1994—; vol. police/city chaplain, capt. City of Riverdale, Ga. Sgt. U.S. Army, 1970-77; hosp. adminstr. Ga. Dept. Def., Ga. State Def. Force, Air Med. Detachment, Savannah, Ga., 2003—. Scholar, Columbia Pacific U., 1982. Fellow Am. Bd. Disability Analysts; mem. Internat. Soc. Poets (disting.), Am. Coll. of Profl. Mental Health Practitioners (diplomate), Nat. Assn. of Forensic Counselors, Am. Acad. of Profl. Sociological Practitioners. Democrat. Avocations: hunting, fishing, swimming, boating, camping. Home: 324 Green Oak Rd Lyons GA 30436 E-mail: annbob@stealthport.com., dafann@stealthport.com., dafbob@stealthport.com.

FREY, BRUCE E. radiation oncologist; b. N.Y.C., Jan. 29, 1945; m. Laura S. Hansen, Aug. 21, 1979; children: Peter, Julia. BS, Cornell U., 1967; PhD, Oreg. State U., 1977; MD, Oreg. Health Sci. U., 1988. Diplomate Am. Bd. Radiation Oncology. Attending physician Good Samaritan Hosp., Corvallis, Oreg., 1992—. Avocations: kayaking, sailing, skiing, bicycling. Office: Good Samaritan Hosp 3600 NW Samaritan Dr Corvallis OR 97330-3700

FREY, DALE FRANKLIN, financial investment company executive, manufacturing company executive; b. Lancaster, Pa., Aug. 14, 1932; s. Franklin W. and Mary A. (Strickler) F.; m. Betty Ann Heistand, Aug. 22, 1953; children—Scott, Philip, Kyle, Susan BS in Econs., Franklin and Marshall Coll., 1954; MBA, NYU, 1957. With GE, Fairfield, Conn., 1957-97, mgr. group fin. ops., 1975-77, internat. and Can. group staff exec., internat. sector, 1977-80, v.p., treas., 1980-84, 86-93; chmn. bd., pres. GE Investment Corp., Stamford, Conn., 1984-97. Bd. dirs. Praxair Inc., Danbury, Damon Runyon-Walter Winchell Cancer Rsch. Fund, Roadway Express, Akron, After Market Tech., Chgo., Cmty. Health Sys., Go Co-op, Maitland, Fla., Yankee Candle, South Deerfield, Mass., McLeod USA, Cedar Rapids, Iowa; mem. adv. bd. NYU Stern Sch. Trustee Franklin and Marshall Coll. Capt. USAF, 1955-57. Mem.: Bent Creek Golf Club (Lititz, Pa.), Bald Peak Golf Club (Melvin Village, N.H.), Medalist Golf Club (Hobe Sound, Fla.), Old Marsh Golf Club (Palm Beach Gardens, Fla.), Aspetuck Valley Country Club (Weston, Conn.). Office: care Michael Allen Co One Gorham Island Westport CT 06880

FREY, DONALD NELSON, industrial engineer, educator, retired manufacturing executive; b. St. Louis, Mar. 13, 1923; s. Margaret Bryden (Nelson) Frey; m. Bonnie A. Gore, May 28, 1989 (dec. Sept. 2002); children: Donald Nelson, Judith Kingsley(dec.), Margaret Bente, Catherine, Christopher, Elizabeth; m. Helen-Kay Eberley, Feb. 14, 2003. Student, Mich. State Coll., 1940—42; BS, U. Mich., 1947, MS, 1949, PhD, 1950, DSc (hon.), 1965; DSc, U. Mo., Rolla, 1966. Instr. metall. engring. U. Mich., 1949—50, asst. prof. chem. and metall. engring., 1950—51; rsch. engr. Babcock & Wilcox Tube Co., Beaver Falls, Pa., 1951; various rsch. positions Ford Motor Co. (Ford div.), 1951—57, various engring. positions, 1958—61, product planning mgr., 1961—62, asst. gen. mgr., 1962—65, gen. mgr., 1965—68, co. v.p. for product devel., 1965—67; pres. Gen. Cable Corp., N.Y.C., 1968—71, Bell & Howell Co., Chgo., 1973—81, chmn., CEO, 1971—88, also bd. dirs.; prof. of indsl. engring. and mgmt. sci. Northwestern U., Evanston, Ill., 1988—. Mem. exec. bd. World Bank, Washington; bd. dirs. Cin. Milacron, Clark Equipment Co., Packer Engring., My Own Meals, Hyatt Corp., Springs Industries, Quintar, 20th Century Fox Corp.; co-chair Japan study multinats. NRC, 1992—94; surveyor World Book, Poland, 1990. Co-chmn. Gov.'s Commn. of Sci. and Industry, Ill., 1988—; exec. bd. mem. World Bank, 2003. With U.S. Army, 1942—46. Named Young Engr. of Yr., Engring. Soc. Detroit, 1953, Outstanding Alumni, U. Mich. Coll. Engring., 1957, Outstanding Young Man of the Yr., Detroit Jr. Bd. of Commerce, 1958, Man of the Yr., Weizmann Inst., 1988; recipient Nat. medal for tech., 1990; Inaugural fellow, INFORMS, 2002. Fellow: INFORMS, AAAS; mem.: ASME, Coun. on Fgn. Rels., Detroit Engring. Soc. (pres., bd. dirs. 1962—65), Soc. Automotive Engrs. (vice chmn. Detroit 1958, Russell Springer award 1956), Nat. Acad. Engring. (mem. coun. 1972), Am. Soc. Metals, Am. Inst. Mining and Metall. Engrs. (chmn. Detroit chpt. 1954, chmn., editor Nat. Symposium on Sheet Steels 1956), Econ. Club, Saddle and Cycle Club, Chgo. Club, Hundred Club Cook County, Chgo. Commonwealth Club, Phi Delta Theta, Tau Beta Pi, Phi Kappa Phi, Sigma Xi. Achievements include established Margaret and Muir Frey Prize for innovation in engring., Northwestern Univ., 2002. Home: 2758 Sheridan Rd Evanston IL 60201-1728 Office: Northwestern U 2145 Sheridan Rd Rm M237 Evanston IL 60208-0834

FREY, DONALD RAY, medical educator, administrator; b. Leavenworth, Kans., Jan. 7, 1952; s. Raymond Donald and Emma Margaret (Beach) F.; m. Leticia Darlene Schneider, June 6, 1975; children: Zachary, Dustin. BA, William Jewell Coll., 1974; MD, U. Mo., 1978. Am. Bd. Family Practice with cert. added qualification in Geriat. Physician Savannah (Mo.) Med. Ctr., 1981-84; family practice residency dir. United Hosp. Ctr., Clarksburg, W.Va., 1984-89; residency devel. dir. Clarkson Hosp., Omaha, 1989-90; v.p. med. affairs United Hosp. Ctr., 1990-93; family practice residency dir. Creighton U. Sch. Medicine, Omaha, 1993-95, family practice dept. chmn., 1995—. Mem. Nebr. Rural Health Commn., 1998—. Maternal Mortality Rev. Panel W. Va. Dept. of Health, Charleston, 1989, med. adv. comm., Child Health, 1991-93; mem. rural health adv. commn. Nebr. Dept. Health, 1998—. Named Ronald L. Kleeberger Endowed Chair Creighton Univ, Omaha, 1996—; recipient Creighton U. Disting. Continuing Edn. award, 1997. Fellow Am. Acad. Family Physicians; mem. Am. Bd. Family Practice, Nebr. Med. Assn., Soc. Tchrs. Family Medicine. Office: Creighton Univ Dept Family Practice 601 N 30th St Ste 6720 Omaha NE 68131-2137 Fax: 402-280-5165. E-mail: dfrey@creighton.edu.

FREY, DOUG R. electrical engineering educator, consultant; b. Rahway, N.J., May 4, 1952; s. William Francis Frey and Marjorie Ann Morgan; m. Patricia Ann Frey, May 11, 1985; 1 child, Rebecca Leigh. BSEE, Lehigh U., 1973, MSEE, 1974, PhDEE, 1977. Profl. engr. Pa. Prof. Lehigh U., Bethlehem, Pa., 1977—; design engr. Silicon Labs., Austin, Tex., 2000—. Cons. Solid State Chargers, Cockeysville, Md., 1985-90, Analog Devices, Santa Clara, Calif., 1990-2000; expert witness Lucent Technologies, 1997-98; design engr. Micrometronics, Clifton, N.J., 1993-84. Contbr. over 75 articles to profl. publs.; patentee in field. Mem. Zoning Hearing Bd., Hanover Twp., Bethlehem, 1996—. Rsch. grantee NSF, 1997—. Mem. IEEE (sr.), Audio Engring. Soc. Avocations: music, basketball. Office: Lehigh U EECS Dept 19 Memorial Dr W Bethlehem PA 18015-3006 E-mail: drf3@lehigh.edu.

FREY, FREDERICK AUGUST, geochemistry researcher, educator; b. Milw., Apr. 1, 1938; s. Frederick August and Evelyn Dorothy (Lange) F.; m. Julie Ann Golden; 1 child, Oren. BSCE, U. Wis., 1960, PhD in Chemistry, 1967. Prof. dept. earth, atmospheric and planetary scis. MIT, Cambridge, 1966—, Francqui Found. prof., 1996-97. Assoc. editor: Geochimica et Cosmochimica Acta; contbr. over 185 articles to profl. jours. Fellow Geochem. Soc., European Assn. Geochemist, Am. Geophys. Union (pres. VGP sect. 2000-2002, VGP Bowen award 1986); mem. Geol. Soc. Am., European Union Geoscis. Office: MIT Dept Earth Atmos & Plan Sci 54 # 1226 Cambridge MA 02139

FREY, GERRARD RUPERT (GARY FREY), management executive, consultant; b. Medicine Hat, Alta., Can., June 7, 1943; s. Walter and Margaret (Materi) F.; m. Karen Martha Johnson, Aug. 27, 1968; children: Samantha Elizabeth, Jonathan Edward. B of Comm. with Distinction, U. Calgary, Alta., 1970; MBA, Harvard U., 1972. Sr. exec. Prin. Group, Edmonton, Alta., 1972-73; dir., v.p. Collective Securities Ltd., Edmonton, 1972-73; program mgr. Banff (Alta.) Ctr. for Mgmt., 1974-75; mgr. fin. svcs. The Banff Ctr., 1976-81, v.p. fin. and adminstrn., 1981-87; v.p. Banff Ctr. for Mgmt., 1981-83; acting pres. The Banff Ctr., 1991-93, exec. v.p., 1987-99; prin. Presidents Network Inc., 1999—. Chmn., pres., Exdev Cons. Ltd., Banff, 1974—; chmn. Sunshine Village Corp., Banff, 1983-89. Councillor Can. West Found., Calgary, 1983-95; founding dir., chmn. Banff/Lake Louise Tourism Bur., 1990-91; chmn. Assn. for Mountain Parks Protection and Enjoyment, 1994-96; elected trustee Banff Sch. Dist., 1990-92. Capt. Royal Can. Armoured Militia Corps, 1967-70. Recipient Commemorative medal 125th Anniversary of Can. Confedn., 1992. Mem. Banff-Lake Louise C. of C. (pres. 1988-90), Banff Springs Golf Club (pres. 1995-98), Harvard Bus. Sch. Club of Calgary, Riverside Golf and Country Club, Skal Club of the Can. Rockies. Avocations: golf, music, books. Home: Box 698 118 Mountain Ave Banff AB Canada TIL IA7 Office: Presidents Network Inc 1311 Howe St Ste 200 Vancouver BC Canada V6Z 2P3

FREY, GLENN, songwriter, vocalist, guitarist; b. Detroit, Nov. 6, 1948; Performed with Bo Diddly and Linda Ronstadt, founding mem. mus. group Longbranch Penny Whistle, Eagles, songs include Take it Easy, (with Eagles albums) Desperado, 1973, On the Border, 1974, One of These Nights, 1975, Hotel California (Grammy award for album of yr., 1977), The Long Run, Hell Freezes Over, solo artist (albums) No Fun Aloud, 1982, The Allnighter, 1984, Soul Searchin', 1988, Strange Weather, 1992, Glen Frey Live, 1993, Solo Collection, 1995; composer (theme song): (TV series) Miami Vice, Body by Jake, 1988; TV appearance Wiseguy, 1988; actor: (TV series) South of Sunset, 1993; (films) Jerry Maguire, 1996. Co-recipient Grammy award for Lyin' Eyes 1975, for New Kid in Town 1977; named (with Eagles) to Rock and Roll Hall of Fame, 1998. Home: 5020 Brent Knoll Ln Suwanee GA 30024-1376

FREY, HARLEY HARRISON, JR., anesthesiologist; b. Toledo, Feb. 22, 1920; s. Harley Harrison and Mina Rosina (Wiedemann) F.; m. Jane Luceia Murray, Aug. 28, 1944 (dec. 1964); children: Richard E., Martha J., Thomas C.; m. Emma Jean Hamilton, Apr. 15, 1966; 1 stepchild, Rick A. Gregory. BS, U. Toledo, 1942; MD, U. Cin., 1945. Diplomate Am. Bd. Anesthesiology. Intern Akron City Hosp., Ohio, 1946—47; fellow anesthesia U. Minn., Mpls., 1950; hon. mem. staff St. Elizabeth Hosp. Med. Ctr., Lafayette, Ind., 1950—, Lafayette Home Hosp., 1950—. Bd. dirs. Lafayette Symphony Orch., 1952-54; counselor, committeeman Lafayette coun. Boy Scouts Am., 1955-63; ruling elder Presbyn. Ch., 1964-67, active deacon, 1991-94; bd. dirs. Lafayette Citizens Band, 1997-2000. Capt. U.S. Army, 1947—49. Fellow Am. Coll. Anesthesiology; mem. Am. Soc. Anesthesiology (bd. dirs. 1965-74), Ind. Soc.

Anesthesiology (pres., bd. dirs. 1961-74, Disting Svc. award 1992), Ind. State Med. Soc. (Cert. Distinction 1995), Tippecanoe County Med. soc. (pres. 1961), Rotary (bd. dirs. 1992-95) Lafayette Country Club (bd. dirs. 1963-65). Avocations: music, painting. Home and Office: 3513 Creek Ridge Lafayette IN 47905-5619 *Personal philosophy: My philosophy of life is simple, whatever talent or wisdom I may have has been given to me by God as a gift. In any task I undertake, this gift should be used to the best of my ability, be fair, build goodwill, better friendships, exhibit truth and benefit all concerned.*

FREY, JAMES MCKNIGHT, government official; b. Mattoon, Ill., Dec. 7, 1932; s. Raymond Matthew and Virginia Laurel (McKnight) F.; m. Jean Meyer, June 18, 1954 (div. 1977); children— Katherine Marie Frey Glenn, Nancy Elizabeth Frey Longo; m. Nancy E. Hitt, Apr. 28, 1978. AB, Harvard U., 1954, MBA, 1956. With Bur. of Budget, 1954-62, 65-70, mgmt. analyst internat. programs, 1960-62, dir. internat. programs div., 1970-75; asst. to spl. asst. to Pres. U.S.; also staff mem. Nat. Security Council, 1962-64; spl. asst. for policy coordination to asst. sec. state inter-Am. affairs, also policy planning officer Bur. Inter-Am. Affairs, State Dept., 1964-65, chief internat. programs div., 1970-75; asst. dir. for legis. reference U.S. Office Mgmt. and Budget, Washington, 1975-88. Mem. Pres.'s Task Force Govt. Reorgn., 1964; ret., 1988; participant Internat. Symposium on Pub. Adminstrn. Reform in China, Beijing, 1989. Mem. Harvard Club (Washington), Cosmos Club, Scottish Terrier Club of Greater Washington. Home: 8106 Inverness Ridge Rd Potomac MD 20854-4013 E-mail: bucrat@aol.com.

FREY, JAMES SEVERIN, educational association executive; b. Milw., Mar. 1, 1938; s. Severin Anthony and Marian Clarice (Blattner) F.; m. Margo Walther, June 29, 1963; children: Michelle Marie Frey Loberg, David James Frey. BA, Marquette U., 1960, MA, 1967; EdD, Ind. U., 1976. Asst. to dir. admissions Marquette U., Milw., 1961-66; dir. fgn. student svcs. U. Wis., Milw., 1966-71; cons. U.S. Ednl. Commn. in Japan, Tokyo, 1971-72; asst. dir. of admissions Ind. U., Bloomington, 1972-76; exec. dir. World Edn. Svcs., Inc., Milw., 1977-80; pres. Ednl. Credential Evaluators, Inc., Milw., 1980—. Cons. New Zealand Qualifications Authority, Wellington, 1990, 92, So. Africa Devel. Coordinating Coun., Mbabane, Swaziland, 1983; acad. specialist U.S. Info. Agy., Iraq, 1987; field svc. cons. NAFSA, Washington, 1968-74. Author: The Educational System of Turkey, 1972, 92, Iraq, 1988; co-author, editor: The Admission and Placement of Students from Canada, 1989; co-author: Israel, 1976. Grantee Internat. Fdn. Rsch. Found., 1975. Mem. NAFSA (Homer Higbee award 1991), European Assn. for Internat. Edn. Avocations: travel, reading history, racquetball, card playing, gardening. E-mial. Office: Ednl Credential Evaluators Inc PO Box 514070 Milwaukee WI 53203-3470 E-mail: jimfrey@ece.org.

FREY, JEFFERY PAUL, internist, geriatrician; b. Ossining, N.Y., Mar. 23, 1948; s. John Joseph and Barbara (Gerlach) F.; m. Linnea Raye Hollis; children: Jeffery W., Charles, Benjamin B. BA, Cornell U., 1970; MD, SUNY, Syracuse, 1974. Diplomate Am. Bd. Internal Medicine, Am. Bd. Geriatrics with added qualifications. Intern Syracuse Med. Ctr., 1974-75, asst. med. resident, 1975-76, resident, 1976-77; clin. assoc. prof. Tulane U. Sch. Medicine, New Orleans, 1979-91; clin. asst. prof. La. State U. Med. Ctr., New Orleans, 1981-91; clin. asst. prof. medicine U. Mo., Columbia, 1991—; staff physician Ochsner Clin., New Orleans, 1981-91; pvt. practice Columbia, 1991—. Staff Columbia Regional Hosp., 1991 , Boone Hosp. Ctr., Columbia, 1991—. Contbr. articles to profl. jours.; presenter in field. Lt. commdr. USPHS, 1977-81. Fellow ACP; mem. So. Med. Assn., Mo. State Med. Soc., Boone County Med. Soc. Episcopalian. Avocations: sailing, skiing, vegetable gardening. Office: 201 W Broadway Columbia MO 65203-3842 E-mail: freydoc@aol.com.

FREY, JOANNE ALICE TUPPER, art educator; b. Wakefield, Mass., Jan. 16, 1931; d. Arthur Andrew Tupper, Elva June Goddard, Joanne Alice Tupper; m. John Oscar Frey, June 14, 1953 (dec. Oct. 2000); children: David J., Donald A., Dale R., Alexandria Brennan. Grad. honors, Vesper George Sch. Art, Boston, 1951; student art history, NTL Art Gallery, London, 1979. Tchr. art Wishing Well Cards, Everett, Mass., 1951—54, Sarrin Studio, Wakefield, Mass., 1960—96; tchr. art oil, acrylic, and watercolor Wakefield H.S., Wakefield, 1997—. Antique and current doll authority; lectr. in field. Asst. resident dir. Boit Home for Women, Wakefield, Mass., 1996—; bd. dirs. The Hartshorne House. Mem.: Collie Rescue League of N.E., The Kosmos Club (decorator 1997—). Republican. Congregationalist. Avocations: painting, reading, walking, gardening, art history. Home: 701 Haverhill St Reading MA 01867

FREY, JOHN WARD, landscape architect; s. Philip Rockel and Sarah Helen (Dempwolf) F.; m. Wilma Emma Weggel, Feb. 11, 1961; children: Holly Frances, Allison Margaret, Frederika Elizabeth, Marietta Isabel. BA in Math., Coll. of Wooster, 1952; MLA, Harvard U., 1955. Urban designer The Architects Collaborative, 1955; assoc., designer Sasaki (Walker) Assocs., Inc., 1957-62; ptnr. Mason and Frey, Landscape Architects, 1963—. Registered landscape architect N.Y., Conn., Mass. Prin. works include Arlington (Mass.) Bicentennial Park, 1975, S.W. Corridor Park, Sect. III, Jamaica Plain, Boston, 1988, State U. Agricultural and Tech. Coll., Farmingdale, N.Y., 1963-71, State U. Coll., Geneseo, N.Y., 1963-73, Fulton Montgomery C.C., Johnstown, N.Y., 1967-70, Burlington (Mass.) High Sch., 1968-74, Wellesley Coll. Sci. Ctr., 1973, Lexington Ctr. Mall, 1967, Murray Hill, Manchester, 1973, Polaroid Corp., Waltham, Mass., 1970, Sandoz Pharm., East Hanover, N.J., 1964, 73, others incl. indsl., comml. office bldgs., land devel. and pvt. res. Adv. com. to planning bd. Lexington Design, 1973-76; mem. Revere Beach Design Rev. Bd., 1976-78, Lexington Tree Com., 1990—, Lexington Minuteman Commuter Bikeway Com., 1993-95, Mass. Recreational Trails Adv. Com., 1993—; chmn. Design Adv. Com., Lexington, 1988—. Recipient Boston Soc. of Architects award 1973, "A" Citation, Mass. Audubon Soc., 1968, Indsl. Plant Beautification award Govs. Conf. on Natural Beauty, 1967, NEA Presdl. Design award Fed. Design Achievement award, 1988. Fellow Am. Soc. of Landscape Architects (Merit award 1973, trustee Boston chpt. 1980-83); mem. BSLA (treas. 1966-67, program com. 1966-67, com. landscape architectural registration in Mass. 1966-67, pub. svc. com. 1963-71, examining bd. 1971-75, others) Charles River Watershed Assn., Appalachian Mountain Club, Appalachian Trail Conf., The Nature Conservancy, Mass. Audubon Soc., Rails to Trails Conservancy. Avocations: gardening, bicycling, hiking, canoeing, jogging. Home: 1133 Massachusetts Ave Lexington MA 02420-3818 Office: Mason & Frey Landscape Architects 1133 Massachusetts Ave Lexington MA 02420-3818 E-mail: jwfrey2@aol.com.

FREY, JULIA BLOCH, French language educator, art historian educator; b. Louisville, July 25, 1943; d. Oscar Edgeworth and Jean Goldthwaite (Russell) Bloch; m. Roger G. Frey, Dec. 27, 1968 (div. Mar. 1976); m. Ronald Sukenick, Mar. 9, 1992. BA, Antioch Coll., 1966; MA, U. Tex., 1968; MPhil, Yale U., 1970, PhD, 1977. Instr. Brown U., Providence, 1972-73; chargé de cours U. Paris, 1974-75; lectr. Yale U., New Haven, 1975-76; prof. Inst. Internat. Comparative Law, U. San Diego, Paris, 1979-89, adminstrv. dir., 1989; prof. French, art history U. Colo., Boulder, 1976—2001, prof. emeritus, 2002—, dir. undergrad. studies, 1985-95, assoc. chmn. for grad. studies, 1996-97, 98-99, chmn., 1999. Guest prof. Sarah Lawrence Coll., Bronxville, N.Y., 1983; curator Toulouse-Lautrec Met. Mus. Art Denver Art Mus., 1999. Author: Toulouse-Lautrec, a life, 1994, Toulouse-Lautrec l'homme qui aimait les femmes, 1996; editor: Gustave Flaubert's La Lutte du Sacerdoce et de L'Empire (1837), 1981; contbr. articles and monographs to profl. publs., chpts. to books; translator: René. Recipient Conn. Grad. Study award, 1970-73; grantee NDEA, 1967, Brown U. Research and Travel, 1973, Boulder Arts Com., 1979, 80, Ctr. for Applied Humanities, 1985, S.W. Inst. for Research on Women, 1985-86, NEH, 1986; fellow NDEA, 1966-68, Yale U., 1968-72, Gilbert Chinard, Inst. Français de Washington, 1977, Big 12 2000, Humanities Rsch. Ctr., Australian Nat. U., 2000; Pen Ctr. USA West Lit. award for non-fiction, 1995; Finalist Nat. Book Critics Cir. award for Biography, 1994. Mem. MLA, PEN U.S.A., Coll. Art Assn., Yale Club. Unitarian Universalist. Home: 200 Rector Place Apt 26B New York NY 10280 E-mail: julia.frey@aya.yale.edu.

FREY, KATIE MANCIET, education educator; b. Tucson, Ariz., Dec. 31, 1952; d. Hector Encinas and Lilian Eloisa (Hanna) Manciet; m. Richard Patrick Frey, Jul. 20, 1974; 1 child, Stacy Ann. BS, U. Ariz., 1974, MEd, 1982, PhD, 1987. Tchr. physical edn. Amphitheater Pub. Schs., Tucson, 1974-81, rsch. specialist, 1982-85, dir. rsch. & devel., 1985-88, asst. supt., 1988-89, assoc. supt., 1989—2001; tng. coord. LINKS U. Ariz., 2002—03. Gymnastics coach Amphitheater Pub. Schs., Tucson, 1974-81, rsch chair Ad Hoc Adv. Coun. on Sch. Dropouts, Ariz., 1987, mem. Gov. Edn. Conf., Ariz., 1989, mem. State Supr. Task Force on Sch. Violence, Ariz., 1993-94, Mayor's Sch. Dist. Action Task Force, Tucson. 1993—; mem. NCAA recertification equity subcom. U. Ariz., 1997-98. Mem. APEX, Tucson, 1987-99, Traveler's Aid Soc. of Tucson, 1993-98, Citizen's Adv. Coun. U. Ariz., 1994-96; mem. tech. adv. bd. Town of Oro Valley, 1995-96; mem. exec. steering com. K-16 Edn. Coun. So. Ariz., 1995-96; bd. dirs. YWCA, 1999—; chair Tucson Resiliency Initiative, 1999—. Recipient APEX Apple award U. Ariz., 1994, Women on the Move award, 2000. Mem.: AAUW, NOW, U. Ariz. Hispanic Alumni Assn., U. Ariz. Letterwinners Assn. Avocations: reading, travel, family, Tai Chi, landscaping. E-mail: tucsonkatie@aol.com.

FREY, LOUIS, JR., lawyer, federal and state government official; b. Jan. 11, 1934; m. Marcia Turner, 1956; children: Julie, Lynne, Louis III, Lauren, Christine. BA cum laude, Colgate U., 1955; JD, U. Mich., 1961; LLD (hon.), Jowez U. Bar: Fla. 1961, U.S. Supreme Ct. 1969. Asst. county solictor Orange County, Fla., 1961-63; gen. counsel Fla. State Turnpike Authority, 1966-67; congressman U.S. Ho. of Reps., 1969-79, Rep. leader, 1973-76, mem. interstate and fgn. commerce com., sci. and tech. com., select com. on narcotics, sub-com. on communications, sub-com. on energy research; ptnr. Lowndes, Drosdick, Doster, Kantor & Reed, P.A., Orlando, Fla., 1987—; commr. Dept. of Lottery State of Fla., 1987-88; founder Lou Frey Inst. Politics and Govt., U. Ctrl. Fla., 2002—. Del. or alternate del. to most Rep. Conv., 1968—; Rep. State Chmn. Pres. Ford, 1976—; nat. co-chmn former mem. for Regan, 1980; nat. fin. com. Bush, 1988—92; state fin com. President Bush, 2000; counsellor to sec. H.U.D., 2001. Author, editor: Inside The House Former Members Reveal How the House Works, 2001. Chmn. Fla. Fedn. of Young Reps., 1965-66; treas. Rep. Party Fla., mem. state exec. com., 1966; past chmn., mem. exec. com. Fla. Coun. on Econ. Edn., 1991—; chmn. Former Mems. Congress, 1992-94, bd. dirs., 1992—; founder The Lou Frey Inst. on Polit. and Govt. Attys. Univ. Ctrl. Fla., 2001—; candidate Fla. Gov., US Senate. Served with USN, 1955-58, capt. Res. ret. Recipient Watchdog of Yr. Treasury award, 1970, 72, 74, 76, 78, Guardian of Small Bus. award, Disting. Service award Ams. for Constitutional Action, Man of Yr. award Fla. Assn. Broadcasters, 1977, Masada award, Hope for Congress, Life Mag., 1975; elected to Sr. Citizen's Hall of Fame; named As one of 200 Rising Leaders in the U.S., Time Mags., 1974. Mem. Order of the Coif, Phi Gamma Delta, Phi Delta Phi. Lutheran. Home: 139 Genius Dr Winter Park FL 32789-5103 Office: Lowndes Drosdick Doster Kantor & Reed PA 215 N Eola Dr # 2809 Orlando FL 32801-2095 E-mail: Lou.Frey@Lowndes-law.com.

FREY, LUCILLE PAULINE, social studies educator, consultant; b. Huggins, Mo., Aug. 1, 1932; d. Albert Raymond and Gladys Pearl (Maxville) F. BS in Edn., Southwest Mo. State U., 1955; MA in English, Mo. U., 1963; MAT, Ala. Pacific U., 1975; PhD in Women's Studies, Union Grad. Inst., 1985. Tchr. Tex. County Rural Schs., Plato, Mo., 1949-53, Sullivan (Mo.) Pub. Schs., 1953-57, Anchorage Pub. Schs., 1957-70, social studies coord., 1970-75; ednl. cons. The Learning Tree, Alaska, 1975-85. Adj. prof. U. Alaska, 1970-77; owner Women's Bookstore, Anchorage, 1981-84; comml. fisherwoman Net Prophets, Bristol Bay, Alaska, 1980-85; real estate salesperson Dynamic Properties, Anchorage, 1989-94, Century 21 Peterson, Hermitage, Mo. 1995— Author: (textbook) Eyes Toward Icebergia, 1963; editor: Women of Alaska Workbook, 1974, Alaska Studies Curriculum, 1975, Athabaskan Curriculum, 1980. Founding mem. Alaska Women's Edn. Caucus, Anchorage, 1970; mem. Alaska Women's Polit. Caucus, Anchorage, 1972; organizer various state edn. confs., 1976-83, women's conf., Alaska, 1982. Recipient Gov's. Vol. award, Alaska, 1984; named to Women's Hall of Fame, Alaska, 1991. Mem. NEA (Women's Right award 1979, Renowned Alaskan award, 1986), Profl. Women's Assn. (sec.), Mo. Realtor's Assn., Union Grad. Inst. (mem. doctoral com.), Ozark Bd. Realtors, Lake Area Friendship Club. Democrat. Avocations: gardener, bird-watcher, historian, political activist. Home: RR 1 Box 1965 Urbana MO 65767-9639

FREY, MARGO WALTHER, career counselor, columnist; b. Watertown, Wis., July 1, 1941; d. Lester John and Anabel Marie (Bergin) Walther; m. James Severin Frey, June 29, 1963; children: Michelle Marie Frey Loberg, David James. BA in French, Cardinal Stritch Coll., 1963; MS in Ednl. Psychology, U. Wis., Milw., 1971; EdD in Adult Edn., Nova U., 1985. Nat. bd. cert. career counselor; approved profl. counselor, Wis. Acad. counselor biology dept. Ind. U., Bloomington, 1975-76; dir. career planning and placement Cardinal Stritch Coll., Milw., 1977-89; pres. Career Devel. Svcs., Inc., Milw., 1989—. Weekly columnist Milw. Journ. Sentinel, 1994-95, 98—. Mem. Bloomington (Ind.) women's commn. com. on employment assessment Displaced Homemakers Task Force, 1975. Named to Practitioner's Hall of Fame, Nova U., 1985. Mem. ASTD (bd. dirs. 1992), Wis. Career Planning and Placement Assn. (bd. dirs. 1987), Wis. Assn. Adult and Continuing Edn. (bd. dirs. 1983-85), Milw. Coun. Adult Learning, Human Resource Mgmt. Assn., Tempo (bd. dirs. 1995-97). Avocations: reading, swimming. E-mail: margocds@execpc.com.

FREY, MARTIN ALAN, lawyer, educator; b. Rochester, NY, Feb. 26, 1939; s. Morrey and Betty (Weinstein) F.; m. Phyllis Sue Hurley, Apr. 19, 1966; 1 child, David Andrew. BS in Mech. Engring., Northwestern U., 1962; JD, Washington U., St. Louis, 1965; LLM, George Washington U., 1966. Bar: Mo. 1965, Okla. 1976, U.S. Dist. Ct. (no. dist.) Okla. 1983. Asst. prof. law Drake U., Des Moines, 1966-67; prof. law Tex. Tech. U., Lubbock, 1967-76, U. Tulsa, 1976—2001, assoc. dean, 1981-84, prof. emeritus, 2001—. Vis. prof. law U. Maine, Portland, 1974—75, Washington U., St. Louis, 1986—87, U. Ala., Tuscaloosa, 2003; adj. settlement judge US Dist Ct and US Bankruptcy Ct. (no. dist.) Okla., 1988—; reporter adv. group Civil Justice Reform Act, U.S. Dist. Ct. (no. dist) Okla., 1991—97; dir. Ctr. Dispute Resolution U. Tulsa Coll. Law, 1994—2000. Author: Alternative Methods of Dispute Resolution, 2003; author: (with T. Bitting) An Introduction to Contracts and Restitution, 1988; author: (with T. Bitting and P.H. Frey) 2d edit., 1993, study guide, 1994; author: (with McConnico and P.H. Frey) An Introduction to Bankruptcy Law, 1990; co-author: West's Bankruptcy Practice Systems, 1991, 3d edit., 1997; author (with Bitting and Frey): An Introduction to the Law of Contracts, 3d edit., 1999; author: (with P.H. Frey) Essentials of Contract Law, 2000; founder, advisor: Tex. Tech. Law Rev., 1967—71; contbr. articles to profl. jours.; author (with B. Bucholtz and M. Tatum): The Little Black Book: A Do-It Yourself Guide For Law Student Competitions, 2001. Mem.: ABA (accreditation site evaluation teams 1978—2000), Am. Inns of Ct. (master emeritus W. Lee Johnson chpt.). Democrat. Jewish. Office: U Tulsa Coll Law 3120 E 4th Pl Tulsa OK 74104-2418 E-mail: martin_a_frey@yahoo.com., martin-frey@utulsa.edu.

FREY, MARY ELIZABETH, artist; b. Yonkers, N.Y., Nov. 25, 1948; d. Harold and Matilda F.; m. William M. Bennett, Jan. 31, 1976; children: Jacob F. and Nicholas F. BA in Fine Arts, Coll. New Rochelle, 1970; postgrad., Pratt Inst., 1970-71; MFA in Photography, Yale U., 1979. Instr. photography Project Art Ctr., Cambridge, Mass., 1975-77, dir. photography, 1976-77; prof. photography Hartford Art Sch., West Hartford, Conn., 1989—. NEA, Washington, 1994; vis. artist Harvard U., Cambridge, 1984, Cooper Union, N.Y.C., 1985, Yale U., New Haven, 1986, NYU, N.Y.C., 1987, Cornell U., Ithaca, N.Y., 1988, Northfield Mt. Hermon, Northfield, Mass., 1989, Mills Coll., Oakland, Calif., 1989, Hampshire Coll., 1992; Harnish vis. artist Smith Coll., Northampton, Mass., 1994-95; guest lectr. Hudson River Mus., Yonkers, N.Y., 1984, Hartford Art Sch., 1988, Smith Coll. Mus. Art, Northampton, 1994. One-woman shows include Panopticon Gallery, Boston, 1974, Hollins College (Va.) Art Gallery, 1977, Project Art Ctr., Cambridge, Mass., 1979, Hudson River Mus., Yonkers, N.Y., 1984, Blue Sky Gallery, Portland, 1985, ZONE Art Ctr., Springfield, Mass., 1988, Ledel Gallery, N.Y.C., 1989, Arno Maris Gallery, Westfield, Mass., 1991, Springfield (Mass.) Mus. of Fine Arts, 1993, Ariz. State U., 1994, Laelia Mitchell Gallery, Boston, 1995, Marlboro (Vt.) Coll., 1998; group shows include Commonwealth Armory, Boston, 1974, Project Art Ctr., Cambridge, 1975, Boston City Hall, 1976, Yale U., New Haven, 1977, Webb & Parsons Gallery, New Bedford, Mass., 1978, Pleasant St. Gallery, Amherst, Mass., 1979, Hampshire Coll., Amherst, 1980, Light Gallery, N.Y.C., 1981, Memphis Acad. Art, 1982, Carpenter Ctr. for Visual Arts, Cambridge, 1984, Blue Sky Gallery, Portland, 1985, Mus. Modern Art, N.Y.C., 1986, Aperture Gallery, N.Y.C., 1986, 87, Real Art Ways, Hartford, Conn., 1988, MS Gallery, Hartford, 1990, Smith Coll. Mus. Art, Northampton, 1992, 100 Pearl St. Gallery, Hartford, 1993, Artspace, New Haven, 1994, ICP-Midtown Eye of the Beholder, 1997, Coll. of N.J., 2002, Smithsonian Instn., 2001, others; represented in permanent collections at Art Inst. Chgo., Mus. Fine Arts, Houston, Smith Coll. Mus. Art, Northampton, Internat. Polaroid Collection, Cambridge, Mus. Modern Art, N.Y.C., Coca-Cola Corp., Atlanta, Bank of Boston, Springfield Tech. C.C., Avon Corp., others. Home: 70 Firglade Ave Springfield MA 01108-2531

FREY, PERRY A. biochemistry educator; b. Plain City, Ohio, Nov. 14, 1935; s. John Edward and Inez (Kramer) F.; m. Carolyn M. Scott, Feb. 11, 1961; children: Suzanne, Cynthia. BS in Chemistry, Ohio State U., 1959; PhD in Biochemistry, Brandeis U., 1968. Teaching asst. Ohio State U., Columbus, 1959-60; chemist USPHS, Cin., 1960-64; asst. prof. chemistry Ohio State U., 1969-74, assoc. prof. chemistry, 1974-79, acad. vice chair chemistry, 1977-80, prof. chemistry, 1979-81; prof. biochemistry U. Wis., Madison, 1981—. Wellcome vis. prof. Emory U., Atlanta, 1995—96; cons. in field. Co-author: (with Abeles and Jencks) Biochemistry, 1992; contbr. articles to profl. jours.; assoc. editor: Biochemistry, 1992—; mem. editl. bd. Bioorganic Chemistry, 1986—, Jour. Biol. Chemistry, 1983-88. With U.S. Army, 1954-56. Alexander von Humboldt fellow, 1995; recipient Repligen award, Am. Chemical Soc., 2000. Fellow AAAS; mem. Biochem. Soc., Am. Chem. Soc., Am. So. Biochem. & Molecular Biology, The Protein Soc., Nat. Acad. Scis. (life). Avocations: travel, reading, hiking. Home: 209 Eddy St Madison WI 53705-4423 Office: U Wis Dept Biochemistry 1710 University Ave Madison WI 53726 E-mail: frey@biochem.wisc.edu.

FREY, RUTH LAZETTA, historian, educator; b. Balt., Jan. 20, 1945; d. Robert Ketterman and Bertha Lazetta (Eberhart) Frey. BA, Goucher Coll., 1966; MA, Columbia U., 1968. Cert. tchr. Md. Dept. Edn. Tchr. social studies Overlea HS, Balt., 1968—83, Pikesville (Md.) HS, 1983—2003; libr. Milford Mill Acad., 2003—. Student advisor Am. Field Svc., Overlea, Md., 1970—75, chpt. officer, 1970—75. Student advisor Nat. History Day, Md., 1988—2003, regional and nat. judge, 1988—; U.S. del. World Coun. Chs. Assembly, Uppsala, Sweden, 1968; active Salem Luth. Ch., Catonsville, Md., 1965—; pres. Luth. Student Assn. Am., 1965—66. Mem.: Nat. Coun. History Edn., Orgn. Am. Historians, Am. Hist. Assn., Md. Combined Tng. Assn. (sec. 1976—77, v.p. 1977—, newsletter 1977—, Horse of the Yr. award 1983, Vol. of Yr. award 1985), Kappa Delta Pi, Phi Beta Kappa. Avocation: equestrian sports. Office: Milford Mill Acad 3800 Washington Ave Baltimore MD 21244 E-mail: rfrey@bcps.org.

FREY, STUART MACKLIN, automobile manufacturing company executive; b. Peoria, Ill., Feb. 13, 1925; s. Muir Luken and Margaret Bryden (Nelson) F.; m. Lillian Maxine Paxton, 1951; children: Mellissa June, Muir Paxton. BS in Mech. Engring, U. Mich., 1949; SM in Indsl. Mgmt, MIT, 1961. With Budd Co., 1949-53; with Ford Motor Co., 1953—, chief car research engr., 1974-75, chief vehicle engr., 1975-80, v.p. car engring., 1980-83, v.p. car product devel., 1983-87, v.p. engring. and mfg. staff, 1987-88, v.p. tech. affairs, 1988-90; with TRW, 1990—; v.p. auto tech. affairs, 1990-94. Contbr. articles to profl. jours. Served as officer AUS, 1943-46, 51-52. Sloan fellow, 1960-61 Fellow Soc. Automotive Engrs., Engring. Soc. Detroit; mem. Am. Soc. Body Engrs., Tau Beta Pi, Pi Tau Sigma. Home: 3790 Darlington Rd N Bloomfield Hills MI 48301-2000 *The key ingredient that has contributed most importantly to my success has been the understanding and employment of the principles of employee involvement and participative management.*

FREY, WILLIAM H. demographer, educator; b. Allentown, Pa., June 21, 1947; s. Elwood H. and Loretta C. Frey. BS, Ursinus Coll., 1969; PhD, Brown U., 1974 Sociology lectr. Rutgers U., New Brunswick, N.J., 1973-74; rsch. assoc. Ctr. for Studies in Demography and Ecology U. Wash., Seattle, 1974-75; project dir., assoc. Ctr. for Demography and Ecology U. Wis., Madison, 1975-81; rsch. scientist Population Studies Ctr. U. Mich., Ann Arbor, 1981-98, 2000—; prof. sociology SUNY, Albany, 1998-2001; sr. fellow Milken Inst., Santa Monica, Calif., 1998—. Vis. rsch. scholar Internat. Inst. Applied Sys. Analysis, Laxenburg, Austria, 1980-81; vis. fellow The Brooking Inst., Washington, D.C., 2003—; Andrew W. Mellon vis. scholar Popular Ref. Bur., Washington, 1988-89; cons. U.S. Census Bur., Population Divsn., Washington, 2000-; dir. ednl. devel. Pub. Data Queries, Inc., Ann Arbor, Mich., 1998-; pres. Frey-First Demographic Networks Inc., Ann Arbor, 1999-. Author: America by the Numbers: A Fieldguide to the U.S. Population, 2001, Regional and Population Growth and Decline in the U.S., 1988; contbr. articles to profl. jours. including Am. Sociol. Rev., Population and Devel. Rev., among others. Grantee Population Ref. Bus., 1998—, Nat. Inst. Aging, 1994-2000, Nat. Inst. child Health and Human Devel. Ctr. for Population Rsch., 1982-87, 1994-2000, NSF, 1996-2001, Russell Sage Found., 1992-93, Child Trends, Inc., 1995, others; vis. fellow Brookings Inst., 2003—. Fellow Urban Land Inst.; mem. Am. Sociol. Assn. (chair com. on nat. statistics 1997-99), Population Assn. Am. (com. on population statistics 1995-2001), Internat. Union for the Sci. Study Population. Avocations: cycling, hiking, website creation. Office: The Univ Michigan 426 Thompson St Ann Arbor MI 48104-2321 Fax: (888) 257-7244. E-mail: bill.frey@usa.net.

FREY, JR. SHERWOOD CHARLES, education educator, consultant; b. Wash., DC, Nov. 7, 1942; s. Sherwood Charles and Mazy Goss Frey; m. Marietta Kirkup, Oct. 11, 1969; children: Christopher Eldon Frey, Matthew Joseph Frey. MS in Engring. Sci., U. of Calif., Berkeley, 1964—65, AB in Math., 1960—64; PhD, The Johns Hopkins U., 1965—69. Faculty Internat. Teachers Program, Versailles, France, 1963—86; cons. Kappa Systems, Rosslyn, Va., 1968—70; assoc. prof. of bus. adminstrn. Harvard Bus. Sch., 1970—79; ethyl corp. prof. of bus. adminstrn. U. of Va. - Darden GSBS, 1979—; vis. prof. Ivey Bus. Sch., London, Canada, 1998—99. Consulting Sherwood C. Frey, Jr. & Associates, Charlottesville, Va., 1979—; treas. and mem. of the bd. Mgmt. Edn. Alliance, Boston, 1995—. Author: (textbook) Quantitative Bus. Analysis - Text and Cases, Quantitative Bus. Analysis Casebook, Quantitative Methods in Mgmt., (jour. articles) Mgmt. Sci., Ops. Rsch. Avocations: hiking, scuba diving, cooking, woodworking. Office: U of Virginia - Darden GSBA Box 6550 Charlottesville VA 22906-6550 E-mail: scf@virginia.edu.

FREYD, PETER JOHN, mathematician, computer scientist, educator; b. Evanston, Ill., Feb. 5, 1936; s. Paul Robert and Pauline Margaret (Pattinson) F.; m. Pamela Parker, Jan. 1, 1957; children: Jennifer Joy, Gwendolyn Ann. AB magna cum laude, Brown U., 1958; MA (Woodrow Wilson fellow), Princeton U., 1959, PhD, 1960. J.F. Ritt instr. math. Columbia U., N.Y.C., 1960-62; faculty U. Pa., Phila., 1962—, prof. math., 1968—, chmn. grad. group math., 1982-87, prof. computer info. sci., 1987—; dir. Lab. for Logic and Computation, 1993—. Adviser Pahlavi U., Shiraz, Iran, 1968; lectr. Canadian Nat. Rsch. Seminar, 1974; vis. rschr. Swiss Fed. Inst. Tech., Zurich, 1969; vis. researcher U. Mex., 1975, U. Sydney, 1985, U. Milan, 1986, U. Parma, 1990; vis. prof. U. Chgo., 1980, U. Louvain, Belgium, 1981; vis. prof. in computer sci. Carnegie Mellon U., 1988-89. Author: Abelian Categories, 1964; (with Andre Scedrov) Categories, Allegories, 1990; founder Jour. Pure and Applied Algebra, 1970; editor Theoretical Computer Sci., 1988—, Math. Structures in Computer Sci., 1989—, Internat. Jour. Algebra and Computation, 1990—, Jour. Knot Theory and its Ramifications, 1991—. Fulbright scholar Australia, 1971; fellow St. John's Coll., Cambridge U., Eng., 1980-81 Mem. Isaac Newton Inst. 1995, Phi Beta Kappa, Sigma Xi. Home: 2020 1/2 Addison St Philadelphia PA 19146-1307 Office: U Pa Dept Maths 33 E Walnut Ln Philadelphia PA 19144-2002

FREYD, WILLIAM PATTINSON, fund raising executive, consultant; b. Chgo., Apr. 1, 1933; s. Paul Robert Freyd and Pauline Margaret (Pattinson) Gardiner; m. Diane Marie Carlson, May 19, 1984. BS in Fgn. Svc., Georgetown U., 1960. Field rep. Georgetown U., Washington, 1965-67; campaign dir. Tamblyn and Brown, N.Y.C., 1967-70; dir. devel. St. George's Ch., N.Y.C., 1971; assoc. Browning Assocs., Newark, 1972-73; regional v.p. C.W. Shaver Co., N.Y.C., 1973-74; founder IDC, Henderson, Nev., 1974—. Bd. dirs. Nev. Symphony Orch., 1994-99, N.J. Symphony Orch., 1991-94; apptd. Nev. Charitable Solicitation Task Force, 1994, pres.'s circle adv. coun. U.S. Naval Acad., 2003. Mem. Assn. Fundraising Profls. (nat. treas. 1980-81, pres. N.Y. chpt. 1974-76, cert. 1982), Am. Assn. Fund Raising Counsel (sec. 1984-86, designated Sage 2000), World Fund Raising Coun. (bd. dirs. 1995-99, treas. 1998-99), Georgetown U. (regional club coun.), N.Y. Yacht Club, Union League Club N.Y., Masons, Nassau Club, Circumnavigators Club. Achievements include invention of phone mail program. Office: IDC IDC Ctr 2500 Paseo Verde Pky Henderson NV 89074 E-mail: wfreyd@aol.com., wfreyd@goidc.com.

FREYER, TONY ALLAN, historian, educator; b. Indpls., Dec. 28, 1947; s. Robert Albert Freyer and Ida Marie Hadley; m. Marjorie Faller, Aug. 12, 1976; 1 child, Allan. AB hist., San Diego State Univ., San Diego, Calif., 1970; MA hist., Ind. Univ., Bloomington, Ind., 1972, PhD hist., 1975. Lectr. in law Ind. Univ. Sch. of Law, Bloomington, Ind., 1974—75; asst. to assoc. prof. hist. Univ. Ark., Little Rock, 1976—81; asst. to full prof. hist. & law Univ. Ala., Tuscaloosa, Ala., 1981—90, Univ. rsch. prof. hist. & law, 1990—. Vis. prof. econ. hist London Sch. of Econ., London, 1986; vis. prof. constl. hist. Univ. Calif., L.A., 1987; bus. hist. rev. editl. bd. Harvard Bus. Sch., Boston, 1985—. Author: Producers Versus Capitalists Rights: Constitutional Conflict in Antebellum America, 1994, Regulating Big Business: Antitrust in Great Britian and America, 1880 to 1990, 1992, Hugo L. Black and the Dilemma of American Liberalism, 1990, The Little Rock Crisis, 1984, Harmony & Dissonance: The Swift & Erie Cases in American Federalism, 1981, Forums of Order: The Federal Courts and Business in American History, 1979; co-author (with Timothy Dixon): Democracy and Judicial Independence: Federal Courts in Alabama, 1820-1994, 1995; editor: Defending Constitutional Rights: Frank M. Johnson, 2001; contbr. chapters to books, articles to encyclopedias, to profl. jour.; rev. (70 books to profl. jour.). PFC USMC Res., 1970—72. Recipient Burnam Disting. Faculty award, Univ. Ala., 1991, Martin Luther King. Jr. Lectr., Vanderbilt Univ., 1991, Abe Fellow-Japan, Ctr. for Global Partnership, 1995—96; grantee Nat. Endowment for the Humanities, Summer Stipends, 1978, 1985, Rsch. Grants Com., Univ. Ala., 1983, 1985, Jud. Conf. of the U.S., Com. on the Bicentennial of the Constn. Summer Rsch. Grant, 1991, Ark. Endowment for the Humanities Rsch. Grants, 1978, 1980, 1981; Earhart Found. Fellowships, 1982, 1985, 1994—95, 2002—03, postdoctral fellow, Project '87, 1980, Hagley Mus. and Libr. Fellowship, 1979—80, Newcomer Fellowship, Harvard Bus. Sch., 1975—76, Charles Warren Fellowship, Harvard U., 1981—82, Fulbright Sr. Scholar award, U.K., 1986, Australia, 1993, Fulbright Disting. Chair Am. Studies, Warsaw Univ., Poland, 2000. Mem.: Ogrn. of Am. Hist., Am. Soc. for Legal Hist., Am. Hist. Assn. Independent. Christian Sci. Avocations: travel, reading, execrise. Office: Univ Ala Sch Law Box 870382 Tuscaloosa AL 35487 Home Fax: 205-348-3917. E-mail: tfreyer@law.ua.edu.

FREYER, VICTORIA C. fashion and interior design executive; b. Asbury Park, N.J.; d. Spiros Steven and Hope (Pappas) Pappaylion; m. Cyril Steven Arvanitis, Dec. 26, 1950 (div. 1975); children: Samuel James, Hope Alexandra. BA, Georgian Court Coll., 1950; student, N.Y. Sch. Interior Design, 1971-72. Mgr. Homestead Restaurant, Ocean Grove, N.J., 1946-58; art supr. Lakewood (N.J.) Pub. Schs., 1950-51; interior designer London, 1975-76, F. Korasic Assocs., Oakhurst, N.J., 1977-78; owner, operator Virginia Interiors, McLean, Va., 1974-90; interior designer Anita Perlut Interiors, McLean, 1986; owner, operator Victoria Freyer Interiors, McLean, 1986—; fashion cons. Nordstrom Splty. Store, McLean, 1988-92, fashion seminar coord. Tysons Corner, Va., 1992—. Lectr. Girl Scouts U.S., Rep. Women of Capitol Hill, Washington Hosp. Ctr., Women's Am. ORT, Nat. Assn. Cath. Women, Bethesda Naval Hosp., NIH, others. Pres. Monmouth County Med. Aux., 1964; originator 1st lecture series Monmouth Coll., Long Branch, N.J., 1965; guest moderator Alexandria (Va.) Hosp. Series, 1988; mem. Women's Symphony Com., Washington, 1988—; guest speaker Girl Scouts U.S. Coun. Nation's Capitol, 1988-90, Nuclear Energy Coun., 1989, pers. dept. CIA, 1989-90, Internat. Women's Group Washington, 1989-90. Recipient Recognition awards Girl Scout Coun. Nation's Capitol, 1991, No. Region Beta Pi, 1991, Beta Sigma Pi, 1991. Mem. AAUW (program chmn. 1968, guest speaker many orgns.). Greek Orthodox. Avocations: greek and roman archeology and antiquities, painting, gourmet cooking, traveling. Home and Office: 7630 Provincial Dr Mc Lean VA 22102-7652

FREYERMUTH, CLIFFORD L. structural engineering consultant; BS in Civil Engring., State U. Iowa, 1956, MS in Structural Engring., 1958. Registered structural engr., Ariz. Consulting engr. structural design Ned L. Ashton, 1955-57; grad. teaching asst. structural mechanics State U. Iowa, 1957-58; with bridge divsn. Ariz. State Hwy. Dept., 1958-64; with Portland Cement Assn., Chgo., Skokie, Ill., 1964-71; dir. post-tensioning divsn. Prestressed Concrete Inst., 1971-76; mgr. Post-Tensioning Inst., 1976-88; pres. Clifford L. Freyermuth, Inc., 1988—. Mem. cable-stayed bridges com. Post-Tensioning Inst, editor various publs.; prin. investigator Nat. Coop. Hwy Rsch. Project, Washington, 1988. Contbr. articles to profl. jours. Recipient Martin P. Korn award Prestressed Concrete Inst., 1969, George C. Zollman award Precast/Prestressed Concrete Inst., 1999. Fellow Am. Concrete Inst. (prestressed concrete com., standard bldg. code com., bd. dirs. 1991—, Henry C. Turner medal 1992); mem. ASCE (prestressed concrete com.), Internat. Assn. Bridge and Structural Engrs., Structural Engrs. Assn. Ariz., Chi Epsilon. Office: Clifford L Freyermuth Inc 9201 N 25th Ave Ste 150B Phoenix AZ 85021-2721 E-mail: asbi@earthlink.net.

FREYRE, FABIO, publishing executive; Assoc. pub., advtsg. sales dir. Sports Illustrated Time Inc., New York, 1996-99, pub. Sports Illustrated mag., 1999—. Office: Time Inc Sport Illustrated Bldg 135 West 50th St 3rd Fl New York NY 10020-1393*

FREYTAG, DONALD ASHE, management consultant; b. Chgo., Apr. 17, 1937; s. Elmer Walter and Mary Louise (Mayo) F.; m. Elizabeth Ritchie Robertson, Dec. 19, 1964; children: Donald C., Gavin K., Alexander M. BA, Yale U., 1959; MBA, Harvard U., 1963. Pres. Mgmts. West, LaJolla, Calif., 1963-65; mktg. asst. Norton Simon, Inc., Fullerton, Calif., 1965-67; product mgr. Warner-Lambert, Inc., Morristown, N.J., 1967-70; group mgr. mktg.-planning dir. advt. Pepsi-Cola Co., Purchase, N.Y., 1970-72; from v.p. mktg. to exec. v.p. Beverage Mgmt., Inc., Columbus, Ohio, 1972-76, pres., 1976-79, vice-chmn., 1979-80; pres. Freytag Mgmt. Co., Columbus, 1980-82, 84—, G.D. Ritzy's, Inc., Columbus, 1982-84. Bd. dirs. Antolino & Assoc., Atlas-Butler, Barney Corp., Century Resources, Contract Sweepers, Contrack Corp., Inc., Columbus Showcase Co., Columbus Paper and Copy Supply Co., Eastway Supplies, Inc., Greencrest Mktg., Ohio Full Ct. Press, Inc., Reitter Stucco, Inc., Profitworks Ltd., Paul Werth & Assoc., Coughlin Automotive Group, Newark, Hugo Bosca Co., Springfield, Ohio, Fenton Art Glass Co., Inc., Williamstown, W.Va., Scioto Properties, LLC, Columbus; ctrl. region dir. Ohio Com. for Employer Support of the Guard and Res., 1992—95. Pres. Cen. Ohio Ctr. for Econ. Edn., 1978-80, 81-87; bd. dirs. Columbus Acad., 1982-84. Capt. U.S. Army, 1959-61. Recipient Roman F. Warmke award, Ohio Coun. on Econ. Edn., 1991. Mem. Nat. Assn. Corp. Dirs., HBS Club Columbus, Yale Club. Avocations: bicycling, scuba diving, golf, reading. Office: 7955 Riverside Dr Dublin OH 43016-8234

FREYTAG, RICHARD ARTHUR, banker; b. Chgo., Oct. 26, 1933; s. Elmer Walter and Mary Louise (Mayo) F.; m. Pamela Burge, Feb. 11, 1989; children: Richard Christopher Hughes Freytag, Bliss Louise Mayo Smith. AB, Trinity Coll., Hartford, Conn., 1955; MBA, Harvard U., 1961; MS, MIT, 1971. Map salesman Rand McNally & Co., Chgo., 1955-56; internat. salesman Diversey Corp., Chgo., 1959-60; with Citibank, Japan, Taiwan, Korea, 1962-70, v.p., sr. credit officer, 1971-73, sr. officer Hong Kong, China, Vietnam, 1973—76, investor rels. and problem loan recovery mgmt., 1977-84; pres. Citicorp Holdings, Inc., Citibank Overseas Investment Corp., 1984-96, vice chmn., dir., 1996-98; pres., CEO Citicorp Banking Corp., New Castle, Del., 1984-96, vice-chmn., dir., 1996-98; pres. Citibank Del., 1989-96, vice-chmn., dir., 1996-98. Vice-chmn. Far East Bank, Ltd., Hong Kong, 1973-76, sr. ptnr. Washington Capital Ptnrs., 1999-2002; bd. dirs. Citicorp Capital Investors Europe Ltd., The Thomas Group, Inc., Irving, Tex.; mem. Expanded Sr. Panel on N.E. Asian Ltd. Nuclear Arms Agreement, 1992—. Trustee Med. Ctr. of Del.; bd. visitors Nat. Def. U., 1988-93, 2002—; chmn. Nat. Def. U. Found., 1993-99, chmn. emeritus, 1999—; mem. Gov.'s Coun. on Banking, 1994-97. 1st lt. USAF, 1956-59, maj. gen. USAFR, 1959-93, fighter pilot operational in F-100 "supersaber". Decorated Air Force DSM, 1993, Medal for Disting. Pub. Svc. Dept. Def., 2000; recipient Brooks prize MIT, 1971; Alfred Sloan fellow The Nat. City Found., N.Y.C., 1969. Mem. Nat. Air Force Salute Found. (pres. 1988-90, chmn. 1990-92), Air Force Assn. (Iron Gate chpt. pres. 1988-90, chmn. 1990-92, Ira Eaker fellow 1991, Medal of Merit 1990, Exceptional Svc. award 1989), Coun. on Fgn. Rels., Falcon Found. (trustee), Del. Bankers Assn. (dir., pres. 1992-97), Del. Bus. Roundtable (vice chmn. 1994-96). Episcopalian. Office: PO Box 921 Montchanin DE 19710-0921

FREYTAG, SHARON NELSON, lawyer; b. May 11, 1943; d. John Seldon and Ruth Marie (Herbel) Nelson; children: Kurt David, Hillary Lee. BS with highest distinction, U. Kans., Lawrence, 1965; MA, U. Mich., 1966; JD cum laude, So. Meth. U., 1981. Bar: Tex. 1981, U.S. Dist. Ct. (no. dist.) Tex. 1981, U.S. Ct. Appeals (5th cir.) 1982, U.S. Supreme Ct. 1993, U.S. Dist. Ct. (so. dist.) Tex. 2001, U.S. Ct. Appeals (8th cir.) 2001, U.S. Ct. Appeals (fed. cir.) 2002. Tchr. English, Gaithersburg (Md.) H.S., 1966—70; instr. English, Eastfield Coll., 1974-78; law clk. U.S. Dist. Ct. (no. dist.) Tex., 1981-82, U.S. Ct. Appeals (5th cir.), 1982; ptnr., chmn. appellate practice sect. Haynes and Boone, Dallas, 1983—. Vis. prof. law So. Meth. U., 1985-86; faculty Appellate Adv. program NITA. Editor-in-chief Southwestern Law Jour., 1980-81; contbr. articles to profl. jours. Dir. Ctr. for Brain Health; dir. devel. bd. U. Tex. at Dallas. Woodrow Wilson fellow; recipient John Marshall Constl. Law award, Baird Cmty. Spirit award, 1995. Mem. ABA (litigation sect., co-chmn. subcom. on appellate rules), Fed. Bar Assn. (co-chmn. appellate practice and adv. sect. 1990-91), Tex. Bar Assn. (appellate coun. 1995-98), State Bar Tex. (bd. dirs., exec. com. 1997-2001), Dallas Bar Assn. (appellate coun.), Higginbotham Inn of Ct. (former barrister), Order of Coif, Phi Beta Kappa. Lutheran. Office: Haynes & Boone 3100 Bank of America Plz Dallas TX 75202 E-mail: freytags@haynesboone.com.

FREZZA, ERMENEGILDO ELDO, physician, surgeon; b. Venice, Italy, Apr. 17, 1964; came to U.S., 1992; s. Giovanni Benito and Rosa (Savino) F.; m. Patrizia Costa, June 24, 1995; children: Eduardo, Gian Marco. MD, U. Padova, Italy, 1989. Resident in surery U. Padova, 1989-94; rsch. fellow U. Pitts., 1992-94, liver fellow, 1999—, laparoscopic fellow, 2000—; surg. intern Howard U. Hosp., Washington, 1994-95, Morristown (N.J.) Meml. Hosp., 1995-97; surg. chief resident Staten Island (N.Y.) U. Hosp., 1997-99. Contbr. article Am. Coll. Surgeon (Best Essay award). With Italian Army, 1990-91. Recipient Best Rsch. award Italian Rsch. Inst., 1990. Mem. ACS (Best Essay award 1998). Avocations: journalism, basketball. Office: UDMC Presbyterian C800 200 Lothrop St Pittsburgh PA 15213-2546 E-mail: eldopatri@aol.com.

FRI, ROBERT WHEELER, retired museum director; b. Kansas City, Kans., Nov. 16, 1935; s. Homer O. and Cora Ruth (Wheeler) F.; m. Jean Landon, Jan. 16, 1965; children— Perry, Sean, Kirk. BA, Rice U., 1957; MBA, Harvard U., 1959. Assoc. McKinsey & Co., Washington, 1963-68, prin., 1968-71, 73-75; dep. adminstr. EPA, Washington, 1971-73, acting adminstr., 1973; dep. adminstr. ERDA, Washington, 1975-77, acting adminstr., 1977; head U.S. delegation to IAEA, 1977; pres. Energy Transition Corp., 1978-86, Resources for the Future, 1986-95, sr. fellow, 1995—; dir. Nat. Mus. Natural History, 1996-2001. Bd. dirs. Am. Electric Power Co., Sci. Svc., Inc., Electric Power Rsch. Inst.; mem. Nat. Petroleum Coun. Lt. USNR, 1959-62. Baker scholar. Mem. Phi Beta Kappa, Sigma Xi. Republican. Presbyterian.

FRIARS, EILEEN M. bank executive; b. Holden, Mass., June 3, 1950; d. Gordon Edward and Marjorie Ella Friars. BA, Simmons Coll., 1972; MBA, Harvard U., 1974. Mgmt. asst. U.S. Govt. Office Mgmt. and Budget, Washington, 1974-76; sr. v.p., dir. fin. svcs. practice The MAC Group, Chgo., 1976-90; sr. exec. v.p. C&S/Sovran, Virginia Beach, Va., 1990-92; pres. card svcs. Nations Bank, Charlotte, N.C., 1992-98; pres. consumer credit card svcs. Bank of Am., Charlotte, 1998-99. Mem. vis. com. Harvard Bus. Sch., 2000-. Editor: Financial Services Handbook; contbr. articles to profl. jours. Pres. Charlotte Repertory Theatre, 1997-98; bd. dirs., chair edn. Com. of 200, Chgo., 1997-; trustee, chair fin. com. Simmons U., Boston, 1997-. Named Outstanding Bus. Leader, Northwood U., Palm Beach, Fla., 1998. Mem. Harvard Bus. Sch. Club Charlotte, Charlotte C. of C. (edn. com.). Avocations: theatre, hiking, writing, yoga.

FRIAS, JAIME LUIS, pediatrician, educator; b. Concepcion, Chile, Mar. 20, 1933; came to U.S., 1970; s. Luis Humberto and Olga Ana (Fernandez) F.; m. Jacqueline May Steel, Apr. 8, 1961; children: Jaime Arturo, Juan Pablo, Patricio Andres, Maria Josefina. MD, U. Chile, 1959. Diplomate Am. Bd. Pediatrics, Am. Bd. Human Genetics. Intern Hospital Regional, Concepcion, 1958-59; resident in pediatrics Calvo Mackenna Hosp., Santiago, Chile, 1960-62; clin. genetics and dysmorphology fellow U. Wis., Madison, 1965-66, U. Wash., Seattle, 1966-67; asst. prof. pediatrics U. Concepcion, 1967-69, U. Fla. Coll. Medicine, Gainesville, 1970-74, assoc. prof., 1974-77, prof., 1977-86, chief divsn. genetics, 1977-86, chmn. med. sch. admissions com., 1983-86; prof., chmn. dept. pediatrics U. Nebr. Med. Ctr., 1986—91; prof. pediatrics U. South Fla. Coll. Medicine, Tampa, 1991—, chmn. dept. pediatrics, 1991-99, dir. Birth Defects Ctr., 1999—. Chmn. Com. for Protection of Human Subjects, 1975-78; chmn. Fla. Com. on Prevention Devel. Disabilities, 1979-82, chmn. infant hearing screening adv. coun., 1982-86; cons. Spanish Collaborative Project on Congenital Malformation, Madrid, 1983—. Contbr. chpts. to books, articles to profl. jours. Trustee All Children's Hosp., 1991-99, Ronald McDonald Charities Tampa Bay, 1999-2001; exec. com. Assn. Med. Sch. Pediat. Dept. Chmn., 1993-96; steering com. Nat. Folic Acid Coun., 1999-2003. Named Tchr. of Yr., U. Fla. Coll. Medicine, 1978-79, Lewis A. Barness Endowed Chair Pediatrics, 1994-99. Mem. ACP (affiliate; W.K. Kellogg fellow 1965-67), Am. Acad. Pediatrics (com. genetics 1995-2002), Am. Pediatric Soc., Am. Soc. Human Genetics, Assn. Clin. Scientists, Tampa Yacht and Country Club. Democrat. Roman Catholic. Office: U South Fla Dept Pediat 17 Davis Blvd Ste 200 Tampa FL 33606-3438 E-mail: jfrias@hsc.usf.edu.

FRIBERG, GEORGE JOSEPH, electronics company executive; m. Mary Seymour; children: Fane George, Felicia Lynn Friberg Clark. BSME, U. N.Mex., 1962, MBA, 1982, postgrad. Sales engr. Honeywell, L.A., 1962-64; liaison engr. ACF Industries, Albuquerque, 1964-66; quality assurance mgr. data sys. divsn. Gulton Industries Inc., Albuquerque, 1966-72, mgr. mfg. Femco divsn. Irwin (Pa.), High Point (N.C.), 1972-77, v.p. mfg. data sys. divsn. Albuquerque, 1977-86; pres., CEO Tetra Corp., Albuquerque, 1986-92, also bd. dirs.; pres., CEO Laguna Industries Inc., Albuquerque, 1992-96; dir. programs Tech. Ventures Corp., Albuquerque, 1996—. Adj. prof. U. N.Mex. Mgmt. Tech., 1998—, Dept. Mech. Engring., 2003—; bd. dirs. Noonday, Inc. Mem. editl. bd. N.Mex. Bus. Jour., 1995-97. Mem. N.Mex. R & D Gross Receipts Task Force, 1988-89; mem. Econ. Forum of Albuquerque; bd. dirs. Technet, 1983-97, pres., 1983-84, 88-89; bd. dirs. Lovelace Insts., 1988—, U. N.Mex. R.O. Anderson Bus. Sch. Found., 1988-92, N.Mex. Bus. Innovation Ctr., 1986-92, U. N.Mex. Found., 1999—, N.Mex. Golden Apple Found., 1998—, pres., 2003—; bd. dirs. N.Mex. Natural History Mus. Found., 1999— (sec. 2002-), N.Mex. First, 2001—, United Way, N.Mex., 2001-02; grad. Leadership N.Mex., 1998; mem. mech. engring. adv. coun. U. N.Mex., 1999—. Inducted Anderson Sch. of Bus. Hall of Fame, 1996, U. N.Mex. Athletic Hall of Honor, 2003; recipient Zia award U. N.Mex., 1998, Regents medal U. N.Mex., 1998, Lockheed Martin Nova award, 1998, Albuquerque High Harrington award, 2000; named to All-Time Football Team Albuquerque H.S., 2001. Mem. Albuquerque C. of C. (bd. dirs. 1985—, polit. action com. 1983-84, chair Buy N.Mex. chpt. 1986-87, vice chmn. econ. affairs planning coun. 1987—, chmn. bd. 1990-91), N.Mex. Alumni Lettermen's Club, U. N.Mex. Alumni Assn. (bd. dirs. 1995-2001, pres.-elect 1997, pres. 1997-98). Home: 13234 Sunset Canyon Dr NE Albuquerque NM 87111-4220

FRIBOURG, PAUL J. grain company executive; BA, Amherst Coll.; Advanced Mgmt. degree, Harvard U. 1994exec. v.p., group pres. commodity mktg. Continental Grain Co., N.Y.C., 1990; CEO Conti Group Cos (formerly Continental Grain Co), N.Y.C., 1994—97, 1997—. Office: Continental Grain Co 277 Park Ave Fl 49 New York NY 10172-0003*

FRIBOURGH, JAMES HENRY, university administrator; b. Sioux City, Iowa, June 10, 1926; s. Johan Gunder and Edith Katherine (James) F.; m. Cairdenia Minge, Jan. 29, 1955; children: Cynthia Kaye, Rebecca Jo, Abbie Lynn. Student, Morningside Coll., 1944-47; BA, MA, U. Iowa, 1949, PhD, 1957; LHD (hon.), DHL (hon.), Morningside Coll., 1989. Instr. Little Rock Jr. Coll., 1949-56; assoc. prof. biology Little Rock U., 1957-60, prof., chmn. div. life scis., 1960-69; vice chancellor U. Ark., Little Rock, 1969-72, interim chancellor, 1972-73, exec. vice chancellor for acad. affairs, 1973-82, interim chancellor, exec. vice chancellor for acad. affairs, 1982, provost, exec. vice chancellor, 1983—, disting. prof., 1984-94, disting. prof. emeritus, 1994—. Cons. in field; assoc. Marine Biol. Lab., Woods Hole, Mass. Contbr. articles to profl. jours. Mem. Ark. Gov.'s Com. on Sci. and Tech., 1969-71; bd. dirs., mem. nat. adv. bd. Nat. Back Found., 1979; vice chmn. NCCJ, 1981-82; div. rep. United Way of Pulaski County, 1980-82; bd. dirs. Ark. Dance Theatre, Little Rock, 1980-82; vestryman Good Shepherd Episcopal Ch.; del. Episcopal Diocese of Ark.; fellow Ark. Mus. Sci. and History, 1987. Fribourgh Hall named in his honor, U. Ark., Little Rock, 1994; NSF fellow History of Sci. Inst., 1959-60. Fellow AAAS, Coll. Preceptors (London), Am. Inst. Fishery Rsch. Biologists, Ark. Mus. Sci. and History; mem. Am. Fisheries Soc. (chmn. com. on internationalism cert. fisheries scientist), AAUP (pres. Ark. conf.), Electron Microscopy Soc. Am., Am. Soc. Swedish Engrs. (corr. mem.), Ark. Acad. Sci. (pres. 1966), Ark. Dean's Assn. (pres. 1982), Am. Assn. State Colls. and Univs., Am. Swedish Inst., Swedish Club (Chgo.), Rotary (Paul Harris fellow), Vasa Order Am. Lodge, Sigma Xi, Phi Kappa Phi. Clubs: Swedish, Vasa Order Am. Lodges: Rotary (Paul Harris fellow). Democrat. Office: U Ark 33rd and University Ave Little Rock AR 72204 E-mail: jhfribourgh@ualr.edu.

FRICANO, SCOTT D. counselor; b. Grosse Point, Mich., Feb. 1, 1974; s. James M. and Elaine M. Fricano. BA, U. Mich., 1999; MAE, The Citadel, 2004. Counselor SC Commn. Blind, Columbia, 2002—. Contbr. articles to sch. jour. Mem. SC Rep. Party. Republican. Avocations: nature, travel, politics. Home: 1025 Riverwoodsplace 105 Charleston SC 29412

FRICK, ARTHUR CHARLES, art educator; b. Milw., Oct. 15, 1923; s. Arthur Clement and Nola Ann (Mangum) F.; m. Fay Arrieh, June 11, 1948 (div. 1966); children: Arthur James Frederick, Sumaya; m. Aida Moukheibir, June 7, 1968; children: Nola Ann, Delia Anne. BS in Art, U. Wis., Milw., 1948; postgrad., Ox-Bow, Saugatuck, Mich., 1948-49; MS in Art, U. Wis., 1949; postgrad., Escuela de Pintura y Escultura, Mex., 1950-51, Art Student's League of N.Y., 1994-95. Instr. Berea (Ky.) Coll., 1949-50, Stephens Coll., Columbia, Mo., 1951-56; prof., chmn. dept. fine arts Am. U. Beirut, Lebanon, 1957-76; prof., chmn. dept. art Wartburg Coll., Waverly, Iowa, 1976-95; prof. emeritus, 1995—. Instr. U. Wis., Madison, 1949, Ox-Bow, Saugatuck, Mich., 1949-51, 54-56; vis. prof. Am. Coll., Lugano, Switzerland, U. Wis., Green Bay, 1967-68, U. Wis., Milw., 1972-73; curator Mooney Print Collection, Charles City, Iowa, 1996; cons., lectr. various countries, orgns. Exhbns. include Art Inst. Chgo., 1950, City Art Mus., St. Louis, 1955-57, Cleve. Mus. Art, Sursock Mus., Beirut, Palais de UNESCO, Lebanon, numerous others; co-author: Graphic Arts Processes, 1957; contbr. articles to profl. jours. Pres. League Milw. Artists, 1949-51. Rsch. grantee Am. U. Beirut, 1960-61, 63-64, 67-68, 70-72, 74-75, Rockefeller Found., 1963-64, 66-68, Harvard U., 1960-61, Wartburg Coll. 1980. Mem. VFW, Coll. Art Assn. Am., Mid-Am. Coll. Art Assn., Mid-West Art History Soc. Mid-West Fedn. Chaparral Poets, Iowa Watercolor Soc., Iowa Poetry Assn., Waterloo Art Assn., Am. Legion. Republican. Methodist. Avocations: travel, archeology, sailing, marksmanship, jogging. Home: 212 2nd Ave NW Waverly IA 50677-2502

FRICK, BENJAMIN CHARLES, lawyer; b. Overbrook, Pa., Feb. 23, 1960; s. Sidney Wanning and Marie Pauline Frick; m. Stephanie Ann Sears, June 1, 1991; children: Sarah Marie, Anna Elizabeth, Charles Andrew. BA, Cornell U., 1982; JD, U. Richmond, 1985; LLM in Taxation, Villanova U., 1994. Bar: Pa. 1985. Clk. to Hon. John B. Hannum US dist. ct., 1984; trust officer Provident Nat. Bank, Phila., 1985-89; sole practice Bryn Mawr, Pa., 1989—. Deacon, elder, Ardmore (Pa.) Presbyn. Ch. Mem.: S.R. (bd. dirs. Pa. Soc. 1987—, sec. 1991—95, treas. 1995—97, v.p. 1997—), ABA, Phila. Bar Assn., Pa. Bar Assn., Mil. Order Loyal Legion US (sec. 1993—95, v.p. 1995—97, comdr. 1997—99, judge adv.-in-chief 1997—2001, nat. v.p. 2001—), St. Andrew's Soc. Phila., Colonial Soc. Pa. (treas. 2000—03, v.p. 2003—), Soc. Mayflower Desc., Soc. Colonial Wars (bd. dirs. Pa. chpt. 1999—), The Phila. Club, Athenaeum Phila., Alpha Delta Phi, Phi Alpha Delta. Republican. Presbyterian. Office: Bldg 1 Ste 303 919 Conestoga Rd Bryn Mawr PA 19010-1352

FRICK, GENE ARMIN, university administrator; b. Huntingburg, Ind., Oct. 13, 1929; s. Armin John and Naomi S. (Kemp) F.; m. Barbara Sue Partenheimer, Feb. 12, 1955; children: David Alan, Barbara Jean. BS in Acctg., Butler U., 1951. Acct. Huntingburg Machine Works, 1947-51; auditor Army Audit Agy., Louisville, 1952-53; property acct. E.I. DuPont, Louisville, 1954; acting internal auditor Purdue U., West Lafayette, 1955-57, contract adminstr., 1957-76, dir. contracts, 1976-93, dir. emeritus, 1993—. Treas. Purdue Calumet Devel. Found., East Chicago, Ind., 1955-57; sec., treas. East Chicago Housing Corp., 1955-57; mem. com. on contracts Coun. Govt. Rels., Washington, 1975-82, com. on costing, 1982-84, bd. dirs., 1978-84; lectr. Nat. Grad. U., 1976-80. Cpl. U.S. Army, 1951-53. Named Outstanding Regional Dir., Toastmaster Internat., 1978, Ky. Col., 1989, Sagamore of the Wabash, State of Ind., 1993. Mem. Elks, Lafayette Country Club, John Purdue Club, Sigma Nu (pres. housing corp. 1977-87). Republican. Avocations: golf, spectator sports, reading. Home: 2166 Tecumseh Park Ln West Lafayette IN 47906-2182 Office: Purdue U Hovde Hall West Lafayette IN 47905

FRICK, IVAN EUGENE, college president emeritus, education consultant; b. New Providence, Pa., May 19, 1928; s. Charles George and Lillie Jane (Miller) F.; m. Ruth Hudson, July 16, 1950; children: David Alan, Daniel Eugene, Susan Marie. AB, Findlay (Ohio) Coll., 1949; B.D., Lancaster Theol. Sem., 1952; S.T.M., Oberlin Coll., 1955; PhD, Columbia U., 1959; L.H.D. (hon.), Findlay Coll., 1976. Mem. faculty Findlay Coll., 1953-71, asst. to pres., 1963-64, pres., 1964-71, Elmhurst (Ill.) Coll., 1971-94, pres. emeritus, 1994—; cons. Ivan E. Frick, Cons. in Higher Edn., Oak Brook, Ill., 1994—. Vice chmn. Fedn. Ind. Ill. Colls. and Univs., 1979-81, chmn., 1983-85; pres., chmn. exec. com. Associated. Colls. of Ill., 1991-93; chmn. West Suburban Regional Acad. Consortium, 1991-92. Mem. Am. Coun. on Edn. Commn. on Govtl. Rels., 1986-89; bd. dirs. United Cmty. Fund Findlay, 1965-71, Lizzadro Mus. Lapidary Art, Elmhurst, Elmhurst YMCA, 1971-84; mem. found. bd. Ray Graham Assn. for People With Disabilities, 1995; chmn. non-pub. adv. com. Ill. Bd. Higher Edn., 1990-94. Danforth Found. fellow, 1959, Paul Harris fellow, 1988; recipient Disting. Alumnus award Findlay Coll., 1964, Outstanding Young Man award U.S. Jr. C. of C., 1964 Mem. Econ. Club Chgo. E-mail: i.frick@comcast.net. *Mentors have played a significant role in my life; these mentors have been teachers, older friends, father figures and administrative colleagues. They have supported, challenged and stimulated me and sometimes they have presented an opposite view or role model against which I have reacted. In all, they have helped me immeasurably.*

FRICK, OSCAR LIONEL, physician, educator; b. N.Y.C., Mar. 12, 1923; s. Oscar and Elizabeth (Ringger) F.; m. Mary Hubbard, Sept. 2, 1954. AB, Cornell U., 1944, MD, 1946; M.Med. Sci., U. Pa., 1960; PhD, Stanford U., 1964. Diplomate: Am. Bd. Allergy and Immunology (chmn. 1967-72). Intern Babies Hosp., Columbia Coll. Physicians and Surgeons, N.Y.C., 1946-47; resident Children's Hosp., Buffalo, 1950-51; pvt. practice medicine specializing in pediatrics Huntington, N.Y., 1951-58; fellow in allergy and immunology Royal Victoria Hosp., Montreal, Que., Can., 1958-59; fellow in allergy U. Calif.-San Francisco, 1959-60, asst. prof. pediatrics, 1964-67, assoc. prof., 1967-72, prof., 1972—, dir. allergy tng. program, 1964—; fellow immunology Inst. d'Immunobiologie, Hosp. Broussais, Paris, France, 1960-62. Contbr. articles papers to profl. pubs. Served with M.C., USNR, 1947-49. Mem. Am. Assn. Immunologists, Am. Acad. Pediatrics (chmn. allergy sect. 1971-72, Bret Ratner award 1982), Am. Acad. Allergy (exec. com. 1972—, pres. 1977-78), Internat. Assn. Allergology and Clin. Immunology (exec. com. 1970-73, sec. gen. 1985—), Am. Pediatric Soc. Clubs: Masons. Home: 370 Parnassus Ave San Francisco CA 94117-3609

FRICK, ROBERT HATHAWAY, lawyer; b. Cleve., June 28, 1924; s. Claude Oates and Urshal May (Hathaway) F.; m. Lenore M. Maurin, Aug. 16, 1947 (dec. Sept. 1993); children: Elaine D. Frick, Barbara A. Frick Bundick, Catherine L. Frick Cayer. BBA, U. Mich., 1948, JD, 1950; postgrad. Harvard Bus. Sch., 1965. Bar: Mich. 1951, Ill. 1951, Ohio 1952, N.Y. 1962, U.S. Supreme Ct. 1981. Atty., Amoco Corp. (formerly Standard Oil Co. Ind.), Chgo., 1950, 52-60, Paris, 1960-62, N.Y.C., 1962-68, Chgo., 1968-71, assoc. gen. counsel, Chgo., 1972-87; pvt. practice, Cleve., 1951-52. Served with USAAF, 1943-46. Mem. ABA, Am. Soc. Internat. Law, Assn. of Bar of City of N.Y., Ill. Bar Assn., Chgo. Bar Assn., Order of Coif, Westmoreland Country Club, Meadows Country Club, Univ. Club Chgo., Mid Am. Club, Sigma Phi Epsilon. Republican. Home: 921 Westerfield Dr Wilmette IL 60091-1810

FRICK, STEPHEN N. astronaut; b. Pitts., Pa., Sept. 30, 1964; married. BSc in Aerospace Engring., U.S. Naval Acad., 1986; MSc in Aero. Engring., U.S. Naval Postgraduate Sch., 1994. Commd. 2d lt. USN, 1986, advanced through grades to comdr.; with strike fighter squadron Naval Air Sta., Cecil Field, Fla.,

1988—91; various assignments USN, 1991—94; project officer, test pilot carrier suitability dept. Strike Aircraft Test Squadron, Patuxent River, 1994—96; pilot NASA, Houston, 1996—. Decorated Air medal with 2 strike flight awards USN, 3 Commendation medals one with combat V, Nat. Defense Svc. medal. Mem.: Assn. Naval Aviators, Soc. Exptl. Test Pilots, U.S. Naval Acad. Alumni Assn. Avocations: skiing, bicycling, hiking, camping. Office: Astronaut Office CB NASA Johnson Space Center Houston TX 77058

FRICKE, MARTIN PAUL, science company executive; b. Franklin, Pa., May 18, 1937; s. Frank Albert and Pauline Jane (Wentz) F.; m. Barbara Ann Blanton, Jan. 3, 1959. BS, Drexel U., Phila., 1961; MS, U. Minn., 1964, PhD, 1967. Program mgr., group leader Gen. Atomics, San Diego, 1968-73; program mgr., divsn. mgr. Sci. Applications Internat. Corp., La Jolla, Calif., 1973-77, v.p., 1977-80, corp. v.p., 1980-84; sr. v.p. Systems Group, The Titan Corp., San Diego, Calif., 1984-87, exec. v.p. Techs Group, 1987-89, sr. v.p. corp. ops., 1989-93; program adminstr. San Diego Supercomputer Ctr., 1995-97; ind. cons., 1997—. Mem. cross sect. evaluation working group, Upton, L.I., N.Y., 1970-73, U.S. Nuclear Data Com., Washington, 1970-73. Author publs. in field. Recipient postdoctoral fellowship U. Mich., Ann Arbor, 1967-68, scholarship Pa. Indsl. Chem. Co., 1956-60; grad. fellow Oak Ridge (Tenn.) Assoc. Univs., 1964-67. Fellow Am. Phys. Soc. (panel on pub. affairs 1982-84); mem. Phi Kappa Phi. Roman Catholic. Achievements include first measurements and theoretical analysis of certain polarization phenomena in nucleon-nucleus inelastic scattering. Home and Office: 14929 Caminito Ladera Del Mar CA 92014 E-mail: mfricke@adelphia.net.

FRICKE, RAYMOND W. religious school administrator; b. Mt. Olive, Ill., May 6, 1931; s. Walter H. and Corinne L. Fricke; m. Marlene M. Fricke, Oct. 15, 1955; children: Michael, Debra, Mark, Donna, Barbara, Timothy. BS, Concordia Coll., River Forest, Ill., 1955, MA, 1977. Cert. tchr., supr. and adminstr. Tchr. Trinity Luth. Sch., Cole Camp, Mo., 1951-52, St. Matthew Luth. Sch., Chgo., 1952-55, Immanuel Luth. Sch., Glenview, Ill., 1955-58, Elmhurst, Ill., 1958-62; from tchr. to prin. St. Luke Luth. Sch., Itasca, Ill., 1962-77; asst. prin. Walter Luth. H.S., Melrose Park, Ill., 1977-82; prin. Immanuel Luth. Sch., Palatine, Ill., 1982-91, Prince of Peace Christian Sch., Carrollton, Tex., 1991-98, devel. dir., 1998—. Bd. dirs. Itasca Pub. Libr., 1967-84. Recipient Prin. of Nat. Exemplary Sch. award U.S. Dept. Edn., 1988, Nat. Disting. Prin. award, 1991. Mem. Luth. Edn. Assn. Republican. Home: 3121 Fairgate Dr Carrollton TX 75007 Office: Prince of Peace Christian Sch 4000 Midway Carrollton TX 75007 E-mail: rfricke@popcs.net.

FRICKE, REINER, education educator; b. Wesermuende, Germany, July 16, 1940; s. Arnold and Inga (Mueller) F.; m. Astrid Wilke, Apr. 14, 1965; children: Gerald, Maila. Diploma in Psychology, U. Hamburg, Germany, 1968; PhD, Tech. U., Braunschweig, Germany, 1972. Prof. Tech. U., Braunschweig, Germany, 1972-78, Hannover, Germany, 1978, Braunschweig, 1985. Author: Schulleistungsmessung, 1973, Kriteriumsorientierte Leistungsmessung, 1974, Einfuehrung in die Metaanatyse, 1985; editor: Psychologie fuer die Erwachsenenbildung, 1986. Office: Tech Univ Braunschweig Wendenring 1 38114 Braunschweig Germany E-mail: r.fricke@tu-bs.de.

FRICKE, RICHARD JOHN, lawyer; b. Ithaca, N.Y., Apr. 17, 1945; s. Richard I. and Jeanne L. (Hines) F.; m. Carol A. Borelli, June 17, 1967 (div. 1990); children: Laura, Richard, Amanda; m. Penny Yrizarry, Dec. 29, 1990 (div. 1999); children: Stephanie, Matthew, Tyler. BA, Cornell U., 1967, JD, 1970. Bar: Conn. 1970. Assoc. Gregory & Adams, Wilton, Conn., 1970-73; ptnr. Crehan & Fricke, Ridgefield, Conn., 1973-90; gen. counsel Connex Internat. Inc.; corp. counsel, pres. Safe Alternatives Corp. of Am., Inc.; pres., gen. counsel, dir. T.F.I. Industries, Inc.; gen. counsel, dir. Gold Mustache Pub. Corp., Inc.; sec., dir. DXTC.COM, Inc.; dir. Village Bank & Trust Co.; town atty. Town of Ridgefield, 1973-81. Bd. dirs. Gold Mustache Pub. Corp., Inc.; mem. Closing Mgmt. Svcs. LLC. Co-patentee low reactive pressure foam, polyurethane foam for cellulostic products. Bd. dirs. Ridgefield Community Ctr., Ridgefield Montessori, Ridgefield Community Kindergarten; founder, pres. Ridgefield Lacross League; constable Town of Wilton, Conn.; mem. Conn. Bar Commn. on Women, 1976. Mem. ABA, Conn. Bar Assn., Danbury Bar Assn. Democrat. Roman Catholic. Address: 440 Main St Ridgefield CT 06877-4525 E-mail: rickfricke@aol.com.

FRICKEY, PHILIP PAUL, law educator; b. Oberlin, Kans., June 29, 1953; s. Carl Lewis and Doreen Lydia (Nitsch) F.; m. Mary Ann Bernard, May 7, 1983; children: Alexander, Elizabeth. BA in Polit. Sci. with distinction, U. Kans., 1975; JD magna cum laude, U. Mich., 1978. Bar: D.C. 1980. Law clk. to Judge John Minor Wisdom U.S. Ct. Appeals (5th cir.), New Orleans, 1978-79; law clk. to Justice Thurgood Marshall U.S. Supreme Ct., Washington, 1979-80; assoc. Shea & Gardner, Washington, 1981-83; from assoc. prof. law to prof. U. Minn. Law Sch., Mpls., 1983—91, Faegre and Benson prof. law, 1991—98; Irving Younger prof. law U. Calif., Berkeley, Calif., 1998—2000, Richard W. Jennings prof. law, 2000—. Vis. assoc. prof. law U. Kans. Law Sch., Lawrence, 1980; vis. prof. law Harvard U. Law Sch., Cambridge, Mass., 1996. Author (with Daniel A. Farber): Law and Public Choice: A Critical Introduction, 1991; author: (with William N. Eskridge Jr. and Elizabeth Garrett) Cases and Materials on Legislation: Statutes and the Creation of Public Policy, 2001; author: (with Daniel A. Farber and William N. Eskridge Jr.) Cases and Materials on Constitutional Law: Themes for the Constitution's Third Century, 2003; author: others; co-editor: Issues in Legal Scholarship, 2002—; contbr. articles to profl. jours. Mem.: Am. Acad. Arts and Scis., Am. Law Inst., Order of Coif, Phi Beta Kappa. Office: Univ Calif Berkeley Boalt Hall Berkeley CA 94720

FRICKLAS, ANITA ALPER, retired religious organization administrator; b. Perth Amboy, N.J., Nov. 2, 1937; d. William and Dotty (Finkel) Alper; m. Richard Leon Fricklas, Dec. 22, 1957; children: Michael, Kenneth, Susan. A in Comml. Sci., Boston U., 1957; BBA, Upsala Coll., 1959; MA in Religion, Iliff Sch. Theology, Denver, 1985. Reform Jewish educator. Instr. Somerset County Coll., Somerville, NJ, 1970—72; dir. edn.-programming Temple Sinai, Denver, 1973—90; prof. Iliff Sch. Theology, Denver, 1986—91; exec. dir. Am. Jewish Com., Denver, 1990—2001; ret., 2001. Author: (book) Guide for Interfaith Families, 1993; co-author: Jewish Principal's Handbook, 1984; columnist: Lupus Found. Colo. Mem. Colo. Social Legis. Commn.; rep. Martin Luther King Jr. Meml. Commn.; sec.-treas. Mainstream Colo. Coalition, Cmty. Rels. Coun.; founding mem., chair Coloradans United Against Hatred; sec.-treas. Jewish Agy. Exec. Coun.; founder Muslim-Jewish Dialogue; bd. dirs. N.W. Coalition Human Dignity, Nat. Lupus Rsch. Inst.; sec. Hunter Hill Homeowners Assn., Englewood, Colo., 1973—74; founder Latino-Jewish Coalition. Recipient Disting. Leadership award, 1989—90, Mayor's Cmty. Achievement award, 1999. Mem.: LWV (pres. Somerset County chpt. 1967, Bridgewater Twp. chpt. 1968—70), ASCD, Jewish Educators Coun. Denver (pres. 1984—88), Nat. Assn. Temple Educators (cons. 1982—, bd. dirs. 1987—91), Hadassah, Iliff Sch. Theology Alumni Assn. (trustee, chair), Nat. Coun. Jewish Women. Avocations: travel, aerobic walking, reading. E-mail: anita@fricklas.com. *Respect diversity-but look for more things that unite people than that divide them.*

FRICKLAS, MICHAEL DAVID, lawyer; b. Somerville, N.J., Jan. 9, 1960; s. Richard L. and Anita (Alper) F.; children: Shanna E., Jaimee G., Gabriella S.; m. Donna J. Astion, Jan. 14, 1996. BSEE, U. Colo., 1981; JD magna cum laude, Boston U., 1984. Bar: Calif. 1987, Colo. 1990, N.Y. 1993. Assoc. Ware & Freidenrich, Palo Alto, Calif., 1984-87, Shearman & Sterling, N.Y., San Francisco, 1987-90; v.p., gen. counsel Minorco (U.S.A.) Inc., Denver, 1990-93; sr. v.p., dep. gen. counsel, mem. ops. com. Viacom, Inc., N.Y.C., 1993-98, sr. v.p., gen. counsel, sec., 1998-2000, exec. v.p., gen. counsel, sec., 2000—. Trustee Jazz at Lincoln Ctr., 1995—, Am. Jewish Com., N.Y. chpt., 1998—; mem. bd. vis. Boston U. Sch. Law, 1997—. Mem. ABA (exec. com. of gen. counsel com.), Am. Assn. Corp. Secs., Assn. Gen. Counsel. Office: Viacom Inc 1515 Broadway New York NY 10036-8901

FRICKLAS, RICHARD LEON, roofing educator, educational institute administrator; b. Sept. 30, 1934; s. Irving and Sarah (Brust) Fricklas; m. Anita Janet Alper; children: Michael David, Kenneth Neil, Susan Lee. BA, Hofstra U., 1955; MS, Rutgers U., 1972. Rsch. chemist Johns-Manville, NJ and Denver, 1957—79, Riegel Paper Co., Milford, NJ, 1963—64; dir. Roofing Industry Ednl. Inst., Englewood, Colo., 1979—96. Co-author: Manual of Low Slope Roofing Systems, 1995; columnist: RSI Mag., Buildings.com website. 1st lt. U.S. Army, 1955—56. Recipient James Q. McCawley award, Midwest Roofing Contractors Assn., 1991, J.A. Piper award, Nat. Roofing Contractors Assn., 1999, award, Inst. Roofing and Waterproofing Cons., 1999. Mem.: ASTM (chmn. subcom. 1964—81, Walter A. Voss award 1991), Roof Cons. Inst. (hon.). Jewish.

FRICKS, ERNEST EUGENE, management consultant; b. Knoxville, Tenn., Jan. 16, 1948; s. Ernest E. Fricks and Barbara (Clark) Griffey; m. Dorothy Stanton; children: Natalie, Karen. AB, BSME, Rutgers U., 1970; MS, Pa. State U., 1974; graduate, Air War Coll., 1986, U. Pa. Wharton Sch. exec. mgmt, 1988. Lead engr. Pub. Svc. Electric & Gas Co., Newark, 1972-76, Stone & Webster Engrng. Corp., Cherry Hill, N.J., 1976-78, mgr. licensing, 1978-79, bus. devel., 1979-85, mgr. govt. mktg., 1985-90, project mgr., 1990—2002; adj. lectr. ethics Rutgers U., N.J., 2001; pres. Ernest E. Fricks, L.L.C., 2002—. Cons. Office Sec. of Navy, 1975; profl. ethics reviewer Jour. Engrng. Mgmt., 2001—, mem. peer review panel Jour. Mil. History; chair N.J. Knight Templar Edn. Found., 2003—. Author: The Thermodynamic Effect in Developed Cavitation in Freon 113, 1974. Trustee Camden County (N.J.) Hist. Soc., 1988-92. Lt. col. USAFR, 1970-92. Named Outstanding Augmentee Officer, Mil. Airlift Command, 1977. Fellow ASME (chmn. tech. and society divsn. 1996-98, Tech. Interests Activities award 1998), Soc. Am. Mil. Engrs. (life, pres. Phila. chpt. 1994-95), Royal Philatelic Soc. (London); mem. Royal Aero. Soc. U.K., Am. Philatelic Soc. (v.p. 1977-80), Rutgers Alumni Assn. (chmn. budget and audit coms. 1999—), Rutgers U. Alumni Fedn. (treas. 1985-86, univ. sen. 1986-88, Meritorious Svc. award 2003), Rutgers Engrng. Soc. (pres. 1976-77, sec. 1998-99, treas. 2001—), Newcomen Soc. (vice chmn. N.J. 1992-94, 96-99), Collectors Club (N.Y.C.), Masons (past master, past state grand sec., 33 deg., Order Purple Cross 2001, Grand Gov. York Rite Coll. N.J. 2002). Baptist.

FRIDAY, ELBERT WALTER, JR., federal agency administrator, meteorologist; b. DeQueen, Ark., July 13, 1939; s. Elbert Walter and Mary Elizabeth (Ward) F.; m. Karen Ann Hauschild, Nov. 14, 1959; children: Kristine Ann, Kelly Sue. BS in Engrng. Physics, U. Okla., Norman, 1961, MS in Meteorology, 1967, PhD in Meteorology, 1969. Commd. 2d lt. USAF, 1961, advanced through grades to col., weather officer, 1961-81, dir. environ. and life scis., Dept. Def., 1978-81, ret., 1981; dep. dir. Nat. Weather Svc., Silver Spring, Md., 1981-87, dir., 1987-97; asst. adminstr. Office Oceanic and Atmospheric Rsch., Silver Spring, 1997-98; dir. Nat. Acad. Scis., 1998—2002, mem. bd. atmosphere in scis. and climate, 2002—; Weather News prof. applied meteorology U. Okla., 2002—. Mem. com. on low level wind shear NAS, Washington, 1985-86; U.S. permanent rep. to UN World Meteorol. Orgn., 1988-98, mem. exec. coun., 1988-98; adj. prof. U. Okla., 1998; bd. dirs. Atmospheric Sci. and Climate, NRC, NAS, 1998-2002. Contbr. articles to prof. jours. Elder Calvary Chrisitan Ch., Burke, Va., 1985-89, 2002—, trustee, 1989-93, chmn. bd., 1998-2002. Decorated Bronze Star; recipient Superior Svc. medal Dept. Def., 1981, Presdl. Rank award, 1988, Disting. Achievement award U. Okla., 1992, Fed. Exec. of Yr. award Fed. Exec. Inst. Alumni Assn., 1993. Fellow Am. Meteorol. Soc. (councilor 1988 90, pres. 2003, Cleve. Abbe award 1997); mem. AAAS, Nat. Weather Assn., Sigma Xi. Office: National Research Council 500 5th St NW Washington DC 20001

FRIDAY, GILBERT ANTHONY, JR., pediatrician; b. Pitts., Apr. 16, 1930; s. Gilbert Anthony and Susan Dorothy (Kumer) F.; m. Christina Cecilia McShane, Sept. 12, 1959; children: Martin, Peter, Martha, Timothy, Amy, Anne, Robert. BS, Bucknell U., 1952; MD, Temple U., 1956. Diplomate Nat. Bd. Med. Examiners. Rotating intern Phila. Gen. Hosp., 1956-57; pediatric resident Children's Hosp. of Phila., 1960-62, Children's Hosp. of Pitts., 1962-63, asst. med. dir. ops., 1963-66, preceptorship in allergy/immunology, 1962-67; clin. instr. to asst. prof. U. Pitts., 1963-87, clin. assoc. prof., 1987, prof. pediatrics, 1987—2001, clin. prof., 2001—. Chmn. bd. dirs. Pa. Blue Shield, Camp Hill, 1992-96. Contbr. articles to profl. jours., chpts. to books. Lt. comdr. USN MC, 1956-66. Wyeth Pediatric scholar. Fellow Am. Coll. Allergy, Asthma, and Immunology, Am. Acad. Allery, Asthma, and Immunology, Am. Acad. Pediats.; mem. AMA, Allegheny County Med. Soc. (pres. 1987), Pa. Med. Soc., Pa. Allergy Soc. (pres. 1975), Alpha Omega Alpha. Republican. Roman Catholic. Avocations: boating, fishing. Home: 1901 Highgate Rd Pittsburgh PA 15241-2210 Office: Allergy and Immunology Assocs 180 Fort Couch Rd Pittsburgh PA 15241-8811 E-mail: friday1901@aol.com.

FRIDAY, KATHERINE ORWOLL, artist; b. Granite Falls, Minn., Dec. 3, 1917; d. Melvin Sylvester and Anna Elizabeth (Hustvedt) Orwoll; m. Erling Bjarne Struxness, May 8, 1943 (div. 1961); children: John Eric, Mimi Ann McNicholas, Mari Struxness; m. George Edward Friday, Apr. 12, 1969 (dec. Jan. 1997). Student, U. Minn., 1935-36, 40-41, Frederick Mizen Sch. of Art, Chgo., 1941. Designer, illustrator Josten's, Owatonna, Minn., 1936-39, 42-43; layout artist Tempo Inc., Chgo., 1941-42, Vogue-wright Studios, Chgo., 1943-44; layout, illustration Allan D Parson Advt. Agy., Chgo., 1945, Ad-Art, Wichita, Kans., 1952-54, 63; indsl. designer Harold W. Darr Assoc., Mpls., 1959-61; layout, illustration Lydiard Assoc., Mpls., 1961—62; owner Skyline Studio, Mpls., 1962—66; layout, illustration Comm. Cons., Wilmington, Del., 1971; freelance illustration, med. illustration dept. pathology U. Chgo., Chgo., 1946-48; freelance illustrator Hutchinson, Kans., 1948—52, 1954—58; art dir. SPF Adv., Intermedia, Mpls., 1966-69, Arne Westerman Adv., Portland, Oreg., 1970-71, Battle Advt., Wyncote, Pa., 1971-72; creative dir., owner A'La Carte Advt./Art, Bellevue, Wash., 1973-77; graphic illustration Courseware, Moffat Field, Mountain View, Calif., 1978, Quantic, Los Altos, Calif., 1979—; ret., 1982; represented by Belinki-Duprey Art Gallery, Portland Art Mus. Rental Gallery. Tchr. watercolor, colored pencil, pastel techniques; curator, judge internat. miniature art exhibit Festival of the Arts, Lake Oswego, Oreg., 2002. Exhibitions include Westminster Gallery, London, 1995, Hobart, Tasmania, 2000. Recipient Best of Show award, Internat. Miniature Art Show, Kirkland, Wash., 1997, hon. mention, 1998, 4th pl., 1999, 3d pl., 2001. Mem.: N.W. Artists' Support Group, Oreg. Soc. Artists, Main St. Art. Soc. (Best of show, 1st pl. and 2d pl. awards 2002, Best of Show, 1st and 2d pl. awards, 3d pl., Merit award, Best of Show, 1st pl. oil, 1st pl. watercolor 2003), Painters Showcase (Grand award 1999, Judges Choice award 2000—02), Oreg. Colored Pencil Soc. (2d pl N.W. Regional show 2000—02), Watercolor Soc. Oreg. (Achievement award 1998, 2002), Cider Painters of Am. (award of excellence 1992—94, 1st in floral 1993, still life 1995, portrait 1995, award of excellence 1997, portrait 1998, Pres. award 1999, award of excellence 2001, Pres. award 2002, signature mem.), Ga. Miniature Artists Soc. (2d pl. and 3d pl. 1990, 1st pl. 1991, 1994, Merit award 1997), Miniature Art Soc. Fla. (1st pl. 1989—90, 2d pl. 1994—95, 1st pl. 1997—98, 2d pl. 1999, 1st pl. 2002—03), Miniature Artists of Am. (hon. signature), Colored Pencil Soc. Am., N.W. Watercolor Soc. (assoc.), Miniature Painters, Sculptors, Gravers Soc. (assoc. 3d pl. 1990, 1st pl. 1996, 1st of show 1998, 2d and 3d pl. 1999, Grumbacher award, 2d pl. 2001). Avocations: painting, drawing, reading, music.

FRIDLEY, ROBERT BRUCE, agricultural engineer, educator; b. Burns, Oreg., June 6, 1934; s. Gerald Wayne and Gladys Winona (Smith) Fridley; m. Jean Marie Griggs, June 12, 1955; children: James Lee, Michael Wayne, Kenneth Jon. BSME, U. Calif., Berkeley, 1956; MS in Agrl. Engrng., U. Calif., Davis, 1960; PhD in Agrl. Engrng., Mich. State U., East Lansing, 1973; D (hon.), U. Poly., Madrid, 1988. Asst. specialist U. Calif., Davis, 1956-60, prof. agrl. engrng., 1961-78, prof. emeritus, 1994—, acting assoc. dean engring., 1972, chmn. dept. agrl. engrng., 1974-76, dir. aquaculture and fisheries program, 1985-89, exec. assoc. dean agrl. and environ. scis., 1989-94; dept. mgr. R & D Weyerhaeuser Co., Tacoma, 1977-85. Vis. prof. Mich. State U., East Lansing, 1970—71; NATO vis. prof. U. Bologna, 1975; bd. agrl. and natural resources NRC, 2000—02. Co-author: (book) Principles and Practices for Harvesting and Handling Fruits and Nuts, 1973; contbr. articles to profl. jours. Recipient Charles G. Woodbury award, Am. Soc. Hort. Sci., 1966, Alumni citation, Calif. Aggie Alumni Assn., 1990. Fellow: Am. Soc. Agrl. Engrs. (v.p. Found. 1989—93, pres. Found. 1993—96, pres. 1997—98, Young Rschrs. award 1971, Concept of the Yr. award 1976, Outstanding Paper award 1966, 1968, 1969, 1976, 1986, Disting. Svc. award 1988, 1997, 1999); mem.: NAE. Achievements include patents in field.

FRIDLEY, SAUNDRA LYNN, private investigator; b. Columbus, Ohio, June 14, 1948; d. Jerry Dean and Esther Eliza (Bluhm) F. BS, Franklin U., 1976; MBA, Golden Gate U., 1980. Accounts receivable supr. Internat. Harvester, Columbus, Ohio, San Leandro, Calif., 1972-80; sr. internal auditor Western Union, San Francisco, 1980; internal auditor II County of Santa Clara, San Jose, Calif., 1980-82; sr. internal auditor Tymshare, Inc., Cupertino, Calif., 1982-84, divsn. contr., 1984; internal audit mgr. VWR Scientific, Brisbane, Calif., 1984-88, audit dir., 1988-89; internal audit mgr. Pacific IBM Employees Fed. Credit Union, San Jose, 1989-90, Westaff, Inc., Walnut Creek, Calif., 1990—2002; lic. pvt. investigator, owner Fridley & Assoc., 2000—. Dir. quality assurance, 1992-98, v.p. audit and investigations, 1998-2002; owner Dress Fore the 9's, Brentwood, Calif., 1994—; pres., founder Bay Area chpt. Cert. Fraud Examiners, 1990. Apptd. Brentwood Art Commn., 2003—; mem. Brentwood Bus. Alliance. Mem. NAFE, Calif. Assn. of Lic. Investigators, No. Calif. Fraud Investigators Assn., Friends of the Vineyards, Internal Auditors Speakers Bur., Assn. Cert. Fraud Examiners (founder, pres. Bay area chpt., we. regional gov. 1996-97, Disting. Achievement award 1997, 98), Inst. Internal Auditors (pres., founder Tri-Valley chpt., internat. seminar com., internat conf. com.) Avocations: woodworking, gardening, golfing. Home: 19 Windmill Ct Brentwood CA 94513-2502 Office: Fridley & Assocs 613 1st St # 19 Brentwood CA 94513 also: Dress Fore The 9's 613 1st St Ste 19 Brentwood CA 94513-1322 E-mail: saunief@aol.com.

FRIDOVICH, IRWIN, biochemistry educator; b. N.Y.C., Aug. 2, 1929; s. Louis and Sylvia (Appelbaum) F.; m. Mollie Finkel; children: Sharon E., Judith L. BS, CCNY, 1951; postgrad., Cornell U. Med. Coll., 1951-52; PhD, Duke U., 1955; hon. doctorate, U. Rene Descartes, Paris, 1980. Instr. biochemistry Duke U., Durham, N.C., 1956-58, assoc., 1958—; vis. research assoc. Harvard U., Cambridge, Mass., 1961-62; asst. prof. biochemistry Duke U., 1961-66, assoc. prof., 1966-71, prof., 1971—, James B. Duke prof., 1976—, emeritus, 1996—. Mem. study sect. Am. Cancer Soc., mem. adv. com. biochemistry and chem. carcinogenesis Mem. editorial bd. Jour. Biol. Chemistry, Biochemica Biophysica Acta, Archives of Biochemistry and Biophysics, Biochem. Jour., Bioinorganic Chemistry, Biochemistry, Biochem. Pharmacology, Analytical Biochemistry; contbr. articles to sci. jours. Recipient Founders' award Chem. Industry Inst. Toxicology, 1980, Sr. Passano award Passano Found., 1987, Herty award Ga. sect. Am. Chem. Soc., 1980, Research Career Devel. award NIH, 1959-69, Cressy A. Morrison award N.Y. Acad. Sci., 1984, Townsend Harris medal City U. N.Y., 1990, co-recipient Cresson medal, Franklin Inst., 1997, City of Medicine award, Durham, N.C., 1998, Anlyan Lifetime Achievement award Duke Med. Ctr., 1998. Mem. NAS, Am. Acad. Arts and Scis., Am. Soc. Biol. Chemists (pres. 1982), N.C. Acad. Scis., Oxygen Soc. (pres. 1990), Soc. for Free Radical Rsch. Internat., (pres. 1992), Phi Beta Kappa, Sigma Xi Home: 3517 Courtland Dr Durham NC 27707-5134 Office: Duke U Med Center PO Box 3711 Durham NC 27710-0001 E-mail: fridovich@biochem.duke.edu.

FRIDSON, MARTIN STEVEN, finance executive; b. Highland Park, Mich., Sept. 4, 1952; s. Harry Yale and Mariann (Rodd) F.; m. Elaine Rochelle Sisman, June 14, 1981; children: Arielle Amanda, Daniel Wolfe. BA cum laude in History, Harvard U., 1974; MBA, Harvard U., Boston, 1976. CFA. Trader Mitchell, Hutchins Inc., N.Y.C., 1976-77; asst. v.p. Scandinavian Securities Corp., N.Y.C., 1977-79; v.p. Paine Webber Jackson & Curtis, Inc., N.Y.C., 1980-81, Salomon Bros., Inc., N.Y.C., 1981-84; prin. Morgan Stanley & Co., Inc., N.Y.C., 1984-89; mng. dir. Merrill Lynch & Co., Inc., N.Y.C., 1989—. Cons. bd. govs. Fed. Res.; mem. Harvard Com. on Univ. Resources, 2002—. Author: High Yield Bonds, 1989, Financial Statement Analysis, 1991, Investment Illusions, 1993, It Was a Very Good Year, 1998, How to Be a Billionaire, 2000; co-editor, The Yearbook of Fixed Income Investing, 1996, editor, Extraordinary Popular Delusions and the Madness of Crowds and Confusion de Confusiones, 1996; contbr. articles to profl. jours.; author light verse pub. in Playbill, N.Y. Times, Wall St. Jour., Graham and Dodd Scroll for Excellence in Financial Writing, 1994; mem. editl. bd. Fin. Analysts Jour., 1989—, CFA Digest, 1991—, Fin. Mgmt., 1993-99. Participation chmn. Harvard Coll. Fund, Class of 1974, 1991—, mem. spl. gifts com., 1992—; dir. The Intersch. Orch. of N.Y., N.Y.C., 1991, trustee, 1992—; v.p. Jane St. Block Assn., N.Y.C., 1979; bd. dirs. Candlewood Landing Condominium Assn., 1991—; adv. coun. Salomon Ctr., NYU, 1991-97; mem. exec. com. wall st. divsn. United Jewish Appeal Fedn., 2000—. Mem. Fixed Income Analysts Soc. (pres. 1984-85, named to Hall of Fame 2000), Harvard Bus. Sch. Club (v.p. 1983-84), N.Y. Soc. Security Analysts (Vol.-of-Yr. award 1991-92), Fin. Mgmt. Assn. (practitioner dir. 1994-96, Outstanding Fin. Exec. award 2002), Ea. Fin. Assn., Midwest Fin. Assn., Inst. Chartered Fin. Analysts (trustee 1997-98, editl. bd. Jour. Fin. Statement Analysis, 1995-98), Assn. for Investment Mgmt. and Rsch. (bd. govs. 1997-2001), Harvard Club of N.Y. (mem. Harvard com. on univ. resources 2002—), New Milford Racquet and Swim Club. Democrat. Jewish. Avocations: tennis, theater, opera. Home: 440 W End Ave Apt 10A New York NY 10024-5358 Office: Fridson Vision LLC 110 Plaza 250 W 34th St Ste 3610 New York NY 10119 E-mail: martin_fridson_ab74@post.harvard.edu.

FRIED, ANDREW MICHAEL, radiologist, educator; b. Waterbury, Conn., Jan. 5, 1943; s. Sandor David and Eleanor Lilien (Bernhardt) F.; m. Barbara Perel, July 31, 1966; children: Joshua David, Emily Elizabeth. BA, Cornell U., 1964; MD, U. Ala., 1968. Diplomate Am. Bd. Radiology. Intern U. Cin., 1969, resident in gen. surgery, 1970; resident in diagnostic radiology U. Ky., Lexington, 1972-75, from asst. prof. to assoc. prof. diagnostic radiology, 1975-85, prof. diagnostic radiology, 1985—. Dir. residency tng. U. Ky., Lexington, 1992—. Contbr. articles to profl. jours. Maj. U.S. Army, 1970-72, Vietnam. Named Outstanding Tchr. of Yr., U. Ky. Radiology Residents, 1979, 82, 87, 89, 95. Fellow Am. Coll. Radiology, Soc. Radiologists in Ultrasound; mem. Am. Inst. Ultrasound Medicine (sr. mem.), Radiologic Soc. N.Am. Jewish. Avocations: classical guitar, woodworking, skiing. Office: Univ Ky Med Ctr 800 Rose St Lexington KY 40536-0001

FRIED, ARTHUR, lawyer; m. Kym Vanderbilt. JD magna cum laude, Cornell U., 1975. Bar: N.Y. Law clk. to Hon. John M. Cannella U.S. Dist. Ct. (so. dist.) N.Y., 1975-77; with The Legal Aid Soc. N.Y.C., 1977-90; acting gen. counsel, dep. gen. counsel N.Y.C. Human Resources Adminstrn.; gen. counsel N.Y.C. Dept. Housing Preservation and Devel., to 1995, Social Security Adminstrn., Balt., 1995—2000; exec. dir. NYU Ctr. Excellence in N.Y.C. Governance. Mem. Order of Coif. Office: NYU 269 Mercer St Rm 203 New York NY 10003 Business E-Mail: arthur.fried@nyu.edu.

FRIED, BELLE WARSHAVSKY, education educator; b. N.Y.C., Apr. 14, 1917; d. Maurice and Sarah (Brown) Bennett; m. Henry Warshavsky, Feb. 22, 1941 (dec.); children Barry Alyn, Beth, Benes; m. Joseph Fried, Jan. 13, 1986. BBA, St. Johns U., 1940; MSEd, Hofstra U., 1957; postgrad., NYU, 1962, profl. diploma in reading, 1965; PhD, Walden U., 1975; postgrad., C.W. Post U., 1994. Cert. gerontologist. Pvt. sec. real estate div. Home Owners Loan Corp., N.Y.C., 1935-39; pers. interviewer N.Y. State Arsenal, Bklyn., 1940-41; brokerage agt. Mut. Trust Life Ins. Co., N.Y.C., 1950-55; instr. Cen. Sch. Dist. No. 4, Plainview, N.Y., 1955-60, cons. in reading, 1961-85, dir. summer reading program, 1962-85. Instr. Kindergarten Workshops, 1961-63, Hofstra U. Reading Clinic, 1965-66; adj. instr. Queensboro C.C., 1970-79, asst. prof. 1994—, adj. prof., 1994—. Contbg. author: The Non-graded Primary—A Case History, 1986. Vice chmn. Nassau County Rep. Com., 1981; vice chmn. Rep. Com. Town of North Hempstead, 1983—; exec. leader Great Neck North Rep. Com.; mem. presdl. Task Force; leader Girl Scouts U.S., 1940-42; instr. 1st aid course for adults CD, 1941; aid welfare commr. Saddle Rock Civic Assn., 1962-80; rep. Long Term Care Ins. Mem. NEA, Nat. Soc. Study Edn., N.Y. State Tchrs. Assn., Nassau County Tchrs. Assn., Classroom Tchrs. Assn. (v.p., sec. 1958-60), Great Neck Edn. Assn. Nassau County, Internat. Reading Assn., Internat. Platform Assn., Sigma Tau Delta, Phi Delta Kappa. Home: 35 Cooper Dr Great Neck NY 11023-1908 Address: 4302 Martinique Cir Coconut Creek FL 33066-1482

FRIED, BERNARD, parasitologist, biology educator; b. N.Y.C., Aug. 17, 1933; s. Harry and Anna (Bergstein) F.; m. Janet Avery, Aug. 25, 1959 (div.); 1 child, Neil; m. Grace Jean Evans, Jan. 31, 1969; 1 stepchild, David. AB, NYU, 1954; MS, U. N.H., 1956; PhD, U. Conn., 1961. NIH postdoctoral fellow parasitology Emory U., Atlanta, 1961-63; asst. prof. Lafayette Coll., Easton, Pa., 1963-69, assoc. prof., 1969-75, Kreider prof. biology, 1975-2000, Kreider prof. emeritus, 2000—. Cons. thin-layer chromatography Ctr. Profl. Advancement, East Brunswick, N.J., Kontes Glassware, Vineland, N.J. Author: Thin Layer Chromatography, 1982, 4th edit., 1999, Handbook of Thin Layer Chromatography, 3d edit., 2003, Practical Thin Layer Chromatography--A Multidisciplinary Approach, 1996, Advances in Trematode Biology, 1997, Echinostomes as Experimental Models for Biological Research, 2000; mem. editl. jour. Helminthology; contbr. more than 450 articles to profl. jours. Grantee

NIH, NSF Rsch. Corp., Wellcome Trust Fund. Mem. Am. Soc. Parasitologists (exec. coun.), Am. Micros. Soc., Helminthol. Soc. Washington, Pa. Acad. Sci. (pres. 1972-73), Internat. Soc. Chem. Ecology. Office: Lafayette Coll High St Easton PA 18042

FRIED, BRUCE MERLIN, health services director; BA, JD, U. Fla. With Fla. Legal Svcs., 1975-81, Nat. Sr. Citizens Law Ctr., 1981-86; exec. dir. Nat. Health Care Campaign, 1986-90; exec. v.p. The Wexler Group, 1990-94; chief coord. Clinton/Gore Campaign's Health Care Adv. Group, 1992; v.p. fed. affairs FHP Internat. Corp., 1994-95; dir. Office Managed Care, 1995-97; dir. Health Care Fin. Adminstrn. U.S. Dept. Health and Human Svcs., Balt., 1997-98; ptnr. Shaw Pittman, Washington, 1998—2003, Sonnenschein Nath & Rosenthal, Washington, 2003—. Office: Sonnenschein Nath & Rosenthal 1301 K St NW Ste 600 E Washington DC 20005

FRIED, BURTON THEODORE, lawyer; b. N.Y.C., Feb. 26, 1940; s. Meyer S. and Minnie (Grossberg) F.; m. Gail K. Morgenstern, July 25, 1964; children: Marsha, Howard, Shari. BS, NYU, 1961; LL.B., Bklyn. Law Sch., 1964. Bar: N.Y. 1964, U.S. Dist. Ct. (ea. and so. dists.) N.Y. 1971. Assoc. atty. H. Bermack, N.Y.C., 1964-66, I. Towbis, N.Y.C., 1966-68; gen. counsel Medispas, Inc., N.Y.C., 1968-72; real estate counsel Michael Industries, Inc., N.Y.C., 1972-74, exec. v.p., gen. counsel and sec., 1974-86, The LVI Group, Inc., N.Y.C., 1982-85, vice chmn., gen. counsel, dir., 1985-91; pres. The LVI Group Inc., N.Y.C., 1991-93; pres., CEO LVI Svcs. Inc., N.Y.C., 1986—; chmn. LVI Holding Corp., N.Y.C., 1993—. Trustee Optometric Ctr. N.Y., 1993-99. Vice chmn. sch. bd. Forest Hills Jewish Ctr. Religious Sch., N.Y., 1983-84, chmn. sch. bd., 1984-85, trustee, 1985-88. Mem.: K.P. (Chancellor comdr. 1972-73). Office: LVI Svcs Inc 80 Broad St New York NY 10004

FRIED, CHARLES, law educator; b. Prague, Czechoslovakia, Apr. 15, 1935; came to U.S., 1941, naturalized, 1948; s. Anthony and Marta (Winterstein) F.; m. Anne Sumerscale, June 13, 1959; children: Gregory, Antonia. AB, Princeton U., 1956; BA, Oxford (Eng.) U., 1958, MA, 1961; LLB, Columbia U., 1960; LLD (hon.), New Eng. Sch. of Law, 1987, Pepperdine U., 1994, Suffolk U., 1996. Bar: D.C. 1961, Mass. 1966. Law clk. to Hon. John M. Harlan U.S. Supreme Ct., 1960; from asst. prof. to prof. law Harvard U., Cambridge, 1961-85, Carter prof. gen. jurisprudence, 1981-85, 89-95, Carter prof. emeritus, disting. lectr. Law Sch., 1995-99, Beneficial prof. law, 1999—; assoc. justice Supreme Jud. Ct. Mass., Boston, 1995-99. Spl. cons. Treasury Dept., 1961—62; cons. White House Office Policy Devel., Washington, 1982, Dept. Transp., Washington, 1981—82, Dept. Justice, 1983; solicitor gen. U.S., 1985—89. Author: An Anatomy of Values, 1970, Medical Experimentation: Personal Integrity and Social Policy, 1974, Right and Wrong, 1978, Contract as Promise: A Theory of Contractual Obligation, 1981, Order and Law: ArgSayiuing the Reagan Revolution, 1991, (with David Rosenberg) Making Tort Law: What Should Be Done and Who Should Do It, 2003, Saying What The Law Is: The Constitution in The Supreme Cour, 2004; contbr. legal and philos. jours. Guggenheim fellow, 1971-72 Fellow Am. Acad. Arts and Scis.; mem. Inst. Medicine, Am. Law Inst., Century Assn., Mass. Hist. Soc., Phi Beta Kappa. E-mail: fried@law.harvard.edu.

FRIED, CHARLES A. accountant, financial executive; b. N.Y.C., Jan. 31, 1945; s. Jerome M. and Florence (Silverman) F.; m. Denise Helaine Krafte, Sept. 2, 1965; children: Marc Steven, Shari Lynne. BS in Acctg., Queens Coll., CUNY, 1965. From staff acct. to sr. acct. Klein Hinds & Finke CPAs, N.Y.C., 1965-69; from sr. acct. to mgr. Alexander Grant & Co., N.Y.C., 1969-73; treas. Raybestos-Manhattan, Inc., Trumbull, Conn., 1974-79, v.p., 1979-80; pres. Creative Output, Inc., Milford, Conn., 1980-87; exec. v.p., CFO Home-Med Services Inc., San Diego, 1987-88; asst. v.p. Aetna Life and Casualty, Hartford, Conn., 1988-89; exec. v.p. Avraham Y. Goldratt Inst., New Haven, 1989—. Instr. acctg. L.I. U., 1973, Fairfield U., 1977-81 Vice chair local bd. Selective Svc. Commn., 1988-2002; rep., dist. fin. chmn. Fairfield Rep. Town. Commn., 1975-79; chmn., vice-chmn., dir., v.p., treas. Parents and Friends of Retarded Citizens (Kennedy Ctr.), 1975—; campaign worker United Way, 1976-77, United Jewish Appeal, 1976-78; dir., v.p. exec. com. Conn. affiliate Am. Diabetes Assn., 1977-2002; dir. Fairfield County chpt. Am. Diabetes Assn., 1992-2002, pres. 1994-95, bd. dirs. ea. region, 1998; chmn. adv. coun. Fairfield U. Bus. Bur., 1978-80; vice-chmn. combined health appeal So. Ctrl. Conn., 1991-2001; bd. dirs. Cmty. Health Charities, 1999—, Prevent Blindness, Conn., 2000—2003; bd. dirs. ARZA/N.Am. bd. World Union Progressive Judaism, 1995—2003; bd. dirs., v.p. N.E. coun. Union of Am. Hebrew Congregations, 1992—, Jewish Fedn. Greater Bridgeport, 1992-95; mem. mktg. com. New Haven United Way, 1994-96; trustee, pres. Congregation B'nai Israel, 1986—. Mem. AICPA, N.Y. State Soc. CPA's, Conn. Soc. CPA's, Inst. Mgmt. Accts., Risk Ins. Mgrs. Soc., Conn. Bus. and Industry Assn., Probus Club (bd. dirs., various offices local chpt., nat. asst. treas. 1974-86). Jewish. Home: 140 Canterbury Ln Fairfield CT 06432-2314 Office: 442 Orange St New Haven CT 06511-6201 E-mail: cfried@aol.com.

FRIED, DANIEL, ambassador; b. Sept. 19, 1952; m. Olga Karpiw; children: Hannah, Sophie. BA in History magna cum laude, Cornell U., 1974; MA, Columbia U., 1977. Fgn. svc. officer, 1977—; jr. officer East-West Trade office Econ. Bus. Bur. State Dept., 1977-79; with Consulate Gen. Office, Leningrad, 1980-81; polit. officer U.S. Embassy, Belgrade, 1982-85; reg. affairs officer Soviet Desk State Dept., Washington, 1985-87; Polish desk officer State Dept., Washington, 1987-89; polit. counselor U.S. Embassy, Warsaw, 1990-93; dir. European affairs NSC, Washington, 1993-95, spl. asst. to pres., sr. dir. ctrl. and Ea. Europe, 1995—; amb. to Poland Warsaw, 1997—. Office: Am Embassy Warsaw Poland Dept Of State Washington DC 20521-0001

FRIED, DONALD DAVID, lawyer; b. N.Y.C., Feb. 28, 1936; s. Fred and Sylvia (Falk) F.; m. Joan Hilbert, Sept. 15, 1963; children: Neil, Derek. BA, CCNY, 1956; JD, Harvard U., 1959. Bar: N.Y. 1959. Assoc. Conboy, Hewitt, O'Brien & Boardman, N.Y.C., 1960-68, ptnr., 1968-86, Hunton & Williams, N.Y.C., 1986-88, 92-96; sr. counsel, 1996—; v.p., sec., assoc. gen. counsel Philip Morris Cos., Inc., N.Y.C., 1988-91. Home: 37 W 12th St New York NY 10011-8502 Office: Hunton & Williams 200 Park Ave Rm 4400 New York NY 10166-0091 E-mail: dfried@hunton.com.

FRIED, ELEANOR REINGOLD, psychologist, educator; b. Quantico, Va., Jan. 4, 1943; d. Morris and Eleanor (Wilson) R.; divorced, 1984; children: Joshua Mark, Noah Seth, Adam Lawrence. BS cum laude, Boston U., 1964; MS in Clin. Sch. Psychology, CUNY, 1971; postgrad. Fordham U., 1971-73; MA in Clin. Psychology, The Fielding Inst., 1980, PhD in Clin. Psychology, 1981. Lic. psychologist, N.J. Psychology intern Roosevelt Hosp., N.Y.C., 1971-73; cons. Inwood House, N.Y.C., 1971-83; staff therapist Univ. Consultation Center Mental Hygiene, Bronx, N.Y., 1974-79, clin. instr., 1976-80; sr. clin. psychologist moderate security unit North Princeton Developmental Ctr., 1983-98; cons. Early Childhood Learning Center, Paramus, N.J., 1978-80, Found. for Religion and Mental Health, Briarcliff Manor, N.Y., 1979-82, Inwood House, N.Y.C., 1981-83, prin. clin. psychologist Ewing Residential Ctr., Trenton, N.J., 1987-88, Ind. Child Study Teams, East Orange, N.J; pvt. practice, Princeton, N.J.; ct. expert in forensic psychology; exec. dir. Ea. Profl. Group. Fellow Am. Bd. Forensic Examiners; mem. APA (assoc.), N.J. Psychol. Assn., Nat. Assn. Treatment Sex Offenders, Kappa Tau Alpha. Office: Ea Profl Group 601 Ewing St Ste C20 Princeton NJ 08540-2758 E-mail: fried@nerc.com .

FRIED, EMANUEL JOSEPH, actor, writer; b. Brooklyn, Ny, Mar. 1, 1913; s. Solomon and Pauline Newman Fried; children: Lorrie, Melinda. PhD, U. of Buffalo, Buffalo, NY, 1974. Educator emeritus Buffalo State Coll., Buffalo, 1972—. Bd. mem. Crisis Services, Buffalo. 1st lt. US Army, 1944—46, US & Korea. Recipient One of One Hundred Most Influential Western New Yorkers in The Twentieth Century, WGRZ-TV, Individual Artist Award, Greater Buffalo Chamber of Commerce, Joe Hill Award, AFL-CIO sponsored Labor Heritage Found., Peace award, Western NY Peace Ctr., Outstanding Story of the Yr. award, Pushcart Press, Name embedded in star on sidewalk in Buffalo's Walk of Fame, Western NY Best Actor award, Lifetime Achievement award, Coalition for Econ. Justice. Mem.: Greater Buffalo AFL Council-CIO Coun., Erie Niagara Sr. Citizens Coun. Achievements include first to International reprsentative for Western New York's 30,000 union members.

FRIED, HERBERT DANIEL, advertising executive; b. Chgo., May 27, 1928; s. Herbert D. and Beatrice (Frank) F.; m. Ninon Connart, Mar. 7, 1953; children: Bruce M., William F. Student, U. N.Mex., 1946-48, U. Ill., 1948. Account exec. Foote, Cone & Belding, Chgo., 1948-54, Weiss & Geller, Chgo., 1954-55; account exec., gen. mgr. W.B. Doner & Co., Balt., 1955-56, v.p., 1956-68, pres., 1968-73, chmn. bd., chief exec. officer, 1973—. Bd. dirs. Nat. Advt. Rev. Bd., 1987. Divsn. chmn. Comty. Chest-ARC-United Appeal, 1964, United Fund, 1977; bd. dirs. comm. divsn. United Way, 1978-79; dir. Sinai Hosp., Balt., 1994—, Greater Balt. Com., Balt. Zool. Soc., The Associated, Jewish Comty. Fedn. Balt., 1992—; mem. adv. bd. Ctr. for Advt. History Nat. Mus. Am. History Smithsonian Mus.; bd. dirs. U.S.S. Constellation Fund, 1995—. With USNR, 1946. Recipient award Chgo. Federated Advt. Club, 1949; inducted Advt. Hall of Fame, Advt. Assn. Balt., 1987; named Disting. Marylander of Yr. Advt. and Profl. Club Baltimore, 1991. Mem. Am. Assn. Advt. Agys., Inc. (bd. govs. Chesapeake coun. 1960, regional dir. 1963, chmn. govt. rels. com. 1987-90, bd. dirs. 1987-90), Nat. Advertising Review Bd., Advt. Club Balt., Kappa Sigma. Clubs: Center (Balt.); Suburban of Baltimore County (Pikesville, Md.). Home: Admirals Cove 121 Spinnaker Ln Jupiter FL 33477-4003 Office: W B Doner & Co 400 E Pratt St Baltimore MD 21202-3116

FRIED, JEFFREY MICHAEL, health care administrator; b. Kansas City, Mo., Apr. 9, 1953; s. Harvey J. and SuEllen (Weissman) F.; m. Rosalyn Sue Matz. Student, Drake U., 1971-73; BGS, U. Kans., 1975; MHA, Washington U., St. Louis, 1979. Adminstrv. asst. Rsch. Med. Ctr., Kansas City, Mo., 1979-80; asst. to pres. Rsch. Health Svcs., Kansas City, 1980-81; asst. v.p. Sinai Hosp. Balt., 1981-83, Lancaster (Pa.) Gen. Hosp., 1983-85; v.p., chief oper. officer Lancaster (Pa.) Gen. Svcs. Corp., 1985-86, pres., 1986-88; sr. v.p. Lancaster Gen. Hosp., 1989-91, chief operating officer, 1992-94; pres., CEO Beebe Med. Ctr., Lewes, Del., 1994—. Pres., bd. dirs. Lancaster Med. Equipment, Barge Ganse Vena Care; sec., bd. dirs. Preferred Health Care, Lancaster; bd. dirs. Lancaster Diagnostic Imaging, Inc., Del. Nat. Bank; v.p., bd. dirs., pres. Welsh Mountain Med. and Dental Ctr., Lancaster, 1989-94; mng. ptnr. Roherstown Imaging Assocs., Lancaster, 1986-94; part-time mem. faculty dept. health adminstrn. and devel. Pa. State U., 1988-94, Coll. of St. Francis, 1988-94; mem. bus. adv. coun. Goodwill Industries, 1989-94; asst. prof. Lebanon Valley Coll., 1994—; mem. MBA program adv. bd. Wilmington Coll., 1996—; adj. faculty Wilmington Coll. Grad. Bus. Program, 1996—. Mem. Leadership Lancaster, 1987-88; pres. bd. dirs. Welsh Mt. Med. and Dental Ctr., 1989-94; pres. bd. dirs. Lancaster chpt. Nat. Commn. for Prevention of Child Abuse, 1986-89; treas., bd. dirs. Lancaster Jewish Fedn., 1986-89; bd. dirs. Lancaster Jewish Cmty. Ctr., 1989-94, DE Nat. Bank, 2002—, Temple Shaarai Shomayim, Clinic for Spl. Children, 1991-94, Pa. Acad. Music, 1994-96, Del. Hospice, 1996-99, Rehoboth Art League, 1996-2000, Dewey Beach Lions Club, 2001—, Lewes C. of C., 1999—, Slam Dunk to the Beach, 2001—. Fellow Am. Coll. Healthcare Execs. (com. on ethics 1991-93, credentials com. 1995-98); mem. Am. Hosp. Assn. (ho. of dels. 1998-2000), Assn. Del. Hosps. (bd. dirs. 1995—), Lancaster County Bus. Group on Health (legis. com. 1992-94), Ctrl. Pa. Health Care Adminstrs, Young Pres. Orgn., World Pres. Orgn., Lewes C. of C. (v.p. 2001-03, pres. 2003—), Dewey Beach Lions Club. Jewish. Avocations: tennis, jogging, cooking, reading. Home: 17 Patriots Way Rehoboth Beach DE 19971-1057 Office: Beebe Med Ctr 424 Savannah Rd Lewes DE 19958-1490

FRIED, LOUIS LESTER, information technology and management consultant; b. N.Y.C., Jan. 18, 1930; s. Albert and Tessie (Klein) F.; m. Haya Greenberg, Aug. 15, 1960; children: Ron Chaim, Eliana Ahuva, Gil Ben. BA in Pub. Adminstrn., Calif. State U., Los Angeles, 1962; MS in Mgmt. Theory, Calif. State U., Northridge, 1965. Mgr. br. plant data processing Litton systems, Inc., Woodland Hills, Calif., 1960-65; dir. mgmt. info. systems Bourns, Inc., Riverside, Calif., 1965-68, Weber Aircraft Co., Burbank, Calif., 1968-69; v.p. mgmt. services T.I. Corp. of Calif., Los Angeles, 1969-75; dir. advanced computer systems dept. Stanford Research Inst., Menlo Park, Calif., 1976-85, dir. ctr. for info. tech., 1985-86, dir. worldwide info. tech. practice, 1987-90; v.p. info. tech. cons. Stanford Rsch. Inst., Menlo Park, Calif., 1990-97; spl. advisor to pres. TELUS Corp., Edmonton, Alta., Can., 1997-98; info. tech. mgmt. cons., 1998—. Lectr. U. Calif., Riverside, 1965-69, lectr. mgmt. and EDP. Contbr. numerous articles to profl. jours., 2 textbooks. Home: 788 Loma Verde Ave Palo Alto CA 94303-4147 also: King George V St 16B 7th Fl #14 Jerusalem 94229 Israel Fax: 650-493-8712. E-mail: LLFRIED@aol.com.

FRIED, MARC B. writer; b. N.Y.C., Apr. 25, 1944; s. Bernard J. and Celia Paisner Fried. BS in History, SUNY, New Paltz, 1968. Freelance writer, Gardiner, NY, 1974—. Author: The Early History of Kingston and Ulster County, N.Y., 1974, Tales from the Shawangunk Mountains, 1981, The Huckleberry Pickers:A Raucous History of the Shawangunk Mountains, 1995, Shawangunk: Adventure, Exploration, History and Epiphany from a Mountain Wilderness, 1998, musician. Chmn. Town of Shawangunk Dem. Com., Wallkill, NY, 1973—76. Green Party. Avocations: gardening, travel, wilderness, Rainbow gatherings. Home: 766 Sand Hill Rd Gardiner NY 12525

FRIED, MORRIS LOUIS, retired humanities educator; b. N.Y.C., Jan. 26, 1925; s. Abraham and Tillie (Marrus) F.; m. Helen Gorson, Feb. 26, 1949; children: Stephanie Fried, Pamela Crawford. BA, U. Buffalo, 1951; MA, New Sch. for Social Rsch., N.Y.C., 1958; PhD, New Sch. for Social Rsch., 1964. Verbatim reporter UN Security Coun./U.S. Dist. Cts., N.Y.C., 1958-62; lectr. in Sociology Fairleigh Dickinson U., Teaneck, N.J., 1962-64; lectr. in Labor Rels. Cornell U./Western N.Y. Dist. Internat. Labor Rels. Sch., Buffalo, 1972-78; vis. prof. Leicester (Eng.) U., 1970-71; asst., assoc. prof. Sociology SUNY, Buffalo, 1964-78; prof. Labor Studies & Sociology Ga. State U., Atlanta, 1978-81; ext. prof. continuing edn., adj. prof. sociology U. Conn., Storrs, 1981-92, ext. prof. emeritus, 1992—. Dir. Office of Pub. Svc. & Applied Rsch., U. Conn., 1988-92 Contbr. articles to profl. jours. Bd. dirs. Conn. Joint Coun. on Economic Edn., Storrs, 1987-91, Indsl. Rels. Rsch. Assn., Hartford, Conn. (pres. 1983-85); nat. chair Am. Hist. and Cultural Inst., N.Y.C., 1982-84; cons. Conn. State Dept. Labor, Hartford, 1987-89. Active in educating seniors and related persons Shepherd's Ctr., Columbia, S.C., 1998—, Emory U., Atlanta, 1997, U. Conn., 1988-91. Named prin. investigator constrn. industry OSHA, 1978-81, mining industry Mine Safety & Health Adminstrn., 1982-88. Mem. Ctr. for Learning in Retirement (life). Avocations: computers, teaching, writing, developing new ideas for seniors. Home: 147 Old Hampton Ln Columbia SC 29209-1981 E-mail: MLFLCTR@earthlink.net.

FRIED, RICHARD PETER, physician; b. N.Y., Feb. 4, 1943; s. Samuel and Geraldine (Levine) F.; m. Jane Eliot, Sept. 3, 1967; children: Joanna, Adam, Jessica. AB, Brown Univ., 1964; MD, Columbia Univ., 1968. Diplomate Am. Bd. Internal Medicine, Am. Bd. Infectious Disease. Physician Palo Alto Medical Clinic, Palo Alto, Calif., 1975-79; dir. infectious disease Bergen Pines Hosp., Paramus, N.J., 1979-80; physician N.Y., 1980—; assoc. clinical prof. medicine Columbia Univ., N.Y., 1980—. Bd. dirs. Group Health Ins. of N.J., 1979-80. Contbr. articles to profl. jours. Bd. trustees St. Luke's Roosevelt Hosp. Ctr., 1994-2000, pres. medical bd., 1996-98. With US Army, 1972-73. Mem. Am. Coll. Physicians, Infectious Disease Soc. Am. Office: 15 W 72nd St New York NY 10023-3402

FRIED, WALTER, hematologist, educator; b. Frauenkirchen, Austria, Mar. 21, 1935; came to U.S., 1938; s. Alexander and Aurelia (Haberfeld) F.; m. Judith April Weininger, Dec. 13, 1965; children: Deborah, Jennifer. BA, U. Chgo., 1954, MD, 1958. Diplomate Am. Bd. Internal Medicine, Am. Bd. Hematology. Clin. investigator VA Hosp., Chgo., 1965-67; asst. prof. Dept. Med. U. Ill., 1967-70; prof. medicine, dir. hematology U. Ill., Chgo., 1970-76; prof. U. Chgo., 1976-82; prof., assoc. dean med. scis. Rush Med. Coll., Chgo., 1982-92; mem. hematology/oncology divsn. Luth. Gen. Hosp., Park Ridge, Ill., 1995—. Mem. hematology study sect. NIH, Bethesda, Md., 1976-80, 83-87; acting chmn. dept. medicine Michael Reese Hosp., Chgo., 1980-82. Contbr. articles to profl. jours. Vol. Care-Medico, Malaysia, 1963, Am. Dr., Guatemala, 1970; v.p. Ill. divsn. Leukemia Soc., 1982—. Lt. USN, 1959-61. Mem. AMA (house dels. 1989—), Am. Soc. Hematology (del. to AMA 1988—), Internat. Soc. Exptl. Hematology (pres. 1983), Chgo. Soc. Int. Medicine (pres. 1979). Jewish. Home: 2050 N Mohawk St Chicago IL 60614-4535 Office: Luth Gen Hosp Cancer Care 1700 Luther Ln Park Ridge IL 60068-1270

FRIED, WALTER JAY, lawyer; b. N.Y.C., May 27, 1904; s. Joseph and Flora V. (Shamberg) F.; m. Louise E. Goldman, June 8, 1934; 1 son, Michael W.; m. Brita Digby-Brown, July 8, 1948. BA magna cum laude, Harvard, 1924; LL.B., Columbia U., 1928. Bar: N.Y. 1929, D.C. 1966. Practiced in, N.Y.C., 1929—; former mem. firm, now counsel Fried, Frank, Harris, Shriver & Jacobson; mem. faculty Bklyn. Law Sch., 1931-39. Dir. Salant Corp., 1969-93. Former chmn. Am. Chess Found.; hon. trustee Guild Hall, East Hampton, N.Y., chmn., 1974-78; former trustee Southampton Hosp. Served to maj. AUS, 1942-45. Decorated Legion of Merit. Mem. Assn. Harvard Chemists, Phi Beta Kappa Clubs: Maidstone (East Hampton), Harvard (N.Y.C.), Manhattan Chess (N.Y.C.) (hon. dir.). Home: 14 E 75th St New York NY 10021-2657 also: 18 Lily Pond Ln East Hampton NY 11937 Office: 1 New York Plz New York NY 10004-1901

FRIED, WILLIAM C. lawyer; b. Saginaw, Mich., Apr. 7, 1938; m. Barbara J. Benham, June 20, 1965; children: Marcus W., Kristina L., Jason A., Rebecca E. BBA in Acctg., U. Mich., 1960, LLB, 1963, MBA in Fin., 1964. Bar: Mich. 1964, U.S. Dist. Ct. (ea. dist.) Mich. 1981, U.S. Ct. Appeals (6th cir.) 1982, U.S. Tax Ct. 1979, U.S. Claims Ct. 1987. With tax dept. Arthur Young & Co., Detroit, 1964-74; tax assoc., ptnr. R.J. Dickshott & Co., Livonia, Mich., 1974-79; assoc. Robert Heritier, Detroit, 1979-80; ptnr. Fried & Mies, P.C., Livonia, 1980-92. Sec. Livonia Spree-51 com., Livonia Cmty. Found., Livonia Heart Fund,; bd. dirs. Livonia Bldg. Authority; v.p. Livonia Symphony Orch. Mem.: Livonia C. of C., Livonia Bar Assn., Mich. Soc. CPA's, AICPA, Detroit Bar Assn., Mich. Bar Assn., ABA, Rotary (pres. elect 2001—). Home: 16009 Riverside St Livonia MI 48154-2460 Office: Fried & Assocs 32900 5 Mile Rd Ste 204 Livonia MI 48154-3083

FRIEDBERG, ALAN CHARLES, lawyer; b. Ft. Leavenworth, Kans., Dec. 22, 1945; s. Arnold Millard and Gisela Claire (Newkirk) F.; m. Jean Anderson, June 23, 1973; children: John, Michael. BA with honors, U. Va., 1967; JD, Yale U., 1970. Bar: Va. 1970, Colo. 1973, U.S. Supreme Ct. 1994. Law clk. U.S. Ct. Appeals (10th cir.), Denver, 1974-75; dir. Pendleton, Friedberg, Wilson & Hennessey, P.C., 1975—, pres., 1995—97. Mem. faculty Nat. Inst. for Trial Adv., 1984, 85, 86; lectr. Continuing Legal Edn. of Colo., 1986—; adj. prof. law U. Denver, 1989-2001. Mem. ch. coun. Mt. Calvary Luth. Ch., Boulder, Colo., 1980-82, 89-91. Capt. JAG U.S. Army, 1970-74. Decorated Bronze Star, Army Commendation medal, Vietnamese Cross of Gallantry, Vietnam Svc. medal. Mem. ABA, Denver Bar Assn. (vol. atty. pro bono program, Outstanding Young Lawyer of Yr. award 1981, past. mem. interprofl. jud. selection and benefits com. jud. survey taks force, pub. interest law com., exec. counsel young lawyers sect., chmn. 1979-80; chmn. legal svc. com. 1982-84), Colo. Bar Assn. (med. bd. govs. 1992-94, mem. availability of legal svcs. com.), Colo. Trial Lawyers Assn. (comml. law editor Trial Talk mag. 1989—), Assn. Trial Lawyers Am., Nat. Inst. Trial Advocacy (mem. faculty, nat. sessions 1984-85, regional sessions 1984-86, deposition program 1988), Denver Law Club, Meadows. Democrat. Home: 275 Pawnee Dr Boulder CO 80303-3730 Office: Pendleton Friedberg Wilson & Hennessey PC 303 E 17th Ave Ste 1000 Denver CO 80203-1263

FRIEDBERG, BARRY SEWELL, investment banker; b. Atlantic City, Jan. 4, 1941; s. Herbert and Mildred (Salit) F.; m. Charlotte A. Moss, Oct. 10, 1985; children: Benjamin, James. BA, Princeton U., 1962. Trainee Chem. Bank, N.Y.C., 1963-64; with A.G. Becker, N.Y.C., 1964-84, mgr. mergers and acquisitions dept., 1980-83, mng. dir., 1974-84, mgr. investment banking div., 1984; mng. dir. Merrill Lynch & Co., N.Y.C., 1984—; mgr. investment banking div. Merrill Lynch Pierce Fenner & Smith Inc., N.Y.C., 1985-93, chmn. investment banking divsn., 1993—2003; exec. v.p., mem. exec. com. Merrill Lynch & Co., Inc., 1990—2003; pres. Friedberg Milstein, 2003—. Bd. dirs. N.Y.C. Ballet Co., 1988-96, 97—, chmn., 2003—; bd. dirs. Boys Harbor, Inc., Am. Hosp. Paris Found. Mem. Princeton Club, Econs. Club. Office: Friedberg Milstein 575 Madison Ave 3d Fl New York NY 10022

FRIEDBERG, ERROL CLIVE, pathology educator, researcher; b. Johannesburg, Oct. 2, 1937; s. Edward and Rena (Berman) F.; children: Malcolm, Andrew, Jonathan, Lawrence. BSc, Witwatersrand U., Johannesburg, 1957, MB BCh, 1961. Intern King Edward VIII Hosp./U. Natal, Durban, South Africa, 1962; resident pathologist Witwatersrand U., 1963-64, Cleve. Met. Gen. Hosp., 1965; postdoctoral fellow dept. biochemistry Case Western Res. U., Cleve., 1966-68; rsch. investigator divsn. nuclear medicine Walter Reed Army Inst. Rsch., Washington, 1969-70; asst. prof. pathology Stanford (Calif.) U., 1971-77, assoc. prof. pathology, 1977-84, prof. pathology, 1984-90; prof., chair dept. pathology U. Tex. Southwestern Med. Ctr., Dallas, 1990—, Senator Betty and Dr. Andy Andujar chair pathology, 1990-93, Senator Betty and Dr. Andy Andujar disting. chair pathology, 1993—. Co-organizer symposia and confs. in field. Editor or co-editor: DNA Repair Mechanisms, 1978, DNA Repair: A Laboratory Manual of Research Procedures, Vol. 1, 1981, Cellular Responses to DNA Damage, 1983, DNA Repair: A Laboratory Manual of Research Procedures, Vol. 2, 1983; author: DNA Repair, 1984; editor-in-chief:, editor or co-editor: Scientific American Reader: Cancer Biology, 1985, Mechanisms and Consequences of DNA Damage Processing, 1988, DNA Repair: A Laboratory Manual of Research Procedures, Vol. 3, 1988; author: Cancer Answers: Encouraging Answers to 25 Questions You Were Always Afraid to Ask, 1992, 1993; author: (with others) DNA Repair and Mutagenesis, 1995; author: Correcting the Blueprint of Life, 1997; author: (with others) Sydney Brenner: My Life in Science, 2001; author: The Writing Life of James D. Watson, Professor, Promotor, Provacateur, 2003; contbr. numerous articles to profl. publs. Recipient Rsch. Career Devel. award USPHS, 1974-79, Merit award USPHS, 1988—, Rous-Whipple awrd Am. Soc. Investigative Pathology, 2000; Andrew W. Mellon Found. rsch. fellow, 1973-76; Joshua Macy Jr. Found. faculty scholar, 1978-79. Fellow: Royal Coll. Pathology; mem.: Am. Acad. Microbiol. Office: U Tex Southwestern Med Ctr Dept Path 5323 Harry Hines Blvd Dallas TX 75390-7208

FRIEDBERG, FELIX, biochemist, educator; b. Copenhagen, Apr. 3, 1921; came to U.S., 1938; s. Abram F.; m. Gladys E. Chester, Aug. 16, 1971. BS in Chemistry, U. Denver, 1944; PhD in Biochemistry, U. Calif., Berkeley, 1947. Instr. dept. biochemistry Howard U. Coll. Medicine, Washington, 1948-52, asst. prof., 1953-57, assoc. prof., 1957-61, prof. dept. biochemistry, 1961—. Vis. lectr. Cath. U. Am. Dept. Biology, 1950-52; resident rsch. assoc. Argonne Nat. Lab., 1956. Author: Thoughts About Life, 1954, Caveat Homo sapiens: The Furtive Mind, 2000; contbr. articles to profl. jours. Recipient USPHS Sr. Rsch. fellow U. Calif., Berkeley, 1947-48, Abraham Rosenberg Rsch. fellow, U. Calif., 1946-47, fellow Nat. Found. for Infantile Paralysis Enzyme Inst. U. Wis., 1954, Commonwealth Fund fellow U. Upsala, Sweden, 1956. Mem. Am. Soc. Biochemistry and Molecular Biology, Phi Beta Kappa, Sigma Xi, Phi Lambda Upsilon. Office: Howard U Biochem Dept 520 W St NW Washington DC 20001-2337

FRIEDBERG, MARK, ophthalmologist; b. N.Y.C., Feb. 2, 1960; s. George and Arlene Janice (Katz) F.; m. Ronda Gail Horowitz, June 8, 1985. BSc, Brown U., 1982; MD, U. Pa. Sch. Medicine, 1986. Diplomate Am. Bd. Ophthalmology. Resident Wills Eye Hosp., Phila., 1987-90; vitreo-retinal fellow Washington Nat. Eye Ctr., 1990-91; ophthalmologist Midatlantic Ophthalmology, Red Bank, N.J., 1991—. Lectr. in field. Editor, contbg. author: Wills Eye Hospital: Office and Emergency Room Diagnosis and Treatment of Eye Disease, 1991; contbr. articles to profl. jours. Mem. AMA, Am. Acad. Ophthalmologists, N.J. Acad. Ophthalmology, Retina Soc. N.J., Monmouth County Med. Soc. Avocations: tennis, lecturing, swimming, weight lifting. Office: MidAtlantic Ophthalmology 70 E Front St Red Bank NJ 07701-1851

FRIEDBERG, MICHAEL A. healthcare executive; b. N.Y.C., May 27, 1940; s. Gerald J. and Nettie J. Friedberg; m. Donna K. Friedberg, Sept. 18, 1993; children: Craig, Charles, Emily. BA, Williams Coll., 1960; MD, Columbia U., 1964. Diplomate Am. Bd. Surgery. Pvt. practice gen. surgery Strauss Surg. Group, Chgo., 1973-91; pvt. practice Chgo., 1991-94; assoc. med. dir. United Health Care, Chgo., 1994-96; v.p., regional med. dir. OneHealth Plan, St. Louis, also Rosemont, Ill., 1996—. Capt. USAF, 1965-67. Fellow ACS; mem. Ill. State Med. Soc., Chgo. Med. Soc. Office: Great West Life 13045 Tesson Ferry Rd Saint Louis MO 63128

FRIEDBERG, THOMAS HAROLD, insurance company executive; b. N.Y.C., Aug. 25, 1939; s. Henry R. and Ursula J. (Cale) F.; m. Cynthia K. Thisius; children: Donald Henry, Sharon Elizabeth, Linda Lee. Student, Oberlin (Ohio) Coll., 1956-57, Western Res. U., 1959-61; MBA, U. Chgo., 1971. Asst. v.p. CNA Ins. Co., Chgo., 1961-71; v.p. worldwide automobile ins. ops. Am.

Internat. Group, N.Y.C., 1971-74; pres., dir. Thurston F & C Ins. Co., Tulsa, 1974-75, Am. Inst. Mktg. Corp., Falls Church, Va., 1975-76; v.p. Hartford Ins. Group, Conn., 1976-79, sr. v.p., 1979-81, Reliance Ins. Cos., Phila., 1981-83; v.p. Intermediaries of Am., Inc., 1983-85; pres. Transprotection Service Co./Vanliner Ins. Co., Fenton, Mo., 1985-87; exec. v.p. Chase Ins. Enterprises, 1987-93; chmn., pres., chief exec. officer Ranger Ins. Co., 1987-95; chmn., CEO Accel Internat. Corp., Stafford, Tex., 1995-98; pres., CEO Nobel Ins. Co., Dallas, 1999—2001; pres. Renaissance U.S. Holdings, Inc., 2001—. With AUS, 1957-58. Recipient Disting. Svc. award Park Forest Jaycees, 1967, Jefferson award for pub. svc., 1989, Outstanding Leadership in Edn. award, 1990, Pres.'s award NAACP, 1993, Unity award NAACP, 1994, Hero for Children, Tex. State Dept. of Edn., 1995. Home and Office: 2 Stirling Way Lumberton NJ 08048-5205

FRIEDBERG, WALLACE, biologist, researcher; b. NYC, Apr. 12, 1927; s. Isidor and Mae Doris Friedberg; m. Betsy House, Aug. 17, 1957; children: Susan Clark, Jacqueline Bist, Daniel. AB, Hope Coll., 1949; MS, Mich. State U., 1951, PhD, 1953. Grad. asst. Mich. State U. Dept. Physiology, East Lansing, 1949-53; postdoctoral rsch. fellow Ind. U. Chemistry Dept., Bloomington, 1953-54; rsch. assoc. U. Pa. Children's Hosp. Phila., Pa., 1954-55, Oak Ridge Nat. Lab., Tenn., 1955-56, postdoctoral rsch. fellow, 1957-58, assoc. biologist, 1958-59, biologist, 1959-60; team coord. radiobiology rsch. Civil Aerospace Med. Inst. FAA, Okla. City, 1960—. Vis. investigator Oak Ridge Nat. Lab., 1969—79; assoc. biology Oklahoma City U., 1968—70, 1974—75; adj. prof. zoology U. Okla., Norman, 1971—94; asst. prof. rsch. biochemistry U. Okla. Health Scis. Ctr., Oklahoma City, 1961—64, assoc. prof. rsch. biochemistry, 1964—69, prof. rsch. biochemistry and molecular biology, 1969—94, rsch. prof. parasitology and lab. practice, 1969—74. Contbr. articles to profl. jours. With USN, 1945-46. Recipient Outstanding Innovator award Office of Aviation Medicine, 1996, 2003. Mem. AAAS, Am. Chem. Soc., Am. Physiological Soc., Radiation Rsch. Soc., Bioelectromagnetics Soc., Sigma Xi, Sigma Pi Sigma. Jewish. Avocation: fencing. Home: 7805 NW 26th St Bethany OK 73008 Office: Civil Aerospace Med Inst FAA Mail Rte AAM-610 PO Box 25082 Oklahoma City OK 73125-5006 Fax: 405-954-1010. Personal E-mail: wfriedberg@cox.net. Business E-Mail: wallace.friedberg@faa.gov.

FRIEDE, SAMUEL A(RNOLD), health care executive; b. Starnberg, Fed. Republic Germany, Oct. 17, 1946; s. Simon and Faye F.; m. Andrea Mednick, Aug. 31, 1972; children: David, Rachel. AB, Columbia U., 1969; MBA, U. Chgo., 1975. Adminstrv. liaison to medicine Northwestern Meml. Hosp., Chgo., 1975-76; exec. adminstr. medicine Michael Reese Hosp. and Med. Ctr., Chgo., 1976-81; assoc. dir. patient care services Strong Meml. Hosp. of U. Rochester, N.Y., 1981-84; v.p. ops. Allegheny Gen. Hosp., Pitts., 1984-86; v.p. med. staff affairs and patient mgmt. services Shadyside Hosp., Pitts., 1986-94; dir. cons. and trustee svcs. Hosp. Coun. of Warrendale, Pa., 1994-98; mgr. governance initiative Health Policy Inst., U. Pitts., Pa., 1998—. Sec., treas. Chgo. Health Execs. Forum, 1979, pres., 1980; mem. Alumni Council Exec. Com., Chgo., 1977-80, health adminstrn. program U. Chgo.; preceptor grad. program in hosp. adminstrn. U. Chgo., 1978-81; adj. instr. grad. sch. pub. health U. Pitts., 1993—; mem. ethics com. St. Clair Hosp., 1995—; bd. dirs. Armstrong County Meml. Hosp., 1998—. Sec. bd. dirs. Hyde Park-Kenwood Community Health Ctr., Chgo., 1980-81. Fellow Am. Coll. Healthcare Execs. (regent western Pa. 1993-98), Health Exec. Forum Southwestern Pa. (sec. 1986, treas. 1987, v.p. 1988). Avocations: walking, tennis, coaching basketball. Office: Health Policy Inst U Pitts Crabtree Hall A665 130 DeSoto St Pittsburgh PA 15261 E-mail: friede@pitt.edu.

FRIEDEBERG, PEDRO, painter, sculptor, designer; b. Florence, Italy, Jan. 11, 1937; s. Erwin and Gerda (Landsberg) F. Architecture degree, U. Iberomaericana, Mexico City, 1962. Exhibited in numerous one man exhbns. including Byron Gallery, N.Y.C., 1964, 66, 67, Souza Gallery, Mexico City, 1962, 64, 66, 68, Misrachi Gallery, Mexico City, 1970, 72, 74, Galerie Pecanins, Barcelona, 1976, Ft. Worth Art Ctr., 1979, Harcourts Gallery, San Francisco, 1980, Needleman Gallery, Chgo., 1981, Llewellyn Gallery, New Orleans, 1985, Museo de Arte Moderno Mex., 1986, Vorpal Gallery, N.Y.C., Museo Biblioteca Pape, Monclova, Mex., 1989, Galeria de Arte Mexicano, Mexico City, 1990; exhibited in numerous group shows including Biennale of São Paulo, 1964, Biennale of Paris, 1964, Labyrinthe, Berlin, 1968, Mus. of Modern Art, Toronto, Ottawa and Montreal, 1973-75, Biennale of San Juan, P.R., 1977-79, Bienal Coltejer, Medellin, Colombia, 1978, Llewellyn Gallery, New Orleans, 1989, Microbienal, Mexico City, Vorpal Gallery, N.Y.C., 1987, Museo de Arte Moderno, Mexico City, 1988, Hokin Galleries, Fla., 1988, 92, R.E.F. Studios, Houston; respresented in numerous mus. in Am., Europe, Argentina, Israel, including Musée Des Arts Decoratifs Du Louvre, Paris, Mus. Contemporary Art, New Orleans, Worcester (Mass.) Art Mus., Brandeis U., Washington and Lee U., Toronto Sci. Mus., Mus. Contemporary Art of Jerusalem and Tel Aviv, Mus. Modern Art of Mexico City, Mus. Modern Art, Bagdad, Iraq, Buenos Aires Mus. Modern Art, Casa de las Americas, Havana, Cuba, Nat. Rsch. Libr., Ottawa, Libr. of Congress, Washington, Museo Marco, Monterrey, Mex., others; Art editor: Mexico This Month, 1960-64; subject of book: Pedro Friedeberg (Ida Rodriguez), 1972, Pedro Friedeberg (A. Neuvillate). Recipient 1st prize Biennale of Córdoba, Argentina, 1967; 2d prize Exposición Solar, Mex., 1968; 1st prize Biennale of San Juan, P.R., 1979; 2d prize Triennale of Buenos Aires, 1979 Mem. Foro de Arte Contemporáneo, Accademia Italia delle Arti e del Lavoro, Gallery La Chinche Mexico City (dir.). Home: Recreo 48 San Miguel Allende 37700 Guanajuato Mexico Office: Apartado Postal 6-613 06600 Mexico City Mexico

FRIEDEL, JACQUES, physics educator; b. Paris, Feb. 11, 1921; s. Edmond and Jeanne (Bersier) F.; m. Mary Horder, June 2, 1952; children: Jean, Paul. Degree in engring., Ecole Polytechnique, Paris, 1946; post grad., Ecole des Mines, 1948; doctorate, U. Paris., 1954; PhD in Physics., U. Bristol, Eng., 1952; doctorat (hon.), Ecole Polytechnique, Lausanne, Bristol U., Geneva U., Zagreb U., Cambridge U. Engr. Ecole des Mines, Paris, 1948-56; prof. physics U. Paris, 1956-89; ret. Pres. Cons. Scientifique France Telecom Paris, 1991-98, Obs. Nat. la Lectr., 1994-2001; pres. Comite Consultatif de la Rechereche Scientifique et Technique, 1979-81. Author: Dislocations, 1956, 64, Graine de Mandarin, 1994; contbr. articles to profl. jours. With French Cavalry, 1944. Decorated grand officer Legion of Honor, comdr. Order Nat. Merit; recipient Gold medals CNRS, Ste. Française Metallurgie Paris, Acta Metallurgica, prize Holweck French Soc. Physics and Inst. of Physics, Dannie Heineman prize Acad. Göttingen, von Hippel and Italgas awards. Mem. Acad. des Scis. (past pres.), Swedish Royal Acad. Scis. (hon.), Royal Soc. London (hon.), Am. Acad. Arts and Scis. (hon.), Leopoldina (hon.), Inst. Physics London (hon.), Am. Phys. Soc. (hon.), Nat. Acad. Sci. (hon.), Royal Belgian Acad. Sci. (hon.), Brazilian Acad. Sci. (past pres.), European Phys. Soc. (past pres.), Max Planck Gesellschaft (hon.). Avocation: gardening. Home: 2 rue Jean-Francois Gerbillon 75006 Paris France Office: Physique des Solides U Paris Sud 91405 Orsay France

FRIEDEL, ROBERT OLIVER, physician; b. Corona, N.Y., Aug. 4, 1936; s. August W. and Denise G. (D'Aoust) F.; m. Susanne Weber, June 30, 1961; children— Christine, Scott, Karin, Linda. BS, Duke U., 1958, MD, 1964. Diplomate: Am. Bd. Psychiatry and Neurology. Intern Duke U. Med. Ctr., Durham, N.C., 1964-65, resident in psychiatry, 1967-70, asst. prof. psychiatry and pharmacology dept. psychiatry, 1970 73, assoc. prof. psychiatry and asst. prof. pharmacology, 1973-74; assoc. prof. psychiatry and pharmacology U. Wash. Sch. Medicine, Seattle, 1974-77, dir. div. psychopharmacology, 1974-77, vice chmn., dir. clin. services dept. psychiatry and behavioral scis., 1975-77; prof., chmn. dept. psychiatry Med. Coll. Va.-Va. Commonwealth U., Richmond, 1977-84; prof., chmn. dept. psychiatry, exec. dir. Mental Health Rsch. Inst. U. Mich., Ann Arbor, 1984-85; v.p. psychiat. medicine and rsch. Charter Med. Corp., Macon, Ga., 1985-90, psychiatrist in chief, 1987-90, sr. v.p. clin. svcs. and rsch., 1990, physician in chief, 1990, also bd. dirs.; prof., chmn. dept. psychiatry U. Ala., Birmingham, 1992-2001; disting. clin. prof., dept. psychiatry Va. Commonwealth U., Richmond, 2001—. Mem. sci. adv. bd. Nat. Edn. Alliance for Borderline Personality Disorder. Author: Emotional Storms: Learning to Control the Symptoms of Borderline Personality Disorder, (with others) Behavioral Science: A Selective View, 1972; editor (with L.R. Baxter) Current Psychiatric Diagnosis and Treatment, 1999, (with D. Evans) Current Psychiatry Reports, mem. editl. bd. Jour. Clin. Psychopharmacology, Hosp. and Cmty. Psychiatry, 1986-92; contbr. book chpts. and articles. Bd. dirs. Nat. Mental Health Assn., 1987-92. Served to lt. comdr. USPHS, 1965-67. Fellow Am. Psychiat. Assn. (life); mem. AMA, Am. Coll. Psychiatrists, Soc. Biol. Psychiatry, Med. Soc. Va., Am. Coll. Neuropsychopharmacology (life), Alpha Omega Alpha. Home: 13722 Hickory Nut Point Midlothian VA 23112

FRIEDELL, GILBERT HUGO, pathologist, hospital administrator, educator, cancer center director; b. Mpls., Feb. 28, 1927; s. Aaron and Naomi (Kepman) F.; m. Janet Newell Nelson; children: Mark Lowry, Benjamin Newell, Anne, James Gilbert, Sarah Jane. Student, Harvard Coll., 1943-45; BS, U. Minn., 1947, M.B., 1949, MD, 1950. Diplomate Am. Bd. Pathology. Intern Mpls. Gen. Hosp., 1949-50; resident in pathology Boston City Hosp., 1950-52, Free Hosp. for Women, 1952-53, Salem (Mass.) Hosp., 1953-54, Pondville Hosp., 1954-55; pathologist Mass. Meml. Hosps., 1958-61, New Eng. Deaconess Hosp., 1962-67, Boston City Hosp., 1967-69; chief pathology St. Vincent Hosp., Worcester, Mass., 1969-78, med. dir., 1978-82; dir. Lucille Parker Markey Cancer Ctr., Lexington, Ky., 1983-90, dir. cancer control program, 1990—98; assoc.in pathology Boston U., 1958-61, assoc. prof. pathology, 1967-70; instr. Harvard U., 1962-67, lectr., 1967-69; prof. U. Mass., 1971-83, acting chmn. dept. pathology, 1973; prof. U. Ky., 1983—98. Mem. breast cancer task force Nat. Cancer Inst., 1968-72, dir. nat. bladder cancer project, Nat. Cancer Inst., 1971-84. Author: (with others) Carcinoma in Situ of the Uterine Cervix, 1960; contbr. numerous articles on cancer, cancer research and other pathologic-med. topics to sci. jours. Vice chmn. Mass. Com. on Medico-Legal Investigation, 1977-80; mem. breast cancer adv. com. Ky. Dept. Health, 1990—; mem. Intercultural Cancer Coun. Served with USNR, 1955-57. USPHS spl. research fellow, 1961-62; grantee Nat. Cancer Inst., Am. Cancer Soc. Mem. Mass. Soc. Pathologists (pres. 1975-76, exec. com. 1974-77), New Eng. Cancer Soc. (exec. com. 1975-78), Worcester Dist. Med. Soc. (exec. com. 1980-81), Mass. Med. Soc. (councillor 1980-81), Assn. Cmty. Cancer Ctrs. (trustee 1978-82), Ky. Med. Assn., Am. Assn. for Cancer Rsch., Am. Soc. Clin. Oncology, N.Am. Assn. Ctrl. Cancer Registries (exec. bd. 1991-94), Athenaeum Club (London). Office: Lucille Parker Markey Cancer Ctr 2365 Harrodsburg Rd Ste A230 Lexington KY 40504

FRIEDEN, BERNARD JOEL, urban studies educator; b. N.Y.C., Aug. 11, 1930; s. George and Jean (Harris) F.; m. Elaine Leibowitz, Nov. 23, 1958; 1 child, Deborah Susan. BA, Cornell U., 1951; MA, Pa. State U., 1953; MCP, MIT, 1957, PhD, 1962. Asst. prof. urban studies and planning MIT, Cambridge, 1961-65, assoc. prof., 1965-69, prof., 1969—, Ford prof. urban devel., 1989—, assoc. dean architecture and planning, 1993—; dir. rsch. Ctr. for Real Estate Devel., mem. faculty com. Ctr. for Real Estate, Cambridge, 1985-87; chmn. faculty MIT, 1987-89; dir. MIT-Harvard U. Joint Center for Urban Studies, 1971-75, mem. exec. com., 1975-82. Cons. HUD, 1966-68, DOD, 1994—; staff Pres. Johnson's Task Force Urban Problems, 1965; mem. Pres. Nixon's Task Force Urban Problems, 1968, The White House Task Force Model Cities, 1969, Pres. Carter's Urban Policy Adv. Com., 1977-80; vis. scholar U. Calif., Berkeley, 1990-91, 96. Author: The Future of Old Neighborhoods, 1964, Metropolitan America, 1966, (with Robert Morris) Urban Planning and Social Policy, 1968, (with William W. Nash) Shaping an Urban Future, 1969, (with Marshall Kaplan) The Politics of Neglect, 1975, 77, (with Wayne E. Anderson and Michael J. Murphy) Managing Human Services, 1977, The Environmental Protection Hustle, 1979, (with Lynne B. Sagalyn) Downtown, Inc., 1989; editor: Jour. Am. Inst. Planners, 1962 65; contbr. to various books and encys. Bd. dirs. Citizens Housing and Planning Assn., 1966-75. Served with AUS, 1952-54. Guggenheim fellow U. Calif., Berkeley, 1975-76, rsch. fellow Urban Land Inst., 1978-89, sr. fellow, 1989-98. Mem. Am. Inst. Cert. Planners, Am. Planning Assn. Jewish. Home: 7 Diamond Rd Lexington MA 02420-1610 E-mail: bfrieden@mit.edu.

FRIEDEN, BRENDA JOYCE, secondary school educator; MS in Ednl. Tech., Pitts.(Kans.) State U., 1997; EdD, St. Louis U., 2002. Tchr. Lamar Sch. Dist. R-1, Mo., 1971—94, tech. dir., 1995—99; asst. prof., dir. of Instr. Tech. Pitts. State U., Kans., 2000—. Contbr. articles to profl. publs. Recipient Putting Kids First award, SE Kans. Edn. Svc. Ctr., 1999. Mem.: Nat. Bus. Edn. Assn., Assn. for Advancement of Computing in Edn., Assn. for Ednl. Comm. and Tech., Internat. Soc. for Tech. in Edn., Kans. Assn. for Edn. Comm. and Tech. (pres. elect 2002—03), Delta Kappa Gamma, Phi Kappa Phi.

FRIEDEN, CARL, biochemist, educator; b. New Rochelle, N.Y., Dec. 31, 1928; s. Alexander and Evelyn (Gutman) F.; m. Sari Ann Schneider, Dec. 20, 1953; children: Amy, Eric, Karen. BA, Carleton Coll., 1951; PhD, U. Wis., 1955. Mem. faculty biochemistry and molecular biophysics Washington U., St. Louis, 1957—, prof. biol. chemistry, 1963—, interim dept. head, 1986—89, 1996—2000, Alumni Endowed prof., 1994-2000, dir. med. scientist tng. program, 1986-91, Wittcoff prof., head, 2000—. Mem. NIH study sect., biochemistry, 1969-74, cellular molecular basis of disease, 1992-96. Mem. editorial bd.: Jour. Biol. Chemistry, 1963-68, 75-80, Archives Biochemistry and Biophysics, 1973-79, Biochemistry, 1975—. Protein Sci., 1992-96. Fellow AAAS; mem. Nat. Acad. Sci., Am. Soc. Biochemistry and Molecular Biology, Am. Chem. Soc. (St. Louis award 1976), Am. Soc. Cell Biology, Biophys. Soc., Protein Soc., Sigma Xi. Research, publs. on mechanism of enzyme action including correlation of protein structure to catalytic function, protein folding, devel., application of kinetic theory with respect to enzymes; properties of actin. Home: 7452 Wellington Way Saint Louis MO 63105-2926 E-mail: frieden@biochem.wustl.edu.

FRIEDEN, CHARLES LEROY, university library administrator; b. West Bend, Iowa, Feb. 25, 1941; s. Ernest Leo and Loraine Margaret (Klepper) F.; m. Janet Catherine Cronin, Aug. 16, 1969; children— Christopher Charles, Sara Catherine BABA, Mankato State U., 1963; MA in Polit. Sci., U.Iowa, 1966, MA in Library Sci., 1969. Tchr. Lewis-Central Schs., Council Bluffs, Iowa, 1966-68; serials librarian Coe Coll., Cedar Rapids, Iowa, 1969-72; asst. dir. circulation services U. Va., Charlottesville, 1972-77, dir. circulation services, 1978-94, dir. adminstrv. svcs., 1995—. Co-author: Reference/Information Services in Iowa Libraries, 1969 Mem. ALA, Va. Libr. Assn., Greencroft Club (bd. dirs. 1988—, sec. 1988-90, pres. 1990-91, sec. 1991-92), Ivy Farms Neighborhood Assn. (pres. 1994-95). Roman Catholic. Home: 1903 Stillhouse Rd Charlottesville VA 22901-8837 Office: U Va Alderman Libr Mccormick Rd Charlottesville VA 22904-0001

FRIEDEN, CLIFFORD E. lawyer; b. L.A., Mar. 8, 1949; s. Sidney S. and Norma (Stern) F.; m. Dinah S. Baumring, June 20, 1971; children: Jamie, Kari, Curtis. BA, UCLA, 1971; JD, U. Calif., Berkeley, 1974. Bar: Calif. 1974, U.S. Dist. Ct. (so. dist.) Calif. 1974, U.S. Dist. Ct. (cen. dist.) Calif. 1977. Ptnr. Rutan & Tucker, Costa Mesa, Calif., 1974—. Mem. Orange County chpt. ARC, 1995-2001. Mem. Orange County Bar Assn. (del. state conv. 1983-95, chair judiciary com. 1987-88, bd. dirs. 1989-91), Order of Coif, Phi Beta Kappa. Avocations: sports, jogging. Office: Rutan & Tucker PO Box 1950 611 Anton Blvd Ste 1400 Costa Mesa CA 92626-1931

FRIEDEN, JANE HELLER, art educator; b. Norfolk, Va., Aug. 25, 1926; d. Samuel Ries and Saida (Seligman) Heller; m. Joseph Lee Frieden, Dec. 23, 1950 (dec. 1990); children: Nancy Frieden Crowe, Robert M., Andrew M. AA, Coll. of William and Mary, Norfolk, Va., 1945; BA, Coll. of William and Mary, Williamsburg, Va., 1947; MA, Columbia U., 1950. Lic. pvt. pilot. Tchr. art City of Norfolk Pub. Schs., 1947-48, Hudson Day Sch., New Rochelle, N.Y., 1948-49, Mt. Vernon (N.Y.) Pub. Schs., 1949-50, City of Norfolk Pub. Schs., 1950-51; prof. art Coll. William and Mary Extension, Williamsburg, 1957-72, U. Va. Extension, Norfolk, 1972-78, Cmty. Colls. State of Va., Chesapeake and Hampton, 1978-82, St. Leo Coll., Norfolk, 1982-95; advocate Chrysler Mus. Art, 2003—. Travel agt., 1977-89. Author: (dictionary) A is For Art, 1978-82; artist water color paintings and ink drawings at several shows. Asst. Gen. Douglas MacArthur Meml. Archives, Norfolk, 1945—95; vol. Chrysler Mus. Art, Norfolk, 1991—, advocate, 2003—; vol. Va. Symphony Aux., 1992—98, Norfolk Little Theatre Box Office, 1991—, Meals on Wheels, 1962—66, Make a Wish Found., 1996, ARC, 1953—95, Grey Lady Project, 1956—62, Bloodmobile Project, 1966—80, Va. Zool. Soc., 1996; tchr. drawing Ghent Venture, 1993; reader for the visually handicapped Intouch Network WHRO-Radio, 1991—; archives com. Ohef Sholom Temple; bd. dirs. Norfolk Little Theatre, 1996; vol. career svcs. Coll. William and Mary, 1992—; drawing tchr. Norfolk Sr. Ctr., 1998—99; vol. docent USS Wisconsin BB 64, Hampton Roads Naval Mus., 2001—. Mem. Ninety-Nines (treas. 1978-85), Tidewater Artists Assn. (bd. dirs. 1975-80, 91—, treas. membership com.), Tidewater Orchid Soc., Am. Orchid Soc., Norfolk Soc. Arts, United Daus. Confederacy, Hermitage Soc., Norfolk Ex Libris Soc. Coll. William & Mary (steering com. 1993—), Va. Belles (reunion com. 1993—), Chesapeake Watercolor Soc. Republican. Jewish. Avocations: drawing and water color painting, raising orchids, travel. Home: 221 Oxford St Norfolk VA 23505-4354 E-mail: flymum@earthlink.net.

FRIEDEN, JONATHAN DAVID, lawyer; b. Albemarle County, Va., May 3, 1971; s. David Ralph and Katherine Louise (Pennington) F. BS in Sys. Engring., U. Va., 1994; JD, U. Richmond, 1997. Bar: Va. 1997, U.S. Dist. Ct. (ea. dist.) Va. 1998. Prin. Odin, Feldman, and Pittleman, P.C., Fairfax, Va., 1997—. Adj. prof. bus. adminstrn. Marymount U., 1999—. Author: Medicaid Eligibility Planning for Aged Clients in Virginia, 1997. Midshipman U.S.N., 1989-90. Recipient Lewis F. Powell Medal for Excellence in Advocacy, Am. Coll. of Trial Lawyers, 1996. Avocation: martial arts. Office: Odin Feldman and Pittleman PC 9302 Lee Hwy Ste 1100 Fairfax VA 22031-1215 Fax: 703-218-2160. E-mail: jdf@ofplaw.com.

FRIEDEN, LEX, government agency administrator; m. Joyce Frieden. Degree, Tulsa U.; M in social psychology, U. Houston. Chmn. Nat. Coun. Disability, Washington, 2002—; sr. vp The Inst. for Rehab. and Rsch., Houston, dir of indep. living rsch. utilization; prof. Baylor Coll. of Med.; pres. Rehabilitation Internat.; mem. UN panel of experts Std. Rules for Disability; exec dir Nat. Coun. on Handicapped, Washington, 1984—88; chmn. Am. Assn. People with Disabilities; cons. panel mem. US House of Reps. Com. on Sci. and Tech., 1976—78; rep. employment panel Org. for Econ. Cooperation and Devel., Paris, 1989—90. Named one of Am. Ten Outstanding Young Men, 1983; recipient Henry B. Betts award, 1998. Office: 1331 F St NW Ste 850 Washington DC 20004*

FRIEDEN, THOMAS R. public health physician; b. N.Y.C. BA, Oberlin Coll., 1982; MD, MPH, Columbia U., 1986. Diplomate in internal medicine and infectious diseases Am. Bd. Internal Medicine. Resident in medicine Columbia Presbyn. Hosp., N.Y.C., 1986-89; fellow in infectious disease Yale U., New Haven, 1989-90; med. epidemiologist CDC/N.Y.C. Dept. Health, 1990-92, asst. commr., 1992-96; med. officer CDC/WHO, New Delhi, 1996—; Commr. Health and Mental Hygiene NYC Dept. of Health and Mental Hygiene, New York, NY, 2002—. Contbr. chpts. to books, articles to profl. jours. Office: Dept Health & Mental Hygiene 125 Worth Street New York NY 10013

FRIEDENBERG, DANIEL MEYER, financial investor, writer; b. Mt. Vernon, N.Y., Feb. 24, 1923; s. Samuel and Rose Abravanel (Klein) F.; m. Maria del Carmen Joy, May 1, 1956 (div. June 1964); children: Samuel Clark, Danielle Joy; m. June Meredith Daniels, Apr. 12, 1965 (div. May 1986); children: Jay Daniels, Bertrand Russell. BS, U. Pa., 1943. With John-Platt Enterprises, Inc., N.Y.C., 1947—, pres., 1957—. Curator coins and medals Jewish Mus., N.Y.C., 1960-83, emeritus, 1983—; guest lectr. Columbia U., N.Y.C., Yale U., New Haven, Swarthmore Coll., Hebrew U., Jerusalem. Author: Great Jewish Portraits in Metal, 1963, Jewish Medals from the Renaissance to the Fall of Napoleon, 1970, Jewish Mint Masters & Medalists, 1976, Medieval Jewish Seals from Europe, 1987, Life, Liberty and the Pursuit of Land, 1992, Sold to the Highest Bidder: The Presidency from Dwight D. Eisenhower to George W. Bush, 2002; contbr. articles to profl. jours. Exec. dir. N.Y. County Liberal Party, 1945; sec. Young Dems., N.Y.C., 1952. Served with AUS, 1943-44. Recipient spl. achievement award Loeb Mag., 1962, Loeb Newspaper, 1965, Heath Lit. award for disting. numismatic achievement, 1969, Nat. Jewish Book award, 1988, 3d prize Nat. Libr. Poetry, 1997. Fellow Am. Numismatic Soc. (life); mem. Am. Numismatic Assn. Home: 79 Byram Shore Rd Greenwich CT 06830-6906 Office: 55 Central Park W New York NY 10023-6003

FRIEDENBERG, GARY HOWARD, lawyer; b. N.Y.C., Oct. 15, 1940; s. Lester A. and Mildred (Handelman) F.; m. Carol M. Goldblatt, July 8, 1967; children: Joann M., Steven G. AB in Acctg., Franklin & Marshall Coll., 1962; JD, Bklyn. Law Sch., 1965; LLM in Corp. Law, LLM in Taxation, NYU, 1967. Acct. Jacob M. Kessler & Co., Rockville Centre, N.Y., 1962-67; tax atty. CBS, Inc., N.Y.C., 1967-70; assoc. Morris A. Kaplan, P.C., Huntington, N.Y., 1970-72; pvt. practice Lake Success, N.Y., 1972-74; prin. Porter & Friedenberg, P.C., Lake Success, 1974-93; mng. prin. estates, trusts and taxation divsn. Berkman, Henoch, Peterson & Peddy, P.C., Garden City, N.Y., 1993—. Bd. dirs. Testing Machines, Inc., Islandia, N.Y. Chmn. estate and fin. planning conf. United Jewish Appeal of L.I., 1994—. Mem. N.Y. State Bar Assn., Nassau County Bar Assn. (chmn. tax com. 1981-83, 85-87), N.Y. State Soc. CPAs (Nassau chpt., exec. bd. 1990-92, chmn. estate planning 1988-90, 92-94), Pension Coun. of L.I. Inc. (pres. 1987). Home: 52 Woodmont Rd Melville NY 11747-3319 Office: Berkman Henoch Peterson & Peddy PC 100 Garden City Plz Garden City NY 11530-3203 E-mail: G.Friedenberg@bhpp.com.

FRIEDENBERG, MIKE, publishing executive; Mem. sales staff Cardinal Bus. Media; pub. Internetwork Mag., Midrange Sys., DEC Profl., ENT Mag.; from dist. mgr. to pub. Info. Week, Manhasset, NY, 1996—2000, pub., 2000—; v.p. Camp Media LLC, Manhasset, 2000—. Office: CMP Media Inc 600 Community Dr Ste 1 Manhasset NY 11030-3875*

FRIEDENBERG, RICHARD MYRON, radiology educator, physician; b. N.Y.C., May 6, 1926; s. Charles and Dorothy (Steg) F.; m. Gloria Geshwind, Jan. 22, 1950; children: Lisa, Peter, Amy. AB, Columbia, 1946; MD, L.I. Coll. Medicine, 1949. Diplomate: Am. Bd. Radiology. Intern in medicine Maimonides Hosp., Bklyn., 1949-50; resident in radiology Bellevue Hosp., N.Y.C., 1950-51, Nat. Cancer fellow, 1951-52; fellow radiology Columbia-Presbyn. Hosp., 1952-53; cons. radiologist 3d Air Force, London, Eng., 1953-55; asst. prof. radiology Albert Einstein Coll. Medicine, 1955-66, assoc. clin. prof. radiology, 1966-68; dir., chmn. dept. radiology Bronx Lebanon Hosp. Center, 1957-68; prof., chmn. dept. radiology N.Y. Med. Coll., 1968-80; prof., chmn. dept. radiol. scis. U. Calif., Irvine, 1980—92, emeritus prof. radiol. scis., 1992—. Dir. radiology Flower Fifth Ave. Hosp., Met. Hosp. Ctr., Bird S. Coler Hosp., N.Y.C., Westchester County Med. Ctr., 1968—80. Author: (with Charles Ney) Radiographic Atlas of the Genitourinary System, 1966, 2d edit., 1981; Contbr. (with Charles Ney) articles to profl. jours. Fellow Am. Coll. Radiology, N.Y. Acad. Medicine; mem. Assn. Univ. Radiologists, Radiol. Soc. N.Am., Am. Roentgen Ray Soc., N.Y. Acad. Scis., Assn. Am. Med. Colls., AMA, Soc. Chairmen Acad. Radiology Depts. (past pres.), N.Y. Roentgen Soc. (past pres.), Orange CTY Radiology Soc. (past pres.). Home: 18961 Castlegate Ln Santa Ana CA 92705-2801 Office: U Calif Dept Radiology Irvine CA 92697-0001 E-mail: rmfriede@uci.edu.

FRIEDER, GIDEON, computer science and engineering educator; b. Zvolen, Czechoslovakia, Sept. 30, 1937; came to U.S., 1975; m. Dalia Bogler, Apr. 3, 1960; children— Ophir, Tally, Gony B.Sc., Israel Inst. Tech., Haifa, Israel, 1959, M.Sc., 1961, D.Sc., 1967. Staff mem. Israel Dept. Def. Research and Devel., Haifa, Israel, 1959-68, dir. computer sci., 1968-70; staff mem. IBM Sci. Ctr., Haifa, Israel, 1973-75; assoc. prof., then prof., chmn. SUNY, Buffalo, 1975-81; prof., chmn. dept. elec. engring. and computer sci. U. Mich., Ann Arbor, 1981-86; dean sch. computer info. science Syracuse (N.Y.) U., 1987-92; dean Sch. Engring. and Applied Sci., A. James Clark prof. George Washington U., 1992-97, A. James Clark chair, prof. engring., applied scis., 1997—. Cons. various industries; chief architect computers Nanodata Corp., Buffalo, 1976-80; expert witness patent and copyright cases; lectr. Contbr. articles to profl. jours.; patentee in field of computers, memory and orgn. Mem. Assn. Computing Machinery, IEEE Computer Soc. Office: 8012 Matterhorn Ct Potomac MD 20854-4058

FRIEDERICHS, NORMAN PAUL, lawyer; b. Ft. Dodge, Iowa, Sept. 13, 1936; s. Norman Paul and Dorothy Mae (Vinsant) F.; m. Marjorie Darlene Farrand, Aug. 23, 1959 (dec. July 10, 2000); children: Laurie Lynne, Norman Paul, Stacie Lynne; m. Kathryn Anne Nyblad, June 8, 2002, stepchildren: Michael Stephen Anderson, Mark Burton Anderson, Timothy David Anderson; AA, Ft. Dodge Community Coll., 1956; BA, Wartburg Coll., 1959, JD, U. Iowa, 1966. Bar: Iowa 1966, Mich. 1968, Minn. 1974, U.S. Ct. Appeals (2nd, 7th, 8th and fed. cirs.) 1978, Wis. 1993. Tchr. chemistry Janesville Sch. Dist., Iowa, 1960-63; mem. Woodhams, Blanchard & Flynn, Kalamazoo, 1966-68; atty. PPG Industries, Pitts., 1968-69, Gen. Mills, Inc., Mpls., 1969-76; mem. Merchant, Gould, Smith, Edell, Welter & Schmidt, Mpls., 1976-90, Kinney & Lange P.A., Mpls., 1990-93, pres., bd. dirs. Friederichs Law Firm PLC Mpls., 1993—; pres., bd. dirs. AdSatNet, Inc., JB2 Inc. Editor: (booklet) Report of

Economic Survey, 1983. Mem. Minn. Rep. Cen. Com.; chmn. St. Louis Park Sch. Dist., Minn., 1973; mem. Suburban Hennepin Vocat.-Tech. Bd., 1980-84, chmn. 1982-84. Mem. ABA, Acad. Trial Lawyers, Eden Prairie C. of C. (bd. dirs. 1979-88, pres. 1989), Am. Trial Lawyers Assn. (advocate), Am. Patent Law Assn. (com. chmn. 1980-84), Minn. Patent Law Assn. (chmn. small bus. com.), Optimists (pres. 1971-72, lt. gov. 1976-77), Masons. Baptist. Home: 6421 Kurtz Ln Eden Prairie MN 55346-1609 Office: Friederichs Law Firm Plc 425 Pillsbury Dr SE Minneapolis MN 55455

FRIEDHEIM, JAN V. education administrator; b. Corpus Christi, Tex., Oct. 20, 1935; d. Roy Lee Conyers and Bertha Victoria (Ostrom) Hamm; m. John R. Eisenhour, Nov. 22, 1962 (div. 1983); m. Stephen B. Friedheim, Sept. 1, 1984; children: Neenah, Stephen II, Robert. BS, U. Tex., 1957; PhD (hon.), Constantinian U., Malta, 1994. Chmn. bd. Exec. Secretarial Sch., Dallas, 1960—2001; ptnr. Edn. Sys. and Solutions, 2001—. Vice-chmn. Tex. Vocat.Adv. Bd., Austin, 1979-86; mem. adv. com. Dept. Edn., Washington, 1980-84; commr. So. Assn. Colls. and Schs. Commn. on Occupl. Edn. Instns., 1994-97; adv. com. State Postsecondary Rev. Entity, 1994; bd. dirs. Tex. Assn. Pvt. Schs., Career Coll. and Schs. of Tex.; commr. Coun. on Occupl. Edn., 1995-2001. Bd. dirs. Career Colls. and Schs. of Tex., 1995—. Named Disting. Evaluator, Accrediting Coun. Ind. Coll. Schs., 1999. Mem. Career Coll. Assn. (bd. dirs. 1999—), Assn. Ind. Colls. and Schs. (chmn. bd. dirs. 1980-81, commn. 1978-79, commr. 1974-79, Disting. Mem. 1974, 81, Mem. of Yr. 1979), Southwestern Assn. Pvt. Schs. (pres. 1982), Metroplex Assn. Pvt. Schs. (pres. 1989-90, 92-93), So. Assn. Colls. and Schs. (trustee 1981-85, commn. on occupational edn. instns. 1994-97), Tex. Assn. Pvt. Schs. (bd. dirs. 1992—), Career Colls. and Schs. Tex. (bd. dirs. 1995—, chmn.-elect 1998, chmn. 1999). Home: 6450 Patrick Dr Dallas TX 75214-2444

FRIEDHEIM, JERRY WARDEN, museum consultant; b. Joplin, Mo., Oct. 7, 1934; s. Volmer Havens and Billie Alice (Warden) F.; m. Shirley Margarette Beavers, Oct. 17, 1956; children: Daniel Volmer, Cynthia Diane, Thomas Eric. BJ, U. Mo., 1956, AM, 1962. Reporter, editor, editorial writer Neosho (Mo.) Daily News, Joplin (Mo.) Globe, Columbia Missourian, 1956-61; instr. journalism U. Mo., Columbia, 1961-62; aide to Congressman Durward Hall from Mo., Washington, 1962-63; legis. asst., pres. sec., exec. asst. to U.S. Senator John Tower from Tex., Washington, 1963-69; dep. asst. Sec. Def. for Pub. Affairs, U.S. Dept. Def., Washington, 1969-72; asst. Sec. Def. for Pub. Affairs, Washington, 1973-74; v.p. pub. and govt. affairs AMTRAK, 1974-75; exec. v.p., gen. mgr. Am. Newspaper Pubs. Assn. and ANPA Found., Washington, 1975-87, pres., 1987-91; pub. Presstime mag., 1980-90; v.p. pub. affairs The Freedom Forum, Arlington, Va., 1991-95; exec. dir. The Freedom Forum Newseum, 1991-93; dep. dir. The Newseum, Arlington, Va., 1995-97, mem. adv. com., 1998—. Bd. dirs. World Press Freedom Com; past chmn. Nat. Press Found. Author: Where are the Voters, 1968. Congl. fellow Am. Polit. Sci. Assn.; recipient Disting. Svc. medal Dept. Def., 1972, 74. Home: 46865 Grissom St Sterling VA 20165-3575 E-mail: friedheim1@msn.com.

FRIEDHEIM, STEPHEN BAILEY, educational consultant; b. Joplin, Mo., Nov. 13, 1934; s. Robert Wray and Virginia Grace (Bailey) F.; m. Jan V. Eisenhour, Sept. 1, 1984; children; Neenah Marie, Stephen Bailey II, Robert William. BA, U. Ark., 1956; DBA (hon.), Johnson and Wales U., Providence, 1978; DAM (hon.), Ctrl. New Eng. Coll., Worcester, Mass., 1984. Announcer Sta. KBRS, Springdale, Ark., 1956-57; newsman Sta. KFSB, Joplin, 1957; dir. pub. rels. Am. Pers. and Guidance Assn., Washington, 1961-66; exec. v.p. Am. Soc. Med. Tech., Houston, 1966-76; pres. Assn. Ind. Colls. and Schs., Washington, 1976-84; sr. v.p. Campbell Comm., Bethesda, Md., Dallas, 1984-90, King Edn. Svcs., 1984-89; pres. ESS Coll. Bus. (formerly Exec. Secretarial Sch.), Dallas, 1984-2001; prin. Edn. Solutions for Students LLC, 1991—2001; founder Edn. Systems & Solutions, LLC, 2001—. Cons. Profl. Scs., Internat., 1980-82, South-Western Pub. Co., 1984-88, Career Com Corp., 1984-91, Richard D. Irwin, Inc., Paradigm Pub., 1999, Masters Inst., 1997, Johnson & Wales U., 2002—, Coll. Am., 2002—, KD Studio Actors Conservatory of SW, 2002—; task force on transfer credit Coun. on Postsecondary Accreditation, 1977-78; mem. Nat. Task Force on Image of the Sec., 1980-97; pres. Am. Edn. Alliance, 1988-90; mng. dir. EdVerify, 1998-2000, Johnson and Wales U., 2001--, CollAm, 2002--, KP Studio, 2002 . Editor: The Lead Generation, 1984—90, Tex. Times, 1994—. Bd. dirs. St. Aidan's Sch., Alexandria, Va., 1979-82, Trinity River Arts Ctr., 2002—; trustee Dollars for Scholars, 1982-84; vestry man Ascension Ch., Houston, 1973-76, sr. warden, 1976; narrator Minn. Symphony Orch., 1972; founding mem. local county workforce devel. bd. Dallas County, 1996-2001, chmn., vice-chmn., bd. dirs., 1999, chmn., 2000; bd. dirs., exec. com. Tex. Discovery Gardens, 2000-01; vice-chmn. Workforce Leadership Tex., 2000-01. With U.S. Army, 1957-61. Recipient Freedoms Found. award, 1960, 62, Broadcasting award Am. Legion Aux., 1963. Fellow Australasian Coll. Bio-med. Scientists; mem. Am. Soc. Assn. Execs. (cert.), Nat. Assn. Trade and Tech. Schs. (Outstanding Svc. award 1984), Assn. Ind. Colls. and Schs. (Disting. Svc. award 1991), Washington Soc. Assn. Execs., Work Force Commn. Creative Svc. (1st pl. award 1990, 91), Southwestern Assn. Ind. Colls. and Schs. (bd. dirs. 1985-92, pres. 1989-91), Met. Assn. Career Schs. (bd. dirs. 1985-86, pres. 1999), Assn. Ind. Colls. and Schs. (treas. 1985-89, bd. dirs. 1985-91, chmn. bd. 1990-91), Career Coll. Assn. (bd. dirs. 1991-9, 1st chmn. bd. 1991-94, past chmn. bd. 1994-95), Nat. Ct. Reporters Assn. (strategic alliance com. for edn. 1994-95), Nat. Alliance of Bus. (bus. adv. com. 1994—, S.W. regional bd. dirs. 1996-98), Career Tng. Found. (bd. dirs. 1992-95, trustee 1995—), Am. Assn. Higher Edn., Am. Vocat. Assn., Nat. Bus. Edn. Assn., Nat. Assn. Workforce Bds. (bd. dirs. 2000-01), Am. Vocat. Assn., Nat. Assn. Execs., Nat. Assn. Concerned Vets., Career Coll. Assn., Career Colls. and Schs. of Tex., U.S. C. of C. (edn., employment and tng. com. 1980-92, adv. bd. 1991-95), Ctr. Workforce Preparation and Quality Edn. Home: 6450 Patrick Dr Dallas TX 75214-2444 E-mail: sfriedheim@aol.com.

FRIEDL, RANDALL RAYMOND, environmental scientist; b. San Fernando, Calif., Jan. 18, 1957; s. Raymond Joseph and Ione Louise (Anderson) Friedl; m. Myrna Wijmer, Dec. 20, 1980 (dec.); m. Lisa Melton, Nov. 30, 2002. BS, UCLA, 1978; MA, Harvard U., 1980, PhD, 1984. From rsch. assoc. to group supr. Jet Propulsion Lab., Pasadena, Calif., 1984-94, rsch. scientist, 1997—, lead scientist, 1998-2000, chief scientist for earth sci. and tech. directorate, 2001—; project scientist NASA, Washington, 1994-96, flight scientist, Cirrus Regl. Study of Tropical Anvils and Cirrus Layers - Fla. Area Cirrus Expt., 2002. Co-mission scientist NASA/NOAA/Air Force sponsored field experiment, Atmospheric Chemistry of Combustion Emissions Near the Tropopause, 1999. Assessment chairperson (NASA publ.) Atmospheric Effects of Subsonic Aircraft, 1997; coord. lead author: Intergovernmental Panel on Climate Change Special Report on Aviation and the Global Environment, 1999; contbr. over 30 articles to profl. jours., chpts. to books. Mem. ACS, Am. Geophys. Union, Sigma Xi. Achievements include research on chemistry of importance to understanding anthropogenic impacts on earth's atmosphere. Office: Jet Propulsion Lab Mailstop 183-901 4800 Oak Grove Dr Pasadena CA 91109-8001 E-mail: rfriedl@jpl.nasa.gov.

FRIEDL, RICK, lawyer, former academic administrator; b. Berwyn, Ill., Aug. 31, 1947; s. Raymond J. and Ione L. (Anderson) F.; m. Dawn Friedl; children: Richard, Angela, Ryan, Ariana. BA, Calif. State U., Northridge, 1969; MA, UCLA, 1976, postgrad., 1984; JD, Western State U., 1987. Bar: Calif. 1988, U.S. Dist. Ct. (ctrl. dist.) Calif. 1992. Dept. mgr. Calif. Dept. Indsl. Rels., 1973-78; mem. faculty dept. polit. sci. U. So. Calif., 1978-80; pres. Pacific Coll. Law, 1981-86; staff counsel state fund Calif., 1988-89; prin. Law Offices of Rick Friedl, 1989—. Author: The Political Economy of Cuban Dependency, 1982; tech. editor Glendale Law Rev., 1984; contbr. articles to profl. jours. Calif. State Grad. fellow, 1970-72. Mem. ABA, Calif. State Bar Assn., Los Angeles County Bar Assn., Am. Polit. Sci. Assn., Latin Am. Studies Assn., Acad. Polit. Sci., Pacific Coast Coun. Latin Am. Studies, Calif. Trial Lawyers Assn. Home: PO Box 2095 California City CA 93504-0095

FRIEDLAENDER, FRITZ JOSEF, electrical engineering educator; b. Freiburg/Breisgau, Germany, May 7, 1925; came to U.S., 1947, naturalized, 1953; s. Ludwig and Frieda (Murzynski) F.; m. Gisela Triebe, Aug. 7, 1969; 2 children. BS, Carnegie Mellon U., 1951, MS, 1952, PhD, 1955; Dr.-Ing. (E.h.), Ruhr-Universität Bochum, Germany, 1992. Asst. prof. Columbia, 1954-55, Purdue U., West Lafayette, Ind., 1955-59, assoc. prof., 1959-62, prof. elec. and computer engring., 1962-2000; guest prof. Max-Planck Institut Metallforschung, Tech. U. Stuttgart, Fed. Repubic Germany, 1964-65; Humboldt award and guest prof. Institut für Werkstoffe der Elektrotechnik, Ruhr-Universität, Bochum, West Germany, 1972-73; Japan Soc. for Promotion Sci. fellow and guest prof. Nagoya U., summer 1980; guest prof. U. Regensburg (Fed. Republic Germany), 1981-82; Meyerhoff vis. prof. Weizmann Inst. Sci., Rehovot, Israel, Jan.-June 1990; prof. emeritus, 2001—. Cons. Gen. Electric Corp., Ft. Wayne, Ind., 1956-58, Components Corp., Chgo., 1959-61, Lawrence Radiation Lab., U. Calif. at Livermore, 1967-69, P.R. Mallory & Co., 1974-78, Oakridge Nat. Lab., 1979-82 Adv. editor Jour. Magnetism and Magnetic Materials, 1975—; co-editor Magnetic Separation News, 1983-91, Magnetic and Electrical Separation, 1991-2002; mem. editl. bd. Proc. IEEE, 1975-78; contbr. articles to profl. jours. Recipient Carnegie Mellon U. Alumni Merit award, 2001. Fellow IEEE (revs. editor trans. Magnetics 1965-67, editl. bd. jour. 1968—, chmn. awards Magnetics Soc. 1966-74, 85—, achievement award Magnetics Soc. 1986, chmn. Intermag 1975, London, program co-chmn. Intermag 1978, Florence, Italy, v.p. Magnetics Soc. 1975-76, pres. 1977-78, chmn. Central Ind. sect. 1979-80, J. Fred Peoples award 1989, disting. lectr. 1991-93, IEEE Magnetics Soc., 3d Millennium medal 2000, 8th Internat. Conf. on Ferrites Spl. award 2000, Spl. Recognition award Magnetics Soc. 2001), Am. Phys. Soc., Am. Soc. Engring. Edn.: mem. Magnetics Soc. of Japan (hon.), Arbeitsgemeinschaft Magnetismus, Sigma Xi, Phi Kappa Phi, Tau Beta Pi, Eta Kappa Nu, Beta Sigma Rho. Achievements include research in magnetics, magnetic devices and memories, high gradient magnetic separation, magnetic bubble dynamics, Vertical Bloch Lines, microwave ferrites, Ni-Fe tape magnetization processes. Home: 150 Colony Rd West Lafayette IN 47906-1209 Office: Purdue U Sch Elec and Computer Engrn Bldg 1465 Northwestern ave West Lafayette IN 47907-2035 E-mail: fritzj@ecn.purdue.edu.

FRIEDLAENDER, GARY ELLIOTT, orthopedist, educator; b. Detroit, May 15, 1945; s. Alex Seymour and Eileen Adrianne (Berman) Friedlaender; m. Linda Beth Krohner, Mar. 16, 1969; children: Eron Yael, Ari Seth. BS, U. Mich., 1967, MD, 1969; MA (hon.), Yale U., 1984. Diplomate Am. Bd. Orthop. Surgery. Intern, then resident in surgery U. Mich., Ann Arbor, 1969-71; resident in orthop. Yale New Haven Hosp., 1971-74, fellow in musculoskeletal oncology Mass. Gen. Hosp., Boston, 1983; dir. tissue bank Naval Med. Rsch. Inst., Bethesda, Md., 1974-76; instr. surgery Yale U., New Haven, 1974, asst. prof., 1976-79, assoc. prof., 1979-84, prof., chief orthop., 1984-86, prof. chmn. dept. orthop. and rehab., 1986—, Wayne O. Southwick prof. of orthop. and rehab., 1997—. Mem. orthop. and musculoskeletal study sect. NIH, 1986—89, mem. nat. adv. bd. arthritis and musculoskeletal and skin diseases, 1991—95, chmn., 1993—95; mem. blood products adv. com. FDA, 1995—97; mem. adv. coun. Nat. Inst. Arthritis and Musculoskeletal and Skin Diseases, 1998—2001. Mem. bd. cons. editors: Jour. Bone and Joint Surgery, 1981—89, mem. bd. assoc. editors: Clin. Orthop. and Related Rsch., 1986—97, dep. editor:, 1997—, mem. bd. assoc. editors: Modern Medicine, 1988—; editor: Rheumatology Digest, 1986—95; mem. editl. bd.: Transplantation Scis., 1991—, Jour. Cancer, 1994—; contbr. articles to profl. jours. Served to lt. comdr. USN, 1974—76. Recipient Outstanding Rsch. award, Kappa Delta, 1982, Nicholas Andry award for Outstanding Orthoped. Rsch., 1995. Fellow: ACS, Am. Acad. Orthop. Surgeons (chmn. com. biol. implants 1987—93, chmn. com. rsch. 1999—2002, bd. dir. 1999—2002, chmn. com. academic advocacy 2001—, chair musculoskeletal splty. soc. 2001—02); mem.: NIH (orthop. and musculoskeletal study sect. 1986—89, mem. nat. adv. bd. arthritis and musculoskeletal and skin diseases 1991—95, chmn. 1993—95), AMA, Acad. Orthop. Soc. (pres. 1995—96, chmn. com. rsch. 1999—2002), Assn. Bone and Joint Surgeons (pres. 2001—02), Am. Orthop. Assn., Am. Soc. Transplant Surgeons, Soc. for Surg. Oncology, Am. Coun. on Transplantation (pres. 1983—85), Musculoskeletal Tumor Soc., Transplantation Soc., Orthop. Rsch. Soc. (pres. 1994—95), Am. Assn. Tissue Banks (pres. 1983—85, Disting. Svc. award 1996), Alpha Omega Alpha. Jewish. Home: 15 Old Still Rd Woodbridge CT 06525-1101 Office: Yale U Dept Orthopedics and Rehab PO Box 208071 New Haven CT 06520-8071 E-mail: gary.friedlaender@yale.edu.

FRIEDLAND, BERNARD, engineer, educator; b. Bklyn., May 25, 1930; s. Irving and Beckie (Kissen) F.; m. Zita Isa Silverman, Aug. 16, 1959; children: Barbara, Irene, Shelly. AB, Columbia U., 1952, BSEE, 1953, MSEE, 1954, PhD, 1957. Registered profl. engr., Calif. Instr. Columbia U., N.Y.C., 1953-57, asst. prof., 1957-61; head control lab. Melpar, Inc., Watertown, Mass., 1961-62; prin. scientist Kearfott Guidance and Navigation Corp. (formerly The Singer Co.), Little Falls, N.J., 1962-90; disting. prof. N.J. Inst. Tech., Newark, 1990—. Adj. prof. Columbia U., 1965-72, NYU, 1970-73, Poly. U. (formerly Poly. Inst. N.Y.) Bklyn., 1974-90; Lady Davis vis. prof. Technion (Israel Inst. Tech.), 1996-97. Author: Control System Design, 1986, Advanced Control System Design, 1996; co-author: Principles of Linear Networks, 1961, Linear Systems, 1965; contbr. more than 90 articles to profl. jours. Chmn. The Hilary Sch., Newark, 1965. Named to Bklyn. Tech. H.S. Hall of Fame, 1998. Fellow ASME (various offices, Oldenburger medal 1982), IEEE (disting. mem., various offices, recipient 3d millennium medal), AIAA (assoc.; assoc. editor jour.). Democrat. Jewish. Avocations: skiing, swimming, tennis, reading, sculpture. Office: NJ Inst Tech Dept Elec and Computer Engring Newark NJ 07102 E-mail: bf@njit.edu.

FRIEDLAND, BILLIE LOUISE, former human services administrator; b. Los Alamos, N.Mex., Jan. 6, 1944; d. William Jerald and Harriet Virginia (Short) Van Buskirk; m. David Friedland. BS in Edn., California U. of Pa., 1972, MS in Psychology, 1986; EdD, W.Va. U., 1998. Sales mgr., buyer Friedland's Ladies Ready-To-Wear, Monessen, Pa., 1969-72; tchr. Belle Vernon (Pa.) Area Schs., 1973-74; head social scis. dept. Yeshiva Achei Tmimim, Pitts., 1974-75; caseworker, outreach to children and their families project Fayette County Mental Health and Mental Retardation Clinic, Uniontown, Pa., 1975, ctr. supr. outreach to children and their families project, 1976; case mgr., family support svcs. coord. Diversified Human Svcs. Inc., Monessen, 1978-89, supr. cmty. living arrangements, 1989-92; grad. asst. Affiliated Ctr. for Devel. Disabilities W.Va. U., Morgantown, 1992-93, grad. asst. dept. spl. edn., 1993-98, coord. inclusive schooling project, 1998-99; asst. prof. spl. edn. Ea. Ill. U., Charleston, 1999—2002, Del. State U., 2002—. Founder 1st Infant/Toddler Day Care Project, Fayette County, 1976-78. Mem. NAACP, CEC (sponsor student chpt.), Am. Assn. Mental Retardation, Assn. Supervision & Curriculum Devel., Am. Conf. Rural Spl. Edn. (reviewer RSEQ), W.Va. Fedn. Coun. for Exceptional Children (past pres. divsn. mental retardation/devel/disabilites), Phi Delta Kappa, Sigma Rho Epsilon. Avocations: cross country skiing, canoeing, backpacking, hiking, bicycling. Office: Del State U EH 233 Edn & Human Performance 1200 N Dupont Hwy Dover DE 19901 E-mail: bfriedla@dsc.edu.

FRIEDLAND, DAVID L. industrial and organizational psychologist; b. Long Beach, Calif. BA, MS, Calif. State U., Long Beach; PhD, U. So. Calif., 1975. Instr. Calif. Sch. Profl. Psychology, L.A., 1978; personnel rsch. analyst County of Los Angeles, 1967-72; head personnel rsch. City of Los Angeles, 1972-81; prin. Friedland Assocs., 1981—. Cons. in field. Mem. Calif. Psychol. Assn. (chair divsn. indsl./orgnl. psychology 1999-2001), personnel Testing Coun. So. Calif. (bd. dirs., pres. 1986, 96), Internat. Personnel Mgmt. Assn. Assessment Coun. (bd. dirs. 1985), Western Region Intergovtl. Personnel Assessment Coun. (bd. dirs.). Avocations: golf, skiing, photography, travel. Office: Friedland & Assocs 4611 Maytime Ln Culver City CA 90230-5070 E-mail: david@FriedlandAssociates.net.

FRIEDLAND, LILLI, psychologist; b. Bad Gastein, Austria, Feb. 24, 1947; came to U.S., 1950, naturalized, 1956; d. Joseph and Marie (Bjerkenhejm) Rebhun; m. David Lee Friedland, Feb. 22, 1969; children: Jered, Elana, Ari, Micah. BA, U. Oreg., 1966; PhD, U. So. Calif., 1975. Diplomate Am. Bd Profl. Psychology. Rsch. asst. Rsch. Svc. Bur., L.A., 1968-70; cons. to Coun. Jewish Fedn., N.Y.C., 1969-70; research analyst L.A. Mental Health Dept., 1970-73; chief planning div. Office of Alcohol Abuse and Alcoholism, L.A. County, 1973-74, chief program and system evaluation, 1973-74; chief drug abuse planning L.A. County Dept. Health Svcs., 1973-76; dir. family devel. program Suicide Prevention Center, L.A., 1975-77; pres. Friedland Psychol. Assos., Inc., L.A., 1975—; cons. to pvt. secondary schs., Calif., 1973—; condr. workshops. Chairperson Devel. Disabilities Area Bd., Calif., 1977-79, Program Planning and Evaluation Com. Area Bd., 1975-77; mem. exec. com., cmty. svc. com., leadership devel. com., mem. program planning and budgeting com. Jewish Fedn. Coun., 1981—. Recipient certs. of appreciation Bd. Suprs. L.A. County, 1980, L.A. County Narcotics and Dangerous Drugs Commn., 1975; named one of Women Yr. Cetury City C. of C., 1988. Mem. APA (dir. 1986—, pres. pub. info. com., pres. media psychology divsn.), Bd. Psychology State Calif., Calif. State Psychol. Assn. chairperson div. VI media psychology, chairperson pub. info. com. 1985-87), L.A. County Psychol. Assn. (pres. 1985, bd. dirs. 1986—), L.A. County Clin. Psychol. Assn. (dir. 1980—), Assn. for Media Psychology (sec.), Women in Bus., Women's Referral Svc., Hadassah. Republican. Jewish. Home: 1216 Daniels Ave Los Angeles CA 90035-1104 Office: 2080 Century Park E Ste 1403 Los Angeles CA 90067-2017

FRIEDLAND, LOUIS N. retired communications executive; b. 1913; m. Billie Belenko; children: Eric, Joanne Roberts. BS, Bklyn. Coll., 1934; MA, NYU, 1936. Instr. psychology, 1936-41; chief adminstrn. officer VA, 1946-48; gen. mgr. U.S. Microfilm Co., 1948-52; with MCA, Inc., N.Y.C., 1952—, v.p., 1953, corp. v.p., 1968-86; v.p. MCA, Inc. (MCA TV div., distbr. Universal Studios TV programs), 1953-73; pres. MCA TV div., distbr. Universal Studios TV programs MCA, Inc., 1963-78, chmn. bd. TV div., 1978-86; retired, 1986. Past chmn. Nat. Hemphilia Found. Served as lt. USCG, 1942-46. Recipient citation for bldg. balanced and effective crews, Naval Manning Operation, 12th Naval Dist., USCG, 1946. Home: 10 Steven Ln Great Neck NY 11024-1535

FRIEDLAND, ROGER, religious studies educator, writer; b. N.Y.C., N.Y., June 20, 1947; s. Harry and Helen Friedland; m. Debra Kurtzman, July 12, 1982; children: Sarah, Hannah. PhD, U. of Wis., 1977. Prof. religious studies and sociology U. Calif., Santa Barbara, 1978—. Author: (book) To Rule Jerusalem, 2000; author: (with Robert Alford) Powers of Theory, 1985. Office: U Calif Dept Religious Studies Santa Barbara CA 93108

FRIEDLANDER, ARTHUR HENRY, oral and maxillofacial surgeon, researcher; b. Bklyn., Feb. 8, 1942; s. Edward and Nettie (Hardbrod) F.; m. Ida Kreinik, June 17, 1967; 1 child, Mark David. BA, CUNY, Bklyn., 1963; DMD, Temple U., 1967. Diplomate Am. Bd. Oral and Maxillofacial Surgery. Resident in oral and maxillofacial surgery VA Med. Ctr., Bklyn., 1967-71, chief oral and maxillofacial surgery Northport, N.Y., 1971-82; assoc. prof. surgery SUNY, Stony Brook, 1971-82; chief dental svc. VA Med. Ctr., West Los Angeles, Calif., 1982-89; prof. surgery Dental Sch. UCLA, 1982—; dir. quality assurance Hosp. Dental Svc. UCLA Med. Ctr., 1986—; chief dental, oral and maxillofacial surgery VA Med. Ctr., Sepulveda, Calif., 1989—, chief staff, 1994-96; chief dental and oral and maxillofacial surgery VA So. Calif. Sys. Clinics, 1996-99; assoc. chief staff dir. grad. med. edn. VA Greater L.A. Healthcare Sys., 1999—; prof. oral and maxillofacial surgery UCLA Sch. Dentistry, 1999—. Mem. peer review com. UCLA Med. Ctr., 1989—, mem. quality of care assessment com., 1990—; mem. admission com. UCLA Dental Sch., 1989-92. Contbr. numerous rsch. articles to profl. jours. Fellow Am. Assn. Oral and Maxillofacial Surgeons (ho. of dels. 1980-88); mem. Am. Coll. Oral and Maxillofacial Surgeons (founder 1977), N.Y. State Soc. Oral and Maxillofacial Surgeons (sec. 1979-82). Avocation: vegitarianism. Home: 12459 Marva Ave Granada Hills CA 91344-1527 Office: VA Med Ctr Chief Grad Med Edn Los Angeles CA 90073 E-mail: arthur.friedlander@med.va.gov.

FRIEDLANDER, CHARLES DOUGLAS (CHUCK FRIEDLANDER), space consultant; b. N.Y.C., Oct. 5, 1928; s. Murray L. and Jeane (Sottosanti) F.; m. Diane Mary Hutchins, May 12, 1951; children: Karen Diane, Lauren Patrice, Joan Elyse. BS, U.S. Mil. Acad., 1950; exec. mgmt. program, NASA, 1965; grad., Command and Staff Coll. USAF, 1965, Air War Coll. USAF, 1966. Commd. 2d lt. U.S. Army, 1950, advanced through grades to 1st lt., officer inf., 1950-51, resigned, 1954; mem. staff UN Forces, Trieste, Italy, 1953-54; chief astronaut support office NASA, Cape Canaveral, Fla., 1963-67; space cons. CBS News, Cape Canaveral, Fla., 1967-69; exec. asst. The White House, Washington, 1969-71. V.p. bd. dirs. Internat. Aerospace Hall of Fame, San Diego; space program cons., various cos., Boca Raton, Fla., 1967-69; mem. staff First Postwar Fgn. Ministers Conf., Berlin, 1954; radio/TV cons. space program. Author: Buying & Selling Land for Profit, 1961, Last Man at Hungnam Beach, 1952. V.p. West Point Soc., Cape Canaveral, Fla., 1964. Served to lt. col. USAFR, maj. USAR. Decorated Bronze Star V, Combat Inf. badge; co-recipient Emmy award CBS TV Apollo Moon Landing, 1960; recipient medal of honor N.Y.C., 1951. Mem. Explorer's Club, West Point Soc., Chosin Few Survivors Korea, NASA Alumni League, Nat. Space Soc. Avocations: fishing, travel.

FRIEDLANDER, D. GILBERT, lawyer; b. Hazleton, Pa., Sept. 10, 1946; BA, U. Tex., 1968, JD, 1971. Bar: Tex. 1972, N.Y. 1973. Sr. shareholder, bd. dirs. Johnson & Gibbs, 1973-91; gen. counsel Electronic Data Systems Corp., Plano, Tex., 1991—, sr. v.p., corp. sec., CSU for legal affairs, 1991—. Mem. ABA, N.Y. State Bar Assn., State Bar Tex. (corp. com., corp. banking and bus. law sect. 1980—, chmn. com. for rev. corp. tax law 1983-85), Dallas Bar Assn., Dallas Assn. Young Lawyers. Office: Electronic Data Systems Corp Mail Stop H3-3A-05 5400 Legacy Dr Plano TX 75024-3199

FRIEDLANDER, EDWARD JAY, journalist, educator; b. Portland, Maine, Apr. 24, 1945; s. Otto and Marguerite Evelyn (Smith) Friedlander; m. Roberta Kay Burford, July 12, 1975; 1 child, Erika Anne. BS, U. Wyo., 1967; MA, U. Denver, 1970; EdD, U. No. Colo., 1973. Reporter Denver Post, 1967-68, USIA, Washington, 1968-69; publicist Universal Pictures, N.Y.C., 1969-70; mag. editor Daily Times-Call, Longmont, Colo., 1970-71; media coord. Centaurus HS, Lafayette, Colo., 1972-73; asst. prof. mass communication Ctrl. Mo. State U., Warrensburg, 1973-75; from asst. prof. to assoc. prof. dept. journalism U. Ark., Little Rock, 1975—81, prof., 1981-95, chairperson dept. journalism, 1988-95; dir., prof. U. South Fla. Sch. Mass Comm., Tampa, 1995—. Cons. Bur. Indian Affairs, Washington, 1979, Ark. Press Assn., Little Rock, 1980—85; cons., editor FCC, Washington, 1979—81; adminstr. Waldo Proffitt award, 1998—. Author: (book) Excellence in Reporting, 1987, Feature Writing for Newspapers and Magazines, 1988, Feature Writing for Newspapers and Magazines, 5th edit., 2004, Modern Mass Media, 1990, Modern Mass Media, 2d rev. edit., 1994, Medios de Comunicación Social, 1992. German Acad. Exch. Svc. fellow, Bonn, 1982, European Acad. fellow, Berlin, 1984. Mem.: Soc. Profl. Journalists (officer exec. bd. Ark. profl. chpt. 1986—89, 1992—94, v.p. 1989—91, pres. 1991—92), Assn. Schs. Journalism and Mass Comm. (exec. com. 1997—2000), Assn. Edn. Journalism and Mass Comm., Kappa Tau Alpha. Office: U South Fla Sch Mass Comms CIS # 1040 4202 E Fowler Ave Tampa FL 33620-8000

FRIEDLANDER, EDWARD ROBERT, pathologist; b. Evanston, Ill., Jan. 9, 1952; s. Robert and Joanne (Hiscox) F. AB, Brown U., 1973; MD, Northwestern U., Chgo., 1977. Diplomate Am. Bd. Pathology. Pathologist, Kansas City, 1988—; chmn. dept. pathology Univ. of Health Scis. Lectr. in field; operator free disease info. svcs. online. Author: (booklets) Christian Perspectives on Evolution, 1985, William Blake's Visions, 1986. Foster parent Juvenile Corrections, Johnson City, Tenn., 1984-85; bd. dirs. Tenn. Assn. Vols. Criminal Justice, 1983-86; prison vol. Yoke Fellow, Winston Salem, 1982-83. Fellow Coll. Am. Pathologists, Am. Soc. Clin. Pathologists, Lambda Chi Alpha. Home: 7909 Tauromee Ave Kansas City KS 66112-2639 Office: 1750 Independence Ave Kansas City MO 64106-1453

FRIEDLANDER, GERHART, nuclear chemist; b. Munich, July 28, 1916; came to U.S., 1936, naturalized, 1943; s. Max O. and Bella (Forchheimer) F.; m. Gertrude Maas, Feb. 6, 1941 (dec. 1966); children: Ruth Ann F. Huart, Joan Claire F. Hurley; m. Barbara Strongin, 1983. BS, U. Calif., Berkeley, 1939, PhD, 1942; hon. docorate, Clark U., 1991; hon. doctorate, U. Mainz, Germany, 1992. Instr. U. Idaho, Moscow, 1942-43; staff Los Alamos Sci. Lab., 1943-46; research assoc. Gen. Electric Co. Research Lab., Schenectady, 1946-48; vis. lectr. Washington U., St. Louis, 1948; chemist Brookhaven Nat. Lab., Upton, N.Y., 1948-52, sr. chemist, 1952-81, 89-91, cons., 1981-89, 91-93, chmn. chemistry dept., 1968-77. Chmn. Gordon Rsch. Conf. on Nuclear Chemistry, 1954. Author: (with J.W. Kennedy) Introduction to Radiochemistry, 1949, Nuclear and Radiochemistry, 1955, (with J.M. Miller), 1964, (with E.S. Macias), 1981; editor-in-chief Sci. Spectra, 1993-2000; editor Radiochimica Acta, 1972-73; assoc. editor Ann. Rev. Nuc. Sci., 1958-67; contbr. articles to profl. jours. Recipient Alexander von Humboldt award Institut für Kernchemie, Mainz, Fed. Republic of Germany, 1978-79, 87, 92, 93. Fellow AAAS; mem. Hungarian Acad. Scis. (hon.), Nat. Acad. Sci., Am. Acad. Arts and Scis., Am. Chem. Soc. (chmn. divsn. nuclear chemistry and tech. 1967, award for nuclear applications in chemistry 1967). Achievements include research in chemical effects of nuclear transformations, properties of radioactive isotopes, mecha-

nisms of nuclear reactions, especially those induced by protons of very high energies; solar neutrino detection; cluster impact phenomena. Home: 22 St Charles Pl South Setauket NY 11720 E-mail: gerfried@earthlink.net.

FRIEDLANDER, JAMES STUART, lawyer; b. Chgo., Mar. 25, 1942; s. Earle E. and Sally J. (Meyer) F.; m. Sherfunissa Hassen, Sept. 27, 1969 (div. 2001); children: Samantha, Melissa, Natasha, Davina. BA, U. Wis., 1963; JD, Harvard U., 1966. Bar: Ill. 1966, D.C. 1979. Internat. legal advisor ministry external affairs Govt. of Malawi, Blantyre, 1968-71; counsel World Bank, Washington, 1972-73; mgr. Citibank, N.A., Nairobi, Kenya, 1973-78; assoc. Duncan, Allen and Mitchell, Nairobi, 1978-80, ptnr. Washington, 1980-88, Mitchell, Friedlander & Gittleman, Washington, 1988-91, Akin, Gump, Strauss, Hauer & Feld, LLP, Washington, 1991—2000, resident ptnr. Moscow, 1994-97. Bd. dirs. DAMconsult Ltd., Washington, Internat. Eye Found., Washington, 1990-94. Editor: Malawi Treaty Series, 1964-71, 1971. Vice chmn. Kenya Lawn Tennis Assn., Nairobi, 1981-83; vol. Peace Corps, Blantyre, 1966-68. Mem. ABA, Am. Soc. Internat. Law, Fed. Bar Assn. (chmn., sub-com. on internat. investment 1987-88), Westwood Country Club. Jewish. Avocations: tennis, piano, travel.

FRIEDLANDER, JOHN BENJAMIN, mathematician, educator; b. Toronto, Can., Oct. 4, 1941; s. Daniel Theodore and Beatrice Adele (Axler) Friedlander; m. Cheryl Lynn Thompson, Sept. 1, 1974; children: Jonathan, Diana, Amanda, Keith. BSc, U. Toronto, 1965; MA, U. Waterloo, Ont., Can., 1966; PhD, Pa. State U., 1972. Asst. to A. Selberg, Inst. Advanced Study, Princeton, NJ, 1972-73, mem. Sch. Math, 1973-74, 83-84, 95-96, 99-2000; lectr., dept. math MIT, Cambridge, 1974-76; vis. prof. Scuola Normale Superiore, Pisa, Italy, 1976-77; from asst. prof. to assoc. prof. U. Toronto, 1977—82, prof. math, 1982—, chair dept. math., 1987-91; lectr. U. Ill., Urbana, 1979-80; rsch. prof. Math Sci. Rsch. Inst., Berkeley, Calif., 1991-92. Mem. grant selection com. Nat. Scis. and Engring. Rsch. Coun. Can., 1991—94; lectr. ICM, 1994; mem. sci. adv. bd. Field Inst. Rsch. Math. Sci., 1996—2000; math. convenor Royal Soc. Can., 1990—93; mem. gen. assembly Internat Math. Union, 1994; lectr. in field. Mem. editl. bd. 3 jours. in field; contbr. articles and revs. to profl. jours. Recipient CRM Fields prize, 2002; Acad. Sci. fellow, Royal Soc. Can., 1988—, Killam Rsch. fellow, 2003—. Mem.: Can. Math. Soc. (Jeffery-Williams prize lectr. 1999), Am. Math. Soc. Avocations: bridge, chess, sailing, barbecue. Home: 22 Stonemanse Ct Scarborough ON Canada M1G 3V3 Office: U Toronto Dept Math Toronto ON Canada M5S 3G3 also: Scarborough Coll Dept of Math Scarborough ON Canada M1C 1A4 Fax: (416) 978-4107. E-mail: frdlndr@math.toronto.edu.

FRIEDLANDER, MICHAEL WULF, physicist, educator; b. Cape Town, South Africa, Nov. 15, 1928; came to U.S., 1956; m. Jessica R. Friedlander; 2 children. BS in Physics, U. Cape Town, 1948, MS with 1st class honors, 1950; PhD in Physics, U. Bristol (Eng.), 1955. Jr. lectr. U. Cape Town, 1950-52; rsch. assoc. U. Bristol, 1954-56; asst. prof. physics Washington U., St. Louis, 1956-61, assoc. prof., 1961-67, prof., 1967—. Author: The Conduct of Science, 1972, Astronomy: From Stonehenge to Quasars, 1985, Cosmic Rays, 1989, At the Fringes of Science, 1995, A Thin Cosmic Rain, 2000; contbr. articles to Ency. Brit. and profl. jours. Guggenheim Found. fellow, vis. prof. Imperial Coll., London, 1962-63. Mem. AAUP (2d v.p. 1978-80, mem. nat. coun. 1975-78, 86-89), AAAS, Am. Phys. Soc., Am. Astron. Soc., History of Sci. Soc. Achievements include research in elementary particles, cosmic rays, infrared astronomy, and gamma ray astronomy. Office: Washington U Dept Physics One Brookings Dr Saint Louis MO 63130

FRIEDLANDER, PATRICIA ANN, marketing professional, writer; b. Chgo., May 9, 1944; d. James Farrell and Therese Mary (Pfeiler) Crotty; m. Daniel B. Friedlander, July 3, 1971 (div. Apr. 1978); children: Michael Derek, David Colin; m. Lisa Tolva, Sept. 23, 2000. BA, Cardinal Stritch Coll., 1966; MA, U. Wis., Milw., 1968; postgrad., U. Chgo., 1968-69, U. London, 1968—. Instr. U. Wis., Milw., 1966-68, Chgo. State U., 1968-71, Argo Cmty. H.S., Summit, Ill., 1971-73, Park Dist., Park Forest South, Ill., 1973-77; counselor Will County Mental Health Clinic, Park Forest South, 1977-78; sales rep. Prentice-Hall, Inc., Englewood Cliffs, N.J., 1978-84; nat. sales mgr. Dow Jones-Irwin, Homewood, Ill., 1984-87; dir. mktg. Nat. Textbook Co., Lincolnwood, Ill., 1987-88; mgr. mktg. Scott Foresman & Co., Glenview, Ill., 1988-90; corp. advt. dir. Giltspur, Inc., Itasca, Ill., 1990-96; dir. Mktg. Comms. Exhibitgroup/Gitspur, Roselle, Ill., 1996-98; sales exec. Derse Exhibits, Chgo., 1998-99; dir. mktg. Exhibitor Mag. Group, 1999-2000; pres. Word-Up! Comms., 2000—. Dir. Printer's Row Bookfair, Chgo., 1985; cons.; spkr. and author in trade show. Den mother Cub Scouts Am., Park Forest South, 1981-84. Mem. Bus. Mktg. Assn., Health Care Conv. and Exhibitors Assn., Trade Show Exhibitors Assn. Avocations: piano, reading, cycling, swimming. Home and Office: Word-Up! 2320 W Farwell Ave Chicago IL 60645-4735 E-mail: pat@patfriedlander.com.

FRIEDLANDER, SHELDON KAY, chemical engineering educator; b. N.Y.C., Nov. 17, 1927; s. Irving and Rose (Katzewitz) F.; m. Marjorie Ellen Robbins, Apr. 16, 1934; children: Eva Kay, Amelie Elise, Antonia Zoe, Josiah. BS, Columbia U., 1949; SM, MIT, 1951; PhD, U. Ill., 1954. Asst. prof. chem. engring. Columbia U., N.Y.C., 1954-57, Johns Hopkins, Balt., 1957-59, assoc. prof. chem. engring., 1959-62, prof. chem. engring., 1962-64; prof. chem. engring., environ. health engring. Calif. Inst. Tech., Pasadena, 1964-78; prof. chem. engring. UCLA, 1978—, Parsons prof., 1982—, chmn. dept. chem. engring., 1984-88, chmn. steering com. Ctr. for Clean Tech., 1989-92. Chmn. EPA Clean Air Sci. Adv. Com., 1978-82. Author: Smoke, Dust, and Haze: Fundamentals of Aerosol Dynamics, 2nd edit., 2000. Served with U.S. Army, 1946-47. Recipient Sr. Humboldt prize Fed. Republic of Germany, 1985, Internat. prize Am. Assn. for Aerosol Rsch./Gesellschaft für Aerosolforschung/Japan Assn. for Aerosol Sci. and Tech., Fuchs Meml. award, 1990, Christian Junge award European Aerosol Assn., 2000; Fulbright scholar, 1960-61; Guggenheim fellow, 1969-70. Mem.: AIChE (Colburn award 1959, Alpha Chi Sigma award 1974, Walker award 1979, Lawrence K. Cecil award in environ. chem. engring. 1995, Particle Tech. Forum Lifetime Achievement award 2001), NAE, Am. Assn. for Aerosol Rsch. (pres. 1984—86). Office: UCLA Dept Chem Engring 5531 Boelter Hl Los Angeles CA 90095-0001

FRIEDMAN, ALAN E. lawyer; b. N.Y.C., May 5, 1946; BA, Amherst Coll., 1967; JD, Stanford U., 1970. Bar: Calif. 1971. Ptnr. Tuttle & Taylor, L.A., 1970—. Note editor: Stanford Law Rev., 1969-70 Office: Ste 4600 555 W 5th St Los Angeles CA 90013-3002

FRIEDMAN, ALAN HERBERT, ophthalmologist; b. N.Y.C., 1937; m. Sandra Yasser, 1960; children: David, Jonathan, Lisa, Jennifer. BA in Chemistry with honors, Cornell U., 1959; MD, NYU, 1963. Diplomate Am. Bd. Ophthalmology (assoc. examiner). Intern in medicine Bellevue Hosp., N.Y.C., 1963-64; resident in ophthalmology NYU Med. Ctr., 1966-69, fellow ophthalmic pathology, 1969-70; rsch. fellow histochemistry Royal Postgrad. Med. Sch., London, 1972; practice medicine specializing in ophthalmology N.Y.C., 1970—; attending ophthalmologist and pathologist Mt. Sinai Hosp.; attending ophthalmologist Beth Israel Med. Ctr.; clin. prof. ophthalmology and pathology, dir. eye path. lab. Mt. Sinai Sch. Medicine. Cons. in field. Contbr. numerous articles to profl. publs. With M.C. USAR, 1964-66. Recipient Summer fellow NIH, 1960, 62-63). Fellow ACS, Royal Coll. Ophthalmologists London, Am. Acad. Ophthalmology (Sr. Honor award 1991), N.Y. Acad. Medicine, N.Y. Acad. Scis., Royal Soc. Medicine; mem. AMA, Am. Ophthal. Soc., French Ophthalmology, Am. Assn. Ophthalmic Pathologists (pres. 1992-94), N.Y. County Med. Soc., Med. Soc. State N.Y., Verhoeff Soc., Eastern Ophthalmic Pathology Soc., Pan Am. Assn. Ophthalmology. Address: Mt Sinai Sch Medicine Box 1183 1 Gustave L Levy Pl New York NY 10029-6500 also: 888 Park Ave New York NY 10021-0235

FRIEDMAN, ALAN HOWARD, writer, educator; b. N.Y.C., Jan. 4, 1928; s. Harry Morris and Mina F.; m. Lenore Ann Helman Friedman, Aug. 1, 1950 (div. July 15, 1967); 1 child, Gregory Lawrence Friedman; m. Kate Miller Gilbert Friedman, Oct. 30, 1977; 1 child, Alexander Nicholas Friedman. BA magna cum laude, Harvard Coll., Cambridge, Mass., 1949; MA, Columbia U., N.Y.C., 1950; PhD, U. Calif. Berkeley, 1964. Asst. prof. Columbia U., N.Y.C., 1965-67; assoc. prof. Swarthmore (Pa.) Coll., 1967-70; vis. assoc. prof. Queens Coll., CUNY, 1973-75; prof. U. Ill. at Chgo., 1978-99. Exec. bd. mem. Am. Pen Midwest, Chgo., 1985-89. Author: Hermaphrodeity, 1972, The Turn of the Novel, 1966, (book reviews) N.Y. Times Book Review, 1972-91, contbr. chpts. to books; author of short stories, poems and articles. Nominee Nat. Book award, 1972; recipient D.H. Lawrence fellowship, 1974, award, Nat. Endowment in the Arts, 1975, PEN Syndicated Fiction Project, 1987; Ill. Arts Coun., 1992, Grand prize, Nat. Libr. Poetry, 1998, Best Actor award, ACT, 2001. Home: 3530 Monte Real Escondido CA 92029-7910

FRIEDMAN, ALAN ROY, lawyer; b. N.Y.C., Mar. 18, 1953; s. Oscar B. and Helen (Rosenkrantz) F.; m. Maya Memling, Sept. 3, 1978; 1 child, Charles. AB, Hamilton Coll., 1973; JD, Yale U., 1976. Law clk. to Hon. M. Joseph Blumenfeld U.S. Dist. Ct., Hartford, 1976-77; assoc. Kramer Levin Naftalis & Frankel LLP, N.Y.C., 1977-84, ptnr., 1984—. Office: Kramer Levin Naftalis & Frankel LLP 919 3rd Ave New York NY 10022-3902 E-mail: afriedman@kramerlevin.com.

FRIEDMAN, ALAN WARREN, humanities educator; b. Bklyn., June 8, 1939; s. Leon and Anne (Markowitz) F.; m. Elizabeth Butler Cullingford, Nov. 22, 1985; children: Eric Lawrence, Scot Bradley, Lorraine Eve, Daniel Butler. Student, U. Edinburgh, Scotland, 1960-61; BA, Queens Coll., 1961; MA, NYU, 1962; PhD, U. Rochester, 1966. Grad. teaching asst. U. Rochester, 1963-64; from instr. English to prof. U. Tex., Austin, 1964—2001, dir. honors program, 1972-76, chmn. faculty senate, 1987-89, endowed prof., 2001—. Sr. Fulbright prof. U. Lancaster, Eng., 1977-78, Univ. Coll., Galway, Ireland, 1995; exch. prof. Universite Paul Valery, Montpellier, France, 1985, U. Paris, Sorbonne, 2000. Author: Lawrence Durrell and the Alexandria Quartet, 1970, Multivalence: The Moral Quality of Form in the Modern Novel, 1978, William Faulkner, 1984, Fictional Death and the Modernist Enterprise, 1995, Beckett in Black and Red: The Translations for Nancy Cunard's "Negro", 2000; editor books; contbr. essays and revs. to profl. jours. Chair Dem. Precinct Com.; del. state convs.; founder, 1st pres. Neighborhood Assn., Austin, 1973-74; bd. dirs. Peace Edn. Ctr., Hillel Found., Austin Hospice, Frontline Theatre Co. Recipient Fulbright Rsch. award, 1995, 1984-85, Travel award France, 1990; NEH fellow, 1970-71. Mem. MLA (del. assembly 1977-79, 82-84, 94-96, exec. com. divsn. on 20th century English lit. 1992-96), AAUP (pres. U. Tex. chpt. 1979-84, nat. coun. 1989-92, nat. exec. com. 1991-92, chair com. governance 1992-95), Tex. Higher Edn. Coord. Bd. (chair faculty adv. com. 1992-95), Tex. Assn. Coll. Tchrs., Nat. Collegiate Honors Coun., Fulbright Alumni Assn. (pres. ctrl. Tex. chpt.), Omicron Delta Kappa. Democrat. Jewish. Office: U Tex Dept English Austin TX 78712 E-mail: friedman@uts.cc.utexas.edu.

FRIEDMAN, ALVIN, lawyer; b. Bklyn., June 19, 1931; s. Isidor and Freda F.; m. Maryann Kallison, Mar. 27, 1955; children: Alan K., Margot N. BA with honors in Polit. Sci, Cornell U., 1952; LL.B. cum laude (editor Law Jour. 1956-57), Yale U., 1957. Bar: Tex. 1957, D.C. 1957. Asso. firm Covington & Burling, 1957-63; spl. asst. to gen. counsel Dept. Def., 1963-64, spl. asst. to asst. sec. def. for def. for internat. security affairs, 1964, dep. asst. sec. def. for internat. security affairs Far East and Latin Am., 1964-66; ptnr. Ginsburg & Feldman, Washington, 1966-67, Friedman and Medalie and predecessor firms, Washington, 1967-87; pvt. practice law Washington, 1988—. Served as 1st lt. USAF, 1952-54. Mem. Tex., D.C. bar assns. Office: 700 New Hampshire Ave NW Washington DC 20037-2406

FRIEDMAN, ALVIN EDWARD, investment executive; b. N.Y.C., Aug. 8, 1919; s. Harry and Frances (Levin) F.; m. Pesselle Rothenberg, Feb. 2, 1943; children: Jeffrey F., Joan M. BBA, CCNY, 1942, MBA, NYU, 1949. Ptnr. Kuhn Loeb & Co., N.Y.C., 1951-78; sr. mng. dir. Lehmann Bros. Kuhn Loeb, N.Y.C., 1978-84; dir. Dillon Read & Co., N.Y.C., 1984-86, sr. advisor, 1986—. Bd. dirs. Dreyfus Corp., Avnet, Inc. Pres. Hebrew Arts Sch., N.Y. Served to 1st lt. USAAF, 1943-46, PTO. Home: 101 Del Pond Dr Canton MA 02021-2753 Office: Dillon Read & Co 535 Madison Ave New York NY 10022-4212

FRIEDMAN, ANDREW MITCHELL, director housing and neighborhood preservation; b. N.Y.C., Jan. 29, 1950; BA, Antioch U., 1972; MS, U. Wis., 1984. Asst. dir. ARC, Green Bay, Wis., 1982-86; analyst City of Va. Beach, Va., 1986-89, housing devel. adminstr., 1989-93, dir. housing and neighborhood preservation, 1993—. Mem. allocations com. United Way of S. Hampton Rds., Norfolk; pres. Va. Assn. Housing and Cmty. Devel. Ofcls., 2001—. Office: City of Va Beach Mcpl Ctr Bldg 18A Virginia Beach VA 23456 E-mail: afriedma@vbgov.com.

FRIEDMAN, ARNOLD CARL, radiologist; b. Bronx, N.Y., Nov. 17, 1951; s. Isidore and Helen (Lowenthal) Friedman; m. Poornima Mukerji; children: Jeffrey, Jonathan, Leela. BA in Chemistry, Cornell U., 1972; MD, Albert Einstein Coll., 1975. Intern Mt. Sinai Hosp., Hartford, Conn., 1975-76; resident Montefiore Hosp., Bronx, 1976-79; asst. prof. Uniformed Svcs. U., Bethesda, Md., 1979-83; assoc. prof. George Washington U., Washington, 1983-84, Temple U., Phila., 1984-88, prof. radiology, 1989-92; prof. Med. Coll. Pa. Hahnemann U., Phila., 1992-96, acting chmn. radiology scis., 1992-93, chmn. radiology scis., 1993-95, dir. radiology rsch. Med. Coll., 1996-97; chief radiology svcs. Med. Coll. Pa. Hosp., 1996-97; prof. radiology Allegheny U. Health Scis., 1996-97; assoc. chmn. dept. radiology Beth Israel Med. Ctr., N.Y.C., 1997-99, U. Fla., 2000—; chmn. dept. radiology Shands-Jacksonville Hosp., 2000—. Editor: (book) Radiology of Liver, Spleen, Pancreas, Billiary Tract, 1987, Radiology of the Liver Billiary Tract and Pancreas, 1993. Fellow: Am. Coll. Radiology; mem.: Soc. Gastrointestinal Radiology, Assn. Ultrasound Medicine, Assn. Univ. Radiologists, Am. Roentgen Ray Soc., Radiologic Soc. N.Am. Avocations: tennis, basketball, ice skating, skiing, fitness. E-mail: arnief51@yahoo.com.

FRIEDMAN, ARTHUR DANIEL, electrical engineering and computer science educator, investment management company executive; b. Bronx, N.Y., Apr. 24, 1940; s. Henry and Yetta Friedman; m. Barbara Allyn Bernstein, Mar. 31, 1968; children: Michael Kenneth, Steven David. BA, Columbia U., 1961, BS, 1962, MEE, 1963, PhD, 1965. Tech. staff Bell Labs., Murray Hill, N.J., 1965-72; assoc. prof. elec. engring. and computer sci. U. So. Calif., L.A., 1972-77; prof. George Washington U., Washington, 1977-97, dept. chmn., 1980-84, prof. emeritus, 1997—. Vis. prof. U. Calif., San Diego, 1999, 2002, 03; chmn. bd., co-founder Computer Sci. Press of W.H. Freeman and Co., Rockville, Md., 1974-88, co-editor-in-chief, 1988-89; dir. Gen. Microwave Corp., 1987-94; co-founder, pres. investment mgmt. co. ABF Enterprises, Friedman Family Found. Inc., ABF Capital Mgmt.; pres. Market Mavens, 1998-2001; gen. ptnr. Potomac Ptnrs. LP, 1991; mem. Aztec Venture Networks, 2000-2001, Tech Coast Angels, 1999-2001; mem. adv. com. on elec. engring. San Diego (Calif.) State U., 2003—. Author: (with Premanchandra Menon) Fault Detection in Digital Circuits, 1971, Theory and Design of Switching Circuits, 1975, Logical Design of Digital Systems, 1975, Fundamentals of Logic Design and Switching Theory, 1986; (with Melvin Breuer) Diagnosis of Digital Systems, 1976; (with Miron Abramovici and Melvin Breuer) Digital System Testing and Testable Design, 1990, 2d edit., 1995. Pres. Friedman Family Found. Inc. Fellow IEEE; mem. Market Mavens. Avocations: tennis, reading, swimming. Home: 4969 Beauchamp Ct San Diego CA 92130-2742

FRIEDMAN, AVERY S. lawyer; b. Walla Walla, Wash., Aug. 5, 1945; s. Joseph H. and Marjorie (Greentree) F.; m. Betsey Nims, Dec. 28, 1968; children: Erika Grace, Joey Nims, Tyler Joseph. BA, U. Louisville, 1968; JD, Cleve. State U., 1973. Bar: U.S. Ct. Appeals (6th cir.) 1974, U.S. Ct. Appeals (4th cir.) 1986, U.S. Ct. Appeals (1st cir.) 1987, U.S. Supreme Ct. 1977. Assoc. dir. Lawyers for Housing, 1972-75; chief counsel The Housing Advocates, Inc., 1975-82, Fair Housing Coun. N.E. Ohio, 1990—; atty. Friedman & Assocs., Cleve. Adj. law faculty Cleve. State U., 1973-75, asst. adj. prof. urban affairs, 1975—; vis. lectr. U. Mich., Stanford U., Duke U., U. Calif., Berkeley, U. Tex., U. N.C., U. Hawaii, U. Wis., numerous others; cons. to HUD, EEOC, State of Tex., also various human rights commns. and couns. on civil rights, others; legal cons. Office of Gen. Counsel, Nat. NAACP, 1986; spl. counsel State of Tex. Atty. Gen. and Commn. on Human Rights, 1992—; spl. counsel to pres. Internat. Assn. Office Human Rights Agys., 1996—. Office: 701 City Club Bldg 850 Euclid Ave Cleveland OH 44114-3358

FRIEDMAN, AVNER, mathematician, educator; b. Petah-Tikva, Israel, Nov. 19, 1932; arrived in U.S., 1956; s. Moshe and Hanna (Rosenthal) Friedman; m. Lilia Lynn, June 7, 1959; children: Alissa, Joel, Naomi, Tamara. MSc, Hebrew U., Jerusalem, 1954, PhD, 1956. Prof. math. Northwestern U., Evanston, Ill., 1962—85; prof. Purdue U., West Lafayette, Ind., 1985—87, dir. Ctr. Applied Math., 1985—87; prof. math., dir. Inst. Math. and Its Applications U. Minn., Mpls., 1987-97, dir. Minn. Ctr. for Indsl. Math., 1994—2002; prof. Ohio State U., Columbus, 2002—; dir. Math. Bioscis. Inst., 2002—. Author: (book) Generalized Functions and Partial Differential Equations, 1963, Partial Differential Equations of Parabolic Type, 1964, Partial Differential Equations, 1969, Foundations of Modern Analysis, 1970, Advanced Calculus, 1971, Differential Games, 1971, Stochastic Differential Equations and Applications, Vol. 1, 1975, Vol. 2, 1976, Variational Principle's and Free Boundary Problems, 1983, Mathematics in Industrial Problems, 10 vols., 1988—98; author: (with D.S. Ross) Mathematical Models in Photographic Science, 2001; contbr. articles to profl. jours. Recipient Creativity award, NSF, 1983—85, 1990—92; fellow, Sloan Found., 1962—65, Guggenheim, 1966—67. Mem.: NAS, AAAS, Soc. Indsl. Applied Math. (pres. 1993, 1994, chmn bd. math. scis. 1994—97), Am. Math. Soc. Office: Ohio State U Math Dept 231 18th Ave Columbus OH 43210 Business E-Mail: afriedman@mbi.osu.edu.

FRIEDMAN, BARBARA BERNSTEIN, investor, money manager, glass artist, speaker; b. N.Y.C., June 6, 1946; d. Allan Charles and Frances Bernstein; married Mar. 31, 1968; children: Michael Kenneth, Steven David. BA in Polit. Sci., NYU, 1968; Student, Rutgers U., 1968—69, U. So. Calif., 1974. Computer programmer Prudential Life Ins., Newark, N.J., 1968; co-founder, publisher, pres. Computer Sci. Press, Inc., Rockville, Md., 1976-88; editor in chief Computer Sci. Press, W. H. Freeman and Co., 1988-89; co-founder, chmn. of bd., v.p. ABF Ent., Inc. doing bus. as Potomac Ptnrs., Potomac, 1991—97; gen. ptnr. Potomac Ptnrs., 1991—; mem. San Diego Chmn.'s Roundtable, 2001—. Judge student bus. plan competition San Diego (Calif.) State U., 2002—03; spkr. in field. Sec., Nat. Children's Book coun., N.Y.C., 1964. N.Y. State Regents scholar, 1964; recipient 2d pl. Hot Glass, "Glass Art 92," Longview (Tex.) Mus. Mem. IEEE (assoc.), Pi Sigma Alpha (pres. 1968). Avocations: reading, fused glass, holography, metal sculpture. Home: 4969 Beauchamp Ct San Diego CA 92130-2742 E-mail: adfbbf@san.rr.com.

FRIEDMAN, BARRY DAVID, political scientist, educator; b. Meriden, Conn., Sept. 29, 1953; s. Edward Louis and Esia (Baran) F.; m. Cynthia Joy Landis, July 8, 1990 (div. Feb. 17, 2003). BA in Polit. Sci., BS in Engring., U. Hartford, 1976; MPA, MBA, U. Conn., 1983, PhD in Polit. Sci., 1991. Forecasting analyst Northeast Utilities, Berlin, Conn., 1976-82; pers. specialist ARC, Fairfax, Va., 1986-87; asst. prof. polit. sci. Valdosta (Ga.) State U., 1987-92; prof. polit. sci. North Ga. Coll. & State U., Dahlonega, 1992—; dir. MPA program North Ga. Coll., Dahlonega. Conf. presentations, 1988—. Author: Regulation in the Reagan-Bush Era: The Eruption of Presidential Influence, 1995; book rev. editor Internat. Social Sci. Rev., 2002—; contbr. articles to profl. jours. Nat. instr.-trainer ARC 1990-96. Recipient Outstanding Lt. Gov. award New Eng. dist. Key Club Internat., 1971, Phi Kappa Phi Promotion of Excellence in Higher Edn. award, 1999, Disting. Prof. award North Ga. Coll. and State U. Alumni Assn., 1997, 2002; named Bd. Mem. of Yr., ARC, Valdosta, 1991. Mem. ASPA (life, sec.-treas., pres., editor Ga. chpt. 1994—), Ga. Polit. Sci. Assn. (exec. bd. 1997-99), Am. Red Magen David for Israel (internat. life, nat. adv. coun., 2002—), Phi Beta Kappa, Phi Kappa Phi (chpt. pres. 1989-90), Pi Alpha Alpha, Pi Sigma Alpha, Pi Gamma Mu (gov. Ga. 1995-2002, vice chancellor Atlantic region 1999-2002, chancellor, 2002—), Beta Gamma Sigma, Alpha Chi, Kappa Mu, Omicron Delta Kappa, Alpha Kappa Delta. Jewish. Office: North Ga Coll & State U Dept Polit Sci Dahlonega GA 30597-0001 E-mail: bfriedman@ngcsu.edu.

FRIEDMAN, BARRY HOWARD, lawyer, physician; b. Joplin, Mo., Mar. 18, 1945; s. Marion and Esther (Lerner) Friedman; m. Marshal Lee Rosenthal, June 25, 1967; children: Heather Michelle, Jarrod David. BA, Western Md. Coll., 1965; MD, U. Md., 1969; JD, U. Balt., 1987, 1987; MBA, U. Balt., 1999. Bar: Md. 1987, Pa. 1987; diplomate Am. Bd. Radiology, Am. Bd. Nuc. Medicine, Am. Bd. Legal Medicine, Nat. Bd. Medicine Examiners. Intern Washington Hosp. Ctr., 1969-70; resident Sinai Hosp., Balt., 1970-73, fellow in diagnostic radiology, 1982-83; fellow in nuclear medicine Johns Hopkins Hosp., Balt., 1973-74, assoc. attending radiologist, 1983-88; pres. Chesapeake Imaging Specialists, Pikesville, Md., 1986-89; attending radiologist Northwest Hosp. Ctr., 1988-95, MRI Ctr. at Northwest Hosp. Ctr., 1990-98; physician adminstr. dept. health and mental hygiene State of Md., 1998—. Adj. prof. bus. law U. Balt., 1999—. Scholar France-Berrick Grad. Bus. scholar, 1997, 1998. Fellow: Am. Coll. Angiology, Am. Coll. Legal Medicine; mem.: ABA, Bar Assn. Balt. City, Baltimore County Med. Soc., Md. Soc. Radiology, Md. Trial Lawyers, Radiol. Soc. N.Am., Soc. Nuc. Medicine, Am. Coll. Radiology, Am. Coll. Physician Execs., Sigma Iota Epsilon. Home: 6 Green Heather Ct Pikesville MD 21208-1516 Office: DHMH Rm 135 212 W Preston St Baltimore MD 21201-2323

FRIEDMAN, BART, lawyer; b. NYC, Dec. 5, 1944; s. Philip and Florence (Beckerman) F.; m. Wendy Alpern Stein, Jan. 11, 1986; children: Benjamin Alpern, Jacob Stein. AB, L.I. U., 1966; JD, Harvard U., 1969. Bar: N.Y. 1970, Mass. 1972. Rsch. fellow Harvard U. Bus. Sch., Cambridge, Mass., 1969-70; assoc. Cahill, Gordon & Reindel, N.Y.C., 1970-72, 77-80, ptnr., 1980—; spl. counsel SEC, Washington, 1974-75, asst. dir., 1975-77. Bd. dirs. Calif. Inst. for the Arts. Active Ind. Task Force on Post-Conflict Iraq, 2003—; vis. com. Harvard U. Grad. Sch. Edn., 1995—2001, com. on univ. resources, 1996—; trustee Juilliard Sch., 1988—2001, vice chmn., 1994—2001; trustee Brookings Inst., 1997—, chmn. N.Y. adv. com., 1997—2001, mem. coun. fgn. rels., 1995—, joint task force on resources for fgn. affairs, ind. task force on non-lethal weapons; del. NATO Hdqrs. and Field, 1998, 2003; adv. bd. Remarque Inst. NYU, 1997—2002, Internat. Inst. for Strategic Studies, 2000; bd. dirs. Lincoln Ctr. for Performing Arts, 2002—, trustee, 2002—, Bretton Woods Com., 2003—. Mem. Assn. Bar City of N.Y., Coun. Fgn. Rels., Explorers Club, The River Club, Links Club, The Tuxedo Club, Century Assn., The Met. Club (Washington). Home: 1172 Park Ave Apt 5B New York NY 10128-1213 Office: Cahill Gordon & Reindel 80 Pine St Fl 17 New York NY 10005-1790

FRIEDMAN, BARTON ROBERT, English educator; b. Bklyn., Feb. 5, 1935; s. Abraham Isaac and Mazie Diana (Cooper) F.; m. Sheila Lynn Siegel, June 22, 1958; children— Arnold, Jonathan, Daniel, Esther. BA, Cornell U., 1956, PhD (univ. dissertation fellow), 1964; MA, U. Conn., 1958. Instr. Bowdoin Coll., Brunswick, Maine, 1961-63; from instr. to prof. English lit. U. Wis., Madison, 1963-78; prof. English lit. Cleve. State U., 1978-97, chmn. dept. English, 1978-87, prof. emeritus, 1997—. Visitor Psychoanalytic Inst. Cleve. Author: Adventures in the Deeps of the Mind: The Cuchulain Cycle of W.B. Yeats, 1977, You Can't Tell the Players, 1979, Fabricating History: English Writers on the French Revolution, 1988 (Nancy Dasher award for best scholarly book by mem. Coll. English Assn. Ohio 1989); mem. editl. bd. Irish Renaissance Ann., 1980-84, Lit. Monographs, 1970-76. Recipient William Kiekhofer Teaching Excellence award U. Wis., 1967, Disting. Scholar award Cleve. State U., 1990. Mem. MLA, Am. Com. Irish Studies, Coll. English Assn. Ohio (bd. govs. 1980-81), Soc. Lit. and Sci. (bibliographer Bibliography of Lit. and Sci. in Configurations 1996-98), Phi Kappa Phi. Jewish. Home: 2916 E Overlook Rd Cleveland OH 44118-2434 Office: Cleve State Univ Dept English Cleveland OH 44115 E-mail: sheilaf@stratos.net.

FRIEDMAN, BENJAMIN MORTON, economics educator; b. Louisville, Ky., Aug. 5, 1944; s. Norbert and Eva (Lipsky) F.; m. Barbara Allan Cook, Dec. 17, 1972; children: John Norton, Jeffrey Allan. AB summa cum laude, Harvard U., 1966, AM, 1969, PhD, 1971; MSc King's Coll., Cambridge U., 1970. Economist Morgan Stanley & Co., N.Y.C., 1971-72; asst. prof. econs. Harvard U., Cambridge, Mass., 1972-76, assoc. prof., 1976-80, prof., 1980-89, William Joseph Maier prof. polit. economy, 1989—, chmn. dept. of econs., 1991-94. Dir. fin. markets and monetary econs. Nat. Bur. Econ. Rsch., Cambridge, 1977—93; dir. Pvt. Export Funding Corp., NYC, 1981—, Britannica.com, 2000—. Author: Economic Stabilization Policy, 1975, Monetary Policy in the United States, 1981, Day of Reckoning, 1988; co-author: Does Debt Management Matter?, 1992; editor: New Challenges to the Role of Profits, 1978, The Changing Roles of Debt and Equity in Financing U.S. Capital Formation, 1982, Corporate Capital Structures in the United States, 1985, Financing Corporate Capital Formation, 1986, Handbook on Monetary Economics, 1990; assoc. editor Jour. Monetary Econs., 1977-95. Trustee Coll. Retirement Equities Fund, N.Y.C., 1978-82, Standish Mellon Investment, 1989—; dir. Am. Friends of Cambridge U., 1994-2000. Marshall scholar Cambridge U., 1966-68; Soc. Fellows jr.

fellow Harvard U., 1968-71. Mem. Coun. Fgn. Rels., Brookings Panel Econ. Activity, Am. Econ. Assn., Harvard Club N.Y.C. Home: 74 Sparks St Cambridge MA 02138-2238 Office: Harvard U 127 Littauer Center Cambridge MA 02138

FRIEDMAN, BERNARD ALVIN, federal judge; b. Detroit, Sept. 23, 1943; s. David and Rae (Garber) F.; m. Rozanne Golston, Aug. 16, 1970; children: Matthew, Megan. Student, Detroit Inst. Tech., 1962-65; JD, Detroit Coll. Law, 1968. Bar: Mich. 1968, Fla. 1968, U.S. Dist. Ct. (ea. dist.) Mich. 1968, U.S. Ct. Mil. Appeals 1972. Asst. prosecutor Wayne County, Detroit, 1968-71; ptnr. Harrison & Friedman, Southfield, Mich., 1971-78, Lippitt, Harrison, Friedman & Whitefield, Southfield, 1978-82; judge Mich. Dist. Ct. 48th dist., Bloomfield Hills, 1982-88; U.S. dist. judge Ea. Dist. Mich., Detroit, 1988—. Lt. U.S. Army, 1967-74. Recipient Disting. Service award Oakland County Bar Assn., 1986. Avocation: running. Office: US Dist Ct US Courthouse Rm 238 231 W Lafayette Blvd Detroit MI 48226-2700

FRIEDMAN, B(ERNARD) H(ARPER), writer; b. N.Y.C., July 27, 1926; s. Leonard and Madeline (Uris) F.; m. Abby Noselson, Mar. 6, 1948; children: Jackson, Daisy. BA, Cornell U., 1948. With Cross & Brown Co., 1949-50; v.p., dir. Uris Bldgs. Corp., N.Y.C., 1950-63; lectr. creative writing Cornell U., 1966-67; staff cons., dir. Fine Arts Work Center, Provincetown, Mass., 1968-82. Founding mem. Fiction Collective, 1973—; adv. council Cornell U. Coll. Arts and Scis., 1968-83, Herbert F. Johnson Mus., 1972-87. Author: (novels) Circles, 1962 (reprinted as I Need to Love, 1963), Yarborough, 1964, Whispers, 1972, Museum, 1974, Almost A Life, 1975, The Polygamist, 1981; (stories) Coming Close, 1982, Between the Flags, 1990, Swimming Laps, 1999; (biographies) Jackson Pollock: Energy Made Visible, 1972, (with Flora Miller Biddle) Gertrude Vanderbilt Whitney, 1978, Tripping: A Memoir of Timothy Leary & Co., 2003; (plays) In Search of Luigi Pirandello, 1983 (revised as My Small Self, 1998), The Critic, 1986, Beauty Business, 1987, Tony's Case, 1991 (revised as Case History, 1994), Heart of a Boy, 1993 (adapted as screenplay with M. Benderoth, 1997), Married Moments, 1999 (revised as Should I Marrry Her?, 2003), Eros and Psyche, 2000; editor: School of New York, 1959, Morton Feldman Collected Writings 2001; mem. adv. bd. Cornell Rev., 1977-79; contbr. articles to mags., anthologies and reference vols. Trustee Am. Fedn. Arts, 1958-64, Whitney Mus. Am. Art, 1961—, Broida Mus., 1983-86. With USNR, 1944-46. Recipient awards for short stories, including Nelson Algren award, 1983; fellow Camargo Found., 1991. Mem. PEN, Authors Guild, Dramatists Guild. Clubs: Century Assn. (N.Y.C.). Home: 439 E 51st St New York NY 10022-6473 also: PO Box 338 Wainscott NY 11975-0338

FRIEDMAN, BETSY SUE, artist; b. Bklyn., Dec. 2, 1955; d. Murry Nathan and Elinor Lee (Bloom) F.; m. Robert Baker Rorick Jr., May 7, 1983. BFA, Washington U., 1978. Exhibited in group shows at Like Young, 12 N.Y. Painters Three River Arts Festival, Pitts., 1995, Work for a Funhouse E.S. Van Dam, N.Y.C., 1995, Comic Inspirations Adam Baumgold Fine Art and Simon Capstick-Dale Fine Art, 1996, Benefit Exhbn. White Columns, 1996, Scratch Thread Waxing Space, 1996, Works on Paper 7th Regiment Armory, 1996, Art Exch., 1996, 1997, Invitational Plus Adam Baumgold Fine Art, 1997, Geoffrey Young Gallery, Gt. Barrington, Mass., 2001, Adam Baumgold Gallery, N.Y.C., 2002, numerous others, one-woman shows include White Columns, N.Y.C., 1983, Mary Delahoyd Gallery, 1986, 1987, 1988, 1991, Maranushi Lederman Prodns., 1993, Adam Baumgold Fine Art, 1997.

FRIEDMAN, COLLETTE SWEET, kitchen and interior designer; b. LA, Feb. 25, 1933; children: Scott D., Brian C., Victoria A., Valaree L., Collette. Student, Los Angeles Valley Coll., 1961-63, Calif. State U., Northridge, 1964, Pierce Coll., 1965-67, UCLA, 1968-70. Lic. gen. contractor. Interior designer, North Hollywood, Calif., 1962-76; owner, designer Better Homes and Kitchens, Westlake Village, Calif., 1976—. Recipient award, Bank of Am., 1951. Mem.: Nat. Assn. Women in Constrn., Conejo Assn. Profl. Interior Designers, Nat. Kitchen and Bath Assn., Zonta Internat., Thousand Oaks-Westlake Village C. of C. Office: 32147 Beachlake Ln Westlake Village CA 91361-3607

FRIEDMAN, DANIEL MORTIMER, federal judge; b. N.Y.C., Feb. 8, 1916; s. Henry Michael F. and Julia Freedman Friedman; m. Leah Lipson, Jan. 16, 1955 (dec. Dec. 1969); m. Elizabeth Ellis, Oct. 19, 1975 (dec. June 2002). AB, Columbia U., 1937, LLB, 1940. Bar: N.Y. 1941. Practice law, N.Y.C., 1940—42; with SEC, Washington, 1942—51, Justice Dept., Washington, 1951—59, asst. to solicitor gen., 1959—62, 2d asst. to solicitor gen., 1962—68, 1st dep. solicitor gen., 1968—78; chief judge Ct. Claims and U.S. Ct. Appeals, Washington, 1978—89, sr. judge, 1989—. With U.S. Army, 1942—46. Recipient Exceptional Svc. award, Atty. Gen., 1969. Office: US Ct Appeals Federal Circuit 717 Madison Pl NW Washington DC 20439-0002

FRIEDMAN, DAVID BERNARD, psychiatrist, educator; b. N.Y.C., Nov. 15, 1922; s. Isidore and Dora (Abramowitz) F.; m. Anita Salan, Mar. 30, 1947 (dec. July 1967); children: Douglas, Andrew; m. Nancy Ryk, May 3, 1968; 1 child, Tanya. BA, NYU, 1942, MD, 1945. Diplomate Am. Bd. Psychiatry and Neurology. Asst. prof. NYU Sch. Medicine, N.Y.C., 1961-68, assoc. prof., 1968—; pvt. practice N.Y.C., 1951—. Author: The Analyst's Role, 1963; contbg. author: The Experience of Dying, 1967; contbr. sci. papers to profl. jours. Capt. U.S. Army, 1946-48. Fellow Am. Psychiat. Assn. (life), Am. Acad. Psychoanalysis; mem. Soc. Med. Psychoanalysts (pres. 1967), Phi Beta Kappa. Jewish. Avocations: photography, tennis, reading, computing. Home: 30 E 72nd St New York NY 10021-4265 Office: 20 Park Ave New York NY 10016-3893 E-mail: fried001@aol.com.

FRIEDMAN, DAVID SAMUEL, lawyer; b. Flushing, N.Y., Feb. 21, 1971; s. Stanley and Lita June (Fine) F.; m. Jennifer Katherine Sun; 1 child, Daniel James Sun-Friedman. BA magna cum laude, Harvard U., 1993; JD magna cum laude, Harvard Law Sch., 1996. Bar: Mass. 1997, N.Y. 1997, U.S. Dist. Ct. Mass. 1998, U.S. Ct. Appeals (1st cir.) 1999. Editor Harvard Law Rev., Cambridge, Mass., 1994-96, pres., 1995-96; law clerk to Justice John Paul Stevens Supreme Court, 1997-98; law clk. to Judge Michael Boudin First Cir. Ct. Appeals, 1996-97; litigation assoc. Hill & Barlow, Boston, 1998—2002; counsel, chief policy advisor Office of Senate Pres., Boston, 2002—. Line editor Environ. Law Rev., 1993-94. Election atty. Gore-Lieberman Recount Com., 2000; press sec. Mass. Dem. Party, 2000, vice-chair pub. policy com., 2001—. Harvard Nat. scholar, 1993; named World Univs. Debating Champion, 1993. Mem. ABA (vice-chair environ. justice com. 2000-02), Phi Beta Kappa. Democrat. Jewish. Avocations: cooking, tennis, football, basketball, golf. Home: 116 Lake St Brighton MA 02135 Office: State House Rm 332 Boston MA 02133

FRIEDMAN, DEBORAH LESLIE WHITE, educational administrator; b. Grand Rapids, Mich., July 5, 1950; d. Edward Charles and Luella Jane (Carr) White; children: Karen Elizabeth, David Edward. BS, Cen. Mich. U., 1972; MBA, U. Toledo, 1980; D in Higher Ednl. Adminstrn., N.C. State U., 1995. Traffic mgr. WTOL-TV, Toledo, 1972-74; catering cons. Gladieux Food Svcs., Toledo, 1974-75; mktg. rsch. analyst Owens-Ill., Toledo, 1978; instr. Sampson C.C., Clinton, N.C., 1980-81, chmn. acctg., bus. adminstrn., real estate, 1981-98, divsn. chair bus. and pub. svc. programs, 1998-2001; dean bus. programs Fayetteville Tech. C.C., 2001—03, v.p. for human resources, 2003—. Faculty advisor Phi Beta Lambda, 1981-88; adj. trainer N.C. Dept. Community Colls., Raleigh, 1989-2001; bd. dirs. Sampson County United Way, Inc., 1995-1998, State Employees Credit Union, Clinton br., 1998-2001. Bd. dirs. Found. for Edn., 1984-89, appropriations chmn., 1984-88, sec., 1988-89; com. mem. Clinton City Schs. Com. on Stds. of Excellence, 1986-87; vol. Girl Scouts Am., Clinton, 1983, 85; mem. N.C. C.C. Leadership Program, 1990; pres. Sunday Sch. Class, 1997-98; bd. ch., Acad. of Fin., 2001—, bd. chair, 2002—; mem. Leadership Fayetteville, 2001-02; mem. faculty for leadership Fayetteville and Leadership Fayetteville Youth Acad., 2002-03. Named Outstanding Young Educator, Clinton Jaycees, 1985; recipient Outstanding Svc. award Clinton Student Govt. Assn., 1982, Excellence in Tchg. award N.C. State Bd. C.C., 1989, 98, Cert. of Appreciation, State of N.C. for Vol. Svcs., 1987, Leadership Challenge awrd Fayetteville C. of C., 2002. Mem. Am. Assn. Women in Cmty. Colls. (membership dir. 1988-89), N.C. Assn. Bus. Chair and Dept. Heads (pres. 1997-99), Am. Bus. Women Assn. (pres. 1983-84, Sampson County Woman of Yr. 1984), Kiwanis, NetWorth, Beta Gamma Sigma, Phi Kappa Phi, Phi Theta Kappa. Avocations: tennis, running, golf. Home: 585 Broyhill Rd Fayetteville NC 28314-2522 Office: Fayetteville Tech CC PO Box 35236 Fayetteville NC 28303 E-mail: friedmad@faytechcc.edu.

FRIEDMAN, EDWARD DAVID, lawyer, arbitrator; b. Chgo. s. Jacob C. and Bessie (Levison) F.; m. Mary Louise Melia, Nov. 1, 1947 (dec. Feb. 1997); children: Michael, Daniel, Mary Eleanor, Elizabeth; m. Carol Green, Nov. 26, 1999. AB with honors, U. Chgo., 1935, JD cum laude, 1937. Bar: Ill. 1937, U.S. Ct. Appeals 1950, D.C. 1969, U.S. Supreme Ct. 1969. Law clk. to fed. master in chancery, Chgo., 1937-38; assoc. Rosenberg, Toomin & Stein, Chgo., 1938-39; gen. counsel staff SEC, 1939-42; chief counsel OPA, 1942-43; spl. asst. to dep. solicitor and solicitor Dept. Labor, Washington, 1943-48, dep. solicitor of labor, 1965-68, acting solicitor of labor, 1969; ptnr. Bernstein, Alper, Schoene & Friedman, Washington, 1969-75, Highsaw, Mahoney & Friedman, Washington, 1975-80, Friedman & Wirtz, 1980-90; chief law officer 5th regional office, also asst. gen. counsel NLRB, 1948-60; labor counsel to Senator John F. Kennedy, 1960-61, Senator Wayne Morse, 1961-65, U.S. Senate Labor and Pub. Welfare Com., 1961-65; counsel to majority and minority floor mgrs. Senators Clark and Case on Title VII of Civil Rights Bill, 1964; spl. asst. sec. labor fgn. farm labor program, 1965; counsel compaign conduct adminstrv. com. United Steelworkers Am., 1980-89. U.S. del. to OECD, Paris, 1968. Mem. editl. bd. U. Chgo. Law Rev, 1936-37. Mem. town coun., Garrett Park, Md., 1954-58, mayor, 1960-66; mem. Truro (Mass.)Zoning Bd. Appeals, 1999—. U. Chgo. James Nelson Raymond fellow, 1937. Mem. ABA, D.C. Bar Assn., Fed. Bar Assn., Order of Coif, U. Chgo. Alumni Club. Home: 24 Gospel Path PO Box 1123 Truro MA 02666-1123 also: 1300 N Placita Parasol Green Valley AZ 85614-3643

FRIEDMAN, ELAINE FLORENCE, lawyer; b. N.Y.C., Aug. 22, 1924; d. Henry J. and Charlotte Leah (Youdelman) F.; m. Louis Schwartz, Apr. 10, 1949; 1 child, James Evan. BA, Hunter Coll., 1944; JD, Columbia U., 1946. Bar: N.Y. 1947, U.S. Dist. Ct. (so. and ea. dists.) N.Y., U.S. Ct. Appeals (2d cir.), U.S. Supreme Ct. 1954. Assoc. Oseas, Pepper & Siegel, N.Y.C., 1947-48, Bernstein & Benton, N.Y.C., 1948-51, Copeland & Elkins, N.Y.C., 1951-53; sole practice N.Y.C., 1953—. Bd. dirs. Health Ins. Plan of Greater N.Y. Mem. Fedn. Internat. des Femmes Juristes (v.p. U.S. chpt. 1993-95), N.Y. State Bar Assn., Hunter Coll. Alumni Assn., Columbia Law Sch. Assn. Jewish. Avocation: poetry. Home: 2 Agnes Cir Ardsley NY 10502-1709 Office: 60 E 42nd St New York NY 10165-0006

FRIEDMAN, ELI A. nephrologist, educator; b. N.Y.C., Apr. 9, 1933; s. Israel and Ida (Gutman) F.; widowed; children: Amy Louise, Rebecca Alicia, Sara Jo. BS, Bklyn. Coll., 1953; MD, SUNY Downstate Med. Center, 1957; DSc (hon.), Maduri Kamaraj U., India, 1985, L.I. U., 1991. Intern in medicine Harvard Med. Sch., 1957-58; resident in medicine Peter Bent Brigham Hosp., Boston, 1960-61; Am. Heart Assn. rsch. fellow Harvard U., 1958-60; mem. faculty, chief divsn. renal disease Downstate Med. Ctr., Bklyn., 1963—; prof. Health Sci. Ctr. SUNY, Bklyn., 1972—, Disting. Tchg. prof., 1992—. Bd. dirs. Am. Bur. Med. Aid to China, 1979—, Cleve. Found., 1979—, Bklyn. Nephrology Found., 1978—; Kasperzak lectr. Cleve. Clinic, 1998; Alpha Omega Alpha lectr. SUNY Health Sci. Ctr., Bklyn., 1999; Conrad Pirani lectr. Columbia Coll. Physician and Surgeons, 2000; Helen and Payne Whitney lectr. N. Shore Univ. Hosp., 2001; excellence in dialysis participant, Karachi, Pakistan, 00; mem. faculty masters in nephrology U. Naples, Italy, 2001; rsch. grants coun. reviewer Nat. Natural Sci. Found. of China, 2001; George E. Schreiner lectr. Canisus Coll., Buffalo, 2003. Author: Acute Renal Failure, 1973, Strategy in Renal Failure, 1978, Diabetic Renal-retinal Syndrome, 1980, Diabetic Renal-retinal Syndrome 3 Therapy, 1986, Diabetic Nephropathy, 1986, Diabetic Renal-retinal Syndrome 4: Management Strategy, 1987; editor: Journal of Diabetic Complications, 1986—. Mem. adv. bd. Nat. Kidney Found. Singapore, 1999. Lt. comdr. USPHS, 1961-63. Named master, ACP, 1996; named one of Best Drs. in N.Y., N.Y. Mag., 2000, 2001, Am.'s Top Drs., 2001, 2002; recipient Hoenig award, Nat. Kidney Found., 1986, Silver medal, U. Bologna, 1988, Disting. Svc. to Black Kidney patients award, Howard U., 1989, Physicians award, Am. Assn. Kidney Patients, 1989, Alumni medal, SUNY Downstate Med. Coll., William Dock Master Tchr. award, Alumni Assn. SUNY Health Scis. Ctr., 1992, Recognition award, N.Y. Regional Transplant Program, 1994, Am. Kidney Fund Nat. Torchbearer award, 1995, Juvenile Diabetes Found./Bklyn. award honoree, 1995, medal of excellence, Am. Kidney Fund, 1996, Torchbearer award, Organ Transplantation and Kidney Disease, 1998, Internat. Torchbearer award, India, 1998, Samuel L. Kountz award, Howard U., 1999, Peter Lundin award, Am. Assn. Kidney Patients, 2001, Medal of Excellence award, 1996, alumni award in nephrology, Downstate Med. Ctr., 2002, Excellence in Postgrad. Tchg., 2002, Best Doctors in N.Y., N.Y. Mag., 2002; grantee, NIH, USPHS, N.Y. Kidney Found., N.Y. State Kidney Disease Inst., Am. Kidney Fund; Paul Teschan Vis. Professorship, Vanderbilt U., 2002. Fellow Explorers Club (1st prize photo competition 1995); mem. ACP (Master 1996), Am. Soc. Nephrology, Internat. Soc. Nephrology, Am. Soc. Artificial Internal Organs (pres. 1987—, editor Transactions 1985—), Am. Soc. Immunology, Transplantation Soc., Assn. Am. Physicians, Internat. Soc. Artificial Organs (pres. 1986), Italian Soc. Nephrology (hon.), Royal Soc. Medicine Belgium (corres. mem.), German Soc. Clin. Nephrology (hon.). Home: 1049 E 17th St Brooklyn NY 11230-4412 Office: 450 Clarkson Ave Brooklyn NY 11203-2056 E-mail: elifriedmn@aol.com. *Achievement is as much a function of unswerving persistence, which is a learned behavior pattern, as it is of intellectual endowment, over which we have no control. Effective individuals, though often very bright, have learned to stick with it even after initial or repetitive failure. All of us lose some or even most of the time indicating the need to extract maximal joy from our wins no matter how infrequent the event.*

FRIEDMAN, EMANUEL A. medical educator; b. N.Y.C., June 9, 1926; s. Louis and Pauline (Feldman) F.; m. E. Judith Salomon, June 6, 1948; children: Lynn Alice, Meryl Ruth, Lee Martin. AB, Bklyn. Coll., 1947; MD, Columbia U., 1951, ScD, 1959; MA, Harvard U., 1969. Diplomate Am. Bd. Ob-Gyn. Intern Bellevue Hosp., N.Y.C., 1951-52; resident Columbia-Presbyn. Hosp., N.Y.C., 1952-57; instr. Columbia Coll. Physicians and Surgeons, 1957-59, asst. prof., 1960-62, assoc. prof., 1962-63; prof., chmn. dept. ob-gyn Chgo. Med. Sch., 1963-69; chmn. dept. ob-gyn Michael Reese Hosp., Chgo., 1963-69; prof. ob-gyn Harvard U., 1969-90, prof. emeritus, 1990—; obstetrician-gynecologist-in-chief Beth Israel Hosp., Boston, 1969-90, obstetrician-gynecologist in chief emeritus, 1990—; prof. ob-gyn Einstein, 1991—. Author: Labor: Clinical Evaluation and Management, 1967, 2d edit., 1978, Rh-Isoimmunization and Erythroblastosis Fetalis, 1969, Lymphatic System of Female Genitalia, 1971, Biological Principles and Modern Practice of Obstetrics, 1974, Blood Pressure, Edema and Proteinuria in Pregnancy, 1976, Pregnancy Hypertension, 1977, Uterine Physiology, 1979, Advances in Perinatal Medicine, 1981, 5th edit., 1986, Obstetrical Decision Making, 1982, 2d edit., 1987, Management of Labor, 1983, 2d edit., 1988, Gynecological Decision Making, 1983, 2d edit., 1987, Labor and Delivery Impact on Offspring, 1987, Legal Principles and Practice in Obstetrics and Gynecology, 1988, Vol. 2, 1990. Served with USNR, 1944-46. Recipient Joseph Mather Smith research prize Columbia U., 1958, Disting. Alumnus award Bklyn Coll., 1964, Bicentennial commemorative silver medallion award Columbia U., 1967 Fellow ACS, Am. Coll. Ob-Gyn, N.Y. Acad. Medicine; mem. N.Y. Acad. Scis., Soc. Exptl. Biology and Medicine, Soc. Gynecologic Investigation, AAUP, AAAS, Alpha Omega Alpha. Office: One Lincoln Pla New York NY 10023 E-mail: eafriedman@post.harvard.edu.

FRIEDMAN, ERNEST HARVEY, physician, psychiatrist; b. Cleve., Jan. 8, 1931; s. Sol and Ann (Nittskoff) F.; m. Anita Rose Bogdanow, Oct. 26, 1962; children: Rachel Samantha, Sarah Ann, Eric Daniel, Jessica Emily. BS, Case Western Res. U., 1952; MD, Ohio State U., 1956. Diplomate Am. Bd. Psychiatry and Neurology. Intern U. Ill. Hosps., Chgo., 1956-57; psychiat. resident U. Hosps. of Cleve., 1957-60; clin. instr. Case Western Res. U., Cleve., 1974-86, asst. clin. prof., 1983—; vis. psychiatrist Mt. Sinai Hosp., Cleve., 1963-70, sr. vis. psychiatrist, 1970-97; pvt. practice psychiatry, medicine Cleve., 1962—; owner, computer mfr. Voxaflex Co., East Cleveland, Ohio, 1986—; active staff Huron Hosp., East Cleveland, 1971—, Euclid (Ohio) Hosp., 2000—. Chmn. ad hoc com. on stress Am. Heart Assn., Cleve., 1977; cons. psychiatrist Nat. Exercise and Heart Disease Study, Washington, 1972-75. Mem. editorial bd. Heart and Lung, 1974-80; patentee computer software and hardware; reviewer Am. Jour. Cardiology, 2000—. Served as lt. comdr. M.C., USNR, 1960-62. Grantee-in-aid Am. Heart Assn., Cleve., 1964, 65, 75. Fellow Am. Psychiat. Assn. (disting. life). Jewish. Avocations: tennis, photography, bicycling. Office: Voxaflex Co 1831 Forest Hills Blvd Cleveland OH 44112-4313 E-mail: friedman@en.com.

FRIEDMAN, EUGENE STUART, lawyer; b. N.Y.C., Apr. 5, 1941; s. Abe and Etta (Fischer) F.; m. Karin L. Mehlem, Feb. 3, 1968; children: Gabrielle, Douglas, Jason. AB, NYU, 1961; LLB, Columbia U., 1964. Bar: N.Y. 1965, U.S. Supreme Ct. 1979. Atty. NLRB, San Francisco, 1965-67; assoc., ptnr. Cohen, Weiss & Simon, N.Y.C., 1968-86; sr. ptnr. Friedman & Wolf, N.Y.C., 1987—. Lectr. Ill. Inst. Continuing Legal Edn., Chgo., 1982-84, NYU Conf. Labor & Practicing Law Inst., N.Y.C., 1983-85; adv. bd. for labor and employment law ctr. NYU Law Sch. Contbr. articles to profl. jours. Active N.Y. State Task Force Plant Closings, N.Y.C., 1984. With USN, 1964-65. Mem. N.Y. State Bar Assn., Assn. of Bar of City of N.Y. (chmn. labor & employment law com. 1987-90), Am. Arbitration Assn. (law com.). Democrat. Jewish. Avocation: scuba diving. Home: 277 W End Ave New York NY 10023-2604 Office: Friedman & Wolf 1500 Broadway Ste 2300 New York NY 10036-4056

FRIEDMAN, EUGENE WARREN, surgeon; b. N.Y.C., Mar. 10, 1919; s. Isadore and Dora (Abramowitz) F.; m. Geraldine F. Gewirtz, Nov. 11, 1945; children: John Henry, Robert James. AB, NYU, 1939, MD, 1943. Diplomate: Am. Bd. Surgery, Am. Bd. Laser Surgery (bd. dirs. 1986—). Intern, resident in surgery Morrisania City Hosp., N.Y.C., 1943-45; resident in surgery Mt. Sinai Hosp., N.Y.C., 1947-48, attending surgeon, chief div. head and neck surgery, 1952—, clin. prof. surgery Sch. Medicine, 1967—, Hess Found./Friedman prof. surgical oncology, 1991. Resident and fellow in surgery Meml. Sloan-Kettering Cancer Ctr., N.Y.C., 1948-52; attending surgeon tumor surgery Manhattan State Hosp., N.Y.C., 1960-72; attending surgeon, co-dir. head and neck surgery French Polyclinic Med. Ctr., N.Y.C., 1965-72; cons. head and neck surgery Bronx-Lebanon Hosp. Ctr., N.Y.C., 1960—, Peninsula Hosp. Ctr., N.Y.C., 1960—, Bronx VA Hosp., N.Y.C., 1960— ; attending surgeon Beth Israel Hosp. North (formerly Doctors Hosp.), N.Y.C., 1960— ; cons. surgeon Lenox Hill Hosp., N.Y.C., 1976— ; lectr. Founding co-editor-in-chief Lasers in Surgery and Medicine, 1980-87; editor-in-chief Jour. Clin. Laser Medicine and Surgery (formerly Laser Medicine and Surgery News and Advances), 1988-97; contbr. chpts. to books and articles in field to profl. jours. Mem. sci. adv. bd. Chemotherapy Found., N.Y.C.; mem. sci. adv. bd. Samuel Waxman Rsch. Fund, Israel Cancer Rsch. Fund; bd. dirs. N.Y. City divsn. Am. Cancer Soc., 1976—; med. dir. Greater N.Y. Area State of Israel Bonds, 1976-00; hon. police surgeon, City of N.Y., 1968—. Capt. AUS, 1945-47. Recipient 2nd annaward Israel Cancer Research Fund, 1981m Jacobi medallion Alumni Assn. Mt. Sinai Hosp., N.Y.C., 1988. Fellow ACS, N.Y. Acad. Medicine, Am. Soc. Lasers in Medicine and Surgery; mem. AMA, N.Y. Surg. Soc., N.Y. Cancer Soc., N.Y. Head and Neck Soc., Am. Head and Neck Soc., Soc. Surg. Oncology, Am. Soc. Clin. Oncology, Internat. Soc. Lasers in Surgery and Medicine (sec.-treas. 1980-82), N.Y. County Med. Soc., N.Y. State Med. Soc., Univ. Club, Lotos Club. Democrat. Jewish. Office: 45 Sutton Pl S New York NY 10022

FRIEDMAN, FRANCES, public relations executive; b. NYC, Apr. 8, 1928; d. Aaron and Bertha (Itzkowitz) Fallick; m. Clifford Jerome Friedman, June 17, 1950; children— Kenneth Lee, Jeffrey Bennett. BBA, CCNY, 1948. Dir. pub. relations Melia Internat., Madrid, N.Y.C., 1971-73; sr. v.p. Lobsenz-Stevens, N.Y.C., 1973-75; exec. v.p. Howard Rubenstein Assocs., N.Y.C., 1975-83; pres., prin. Frances Friedman Assocs., N.Y.C., 1983-84; pres., chmn. bd. dirs. GCI Group Inc., N.Y.C., 1984-91, pub. rels. and editorial cons., 1991-93; mng. dir. L.V. Power & Assoc., Inc., 1993-97; pub. rels. cons. N.Y.C., 1997—. Media cons. White House on Women's Issues, 1995; participant in Vital Voices Confs., Hillary Clinton's program for women in emerging democracies, 1996. Bd. dirs. United Nations Assn. (NW Ct. chpt.), 2003, Morris-Jumel Mansion, 1999-2001, Contemporary Guidance Svcs, 1999, 2001, City Coll. Fund, N.Y.C., 1970-79; mem. adv. bd. League for Parent Edn., N.Y.C., 1961-65; editor South Shore Democratic Newsletter, North Bellmore, N.Y., 1958-61, press sec. N.Y. State Assembly candidate, 1965, N.Y. State Congl. candidate, 1968; officer Manhasset Dem. Club, N.Y., 1965-69; mem. adv. com. N.Y.C. Council candidate, 1985. U. New Haven Bartels fellow, 1993. Mem. Pub. Relations Soc. Am., Women in Communications (Matrix award for pub. relations 1989), The Counselors Acad., Pride and Alarm, City Club N.Y. Democrat. Jewish. Home: 30 Appalachian Rd Kent CT 06757-1009 E-mail: ffried2078@aol.com.

FRIEDMAN, FRANCES WOLF, political fund raiser; b. Ft. Worth, June 14, 1940; d. Tobian Alexander and Ann (Katz) Wolf; m. Christopher I. Newman (div. 1984); children: Peter A., J. Hope; m. Frederick Friedman Sr., Jan. 3, 1986; stepchildren: Danielle F., David J. BA in Polit. Sci., Tulane U., 1961. Motion picture film prodn. office coord. Columbia Pictures Corp. Paramount Pictures, N.Y.C., 1965-72, Metro Goldwyn Mayer, N.Y.C., 1965-72; dir. vols. Congressman Bill Green, N.Y.C., 1984-86, fin. dir., 1988-92; nat. dir. Modrnpac, N.Y.C., 1993-2001. Bd. dirs. Family Connections, 1998—; domestic violence task force chair Adv. Bd. on the Status of Women-Essex County, Newark, 1997-2000; mem., co-founder Essex County Coalition on Domestic Violence Svc. Providers, Newark, 1997—. Mem. pub. rels. Concert Artists Guild, N.Y.C., 1982-84, LWV, Millburn-Short Hills, N.J., 1996—; v.p. Rep. Club, Millburn-Short Hills, 1996—; freeholder-at-large candidate Rep. Party, Essex County, N.J., 1996. Avocation: gardening. Home: 14 Cross Gates Short Hills NJ 07078-2106

FRIEDMAN, FRANK BENNETT, lawyer; b. Newark, May 1, 1940; s. Martin and Gertrude (Tow) F.; m. Esta Kossack, June 2, 1962; children: Amy, Emily. AB, Columbia U., 1962, JD, 1965. Bar: D.C., Pa., Colo., Calif. Atty. FCC, Washington, 1965-67, Dept. Justice, Washington, 1967-70; counsel ATlantic Richfield Co., Phila., 1970-71, Denver, 1971-73, L.A., 1973-78; dir. environ. health and safety ARCO Chem. Co., Phila., 1978-79, mgr. external affairs occupation and environ. protection L.A., 1979-81; v.p. health, environ. and safety Occidental Petroleum Corp., L.A., 1981-93; ptnr. McClintock, Weston, Benshoff, Rocheford, Rubalcava &MacCuish, L.A., 1993-94; sr. v.p. health, environ. and safety Elf Atochem N.Am., Phila., 1994—; v.p. health safety and environ. Elf Aquitaine, Inc., Washington, 1998—. Mem. exec. com., bd. dirs. Environ. Law Inst., 1979-95, 99—, adv. bd., 1996—. Author: Practical Guide to Environmental Management, 3d edit., 1991, 5th edit., 1993, 6th edit., 1995, 7th edit., 1997. Mem. ABA (natural resources sect. energy and environ. law, chmn. air quality commn. 1975-78, coun. nat. resource energy and environ. law sect. 1978-81, 91-94, internat. environ. law 1989-91), Am. Law Inst., Nat. Environ Devel. Assn. (bd. dirs. 1984-93, 96—), Nat. Safety Coun. (bd. dirs. 1991-93). Office: Elf Aquitaine Inc 910 17th St NW Ste 800 Washington DC 20006-2606

FRIEDMAN, GARY DAVID, epidemiologist; b. Cleve., Mar. 8, 1934; s. Howard N. and Cema C. F.; m. Ruth Helen Schlein, June 22, 1958; children: Emily, Justin, Richard. Student, Antioch Coll., 1951-53; BS in Biol. Sci., U. Chgo., 1956, MD with honors, 1959; MS in Biostats., Harvard Sch. Pub. Health, 1965. Diplomate Am. Bd. Internal Medicine. Intern, resident Harvard Med. Svcs., Boston City Hosp., 1959-61; 2d yr. resident Univ. Hosps. Cleve., 1961-62; med. officer heart disease epidemiology study Nat. Heart Inst., Framingham, Mass., 1962-66; chief epidemiology unit, field and tng. sta., heart disease ctrl. program USPHS, San Francisco, 1966-68; sr. epidemiologist divsn. rsch. Kaiser Permanente Med. Care Program, Oakland, Calif., 1968-76, asst. dir. epidemiology and biostats., 1976-91, dir., 1991-98, sr. investigator, 1998-99, adj. investigator, 1999—; cons. prof. Dept. Health Rsch. and Policy Stanford U. Sch. Medicine, 1998—. Rsch. fellow, then rsch. assoc. preventive medicine Harvard Med. Sch., 1962-66; lectr. dept. biomed. and environ. health scis., sch. pub. health U. Calif. Berkeley, 1968-95; lectr. epidemiology and biostats. U. Calif. Sch. Medicine, San Francisco, 1980-2000, asst. clin. prof. 1967-75, assoc. clin. prof., 1975-92 depts. medicine and family and cmty. medicine; US-USSR working group sudden cardiac death NHLBI, 1975-82, com. on epidemiology and veterans follow-up studies Nat. Rsch. Coun., 1980-85, subcom. on twins, 1980-94, epidemiology and disease ctrl. study sect. NIH, 1982-86, US Preventive Svcs. Task Force, 1984-88, scientific rev. panel on toxic air contaminants State of Calif., 1988—, adv. com. Merck Found./Soc. Epidemiol. Rsch., Clin. Epidemiology Fellowships, 1990-94; sr. advisor expert panel on preventive svcs. USPHS, 1991-96. Author: Primer of Epidemiology, 1974, 4th edit., 1994; assoc. editor, then editor Am. Jour. Epidemiology, 1988-96, 99—; mem. editl. bd. HMO Practice, 1991-98, Jour. Med. Screening, 1997—; contbr. over 280 articles to profl. jours., chpts. to books; composer: Autumn for oboe and piano (First prize Composers Today Competition Music Tchrs. Assn. Calif. 1999), Fugue for Four Winds (Second prize Music Tchrs.

Assn. Calif. 2000). Oboist San Francisco Civic Symphony, 1990—, Symphony Parnassus, 1994—, Bohemian Club Band, 1994—; bd. dirs. Chamber Musicians No. Calif., Oakland, 1991-98. Sr. surgeon USPHS, 1962-68. Recipient Roche award for Outstanding Performance as Med. Student; Merit grantee Nat. Cancer Inst., 1987, Outstanding Investigator grantee, 1989, 94; named to Disting. Alumni Hall of Fame Cleve. Heights High Sch., 1991. Fellow Am. Heart Assn. (chmn. com. on criteria and methods 1969-71, chmn. program com. 1973-76, coun. epidemiol.), Am. Coll. Physicians; mem. APHA, Am. Epidemiol. Soc. (mem. com. 1982-86, pres. 1999-2000), Am. Soc. Preventive Oncology, Internat. Epidemiol. Assn., Soc. Epidemiologic Rsch. (exec. com. 1998-2001), Med. Biol. Alumni Assn. U. Chgo. (Disting. Svc. award 2000), Phi Beta Kappa, Alpha Omega Alpha, Delta Omega. Achievements include research on cancer, cardiovascular disease, gallbladder disease, effects of smoking, alcohol and medicinal drugs, evaluation of health screening tests. Office: Stanford U Sch Medicine Dept Health Rsch and Policy Redwood Bldg Rm T210 Stanford CA 94305-5405 E-mail: gdf@stanford.edu.

FRIEDMAN, GARY E. lawyer; married. AB in Econs. with sr. honors, Washington U., St. Louis, 1969; JD, U. Calif., Berkeley, 1973, MBA in Acctg. and Real Estate, 1974; LLM in Taxation, U. San Diego, 1982. CPA Colo.; bar: Calif. 1974, Mo. 1974, cert.: (specialist in taxation law). Assoc. Higgs, Fletcher & Mack, San Diego, 1975—76; sr. tax analyst San Diego Gas & Electric Co., 1976—79; assoc. Jenkins & Perry, 1979—82, Augustine & Rose, 1982; prin. Friedman, Jay & Cramer A.P.C., 1982—. Lectr. taxation U. So. Calif. Tax Inst., C.P.A. Found., others. Author textbook series on real estate taxation; contbr. articles to legal jours. Mem.: San Diego County Bar Assn. (chmn. taxation sect. 1983), Calif. Bar (exec. com. taxation sect. 1984—). Office: 111 Elm St Suite 400 San Diego CA 92101

FRIEDMAN, GEORGE JERRY, aerospace engineer, executive; b. N.Y.C., Mar. 22, 1928; s. Sander and Ruth (Oberlander) F.; m. Ruthanne Goldstein, Sept. 7, 1953; children— Sanford, Gary, David BS, U. Calif.-Berkeley, 1949; MS, UCLA, 1956, PhD, 1967. Registered profl. mech. engr., controls engr., Calif. Mech. engring. assoc. Dept. Water and Power, Los Angeles, 1949-56; devel. engr. Servo Mechanisms, Hawthorne, Calif., 1956-60; v.p. Northrop Corp., Los Angeles, 1960-94; exec. v.p., rsch. dir. Space Studies Inst., Princeton, N.J., 1994—. Mem. indsl. adv. group NATO, Brussels, 1977-78; guest lectr. UCLA, 1983—, Calif. State U., Northridge, 1983—, dir. trust fund, 1984-89; cons. to sci. adv. bd. USAF, Washington, 1985—, bd. govs. Aerospace and Elec. Sys. Soc., L.A., 1985—, v.p. publs., 1999-2001; adj. prof. U. So. Calif., L.A., 1994—; pres. Internat. Coun. on Sys. Engring., 1994, fellow 1998. Contbr. articles to profl. jours. Served as pfc. U.S. Army, 1950-52 Recipient Engring. Excellence award San Fernando Valley Engring. Council, 1983 Fellow IEEE (Baker award 1970), AIAA (assoc.; chmn. planetary def. subcom. 1995-97); mem. Am. Def. Preparedness Assn. (exec. com., preparedness award 1985). Democrat. Jewish. Home and Office: 5084 Gloria Ave Encino CA 91436-1529 E-mail: gfriedma@usc.edu.

FRIEDMAN, GERALD MANFRED, geologist, educator; b. Berlin, July 23, 1921; came to US, 1946, naturalized, 1950; s. Martin and Frieda (Cohn) F.; m. Sue Tyler Theilheimer, June 27, 1948; children: Judith Fay Friedman Rosen, Sharon Mira Friedman Azaria, Devorah Paula Friedman Zweibach, Eva Jane Friedman Scholle, Wendy Tamar Friedman Spanier. Student, U. Cambridge, Eng., 1938-39; BSc, U. London, Eng., 1945, DSc, 1977; student, U. Wyo., 1949; MA, Columbia U., 1950, PhD, 1952; DSc (hon.), U. Heidelberg, Fed. Republic Germany, 1986. Agrl. laborer, England, 1938-39; baker, 1940-42; internee Brit. Army, 1940; lectr. Chelsea Coll., London, 1944-45; analytical chemist J. Lyons & Co., 1945—46, E.R. Squibb & Sons (now Bristol Myers-Squibb), New Brunswick, 1946—49; asst. geology Columbia U., 1950; temp. geologist NY State Geol. Survey, 1950; from instr. to asst. prof. geology U. Cin., 1950-54; cons. geologist Sault Ste. Marie, Ont., Can., 1954-56; from sr. rsch. scientist to supr. sedimentary geology rsch. Pan Am. Petroleum Corp. (now BP), 1956-64; Fulbright vis. prof. geology Hebrew U., Jerusalem, 1964; prof. geology Rensselaer Poly. Inst., 1964-84, prof. emeritus, 1984—; prof. geology Bklyn. Coll., 1984—88, Disting. prof. geology, 1988—; prof. earth and environ. sci. Grad. Sch. CUNY, 1984—88, disting. prof. earth and environ. sci., 1988—, dep. exec. officer, 1992-94; pres. Gerry Exploration Inc., 1982-88. Rsch. sci. Hudson Labs., Columbia, 1965-69, rsch. assoc. dept. geology Lamont Geol. Obs., 1968-73; vis. prof. U. Heidelberg, 1967; cons. sci. Inst. Petroleum Rsch. and Geophysics, Israel, 1967-71; lectr. Oil & Gas Cons. Internat., 1968-98; pres. Northeastern Sci. Found. Inc., 1979—; vis. scientist Geol. Survey of Israel, 1970-73, 78; mem. Com. Sci. Soc. Pres., 1974-76; Gerald M. Friedman fellow Inst. Earth Sci., Hebrew U., Israel, 1990—; vis. prof. Martin-Luther-Univ., Halle-Wittenberg, Germany, 1998. Co-author: Principles of Sedimentology (Outstanding Acad. Books, Choice, 1978/79), 1978, Exploration for Carbonate Petroleum Reservoirs, 1982, Exercises in Sedimentology, 1982, Principles of Sedimentary Deposits: Stratigraphy and Sedimentology, 1992; pub. Northeastern Environ. Sci., 1982-90; editor: Jour. Sedimentary Petrology, 1964-70 (Best Paper award 1961, hon. mention 1964, 66), Northeastern Geology (now Northeastern Geology and Environ. Sci.), 1979—, Earth Sci. History, 1982-93, Carbonates and Evaporites, 1986—, 10th Internat. Congress on Sedimentology, 1978, Oil Industry History, 1999-2003; sect. co-editor: Chem. Abstracts (Mineralogical and Geol. Chemistry), 1962-69, abstractor, 1952-69; editl. bd. Jour. Geol. Edn., 1951-55, Sedimentary Geology, 1967-95, Israel Jour. Earth Sci., 1971-76, Coral Reef Newsletter, 1973-75, Jour. Geology, 1977—, GeoJour., 1977-83, Facies, 1987—; mng. editor Sedimentology for Earth Sci. Revs., 1992—; contbg. co-editor: Carbonate Sedimentology in Central Europe, 1968, Hypersaline Ecosystems: The Gavish Sabkha, 1985, editor, contbr.: Depositional Environments in Carbonate Rocks, 1969; co-editor: Modern Carbonate Environments, 1983, Lecture Notes in Earth Sci., 1985—; founding editor: Earth Sci. History, 1982, hon. life mem.; contbr. articles to profl. jour.; patentee in field. Phys. edn. com., judo instr. Tulsa YMCA, 1958-64, chmn. awards com., 1962-64; adviser, instr. Judo Club, Rensselaer Poly. Inst., 1964-84; bd. dir. Troy Jewish Cmty. Coun., 1966-72, 74-77; v.p. Temple Beth El, 1986-89, pres., 1989-91, bd. dir., 1965-76; bd. dir. Leo Baeck Inst., NYC, 1986—; v.p., chmn. pub. com. Drake Well Found., 1998-2003, v.p., 2002—. Recipient award for devoted svc. Tulsa YMCA, 1963, Hon. W Va. award, 1998; named hon. alumnus dept. geology Bklyn. Coll., 1989; grantee Office Naval Rsch., AEC, Dept. Energy, Petroleum Rsch. Fund, NY Gas Assn., NY State Energy Rsch. and Devel. Authority. Fellow: AAAS (councillor 1979—80, soc. rep. geology/geography sect. 1989—97), Soc. Econ. Geologists, N.Y. Acad. Sci. (vice chair geol. sci. sect. 1993—94, chmn. 1994—96, vice chair geol. sci. sect. 1996—97, chmn. 1997—2001), Geol. Assn. Can., Geol. Soc. London (life, chartered geologist, hon. fellow 1996), Mineral Soc. Am. (mem. nominating com. fellows 1967—69, mem. awards com. 1977—78), Mineral Soc. Gt. Brit. (abstractor mineralogical abstracts 1963—64), Geol. Soc. Am. (sr. chmn. sect. program com. 1969, candidate sect. chmn. 1969, publ. com. 1980—82, chmn. overseas pub. rels. com. internat. divsn. 1996—97, vice chair history geology divsn. 1997—99, chair 1999—2000, mem. awards nom. com. sedimentary geol. divsn. 1999—2000, chair history geology awards com. 2000—01); mem.: So. Venezolana Historia Geociencias (internat. corr. mem.), Sigma Xi, Sigma Gamma Epsilon (nat. pres. 1982—86), Kodokan, Empire State Judo Assn., Amateur Athletic Union (judo com. 1963, Okla.), Okla. Judo Fedn. (pres 1959—60, v.p. 1961—64), U.S. Judo Fedn. (San Dan, cert. judo tchr.), Cin. Mineral Soc. (v.p. program chmn. 1953—54), N.Y. State Mus.-N.Y. State Geol. Survey (James Hall medal 1997), N.Y. State Geol. Assn. (pres. 1978—79, bd. dir. 1979—84), Geosci. Info. Soc. (mem. membership com. 1983—85, ad hoc com. to devel. criteria for reviewing geosci. jour. 1985—86), Assn. Earth Sci. Editors (v.p. 1970—71, pres. 1971—72, host 1991, Outstanding Editorial Pub. Contributions Award 1993), Nat. Assn. Geosci. Tchr. (nat. treas. 1951—55, subscription and circulation mgr. 1951—55, chmn. organizing and nominating com. establish east-ctrl.sect. 1952—53, assoc. editor Jour. of Geosci. Edn. 1953—55, pres. Okla 1962—63, pres. Ea. sect. 1983—84, Disting. Svc. Award 2001), Geol. Vereinigung, Deutsche Geol. Gesellschaft, Soc. Venezolana Historia Geociencias (intenat. corr. mem.), Indian Assn. Sedimentologists (mem. governing coun. 1978—82), Serbian Yugoslavian Geol. Soc. (hon. 1998), History of the Earth Sci. Soc. (hon.; co-founder 1981), Geol. Soc. Israel (hon. 1992), Internat. Assn. Sedimentologists (nat. corr. USA 1971—73, v.p. 1971—75, pres. 1975—78, program com. Internat. Sedimentological Congress 1978, excursion com. Internat. Sedimentological Congress 1982, hon. mem. 1986), Geologists' Assn. (life), Am. Geol. Inst. (governing bd. 1971—72, 1974—75), New Eng. Intercollegiate Geol. Conf. (convenor, editor 1979), Capital Dist. Geologists Assn. (chmn. program 1966—73), Hudson-Mohawk Profl. Geologists Assn. (bd. dir. 1995—2001, program com. 1996—97, chmn. program com. 1997—2001), Paleontological Soc. (hon. mention to Outstanding Paper award Jour. Paleontology 1971, Twenhofel medal 1997), Soc. for Sedimentary Geology (sect. pres. pro tem 1966—67, chmn. Shepard award selection com. 1966—67, sect. pres. 1967—68, pres. 1974—75, Best Paper award Gulf Coast sect. 1974, Twenhefel medalist 1997), Am. Assn. Petroleum Geologists (chmn. carbonate rock com. 1965—69, mem. rsch. com. 1965—71, lectr. continuing edn. program 1967—88, chmn. Persian Gulf liaison com. 1968—70, mem. marine geology com. 1970—74, Disting. lectr. 1972—73, adv. coun. 1974—75, mem. disting. lectr. com. 1975—78, mem. rsch. com. 1976—82, ho. of dels. 1977—80, Eastern Section sect. sec. 1979—80, sect. treas. 1980—81, alt. del. 1980—83, sect. v.p. 1981—82, sect. pres 1982—83, mem. vis. geologists program com. 1982—85, membership com. 1982—87, div. profl. affairs rep. from Eastern sect. 1983—84, hon. mem. Eastern sect. 1984, com. on convs. 1984—85, nat. v.p. 1984—85, ho. of dels. 1984—87, mem. select com. on future petroleum geologist 1985—86, chmn. sect. awards com. 1989—92, nat. hon. mem. 1990, ho. of dels. 1991—93, alt. del. 1993—98, sect. chmn. tech. program com. 1994—95, vice chair standing com. hist. petroleum geology 1997—2000, chair 2000—01, ho. of dels. 2002—, John T. Galey Meml. Award medal 1993, sect. cert. of merit 1995, Disting. Educator award 1996, Nat. Disting. Svc. award 1998, Sidney Powers Meml. award 2000, Divsn. Environ. Scis. Tchg. award 2001, award for excellence and dedication in tchg. environ. geology 2001), Am. Chem. Soc. (group leader 1962—63), Am. Inst. Profl. Geologists (cert.), Russian Acad. Nat. Sci. US sect. (Kapitsa Gold medal of honor 1996), Ky. Cols., Explorers Club NY. Home: 32 24th St Troy NY 12180-1915 Office: Bklyn Coll/Grad Sch CUNY Dept Geology Brooklyn NY 11210 E-mail: gmfriedman@juno.com.

FRIEDMAN, GREGORY H. energy administrator; BBA, Temple U.; MBA, Fairleigh Dickinson U. Sr. auditor U.S. Army Audit Agy., 1968-74; dep. dir. Office of Contingency Planning, FEA, Washington, 1974-80, assoc. dir. Gasoline Rationing Implementation Office, 1980-82; with Office of Insp. Gen. Dept. of Energy, Washington, 1982—, dep. asst. insp. gen. for audit ops., 1985-94, dep. insp. gen. for audit svcs., 1994-97, prin. dep. insp. gen., 1997-98, acting insp. gen., 1998, insp. gen., 1998—. Guest lectr. audit matters and govtl. affairs Princeton U., George Washington U. Office: Dept of Energy Insp Gen 1000 Independence Ave SW Washington DC 20585-0002

FRIEDMAN, HANS ADOLF, architect; b. Hamburg, Germany, June 10, 1921; came to U.S., 1939, naturalized, 1942; s. Sally and Erna (Samson) F.; m. Maxine Oppenheimer, May 31, 1952; children: Eric, Katy, John, Paul. B.Arch., Ill. Inst. Tech., 1950. Chief architect DeLeuw, Cather & Co., Chgo., 1951-61; sr. partner Friedman, Omarzu, Zion & Lundgoot, Chgo., 1961; pres. A.M. Kinney Assocs., Inc., Chgo., 1961-87, vice chmn., 1988-92; partner A.M. Kinney Assocs., Cin., 1961-93; cons., pvt. practice Evanston, Ill., 1992—. V.p. Kintech Svcs., Inc., 1975-93; lectr. So. Ill. U., 1959. Editor: Inland Architect, 1958-64. Mem. Evanston (Ill.) Preservation Commn., 1978-85, chmn., 1981-82; mem. Evanston Site Plan and Appearance Rev. Com., 1996—. Recipient Distinguished Bldg. awards Chemplex Co., Rolling Meadows, Ill., 1969, Distinguished Bldg. awards S.C. Johnson & Sons, Wind Point, Wis., 1969, Distinguished Bldg. awards Quaker Oats Co., Jackson, Tenn., 1973, Disting. Bldg. awards Moore Bus. Forms, Inc., Glenview, Ill., 1973; Lab. of Yr. award Am. Critical Care, 1980; Disting. Pub. Service award City of Evanston, 1985 Fellow AIA (emeritus); mem. Nat. Trust for Historic Preservation, Landmarks Preservation Council of Ill. Home and Office: 1501 Hinman Ave Evanston IL 60201

FRIEDMAN, HAROLD EDWARD, lawyer; b. Cleve., Apr. 7, 1934; s. Joseph and Mary (Schreibman) F.; m. Nancy Schweid, Aug. 20, 1961; children: Deborah, Jay, Susan. BS, Ohio State U., 1956; LL.B., Case Western Res U., 1959. Bar: Ohio 1960. Practiced in, Cleve., since 1960; ptnr. Simon, Haiman, Gutfeld, Friedman & Jacobs, 1967-80, Ulmer & Berne, 1981—; chair real property practice group. Sec., trustee Harry K. and Emma R. Fox Charitable Found.; pres. Jewish Vocat. Svcs., Cleve.; pres. Internat. Assn. Jewish Vocat. Svcs.; pres. Cleve. Hillel Found.; vice chmn. endowment fund Jewish Cmty. Fedn. Cleve., bd. dirs.; pres. Metro Health Found.; bd. dirs. Bur. Jewish Edn., Jewish Convalescence and Rehab. Ctr., Big Bros. Greater Cleve., Jewish Cmty. Fedn. Cleve., Jewish Family Svc. Assn., YES, Inc., Bellefaire/Jewish Children's Bur. Recipient Kane Leadership award Jewish Community Fedn. Cleve., 1974 Mem. ABA, Ohio Bar Assn., Cleve. Bar Assn., Oakwood Country Club. Home: 23149 Laureldale Rd Cleveland OH 44122-2101 Office: 900 Bond Ct Bldg Cleveland OH 44114 E-mail: hfriedman@ulmer.com., hedwfried@aol.com.

FRIEDMAN, HARVEY MICHAEL, infectious diseases educator; b. Montreal, May 29, 1944; came to U.S., 1971; s. Sidney and Sybil (Garfinkle) F.; m. Cynthia Diane Mickey, Apr. 12, 1980; children: Lisa, Steven, Julie. BS, McGill U., 1965, MD, 1969. Intern, resident Jewish Gen. Hosp., Montreal, 1969-71; fellow in virology Wistar Inst., Phila., 1971-73; fellow in infectious disease U. Pa. Hosp., Phila., 1973-75; asst. prof., assoc. prof. Med. Sch. U. Pa., Phila., 1975-91, prof. Med. Sch., 1991—. Med. dir. Clin. Virology Lab. Children's Hosp., Phila., 1975—96; chief infectious diseases U. Pa., 1990—. Contbr. numerous papers and book chpts. Grantee NIH, Found., 1978—. Fellow: Infectious Disease Soc. Am.; mem.: AAAS, Am. Clin. and Climatological Assn., Assn. Am. Physicians, Am. Soc. Clin. Investigation. Achievements include description of novel mechanisms used by herpes simplex virus glycoproteins that favor virus escape from immune attack. Office: U Pa Med Sch 502 Johnson Pavilion Philadelphia PA 19104-6073 E-mail: hfriedma@mail.med.upenn.edu.

FRIEDMAN, HERBERT A. rabbi, educator, fund raising executive; b. New Haven, Sept. 25, 1918; s. Israel and Rae (Aaronson) F.; children from previous marriage: Judith Rae, Daniel Stephen, Joan Michal; m. Francine Bensley, June 28, 1963; children: David Herbert, Charles Edward. BA, Yale U., 1938; MHL, Jewish Inst. Religion, 1943; DD (hon.), Hebrew Union Coll., 1969; PhD (hon.), Tel Aviv Univ., 2002. Ordained rabbi, 1944. Rabbi Temple Emanuel, Denver, 1943-52, Milw., 1952-55; exec. chmn. Nat. United Jewish Appeal, N.Y.C., 1955-75; pres. Am. Friends of Tel Aviv U., N.Y.C., 1982-85, Wexner Heritage Found., 1985-95, founding pres. emeritus, 1995—. Author: Collected Speeches, 1971, Roots of the Future, 1999. Chaplain (capt.) U.S. Army, 1944—47, ETO. Mem. Central Conf. Am. Rabbis, Yale Club (N.Y.C.). Home: 500 E 77th St Apt 2519 New York NY 10162-0008 Office: Wexner Heritage Found 551 Madison Ave New York NY 10022-3212

FRIEDMAN, HERBERT SHELDON, urologist; b. Chicago, Ill., Dec. 30, 1928; s. Harry and Rose (Brown) F.; m. Miriam Gabel Kranz, Dec. 27, 1953; children: Saul B., Daniel B., Naomi G. Student, Wright Coll., 1946-47; AB, U. Ill., 1950, MD, 1952. Diplomate Am. Bd. Urology. Intern Indpls. Gen. Hosp., 1952-53; resident in urology Michael Reese Hosp., Chgo., 1953-55, Sinai Hosp., Balt., 1957-58; pvt. practice Albuquerque, 1958—97; ret. Mem. exec. com. med. staff St. Joseph Hosp., Albuquerque, 1975-84, pres., 1981-82; bd. dirs. Lectronsonics Corp., Albuquerque. Mem. N.Mex. Gov.'s Adv. Coun. on Vocat. Rehab., 1967; trustee Congregation Albert, Albuquerque; bd. dirs. Albuquerque Dance Theater, 1979-84; pres. Jewish Fedn. Greater albuquerque, 1983-84. Mem. N.Mex. Med. Soc. (pres. 1988-89), Am. Urological Assn. (pres. South Ctr. sect. 1994-95). Avocations: tennis, skiing, performing and graphic arts. Home: 347 Paint Brush Dr NE Albuquerque NM 87122-1414

FRIEDMAN, HOWARD MARTIN, law educator; b. Springfield, Ohio, Sept. 26, 1941; s. Sam and Ida (Rubinoff) F.; m. Sharon Eve Kaufman, June 15, 1969; 1 child, Leah. BA, Ohio State U., 1962; JD, Harvard U., 1965; LLM, Georgetown U., 1967. Bar: Ohio 1965, S. Supreme Ct. 1970, U.S. Dist. Ct. (no. dist.) Ohio 1973. Atty. SEC, Washington, 1965-67; asst. prof. U. N.D., Grand Forks, 1967-69; atty. U.S. Indian Claims, Washington, 1969-70; assoc. prof. law U. Toledo, 1970-74, prof. law, 1974—, dir. Cybersecurities Law Inst., 2000—. Of counsel Eastman and Smith, Toledo; vis. prof. Case Western Res. U., spring 1990, St. John's U., fall 1995, Notre Dame U., fall 1999; mem. Supreme Ct. Commn. on Cert. of Specialists, 1994-99. Author: Securities and Commodities Enforcement, 1981, Ohio Securities Law and Practice, 1987, 2d edit., 1996, Securities Regulation in Cyberspace, 1997, 3d edit., 2001; contbr. articles to profl. jours. Trustee ACLU of N.W. Ohio, 1982-89, pres. Toledo Bd. Jewish Edn., 1984-86, Temple B'Nai Israel, Toledo, 1991-93; v.p. govt. affairs com. Ohio Jewish Cmty., 1993-96, pres., 1996-98; mem. exec. com. Nat. Jewish Cmty. Rels. Adv. Coun., 1993-95, United Jewish Coun. Greater Toledo, 2000-03. Mem. ABA, Ohio State Bar Assn. (chmn. specialization com. 1991-94), Toledo Bar Assn. (chmn. corp. and securities law com. 1991-92). Democrat. Jewish. Home: 3715 Sylvanwood Dr Sylvania OH 43560-3925 Office: U Toledo Coll Law Toledo OH 43606 E-mail: howard.friedman@utoledo.edu.

FRIEDMAN, IRA HUGH, surgeon; b. N.Y.C., July 17, 1933; s. Leonard Seymour and Ruth (Binder) F.; m. Erika Berger, Oct. 22, 1961; children— Richard Lawrence, Joanne Beth BA, NYU, 1953, MD, 1957. Diplomate Am. Bd. Surgery, Nat. Bd. Med. Examiners. Intern, resident in surgery Beth Isreal Med. Ctr., N.Y.C., 1957-59, 61-63; surg. resident Bellevue Hosp., N.Y.C., 1959-60; practice medicine specializing in surgery N.Y.C., 1963—. Attending surgeon Beth Israel Med. Ctr., pres. med. bd., 1981-82; assoc. clin. prof. surgery Albert Einstein Coll. Medicine; med. adv. to N.Y.C. dir. SSS, 1968. Contbr. articles to profl. jours. Bd. dirs. Union Orthodox Jewish Congregations Am., Am. Com. for Shaare Zedek Hosp. of Jerusalem, Yeshiva Sha-alvim, Isreal, P'Tach; co-chmn. bd. dirs. Yeshiva Chofetz Chaim, N.Y.C. Recipient Koach award Israel Bond Orgn., 1977; N.Y. Heart Assn. fellow, 1960-61 Fellow ACS (elected gov. 1996), Am. Coll. Gastroenterology, Am. Soc. Colon and Rectal Surgeons, Royal Soc. Medicine; mem. AMA, N.Y. Acad. Medicine, N.Y. Surg. Soc., Soc. Surgery of Alimentary Tract, Soc. Am. Gastrointestinal Endoscopic Surgeons, Am. Gastroent. Assn., Am. Soc. Gen. Surgeons, Am. Hernia Soc., Am. Soc. Breast Surgeons, N.Y. Gastroent. Assn., N.Y. Cancer Soc., N.Y. Soc. Colon and Rectal Surgeons, Collegium Internationale Chirugiae Digestive, N.Y. State Med. Assn., N.Y. County Med. Assn. Home: 1175 Park Ave New York NY 10128-1211

FRIEDMAN, IRWIN, medical and pharmaceutical educator; b. N.Y.C., Dec. 15, 1929; s. Dave and Lillie (Shapiro) F.; m. Iris Ann Zelikofsky, June 23, 1953; children: Robin, Michael, Scott. BS, Union Coll., Schenectady, 1951; MD, NYU, 1955. Intern Buffalo Hosp., 1955-56; resident U. Utah/Mary Imogene Brandt Hosp., 1958-60; clin. prof. medicine SUNY, Buffalo, N.Y., 1961—, clin. assoc. prof. pharmacy. Capt. U.S. Army, 1956-58, Okinawa. NIH fellow, 1960-61. Home: 4 Fox Chapel Rd Buffalo NY 14221-4515 E-mail: irwinfrd@aol.com.

FRIEDMAN, J. ROGER, publisher; b. N.Y.C., Oct. 26, 1933; s. Arnold Darcy and Judith (Scheinberg) F.; m. Patricia Mosle, Dec. 1, 1962; children: Amanda, Randall. BA in English, Williams Coll., 1955. Salesman Chain Store Age, Drug Editions, N.Y.C., 1957-61; founder, sales mgr. Discount Store News, N.Y.C., 1961-63, publ. dir., 1963-65; v.p. sales Lebhar-Friedman, Inc., N.Y.C., 1965-68, exec. v.p., 1968-70, pres., 1970—; sec. Chain Store Guide, N.Y.C., 1970—. Bd. dirs. Upper Pecos Assn., N.Mex., 1971, Brush Ranch Sch., N. Mex., 1974, pres., 1997—; bd. dirs. Students in Free Enterprise, 1977—, Am. Bus. Press, 1994—, Freedom Communications, 2000—; trustee, chmn. Bus. Press Ednl. Found., McElvain Oil & Gas Co.; hon. trustee Temple Rodeph Shalom, N.Y.C., 1987. Mem. Lotos (pres. 1983-87), Williams (N.Y.C.) (pres. 1991-95, hon. bd. mem.). Office: Lebhar-Friedman Inc 425 Park Ave Ste 501 New York NY 10022-3549

FRIEDMAN, JAMES DENNIS, lawyer; b. Dubuque, Iowa, Jan. 11, 1947; s. Elmer J. and Rosemary Catherine (Stillmunks) F.; m. Kathleen Marie Maersch, Aug. 16, 1969; children: Scott, Ryan, Andrea, Sean. AB in Polit. Sci., Marquette U., 1969; JD, U. Notre Dame, 1972. Bar: Wis. 1972, U.S. Ct. Appeals (D.C. cir.) 1973, U.S. Ct. Appeals (7th cir.) 1976, U.S. Supreme Ct. 1978, U.S. Ct. Appeals (6th cir.) 1989, Ill. 1996, U.S. Tax Ct. 1997. Pvt. practice, Milw., 1972—81; ptnr. Quarles & Brady, Milw., 1981—. Presenter in field; mem. legis. coun. spl. study com. on regulation of fin. instns. State of Wis., 1986-87; bd. dirs. Concours Motors, Inc., Wis. Equal Justice Fund, Inc.; mem. dept. fin. instns. task force on fin. competitiveness 2005, State of Wis., 2000; mem., vice chair State of Wis. Supreme Ct., Office of Lawyer Regulation Preliminary Rev. Com., 2000—; mem. Gov.'s Adv. Coun. on Jud. Selection of the State of Wis., 2002. Mng. editor: Notre Dame Law Rev., 1971—72; contbr. articles to profl. jours. Alderman 4th and 7th dists. Mequon, Wis., 1979-85, pres. common coun., 1980-82, bd. ethics 1996-98, 2000—, chair blue ribbon visioning com. 1998-99; bd. dirs. Weyenrg, Pub. Libr. Found. Inc., 1983—, pres., 1984—; bd. dirs. Ptnrs. Advancing Values in Edn. Inc., 1987—, Wis. Law Found., 1998—; bd. visitors Marquette U. Ctr. for Study of Entrepreneurship, Milw., 1987-95; bd. dirs. Ozaukee Family Svcs., 1983-99, sec., 1993-98; bd. dirs. Notre Dame Club of Milw., 1984-88, sec., 1978, v.p., 1986-88; bd. dirs. Marquette Club of Milw., 1987-88; chair attys. unit United Way Fund Dr. Greater Milw., 1987; mem. St. James Ch., Mequon. Named Outstanding Sr., Coll. of Liberal Arts, Marquette U., 1969. Fellow Wis. Law Found., Am. Bar Found.; mem. ABA (banking law com. sect. bus. law); State Bar Wis. (chair bd. govs. 1999-2000, chair exec. com. 1999-2000, fin. com. 1997-98, strategic planning task force 1997-98, bd. govs. 1996-2000, exec. com. 1998-2000, internat. transactions sect. bd. dirs. 1984-99, sec. and chair-elect 1988-89, chair 1989-90, del. to ABA Ho. of Dels. 1980-82, standing com. on adminstrn. justice and judiciary 1979-81, legal edn. and bar admissions com. 1984-89, com. on minority lawyers 1992-99, chmn. 1997-1999, bd. dirs. young lawyers divsn. 1978-82, chmn. bar admission stds. and requirements com. 1979, So. Regional chair capital fund campaign 1998-99), Milw. Bar Assn., Wis. Acad. Trial Lawyers (bd. dirs. 1980-82), Wis. Bankers Assn., Milw. Country Club. Roman Catholic. Avocations: tennis, golf. Office: Quarles & Brady LLP 411 E Wisconsin Ave Ste 2040 Milwaukee WI 53202-4497 E-mail: jdf@quarles.com.

FRIEDMAN, JAMES WINSTEIN, economist, educator; b. Cleve., Sept. 25, 1936; s. Theodore and Gertrude (Winstein) F.; m. Marcia Sherman, Aug. 11, 1957; children: Nancy Elizabeth, Robert U. Student, MIT, 1954-56; BA, U. Mich., 1959; MA, Yale U., 1960, PhD, 1963. Instr., then asst. prof. econs. Yale U., 1963-68; assoc. prof. U. Rochester (N.Y.), 1968-72, prof. econs., 1972-83; prof. Va. Poly Inst., Blacksburg, 1983-85; Kenan prof. U. N.C., Chapel Hill, 1985-2001, Kenan prof. emeritus, 2001—. Mem. rsch. staff Cowles Found., 1963-68, asst. dir., 1964-66; vis. prof. U. Bielefeld, Fed. Republic Germany, 1976, 87-88, Hebrew U., Jerusalem, 1979, Cath. U. Louvain, Belgium, 1987, 91, 99, U. Paris, 1991, 93, 2000, U. Alicante, Spain, 1992, U. Kobe, Japan, 1994. Author: Oligopoly and the Theory of Games, 1977, The Theory of Oligopoly, 1983, Game Theory with Applications to Economics, 1986, 2d edit., 1990; co-author: An Experiment in Noncooperative Oligopoly, 1979; editor: Problems of Coordination in Economic Activity, 1994; assoc. editor Japanese Econ. Rev., 1994—, Regional Sci. and Urban Econs., 1997—, Games and Econ. Behavior, 1998—; contbr. articles to profl. jours. Fellow Econometric Soc. (assoc. editor jour. 1975-81); mem. Am. Econ. Soc. Avocation: hiking. Office: U NC Dept Econs Cb # 3305 Chapel Hill NC 27599-0001

FRIEDMAN, JANE, publishing executive; BA in English, NYU, 1967. Joined Random House, 1968, with publicity dept., exec. v.p. Knopf Pub. Group, pub. Vintage Books, founder, pres. Random House Audio, exec. v.p. Random House Inc., mem. exec. com.; pres., CEO HarperCollins, N.Y.C., 1997—. Co-chair pub. divsn., vice chair entertainment, media and comms. divsn. UJA; mem. Am. adv. com. Jerusalem Internat. Book Fair; chmn. bd. dirs., adv. com. Assn. Am. Pubs.; bd. dirs. Poets and Writers; adv. com. Literacy Ptnrs., Yale U. Press. Named Person of Yr., LMP, 1999; named one of 200 Women Legends, Leaders and Trailblazers, Vanity Fair, 1998, N.Y.'s 100 Most Influential Women in Bus., Crain's N.Y. Bus., 1999, Am.'s 100 Most Important Women, Ladies Home Jour., 1999, 101 Most Important People in Entertainment, Entertainment Weekly, 1999—2002; recipient Matrix award, Women Who Change the World, 2001. Office: HarperCollins 10 E 53rd St New York NY 10022-5299

FRIEDMAN, JANET TERI, mortgage company executive; b. Houston, Aug. 21, 1957; d. Ben and Susanna Ruth (Stern) Friedman. BS in Elem. Edn. magna cum laude, U. Houston, 1978; JD, S. Tex. Coll. Law, 2000. Cert. real estate broker Tex., tchr. Tex., airline sales agt. Tex., fraud examiner, expert witness. Sales rep. Continental Airlines/Tex. Internat. Airlines, 1978-82; pvt. practice real estate broker, buyer's agt., renovator, 1982; sr. residential loan originator Richard Gill Co./Gill Savs. and Loan, 1983-84; prodn. mgr., secondary mktg. coordinator, mem. orgn. team Devel. Mortgage Group, Inc., 1984-85; pres., mortgage broker, real estate and fin. cons. Friedman Fin. Services, Inc., Houston, 1985-94; pres. J. Friedman Mortgage, Houston, 1994—. Expert witness, mem. bus. devel. bd. Lockwood Nat. Bank, Houston, 1990. Author: (book) Safecracking the Mortgage Secrets: The Complete Guide to Home Loans, 1987; syndicated columnist: Dear Ms. Mortgage; contbr. articles to profl. jours. Vol. Crisis Intervention Houston; chmn. Houston Proud's Continuing Edn. and C.A.R.E. seminars. Mem.: Houston Bd. Realtors (subcom. chmn.

Burning Issues seminars, edn. com., spkrs. bur.), Tex. Realtors Assn. (edn. com.), Am. Bus. Women, Houston Assn. Profl. Mortgage Women, Greater Home Builders Assn. Houston, Kappa Delta Phi, Phi Kappa Phi. Office: 6060 Richmond Ave Ste 226 Houston TX 77057-6205

FRIEDMAN, JEROME ISAAC, physics educator, researcher; b. Chgo., Mar. 28, 1930; married, 1956; 4 children. AB, U. Chgo., 1950, MS, 1953, PhD in Physics, 1956. Research assoc. in physics U. Chgo., 1956—57; research assoc. in physics Stanford U., Calif., 1957—60; from asst. prof. to assoc. prof. MIT, Cambridge, 1960—67, prof. physics, 1967—, dir. lab. nuclear sci., 1980—83, head dept. physics, 1983—88, William A. Collidge prof., 1988—90, inst. prof., 1990—. Recipient Nobel prize in Physics, 1990. Fellow: AAAS, Am. Phys. Soc. (co-recipient W.H.K. Panofsky prize 1989); mem.: NAS, Am. Acad. Arts and Scis. Office: MIT Room 24-512/Dept Physics 77 Massachusetts Ave Cambridge MA 02139-4307*

FRIEDMAN, JOAN M. accounting educator; b. N.Y.C., Nov. 30, 1949; d. Alvin E. and Pesselle Gail (Rothenberg) F.; m. Charles E. Blair III, Sept. 20, 1992. AB magna cum laude, Harvard U., 1971; MA, Courtauld Inst., U. London, 1973; MS with honors, Columbia U., 1974; MAS, U. Ill., 1993. CPA, Ill. Asst. research librarian Beinecke Library, New Haven, Conn., 1974-75; asst. research librarian Yale Ctr. for Brit. Art, New Haven, Conn., 1975-76, curator of rare books, 1976-90; computer cons., teaching asst. dept. accountancy U. Ill., Champaign, 1990-95; vis. asst. prof. acctg. Ill. Wesleyan U., Bloomington, Ill., 1995-99, asst. prof. acctg., 1999—. Cons. Johns Hopkins U., Balt., 1983; tchr. Sch. Library Service Columbia U., 1983-88, Sysop WordPerfect Users Forum on CompuServe, 1987-2000, Sysop, Tapcis Forum on CompuServe, 1988-95. Author: Color Printing in England, 1978; contbr. articles in field Recipient student achievement award Fedn. Schs. Accountancy, 1993; Nat. Merit scholar Harvard U., 1967; Moss Accountancy fellow U. Ill. 1990. Mem. ALA (chmn. rare books and manuscripts sect. 1982-83), Bibliog. Soc. Am. (coun. 1982-86, sec. 1986-88), Am. Printing History Assn., Phi Beta Kappa, Beta Phi Mu. Clubs: Grolier (N.Y.C.); Elizabethan (New Haven). Jewish. Avocations: microcomputers, bicycling. Office: Ill Wesleyan U Divsn Bus & Econs PO Box 2900 Bloomington IL 61702-2900 E-mail: jfriedma@titan.iwu.edu.

FRIEDMAN, JOEL WILLIAM, law educator; b. Mar. 16, 1951; s. Max Aaron and Muriel (Yudien) F.; m. Vivian Stoleru, Apr. 5, 1987; children: Alexa Erica, Chloe Gabriella, Max Aaron. BS, Cornell U., 1972; JD, Yale U., 1975. Bar: Calif. 1975, U.S. Dist. Ct. (cen. dist.) Calif. 1975. Asst. prof. Tulane U., New Orleans, 1976-79, assoc. prof., 1979-82, prof. law, 1982—, C.J. Morrow prof. law, 1985-86, Jack M. Gordon prof. procedural law and jurisdiction, 2002—, dir. tech., 1996—, dir. ITESM PhD program, 2000—. Vis. prof. law U. Tel Aviv, Israel, 1983, U. Tex. Law Sch., 1985-86, Chuo Law Sch., Tokyo, 1988, Hebrew U. of Jerusalem Law Sch., 1990; lectr. Fed. Jud. Ctr., Washington, 1987—; cons. La. Ho. of Reps., Baton Rouge, 1982-85, West Group, 1996—; bd. dirs. Ctr. for Computer-Assisted Legal Instrn., 1996-99; spl. master Pasadena Ind. Sch. Dist., Houston, 1987-93. Editor: Cases and Materials on Law of Employment Discrimination, 1983, 5th edit., 2001, The Law of Civil Procedure: Cases and Materials, 2002; contbr. articles to law revs. Pres., bd. dirs. Woldenberg Village, Inc., 1995-97; pres., bd. dirs., Jewish Fedn. Greater New Orleans, 2001—. Recipient Felix Frankfurter Faculty award for disting. tchg. Tulane Law Sch., 1989; Fulbright scholar, Israel, 1990. Mem. Am. Assn. Law Schs. (chair sect. on employment discrimination law 1987-88), Am. Law Inst., B'nai B'rith Hillel Found. (pres. New Orleans 1987-91), Internat. Assn. of Jewish Lawyers and Jurists La. Br. (pres. 1994-95). Democrat. Avocations: running, squash, scuba diving, skiing. Home: 1230 State St New Orleans LA 70118-6027 Office: Tulane Law Sch 6329 Freret St New Orleans LA 70118-6231 E-mail: jfriedman@law.tulane.edu.

FRIEDMAN, JOHN MAXWELL, JR., lawyer; b. N.Y.C., Oct. 31, 1944; s. John M. and Jane (Blum) F.; m. Laurie Suzanne Nevin, July 8, 1973 (div. 1988); children: David, Michael; m. Judith Zuckerman, Mar. 5, 1989; 1 child, Julia. AB, Princeton U., 1966; MA, U. Sussex, Brighton, Eng., 1967; JD, U. Chgo., 1970. Bar: N.Y. 1971, U.S. Ct. Appeals (2d cir.) 1971, U.S. Dist. Ct. (so. and ea. dist.) N.Y. 1972, U.S. Supreme Ct. 1974. Assoc. Dewey Ballantine, N.Y.C., 1970-78, ptnr., 1978-96. Home: 80 Rocky Mountain Rd Roxbury CT 06783-1623 E-mail: johnmfriedman@earthlink.net.

FRIEDMAN, JONATHAN BLOCK, architect, educator, writer; b. Washington, Jan. 14, 1946; s. Charles and Bernice Block Friedman; m. Marilyn Turtz, July 1, 1982; children: Charles Michael, David Lawrence. Diplomate in Architecture, Cambridge U., 1967—68; BA cum laude, Princeton U., 1963—67, MArch, 1967—70. Cert. NCARB, Nat. Coun. of Archtl. Rev. Boards, 1977, registered Architect, Ky. State Bd. of Architects, 1977. Summer intern The Office of Mayor John Lindsay, NYC, 1968; archtl. designer Richard Meier and Associates, NYC, 1969; editor Big Rock Candy Mountain Portola Inst., Menlo Park, Calif., 1970; project arch. Jules Gregory FAIA at Uniplan, Princeton, NJ, 1971; garden designer/builder Richard W. Painter, Landscape Designer, Lake Oswego, Oreg., 1972; job capt. Kimura Garfinkel Architects, Palo Alto, Calif., 1973; asst. prof. of architecture U. of Ky., 1973—78; archtl. designer Kibbutz Degania, Israel, 1974; assoc. prof. of architecture U. of Ky., 1979—80, prof. of architecture, 1980—83, NY Inst. of Tech., 1991—, dean, sch. of architecture and design, 1992—2000. Invited spkr. French Nat. Space Agy., 1981, Internat. Conf. on Energy Efficient Buildings with Earth Sheltered Protection, Sydney, Australia, 1983; colloquium presenter Math. Dept., Calif. State U., 1985; invited mem. of the sci. com. Internat. Joint Conf. on CAD and Robotics in Architecture and Constrn., Marseilles, 1986; poster paper presenter 14th Internat. Symposium on Remote Sensing of the Environment, San Jose, Costa Rica, 1990; keynote spkr. Seventh Nat. Conf. on The Beginning Design Student, Santa Fe, 1990; invited critic U. of Wash., Sch. of Architecture, 1990, U. of Pa, Grad. Sch. of Architecture, 1991; keynote spkr. AIA, LI Chpt., Carle Place, NY, 1992; conf. organizer, environ. edn. and awareness symposium NY State Dept. of Environ. Protection, 1996; fellow Inst. for Urban Design, NYC, 1999—; plenary panelist 16th Nat. Conf. on the Beginning Design Student, Las Vegas, 1999. Author: (scholarly text) Creation in Space 1: Architectonics, Creation in Space Volume 2: Dynamics; nat. space habitat design competition, Earthlight Lodge Lunar Natural Pk. (Hon. Mention, 1989), nat. design competition, Home For Generations (Hon. Mention, 1993); project architect East Orange Mid. Sch., NJ (Design Award, NJ. Soc. of Architects, 1971); historic railroad station renovation, Project Railrest Nat. Endowment for the Arts Nat. Competition (First Prize Winner, Nat. Endowment of the Arts Nat. Design Competition, 1977), exhibition, Synagogue Bayt; project in series Idea About Synagogue, Synagogue Aleph; project in series Idea About Synagogue. Recipient First Ann. Outstanding Tchr. award, U. of Ky. Coll. of Architecture, 1977, President's Svc. award, NY Inst. of Tech., 1997; Nat. Merit scholar, Nat. Merit Scholarship Corp., 1963, U. Grad. fellow, Princeton U., 1970, Faculty Rsch. grant, U. of Ky., 1978, Rsch. grant, NY State Coun. on the Arts, 1986, grant, Anna M. Rockefeller Found., 1992, MacDowell fellow, The MacDowell Colony, 1994. Achievements include patents for earth photo globe; cloud cover overlay; illuminating support assembly; design of Evolution of a Campus: 250 years of Princeton University originator and co-principal investigator of 4-dimensional interactive model of Princeton University, with Interactive Computer Graphics Lab. Home: 6 Sunset Ave Glen Cove NY 11542 Office: NY Inst of Tech Education Hall Old Westbury NY 11568 Personal E-mail: friedman2k@aol.com.

FRIEDMAN, JOSEPH HAROLD, neurologist; b. N.Y.C., Nov. 16, 1948; s. William and Henrietta (Feuerstein) F.; m. Susan M. Mates, Dec. 10, 1978; children: Rebecca, Deborah, William. BA, U. Chgo., 1969; MA, Washington U., St. Louis, 1973; MD, Columbia U., 1978; MA (ad eundem), Brown U., Providence, 1988. Med. intern Mt. Sinai Hosp. N.Y., N.Y.C., 1978-79; neurology resident Neurol. Inst. N.Y., N.Y.C., 1979-82; asst. prof. neuroscis. Brown U. Sch. Medicine, Providence, 1982-88, assoc. prof., 1988-94, prof., 1994—. Editor-in-chief: jour. Medicine & Health, mem. editl. bd.: Movement Disorders. Vol. physician Traveller's Aid, Providence, 1986-92; mem. Barrington Ednl. Found., 1992-94; mem. edn. com. Temple Habonim, Barrington, 1989-93. Recipient Point of Light award Pres. of U.S./R.I. Parkinson's Support Assn., 1990. Fellow Am. Acad. Neurology and Psychiatry (exec. com. Parkinson's Study Group, 1999-2001); mem. Am. Neurol. Assn., Movement Disorders Soc. Jewish. Achievements include research in the role of dopamine withdrawal in neuroleptic malignant like syndrome in Parkinsons's disease; early advocate for role of clozapine in treating drug-induced psychosis in Parkinson's. Avocation: chamber music. Office: Meml Hosp RI 111 Brewster St Pawtucket RI 02860-4499 E-mail: Joseph_Friedman@mhri.org.

FRIEDMAN, JULIAN RICHARD, lawyer; b. Savannah, Ga., Oct. 9, 1936; s. W. Leon and Evelyn B. F.; m. Deborah I. Shaw, Sept. 12, 1963; m. Em Olivia Bevis, Dec. 27, 1974; children: Sheldon A., Esther B. AA cum laude, Armstrong State Coll., 1954; BA, Emory U., 1956; JD cum laude, U. Ga., 1959; LLM in Taxation, NYU, 1964. Bar: Ga. 1958, S.C. 1980. Assoc. W. Leon Friedman, Savannah, 1959, 61-63, Cheatham, Bergen & Sparkman, Savannah, 1960, Adams, Adams, Brennan & Gardner, Savannah, 1965-68, ptnr., 1968-82, Oliver Maner & Gray, LLP, Savannah, 1982-2000, of counsel, 2000—. Mem. Ga. del. S.E. Liaison Tax Com., 1971-73, chmn. Ga. del., 1972-73; mem. Ga. Fiduciary Law Revision Study Com., 1976-81, Ga. Probate Code Revision Com., 1992-97; mem. Ga. Trust Code Revision Com., 2003—. Contbr. articles to profl. publs.; asst. editor-in-chief student editl. bd. Ga. Bar Jour., 1958-59. Pres. Congregation, Mickve Israel Synagogue, Savannah, 1998-2001; pres. Ga. Pub. Radio, 1984-86, Ga. Trust Law Revision Study Com., Served to capt. USAFR, 1961-68. Recipient Outstanding Grad. award Phi Delta Phi, 1959, Henry Shinn Meml. award Phi Alpha Delta, 1959. Mem. ABA, Am. Coll. Trust and Estate Counsel, Am. Coll. Tax Counsel, Savannah Estate Planning Coun. (pres. 1972-73), Fed. Bar Assn. (pres. Savannah chpt. 1971-72), State Bar Ga. (chmn. sect. taxation 1971-72, chmn. fiduciary law sect. 1975-76), State Bar S.C., Savannah Bar Assn., Phi Beta Kappa, Phi Kappa Phi, Omicron Delta Kappa, Pi Sigma Alpha. Clubs: B'nai B'rith (pres. Savannah lodge 1968-69). Home: 7 Rose Dhu Dr Bluffton SC 29910-6801 Office: Oliver Maner & Gray 218 W State St Savannah GA 31401-3232 E-mail: jfriedlaw@aol.com.

FRIEDMAN, K. BRUCE, lawyer; b. Buffalo, Jan. 1, 1929; s. Bennett and Florence Ruth (Israel) Friedman; m. Lois G. Rosoff, June 15, 1986. AB, Harvard U., 1950; LLB, Yale U., 1953. Bar: N.Y. 1955, DC 1956, Calif. 1958. Atty. CAB, Washington, 1955-57; pvt. practice San Francisco, 1958—; mem. Zang, Friedman & Damir, 1969-78, Cotton, Seligman & Ray, 1978-79, Friedman, McCubbin, Spalding, Bilter, Roosevelt, & Montgomery, San Francisco, 1980—. Pres. Econ. Roundtable San Francisco, 1964; lectr. law U. Calif. Berkley, 1966—76. Trustee World Affairs Coun. No. Calif., San Francisco, 1970—76; pres. San Francisco Estate Planning Coun., 1973—74; bd. dirs. Am. Coll. Trust and Estate Counsel Found., 2000—; bd. dirs. San Francisco chpt. Am. Jewish Com., 1960—76; regional dir. No. Calif. Assn. Harvard Alumni, 1981—84. With U.S. Army, 1953—55. Fellow: Am. Bar Found., Am. Coll. Trust and Estate Counsel; mem.: ABA, U. Calif. San Francisco Found., San Francisco Com. Fgn. Rels., Am. Law Inst., Internat. Acad. Estate and Trust Law (treas. 1996—), San Francisco Bar Assn., State Bar Calif., Harvard Club San Francisco (pres. 1976—78), Commonwealth Club Calif., Calif. Tennis Club, Univ. Club, Rotary. Jewish. Office: Friedman McCubbin Spalding Bilter Roosevelt & Montgomery 425 California St Ste 2500 San Francisco CA 94104-2207 E-mail: kbrucefriedman@fomlaw.com.

FRIEDMAN, LAWRENCE M. law educator; b. Chgo., Apr. 2, 1930; s. I. M. and Ethel (Shapiro) F.; m. Leah Feigenbaum, Mar. 27, 1955; children: Jane, Amy. AB, U. Chgo., 1948, JD, 1951, LLM, 1953; LLD (hon.), U. Puget Sound, 1977, CUNY, 1989, U. Lund, Sweden, 1993, John Marshall Law Sch., 1995, U. Macerata, Italy, 1998. Mem. faculty St. Louis U., 1957-61, U. Wis., 1961-68; prof. law Stanford U., 1968—, Marion Rice Kirkwood prof., 1976—; David Stouffer Meml. lectr. Rutgers U. Law Sch., 1969; Sibley lectr. U. Ga. Law Sch., 1976; Wayne Morse lectr. U. Oreg., 1985; Childress meml. lectr. St. Louis U., 1987. Jefferson Meml. lectr. U. Calif., 1994; Higgins vis. prof. Lewis and Clark U., 1998; Tucker lectr. Washington and Lee U., 2000. Author: Contract Law in America, 1965, Government and Slum Housing, 1968, A History of American Law, 1973, 2d edit., 1985, The Legal System: A Social Science Perspective, 1975, Law and Society: An Introduction, 1977, American Law, 1984, Total Justice, 1985, Your Time Will Come, 1985, The Republic of Choice, 1990, Crime and Punishment in American History, 1993, The Horizontal Society, 1999, Law in America: A Short History, 2002; author (with Robert V. Percival) The Roots of Justice, 1981; co-editor (with Stewart Macaulay): Law and the Behavioral Sciences, 1969, 2d edit., 1977; co-editor: (with Stewart Macaulay and John Stookey) Law and Society: Readings on the Social Study of Law, 1995; co-editor: (with Harry N. Scheiber) American Law and the Constitutional Order, 1978; co-editor: Legal Culture and the Legal Profession, 1996; co-editor: (with George Fisher) The Crime Conundrum, 1997; contbr. articles to profl. jours. Served with U.S. Army, 1953-54. Recipient Triennial award Order of Coif, 1976, Willard Hurst prize, 1982, Harry Kalven prize, 1992, Silver Gavel award ABA, 1994, Rsch. award Am. Bar. Found., 2000-01; Ctr. for Advanced Study in Behavioral Sci. fellow, 1974-75, Inst. Advanced Study fellow, Berlin, 1985. Mem. Law and Soc. Assn. (pres. 1979-81), Am. Acad. Arts and Scis., Am. Soc. for Legal History (v.p. 1987-89, pres. 1990-91), Soc. Am. Historians, Rsch. Com. Sociology of Law (hon. life, pres. 2003—). Home: 724 Frenchmans Rd Palo Alto CA 94305-1005 Office: Stanford U Law Sch Nathan Abbott Way Stanford CA 94305-9991 Business E-Mail: lmf@stanford.edu.

FRIEDMAN, LAWRENCE MILTON, lawyer; b. Chgo., Apr. 2, 1945; s. Armin C. and Mildred Friedman; m. Linda M. Friedman, June 25, 1967; children: Benjamin J., David K. BA, U. Ill., 1966; JD, Ohio State U., 1969. Bar: Ill. 1970, U.S. Tax Ct. 1970; CPA, Md., Ill. Ptnr. Coopers & Lybrand, Chgo., 1969-85, Lord, Bissell & Brook, Chgo., 1985—. Adj. prof. law IIT Chgo. Kent Coll. Law, Chgo., 1990—; mem. adv. bd. Hartford Inst. Ins. Tax, 1995-2000; spkr. on mergers, aquisitions and taxation. Mem. adv. bd. Ins. Tax Rev., 1987—; contbr. articles to law jours. Sec.-treas., dir. North Shore Performing Arts Ctr. Found. in Skokie, Ill., 1993-97; vice chmn., dir. Jewish Fedn. Met. Chgo., 1992-99. Mem. ABA, AICPA, Chgo. Fed. Tax Forum. Office: Lord Bissell & Brook 115 S La Salle St Ste 3200 Chicago IL 60603-3902

FRIEDMAN, LAWRENCE SAMUEL, gastroenterologist, educator; b. Newark, May 11, 1953; s. Maurice and Esther (Slansky) F.; m. Mary Jo Cappuccilli, Apr. 12, 1981; 1 child, Matthew Jacob. Student, Princeton U., 1971-73; BA, Johns Hopkins U., 1975, MD, 1978. Diplomate in internal medicine and gastroenterology Am. Bd. Internal Medicine. Intern dept. medicine Johns Hopkins Hosp., Balt., 1978-79, resident dept. medicine, 1979-81; fellow Mass. Gen. Hosp./ Harvard Med. Sch., Boston, 1981-84; asst. prof. Jefferson Med. Coll., Phila., 1984-87, assoc. prof., 1987-93, vice chmn., 1987-92; assoc. prof. Harvard Med. Sch., Boston, 1993-2001, prof. medicine, 2001—; physician Mass. Gen. Hosp., Boston, 1993—; chief Bauer Firm, 1997—2003; chmn. dept. medicine Newton-Wellesley Hosp., Newton, Mass., 2003—. Chmn. Gastroenterology Leadership Coun. Tng. Com., 1994. Editor: Gastrointestinal Disorders in the Elderly, 1990, 2001, Gastrointestinal Bleeding I, 1993, Gastrointestinal Bleeding II, 1994, Viral Hepatitis, 1994, Training in Endoscopy, 1995, Management of Chronic Liver Disease, 1996, Handbook of Liver Disease, 1998, Sleisenger & Fordtran's Gastrointestinal and Liver Disease, 2002; contbr. articles. Fellow ACP, Am. Coll. Gastroenterology, Coll. Physicians of Phila.; mem. Am. Assn. for Study of Liver Diseases, Am. Fedn. for Med. Rsch., Am. Soc. Gastrointestinal Endoscopy (treas. 1998-2000, Disting. Svc. award 2001), Am. Gastroenterol. Assn., Am. Liver Found., Assn. Subsplty. Profs., Crohn's and Colitis Found. Am., Am. Bd. Internal Medicine Gastroenterology (chair 2003—). Jewish. Avocations: american history, woodwind instruments, travel, basketball. Office: Mass Gen Hosp GI Unit 456D Baker St Boston MA 02132-4235

FRIEDMAN, LAWRENCE STUART, internist, pediatrician, educator; b. Bridgeport, Conn., Aug. 31, 1951; s. Alvin and Steffi (David) F. BA, Dickinson Coll., Carlisle, Pa., 1973; MS, Georgetown U., 1976, MD, 1983. Diplomate Am. Bd. Internal Medicine. Intern, resident Deaconess Hosp., Boston, 1983-86; fellow Harvard U., Boston, 1986-88; instr. medicine Harvard Med. Sch., Boston, 1988-92, asst. prof., 1992-94; chief primary care pediat. and adolescent medicine U. Calif., San Diego, 1994—, prof. pediat., 1994—; med. dir., primary and ambulatory care U. Calif. San Diego Med. Group, 1998—. Co-editor: Source Book on Substance Abuse and Addictions, 1996; contbr. articles to profl. jours. Mem. Soc. Adolescent Medicine (pres. 1995—). Office: U Calif San Diego Med Ctr 200 W Arbor Dr San Diego CA 92103-8449

FRIEDMAN, LESTER DAVID, humanities educator; b. N.Y.C., N.Y., Oct. 11, 1945; s. Eugene and Eva Friedman; m. Rae-Ellen Webb, Oct. 22, 2001; children: Marc Ian, Rachel Elizabeth. PhD, Syracuse U., 1975. Prof. Upstate Med. U., Syracuse, NY, 1977—2000; sr. lectr. Northwestern U., Chgo., 2000—. Author: (scholarly book) Arthur Penn's Bonnie and Clyde, 2000. Recipient Nat. Jewish Book award, Jewish Nat. Book Coun., 1987. Mem.: Soc. Cinema and Media Studies. Avocation: tennis. Home: 5D 3800 N Lake Shore Dr Chicago IL 60613 Office: Northwestern U ABA 627 750 N Lake Shore Dr Chicago IL 60611 Office Fax: 312-503-0574. Personal E-mail: l-friedman@northwestern.edu. E-mail: l-friedman@northwestern.edu.

FRIEDMAN, LYNN JOSEPH, counselor; b. New Orleans, Jan. 12, 1949; d. Leonard Cerf and Paula Rose (Levy) Joseph; children; Rebecca, Naomi. BS, La. State U., 1970; MEd, U. Tex., 1971; PhD, U. New Orleans, 1995. Tchr. Orleans Parish Schs., New Orleans, 1971-73; rehab. counselor L.A. Div. Rehab. Svcs., Metairie, 1973-87, Intracorp, Metairie, 1987-91, GAB Robins/Med Insights, Metairie, 1991—. Counselor Metro Battered Women, Metairie, 1990-92; edn. dir. Congregation Gates of Prayer, New Orleans, 1971-75; nat. mgr. Crisis Intervention Program. Contbr. articles to profl. jours. Named Counselor of Yr. Goodall Rehab., 1980; recipient Cert. Appreciation Nat. Assn. Ret. Citizens, 1974, Magnolia Sch., 1976. Mem. ACA (La. Grad. Student of Yr. 1991), Nat. Rehab. Assn. (La. Counselor of Yr. 1979), Chi Sigma Iota (treas. 1990-91, v.p. 1991-92). Democrat. Jewish. Home: 4721 Loveland St Metairie LA 70006-4027 Office: GAB Robins/Med Insights 4721 Loveland St Metairie LA 70006-4027

FRIEDMAN, MALCOLM, consultant; b. N.Y.C., Sept. 29, 1928; s. Martin and Anna (Schoen) F.; children: Marci, Carestia. BA, NYU, 1949; MA, Bklyn. Coll., 1952; PhD, Yeshiva U., 1957; advanced study, Alfred Adler Inst. Psychotherapy, 1980. Cert. ednl. adminstr., N.Y. Dir. team teaching N.Y.C. Bd. Edn., 1962-66, dir. reading, 1977-79, dir. spl. programs, 1980-84; prin. Pub. Sch. #14, S.I., N.Y., 1966-77; prof. Hunter Coll., N.Y.C., 1966-73; dean L.I. U., Bklyn., 1984—94; dir. Leadership Inst. for Edn., 1995-2000; v.p. Cardialert, 2002—. Adj. prof. St. John's U., N.Y.C., 1975-76, Hunter Coll., Staten Island (N.Y.) Coll.; asst. examiner Bd. Examiners, N.Y.C., 1966-84. Mem. Am. Assn. Colls. for Tchr. Edn., N.Y. Acad. Pub. Edn., Internat. Reading Assn., Assn. Tchr. Educators, Phi Delta Kappa. Avocations: boating, tennis. Home and Office: 44 Island Rd Stonington CT 06378 Address: 3905 S Ocean Blvd Palm Beach FL 33480

FRIEDMAN, MARCIA L, photographer, writer; b. Madison, Wis., Sept. 13, 1942; d. Stanleigh and Eleanor Friedman. BA, U. Wis., Madison, WI, 1964. Legal sec. Melvin Belli, San Francisco, 1965—65; flight attendant World Airways, Oakland, Calif., 1965—67; ground hostess TWA, Tel Aviv, 1967—69; mgr. Roland Agy., Los Angeles, Calif., 1970—72; owner, mgr. M. Friedman Agy., Los Angeles, Calif., 1972—76; fashion designer/owner Le Bag Swimwear, Los Angeles, Calif., 1976—83; design educator Otis Parsons Sch. Design, Los Angeles, Calif., 1979—79; free lance writer various, Los Angeles, Calif., 1982—90; writer The Jewish Press, New York, NY, 1999—; pvt. practice Madison, Wis., 1992—. Fashion cons. Adrienne Vitiadini, New York, NY, 1985. Photographer (book) Cuba: The Special Period. Fundraising dir. Friends Jerusalem Coll., Los Angeles, Calif., 1989; tribute jour. chmn. Pacific Jewish Ctr., Los Angeles, Calif., 1987. Mem.: Mensa. Jewish. Avocations: reading non-fiction, animal interaction.

FRIEDMAN, MARK JOEL, cardiologist, educator; b. N.Y.C., 1944; s. Hyman and Sylvia (Baumgarten) F.; m. Barbara Lynn Rauch, Oct. 11, 1969; 1 child, Gregory N. BA cum laude, Syracuse U., 1967; MD, N.Y. Med. Coll., 1971. Cert. in internal medicine, specialty in cardiovasc. disease. Intern Mt. Sinai Hosp., N.Y.C., 1971-72, resident in medicine, 1972-74; fellow in cardiology U. Ariz., 1976-78; active staff St. Francis Hosp., Tulsa, 1981—. Prof. medicine U. Okla. Tulsa Med. Coll., 1982—. Contbr. articles to profl. jours. Fellow Am. Coll. Cardiology, Am. Heart Assn.; mem. AMA, Alpha Omega Alpha. Office: Springer Clinic Cardi 6151 S Yale Ave Tulsa OK 74136-1907 E-mail: marktul@email.msn.com.

FRIEDMAN, MARLA LEE, marketing professional; b. Chgo., May 26, 1953; d. Martin P. and Charlotte K. (Beilenson) F. BSC in Commerce, DePaul U., Chgo., 1977; MBA with honors, Roosevelt U., Chgo., 1985. Gen. mgr., adminstr. Chgo. Ctr. for Devel. Learning, Inc., Ill., 1975—77; dist. health claims adminstrn. analyst Washington Nat. Ins. Co., Evanston, Ill., 1977—80; unit coord. computer resource liaison Luth. Gen. Hosp., Pk. Ridge, Ill., 1980—99; pres., owner Dancing By Candlelight, 1995—; media & investor rels. prof.. IPA, Buffalo Grove, Ill., 2000—01; dir. mktg. programs Samples & Surveys, Northbrook, Ill., 2001; acting dir. mktg. & publ. rels. Penworthy Ctrl., Glenview, Ill., 2002; scheduling coord. Nurse Staffers, Rosemont, Ill., 2003—. Mem. associated writing programs George Mason U. Contbr. prose poem Chips Off the Writer's Block, 1992, columnist, 1994; contbr. poem Guided By Voices Anthology, 1998, Best Poets of the 20th Century, 2000, Best Poets of 2000, 2000, Sound of Poetry, 2001; author short stories, children's stories, novels and articles. Recipient Editors Choice award N.Am. Poetry Open Competition, 1998, awards for nonfiction articles. Fellow Life Mgmt. Soc. (cert. fin. scis.); mem. NAFE, Acad. Am. Poets. Avocations: drama, music, creative cookery. E-mail: beyondpage2@yahoo.com.

FRIEDMAN, MARTIN, museum director, arts adviser; b. Pitts., Sept. 23, 1925; s. Israel and Etta (Louik) F.; m. Mildred Shenberg, Sept. 3, 1949; children: Lise, Ceil, Zoe. Student, U. Pa., 1943-45; BA, U. Wash., 1947; MA, UCLA, 1949; postgrad., Columbia, 1956-57, U. Minn., 1958-60, LHD (hon.), 1990, Bates Coll., 1983; DFA (hon.), Macalester Coll., 1983; LHD (hon.), Md. Inst., 1983; DFA (hon.), Hamline U., 1987, Phila. Coll. of Art and Design, 1989. Instr. art, curriculum cons. L.A. City Schs., 1949-56; instr. art U. Calif. Extension, L.A., 1950-51; fellow Bklyn. Mus., 1956-57; grantee Belgian-Am. Ednl. Found., Brussels, 1957-58; fellow Am. art U. Minn., 1959-60; curator Walker Art Center, Mpls., 1958-60, dir., 1961-90, dir. emeritus, 1990—. Mem. mus. adv. com. NEA, 1973-78, adv. coun. internat. exhbns., 1987-91, Nat. Coun. Arts, 1978-84, Smithsonian Coun., 1988-93; adv. Am. Ctr. Paris, 1990-92, Fed. Art Com. Internat. Exhbns., 1987-91; adviser art program Hall Family Found., Kansas City, 1991—, Nat. Gallery Art, Washington, 1991-92, Nelson Atkins Mus. Art, Kansas City, Mo., 1991-92, contemporary art Va. Mus. Fine Arts, Richmond, 1992-93; guest curator Landscape as Metaphor exhbn. Denver Art Mus., 1992-94, Columbus Mus. Art, 1992-94; Am. fine arts commr. São Paulo Bienal, 1963; mem. Nat. Collection Fine Arts Commn., Washington, Commn. on Founds. and Pvt. Philanthropy; hon. mem. commn. Nat. Mus. Am. Art, Washington; mem. adv. bd. on environ. planning Bur. Reclamation, Washington, 1965-69; art adv. com. Japan House Gallery, N.Y.C., 1999-2000; adviser Ind. Curators, Inc., N.Y. Author numerous catalogues on internat. contemporary art, also books, articles; dir. numerous mus. exhbns. Trustee Spring Hill Found., Minn., 1970—81, Am. Fedn. Arts, 1972—85, Socrates Sculpture Pk., NY, 2000—02; mem. Internat. Mus. Com., Washington, 1976—78; mem. vis. com. J. Paul Getty Mus., Malibu, Calif., 1990—95. Ford Found. fellow, 1961-62; artist fellow Aspen Inst. Humanistic Studies, 1980, Intellectual Interchange fellow, Tokyo, 1982, Japan Found. fellow, 1991; Asian Cultural Coun. grantee, 1995; recipient Disting. Svc. award Mid-Am. Coll. Art Assn., 1987, Nat. Medal of Arts, White House, 1990, Lifetime Achievement award Internat. Sculpture Ctr., 1999; decorated officer Arts et Lettres (France); honoree DIA Ctr. for the Arts, 1997. Mem. Coll. Art Assn., Assn. Art Mus. Dirs. (pres. 1978-79, trustee 1979-81, citation for disting. svc. 1990). E-mail: mlfnyc@mindspring.com.

FRIEDMAN, MARTIN BURTON, chemical company executive; b. N.Y.C., June 21, 1927; s. William L. and Ella (Holstein) F.; m. Rita Fleischman, Mar. 19, 1950; children— Jay Edward, Ellen Jane. Student, Mt. St. Mary's Coll., 1943-44, Cornell U., 1944-45; BA, Pa. State U., 1949. Mgr. advt. and promotion chems. group Sun Chem. Corp., N.Y.C., 1949-54; mgr. advt. and promotion textile chems. dept. Am. Cyanamid Co., N.Y.C., 1954-58, mgr. advt. and promotion, organic chems. div., 1958-60, gen. merchandising mgr., fibers div., 1961-64, dir. sales, 1964-65, dir. mktg., 1965-69, asst. gen. mgr. fibers div., 1969-72; v.p. IRC Fibers Co. (subs.), 1969-72; exec. v.p. Formica Corp., Cin., 1972-73, pres., 1973-80; pres. fibers div. Am. Cyanamid, 1980-84, corp. v.p., 1984-90. Chmn. bd. 4th Dist. Fed. Res. Bank, Cin.; adj. prof. Ramapo Coll., 1990-98; chmn. Mgmt. Decision Lab., NYU Grad. Sch. Bus., 1990-98. Author: The Leadership Myth; contbr. articles to textile and tech. publs. Served with USNR, 1945-46. Mem. Am. Chem. Soc., Am. Assn. Textile Chemists and Colorists. Clubs: Chemists (N.Y.C.). Home: 777 Butternut Dr Franklin Lakes

NJ 07417-2281 E-mail: friedmanm@prodigy.net. *Integrity should permeate every discussion of every facet of leadership. Integrity is the basic quality to be sought in consideration of any person's qualifications for assuming a position of trust and responsibility.*

FRIEDMAN, MARTIN PHILIP, applied behavior sciences specialist, education educator; b. N.Y., Nov. 20, 1956; s. Robert and Irma (Juroff) Friedman. BS, SUNY, Cortland, 1978, MS, 1983. Tchg. asst. SUNY, Cortland, 1980—81; adj. lectr. Tompkins-Cortland C.C., Dryden, NY, 1982; behavior specialist Albany ARC, NY, 1983—84; sr. behavior specialist Ctr. for the Disabled, Albany, 1984—95; staff tng. specialist Camary Statewide Svc., Albany, 1995—96; applied behavior sci. specialist Schenectady County ARC (Ridge Health Svcs.), Schenectady, NY, 1996—99; adj. lectr. The Coll. St. Rose, Albany, 2000—. Rsch. asst. SUNY, Cortland, 1976—83. Mem.: Media Ecology Assn. Jewish. Avocations: music, book and music collecting, advocating for people with disabilities.

FRIEDMAN, MARVIN ROSS, lawyer; b. Mpls., July 13, 1941; s. H. W. and Katherine F.; widowed; children: Natasha E., Chloe J. BBA, U. Miami, 1966, JD, 1969. Bar: Fla. 1969. Pvt. practice, Coral Cables, Fla., 1970—. Founder Diabetes Rsch. Found.; hon. trustee Lowe Art Mus., Mus. Contemporary Art, Wolfsonian Mus., F.I.U. Art Mus.; Tri-county v.p. Miami City Ballet; hon. trustee Friends of the Libr., Met. Opera, N.Y.C., Mus. Modern Art, N.Y.C., Whitney Mus., N.Y.C., Guggenheim Mus., NY, Miami Art Mus. Mem.: ABA, ATLA, Am. Coll. Barristers, Million Dollar Advocates Forum, Dade County Trial Lawyers Assn., Fla. Acad. Trial Lawyers, Coral Gables Bar Assn., Dade County Bar Assn., Fla. Bar, English Speaking Union, Guild Hall Club, East Hampton (NY) Tennis Club, Fisher Island Club. Office: Friedman & Friedman 2600 S Douglas Rd Ste 1011 Coral Gables FL 33134-6142

FRIEDMAN, MATTHEW JOEL, psychiatrist, pharmacologist, educator; b. Newark, N.Y., Mar. 10, 1940; s. Harry and Gertrude (Plaine) F.; divorced; children: Abigail Jewell, Ezra Richard; m. Gayle Marie Smith, Oct. 3, 1976; children: Jessica Kate, Rebecca Marie. AB summa cum laude, Dartmouth Coll., 1961; PhD in Pharmacology, Albert Einstein Coll. Medicine, 1967; MD, U. Ky., 1969. Intern U. Ky. Med. Ctr., Lexington, 1969-70; resident in psychiatry Mass. Gen. Hosp., Boston, 1970-72, Dartmouth-Hitchcock Med. Ctr., Hanover, N.H., 1972-73; asst. prof. psychiatry and pharmacology Dartmouth Med. Sch., Hanover, 1973-78, assoc. prof., 1978-88, prof., 1988—; staff psychiatrist VA Hosp., White River Juction, Vt., 1973-78, chief psychiatry, 1978-89; exec. dir. Nat. Ctr. for Post-Traumatic Stress Disorder, White River Juction, Vt., 1989—; attending staff Dartmouth-Hitchcock Med. Ctr., Hanover, 1980—. Chmn. VA chief med. dirs. spl. com. post-traumatic stress disorder, 1984-89; mem. Persian Gulf expert sci. com. VA/Dept. Def./HHS, 1993-98; mem. clin. practice guidelines com. VA/Dept. Def., 2002—. Contbr. books, chpts. for books, articles for profl. jours. Recipient Nat. Comdr.'s award DAV, 1975, 83, cert. for significant achievement Hosp. and Community Psychiatry Inst., 1988, William C. Porter award Assn. Mil. Surgeons U.S., Spl. Recognition award Vietnam Vets. Am., 1993, Patrick J. Leahy VA Rsch. award, 1996; named an Outstanding Fed. Employee of Vt., 1989; grantee VA, 1975—, NIH, 1996. Fellow Am. Psychiat. Assn. (diagnostic and statis. manual IV task force on post-traumatic stress disorder); mem. Internat. Soc. Traumatic Stress Studies (co-chmn. psychiat. curriculum com. 1988-90, bd. dirs. 1991—, exec. com. 1991—, pres. 1995-96, Lifetime Achievement award 1999), Anxiety Disorders Assn. Am. (sci. adv. bd. 2000—), Nat. Assn. VA Chiefs Psychiatry, Physicians for Social Responsibility. Avocations: alpine skiing, nordic skiing, gardening, running, horses. Home: 2326 Cox Dist Rd Woodstock VT 05091-9717 Office: Nat Ctr for Post-Traumatic Stress Disorder VA Hosp 215 N Main St White River Junction VT 05009 E-mail: matthew.friedman@dartmouth.edu.

FRIEDMAN, MAURICE STANLEY, religious educator; b. Tulsa, Dec. 29, 1921; s. Samuel Herman and Fanny (Smirin) F.; m. Eugenia Chifos, Jan. 1947 (div. 1974); children: David Michael, Dvora Lisa; m. Aleene Maree Wright Dorn, Sept. 29, 1986. SB in Econs. magna cum laude, Harvard U., 1943; MA in English, Ohio State U., 1947; PhD in History of Culture, U. Chgo., 1950; LLD (hon.), U. Vt., 1961; MA in Psychology, Internat. Coll., 1983; LHD (hon.), Profl. Sch. Psychol. Studies, San Diego, 1986, Hebrew Union Coll., 1998. Prof. philosophy and lit. Sarah Lawrence Coll., 1951-54, prof. philosophy, 1954-64; prof. philosophy and religion Manhattanville Coll. of the Sacred Heart, Purchase, N.Y., 1966-67, Vassar Coll., Poughkeepsie, N.Y., 1967; prof. religion Temple U., Phila., 1966-73, also dir. PhD programs in religion and psychology and religion and lit.; prof. religious studies, philosophy and comparative lit. San Diego State U., 1973-91, ann. Maurice Friedman lectureship in modern Jewish thought, 1992—, prof. emeritus, 1991—; human sci. program dir., faculty Calif. Inst. for Human Sci., San Diego, 1995-97; disting. consulting faculty Saybrook Grad. Sch., 1998—. Tutor Internat. Coll., L.A., 1976-86, William Lyon U., 1986-92, Am. Commonwealth U., 1992-95; vis. prof. religious philosophy Hebrew Union Coll.-Jewish Inst. Religion, Cin., 1956, Union Theol. Sem., N.Y.C., 1965, 67, dept. religion U. Hawaii, 1975; mem. faculty New Sch. for Social Rsch., N.Y.C., 1954-66, Washington Sch. Psychiatry, 1957-59, Pendle Hill, Quaker Ctr. for Study, Wallingford, Pa., 1959-60, 64-65, 67-73; guest lectr. William Alanson White Inst. Psychiatry, Psychoanalysis and Psychology, 1958-60; core faculty Calif. Sch. Profl. Psychology, San Diego, 1973-75; univ. rsch. scholar San Diego State U., 1984-85; sr. Fulbright lectr. Hebrew U., Jerusalem, 1987-88; vis. prof. Indira Gandhi Nat. Ctr. for Arts, New Delhi, 1992; vis. prof. edn. U. San Diego, 2003; fellow com. on the history of culture U. Chgo., 1947-49; co-dir. Inst. for Dialogical Psychotherapy, San Diego, 1984-2000; vis. prof. Trinity Coll. Grad. Studies, 1999, 2001; prof. philosophy Acad. for Jewish Religion, 2001—. Author: Martin Buber: The Life of Dialogue, 1955, 4th edit., 2002Problematic Rebel: Melville, Dostoievsky, Kafka, Camus, 1963, rev. edit. 1970, The Worlds of Existentialism: A Critical Reader, 1964, To Deny Our Nothingness: Contemporary Images of Man, 1967, Touchstones of Reality: Existential Trust and the Community of Peace, 1972, The Hidden Human Image, 1974, The Human Way: A Dialogical Approach to Religion and Human Experience, 1982, The Confirmation of Otherness: In Family, Community and Society, 1983, Martin Buber's Life and Work: The Early Years 1878-1923, 1982, The Middle Years, 1923-45, 1983, The Later Years 1945-65, 1984 (Nat. Jewish Book award for biography 1985), Contemporary Psychology: Revealing and Obscuring the Human, 1984, The Healing Dialogue In Psychotherapy, 1985 (main selection of Psychotherapy and Social Sci. Book Club, Mar. 1985), Martin Buber and The Eternal, 1986, Abraham Joshua Heschel and Elie Wiesel: "You are my Witnesses", 1987, A Dialogue with Hasidic Tales: Hallowing the Everyday, 1988, Encounter on the Narrow Ridge: A Life of Martin Buber, 1991, Dialogue and the Human Image: Beyond Humanistic Psychology, 1992, Religion and Psychology: A Dialogical Approach, 1992, A Heart of Wisdom: Religion and Human Wholeness, 1992, Encuentro en el Desfiladero: Una Vida de Martin Buber, 1993, Intercultural Dialogue and the Human Image: Maurice Friedman at the Indira Gandhi National Centre for the Arts, 1995; Editor-in-Chief, Martin Buber and the Human Sciences, 1996, The Affirming Flame: A Poetics of Meaning, 1999, Begegnung auf dem schmalen Grat: Ein Leben Martin Bubers, 1999, Narrow Ridge: A Life of Martin Buber, two vol. Japanese trans., 2000; contbr. numerous articles to profl. jours. Recipient Outstanding Faculty award San Diego State U., 1980, Humanist Scholar of Yr. award Saybrook Grad. Sch., 1995. Mem. Religious Edn. Assn. (past bd. dirs., past edit. bd.), Am. Philol. Assn., Am. Acad. Religion, Am. Soc. Study Religion, Fellowship of Reconciliation, Jewish Peace Fellowship, Assn. Humanistic Psychology (edit. bd. Jour. Humanistic Psychology and Person-Centered Rev.). Home: 421 Hilmen Pl Solana Beach CA 92075-1318

FRIEDMAN, MAX PAUL, education educator; b. Boston, Sept. 21, 1967; s. Martin Boris Friedman and Adele Charlene Bernstein; m. Katharina Vester, Oct. 19, 2001. BA, Oberlin Coll., 1989; MA, Univ. Calif., Berkeley, 1995, PhD, 2000. Asst. prodr. Nat. Pub. Radio, Washington, 1989—92; freelance writer N.Y., 1992—94; graduate fellow Univ. Calif., Berkeley, Calif., 1994—2000; Woodrow Wilson postdoctoral fellow Univ. Colo., Boulder, Colo., 2000—02; asst. prof. Fla. State Univ., Tallahassee, 2002—. Author: Nazis and Good Neighbors, 2003 (Littauer, 2003); contbr. articles to profl. jours. Bendix fellowship, Berlin, Germany, 1996, German Hist. Inst. fellowship, Cologne, Germany, 2003. Mem.: Soc. for Hist. of Am. Foreign Rels. (Holt Fellowship 1998), Am. Hist. Assn. Office: Fla State Univ Hist Dept 401 Bellamy Tallahassee FL 32306-2200

FRIEDMAN, MERTON HIRSCH, retired psychologist, educator; b. Boston, Apr. 12, 1925; s. Isadore and Frances (Ponack) F.; m. Judith Lee Freeman, Nov. 27, 1955; 1 child, Eric Lund. BS, Coll. William and Mary, 1945; MA, U. Pa., 1947; PhD, U. Ill., 1952. Lic. psychologist, N.J., Mass. Psychology intern Conn. Valley Hosp., Middletown, 1947-48; postdoctoral intern Dept. Vet. Affairs Mental Health Clinic, Phila., 1952-53; staff psychologist Dept. Vet. Affairs Med. Ctr., Boston, 1953-59, chief psychology svc. Providence, 1959-62; chief psychologist Cmty. Mental Health Ctr., Brookline, Mass., 1962-64; dir. clin. svcs. Jewish Vocat. Svc., Milw., 1966-67; clin. assoc. prof. psychiatry U. Medicine and Dentistry N.J., 1968-92; chief psychology svc. Dept. Vet. Affairs Med. Ctr., East Orange, N.J., 1967-96; ret., 1996. Vis. lectr. Fulbright program Lund U., Sweden, 1964-66. Contbr. articles to profl. jours. USPHS Rsch. fellow NIMH, U. Ill., 1951-52. Fellow Am. Orthopsychiat. Assn.; mem. APA, Mass. Psychol. Assn., N.J. Psychol. Assn., Sigma Xi (U. Ill. chpt.). Democrat. Jewish. Avocations: piano, hiking, philately, classical music. Home: 79 Falcon Rd Livingston NJ 07039-4414

FRIEDMAN, MICHAEL, pharmaceutical executive; BA, Bklyn. Coll.; MBA, U. Conn. Various pos., including v.p. mktg. and COO pneumatic fastening systems divsn. Hilti, Inc.; v.p., asst. to pres. and chmn. Purdue Pharma, Stamford, Conn., 1985—88, group v.p., 1988—99, exec. v.p., COO, 1999—2002, pres., CEO, 2003—. Office: Purdue PHrma 1 Stamford Forum Stamford CT 06901*

FRIEDMAN, MILDRED, architectural and design educator, curator, consultant; b. L.A., July 25, 1929; d. Nathaniel and Hortense (Weinsveig) Shenberg; m. Martin Friedman; children: Lise, Ceil, Zoe. BA, UCLA, 1951, MA, 1952; DFA (hon.), Mpls. Coll. Art, 1984; DFA, Hamlin U., 1987. Instr. design L.A. City Coll., 1952-54; archtl. designer Cerny Assocs., Mpls., 1957-69; design curator Walker Art Ctr., Mpls., 1970-90; freelance cons. N.Y.C., 1990—. Mem. arch. and design panel Nat. Endowment Arts, 1975—78, mem. policy panel design arts, 1979—82, mem. presdl. design awards jury, 1991; mem. vis. com. Sch. Arch. and Planning MIT, 1985—88; mem. vis. com. Grad. Sch. Design Harvard U., 1994—; bd. dirs. Internat. Design Conf., Aspen, 1989—91, Chgo. Inst. Arch. and Urbanism, 1990—93, Nat. Inst. Archtl. Edn., 1993—; mem. design jury Am. Acad. Rome, 1991; guest instr. UCLA, 1992; mem. jury to select architect for Whitehall Ferry Terminal, N.Y.C., 1992; vis. instr. Harvard U., 1993; cons. Battery Park City Authority, N.Y.C.; guest curator Bklyn. Mus., 1992—2002; guest curator for Frank Gehry retrospective exhbn. Solomon R. Guggenheim Mus., N.Y.C., 2001; guest curator for Vital Forms exhbn. Bklyn. Mus. Art, 2001—02. Author, editor: Gehry Talks, 1999; editor Design Quar., 1970-91, numerous catalogues. Recipient Outstanding Achievement award YWCA, 1984, Outstanding Svc. award U. Minn., 1991; fellow Intellectual Interchange program Japan Soc., 1982, Chrysler Design award, 2002; grantee Nat. Endowment Arts, 1992-93, Graham Found. for Advanced Studies in Fine Arts, 1997; recipient Graham Found grant for Design Quar. Anthology. Mem. AIA (hon., nat. awards jury 1981, 87, bd. dirs. Minn. chpt. 1984-86, Inst. Honors 1994).

FRIEDMAN, MILTON, economist, educator; b. Bklyn., July 31, 1912; s. Jeno Saul and Sarah Ethel (Landau) Friedman; m. Rose Director, June 25, 1938; children: Janet, David. AB, Rutgers U., 1932, LLD (hon.), 1968; AM, U. Chgo., 1933; PhD, Columbia U., 1946; LLD (hon.), St. Paul's (Rikkyo) U., 1963; LLD (hon.), Loyola U., 1971; LLD (hon.), U. N.H., 1975; LLD (hon.), Harvard U., 1979, Brigham Young U., 1980; LLD (hon.), Dartmouth Coll., 1980, Gonzaga U., 1981; DSc (hon.), Rochester U., 1971; LHD (hon.), Rockford Coll., 1969, Roosevelt U., 1975, Hebrew Union Coll., L.A., 1981, Jacksonville U., 1993; LittD (hon.), Bethany Coll., 1971; PhD (hon.), Hebrew U., Jerusalem, 1977; DCS (hon.), Francisco Marroquín U., Guatemala, 1978; D honoris causa (hon.), Econ. U. Prague, 1997. Assoc. economist Nat. Resources Com., Washington, 1935—37; mem. rsch. staff Nat. Bur. Econ. Rsch., N.Y.C., 1937—45, 1948—81; vis. prof. econs. U. Wis., Madison, 1940—41; prin. economist, tax research div. U.S. Treasury Dept., Washington, 1941—43; assoc. dir. research, statis. research group, War Research div. Columbia U., N.Y.C., 1943—45; assoc. prof. econs. and statistics U. Minn., Mpls., 1945—46; assoc. prof. econs. U. Chgo., 1946—48, prof. econs., 1948—62, Paul Snowden Russell disting. service prof. econs., 1962—82, prof. emeritus, 1983—; Fulbright lectr. Cambridge U., 1953—54; vis. Wesley Clair Mitchell research prof. econs. Columbia U., N.Y.C., 1964—65; fellow Ctr. for Advanced Study in Behavioral Sci., 1957—58; sr. research fellow Hoover Inst., Stanford U., 1977—. Mem. Pres.'s Commn. All-Vol. Army, 1969—70, Pres.'s Commn. on White House Fellows, 1971—74, Pres.'s Econ. Policy Adv. Bd., 1981—88; vis. scholar Fed. Res. Bank, San Francisco, 1977. Author (with Carl Shoup and Ruth P. Mack): Taxing to Prevent Inflation, 1943; author: (with Simon S. Kuznets) Income from Independent Professional Practice, 1946; author: (with Harold A. Freeman, Frederic Mosteller, W. Allen Wallis) Sampling Inspection, 1948; author: Essays in Positive Economics, 1953, A Theory of the Consumption Function, 1957, A Program for Monetary Stability, 1960, Price Theory: A Provisional Text, 1962; author: (with Rose D. Friedman) Capitalism and Freedom, 1962; author: (with Anna J. Schwartz) A Monetary History of the United States, 1867-1960, 1963; author: Inflation: Causes and Consequences, 1963; author: (with Robert Roosa) The Balance of Payments: Free vs. Fixed Exchange Rates, 1967; author: Dollars and Deficits, 1968, The Optimum Quantity of Money and Other Essays, 1969; author: (with Walter W. Heller) Monetary vs. Fiscal Policy, 1969; author: (with Schwartz) Monetary Statistics of the United States, 1970; author: A Theoretical Framework for Monetary Analysis, 1972; author: (with Wilbur J. Cohen) Social Security, 1972; author: An Economist's Protest, 1972; author: (with Robert J. Gordon et al) Milton Friedman's Monetary Framework, 1974; author: There's No Such Thing as a Free Lunch, 1975, Price Theory, 1976, Tax Limitation, Inflation and the Role of Government, 1978; author: (with R.D. Friedman) Free to Choose, 1980; author: (with Schwartz) Monetary Trends in the U.S. and the United Kingdom, 1982; author: Bright Promises, Dismal Performance, 1983; author: (with R.D. Friedman) Tyranny of the Status Quo, 1984; author: Monetarist Economics, 1991, Money Mischief, 1992; author: (with Thomas S. Szasz) Friedman & Szasz on Drugs: Essays on the Free Market and Prohibition, 1992; author: (with R.D. Friedman) Two Lucky People: Memoirs, 1998; editor: Studies in the Quantity Theory of Money, 1965; bd. editors: Am. Econ. Rev., 1951—53, Econometrica, 1957—69, adv. bd.: Jour. Money, Credit and Banking, 1968—94, columnist: Newsweek Mag., 1966—84, contbg. editor:, 1971—84; contbr. articles to profl. jours. Chmn. bd. dirs. Milton and Rose D. Friedman Found.; mem. adv. bd. Calif. Parents for Ednl. Choice, 1999—. Decorated Grand Cordon of the 1st Class Order of the Sacred Treasure Japan; named Chicagoan of Yr., Chgo. Press Club, 1972, Educator of Yr., Chgo. Jewish United Fund, 1973; recipient Nobel prize in econs., 1976, Pvt. Enterprise Exemplar medal, Freedoms Found., 1978, Presdl. medal of Freedom, 1988, Nat. Medal of Sci., 1988, Prize in Moral-Cultural Affairs, Instn. World Capitalism, 1993, Earl M. Combs Jr. award, Chgo. Bd. Trade Ednl. Rsch. Found., 1991, Source award for lifetime achievement, The Primary Source, Tufts U., 1997, Robert Maynard Hutchins History Maker award for distinction in edn., Chgo. Hist. Soc., 1997, Templeton Honor Rolls Lifetime Achievement award, 1997, Goldwater award, 1997, James U. Blanchard III Freedom award, Jefferson Fin., 2001, Abraham Lincoln award, Am. Hungarian Found., 2002, Statesmanship award, Claremont Inst., 2002. Fellow: Econometric Soc., Am. Statis. Assn., Inst. Math. Stats.; mem.: NAS, Mont Pelerin Soc. (bd. dirs. 1958—61, pres. 1970—72), Am. Philos. Soc., Royal Econ. Soc., Western Econ. Assn. (pres. 1984—85), Am. Enterprise Inst. (adv. bd. 1956—79), Am. Econ. Assn. (exec. com. 1955—57, pres. 1967, John Bates Clark medal 1951), Quadrangle Club. Office: Stanford U Hoover Instn Stanford CA 94305-6010

FRIEDMAN, MONROE, psychologist, educator; b. NYC, Oct. 16, 1934; s. Isadore and Pearl Friedman; m. Rita Joyce Shaffer, Sept. 2, 1956; children: Ethan, Mark, Jordan. BS, Bklyn. Coll., 1956; PhD, U. Tenn., 1959. Human factors scientist Sys. Devel. Corp., Santa Monica, Calif., 1959-64; prof. Ea. Mich. U., Ypsilanti, 1964—, dir. Contemporary Issues Ctr., 1970—79. Vis. prof. Tilburg (The Netherlands) U., 1982—83, U. Leuven, Belgium, 1990—91; cons. Pres.'s Com. (Lyndon Johnson) on Consumer Interests, Washington, 1966, Consumer Interests Found., Washington, 1972—73; cons. NSF, Washington, 1973—74, U.S. Gen. Acctg. Office, Washington, 1973—74, FTC, Washington, 1976—77, ACLU Found., NY, 2001—02; bd. dirs. Consumer Interest Rsch. Inst., Washington; presenter in field. Author: A Brand New Language, 1991, Consumer Boycotts, 1999 (Outstanding Acad. Title of Yr., Assn. for Coll. and Rsch. Librs. 2000); contbr. Jour. Consumer Affairs, 1998; issue editor Jour. Social Issues, 1991; co-editor: Frontier of Research in the Consumer Interest, 1988; contbr. over 100 articles to profl. publs.; editl. bd. Jour. Consumer Affairs, Jour. Consumer Rsch., Jour. Consumer Policy; editor: Jour. Consumer Affairs, 1980-84. Pres. Am. Coun. Consumer Interests, 1989—90. Rsch. grantee AARP Andrus Found., 1990, 92, Mich. Coun. for Humanities, 1975; Congl. fellow Am. Polit. Sci. Assn., 1966-67; recipient Disting. Faculty award Mich. Bd. Regents, 1983. Fellow APA (divsn. Population and Environ. Psychology, divsn. Tchg. of Psychology, divsn. Internat. Psychology, divsn. Media Psychology and divsn. Adult Devel. and Aging), Am. Psychol. Soc. (charter), Am. Assn. Applied and Preventive Psychology (charter), Am. Coun. on Consumer Interests (disting., Applied Consumer Econs. award, 1991, 97), Soc. for Consumer Psychology, Soc. for the Psychol. Study of Social Issues, Soc. for Psychology of Aesthetics, Creativity, and the Arts, Soc. for the Study of Peace, Conflict and Violence; mem. Internat. Assn. for Rsch. in Econ. Psychology (U.S. rep. bd. trustees 1982—), Internat. Assn. Applied Psychology (U.S. rep. bd. trustees econ. psychology divsn. 1988—). Home: 1613 E Stadium Blvd Ann Arbor MI 48104-4452 Office: Ea Mich U Psychology Dept Ypsilanti MI 48197

FRIEDMAN, MORTON LEE, lawyer; b. Aberdeen, S.D., Aug. 4, 1932; s. Philip and Rebecca (Feinstein) F.; m. Marcine Lichter, Dec. 20, 1955; children— Mark, Philip, Jeffrey. Student, U. Mich., 1950-53; AB, Stanford U., 1954, LL.B., 1956. Bar: Calif. bar 1956. Mem. firm Kimble, Thomas, Snell, Jamison & Russell, Fresno, 1957, Busick & Busick, Sacramento, 1957-59; sr. ptnr. firm Friedman, Collard & Poswall (name now Friedman, Collard & Panneton), Sacramento, 1959—. Lectr. various law schs. and seminars; mem. Calif. Bd. Continuing Edn. Pres. Mosaic Law Congregation, 1977-80, 97-99; v.p. Sacramento Jewish Fedn., 1980-82; chmn. Sacramento campaign United Jewish Appeal, 1981; bd. dirs., former nat. v.p. Am. Israel Pub. Affairs Com.; mem. bd. Calif. State U. Inst., 1995-99; bd. dirs. Nat. Bd. AntiDefamation League. 1st lt. USAF, 1956. Recipient Sacramento Businessman of Yr. award Sacramento Met. C. of C., 1991, Best Lawyers in Am. award, Outstanding Philanthropists award Nat. Soc. Fund Raising Execs., 1999; Fulbright candidate Stanford Law Sch., 1956. Fellow Am. Coll. Trial Lawyers; mem. ABA, ATLA, Calif. Bar Assn., Sacramento County Bar Assn. (pres. 1976, Lawyer of Yr. 1999), Calif. Trial Lawyers Assn. (v.p. 1973-75), Capitol City Lawyers Club (past pres.), Am. Bd. Trial Advocates (adv., pres. 1977, Calif. Trial Lawyer of Yr. 1988, SCALE award 2002), West Sacramento C. of C. (dir.), Order of Coif. Democrat. Home: 1620 McClaren Dr Carmichael CA 95608-5936 Office: Friedman Collard & Panneton 7750 College Town Dr Ste 300 Sacramento CA 95826 2386

FRIEDMAN, MURRAY, civil rights official, historian; b. N.Y.C., Sept. 15, 1926; s. Benjiman and Eva (Greenspan) F.; m. Eve Rosenfeld, July 23, 1949 (dec. 1997); children: Oren L., Keith M., Tamima Beth; m. Marha Varbald, Feb. 1998. BA, Bklyn. Coll., 1948; MA, NYU, 1949; PhD, Georgetown U., 1958. Historian Office Chief Mil. History, Washington, 1949—52; asst. to dir. Washington Housing Assn., 1952—53; dir. Va.-N.C. office Anti-Defamation League, Richmond, Va., 1954—59; dir. Mid Atlantic region Am. Jewish Com., Phila., 1959—2002. Dir. Myer and Rosaline Feinstein Ctr. for Am. Jewish History, Temple U., Phila., 1990—; lectr. USIA, Africa, India, 1974. Author: The Utopian Dilemma, American Judaism and Public Policy: What Went Wrong? The Creation and Collapse of the Black Jewish Alliance, 1995; editor: Overcoming Middle Class Rage, 1971, New Perspectives on School Integration, 1979, Jewish Life in Philadelphia, 1983, When Philadelphia Was the Capitol of Jewish America, 1994, (with Nancy Isserman) The Tribal Basis of American Life, 1998; editor: (with A. Chernin) A Second Exodus: The American Movement to Free Soviet Jews, 1999, Philadelphia Jewish Life, 1940-2000, 2d edit., 2003; guest editor (spl. issue) Am. Jewish History Am. Jewish Polit. Conservatism, June 1999 and Nov. 1999. Bd. dirs. Pa. Humanities Coun., Phila., 1984-88, Landmark Legal Found. Ctr. for Civil Rights; bd. dirs., past co-chmn. Greater Phila. Urban Affairs Coalition; vice chmn. U.S. Commn. on Civil Rights, Washington, 1986-89. With USMC, 1945. Mem. Am. Hist. Assn., Am. Jewish Hist. Assn. Democrat. Jewish. Avocation: tennis. Home: Apt 11A5 2401 Pennsylvania Ave Philadelphia PA 19130 Office: Temple Univ Rm 203 1515 Market St Philadelphia PA 19103 E-mail: murrayfrie@aol.com.

FRIEDMAN, MYLES IVAN, education educator; b. Chgo., Apr. 5, 1924; s. Max Edward and Ethel (Goldman) F.; m. Betty Ann McDowell, July 4, 1978; children: Gregg Alan, Myles Ivan Jr. MA, U. Chgo., 1957, PhD, 1959. Real estate, home builder, 1946-58; asst. prof. edn. Northwestern U., 1958-60, assoc. prof., 1960-64; chaired prof. edn. U. S.C., 1964—99; vis. prof. U. Calif., Berkeley, summer 1968. Cons. in field; dir. Head Start Evaluation and Rsch. Ctr.; dir. rsch. Regional Edn. Lab., Carolinas and Va.; pres. Inst. for Evidence-Based Decision-Making in Edn., 1995—. Author: Rational Behavior, 1975, Teaching Reading and Thinking Skills, 1979; sr. author: Improving Teacher Education, 1979, Human Nature and Predictability, 1981, Teaching Higher Order Thinking Skills to Gifted Students, 1983, The Psychology of Human Control, 1991, Taking Control: Vitalizing Education, 1993, Improving the Quality of Life, 1997, Handbook on Effective Instructional Strategies, 1998, Ensuring Student Success, 2000, Educators' Handbook on Effective Testing, 2003; contbr. articles to profl. jours. Served with USAAF, 1942-46. Mem. APA. Home: 1709 Seay Ct Columbia SC 29206-3117

FRIEDMAN, PAUL JAY, radiologist, educator; b. N.Y.C., Jan. 20, 1937; s. Louis Alexander and Rose (Solomon) Friedman; m. Elisabeth Clare Richardson, June 18, 1960; children: Elizabeth Ruth Coley, Deborah Anne Yeager, Matthew Alexander Xu-Friedman, Rachel Clare Lentz. BS, U. Wis., 1955; postgrad., Oxford (Eng.) U., 1957-58; MD, Yale U., 1960. Intern Einstein Med. Sch., N.Y.C., 1960-61; resident in radiology Columbia-Presbyn. Hosp., N.Y.C., 1961-64; asst. prof., assoc. prof. U. Calif. San Diego Med. Sch., 1968-75, prof. radiology, 1975-2001, from assoc. dean to dean acad. affairs, 1982-95, prof. emeritus, 2001—. Cons. VA Hosp., 1971-2001; vis. scholar Inst. Med./NAS, AAMC, 1988-89; adv. com. on rsch. integrity Dept. Health & Human Svcs., 1991-93; cons. 26th, 27th and 28th edit. Stedman's Med. Dictionary; specialist in chest radiology and rsch. ethics, tenure and retirement issues; bd. dirs. Am. Coun. Edn., 1996-97. Mem. editl. bd. Investigative Radiology, 1976-87, Am. Jour. Roentgenology, 1986-88; contbr. articles to profl. jours. Bd. dirs. La Jolla Symphony Assn., 1987—92. Lt. cmdr. M.C. USNR, 1964—66. Markle scholar acad. medicine, 1969-74; Picker Found. advanced acad. fellow and scholar, 1966-69 Fellow Am. Coll. Chest Physicians, Am. Coll. Radiology; mem. AAUP, Assn. of Am. Med. Colls. (disting. svc. mem.), Internat. Soc. for Magnetic Resonance in Medicine, Assn. Univ. Radiologists (rep. to coun. acad. socs. Assn. Am. Med. Colls. 1985-97), Soc. for Computer Applications in Radiology, Fleischner Soc. (pres. 1994-95), Radiol. Soc. N.Am. (emeritus), Roentgen Ray Soc. (emeritus), Nat. Conf. Lawyers and Scientists, Phi Beta Kappa, Alpha Omega Alpha. Avocations: choral singing, computers, gardening. Home: 5644 Soledad Rd La Jolla CA 92037-7048 Office: U Calif Sch Medicine Dept Radiology 200 W Arbor Dr San Diego CA 92103-9000

FRIEDMAN, PAUL RICHARD, lawyer; b. Washington, Mar. 25, 1944; s. Herbert and Gertrude (Miller) F.; m. Ronna Lee Beck; children: Mali, Luke, Jed. BA, Princeton U., 1965; MA, Trinity Coll., Cambridge U., England, 1967; JD, Yale U., 1970; postgrad., Balt./D.C. Inst. Psychoanalysis, 1971-78. Bar: D.C. 1972, U.S. Ct. Appeals (3d - 1984, 4th - 1979, and D.C. cirs. - 1972), U.S Supreme Ct. 1975. Law clk. to Hon. J. Skelly Wright U.S. Ct. Appeals (D.C. cir.), Washington, 1970-71; fellow Ctr. for Law and Social Policy, Washington, 1971-72; dir. Mental Health Law Project, Washington, 1972-81; mng. ptnr. Ennis, Friedman, Bersoff and Ewing, Washington, 1981-88; pvt. practice, Washington, 1996—; dep. assoc. atty. gen. Dept. of Justice, Washington, 1993-96; of counsel Shea and Gardner, 2002—. Ct.-apptd. mediator and early neutral evaluator, 1988-89; chmn. Practicing Law Inst. Nat. Seminars on Legal Rights of Mentally Disabled Persons, 1979-80; coord. task panel on legal and ethical issues Pres.'s Commn. on Mental Health, 1977-78; mem. adv. com. on procedures U.S. Ct. Appeals (D.C. cir.) 1977-78; mem. steering com. Ctr. for Y2K & Soc., 1998-2000. Author: The Rights of Mentally Retarded Persons - An American Civil Liberties Handbook, 1976; editor: Legal Rights of Mentally Disabled Persons, 3 vols., 1979; note and comment editor Yale Law Jour., 1969-70, bd. editors 1967-69; contbr. articles to profl. publs. Trustee The Green Door, 1977-83. Nat. Merit scholar, Univ. scholar; Woodrow Wilson fellow, Keasbey fellow. Mem. ABA (mem. comm. on mentally disabled 1981-82), D.C. Bar, Am. Psychoanalytic Assn (affiliate), 1971 78, Phi Beta Kappa. Avocations: tennis and other racquet sports, computers, photography. E-mail: pfriedman@sheagardner.com.

FRIEDMAN, PAULINE POPLIN, civic worker, consultant; b. Scranton, Pa., Apr. 2, 1930; d. Harry and Lillian (Kushner) Poplin; m. Sidney Friedman, Aug. 3, 1952; children: Anne Friedman Glauber, Robert. BS, Pa. State U., 1952. Cons. AID, Washington, 1993—. Trustee Temple Israel, 1985-87, Jewish Cmty. Ctr., 1992—; mem. coun. King's Coll., 1992—; pres. Home Health Svcs.-vis. Nurse Assn., Kingston, Pa., 1987-88, Coun. Family Agys., Harrisburg, Pa., 1987-88, Family Svc. Wyoming Valley, Wilkes-Barre, 1988-90; mentor Leadership Wilkes-Barre; mem. pres.' coun. Wilkes U., 1991—, King's Coll.; v.p. United Way, Interfaith Coun. Wyoming Valley; bd. dirs. Ethics Inst. N.E. Pa., Dallas, 1994—, St. Vincent De Paul Soup Kitchen, Prevent Child Abuse Pa.; bd. alumni coun. Pa. State U.; mem. Jewish Cmty. Bd. Wyoming Valley; chairwoman United Jewish Campaign, Wyoming Valley, 1998-99; chair Speak-Out Day U.S.A., Luzerne County, First Cantorial Concert for Wilkes Barre, Scranton and Northeat Pa. Recipient Humanitarian award Interfaith Coun. Wyoming Valley, 1989, Phillip Mitchell Cmty. Svc. award Pa. State U., 1990, Woman of Yr. award Family Svc. Wyoming Valley, 1993, Pathfinders award Luzerne County Women's Conf., 1995, Disting. Svc. award B'nai Brith, 1996, Svc. award to Women, N.E. Pa. Boy Scouts Coun. Avocations: golf, tennis, travel. Home: 796 Milford Dr Kingston PA 18704-5308

FRIEDMAN, PENNY, lawyer; b. Cleve., Dec. 24, 1951; d. Harold Emanuel and Ruth (Resnick) F.; children: Rachel, Leah. AB in Econs. with high honors, U. Mich., 1973, JD cum laude, 1977. Bar: Ohio 1977. Atty. Taft, Stettinius & Hollister, Cin., 1977-80; v.p. property devel. Gt. Am. Broadcasting Co. (formerly Taft Broadcasting Co.), Cin., 1980-88; real estate portfolio mgr. Bartlett & Co., Cin., 1988-98; pres. Benefactors, LLC, 1998—. Mem. Cin. Downtown Progress Com., 1991-95, mem. exec. com., 1993-95; v.p. Cin. chpt. Am. Jewish Com., 1992-96, pres. 1996-98, mem. exec. com., 1990—; v.p. Leadership Cin. Alumni Assn., 1987-89; chmn. Family Svc. Cin. Area, 1991-92, pres., 1988-90, v.p., 1985-88, trustee, 1979-93, trustee emeritus, 1993—; vice-chmn. Cin. Devel. Fund, 1989-95; vice chmn. Devel. Corp. Cin., 1990-92, trustee, 1989-92; bd. dirs. Cin. Ctr. for Devel. Disorders, 1979-85, Seven Hills Neighborhood Houses, 1981-86; trustee Cin. Arts Assn., 1992—, mem. exec. com. 1994—; trustee Downtown Cin., Inc., 1998—, Cin. Psychoanalytic Inst., 1994-2002, The Wellness Cmty., 1999-2002; vice chair, trustee Knowledgeworks Found., 1999—; trustee Found. Family Svc., 2000— (v.p. 2002—), Greater Cin. Arts and Edn. Ctr., 1999—; trustee Project Grad. Cin., 2003—. Mem. Cin. Bar Assn., Phi Beta Kappa. Office: BeneFactors LLC 312 Walnut St Ste 3560 Cincinnati OH 45202-4026 E-mail: benefactors@fuse.net., psoul@aol.com.

FRIEDMAN, RICHARD ALAN, psychiatrist; b. N.Y.C., Sept. 11, 1956; s. Jerome G. and Frances B. F. BA, Duke U., Durham, N.C., 1978; MD, Robert Wood Johnson Med. Sch., N.J., 1982. Assoc. prof. psychiatry Cornell U. Med. Coll., N.Y.C., 1987—. Fellow Am. Psychiat. Assn. Avocations: pianist, swimming, chamber music. Office: The New York Hosp Payne Whitney Clinic 535 E 68th St New York NY 10021-4870 E-mail: rafriedm@med.cornell.edu.

FRIEDMAN, RICHARD LLOYD, lawyer; b. Bklyn., Feb. 17, 1943; s. H. Martin and Naomi (Ortman) F.; m. Carole Anne Greenhause, Aug. 28, 1966; children: Melissa Joy, Jonathan Scott. BA, Rutgers U., 1964; JD, U. Calif., Berkeley, 1967; LLM, NYU, 1972. Bar: N.Y. 1968, U.S. Dist. Ct. (so. and ea. dists.) N.Y. 1968, U.S. Ct. Appeals (2d cir.) 1968, U.S. Suprme Ct. 1971, N.J. 1972, U.S. Dist. Ct. N.J. 1972, U.S. Ct. Appeals (3d cir.) 1982, U.S. Ct. Appeals (11th cir.), 1986; cert. criminal trial atty., civil trial atty. Asst. dist. atty. Office N.Y. County Dist. Atty., N.Y.C., 1967-71; ct. planner Appellate Divsn., N.Y.C., 1971-72; exec. dir. Dist. Atty.'s Assn., N.Y.C., 1972-74, Office Prosecutorial Svcs., N.Y.C., 1974-75; asst. U.S. atty., Newark, 1975-82; officer Giordano, Halleran & Ciesla, Middletown, N.J., 1982—. Lectr., advisor Inst. for Continuing Legal Edn., 1982—; lectr. Nat. Inst. Trial Advocacy; mem. Supreme Ct. Criminal Practice Com., Trenton, 1983-86, Supreme Ct. Women in Cts. com., 1994—, Mayor's Anti-Rape Task Force, N.Y.C., 1973-75; adj. assoc. prof. John Jay Coll. Criminal Justice, N.Y.C., 1973-74. Editor Dist. Atty. Newsletter, 1972-75, Criminal Law Sect. Newsletter, 1978-81. Recipient Dir.'s award Dept. Justice, 1982, spl. commendation award, 1983, spl. achievement awards, 1978, 80. Mem. NACDL, N.J. Bar Assn. (chmn. criminal law sect. 1983=84), Monmouth County Bar Assn., N.Y. State Bar Assn. (sec. criminal justice sect. 1974-75), N.J. Assn. Criminal Def. Lawyers (v.p., trustee, editor newsletter). Office: Giordano Halleran & Ciesla PC PO Box 190 Middletown NJ 07748-0190 E-mail: carrich21@aol.com., rfriedman@ghclaw.com.

FRIEDMAN, RICHARD NATHAN, lawyer; b. Phila., June 13, 1941; s. Martin Harry Friedman and Caroline (Fruchtman) Shaines; m. Nini; 1 child, Melissa Danielle. BA, U. Miami, 1962, JD, 1965; LLM in Taxation, Georgetown U., 1967. Bar: Fla. 1965. Staff atty. SEC, Washington, 1965-66; pvt. practice Washington, 1966-67; individual practice law Miami, Fla., 1968—; CEO All-State Sports Agts., Inc., 1996—99; player agt. NBPA, 1996-99; spl. asst. village atty. Village of Pinecrest, 2001. Adj. prof. U. Miami, 1972-76; arbitrator N.Y. Stock Exch., 1973—, AAA, 1988-2000, AMEX, NASD, 1988—; founder, pres. All-Star Music Corp., 1996—. Columnist Cmty. Newspapers, Miami, 1989—; featured performer motion picture Lenny 1974, other TV and theatrical films; rec. artist, The Singing Attorney, For Love of Country, 1996, All My Love, 2001; author numerous pub. poems. Founder, pres. Am. Stockholders Assn., Inc., 1971-74, Stop Transit-Over People, Inc., 1975-87; chmn. Sales Taxes Oppressing People, Fla., 1987—; mem. endowment com. U. Miami, 1970—; mem. Soc. Univ. Founders, U. Miami, 1980; co-chmn. sports com. Fla. Bar, 1997-99. Recipient Merit cert. Dade County Bar Assn., 1972-73; numerous certs. of appreciation Rotary Internat., Kiwanis and other svc. orgns., 1970—; Richard N. Friedman Week held in his honor City of Homestead, Fla., Apr. 1978; named Hon. Citizen State of Tenn., 1970, Citizen of Day Dade County (Fla.), Radio Sta. WINZ, 1980; recipient Leaders award Sunrise Cmty., 1986. Mem. NARAS, Unified Bar D.C. Office: 9655 S Dixie Hwy Ste 209 Miami FL 33156-2813 E-mail: busorgs@aol.com.

FRIEDMAN, ROBERT BARRY, physician; b. Bklyn., Dec. 28, 1953; s. Roy and Bernice (Berger) F. BA, SUNY, Stony Brook, N.Y., 1975; MD, SUNY Health Sci. Ctr., Bklyn., 1980. Bd. Cert. Diplomate Am. Bd. Neurol. Surgery. Gen. med. officer USPHS Indian Health Svc., Sacaton, Ariz., 1981-82; neurosurgeon USAF, Wright Patterson AFB, Ohio, 1989-91, South Broward Neurosurg. Assn., Pembroke Pines, Fla., 1991-95, Cleve. Clinic Fla., Ft. Lauderdale, 1995-97, Spectrum Neurosurg. Specialists, Marietta, Ga., 1997-98, Henry Neurosurg. Specialists, P.C., Stockbridge, Ga., 1998—. Med. staff fellow Nat. Inst. Health, Bethesda, Md., 1986-88. Contbr. articles to profl. jours. Maj. U.S.A.F., 1988-91. Recipient Neuroscience award U. Pitts., 1989. Fellow Am. Coll. Surgeons; mem. Am. Assn. Neurol. Surgeons, Congress of Neurol. Surgeons, Southern Med. Assn., Fla. Med. Assn., AMA. Avocation: private pilot. Home: 602 Redbud Ln Stockbridge GA 30281 Office: c/o Henry Neurosurg Specialists PC 297 Country Club Dr Stockbridge GA 30281-7350

FRIEDMAN, ROBERT LAURENCE, investment professional; b. Mt. Vernon, NY, Mar. 19, 1943; s. Alvin S. and Frances (Feinsod) F.; m. Barbara Lander, Dec. 25, 1964; children: Lisa, Andrew. AB, Columbia Coll., 1964; JD, U. Pa., 1967. Bar: NY 1968. Assoc. Simpson, Thacher & Bartlett, NYC, 1967—74, ptnr., 1974—99; sr. mng. dir. The Blackstone Group LP, NYC, 1999—2002, sr. mng. dir., chief adminstrv. officer, chief legal officer, 2003—. Office: The Blackstone Group LP 345 Park Ave Fl 31 New York NY 10154-0004

FRIEDMAN, ROBERT LEE, film company executive; s. Edward A. and Claire (Seidenberg) F.; m. Marlene Saltz; children: Marc, Lisa. Sales Universal Pictures, N.Y.C., 1948-52, 54-59; exec. v.p., distbn. & mktg. United Artists Corp., N.Y.C., 1959-79; pres., distbn. Columbia Pictures, Burbank, Calif., 1979-82; pres. AMC Entertainment Internat., L.A., 1984-92, pres. motion picture group, 1992-99; pres. RLF Entertainment, Beverly Hills, Calif., 1999—; CEO, pres. Stereo Vision Entertainment, Beverly Hills, 2000—. Radio announcer The Bob Friedman Hour, 1952-54; cons. RLF Prodns., Beverly Hills, Calif., 1982-84; entertainment advisor, cons. Chanin Capital Ptnrs. Exec. prodr., appeared in (motion picture) 9 Deaths of the Ninja, 1984; appeared in (motion picture) Stardust Memories, 1980. Bd. dirs., chmn. Entertainment Industry com. Century City C. of C., L.A., 1988—; chmn. Will Rogers Hosp., 1980-81, also bd. dirs.; bd. dirs. Dare Am.; mem. vision fund The Lighthouse for the Blind. With U.S. Army, 1952-54. Named Man of Yr. N.Y. State Nat. Assn. Theatre Owners, 1981, Va., Md., Washington D.C. Assn. Theatre Owners, 1980. Mem. Acad. Motion Picture Arts & Scis. (bd. dirs. endowment fund, 1979—), Variety Club Am. (L.A.), Motion Picture Pioneers Am., Motion Picture Assocs. Found. (pres. 1970-73), L.A.-Century City C. of C. (Citizen of Yr., 1994) Avocations: going to movies, playing tennis, exercising, photography, spending time with my wife and grandchildren. Office: RLF Entertainment 2216 Summitridge Dr Beverly Hills CA 90210-1526

FRIEDMAN, ROBERT MORRIS, pathologist, molecular biologist; b. N.Y.C., Nov. 21, 1932; s. Jack and Rose M. (Weiss) F.; m. Ina Reichler, Dec. 15, 1989 (dec. Aug. 1992); children: Thomas, Deborah, Antony; m. Harriet H. Schisgall, Jan. 9, 1994. BA with honors, Cornell U., 1954; MD, NYU, 1958. Intern Mt. Sinai Hosp., NYC, 1958-59; resident The Clinical Ctr., NIN, Bethesda, Md., 1961-63; pathologist NIH, Bethesda, Md., 1963-73, lab. chief, 1973-80; chmn. dept. pathology Uniformed Svcs. U., Bethesda, Md., 1981—. Vis. scientist Nat. Inst. for Med. Rsch., Mill Hill, London, 1963-64, 71-73; vis. prof. Warwick U., Coventry, U.K., 1981, The Cleve. Clinic Found., 1993; adj. prof. pathology Georgetown U. Med. Sch., 1992—; pres. Internat. Soc. for Interferon and Cytokine Rsch., 1996-98. Author: The Interferons: A Primer, 1981, Interferons, 1982, Interferons as Cell Growth Inhibitors & Anti-tumor Factors, 1986, (novel) Love, Loss and Interferon, 1998. Capt. USPHS, 1979-90. Recipient Hon. award for 20 yr. contbn., U.S. Embassy, New Delhi. Fellow Coll. Am. Pathologists; mem. Am. Soc. for Investigative Pathology, Am. Soc. for Microbiology, Internat. Acad. Pathology, Internat. Soc. for Interferon and Cytokine Rsch. (sec. 1994-95, pres. 1996-98), Phi Beta Kappa, Phi Kappa Phi, Alpha Omega Alpha. Democrat. Jewish. Achievements include research in replication of arboviruses, mechanism of antiviral activity of interferons, mechanism of action of tumor suppressor genes. Office: Uniformed Services Univ Dept Pathology 4301 Jones Bridge Rd Dept Bethesda MD 20814-4799

FRIEDMAN, ROBERT SIDNEY, political science educator; b. Balt., Mar. 1, 1927; s. Harry N. and Eva (Cohen) F.; m. Renee Cohen, Aug. 11, 1953 (dec. Oct. 4, 2002); children: Helene, David. BA, Johns Hopkins U., 1948; MA, U. Ill., 1950, PhD, 1953. Rsch. asst. Bur. Govt. Rsch., Md., 1953-55; instr. govt. and politics U. Md., 1955-56; from instr. to assoc. prof. govt. La. State U., 1956-61; rsch. assoc. Inst. Pub. Adminstrn., U. Mich., 1961-67, acting dir., 1967-68; assoc. prof. polit. sci. U. Mich., 1961-66, prof., 1966-68; prof., head dept. polit. sci. Pa. State U., 1968-78; dir. Center for Study Sci. Policy, Inst. for Policy Research and Evaluation, 1978-88, dir. policy analysis program, 1991-94; prof. emeritus, 1994—. Cons. in field. Co-author: Local Government in Maryland, 1955, Government in Metropolitan New Orleans, 1959, Political Leadership and the School Desegration Crisis in New Orleans, 1963; author: The Michigan Constitutional Convention and Administrative Organization: A Case Study in the Politics of Constitution-Making, 1971; contbg. author: Politics in the American States, 1965, 5th edit., 1990; contbr. articles to profl. jours. Bd. dirs. Pa. Civil Liberties Union, 1969-72; mem. State College (Pa.) Zoning Hearing Bd., 1976-79; chmn. study com. State College Mcpl. Govt., 1991-93; active State College Planning Commn., 1996-99; safety adv. bd. Three Mile Island-2 Cleanup, 1981-89; Pa. bd. Common Cause, 1998—; pres. Friends of Schlow Meml. Libr., 1999-2002, trustee, 2002—. With AUS, 1945-46. Recipient McKay Donkin award for disting. svc., 1980. Mem. Am. Polit. Sci. Assn. Home: 205 Horizon Dr State College PA 16801-8615 Office: Pa State U Burrowes Bldg University Park PA 16802 E-mail: rsf3@psu.edu.

FRIEDMAN, RODGER, antiquarian bookseller, consultant; b. Detroit, Nov. 10, 1951; s. Stanley B. and Miriam Elizabeth (Levin) F.; m. Kiki Nelson, July 1, 1983. BA, Kalamazoo Coll., 1973; MA, U. N.Mex., Albuquerque, 1979, CUNY, 1987, PhD, 1989; MLS, Pratt Inst., 1996. Libr. Century Assn., N.Y.C., 1982—88, Union League Club, N.Y.C., 1989—96. Mem. editl. bd. Ballet Rev., 1983-96; translator: Posthumous People by Massimo Cacciari, 1996; Quar. catalogue of rare books; contbr. articles to profl. jours. Recipient Frederick II medal U. Naples, 1991. Mem. Antiquarian Booksellers Assn. Am., Assn. Internat. Studi di Lingua Letteratura Italiana, Internat. Assn. for Neo-Latin Studies, The Sterling Forest Partnership. Home: 1 Mystic Cir Tuxedo Park NY 10987-5027 E-mail: rf@rarebookstudio.com.

FRIEDMAN, RONALD MICHAEL, judge; b. Miami, Fla., June 11, 1942; s. Milton and Sylvia S. (Stern) F.; m. Janyce L. Friedman, May 23, 1981; stepchildren: Lisa, David. BSBA, U. N.C., 1964; JD, U. Miami, 1967; LLM in Taxation, NYU, 1969. Bar: Fla. 1967, Calif. 1969. Assoc. Wyman, Bautzer, Rothman & Kuchel, L.A., 1968-71, Lederer & Jacobs, Beverly Hills, Calif., 1971-73; ptnr. Sankary & Friedman, L.A., 1973-76, Freidin, Silber & Friedman, Miami, 1976-77; pvt. practice law Coral Gables, Fla., 1977-85; cir. ct. judge State of Fla., Miami, 1985—. Adminstrv. judge appellate divsn., 11th Jud. Cir., 2000-01; instr. law sch. Northrop U., 1975-76; arbitrator Am. Arbitration Assn.; lectr. in field. Author: How to Prove a Profit Motive in Horse Breeding, 1976; contbr. articles to profl. jours. Past bd. dirs. South Fla. Epilepsy Found.; past bd. dirs. Greater Miami Jewish Fedn., leadership coun.; past chmn. tax com. L.A. Bar Assn., Beverly Hills Bar Assn.; past mem. bd. dirs. Jewish Family and Children's Svcs.; past trustee U. Miami Alumni Assn.; bd. dirs. The Spellman-Hoeveler Am. Inn of Ct., others. Mem. Fla. Bar Assn., Calif. Bar Assn., Dade County Bar Assn., B'nai Brith (past pres., couns., South Dade chpt., past pres., state v.p. youth adult bd., past pres. Bench and Bar South Dade adult bd., past nat. youth commr., Outstanding Man of Yr. award Koach chpt. 1981), Fla. Bar (bd. govs., cir. com.), U. Miami Law Alumni Assn. (judicial dir., Thomas Davison III Svc. award, 1993). Democrat. Office: 1304 Dade County Courthouse 73 W Flagler St Miami FL 33130-1731

FRIEDMAN, ROSELYN L. lawyer, mediator; b. Cleve., Dec. 9, 1942; d. Charles and Lillian Edith (Zalzneck) F. BS, U. Pitts., 1964; MA, Case Western Res. U., 1967; JD cum laude, Loyola U., Chgo., 1977. Bar: Ill. 1977, U.S. Dist. Ct. (no. dist.) Ill. 1977. Mem. legal dept. No. Trust Co., Chgo., 1977-79; assoc. Rudnick & Wolfe, Chgo., 1979-84, ptnr., 1984-95, Sachnoff & Weaver, Ltd., Chgo., 1995—, ptnr., chmn. dept. estates and trusts, 2002—. Mem. Loyola U., Chgo. law rev.; mem. profl. adv. com. Chgo. Jewish Fedn., chmn., 1999-2001; mem. profl. adv. com. Chgo. Cmty. Trust, 2001-. Trustee Jewish Women's Found., 1997—2001; mediator Ctr. for Conflict Resolution, 2000—. Fellow Am. Coll. Trust and Estate Counsel; mem. ABA, Am. Jewish Congress (gov. coun. Midwest region 1995-97), Chgo. Bar Assn. (cert. appreciation continuing legal edn. program 1984, chmn. trust law com. 1989-90), Chgo. Estate Planning Coun. (program com. 1992-94, 98-2000, membership com. 1997-98, bd. dirs. 2001-2003), spkr. Ill. Inst. CLE, Chgo. Fin. Exch. (bd. dirs. 1995-97, sec. 1996-97). Office: Sachnoff & Weaver Ltd 30 S Wacker Dr Ste 2900 Chicago IL 60606-7413 E-mail: rfriedman@sachnoff.com.

FRIEDMAN, S. LILA, librarian; b. Bklyn., Sept. 25, 1926; d. Ephraim Eliezer and Naomi (Weisdorff) Ritter; m. S. Lester Friedman, Jan. 25, 1946; children—Matthew, Joel, Amy. B.A., Bklyn. Coll., 1948; M.L.S., L.I. U., 1975. Cert. library media specialist, secondary sch. tchr. library, N.Y. Librarian, Hunter Coll. High Sch., N.Y.C., 1973-74, Hawthorne (N.Y.) Cedar Knolls Sch., 1976, Samuel Tilden High Sch., Bklyn., 1978-79, Bellerose Jewish Ctr., Floral Park, N.Y., 1980—, dir. library, 1980— ; librarian Katharine Gibbs Sch., Huntington, N.Y., 1984— . Area chmn. Queens United Cerebral Palsy, 1969, 71. Recipient 25th Anniversary award State of Israel Bonds, 1975, Youth Services award B'nai B'rith, 1983. Mem. ALA, Assn. Jewish Libraries, L.I. Assn. Jewish Libraries (charter mem.), Am. Assn. Sch. Librarians. Jewish. Home: 80 49 252d St Bellerose NY 11426 Office: Bellerose Jewish Ctr 25404 Union Tpke Floral Park NY 11004-1293

FRIEDMAN, SAMUEL SELIG, lawyer; b. N.Y.C., July 25, 1935; s. Nathan and Anne M. (Sobel) F.; m. Maxine E. Goldfarb, Jan. 7, 1961; 1 child, Alison J. BS, MIT, 1956; MBA, U. Pa., 1959; LLB, Columbia U., 1965. Bar: N.Y. 1965, U.S. Dist. Ct. (so. and ea. dists.) N.Y. 1967, U.S. Supreme Ct. 1984. Assoc. Lord, Day & Lord, N.Y.C., 1965-72; ptnr., mem. exec. com. Lord Day & Lord, Barrett Smith and predecessor firm, N.Y.C., 1972-94; ptnr. Morgan, Lewis & Bockius LLP, N.Y.C., 1994—. Vice chmn., dir., mem. exec. com. Times Square Bus. Improvement Dist., 1992-95. 1st lt. U.S. Army, 1959-62. Mem. ABA, N.Y. State Bar Assn., Assn. of Bar of City of N.Y., MIT Club N.Y., The Penn Club, Phi Delta Phi. Avocations: travel, wine, sports. Office: Morgan Lewis & Bockius LLP 101 Park Ave New York NY 10178-0060

FRIEDMAN, SANFORD, literature educator, writer; b. N.Y.C., June 11, 1928; s. Leonard and Madeline Friedman. BFA, Carnegie Inst. Tech., 1949. Asst. tchr. drama divsn. Julliard Sch., N.Y.C., 1977—78; tchr. writing workshop Sr. Action in a Gay Environment, N.Y.C., 1987—. Bd. mem. PEN Am. Ctr., N.Y.C., 1985—96, com. mem., 1997—. Author: (novels) Totempole, 1965 (O. Henry award, 1965), A Haunted Woman, 1968, Still Life, 1975, Rip Van Winkle, 1980. Cpl. U.S. Army, 1951—53, Korea. Recipient award in lit., Am. Acad. and Inst. Arts and Letters, 1984, Manhattan Borough Pres. cert. for volunteerism, 1997. Home: Apt 10F 37 W 12th St New York NY 10011-8544

FRIEDMAN, SANFORD HOWARD, information scientist; b. L.A., Oct. 24, 1955; s. George Jerry and Ruthanne (Goldstein) F.; m. Shelley Jane Keer, June 15, 1980.; 1 child, Julia Gail. BS, UCLA, 1978; MS, U. Iowa, 1981; MBA, Boston U., 1985. Cert. fellow in prodn. and inventory mgmt.; cert. in integrated resource mgmt. Teaching asst. dept. zoology U. Iowa, Iowa City, 1978-80, rsch. asst. dept. pediatrics, 1981-83; project mgr. Northrop Electronics Systems Div., Hawthorne, Calif., 1985-90; mgr. Northrop Info. Svcs. Ctr., Hawthorne, 1991-92; cons. Western Data Systems, Calabasas, Calif., 1992-93; mgr. Integration Systems Merisel, Inc., El Segundo, Calif., 1993-96; dir. mgmt. edn. Functional Infosystems, Costa Mesa, Calif., 1996—2002; project mgr. La Jolla Pharm. co., 2002—. Contbr. articles to profl. conf. proc. Fellow Am. Prodn. and Inventory Control Soc. (v.p. publs. L.A. chpt. 1989-95, pres. 2001-02); mem. L.A. Aerospace and Def. Spl. Interest Group (dir. publs. 1990-93), Coun. Logistics Mgmt., Internat. Coun. Sys. Engring. Democrat. Jewish. Achievements include design, development and implementation of several computer-aided engineering and manufacturing systems, including Adanced Integrated Manufacturing System, Product Data Management System, CALS-compliant on-line Configuration Management and Traceability System, FDA & GMP compliant enterprise resource planning systems, and Business Process Re-engineering programs for a wide variety of tech., scientific and commercial manufacturing and distribution environs. E-mail: sandyf@ix.netcom.com.

FRIEDMAN, SCOTT EDWARD, lawyer, author, business consultant; b. Salt Lake City, Sept. 17, 1958; BA, Trinity Coll., Hartford, Conn., 1980; JD, Washington U., St. Louis, 1983; LLM, U. Pa., 1984. Bar: N.Y. 1984, Pa. 1984. Ptnr. Lippes Silverstein Mathias & Wexler, LLP, Buffalo, 1994—. Mem. Canyon Ranch Family Bus. Group; pres. Niagra Gorge Ptnrs., LLC. Author: Sex Law, 1991, The Law of Parent-Child Relationships, 1992, How to Run a Family Business, 1993, How to Profit by Forming Your Own Limited Liability Company, 1995, The Successful Family Business, 1998; contbr. articles to profl. jours. Mem. ABA, N.Y. Bar Assn., Erie County Bar Assn. Office: Lippes Silverstein Mathias & Wexler 28 Church St Buffalo NY 14202-3908

FRIEDMAN, SHELLY ARNOLD, cosmetic surgeon; b. Providence, Jan. 1, 1949; s. Saul and Estelle (Moverman) F.; m. Andrea Leslie Falchook, Aug. 30, 1975; children: Bethany Erin, Kimberly Rebecca, Brent David, Jennifer Ashley. BA, Providence Coll., 1971; DO, Mich. State U., 1982. Diplomate Nat. Bd. Med. Examiners, Am. Bd. Dermatology. Intern Pontiac (Mich.) Hosp., 1982-83, resident in dermatology, 1983-86. Assoc. clin. prof. dept. internal med. Mich. State U., 1984-89, adj. clin. prof., 1989—; med. dir. Inst. Cosmetic Dermatology, Scottsdale, Ariz., 1986—; pres. Am. Bd. Hair Restoration Surgery. Contbr. aritcles to profl. jours. Mem. B'nai B'rith Men's Council, 1973, Jewish Welfare Fund, 1973. Am. Physicians fellow for medicine, 1982. Mem. AMA, Am. Osteopathic Assn., Am. Assn. Cosmetic Surgeons, Am. Acad. Cosmetic Surgery, Internat. Soc. Dermatologic Surgery, Internat. Acad. Cosmetic Surgery, Am. Acad. Dermatology, Am. Soc. Dermatol. Surgery, Frat. Order Police, Sigma Sigma Phi. Jewish. Avocations: Karate, horseback riding. Office: Scottsdale Inst Cosmetic Dermatology 5206 N Scottsdale Rd Scottsdale AZ 85253-7006

FRIEDMAN, SIDNEY A. financial services executive; b. Bklyn., Mar. 7, 1935; s. Benjamin and Celia (Jacobs) F.; m. Sue Helen Mansbach, May 2, 1965; children: Lori Beth, Wendi Ellen. BS, NYU, 1957; student, Bklyn. Law Sch., 1958. CLU, ChFC, MSFS; registered health underwriter. Pres. Corp. Fin. Services, Phila., 1970-99, pres., chmn. bd., 1988—; past pres. Phoenix Mut. Adv. Council; motivational speaker; cons. life ins. orgns.; past pres. Top of the Table/25 Million Dollar Forum. Author: How to Make Money Tomorrow Morning, 1991, Success Systems, It's About Time. Bd. dirs. Fight for Sight, 1983; bd. dirs. Phila. Variety Club, 1993. Mem. Million Dollar Round Table; mem. Top of the Table, 25 Million Dollar Forum; recipient Nat. Quality award, 1983, 95. Mem. Am. Coll. Life Underwriters (pres. 1971-72), Health Underwriters, Nat. Assn. Security Dealers (registered investment advisor), Assn. Advanced Underwriters, Phila. Assn. Life Underwriters, Gen. Agts. and Mgrs So. N.J. (past pres.), CLUs So. N.J. (past pres.), Gen. Agts and Mgrs. Assn. Democrat. Office: Corp Fin Svcs Inc 1700 Market St Philadelphia PA 19103-3913

FRIEDMAN, SIMON, lawyer; b. Novosibirsk, USSR, Aug. 30, 1945; came to U.S., 1954; s. Ozjasz and Luba (Zinkowskaya) F.; m. Linda S. Mandeville, Feb. 25, 1984; children: Scott L. M., Lisa G. M. BA, Columbia U., N.Y.C., 1965, King's Coll., Cambridge, Eng., 1967; PHD, Yale U., 1972, JD, 1980. Bar: N.Y. 1981, Calif. 1998; U.S. Dist. Ct. (so. dist.) N.Y. 1989. Asst. prof. English Reed Coll., Portland, Oreg., 1971-77; assoc. Cravath, Swaine & Moore, N.Y.C., 1980-88, Milbank, Tweed, Hadley & McCloy, N.Y.C., 1988-93, of counsel, 1993-97, ptnr. L.A., 1997—. Home: 3841 Keswick Rd La Canada CA 91011-3945 Office: Milbank Tweed Hadley McCloy 601 S Figueroa St Los Angeles CA 90017-5704 E-mail: sfriedma@milbank.com.

FRIEDMAN, STANLEY, insect physiologist, educator; b. N.Y.C., Dec. 11, 1925; s. Nathan and Eva (Rothstein) F.; m. Frances Ray Shapiro, May 21, 1955; children: David, Douglas, Catherine, Matthew. Student, CCNY, 1941-43; BA, U. Ill., 1948; PhD, Johns Hopkins U., 1952. Rsch. assoc. U. Ill., 1953-56; biochemist NIH, 1956-58; asst. prof. entomology Purdue U., 1958-62; rsch. fellow London Sch. Hygiene and Tropical Medicine, 1962-63; assoc. prof. entomology Purdue U., 1963-64, U. Ill., Urbana, 1964-68, prof., 1968-92, prof. emeritus, 1992—, head dept., 1976-92, assoc. dir. Sch. Life Scis., 1989-92. With USN, 1943-46. Fellow AAAS; mem. Am. Soc. Zoology, Am. Soc. Biol. Chemists, Entomol. Soc. Am., Federated Socs. Exptl. Biology and Medicine, Sigma Xi. Office: 320 Morrill Hall 505 S Goodwin Ave Urbana IL 61801-3707

FRIEDMAN, STEPHEN J, lawyer; b. Mar. 19, 1938; s. A.E. Robert and Janice Clara (Miller) F.; m. Fredrica L. Schwab, June 25, 1961; children: Vanessa V., Alexander S. AB magna cum laude, Princeton U., 1959; LLB magna cum laude, Harvard U., 1962. Bar: N.Y. 1962, D.C. 1982. Law clk. to justice William J. Brennan Jr. U.S. Supreme Ct., 1963-64; spl. asst. to maritime adminstr. Maritime Adminstrn., Dept. Commerce, 1964-65; assoc. Debevoise & Plimpton, NYC, 1965-70, ptnr., 1970-77, 81-86, 93—; dep. asst. sec. for capital markets policy Dept. Treasury, Washington, 1977-79; commr. SEC, 1980-81; exec. v.p., gen. counsel E.F. Hutton Group Inc., NYC, 1986-88, Equitable Life Assurance Soc., NYC, 1988-93; ptnr. Debevoise & Plimpton, NYC, 1994—. Lectr. law Columbia U., N.Y.C., 1974—77, 1982—85. Author: An Affair With Freedom, the Opinions and Speeches of William J. Brennan, Jr., 1967; contbr. articles on legal and policy aspects of fin. inst. to profl. jours. Active Coun. on Fgn. Rels.; trustee, chmn. emeritus Am. Ballet Theatre, N.Y.C.; dir. United Way N.Y.C.; pres., trustee Practising Law Inst.; mem. bd. govs. NASD, 1991-94, Chgo. Bd. Options Exch., 1982-88; pres. Practicing Law Inst.; chmn. Asian U. for Women Support Found. With USAR, 1962-68. Mem. ABA, Assn. of Bar of the City of N.Y. (chmn. com. on securities regulation), Univ. Club. Office: Debevoise & Plimpton 919 3rd Ave 45th Fl New York NY 10022-6225

FRIEDMAN, STEVEN ERIC, communications executive; b. N.Y.C., Apr. 21, 1954; s. Lawrence and Thelma (Hahn) F.; m. Linda Hutkof, Apr. 1, 1978; children: Elizabeth, Jeremy, Abby. BA, SUNY, Stony Brook, 1975; MA, N.Y. Inst. Tech., 1984. Pres. Artica Films, Inc., Merrick, N.Y., 1973-76; instr. N.Y. Inst. Tech., Westbury, 1976-77; various positions USIA, Washington, 1978—, dir. video library programs, 1986-87, chief of program acquisition, 1987-89; chief of acquisition TV Marti, Washington, 1989-91, dir. ops., 1991-96; chief broadcast ops. Worldnet, Washington, 1996-2000, program dir., 2000—. Bd. dirs. Montgomery (Md.) Cmty. TV, Inc. Author, dir. book/video Psychic Express; dir. film They Know Where They're Going, 1975; contrb. articles to profl. journals. Bd. dirs. Montgomery Cmty. TV Inc., 1994—, Potomac Soccer Assn., 1996-97; chmn. Montgomery County (Md.) Recreation Bd., 1983-86; v.p. Flints Grove Homeowners Assn., 1994-97. Mem. Soc. Motion Picture TV Engrs., Interdepartmental Com. Visual & Auditory Materials for Distbn. Abroad (rep.), Council for Internat. Non-Theatrical Events (rep., Gold Eagle awards

1981, 82, 83). Jewish. Avocations: golf, playing bridge. Home: PO Box 625 Gaithersburg MD 20884-0625 Office: IBB-TV 300 C St SW Washington DC 20547-0001 E-mail: Sfriedma@IBB.gov.

FRIEDMAN, STEVEN M. investment company executive; b. 1955; BA, MA, U. Chgo.; JD, Bklyn. Law Sch. Former v.p. Citibank; gen. ptnr. Odyssey Ptnrs. LLP, 1983—93, EOS Ptnrs., N.Y.C., 1993—. Office: EOS Ptnrs 320 Park Ave Fl 22D New York NY 10022-6815

FRIEDMAN, SUE TYLER, technical publications executive; b. Nürnberg, Germany, Feb. 28, 1925; came to U.S., 1938; d. William and Ann (Federlein) Tyler (Theilheimer); m. Gerald Manfred Friedman, June 27, 1948; children: Judith Fay Friedman Rosen, Sharon Mira Friedman Azaria, Devora Paula Friedman Zweibach, Eva Jane Friedman Scholle, Wendy Tamar Friedman Spanier. Student, Beth Israel Sch. Nursing, 1941-43. Exec. dir. Ventures and Publs. Gerald M. Friedman, 1964-90; owner Tyler Publs., Watervliet and Troy, N.Y., 1978-86; treas., dir. Northeastern Sci. Found., Inc., Troy, 1979—; treas. Gerry Exploration, Inc., Troy, 1982-88; office mgr. Rensselaer Ctr. Applied Geology, Troy, 1983—. Pres. Pioneer Women/Na'amat, Tulsa, 1961-64, treas., Jerusalem, Israel, 1964, pres., Albany, N.Y., 1968-70; bd. dirs. Temple Beth-El, 1965—, dir. Hebrew Sch., 1965-80; mem. social program com. Internat. Sedimentological. Congress, 1979. Named Hon. Alumna, Dept. Geology, Bklyn. Coll. at CUNY, 1989; Sue Tyler Friedman medal for distinction in history of geology created in her honor Geol. Soc. London, 1988; recipient Disting. Svc. award Temple Beth-El, 1991, Scroll of Honor, State of Israel Bonds, 1981. Mem. Geology Alumni Assn. (hon.). Avocation: world travel. Office: Northeastern Sci Found Inc/Bklyn Coll CUNY Rensselaer Ctr Applied Geology PO Box 746 Troy NY 12181-0746

FRIEDMAN, SUSAN LYNN BELL, economic development professional; b. May 23, 1953; d. Virgil Atwood and Jean Loree (Wiggins) B.; m. Frank H. Friedman, July 31, 1976; 1 child, Alex Charles. BA, Purdue U., 1975; MSc, Ind. State U., 1981. Asst. dir. pub. rels. Vincennes U. Jr. Coll., Ind., 1977-83; dir. Knox County C. of C., Vincennes, 1983-84; asst. to pres. Am. Assn. Cmty. and Jr. Colls., Washington, 1985-87; owner, pres. SBF Promotions, 1987—; mgr., program developer Family Resources, Inc., 1988-89; partnership coord. Beaufort (S.C.) County Sch. Dist., 1989-90; job tng. coord. Heart of Ga. Tech. Inst., 1990-92, v.p. econ. devel., 1992-96; exec. dir. Tex. Assn. Ptnrs. in Edn., 1996-98; dir. regional bus. assistance Thomas Jefferson Partnership for Econ. Devel., 1999—. Mem. Leadership Class, Charlottesville, Va., 2000; pres. Annandale BPW, Vincennes, Ind., BPW Dublin and Capital City; newsletter adv. coord. Focus Women's Ctr.; mem. Albemarle Pub. Schs. Equity and Diversity Com. Va.; bd. dirs. Focus Women's Ctr., 2002—, I Have A Dream Found., 2001—. Scholar, Hoosier scholar, 1971, 1972. Mem. NAFE, LWV (v.p. chpt. 1982-84, pres. 2000-2002), ACLU, Nat. Assn. Ptnrs. in Edn., NOW, Kiwanis (v.p. 2000-01). Home: 2544 Brandermill Pl Charlottesville VA 22911-8253 Office: PO Box 1525 Charlottesville VA 22902

FRIEDMAN, SUSAN MARIE, geriatrician, educator, medical researcher; b. Madison, Wis., Dec. 1963; d. Alexander and Gertrud Friedman; m. Robert Paine, July 16, 2000; 1 child, Alexander Paine. MD, Northwestern U., Chgo., 1988, MPH, 1992. Diplomate Am. Bd. Internal Medicine, Am. Bd. Geriatrics. Asst. prof. medicine Johns Hopkins U., Balt., 1996—2000, intern, resident Bayview Primary Care Internal Medicine program, 1988—91, fellow in geriatric medicine, 1992—95; asst. prof. U. Rochester, NY, 2000—. Geriatric fellow, Nat. Coun. Aging/Travelers, 1984, Postdoctoral fellow, Am. Geriat. Soc./Pfizer, 1996—98, K23 Career Devel. fellow, Nat. Inst. Aging, 2000—. Mem.: Nat. PACE Assn. (mem. rsch. com. 1999—2002), Am. Geriat. Soc. (mem. pub. edn. com. 1998—2001). Achievements include research in evaluated predictors of falls and fear of falling; long-term care models. Office: Highland Hosp 1000 South Ave Box 58 Rochester NY 14620

FRIEDMAN, SUSAN R. foundation administrator, consultant; b. Cin., June 22, 1949; m. Joel M. Friedman; children: Adam, Benjamin. BA, Stern Coll., 1971; M in Social Scis., Bryn Mawr Grad. Sch. Social Sci., 1975; postmasters cert. in gerontology, Hunter Coll.; postmasters cert. in grantsmanship, The Grantsmanship Ctr., L.A. Program planner/analyst The Cmty. Svc. Soc., 1975—81; corp./found. campaign mgr. City Meals on Wheels, N.Y.C., 1981—87; dir. program devel. N.Y.C. Dept. Aging, 1988—95; exec. dir. The Grotta Found., South Orange, NJ, 1995—. Staff dir. New Sch. for Social Rsch., Commn. on the Status of Older Students, 1994—95; chair adv. com. Synagogue Hope, West Orange, NJ, 1996—; cons. The Silverman Charitable Trust, N.Y.C., 2000—; co-chair PBS Adv. Bd., N.Y.C., 2001—02; mem. pub. policy com. Forum of Regional Assn. Grantmakers, 2001—02; mem. task force Senator Jon Corzine's Sr. Issues Task Force, 2002—. Author: Public/Private Partnerships: A Technical Assistance Guide; contbr. chapters to books, articles to profl. jours. Chair Micky Fried Nursery, South Orange, 1986; chair devel. com. Solomon Schechter Sch., West Orange, 1993; mem. planning com. Coalition to Preperal South Orange, 2000—01; treas. Oheb Shalom Congregation, South Orange, 1995; mem. adv. bd. Brookdale Ctr. on Aging, 2000—. Recipient Cmty. Svc. award, Health Career Acad., West Orange, 2000, Phila. Press Club award for documentary excellence, Phila., 2003. Mem.: Coun. N.J. Grantmakers, Nat. Grantmakers Agy. (mem. program planning com. 2000—). Office: The Grotta Found Ste 305 76 S Orange Ave South Orange NJ 07079

FRIEDMAN, SYDNEY M. anatomy educator, medical researcher; b. Montreal, Que., Can., Feb. 17, 1916; s. Jacob and Minnie (Signer) F.; m. Constance Livingstone, Sept. 23, 1940. B.Sc., McGill U., Montreal, Can., 1938, MD, C.M., 1940, M.Sc., 1941, PhD, 1946. Med. licentiate, Que. Teaching fellow anatomy McGill U., Montreal, Que., Can., 1940-42, asst. prof. anatomy, 1944-48, assoc. prof. anatomy, 1948-50; prof., head dept. anatomy U. B.C., Vancouver, Can., 1950-81, prof. anatomy, 1981-85, prof. emeritus, 1985—. Mem. panel on shock Def. Research Bd., Ottawa, Can., 1955-57; sci. subcom. Can. Heart Found., 1962-66, Am. Heart Assn., 1966-68, B.C. Heart Found., Vancouver, founding mem. Author: Visual Anatomy. Served as flight lt. RCAF, 1943-44. Recipient Premier award for rsch. in aging CIBA Found., 1955, Outstanding Svc. award Heart Found. Can., 1981, Disting. Achievement award Can. Hypertension Soc., 1987; Commemorative medal 125th Anniversary Can. Confedn.; Pfizer travel fellow Clin. Rsch. Inst., Montreal, 1971. Fellow Royal Soc. Can., Coun. High Blood Pressure Rsch.; mem. Am. Anatomical Assn. (exec. com. 1970-74), Can. Assn. Anatomists (pres. 1965-66, J.C.B. Grant award 1982), Internat. Soc. Hypertension, Am. Physiol. Soc., Royal Vancouver Yacht Club, Vancouver Club. Avocation: painting. Home: 4916 Chancellor Blvd Vancouver BC Canada V6T 1E1

FRIEDMAN, THOMAS LOREN, foreign correspondent; b. Mpls., July 20, 1953; s. Harold Abraham and Margaret (Phillips) F.; m. Ann Louise Bucksbaum, Nov. 23, 1978. BA, Brandeis U., 1975; M.Phil., St. Anthony's Coll., Oxford U., 1978. Staff corr. UPI, London, 1978-79, Middle East corr. Beirut, 1979-81; reporter Bus. Day. sect. N.Y. Times, N.Y.C., 1981-82, Beirut bur. chief, 1982-84, Jerusalem bur. chief, 1984-89, chief diplomatic corr., 1989—, fgn. affairs columnist, 1995—. Recipient Pulitzer prize, 1983, 1988, George Polk award L.I. U., 1982, Livingston award Livingston Found., 1983, Overseas Press Club award, 1980, Robert D. Heinl Jr. Meml. award Marine Corps History, 1985, Page 1 award N.Y. Newspaper Guild, 1984, Nat. Book award 1989 for "From Beirut to Jerusalem". Jewish. Office: NY Times 1627 I St NW Washington DC 20006

FRIEDMAN, TULLY MICHAEL, investment banker; b. Chgo., Jan. 9, 1942; s. Louis P. and Dorothy G. Friedman; m. Elise Woolsey Dorsey; children: Albert Evans Walker (dec.), Abigail Fay, Alexander Louis, Allegra Woolsey. AB, Stanford U., 1962; JD, Harvard U., 1965. Bar: Calif. 1965, Ill. 1967. With Charles Percy for Senator Com., Chgo., 1966; assoc. Sidley & Austin, Chgo., 1967-70; corp. fin. assoc. Salomon Bros., N.Y.C., 1970-71, v.p., dir. West Coast corp. fin. San Francisco, 1972-79, gen. ptnr., 1979-81, mng. dir., 1981-84; founding ptnr. Hellman & Friedman, San Francisco, 1984-97; chmn., CEO Friedman, Fleischer & Lowe, LLC, San Francisco, 1997—. Bd. dirs. The Clorox Co., Mattel, Inc., Levi Strauss Assocs., McKesson Corp., Archimedes Tech. Group, CapitalSource Holdings LLC. Trustee, treas. Am. Enterprise Inst., 1988—; trustee Katherine Delmar Burke Sch., 2001—, dir., The Telluride Found., 2001—. Office: One Maritime Pla 1 Maritime Plz Ste 1000 San Francisco CA 94111-3413 E-mail: tfriedman@fflpartners.com.

FRIEDMAN, VICTOR ALLEN, linguist, educator; b. Chgo., Oct. 18, 1949; s. Norman and Lorraine Friedman. BA, Reed Coll., 1970; MA, U. Chgo., 1971, PhD, 1975; golden plaque (hon.), U. Skopje, Macedonia, 1991. From asst. prof. to prof. U. N.C., Chapel Hill, 1975-93; prof. U. Chgo., 1993—, Andrew W. Mellon prof., 2001—. Cons. Internat. Rsch. and Exch. Bd., 1981-99; mem. joint com. on Eastern Europe Am. Coun. Learned Socs., 1992-97, fellow, 1986, 2000-2001. Author: Grammatical Categories of the Macedonian Indicative, 1977; translator: Macedonian Historical Phonology, 1983; contbr. numerous articles to profl. jours. Decorated medal (Bulgaria); fellow NEH, 1980-81, 2001. Mem. Am. Com. Slavists (v.p. 1994—), Am. Assn. Southeast European Studies (pres. 1990-92), Soc. Albanian Studies (v.p. 1978-81), Bulgarian Studies Assn. (nominating com. 1984-90), Macedonian Acad. Arts and Scis. Jewish. E-mail: vfriedm@midway.uchicago.edu.

FRIEDMAN, VICTOR STANLEY, lawyer; b. N.Y.C., May 9, 1933; s. Harry and Rose (Cohen) F.; m. Sara Ann Riesner, June 21, 1958 (div.); children: Eric H., Diana B., Michael C.; m. Victoria Schonfeld, Mar. 7, 1984; children: Jared D., Rumyana L. AB, Harvard U., 1954; LLB, Yale U., 1957. Bar: N.Y. 1958, U.S. Dist. Ct. (so. dist.) N.Y. 1964, U.S. Dist. Ct. (ea. dist.) N.Y. 1966, U.S. Ct. Appeals (2nd cir.) 1966, U.S. Ct. Appeals (4th cir.) 1981, U.S. Ct. Appeals (3rd cir.) 1972, U.S. Ct. Appeals (8th cir.) 1970, U.S. Ct. Appeals (10th cir.) 1987, U.S. Supreme Ct. 1974. Asst. to dep. atty. gen. Dept. Justice, Washington, 1958-60; assoc. firm Fried, Frank, Harris, Shriver & Jacobson, N.Y.C., 1960-66, ptnr., 1967-99, of counsel, 1999—. Served with USAR, 1958-59 Mem. Assn. of Bar of City of N.Y., Am. Coll. Trial Lawyers. Office: Fried Frank Harris 1 New York Plz Fl 22 New York NY 10004-1980

FRIEDMAN, W. ROBERT, JR., investment banker; b. N.Y.C., Jan. 5, 1942; s. William Robert and Erica DeMeuron Friedman; children: Douglas, Brian, Catherine. BA, U. Pa., 1965, MBA, 1970. First team institutional investor L.F. Rothschild Untenberg Towbin; gen. ptnr. Montgomery Securities; co-founder Montgomery Med. Ventures; mng. dir. health care-corp. fin. group Prudenital Bache Capital Funding; mng. dir. Deutsche Morgan Grenfell; head internat. health care corp. fin. Robert Fleming & Co. Ltd.; sr. mem. health care corp. fin. group Furman Selz; sr. mng. dir. Dominick & Dominick, N.Y.C., 1996—. Bd. dirs. MaxiCare Health Plans, Inc., Alta Bates Hosp., Health Care Corp., Berkeley, Calif., The Mount Zion Hosp. and Med. Ctr., San Francisco, The Plan of Calif. Bd. dirs. Children's Health Fun, N.Y., Citizen's Com. for N.Y.C., Inc.; trustee The Health Care and Biotech. Venture Fund, Toronto, Can. Fellow of The Inst. of Dirs., London, 1997. Office: Dominick & Dominick LLC 32 Old Slip New York NY 10005-3504 Fax: 212-785-0541.

FRIEDMAN, WILBUR HARVEY, lawyer; b. N.Y.C., May 2, 1907; s. Isador Peter and Zara (Sloat) F.; m. Frances Margolis, May 21, 1943. AB, Columbia U., 1927, LLB, 1930. Bar: N.Y. 1931. Law sec. U.S. Supreme Ct. Justice Harlan F. Stone, 1930-31; staff atty. Office of U.S. Solicitor Gen., 1931-32; mem. firm Proskauer Rose Goetz & Mendelsohn (now Proskauer Rose LLP), N.Y.C., 1932-40; ptnr. Proskauer, Rose, Goetz, & Mendelsohn, N.Y.C., 1940—. Lectr. Inst. on Fed. Taxation, NYU, 1943-65, lectr. Sch. Gen. Edn., 1955-60; bd. dirs., sec. Lawrence M. Gelb Found.; bd. dirs. Cancer Rsch. Inst., 1983-99; chmn. exec. com. bd. visitors Law Sch., Columbia U., 1977-91. Contbr. articles to profl. jours. Chmn. bd. overseers Edith C. Blum Art Inst. at Bard Coll., 1985-93; mem. Rockefeller U. Coun., 1986—; mem. med. ctr. adv. bd. N.Y. Hosp.-Cornell Med. Ctr., 1986—. Mem. ABA (mem. ho. dels. 1978-87), N.Y. State Bar Assn. (mem. exec. com. sect. taxation 1968-76), Assn. of Bar of City of N.Y. (chmn. com. on mgmt. and operation of profl. practice 1981-85), N.Y. County Lawyers Assn. (pres. 1975-77, mem. exec. com. 1977-79, chmn. com. on taxation 1948-54, chmn. com. on group ins. 1960-74, chmn. spl. com. on consumer agreements 1977-83), Lotos Club, Princeton U. Club, Phi Beta Kappa, Phi Beta Kappa Assocs., Tau Delta Phi. Home: 1016 5th Ave Apt 2D New York NY 10028-0132 Office: Proskauer Rose LLP 1585 Broadway Rm 2016 New York NY 10036-8299 E-mail: wfriedman@proskauer.com.

FRIEDMAN, WILFRED T. lawyer; b. N.Y.C., Mar. 26, 1932; s. Samuel Paul Friedman and Sylvia Jeanette Tunis; m. Sandra Kayla Copp, 1972 (div. 1986); 1 child, Carrie Samantha; m. Ann M. Woods, Oct. 11, 1992; 1 child, Bethany Ann. AB, Hiram Coll., 1953; JD, NYU, 1958. Bar: N.Y. Pvt. practice, N.Y.C. 1st lt. USAR, 1953-55. Office: 36 W 44th St 8th Fl New York NY 10036-8102

FRIEDMAN, Y. ZAK, process control consultant; b. Tel Aviv; came to U.S., 1971; s. Jacob and Sabine Friedman; m. Tova Beck; children: Adie, Barak. BSc cum laude, Technion, Haifa, Israel, 1967; PhD, Purdue U., 1973. Process engr. Haifa Refineries, 1967-71; instr. Purdue U., West Lafayette, Ind., 1971-73; control mgr. Sci. Energy Systems, Watertown, Mass., 1973-77; staff engr. Exxon Rsch. and Engring., Florham Park, N.J., 1977-86; prin. cons. KBC Process Automation (now Honeywell), Southampton, Eng., 1986-92, Petrocontrol, N.Y.C., 1992—. Contbr. articles to profl. jours.; inventor in field. Office: Petrocontrol 34 E 30th St New York NY 10016 E-mail: zak@petrocontrol.com.

FRIEDMAN-BARONE, RONNIE EVA, b. Bklyn., Oct. 28, 1946; d. Sol and Sylvia Friedman; m. Joseph Peter Barone; 1 child, Dmitry. BA in English, Emerson Coll., 1966; MS in Counseling, CCNY, 1979; Ed.M., Harvard U., 1985. Chair religious outreach Mass. Citizens Against Death Penalty, Boston, 1986—2000, exec. dir., 1995—2000; v.p. Wash. Coalition to Abolish Death Penalty, Seattle, 2002—. Mem. steering com. Wash. Coalition to Abolish Death Penalty, Seattle, 2000—; mem. adj. faculty Harvard Div. Sch., Cambridge, Mass., 1992—99. See career and voluntary resume. Named Luce fellow in Urban Ministry, Harvard Div. Sch., Cambridge, 1997—2000. Office: Wash Coalition to Abolish Death Penalty PO Box 3045 Seattle WA 98114 Personal E-mail: rfriedbar@earthlink.net. Business E-Mail: info@abolishdeathpenalty.org.

FRIEDMANN, ELIZABETH CARROLL, writer, editor; b. Nashville, Tenn., Jan. 3, 1941; BA, U. Tenn., 1962; MA, U. Fla., 1979. Freelance travel writer mags. and newspapers, Jacksonville, Fla., 1979—85; reporter and feature writer Florida Times-Union, Jacksonville, 1965—68; lectr. to adj. asst. prof. of English Jacksonville U., 1979—86; book reviewer Florida Times-Union, Jacksonville, 1975—88; columnist and feature writer Jacksonville Mag., Jacksonville, 1979—88; ind. scholar and rschr., 1988—. Mem. Laura (Riding) Jackson Bd. Literary Mgmt., 1991—; project dir. Kalliope On the Air/Cable TV series, 1980—88; founding editor, project dir. Kalliope: A Jour. of Women's Art, 1978—88; numerous other coms., panels in field. Co-editor: Four Unposted Letters to Catherine, by Laura Riding, 1993; co-editor: (with Alan J. Clark) The Word "Woman" and Other Related Writings, by Laura (Riding) Jackson, 1993; co-editor: (with Alan J. Clark and Robert Nye) First Awakenings, The Early Poems of Laura Riding, 1992. Home: 2355 South Ponte Vedra Blvd Ponte Vedra Beach FL 32082

FRIEDMANN, E(MERICH) IMRE, biologist, educator; b. Budapest, Hungary, Dec. 20, 1921; came to U.S., 1965; s. Hugo and Gisella (Singer) Friedmann; 1 child, Daphna; m. Roseli Ocampo, July 22, 1974. PhD, U. Vienna, 1951. Instr., lectr. Hebrew U., Jerusalem, 1952-66; assoc. prof. Queens U., Kingston, Ont., Can., 1967-68, Fla. State U., Tallahassee, 1968-76, prof., 1976-01, Robert Lawton Disting. prof., 1991-01, dir. Polar Desert Rsch. Ctr., 1985-01, sr. NRC rsch. fellow NASA Ames Rsch. Ctr., Moffett Field, Calif., 2001—. Concurrent prof. Nanjing U., People's Republic of China, 1987—; vis. prof. Fla. State U., Tallahassee, 1966-67, U. Vienna, 1975; disting. sr. vis. scientist Jet Propulsion Lab., 1999-2000. Editor Antarctic Microbiology, 1993; contbr. articles to profl. jours. Recipient Congl. Antartic Service medal NSF, 1979, Alexander v. Humboldt award, 1987, resolution of commendation Gov. of Fla., 1978, Procter & Gamble award Am. Soc. Microbiology, 1998, Bergey's medal Bergey's Manual Trust, 2001. Fellow: AAAS, Am. Acad. of Microbiology, Am. Soc. Microbiology (Procter and Gamble award in environ. microbiology 1998), Royal Microsc. Soc., Linnean Soc. London, Exploreres Club; mem.: Internat. Soc. Study of Origins of Life, Soc. Phycol. France, Hungarian Algological Soc. (hon.), Internat. Phycol. Soc., Am. Phycol. Soc. (award of Excellence 2002), Indian Phycol. Soc., Brit. Phycol. Soc., Hungarian Acad. Scis. (fgn.). Jewish. Achievements include co-discovery of micro-organism (cryptoendolithic lichens) living in Antarctic rocks, 1976. Discovery of fossil bacteria in the Martian meteorite ALH 84001, 2001. Home: 300 E 59th St Apt 1402 New York NY 10022 Office: Space Sci Divsn 245-3 NASA Ames Rsch Ctr Moffett Field CA 94035

FRIEDMANN, PATRICIA ANN, writer; b. New Orleans, La., Oct. 29, 1946; d. Werner and Marjorie Sybil (Cahn) F.; m. Robert E. Skinner, Mar. 17, 1979 (div. Nov. 1996); children: Esme Friedmann, Werner Skinner; m. Edward G. Muchmore, Nov. 11, 1999. AB, Smith Coll., 1968; MEd, Temple Univ., 1970; ABD, Univ. Denver, 1975. Fiction workshop facilitator, New Orleans, 1994—99; writer-in-residence Tulane U., 2001; reviewer Publishers Weekly, Brightleaf, Times-Picayune, 1993—99; spkr. in field. Author: Too Smart to Be Rich, 1988, The Exact Image of Mother, 1991, Eleanor Rushing, 1999 (Barnes & Noble Discover Great Writers selection, Borders Original Voices selection), Odds, 2000, Secondhand Smoke, 2002 (Book Sense 76 selection), (play) The Accidental Jew as part of Native Tongues, 1994, Lovely Rita as part of Native Tongues, 2000; short stories. Mem. Authors Guild. Home: 8330 Sycamore Pl New Orleans LA 70118-2941 E-mail: afreelunch@aol.com.

FRIEDMANN, PAUL, surgeon, educator; b. Vienna, Dec. 2, 1933; came to U.S., 1938; s. Erich and Rochelle (Behar) F.; m. Janee Armstrong, Apr. 24, 1962; children: Pamela, Cynthia. BA, U. Pa., 1955; MD, Harvard U., 1959. Diplomate Am. Bd. Surgery, Am. Bd. Vascular Surgery. Chmn. dept. surgery Baystate Med. Ctr., Springfield, Mass., 1971-98, sr. v.p. acad. affairs, 1996—; prof. surgery Sch. Medicine Tufts U., Boston, 1985—. Prof. of surgery, Tufts U. Sch. Medicine, Boston, 1985—, chmn. ad interim dept. surgery, 1996-2001; mem. residency rev. com., 1985-91, chmn., 1989-91; chmn. RRC Coun., Accreditation Coun. for Grad. Med. Edn., 1989-91, mem., 1994-2000. Contbr. articles to profl. jours. Served to capt. USAF, 1961-63. Fellow ACS (bd. govs. 1978-84, 94—, vice chmn., 1998-99, pres. Mass. chpt. 1987, exec. com. bd. govs. 1996-99, adv. coun. for gen. surgery 1996—, chmn. 2001—); mem. Am. Surg. Assn., Assn. Program Dirs. in Surgery (sec. 1985-87, pres. 1987-89), Coun. Med. Specialty Socs. (bd. dirs., sec. 1995-96, pres. elect 1996-97, pres. 1997-98), New Eng. Soc. Vascular Surgery (recorder 1989-90, pres.-elect 1990-91, pres. 1991-92), New Eng. Surg. Soc. (treas. 1991-95, pres.-elect 1995-96, pres. 1996-97), Accreditation Coun. for Grad. Med. Edn. (exec. com. 1995—, chmn. designate 1997-98, chmn. 1998-2000, John Gienapp award 2003). Office: Baystate Med Ctr 759 Chestnut St Springfield MA 01199-1001 E-mail: paul.friedmann@bhs.org.

FRIEDMANN, PAUL GARSON, control engineer, editor; b. Millburn, N.J., May 29, 1932; s. Ludwig and Libby (Serkau) F.; m. Mary Elizabeth Anderson, Dec. 4, 1961; 1 child, John Harold. BS in Chem. Engring., U. Mich., 1953; MS in Engring., U. Pa., 1965. Devel. engr. Mobil Oil, Paulsboro, N.J., 1957-63; sr. scientist Leeds & Northrup, North Wales, Pa., 1963-74; sr. cons. Allied Signal, Morristown, N.J., 1974-86; sr. engr. John Brown, Stamford, Conn., 1986-88; cons. CRB Sys., Norwalk, Conn., 1988-92; ind. cons., 1992—. Author: Economics of Control Improvement, 1994; editor: Continuous Process Control, 1996, Control Valves, 1998, Instrumentation, Systems, and Automation Dictionary, 2002. With U.S. Army, 1955-57. Mem. Instrument Soc. Am., Tau Beta Pi. Achievements include patents on pH control, adaptive control; research on control application and algorithms; development of controls for high speed continuous casting of amorphous metal. Home and Office: 3 Wildwood Park Rd Clinton CT 06413

FRIEDMANN, PERETZ PETER, aerospace engineer, educator; b. Timisoara, Romania, Nov. 18, 1938; arrived in U.S., 1969, naturalized, 1977; s. Mauritius and Elisabeth Friedmann; m. Esther Sarfati, Dec. 8, 1964. DSc, MIT, 1972. Research asst. dept. aeronautics and astronautics MIT, Cambridge, 1969-72; asst. prof. mech. and aerospace engring. dept. UCLA, 1972-77, assoc. prof., 1977-80, prof., 1980-98, chmn. dept. mech. and aerospace engring., 1988-91; François-Xavier Bagnoud prof. aerospace engring. dept. U. Mich., Ann Arbor, 1999 . Editor in chief Vertica-Internat. Jour. Rotocraft and Powered Lift Aircraft, 1980-90; contbr. numerous articles to profl. jours. Grantee NASA, Air Force Office Sci. Rsch., U.S. Army Rsch. Office, NSF. Fellow AIAA (recipient Structures, Structural Dynamics and Materials award 1996, Structures, Structural Dynamics and Materials Lectr. award 97); mem. ASME (Structures and Materials award 1984, Spirit of St. Louis medal, 2003), Am. Helicopter Soc., Sigma Xi. Jewish. Office: U Mich Aerospace Engring Dept 3001 FXB Bldg Ann Arbor MI 48109-2140 E-mail: peretzf@umich.edu.

FRIEDMANN, THEODORE, physician; b. Vienna, June 16, 1935; s. Eric and Rochelle (Behar) Friedmann; m. Ingrid Anna Stromberg, Jan. 3, 1965; children: Eric, Carl. BA, U. Pa., 1956, MD, 1960, MA, 1994. Diplomate Nat. Bd. Med. Examiners. Staff scientist NIH, Bethesda, Md., 1965-68; from asst. to full prof. pediatrics U. Calif. San Diego, La Jolla, 1970—, prof. pediatrics, dir. gene therapy, bd. dirs. Newton Abraham vis. prof., fellow Lincoln Coll., U. Oxford, England, 1994; mem. Congrl. Biomed. Ethics Adv. Com., U.S. Congress, Washington, 1988—92, Exptl. Virology Study Sect./NIH, 1986—90; Muriel Jeannette Whitehill chair biomed. ethics U. Calif., San Diego, 1989—; mem. com. on human cloning State of Calif., 2000—; mem. com. on medicine, health & rsch. IOC, World Anti Doping Agy., 2000—; mem. Recombinant DNA Adv. Bd./NIH, 1998—, chmn., 2002—. Author: (monograph) Gene Therapy: Fact and Fiction, 1993; editor: (book series) Molecular Genetic Medicine, 1989—; patentee in gene therapy. Recipient H.C. Jacobeaus prize, Nordic Rsch. Com., Sweden, 1995, Cross of Honor for Sci. and the Arts, Austria, 1996. Mem.: AAAS (chmn. adv. com. germ line gene therapy 1995—), NIH (chmn. DNA adv. com. 2001—). Avocation: music. Office: Univ Calif San Diego CMG Rm 122 9500 Gilman Dr La Jolla CA 92093-0634 E-mail: tfriedmann@ucsd.edu.

FRIEDRICH, CHARLES WILLIAM, corporate executive; b. Elgin, Ill., Aug. 30, 1943; s. Charles Kenneth and Veronica Elizabeth (Sharpe) F.; m. Janet Lee West, June 20, 1970; children: Joan Elizabeth, Charles Kenneth II. Student, Loras Coll., 1961-63; BA, Parsons Coll., 1967. Salesman Bendix Corp., South Bend, Ind., 1967; safety dir., asst. pers. mgr. Nat. Castings divsn. Midland Ross, Cicero, Ill., 1968-69; pers. mgr. Continental Tube Co. divsn. Hofmann Industries, Bellwood, Ill., 1969, asst. mgr. indsl. rels., 1971-73, Midwest dir. indsl. rels. parent co., 1971-73; dir. indsl. rels., gen. mgr. Lemont (Ill.) Shipbldg. and Repair Co., 1973-75; indsl. rels. exec. Modern Mgmt. Methods, Inc., Deerfield, Ill., 1975-77; pres. Std. Cons. Svcs. Co., Inc., Hinsdale, Ill., 1977-88; chmn. bd. dirs., pres. B.I. Industries, Inc., Blue Island, Ill., 1986—2002, Brulé Pollution Control Co., Blue Island, 1986—2002, Radiant Products Co., Blue Island, 1986—2002. Past Ill. Pres., Burr Ridge (Ill.) Park Dist. Bd.; scoutmaster Boy Scouts Am., 1982-88; past treas. Palisades Sch. Dist. Mem. Packard Automobile Classics Club (pres. 1996—), Classic Car Club Am., Antique Automobile Club Am., Kiwanis, KC (former grand knight, trustee Mayslake coun.), Alpha Phi Omega. Home: 10 S 431 Glenn Dr Burr Ridge IL 60527-6859 Office: 8412 Wilmette Ave Darien IL 60561 E-mail: brulecee@aol.com.

FRIEDRICH, CRAIG WILLIAM, lawyer; b. Oshkosh, Wis., Oct. 25, 1946; s. William Harold and Lorraine June (Pugh) F. AB, U. Wis., Madison, 1968; JD cum laude, Harvard U., 1972. Bar: N.Y. 1973, U.S. Tax Ct. 1973, U.S. Dist. Ct. (so., ea. dists.) N.Y. 1979, U.S. Ct. Internat. Trade 1980, Maine 1986. Atty., advisor Office Tax Legis. Counsel U.S. Treasury Dept., Washington, 1974-76; assoc. Weil, Gotshal and Manges, N.Y.C., 1972-74, 1976-77, Debevoise and Plimpton, N.Y.C., 1977-81; assoc. prof. N.Y. Law Sch., N.Y.C., 1981-83; counsel Schoeman, Marsh, Updike and Welt, N.Y.C., 1982-83, ptnr., 1983-86, Bernstein, Shur, Sawyer & Nelson, Portland, Maine, 1986—. Cons. Bank Tax Inst., 1981-83; subject specialist Council Non Collegiate Continuing Edn., 1982. Mem. bd. contbg. editors, advisors Jour. Corp. Taxation, 1980—, author column, 1980—; contbr. articles to profl. jours. Mem. N.Y. State Bar Assn., Maine Bar Assn., Am. Soc. Internat. Law, N.Y.C. Bar Assn., Cumberland Club, Purpoodock Club, Phi Beta Kappa, Phi Kappa Phi, Phi Eta Sigma. Republican. Congregationalist. Home: 1 Ellie Ave Scarborough ME 04074-8549 Office: Bernstein Shur Sawyer & Nelson PO Box 9729 Portland ME 04104-5029

FRIEDRICH, PAUL, anthropologist, linguist, poet; b. Cambridge, Mass., Oct. 22, 1927; s. Carl Joachim and Lenore Louise (Pelham) F.; m. Lore Bucher, Jan. 6, 1950 (div. Jan. 1966); children: Maria Elizabeth, Susan Guadalupe, Peter Roland; m. Margaret Hardin, Feb. 26, 1966 (div. June 1974); m. Deborah Joanna Gordon, Aug. 9, 1975 (div. Nov. 1996); children: Katherine Ann, Joan Lenore; m. Domnica Radulescu, Nov. 10, 1996; 1 child, Nicholas. BA, Harvard Coll., 1950; MA, Harvard U., 1951; PhD, Yale U., 1957. Instr. U. Conn., Storrs, 1956-57; asst. prof. Harvard U., Cambridge, Mass., 1957-58; jr. linguistic scholar Deccan Coll., Poona, India, 1958-59; asst. prof. anthropology U. Pa., Phila., 1959-62; assoc. prof. anthropology U. Chgo., 1962-67, prof. anthropology, linguistics and soc. thought, 1967-96, prof. emeritus (active), 1996—. Vis. prof. linguistics Georgetown U., winter, 1998-2001, U. Va., 2002. Author:

Proto-Indo-European Trees, 1970, Agrarian Revolt in a Mexican Village, 1970, The Meaning of Aphrodite, 1978, Bastard Moons, 1979, Language, Context and Imagination, 1979, The Language Parallax, 1986, The Princes of Naranja, 1987; co-editor: Russia and Eurasia-China, 1994, Music in Russian Poetry, 1998. Served to pfc. U.S. Army, 1946-47, Germany. Grantee Wenner-Gren Found., 1955; grantee NIMH, summers 1961-62; fellow Social Sci. Rsch. Coun., 1966-67; Guggenheim fellow, 1982-83 Mem.: Am. Acad. Arts and Scis., Linguistic Soc. Am. (chmn. program com. 1972, chmn. nominating com. 1975, mem. exec. com. 1981—83). Home: 5500 S South Shore Dr Apt 1609 Chicago IL 60637-1986 Office: U Chgo Dept Anthropology 1126 E 59th St Chicago IL 60637-1580

FRIEDRICH, SU G. filmmaker, educator; b. New Haven, Dec. 12, 1954; d. Paul William and Lore (Bucher) Friederich; life ptnr. Cathy Quinlan. BA, Oberlin (Ohio) Coll., 1975. Instr. film prodn. U. Wis., Milw., 1989, The New Sch., NYC, 1993—98, NYU, 1998—99; prof. video and film Princeton U., NJ, 1999—. (films) Gently Down the Stream, 1981; The Ties That Bind, 1984; Sink or Swim, 1990 (Charlotte Film and Video Festival Gold Jurors Choice award, 1993, Melbourne Film Festival Grand Prix, Kino Awards, 1991, San Francisco Film Festival Golden Gate award, Best of New Visions Category, 1991); First Comes Love, 1991; Rules of the Road, 1993; Hide and Seek, 1996 (LA Outfest Outstanding Documentary award, 1997, Athens Film Festival Best Narrative award, 1997); The Odds of Recovery, 2002. Recipient Peter S. Reed Lifetime Achievement award, 2000, Alpert Award in the Arts, 1996; fellow, John Simon Guggenheim Meml. Found., 1989; grantee, Nat. Endowment Arts; Ind. TV Svc., 1994, Rockefeller Found. fellowship, 1990. Democrat.

FRIEDRICHS, ARTHUR MARTIN, manufacturing company executive, retired; b. N.Y.C., May 8, 1911; s. Arthur C. and Olga A. (Knoepke) F.; m. Juanita Elizabeth Barrett, Nov. 2, 1968. Student, Union Coll., 1930-31; BS, NYU, 1935. Bookkeeper Corn Exchange Bank, N.Y.C., 1935-37; with E.H. & A.C. Friedrichs Co., 1937-71, pres., 1958-71. Bd. dirs. Fredrix Artists Canvas, Inc., Lawrenceville, Ga. Bd. dirs. Wartburg Home, Mt. Vernon, N.Y., 1974-96; pres. Artists Material Mfrs. Assn., 1965-68; life mem. Imperial Point Hosp. Aux., Ft. Lauderdale, No. Broward Hosp. Aux.; mem. Norwalk Hosp. Vols. Mem. Artists Fellowship, Pompano Beach Hist. Soc., Met. Opera Guild, Art Material Mfrs. Assn. N.Y. (past pres.), Salamagundi Club (N.Y.C., life), Lighthouse Point Yacht and Racquet Club, Corinthians Clubs; Salmagundi (life) (N.Y.C.); Lighthouse Point Yacht and Racquet (Fla.); Corinthians. Home: 2510 NE 35th St Lighthouse Point FL 33064

FRIEDRICHS, DAVID O. legal educator; b. White Plains, N.Y., Oct. 31, 1944; s. Kurt O. and Nellie (Bruell) F.; m. Jeanne A. Windle, June 5, 1976; children: Jessica Pauline, Bryan Patrick. AB, NYU, 1966, MA, 1970, ABD. Lectr., asst. prof. CUNY, Staten Island, 1969-77; from asst. to prof. U. Scranton, Pa., 1977—. Vis. lectr. Sch. Law U. S. Africa, 1988, Ohio U., 1991, Rufus Putnam lectr., 1991; pres. White Collar Crime Rsch. Consortium, 2002— Author: Trusted Criminals: White Collar Crime in Contemporary Society, 1996, Law in Our Lives: An Introduction, 2001; editor State Crime, Vols. I and II, 1998; mem. editl. bd. Justice Quarterly, 1996-98, The Am. Sociologist, 1997—; contbr. articles to profl. jours. Bd. dirs. Friends of the Library, Scranton, 1979-84, Pa. Citizens for Better Libraries, Harrisburg, Pa., 1983-85. Faculty rsch. grantee CUNY, 1972, U. Scranton, 1983-2000. Mem. Assn. for Humanist Soc. (v.p. 1983), Acad. Criminal Justice Scis. (com. chmn. 1982-86), Am. Legal Studies Assn. (editor Legal Studies Forum 1985-89), Am. Soc. Criminology (vice chair divsn. crit. criminology 1998, awards chair 2000), Law and Society Assn., Pi Gamma Mu (Frank Brown scholarship medal 1984). Office: U Scranton Dept Sociology and Crim Justice Scranton PA 18510

FRIEDRICHS, EDWARD CHARLES, architect; BA, Stanford U., 1965; MArch, U. Pa., 1968. Lic. architect Calif., Nev., Utah, Hawaii, N.Y., N.J., Ind. Architect M. Arthur Gensler Jr. & Assocs., San Francisco, 1969—, dir. projects, 1973-76, mng. prin. L.A., 1976-95; pres. Gensler, San Francisco, 1995—, CEO, 2000—, also bd. dirs., mem. mgmt. com. Mem. exec. bd. San Francisco Bay Area Coun., Boy Scouts Am. Fellow AIA, Internat. Interior Design Assn.; mem. Nat. Coun. Archtl. Registration Bds., Urban Land Inst. Office: Gensler 2 Harrison Street Ste 400 San Francisco CA 94105

FRIEL, BRIAN (BERNARD PATRICK FRIEL), author; b. Omagh, County Tyrone, No. Ireland, Jan. 9, 1929; s. Patrick and Christina (MacLoone) F.; m. Anne Morrison, Dec. 27, 1955; children: Paddy, Mary, Judy, Sally, David. Student, St. Columb's Coll., 1941-46; BA, St. Patrick's Coll., Maynooth, Ireland, 1948; postgrad., St. Joseph's Tchrs. Tng. Coll., Belfast, Ireland, 1949-50; Litt.D. (hon.), Dominican Coll., Chgo., Nat. U. Ireland, New U. Ulster, Trinity Coll., Dublin, Ireland, Georgetown U. Tchr. various schs., Derry City, No. Ireland, 1950-60; freelance writer, 1960—; with Tyrone Guthrie Theatre, 1963; co-founder Field Day Theatre Co., Derry, No. Ireland, 1980. Author: (short stories) A Saucer of Larks, 1964, The Gold in the Sea, 1966, The Diviner: Brian Friel's Best Short Stories, 1983, (plays) This Doubtful Paradise, 1960, The Enemy Within, 1962, The Blind Mice, 1963, Philadelphia, Here I Come!, 1964, The Loves of Cass McGuire, 1966, Lovers, 1967, Crystal and Fox, 1968, The Mundy Scheme, 1969, The Gentle Island, 1971, The Freedom of the City, 1972, Volunteers, 1975, Living Quarters, 1977, Faith Healer, 1979, Aristocrats, 1979 (London Evening Standard Best Play award 1988, Best Fgn. Play award N.Y. Drama Critics Circle 1989), Translations, 1980 (Christopher Ewart-Biggs Meml. prize Brit. Theatre Assn. 1981, Plays and Players Best New Play award 1981), American Welcome, 1980, The Communication Cord, 1982, Making History, 1988, Dancing at Lughnasa, 1990 (Tony Best Play award 1992), Wonderful Tennessee, 1993, Molly Sweeney, 1994, Give Me Your Answer, Do!, 1997, The Yalta Game, 2001, Two Plays After, 2002; (translator) Three Sisters (Anton Chekhov), 1981, Uncle Vanya, 1998, Two Plays After, 2002, Performances, 2003; translator: Fathers and Sons (Ivan Turgenev); (screenplay) Philadelphia, Here I Come!, 1970; (version) A Month in the Country, Performances, 2003; editor: The Last of the Name; contbr. short stories to New Yorker. Mem. Irish Senate, 1987. Recipient Macauley fellow Irish Arts Coun., 1963; hon. fellow U. Coll., Dublin. Fellow Royal Soc. Literature; mem. Nat. Assn. Irish Artists, Am. Acad. Arts and Letters. Office: Drumaweir House Greencastle Donegal Ireland

FRIEL, DANIEL DENWOOD, SR., manufacturing executive; b. Queenstown, Md., Aug. 11, 1920; s. Samuel Edward Whiting and Martha Washington (Reynolds) F.; m. Helen June Hennessy, May 1, 1943; children: Barbara Friel Holme, Martha Friel Wilson, Patricia, Daniel D. Jr. BChemE, Johns Hopkins U., 1942. Supr. optical instruments Manhattan Project, U. Chgo., 1943-45; dir. applied physics E.I. du Pont, Wilmington, Del., 1945-61, mgr. investments, 1961-69, dir. electronic products, 1974-77, dir. instrument products, 1977-82; pres. Holotron Corp., Wilmington, 1969-71; pres., chmn. Edgecraft Corp., Wilmington, 1983-91, chmn. bd., chief exec. officer Avondale, Pa., 1991—. Chmn. Mt. Cuba Astron. Obs., Wilmington, 1960—. Co-author: Process Instruments and Control, 1960; contbr. articles to profl. jours. Trustee Tatnall Sch., Wilmington, 1967-74. Mem. Phys. Soc. Am., Optical Soc. Am., Instrument Soc. Am., Ams. for Competitive Enterprise System (bd. dirs.), Tau Beta Pi. Achievements include patents for radiation measurement, instruments, and household appliances; invention of radiation detection and analysis devices. Office: Edgecraft Corp 825 Southwood Rd Avondale PA 19311-9765

FRIELING, GERALD HARVEY, JR., specialty steel company executive; b. Kansas City, Mo., Apr. 29, 1930; s. Gerald Harvey and Mary Ann (Coons) F.; m. Joan Lee Bigham, June 14, 1952; children: John, Robert, Nancy. BS in Mech. Engring., U. Kans., 1951. Application engr. Westinghouse Elec. Corp., Pitts., 1951-53; mfg. mgr. Madison-Faessler Tool Co., Moberly, Mo., 1956-60; gen. mgr. wire and tubing Tex. Instruments Inc., Attleboro, Mass., 1960-69; v.p. Air Products & Chems. Co., Allentown, Pa., 1969-79; pres., chief exec. officer, chmn. bd. Nat. Standard Co., Niles, Mich., 1979-89, retired. CEO Tokheim Corp., 1990—91, chmn. bd., 1990—96, vice chmn., 1997—2000; bd. dirs., lead dir. Superior Metal Products; bd. dirs. Mossberg Printing Co., CTS; pres. Frieling & Assocs.; instr. Brown U., 1965—68; adj. prof. U. Notre Dame, Mendoza Sch. Bus., 1990—; mem. adv. bd. U. Kans. Sch. Engring., 1983—96. Author; patentee in field. Served to lt. USNR, 1953-56, Korea. Recipient Wire Assn. medal, 1966, Disting. Engring. Service award U. Kans., 1986. Mem.: Union League (Chgo.), Signal Point Country, Summit. Presbyterian. E-mail: nordict6@aol.com.

FRIEND, DAVID, publishing executive; b. Chgo., Jan. 31, 1955; m. Nancy Paulsen; children: Sam and Molly (twins). BA summa cum laude, Amherst Coll., 1977. Corr. Life mag., 1978-86, sr. editor, 1987-92, dir. photography and new media, 1992-98, dir. photography, asst. mng. editor, 1998; editor creative devel. Vanity Fair, 1998—. Mem. numerous nat. and internat. photography award juries; co-curator numerous photog. exhbns. including Somalia's Cry; videos include LIFE at Woodstock; prodr. CD-ROM The Face of LIFE, 1936-72; helped place 1st ind. photog. exhbn. on genocide in Bosnia at U.S. Holocaust Meml. Mus., Washington. Author: The Meaning of Life, More Reflections on the Meaning of Life, (juvenile) Baseball, Football, Daddy and Me; contbr. articles to London Sunday Times, Playboy, Nat. Lampoon, Contemporary Lit. Criticism, Life, N.Y. Times Sunday Mag.; editl. dir. LIFE's Web site. Recipient photojournalism editing award Nat. Press Photographers Assn. Mem. Internat. Ctr. Photography (pres. coun.), Overseas Press Club. Office: Vanity Fair 4 Times Sq 7th Fl 350 Madison Ave New York NY 10036

FRIEND, DONALD AGAR, geographer, geomorphologist, educator; b. San Francisco, June 26, 1960; s. Edward Armand Friend and Nancy Jaicks Alexander; m. Lisa Mitchell, Mar. 19, 1994; children: Scanlon Parker, Reilly Rose. BS in Conservation of Natural Resources, U. Calif., Berkeley, 1984; MA in Geography, U. Colo., 1988; PhD in Geography, Ariz. State U., 1997. Instr. Colo. Outward Bound Sch., Denver, 1987-94; dir. earth scis. program, tchg. scholar fellow Minn. State U., Mankato, 1997—, asst. prof. geography, 1997-2001, assoc. prof. geography, 2001—. U.S. rep. Internat. Commn. on Diversity in Mountain Sys. Internat. Geog. Union, Rome, 2000—; adv. bd. Mountain Studies Inst., Silverton, Colo., 2002—; sr. instr. Mountain Inst., Washington, 2002—; mem. adv. bd. for phys. geography and earth scis. McGraw-Hill Pubs., 2002—. Editor (guest): Geog. Rev., 2002; contbr. articles to profl. jours. Preparing Tomorrow's Tchrs. to Use Tech. grantee, U.S. Dept. Edn., 1999—2000. Fellow Am. Geog. Soc.; mem. Internat. Mountain Soc., Assn. Am. Geographers (founder, adv. bd. 1998—, chair mountain geography specialty group 1998-2001, J. Warren Nystrom award 1999, Internat. Geog. Congress Jr. scholar 2000), Gamma Theta Upsilon. Avocations: mountaineering, running, traveling. Office: Dept Geography Minn State Univ Mankato MN 56001 Office Fax: 507-389-2980. E-mail: donald.friend@mnsu.edu.

FRIEND, EDWARD MALCOLM, III, lawyer, educator; b. Birmingham, Ala., Oct. 12, 1946; s. Edward M. Jr. and Hermione Frances (Curjel) F. BA in History U. Ala., 1968, JD, 1971. Bar: Ala. 1971. Shareholder Sirote and Permutt, P.C., Birmingham, 1971—, pres., 1991-93. Chmn. Birmingham Area C. of C., 1990-91; chmn. dist. bd. dirs. Colonial Bank Ala., Birmingham, 1985-2000; vice chair Colonial Bank Ctrl. Dist., 2000—; adj. prof. U. Ala., Birmingham, 1994—, chmn. adv. bd. Sch. Bus., 2003—. Chmn. Birmingham Area chpt. ARC, 1987-88; chmn. bd. NCCJ, 1983, nat. bd., 1981-88; pres. coun. U. Ala., Birmingham, 1980-94, Birmingham Jewish Fedn., 1984-89, United Way Ctrl. Ala., 1984-99, chmn., 1993-94, gen. campaign chmn., 1989; bd. dirs. Childrens Hosp. Ala., 1986—; exec. com. Ala. Symphony Assn., 1980-82, bd. dirs., 1982-85, Birmingham Festival Arts, 1978-88, pres., 1984-85, chmn., 1985-86; mem. nat. leadership coun. United Way Am.; pres. Big Bros./Big Sisters Greater Birmingham, 1980, chmn., 1981-83; trustee St. Vincent's Hosp., 1982-86, v.p., 1984-86, Ala. Sch. Fine Arts Found., 1985-91; trustee Cmty. Foun. of Greater Birmingham, 2002--; chmn. Leadership Ala., 1993; bd. dirs. Boy Scouts Am., 1996—, Comty. Found. Greater Birmingham, 2002-. Recipient Brotherhood award Nat. Conf. Christians and Jews, 1987; named to Ala. Acad. of Honor; named Lawyer of Yr., Birmingham Legal Secretarial Assn., 1976, Outstanding Alumnus, U. Ala. Sch. Law, 1984. Mem. So. Inst. Health Law (chmn. 1985-87), Nat. Health Lawyers Assn. (bd. dirs. 1992-95), Farrah Law Soc. (chmn. 1982-84). Office: Sirote and Permutt PC 2311 Highland Ave South Birmingham AL 35205-4004 E-mail: efriend@Sirote.com.

FRIEND, HAROLD CHARLES, neurologist; b. Chgo, Nov. 28, 1946; s. Leonard Nathan and Sharlee (Friedman) F.; m. Karenanne; children: Reed, Chad. BA, U. Tex., 1968, MD, 1972. Diplomate Am. Bd. Neurology. Resident Upstate Med. Ctr., Syracuse, NY, 1972-73, Albert Einstein Coll. Medicine, Bronx, NY, 1973-75; mem. staff Boca Raton Cmty. Hosp., Fla., 1975—; pres. Neurosci. Ctr., Boca Raton, Fla., 1984—; rsch. prof. dept. brain sci. Fla. Atlantic U., Boca Raton, Fla., 2002—. Spl. expert witness Fla. Agy. for Health Care Adminstrn.; expert med. advisor divsn. workers compensation Fla. Dept. Labor and Employment Security; bd. dir. Pan Am. Bankcorp; pres. Puget Sound Yellow Taxi, Inc., 1994-95. Author: Territorial Marking, 1968, Bell's Palsy, 1975, Transient Global Amnesia, 1987, exec. bd. (United Way Palm Beach County Agy. Rels. Com., 1992-95; mem. allocation com., 1990-92; bd. dir. Raton Children's Mus. 1989-92.) Mem. exec. bd., v.p. Gulfstream coun. Boy Scouts Am., 1988—93, pres. coun., 1993—95, area I v.p., 1990—92, area IV v.p., 1993—95, area IV pres., 1995—98, mem. so. region exec. bd., 1993—, mem. internat. scouting com., 1998—, chmn. direct svc. com., 1999—, mem. nat. adv. coun., 2000—; benefactor World Orgn. Scout Movements; treas. Interam. Scout Found., 2001—03, pres., 2003—, Interamerican Scout Found., 2003—. Recipient Order of Arrow Vigil Honor award Boy Scouts Am., 1983, Dist. Merit award, 1987, Silver Beaver award, 1990, Wood Badge, 1990, Disting. Commr. award, 1991, Disting. Eagle Scout, 1997, Silver Antelope award, 1997; James West fellow, 1993, 1910 Soc., 1998, Baden Powell fellow, 2000. Fellow: Am. Acad. Neurology; mem.: Fla. Soc. Neurology, So. Clin. Neurol. Soc., NY Acad. Sci. (life), Am. Soc. Neuroimaging (cert.), Internat. Fellowship Scouting Rotarians (N.Am. sect. chmn. 1995—96, internat. sec. 1996—98, internat. vice chair 1998—99, internat. chair 1999—2002, internat. commr. 2002—, Silver Wheel award 2002), Rotary Internat. Fellowship Running and Fitness Rotarians (internat. chmn. 1992—98, internat. treas. 1998—99, internat. sec. 1999—2001, internat. chair 2003—), Boca Raton Road Runners Club (pres. 1992—93), Sierra Club (life), Rotary (bd. dir., pres. Boca Raton Club dist. world fellowship chmn. 1992—94, dist. found. chmn. 1994, gov.'s rep. 1994—95, chmn. dist. conf. 1995, gov.'s rep. 1996—97, dist. gov. 1998—99, chmn. coll. gov. 1999—2000, zone coord. Children at Risk 2000—01, cmty. svc. task force 2001—02, benefactor Rotary Found., Dist. Found. Svc. award 1992, Pres. Salute Commendation 1993, Dist. Found. Svc. award 1995, featured on cover of The Rotarian 2003, Paul Harris fellow), Phi Beta Kappa (photo on the cover of The Rotarian 2003), Alpha Phi Omega, Theta Xi, Phi Kappa Phi. Avocation: marathons. Office: 1500 NW 10th Ave Ste 105 Boca Raton FL 33486-1344

FRIEND, SANDRA ANN COVERT, interior designer; b. Oceanside, N.Y., Feb. 6, 1937; d. Sidney Roscoe and Dorothy (Van Kleek) Covert; m. Howard Friend, Aug. 20, 1960; children: David Sidney, Steven Scott, Laura Jill. AAS in Environ. & Interior Design, Otis Parsons Sch. Design, L.A., 1984; BA in Spanish, Bucknell U., Lewisburg, Pa., 1958. Bi-lingual interpretor Lederle Labs., Pearl River, N.Y., 1958-60; designer Archtl. Interiors, Claremont, Calif., 1980-84; sr. planner Huntington Resource, Pasadena, Calif., 1984-86; project mgr. Wheeler & Wheeler Architects, Claremont, Calif., 1986-89; prin. Berkeley Design Assocs., Claremont, Calif., 1989-94; instr. Calif. Poly. U., Pomona, Calif., 1991; prin. Grape St. Design Assocs., Medford, Oreg., 1995-99. Interior design adv. bd. Calif. Poly. U., Pomona, 1991, Chaffey Coll., Alta Loma, Calif., 1991; mem. ASID nat. legis. adv. coun., 1999-2002, Nat. Strategic Planner, 1998-2000; chmn. Nat. Legis. Coalition on Interior Design. 1992-93. State treas. Calif. Legis. Conf. on Interior Design, 1990-92, v.p. edn. and membership, 1992-94; chmn. Claremont Archtl. Commn., 1991-92; bd. dirs. Schneider Art Mus., Ashland, 1994-2000, pres. 1999-2000. Fellow: Am. Soc. Interior Designers (bd. dirs. 1984—91, chpt. pres. 1989—98, bd. dirs. 1995—97, chpt. treas. 1998—2000, profl.); mem.: AIA (profl. affiliate 1997—99), Nat. Coun. Interior Design Qualifications (chair practicum com. 2000—02), Oreg. Coalition for Profl. Interior Design (co-chair 1998—2000, pres. 2001, legisl. chair 2002—03), Illuminating Engring. Soc. Avocations: swimming, skiing, kayaking, travel. Home and Office: Interior Planning + Design 965 Pinecrest Ter Ashland OR 97520-3425

FRIEND, THEODORE WOOD, III, foundation executive, historian, writer; b. Pitts., Aug. 27, 1931; s. Theodore Wood and Jessica (Holton) F.; m. Elizabeth Groesbeck Pierson, Feb. 20, 1960; children: Theodore Porter, Pierson, Elizabeth Robinson. BA, Williams Coll., 1953, LLD (hon.), 1978; PhD, Yale U., 1958. Mem. faculty SUNY, Buffalo, 1959-73, prof. history, 1966-73; pres. Swarthmore (Pa.) Coll., 1973-82; trustee Eisenhower Exchange Fellowships Inc., 1982—, pres., 1984-96. Author: Between Two Empires, The Ordeal of the Philippines, 1929-46, 65 (Bancroft prize in history 1966), The Blue Eyed Enemy: Japan Against the West in Java and Luzon, 1942-45, 88, Indonesian Destinies, 2003; (novel) Family Laundry, 1986. Dir. Phila. Savings Fund Soc., 1975-90; mem. Truman Scholarships Selection Panel, Pa., N.J., Del., 1993—, chmn., 1997—; mem. bd. advisors U.S.-Indonesia Soc., 2000—; bd. dirs. Metanexus Inst. on Religion and Sci., 2002—. Fulbright grantee, Philippines, 1957-59; Rockefeller Found. internat. rels. fellow, 1961-62; Nat. Def. Fgn. Lang. postdoctoral fellow, 1966-67; Guggenheim fellow, Indonesia, Philippines, Japan, 1967-68; fellow Woodrow Wilson Internat. Ctr., 1983-84, Bellagio Ctr. for Artists and Scholars fellow, 1988; recipient Dwight D. Eisenhower medal, 1997. Mem. Coun. on Fgn. Rels., Am. Hist. Assn., Soc. Historians Am. Fgn. Rels., Asia Soc., Phila. Com. on Fgn. Rels. (chmn. 1985-2000), Fgn. Policy Rsch. Inst. (sr. fellow), Phila. Club, Franklin Inn Club, Phi Beta Kappa. Presbyterian. Achievements include being a nationally ranked sr. squash player, 1983-93, 97—. Home: 264 S Radnor Chester Rd Villanova PA 19085-1306

FRIEND, WILLIAM BENEDICT, bishop; b. Miami, Oct. 22, 1931; s. William Eugene and Elizabeth (Paulus) F.. Student, U. Miami, 1949—52; cert. in philosophy, St. Mary's Coll., St. Mary, Ky., 1955; cert. of ordination, Mt. St. Mary's Sem., Emmittsburg, Md., 1959; MA in Edn., Cath. U. Am., 1965; LLD, St. Leo Coll., 1986. Ordained priest Roman Cath. Ch., 1959. Parish priest, educator, counselor, adminstr., 1959—68; ednl. rsch. adminstr. U. Notre Dame, Ind., 1968—71; vicar for edn., supt. schs. Diocese of Mobile, Ala., 1971—76, chancellor adminstrn., vicar for edn., 1976—79; aux. bishop Diocese of Alexandria-Shreveport, La., 1979—83, diocesan bishop, 1983—86; first bishop of Shreveport La., 1982—85, 1986—. Chmn. campaign for human devel. Nat. Conf. Cath. Bishops, 1982—85; mem. sci. and human values com. Commn. of Bishops and Scholars, 1983—86, chmn., 1986—92, cons., 1993—, sec., 2000—; mem. Pontifical Coun. for Culture. Editor handbooks and study guides for Cath. edn; editor: (with Ford and Daues) Evangelizing the Cultures in A.D. 2000, 1990; co-editor (with J. Anderson): The Culture of Bible Belt Catholics, 1995; contbr. Bd. dirs., v.p. S.E. Regional Hispanic Ctr., Miami, 1986—; trustee Notre Dame Sem., 1976, St. Joseph Coll. Sem., New Orleans, 1976—; bd. councillors Shreveport Cmty. Renewal; mem. rsch. oversight com. Biomed. Rsch. Found. N.W. La.; chmn. bd. Ctr. for Applied Rsch. in the Apostolate, 1997—; mem. adv. bd. The John J. Reilly Ctr. Sci., Tech. and Values U. Notre Dame; sec. U.S. Conf. Cath. Bishops; bd. dirs. La. Interchurch Conf., Ctr. for Bioethics and Law. Decorated Order of Fleur de Lis K.C., knight comdr. with star Knights of Holy Sepulchre of Jerusalem; recipient Presdl. award, Nat. Cath. Ednl. Assn., 1978, O'Neil D'Amour award, Nat. Assn. Bds. Edn., 1982, NCCJ Brotherhood and Humanitarian award, 1987, Human Rels. Coun. award, 2000. Mem.: AAAS, World Futures Soc., N.Y. Acad. Scis., U.S. Acad. Scis., Cath. Acad. Sci., Am. Acad. Religion, KC (state chaplain La. coun.). Roman Catholic. Avocations: hiking, art, music, reading. Office: Diocese of Shreveport Catholic Ctr 3500 Fairfield Ave Shreveport LA 71104-4108

FRIENDLY, ED, television producer; b. N.Y.C., Apr. 8, 1922; s. Edwin S. and Henrietta (Steinmeier) F.; m. Natalie Coulson Brooks, Jan. 31, 1952 (dec. May 9, 2002); children: Brooke Friendly, Edwin S. III. Grad., Manlius Sch., 1941. Radio exec., dir. BBD&O, N.Y.C., 1946-49; sales exec. ABC-TV, N.Y.C., 1949-53; ind. producer and packager N.Y.C., 1953-56; producer, program exec. CBS-TV, N.Y.C., 1956-59; v.p. spl. programs NBC-TV, N.Y.C., 1959-67; pres., founding mem. Ed Friendly Prodns., Los Angeles, 1967—. Co-chmn. steering com. Caucus for Producers, Writers and Dirs. Exec. producer: film Little House on the Prairie; Laugh-In; producer: film Peter Lundy and the Medicine Hat Stallion (Emmy nomination); Young Pioneers; mini-series Backstairs at the White House (11 Emmy nominations); also producer motion pictures and TV spls.; exec. producer/producer: Barbara Cartland's The Flame Is Love. Served to capt., U.S. Army, 1942-45, PTO. Recipient Spl. award Internat. Film and TV Festival N.Y., 1967; Emmy award for Laugh-In, 1968; Producer of Yr. award Producers Guild of Am., 1968; Golden Globe award Hollywood Fgn. Press, 1968; Gold medal of honor Internat. Radio and TV Soc., 1970; Christopher award for motion picture, 1975; Western Heritage award Nat. Cowboy Hall of Fame and Western Heritage Center, for Little House on the Prairie, 1975, for Peter Lundy and the Medicine Hat Stallion, 1978; Scout awards for best weekly series and show of yr. for Laugh-In, 1969 Mem. Calif. Horsemen's Benevolent and Protective Assn. (pres. 1994, former mem. bd. dirs.), Thoroughbred Owners Calif. (founder, pres., chmn. 1993-96, chmn. 1996-97, bd. dirs. 1993-2000), Nat. Thoroughbred Assn. (vice chmn., bd. dirs. 1996-98, founding mem.), Nat. Thoroughbred Racing Assn. (bd. dirs. 1997-99).

FRIES, ARTHUR LAWRENCE, life health insurance broker, disability claim consultant; b. Bklyn., Aug. 21, 1937; s. Jack Edwin and Sophia (Kabat) F.; m. Cindy Ann Blum, Mar. 27, 1960; children: Stacey Jill, Todd Steven. AB, Nichols Coll., 1956; BS, Syracuse U., 1958. Registered health underwriter; diplomate Acad. Cert. Cons. and Experts. Various positions ins. sales and adminstrn. various firms, N.Y.C., 1962-72; life and health ins. agt. Washington Nat. Ins. Co., Los Angeles, 1973-85; pvt. practice, N.Y.C., Los Angeles and Northridge, Calif., 1962-72, Northridge, 1982-95, Newport Beach, Calif., 1996—. Blood chmn. Washington Nat. Ins. Co., 1976-79; spkr., lectr., cons. on individual disability income ins. claims; cons., expert witness and negotiator for non-can disability ins. claims. Contbr. articles to profl. jours. Chmn. memberships Vista Del Mar Men's Assn. for Orphaned Children, 1975. Recipient Nat. Sales Achievement award L.A. Gen. Agts. and Mgrs. Assn., 1965-94, Health Ins. Quality award, 1965-92, 93, Agt. of Yr. award 1976, 78, Nat. Quality award, 1980-91, Disting. Svc. award D.I.T.C. Rsch. Seminar, 1994. Fellow Am. Coll. Forensic Examiners, Inst. for Forensic Experts, Nat. Forensic Ctr., Nat. Assn. Life Underwriters (blood chmn. 1976-79, spkr. ann. conv. 1988, 90, 93 million dollar roundtable), Nat. Assn. Health Underwriters (life leading prodrs. roundtable), Calif. Assn. Life Underwriters, Calif. Assn. Health Underwriters (charter), San Fernando Valley Life Underwriters Assn., Orange County Assn. Ins. and Fin. Advisors, Orange County Assn. Health Underwriters, Forensic Cons. Assn. of Orange County, L.A. Assn. Health Underwriters (conf. spkr., spkrs. chmn. 1983-84, program chmn. 1984, bd. dirs., membership chmn. 1987-88), Am. Diabetic Assn., Am. Bd. Disability Analysts. Republican. Home and Office: 225 Via San Remo Newport Beach CA 92663-5511

FRIES, HELEN SERGEANT HAYNES, civic leader; d. Harwood Syme and Alice (Hobson) Haynes; m. Stuart G. Fries, May 5, 1938. Student, Coll. William and Mary, 1935-38. Bd. mem. Cmty. Ballet Assn., Huntsville, Ala., 1968—; mem. nat. nurses aid com. ARC, 1958-59; dir. ARC Aero Club, Eng., 1943-44; supr. ARC Clubmobile, Europe, 1944-46; mem. women's com. Nat. Symphony Orch., Washington, 1959—, chmn. residential and fund dr. for apts., 1959; bd. dirs. Madison Country Rep. Club, 1969-70; mem. nat. coun. Women's Nat. Rep. Club N.Y., 1963—, chmn. hospitality com., 1963-65; bd. dirs. League Rep. Women, 1952-61; patron mem., vol. docent Huntsville Mus. Art, Huntsville Lit. Assn.; vol. docent Weeden House, Twickenham Hist. Preservation Dist. Assn., Inc., Huntsville; mem. The Garden Guild, Huntsville, The Collectors Guild Constn. Hall Village, Huntsville, Hist. Huntsville Found., Huntsville Mus. Art, Corcoran Art Gallery. Recipient cert. of merit 84th Divsn., U.S. Army, 1945. Mem.: DAR, Assn. Preservation Va. Antiquities, Turkish-Am. Assn., English Speaking Union, Greensboro Soc. Preservation, Nat. Trust Hist. Preservation, Va., Nat., Valley Forge (Pa.), Eastern Shore Va., Nat. Soc. Colonial Dames Am., Daus. Am. Colonists, Huntsville-Madison County hist. socs., Friends of Ala. Archives, Nat. Soc. Lit. and Arts, Va. Hist. Soc., Bot. Garden Club, Heritage Club, Redstone Yacht Club, Garden Club, Army-Navy Country Club, Capitol Hill Club, Washington Club, Army-Navy Club. Address: 6200 Oregon Ave NW Apt 480 Washington DC 20015-1549

FRIES, JAMES FRANKLIN, internal medicine educator; b. Normal, Ill., Aug. 25, 1938; s. Albert Charles and Orpha (Hair) F.; m. Sarah Elizabeth Tilton, Aug. 27, 1960; children: Elizabeth Ann, Gregory James. AB, Stanford U., 1960; MD, Johns Hopkins U., 1964. Diplmate Am. Bd. Internal Medicine. Intern Johns Hopkins Hosp., Balt., 1964-65, resident in medicine, 1965-66, fellow connective tissue disease divsn., 1966-68; resident in medicine Stanford (Calif.) U. Sch. Medicine, 1968-69, instr. in medicine, 1969-71, asst. prof. medicine, 1971-77, assoc. prof. medicine, 1978-93, prof. medicine, 1993—. Dir. Arthritis, Rheumatism, Aging Med. Info. Sys., Stanford, 1975—; chmn. bd. dirs. Healthtrac Found., Menlo Park, Calif.; chmn. Healthtrac, Inc., 1984-2001; exec. com. The Health Project, 1992—. Author: Take Care of Yourself, 1975, 2000, Prognosis, 1981, Living Well, 1997, 1999, Taking Care of Your Child, 1999, The Arthritis Helpbook, 1999, Arthritis, 1999; mem. editl. bd. Jour. Rheumatology, Jour. Clin. Rheumatology. Named Best Med. Specialist in U.S., Town and Country mag., 1984, Best Dr. in U.S., Good Housekeeping mag., 1991, Rsch. Hero, Arthritis Found., 2001; named one of Best Drs. in Am., Woodward-

White, 1995; recipient C. Everett Koop Nat. Health award, 1994. Fellow ACP, Am. Coll. Rheumatology, Am. Coll. Med. Info. Avocations: skiing, running, expedition mountain climbing. Home: 135 Farm Rd Woodside CA 94062-1210 Office: Stanford U Sch Medicine 1000 Welch Rd Ste 203 Palo Alto CA 94304-1808 E-mail: jff@stanford.edu.

FRIES, RAYMOND SEBASTIAN, manufacturing company executive; b. St. Paul, June 19, 1919; s. Jacob H. and Christine Fries; children: Raymond B., John A., Christine. BS, U. Minn., 1948. Vice pres. Honeywell, Mpls., Los Angeles and Phila., 1944-65; v.p. Varian Assos., Palo Alto, Calif., 1965-67; pres. Esterline Angus, Indpls., 1967-71; v.p. Esterline Corp., N.Y.C., 1969-71; pres. Dietzgen Corp., Chgo., 1971-73; v.p. Allegheny Ludlum Industries, Pitts., 1973-80; exec. v.p. Allegheny Internat., Pitts., 1980-86, also dir.; pres., mgmt. consulting assoc. Chematron Corp., Chgo. Dir. Phila. Corp. Contbg. author: Industrial Engineering Handbook. Mem. ASME, Fries Engring. Assn., Fossivile Yacht Club (commodore). Clubs: Duquesne, Pitts. Athletic Assn.

FRIES, ROBERT FRANCIS, historian, educator; b. LaCrosse, Wis., Dec. 16, 1911; s. William James and Laura Merlinda (Olsen) F.; m. Frances Katherine Clements, Jan. 2, 1936 (dec. Jan. 1972); children: Mary Ann, Margaret Frances; m. Elizabeth Zevnik Dunne, Dec. 16, 1972. B.E., LaCrosse State Tchrs. Coll., 1933; Ph.M., U. Wis., 1936, PhD, 1939. Social sci. tchr. Cashton (Wis.) High Sch., 1933-35; asst. in history U. Wis., 1936-38; asst. prof. history De Paul U., Chgo., 1939-43, assoc. prof., 1943-45, prof. history, 1945-80, emeritus prof., 1980—2003, chmn. dept., 1945-56, 67-76, dean univ. coll., 1955-71. Fellow in history U. Wis., 1938-39 Contbr. to hist. jours.; author: Empire in Pine, the Story of Lumbering in Wisconsin, 1951, rev. edit., 1989; Author: Crown and Parliament in Tudor-Stuart England, 1959, European Civilization: Basic Historical Documents, 1965; editor: Readings in European Civilization, 1956. Recipient Via Sapientiae award, 1980 Mem. AAUP (chpt. sec. 1947-48), Am. Hist. Assn., Orgn. Am. Historians, Wis. Hist. Soc. Home: Wilmette, Ill. Died Aug. 27, 2003.

FRIESE, GEORGE RALPH, retail executive; b. Chgo., Feb. 15, 1936; s. George R. and Marie D. (Pilz) F.; m. Patricia J. Brown, Aug. 24, 1957; children: Christine Carol, Kurt Michael. BA, Monmouth Coll., 1956; JD, Chgo. Kent Coll. Law, 1960. Bar: Ill. 1961, U.S. Dist. Ct. Ill. (no. dist.) 1961, U.S. Supreme Ct. 1965. Asst. gen. counsel, v.p. Banner Mut. Ins. Cos., Chgo., 1959-63; ptnr. Madsen & Friese, Park Ridge, Ill., 1963-68; corp. counsel, sec. SCOA Industries, Inc., Columbus, Ohio, 1968-71, v.p. legal, sec., 1971-81, pres., 1981-85; vice chmn., dir. Hills Dept. Stores Inc., Canton, Mass., 1986—95. Propietor Portsmouth (N.H.) Athenaeum, 1993—. Bd. dirs. Columbus Symphony Orch., Greater Columbus Art Coun.; chmn., trustee New Eng. Red Cross; trustee Boy Scouts Am., Columbus, 1981-86, Boston Lyric Opera, 1988-95, Strawbery Banke Mus., 1994—, treas., 1996-98; mem., trustee Greater Piscataqua Cmty. Found., 1995—, vice chmn., 1998-2000, chmn., 2000. Mem. ABA, Ill. Bar Assn., Tau Kappa Epsilon, Phi Delta Phi. Clubs: Athletic (Columbus); Lotos (N.Y.). Unitarian Universalist. Home and Office: PO Box 690 New Castle NH 03854-0690

FRIESE, ROBERT CHARLES, lawyer; b. Chgo., Apr. 29, 1943; s. Earl Matthew and Laura Barbara (Mayer) F.; m. Chandra Ullom; children: Matthew Robert, Mark Earl, Laura Moore. AB in Internat. Rels., Stanford U., 1964; JD, Northwestern U., 1970. Bar: Calif. 1972. Dir. Tutor Applied Linguistics Ctr., Geneva, 1964-66; atty. Bronson, Bronson & McKinnon, San Francisco, 1970-71, SEC, San Francisco, 1971-75; ptnr. Shartsis, Friese & Ginsburg, San Francisco, 1975—. Pres., bd. dirs. Custom Diversification Fund Mgmt., Inc., 1993—; dir.-co-founder Internat. Plant Rsch. Inst., Inc., San Carlos, Calif., 1978-86. Chmn. bd. suprs. Task Force on Noise Control, 1972-78; chmn. San Franciscans for Cleaner City, 1977; exec. dir. Nob Hill Neighbors, 1972-81; bd. dirs. Nob Hill Assn., 1976-78, Palace Fine Arts, 1992-94, San Francisco Beautiful, 1986—, pres., 1988-2000; chmn. Citizens Adv. Com. for Embarcadero Project, 1991—; mem. major gifts com. Stanford U.; bd. dirs. Presidio Heights Neighborhood Assn., 1993—, pres., 1996-98; bd. dirs. Inst. of Range and the American Mustang, 1990—. Mem. ABA, Assn. Bus. Trial Lawyers (bd. dirs.), Calif. Bar Assn., Bar Assn. San Francisco (bd. dirs. 1982-85, chmn. bus. litigation com. 1978-79, chmn. state ct. civil litigation com. 1983-90, new courthouse com. 1993-95), Assn. SEC Alumni (bd. dirs. 1995—, 1st v.p. 2002—), Lawyers Club of San Francisco, Mensa, Calif. Hist. Soc., Commonwealth Club, Swiss-Am. Friendship League (chmn. 1971-79). Office: Shartsis Friese & Ginsburg 1 Maritime Plz Fl 18 San Francisco CA 94111-3404 E-mail: rcf@sfglaw.com.

FRIESECKE, RAYMOND FRANCIS, health company executive; b. Mar. 12, 1937; s. Bernhard P. K. and Josephine (De Tomi) F. BS in Chemistry, Boston Coll., 1959; MSCE, MIT, 1961. Product specialist Dewey & Almy Chem. divsn. W. R. Grace & Co., Inc., Cambridge, Mass., 1963-66; market planning specialist USM Corp., Boston, 1966-71; mgmt. cons. Boston, 1971-74; dir. planning and devel. Schweitzer divsn. Kimberly-Clark Corp., Lee, Mass., 1974-78; v.p. corp. planning Butler Automatic, Inc., Canton, Mass., 1978-80; pres. Butler-Europe Inc., Greenwich and Munich, Conn., Germany, 1980; v.p. mktg. and planning Butler Greenwich Inc., 1980-81; pres. Strategic Mgmt. Assocs., San Rafael, Calif., 1981-96; chmn. Beyond Health Corp., 1994—, Health-E-America Found., 2000—. Bd. dirs. Better Physiology, Ltd., 2000—; corp. clk., v.p. Bldg. R&D, Inc., Cambridge, 1966-68. Host, prodr. The Ounce of Prevention Show, Sta. KEST, San Francisco, 1994—98, Sta. KBZS, 1998—2001, Stas. WRPT and WSRO, 1999—2001; host, prodr. KYCY, 2001—; host, prodr. KRLA, KSBN, KFNX, 2003—; author: Management by Relative Product Quality, 1982, The New Way to Manage, 1983, Never Be Sick Again, 2002; pub.: Beyond Health News, 1995—; contbr. articles to profl. jours. State chmn. Citizens for Fair Taxation, 1972-73; state co-chmn. Mass. Young Reps., 1967-69; chmn. Ward 7 Rep. Com., Cambridge, 1968-70; vice-chmn. Cambridge Rep. City Com., 1966-68; bd. dirs. Kentfield Rehab. Hosp. Found., 1986-88, chmn., 1988-91; Rep. candidate Mass. Ho. of Reps., 1964, 66; pres. Marin Rep. Coun., 1986-91; chmn. Calif. Acad., 1986-88; sec. Navy League Marin Coun., 1984-91, v.p., 1994-2000; bd. dirs. The Marin Ballet, 1996-98; bd. dirs. Insts. for Behavioral Physiology, Seattle, 1999-2000. 1st lt. U.S. Army, 1961-63. Mem. NRA, Nat. Health Fedn., Am. Chem. Soc., Physicians Com. for Responsible Medicine, Marin Philos. Soc. (v.p. 1991-92), Ctr. for Sci. in Pub. Interest, Health Medicine Forum, Assn. of Am. Physicians and Surgeons, Orthomolecular Health Medicine Soc., The World Affairs Coun. Office: 777 Grand Ave Ste 205 San Rafael CA 94901-3509

FRIESEN, HENRY GEORGE, endocrinologist, educator; b. Morden, Man., Can., July 31, 1934; s. Frank Henry and Agnes (Unger) F.; m. Joyce Marylin Mackinnon, Oct. 12, 1967; children: Mark Henry, Janet Elizabeth. BSc, MD, U. Man., 1958. Diplomate: Am. Bd. Internal Medicine. Intern Winnipeg (Man.) Gen. Hosp., 1958-60; resident Royal Victoria Hosp., Montreal, Que., 1961-62; rsch. assoc. New Eng. Centre Hosp., Boston, 1962-65; prof. exptl. medicine McGill U., Montreal, 1965-73; prof. physiology and medicine U. Man., 1973-92, head dept. physiology, 1973-92; pres. Med. Rsch. Coun. Can., 1991-2000; chmn. Genome Can., Winnipeg; disting. prof. emeritus U. Man. Chmn. exec. com. Med. Rsch. Coun. Can., mem. exec. com., 1981-87; pres. Nat. Cancer Inst. Can., 1990-92. Contbr. numerous articles to profl. jours. Decorated Companion Order of Can.; named to, Can. Med. Hall of Fame, 2001; recipient Gairdner award, Gairdner Found., 1977, Wightman award, 2001. Fellow Royal Soc. Can. (McLaughlin medal 1987), Royal Coll. Physicians and Surgeons; mem. AAAS, Am. Physiol. Soc., Endocrine Soc. (Koch award 1987), Can. Soc. Clin. Investigation (pres. 1974, G. Malcolm Meml. award 1982, Disting. Sci. award 1987), Nat. Acad. Scis. (fgn. assoc.), Can. Physiol. Soc., Am. Fedn. Clin. Research, Am. Soc. Clin. Investigation, Can. Soc. Endocrinology and Metabolism (past pres.), Internat. Soc. Neuroendocrinology, U.S. Nat. Acad. Sci. (fgn. assoc.). Mennonite. Office: U Man Ctr Advancement Medicine 753 McDermot Ave Winnipeg MB Canada R3E 0WE Fax: (204) 789-3979. Personal E-mail: hfriesen2@shaw.ca. E-mail: Henry_Friesen@umanitoba.ca.

FRIESEN, JANICE A. social worker; b. L.A., Feb. 15, 1937; d. Alvin B. and Loretta (Auerbach) Lando; m. John B. Friesen, Jr., Aug. 24, 1958; children: Jennifer, Kevin. BA, U. Calif., Berkeley, 1958, MSW, 1965. Lic. clin. social worker. Social worker Alameda County Social Svcs., Oak, Calif., 1959-63; tchr. North Monterey County Unified Sch. Dist., Salinas, Calif., 1961-62; social worker Head Start, Hayward, Calif., 1965-67, Berkeley (Calif.) Health Dept., 1967-69; clin. social worker Hayward and Pleasanton, Calif., 1970—. Trustee Castro Valley (Calif.) Sch. Dist., 1989—. Fellow Calif. Soc. Clin. Social Workers; mem. NASW, LWV, Calif. Sch. Bds. Assn., Nat. Women's Polit. Caucus. Home: 5490 Jensen Rd Castro Valley CA 94552-5010

FRIESEN, RONALD LEE, economics educator; b. Inman, Kans., Mar. 2, 1939; s. J.D. and Hilda Marie (Neufeld) F.; m. Phyllis Ruth Sawatzky, June 2, 1961; children: Janine Renee, Jon Alan, Julie Dyan. BA, Bethel Coll., 1961; MA in Econs., U. Kans., 1962; PhD in Econs., Columbia U., 1973. Tchr. Alliance Secondary Sch., Dodoma, Tanzania, 1962-65; prof. econs. Bluffton (Ohio) Coll., 1969—. Past faculty chmn., past chmn. econ., bus. adminstrn. and acctg. dept. Bluffton Coll.; cons. in field. Contbr. book reviews and articles to profl. jours. and collected vols. Recipient Rsch. and Lectr., C. Henry Smith Trust, 1981-82; scholar faculty U. Kans., Lawrence, 1961-62, faculty fellow Columbia U., N.Y.C., 1965-69; Albert Schweitzer Chair fellow, N.Y.C., 1969. Mem. Am. Econs. Assn., African Studies Assn., Ohio Assn. Economists and Polit. Scientists, Economists Allied for Arms Reduction. Avocations: tennis, stamp collecting, coin collecting, antique collecting. Office: Bluffton Coll Dept Econs Bluffton OH 45817

FRIESS, DONNA LEWIS, children's rights advocate; b. LA, Jan. 16, 1943; d. Raymond W. Lewis, Jr. and Dorothy Gertrude (Borwick) McIntyre; m. Kenneth E. Friess, June 20, 1964; children: Erik, Julina, Daniel. BA in Comm., U. So. Calif., 1964; MA in Comm., Calif. State U., Long Beach, 1966; PhD in Psychology, U.S. Internat. U., San Diego, 1993. Cert. tchr., Calif. Prof. human comm. Cypress (Calif.) Coll., 1966—. Lectr. survivors of abuse, 1990—, mental health profls., 1990—; guest expert (TV) Sally Jessy Raphael, 1993, Leeza Gibbons Talk Show, 1994, Sonja: Live, 1994, Oprah Winfrey Show, 1991, others; presenter, spkr. in field. Author: Relationships, 1995, Just Between Us: A Guidebook for Survivors of Childhood Trauma, 1995, Cry the Darkness, 1993, European edit. 1995, Danish edit., 1999, Korean edit., 1995, Norwegian edit., 1998, Circle of Love: Secrets to Successful Relationships, 1996, 2d edit., 2002, Whispering Waters: The Story of Historic Weesha, 1998, Chronicle of Historic Weesha and the Upper Santa Ana River Valley, 2000; contbr. articles to mags. Del. to round table discussion on victims' issues U.S. Justice Dept., 2002, apptd. consortium for victims affairs, 2003; nat. consortium of victim assistance experts U.S. Dept. Justice, 2003—, adv. bd. Recipient Author's award U. Calif. Friends of Libr., 1996, recognition from U.S. Justice Dept. for outstanding efforts to stop child abuse, 1995, Lee Steelmon award, Recognition cert. for work to prevent child abuse Calif. State Senate, 2000, Orange County (Calif.) Bd. Suprs.' Resolution for Outstanding Efforts for Children, 2000, Outstanding Speech Faculty award Calif. State U., 2001. Mem. Am. Coalition Against Child Abuse (founder), Task Force for ACCA to Educate American Judges on Issues of Sexual Abuse, One Voice, Calif. Psychol. Assn., Western Social Sci. Assn., Child Abuse Listening and Mediating (bd. dirs.), Am. Profl. Soc. on Abuse of Children, Mother Against Sexual Abuse (bd. dirs.), Laura's House for Battered Women (bd. dirs.), Calif. Tchrs. Assn., Faculty Assn. Calif. C.Cs., Speech Communication Assn. of Am., U.S. Internat. U. Alumni Assn. (bd. dirs.). Avocation: painting on porcelain. Office: Cypress College Dept Human Communications Cypress CA 90630 E-mail: donafriess@aol.com.

FRIESZ, MARY LEE, freelance/self-employed poet; b. Little Rock, Ark., Apr. 13, 1940; d. E. Lee and Lala Maurine (Bain) Franklin; m. David Wilson Dubbell, Jan. 28, 1961 (div. Aug. 1982); children: Cheryl Blaine Dubbell Knight, Paul Fremont Dubbell; m. Donald Stuart Friesz; July 5, 1985; children: Mark Allan Friesz, Carol Ann Friesz Leslie. BA in Psychology, U. Ark., 1962. Sec. Stanford U., Palo Alto, Calif., 1962-63; tchr. aide Pedregal Sch., Palos Verdes, Calif., 1974-78; corp. sec. Pel-Freez Biols., Inc., Palos Verdes, Calif., 1978-81; asst. mgr. May Co., Rolling Hills Estates, Calif., 1981-82; investment counselor Am. Savs. & Loan, Redondo Beach, Calif., 1982-84; founder, editor Mustard Seed Poetry, Palos Verdes, 1995—. Author books of poetry. Dir; Poetry By The Sea, Serenos de Point Vicente (televised, 1997-99). Mem. membership com. Assistance League San Pedro/South Bay, 1994-95; leader cmty. Bible study core Palm Desert Cmty. Presbyn. Ch., Palm Desert, Calif., 2003—. Recipient Cmty. Svc. award South Bay Panhellenic Coun., 1996. Mem. Palos Verdes Woman's Club (first v.p.), S.W. Manuscripters, So. Calif. Fedn. Zeta Tau Alpha (pres. 1994-95, pres. local chpt. 1990-91, cert. merit Nat. coun. 1994), Surfwriters (treas. 1994-99), Arts Coun. Torrance (sec.), Phi Beta Kappa. Home: 38 Maximo Way Palm Desert CA 92260 Office: Mustard Seed Poetry 38 Maximo Way Palm Desert CA 92260

FRIGERIO, CHARLES STRAITH, lawyer; b. Detroit, Mar. 8, 1957; s. Louie John and LaVern (Straith) F.; m. Annette Angela Russo, Oct. 18, 1985; 1 child, Charles Anthony. BA, St. Mary's U., 1979, JD, 1982. Bar: Tex. 1982, U.S. Ct. Appeals (5th cir.) 1987, U.S. Supreme Ct. 1987; cert. in personal injury trial law. Pros. atty. City Attys. Office, San Antonio, 1982-84; trial atty. City Atty's. Office, San Antonio, 1984—; litigation chief and chief prosecutor City Atty.'s Office, San Antonio, 1995; pvt. practice law enforcement litigation San Antonio, 1995—. Mem. Dem. Nat. Com., San Antonio, 1976; asst. mgr. local campaigns, San Antonio, 1976-84. Mem.: ABA, Cath. Lawyers Assn., Nat. Bd. Trial Advocacy, San Antono Bar Assn., Fed. Bar Assn., Tex. Bar Assn., Delta Epsilon Sigma. Democrat. Roman Catholic. Home: 317 Cleveland Ct San Antonio TX 78209-5862 Office: Riverview Towers 111 Soledad St Ste 840 San Antonio TX 78205-2219

FRIGGENS, THOMAS GEORGE, state official, historian; b. Pontiac, Mich., July 12, 1949; s. Francis G. and Jane E. (Pettit) F.; m. Mary T. Bahra; children: Christopher P., Michael C. BA, Albion Coll., 1971; MA, Wayne State U., 1973. Contract historian Mich. Dept. Natural Resources, Fayette, 1973; site historian 07 Mich. Dept. State, History Div., Fort Wilkins Hist. Complex, Copper Harbor, 1974-75, site historian 09, 1975-76, site historian 11, 1976-80, site historian VII, 1980-85, Dept. State, Bur. History, Mich. Iron Industry Mus., Negaunee, 1985-87, regional historian VII, 1987-92, regional historian VII supr., 1992-96, historian mgr. XII, 1996-98, history mgr. 13, 1998—2001; history mgr. 13 dept. history, arts and librs. Mich. Hist. Ctr., 2001. Cons. St. Louis County Hist. Soc., Duluth, Minn., 1985, 86. Contbr. articles to jours. in field. Active Hist. Soc. Mich., bd. dirs., 1984-90; active Copper County Heritage Coun., pres., 1982-83; bd. dirs. Marquette County Hist. Soc., 1992-97; mem. Mich. Hist. Preservation Network. Recipient Roy W. Drier award Houghton County (Mich.) Hist. Soc., 1987, Merit award Hist. Soc. Mich., 1983, Disting. Svc. award, 1983, Dwight B. Waldo award No. Mich. U. Dept. History, 1999. Mem. Am. Assn. State and Local History, Nat. Trust for Hist. Preservation, Mich. Mus. Assn., Phi Alpha Theta. Office: Mich Iron Industry Mus 73 Forge Rd Negaunee MI 49866-9532

FRIGO, JAMES PETER PAUL, industrial hardware company executive; b. Iron Mountain, Mich., Jan. 11, 1942; s. Louis and Giustina (Carollo) F.; m. Patricia Mary Nellen, June 21, 1969; children: Christine, Catherine, P.J. Ortiz, Pamela Aks, Steven, Sandy. BBA, U. Miami, 1966. Sales rep. Great Dane Trailers, Miami, 1966-67, Foster Inc., Miami, 1968, Lawson Products Inc., Miami, 1968—; pres. Jim Frigo Inc., Miami, 1972—. Asst. scoutmaster Troop 314 Boy Scouts Am. Mem.: KC. Republican. Roman Catholic. Office: Jim Frigo Inc 7420 SW 175th St Miami FL 33157-6313

FRIIS, ROBERT HAROLD, epidemiologist, health science educator; b. San Jose, Calif., July 15, 1941; s. Harold Hector and Florence Marie (Brant) F.; m. Carol Ann Speer, Oct. 28, 1966; children: Michelle Alanna, Erik Adler. BA, U. Calif., Berkeley, 1964; MA, Columbia U., N.Y.C., 1966, PhD, 1969. Postdoctoral fellow U. Mich., Ann Arbor, 1969-71; asst. prof. Sch. Pub. Health Columbia U., 1971-74, Albert Einstein Coll. Medicine, Bronx, N.Y., 1974-76; assoc. prof. CUNY, Bklyn. Coll., 1976-78; dir. field epidemiology Orange County Pub. Health, Santa Ana, Calif., 1978-79; assoc. clin. prof. U. Calif., Irvine, 1979-93; prof., chairperson dept. health sci. Calif. State U., Long Beach, 1988—, now mem. acad. senate. Vis. rschr. Karolinska Inst., Stockholm, 1993; dir. Joint Studies Inst. Calif. State U. and VA Med. Ctr., Long Beach, 1995—; adv. bd. Ctr. for Health Care Innovation Calif. State U., Long Beach; guest scientist Max Planck Inst. Psychiatry, Munich, 2001; vis. prof. clin. psychology and psychotherapy unit Dresden (Germany) Tech. U., 2001; bd. dirs. Long Beach (Calif.) Global Health Initiative, Ctr. for Health Care Innovation, Long Beach, Long Beach Tobacco Edn. Program; clin. prof. dept. cmty. and environ. medicine U. Calif., Irvine, 2003; cons. in field. Sr. author: Epidemiology Public Health Practice, 1996, 3d edit. 2004; co-author: Introductory Biostatistics for the Health Sciences, 2003; contbr. articles to profl. jours. Faculty mentor Ptnrs. for Success, Long Beach, 1992. Grantee U. Calif., Irvine, 1995, Mexus com. U. Calif., 1988, U. Calif. systemwide, 1988, U. Calif. Tobacco Related Disease Rsch. Program, 1998-2002, 2003—. Mem. APHA, Am. Statis. Assn. (So. Calif. sect.), Soc. Epidemiol. Rsch., Am. Assn. Health Edn., U. Calif. Berkley Alumni Assn., So. Calif. Pub. Health Assn. (bd. dirs.), Eta Sigma Gamma. Democratic. Avocations: reading, travel, coin collecting, computers, gardening. Office: Calif State U Long Beach Dept Health Sci 1250 N Bellflower Blvd Long Beach CA 90840-0006 E-mail: rfriis@csulb.edu.

FRIMAN, ALICE RUTH, poet, English educator; b. N.Y.C., Oct. 20, 1933; d. Joseph and Helen (Friedman) Pesner; m. Elmer Friman, July 3, 1955 (div. Dec. 1975); children: H. Richard, Paul Lawrence, Lillian Elaine; m. Marshall Bruce Gentry, Sept. 24, 1989. BA, Bklyn. Coll., 1954; MA, Butler U., 1971. Instr. English U. Indpls., 1971-74, asst. prof. English, 1974-81, assoc. prof. English, 1981-90, prof. English, 1990-93, prof. emerita, 1993—. Vis. prof. creative writing Ind. State U., Terre Haute, 1982, Ball State U., Muncie, Ind., 1996; writer in residence Curtin U., Perth, Australia, 1989; presenter in field. Author: Reporting from Corinth, 1984, Insomniac Heart, 1990, Driving for Jimmy Wonderland, 1992, Inverted Fire, 1997, Zoo, 1999; editor: Loaves and Fishes: A Book of Indiana Women Poets, 1983; poetry editor The Flying Island, 1993, 96, 2001; author numerous poems. Co-recipient Sheila Margaret Motton prize, New Eng. Poetry Club, 2001; recipient Ezra Pound Poetry award, Truman State U., 1998, 1st place internat. poetry contest, Abiko Quar., Japan, 1994, award of excellence in poetry, Hopewell Rev., 1995, Firman Houghton award, New Eng. Poetry Club, 1996, second prize The Anna David Rosenberg award for poems on the Jewish experience, 1996, 1st prize runner-up, Miriam Lindberg Israel Poetry for Peace Competition, 2000, James Boatwright III prize, Shenandoah, 2001; fellow, Ind. Arts Commn., 1996—97, Creative Renewal fellow, Arts Coun. Indpls., 1999—2000, Ga. Poetry Circuit, 2001—02; Bernheim Found. Fellow, 2003—. Mem. MLA (life), Soc. for the Study Midwestern Lit., Associated Writing Programs, Poetry Soc. Am. (Lucille Medwick Meml. award 1993, Cecil Hemley Meml. award 1990, Consuelo Ford award 1988), Writers' Ctr. Ind. (life, charter), Soc. Midland Authors. Democrat. Jewish. Avocations: travel, reading. Home: 109 Treanor Dr Milledgeville GA 31061 E-mail: alicefriman@alltel.net.

FRIMAN, H. RICHARD, political science educator; b. Ohio; s. Elmer and Alice F.; m. Julie. BA, Ind. U., 1979; PhD, Cornell U., 1987. Instr. polit. sci. Marquette U., Milw., 1986-87, asst. prof. polit. sci., 1987-93, assoc. prof. polit. sci., 1993-99, prof. polit. sci., 1999—, asst. chair, dir. grad. studies dept. polit. sci., 1997-2000, chair dept. polit. sci., 2000—03, Eliot Fitch chair for internat. studies, 2001—. Coord. INIA Major Marquette U., 1988-94, dir. OPTIONS univ. outreach project on internat. security, 1991-94; assoc. dir. Title VI NRC for Internat. Studies U. Wis.-Milw./Marquette U., Milw., 1991-94; acad. assoc. Atlantic Coun. U.S., 1988—; mem. exec. coun. Wis. Inst. Peace and Conflict Stdies, 1991—. Author: Patchwork Protectionism, 1990, NarcoDiplomacy: Exporting the U.S. War on Drugs, 1996; co-editor: the south Slav Conflict, 1996, The Illicit Global Economy and State Power, 1999. Fulbright scholar Japan-US ednl. commn., 1994-95; grantee Am. Coun. Learned Socs., 1991-92, 94, rsch. and workshop grantee Social sci. rsch. coun., 1991 96, German Acad. Exch. Svc., 1998; recipient award for Outstanding Tcgh. in Polit. Sci. Am. Polit. Sci. Assn. and Pi sigma Alpha, 1998 Mem. Am. Polit. Sci. Assn., Internat. Studies Assn., Fulbright Assn., Internat. House of Japan, Phi Beta Kappa (bd. govs. Greater Milw. 1999-2000). Office: Marquette U Dept Polit Sci Milwaukee WI 53201-1881

FRIMERMAN, LESLIE, retired financial services company executive; b. Bklyn., Nov. 25, 1943; s. Abraham and Shirley (Lerner) F.; m. Judith Fogelman, Aug. 17, 1968. BBA in Fin., Baruch Coll., 1974; MBA with distinction, Adelphi U., 1978. From new accounts analyst, sr. systems analyst to v.p. Am. Express Co., N.Y.C., 1965—92; v.p. U.S. systems Am. Express, 1992—2000, ret., 2000; instr. math. Nassau C.C., 2000—. Fin. officer Nat. Computer Conf., 1980-81. Pres. Pebble Cove Homeowner Assn., Inc.; commr. Village of Atlantic Beach, N.Y. Mem. Inst. Mgmt. Scis., KP, Sigma Alpha, Delta Mu Delta. Avocations: skiing, scuba diving, electronics, photography, travel.

FRINK, EUGENE HUDSON, JR., business and real estate consultant; b. Denver, Feb. 6, 1927; s. Eugene Hudson and Maxine Louella (Ingle) F.; m. Catherine Claire Heath, Dec. 27, 1947; children: Douglas Martin, Bryan Clifford, Daniel Neal. BA, Denver U., 1947. Mgr. Frink Creamery Co., Ft. Collins, Colo., 1948-64; co-founder, mgr. ops Aqua-Tec Corp. (Water Pik), Ft. Collins, 1964-66; archtl. designer Gene Frink Designers, Ft. Collins, 1967-84; ptnr. Wakaya Island, Ltd., Fiji, 1968-71; chmn. Beehive Internat., Salt Lake City, 1969-85; prin. Architecture Plus, P.C., Ft. Collins, 1985-88; ptnr. Naindi Plantation, Fiji, 1969—; pres. Ft. Collins Children's Clinic, 1993-99. Councilman, City of Ft. Collins, 1959-63, mayor, 1961-63; mem. Ft. Collins Regional Planning Bd., 1962-64. Mem. Rotary Club. Republican. Episcopalian. Avocations: industrial design, painting, swimming, hiking. Home: 1212 Morgan St Fort Collins CO 80524-3836

FRINTA, MOJMIR SVATOPLUK, art history educator; b. Prague, Czech Republic, July 28, 1922; arrived in U.S., 1951; s. Antonin and Jarmila F.; m. Irena; children: Daniel, Dagmar, Richard. PhD in Art History, U. Mich., 1960. Prof. emeritus SUNY, Albany. Author: The Genius of Robert Campin, 1966, Punched Decoration on Late Medieval Panels & Miniature Painting, 1998; contbr. articles to profl. jours. Rsch. grantee NEH, 1977-78, 82-84; sr. fellow Ctr. Advanced Study Visual Arts, 1984-85, Fulbright fellow, 1987. Mem. Medieval Acad. Am., Internat. Ctr. Medieval Art, Coll. Art Assn. Home: PO Box 854 150 Maple Ave Altamont NY 12009 E-mail: frinta@juno.com.

FRISBEE, DON CALVIN, retired utilities executive; b. San Francisco, Dec. 13, 1923; s. Ira Nobles and Helen (Sheets) F.; m. Emilie Ford, Feb. 5, 1947; children: Ann, Robert, Peter, Dean. BA, Pomona Coll., 1947; MBA, Harvard U., 1949. Sr. investment analyst, asst. cashier investment analysis dept. 1st Interstate Bank Oreg., N.A., Portland, 1949-52; treas. PacifiCorp, Portland, 1958-60, then v.p., exec. v.p., pres., 1966-73, chief exec. officer, 1973-89, chmn., 1973-94; chmn. emeritus PacifiCorp., Portland, 1994-97. Bd. dirs. Wells Fargo Bank. Chmn. bd. trustees Reed Coll.; trustee Safari Game Search Found., High Desert Mus.; mem. cabinet Columbia Pacific coun. Boy Scouts Am.; founder Oreg. chpt. Am. Leadership Forum; mem. exec. com. Oreg. Partnership for Internat. Edn. 1st lt. AUS, 1943-46. Mem. Arlington Club, Univ. Club Multnomah Athletic Club, City Club. Office: 310 SW 4th Ave Ste 510 Portland OR 97204

FRISBIE, CHARLES, lawyer; b. Kansas City, Mo., June 1, 1939; s. A.C. Jr. and Florence (Waddell) F.; m. Julia Louise Ross, June 28, 1969; children: Ross Waddell, Andrew James Louis. AB, Princeton U., 1961; JD, U. Mich., 1964. Bar: Mo. 1964, U.S. Supreme Ct. 1968. Assoc. Lathrop Righter Gordon & Parker, Kansas City, Mo., 1964-70; ptnr. Lathrop & Norquist, Kansas City, Mo., 1971-94; mem. Lathrop & Gage L.C., Kansas City, Mo., 1994—. Lt. USAFR, 1964-70. Mem. ABA, Mo. Bar Assn. (chmn. internat. law com. 1995-97), Kansas City Country Club (sec., bd. dirs. 1981-84). Republican. Episcopalian. Avocations: golf, reading. Home: 808 Romany Rd Kansas City MO 64113-2013 Office: Lathrop & Gage LC 2345 Grand Blvd Ste 2600 Kansas City MO 64108-2617

FRISBIE, CURTIS LYNN, JR., lawyer; b. Greenville, Miss., Sept. 13, 1943; s. Curtis Lynn and Edith L. (Brantley) F.; m. Gena F. Johnson, May 30, 1965; children: Curtis L. III, Mark A. BSBA, U. Ala., 1966; JD, St. Mary's U., San Antonio, 1971. Bar: Tex. 1971; U.S. Dist. Ct. (no. dist.) Ga. 1974, U.S. Dist. Ct. (no. dist.) Tex. 1978, U.S. Dist. Ct. (we. dist.) Tex. 1985, U.S. Dist. Ct. (ea. and so. dists.) Tex. 1986, U.S. Dist. Ct. (ea. dist.) Wis. 1986; U.S. Tax Ct. 1986; U.S. Ct. Appeals (5th cir.) 1975, U.S. Ct. Appeals (10th cir.) 1982, U.S. Ct. Appeals (8th cir.) 1987; U.S. Supreme Ct. 1977. Trial atty. Antitrust divsn. U.S. Dept. Justice, Atlanta, 1971-73; assoc. King & Spalding, Atlanta, 1974-77; ptnr. Gardere Wynne Sewell LLP (formerly Gardere & Wynne LLP), Dallas, 1978—. Assoc. editor St. Mary's Law Jour., 1970-71. Capt. USMC, 1966-69, Vietnam. Named one of Best Lawyers in Dallas, D Mag., 2003. Fellow Tex. Bar Found. (life), Dallas Bar Assn. (life); mem. ABA (antitrust and bus. law sect.), Tex. Bar Assn. (antitrust sect., mem. coun. 1995—, vice chair, chair elect 2000-01, chair 2001-02), Dallas Bar Assn. (pres. antitrust and trade regulation sect. 1993), Coll. State Bar Tex., Phi Alpha Delta. Avocations: scuba diving, fishing, hunting. Home: 5605 Palomar Ln Dallas TX 75229-6417 Office: Gardere Wynne Sewell LLP Thanksgiving Tower 1601 Elm St Ste 3000 Dallas TX 75201-4761 E-mail: cfrisbie@gardere.com.

FRISBIE, RICHARD PATRICK, communications consultant, author; b. Chgo., Nov. 27, 1926; s. Chauncey Osborn and Pearl Genevieve (Harrison) F.; m. Margery Rowbottom, June 3, 1950; children: Felicity, Anne Celeste, Thomas, Ellen, Paul, Patrick, Teresa, Margaret. BA, U. Ariz., 1948. Writer, editor Chgo. Daily News, 1948-55; copy chief Tempo, Inc., Chgo., 1956-57, Cunningham & Walsh, Chgo., 1958-61, Hill, Rogers, Mason & Scott, Chgo., 1961-63; creative dir. Campbell-Ewald Co., Chgo., 1964-66; editor-in-chief Chgo. Mag., 1971-73; owner Frisbie Comms., Chgo., 1966—; exec. sec. Nat. Satellite Cable Assn., Chgo., 1982-83. Author: Family Fun and Recreation, 1964, How to Peel a Sour Grape, 1965, Who Put the Bomb in Father Murphy's Chowder, 1968, It's a Wise Woodsman Who Knows What's Biting Him, 1969, Basic Boat Building, 1979, Daily Meditations for Busy Grandpas, 1998; author: (with wife Margery) The Do-It-Yourself Parent, 1963. Trustee Arlington Heights (Ill.) Meml. Libr., 1967—, treas., 1971-73, pres., 1973-79, 99-2001, v.p. and sec., 1993-97; dir. North Suburban Libr. System, Wheeling, Ill., 1976-77, treas., 1978, pres., 1979-81; dir. Ill. Ctr. for the Book, Chgo., 1989-93, pres., 1991-92. Served with USN, 1945. Recipient Best Mag. Article award Cath. Press Assn., 1957. Mem. ALA, Ill. Libr. Assn., Authors Guild, Soc. Midland Authors (pres. 1985-88, Lifetime Achievement award 2000), Chgo. Press Vets. Democrat. Roman Catholic. Home: 631 N Dunton Ave Arlington Heights IL 60004-5531 E-mail: richardpfrisbie@hotmail.com.

FRISBY, HERBERT RUSSELL, lawyer; b. Balt., Dec. 28, 1950; m. June J. Frisby; children: Herbert R. III, James T. BA in Polit. Sci./Internat. Rels., Swarthmore Coll., 1972; JD, Yale U., 1975. Bar: Md. 1975, D.C. 1979. Asst. gen. counsel Md. Atty. Gen.'s Office, Balt., 1978-79; atty.-advisor FCC, Washington, 1979-80, legal asst., 1980-83; sr. atty. Weil, Gotshal & Manges, Washington, 1983-86; prin. Melnicove, Kaufman, Weiner & Smouse, PA, Washington, 1986-89; ptnr. Venable, Baetjer & Howard, Balt., 1989-95; chmn. Md. Pub. Svc. Commn., Balt., 1995-98; pres. Competitive Telecomm. Assn., Washington, 1998—. Mem. NARUC Comms. Com., Washington, 1995-98. Bd. dirs. United Way of Ctrl. Md., Balt., 1989-97; v.p. Balt. Mus. Art, 1993-95. Recipient Charles Hamilton Houston award Minority Bus. Enterprise Legal Def. and Edn. Fund, 1989, Disting. Alumnus award Fund for Ednl. Excellence, 1991; named to Balt. City Coll. Hall of Fame, 1989. Fellow Md. Bar Found.; mem. ABA (budget officer adminstrv. law sect. 1995-98). Office: CompTel 1900 M St NW Ste 800 Washington DC 20036-3517 E-mail: rfrisby@comptel.org.

FRISBY, JAMES CURTIS, agricultural engineering educator; b. Bethany, Mo., Oct. 22, 1930; s. Jackson Carey and Gladys (Selby) F.; m. Hazel M. Kallenbach, Dec. 20, 1969. BS in Edn., U. Mo., 1952, BSAE, 1956; MS, Iowa State U., 1963, PhD, 1965. Registered profl. engr., Mo. Classroom instr., tech. writer, market analyst Caterpillar Tractor Co., Peoria, Ill., 1956-60; acting mgr. farm services dept. Iowa State U., Ames, 1961-63, instr., 1963-65; asst. prof. agrl. engring. U. Mo., Columbia, 1966-69, assoc. prof., 1969-74, prof., 1974-96, chmn. agrl. engring., 1989-94; prof. emeritus, 1996—. Served to 1st lt. U.S. Army, 1952-54. Recipient award of merit Gamma Sigma Delta, 1976; recipient cert. of appreciation U. Mo. Coll. Engring., 1983, 87. Mem.: NSPE, Am. Soc. Agrl. Engrs. (Mem. of Yr. Mo. sect. 1995, Spl. Svc. award MidCtrl. Conf. 1996), Nat. Assn. Colls. and Tchrs. Agr. (Tchg. award of merit 1994), Am. Soc. Engring. Edn., Am. Soc. Agrl. Engrs. (chmn. mid-ctrl. region 1982—83, dir. mid-ctrl. region 1984—86), Mo. Soc. Profl. Engrs. (pres. ctrl. chpt. 1995—96), Kiwanis Internat. Mem. Ch. of Christ. Home: 1805 Bluff Pointe Dr Columbia MO 65201-6287 E-mail: frisbyj@missouri.edu.

FRISCH, CELIA, violinist, chamber music coach, educator; b. Boston, Dec. 27; d. Nathan and Annie (Bolanzy) Hirschorn; m. Al Frisch; 1 child, Myra Jacqueline Bennett. Grad. high sch., Roxbury, Mass.; student, New Sch., Bklyn. Coll. Pvt. violin tchr., Mass.; chamber music coach; mem. Crystal Strings Trio, Mass., Marjorie Posselt Chamber Group, Boston, Ondricek Ensemble, Boston; freelance violinist under Arthur Fiedler, Milton Katims, Dean Dixon and Lukas Foss, Bklyn. Philharm., Boston and N.Y.; asst. dir. Strings Chamber Music, N.Y.; 1st violinist Brwyn Mawr String Quartet, Boston and N.Y. Pres. Myra Music Co., Tarrytown, N.Y., 1976—; lectr. on music, travel, books and other topics. Author: The Animals Nobody Knows, 1981. Mem.: ASCAP, Ethical Culture Soc. Westchester, Wagner Soc. N.Y., Hudson Valley Music Guild, Chamber Music Am., Songwriters Guild, Great Books Westchester Cmty. Coll., Bohemian Club (N.Y.C.), Rockland County (N.Y.) Book and Discussion Club. Avocations: writing, walking, swimming, reading, music, traveling, accordion. Home and Office: Myra Music Co 177 White Plains Rd Apt 33F Tarrytown NY 10591-5511

FRISCH, HARRY DAVID, lawyer, consultant, investment company executive; b. N.Y.C., June 5, 1954; s. Isaac and Regina (Rottenberg) Frisch; m. Sherry Beth Bannerman, 1992; children: Rachel Michele, Michael Elliot. BS, CCNY, 1976; postgrad., Rutgers U., 1976-77; JD, Pace U., 1980. Bar: N.Y. 1981, U.S. Dist. Ct. (so. and ea. dists.) N.Y. 1981, U.S. Ct. Appeals (2d cir.) 1984, U.S. Supreme Ct. 1986, U.S. Ct. Appeals (5th cir.) 1987. Law clk. Shearson Hayden Stone, Inc., N.Y.C., 1977-80; assoc. gen. counsel Shearson Loeb Rhoades, Inc., N.Y.C., 1980-82; asst. v.p., asst. corp. sec., assoc. gen. counsel Shearson/Am. Express, Inc., N.Y.C., 1982-85; v.p., sr. litigator, assoc. gen. counsel Shearson Lehman Bros., Inc., N.Y.C., 1985-88; 1st v.p., sr. litigator, assoc. gen. counsel Shearson Lehman Hutton, Inc., N.Y.C., 1988-90, Shearson Lehman Bros., Inc., N.Y.C., 1990-93; 1st v.p., sr. litigator, asst. gen. counsel Smith Barney Shearson Inc., N.Y.C., 1993-94; asst. gen. counsel Gruntal & Co. Inc., N.Y.C., 1994-97, Gruntal & Co., L.L.C., N.Y.C., 1997-99; spl. counsel Lubiner & Schmidt, N.Y.C., 1999; sr. v.p., compliance mgr. Datek Online Holdings Corp., Jersey City, 1999—2002, Ameritrade Holding Corp., 2002—. Contbr. articles to profl. jours. Mem.: ABA, Fed. Bar Coun., N.Y. County Lawyers Assn., Assn. Bar City of N.Y., N.Y. State Bar Assn. Democrat. Jewish. Home: 2 Waterview Dr Ossining NY 10562-2442 Office: Datek Online Holdings Corp 70 Hudson St 10th Fl Jersey City NJ 07302 E-mail: hdfrisch@optonline.net.

FRISCH, IVAN THOMAS, computer and communications company executive; b. Budapest, Hungary, Sept. 21, 1937; came to U.S., 1939, naturalized, 1941; s. Laszlo and Rose (Balog) F.; m. Vivian Scelzo, June 6, 1962; children: Brian, Bruce. BS, MS, Columbia U., 1958, PhD, 1962. Asst. prof. elec. engring. and computer sci. U. Calif., Berkeley, 1962-65, assoc. prof., 1965-69; Ford Found. resident engring. practice Bell Labs., Holmdel, N.J., 1965-66; founding mem. Network Analysis Corp., Great Neck, N.Y., 1969—, sr. v.p., 1971—, gen. mgr., 1978-85; v.p. Contel Bus. Networks, 1985-87; dir. Ctr. on Advanced Tech. in Telecommunications, prof. Poly. U., Bklyn., 1987—; provost Polytech. U., 1992—. Adj. prof. computer sci. SUNY, Stony Brook, 1975—, Columbia U., N.Y.C., 1977—; cons. in field. Author: (with Howard Frank) Communication, Transmission and Transportation Networks, 1971; Founding editor-in-chief: Networks, 1971—; contbr. articles to profl. publs. Guggenheim fellow, 1969 Fellow IEEE (Eric E. Sumner award 1999, 3d Millenium award 2000); mem. N.Y. Acad. Scis., Cable TV Assn. Am., Nat. Acad. Engring., Phi Beta Kappa, Tau Beta Pi, Eta Kappa Nu. Office: Poly U Six Metrotech Ctr Rm JB-555 Brooklyn NY 11201-2907

FRISCH, JOSEPH, mechanical engineer, educator, consultant; b. Vienna, Apr. 21, 1921; came to U.S., 1940, naturalized, 1946; s. Abraham and Rachel (Lieberman) F.; m. Joan S. Frisch, May 26, 1962; children— Nora Theresa, Erich Martin, Jonathan David BSME, Duke U., 1946; MS, U. Calif., 1950. Registered profl. engr., Calif. Mem. faculty U. Calif.-Berkeley, 1947—, asst. prof. mech. engring., 1951-57, assoc. prof. mech. engring., 1957—, prof. mech. engring., 1963—, asst. dir. Inst. Engring. Rsch., 1961-63, chmn. div. mech. design, 1966-70, assoc. dean, 1972-75. Cons. to indsl. and govtl. labs. Contbr. articles to profl. jours. Fellow ASME (life); mem. Phi Beta Kappa, Sigma Xi, Tau Beta Pi, Pi Tau Sigma Clubs: U. Calif.-Berkeley Faculty. Office: U Calif Dept Mech Engring Berkeley CA 94720-1740

FRISCH, MORTON JEROME, political scientist, educator; b. Chgo., Jan. 26, 1923; s. Harry Isadore and Gertrude Frisch; m. Joelyn Alice Saltzman, Feb. 20, 1949; children: Hollis, Mark, Seth. BA, Roosevelt U., 1949; MA, U. Chgo., 1949; PhD, Pa. State U., 1953. Asst. prof., assoc. prof. Govt. Coll. William and Mary, Williamsburg, Va., 1953—64; assoc. prof., prof. Polit. Sci. No. Ill. U., DeKalb, 1964—91, prof. emeritus, 1992—. Vis. prof. Polit. Sci. U. Minn., Mpls., 1957—58; Fulbright prof. Statskunskap U. Stockholm, 1963—64; sr. scholar in resident U. Va., Charlottesville, 1977—78; Fulbright Disting. prof. Korea U., Seoul, 1992; tutor U. Coll., Oxford, England, 1984. Author: A. Hamilton and the Political Order, 1991; editor: Selected Writings and Speeches of A. Hamilton, 1985; co-editor: American Political Thought, 1971. T/5 U.S. Army, 1943—46. Grantee, Earhart Found., 1981, 1985, 1988, 1989; Rsch. fellow in polit. ideology, Rockefeller Found., 1956, NEH Bicentennial Challenge grant, Am. Enterprise Inst., 1981—82. Mem.: Am. Polit. Sci. Assn. Home: 1626 Schifly Ln DeKalb IL 60115 Office: Northern Ill Univ DeKalb IL 60115

FRISCH, PAUL ANDREW, librarian; b. Madison, Wis., Oct. 23, 1950; s. Arthur Joseph and Ruth Beverly (Myers) F.; m. Claudia Anna Maria Hirsch, Aug. 1, 1990. BA History, UCLA, 1975, MA History, 1977, MLS, 1986, PhD History, 1992. Social scis. libr. Trinity Univ., San Antonio, 1986-88; head ref. dept., libr. Southwest Mo. State U., Springfield, 1988-92; head of ref. dept., libr. U. Ill., Chgo., 1992-95; head libr. Washington & Jefferson Coll., Washington, Pa., 1995-2000; dir. Old Westbury Libr. SUNY, Old Westbury, NY, 2000—01; dean libr. Our Lady of the Lake, San Antonio, 2001—. Contbr. articles to profl. jours. Treas., trustee Citizens Libr., Washington, Pa., 1995-2000. Summer rsch. grantee S.W. Mo. State U., 1990. Mem. ALA, Assn. Coll. and Rsch. Libs. Office: Sueltenfuss Libr Our Lady of the Lake U San Antonio TX 78207-4689

FRISCH, SIDNEY, JR., lawyer, real estate developer; b. Evanston, Ill., Oct. 25, 1940; s. Sidney and Helen (Hunter) F.; m. Deborah A. King, Aug. 27, 1988. BS in Fin., U. Ill., 1962, JD, 1965. Bar: Ill. 1966, U.S. Dist. Ct. (no. dist.) Ill. 1966, U.S. Ct. Appeals (7th cir.) 1968, Colo. 1977, U.S. Dist. Ct. (mid. dist.) Ga. 1974, U.S. Supreme Ct. 1986. Ptnr. Frisch & Frisch, Chartered, Chgo., 1977—; v.p., gen. counsel Weber-Stephen Products Co., Palatine, Ill., 1966—. Gen. ptnr. Locks Landing Residential Devel., Stuart, Fla.; lectr. seminars in field; mem. sec. of state's adv. com. to revise Ill. Bus. Corp. Act, 1984. Author: Illinois Mechanic's Liens, 1972; Attorney's Guide to Negotiation, 1979. Asst. editlr Ill. Law Forum, U. Ill. Coll. Law, 1964, 65; mem. editorial com. Illinois Business Act Annotated, 1978. Assoc. bd. mem. U. Chgo. Cancer Research Found., 1982, v.p. 1984. Served to lt. USNR, 1962-69. Recipient cert. of appreciation Ill. Inst. for Continuing Legal Edn., 1983. Mem. ABA, Ill. Bar Assn, Chgo Bar Assn (chmn corp law com 1983-84 cert of appreciation 1978, 83), Order of Coif. Clubs: Deans (U. Ill. Coll. Law). Office: Frisch & Frisch Chartered 312 W Randolph St Chicago IL 60606-1721

FRISCHKORN, DAVID EPHRAIM KEASBEY, JR., investment banker; b. Huntington, W.Va., Apr. 11, 1951; s. David Ephraim Keasbey Frischkorn and Permele Elliott (Francis) Booth; m. Anne Cochran, May 9, 1981. BA magna cum laude, Tufts U., 1973; MBA, Columbia U., 1976. Corp. fin. assoc. Rotan Mosle, Houston, 1976-77, asst. v.p., 1977-79, v.p., 1979-82, sr. v.p., 1982-85; v.p. Kidder, Peabody & Co., Houston, 1985-87, Frischkorn & Co. Investment Bankers, Houston, 1988-92; sr. v.p., mng. dir. Rauscher Pierce Refsnes, Inc., Houston, 1993-96; mng. dir. Jefferies & Co. Bd. dirs. Houston Child Guidance Ctr., 1981-88, pres. bd. dirs. 1984-86; trustee The Hill Sch., Pottstown, Pa., 1978-80, Presbyn. Sch., Houston, 1990-94. Mem. N.Y. Athletic Club, Racquest and Tennis, N.Y.C., Houston Country Club, Coronado Club (Houston), Argyle Club (San Antonio), Mill Reef Club (Antiqua, W.I.). Republican. Presbyterian.

FRISCHLING, CARL, lawyer; b. N.Y.C., Feb. 21, 1937; s. Irving and Anna (Klein) F.; m. Adele Frischling, June 21, 1959; children: William, James, Edward. BA, Columbia U., 1958, JD, 1962, MBA, 1963. Bar: N.Y. 1963, U.S. Dist. Ct. N.Y. 1968. Atty. Am. Stock Exchange, N.Y.C., 1963-65; asst. to chmn. Investors Funding, N.Y.C., 1965-67; exec. v.p. and gen. counsel Am. Gen. Capital Mgmt., N.Y.C., 1968-76; ptnr. Alexander Green, N.Y.C., 1976-79; sr. ptnr. Spengler Carlson Gubar Brodsky Frischling, N.Y.C., 1979-92; ptnr. Reid & Priest, N.Y.C., 1992-94, Kramer Levin, N.Y.C., 1994—. Bd. dirs. AIM Mut. Funds, Houston, Cortland Funds. Office: Kramer Levin 919 3rd Ave Rm 3803 New York NY 10022-3902

FRISCHMUTH, ROBERT ALFRED, landscape planner, filmmaker; b. N.Y.C., Dec. 15, 1940; s. Alfred P. and Emma (Glas) F.; m. Marlis Lowenhagen, July 15, 1967 (div. 1979); children: Bettina, Malissa; m. Ana Berti, June 30, 1995. Student, SUNY, Albany, 1958-60; BBA, Pace U., 1973. Cert. nurseryman, N.Y. Statis. analyst N.Y. Ctrl. System, N.Y.C., 1961-68; landscape planner Rosedale Nurseries, Hawthorne, N.Y., 1969-2000; founder RAF Film, 1980—. Prodr. films Gardening: A Brief History, 1979, Tree Transplant, 1980, Florida, 1981, Best of the West, 1982, Kenya Safari, 1983, Of Temples and Tombs, 1984; exhibitor of films, Paramount Ctr., 1987—. Bd. dirs. Paramount Ctr. Arts, 1981-87, pres., 1983-85. With U.S. Army, 1963-65. Mem. Am. Film Inst., Info. Film Producers Am. Home and Office: 31 Ogden Ave Cortlandt Manor NY 10567-4230

FRISCHWASSER, HEINZ FELIX See RA'ANAN, URI

FRISCIA, ARLINE M. assemblywoman; BA in music, Caldwell Coll.; MA in adminstrn. and supervision, Seton Hall U. Councilwoman at large Woodbridge Twp., 1988—91; assemblywoman N.J. Gen. Assembly, 1996—; assoc. minority leader, 1998—2001; asst. majority whip, 2002—; vice chair Woodbridge Twp. Dem. Party. Bd. mgrs. Roosevelt Hosp. Democrat. Office: 245 Main St Woodbridge NJ 07095 E-mail: AswFriscia@njleg.org.*

FRISCO, LOUIS JOSEPH, retired materials science company executive, electrical engineer; b. Patchogue, N.Y., Aug. 21, 1923; s. Anthony Michael and Rose Katherine (Lotito) F.; m. Verona May Kindig, Aug. 20, 1950; children: Richard Samuel, Charles Francis. BSEE, Johns Hopkins U., 1949, MSEE, 1952. Dielectrics lab. dir. Johns Hopkins U., Balt., 1950-64; dielectrics program mgr. GE, Schenectady, N.Y., 1964-65; various tech. and ops. mgmt. positions Raychem Corp., Menlo Park, Calif., 1965-79, dir. corp. product rev., 1979-83, gen. mgr. Wire and Cable div., 1983-89, tech. dir. Electronics Sector, 1989-90. Chmn. Conf. on Elec. Insulation, NAS/NRC, 1963-65; U.S. del. tech. com. TC-15 Internat. Electrotech. Commn., 1963-65, 79-82. Editor Digest of Lit. on Dielectrics, NAS/NRC, 1959, 60.; contbr. numerous articles to profl. jours. Fellow IEEE; mem. ASTM, Electrochem. Soc. (chmn. insulation div. 1957-59, bd. dirs. 1957-59, insulation div. editor jour. 1961-64), Tau Beta Pi, Sigma Xi. Roman Catholic.

FRISELL-SCHRÖDER, SONJA BETTIE, opera producer, stage director; b. Richmond, Surrey, Eng., Aug. 5, 1937; d. Bertel and Helena Margaret (Smith) Frisell; m. Rolf Peter Schröder, Feb. 3, 1976. Licentiate, Guildhall Sch. Music and Drama, London, 1958. Asst. dir. Arena Opera, Verona, Italy, summers 1962-65; from asst. dir. to head of regie and prodn. La Scala Opera Co., Milan, Italy, 1964-79; free-lance producer U.S.A., Can., Argentina, Brazil, Italy, France, Austria, Eng. Producer Ballo in Maschera, Paris Opera, 1981, Andrea Chenier, Miami, 1982, Marriage of Figaro, San Francisco, 1982, Khovanscina, San Francisco, 1984, Agrippina, Venice, 1985, Carmen, Teatro Colon, Buenos Aires, 1985, Salome, Seattle, 1986, Aida, Rio de Janeiro, 1986, Ballo, San Francisco, 1986, Ballo, Phila. (with Pavarotti), 1986, Magic Flute, Edmonton, Winnipeg, 1986, Trovatore, Chgo., 1987, Don Carlos, Tulsa, 1987, Marriage of Figaro, Treviso, 1987, Rigoletto, Seattle, 1988, Otello, Barcelona, 1988, Maometto II, San Francisco, 1988, Aida Met. N.Y., 1988, Ballo, Bologna, 1989, Forza del Destino, Washington, 1989, Don Carlos, Chgo., 1989, Daughter of the Regiment, Calgary, Can., 1990, Otello, P.R., 1990, Don Carlos, L.A., 1990, Siege of Calais, Donizetti Festival Bergamo, 1990, Magic Flute, Washington, 1990, Don Giovanni, Cape Town, South Africa, 1991, Don Carlos, Washington, 1991, Forza, San Francisco, 1992, Otello, Washington, 1992, Ballo, Chgo., 1992, Rigoletto, Goteborg, 1993, Trovatore, Chgo., 1993, Lucia diLammermoor, Calgary, 1994, Eugene Onegin, Calgary, 1996, Don Carlos, Chg., 1996, La Gioconda, Milan, 1997, Elena di Feltre, Wexford, 1997, Magic Flute, Washington, 1998, Turandot, Seville, 1998, Turandot Trieste, Cagliari, Santander, Cordoba, 1999, Eugene Onegin, Tucson, Otello, Washington, 2000, Don Carlos, Washington, Carmen, Iceland, La Traviata, Rio de Janeiro, 2001, Salome, Tucson, Phoenix, 2003. Arts scholar Can. Arts Coun., 1960. Mem. Am. Guild Mus. Artists. Avocations: archaeology, walking, dogs, gardening. Office: care CAMI 165 W 57th St New York NY 10019-2201 E-mail: frisellschroeder@hotmail.com.

FRISHBERG, BENJAMIN M. neurologist; b. St. Paul, Jan. 5, 1952; s. Donald I. and Serene Y. F.; m. Susan B. Frishberg, Oct. 21, 1979; children: Andrea, Charlie. BA summa cum laude, U. Minn., 1974, MD, 1979. Neurologist Neurology Ctr., Washington, 1985-97, La Jolla, Calif., 1997—. Contbr. articles to profl. jours., chpts. to books. Fellow Am. Acad. Neurology, N.Am. Neuro-Ophthalmology Soc.; mem. AMA, Am. Headache Soc., Calif. Med. Assn., Phi Beta Kappa, Alpha Omega Alpha. Avocations: skiing, tennis, numismatics.

FRISHKORN, DAVID LOY, finance company executive; b. Ellwood City, Pa., Nov. 18, 1955; s. Gary Franklin and Evelyn Ruth (Gobrecht) F.; m. Carolyn Ann Getsay, May 28, 1977 (div. Apr. 1989); m. Jack H. Hellaby, Oct. 6, 1991; children: Jessica, Jasmine. BS in Econ., Slippery Rock U., Pa., 1979; MBA in Internat. Bus., Rochester Inst. Tech., N.Y., 1995; diploma in Indsl. Mgmt., Cornell U., 1998. CPA, Fla. Auditor KPMG, Pittsburgh, Harrisburg, Pa., 1979-82; asst. to controller Ampco-Pittsburgh Corp., Pittsburgh, 1982-84; audit supr. Coopers & Lybrand, Tampa, Fla., 1984-85; mgr. internal audit Milton Roy Co., St. Petersburg, Fla., 1985-90; mgr. internal control Xerox Corp., Webster, N.Y., 1990-95, mgr. ops. analysis worldwide mfg., 1995-98, mgr. bus. relations-Japan Stamford, Conn., 1998—. Chair/adv. Galaxe, Rochester, N.Y., 1992-99; leader seminars in field. Adv. Pride Collaborative, San Francisco, 1999; treas. Colleagues, Rochester, 1997-99. Mem. Inst. Mgmt. Accts. (v.p. 1978-99), Fla. Inst. CPA's, Triangle Cmty. Ctr. Home: 208 Richards Ave Norwalk CT 06850-2728 Office: Xerox Corp PO Box 1600 800 Long Ridge Rd Stamford CT 06902-1288 E-mail: davyLF1@aol.com.

FRISHMAN, WILLIAM HOWARD, cardiology educator, cardiovascular pharmacologist, gerontologist; b. N.Y.C., Nov. 9, 1946; s. Aaron and Frances (Fishel) F.; m. Esther Rose Sandowsky, Mar. 11, 1971; children: Sheryl Renée, Amy Helene, Michael Aaron. BA, MD, Boston U., 1969. Diplomate Am. Bd. Internal Medicine, Am. Bd. Cardiovascular Medicine, Am. Bd. Critical Care Medicine, Am. Bd. Clin. Pharmacology, Am. Bd. Geriatrics, Am. Bd. Med. Mgmt. Intern Montefiore Hosp., Bronx, NY, 1969—70, resident in medicine, 1970—71, Bronx Mcpl. and Einstein Hosps., 1971—72; fellow in cardiology N.Y. Hosp.-Cornell U. Med. Coll., N.Y.C., 1972—74, instr., 1974—76; dir. noninvasive cardiac labs. Einstein Hosp. and Montefiore Hosp., 1976—80, dir. cardiology svc. 1980—82, chief medicine 1982—91; prof. medicine and epidemiology, assoc. chmn. dept. medicine Albert Einstein Coll. Medicine Yeshiva U., Bronx, 1991—97; prof. medicine and pharmacology, chmn. dept. medicine N.Y. Med. Coll., Valhalla, 1997—; chief of medicine Westchester Med. Ctr., Valhalla, NY, 1997—. Expert cons. cardiorenal divsn. FDA, Bethesda, Md., 1987—; panel mem. U.S. Pharmacopeial Conv., Rockville, Md., 1990—. Author: (med. book) Clinical Pharmacology of the Beta Blocking Drugs, 1980, 2nd edit., 1984, (med.book) Management of Lipid Disorders, 1992; co-author: Calcium Channel Antagonists in Cardiovascular Disease, 1984, Therapy of Angina Pectoris, 1986, Current Cardiovascular Drugs, 1994, 3d edit., 2000, (med.book) Beta-3 Adrenergic Mechanism, 1995, (med. book) Cardiovascular Pharmacotherapeutics, 1997, 2nd edit., 2003, (med. book) Handbook of Cardiovascular Pharmacotherapeutics, 1998; editor: Yearbook of Medicine: Heart Disease; contbr. chapters to books and articles to profl. jours. Mem. fiscal affairs com. Village of Scarsdale, N.Y., 1991—. Lt. col. M.C., U.S. Army, 1969-90. Named to Boston Collegium of Disting. Alumni, Boston U., 1988, Disting. Alumnus sch. medicine, 1994; teaching scholar Am. Heart Assn., 1979-82; preventive cardiology acad. award Nat. Heart, Lung and Blood Inst., 1980-85; recipient Disting. Tchr. award AAMC-AOA, 1997, Med. Humanism award AAMC, 2001. Master: ACP; fellow: Am. Coll. Chest Physicians, Am. Coll. Cardiology (bd. govs. 1987—91, pres. N.Y. State chpt. 1991); mem.: N.Y. Cardiology Soc. (pres. 1996—97), Assn. Profs. Medicine, Am. Soc. for Clin. Rsch., Am. Soc. for Clin. Pharmacology and Therapeutics (McKeen Cattell award 1990), Scarsdale Town and Village Club, Alpha Omega Alpha (regional councilor). Jewish. Avocations: reading, athletic coaching. Home: 7 White Birch Ln Scarsdale NY 10583-7634 Office: Munger Pavilion NY Med Coll Valhalla NY 10595

FRISINA, ROBERT DANA, sensory neuroscientist, educator; b. Evanston, Ill., Sept. 11, 1955; s. D. Robert and Louise (Boaz) F.; m. Susan Taylor Frisina, July 31, 1982; children: Laurin Taylor, Taylor Robert. AB in Exptl. Psychology summa cum laude, Hamilton Coll., 1977; PhD in Neurosci., Syracuse U., 1983. Rsch. asst. Hamilton Coll., Clinton, N.Y., 1977; Root fellow in sci. Inst. Sensory Rsch., Syracuse (N.Y.) U., 1977-78, NSF grad. fellow, 1978-81, grad. rsch. assoc., 1981-83; NIH rsch. fellow Ctr. Brain Rsch. U. Rochester, N.Y., 1983-85; asst. prof. physiology and otolaryngology U. Rochester, 1985-91, assoc. prof. surgery, neurobiology and anatomy, 1991-99, prof. surgery, neurobiology, anatomy, and biomed. engring., 1999—, dir. rsch. otolaryngology, 1988-92, assoc. chmn. otolaryngology, 1992—; v.p. and founder Auditory System Technologies, Inc., Pittsford, N.Y., 1989-98; adj. assoc. prof. comm. scis. Nat. Tech. Inst. Deaf, 1993—; adj. clin. instr. comm. scis. U. Buffalo, 1998—; disting. rsch. prof. Rochester Inst. Tech., 2003—. Staff mem. Nat. Tech. Inst. for Deaf, Rochester, 1975; charter mem. adv. bd. Internat. Ctr. for Hearing and Speech Rsch., 1988—; assoc. editor, Jour. Acoustical Soc. Am., 1996-99; chmn. study sect. NIH, 2000-02. Author: Hearing, 1989; mem. edit. bd. Hearing Rsch. Jour., 1997—; contbr. articles to profl. jours. Dir. Vols. Hamilton Coll. Aspect of Marcy (N.Y.) Psychiat. Ctr., 1974-77. Recipient 1st Award in Communicative Disorders, NIH, 1988-94. Fellow Am. Acad. Otolaryngology-Head and Neck Surgery, Acoustical Soc. Am.; mem. Assn. Rsch. in Otolaryngology, Soc. Neurosci., Am. Speech-Hearing-Lang. Assn., Acoustical Soc. Found. (charter, bd. dirs. 1996—, gen. sec. and chief fin. officer 1998—), Phi Beta Kappa, Sigma Xi, Psi Chi. Roman Catholic. Achievements include patents for a noise suppression electronic circuit for enhancing speech in the presence of background noise; a hearing aid circuit which can be custom fit to a patient's hearing loss using laser trimming. Office: U Rochester Med Ctr Otolaryngology Divsn Rochester NY 14642-8629 E-mail: rdf@q.ent.rochester.edu.

FRISMAN, ROGER LAWRENCE, industrial sales executive; b. Cleve., Apr. 30, 1952; s. Al and Elsie (Joseph) F. BA, Kent State U., 1974. Sales rep. Lawyers Title Ins. Corp., Cleve., 1977-80, sales mgr., 1980; asst. v.p. sales Midland Title Security, Cleve., 1983-84, sr. v.p. comml. indsl. sales, 1984-90, sr. v.p., mgr. home builder dept., 1990—. Bd. dirs. Ohio Home Builders Assn., mem. exec. com. Advisor YMCA Youth Gov., Stow, 1974; chmn. Nat. Assn. Home Builders Assoc., Build Pac, Wash., 1988—, chmn., 1995, com. vice-chmn., 1996. Recipient Affiliate of the Yr. award Bldg. Industry Assn., 1986, Affiliate of the Yr. award Ohio Home Builders Assn., 1985. Mem. Cleve. Bldg. Industry Assn., Cleve. Bd. Realtors (Affiliate of Yr. award 1982), Mortgage Bankers Assn. Apartment and Home Owners Assn. (Affiliate of Yr. award 1984), Nat. Assn. Home Builders (assocs. com., bd. dirs., exec. com.). Jewish. Avocations: sports watching, playing, softball, baseball, football. Home: 725 Village Club Rd Northfield OH 44067-2333 Office: Revere Title Agy 6480 Rockside Woods South Ste 280 Independence OH 44131

FRISOSKY, ROSARITA MARIE, volunteer nurse; b. Lansing, Mich., July 11, 1918; d. Frank A. and Catherine J. Schmitt; m. Maxwell M. Frisosky, Aug. 24, 1944; children: Julann M., Martin J., James Maxwell, Rodger F., Timothy P., Mary Agnes. Diploma in Nursing, St. Lawrence Sch. Nursing, 1939; postgrad., Lansing C.C. RN, Mich. Ob/gyn. nurse St. Lawrence, Lansing, Mich., 1939, nurse supr., 1940-41; office nurse Dr. Perry Spencer, Lansing, Mich., 1941, L.R. M. Elmurray, M.D., Lansing, Mich., 1941-44; vol. nurse. Assoc. Marionist Mission. Mem. Mich. Nurses Assn., Sons Diamond Boutique (sec./treas. 1987-98), Order of Crusade, Paladins Round Table. Home: 215 Banberry N Lansing MI 48906-1799

FRISQUE, ALVIN JOSEPH, retired chemical company executive; b. Wis., Jan. 27, 1923; s. Henry Louis and Angeline (Thayse) F.; m. Jaye Anzak, June 1, 1950; children: Susan, Alice. BS, U. Wis., 1948, PhD, 1954; MS, U. Iowa, 1951. Sr. scientist Standard Oil Co. Ind., 1954-61; group leader and research mgr., then v.p. div. research Nalco Chem. Co., 1961-73, corp. v.p. research and devel., 1973-82, dir. corp. tech., 1982—. Author, patentee in field. Trustee Ill. Benedictine Coll. Served with USAAF, 1943-46. Decorated Air medal; Croix de Guerre France). Mem. Indsl. Research Inst., Am. Chem. Soc., Sigma Xi, Phi Lambda Upsilon. Home: 129 Acacia Cir Apt 502 Indianhead Park IL 60525-9057

FRISSORA, MARK P. automotive parts manufacturing company executive; BA, Ohio State U.; postgrad., U. Pa., Thunderbird Internat. Sch. Mgmt. With lighting bus. group GE, 1977-87; various mgmt. positions Philips Lighting co., 1987-91; v.p. N.Am. mktg., sales and distbn. Aeroquip-Vickers Corp., 1991-96; v.p. oroginal equipment sales and engring. Walker Mfg., 1996; sr. v.p., gen. mgr. original equipment bus.-program mgmt. Tenneco Automotive, Lake Forest, Ill.,

1996-99, pres., CEO, 1999—, chmn., 2000—. Mem. automobile industry bd. govs. for World Econ. Forum and Bus. Roundtable. Mem. Soc. Automotive Engrs., Automotive Original Equipment Mrfs. Office: Tenneco Automotive 500 N Field Dr Lake Forest IL 60045-2595*

FRIST, THOMAS FEARN, JR., hospital management company executive; b. Nashville, Aug. 12, 1938; s. Thomas Fearn and Dorothy (Cate) Frist; m. Patricia Champion, Dec. 22, 1961; children: Trisha, Thomas Fearn III, Bill. BS, Vanderbilt U., 1961; MD, Washington U., 1966. Chmn., chief exec. officer Hospital Corp. of Am., Nashville; exec. v.p. Hosp. Corp. Am., Nashville, 1968—77, pres., chief oper. officer, 1977—82, pres., chief exec. officer, 1982—85, chmn., 1985—95; vice chmn. Columbia/ Hosp. Corp. of Am. Healthcare Corp., Nashville, 1994—97; chmn., CEO Hosp. Corp. of Am. Healthcare Corp., Nashville, 1995—2001; chmn. HCA Healthcare, The Frist Found., Nashville. Bd. dirs. Columbia Healthcare. Trustee Vanderbilt U., Nashville, 1987, United Way of Am., Alexandria, Va., 1987. Fellow: Am. Coll. Healthcare Execs. (hon.); mem.: Bus. Coun., Bus. Roundtable, Belle Meade Country Club. Presbyterian. Avocations: marathon running, tennis, skiing, flying. Office: The Frist Found 3319 West End Ave, Ste 900 Nashville TN 37203

FRIST, WILLIAM H. senator, thoracic surgeon; b. Nashville, Feb. 22, 1952; m. Karyn Frist; children: Harrison, Jonathan, Bryan. AB, Princeton U. Woodrow Wilson Sch. Pub. and Internat. Affairs, 1974; MD, Harvard U., 1978. Resident Mass. Gen. Hosp. Stanford U., 1978-83, rsch. fellow in surgery, 1983; chief registrar CT Surgery Southampton Gen. Hosp., Eng., 1983; chief resident CT Surgery Mass. Gen. Hosp. Stanford U., 1984-85; chief resident CT Surgery, sr. fellow cardiac transplant svc. Stanford U. Med. Ctr., 1985-86; founder, surgeon Vanderbilt Transplant Med. Ctr., 1986—, asst. prof. surgery, 1986-93, dir. heart and lung transplantation, 1986-93; founder, surgical dir. Vanderbilt Multi-Organ Transplant Ctr., 1989-93; senator from Tenn. U.S. Senate, 1995—; vice chair Alliance for Health Reform, 1995. Mem. U.S. Senate coms. budget, commerce, sci. & transp., fgn. rels., health, edn., labor & pensions, Nat. Bipartisan Comm. on Future of Medicaire, 1998-99; vice chair Alliance for Health Reform. Chmn. Nat. Rep. Senatorial com., 2001—. Republican. Office: US Senate 416 Russell Senate Ofc Bldg Washington DC 20510-4205 E-mail: senator_frist@frist.senate.gov.*

FRISTACKY, NORBERT, computer engineering educator, researcher; b. Puchov, Czechoslovakia, Nov. 8, 1931; s. Eduard and Anna (Janasova) F.; m. Hilda Matejcikova, Feb. 21, 1937; 1 child, Tomas. Dipl.-Ing., Slovak Tech. U., Bratislava, Czechoslovakia, 1954, PhD, 1964. Asst. prof. Slovak Tech. U., 1955-62, 63-70, assoc. prof., 1971-85, full prof., 1985—, head dept. computer engrng., 1978-90, mem. sci. coun., 1988-92. Rschr. Krizik Rsch. Inst., Prague, Czechoslovakia, 1962; vis. lectr. Salford (Eng.) U., 1970-71; vis. prof. Tech. U., Dresden, Germany, 1986; mem. supervisory com. R&D Inst., VUVT Engrng., Zilina, Czechoslovakia, 1990-91. Author: (books) Programmable Logic Controllers, 1981 (Czechoslovakia Tech. Nat. Soc. prize 1981), Logic Circuits, 1986, 90 (Slovak Lit. Fund prize 1986), Digital Computers (Slovak Lit Fund prize, 1994), 1993; editor-in-chief Elec. Engrng. Jour., 1991-2002; mem. editl. bd. Jour. Computers and Informatics, 1981—. Rector Slovak Tech. U., 1990-91. Mem.: IEEE (chmn. Slovak com., Computer Soc. IEEE award Computer Pioneer 1996), Slovak Acad. Soc., Internat. Fedn. Info. Processing (Slovak nat. com., tech. com., working group), Slovak Informatics Soc., Czechoslovak Elec, Engrng. Soc. (chmn. spl. interest group in informatics sci. and engrng. 1977—92), Slovak Soc. Cybernetics and Informatics (v.p. 1991), Slovak Acad. Scis. (sci. com. electronics and cybernetics 1988—96), Am. Czechoslovak Soc. (hon.). Home: JC Hronskeho 14 Bratislava Slovakia Office: Slovenska Tech U Ilkovicova 3 81219 Bratislava Slovakia

FRISTOE, MACALYNE, speech-language pathologist, psychologist, educator, writer; b. Nashville, Mar. 14, 1931; d. George Miller and Brownie Appleton Watkins; m. James Houston Fristoe, June 4, 1953 (div. Nov. 1964); children: James Houston Jr., Andrew McLean; m. John Leiper Freeman, Jr., Jan. 20, 1966 (div. Oct. 1973). BA cum laude, Vanderbilt U., 1953, MS, 1960, PhD, 1972. Lic. speech pathologist, Ind. Health Prof. Bur. Speech clinician East Tenn. Hearing & Speech Ctr., Knoxville, Tenn., 1953—54; speech clinician, speech pathologist Bill Wilkerson Hearing & Speech Ctr., Nashville, 1955—60, asst. dir. speech clinic, 1964—67; instr. speech pathology Sch. Medicine Vanderbilt U., Nashville, 1960, 1964—67, instr. psychology, 1971—72, asst. prof., 1972—74; dir. lang. intervention study project Ctr. Devel. & Learning Disorders Med. Ctr., U. Ala., Birmingham, 1974—76; asst. prof. to assoc. prof. dept. biocomm. U. Ala., Birmingham, 1974—76; dir. speech clinic Purdue U., West Lafayette, Ind., 1976—79, assoc. prof. to prof. dept. audiology & speech scis., 1976—96, dir. grad. programs dept. audiology and speech scis., 1986—90, 1992—96, assoc. dept. head audiology and speech scis., 1993—96, assoc. prof. to prof. dept psychol. scis., 1982—96, prof. emerita, 1996—. Speech clinician Nashville-Davidson County Schs., Nashville, 1955—57; cons. Vanderbilt Hosp., 1957—60, L.B. Wallace Devel. Ctr., Decatur, Ala., 1974—78; rsch. NIH-NIAMDD kidney disease contract Vanderbilt Med. Ctr., 1971—74; mem. adv. bd. Ind. Resource Ctr. for Autism, Ind. U., Bloomington, 1986—94, Steer Speech and Hearing Clinics, Purdue U., 2000—02; reviewer NIH, Bethesda, Md., 1990—96; sci. reviewer Nat. Inst. Neurological and Commn. Disorders and Stroke, NIH, Nat. Inst. Child Health and Human Devel., Nat. Inst. Deafness and Commn. Disorders, Sensory Disorders and Lang. Study sect. NIH, NSF, March of Dimes, Purdue U.; spkr. in field. Assoc. editor Jour. Childhood Comm. Disorders, 1975-78, reviewer, 1978-82; mem. pub. bd. CEC Divsn. Children with Comm. Disorders, 1977-79; editl. cons. Jour. Speech and Hearing Disorders, 1977-79, 1982—, Mental Retardation, 1977-80, Augmentative and Alternative Comm.; cons. editor Am. Jour. Mental Deficiency, 1979-83; reviewer Jour. Applied Rsch. in Mental Retardation; contbr. numerous articles to profl. jours.; co-author, developer: Filmstrip Articulation Test, 1966, Goldman-Fristoe Test of Articulation, 1969, Goldman-Fristoe-Woodcock Test of Auditory Discrimination, 1970, Goldman-Fristoe-Woodcock Auditory Skills Test Battery, 1975, Goldman-Fristoe Test of Articulation 2, 2000; author: Language Intervention Systems for the Retarded, 1975; editor: (book) Four Language Intervention Systems, 1977. Recipient Women in Rsch. award Kennedy Inst. Johns Hopkins U., Balt., 1976; scholar Vanderbilt U., 1952-53; fellow Nat. Def. Edn. Act., 1969; traineeship U. Miami, 1956, Columbia U., 1966, Vanderbilt U., 1969-70, 1970-71. Fellow APA, Am. Speech Lang. Hearing Assn. (cert. clin. competence in speech pathology), Am. Assn. Mental Retardation (v.p. comm. disorders 1985-86, pres. comm. disorders divsn. 1986-87); mem. Nat. Coun. Comm. Disorders (rep.), Phi Beta Kappa, Sigma Xi.

FRISWOLD, FRED RAVNDAL, manufacturing executive; b. Mpls., Jan. 21, 1937; s. Ingolf Oliver and Derrice Ernestine (Anderson) F.; m. C. Marie Martin, Sept. 14, 1957; children— Cynthia, Steven, Barry, Michelle (dec.), Benjamin. BBA with distinction in Fin, U. Minn., 1958. Chartered fin. analyst. With J.M. Dain & Co. (now Dain, Rauscher, Inc.), Mpls., 1958—; exec. v.p. Dain, Bosworth, Inc., 1976-82, pres., CEO, 1982-90, cons., 1990-92; CEO Tonka Equipment Co., Plymouth, Minn., 1992—. Chmn. bd. U. Gateway Corp., UMF Investment Advisors; mem. bd. advisors Otologics L.L.C. Chmn. bd. Met. Mpls. YMCA; trustee U. Minn. Found.; treas. Mpls. Rotary Found. Mem. Twin City Soc. Security Analysts, Wildwood Lodge, Mpls. Rotary (pres. 1997-98). Methodist. Home: 7033 Comanche Ct Minneapolis MN 55439-1004 Office: Tonka Equipment Co 13305 Water Tower Cir Plymouth MN 55441-3803

FRITCH, JOHN WILLIAM, library and information scientist, educator; b. Indpls., Feb. 27, 1963; s. John Martin and Frances Antoinette Fritch. BA, Purdue U., 1987; MLS, Ind. U., 1995. Asst. prof. libr. sci. Purdue U., West Lafayette, Ind., 1998—. Tech. plan cons. Johnson County Pub. Libr., Franklin, Ind., 1997. Contbr. ; author: web-based ednl. material; contbr. articles to profl jours., chpts. to books. Mem.: ALA, Beta Phi Mu (sec. chpt. 2000—). Home: 8265 S1000 East Lafayette IN 47905 Office: Purdue Univ Librs UGRL 504 W State St Lafayette IN 47907-2058 Business E-Mail: jfritch@purdue.edu.

FRITCHER, EARL EDWIN, civil engineer, consultant; b. St. Ansgar, Iowa, Nov. 24, 1923; s. Lee and Mamie Marie (Ogden) F.; m. Dorsille Ellen Simpson, Aug. 24, 1946; 1 child, Teresa. BS, Iowa State U., 1950. Registered civil engr., Calif. Project devel. engr. dept. transp. State of Calif., Los Angeles, 1950-74, traffic engr. dept. transp., 1974-87; pvt. practice cons. engr. Sunland, Calif., 1987—; consulting prin. traffic engr. Parsons DeLeuw Inc., 1990—; cons. traffic engr. DeLeuw Cather Internat., Dubai, United Arab Emerates, 1994. Co-author: Overhead Signs and Contract Sign Plans, 1989; patentee in field. Served to 2d lt. USAF, 1942-46, 50-51. Mem. Iowa State U. Alumni Assn. (life), Lockheed Employees Recreational Club (Burbank), Glendale Numismatic Club. Republican. Methodist. E-mail: allinone@webtv.net.

FRITCHEY, JOHN A. state representative; b. Bossier City, La., Mar. 2, 1964; married; 1 child. BA in Econs., U. Mich., 1986; JD, Northwestern U., 1989. Asst. atty. gen. State of Ill., 1989—91; assoc. ptnr. Barnett, Bornstein, and Blazer Law Offices, 1991—95, counsel Wildman, Harrold, Allen and Dixon Law Offices, 1995—; mem. Ill. Ho. of Reps., 1996—. Mem. Chgo. Gateway Green Com. Mem.: John G. Shedd Aquarium Aux. Soc. (v.p.), Theta Chi. Democrat. Office: 200-7S Stratton Office Bldg Springfield IL 62706 Address: 1547 W Belmont Ave Chicago IL 60657*

FRITH, ANNA BARBARA, artist; b. Fort Collins, Colo., Jan. 3, 1925; d. Adam Christian and Rose Virginia (Ayers) Tepfer; m. Donald Eugene Frith, May 7, 1949; children: Eugenia, Martin, Johanna, Juliet. ABFA in Painting, Colo. Women's Coll., Denver, 1944; Cert. in Illustration, Cleve. Sch. of Art, 1946; BFA in Painting (Hon.), Cleve. Western Reserve U., 1947; MA in Painting, Denver U., 1950; attended, U. Ill., Champaign, 1975-89. Tchr. figure drawing Denver Art Mus.; tchr. figure drawing, summers Chappell House, Denver, 1942, 43, 44, 45; tchr. ceramic sculpture San Bernardino (Calif.) Jr. Coll., 1950, 51, 52; tchr. art H.S. San Bernardino, 1953; part-time tchr. women's classes U. Ill., Champaign, 1955-80. Tchr. Sat. and pvt. classes; conductor workshops in field. Exhbns. include Gilman/Gruen Gallery, Chgo., The Peoria (Ill.) Art Guild, Prairie House Gallery, Springfield, Ill., Mus. Modern Art, N.Y.C., 1950; one-woman shows include Julian McPhee Univ. Gallery, San Luis Obispo, Calif., Calif. Poly. U., 1996, Lompoc, Calif., 1999; participant Mural-in-a-Day, Lompoc, 1998, 99, 2001. Recipient Mary Agnes Page award Cleve. Inst. of Art, 1946, 5th Yr. Scholarship award, 1946, Excellence award for watercolor Picnic Calif. State Fair, 2002. Republican. Presbyterian. Avocations: tennis, swimming, dancing, travel, music. Home: 310 Poppinga Way Santa Maria CA 93455-4204

FRITH, DOUGLAS KYLE, retired lawyer; b. Henry County, Va., Sept. 2, 1931; s. Jacob and Sally Ada (Nunn) F.; m. Ella Margaret Tuck, Sept. 10, 1960; children: Margaret Frith Ringers, Susan Elaine. AB, Roanoke Coll., 1952; JD, Washington and Lee U., 1957. Bar: Va. 1957. Pvt. practice, 1957-58; assoc. Taylor & Young, Martinsville, Va., 1957-58; ptnr. Young, Kiser & Frith, 1960-71, Frith, Gardner & Gardner, 1973-78; pres. Douglas K. Frith & Assocs., P.C., Martinsville, 1979-99; ret., 1999. Bd. dirs. Frith Constrn. Co., Inc., Frith Equipment Corp.; substitute judge 21st Gen. Dist. Ct., 21st Juvenile and Domestic Relations Dist. Ct., 1969-80. Chmn. March of Dimes, 1960, Brotherhood Week, 1960; capt. profl. div. United Fund, 1971. With U.S. Army, 1952-54. Mem. ABA, Am. Bd. Trial Advocates, Va. Bar Assn., Martinsville-Henry County Bar Assn. (pres. 1970-71), Va. Trial Lawyers Assn. (dis. v.p. 1970-71, del. at large 1971-77), Kiwanis. Republican. Baptist. Address: 1409 Whittle Rd Martinsville VA 24112

FRITH, MICHAEL KINGSBURY, artistic director, illustrator, writer, production company executive, actor; b. Grand Rapids, Mich., July 8, 1941; s. Alexander J. and Mary Eleanor (Hefferan) F.; m. Kathryn Mullen; children: Callee Allison, Christina Huston, Jonathan Kingsbury. BA, Harvard U., 1963. Art dir., editor in chief Random House, Beginner Books, N.Y.C., 1963-75; from art dir. to exec. v.p., dir. creative svcs. Jim Henson Prodns., N.Y.C., 1975-96; founding ptnr. Sirius Thinking Ltd., NYC., 1996—2002; design dir. No Strings, Inc., 2003—. Conceptual designer, creative dir., exec. prodr., co-creator Between the Lions, (with Kathryn Mullen) ChucheQhalin, The Little Carpet Boy, a landmine safety project for Afghanistan children, 2003; conceptual designer, co-prodr. Fraggle Rock; creative cons., exec. prodr. Muppet Babies; creative and design cons. The Muppet Show; design cons. five Muppet movies, The Jim Henson Hour, Muppets Tonight; creative prodr. Little Muppet Monsters; Muppet segment prodr. Free to be...A Family; exec. prodr. Jim Henson's Dog City, Mr. Willowby's Christmas Tree; exec. prodr. The Wubbulous World of Dr. Seuss; art dir., curator Miss Piggy's Treasury of Art Masterpieces from the Kermitage Collection, 1984; pres. The Harvard Lampoon. Co-author: Alligator, 1962; author: I'll Teach My Dog 100 Words, 1973; co-author: (with Dr. Seuss as Rosetta Stone), illustrator Because a Little Bug Went Kachoo, 1975; author, illustrator: Some of Us Walk, Some Fly, Some Swim, 1971, My Amazing Book of Autographs, 1974, The Early Bermudians, 1985; illustrator (books by Bennett Cerf): Laugh Day, 1965, Treasury of Atrocious Puns, 1968, The Sound of Laughter, 1970, Stories to Make You Feel Better, 1972; illustrator: The World's Largest Cheese, 1968, The Perils of Penelope, 1973, Insomniacs of the World, Goodnight, 1974; illustrator (series) Animals Do the Strangest Things, Birds Do the Strangest Things, Fish Do the Strangest Things, Insects Do the Strangest Things, Reptiles Do the Strangest Things, Prehistoric Monsters Did the Strangest Things, 1964-74. Mem. NARAS, NATAS, AFTRA, Writers Guild Am. East, Soc. Illustrators, Art Dirs. Club. Office: Trudy Trees Inc 1158 Fifth Ave 6B New York NY 10029

FRITSCH, BILLY DALE, JR., construction company executive; b. Pensacola, Fla., May 10, 1956; s. Billy Dale Fritsch Sr. and Cleta Thiel; children: Mackenzie, Billy Dale III, Jessica. BS, No. Mich. U., 1978. CPA, Ill. Staff acct. Jonet, Fontain, Vande Loo, et al, Green Bay, Wis., 1979; asst. contr. Carpenter Contractors of Am., Pompano Beach, Fla., 1979-81, contr., 1981-84, v.p. fin., 1984-90, exec. v.p., 1990—. Cons. Jade Industries, Coral Springs, Fla., 1983-86; mem. team of taxation and acctg. specialists Citizen Ambassador Program, 1988. Mem. AICPA, Fla. Inst. CPAs, Ill. CPA Soc., Constrn. Fin. Mgmt. Assn., Greater Ft. Lauderdale C. of C. (founding trustee 1990), Internat. Platform Assn. Republican. Avocation: squash. Office: Carpenter Contractors Am 941 SW 12th Ave Pompano Beach FL 33069-4610

FRITSCH, DEREK ADRIAN, nurse anesthetist; b. Cuero, Tex., Sept. 12, 1957; s. Adrian Henry and Virginia Emma (Bernshausen) F.; m. Jacqueline Ann Joyce, June 8, 1985; children: Alexander Derek, Adrienne Joyce. AA, Wharton County Jr. Coll., Wharton, Tex., 1978; BSN, U. Tex. Health Sci. Ctr., 1980; CRNA, Harris County Hosp. Dist., Houston, 1983. Cert. registered nurse anesthetist. Anesthesia tng. Ben Taub Gen. Hosp., The Meth. Hosp., VA Hosp., others, Houston, 1979-88; staff anesthetist Anesthesia Specialists of Houston/The Woman's Hosp. Tex., Houston, 1988-94, 95—. Freelance staff anesthetist Schick Shadel Hosp., Houston, 1990, Gulf Coast Regional Med. Ctr., Wharton, 1994-95; staff anesthetist, anesthesia specialists of Houston/The Woman's Hosp., Houston, 1995—. Colo. County emergency vol. Ambulance Corps, 1976-78; provider anesthesia internat. eye surgery team, Benovolent Missions Internat., Belize, Boliva, El Salvador, 1993-94, 93-95, gen. surgery team, Guatemala, 1996. Recipient Luth. Brotherhood scholarship, 1979, Rotarian scholarship, Houston, 1979, others. Mem. AANA, Tex. Assn. Nurse Anesthetists, Internat. Anesthesia Rsch. Soc., Gulf Coast Assn. Nurse Anesthetists (bd. dirs. 1987-89, pres. 1988-89), Greater New England Acad. Hypnosis, U.S. Parachute Assn., Phi Theta Kappa (State Recognition award, chpt. pres. 1977-78), Sigma Theta Tau. Lutheran. Avocations: fishing, computers, carpentry, skydiving. Home: 410 Lake Bend Dr Sugar Land TX 77479-5804 Office: Anesthesia Specialists Houston 7800 Fannin St Ste 101 Houston TX 77054-2905

FRITSCHE, CLAUDIA, diplomat, ambassador; Personal sec. Liechtenstein Head Gov., 1970-74, Dep. Head Gov., Liechtenstein, 1974-78; diplomatic collaborator Office of Fgn. Affairs, Liechtenstein, 1978-90; dep. Permanent Rep. to Coun. of Europe, Strasbourg, France, 1983-90; first sec. Liechtenstein Embassy, Berne, Switzerland, 1987-89, first sec., chargée d'affaires Vienna, 1989; permanent rep. of Liechtenstein UN, N.Y.C., 1990—2002; Liechtenstein amb. to U.S. Washington, 2002—. Head Liechtenstein Nat. Com. on Equality between Women and Men, 1987 90; sec. Liechtenstein parliamentary del. to the Coun. of Europe, parliamentary del. to the European Free Trade Assn. Office: Embassy of Liechtenstein 1300 Eye St NW Ste 550W Washington DC 20005

FRITTITTA, PETER ANTHONY, health maintenance organization executive; b. Milw., Dec. 12, 1956; s. Agostino and Pietra Fortunata (Balistreri) F.; m. Lucia Antonette Galati, June 12, 1982. BSBA, Marquette U., 1978, MBA, 1988. Sr. fin. acct., then fin. analyst Harley-Davidson Motor Co., Inc., Milw., 1978-81; sr. fin. analyst N.Am. Philips-Centralab, Inc., Milw., 1981-83; ind. bus. cons. Milw., 1984; project analyst, then budget analyst Blue Cross & Blue Shield United of Wis., Milw., 1984-86; mktg. project coord. Compcare Health Svcs. Ins. Corp., Milw., 1986-87; ops. adminstr. MetLife HealthCare Network Wis., Milw., 1987; mgr. mktg. PrimeCare Health Plan, Inc., Milw., 1987-92, mgr. sales, 1992—96, dir. sales and accts. mgmt., 1997—99; v.p. small bus. sales and acct. mgmt. United Healthcare of Wis., Milw., 2000—. Copywriter, direct mail and telemarketing campaign PrimeSize, 1988-90, Met. Milw. Solution, 1991—'; developer first HMO point-of-svc. product in Wis., 1990; speaker in field. Mem. Froedtert Meml. Hosp. Exec. Group. Mem. Internat. Platform Assn., Wis. Direct Mktg. Club, Sales and Mktg. Execs. Milw. (Disting. Sales and Mktg. award 1989). Home: 3866 Cypress Ln Franklin WI 53132-8784

FRITTON, KARL ANDREW, lawyer; b. Olean, N.Y., Mar. 29, 1955; s. William John and Margaret (O'Brian) F.; m. Christine Evelyn Councill, June 9, 1984; children: Katherine Evelyn, Jessica Claire, Rebecca Lee. BS in Econs., SUNY, Albany, 1977; JD, Rutgers U., 1980. Bar: Pa. 1981, N.Y. 1981, U.S. Supreme Ct. 1985. Assoc. Bond, Schoeneck & King, Syracuse, N.Y., 1980-81, Obermayer, Rebmann, Maxwell & Hippel, Phila., 1981-84, Sprecher, Felix, Visco, Hutchinson & Young, Phila., 1984-86, ptnr., 1987-91, Montgomery, McCracken, Walker & Rhoads, Phila., 1991-96, Reed, Smith, Shaw & McLay LLP, Phila., 1996—. Contbr. articles to profl. jours. Active Phila. Vol. Lawyers For Arts, 1981—, Big Brs. Phila., 1981—. Mem ABA (labor law sect.). Democrat. Roman Catholic. Home: 53 Cedarbrook Rd Ardmore PA 19003-1617 Office: Reed Smith Shaw & McLay 2500 One Liberty Pl Philadelphia PA 19103

FRITTS, EDWARD O. broadcast executive; b. Cape Girardeau, Mo., Feb. 21, 1941; m. Martha Dale; children: Kimberley, Timothy, Jennifer. Grad., U. Miss. Pres. Nat. Assn. Broadcasters, Washington, 1982—. Past chmn. joint bd. Nat. Assn. Broadcasters; vice chair U.S. State Dept. Internat. Media Fund. Cons. U.S. C. of C. Assns. Com.; chair media adv. com. U.S. Bicentennial Commn.; vice chmn. White House Pvt. Sector Initiatives Bd., 1985—88; mem. individual investors adv. com. N.Y. Stock Exch.; active Nat. Mus. Women in the Arts; dir. advt. coun., former trustee Mus. TV and Radio; active Wolf Trap Found., Arlington Hosp. Found.; bd. dirs. Nat. Commn. Against Drunk Driving, Partnership for a Drug-Free Am., Ctrs. for Disease Control's Bus. Responds to AIDS program. Recipient Silver Mike award, U. Miss. Mem.: Sigma Alpha Epsilon (Highest Effort award). Avocation: golf. Office: Nat Assn Broadcasters 1771 N St NW Ste 200 Washington DC 20036-2812

FRITTS, HAROLD CLARK, dendrochronology educator, researcher; b. Rochester, N.Y., Dec. 17, 1928; s. Edwin Coulthard and Ava Lee (Washburn) F.; m. Barbara Smith, June 11, 1955 (dec.); children: Marcia L., Paul T.; m. Miriam Colson, July 19, 1982. AB, Oberlin Coll., 1951; MS, Ohio State U., 1953, PhD in Botany, 1956. Asst. prof. botany Eastern Ill. U., Charleston, 1956-60; asst. prof. dendrochronology U. Ariz., Tucson, 1960-64, assoc., 1964-69, prof., 1969-92, emeritus, 1992—; adj. prof. in rsch. Desert Rsch. Inst., U. Nev. Vis. scientist CSIRO forest products divsn., Melbourne, Australia, 1996; owner Dendro-Power, Tucson, 1992—; dir., founder Internat. Tree-Ring Data Bank, 1975-90; NSF faculty, mem. Task Group 3 adv. com. on paleoclimatology, Climate Dynamics Program, 1978-79; lectr. NATO Advanced Study Inst. on Climatic Variability, Sicily, 1980; vis. dir. U. Wyo. Summer Sci. Camp, summer 1956; mem. U. Ariz. del. to People's Republic of China, 1976; participant Nat. Def. U., 1978-79; mem. organizing group internat. conf. on dendroclimatology, Eng., 1980. Author: Tree Rings and Climate, 1976, reprinted 2001, Reconstructing Large-Scale Climate Patterns from Tree-Ring Data, 1991; mem. editorial adv. bd. Quaternary Rsch., 1977-82; contbr. articles to profl. jours. Mem. local sch. bd., 1971-72. Recipient Dendrochronological award of Appreciation Sci. Community, Lund, Sweden, 1990; Grad. fellow Ohio State U., 1954-56, NSF fellow Oreg. Inst. Marine Biology, summer 1957, Guggenheim fellow, 1968-69; grantee NSF 1971-87, U. Calif. Lawrence Livermore Lab., 1978-79, State of Calif., 1979-80, 85-86. Fellow: AAAS; mem.: Am. Meteorol. Soc. (Outstanding Achievement in Bioclimatology award 1982), Am. Inst. Biol. Scis., Ecol. Soc. Am. (editl. bd. 1964—66, chmn. paleoecology sect. 1984, coun. rep.), Am. Assn. Quaternary Environment (coun. 1978—82, adv. com. paleoclimatology), Tree-Ring Soc. (exec. com. 2000—01, mem.-at-large exec. bd.). Home: 5703 N Lady Ln Tucson AZ 85704-3905 E-mail: hfritts@ltrr.arizona.edu.

FRITTS, HARRY WASHINGTON, JR., physician, educator; b. Rockwood, Tenn., Oct. 4, 1921; s. Harry Washington and Hyder (Smith) F.; m. Helen Dyer Goodwin, Aug. 25, 1949; children: John Goodwin, Benjamin Carroll, Patricia Louise. Student, Vanderbilt U., 1941; BS, Mass. Inst. Tech., 1943; MD, Boston U., 1951. Diplomate: Am. Bd. Internal Medicine (mem.). Mem. research staff MIT, 1946-47; intern, then resident Univ. Hosp., Boston, 1951-53; vis. fellow Columbia Coll. Physicians and Surgeons, 1953-56, mem. faculty, 1956-73, prof. medicine, 1967-73, Dickinson W. Richards prof. medicine, 1972-73; prof., chmn. dept. medicine Sch. Medicine, State U. N.Y. at Stony Brook, 1973-87, Edmund D. Pellegrino prof. medicine, 1986-87. William Harris vis. prof. Nat. Med. Sch. Taiwan, 1987-88; vis. physician Bellevue Hosp., 1957-68, Presbyn. Hosp., N.Y.C., 1961-73; vis. physician, cons. Manhattan VA Hosp., 1957-68; vis. prof. U. London, 1982; bd. dirs., adv. council research N.Y. Heart Assn.; mem. sci. council Parker Francis Found.; mem. physiology study sect., mem. cardiovascular tng. com. USPHS; mem. council Nat. Heart, Lung and Blood Inst. Author: On Leading a Clinical Department, 1997; assoc. editor: Jour. Clin. Investigation; mem. editl. bd.: Am. Rev. Respiratory Diseases; contbr. articles to profl. jours. Served to lt. (j.g.) USNR, 1943-46. Guggenheim fellow, 1959-60 Fellow ACP; mem. Am. Physiol. Soc., Am. Soc. Clin. Investigation, Assn. Am. Physicians, Am. Clin. and Climatol. Soc., Alpha Omega Alpha. Home: 79 Bevin Rd Northport NY 11768-1133 Office: SUNY at Stony Brook Dept Medicine Stony Brook NY 11794-0001 E-mail: hwfritts@aol.com.

FRITTS, JOSEPHINE ANN, education educator; b. Olathe, Kans., Apr. 13, 1960; d. John B. and Catherine A. Morris; m. Steven J. Fritts, Nov. 30, 1991. Associates, Johnson County C.C., Kans., 1990; BGS, U. of Kans., 1993, MA in Human Devel. and Family Life, 1997. ACTE-MoEFACS Mo., 1998, NAEYC Wash., DC, 2000, Skills USA Mo., 2001. Prof. Ozarks Tech. C.C., Springfield, Mo., 1997—, phi theta kappa advisor, 1997—. Seminar spkr. Early Childhood Educators, Mo., 1999—. Recipient Advisor Paragon award, Phi Theta Kappa, 2001, Disting. Chpt. Advisor, 2001, Mo. Region Horizon award, 2001. Mem.: ACTE (assoc.), MOEFACS (assoc.), MCCA (assoc.), NAEYC (assoc.). Office: Ozarks Tech CC 933 E Central Springfield MO 65802

FRITZ, BARBARA JEAN, occupational health nurse; b. Helena, Mont., Sept. 16, 1936; d. Marion Caldwell and Clara K. (Bernard) Heffern; m. Bernard John Fritz Sept. 2, 1961; children: Cathleen, Stephen, Elizabeth. Diploma in nursing, Sacred Heart Sch. Nursing, 1957; BS in Nursing, St. Louis U., 1959; postgrad., Oreg. State U., Portland State U., Oreg. Health Scis. U. Cert. occupl. health nurse. Occupl. health nurse Chloride Western Battery, Portland, Oreg., 1984-85; occupl. health nurse unit mgr. Pub. Health Dept. Fed. Occupl. Health, Portland, 1985-86; occupl. health relief nurse James River Corp., Portland, 1986-88; occupl. health nurse Harder Mech./James River Site, Camas, Wash., 1988; health & safety mgr. Armour Foods, Portland, 1988-90; occupl. health cons. Pacific Rim Occupl. Health & Safety Svcs., Portland, 1990—; occupl. health nurse mgr. Toyota Vehicle Processing, Inc., Portland, 1992-95; med. case mgr. Gates McDonald, Beaverton, Oreg., 1995-96; temp. occupl. health mgr. L.S.I. Logic, Gresham, Oreg., 1997. Relief occupl. health cons. Atlas, Copco, Wagner Mining, Portland, 1986 99; instr. in field. Chmn. northeast citizen's adv. Portland Planning Commn., 1988, com. historic landmarks, 1988; mem. Urban Tour Group, Portland; leadership group Mid-County Sewer Project, 1991-92; vol. Portland Ctr. Performing Arts. Recipient Cert. of Appreciation, 25th Anniversary of Urban Tour Group, 1995. Mem. Am. Assn. Occupl. Health Nurses, Oreg. State Assn. Occupl. Health Nurses (registered lobbyist, historian 1992-96, govtl. affairs co-chair 1995-96, chair 1996-97, Nat. Govtl. Affairs award 1996, 98). Democrat. Roman Catholic. Achievements include being instrumental in inclusion of occupational health professionals in Oregon state worksite redesign grant program. Home and Office: 4705 NE Ainsworth St Portland OR 97218-1818 E-mail: prohealthme@msn.com.

FRITZ, EDWARD LANE, dentist; b. Evansville, Ind., Dec. 15, 1932; s. Edward E. and Virginia B. (Lane) F.; m. Bettye J. Samples, July 31, 1954; children: Mary Ann, Sarah Jane. AB, Ind. U., 1954, DDS, 1957; BS, U. Evansville, 1975, MBA, 1978. Pvt. practice dentistry, Evansville, 1959-99; ret.; pres., chmn. bd. Health Resources, Inc., 1986-99, chmn. bd., 1986—. Corp. bd. dirs. Va. Corp., Evansville, 1962-72, Dynatron, Inc., 1980-87. Editor: The Bulletin of the Am. Assn. of Dental Examiners, 1981-85. Capt. U.S. Army, 1957-59. Named Disting. Alumnus Ind. U. Sch. Dentistry, 1991. Fellow Am. Coll. Dentists, Acad. Gen. Dentistry, Acad. Dentistry Internat., Internat. Coll.

Dentists; mem. ADA (continuing edn. com. 1981-83, cons./evaluator 1980), Ind. Dental Assn. (trustee 1983-91, Disting. Svc. award 1996), Vanderburgh County Dental Soc. (pres. 1967, various offices), First Dist. Dental Soc. (pres. 1976-77, various offices), Am. Assn. Dental Examiners (pres. 1989, various offices), Ind. Bd. Dental Examiners (pres. 1982-83, sec. 1980-82), Acad. Operative Dentistry, Internat./Am. Assn. Dental Rsch., Am. Assn. Dental Editors, Acad. Gen. Dentistry, Pierre Fauchard Acad., Sagamores of the Wabash, Ky. Col., Phi Kappa Phi. Home: 12200 Edgewater Dr Evansville IN 47720-8169 E-mail: ebfritz@evansville.net.

FRITZ, ETHEL MAE HENDRICKSON, writer; b. Gibbon, Nebr., Feb. 4, 1925; d. Walter Earl and Alice Hazel (Mickish) Hendrickson; m. C. Wayne Fritz, Feb. 25, 1950; children: Linda Sue, Krista Jane. BS, Iowa State U., 1949. Accredited master flower show judge. Dist. home economist Internat. Harvester Co., Des Moines, 1949-50; writer Wallace's Farmer mag., Des Moines, 1960-64; freelance writer, 1960—. Author: The Story of an Amana Winemaker, 1984, Prairie Kitchen Sampler, 1988, The Family of Hy-Vee, 1989. Chmn. Ariz. Coun. Flower Show Judges, 1983-85; medial rels. Presdl. Inaugural Com., 1988; mem. PEO. Mem. AAUW, Assn. for Women in Comm. (pres. Phoenix profl. chpt., nat. task force com. 1980-82), PEO, Am. Soc. Profl. and Exec. Women, Am. Assn. Family and Consumer Sci., Consumer Sci. Bus. Profls., S.W. Writer's Conf., Ariz. Authors Assn., Phi Upsilon Omicron, Kappa Delta. Republican. Methodist.

FRITZ, HENRY EUGENE, American history educator; b. Garrison, Kans., June 20, 1927; s. Frank Alfred and Esther (Anderson) F.; m. Dolores Ileen Moeller, Sept. 3, 1950; children— Esther Anne, Malin Eugenia, Marie Louise. B.S., Bradley U., 1950, M.A., 1952; Ph.D. in History, U. Minn., 1957. Instr. history U. Wis.-Milw., 1956-58; asst. prof. St. Olaf Coll., Northfield, Minn., 1958-62, assoc. prof., 1962-68, prof. Am. history, 1968—, chmn. history, 1969-84, founder, dir. Am. minorities studies, 1970-72; faculty fellow Newberry Library, Chgo., 1968-69. Author: The Movement for Indian Assimilation, 1860-1890, 1963. Contbr. articles to profl. jours. Served with AUS, 1945-46, ETO. Louis and Maude Hill fellow Hill Found., St. Paul, 1965. Mem. Orgn. Am. Historians (life), Am. Hist. Assn., Western History Assn. (life, chmn. local arrangements 24th ann. meeting 1984, mem. awards of merit com. 1981-84). Republican. Lutheran. Avocations: beef cattle; quarter horses; farming. Home: 805 W 4th St Red Wing MN 55066-2417 E-mail: fritzh@redwing.net.

FRITZ, JACK WAYNE, communications and marketing company executive; b. Battle Creek, Mich., Apr. 22, 1927; s. Charles Lewis and Ruth Marie (Lieb) F.; m. Marilyn Joyce Shingleton, Aug. 26, 1950; children: Jack Wayne II, Dain Thomas, Susan Lynne. BA, U. Mich., 1949. Sales staff Lever Bros., Mich., 1949-51; with sales staff ABC-owned AM and TV stas., Mich. and Ohio, 1951; product mgr. Pepsodent div. Lever Brothers, N.Y.C., 1951-54; salesman, v.p., sales mgr. v.p., gen. mgr. Blair TV div., N.Y.C., 1954-68; with John Blair & Co., N.Y.C., 1954-87, dir., 1968-87, v.p., gen. mgr. broadcasting, 1968-72; pres., chief exec. officer, 1972-87. Bd. dirs. Fritz Broadcasting, Detroit, chmn. Fritz Comms. CIV-Credit Suisse/ Warburg-Pincus Funds, N.Y.C. Past pres. bd. trustees Nat. Mus. Wildlife Art. Served with AUS, 1945-47. Mem. Internat. Radio and TV Soc. (past dir.), Broadcast Pioneers. (past dir.). Clubs: Univ. (N.Y.C.), Teton Pines Country Club (Jackson, Wyo.). Republican. Episcopalian. Address: 2425 N Fish Creek Rd PO Box 1287 Wilson WY 83014-1287

FRITZ, JAMES SHERWOOD, chemist, educator; b. Decatur, Ill., July 20, 1924; s. William Lawrence and Leora Mae (Troster) F.; m. Helen Joan Houck, Apr. 26, 1949 (dec. Oct. 1987); children— Barbara Lisa, Julie Ann, Laurel Joan, Margaret Ellen; m. Miriam Simons Reeves, July 15, 1989. BS, James Millikin U., 1945; MS, U. Ill., 1946, PhD, 1948. Asst. prof. chemistry Wayne State U., Detroit, 1948-51; asst. prof. Iowa State U., Ames, 1951-55, assoc. prof., 1955-60, prof., 1960-90, disting. prof., 1990—. Author: Acid Base Titrations in Nonaqueous Solvents, 1973, An Analytical Solid-Phase Extraction, 1999; co-author: Quantitative Analytical Chemistry, Ion Chromatography, 1982, 3d edit., 2000, Solid Phase Extraction, 1999; contbr. articles to profl. jours. Recipient Minn. Chromatography Forum award, 1987, Dal Nogare award in chromatography, 1991. Mem. Am. Chem. Soc. (award in chromatography 1976, award in analytical chemistry 1985) Methodist. Avocations: tennis, collecting wall hangings. Home: 2018 Greenbriar Cir Ames IA 50014-7820 Office: Iowa State U 322 Wilhelm Ames IA 50011-0001 E-mail: kniss@ameslab.gov.

FRITZ, JAN MARIE, planning educator, mediator, clinical sociologist; b. Cleve., Nov. 4, 1941; d. Andrew and Julia (Zrencsik) F.; m. Richard Lerner; children: Hyunjin, Karin. BA, Bowling Green State U.; MA, Ohio State U.; PhD, Am. U. Cert. clin. sociologist, 1984. Asst. prof. Georgetown U., Washington, 1975-85; sci. assoc. Nat. Cancer Inst., Washington, 1986-89; assoc. prof. Calif. State U., San Bernardino, 1989-93, U. Cin., 1993—. Mem. Nat. Environ. Justice Adv. Coun., U.S. EPA, 2002—. Mediator U.S. Equal Opportunity Commn. U.S. Postal Svc. Grantee U.S. EPA, 1996-97; Kellogg Found. Nat. fellow, 1982-85, NEH fellow, 1991-92, Ohio Campus Compact Faculty fellow, 1999-2000; recipient Peres-Rabin Peace award, 1999. Mem.: AAUP, Internat. Assn. Facilitators, Nat. Network Forest Practioners, Am. Health Planning Assn. (bd. dirs. 1995—2000), Assn. Conflict Resolution, Am. Sociol. Assn., Sociol. Practice Assn. (pres. 1980—82, Disting. Career award 1992), Internat. Sociol. Assn. (pres. clin. sociology divsn. 1992—94, exec. bd. 1994—2002, rep. to UN 1999—2002, v.p. sociotechnics-sociol. practice divsn. 2002—). E-mail: jan.fritz@uc.edu.

FRITZ, MARY ANN, music educator; b. Springfield, Mo. d. James Martin and Mary Lavon Fritz. BA, Drury Coll., 1982; MA in Ednl. Psychology, U. Nebr., 1984; MusM in Piano Performance, Southwestern Bapt. Theol. Sem., 1994, D in Musical Arts in Piano Pedagogy, 1998. Advanced cert. Creative Motion Alliance. Pvt. piano tchr., Ft. Worth, 1975—; piano tchr. Lake Arlington (Tex.) Acad., 1989—99. Adj. prof. piano Howard Payne U., Brownwood, Tex., 1993—94, Dallas Bapt. U., 1997—; tchg. fellow music edn. and piano Southwestern Bapt. Theol. Sem., Ft. Worth, 1994—98, adj. prof. music edn. and piano, 1999—2000; dir. children's choirs Overton Pk. Meth. Ch., Ft. Worth, 1996—; adjudicator piano festivals various music tchr. assns., 1995—; adjudicator piano auditions Am. Coll. Musicians, 1999—; clinician children's creativity camps various chs. and schs., Tex. and La., 1985—. Author: A Piano Pedagogy of Creative Motion, 1998; percussionist : mus. rec. Steal Away Home, 1995; editor: Jour. Creative Motion, 2000—. Pres.' Merit scholar Southwestern Bapt. Theol. Sem., Ft. Worth, 1994. Mem.: Creative Motion Alliance, Inc. (charteR) (pres. 1994—98, clinician/workshop leader 1995—, 1st v.p. 1999—2001), Ft. Worth Music Tchrs. Assn., Ft. Worth Piano Tchrs. Forum (4th v.p. 1998—2002), Am. Coll. Musicians (adjudicator), Choristers Guild. Home: 5881 Chesapeake Pl Fort Worth TX 76132-2659

FRITZ, MELVIN M. physician; b. Huntington, N.Y., June 22, 1935; s. Charles M. and Jean Rosen Fritz; m. Marjorie Fritz; children: Steven, Kevin. AB, Cornell U., 1956; DO, Chgo. Coll. Osteo. Medicine, 1961; MD, Calif. Coll. Medicine, L.A., 1962. Diplomate in family practice and geriatrics Am. Bd. Family Practice. Physician, Huntington, N.Y., 1962—; med. dir. Carillon Nursing and Rehab. Ctr., 1996—. Active Suffolk County Bd. Health, 1980—, Suffolk County Water Authority, 1987—. Fellow Am. Acad. Family Physicians, 1976. Office: 175 E Main St Huntington NY 11743-2911 E-mail: dmfritz@aol.com.

FRITZ, RENE EUGENE, JR., manufacturing executive; b. Prineville, Oreg., Feb. 24, 1943; s. Rene and Ruth Pauline (Munson) F.; m. Sharyn Ann Fife, June 27, 1964; children: Rene Scott, Lanz Eugene, Shay Steven, Case McGarrett. BS in Bus. Adminstrn., Oreg. State U., 1965. Sales mgr. Renal Corp., Albany, Oreg., 1965-66, Albany Machine and Supply, 1965-66; pres. Albany Internat. Industries Inc., 1966-85, Wood Yield Tech. Corp., 1972-85, Albany Internat. DISC, 1972-85, Automation Controls Internat. Inc., 1975-85; co-founder, chmn. Albany Titanium Inc., 1981-89; prin. Torwest Capital, 1989; founder, pres. WY Tech. Corp., 1984-89, R. Fritz & Assocs., 1987-89. Pres. Chief Execs. Forum, 1989—, Fritz Grup, Inc., 1989—; fin. planner, investment banker M&A, Vancouver, Wash., 1991—; chmn. Stormwater Treatment LLC, CSF Treatment Sys., NTP, Wilsonville, Oreg., 1999—, Dentamax, Inc., Vancouver, 1999—, Human Capital Oreg./Wash., Vancouver, 1999—, MindNautilus, Inc., Portland, 2000—; bd. dirs. Max-Viz, Inc., 2001. Patentee computer controlled machinery. Pres. Oreg. World Trade Coun., 1982—; trustee U.S. Naval Acad. Found., Annapolis, Md., 1988—. Mem. Oreg. State Alumni, Forest Products Rsch. Soc., Young Pres. Orgn., Rotary, Elks. Presbyterian.

FRITZ, ROGER JAY, management consultant; b. Browntown, Wis., July 18, 1928; s. Delmar M. and Ruth M. (Sandley) F.; m. Kathryn Louise Goddard, Oct. 13, 1951; children: Nancy Goddard, Susan Marie. BA in Polit. Sci, Monmouth (Ill.) Coll., 1950; MS in Speech, U. Wis., 1952, PhD in Ednl. Counseling, 1956. Asst. dean men, asst. prof. Purdue U., 1953-56; mgr. pub. relations Cummins Engine Co.; also sec. Cummins Engine Found., 1956-59; sec. John Deere Found.; also mem. pub. relations staff Deere & Co., 1959-65, dir. mgmt. devel. and personnel research; also dir. John Deere Found., 1965-69; pres. Willamette U., 1969-72, Orgn. Devel. Cons., Naperville, Ill., 1972—. Bd. dirs. Intelligent Electronics, Inc., List Processing Co., Todays Computers Bus. Ctrs., Entre Computer Ctrs., Inc., Natural Golf, Inc., Quote Me, Optionize, Envisionworks, Inc. Author: A Handbook for Resident Counselors, 1952, The Argumentation of William Jennings Bryan and Clarence Darrow in the Tennesee Evolution Trial, 1952, How Freshmen Change, 1956, The Power of Professional Purpose, 1974, MBO Goes to College, 1975, Practical Management by Objectives, 1976, What Managers Need to Know-A Practical Guide for Management Development, 1978, Performance Based Management, 1980, Productivity and Results, 1981, People Compatibility System, 1983, Rate Yourself as a Manager, 1985, You're in Charge, 1986, Personal Performance Contracts: The Key to Job Success, 1986, Nobody Gets Rich Working for Somebody Else, 1987, Rate Your Executive Potential, 1987, The Inside Advantage, 1987, If They Can-You Can, 1988, Be Your Own Boss, 1988, Managing a Successful Team, 1989, Management Ideas That Work, 1989, Developing A Positive Attitude, 1990, The Entrepreneurial Family, 1991, Think Like a Manager, 1991, How to Export, 1992, How to Get Rich Working for Yourself, 1992, Sleep Disorders-America's Hidden Nightmare, 1993, The Sales Manager's High Performance Guide, 1993, How to Manage Your Boss, 1994, A Team of Eagles, 1994, The Small Business Troubleshooter, 1995, The Field Guide for Boss Types...And How to Deal With Them, 1996, An Idea-A-Day For Promotable People, 1996, Crime Crisis: Bold New Ideas to Fit Punishment with Crimes, 1997, Wars of Succession, 1997, One Step Ahead: The Unused Keys to Success, 1998, Bounce Back and Win, 1999, Fast Track-How to Gain Momentum and Keep It, 1999, Attitude Makes The Difference, 2000, Beyond Commitment: The Skills All Leaders Need, 2000, Family Ties and Business Binds, 2000, Magnet People: Their Secrets and How To Learn From Them, 2001, Little Things-Big Results, 2002, How To Make Your Boss Your Ally and Advocate, 2002, Building a Legacy--One Decision at a Time, 2002, 100 Ways to Bring Out Your Best, 2003, After You-Can Humble People Prevail?, 2003; also articles, papers; columnmist Entrepreneur mag., New Bus. Opportunity mag., 1989, Benefits and Compensation Solutions Mag., Bus. Start Ups Mag.; mgmt. editor Communication Briefings Newsletter, 1989. Mem. com. preparation coll. tchrs. Ill. Bd. Higher Edn., 1965-67, mem. com. med. edn., 1967-68; edn. com. N.A.M., 1967-69; mem. Iowa-Ill. Indsl. Devel. Group, 1964-69; council contbr. Nat. Indsl. Conf. Bd., 1960-65, council devel., edn. and tng., 1966-69; adv. com. solicitations Nat. Better Bus. Bur., 1964-69; v.p. Oreg. Ind. Colls. Assn., 1969-72; mem. Pres. Johnson's Citizens Adv. Bd. on Youth Opportunity, 1968-69, Gov.'s Personnel Grievance Panel, Ill., 1974-77; trustee Monmouth Coll., 1957-79, chmn., 1961-69; trustee Oreg. Colls. Found., 1969-72, Ind. Coll. Funds Am., N.Y.C., 1972, Internat. Coll. Commerce and Econs., Tokyo, 1970-72, U. Chgo. Cancer Research Found., 1973-78. Recipient Achievement award, Monmouth Coll., 2002. Mem. Phi Eta Sigma, Omicron Delta Kappa, Tau Kappa Epsilon, Phi Alpha Theta, Sigma Tau Delta, Pi Kappa Delta. Clubs: Naperville (Ill.) Country. Republican. Methodist. Home: 1113 N Loomis St Naperville IL 60563-2745 Office: 1240 Iroquois Dr Naperville IL 60563-8536 Fax: 630-420-7835. E-mail: R.Fritz3800@aol.com.

FRITZ, STEVEN L, physicist; b. Kans. City, Mo., Aug. 10, 1944; s. John Henry and Barbara Jean Fritz; m. Carmen Ann Fiorella, June 15, 1968; children: John Eric, Stephanie Kristen Savolaine, Melissa Ann. BS in physics, U. of Md., 1967; PhD, U. of Kans., 1979. Asst. prof. So. Ill. U., Springfield, Ill., 1976—77, U. of Kans., 1977—86; assoc. prof. U. of Md., 1986—2000, dir., tech. devel., 1995—97, assoc. v.p., 1997—2000; dir. tech. transfer Md. TEDCO, 2000—. SBIR rev. NIH, Washington DC, 1983—2002; bd. mem. DeJarnette Rsch. Systems, Towson, Md., 1999—. Coord. marriage prep. St. John the Evangelist, Columbia, Md., 2001—; pres. Johnson County Bd. of Cath. Schools, Kans., 1986—88. Comdr. USNR, 1967—94, USA. Recipient DAAD Rsch. visit, German Acad. Exch. Svc., 1997. Mem.: Assn. of U. Tech. Managers. Avocation: aviation. Office: Maryland TEDCO 5575 Sterrett Pl Ste 240 Columbia MD 21044 Business E-Mail: sfrtiz@marylandtedco.org.

FRITZ, TERRENCE LEE, investment banker, strategic consultant; b. Ft. Dodge, Iowa, Mar. 10, 1943; s. George and Julia Evelyn (Katnik) F.; m. Pam Fritz; children: Erich, Kevin, Tanya. BS in Indsl. Engring., Iowa State U., 1967. Registered profl. engr., Colo. Mfg. system analyst Martin-Marietta, Denver, 1967-68; system fin. analyst N.Am. Philips, Denver, 1968-69; mgmt. cons. Denver, 1970-74; exec. dir. Met. Transit Authority-Iowa Dept. Transp., Des Moines, 1974-78; sr. v.p. mktg., strategic planning Holiday Inns, Trailways, Dallas, 1978-80; pres. Strategic Actions, Dallas, 1984-88; regional dir. capital markets group Grant Thornton, Dallas, 1988-90; pres. Capital Mkts. Group, Inc., Dallas, 1990—. Mem. adv. bd. So. Meth. U., 1981-84, local adv. bd. Dallas Fed. Res., 1982-84; advisor transp. rsch. bd. NAS, 1980. Bd. dirs. Dallas-Ft. Worth Adv. bd., 1980-84; cons. Dallas-Ft. Worth Transp. Authority, 1980; mem. Gov.'s Com. on Tech., Austin, 1982-83; Dallas rep. U.S. President's Carribean Initiatives Program to Jamaica, Costa Rica, 1981-83; exec. dir. Japan-Tex. Conf., 1981-84; mem. adv. bd. So. Meth. U. Cox Sch. Bus., 1981-84. Mem. Dallas C. of C. (pres., chief exec. officer 1980-84). Avocations: skiing, sailing, wine collecting. Home: 9347 Briarhurst Dr Dallas TX 75243-6139 Office: Ste 300 2911 Turtle Creek Blvd Dallas TX 75219-6243

FRITZ, THOMAS VINCENT, business executive; b. Pitts., July 6, 1934; s. Zeno and Mary M. (Briley) F.; m. Barbara L. Jacob, Jan. 31, 1959; children: William T., James Z., Juliann W. BBA in Acctg. cum laude, U. Pitts., 1960; JD, Duquesne U., 1964; LLM, NYU, 1966; Advanced Mgmt. Program, Harvard Bus. Sch., 1975. Bar: Pa. 1964, U.S. Supreme Ct. 1969; CPA, Pa. 1962. Ptnr. Ernst & Young (formerly Arthur Young & Co.), Pitts., N.Y.C., Washington, 1970, regional mng. ptnr., vice chmn., 1977-89, vice chmn., 1989-92; pres., CEO, bd. dirs. Pvt. Sector Coun., Inc., Washington, 1992-2000; pres. Thomas V. Fritz & Assocs., Washington, 2000—. Adj. prof. Sch. Law Duquesne U., Pitts., 1966-79; adv. dirs. Pvt. Sector Coun., Washington, 1983—; bd. dirs. Innovative Sys., Inc.; chmn. Alliance for Free Enterprise, Washington, 1987-89. Editor Duquesne U. Law Rev., 1963-64. Active Century Club, Duquesne U.; bd. dirs. Evermay Comty. Assn., pres., 1994-96; bd. dirs. McLean Citizens Assn., 1994-97; co-chmn. U. Pitts. Katz Campaign 3d Century, 1988-91. With U.S. Army, 1955-57. Recipient Gorley award, 1964, Disting. Alumni award U. Pitts., 1981, Advancement Info. Tech. award, 1988, Federal 100 Info. Tech. award, 1997. Mem. AICPA, ACBA, Pa. Inst. CPAs, Duquesne Club, Met. Club, Rolling Rock Club, Avenel Club, Beta Gamma Sigma, Beta Alpha Psi. Office: 6303 Long Meadow Rd Mc Lean VA 22101-2314

FRITZHAND, IRVIN DICK, psychologist; b. Bklyn., Aug. 2, 1936; s. Philip and Hannah Frances (Arbeit) F.; m. Sheila Wynn Block, June 23, 1963; children: Alan, Aaron, Jason. BS, CUNY, Bklyn., 1959; MS, CUNY, N.Y.C., 1962; PhD, Hofstra U., 1974. Lic. psychologist, N.Y.; N.Y. state cert. sch. psychologist; workers compensation bd. cert. authorization. Psychol. examiner NYU, N.Y.C., 1963; grad. tchg. asst. La. State U., Baton Rouge, 1963-64; psychologist children's unit Kings Park (N.Y.) Psychiat. Ctr., 1964-71, supervising psychologist children's unit, 1971-73, treatment team leader, 1973-76, treatment svc. chief, 1983-95; pvt. practice psychology Smithtown, N.Y., 1975—; chief treatment svc. Central Islip (N.Y.) Psychiat. Ctr., 1976-83. Cons. psychologist Advanced Ctr. for Psychotherapy, Hempstead, N.Y., 1966-72; panel psychologist N.Y. Bur. Disability Determination, 1977—; adj. supr. grad. psychology dept. Hofstra U., Hempstead, 1971-75. Mem. editl. bd. Jour. Psychiat. Treatment and Evaluation, 1980-81. Mem. APA, Ea. Psychol. Assn., N.Y. State Psychol. Assn., Suffolk County Psychol. Assn., Assn. for Advancement of Behavior Therapy, Coun. for Nat. Register of Health Svc. Providers in Psychology, Am. Profl. Soc. on Abuse of Children, Obsessive-Compulsive Found., Internat. Acad. Profl. Counseling and Psychotherapy (diplomate in psychotherapy 1983), Am. Acad. Behavioral Medicine (diplomate in behavioral medicine 1980). Jewish. Avocations: swimming, cycling, gardening, travel, chess. Home and Office: 46 Hofstra Dr Smithtown NY 11787-2019 E-mail: DFritzPhD@msn.com.

FRITZSCHE, HELLMUT, physics educator; b. Berlin, Feb. 20, 1927; came to U.S., 1952; s. Carl Hellmut and Anna (Jordan) F.; m. Sybille Charlotte Lauffer, July 5, 1952; children: Peter Andreas, Thomas Alexander, Susanne Charlotte, Katharina Sabine. Diploma in Physics, U. Göttingen, Fed. Republic Germany, 1952; PhD in Physics, Purdue U., 1954, DSc (hon.), 1988. Instr. physics Purdue U., Lafayette, Ind., 1954-55, asst. prof., 1955-56, U. Chgo., 1957-61, assoc. prof., 1961-63, prof., 1963-96, dir. Materials Rsch. Lab., 1973-77, chmn. dept., 1977-86, Louis Block prof. physics, 1989-96. V.p., bd. dirs. Energy Conversionn Devices, Inc., Rochester Hills, Mich., United Solar Systems Corp.; mem. adv. com. Ency. Britannica, 1969—96. Editor: 12 sci. books; assoc. editor Jour. Applied Physics, 1975-80; regional editor Jour. Non-Crystalline Solids, 1987-96; contbr. 270 articles to profl. jours.; patentee in field. Named hon. prof. Shanghai Inst. Ceramics, 1985, Nanjing U., 1987, Beijing U. Astronautics, 1988. Fellow AAAS, Am. Physical Soc. (Oliver Buckley Condensed Matter Physics prize 1989), N.Y. Acad. Scis. (chmn. divsn. condensed matter physics 1979-80). Avocations: the violin, sailing, skiing. Home: 3140 E Camino Juan Paisano Tucson AZ 85718-4206 Office: Energy Conversion Devices Inc 2956 Waterview Dr Rochester Hills MI 48309 E-mail: hellmutf@aol.com.

FRITZSCHE, KATHLEEN (DRAGONFIRE FRITZSCHE), performing arts educator; b. Liverpool, Eng., Apr. 22, 1943; came to U.S., 1964; d. James and Kathleen Honora (Parry) Walker; m. James Dockery, 1966 (div. 1971); 1 child, James Dockery II; m. Francis Frederick Fritzsche, Feb. 14, 1978 (div. 1989); 1 child, Rebecca. Student, L.A. Harbor Coll.; studied with, Lawrence J. Wong, Richard Hatch, Dr. Rodney Oakes. Pvt. tchr. art, L.A., 1996—. Writer, composer, performer, artist in various media. Avocation: walking by ocean. Home: 922 E 118th Pl Los Angeles CA 90059-2819

FRITZSCHE, R(OBERT) WAYNE, corporate executive; b. Woodbury, N.J., Jan. 8, 1949; s. Robert Edward and Mae Frances (Geiger) Fritzsche; m. Laurie Ann Owen, 2000 (dec.); children from previous marriage: Allison Anne, Benjamin Robert, Heather Leigh, Kelsey Marie. BA, Rowan U., 1971; MBA, U. San Diego, 1973. Sales rep. Warner Lambert, Morristown, N.J., 1972-74; group product mgr. Hoechst, San Diego, 1974-79; strategic planning Johnson & Johnson, Raritan, N.J., 1978-79; v.p. Cytogen, Princeton, N.J., 1979-80; sr. analyst Channing Weinberg, Inc., N.Y.C., 1980-81; founder, chmn. Fritzsche Pambianchi & Assocs., Inc., Somerville, NJ, 1981—91; founder Fritzsche & Assocs., Tampa, Fla., 1991—. Founder Immune Response Co., San Diego, 1987—, Cortex Pharm., Irvine, Calif., 1988—90, Med. Bus. Pub. Corp., Sommerville; bd. dirs. Hesed Biomed, Houston, Biokeys, San Diego, Occu-Logix, Tampa, OPEXA Pharms.; pres. Organ Savers Inc., 2002—. Mem.: Am. Assn. Clin. Chemists, Am. Chem. Soc., N.Y. Acad. Sci. Republican. Avocations: piano, running. Office: 18925 Saint Laurent Dr Lutz FL 33558-2808 E-mail: wayneF2000@mindspring.com.

FRITZSCHE, SONJA RAE, humanities educator; b. Alexandria, Va., May 5, 1970; d. David Jerome and Nancy Jean Fritzsche. BA in History and German, Ind. U., 1992; MA in Modern European History, UCLA, 1995; PhD in Germanic Studies, U. Minn., 2001. Asst. prof. Ill. Wesleyan U., Bloomington, 2001—. Recipient Grad. Rsch. fellowship, German Acad. Exch. Svc., 1998—99; grantee, Boje Buck Studios/Polzer Media Group, Berlin, 2001. Mem.: Soc. for Utopian Studies., Women in German, German Studies Assn. Avocations: cycling, speed skating, travel, music. Office: Ill Wesleyan U/MCLL PO Box 2900 Bloomington IL 61702

FRIX, PAIGE LANE, lawyer, accountant; b. Washington, Apr. 13, 1961; d. William Elza Smith Jr. and Janet Helen (Peoples) Davis; m. Kemmy Deane Frix, July 29, 1993; 1 child, Avery Karlin. BBA, U. Okla., 1984, JD, 1987. Bar: Okla. 1987; CPA, Okla. Pvt. practice, Muskogee, Okla., 1987—; sec. Frix Constrn. Co., Inc., Muskogee, 1999—. Instr. Becker CPA Rev. Course, Tulsa, 1988-97; cons. Frix & Foster Constrn. Co., Inc., Muskogee, 1990—. Sunday sch. tchr. Honor Heights Meth. Ch., Muskogee, 1996—; trustee Steve Yaffe Charitable Trust, Muskogee; bd. dirs. Promoting Animal Welfare Soc., Inc., Muskogee, 1992—, Kids Space, Muskogee County Child Advocacy Ctr., Muskogee, 1999—; mem. Five Civilized Tribes Mus. Aux., 1997—; Cub Scout den leader Boy Scouts Am. Mem. Okla. Bar Assn., Muskogee County Bar Assn., Muskogee Edn. Found. Democrat. Home and Office: PO Box 284 Muskogee OK 74402-0284

FRIZELL, DAVID J. lawyer; b. National Park, N.J., Sept. 13, 1948; s. Robert E. and Kathleen S. (Ford) F.; m. Aurelia M. Wright, Aug. 5, 1989; children: Brigid, St. John, Catherine. AB, Rutgers U., 1970, JD (with honors), 1973. Bar: N.J. 1973, U.S. Dist. Ct. N.J. 1973, U.S. Supreme Ct. 1986. Counsel Levin Affiliates, Plainfield, N.J., 1975-77; ptnr. Frizell & Pozycki, Metuchen, 1977-93, Frizell & Samuels, 1993—. Mem. N.J. Legislature Adv. Com. Land Use Law Revisions, 1979-86; lectr. Inst. for CLE, 1983—; pres. Frizell Real Estate Devel. Group, 1994—. Author: New Jersey Land Use Law, 2000; contbr. articles to profl. jours.; editor Land Use Law Newsletter, 1983-92; mem. editl. bd. Housing N.J. Mag., 1990-96. Bd. dirs. First Concern, Inc., 1998—. Mem. ABA, N.J. State Bar Assn. (dir., chmn. land use sect. 1983, dir. 1984-96, Outstanding Svc. award 1983), Metuchen C. of C. Democrat. Avocations: sailing, hiking. Office: PO Box 474 Metuchen NJ 08840-0474 E-mail: david.frizell@verizon.net.

FRIZZELL, GREGORY KENT K. judge; b. Wichita, Kans., Dec. 13, 1956; s. D. Kent and Shirley Elaine (Piatt) F.; m. Kelly Susan Nash, Mar. 9, 1991; children: Benjamin Newcomb, Hannah Kirsten, Robert Nash, David Gregory, Elizabeth Piatt, Jubilee Kathryn. BA, U. Tulsa, 1981; JD, U. Mich., 1984. Bar: Okla. 1985, U.S. Dist. Ct. (no., ea. and we. dists.) Okla. 1985, U.S. Ct. Appeals (10th cir.) 1985, U.S. Supreme Ct. 1990. Jud. clk. to judge U.S. Dist. Ct. for No. Dist. Okla., Tulsa, 1984-86; pvt. practice Tulsa, 1986-95; gen. counsel Okla. Tax Commn., 1995-97; dist. judge Tulsa County, 1997—. Master of the bench Hudson, Hall, Wheaton Chpt. of Amer. Inns of Ct., Tulsa. Counsel bd. dirs. Tulsa Speech and Hearing Assn., 1987-95, pres., 1994-95. Mem. Okla. Bar Assn., Am. Inns of Ct. (past pres. local chpt.), Rotary, Federalist Soc. Office: Tulsa County Courthouse 500 S Denver Ave Tulsa OK 74103-3838

FRIZZELL, LAWRENCE EDWARD, religious studies educator, priest; b. Calgary, Alta., Can., May 28, 1938; arrived in U.S., 1974; s. Walter John Frizzell and Mary Angela Long. Lic. in sacred theology, U. Ottawa, Ont., Can., 1962; lic. in sacred scripture, Pontifical Bibl. Inst., Rome, 1967; PhD, U. Oxford, Eng., 1974. Lectr. St. Joseph's Sem., Edmonton, 1962—64, Newman Theol. Coll., Edmonton, 1967—70; assoc. prof. Seton Hall U., South Orange, NJ, 1974—. Vis. prof. Cath. Bibl. Assn., Jerusalem, 1983, Rome, 90; mem. adv. bd. U.S. Bishops for Cath.-Jewish Rels., Washington, 1983—. Grantee, Can. Coun., 1970—74. Office: Seton Hall U 400 S Orange Ave South Orange NJ 07079 Office Fax: 973-761-9596. E-mail: frizzela@shu.edu.

FRIZZELLE, CHARLES DELANO, JR., military officer, educator; b. Hampton, Va., Sept. 15, 1958; s. Charles Delano Sr. and Betty Ann (Baker) F.; m. Remedios Almanzar Arias, May 5, 1987; children: Robert Thomas, Charles David III. AA, U. Md., Ramstein, Germany, 1978; BSBA, East Carolina U., 1980; MS in Sys. Mgmt., U. So. Calif., 1989; MA in Nat. Security, Georgetown U., 1997; MPA in Pub. Adminstrn., U. So. Calif., 1997, DPA in Pub. Admin., 1998. Cert. master in program mgmt., test and evaluation, acquisition logistics, chief info. officer and comm.-computer sys. Dept. Def. Acquisition Profl. Devel. Program Level III. Commd. 2d lt. USAF, 1980, advanced through grades to lt. col.; acquisition program mgr., test and devel. dir., air liason officer U.S. Army Spl. Forces, AF Sys. Command Wright Patterson AFB, Dayton, Ohio, 1980-85; comdr. space surveillance ops. crew 17th Surveillance Squadron, San Miguel, The Philippines, 1985-87; chief standardization/evaluation 3d Comms. Squadron, Kapaun Air Sta., Germany, 1987-90; space sys. operational test mgr. AF Operational Test and Evaluation Ctr., Kirtland AFB, Albuquerque, 1990-94; acquisition program dir. Office Asst. Sec. Def. Command, Control, Comm., Intell., Washington, 1994-96; prof. Def. Sys. Mgmt. Coll., Ft. Belvoir, Va., 1996-2001; staff asst. for live fire, dir. operational test and evaluation The

Pentagon, Washington, 1999—2001; mil. advisor AC/ST Dept. of State, Washington, 2001—. Assoc. faculty Ga. Inst. Tech., 1997—, U. Tex., Austin, 1999—. Master rescue diver, emergency med. tech. Co. 56, Prince Georges County, Md., 1996—2000, Co. 12, Great Falls County, Va., 2001—03. Mem.: NRA (benefactor), Air Commando Assn., Soc. Flight Test Engrs., Profl. Assn. of Dive Instrs., Jujitsu Am., Interat. Test and Evaluation Assn., 82d Airborne Assn. (life), Va. Sport Shooting Assn. (life), The Mil. Officers Assn. (life), Omicron Delta Epsilon, Pi Alpha Alpha, Phi Alpha Sigma, Sigma Tau Gamma. Avocations: martial arts, rugby, parachuting, running, scuba diving. Home: 9350 Birchfield Way Lorton VA 22079-3440 Office: Dept of State AC/ST Washington DC 20520

FROBEL, RONALD KENNETH, geosynthetic engineer, consultant; b. Middletown, Conn., Oct. 10, 1946; s. Kenneth LeRoy and Hazel (Austin) Frobel; m. Rose M. Frobel; children: Elizabeth Ashley, Nicholas Alexander. AS in Archtl. Engring., Wentworth Inst. Tech., 1966; BS in Civil Engring., U. Ariz., 1969, MS in Geotech. Civil Engring., 1975. Registered profl. engr., Colo., Ariz. Civil engr. NE Utilities, Hartford, Conn., 1969-70; research engr. Engring. Experiment Sta. U. Ariz., Tucson, 1974-75, Water Resources Research Ctr., Tucson, 1975-77; materials engring. specialist U.S. Bur. Reclamation, Denver, 1978-85; tech. mgr. geosynthetics Polyfelt Ges. M.B.H., Denver and Linz, Austria, 1985-88; prin., cons. GeoSynthetics Cons. Inc., Evergreen, Colo., 1988—. Cons. Woodward-Clyde Cons., Chgo., 1982-85. Author: Geosynthetics Terminology, 1987, (with others) Polyfelt Design and Practice, 1987; co-editor: Hydraulic Barriers in Soil and Rock, 1985; editor spl. edit. jour. Geomembrane Quality Assurance, 1986; mem. editorial bd. Internat. Jour. Geotextiles and Geomembranes, 1986—, Geotech. Fabrics Report Mag., 1985—; contbr. over 70 articles to profl. jours. Lt. USN, 1970-73. Mem. ASCE, NSPE, Internat. Stds. Orgn. (U.S. rep.), Internat. Geosynthetics Soc., ASTM (com. chmn.), Internat. Soc. Soil Mechanics and Found. Engrs. Republican. Avocations: sailing, cycling, travel, woodworking, collecting coins and antiques. Office: 1153 Bergen Pky Ste M-240 Evergreen CO 80439-9501

FROBERG, BRENT MALCOLM, classics educator; b. Balt., Apr. 8, 1943; s. Lawrence Oscar and Ruth Louise (Lindner) F.; m. M. Gail Galloway, Feb. 27, 1970. BA, Ind. U., 1964, MA, 1965; PhD, Ohio State U., 1972. Instr. U. Tenn., Knoxville, 1968-69; asst. prof. U. S.D., Vermillion, 1970-74, assoc. prof., 1974-96. Vis. lectr. Baylor U., Waco, Tex., 2001—; cons. Medusa Nat. Mythology Exam, Nat. Greek Exam. Editor: (newsletter) Nuntius, 1978-96; writer Nat. Greek Exam., ATTIC, Level I, 1998-2000. Pres. Friends of the Libr., Vermillion, 1995-97, sec., 1997-99 Mem. Am. Philol. Assn. (award for excellence in tchg. 1994), Am. Classical League, Vergilian Soc. (membership chmn. 1990-94), Classical Assn. Mid. West & South (Ovatio award 1985, chair Manson Stewart scholarship com. 1998), Eta Sigma Phi (exec. sec. 1978-96, hon. life trustee). Avocations: crossword puzzles, travel. E-mail: Brent_Froberg@baylor.edu.

FROBOM, LEANN LARSON, lawyer; b. Ramona, S.D., May 31, 1953; d. Floyd Burdette and Janice Anne (Quist) L.; m. Richard Curtis Finke, May 19, 1973 (div. Jan. 1978); 1 child, Timothy; m. Dwayne Jeffery LaFave, May 31, 1981 (div. 1992); children: Jeffrey, Allison; m. Jerome B. Frobom, Aug. 21, 1999. BS, U. S.D., 1974, JD with honors, 1977. Bar: S.D. 1977, U.S. Dist. Ct. S.D. 1977, U.S. Ct. Appeals (8th cir.) 1977, N.D. 1978, U.S. Dist. Ct. N.D. 1978, Iowa 1998, Nebr. 2001. Asst. atty. gen. State of S.D., Pierre, 1977 78, 79-81; assoc. Bjella, Neff, Rathert & Wahl, Williston, N.D., 1978-79, Tobin Law Offices, P.C., Winner, S.D., 1981-83; assoc. dean, asst. prof. U. S.D. Sch. Law, Vermillion, 1983-86, dir. continuing legal edn., 1983-89, assoc. prof. law, 1986-89; ptnr. Aho & LaFave, Brookings, S.D., 1990-91; pvt. practice Brookings, 1991-92; asst. U.S. atty. U.S. Dist. Ct. S.D., 1992-97; gen. counsel S.D. Auto Group, Inc., Sioux Falls, 1997-98; atty. Hughes Law Offices, Sioux Falls, 1998-99, Cline Williams Wright Johnson & Oldfather, Lincoln, Nebr., 1999—; seasonal tax preparer H&R Block Co., 1999—. Mem. S.D. Bd. Pardons and Paroles, 1987-90, chmn., 1989-90; comml. arbitrator Am. Arbitration Assn., 1985-92; prof. Kilian C.C. Contbr. articles to profl. jours. Mem. planning coun. Nat. Identification Program for Advancement Women in Higher Edn. Adminstrn., Am. Coun. on Edn., S.D., 1984-90; bd. dirs. Mo. Shores Women's Resource Ctr., Pierre, 1980, W.H. Over Mus., Vermillion, 1986-87, S.D. Vol. Lawyers for Arts, 1987-92, Brookings Interagy. Coun., 1990-91, Brookings Women's Ctr., 1990-94; sec. Mediation Ctr., Inc. Named S.D. Woman Atty. of Yr. Women in Law U. S.D., 1985. Mem. Epsilon Sigma Alpha (S.D. coun. sect. 1985-86). Republican. Episcopalian. Avocation: reading. Home: 4911 High St Lincoln NE 68506 3970 Office: 1900 US Bank Bldg 233 S 13th St Lincoln NE 68508

FROCK, J. DANIEL, transportation executive, retired manufacturing company executive; b. Hanover, Pa., Mar. 10, 1940; s. Edmond Burnell and Rebecca Martha (Black) F.; m. Joanne Marie Klunk, Oct. 3, 1939; children: Carole A. Frederick, John D. Frock, Julie M. Crapster. Student, York Coll., 1958-59. Machine operator Hanover (Pa.) Wire Cloth Co., 1957-62, supt., 1962-65, plant mgr., 1965-72, v.p. mfg., 1972-89, v.p., gen. mgr., 1989-91, v.p. ops. Hanover, Pa. and Walterboro, S.C. plants, 1991-93; co-owner, pres., treas. Frock Bros. Trucking, Inc., New Oxford, Pa., 1985—. Bd. dirs. Hanover Bancorp. Charter mem. Hanover Area YMCA, 1972, bd. dirs.; deacon Emmanuel United Ch. of Christ, Hanover, 1973, elder, 1999-2002. Mem. Wire Assn. Internat. (25-yr. plaque 1992), Hanover Area C. of C., Hanover Area Indsl. Mgmt. Club (past officer), Elks. Republican. Avocations: walking, travel, family. Home: 309 Clearview Rd Hanover PA 17331-1313 Office: Frock Bros Trucking Inc PO Box 157 New Oxford PA 17350-0157 E-mail: danfrock@frockbros.com.

FROCK, SCOTT JOSEPH, music educator; b. Lafayette, Ind., Nov. 26, 1958; s. Joseph Raymond and Joline (Paradis) Frock. BA, U. Md., 1981, MusM, 1985; postgrad., U. North Tex., 1993. Teaching fellow in music U. North Tex., Denton, 1987—90; asst. prof. music Jarvis Christian Coll., Hawkins, Tex., 1995—96; instr. piano Brook Mays Music, Plano, Tex., 1996—, Piano Works, Lewisville, Tex., 1997—; instr. music appreciation North Ctrl. Tex. Coll., Corinth, 2001. Actor, singer Denton Cmty. Theater, 1985—; mem. choir Cath. Campus Ctr., Denton, 1985—. Roman Catholic. Avocations: swimming, cycling, jogging, movies, piano. Home: 2409 Charlotte St # 3 Denton TX 76201-5539 Office: Brook Mays Music Co 1729 N Central Expy Plano TX 75075 E-mail: sjf0001@unt.edu.

FROEBE, GERALD ALLEN, lawyer; b. The Dalles, Oreg., Feb. 16, 1935; s. Earl Wayne and Ethelene Alvina (Ogle) F.; m. Olivia Ann Tharaldson, Aug. 31, 1958; children: Dana Lynn, Heidi Ann. BBA, U. Oreg., 1956, LLB, 1961; LLM, NYU, 1962. Bar: N.Y. 1962, Oreg. 1962, U.S. Dist. Ct. Oreg. 1962. Auditor Arthur Andersen & Co., Seattle, 1956-58; lawyer, ptnr. Miller, Nash, Wiener, Hager & Carlsen, Portland, Oreg., 1962—99. Editor-in-chief Oreg. Law Rev., Eugene, 1960-61. Republican. Christian. Avocations: hiking, travel. Home: 1109 SW Ardmore Ave Portland OR 97205-1004 Office: 1109 SW Ardmore Ave Portland OR 97205

FROEBER, SARAH MARJORIE, actor, playwright, educator; b. Hollis, Okla., Dec. 15, 1946; d. Robert Jones and Marjorie Husband F.; m. John Peter Nussbaumer (div.); 1 child, Eric Robert Nussbaumer; m. Jeffrey Charles Lambdin, June 27, 1987. BA, Duke U., 1968; MA, Columbia U., 1969. Psychometrist Child Devel. Rsch. Project, N.Y.C., 1969-71; evaluator street acad. program N.Y. Urban League, N.Y.C., 1971-72; rsch. asst. Program Rsch. Media Assocs., N.Y.C., 1972-73, City Coll. N.Y., N.Y.C., 1973-74; instr. and dir. day care ctr. Vance-Granville C.C., Henderson, N.C., 1977-81; dir. day care ctr. Frank Porter Graham Child Devel. Ctr., Chapel Hill, N.C., 1981-84. Artistic dir., playwright Jelly Ednl. Theater, Carrboro, N.C., 1996-2000; playwright, dir. Scroggs Elem. Sch., Chapel Hill, N.C., 2000, McDougle Elem. Sch., Chapel Hill, 2000; instr. drama program Duke U., Durham, N.C., 1995—; bd. dirs. drama program Duke U., Durham; bd. dirs. Americal Corp., Henderson. Actor regional stage cos., film, radio, and audiotape, 1985—; author (play for children) Samuel and the Wishards, 1996, Melvin the Pelican, 1997, The Prince Who Was Afraid of Peanut Butter, 1997, The Great Nut Hunt, 1998, Wheelchair Dancer, 1999, Spiders on Strike, 2000, Getting Help, 2000, Dolphins and Grolphins and the Keys to Success, 2000, Lovely, Lovely, Lily Pad, 2000. Mem. SAG, Actors Equity Assn. Avocations: yoga, dancing, cross country skiing, singing. Home: PO Box 203 Buxton NC 27920 E-mail: froeber@mindspring.com.

FROEHLE, BRYAN THOMAS, sociologist, director; b. Cin., Dec. 13, 1964; s. Andrew Lee and Kathleen Prendergast Froehle; m. Mary Christman, June 7, 1986; 1 child, Thomas Francis. BS in Fgn. Svc., Georgetown U., 1986; MA in Sociology, U. Mich., 1989, PhD in Sociology, 1993. Lectr. U. Mich., Ann Arbor, Mich., 1987—89; vis. prof. U. Cath. Andrés Bello, Caracas, Venezuela, 1990—91; rsch. assoc. Centro de Investigación, Caracas, 1990—91; asst. prof. U. SC, Spartanburg, 1992—95; sr. rsch. assoc. Ctr. Applied Rsch. in the Apostolate Georgetown U., Washington, 1995—98, exec. dir. Ctr. for Applied Rsch. in the Apostolate, 1998—. Rsch. assoc. prof. Georgetown U., 1998—; bd. dir. Loyola Press, Chgo. Author: A Century and A Half, 1982, Catholicism USA, 2000, Global Catholicism, 2002; contbr. articles to profl. jours. Grantee, NSF, 1989, Interamerica Found., 1995. Mem.: Am. Assn. Pub. Opinion Rsch., Am. Sociol. Assn., Assn. Sociology of Religion (program chmn. 1998—99). Avocations: travel, reading. Home: 3318 19th Street NW Washington DC 20010 Office: CARA 2300 Wisconsin Ave NW Washington DC 20007

FROEHLICH, CONRAD GERALD, museum director, researcher; b. Mpls., Oct. 22, 1958; s. Gerald William and Marie Diane Froehlich; m. Judy Marie Froehlich, Sept. 18, 1995. BA in Anthropology, Classical Humanities and Sociology, Miami U. of Ohio, 1981, MA in Anthropology, 1983. Mus. asst., archaeologist Anthropology Mus. Miami U. of Ohio, 1977-88; mus. dir. Martin and Osa Johnson Safari Mus., Chanute, Kans., 1989—. Spkr. prol. confs.; appeared on ESPN2, History Channel; rschr. Borneo and Kenya. Reviewer: A Museum Guide to Copyright and Trademark, 1999, American Film Institute Catalog of Motion Pictures: Feature Films, 1931-40, 1993; contbr. articles to profl. jours. Trustee Elefence Internat., Cleve., 1998—. Recipient commendation cert. Am. Assn. for State and Local History, 1993; grante Inst. Mus. and Libr. Svcs., Washington, 1995-97, 98-2000, 2000-02. Mem. Am. Anthropol. Assn., Am. Assn. Mus. (lic. and intellectual property coms. 1996-97, 98-99, nat. mus. field rep. for mus. and cmty. initiative 2000-01, Nancy Hanks Meml. award for profl. excellence 1996), Am. Zoo and Aquarium Assn., Internat. Coun. Mus., Kans. Mus. Assn. (conf. spkr. 1998, 99, arrangements chair 1998, ann. mtg. chair 2001, awards com. 1995, 98, v.p. 2000-02, pres. 2002—). Coun. for Mus. Anthropology, Rotary, Mtn.-Plains Mus. Assn. (bd. dirs. 2002—, mem. program com. 2002). Avocations: photography, documentaries, military history, classic films, travel. Office: Martin and Osa Johnson Safari Mus 111 N Lincoln Ave Chanute KS 66720-1819

FROEHLICH, FRITZ EDGAR, communications educator, telecommunications scientist; b. Worms am Rhine, Hesse, Germany, Nov. 12, 1925; arrived in U.S., 1938; s. Julius and Ida (Heilborn) Froehlich; m. Eileen Karch, Dec. 25, 1949; children: Laurence Alan, Georgine K. Froehlich Scharff, Philip Marc. BS in Physics magna cum laude, Syracuse U., 1950, MS in Physics, 1952, PhD in Physics, 1955. Rsch. asst. Syracuse (N.Y.) U., 1950-54; asst. instr. Utica (N.Y.) Coll., 1952-54; with AT&T Bell Labs., 1954-87, tech. staff, 1954-56, supr. data transmission divsn. Murray Hill, NJ, 1956-63, head data theory dept. Holmdel, NJ, 1963-68, head telecom. and data sys. dept., 1968-83; head univ. relations AT&T Info. Sys. and Comm., Lincroft, NJ, 1983-87; prof. telecom. U. Pitts., 1987—2002. Mem. adv. bd. Ctr. Info. and Comm. Scis. Ball State U., Muncie, Ind., 1987—93; nat. telecom adv. coun. U. Pitts., 1992—93. Editor-in-chief: Ency. Telecom., 1988—2000, sr. editor: IEEE Trans. Comm., 1988—94; contbr. articles to profl. jours. Trustee Congl. B'nai Israel, Rumson, NJ, 1970—84, v.p. congregation, 1974—76; v.p. bd. dirs. Isles of Tamarac Homeowners Assn., 1992—2001, pres., 2001—02. With U.S. Army, 1944—46. Named Ann. Fritz Froehlich award in his honor, U. Pitts. Sch. Info. Sci., 1992—; recipient Hon. Alumnus award, Pitts. U., 1992. Fellow: IEEE (chmn. N.J. Coast sect. 1970, mem. data com., trans. sys. com. 1960—95, chmn. comms. terminal com. 1981—84, mem. multimedia, svcs. and terminals com. 1981—89, mem. awards bd. 1992—95), Comm. Soc. IEEE; mem.: Jewish War Vets., Phi Beta Kappa, Pi Mu Epsilon, Sigma Xi Sigma (pres. Syracuse U. chpt. 1949). Achievements include patents in field. Home: 10621 NW 71 Ct Tamarac FL 33321-2215 Office: 743 Slis Bldg 135 N Bellefield Ave Pittsburgh PA 15213-2609 E-mail: fefroehlich@att.net.

FROEHLICH, HAROLD VERNON, judge, former congressman; b. Appleton, Wis., May 12, 1932; s. Vernon W. and Lillian F.; m. Sharon F. Ross, Nov. 20, 1970; children: Jeffrey Scott, Michael Ross. BBA, U. Wis., 1959, LLB, 1962. Bar: Wis. 1962. Staff acct. Ruschlien & Stortreon, CPAs, Madison, Wis., 1958-62; practiced in Appleton, 1962-81; judge Circuit Ct., 1981—; dep. chief judge 8th Jud. Dist. Wis., 1983-85, spl. dep. chief judge, 1985-88, chief judge, 1988-94; sec. Wis. Judicial Conf., 1991-97; mem. Wis. Ho. of Reps., 1963-73, speaker, 1967-71, minority floor leader, 1971-73; mem. 93d Congress from 8th Dist., Wis.; v.p. Black Creek Improvement Corp., Outagamie County Family Ct. Commn., 1975-78. Chmn. Com. Chief Judges, 1992—94; chief adminstrn. judge Outagamie County, 1983—88, 1994—. Rep. precinct committeeman 19th ward, Appleton, 1956-62; chmn. Outagamie County Rep. Statutory Com., 1958-62; sec. Assembly Rep. Caucus, 1965-66; bd. regents Fox Valley Luth. H.S., Appleton, 1990-93. With USN, 1951-55. Mem. ABA, Am. Judges Assn. (bd. govs. 1997-99, asst. treas. 1998-99, treas. 1999—), Wis. Bar Assn., Outagamie County Bar Assns., Wis. Assn. Trial Judges (pres. 1991-2000), Am. Legion, VFW (judge adv. 1963-75, 82-99), Assn. Trial Judges in Wis. (sec. 1984-91, pres. 1991-00), Midwest Coun. State Govts. (vice chmn. 1968-69, chmn. 1969-70), Coun. State Govts. (nat. exec. com. 1970-72), Phi Alpha Delta. Office: 410 S Walnut St Appleton WI 54911-5920 E-mail: harold.froehlich@outagamie.courts.state.wi.us.

FROEHLKE, ROBERT FREDERICK, financial services executive; b. Neenah, Wis., Oct. 15, 1922; s. Herbert O. and Lillian (Porath) F.; m. Nancy Jean Barnes, Nov. 9, 1946; children: Bruce, Jane, Ann, Scott. LL.B., U. Wis., 1949. Bar: Wis. 1949. Assoc. firm McDonald & MacDonald, Madison, 1949-50; mem. faculty U. Wis. Law Sch., 1950-51; with Sentry Ins. Co., 1951-69, exec. v.p., 1968-69; asst. sec. def. for adminstrn. Washington, 1969-71; sec. of army, 1971-73; pres. Sentry Corp., 1973-75, Health Ins. Assn. Am., 1976-80, Am. Council of Life Ins., 1980-82; chmn. bd. Equitable Life Assurance Soc. U.S., 1983-87; pres. IDS Mutual Fund Group, 1987-93. Bd. dirs. Laird Youth Leadership Found.; mem. nat. adv. coun. Marshfield (Wis.) Clinic. Capt. AUS, 1943-46. Mem. Order of Coif, Psi Upsilon. Republican. Presbyterian.

FROEHLY, BERTRAM MARTIN, JR., neurologist; b. St. Louis, Aug. 26, 1947; s. Bertram Martin and Elaine E. (Bost) F.; married; children: Brittany, Courtney. BS with honors in biology, Tulane U., 1969; MD, Cornell U., 1973. Diplomate Am. Bd. Neurology, Am. Bd. Psychiatry and Neurology, Am. Bd. Internal Medicine. Cons. neurologist Riverside (Calif.) Med. Clinic, 1979—. Chmn. bioethics com. Parkview Cmty. Hosp., Riverside, 1995—. Mem. AMA, Am. Acad. Neurology, Calif. Med. Assn., Riverside County Med. Assn., L.A. Acad. of Medicine, Victoria Club. Avocations: golf, astronomy, camping, tennis, chess. Office: Riverside Med Clinic 3660 Arlington Ave Riverside CA 92506-3912

FROELICH, BEVERLY LORRAINE, foundation director; b. Vancouver, B.C., Can., Oct. 23, 1948; came to U.S., 1968; d. Kenneth Martin and Ethel Pulham; m. Eugene Leonard Froelich, Dec. 26, 1971; children: Craig, Grant. Cert. in fundraising, U. So. Calif., 1986; profl. designation in pub. rels., UCLA, 1987. Cert. fund raising exec. Contract analyst Universal Studios, Calif., 1968-71; exec. dir. Olive View, UCLA Med. Ctr. Found., Sylmar, Calif., 1987—. Pres. Beverly Froelich Pub. Rels., Sherman Oaks, Calif., 1988-90; prin. Tracy Susman & Co., Sherman Oaks, 1986-88. Co-author: (program) Overcoming Chronic Arthritis Pain, 1989; contbg. writer hosp. earthquake preparedness guidelines Hosp. Coun. So. Calif., 1991. Founder San Fernando Valley br. Arthritis Found., Encino, 1983, pres., 1983-87, mktg. com.; bd. dirs. health care com. Valley Industry and Commerce Assn. Recipient Nat. Vol. Svc. award Arthritis Found., 1986, Jane Wyman Humanitarian award Arthritis Found., 1991, Disting. Svc. award Arthritis Found., 1990, Marilyn Magaram award for Cmty. Svc., 1997. Mem.: Assn. Fundraising Profls. (pres. San Fernando Valley chpt., Fundraising Profl. of Yr. 2000, Fundraising Profl. of Yr.), Valley Industry and Commerce Assn., UCLA Alumni Assn. Avocations: hockey, music. Office: Olive View Med Ctr Found Cottage J2 14445 Olive View Dr Sylmar CA 91342-1437

FROELICH, ROBIN ANN, systems analyst, educator; b. Salisbury, Md., June 1, 1963; d. Ralph Nathaniel and Mary Esther (Norwood) Krum; m. Richard Paul Froelich, Aug. 25, 1991. BS, Columbia Union Coll., 1985; MBA, Am. U., 1989. Mktg. dir. adult eve. program Columbia Union Coll., Takoma Park, Md., 1985-87; grad. asst. Am. U., Washington, 1987-89; sys. cons. The Orkand Corp., Silver Spring, Md., 1989—. Mem. Am. Soc. Tng. and Devel. Mem. Seventh Day Adventist Ch. Avocations: piano, choral/vocal performance, gardening. Office: The Orkand Corp 7799 Leesburg Pike Ste 700 Falls Church VA 22043-2413

FROEMMING, HERBERT DEAN, retired retail executive; b. Alexandria, Minn., Aug. 19, 1936; s. Herbert Edward and Bertha Anna (Hink) F.; m. Mary Louise Gapinski, Sept. 2, 1961; children— Mark, Traci, Scott. BBA, U. Minn., 1959; MBA, U. Mo. CPA, Minn. Fin. exec. The Kroger Co., various locations, 1960-69; exec. v.p. E.F. MacDonald Shopping Bag, L.A., 1969-73; also dir.; v.p., treas., dir. Western Auto Supply Co., Kansas City, Mo., 1973-78; sr. corp. v.p., controller Gamble-Skogmo Co., Mpls., 1978-80; exec. v.p. Red Owl Food Stores, Inc., 1980-84; v.p. Sullivan Assocs., Inc., 1985-88; sr. v.p.-adminstr., chief fin. officer Braun's Fashions Inc., Plymouth, Minn., 1989-94, pres., COO, 1994-97, vice chmn., 1997-98; chmn., CEO Millennium Plastics Tech., LLC, El Paso, Tex., 1999-2000. Served with AUS, 1955-57. Home: 104 Coventry Ln Edina MN 55435-5634

FROESCHNER, JOHN R. federal judge; b. 1950; BA, Elmhurst Coll., 1972; JD, U. Mo., 1976. Bar: Tex. 1976, U.S. Dist. Ct. (so. dist.) Tex. 1980, U.S. Ct. Appeals (5th cir.) 1985. Pvt. practice, Galveston, Tex., 1977-91; magistrate judge U.S. Dist. Ct. (so. dist.) Tex., Galveston, 1991—. Office: US Dist Ct (so dist) Tex 601 Rosenberg St Fl 5 Galveston TX 77550-1799 Fax: 409-5766-3549.

FROGGE, BEVERLY ANN, nurse, consultant; b. Wichita, Kans., Jan. 1, 1943; d. Owen Elba Frogge and Maudie Frances (Gillette) Surber; m. Jake C. Saubers (sept. 5, 1967 (div. May 1989); 1 child, Jeff Lee. Student, So. Meth. U., 1960-61, St. Mary of Plains Coll., 1961-62; diploma in nursing, Wichita-St. Joseph Hosp., 1964; student, UCLA, 1965. RN, Kans.; cert. health facility surveyor. Instr. LPN Program Neosho C.C., 1970-73; pub. health nurse Woodson Co., Yates Ctr., Kans., 1973-75; health facility surveyor Kans. Dept. Health and Environ., Topeka, 1975-77; nursing dir. Neosho Meml. Hosp., Chanute, Kans., 1977-84, Regency Health Care Ctr., Yates Ctr., 1985-89; psychiatric nurse VA Med. Ctr., Topeka, 1989-98; ret., 1998. Dir. Neosho Meml. Hosp. Home Health Agy., Chanute, 1977-84; instr. Disaster Preparedness, Yates Ctr., 1973-75; cons. in field, 1975-77. Author: (textbook) Anatomy & Physiology Medical Treatment, 1965-67; contbg. author: (poetry) National Anthology of College Poetry, 1961; radio presenter weekly broadcast, 1978-84. Founder, dir., instr. Dresser Sch. U.S. Peace Corps, Makele, Ethiopia, 1965-67, spkr., 1967; adv. com. mem. Vocat. Edn. State Kans., Neosho C.C., Chanute, 1980-81. Avocations: music, writing, hiking, canoeing, painting. Home: 1907 W 24th Ave Apt 13A Emporia KS 66801

FROHLICH, ANTHONY WILLIAM, lawyer, master commissioner; b. Covington, Ky., Dec. 8, 1954; s. Kenneth Raymond and Joan Jude (Laake) F.; m. Candace Powell Robbins, May 31, 1975; children: Kenneth Zane, Matthew Andrew. BS, No. Ky. U., 1976, JD, 1980. Bar: Ky. 1980, U.S. Dist. Ct. (ea. dist.) Ky. 1981. Staff atty. Boone County (Ky.) Child Support Program, 1980-97; city atty. City of Walton, 1980-89; master commr. Boone County Cir. Ct., Burlington, Ky., 1989—; asst. commonwealth atty. 54th Jud. Dist., Burlington, Ky., 1984-89; ptnr. Mathis, Dallas & Frohlich, Florence, Ky., 1980-96, Law Office of Anthony W. Frohlich, Florence, Ky., 1996—. Pres. Soccer Tech., Union, Ky., 1994. Bd. dirs. No. Ky. Soccer Club, Florence, 1994; state coach Ky. Youth Soccer, 1994-96; coaching dir. Ky. Olympic Devel. Program Dist. One, Florence, 1992-94; soccer coach DHL USA men's nat. team, 2000-2001; active Union Town Plan Steering Com., 1999; bd. dirs. Greater Cin. Consumer Credit Counseling, 1999-2002; nominating chmn. Boy Scouts Am., 1999--; mem. steering com. Boone County Parks & Recreation, 2000—. Named Coach of Yr., No. Ky. Soccer Club, 1992. Mem. ATLA, Ky. Bar Assn., Boone County Bar Assn. (treas. 1980), Ky. Acad. Trial Lawyers. Roman Catholic. Avocations: coaching soccer, basketball. Home: 9253 Us Highway 42 Union KY 41091-9470 Office: Law Office Anthony Frohlich PO Box 396 Florence KY 41022-0396 E-mail: awfpsc42@fuse.net.

FROHLICH, EDWARD DAVID, medical educator; b. N.Y.C., Sept. 10, 1931; s. William and May (Zneimer) F.; m. Sherry Linda Fine, Nov. 1, 1959; children: Marjorie, Bruce, Lara. BA, Washington and Jefferson Coll., 1952; MD, U. Md., 1956; MS, Northwestern U., 1963; DSc (hon.), U. Buenos Aires, 2001. Diplomate Am. Bd. Internal Medicine. Intern, resident D.C. Gen. Hosp., 1956-58; resident Georgetown U. Hosp., Washington, 1958—60; clin. investigator VA Rsch. Hosp., Chgo., 1962-64; assoc. in medicine Northwestern U., 1963-64; staff mem. rsch. divsn. Cleve. Clinic, 1964-69; prof. medicine, physiology and biophysics U. Okla., Oklahoma City, 1969-76, George Lynn Cross rsch. prof., 1975-76; prof. medicine and physiology La. State U., 1976—; clin. prof. medicine, adj. prof. pharmacology Tulane U., 1976—. Cons. FDA, 1971—74, VA, 1972—, NIH, 1972—2003, WHO, 1975—82, U.S. Pharmacopeia, 1975—96; gov. La. Am. Col. Cardiology, 1988—91, bd. trustees, 1991—92, 1996—2000; assoc. editor Am. Jour. Physiology, Heart Circulation, 2003—. Editor: Pathophysiology-Altered Regulatory Mechanisms in Disease, 1972, 1976, 1984, Rypins' Medical Licensure Examinations, 13th - 18th edits., 1981—2001, Rypins' Intensive Revs., 13 vols., 1996, Take Heart, 1990, Hypertension: Evaluation and Treatment, 1998; editor-in-chief: jours. Jour. Lab. and Clin. Medicine, 1974—76, Hypertension, 1994—2002; mem. editl. bd. (jours.) Am. Jour. Cardiology, 1982—91, Circulation, 1978—91, Archives of Internal Medicine, 1978—88, Modern Medicine, 1980—2000, Jour. Hypertension, 1994—2003; contbr. chapters to books, articles to profl. jours. Capt. U.S. Army, 1960-62. Cardiovascular Rsch. fellow Georgetown U. Hosp., 1958-59; recipient Honors Achievement award Angiology Rsch. Found., 1964, So. Med. Assn. Annual award, 1971, award of Merit Am. Heart Assn., 1986, Lifetime Achievement award Coun. for High Blood Pressure Rsch., Am. Heart Assn., 1994, Okamoto Internat. award for Hypertension Rsch., 1994. Master ACP (laureate 1996); hon. fellow, Royal Coll. Physicians, Glasgow, 2003, fellow AAAS, Am. Coll. Cardiology, Coun. for High Blood Pressure Rsch. (exec. com. 1972-75, 81-85, vice chmn. 1986-88, chmn. 1989-91)); mem. Internat. Soc. Hypertension (sci. coun. 1974-84, treas. 1980-82, v.p. 1982-84, Astra award 2000), Am. Heart Assn. (dir. La. chpt. 1979-83, chmn. Coun. High Blood Pressure Rsch. 1988-91, award of Merit 1986, Lifetime Achievement award 1993, Okamoto Internat. award 1993), Inter-Am. Soc. Hypertension (Lifetime Achievement award 1999), Soc. Geriatric Cardiology (pres. 2000-01), Am. Soc. Clin. Investigation, Am. Soc. Pharmacology and Exptl. Therapeutics, Am. Soc. Clin. Pharmacology and Therapeutics (past pres.), Am. Physiol. Soc., Am. Soc. Nephrology, Ctrl. Soc. for Clin. Rsch., So. Soc. for Clin. Rsch., Am. Soc. Clin. Investigations, Assn. Am. Physicians, Peruvian Soc. Cardiology, Columbian Soc. Cardiology, Polish Acad. Arts Sci. (faculty medicine), Chi Epsilon Mu, Phi Sigma, Alpha Kappa Alpha. Office: Ochsner Clinic Found 1516 Jefferson Hwy New Orleans LA 70121-2429

FROHLICH, JACK T. lawyer, computer educator, consultant; b. Bklyn., Feb. 18, 1950; s. Arthur Joseph and Florence Helen (Toppel) F.; m. Gladys Yvette Bravo, Nov. 25, 1971 (div. 1980): m. Susan Anna Christiano, Jan. 17, 1989; 1 child, Arthur William. BA, SUNY, Stony Brook, 1973; cert. labor rels., New Sch. Social Rsch., 1986; JD, N.Y. Law Sch., 1993. Bar: N.Y., 1994, N.J., 1995, Calif., 1995. Class B counterman Pudlin Auto Supply, Bronx, N.Y., 1973-74; trackman N.Y.C. Transit Authority, 1974-80, 82-84, track inspector, 1984-85, safety insp., 1980-81, 86 94. Shop steward Internat. Brotherhood Teamsters Local 239, N.Y.C., 1973, Transport Workers Union Local 100, N.Y.C., vice chmn. track divsn., 1980-81, 86-90, dir. ops., 1986-90, rec. sec., 1990-94, adminstrv. dir. union assistance program, 1995-96, staff rep., 1996-98; guest lectr. NYU, 1990-93; lectr. Empire State Coll., SUNY, 1997-99; computer tchr. Thomas Edison Elem. Sch., Daly City, Calif., 2000—. Exec. bd. Community Free Dems., N.Y.C., 1989-90; commr. deeds office city clk. City of N.Y., 1989-96; v.p. Student Bar Assn., N.Y. Law Sch., 1990-92. Mem. ABA, ACLU, Nat. Lawyers Guild. Jewish. Avocations: science fiction, historical novels. Home: Apt 12L 350 Arballo Dr San Francisco CA 94132-2168

FROHLICHSTEIN, ALAN, retinal angiographer; b. Fort Wayne, Ind., Oct. 31, 1953; s. Ben and Juliana Rose (Levey) F.; m. F. Diane Willett, Sept. 2, 1984. BFA, Ohio U., 1975; AS, Rochester (N.Y.) Inst. Tech., 1976, BS, 1977; cert. completion, Rsch. and Holographic Ctr., Chgo., 1983. Intern U. Chgo., 1976; med. photographer Luth. Gen. Hosp., Niles, Ill., 1977-80; cert. retinal angiog-

rapher Wilder & Vygantas MD, Ltd., Niles, 1980-84, C.M. Vygantas MD, Ltd., Des Plaines, Ill., 1984-89; pres. Retinal Angiography Svcs., Morton Grove, Ill., 1989-99. Adj. faculty Triton Coll., River Grove, Ill., 1988-99; lectr. Joint Commn. on Allied Pers. in Ophthalmology; instr. Soc. of Ophthalmic Med. Assts. in Chgo. Ann. Rev. Course, 1991—. Contbg. editor: Jour. Ophthalmic Photography, 1988—; contbr. articles to profl. jours., jour. cover; inventor anaglyphic stereo projection sys. for ophthalmology. Recipient Med. Edn. award Biol. Photographic Assn., 1992. Fellow Soc. Ophthalmic Med. Assts. in Chgo. (treas. 1996—), Ophthalmic Photographers Soc. (elected, bd. dirs. 1994-98, 2000—, v.p. 1984-86, treas. 1998-2000, chmn. sci. exhibit 1988-89, ethics com. 1990—, cert. pres. Chgo. chpt. 1981—, workshop instr. 1983—); mem. Fine Arts Rsch. and Holographic Ctr. Alumni Assn. (charter v.p. 1990—), Mensa, Am. Acad. Ophthalmology (Honor award 1993), Soc. Opthalmic Med. Assts. in Chicago (treas. 1997—). Avocations: holography, theater, movies, music, art.

FROHMAN, LARRY PHILIP, neuro-ophthalmologist; b. N.Y.C., July 14, 1955; s. Peter and Arlene Joan (Horowitz) F.; m. Judith Anne Levy, July 9, 1978; children: Daniel, Charles. BA in Biology, Swarthmore Coll., 1976; MD, U. Pa., 1980. Intern Presbyn.-U. Pa. Med. Ctr., Phila., 1980-1; resident in ophthalmology NYU-Bellevue, 1981-84; fellow in neuro-ophthalmology NYU-Bellevue and N.Y. Eye and Ear Infirmary, 1984-85; assoc. prof. ophthalmology and neurology N.J. Med. Sch., 1992—, vice chair ophthalmolgoy, 1992—, chief neuro-ophthalmology, 1992—. Hunter GruBB scholar, 1976-80. Mem. AMA, Am. Acad. Ophthalmology (Honor award 1995), N.Am. Neuro-Ophthalmology Soc. (pres.-elect), Sigma Xi. Avocations: cooking, photography, mineral and tie collecting. E-mail: LPF2584@aol.com.

FROHMAN, LAWRENCE ASHER, endocrinology educator, scientist; b. Detroit, Jan. 26, 1935; s. Dan and Rebecca (Katzman) F.; m. Barbara Hecht, June 9, 1957; children: Michael, Marc, Erica, Rena. MD, U. Mich., 1958. Diplomate: Am. Bd. Internal Medicine. Intern Yale-New Haven Med. Ctr., 1958—59, resident in internal medicine, 1959—61; asst. prof. medicine SUNY, Buffalo, 1965—69, assoc. prof., 1969—73, prof. medicine U. Chgo., 1973—81; dir. endocrinology Michael Reese Hosp., Chgo., 1973—81; prof., dir. div. endocrinology and metabolism U. Cin., 1981—92; prof. medicine U. Ill., Chgo., 1992—, chmn. Dept. Medicine, 1992—2001; dir. Med. Svcs. U. Ill. Hosp., Chgo., 1992—2001. Dir. Gen. Clin. Rsch. Ctr., 1986-90; mem. sci. rev. com. NIH, Bethesda, Md., 1972-76; mem. sci. rev. bd. VA, Washington, 1979-82; mem. endocrine adv. bd. FDA, Washington, 1982-86; mem. adv. com. Nat. Inst. Diabetes, Digestive and Kidney Diseases, NIH, 1983-94, chmn., 1991-93; mem. sci. adv. bd. Edison Biotech. Inst., Ohio U. Editor: (with others) Endocrinology and Metabolism, 2001; editl. bd. 7 med. and sci. jours., 1970—; contbr. articles to profl. jours. NIH research grantee, 1967-98, Endocrine Soc. Rorer Clin. Investigator award, 1991. Mem.: ACP, Am. Clin. Climatological Assn., Pituitary Soc., Internat. Soc. Neuroendocrinology, Am. Diabetes Assn., Am. Soc. Clin. Investigation, Assn. Am. Physicians, Endocrine Soc. Office: U Ill at Chgo Section Endocrinology M/C 640 1819 W Polk St Chicago IL 60612-7333 E-mail: frohman@uic.edu.

FROHNMAYER, DAVID BRADEN, academic administrator; b. Medford, Oreg., July 9, 1940; s. Otto J. and MarAbel (Braden) F.; m. Lynn Diane Johnson, Dec. 30, 1970; children: Kirsten (dec.), Mark, Kathryn (dec.), Jonathan, Amy. AB magna cum laude, Harvard U., 1962; BA, Oxford (Eng.) U., 1964, MA (Rhodes scholar), 1971; JD, U. Calif., Berkeley, 1967; LLD (hon.), Willamette U., 1988; D Pub. Svc. (hon.), U. Portland, 1989. Bar: Calif. 1967, U.S. Dist. Ct. (no. dist.) Calif. 1967, Oreg. 1971, U.S. Dist. Ct. Oreg. 1971, U.S. Supreme Ct. 1981. Assoc. Pillsbury, Madison & Sutro, San Francisco, 1967-69; asst. to sec. Dept. HEW, 1969-70; prof. law U. Oreg., 1971-81, spl. asst. to univ. pres., 1971-79; atty. gen. State of Oreg., 1981-91; dean Sch. Law U. Oreg., 1992-94, pres., 1994—. Chmn. Conf. Western Attys. Gen., 1985-86; chmn. Am. Coun. Edn. Govtl. Rels. commn, 1996-98; bd. dirs. Umpqua Holding Co. Mem. Oreg. Ho. of Reps, 1975-81; mem. coun. pub. reps. NIH, 1999-2000; bd. dirs. Fred Hutchinson Cancer Rsch. Ctr., 1994-2000, Nat. Marrow Donor Program, 1987-99, Fanconi Anemia Rsch. Fund, Inc., Tax Free Trust of Oreg. Fund; active Oreg. Progress Bd. Recipient awards Weaver Constl. Law Essay competition Am. Bar Found., 1972, 74, Advocacy award Research!Am., 1999, Albert B. Sabin Heroes of Sci. award Ams. for Med. Progress Ednl. Found., 2000; Rhodes scholar, 1962. Fellow Am. Acad. Arts and Scis.; mem. ABA (Ross essay winner 1980), Oreg. Bar Assn., Calif. Bar Assn., Nat. Assn. Attys. Gen. (pres. 1987, Wyman award 1987), Round Table Eugene, Order of Coif, Phi Beta Kappa, Rotary. Republican. Presbyterian. Home: 2315 McMorran St Eugene OR 97403-1750 Office: U Oreg Johnson Hall Office Pres Eugene OR 97403 E-mail: pres@oregon.uoregon.edu.

FROHNMAYER, JOHN EDWARD, lawyer, legal scholar, ethicist, writer; b. Medford, Oreg., June 1, 1942; s. Otto J. and Marabel (Braden) F.; m. Leah Thorpe, June 10, 1967; children: Jason Otto, Jonathan Aaron. BA in Am. History, Stanford U., 1964; MA in Christian Ethics, U. Chgo., 1969; JD, U. Oreg., 1972. Bar: Oreg. 1972, Mont. 1995. Assoc. Johnson, Harrang & Mercer, Eugene, Oreg., 1972-75; ptnr. Tonkon, Torp, Galen, Marmaduke & Booth, Portland, Oreg., 1975-89; 5th chmn. Nat. Endowment for the Arts, Washington, 1989-92; writer, lectr. on art, ethics and politics, 1992—; pvt. practice, 1972-89, 1995—. Mem. Oreg. Arts Commn., 1978-85, chmn., 1980-84; bd. dirs. Internat. Sculpture Symposium, eugene, 1974; chmn. screening com. Oreg. State Capitol Bldg., 1977. Author: Leaving Town Alive, 1993, Out of Tune: Listening to The First Amendment, 1994; editor-in-chief Oreg. Law Rev., 1971-72; singer; appeared in recital, oratorio, mus. comedy and various other mus. prodns. Trustee Holladay Park Pla.; founding mem. chamber choir Novum Cantorum; bd. dirs. Chamber Music Northwest, Western States Arts Found.; mem. Nat. Endowment for the Arts Opera-Mus. Theater, 1982, 83. With USN, 1966-69. Sr. fellow Freedom Forum, 1993; recipient People for the Am. Way Ann. 1st Amendment award, 1992, Oreg. Gov. Arts award, 1993, Intellectual Freedom award Mont. Libr. Assn., 1997, Citation of Merit, Mu Phi Epsilon, 1998. Fellow Am. Leadership Forum; mem. ABA (com. comml. transactions litigation), Oreg. State Bar Assn. (chmn. bar com. domestic law 1975-76, procedure and practice com. 1984-85), Multnomah County Bar Assn., City Club Portland (bd. dirs.), Sta. L. Rowing Club (sec.), Order of the Coif (legal hon. 1972). Home and Office: 14080 Lone Bear Rd Bozeman MT 59715-6620 E-mail: frohn@wtp.net.

FROHOCK, FRED MANUEL, political science educator; b. Perry, Fla., Feb. 7, 1937; s. Fred Clifton and Marie Antonia (Domenech) F.; m. Val Jean Derrick, Sept. 7, 1963; children— Katherine Renee, Christina Marie BA, U. Fla., 1960, MA, 1961; PhD, U. N.C., 1966. Asst. prof. polit. sci. Syracuse U., N.Y., 1965-68, assoc. prof., 1968-74, prof., 1974—, chmn. dept. polit. sci., 1985-89, prof. Florence program, 1969-70, prof., chmn. Madrid program, 1972-74, prof., chmn. London Politics Seminar, 1984—. Author: Nature of Political Inquiry, 1967, Normative Political Theory, 1974, Public Policy, 1979, Abortion: A Case Study in Law and Morals, 1983, Special Care: Medical Decisions at the Beginning of Life, 1986, Rational Association, 1987, Healing Powers, 1992, Public Reason: Mediated Authority in the Liberal State, 1999, Lives of the Psychics: The Shared Worlds of Science and Mysticism, 2000; contbr. numerous articles to profl. jours. Social Sci. Research Council fellow, 1964-65, 67-68; NEH summer fellow, 1988. Democrat. Roman Catholic. Avocations: golf, watching baseball. Home: 4448 Kasson Rd Syracuse NY 13215-9616 Office: Syracuse U Polit Sci Dept Syracuse NY 13244-0001

FROILAND, KATHRYN GRACE, nursing educator; d. Phyllis June and Alfred Wilhelm Froiland. BSN, St. Olaf Coll., Northfield, Minn., 1979; MSN, U. Tex., Houston, 1994. Cert. Wound Ostomy Continence Nursing Soc., 2000, Oncology Nursing Soc., 2001. Asst. head nurse, sta. instr., charge nurse, staff nurse U. Minn. Hosps. and Clinics, Mpls., 1979—88; asst. head nurse Meth. Hosp., Mpls., 1988—89; hospice nurse Mayo Clinic Found., Rochester, Minn., 1989—91; sr. nursing instr. U. Tex. MD Anderson Cancer Ctr., Houston, 1991—94, sr. wound ostomy continence nurse, 1995—2001, program dir./mgr. of wound ostomy continence nurse edn. program, 2001—03; oncology clin. nurse educator Glaxo Smith Kline, 2003—. Vol. Am. Cancer Soc., Houston, Tex., 1991—2003. Named WOCN of the Yr., South Ctrl. Region of the Wound Ostomy Continence Nursing Soc., 2001; recipient Excellence in Patient Care & Clin. Edn. award, MD Anderson Gynecologic Oncology Fellows Class of 2000, 2000, Excellence in Clin. Care award, NurseWeek, 2001, Disting. Alumna award, U. Tex.-Houston Sch. of Nursing, 2002. Mem.: Oncology Nursing Soc. (Houston chpt. sec., pres.-elect, pres., bd. dirs. 1995—2000, Mary Mazzaway Scholarship award 2000), Wound Ostomy Continence Nursing Soc., Sigma Theta Tau. Dfl. Lutheran. Avocations: reading, travel, biking, sewing.

FROLICK, PATRICIA MARY, retired elementary school educator; b. Portland, Oreg., May 17, 1923; d. Fred Anthony and Clara Cecelia (Riverman) F. BS in Edn., Marylhurst Coll., 1960; MS in Edn., Portland State U., 1970; student, U. Oreg., 1975; MA in Theology, St. Mary's Coll., Moraga, Calif., 1977. Joined Roman Cath. Order Sisters of Holy Names of Jesus and Mary, 1943. Left order in 1974. Elem. sch. tchr. Catholic Sch. System, Oreg., 1943-69; tchr., libr. Hood River Pub. Schs., 1970-74, Bend-La Pine (Oreg.) Pub. Schs., 1981-93; ret., 1993. Part-time tchr.'s asst., Portland, 1993—2000. Mem. NEA, Oreg. Edn. Assn., Met. Mus. Art (assoc.), Nat. Mus. Women in Arts (charter). Democrat. Roman Catholic. Avocation: watercolor and oil painting. Home: 3465 SE 153rd Ave Portland OR 97236-2265

FROMAN, SANDRA SUE, lawyer; b. San Francisco, June 15, 1949; d. Jay and Beatrice Froman. AB with honors, Stanford U., 1971; JD, Harvard U., 1974. Bar: Calif. 1974, U.S. Dist. Ct. (cen. dist.) Calif. 1974, U.S. Dist. Ct. (so. dist.) Calif. 1976, U.S. Dist. Ct. (no. dist.) Calif., U.S. Ct. Claims 1979, U.S. Tax Ct. 1984, Ariz. 1985, U.S. Dist. Ct. Ariz. 1985, U.S. Ct. Appeals (9th cir.) 1986, U.S. Supreme Ct. 1986. Assoc. Loeb & Loeb, L.A., 1974-80, ptnr., 1981-84; assoc. Bilby & Schoenhair, P.C., Tucson, 1985, shareholder, 1986-89; ptnr. Snell & Wilmer, Tucson, 1989-99. Vis. asst. prof. law U. Santa Clara, Calif., 1983-85; mem. Pima County Commn. on Trial Ct. Appointments, 1996-98. Trustee NRA Civil Rights Def. Fund, 1992-98, NRA Found., pres. 1997-2000; bd. dirs., 1st v.p. NRA, 1992—. Mem. Ariz. Bar Found. (pres. 1996—), Nat. 4-H Shooting Sports Found. (pres. 2002—), Wildlife for Tomorrow Found. (pres. 1999—). Office: Ste 140 200 W Magee Rd Tucson AZ 85704-6492

FROMBERG, JEAN STERN, school system administrator; b. Roanoke, Va., Jan. 4, 1943; d. Ernest George and Marianne (Stamm) Stern; m. Aug. 26, 1968 (div. 1989); children: Nathan, Eric, Craig, Brian, Laura; m. Zachary Fromberg, Nov. 11, 1990. BA, Coll. William and Mary, 1965; MA, Wichita State U., 1986, specialist degree, 1989. Cert. permanent tchr. German, N.Y., cert. supt. bldg adminstr., Kans., Colo., N.Y., Va., N.H., Ohio, Ariz., Pa., Ky. Rural community devel. vol. Peace Corps, Turkey, 1965-67; tchr. German, Spanish and English Kenmore (N.Y.)-Tonawanda Sch. Dist., 1967-70; tchr. German Grand Island (N.Y.) Sch. Dist., 1978-82, coord. adult edn., prin., 1982; grad. rsch. asst. Wichita (Kans.) State U., 1984-86, instr. German, 1985; asst. prin. Unified Sch. Dist. 259, Wichita, 1986-88; supt., high sch. prin. Unified Sch. Dist. 314, Brewster, Kans., 1988-91; supt. Unified Sch. Dist. 271, Stockton, Kans., 1991-93; dir. edn. Computer Learning Ctr., Alexandria, Va., 1993; sr. dir. distbr. Nat. Safety Assocs., Lorton, Va., 1993-96; dir. KinderCare Learning Ctr., Alexandria, 1994; dir. edn. Gesher Jewish Day Sch. of No. Va., Fairfax, 1994; dir. Kinder Care Learning Ctr., Vienna, Va., 1994-95, Children's World Learning Ctr., Lake Ridge, Va., 1995-98; dir. adminstrn. Sanz Sch., Inc., Washington, 1998—. Mem. sch. community adv. coms., N.Y., Kans., 1975-86; chmn. Com. To Revise Fgn. Lang. Curriculum, Grand Island, 1981-83; judge Kans. Fgn. Lang. Competition, 1987. Contbr. numerous articles on ednl. leadership to profl. jours. Pres. Grand Island Food Coop., 1978-83, Waterford Food Coop., Wichita, 1983-88. Mem. ASCD, Am. Assn. Sch. Adminstrs., Nat. Assn Secondary and Elem. Sch. Prins., Am. Assn. Tchrs. German, Kans. Assn. Sch. Adminstrs., Kans. Unified Sch. Adminstrs., AAUW (active local, regional and state levels 1973—), Phi Kappa Phi, Phi Delta Kappa, Nat. Supts. Acad., Ankadaslar-Returned Peace Corps Vols. of Turkey (bd. dirs. 1993-99, pres. 1996-98, area coord. 1993-2002). Avocations: gourmet cooking and baking, reading, gardening, swimming, sewing. Home: 8513 Farrell Dr Chevy Chase MD 20815-3849 Office: Sanz Sch Inc 2nd Fl 8455 Colesville Rd Silver Spring MD 20910 Fax: 301-608-3685. E-mail: jean@sanzschool.erols.com.

FROME, DAVID HERMAN, dentist; b. Richmond, Va., Jan. 22, 1945; married; 3 children. Student, U. Md., 1962-64, 68; DDS, Georgetown U., 1968; MPH, Johns Hopkins U., 1973. Lic. dentist, Md., D.C. Pvt. practice, Gaithersburg, Md., 1970—. Clin. instr. dental materials Georgetown Sch. Dentistry, 1970-72; clin. instr. pediatric dentistry U. Md., 1970-73; dental dir. Group Health Assn., 1982-86, Md. State Dental Svc. Corp., 1980-81; cons. in field. Contbr. articles to profl. jours. Past pres. Layhill Village East Citizens Assn.; bd. dirs., trustee Hebrew Day Inst., pres., 1986-88; mem. adv. group FDA, 1985, 89-91; bd. dirs. Congregation Har Shalom, 1997-98, 2001-03, fin. sec. 1998-2000, sec. 2000-01, treas. 2001—. Capt. AUS, 1968-70, Vietnam. Nat. Inst. Dentistry Rsch. grantee, 1967; Pub. Health fellow; decorated Purple Heart, Bronze Star, Vietnam Svc. Ribbon, Nat. Def. Svc. Ribbon. Master Acad. Gen. Dentistry (chair dental care 1998-2002, pub. information chair 2002, region 5 treas. 2000—, del. 2003-05, alt. 2000-03); mem. ADA, Md. Dental Assn., So. Md. Dental Soc. Home: 8808 Wooden Bridge Rd Potomac MD 20854-2445 Office: 8 Russell Ave Ste 104 Gaithersburg MD 20877-2962 E-mail: fiefrodds@erols.com.

FROMLET, K. HUBERT, banking economist; b. Stuttgart, Germany, May 22, 1947; arrived in Sweden, 1975; s. Kurt and Marianne (Schnitzler) F.; m. Cristina Lindqvist, June 1, 1979; children: Camilla, Pia. Diploma in bus., U. Würzburg, Fed. Republic Germany, 1971, D. in Polit. Sci., 1975. Researcher Saab-Scania, Södertälje, Sweden, 1975-81, Swedish Coop. Banks, Stockholm, 1981-83, chief economist, 1983-84, Swed Bank, Stockholm, 1984—. Lectr. various univs. Author: Das schwedische Bankensystem, 1975; contbr. articles to profl. jours. Avocations: sports, art.

FROMM, DAVID, surgeon; b. N.Y.C., Jan. 21, 1939; s. Alfred and Hanna F.; m. Barbara Solter, June 13, 1961; children— Marc, Kenneth, Kathleen. BS, U. Calif., Berkeley, 1960, MD, 1964. Diplomate Am. Bd. Surgery. Intern U. Calif. Hosp., San Francisco, 1964-65; resident in surgery U. Calif., San Francisco, 1965-71; asst. prof. surgery Harvard Med. Sch., Boston, 1973-77, asso. prof., 1977-78; prof. chmn. dept. surgery SUNY-Upstate Med. Center, Syracuse, 1978-88; Penberthy prof., chmn. dept. surgery Wayne State U., 1988—; surgeon-in-chief Detroit Med. Ctr., 1988—; chief surgery Harper Hosp., Detroit, 1988. Dir. Am. Bd. Surgery, 1996-2001. Author: Complications of Gastric Surgery, 1977; editor Gastrointestinal Surgery, 1985; contbr. articles to profl. jours. Trustee Karmanos Cancer Inst. With M.C., U.S. Army, 1971-73. NIH career devel. awardee, 1976-79; grantee, 1974— Fellow: ACS (gov. 1977—83); mem.: Detroit Acad. Medicine, Detroit Acad. Surgery, Soc. Surgery Alimentary Tract (sec. 1994—97, pres. 1998, chmn. bd. trustees 1999—2000), Halsted Soc., Am. Surg. Assn., Am. Physiol. Soc., Assn. Acad. Surgery, Soc. Clin. Surgery, Am. Gastroent. Assn., Soc. Univ. Surgeons. Office: Wayne State U 6C Univ Health Ctr 4201 St Antoine St Detroit MI 48201-2153 E-mail: dfsurg@aol.com.

FROMM, ERWIN FREDERICK, retired insurance company executive; b. Kalamazoo, Oct. 24, 1933; s. Erwin Carl and Charlotte Elizabeth (Wilson) F. Student, U. Mich., 1951-52, Flint Jr. Coll., 1952-53; BA, Kalamazoo Coll., 1959; postgrad., Ill. State U., 1970-72. CPCU, CLU; cert. nursing home adminstr. Underwriter State Farm Ins., 1959-72; cons. Met. Property & Liability Ins. Co., Warwick, R.I., 1972-73, dir. underwriting and policyholders svcs., 1973, asst. v.p., 1973-74, v.p., 1974—. Sr. v.p. Royal Ins. Co., Charlotte, N.C., 1979-90; ret., 1990; nursing home exec. Royal Crest Health Care Ctr., Inc., 1990-92; pres. Royal Monarch Cons., Inc., 1990—; past chmn. All Industry Ins. Com. for Arson Control; chmn. Nat. Coun. on Compensation Ins.; past chmn. Comml. Lines Com. Ins. Svc. Office; past mem. adv. com. underwriting program Ins. Inst. Am.; cert. long term care ombudsman, 1998—. Past mem. adv. coun. Bus. Sch., U. R.I.; past bd. dirs. Charlotte Symphony; bd. dirs. N.C. Ins. Edn.; mem. Calif. Sr. Legisature, 2000—, mem. adv. coun. on aging; bd. dirs. Calif. Found. on Aging. Mem. CPCU Assn. (Calif. chpt.), CLU Assn. (Calif. chpt.), Masons, Shriners. Home and Office: 73 Colgate Drive Rancho Mirage CA 92270 E-mail: pssstca@aol.com.

FROMM, FREDERICK ANDREW, JR., lawyer; b. Grosse Pointe Farms, Mich., Aug. 2, 1951; s. Frederick Andrew and Jeanette (Sellars) F.; m. Kathleen Ann Lewis, Sept. 25, 1976; children: Andrew Blair, Jennifer Kathleen. BS, Mich. State U., 1973; JD, U. Detroit, 1976. Bar: Mich. 1976, U.S. Dist. Ct. (ea. dist.) Mich. 1976. Law clk. to M.J. Kelly Mich. Ct. Appeals, Detroit, 1976-77; atty. legal staff GM, Detroit, 1977-92, sr. counsel, atty., practice area mgr., 1997—. V.p., gen. counsel, sec. Delco Electronics Corp., 1992-96. Mem. Mich. Bar Assn., Ind. Bar Assn. Home: 2887 Chestnut Run Dr Bloomfield Hills MI 48302-1105 Office: GM Corp MC 482-C23-D24 300 Renaissance Ctr Detroit MI 48265-3000 E-mail: fred.fromm@gm.com.

FROMM, HANS, gastroenterologist, educator, researcher, hepatologist; b. Hagenow, Germany, Aug. 1, 1939; s. Johannes C. and Irene (Biermann) F.; m. Sharon A. Kleiv, June 8, 1968; children: H. Chris, Martin T. MD, Albert Ludwig U., Freiburg, Fed. Republic Germany, 1964. Intern Meml. Hosp., Worcester, Mass., 1966-67; resident Lemuel Shattuck Hosp., Boston, 1967-68, Albany Med. Ctr., 1968-70; fellow Mayo Clinic, Rochester, Minn., 1970-71; resident/fellow Medizinische Hochschule Hannover, Germany, 1971-74; asst. prof. medicine U. Pitts., 1975-80, assoc. prof. medicine, 1980-84, prof. medicine, 1984, George Washington U., Washington, 1984-99; dir. divsn. gastroenterology and nutrition George Washington Med. Ctr., Washington, 1984-99; prof. medicine Dartmouth Med. Sch., 1999—; dir. Dartmouth-Hitchcock Hepatopancreaticobiliary Disease Ctr., Lebanon, NH, 1999—. Mem. numerous grant rev. coms. including NIH, Merit Rev. Bd., Gastroenterology Med. Rsch. Svc. VA, Washington, 1984—87. Mem. editl. bd.: Hepatogastroenterology, 1981—88, mem. editl. bd.: Hepatology, 1985, 1991—2001; contbr. articles to profl. jours., chapters to books. Mem.: Orgn. Mondiale de Gastro-Enterologie/World Orgn. Gastroenterology (vice chmn. interamerican edn. com. 1998—2001), Am. Assn. Study of Liver Diseases (chmn. pubs. com. 1988—90, mem. com. on admissions 2002—), Am. Gastroent. Assn. (chmn. com. on admissions 1990—91, chmn. internat. liaison com. 1995—98, chmn. biliary disorders sect. 1997—99), Am. Soc. Clin. Investigation. Lutheran. Office: Dartmouth Hitchcock Med Ctr Sect Gastroenterology & Hepatology 1 Medical Center Dr Lebanon NH 03756-0002 E-mail: Hans.Fromm@Dartmouth.edu.

FROMM, HENRY GORDON, retired manufacturing and marketing executive; b. Burlington, Iowa, June 10, 1911; s. Henry Carl and Lillian (Lohmann) F.; m. Elizabeth H. Orthner, July 15, 1936; children— Dan G., Allan P., Martha E., Mark H., Eric C., Lynne M. BSChemE, Iowa State U., 1933; MS (Sloan fellow), MIT, 1950; DHH, Robert Morris Coll., 1998. Gen. plant mgr. Manhattan Soap Co., Bristol, Pa., 1937-44; prodn. mgr. Johnson & Johnson, 1944-55; v.p. ops. Internat. Latex Corp., 1955-61; v.p., gen. mgr. ops. Sun Chem. Corp., N.Y.C., 1961-63; gen. mgr. Crown Cork & Seal Co., Phila., 1963-64; v.p. ops. Marathon Electric Co., Wausau, Wis., 1964-69; pres. Bell & Howell Communications Co., Waltham, Mass., 1969, Bell & Howell Electronics & Instruments Group, Pasadena, Calif., 1969-71; group v.p. Bell & Howell, Chgo., 1971-77; chmn. bd. Ditto, Inc., Chgo., 1977-79; pres. Fromm Services, Inc., Green Bay, Wis., 1973-90, Eau Claire T.A.S., Wis., 1973-89, Gordon Fromm & Assos., Lake Forest, Ill., 1979-87; pres., chief exec. officer Templeton, Kenly & Co., 1979-87, Miller Fluid Power, 1981-87. Mem. gen. council Am. Baptist Conv., Dover (Del.) City Council, 1958-62, Rotary Internat., 1937-87; chmn. Dover City Planning Commn., 1960-62; trustee, treas. Robert Morris Coll., 1982—; mem. Chgo. Exec. Service Corps, 1987—; bd. dirs. Lake Forest Hist. Assn., Lake Forest Sr. Citizens Resources Found. Mem. Midwest Indsl. Mgmt. Assn. (dir.), Am. Mgmt. Assn. (v.p.), Am. Inst. Chem. Engrs., Lake Forest Symphony Assn. (pres. 1988-89), Univ. Club (Chgo.). Home: Lake Forest Pl 1100 Pembridge Dr # 202 Lake Forest IL 60045

FROMM, JEFFERY BERNARD, lawyer; b. Washington, Oct. 9, 1947; s. Seymour Morris and Frances Sylvia (Goldstein) F.; m. Mary Ellen Sommer, Sept. 11, 1971; children: Aaron M., David P. BS in Elec. Engring., BA in Physics, U. Pa., 1970; JD magna cum laude, Widener U., 1981. Bar: Pa. 1982, Calif. 1982, U.S. Ct. Appeals (9th and fed. cirs.) 1982, Colo. 1988. Patent atty. Hewlett-Packard Co., Palo Alto, Calif., 1981-83, sr. patent atty., 1983-85, mng. patent counsel Andover, Mass., 1985-87, sr. mng. counsel intellectual property Ft. Collins, Colo., 1987—2002; pvt. intellectual property legal practice, 2002—. Asst. scoutmaster Boy Scouts Am., Ft. Collins, 1988-96; asst. coach-umpire Little League, Andover and San Jose, Calif., 1983-87. Mem. IEEE, ABA, AIPLA, Pa. Bar Assn., Calif. Bar Assn., Colo. Bar Assn., Phi Delta Phi. Avocations: skiing, golf. Office: PO Box 7399 PMB 332 Breckenridge CO 80424-7399 E-mail: jeff@fromms.ws.

FROMM, JOSEPH, retired magazine editor, foreign affairs consultant; b. South Bend, Ind., Jan. 6, 1920; s. Michael M. and Ethel (Mentzel) F.; divorced; children: Margot, Lisa; 1 stepchild, Erik. Student, U. Chgo., 1937-38, Northwestern U., 1938-39. Reporter S. Bend Tribune, 1935-37, Southtown Economist, Chgo., 1937-39; writer UP, Chgo., 1939-40; radio news bur. chief AP, Chgo., 1940-42; mng. editor air edit. Chgo. Sun, 1942; fgn. corr. U.S. News and World Report, 1946-74, dep. editor, 1974-79, asst. editor, 1979-85, contbg. editor, 1985-88. Cons. to think tanks, U.S. Dept. Def., Nat. Security Coun., CIA, Joint Warfare Analysis Ctr.; lectr. on strategy and internat. rels.; mem. tech. adv. com. Ctr. Naval Analysis. Served with Brit. and Indian armies, 1943-45; honorable discharge U.S. Army, 2002. Served with Brit. Army, 1943, with U.S. Army, 1943—44, commd. capt. Indian Army, 1945. Decorated Order Brit. Empire. Fellow Johns Hopkins Fgn. Policy Inst., Internat. Inst. Strategic Studies (mem. exec. com., vice chmn. U.S. com.); mem. Washington Inst. Fgn. Affairs, Coun. on Fgn. Rels., Midatlantic Club, Fgn. Corr. Club Japan (pres. 1950), Assn. Am. Corrs. in London (pres. 1967), Fgn. Press Assn. London (dir. 1972-74), Arms Control Assn., Cosmos Club Washington. E-mail: joefromm@aol.com.

FROMM, PAUL OLIVER, physiology educator; b. Ramsey, Ill., Dec. 2, 1923; s. August Moltke and Edith Marie (Wollerman) F.; m. Mary Magdalene Shaw, June 15, 1947; children: David, Emily. BS, U. Ill., 1949, MS, 1951, PhD, 1954. Instr. dept. physiology Mich. State U., East Lansing, 1954-58, asst. prof., 1958-62, assoc. prof., 1962-65, prof., 1965-87, prof. emeritus, 1987—. Cons. U.S.-Can. Great Lakes Commn., Windsor, Ont., Can., 1981, Nat. Research Council Can., 1983 Contbr. articles to profl. jours. Served with USMC, 1943-46 Fulbright rsch. scholar Musée Oceanographique Monaco, 1963-64. Mem. N.Am. Benthological Soc. (pres. 1958), Am. Soc. Zoologists, Am. Physiol. Soc., Soc. Exptl. Biology and Medicine Home: 6741 S Lake RR 1 Pentwater MI 49449-9801 Office: Mich State U Dept Physiology East Lansing MI 48824

FROMMELT, JEFFREY JAMES, management consulting firm executive; b. Mpls., July 23, 1940; s. Henry Julius and Inez Vivian (Okins) F.; m. Janet Ruth Parry, Apr. 10, 1965; children: Brian Jeffrey, Craig Henry. BA, Jamestown Coll., 1963; MHA, U. Minn., 1965. Adminstrv. resident R.I. Hosp., Providence, 1964-65; assoc. Herman Smith Assocs., Hinsdale, Ill., 1965-70, prin., 1970-77, pres., 1977-88; ptnr. Coopers & Lybrand, 1988-97; nat. advisor Argus/Arista Assocs., Western Springs, Ill., 1997—. Bd. dirs. LaGrange (Ill.) Meml. Health System. Author: Building A Hospital, 1980; contbr. articles to profl. jours. Bd. dirs. Jamestown (N.D.) Coll., 1984—; elder First Presby. Ch., La Grange, Ill., 1981-84; bd. dirs. Cmty. Meml. Found., 1996—. Fellow Am. Assn. Health Care Cons. (treas. 1980-81, chmn. bd. 1982-83); mem. Inst. Mgmt. Cons., Am. Coll. Hosp. Adminstrs. Lodges: Elks. Republican. Home: 4136 Clausen Ave Western Springs IL 60558-1229

FROMMER, ANN, systems analyst; b. Tamaqua, Pa. m. Robert E. Frommer, Apr. 23, 1990. BS, Fairleigh Dickinson U., 1968, MA, 1975. RN. Cons. Custom Pers. Svc., Convent Station, N.J., 1978-80; coord. Gen. Hosp. Passaic, N.J., 1980-83; mgr. Pocono Hosp., E. Stroudsburg, Pa., 1983-87; dir. utilization mgmt. Morristown (N.J.) Meml. Hosp., 1987-97; mgr. clin. payor sys. Morristown Meml. Hosp., 1998—2001, systems specialist performance improvement, 2001—. Critical path com., Cranberry, N.J., 1995-96, all com. mem. VHA East, Cranberry, N.J., comparative data study com., Cranberry, 1995—, Quality Coun., 1996—, VHA, Cranberry, 1995-96, quality data com.; mem. quality and fin. data com. N.J. Hosp. Assn., Princeton, 1995-96; spkr. in field. Contbr. columns in newspapers; editor: Alert News Mag.; contbr. articles to profl. jours. Mem.: HIMMS, Chatham Bd. Health (pres.), Healthcare Quality Profl. NJ, Healthcare Fin. Mgmt. Assn. NJ, Healthcare Fin. Orgn. NJ, Am. Heart Assn. (bd. dir. 1977—80), Am. Assn. Healthcare Execs., Nat. Healthcare Quality Profls. Avocations: computers, working out, cycling, travel, writing. Home: 24 Coleman Ave E Chatham NJ 07928-2205

FROMMER, DARIO F. state representative; b. Long Beach, Calif. BA, Colgate U., 1985; JD, U. Calif., Davis, 1992. Press sec. Controller Gray Davis, 1988; atty., 1992—; chief of staff Senator Art Torres, 1993; appointments sec. to gov., 1999; mem. Calif. Assembly, 2000—. Democrat. Office: PO Box 942849 Rm 6005 Sacramento CA 94249-0001 Address: 111 E Broadway Ste 205 Glendale CA 91205*

FROMMER, LAWRENCE JULIAN, retired travel company executive; b. Trenton, N.J., Sept. 8, 1917; s. Samuel Alexander Frommer and Fannie Cohen; m. Yolande Irene Foisy, Aug. 22, 1975. BA in Journalism, Ind. U., 1939, MS in Bus. Adminstrn., 1942. Cert. travel counselor. Writer Radio Sta. WOWO, Ft. Wayne, Ind., 1943—44, Radio Sta. WKRC, Cin., 1944—45, Radio Sta. WOL, Washington, 1945—53; travel agy. exec. Frommer Travel Svc., Washington, 1958—91; travel writer Washingtonian Mag., 1969—82, Asta Agy. Mgmt., N.Y.C., Washington, 1973—95; travel and restaurant writer Crystal City Mag., Arlington, Va., 1990—. Mem. travel agy. adv. bd. State Maine, Augusta, 1980, Am. Express, N.Y.C., 1983—90, Access Am., N.Y.C., 1985—88. Contbr. articles to profl. jours. Pres. Louis D. Brandeis Zionist Dist., Washington, 1958—59, Skal Club Travel Execs., Washington, 1975—76; trustee Inst. Cert. Travel Agts., Wellesly, Mass., 1968—90; vol. Animal Welfare League Alexandria; mem. U.S. Holocaust Mus. Named Travel Agt. of Yr., Am. Soc. Travel Agts., Washington, 1985. Fellow: Louis D. Brandeis Zionist Dist. (life; pres.), Skal Club Washington (pres.). Avocations: music, theater, sports, volunteer work. Home: Apt 505 5902 Mount Eagle Dr Alexandria VA 22303-2516

FROMMER, WILLIAM S. lawyer; b. Bklyn., Sept. 27, 1942; s. Herbert S. and Molly S. Frommer; m. Karen Beagle, July 31, 1966; 1 child, Hillary. BEE, Cornell U., 1965; JD, Am. U., 1969. Bar: N.Y. 1970, U.S. Patent Office 1970, U.S. Ct. Customs and Patent Appeals 1975, U.S. Ct. Appeals (fed. cir.) 1982, U.S. Supreme Ct. 1985. Assoc. Marn & Jangarathis, NYC, 1969—73, Curtis, Morris & Safford, P.C., NYC, 1973—76, ptnr., 1976—97; founding ptnr. Frommer, Lawrence & Haug, NYC, 1997—. Mem. Am. U. Law Rev., 1967—69. Mem.: ABA, Internat. Bar Assn., Internat. Patent and Trade Assn., N.Y. State Bar Assn., N.Y. Patent Law Assn. Office: 745 5th Ave New York NY 10151-0099

FRONTIERE, GEORGIA, professional football team executive; b. St. Louis; m. Carroll Rosenblum, July 7, 1966 (dec.); children: Dale Carroll, Lucia; m. Dominic Frontiere. Pres., owner L.A. Rams, NFL, 1979—; now mng. ptnr. St. Louis Rams. Bd. dirs. L.A. Boys and Girls Club, L.A. Orphanage Guild, L.A. Blind Youth Found. Named Headliner of Yr., L.A. Press Club, 1981. Office: St Louis Rams 1 Rams Way Earth City MO 63045-1525 also: Transworld Dome 701 Convention Plz Saint Louis MO 63101

FROOMKIN, JOSEPH, economic consultant; b. Harbin, China, Feb. 7, 1927; came to U.S., 1947; s. Nathan and Rachel (Sineikin) F.; m. Maya Pines, 1959; children: A. Michael, Daniel P. AB, St. John's U., Shanghai, China, 1946; MBA, U. Chgo., 1947, PhD, 1950. Economist various rsch. orgns., Harvard U., Columbia U., 1953-57; exec. DP divsn. IBM, White Plains, N.Y., 1957-66; asst. commr. edn. U.S. HEW, Washington, 1966-69; pres. Joseph Froomkin Inc., 1970-90; dir. Ednl. Policy Ctr. for Higher Edn., 1970-90; ind. econ. cons. Washington, 1990—. Sgt. U.S. Army, 1952-53. Avocation: reading. Home and Office: 4701 Willard Ave Chevy Chase MD 20815-4643

FROSCH, ROBERT ALAN, retired automobile manufacturing executive, physicist; b. N.Y.C., May 22, 1928; s. Herman Louis and Rose (Bernfeld) Frosch; m. Jessica Rachael Denerstein, Dec. 22, 1957; 1 child, Margery Ellen; 1 child, Elizabeth Ann. AB, Columbia U., 1947, A.M., 1949, PhD, 1952; DEng (hon.), U. Miami, 1982, Mich. Technol. U., 1983. Scientist Hudson Labs. Columbia U., 1951—53, asst. dir. theoretical divsn., 1953—54, assoc. dir., 1954—56, dir., 1956—63; dir. nuclear test detection Advanced Rsch. Projects Agy., Office Sec. Def., 1963—65; dep. dir. Advanced Rsch. Projects Agy., 1965—66; asst. sec. navy for rsch. and devel. Washington, 1966—73; asst. exec. dir. UN Environment Programme, 1973—75; assoc. dir. for applied oceanography Woods Hole (Mass.) Oceanographic Instn., 1975—77; adminstr. NASA, Washington, 1977—81; pres. Am. Assn. Engring. Socs., N.Y.C., 1981—82; v.p. in charge Research Labs. Gen. Motors Corp., Warren, Mich., 1982—93; sr. rsch. fellow Ctr. for Sci. and Internat. Affairs John F. Kennedy Sch. Govt., Harvard U., Cambridge, Mass., 1993—. Chmn. U.S. del. to Intergovtl. Oceanographic Commn. meetings UNESCO, Paris, 1967, Paris, 70. Contbr. numerous sci. and tech. articles to profl. jours. Recipient Arthur S. Flemming award, 1966, NASA Disting. Svc. award, 1981, IRI medal Indsl. Rsch. Inst., 1996, Founders medal, IEEE Found. Fellow: IEEE, AIAA, NAE (sr.), AAAS, Am. Astronautical Soc. (John F. Kennedy Astronautics award 1981), Acoustical Soc. Am.; mem.: Royal Acad. Engring. (U.K., fgn.), Engring. Soc. Detroit, Soc. Automotive Engrs., Soc. Naval Architects and Marine Engrs., Am. Phys. Soc., Marine Tech. Soc., Soc. Exploration Geophysicists (spl. commendation 1981), Am. Acad. Arts and Scis., Seismol. Soc. Am., Am. Geophys. Union. Office: Harvard U John F Kennedy Sch Govt BCSIA 79 JFK St Cambridge MA 02138-5801 E-mail: bob_frosch@harvard.edu, rfrosch522@aol.com.

FROSCH, ROBERT J. civil engineer, educator; s. Warren R. and Bessie G. Frosch; m. Maria M. Tuttle, July 10, 1999. BS in Engring., Tulane U., 1991; MS in Engring., U. Tex., 1992, PhD, 1995. Registered profl. engr., Ind., 2002, La., 1997. Asst. engr. Modjeski and Masters, Inc., New Orleans, 1996—97; asst. prof. civil engring. Purdue U., West Lafayette, Ind., 1997—2002, assoc. prof. civil engring., 2002—. Fellow, Kyoto U., 2000. Fellow: Am. Concrete Inst. (sec. cracking com. 1997—, mem. std. bldg. code, safety and serviceability com. 2002—, mem. bond and devel. com. 2000—, Young Members award 2002); mem.: ASCE, Earthquake Engring. Rsch. Inst. Home: 2105 Windflower Pl West Lafayette IN 47906-6616 Office: Purdue Univ 550 Stadium Mall Dr West Lafayette IN 47907-2051 Office Fax: 765-496-1105. E-mail: frosch@purdue.edu.

FROSCH, WILLIAM A. psychiatry educator, psychoanalyst; b. N.Y.C., June 24, 1932; s. Herman L. and Rose (Bernfeld) F.; m. Paula Frosch, Dec. 20, 1953; children: Matthew P., Emily J. AB, Columbia U., 1953; MD, NYU, 1957; cert., N.Y. Psychoanalytic Inst., 1965. Diplomate Am. Bd. Psychiatry and Neurology. Intern in psychiatry Bellevue Hosp., N.Y.C., 1957—58, resident in psychiatry, 1958—61; from instr. to prof. Sch. Medicine NYU, N.Y.C., 1960-75, asst. dean, 1961-63; prof. Coll. Medicine Cornell U., N.Y.C., 1975—. Contbr. articles to profl. jours. Mem. Am. Psychiat. Assn., N.Y. Acad. Medicine, Century Assn., Alpha Omega Alpha. Democrat. Jewish. Home: 15 W 75th St New York NY 10023 Office: Weill-Cornell Med Coll 525 E 68th St New York NY 10021 E-mail: wafrosc@med.cornell.edu.

FROSH, BRIAN ESTEN, lawyer, state senator; b. Washington, Oct. 8, 1946; s. Stanley Benjamin and Judith Lee (Wirkman) F.; m. Marcy Masters, Nov. 19, 1984; children: Elena, Alexandra. Student, U. Stockholm, 1966-67; BA, Wesleyan U., 1968; JD, Columbia U., 1971. Legis. asst. Sen. Harrison Williams U.S. Senate, Washington, 1972-76; ptnr. Kass, Skalet & Frosh, Washington, 1976-79, Bingaman, Davenport & Lovejoy, Santa Fe, 1979-81; pvt. practice Bethesda, Md., 1981—96; ptnr. Karp, Frosh, Lapidus, Wigodsky and Norwind, Washington, 1996—; del. Md. Gen. Assembly, Annapolis, 1987-95, chmn. Montgomery County House del., 1991-93; state senator Md. State Senate, 1995—, dep. majority leader, 2001—02, chmn. jud. procs. com., 2003—; mem. gov.'s task force on energy Md. Gen. Assembly, Annapolis, 1989-94; chmn. environ. subcom. Econ. and Environ. Affairs Com., 1995—2002; mem. Chesapeake Bay Commn., 1995—2002. Legis. acts include Md. Recycling Act, Newspaper Recycling Act, Oil Spills Bill, Bay Protection and Oil Exploration, also others; bd. dirs. State Nat. Bank Md. Bd. dirs. Hebrew Home Greater Washington, 1986-95, Jewish Cmty. Ctr. Greater Washington, 1983-89; mem. Montgomery County Charter Rev. Commn., 1983-86; nat. adv. commn. SBA, 1981-82. Recipient citation Chesapeake Bay Found., 1991, cert. of merit Montgomery County Common Cause Md., 1991; Clean Air award Sierra Club, 1991, Conservationist of Yr. award, 1989; Lawmaker of Yr. award Am. Lung Assn. Md., 1991, Outstanding Svc. award Am. Heart Assn. Md. Mem. Wesleyan U. Alumni Assn. (exec. com. 1986-89). Address: Miller Senate Office Bldg 2E Annapolis MD 21401 Office: Ste 800W 7315 Wisconsin Ave Bethesda MD 20814-3217

FROSS, ROGER RAYMOND, lawyer; b. Rockford, Ill., Mar. 8, 1940; s. Hollis H. and Dorothy (George) F.; m. Madelon R. Rose, Feb. 14, 1970; 1 child, Oliver. AB, DePauw U., 1962; JD, U. Chgo., 1965. Bar: Ill. 1965. Assoc. Norman and Billick, Chgo., 1965-70; ptnr. Lord, Bissell & Brook, Chgo., 1970—, mng. pntr., 1982-87. Bd. dirs. Hyde Park Bank and Trust Co., Chgo., 1975—; pres. Hyde-Park-Kenwood Devel. Corp., 1998—. Bd. dirs. Hyde Park Neighborhood Club, Chgo., 1970—, pres. 1972-73; bd. dirs., mem. exec. com. South East Chgo. Commn., 1978—; mem. Community Conservation Council, Chgo., 1980-99; bd. dirs., sec. Chgo. Metro History Fair, 1991—; bd. dirs. The Joyce Found., 1991—, Lab. Sch. U. Chgo., 1991-94, Citizens Com. of the Juvenile Ct., 1973-96. Rector schlor DePauw U., Greencastle, Ind., 1958-62. Mem. ABA, Ill. Bar Assn., Chgo. Bar Assn. (chmn. com. juvenile delinquents 1972). Office: Lord Bissell & Brook Harris Bank Bldg 115 S La Salle St Ste 3500 Chicago IL 60603-3801

FROST, A. CORWIN, architect, consultant; b. Bronxville, N.Y., Nov. 18, 1934; s. Frederick George Jr. and Gwendolyn Belle (Corwin) F.; m. Rosalie Randolph Halsey, Sept. 26, 1959; children: Frederick Halsey, Anne Randolph. AB, Princeton U., 1956; BS, R.I. Sch. Design, 1959. Registered architect, N.Y., other states. Designer, draftsman Harrison & Abramovitz, N.Y.C., 1959-60; project architect Frederick G. Frost Jr. and Assocs., N.Y.C., 1960-63, assoc., 1963-68; ptnr. Frost Assocs., N.Y.C., 1968-78; assoc. dir. archtl. and engring. services CBS Inc., N.Y.C., 1978-80, dir. planning and design, 1980-86, dir. facilities engring., 1986-88; prin. Frost Assocs. Cons., Bronxville, N.Y., 1988—; dep. dir. dept. design, cons. and mgmt. CUNY, 1992-95; cons. Newark Pub. Schs., 1995—. Chmn. Bronxville Planning Bd., 1990—; trustee Coun. for Arts in Westchester, White Plains, N.Y., 1972-81 (pres. 1974-75), R.I. Sch. Design, 1989-99, 2000—, Westchester County Hist. Soc., 1998—; trustee, mem. exec. com. Westchester Preservation League, 1989-98; mem. Bronxville Adult Sch., 1982-88, Bronxville Planning Commn., 1977-80. Mem. AIA (exec. com. N.Y. chpt. 1974-76, ethics com. 1978-80, corp. architects com. 1980-82, fin. com. 1981-87), Princeton Club, Bronxville Field Club (pres. 1992-96). Home and Office: Frost Assoc Cons 11 Sunset Ave Bronxville NY 10708-2208 E-mail: fiberarch@earthlink.net.

FROST, ADAANI, internist; b. Sydney, Australia, June 5, 1950; d. Archibald Rimmer Frost and Clarice Connolly; m. Wadi Nagib Suki, Jan. 5, 1992. B of Med. Sci., Meml. U. Nfld., St. Johns, Canada, MD, 1973. Diplomate Am. Bd. Internal Medicine, subspecialty in pulmonary medicine Am. Bd. Internal Medicine, cert. subspecialty in critical care medicine Am. Bd. Internal Medicine. Asst. prof. medicine Baylor Coll. Medicine, Houston, 1990—93, assoc. prof., 1993—99, prof., 1999—, med. dir. lung transplant program for Meth. and St. Lukes Epis. Hosps., 1990—2002, dir. pulmonary hypertension, 1992—. Fellow: Royal Coll. Physicians (Can.); mem.: ACCP, Am. Thoracic Soc., Am. Soc. Transplantation, Pulmonary Hypertension Assn. (mem. sci. adv. coun.), Soc. Critical Care Medicine, Internat. Soc. Heart Lung Transplantation. Office: Baylor Coll Medicine SM 1236 6550 Fannin Houston TX 77030 Office Fax: 713-790-3648.

FROST, BARRY WARREN, lawyer; b. Glen Ridge, N.J., Aug. 17, 1947; m. Nancy Teich, Aug. 16, 1970; children: Benjamin, Alison. BS, Bradley U., 1969; JD, N.Y. Law Sch., 1976. Bar: N.J. 1976, U.S. Dist. Ct. N.J. 1976, U.S. Dist. Ct. (so. and ea. dists.) N.Y. 1977, N.Y. 1977. Assoc. Gladstein & Isaac, N.Y.C., 1972-77; ptnr. Teich, Groh & Frost, Trenton, N.J., 1977—. Office: Teich Groh & Frost 691 Highway 33 Trenton NJ 08619-4407 E-mail: teich1g2f3@aol.com.

FROST, CAROL A. clinical social worker, consultant; b. Ridgewood, N.J., Oct. 16, 1952; d. William Pepperell and Carol Anne (Norcross) Frost; m. Robert E. Vercollone, May 8, 1982 (div. 2002). BA summa cum laude, U. Mass., 1974; MSW, U. Albany, 1978. Lic. social work, Mass. Social worker Whitney M. Young Health Ctr., Albany, N.Y., 1976-77; vol. counselor Rape Crisis Counseling Ctr., Albany, 1977-1978; intern family counselor Div. For Youth, Schenectady, N.Y., 1977-78; social worker Children's Health Program, Gt. Barrington, Mass., 1978-79; coord., asst. dir. Resolve, Inc., Arlington, Mass., 1979-83; psychotherapist Pastoral Counseling Ctr., Lowell, Mass., 1983-84; coord. spl. projects Resolve, Inc., Arlington, Mass., 1983-87; pvt. practice Wakefield and Fall River, Mass., 1983—. Co-author: Understanding Artificial Insemination booklet, 1987, Helping the Stork, 1997. Bd. dirs. Resolve Bay State, 1986-89. Mem. NASW, Am. Soc. Reproductive Medicine, Open Door Soc. Address: 56 N Main St Ste 207 Fall River MA 02720

FROST, CAROL D. geology educator; b. Salem, Oreg., May 23, 1957; d. O.W. and Mary D. (Bills) F.; m. Eric W. Nye, Dec. 21, 1980; children: Charles W., Ellen M. AB, Dartmouth Coll., 1979; PhD, U. Cambridge, 1984. From asst. prof. to prof. U. Wyoming, Laramie, 1983—. NSF panelist, 1992-96. Named CASE Prof. of the Yr. for Wyo., 2001. Mem. Mineral. Soc. Am. (Disting. Lectr. award 1997-98), Geochem. Soc., Geol. Soc. Am. (editl. bd. 1990-96). Office: U Wyo Dept Geology/Geophysics Laramie WY 82071-3006

FROST, CHARLES ESTES, JR., lawyer; b. Houston, Aug. 17, 1950; s. Charles Estes and Lucille Fourmey (DeGravelles) F. BS, U.S. Mil. Acad., 1972; MBA, Armstrong State Coll., 1979; JD, U. Tex., 1981. Bar: Tex. 1982, U.S. Dist. Ct. (no. and so. dists.) Tex. Commd. 2d lt. U.S. Army, 1972, advanced through grades to capt., 1979; resigned from active duty, 1979; assoc. Strasburger & Price, Dallas, 1982-84, Chamberlain, Hrdlicka et al, Houston, 1985-88; shareholder Chamberlain Hrdlicka et al, Houston, 1989—. Mem. bd. advocates U. Tex. Law Sch. Note editor: Tex. Law Rev., U. Tex. Law Sch.1981-82. Mem. ethics com. Haris County Rep. Party, 2000. Lt. col. USAR, 1979-98. Mem. Houston Bar Assn. (dir. litigation sect. 2000—). Republican. Avocations: running, church. Office: Chamberlain Hrdlicka et al 1200 Smith St Ste 1400 Houston TX 77002-4401

FROST, DARREL RICHMOND, biologist, administrator; b. Mesa, Ariz., June 12, 1951; s. David Richmond and Lea Charlotte (Caldwell) F.; m. Lynne Celeste Longwell, May 27, 1951. BS, U. Ariz., 1972; MS, La. State U., 1978, MS, 1975; PhD, U. Kans., 1988. From asst. curator to assoc. curator Am. Mus. Natural History, N.Y.C., 1990—2001, curator, 2001—, assoc. dean sci., 1997—, chair divsn. vertebrate zoology, 1999-2000. Adj. rsch. scientist Ctrl. Environ. Rsch. Conservatory, adj. prof. dept. ecol. and evolutionary biology Columbia U. Editor: Amphibian Species of the World, 1985, Herpetol. Monographs, 1994-98; mem. editl. bd. Vestnik Zool., Ukrainian Acad. Sci. Grantee NSF, 1992-98, NASA, 1998--. Fellow Willi Hennig Soc.; mem. Soc. Study Amphibians and Reptiles (pres. 1998), Assn. Systematics Collection (v.p. 1999-2001), Soc. Systematic Biologists (councilor 1989-92, Ernst Mayr award 1987), Herpetologists' League (councilor 1998-2000). Avocation: history. Office: Am Mus Natural History Central Park W at 79th St New York NY 10024

FROST, DAVID, former biology educator, medical editor, consultant; b. Bklyn., Dec. 19, 1925; s. Charles and Regina (Sad) Feivlowitz; m. Ruthann Steinberg, Dec. 24, 1946; children: Michael Joseph, Jane Alice. BS, CCNY, 1945, MED, 1949; MS, NYU, 1952, PhD, 1960. Instr. in biology CCNY, 1946-49; instr. in sci. Rhodes Sch., N.Y.C., 1949-52; asst. prof. biology Rutgers U., Newark, N.J., 1952-59, adj. prof. biology New Brunswick, N.J., 1960-78; sci. editor Squibb Inst. for Med. Rsch., Princeton, N.J., 1959-75. Pvt. practice, Plainfield, N.J., Olmstedville, N.Y., 1975—. Pres. N.J. SANE, 1964-65; co-chmn. Plainfield Joint Def. Com., 1970-85; newsletter editor Cen. Jersey/Masaya, Nicaragua Friendship Cities Project, 1985-97. Mem. Coun. Sci. Editors (pres. 1982-83), Schroon Lake Assn. (v.p., 1980—, pres. 1997—). Office: 1229 E 7th St Plainfield NJ 07062-1907 also: 1637 Hoffman Rd Olmstedville NY 12857-2436

FROST, EDMUND BOWEN, lawyer; b. Pueblo, Colo., Dec. 5, 1942; s. Hildreth and Doris (Bowen) F.; m. Molly Spitzer; children: Julia A., Elizabeth E., Edmund N., Luette S. BA, Dartmouth Coll., 1964; JD magna cum laude, U. Mich., 1967. Bar: Colo. 1967, D.C. 1970, U.S. Supreme Ct. 1980. Assoc. Steptoe & Johnson, Washington, 1969-75; chief legal advisor to commr. ICC, Washington, 1975-76; asst. dir. for gen. litigation Bur. Competition, FTC, Washington, 1976-77; v.p., gen. counsel Chem. Mfrs. Assn., Washington, 1978-82; ptnr. Kirkland & Ellis, Washington, 1982-88, Davis, Graham & Stubbs, Washington, 1988-94; sr. v.p. and gen. counsel Clean Sites, Inc., Alexandria, Va., 1994-99; shareholder, dir. Leonard Frost Levin & Van Court, PC, 1998—; bd. dirs., chmn., bd. environ., health and safety com. Philip Svcs. Co., 2000—. Contbr. articles to profl. jours. Participant pub. policy dialogs on environ. issues Keystone (Colo.) Ctr., 1980—; guest artisan Washington Nat. Cathedral, 1997—; co-pres., bd. dirs., exec. com. Cmty. Coun. for the Homeless at Friendship Place, Wash., DC; pres., bd. dirs. Vincent Palumbo Ctr. for Stonecarving and Indsl. Arts, Inc., 2001—. Capt. U.S. Army, 1967-69. Mem. Cosmos Club Washington. Avocations: sculpture and stone carving, skiing, mountain climbing, tuba and euphonium. Home: 3309 35th St NW Washington DC 20016-3141 E-mail: ebfrost@leonardFrost.com.

FROST, ELIZABETH ANN MCARTHUR, physician; b. Glasgow, Scotland, Oct. 29, 1938; came to U.S., 1963; d. Robert Thomas and Annie M. (Ross) F.; m. Wallace Capobianco, Sept. 4, 1965 (dec. May 1988); children: Garrett, Ross, Christopher, Neil. MBChB, U. Glasgow, 1961. Diplomate Am. Bd. Anesthesiology, Royal Coll. Ob-Gyn., London. Intern in surgery Royal Infirmary, Glasgow, 1961-62; intern in medicine Victoria Infirmary, Glasgow, 1962; intern in obstetrics Royal Maternity Hosp., Glasgow, 1962-63; resident in internal medicine Englewood (N.J.) Hosp., 1963-64; resident in anesthesiology N.Y. Hosp., N.Y.C., 1964-66; instr. in anesthesiology Albert Einstein Coll. Medicine, Bronx, N.Y., 1966-68, asst. prof. to assoc. prof., 1968-81, prof. anesthesiology, 1981-91, mem. dept. history of medicine, 1973-91; prof. dept. anesthesiology N.Y. Med. Coll., Valhalla, N.Y., 1992-99; clin. prof. dept. anesthesiology Mt. Sinai Med. Ctr., N.Y.C., 2000—; attending anesthesiology VA Bronx, 2000—. Book reviewer New Eng. Jour. of Medicine, 1983—; editor Preanesthetic Assessment, Anesthesiology News, 1984—, Gen. Surgery News, 1991; author/contbr. books; contbr. articles to profl. jours. Mem. N.Y. State Soc. Anesthesiologists, Am. Soc. of Anesthesiologists, Assn. of Univ. Anesthesiologists, Soc. of Neurosurg. Anesthesia and Neurologic Supportive Care, Am. Assn. of Neurol. Surgeons, Anesthesia History Assn. Home: 2 Pondview West Purchase NY 10577 E-mail: ElzFrost@aol.com.

FROST, ELLEN ELIZABETH, psychologist; b. N.Y.C. d. John Joseph and Josephine Mary (Cornell) F.; m. Jerry Melnick, Jan. 8, 1982; children: Mariel Frost, Matt James. BA magna cum laude, St. John's U., 1969; MA, Fordham U., 1971, PhD, 1982; candidate NYU Postdoctoral Program for Psychotherapy and Psychoanalysis, 1982-84. Cert. Eye Movement Desensitization Reprocessing tng., 2000. Clin. psychology intern Columbia-Presbyn. Psychiat. Inst., N.Y.C., 1972-73; asst. team leader staff psychologist Bensonhurst inpatient unit South Beach Psychiat. Ctr., Bklyn., 1973-75, sr. psychologist, Bensonhurst outpatient dept., 1975-81, assoc. psychologist, supr., 1982-89; dir. Phobia Svc., 1982-89; pvt. practice, 1983—; clin. supr. New Hope Guild, Bklyn., 1983—2000. Faculty L.I. Inst. Mental Health, 1990-97, supr., 1993-97. N.Y. State regents fellow, 1969-72; USPHS fellow, 1969-72. Mem. Am. Psychol. Assn., EMDR Internat. Assoc., Sigma Xi. Office: 200 E 33rd St Apt 25J New York NY 10016-4831 E-mail: efrostphd@aol.com.

FROST, ELLEN LOUISE, political economist; b. Boston, Apr. 26, 1945; d. Horace Wier and Mildred (Kip) F.; m. William F. Pedersen, Jr., Feb. 2, 1974; 1 son by previous marriage, Jai Kumar Ojha; children: Mark Francis Pedersen, Claire Ellen Pedersen. BA magna cum laude, Radcliffe Coll., 1966; MA, Fletcher Sch. Law and Diplomacy, 1967; PhD, Harvard U., 1972. Teaching fellow, instr. Harvard U., Wellesley Coll., 1969-71; legis. asst. Office of Senator Alan Cranston, Washington, 1972-74; fgn. affairs officer Dept. Treasury, Washington, 1974-77; dep. dir. Office of Internat. Trade Policy and Negotiations, 1977; dep. asst. sec. of def. for internat. econ. and tech. affairs Dept. Def., Washington, 1977-81; dir. govt. programs Westinghouse Electric Corp., Washington, 1981-88; corp. dir., internat. affairs United Techs. Corp., Washington, 1988-91; sr. fellow Inst. for Internat. Econs., Washington, 1992-93, 95-98, vis. fellow; counselor to U.S. Trade Rep., Washington, 1993-95. Author: For Richer, For Poorer: The New U.S.-Japan Relationship, 1987, Transatlantic Trade: A Strategic Agenda, 1997; co-editor: The Global Century, 2001. Trustee Aspen Inst. Berlin, 1990-92. NSF trainee, 1967-69 Mem. Internat. Inst. Strategic Studies, Coun. Fgn. Rels., Phi Beta Kappa.

FROST, EVERETT LLOYD, anthropologist, academic administrator; b. Salt Lake City, Oct. 17, 1942; s. Henry Hoag Jr. and Ruth Salome (Smith) F.; m. Janet Owens, Mar. 26, 1967; children: Noreen Karyn, Joyce Lida. BA in Anthropology, U. Utah, 1965; PhD in Anthropology, U. Oreg., 1970. Field researcher in cultural anthropology, Taveuni, Fiji, 1968-69; asst. prof. in anthropology Ea. N.Mex. U., Portales, 1970-74, assoc. prof., 1974-76, asst. dean Coll. Liberal Arts and Scis., 1976-78, dean acad. affairs and grad. studies, 1978-80, v.p. for planning and analysis, dean rsch., 1980-91, dean grad. studies, 1983-88, pres., 1991-2001, pres. emeritus, prof. anthropology emeritus, 2001—. Cons., evaluator N. Ctrl. Assn. Accreditation Agy. for Higher Edn., 1989-93—, mem. rev. bd., 1993-95—; bd. mem. emeritus N.Mex. First; commr., past pres. Western Interstate Commn. for Higher Edn., 1993—; pres. Lone Star Athletic Conf. Pres.'s Commn., 1992-93; chmn. rsch. com. N.Mex. First, 1989-91. Chmn. N.Mex. Humanities Coun., 1980-88; mem. N.Mex. Gov.'s Commn. on Higher Edn., 1983-86; mem. exec. bd. N.Mex. First, 1987-92; bd. dirs. Roosevent Gen. Hosp., Portales, 1989-92; pres. bd. dirs. San Juan County Mus. Assn., Farmington, 1979-82; vice chair Portales Pub. Schs. Facilities Com., 1990-91. NDEA fellow, 1969-70; grantee NEW, 1979-80, NSF, 1968-69, Fiji Forbes, Ltd., 1975-76, others. Fellow Am. Anthropol. Assn., Am. Assn. Higher Edn., Soc. Coll. and Univ. Planning, Assn. Social Anthropologists Oceania, Anthropol. Soc. Washington, Sch. Am. Rsch., Western Assn. Grad. Deans, Current Anthropology (assoc.) Polynesian Soc., Phi Kappa Phi.

FROST, HELEN MARIE, writer; b. Brookings, S.D., Mar. 4, 1949; d. Reuben Bernhard and Jean Elizabeth (Timmons) F.; m. Chad Lawrence Thompson, July 23, 1983; 1 child, Glen Andrew Thompson; 1 stepchild, Lloyd Samuel Thompson. BS, Syracuse U., 1971; MAT, Ind. U., 1994. Cert. in elem. edn., Alaska, Ind., Mass. Tchr. Kilquhanity House Sch., Castle Douglas, Scotland, 1976-78; prin., tchr. Telida (Alaska) Sch., 1981-84; tchr. White Cliff Sch., Ketchikan, Alaska, 1990-91; tchr. English, dir. Writing Ctr. Ind. U./Purdue U., Ft. Wayne, 1996-97. Cons. numerous schs. and orgns., 1990—; mem. Lane Literary Guild, Eugene, Oreg., 1986-89, pres. 1988-89. Poetry tchr. program for at-risk youth Ft. Wayne Dance Collective, 1995—. Mem. Soc. Children's Book Writers and Illustrators, Tchrs. and Writers Collaborative, Poetry Soc. Am. (Robert Winner award 1992, Mary Carolyn Davies award 1993), Acad. Am. poets, Writers Ctr. Indpls. Avocations: crosscountry skiing, gardening, raising and releasing monarch butterflies. Home and Office: 6108 Old Brook Dr Fort Wayne IN 46835-2438 E-mail: frost-thompson@att.net.

FROST, J. ORMOND, otolaryngologist, educator; b. Ireland, May 18, 1927; came to U.S., 1952, naturalized, 1963; s. James Patrick and Margaret (O'Loghlen) F.; m. Rita Robert, Oct. 1, 1955; 1 dau., Roberta. M.B.B.Ch., Univ. Coll. Dublin, 1952. House officer Mater Hosp., Dublin, Ireland, 1952; intern Loyola U. Mercy Hosp., Chgo., 1953; resident, asst., assoc. prof. Sch. Medicine NYU, N.Y.C., 1953-74, prof. clin. otolaryngology, 1974-89, clin. prof. otolaryngology, 1989—. Mem. AMA, N.Y. Otologic Soc. (pres. 1983-85), ACS, Am. Acad. Otolaryngology (bd. govs. 1985-88), Am. Otol., Rhinol. and Laryngol. Soc., St. George Soc., Irish-Am. Cultural Inst., W.B. Yeats Soc., Amateur Comedy Club. Roman Catholic.

FROST, JAMES ARTHUR, former university president; b. Manchester, Eng., May 15, 1918; came to U.S., 1926, naturalized, 1942; s. Harry Arthur and Janet (Wilson) F.; m. Elsie Mae Lorenz, Sept. 14, 1942 (dec.); children: Roger Arthur (dec.), Janet Linda Frost Naleski, Elise Anita Frost Alair. BA, Columbia U., 1940, MA, 1941, PhD, 1949; LLD, So. Conn. State U., 1993. Tchr. Am. history high sch., Nutley, N.J., 1946-47, instr. SUNY Coll.-Oneonta, 1947-49, asst. to pres., 1949-52, dean, 1952-64; assoc. provost acad. planning Cen. Adminstrn., SUNY, 1964-65, exec. dean for four year colls., 1965-68, vice chancellor for univ. colls., 1968-72; exec. dir. Conn. State Colls., 1972-83; pres. Conn. State U., 1983-85, pres. emeritus, 1985—; instr. Am. history Columbia U., summers, 1947-48; Smith-Mundt prof. Am. history U. Ceylon, 1959-60. Mem. com. on research and devel. Coll. Entrance Exam Bd., 1973-76; mem. adv. bd. Conn. Rev., 1972-76; mem. commn. on higher edn. Middle States Assn. Colls. and Secondary Schs., 1966-72; mem. Nat. Coun. Heads of Systems of Pub. Higher Edn., 1976-85, pres., 1979-80, now hon. mem. Author: Life on the Upper Susquehanna, 1783-1860, 1951; (with David M. Ellis, Harold Syrett, Harry J. Carman) A Short History of New York State, 1957, 2d edit., 1967; (with David M. Ellis and William B. Fink) New York: The Empire State, 1961, 5th edit., 1980; (with R.A. Brown, D.M. Ellis, William B. Fink) A History of the United States: The Evolution of a Free People, 1967, 2d edit., 1969, The Establishment of the Connecticut State University, 1965-85; Notes and Reminiscences, 1991, The Country Club of Farmington, Connecticut, 1892-1995, 1996; mem. editl. bd. SUNY Press, 1964-72; contbr. articles on history and edn. to mags. Treas. Conn. State U. Found., Inc., 1999—2003, bd. dirs., 1983—, treas., 1986—95, 1995—2003, pres., 1995—98, chmn. investment com., 1995—2003; trustee Robinson Sch., Hartford, 1973—77; sponsor Soc. Columbia Scholars, 1997—. Maj. AUS U.S. Army, 1941—46, lt. col. USAFR. Rockefeller grantee, 1959

Fellow N.Y. State Hist. Assn.; mem. Country Club of Farmington, Conn. Congregationalist. Home: 17 Neal Dr Simsbury CT 06070-2801 Office: Conn State U 39 Woodland St Hartford CT 06105-2337

FROST, JEROME KENNETH, lawyer; b. July 4, 1939; s. Carl Kenneth and Madeline May (Michel) F.; m. Carol Ann Brown, May 16, 1967; children: Arthur, Carl, Anya, Jonah, Jerome. BA, Siena Coll., 1962; JD, Boston Coll., 1965. Bar: N.Y. 1965, U.S. Dist. Ct. (no. dist.) N.Y. 1965, U.S. Ct. Appeals (2d cir.) 1982. Assoc. Wagar, Taylor, Howd & Brearton, Troy, N.Y., 1965-66; ptnr. Lee, LeForestier & Frost, Troy, N.Y., 1967-75; sole practice Troy, N.Y., 1976—. Asst. corp. counsel City of Troy, 1970-73, Rensselaer County Pub. Defender, 1995—. Editor Boston Coll. Law Rev., 1965. Player, agt. Lansingburgh Little League, 1982-87. Named one of, Best Lawyers in Am., 2001—02, 2003—; Presdl. scholar, Boston Coll., 1965. Mem. Rensselaer County Bar Assn., Order of Coif, Alpha Sigma Nu, Delta Epsilon Sigma, Alpha Kappa Alpha, Alpha Mu Gamma. Roman Catholic. Avocation: French language. Home: 20 Deepkill Ln Troy NY 12182-9738 Office: 105 Jordan Rd Troy NY 12180-8376 E-mail: jfrost@frostfirm.com.

FROST, JERRY WILLIAM, religion and history educator, library administrator; b. Muncie, Ind., Mar. 17, 1940; s. J. Thomas and Margaret Esther (Meredith) F.; m. Susan Vanderlyn Kohler; 1 son, James. BA, DePauw U., Greencastle, Ind., 1962; postgrad., Yale Div. Sch., 1962-63; MA, U. Wis.-Madison, 1965, PhD, 1968. Instr. Vassar Coll., 1967-68, asst. prof. history, 1968-73; assoc. prof. religion Swarthmore Coll., 1973—, prof. religion, 1980—, Howard M. and Charles F. Jenkins prof. of Quaker history and rsch., 1981—2002, sr. rsch. scholar, 2003—. Author: The Quaker Family in Colonial America, 1973, Connecticut Education in Revolutionary Era, 1974, A Perfect Freedom: Religions Liberty in Pennsylvania, 1990; co-author: The Quakers, 1988, Christianity: A Social and Cultural History, 1998; editor: The Keithian Controversy in Early Pennsylvania, 1980, Ouaker Origins of Antislavery, 1981, Records and Recollections of James Jenkins, 1984, Seeking the Light: Essays in Quaker History, 1987; editor Pa. Mag. of History and Biography, 1981-86; contbr. articles to profl. publs. Bd. dirs. Friends Hist. Assn., 1973—. John Carter Brown Libr. fellow, 1970, Eugene M. Lang fellow, 1980-81, 97, Phila. Ctr. fellow, 1986; U.S. Inst. of Peace grantee, 1992. Mem. Soc. Of Friends. Home: 890 Millington Rd Sudlersville MD 21668 Office: Swarthmore Coll Friends Hist Libr Swarthmore PA 19081

FROST, JOHN ELLIOTT, minerals company executive; b. Winchester, Mass., May 20, 1924; s. Elliott Putnam and Hazel Lavera (Carley) F.; m. Carolyn Catlin, July 12, 1945 (div. 1969); children: John Crocker, Jeffrey Putnam, Teresa Baird, Virginia Nicholl; m. Martha Hicks, June 6, 1969 (div. 1984); m. Catherine Kearns, July 27, 1985 (dec. Jan. 1997); m. Betty Nelson, Sept. 12, 1997. BS, Stanford U., 1949, MS, 1950, PhD, 1965. Geologist Asarco, Salt Lake City, 1951-54; chief geologist, surface mines supt., gen. mgr. Philippine Iron Mines Inc., Larap, Camarines Norte, 1954-60; chief geologist Duval Corp. (Pennzoil Corp.), Tucson, 1961-67; minerals exploration mgr. Exxon Corp., Houston, 1967-71; divsn. minerals mgr. Esso Eastern Inc., 1971-80; sr. v.p. div. Exxon Minerals Co., Houston, 1980-86; pres. Exxon Minerals Internat., Houston, 1980-86, Frost Minerals Internat., Houston, 1986—; v.p. Kalahari Resources, 1996—. Bd. dirs. Abitibi Mining Corp., Sedex Mining Corp., UnitedEngring. Trustees, N.Y.C., chmn. real estate com., 1986-89, v.p., 1989-91, pres., 1991-93. Mem. adv. bd. Earth Scis., Stanford (Calif.) U., 1983-85; pres. SEG Found., 1984, bd. dirs., 1981-84, 94-98. Served to 1st lt. USAAF, 1943-45, PTO. Fellow Geol. Soc. Am., Soc. Econ. Geologists (pres. 1989-90, councilor 1982-84, program com., chmn. nominating com. 1982); mem. AIME (chmn. edn. com. Soc. Mining Engrs. 1971; Charles F. Rand medal 1984, Disting. Mem. award 1984, Disting. Svc. award 1991, named to Legion of Honor 2001), Australian Inst. Mining and Metallurgy, Am. Inst. Profl. Geologists, Sigma Xi. Republican. Presbyterian. Home and Office: 602 Sandy Port St Houston TX 77079-2419

FROST, JUANITA CORBITT, retired hospital foundation coordinator; b. Rockford, Ill., Aug. 4, 1926; d. Mervin Charles and Eva Marie (Moberg) Corbitt; m. Thomas Tapenden Frost, Jan. 3, 1954; children: Annamarie, Thomas Tapenden. Student, Little Rock U., Ark., 1959-61. Med. sec. asst. clin. pathology lab. VA Hosp., Whipple, Ariz., 1951-54; exec. dir. Camp Fire Girls, Temple, Tex., 1967-73; exec. sec. Scott and White Meml. Hosp. Found., Temple, 1973-82; hosp. found. coordinator, exec. asst. to bd. Scott and White Meml. Hosp., Temple, 1982-98, Scott Sherwood and Brindley Found., Temple, 1982-98; ret., 1998. Vestrywoman Episcopal Ch., Temple, 1985-88, sr. warden, 1987, worship com., 1995-97, search com., 1996-97; active Com. on Bishops Address NW Region Diocese Episcopal Ch., Houston, 1988, Bell County Choral Group, Belton, Tex., 1988-92, Tchr. Literacy Coun., Temple, 1988-93, Temple Civic Theatre Guild, 1997; mem. St. Francis Ch. Altar Guild; coord. capital campaign St. Francis Episcopal Ch., Temple, 2000. Mem. Am. Hosp. Assn. Exec. Assts., Dau. of the King (sec. St. Clare chpt. 1998-99). Avocations: choral singing, playing piano and organ, sailing, needlework, reading. Home: 4312 S 31st St Apt 34 Temple TX 76502

FROST, LINDA GAIL, clergyman, hospital chaplain; b. Louisville, Feb. 26, 1950; d. Halqua Mildon and Christena (Crisp) F. BA, Georgetown (Ky.) Coll., 1972; MDiv, So. Bapt. Sem., Louisville, 1978, DMin, 1982. Ordained to ministry Bapt. Ch., 1978; bd. cert. chaplain. Social worker Dept. Pub. Welfare, Corpus Christi, 1972-76; assoc. to pastor Walnut St. Bapt. Ch., Louisville, 1979-89; chaplain, clin. supr. Koala Hosp., Columbus, Ind., 1989-92; dir. chaplain svcs. Caritas Med. Ctr., Louisville, 1993—. Advisor pastoral svcs. Hospice of S.E. Ind., Jeffersonville, 1993—. Author, A Legacy in Missions and Ministry, 1993. Bd. dirs., pres. Neighborhood Devel. Corp., Louisville, 1979-89; mem., sec. Old Louisville Neighborhood Coun., 1979-87; active ARC Disaster Svcs., 1999—. Mem.: Ky. Chaplain Assn. (pres. 1999—).

FROST, (JONAS) MARTIN, III, congressman; b. Glendale, Calif., Jan. 1, 1942; s. Jack and Doris (Marwil) Frost; m. Kathy George Frost; children: Alanna, Mariel, Camille. BA in History, BA in Journalism, U. Mo., 1964; JD, Georgetown U., 1970. Bar: Tex. 1970. Law clk. U.S. Dist. Ct. Judge Sarah T. Hughes, Dallas, 1970-71; legal commentator Sta. KERA-TV, Dallas, 1971-72; pvt. practice law Dallas, 1972-79; mem. 96th-108th Congresses from 24th Tex. dist., Washington, 1979—, Select Com. on Homeland Security. Mem. US Army Reserve, 1966—72. Del. Dem. Commn. on Congl. Mailing Stds. Nat. Conv., 1976, 84, 88, 92, 96; coord. North Tex. Carter-Mondale Campaign, 1976; chmn. Dem. Caucus 1999-2003; Tex. del. chmn. Dem. Nat. Conv., mem. rules com.; del. Dem. Nat. Conv., 2000. Democrat. Office: 2256 Rayburn Ho Office Bldg Washington DC 20515-4324*

FROST, NORMAN COOPER, retired telephone company executive; b. Nashville, Feb. 6, 1923; s. Norman and Anna Martha (Cooper) F.; m. Katherine McDonald Shapard, Nov. 25, 1948; children: Kathy, Norman Cooper Jr. BA, Vanderbilt U., 1943, JD, 1948. Bar: Tenn. 1946, Ga. 1954, N.Y. 1964, D.C. 1965. Practiced in Nashville, 1948-50; trust officer Nashville Trust Co., 1952-53; atty. So. Bell Telephone Co., Atlanta, 1953-61, gen. atty., 1961-62; atty. Am. Tel. & Tel. Corp., N.Y.C., 1962-66, asst. gen. atty., 1966-67; v.p., gen. counsel South Cen. Bell, Birmingham, Ala., 1968-83; exec. v.p., gen. counsel Bell South Corp., Atlanta, 1983-88. Served with USMCR, 1943-46, 50-52. Mem. ABA, Ga. Bar Assn., Tenn. Bar Assn., N.Y. Bar Assn., D.C. Bar Assn., Order of Coif. Methodist. Home: 9955 Huntcliff Trce Atlanta GA 30350-2717 Office: Bell South Corp 533 Southern Bell Ctr Atlanta GA 30375-0001

FROST, ORCUTT WILLIAM, historian, educator; b. Cloquet, Minn., June 3, 1926; s. Orcutt William and Agnes Harriet Frost; m. Mary Denison Bills, June 22, 1954; children: Carol, William, Susan, Robert. BA co-salutatorian, U. Ill., Champaign-Urbana, 1949, MA, 1950, PhD, 1954. Assoc. prof. Willamette U., Salem, Oreg., 1954—63; prof. English Alaska Meth. U., Anchorage, 1963—76; prof. humanities Alaska Pacific U., Anchorage, 1977—91, prof. emeritus, 1991. Acad. dean Alaska Meth. U., Anchorage, 1963—71, 1975—76; exchange prof. Nagoya Gakuin U., Nagoya, Japan, 1969—70; mem. bd. dirs. Alaska Humanities Forum, Anchorage, 1978—84; dir. Bering-Chirikov Conf. Alaska Pacific U., Anchorage, 1991. Author: (Book) Joaquin Miller, 1967, Bering: The Russian Discovery of America, 2003; editor (and co-translator): G. W. Steller Journal of Voyage with Bering, 1988 (Alaskan Historian of Yr., 1989). V.p. Anchorage Native Welcome Ctr., Alaska, 1964—66; pres. Coun. of Chs., Salem, Oreg., 1958—60; bd. dirs. Alaska Lung Assn., Anchorage, 1975—76. Sgt. U.S. Army, 1944—46, Philippines, Japan. Mem.: Soc. for the History of Discoveries, Phi Beta Kappa. Presbyterian. Achievements include research in the history of Russian America, 1741-1867. Avocation: tennis. Home: 1130 Skyline Dr Medford OR 97504-8586

FROST, PHILIP, pharmaceutical executive, dermatologist; MD, Albert Einstein Coll., Bronx, NY, 1961. Former chmn. dept. of dermatology Mt. Sinai Med. Center, Miami, Fla.; chmn. Key Pharmaceuticals, Miami, Fla., 1972—86; founder, chmn., CEO Ivax Corp., Miami, Fla., 1987—. Office: Ivax Corp 4400 Biscayne Blvd Miami FL 33137-3212

FROST, ROBERT EDWIN, chemistry educator; b. Gowanda, N.Y., Feb. 1, 1932; s. Sidney Mauthe and Mary Theresa (Bollinger) F.; m. Janice Ruth Young, May 31, 1958; children— Elizabeth Ann, Nancy Lynn, Barbara Jean. BS, Allegheny Coll., 1953; A.M., Harvard, 1955, PhD, 1957. Research chemist B.F. Goodrich Research Center, Brecksville, Ohio, 1957-61; assoc. prof. SUNY at Albany, 1961-64, prof. chemistry, 1964-95, prof. emeritus, 1995. Kettering vis. lectr. U. Ill., Urbana, 1965-66 Mem. Am. Chem. Soc., Phi Beta Kappa, Sigma Xi. Home: 329 W Highland Dr Schenectady NY 12303-5751

FROST, S. DAVID, retired naval officer; b. Southard, Okla., Apr. 21, 1930; s. Chester William and Martha Leah (Weber) F.; m. Dolores Marie Radja, Oct. 17, 1953; children: Kathleen D., David J., Karen T., Mary C. BS, U.S. Naval Acad., 1953; MBA, Stanford U., 1961; student, Naval War Coll., 1964-65. Commd. officer USN, 1953, advanced through grades to rear adm., 1977; jr. officer USS Henrico, 1953-55; with Navy Fin. Center, Cleve., 1956-58; supply officer USS Rankin, 1958-59; asst. planning officer Navy Ordnance Supply Office, Mechanicsburg, Pa., 1961- 64; with Navy Fleet Material Support Office, 1965-68; supply officer USS America, 1968-70; exec. asst. asst. sec. def. (comptroller) Washington, 1970-74; exec. officer Naval Supply Center, Norfolk, Va., 1974-75; comdg. officer Navy Supply Corps Sch., Athens, Ga., 1975-77; dep. comdr. plans, policy and systems devel. Navy Dept., Washington, 1977-78; dep. comptroller of the Navy, 1978-80, 81-83; comptroller, 1980-81; staff dir. for mgmt. Bd. Govs. FRS, 1983-99; ret., 1999. Pres. Civic League, Virginia Beach, Va., 1969; bd. dirs. N.E. Ga. coun. Boy Scouts Am., 1976-77; bd. dirs. Brent Soc., 1986-92, pres., 1990-91; pres. Oakton Optimist Club, 1986-87, 92-93. Decorated Disting. Service Medal, Legion Merit, Vietnamese Gallantry cross. Mem. Athens C. of C., Optimists Club, Rotary, Knights of Malta, Phi Delta Theta. Roman Catholic. Home: 10870 Meadow Pond Ln Oakton VA 22124-1446 *My life, both personal and professional, has been guided by allegiance to three primary areas: family, Christian faith, and the nation.*

FROST, STERLING NEWELL, arbitrator, mediator, management consultant; b. Oklahoma City, Dec. 21, 1935; s. Sterling Johnson and Eula Dove (Whitford) F.; m. Patricia Joyce Rose, Aug. 18, 1957; children: Patricia Diane Wiscarson, Richard Sterling, Lindy Layne Harrington. BS Indsl. Engring., U. Okla., Norman, 1957; MS Indsl. Engring., Okla. State U., 1966. Registered profl. engr., Okla., Calif. Asst. mgr. acctg. Western Electric, Balt., 1972-73; mgr. indsl. engring. Chgo., 1973-75; mgr. devel. engring., 1975-76; mgr. acct. mgmt., 1976-78; dir. staff Morristown, N.J., 1978-79; gen. mgr. distbn. & repair AT&T Techs., Sunnyvale, Calif., 1979-85; area v.p. material mgmt. svcs. AT&T Info. Systems, Oakland, Calif., 1985-87; ops. v.p. material mgmt. svcs. San Francisco, 1988-89; dir. configuration ops. Businessland, Inc., San Jose, Calif., 1989-90; dir. svcs. support, 1990-91; exec. v.p. Isotek, Tiburon, Calif., 1991; v.p., gen. mgr. Tree Fresh, San Francisco, 1991-92; CFO Prima Pacific, Iinc., Tiburon, 1992-93; mgmt. cons., arbitrator/mediator Sterling Solutions, Santa Cruz, 1992—. Bd. dirs. Contract Office Group, San Jose, 1983-2001, chmn., 1984-2001; arbitrator NASD, N.Y. Stock Exch., Calif. State Mediation and Conciliation Svcs., 1992—; mediator U.S. Postal Svc., 1998—. Bd. dirs. Santa Clara County YMCA, San Jose, Calif., 1981-84, No. Calif. Mediation Assn., 1995-99. Recipient Man of Day citation Sta. WAIT Radio, Chgo. Mem. NSPE (chmn. edn. com. 1969-70), Am. Inst. Indsl. Engrs. (pres. bd. dirs. 1966-68), Okla. Soc. Profl. Engrs. (v.p. 1968-69), No. Calif. Mediation Assn. (bd. dirs. 1996-98), Am. Arbitration Assn. Republican.

FROST, WAYNE N. lawyer; b. Winters, Tex., Nov. 24, 1953; s. J.F. and Dorothy (Martin) F.; m. Susan Amini, Aug. 15, 1981; children: Daniel Morgan, Charlotte Nicole. BA in Criminal Justice, U. Tex., Odessa, 1976; M Criminal Justice Adminstrn., Oklahoma City U., 1978; JD, Detroit Coll. Law, 1984; postgrad., U. Houston, 1987. Bar: Tex. 1986, U.S. Dist. Ct. (we. dist.) Tex. 1990, U.S. Ct. Appeals (5th cir.) 2000. Law clk. U.S. Atty.'s Office, Detroit, 1984; tchg. fellow, dir. moot ct. program Detroit Coll. Law, 1984; asst. dist. atty. Midland County Dist. Atty.'s Office, Midland, Tex., 1984-2000, chief narcotics prosecutor, 1992-99, sr. staff atty., 1986-2000. Pvt. practice, Midland, 1986—; guest lectr. Tex. Crime-Stoppers, West Tex. Area Peace Officers Assn.; instr. Tex. Narcotics Control Program, Police Acad., Ft. Worth, Tex.; hon. co-chmn. Congrl. Bus. Adv. Coun. Contbr. articles to profl. jours. Sunday sch. tchr. 1st Baptist Ch., Midland; hon. dep. Ector County Sheriff's Dept., Odessa, Tex., 1974—; bd. dirs. MADD, Midland, 1993—; hon. co-chmn. Congl. Bus. Adv. Coun. Named Businessman of Yr., Nat. Rep. Congl. Com., 2003. Mem. Nat. Dist. Attys. Assn., Tex. Dist. and County Attys. Assn., Tex. Narcotics Officers Assn. (guest lectr., counsel gen.), Sheriffs Assn. Tex., Midland Scottish Rite Assn. (past pres., trustee scholarship found.), Hon. co-chmn. Congressional Bus. Adv. Coun., Nat. Rep. Congressional Com. (Tex. Businessman of Yr. 2003), U. Tex. Alumni Assn. (life), Masons (32d degree), DeMolay (Legion of Honor), Phi Theta Kappa. Republican. Baptist. Avocations: jogging, hunting, antiques, classical music. Home: 4503 Teakwood Trce Midland TX 79707-1626 also: PO Box 2233 Midland TX 79702-2233 Office: 203 W Wall Ste 205 Midland TX 79701

FROSTIC, FREDERICK LEE, strategic planning and defense policy consultant; b. Detroit; s. Frederick Ralph and Harriet Julia (Stroh) F.; children by previous marriage: Melinda Ann, Frederick Hollis; m. Dianne Kathleen Hughes, May 24, 2003. BS, USAF Acad., 1963; MS in Engring., U. Mich., 1971. Comml. pilot. Fighter pilot USAF, 1963-89, asst. prof. engring. sci., 1971-74, vice comdr. 50th Tactical Fighter Wing, 1984-87, comdr. Northeast Air Def. Sector Griffiss AFB, N.Y., 1987-89; sr. engr., assoc. programming dir. RAND, Santa Monica, Calif., 1989-94; dept. asst. sec. def. Dept. Def., Washington, 1994-97; prin. Booz, Allen & Hamilton, Inc., McLean, Va., 1997—. Mem. Long Range Airpower Panel, 1998—. Author: The New Calculus, 1994. Named Outstanding Young Man Am., 1970. Democrat. Presbyterian. Avocations: sports, reading. Home: 1357 Heritage Oak Way Reston VA 20194 Office: Allen & Hamilton Inc 8283 Greensboro Dr Mc Lean VA 22102-3802 E-mail: frostic_fred@bah.com.

FROST-KNAPPMAN, ELIZABETH (LINDA ELIZABETH FROST-KNAPPMAN), editor, author, executive; b. Washington, Oct. 1, 1943; d. Edward Laurie and Lorena (Ameter) Frost; m. Edward William Knappman, Nov. 6, 1965; 1 child, Amanda. BA, George Washington U., 1965; postgrad., U. Wis., 1966, NYU, 1966. Editor Natural History Press, N.Y.C., 1967-69, William Collins and Sons, London, 1970-71; sr. editor Doubleday and Co., N.Y.C., 1972-80, William Morrow and Co., Inc., N.Y.C., 1980-82; founder, pres. New Eng. Pub. Assocs. Inc., Chester, Conn., 1982—. Lectr. New Eng. colls. and univs. Author: The World Almanac of Presidential Quotations, 1993, The ABC-CLIO Companion to Women's Progress in America, 1994 (Outstanding Acad. Book-Reference of Yr. award ALA), The Quotable Lawyer, 1986, 1998, Women Suffrage in America: An Eyewitness History, 1992, Courtroom Dramas, 3 vols., 1997; gen. editor: (CD-ROM) American Journey: Women in America, 1994, Women's Rights on Trial, 1998. Mem. Assn. Authors Reps., Authors Guild, Am. Soc. Journalists and Authors. Avocations: knitting, tennis, travel, reading, piano. Home: 59 Parker Hill Rd PO Box 805 Higganum CT 06441-0805 Office: New Eng Pub Assocs Inc PO Box 5 Chester CT 06412-0005 E-mail: nepa@nepa.com.

FROTHINGHAM, THOMAS ELIOT, pediatrician; b. Boston, June 21, 1926; s. Channing and Clara Morgan (Rotch) F.; m. Phyllis Mary Steiner, June 12, 1954 (div. 1983); children: Phyllis Eliot, Thomas Dean, Benjamin Rotch, David Griffith; m. Barbara Mathis, Dec. 28, 1987 (div. 2002). Student, Harvard U., 1944-46, MD, 1951. Intern Bellevue Hosp., N.Y.C., 1951-52; resident, rsch. fellow in infectious diseases Children's Hosp., Boston, 1955-59; asst. prof. epidemiology Tulane U. Med. Sch., 1959—60; assoc. mem. Pub. Health Rsch. Inst., City of N.Y., 1960-61; asst. prof., then assoc. prof. tropical pub. health Sch. Pub. Health Harvard U., 1961-69; pediatrician Corvallis (Oreg.) Clinic, 1969-73; prof. pediat., family and cmty. medicine Duke U. Med. Ctr., 1973-94, prof. emeritus, 1994—. Contbr. articles to profl. jours. Co-founder Ctr. for Child and Family Health, N.C., 1996—. With USNR, 1944-46, 52-55. Mem. Am. Soc. Tropical Medicine and Hygiene, Am. Acad. Pediatrics. Home: 26 Lucy St Dartmouth MA 02748

FROULA, CHRISTINE, English literature educator; b. Louisville, Mich., Mar. 24, 1950; d. James C. and Helen B. Froula; m. John Bradbury Austin, Sept. 4, 1988. BA, U. Chgo., 1971; MA, U. Chgo., 1972, PhD, 1977. Asst. prof. U. Ala., Tuscaloosa, 1977—78, Yale U., New Haven, 1978—83, assoc. prof., 1987—91, Northwestern U., Evanston, Ill., 1987—91, prof., 1991—. Hurst vis. prof. Washington U., St. Louis, 2000; faculty Internat. James Joyce Summer Sch., Dublin, 1996, Internat. Yeats Summer Sch., Sligo, Ireland, 1993. Author: (books) Modernism's Body: Sex, Culture and Image, 1996, To Write Paradise: Ezra Pound's Cantos, 1984, A Guide to Ezra Pound's Selected Poems, 1983; contbr. articles to profl. jours. Co-chair Orgn. Women Faculty, Northwestern U., 2001—02. Named Herman & Beulah Pearce Miller Rsch. prof., Northwestern U., 1992—94, Alice Buline Kaplan Humanities fellow, 2002—03; fellow, Guggenheim Found., 1990—91. Mem.: AAUW, MLA, Internat. Virginia Woolf Soc. (pres. 1997—2000). Home: 2801 Girard Ave Evanston IL 60201 Office: Northwestern U English Dept 1897 Sheridan Rd Evanston IL 60208

FROULA, JAMES DEWAYNE, national honor society executive, engineer; b. Oak Park, Ill., May 17, 1945; s. James Clarence and Helen Barbara (Tanana) F.; m. Barbara Jean Leftwich, June 8, 1968; children: James Matthew, Anna Katherine. BSME, U. Tenn., 1967, MS, 1968. Lic. profl. engr., Tenn. Engr. IBM Corp., Lexington, Ky., 1970-74, engring. mgr. Boulder, Colo., 1974-82; exec. dir., sec.-treas., editor Tau Beta Pi, Knoxville, Tenn., 1982—; pres. Assn. Coll. Honor Socs., 1991-93. Editor The Bent of Tau Beta Pi, 1982—; patentee magnetic brush roll. 1st lt. U.S. Army, 1968-70, Vietnam. Decorated Bronze Star; fellow Nat. Sci. Found., 1967-68. Mem. ASME, NSPE (bd. dirs. Knoxville chpt. 1988-94, Outstanding Engr. 1994), Coun. Engring. and Sci. Soc. Execs., Tenn. Soc. Profl. Engrs. (chair divsn. profl. engrs. in edn. practice 1993-96), Am. Assn. Engring. Socs. (awards com. 1997-2000). Roman Catholic. Avocations: mountain climbing, hiking. Office: Tau Beta Pi PO Box 2697 Knoxville TN 37901-2697

FROW, RICHARD G. retired librarian; b. Miami, Fla., May 7, 1932; s. Franklin John Frow and Edith M. Pearce. AB in French, magna cum laude, U. Miami, 1954; MA in Libr. Sci., Fla. State U., 1961. Cert. libr. and tchr. social studies Fla. Tchr., libr. Dade County Pub. Schs., Miami, 1957—58; head libr. Miami Jackson H.S., 1958—64; summer intern libr. econs., divsn. NY Pub. Libr, NYC, 1962; asst. editor Pub. Affairs Info. Svc. Bull., N.Y.C., 1964—77; libr. planning dept. Metro-Dade County, Miami, 1978—79; head ref. libr. urban affairs sect. Miami-Dade Pub. Libr. Sys., 1979—92; ret., 1992. Editor: Urban Affairs Newsletter, 1979—92. Mem.: Am. Horticultural Soc., Am. Assn. Individual Investors, Nat. Audubon Soc., Am. Orchid Soc., Nat. Trust for Hist. Preservation, Phi Eta Sigma, Pi Delta Phi, Kappa Delta Pi, Beta Phi Mu, Phi Kappa Phi. Democrat. Baptist. Avocations: gardening, reading, music, studying foreign languages. Home: 406 SE 28 Ave Ocala FL 34471

FRUCHER, MEYER S. (SANDY FRUCHER), brokerage house executive; BS in govt., Columbia U.; MPA, John F. Kennedy Sch. Govt., Harvard U. Chief labor negotiator State of N.Y., 1978—83; pres. and CEO Battery Park Authority, N.Y.C., 1984—88; exec. v.p. devel. Olympia and York (now World Fin. Properties, Inc.), 1988—96; chmn. and CEO Phila. Stock Exch., 1998—. Mgmt. cons. Chmn. bd. Mass. Mus. Contemporary Art. Office: Phila Stock Exch 1900 Market St Philadelphia PA 19103*

FRUCHTER, JONATHAN SEWELL, research scientist, geochemist; b. San Antonio, June 5, 1945; s. Benjamin and Dorothy Ann (Sewell) F.; m. Cecelia Ann Smith, Mar. 31, 1973; children: Diane, Daniel. BS in Chemistry, U. Tex., 1966; PhD in Geochemistry, U. Calif., San Diego, 1971. Research assoc. U. Oreg., Eugene, 1971-74; research scientist Battelle Northwest, Richland, Wash., 1974-79, mgr. research and devel., 1979-87, staff scientist, 1987-91, 94—, tech. group leader, 1991-94. Contbr. numerous articles to profl. jours. Recipient R&D 100 Awd., 1998. Mem. AAAS, Am. Chem. Soc., Phi Beta Kappa, Phi Kappa Phi. Avocations: fishing, skiing, boating. Office: Battelle NW PO Box 999 Richland WA 99352-0999

FRUDAKIS, EVANGELOS WILLIAM, sculptor; b. Rains, Utah, May 13, 1921; s. William and Christina (Legerakis) F.; children— Anthony, Jennifer; m. Gerd Hesness, 1982 Student, Greenwich Work Shop, N.Y.C., 1935-39, Beaux Arts Inst. Design, 1940-41, Pa. Acad. Fine Arts, 1941-42, 45-49, Am. Acad. in Rome, 1950-52. Founder, instr. Frudakis Acad. Fine Arts, Phila., 1976-90. One-man shows include Atlantic City Art Center, 1956, 61, Woodmere Art Gallery, 1957, 62, Phila. Art Alliance, 1958, Pa. Acad. Fine Arts, 1962, Briarcliff Coll. Mus. Art, 1975, numerous group shows, 1940—, including, Pa. Acad. Fine Arts anns., N.A.D. anns., Am. Acad. in Rome, Audubon Artists, Phila. Mus. Art, Allied Artists Am., Nat. Arts Club, Pennsylvania Treasures show, Gov.'s Mansion, 1982; represented in permanent collections Pa. Acad. Fine Arts, Lehigh Valley Art Alliance, Woodmere Art Gallery, also pvt. collections; tchr., demonstrator sculpture, Nat. Acad. Design, N.Y.C., 1969-76, sculptor John F. Kennedy meml. monument Atlantic City Conv. Hall, 1964, Statesmen in Medicine Awards; portrait works Brian Brewer Blades, 1969, Melvin R. Laird, 1970, Barnes Woodhall, 1971, Aharon Katzir and Ephraim Katzir for Weizmann Inst., Israel, 1978, Dr. William Feinbloom, Pa. Coll. Optometry, 1989, Stephen E. Hyde, Trump Castle, Atlantic City, 1990; coins and medals Ted Shawn and Ruth St. Denis medal, Jacobs Pillow, Mass., Gemini Space Flights Nat. Commemorative Soc., 1966, Dacron medallion, Dupont, Wilmington, Del., Capt. James Cook medal, Hawaii Festival, Dolly Madison coin, medal Sociéte Commemorative de Femmes Celebres, 1967, Joseph Brant coin, Internat. Fraternal Commemorat Soc., 1968, Paul Lawrence Dunbar medal, Am. Negro Commemorative Soc., 1969, St. Damasus I medal, Cath. Commemorative Soc., Life of Christ series 12 coin medals, 1968-70, Alfred the Great medal, Britannia Commemorative Soc., 1970, Prince of Peace medal, Cath. Commemorative Soc., Scapular medal, Cath. Art Guild, 1970, St. John the 4th Apostle 12 Apostle series, Cath. Commemorative Medal Soc., 1970, John Quincy Adams and Lillian Wald medals, Hall of Fame for Great Ams., 1971, Brian Brewer Blades award medal Statesmen in Medicine, 1970, Richardson Dilworth Meml. Plaque, Phila., 1978, Deng Xioping Portrait Medal, 1979, Fishing Bear fountain, Phila. Zool. Gardens., The Signer, Independence Nat. Hist. Park, Phila., 1982, Naiad Fountain, Phila. Civic Ctr., 1982, Statue of Liberty Greek Relief, Ellis Island, 1986; Welcome Fountain, The Ritten House, Phila., 1989, The Minute Man, Nat. Guard Bld., Washington, 1991, 9' Minute Man, Nat. Guard Readiness Ctr., Arlington, Va., 1995, Reaching Fountain, Brookgreen Gardens, S.C., 1997; mem. coins and medals Art Commn., Atlantic City, Served with AUS, World War II, ETO. Decorated Bronze Battle Star (3); recipient 2 1st prizes Greenwich Work Shop 1939, Beaux Art Inst. 1941, 1st Julian B. Slevin prize Pa. Acad. Fine Arts 1941, Stimson prize 1947, Stewardson prize 1947, Cresson European scholarship 1947, spl. citation achievement 1948, 1st hon. mention fellowship 1948, Fellowship gold medal 1949, 55, 56, Henry Scheidt Meml. scholarship 1949, 1st hon. mention Prix de Rome 1942, Prix de Rome 1950, 51, Helen Foster Barnett prize N.A.D. 1948, Thomas R. Proctor prize 1957, Eben Demarest Trust Fund prize 1949, Louis Comfort Tiffany scholarship 1949, Sculpture House award Allied Artists Am. 1959, best portrait sculpture award Nat. Sculpture Soc.-Nat. Art Club 1961, John Gregory award Nat. Sculpture Soc. 1963, Nat. Fountain Competition award Little Rock 1965, Elizabeth N. Watrous gold medal N.A.D., N.Y.C. 1968, Dessie Greer prize N.A.D., N.Y.C. 1970, Artists Fund prize 1975, 77, 90, Therese and Edwin H. Richards prize Nat. Sculpture Soc., N.Y. 1972, Gold medal 1972, Francis Keally prize 1974, Herbert Adams Meml. medal 1976), N.S.S. Meiselman prize, 1981; gold medal NAD, 1984 N.A. Fellow Pa. Acad. Fine Arts, Am. Acad. in Rome, Nat. Sculpture Soc. (council), founding mem. Acad. Scis. Phila.; mem. Allied Artists Am.; hon. men. Am. Inst. Commemorative Art. Address: 312 Valley Dr Kerrville TX 78028-3910 E-mail: gareth@ktc.com.

FRUDAKIS, ROSALIE, small business owner; b. Bloomsburg, Pa., May 29, 1952; d. Jacob Louis and Mary (Kalish) Gluchoff; m. Zenos Antonios Frudakis, Jan. 9, 1976. BA in Social Work, Elizabethtown Coll., 1973; postgrad., Temple U., 1974. Art therapist Inst. of Pa. Hosp., Phila., 1974-75; dir. art therapy Bacharach Rehab. Ctr., Pomona, N.J., 1975-76; co-founder, officer of found.

Frudakis Acad. Fine Arts, Phila., 1976-85; founding ptnr., pres. Frudakis Gallery, Phila., 1976-85; founding ptnr. The Support System, Inc., Phila., 1984-87; ptnr. Frudakis Studio, Glenside, Pa., 1985—. Devel. cons. Mus. at Drexel U., Phila., 1988-91. Patentee for game and method for encouraging self-improvement. V.p. fin. and adminstrn. Bach Festival, Phila., 1992-93; mng. dir. Convergence Dancers and Musicians, 1993-2001; mgr. Pa. Pro Musica, 1995-97, Revisions, 1997-98; v.p. Phila. Cmty. Found., 1997—; pres. Frudakis Studio, Inc., 2002. Mem. Nat. Sculpture Soc. (allied profl. mem., devel. cons. 1985—, exhbn. project mgr 1987), mem. Lotos Club, NYC, 2003. Avocation: dance. Home: 2355 Mount Carmel Ave Glenside PA 19038-4103

FRUDAKIS, ZENOS ANTONIOS, sculptor, artist; b. San Francisco, July 7, 1951; s. Vasili and Kassiani (Alexis) F. Student, Pa. Acad. Fine Arts, Phila., 1973-76; BFA, U. Pa., 1982, MFA, 1983. Co-adj. prof. sculpture and drawing Rutgers U., 1984-85, 1993. Guest lectr. anatomy and sculpture Med. Coll. Pa., Phila., 1986-87; invited artist Utsukushi-Ga-Hara Open Air Mus., Japan, 1990. Exhibitions include Nat. Sculpture Soc., 1979—97, Allied Artists Am., N.Y.C., 1980—81, NAD, 1980, 1984, 1986, 1990, 1997, Pa. Acad. Fine Arts, 1981, Inst. Contemporary Art, Phila., 1981—83, Rutgers U., 1984—86; (numerous commd. works including) Air Force Meml., Arlington, Va., Richard Tufts Payne Stewart, Pinehurst, N.C., Frank Rizzo, Richardson Dilworth, Phila., Freedom, GSK, 16th Vinc Sts, Phila., Ga. Gov. Ellis Arnall, Atlanta, Elephant Fountain, Burlington, N.J., 1993. Recipient Hakone award, Rodin Grand prize Hakone Open Air Mus., Japan, 1990; inducted into Bobby Jones and Arnold Palmer, Ga. Golf Hall of Fame; devel. grantee Nat. Endowment for Arts, 1985, USIA travelling grantee, 1988-89. Fellow Nat. Sculpture Soc. (bd. dirs. 1988—, Art-in-Architecture award 1990, editor pro-tem Nat. Sculpture Rev. 1991-2002); mem. NAD (acad.), Academia Internat. per L'Unita della Cultura (Rome, academician), Lotos Club. Home: 2355 Mount Carmel Ave Glenside PA 19038-4103

FRUE, WILLIAM CALHOUN, lawyer; b. Pontiac, Mich., Dec. 29, 1934; s. William Calhoun and Evelyn Laura Frue; m. Eloise Saunders, June 22, 1956 (div. Dec. 1989); m. Jane Torres Fletcher, Dec. 30, 1989; children: William C. III, John C., Michael C., Victoria. BA, Washington & Lee U., 1956; LLB, U. N.C., 1960. Bar: N.C. 1960, U.S. Dist. Ct. (we. dist.) N.C. 1961, U.S. Tax Ct. 1968, U.S. Ct. Appeals (4th cir.) 1988. Rsch. asst. Inst. of Govt., Chapel Hill, N.C., 1958-60; assoc. Wright & Shuford, Asheville, N.C., 1961-69; ptnr. Shuford, Frue & Sluder, Asheville, 1969-72, Shuford, Frue & Best, Asheville, 1973-84, The Frue Law Firm, Asheville, 1984—. Editor Popular Govt. mag., 1958-60. Chmn. Asheville Police Retirement Fund, 1973-83, Morehead Scholarship Selectincom., 1965-90, Asheville Planning and Zoning Commn., 1982-92. Mem. N.C. Bar Assn., Buncombe County Bar Assn., (sec., v.p. 1978-92), Trout Unl d. (N.C. coun. 1965). Democrat. Episcopalian. Avocations: fishing, camping. Office: PO Box 7627 Asheville NC 28802-7627

FRUEH, BARTLEY RICHARD, surgeon; b. Cleve., Sept. 1, 1937; s. Lloyd Walter and Elizabeth Virginia (Scott) F.; m. Frances Olive Beach, June 10, 1961 (div. Dec. 1976); children: Bartley Christopher, Dylan Beach (dec.), Walter Terry; m. Frances Mallet-Prevost Gaston Sargent, Dec. 31, 1976 (div. Oct. 1997); stepchildren: Eric Winslow Sargent, Laura Elizabeth Sargent; m. Cheryl Lynn Terpening, June 1, 2002; 1 stepchild, Cherilyn Marie Smith. BChemE, Cornell U., 1960; MD, Columbia Coll. Phys./Surgeons, 1964; MS Ophthalmology U. Mich., 1970. Diplomate Am. Bd. Ophthalmology. Surg. intern N.C. Meml. Hosp., Chapel Hill, N.C., 1964-65; resident in ophthalmology U. Mich., Ann Arbor, 1967-70; fellow eye plastic surgery Alston Callahan, Birmingham, Ala., 1970; asst. prof. ophthalmology, eye plastic surgery U. Mo., Columbia, 1971-72, asst. clin. prof. ophthalmology eye plastic surgery, 1972-76, assoc. clin. prof. ophthalmology eye plastic surgery, 1976-79; pvt. practice, ophthalmology Columbia, 1972-79; assoc. prof. ophthalmology, eye plastic and orbital surgery U. Mich., Ann Arbor, 1979-86, prof. ophthalmology, 1986—. Cons. med. staff U. Mo. Med. Ctr., Columbia, 1971-79, Meml. Hosp., Jefferson City, 1971-73, Boone County Hosp., Columbia, 1972-79, Harry S. Truman Meml. Vet.'s Hosp., Columbia, 1971-79; med. staff Columbia Regional Hosp., Columbia, 1974-79, U. Mich. Med. Ctr., 1979—, VA Med. Ctr., 1979—; hon. guest spkr. Royal Australian Coll. Ophthalmology, 1995, Peter Rogers lectr., 1999, Bruce Frolick lectr. 2003; lectr. in field. Author: Transactions, American Ophthalmological Society, 1984; editor/author: Surgery of the Eye, 1988; editl. bd.: Ophthalmic Surgery, 1980-87, Am. Acad. Ophthalmology Clin. Modules, 1983-86, Ophthalmic Plastic and Reconstructive Surgery, 1984-98, Orbit; contbr. articles to profl. jours./publs., books in field. Capt. USAF, 1965-67, Taiwan. Grantee in field. Fellow Am. Acad. Ophthalmology (Wendell Hughes lectr. 1993, Sr. Honor award 1990); mem. Am. Soc. Ophthal. Plastic and Reconstructive Surgery (sec. 1973-74, pres. 1976), Am. Ophthalmol. Soc., Orbital Soc., Australasian Soc. Ophthalmic Plastic Surgeons (hon.), European Soc. Ophthal. Plastic and Reconstructive Surgeons (hon.). Avocations: pocket billiards, model t fords and old morgans, wine, violin. Office: WK Kellogg Eye Ctr U Mich 1000 Wall St Ann Arbor MI 48105-1986 E-mail: frueh@umich.edu.

FRUEHWALD, KRISTIN G. lawyer; b. Sidney, Nebr., May 15, 1946; d. Chris U. and Mary E. (Boles) Bitner; m. Michael R. Fruehwald, Feb. 23, 1980; children: Laurel Elizabeth, Amy Marie. BS with highest distinction in History, U. Nebr., 1968; JD summa cum laude, Ind. U., 1975. Bar: Ind. 1975, U.S. Dist. Ct. (so. dist.) Ind. 1975. Assoc. Barnes & Thornburg, Indpls., 1975-81, ptnr., 1982—. Spkr. in field. Contbr. articles to profl. jours. Trustee The Orchard Sch., 1993—, chmn., 1997—98; bd. dirs. Indpls. Parks Found., 1995—2000, Arts Ind., 1994—98, Ind. Continuing Legal Edn. Forum, 1993—2001, pres., 2000—01; bd. dirs. Indpls. Bar Found., 1992—, chmn., 1997—99; bd. dirs. James Whitcomb Riley Meml. Assn., 1995—, treas., 2000—; bd. dirs. Planned Giving Group Ind., Fedn. Cmty. Defenders, Inc., 1993—99, pres., 1999—2001; bd. dirs . Ind. affiliate Am. Heart Assn., 1977—81, vice chmn. Marion County chpt., 1981; bd. dirs. Indpls. Bar Found., 2003—. Fellow: ABA (chmn. distributable net income subcom 1985—91, sect. taxation, mem. real property, probate and trust sect.), Ind. State Bar Assn. (chmn. probate, trust and real property sects. 1987—88, mem. ho. of dels. 1987—, bd. mgrs. 1989—90, treas. 1996—97, chair ho. of dels. 1998—99, pres. 2001—02, mem. sect. taxation), Ind. Bar Found. (bd. dirs. 2003—), Am. Coll. Trust and Estate Counsel (chmn. Ind. state laws com. 1992—95); mem.: Ind. Code Study Commn., Internat. Assn. Fin. Planners, Indpls. Estate Planning Coun., Indpls. Bar Assn. (chmn. estate planning and adminstrn. sect. 1982—83, chmn. long range fin. planning com. 1988—89, pres. 1993). Office: Barnes & Thornburg 11 S Meridian St Indianapolis IN 46204-3535 E-mail: kris.fruewald@btlaw.com.

FRUGOLI, ANTHONY FRANCIS, priest, educator; b. San Francisco, Feb. 16, 1914; s. Anton Ferdinand Frugoli and Mae Ellen Beechinor. MA, Gonzaga U., Spokane, Wash. Ordained priest Roman Cath. Ch., 1945. Tchr. Loyola H.S., L.A., 1937—42; tchr., adminstr. Bellarmine Coll. Prep., San Jose, Calif., 1947—49; tchr., chaplain Loyola H.S., L.A., 1949—56; asst. pastor St. Joseph's Ch., San Jose, 1956—57; v.p., student conselor Santa Clara (Calif.) U., 1957—66; student counselor St. Ignatius Coll. Prep., San Francisco, 1966—98; cruise ship chaplain 38 ships on 458 cruises to date, 1950—2003. Avocations: reading, world travel. Home: Sacred Heart Jesuit Ctr 300 College Ave Los Gatos CA 95031-0128

FRÜHBECK DE BURGOS, RAFAEL, conductor; b. Burgos, Spain, Sept. 15, 1933; s. Guillermo and Estefania (Ochs) Frühbeck de Burgos; m. Maria Carmen Martinez, Dec. 21, 1959; children: Rafael, Gema. Attended, Bilbao Conservatory, Madrid Conservatory, HS for Music, Munich; student, U. Munich, Richard Strauss Price, 1958, U. Madrid; D (hon.), U. Navarra, Pamplona, Spain, 1994, U. Burgos, 1998. Chief condr. Mcpl. Orch., Bilbao, Spain, 1958—62, Nat. Orch., Madrid, 1962—78, hon. condr., 1998, gen. music dir. Dusseldorf Symphony, Germany, 1966—71, music dir. Montreal Symphony, Can., 1974—76, Vienna Symphony, Austria, 1991—96, Deutsche Oper, Berlin, 1992—97, Rundfunk Symphony Orch. Berlin, 1994—2000, RAI Nat. Symphony Orch., Turin, Italy, 2001—, prin. guest condr. Nat. Symphony, Washington, 1980—90, Dresden (Germany) Philharm. Orch., 2003—, Yomiuri Nippon Symphony Orch., Tokyo, 1980—90, hon. condr., 1991. Decorated Encomienda Orden de Alfonso X El Sabio (Spain), Gran Cruz Orden del Merito Civil (Spain); recipient Prize of Musical Interpretation, Larios CEOE, Madrid, 1992, Ehrenmedaille in Gold, Burgermeister, Vienna, 1995, State of Vienna, Austria, 2000, Gold medal to the Civil Merit of Austria, 1996, Gold medal, Internat. Gustav Mahler Soc., Vienna, 1996, Fundacion Guerrero prize of Spanish Music, Madrid, 1996, Big Cross to the Civil Merit, Republic of Germany, Berlin, 2001. Mem.: Real Acad. de Bellas Artes de San Fernando (Madrid). Office: care Musiespaña Jose Marañón 10 E-28010 Madrid Spain also: CAMI Columbia Artists Mgmt Inc 165 W 57th St New York NY 10019-2276 also: care Harold Holt Ltd 122 Wigmore St London W1H ODJ England

FRUIHT, DOLORES GIUSTINA, artist, educator, poet; b. Portland, Oreg., Mar. 9, 1923; d. Erminio and Irene (Onorato) Giustina; m. Thos. Herman Fruiht, Dec. 20, 1947 (div. 1976); children: Justina, Bryce, Bradford, Erica, Renee. BS, RN, U. Portland, 1944; attended, U. San Francisco, 1971. Nurse, Nurse Corps U.S. Army, 1944-46; intravenous nurse St. Vincent's Hosp., Portland, 1946; staff nurse Dr. Shepard, Eugene, Oreg., 1947-49; surg. nurse Sacred Heart Hosp., Eugene, Oreg., 1949-52; tchr. Ursulina High Sch., Santa Rosa, Calif., 1976-78; artist Angela Ctr. for Adult Edn., Santa Rosa, Calif., 1978-88. Juror Bodega Bay Fisherman's Festival, Calif., 1992, Sebastopol Ctr. for the Arts, 1995. One woman shows include: "Expressions in Art", Abstract Photography, Paintings, and Images in Clay, Sonoma County Mus., Santa Rosa, 1992, Pottery Exhibit, Angela Ctr., 1980, Sonoma, 1976; exhibited in group shows at: Oreg. State U., 1999, Cultural Arts Coun. Sonoma County, 1998, Sebastopol Libr., 1992, Bodega Bay Allied Arts, 1991, 93-96, Nor Cal. State Art Exhibit, Nat. League of Am. Pen Women, Souverain Winery, 1985, "Tibetan Faces", Photography, Calif. Mus. of Art, Santa Rosa, 1985, Photography Exhibit, Angela Ctr., 1982, "The Healing Celebration of Art", Photography, San Francisco Civic Auditorium, 1981, Photography Show, Angela Ctr., 1980, Pottery Exhibit, 1975; contbr. articles to numerous profl. jours.; disting. lectr. Diplomat City of Sonoma, Russia, 1988. 1st Lt. U.S. Army Nurse Corps, 1944-46. Decorated Bronze Star for Luzon Campaign U.S. Army. Mem. Nat. League of Am. Pen Women (Biennial Selection award, 1986, Excellence award, 1985). Roman Catholic. Avocations: hiking, golfing, reading. Office: PO Box 823 Bodega Bay CA 94923-0823

FRUISEN, CATHERINE MYLER (VIOLET LEMAY), illustrator; b. Belleville, Ill., Oct. 11, 1966; d. Roy Ellington and Marianne Mohrmann Myler; m. Frederick Graham Fruisen, June 23, 1995; 1 child, Graham Myler. BFA in theater design, Webster U., St. Louis, 1989; MFA in illustration, Savannah (Ga.) Coll. of Art and Design, 1996. Freelance theater design asst., NYC, 1990—94; scenery and costume designer Nat. Theater of the Deaf, Chester, Conn., 1991; scenic designer Maine State Music Theater, Brunswick, 1990; summer asst. scenic designer St. Louis Mcpl. Opera, 1987—93; prof. illustration Savannah Coll. of Art and Design, 1998—2002; author-illustrator Design Press / Cedco, Savannah, Ga., 1999—2000; illustrator Anna Goodson Mgmt.,Inc., Savannah, 2000—. Author (and illustrator): (children's books) My Mother's Pearls, 2000; illustrator: children's books Rick and Rocky, 2000, Alice and Her Fabulous Tooth, 2000, illustrator as Violet LeMay: editorial illustrations in periodicals. Vol. reader for libr. and sch., 2000—02. Recipient ann. competition, Am. Illustration, NYC, 2001, 2002, RSVP Directory of Illustration, NYC, 2000, 2002, Applied Arts Mag., 2002. Mem.: Graphic Artists Guild, Soc. of Illustrators, LA chpt. Avocation: running. E-mail: violetlemay@bellsouth.net.

FRUITMAN, FREDERICK HOWARD, investment banker; b. Toronto, Oct. 8, 1950; s. Herbert Lance and Libby (Kamin) Fruitman; m. Marlin Sue Potash, Nov. 21, 1981 (div. Dec. 1996); children: Laura, Hilary; m. Susan Beth Levinsohn, Apr. 19, 1998, 1 child, Charles. SB, MIT, 1972; BA, Oxford (Eng.) U., 1974, MA, 1981; LLB, U. Toronto, 1976; MBA, Harvard U., 1981. Assoc. Davies, Ward & Beck, Toronto, 1976-77, Merrill Lynch White Weld Capital Markets Group, N.Y.C., 1978-79; cons. Bain & Co., Boston, 1981-82; v.p. Investors in Industry Corp., Boston, 1982-84; assoc. E.M. Warburg, Pincus & Co. Inc., N.Y.C., 1984-86; sr. v.p. The Stuart James Co. Inc., N.Y.C., 1986-89; mng. dir. Loeb Ptnrs. Corp., N.Y.C., 1990—. Mem. Law Soc. Upper Can., Can. Soc. of N.Y., Harvard Club (N.Y.C.), Tuxedo Club. Office: Loeb Ptnrs Corp 61 Broadway New York NY 10006-2701

FRUMENTO, ROBERT JAMES, anesthesiologist, educator, clinical researcher; b. New Haven, Conn., Nov. 27, 1968; s. Gennaro and Elizabeth Regina (Lynch) Frumento; m. Christine Bilello, Aug. 19, 1995; 1 child, Aedan Richard. MPH, Yale U, New Haven, CT, 1991—93. Asst. prof. Columbia U/ Dept. Anesthesiology, New York, NY, 2002—; sr. clin. rsch. officer Albert Einstein Coll. of Medicine, New York, NY, 1998—2000. Cons. Scientia, Trumbull, Conn., 2002—. Author: (presentation) A Comparison Of Four Routinely Used Intravenous Fluids On Clin. (Internation Rsch. Award, 2001). Recipient Nat. Rsch. Award, Soc. for the Advancement of Blood Mgmt., 2002. Mem.: Soc. Cardiovasc. Anesthesiology. Independent. Office: Columbia Univ Dept Anethesiology PH5-505 - 630 W 168th St New York NY 10032 Office Fax: 212-342-2211. E-mail: rf356@columbia.edu.

FRUMKIN, SIMON, political activist and columnist; b. Kaunas, Lithuania, Nov. 5, 1930; came to U.S., 1949; s. Nicholas and Zila (Oster) F.; m. Rhoda Hirsch, June 1953 (div. 1978); children: Michael Alan, Larry Martin; m. Kathy Elizabeth Hoopes, June 22, 1981 (dec. 1994); m. Ella Zousman, Dec. 11, 1995. BA, NYU, 1953; MA in History, Calif. State U., Northridge, 1964. Pres., chief exec. officer Universal Drapery Fabrics, Inc., Los Angeles, 1953-87; chmn. Southern Calif. Council for Soviet Jews, Studio City, 1969—. Lectr. Simon Wiesenthal Ctr. for Holocaust Studies, Los Angeles, 1980—; chmn. Union of Councils for Soviet Jews, 1972-73. Columnist Heritage, numerous other So. Calif. newspapers, 1980—; corr. to columnist Panorama, U.S.A. Russian Lang., 1985—; contbr. articles to newspapers. Pres. Media Analysis Found., Los Angeles, 1988; chmn. Ams. for Peace and Justice, 1972-74; mem. Pres.' Senatorial Inner Circle, U.S. Senatorial Club. Honored by Calif. Govt., Los Angeles City Council, Los Angeles Office of City Atty., numerous Jewish orgns. Mem. Assn. Soviet Jewish Emigre's (pres. 1987—), Zionist Orgn. Am., Am. Israel Polit. Action Com., Russian Republican Club, Mensa. Avocations: writing, photography, skiing, fitness. Home and Office: 3755 Goodland Ave Studio City CA 91604-2313

FRUNDT, HENRY JOHN, sociologist, educator; b. Blue Earth, Minn., May 22, 1940; s. John Henry and Mary Ellen (Kane) F.; m. Bette Jule Swatzki, June 13, 1970; children: Michael, Laura, James, Daniel, Janine, Paul. BA, St. Louis U., 1964, MA, PhL, 1967; PhD, Rutgers U., 1975. Tchr. Creighton Prep. Sch., Omaha, 1965-68; program developer U.S. Dept. Labor, Omaha, 1969; instr. sociology U. Wis., Superior, 1969-71; cons. UN, N.Y.C., 1978-85; prof. sociology Ramapo Coll., Mahwah, N.J., 1973—, dir. sch. social sci., assoc. dean, 1989-93, convenor Latin Am. studies, 1995-2000, convenor sociology, 2000—01. Rsch. assoc. conservation of human resources Columbia U., N.Y.C., 1980-82; rsch. assoc. inter-Am. devel. program Am. U., Washington, 1982-84; Fulbright lectr. U. Rafael Landivar, Guatemala City, 1987-88, 2002; Fulbright sr. specialist peer rev. com., 2003. Author: Agribusiness Manual, 1978, Refreshing Pauses, 1987, Trade Conditions and Labor Rights, 1998 (Whitaker prize: Outstanding Book award labor sect. Latin Am. Studies Assn.); contbr. articles to profl. jours. Co-chair N.J. Labor Com. on Ctrl. Am., 1987-93; bd. dirs. U.S./Labor Edn. in Americas Project, 1990—; choral singer N.J. Oratorio Soc., Essex County, N.J., 1994—, pres., 2003—; commr. commn. on disarmament edn. UN, 1995-2002. Orgn. Am. States fellow, 1982, Faculty fellow NYU, 1996-97; grantee Soc. for the Psychol. Study of Social Issues, 2002. Mem. Soc. for Psychol. Study of Social Issues, Latin Am. Studies Assn., Guatemala Scholars Network, Am. Fedn. Tchrs. (local pres. 1984-87, coun. del. 1997—). Roman Catholic. Office: Ramapo Coll Mahwah NJ 07430

FRUTH, BERYL ROSE, physician; b. Carey, Ohio, Mar. 27, 1952; d. Oscar W. and Alice (Arnett) Fruth. BA in Chemistry magna cum laude, Asbury Coll., 1973; MD, Ohio State U., 1977. Diplomate Am. Acad. Family Practice. Intern Grant Hosp., Columbus, Ohio, 1977-78, resident, 1978-79, chief resident, 1979-80; pvt. practice Columbus, 1980-93; family physician Columbus Community Physicians, Inc., Grove City, Ohio, 1993—; med. dir. Meml. Physicians Inc. Urgent Care, Marysville, Ohio, 1998—, Vets. Med. Ctr., Chillicothe, Ohio, 2000-01, primary care team physician, 2000—; ambulatory care physician VA Med. Ctr., Miami, 2003—. Asst. dir. family practice residency Grant Hosp., 1980-81; med. dir. Columbus Dispatch, 1983-93, St. Anthony Breast Evaluation Ctr., 1986—, Physicians House Call, Columbus, 1998—; lectr. Columbus Cancer Clinic, 1984; mentor family practice dept. Ohio State U., physician preceptor Sch. Medicine. Contbr. Ohio State U. Med. Sch. Learning Module in Alcoholism, 1983-84. Named Alumna of Yr. Vanlue Sch., Ohio. Fellow Am. Acad. Family Physicians; mem. AMA, Am. Med. Women's Assn., Acad. Family Practice. Address: 17273 Rt 4 Chillicothe OH 45601

FRUZZETTI, ALAN E. psychologist, educator; b. Weymouth, Mass., Dec. 23, 1959; s. Albert E. and Phyllis Lander Fruzzetti; m. Armida Rubio Fruzzetti, July 0, 2000; children: Samuel D., Rachel A., Benjamin A., Carlos P. I. BA, Brown U., 1982; PhD, U. Wash., 1993. Assoc. prof. U. Nev., Reno, 1994—. Dir. Dialectical Behavior Therapy and Rsch. Program, Reno, 1994—. Contbr. chapters to books, articles to profl. jours. Rsch. advisor Nat. Ednl. Alliance for Borderline Personality Disorder, N.Y.C., 2001—03. Mem.: APA, Internat. Soc. for Dialectical Behavior Therapy, Assn. for the Advancement Behavior Therapy. Office: Dept Psychology 298 Univ Nevada Reno NV 89557

FRY, ALBERT JOSEPH, chemistry educator; b. Phila., May 12, 1937; s. Russell Mayne and Margaret (McCann) F.; m. Melissa Grant Betton, July 30, 1966; children: Anne Margaret, Peter, Jonathan. BS, U. Mich., 1958; PhD, U. Wis., 1963; MA, Wesleyan U., 1978. Postdoctoral fellow Calif. Inst. Tech., Pasadena, 1963-64, Wesleyan U., Middletown, Conn., 1964-65, asst. prof., 1965-72, assoc. prof., 1972-77, prof. chemistry, 1977—, E.B. Nye prof. chemistry, 1993—. Author: Synthetic Organic Electrochemistry, 1972, 2d edit., 1989; editor: Topics in Organic Electrochemistry, 1986, New Directions in Organic Electrochemistry, 2000; contbr. articles to profl. jours. Fellow Chem. Soc. London; mem. Am. Chem. Soc., Conn. Acad. Sci. and Engring., Electrochem. Soc., Internat. Soc. Electrochemistry, Sigma Xi, Alpha Chi Sigma, Phi Lambda Upsilon Roman Catholic. Home: 116 Maple Shade Rd Middletown CT 06457-5188 Office: Wesleyan Univ Dept Chemistry Middletown CT 06459-0001

FRY, AMELIA ROBERTS, biographer, oral historian; b. Abilene, Tex. d. Clarence Rufus and Mary Belle (McKeown) Roberts; m. Hilary G. Fry, Dec. 27, 1947 (div. 1971); children: Gary G., Randal B., Hilary Byron; m. Rex Darwin Davis, Oct. 6, 1980. BA, U. Okla., 1947; MA, U. Ill., 1952. English instr. U. Ill., Urbana, 1947-48, Hiram Coll., 1953-54; instr. Oral History Inst. U. Vt., summers 1975-79. Rschr., interviewer, editor, prodr. oral history memoirs U. Calif., Berkeley, 1959-2000, project dir. oral history polit. series, 1969—. Oral History Dept. editor Jour. Libr. History, 1969-74; polit. reporter, feature writer San Leandro Morning News, 1966-67; contbr. articles to profl. jours., chpts. to books.; cons., interviewee for documentaries and movies; biographer of Alice Paul. Bd. dirs. Nat. Woman's Party, William Penn House, Washington, 1999—. Grantee Nat. Endowment for Humanities, Rockefeller Found., Radcliffe Coll. Support Program, others, 1965—; recipient Chancellor's Outstanding Performance award U. Calif., 1972. Mem. Orgn. Am. Historians, Nat. Oral History Assn. (bd. dirs.). Avocations: playing violin, kayaking, bicycling. E-mail: ameliafry@aol.com.

FRY, ANNE EVANS, zoology educator; b. Phila., Sept. 11, 1939; d. Kenneth Evans and Nora Irene (Smith) F. AB, Mount Holyoke Coll., 1961; MS, U. Iowa, 1963; PhD, U. Mass., 1969. Instr. Carleton Coll., Northfield, Minn., 1963-65; asst. prof. Ohio Wesleyan U., Delaware, 1969-74, assoc. prof., 1974-80, prof., 1980—. Helen Whitelaw Jackson univ. prof., 1999—. Contbr. articles to profl. jours. Recipient Welch Teaching award Ohio Wesleyan U., 1976. Mem. AAAS, Am. Inst. Biol. Scis., Soc. for Integrative and Comparative Biology, Ohio Acad. Sci., Soc. Devel. Biology, Sigma Xi. Office: Ohio Wesleyan U Delaware OH 43015 E-mail: AEFry@owu.edu.

FRY, CHARLES GEORGE, theologian, educator; b. Piqua, Ohio, Aug. 15, 1936; s. Sylvan Jack and Lena Freda (Ehle) F. BA, Capital U., 1958; MA, Ohio State U., 1961, PhD, 1965; BD, Evang. Lutheran Theol. Sem., 1962, MDiv, 1977; DMin, Winebrenner Theol. Sem., 1978; DD, Cranmer Sem., 2001; M of Sacred Theology, Holy Trinity Coll. and Sem., 2002, M in Religions Edn., 2003. Ordained to ministry Lutheran Ch. U.S.A, 1963; diplomate Am. Psychotherapy Assn. Pastor St. Mark's Luth. Ch. and Martin Luther Luth. Ch., Columbus, Ohio, 1961-62, 63-66; instr. Wittenberg U., 1962-63, 71-72, Capital U., 1963-75, asst. prof. history and religion, 1966-69, assoc. prof., 1969-75; theologian-in-residence North Community Luth. Ch., Columbus, 1971-73; assoc. prof. hist. theology, dir. missions edn. Concordia Theol. Sem., Ft. Wayne, Ind., 1975-84; sr. minister First Congl. Ch., Detroit, 1984-85; Protestant chaplain St. Francis Coll., Fort Wayne, 1982-92; prof. philosophy and theology Luth. Coll. of Health Professions, Ft. Wayne, 1992-98, U. St. Francis, Ft. Wayne, 1998-99, Winebrenner Theol. Sem., U. Findlay, Ohio, 1999—. Interim min. Arbor Grove Congl. Ch., Jackson, Mich., 1980, hon. minister emeritus 1996, First Presbyn. Ch., Huntington, Ind., 1988-89, St. Luke's Luth. Ch., Ft. Wayne, 1989-90, Mt. Pleasant Luth. Ch., 1990-91, St. Mark's Luth. Ch., 1990-91, Mt. Zion Luth. Ch., Ft. Wayne, 1991-93; interim min. Cmty. Christian Ch., New Carlisle, Ind., 1993-94, First Luth. Ch., Stryker, Ohio, 1994-95, Zion Luth. Ch., West Jefferson, Ohio, 1994-97, 98-2000, Agape Congl. Ch., Bowling Green, Ohio, 1997-98; interim min. Fairfield Parish, Lancaster, Ohio, 2000—; vis. prof. Damavand Coll., Tehran, 1973-74, bd. dirs., 1976-94; vis. prof. Ref. Bible Coll., 1975-80, Concordia Luth. Sem. at Brock U., summers 1977, 79, Grad. Sch. Christian Min., Huntington (Ind.) Coll., 1986-89, Wheaton Coll., 1987-88; vis. scholar Al Ain U., United Arab Emirates, 1987; theologian-in-residence, tchg. theologian Queenstown Luth. Ch., Singapore, 1991, 99, 2000, 02; adj. faculty history Ind. U./Purdue U., Ft. Wayne, 1982-98, Winebrenner Theol. Sem., Findlay, Ohio, 1992, 99, 2000, Holy Trinity Coll. and Sem., 1999—, Tung Ling Bible Coll., Singapore, 2000, 02, North Tenn. Bible Inst., 1998—; pastor-in-residence Wittenberg U., Springfield, Ohio, 1992, Deaconess Cmty. Evang. Luth. Ch. Am., Phila., 1993. Author books including Age of Lutheran Orthodoxy, 1979, Lutheranism in America, 1979, Islam, 1980, 2d edit. 1982, The Way, The Truth, The Life, 1982, Great Asian Religions, 1984, Francis: A Call to Conversion, 1988, Brit. edit., 1990, The Middle East: A History, 1988, Congregationalists and Evolution: Asa Gray and Louis Agassiz, 1989, Pioneering a Theology of Evolution: Washington Gladden and Pierre Teilhard de Chardin, 1989, Avicenna's Philosophy of Education: An Introduction, 1990, Explorations in Protestant Theology, 1992, Life's Little Lessons, 1997, Kant's Three Questions, 1997, Four Little Words, 1997, Goethe: Life and Truth, 2001, Washington Gladden as a Preacher of the Social Gospel, 1882-1918, 2003, others; co-producer Global Perspectives, IPFW-TV, Ft. Wayne, 1987-97. Bd. dirs. Luth. Liturgical Renewal, 1983-90, 94-2000, pres., 1999-2000; v.p. Internat. Luth. Fellowship, 1995-98, pres., 1998-2001; consecrated bishop, so. region Internat. Luth. Fellowship, 1996; assoc. St. Augustine's Fellowship, 1996—; bd. dirs. Zwemer Inst., Ft Wayne, Ind., 1997—. Recipient Praestantia award Capital U., 1970, Concordia Hist. Inst. citation, 1977, Archbishop Robert Leighton award Nat. Anglican Ch., 1997; Regional Coun. for Internat. Edn. rsch. grantee, 1969; Joseph J. Malone postdoctoral fellow Egypt, 1986, Malone postdoctoral fellow, United Arab Emirates, 1987; named Ky. Col., 1999. Fellow Brit. Interplanetary Soc., Coll. Pastoral Counseling (diplomate), Am. Assn. Integrated Medicine (diplomate, bd. coll. pastoral counseling 2001-), Oxford Soc. Scholars; mem. Am. Hist. Assn., Am. Acad. Religion, Mid. East Inst. Gen. Soc. War of 1812 (compatriot 1994—, chaplain Ohio chpt. 1996—, chaplain gen. 2001-), German Soc. Md., Mil. and Hospitaller Order of St. Lazarus of Jerusalem (chaplain 2000—), Phi Alpha Theta. Democrat. Home: 158 W Union St Circleville OH 43113-1965 Office: 950 N Main Street Findlay OH 45840-4416

FRY, CLARENCE HERBERT, retired retail executive; b. Pottstown, Pa., June 27, 1926; s. Clarence H. and Rosa B. (Savage) F.; m. Barbara Ruth McGuire, Aug. 28, 1950; children: James Nathan, David Andrew, Joel Timothy, Ann Elizabeth. BS magna cum laude, Syracuse U., 1950. C.P.A., Pa. Accountant Peat, Marwick, Mitchell & Co., Phila., 1950-56, supr., 1956-60, mgr., 1960-69; controller Acme Markets, Inc. (now Am. Stores Co.), Phila., 1969-73; chief acctg. officer Am. Stores Group Services, Inc., Phila., 1974-78, contr., 1974-75, v.p., 1975-78; v.p., contr. Am. Stores Co., Wilmington, Del., 1979, v.p. contr., 1979-80; v.p., contr. Acme Markets, Inc. subs. Am. Stores Co., Phila., 1980-83, sr. v.p., treas., contr., 1983-87; sr. v.p. fin. Am. Superstores Inc. subs. Am. Stores Co., Wilmington, 1987-89; ret., 1990. Mem. food merchandisers LIFO adv. com. Food Mktg. Inst., 1975-82 Mem. Easttown Twp. Tricentennial Com., 2001—; bd. dirs. Tredyffrin Historic Preservation Trust, 2003—. With 69th Inf. Div. AUS, 1944-46. Mem. AICPA, Pa. Inst. CPAs, Chester County Hist. Soc.; pres. Tredyffrin-Easttown History Club, 1992-95, editor quar., 1996—. Presbyterian. Avocations: historical research, motorsports. Home: 519 Daventry Rd Berwyn PA 19312-1740

FRY, DAVID DONALD, civil engineer, consultant; b. Canton, Ohio, Oct. 4, 1924; s. Don David and Mary J. (Petch) F.; student Kans. State Coll., 1943-44; B.S.C.E., Case Inst. Tech., 1949; m. Ann Selden Nicholson, Apr. 25, 1958; 1 child, Constance Louise. Engr., Ohio Dept. Hwys., Ravenna, 1949-53; engr.

Peter Kiewit Sons Co., Portsmouth, Ohio, 1953-54; area engr. Arabian Am. Oil Co., Dhahran, S.A., 1954-56; design engr. M. H. Connell & Assoc., Inc., Miami, 1956-60; asst. dir. pub. works City of Coral Gables (Fla.), 1960-67; v.p. charge Fla. office Brighton Engring. Co., 1967-69; project engr. Clarkeson, Kononoff & Smith, Inc., Coral Gables, 1970-71; chief engr., gen. mgr. Pavlo Engring. Co., Inc., Coral Gables, 1971-85; cons., 1986—. Registered profl. engr., Ohio, Fla. Mem. Theta Chi. Presbyterian. Home: 6001 SW 81st St Miami FL 33143-8121 Office: 2780 S Douglas Rd Miami FL 33133-2740

FRY, DONALD LEWIS, physiologist, educator; b. Des Moines, Dec. 29, 1924; s. Clair V. and Maudie (Long) F.; children— Donald Stewart, Ronald Sinclair, Heather Elise, Laurel Virginia. MD, Harvard U., 1949. Rsch. fellow Univ Minn Hosp., Mpls., 1952-53; sr. asst. surgeon gen. NIH, Bethesda, Md., 1953-56, surgeon, 1956-57, sr. surgeon, 1957-61, med. dir., 1961-80; prof. Ohio State U., Columbus, 1980—. Contbr. numerous articles and papers on physiology and biophysics of pulmonary mechanics, blood vascular interface, transvascular mass transport and the genesis of atherosclerosis to profl. jours., books. Mem. AAAS, Am. Physiol. Soc., Am. Soc. Clin. Investigation, Biophys. Soc., N.Y. Acad. Scis. Office: Ohio State U Coll Medicine 2025 Wiseman Hall 400 W 12th Ave Columbus OH 43210-1214

FRY, DONALD OWEN, broadcasting company executive; b. Headlee, Ind., Mar. 5, 1921; s. George Mason and Nima E. (Ulrey) F.; m. Phyllis Amy McMillan, Feb. 2, 1947. BS, Calif. Coll. Commerce, 1953. Chief acct. Philco Dist., Inc., Los Angeles, 1953-58, Pacific Ocean Park (Calif.), 1958-59; controller Eleven-Ten Broadcasting, Pasadena, Calif., 1959-63, Los Angeles Standard, 1963-69; treas. Oak Knoll Broadcasting Corp., Pasadena, 1969—, v.p., gen. mgr., 1976-82, pres., chmn. bd., 1982—, dir., 1974—. Trustee, pres., chmn. bd. Broadcast Found. of Calif., Pasadena. Served with U.S. Army, 1940-45. Decorated Bronze star (2). Mem.: Masons, Scottish Rite, Shriners. Home: 401 E Live Oak St Apt 11 San Gabriel CA 91776

FRY, DONNA MARIE, military officer, educator; b. Altadena, Calif., Oct. 16, 1947; d. Hampton Scott and M. Genevieve (Wolff) F.; 1 child, Alicia Fay. BA, Rutgers U., 1981; MS, Air Force Inst. Tech., 1986. Enlisted USAF, 1968, advanced through grades to master sgt., 1981, commd. 2d lt., advanced through grades to capt., staff cost analyst Cost Rsch. Office, 1986-88, instr. Air Force Inst. Tech. Wright-Patterson AFB, Ohio, 1989-91, chief divsn. exec. communications Maxwell AFB, Ala., 1991-92, chief divsn. analysis for resource mgrs., 1992-95, instr. Ctr. Profl. Devel., Profl. Mil. Comp. Sch., 1991-95, ret., 1995; sr. analyst, curriculum developer Budget Info. Sys. FIRST, MCR Fed., Inc., Maxwell AFB, Montgomery, Ala., 1999-2000; v.p. curriculum devel. Knowledge Mgmt. Solutions, Prattville, Ala., 2000—02; substitute tchr. Lighthouse Christian Acad., 2001—, Evangelical Christian Acad., 2001—, Montgomery Cath. Prep. Sch., 2001—. Tchr. speech/pub. speaking, computers Covenant Acad., 1995-97; adj. faculty J. Patterson State Tech. Coll. (now H. Coun. Trenholm State Coll.), 1996—; cons. in field. Mem. NAFE, Am. Soc. Mil. Comptrollers (v.p., project officer 1988-91, v.p. for Profl. Mil. Comptrollers' Sch. 1992), Air Force Assn. (life), Soc. Cost Estimating and Analysis, SALSAW (pres. Dayton chpt. 1990-91), Res. Officers Assn. (life), Non-Commd. Officers Assn. (life), Rutgers U. Alumni Assn. Republican. Roman Catholic. Avocations: travel, costume design, reading, swimming, knitting. Home: 7537 Halcyon Forest Trl Montgomery AL 36117-3493 E-mail: wafretiree@aol.com.

FRY, EARL HOWARD, political scientist, educator; b. Oakland, Calif., May 19, 1947; s. Harvey Wallace and Alice (Horlacher) F.; m. Elaine Fisher, May 29, 1971; children: Christopher, Lisa, Leanna, Kimberly, Steven, Kristen. BA, BA, Brigham Young U., 1971, MA, 1972; PhD, UCLA, 1976. Fulbright prof. U. Sorbonne, Paris, 1974-75; asst. prof. Boise State U., Idaho, 1976-79; assoc. prof. SUNY, Plattsburgh, 1979-80, Brigham Young U., Provo, Utah, 1980-83, prof. dept. Polit. Sci., Endowed prof. Canadian studies, 1989—, dir. the Washington Seminar, 1999-2000; spl. asst. Office U.S. Trade Rep., Washington, 1983-84. Asst. dir. Brigham Young U.-U Grenoble Semester Abroad Program, 1972; vis. rschr. UN, Geneva, 1974; asst. prof. Boise State U., 1976-79; chmn. BSU Faculty Rsch. com., 1977-78; vis. prof. U. B.C., 1977; prin. investigator Idaho Internat. Trade directory Pacific northwest Regional Commn., 1979; assoc. prof. SUNY Plattsburgh, 1979-80, dir. Internat. Edn., Canadian Studies, 1979-80; vis. prof. U. Montreal, 1989, Ecole des Hautes Etudes en Scis. Sociales, Paris, 1990; review com. Internat. Proposals U.S. Dept. Edn., 1985-88; Utah State Tax Commn. Task Force on Unitary Taxation, 1985; chmn. Canadian Studies, Brigham Young U., 1980—; Univ. rep. Atlantic Coun. U.S., 1987—; fellowship com. Coun. Fgn. Rels., 1989-93, fellow 1983-84; dir. Grad. Studies, Rsch., Publs., David M. Kennedy Ctr. Internat. Studies, 1987-90; Fulbright Commn. review com., 1991; vis. fellow Ams. Soc., N.Y.C., 1991-93; acad. assoc. Atlantic Coun., Washington, 1987—; dir. The Washington Seminar, 1999-2000; lectr., cons. and spkr. in field. Author: Financial Invasion of the U.S.A., 1980, Canadian Government and Politics in Comparative Perspective, 1983, The Canadian Political System, 1991, Canada's Unity Crisis: Implications for U.S.-Canadian Economic Relations, 1992; co-author Idaho's Foreign Relations: The Transgovernmental Linkages of an American State, 1978, The Other Western Europe: A Comparative Analysis of the Smaller Democracies, 1980, The Other Western Europe, 1983, America the Vincible: U.S. Foreign Policy for the Twenty-First Century, 1994, The Expanding Role of State and Local Governments in U.S. Foreign Affairs, 1998; co-editor The Canada/U.S. Free Trade Agreement: The Impact on Service Industries, 1988, Investment in the North American Free Trade Area: Opportunities and Challenges, 1992; gen. editor Canadian Studies Curriculum Guide, 1980; contbr. numerous articles to profl. jours. Bd. dirs. Fulbright Assn., 1995-98. Recipient Can. Studies Sr. Fellowship award, 1983, Karl G. Maeser Rsch. and Creative Arts award, 1989; rsch. grantee Coll. Family, Home and Social Scis., 1986, 88, 89, 92; rsch. and conf. grantee Can. govt., 1985-92; Fulbright lectr. U. Paris (La Sorbonne), 1974-75; Bissell-Hyde-Fulbright chair U. Toronto, 1995-96; Elliot/Winant Lecture fellow UK, 1993, Coun. Fgn. Rels. Internat. Affairs fellow, 1983, David M. Kennedy Rsch. fellow Brigham Young U., 1985-86, Rsch. grantee, 1987-89; Atlantic Coun. Travel grantee, 1988; Presdl. fellow Am. Grad. Sch. Internat. Mgmt., 1993; Thomas O. Enders fellow McGill U., 2002. Mem. Internat. Polit. Sci. Assn., Assn. Can. Studies in U.S. (Washington v.p. 1989-91, pres. 1991-93, exec. coun. 1985—, Bissell-Hyde Fulbright chair U. Toronto 1995-96), Fulbright Assn. (bd. dirs. 1995-97), Coun. Fgn. Rels. Mem. Lds Ch. Office: Brigham Young U Dept Pol Scis Provo UT 84602 E-mail: earl_fry@byu.edu.

FRY, EDWARD BERNARD, education educator, retired; b. L.A., Apr. 4, 1925; s. Eugene Bernard and Frances (Dreier) F.; m. Carol Addison Adams, 1950 (div. 1970); m. Cathy Ruwe, Jan. 8, 1974; children: Shanti, Christopher. BA, Occidental Coll., 1949; MS in Edn., U. So. Calif., 1954, PhD, 1960. Asst. prof. Loyola U., L.A., 1953-63; prof. edn. Rutgers U., New Brunswick, N.J., 1963-86, prof. emeritus, 1986—; pub., author Tchr. Created Materials Jamestown Glenoe McGraw-Hill. Fulbright lectr., Uganda, 1961, Zimbabwe, 1985; pub., owner Laguna Beach Ednl. Books, 1991-98; founder Africa Univ. Press, 1999. Author: How to Teach Reading, 1992; co-author: Reading Teachers Book of Lists, 4th edit., 2000; author of over 25 textbooks for schs. and colls. With U.S. Mcht. Marine, 1943-46. Recipient Disting. Svc. award N.J. Reading Assn., 1979. Mem. Nat. Reading Conf. (pres. 1974-76, Oscar Causey award 1980), Internat. Reading Assn. (Reading Hall of Fame 1992). Democrat. Methodist. Avocations: skiing, docent in laguna coast wilderness park. Home: 245 Grandview St Laguna Beach CA 92651-1518

FRY, EVA MARGARET, entertainer, writer; b. Calgary, Alta., Can. d. John Robert and Edith Marion (Duckworth) Maeers; m. Albert Norman Fry, Mar. 14, 1959; children: Laurie Elizabeth Poirier, Linda Marie Wright, Kevin Alan. Developer, spkr. juvenile motivational program Be A Winner In Life, San Diego, 1998—. Author: Be a Winner in Life, 1998, You Must Have a Dream, 2001; singer: (albums) Remember, 2002, Oh What Joy Christmas, 2002. Named Vol. of Jr., Juvenile Instns., 1997. Mem.: WCTU, Phi Rho Pi. Republican. Mem. Lds Ch. Avocation: Avocations: singing, songwriting and performing for senior citizens, reading writing. Home: 12115 Fry Ln Valley Center CA 92082-5700

FRY, EVELYN LEONA, clinical social worker; b. Melrose Park, Ill., Feb. 6, 1952; d. James Herbert and Mary Grace (Anthony) Zimmermann; m. John David Fry, Nov. 9, 1974; children: Kathleen Ann, Jennifer Marie. BA in Psychology, So. Ill. U., 1975; MSW, Aurora (Ill.) U., 1987. Lic. clin. social worker, Ill. Pub. aid caseworker Ill, Ill. Dept. Pub. Aid, Aurora, 1980-81; social worker Carol Stream (Ill.) Police Dept., 1987-90, Cen. DuPage Hosp., Winfield, Ill., 1990; social worker, clin. coord. Rapha Christian Group, Forest Park, Ill., 1991-93; clin. dir. Living Hope Inst., Elk Grove Village, Ill., 1994; psychotherapist in pvt. practice Peace of Mind Counseling Ctr., Roselle, Ill., 1993—98, also bd. dirs.; psychotherapist in pvt. practice Maryville-Herrick House, Bartlett, Ill., 1993—98; program therapist Riveredge Hosp., Forest Park, Ill., 1998—2001; psychotherapist Elmhurst (Ill.) Meml. Guidance Svcs., 2001—. On call mental health specialist and tng. officer Nat. Disaster Med. Sys., 2002—; field instr. Aurora U., 1987-90; mem. adv. com. U-46 In Touch/Drug Free Task Force, Elgin, Ill., 1987-90; mem. steering com. Warrenville Youth and Family Svcs., 1989—; treas. NW DuPage Human Svcs. Coordinating Com., Bloomingdale, Ill., 1990—. Treas. Edgebrook Homeowners Assn., Warrenville, 1986—87; campaign worker Paul Simon for U.S. Senate, Lombard, Ill., 1980—; committeeman 27th precinct Winfield Twp. Dem. Orgn., Warrenville, Ill., 1985—92; active local polit. campaigns, 1985, 1989, 1993; chmn. united thank officer Episcopal Churchwomen, St. Mark's Ch., Geneva, Ill., 1989—90. Mem. NASW, Soc. Clin. and Exptl. Hypnosis (assoc.), Milton Erickson Inst. No. Ill. Avocations: music, golf, travel, snow skiing. Office: Elmhurst Meml Guidance Svcs 183 N York Rd Elmhurst IL 60126

FRY, HEDY, member of parliament; 3 children. MD, Royal Coll. Surgeons, Dublin, Ireland, 1968. Pvt. practice; mem., sec. of state (multiculturalism) (status of women) Can. Parliament/Vancouver Ctr., Ottawa, 1996—2002; chair B.C. Caucus, 2002—; mem. spl. com. on non-med. use of drugs, mem. standing com. on health, standing com. on justice and human rights Can. Parliament, Ottawa, Canada, 2002. Dr. Hirsh Rosenfeld Disting. Lectr. in family medicine McGill U., 1994; featured on Doctor-Doctor, CBC TV series, 1985-89. Mem. editl. bd. Med. Post. Mem. com. Royal Commn. on Reproductive Technologies.dn. Learning for Living Adv. Bd.; mem. Mayor's Spl. Com. on Urban Natives; bd. dirs. St. George's sch., 1989-91; adv. bd. B.C. Physicians Against Nuclear War; co-chair Liberal Party Health and Social Issues sect., Aylmer Conf., 1992, mem. Leader's Nat. Task Force on Women, 1992-93; parliamentary sec. Min. of Health, 1993-96, mem. task force on reform of social security sys., 1994, standing com. on health, 1994, subcom. on AIDS, mem. caucus com. on social policy. Recipient Cmty. Svc. award Commonwealth Caribbean Club, 1991, Black Achievement award, 1994, Congress of Black Women award, 1994. Mem. B.C. Fedn. Med. Women (pres. 1977), Vancouver Women's Network, Vancouver Med. Assn. (pres. 1988-89), B.C. Med. Assn. (pres. 1990-91, chief negotiator 1991-93), Can. Med. Assn. (chair obstetrics task force 1986-87, chair multiculturalism com. 1992-93), Coun. of Healthcare and Promotion (B.C. rep. 1984-92). Avocations: travel, gardening, reading.

FRY, JOHN, magazine editor; b. Montreal, Jan. 22, 1930; s. J. Stevenson and Beatrice (Pratt) F.; m. Marlies Strillinger, Feb. 19, 1965; children— Leslie, William, Nicole. Student, Lower Can. Coll., Montreal, 1936-47; BA, McGill U., 1951. Writer Forster McGuire & Co. Ltd., Montreal, 1951-57; assoc. editor to mng. editor Am. Metal Market, 1957-63; editor-in-chief Ski mag., N.Y.C., 1964-74, editl. dir., 1975-79, Ski Bus., 1964-79, 92—, Golf mag., 1968-71, 77-79, Outdoor Life, 1975-79, Cross Country Ski mag., 1975—; dir. publs. devel. Times Mirror Mags., 1979-83; editl. and publs. cons., 1983—; founding editor Snow Country mag., 1987-98; editor for new mag. devel. N.Y. Times mag. group, N.Y.C., 1995-97. Mem. World Cup com. Internat. Ski Fedn., 1970-75. Author: (with Phil and Steve Mahre) No Hill Too Fast, 1985. Bd. dirs. Beaver Dam Sanctuary, Chambers Found. Recipient Lifetime Achievement award Internat. Skiing History Assn., 1996; named to U.S. Nat. Ski Hall of Fame, 1995. Mem.: Internat. Skiing History Assn. (bd. dirs. 1995—, pres. 2001—), Overseas Press Club of Am. Achievements include being the founder of the National Standard Ski Race and the Nations Cup of Alpine Skiing. Office: 23 E Lake Dr Katonah NY 10536-3501 E-mail: snowfry@worldnet.att.net.

FRY, JOHN, electronics executive; CEO Fry's Electronics Inc., San Jose, Calif., 1985—; owner San Jose SaberCats, 1994—. Office: Frys Electronics Inc 600 E Brokaw Rd San Jose CA 95112-1006*

FRY, JOHN CRAIG, JR., portfolio manager; b. Phila., July 6, 1953; s. John C. and Tanya A. (Ojeda) Fry; m. Karin U. Fry, Nov. 5, 1983; children: Matthew, Kirsten. BA in Econs., George Washington U., 1980, postgrad., 1983. Cert. fin. analyst. Economist World Bank, Washington, 1981-82; account exec. Merrill Lynch, Washington, 1983-88; asst. br. mgr. Hutton/Shearson, Washington, 1988-90; br. mgr. Janey Montgomer Scott, Washington, 1990-91, Ferris, Baker, Watts, Washington, 1991; v.p. investments Prudential Securities, Washington, 1991-92; portfolio mgr. Wheat First Union, NYC, 1992-98, Evans Capital Mgmt., Seattle, 1998-99, Laird Norton Trust Co., 2000—02, Citigroup Pvt. Bank, 2002—. V.p. Tuxedo (NY) Bd. Edn., 1994—98; dir. Mercer Island Sch. Bd., 2001—. Mem.: Assoc. for Invest. Mgmt. and Rsch. (AIMR), Seattle Soc. Fin. Analysts, Tuxedo Park Club, Coryanthian Yacht Club. Avocations: sailboat racing, rock climbing, skiing. Home: 8648 SE 76th Pl Mercer Island WA 98040-5709 Office: Citigroup Pvt Bank 601 Union St Ste 3700 Seattle WA 98101

FRY, LOUIS EDWIN, JR., architect; b. Prairie View, Tex., Sept. 11, 1928; s. Louis Edwin and Obelia (Swearingen) F.; m. Genelle Wiley, Nov. 7, 1955; children— Jo Nisa, Louis Edwin, Vicki-Lynn, A'lexa AB, Howard U., 1949; B.Arch., Harvard U., 1953, M.Arch., 1954, M.Arch. in Urban Design, 1962. Registered profl. architect, D.C., Va., Md., Mass., Mich., Ala., Ga., Pa., Calif. Architect McGowan & Johnson, Washington, 1955-59; architect Fry & Welch Assoc. PC, Washington, 1959—. Vis. critic Harvard U., Cambridge, Mass., 1970-74; bd. dirs. Mid Atlantic NCARB, Washington, 1979-81; pres. D.C. Arch. Registration Bd., 1979-84; mem. Redevel. Land Agy., 1978— ; mem. design com. Harvard U., 1980—, vis. mem. Grad. Sch. Design Mem. Shepherd Park Community Assn., Washington, Georgia Ave. Profl. and Civic Assn., Washington Fulbright fellow, Holland, 1954-55 Fellow AIA; mem. Nat. Orgn. for Minority Architects, Omega Psi Phi Democrat. Avocation: breeding saltwater fish. Office: Fry and Welch Assocs PC 7100 Alaska Ave NW Washington DC 20012-1544

FRY, MALCOLM CRAIG, retired clergyman; b. Detroit, June 6, 1928; s. Dwight Malcolm and Adrienne (Craig) F.; m. Myrtle Mae Downing, June 5, 1948 (dec.); children: Pamela Mae, Malcolm Craig Jr., Rebecca Fry Gwartney, Matthew Dwight. Student, Bible Bapt. Sem., 1950; Th.B., Am. Div. Sch., Chgo., 1959; student, McNeese State Coll., Lake Charles, La., 1958-61; BS, Austin Peay State Coll., 1962; M.Ed., U. Ariz., 1969; D. Laws and Letters (hon.), Clarksville Sch. Theology, 1974; D.Ministry, Luther Rice Sem., 1978. Ordained to ministry Free Will Bapt. Ch., 1955. Asst. jewelery store mgr. Sonne Bros., Norwich, N.Y., 1948-50; pastor in Lake Charles, La., 1955-58, 59-61, Bryan, Tex., 1958-59, Ashland City, Tenn., 1961-62; asst. pastor in Royal Oak, Mich., 1962-64; pastor First Free Will Bapt. Ch., Tucson, 1964-71; dir. curriculum and rsch. Bd. Ch. Tng. Svc. Nat. Assn. Free Will Baptists, Nashville, 1971-72; gen. dir., treas. Bd. Ch. Tng. Svc., 1972-78; dir. Nat. Youth Conf., 1972-83; asst. dir. Bd. Sunday Sch. and Ch. Tng., 1978-83; pastor Unity Free Will Bapt. Ch., Smithfield, N.C., 1983-89, Goodlettsville Free Will Bapt. Ch., Goodlettsville, Tenn., 1991-96; asst. dir. Randall House Publs., 1989—96; ret., 1996. Program writer, teen tng. mgr. Nat. Assn. Free Will Bapts., 1963-78, clk., 1965-67, chmn. stewardship commn., 1962-67, editor in chief bd. Sunday Sch. and Ch. Tng., 1989-95. Author: Total Involvement, 1964, Why Worry?, 1967, Precepts for Practice, 1971, Discipling and Developing, 1971, The Teacher-in-Training, 1972, Contemporary Topical Studies, 1973, rev. edit., 1991, The Ministry of Music, 1974, Balancing Christian Education, 1977, Leader's Guide Discipling and Developing, 1979, Leader's Guide the Ministry of Ushering, 1980. Served with AUS, 1946-48; with USAF, 1951-57, Korea. Mem. Evang. Philos. Soc., Kiwanis, Civitan, Phi Delta Kappa.

FRY, MARY BETH, librarian; b. McKeesport, Pa., June 17, 1961; d. Charles Theodore and Olga (Maha) F. BS in Libr. Sci., Edinboro (Pa.) U., 1984; MLS, U. Md., 1989. Acquisitions asst. Am. U., Washington, 1985-90; acquisitions librarian The Brookings Instn., Washington, 1990-93, reference librarian, 1993—. Mem. D.C. Libr. Assn. Avocations: travel, watercolor painting, needlework. Office: The Brookings Instn Libr 1775 Massachusetts Ave NW Washington DC 20036-2103

FRY, MEREDITH WARREN, civil engineer, consultant; b. Bedford, Ind., Mar. 9, 1924; s. Cornelius Alexander and Ruby Estel (Jackson) F.; m. Mary Louise Henley, Dec. 25, 1952; children: James Owen, Robert Dail, Marvin Lee. BSCE, Tri-State U., 1952; MA in Econs., Ball State U., 1985. Registered profl. engr., Mo., Ind., registered land surveyor, Ind. Designer, design squad chief, traffic control designer Mo. State Hwy. Dept., Jefferson City, 1952-62; project engr., dist. traffic engr. Ind. State Highway Commn., Greenfield, 1962-66; engr. of traffic signs Ind. State Hwy. Commn., Indpls., 1967-69; city traffic engr. City of Muncie, Ind., 1966-67; supt. of planning Ball State U., Muncie, 1969-80, supt. of planning and constrn., 1980-88; civil engr., pres. M.W. Fry, Inc., Chesterfield, Ind., 1988—. Cons. Ball State U., 1988—. Muncie Sanitary Dist., 1988-91. Trustee Town Bd., Chesterfield, 1972-76; mem. traffic com. 500 Mile Speedway Race, Indpls., 1962-66, ad hoc com. for handicapped Ball State U., 1963-87, Del.-Muncie planning commn. tech. com., 1963-87; internat. student host family mem. Ball State U., 1979—; mem. The Heritage Found.; certification team Christian Theol. Sem. With USMC, 1944, World War II. Recipient Cert. of Appreciation Ind. Nat. Guard, Indpls., 1965, Disabled Student in Action of Ball State U., 1975, Disting. Svc. award Tri-State U., 1978, Grand Cross of Color, Supreme Assembly-Rainbow for Girls, Oklahoma City, 1961, Outstanding Alumni award Needmore H.S. Alumni Assn., 1995. Mem. NSPE, Inst. Transp. Engrs., Ind. Soc. Profl. Engrs. (pres. Delta chpt. 1979, 92, Engr. of Yr. 1992), Tri-State Alumni (bd. govs. 1992—), First Marine Divsn. Assn. (life), Chesterfield Optimist Club (pres. 1978), Masons (master 1961), Order of Eastern Star. Republican. Mem. Christian Ch. Avocations: travel, music, reading, education. Home and Office: MW Fry Inc 917 Hampton Ln Chesterfield IN 46017-1446 E-mail: mwfry@att.net.

FRY, MICHAEL GRAHAM, historian, educator; b. Brierley, Eng., Nov. 5, 1934; s. Cyril Victor and Margaret Mary (Copley) F.; m. Anna Maria Fulgoni; children: Michael Gareth, Gabrielle, Margaret Louise. B.Sc. in Econs. with honors, U. London, 1956, PhD, 1963. Dir. Norman Paterson Sch. Internat. Affairs, Carleton U., Ottawa, Ont., 1973-77; dean, prof. internat. relations Grad. Sch. Internat. Studies, U. Denver, 1978-81; dir., prof. Sch. Internat. Relations, U. So. Calif., Los Angeles, 1981—. Vis. prof. Middle East Center, U. Utah, 1979, U. Leningrad, 1976 Author: Illusions of Security: North Atlantic Diplomacy, 1918-1922, 1972, Freedom and Change, 1975, Lloyd George and Foreign Policy, Vol. I, The Education of a Statesman, 1890-1916, 1977, Despatches from Damascus, 1933-39, 1986, History and International Studies, 1987, History, The White House and the Kremlin: Statesmen as Historians, 1991, Power, Personalities and Policies, 1992, The North Pacific Triangle: Canada Japan and the U.S. at Century's End, 1998, Guide to International Relations and Diplomacy, 2002. NATO rsch. fellow, 1970-71, rsch. fellow Annenberg Program, Washington, 1986-87; grantee Can. Coun. Fellow Royal Hist. Soc. Roman Catholic. Home: 1358 Cassins St Carlsbad CA 92009-4856 Office: U So Calif Sch Internat Rels Los Angeles CA 90084-0001

FRY, MORTON HARRISON, II, lawyer; b. N.Y.C., May 15, 1946; s. George Thomas Clark and Louise Magdalen (Cronin) F.; m. Patricia Laylin Coffin, May 29, 1971. AB, Princeton U., 1968; JD, Yale U., 1971. Bar: N.Y. 1973, U.S. Ct. Mil. Appeals 1973, U.S. Dist. Ct. (so. and ea. dists.) N.Y. 1975, U.S. Ct. Appeals (2d cir.) 1975. Assoc. Cravath, Swaine & Moore, N.Y.C., 1971-72, 75-79; dep. gen. counsel Columbia Pictures Industries, Inc., N.Y.C., 1979-81; v.p., gen. counsel Warner Home Video Inc., N.Y.C., 1982-83; exec.v.p. Warner Electronic Home Svcs., N.Y.C., 1983-84; sr. counsel corp. and new techs. Warner Comms. Inc., N.Y.C., 1984-85; pres., CEO, bd. dirs. The Congress Video Group, Inc., 1985-87; pres., cons. Fry Assocs., 1987-89; ptnr. Marshall, Morris, Bomser & Fry, N.Y.C., 1990-94, Rubin, Bailin, Ortoli, Mayer, Baker & Fry, N.Y.C., 1995-2000; of counsel Stairs, Dillenbeck, Finley & Rendon, N.Y.C., 2000—. Mem. Dem. Nat. Fin. Com. Capt. USMC, 1966-75. Democrat. Congregationalist. Home: 310A E 18th St New York NY 10003 E-mail: frylaw@mindspring.com.

FRY, RANDY DALE, emergency medical technician, paramedic; b. Houston, Feb. 3, 1957; s. LeRoy D. Fry and Ardria Faye (Stegall) Boyd; m. Robbie Ruth Rippy, June 4, 1982. Paramedic Panola County Ambulance, Carthage, Tex., 1979-87; cardiac monitor tech. Bossier Med. Ctr., Bossier City, La., 1991—. Instr. CPR, PALS Bossier Med. Ctr.; instr. EMS, coord. Panola Jr. Coll., Carthage. Home: 770 CR 3341 Joaquin TX 75954-4962 Office: Bossier Med Ctr Bossier City LA 75954

FRY, RONALD SYLVAN, music educator, director; b. Charleston, S.C., Apr. 2, 1948; s. Philip Henry and Effie Evelyn Fry; m. Cheryl Anne LeHeup, Aug. 23, 1975; 1 child, Loren Matthew. AA, The Coll. of Orlando, 1970; BA, U. South Fla., 1972; MA in Tchg., Rollins Coll., 1981. Cert. profl. tchr. State of Fla., 1973. Instr. adult basic edn. Osceola County Dist. Schs., Kissimmee, Fla., 1985—87, music edn. tchr., 1987—91; choral dir., 1987—91; music edn. tchr. Pasco County Dist. Schs., Land-O-Lakes, Fla., 1991—, choral dir., 1991—, Fox Hollow Elem. Sch., Port Richey, Fla., 1998—, music edn. tchr. Substitute tchr. Osceola County Dist. Schs., 1973—76, 1986—87; pvt. music instr., Port Richey, Fla., 1974—; condr. and dir. Osceola (Fla.) Civic Orch., Kissimmee, 1975—78; mem. dist. level instrument com. Pasco County Dist. Schs., 1994—95; chmn. open house com. Hudson (Fla.) Elem. Sch., 1993—94; mem. sch. discipline com. Hudson (Fla.) Elem. Sch., 1997—98, Fox Hollow Elem. Sch., Port Richey, 1999—2000; mem. sch. safety com. Hudson (Fla.) Elem. Sch., 1994—96, Fox Hollow Elem. Sch., 2001—02, mem. sch. environ. com., 2001—02; mem. youth motivational program Osceola County Dist. Schs., 1989—90; mem. sch. leadership coun. Hudson (Fla.) Elem. Sch., 1993—94, 1996—97. Musician: George Grey Combo, 1970—85. Mem.: Kappa Delta Pi, Phi Mu Alpha (chpt. v.p. 1971—72). Democrat. Avocations: reading, walking, history, movies, travel. Home: 8822 Forest Lake Drive Port Richey FL 34668-5819 Office: Fox Hollow Elementary 8309 Fox Hollow Drive Port Richey FL 34668

FRY, ROY H(ENRY), librarian, educator; b. Seattle, June 16, 1931; s. Ray Edward and Fern Mildred (Harmon) F.; m. Joanne Mae Van de Guchte, Sept. 12, 1970; 1 child, Andrea Joy. BA in Asian Studies, BA in Anthropology, U. Wash., 1959; MA in Libr. Sci., Western Mich. U., 1965; MA in Polit. Sci., Northeastern Ill. U., 1977; archives cert., U. Dever, 1970; advanced studies program cert., Moody Bible Inst., 1990. Cert. tchr., Wash.; cert. pub. libr., N.Y.; cert. Med. Libr. Assn. Libr. and audio-visual coord. Zillah (Wash.) Pub. Schs., 1960-61; libr. Mark Morris H.S., Longview, Wash., 1961-64; evening reference libr. Loyola U. of Chgo., 1965-67, head reference libr., 1967-73, bibliog. svcs. libr., 1973-74, head circulation libr., 1974-76, coord. pub. svcs., 1976-85, gov. documents libr., 1985-91; ind. libr. cons., 1991-94; ref. libr. Trinity Evang. Divinity Sch., Deerfield, Ill., 1994—2001, reference and archives libr., 2001—. Tchg. asst. in anthropology Loyola U. of Chgo., 1966-67, instr. libr. sci. program for disadvantaged students, 1967, 68, univ. archivist, 1976-78, bibliographer for polit. sci., 1973-91, instr. corr. study div., 1975-85. Mem. Niles Twp. Regular Rep. Orgn., Skokie, Ill., 1982-98, sec. 1986-98; mem. Skokie Caucus Party, 1981-98; vol. Dep. Registration Officer, 1986—; mem. Skokie Traffic Safety Commn., 1984—, Skokie 4th July Parade com., 1986—; election judge Niles Twp., 1983-98, Avon Twp., 1999—. With USNR, 1951-52. Mem. Nat. Librs. Assn. (founding mem., bd. dirs. 1975-76), Asian/Pacific Am. Librs. Assn. (founding mem.), Chgo. Area Theol. Librs. Assn., Pacific N.W. Libr. Assn., Chgo. Area Archivists (founding mem.), Midwest Archives Conf. (founding mem.), ALA, Assn. Coll. and Rsch. Librs., Ill. Prairie Path Assn., Royal Can. Geog. Soc., Skokie Hist. Soc. (recording sec. 1986—), Ballard Hist. Soc. (Seattle), Macon County Hist. Soc. (Decatur, Ill.), Nat. Right to Life Com., Ill. Fedn. for Right to Life, Am. Legion, VFW, Korean War Vets. Assn., Pi Sigma Alpha. Republican. Evangelical Free. Office: Trinity Evang Divinity Sch Rolfing Meml Libr 2065 Half Day Rd Deerfield IL 60015-1241 Address: 335 S Arrowhead Ct Round Lake IL 60073-4209 E-mail: rfry@tiu.edu, lexifry@netzero.net.

FRY, TERRY L. retired English educator; b. Roodhouse, Ill., Oct. 10, 1942; s. Junior Earl and Elizabeth Ann (Nalefski) F.; m. Rochelle Lynne Morris Fry, Aug. 8, 1964; children: Howard Earl, Suzanne Fry Dees; m. Dolores Neps Fry, Jan. 7, 1989; children: Anthony Neps, Gregory Neps. BSEd, Ill. State U., 1965, MS in English, 1969, EdD in Edn., 1976. Tchr. English St. Anne (Ill.) Comm. H.S., 1965—68, Bloomington (Ill.) H.S., 1968—2003; ret., 2003; assoc. prof. English U. Ill., Urbana, 1977—78. Author: (textbook) Public Speaking, 1972. Deacon 2nd Presbyn. Ch., 1994-97. Mem. NEA, Bloomington Edn. Assn. (negotiator, pres. bd. dirs., del. 1968—), Ill. Edn. Assn., Moose, Masons. Avocations: vol. hist. interpreting, travel, reading, music, golf. Home: 500 S Blair Dr Normal IL 61761-3110 E-mail: fryt@district87.org.

FRY, VIRGINIA MILNE, artist, poet; b. Mpls., June 14, 1929; d. Stewart James and Cora Woodward Milne; m. Donald Lewis Fry, Sept. 13, 1947 (div. Feb. 0, 1992); children: Donald Stewart, Ronald Sinclair, Heather Fry Raymond, Laurel Fry Erickson. MA, Am. U., Washington, DC, 1980; Grad. in Tech. Illustration, Columbia Tech. Inst., Arlington, Va., 1969. Tech. illustrator Dames & Moore Environ. Engring. Cons., Bethesda, Md., 1973—. Author: (book of poems and prints) Things Done Alone, (book of poetry) Best Poems of 1988; Exhibited in group shows at The Ohio State Fair Profl. Divsn., The West Annapolis Gallery, Annapolis, Md., St. John's Coll., The Columbus (Ohio) Mus. Art, The Copley Soc., Boston, The Columbus (Ohio) Art League Exhbns., The Columbus (Ohio) Cultural Art Ctr., one-woman shows include The Zanesville (Ohio) Art Ctr., Mount Carmel Hosp. East, Columbus, Ohio, Capital U., Franklin U., The Canal House Gallery, Washington, D.C., The Cosmos Club, Washington, The Online Computerized Libr. Ctr., Dublin, Ohio. Leader Girl Scouts Am., Bethesda, Md., 1962—63; rec. studio narrator Md. Libr. Blind, Balt., 1992—2003; ICU vol. Ohio State U. Hosp., Columbus, 1980—85; vol. Shelter Homeless, Annapolis, Md., 2001—02; pres. Ohio State U. Women's Club Poetry Group, Columbus, 1985—92. Recipient 3d Pl. award, Internat. Libr. of Poetry. Mem.: Annapolis Chorale, The Annapolis Kiwanis Club (pres. 1997—98, Disting. 1998). Presbyterian. Avocations: choral soprano, tutoring, art judge. Home: 129 Bay Shore Avenue Annapolis MD 21403 Personal E-mail: gfkitty@aol.com.

FRY, W. LOGAN, artist; b. Columbus, Ohio, Sept. 2, 1944; s. Walter Logan and Frieda Mae Fry; m. Joanne Shapiro, Mar. 29, 1969; children: Rachel Megan Mitton-Fry, Matthew Logan, Elizabeth Anne, Michael William. Founder, dir. Digital Mus. Modern Art, Richfield, Ohio. Weaving, Evolutionary Fantasy (Kimono), The Renwick Gallery, Smithsonian Am. Art Mus., 1997, Untitled (Rubychip Vi), Cleve. Art Mus., 1999, Microhip Series 2:A, Mpls. Inst. Arts, 2001, Digital Interface, 2001, Circuit Board Series 3: 1Yg, 2001, Cosmic Code: Geometry, 2001, Microchip Series 2: Poly, Fine Arts Mus. San Francisco, M.H. de Young Meml. Mus., 2002, exhibitions include Cleve. Art Mus., 1988, Textile Arts Ctr., Chgo., 1990, Butler Inst. Am. Art, Youngstown, 1991, Moos Gallery, Western Res. Acad., 1993, Sch. Visual Arts, N.Y.C., 1995, The Textile Mus., Washington, 1996, Dixon Gallery and Gardens, Memphis, 1996, The Parish Mus., Southampton, N.Y., 1997, Csongrad & Szegad, Hungary, 1998, Tomsk & Novosibirsk, Russia, 1988, Textile Festival, 2000, Mus. Quilts & Textiles, San Jose, Calif., 2001, Mpls. Inst. Arts, 2001, Millworks Gallery, Akron, 2001, Flaten Gallery, St. Olaf Coll., Northfield, Minn., 2003. Creative Arts fellow, Ohio Arts Coun., 1993. Studio: PO Box 249 Richfield OH 44286

FRYAUFF, DAVID J. military officer, research scientist, microbiologist; b. St. Paul, Minn., Mar. 15, 1952; s. Robert Joseph Fryauff and Marilee Jane Hutchinson; m. Pasimani Pa'ane, June 25, 1981; children: Leilani Marie, Michael Jeffery, Krista Caroline. ScD, Johns Hopkins Sch. of Hygiene & Pub. Health, Balt., MD, 1982—87; MSc, Rutgers U., New Brunswick, NJ, 1976—78; BSc, Wagner Coll., Staten Island, NY, 1971—75. Good Clinical Practice (GCP) NIH, 2002; Good Laboratory Practice (GLP) Dept. of Def., 2002. Rsch. asst., mosquito rsch. & control Rutgers U. Dept. of Entomology, New Brunswick, NJ, 1979—78; vol., disease control US Peace Corps, Nuku'alofa, 1978—80; cons., german-samoan plant protection program GTZ, Apia, Western Samoa, 1981—81; project mgr. USAID Onchocerciasis Study, Robertsfield, Liberia, 1983—84; cons. Liberian Inst. for Biomedical Rsch./New York Blood Ctr., Roberstfield, Liberia, 1984—85; rsch. entomologist/commd. officer US Naval Med. Rsch. Unit No. 3, Cairo, Egypt, 1985—92; dept. head, parasitology US Naval Med. Rsch. Unit No. 2, Jakarta, Indonesia, 1992—99; dir., overseas malaria rsch. Malaria Program, Naval Med. Rsch. Ctr., Silver Spring, 1999—. Cons. Vector Biology & Control (USAID), Roslyn, Va.; infectious disease rsch. team leader Multinational Forces & Observers, North Sinai, Egypt, 1985—92; team mem., disease threat assessment US Navy, Kuwait City, Kuwait, 1991—92. Author: (infectious disease research.) Lancet, Vaccine, Jour. of Parasitology, Am. Jour. of Tropical Medicine & Hygiene, Emerging Infectious Diseases, Jour. of Infectious Diseases, Clin. Infectious Diseases, etc. Coach Youth Sports Assoc., Scouts, Jakarta, Indonesia, 1995—99. Comdr. USN, 1984. Decorated Navy Achievement Medal, Navy Commendation Medal, Navy Meritorious Unit Citation Medal, Dept. of Def.; scholar US Pub. Health Svc. Academic Scholarship, Johns Hopkins Sch. of Hygiene & Pub. Health, 1982-1983. Mem.: Am. Soc. of Tropical Medicine & Hygiene. Church Of Jesus Christ Of Latter Day Saints. Achievements include research in Carried out original epidemiological research on human diseases in Polynesia (Bancroftian filariasis), West Africa (Onchocerciasis), East Africa & the Middle East (Leishmaniasis), Asia (Malaria)); development of Principal Investigator in trials demonstrating the safety and efficacy of antimalarial drugs (Primaquine, Malarone). Avocations: swimming, diving, bicycling, gardening, hiking. Home: 24109 Sugarcane Ln Gaithersburg MD 20882 Office: Naval Med Rsch Center 503 Robert Grant Ave Silver Spring MD 20910 Office Fax: 301-319-7545. E-mail: fryauffd@nmrc.navy.mil.

FRYBURGER, LAWRENCE BRUCE, lawyer, mediator, writer; b. Cin., Apr. 7, 1933; BA, U. Cin., 1956; LLB with nat. honors, U. Tex., 1958. Bar: Tex. 1959, U.S. Dist. Ct. (we. dist.) Tex. 1961, U.S. Ct. Appeals (5th cir.) 1962, U.S. Supreme Ct. 1963, U.S. Dist. Ct. (so. dist.) Tex. 1972, U.S. Dist. Ct. (no. dist.) Tex. 1981, U.S. Ct. Appeals (11th cir.) 1981; bd. cert. labor and employment law Tex. Bd. Legal Specialization. Pvt. practice, San Antonio, 1959—. Spl. prof. labor relations law San Antonio Coll., 1968; originator Tex. Young Lawyer's Inst. Author: Policies, Procedures and People: A Blueprint for Human Resources, 1997; contbr. articles to law jours.; mem. editorial bd. Tex. Lawyers Practice Guide, 1964. Mem. San Antonio Bd. Adjustment, 1969-72; chmn. lawyer's div. United Fund, San Antonio and Bexar County, 1967-68. Sutphin scholar U. Cin., 1956. Mem. ABA, Tex. Bar Assn. (program chmn. current devels. in labor law inst. 1978, mem. coun. labor law sect. 1978-80), San Antonio Bar Assn. (chmn. lawyer reference plan 1970-73), Tex. Young Lawyers Assn. (bd. dirs. 1964-66), San Antonio Young Lawyers Assn. (pres. 1963-64, Outstanding Young Lawyer award 1967), Tex. Assn. of Residential Care Communities (spl. labor law counsel 1996—), Phi Delta Phi, Sigma Chi.

FRYBURGER, VERNON RAY, JR., advertising and marketing educator; b. Cin., June 9, 1918; s. Vernon Ray and Florence Rose (Steding) F.; m. Marjorie Anne Clarke, June 19, 1948; 1 dau., Candace. BS in Bus. Adminstrn., Miami U., Oxford, Ohio, 1939; PhD in Econs., U. Ill., 1950. Salesman U.S. Printing & Lithograph Co., 1940-41; instr. mktg. Miami U., 1941-43; assoc. rsch. dir. Nat. Assn. Broadcasters, 1946; asst. prof. journalism U. Ill., 1947-53; faculty Northwestern U., 1953-86, prof. advt. and mktg., chmn. dept. advt., 1959-84, ednl. dir. Inst. Advanced Advt. Studies, 1963-85, prof. emeritus, 1986—; nat. assoc. dean Am. Acad. Advt., 1964-65, nat. dean, 1965-66, chmn. bd.; cons. to bus., 1954—; adviser Advt. Ednl. Found., 1972-84. Vis. prof. U. Hawaii, 1965; cons. advt. U.S. Army, 1983-91. Author: (with C.H. Sandage and K. Rotzoll) Advertising Theory and Practice, 12th edit., 1989, (with Boyd and Westfall) Cases in Advertising Management, 1964; editor: (with C.H. Sandage) The Role of Advertising, 1960. Bd. dirs. Lake Forest Library. Served to lt., submarines USNR, 1943-46, PTO. Mem. Am. Mktg. Assn., Internat. Advt. Assn., Assn. Edn. Journalism, Beta Gamma Sigma, Kappa Tau Alpha, Delta Tau Delta, Delta Sigma Pi, Artus. Presbyterian. Home: 1921 Shore Acres Dr Lake Bluff IL 60044-1342

FRYE, CLAYTON WESLEY, JR., finance executive; b. L.A., May 18, 1930; s. Clayton Wesley Sr. and Mary Virginia (Briggs) F.; m. Dorothy Rumsfeld, Jan. 14, 1957; children: Carolyn Frye Halloran (dec.), Diane Frye Tanner. AB, Stanford U., 1953, MBA, 1959. Pres. Sutter Hill Devel. Co., Palo Alto, Calif., 1962-69; gen. ptnr. Johnson & Frye Investment Co., San Antonio, 1970-73; sr. assoc. Laurance S. Rockefeller, N.Y.C., 1973—. Ptnr. Rockefeller & Assocs. Realty, L.P., San Francisco, 1990-99, Pacific Property Svcs., San Francisco, 1984-98; bd. dirs. Col. Williamsburg (Va.) Co., Woodstock Resort Corp., Vt., chmn.; dir. Tejon Ranch Co., L.A., 1975-98, Rockefeller Ctr. Inc., 1976-81, Times Mirror Co., L.A., 1988-2000, King Ranch, Inc., Tex., 1996-2000. Trustee Hist. Hudson Valley, Tarrytown, N.Y.; trustee, chmn. Jackson Hole Preserve, Inc., Woodstock Found., White House Hist. Assn., bd. dirs.; vice-chmn., former trustee South St. Seaport Mus., N.Y.C.; vice-chmn., bd. dirs. Rockresorts, Inc., N.Y.C., 1973-87. Office: 30 Rockefeller Plz Rm 5600 New York NY 10112-0002

FRYE, DELLA MAE, portrait artist; b. Roanoke, Va., Feb. 16, 1926; d. Henry Vetchel and Helen Lavinia Theradosia (Eardley) Pearcy; m. James Frederick Frye, Nov. 1, 1944; children: Linda Jeanne Frye, James Marvin, David Scott. Student, Hope Coll., 1968, Grand Valley State Coll., 1969-71. Asst. med. records librarian Bapt. Hosp., Little Rock, 1944; receptionist, sec. Stephens Coll., Columbia, Mo., 1945-46; art tchr. Jenison (Mich.) Christian Sch., 1965-67, pvt. classes, 1964-74; realtor, 1978-80; with Diversified Fin., 1979-82; portrait artist, 1967 . Cons. World Traders, Grand Rapids, Mich., 1986—. Author various poems; exhbns. include Salon Des Nations (cert. honor), 1984, Ann Arbor (Mich.) Art Guild, Kalamazoo Artists, Internat. Art Gallery, Hawaii, La Mandragore Gallery Internationale D'Art Contemporain, songwriter: (album) I Love America, 2000-2002 Pres. mother's club Jenison Christian Sch., 1965-66; treas. Band Boosters, Jenison, 1966. Recipient awards for nat. contests in portrait painting. Republican. Baptist. Avocations: songwriting, swimming. Home: 7677 Steele Ave Jenison MI 49428 also: 8901 SE 120th Pl Belleview FL 34420 Mailing: PO Box 2484 Grand Rapids MI 49501-2484

FRYE, EDWARD MOSES, law educator; b. Sallisaw, Okla., Jan. 28, 1920; s. Edward Moses and Mattie Lucille (Watts) F.; m. Mary Lois Rulifson, Aug. 15, 1953; children— Lynette, Camille, Renee. Student Muskogee Jr. Coll., 1937-39; B.A., U. Okla., 1941; J.D., Oklahoma City U., 1957. Bar: Okla. 1957, U.S. Dist. Ct. (we., no. and so. dists.) Okla. 1957, U.S. Ct. Appeals (10th cir.) 1960, U.S. Supreme Ct. 1962. Tax agt. Okla. Tax Commn., Oklahoma City, 1954-57, legal counsel, 1957-62; legal counsel bd. regents A&M Colls., Stillwater, Okla., 1962-75; prof. law Okla. State U., Stillwater, 1975— . Author: Oklahoma Higher Education Law, 1976; Oklahoma Public School Law, 1976; Teacher and the Law, 1977. Bd. dirs. Okla. Hist. Soc., 1972-81; dep. chief Cherokee Nation of Okla., Tahlequah, 1976, Cherokee Council, 1978—, mem. supreme ct., 1980, mem. council, 1982. Served to brig. gen. AUS (Ret.). Mem. ABA, Okla. Bar Assn., Payne County Bar Assn. Republican. Presbyterian. Home: 702 W Lakeshore Dr Stillwater OK 74075-1335 Office: Coll Edn Okla State U Rm 309 Stillwater OK 74078-0001

FRYE, HELEN JACKSON, federal judge; b. Klamath Falls, Oreg., Dec. 10, 1930; d. Earl and Elizabeth (Kirkpatrick) Jackson; m. William Frye, Sept. 7, 1952; children: Eric, Karen, Heidi; 1 adopted child, Hedy; m. Perry Holloman, July 10, 1980 (dec. Sept. 1991). BA in English with honors, U. Oreg., 1953, MA, 1960, JD, 1966. Bar: Oreg. 1966. Public sch. tchr., Oreg., 1956-63; with Riddlesberger, Pederson, Brownhill & Young, 1966-67, Husband & Johnson, Eugene, 1968-71; trial judge State of Oreg., 1971-80; U.S. dist judge Dist. Oreg. Portland, 1980-95; sr. judge U.S. Dist. Ct., Portland, 1995—. Mem. Phi Beta Kappa. Office: 1107 US Courthouse 1000 SW 3rd Ave Portland OR 97204-2930

FRYE, HENRY E. retired state supreme court chief justice; b. Ellerbe, N.C., Aug. 1, 1932; s. Walter A. and Pearl Alma (Motley) F.; m. Edith Shirley Taylor, Aug. 25, 1956; children: Henry Eric, Harlan Elbert. BS in Biol. Scis., A & T U., N.C., 1953; JD with honors, U. N.C., 1959. Bar: N.C. 1959. Asst. U.S. atty. (middle dist.), N.C., 1963-65; prof. law N.C. Central U., Durham, 1965-67; practice law Greensboro, N.C., 1967-83; rep. N.C. Gen. Assembly, 1969-80, N.C. Senate, 1980-82; assoc. justice N.C. Supreme Ct., Raleigh, 1983-99, chief justice, 1999—2001; of counsel Brooks, Pierce, McLendon, Humphrey & Leonard, LLP, Greensboro, NC, 2001—. Organizer, pres. Greensboro Nat. Bank, 1971-80. Deacon Providence Baptist Ch. Capt. USAF, 1953-55. Mem. ABA, N.C. Bar Assn., Greensboro Bar Assn., Nat. Bar Assn., Am. Judicature Soc. (chair bd. dirs. 1995-97), Kappa Alpha Psi. Office: Brooks Pierce McLendon humphrey & Leonard LLP 2000 Renaissance Plaza 230 N Elm St PO Box 26000 Greensboro NC 27420-1841 Fax: 336-378-1001. E-mail: hfrye@brookspierce.com.

FRYE, LINDA BETH (LINDA BETH HISLE), elementary, secondary education educator; b. Apr. 15, 1947; d. Roland Earl Jr. Hisle and Paralee M. Jones; m. Dennis Franklin Frye; children: Byron Franklin, Cody Earl, Matthew Cole. BA in Art and Elem. Edn., E. Ctrl. State U., Ada, 1970; M.Ed. in Elem. Edn., E. Tex. State U., Commerce, 1975. Tchr. Sherman (Tex.) Ind. Sch. Dist., 1969—2002. Specialist in lang., learning disabilities in spl. edn. Recipient Tex. Instrument Invention Conv. award, Tchr. award, Tex. Instrument Invention Convention; grantee Ada City Sch. Foundation, Ada City Sch. Foun. Mem.: Church of Christ. Home: 8380 CR 3510 Ada OK 74820-9619 Office: P O Box 2015 Ada OK 74821-1701

FRYE, MARY CATHERINE, prosecutor; b. Amarillo, Tex., Feb. 9, 1950; d. John Gristy and Estelle Angelina (Ashton) F.; m. Irwin Allen Popowsky, Dec. 18, 1977; children: Matthew Frye, Rebecca Susan. AB, Oberlin Coll., 1972; JD, U. Pa., 1977. Bar: Pa. 1977. Law clk. Phila. Orphans' Ct., 1977-79; assoc. Reager, Selkowitz & Adler, Harrisburg, Pa., 1980-89; staff atty. Pa. State Edn. Assn., Harrisburg, 1989-92; chief counsel Pa. Assn. Elem. and Secondary Sch. Prins., Harrisburg, 1992-94; chief civil divsn./asst. U.S. atty. U.S. Atty.'s Office (mid. dist.) Pa., Harrisburg, 1994—2002, sr. litig. counsel, 2002—. Adj. prof. law Widener U., Harrisburg, 1994-94. Author: Sexual Harassment: A Guide for Administrators, 1993. Democrat. Home: 4218 Kirkwood Rd Harrisburg PA 17110-3122 Office: US Atty's Office 228 Walnut St Harrisburg PA 17101-1714

FRYE, RICHARD ARTHUR, lawyer; b. Akron, Ohio, Sept. 3, 1948; s. Virgil Arthur and Margaret (Mullen) F.; children: Kathleen, Emily, Abigail. BA, Wittenberg U., 1970; JD, Ohio State U., 1973. Bar: Ohio 1973, U.S. Dist. Ct. (so. dist.) Ohio 1974, U.S. Ct. Appeals (6th cir.) 1978, U.S. Supreme Ct. 1980, U.S. Ct. Appeals (fed. cir.) 1987, U.S. Ct. Appeals (9th cir.) 1998. Ptnr. Chester, Willcox & Saxbe LLP, Columbus, 1996—. Co-author: Ohio Eminent Domain Practice, 1977, Personal Injury Litigation in Ohio, 1985. Bd. dirs. Am. Heart Assn., Franklin County, Ohio, 1985-87, J. Ashburn Youth Ctr., 1996-2000; bd. dirs. Legal Aid Soc. Columbus, 1996—, pres., 2003—; chmn. adv. com. on local rules U.S. Dist. Ct. for So. Dist. Ohio, 1990—; chmn. com. to rev. reporting of opinions Supreme Ct. of Ohio, 2000-03; life mem. 6th Cir. Jud. Conf., ctrl. com. Franklin County Dem. Party, 2000—. Fellow Am. Coll. Trial Lawyers, Columbus Bar Found., Ohio State Bar Found.; mem. Fed. Bar assn. (pres. Columbus chpt. 1991). Methodist. Office: Chester Willcox & Saxbe LLP 65 E State St Ste 1000 Columbus OH 43215 E-mail: rfrye@cwslaw.com.

FRYE, ROLAND MUSHAT, JR., lawyer; b. Princeton, N.J., Feb. 8, 1950; s. Roland Mushat and Jean (Steiner) F.; m. Susan Marie Pettey, Jan. 23, 1988. AB cum laude, Princeton U., 1972; JD, Cornell U., 1975. Bar: Pa. 1975, D.C. 1978, U.S. Ct. Appeals (D.C. cir.) 1991, U.S. Supreme Ct. 1991. Litigation assoc. White and Williams, Phila., 1975-77; litigation atty. U.S. Dept. Energy, Washington, 1977-79, asst. solicitor, 1979-80; presiding officer Fed. Energy Regulatory Commn., Washington, 1980-83, chief presiding officer, 1983-85, supervisory atty., 1985-88, adv. atty., 1988-91; energy atty. Pepper, Hamilton & Scheetz, Washington, 1991-92; sr. atty. Office Commn. Appellate Adjudication U.S. Nuclear Regulatory Commn., Washington, 1992—. Mediator Ctr. for Cmty. Justice, D.C. Superior Ct., 1984-86. Editor Cornell Law Rev., 1974-75; mem. editl. bd. Sidwell Friends Sch. Alumni Mag., 1994-2003; contbr. articles to profl. jours. Mem. schs. and ann. giving coms. Princeton U., Washington and Phila., 1978-91; arbitrator Better Bus. Bur. Greater Washington, 1983-86, Phila. Ct. Common Pleas, 1975-77; mem. Sidwell Friends Sch. Parents Assn., treas. 2001-03. Capt. USAR. Recipient Outstanding Young Man Am. award U.S. Jaycees, 1979. Mem. ABA, D.C. Bar Assn. (fee arbitration panel 1983-89, com. on alt. dispute resolution 1983-87), Fed. Bar Assn., Fed. Energy Bar Assn. (adminstrv. practice com. 1991-92), Sidwell Friends Sch. Alumni Assn. (exec. com. 1985-93, 94-2003, v.p. 1987-89, pres. 1989-93, Newmyer award), Soc. Cin., St. Andrews Soc., Prettyman-Leventhal Am. Inn of Ct. (barrister 1989-92, master 1992-99, exec. com. 1992-99, program chmn. 1993-95, counsellor 1995-96, pres.-elect 1996-97, pres. 1997-98, nat./emeritus mem. 1999—), Cosmos Club. Presbyterian. Avocations: trout fishing, singing, travel. Home: 220 N Royal St Alexandria VA 22314-3329 Office: US Nuclear Regulatory Commn 11555 Rockville Pike Rockville MD 20852-2739 E-mail: rmf@nrc.gov.

FRYE, WILBUR WAYNE, retired soil science educator, researcher, administrator; b. Finger, Tenn., Aug. 6, 1933; s. Alfred D. and Lela E. (Rouse) F.; m. Martha Hoskins, Apr. 20, 1957; children: Thomas W., John D. BS, U. Tenn., 1961, MS, 1964; PhD, Va. Tech, 1969. Cert. profl. soil scientist, cert. crop advisor. Air traffic controller FAA, Memphis, 1957-58; instr. Tenn. Tech. U., Cookeville, 1963-74; asst. prof. U. Ky., Lexington, 1975-78, assoc. prof., 1978-84, prof., 1984-2000, prof. emeritus, 2000—. Contbr. numerous articles to profl. jours. and chpts. to books; editor books. Chmn. troop commn. Boy Scouts Am., Lexington, 1976-81; chmn. adminstrv. bd. Trinity Hill United Meth. Ch., Lexington, 1977-79; lay del. to Ky. Conf. United Meth. Ch., 1994-96. Recipient Sci. Faculty Fellowship award NSF, 1967, Master Tchr. award Gamma Sigma Delta, 1978, Great Tchr. award U. Ky. Alumni Assn., 1980, Pres.'s Citation Soil & Water Conservation Soc., 1976, 78; named Danforth Assoc., 1981. Fellow Soil and Water Conservation Soc. (bd. dirs. 1975-79), Soil Sci. Soc. Am. (bd. dirs. 1989-90, assoc. editor Jour. 1990-93, Soil Sci. Edn. award 1995), Am. Soc. Agronomy (Agronomic Resident Edn. award 1995); life mem. Coun. for Agrl. Sci. and Tech. (life, bd. dirs. 1991-99), Assn. Am. Feed Control Ofcls. (life, bd. dirs. 1995-97), Assn. Am. Plant Food Control Ofcls. (life), Lexington Lions Club Melvin Jones Fellow (chmn. program com. 2002--). Methodist. Office: U Ky Dept Agronomy Lexington KY 40546-0091 E-mail: wfrye@uky.edu., wilburfrye@cs.com.

FRYE-MOQUIN, MARSHA MARIE, social worker; b. Tecumseh, Mich., Aug. 1, 1950; d. Jesse Roberts Gray and Evelyn Marie Binns Wade; children: Dawn M. Savidge, James M. Savidge Jr., David R. Frye. AS, Monroe County C.C., Monroe, Mich., 1976; ADN, U. Vt., 1988; BA in Sociology, North Adams (Mass.) State Coll, 1992; MSW, SUNY, Albany, 1994; cert. case mgmt., New Eng. Healthcare Assembly, 1997. Cert. social worker, Mass.; lic. ind. cert. social worker, Mass., clin. hypnotherapist. Sales clk./cashier Woolworth's dept. Store, Burlington, Vt.; clk./typist New Eng. Telephone, Burlington, 1978-80; unit sec. Prince Georges Hosp., Cheverly, Md., 1969-72, Fairfax Hosp., Falls Church, Va., 1972-73; nurses aide Burlington Convalescent Ctr., 1976-77; EEG technician Med. Ctr. of Vt., Burlington, 1980-88; lab. technician U. Vt., Burlington, 1987-88; staff nurse Berkshire Med. Ctr., Pittsfield, Mass., 1988-90, charge nurse, 1989-90; intern Women's Svcs. Ctr./Battered Women's Shelter, Pittsfield, Mass., 1991, No. Berkshire Health and Human Svcs. Coalition, North Adams, 1992, Hillcrest Ednl. Ctr., Lenox, Mass., 1992-93, Dept. Vet. Affairs Med. Ctr., Northampton, Mass., 1993-94; med. social worker Fairview Hosp., Great Barrington, Mass., 1994—, dir. mgmt., social svcs., patient adv., 1995—; nurse, med. social worker Vis. Nurses Assn. No. Berkshire, Williamstown, Mass., 1991-95. Faculty Mildred Elley Sch., Inc., 2001. Vol. Am. Cancer Soc., 1995—; adv. bd. pres. United Cerebral Palsy Assn. Berkshire County, Inc. Recipient Clin. Excellence award The Vt. State Nurses Assn., Cert. of Honor for vol. svc. Women's Svc. Ctr., 1991, Cert. of Appreciation, No. Berkshire Health and Human Svcs. Coalition, 1991. Mem. NASW, New England Sociological Assn., Alpha Chi. Avocations: concerts, theater, movies. Home: 9 Prescott Ln Apt 1 Monterey MA 01230

FRYER, APPLETON, publisher, sales executive, lecturer, diplomat; b. Buffalo, Feb. 25, 1927; s. Livingston and Catherine (Appleton) F.; m. Angeline Dudley Kenefick, May 16, 1953; children: Appleton, Daniel Kenefick, Robert Livingston, Catherine Appleton. AB cum laude, Princeton U., 1950. Head interpreter Hewitt-Robins, Inc., Buffalo, 1950-51; with advt. dept. Buffalo Evening News, 1953-55; field rep., advt. Ketchum, MacLeod & Grove, Inc., 1955-56; pres. Duo-Fast of We. N.Y., Inc., Buffalo, 1956-84; pub. Buffalo Bus. Jour., 1984-86; travel cons. Pieper Travel Bur., 1990; hon. consul gen. Japan, Buffalo, 1979—2002. Task force Inner Harbor Hist. Interpretation, Buffalo, 2000—, Dep. sherif Erie County, N.Y., 1954-60, adv. bd. Children's Hosp. Buffalo; mem. Cmty. Welfare Coun. Buffalo and Erie county; co-chmn. corp. divsn. Episcopal Charities, 1988, chmn. devel. com., 1989; mem. bd. Erie County Sesquicentennial Commn., 1970-71, 74-76, chmn. devel. com., 1988-89; adv. City Buffalo Environ. Mgmt. Commn., 1973-75; trustee Theodore Roosevelt Inaugural Nat. Hist. Site Found., 1969-87; bd. dirs. Zool. Soc. Buffalo, 1972-78, Buffalo Fine Arts Acad., Albright-Knox art Gallery, 1973-76; chmn. Buffalo-Kanazawa Sister Cities Com., 1978-79; pres. Arboretum Met. Buffalo, 1977-78; mem. Pan Am. Contennial com., 1998-2002; bd. dirs. Maud Gordon Holmes Arboretum, 1974-88, pres., 1976-78; mem. Buffalo Landmark and Preservation Bd., 1978-87, Erie County Preservation Adv. Bd., 1978-82; mem. coun. Charles Burchfield Ctr., 1974-92, Cen. Erie deanery Diocese We. N.Y., 1970, Young Life on Niagra Frontier, 1971-72; mem. Erie Canal Heritage Corridor Com., 2001--; chmn. planning com. Venture in Mission, 1979, mem. campaign exec. com., 1979-80; chmn. N.Y. State sect. ann. giving Princeton U., 1979-82, We. N.Y. ann. giving regional com., 1978-79, mem. nat. ann. giving com.; exec. dir. Landmark Soc. Niagara Frontier, 1998—; mem. adv. bd. Erie County Cultural Resources, 1986-92, Concerned Ecumenical Ministry (West Side), 1986-98; chmn. devel. com. Crane Cutting Ctr., 1987-90; comdr. Lorenzo Burrows post Am. Legion, 1988-89; mem. N.Y. State coms. Bicentennial French Revolution, 1988-90; historian We. N.Y. commandery Naval Order U.S., 1991-99, vice comdr., 1999-2001, comdr., 2001—; patients' rep. Buffalo Gen. Hosp., 1996—; mem. Navy League of U.S. (Niagara region), 1999—, The New Millennium Group of W. N.Y., 2000—, Martin House Restoration Corp., 1999—, Military Order of Fgn. Wars of U.S., 1998—. With USNR, 1945-46, to 1st lt. AUS, 1951-52. Recipient Key to City of Buffalo, Mayor Anthony Masiello, 1996, Long and Dedicated Svc. award, Buffalo-Kanazawa Sister City Com., 1997, Order of the Sacred Treasure, Gold Ray with ribbon, Govt. of Japan, 2002. Mem.: Buffalo Soc. Natural Scis., Am. Assn. Mus. (trustee 1978—81), SAR (Buffalo chpt. v.p. 1993—94, pres. 1995—96), Bi-Nat. Bridge Task Force (Peace Bridge), Princeton U. Alumni Assn. (chmn. schs. com. We. N.Y. area 1974—77), Old Ft. Niagara Assn. (dir. 1980—90), Buffalo and Erie County Hist. Soc. (bd. mgrs. 1969—, v.p. 1977—82, pres. 1982—84), Soc. Colonial Wars, Buffalo Area C. of C. (Buffalo Beautiful com.), Mil. Order Fgn. Wars U.S., Navy League U.S., Niagra Frontier Indsl. Distbrs. Assn., Soc. Mayflower Descendants (regent Buffalo colony 1961—65), Holland Soc. N.Y. (pres. Niagra Frontier br. 1969—79), Landmark Soc. Niagara Frontier (pres. 1969—73, Outstanding award 1979, Landmarker award 2000, Appleton Fryer Founder award 2003), Order Colonial Lords of Manors, Canal Soc. N.Y. State, Saturn Club, Scriptores, Porcupine Club (gov. 1969—73), U. Cottage Club, Nassau Club, Saturn Club (vice dean 1963, 1986, dean 1990), Princeton Club of We. N.Y. (pres. 1960), Princeton Club, Rotary of Buffalo (internat. svc. com. 1978—90, bd. dirs. 1983—86), Masons. Episcolpalian (warden, lic. lay reader). Home: 85 Windsor Ave Buffalo NY 14209-1018

FRYER, THOMAS WAITT, JR., writer and editor; b. Martinsville, Va., Oct. 6, 1936; s. Thomas Waitt and Wilma Pauline (Harp) F.; m. Mary Margaret Allshouse, Jan. 5, 1980; children— Laura Elizabeth, Matthew Thomas, John Anderson. AA, Mars Hill Coll., 1956; BA, Wayland Coll., 1958; MA (Ford Found. fellow), Vanderbilt U., 1959; PhD (Kellogg Found. fellow), U. Calif., Berkeley, 1968. Instr. in English Daytona Beach Jr. Coll., 1959-61; assoc. dean instrn. Chabot Coll., 1965-67; v.p., chief campus adminstr. Miami-Dade Community Coll., 1967-73; chancellor Peralta Colls., 1973-78; chancellor, dist. supt. Foothill-De Anza Community Coll. Dist., 1978-92; vice chmn. bd. dirs. Am. Council on Edn., 1979-80. Vis. prof. U. Calif. at Berkeley, 1988-92; pres. Fla. Assn. Community Colls., 1971-73. Chmn. WASC Accred Com. for Community and Jr. Colls., 1984-86; pres. chief exec. officers Calif. Community Colls., 1986-87; trustee Fla. C.C. Jacksonville, 1999. Recipient Communication and Leadership award Toastermasters Internat., 1977, selected a Young Leader of Acad., 1978; named one of Most Effective Coll. Pres. in Nation Exxon Edn. Found., 1986, one of 50 best community coll. CEO's by U. Tex., Austin, 1988. Mem. Nat. Soc. Study Edn., Am. Assn. Higher Edn. (dir. 1975-78), Assn. for Study of Higher Edn. Phi Delta Kappa. Clubs: Commonwealth of Calif., Rotary.

FRYKENBERG, ROBERT ERIC, historian, educator; b. India, June 8, 1930; s. Carl Eric and Doris Marie (Skoglund) F.; m. Carol Enid Addington, July 1, 1952; children: Ann Denise Leinis, Brian Robert, Craig Michael. BA, Bethel Coll., Minn., 1951; MA, U. Minn., 1953; M.Div., Bethel Theol. Sem., 1955; PhD (Rockefeller fellow 1958-61), London U., 1961. Research asst. U. Calif., Berkeley, 1955-57; instr. Oakland (Calif.) Jr. Coll., 1957-58; Ford and Carnegie research and teaching fellow U. Chgo., 1961-62; mem. faculty U. Wis., Madison, 1962—, prof. history and S. Asian studies, 1971-97, emeritus prof. history and South Asian studies, 1997—, chmn. dept., dir. Center S. Asian Studies, 1970-73. Vis. prof. U. Hawaii, summer 1968; Radhakrishwan Meml. lectr. Oxford U., 1998; dir. Pew India Rsch. Advancement Projects, 1994-01. Author: Guntur District, 1978-1848: A History of Local Influence and Central Authority in South India, 1965, History and Belief: The Foundations of Historical Understanding, 1996; editor: Land Control and Social Structure in Indian History, 1969, 77, Land Tenure and Peasant in South Asia: An Anthology of Recent Research, 1977, Studies of South India, 1985, Delhi Through the Ages, 1986, 93; co-editor: Studies in the History of Christian Missions series, 1997—; contbr. articles to revs. and profl. publs. Trustee Am. Inst. Indian

Studies, 1971-81; dir. summer seminar NEH, 1976. Rsch. fellow Am. Coun. Learned Socs.-Social Sci. Rsch. Coun. 1962-63, 67, 73-74, 83-84, 88-89, Guggenheim fellow, 1968-69, HEW Fulbright Hays sr. fellow, 1965-66, NEH fellow, 1975, fellow Wis. Inst. Rsch. Humanities, 1975, Wilson Ctr., 1986, 91-92, Pew Rsch. fellow, 1997. Fellow Royal Hist. Soc., Royal Asiatic Soc.; mem. Internat. Conf. and Seminars, Soc. S. Indian Studies (pres. 1968-70, 82-84), Am. Hist. Assn. (pres. conf. faith and history 1970-72), Assn. Asian Studies, Inst. Hist. Studies India, Inst. Asian Studies India, Assn. South Asian Studies Australia, Inst. Advanced Christian Studies (dir. 1979-83, 87-91, pres. 1981-83) Office: Univ Wis 4134 Humanities Bldg Madison WI 53706 E-mail: frykenberg@mhub.history.wisc.edu.

FRYLING, VICTOR J. energy company executive; Pres., COO CMS Energy Corp., Dearborn, Mich., 1991—. Office: CMS Energy Corp Fairlane Plz S Ste 1100 330 Town Center Dr Dearborn MI 48126

FRYMAN, DAVID TRAVIS, professional baseball player; b. Lexington, Ky., Mar. 25, 1969; With Detroit Tigers, 1987—97, Cleveland Indians, 1998—. Recipient Silver Slugger award, 1992; mem. Sporting News All-Star Team, 1993, Am. League All-Star Team, 1992-93, 94, 96. Office: Cleveland Indians Jacobs Field 2401 Ontario St Cleveland OH 44115-4003

FRYMAN, VIRGIL THOMAS, JR., lawyer; b. Maysville, Ky., Apr. 9, 1940; s. Virgil Thomas and Elizabeth Louis (Marshall) F. AB cum laude, Harvard U., 1962, LLB, 1966. Bar: N.Y. 1967, U.S. Ct. Appeals (2d cir.) 1967, U.S. Dist. Ct. (so. and ea. dists.) N.Y. 1968, U.S. Supreme Ct. 1970, U.S. Ct. Appeals (6th cir.) 1988,U.S. Ct. Appeals (11th cir.) 2002, U.S. Dist. Ct. (ea. and we. dists.) Ky. 1988. Assoc. Cravath, Swaine & Moore, N.Y.C., 1966-73; asst. U.S. atty. U.S. Dist. Ct. (so. dist.) N.Y., N.Y.C., 1973-78; assoc. gen. counsel Price Waterhouse, N.Y.C., 1978-86; staff counsel select com. to investigate covert arms transactions with Iran, U.S. Ho. Reps., 1987; mem. Greenebaum, Doll & McDonald PLLC, Lexington, Ky., 1988—. Contbr. to Proving Federal Crimes, 6th edit., 1976. Mem. ABA, Assn. Bar City of N.Y., Ky. Bar Assn., Fayette County Bar Assn., Harvard Club, Idle hour Country Club. Democrat. Episcopalian. Home: Fed Hill Washington KY 41096-0173 Office: Greenebaum Doll & McDonald PLLC 300 W Vine St Ste 1100 Lexington KY 40507-1665

FRYMER, MURRY, writer, theater and film critic; b. Toronto, Ont., Can., Apr. 24, 1934; came to U.S., 1945; s. Dave and Sylvia (Spinrod) F.; m. Barbara Lois Grown, Sept. 4, 1966; children: Paul, Benjamin, Carrie. BA, U. Mich., 1956; student, Columbia U., 1958; MA, NYU, 1964. Editor Town Crier, Westport, Conn., 1962-63, Tribune, Levittown, N.Y., 1963-64; viewpoints editor, critic Newsday, L.I., N.Y., 1964-72; asst. mng. editor Rochester Democrat & Chronicle, N.Y., 1972-75; Sunday and feature editor Cleve. Plain Dealer, 1975-77; editor Sunday Mag. Boston Herald Am., 1977-79; film and TV critic San Jose Mercury News, Calif., 1979-83, theater critic, 1983—, columnist, 1983—, San Jose Mag., 2000—. Instr. San Jose State U., Cleve. State U., judge Emmy awards NATAS, 1968; co-founder, sr. writer TheColumnists.com.; staff mem. Pulitzer Prize, 1990. Author: They are Coming for My Mattress, 1999; author, dir. musical revue Four by Night, N.Y.C., 1963; author (play) Danse Marriage, 1955 (Hopwood prize 1955); author, dir. 6th U.S. Army show A Dozen and One, 1958. Served with U.S. Army, 1956-58. Recipient Best Columnist/Critic award Calif. Publishers Assn., 1993; named Best Columnist, Peninsula Calif. Press Club, 1993. E-mail: mfrymer@yahoo.com.

FRYREAR, DONALD WILLIAM, agricultural engineer, researcher; b. Haxtun, Colo., Dec. 8, 1936; s. William Alfred and Majorie (Adams) F.; m. Sherry Janice Watson, Sept. 16, 1956; children: Debra Lou, Kenneth William. BSAE, Colo. State U., 1959; MSAE, Kans. State U., 1962. Registered profl. engr., Tex. Engr. USDA-Agrl. Rsch. Svc., Akron, Colo., 1959-60, Manhattan, Kans., 1960-62, rsch. engr. Temple, Tex., 1962-65, rsch. leader Big Spring, Tex., 1965-97. Erosion cons. UNESCO, Medmine, Tunisia, 1983, Pretoria, South Africa, 1985; project leader for devel. of Revised Wind Erosion Equation. Contbr. articles to profl. jours. Recipient Appreciation award Howard Coll., 1977; Soil Conservation Soc. Am. fellow, 1982. Mem. Am. Soc. Agrl. Engrs. (assoc. editor 1974, SW Dirs. citation 1996), Soil and Water Conservation Soc. (charter pres. 1972), Am. Soc. Agronomy (state pres. 1977), N.Y. Acad. Sci. Baptist. Achievements include development of graded furrow concept for controlling water erosion, techniques for analyzing field erosion data; design and construction of five wind tunnels; design of first field equipment for measuring wind erosion. Office: Custon Products and Cons 7204 S Service Rd Big Spring TX 79720-0546 E-mail: dfryrear@crcom.net.

FRYS, RUSSELL N. obstetrician-gynecologist; b. St. Paul, Minn., Nov. 13, 1922; MD, Med. Coll. Wis., 1946. Diplomate Am. Bd. Ob-Gyn. Intern Ancker Hosp., St. Paul, Minn., 1947-48, resident in pathology, 1948-49; resident in ob-gyn. Northwestern Hosp., Mpls., 1949-51, Loyola U. Hosps., Chgo., 1951-52; hosp. staff Fairview Southdale Hosp., Mpls., North Meml. Med. Ctr., Mpls. Fellow ACS, Am. Coll. Ob-Gyn. Home: 6400 Glacier Pl Edina MN 55436-1808

FRYSTAK, SHANNON LEE, historian, researcher; b. Sumter, SC, Oct. 7, 1968; d. Jerry Albert Frystak and Charlotte Marie Seifert. BS, Bowling Green State U., 1986—90; MA, U. of New Orleans, 1994—97; ABD, U. of NH., 1997—2003. Adj. prof. Merrimack Coll., Andover, Mass., 2000; instr. U. of NH., 1997—2001; vis. scholar Newcomb Coll. Ctr. for Rsch. on Women, New Orleans, 2001—. Contbr. historical collection. Mem. NAACP, Washington, 1995—2003, So. Poverty Law Ctr., 2001—03; activist/mem. Internat. ANSWER, Washington, 2002—03; vol./activist Cmty. for Creative Non-Violence, Washington, 1987—91. Grantee Rsch. money, Boebel Found., 1996. Mem.: So. Assn. of Women Historians, Peace History Soc., So. Hist. Assn., Orgn. of Am. Historians, Am. Hist. Assn. Green Party. Avocations: artist, political activist. Home: 3445 Mt Pleasant St NW - A Washington DC 20010 Office: Newcomb-Ctr for Rsch on Women Caroline Richardson Hall- Tulane New Orleans LA 70118 Personal E-mail: sfrystak@aol.com.

FRYT, MONTE STANISLAUS, petroleum company executive, speaker, advisor; b. Jackson, Mich., Aug. 3, 1949; s. Marion S. and Dorothy A. (Fischman) F.; m. Pollyanna Hayes, May 26, 1990. BS in Aerospace Engring., U. Colo., Boulder, 1971; MBA in Mgmt., U. Colo., Denver, 1988. Field engr. Schlumberger Well Svcs., Bakersfield, Calif., 1971-75, computer R & D engr. Houston, 1975-77, account devel. engr. L.A., 1977-78, dist. mgr. Abilene, Tex., 1978-80, Williston, N.D., 1980-81; v.p. ops. Logmate Svcs. Inc., Calgary, Alta., Can., 1981-84; pres. Fryt Petroleum Inc., Denver, 1984-91; mgr. petrophysics Am. Hunter Exploration, Ltd., Denver, 1991-92; prin. Reservoir Evaluations Group, Denver, 1992-99; ptnr., mgr. Monteray Energy LLC, Denver, 1994-98; mgr. tech. Anschutz Exploration Corp., 1995—2003. Mem. Colo. Rep. Com., 1990—, Rep. Nat. Com., Colo. Rep. Leadership Program, 1992-93; mem. exec. com. Colo. Rep. Bus. Coalition, 1993-2002, vice-chmn., 1996-97, chmn., 1997-99. Mem. Am. Assn. Petroleum Geologists, Soc. Petroleum Engrs., Rocky Mountain Assn. Geologists, Elks, Rockies Venture Club, Independence Inst. Roman Catholic. Avocations: mountain climbing, skiing, running, cultural and political reading, Tae Kwon Do. Home and Office: 7400 S Curtice Ct Littleton CO 80120-3951

FRYXELL, DAVID ALLEN, publishing executive; b. Sioux Falls, S.D., Mar. 8, 1956; s. Donald Raymond and Lucy (Dickinson) F.; m. Lisa Duaine Forman, June 16, 1978; 1 child, Courtney Elizabeth. BA, Augustana Coll., 1978. Assoc.-sr. editor TWA Ambassador, St. Paul, 1978-80, mng. editor, 1980-81; sr. editor Horizon, Tuscaloosa, Ala., 1981-82; circuit writer Telegraph Herald, Dubuque, Iowa, 1982-85; contbg. editor Horizon mag., 1982-85; dir. publs., exec. editor Pitt mag. U. Pitts., 1985-90; editl. dir. Quad/Creative Group Milwaukee Mag., 1991-92; exec. features editor, dir. new ventures St. Paul Pioneer Press, 1992-95, sr. editor technology and new ventures, 1995-96; sr. editor bus. and tech., 1996; exec. producer Twin Cities Sidewalk Microsoft Corp., 1996-98; mag. editl. dir. F & W Publs., Cin., 1998—2001, editor-in-chief, 2001—03; editor and pub. Desert Exposure, 2003—. Chief judge mags. Golden Quill awards, Pitts., 1980; nonfiction columnist Writer's Digest, 1994—; faculty Maui Writers Conf., 2000—. Author: Double-Parked on Main Street, 1988, How to Write Fast While Writing Well, 1992, Elements of Article Writing: Structure and Flow, 1996, Write Faster, Write Better, 2004; editor: Family Tree Mag., 2000-03, Comair Navigator Mag., 2001-02; contbr. articles to mags. including Travel & Leisure, Playboy, Passages, AAA World, Savvy, Online Access, Diversion, Easy Living, Readers Digest, Link Up, others. Chief writer Anderson for Pres. Com., Minn., 1978. Mem. Iowa Newspaper Assn. (2d award master columnist 1983, 2d award best feature writing 1983, 2d award best series 1983), Chgo. Art Dirs. Club (Merit award for editing 1981), Coll. and Univ. Pub. Relations Assn. of Pa., Council for Advancement and Support of Edn. (Periodicals Improvement award 1987, 90, 91, Top Ten Mag. award 1990, 91, Articles of Yr. award 1990, Periodical Spl. Issues award 1991, Instl. Rels. Publs. award 1991, Periodical Resource Mgmt. award, 1990, 91), Augustana Coll. Fellows, Augustana Alumni Assn. (Decades of Leadership award 1978), Blue Key, Internat. Assn. Bus. Communicators (Golden Triangle award 1987, 89, best spl. publ. award 1988), Women in Communications (Matrix award 1990, hon. mention 1990, 91), City and Regional Mag. Assn. (Gen. Excellence award 1992, Spl. Sect. award 1992, Commentary award 1992, Investigative Writing award 1992), Mo. Lifestyle Awards (2d Gen. Excellence award 1994, 95). Democrat. Unitarian Universalist. Office: PO Box 191 Silver City NM 88062 E-mail: editor@desertexposure.com.

FTHENAKIS, EMANUEL JOHN, diversified aerospace company executive; b. Greece, Jan. 30, 1928; came to U.S., 1952, naturalized, 1956; s. John and Evanthia (Magoulakis) F.; m. Hermione Jane Coates, 1972; children: John, Basil. Diploma mech. and elec. engring., Tech. U. Athens, 1951; MS in Elec. Engring., Columbia U., 1954; postgrad., U. Pa., 1961-62. Mem. tech. staff Bell Tel. Labs., 1952-57; dir. engring. missile and space div. G.E., Phila., 1957-61; v.p., gen. mgr. space and re-entry div. Philco-Ford Co., Palo Alto, Calif., 1961-69; pres. ITT Aerospace Co., L.A., 1969-70; chmn. Am. Satellite Corp., Germantown, Md., 1971-85; v.p. Fairchild Industries, Germantown, 1971-80, sr. v.p., 1980-84, exec. v.p., 1984, pres., chief exec. officer Chantilly, Va., 1985-86, chmn., chief exec. officer, 1986-91; pres., COO Fairchild Corp., Chantilly, 1990-91, also bd. dirs.; chmn., chief exec. officer CEF Corp., Potomac, Md., 1991—. Adj. prof. U. Md., 1981-84; mem. Pres.'s Nat. Security Telecomms. Adv. Coun., 1982-91; chmn., CEO, Olympic Airways, 1993. Author: A Manual of Satellite Communications, 1984; patentee in field. Mem. bd. visitors Coll. Engring., U. Md., 1980—; bd. dirs. Challenger Ctr. for Space Sci. and Edn., 1988-96, U. Md. Found., 1989—; chmn. bd. Challenger Ctr. for Space Sci. and Edn., 1994-96; trustee Univs. Rsch. Assn., Inc., 1990—. Named Man of Yr., Electronics & Aerospace Systems Conf., 1982. Fellow IEEE; mem. AIAA (assoc.), The George Town Club. Greek Orthodox. Office: CEF Corp PO Box 59708 Rockville MD 20859-9708

FTHENAKIS, VASILIS, chemical engineer, consultant, educator; b. Chania, Crete, Greece, July 21, 1951; came to U.S., 1976; naturalized, 1986; s. Menelaos and Antonia Korkidis; m. Christina Georgakopoulos, Feb. 6, 1982; children: Antonia, Menelaos. Diploma in Chemistry, U. Athens, 1975; MS in Chem. Engring., Columbia U., 1978; PhD in Fluid Dynamics & Atmospheric Sci., NYU, 1991. Rsch. analyst Columbia U., N.Y.C., project engr.; sr. chem. engr. Brookhaven Nat. Lab., Upton, N.Y., 1980—. Cons. in chem. engring., 1986—, semiconductor and photovoltaic cons., 1987—, petroleum and petrochemical cons., specialist on prevention of hazardous gas releases, 1989—; founder, pres. EnviroConsultants Inc., Upton, N.Y., 1991; chmn. confs.; adj. prof. environ. engring., chem. engring. CCNY, 1992-96, Columbia U., 1993—; expert witness on chem. process safety and environ. cases, 1997—. Author: Prevention and Control of Accidental Releases of Hazardous Gases, 1993; editor Fossil Energy and the Environ. newsletter, 1991-93; mem. editl. bd. Progress in Photovoltaics, 1996—, Jour. Loss Prevention, 1998—; contbr. over 170 articles to sci. jours., chpts. to books. Recipient Sci. Excellence award, EENS, 2002. Fellow AIChE; mem. Ctr. Chem. Process Safety (panel experts), Semiconductor Safety Assn, Am. Meteorol. Soc., Am. Chem. Soc. Home: 9 Lucille Ln Dix Hills NY 11746-5848 Office: Brookhaven Nat Lab Environ Scis Dept Ctr Bldg 830 Upton NY 11973 E-mail: vmf@bnl.gov.

FU, DON HONGBIN, software engineer; b. Zhaotong, Yunnan, China, Apr. 2, 1961; came to U.S., 1987; s. Yusheng Fu and Donghua Zhou; m. Cindy Lihong Que, Feb. 20, 1996; children, Kristy Y., Valerie T. BS in Engring., Xian (China) Inst. Metallurgy, 1982; MS in Mech. Engring., Worcester Poly. Inst., 1990, PhD in Mfg. Engring., 1993. Sr. product engr. Baystate Techs., Marlborough, Mass., 1993-95; sr. software engr. Bentley Sys., Inc., Exton, Pa., 1995—. Mem. ASME (assoc.), Sigma Xi. Home: 111 Stetson Dr Elverson PA 19520-9195 Office: Bentley Sys Inc 685 Stockton Dr Exton PA 19341-1151 E-mail: Don.Fu@Bentley.com.

FU, GONGKANG, civil engineering educator; b. Shanghai; s. Jixin and Zesheng (Yang) F.; m. Xiaojian Wang; children: Clementine, Gratiana. PhD, Case Western Res. U., 1987. Registered profl. engr., N.Y., Mich. Head structures rsch. N.Y. State Dept. Transp., Albany, 1990-96; assoc. prof. Wayne U., Detroit, 1996—2001; prof. Wayne State U., Detroit, 2002—; dir. Ctr. Advanced Bridge Engring. Cons. for industry and govt. agencies. Contbr. articles to profl. jours. Mem. ASCE, ASTM, Am. Acad. of Mechanics, Structural Stability Rsch. Coun., Am. Inst. of Concrete. Achievements include development of structural design and evaluation methods and specifications. Office: Wayne State U Civil Engring 5050 Anthony Wayne Dr Detroit MI 48202-3902 E-mail: gfu@ce.eng.wayne.edu.

FU, I-PING PHYLLIS, language educator, researcher; b. Taiwan, Apr. 29, 1963; d. Chan Lu and I-Feng Fu; m. Szetsen Steven Lee, Nov. 18, 1993 (div. Mar. 15, 2000); children: Shannon Lee, Serena Lee. BA, U. of Calif., Berkeley, 1986; MPA, U. of Wash., 1990; PhD, Va. Tech, 2000—. Cert. Chinese Instr. Union Chinese Sch., N.J., 1995, Effective Chinese Language Tchg. III Chinese Am. Cultural Assn. Edn. Rsch. Ctr., N.J., 1996, English Lang. Instr. Nat. Taiwan Normal U., 1999, Tchg. Chinese as a Second Lang. Nat. Taiwan U., 2001. Adj. faculty Radford U., Va., 2000—; Chinese lang. instr. Va. Tech, Blacksburg, 2000—, asst. to chair, 2002—; Chinese lang. and cultural instr. Chinese Sch. of VPI, Blacksburg, Va., 2002—. Lang. consulting State and City Courts, Roanoke, Va., 2000—; lang. cons. Pulaski Furniture Corp., Va., 2003. Fellow Assn. for Internat. and Mgmt., Grad. Sch. of Pub. Policy, U.C. Berkeley, 1995, John F. Kennedy Sch. of Govt., Harvard U., 1986, Grad. Sch. of Pub. Affairs, U. of Wash., 1987—88; grantee Rsch. Grant, Sapinia Culture and Edn. Found., 2002. Mem.: Tchr. Devel. Spl. Interest Group, Va. Tchrs. of English to Speakers of other Lang., Chinese Lang. Tchrs. Assn., Chinese Lang. Assn. of Secondary-Elem. Sch., Am. Coun. for Tchrs. of Fgn. Lang. (assoc.). Home: PO Box 602 Christiansburg VA 24068 Personal E-mail: ifu@vt.edu.

FU, JIE, biopolymer scientist, educator; d. Xiang Kun Meng and Cun Zhi Fu; m. Jun Wang; 1 child, Lu Wang. BS, Wuhan U., China, 1985; MS, Peking U., China, 1988; PhD, Wuhan U., China, 1996. Tchr. Wuhan U. Tech., China, 1988—90, lectr., 1990—97, assoc. prof., 1997—2000; postdoctoral rsch. fellow Johns Hopkins U., Balt., 2000—02, assoc. rsch. scientist, 2002—. Mem.: Biomed. Engring. Soc. (assoc.), Controlled Drug Release Soc. (assoc.). Achievements include patents pending for new polymer for pulmonary drug delivery; design of new biodegradable polymer for Lung drug delivery; new biodegradable polymer for non virus gene delivery; development of biodegradable Nano and microsphere for protein and DNA delivery. Home: 105-c Dumbarton Rd Baltimore MD 21212 Office: Johns Hopkins U 226 Maryland Hall 3400 N Charles St Baltimore MD 21218 Office Fax: 410-516-5510.

FU, KAREN KING-WAH, radiation oncologist; b. Shanghai, Oct. 15, 1940; came to U.S., 1959, naturalized, 1975; d. Ping Sen and Lein Sun (Ho) F. Student, Ind. U., 1959-61; AB, Barnard Coll., Columbia U., 1963, MD, 1967. Cert. radiation oncologist. Intern Montreal Gen. Hosp., Que., Can., 1967-68; resident Princess Margaret Hosp., Toronto, Ont., Can., 1968-69, Stanford U. Hosp., Calif., 1969-71; instr. U. Utah, 1971-72; clin. instr. U. Calif., San Francisco, 1972-73, asst. prof., 1973-76, assoc. prof., 1976-82, prof., 1982—2000, prof. emeritus, 2000—, vice chmn., 1994-95, rsch. assoc. Cancer Research Inst., 1973-96. Contbr. articles to profl. jours. Mem. San Francisco Opera Guild, San Francisco Symphony Assn., San Francisco Ballet, Calif. Acad. Sci., De Young Mus. Grantee Am. Cancer Soc., 1982, 86, NIH, 1982, 87. Fellow Am. Coll. Radiology; mem. Am. Soc. Therapeutic Radiologists, Am. Med. Women's Assn., Calif. Radiation Therapy Assn., Calif. Radiol. Soc., No. Calif. Acad. Clin. Oncology, Radiation Research Soc., Am. Soc. Clin. Oncologists, Assn. Women in Sci. Office: U Calif San Francisco Dept Radiation Oncology PO Box 226 San Francisco CA 94143-0226

FU, LEE-LUENG, oceanographer; b. Taipei, Republic of China, Oct. 10, 1950; s. Yi-Chin and Er-Lan (Chen) F.; m. Cecilia C. Liu, Mar. 26, 1977; 1 child, Christine. BS, Nat. Taiwan U., Taipei, 1972; PhD, MIT, 1980. Postdoctoral assoc. MIT, Cambridge, Mass., 1980; mem. tech. staff Jet Propulsion Lab., Pasadena, Calif., 1981-85, tech. group supr., 1986-93, project scientist, 1988—, lead scientist/ocean scis., 1994, sr. rsch. scientist, 1994. Chmn. Jason sci. working team NASA, Washington, 1988—; mem. sci. steering com. U.S. World Ocean Experiment Circulation, 1998—; vis. prof. Ocean U. Qingdao, China, 2002. Contbr. articles to profl. publs. Recipient Laurels award Aviation Week and Space Tech., 1993, CNES medal French Space Agy., 1994, Exceptional Scientific Achievement medal NASA, 1996, Verner E. Suomi award, Am. Meteorolgocial Soc., 2002. Fellow: Am. Meteorol. Soc., Am. Geophys. Union; mem.: Oceanography Soc. Office: Jet Propulsion Lab MS 300-323 4800 Oak Grove Dr Pasadena CA 91109-8001

FU, LEI, materials scientist, research scientist; b. China; PhD, Tsinghua U., Beijing, 1993—97. Rsch. scientist Northwestern Univ., Evanston, Ill., 2000—03; rsch. fellow Nanyang Technol. Univ., Singapore, Singapore, 1997—99. Rsch. assoc. Tsinghua Univ., Beijing, 1993—96. Mem.: Materials Rsch. Soc. (Silver awards for Poster Presentation 2001), Am. Ceramic Soc. (The first Pl. for Ceramographic Exhibit 2002, The third Pl. for Ceramographic Exhibit 2003), Materials Rsch. Soc. (Silver awards for rsch. presentation 2002). Home: 818 Noyes St Apt 2A Evanston IL 60201 Office: Northwestern University 2220 Campus Dr Evanston IL 60208 E-mail: flei_david@yahoo.com.

FU, LI MIN, biomedical and computer science educator; b. Taipei, Taiwan, Dec. 8, 1953; came to U.S., 1987; s. Tsai-Yi and Jen-Yui (Huang) F.; m. Lienfen Yueh, May 22, 1989; children: Katherine, Edward. MD, Nat. Taiwan U., 1978; MS, Stanford U., 1983, PhD, 1985. Assoc. prof. Nat. Taiwan U., Taipei, 1985-87; rsch. scientist Allied Signal Inc., Washington, 1988; asst. prof. U. Wis., Milw., 1988-90; asst. and assoc. prof. biomed.-computer sci. U. Fla., Gainesville, 1990—2000, prof. bioinformatics-genomics, 2000—; pres. Pacific TB & Cancer Rsch. Orgn., Calif., 2002—. Author: Neural Networks in Computer Intelligence, 1994; patentee neural network invention, 1995. Recipient Dr. T.M. Du's award Med. Soc. Taiwan, 1978, Overseas Outstanding Young Man medal Fedn. Overseas Chinese Assn., 1994. Mem. AAAS, IEEE, Am. Assn. Artificial Intelligence, Computer and Medicine Assn. (v.p. 1993—Disting. Svc. award 1993), N.Y. Acad. Sci., Sigma Xi. Avocations: swimming, tennis, music, movies. Office: Pacific TB and Cancer Rsch Orgn 10 Congress St Ste 201 Pasadena CA 91105 E-mail: lifu@patcar.org.

FU, MICHAEL C. management science educator; s. Yuen-Sun and Ruth H. Fu; m. Fan Chen, June 24, 1989; children: Lara, David. SB, SM, MIT, 1985; MS, PhD, Harvard U., 1989. Prof. U. Md., College Park, 1989—. Author: Conditional Monte Carlo: Gradient Estimation and Optimization Applications, 1997. Recipient Ops. Rsch. Divsn. award Inst. for Indsl. Engr., 1999, Best Paper award, 1998. Mem. Inst. Ops. Rsch. and Mgmt. Sci. (Outstanding Pub. award 1998). Office: U Md Van Munching Hall College Park MD 20742-1815

FU, QIANJIE, research scientist; b. Dongyang, Zhejiang, China; s. Xiaosong Wang; married; 1 child, William. BS, U. Sci. Tech. China, Hefei, 1991; MS, U. Sci. Tech. China, 1994; PhD, U. So. Calif., 1997. Rsch. assoc. House Ear Inst., L.A., 1996-98, scientist I LA, 1998—2001, scientist II, 2001—. Tchg. asst. U. So. Calif., L.A., 1994-95. Contbr. articles to profl. jours. NIH grantee, 1998-2001, 2001-2006. Mem. IEEE, Acoustical Soc. Am., Assn. Rsch. Otolaryngology. Office: House Ear Inst 2100 W Third St Los Angeles CA 90057

FU, SHOUCHENG JOSEPH, biomedicine educator; b. Beijing, Mar. 19, 1924; s. W.C. Joseph and W.C. (Tsai) F.; m. Susan B. Guthrie, June 21, 1951; children: Robert W.G., Joseph H.G., James B.G. BS, MS, Cath. U., Beijing, 1944; PhD, Johns Hopkins U., 1949. Postdoctoral fellow Nat. Insts. Health, Bethesda, Md., 1949—51, scientist, 1951—55; Gustav Bissing fellow Johns Hopkins U. at Univ. Coll. London, 1955—56; chief enzyme and bioorganic chemistry lab. Children's Cancer Rsch Found (now Dana Farber Cancer Inst.), 1956—65; rsch. assoc. Harvard U. Med. Sch., Boston, 1956—65; prof., chmn. bd. chemistry Chinese U., Hong Kong, 1966—70, dean sci. faculty, 1967—69; vis. prof. Coll. Physicians and Surgeons Columbia U., N.Y.C., 1970—71; prof. biochemistry and molecular biology U. Medicine and Dentistry of N.J., Newark, 1971—2003, prof. emeritus, 2003—, asst. dean, 1974—77; acting dean Grad. Sch. Biomed. Scis., 1977—78, prof. ophthalmology, 1989—2003, prof. emeritus, 2003—. Founder, pres. CMDNJ Credit Union (now North Jersey Fed. Credit Union), 1974-75. Contbr. articles to profl. jours. Capt. USPHS Res., 1959—. Named Hon. Disting. Prof. and Acad. Advisor Inner Mongolia Med. U., Huthot, Peoples Republic of China, 1988—. Fellow AAAS, Royal Soc. Chemistry (U.K.); mem. Royal Hong Kong Jockey Club, Am. Club Hong Kong, Sigma Xi (Newark chpt. pres. 1976-80, sec. 1974-76, 81-82). Home: 693 Prospect St Maplewood NJ 07040-3105 Office: U of Medicine and Dentistry NJ Med Sch Med Sci Bldg 185 S Orange Ave Newark NJ 07103-2757 E-mail: fujo@umdnj.edu.

FU, ZHIWEI, information technology manager, consultant; b. Jinan, Shandong, China, Sept. 22, 1967; s. Tonglu Fu, Yanshu Yu; m. Zhongfei Yu; 1 child, Matthew. PhD, U. Md., 2000. Lectr., rschr. U. Md., College Park, 1995—2000; mgr. Fannie Mae, Washington, 2000—. Mem.: Am. Statis. Assn., Am. Assn. Artificial Intelligence, IEEE, Inst. for Ops. Rsch. and Mgmt. Sci. Home: 9412 Wooden Bridge Rd Potomac MD 20854 Office: Fannie Mae 3900 Wisconsin Ave NW Washington DC 20016 Office Fax: 202 752 4694. Business E-Mail: zhiwei_fu@fanniemae.com.

FUCCI, JOSEPH LEONARD, architect, librarian, editor; b. Mt. Vernon, N.Y., Jan. 31, 1950; s. Joseph Vito and Roselyn (Pecoraro) F.; m. Adrianne Darway, Aug. 7, 1977. AA, Bronx Community Coll., 1971; BA in English Lit., Herbert H. Lehman Coll., 1972; MLS, Columbia U., 1974; BArch, Pratt Inst., 1985. Head serials dept. Sarah Lawrence Coll. Library, Bronxville, N.Y., 1974-76; head circulation dept., Westchester Med. Ctr. Library, N.Y. Med. Coll., Valhalla, N.Y., 1976-77; head periodicals dept. Orange County Community Coll. Library, Middletown, N.Y., 1977-82; owner Archtl. Editing, Graphics & Info. Services, Middletown, 1982-90; asst. prof. of reader svcs. Sullivan County C.C., 1990-94, head reader svcs., 1992-94; prin., architect Aegis Design, Middletown, 1990—; asst. prof. bibliographic instrn. Westchester C.C., 1994-96. Home improvement consulting editor, Creative Homeowner Press, Upper Saddle River, N.J., 1998-2000; architect Sullivan Co. Dept. Pub. Works, 2001-02; mem. curriculum com. Orange County C.C., 1978-81, mem. acad. affairs bd., 1978-81, chair Info. Lit. and Bibliographic Instrn. Com. Sullivan County C.C., 1993-94; mem. environ. com. Westchester C.C., 1994-96. Editor: Architecture: Classified Bibliography, 1980, 3d. rev. ed., 1982, Quick Guide to Siding, 1999, Adding Value to Your Home, 1999, Home Wiring: Basic & Advanced Projects, 2000. Mem. St. John's Luth. Ch. coun., 2002—. Regents scholar, N.Y. State, 1968-72, Myra E. Sayer Meml. scholar in English, CUNY, 1970; recipient commencement scholarship awards in French, English, CUNY, 1971, cert. of merit in archtl. tech., SUNY, 1982. Mem. AIA (Westchester/Mid-Hudson chpt., mem. interprofl. com. for environ. design 1988-92), SUNY L.A., 1994-96. Lutheran. Avocations: reading, writing, design, environmentalism, mountain hiking. Home and Office: 38 Roosevelt Ave Middletown NY 10940-4635

FUCHS, ALFRED HERMAN HERMAN, psychologist, educator; b. Englewood, NJ, Nov. 29, 1932; s. Herman and Wilhemine Katharine (Dieling) F.; m. Phyllis Elizabeth Rocke, Aug. 27, 1955; children: Christopher Frederick, Jeffrey Alfred, Lisa Marie, Eric William. AB, Rutgers U., 1954; MA, Ohio U., 1958; PhD, Ohio State U., 1960. Psychologist, scientist Gen. Dynamics/Electric Boat Co., 1961-62; asst. prof. psychology Bowdoin Coll., Brunswick, Maine, 1962-66, assoc. prof., 1966-72, prof., 1972-98, prof. emeritus, 1998—, chmn. dept., 1965-75, 94-97, dean faculty, 1975-91. Summer research participant NSF, 1963, 64 Contbr. articles to profl. jours. NSF grantee, 1963-64, 64-65 Fellow APA (pres.-elect divsn. 26 1997-98, pres. 1998-99); mem. History of Sci. Soc., Internat. Soc. History Behavioral Scis., Sigma Xi. Democrat. Home: 5 Longfellow Ave Brunswick ME 04011-2535 Office: Bowdoin Coll Dept Psychology 6900 College Station Brunswick ME 04011

FUCHS, ANNE SUTHERLAND, magazine publisher; b. Volta Redonda, Brazil, Apr. 19, 1947; d. Paul Warner and Evelyn Coffman; m. James E. Fuchs, Feb. 6, 1982 Student, U. Paris at Sorbonne, 1967-68, Western Coll. for Women, 1966-67; BA, NYU, 1969. Registered architect. V.p., pub. Woman's Day Spl. Interest Mags.-CBS Mags., N.Y.C., 1980-82, Cuisine Mag., CBS Mags., N.Y.C., 1982-84; v.p., pub. Woman's Day mag. DCI Comm., Inc., N.Y.C., 1985-88; sr. v.p., pub. ELLE mag., N.Y.C., 1988-90, Vogue, N.Y.C., 1991—94; group pub. dir., sr. v.p. Harper's Bazaar/Hearst Mag., N.Y.C., 1994—2001; global CEO, chmn., mgmt. bd. Phillips, dePUry & Luxembourg, 2001—02; exec. v.p. LVMH Group, 2002; cons., 2003—. Chmn. mag. and print com. U.S. Info. Agy., 1989—. Author: (other) The Modular Pattern, 1945, British Prefabricated School Construction, 1962; other, Sch. Constrn. Systems Devel., 1964; contbr. numerous articles to profl.jours; other, De Laveaga Elem. Sch., Santa Cruz, Calif., 1966, Silvercreek High Sch., San Jose, Calif., 1969, Canady Hall Harvard U., 1974, Aaron Davis Hall, CCNY, 1978. Chmn. women's bd. Madison Sq. Boys and Girls Club, N.Y.C.; mem. Com. 200, USIA; bd. dirs. N.Y.C. Partnership, N.Y.C. Partnership Found. Recipient Innovation in Bldg. award, Am. Builder, 1965, Services to Building Industry award, Engring. News Record, 1966, Gov.'s Design award, State of Calif., 1966, Quarter Century award, Bldg. Rsch. Adv. Coun., 1977, named Constrn. Man of Yr., Engring. News Record, 1968; fellow Fulbright fellow, England, 1955—56. Mem. Fin. Women's Assn. N.Y., N.Y. Jr. League, Advt. Women of N.Y., Women in Communications, Women's Forum, Com. of 200, Fin. Women's Assn. N.Y. Clubs: Economic (N.Y.C.). E-mail: afuchs@hearst.com.

FUCHS, BETTY CORCORAN, retired fundraising consultant; b. Tulsa, Oct. 20, 1930; d. Harold Francis and Angela Mary (Dawson) Corcoran; m. Lawrence Howard Fuchs, Sept. 12, 1970. BA, Antioch Coll., 1953. Course asst. Harvard Bus. Sch., Cambridge, Mass., 1953-55; instr. U. Mich. Sch. Bus. Adminstrn., 1957-61; rsch. asst., editl. asst. Harvard Bus. Sch., 1966-73; dean admissions, v.p. devel. Wheelock Coll., Boston, 1973-83; dir. devel. (on leave) Gallaudet Coll., Washington, 1980-81; dir. devel., sr. devel. officer Wellesley (Mass.) Coll., 1983-90; exec. dir. devel., alumni and external affairs Boston U. Law Sch., 1990-92; fundraising counsel for nonprofit instns., Weston, Mass., 1993—2001. Trustee Wheelock Coll., 1983-2000, corp. mem., 2000—; mem. adv. bd. Ctr. Women in Politics, U. Mass., Boston, 1995-02; mem. founding bd. dirs. Gem List, women's Dem. polit. orgn., Boston, 1993-94; trustee Antioch U., 1999-2001. Mem. Antioch Coll. Alumni Assn. (bd. dirs. 1994-99).

FUCHS, ERAN, oceanographer, researcher; s. Uzi and Ayala Fuchs. BSc, Technion, Haifa, 1986; MS, MIT, 1996, PhD, 1999. Rschr. Scripps Instn. of Oceanography, San Diego, 1999—2002, Harbor Br. Oceanographic Instn., Fort Pierce, Fla., 2002—. Capt. Air Force, 1986—90, Israel. Office: Harbor Br Oceanographic Instn 5600 US 1 N Fort Pierce FL Office Fax: 772-468-0757. E-mail: eran@hboi.edu.

FUCHS, HENRY CARL, music educator, pianist; b. Miami Beach, Fla., Aug. 14, 1938; s. Henry Fuchs and Ella Gebauer; m. Jo Ann McNaughton. MusB, Eastman Sch. Music, 1960; MusM, U. Mich., 1961. Prof. music U. R.I., Kingston, 1968-2000, dir. Great Performances concert series, 1982-98. Concert presenter. Office: U RI Dept Music Kingston RI 02881

FUCHS, JEROME HERBERT, management consultant; b. N.Y.C., Jan. 7, 1922; s. Berthold and Fannie (Neuschotz) F.; m. Eleanor May DeRoo, May 26, 1945; children: Jerome S. Taylor, Susan Fuchs Decker, Sandra Fuchs Lombino. BS in Mktg. with honors, Syracuse U., 1950, MBA, 1951. Systems and methods analyst Carrier Corp., 1951-52; supr. systems and methods Lukens Steel, Coatesville, Pa., 1952-54; mgr. systems and methods PennWalt Co., Phila., 1955-57, mgr. systems and methods and office svcs. Amax, Inc., Greenwich, Conn., 1958-60; exec. asst. to pres. Rockbestos Wire & Cable Co., 1960-61; v.p. mfg. United Aircraft Products, Dayton, Ohio, 1970-71; exec. v.p. Bus. Supplies Corp. Am., N.Y.C., 1972; sr. ptnr. Fuchs Assocs., East Meadow, N.Y., 1960—2001; indsl. rsch. asst., Syracuse (N.Y.) U., 1949-51; adj. prof. Syracuse U., 1950-52, John Hopkins U., Balt., 1953-54, Drexel, Phila., 1955-57, Queens Coll., N.Y.C., 1963-65, SUNY, Stony Brook, 1987-91, Hofstra U., 1988—. Author: Making the Most of Management Consulting Services, 1975; Management Consultants in Action, 1975; Computerized Cost Control Systems, 1976; Computerized Inventory Control Systems, 1977; Administering the Quality Control Function, 1979, The Prentice-Hall Illustrated Handbook of Advanced Manufacturing Methods, 1988. Served as 2nd lt. AC, U.S. Army, 1943-46. Mem. Soc. Profl. Mgmt. Cons. (charter, pres. 1977-79), Inst. Mgmt. Cons. (cert., founding mem.), Sigma Iota Epsilon. Home and Office: 1612 Salisbury Park Dr East Meadow NY 11554-5522

FUCHS, JOSEPH LOUIS, retired magazine publisher; b. Bklyn., Nov. 23, 1931; s. Sol and Yetta (Stein) F.; m. Carol Polner, Feb. 7, 1955; children— Beth, Randy, Sheryl. BA, Baruch Sch., CCNY, 1954. Advt. dir. House and Garden mag., N.Y.C., 1958-73; assoc. pub. House and Garden Guides, N.Y.C., 1973-75; pub. Brides mag., N.Y.C., 1975-77, Mademoiselle mag., 1977-85; v.p. Condé Nast Pubs., 1985-87, exec. v.p., 1987-97; ret., 1997. Served with AUS, 1956-58. Mem. Ballen Isles, Engrs. Country Club, Sky Club, Alpha Delta Sigma.

FUCHS, LAWRENCE HOWARD, government official, educator; b. N.Y.C., Jan. 29, 1927; s. Alfred F. and Frances S. (Scheiber) F; m. Betty Corcoran Sept. 12, 1970; 1 adopted child, Carole Hooven; stepchildren: Michael Hooven, Fred Hooven, John Hooven; children by previous marriage: Janet Pearl, Frances Sarah, Naomi Ruth. BA, N.Y. U., 1950; PhD, Harvard U., 1955; DHL (hon.), Brandeis U., 2002. Teaching fellow Harvard U., Cambridge, Mass., 1950-51; mem. faculty Brandeis U., Waltham, Mass, 1951—, chmn. dept. politics, 1959-60, dean faculty, 1960-61, prof. Am. civilization and politics, chmn. Dept. Am. Studies, 1970-86. On leave as dir. Peace Corps, Phillippines, 1961-63; exec. dir. U.S. Select Commn. on Immigration and Refugee Policy, 1979-81; vice chmn. U.S. Commn. on Immigration Reform, 1992-97; part-time radio-TV news commentator for stas. WCRB and WGBH, Boston, 1951-59. Author: The Political Behavior of American Jews, 1955, Hawaii Pono: A Political and Ethnic History, 1961, John F. Kennedy and American Catholicism, 1967, Those Peculiar Americans: Peace Corps and American National Character, 1967, American Ethnic Politics, 1968, Family Matters, 1972, The American Kaleidoscope: Race, Ethnicity and the Civic Culture, 1990, Beyond Patriarchy: Jewish Fathers and Families, 2000. Former mem. nat. adv. bd. commn. law and social action Am. Jewish Congress; former mem. nat. adv. council Mexican Am. Lega Def. and Edn. Fund; Mass. Cong. Racial Equality; mem. exec. council Am. Jewish Hist. Soc.; former vice chmn. Facing History & Ourselves; 1st chmn. Commonwealth Service Corps Commn.; former chmn. exec. com. sch. and soc. program Edn. Devel. Ctr., Inc.; founding pres. Self-Devel. Group, Inc. Served with USNR, 1945-47. Recipient Decade Humanity award Facing History and Ourselves, John Carroll Centennial award, John Hope Franklin award, 1991, Theodore Saloutos award, 1991, Carey McWilliams award, 1992; Woodrow Wilson fellow; grantee Social Scis. Rsch. Coun., East-West Ctr., Rockefeller Found., Ford Found., Exxon Found., Jaffe Found., Sloan Found. Mem. Phi Beta Kappa. Home: 202 Del Pond Drive Canton MA 02021

FUCHS, MICHAEL JOSEPH, television executive; b. N.Y.C., Mar. 9, 1946; s. Charles and Sue (Wile) Fuchs. BA in Polit. Sci., Union Coll., 1967; JD, NYU, 1971. Bar: N.Y. 1971. Assoc. Marshall, Bratter, Greene, Allison & Tucker, N.Y.C., 1971—74; assoc. Bomser & Oppenheim, N.Y.C., 1974—75; dir. bus. affairs William Morris Agy., N.Y.C., 1975—76; dir. spl. programming Home Box Office, N.Y.C., 1976—77, v.p. spls. & sports, 1977—79, v.p. programming, 1979—80, sr. v.p. programming, 1980—82, exec. v.p. programming, 1982—83, pres. entertainment group, 1983—84, pres., COO, 1984, chmn., CEO, 1984—95, chmn. New York, 1995; chmn., CEO Warner Music Group, New York, 1995, Jeffrey Bewkes, 1995—; chmn., interi CEO MyTurn.com. Trustee Simon Wiesenthal Ctr.; bd. dirs. Am. Found. AIDS Rsch., Creative Coalition, Alzheimer's Assn., Hebrew Home for Aged at Riverdale; chmn. Bryant Park Restoration Corp. Named to Broadcasting and Cable Mag. Hall of Fame, 1994; recipient Van Guard award, NCTA, 1988, Disting. Svc. award, Simon Wiesenthal Ctr., 1989, Humanitarian award, 1996, Cable Ace Govs. award, 1994, Nott medal, Union Coll., 1995, Spirit of Liberty award, People for the Am. Way, 1996. Mem.: Mus. Modern Art (mem. bus. com.), Acad. Motion Picture Arts and Scis. (mem. execs. br. 1984—), Met. Mus. Art, Am. Mus. Moving Image (trustee 1988—), Bronx Mus. Arts (trustee 1983—95), Bklyn. Acad. Music (trustee 1983—), N.Y. State Motion Picture and TV Adv. Bd. (bd. dirs. 1984—94), Am. Film Inst. (trustee 1982—). Democrat. Jewish. Avocations: tennis, travel, reading, art collecting.

FUCHS, OLIVIA ANNE MORRIS, lawyer; b. Louisville, Ky., May 2, 1949; d. H.H. Morris Jr. and Betty Jean Wills Saltkill; m. Robert Edward Fuchs, Dec. 27, 1969. BA, U. Louisville, 1977; JD cum laude, 1980. Bar: Ky. 1980, Ind. 1987, U.S. Dist. Ct. (we. dist.) Ky. 1985, U.S. Tax. Ct. 1987. Assoc. Brown, Todd & Heyburn, Louisville, 1981-87; mem. Conliffe, Sandmann & Sullivan PLLC, Louisville, 1987-97; pvt. practice Louisville, 1997—. Notes editor Jour. Family Law, 1979-80. Vol. advocate R.A.P.E. Relief Ctr. YWCA, Louisville, 1981-87. Mem. ABA, Ind. Bar Assn., Ky. Bar Assn., Louisville Bar Assn. (probate sect. chmn. 1990, profl. responsibility com., com. chmn. 1988), U. Louisville Law Alumni Coun. (bd. dirs., pres. 1997-98), Exec. Club Louisville (pres. 1996-97), Jefferson Club, Citizens for Better Judges, Phi Alpha Delta. Democrat. Presbyterian. Office: Ogden & Ogden 500 W Jefferson St Ste 1610 Louisville KY 40202-2816

FUCHS, ROLAND JOHN, geography educator, university science official; b. Yonkers, N.Y., Jan. 15, 1933; s. Alois L. and Elizabeth (Weigand) F.; m. Gaynell Ruth McAuliffe, June 15, 1957; children: Peter K., Christopher K., Andrew K. BA, Columbia U., 1954, postgrad., 1956-57, Moscow State U., 1960-61; MA, Clark U., 1957, PhD, 1959, DSc (hon.), 1995. Asst. prof. to prof. emeritus U. Hawaii, Honolulu, 1958—, chmn. dept. geography, 1964-86, asst. dean to assoc. dean coll. arts and scis., 1965-67, dir. Asian Studies Lang. and Area Ctr., 1965-67, adj. rsch. assoc. East West Ctr., 1980—, spl. asst. to pres., 1986; vice rector UN U., Tokyo, 1987-94; dir. Internat. Start Secretariat, 1994—. Vis. prof. Clark U., 1963-64, Nat. Taiwan U., 1974; mem. bd. internat. orgns. and programs Nat. Acad. Scis., 1976-81, chmn., 1980-81, mem. bd. sci. and tech. in devel., 1980-85; mem. U.S. Nat. Commn. for Pacific Basin Econ. Coop., 1985-87; sr. advisor United Nations U., 1986. Author, editor: Geographical Perspectives on the Soviet Union, 1974, Theoretical Problems of Geography, 1977, Population Distribution Policies in Development Planning, 1981, Urbanization and Urban Policies in the Pacific-Asia Region, 1987, Megacities: The Challenge of the Urban Future, 1994, Global-Regional Linkages in the Earth System, 2002; asst. editor Econ. Geography, 1963-64; mem. editl. adv. com. Soviet Geography: Rev. and Translation, 1966-85, Geoforum, 1988-96, African Urban Quar., 1987, Global Environ. Change, 1990—, Asian Geographer, 1991-98. Ford Found. fellow, 1956-57; Fulbright Rsch. scholar, 1966-67 Mem. Assn. Am. Geographers, Am. Geophys. Union, Internat. Geog. Union (v.p. 1980-84, 1st v.p. 1984-88, pres. 1988-92, past pres. 1992-96), Assn. Am. Geographers (Hon. award 1982), Am. Assn. Advancement of Slavic Studies (bd. dirs. 1976-81), Pacific Sci. Assn. (mem. coun. 1978—, mem. exec. com. 1986-99, sec. gen-treas. 1991-99), Acad. Europaea (elected fgn. mem.). Home: 1200 N Nash St Arlington VA 22209-3616 E-mail: rfuchs@agu.org.

FUCHS, VICTOR ROBERT, economist, educator; b. New York, Jan. 31, 1924; s. Alfred and Frances Sarah ((Scheiber)) Fuchs; m. Beverly (Beck), Aug. 29, 1948; children: Nancy, Frederic, Paula, Kenneth. BS, N.Y. Univ., 1947; MA, Columbia Univ., 1951, PhD, 1955. Internat. fur broker, 1946—50; lectr. Columbia Univ., N.Y.C., 1953—54, instr., 1954—55, asst. prof. econ., 1955—59; assoc. prof. econ. N.Y. Univ., N.Y.C., 1959—60; program assoc. Ford Found. Program in econ., devel., and adminstrn., 1960—62; mem. sr. rsch staff Nat. Bur. Econ. Rsch., 1962—; prof. econ. Grad. Ctr. City Univ. of N.Y., N.Y.C., 1968—74; prof. cmty. medicine Mt. Sinai Sch. Medicine, 1968-74; v.p. rsch. Nat. Bur. Econ. Rsch., 1968—78; prof. econ. Stanford U., Stanford Med. Sch., 1974—95; Henry J. Kaiser Jr. prof. Stanford U., Stanford Med. Sch., 1988—95, prof. emeritus, 1995—. Author: The Economics of the Fur Industry, 1957; co-author (with Aaron Warner): Concepts and Cases in Econ. Analysis, 1958; author: Changes in the Location of Mfg. in the U.S. Since 1929, 1962, The Svc. Economy, 1968, Production and Productivity in the Svc. Industries, 1969, Policy Issues and Rsch. Opportunities in Indsl. Orgn., 1972, Essays on the Economics of Health and Med. Care, 1972, Who Shall Live? Health, Economics, and Social Choice, 1975; co-author (with Joseph Newhouse): The Economics of Physician and Patient Behavior, 1978; author: Economic Aspects of Health, 1982, How We Live, 1983, The Health Economy, 1986, Women's Quest for Econ. Equality, 1988, The Future of Health Policy, 1993, Individual and Social Responsibility: Child Care Edn., Med. Care, and Long-term Care in Am., 1996, Who Shall Live? Health, Economics and Social Choice, expanded edit., 1998; contbr. articles to profl. jour. Served in USAF, 1943—46. Fellow: Am. Econ. Assn. (disting., pres. 1995), Am. Acad. Arts and Sci.; mem.: Am. Philos. Soc. (John R, Commons award), Am. Inst. Medicine of NAS, Beta Gamma Sigma, Sigma Xi. Home: 796 Cedro Way Stanford CA 94305-1032 Office: NBER 30 Alta Rd Stanford CA 94305-8006

FUCHS, WAYNE SCOTT, medical educator; b. N.Y.C., NY, Sept. 4, 1954; married. BA magna cum laude, NYU, 1975; MD, Mt. Sinai U., 1979. Intern in internal medicine U. Miami (Fla.) Hosps., 1979-80; resident in ophthalmology Mt. Sinai Med. Ctr., N.Y.C., 1980-83, assoc. clin. prof., 1991—2002, clin. prof., 2002—. Treas. Profl. Offices, N.Y.C., 1994-2002; lectr. in field.; med. adv. bd. PXE Internat. Contbr. articles to profl. jours. Mem. med. adv. bd. Nat. Assn. Visually Handicapped, N.Y.C., 1989, Nat. Assn. Pseudoxanthoma Elasticum. N.Y. Hosp. Cornell Med. Ctr. fellow, 1983-84. Fellow Am. Acad. Ophthalmology; mem. AMA, Nat. Assn. for Visuallly Handicapped (med. adv. bd.), N.Y. State Ophthalmological Soc., N.Y. County Med. Soc., Med. Soc. of State of N.Y., Soc. of Retina Specialists, Mt. Sinai Alumni Assn. (v.p. 1995-97, treas. 1991-95, pres. 1997-99), Alpha Omega Alpha, Phi Beta Kappa. Office: 121 E 60th St New York NY 10022-1102 E-mail: wsfuchs@aol.com.

FUCHSBERG, LAWRENCE J. writer, editor, performing arts association administrator, consultant; b. N.Y.C., 1950; m. Janika Vandervelde. Student, Yale Coll., 1967—69, Columbia U., 1972—73; BA, New Sch. for Social Rsch., 1973; postgrad., U. Chgo., 1973—77. Faculty New Sch. for Social Rsch., N.Y.C., 1975—85; fgn. svc. officer USIA, Washington, 1987—93; exec. co-dir. Zeitgeist, St. Paul, 1994—95, pres., 1998—2003; co-exec. prodr. The Composer's Voice, St. Paul, 1996—98. Contbg editor Willamette Week, Portland, Oreg., 1985—86; exec. prodr. arts-culture-technology '98 Internat. Telecom. Union Plenipotentiary Conf., Mpls., 1998; freelance music reviewer Mpls. Star Tribune, 2001—. Recipient First Pl. Arts and Criticism category, Soc. Profl. Journalists, Pacific NW Chpt., 1986. Avocation: oenology. Personal E-mail: mammouth@visi.com.

FUCUALS, RONALD H. conductor, director; b. L.A., Calif., May 6, 1957; s. Walter Lee and Edna Mildred Fucuals. AS in Math Phys. Sci., Am. River Coll., 1984; BA in Music Edn., U. N. Tex., 1994; MA in Mgmt., Nat. U., 2000. From musician to dir. USMC, Iwakuni, Japan, 1975—89, band dir., prin. condr. Jacksonville, Fla., 1989—. Featured in: Guitar Player Mag., 1984. Vol. Navigators Ministry, 1977—. Recipient Top Gun award, Army Nat. Guard, 1983. Mem.: Nat. Naval Officers Assn. (treas. 1995—96), Internat. Assn. Jazz Educators, Music Educators Nat. Conf. Avocations: bowling, tennis, martial arts, running, exercise.

FUDA, SIRI NARAYAN K.K. (ELAINE T. BARBER), educator, clergy, writer; b. Albany, N.Y., June 13, 1941; d. Adam Henry and Anna Mae Farrell Barber; m. Michael G. Fuda, Nov. 23, 1962; children: Meredith-Anne Costello, Melanie Elsie Henderson, Michelle Germanne Buscaglia. BA in English with honors, SUNY, Albany, 1963, MA in English Lang. and Lit., 1965; postgrad., SUNY, Buffalo, 1967; MS in Exceptional Edn., Buffalo State Coll., 1982. Tchr. Albany Pub. Sch. Sys., 1964-67, curriculum developer, 1966-67; tchr. Buffalo Pub. Schs., 1981-99; dir. Ctr. for Healthy, Happy, Holistic Living, Buffalo, 1987—. Adj. prof. Buffalo State Coll., 1993—; edn. cons. just buffalo lit. ctr., 1990-99; yoga tchr. Women's Wellness Ctr. Western N.Y., 1999—, others; cons. SUNY, Buffalo, 1999; coord. Buffalo State Coll./Buffalo Pub. Schs. coop. program, 1993-99; writer-in-residence Khalsa Women's Tng. Camp, Espinola, N.Mex., 1993-94, just buffalo lit. ctr., 1994; developer, instr. Creative Writing Workshops, Buffalo, Santa Fe; reader Erie and Niagara County Writers Assn.; presenter workshops on yoga for personal stress reduction, expectant mothers and infants, and as metatherapy for emotionally disturbed students. Contbg. editor to lit. anthology Life Junkies: On Our Own, 1990; author: (poetry collections) Unconditional Love: The Sapphire Poems, 1992, Dancing with the Guru, 1994.; contbr. articles to profl. jours., poetry to Buffalo News, others. Founding mem. Lexington Real Foods Co-op, Buffalo, 1971; bd. dirs. Elmwood Ave. Bus. Assn., Buffalo, 1980-83; founder Children's Rm. Co-op Day Care Ctr., Buffalo, 1972-73. Recipient Labor in Lt. award AFL-CIO, Buffalo, 1995; grantee Arts Coun., Buffalo and Erie County, 1990. Mem. Buffalo Tchrs. Fedn. (coun. of dels. 1984-91), just buffalo lit. ctr., Internat. Kundalini Yoga Tchrs. Assn. Democrat. Sikh. Avocation: gardening. Home: 460 Ashland Ave Buffalo NY 14222-1502 Office: Ctr for Healthy Happy Holistic Living 460 Ashland Ave Buffalo NY 14222-1502 E-mail: SiriNarayan@aol.com.

FUDENBERG, HUGH, neuroimmunologist, educator; b. NYC, Oct. 24, 1928; s. Nathan and Frances (Chackowitz) F.; m. Betty Roof, June 1956 (div.); children: Drew, Brooks, David, Haskell. AB, UCLA, 1949; MD, U. Chgo., 1953; MA, Boston U., 1958. Diplomate Am. Bd. Med. Lab. Immunology. Intern U. Utah Hosp., 1953-54; trainee in hematology New Eng. Ctr. Hosp., Tufts U., Boston, 1954-56; resident Mt. Sinai Hosp., N.Y.C., 1956-57, Peter Bent Brigham Hosp., Harvard U., Boston, 1957-58; rsch. assoc. Rockefeller Inst., NYC, 1958-60; asst. prof. medicine U. Calif. Sch. Medicine, San Francisco, 1960-62, assoc. prof. medicine, 1962-66, prof., 1966-75; assoc. prof. immunology U. Calif., Berkeley, 1965-66, prof. bacteriology and immunology, 1966-75; prof., chmn. dept. basic and clin. immunology and microbiology Med. U. SC, Charleston, 1974-85, prof. medicine, immunology, 1974-88; dir. rsch. NeuroImmunoTherapeutic Rsch. Found., Spartanburg, SC, 1988—. Adj. prof. pub. health U. Calif., Berkeley, 1966-75; adj. prof. epidemiology U. NC, Chapel Hill, 1977—; vis. prof. univs. and rsch. insts. in US and Europe, including Karolinska Inst., Sweden, Middlesex Hosp., Eng., Harvard U., Yale U., Princeton U., NYU, U. Ala., Wayne State U., U. So. Calif., U. Amsterdam, U. Leiden, U. Paris, U. Glasgow, U. Edinburgh, U. PR, U. Medellin, Colombia, Caracas, Venezuela, U. Innsbruck, Weismann Inst., Israel, Weifang Med. Sch., China, U. Norway, U. Helsinki, also Cancer Rsch. Inst., France, Italy, Russia, and The Netherlands; spkr. in field; mem. nat. adv. coun. Nat. Inst. Allergy and Infectious Diseases, 1981-85; mem. expert adv. panel on immunology WHO, 1962-82; mem. panel biomed. manpower NRC, 1974-78, mem. com. on immunization, 1978-80; mem. nat. task force on multiple myeloma and chronic leukemia NIH, 1966-71; chmn. external evaluation sci. com. U. Merida, Venezuela, 1982-86; mem. sci. adv. bd. UNESCO Internat. Ctr. for Immunology, Lyon, France, 1982-88; chmn. sci. adv. bd. Integra Inst., 1988-92; chmn. bd. sci. direction Inst. Immunology, Weifang Med. Coll., Changdong, China, 1988—; v.p. rsch. Neuro Immunology Therapeutic Rsch. Found. Author: (with others) Basic Immunogenetics, 1972, 3d edit., 1984, Basic and Clinical Immunology, 1974, 4th edit., 1982 (transl. into 12 lang.), Introduction to Medical Immunology, 1986, 2d edit., 1990; editor: (with others) Phagocytic Mechanisms in Health and Disease, 1972, Biomedical Scientists and Public Policy, 1978; editor: Biomedical Institutions, Biomedical Funding, and Public Policy, 1983; past mem. 35 editl. bds. including African Jour. Clin. and Exptl. Immunology, Annals Allergy, Biomedicine and Pharmacotherapy, Clin. and Exptl. Immunology, Folia Allergologica et Immunologica Clinica, Alzheimer's Longevity and Aging, Hosp. Practice, Jour. Irreproducible Results; co-editor in chief Internat. Jour. Clin. Investigation; contbr. 850 articles to sci. jour.; patentee in field. Mem. nat. adv. coun. Nat. Inst. Allergy and Infectious Diseases, 1981-85; mem. expert adv. panel immunology WHO, 1962-82; mem. panel biomed. manpower Nat. Rsch. Coun., 1974-78, mem. com. on immunization, 1978-80; mem. nat. task force on multiple myeloma and chronic leukemia NIH, 1966-71; chmn. external evaluation sci. com. U. Merida, Venezuela, 1982-86; mem. sci. adv. bd. UNESCO Internat. Ctr. for Immunology, Lyon, France, 1982-88; chmn. sci. adv. bd. Integra Inst., 1988—; chmn. bd. sci. dir. Inst. Immunology, Weifang Med. Coll., Shandong, People's Republic of China, 1988—; v.p. rsch. Neuro Immunology Therapeutic Rsch. Found.; mem. adv. bd. Cambridge Internat. Biog. Centre, 1992; numerous others. Recipient Pasteur medal Inst. Pasteur, 1962, Robert A. Cook medal Am. Acad. Allergy, 1966, Berman medal Am. Acad. Dermatology, 1973, Disting. Svc. award U. Chgo. Med. Alumni, 1973, Petrov Cancer medal Govt. USSR, 1976, Carl Neuberg medal Virchow-Pirquet Med. Soc., 1980, Koch medal German Soc. Microbiology, 1980, von Behringer medal, 1981, Semmelweis medal Hungarian Soc. Immunology, 1981, Metchnikoff Centennial, 1983, Phagocytosis medal Italian Soc. Immunology, 1983, Danish Cancer Soc., 1988, Castelloa di Pietrarossa award, Italy, 1991, Internat. First Prize, Frontiers in Medicine, Italy, 1992, 1st prize Biomed. Rsch. Italian Acad. Arts and Sci., 1992, 20th Century award rsch. sci. med. rsch. and edn., 1993; decorated Order of San Ciriaco, Italy, 1993, Internat. 1st prize in Exptl. Medicine, Italian Govt., 2000; named hon. prof. U. Kuopio, Finland, 1982, U. Claude Bernard, France, 1985, Free Sci. U. Bologna, Italy, 1985, Weifang Med. Coll. Fellow AAAS, Am. Acad. Microbiology; mem. Am. Assn. for Cancer Rsch., Am. Assn. Immunologists (com. for congl. liaison for HEW appropriations, long range planning com.), Am. Rheumatism Assn., Am. Soc. for Clin. Investigation (chmn. com. on pub. info. 1971-74), Am. Soc. Hematology (pres. subdivision on immunohematology and immunogenetics 1970, 74, subcom. rsch in teaching methods 1961-65), Am. Soc. for Human Genetics (exec. coun. 1969-72), Assn. Am. Sch. Microbiology (chmn., pub. affairs com.), Assn. Am. Physicians, Genetics Soc. Am., Internat. Soc. Blood Transfusion (exec. councillor 1965-71), Internat. Soc. Environ. Toxicology and Cancer (bd. councilors), Internat. Soc. Hematology, Internat. Union Immunolog. Socs. (immunoglobin subcom. 1977), Internat. Platform Assn., Midwinter Conf. Immunologists (founder, past pres.), Royal Soc. Medicine (assoc.), Soc. Clin. Immunology, Am. Soc. Med. Labs., Med. Immunology, Sigma Xi. Office: NeuroImmunoTherapeutics Rsch Found 8800 Hwy 9 Inman SC 29349-2247

FUDGE, ANN MARIE, advertising executive; b. Washington, Apr. 23, 1951; d. Malcolm R. and Bettye (Lewis) Brown; m. Richard E. Fudge, Feb. 27, 1971; children: Richard Jr., Kevin. BA, Simmons Coll., 1973; MBA, Harvard U., 1977; DHL (hon.), Adelphi U., 1995, Howard U., 1998, Simmons Coll., 1998, Marymount Coll., 1999. Manpower specialist GE, Bridgeport, Conn., 1973-75; mktg. asst. Gen. Mills, Mpls., 1977-78, asst. product mgr., 1978-80, product mgr., 1980-83, mktg. dir., 1983-86; assoc. dir., strategic planning Gen. Foods, White Plains, N.Y., 1986-87, mktg. dir., 1987-89, v.p. mktg. and devel., 1989-91, exec. v.p., gen. mgr., 1991-94; exec. v.p. Kraft Foods, 1994-97; pres. Maxwell House Coffee Co., White Plains, N.Y., 1994-97, Maxwell House Coffee and Post Cereal, Tarrytown, NY, 1997—2001; chmn., CEO Young & Rubicam, Inc., Y&R Advt. Bd. dirs. GE, Marriott Internat.; trustee Am. Grad. Sch. Internat. Mgmt., Brookings Instn. Bd. dirs. Women's Econ. Devel. Corp., St. Paul, 1984-86; chair allocations panel United Way, Mpls., 1983-86; vol. Big Sisters/Big Bros., Fairfield County, Conn., 1988-90; bd. govs. Boys and Girls Clubs Am. Recipient Leadership award YWCA, Mpls., 1980, Black Achievers award Harlem YMCA, 1988, Candace award Nat. Coalition of 100 Black Women, 1991-92, Corp. Women's Network award, 1994, She Knows Where She's Going award Girls, Inc., 1994, Alumni Achievement award Harvard Bus. Sch., 1998; named Woman of Yr., Glamour Mag., 1995, Ad Woman of Yr., Advt. Women of N.Y., 1995, Sara Lee Frontrunner award, 1999, one of 50 Most Powerful Women in Am. Bus., Fortune mag. Mem. Exec. Leadership Coun. (pres. 1994-96, Achievement award 2000), Com. of 200, NY Women's Forum, Coun. on Fgn. Rels. Office: Y&R Advt 285 Madison Ave New York NY 10017-6486

FUDGE, MARY ANN, vocational school educator; b. Traverse City, Mich., July 21, 1947; d. Thomas C. and Mildred M. (Garey) Moran; m. Lew Fudge, June 28, 1969; children: Brian M., Cheryl M. BS, Cen. Mich. U., 1969; MA, Ea. Mich. U., 1975. Jr. HS tchr. math. St. Charles Sch., Mich., 1969-71; mid. sch. tchr. Gallatin County Sch., Bozeman, Mont., 1972-73; substitute tchr. Lincoln Consol. Sch., Ypsilanti, Mich., 1973-77; tchr. adult edn. Benton Harbor Area Sch., Mich., 1980-82; instr. math. Southwestern Mich. Coll., Dowagiac, Mich., 1983-84; high sch. tchr. math. Coloma Pub. Sch., Mich., 1984-86; tchr. adult edn. math. Van Buren Technology Ctr., Lawrence, Mich., 1982-83, math. cons., coord., 1986-99, tech. coord., 1999—. Dep. clk. Hagar Twp., Riverside, Mich., 1987-88. Mem. Nat. Coun. Tchr. Math., Mich. Coun. Tchr. Math. Roman Catholic. Home: 25403 63rd Ave Mattawan MI 49071-9594 Office: Van Buren Intermediate Sch Dist 490 S Paw Paw St Lawrence MI 49064-9599 E-mail: mfudge@vbisd.org.

FUENTEALBA, VICTOR WILLIAM, professional society administrator; b. Balt., Sept. 1, 1922; s. Manuel Lagos and Antonia (Lengler) F.; m. Viola J. Henderson, Jan. 26, 1952; children: Victoria, Mary Lee, Donna Jean, Patricia. Student, Loyola Coll., 1946-47; JD, U. Md., 1950. Bar: Md. 1950, U.S. Supreme Ct. 1950. V.p. Musicians Union Met. Balt., 1951-53, sec., treas., 1953-58, pres., 1958-78; mem. internat. exec. bd. Am. Fedn. Musicians, N.Y.C., 1967-70, v.p., 1970-78, pres., 1978-87, pres. emeritus, 1987—. Bd. dirs. Hearing and Speech Agy., Balt., 1973-78; mem. Pres.' Com. on Employment of

Handicapped; adv. council Ctr. Labor and Indsl. Relations of N.Y. Inst. Tech., Assn. Concert Bands, Van Cliburn Internat. Piano Competition; chmn. bd. Nat. Music Council; v.p. Muscular Dystrophy Assn.; adv. bd. Music Industry Educators Assn. Served with inf. U.S. Army, World War II; judge Adv. Gen. Vets. Fgn. Wars of U.S., 2001-2002. Decorated Purple Heart. Mem. Am. Bar Assn., Delta Theta Phi. Democrat. Roman Catholic. Home: 4501 Arabia Ave Baltimore MD 21214-3306 Office: 805 Court Sq Bldg 200 E Lexington St Baltimore MD 21202-3530

FUENTES, CARLOS, writer, former ambassador; b. Mexico City, Nov. 11, 1928; s. Rafael Fuentes Boettiger and Berta Macías Rivas; m. Rita Macedo, 1959 (div. 1969); 1 dau., Cecilia; m. Sylvia Lemus, 1973; children: Carlos, Natasha Ed., U. Mex., Institut des Hautes Etudes Internationales, Geneva; hon. degrees, Columbia Coll., Chgo. State U., Cambridge U., Essex U., Harvard U., Dartmouth Coll., Bard Coll., New Sch., Georgetown U., Washington U., St. Louis, Borwn U. Mem. Mexican del. ILO, Geneva, 1950-52; asst. chief press sect. Mexican Ministry Fgn. Affairs, 1954; asst. dir. cultural dissemination U. Mex., 1955-56; head dept. cultural rels. Mexican Ministry Fgn. Affairs, 1957-59; fellow Woodrow Wilson Internat. Ctr. for Scholars, Washington, 1974; Mexican ambassador to France, 1975-77; prof. English and romance langs. U. Pa., 1978-83; prof. comparative lit. Harvard U., 1984-86, Robert F. Kennedy prof., 1987-89; prof.-at-large Brown U., Providence, 1995—; asst. chief Madrid U, Spain, Salamanca U, Spain, Veracmz U, Mexico, Puebla U, Spain. Norman Maccoll lectr. Cambridge U., 1977, Simon Bolivar prof., 1986-87; Virgina Gildersleeve prof. Barnard Coll., 1977; Henry L. Tinker lectr. Columbia U., 1978; pres. Modern Humanities Rsch. Assn., 1989—; prof. at large Brown U., 1995—. Author: Los diás enmascarados, 1954, La región más transparente, 1958 (ub. as Where the Air Is Clear, 1960), Las buenas conciencias, 1959 (pub. as The Good Conscience, 1961), Aura, 1962, La muerte del Artemio Cruz, 1962 (pub. as The Death of Artemio Cruz, 1964), The Argument of Latin America: Words for North Americans, 1963, Cantar de ciegos, 1964, Zona sagrada, 1967 (pub. as Holy Places, 1972), Cambio de piel, 1967 (pub. as A Change of Skin, 1968; Biblioteca Breve prize Barcelona 1967), Paris: la revolución de mayo, 1968, La nueva novela hispanoamericana, 1969, Cumpleaños, 1969, El mundo de José Luis Cuevas, 1969, Casa con dos puertas, 1970, Tiempo mexicano, 1971, Poemas de amor: cuentos del alma, 1971, Cuerpos y ofrendas, 1972, Chac Mool y otros cuentos, 1973, Terra Nostra, 1975 (Rómulo Gallegos prize Venezuela 1977), Cervantes: o, La crítica de la lectura, 1976 (pub. as Don Quixote: or, The Critique of Reading, 1976), La cabeza de la hidra, 1978 (pub. as The Hydra Head, 1978), Una familia lejana, 1980 (pub. as Distant Relations, 1982), Agua quemada, 1981 (pub. as Burnt Water, 1981), High Noon in Latin America, 1983, Juan Soriano y su obra, 1984, Of Human Rights: A Speech, 1984, El gringo viejo, 1985 (pub. as The Old Gringo, 1986; LA Times Book award nomination 1986, Rubén Darío prize 1988, Italo-Latino Americano Instituto prize 1988), Latin America: At War with the Past, 1985, Palacio Nacional, 1986, Cristóbal Nonato, 1987 (pub. as Christopher Unborn, 1989), Gabriel García Marquez and the Invention of America, 1987, Myself with Others: Selected Essays, 1988, Constancia, y otras novelas para vírgenes, 1989 (pub. as Constancia and Other Stories for Virgins, 1990), La campaña, 1990 (pub. as The Campaign, 1991), Valiente Mundo Nuevo, 1991, The Buried Mirror: Reflections on Spain and on the New World, 1992, Witnesses of Time, 1992, Return to Mexico: Journeys Beyond the Mask, 1992, El Naranjo, 1993 (pub. as The Orange Tree, 1993), Geografia de la Novela, 1993, Diana the Goddess Who Hunts Alone, 1995, The Crystal Frontier, 1995, La Edad del Tiempo, 1994—, A New Time for Mexico, 1994, Por un Progreso Incluyente, 1997, Retratos en el Tiempo, 1998, Los Anos con Laura Diaz, 1999; Inez, 2000, Los cinco soles de Mexico, 2001, La silla del áquila, 2003; (plays) Todos los gatos son pardos, 1970, El tuerto es rey, 1970, Los reinos originarios, 1971, Orquídeas a la luz de la luna, 1982 (pub. as Orchids in the Moonlight, 1982; Mexican Nat. award for lit. 1984); screenwriter: (films) Pedro Paramo, 1966, Tiempo de morir, 1966, Los Caifanes, 1967, (TV series) The Buried Mirror, 1991; contbr. to mag. and newspapers including Los Angeles Times, NY Times, Newsweek; editor: Revista Mexicana de Literatura, 1954-58, El Espectador, 1959-61, Siempre, 1960—, Política, 1960—, Los signos en rotación y otra ensayos, 1971. Trustee NY Pub. Library, mem. Mexican Nat. Commn. Human Rights, 1991—. Recipient Centro Mexicano de Escritores fellowship, 1956-57, Xavier Villaurrutia prize (Mex.), 1975, Alfonso Reyes prize (Mex.), 1979, Miguel de Cervantes Lit. prize Spanish Ministry of Culture, 1987, Medal of Honor for Lit., Nat. Arts Club, NYC, 1988, Rector's medal U. Chile, 1991, Casita Maria medal, 1991, UCLA medal, 1993, Order of Merit (Chile), 1992, French Legion of Honor, 1992, Menèndez Pelayo Internat. award U. Santander, 1992, Picasso medal UNESCO, 1994, Principe de Asturias prize, 1994, Premio Grinzane-Cavour, 1994; named hon. citizen Santiago de Chile, 1993, Buenos Aires, 1993, Veracruz, 1993, Order of the So. Cross (Brazil), 1997, French Order of Merit, 1998, Latin Civilization prize French and Brazilian Acad., 1999;Mexican Senate Award, 2000, Delaware Commonwealth Award, 2002. Mem. Am. Acad. and Inst. Arts and Letters, Nat. Coll. Mex., Inst. Nat. Strategy (bd. dir.).

FUENTES, JULIO M. federal judge; b. Humacao, PR, 1946; BA, So. Ill. U., 1971; MA, NYU, 1972; JD, SUNY, Buffalo, 1975; MA, Rutgers U., 1993. Private practice, Newark, 1975—81; superior ct. judge State NJ Essex County, 1979—87; judge U.S. Ct. Appeals 3rd Cir., 2000—. Office: US Ct Appeals 3rd Cir M L King Jr Fed Bldg & Cthse 50 Walnut St Rm 5032 Newark NJ 07102*

FUENTES, MARTHA AYERS, playwright; b. Ashland, Ala., Dec. 21, 1923; d. William Herny and Elizabeth (Dye) Ayers; m. Manuel Solomon Fuentes, Apr. 11, 1943. BA in English, U. South Fla., 1969. Lectr., instr. workshops on drama, writing for TV. Author: The Rebel, 1970, Mama Don't Make Me Go To College, My Head Hurts, 1963, Two Characters in Search of An Agreement, 1970, A Cherry Blossom for Miss Chrysanthemum; contbr. articles to local, regional and nat. newspapers, feature artcles to nat. mags.; author TV plays and feature articles for children and young adults. Recipient George Sergel drama award U. Chgo., 1969. Mem. AAUW, NAFE, S.E. Playwrights Project, The Alliance of Resident Theatres, Stageworks, Authors Guild, Dramatists Guild, Romance Writers Am., Southeastern Writers Assn., Fla. Studio Theatre, United Daus. Confederacy. Roman Catholic. Avocations: reading, animal rights, environmental protection, theater, travel. Home and Office: 102 3rd St Belleair Beach FL 33786-3211 E-mail: fuentes8530@s.com.

FUENTES-HENRIQUEZ, FERNANDO NEFTALI, finance educator, researcher; b. Parral, Chile, Feb. 26, 1969; s. Daniel Fuentes-Falcon and Maria Henriquez-Ponce; m. Jessica Victoria Quezada-Arias; children: Nehemias Esteban Fuentes-Quezada, Eliezer Isaac Fuentes-Quezada, Josue Andres Fuentes-Quezada. BS in Econs. and Mgmt., Universidad de Concepcion, Chile, 1993; PhD in Mgmt., U. Ark., 2003. Instr. Universidad de Concepcion, Concepcion, Chile, 1993—95, direct adviser to pres., 1995—2000; asst. prof., rchr. U. Ark., Fayetteville. Author: Cases of Study in Marketing and Sales. Dir. Evang. Pentecostal Ch., Fayetteville, Ark., 2000—02. Mem.: Comml. Engring. Assn., Strategic Mgmt. Soc. (assoc.), Acad. of Mgmt. (assoc.). Home: 705 Putman St Apt H2 Fayetteville AR Office: U Ark Sam M Walton Coll Bus Fayetteville AR 72701 E-mail: fnfuentes@walton.uark.edu.

FUENTEVILLA, MANUEL EDWARD, chemical engineer; b. Havana, Cuba, Feb. 17, 1923; s. Fernando and Edith Agnes (Pira) F.; m. May Belle Tutwiler, Oct. 18, 1945; children: William F., Diane G., Austin D., Eve J., Inez M. BChemE, Poly. Inst. Bklyn., 1947; MS, Drexel U., 1954. Sr. engr. Catalyic Inc., Phila., 1951-60; chief engr. Stokes Equipment divsn. Pennwalt Corp., 1960-67; asst. mgr. mfg. Esso Eastern, Tokyo, 1967-69, tech. supt. Okinawa, Japan, 1969-72; project mgr. Jacobs Engring. Co., Cherry Hill, N.J., 1972-75, Stauffer Japan Ltd., Tokyo, 1975-77; dir. process devel. Alfa Laval Process, Mt. Laurel, N.J., 1977-79; tech. dir., sr. project mgr. Synergo, Inc., Phila., 1979-82; chief mech. engring. Kling/Lindquist, Inc., Phila., 1982-2000, Cerus, Inc., Cherry Hill, N.J. Process and tech svc. pharm. and chem. applications. Served with USNR, 1943-46. Mem. Am. Inst. Chem. Engrs., Soc. History of Tech., Phi Lambda Upsilon. Achievements include patentee in indsl. processes. Home: 314 Tearose Ln Cherry Hill NJ 08003-3524 E-mail: m.fuentevilla@worldnet.att.net.

FUERST, ADOLPH, consultant; b. Linz, Austria, Sept. 11, 1925; came to U.S., 1939; s. Siegfried and Anna (Strassberger) F.; m. Shirley Rita Miller, July 6, 1951; children: David Jonathan, Ellen Laura. BS in Chemistry, CCNY, 1949; MA in Chemistry, Bklyn. Coll., 1957. Chem. lab. technician Mt. Sinai Hosp., N.Y.C., 1949-50; asst. prodn. chemist U.S. Vitamin Corp., N.Y.C., 1950-52; pigment chemist Ansbacher-Siegle Corp., Rosebank, N.Y., 1952-55; pigment and dyestuff chemist Gen. Aniline & Film Corp., Linden, N.J., 1955-58; from group leader to R&D mgr. Sinclair & Valentine Co., N.Y.C. and Elmsford, N.Y., 1958-74; mgr. spl. svcs. Graphic Arts Labs. Sun Chem. Corp., Carlstadt, N.J., 1974-86; cons. Adolph Fuerst Cons., Bklyn., 1986—94. Mem. Nat. Assn. Printing Ink Mfrs. gloss project steering com., N.Y. and N.J., 1984-85; chmn. adv. bd. PCI Ink Complaint Handbook System, N.Y., N.J. and Pa., 1986-87. Co-author: Fountain Solution Composition & Its Effect on Printing Ink and Paper, 1986; co-reviser: The Printing Ink Handbook, 1988; co-developer: The Printing Ink Complaint Handbook System, 1988. V.p. Friends of the Libr., Cortelyou Rd., Br., Bklyn. Pub. Libr., 1984; garden guide Bklyn. Botanic Garden, 1990—; judge Sci. Fair, N.Y. Acad. Scis., Bklyn., 1967—, chairperson garden guide com., 1990-92. With U.S. Army, 1944-45, ETO. Fellow Am. Inst. Chemists, N.Y. Microscopical Soc. (rec. sec. 1989-91, pres. 1992-93); mem. Am. Chem. Soc., N.Y. Pigment Club (pres. 1965-66, Gavel 1966), Recording for the Blind and Dyslexic (reader 1997—). Achievements include patents in Improvements in or Relating to Coloring of Anodized Aluminum, Pigment Dispersions, Heat Transfer Method of Coloring Anodized Aluminum; development of paper and ink tests for predicting on-press performance, rheological testing of ink, organic pigment synthesis. Home: 266 Marlborough Rd Brooklyn NY 11226-4512

FUERST, STEVEN BERNARD, lawyer; b. Somerville, N.J., Sept. 18, 1945; s. Ernest S. and Else (Loewengart) F.; m. Elizabeth Yusem, Aug. 2, 1970; 1 dau., Emma. B.S. in Econs., U. Pa., 1967, J.D., 1970. Bar: N.J. 1970, U.S. Dist. Ct. N.J. 1970. Law clk. to judge N.J. Appellate Ct., Somerville, 1970-71; sr. mem. Fuerst, Yusem & Boehmer and predecessor firms, Somerville, N.J., 1973— ; sec. FCS Industries, Inc., N.J. and Ariz., 1981— ; mem. N.J. Supreme Ct. Dist. 7 ethics com. 1978-81. Bd. dirs. Somerset City Spl. Olympics Com., 1978-83. Served to maj. USAR, 1970— . Mem. Somerset County Bar Assn. (pres. 1984). Jewish. Office: Lowenstein Sandler Kohl Fisher & Boylan PO Box 1113 Somerville NJ 08876-1113

FUERSTENAU, DOUGLAS WINSTON, mineral engineering educator; b. Hazel, S.D., Dec. 6, 1928; s. Erwin Arnold and Hazel Pauline (Karterud) Fuerstenau; m. Margaret Ann Pellett, Aug. 29, 1953; children: Linda(dec.), Lucy, Sarah, Stephen. BS, S.D. Sch. Mines and Tech., 1949; MS, Mont. Sch. Mines, 1950; ScD, MIT, 1953; Mineral Engr., Mont. Coll. Mineral Sci. and Tech., 1968; hon. doctorate degree, U. Liege, Belgium, 1989; D of Technology (hon.), Lulea U. Tech., Sweden, 2001. Asst. prof. mineral engring. MIT, 1953-56; sect. leader, metals research lab. Union Carbide Metals Co., Niagara Falls, N.Y., 1956-58; mgr. mineral engring. lab Kaiser Aluminum & Chem. Corp., Permanente, Calif., 1958-59; assoc. prof. metallurgy U. Calif., Berkeley, 1959-62, prof. metallurgy, 1962-86, P. Malozemoff prof. of mineral engring., 1987-93, prof. grad. sch., 1994—, Miller rsch. prof., 1969-70, chmn. dept. materials sci. and mineral engring., 1970-78; hon. prof. Huainan Inst. Tech., 2000—. Mem. Nat. Mineral Bd., 1975—78; Am. rep. Internat. Mineral Processing Congress Com., 1978—97. Editor: Froth Flotation-50th Anniversary Vol., 1962; co-editor-in-chief: Internat. Jour. Mineral Processing, 1974—98, hon. editor-in-chief:, 1998—; contbr. articles to profl. jours. Named Douglas W. Fuerstenau professorship at S.D. Sch. of Mines and Tech., 1998; recipient Alexander von Humboldt Sr. Am. Scientist award, Germany, 1984, Frank F. Aplan award, Engring. Found., 1990, Lifetime Achievement award, Internat. Mineral Processing Congress, 1995; fellow Rsch., Japan Soc. Promotion Sci., 1993. Fellow: Indian Nat. Acad. Engring. (fgn.), Australian Acad. Tech. Scis. and Engring. (fgn.); mem.: AIChE, NAE, Russian Fedn. Acad. Natural Scis. (fgn. mem.), Am. Chem. Soc., Soc. Mining Engrs. (bd. dirs. 1968—71, Disting. mem.), Am. Inst. Mining and Metall. Engrs. (chmn. mineral processing divsn. 1967, Robert Lansing Hardy gold medal 1957, Rossiter W. Raymond award 1961, Robert H. Richards award 1975, Antoine M. Gaudin award 1978, Mineral Industry Edn. award 1983, Henry Krumb disting. lectr. 1989, hon. 1989), Theta Tau, Sigma Xi. Congregationalist. Home: 1440 Le Roy Ave Berkeley CA 94708-1912 E-mail: dwfuerst@socrates.berkeley.edu.

FUERSTNER, FIONA MARGARET ANNE, ballet company executive, ballet educator; b. Rio de Janeiro, Apr. 24, 1936; d. Paul G. and Agnes Ethel (Stothard) F.; m. Dane LaFontsee, June 7, 1969 (div. 1992); 1 child, Liana Marie. Studied with San Francisco Ballet, Royal Ballet (London), Ballet Rambert (London) Ballet Theatre Sch. (N.Y.C.), Sch. Am. Ballet (N.Y.C.). With corps de ballet San Francisco Ballet, 1952-55, soloist, 1955-58, prin. dancer, 1958-62; toured with Walter Terry's Am. Dances, 1962-63; prin. dancer Les Grands Ballets Can., Montreal, 1963-64, Am. Choreographer's Co. of N.Y., 1964, Pa. Ballet, 1965-68, 1968-74, ballet mistress, instr. co. class, apprentice class, 1974-77, ballet mistress, instr. co. class, 1977—86; ballet mistress Nashville Ballet, 1986-87, ballet mistress, asst. to artistic dir., 1987-91; ballet mistress Milw. Ballet, 1990-95, asst. to artistic dir. ballet mistress, 1995—2003. Guest dancer Ballet Concerto, Miami, 1967, 68, Erie Civic Ballet, 1969; guest instr. Marsha Woody Dance Acad., Beaumont, Tex., 1974, U. Louisville, 1977-78, co. class San Francisco Ballet, 1985, Tenn. Assn. Dance Nashville Conf., 1988, So. Regional Workshop Chgo., Nat. Assn. Dance Masters in Nashville, 1989, BalletMet, 1991, Memphis Classical Ballet, 1992, 97, 99, Nashville Ballet, 1992; guest ballet mistress BalletMet, 1993; faculty tchr. Sch. of Pa. Ballet, 1977-78, 78-86; organized concert group, ballet mistress, dancer Pa. Ballet, 1971; mem. dance panel Nat. Found. Advancement in the Arts, 1995-98; master tchr. South Eastern Regional Ballet Assn. Festival, 1998, Nat. Found. for Advancement in the Arts, 1999, 2001; guest tchr. Ind. U. Ballet Dept., 2000, Western Mich. U., Mar. and Oct. 2002; dance panelist Midwest Regional, Nat. Found. for Advancement in the Arts, May and July 2001, 02. Staged Allegro Brillante, Sch. Pa. Ballet Student Showcase, 1986, Nashville Ballet, 1988, Madrigalesco, Pacific NW Ballet, 1981, (parts) Nutcracker, Nashville Ballet, 1989, Carmina Burana (Butler), Milw. Ballet, 1989, Scotch Symphony, Pa. Ballet, 1993, Carmina Burana, Alberta Ballet, 1993, Concerto Barocco, Ballet Omaha, 1994, Ballet Met, 1995, Serenade, Milw. Ballet Sch., 1994, 95, 96, Serenade Milw. Ballet, 1998-99, Serenade Western Mich. U., 1999-2000; staged Concerto Barocco, The Four Temperaments for Milw. Ballet, 1999-2000, Allegro Brillante, 2000-01.

FUESS, BILLINGS SIBLEY, JR., advertising executive; b. N.Y.C., Mar. 11, 1928; s. Billings Sibley and Lucile (McNeill) F.; m. Doris Vannoy, July 19, 1952; children: Billings Sibley III, Doris Jr., Frederick, Lucile. AB in Journalism, U. N.C., 1949. Analyst Gallup & Robinson, Princeton, N.J., 1952-53; writer Kenyon & Eckhardt, N.Y.C., 1953-59, Batten, Barton, Durstine & Osborn, N.Y.C., 1959-65; creative dir. Ogilvy & Mather, N.Y.C., 1965-89; pres. Billings S. Fuess Advt., Summit, N.J., 1989—. Mem. selection com. N.C. Advt. Hall of Fame award. Author, editor: How to Use the Power of the Printed Word, 1985. Mem. N.Y. Philharmonic Vol. Coun., 1976—. Recipient Grand award Internat. Film and Television Festival N.Y., 1984, Stephen E. Kelly award Mag. Pubs. Assn., N.Y.C., 1983, Gold award Art Dirs. Club N.J., numerous top industry awards; elected to N.C. Advt. Hall of Fame, U. N.C., Chapel Hill, 1995. Mem. Art Dirs. Club of N.J. (bd. trustees 1995—, treas. 1996—). Home: 19 Highland Dr Summit NJ 07901-3108

FUFUKA, NATIKA NJERI YAA, business executive; b. Cleve., Feb. 21, 1952; d. Russell and Mindoro Reed. AA, AAB, Cuyahoga Community Coll., Cleve., 1973; BA, Mich. State U., 1975; postgrad., Cleve. State U. Asst. pers. dir. May Co., Cleve., 1975-78; merchandiser J.C. Penney, Cleve., 1978-80; sports mgr. Joseph Hornes, Cleve., 1980-81; fashion buyer Higbee, Cleve., 1981-86; exec. v.p. Mindoro & Assocs., 1982—; merchandise exec. Fashion Bug, Euclid, Ohio, 1986-92; pres., CEO Mindy's Return to Fashion, Cleve., 1993—. Vice chair Joint Com. on Medicaid Provider Impact for State of Ohio, 1992; mem. Mayor's Census Task Force, Cuyahoga County Women Bus. Enterprise Adv. Coun., Cleve. Female Bus. Enterprise Adv. Coun., Greater Cleve. Growth Assn. (pub. affairs com.), Displaced/Single Parent Homemakers Adv. Coun., Cuyahoga Cmty. Coun., Cuyahoga Hills Boys Adv. Coun., Black Aspiration Week Celebrationcom. Cleve. State U., 1990, cmty. rels. coun. Cleve. Job Corp., 1996, African Am. com. Cleve. Found., 1996, nat. nomination com. Outstanding Young Woman of Am., 1998, Outstanding Young Man of Am., 1998; chair Centralized Resource Referral Svc. Panel United Way, 1993, mem. Gen. Assembly, 1993—, United Way Appeal Com., 1996, leadership devel. program; active Citizen League, Cleve. Mus. Art, Playhouse Square Found., Women in Apptd. Office Project, Planned Parenthood Greater Cleve., WCPN Radio.; bd. dirs. Ohio Youth Adv. Coun., Women Cmty. Found., 1993—, Career Beginning Program Bd., 1993—, Nat. Ctr. Non-Profit; mem. Nat. Coun. Christians and Jews, 1996. Ford Found. scholar, 1975; recipient Jesse Jackson Voter Registration award, 1984, Leadership award United Way, 1991, Cert. Appreciation award, 1998, 2001, Vol. Leadership recognition City of Cleve., 1991, Cmty. Rels. Coun. Svc. award Cleve. Job Corps., 1998. Mem. NAFE, Nat. Nominating Bd. Outstanding Ams., Assn. MBA Execs., Black Profl. Assn., Nat. Assn. Negro Bus./Profl. Women, Am. Profl. Exec. Women, Am. Women Bus. Assn., Nat. Assn. Black Female Entrepreneurs, Severance Merchant Mall Orgn., Op. Big Vote, Nat. Coun. Negro Women, Nat. Polit. Congress Black Women (nat. founder mem., founder mem. Ohio state chpt.), Nat. Hook-Up, 100 Black Women Coalition, Black Congl. Caucus Braintrust, Small Minority Bus. Braintrust, Corp. Braintrust, Nat. Non-Profit Bds., Black Women Agenda, Black Women Roundtable, Black Focus (pres. bd. trustees), 21st Congl. Dist. Caucus (exec. bd. mem., chair bus. women com., certs. of appreciation for outstanding svc. 1985, 86), Urban League Greater Cleve., Op. Push of Greater Cleve. (bd. dirs.), Project Vote (asst. dir., Voter Registration award 1984), Midwest Vote Project, Women Vote Project, WomenSpace, United Black Fund, Greater East Cleve. Dem. Club, Minority Women Polit. Action Com., LWV, Cuyahoga Women Polit. Caucus, Ohio Pub. Interest Campaign, Ohio Rainbow Coalition, Ohio Dem. Women Com., Network Together, Black Elected Dem. Ofcls. Ohio, Cleve. City Club, 16th Dist. Club, Project M.O.V.E, Kinsman Youth Devel. Program and Scholarship Cmty. Liasion. Democrat. Pentecostal. Avocations: collecting african art, golf. Office: One Chagrin Highlands 2000 Auburn Drive Ste 200 Beachwood OH 44122

FUGARO, ANTHONY JOSEPH, anesthesiologist; b. Camden, N.J., Aug. 18, 1939; s. Joseph and Rose (Bocco) F.; m. Delia C. Settanni, Feb. 24, 1940; children: Joseph, Michael, Christopher. AB in Biology, LaSalle Coll., Phila., 1962; DO, Phila. Coll. Osteopathy, 1966. Intern Detroit Osteo. Hosp., 1966-67; resident in internal medicine Cooper Hosp., Camden, N.J., 1970-72; resident in anesthesiology Temple U. Hosp., Phila., 1972-74, anesthesiologist, 1974-77, asst. prof. anesthesia, 1977-78, assoc. prof., 1978-81; dir. anesthesiology Episcopal Hosp., 1977-81, chmn. dept. anesthesia, 1977-81; staff anesthesiologist, instr. Lankenau Hosp., Phila., 1981—. Maj. U.S. Army, 1968-70. Roman Catholic. Mem. AMA, ACS, ACP, Am. Soc. Anesthesiology, Soc. Obstetrics Anesthesia and Perinatology, Montgomery County Med. Soc., Phila. Soc. Anesthesia (sec. 1996-97, pres. 1997-99), Am. Heart Assn., Pa. Soc. Anesthesiologists, Soc. Obstetrics Anesthesiologists and Perinatologists, Soc. Ambulatory Anesthesia. Office: United Anesthesia Services 100 E Lancaster Ave # 100 Wynnewood PA 19096-3450

FUGATE, CHARLES ROYCE, SR., civil engineer; b. Pomona, Mo., Aug. 13, 1935; s. Charles and Margaret Norene Fugate; m. Rita Sharon Fugate, July 10, 1965; 1 child, Charles Royce Jr. BS in Civil Engring., U. Kans., 1958. Registered profl. engr., Kans., Mo. Various positions Mo. Dept. Transp., Jefferson City, Kansas City, Macon, 1959-90, dist. engr. Willow Springs, 1990-96, divsn. engr. rsch. devel. tech. Jefferson City, 1996—; city adminstr., engr. City of West Plains, Mo., 1996—. Fellow ASCE (sect. pres.); mem. NSPE (past nat. dir.), Mo. Soc. Profl. Engrs. (pres.), Rotary (Macon pres.-elect 1971, Jefferson City West charter sec. 1974, Wiilow Spring pres. 1994). Republican. Roman Catholic. Avocations: quail hunting, golf. Office: City of West Plains 1910 N Holiday Ln West Plains MO 65775-8000

FUGATE, IVAN DEE, banker, lawyer; b. Blackwell, Okla., Dec. 9, 1928; s. Hugh D. and Iva (Holmes) F.; m. Lois Unita Rossow, June 3, 1966; children: Vickie Michelle, Roberta Jeanne, Douglas B., Thomas P. AB, Pittsburg (Kans.) State U., 1949; LLB, U. Denver, 1952, JD, 1970. Bar: Colo. 1952. Exec. sec., mgr. Jr. C. of C. of Denver, 1950-52; also sec. Colo. Jr. C. of C.; individual practice law Denver, 1954—; chmn. bd., pres. Green Mountain Bank, Lakewood, Colo., 1975-82; chmn., pres. Western Nat. Bank Denver (now Vectra Bank of Colorado); chmn. exec. com. North Valley Bank, Thornton, Colo., 1962—, chmn., pres., 1981-2000, chmn., 2000—; founder, chmn. emeritus Ind. State Bank of Colo. (now Bankers Bank of West), 1978—, Ind. Bankers of Colo., 1973—. Former bd. dirs. Kit Carson State Bank, Colo.; sec. First Nat. Bank, Burlington, Colo.; owner, farms, ranches, Kans., Colo.; instr. U. Denver Coll. Law, 1955-60; mem. Colo. Treas's. Com. Investment State Funds, 1975—. Treas. to Rep. Assos., Colo., 1959-61, trustee, 1959-64. Maj. USAR, 1952-54. Mem. ABA, Colo. Bar Assn., Denver Bar Assn. (trustee 1962-65), Colo. Bankers Assn. (bd. dirs.), Colo. Cattlemen's Assn., Ind. Bankers Assn. Am. (pres. 1978, adminstrv. com. 1976—, bd. dirs. fed. legis. com., chmn. spl. tax com.), instr. One Bank Holding Co. seminars 1976—), Lakewood Country Club, Phi Alpha Delta. Methodist. Home: 12015 W 26th Ave Lakewood CO 80215-1110

FUGATE-WILCOX, TERY, artist; b. Kalamazoo; Represented in permanent collections Solomon R. Guggenheim Mus., N.Y.C., Australia Nat. Gallery, Canberra, Mus. Modern Art, N.Y.C., Western Mich. U., J. Hood Wright Park, N.Y.C., J. Patrick Lannan Found. Mus., Palm Beach, Fla., Nat. Shopping Ctrs., Harrisburg, Pa., Prudential Ins. Co., Newark, Damson Oil Co., N.Y.C., N.Y.C. Dept. Parks and Recreations, Princess Gloria von Thurn and Taxis, Regensburg, Germany; sculpture located 7th Ave and Waverly, N.Y.C., City Wall, Lafayette, Houston, N.Y.C., Holland Tunnel Entrance, N.Y.C., 40-ft. sculpture Riverside Dr. and Jay Hoodwright Park, N.Y.C., 30-ft. self-watering sculpture The Prudential Gateway 4, Newark. Named laureate Nat. Endowment for Arts. Address: 500 Canal St New York NY 10013 *Actual art includes in its statement the long-suppressed dimension of time, in the context of the naturally occurring changes that are part of the life of any material and make it part of the life of the work of art incorporating that material.*

FUGGI, GRETCHEN MILLER, education educator; b. Westerly, R.I., Aug. 26, 1938; d. John Louis and Harriet (Scheid) M.; m. William Joseph Fuggi, Aug. 15, 1960; children: Gretchen, Juliann, John, Kristen. BS, So. Conn. State U., 1960, MS, 1969, 6th yr. diploma, 1991, 6th yr. Ednl. Leadership diploma, 1994. Reading cons. Washington Magnet Sch., West Haven, Conn., 1974—; adj. prof. So. Conn. State U., New Haven, 1988—. Pres. Cath. Charity League of Greater New Haven, 1989-90; bd. dirs. New Haven Symphony Aux., 1992—. Named Tchr. of Yr., West Haven Fedn. Tchrs., 1998-99. Mem. AAUP, Internat. Reading Assn., Conn. Reading Assn., Stonington Hist. Soc. of Conn., Delta Kappa Gamma Soc. Internat., Grad. Club New Haven. Roman Catholic. Home: 19 Westview Rd North Haven CT 06473-2013 E-mail: Fuggi@Juno.com.

FUGIEL, FRANK PAUL, insurance company executive; b. Chgo., Aug. 23, 1950; s. Richard A. and Sally (McKinney) F.; m. Nancy Campbell, Sept. 15, 1973; children: Michele, Rachelle. Student, SUNY, Albany. CLU; cert. managed healthcare profl. Individual underwriter Prudential Ins. Co., Merrillville, Ind., 1971-80, group claims mgr., 1980-82, underwriting mgr., 1982-84; group claims officer Employers Health Ins. Co., Green Bay, Wis., 1984-86, underwriting officer, 1986-88, managed care officer, 1988; 2d v.p. individual health ins. Washington Nat. Ins. Co., 1988-90, v.p. ops., 1990; exec. v.p. Oak Brook (Ill.) group divsn. Aegon U.S.A., 1990-94; exec. v.p. TPA divsn. Centennial Life Ins. Co., Merriam, Kans., 1994-95; v.p. managed care adminstrn. United Chambers HealthCare Corp., Naperville, Ill., 1995-96; v.p. bus. devel. Insurers Adminstrv. Corp., Phoenix, 1996—. Councilman Hobart, Ind. C. of C., 1981. Served as sgt. USMC, 1970-76. Fellow Life Office Mgmt. Inst., Acad. Life Underwriting; mem. Internat. Claims Assn. (assoc. life and health claims), Life Underwriting Edn. Com., Inst. Home Office Underwriters. Home: 22255 N 51st St Phoenix AZ 85054-7126 Office: Insurers Adminstrv Corp VP Bus Devel 2101 W Peoria Ave Phoenix AZ 85029-4925 E-mail: frankazusa@yahoo.com.

FUGLESONG, CHRISTER, astronaut; b. Stockholm, Mar. 18, 1957; arrived in U.S., 1996; m. Elisabeth Walldie; 3 children. MSc in Engring. Physics, Royal Inst. Tech., Sweden, 1981; PhD in Exptl. Particle Physics, U. Stockholm, 1987; PhD (hon.), Umea U., Sweden, 1999. Fellow European Rsch. Ctr. Particle Physics, Geneva, 1988—89; with Manne Siegbahn Inst. Physics, Stockholm, 1990—92; with astronaut corp. European Space Agy., Cologne, Germany, 1992—96; mission specialist NASA, Houston, 1996—. Instr. in math. Royal Inst. Tech., 1980—92; with Euromir 95 mission European Space Agy., 1993, mem. crew 2 Euromir 95 mission, 95. Avocations: sports, sailing, skiing, frisbee, reading. Office: Astronaut Office CB NASA Johnson Space Center Houston TX 77058

FUGUITT, GLENN VICTOR, sociologist; b. Clearwater, Fla., Feb. 27, 1928; s. Greene Victor and Surrilda Holliday Fuguitt.; m. Martha Tison, Aug. 31, 1951; children: Phyllis Gayle, Graham Victor. BA with honors, U. Fla., 1950, MA in Sociology, 1952; PhD in Sociology, U. Wis., 1956. Asst. prof. rural sociology U. Wis., Madison, 1956-61, assoc. prof. rural sociology, 1961-65, prof. rural sociology and sociology, 1965-93, prof. emeritus, 1993— Co-author: The Changing Rural Village, 1984, Rural and Small Town America, 1989. Mem.: Internat. Rural Sociol. Assn. (pres. 1976—80), Rural Sociol. Soc. (disting., pres. 1970—71), Population Assn. Am., Assn. Am. Geographers, Am. Sociol. Assn. Baptist. Home: 5062 La Crosse Ln Madison WI 53705 Office: 350 Agricultural Hall 1450 Linden Dr Madison WI 53706

FUHLRODT, NORMAN THEODORE, retired insurance executive; b. Wisner, Nebr., Apr. 24, 1910; s. Albert F. and Lena (Schafersman) F.; student Midland Coll., 1926-28; A.B., U. Nebr., 1930; M.A., U. Mich., 1936; m. Clarice W. Livermore, Aug. 23, 1933; 1 son, Douglas B. Tchr., athletic coach high schs., Sargent, Nebr., 1930-32, West Point, Nebr., 1932-35; with Central Life Assurance Co., Des Moines, 1936-74, pres., chief exec. officer, 1964-72, chmn. bd., chief exec. officer, 1972-74, also dir. Named Monroe St. Jour. Alumnus of Month, U. Mich. Grad Sch. Bus. Adminstrn. Gen. chmn. Greater Des Moines United campaign United Community Service, 1969-70. Former bd. dirs. Des Moines Center Sci. and Industry. Fellow Soc. Actuaries. Home: 760 E Bobier Dr # 116B Vista CA 92084-3806

FUHR, GRANT, hockey player; b. Spruce Grove, Alta., Canada, Sept. 28, 1962; m. Candice Fuhr, July 28, 1995; children: Kendyl, R. J., Rochelle, Janine. Player Edmonton Oilers, 1981-91, Toronto Maple Leafs, 1991-93; goalie Buffalo Sabers, 1993-95, St. Louis Blues, 1996-99, Calgary Flames, 1999—. Mem. NHL All-Star 2d Team, 1981—82, Sporting News All-Star Team, 1987—88, NHL All-Star Team, 1987—88, All-Star 1st Team, 1979—80, 1980—81, Stanley Cup Championship Team, 1984, 85, 87, 88, 90; player All-Star Game, 1982, 1984—86, 1988—89. Named Sporting News All-Star 2d Team, 1981—82, 1985—86, All-Star MVP, 1986; recipient Vezina Trophy (top NHL Goaltender), 1987—88, Stewart (Butch) Meml. Trophy, 1979—80, Top Goaltender Trophy, 1980—81. Office: Calgary Flames PO Box 1540 Station M Calgary AB Canada T2P3B9

FUHRER, LARRY, management consultant, management educator, finance company executive; b. Sept. 23, 1939; m. Linda Larsen; 1 child, Lance. AB, Taylor U., 1961; MS, No. Ill. U., 1966, MBA, 1993, Benedictine U., 1988, MS in Mgmt. and Orgnl. Behavior, 2001; MA, Wheaton Coll., 2001. Founder, chmn. Presdl. Svcs. Ltd., 1965—; founder, pres. Rockford Equities Ltd. and Rockford CyberShoppes.Com., 1981—, The L. Fuhrer Co. LLC, 1997—. Pubs. mgr. Campus Life Mag., 1962-65, editl. bd., 1966-70; pres. Killian Assocs. Inc., 1973-75; dir. Gamel Broadcasting Inc., WFXW, Geneva, Ill., 1985-88; joint venture ptnr. INEX Trading Co. Pte. Ltd., Singapore, 1987-89; corp. devel. The Lady D Group Inc., 1987-93; chmn. Mt. Vernon Properties Inc., 1990-91; adj. faculty bus. and info. sys. divsn. Waubonsee C.C., 1991—2003, mem. adj. faculty bus. and svcs. divsn. Coll. of DuPage, 1999—; adj. prof. mktg. Grad Sch. Mgmt., Coll. Bus., Lewis U., 1999—2003; ednl. dir. Halls of Ivy.net.; adj. faculty in mktg. and mgmt. Aurora U., 2000-02; instr. mgmt. Keller Grad. Sch. Mgmt., 2000—; program chmn. U. Phoenix, Chgo., Ill., campus coll. chmn. Exec. club dir. Youth for Christ, Marion, Ind., 1961-62, dir. devel., 1962; chmn. Washington Conf., 1980; mem. Cmty. Task Force for Econ. Devel. Coll. of DuPage, 1988-89; vol. Pathfinders Bible Studies, 1988—; chmn. Ill. Rsch. & Devel. Corridor Coun., 1988-89; founding chmn. Ill. Assn. of Corridor Coun., 1989-90; vice chmn., co-founder Dakota Ptnrshp., 1989-95; mem. mission & steward com. Presbytery of Chgo., 1990-95, congregational mission planning and strategy coun., 1993-95; pres. Internat. Christian Broadcasters, 1990-95; chmn., co-founder Naperville Conf.; bd. dirs. DuPage Prevention Ptnrshp., 1993; dir. Urban Min. San Marcos, 1997-98; chmn. adult edn. team Good Shepherd Luth. Ch., Naperville, Ill. Mem. Am. Soc. for Quality (dir. human devel. and leadership 1999, vice chmn. 2001). Home and Office: 2808 Willow Ridge Dr Naperville IL 60564-8938

FUHRMAN, GWENDOLYN SUE, secondary school educator; BS in Home Econs. Edn., Mansfield U., 1975, M, 1994. Cert. family and consumer scis. tchr., Pa. Famiy and consumer sci. tchr. Conrad Weiser Sch. Dist., Robesonia, Pa., 1975—. Chair Renaissance Program, Robesonia, 1996—; textiles cons. 4-H, Lebanon County, Pa., 1989-91; leader Girl Scouts U.S., Lebanon County, 1985-93; cub scout leader, mem. com. Boy Scouts Am., Lebanon County, 1994-98, asst. scoutmaster, 1998—; venture crew adv., 1999. Grantee NEA, 1992, State of Pa., 1998. Mem. Am. Assn. Familly and Consumer Sci., Pa. Assn. Family and Consumer Sci., Pa. State Edn. Assn. (External Comm. grant 1993, Intergroup award 1996, 98), Conrad Weiser Edn. Assn. Office: Conrad Weiser Sch ist 44 Big Spring Rd Robesonia PA 19551

FUHRMAN, RUSSELL L. career officer; b. Shawano, Wis. BA, West Point Acad., 1968; M in Chem. Engring., Pa. State U. Commd. 2d lt. U.S. Army, 1968, advanced through grades to maj. gen.; dir. civil works U.S. Army C.E., Washington, 1996-99, dep. chief engrs., dep. comdg. gen., 1999—. Office: Office of Army CE 20 Massachusetts Ave NW Washington DC 20314-0001

FUHRMANN, CHARLES JOHN, II, strategic and finance consultant; b. Seattle, Feb. 21, 1945; s. Carl I. and Darlene (Reynolds) F.; m. Eugenie A. Livanos, June 24, 1967 (div. 1982); children: Katharine Reynolds, Alexandra Livanos; m. Martha M. Harris, Oct. 17, 1987; children: Arianna Taylor, Charles J. III. AB summa cum laude, Harvard Coll., 1967, MBA with honors, 1969. Sr. v.p. White Weld & Co., Inc., N.Y.C., 1969-78; mng. dir. Merrill Lynch Capital Markets, N.Y.C., 1978-91; pres., CEO 50-Off Stores, Inc., 1996-97, Lot$Off Corp., 1997-99. Chmn. bd. dirs. Lot$Off Corp., 1997-99; chmn. Healthy Pl. Co., Inc., 1999—, Texace Ltd., 2001-2003. Vestry, St. James' Episcopal Ch., N.Y.C., 1979-84, treas. 1981-84; bd. trustees San Antonio Mus. Art, 1994-97, San Antonio Mus. Assn., 1993-95, The Witte Mus., 1994—, San Antonio Pub. Libr. Found., 1995-99; bd. dirs. The Sunshine Cottage, 1993-97, Children's Rehab. Ctr., 1996-99, Charity Ball Assn., 2003—. Mem. River Club (N.Y.C.), Delphic Club (Cambridge, Mass.), Country and Yacht Clubs (Prout's Neck, Maine), San Antonio Country Club, Argyle Club, Majestic Club (chmn. 1994-96), Order of the Alamo. Home: 110 Wyckham Rise San Antonio TX 78209 Office: 402 W Nueva San Antonio TX 78207 E-mail: cj2mhf@swbell.net.

FUHS, TERRY LYNN, emergency room nurse, educator; b. Gallup, N.Mex., Aug. 21, 1957; d. Louie Rube and Wilda (Boardman) Orr; m. Loren Bruce Fuhs, Dec. 11, 1981; children: Melissa Marincell, Misty Fuhs. ADN, U. N.Mex., Gallup, 1979; BSN, U. N.Mex., 1990. Cert. emergency nurse, TNCC-I, ENPC-I, ACLS-I, PALS-I; RN, N.Mex. Med./surg. staff/chg. nurse Rehoboth McKinley Christian Hosp., Gallup, 1979-83, chg. nurse emergency dept., 1983—, critical care educator, 1992—. Affiliate faculty PALS/ACLS, N.Mex. chpt. Am. Heart Assn., 1991—, mem. emergency cardiac care com., 1993—, mem. PALS nat. faculty, 1995-97. Presenter/coord. Emergency Nurses Cancel Alcohol Related Emergencies, Gallup, 1994—, Safe Sitter Program, Gallup, 1994—. Recipient Meritorious award N.Mex. Hosp. Assn., 1994, Family Educator of Yr. award, 1998. Mem.: ANA, Emergency Nurses Assn. (N.Mex. chpt. trauma com. chmn. 1994—). Democrat. Methodist. Avocations: reading, movies, travel. Home: 1117 Ridgecrest Ave Gallup NM 87301-4980 Office: Rehoboth McKinley Hosp 1901 Redrock Dr Gallup NM 87301-5683 E-mail: tfuhs@rmchcs.org.

FUJIKAWA, DENSON GEN, neurologist, researcher; b. Denson, Ark., Oct. 23, 1942; s. Yoshihiko Fred and Alice May (Aoki) F.; m. Christine Margaret Nelson, Dec. 2, 1964 (div. 1967); m. Lilla Rose Smithline, Dec. 12, 1976 (div. 1995); m. Bonita Weavingearth, May 24, 1997. AB magna cum laude, Harvard U., 1964; MD, U. So. Calif., 1969. Diplomate Am. Bd. of Psychiatry and Neurology. Intern surgery Columbia Presbyn. Med. Ctr., N.Y.C., 1969-70, resident in surgery, 1970-71; resident in neurosurgery UCLA Med. Ctr., 1971-73; resident in neurology Harbor UCLA Med. Ctr., Torrance, 1978-81; rsch. fellow VA Med. Ctr., Sepulveda, Calif., 1981-83, dir. EEG & evoked potentials lab. dir., 1983—2000. Head Seizure Clinic, Sepulveda, 1983—; adj. instr. neurology UCLA Sch. Medicine, 1981-83; asst. adj. prof. neurology, 1983-90, assoc. adj. prof. neurology, 1990-96, adj. prof. neurology, 1996—. Contbr. articles to profl. jours. Grantee VA, 1984-85, 87—, Epilepsy Found. Am., 1985-87, biomed. research support grantee NIH, 1986-87, Am. Heart Assn. We. States Affiliate, 1998-2003. Fellow Am. Acad. Neurology; mem. Soc. for Neurosci., Internat. Soc. Cerebral Blood Flow and Metabolism, Am. Neurol. Assn., Am. Epilepsy Soc., Am. Soc. for Neurochemistry, Harvard Club of So. Calif. (L.A.). Office: Neurology Service (127) VA Greater Los Angeles Healthcare Sys 16111 Plummer St Sepulveda CA 91343

FUJIMOTO, JUNICHIRO, pathologist; b. Osaka, Japan, May 25, 1951; MD in Medicine, Gifu (Japan) U., 1977; PhD in Medicine, Sapporo U., Hokkaido, Japan, 1984. Sr. investigator dept. pathology Nat. Children's Med. Rsch. Ctr., Tokyo, 1985-89, dir. dept. pathology, 1989—2002; dir. dept. devel. biology Nat. Rsch. Inst. Child Health Devel., 2002—. Avocation: driving. Office: Nat Rsch Inst Child Health Devel 3-35-31 Taishido Setagaya Tokyo 154-8567 Japan Fax: 81-3-3487-9669. E-mail: jfujimoto@nch.go.jp.

FUJINAMI, ROBERT SHIN, neurology educator; b. Salt Lake City, Dec. 8, 1949; BA, U. Utah, 1972; PhD, Northwestern U., Chgo., 1977. Instr. microbiology and immunology Northwestern U., Chgo., 1973-76; rsch. fellow immunopathology Scripps Clinic and Rsch. Found., La Jolla, Calif., 1977-80, rsch. assoc. immunopathology, 1980-81, asst. mem., asst. prof. dept. immunology, 1981-85, vis. investigator dept. immunology, 1985-89; vis. investigator dept. neuropharmacology divsn. virology Scripps Rsch. Inst. (formerly Scripps Clinic and Rsch. Found.), La Jolla, 1989-90; rsch. immunopathologist dept. pathology U. Calif., San Diego, 1980-82, assoc. prof. pathology, 1985-90; prof. neurology U. Utah, Salt Lake City, 1990—, adj. prof. dept. pathology divsn. cell biology and immunology, 1991—. Mem. Weber immunology adv. com., dept. pathology U. Utah, Salt Lake City, 1991—, mem. neurosci. steering com., 1992-96, mem. biosafety com., 1992-96, chmn., 1994-96, chmn. safety com., dept. neurology, 1993—, chmn. promotion, retention and tenure com., 1993-96, mem. univ. promotions and tenure adv. com., 1995-98, chair oversight com. Fluorescence Activated Cell Sorter (FACS) Sch. Medicine, 1996-99, mem. univ. rsch. com., 1999—, disting. rsch. award subcom., 1999—, senate task force on RPT procedures, 1999—, adv. com. core facilities Huntsman Cancer Inst., 1999—, dir. grad. studies pathology PhD program, 1999—, chmn. tenured faculty rev. com., dept. neurology, 1999—. Contbr. chpts. to books, 110 articles to profl. jours. Recipient New Investigator award NIH, 1981-83; NIH scholar, 1989-96. Fellow AAAS; mem. Nat. Multiple Sclerosis Soc. (bd. dirs. Utah chpt. 1992-99—, Hary M. Weaver Neurosci. award 1982-86). Office: U Utah Dept Neurology 30 N 1900 E Salt Lake City UT 84132-0001

FUJIOKA-ITO, NORIKO, language educator; d. Keizo and Harue (Sawai) Fujioka; m. Hiroshi Ito, Apr. 21, 1965. BA, Chuo U., Tokyo, 1988; MA, Ohio State U., Columbus, 1993, PhD, 2000. Cert. tchr. fgn. lang. Ministry of Edn., Japan, libr. Ministry of Edn., Japan, sch. libr. Ministry of Edn., Japan. Part-time lectr. NC State U., Raleigh, 1989—90; instr. Japan Ctr., NC State U., Raleigh, NC, 1989—90; adj. instr. U. of Cin., Cincinnati, Ohio, 1996—97; head of jr. h.s. divsn. Japanese Lang. Sch. of Greater Cin., Highland Heights, Ky., 1999—2000; adj. asst. prof. U. Cin., Ohio, 1997—. Vis. instr. Duke U., Durham, NC, 1989—90. Contbr. articles to profl.jours. Recipient Scholarship, Centers for Internat. Bus. Edn. and Rsch., 2002; grantee Faculty Devel. Grant, Devel. Coun., U. of Cin., 2002, 1998, Japanese Language Tchg. Materials Grant, Japan Found. & Lang. Ctr., 2001, 1999, 1998, 1997, NE Asia Coun. Assn. for Asian Studies/Japan-US Friendship Commn., 1997. Mem.: AAUP, Assn. of Teachers of Japanese, Assn. for Asian Studies, Am. Coun. Tchg. of Fgn. Languages, Am. Ednl. Rsch. Assn., Am. Assn. for Applied Linguistics. Avocations: computer, reading, swimming, travel, ice skating. Office: Univ Cin 719A Old Chemistry Cincinnati OH 45221-0372 Office Fax: 513-556-1991. Personal E-mail: norikofujioka1@aol.com. E-mail: noriko.fujioka@uc.edu.

FUJISHIRO, KATAKAZU KENNETH, retired urban/regional planner, engineer; b. Cambridge, Mass., Sept. 25, 1932; s. Shinji and Yasu (Matsudaira) Fujishiro; m. Jane Foster Eubanks, Nov. 22, 1973 (dec. 1991); 1 child, Joni; m. Daisy E. Semling, Sept. 29, 2001. BSCE, U. S.C., 1964; postgrad., Rensselaer Poly. Inst., 1969, Ga. Inst. Tech., 1970, Mich. Tech. U., 1972, Naval War Coll., 1996-97. Casualty underwriter Am. Internat. Underwriters Corp., Tokyo and N.Y.C., 1948-57; engr./expeditor Charles J. Craig Constrn. Co., Columbia, S.C., 1958-65; planner/engr. Lyles Bissett Carlisle and Wolff, Columbia, 1965-73; environ. planner, dir. Berkeley-Charleston (S.C.)-Dorchester Regional Planning Coun. and Charleston County Planning Bd., 1973-76; chief water pollution control, prin. planner Met. Washington Coun. Govts., 1976-79; sr. program engr. Advanced Tech., Inc., McLean, Va., 1979-83; gen. engr. region 3 Fed. Emergency Mgmt. Agy., Phila., 1983-84; civil engr. USCG Hdqrs., Washington, 1984-98. Course dir. architects and engrs. profl. devel. program Def. Civil Preparedness Agy., 1967-73; evening div. instr. Midlands Tech. Coll., Columbia, 1965, 66. Contbr. articles to profl. jours. Served with 101st Airborne Inf. U.S. Army, 1954-56. Recipient ASCE award U. S.C., 1963; Mich. Tech. U. fellow, 1972. Fellow Soc. Am. Mil. Engrs.; mem. Am. Planning Assn. (svc. award Nat. Capitol area chpt. 1979), Am. Inst. Cert. Planners, Asian Pacific Am. Fed. Fgn. Affairs Coun. (vice-chair 1995-99). Home: #821 19375 Cypress Ridge Terr Lansdowne VA 20176 E-mail: kfujishiro@worldnet.att.net.

FUJITA, JAMES HIROSHI, history educator; b. Honolulu, July 24, 1958; s. George Hideo and Teruko (Miyano) F. BA, U. Hawaii, 1980, MA, 1983. Grad. asst. U. Hawaii at Manoa, Honolulu, 1980-85, lectr. history, 1986—, Kapiolani C.C., Honolulu, 1987-97; adj. staff Hawaii Pacific U., Honolulu, 1998—. Lectr. Elderhostel Program, Honolulu, 1992, Leeward C.C., 1997—; adj. staff Chaminade U., Honolulu, 1998—. Mem. NEA, World History Assn., U. Hawaii Profl. Assembly, Phi Alpha Theta. Office: Hawaii Pacific U 1188 Fort Street Mall Honolulu HI 96813-2713

FUJITA, SEI, political economist, educator; b. Kyoto, Mar. 20, 1928; s. Keizo and Hisa (Matsuzaki) F.; m. Hiroko Murotani, Mar. 20, 1962; 1 child, Reo. MS in Sociology, Hitotsubashi U., Tokyo, 1957, PhD in Sociology, 1961. Instr. in econs. Osaka (Japan) City U., 1963-66, assoc. prof. econs., 1966-75, prof. econs., 1975-91, prof. emeritus, 1991—; prof. econs. Osaka U. Econs. and the Law, Yao, Japan, 1991—. Co-dir. Assn. Ann. scientific Exch. with Scholars of the Far-East Region of the Russian Fedn., Osaka, 1984—95; dean faculty of econs. Osaka City U., 1981—82, Osaka U. Econs. and the Law, 1993—97, pres., 2001—. Author: Socialist Economy and the Law of Value, (in Japanese) 1967, Soviet Commodity Production: Its Semi-permanent Continuation, (in Japanese) 1991, The Soviet Economy as a Social Experiment: Lessons from the 20th Century, 1999, Fundamental Reform of the Credit System in Japanese Universities: A Proposal (in Japenese), 2000; contbr. articles to profl. jours. Chmn. Movement Against Comml. Advt. through Loudspkr. in the Mcpl. Subway, Osaka, 1976-77. Recipient 3d Niigata prize, Prefectural Office of Niigata, Japan, 1997. Mem. Japan Assn. Comparative Econ. Studies (pres. 1993-95), Assn. Sci. of Thought, Assn. Evolutionary Econs., Internat. Ho. of Japan, Inc., Amnesty Internat., Japan Braille Libr. Buddhist. Avocations: Go, gardening, art appreciation. Home: 4-5-11 Mukogaoka Uenoshiba Sakai 593-8303 Japan Fax: 072-278-0146. E-mail: fujitash@muc.biglobe.ne.jp.

FUJITANI, MARTIN TOMIO, software engineer; b. Sanger, Calif., May 3, 1968; s. Matsuo and Hasuko Fujitani; m. Augustina Nguyen; children: Amber, Natasha, Olivia. BS in Indsl. and Sys. Engring., U. So. Calif., 1990. Sec. Kelly Svcs., Inc., Sacramento, 1987; receptionist Coudert Bros., L.A., 1988; rsch. asst. U. So. Calif., L.A., 1988-89; math. aide Navy Pers. Rsch. and Devel. Ctr., San Diego, 1989; quality assurance test technician Retix, Santa Monica, Calif., 1989-90; software engr. Quality Med. Adjudication, Inc., Rancho Cordova, Calif., 1990-92; test engr. Worldtalk Corp., Los Gatos, Calif., 1993-94; quality engr. Lotus Devel. Corp., Mountain View, Calif., 1994-95, Gen. Magic, Sunnyvale, Calif., 1995-96; software engr. Sun Microsys. Inc., Palo Alto, Calif., 1996-99, Cisco Sys. Inc., San Jose, Calif., 1999—. Assemblyman Am. Legion Calif. Boys State, 1985. Recipient Service Above Self award East Sacramento Rotary, 1986. Mem. Gen. Alumni Assn. U. So. Calif. (life). Avocations: dancing mambo, watching ballet, listening to jazz music, bicycling, windsurfing, cooking.

FUJITO, WAYNE TAKESHI, international business company executive; b. Stockton, Calif., Nov. 9, 1938; BA, San Jose State U., 1961; MS, U. So. Calif., 1982. Commd. 2d lt. U.S. Army, 1961, advanced through grades to col., U.S. Army attache to Japan, 1983-87, chief of staff Strategic Def. Command, 1988-90, ret., 1990; v.p. Internat. Tech. & Trade Assocs., Washington, 1990-93, sr. v.p., 1994-95, exec. v.p., 1995—, pres., 2000—02; pres. internat. divsn. Decisive Analytics Corp., Arlington, Va., 2002—. Vol. advisor CARE Internat., Atlanta, 1993—. Decorated Legion of Merit with oak leaf cluster, Bronze Star, Imperial Order of Scared Treasure, Govt. of Japan. Mem. Army and Air Force Mut. Aid Assn. (bd. dirs. 1994—), Asia Soc., Japan-Am. Soc. of Washington, D.C., Armed Forces Commn. and Electronics Assn., Nat. Def. Indsl. Assn. Avocations: skiing, reading, stock market, internet. Home: 1217 Delta Glen Ct Vienna VA 22182-1321 Office: Decisive Analytics Corp 1213 Jefferson Davis Hwy Arlington VA 22202

FUJIWARA, CHRIS, writer; Bassist Cul de Sac, Cambridge, Mass., 1992—97; contbg. editor Hermenaut, Jamaica Plain, 1997—. Vis. prof. film studies program Yale U., New Haven, 2001; adj. prof. dept. visual and media arts Emerson Coll., Boston, 2001—. Author: Jacques Tourneur: The Cinema of Nightfall; contbr. articles to profl. jours. Mem.: AAUP, Boston Soc. Film Critics. Home: 88 Boston St Somerville MA 02143 Personal E-mail: chris.fujiwara@verizon.net.

FUJIWARA, HIDEJI, chemist, researcher; b. Tamano, Okayama, Japan, Nov. 19, 1943; s. Motoyoshi and Sumiko Fujiwara; m. Mieko Ogawa, Apr. 29, 1978; children: Kenichiro, Mikiko Kay. BS, Sci. U. Tokyo, 1967; MS, Stevens Inst. Tech., 1969, PhD, 1974. Postdoctoral fellow Stevens Inst. Tech., 1974-75, rsch. scientist, 1975-77; rschr. Exxon br. Tao Nenryo Kogyo KK, Saitam, Japan, 1962-67; sr. rsch. chemist (specialist) Monsanto Co., St. Louis, 1977-87, assoc., full sci. fellow, 1987-2000; sci. fellow Pharmacia Co., Chesterfield, Mo., 2000—. Contbr. articles to sci. jours., includinfg Jour. Agrl. Food Chemistry, Chem. and Engring. News. Trustee Bethany Bapt. Ch., 1990—. Schering postdoctoral fellow Stevens Inst. Tech., 1975-76. Em. Am. Chem. Soc., Am. Soc. for Mass Spectrometry, N.Y. Acad. Scis., St. Louis Japan Soc., Toastmasters (treas. Life Scis. chpt. 1999-2000), Sigma Xi. Home: 1247 Ticonderoga Dr Chesterfield MO 63017-2435 Office: Pharmacia Co 700 Chesterfield Pky Chesterfield MO 63017 Fax: 636-737-7099. E-mail: hideji.fujiwara@pharmacia.com.

FUJIWARA, MITSUKO, chemist, researcher, chemist, educator; b. Okayama, Japan, Dec. 7, 1966; came to U.S., 1979; d. Akira and Masako (Kitao) F. BA summa cum laude, Cornell U., 1988; PhD, Calif. Inst. Tech., 1993. Lab. technician Cornell Med. Coll., N.Y.C., summer 1986, 87, Bayer, A.G., Leuerkusen, Germany, summer 1988; undergrad. rsch. asst. Cornell U., Ithaca, N.Y., 1986 88; grad. rsch. asst. Calif. Inst. Tech., Pasadena, 1989-93, grad. tchg. asst., 1989-91, grad. lab. asst., 1992-93; prin. rsch. chemist Unilever Rsch., Edgewater, NJ, 1993-95, rsch. scientist, 1995-96; instr. Parkland Coll., Champaign, Ill., 1997—; acad. hourly U. Ill, Urbana, 1998—. Cons. Cryopharm Corp., Pasadena, 1990-92. Author abstracts in field; contbr. article to profl. jour.; patentee in field. Mem. Am. Chem. Soc., Phi Beta Kappa, Phi Kappa Phi. Achievements include development of antibacterial skin cleansing formulations. Home: 2310 E Shurts Cir Urbana IL 61801-6748

FUJIYAMA, WALLACE SACHIO, lawyer; b. Honolulu, Aug. 8, 1925; s. George Susumu and Cornelia (Matsumoto) F.; m. Mildred Hatsue Morita, Jan. 24, 1959; children— Rodney Michio, Susan Misao, Keith Susumu. B.A., U. Hawaii, 1950; J.D., U. Cin., 1953. Bar: Hawaii 1954. Dep. atty. gen. State of Hawaii, Honolulu, 1954-56, examiner employment relations bd., 1956-59; ptnr. Chuck & Fujiyama, 1959-74; pres. Fujiyama, Duffy & Fujiyama, Honolulu, 1974— ; dir. 1st Hawaiian Bank; chmn. adv. bd. Duty Free Shoppers Ltd., 1982—, lectr. William S. Richard Sch. Law, Honolulu, 1981— . Mem. Hawaii Statehood Commn., Honolulu, 1957-59; regent U. Hawaii, 1974-82; bd. dirs. Honolulu Symphony, 1983—, Hawaii Imin Centennial Corp., 1983— ; mem. Palama Settlement Exec. Campaign Com., 1981—, Stadium Authority, 1982— . Served to pvt. U.S. Army, 1944-46. Mem. Hawaii Bar Assn. (bd. bar examiners 1962-82, pres. 1973, jud. appointments com. 1975), ABA mem. ho. of dels. 1973, active com. mem.), Hawaii Trial Lawyers Assn. (pres. 1971-79), Assn. Trial Lawyers Am., Calif. Trial Lawyers Assn., Fedn. Ins. Counsel, Def. Research Inst., Am. Judicature Soc., Trial Attys. Am., Am. Bd. Trial Advocates (pres. Hawaii chpt. 1980—), Am. Inn of Ct. (bencher 1982—), Hastings Ctr. Trial and Appellate Advocacy (bd. dirs. 1977—), Order of Coif, Phi Alpha Delta. Clubs: Honolulu Internat. Country (dir., gen. counsel), Waialae Country, Plaza (bd. dirs. 1985—). Home: 1803 Laukahi St Honolulu HI 96821-1333 Office: Fujiyama Duffy & Fujiyama 1001 Bishop St 2700 Pauahi Tower Honolulu HI 96813

FUKASAWA, KENJI, medical researcher; s. Fukuyo and Isamu Fukasawa. PhD, Columbia U., New York City, 1987—91. Rsch. scientist Nat. Cancer Inst., Frederick, Md., 1991—97. Fellow, Nat. Cancer Inst., 2001—02; Ruth Lyon Cancer Rsch. Found., 1998. Office: U Cin 3125 Eden Ave PO Box 670521 Cincinnati OH 45267-0521 Office Fax: 513-558-4454. E-mail: kenji.fukasawa@uc.edu.

FUKASAWA, NATSUKI, music educator; d. Yukio and Takako Fukasawa; m. Richard Cionco, Sept. 5, 1998. MusB, Juilliard Sch., N.Y., 1992, MusM, 1994. Cert. music Prague Acad. of Music, Czech Republic, 1995. Jalina Piano Trio, Denmark, 1995—; pvt. music tchr., 1998—. Recipient 1st Prize, Trapani Internat. Music Competition, Italy, 1999, 2nd Prize, Osaka Internat. Chamber Music Competition, Japan, 2002; scholar Fulbright Scholarship, Fulbright Commn., 1994—95. Mem.: Calif. Assn. of Profl. Music Tchrs., Music Tchrs. Assn. of Calif.

FUKATSU, TANEFUSA, retired Chinese classics educator; b. Toyota, Aichi, Japan, Apr. 23, 1923; s. Kingo and Shizu (Noba) F.; m. Michiko Kato, Jan. 17, 1954 (dec. 1981); children: Tomonao, Arikata. BA, Tokyo U., 1951. Tchr. Chinese classics Musashi High Sch., Tokyo, 1957-89; asst. prof. Chinese classics Musashi U., Tokyo, 1971-74, prof. Chinese classics, 1974-85; retired, 1989—. Lectr. Chinese classics Nisho-Gakusha U., Tokyo, 1967-93, guest prof., 1993—. Author: Juzi Tongbian Jingdianshiwen, 1978, Lunyu Xidu, 1990, Laozi Xidu, 1994, Thought and Life of the Ancient Chinese-Mirror-, 1996, Japanese Culture and Chinese Culture-White Chrysanthemum and Yellow Chrysanthemum, 1997, Studies on the Latent Thought in Chinese Characters and Poetry, 1997, Chinese Thought and Culture, 1998, Studies of the Book of Laozi, 1999, Thought and Life of the Ancient Chinese-Cock-, 1999, Thought and Life of the Ancient Chinese—The Source and Course of the Thought of "The Book of Laozi", 2000. Mem. Nippon-Chugoku-Gakkai, Shibunkai (dir. 1990-93, councilor 1993—). Home: 86-1-501 Konya-Cho Saiwai-Ku Kawasaki-Shi Kanagawa-Ken 212-0026 Japan

FUKS, BORIS BORISOVICH, immunologist, researcher; b. Tomsk, Russia, Oct. 18, 1926; came to U.S., 1996; s. Boris Ilyich and Zinaida Lvovna Fuks; m. Irina Vitalyevna Konstantinova, Sept. 9, 1949 (dec. Aug. 1998); 1 child, Alexandr Borisovich Konstantinov; m. Susanna E. Staroselsky. MD, Med. Inst., Novosibirsk, Russia, 1948; PhD, Med. Inst., Tomsk, 1951, DSc, 1960. Asst. for chair of pathology Inst. Postgrad. Tng., Novokuznetsk, Russia, 1951-53; head of lab. of cytochemistry Rsch. Inst. Traumatology and Orthopaedics, Novosibirsk, 1953-58; head of lab. of histochemistry Inst. Exptl. Biology/Medicine Siberian br. USSR Acad. Sci., Academishen Town, 1958-63; prof. for chair med. biology Siberian U., Novosibirsk, 1960-63; head dept. exptl. biology Inst. Cytology and Genetics Siberian br. USSR Acad. Sci., Novosibirsk, 1962-64; head lab. of cellular immunology and biotech. Rsch. Inst. Human Morphology, Russian Acad. Med. Sci., Moscow, 1964-96; v.p. N-DIA, Inc., Plainsboro, N.J., 1991—; pres. Calif. Rsch. LLC, Mountain View, Calif., 1996-98. Author: (books) The Immune System in Space and Other Extreme Conditions, 1991, Glycoconjugates as Modifiers of Antitumor Immunity, 1991; contbr. articles and monographs to profl. jours.; patentee in field. Named Honored Scientist of Russia, Pres. of Russia, 1994. Mem. Nat. Soc. Immunologists (head immunol. br., mem. presidium). Achievements include research in reduction of human T-cells and NK activity and alteration of lymphokine production in outer space; phenomenon of tumor cell toxicity for lymphocytes and NK; conception: escape of tumor cells out of immune control. Home: Apt 335 1 Kulas Ln Parlin NJ 08859 E-mail: foux2000@aol.com.

FUKUI, GEORGE MASAAKI, microbiology consultant; b. San Francisco, May 25, 1921; s. Tsunejiro and Kimiko (Wada) F.; m. Yuri Lillyn Kenmotsu, Sept. 23, 1944; children: Lisa Jo, Tenley Kay. BS, U. Conn., 1945, MS, 1948; PhD, Cornell U., 1952. Instr. bacteriology U. Conn., Storrs, 1948-49; lab. instr. Cornell U., Ithaca, N.Y., 1949-52, mem. adv. bd. microbiology dept., 1985-88; asst. br. chief U.S. Army, Frederick, Md., 1952-60; dir. microbiology and

immunology Wallace Labs., Cranbury, N.J., 1960-77, Hazelton Labs., Vienna, Va., 1977-78; dir. microbiology Abbott Labs., North Chicago, Ill., 1978-79, rsch. microbiologist Irving, Tex., 1979-86; pres. Internat. Cons. in Microbiology, Irving, 1986—. Contbr. articles to sci. jours. Asst. scoutmaster troop 712, Boy Scouts Am., Topaz, Utah, 1943; recruiter Cornell U., Princeton, N.J., 1964-69. With U.S. Army, 1945-46. Recipient commendation Rsch. Soc. Am., 1959, medal for sci. achievement Hiroshima (Japan) U., 1973, Gran Amigo de Mex. commendation Nat. U. Mex., 1982, commendation Tohoku U., Sendai, Japan, 1983. Fellow Am. Acad. Microbiology (charter, diplomate); mem. Am. Soc. for Microbiology, Rutgers Soc. Japan (hon.), Phi Beta Kappa, Sigma Xi. Republican. Episcopalian. Achievements include patents for Non-Allergenic Penicillin; Phenoxypropanediols on Reduction of Penicillin Allergy; Synthetic Penicillin, Non-Allergenic; Suppression of Histamine Release; Salicylates for Quantification of Antibiotics in Sera. E:mail. Home and Office: 3813 E Greenhills Ct Irving TX 75038-4819 E-mail: g.fukui@verizon.net.

FUKUI, HATSUAKI, electrical engineer, art historian; b. Yokohama, Japan, Dec. 14, 1927; came to U.S., 1962, naturalized, 1973; s. Ushinosuke and Yoshi (Saito) F.; m. Atsuko Inamoto, Apr. 1, 1954 (dec. 1973); children: Mayumi, Naoki; m. Kiku Kato, Dec. 12, 1975. Diploma, Miyakojima Tech. Coll. (now Osaka City U.), 1949; BS, Sci. U. Tokyo; D.Eng., Osaka U., 1961. Rsch. assoc. Osaka City U., 1949-54; engr. Shimada Phys. and Chem. Indsl. Co., Tokyo, 1954-55; sr. engr. to mgr. semi-condr. divsn. Sony Corp. (formerly Tokyo Tsushin Kogyo KK), Tokyo, 1955-61; mgr. engring. div. Sony Corp., 1961-62; mem. tech. staff Bell Telephone Labs., Murray Hill, N.J., 1962-69, supr., 1969-73; v.p. Sony Corp. Am., N.Y.C., 1973; asst. to chmn. Sony Corp., Tokyo, 1973; staff mem. Bell Labs., Murray Hill, N.J., 1973-81, supr., 1981-83, Lucent Techs. (formerly AT&T Bell Labs.), 1984-89. Lectr. Tokyo Met. U. (part-time), 1962 Author: Esaki Diodes, 1963, Solid-State FM Receivers, 1968; contbr. to: Semiconductors Handbook, 1963, GaAs FET Principles and Technologies, 1982; editor: Low-Noise Microwave Transistors and Amplifiers, 1981; contbr. articles to profl. jours.; patentee in field. Fellow IEEE (life; standardization com. 1970-82, edit. bd. IEEE Transactions on Microwave Theory and Techniques 1980-90, com. on U.S. competitiveness 1988-90); mem. Inst. Electronics, Info. and Comm. Engrs. Japan (Inada award 1959), IEEE Comms. Soc., IEEE Electron Devices Soc., IEEE Lasers and Electro-Optics Soc., IEEE Microwave Theory and Techniques Soc. (Microwave prize 1980, Pioneer award 1990), Electromagnetics Acad., Japan Soc. Applied Physics, Inst. TV Engrs. Japan (tech. steering com. 1973-74), Medieval Acad. Am., Assn. Art History, Am. Assn. Museums, Gakushikai, Internat. House Japan. Home: 53 Drum Hill Dr Summit NJ 07901-3141 also: 1-21-16-802 Nakane Meguro Tokyo 152-0031 Japan

FUKUI, YOSHIO, biology educator; b. Shinagawa, Tokyo, Japan, Jan. 4, 1942; came to U.S., 1985; s. Shizuo and Momoko Fukui; m. Yumiko Fukui, Mar. 12, 1978; children: Ibuki, Maya. BA, Internat. Christian U., 1966; MS, Osaka (Japan) U., 1969, PhD, 1972. Rsch. assoc. prof. Osaka U., 1972-74, asst. prof., 1974-77; rsch. assoc. Princeton (N.J.) U., 1977-78; assoc. prof. Osaka U., 1978-85; vis. assoc. prof. Northwestern U., Chgo., 1985-89, assoc. prof. cell, molecular, structural biology (tenured), 1989—. Prof. cell molecular biology, Yamada exch. scientist Yamada Sci. Found., Osaka, 1978; Yoshida exch. visitor Yoshida Chem. Found., Tokyo, 1983. Contbr. articles to profl. jours. including Nature, Proc. Nat. Acad. Sci. Jour. Cell Biology, Internat. Rev. Cytology, others. Recipient Matsunaga Rsch. award Matsunaga Meml. Found., Tokyo, 1976; rsch. grantee NIH, 1988—. Mem. Cooperation of Marine Biol. Lab. (Woods Hole, Mass.), Am. Soc. for Cell Biology, Soc. Advancement of Sci., N.Y. Acad. Scis. (elected), Japan Soc. for Cell Biologist (Tokyo). Office: Northwestern Med Sch 303 E Chicago Ave Chicago IL 60611-3008 E-mail: y-fukui@northwestern.edu.

FUKUMA, TOSHIKATSU, investment banking executive; CFO Mitsui & Co., Tokyo. Mem. Internat. Acctg. Stds. Com., 2000. Office: Mitsui & Co 12-1 Ohtemachi Chiyoda-ku Tokyo 100 0004 Japan

FUKUMOTO, LESLIE SATSUKI, lawyer; b. L.A., Mar. 10, 1955; parents: Robert Fukumoto and Florence Teruko Kodama Kuroda. BA, U. Hawaii, 1977; JD, William S. Richard Sch. Law, 1980. Bar: Hawaii 1980, U.S. Dist. Ct. Hawaii 1980, U.S. Ct. Appeals (9th cir.) 1981. Dep. pub. defender State of Hawaii, Honolulu, 1980-81; assoc. Pyun, Kim & Okimoto, Honolulu, 1981-83; ptnr. Pyun, Okimoto & Fukumoto, Honolulu, 1983-84; sole practice Honolulu, 1984-85; ptnr. Fukumoto & Wong, Honolulu, 1985-93, Tanaka & Fukumoto, Honolulu, 1993-94; prin. Fukumoto Law Corp., Honolulu, 1994—. Bd. dirs. Ichiryo Enterprises, Inc., Honolulu. Assoc. editor U. Hawaii Law Rev., 1979-80. Mem. ATLA, Honolulu Club. Office: 841 Bishop St Ste 1711 Honolulu HI 96813-3924 E-mail: fukulaw@mail.com.

FUKUNAGA, CAROL A. state legislator, lawyer; b. Dec. 12, 1947; BA, JD, U. Hawaii. Pvt. practice, Honolulu; mem. Hawaii Ho. of Reps., Honolulu, 1978-82, 86-92, Hawaii Senate, Dist. 12, Honolulu, 1992—; co-chair ways and means com., mem. health and human svcs. Hawaii Senate, Honolulu, mem. labor and environment com. Exec. officer Office of the Lt. Gov., Honolulu, 1982-86; hearings officer Hawaii Pub. Employees Rels. Bd.; mem. coord. com. Hawaii Dem. Action, 1985; platform co-chair State Dem. Conv., 1984; bd. dirs. Hawaiian Air; mem. Japanese Am. Citizens League, Sex Abuse Treatment Ctr. Mem. Hawaii Women Lawyers. Democrat. Office: State Capitol 415 S Beretania St Rm 210 Honolulu HI 96813-2407*

FUKUSHIMA, BARBARA NAOMI, financial advisor; b. Honolulu, Apr. 5, 1948; d. Harry Kazuo and Misayo (Kawasaki) Murakoshi; m. Dennis Hiroshi Jr. (div. 2001). BA with high honors, U. Hawaii, 1970; postgrad., Oreg. State U., 1971, 73, U. Oreg., 1972. Intern Coopers & Lybrand, Honolulu, 1974; auditor Haskins & Sells, Kahului, Hawaii, 1974-77; pres. Book Doors, Inc., Pukalani, Hawaii, 1977-97, Barbara N. Fukushima CPA, Inc., Wailuku, Hawaii, 1979-86, sec. treas. Target Pest Control, Inc., 1979-96; internal auditor, acct. Maui Land & Pineapple Co., Inc., Kahului, Hawaii, 1977-80; auditor Hyatt Regency, Maui, Hawaii, 1980-81; ptnr. D & B Internat., Pukalani, Hawaii, 1980-91; instr. Maui C.C., 1982-85; fin. advisor Merrill Lynch, Pierce, Fenner & Smith, Inc., 1986—. Recipient Phi Beta Kappa Book award, 1969. Mem.: AICPA, Hawaii Soc. CPAs, C. of C. of Hawaii, Phi Beta Kappa. Christian. Home: 1088 Bishop St Apt 1117 Honolulu HI 96813-3134 Office: 1001 Bishop St PH Honolulu HI 96813-3429 E-mail: barbnf@yahoo.com.

FUKUSHIMA, KIYOHIKO, economist; b. Nishinomiya, Hyogoken, Japan, Dec. 6, 1944; s. Tohta and Yasuko Fukushima; m. Chizuko Yamauchi, Nov. 2, 1970; children: Izumi, Nobuhiko. BA in Econs., Hitotsubashi U., Tokyo, 1967, MA, 1969. Econ. corr. Mainichi Shinbun, Tokyo, 1969-77; sr. economist Nomura Rsch. Inst., Tokyo, 1978-80; guest scholar Brookings Instn., Washington, 1980-81; sr. economist Nomura Rsch. Inst., N.Y.C., 1981-83, gen. mgr. Washington, 1983-86, dep. dir. econ. rsch. Tokyo, 1986-89, dir. policy rsch. dept., 1989-92, gen. mgr., sr. economist, 1992-94, chief economist, 1996—, chief economist Tokyo hdqrs., 2002—; pres. Nomura Rsch. Inst. Europe, Ltd., 1999—2002; professorial lectr. sch. advanced internat. studies Johns Hopkins U., Washington, 1994-96. Vis. fellow Princeton (N.J.) U., 1976-77. Author: Regionalism and Foreign Direct Investment, 1993, The Age of the Pacific, 1994. Recipient Takahashi Kamekichi award Toyo Keizai Pubs., Inc., 1984, Okita Saburo award Econ. Planning Agy., 1995. Mem. Inst. Internat. Strategic Studies (Japan com. 1992—), Policy Rsch. Com. Avocations: athletics, jogging, movies. Home: 5 20 Higashi 4 Chome Kunitachi shi Tokyo 186-0002 Japan

FUKUSHIMA, TEIICHIRO, obstetrician, educator, gynecologist; b. São Paulo, Brazil, June 20, 1942; came to U.S., 1977; MD, Escola Paulista de Med., Sao Paulo, 1968. Cert. in ob-gyn., specialty in maternal-fetal medicine. Intern King-Drew Med. Ctr., L.A., 1977-78, resident in ob-gyn., 1978-81, fellow in maternal-fetal medicine, 1981-83, chief divsn. obstetrics, 1991-97; assoc. prof. Charles R. Drew Med. Scis., 1993-94, vice chmn., 1994-97, chmn., 1997—; assoc. prof. UCLA, 2001—; vice chmn. ob-gyn. UCLA Sch. Medicine, 1997—. Mem. ACOG, AMA, L.A. Ob-Gyn. Soc., Pacific Coast Obstet. and Gynecol. Soc., Soc. Maternal-Fetal Medicine. Office: King-Drew Med Ctr Dept Ob-Gyn 12021 Wilmington Ave Los Angeles CA 90059-3019 E-mail: tefukush@cdrewu.edu.

FUKUYAMA, FRANCIS, political scientist, educator; b. Chgo., Oct. 27, 1952; m. Laura Holmgren; 3 children. BA in Classics, Cornell U., 1974; PhD in Soviet Fgn. Policy, Harvard U., 1981; Doctorate (hon.), Conn. Coll., 1995, Doane Coll., 2001. Intern U.S. Arms Control and Disarmament Agy., 1976; cons. Pan Heuristics, Inc., L.A., 1978—79; assoc. social scientist The RAND Corp., Santa Monica, Calif., 1979—81, sr. staff mem. polit. sci. dept., 1983—89, cons., 1990—94, sr. social scientist, 1995—96; policy planning staff U.S. Dept. State, Washington, 1981—82, dep. dir. policy planning staff, 1989—90; dir. Intenrat. Commerce and Policy Program, Inst. Pub. Policy Ga. Mason U., 1996—2001; Bernard Schwartz prof. internat. polit. economy Johns Hopkins U., Paul H. Nitze Sch. Advanced Internat. Studies, 2001—. Mem. adv. bd. New Am. Found., Nat. Interest; vis. lectr. dept. polit. sci. UCLA, 1986, 89; fellow Fgn. Policy Inst. Johns Hopkins Sch. Advanced Internat. Studies, 1994—96, dir. SAIS Telecom. Project, 1994—96, dir. New Scis. Project, 1996—99; co-dir. Project on the Info. and Biol. Revolution RAND/Ga. Mason U., 1996—99. Author: Moscow's Post-Brezhnev Reassessment of the Third World, 1986, Soviet Civil-Military Relations and the Power Projection Mission, 1987, Gorbachev and the New Soviet Agenda in the Third World, 1989, The End of History and the Last Man, 1992, Trust: The Social Virtues and the Creation of Prosperity, 1995, The End of Order, 1997, The Great Disruption: Human Nature and the Reconstitution of Social Order, 1999; co-author (with Kongdan Oh): The U.S.-Japan Security Relationship Aftern the Cold War, 1993; co-author: (with Abram Shulsky) The Virtual Corporation and Army Organization, 1997; co-editor (with Caroline S. Wagner): Information and Biological Revolutions: Global Governance Challenges-Summary of a Study Group, 1999; mem. editl. bd.: Jour. Democracy; contbr. chapters to books, articles to profl. jours. Grad. fellow, Ctr. for Sci. and Internat. Affairs, Harvard U., 1978—79, Nat. Security Program, Ctr. for Internat. Affairs, Harvard U., 1979. Mem.: Coun. on Civil Soc., Nat. Endowment for Democracy (bd. dirs.), Global Bus. Network, Pacific Coun. on Internat. Policy (founding mem.), Am. Polit. Sci. Assn., Coun. on Fgn. Rels. Office: Johns Hopkins U 1619 Massachusetts Ave NW Washington DC 20036

FULBRIGHT, HARRIET MAYOR, educational association administrator; b. N.Y.C., Dec. 13, 1933; d. Brantz and Evelyn (Griswold) M.; m. William Watts, Aug. 4, 1954 (div. 1975); children: Evelyn G. Ward, Shelby Funk, Heidi H. Mayor; m. J. William Fulbright, Mar. 10, 1990. BA, Radcliffe Coll., Cambridge, Mass., 1955; MFA, George Wash. U., 1975; LLD (hon.), U. Scranton, 1986; LHD (hon.), L.I. U., Bank St. Coll. Chair art dept. Maret Sch., Washington, 1975-80; asst. dir. Congl. Arts Caucus, Washington, 1980-82, Alliance of Ind. Coll. Art, Washington, 1982-84; exec. sec. Internat. Congress Art History, Washington, 1984-87; exec. dir. Fulbright Assn., Washington, 1987-91; pres. The Ctr. for Arts in the Basic Curriculum, Washington, 1991-96; exec. dir. Pres.'s Com. on the Arts and the Humanities, 1997-2000. Vice chair Reves Internat. Ctr., 1994—97, chmn. 1997-; mem. J.W. Fulbright Fgn. Scholarship Bd., 1992-98, Acad. for Ednl. Devel., 1995—; pres. Fulbright Internat. Ctr., 1996—; unofficial amb. Fulbright Program's 50th Ann. Author: How To Get Your Own Pre-School Play Group; editor: Fulbrighters Newsletter. Pres. Maret Sch. Bd., 1975; exec. dir. Pres.'s Com. for Arts and Humanities, 1997—2000; pres. Maret Sch. Bd., 1975; mem. U.S. Cuba Policy Project, Ctr. for Nat. Policy, 2001—. Honoree, Young Audiences, 1994; recipient El Orden de Manuel Amador Querrero (Panama's highest civilian award), 1997, Arts in Edn. award Fillmore Arts Ctr., 2001, Medal Cross of the Order of Merit, Hungary, 2002. Mem. Nat. Coun. Stds. in the Arts.

FULBRIGHT-BROCK, VIVIAN, supervisory probation officer; b. Paris, Tex., July 30, 1959; d. David Arthur and Dorothy Jean (Fluckus) Fulbright; m. Melvin Brock, Mar. 25, 1989; 1 child, Grace Elizabeth. BA, Austin Coll., 1981; MA in Commerce, Texas A&M U., 1983. Lic. profl. counselor, D.C.; cert. domestic violence counselor. Counselor, asst. dir. Vols. of Am., Ft. Worth, 1985-86; outreach counselor Sasha Bruce Youth Walks, Inc., Washington, 1986-88; diagnostic assessor Consortium for Youth Alternatives, Washington, 1988-90; probation officer D.C. Supr. Ct., 1990-96; supr. D.C. Supr. Ct. Juvenile Intake Office, 1996—. Mem. Delta Phi Nu.

FULCI, FRANCESCO PAOLO, diplomat; b. Messina, Italy, Mar. 19, 1931; s. Sebastiano and Enza (Sciascia) F.; m. Claris Glathar, 1965; children: Sebastiano, Marie Sol, William. LLD, U. Messina, Italy, 1953; M in Comparative Law, Columbia U., 1955; diploma, Acad. Internat. Law, The Hague, The Netherlands, 1956; LLD (hon.), U. Windsor, Ont., Can., 1981, St. Thomas Aquinas Coll., 1996, St. John's U., 1998. Joined Italian Fgn. Svc., 1956, attache directorate gen. for econ. affairs N.Am. desk, 1956-58, 1st sec. directorate gen. for polit. affairs Soviet and Ea. European desk, 1963-65, liaison officer with Parliament in Cabinet, 1965-68; 1st vice consul Consulate Gen. Italy, N.Y.C., 1958-61; 2nd sec. Italian Embassy, Moscow, 1961-63, counsellor, 1st counsellor Paris, 1968-74, min. counsellor Tokyo, 1974-76; mem. Italian del. UN Gen. Assembly, N.Y.C., 1965; chief of cabinet to Hon. Amintore Fanfani Italian Senate, Rome, 1976-80; amb. to Can. Ottawa, 1980-85; amb. and permanent rep. of Italy NATO, Brussels, 1985-91; sec. gen. of exec. com. for intelligence and security CESIS, 1991-93; permanent rep. of Italy UN, N.Y.C., 1993-99; head, Italian del. UN Security Coun., New York, 1995-96; first v.p. ECOSOC, New York, 1998-99, pres., 1999-2000; v.p. Ferrero Internat., Luxembourg, 2000—. Pres. Campiello Nat. Lit. Prize, Venice, 1999; mem. UN Com. for Rights of the Child, Geneva, 1998-2001. Editorialist La Stampa, Turin, 2000—. Decorated Cross of Merit (Germany), officer Legion of Honor (France), comdr. Imperial Order of Rising Sun (Japan), knight Gt. Cross of Order of Merit (Italy), knight Mil. Order of Malta, Grand Cross Portuguese Rep., Knight Grand Cross Piano Order, Holy See; Fulbright scholar Columbia U., 1954-55. Office: Salita S Nicola da Tolentino 1b 00187 Rome Italy

FULCO, ARMAND JOHN, biochemist; b. L.A., Apr. 3, 1932; s. Herman J. and Clelia Marie (DeFeo) F.; m. Virginia Loy Hungerford, June 18, 1955 (div. July 1985); children: William James, Lisa Marie, Linda Susan, Suzanne Yvonne; m. Doris V.N. Goodman, Nov. 29, 1987. BS in Chemistry, UCLA, 1957, PhD in Physiol. Chemistry, 1960. NIH postdoctoral fellow Lipid Labs. UCLA, 1960-61; NIH research fellow dept. chemistry Harvard U., Cambridge, Mass., 1961-63; biochemist, prin. investigator Lab. Nuclear Medicine and Radiation Biology, UCLA, 1963-80; asst. prof. dept. biol. chemistry UCLA (Med. Sch.), 1965-70, assoc. prof., 1970-76, prof., 1976—, prin. investigator lab. biomed. and environ. scis., 1981-93; prin. investigator lab. structural biology/molecular med. UCLA-Dept. of Energy, 1993-95. Cons. biochemist VA, Los Angeles, 1968-79; mem. UCLA Molecular Biology Inst., 1991—; co-dir. Lipid-Hormone Core Lab., UCLA, 1989-96; mem. Jonsson Comprehensive Cancer Ctr. UCLA, 1994—. Author: (with J.F. Mead) The Unsaturated and Polyunsaturated Fatty Acids in Health and Disease, 1976; contbr. over 90 articles to sci. jours. Served with U.S. Army, 1952-54. Mem. AAAS, Am. Chem. Soc., Am. Soc. Biol. Chemistry and Molecular Biology, Am. Soc. Microbiology, Internat. Soc. for Study of Xenobiotics, Harvard Chemists Assn., Sigma Xi. Office: UCLA Sch Medicine Dept Biol Chemistry PO Box 951737 Los Angeles CA 90095-1737 E-mail: fulco@mednet.ucla.edu.

FULD, FRED, III, computer consultant, financial consultant; b. San Pedro, Calif., July 31, 1952; s. Fred Jr. and Gloria Mary F.; m. Sharon Elizabeth Fuld; 1 child, Fred IV. BA in Bus., BA in Econs., Rockford Coll., 1974; postgrad., Heriot-Watt U., Berkeley/Edenburgh. Cert. tchr. credential, Calif.; Registered Investment Advisor, SEC, 1981. Investment mgr. San Diego Securities, 1974-78; market maker Pacific Stock Exch., San Francisco, 1978-79; v.p. CGR Conss., San Francisco, 1979-83; pvt. practice fin., computer cons. Concord, Calif., 1983—; exec. prodr. Mt DTV Ednl. TV series. Adj. prof. dept. computer information systems, sch. bus., Calif. State U., Hayward, 1997—; computer mgr. Calif. State U., Hayward, 1999—. Author: (software) Personal Financial Planning, 1984, (software) Asset Allocation, 1986, (software) Business Valuation, 1986; author: Stock Market Secrets, 1985, 101 Most Asked Questions about the MAC, 1992. Mem. Mensa Soc. (life), The Magic Castle (life). Avocations: swimming, jogging, collecting antique stock certificates. Office: 3043 Clayton Rd Concord CA 94519-2730

FULD, RICHARD SEVERIN, JR., investment banking executive; b. N.Y.C., Apr. 26, 1946; s. Richard Severin and Elizabeth (Schwab) F.; m. Kathleen Ann Bailey, Sept. 24, 1978; children: Jacqueline, Christine, Richard S. III. BS, U. Colo., 1969; MBA, NYU, 1973. Mng. dir. Lehman Bros., N.Y.C., 1969-84; vice chmn. Shearson Lehman (merger Shearson and Lehman Bros.), N.Y.C., 1984-90; CEO, pres. Lehman Bros., N.Y.C., 1990—93; chmn. bd., CEO, pres. Lehman Bros. Holdings, N.Y.C., 1994—. Mem. PSA Govt. and Fed. Agy. Securities Com. Trustee Mt. Sinai Med. Ctr., N.Y.C.; former chmn. Mt. Sinai Children's Ctr. Found., mem. exec. com.; bd. dirs. Ronald McDonald House. Avocations: squash, photography.

FULD, STEVEN ALAN, financial advisor, insurance specialist; b. Balt., Aug. 20, 1963; s. George Joseph Fuld and Nancy (Morstein) Boltz; m. Julie Michelle Glaser, Jan. 21, 1989; children: Zachary Aaron, Jessica Sydney. Student, Calif. State U., Northridge, 1981-85; MBA, Northfield U., 1998, PhD, 2003. CLU, ChFC, accredited estate planner. Agt. Lincoln Nat. Life, Tarzana, Calif., 1984-85; mng. ptnr. The Skyline Group, Encino, Calif., 1985—; extended faculty Am. Coll., 1990-92. Lectr. Assn. for Advanced Life Underwriting, The Arthritis Found., Georgetown U., Nat. Assn. Health Underwriters, Nat. Assn. Life Underwriters, Calif. Soc. CPAs, Internat. Soc. Appraisers, March of Dimes, City Nat. Bank, L.A. Bus. Jour., Forth Fin. Network, others; bd. advisors Manulife, 1996-97, chmn. MFP tech. com., 1996-97; bd. dirs. Case Fin., Inc.; co-host TV series: Strategies of the Rich and Smart, 1995—. Contbg. author: Business Insurance Law and Practice, 1989; contbr. articles to profl. jours. Trustee Arthritis Found. Am., 1999—, Calif. State U. Found.; trustee, bd. govs. So. Calif. chpt. Arthritis Found., 1995—, planned gift com., exec. com., 1996—, mem. nat. breakthrough century com., chmn. estate planning day, 1996, chmn. bd. dirs., 2000-01; res. officer L.A. City Police Dept., 1996—; nat. resource devel. com., chair CEO task force, chair major gifts conf., chmn. So. Calif. chpt. Arthritis Found., 2000—; dean's coun. of bus. advisors CSUN, 1999—. Named Man of Yr., Pacific S.W. Region, Fedn. Jewish Men's Clubs, 1993; recipient Disting. Svc. award Arthritis Found., 1995, Nat. Vol. Svc. citation, 1997. Mem. Am. Soc. CLU and ChFC (lectr., bd. dirs. San Fernando Valley chpt. 1989-92, Disting. Svc. award 1990, 92), Beverly Hills Estate Counselors Forum (bd. dirs. 1992-95), Conejo Valley Estate Counselors Forum (founder), Nat. Assn. Life Underwriters, Assn. for Advanced Life Underwriting, Temple Beth Haverim Men's Club (pres.), Temple Beth Haverim (trustee, v.p. ways and means 1993-95). Office: 21333 Oxnard St Woodland Hills CA 91367 E-mail: stevenfuld@skylinegroup.net.

FULDA, MICHAEL, space policy researcher; b. Liverpool, Eng., Apr. 21, 1939; came to U.S., 1962, naturalized, 1966; s. Boris and Catherine (Von Dehn) F.; m. Rosa Bongiorno, July 19, 1970; children: Robert, George. Student, Polytechnique, Grenoble, France, 1956-57, Tech. U., West Berlin, Germany, 1957-58, Karl Eberhardt U., Tubingen, Germany, 1963-66; MA, Am. U., 1968, PhD in Internat. Studies, 1970. Prof. polit. sci. Fairmont State Coll., W.Va., 1971—. Vis. prof. Bauman Moscow State Tech. U., 2002; internat. rels. specialist NASA, Washington, 1979. Author: Oil and International Relations, 1979; (with others) United States Space Policy, 1985; contbr. articles to profl. jours. Bd. dirs. Fairmont Chamber Music Soc., 1983—; W.Va. state com. chmn., dir. space policy Nat. Unity Campaign for John Anderson, 1980; mem. nat. adv. com. John Glenn Presdl. Com., 1984, space policy group Dukakis/Bentsen Com., 1988; dist. advancement com. Boy Scouts Am.; active psychol. ops. Vets. Assn. With U.S. Army, 1962-66. Fellow NASA Marshall Ctr., Huntsville, Ala., 1977, Langley Ctr., Hampton, Va., 1976, Woodrow Wilson Found., 1969-70; grantee Humanities Found. W.Va., 1978-80, NASA W.Va. Space Grant Consortium, 1991—; named del. to Aerospace States Assn. by Gov. of W.Va., 2001. Fellow AIAA (assoc.), Brit. Interplanetary Soc.; mem. Am. Astronautical Soc., Nat. Space Soc. (dir. 1991-93), German Assn. for Luft and Raumfamrt, Soc. Espacial Mexicana, Nat. Space Club, Assn. Argentina Tech. Space, Inst. for Social Sci. Study of Space (pres. 1988—), Fairmont Elks Lodge (edn. com.). Avocations: physical fitness, weightlifting, tango, triathlons. Home: 2 Briarwood Terr Fairmont WV 26554-1331 E-mail: mfulda@mail.fscwv.edu.

FULKER, EDMUND NORMAN, management consultant; b. Pittsfield, Mass., June 14, 1927; s. Herbert Ernest Creal Fulker and Albina Archambault; m. Jeanette Ruth Fletcher, July 31, 1948; children: Pamela J. Fulker Leonard, Glen Herbert. BS, Purdue U., 1951, MS in Psychology, 1952; EdD in Adult Edn., Am. U., 1970. Lic. psychologist, D.C. Instr. Purdue U., Indpls., 1952-54; tng. officer USAF Hdqrs., Pentagon, Washington, 1954-57, Hdqrs. USDA, Washington, 1957-59; asst. dir. USDA Grad. Sch., Washington, 1959-80, dir., 1980-85; cons. The World Bank, Washington, 1987-99. Adj. faculty Am. U., Washington, George Washington U., Ctrl. Mich. U., Nat. Cheng Chi U., Taiwan; pres. Washington chpt. ASPA, 1977-78, nat. coun. mem., 1979-81. Contbr. articles to profl. jours. Mgmt. cons. U. Mich., Taipei, Taiwan, 1963, Ford Found., New Delhi, India, Nepal, 1970-71, Ohio State U., Ankara, Turkey, 1993, Egypt Gen. Petroleum Co., Cairo, 1996-99. With USNR, 1945-47. Recipient Outstanding Pub. Adminstr. award ASPA, Washington, 1984. Mem. ASTD (pres. chpt. 1964-65, Outstanding Trainer award 1963), Royal Palm Yacht Club (Ft. Myers, Fla.). Avocations: boating, golfing, traveling. Home: 15240 Sam Snead Ln Fort Myers FL 33917-3260 E-mail: edfulker@aol.com.

FULKERSON, SUE ELLEN, poet; b. Zanesville, Ohio, Dec. 14, 1943; d. Arthur Amos and Helen Marie Bryan; m. Larry Dean Fulkerson, Apr. 5, 1968; children: Rebecca, Matthew. BA in Social Work, Valparaiso U., Ind., 1966. Probation officer Muskingum County Juvenile Ct., Zanesville, Ohio, 1966—67; caseworker Muskingum County Welfare Dept., Zanesville, 1967—68; social worker Franklin County Children Svcs., Columbus, Ohio, 1968—70; income maint. worker Muskingum County Welfare Dept., Zanesville, 1977—80; foster care coord. Muskingum County Children Svcs., Zanesville, 1980—81; social worker ODC Nursing Home, Zanesville, 1987—88; ret., 1988. Author: (book of poetry) Poems for Life's Seasons, 1999; contbr. Vol. Assisted Living Cmty., Zanesville; mem. Rep. Nat. Com., 2000—03. Recipient Editors Choice award for poem Autumn, Nat. Libr. Poetry, 1993, Editor's Choice award for poem Summer's Farewell, 1997, Editor's Choice award for outstanding achievement in poetry for poem The Autumn Leaves, 2002, Poetry Cert. of Recognition, Famous Poet Soc., 2001. Mem.: Gideons Internat. (sec. 1985—99). Avocations: reading, making bookmarks, photography. Home: 3275 Buena Vista Cir Zanesville OH 43701 E-mail: verse_maker@msn.com.

FULKS, ROBERT GRADY, computer executive; b. Kansas City, Mo., Apr. 8, 1936; s. Hilburne Grady and Dora Elouise (Johnson) F.; children— Stephanie, Scott Grady. BSEE, MIT., 1958, MSEE, 1959. Engr., chief engr. v.p. engring. and product mktg. GenRad, Inc. (formerly Gen. Radio Co.), Concord, Mass., 1959-73; pres. Mirco Systems, Inc., 1973-75, Omnicomp, Inc., Phoenix, 1975-80, gen. mgr. advanced tech div. (formerly Omnicomp, Inc.) GenRad, Inc., Phoenix, 1980-86, also v.p. parent co.; v.p. engring. Telesis Systems Corp., Chelmsford, Mass., 1986-87; v.p., gen. mgr. Valid Logic Systems PCB CAD div., 1987-89, group v.p. product divs., 1989-91; v.p. Cadence Design Systems, 1992—; bd. dirs. Cirrus Sigma Ltd., Fareham, Eng., Texcon Corp., Phoenix, Custom Data Mgmt. Inc., Phoenix, Markwood, Inc., Phoenix, Office Tech. Ltd., Boston. Mem. IEEE, Assn. Computing Machinery, Concord C. of C. (former bd. dirs., chmn. fin. com.), Sigma Xi. Contbr. articles tech. jours. Patentee in field. Office: 270 Billerica Rd Chelmsford MA 01824-4140

FULLAM, JOHN P. federal judge; b. Gardenville, Pa., Dec. 10, 1921; s. Thomas L. and Mary Nolan F.; m. Alice Hilliar Freiheit, Apr. 15, 1950; children: Nancy, Sally, Thomas, Jeffrey. BS, Villanova U., 1942; JD, Harvard U., 1948. Atty., Bristol, Pa., 1948-60; judge Pa. Ct. Common Pleas, 7th Jud. Dist., 1960-66, U.S. Dist. Ct. (ea. dist.) Pa., Phila., 1966—, chief judge, 1986-90; now sr. judge. Lectr. in law U. Pa. Law Sch., Phila., Temple U. Law Sch., Phila.; mem. adv. com. Codes of Conduct of Jud. Conf. U.S., mem. adminstrn. magistrates sys., mem. com. to rev. jud. coun. disciplinary and disability orders. Democratic candidate for U.S. Congress, 1954, 56 Mem. Am. Law Inst., Pa. Bar Assn., Bucks County Bar Assn., Phila. Bar Assn. Office: 15614 US Courthouse Ind Mall W 601 Market St Philadelphia PA 19106-1713

FULLENLOVE, CARMEN MILLAY (KIT FULLENLOVE), public relations executive; b. Louisville, Aug. 27, 1959; d. Joseph Claude Millay and Erma Louise Fleischmann; m. William Burnley Wolfe, Oct. 10, 1981 (div. June 1986); m. James Martin Fullenlove Sr., Sept. 12, 1987; 1 child, Rachel Reneé. BS in Journalism and Polit. Sci., Murray State U., 1980. City editor Mt. Vernon (Ind.) Dem., 1980-81; editor Softball Watch, Marietta, Ga., 1982; reporter, photographer The Sentinel-News, Shelbyville, Ky., 1983-84; editor The Oldham Era, La Grange, Ky., 1984-97; pub. rels. mgr. Bapt. Hosp. East, Louisville, 1997—. Mem. Oldham County Bd. Edn., La Grange, 1998-2002. Recipient Sch. Bell award Ky. Edn. Assn., 1997. Mem.: Exec. Quality Coun., Soc. Profl. Journalists

(membership chair, pres. 1991—92, mem. chmn. 2003—), Ky. Edn. Assn. (Sch. Bell Award 1997). Office: Bapt Hosp East 4000 Kresge Way Louisville KY 40207-4676 E-mail: kfullenlove@bhsi.com.

FULLENWEIDER, DONN CHARLES, lawyer; b. Milw., Jan. 25, 1935; s. Russell Charles and Anne Mae (Murphy) F.; m. Wendy Lattimer; 1 child, Keith Rabon. BS, U. Houston, 1957, JD, 1958. Bar: Tex. bar 1958; Cert. in family law and civil trials Tex. Bd. Legal Specialization. Assoc. Fred Parks, Houston, 1958-65; partner Haynes & Fullenweider, Houston, 1965-89; pvt. practice, Houston, 1989-93; ptnr. Fullenweider and Wardell L.L.P., 1993-97, The Fullenweider Firm, 1997—. Adj. assoc. prof. law U. Houston Bates Coll. Law, 1972-74 Mem. 43d Joint Civilian Orientation Conf., 1973; mem. Tex. Bd. Legal Specialization, 1977-98. Recipient Emison award Tex. Acad. Family Specialists, 1993. Fellow Am. Bar Found., Houston Bar Found., Tex. Bar Found. (dir. 1973-76), Am. Acad. Matrimonial Lawyers (pres. Tex. chpt. 1979-81, bd. dirs. 1981-84, treas. 1985-88, pres.-elect 1988-89, pres. 1990-91); mem. ABA, Am. Bd. Trial Advocacy (advocate), Houston Bar Assn. (treas. 1961-62, 2d v.p. 1962-63, dir. 1971, 73, 1st v.p. 1970-73, Outstanding Svc. award 1974), Am. Coll. Family Trial Lawyers (diplomate 1994—), State Bar Tex. (dir. 1973-76, chmn. bd. 1975-76, exec. com. 1976-77, chmn. litigation sect. 1979-81), Am. Trial Lawyers Assn., Houston Trial Lawyers Assn. (v.p. 1971), Def. Orientation Conf. Assn., Houston C. of C., River Oaks Country Club, Sigma Chi, Phi Delta Phi. Home: 5502 Fieldwood Dr Houston TX 77056-2719 Office: 4265 San Felipe St Ste 1400 Houston TX 77027-2999

FULLENWIDER, NANCY VRANA, music composer, dance educator, pianist; b. Sheridan, Wyo., May 9, 1940; d. Jacob Allen and Edith Martha (Tripp) Fullenwider; m. Linsfred Leroy Vrana, Apr. 26, 1980. BA summa cum laude, U. Denver, 1962, MA, 1971, postgrad., 1974. Prin. dancer, instr. Colo. Ballet and Colo. Ballet Ctr., Denver, 1958-80; owner, instr. Idaho Springs (Colo.) Sch. Ballet, 1962-67, Sch. Ballet, Parker, Colo., 1974-79. Curriculum developer Career Edn. Ctr., Denver Pub. Schs., 1973; grad. asst. U. Denver, 1974; guest artist, choreographer, composer Young Audiences, Denver, 1975-80; instr. ballet Ballet Arts Ctr., Denver, 1992-98, Colo. Dance Ctr., Littleton, 1992—; music dir., accompanist for Western Chamber Ballet, Denver, 1994-98, Colo. Ballet, 1999, Arvada Ctr., 1998, Ballet Arts, 1998, Internat. Sch. Ballet, 2000. Composer (CD's) To the Pointe, 1997, Brava!, 1999, Curtain Call, 2000, Inner Dance, 2002; commissioned ballet works performed at Auditorium Theatre, Denver, 2000, Arvada Ctr. for Performing Arts, Colo., 1991, Aurora (Colo.) Fox Arts Ctr., 1989-92, Buell Theatre, Colo., 1993, Cleo Parker Robinson Dance Theatre, Colo., 1992, 2003, Colo. Springs Fine Arts Ctr., 1991, Houston Fine Arts Ctr., Colo., 1971, San Luis Arts Festival, Colo., 1990, Bonfils Theatre, Colo., 1971, Denver Civic Theatre, 2000, Auditorium Theatre, Denver, 2000, 01, (TV series) Providence, 2000. Grantee Douglas County Schs., Colo., 1998. Mem. Phi Beta Kappa, Alpha Lambda Delta. Avocations: hiking, fly fishing, theatre, concerts.

FULLER, ANNE ELIZABETH HAVENS, English language and literature educator, consultant; b. Pomona, Calif., Jan. 20, 1932; d. Paul Swain and Lorraine Elizabeth (Hamilton) Havens; m. Martin Emil Fuller, II, June 17, 1961; children: Katharine Hamilton, Peter David Takashi. AB, Mount Holyoke Coll., 1953; BA (Fulbright scholar), Somerville Coll., Oxford U., 1955, MA, 1959; PhD (Univ. fellow), Yale U., 1958. Instr. English, Mount Holyoke Coll., 1957-59; instr. Pomona Coll., 1959-61; asst. prof. U. Fla., Gainesville, 1961-63; lectr. U. Denver, 1964-68, 71-73; assoc. prof., chmn. center for lang. and lit. Prescott (Ariz.) Coll., 1968-70; tchr. Colo. Rocky Mountain Sch., 1970-71; dean of faculty Scripps Coll., Claremont, Calif., 1973-80, prof. English, 1973-80; spl. asst. to pres., sec. to corp. Claremont U. Center, 1981-83; v.p. for acad. affairs Austin Coll., Sherman, Tex., 1982-84, faculty mem., 1984-96. Mem. SW dist. Rhodes Scholar Selection Com., 1975-83 Bd. dirs. Am. Council on Edn., 1979-81. Mem. Assn. Am. Colls. (dir. 1977-81, chmn. 1980-81), Am. Conf. Acad. Deans (dir. 1976-79), Commn. on Women in Higher Edn., Am. Assn. Higher Edn., Modern Lang. Assn. Am. Democrat. Episcopalian. Home: 11304 Pinos Altos Ave NE Albuquerque NM 87111-5701 E-mail: ahnefu@nmia.com.

FULLER, BRUCE E. mechanical engineer; b. Wellsville, N.Y., Nov. 5, 1960; s. Robert J. and Beuna M. Fuller; m. Marett D. Silsby, July 17, 1982; children: Brittany D., Caitlin M., Alyssa M. AAS in Applied Sci. and Engring. Tech., SUNY Coll. Tech., Alfred, 1980; BTech in Mech. Engring. Tech., Rochester Inst. Tech., 1985; MS in Mech. Engring., N.J. Inst. Tech., 1989. Programmer I Air Preheater, Wellsville, NY, 1980—85; mem. of tech. staff AT&T Bell Labs., Whippany, NJ, 1985—92; asst. prof. mech. engring. tech. SUNY Coll. of Tech. at Alfred, 1992—94; sr. devel. engr. Dresser-Rand, Wellsville, NY, 1994—2000; dept. chair, mech. engring. tech. SUNY Coll. of Tech. at Alfred, Alfred, NY, 2000—02; sr. devel. engr. Dresser-Rand, Wellsville, NY, 2002—. Sec. Alfred Sta. Fire Co. Assn., Alfred Station, NY, 1999. Mem.: ASME (assoc.; sec. 1999—2000). Achievements include patents pending for easily installed labyrinth seal that closes with increasing pressure drop. Home: 1299 State Route 244 Alfred Station NY 14803 Office: Dresser-Rand 37 Coats St Wellsville NY 14895

FULLER, CHARLES H, JR., playwright; b. Phila., Mar. 5, 1939; s. Charles Henry and Lillian (Anderson) Fuller; m. Miriam A. Nesbitt, Aug. 4, 1962; children: Charles III, David. Student, Villanova U., 1956-58, hon. degree, 1983; student, LaSalle Coll., 1965-67, hon. degree, 1982, Chestnut Hill Coll., 1985. Co-founder, co-dir. Afro-Am. Arts Theatre, Phila., 1967-71; writer, dir. The Black Experience Sta. WIP-Radio, Phila., 1970-71; prof. African-Am. studies Temple U., Phila., until 1993. Author: (plays) The Village: A Party, 1968, rev. as The Perfect Party, 1968, In My Names and Days, 1972, Candidate, In the Deepest Part of Sleep, First Love, 1974, The Lay Out Letter, 1975, The Brownsville Raid, 1976, Sparrow in Flight, 1978, Zooman and the Sign, 1981 (Obie award, 1981, Audelco award, 1981), A Soldier's Play, 1982 (Pulitzer prize in drama, 1982, N.Y. Drama Critics award best Am. play, 1982, Outer Circle Critics award best off-Broadway play, 1982, Audelco award, 1982, Theatre Club award, 1982), Sons of the Same Lion, 1991, (play series) We Part I "Sally", 1988, Part II "Prince", 1988, Part III "Jonquil", 1989, Part IV "Burner's Frolic", 1990; contbr. ; author: (TV miniseries) Roots, Resistance and Renaissance, 1967, (TV series) The Sky is Gray, 1987, (screenplays) A Soldier's Story, 1984 (Academy award nominations best picture and best screenplay adaptation, 1984, Edgar Allen Poe Mystery award, 1985), (TV films) A Gathering of Old Men, 1987; dir.: (TV films) Zooman, 1995, The Black Experience, 1970—71; prodr.: (TV films) Love Songs, 1998; author: (screenplays) (TV Films) Love Songs. Bd. dirs. Adolp Caesar Meml. Fund. Served with USAF, 1959—62. Recipient Creative Artists Pub. Svc. award, 1974, Hazelitt award Pa. State Coun. Arts, 1984; NEA grantee, 1976, Rockefeller Found. grantee, 1976, Guggenheim Found. fellow, 1977—78. Mem.: PEN (bd. dirs. Am. div.), Writers Guild Am. East, Dramatists Guild. Roman Catholic. *I have always sought wisdom and humility, using one to counterbalance the other.*

FULLER, DAVID OTIS, JR., lawyer; b. Grand Rapids, Mich., May 28, 1939; s. David Otis and Virginia Chapin (Emery) F.; m. Isabelle Patrice Gigout, July 5, 1968; children: Thomas Andrew, Christian Scott, Pierre Emery, Margaret Isabelle. BA, Wheaton Coll., 1961; JD, Harvard U., 1964; postgrad., George Washington U., 1963, U. Paris, 1966. Bar: Mich., 1964, N.Y., 1967, U.S. Supreme Ct., 1968. Law clk. U.S. Ho. of Reps. Judiciary Com., 1963; assoc. Amberg, Law & Fallon, Grand Rapids, 1964-65; asst. dist. atty. N.Y. County, 1966-72, law sec. to justice, 1972-73; corp. atty. Pan Am. World Airways, Inc., 1973-74; dep. gen. counsel Reader's Digest Assn., Inc., 1974-84; pvt. practice N.Y.C., 1984-87; ptnr. Baker, Nelson & Williams, N.Y.C., 1987-94, Bosworth, Gray & Fuller, Bronxville, N.Y., 1994—; justice Tuckahoe Village, N.Y., 1986—. Lectr. Am. Bar Assn., Practicing Law Inst., Bronx C.C. Editor: Harvard Jour. on Legislation, 1962-64; contbr. articles to profl. jours. Warden Episc. Ch., 1991-97. Mem.: ABA, Fed. Bar Coun., Westchester County Magistrates Assn. (pres. 1993—94), Westchester County Bar Assn., NY State Magistrates Assn. (v.p. 2002—), Am. Arbitration Assn. (arbitrator 1983—96), Assn. Bar City NY (comms. law com. 1984—87), NY State Bar Assn. (chmn. privacy com. 1982—84), Internat. Bar Assn., Harvard Club (N.Y.C.). Republican. Avocations: fishing, skiing, coins, racquet sports, French. Office: Bosworth Gray & Fuller 116 Kraft Ave Bronxville NY 10708-3810 E-mail: dofjr@aol.com.

FULLER, DAVID RALPH, lawyer; b. Pittsfield, Mass., Feb. 12, 1932; s. Everett Joseph and Myrtle Thankfull (Bellinger) F.; m. Joanne Morris, Aug. 15, 1953; children: Susan Anne, Thomas Edward, Mary Elizabeth. AB, U. Calif., Berkeley, 1953, JD, 1956. Bar: Calif. 1956, U.S. Ct. Appeals (9th cir.) 1956, U.S. Supreme Ct. 1972. Atty. Pacific Gas and Electric, San Francisco, 1956-62, Peters, Fuller, Rush et al, Chico, Calif., 1962-97; retired, 1997. Pres. Chico C. of C., 1968; trustee Chico Unified Sch. Dist., 1967-71, Butte Community Coll., Chico, 1976-90. Recipient Disting. Svc. award Chico Jr. C. of C., 1970. Mem. No. Calif. Def. Counsel Assn. (bd. dirs. 1980—), Assn. Def. Trial Lawyers, Am. Bd. Trial Advs. (assoc.), Rotary (Chico club pres. 1978, Paul Harris fellow 1984. Republican. Presbyterian. Avocations: skiing, gardening, hiking. Home: 5 Canterbury Cir Chico CA 95926-2411

FULLER, DAVID WILLIAM, music educator; b. Melrose, Mass., Sept. 25, 1952; s. Clarence William and Anora Peavey Fuller; m. Susan Carol Fuller, Oct. 27, 1979; children: Sara Rathman, Rachael Anora. MusM, Boston Conservatory Music, 1978. Voice instr. divsn. spl. programs Boston Conservatory, 1992—94, Fairmount Fine Arts Ctr., Novelty, Ohio, 1995—; coord. music St. Anselm Ch., Chesterland, Ohio, 2002—. Apprentice artist: Santa Fe Opera Co., 1976. Finalist New Eng. Regional Met. Opera Auditions, Met. Opera Nat. Coun., N.Y.C., 1976, 1977. Mem.: Am. Guild Musical Artists, Nat. Assn. Tchrs. Singing. Home: 13466 Hotchkiss Rd Burton OH 44021

FULLER, DIANA CLARE, lawyer; b. Omaha, Jan. 26, 1953; d. William Thomas and Dorothy Louise (Gallen) F.; m. James E. O'Connor, 1984; 1 child, Elizabeth Rose. BA, U. Nebr., Omaha, 1974; JD, Creighton U., 1977. Bar: Nebr. 1977, U.S. Dist. Ct. Nebr. 1977. Law clk. to presiding justice Nebr. 4th Jud. Dist., Omaha, 1978-79; atty. United Omaha subs. Mut. Omaha, 1979-83; assoc. corp. counsel Mut. of Omaha, 1983-85; asst. v.p. Actuarial United of Omaha subs. Mut. of Omaha, 1985—. Explorers leader Boy Scouts Am., 1978-84; mem. membership com. bd. dirs. Campfire, Inc., Omaha, 1982-83; trustee Cen. Presbyn. Ch., Omaha, 1984-87; mem. Leadership Omaha Program, 1986. Recipient award Boy Scouts Am., 1984, Merit award Boy Scouts Am., 1986; named one of 10 Outstanding Young Omahans, 1985. Mem. Omaha Fin. Planners (pres. 1982-83), Omaha Bar Assn. (pub. service com. 1983—), Nebr. Bar Assn., Urban Housing Found. (bd. dirs.), Rotary. Democrat. Office: Mut Omaha Law Div Mutual Of Omaha Plz Omaha NE 68175-0001

FULLER, DIANA LYNN, lawyer; b. Morgantown, W.Va., Nov. 16, 1952; d. William Fleming and Amelia Marie (Lattanzi) F.; m. Robert Deeb Batey, July 21, 1979. B.S., W.Va. U., 1972, J.D., 1977. Bar: W.Va. 1977, U.S. Dist. Ct. (so. dist.) W.Va. 1977, Fla. 1978, U.S. Dist. Ct. (no.; mid. and so. dists.) Fla., U.S. Ct. Appeals (5th and 11th cirs.). Law clk., ct. crier to chief judge U.S. Dist. Ct. (mid. dist.) Fla., Tampa, 1977-79, arbitrator arbitration program; ptnr. Fowler, White, Gillen, Boggs, Villareal & Banker, P.A., Tampa, 1979-85; ptnr. Smith & Fuller, P.A., Tampa, 1985—; lectr. in area of constrn. law. Contbr. articles to profl. jours. Mem. ABA (del. gen. assembly 1984, litigation sect., construction litigation com.), Forum on the Construction Industry, Am. Judicature Soc., Fed. Bar Assn., Hillsborough County Bar Assn., W.Va. Trial Lawyers Assn., Greater Tampa C. of C., Nat. Coun. of W.Va. U. Coll. of Law, Phi Alpha Delta. Home: 2418 W Palm Dr Tampa FL 33629-7312 Office: 101 E Kennedy Blvd Ste 1800 Tampa FL 33602-5148

FULLER, EDWIN DANIEL, hotel executive; b. Richmond, Va., Mar. 15, 1945; s. Ben Swint and Evelyn (Beal) F. Student, Wake Forest U., 1965; BSBA, Boston U., 1968; postgrad., Harvard Sch. Bus., 1987. Security officer Pinkerton Inc., Boston, 1965-68; with sales dept. Twin Bridges Marriott Hotel, Arlington, Va., 1972-73; nat. sales mgr. Marriott Hotels & Resorts, NYC, 1973-76, dir. nat. and internat. sales Washington, 1976-78, v.p. mktg., 1978-82, gen. mgr. Hempstead, NY, 1982-83, Marriott Copley Pl., Boston, 1983-85; v.p. ops. Midwest region Marriott Corp., Rosemont, Ill., 1985-89, v.p. ops. Western and Pacific regions Santa Ana, Calif., 1989-90; sr. v.p., mng. dir. Marriott Hotels & Resorts-Internat., Washington, 1990-93; exec. v.p., mng. dir. internat. lodging Marriott Lodging Internat., Washington, 1994-97, pres., mng. dir., 1997—. Chmn. bd. dir. SNR Reservation Sys., Zurich, Switzerland, 1979-81; bd. dirs. Boston U. Hotel Sch., 1984—, Barnby Books, Barnaby Books, Honolulu, 1997—; treas. MEI Pacific Honolulu, 1985—; chmn. Pres. Boston U. Gen. Alumni Assn., 1993-1996, v.p., 1990-93; v.p. Boston U. Sch. Mgmt. Alumni Bd., 1985—; mem. adv. bd. Boston U. Hospitality Mgmt. Sch., 1985—; trustee Boston U., mem. exec. com. bd. trustees, 1994—,dir., Prince of Whales Hotel Environ. Org., 1995-pres., dir. Internat. bd. of United Way; Capt. US Army, 1968-72, Vietnam. Decorated Bronze Star. Mem. Boston U. Alumni Coun. (v.p.), Harvard Sch. Bus. Advanced Mgmt. Program (fund agt.), Sigma Alpha Epsilon, Delta Sigma Pi. Republican. Avocations: real estate, travel, golf, history. Home: 25362 Derbyhill Dr Laguna Hills CA 92653 Office: Marriott Hotels & Resorts 1 Marriott Dr Washington DC 20058-0001

FULLER, G. M. lawyer; b. Anadarko, Okla., Aug. 6, 1920; s. G.M. and Alma (Tabor) F.; m. Alta Duncan, June 18, 1948; 1 dau., Teresa Ann. AB, Okla. U., 1941, LLB, 1946. Bar: Okla. 1942, U.S. Tax Ct. 1957, U.S. Supreme Ct. 1961. Pvt. practice law, Oklahoma City, 1946-64; ptnr. Fuller, Tubb & Pomeroy, Oklahoma City, 1964-74, pres., 1974-97, ptnr. Fuller, Tubb, Pomeroy, Kirschner, Bickford & Stokes, 1997—. State rep. Okla. Legislature, 1952-60; state chmn. YMCA Youth and Govt. Com., Oklahoma City, 1960-90; commr. Nat. Conf. Commrs. Uniform State Laws, 1961-67. Maj. USAF, 1942-45. Recipient Jour. Record award, 1991. Fellow Am. Bar Found. (life); mem. ABA, Oklahoma County Bar Assn. (pres. 1959-60), Okla. Bar Assn., Okla. Bar Found., Am. Judicature Soc., Order of Coif, Oklahoma City Golf and Country Club, Beacon Club. Democrat. Methodist. Home: 6429 Grandmark Dr Oklahoma City OK 73116-6534 Office: Fuller Tubb Pomeroy et al 3300 Bank One Tower 100 N Broadway Ave Oklahoma City OK 73102-8606

FULLER, GLENN R. park ranger; b. Van Nuys, Calif., Sept. 1, 1946; s. Earl D. and Virginia (Allen) F. Masters, Calif. State U., Sacramento, 1972. Park ranger Grand Canyon (Ariz.) Nat. Park, 1975-80, Cape Cod Nat. Park, Wellfleet, Mass., 1980-81, Rocky Mountain Nat. Park, Estes Park, Colo., 1981-82, Golden Gate NRA, San Francisco, 1982-83; park supt. Muia Woods Nat. Monument, Mill Valley, Calif., 1983—; supt. Eugene O'Neill Nat. Hist. Site, Danville, CA. Sgt. U.S. Army, 1970-68. Mem. Friends of the River, Assn. Nat. Park Rangers. Office: Muir Woods NM Mill Valley CA 94941

FULLER, JACK WILLIAM, writer, publishing executive; b. Chgo., Oct. 12, 1946; s. Ernest Brady and Dorothy Voss (Tegge) Fuller; children: Timothy, Katherine. BS, Northwestern U., 1968; JD, Yale U., 1973. Bar: Ill. 1974. Reporter Chgo. Tribune, 1973—75, Washington corr., 1977—78, editl. writer, 1978—79, dep. editl. page editor, 1979—82, editl. page editor, 1982—87, exec. editor, 1987—89, v.p. and editor, 1989—93, pres., CEO, 1993—97, pub., 1994—97; pres. Tribune Pub. Co., 1997—. Spl. asst. to atty. gen. U.S. Dept. Justice, Washington, 1975—77. Author: Convergence, 1982 (Cliff Dwellers award, 1983), Fragments, 1984 (Friends of Am. Writers award, 1985), Mass, 1985, Our Fathers' Shadows, 1987, Legends' End, 1990, New Values, 1996, The Best of Jackson Payne, 2000. Mem. Pulitzer Prize Bd., 1991—2000; trustee U. Chgo., Field Mus.; bd. dirs. McCormick Tribune Found. With U.S. Army, 1969—70, Vietnam corr., Pacific Stars and Stripes. Recipient Gavel award, ABA, 1979, Pulitzer prize for editl. writing, 1986. Fellow: Am. Acad. Arts and Scis.; mem.: Inter-Am. Press Assn. (v.p.), Inter-Am. Dialogue, Newspaper Assn. Am., Am. Soc. Newspaper Editors, Comml. Club Chgo. Office: Chgo Tribune Co 435 N Michigan Ave Chicago IL 60611-4066

FULLER, JACK GLENDON, JR., retired plastics engineer; b. Ft. Lewis, Wash., Feb. 25, 1923; s. Jack Glendon and Matilda Margaret (Kindschi) F.; m. Nancy Dorr Tatnall, May 14, 1945; children: Jack Glendon III, Margaret Tatnall Fuller-Scott, Pamela Dorr Fuller, Joellen Swift Fuller Gargaly, Charlotte Mahaffy Fuller-Pietrak. BS, Dickinson Coll., 1947; postgrad. in high polymer chemistry, U. Del., 1947-48. Prodn. engr. Master Plastics, Wilmington, Del., 1946-48; research chemist Hercules Powder Co., Parlin, N.J., sr. tech. rep. Boston and Wilmington, mgr. plastics sales Los Angeles, 1948-58; v.p. sales and gen. mgr. Chemtrol div. Rexall Drug & Chem. Co., 1958-60; nat. sales mgr. Ankerwerk Internat., 1960-62; pres. Polymer Machinery Corp., Berlin, Conn., 1962-82, chmn. bd., 1983-84; pres., dir. Wilmington Terminal Co., Inc., Wilmington, Del., 1967-75; exec. v.p., dir. Molding Systems, Inc., Berlin, 1968-82. Chmn. bd. dirs. Plastics Edn. Found., 1973-74 Author numerous tech. papers. 1st lt. AUS, 1943-46. Mem. Soc. Plastics Engrs. (disting. mem.; nat. council 1959, 60, treas. 1962, internat. pres. 1963), Soc. Plastics Industry (nat. dir. at large 1976-79, 80-82, exec. com. machinery div. 1973-84, chmn. machinery div. 1980-82), Plastic Pioneers. Home: 432 Bayberry Ln West Grove PA 19390-9491

FULLER, JAMES CHESTER EEDY, retired chemical company executive; b. Toronto, Can., June 5, 1927; came to U.S., 1968; s. James Clifford and Marion Winifred (Eedy) F.; m. Doris Shirley Johnson, June 16, 1951 (dec. June 1992); children— Hilary, John; m. Shirley Patricia Honeyman, Feb. 8, 1993. BSA., U. Toronto, 1948; MBA, U. Western Ont., 1955. Sales and mktg. ofcl. Uniroyal Chem. Co., Man. and Ont., Can., 1948-53, 55-64; with Akzo Chemicals and affiliates, 1964-90; gen. mgr. Armour Indsl. Chems., Toronto, 1964-68, nat. sales mgr., asst. to pres., internat. dir. Chgo., 1968-70; mng. dir. Armour-Hess Ltd., Harrogate, Yorkshire, Eng., 1970-73; exec. v.p. Akzo Chemie Am., Chgo., 1973-74, pres., 1975-87; exec. v.p. Akzo Chemicals B.V., Amersfoort, The Netherlands, 1988-90. Mem. Chem. Inst. Can. Clubs: Farmers (London). Home: 403-2605 Windsor Rd Victoria BC V8S 5H9 Canada E-mail: jfuller@vicsurf.com

FULLER, JAMES WILLIAM, financial director; b. Rochester, Ind., Apr. 3, 1940; s. Raymond S. and Mildred (Osteimeier) F.; children: Kristen Anne, Glen William. AA, San Bernardino (Calif.) Valley Coll., 1960; BS, San Jose (Calif.) State U., 1962; MBA, Calif. State U., 1967. V.p. Dean Witter, San Francisco, 1967-71, Shields & Co., San Francisco, 1971-74; dir. fin. programs SRI Internat., Menlo Park, Calif., 1974-77; sr. v.p. N.Y. Stock Exch., N.Y.C., 1977-81, Charles Schwab & Co., San Fransico, 1981-85; pres. Bull & Bear Corp., N.Y.C., 1985-87; dir. Bridge Info. Systems, San Fransico, 1987—. Bd. dirs. Action Trac Inc., L.A., Current Techs. Inc., Vancouver, B.C., Environ. Scis. Inc., San Diego; chmn. bd. dirs. Pacific Rsch. Inst., 1992—. Dir. Securities Industry Protection Corp., Washington, 1981-87, Global Econ. Action Inst., N.Y.C., 1989—; trustee U. Calif., Santa Cruz. Lt. USN, 1963-66. Mem. The Family Club (San Francisco), Olympic Club (San Francisco), Jonathon Club (L.A.), Univ. Club (N.Y.C.), The Lincoln Club (San Francisco), Polit. Com. for Econ. Growth, Internat. Platform Assn., Newcomer Soc., World Affairs Coun., Coun. on Formulations (San Francisco com.), Commonwealth Club. Republican. Presbyterian. Avocations: tennis, politics, public affairs. Home: 2584 Filbert St San Francisco CA 94123-3318 Also: Bridge 44 Montgomery St Ste 2410 San Francisco CA 94104-4711

FULLER, JOHN G.C. food and drug company executive; b. Phila., Dec. 16, 1930; s. William Duncan and Katherine Harper (Campbell) F.; m. Elizabeth Ann Dobbins, Nov. 29, 1969; 1 dau., Sarah. AB, Harvard U., 1952, MBA, 1958. Engaged in mktg. and distbn. Acme Markets, Inc., Phila., 1958-66, asst. treas., 1966-69, treas., 1969-73; v.p. finance, treas. Am. Stores Co., 1973—. Bd. dirs. Phila. Port Corp. Trustee, Treas. Germantown Hist. Soc.; overseer William Penn Charter Sch. Served with Naval Intelligence USNR, 1952-56. Mem.: Harvard (Phila.), Cricket (Phila.). Republican. Episcopalian. Home: 3910 Vaux St Philadelphia PA 19129-1415 Office: Gibbs Bldg 300 W School House Ln Philadelphia PA 19144-3929

FULLER, JOSEPH, JR., aeronautical engineer; b. Houston; BS in Physics, Tex. So. U.; MBA, U. Houston. Founder, pres., CEO Futron Corp., Bethesda, Md.; aerospace sys. engr., project mgr., sr. exec. NASA. Bd. dirs. Aero. and Space Engring. Bd.; mem. indsl. adv. bd. U. Md., Balt. Office: Futron Corp 7315 Wisconsin Ave Ste 900W Bethesda MD 20814

FULLER, KATHRYN SCOTT, environmental association executive, lawyer; b. N.Y.C., July 8, 1946; d. Delbert Orison and Carol Scott (Gilbert) F.; m. Stephen Paul Doyle, May 29, 1977; children: Sarah Elizabeth Taylor, Michael Stephen Doyle, Matthew Scott Doyle. BA English, Am. Lit., Brown U., 1968, LHD (hon.), 1992; JD with honors, U. Tex., 1976; postgrad., U. Md., 1980-82; DSci. (hon.), Wheaton Coll., 1990; LLD (hon.), Knox Coll., 1992. Bar: Tex. 1977, D.C. 1979. Rsch. asst. Yale U., New Haven, Conn., 1968-69, Am. Chem. Soc., 1970-71, Harvard U. Mus. Comparative Zoology, Cambridge, Mass., 1971-73; law clerk Dewey, Ballantine, Bushby, Palmer & Wood and Vinson & Elkins, N.Y.C., Houston, 1974-76, U.S. Dist. Ct. (so. dist.), Tex., 1976-77; atty., advisor Office Legal Counsel Dept. Justice, Washington, 1977-79, atty. Wildlife and Marine Resources sect., 1979-80, chief Wildlife and Marine Resources sect., 1981-82; exec. v.p., dir. Traffic USA, pub. policy, gen. counsel World Wildlife Fund, Washington, 1982-89, pres., CEO, 1989—. Contbr. articles to profl. jours. Adv. com. Trade Policy and Negotiations; Pres'. Commn. Environ. Quality; bd. dirs. Brown U.; trustee The Ford Found.; mem. World Bank Adv. Com. on Sustainable Devel. Recipient William Rogers Outstanding Grad. award Brown U., 1990, UN Environment Programme Global 500 award, 1990; outstanding woman law student Tex. scholar, 1975. Mem. State Tex. Bar, D.C. Bar (coun. fgn. rels., internat. coun. environ. law, overseas devel. coun.), Zonta Internat. (hon.). Avocations: squash, trekking, scuba diving, gardening, fishing. Office: World Wildlife Fund 1250 24th St NW Fl 6 Washington DC 20037-1193

FULLER, KATHY J. special education educator, consultant, researcher; b. Lamar, Colo., Oct. 24, 1957; d. Alfred L. and Leona M. Fuller; 1 child, Samantha Devon Blake. MA, Calif. State U., Northridge, 1993; postgrad., U. Calif., L.A., 1997. Prof. UCLA ext., L.A., 1999—, Pacific Oaks Coll., Pasadena, Calif., 2002—; cons. L.A. County of Edn., Calif., 2002—. Tchr. Pasadena Unified Sch. Dist., Calif., 1992—94; tchr., full inclusion specialist LA Unified Sch. Dist., 1994—2000; prof. Calif. State U., 1999—2002; presenter in field. Musician: (singer) New Life - Kora Music for the 21st Century (Prince Diabate CD); poet (poem) Helpless Hoping; contbr. articles to profl. jours. Pet therapist Love on 4 Paws, L.A., 2002. Recipient 1st place Edn. award, 2001, 2d place Behavioral/Social Scis. award, 2002. Mem.: Am. Ednl. Rsch. Assn., Coun. for Exceptional Children (assoc.), Phi Lambda Theta. Achievements include design of Fuller-Blake Academic Inventory. Home: 790 Monterey Rd South Pasadena CA 91030 Personal E-mail: kfullerbla@aol.com. E-mail: pacificoaks@edu.com.

FULLER, KENT RALPH, mathematician, educator; b. Northfield, Minn., Feb. 15, 1938; s. Ralph Edwin and Evelyn Janet Fuller; m. Gretchen Helen Absenmacher, July 6, 1958; 1 child, Dawn. BS, Mankato State Coll., Minn., 1960; MS, Mankato State Coll., 1962; PhD, U. Oreg., 1967. Asst. prof. math. U. Iowa, Iowa City, 1967—71, prof., 1971—75, prof. math., 1975—. Vis. prof. U. Hawaii, Honolulu, 1979—80, 1984—85, 1988—89, 1989—95. Co-author: (book) Rings and Categories of Modules, 1973, 1992; mem. editl. bd. Jour. of Algebra; contbr. NSF grantee, 1972—74, 1977—79, NATO grantee, 1992—2001. Mem.: Am. Math. Soc. Democrat. Avocations: reading, gardening. Office: Univ of Iowa Dept Math Iowa City IA 52242

FULLER, MARGARET JANE, medical technologist; b. Park Rapids, Minn., Jan. 29, 1947; d. Rudolph Kenneth and Jean Ellen (Klenk) Haas; m. Phillip Fuller, Aug. 7, 1970; 1 child, Sharon Dawn. BS in Chemistry, Muhlenberg Coll., 1969; diploma in med. tech., Allentown (Pa.) Hosp., 1972; MPA, Angelo State U., 1988; MS in Microbiology, Tex. Tech. U., 1992. Lab. dir. San Angelo-Tom Green County Health Dept., 1984-89; outpatient lab. supr. Meth. Hosp., Plainview, Tex., 1995-96; lab. mgr. Highland Med. Ctr., Lubbock, Tex., 1996-98; instr. microbiology Great Basin Coll., Ely, Nev. Mem. med. adv. bd. Planned Parenthood West Tex., San Angelo, 1987-89; scientist-by-mail, assoc. Children's Mus. Houston, 1991-92; direct patient vol. Hospice of Lubbock, 1993-98. Bd. dirs. El Camino coun. Girl Scouts U.S.A.; sec. Big. Bros.-Big Sisters Ely, 2002-2003. Recipient Thanks Badge, El Camino coun. Girl Scouts U.S.A., 1986. Mem. AAUW, Am. Soc. Microbiology, Am. Soc. Clin. Lab. Sci., Am. Soc. Clin. Pathologists (assoc., cert. med. technologist), Clin. Lab. Mgmt. Assn., Mensa, Beta Beta Beta, Sigma Theta Tau. Episcopalian. E-mail: pfuller@yahoo.com.

FULLER, MAXINE COMPTON, retired secondary school educator; b. Tiny, Va., Aug. 23, 1921; d. Perry and Lillie (Sutherland) Compton; m. David Thompson Fuller Jr., 1946 (dec. Mar. 1975); children: Davine Miller, Patricia Machen, Shirley Brodeur, Dorothy Brunson, David Thompson III. BS, Longwood Coll., 1943; MA, U. Ala., 1966; AA in Edn., U. Ala., Birmingham, 1980. Receptionist Goodyear Tire and Rubber Co., Richmond, Va., 1943, office mgr. trainee Selma, Ala., 1943-44; office mgr. Goodyear Service, Bessemer, Ala., 1944-46; sec., ops. mgr. Birmingham So. Coll., 1966; tchr. Hanpower-Bessemer State Tech. Coll., 1966-68, McAdory H.S., 1968-71; bus. edn. coord.

Hueytown (Ala.) H.S., 1971-88; ret. Hueytown H.S., 1988. Vis. com. mem. So. Assn. Secondary Schs. and Colls., 1980, 84. Sunday sch. tchr. Pleasant Ridge Bapt. Ch., Hueytown, 1962-88, pers. com., 1980-83; mem. Hueytown High PTA, 1986-87; liaison officer Adopt-A-Sch. program Hueytown High/Lloyd Noland Hosp., 1987-88; chmn. bus. edn. dept. Hueytown H.S., 1971-88. Mem. NEA, Nat. Ret. Tchrs. Assn., Ala. Ret. Tchrs. Assn., former mem. Echo Study Club (pres. 1987-88, sec. 1991-92), former mem. Culture Club of Hueytown (pres. 1994-96), Longwood Coll. Alumni Assn., former mem., Alpha Delta Kappa (corr. sec. XI chpt. 1982-84), Delta Kappa Gamma (treas. Gamma Lambda chpt. 1976-80). Baptist.

FULLER, MELVIN STUART, botany educator; b. Livermore Falls, Maine, May 5, 1931; s. George Raymond and Hilda Gordon (Pike) F.; m. Barbara Paul Newman, Apr. 2, 1955; children: Erica Ann, Scott Eliot, Amy Elizabeth. BS, U. Maine, 1953; MS, U. Nebr., 1955; PhD, U. Calif., 1959; Master's ad eundum, Brown U., 1963. Instr. Brown U., 1959, asst. prof., 1960-63, assoc. prof., 1963-64; asst. prof. U. Calif., 1964-65, assoc. prof., 1965-68; prof. botany U. Ga., 1968—, head dept., 1968-73, 86-89, univ. prof., 1990—; vis. agrl. rsch. biologist Sandoz Ltd., Basel, Switzerland, 1983; vis. rsch. prof. U. Uppsala, Sweden, 1985, 86; adj. prof. botany U. Maine, 1992—; emeritus univ. prof. and emeritus prof. botany U. Ga., 1995—. Mem. editorial bd. for publs. in biology McGraw Hill; sec. 2d Internat. Mycol. Congress; organizer Fifth Internat. Fungus Spore Meeting, 1991. Author: The Science of Botany, 1962, Lower Fungi in the Laboratory, 1978, Zoosporic Fungi in Teach. and Research, 1987. Fellow British Mycological Soc.; mem. Bot. Soc. Am., Mycol. Soc. Am. (counselor 1966-68, 70-72, pres. 1975, Disting. Mycologist Award, 1992), Soc. Study of Growth and Devel., Am. Phythopath. Soc., Gulf of Maine Found. (pres. 1997-99). Achievements include research on growth and development of aquatic fungi, ultrastructure, mechanism of action of fungicides. Home: 48 Water St Damariscotta ME 04543

FULLER, MILLARD DEAN, charitable organization executive, lawyer; b. Lanett, Ala., Jan. 3, 1935; s. Render and Estin (Cook) F.; m. Linda Caldwell; children: Christopher, Kimberly, Faith, Georgia. BS in Econs., Auburn U., 1957; LLB, U. Ala., 1960; LHD (hon.), Ea. Coll., Pa., 1985, Ottawa U., 1987, Susquehanna U., 1989; D Pub. Svcs. (hon.), DePauw U., 1988; HHD (hon.), Coll. of Wooster, 1989, Wake Forest U., 1990, Mercer U., 1990, Westminster Coll., 1990, Whitworth Coll., 1990, Dallas Bapt. U., 1994, Lynchburg Coll., 1992, North Park Coll., 1992, Tech. U. Nova Scotia, 1992, U. North Ala., 1994, Providence Coll., 1994, Presbyn. Coll., Clinton, S.C., 1995, Bluffton Coll., 1995, Elon Coll., 1995, Nova Southeastern U., 1996. Bar: Ala. 1960, Ga. 1972. Co-founder Fuller and Dees Mktg. Group, Inc., Montgomery, Ala., 1960, pres., 1960-65; ptnr. Fuller and Dees (law firm), Montgomery, 1960-65; devel. dir. Tougaloo (Miss.) Coll., 1966-68; dir. Koinonia Ptnrs., Inc. (developer various bus. ops. for Koinonia Christian community), Americus, Ga., 1968-72; dir. devel. Ch. of Christ, Zaire, Equator region Africa, 1973-76, initiator housing project for low-income families, Mbandaka, Zaire; founder, pres. Habitat for Humanity Internat., Inc., Americus, 1976—. Author: Bokotola, 1977, Love in the Mortar Joints, 1980, No More Shacks!, 1986, The Excitement is Building, 1990, Theology of the Hammer, 1994, A Simple, Decent Place to Live, 1995, More than Houses, 2000, Building Materials for Life, 2002. Adv. com. Albert Schweitzer Fellowship of Am., 1992. Lt. U.S. Army, 1960. Recipient Outstanding Achievement award Coun. State Housing Agys., 1986, Clarence Jordan Exemplary Chistiran Svc. award So. Bapt. Theol. Sem., 1986, Dr. Marting Luther King, Jr. Humanitarian award, 1987, Disting. chrisitan Svc. in Social Welfare award N.Am. Assn. christians in Social Work, 1988, Internat. Humanity Svc. award Am. Overseas Assn. ARC, 1989, Pub. Svc. Achievement award Common Cause, 1989, M. Justin Herman Meml. award Nat. Assn. Housing and Devel. Ofcls., 1989, The Temple award for Creative Altruism, 1990, Joseph C. Wilson award Rochester Assn. for the UN, 1990, Amicus Certus award Luth. Social Svcs. Ill., Martin Luther Jr. Humanitarian award Ga. State Holiday Commn., 1992, Profl. Achievement award Partnership Affordable Housing, 1993, Harry S. Truman Pub. Svc. award City of Independence, 1994, The McConnell award Truett-McConnell Coll., Ga., 1995, Faithful Servant award Nat. Assn. of Evangelicals, 1996, Spirit of Ga. award, 1996; named Builder of Yr. Profl. Bldr. mag., 1995, Nat. Housing Hall of Fame, 1996, Presdl. Medal of Freedom, 1996, Jefferson award 1999. Mem. Ala. Bar Assn., Ga. Bar Assn., The Am. Works Partnership (bd. dirs.). Baptist. Avocations: reading, walking. Office: Habitat for Humanity Internat 121 Habitat St Americus GA 31709-3498

FULLER, MITCHELL FRANKLIN, II, political scientist, educator; b. Okla. City, Okla., Oct. 3, 1967; s. Mitchell Franklin Fuller, Sr. and Alpha Ann Fields; m. Sherri Louise Manning, Dec. 15, 2001; children: Madison Taylor, Braxton Alexander. BA in Polit. Sci., S.W. Okla. State U., 1995; MPA, U. Okla., 1999. Spl. asst. to exec. dir. Internat. Programs Ctr. U. Okla., Normon, Okla., 1997—2000; asst. prof. polit. sci. Johnson County C.C., Overland Park, Kans., 2001—. 1st lt. USAR, 1995—. Mem.: Res. Officers Assn., Shawnee Kiwanis Club, Overland Park Masonic Lodge. Methodist. Home: 2707 Zambia Dr Cedar Park TX 78613 E-mail: mfuller@jccc.net.

FULLER, PAMELA DORR, software engineer; b. Monrovia, Calif., July 23, 1956; d. Jack Glendon and Nancy (Tatnall) F.; m. Timothy Seth Daniel, July 5, 1985 (div. Dec. 1999). BS in Computer Sci., Coll. William and Mary, 1978; MS in Computer Sci., Va. Poly. Inst. and State U., 1989. Programmer/analyst United Info. Svcs., Falls Church, Va., 1978-83; software engr. Hadron, Inc., Fairfax, Va., 1983-88, Wollongong Group, McLean, Va., 1988-96, Attachmate Corp., McLean, 1996-99, Vignette Corp., Gaithersburg, Md., 1999—2003. Avocations: sailing, scuba diving, travel, weaving. E-mail: pdfuller@bigfoot.com.

FULLER, PERRY LUCIAN, lawyer; b. Central City, Nebr., Oct. 26, 1922; s. Perry L. and Ruth (Howorth) F.; m. Alice Moorman, Mar. 6, 1948; 1 child, Leslie Ann Fuller. Student, U. Chgo. Law Sch., 1946-47; AB, U. Nebr., 1947, JD, 1949. Bar: Ill. 1950, U.S. Supreme Ct. Mem. staff Chgo. Crime Commn., 1949; sr. ptnr. Hinshaw & Culbertson and predeccessors, Chgo., 1956—. Lectr. in law U. Chgo., 1970-76, mem. vis. com., 1991-93. Vice chmn. exec. com. Law in Am. Soc. Found., 1966, chmn., 1967—69, pres., 1969—95; chmn. Cook County CSC, 1967—69; mem. Ill. Law Enforcement Commn., 1971—72; v.p. Fed. Defender, Inc., 1964; trustee Village of Winnetka, 1992—96; bd. dir. Winnetka Cmty. Chest, Ill., 1966—69, Ill. Humane Soc., 1978—, pres., 1986. 1st lt. USMC, 1942—46, Capt. USMC, 1952—53. Decorated Air medal. Fellow Am. Coll. Trial Lawyers (state chmn. 1972-74), Am. Bar Found., Ill. Bar Found.; mem. ABA (chmn. pub. relations com. 1968-69, gavel awards com. 1974-77, chmn. 1976-78), Ill, Fed., 7th Cir. Chgo. (bd. mgrs. 1967-69) bar assns., Am. Law Inst., Am. Judicature Soc., Internat. Assn. Def. Counsel (chmn. Continuing Legal Edn. bd. 1982-86, exec. com. 1983-86), Soc. Trial Lawyers Ill. (bd. dirs. 1967-68, 73-74, sec. 1975-76, pres. 1977-78), Def. Rsch. Inst. (chmn. insts. com. 1986-90), Scribes, Legal Club, Law Club (pres. 1987-88). Republican. Home: 1093 Fisher Ln Winnetka IL 60093-1503 Office: Hinshaw & Culbertson 222 N La Salle St Ste 300 Chicago IL 60601-1081

FULLER, PHILLIP ROLAND, finance educator; b. LaGrange, Ga., Jan. 27, 1955; s. Barney Elbert Fuller Sr. and Sara Fuller. BBA, West Ga. Coll., 1977, MBA, 1979; DBA, Miss. State U., 1990. Asst. prof. Fin. Delat State U., Cleveland, Miss., 1985—86; prof. Fin. Jackson State U., Jackson, Miss., 1986—. Co-editor: Jour. Acctg. and Fin. Rsch., 1992—. Nissan fellow, U. Chgo., 1994. Mem.: Internat. Acad. Bus. Discipline. Avocations: hiking, reading, fishing. Office: Jackson State Univ Lynch St Jackson MS 39217*

FULLER, RENEE NUNI, psychologist, educational publisher; b. Mannheim, Germany, Apr. 14, 1929; came to U.S., 1938; d. Eric Woldemar and Fridel Gronau (Henning) Stoetzner; widowed. Student, Swarthmore (Pa.) Coll., 1947-49; BA, Hunter Coll., 1951; MA, Columbia U., 1953; PhD, NYU, 1963. Research scientist Letchworth Village N.Y. State Dept. Mental Hygiene, Thiells, 1961-67; project dir. Staten Island (N.Y.) Soc. Mental Health, 1967-68; chief psychol. services Rosewood Hosp. Ctr., Owings Mills, Md., 1968-75; pres. Ball-Stick-Bird Publs. Inc., Williamstown, Mass., 1975—. Author: In Search of the IQ Correlation, 1977, (reading series) Ball-Stick-Bird; contbr. articles to profl. jours. Recipient Disting. Achievement award Fairleigh-Dickinson U., N.J., 1979. Fellow Am. Psychol. Soc.; mem. APA, Soc. for Rsch. in Child Devel. Office: Ball Stick Bird Publs Inc PO Box 429 Williamstown MA 01267 E-mail: info@ballstickbird.com.

FULLER, RICHARD KENNETH, retired alcohol/drug abuse services professional; b. Chgo., Apr. 2, 1935; s. Marc Cornelius and Edna Jane (Gibson) F.; m. Kathleen Julia Brain, Oct. 22, 1960; children: Julia, Douglas. BA, Monmouth Coll., 1957; MD, Western Res. U., 1962; MS, Case Western Res. U., 1971. From staff physician to asst. chief GI sect. VA Hosp., Cleve., 1971-90; dir. divsn. of clin. and prevention rsch. Nat. Inst. on Alcohol Abuse and Alcoholism, Rockville, Md., 1990—2003; ret., 2003. Asst. prof., assoc. prof. medicine Case-Western Res. U., Cleve., 1974-90, asst. prof. biometry, 1972-90. Contbr. chpts. in books and articles to profl. jours. Capt. USAF, 1964-66.

FULLER, ROBERT KENNETH, architect, urban designer; b. Denver, Oct. 6, 1942; s. Kenneth Roller and Gertrude Ailene (Heid) F.; m. Virginia Louise Elkin, Aug. 23, 1969; children: Kimberly Kirsten, Kelsey Christa. BArch, U. Colo., 1967; MArch and Urban Design, Washington U., St. Louis, 1974. Registered profl. arch., Colo. Archtl. designer Fuller & Fuller, Denver, Marvin Hatami Assocs., 1968-69; architect, planner Urban Research and Design Ctr., St. Louis, 1970-72; urban designer Victor Gruen & Assocs., 1973-75; prin. Fuller & Fuller Assocs., Denver, 1975—. Past pres. Denver East Ctrl. Civic Assn., Country Club Hist. Dist.; bd. dirs. Cherry Creek Steering Com., Cherry Creek Found.; pres. Horizon Adventures, Inc.; permanent sec.-treas. Archtl. Edn. Found., AIA Colo. Sgt. USMCR, 1964-70. Mem.: AIA (past pres. Denver chpt.), Rocky Mountain Vintage Racing Assn., Colo. Arlberg Club (past pres.), Delta Phi Delta, Phi Gamma Delta. Home: 2244 E 4th Ave Denver CO 80206-4107 Office: 3320 E 2nd Ave Denver CO 80206-5302

FULLER, SAMUEL ASHBY, retired lawyer, mining company executive; b. Indpls., Sept. 2, 1924; s. John L.H. and Mary (Ashby) F.; m. Betty Winn Hamilton, June 10, 1948; children— Mary Cheryl Fuller Hargrove, Karen E. Fuller Wolfe, Deborah R. BS in Gen. Engring, U. Cin., 1946, JD, 1947; cert. fin. planner, Coll. for Fin. Planning, 1989. Bar: Ohio 1948, Ind. 1951, Fla. 1984. Cleve. claims rep. Mfrs. and Mchts. Indemnity Co., 1947-48; claims supr. Indemnity Ins. Co. N.Am., 1948-50; with firm Stewart, Irwin, Gilliom, Fuller & Meyer (formerly Murray, Mannon, Fairchild & Stewart), Indpls., 1950-85, Lewis Kappes Fuller & Eads (name changed to Lewis & Kappes), Indpls., 1985-89, of counsel, 1990—2000; pres., dir. Irsugo Consol. Mines, Ltd., 1953-80; ret., 2000. Dir. Ind. Pub. Health Found., Inc., 1972-84; staff instr. Purdue U. Life Ins. and Mktg. Inst., 1954-61; instr. Am. Coll. Life Underwriters, Indpls., 1964-74; mem. Ind. State Bd. Law Examiners, 1984-96, treas. 1987-88, Bd. dirs. Southwest Social Centre, Inc., 1965-70; pres., dir. Westminster Village North, Inc., 1981-89. Fellow: Indpls. Bar Found.; mem.: Fla. Bar, 7th Cir. Bar Assn., Ind. State Bar Assn. (bd. mgrs. 1986—88), Lincoln Hills Golf Club, Sun City Ctr. Golf and Racquet Club, Masons, Beta Theta Pi. Republican. Roman Catholic. Home: 306 Thornhill Pl Sun City Center FL 33573-5842 E-mail: samuel105@peoplepc.com.

FULLER, S(HERI) MARCE, energy executive; BSEE, U. Ala.; MS in Power System Engring., Union Coll. Student engr. Ala. Power (subs. The So. Co.), 1980-83; engr. power system engring. dept. GE, 1983-85; electric system planning engr. Ala. Power (subs. The So. Co.), 1985-87; sr. fin. analyst corp. finance So. Co. Svcs., 1987-89, prin. strategic planning, asst. to pres., 1989-91; bus. devel. mgr. So. Electric (subs. The So. Co.), 1991; v.p. domestic bus. devel. So. Electric, 1994-96, sr. v.p. domestic ops., 1996; pres., CEO Mirant Corp., Atlanta, 1999—. Bd. dirs. Curtiss-Wright Corp., Earthlink. Trustee Atlanta Internat. Sch. Office: Mirant 1155 Perimeter Ctr W Atlanta GA 36338

FULLER, STEPHEN HERBERT, business administration educator; b. Columbus, Ohio, Feb. 4, 1920; s. Josiah Allen and Mary Ellen (Quinn) F.; m. Frances Mulhearn, Jun 23, 1951; children: Teofilo M., Rogelio M., Mark B., Joseph B. BA, Ohio U., 1941, PhD, 1977; grad. Indusl. Adminstr., Harvard U., 1941-43, MBA, 1947, D in Bus. Adminstrn., 1958; PhD, Ateneo de Manila, Philippines, 1964, De LaSalle Coll., Manila, 1971, Lawrence Inst. Tech., 1978. From instr. to assoc. prof. in bus. adminstrn. Harvard U., Boston, 1947-61, prof. in bus. adminstrn., 1961-71, assoc. dean. for external affairs, 1964-69, Chua Tiampo prof. in bus. adminstrn. Cambridge, Mass., 1982-85; pres. Asian Inst. Mgmt., Manila, 1969-71; v.p. personnel adminstrn. and devel. staff Gen. Motors Corp., Detroit, 1971-82; chmn., CEO, World Book Inc., Chgo., 1985-92; instr. econs. and labor rels. Ohio U., Athens, 1977, prof. bus. adminstrn., 1992-97. Author: (with others) Problems in Labor Relations, 1950, 3d edit. 1964. Served to capt. AUS, 1943-46. Recipient Presl. Medal Merit, Republic Philippines, 1971. Mem. Internat. Acad. Mgmt., Nat. Mgmt. Assn., Philippine Am. Soc., Phi Beta Kappa, Phi Eta Sigma, Omicron Delta Kappa, Beta Gamma Sigma, Delta Tau Delta, Sigma Iota Epsilon. Clubs: Bald Peak Colony (Melvin, N.H.); Chicago; Harvard (N.Y.C.). Republican. Roman Catholic. Avocations: theatre, travel, reading. Home (Summer): 35 Lantern Rd Belmont MA 02478

FULLER, STEPHEN W. science educator; b. Port Chester, NY, Mar. 14, 1945; s. Edouard W. and Dorothy R. Fuller; m. Anne Gray Jones, June 22, 1974; children: Ross S., Sarah Anne. BS, Cornell U., Ithaca, NY, 1967; PhD, U. N.H., Durham, N.H., 1971. Asst. prof. biol. sci. Mary Washington Coll., Fredericksburg, Va., 1972—77, chmn. dept. biol. sci., 1976—88, assoc. prof. biol. sci., 1977—84, prof. biol. sci., 1984—. Mem.: Estuarine Rsch. Fedn. (mem. governing bd. 2002—), Atlantic Estuarine Rsch. Soc. (ores. 2002—04).

FULLER, THEODORE, retired insurance executive; b. Yonkers, N.Y., Dec. 7, 1918; s. Clarence Wendel and Mary Edgar (Denniston) F. AB cum laude, Princeton U., 1941; LLB, Columbia U., 1948. Bar: N.Y. 1948. With Savs. Bank Life Ins. Fund, N.Y.C., 1948-83, exec. v.p., 1964-65, pres., 1965-83. Former mem. N.Y. State Adv. Bd. Life Ins.; cons. Nat. Exec. Svc. Corps, Svc. Corps Retired Execs. Tax counselor Am. Assn. Ret. Persons. Comdr. USNR, World War II, Korea. Mem. Assn. of Bar of City of N.Y., Princeton Club, Univ. Glee Club, Indian Harbor Yacht Club, Retired Men's Assn. (former pres.), Ea. Packard Club, Antique Automobile Club Am., Classic Car Club Am. (former bd. dirs.), Rolls Royce Owners Club, Pierce Arrow Club, Sound Investments Club. Home: 3 Mercia Ln Greenwich CT 06830-7068

FULLER, WAYNE ARTHUR, statistics educator; b. Corning, Iowa, June 15, 1931; s. Loren Boyd and Eva Gladys (Darrah) F.; m. Evelyn Rose Steinford, Dec. 22, 1956; children: Douglas W., Bret E. BS, Iowa State U., 1955, MS, 1957, PhD, 1959. Asst. prof. Iowa State U., Ames, 1959-62, assoc. prof., 1962-66, prof., 1966-83, disting. prof. stats., 1983—2001, disting. prof. emeritus, 2001—. Cons. Doane Mktg. Rsch., Inc., St. Louis. Author: Introduction to Statistical Time Series, 1976, 2nd ed. 1996, Measurement Error Models, 1987; also articles. Served as cpl. U.S. Army, 1952-54 Fellow Am. Statis. Assn. (v.p. 1991-93), Inst. Math Stats., Econometric Soc.; mem. Internat. Statis. Inst. Biometric Soc., Royal Statis. Soc., Am. Agr. Econ. Assn. Home: 3013 Briggs Cir Ames IA 50010-4705 Office: Iowa State U Statis Lab 221 Snedecor Hall Ames IA 50010 E-mail: waf@iastate.edu.

FULLER, WILLIAM SIDNEY, lawyer; b. Auburn, Ala., Aug. 9, 1931; s. William Melton and Ernestine (Torbert) F.; m. Joyce Jeffrey, Nov. 5, 1953; children: Jeffrey Melton, Barbara Rush. BS, Auburn U., 1953; LLB, U. Ala., 1956, JD, 1969. Bar: Ala. 1956. Student asst. to dean U. Ala. Law Sch., 1954—55; law clk. to U.S. dist. judge, Montgomery, Ala., 1956—57; practice law Andalusia, 1957—; former city atty. City of Andalusia. Dir., sec. Covington County Bank; lectr. Southeastern Trial Inst.; mem. grievance com. Ala. State Bar, 1968-71, mem. bd. commrs., 1979-81; mem. law and contemporary affairs adv. council Auburn U. Author: Personal Injury Treatises. Mem. ABA, Ala., Covington County bar assns., Am. Trial Lawyers Assn., Am. Bd. Trial Advocates, Ala. Plaintiff Lawyers Assn., Ala. Trial Lawyers Assn. (pres. 1968), Phi Delta Phi, Kappa Alpha, Alpha Phi Omega. Presbyterian (elder, trustee, past chmn. bd. deacons Sunday sch. tchr.). Club: Andalusia (dir., pres. 1972), Topsl Beach and Racket (Destin, Fla.). Home: 100 S Ridge Rd Andalusia AL 36420-4214 Office: 28 S Court Sq Andalusia AL 36420-3918

FULLER-MCCHESNEY, MARY ELLEN, sculptor, writer, publisher; b. Wichita, Kans., Oct. 20, 1922; d. Edward Emory and Karen Mabel (Rasmussen) Fuller; m. Robert Pearson, Dec. 17, 1949. AA, U. Calif., Berkeley, 1943. Staff writer Currant; rschr. Archives of Am. Art; publisher Sonoma Mt. Publishing Co. Author: (art book) A Period of Exploration, 1973, Robert McChesney: An American Painter, 1996, 3 mystery novels, short stories, poems, articles; exhibitions include Syracuse (N.Y.) Mus., San Francisco Mus., Oakland (Calif.) Mus., Calif. State U., Sonoma, Santa Rosa Civic Ctr., U. Calif., Davis, San Jose (Calif.) State U., U. Calif. Ctr. U. Oaxaca, San Francisco art festivals, galleries, prin. works include Dos Leones, San Francisco Gen. Hosp., 1974, Children's Sculpture Park, Salinas Cmty. Ctr., 1976, Falcon, Andrew Hill High Sch., San Jose, Calif., 1977, Yuba Totem,Yuba Lion, Dept. Motor Vehicles Bldg., Calif., 1983, Playground, Portsmouth Square, San Francisco, 1982, Olympic Lions, Squaw Valley, Calif., 1983, Stratford Meml. Lion and Bear, Petaluma (Calif.) Libr., 1983, Anshen-Mays Birdbath, Sausalito, Calif., 1984, West Side Pump Sta., San Francisco, 1979, 4 garden sculptures, L.A. State Office Bldg., 1987, Walnut Creek Totem, 1992, Seach Park, Santa Cruz, Calif., 1993, Utah Arts coun. Bear v Rams, Salt Lake City, 1999, sculptures, Becky Temko Park, Berkeley, Calif., 2000, Rainbow Ridge Park, Reno, Nev., 2001, Gala Chamberlain Fountain, Santa Rosa, Calif., 2002, Garden Lion, Sonoma State U., Rohnert Park, Calif., 2002, Lady of the Beasts sculpture, Animal Shelter, Petaluma, Calif., 2003. Ford Found. fellow, 1965-66; Nat. Endowment Arts grantee, 1975. Home: 2955 Sonoma Mt Rd Petaluma CA 94954

FULLERTON, CHARLES WILLIAM, retired insurance company executive; b. Columbus, Ohio, May 18, 1917; s. Paul O. and Marvina (Groom) F.; m. Anne Hoddy, Jan. 21, 1940; children— Gary, Lynn Fullerton Johnson. BS, Ohio State U., 1938. C.P.A., Ohio. Dist. financial dir. FSA, Columbus, 1938-40; office mgr. Goodyear Tire & Rubber Co., Huntington, W.Va., 1940-41; chief accountant to v.p. finance Landmark Farm Bur., Columbus, 1941-66; v.p., sec., treas. Nationwide Devel. Co., Columbus, 1966-71; with Nationwide Ins. Affiliates, Columbus, 1971-82, exec. v.p., 1972-73, pres., 1973-82; v.p. Nationwide Ins. Co., 1973-82. Dir. Nationwide Devel. Co., Nationwide Comm., Inc., Nationwide Consumer Svcs., Inc., Heritage Securities, Inc.; bd. govs. Investment Co. Inst., Washington. Mem. steering com. Devel. Com. for Greater Columbus, 1977-79; bd. dirs. Greater Columbus Arts Coun., Ohio Dominican Coll., Players Theatre of Columbus; active Downtown Action Com., Capitol Sq. Com. Mem. AICPA, Ohio Soc. CPA, Treas. Club of Columbus (past pres.), Nat. Soc. Accts. for Coops. (past pres.), Ohio Coun. Farmer Coops. (v.p.), Columbus Contrs. Club. Clubs: Masons. Methodist. Home: Apt 331 4590 Knightsbridge Blvd Columbus OH 43214-4334 *To achieve the goals and objectives established for a business enterprise, I strive to set tasks and priorities in concert with the persons responsible for the results. This process is carried on in a manner that assists those persons to grow as individuals while the organization becomes stronger through the successful performance of those goals and objectives.*

FULLERTON, GAIL JACKSON, university president emeritus; m. Stanley James Fullerton, Mar. 27, 1967; children by previous marriage— Gregory Snell Putney, Cynde Putney Mitchell. BA, U. Nebr., 1949, MA, 1950; PhD, U. Oreg., 1954. Lectr. sociology Drake U., Des Moines, 1955-57; asst. prof. sociology Fla. State U., Tallahassee, 1957-60, San Jose (Calif.) State U., 1963-67, asso. prof., 1968-71, prof., 1972-91, dean grad. studies and research, 1972-76, exec. v.p. univ., 1976-78, pres., 1978-91; ret., 1991. Bd. dirs. Assn. Western Univs., Inc., 1980-91; mem. sr. accrediting commn. Western Assn. Schs. and Colls., 1982-88, chmn., 1985-86; mem. Pres.'s Commn. Nat. Collegiate Athletic Assn., 1986-91; bd. dirs. Am. Coll. Assn., 1991. Author: Survival in Marriage, 2d edit, 1977, (with Snell Putney) Normal Neurosis: The Adjusted American, 2d edit, 1966. Carnegie fellow, 1950-51, 52-53; Doherty Found. fellow, 1951-52 Mem. Phi Beta Kappa, Chi Omega. *Our lives are the summations of the choices we make, one at a time, by intention or by default. I have tried to choose by deliberate and rational intent, so that even when the choice proves wrong, it is clear to me that I am responsible for myself.*

FULLERTON, JOHN C., III, surgeon; b. Durham, N.C., 1951; MD, U. Va., 1977. Diplomate Am. Bd. Surgery. Intern William Beaumont AMC, El Paso, Tex., 1977-78, resident, 1978-82; pvt. practice Arkadelphia, Ark.; attending Bapt. Med. Ctr., Arkadelphia. Fellow ACS; mem. Tex. Med. Assn., Soc. of Am. Gastrointestinal Endoscopic Surgeons, Ark. Med. Soc. Office: 2910 Cypress Rd Arkadelphia AR 71923-4227

FULLERTON, R. DONALD, banker; b. June 7, 1931; married. BA, U. Toronto, 1953. With Can. Bank of Commerce, Vancouver, 1953—, exec. v.p., chief gen. mgr., 1973, dir. of bank, 1974—, pres., COO, 1976, chmn., CEO, 1984, ret. chmn., CEO, 1992, chmn. exec. com., 1992-99. Bd. dirs. CIBC, George Weston Ltd., Hollinger, Inc., Asia Satellite Telecomms. Holding, Ltd., Husky Energy, Ptnr. Comm. Co. Ltd. Avocations: skiing, golfing. Office: CIBC Commerce Ct W Toronto ON Canada M5L 1A2

FULLERTON, ROBERT VICTOR, lawyer; b. Lakewood, Ohio, Mar. 30, 1918; s. Victor G. and Gertrude H. (Horsley) F.; m. Frances Riebel Aug. 23, 1941 (dec. Mar. 1989); children: Susan Anne, Thomas George; m. Margaret Paver Van Voorhis, Feb., 1991. BS in Bus., Miami U., Oxford, Ohio, 1939; LL.B., JD, Case Western Res. U., 1941. Bar: Ohio 1941, Calif. 1945, U.S. Dist. Ct. (ctrl. dist.) Calif. 1945, U.S. Dist. Ct. (so. dist.) Calif. 1974, U.S. Ct. Appeals (9th cir.) 1974, U.S. Tax Ct. 1952, U.S. Supreme Ct. 1974. Spl. agt. FBI, 1941-46; dep. dist. atty. San Bernardino County (Calif.), 1946; asst. dist. atty., 1946-47; individual practice law, 1947—. Chmn. San Bernardino County U.S. Savs. Bond Com. Dept. Treasury, 1963— Pres. United Fund, San Bernardino, 1961-62; trustee Found. for Calif. State U., San Bernardino, 1981—, v.p., 1986—; bd. dirs. Inland Action, 1974-90; trustee Inland Area Symphony Assn., 1983—, v.p. endowments, 1986; bd. dirs. Estate Planning Coun. San Bernadino County, 1984-92, pres., 1990-91; chmn. planning divsn. United Cmty. Svcs., San Bernardino, 1966-69; mem. adv. bd. Auto. Club So. Calif., 1969-80. Recipient Citizens of Yr. award San Bernardion Realtors, 1967. Mem. ABA, State Bar Calif. (asst. sec. San Bernardino County 1953-56, conf. coord. com. on fed. rules 1954-57), Am. Judicature Soc., Air Force Assn. (pres. local chpt. 1969-70), San Bernardino C. of C. (pres. 1968-69), Kiwanis (pres. local club 1959-60), Arrowhead Country. Republican. Home: 3255 Valencia Ave San Bernardino CA 92404-2418 Office: 215 N D St San Bernardino CA 92401-1733 E-mail: rfullerton@inlandbusinesslaw.com.

FULLERTON, STUART LATIMER, corporate lawyer; b. Washington, July 13, 1960; s. George Latimer and Dorothy H. (Mallan) F.; m. Shelby Lynn Haverson, June 18, 1989; children: Maisie Haverson, Sallie Mallan. BA, U. Calif., Berkeley, 1983; JD, Georgetown U., 1987. Bar: NY 1988, DC 1990, Pa. 1994. Assoc. Curtis, Mallet-Prevost, Colt & Mosle, N.Y.C., 1987-88, O'Melveny & Myers, Washington, 1988-90; trial atty. U.S. Dept. of Justice, Washington, 1990-93; assoc. Harkins Cunningham, Phila., 1993-95; sr. counsel AstraZeneca Pharms., Wilmington, Del., 1995—. Democrat. Episcopalian. Home: 358 Valley Rd Merion Station PA 19066-1520 Office: AstraZeneca Pharmaceuticals LP 1800 Concord Pike Wilmington DE 19803-2910

FULLERTON, THOMAS MANKIN, JR., economist; b. Ft. Worth, Aug. 31, 1959; s. Thomas Mankin and Katherine Jane (Copeland) F.; m. Lourdes Licon; children: Kristy, Steven, Brett. BBA, U. Tex., El Paso, 1981; MS, Iowa State U., 1984; MA, U. Penn., 1988; PhD, U. Fla., 1996. Assoc. economist El Paso (Tex.) Electric Co., El Paso, 1981-83; economist Exec. Office of the Gov., Boise, Idaho, 1984-87; internat. economist Wharton Econometrics, The WEFA Group, Bala Cynwyd, Pa., 1988-91; sr. economist U. Fla., Gainesville, 1991-96; rsch. assoc. U. Fla. Ctr. for Latin Am. Studies, Gainesville, 1991-96; assoc. prof. U. Tex. El Paso, 1996—, coord. border region modeling project, 1996—. Alternate, Nat. Gov.'s Assn. Energy Com., Boise, 1985-86; Idaho state expert, Wharton Econometrics Regional Network, Boise, 1986-87; Idaho coord., Fed. Program Population Estimates, Boise, 1985-87; broadcaster, Radio YSKL, San Salvador, El Salvador, 1976-77. Sponsor Save the children, Bogota, Colombia, 1985—; commr. U. Tex. Student Election Bd., El Paso, 1978-79, mortar bd. U. Tex., El Paso, 1981. Dean's fellow, Wharton Sch., 1987-88. Mem. Nat. Assn. Bus. Economists (policy panel 1989—, forecast panel 1984-88), Rio Grande Econs. Assn., Wharton Alumni Assn., Beta Gamma Sigma, Phi Kappa Phi, Alpha Chi. Presbyterian. Office: U Tex Dept Econs And Fin El Paso TX 79968-0543 E-mail: tomf@utep.edu.

FULLINGTON, CYNTHIA JANETTE, pediatric nurse; b. Little Falls, N.Y., Nov. 19, 1960; d. Lloyd Douglas and Janette Elizabeth (Trumble) VanAlstine; m. Bruce Fullington, Sept. 8, 1984; children: Scott H., Beth Lindsey. Lic. practical nurse, Otsego Area Occupational Ctr., Milford, N.Y., 1979; AS in Nursing with honors, Fulton-Montgomery Community Coll., Johnstown, N.Y., 1989. RN, N.Y.; cert. BLS, ACLS, PALS; cert. pediatric nurse. Practice nurse surg. med. unit and ICU Mary Imogene Bassett Hosp., Cooperstown, NY, 1979—84, practical nurse emergency rm., 1984—89, RN emergency room, 1989—91, pediatric clinic RN-triage nurse, 1991—, part-time allergy nurse,

1997—98. Treas. Cherry Valley-Springfield Ctrl. Sch. PTO, 2000—01; sec. Cherry Valley-Springfield PTO, 1999—2000; tchr. Sunday Sch., 1992—99. Home: 1834 Clinton Rd Fort Plain NY 13339-4607 Office: Mary Imogene Bassett Hosp 1 Atwell Rd Cooperstown NY 13326-1394

FULLMER, DANIEL WARREN, former psychologist, educator; b. Spoon River, Ill., Dec. 12, 1922; s. Daniel Floyd and Sarah Louisa (Essex) F.; m. Janet Satomi Saito, June 1980; children: Daniel William, Mark Warren. BS, Western Ill. U., 1947, MS, 1952; PhD, U. Denver, 1955. Post-doctoral intern psychiat. div. U. Oreg. Med. Sch., 1958-61; mem. faculty U. Oreg., 1955-66; prof. psychology Oreg. System of Higher Edn., 1958-66; faculty Coll. Edn. U. Hawaii, Honolulu, 1966-95, retired, 1995, prof. emeritus, 1974—; pvt. practice psychol. counseling. Cons. psychologist Grambling State U., 1960-81; founder Free-Family Counseling Ctrs., Portland, Oreg., 1959-66, Honolulu, 1966-74; co-founder Child and Family Counseling Ctr., Waianae, Oahu, Hawaii, Kilohana United Meth. Ch., Oahu, 1992, v.p., sec., 1992; pres. Human Resources Devel. Ctr., Inc., 1974—; chmn. Hawaii State Bd. to License Psychologists, 1973-78. Author: Counseling: Group Theory & System, 2d. edit., 1978, The Family Therapy Dictionary Text, 1991, MANABU, Diagnosis and Treatment of a Japanese Boy with a Visual Anomaly, 1991; co-author: Principles of Guidance, 2d. edit., 1977; author (counselor/cons. training manuals) Counseling: Content and Process, 1964, Family Consultation Therapy, 1968, The School Counselor Consultant, 1972, Family Therapy as the Rites of Passage, 1998; editor: Bulletin, Oreg. Coop Testing Service, 1955-57, Hawaii P&G Jour., 1970-76; assoc. editor: Educational Perspectives, U. Hawaii Coll. Edn. Served with USNR, 1944-46. Recipient Francis E. Clark award Hawaii Pers. Guidance Assn., 1972, Thomas Jefferson award for Outstanding Pub. Svc., 1993; named Hall of Fame Grambling State U., 1987. Mem. Am. Psychol. Assn., Am. Counseling Assn. (Nancy C. Wimmer award 1963), Masons. Methodist. Office: 1750 Kalakaua Ave Apt 809 Honolulu HI 96826-3725 *I grew up along Spoon River. The people of Spoon River had a principle of life: Improve on what you are. The purpose is to be able to help others help themselves. From here, it is like stepping into a river of life; the deeper you got, the stronger the current. Then, suddenly, here you are nearing the delta. Just ahead lies a beautiful ocean.*

FULLMER, HAROLD MILTON, dentist, educator; b. Gary, Ind., July 9, 1918; s. Howard and Rachel Eva (Tiedge) F.; m. Marjorie Lucile Engel, Dec. 31, 1942 (dec. Apr. 1983); children: Angela Sue, Pamela Rose; m. Shirley Ford Davis, Mar. 28, 1987. BS, Ind. U., 1942, D.D.S., 1944; hon. doctorate, U. Athens (Greece), 1981. Diplomate: Am. Bd. Oral Pathology. Intern Charity Hosp., New Orleans, 1946-47, resident, 1947-48, vis. dental surgeon, 1948-53; instr. Loyola U., New Orleans, 1948-49, asst. prof., 1949-50, assoc. prof. gen. and oral pathology, 1949-53; cons. pathology VA hosps., Biloxi and Gulfport, Miss., 1950-53; asst. dental surgeon Nat. Inst. Dental Research, NIH, Bethesda, Md., 1953-54, dental surgeon, 1954-56, sr. dental surgeon, 1956-60, dental dir., 1960-70; chief sect. histochemistry Nat. Inst. Dental Research, 1967-70, chief exptl. pathology, 1969-70, cons. to dir., 1971-72; mem. dental caries program adv. com. HEW, 1975-79, chmn., 1976-79; dir. Inst. Dental Research; prof. pathology, prof. dentistry, assoc. dean Sch. Dentistry, U. Ala. Med. Center, Birmingham, 1970-87; prof. emeritus, 1987—; sr. scientist cancer research and tng. program, sci. adv. com. Sch. Dentistry, U. Ala. Med. Center (Diabetes Research and Tng. Center), 1977-87. Mem. med. rsch. career devel. com. VA 1977-81; mem. com grants and allocations Am. Fund for Dental Health, 1977-83. Editor: (with R.D. Lillie) Histopathologic Technic and Practical Histochemistry, 1976; editor in chief, founder Jour. Oral Pathology, 1972-90, Tissue Reactions, 1976-88; assoc. editor Jour. Cutaneous Pathology, 1973-83, Oral Surgery, Oral Medicine, Oral Pathology, 1970. Served to capt. AUS, 1944-46. Recipient Isaac Schour award for outstanding research and teaching in anat. scis. Internat. Assn. Dental Research, 1973, Disting. Alumnus of Yr. award Ind. U. Sch. Dentistry, 1978; Disting. Alumnus of Yr. award, Ind. U., 1981; Disting. Faculty Lectr. award, U. Ala. Med. Ctr., Birmingham, 1989—, Disting. Scientist award Am. Assn. Dental Rsch, 1990. Fellow Am. Coll. Dentists, Am. Acad. Oral Pathology (v.p. 1984-85, pres.-elect 1985-86, pres. 1986-87), AAAS (chmn. sect. 1976-78, sec. sect. 1979-87); mem. ADA (cons. Coun. Dental Rsch. 1973-74), Internat. Assn. Dental Rsch. (v.p. 1974-75, pres. 1976-77, pres. Exptl. Pathology Group 1985-86), Am. Assn. Dental Rsch. (pres. 1976-77), Internat. Assn. Pathologists, Histochem. Soc., Nat. Soc. Med. Rsch. (dir. 1977-79), Biol. Stain Commn. (trustee 1977—), Commd. Officers Assn., Internat. Assn. Oral Pathologists (co-founder, 1st pres. 1979-81, 1st editor 1971-89), Brit. Soc. Oral Pathologists (hon.), Exchange Club (Birmingham, pres. New Orleans 1952-53). Home: 3514 Bethune Dr Birmingham AL 35223-1418

FULLMER, LEE WAYNE, retired minister; b. Victor, Iowa, Jan. 12, 1931; s. Joseph Jacob and Hazel Fannie (Carl) F.; m. Hazel June Shook, June 30, 1956; children: Carey Lee, Daniel Ray. Pastoral Dipl., Moody Bible Inst., Chgo., 1954; AB in History, Wheaton (Ill.) Coll., 1956; ThB in Theology, Bapt. Bible Sem., Johnston City, N.Y., 1958. Ordained to ministry Gen. Assn. of Regular Bapt. Chs., 1958. Min. Waneta Lake Bapt. Ch., Hammondsport, NY, 1957-61, Panama Bapt. Ch., NY, 1961-63, Shoaff Pk. Bapt. Ch., Ft. Wayne, Ind., 1963-69; minister Mt. Tabor Bapt. Ch., Beckley, W.Va., 1970-79; min. Norwood Bapt. Ch., Cin., 1979-93; pastor Maranatha Bapt. Ch., Springfield, Ohio, 1993—2002. Tchr. Norwood Bapt. Christian Sch., Cin., 1980-93; trustee Scioto Hills Bapt. Camp, Wheelersburg, Ohio, 1982-93; prof. Appalachian Bible Coll., Bradley, W.Va., part-time, 1970s; min. Philippine Islands, 1998. Republican. *The great need of our troubled society is a return to the Biblical Christianity based upon a renewal of a healthy fear of God.*

FULLMER, PAUL, public relations counselor; b. Evanston, Ill., June 4, 1934; s. Joseph Charles and Marie (Guirsch) F.; m. Sandra Lewars Clifford, Apr. 22, 1961; children: Monica, David. AB, U. Notre Dame, 1955. Newspaper reporter Aurora (Ill.) Beacon News, 1955-57; account exec. Selz/Seabolt Comms., Chgo., 1957-64; v.p. Selz/Seabolt Comms., Inc., Chgo., 1964-72, exec. v.p., 1972-79, pres., 1979-99, chmn., 1999-2000, Publicis Dialog Chgo., 2000—. Bd. dirs. Pinnacle Worldwide, pres. 1990-92, chmn., 1992-93. Pres. Notre Dame Club Chgo., 1964-65, hon. pres., 1992-93; co-chmn. jr. bd. NCCJ, Chgo., 1962; chmn. Amate House, Chgo., 1985-87; chmn. bd. trustees St. Mary's Acad., 1985-88; co-chmn. Bus. Execs. for Econ. Justice, 1992-94; chmn. exec. com. Holy Family Ch., 1989-93. Sgt. USAR, 1957. Fellow Pub. Rels. Soc. Am. (pres. Chgo. chpt. 1988-89); mem. Internat. Pub. Rels. Assn. Roman Catholic. Home: 87 Heatherdowns Ln Galena IL 61036 Office: Publicis Dialog Chicago 111 E Wacker 18th Fl Chicago IL 60601 E-mail: paul.fullmer@publicis-USA.com.

FULLMER, STEVEN MARK, engineering executive; b. San Francisco, Mar. 15, 1956; s. Thomas Patrick and Patricia Ann (Carroll-Boyd) Fullmer; m. Rhonda Lynnette Bush, Nov. 8, 1992; children: Wesley Stevenson, Sierra Marin. BA in Chemistry, BA in Biology, Willamette U., 1978; MBA, Ariz. State U., 1993. Sr. engr., project leader Honeywell Large Computer Products, Phoenix, 1981—86; bank officer, cons., infosecurity cons. First Interstate Bank/Wells Fargo Bank, Phoenix, 1987—96; project mgr. Wells Fargo Bank, 1996; sr. engr. AG Comm. Sys./ Lucent Technologies, Phoenix, 1996—. Cons. J. A. Boyd & Assoc., San Francisco, 1985—96, ImaginInc. Consulting, Phoenix, 1985—. Mem. exec. bd. Grand Canyon coun. Boy Scouts Am., scoutmaster, 1983—88, commr., 1988—92, dist. chmn., 1995—96; founder, lt. comdr. Maricopa County Sheriff's Adj. Posse, 1982—93; pres. Heard Mus. Coun., 1995—96; dept. head, lead Liberty Wildlife. Recipient Order of Merit, Boy Scouts Am., 1988, Nat. Disting. Commr. award, 1991, Silver Beaver award, 1994. Mem.: Am. Inst. Cert. Computer Profls. (cert. data processor 1985), Mensa, Knights Cross (Sovereign Order of St. Stanislas), SAR, KC (membership dir. 1988), Beta Gamma Sigma, Sigma Iota Epsilon, Alpha Chi Sigma, Kappa Sigma (asst. dist. grand master 2001—), Phi Eta Sigma, Phi Lambda Upsilon. Republican. Roman Catholic. Avocations: American Indian history, science fiction, scuba diving, hiking, camping. Office: Lucent Techs 2500 W Utopia Rd Phoenix AZ 85027-4129 E-mail: sfullmer@lucent.com.

FULMER, DANIEL A. music educator, composer; b. Apr. 4, 1964; s. James B. and Martha G. Fulmer; m. Sharee Fulmer, July 20; children: Maeghan, Micah. B.Music Theory, Stetson U., DeLand, Fla., 1991; M.Music Composition, Fla. State U., 1994; DMA, U. Miami, 1998. Tchg. asst. adj. U. Miami, Coral Gables, Fla., 1994—97; asst. prof. Trinity Bible Coll., Ellendale, ND, 1997—98; adj. interim prof. music composition Middle Tenn. State U., Murfreesboro, 1998; adj. prof. music Volunteer State C.., Gullatin, Tenn., 1999—2000; asst. prof. music Southwestern U., Waxahachie, Tex., 2000—. Composer: (classical concert music) A Mortuis Excitare Et Obviam Domino in Aera (Symphony No. 4), 2002, (for band) March to Babylon, 2002, (concert music) Quintet for Bassoon and Strings, 2000, Symphony No. 2, 1997, (for soprano and 13 instruments) Set Me as a Seal, 1995, (for soprano, mixed chorus and eighteen instruments) Lamentum, 1994, (for large orch.) Lacrymosa, 1991, (for orch.) Symphony No. 3, numerous others. Recipient ASCAP-Raymond Hubbell Music scholar, 1996; grantee U. Miami grantee, 1997. Mem.: ASCAP (award for composition 1997—2002), Pi Kappa Lambda. Office: Southwestern Univ 1200 Sycamore St Waxahachie TX 75165-2397

FULMER, DOUGLAS ALAN, political consultant, journalist; b. Akron, Ohio, June 12, 1959; s. Gordon Lozier and Marjorie Helen (Glandorf) F.; m. Alice Marie Fry, Aug. 16, 1980 (div. Aug. 16, 1982). BA, Mt. Union Coll., Alliance, Ohio, 1981; MA, Syracuse U., 1982. Dir. state and local affairs Coalition for Scenic Beauty, Washington, 1987-89; internat. field coord. Nat. Space Soc., Washington, 1989-91; exec. dir. Com. To Preserve Assateague Island, Towson, Md., 1991; sr. assoc. Phil Noble and Assocs., Towson, 1991-92; pres. Douglas Fulmer and Assocs., Hermitage, Tenn., 1993—; freelance journalist Hermitage, Tenn., 1990—. Contbr. articles to periodicals, newspapers, mags., and Web sites. Vol. numerous polit. campaigns, 1972-80; mem. campaign staff numerous polit. campaigns, 1982-86; field rep. Am. Fedn. State, County and Mcpl. Employees, Indpls., 1986; campaign cons. Md. State Tchrs. Assn., Annapolis, Md., 1986; field rep. Am. Fedn. State, Jersey City, 1985; dir. del. selection George McGovern for Pres., Washington, 1984; field dir. Lane Evans for Congress, Rock Island, Ill., 1984; field coord. Elain Lytel for Congress, Syracuse, 1982. Home: 4100 Central Pike # 1420 Hermitage TN 37076 Office: Douglas Fulmer and Assocs 4100 Central Pike # 1420 Hermitage TN 37076 Fax: 615-391-9013. E-mail: Fulmerd@aol.com.

FULMER, HUGH SCOTT, physician, educator; b. Syracuse, N.Y., June 18, 1928; s. Herbert C. and Emily (Price) F.; m. Zola M. Jones, July 12, 1952; children: James, Kim, Scott. AB, Syracuse U., 1948; MD, SUNY-Syracuse, 1951; M.P.H., Harvard U., 1961. Intern R.I. Hosp., 1951-52; resident internal medicine SUNY-Syracuse, 1954-57; fellow pulmonary medicine SUNY, Syracuse, 1957-58; asst. dir., rsch. assoc. Navajo-Cornell Field Health Research Project, 1958-60; instr. pub. health and preventive medicine Cornell U. Coll. Medicine, 1958-60; asst. prof. community medicine U. Ky. Coll. Medicine, 1960-64, assoc. prof., 1964-66, prof., 1966-68, dir. sr. med. student internat. cross-cultural program, 1964-68, dir. preventive medicine residency program, 1964-68; tech. cons. health Peace Corps, Malaysia, 1968-69; prof., chmn. dept. community and family medicine U. Mass. Med. Sch., 1969-77, asso. dean for clin. edn. and primary care, 1975-79, chief sect. gen. medicine, dept. medicine, 1978-83; dir. ambulatory and community svcs. Carney Hosp., Boston, 1983-88, dir. community-oriented primary care program, 1988-93, dir. preventive medicine residency, 1988-93; exec. dir. Ctr. for Cmty. Reponsive Care, Boston, 1992—, dir. preventive medicine residency & COPC fellowship program, 1992—. Adj. prof. socio-med. scis., cmty. medicine and pub. health Boston U. Sch. Medicine and Pub. Health, 1983-96. Served with M.C., USAF, 1952-54. Mem. AMA, APHA, Mass. Med. Soc., Assn. Tchrs. Preventive Medicine (past pres., Outstanding Tchr. award 1993), Am. Assn. Pub. Health Physician, Am. Coll. Physician Execs., Am. Coll. Preventive Medicine (bd. regents 1988-94). Achievements include research on community responsive care. Home: 61 Cherlyn Dr Northborough MA 01532-1135 E-mail: copc1@aol.com.

FULMER, MICHAEL CLIFFORD, food company administrator; b. Cin., May 8, 1954; s. William George and Mirella Martha (Kloeker) F. BBA, U. Cin., 1980. Aux. police City of Norwood, Ohio, 1977-79, councilman, 1980-85, 92-93, 96—; asst. dock supr. Lee Way Motor Freight, Inc., Cin., 1981; supr. Serv-A-Portion div. Di Giorgio Corp., Cin., 1981-85, shift mgr., 1986-88; prodn. supt. Borden, Cin., 1988-91; prodn. adminstrn. Pierre Frozen Foods, 1992—. Lector St. Matthew Ch., Norwood, 1978-94; precinct exec. Norwood Centennial Com., 1987-88, 90—; pres. St. Matthew Parish Coun., Norwood, 1979-80; precinct exec., 1990—; chmn. fin. City of Norwood, 1982-83. Named Sailor of Yr. USN, 1976. Mem. Nat. Audubon Soc., Lighthouse Preservation Soc., Wilderness Soc., Sierra Club, U. Cin. Bus. Tribunal (pres. 1979-80, award 1980), Kiwanis (bd. dirs. 1991-92). Roman Catholic. Avocations: photography, jogging, gardening, reading, hiking. Home: 3737 Hazel Ave Cincinnati OH 45212-3823 Office: Pierre Frozen Foods 9990 Princeton Rd Cincinnati OH 45246

FULMER, PHILLIP, university football coach; b. Winchester, Tenn., Sept. 1, 1950; m. Vicky Morey; children: Phillip Jr., Courtney, Brittany, Allison. BA, U. Tenn., 1972. Offensive line coach Wichita (Kans.) State U., 1974, 77-78, linebacker coach, 1975-76; asst. football coach Vanderbilt U., Nashville, 1979; grad. asst. U. Tenn., Nashville, 1972, defensive coord. freshman team, 1973, asst. coach, 1980-91, head coach, 1992—. Head coach East-West Shrine Game, 1998; coach Fla. Citrus Bowl, 1993, Orange Bowl, 1997. Led U. Tenn. Vols. to Southeastern Conf. championship, 1997. Mem. Am. Football Coaches Assn. (trustee 1996—, mem. Hall of Fame com., I-A coaches legis. issues com., Kodah Region 2 Coach of Yr. award 1993). Office: care Am Football Coaches Assn 5900 Old Mcgregor Rd Waco TX 76712-6166

FULMER, VINCENT ANTHONY, retired college president; b. Alliance, Ohio, Oct. 23, 1927; s. Anthony and Catherine (Long) F.; m. Mary Alma Pineau, Dec. 27, 1950; children: Kevan, Kristine, David, Amy, Charles, Alma Leigh. AB cum laude, Miami U., Oxford, Ohio, 1949; postgrad., Harvard U., 1950; S.M., MIT, 1963; LL.D., Suffolk U., 1971; D.Sc., Fla. Inst. Tech., 1982; Ed.D., Hawthorne Coll., 1988. Mem. staff MIT, 1951-86, exec. asst. office chmn., 1960-63, v.p., 1963-73, sec. inst., 1963-85; v.p. adminstrn. William Underwood Co., 1973-75; sec. M.I.T. Corp., 1979-85; v.p., dir. Video Optics Corp., Waltham, Mass., 1985-86; pres. Hawthorne Coll., Antrim, N.H., 1986-88, pres. emeritus, 1988—. Bd. dirs. Barbour Stockwell, Inc., Control Air, Inc., Fiberspar Corp., Tech. Capital Network, Inc.; instr. econs. Williams Coll., 1952. Contbr. chpts. to books and mags. Bd. dirs. Planning Office for Urban Affairs, Archdiocese of Boston, 1968-93; trustee Suffolk U., 1972—, chmn., 1976-81; trustee Hawthorne Coll., 1982-92, chmn., 1985-92; corporator New Eng. Coll. Optometry, 1985-87, trustee, 1987-93; bd. dirs. Sml. Bus. High Tech. Inst., Washington, 1982—; mem. exec. com. MIT Enterprise Forum, 1978—, vice-chmn. 1992-93. With USNR, 1944-46. Mem. Am. Econ. Assn., AAAS, Ops. Research Soc. Am., Inst. Mgmt. Scis., Phi Beta Kappa, Sigma Chi, Omicron Delta Kappa. Home and Office: 26 Kimball Rd Arlington MA 02474-1206 *While individuals may address themselves exclusively to high personal attainments within the existing framework of our institutions, or devote prodigious efforts to improve or restructure those institutions, in the end it is our lifetime example that counts more heavily than all else.*

FULOP, MILFORD, physician; b. N.Y.C., Nov. 7, 1927; s. Herman and Adele (Karl) F.; m. Christine Lawrence, Aug. 4, 1957; children: Michael Alain, Tamara Ann. AB, Columbia U., 1946, MD, 1949. Intern, then resident in medicine Presbyn. Hosp., N.Y.C., 1949-51, 53-55; chief resident Bronx Mcpl. Hosp. Ctr., 1955-56; practice medicine specializing in internal medicine N.Y.C., 1955—; mem. faculty Albert Einstein Coll. Medicine, Bronx, N.Y., 1956—, Gertrude and David Feinson prof. internal medicine, 1968—, acting chmn. dept. medicine, 1975-80, vice chmn. dept. medicine, 1980—, disting. univ. prof. medicine, 1994—. Mem. staff Bronx Mcpl. Hosp., Hosp. of Einstein Coll. Medicine. Served with M.C. USAF, 1951-53. Recipient Commendation medal, Pulitzer scholar Columbia Coll., Lifetime Achievement award for excellence in clin. tchg. Albert Einstein Coll. Medicine, 2000. Master ACP (laureate N.Y. State chpt.); mem. Assn. Am. Physicians, Phi Beta Kappa, Alpha Omega Alpha. Home: 630 W 246th St Bronx NY 10471-3631 Office: 1300 Morris Park Ave Bronx NY 10461-1926

FULP, ERRIN, computer science educator; PhD in Computer Engring., N.C. State U., 1999. Rsch. asst. N.C. State U., Raleigh, 1999—2000; asst. prof. computer sci. Wake Forest U., Winston-Salem, 2000—. Rsch. asst. NEC C&C Rsch. Laboratories, Princeton, NJ, 1997—97. Contbr. scientific papers to profl. jours. Vol. N.C. Mus. Art, Raleigh, 1985—2002. Mem.: ACM, IEEE, Upsilon Pi Epsilon, Phi Kappa Phi. Achievements include patents for Computer Network with Microeconomic Flow Control, Patent No. 6, 055, 571.

FULRATH, ANDREW WESLEY, retired small business owner; BA summa cum laude, Trinity Internat. U., Deerfield, Ill., 1989, MA magna cum laude, 1996; Cert. profl. edn., Coll. for Fin. Planning, Denver, 1995. CFP licensee. V.p. trust bus. devel. First Citizens Bank, Wilmington, N.C., 1998-2000; v.p., fin. cons. First Citizens Investor Svcs., Jacksonville, NC, 2000—03. Methodist. Avocations: personal fitness, hiking, life planning, jazz and blues music. E-mail: fulrath@hotmail.com.

FULSHER, ALLAN ARTHUR, lawyer; b. Portland, Oreg., July 5, 1952; s. Rémy Walter and Barbara Lee (French) F.; m. Karen Louise Schmid, Dec. 28, 1974 (dec. Sept. 1990); children: Brian Rémy, Louise Katherine, Elizabeth Alane. BA in Biology, U. Oreg., 1974, BA in Econs., 1976; JD, U. of Pacific, 1979. Bar: Oreg. 1979, Calif. 1980, U.S. Dist. Ct. Oreg. 1980, U.S. Dist. Ct. (ea. dist.) Calif. 1981, U.S. Ct. Appeals (9th cir.) 1982, U.S. Dist. Ct. (no. dist.) Calif. 1985, U.S. Dist. Ct. (so. dist.) Calif. 1986. Assoc. Law Offices of Jacques B. Nichols PC, Portland, 1979-82, Ragen, Roberts, O'Scannlain, Robertson & Neill, Portland, 1982-83; shareholder Bauer, Hermann, Fountain & Rhoades PC, Portland, 1983-87, v.p., 1984-87; shareholder, v.p. Fulsher and Weatherhead PC, Portland, 1987-88, pres., 1988—2001; gen. counsel Peregrine Holdings, Ltd., Beaverton, Oreg., 1993-97, Peregrine Capital, Inc., Beaverton, 1993-2000; mgr. Stamford Bridge, LLC, 1995—; gen. counsel Redfire, Inc., 2000—02, Serra Pacific Acceptance, LLC, Portland, 2001—, Serra Capistrano Funding, LLC, Portland, 2002—. Pres., mgr. ProSoccer, LLC, Tigard, Oreg., 1998-2001; gen. counsel World Indoor Soccer League, LLC, Dallas, 1998-2000. Republican. Roman Catholic. Avocations: basketball, automobile racing and restoration, coaching youth and adult sports. Home: 16399 SE Sager Rd Portland OR 97236-5509 Office: Serra Capistrano Funding LLC 8525 N Lombard St Ste 212 Portland OR 97203-3156

FULTON, JANE, health science institution administrator; b. Edmonton, Alta., Can., July 12, 1947; came to U.S., 1998; d. James Blair Fulton and Margaret Anna Massie; children: Jean, Amy, Sarah, Lila. B of Home Econs. with honors, U. B.C., 1969, MS in Health Svcs. Planning, 1982, PhD, 1986. Cert. secondary edn., B.C., 1979. Prin. The Health Group, Ottawa, 1978—96, pres., 1996-98; asst./assoc. prof. faculty of adminstrn. U. Ottawa, Ont., Can., 1986-95; dep. minister of health Alta., 1995-96; prof., dir. MS program in health svcs. adminstrn. Sch. Natur Barry U., Miami, Fla., 1998-99; exec. dir. Cleve. Health Inst., 1999—2001; dean Coll. of Health Slippery Rock U., Pa., 2001—. Mem. faculty Banff Sch. Advanced Mgmt.; mem. com. on health law Can. Bar Assn.; mem. Emergency Med. Svcs. Rev. Commn. of Ont.; mem. dean's com. on strategic plannng for faculties of medicne and health scis. U. Ottawa; mem. lithotripsy proposal rev. com. Ministry of Health of Ont.; mem. com. on grants program Med. Rsch. Coun. of Can.; mem. econs. com., genetics program Sci. Coun. of Can.; lectr., presenter in field. Author: The Regulation of Emerging Health Care Occupations, 1988, Canada's Health System: Bordering on the Possible, 1993; co-author: (with Ralph Sutherland) Health Care in Canada: A Description and Analysis of Canadian Health Services, 1988, 3d printing, 1992, Spending Smarter and Spending Less: Policies and Partnerships for Health Care in Canada, 1994; contbr. articles to profl. jours., chpts. to books; mem. editl. bd. Internat. Jour. Humane Medicine, Can. Jour. Program Evaluation, reviewer New Eng. Jour. Medicine, Health Mgmt. Forum. Bd. dirs., mem. internat. coun. Enterprise Internat., Fairfax, Va., 1998—; bd. dirs. Elizabeth Bruyere Health Ctr., Ottawa, 1988-92; former bd. dirs., former mem. exec. com. Nat. Inst. for Disability Mgmt. and Rsch., 1996-98. Social Scis. and Humanities doctoral fellow, 1982-86; grantee U. Ottawa, 1986, Can. Inst. Pub. Health Insps., 1987, demonstration grantee NHRDP, 1987-89; grantee Can. Coun. on Hosp. Accreditation, 1988, U. Ottawa and Fed. Task Force on Barriers to Women in Pub. Svc., 1988, Can. Ctr. for Philanthropy and Ryerson U., 1989, Workers Compensation Bd. of B.C., 1993, Ministry of Edn. of Ont., 1994, Ohio Bd. of Regents Grant (PI), 1999. Mem. Am. Coll. Healthcare Execs. (assoc.), Can. Assn. Radiologists (hon., life). Office: Slippery Rock U PT 325 Slippery Rock PA 16057 Fax: 724-738-2881. E-mail: jane.fulton@sru.edu.

FULTON, NEIL, lawyer; b. Huron, S.D., July 18, 1971; s. Tex Ray and Mary Ann Fulton. BA, Yale U., 1994; JD summa cum laude, U. Minn., 1997. Bar: S.D., U.S. Dist. Ct. S.D., U.S. Ct. Appeals (8th cir.), U.S. Supreme Ct., Rosebud Sioux Tribal Ct., Cheyenne River Sioux Tribal Ct. Law clk. to Judge Diana Murphy U.S. Ct. Appeals 8th cir., Mpls., 1997-98; atty. May Adam Gardes and Thompson, Pierre, S.D., 1998—. Mem. Am. Judicature Soc., Western S.D. Buckaroos. Democrat. Roman Catholic. Office: May Adam Gardes and Thompson LLP 503 S Pierre St Pierre SD 57501 E-mail: nkf@magt.com.

FULTON, NORMAN ROBERT, credit manager; b. L.A., Dec. 16, 1935; s. Robert John and Fritzi Marie (Wacker) F.; m. Nancy Butler, July 6, 1966; children: Robert B., Patricia M. AA, Santa Monica Coll., 1958; BS, U. So. Calif., 1960. Asst. v.p. Raphael Glass Co., L.A., 1960-65; credit adminstr. Zellerbach Paper Co., L.A., 1966-68; gen. credit mgr. Carrier Transicold Co., Montebello, Calif., 1968-70, Virco Mfg. Co., L.A., 1970-72, Superscope, Inc., Chatsworth, Calif., 1972-79; asst. v.p. credit and adminstrn. Inkel Corp., Carson, Calif., 1980-82; corp. credit mgr. Gen. Consumer Electronics, Santa Monica, Calif., 1982-83; br. credit mgr. Sharp Electronics Corp., Carson, Calif., 1983-96; credit mgr. Rocheux Internat., Inc., Carson, 1997-99; with Barron Chestney, Internat., 2000—. With AUS, 1955-57. Fellow Nat. Inst. Credit (cert. credit exec.). Home: 12635 Hildago St Desert Hot Springs CA 92240

FULTON, THOMAS, theoretical physicist, educator; b. Budapest, Hungary, Nov. 19, 1927; came to U.S., 1941; s. Michael and Irene (Weisz) F.; m. Babette Pilzer, June 14, 1952; children: Ruth Carol, Judith Pamela. BA, Harvard U., 1950, MA, 1951, PhD, 1954. Prof. emeritus Johns Hopkins U., Balt., 2000—; Frank B. Jewett Found. postdoctoral fellow Inst. Advanced Studies, Princeton, N.J., 1954-55; NSF postdoctoral fellow Princeton, N.J., 1955-56; from asst. prof. to assoc. prof. physics Johns Hopkins U., Balt., 1956-64, prof., 1964-2000. Rsch. cons. and vis. scientist numerous orgns., 1954—. Author: (with others) Resonances in Strong Interaction Physics, 1963; assoc. editor Jour. Math. Physics, 1968-71; contbr. over 100 articles to profl. jours. Bd. dirs. Shriver Hall Concert Series, Balt., 1981-91. With U.S. Army, 1946-47. John Simon Guggenheim Found. fellow, U. Vienna, 1964-65, Fulbright sr. rsch. fellow, 1964-65; prin. investigator rsch. grantee NSF, Johns Hopkins U., 1960-92. Fellow Am. Phys. Soc.; mem. Archeol. Inst. Am., Sigma Xi. Home: 5600 Roxbury Pl Baltimore MD 21209-4502 Office: Johns Hopkins U Dept Physics And Astro Baltimore MD 21218

FULTON-QUINDOZA, DEBRA ANN, nurse practitioner; b. Anne Arundel, Md., Dec. 16, 1961; d. William D. and Patricia A. (Rensel) Fulton; m. Stephen S. Quindoza, Nov. 17, 1997; children: William Benjamin Quindoza, Allison Marie Quindoza 1 stepchild, Costas Quindoza. BSN, U. Tex., Galveston, 1983, MSN, 1986. Cert. advanced RN practitioner Fla., profl. nurse practitioner, profl. coder AAPC. Clin. nurse specialist Arnold Palmer Hosp. for Childen and Women, Orlando, Fla., 1989-90; pediatric and internal medicine nurse practitioner Office of Dr. Shirley Nagel, Mt. Dora, Fla., 1990-91; project leader in med. policy-med. rev. Medicare of Fla., Jacksonville, 1991-93; med. cons., outreach educator, project mgr. Medicare Fraud Br., Jacksonville, Fla., 1993-98; advanced RN practitioner part time Dr. Perry G. Carlos, 1995-2000; sr. healthcare data analyst dept. benefits/program integrity divsn. Medicare Fla., 1998-2000, mgr., 2000—. Adj. instr. Coll. Continuing Edn. U. North Fla., 2001; med. cons. in field. Home: 12638 Point Park Dr Jacksonville FL 32225-5508 Office: Medicare Program Safeguards/SMDA 532 Riverside Ave Jacksonville FL 32202

FULTS, DANIEL WEBSTER, III, neurosurgeon, educator; b. Washington, Aug. 22, 1953; s. Daniel W. Jr. and Helen (Hobbs) F.; m. Carol Gibson, June 16, 1979; children: Erin Marie, Robin Diane. BS in Chemistry, U. Tex., 1975; MD, Southwestern Med. Sch., Dallas, 1979. Resident in neurosurgery Wake Forest U., Winston-Salem, NC, 1979-85; rsch. assoc. dept. biochemistry U. N.C., Chapel Hill, 1985-87; asst. prof. neurosurgery U. Utah, Salt Lake City, 1987-92, assoc. prof. neurosurgery, 1992—2000, prof. neurosurgery, 2000—. Contbr. numerous articles to profl. jours. Assn. for Brain Tumor Rsch. fellow, 1985-87; recipient Clin. Investigator award NIH Nat. Cancer Inst., 1985-90, First award, 1990—. Mem. Am. Assn. Neurol. Surgeons, Am. Acad. Neurol. Surgeons, Utah State Soc. Neurol. Surgeons (pres. 1989). Avocations: skiing, guitar playing and composing, restoring antique automobiles. Office: U Utah Sch Medicine 50 N Medical Dr Salt Lake City UT 84132-0001

FULTZ, BRENT THOMAS, materials scientist, educator, researcher; b. Troy, NY, Feb. 24, 1955; s. Stanley Charles and Esther Doris (Richert) F.; m. Colleen Jaye O'Hara, Sept. 30, 1984; children: Emily Elise, Eric Michael, Elissa Katherine. BSc in Physics, MIT, 1975; MSc in Materials Sci., U. Calif., Berkeley, 1978, PhD in Materials Sci., 1982. Staff scientist Lawrence Berkeley (Calif.) Lab., 1982-85; asst. prof. materials sci. Calif. Inst. Tech., Pasadena, 1985-90, assoc. prof., 1991-97, prof., 1997—. Prof. U. Udine, Italy, 1992; cons. Everett Charles Technologies, Pomona, Calif., 1986-96, Def. Sci. Study Group, Alexandria, Va., 1994-95, Def. Sci. Bd., Washington, 1996; Los Alamos Nat. Lab., 1997—. Author 1 book; editor 7 books; contbr. over 230 articles to profl. jours.; patentee in field. Recipient Faculty Devel. award IBM, 1986, 87; NSF Presdl. Young Investigator, 1988-93; Xerox Found. grantee, 1986; Wallenberg Found. scholar, 1988. Mem. Am. Soc. Metals (chmn. atomic transport com. 1994-97), Am. Phys. Soc., Minerals Metals Materials Soc. (chmn. chemistry and physics com. 1996—), Internat. Bd. for Applications of Mössbauer Effect, 1998—. Home: 269 S Berkeley Ave Pasadena CA 91107-4734 E-mail: btf@caltech.edu.

FULTZ, PHILIP NATHANIEL, management analyst; b. N.Y.C., Jan. 29, 1943; s. Otis and Sara Love (Gibbs) F.; m. Anita Neu, Nov. 8, 1998. AA in Bus., Coll. of the Desert, 1980; BA in Mgmt., U. Redlands, 1980, MA in Mgmt., 1982. Enlisted USMC, 1967, advanced through grades to capt., 1972, served in various locations, 1964-78, resigned commn., 1978; CETA coord. County of San Bernardino, Yucca Valley, Calif., 1978-85; mgmt. analyst Advanced Technology, Inc., Twentynine Palms, Calif., 1985-88; spl. transit analyst Omintrans, San Bernardino, Calif., 1988-89; tech. analyst Atlantic Rsch. Corp. (formerly Calculon Corp.), Twentynine Palms, Calif., 1988—; mgmt. analyst Marine Corps Base, Twentynine Palms, Calif., 1991—. Adj. asst. prof. mgmt. Chapman U., Orange, Calif., 1992—. Founding dir. Unity Home Battered Women's Shelter, Joshua Tree, Calif., 1982, Morongo Basin Adult Literacy; bd. dirs. Twentynine Palms Water Dist., 1991-95; bd. trustees Copper Mountain C.C., 1999—. Mem. Rotary (sec. Joshua Tree chpt. 1983-85). Republican. Home: 73477 Desert Trail Dr Twentynine Palms CA 92277-2218 Office: Morale Walfare & Recreation Marine Corps Base Twentynine Palms CA 92277-2302 E-mail: maqpes@thegrid.net.

FULTZ, ROBERT EDWARD, lawyer; b. Columbus, Ohio, May 24, 1941; s. Clair Ervin and Isabelle (Eichelberger) F.; m. Judith Ann McClannan, June 15, 1963; children: Cynthia, Jennifer, Stephen. BA cum laude, Ohio State U., 1963; JD with distinction, U. Mich., 1965. Ohio 1966, U.S. Supreme Ct. 1970. Assoc. Porter, Wright, Morris & Arthur, Columbus, 1966—70, ptnr., 1970—2001. Past trustee Columbus Symphony Orch. and Ballet; past trustee, sec. United Cerebral Palsy of Columbus; past trustee, treas. Goodwill Industries; past trustee, pres. Cen. Community House; former advisor, bd. dirs. United Negro Coll. Fund; past trustee Columbus Assn. for Performing Arts, Columbus Law Libr. Assn. Mem. Phi Beta Kappa, Delta Upsilon (treas.). Home: 717 Pineside Ln Naples FL 34108

FULWILER, ROBERT NEAL, oil company executive; b. Belton, Tex., Nov. 5, 1937; s. Charles Calvin and Luella (Smith) F.; m. Sylvia Jean Marshall, Dec. 26, 1959; 1 child, Roger Neal. AA, Temple Jr. Coll., 1959; BBA, U. Tex., 1961. Statis. asst. Tex. Eastern Transmission Corp., Houston, 1961-62; adminstrv. asst. subs. LaGloria Oil & Gas, Houston, 1969-76, v.p., 1976; exec. v.p. La Jet, Inc., Houston, 1976-81, pres., 1981-82; chmn. bd. dirs. EnJet Inc., 1982-88; chief exec. officer Trend Energy, Houston, 1989—. Bd. dirs. BFC Assocs., Inc. Author: Competition and Growth in American Energy Markets, 1947-1985, 1968. Mem. Aspen Found., Colo. Mem. Knights of Momus., The Aspen Inst. (assoc.), Houston Mus. Fine Arts. Republican. Mem. Ch. of Christ. Office: Trend Energy 5100 Westheimer Rd Ste 200 Houston TX 77056-5597 E-mail: RFTrend@compuserve.com.

FUMAGALLI, BARBARA MERRILL, artist, printmaker; b. Kirkwood, Mo., Mar. 15, 1926; d. Harold C. and Mary Louise (Fitch) Ellison; m. Orazio Fumagalli, Aug. 15, 1948; children: Luisa, Piera, Elio. BFA, State U. Iowa, 1948, MFA, 1950; student, Mauricio Lasansky, Iowa City, 1945-50, Garo Antreasian, John Sommers, Jim Kraft, Albuquerque, 1980-81. Solo shows, Tweed Gallery, U. Minn., Duluth, 1955, 82, U. Minn., St. Paul, 1964, Mpls., 1965, Concordia Coll., Moorhead, Minn., 1965, Suzanne Kohn Gallery, St. Paul, 1967, Hamline U., St. Paul, 1969, 84, Paine Art Center and Arboretum, Oshkosh, Wis., 1973, Cork Gallery, Lincoln Ctr., N.Y.C., 1982, St. Johns U., Collegeville, Minn., 1984, U. Louisville, 1993; group shows, Baylor U., Waco, Tex., 1990, Abilene (Tex.) Christian U., 1991, Multnomah County Libr., Portland, Oreg., 1991, Hesston (Kans.) Coll., 1991, Henry Ford C.C., Dearborn, Mich., 1991, Grinnell (Iowa) Coll. Gallery, 1993, One West Contemporary Arts Ctr., Ft. Collins, Colo., 1994, Tarleton State U., Stephenville, Tex., 1994, Chadron (Nebr.) State Coll., 1994, Waldorf Coll., Forest City, Iowa, 1995, Ctrl. Coll., Pella, Iowa, 1996, Mo. Western State Coll., St. Joseph, 1996, Highland (Kans.) C.C., 1997, Indian Hills C.C., Ottumwa, Iowa, 1997, 98, Tex.-Dallas, Richardson, 1997, Truman State U., Kirksville, Mo., 1998, S.E. Mo. State U., Cape Girardeau, 1999, Albrecht-Kemper Mus. Art, St. Joseph, Mo., 2000, Butler C.C., El Dorado, Kans., 2000, U. Ctrl. Ark., Conway, 2001, Focus On the Masters, Ventura, Calif., 2002, others; represented in permanent collecions Mus. Modern Art, N.Y.C., Nelson A. Rockefeller Collection, N.Y.C.illustrator: Swing Around the Sun (Barbara J. Esbensen), 1965.

FUMASOLI, JOHN, music educator; b. Poughkeepsie, N.Y., July 30, 1954; s. Maurice Albert Fumasoli and Helen Bogdanffy; m. Anne Marie Bach, June 28, 1982; children: Jessica, Christian. BS in Mus. Performance summa cum laude, BS in Music Edn. cum laude, U. Bridgeport, 1977, MS in Music Edn., 1982. Cert. tchr. Conn., N.Y. Pvt. tchr., Rye, NY, 1972—; tchr. Fairfield (Conn.) Pub. Schs., 1978—. Prof. U. Bridgeport, 1989—96, Fairfield U., 1993—. Contbr. articles to profl. jours. Coach CYO Basketball, Rye, 1999—2001; mgr. Little League Baseball, Rye, 2000—02. Grantee Sharing Diversity grant, Cooperative Edn. Svcs., Trumbull, Conn., 1998—2003. Mem.: Musicians Union, Music Educators Nat. Conf., Internat. Assn. Jazz Educators. Democrat. Roman Catholic. Avocations: basketball, auto racing, bicycling, coaching basketball and baseball. Home: 166 Soundview Ave Rye NY 10580

FUMENTO, ROCCO, retired English and film educator; b. North Adams, Mass., Feb. 12, 1923; s. Mauro-Vincenzo and Antonia Cifrese Fumento; m. Tobey Baer Fumento, Mar. 10, 1956; children: David, Michael, Andrew, Matthew. BS, Columbia U., 1950; MFA, U. Iowa, 1952. Prof. English and film U. Ill., Urbana, 1952—92; ret. Author: (novels) Devil By the Tail, 1953, Tree of Dark Reflection, 1964, A Decent Girl Always Goes to Mass on Sunday, 2002, short stories; contbr. articles to profl. jours. Staff sgt. U.S. Army, 1944—46. Mem.: Italian-Am. Orgns. (film festival organizer Oct. celebrations 2001—02). Avocations: traveling, reading, film studios. Home: 1100 Main St Dalton MA 01226-2202

FUMERTON, RICHARD ANTHONY, philosopher, educator; b. Toronto, Ontario, Can., Oct. 7, 1949; s. Robert Carl and Mabeleine (Reay) F.; m. Patricia C. Rowe, Apr. 18, 1948; children: Tara A., Robert A. BA, U. Toronto (Ont.), 1971; MA, Brown U., 1973, PhD, 1974. Asst. prof. philosophy U. Iowa, Iowa City, 1974-79, assoc. prof., 1979-85, prof., 1985—, prof. chmn., 1988—. Vis. prof. U. Minn., Mpls., Fall 1978. Author: Metaphysical and Epistemological Problems of Perception, 1985, Reason and Morality, 1990, Metaepistemology and Skepticism, 1995. Recipient Woodrow Wilson fellow, 1971-72, Can. Coun. fellow, Canadian govt., 1973-74. Home: 608 Whiting Ave Iowa City IA 52245-5640 E-mail: richard_fumerton@uiowa.edu.

FUNARI, ROBERT GLENN, health care services executive; b. Pitts., Sept. 20, 1947; s. Mario Ronald and Virginia Alice Funari; m. Marilyn Romcea, July 18, 1970; children: Carla Marie, Michael Anthony. BSME, Cornell U., 1969; MBA, Harvard U., 1975. Dir. distbn. Baxter Internat., Deerfield, Ill., 1977-79, v.p. materials mgmt., 1979-83; pres. Medcom, Inc., Garden Grove, Calif., 1983-86, Paramax Sys. Baxter Internat., Irvine, Calif., 1986-89; corp. v.p. and pres. Pharmaseal divsn. Baxter Internat., Valencia, Calif., 1989-93; exec. v.p., COO Syncor Internat., Woodland Hills, Calif., 1993-96, pres., CEO, 1996—2002. Bd. dirs. Bay Cities Nat. Bank, Redondo Beach, Calif., Cmty. First Group, English, Ind., Pope and Talbot Inc.; chmn. exec. coun. Adaptive Bus. Leaders, Newport Beach, Calif., 1998-99; mem. Rand Health Bd. of Advisors. Baker scholar, 1975. Mem.: Ctr. for Corp. Innovation. Home: 25615 Melbourne Ct Calabasas CA 91302-3165 Office: Syncor Internat 6464 Canoga Ave Woodland Hills CA 91367-2407

FUNCHION, MICHAEL F. historian, educator; b. N.Y.C., Oct. 4, 1943; s. Richard Funchion and Mary Lynch; m. Margaret Claire Bullers, July 25, 1976; children: John, Maura. BA, Iona Coll., New Rochelle, N.Y., 1966; MA, Loyola U., Chgo., 1968, PhD, 1973. Asst. prof. history S.D. State U., Brookings, 1973—76, assoc. prof. history, 1976—83, prof. history, 1983—. Author: Chicago's Irish Nationalists, 1976; editor: Irish American Voluntary Organizations, 1983; co-author: The Irish in Chicago, 1987. Mem.: Immigration History Soc., Am. Conf. Irish Studies, Orgn. Am. Historians. Democrat. Roman Catholic. Home: 1424 Wisconsin St Brookings SD 57006 Office: S D State U Box 504 Brookings SD 57007 E-mail: Michael_Funchion@sdstate.edu.

FUNCK, DENNIS LIGHT, chemist, researcher; b. Palmyra, Pa., Nov. 30, 1926; s. Ammon Book and Edna May (Light) F.; m. Betty K. King, Sept. 3, 1949; children: Pamela Kay Abrams, Patricia Kay Kremer. ASTRP Cert., Pa. Mil. Sch., Chester, Pa., 1944; BS in Chemistry, Lebanon Valley Coll., Annville, Pa., 1949; MS in Organic Chemistry, U. Del., Newark, Del., 1950, PhD, 1952. From rsch. chemist to sr. rsch. assoc. E. I. DuPont DeNemours, Wilmington, 1952—86, ret., 1986; cons. DLight & Assocs., Inc., Wilmington, Del., 1986—98. Co-author: scientific publications. Deacon, trustee, elder, clk. of session, fin. sec. Concord Presbyn. Ch., Wilmington, 1955—2003. Served with U.S. Army, 1945—46. Recipient Alumni Assn. Citation, Lebanon Valley Coll., 1970; DuPont fellowship, U. Del., 1952. Mem.: ACS (life), Soc. Plastic Engineers (life), Sigma Xi (assoc.). Republican. Presbyterian. Achievements include patents for 9 US patents and foreign equivalents on a number of them. Avocations: swimming, golf, travel.

FUNDERBURK, DAVID BRITTON, former congressman and ambassador, consultant; b. Langley Field, Va., Apr. 28, 1944; married; 2 children. BA, Wake Forest Coll., 1966; MA, Wake Forest U., 1967; PhD, U. S.C., 1974. Instr. Wingate (NC) Coll., 1967—69, U. SC, Columbia, 1969—70; assoc. prof. history Hardin-Simmons U., Abilene, Tex., 1972—78; prof. history Campbell U., Buies Creek, NC, 1978—81, 1985—86; U.S. amb. to Romania Bucharest, 1981—85; cons. U.S. Dept. Edn., 1987—88; mem. Nat. Edn. Com. on Internat. Ednl. Programs, 1987—90, 104th Congress from 2nd N.C. dist., Washington, 1994—96. Candidate for U.S. Senate from N.C., 1986; exec. dir. Conservatives for Freedom Polit. Action Com., 1988-94; chmn. Internat. Romanian Relief Fund, 1990-94; mem. U.S. Congress, 1994-96. Republican. Office: 130 Canter Ln Pinehurst NC 28374 E-mail: ambromdf@aol.com.

FUNDERBURK, RAYMOND, judge; b. Phila., Mar. 2, 1944; s. Walter and Inez (Prince) F. AA, Olive-Harvey Coll., 1972; BA, U. Ill., 1974; MPA, Roosevelt U., 1975; JD, U. Ill., 1978. Bar: Ill. 1979, U.S. Dist. Ct. (no. dist.) Ill. 1979, U.S. Ct. Appeals (7th and fed. cirs.) 1983, U.S. Supreme Ct. 1983. Staff atty. Cook County Legal Assistance, Harvey, Ill., 1978-80, mng. atty., 1980-82; assoc. O. Kenneth Thomas Ltd., Harvey, 1982-83, Jones, Ware & Grenard, Chgo., 1983-88, Earl L. Neal and Assocs., Chgo., 1988-93; judge Cir. Ct. of Cook County, Chgo., Ill., 1993—. Bd. dirs. Cook County Legal Assistance Found., Oak Park, Ill., chmn. 1985-87; active legal adv. bd. Thornton Community Coll., South Holland, Ill., 1982—, Aunt Martha's Service, Park Forest, Ill., 1981-83. Chmn. Zoning Bd. of Appeals, Park Forest, 1988-99, Housing Bd. of Appeals, Park Forest, 1988-99, Equal Employment Opportunity Bd., Park Forest, 1988-99, Housing Rev. Bd., Park Forest, 1988-99; bd. dirs. Park Forest Pub. Library, 1982. Served with U.S. Army, 1965-67. Recipient Cert. of Appreciation Aunt Martha's Youth Svc., 1980, Thornton C.C., 1985, Wendell Phillips H.S., 1985, South Suburban YMCA, 1986, 1987, City Ptnr. award U. Ill. Chgo., 1995; named Disting. Grad., U. Ill. Coll. of Law, 1998-99, Olive-Harvey Jr. Coll., 2001. Mem. ABA, Chgo. Bar Assn., Cook County Bar Assn., Ill. Jud. Coun., Ill. Judges Assn., Phi Alpha Delta, Alpha Phi Alpha. Democrat. Avocations: running, chess, tennis. Office: Cir Ct of Cook County Ill Rm 2600 Richard J Daley Ctr Dearborn & Randolph Sts Chicago IL 60602

FUNDIS, LOIS ALETA, librarian; b. Wilkinsburg, Pa., Nov. 18, 1950; d. Jack William Lewis Fundis, Dorothy Lois Smith. BA, U. Pitts., 1972, MLS, 1974. Cataloger Mary H. Weir Pub. Libr., Weirton, W.Va., 1974—81, reference libr., 1981—. Chairperson W.Va. Govt. Documents Roundtable W.Va. Libr. Assn., Charleston, 1999—2000. Author: Stumpers!: Answers to Hundreds of Questions That Stumped the Experts, 1998. Office: Mary H Weir Pub Libr 3442 Main St Weirton WV 26062 Office Fax: 304 797-8526.

FUNDORA, THOMAS, artist, journalist, composer; b. Havana, Cuba, Mar. 7, 1935; came to U.S., 1960; s. Evangelio and Juana Evangelina (Rodriguez) F.; m. Marlene Delgado, Feb. 10, 1954 (div. June 1957). Degree in art journalism, Candler Coll., 1953; degree in modern art and restoration, Escola Arte Bologna, Italy, 1961; student, Escuela San Alejandro, Havana, 1950. Dir. gen., dir. exhbns. Fundora Gallery, Miami, Fla. Pres., bd. dirs. Song Festival, N.Y.C., Internat. Song Festival, Trujillo, Internat. Song Festival, Chiclayo, Festival of Song, Buenos Aires, Internat. Song Festival, Viña del Mar, Miami, others; former sr. v.p. Record World, Internat. Music Rev. mag.; pub., editor USA 23 Millones, Miami. Author: Union Panamericana, Washington, 1959, Galeria Duneen Graham, N.Y.C., 1959, Condon Relley Gallery, N.Y., 1959, Muestra Arquitectonica Neocolonial Colegio de Arquitectos, Havana, 1959, Emociones, 1963 (award 1964), Lo Mejor de Mi Vida, 1984, Inquietudes, 1988 (award 1990), Tu y Ellos, 1989; exhbns. include Lyceum de La Havana, 1949, Asociacion de Reporters, Havana, 1954, Galeria Gratacielo, Milan, 1961, Galeria del Canale, Venice, Los Grandes de Am., Hotel Woodstock, N.Y., 1964, Mamma Leones Art Show, N.Y., 1965 (Internat. Grand prize 1966), Glovier Club, N.Y., 1965, Exposition of Contemporary Art, Hotel Turistas, Trujillo, Peru, 1965, IRT Art Exhibit, Bklyn., 1966 (medalla de plata), Internat. Exhibition Friends of P.R., N.Y.C., 1967, Bienal de Sao Paulo, 1967, Roland de Aenlle Gallery, N.Y., 1967, Cayre Art Exhibit, 1968, Inst. Arte Latino, Washington, 1968, Inst. P.R., N.Y., 1969, Internat. Art Gallery, Miami, 1989, Strokes and Motion of Light and Matter, Miami, 1989-90, Martin's Art Gallery, Coral Gables, Fla., 1990, Catalina Art Gallery, Kendall, Fla., 1996, 98, Domingo Padron Art Gallery, Coral Gables, 1997, Frame USA Gallery, Kendall, 1997, Izzo's Artery Gallery, Chgo., 1998, 2001, Fundora Art Show, Ocean Reef Art League, Key Largo, Fla., Estefan Enterprises, Inc.m Bongos Cuban Cafe, Miami, Fla., 2002, Named Artist of the Yr. Carteles Mag., 1967. Mem. Assn. Painters N.Y. (pres. 1969-73), Assn. Latin Am. Painters N.Y., Cir. Painters Miami, Monroe Coun. Arts (mem. adv. bd.). Republican. Avocations: fishing, boating, traveling. Home: 205 Camelot Dr Tavernier FL 33070-2805 Office: Fundora Art Gallery 103400 Overseas Hwy Key Largo FL 33037-2834 E-mail: thomasfund@aol.com.

FUNES, PABLO JOSE, computer science researcher; b. Cordoba, Argentina, Apr. 18, 1966; came to U.S., 1995; s. Everest Santiago Funes and Maria Del Carmen Arguello. Degree in math., U. Buenos Aires, 1994; PhD in Computer Sci., Brandeis U., 2001. Cons. in sys. FAO (UN), Mex., 1983-95; sys. mgr. UAPE, Buenos Aires, 1986-93; CTO MAPA Sys., Buenos Aires, 1991-93; cons. in modeling Ministry of Economy, Argentina, 1995; evolutionary scientist Icosystem Corp., 2001—. Inventor in field of modular structures evolution. Office: Icosystem 10 Fawcett St Cambridge MA 02138 E-mail: pablo@icosystem.com.

FUNG, AMY SHU-FONG, accountant; b. Hong Kong, Sept. 23, 1949; came to U.S., 1970; d. Wing-Chee and Fung-Siu (Tsang) Leung; m. Gee-You Fung, Mar. 17, 1970; children: Alice, Deborah. BS in Acctg., CUNY, 1982. Acct. Cath. Charities Diocese of Bklyn. Inc., N.Y.C., 1982-83; sr. acct. Beth Israel Med. Ctr., N.Y.C., 1983-85, St. John Episcopal Home for Aged and Blind, N.Y.C., 1986-87, Internat. Ctr. for Disabled, N.Y.C., 1988-91, United Jewish Appeal-Fedn. Jewish Philanthropies N.Y., N.Y.C., 1992-94. Avocations: music, cooking, theater, travel. Home: 359 Colon Ave Staten Island NY 10308-1415

FUNG, BING MAN, chemistry educator; b. Hong Kong, China, Aug. 15, 1939; came to U.S., 1963; m. Mildred W.Y. Mah, Aug. 26, 1967; 1 child, Archon. Diploma, Chung Chi Coll., Hong Kong, 1963; PhD, Calif. Inst. Tech., Pasadena, 1967. Asst. prof. Tufts U., Medford, Mass., 1966-72; assoc. prof. U. Okla., Norman, 1972-76, prof. chemistry, 1976-95; George Lynn Cross prof., 1995—. Contbr. articles to profl. jours. Recipient Career Devel. award NIH, 1975-80.

FUNG, CHI-KEUNG VICTOR, music educator, researcher; b. Hong Kong, Feb. 22, 1966; s. Hoi and Pik Lin F. Hon. Diploma, Hong Kong Bapt. U., 1988; MM, Baylor U., 1990; PhD, Ind. U., 1993; MBA, U. Leicester, 2003; licentiate, Trinty Coll. of Music, 1986. Asst. prof. U. Minn., Mpls., 1993-96; instr. I Chinese U. Hong Kong, 1997-98; asst. prof. Hong Kong Bapt. U., 1996-98, Bowling Green (Ohio) State U., 1998-2001, assoc. prof., 2001—, chair music edn., 2002—. External examiner in music Hong Kong Inst. Edn., 2000—03; bd. mem. Coll. Music Soc., 2004—; assessment cons. St. Paul Chamber Orch., 1995—96. Mem. editl. bd. Jour. Rsch. in Music Edn., 1998-2004, Asia-Pacific Jour. for Arts Edn., 2001—. Mem. music subject com. Hong Kong Exams. Authority, 1996-98; contbr. Arts for Bus., N.Y., 1999, 2000, 01; mem. external validation com. Hong Kong Coun. Academic Accreditation, 1998-2001. Mem. Internat. Soc. Music Edn., European Soc. Cognitive Scis. of Music, Soc. Ethnomusicology, Music Educators Nat. Conf., Coll. Music Soc., Assn. for Tech. in Music Instrn. Office: Bowling Green State U Coll Musical Arts Bowling Green OH 43403-0290

FUNG, HENRY CHI-HANG, physician, medical researcher; b. Hong Kong, Nov. 4, 1963; came to the U.S., 1996; s. Norman W. and Ann O. Fung; m. Grace W. Fung, June 2, 1990; 1 child, Germaine. MB, BChir, Chinese U. Hong Kong, 1987. Cert. clin. rsch. investigator. Intern Prince of Wales Hosp., 1987-88; resident Queen Mary Hosp., 1988-92, clin. fellow, 1992-94; clin. instr. U. B.C., Vancouver, Can., 1994-96; staff physician Vancouver Hosp. and Health Sci. Ctr., 1994-96, B.C. Cancer Agy., Vancouver, 1994-96; mem. Leukemia/BMT Program B.C., Vancouver, 1994-96; staff physician, clin. rsch. divsn. hematology/BMT City of Hope Nat. Med. Ctr., Duarte, Calif., 1996—. Author articles and abstracts related to malignant hematology and BMT. Fellow Royal Coll. Physicians (Edinburgh); mem. European Soc. Clin. Oncology, Am. Soc. Hematology, Am. Soc. Clin. Oncology, Am. Soc. Blood and Marrow Tranplantations. Avocations: research, music, reading. Office: City Hope Nat Med Ctr 1500 Duarte Rd Duarte CA 91010-3012 E-mail: hfung@coh.org.

FUNG, PAUL, JR., cartoonist, illustrator; b. Seattle, Mar. 9, 1923; s. Paul Fung and Mabel Seung; m. Carol Lorraine M. Fung; children: Lorraine Mae Gardephy, Paul Randall. BA, Pratt Inst., Bklyn., 1946. Artist Richard & Gunther Advt. Agy., N.Y.C., 1947-48; artist, prodn. mgr. Dowd, Redfield, Johnstone Advt. Agy., N.Y.C., 1947-48; prodn. mgr. Theatre Arts Mag., N.Y.C., 1947-49; cartoonist King Features Syndicate, N.Y.C., 1949-79, Pines Pub. Co., N.Y.C., 1948-49, Charlton Pub. Co., Derby, Conn., 1960-78, Western Printing & Pub. Co., N.Y.C., 1968-72. Artist Advt. Club N.Y., 1954-68, Lambs Club, N.Y.C., 1949-53. Writer, illustrator more than 495 Blondie and Hong Kong Phooey comic books; drawings include Blondie, Bulwinkle and Rocky, George of the Jungle, Hong Kong Phooey; exhibits include Libr. Congress, Washington, D.C., Smithsonian Inst., Washington, D.C., Mus. Modern Art, N.Y.C., N.Y., N.Y.C. (N.Y.) Libr., Internat. Mus. Cartoon Art, Boca Ratan, Fla., Cartoon Art Mus., Chgo., Ill., Cartoon Art Mus., San Francisco, Calif., Cartoon Art Mus., Orlando, Fla., Ohio State U. Art Libr. With USAF, 1941—46. Recipient medal, ASPCA, 1934; named Best Comic Book Cartoonist Nat. Cartoonist Soc., 1964, named Best Comic Book Humorist Nat. Cartoonist Soc., 1980. Mem. Nat. Cartoonist Soc. (Best Comic Book Cartoonist of Yr. award 1964, Best Comic Book Humorist award 1980), Masons (freelance artist 1969—), Greenwich (N.Y.) Lions Club (dir. 1968-2001, 30 Yr. award 1999). Republican. Episcopalian. Avocations: cooking, gardening, hunting and fishing, swimming. Home: 227 Langley Hill Rd Greenwich NY 12834

FUNG, PETER E. H. actor, martial arts educator, apparel designer; b. Honolulu, June 14, 1961; s. James Fung and Edigma Yap; m. Laurie Chin Fung, July 8, 1998; 1 child, May Lin Chin. Tchr. Bruce Lee Ednl. Inst., San Francisco, L.A., 1998—2003; mechanic Sequoia Auto Inst., Fremont, Calif.; teller Bank of Am., San Francisco, 1989—91. Actor: (films) Matrix II, 2003, Chona, 2003; designer (clothing), 2003—. Sunday sch. tchr. asst. St. Xavier's Ch., San Francisco, 1995—2000; tchr. Bruce Lee Ednl. Inst., San Francisco, 1998—. Recipient Karate Brown Belt, Sid Campbell's Karate, 1970, Kung Fu Black Sash, Jack Man Wong Kung Fu, 1979. Mem.: Bruce Lee Ednl. Found. Avocations: martial arts, self learning, religions. Home: Apt 612 685 Lucas Ave Los Angeles CA 90017-1929

FUNG, RICHARD LAP CHUNG, business executive; b. Hong Kong, May 13, 1953; s. Kit Fung and Nora Fung-Ng; m. Aleen Lo, Feb. 22, 1987; children: Kendrick, Carson. BA in Applied Sci., U. Toronto, 1977; PhD (hon.), Pacific So. U., 1997. Profl. engr. Chief exec. Hong Kong Standards and Testing Ctr., Hong Kong, 1992—. Home: 34 Hong Lok Rd West Hong Lok Yuen Taipo Hong Kong E-mail: richard_fung@hkstc.com.

FUNG, ROSALINE LEE, educator; b. China, May 14, 1944; came to U.S., 1963; d. Frank Kwok-Wai and Teresa Wai-Hing (Cheung) Lee; m. Stephen Ying-Chung Fung, Aug. 23, 1968. BA, Briar Cliff Coll., 1966; MA, Idaho State U., 1968. Instr. Highland C.C., Freeport, Ill., 1968-69, Merced (Calif.) Coll., 1969-70; tchr. Linden (Calif.) High Sch., 1970-84; prof. San Joaquin Delta Coll., Stockton, Calif., 1984—. Cons. in field. Author: (textbooks) ESL Writing Manual, 1992, Patterns for Success, 4 vols., 1997, Basic Composition, 1997, Writing Essays, 1998, Writing Paragraphs, 1999. Coord. cultural exch. San Joaquin Delta Coll., 1995, 96, 98. Mem. NEA, Calif. Tchrs. Assn. Avocations: reading, writing, concerts, theater, surfing the net. Office: San Joaquin Delta Coll 5151 Pacific Ave Stockton CA 95207-6304 E-mail: rfung@deltacollege.edu.

FUNG, YUAN-CHENG BERTRAM, bioengineering educator, writer; b. Yuhong, Changchow, Kiangsu, China, Sept. 15, 1919; came to U.S., 1945, naturalized, 1957; s. Chung-Kwang and Lien (Hu) F.; m. Luna Hsien-Shih Yu, Dec. 22, 1949; children: Conrad Antung, Brenda Pingsi. BS, Nat. Central U., Chungking, China, 1941, MS, 1943; PhD, Calif. Inst. Tech., 1948; DSc (hon.), Hong Kong U. Sci. and Tech., 1992, Drexel U., 2001, Nat. Central U., 2002, Sichuan U., 2002. Research fellow Bur. Aero. Research China, 1943-45; research asst., then research fellow Calif. Inst. Tech., 1946-51, mem. faculty, 1951-66, prof. aeros., 1959-66; prof. bioengring. and applied mechanics U. Calif., San Diego, 1966—2000, prof. emeritus bioengring., 2000—. Cons. aerospace indsl. firms, 1949—; prof. (hon.) 15 univs. China; hon. chair World Coun. Biomechanics, 1998. Author: The Theory of Aeroelasticity, 1955, 69, 93, Foundations of Solid Mechanics, 1965, A First Course in Continuum Mechanics, 1969, 77, 93, Biomechanics, 1972, Biomechanics: Mechanical Properties of Living Tissues, 1980, 1993, Biodynamics: Circulation, 1984, Biomechanics: Circulation, 1996, Biomechanics: Motion, Flow, Stress and Growth, 1990, Selected Works on Biomechanics and Aeroelasticity by Y.C. Fung, 1997, Classical and Computational Solid Mechanics, 2001, Introduction to Bioengineering, 2001; also papers; editor Jour. Biorheology, Jour. Biomech. Engring. Bd. trustees (hon.) Chongqing U.; chair (hon.), bd. trustees Nanjing U., China. Recipient Achievement award Chinese Inst. Engrs., 1965, 68, 93, Landis award Microcirculatory Soc., 1975, Poiseuille medal Internat. Soc. Biorheology, 1986, Engr. of Yr. award San Diego Engring. Soc., 1986, von Karman medal ASCE, 1976, ALZA award Biomed. Engring. Soc., 1989, Borelli award Am. Soc. Biomechanics, 1992; Guggenheim fellow, 1958-59, Melville medal Am. Soc. of Mechanical Engineers, 1994, Founders award, Nat. Acad. Engring. U.S., 1998, U.S. Nat. Medal of Sci., 2000. Fellow AIAA, ASME (hon., Lissner award 1978, Centennial medal 1978, Worcester Reed Warner medal 1984, Timoshenko medal 1991, Melville medal 1994); mem. Japan Soc. Mech. Engrs. (Bioengring. award 1995), NAS, NAE, Inst. Medicine, Soc. Engring. Sci., Microcirculatory Soc., Am. Physiol. Soc., Nat. Heart Assn., Acad. Sinica, Chinese Acad. Scis. (fgn. mem.), Basic Sci. Coun., Sigma Xi; hon. mem. ASME, 1996. Home: 2660 Greentree Ln La Jolla CA 92037-1148 Office: U Calif Dept Bioengring 9500 Gilman Dr La Jolla CA 92093-0412

FUNK, CARLA JEAN, library association executive; b. Wheeling, W.Va., Sept. 21, 1946; d. David H. and Jean (Duffy) Belt. BA in Psychology, Northwestern U., 1968; MLS, Ind. U., 1973; MBA, U. Chgo., 1985. Libr. adult svcs. Northbrook (Ill.) Pub. Libr., 1973-77; dir. Warren-Newport Pub. Libr. Dist., Gurnee, Ill., 1977-80; cons. Suburban Libr. Sys., Burr Ridge, Ill., 1980-83; dir. automation and tech. svcs., med. student svcs. AMA, Chgo.,

1983-92; exec. dir. Med. Libr. Assn., Chgo., 1992—. Adj. faculty Dominican U., 1986—; adv. com. Bicentennial Campaign U. S.C. Coll. Libr. and Info. Sci., Dominican U. Health Sci. com. Contbr. articles to profl. jours. Mem. Internat. Fedn. Libr. Assns. and Insts. (treas., U.S. nat. organizing com.), Am. Soc. Assn. Execs. (cert. assn. exec.), Ill. Libr. Assn., Assn. Forum of Chicagoland, Beta Phi Mu, Delta Zeta. Home: 345 W Fullerton Pkwy #2707 Chicago IL 60614 Office: 65 E Wacker Pl Ste 1900 Chicago IL 60601-7246 E-mail: funk@mlahq.org.

FUNK, CYRIL REED, JR., agronomist, educator; b. Richmond, Utah, Sept. 20, 1928; s. Cyril Reed and Hazel Marie (Jensen) F.; m. Donna Gwen Buttars, Feb. 2, 1951; children: Bonnie Arlene, David Christopher, Carol Jean. BS (Scholarship A 1955), Utah State U., 1952, MS, 1955; PhD, Rutgers U., 1961; DAgr (hon.), Utah State U., 1994. Mem. faculty Rutgers U., New Brunswick, NJ, 1956—, rsch. prof. turfgrass breeding plant biology and pathology dept., 1969—, also instr. grad. faculty. Author, patentee in field. Served to 1st lt. AUS, 1952-54. Recipient Green Sect. award U.S. Golf Assn., 1980, Achievement award Lawn Inst., 1977; named to Hall of Disting. Alumni, Rutgers U. Fellow Crop Sci. Soc. Am., Am. Soc. Agronomy (research award N.E. sect. 1979); mem. AAAS (fellow 1992), Am. Sod Producers Assn. (hon.), Golf Course Supts. Assn. (hon. mem.; Disting. Service award 1979), Internat. Turfgrass Soc., N.J. Turfgrass Assn. (Achievement award 1976, Hall of Fame award 1984), N.J. Golf Course Supts. Assn. (hon.), N.J. Acad. Scis., Sigma Xi, Phi Kappa Phi, Acad. Scis. Uzbekistan (hon.), Acad. Agrl. Scis. Kyrgyzstan (hon.). Mem. Lds Ch. Achievements include developing numerous turfgrasses. Home: 4 Delaware Dr East Brunswick NJ 08816-3255 Office: Rutgers U Cook Coll New Brunswick NJ 08901 E-mail: reedonna1@comcast.com.

FUNK, DAVID ALBERT, retired law educator; b. Wooster, Ohio, Apr. 22, 1927; s. Daniel Coyle and Elizabeth Mary (Reese) F.; children— Beverly Joan, Susan Elizabeth, John Ross, Carolyn Louise; m. Sandra Nadine Henselmeier, Oct. 2, 1976 Student, U. Mo., 1945-46, Harvard Coll., 1946; BA in Econs., Coll. of Wooster, 1949; MA, Ohio State U., 1968; JD, Case Western Res. U., 1951, LLM, 1972, Columbia U., 1973. Bar: Ohio 1951, U.S. Dist. Ct. (no. dist.) Ohio 1962, U.S. Tax Ct. 1963, U.S. Ct. Appeals (6th cir.) 1970, U.S. Supreme Ct. 1971. Ptnr. Funk, Funk & Eberhart, Wooster, Ohio, 1951-72; assoc. prof. law Ind. U. Sch. Law, Indpls., 1973-76, prof., 1976-97, prof. emeritus, 1997—. Vis. lectr. Coll. of Wooster, 1962-63; dir. Juridical Sci. Inst., Indpls., 1982—. Author: Oriental Jurisprudence, 1974, Group Dynamic Law, 1982; (with others) Rechtsgeschichte und Rechtssoziologie, 1985, Group Dynamic Law: Exposition and Practice, 1988; contbr. articles to profl. jours. Chmn. bd. trustees Wayne County Law Library Assn., 1956-71; mem. Permanent Jud. Commn., Synod of Ohio, United Presbyn. Ch. in the U.S., 1968. Served to seaman 1st class USNR, 1945-46 Harlan Fiske Stone fellow Columbia U., 1973; recipient Am. Jurisprudence award in Comparative Law, Case Western Res. U., 1970 Mem. Assn. Am. Law Schs. (sec. comparative law sect. 1977-79, chmn. law and religion sect. 1977-81, sec.-treas. law and social sci. sect. 1983-86), Am. Soc. for Legal History, Pi Sigma Alpha. Republican. Home: 6208 N Delaware St Indianapolis IN 46220-1824

FUNK, JAMES WILLIAM, JR., insurance agency administrator, business owner; b. Vincennes, Ind., May 31, 1947; s. James William and Elizabeth (Bauer) F.; m. Janis Burrell, Aug. 11, 1973; children: Christopher James, Kelly Elizabeth. BA, Butler U., Indpls., 1969. Cert. ins. counselor, 1991, cert. profl. ins. agt., 1999; chartered property casuality underwriter, 2002. Mem. campaign staff U.S. Senator Birch Bayh, Indpls., 1968; bus. cons. Dun & Bradstreet, Inc., Indpls., 1969-71; dir. ops. Terry Properties, Inc., Springfield, Ill., 1971-72; pers. mgr. Am. Underwriters, Inc., Indpls., 1972-73, adminstrv. asst. to pres., 1973-75, asst. sec., 1975-78, v.p. pub. rels., 1978-79; adminstrv. mgr. Affiliated Agys., Inc., Indpls., 1979-93; ind. agt., v.p., sec. Ctrl. Ins. Assocs., Inc., 1993-98, pres., 1999—. Owner Bauer Bros. Exploration Co.; lectr., instr. A.D. Banker Co., 1997-2001 Sec., treas. Ctrl. North Civic Assn., Indpls., 1976, pres. 1977-78; bd. dirs. Ind. Amateur Baseball Assn., 1993—, sec. 1999; active Bishop Chatard H.S. PTO, 1995-97, pres. 1997—; bd. dirs. Clearwater Cove Homeowners Assn., 1999-2000, pres., 2000. Mem. Ind. Soc. Chgo., Profl. Ins. Agts Ind. (v.p. 1984-85, pres. 1986-87, chmn. legis. com., treas. polit. action com., bd. dirs. 1982-88, 99—, pres.-elect 2002, pres. 2003, agt. of yr. 1990, v.p. 2001—), Preussian Benefit Soc., Heimaths Benefit Soc., Butler Univ. Pres.'s Club, K.C. Roman Catholic. Home: 6491 N Sherman Dr Indianapolis IN 46220 Office: 3520 E 96th St Ste A-2 Indianapolis IN 46240-3782 E-mail: jwfunkjr@aol.com.

FUNK, PHILLIP E. immunologist, biology educator; b. Jerseyville, Ill. m. Wendy Siegel, July 23, 1989. BS, U. Ill., 1987; PhD, Loyola U., Chgo., 1993. Asst. prof. DePaul U., Chgo., 1998—. Office: DePaul U Dept Biology 2325 N Clifton Chicago IL 60614 E-mail: pfunk@depaul.edu.

FUNK, ROBERT ALLEN, personnel executive; b. Duvall, Wash., May 14, 1940; s. A. Roy and Dorothy Ellen (Herman) F.; m. Nedra Ruth Pitcher, Nov. 16, 1963; children: Julie Ann, Robert Allen. BA in Bus., Seattle Pacific U., 1962, MA in Bus., 1969; postgrad., U. Edinburg, 1962-63. Ordained to ministry Evangelical Meth. Ch., 1967, So. Baptist Ch., 1980. Minister Evangelical Meth. Ch., Duvall, Wis., 1967—, So. Baptist Ch., Piedmont, Okla., 1980—; 1st v.p. ACME Personnel Svcs., Oklahoma City, 1965-83; co-founder, CEO, chmn. bd. Express Pers. Svcs., Oklahoma City, 1983—. Mem. pub.'s adv. panel Fortune mag., 1989. Pres. sch. bd. Piedmont Sch. Dist, 1974-85; deacon Piedmont Baptist Ch., 1980—. Named to Hall of Fame, Sales and Mktg. Execs. Internat., 1990, Inc 500, Inc Mag., 1988, 89, Entrepreneur of Yr., Okla. Venture Forum, 1989, Paul Harris Fellow, Rotary Internat., 1989, Entrepreneur of Yr. Finalist, Arthur Young, 1989. Mem. Nat. Assn. Temporary Svcs. (bd. dirs. 1990—), Nat. Assn. Personnel Cons., Sales and Mktg. Execs. Assn. (trustee 1990—), Adminstrv. Mgmt. Soc. (pres. 1977), Okla. Personnel Assn. (pres. 1978). Republican. Avocations: farming, tennis, fishing. Office: Express Personal Svcs 8516 Internat Expressway Oklahoma City OK 73162*

FUNK, SHERMAN MAXWELL, former government official, writer, consultant; b. N.Y.C., Nov. 13, 1925; s. Bernard and Dorothy (Arkin) F.; m. Elaine Myrl Bayer, Mar. 6, 1953 (dec. 1977); children: Katherine Sara, Bernard Eugene; m. Sylvia Grunbaum Straka, June 3, 1978; children Eric, Marc, Paul. AB, Harvard U., 1950; postgrad., Columbia U., 1956, U. Ariz., 1958. Salesman, sales exec. Bernard Funk Co., N.Y.C., 1950-54; history tchr. Catskill (N.Y.) High Sch., 1954-57; polit. sci. teaching asst. U. Ariz., Tucson, 1957-58; mgmt. intern USAF Hdqrs., Washington, 1958, war planning officer, mgmt. analyst, 1958-63, chief Air Force Mgmt. Improvement Programs Office, 1963-67, chief Air Force Cost Reduction Office, 1967-70; successively asst. dir. adminstrn. and program devel., dir. rsch. and program devel., asst. dir. planning and evaluation Office Minority Bus. Enterprise, Dept. Commerce, 1970-79; spl. asst. for small bus. Dept. Energy, 1979-81; insp. gen. Dept. Commerce, 1981-87, Dept. State, 1987-94, adviser to fgn. govts. on anti-corruption efforts, 1994—; vice chmn. Pres.'s Coun. on Integrity and Efficiency, 1989-90. TV commentator. Contbr. articles to profl. jours., major newspapers. Mem. Bowie City Council, (Md.), 1963-65, chmn. human relations com., 1964-65, chmn. charter rev. com., 1968; pres. Bethesda Jewish Congregation, 1986. Served with inf. AUS, 1943-46. Decorated Purple Heart; recipient Presdl. Unit Citation, spl. award Sec. Air Force, 1968, prizes Washington-Md.-Del Press Assn., 1970, 71, 73, 75, Silver medal Commerce Dept., 1972, Disting. honor award State Dept., 1992. Mem. Fed. Investigators Assn. Mailing: 2982 Salem Dr Ann Arbor MI 48103-6811 *My years in government were marked by paradox: I worked with some extraordinarily able people and with important and challenging programs. Yet I increasingly came to doubt the ability of these and other federal programs to solve many national ills. Too many of them are subverted externally by political pork and internally by waste, fraud and don't-rock-the boat thinking. As an Inspector General, under three pres., I tried to fight such abuse, and to help change the poor image of federal service-both appointive and career-which scares off exactly the kind of bright and aggressive talent needed in government. As a private citzen now, free of the constraints levied on appointees, I shall continue this fight with redoubled vigor.*

FUNK, VICKI JANE, librarian; b. Frankfurt am Main, Hesse, Federal Republic of Germany, Apr. 7, 1951; d. George N. and Maymie Lou Funk; m. David Robert Koble, July 11, 1986. BS, Ind. State U., 1971; MLS, Okla. U., 1975; cert. in comparative libraries, Oxford U., Eng., Summer 1978; cert. in Scottish lit., St. Andrews U., Scotland, Summer 1985. Elem. open concept team tchr. Plainfield (Ind.) Pub. Schs., 1971-72; media specialist, tchr. elem. schs. Enid (Okla.) Pub. Schs., 1972-73, librarian, 1973-74; libr. media specialist Bartlesville (Okla.) Sr. H.S., 1975-96. Chmn. library evaluation teams North Cen. Assn., Okla., 1982-86; pres. V.I.E.W. adv. bd. Okla. State Dept. Vocat. Edn., 1980-81; tchr. pub. library continuing adult edn. program, Bartlesville, 1986. Storyteller Ednl. TV Bartlesville Cable, 1975-77, Oral Children's Program Pub. Library, 1985-86; book reviewer Okla. State Dept. Libraries "Gushers and Dusters", 1986-87; mem. book rev. selection com. Bartlesville Pub. Library. V.P Friends of the Pub. Library, Bartlesville, 1986. Recipient Outstanding Svc. award Okla. Dept. Vocat. Edn., 1981; Emiline Libr. scholar Ind. State U., 1970; Innovative Edn. grantee Bartlesville Pub. Edn. Found., 1990, 91. Mem. NEA, AAUW (edn. officer 1980-81), Okla. Edn. Assn., Bartlesville Edn. Assn., Bartlesville Art Assn., Okla. Libr. Assn., Kappa Kappa Iota (v.p. 1990-91, secd. 1996-98). Democrat. Presbyterian. Avocations: bridge, traveling, skiing, acting, oil painting.

FUNK, WILLIAM F. lawyer, educator; b. Boston, Nov. 29, 1945; s. Ward I. and Mary Roberts (Fergusson) F.; m. Renate Dieckmann, June 5, 1971; children: Andrew Christopher, Jonas Peter, Rebecca Matthea. BA, Harvard U., 1967; JD, Columbia U., 1973. Bar: N.Y. 1974, D.C. 1979, U.S. Supreme Ct. 1983. Law clk. to Hon. James Oakes U.S. Ct. Appeals 2d Cir., Brattleboro, Vt., 1973-74; atty. advisor Office Legal Counsel Dept. Justice, Washington, 1974-77; prin. staff Intelligence Com. U.S. Ho. of Reps., Washington, 1977-78; asst. gen. counsel U.S. Dept. Energy, Washington, 1978-83; assoc. prof. Lewis and Clark Coll. Law Sch., Portland, Oreg., 1983-86, prof., 1986—. Cons. U.S. Dept. Energy, Washington, 1983-84, U.S. Adminstrn. Conf., Washington, 1985-86. 1st lt. U.S. Army, 1967-70. Mem.: ABA (sect. chair). Home: 22 Grouse Terr Lake Oswego OR 97035 Office: Lewis and Clark Law Sch 10015 SW Terwilliger Blvd Portland OR 97219-7768 E-mail: funk@lclark.edu.

FUNK, WILLIAM HENRY, retired environmental engineering educator; b. Ephraim, Utah, June 10, 1933; s. William George and Henrietta (Hackwell) F.; m. Ruth Sherry Mellor, Sept. 19, 1964 (dec.); 1 dau., Cynthia Lynn; m. Lynn Bridget Robson, Mar. 30, 1996. BS in Biol. Sci, U. Utah, 1955, MS in Zoology, 1963, PhD in Limnology, 1966. Tchr. sci., math. Salt Lake City Schs., 1957-60; research asst. U. Utah, Salt Lake City, 1961-63; head sci. dept. N.W. Jr. High Sch., Salt Lake City, 1961-63; mem. faculty Wash. State U., Pullman, 1966-99, assoc. prof. environ. engring., 1971-75, prof., 1975-99, chmn. environ. sci./regional planning program, 1979-81; dir. Environ. Research Center, 1980-83, State of Wash. Water Research Ctr., 1981-99; ret., 1999. Cons. U.S. Army C.E., Walla Walla, Wash., 1970—74, Harstad Engrs., Seattle, 1971—72, Boise Cascade Corp., Seattle, 1971—72, Wash. Dept. Ecology, Olympia, 1971—72, ORB Corp., Renton, Wash., 1972—73, U.S. Civil Svc., Seattle, Chgo., 1972—74; mem. High Level Nuclear Waste Bd., Wash., 1986—89, Wash. 2010 Com., 1989, Pure Water 2000 Steering Com., 1990; co-dir. Inst. Resource Mgmt.; co-founder Terrene Inst., Washington, 1991, pres., 1993—2002. Author publs. on water pollution control and lake restoration. Served to capt. USNR, 1955-88. Grantee NSF Summer Inst., 1961, U.S. Army C.E., 1970-74, 94-96, 97-98, Office Water Resources Rsch., 1971-72, 73-76, EPA, 1980-83, 93-94, 95-96, U.S. Geol. Survey, 1983-94, 95-96, 97-98, 99-00, Nat. Parks Svc., 1985-87, Colville Confederated Tribes, 1990-92, Nez Pierce Tribe, 1992-95, Wash. Conservation Commn., 1992-95, Clearwater Co., 1992-93, Idaho Dept. Environ. Quality, 1995-96, U.S. Bur. Reclamation, 1995-98; USPHS fellow, 1963; recipient Pres.'s Disting. Faculty award Wash. State U., 1984. Mem. Naval Res. Officers Assn. (chpt. pres. 1969), Res Officers Assn. (U.S. Naval Acad. info. officer 1973-76), N.Am. Lake Mgmt. Soc. (pres. 1984-85, Secchi Disk award 1988), Pacific N.W. Pollution Control Assn. (editor 1969-77, pres.-elect 1982-83, pres. 1983-84), Water Pollution Control Fedn. (Arthur S. Bedell award Pacific N.W. assn. 1976, nat. bd. dirs. 1978-81, bd. dirs. Rsch. Found. 1990-92), Nat. Assn. Water Inst. Dirs. (chair 1985-87, bd. dirs. univ. council on water resources 1986-89), Wash. Lakes Protection Assn. (co-founder 1986, Friend of Lakes award 1999), Am. Water Resources Assn. (v.p. Wash. sect. 1988), Am. Soc. Limnology and Oceanography, Am. Micros. Soc., N.W. Sci. Assn., North Am. Lake Mgmt. Soc. (co-founder 1972), Sigma Xi, Phi Sigma. Home: 330 SW Kimball Ct Pullman WA 99163-2176

FUNKHOUSER, ERICA, writer, educator, communications educator; b. Cambridge, Mass., Sept. 17, 1949; d. Elmer Newton and Gladys McFeeley Funkhouser; children: Justin, Sophie. BA, Vassar Coll., 1971; MA, Stanford U., 1973. Part-time lectr. dept. writing and humanistic studies MIT, Cambridge, Mass., 1998—. Author: Sure Shot and Other Poems, 1992, The Actual World, 1997, Pursuit, 2002. Fellow, McDowell Found., 1994. Mem.: Acad. Am. Poets, Poetry Soc. Am., PEN New Eng.

FUNKHOUSER, JOHN JEREMIAH, urologist; b. Indpls., July 1, 1937; s. James Bauer and Gene Marie (Smith) F.; m. Margaret Avery Thompson, June 22, 1963; children: Christopher, Stewart, Margaret. BA, Yale U., 1959; MD, U. Va., 1963. Diplomate Am. Bd. Urology. Resident Barnes Hosp., Saint Louis, 1963-64; med. officer USS Oglethorpe, 1964-65, NAS Oceana, 1965-66; resident Naval Hosps., Phila., Portsmouth, Va., 1966-70; chief urology Naval Hosp., St. Albans, N.Y., 1970-71; pvt. practice urology, Falmouth, Mass., 1971—. Chief of surgery Jordan Hosp., Plymouth, 1974-79; pres. med. staff Falmouth Hosp., 1991-93. Pres. Hist. Commn., Kingston, Mass., 1973-77. Fellow ACS (cancer liaison fellow 1983-2002), New Eng. Cancer Soc.; mem. Am. Urol. Assn., Mass. Med. Soc., West Falmouth Civic Assn. (pres. 1989-95), Harbor Head Tennis Club, Woods Hole Golf Club. Office: 17 Bramblebush Park Falmouth MA 02540-2325

FUNKHOUSER, LAWRENCE WILLIAM, retired geologist; b. Napoleon, Ohio, June 9, 1921; s. Edward A. and Margaret M. (Reinking) F.; m. Jean Garnet Cooper, June 1, 1946 (dec. Feb. 27, 2003); children: Donald W., Thomas E., David P., Karen J. AB in Geology, Oberlin Coll, 1943; MS in Geology, Stanford U., 1948; DSc (hon.), Oberlin Coll., 1990. Geologist, dist. geologist The Calif. Co., New Orleans, 1948-58, div. exploration supt., 1958-61; div. exploration supt., v.p. exploration Standard Oil Co. Tex., Midland and Houston, 1961-66; v.p. exploration Standard Oil Co. Calif., San Francisco, 1968-73, dir., v.p. exploration, 1973-77; dir., v.p. exploration and prodn. Chevron Corp., San Francisco, 1978-86, ret., 1986; v.p., dir. Energy Exploration Mgmt. Co., Houston, 1989-92. Mem. Nat. Research Council Commn. on Physical Sci., Math. and Resources, 1987-90. Named to Hall of Fame, Offshore Energy Ctr., 2002. Mem. Am. Assn. Petroleum Geologists (hon., pres.-elect 1986-87, pres. 1987-88), Am. Assn. Petroleum Geologists Found. (chmn. 1991-2001), Geol. Soc. Am., Phi Beta Kappa, Sigma Xi. Presbyterian. Home: 283 Park Ln Atherton CA 94027-5448 Office: PO Box 1088 Menlo Park CA 94026-1088 E-mail: lwfexpl@aol.com.

FUNKHOUSER, ROBERT BRUCE, lawyer; b. Calgary, Alta., Can., Jan. 3, 1959; AB, Harvard U., 1981; JD, Fordham U., 1987. Bar: N.Y. 1988, D.C. 1993. Law clk. Hon. Lloyd F. MacMahon, N.Y.C., 1987-88; assoc. Hughes Hubbard & Reed, N.Y.C., 1988-92, Washington, 1992-97, counsel, 1997—. Editor Fordham Law Rev., 1986-87. Mem. ABA (antitrust and litigation sects.). Office: Hughes Hubbard & Reed LLP 1775 I St NW Washington DC 20006-2402 E-mail: funkhous@hugheshubbard.com.

FUNNELL, CHRISTINA MARY, non-profit consultant; b. Wakefield, Eng., Aug. 24, 1947; d. Norman and Joanna Christina (Lenes) Beaumont; m. Ivan Neil Funnell (div. May 1994); children: Laura Jane, Thomas William. Student, Southgate, London, 1968-71; BA with spl. honors, Hull U., Yorkshire, Eng., 1968. Adminstrv. sec. Meth. Assn. Youth Clubs, London, 1965-68; organiser Orgn. for Vol. Youth Orgns., London, 1971-74; CEO Nat. Eczema Soc., London, 1982-96; cons. The Meth. North Bank Estate, London, 1999—. Founder Long Term Med. Conditions Alliance, London, 1993, chmn., 1995-96; patient advisor All Party Parliamentery Group on Skin, 1994-97; CEO Skin Care Campaign, London, 1995-97; cons. in field. Active NHS Exec. Patient Partnership Strategy Working Group, London, 1994-97, Standing Adv. Group on Consumer Involvement in the NHS R&D Programme, 1996-98; exec. mem. Christian Socialist Movement, 1997-2003; assoc. mem. The Iona Cmty.; steward Wesleys Chapel, London; chmn. Consumer Health Info. Centre, 1998-2003, Sec. Health Coalition Initiative, New Generation Project Reference Group, 2003; coord. Patients Info. Forum; lay mem., nursing, midwifery coun.; non-exec. bd. Nat. Clin. Assessment Authority; patient and pub. involvement cons. NHS Modernisation Agy. Rapid Response Unit, 2003— Mem.: Socialist Health Assn. Mem. Labour Party. Methodist. Avocations: travel, human rights, history, current affairs, gardening. Home: 28 Queensbury St London N1 3AD England Fax: 020-7704-9697. E-mail: tinafunnell@btopenworld.com.

FUNSETH, ROBERT LLOYD ERIC MARTIN, international consultant, lecturer, retired senior foreign service officer, foundation administrator; b. International Falls, Minn., May 10, 1926; s. Martin Emmanuel and Agnes Evangeline (Guibault) F.; m. Marilyn Ann Schuelke, Mar. 23, 1957; 1 child, Eric Christian. BA, Hobart Coll., 1948, postgrad., 1950-51, Cornell U., 1950, 51, Sch. Advanced Internat. Studies, Johns Hopkins U., 1951-52; MS, George Washington U., 1969; LL.D, Hobart and William Smith Colls., 1978. Editor Coachella Desert Barnacle, (Calif.), 1948; mng. editor Anaheim Gazette, (Calif.), 1948-50; corr. AP, 1950; resident tutor Hobart Coll., 1950-51; info. officer U.S. Mut. Security Agy., 1952-53; editor USIA, 1953-51; joined U.S. Fgn. Service, 1954; advanced to rank of minister-counselor Career Sr. Fgn. Service; vice consul Tehran, Tabriz, Azerbaijan and Kurdistan, Iran, 1954-56; 3d sec. Am. embassy, Beirut, 1957-59; UN polit. affairs officer Dept. State, 1959-61; Am. consul (Bordeaux), France, 1961-64; Portuguese desk officer Dept. State, Washington, 1964-66; mem. U.S. del. 20th UN Gen. Assembly, 1965; dep. dir. Iberian affairs Dept. State, 1966-68; assigned to Nat. War Coll., 1968-69; dir. mgmt. U.S. diplomatic and consular posts Dept. State, Mex. and Central Am., 1969-70, coordinator Cuban affairs, 1970-72, sr. fgn. service insp., 1972-73; counselor Am. embassy, Ottawa, Ont., Can., 1973-74; dep. dept. spokesman and dir. office of press relations Dept. State, Washington, 1974-75, dept. spokesman and spl. asst. to sec. of state for press relations, 1975-77, dir. office No. European affairs, 1977-82, dep. asst. sec. for refugee resettlement, 1982-83, sr. dep. asst. sec. Bur. Refugee Programs, 1983-91, cons., 1991—; trustee, pres. Diplomatic and Consular Officers Ret.-Bacon House Found., Washington. Detailed to U.S. Falkland Island Peace Mission to London and Buenos Aires, 1982; vis. disting. alumni scholar in residence Hobart and William Smith Colls., 1978, Nat. Cathedral Assn.; vis. fellow Woodrow Wilson Found., Princeton U.; lectr. Am. studies U. Tabriz, 1955-56; mem. numerous U.S. Delegations, 1976-89 including NATO Ministerial Meetings in Ottawa, Brussels, Oslo, U.S. China Consultations, Beijing, former Pres. Ford's 1975 visit to Philippines, OECD, Paris, SALT, Moscow, U.S.-So. Africa Initiative, Nairobi, Dar es Salam, Lusaka, Kinshasa, Monrovia, Dakar, UN Trade and Devel. Conf., Kenya, OAS Ministerial Meeting, Santiago, Chile, 1976 econ. summit former Pres. Ford Puerto Rico, 1st U.S. South African Ministerial meeting, Grafenau, Germany, U.S.-Iran Joint Commn., Tehran, U.S. Bilateral Consultations with Afghanistan and Pakistan, 1976 Inauguration Mexican Pres. Lopez-Portillo; head U.S. dels. U.S.-Vietnamese Refugee Consultations, Geneva, Switzerland, 1982-90; head U.S. del., U.S.-Vietnamese negotiations, Resettlement Vietnamese Polit. Prisoners, Hanoi, Vietnam, 1988, 89, 2d internat. conf. Indochinese Refugees, Geneva, 1989. U.S. observer Internat. Cath. Migration Commn. Conf., Vatican City, 1990; bd. dirs. Episcopal Ch. Presiding Bishop's Fund for World Relief; mem. peace commn. Episcopal Diocese of Washington. Lt. (j.g.) USNR, 1943—46, PTO. Recipient Outstanding Service commendation Am. Forces Spl. Command, Middle East, 1958, Disting. and Superior Honor Group awards Dept. State, 1959, 61, 70, Superior Honor award Dept. State, 1977, Sesquicentennial award Hobart Coll., 1972, Presdl. honor awards Sr. Fgn. Svc., 1986, 88, 91, Disting. Honor award Dept. State, 1989, Resolutions of Commendation Calif. State Senate, 1989, 91, Wilbur Carr disting. svc. award Dept. State, 1991, medal of excellence Hobart Coll. Alumni Assn., 1997, Hero of the Vietnamese Polit. Prisoners award Fedn. of U.S. Assns. of Vietnamese Polit. Prisoners, 1999. Mem.: Johns Hopkins Alumni Assn. (exec. coun. 1968—70), Diplomatic and Consular Officers Ret. (bd. govs. 1999—2001, sec., v.p. 2001—03, pres. 2003—, pres. Dacor-Bacon House Found.), Assn. Diplomatic Studies, Am. Fgn. Svc. Assn., Journalism Soc. (hon.), Mil. Order of Carabao, Nat. War Coll. Alumni Assn., Sch. Advanced Studies Alumni Assn. (mem. adv. coun. 1969, 1970, pres.), Hobart Coll. Alumni Assn. (medal of excellence 1997), George Washington U. Alumni Assn., Ebenezer Sch. Alumni Assn., West Seneca (N.Y.) Hist. Soc., Am. Fgn. Svc. Club, Phi Delta, Phi Sigma Kappa. Office Fax: 202-842-3295.

FUOCO, PHILIP STEPHEN, lawyer; b. Riverside, N.J., Oct. 28, 1946; s. Francis and Mary Helen Fuoco; m. Carol Freeman, June 7, 1969; 1 child. BA in Philosophy, U. Notre Dame, 1968; JD, Villanova (Pa.) U., 1971. Bar: N.J. 1972, U.S. Dist. Ct. N.J. 1972, Pa. 1973, U.S. Dist. Ct. (ea. dist.) Pa. 1975, U.S. Ct. Appeals (3d cir.) 1977, U.S. Supreme Ct. 1980; cert. criminal trial atty. N.J. Supreme Ct. Trial atty. civil rights div. U.S. Dept. Justice, Washington, 1971-75; asst. U.S. atty. U.S. Dist. Ct. (ea. dist.) Pa., Phila., 1975; pvt. practice N.J., 1975—. Adj. prof. law Rutgers U., Camden, 1997-2000. Contbr. articles to profl. jours. and law revs. Mem. Haddonfield Environ. Commn., 1991—93; apptd. mem. com. on model jury charges-criminal N.J. Supreme Ct., 1996—2002, apptd. mem. dist. IV ethics com., 1997—2001, apptd. mem. com. on character, 2001; mem. steering com. First Night Haddonfield, 1999; bd. dirs. Steininger Ctr., 1990—92, Haddonfield Zoning Bd., 1984—88. Recipient Stivale d'Italia award for excellence Italian Tribune of Newark, N.J., 2003; NEH fellow, 1978. Mem. ABA, ACLU, Nat. Assn. Dist. Attys., Nat. Assn. Criminal Def. Lawyers, Camden County Bar Assn. (trustee 1986-89), N.J. Bar Assn., Lions (Haddonfield pres. 1986-87). Office: 24 Wilkins Place Haddonfield NJ 08033-2406

FUQUA, CHARLES JOHN, retired classics educator; b. Paris, Oct. 5, 1935; s. John Howe and Gillian Elynor (Quennell) F.; m. Mary Louise Morse, Aug. 26, 1961; children— Andrew Morse, David Reed, Gillian Quennell. BA magna cum laude, Princeton, 1957; MA, Cornell U., 1962, PhD, 1964. Instr. classics Dartmouth Coll., Hanover, NH, 1964, asst. prof., 1965-66; assoc. prof. classics, chmn. dept. classics Williams Coll., Williamstown, Mass., 1966-72, Garfield prof. ancient langs., chmn. dept. classics, 1972-86, ret., 2003. Mem. adv. council Am. Acad. in Rome, 1966, chmn. exec. com., 1974 Served to lt. (j.g.) USNR, 1957-60. Mem.: Vergilian Soc., Classical Assn. Mass., Classical Assn. New Eng., Am. Philol. Assn., Phi Beta Kappa, Phi Kappa Phi. Home: 96 Grandview Dr Williamstown MA 01267-2528 E-mail: cfuqua@williams.edu.

FUQUA, JOHN BROOKS, retired consumer products and services company executive; b. Prince Edward County, Va., June 26, 1918; s. J.B. Elam and Ruth F.; m. Dorothy Chapman, Feb. 10, 1945; 1 son, John Rex. Grad. high sch., Prospect, Va.; LLD (hon.), Hampden-Sydney Coll., 1972, Duke U., 1973, Fla. Meml. Coll., 1982, Oglethorpe U., 1986; LHD (hon.), Queens Coll., 1987, Longwood Coll., 1990; LLD (hon.), U. Tulsa, 1991, Mercer U., 1991; DHL (hon.), Queens Coll., Charlotte, 1995; D in Adminstrn. (hon.), Cumberland Coll., 1995. Chmn. Fuqua Industries, Inc., Atlanta, 1965-89. Mem. adv. bd. Norfolk So. Corp.; established Ctr. for USSR Mgr. Devel., tng. program for top Soviet mgrs. at Fuqua Sch. Bus. Duke U., 1990. Author: Fuqua-A Memoir, 2002. Mem. Augusta Aviation Commn., 1945-67; past mem., fin. chmn. Augusta Hosp. Authority; past mem. Ga. Sci. and Tech. Commn.; mem. Ga. Ho. of Reps., 1957-62, chmn. House Banking Com., 1959-63; mem. Ga. Senate, 1963-65, chmn. Senate Banking and Fin. Com., Dem. Party and Exec. Com. Ga., 1962-66; bd. visitors Emory U., 1970-76; former mem. adv. council Ga. State U.; former trustee Ga. State U. Found.; trustee Duke U., 1974-87; trustee Hampden-Sydney Coll., 1976-91, bd. dirs. Horatio Alger Assn. Disting. Americans, bd. dirs. Lyndon B. Johnson Found; bd. visitors Fuqua Sch. Bus., Duke U.; past dir. Atlanta C. of C.; donor $10 million to found Fuqua Sch. Bus., Duke U., 1980, $5.5 million to build the Dorothy Chapman Fuqua Conservatory, Atlanta Bot. Gardens, 1989, $10 million to establish Fuqua Sch., Va., 1993, $3 million to establish the Fuqua Heart Ctr. of Atlanta at Piedmont Hosp., 1995, $1.5 million to Atlanta Com. for Spl. Games, 1996, $4 million to Jr. Achievment Internat., 2001, $1 million to PACE Acad., Atlanta, 2002, $1 million to The Wesley Woods Found., 2002, $1 million to The Nuc. Threat Initiative, 2002; established Fuqua Internat. Christian Comm., Crystal Cathedral, 1991, Fuqua Orchid Ctr. for Conservation and Edn., 1997, Fuqua Ctr. Late-Life Depression at Wesley Woods Geriatric Ctr., 1997, J.B. Fuqua chair pub. speaking, Pace Acad., 1999. Recipient Horatio Alger award, 1984, award U. Pa. Wharton Grad. Sch. Bus., 1985, Disting. Entrepreneurship award, 1985, Free Enterprise medal Entrepreneur of Yr. Shenandoah Coll., 1991, Pinnacle award Sales and Mktg. Execs. Internat. Acad. Achievement, 1993, Fellow of the Coll. award Capitol Coll., 1994, Shining Light award Atlanta Gas Light & WSB, 2000, Disting. Georgian award Augusta State U., 2002, Philanthropist of the Yr. award Bus. to Bus. Mag., 2003; named Boss of Yr. Augusta Jaycees, 1960, Broadcaster-Citizen of Yr. Ga. Assn. Broadcasters, 1963, Broadcast Pioneer of Yr., 1979, Outstanding Bus. Leader Northwood Inst., 1986, Mktg. Statesman Sales and Mktg. Execs. Internat., 1986, Bus. Statesman Harvard Bus. Sch. Club Met. Atlanta, 1987, Georgian of Yr., 1989, Philanthropist of Yr. Ga. chpt. Nat. Soc.

Fund Raising Execs., 1989, Philanthropist of Yr. Nat. Assn. Fund Raising Execs., 1993, Entrepreneur of Yr. Stanford Bus. Sch. Alumni Assn., 1992; The Fuqua Heart Ctr. of Atlanta at Piedmont Hosp. named in his honor; inducted into J. Mack Robinson Coll. of Bus. Hall of Fame, Ga. State U., 2001, Atlanta Bus. Hall of Fame, Jr. Achievement Ga., 2002, Bus. Hall of Fame, Jr. Achievement Nat., 2002. Mem.: Chief Exec. Orgn. Home: 3574 Tuxedo Rd NW Atlanta GA 30305-1049 Office: The Fuqua Cos 1201 W Peachtree St NW Ste 5000 Atlanta GA 30309-3467

FUQUA, JUDY See FOUQUET, ANNE

FURASH, EDWARD ELLIOTT, banker, investment company executive, writer, lecturer, theater producer; b. Boston, Oct. 31, 1934; s. Moses Harry Furash and Sara (Jacobs) Dorfman; m. Elizabeth Louise Wilson, Jan. 2, 1959; children: Jennifer Lee, Jonathan Wilson, James Shortlidge. AB magna cum laude, Harvard Coll., 1956; MBA, U. Pa., 1958; postgrad., Harvard Bus. Sch., Boston, 1959-67. Rsch. asst. Harvard Grad. Sch. Bus., Boston, 1958-59; asst. editor Harvard Bus. Review, Boston, 1959-62; instr. bus. adminstrn. Harvard Grad. Sch. Bus., Boston, 1961-62; sec. com. on. space Am. Acad. Arts & Scis., Boston, 1962-64; sr. staff assoc., bus. mgr. Arthur D. Little, Inc., Cambridge, Mass., 1964-67; v.p. mktg. Nat. Shawmut Bank Boston, 1967-72, sr. v.p. mktg., 1972-74; sr. v.p. corp. planning Shawmut Corp. Boston, 1972-78; mng. dir. Golembe Assocs., Washington, 1978-80; chmn. Furash & Co., Washington, 1980-98; vice chmn. dir. Headway Corp. Resources, Inc., N.Y.C., 1995-98; CEO Furash Holdings, Washington, 1994-2000; chmn. Monument Fin. Group, Alexandria, Va., 1999—, Effinity Fin. Corp., Alexandria, 1999—, Treasury Bank, 2000—03. Bd. dirs. Inova Alexandria Hosp. Found., Metrostage, Pa. Bus. Bank, City First Bank, Washington, Online Resources; interviewed on TV ABC, CBS, CNBC, PBS; lectr. Williams Sch. of Banking, 1974—78, Am. Inst. Banking, 1968—98, Stonier Sch. Banking, 1994, 95. Gen. editor: Technology Space & Soc.; contbr. (newspapers, mags.) including Wall St. Jour., Bus. Week, Bankers Mag., Am. Banker, RMA Jour. Credit and Risk Mgmt., and many others; contbr. to profl. jours. Chmn. appropriations com. Town of Lexington, Mass., 1967-78; participant Lexington Town Meetings, 1969-78; trustee The Carroll Sch., Lincoln, Mass., 1970-; Shell Oil Found. fellow U. Pa., 1957-58. Mem. Am. Assn. Bank Dirs. (bd. dirs. 1998—), Cosmos Club, City Club Washington, Harvard Club, Nat. Press Club, Harvard Club of Boston, Belle Haven Country Club, The Penn Club, Beta Gamma Sigma. Republican. Office: Effinity Fin Corp 1199 N Fairfax St Ste 500 Alexandria VA 22314-1437 E-mail: ed_furash@treasurybank.com., efurash@aol.com.

FURBUSH, DAVID MALCOLM, lawyer; b. Palo Alto, Calif., Mar. 25, 1954; s. Malcolm Harvey and Margaret (McKittrick) F. BA, Harvard U., 1975, JD, 1978. Bar: Calif. 1978, U.S. Dist. Ct. (no. dist.) Calif. 1978, U.S. Ct. Appeals (9th cir.) 1987, U.S. Supreme Ct. 1990. Assoc. Chickering & Gregory, San Francisco, 1978-81, Brobeck, Phleger & Harrison, San Francisco, 1981-85, ptnr. Palo Alto, Calif., 1985—. Office: Brobeck Phleger & Harrison 2000 University Ave East Palo Alto CA 94303

FURBUSH, MARY CHAPMAN, clubwoman; b. Danville, Va., Feb. 16, 1913; d. Fred L. and Martha L. (Hubbard) C.; m. Spencer Sanderson Furbush, Aug. 24, 1940. Grad. Chatham Hall, 1929; student Goucher Coll., 1929-32. N.H. state chmn. Flag of the U.S.A. com. DAR, 1959-62, state rec. sec. N.H., 1962-65, chpt. regent, 1960-62, state chmn. sch. com., 1974-77, nat. vice chmn. motion picture com., 1968-71, Constn. Week com., 1977-80, vice chmn. 1986-87; gov. N.H., Gen. Soc. Mayflower Descs., 1965-67, asst. gen., 1969-78, dep. gov. gen., 1978— ; v.p. N.H. soc. Nat. Soc. Daus. Colonial Wars, 1968-71, pres. N.H. soc., 1971-74, nat. chaplain, 1974-77, nat. 1st. v.p., 1977-80; mem. Orders of Distinction com. Nat. Soc. Daus. of Barons of Runnymede, surety, 1974-79, 87—. Mem. Sch. Bd. Somersworth (N.H.), 1946-49; trustee Trust Funds City of Somersworth, 1954-66, Forest Glade Cemetery, 1946-65. Recipient Valuable Service award Pres. U.S., 1948. Mem. Order of Americans of Armorial Ancestry, Nat. Hist. Soc., N.H. Hist. Soc., Somersworth Hist. Soc., Smithsonian Assos., N.H. Huguenot Soc. (state pres. 1984—), N.H. Soc. DAR (state program chmn. com. 1985-86), Mass. Huguenot Soc., Strawbery, Banke, Nat. Soc. Daus. Am. Colonists, Huguenot Soc. N.H. (v.p.), Piscataqua Pioneers (v.p. 1970-75), Nat. Soc. Dames of Ct. of Honor (N.H. v.p. 1975-79, 82—), Jamestowne Soc., Nat. Soc. Colonial Dames XVII Century, Nat. Soc. Daus. Colonial Wars (nat. chaplain 1974-77, 1st v.p. 1977-80, nat. chmn. awards com. 1983—). Democrat. Episcopalian. Deceased.

FURBUSH, STEVEN DEAN, financial executive; b. Seattle, Nov. 18, 1958; s. Erving Ainsworth and Dorothy (Ranns) F.; m. Helen Rae Holcomb, Sept. 13, 1980; children: Julie Rae, Jamie Lynne, Lauren Dean, Ross Alan. BA, U. Wash., 1981; MA, U. Md., 1988, PhD, 1990. Jr. economist exec. office of pres. Council Econ. Advisers, Washington, 1985-87; rsch. economist SEC, Washington, 1987-89; econ. advisor to the chmn. Commodity Futures Trading Comm., Washington, 1989-90; sr. economist Economists Inc., 1990-95; sr. v.p., chief economist Nat. Assn. Securities Dealers, 1995-2000; dir. strategic planning Nat. Assn. Securities Dealers/NASDAQ Stock Markets, 1997-2000; exec. v.p. NASDAQ Transaction Svcs., 2000—. Adj. prof. econs. Va. Polytech. Inst. and State U., 1990-92; rsch. assoc. Ctr. Naval Analyses, Alexandria, Va., 1982-85 Chmn. Coll. Summit, helping economically disadvantaged to enter college, 1995—. Mem. Am. Econ. Assn. Christian Scientist. Avocations: tennis, soccer. Office: NASDAQ Stock Market Inc 1 Liberty Plaza 49th Flr New York NY 10006 Home: 1034 Old White Plains Rd Mamaroneck NY 10543-1118

FURCHES, W. RALPH, JR., writer; s. W R and Ethel Alexander Furches; m. Alicia Furches, Dec. 7, 1950; children: Paulo, Melanie, Amanda, Monica, Alicia-Michelle, Raul-Antonio. AA, Chipola Jr. Coll., Mariannna, Fla., 1970. Prof. Pontifical Cath. U. of Peru, Lima, Peru, 1971—73, Peruian-Am.Cultural Inst., Lima, Peru, 1971—74; mgr. Asheville, NC, 1975—. Author: (book of short stories) Reminiscent Pendezvous, (3 novellas) Gemstones, (short stories, novellas) Journeys to the far places, From the Quill. Home: 15 Lance Rd Candler NC 28715 Personal E-mail: avespirit@juno.com.

FURCHGOTT, ROBERT FRANCIS, pharmacologist, educator; b. Charleston, S.C., June 4, 1916; married, 1941; 3 children. BS, U. N.C., 1937; PhD in Biochemistry, Northwestern U., 1940; DM (hon.), Autonomous U., Madrid, 1984, U. Lund, 1984; DSc (hon.), U. N.C., 1989, U. Ghent, 1995; degree (hon.), Mt. Sinai Med. Sch., 1995, Ohio State U., 1996, Med. U. S.C., 1997, Med. Coll. Ohio, 1997, Northwestern U., 1998, U. Coll., London, 1998, Washington U., 2001, Charles U., Prague, 2003. Rsch. fellow medicine Med. Coll. Cornell U., 1940—43, rsch. assoc., 1943—47, instr. physiology, 1943—48, asst. prof. med. biochemistry, 1947—49; from asst. prof. to assoc. prof. pharmacology Med. Sch. Wash. U., 1949—56; chmn. dept. pharmacology SUNY Health Sci. Ctr., Bklyn., 1956—83, Univ. Disting. prof., 1988—90, emeritus prof. pharmacology, 1990—. Mem. pharmacol. tng. com. USPHS, 1961—64, mem. pharmacotoxicol. rev. com., 1965—68; Commonwealth fellow, 1962—63; vis. prof. U. Geneva, 1962—63, U. Calif., San Diego, 1971—72, Med. U. S.C., 1980, UCLA, 1980; adj. prof. pharmacology, Sch. Medicine U. Miami, 1989—2001; disting. vis. prof. Med. Univ. South Carolina, 2001—. Recipient rsch. achievement award, Am. Heart Assn., 1990, Bristol-Myers Squibb award for achievement in cardiovasc. rsch., 1991, Gairdner Fund Internat. award, 1991, medal, N.Y. Acad. Medicine, 1992, Roussel Uclaf prize for rsch. in cell communication and signalling, 1994, Wellcome Gold medal, Brit. Pharmacology Soc., 1995, ASPET award for exptl. therapeutics, 1996, Gregory Pincus award for rsch., 1996, Lasker award for med. rsch., 1996, Lucian award, 1997, Nobel prize for Medicine, 1998. Mem.: NAS, AAAS, Harvey Soc., Am. Soc. Pharmacology and Exptl. Therapeutics (pres. 1971—72, Goodman and Gilman award 1984), Am. Soc. Biochemistry, Am. Chem. Soc., Am. Acad. Arts and Scis., Polish Physiol. Soc. (hon.), Sigma Xi. Office: SUNY Health Sci Ctr Dept of Pharmacology 450 Clarkson Ave # 29 Brooklyn NY 11203-2056

FURCON, JOHN EDWARD, management and organizational consultant; b. Mar. 17, 1942; s. John F. and Lottie (Janik) F.; children: Juliana, Annalisa, Diana; m. Orisha Agatha Kulick, Oct. 28, 1995. BA, DePaul U., 1963, MA, 1965; MBA, U. Chgo., 1970. With Human Resources Ctr. Chgo. U., 1963-81, project dir., 1966-70, rsch. psychologist, divsn. dir., 1970-81; with orgn. change practice Harbridge House, Inc., Northbrook, Ill., 1981—93, v.p., 1987-93; ptnr. human resource adv. group Coopers & Lybrand, 1993-98; ptnr. Global Human Resource Solutions PricewaterhouseCoopers LLP, 1998—2001, prin., 2001—; regional practice leader, human resource mgmt. cons. Mellon Human Resources and Investor Solutions (formerly Buck Cons.), Chgo., 2002—. Mem. faculty Traffic Inst., Northwestern U., 1969-84, DePaul U. Sch. for New Learning, 1974-82; cons. bus., ednl. and govt. orgns.; bd. dirs. Bur. of Testing Svcs., 1975-77, Harbridge House, Inc., 1991-97; lectr. in field. Contbr. articles on pers. mgmt. and human resources planning to profl. jours. Active parents bd. Marquette U., 1988-89. Served to lt. AUS, 1963-65. Mem. Soc. Indsl. and Orgnl. Psychology, Indsl. Psychology Assn. Chgo. (chmn. 1973-75), Internat. Assn. Chiefs of Police, Chgo. Coun. Fgn. Rels., World Future Soc., Human Resource Mgmt. Assn. Chgo. Office: Mellon Human Resources and Investor Solutions One N Dearborn St Chicago IL 60602 E-mail: furcon.j@buckconsultants.com.

FURDA, IVAN, chemist, consultant; b. Trnava, Czechoslovakia, Apr. 29, 1938; came to U.S., 1971; s. Juraj and Petronila (Didolicova) F.; m. Jana Stuchlikova, June 20, 1964; children: Peter Mark, Thomas Ronald. MS in Analytical Chemistry, Tech. U. Chem. Faculty, Bratislava, Czechoslovakia, 1960; PhD in Organic Chemistry, Czechoslovak Acad. Scis., Bratislava, Czechoslovakia, 1967. Post doctorate fellow Nat. Rsch. Coun. Canada, Ottawa, Ont., 1968-69, Trent U., Peterborough, Ont., Canada, 1969-70; project specialist Gen. Foods Corp., Tarrytown, N.Y., 1971-78; prin. scientist Gen. Mills Inc., Mpls., 1978-94; pres. Furda & Assocs. Inc. Internat. Consulting, Wayzata, Minn., 1994—. Adv. bd. CRC Press Inc. Handbook of Dietary Fiber in Human Nutrition, Boca Raton, Fla., 1984-1986. Author, editor: Unconventional Sources of Dietary Fiber, 1983, New Developments in Dietary Fiber, 1990; patentee in field; inventor of fat-binding dietary fiber. Mem. Am. Chem. Soc., Am. Chitoscience Soc., Czechoslovak Soc. Arts and Scis. Avocations: swimming, tennis, music, economics. Home and Office: 16664 Meadowbrook Ln Wayzata MN 55391-2960 E-mail: furdaconsult@msn.com.

FUREY, JAMES MICHAEL, lawyer; b. East Rockaway, N.Y., May 2, 1927; s. Francis Leo and Loretta (Kenney) F.; m. Dolores Solosky, Aug. 4, 1956; children: James, Dennis, Kathleen Furey Tran, Sheila Furey O'Malley. BA, St. John's U., 1951, JD, 1957. Bar: N.Y. 1957, U.S. Dist. Ct. (so. and ea. dists.) N.Y. 1958, U.S. Ct. Appeals (2d cir.) 1975. Atty. Lawless & Lynch, N.Y.C., 1956-61; ptnr. Schaffner & Furey, N.Y.C., 1961-64, Clune & Furey, Mineola, N.Y., 1964-68, Furey & Mooney, Hempstead, N.Y., 1968-80; atty. Furey & Furey, Hempstead, N.Y., 1980—. Lectr. numerous med. orgns., 1975-84; pres. Realty Corp. North Hills, 1999-2000. Candidate Mayor, Village of Mineola, 1974. With USN, 1945-46. Mem. Am. Bd. Profl. Liability (chmn. 1990—), Nassau Suffolk Trial Lawyers (pres. 1980-81), Nassau County Bar Assn. (bd. dirs. 1986-89), N.Y. State Bar Trial Lawyers (chmn. malpractice sect. 1990—, spokesman legis. com. 1973, spokesman legis. hearing 1986), North Hills Country Club (bd. govs. 1992), Bay View Oaks Assn. (pres. 1972). Home: 220 Cherry Valley Ave Garden City NY 11530-1528 Office: Furey & Furey 600 Front St Hempstead NY 11550-4494

FUREY, JOHN J. lawyer; b. Coaldale, Pa., Nov. 3, 1949; s. James J. and Georgene C. (Young) F.; m. Jill A. Luscombe, Nov. 23, 1975; children: Matthew J., Andrew S. BS, Villanova U., 1971, JD, 1975, LLM, 1984. Bar: Pa. 1975, Fla. 1994; CPA, Pa. VISTA vol. Vols. in Service to Am., Rose Hill, N.C., 1971-72; staff atty. Legal Services N.E. Pa., Wilkes-Barre, 1975-77; atty. Legal Services Corp., Phila., 1977-80, dep. regional dir., 1980-81; assoc. corp. counsel Mrs. Paul's Kitchen's, Phila., 1981-82; asst. counsel, asst. sec. Campbell Soup Co., Camden, N.J., 1982-85, assoc. counsel, asst. sec., 1985-89, assoc. counsel, dep. corp. sec., 1989-90; corp. counsel, dep. corp. sec., 1990-92; corp. sec., corp. counsel Campbell Soup Co., Camden, N.J., 1992-97, corp. sec., 1997—. Office: Campbell Soup Co Campbell Pl Camden NJ 08103*

FURGASON, ROBERT ROY, university president, engineering educator; b. Spokane, Wash., Aug. 2, 1935; s. Roy Elliott and Margaret (O'Halloran) F.; m. Gloria L. Althouse, June 14, 1964; children: Steven Scott, Brian Alan. BSChemE, U. Idaho, 1956, MSCE, 1958; PhD in Chem. Engring., Northwestern U., 1961; postdoctoral, U. Wis., 1961. Registered profl. engr., Idaho. Design engr. Phillips Petroleum Co., Bartlesville, Okla., 1956; rsch. engr. Martin Marietta Co., Denver, 1958; instr. chem. engring. U. Idaho, Moscow, 1957-59, asst. prof., 1961-63, assoc. prof., 1963-67, acting head dept. chem. engring., 1964-65, chmn. dept. chem. engring., 1965-74, prof., 1967-84, dean Coll. Engring., 1974-78, v.p. acad. affairs and rsch., 1978-84; prof., vice chancellor acad. affairs U. Nebr., Lincoln, 1984-90; prof., pres. Tex A&M U.-Corpus Christi, 1990—. NSF advisor scientists and engrs. in econ. devel. program Escuela Politecnica Nacional, Quito, Ecuador, 1973-74, 76; proposal reviewer NSF, 1965-84; program reviewer Clearwater Econ. Devel. Assn., 1978-84; mem. long-range planning commn. Idaho State Bd. Edn., 1978-80, Gov.'s Com. Faculty Salary Equity, 1980, State of Idaho Energy Policy Bd., 1980-84, adv. com. Northwest Power Policy Coun., 1982-84, engring. accreditation commn. Accreditation Bd. Engring. and Tech., 1981-96, exec. bd., 1984-89, vice chmn., 1985-87, chmn., 1988-89, bd. dirs., 1989-95, fellow, 1990, pres., 1993-94; bd. dirs. Hanover Cos.; adv. bd. dirs. Am. Bank. Bd. of trustees, Driscoll Hospital Found., 2002— . Contbr. articles to profl. jours. Chmn. Idaho-Ecuador Ptnrs. of Ams., 1975-77; commr. Moscow Parks and Recreation Commn., 1977-81; mem. charter revision commn. City of Lincoln, 1989-90; chair Nebr. Energy Mgmt. Plan Adv. Com., 1989-90; mem. chem. engring. vis. com. Colo. Sch. Mines, 1989-99; exec. adv. bd. Coastal Bend United Way, 1991-93; bd. dirs. S.W. Moscow Cmty. Assn., 1977-84, Am. Festival Ballet, 1978-80, Lincoln Cancer Ctr., 1988-90, Tex. Econ. Edn. Commn., 1991-2001, Ada Wilson Children's Rehab. Ctr., 1993-96, Tex. State Aquarium, 1994—; adv. bd. Sta. KEDT-TV, Sta. KEDT-FM. Recipient Pub. Svc. award Idaho State Libr. Assn., 1978, Phillip Carrol Nat. award Soc. Advanced Mgmt., 1996, Grinter award Accreditation Bd. Engring. and Tech., 1996, Baldwin award Corpus Christi C. of C., 2000; named Citizen of Yr. Kappa Sigma, 1980, Newsmaker of the Yr., Corpus Christi Caller-Times, 1997, Newsmaker of the Decade, 2000; CASE Chief Exec. Leadership award, 2001; Walter P. Murphy fellow. Fellow AIChE (chmn. nat. tech. sessions 1967, sec. dept. heads forum 1971-72, chmn. 1981, nat. vis. lectr. 1977-79, edn. and accreditation com. 1981-92, chair 1989-91, accreditation visitation group 1977—); mem. Am. Soc. Engring. Edn. (Pacific Northwest coord. effective tchg. 1962-64, bd. dirs. chem. engring. divsn. 1974-77, Centennial medal 1993), Idaho Soc. Profl. Engrs. (No. Idaho chpt. pres. 1970, state pres. 1980, Idaho's Young Engr. of Yr. 1967), Northwest Coll. and Univ. Assn. Scis. (exec. com. bd. dirs. 1976-80, 81-84, chmn. bd. dirs. 1979-80), Corpus Christi C. of C. (bd. dirs. 1990-94), Crucible Club, Wranglers Club, Lions (program chmn., corr. sec., bd. dirs.), Rotary, Sigma Xi, Phi Kappa Phi, Phi Eta Sigma, Sigma Tau. Avocations: piloting, skiing, camping, woodworking. Home: 1334 Sandpiper Dr Corpus Christi TX 78412-3818 Office: Tex A&M U Office of Pres 6300 Ocean Dr Corpus Christi TX 78412-5503 E-mail: furgason@tamucc.edu.

FURGESON, WILLIAM ROYAL, federal judge; b. Lubbock, Tex., Dec. 9, 1941; s. W. Royal and Mary Alyene (Hardwick) F.; m. Marion McElroy, Aug. 15, 1964 (div.); m. Juli Ann Bernat, July 29, 1973; children— Kelly Lynn, Houston, Joshua, Seth, Jill BA in English, Tex. Tech Coll., 1964; JD with honors, U. Tex., 1967. Bar: Tex. 1969, U.S. Dist. Ct. (we. dist.) Tex. 1971, U.S. Ct. Appeals (5th cir.) 1974, U.S. Supreme Ct. 1976. Law clk. to presiding judge U.S. Dist. Ct. for No. Dist. Tex., 1969-70; ptnr. Kemp, Smith, Duncan & Hammond, El Paso, Tex., 1970-94; judge U.S. Dist. Ct. (we. dist.) Tex., Midland/Odessa, 1994—. Gen. campaign chmn. El Paso United Way, 1979, 1st v.p., 1980, pres., 1981; mem. Jewish Fedn., El Paso, 1980-86; trustee Baylor U. Coll. Dentistry, 1982-86; chmn. YWCA Capital Devel. Campaign, 1986-87. Served to capt. U.S. Army, 1967-69 Decorated Bronze Star; recipient Service award Social Workers of El Paso, 1982, Faculty award U. Tex. Law Sch., 1983, Dean Leon Green award Tex. Law Review, 2001, Mem. El Paso Bar Assn. (pres. 1982-83, Outstanding Young Lawyer award 1972), Am. Law Inst., U. Tex. Law Sch. Assn. (pres. 1978), U. Tex. Law Rev. Assn. (pres. 1982-83), El Paso Legal Assistance Soc. (bd. dirs. 1972-78), NCCJ (chmn. El Paso region 1980), ABA, Fed. Bar Assn. (pres. West Tex. chpt. 1987), Am. Law Inst., Tex. Bar Assn. (sec., treas., chair anti-trust and trade regulation sect. 1985-86), Am. Bar Found., Tex. Bar Found. Democrat. Jewish. Office: US Dist Ct 200 E Wall St Ste 301 Midland TX 79701-5248

FURGURSON, ERNEST BAKER, JR., (PAT FURGURSON), writer; b. Danville, Va., Aug. 29, 1929; s. Ernest Baker and Passie Durham (Ferguson) F.; m. Mary Louise Stallings (div.); children— Ernest Baker III, Elisabeth Glyn; m. Cassie Woodward Thompson, Apr. 21, 1973. Student, Averett Coll., 1948-50; AB, Columbia, 1952, MS, 1953. Reporter Danville Comml. Appeal, Sta. WDVA, 1948-51; with Roanoke (Va.) World-News, 1952, Richmond (Va.) News Leader, 1955-56; reporter, Washington corr. Balt. Sun, 1956-61, chief Moscow bur., 1961-64, White House corr., nat. polit. corr., Saigon corr., nat. affairs columnist, 1964-92, chief Washington bur., 1975-87, assoc. editor, 1987-92; syndicated by L.A. Times Syndicate, 1970-90. Author: Westmoreland: The Inevitable General, 1968, Hard Right: The Rise of Jesse Helms, 1986, Chancellorsville 1963: The Souls of the Brave, 1992, Ashes of Glory: Richmond at War, 1996, Not War But Murder: Cold Harbor 1864, 2000; contbg. editor Washingtonian mag., 1973-83, Mid-Atlantic Country mag., 1983-96. 1st lt. USMC, 1953-55. Mem. Gridiron Club, Cosmos Club. Home: 4812 Tilden St NW Washington DC 20016-2330

FURINO, ANTONIO, economist, educator; b. Rome; JD, U. Rome, 1955; MA, U. Houston, 1965, PhD, 1972. Asst. prof. to assoc. prof. econs. St. Edwards U., Austin, Tex., 1967-70; dir. regional analysis Alamo Area Council Govts., San Antonio, 1970-73; prof. econs. U. Tex., San Antonio, 1973-90, dir. Ctr. for Studies in Bus., Econs. and Human Resources, 1973-78, dir. human resource mgmt. and devel. program, 1978-82; sr. ptnr., dir. Devel. Through Applied Sci., San Antonio, 1972—; prof. econs. U. Tex. Health Sci. Ctr., San Antonio, 1985—, dir. Ctr. for Health Econs. and Policy, 1987—, dir. Regional Ctr. for Health Workforce Studies at Ctr. for Health Econs. and Policy, 2001—; sr. rsch. fellow U. Tex. IC 2 Inst., Austin, 1986—. Econ. cons. Home: 16114 Robinwood Ln San Antonio TX 78248-1744

FURLAND, JOSEPH, engineering educator; b. Berlin, Jan. 26, 1923; came to U.S., 1940; s. Otto Rosenthal and Henny (Meyer) Gurland; m. Doris Hurwitch, 1948; children: Lisa, Johanna. B. Engring., NYU, 1944, M.E., 1947; Sc.D., MIT, 1951. Research engr. Battelle Meml. Inst., Columbus, Ohio, 1947-48; rsch. engr., mgr. basic research Firth Sterling, Inc., Pitts., 1951-55; asst. prof. engring. Brown U., Providence, R.I., 1955-57, assoc. prof., 1957-64, prof., 1964-87, prof. emeritus, 1988—. Disting. vis. scientist Boston U. Mfg. Engring. Dept., 1990—. Co-editor: Science of Hard Materials, 1983; contbr. articles on materials sci. and engring. to profl. jours. Served with U.S. Army, 1944-46. Recipient Plansee medal Internat. Plansee Soc. Powder Metallurgy, 1989, Civil Libertarian of Yr. award R.I. Civil Liberties Union, 1990; NSF fellow, 1961, NATO fellow, 1970. Fellow Am. Soc. for Metals; mem. AIME, Internat. Metallographic Soc., Internat. Soc. Stereology. Jewish. Office: Brown U Divsn Engring PO Box D Providence RI 02912-0001

FURLAND, LOREN P. civil and environmental engineer; b. Marshalltown, Iowa, Nov. 22, 1945; s. Paul L. and Mildred M. (Williamson) F.; m. Nancy A. Newton, Feb. 17, 1979; children: Thomas L., Ashley E. BS in Civil Engring. Iowa State U., 1968; MS, U. Iowa, 1976. Registered profl. engr., Iowa, Ill., Ga., N.Mex., Tex., Ark., Fla. Design mgr. Stanley Cons., Inc., Muscatine, Iowa, 1968-77, Atlanta, 1977-83, project mgr. Albuquerque, 1983-85; sr. project mgr. Engring. Sci., Inc., Austin, Tex., 1985-87; tech. svcs. mgr. Ralph M. Parsons Co., Tampa, Fla., 1987-88; Fla. ops. mgr. Parsons Engring. Sci., 1988-90; projects and client svcs. mgr. Parsons Infrastructure & Tech., Tampa, 1990—; project mgr. Tampa Bay Regional Water Treatment Plant, 1998—2003. Cons. West Coast Regional Water Supply Authority/Tampa Bay Water, Clearwater, Fla., 1989—; cons. Pasco County Utilities, New Port Richey, Fla., 1992—. Fellow ASCE (dir. Tri City sect. 1971-72); mem. Water Environment Fedn. (chair West Coast chpt. 2002-03), Am. Waterworks Assn., Am. Acad. Environ. Engrs. (diplomate). Presbyterian. Home: 736 S Lakeshore Blvd Lake Wales FL 33853-4220 Office: Parsons Infrastructure & Tech Ste 345 3450 Buschwood Park Dr Tampa FL 33618-4572 E-mail: loren.furland@parsons.com.

FURLANE, MARK ELLIOTT, lawyer; b. Joliet, Ill., Aug. 2, 1949; s. Francis Emilio and Tosca (Cipriani) F.; m. Susan M. Keegan, July 4, 1987; children: Gahan Patricia, Michael Keegan. BA magna cum laude, Ctrl. Coll., 1971; JD with honors, George Washington U., 1974; MBA in Finance Specialization, U. Chgo., 1982. Bar: Ill. 1974, U.S. Dist. Ct. (no. dist.) Ill. 1979, U.S. Ct. Appeals (5th, 6th, 7th, 9th and 11th cirs.), U.S. Ct. Mil. Appeals, U.S. Supreme Ct. 2001. Ptnr. Gardner Carton & Douglas, Chgo., 1979—. Bd. mem. Ctr. for Disability and Elder Law, 2000—, Pub. Interest Law Initiative, 2001—, Abraham Lincoln Local Sch. Coun.; bd. dirs. Friends of Lincoln; local sch. counsel Lincoln Elem. Sch. Capt. USMCR. Mem. FBA (labor and employment com. 1996—, trustee 1999—), Chgo. Bar Assn. (chmn. labor and employment com. 1994-95), GSB Chgo. Club. Democrat. Roman Catholic. Office: Gardner Carton & Douglas 191 N Wacker Dr Chicago IL 60606-1698 E-mail: mfurlane@GCD.com.

FURLAUD, RICHARD MORTIMER, pharmaceutical company executive; b. N.Y.C., Apr. 15, 1923; s. Maxime Hubert and Eleanor (Mortimer) F.; children: Richard Mortimer, Eleanor Jay, Elizabeth Tamsin; m. Isabel Phelps Furlaud. Student, Institut Sillig, Villars, Switzerland; AB, Princeton U., 1944; LLB, Harvard U., 1947. Bar: N.Y. 1949. Assoc. Root, Ballantine, Harlan, Bushby & Palmer, 1947-51; with legal dept. Olin Mathieson Chem. Corp., 1955-56, asst. to exec. v.p. for finance, 1956-57, asst. pres., 1957-59, v.p., 1959-64, gen. counsel, 1957-60, gen. mgr., v.p. internat. div., 1960-64, exec. v.p., 1964-66, now dir., 1964-94; pres., dir. E. R. Squibb & Sons, Inc., 1966-68; pres., chief exec., dir. Squibb Beech-Nut, Inc. (renamed Squibb Corp. 1971), Princeton, N.J., 1968-74; chmn., chief exec., dir. Squibb Corp. (merged with Bristol-Myers Co.), N.Y.C., 1974-89; pres., bd. dirs. Bristol-Myers Co. (renamed Bristol-Myers Squibb Co.), N.Y.C., 1989-91. Mem. profl. staff Ho. of Reps. Com. Ways and Means, 1954; chmn. Rockefeller U. Coun.; trustee John M. Olin Found. 1st lt. JAGC U.S. Army, 1951-53. Mem. Assn. Bar City of N.Y., Coun. on Fgn. Rels., Links Club, River Club. Home: PO Box 478 East Hampton NY 11937-0478 Office: Bristol-Myers Squibb Co 150 E 52nd St Fl 12 New York NY 10022-6017

FURLONG, EDWARD V., JR., paper company executive; b. Phila., Feb. 15, 1937; s. Edward V. and Joy (Sadler) Furlong; m. Rosemary Cerne, Apr. 1968; children: Tracy L., Edward V. III. BA, Princeton U., 1959; MBA, Harvard U., 1963. Successively asst. to pres., treas., exec. v.p. WWF Paper Corp., Bala Cynwyd, Pa., 1963—72, pres., 1972—. Served to lt. j.g. USN, 1959—61. Mem.: Inst. Dirs. London, Nat. Paper Trade Assn. (bd. dirs.), The Ivy Club, Union League Club, Merion Cricket Club. Republican. Methodist. Avocations: sailing, tennis, squash. Home: 318 Julip Run Wayne PA 19087-4731 Office: WWF Paper Corp 2 Bala Plz Bala Cynwyd PA 19004-1501

FURLONG, GEORGE MORGAN, JR., museum foundation consultant, retired naval officer; b. Muskogee, Okla., Nov. 23, 1931; s. George M. and Anna (Moore) F.; m. Ryland Hagood Blakey, June 5, 1956; children: Morgan, William. BS in Naval Sci., U.S. Naval Acad., 1956; BS in Aero. Engring., U.S. Naval Postgrad. Sch., 1963. Commd. ensign U.S. Navy, 1956, advanced through grades to rear adm. (upper half), 1981; F-14 program mgr. Comdr. Naval Air Forces, U.S. Pacific Fleet, 1973-74; wing comdr. Attack Carrier Air Wing 14, USS Enterprise, 1974-75; comdg. officer USS Ponchatoula, Pearl Harbor, Hawaii, 1975-76, USS Independence, Norfolk, Va., 1977-78; chief of staff U.S. Sixth Fleet, Gaeta, Italy, 1978-80; dir. Air Warfare Systems Analysis Staff, Office Chief of Naval Ops., Washington, 1980-81; comdr. Fighter Airborne Early Warning Wing. U.S. Pacific Fleet, Naval Air Sta., Miramar, San Diego, 1981-83; dep. chief Naval Edn. and Tng., Pensacola, Fla., 1983-85; ret., 1986; exec. v.p. Naval Aviation Mus. Found., Pensacola, 1986-96; dir. devel. Bapt. Health Care Found., Pensacola, 1997—2001; cons. Naval Aviation Mus. Found., 2001—. Deocorated Legion of Merit with gold star; recipient John Paul Jones award Nat. Navy League Assn., 1971 Office: Naval Aviation Mus Found Inc 1750 Radford Blvd Ste B Pensacola FL 32508- E-mail: skipone@aol.com.

FURLONG, PATRICK DAVID, educator, researcher; b. Cleve., Sept. 27, 1948; s. Harold Joseph and Jean Ann (Blair) F. BS magna cum laude, Lake Erie Coll., Painesville, Ohio, 1975. Staff psychometrist VA Med. Ctr., North Chicago, Ill., 1975-78; psychometrist Northwestern U. Med. Sch., Chgo., 1978-80, 1987-93; counselor/coord. vets. affairs Columbia Coll., Chgo., 1980-81; assoc. coord. internat. edn. Roosevelt U., Chgo., 1981-84; dir. accreditation Nat. Commn. on Correctional Health Care, Chgo., 1984-85; sch. counselor/coord. student support svcs. United Edn. and Software, Chgo., 1985-87; asst. adminstr. Assessment Sys., Inc., Chgo., 1993-94; lead ctr. adminstr. Sylvan Learning Sys., Inc., Chgo., 1994-96; benefit analyst Dept. Health and Human Svcs., Chgo., 1996—2001, Dept. Vets. Affairs, 2001—. With USN, 1967—71, Vietnam. Decorated Navy Achievement medal with combat V. Mem.: Psi Chi. Home: 15 Dignon Rd Billerica MA 01821-2146

FURLONG, PATRICK J. historian, educator, university administrator; b. Lexington, Ky., Feb. 7, 1940; s. Dennis A. and Anna (Carollo) F.; m. Gertrude Alice Griffin, Aug. 21, 1965; children: Elizabeth, Joseph. AB, U. Ky., 1961; MA, Northwestern U., 1962, PhD, 1966. Prof. history Ind. U., South Bend, 1967—, dir. MLS program, 1995—2002, chmn. dept. history, 1997—. Author: Indiana: An Illustrated History, 1985, rev. edit., 2001; rsch. dir. TV documentary Studebaker: Less Than They Promised, 1983; contbr. articles to profl. jours. Bd. dirs. Southhold Preservation, Inc., South Bend, 1965-91, 93-98, Discovery Hall Assocs., Inc., South Bend, 1977-85. Recipient Lundquist award Ind. U. South Bend, 1988. Mem. Am. Hist. Assn., Orgn. Am. Historians, Ky. Col. Avocation: travel. Home: 1320 Sunnymede Ave South Bend IN 46615-1018 Office: Ind U South Bend PO Box 7111 South Bend IN 46634-7111 E-mail: pfurlong@iusb.edu.

FURLONG, RICHARD W. structural engineer, educator; b. Norwalk, Ohio, Mar. 30, 1929; s. Norman Burr and Dorothy May (Wilson) Furlong; m. Helen Corinne Prince, Sept. 7, 1951; children: John Norman, Sara Catherine(dec.). BS in Civil Engring., So. Meth. U., 1952; MS in Civil Engring., Washington U., 1957; PhD, U. Tex., 1963. Drafter Austin Bros. Steel, Dallas, 1949—52; engr. McDonnell Aircraft, St. Louis, 1952—53, F. Ray Martin, Inc., St. Louis, 1954—58; asst. prof. U. Tex., Austin, Tex., 1958—65, assoc. prof., 1965—71; pvt. practice Austin, Tex., 1967—; prof. U. Tex., 1971—99, prof. emeritus, 1999—. Vis. prof. Canterbury U., Christ Ch., New Zealand, 1973, U. Toronto, Canada, 1978—79. Editor: Tex. Civil Engr., 1979—85 (award, 1985); author: (computer software) Reinf Concrete Design Helper, 1992; contbr. articles to profl. jours. (Ray Reese award, 1992); author: (textbook) Basic Decisions for Design of Reinforced Concrete, 2002. Pres. vol. coun. Austin (Tex.) State Sch., 1981. Mem.: ASCE (hon.; dist. dir. 1989—92), Tex. ASCE (pres. 1997), Am. Concrete Inst. (bd. dirs. 1978—82). Presbyn. Avocations: golf, music, travel. Home and Office: 6305 Mountain Park Cove Austin TX 78731

FURLOW, MACK VERNON, JR., retired financial executive, treasurer; b. Summit, Miss., Aug. 20, 1931; s. Mack Vernon and Trudie Dena (Ratcliff) F.; m. Barbara Elaine Rolfs, Mar. 20, 1954 (div. Dec. 1985); children— David Wayne, Kevin Rolfs. BS, La. State U., 1953; grad., advanced mgmt. program Harvard, 1968. Financial and systems analyst Humble Oil & Refining Co., Baton Rouge, 1957-61; asst. controller Skyland Internat. Corp., Chattanooga, 1961-65; v.p., corp. controller Blount, Inc., Montgomery, Ala., 1965-71; pres. Pipeco Steel Co., Inc., Wilmington, Del., 1971-73; v.p. fin., treas. Huber, Hunt & Nichols, Inc., Indpls., 1973-96, dir., 1977-96. Asst. treas. 54th Advanced Mgmt. Program class Harvard Bus. Sch., 1968— Served to 1st lt. AUS, 1953-57. Mem. La. State U. Alumni Assn. (mem. adv. com. Montgomery chpt. 1967-71), Nat. Assn. Accts. (nat. bd. dirs. 1976-78), Fin. Execs. Inst. (nat. bd. dirs. 1994-97). Republican. Lutheran. Home: 9337 Spring Forest Dr Indianapolis IN 46260-1269 *The creation of a management climate or environment which causes people to want to excel and perform to their fullest capabilities is a far superior approach than is a management style which causes people to perform because they are constantly afraid of the consequences of failing to perform.*

FURLOW, WILLIAM LAWRENCE, manufacturing and financial consultant; b. Castroville, Tex., July 19, 1944; s. William Elmer and Mary Ellen (Griffin) F.; m. Patricia Mary Nevins, July 20, 1974; 1 child, Christopher Randolf. Student, U. Ky., 1962-64, Santa Monica City Coll., Calif., 1966, La. Poly., 1972. Shipping clk. Coastal Dynamics Corp., Venice, Calif., 1964; sr. PC clk. Vol-Shan Mfg. Co., Culver City, Calif., 1965-68; materials coord. Hughes Aircraft, Culver City, 1969-70; PC clk. Everest & Jennings Inc., L.A., 1970-72; supr. Audio Magnetics Corp., Compton, Calif., 1973-74, Am. Safety Corp., Pacoima, Calif., 1975-76; agent Combined Ins. Co. Am., Virginia Beach, Va., 1977; buyer Perma-Bilt Industries, Torrance, Calif., 1978-80; gen. mgr. Cweco, Gardena, Calif., 1980-83, Saferail Inc., Gardena, 1980-83; PC mgr. DB Products Inc., Pasadena, Calif., 1984-92; CFO Bulltek Ltd., Running Sprints, Calif., 1996—; also bd. dirs. Cons. in field, Ocean Springs, Miss., 2000—; affiliate Maple Leaf Meds, Kirkland, Wash., 2003—; owner householdsolutions.net, 2001—, 4her2shop.com/27194, 2001—; owner householdsolutions.net, 4her2ship.com Author poems. Enumerator U.S. Census Bur., Gulfport, Miss., 2000. Pfc USAR, 1963—69. Mem. Nat. Splty. Merchandisers Assn., eMcht. Club, Am. Legion, Internat. Soc. Photographers, Internat. Soc. Poets, NRA Golden Eagles, Historic Ocean Springs Assn., Lions. Republican. Methodist. Avocations: coin collecting, stamp collecting, writing, photography. Home: 1119 Halstead Bayou Dr Ocean Springs MS 39564 Office: 1119 Halstead Bayou Dr Ocean Springs MS 39564 E-mail: furlow_nevins@msn.com.

FURMAN, HOWARD, mediator, arbitrator, lawyer; b. Newark, Nov. 30, 1938; s. Emanuel and Lilyan (Feldman) F.; m. Elaine Sheitleman, June 12, 1960 (div. 1982); children: Deborah Toby, Naomi N'chama, David Seth; m. 2d Janice Wheeler, Jan. 14, 1984. BA in Econs., Rutgers U., 1966; JD cum laude, Birmingham Sch. Law, 1985. Bar: Ala. 1985, U.S. Dist. Ct. (no. dist.) Ala. 1986, U.S. Dist. Ct. (so. dist.) Ala. 1996. Designer/draftsman ITT, Nutley, N.J., 1957-61; pers. mgr. Computer Products Inc., Belmar, N.J., 1962-64, Arde Engring. Co., Newark, 1964-66; econs. instr. Rutgers U., New Brunswick, N.J., 1966-74; dir. indsl. rels. Harvard Ind. Frequency Engring. Labs. Divsn., Farmingdale, N.J., 1966-74; commr. Fed. Mediation and Conciliation Svc., Birmingham, 1974-96; pvt. practice Birmingham, 1985—. Instr. bus. law Jefferson State C.C., 1989-95; instr. human resources mgmt. Nova U., 1993; prof. personal property, adminstrv. law, sales and alternative dispute resolution Birmingham Sch. Law, 1993—. Pres. Ocean Twp. Police Res. (N.J.), 1968. Recipient ofcl. commendation Fed. Mediation and Conciliation Svc., 1979, 81-82, 88. Mem. ABA, Ala. Bar Assn., Birmingham Bar Assn., Soc. Profls. in Dispute Resolution, Fed. Soc. Labor Rels. Profls., Indsl. Rels. Rsch. Assn., Sigma Delta Kappa. Jewish. Home: 900 Kathryne Cir Birmingham AL 35235-1722 E-mail: hfesq@bellsouth.net.

FURMAN, MARK EVAN, human performance scientist; b. Bronx, Mar. 14, 1962; s. Edward and Charlotte F.; m. Beth Ann Schad, Aug. 9, 1987; children: Lauren Ashley, Jonathan Cyle. BA in Behavioral Scis./Psychology, Coll. of S.I., 1984. Cert. practitioner of neuro-linguistic programming. Dir. edn. and rsch. Assoc. Schs. Music, Inc., Cooper City, Fla., 1988-97; spkr., author, human performance cons., 1990—; founder, exec. dir. Furman Rsch. Assocs., Boca Raton, Fla., 1987—; dir. edn. and rsch. The Keys to Success, Inc., Coral Springs, Fla., 1992—2000, Ozone Park, NY, 1992—2000; human performance cons. Interactive Response Techs., 2001—. Lectr. in field of neurosci.; founder, exec. dir. Furman Rsch. Assocs.; designer comm. program Jewish Ednl. Found. of Am., theoretical tng. model Syntonics Ednls., Switzerland; cons. Keys to Success Music Sch., N.Y., Century 21, Fla.; founder Internat. Soc. for Edn. Neurosci.; developer Intelligent Learning Systems, Neuroprint, Human Performance Modeling & Engineering; numerous others application models. Author: Mind in Motion, The Human Performance Technology for the Next Millenum, 1996; author: Jour. for the Soc. of Neuro-Linguistic Programming, 1995-2002, The Neurophysics of Human Behavior: Explorations at the Interface of Brain, Mind, Behavior and Information, 1999; contbg. author: Energy Psychology in Psychotherapy, 2002; contbr. articles to profl. jours. Mem.: APA (affiliate, divsn. 48, divsn. peace psychology), AAAS, Soc. for Study of Peace, Conflict and Violence, Internat. Soc. for Cognitive Neurophysics (founder). Achievements include developing intelligent learning systems (ILS); currently pioneering coordinated research and development efforts in the field of education neuroscience, studying the neurophysics of human information processing and its application to the field of human education, psychotherapy and the management sciences, advanced standard theory: Pattern-Entropy dynamics of matter and energy interaction; formerly established the interdisciplinary branch of science known as cognitive neurophysics. Home: 9559 Trivolo Pl Boca Raton FL 33434-2057 Office: Furman Rsch 9559 Trivolo Pl Boca Raton FL 33434

FURMAN, ROBERT RALPH, real estate developer; b. Trenton, N.J., Aug. 21, 1915; s. William Amies and Lelia Ficht F.; m. Mary Eddy, Dec. 21, 1951; children: martha, Julia, David, Serena. BSE, Princeton U., 1937; D in Pub. Svc. (hon.), Carroll C.C., 1999. Prin., owner Furman Bldrs., Inc., Rockville, Md., 1946-83, Greentree Assocs., Inc., Rockville, Md., 1983—. Chmn. bldg. adv. bd. Prince George's C.C., 1988-98; exec. officer for construction The Pentagon Bldg. U.S. Army Engrs., 1942-43; spl. asst. Lt. Gen. Leslie R. Groves Manhattan Dist. U.S. Army Engrs., 1943-45. Lt. Col. U.S. Army, 1940-46. Mem. United Way (pres. 1970), Bethesda Chevy Chase Rotary (pres. 1960), Bethesda Chevy Chase C. of C. (pres. 1955), Edgemoor Tennis Club (pres. 1966). Republican. Episcopalian. Office: Greentree Assocs Inc 5818B Hubbard Dr Rockville MD 20852-4818

FURMAN, ROY LANCE, investment banker; b. N.Y.C., Apr. 19, 1939; s. Joseph M. and Frances L. (Kurlander) F.; m. Frieda Anne Bueler, Nov. 7, 1965; children: Jill Tracy, Stephanie Gail. AB, Bklyn. Coll., 1960; LL.B., Harvard U., 1963. Atty. Western Electric Co., N.Y.C., 1964-67; v.p. Continental Tel. Supply Co., N.Y.C., 1967-68; with Seiden & de Cuevas, Inc., N.Y.C., 1968-73, pres., 1972-73; co-founder, pres. Furman Selz LLC, N.Y.C., 1973-98, also bd. dirs., 1973-98; chmn., CEO Livent Inc., N.Y.C., 1998-99; vice chmn. Furman Selz LLC, N.Y.C., 1997-99, ING Barings, N.Y.C., 1999—2001, Jefferies and Co., N.Y.C., 2001—; chmn. Jefferies Capital Mgmt., N.Y.C., 2001—. Former nat. fin. chmn. Dem. Nat. Com.; past chmn. splty. firms adv. com. N.Y. Stock Exch.; bd. dirs. Westfield Am., Broadway TV Network. Chmn. emeritus Film Soc. of Lincoln Ctr.; v.p. N.Y.C. Opera; vice chmn. Lincoln Ctr. for Performing Arts; past nat. chmn. Harvard Law Sch. Fund; chmn. Bklyn. Coll. Found., 2001-; vice-chmn. dean's adv. bd. Harvard Law Sch. Mem.: East Hampton Golf Club, Palm Beach Country Club (Fla.), Harmonie Club (NYC). Office: Jefferies and Co 520 Madison Ave New York NY 10022

FURNAD, V. ROBERT (BOB FURNAD), television news executive; BA in Radio/TV, American U. Fl. dir., film editor, assoc. dir., prodr. Sta. WMAL-TV, Washington; with ABC News, 1964-68, 69-83; from polit. news dir. to exec. v.p. and sr. exec. prodr. CNN, 1983—, now pres. Headline News network, 1997—. Recipient George Foster Peabody award, Acad. for cable Excellence Golden-ACE, Emmy award, Overseas Press Club award, Alfred I. duPont award. Office: CNN Headline News One CNN Ctr PO Box 105366 Atlanta GA 30348-5366

FURNAS, DAVID WILLIAM, plastic surgeon, educator; b. Caldwell, Idaho, Apr. 1, 1931; s. John Doan and Esther Bradbury (Hare) F.; m. Mary Lou Heatherly, Feb. 11, 1956; children: Heather Jean, Brent David, Craig Jonathan. AB, U. Calif.-Berkeley, 1952, MS, 1957, MD, 1955. Diplomate Am. Bd. Plastic Surgery, Royal Coll. Surgeons. Intern U. Calif. Hosp., San Francisco, 1955-56, asst. resident in surgery, 1956-57; asst. resident in psychiatry, NIMH fellow Langley Porter Neuropsychiat. Inst. U. Calif., San Francisco, 1959-60; resident in gen. surgery Gorgas Hosp., Panama Canal Zone, 1960-61; asst. resident in plastic surgery N.Y. Hosp., Cornell Med. Center, N.Y.C., 1961-62; chief resident in plastic surgery Cornell U. Svc., VA Hosp., Bronx, N.Y., 1962-63; registrar Royal Infirmary and Affiliated Hosps., Glasgow, Scotland, 1963-64; assoc. in hand surgery U. Iowa, 1964-68, sr. resident, faculty assoc. in surgery, 1964-65, asst. prof. surgery, 1966-68, assoc. prof., 1968-69; assoc. prof. surgery, chief div. plastic surgery U. Calif., Irvine, 1969-74, prof., chief div. plastic surgery, 1974-80, clin. prof., chief div. plastic surgery, 1980-99, clin. prof. plastic surgery, 1999—2002, emeritus prof. plastic surgery, 2002—. Surgeon East Africa Flying Drs. Svc., African Med. and Rsch. Found., Nairobi, Kenya, 1972-73; plastic surgeon S.S. Hope, Nicaragua, 1966, Sri Lanka, 1968; mem. Balakbayan med. mission Mindanao and Sulu, The Philippines, 1980-82; overseas vis. prof. plastic surgery Ednl. Found., 1994; Godrej vis. prof. Assn. Plastic Surgeons of India, 2000; keynote spkr. Pan African Assn. Plastic Surgeons, 2000; dir. Am. Bd. Plastic Surgeons, 1979-85; trustee Royal Coll. Surgeons Found., 1995-2002. Contbr. chpts. to textbooks, articles to profl. jours.; author, editor 5 textbooks; mem. edit. bd. Jour. Hand Surgery, Annals of Plastic Surgery, Jour. Craniofacial Surgery; reviewer Plastic and Reconstructive Surgery. Expedition leader Flag 171 Skull Surgeons of the Kisii Tribe Explorer's Club, Kenya, expedition leader Flag 44 Skull Surgeons of the Marakwet Tribe, 1987; bd. govs. Bowers Mus. Cultural Art, 2000—02. Capt. M.C. USAF, 1957—59, col. M.C. USAR, 1989—92. Recipient Golden Apple award U. Calif.-Irvine Sch. Medicine, 1980, Kaiser-Permanente award U. Calif.-Irvine Sch. Medicine, 1981, Humanitarian Svc. award Black Med. Students, U. Calif. Irvine, 1987, Sr. Rsch. award (Basic Sci.) Plastic Surgery Ednl. Found., 1987, Cert. of Spl. Recognition, U.S. Congress, 1998; named Orange County Press Club Headliner of Yr., 1982, Physician of the Year, Orange County Med. Assn., 1998. Fellow ACS, Royal Coll. Surgeons Can., Royal Soc. Medicine, Explorers Club (chmn. So. Calif. chpt. 2001-02), Royal Geog. Soc.; mem. AMA (Disting. Svc. award 2002), Calif. Med. Assn., Orange County Med. Assn. (Physician of Yr. 1998), Am. Soc. Plastic Surgery (bd. dirs. 1970-73), Am. Soc. Reconstructive Microsurgery, Soc. Head and Neck Surgery, Am. Cleft Palate Assn., Am. Soc. Surgery of Hand, Soc. Univ. Surgeons, Am. Assn. Plastic Surgeons (trustee 1983-86, treas. 1988-91, v.p. 1993-94, pres.-elect 1994, pres. 1995, Godrej vis. prof. 2000), British Assn. Plastic Surgeons (hon.), Am. Soc. Craniofacial Surgery, Am. Soc. Aesthetic Plastic Surgery, Am. Soc. Maxillofacial Surgeons, Assn. Acad. Chairmen Plastic Surgery (bd. dirs. 1986-89), Assn. Surgeons East Africa, Assn. Plastic and Reconstructive Surgeons So. Africa (hon.), Pacific Coast Surg. Assn., Internat. Soc. Aesthetic Plastic Surgery, Internat. Soc. Reconstructive Microsurgery, Internat. Soc. Craniomaxillofacial Surgery, Pan African Assn. Neurol. Sci., African Med. and Rsch. Found. (bd. dirs. U.S.A. 1987-2002, team leader Reconstruct! mission for victims of Am. Embassy bombing, Nairobi, Kenya, 1999), Muthaiga Club, Ctr. Club, Club 33, Univ. Club, Phi Beta Kappa, Alpha Omega Alpha. E-mail: daktari1@cox.net. *A crisis, at the outset, usually augurs nothing but ill. In the long run, however, my crises have more often than not marked a new course for my life, which is more fulfilling, and more exciting than anything in the past. Yes, a bit of good luck is needed, but the special feature of a crisis is that you are suddenly cut off from past patterns, habits, and interdependencies. Along with the distress and pain is freedom! Freedom to build again, with a new foundation and modern structure, using wisdom you didn't have the last time you built.*

FURNAS, HOWARD EARL, business executive; b. Battle Creek, Mich., Jan. 29, 1919; s. Howard Earl and Dorothy Anna (Collings) F.; m. Gail Abbott, May 14, 1942; children: Howard Earl III, Paul Abbott, Christopher Collings. AB, Hillsdale (Mich.) Coll., 1940; postgrad., Harvard U., 1945-47. Joined Fgn. Svc. Dept. State, 1947; assigned to embassy, Paris, 1948—49; asst. to spl. asst. to sec. state for intelligence, 1949-52, 54-57; assigned to U.S. mission to NATO, Paris, 1952-54; mem. policy planning staff, also alternate Dept. State rep. to plannning bd. NSC, 1957-61; dep. spl. asst. to sec. state for atomic energy and outer space, 1961-62; dept. exec. sec. Dept. State, 1962-63; del. 2d Nat. Conf. Peaceful Uses Space, Seattle, 1962; dep. spl. asst. to sec. state for multilateral force negotiations, 1963-64; spl. asst. to sec. state, 1964-65; mem. VIII sr. seminar in fgn. policy, 1965-66; assigned Office Undersec. State Polit. Affairs, 1966-69; spl. asst. to dir. ACDA, 1969-71, spl. adviser to chmn. gen. adv. com. on arms control and disarmament, 1969-71; prof. internat. rels. Windham Coll., Putney, Vt., 1971-76, also trustee; pres. Unipro Tennis Svcs., Howard Furnas Assocs., Windsor, Vt., 1974—, Chuckle Hill, Ltd., 1975-76. Pres. The Vermont Group, Internat. Cons., 1989-90. Contbr. articles to profl. jours. and newspaper columns. Bd. dirs. Montgomery County (Md.) Scholarship Fund, 1954-60; trustee Woodstock (Vt.) Country Sch., 1973-75; vestryman St. James Ch., Woodstock, Vt.; justice of peace West Windsor, Vt., 1986-95, U.S. joint chief of staff, Washington, DC, 1945. Maj. USAAF, 1942-45, ETO. Recipient Alumni Achievement award Hillsdale Coll., 1957. Mem. Kenwood Golf and Country Club (Washington), Woodstock Country Club, Twin States Valley Club, The Round Table, Delta Tau Delta. Episcopalian. Home and Office: 1360 Sheddsville Rd Windsor VT 05089-9664 E-mail: bluestar@vermontel.com.

FURNESS, PETER JOHN, lawyer; b. Providence, Jan. 30, 1956; s. Robert I. and Elsie R. (Mooradian) F.; m. Alison M. Furness; children: Lindsey Elizabeth, Jonathan Peter. BA, U. R.I., 1979; JD, U. Pitts., 1982. Bar: Pa. 1982, U.S. Dist. Ct. (we. dist.) Pa. 1982, R.I. 1987, Mass. 1989, U.S. Dist. Ct. Mass. 1989. Ptnr. Nixon Peabody LLP, Boston/Providence, 1991—. Lectr. Nat. Bus. Inst., Inc., 1986—. Author: (seminar books) NBI Foreclosure in Rhode Island, 1986, NBI Basic Bankruptcy in Rhode Island, 1988, NBI Protection of Secured Interests in Bankruptcy, 1989. Mem. ABA, Am. Bankruptcy Inst., Fed. Bar Assn., Pa. Bar Assn., R.I. Bar Assn., Mass. Bar Assn., Comml. Law League, Phi Beta Kappa, Phi Kappa Phi. Avocations: photography, golf, vol. work with nonprofit orgns. Office: Nixon Peabody LLP 1 Citizens Plz Providence RI 02903-1344 E-mail: pfurness@nixonpeabody.com.

FURNISH, DALE BECK, lawyer, educator; b. Iowa City, Iowa, Feb. 11, 1940; s. William Madison and Eula Bernice (Beck) F.; m. Roberta Rae Mahnke, Aug. 23, 1963 (div. Oct. 1975); 1 child, Katherine Elizabeth; m. Hannah Rose Arterian, May 27, 1978 (div. May 1994); children— William, Susannah, Diana, Cordelia; m. Diane Larkey, June 11, 1994. B.A., Grinnell Coll., 1962; J.D., U. Iowa, 1965; LL.M., U. Mich., 1970. Bar: Iowa, 1965; U.S. Ct. Appeals (8th cir.) 1966, Ariz. 1973, U.S. Ct. Appeals (9th cir.), Ariz. 1992; U.S. Dist. Ct. Ariz. 1976. Law clk. U.S. Ct. Appeals (8th cir.), Sioux City, Iowa, 1965-66; asst. prof. law U. Iowa, Iowa City, 1966-68; vis. prof. law Ford Found. Internat. Legal Ctr., Santiago, Chile, 1969-70; prof. law Ariz. State U., Tempe, 1970— ; ptnr. Molloy, Jones & Donahue, P.C., 1988-92; vis. prof. law U. Nacional Autonoma de Mexico, Mexico City, 1974-75; Fulbright prof. Pontificia U. Católica del Peru, 1984, 88, prof. law U. of Sonora, Mexico, 1994—; lectr. USIA, Latin Am., 1972—; chmn. Ariz. Supreme Ct. Project on Judicial Cooperation with Sonora, Mex., 1993—, Nat. Law Ctr. Inter-Am. Free Trade, 1991—. Author: Usury and the Monetary Control Act of 1980, 1981, Legal Aspects of the North American Free Trade Agreement, 1992. Bd. editors Am. Jour. Comparative Law, 1972-89, 96—, Revista Peruana del Derecho Internat., 1979— . Mem. Fgn. Relations Com., Phoenix, 1979—, mem. exec. bd. 1986-91; mem. Gov.'s Ariz.-Mex. Commn., 1981—, chmn. legal adv. com., 1988-93. Mem. Am. Assn. Law Schs. (chmn. creditor debtor sect. 1978, chmn. comparative law sect. 1979), ABA, Ariz. Bar Assn., Iowa Bar Assn., Interam. Bar Assn., Am. Bankruptcy Inst. (bd. dirs. 1984-91), Order of Coif. Republican. Office: Ariz State U Coll Law Tempe AZ 85287-7906

FURNISH, SHEARLE LEE, English and modern languages educator; b. Denver, Mar. 30, 1953; s. C. Wilbur and Ruth S. Furnish; m. Carolyn D. Beck, Jan. 2, 1998. AB in English Lit., Transylvania U., 1975; MA in English Lit., U. Ky., Lexington, 1978, PhD in English Lit., 1984. Teaching asst. dept. English U. Ky., 1975-81, instr., 1981-84; vis. asst. prof. dept. lit., lang. and comm. U. N.C., Asheville, 1984-86; asst. prof. dept. English Meredith Coll., Raleigh, N.C., 1986-89; asst. prof. dept. English and modern langs. West Tex. State U. (now West Tex. A&M U.), Canyon, 1989-93, assoc. prof., 1993-97, prof., 1997—, dir. composition, 1996—2002, head dept., 2001—. Presented papers various confs. Publs. com. Panhandle-Plains Hist. Rev., 1991-98; editorial bd. KPA Bull., 1985; contbr. articles to profl. jours., including Am. Benedictine Rev., Dictionary of LIt. Biography. Manuscriptor, Mediaevedia, others. Bd. dirs. Friends of the Cornette Libr., West Tex. A&M U., 1993-96. Grantee West Tex. State U., 1990, West Tex. A&M U., 1994, 98, 2000. Mem. MLA, Southeastern Medieval Assn., Conf. Coll. Tchrs. English, Assn. Literary Scholars and Critics, Panhandle-Plains Hist. Soc., Assn. for Study Lit. and Environ., New Chaucer Soc., Medieval and Renaissance Drama Soc., Tex. Medieval Assn., Medieval Acad. Democrat. Home: 4507 W 2nd Ave Amarillo TX 79106-5205 Office. West Tex A&M U PO Box 60908 Canyon TX 79015-0908 E-mail: sfurnish@mail.wtamu.edu.

FURR, QUINT EUGENE, marketing executive; b. Concord, N.C., Sept. 21, 1921; s. Walter Luther and Mary (Barnhardt) F.; m. Helen Wilson, Dec. 30, 1961; children: Tiffany Grantham, Quentin, Robert; stepchildren: Pamela Erickson, Erik Erickson. Grad. Belmont Abbey Coll., BA, U. N.C., Chapel Hill, 1943, postgrad. Law Sch., 1946-47. Promotion rep. Sears, Roebuck & Co., Atlanta and Greensboro, N.C., 1947-49; nat. advt. and sales promotion mgr. Western Auto Supply Co., Kansas City, Mo., 1949-61; regional mgr. J.F. Pritchard Co., Charlotte, N.C., 1961-63; gen. mgr. Hogan Rose Advt., High Point, N.C., 1963-65; regional mgr. Top Value Enterprises, Washington, 1965-67; v.p. corp. mktg. Textilease Corp., Beltsville, Md., 1967-85; v.p. sales and mktg. Am. Directory Service Agy., Bethesda, Md., 1985-88; Marketing Consultant, 1988—. Lt. USNR, World War II, Korea. Recipient Mktg. award Textile Leasing Industry, 1970-74. Mem. Sales and Mktg. Execs. Internat., Inst. Indsl. Laundries (past chmn. mktg. com.), Am. Legion, VFW, Pi Kappa Alpha. Roman Catholic. Club: AD (Washington). Lodges: Moose, Elks. Home and Office: 32 Obsidian Dr Chambersburg PA 17201-8207

FURRER, JOHN RUDOLF, retired chemicals executive; b. Milw., Dec. 2, 1927; s. Rudolph and Leona (Peters) Furrer; m. Annie Louise Waldo, Apr. 24, 1954; children: Blake Waldo, Kimberly Louise. BA, Harvard U., 1949. Spl. rep. ACF Industries, Madrid, 1949-51, dir. product devel. N.Y.C., 1954-59; asst. supr. thermonuclear devel. and test Los Alamos, 1952-53; dir. machinery systems group, central engring. labs. FMC Corp., San Jose, Calif., 1959-68, gen. mgr. engineered systems div., 1968-70, v.p. in charge planning dept., ctrl. engring. labs. and engineered sys. divsn. Chgo., 1970-71, v.p. material handling group, 1971-77, v.p. corp. devel., 1977-88, sr. v.p., 1988-90; ret., 1990. Trustee Ravinia Festival, 1986—90, Grand Teton Music Festival, 2002—. With USN, 1945—46. Mem.: ASME, Coun. Planning Execs. (chmn. conf. bd. 1986—87). Achievements include patents in field. Home: PO Box 10849 Jackson WY 83002-0849 also: 203 Spinnaker Dr Vero Beach FL 32963-2953 E-mail: jrfurrer@aol.com.

FURROW, JOHN MAYO, secondary school educator; b. Alexandria, Va., Apr. 6, 1964; s. Hayden Mayo and Catherine Furrow; m. Beverley Elaine Vidger; children: Lindsay, Caleb, Joshua. B in Music Edn., BS in Bible, Phila. Bibl. U., 1987; MEd in Adminstrn., Columbia (S.C.) Internat. U., 2000. Cert. all-levels tchr. Assn. Christian Schs. Internat., all-levels prin. Assn. Christian Schs. Internat. Dir. of bands Riverdale Bapt. Sch., Upper Marlboro, Md., 1988—92, Roanoke (Va.) Valley Christian Sch., 1992—97; asst. prin. and dir. of fine arts Southside Christian Sch., Simpsonville, SC, 1997—; worship leader New Hope Bapt. Ch., Mauldin, SC, 2001—. Seminar and conf. spkr. Assn. Christian Schools Internat., 1999—. Recipient Roy W. Lowrie Jr. Christian Sch. Leadership award, Columbia Internat. U., 2000. Mem.: Christian Instrumental Dirs. Assn., S.C. Music Educators, Nat. Assn. Music Educators. Office: Southside Christian Sch 2211 Woodruff Rd Simpsonville SC 29681

FURSE, CLARA, stock exchange executive; married; three children. Dept. chmn. Liffe; CEO London Stock Exchg. Ltd., London, 2001—. Office: London Stock Exchg Ltd Dexter House Royal Mint Ct London EC3N 4QN England

FURSE, ELIZABETH, former congresswoman, small business owner; b. Nairobi, Kenya, 1936; came to U.S., 1958, naturalized, 1972; m. John Platt; 2 children (from previous marriage). BA, Evergreen State Coll., 1974; postgrad., U. Wash., Northwestern U., Lewis & Clark Coll. Dir. Western Wash. Indian program Am. Friends Svc. Com, 1975-77; coord. Restoration program for Native Am. Tribes Oreg. Legal Svc., 1980-86; co-owner Helvetia Vineyards, Hillsboro, Oreg.; mem. 103rd-105th Congresses from 1st Oreg. dist., 1993-98, mem. commerce, fin. and hazardous materials, health and environment, energy and power coms., mem. telecomm. and finance com. Assoc. dir. tribal programs Inst. Tribal Govt., Portland Co-Founder Oreg. Peace Inst., 1985. Address: 22485 NW Yungen Rd Hillsboro OR 97124-8146 also: Inst Tribal Govt PO Box 751 Portland OR 97207

FURST, ALEX JULIAN, thoracic and cardiovascular surgeon; b. Augusta, Ga., Aug. 21, 1938; m. George Alex and Ann (Segall) F.; m. Elayne Kobrin, Aug. 11, 1962; children: James Andrew, Jeffrey Michael, Joseph Robert. Student, U. Fla., 1963; MD, U. Miami, 1967. Intern U. Miami Hosp., 1967-68, resident, 1968-72, clin. instr. dept. surgery, 1974-91; chief resident in thoracic and cardiovascular surgery Emory U. Hosp., Atlanta, 1972-73, sr. surg. registrar of thoracic unit, 1972-73, Hosp. for Sick Children, London, 1973-74; practice medicine specializing in thoracic and cardiovascular surgery Miami, Fla.; clin. assoc. prof. surgery and cardiology, chief surg. svc. Miami VA Med. Ctr., 1991—, clin. prof., surgery and medicine, chief of surgery; chief surgeon West Palm Beach Med. Ctr., Va., 2000—02. Chief thoracic surgery, pres. med. staff Mercy Hosp.; mem. staff Bapt. Hosp., South Miami Hosp., Doctor's Hosp. (all Miami), North Ridge Gen. Hosp., Ft. Lauderdale; program dir. cardiothoracic surgery U. Miami Sch. of Medicine, 1998-2000. Fellow Am. Coll. Cardiology, Am. Coll. Chest Physicians, A.C.S.; mem. Dade County Med. Assn., Fla. Med. Assn., Heart Assn. Greater Miami, Soc. Thoracic Surgeons, So. Thoracic Surg. Assn. Home: 8802 Arvida Dr Miami FL 33156-2302

FURST, ARTHUR, toxicologist, educator; b. Mpls., Dec. 25, 1914; s. Samuel and Doris (Kolochinsky) F.; m. Florence Wolovitch, May 24, 1940; children: Carolyn, Adrianne, David Michael, Timothy Daniel. AA, L.A. City Coll., 1935; AB, UCLA, 1937, AM, 1940; PhD, Stanford U., 1948; ScD, U. San Francisco, 1983. Mem. faculty, dept. chemistry San Francisco City Coll., 1940-47; asst. prof. chemistry U. San Francisco, 1947-49, assoc. prof. chemistry, 1949-52; assoc. prof. medicinal chemistry Stanford Sch. Medicine, 1952-57, prof., 1957-61; with U. Calif. War Tng., 1943-45, San Francisco State Coll., 1943; rsch. assoc. Mt. Zion Hosp., 1952-82; clin. prof. pathology Columbia Coll. Physicians and Surgeons, 1969-70; dir. Inst. Chem. Biology; prof. chemistry U.

San Francisco, 1961-80, prof. emeritus, 1980—, dean grad. div., 1976-79. Vis. fellow Battelle Seattle Research Center, 1974; Michael vis. prof. Weizmann Inst. Sci., Israel, 1982; cons. toxicology, 1980—; cons. on cancer WHO; mem. com., bd. mineral resources NRC; emeritus mem. scientific advisory bd. Golden Neo Life Diamite Internat., Fremont, Calif. Author: Toxicologist as Expert Witness, 1997; contbr. over 300 articles to profl. and ednl. jours. Recipient Klaus Schwartz Commemorative medal Internat. Toxological Congress, Tokyo, 1986, Profl. Achievement award UCLA Alumni Assn., 1992, Henry Hall Clay award U. San Francisco, 1977; ann. lectureship named in his honor Stanford U. Health Libr. Fellow Acad. Toxicological Scis. (diplomate), AAAS, Am. Coll. Nutrition, Am. Coll. Toxicology (nat. sec., pres. 1985, Lifetime Contbn. award 2001), N.Y. Acad. Scis., Am. Inst. Chemists; mem. Am. Soc. Pharmacology and Exptl. Therapeutics, Am. Chem. Soc., Am. Assn. Cancer Research, Soc. Toxicology, Sigma Xi, Phi Lambda Upsilon. Achievements include research activities on organic synthesis, chemotherapy cancer, carcinogenesis of metals and hydrocarbons. Home: 23500 Cristo Rey Dr Unit 211D Cupertino CA 95014-6524 Office: U San Francisco Inst Chem Biology San Francisco CA 94117-1080 Fax: 650-967-4488. E-mail: artfurst@aol.com.

FURST, E. KENNETH, accountant; b. Oct. 11, 1946; BS in Econs., U. Pa., 1968, MS in Acctg., 1969. CPA, N.J. V.p. fin. Sea-Land Corp., Edison, N.J., 1971-89; CFO, dir., owner Toledo, Peoria (Ill.) & Western Railway, 1989-96; CFO, v.p. Golden Eagle Network, Bethel, Conn., 1996-97; owner E. Kenneth Furst, CPA, Short Hills, NJ, 1982—. Mem. N.J. Soc. CPAs (trustee, 1997-2000, pres. Essex chpt., 1995-96), Ct. Apptd. Spl. Adv. (trustee 2000—, treas. 2000-03), U. Penn. Club Metro. N.J. (pres. 1995-96, trustee 1971—). E-mail: furstk@att.net.

FURST, WARREN ARTHUR, retired holding company executive; b. Chgo., May 2, 1924; s. Joseph and Elizabeth (Pratscher) Furst; m. Billie L. Arvidson, Dec. 1, 1951; children: Ronald, Jeanette, Shirley, Mary, Kathryn. BS, Ill. Inst. Tech., 1944; JD, John Marshall Law Sch., 1950; MBA, U. Chgo., 1962. Mgr. indsl. rels. Am.-Marietta/Martin Marietta, Chgo., 1952—65; v.p. Wedron Silica Sand Co., Chgo., 1965—68; mgr. indsl. rels. MSL Industries, Chgo., 1968; v.p. indsl. rels. Consol. Packaging Corp., Chgo., 1969; v.p., sec. Katy Industries, Inc., Elgin, Ill., 1970—93; ret., 1993. Lt. (j.g.) USNR, 1943—46. Mem.: Ill. Bar Assn. Republican. Presbyterian. Home: 277 Otis Rd Barrington IL 60010-5123

FURSTE, WESLEY LEONARD, II, surgeon, educator; b. Cin., Apr. 19, 1915; s. Wesley Leonard and Alma (Deckebach) F.; m. Leone James, Mar. 28, 1942; children: Nancy Dianne, Susan Deanne, Wesley Leonard III. AB cum laude (Julius Dexter scholar 1933-34); Harvard Club scholar 1934-35), Harvard U., 1937, MD in Anatomy, 1941. Diplomate: Am. Bd. Surgery. Intern Ohio State U. Hosp., Columbus, 1941-42; fellow surgery U. Cin., 1945-46; asst. surg. resident Cin. Gen. Hosp., 1946-49; sr. asst. surg. resident Ohio State U. Hosps., 1949-50, chief surg. resident, 1950-51; limited practice medicine specializing in surgery Columbus, 1951—; instr. Ohio State U., 1951-54, clin. asst. prof. surgery, 1954-66, clin. assoc. prof., 1966-74, clin. prof. surgery, 1974-85, clin. prof. emeritus, 1985—. Mem. surg. staff Mt. Carmel Med. Center, chmn. dept. surgery, 1981-85, dir. surgery program, 1981-82; mem. surg. staff Children's, Grant Med. Ctr., Univ., Riverside, Meth. Hosps., St. Anthony Med. Ctr., Park Med. Ctr. (all Columbus); surg. cons. Dayton (Ohio) VA Hosp., Columbus State Sch., Ohio State Penitentiary, Mercy Hosp., Benjamin Franklin Hosp., Columbus, Columbus Cmty. Hosp.; regional adv. com. nat. blood program ARC, 1951-68, chmn., 1958-68; invited participant 2d Internat. Conf. on Tetanus, WHO, Bern, Switzerland, 1966, 3d, São, Paulo, Brazil, 1970, 4th, Dakar, Sénégal, 1975, 5th, Ronneby Brunn, Sweden, 1978, 6th, Lyon, France, 1981, 7th, Copanello, Italy, 1984, 8th, Leningrad, USSR, 1987, 9th, Granada, Spain, 1991; invited rapporteur 4th Internat. Conf. on Tetanus, Dakar, Sénégal, 1975; mem. med. adv. com. Medic Alert Found. Internat., 1971-73, 76-80, bd. dirs., 1973-76; Douglas lectr. Med. Coll. of Ohio, Toledo; founder Digestive Disease Found; lectr. U.S. Army M.C. on WWII Chinese activities during 1943-46; invited orator for new citizens at naturalization ceremonies U.S. Dist. Ct. (so. dist.) Ohio. Prime author: Tétanos; Tetanus: A Team Disease; contbg. author: Advances in Military Medicine, 1948, Management of the Injured Patient, Immediate Care of the Acutely Ill and Injured, 1978, Anaerobic Infections, 1989, Procs. of Internat. Tetans Confs. in Switzerland, Brazil, Sweden, Sénégal, France, Italy, USSR, Current Therapy in Emergency Medicine, Surgical Infectious Diseases (3 edits.), Currenty Emergency Therapy, Surgical Infections, Current Diagnosis (multiple edits.), Current Therapy (multiple edits.), Surgical Infections, 5 Minute Clinical Consult, 8 edits. (4 and 5 CD-Rom, Internet), Medical Microbiology and Infectious Diseases, editor Surgical Monthly Review; contbr. articles to profl. jours. Mem. Ohio Motor Vehicle Med. Rev. Bd., 1965-67, Pres. Club, Ohio State Univ.; bd. dirs. Am. Cancer Soc. Franklin County, pres., 1964-66; adv. coun. Upper Arlington Sr. Ctr., 2000. Served to maj., M.C. AUS, 1942-46, CBI, 1951-53. Recipient China Liberation medal, 2 commendations for surg. service in China U.S. Army; cert. of merit Am. Cancer Soc.; award for outstanding achievement in field clostridial infection dept. surgery Ohio State U. Coll. Medicine, 1984, Outstanding Service award, 1985; award for outstanding and dedicated service Mt. Carmel Med. Ctr., 1985; award for over 25 yrs. service St. Anthony Med. Ctr., U.S.A. Nat. Softball Squash Champion for age group, (1975—), Houston, 1992, (1980—), Denver, 96. Mem. AMA, AAAS, APHA, Cen. Surg. Assn., Surgical Infection Soc., Internat. Biliary Assn., Shock Soc., Soc. Am. Gastrointestinal Endoscopic Surgeons (com. on stds. of practice, resident and fellow edn., com. legis. review), Soc. Surgery of Alimentary Tract, A.C.S. (gov.-at-large, chmn. Ohio com. trauma; nat. subcom. prophylaxis against tetanus in wound mgmt., Ohio chapter Disting. Service award 1987; regional credentials com.), Am. Assn. Surgery of Trauma, Internat. Fedn. of Surg. Colls., Ohio Surg. Assn., Columbus Surg. Assn. (hon. mem.; pres. 1983), Am. Trauma Soc. (founding mem., dir.), Ohio Med. Assn., Acad. Medicine Columbus and Franklin County (Award of Merit for 17 yrs. service, chmn. blood transfusion com., 50 Year Svc. award), Acad. Medicine Cin., Am. Med. Writers Assn., Grad. Surg. Soc. U. Cin., Robert M. Zollinger Surg. Ohio State U. Surg. Soc., Mont Reid Grad. Surg. Soc., Am. Geriatrics Soc., N.Y. Acad. Scis., Assn. Program Dirs. in Surgery, Assn. Physicians State of Ohio, Collegium Internationale Chirurgiae Digestivae, Assn. Am. Med. Colls., Internat. Soc. Colon and Rectal Surgeons, Soc. Internat. de Chirurgie, Am. Assn. Sr. Physicians, Société Internationale sur le Tétanos, Am. Physicians Art Assn., Am. Assn. Retired Persons (bd. dirs. Franklin County Unit), China-Burma-India Vets., Assn. Columbus Basha (vice comdr. 1992-93, comdr. 1993-94, V-J Day coord., surgeon gen. 1994—), Am. Legion NW Post # 443, Am. Med. Golfing Assn., Internat. Brotherhood Magicians, Soc. Am. Magicians, N.Y. Cen. System Hist. Soc., U.S. Squash Racquets Assn. (mem. ranking com., med. adv. com., Nat. Softball Champion, 1992, 1996), Am. Platform Tennis Assn., Columbus Squash Racquets Assn. (bd. dirs.), VFW of U.S. (lectr.), Pres.'s Club (Ohio State U.). Presbyterian. Home and Office: Ohio State Univ 3125 Bembridge Rd Columbus OH 43221-2203 Fax: 614-457-5119. E-mail: wfursteii@aol.com.

FURSTMAN, SHIRLEY ELSIE DADDOW, advertising executive; b. Butler, N.J., Jan. 26, 1930; d. Richard and Eva M. (Kitchell) Daddow; grad. high sch.; m. Russell A. Bailey, Oct. 1, 1950 (div. Oct. 1967); m. William B. Furstman, Dec. 24, 1977. Asst. corporate sec. Hydrospace Tech., West Caldwell, N.J., 1960-62; sec. to pres. R.J. Dick Co., Totowa, N.J., 1962-63, Microlab, Livingston, N.J., 1963; asst. corporate sec. Astrosystems Internat., West Caldwell, N.J., 1963-65; corporate sec. Internat. Controls Corp., Fairfield, N.J., 1965-73; sec. to pres. Global Financial Co., Nassau, Bahamas, 1974-75; office mgr. Internat. Barter, Nassau, 1975-76; sec. to pres., corp. sec. Haas Chem. Co., Taylor, Pa., 1976-77; asst. to pres., pub. Am. Home mag., N.Y.C., 1977-78; v.p., office mgr. Gilbert, Whitney & Johns, Inc., Whippany, N.J., 1979-95; ret., 1996. Home: 4 Oceans West Blvd Apt 606D Daytona Beach FL 32118-5977

FURTADO-LAVOIE, JULIA, new business startup consultant, accountant; b. Fall River, Mass., July 22, 1964; d. Manuel Lawrence and Mary Gloria (Mello) Furtado; m. Michael Cavoie. Student, U. Mass., Dartmouth, 1987, Emerson Coll., Boston, 1987-89. Dist. sales mgr. InterPay Inc., Mansfield, Mass., 1996—2003; sales payroll cons. Paychex, Inc., Providence, 2003—. Cons. Start Me Up, Dartmouth, 1993—. Recipient Freedom Torch award ABC6 and Providence Jour., 1996. Mem. C. of C. (amb.). Avocations: reading, cats, theatre, opera. Home: 6 Ashley St South Dartmouth MA 02748-2808 Office: 501 Wampanoag Tr East Providence RI 02915

FURTH, FREDERICK PAUL, lawyer; b. West Harvey, Ill., Apr. 12, 1934; s. Fred P. and Mamie (Stelmach) F.; children: Darby, Ben Anthony, Megan Louise; m. Peggy Wollerman, July 19, 1986. Student, Drake U., 1952-53; BA, U. Mich., 1956, JD, 1959; postgrad., U. Berlin, 1959, U. Munich, Fed. Republic Germany, 1960. Bar: Mich. 1959, N.Y. 1961, D.C. 1965, U.S. Supreme Ct. 1965, Calif. 1966. Assoc. Cahill, Gordon, Reindel & Ohl, N.Y.C., 1960-64; with Kellogg Co., Battle Creek, Mich., 1964-65; assoc. Joseph L. Alioto, San Francisco, 1965-66; sr. ptnr. The Furth Firm LLP, San Francisco, 1966—. Bd. dirs. Robert Half Internat.; chmn., propr. Chalk Hill Winery. Trustee, chmn. bd. Furth Family Found., San Francisco; bd. dirs. Franklin and Eleanor Roosevelt Inst., 1996—, The Ctr. for Democracy, Washington; chmn. Internat. Jud. Conf., Strasbourg, France, 1992-. Mem. ABA, Internat. Bar Assn., N.Y. Bar Assn., San Francisco Bar Assn., State Bar Calif., Assn. of Bar of City of N.Y., St. Francis Yacht Club, Olympic Club. Office: The Furth Firm LLP 201 Sansome St San Francisco CA 94104-2303 E-mail: fpfurth@aol.com.

FURTH, JOHN JACOB, molecular biologist, pathologist, educator; b. Phila., Jan. 25, 1929; s. Jacob and Olga (Berthauer) F.; m. Mary Autry, June 24, 1959; children: Karen, Susan, Robin. BA, Cornell U., 1950; student, Yale Law Sch., 1950-51; MD, Duke U., 1958; MA, U. Pa., 1972. Intern Bellevue Hosp., N.Y.C., 1958-59; resident in pathology NYU Sch. Medicine, N.Y.C., 1959-60, postdoctoral fellow dept. microbiology, 1960-62; mem. faculty dept. pathology U. Pa. Med. Sch., Phila., 1962—, prof., 1978—2001, emeritus prof., 2001—. Contbr. articles to profl. jours. Bd. dirs., chmn. hist. sites com. Darby Creek Valley Assn., 1984-96, 1st v.p. 1997—; bd. dirs., founder Friends of the Swedish Cabin (constructed circa 1654), Upper Darby, Pa., 1987, pres. 2002—; bd. dirs. Fair Housing Coun. of Suburban Phila., 1995-97, 2d dist. leader Upper Darby Democratic Party, 1994—2002, chmn., 2002—; candidate for Congress, 7th Dist. Pa. 2d lt. Q.M.C., U.S. Army, 1951-53. Recipient Hoffman LaRoche award, 1958; Eleanor Roosevelt fellow, 1977-78. Mem. AAAS, Am. Soc. Biol. Chemists and Molecular Biologists, Am. Assn. Cancer Rsch., Am. Assn. Pathologists. Democrat. Mem. Soc. Of Friends. Achievements include codiscovery of RNA polymerase. Home: 43 Roselawn Ave Lansdowne PA 19050-2317 Office: U Pa Sch Medicine Dept Pathology and Lab Med Philadelphia PA 19104-6082 E-mail: jjfurth@mail.med.upenn.edu.

FURTH, KAREN J. artist, art educator; BA in Am. History, U. Pa., 1983; MA in Photography, NYU, 1988. Biomed. photographer Rockefeller U., 1988—89; photographer Smithsonian Instn., 1989—94; tchr. Trinity Sch., 1990; freelance photographer, 1994—; tchr., cons. Ctr. Urban Cmty. Svcs. The Times Sq., 1994—; tchr. Internat. Ctr. Photography at The Point, N.Y.C., 1998—. One-woman shows include Washington Sq. East Galleries, N.Y.C., 1988, 494 Gallery, 1991, 1992, 1994, Pulse Art Gallery, 1997, exhibited in group shows at Oswego Civic Art Ctr., 1988, 494 Gallery, 1991, 1992, Synchronicity Space, 1995, Pulse Art Gallery, 1996, Golin/Harris, 1998, others, curatorial projects include, The Times Sq. Photography Project, Met. Transp. Authority, 1999; presenter in field; contbr. ; Represented in permanent collections J.P. Morgan, Mt. Sinai Hosp., others. Recipient Gilbert Graphic Paper award, 1993; fellow Open Soc. Inst. Individual Project fellow, Soros Found., 1997; scholar Faculty scholar, U. Pa., 1979—83; Internat. Outreach grante, 1993—94.

FURTH, YVONNE, advertising executive; Asst. account exec. Draft Worldwide, 1981—88, gen. mgr., 1988—92, pres. of Chicago office, 1992—96, pres. & COO US operations, 1996—2001, pres. & CEO, 2002—. Office: Draft Worldwide 142 E Ontario St Chicago IL 60611-2818

FURUBOTN, EIRIK GRUNDTVIG, economics educator; b. N.Y.C., Apr. 18, 1923; s. Konrad Martin and Caroline (Grundtvig) F.; m. Florence Birkby Duckworth; children— Karin Florence, Erik Grundtvig, Kristian George BA, Brown U., 1948; MA, Columbia U., 1950, PhD, 1959. Instr. Wesleyan U., Middletown, Conn., 1953-55; asst. prof. Lafayette Coll., Easton, Pa., 1958-60; assoc. prof. Emory U., Atlanta, 1960-63; prof. SUNY, Binghamton, 1963-67, Tex. A&M U., College Station, 1967-82; James L. West prof. econs. U. Tex., Arlington, 1982-96; rsch. fellow pvt. enterprise rsch. ctr. Tex. A&M U., College Station, 1996—. Com. mem. Tex. A&M Univ. Press, College Station, 1974-82; co-dir. Ctr. for Study of New Instl. Econs., U. Saarland, W.Ger., 1986—; mem. bd. advs. Utrecht Sch. Econs., Utrecht U., Netherlands, 2002. Co-author: (with R. Richter) Neue Institutionen Okonomik, 1996, The Evolution of Modern Demand Theory, 1972; co-editor: The Economics of Property Rights, 1974, The New Institutional Economics: An Assessment, 1991, Institutions and Economic Theory, 1997; mem. editl. bd. Applied Econs., London, 1971-72; mem. bd. editors So. Econ. Jour., 1979-81, Zeitschrift für die gesamte Staatswissenschaft, 1984—; contbr. articles to profl. jours. Trustee Allen Acad., Bryan, Tex., 1974-76; mem. adv. coun. Polit. Economy Rsch. Ctr., Bozeman, Mont., 1984-92; mem. nat. adv. bd. Nat. Ctr. for Privatization, Wichita, Kans., 1985-95. Cpl. U.S. Army, 1942-46, ETO. Francis Wayland scholar Brown U., 1948; named Honorarprofessor für Volkswirtschaftslehre U. Saarland, Fed. Republic of Germany. Mem. Am. Econ. Assn., So. Econ. Assn. (exec. com. 1975-77), Can. Econ. Assn., Phi Beta Kappa, Omicron Delta Epsilon, Beta Gamma Sigma, Omega Rho. Republican. Episcopalian. Avocations: antiques, travel. Home: 750 N Rosemary Dr Bryan TX 77802-4307 Office: Tex A&M U Pvt Enterprise Rsch Ctr PO Box 3327 College Station TX 77841-3327 E-mail: perc@tamu.edu.

FURUMOTO, HORACE WATARU, medical products company executive; b. Honolulu, Dec. 13, 1931; s. Kitaru and Shizuko (Okita) F.; m. Laurel Waishnor, June 10, 1959; children: Robin, Jill. BS, Calif. Inst. Tech., 1955; PhD, Ohio State U., 1963. Mem. staff research and devel. div. Avco, Wilmington, Mass., 1963-66; asst. br. chief NASA, Cambridge, Mass., 1966-70; mem. staff U.S. Dept. Transp., Cambridge, Mass., 1970-72; dep. dir. isotopes rsch. Avco Everett (Mass.) Rsch. Lab., 1972-77; pres. Candela Laser Corp., Wayland, Mass., 1977-91, Cynosure, Inc., Bedford, Mass., 1991—97. Bd. dirs. Mass. Tech. Devel. Corp., Boston. Contbr. articles to profl. jours.; patentee in field. Served to 1st lt. USAF, 1955-57. Fellow Am. Soc. Laser Medicine and Surgery; mem. IEEE, Am. Phys. Soc., Laser Inst. Am., Optical Soc. Am. Democrat. Home: 14 Woodridge Rd Wellesley MA 02482-7033 Office: Cynosure Inc 10 Elizabeth Dr Chelmsford MA 01824-4145

FURUYAMA, RENEE HARUE, association executive; b. Honolulu, Feb. 15, 1957; d. Walter Tadashi and Jane Machie (Kamada) F.; m. Joel Fischer, Oct. 31, 1991; children: Lisa, Nicole. Grad., Tohoku U., Sendai, Japan, 1984; MSW, U. Hawaii, 1988, M.Urban and Regional Planning, 1993. Lic. social worker, Hawaii. Geriatric case mgr. Dept. Human Svcs., Honolulu, 1992-95; pub. policy dir. Mental Health Assn. Hawaii, Honolulu, 1995-98; instr. U. Hawaii Sch. Social Work, 1998—. Lectr., spkr. in field. Bd. dirs. Waianae Clubhouse, Miyagi Kenjinkai, Am. Friends Svc. Com.; mem. Unity Organizing Com.; chmn. Hawaii Commn. for Africa. Tohuku U. scholar; recipient numerous scholarships and awards. Mem. NASW (v.p. 2001-03), UN Assn. Hawaii (treas. 1988-91). Democrat. Avocation: Buddhist sculpture. Home: 1371-4 Hunakai St Honolulu HI 96816-5501

FURZE, EDWARD WILLIAM, fundraising consultant; b. Syracuse, NY, Jan. 7, 1938; s. John T. and Marion Joy (Gieselman) F.; m. Joanne M. Sojewicz, Aug. 4, 1962 (div. 1992); children: David John, Jeffrey Paul, Daniel Edward. BS in History, LeMoyne Coll., 1961. Exec. dir. agy. ops. United Way Cen. N.Y., Syracuse, 1965-70; exec. dir. Community Found., Syracuse, 1968-70; dir. devel. and community rels. LeMoyne Coll., Syracuse, 1970-83; v.p. Mt. St. Mary's Coll., Emmittsburg, Md., 1983-85; sr. devel. officer Pa. State U., Harrisburg, 1985-87, Fairleigh Dickinson U., Rutherford, N.J., 1987-90; exec. dir. for found., asst. v.p. devel. Gen. Hosp. Ctr., Passaic, N.J., 1990-92; fundraising cons. Ketchum, Inc., Pitts., 1992—; resource devel. dir. Boys and Girls Club of Syracuse, N.Y., 1995-97. Cons. Cyo-Brighton Family Ctr., Syracuse, 1972-73, Christ the King Retreat House, Syracuse, 1972-95, 2003. Vol. Ctr., Newark, 1990-91, Ketchum, Inc., Pitts., 1989-90; trustee St. Camillus Extended Care, Syracuse, 1972-83. Alt. del. Rep. Nat. Conv., Detroit, 1980. Mem.: Nat. Soc. Fundraising Execs., Pub. Rels. Soc. Am., Rotary (pres. 1991). Home: 700 Danforth St Apt 2 Syracuse NY 13208-1612

FUSARO, RAMON MICHAEL, dermatologist, researcher; b. Bklyn., Mar. 6, 1927; s. Angelo and Ida (Pucci) F.; m. Lavonne Johnsen, Nov. 6, 1971; children: Lisa Ann, Toni Ann; stepsons: Jeff, Scott. BA, U. Minn., 1949, BS, 1951, MD, 1953, MS, 1958, PhD, 1965. Diplomate Am. Bd. Dermatology. Intern Mpls. Gen. Hosp., 1953-54, resident in dermatology, 1954—57; from instr. to assoc. prof. U. Minn., 1957-70, dir. outpatient dermatology clinic, 1962-70; prof., chmn. dept. dermatology U. Nebr. Med. Center, Omaha, 1970-82; prof. dermatology sect. dept. internal medicine U. Nebr. Med. Ctr., Omaha, 1982-91, acting chief sect. dermatology, 1991-94; prof., chmn. dept. dermatology Creighton U., Omaha, 1975-87; prof. dermatology dept. internal medicine Creighton U. Sch. Medicine, Omaha, 1983-89; prof. Creighton U., Omaha, 1989—; dir. dermatology residency program Creighton/Nebr. Univs. Health Found., 1975-83; prof. dept. pub. health and preventive medicine Hereditary Cancer Inst., Creighton U., 1984—. Contbr. over 300 articles to profl. jours., 25 chpts. to books. With USN, 1944-46. Mem. Am. Acad. Dermatology, Sigma Xi. Home: 908 Beaver Lake Blvd Plattsmouth NE 68048-4500 Office: 984360 Nebr Med Ctr Omaha NE 68198-4360 also: Creighton U Med Sch Criss III Dept Prev Med 2500 California Plz Omaha NE 68178-0403 E-mail: rmfusaro@Creighton.edu.

FUSCO, ANDREW G. lawyer; b. Punxsutawney, Pa., Jan. 11, 1948; s. Albert G. and Virginia N. (Whitesell) F.; m. Deborah K. Lucas; children: Matthew, Geoffrey, David. BS in Bus. Adminstrn. and Fin., W.Va. U., 1970, JD, 1973. Bar: W.Va. 1973, U.S. Ct. Appeals (4th cir.) 1974, U.S. Supreme Ct. 1977, U.S. Ct. Appeals (fed. cir.) 1985, U.S. Tax Ct. 1995. Pvt. practice, Morgantown, W.Va., 1973-85; prin. Fusco & Newbraugh, L.C., Morgantown, 1985-98, The Fusco Legal Group, L.C., Morgantown, 1998-2001; mem. Eckert Seamans Cherin & Mellott, LLC, 2001—. Pros. atty. Monongalia County, W.Va., 1977-81; instr. Coll. Bus. and Econs., Law Ctr., W.Va. U., 1975-76, instr. W.Va. U. Sch. Journalism, 1997—; dir. Pitts. Environ. Systems Inc., 1983-86. Author: Antitrust Law (West Virginia Practice Handbook), 1991; editor, contbg. author: Twenty Feet From Glory (John R. Goodwin), 1970, Business Law (John R. Goodwin), 1972, Beyond Baker Street (Michael Harrison), 1976. Bd. dirs. W.Va. Career Colls., 1971-76; mem. profl. adv. bd. Childbirth and Parent Edn. Assn., 1975-82, Rape and Domestic Violence Info. Ctr., 1977-81; mem. W.Va. Sec. State's Tribunal on Election Reform, 1977-81; chmn. Monongalia County Drug Edn. Task Force, 1978-80; mem. bd. advisors Nat. Smokers Alliance, 1998-99; mem. vis. com. W.Va. U. Coll. Law, 2000—. Recipient Am. Jurisprudence award Bancroft-Whitney Publ. Co., 1971; named Outstanding Young Man of Morgantown, 1979. Mem. ABA (Civil RICO com., antitrust law sect.), Monongalia County Bar Assn., Am. Judicature Soc., W.Va. Bar Assn., Baker St. Irregulars of W.Va. Sherlock Holmes Soc. London, Bootmakers of Toronto, Nat. Dist. Attys. Assn., Sons of Italy, W.Va. Law Sch. Assn., Monongalia Arts Ctr. (pres., treas., vice-chmn., trustee). Democrat. Roman Catholic. Home: 2054 Iron Bridge Cir Morgantown WV 26508 Office: Eckert Seamans Cherin & Mellott 2400 Cranberry Sq Morgantown WV 26508-9209 Fax: 304-594-1181. E-mail: agf@escm.com.

FUSCO, JOHN ANTHONY, lawyer; b. N.Y.C., Sept. 7, 1937; s. Michael and Rose (Marinelli) F.; m. Carol Ann Odessa, July 21, 1967; children— Michael John, Michelle Lynn. B.S., St. Peters Coll., 1959; J.D., New Eng. Sch. Law, Boston, 1963. Bar: Mass. 1963, N.Y. 1967, U.S. Supreme Ct. 1972, U.S. Dist. Ct. (ea. and so. dists.) N.Y. 1975, U.S. Ct. Appeals (2d cir.) 1975. Claims adjuster Allstate Ins. Co., N.Y.C., 1965-68; law sec. N.Y. State Supreme Ct., N.Y.C., 1969-71; ptnr. Russo, Fusco, Scano, Scamardella & Fredreck, S.I., N.Y., 1972— ; civil ct. arbitrator, 1982— . Law chmn. Richmond County Republican Com., 1971, vice chmn. 1973; mem. S.I. Heart Assn. Mem. ABA, Richmond County Bar Assn. (past dir.), N.Y. State Bar Assn. Republican. Roman Catholic. Clubs: Italian (S.I.); Holy Name Soc. Lodge: Lions. Home: 2314 Richmond Rd Staten Island NY 10306-2562 Office: Russo Fusco Scano et al 1010 Forest Ave Staten Island NY 10310-2415

FUSCO, RICHARD, English literature educator; b. Phila., Apr. 27, 1952; BA, U. Pa., 1973, MA, 1974, U. Miss., 1982; PhD, Duke U., 1990. Instr. English St. Joseph's U., Phila., 1988-91, asst. prof. English, 1997—2003, assoc. prof. English, 2003—. Author: Maupassant and the American Short Story: The Influence of Form at the Turn of the Century, 1994, (pamphlet) Fin de millénaire: Poe's Legacy for the Detective Story, 1993; contbr. articles to profl. jours. Served as intelligence officer U.S. Navy, 1975-79. Mem. MLA. Home: 2237 S 23rd St Philadelphia PA 19145-3321 Office: Dept English St Joseph's U 5600 City Ave Philadelphia PA 19131-1308 E-mail: fusco@sju.edu.

FUSEK, SERENA REBECCA, poet; b. East Orange, N.J., Apr. 28, 1948; d. John Henry Vreeland and Serena May Brown; m. John Stephen Fusek, June 11, 1946. Editor: Orphic Lute/Proof Rock, 1982—86, 1986—91; author: (chapbook) The Color of Poison, 1991, Night Screams with Jaguars Voice, 1998, poems, short stories, articles. Avocations: reading, travel, wildlife study. Home: PO Box 3095 Newport News VA 23603-0095

FUSELIER, HAROLD ANTHONY, JR., physician, urologist; b. Abbeville, La., Dec. 1, 1942; s. Harold Anthony and May Elizabeth (Fowler) F.; m. Ann Valentino, May 17, 1968; children: Harold Anthony III, F. Scott, J. Prentice, Mims Michael. BS, La. State U., Baton Rouge, 1964; MD, La. State U., New Orleans, 1967. Diplomate Am. Bd. Urology. Internship Charity Hosp., New Orleans, 1967-68; residency urology Alton Ochsner Medical Found., 1970-74; mem. dept. urology Ochsner Clinic Found., New Orleans, 1974—, chmn. dept. urology, 1989—2002; med. dir. surgery Ochsner Found. Hosp., New Orleans, 1990—; clin. prof. urology Tulane U. Med. Ctr., New Orleans, 1988—, La. State U. Med. Ctr., New Orleans, 1990—. Program dir. La. State U./Ochsner Urology Tng. Program, 1991—. Contbr. articles to profl. jours. Capt. USAF, 1968-70. Fellow ACS; mem. Am. Urol. Assn., Soc. Internat. d'Urologie, Soc. for Study of Impotence, Soc. Univ. Urologists. Roman Catholic. Avocations: golf, hunting, fishing. Office: Ochsner Clinic 1514 Jefferson Hwy New Orleans LA 70121-2483 E-mail: hfuselier@ochsner.org.

FUSFELD, DANIEL ROLAND, economist; b. Washington, May 23, 1922; s. Irving Sidney and Cecile (Leban) F.; m. Harriet Miller, Aug. 30, 1947; children: Robert, Sarah, Yaakov Sadeh. BA, George Washington U., 1941; MA, Columbia U., 1947, PhD, 1953. Instr. Hofstra Coll., Hempstead, N.Y., 1947-53, asst. prof., 1953-56, Mich. State U., East Lansing, 1956-60; assoc. prof. U. Mich., Ann Arbor, 1960-64, prof., 1964-87, prof. emeritus, 1987—. Lectr. USAF Inst. Tech., Dayton, Ohio, 1958-59; vis. assoc. prof. Columbia U., N.Y.C., 1960; bd. dirs. Spectrum Human Svcs., 1992-98, Avalon Housing, Inc. *The mission of Avalon Housing, Inc. is to develop, own and/or manage permanent leased housing that is affordable to people with low incomes, including those in minimum/low-wage employment or on limited fixed incomes. Avalon Housing is committed to the inclusion of persons with disabilities and special needs who are underserved in the housing market. In operating housing, Avalon utilizes and enhanced management approach, which maximizes problem solving with tenants, minimizes eviction, and insures financial viability, property maintenece and safety.* Author: Economic Thought of Franklin D. Roosevelt, 1956, The Age of the Economist, 1966, 9th edit. 2001, Economics, 1972, The Basic Economics of the Urban-Racial Crisis, 1973, Rise and Repression of Radical Labor, 1877-1918, 1985; co-author: The Political Economy of the Urban Ghetto, 1984; co-editor: The Soviet Economy, 1962; also articles. With U.S. Army, 1943—46. Mem. Am. Econ. Assn., Assn. for Evolutionary Econs. (v.p. 1970, pres. 1971), Internat. Network for Econ. Method (chmn. 1989-92), Hist. Econ. Soc. Home: Apt 324 4001 Glacier Hills Dr Ann Arbor MI 48105 Office: U Mich Dept Econs Ann Arbor MI 48109 E-mail: hadafusf@yahoo.com.

FUSILLO, THOMAS VICTOR, environmental engineer; b. Bklyn., Feb. 17, 1953; s. Pat and Catherine (Notarnicola) F.; m. Michele Fran Lipman, June 24, 1979; children: Jennifer Lynn, Steven Joseph, Alyssa Nicole. BS in Environ. Sci., Rutgers U., 1975, MS in Agrl. Engring., 1977. Cert. groundwater profl. Rsch. intern Rutgers U., New Brunswick, N.J., 1975-77, adj. instr., 1976-77; hydrologist U.S. Geol. Survey, Trenton, 1977-87, dist. geochemistry specialist, 1983-87; sr. assoc. Environ. Corp., Princeton, N.J., 1987-89, project mgr., 1989-91, mgr., 1991-94, prin., 1994—, mng. principal, 2003—. Mem. Am. Geophys. Union, Assn. Groundwater Scientists and Engrs., Sigma Xi, Alpha Zeta. Home: 1228 Bridle Estates Dr Yardley PA 19067-3957 Office: 214 Carnegie Ctr Princeton NJ 08540-6237 E-mail: tfusillo@environcorp.com.

FUSS, MELVYN ALLAN, educator, researcher; b. Kitchener, Ont., Can., Mar 29, 1940; s. Abraham Bernard and Florence (Rosenberg) F.; m. Evelyn Susan Kaufman, Oct. 10, 1974; 1 child, Adina. B.Sc., U. Toronto, 1963, M.A., 1965 Ph.D., U. Calif.-Berkeley, 1970. Asst. prof. econs. Harvard U., Cambridge Mass., 1969-72; vis. prof. econs. Hebrew U., Jerusalem, 1972-73; assoc. prof econs. U. Toronto, 1972-79, prof., 1979—, assoc. chmn. econs., 1984-85, chmn

econs., 1985-90, 2000-01; cons. Gulf Can., Toronto, 1981-84, U.S. Dept. Justice, Washington, 1983-84, U.S. Postal Service, Washington, 1982—, Chrysler Corp., Detroit, 1984-85. Author: Costs and Productivity in Automobile Production, 1992; editor: Production Economics, 1978; also articles. Mem. Econometric Soc., Can. Econ. Assn., Am. Econ. Assn. Avocations: golf; tennis; music listening; reading. Office: U Toronto, 150 St George St, Toronto ON Canada M5S 3G7 E-mail: fuss@chass.utoronto.ca.

FUSSELL, CATHARINE PUGH, biological researcher; b. Phila., July 13, 1919; d. Milton H. and Isabel R. (Pugh) F. AB, Colby Coll., 1941; MS, Cornell U, 1958; PhD, Columbia U., 1966. Administrv. asst. Am. Friends Svc. Commn., Phila., 1947-55; rsch. asst. Brookhaven Nat. Lab., Upton, N.Y., 1957-60; rsch. assoc. Inst. Cancer Rsch. Fox Chase, Phila., 1966-67; postdoctoral fellow Fels Rsch. Inst., Phila., 1967—68; from asst. prof. to assoc. prof. Pa. State U., McKeesport, 1968-77; sabbatical leave at Med. Rsch. Coun. Population and Cytogenetics Unit, Edinburgh, 1975-76; assoc. prof. Pa. State U., Abington, 1977-88, rsch. scientist, 1988-89. With Marine Biol. Lab., Woods Hole, Mass., 1972—74, 1977—82, 1986—92. Contbr. articles to profl. jours. Bd. dirs. The Woodlands Trust for Hist. Preservation, 1998-2001, pres., 1998-2001. Vis. scholar, U. Pa. Med. Sch., Phila., 1990—96. Mem. AAAS, AAUW (pres. 1985-87, Northeastern Montgomery County br.), Bot. Soc. Am., Genetics Soc. Am., Woodlands Cemetery Co. of Phila. (chief operating officer 1997-98, v.p. 1996-2000, bd. dirs. 1991-2000). Avocations: gardening, historic preservation. Home: 179 Kendal Dr Kennett Square PA 19348-2333

FUSSELL, PAUL, author, English literature educator; b. Pasadena, Calif., Mar. 22, 1924; s. Paul and Wilhma Wilson (Sill) F.; m. Betty Ellen Harper, June 17, 1949 (div. 1987); children: Rosalind, Samuel; m. Harriette Behringer, Apr. 11, 1987. BA, Pomona (Calif.) Coll., 1947, LittD (hon.), 1981; MA, Harvard U., 1949, PhD, 1952; MA (hon.), U. Pa., 1983; LittD (hon.), Monmouth U., N.J., 1985. Instr. English, Conn. Coll., 1951-55; mem. faculty Rutgers U., 1955—, John DeWitt prof. English lit., 1976-83; Donald T. Regan prof. English lit. U. Pa., Phila., 1983-94, prof. emeritus, 1994—. Cons. editor Random House, 1963-64; lectr. Am. univs., 1965—; vis. prof. Kings Coll., London, 1990-92. Author: The Rhetorical World of Augustan Humanism, 1965, Poetic Meter and Poetic Form, 1965, rev., 1979, Samuel Johnson and The Life of Writing, 1971, The Great War and Modern Memory (Nat. Book Critics Circle award 1975, Nat. Book award 1976), Abroad: British Literary Traveling Between the Wars, 1980, The Boy Scout Handbook & Other Observations, 1982, Class: A Guide through the American Status System, 1983, Thank God for the Atom Bomb & Other Essays, 1988, Wartime: Understanding and Behavior in the Second World War, 1989; BAD: or The Dumbing of America, 1991, The Anti-Egoist: Kingsley Amis, Man of Letters, 1994, Doing Battle: The Making of a Skeptic, 1996, Uniforms: Why We Are What We Wear, 2002; contbg. editor Harper's, 1979-83, The New Republic, 1979-85. Served with AUS, 1943-46. Decorated Purple Heart, Bronze Star; recipient James D. Phelan award Phelan Found., 1964; Lindback Found. award, 1971; Ralph Waldo Emerson award Phi Beta Kappa, 1976; sr. fellow Nat. Endowment Humanities, 1973-74; Guggenheim fellow, 1977-78; Rockefeller Found. fellow, 1983-84 Fellow Royal Soc. Lit., Soc. Am. Historians; mem. MLA, Acad. Lit. Studies. Home: 2020 Walnut St Philadelphia PA 19103-5635

FUSTÉ, JOSÉ ANTONIO, federal judge; b. San Juan, Puerto Rico, Nov. 3, 1943, BBA, U. P.R., San Juan, 1965, LLB cum laude, 1968. Ptnr. Jimenez & Fuste, Hato Rey, P.R., 1968-85; judge U.S. Dist. Ct. P.R., San Juan, 1985—. Prof. U. P.R., 1972-85, 96-2002. Office: US Courthouse CH-133 150 Ave Carlos Chardon San Juan PR 00918-1758

FUSTER, JAIME B. supreme court justice; b. Guayama, P.R., Jan. 12, 1941; s. Jaime L. and Maria Luisa (Berlingeri) Fuster; m. Mary Jo Fuster, Dec. 19, 1966; children: Maria Luisa, Jaime. BA, Notre Dame U., 1962; JD, U. P.R., 1965; LLM, Columbia U., 1966; SJD, Harvard U., 1974; LLD (hon.), Temple U., 1985. Bar: P.R. 1966. Prof. law U. P.R., 1966—73, 1978—80; project dir. Study on Legal Profession of P.R. Ctr. Social Rsch., 1970—73; dean Law Sch. U. P.R., 1974—78; ednl. cons. Office of Cts. Adminstrn. Govt. of P.R., 1978—80; dep. asst. atty. gen. U.S. Dept. Justice, Washington, 1980—81; pres. Cath. U. P.R., 1981—84; mem. Congress from P.R., Washington, 1984—92; resident commr. Commonwealth of P.R., 1984—92; assoc. justice P.R. Supreme Ct., 1992—. Cons., lectr. in field. Author: Political and Civil Rights in Puerto Rico, 1968, The Duties of Citizens, 1973, The Lawyers of Puerto Rico: A Sociological Study, 1974, Law and Problems of Elderly People, 1978; editor-in-chief: U. P.R. Law Rev., 1964—65; contbr. chapters to books, articles to profl. jours. Named One of Outstanding Young Men of Am., U.S. Jr. C. of C., 1978. Mem.: Interam. Bar Found. (bd. dirs. 1975—79), Assn. Am. Colls. (adv. bd. 1980—84). Democrat. Roman Catholic. Avocation: tennis. Office: PO Box 2392 San Juan PR 00902-2392 E-mail: jaimefb@tribunales.prstar.net.

FUTCH, ARCHER HAMNER, retired physicist; b. Monroe, N.C., Mar. 21, 1925; s. Archer Hamner and Emma Lee (Covington) F.; m. Patricia West, June 13, 1953; children: Lisa Stewart, Jacqueline Lee, Tina Corine. BS, U. N.C., 1949, MS, 1951; PhD, U. Md., 1955. Physicist E.I. Du Pont de Nemours Co., Aiken, S.C., 1955-58, Lawrence Livermore (Calif.) Nat. Lab., 1959-91. Mem. Livermore Planning Commn., 1968-72, Livermore City Coun., 1972-76; mayor City of Livermore, 1976; bd. dirs. Alameda County Water Dist., 1976-80, South Livermore Valley Agric. Land Trust, 1995—. Mem. Am. Phys. Soc., Phi Beta Kappa, Sigma Xi, Sigma Pi Sigma. Republican. Home: 1252 Westbrook Pl Livermore CA 94550-6430 E-mail: ahfutch@yahoo.com.

FUTCH, DOROTHY HELEN, librarian, paralegal; b. Alachua, Fla., Aug. 17, 1931; d. David Malcolm and Burdine (Slaughter) Futch. BA, Fla. State U., 1951; MS, Simmons Coll., 1960; cert. paralegal, City Coll. San Francisco, 1980. Cataloger Oakland (Calif.) Pub. Libr., 1961—76; file supr. Orrick, Herrington & Sutcliffe, San Francisco, 1977—80; probate paralegal R.E. Neuman Probate Referee, San Francisco, 1982—89; database mgr. Natkin, Weisbach, Higginbothan, San Francisco, 1990—93; adminstr. Cool Shades Internat., San Francisco, 1995—. Editor: (newsletter) Oak Leaves, 1969—76; translator: Astucia, 1995—2000. Pres. Oakland Pub. Libr. Staff Assn., 1973; active Rep. Nat. Com., 2003—. Lewis State Tchrs. scholar, State of Fla., Tallahassee, 1948—51. Mem.: Luis Inclan Soc. (pres. 2003—), Gamma Phi Beta. Republican. Baptist. Home: Apt 212 631 O'Farrell San Francisco CA 94109

FUTCHER, PALMER HOWARD, physician, educator; b. Balt., Sept. 13, 1910; s. Thomas Barnes and Gwendolen Marjorie (Howard) F.; m. Mary Viola Rightor, Nov. 21, 1942 (dec. Mar. 1985); children: Marjorie Rightor, Jane Pillow. AB, Harvard U., 1932; MD, Johns Hopkins U., 1936. Diplomate Am. Bd. Internal Medicine (exec. dir. 1967-75). Intern, then asst. resident and chief resident Johns Hopkins Hosp., 1936-39, 41; asst. resident Rockefeller Inst. Hosp., 1939-41; asst. prof. medicine Washington U., St. Louis, 1946-48; assoc. prof. medicine Johns Hopkins U., Balt., 1948-66, U. Pa., Phila., 1967-89, prof., 1989-94, asst. dean John Hopkins U. Sch. Medicine, 1959-62, dir. health svcs. med. instns., 1962-66. Physician in charge pvt. outpatient svc. Johns Hopkins Hosp., 1948-57. Author: Giants and Dwarfs, 1933; contbr. numerous articles to profl. jours. Comdr. M.C. USNR, 1941—46. Fellow Coll. Physicians Phila.; mem. Am. Soc. Clin. Investigation, Endocrine Soc., Am. Diabetes Assn., Am. Clin. and Climatol. Assn., Am. Osler Soc., World Federalist Assn., 14 West Hamilton St. Club (Balt.), Phi Beta Kappa. Democrat. Episcopalian. Avocations: tennis, golf, sailing, fishing, world peace affairs. Home: 13801 York Rd Apt D11 Cockeysville Hunt Valley MD 21030-1860

FUTRELL, JOHN WILLIAM, environmental agency executive, lawyer; b. Alexandria, La., July 6, 1935; s. J.W. and Sarah Ruth (Hitesman) F.; m. Iva Macdonald, Aug. 13, 1966; children: Sarah, Daniel. BA, Tulane U., 1957; postgrad., Free U. Berlin, 1958; LLB, Columbia U., 1965. Bar: La. 1966. Atty. Lemle & Kelleher, New Orleans, 1966-71; prof. law U. Ala., 1971-74, U. Ga., 1974-80; pres. Environ. Law Inst., Washington, 1980—. Lectr. USIA, Japan and India, 1978, Austria, 1979, Sweden, Germany, U.K. and Ireland, 1980, Argentina, 1988, Brazil, 1991, Mex., 1992, Germany and Chile, 1993, India, 1997, 2000; Woodrow Wilson fellow Smithsonian Instn., Washington, 1978-80. Co-author: Sustainable Environmental Law, 1993. Pres. Sierra Club, San Francisco, 1977-78, nat. bd. dirs., 1971-81; del. UN Conf. on Water, 1977, White House Conf. Inflation, 1974. Capt. USMC, 1957-62. Fulbright scholar, 1958 Mem.: AAAS, ABA, Am. Law Inst., Cosmos Club, Marines' Meml. Club, Phi Beta Kappa, Order of Coif. Home: 4600 7th St N Arlington VA 22203-2011 Office: Environ Law Inst 1616 P St NW Washington DC 20036-1434 E-mail: futrellfam@aol.com.

FUTROVSKY, CHERYL JEAN, foundation administrator, performing company executive; b. Santa Paula, Calif., Oct. 31, 1946; d. Ralph Vernon and Mary Emadee Mashburn; m. John Henry Ablard, Aug. 26, 1965 (div. Sept. 30, 1991); children: James Vernon Ablard, Tracie Jean Grant; m. Steven Henry Futrovsky, Jan. 22, 2000. Student, Ventura Jr. Coll., 1964—65, Ottawa U., 1965—66, U. Md., Eng., 1976—77, Mont. Coll., 1987—88. Cert. Notary Pub., Md., 1991-. Mgr. purchasing Choice Hotels Internat., Silver Spring, Md., 1978—83; mgr. office Audy Group, Inc., Silver Spring, 1985—91, Eric B. Cohen, P.C., Rockville, Md., 1992—93; events mgr., devel. assoc. Jewish Found. Group Homes, Inc., Rockville, 1993—. Bd. dirs. devel. com. Jewish Found. Group Homes, Inc., Rockville, 2001—, com. employee recognition, 2002—; cons. events Cmty. Svs. Autistic Adults and Children, Rockville, 2001—. Author, editor: newsletter Audy Group, 1987—91, Home Notes, 2001—02. Troop leader Boy Scouts Am., England, 1975—77, mem. coun., 1978—82; leader troop Girl Scouts Am., Silver Spring, 1978—83; organizer Desert Storm Benefit, Silver Spring, 1991; vol. United Jewish Fedn. Greater Wash., Rockville, 1993—; coord. United Way/CFC, Rockville, 2001—; mem. campaign staff Joel Chasnoff County Coun., Silver Spring, 1982, Isiah Leggett County Coun., Silver Spring, 1983; vol. Homeless Shelter Christ Congl. Ch., Silver Spring, 1981—83, Helping Hand, Silver Spring, 1985—87; facilitator Coop. Edn. Programs Mont. County Pub. Schs., Silver Spring, 1986—88; vol., tech. crew Burtonsville Cmty. Theatre, Md., 1988—89; creator, facilitator comparative religions Christ Congl., Silver Spring, 1981—82, developer lead travel program, 1983—85, creator, leader jr. ch., 1985—87; pres. Protestant Women Chapel, Germany, 1974—75. Recipient Cert. of Honor, European Congress Am. Parents and Tchrs., Frankfurt, Germany, 1975, Award of Excellence, Award of Excellence, Manor Care, Inc., Silver Spring, 1983. Mem.: Assn. Fundraising Profls. Democrat. Congregationalist. Avocations: golf, reading, travel, knitting. Office: Jewish Found Group Homes 6010 Executive Rd #800 Rockville MD 20852-3814 E-mail: cfutrovsky@jfgh.org.

FUTTER, ELLEN VICTORIA, museum administrator; b. N.Y.C., Sept. 21, 1949; d. Victor and Joan Babette (Feinberg) F.; children— Anne Victoria, Elizabeth Jane. Student, U. Wis., 1967-69; AB magna cum laude, Barnard Coll., 1971; JD, Columbia U., 1974, LLD (hon.), 1984, Hamilton Coll., 1985, N.Y. Law Sch.; DHL (hon.), Amherst Coll., Hofstra U., 1994, CCNY, 1996, L.I. City Coll., 1995, Yale U., 2000; DL, Columbia U. Bar: N.Y. 1975. Assoc. Milbank, Tweed, Hadley & McCloy, N.Y.C., 1974-80; acting pres. Barnard Coll., N.Y.C., 1980-81, pres., 1981-93, Am. Mus. Natural History, N.Y.C, 1993—. Bd. dirs. Bristol Myers Squibb, Am. Internat. Group, JP Morgan Chase, Consol. Edison of N.Y., Overseer Meml. Sloan Kettering Cancer Ctr., N.Y.; trustee Am. Mus. Natural History. Recipient L. Sachar award Brandeis U., Elizabeth Cutter Morrow, Distinction medal Barnard Coll., Excellence medal Columbia U., Gold medal award Nat. Inst. Social Scis., Legacy Conservation award Theodore Roosevelt Sanctuary, Visionary award New Vision in Pub. Sch. Mem. ABA, Am. Acad. Arts and Scis., N.Y. State Bar Assn., Assn. Bar City N.Y., Nat. Inst. Social Scis., Coun. Fgn. Rels., Cosmopolitan Club, Century Club, Phi Beta Kappa. Office: Am Mus Natural History Central Park West at 79th New York NY 10024

FUTTER, JOAN BABETTE, former school librarian; b. N.Y.C., Nov. 15, 1921; d. Samuel S. and Helen (Mosher) Feinberg; m. Victor Futter, Jan. 26, 1943; children: Jeffrey Leesam, Ellen Victoria, Deborah Gail Futter Cohan. AB, NYU, 1941; MS, L.I. U., 1966. Sch. libr. Carrie Palmer Weber Jr. High Sch., Port Washington, N.Y., 1966-91. Mem. LWV, AAUW, L.I. Sch. Media Assn., C.W. Post Libr. Assn., Cold Spring Harbor Beach Club, Manhasset Bay Yacht Club. Home: 17 Sunnyvale Rd Port Washington NY 11050-4519

FUTTER, VICTOR, lawyer; b. N.Y.C., Jan. 22, 1919; s. Leon Nathan and Merle Caroline (Allison) F.; m. Joan Babette Feinberg, Jan. 26, 1943; children: Jeffrey Leesam, Ellen Victoria Futter, Deborah Gail Futter Cohan. AB in Govt. and English with honors, Columbia U., 1939, JD, 1942. Bar: N.Y. 1942, U.S. Supreme Ct. 1948. Assoc. Sullivan & Cromwell, 1946-52; with Allied Corp. (now Honeywell Internat.), Morristown, N.J., 1952-84, assoc. gen. counsel, 1976-78, v.p., sec., 1978-84; dir. Allied Chem. Nuclear Products, 1977-84; gen. counsel, sec. to bd. trustees Fairleigh Dickinson U., 1984-85. Spl. prof. law Hofstra Law Sch., 1976-78, 88-89, 94—, spl. cons. to the dean, 1997—; lectr., seminar on corp. in modern soc. Columbia U. Law Sch., 1986-98. Editor: Columbia Law Rev.; editor-in-chief: Nonprofit Governance and Management, 2002; contbr. articles to profl. jours. Trustee, dep. mayor Village of Flower Hill, N.Y., 1974-76; mem. senate Columbia U., 1969-75; chmn. bd. Columbia Coll. Fund, 1970-72; pres. parents and friends com. Mt. Holyoke Coll., 1978-80; pres. Flower Hill Assn., 1968-70; bd. dirs. N.Y. Young Dems., 1948-52, Nat. Exec. Svc. Corps, 1997-2003, Soc. Columbia Grads., 1998-2003; co-chmn. fund drive Port Washington Cmty. Chest, 1965-66, bd. dirs., 1965-75; mem. coun. overseers C.W. Post, 1984-85; bd. dirs. Acad. Polit. Sci., 1986-94; bd. dirs. Greenwich House, 1985—, vice chair, 1999—; bd. dirs. Nat. Assn. Local Arts Agys.-Arts for Am., 1989-91, Am. Soc. Corp. Secs., 1987-90, pres. N.Y. chpt., 1983-84; chmn. Com. on Nonprofits, 1992-97; bd. dirs. Justice Resource Ctr., 1992-97; chair ad hoc Lunch Group for Nonprofits, 1993—. Maj. AUS. Recipient Alumni medal Columbia U., 1970, Disting. Svc. award Am. Soc. Corp. Secs., 1994; James Kent scholar. Fellow Am. Bar Found.; mem. ABA (coun. sr. lawyers divsn. 1989-97, chair 1995-96, chair editl. Bd. Experience, 1989-95, liaison to ABA CEELI program 1990-99, sec. on bus. law, corp. laws com., com. on non-profit corps., com. on corp. govs., sect. on internat. law and practice 1990—, bd. govs., program and planning com. 1999-2002), Assn. of Bar of City of N.Y. (com. on internat. human rights 1983-85, com. on 2d century 1985-89, sr. lawyers com. 1989-2002, chair 1992-95, nonprofit com. 1995-96, Disting. Svc. award Individual Mentor Program 1995), Am. Law Inst. (consultative group for restatement of law governing lawyers 1987-98, consultative group for prins. of non profit orgns.), Nat. Assn. Corp. Dirs. (pres. N.Y. chpt. 1988-89), Nat. Assn. Coll. Univ. Attys. (sec. on personal rels., tenure and retirement programs 1984-86), Am. Judicature Soc., N.Y. Lawyers Alliance for World Security, Columbia Coll. Alumni Assn. (pres. 1972-74, Pres.'s Cup award 1999), The Supreme Ct. Hist. Soc., Playwrights First, U.S. Lawn Tennis Assn., Am. Philatelic Soc., Univ. Club (coun. 1996-99, chair spl. events com. 1993-2000, chair club activities com. 1996-99), Manhasset Bay Yacht Club, Cold Spring Harbor Beach Club, Village Club of Sands Point (golf com. 1999-2000), Phi Beta Kappa. E-mail: vandjfut@optonline.net.

FUZESI, STEPHEN, JR., lawyer, communications executive; b. Budapest, Hungary, Hungary, Aug. 3, 1948;, naturalized, US, 1963; s. Stephen Sr and Marta Fuzesi; m. Nancy J Steinhardt, Apr. 5, 1975; children: Stephen Joseph, Timothy Roger. AB, Princeton U., 1970; JD, U. Pa., 1974. Bar: NY 1975, DC 1982. Atty. Davis, Polk & Wardwell, N.Y.C., 1974-82; ptnr./of counsel Reid & Riege, PC, Hartford, Conn., 1982-83; 1st. sr. v.p., gen. counsel and sec. Am. Savings Bank, FSB, N.Y.C., 1984-87; sr. v.p., gen. counsel, sec. Stamford Capital Group, Inc., 1987-90; of counsel White & Case, N.Y.C., 1990-94; v.p., sec., chief counsel Newsweek, N.Y.C., 1994—. Contbr. articles to profl jours, newspapers. Mem Coun Foreign Relations, NY, 1976—81, Am Coun Germany, 1977—80, Greenwich Bd Educ, Conn., 1987—91, Greenwich Dem Town Comt, Conn., 1985—94; cand 36th dist Conn State Senate, 1986; bd dirs Greenwich Soccer Asn, 1989—94. Recipient Keedy Law Rev Award, Univ Pa Law Sch, 1974. Mem.: Mgg. Pubs. Assn. (legal affairs comt 1994—, chmn bus affairs subcommittee 1995—99), Assn. Bar City N.Y. (comt int human rights 1979—81, banking law comt 1987—90, comt communications and media law 2002—). Office: Newsweek 251 W 57th St New York NY 10019-1802

FYE, W. BRUCE, III, cardiologist; b. Meadville, Pa., Sept. 25, 1946; s. W. Bruce Jr. and Anne Elizabeth (Schreck) F.; m. Lois Eileen Baker, May 10, 1969; children: Katherine Anne, Elizabeth Jane. AB, Johns Hopkins U., 1968, MD, 1972, MA in Med. History, 1978. Diplomate Am. Bd. Internal Medicine, Am. Bd. Cardiovascular Diseases. Intern N.Y. Hosp.—Cornell Med. Ctr., N.Y.C., 1972-73, asst. resident, 1973-74, sr. asst. resident, 1974-75, fellow cardiology, 1975; fellow in cardiology Johns Hopkins U. Sch. Medicine, Balt., 1975-77, postdoctoral fellow in med. history, 1976-78, instr. in medicine, 1977-78; dir. cardiographics lab. Marshfield (Wis.) Clinic, 1978-99, chmn. dept. cardiology, 1981-99, dir. noninvasive cardiology, 1999; assoc. prof. medicine Med. Coll. Wis., Milw., 1988-99; prof. medicine and history medicine Mayo Med. Sch., Rochester, Minn., 2000—. Vice chief of staff St. Joseph's Hosp., Marshfield, 1989-99, exec. com., bd. dirs., 1994-97; clin. prof. medicine, adj. prof. history medicine U. Wis., Madison, 1990—; sr. assoc. cons. Mayo Clinic, Rochester, 2000, cons., 2001—. Author: The Development of American Physiology, 1987; editor: William Osler's Collected Papers on the Cardiovascular System, 1985, Classic Papers on Coronary Thrombosis and Myocardial Infarction, 1991; editor-in-chief: Classics of Cardiology Library, 1985—; author: American Cardiology; The History of a Specialty and Its College, 1996; mem. editl. bd. Marshfield Med. Bull., 1985-95, Am. Jour. Cardiology, 1990—, Clin. Cardiology, 1994—. Fellow Am. Coll. Cardiology (chmn. libr. com. 1991, historian 1991—, gov. Wis. chpt. 1993-96, steering com. bd. govs., 1994—, nominating com., 1994-96, chair govt. rels. com. 1996-99, trustee 1997—, v.p. 1999—, pres. 2002—); mem. Am. Assn. for History of Medicine (program chair 1987), State Med. Soc. Wis. (alt. del. 1990-94), Am. Hist. Assn., Am. Osler Soc. (pres. 1988-89), Am. Heart Assn. (exec. com. coun. on clin. cardiology 1991-97, chmn. membership com. coun. on clin. cardiology 1994-97, chair credentials com. coun. on clin. cardiology 1994-97), Inst. for Study of Cardiovascular Medicine (bd. dirs. 1994—), Phi Beta Kappa, Alpha Omega Alpha, Grolier Club. Presbyterian. Avocation: collecting and selling antiquarian medical books. Home: 1533 Seasons Ln SW Rochester MN 55902 Office: Mayo Clinic 200 1st St SW Rochester MN 55905-0002 Office Fax: 507-284-3968. E-mail: fye.bruce@mayo.edu.

FYFE, DORIS MAE, elementary school educator; b. Shelby, Nebr., Sept. 5, 1930; d. Harold William Fyfe and Mae Emma Schmid. Assoc. in Elem. Edn., Scottsbluff Jr. Coll., Nebr., 1957; BS in Elem. Edn., Peru State Tchrs. Coll., Nebr., 1963; M in Urban Edn., U. Nebr., Omaha, 1980. Cert. K-12 tchr. Nebr. Tchr. K-8, Polk County Schs., Shelby, 1947—50, Banner County Schs., Harrisburg, Nebr., 1950—53; tchr. 2d grade Albin Consol. Schs., Albin, Wyo., 1953—57; prin., tchr. K-2, Union Pub. Schs., Nebr., 1957—61; tchr. 2d grade Nebraska City Pub. Schs., Nebr., 1961—63; intermediate tchr. Omaha Pub. Schs., 1963—90, substitute tchr., 1990—; adj. faculty Grace U., Omaha, 1984—. 4-H leader Agr. Coll. Ext. Svc. Polk County, 1947—50; vol. tutor Uta Halee Girls' Village, Omaha, 1995—; active Harvey Oaks Bapt. Ch., 1962—; dir. Midway Bible Camp, Thompson, Canada, 1970—90. Mem.: Omaha Area Ret. Tchrs. Assn., Olympian Club. Republican. Avocations: philately, doll collecting, pencil collecting. Home: 6222 Ponderosa Dr Omaha NE 68137-4231

FYFE, WILLIAM SEFTON, geochemist, educator; b. New Zealand, June 4, 1927; s. Colin Alexander and Isabella Fyfe; m. Patricia Walker, Feb. 27, 1981; children: Christopher, Catherine, Stefan. BSc, U. Otago, New Zealand, 1948, MS, 1949, PhD, 1952; DSc (hon.), Meml. U., Lisbon, Portugal, 1989, 90, Lakehead U., 1992, Guelph U., 1994, St. Mary's U., Otago, New Zealand, 1994, Otago U., New Zealand, 1995, U. Western Ont., 1995. Prof. chemistry in, N.Z., 1955-58; prof. geology U. Calif., Berkeley, 1958-66; research prof. Manchester U. and Imperial Coll., London, 1966-72; chmn. dept. geology Western Ont. U., 1972-84, prof. dept. geology, 1984-92, prof. emeritus dept. earth sci., 1992—, dean faculty sci., 1986-90. Decorated companion Order of Can.; Commemorative medal (New Zealand), Commemorative medal (Canada); recipient Logan medal Geol. Assn. Can., Arthur Holmes medal European Union of Geoscis., Can. Gold medal for Sci. and Engring., 1991; Guggenheim fellow, 1964, 83; named hon. prof. U. Beijing. Fellow Geol. Soc. London (hon.; Wollaston medal 2000), Royal Soc. London, Geol. Soc. Am. (hon. life, Day medal), Mineral Soc. Am. (Roebling medal); mem. AAAS (chmn. geology geography sect. 2000—), Internat. Union Geoscis. (pres. 1992-96, Grand Cross Ordem Nacional do Merito Cientifico, Brazil, 1996), Nat. Sci. and Engring. Rsch. Coun. Can., Royal Soc. Can., Acad. Sci. Brazil, Brit. Chem. Soc., Russian Acad. Sci., Indian Acad. Sci., Chinese Acad. Sci. Home: 1197 Richmond London ON Canada N6A 3L3 Office: U Western Ont Dept Earth Scis London ON Canada N6A 5B7 Fax: 519-661-2179. E-mail: pjfyfe@uwo.ca.

FYLER, CARL JOHN, dentist; b. Spearville, Kans., May 14, 1921; s. John Henry and Helen Elsie (Parthie) F.; m. Marguerite E. Burris, Feb. 14, 1946. DDS, U. Mo., Kansas City, 1950. Practice dentistry, Topeka, Kans., 1950-92; ret., 1992. Author: Staying Alive. Served to maj. USAF, 1942-46, ETO. Decorated Purple Heart, Silver Star, 4 Air Medals, D.F.C., Prisoner of War medal. Mem. ADA (life), Kans. Dental Assn., Shawnee County Dental Assn., Internat. Fedn. Dentists, Am. Ex-Prisoners of War (nat. dir. 1974-85, nat. jr. vice comdr. 1984-85), Kans. Ex-Prisoners of War (Gov.'s adv. com. 1978-86), 303d H.B.G. Assn. (pres. 1987-89), Eighth Air Force Hist. Soc. (bd. dirs. 1989-92, heavy bomb group), Mil. Order of World Wars (pres. Topeka chpt. 1996—), Distinguished Flying Cross Soc., Am. Legion, D.A.V., Am. Vets. Republican. Presbyterian. Avocations: flying, lapidary, rock hunting. Home: 300 SW Yorkshire Rd Topeka KS 66606-2260

FYLER, JOHN MORGAN, English language educator; b. Chgo., Sept. 17, 1943; s. Earl Harris and Harriet (Morgan) F.; m. Julia Ann Genster, Aug. 5, 1978; children: Amanda, Lucy. AB, Dartmouth Coll., 1965; MA, U. Calif., Berkeley, 1967, PhD, 1972. Asst. prof. Tufts U., Medford, Mass., 1972-78, assoc. prof., 1978-88, prof., 1988—. Author: Chaucer and Ovid, 1979; contbg. editor: Riverside Chaucer, 1986. ACLS fellow, 1975-76, Guggenheim fellow, 1982-83, Camargo Found. fellow, 2002; fellow Clare Hall, U. Cambridge, 2003. Home: 126 Central St Concord MA 01742-2911 Office: Dept English Tufts U Medford MA 02155 E-mail: john.fyler@tufts.edu.

GAAB, JEFFERY S. history educator; b. New York, Mar. 22, 1963; BA History, Hofstra U., Hempstead, NY., 1985; MA History, SUNY, Stony Brook, NY., 1987, PhD. History, 1992. Instr. SUNY, Farmingdale, NY, 1991—92, asst. prof., 1992—2000, assoc. prof. Farmingdale, NY, 2000—; adj. prof. history Hofstra U., Hempstead, NY, 1997—. Author: Justice Delayed, 1999. Office: History Dept Farmingdale State U Rt 110 Farmingdale NY 11735 Business E-Mail: Gaabjs@farmingdale.edu.

GAADT, SUZANNE DEMOTT, graphic designer; b. Phila., Apr. 13, 1965; d. Evard O. and Anne (Stevens) DeMott; m. John Michael Gaadt, Apr. 4, 1992, children: Giulia, Ian. BFA cum laude, Temple U., 1987. Graphic designer Bailey/Spiker Inc., Phila., 1987-89; art dir. Ardmoor Corp., Chadds Ford, Pa., 1989-90; publ. dir. Brandywine River Mus., Chadds Ford, 1990-93; ptnr. Gaadt Perspectives, LLC, Chadds Ford, Pa., 1993—. Designer publs. and materials Winterthur Mus., Garden and Libr., Swarthmore Coll., Chester County Hist. Soc. Mem. Am. Inst. Graphic Artists, Am. Assn. Mus., Univ. and Coll. Designers Assn., Greater West Chester C. of C., Art Dirs. Club. Democrat. Roman Catholic. Avocations: reading, writing, travel, music, arts. Home: 251 Fairville Rd Chadds Ford PA 19317-9438

GAAL, JOHN, lawyer; b. Flushing, N.Y., Oct. 10, 1952; s. Stephen Alfred and Marjorie (Lappin) G.; m. Barbara Jeanne Zacher, Aug. 5, 1973; children: Bryan A., Adam C., Benjamin Z. BA cum laude, U. Notre Dame, 1974, JD magna cum laude, 1977. Bar: N.Y. 1978, U.S. Ct. Appeals (D.C. cir.) 1978, U.S. Dist. Ct. (no. dist.) N.Y. 1979, U.S. Supreme Ct. 1986. Law clk. to judge U.S. Ct. Appeals (D.C. cir.), Washington, 1977-78; assoc. Bond, Schoeneck & King, Syracuse, N.Y., 1978-85, ptnr., 1986—. Bd. dirs. Legal Svcs. of Ctrl. N.Y., Syracuse, 1981-87, 94-2000, pres. 1999-2000—; adj. prof. Sch. of Mgmt., Syracuse U., 1989-92, Coll. of Law, 2001. Editor: Senior Citizens Handbook, 1988; contbg. author: Public Sector Labor and Employment Law, 1988; co-chair editl. bd. Jour. Coll. and Univ. Law, 2000-02; columnist The Bus. Jour., 1998-2000; mem. bd. advs. N.Y. Employment Law Practice Newsletter, 2001-; contbr. articles to profl. publs. Bd. dirs. Transitional Living Svcs., 2001—. Fellow Am. Bar Found.; mem. ABA (labor and employment law sect.), N.Y. State Bar Assn. (exec. com. labor and employment law sect., chair young lawyer sect. 1989-90, spl. com. on AIDS and the law 1988, spl. com. on mandatory pro bono svc. 1989, ho. of dels. 1987-89, 90-91, co-chair adhoc com. ethics 1999—). Democrat. Roman Catholic. Home: 8006 Austrian Pine Cir Manlius NY 13104- Office: Bond Schoeneck & King 1 Lincoln Ctr Fl 18 Syracuse NY 13202-1324 E-mail: jgaal@bsk.com.

GAAL, VIOLETTA, retired social worker, massage therapist; b. Bucharest, Romania, May 1, 1931; came to the U.S., 1957; d. Gábor and Rozália (Turzai) G.; m. Alex Balogh, Sept. 14, 1953 (div. May 1965); 1 child, Gábor. BA, Sacramento State U., 1962. Cert. social worker, Calif.; cert. massage therapy, Calif. Adminstr. State Planning Bur., Budapest, Hungary, 1950-54; stock clk.

Ladies Dress Shop, Sacramento, Calif., 1957-61; social worker Welfare Dept., Sacramento, 1963-65, Oakland, Calif., 1965-80; pvt. practice massage therapist San Francisco, 1986—. Mil. contractor, watch-clock repair, 1978-81. Author: Spiral; Translator: Idegen a Királyok Völgyében, 1993, Jézus Misztikus élete, 1993, The Boys of Pal Street, 1994, Fehér Sierrak, 1994. Republican. Avocations: watercolor, ceramics. Home: 4099 Howe St Apt 101 Oakland CA 94611-5204

GAAR, MARILYN AUDREY WIEGRAFFE, political scientist, educator, property manager; b. St. Louis, Sept. 22, 1946; d. Arthur and Marjorie Estelle (Miller) W.; m. Norman E. Gaar, Apr. 12, 1986. AB, Ind. U., 1968, MA, 1970, MS, 1973. Mem. faculty Stephens Coll., Columbia, Mo., 1971-73, Johnson County CC, Overland Park, Kans., 1973—. Interviewer Fulbright Hayes Tchr. Exch. fellowship candidates, Kansas City, Mo., 1982-92; mem. state selection com. Congress Bundestag Youth Exch. Program, Kans., 1985; pres. faculty del. Kans. Assn. C.C.s, 1984-85; gov.'s appointee, admissions interviewer, mem. selection panel Sch. Medicine U. Kans., 1991-95, mem. admissions criteria and admissions process rev. com., 1992. Author: Profile of Kansas Government, 1990; contbg. editor to instr.'s manual Am. Democracy (by Thomas Patterson). Pres. LWV Johnson County, 1987—89, prodr. candidates forum, mem. governing bd., 1993—95; mem. Johnson County Elder Net Coalition, 1988; mem. governing bd. Johnson County Mental Health Ctr., 1981—86, chmn., 1985—86; vol., translator Russian Refugee Resettlement Program of Jewish Family and Children Svcs., Kansas City, 1979—81; treas. Heart of Am., Japan Am. Soc., 1979; hon. dir. Rockhurst Coll., Kansas City; sec. Ctrl. Slavic Conf., 2000—; alt. mem. Rep. State Com., Kans., 1984—86; chmn. Rep. City Com., Shawnee, Kans., 1982—86; program chmn. Kans. Fedn. Rep. Women, 1984—87; bd. dirs. Internat. Rels. Coun. Kansas City, 2001—, Substance Abuse Ctr., Johnson County, 1983—85, Huntington Farms Homes Assn., Leawood, Kans., 1984—87. Grantee Europaische Akademie, West Berlin, 1984, 92, 97, Fulbright Hayes, The Netherlands, 1982, Japan, 1975; Univ. fellow NEH, 1990; Scholars in Residence grant, Johnson County C.C., 1998, 1999, 2001, 2003. Mem. Russian and Am. Internat. Studies Assn. (sec. 1999—), C.C. Humanities Assn., Kans. Polit. Sci. Assn., Internat. Rels. Coun., Assn. Russian and Am. Historians (sec. 1998-99), Ctrl. ASsn. Russian Tchrs. Am. (bd. dirs. 2003—), People to People, Soc. Fellows, Nelson-Atkins Mus. Arts, Dobro Slovo Nat. Slavic Honor Soc., Phi Beta Kappa, Phi Sigma Alpha. Episcopalian. Avocations: piano, gardening. Office: Johnson County C C 12345 College Blvd Shawnee Mission KS 66210-1283

GAAR, NORMAN EDWARD, lawyer, former state senator; b. Kansas City, Mo., Sept. 29, 1929; s. William Edward and Lola Eugene (McKain) G.; children: Anne, James, William, John; m. Marilyn A. Wiegraffe, Apr. 12, 1986. Student, Baker U., 1947-49; AB, U. Mich., 1955, JD, 1956. Bar: Mo. 1957, Kans. 1962, U.S. Supreme Ct. 1969. Assoc. Stinson, Mag, Thomson, McEvers & Fizzell, Kansas City, 1956-59; ptnr. Stinson, Mag & Fizzell, Kansas City, 1959-79; mng. ptnr. Gaar & Bell, Kansas City, St. Louis, Overland Park, Wichita, Kans., 1979-87; ptnr. Burke, Williams, Sorensen & Gaar, Overland Park, L.A., Camarillo, Fresno, Costa Mesa, Calif., 1987-96; shareholder McDowell, Rice, Smith & Gaar, Overland Park, 1996—. Mem. Kans. Senate, 1965-84, majority leader, 1976-80; faculty N.Y. Practising Law Inst., 1969-74; adv. dir. Panel Pubs., Inc., N.Y.C. Mcpl. judge City of Westwood, Kans., 1959-63, mayor, 1963-65. With USN, 1949-53. Decorated Air medal (2); named State of Kans. Disting. Citizen, 1962. Fellow Am. coll. Bd. Coun.; mem. ABA, Am. Radio Relay League, Nat. Assn. Bond Lawyers, Calif. Assn. Bond Lawyers (charter), Russian-Am. Internat. Studies Assn. (dir. 2000--), Flying Midshipmen Assn., Assn. Naval Aviators, Tailhook Assn., Antique Airplane Assn., Exptl. Aircraft Assn., People to People. Republican. Episcopalian. Office: 7101 College Blvd Ste 200 40 Executive Hills Shawnee Mission KS 66210-1891 E-mail: ngaar@earthlink.net., ng@mrsg.com.

GABARRA, CARIN LESLIE, professional soccer player, professional soccer coach; b. East Orange, N.J., Jan. 9, 1965; m. Jim Gabarra. Degree in bus. mgmt., U. Calif., Santa Barbara, 1987. Mem. U.S. Nat. Women's Soccer Team, 1987—96; head coach, women's soccer Westmont Coll., 1987—88; assist. coach, women's soccer Harvard U., Boston, 1988—93; head coach, women's soccer Navy, 1993—. Mem. U.S. Olympic World Festival team, 1986—89; mem. women's soccer U.S. Naval Acad., 1993. Named U.S. Soccer's Female Athlete of Yr., 1987, 1992; named to, U. Calif.-Santa Barbara Athletic Hall of Fame; recipient Golden Ball, FIFA Women's World Championship, China, 1991, gold medal, Atlanta Summer Olympic Games, 1996. Achievements include ranked as 3d-leading goal scorer in U.S. women's history; mem. CONCACAF Championship team, 1993, 94. Office: c/o US Soccer Fedn 1801 S Prairie Ave # 1811 Chicago IL 60616-1319

GABASHVILI, IRENE, biophysicist; b. Sochi, USSR, Nov. 14, 1967; d. Sergo and Ludmila Gabashvili. BS equivalent, Tbilisi State U., Georgia, USSR, 1987, MS equivalent, 1989; PhD equivalent, Inst. Physics, Acad. Scis., Tbilisi, 1992. Scientific rschr., lab. math. modeling and expert systems Ctr. Genetic Ecology, Tbilisi, Georgia, 1992-93, sr. rschr., 1993, head of Lab. for Med. and Biol. Problems, 1994-95; vis. scientist Ctr. Photobiophys. Rsch., U. Que., Trois-Rivieres, Que., Can., 1995; postdoctoral fellow U. Tex. Health Sci. Ctr., San Antonio, 1995-97; rsch. affiliate Wadsworth Ctr., State Dept. Health, Albany, N.Y., 1997-98, rsch. scientist, 1998-2001; rsch. fellow Med. Dept., Stanford (Calif.) U., 2001—03; tech. lead comp. bioscis. group Hewlett-Packard Lab., 2001—03. Contbr. articles to profl. jours., chpts. to books. Mem.: IEEE, Quantitative Structure-Activity Relationships and Molecular Modelling Soc., Biophys. Soc., Am. Med. Informatics Assn. Office: HP Labs 1501 Page Mill Rd Palo Alto CA 94304 E-mail: igabashvili@yahoo.com.

GABAY, DONALD DAVID, lawyer; b. Bklyn., Apr. 1935; s. Harry I. and Rachel Gabay. BBA, CCNY, 1956; LLB, Bklyn. Law Sch., 1961. Bar: N.Y. 1962. Pvt. practice law, N.Y.C., 1962-75; chief counsel N.Y. State Assembly Com. on Ins., Albany, 1975-78; 1st dep. supt. N.Y. State Ins. Dept., N.Y.C., 1978-84; ptnr. Stroock & Stroock & Lavan, LLP, N.Y.C., 1984—. Pres. Ins. Fedn. N.Y., 1994-98, 99—, chmn. Served with U.S. Army, 1956-58. Named Ins. Man of Yr., Ind. Ins. Brokers Assn., 1973; recipient Pub. Service award Bklyn. Ins. Brokers Assn., 1977, ann. achievement award Council Ins. Brokers, 1981, Outstanding Achievement award CCNY Alumni Assn., 1981, Pub. Service award Ind. Ins. Agts. Assn., 1984, Torch of Liberty award ins. div. Anti-Defamation League, 1984. Office: Stroock Stroock & Lavan LLP 180 Maiden Ln New York NY 10038-4925 E-mail: dgabay@stroock.com.

GABAY, ELEONORA V. mechanical engineer, educator; b. Leningrad, Russia, Apr. 20, 1938; arrived in US, 1991; d. Victor N. and Antonina V. Gabay; m. Natan A. Kogan, May 27, 1961; 1 child, Leon N. Kogan. BS in Mech. Engring., U. Cinema Engring., St. Petersburg, 1959, MS in Mech. Engring. (with hons.), 1961. Author: (tchrs.' tool) FeedBack Cards (Diploma of All-Union contest on instrnl. tools, 1986), (instrnl. tool) Hands-on COLORIDE workbooks, 1999. Coord. Russian Leadership Com., Edison, NJ, 2001—03. Achievements include patents for Workbook with movable colored tabs. Home: 1412 Stone Ridge Cir Helmetta NJ 08828 Home Fax: 732-605-0956. Personal E-mail: nevka@comcast.net.

GABBARD, DOUGLAS, II, (JAMES GABBARD), judge; b. Lindsay, Okla., Mar. 27, 1952; s. James Douglas and Mona Dean (Dodd) G.; m. Connie Sue Mace, Dec. 30, 1977 (div. Feb. 1979); m. Robyn Marie Kohlhaas, June 18, 1981 (div. Aug. 2003); children: Resa Marie, David Ryan, James Douglas III, Michael Drew. BS, Okla. U., 1974, JD, 1977; grad., Nat. Jud. Coll., 1987, U. Kans. Law Orgnl. Econs., 1997. Bar: Okla. 1978. Ptnr. Stubblefeild & Gabbard, Atoka, Okla., 1978; sole practice Atoka, 1979; asst. dist. atty. State of Okla., Atoka, 1979-82, 1st asst. dist. atty. Atoka, Durant and Coalgate, 1982-85; dist. judge 25th Jud. Dist. State of Okla., Atoka and Coalgate, 1985—; presiding judge South East Adminstrn. Dist., Okla., 1992—, State Ct. Tax Review, Okla., 1992—. Presiding judge of emergency panel of State Ct. Criminal Appeals, State Ct. on Judiciary Trial divsn., 1997—, vice-presiding judge 2003—; mem. Supreme Ct. Com. on Civil Jury Instructions, 2002—; dir. Okla. Trial Judges Assn., 1996-; mcpl. judge City of Atoka, 1978-79; chmn. Chickasaw Nation Ethics Commn., 2003—. Mem. Bryan County/Durant Arbitration Com., 1984; negotiator Bryan Meml. Hosp. Bd., Durant, 1984-85. Mem. Okla. Bar Assn. (legal ethics com. 1988-90, jud. adminstrv. com. 1988-90, resolutions com., 1998, long range planning com., bench and bar com. 1999), Okla. Jud. Conf., Am. Judges Assn., Masons. Democrat. Methodist. Avocations: painting, carpentry, reading. Home: 1401 S Walker Dr Atoka OK 74525-3611 Office: County Ct House Atoka OK 74525

GABBARD, GLEN OWENS, psychiatrist, psychoanalyst; b. Charleston, Ill., Aug. 8, 1949; s. Earnest Glendon and Lucina Mildred (Paquet) G.; children: Matthew, Abigail, Amanda, Allison; m. Joyce Eileen Davidson, June 14, 1985. BS, Eastern Ill. U., 1972; MD, Rush Med. Coll., 1975; degree in psychoanalytic tng., Topeka Inst. for Psychoanalysis, 1984. Diplomate Am. Bd. Psychiatry and Neurology. Resident in psychiatry Menninger Sch. Psychiatry, Topeka, 1975-78, mem. faculty, 1978—; staff psychiatrist C.F. Menninger Hosp., Topeka, 1978-83, sect. chief, 1984-89. Med. dir., 1989-94; tng. analyst Topeka Inst. for Psychoanalysis, 1989-2001, dir., 1996-2001; v.p. for adult svcs. Menninger Clinic, 1991-94; clin. prof. psychiatry U. Kans. Med. Sch., 1991-2001; Callaway Disting. prof. Menninger Clinic and Karl Menninger Sch. Psychiatry, 1994-2001; prof. psychiatry Baylor Coll. Medicine, 2001—, Brown Found. chair psychoanalysis, 2003—. Author: With the Eyes of the Mind, 1984, Psychiatry and the Cinema, 1987, 2d edit., 1999, Medical Marriages, 1988, Sexual Exploitation in Professional Relationships, 1989, Psychodynamic Psychiatry in Clinical Practice, 1990, Portuguese transl., 1992, Italian transl., 1992, 2d edit., 1994, Korean transl., 1996, Japanese transl., 1997, 3rd edit., 2000, Treatments of Psychiatric Disorders: the DSM-IV Edition, 1995; meml. editl. bd. Am. Jour. Psychiatry, Am. Psychiat. Press; joint editor-in-chief Internat. Jour. Psychoanalysis; contbr. articles to profl. jours. V.p. Topeka Civic Theatre, 1981-82, pres. 1982-83, bd. dirs. 1981-83. Named one of Outstanding Young Men in Am. U.S. Jaycees, 1984. Mem. AAAS, Am. Psychoanalytic Assn. (assoc. editor jour., mem. editl. bd.), Am. Psychiat. Assn. (Falk fellow 1976, Edward A. Strecker award 1994, Disting. Psychiatrist lectr. 1995, C. Charles Burlingame award 1997, Mary S. Sigourney award 2000, Disting. Svc. award 2002), Sch. Psychotherapy Rsch., Menninger Sch. Psychiatry Alumni Assn. (pres. 1982-83), Alpha Omega Alpha. Avocations: theater, music. Home: 1290 Jimmy Phillips Blvd Angleton TX 77515 Office: Dept Psychiatry Baylor Coll Medicine One Baylor Plz MS 350 Houston TX 77030

GABBAY, ROBERT ABRAHAM, physician, educator; b. N.Y.C., Dec. 24, 1957; s. Harry and Rachel G.; 1 child, Juliana. BA, McGill U., 1978; PhD, U. Wis., 1985; MD, SUNY, Bklyn., 1990. Chief resident N.Y. Downtown Hosp N.Y.C., 1994—95; assoc. physician Rockefeller U., N.Y.C., 1994-95; resident Cornell U. Med. Ctr., N.Y.C., 1997—98; instr. Harvard Med. Sch., Boston, 1998—99; dir. diabetes program Pa. State Coll. of Medicine, Hershey, 1999—; assoc. prof. Pa. State Coll. Medicine, Hershey, 2001—. Harvard Med. Sch. fellow, 1995-97. Office: Pa State Coll of Medicine Milton S Hershey Med Ctr Sect Endocrine Diabetes Hershey PA 17033

GABBE, STEVEN GLENN G. dean, obstetrician, gynecologist, educator; b. Newark, Dec. 1, 1944; s. Charles Paul and Marcia May Gabbe; m. Jessica Gabbe, June 26, 1966 (div. 1980); children: Amanda, Daniel; m. Patricia Temple, July 26, 1981. BA, Princeton U., 1965; MD, Cornell U., 1969; MA (hon.), U. Pa., 1983. Diplomate Am. Bd. Ob-Gyn (examiner 1980—), Am. Bd. Maternal-Fetal Medicine (examiner 1979-89). Intern in medicine N.Y. Hosp., N.Y.C., 1969-70; rsch. fellow reproductive medicine Boston Hosp. for Women, 1970-71, resident in ob-gyn, 1972-74; rsch. fellow in biol. chemistry Harvard Med. Sch., Boston, 1970-71, clin. fellow ob-gyn., 1972-74; asst. prof. ob-gyn U. So. Calif., L.A., 1975-77; assoc. prof. U. Colo. Sch. Medicine, Denver, 1977-78; assoc. prof. ob-gyn. and pediatrics U. Pa. Sch. Medicine, Phila., 1978-87, prof. radiology, 1987; mem. staff Hosp. of U. Pa., Phila., 1978-87, dir. Jerrold R. Golding divsn. fetal medicine, 1978-87, mem. med. bd. and numerous coms., 1984-87; prof. U. Pa. Sch. Nursing, Phila., 1982-87; prof., chmn. dept. ob-gyn Ohio State U. Coll. Medicine, Columbus, 1987-96; prof., chmn. dept. ob/gyn. U. Wash. Sch. Medicine, Seattle, 1996—2001; dir. Jerrold R. Golding divsn. fetal medicine Hosp. of U. Pa., Phila., 1978-87, mem. med. bd. and numerous coms., 1984-87; dean Sch. of Medicine Vanderbilt U., Nashville, 2001—. Vis. prof. ob-gyn King's Coll. Hosp., London, 1985-86; dir. maternal and infant care program Phila. Dept. Health, Disease Prevention and Health Promotion, 1982-87; mem. maternal and infant care adv. coun. Dept. Pub. Health, Phila., 1983-87; mem. subcom. on pregnancy and weight gain NRC, NAS, 1981; mem. internat. sci. bd. Reproductive Toxicology Ctr., 1984—; bd. dirs., med. adv. bd. Diabetes Treatment Ctrs. Am., 1984, others; mem. Coun. Univ Chairs of Ob-Gyn., 1996—; chair Maternal Fetal Medicine Rsch. Network Nat. Inst. Child and Human Devel. Author: Clinical Obstetrics and Gynecology: Diabetes and Pregnancy, 1985, Clinical Obstetrics and Gynecology: Obstetric Ultrasound Update, 1988; (with J.R. Niebyl and J.L. Simpson) Obstetrics: Normal and Problem Pregnancies, 1986, 2d edit., 1991; contbr. numerous articles to profl. jours. and chpts. to books; editor i chief Am. Jour. Perinatology, 1983—; mem. numerous editorial bds. Mem. Pa. Diabetes Task Force, 1981-87, Ohio Diabetes Task Force, 1987—; bd. dirs. UNITE, Jeanes Hosp., 1980-87. Recipient Sr. Resident's award for Excellence in Tng., L.A. County Women's Hosp., 1976, Disting. Tchr. award from Graduating Class, U. Wash., 1999; grantee Juvenile Diabetes Found., 1981, HHS, 1984, 1985, Diabetes Treatment Ctrs. Am., 1986. Fellow Am. Coll. Obstetricians and Gynecologists (mem. PROLOG self assessment program task force 1981-82, chmn. 1986, mem. PROLOG subcom. 1986—); mem. Am. Gynecol. and Obstet. Soc., Am. Inst. Ultrasound in Medicine, Perinatal Rsch. Soc., Soc. Gynecologic Investigation, Soc. Perinatal Obstetricians (v.p. 1986, pres. 1987-88, bd. dirs. 1983-88, chmn. credentials, constn. and by-laws com. 1983-87), Am. Diabetes Assn. (mem. nat. rsch. bd. 1981-83, chmn. coun. on diabetes in pregnancy 1985, com. on food and nutrition 1976-80), Juvenile Diabetes Found. (mem. med. sci. rev. com., med. sci. adv. bd. 1981-83), Phila. Neonatal Soc., Obstet. Soc. Phila. (program chmn. 1986-87), Phila. Perinatal Soc. (pres. 1982-84), Columbus Ob-Gyn Soc., Pa. Diabetes Acad. (acad. steering com. 1986—, editorial rev. com. 1986—), Union League (Phila.), Phi Beta Kappa, Alpha Omega Alpha. Avocations: sports, running. Office: Vanerbilt U Sch of Medicine 21st Ave South at Garland Ave Nashville TN 37232 E-mail: steven.gabbe@mcmail.vanderbilt.edu.

GABBOUR, ISKANDAR, city and regional planning educator; b. Mansura, Egypt, Feb. 6, 1929; s. Iskandar Gabbour and Mathilde Louli; m. Amy Surur, Feb. 4, 1956; children: May, Tamer, Rami. B.Arch. with honors, Cairo U., 1953; M.Arch., M.C.P., U. Pa., 1963, PhD, 1967. Arch., chief designer Devel. & Popular Housing Co., Cairo, 1954-61; rschr. assoc. U. Pa., Phila., 1966-67; prof. city and regional planning U. Montreal, Que., Can., 1967-97, vice dean acad. affairs, faculty environ. design, 1993—97, hon. prof., 1997—, interim chmn. dept. landscape architecture, 2000—02. Cons. UN Ctr. for Human Settlements, Nairobi, Kenya, 1985; vol. advisor Tech. Studies and Devel. Office, Abidjan, Ivory Coast, 1998. Contbr. numerous articles to profl. jours. Mem. Am. Planning Assn. (charter), Am. Inst. Cert. Planners (charter), Can. Inst. Planners, Royal Archtl. Inst. Can., Assn. Collegiate Schs. Planning, Order Urbanists of Que. Home: 5510 Ashdale Ave Montreal QC Canada H4W 3G4 Fax: (514) 484-8245. E-mail: iskandar.gabbour@umontreal.ca.

GABEL, CONNIE, chemist, educator; b. Green Bank, W.Va. d. William Ashby and Marie Lowry; m. Richard Gabel; children: Greg, Keith, Debbie. BS in Chemistry magna cum laude, James Madison U.; MA in Ednl. Adminstrn. summa cum laude, U. Colo., 1984, PhD in Ednl. Leadership and Innovation, 2001. Tchg. asst. U. Wis., Madison, 1969-70, specialist endocrinology, 1970-71; tchr. Dept. Def. Schs., Tokyo, 1972-74, Poudre R-1 Schs., Ft. Collins, Colo., 1975-78, Boulder (Colo.) Valley Schs., 1985-87, 96-98, intern asst. prin., 1984-85; intern supt. Jefferson County Schs., Golden, Colo., 1992; tchr. Mapleton Pub. Schs., Thornton, Colo., 1992-95; internat. studies Egyptian program Regis U., Denver, 1994; instr. chemistry Colo. Sch. Mines, 1995-98; dean students Horizon HS, Thornton, Colo., 1995-96; project 2061 coord. dept. chemistry/edn. U. Colo., Denver, 1998-2000; instr. St. Mary's Acad., Englewood, Colo., 2000—. Cons. sch. fin. Colo. Dept. Edn., Denver, 1984; rschr. AMC Cancer Rsch. Ctr., Denver, 1993, Colo. U. Med. Ctr., Denver, 1994; display tech. Boulder-Chemistry Rsch., 1995. Charter mem., pres. Friends Louisville (Colo.) Libr., 1985—; charter mem. Nat. Women's History Mus.; charter mem., pres., v.p. Coal Creek Rep. Women, Louisville, 1987—; sec., mem. Boulder County Reps., 1988—98, precinct chair; mem. Nat. Rep. Women, Washington, 1987—; sec. Dist. 17 Colo. Senate, Dist. 13 Colo. Ho., 1993—2002; mem. Colo. Fedn. Rep. Women, 1987—, Colo. Rep. Ctrl. Com. Mem.: AAUW, AAAS, ASCD, N.Y. Acad. Scis., Math., Engring. and Sci. Achievement (dir., advisor 1992—97, mem. state level adv. bd. 1992—96), Colo. Chemistry Tchrs. Assn., Colo.-Wyo. Acad. Sci., Colo. Assn. Sci. Tchrs., Nat. Soc. Study Edn., Nat. Assn. Rsch. Sci. Tchg., Am. Chem. Soc., Nat. Assn. Sci. Tchrs., Am. Ednl. Rsch. Assn., Phi Delta Kappa. Avocations: reading, hiking, gardening. Office: St Marys Academy 4545 S University Blvd Englewood CO 80110-6099 E-mail: connie_gabel@ceo.cudenver.edu.

GABEL, CREIGHTON, retired anthropologist, educator; b. Muskegon, Mich., Apr. 5, 1931; s. Kenneth Alonzo and Edith Myrtle (Creighton) G.; m. Jane Whitfield, Sept. 6, 1952; children: James, Anne, Molly. BA, U. Mich., 1953, MA, 1954; PhD, U. Edinburgh, Scotland, 1957. Instr. Northwestern U., 1956-58, asst. prof., 1958-63; asso. prof. Boston U., 1963-69, prof., 1969-96, prof. emeritus, 1996—; research assoc. Boston U. African Studies Center, 1963-96, chmn. anthropology dept., 1970-72, 76-79. Author: Stone Age Hunters of the Kafue, 1965, Analysis of Prehistoric Economic Patterns, 1967; editor: Man Before History, 1964; editor: Reconstructing African Culture History, 1967, Jour. Field Archaeology, 1985-95. NSF grantee, 1960-61, 66-67; Fulbright grantee, 1973; Social Sci. Research Council grantee, 1963-64 Mem. Comm. Internat. Exchange of Scholars (chmn. discipline screening com. in archaeology 1985-88)

GABEL, GEORGE DESAUSSURE, JR., lawyer; b. Jacksonville, Fla., Feb. 14, 1940; s. George DeSaussure and Juanita (Brittain) G.; m. Judith Kay Adams, July 21, 1962; children: Laura Gabel Hartman, Meredith Gabel Harris. AB, Davidson Coll., 1961; JD, U. Fla., 1964. Bar: Fla. 1964, D.C. 1972. With Toole, Taylor, Moseley, Gabel & Hair, Jacksonville, 1966-74, Gabel & Hair (formerly Wahl & Gabel), Jacksonville, 1974-98; ptnr., mem. dirs. com. Holland & Knight, Jacksonville, 1998—2001, exec. ptnr., 2002—. Mem. Fla. Jud. Nominating Commn., 4th cir., 1982-86. Pres. Willing Hands, Inc., 1971-72; chmn. N.E. Fla. March of Dimes, 1974-75; mem. budget com. United Way, 1972-74, chmn. rev. com., 1976; bd. dirs. Ctrl. and So. brs. YMCA, 1973-79, Camp Immokalee, 1982-86; elder Riverside Presbyn. Ch., 1970-77, 80-86, 90-92, 97—, clk. session, 1975-76, 85-86, trustee, 1988-91; pres. Riverside Presbyn. Day Sch., 1977-79; chmn. Nat. Eagle Scout Assn., 1974-75; pres. Boy Scouts Am., North fla. Coun. 1993-96, silver Beaver award, 1978; trustee Davidson Coll., 1984-95; Norwegian Consul, 1989—; pres. Jacksonville Consular Corps, 1992-93, 96—. Capt. U.S. Army, 1964-66. Named Internat. Person of Yr., Jacksonville Area C. of C., 2002. Fellow Am. Coll. Trial Lawyers, Am. Bar Found., mem. ABA (chmn. admiralty and maritime law com., 1980-81. chmn. media law and defamation torts com. 1988-89. tort and ins. practice sect.) ATLA, Am. Counsel Assn. (bd. dirs. 1980-82, pres. 1992-93), Maritime Law Assn. U.S. (bd. dirs. 1994-97), Assn. Average Adjusters (overseas subscriber), Fla. Bar (chmn. grievance com. 1973-75, chmn. admiralty law com. 1978-89, chmn. media and comms. law com. 1990-91), Southeastern Admiralty law Inst. (bd. govs. 1973-75), Duval County Legal Aid Assn. (bd. dirs. 1971-74, 81-84), Am. Inn of Ct. (master of bench, sec.-treas. 1990-95), Rotary of Jacksonville (bd. mem. 1982-84, 88-89, pres. 87-88), World Affairs Coun. of Jacksonville (exec. com. 2001—). Democrat. Home: 1850 Shadowlawn St Jacksonville FL 32205-9430 Office: Holland & Knight 50 N Laura St Ste 3900 Jacksonville FL 32202-3622

GABEL, KATHERINE, retired academic administrator; b. Rochester, N.Y., Apr. 9, 1938; d. M. Wren and Esther (Conger) G.; m. Seth Devore Strickland, June 24, 1961 (div. 1965). AB, Smith Coll., Northampton, Mass., 1959; MSW, Simmons Coll., 1961; PhD, Syracuse U., 1967; JD, Union U., 1970; bus. program, Stanford U., 1984. Psychol. social worker Cen. Island Mental Health Ctr., Uniondale, N.Y., 1961-62; psychol. social worker, supt. Ga. State Tng. Sch. for Girls, Atlanta, 1962-64; cons. N.Y. State Crime Control Coun., Albany, 1968-70; faculty Ariz. State U., Tempe, 1972-76; supt. Ariz. Dept. of Corrections, Phoenix, 1970-76; dean, prof. Smith Coll., 1976-85; pres. Pacific Oaks Coll. and Children's Sch., Pasadena, Calif., 1985-98; western region v.p. Casey Family Program, Pasadena, 1998—2001; cons. svcs., 2001—. Advisor, del. UN, Geneva, 1977; mem. So. Calif. Youth Authority, 1986-91. Editor: Master Teacher and Supervisor in Clinical Social Work, 1982; author report Legal Issues of Female Inmates, 1981, model for rsch. Diversion program Female Inmates, 1984, Children of Incarcerated Parents, 1995. Vice chair United Way, Northampton, 1982-83; chair Mayor's Task Force, Northampton, 1981. Mem. Nat. Assn. Social Work, Acad. Cert. Social Workers, Nat. Assn. Edn. Young Children, Western Assn. Schs. and Colls., Pasadena C. of C., Athenaeum, Pasadena Rotary Club. Democrat. Presbyterian. Avocations: collecting, S.W. Indian art, aviary. Fax: 626-449-8501. E-mail: gabelk@prodigy.net.

GABEL, RONALD GLEN, telecommunications executive; b. Allentown, Pa., Nov. 22, 1937; s. Glen Harry and Mary (Oberlin) G.; m. Claire A. Hollern (div.); children: Debra K., Jeffrey A., Stacy L.; m. Elaine M. Petro, Sept. 29, 1988. Student, Pa. State U., 1957-58. Cert. elec. and electronic mfg. engr. Design draftsman Mack Trucks Inc., Allentown, 1958-62, Bell Telephone Labs., Allentown, 1962-66; indsl. engr. Western Electric, Allentown, 1966-84; sr. engr. AT&T, Allentown, 1984-95, Lucent Technologies, Allentown, 1995-97. Cons. expert Man at Arms Mag.; gen. chmn. Engrs.' Week Joint Planning Coun., Lehigh Valley, 1981; cost reduction coord. Western Elec. Allentown Works, 1982-86; Western Electric Speakers Bureau, 1972-83; adminstr. Tel. Pioneers Am., Allentown, 1987-94. Co-author: Work Simplification by Motion Economy Handbook, 1982; coord. Western Elec. Allentown Works Indsl. Engring. newsletter, 1973-85. Advisor Lehigh County Dept. Human Svcs., 1989—93; solicitor United Way, 1974, 1982, 1989, 1990; dir. Lehigh County Hist. Soc., 1999—2000; v.p. Jacobsburg Hist. Soc., 1999—2000, pres., 2000—01; dir. Lehigh County Mus. Commn., 1977—81; sec. devel. and prodn. com. Lehigh County Bicentennial Commn., 1977; pres. Indian Guides Allentown YMCA, 1972, v.p., 1971; sec. ch. coun. St. James Luth. Ch., 1964—67; advisor St. James Luther League, 1964—67. Mem.: Am. Inst. Indsl. Engrs. (pres. 1976—77, editor nat. mfg. sys. divsn. newsletter 1979—80, dir. Lehigh Valley chpt. 1983, Outstanding Svc. award 1978, 5 nat. awards for profl. soc. newsletters 1971—75), Internat. Inst. Indsl. Engrs., Ducks Unltd., Tex. Gun Collectors Assn., Am. Soc. Arms Collectors (bd. dirs. 1988—91, v.p. 1991—94, pres. 1994—95), Forks of Del. Weapons Assn., Pa. Antique Gun Collectors Assn. (bd. dirs. 1996—97, v.p. 1998—99, sec./treas. 1999—, editor Bugle newsletter 2001—), Ky. Rifle Assn. Found. (pres. 1972—73), NRA, U.S. Power Squadrons (dist. lt. D-5 1991—95), Delhigh Power Squadron (comdr 1990—91, pres. past comdr. club 2000—01), Nat. Soc. Pershing Rifles, Pa. Antiques Appraisers Assn., Ky. Rifle Assn. (newsletter editor 1974—), Mercedes Benz Club (v.p. N.E. Pa. sect. 2002—03), Shriners, Knights Templar, Lions (pres. 1987—2003), Rajh Temple Upper Lehigh, Internat. Order DeMolay. Republican. Avocation: antique firearms. E-mail: rggabel@fast.net.

GABELICH, CHRISTOPHER JAMES, environment specialist, researcher; s. James Frederick and Michele Antoinette Gabelich; m. Christian Lin, Dec. 11 1999; 1 child, Miles Frederick. BS in Environ. Sci., U. of Calif., Riverside 1993; MS in Environ. Chemistry, UCLA, 1995, D of Environ. Sci. and Engring., 2001. Environ. specialist Met. Water Dist. of So. Cal., La Verne Calif., 1997—. Mem.: Internat. Desalination Assn. (assoc.), Am. Water Works Assn. (assoc.), Am. Chem. Soc. (assoc.). Liberal. Avocations: volleyball mountain biking, snow skiing. Office: Met Water Dist So Calif 700 Moreno Ave La Verne CA 91750 Office Fax: 909-392-5166. E-mail cgabelich@mwdh2o.com.

GABELNICK, HENRY LEWIS, medical research director; b. Boston, May 10, 1940; s. Murray and Lillian G.; m. Faith Schectman, June 17, 1962 children: Deborah Anne, Tamar Miriam; m. Clare Ann Donaher, May 22, 1987 m. Judith Andai, Mar. 15, 2003. BS, MIT, 1961, MS, 1962; PhD, Princeton U. 1966. Sr. chem. engr. Monsanto Co., Springfield, Mass., 1966-68; biomed. engr NIH, Bethesda, Md., 1968-1986; dir. extramural rsch. CONRAD Program Ea Va. Med. Sch., Arlington, 1986-89, dep. dir. CONRAD Program, 1989-90, dir CONRAD Program, 1990—. Pres. Reprodn. Rsch. Inst., 1997—2001; tech advisor WHO, Geneva, 1977—; tech. expert UN Devel. Program, Haifa, Israel 1973. Editor: Rheology of Biological Systems, 1973, Drug Delivery Systems 1976, Heterosexual Transmission of AIDS, 1990, Barrier Contraceptives, 1993 Biology, Pharmacology, and Clinical Applications of Androgens, 1996, Rotary Club Internat. Fellow Textile Resch. Inst.; mem. APHA, N.Y. Acad. Scis., Am Chem. Soc., Controlled Release Soc., Soc. for Reproductive Care (bd. dirs 2000—, v.p. 2001-02, pres. 2002—), Cosmos Club, Sigma Xi. Avocation nature photography. Home: 6315 Swords Way Bethesda MD 20817 E-mail hgabelnick@conrad.org., hgabelnick@alum.mit.edu.

GABER, ROBERT, psychologist; b. N.Y.C., Nov. 5, 1923; s. William and Freda (Harris) Gaber; m. Heidi Walters, Apr. 3, 1967 (div. Jan. 5, 1976); 1 child, Nathan. BA, NYU, 1949, MA, 1951; PhD, Columbia Pacific U., San Rafael, Calif., 1982. Psychotherapist Nat. Hosp. Speech Disorders, N.Y.C., 1954-57; psychologist Indsl. Home for the Blind, N.Y.C., 1957-58; sch. psychologist Roosevelt Sch., Stamford, Conn., 1958-60; sr. clin. psychologist N.Y. State Dept. Mental Hygiene, Thiells, 1960-64; staff psychologist N.Y. Med. Coll., N.Y.C., 1965-66; cons. psychologist Salvation Army, Phila., 1971-72; psychologist Md. Dept. Mental Hygiene, 1975-76, Dept. Corrections, Balt., 1979-80; CEO Axxiom De-Stress Ctrs., Balt., 1980—; dir. Ctr. Stress Rsch., Norristown, Pa., 1994—. Dir. mental health, nursery divsn. Dept. Welfare, N.Y.C., 1953—56; cons. Gov., Pa. Dept. Corrections, 1971, Family Crisis Ctr. Balt., 1973—74. Author: (book) The Experience of Enlightenment, 1980, Federal Prisoners' Attitudes Toward Crime and Confinement, 1982, Personality Traits and Behaviorisms of a Well-Adjusted Person, 1993, What Kind of Person is the Drug Addict?, 1996, The Psychodynamics of Self-Hypnosis, 1998, The SEEP Factors in Crime, 1999, (booklet) Comprehensive Therapy Questionnaire, 1978; contbr. articles to profl. jours. With USAF, 1942—46, PTO. Mem.: APA. Democrat. Avocations: golf, horseback riding, skiing, water-skiing, tennis. also: Ctr for Stress Rsch 11 W Lafayette St Norristown PA 19401-4709 E-mail: gab7rob@netzero.com.

GABERINO, JOHN ANTHONY, JR., lawyer; b. Tulsa, Aug. 6, 1941; s. John A Sr and Elizabeth (McCafferty) Gaberino; m. Marjory Ann Diamond, Aug. 21, 1965; children: Christina M, Megan E, Courtney L, John A III, Kathleen A. AB cum laude, Georgetown U., 1963, JD, 1966. Bar: Okla 1966, US Dist Ct (no & we dists) Okla, US Ct Appeals (10th cir) 1968, US Tax Ct 1968, US Supreme Ct 1994. Assoc. Huffman, Arrington & Kihle, Tulsa, 1968-75; ptnr. Arrington, Kihle, Gaberino & Dunn, Tulsa, 1975-87, also bd. dirs., 1987-97; sr. v.p., gen. counsel ONEOK, Inc., 1998—. Counsel, bd dirs St Francis Health Sys, Inc, Tulsa, Okla., 1989—97. Chmn. Law Ctr. Alumni Bd. Georgetown U., 1990—92, bd. govs., 1990—, chair, 2000—02, bd. dirs., 2000—02; pres. Georgetown U. Club Okla; past chmn. Georgetown U. AAP Okla.; bd. regents Georgetown U., 2002—; past chmn Christ the King Bd Educ; past pres. bd. trustees Monte Cassino Sch.; past chmn. bd. trustees Monte Cassino Sch. Endowment Fund; bd. dirs. W K Warren Found, Tulsa Area United Way, Tulsa Pub. Schs. Found.; chmn. bd. dirs. Operation Aware Inc, 1991; bd. dirs. The Salvation Army-Tulsa Region, 2002—. Capt U.S. Army, 1966—68. Recipient John Carroll Medal, Georgetown Univ, 1993. Fellow: Am. Bar Found. (life; chair 2000—01); mem.: NCCJ (bd dirs Tulsa chpt, pres 1993—95, Ann. Dinner honoree 2003), Okla. Fellows of the Am. Bar Found. (chair 2000—01), Tulsa County Bar Found (bd dirs 1993—99, pres 1994), Tulsa Bar Asn (secy 1988, chmn construction and bylaws comt, bd dirs 1989, 1991—94, pres 1993), Okla Bar Asn (mem bd govs 1990—92, 1995, vpres 1995, mem bd govs 1997—99, pres 1998), Metropolitan Tulsa CofC (bd dirs 1996—, chair 2001), Southern Hills Country Club (mem bd govs 1990—95, 1st vpres 1991—93, pres 1994), Knights Holy Sepulchre (hon soc Cath ch, chair Tulsa Diocese rev. bd. 2002—), Phi Beta Kappa. Republican. Roman Catholic. Avocations: golf, tennis. Office: ONEOK Inc 100 W 5th St Tulsa OK 74103-4240

GABERMAN, HARRY, retired lawyer; b. Springfield, Mass., May 6, 1913; s. Nathan and Elizabeth (Binder) G.; m. Ingeborg Luise Gruda, Sept. 24, 1953; children: Claudia, Natalie Gaberman Razzook, Victor Lucius. JD, George Washington U., 1941; LLM, Cath. U. Am., 1954. Bar: D.C. 1942. Priorities analyst War Prodn. Bd., 1942, asst. indsl. and indsl. analyst, 1943-45; asst. chief industry control sect., legal and intercorp. rels. analyst U.S. Mil. Govt. and U.S. High Commn. for Germany, Berlin, Frankfurt, Bonn; atty.-investigator, atty-advisor; indsl. specialist, bus. economist U.S. Mil. Govt. and U.S. High Commn. for Germany, Berlin, Frankfurt, Bonn, 1945—53; asst. legal advisor, attache, dep. U.S. agt. Italian-U.S. Conciliation Commn., Am. Embassy, Rome, 1953; pvt. practice Washington, 1953-55; intelligence analyst Army Transp. Intelligence Agy., Gravelly Point, Va., 1955-56; supervisory atty.-advisor, atty.-advisor Air Force Sys. Command, Andrews AFB, Md., 1956-75; ret. Asst. to U.S. mem. Four-power liquidation of German War Potential Com., Berlin, 1946; chief deconcentration br. U.S. High Commn., Frankfurt, 1949; acting dep. U.S. mem. law com. Allied Kommandatura, Berlin, 1951; U.S. mem. 3-power Film Reorgn. Com., Bonn, 1949-50. Contbr. articles to profl. jours. Recipient Profl. Achievement award George Washington U. Law Assn., 1983. Mem. Fed. Bar Assn. (dep. coun. and com. coord. 1982, coun. and com. coordinating 14 substantive law couns. containing 83 constituent coms. 1983, chmn. coun. on govt. contracts 1970-75, 80-81, chmn. internat. procurement com. 1977-79, dep. chmn. sect. on internat. law and its newsletter editor 1984-97, dep. chmn. sect. on internat. law and its newsletter contbg. editor 1998-99, found. advisor 1996-2000; numerous Disting. Svc. and other awards), D.C. Bar Assn. (chmn. govt. contracts com. 1964-66), Diplomatic and Consular Officers Ret. (charter mem., DACOR House), Am. Fgn. Svcs. Assn., Air Force Assn. Avocations: walking, reading, listening to classic and semi-classic music.

GABI, MARK, engineering and management educator, consultant, researcher; b. Damascus, Syria; m. Mary Gabi, 1993; 1 child, Maya. BS, Ark. State U., 1985; MS, Ctrl. Mo. State U., 1987, EdD, 1989; PhD, Wichita State U., 1990. Rschr. Ctrl. Mo. State U., Warrensburg, 1986-89; asst. prof. Wichita (Kans.) State U., 1989-90; writer World Info. Svcs., Washington, 1990-92; indsl. hygienist OSHA, Washington, 1992-94; assoc. prof. U. Md., College Park, 1992—; sr. engr. Goddard Space Flight Ctr. NASA, Greenbelt, Md. Advisor Grad. Sch. Tech. and Mgmt. U. Md., College Park, 1992—; contractor Dept. of Def., 1999—; cons., Washington, D.C. Writer Arabuter, 1990. Coord. Rohrkemper for Congress, Vienna, 1992. Avocations: reading, sports, computers, cooking. Home: 1220 E West Hwy Apt 201 Silver Spring MD 20910-6200 E-mail: markg@myway.com.

GABIG, JEROME S., JR., lawyer; BS in Engring., U.S. Mil. Acad., 1972; JD, U. Calif., 1977; CSS in Mgmt., Harvard U., 1986. Dir. telecom. law USAF Comm. Command, 1980—83; with USAF Computer Acquisition Ctr., 1983—87; dir. contract law USAF Armament Divsn., 1987—90; dep. SJA USAF Electronic Systems Ctr., 1990—92; ptnr. Venable, Baetjer, Howard and Civiletti, 1992—99; gen. counsel Time Domain Systems, Inc., Huntsville, Ala., 1999—. Mem. Army Sci. Bd.; mem. procurement process action team NASA, 1997—2000. Named Outstanding Young Mil. Lawyer in Air Force, 1985. Fellow: Nat. Contract Mgmt. Assn. (Delaney award 1993); mem.: ABA (chair info. systems com., pub. contract law sect.). Office: Time Domain Corp 7075 Old Madison Pike Huntsville AL 35806

GABLE, CAROL BRIGNOLI, health economics researcher; b. N.Y.C., Dec. 28, 1945; d. Peter Joseph and Frances Veronica (Guma) Abatemarco; m. Frank Giovanni Brignoli, May 19, 1968 (div. Nov. 1981); children: Barbra, James; m. Raymond Lewis Gable, Jan. 8, 1983; 1 child, Matthew. BS, CUNY, 1968; PhD in Chemistry, U. Md., 1973, MA in Statistics, 1986. Chemist N.Y. Rsch. Inst., N.Y.C., 1967-68; grad. asst. U. Md., College Park, 1968-73; lectr. Montgomery Coll., Takoma Park, Md., 1972-75; rsch. assoc. USDA/CFEI, Hyattsville, Md., 1974-76; chemist FDA, Washington, 1977-89; rsch. dir. pharmacoepidemiology Systemetrics/McGraw Hill, Washington, 1989-92; project dir. Degge Group Ltd., Arlington, Va., 1992-93; dir. Health Econs. State and Fed. Assocs., Alexandria, Va., 1994-96, v.p., 1996; dir. outcomes rsch. Pfizer, Inc., U.S. Pharms. Group (PPG), N.Y.C., 1996—99; rschr. HIV/AIDS Westchester County Dept. Health, NY, 2001—. Contbr. articles to profl. jours. including Biophys. Chemistry, Nutrition, Risk Assessment, Pharmacoepidemiology, Pharmacoeconomics, Jour. AMA. N.Y. State Regents scholar, 1963-67; recipient NSF traineeship, 1969-73. Mem. Am. Chem. Soc., Am. Assn. Pharm. Scis. (mem. econ. mktg. and mgmt. sect., vice chmn. 1992-93, chmn.-elect 1993-94, chmn. 1994-95), Soc. for Risk Analysis, Internat. Soc. for Pharmacoepidemiology, Drug Infos. Assn., Assn. Health Svcs. Rsch., Assn. Pharms. Outcomes Rsch. Democrat. Methodist. Avocation: jogging. Office: Westchester County DOH Planning & Evaluation 145 Huguenot St New Rochelle NY 10801 E-mail: gablecarol@aol.com.

GABLE, EDWARD BRENNAN, JR., lawyer; b. Shamokin, Pa., Mar. 15, 1929; s. Edward Brennan and Kathleen (Welsh) G. B.S., Villanova U., 1953; J.D., Georgetown U., 1957; m. Judy Lipshy July 17, 1981; children by previous marriage: Karen Lynn, Kimberly Ann, Katherine Rebel; stepchildren: Steven H., Karen Sue, Scott Michael. Bar: D.C. 1957, U.S. Dist. Ct. D.C. 1957, U.S. Ct. Appeals (D.C. cir.) 1957, U.S. Ct. Customs and Patent Appeals, 1959, U.S. Customs Ct., 1961, U.S. Ct. Mil. Appeals, 1966, U.S. Supreme Ct., 1967, U.S. Ct. Appeals (fed. cir.) 1982. With U.S. Customs Svc., Treasury Dept., Washington, 1958-88, chief documentation br., 1965-66, chief carrier rulings br., 1966-76, chief penalties br., 1976-78, spl. asst. to asst. commr. Office of Regulations and Rulings, 1978-82, dir. carriers, drawback and bonds div., 1983-88, legal cons. in martime law, Washington, 1988—; mem. U.S. del. Intergovtl. Maritime Cons. Orgn., London, 1972-75, U.S. rep., inter-sessional meeting, Hamburg, Fed. Republic Germany, 1973. Pres., Customs Fed. Credit Union, 1967-69. Recipient Superior Performance award Treasury Dept., 1962, commendation letter from asst. sec. treasury, 1964, Customs Outstanding Performance award, 1983, Customs Cash Performance award, 1984, 85. Mem. Customs Lawyers Assn. (pres. 1965-66), Fed. Bar Assn., Propeller Club U.S., United Seamen's Svc. (council of trustees 1986-88), Nat. Lawyers Club, Elks, Delta Pi Epsilon, Delta Theta Phi. Roman Catholic. Home and Office: 955 26th St NW Washington DC 20037-2009 E-mail: edwardbgable@aol.com.

GABLE, JOHN ALLEN, historian, association executive, educator; b. Rockford, Ill., Nov. 14, 1943; s. Allen Herman and Mary Jane (Kirkpatrick) G. AB, Kenyon Coll., 1965; PhD in History, Brown U., 1972. Asst. prof. history Briarcliff Coll., Briarcliff Manor, N.Y., 1974-77; exec. dir. Theodore Roosevelt Assn., Oyster Bay, N.Y., 1974—; adj. assoc. prof. C.W. Post L.I. U., Greenvale, N.Y., 1977-89; adj. prof. New Coll. Hofstra U., Hempstead, N.Y., 1989—. Editor, founder Theodore Roosevelt Assn. Jour., 1975—; author, editor 6 books in field; contbr. articles to profl. jours. Vestry Christ Ch., Oyster Bay, 1979-2002. Mem. Orgn. Am. Historians. Episcopalian. Home: 64T Glen Keith Rd Glen Cove NY 11542-3515 Office: Theodore Roosevelt Assn PO Box 719 Oyster Bay NY 11771-0719 E-mail: tra_gable@sprynet.com.

GABLE, KAREN ELAINE, health science educator; b. Des Moines, Nov. 12, 1939; d. John E. and Mabel I. (Davis) Clay; m. Robert W. Gable, Jr., Feb. 4, 1961; children: Susan Kay, Barbara Lynne, R. J. Kent. AS, 1969; BS in Edn., Ind. U., Indpls., 1976, MS in Edn., 1979, EdD, 1985. Registered dental hygienist Ind. U., cert. dental asst. Ind. U. Clin. instr. dental hygiene program Sch. Dentistry Ind. U., Indpls., 1976, asst. prof., coord. program dir. health scis. edn. Sch. Medicine, 1977-81, asst. prof. Sch. Edn., 1981-94, assoc. prof. health scis. edn. Sch. Allied Health & Medicine, 1994—, program dir., 1994—. Contbr. articles to profl. jours. Recipient Disting. Dental Hygiene Alumna award, Ind. U. Sch. Dentistry. Mem.: ACTE/Health Occupations Edn. (mem. policy bd. 2002—), Ind. Career and Tech. Edn. Assn. (Outstanding Svc. awards), Ind. Dental Hygienists Assn. (sec.), Ind. Health Careers Assn. (pres.-elect, pres.), Health Occupations, Supvs. and Tchr. Educators Coun. (treas., pres.), Sigma Phi Alpha.

GABLE, ROBERT ELLEDY, real estate investment company executive; b. N.Y.C., Feb. 20, 1934; s. Gilbert E. and Paulina (Stearns) G.; m. Emily Brinton Thompson, July 5, 1958; children: James, Elizabeth, John. BS, Stanford U., 1956. Asst. to pres. The Stearns Co. Ltd. (formerly Stearns Coal & Lumber Co. Inc.), Lexington, KY, 1958-60, sec., 1960-70, treas., 1961-62, v.p., 1962-70, chmn. bd., 1970—, pres., dir., 1975-78. Past chmn. bd., dir. Ky. & Tenn. Railway, Stearns, Ky., Lexington; past chmn. bd. Lumber King Inc., Stearns; past dir., audit com. Kuhn's Big K Stores Corp., Nashville, 1979-81; dir. emeritus Blue Cross and Blue Shield Ky.; past dir. Bank of McCreary County. Commr. Ky. Dept. Parks, 1967-70; mem. pub. lands com. Interstate Oil Compact Commn., 1968-70; mem. adv. com. Ky. Ednl. TV, 1971-75; former mem. Breaks Interstate Park Commn.; past pres., past dir. McCreary County Indsl. Devel. Corp.; former trustee Stearns Recreational Assn., Inc.; mem. S.E. regional adv. com. Nat. Park Service, 1973-78, sec., 1977-78; former bd. dirs. Ky. Mountain Laurel Festival Assn., v.p., 1974-75; mem. McCreary County Air Bd., 1967-81; mem. adv. bd. U. Ky. for Somerset Cmty. Coll., 1965-73; Republican candidate for U.S. Senate from Ky., 1972; Ky. co-chmn. Finance Com. for Re-election of Pres., 1972; mem. Rep. Nat. Com., 1986-94, mem. budget com., 1989, Rep. Nat. Fin. Com., 1971-76; rep. state finance chmn. 1973-75, 86; mem. Ky. Rep. Central Com., 1974-94; state chmn. Rep. Party Ky., 1986-94; Rep. nominee for gov. Ky., 1975, 1995; trustee George Peabody Coll. for Tchrs., Nashville, 1970-79, mem. exec. com., 1976-79, chmn. bd. 1979; former trustee Capital Day Sch., Frankfort, Ky.; bd. dirs., past chmn., past pres., founder Ky. Coun. on Econ. Edn., Inc.; mem. bd. founders Nat. Coun. Econ. Edn. (formerly Joint Coun. Econ. Edn.) N.Y.C., 1982—; trustee Ky. State U. Found., 1979-82; Vanderbilt U., Nashville, 1979-87, former mem. budget com.; past mem. bd. dirs. Ky. Better Roads Coun., Inc., vice chmn., 1976-79; former mem. missions bd. Episcopal Diocese of Lexington; bd. dirs. Lexington Conv. and Tourist Bur., 1982-85, Ky. Opera Assn., 1982—2002, pres., 2000-03, Frazier Rehab. Found., Inc., Louisville, 1982-84, Headley-Whitney Mus., Lexington, 1985-90; bd. trustees Epworth Assembly, Ludington, Mich., 1995-2001, treas. 1995-2000, pres. 2000-2001; founding bd. Lexington Fund for the Arts, 1984-86; So. Assn. Rep., 1987-94, state chmn.; appointed Pres. Adv. Com. Arts, 1992-93; mem. Nat. Com. for Performing Arts, John F. Kennedy Ctr. for Performing Arts, Washington, 1993—, pres., CEO, 1993-97; mem. nat. leadership coun. Rep. Exchange Satellite Network, Nashville, Tenn., 1993-95; pres. & CEO Kentuckians for Fair Redistricting, Inc., 2001-. Served to lt. (j.g.) USNR, 1956-58. Named Ky. Col., Mr. Coal of Ky., 1970. Mem. Ky. Coal Assn. (dir. 1972-86, exec. com. 1974-78, sec. 1979-86), Ky. C. of C. (regional v.p., 1971-72, 76-80, exec. com. 1971-72, 76-80, dir. 1971-80, fin. com. 1978-79), Lexington C. of C. (dir. 1982, 84-87), Frankfort Country Club, Keeneland Club, Lafayette Club, Thoroughbred Club, Lexington Club, Bluegrass Auto Club (former bd. dirs.), Pendennis Club, River Valley Club, Capitol Hill Club, Coral Beach Club, Tau Beta Pi, Alpha Kappa Lambda (past chpt. pres.). Home: 1715 Stonehaven Dr Frankfort KY 40601-8624 Office: 200 W Vine St Ste 600 Lexington KY 40507-1616

GABLIK, SUZI, art educator, writer; b. N.Y.C., Sept. 26, 1934; d. Anthony Julius and Geraldine (Schwartz) G. BA, Hunter Coll., 1955. Vis. prof. art Sydney Coll. Arts, 1980, U. of the South, Sewanee, Tenn., 1982, 84, U. Calif., Santa Barbara, 1985, 86, 88, Va. Commonwealth U., Richmond, 1987, Va. Tech., Blacksburg, 1990, U. Colo., Boulder, 1990. Endowed lectr. U. Victoria, B.C., 1983, Colo. Coll., 1983, U. Santa Barbara, 1985, Va. Tech., 1989. Author: Magritte, 1979, Has Modernism Failed?, 1984, The Reenchantment of Art, 1991, Conversations Before the End of Time, 1995, Living the Magical Life, 2002. Recipient Lifetime Achievement award, Women's Caucus for Art, 2003. Home: 3271 Deer Run Rd Blacksburg VA 24060-9075 E-mail: suzi@swva.net.

GABOR, FRANK, insurance company executive; b. Apr. 15, 1918; Pres. Gabor & Co., Inc., 1948-83, Anglo-Am. Agrl. Underwriters, Inc., Havana, Cuba, 1950-52; v.p., dir. Wilson Nat. Life, 1957-73; pres. Fla. Assn. Health Underwriters, 1960-66, Variable Income Planning Co., 1966, Bent Tree Farm, Inc., 1971—. Dir., mem. exec. com. Stanwood Corp., Charlotte, NC, 1975—89; pres. Gabor Reins. Mgmt Corp, 1975—93; pres. Ins. Svc. Agy. Inc; chmn. Gabor Agy. Inc., 1983—2000; underwriting mgr., cons. Life Disability, Property & Casualty Ins Cos. Home: 600 Biltmore Way Coral Gables FL 33134-7541 Office: 7270 NW 12th St Ste 130 Miami FL 33126-1928 E-mail: fgabor@gaborinsurance.com.

GABOR, JEFFREY ALAN, insurance and financial services executive; b. Cambridge, Mass., July 7, 1942; s. Frank and Selma (Cluck) G.; m. Ann Steinholtz, June 15, 1963; children: Elissa, Andrea, William. Student, U. Miami, 1960-64. CFP; CLU. Pres. The Gabor Agy., Inc., Tallahassee, 1964-2000, chmn., CEO, 2000—; v.p. and dir. Investar Holdings, Inc., Tallahassee, 2000—; also bd. dirs. Mem. Nat. Assn. Life Underwriters, Tallahassee Life Underwriters Assn. (bd. dirs. 1985—), Inst. CFP, Nat. Structured Settlements Trade Assn., Gen. Agts. and Mgrs. Assn. (pres. 1983-84), Million Dollar Round Table (life). Home: 3050 Fermanagh Dr Tallahassee FL 32309-3333 Office: 3500 Financial Plz Tallahassee FL 32312 E-mail: jgabor@gaboragency.com.

GABOR-HOTCHKISS, MAGDA, research scientist, librarian; b. Paris, Mar. 21, 1934; arrived in U.S., 1967; d. Andor and Olga (Halpern) Gabor; m. Rollin D. Hotchkiss, May 21, 1967. D of Natural Scis. summa cum laude, Eotvos Lorand Sci. U., 1963. Intern Plant Physiology Humboldt U., Berlin, 1957—58; rsch. asst., rsch. assoc. Inst. Genetics Hungarian Acad. Scis., Budapest, 1959—67; rsch. assoc. Rockefeller U., N.Y.C., 1967—82; asst., assoc. libr. Hancock Shaker Village Mus., Pittsfield, Mass., 1985—94, coord. libr. collections, 1995—99, vol. libr., archivist, 2000—. Postdoctoral Bacterial Genetics, Animal Viruses Cold Spring Harbor Lab. of Quantitative Biology, NY, 1965; guest investigator Rockefeller U., N.Y.C., 1964—66; mem. adv. bd. We. Mass. Libr. Assn., Hadley, 1996—97. Author, compiler: Guide to Hancock Shaker Village Library Collections, 2001—03, annotator, editor: The Shaker Image, 1994; contbr. articles to profl. jours., chapters to books. Vol. libr. Berkshire Mus., Pittsfield, 1998—; tutor ESL Lit. Vols. Am., Pittsfield, 2001—. Mem.: N.Y. Acad. Scis., Genetics Soc. Am., Sigma Xi. Achievements include discovery of entry of various forms of purified DNAs into bacterial cells of pneumococcus progresses in a linear fashion; recombination patterns of induced bacterial diploids (via protoplast fusion in Bacillus subtilis) follow the classical mechanism found in eucaryotic cells. Avocations: reading, photography, yoga, languages, stained glass.

GABOVITCH, STEVEN ALAN, lawyer, accountant; b. Newton, Mass., Feb. 7, 1953; s. William and Annette (Richman) G.; m. Rhonda Merle Kitover, Aug. 6, 1978; childre: Daniel J., Lindsey D. BS in Acctg., Boston Coll., 1975, JD, 1978; LLM in Taxation, Boston U., 1982. Bar: Mass. 1978, R.I. 1979, U.S. Dist. Ct. R.I. 1979, U.S. Tax Ct. 1980, U.S. Ct. Appeals (1st cir.) 1980, U.S. Dist. Ct. Mass. 1981, U.S. Ct. Appeals (fed. cir.) 1982, U.S. Supreme Ct. 1983; CPA, Mass. Tax specialist Peat, Marwick, Mitchell & Co., Providence, 1978-80; prin. William Gabovitch & Co., Boston, 1980-97; pvt. practice Stoughton, Mass., 1998—. Lectr. on bankruptcy taxation. Contbr. articles to profl. jours. Mem.: Boston Bar Assn., Mass. Bar Assn., R.I. Bar Assn., Nat. Soc. Tax Profls., Beta Gamma Sigma. Office: 378 Page St 3 Deerfield Corp Ctr Stoughton MA 02072 E-mail: steve@gabovitch.com.

GABOVITCH, WILLIAM, lawyer, accountant; b. June 18, 1922; s. Ezra and Lena Ruth (Elkins) Gabovitch; m. Annette Richman, Feb. 7, 1951; children: Steven A., Ellis. BSBA, Boston U., 1943; JD, Boston Coll., 1949; LLM in Taxation, NYU, 1950. CPA Mass.; bar: Mass. 49, U.S. Dist. Ct. Mass., U.S. Dist. Ct. R.I., U.S. Ct. Appeals (1st cir.), U.S. Tax Ct., U.S. Ct. Claims, U.S. Ct. Appeals (fed. cir.), U.S. Supreme Ct. Sr. ptnr. William Gabovitch & Co., CPAs, Boston, 1962—. Lectr. in legal acctg. and taxation Boston Coll. Law Sch., 1959—70; examiner and trustee in bankruptcy, state ct. receiver. Campaign treas. Congressman Robert F. Drinan, 1970—84. Lt. (s.g.) USNR, 1943—46. Mem.: ABA, Mass. Soc. CPAs, Boston Bar Assn., Mass. Bar Assn., ALTA, Mensa, Masons. Home: 33 Old Nugent Farm Rd Gloucester MA 01930-3169 Office: 256 Hanover St Boston MA 02113-2337

GABOW, PATRICIA ANNE, internist; b. Starke, Fla., Jan. 8, 1944; m. Harold N. Gabow, June 21, 1971; children: Tenaya Louise, Aaron Patrick. BA in Biology, Seton Hill Coll., 1965; MD, U. Pa. Sch. Medicine, 1969. Diplomate Am. Bd. Internal Medicine, Am. Bd. Nephrology, Nat. Bd. Med. Examiners; lic. Colo. Internship in medicine Hosp. of U. of Pa., 1969-70; residency in internal medicine Harbor Gen. Hosp., 1970-71; renal fellowship San Francisco Gen. Hosp. and Hosp. of U. Pa., 1971-72, 72-73; instr. medicine divsn. renal diseases, asst. prof. U. Colo. Health Scis. Ctr., 1973-74, 74-79, assoc. prof. medicine divsn. renal diseases, prof., 1979-87; chief renal disease, clin. dir. dept. medicine Denver Gen. Hosp., 1973-81, 76-81, dir. med. svcs., 1981-91; CEO, med. dir. Denver Health and Hosps., 1992—. Intensive care com. Denver Gen. Hosp., 1976-81, med. records com., 1979-80, ind. rev. com., 1978-81, continuing med. edn. com., 1981-83, animal care com., 1979-03, student adv. com. U. Colo. Health Scis. Ctr., 1982-87, faculty senate, 1985, 86, internship adv. com., 1977-92; exec. com. Denver Gen. Hosp., 1981—, chmn. health resources com., 1988-90, chmn. pathology search com., 1989, chmn. faculty practice plan steering com., 1990-92. Mem. editorial bd. EMERGINDEX, 1983-93, Am. Jour. of Kidney Disease, 1984-96, Western Jour. of Medicine, 1987-98, Annals of Internal Medicine, 1988-91, Jour. of the Am. Soc. of Nephrology, 1990-97; contbr. numerous articles, revs. and editorials to profl. publs., chpts. to books. Mem. Mayor's Safe City Task Force, 1993; mem. sci. adv. bd. Polycystic Kidney Rsch. Found., 1984-96, chmn., 1991; mem. sci. adv. bd. Nat. Kidney Found., 1991-94; mem. Nat. Pub. Health and Hosps. Inst. Bd., 1993-2001. Recipient Sullivan award for Highest Acad. Average in Graduating Class, Seton Hill Coll., 1965, Pa. State Senatorial scholarship, 1961-65, Kaiser Permanente award for Excellence in Teaching, 1976, Ann. award to Outstanding Woman Physician, 1982, Kaiser Permanente Nominee for Excellence in Teaching award, 1983, Seton Hill Coll. Disting. Alumna Leadership award, 1990, Florence Rena Sabin award U. Colo., 2000, Nathan Davis award AMA, 2000, Good Housekeeping Women in Govt. award, 2002; named one of The Best Doctors in Am., 1994-95, 2002; grantee Bonfils Found., 1985-86, NIH, 1985-90, 91-96, 96-2000, W.K. Kellogg Found., 1997—, AHRQ, 2000-03. Mem. Denver Med. Soc., Colo. Med. Soc., Am. Soc. Nephrology, Internat. Soc. Nephrology, Am. Coll. Physicians, Am. Fedn. Clin. Rsch., Am. Physiol. Soc., Polycystic Kidney Disease Rsch. Found. (sci. advisor 1984-96), Western Assn. Physicians, Nat. Kidney Found. (sci. adv. bd. 1987-91), Women's Forum of Colo., Inc., Assn. Am. Physicians. Roman Catholic. Office: Denver Health 660 Bannock St Denver CO 80204-4506

GABRIA, JOANNE BAKAITIS, health and education volunteer, former information processing systems equipment company executive; b. Washington, Pa., Jan. 16, 1945; d. Vincent William and Mary Jo (Cario) Bakaitis. BA in English, U. Dayton, 1965, MA in Mktg. Comm., 1973, MBA, 1979. Advt. writer Dancer-Fitzgerald-Sample, Dayton, Ohio, 1969-72; advt. coord. Monarch Marking Sys., Dayton, 1972-73; product tech. editor Frigidaire divsn. GM, Dayton, 1973-77; dir. tech. comm. Mead Tech. Lab., Dayton, 1977-79; publs. mgr. NCR Corp., Dayton, 1979-81, internat. product mgr., 1981-86, mgr. internat. market analysis, 1986-87, mgr. internat. market rsch., 1987-93, mgr. European info. resources, 1993-94. Patient adv. coun. rep. Renal Network, Inc., 2002—. Author: Microwave Cooking in 3 Speeds, 1976, Communications Standards, 1978, Retail Operations, 1982; editor Ivy Jour., 1980-82; editor patient forum newsletter Miami Valley Hosp., 2001—. Chair numerous coms. St. Leonard Cmty., Centreville, Ohio, 1978-88; tel. vol. Contact-Dayton Crisis Intervention, 1982-86; big sister Big Bros./Big Sisters, Dayton, 1985-86; bd. dirs. Miami Valley chpt. Nat. Kidney Found. Ohio, 1987-91, spkrs. bur., 1995—; mem. Ohio Patient adv. com. Renal Network, Inc., 1989-91, Patient Leadership Com., Renal Network, 1997-99; bd. dirs. Contact-Dayton, 1984-85; local coord. Friends of Polycystic Kidney Rsch. Found., 1994-99; mem. leadership com. PKD Found., Dayton-Cin. chpt., 2002—; tutor Miami Valley Literacy Coun., Proliteracy Worldwide, 1997—; liaison Nat. Kidney Found., Patient and Family Coun., 2000—; moderator Inst. for Learning in Retirement, U. Dayton, 2001—. Recipient Disting. Achievement award Contact-Dayton, 1985, Outstanding Svc. award Miami Valley chpt. Nat. Kidney Found. Ohio, 1988, Edn. award, 1990. Mem. Marianist Affiliates (co-chmn. 1981-86), Leo Meyer Soc. Democrat. Roman Catholic. Avocations: nature, classical music. E-mail: jgabria@prodigy.net.

GABRICK, ROBERT WILLIAM, secondary education educator; b. Mpls., Nov. 11, 1940; s. Michael Jr. and Helen Marie (Lendt) G.; children: Brad William, Ross Michael. BS, U. Minn., 1962, postgrad., 1962, 63; MEd, Macalester Coll., 1969; postgrad., U. Wis., River Falls, 1968-69, 71, 84, U. Va., 1988, UCLA, summer 1990, U. Minn., 1991, U. Mass., 1995. Cert. social studies tchr. Tchr., River Falls, Wis., 1962-70, White Bear Lake (Minn.) Schs., 1970-84, 87—, social studies curriculum leader, 1994—; tchr. Blaine (Minn.) Sr. H.S., 1984-87. Cons. teaching Ednl. Growth, 1974—; reviewer, panelist tchr. scholar program NEH, 1989, mem. summer seminar, 1993; cons. Ednl. Testing Svc., Tex. Assessment of Acad. Skills, Austin, 1990; adj. faculty history U. Minn., 1989—; reviewer, panelist innovative projects tech. U.S. Office Edn., 1993; reviewer Minn. State rev. com. Nat. Stds. Civics and Govt., 1993-94; reviewer, panelist NEH, Humanities Focus grant, 1995, 98, Tchg. Am. History Grant Program, U.S. Office Edn., 2001; judge Nat. History Day, 1996—; congl. dist. coord. We the People program Ctr. Civic Edn., 1998-2003, judge state finals, 1998; summer inst. participant Nat. Gallery of Art, 1999; adv. bd. Coll. in the Schs., U. Minn., 2002—; rsch., evaluation and assessment com. LA County Office Edn., 2002—; presenter in field. Author: Humanities Focus grant: Victorian America: The Birth of Modern American Culture, 1860-1915, 1995-96, Autocar Trucks, 1950-1987, Photo Archive, 2002, Freightliner Trucks, 1937-1981, Photo Archive, 2003; co-author (curriculum for website): Thank You, Mr. Edison: Electricity, Innovation and Social Change; co-author: The Great Depression and the Arts, 1998; contbr. articles to profl. jours. Scholar Am. Studies Inst., COE Found., 1965, NDEA Fgn. Policy Inst., U. Wis., 1968, Inst. for Staff Devel., White Bear Lake Schs., 1972-73, Minn. History Tchg. Alliance, 1987-88, Monticello-Stratford Hall Seminar for Tchrs., 1988, Fgn. Policy Rsch. Inst., 1998, 2000, Nat. Archives, 1998; Allen J. Ellander fellow Close-Up Program, 1973, Nat. fellow Coun. for Basic Edn., 1988, Montpelier Program Nat. Trust for Hist. Preservation fellow, 1989, Ctr. for Civic Edn./UCLA fellow, 1990; grantee NEH, 1989-90, 2000, 02-03, Minn. Humanities Commn.,

1990-91, Bill of Rights Summer Inst., U. Minn., 1991, Bill of Rights Edn. Collaborative, 1991-92, NEH Summer Inst., 1992, 94-96, U.S. Dept. Edn., 2003-05; Am. Memory fellow Libr. of Congress, 1999, Gilder Lehrman Summer Seminar for Tchrs., 2002, Assumption Coll., 2003.. Mem. NEA, Assn. Tchr. Educators, Orgn. Am. Historians (presenter ann. mtg. 1995, 98, 2001), Nat. Coun. Social Studies, Nat. Coun. History Educators, Wis. Assn. Tchr. Educators (exec. bd. 1984-90, pres. 1989-90), St. Croix Valley Assn. Tchr. Educators (pres. 1984-86, 95-97), Minn. Assn. History Educators (v.p. 1994—), Minn. Edn. Assn., Phi Delta Kappa (chpt. pres. 1986-88, v.p. pres. membership 1998-2001, found. rep. 2001-2003). Home: 424 165th Ave Somerset WI 54025-7011 Office: White Bear Lake Pub Sc Saint Paul MN 55110 E-mail: rwgabrick@aol.com.

GABRIEL, EBERHARD JOHN, lawyer; b. Bucharest, Romania, Mar. 22, 1942; arrived in U.S., 1952, naturalized, 1955; s. William and Margaret (Eberhart) Krzyzewski; m. Janice Josephine Jedrzejewski, Aug. 21, 1965; children: John, Stephanie, Christopher. BA in English, St. Joseph's Coll. of Ind., 1963; JD, Georgetown U., 1966. Bar: Md. 1966, Minn. 1993, U.S. Supreme Ct. 1972. Staff atty. Fgn. Claims Settlement Commn., Washington, 1966-68; sr. v.p., gen. counsel Govt. Employees Fin. Corp., Denver, 1968-87; pres., CEO MNC Am. Indsl. Banks, Denver, 1987-89; v.p., asst. gen. counsel and compliance officer ITT Consumer Fin. Corp., Mpls., 1989-94; pvt. practice Mpls., 1994-95; coun. Comml. Credit Co., Balt., 1995-99; sr. v.p., gen. counsel Citibank USA, Wilmington, Del., 1995—2002; assoc. gen. counsel Citi Fin., Balt., 2002—. Fellow St. Joseph's Coll.; pres. Indsl. Bankers Assn. Colo., 1985-89; sec., treas. Indsl. Bank Savs. Guaranty Corp. Colo., 1973-83, pres., 1983-87; lectr. advanced mgmt. program Am. Fin. Svcs. Assn., 1974-81, 85, 87, law com. 1978-89, bd. dirs., 1988-89. Bd. dirs. Jeffco/Lakewood (Colo.) C. of C., 1974-80, 82-86, chmn., 1984-85; mem. Jefferson County DA Adult Diversion Coun., 1985-89; mem. Jefferson Found., 1985-87; mem. adv. coun. Colo. Office Regulatory Reform, Colo. Dept. Regulatory Agys., 1984-89; trustee Lakewood Polit. Action Com., 1978-89, chmn., 1986-87, Lakewood on Parade, 1980, chmn. bd. govs., 1982; vice chmn. fin. divsn. United Way Metro Denver, 1982. Mem. ABA, Am. Corp. Counsel Assn., Md. Bar Assn., Phi Alpha Delta. Roman Catholic. Home: 6178 Mississippi Ln New Market MD 21774-6247 E-mail: gabelex@aol.com., gabrielg@citifinancial.com.

GABRIEL, EDWIN ZENITH, consulting engineer; b. Union City, N.J., Aug. 26, 1913; s. Enoch H. and Louise Beatrice (Seraydarian) G. BSME, N.J. Inst. Tech., 1936, ME, 1939, MSEE, 1952; postgrad., MIT, 1949-50. Registered profl. engr. N.J.; lic. Am. Bd. Profl. Engrs. and Land Surveyors. Heating systems engr. Webster-Talmadge Co., N.Y.C., 1938-39; efficiency engr. Prudential Ins. Co. of Am., Newark, 1939-41; mech. and elec. engr. U.S. Govt., 1941-52; project engr. Wright Aeronautical Corp., Caldwell, N.J., 1952-53, Kearfott (Singer Corp.), Clifton, N.J., 1953-55; asst. prof. elec. engring. Lehigh U., Bethlehem, Pa., 1955-56, Villanova (Pa.) U., 1956-60, Fairleigh Dickinson U., Teaneck, N.J., 1960-62; assoc. prof. weapons and engring. dept. U.S. Naval Acad., Annapolis, Md., 1962-64; electronic engr. Avionics Lab, Fort Monmouth, N.J., 1965-73. Presenter papers at profl. confs. Author: Automatic Control Systems, 1965, Computer Cookbook Approach to Digital Circuits and Computers, 1984, Cookbook Approach to Analog Circuits, 1985; numerous patents on computers and handling equipment in U.S., Can., Australia. Cubmaster, asst. scoutmaster Boy Scouts Am., Eatontown, N.J., 1946-48; sec. men's club Community Ch., Eatontown, 1946-48; founder, leader Search for Truth by Youth, Ocean Grove, N.J., 1985-87; Bible study tchr., Asbury Park, 1987-89; Bible tchr. Drop-in-Ctr., Thornley Chapel, Ocean Grove, 1989-90. With AUS, 1943-45. Recipient cert. of merit Internat. Inventor's Expn., 1965; grantee NSF, Stevens Inst. Tech., 1962, U. Notre Dame, 1963. Mem. IEEE (life), ASME (acting sec. materials handling div. 1939-42), Am. Helicopter Soc., N.J. Inst. Tech. Alumni Assn. Republican. Baptist. Achievements include patents for on aircraft and boat crash avoidance systems; patents pending for on auto collision avoidance and protection systems. Avocations: photography, choir singing, bible study leader, exercising. Home and Office: 91 Mt Tabor Way Ocean Grove NJ 07756-1437

GABRIEL, JEANETTE HANISEE, curator, art historian; b. Long Beach, Calif., Jan. 12, 1940; d. William Edward and Lorena (Mansell) Lester; m. Robert Maxwell Hanisee, Sept. 28, 1973 (div. 1986); children: Robb Andrew Hanisee, Michele Alpoente Hanisee, Leigh Mathilde Hanisee, Caleb Joseph Hanisee, Patricia Lorena Hanisee, Molly Beverly Hanisee; m. Angelo Julius Gabriel, Oct. 1, 1992. BS, MS, Calif. State U., Northridge, 1978; MA, U. Calif., Santa Barbara, 1988. Instr. Ventura (Calif.) Coll., 1979-81; dir., founder Adoptions Unltd., Ontario, Calif., 1981-83; curator L.A. County Mus. Art, 1988-92, Gilbert Collection, L.A. and London, 1994—; dir. art collections Gilbert Found., L.A., 2001—02. Author: The Gilbert Collection Micromosaics, 2000, The Gilbert Collection Hardstones; co-author: By Judgement of the Eye: The Varya and Hans Cohn Collection at the Los Angeles County Museum of Art, 1991, The World of Jade, 1992. Mem. Internat. Churchill Soc., The Churchill Ctr. (founding mem., Clementine Churchill assoc. 1998), Reform Club London. Avocations: antique collecting, movie memorabilia and autographs, gardening. Office: 2461 Santa Monica Blvd #323 Santa Monica CA 90404 also: Gilbert Collection Somerset House Strand London WC2R 1LA England Fax: 310-271-1854. E-mail: jeanettegabriel@aol.com.

GABRIEL, JUDITH A. bodywork therapist, educator, writer; b. Reading, Pa., July 14, 1949; d. Daniel Jacob and Alma Geraldine (Wengel) Tobias; m. Cleon Jay Hertzog, Oct. 5, 1974 (div. 1987). BS, Kutztown U., 1971, MEd, 1977; cert. massage therapist, Pa. Sch. Muscle Therapy, Phila., 1989; further tng., U.S. and Sweden. Cert. tchr. Pa., bodywork therapist. Tchr. Hamburg (Pa.) Area Sch. Dist., 1971-96; bodywork therapist, owner, operator Judith Gabriel Integrational Bodywork, Reading, Pa., 1989—; Rebirther (breathwork counseling) Reading, Pa., 1988—. Presenter WIOV Radio, 1997; asst. Patrick Collard's Internat. Apprenticeship, 1997, 98, 99; prodr. concert A Tribute to John Denver: The Man and His Music, Kempton, Pa., 2000; prodr. A Tribute to John Denver: The Man and His Music concert, Kempton, Pa., 2001; organizer Hibernia County Park, Pa., 2002; pres., CEO, The John Denver Meml. Found., Inc.; presenter Tuly's Conf. for Women, Reading, Pa., 2003; prodr., pres./CEO John Denver Meml. Found., Inc.; prodr. concert A Tribute to John Denver: The Man and His Music, Hibernia County Park, Pa., 2002; presenter Tulip Conf. for Women, Reading, Pa., 2003. Choir singer various chs., Reading; stress mgmt. demonstrator Berks Advocates Against Violence, Reading, 1997. Recipient Corp. Achiever award, Multiple Sclerosis Found., 2002. Mem.: Berks C. of C., Assoc. Bodyworkers and Massage Profls. (cert. massage therapist, cert. bodywork therapist). Avocations: reading, walking, singing, meditation, travel.

GABRIEL, MARTIN GEORGE, engineering consultant; b. Chgo., Sept. 21, 1926; M. Marie T. DeBlasio, June 25, 1949; children: Martin, James, Kathleen, Jeanne, Mary. BSME, Ill. Inst. Tech., 1947; MS in Engring. Mechanics, U. Mich., 1955. Engr. Borg Warner Corp., Chgo., 1947-50; rsch. engr. Ford Motor Co. Rsch. Lab., Dearborn, Mich., 1950-52; supr. automatic transmissions Ford Motor Co., Livonia, Mich., 1952-75; reliability engr., supr. Ford Car product Devel., Livonia, Mich., 1975-91; sr. reliability engr. Ford Powertrain Ops., Dearborn, 1991-95; ret., 1995; pres. Martin G. Gabriel and Assocs., Inc., Bloomfield Hills, MI, 1995—. Instr. automotive dynamics Oakland U., Rochester, Mich., 1965-68. Patentee in field, contbr. articles to profl. jours. Past pres. Cath. Youth Orgn., Detroit, 1992-93; bd. dirs. Detroit Area Coun. Boy Scouts. Am., 1969—. Recipient Outstanding Engr. award Profl. Engrs. Industry, Mich., 1988, Pres.'s citation Ill. Inst. Tech., 1992, Silver Beaver award, 1979. Fellow NSPE (Engr. of Yr. 1994); mem. ASME (life), Soc. Automotive Engrs. (life, elected bd. dirs. 1996-99, chmn. engring. meetings bd. 1994-95, Forest McFarland award 1986), Mich. Soc. Profl. Engrs. (pres. 1991-92), Sokol Detroit, Sr. Men's Club of Birmingham. Roman Catholic. Avocations: violin, portrait painting, golf, small fruit orchard. Home: 4396 Geisler Ct Bloomfield Hills MI 48301-1233 E-mail: Hornblwr1@aol.com.

GABRIEL, MICHAEL, psychology educator; b. Phila., May 5, 1940; s. Michael and Josephine (Alesio) G.; m. Linda Prinz, June, 1967 (div.); 1 child, Joseph Michael; m. Sonda S. Walsh, 1984. AB in Psychology, St. Joseph's Coll., 1962; MA, U. Wis., 1965, PhD, 1967. Asst. prof. Pomona Coll., Claremont, Calif., 1967—70; staff psychologist Pacific State Hosp., Pomona, Calif., 1968-70; NIMH sr. postdoctoral fellow U. Calif.-Irvine, 1970-72; asst. prof. U. Tex.-Austin, 1973-77, assoc. prof., 1977-82; prof. psychology U. Ill., Urbana, 1982—, appointee Ctr. for Advanced Study, 1990-91. Area chmn. Biol. Psychology Program, U. Tex., Austin, 1979-82; mem. rev. panel in behavioral and neural scis. NSF, 1988-91, prin. investigator database system for neuronal pattern analysis project, 1992—, ad hoc mem. biopsychology rev. panel, 1997-98; faculty Beckman Inst., U. Ill., Urbana, 1989—; chmn. Neuronal Pattern Analysis Group, Beckman Inst., mem. neuroinformatics rev. panel, NIH, 2000-. Co-editor: (with J. Moore) Learning and Computational Neuroscience: Foundations of Adaptive Networks, 1989, (with B. Vogt) Neurobiology of Cingulate Cortex and Limbic Thalamus, 1993; mem. editl. bd. Neural Plasticity, Neurobiology of Learning and Memory. Grantee NIMH, 1978-88, 98—, NIH, 1988—, Air Force Office Sci. Rsch., 1988-91, NSF, 1992—, NIDA, 1996-2001. Fellow Am. Psychol. Soc., Internat. Behavioral Neurosci. Soc.; mem. Sigma Chi. Office: U Ill Beckman Inst 405 N Mathews Ave Urbana IL 61801-2325 E-mail: mgabriel@uiuc.edu.

GABRIEL, MORDECAI LIONEL, biologist, educator; b. N.Y.C., Mar. 18, 1918; s. Joseph and Bertha (Fram) G.; m. Elinor Rosenstein, Nov. 11, 1945; children— Alisa, Jessica. AB, Yeshiva U., 1938; MA, Columbia, 1938, PhD, 1944. Instr. genetics U. Conn., 1943-45; mem. faculty Bklyn. Coll., 1945—, prof. biology, 1963—, chmn. dept., 1965-71; dean Bklyn. Coll. (Sch. Sci.), 1971-76, acting v.p. for acad. affairs, 1981-82; assoc. provost Bklyn. Coll., 1982-88, assoc. provost emeritus, 1988—. Vis. prof. Columbia, 1956; Fulbright lectr., vis. prof. U. Tel Aviv, 1959-60; mem. Marine Biol. Lab., Woods Hole, Mass., 1950— Author: (with S. Fogel) Great Experiments in Biology, 1956. Ford Found. faculty fellow, 1955-56 Fellow AAAS; mem. Am. Soc. Zoologists, Am. Assn. Anatomists, N.Y. Acad. Scis., Soc. Study Evolution, Vertebrate Paleont. Soc., AAUP (pres. Bklyn. Coll. chpt. 1964-66), Phi Beta Kappa, Sigma Xi. Home: 120 Old Mill Rd Great Neck NY 11023-1936 Office: Brooklyn Coll Brooklyn NY 11210

GABRIEL, PETER PAUL, educator; b. Halle, Germany, July 11, 1929; s. Paul and Eva Wernecke G.; m. Linea Elizabeth Larson, Sept. 9, 1950; children: Paul Lawrence, John Peter, Kathryn Anne, Christina Eva. MBA, Harvard U., 1962, DBA, 1965. Various adminstrv. positions, Germany, France, S. Am., 1948-60; assoc. McKinsey & Co., N.Y.C., 1966-69, ptnr., 1969-73; prof. of mgmt., dean Sch. of Mgmt. Boston U., 1972-76; prof. bus. adminstrn. U. Ulm, Germany, 1989-92. Contbr. articles and essays to publs. in field. Recipient G.M. Loeb award for Disting. Writing in Bus. and Fin., U. Conn., 1967, Horace G. Crockett award McKinsey & Co., N.Y., 1966. Home: 240 Beldingville Rd Ashfield MA 01330

GABRIEL, RENNIE, financial counselor, author, publisher; b. L.A., 1948; m. Judi Robbins, Nov. 24, 1968 (div. Feb. 1989); children: Ryan, Davida; m. Lesli Gilmore, May 5, 1990 (div. Aug. 1998); m. Dianne Merryl, Aug. 28, 1999. BA, Calif. State U., Northridge, 1971; CLU, Am. Coll., 1979, Cert. Fin. Planner, 1988. Ins. agt. Prudential and Provident Mutual, Encino, Calif., 1972-78; pension cons. Shadur LaVine & Assocs., Encino, 1978-81; owner Artist Corner Gallery Inc., Encino, 1977-82; pension and fin. planner Gabriel Tolleson & Stroum, Tarzana, Calif., 1983-87; pension cons., fin. planner Shadur LaVine/Integrated Fin., Encino, 1987-90; dir. pensions U.S. Life of Calif., Pasadena, Calif., 1983; fin. planner Pension Alternatives, Encino, 1990-92, The Fin. Coach Inc., Encino, 1993—. Instr. UCLA, 1992—; pub. Gabriel Publs., 1996—. Author: Wealth On Any Income, 1999, You Too Can Create Wealth, 1999; contbr. articles to fin. publs. Mem. Internat. Assn. Fin. Planning (pres. San Fernando Valley chpt. 1992), Nat. Assn. Life Underwriters (Achievement award 1974, Nat. Quality award 1975, Million Dollar Round Table 1990), Internat. Assn. Fin. Planning, CLUs, Inst. Cert. Fin. Planners, Employee Assistance Profls. Assn. (treas. San Fernando Valley chpt. 1992), Apt. Assn. San Fernando Valley-Ventura County (bd. mem. 1992). Avocations: jogging, skiing, real estate management, psychology. E-mail: renniecoach@earthlink.net.

GABRIEL, RONALD SAMUEL, child neurologist; b. Monterey, Calif., Mar. 19, 1937; s. Philip Louis and Theresa Shaheen Gabriel; children: Philip Louis III, Paula Shaheen, Matthew William. BA with honors, Yale U., 1959; MD, Boston U., 1963. Diplomate Am. Bd. Psychiatry and Neurology (examiner 1978-88), Am. Bd. Pediatrics. Intern, resident in pediatrics Los Angeles County Gen. Hosp., 1963-66; fellow in neurology and pediatric neurology UCLA med. ctr., 1966-68, 70-71; head physician, cons. Calif. Children's Svcs., 1970—; clin. prof. neurology/pediatrics UCLA Sch. Medicine, 1971—, dir. pediat. neurology/outpatient, 1971-76. Cons. Regional Ctr.-Calif., 1971—; vis. prof. Prince of Wales, Royal Children's Hosp., Sydney and Melbourne, Australia, 1978; mem. expert panel L.A. Superior Ct., 1992—; founding and mng. gen. ptnr. Med. Imaging of So. Calif., L.A., 1980-94; mng. dir. GFA Cattle and Farm Co. Author: The 410 Shotgun, 2000, Diary of a Mountain Hunter, 2000; contbr.: Textbook of Child Neurology, 1974, 4 edits., 1990, Difficult Diagnoses in Pediatrics, 1990, Founders of Child Neurology, 1990. Mng. dir. GFF Natural History Mus. Maj. U.S. Army, 1968-70. Spl. fellow Nat. Inst. Neurol. Disease/Stroke, 1966-68, 70-71. Fellow Am. Acad. Pediatrics, Am. Acad. Neurology; mem. Calif. Med. Assn. (mem. sci. adv. panel 1987-94, chmn. sci. adv. com. 1989-90). Roman Catholic. Avocations: writing, mountaineering, hunting. Office: Neurology-Pediat Neurology Assocs 2080 Century Park E Ste 203 Los Angeles CA 90067-2005 Fax: (310) 277-9285.

GABRIELE, CHARLES, composer, educator; b. N.Y.C., May 31, 1921; s. Benedict and Rose Tese Gabriele; m. Dina Kurochkin; 1 child, Joanna (dec.). BA, NYU, 1943, MA, 1944; PhD, Marshall Grad. Sch., Jersey City, N.J., 1948; D Music (hon.), Coll. Music, Rome, 1981. Tchr. Rice HS, N.Y.C., 1945—46; instr. St. Peters Coll., Jersey City, 1946—48; assoc. prof. Monmouth Coll., Highland Park, NJ, 1948—50; prof. Rutgers U., New Brunswick, NJ, 1950—57; pub. affairs officer U.S. Dept. Def., Washington, 1960—77; composer Comet Press, Bowie, Md., 1978—93; composer in residence U.S. Naval Acad. Band, Annapolis, Md., 1976—81, Venice Concert Band, Venice, Fla., 1994—. Composer: Christopher Columbus March, 1976 (medal, 1977), Clarinet Concertino, 1992 (plaque, 1992), Lilia Craige Overture, 1995 (trophy, 1996). Lt. USN, 1957—60. Recipient Knighthood in Order of Merit award, Rep. Italy, 1979, honor, U.S. Congress, 1980, 1991, namesake for Gabriele Pavilion, Daytona Beach Coll., 1992. Mem.: Am. Assn. Composers Authors. Democrat. Roman Catholic. Avocation: model railroading. Home: 864 Connemara Cir Venice FL 34292-2260

GABRIELI, ANNA, voice educator; d. Richard Hendrickson and Dorothy Colman Wallace; m. Peter Elvins, May 8, 1957; children: Elisabeth, Eleonora, Laura. MusB, Manhattan Sch. Music, 1993; MusM, New Eng. Conservatory, 1995. Opera singer numerous world wide Opera Houses, 1968—89; voice tchr. Longy Sch. Music, Cambridge, Mass., 1996—; pvt. studio Belmont, 1980—; voice tchr. Washington Opera Young Artist Program, Washington, 2002—. Bd. mem. Powers Music Sch., Belmont, 1995—99. Mem.: Nat. Assn. Tchrs. of Singing (competition judge 1995—). Episcopal. Avocations: reading, theater, concerts, dance. Home: 710 Pleasant St Belmont MA 02478

GABRIELSON, CHARLES, publishing executive; Various mgt. pos. Gannett Co., Inc., 1971—84; formerly advert. dir. Bambergers Co., NY; mkt. sales dir. Advert. Age, 1986—89; exec. V.P., USA Weekend Gannett Co., Inc., 1989—96, pub. USA Weekend, 1996—. Office: Gannett Co Inc 535 Madison Ave Fl 21 New York NY 10022-4212*

GABRIELSON, IRA WILSON, physician, educator; b. N.Y.C., Nov. 27, 1922; s. Benjamin and Lily (Baran) G.; m. Mary Putnam Oliver, Sept. 4, 1948; children: Deborah Anne, David Dwight, Hugh Wilson, Carl Oliver. BA, Columbia U., 1944, MD, 1949; MPH, Johns Hopkins U., 1959. Diplomate: Am. Bd. Pediatrics, Nat. Bd. Med. Examiners. Adminstrv. asst., asst. dir. Johns Hopkins Hosp., 1953-57; dir. community program retarded children New Haven, 1959-61; asst. attending pediatrician Yale-New Haven Community Hosp., 1959-68; asst. prof. public health Yale, 1961-68, exec. officer dept. epidemiology and public health, 1962-67; clin. prof. U. Calif., Berkeley, 1968-71; prof., chmn. dept. community and preventive medicine Med. Coll. Pa., 1971-89, prof. pediatrics, 1987-90, prof. emeritus, 1990—. Adj. prof., exec. dir. physician asst. program Springfield (Mass.) Coll., 1994-97; cons. in field. Editor Medicine Looks at the Humanities, 1987. With AUS. Fellow Nat. Found., 1958 Fellow Am. Acad. Pediatrics, Am. Public Health Assn., Coll. Physicians Phila. (pub. health com. 1976-90); mem. Phila. Pediatric Soc. (chmn. sch. health com. 1983-90), Sigma Xi, Delta Omega. Clubs: Appalachian Mountain (Boston). Avocations: photography, hiking. Home: 85 Old Goshen Rd Williamsburg MA 01096-9707 Office: Med Coll Pa Dept Cmty & Preventive Med 1505 Race St # Ms644 Philadelphia PA 19102-1119

GABRIELSON, SHIRLEY GAIL, nurse; b. San Francisco, Mar. 17, 1934; d. Arthur Obert and Lois Ruth (Lanterman) Ellison; m. I. Grant Gabrielson, Sept. 11, 1955; children: James Grant, Kari Gay. BS in Nursing, Mont. State U., 1955. RN, Mont. Staff and operating room nurse Bozeman (Mont.) Deaconess Hosp., 1954-55, 55-56; staff nurse Warm Springs State Hosp., 1955; office nurse, operating room asst. Dr. Craft, Bozeman, 1956-57; office nurse Dr. Bush, Beach, N.D., 1957-58; pub. health nurse Wibaux County, 1958-59; staff and charge nurse Teton Meml. Hosp., Choteau, Mont., 1964-65; staff pediatric and float nurse St. Patrick Hosp., Missoula, Mont., 1965-70; nurse, insvc. dir. Trinity Hosp., Wolf Point, Mont., 1970-79; ednl. coord. Community Hosp. and Nursing Home, Poplar, Mont., 1979-96; coord. staff devel. Faith Luth. Home, Wolf Point, 1980-81; risk mgr. Northeast Mont. Health Svcs., Inc., Poplar, 1996—. CPR instr. ARC, Am. Heart Assn., Great Falls, Mont., 1979-97; condr. workshops and seminars; program coord., test proctor for cert. nursing assts., 1989-96; risk mgr. N.E. Mont. Health Svcs., Poplar, Wolf Point, 1996—; preceptor for student nurses in rural health nursing clin. U. N.D., 1993-96. Author: Independent Study for Nurse Assistants, 1977. Former asst. camp leader Girl Scouts U.S.A.; former mother advisor, bd. dirs. Rainbow Girls; pres. Demolay Mothers Club, 1977; bd. dirs. Mont. div. Am. Cancer Soc., 1984-90, mem. awards com., 1986-89; founder Tri-County Parkinson's Support Group, N.E. Mont.; mem. Lewis & Clark Bicentennial com. Recipient Lifesaver award Am. Cancer Soc., 1987, Svc. award ARC, 1989, Health and Human Svcs. award Mont. State Dept., 1990, U.S. Dept. Health award, 1990, Outstanding award, U.S. HHS, Mont. Health Promotion award Dept. Health and Environ. Scis. Mem. ANA, Mont. Nurses Assn. (mem. commn. on continuing edn. 1977-91, chmn. 1984-86), Order Eastern Star (Worthy grand matron 1995-96), Alpha Tau Delta (alumni pres. 1956). Presbyterian. Avocations: music, travel, writing prose and poetry, gardening, interior decorating. Home: 428 Hill St Wolf Point MT 59201-1244 Office: NE Mont Health Svcs Inc PO Box 38 Poplar MT 59255-0038

GABRILOVE, JACQUES LESTER, physician; b. N.Y.C., Sept. 21, 1917; s. Benjamin and Pauline (Levine) G.; m. Hilda R. Weiss, May 19, 1946; children: Sandra Leslie Saltzman, Janice Lynn Gabrilove Dirzulaitis. BS magna cum laude, CCNY, 1936; MD, NYU, 1940. Diplomate Am. Bd. Internal Medicine. Intern Mt. Sinai Hosp., N.Y.C., 1940-41, rotating intern, 1941-43, vol. radiology, 1943, resident medicine, 1943-44, Blumenthal fellow medicine, 1946-48, research asst. medicine, 1949-51, asst. attending physician, 1952-60, assoc. attending physician, 1960-68, attending physician, 1969—. Clin. prof. medicine Mt. Sinai Sch. Medicine, 1969-82, chief endocrine clinic, 1969-92, Baumritter prof., 1982-90, Baumritter prof. emeritus, 1990—, prof., 1995—, cting dir. divsn. endocrinology, 1985, assoc. dir. divsn., 1986—, dir. endocrine fellowship program, 1986—; Libman fellow in medicine Yale U., 1945; clin. asst. prof. SUNY Coll. Medicine, N.Y.C., 1957-59, clin. assoc. prof., 1959-66, clin. prof., 1966-69, professorial lectr., 1969—; cons. endocrinology VA Hosp., East Orange, N.J., 1958-66, Elizabeth A. Horton Hosp., Middletown, N.Y., 1961—, VA Hosp., Bronx, N.Y., 1969—, Norwalk (Conn.) Hosp., 1974—, Elmhurst (N.Y.) City Hosp., St. Francis Hosp., Port Jervis, N.Y.; mem. panel on metabolic and rheumatoid diseases U.S. Pharmacopeia, 1956; mem. spl. com. on rsch. tng. grants in diabetes, endocrinology and metabolism NIH, 1976-79, mem. com. on diabetes rsch. and tng. ctrs., 1977-79; Saltzman lectr. Mt. Sinai Hosp., Cleve., 1974; cons. Jour. Urology, 1984-89. Author, contbr. to books in field, also articles to med. jours.; mem. editl. bd. Mt. Sinai Jour. Trustee, v.p. area Jewish synagogue. Recipient Globus prize Mt. Sinai Jour., Townsend Harris medal CCNY Alumni Assn., 1998; J. Lester Gabrilove award established in his honor, 1988; named to Hall of Fame Alumni Assn. Townsend Harris H.S. Fellow ACP, Am. Coll. Endocrinology (Disting. Clin. Endocrinologist award 1996, Festschrift in his honor on 80th birthday), N.Y. Acad. Medicine, Phi Beta Kappa; mem. AMA, AAAS, Am. Assn. Clin. Endocrinologists (Disting. Clin. Endocrinologist award 1996), Am. Diabetes Assn., Harvey Soc., Endocrine Soc., Royal Soc. Medicine, Pan Am. Med. Assn. (v.p. N.Am. endocrinology), Peruvian Endocrine Soc. (hon.), N.Y. Acad. Scis., N.Y. County Med. Soc., N.Y. Diabetes Assn., Mt. Sinai Alumni Assn. (pres. 1970, Jacobi medallion 1973), Lotos Club (bd. dirs.), Alpha Omega Alpha. Achievements include research in delineaton of hyperfunctioning and hypofunctioning endocrine disorders of the adrenal cortex and gonads; mechanism of gynecomastia; medical treatment of thyrotoxicosis; med. treatment of benign prostatic hyperplasia; pathogenesis of the polycystic ovary syndrome. Home: 25 E 86th St New York NY 10028-0553 E-mail: Lester.gabrilove@MSSM.edu.

GABRIS, GEORGE STEVEN, sculptor, welder; b. N.Y.C., Jan. 2, 1953; s. Stephen John and Kveta (Rybička) G.; m. Stephanie Anne Mazanek, Dec. 30, 1989. Cert. in Welding, Albuquerque Tech. Vocat. Inst., 1979. Tchr. art, recreation instr. N.Y.C. Housing Authority, 1975-76; artist, 1977; prodn. welder Environ. Bldg. Products, Albuquerque, 1979-81, H&L Iron Works, Albuquerque, 1982, Hemisphere Steel Co., Bklyn., 1984-85; test welder R&D Eutectic Corp. of Eutectic and Castolin Inc. Internat., Flushing, N.Y., 1985-88; car maintainer in train overhaul shop N.Y.C. Transit Authority, 1988—. Group exhbns. include Lever House, N.Y.C., 1964, 75, A.S.A. Gallery, Albuquerque, 1981, 82, Gelabert Studios, N.Y.C., 1992, Abney Gallery, N.Y.C., 1992, Crossland Svs. Bank, L.I. and Manhattan, N.Y., 1993, Limner Gallery, N.Y.C., 1993, 94, Westbeth Gallery, N.Y.C., 1974, 94, 97, Art Initiatives, N.Y.C., 1996, Broome St. Gallery, N.Y.C., 1996, Stephen Gang Gallery, N.Y.C., 1997, (website) Internat. Artists Interface, 1996—, Americas Towers Lobby, 1998-99; represented in numerous pvt. collections; published in Creative INsight, 2000. Vol. dept. social and cmty. svcs. N.Y.C. Housing Authority, 1974, 75; youth project coord. Visions/Urban Youth Project, N.Y.C., 1976. Recipient Critics' Pix award Manhattan Arts Internat. Mag., 1994, Showcase award, 1996, award of excellence, 1998, 99, 2000; 1st prize Internat. Art League, 1998. Mem. Nat. Sculpture Soc., Am. Welding Soc. (cert.), Orgn. Ind. Artists, Transit Workers Union (local 100), N.Y. Artists Equity Assn., Inc., Artists Talk on Art. Democrat. Avocations: art collector, bread baker, gourmet cook, exotic birds, "good" cigars. Home: 1123 Ave K Apt D-1 Brooklyn NY 11230-4124 E-mail: gssculp@aol.com.

GACEM, DEBRA ANN, critical care nurse; b. St. Louis, Aug. 19, 1955; d. Roy Leo and Nina Lee (Sutton) Case; 1 child, Sam Gacem. Diploma, Barnes Hosp. Sch. Nursing, St. Louis, 1975. Cert. critical care nurse. Staff nurse Barnes-Jewish Hosp., St. Louis; asst. head nurse post-anesthesia care unit Barnes Hosp., St. Louis, staff nurse post-anesthesia care unit, unit based clin. educator for cardiothoracic post-anes care. Mem. Am. Soc. Post Anesthesia Nurses, Ill. Soc. Post Anesthesia Nurses, Barnes Hosp. Sch. Nursing Alumni Assn. Home: 3210 Yorkchester Dr Saint Louis MO 63129-1736 E-mail: debgcm@bigfoot.com.

GACK, KENNETH DAVID, lawyer; b. Bucyrus, Ohio, July 28, 1951; s. William E. and Vera Ann (Welsh) G.; children: Vanessa Theodora (dec.), Colin David, Lily Elizabeth, Remington John. BA in Anthropology, Calif. State U., Dominguez Hills, 1973; JD, Pepperdine U., 1976. Bar: Calif. 1976, U.S. Dist. Ct. (cen. dist.) Calif. 1977, U.S. Dist. Ct. (ea. dist.) Calif. 1982, U.S. Dist. Ct. (no. dist.) Calif. 1983, U.S. Ct. Appeals (9th cir.) 1977. Assoc. Law Office Robert L. Charbonneau Inc., Newport Beach, Calif., 1976-78; pvt. practice Sebastopol, Calif., 1978-80; assoc. Spridgen, Barrett et al, Santa Rosa, Calif. 1980-82; ptnr. James, Gack, Bernheim & Hicks, Santa Rosa, 1982-94; pvt. practice Santa Rosa, 1994-96, 96—; mediator. arbitrator JAMS (Jud. Arbitration and Mediation Svs.), 1996—. Planning commr. City of Sebastopol, 1979-80 Mem. Am. Trial Lawyers Assn., Calif. Trial Lawyers Assn. Democrat. Office: JAMS/Endispute 418 B St Ste 200 Santa Rosa CA 95401-8500

GAD, LANCE STEWART, investment advisor, lawyer, private investor; b. Peekskill, N.Y., Dec. 11, 1945; s. Martin Harold and Claire (Entner) G.; m. Helen Alexandra Grevey, Jan. 14, 1972 (div. 1978); m. Janiece Lee Feiden, Feb. 14, 1987. BA cum laude, SUNY, Stony Brook, 1967; JD, Cornell U., 1970 MBA, 1971; LLM in Taxation, NYU Law Sch., 1975. Assoc. Spear & Hill N.Y.C., 1971-72, Wien, Malkin & Bettex, N.Y.C., 1972-74; mgr. Wheelabrator-Frye, N.Y.C., 1974-75, Citicorp, N.Y.C., 1975-86, Citibank N.A., N.Y.C. 1975-77, asst. v.p., 1977-79, v.p., 1979-86; v.p., gen. counsel and sec. Citicorp Services, Inc., N.Y.C., 1980-85; v.p. Citicorp Investment Bank, N.Y.C., 1985

86; investment advisor WR Family Assocs., N.Y.C., 1986-90, Am. Securities Corp., N.Y.C., 1986-90; chmn., mng. dir., chief investment officer Greenfield Hill Capital Mgmt., 1991—; chmn., pres., treas., dir. The Lance and Janiece Gad Found., Inc., 1987—. Mem deans spl. leadership com. Cornell Law Sch., 2000—; co-pres. family coun. The Jewish Home for the Elderly, 2001—. Mem. N.Y. State Bar Assn., Cornell Law Assn., Johnson Sch. Mgmt. Alumni Assn., NYU Grad. Sch. Law Alumni Assn., Cornell Club of N.Y. Home and Office: 1250 Fence Row Dr Fairfield CT 06824 also: 6 Peter Cooper Rd Apt 8F New York NY 10010-6709 also: 14 N Hollow Dr East Hampton NY 11937 E-mail: lancegad@optonline.net.

GADALA-MARIA, FRANCIS ARTURO, chemical engineering educator; b. San Salvador, El Salvador, Nov. 6, 1952; s. Salvador Gadala-Maria and Mary Issa; m. Sylvia Roxana Nasser, June 18, 1983; children: Daniel, Patrick. BSE, Princeton U., 1973; MS, Stanford U., 1974, PhD, 1979. Registered profl. engr., S.C. Tech. mgr. Kontein divsn. of Sigma, S.A., El Salvador, 1979-81; asst. prof. U. S.C., Columbia, 1982-92, asst. chmn. dept. chem. engring., 1991-96, assoc. prof., 1992—. Contbr. articles to profl. jours. Recipient Excellence in Tchg. award Mortar Bd. Soc., 1990. Mem. AIChE (chmn., vice chmn., sec., treas. Palmetto sect.), Soc. Rheology, Am. Chem. Soc., Phi Beta Kappa, Sigma Xi, Tau Beta Pi (chief faculty advisor 1995—). Office: U SC Dept Chem Engring Columbia SC 29208 E-mail: gadala-m@engr.sc.edu.

GADALLA, FARIDA, anesthesiologist; b. Alexandria, Egypt, Feb. 18, 1951; came to U.S., 1976; d. Mohamed Fahmy Gadalla and Thelma Burnley Fox; m. Mahmoud Towayer, 1974 (dec. Feb. 1979); m. Anthony Potulicki, June 29, 1984; children: Alexander, Julian, Peter. MBChB, Faculty of Medicine, 1974. Bd. cert. anesthesiologist. Intern faculty of medicine Alexandria U., 1975-76; resident in surgery Brookdale Hosp., Bklyn., 1976-77; resident in anesthesia N.Y. Hosp., N.Y.C., 1977-79, anesthesia fellow, 1979-80, attending anesthesioligst, 1980—, assoc. prof. clin. anesthesiology, 1980—. Mem. Am. Soc. Anesthesiology, Am. Soc. of Regional Anesthesiology, Soc. of Obstetrical Anesthesia and Perinatology, N.Y. State Soc. of Anesthesiology. Home: 80 Warren St Apt 47 New York NY 10007-1023 Office: NY Presbyn Hosp 525 E 68th St New York NY 10021-4870 E-mail: fgadalla@med.cornell.edu.

GADAPEE, BRETT RONALD, English language educator, coach; b. Berlin, Vt., Feb. 3, 1970; s. Richard H. and Patsy (Fleming) G.; m. Amy Katherine Adams, Aug. 1, 1997. BA in English, U. Fla., 1992, MA in Secondary English. Edn., 1993. Cert. secondary tchr., Fla., nat. bd. cert. tchr., 2003. English lang. tchr. Astronaut HS, Titusville, Fla., 1993-96, Orange Pk. HS, Fla., 1996-2000, Madison Mid. Sch., 2000—. Head coach jr. varsity football, Astronaut HS, Titusville, Fla., 1993-96, jr. varsity basketball, 1993-95, jr. varsity baseball, 1996, girls softball, Orange Park (Fla.) HS, 1997, asst. varsity football, 1997-2000, head jr. varsity softball, 1997, 98; asst. varsity football Astronaut, 2000—; track coach, head basketball coach Madison Middle Sch., 2000—. Methodist. Avocations: reading, golf. Home: 846 Willowwood Ave Titusville FL 32796-2254 Office: 3400 Dairy Rd Titusville FL 32796-1514

GADBERRY, VICKI LYNN HIMES, librarian; b. Frederick, Md., Jan. 3, 1950; d. Guilford Swisher and Eloise Alberta (Twentey) Himes; m. Eric Brett Gadberry, Aug. 15, 1971. BS, U. Md., 1971; MLS, U. S.C., 1974; postgrad., Penland Sch. Crafts, 1989, 96, Sul Ross State U., 1997-98. Cert. media coord. N.C. Dept. Pub. Instrn. Media coord. N.C. Pub. Schs., Fayetteville, 1976-78, Hendersonville, 1980-85, Asheville, 1985-88; pub. svcs. coord. Mars Hill (N.C.) Coll., 1990-92, reference svcs. libr., 1992-97; asst. exec. dir., adminstrn. Fort Davis (Tex.) C. of C., 1998—; owner Off The Wall Photos & Art, 2001—. On-site dir. Children's Art in the Mountains Program, Marshall, N.C., summer 1992, tchr. fiber art, summer 1990; artist-in-residence Mountain Arts Program, Waynesville, N.C., 1990. Project designer book: Molas!, 1998; contbr. articles, revs., index to profl. publs. Mem. planning com. Beacon Handloom Weaving Show, Asheville, N.C., 1988, 90-92, chair, 1989; bd. dirs. Children's Art in the Mountains Program, Marshall, N.C., 1991-93. Mem. Handweaver's Guild Am. (orgnl. C.O.E. Weaving com. co-chair 1992-94). Avocations: weaving, photography. Home: PO Box 393 Fort Davis TX 79734-0393 E-mail: gadberry@overland.net.

GADDES, RICHARD, performing arts administrator; b. Wallsend, Northumberland, Eng., May 23, 1942; s. Thomas and Emilie Jane (Rickard) G. L.T.C.L. in piano, L.T.C.L. for sch. music; G.T.C.L., Trinity Coll. Music, London, 1964; D. Mus. Arts (hon.), St. Louis Conservatory, 1983; D.F.A. (hon.), U. Mo.-St. Louis, 1984; D.Arts (hon.), Webster U., 1986. Founder, mgr. Wigmore Hall Lunchtime Concerts, 1965; dir. Christopher Hunt and Richard Gaddes Artists Mgmt., London, 1965-66; bookings mgr. Artists Internat. Mgmt., London, 1967-69; artistic adminstr. Santa Fe Opera, 1969—75, assoc. gen. dir., 1995—98; gen. dir. Opera Theatre of St. Louis, 1975-85, bd. dirs., 1985—; gen. dir. Sante Fe Opera, 1998. Bd. dirs. Grand Ctr., Inc., 1988—, pres., 1988-95; bd. dirs. William Matheus Sullivan Found. Mem. bd. advisors Royal Oak Found. Recipient Lamplighter award, 1982, Mo. Arts award, 1983, St. Louis award, 1983, Human Relations award Jewish-Am. Com., St. Louis, 1985, Nat. Inst. for Music Theatre award, 1986, Cultural Achievement award Young Audiences, 1987. Office: Santa Fe Opera PO Box 2408 Santa Fe NM 87504-2408

GADDIS, EVAN R. army officer; m. Bonnita Gaddis; children: Brent, Renee. BSBA, Cameron U.; MBA, Nat. U.; grad., Army Command-Gen. Staff Coll., Nat. War Coll. Commd. 2d lt. U.S. Army, 1968-2000, advanced through grades to maj. gen., 1999; various staff and command positions, forward observer Republic Vietnam, Vietnam; battery comdr. 37th F.A., Republic of Korea; bn. comdr. 5-15 F.A., Ft. Ord, Calif.; divsn. arty. comdr., chief staff 10th Mountain Divsn., Ft. Drum, N.Y.; sr. joint exercise planner Joint Staff U.S. Army; exec. asst. to chief staff of Army Pentagon, Washington; asst. divsn. comdr. (support) 25th Inf. Divsn., Hawaii; comdr. U.S. Army Family and Cmty. Support Ctr., Alexandria, Va.; comdg. gen. Recruiting Command U.S. Army, Ft. Knox, Ky., 1998—. Decorated Legion of Merit with four oak leaf cluster, Bronze Star, Purple Heart, others; recipient Def. Superior Svc. medal. Office: US Army Recruiting Command 1307 3d Ave Fort Knox KY 40121

GADDIS, JOHN LEWIS, history educator; b. Cotulla, Tex., Apr. 2, 1941; m. Toni Dorfman. BA, U. Tex., 1963, MA, 1965, PhD, 1968. Asst. prof. Ind. U. S.E., Jeffersonville, 1968-69; asst. prof. history Ohio U., Athens, 1969-71, assoc. prof., 1971-76, prof., 1976-83, disting. prof. history, 1983-97, dir. Contemporary History Inst., 1987-93; Robert Lovett prof. history Yale U., New Haven, 1997—. Vis. prof. Naval War Coll., 1975-77; Bicentennial prof. Am. history, U. Helsinki, 1980-81; vis. prof. politics Princeton U., 1987; Harmsworth prof. Am. History Oxford U., 1992-93, Eastman prof., 2000-01. Author: The United States and the Origins of the Cold War, 1941-47, 1972, Russia, the Soviet Union, and the United States: An Interpretive History, 1978, 2d edit., 1990, Strategies of Containment: A Critical Appraisal of Postwar American National Security Policy, 1982, The Long Peace: Inquiries into the History of the Cold War, 1987, The United States and the End of the Cold War, 1992, We Now Know: Rethinking Cold War History, 1997; The Landscape of History: How Historians Map the Past, 2002. Fellow Woodrow Wilson Ctr., 1995-96; recipient Bancroft prize, 1973, Stuart L. Bernath prize, 1973, Nat. Hist. Soc. prize, 1973. Mem. Am. Hist. Assn., Orgn. Am. Historians, Soc. for Historians of Am. Fgn. Rels., Coun. on Fgn. Rels.

GADDIS, JOHN ROBERT, music educator; b. Greenville, Ky., Nov. 14, 1949; s. Millard and Dorothy Louise (Lovell) G.; m. Anna Jeanne Berry, Dec. 17, 1971; children: John Mark, Charles Nathan, Jessica Dawn. BMus, Western Ky. U., 1972, MA in Edn., 1981; EdD, U. Ky., 1992. Choral and band dir. Elizabethtown (Ky.) High Sch., 1972—73; band and choral dir. Ctrl. City (Ky.) H.S., 1973—77; band dir. Franklin (Ky.)-Simpson H.S., 1977-79; asst. band dir. Western Ky. U., Bowling Green, Ky., 1981-82; prof. music, dean Sch. Music Campbellsville (Ky.) U., 1982—. Pres. Ky. Music Educators Assn. Adjudicator for band festivals and contests, guest conductor for honors bands and choirs, tuba soloist; youth choir dir. Forest Park Bapt. Ch., Bowling Green, 1970-71; min. of music Mill Creek Bapt. Ch., Radcliff, Ky., 1973, Calvary Bapt. Ch., Franklin, Ky., 1979-82, First Bapt. Ch., Albany, Ky., 1987-88, Lebanon Bapt. Ch., 1990-. Mem. Nat. Assn. for Coll. Wind and Percussion Instrs., Music Educators Nat. Conf., Soc. for Music Tchr. Edn. (state chmn. 1991-), Ky. Music Educators Assn. (bd. dirs. 1989-), Ky. Coalition for Music Edn. (bd. dirs. 1992-). Republican. Baptist. Avocations: golf, fishing, camping. Home: 109 Canterbury Way Campbellsville KY 42718-9546 Office: Campbellsville Univ One University Dr Campbellsville KY 42718

GADDIS, LARRY ROY, lawyer; b. Pratt, Kans., Nov. 8, 1941; s. Wade G. and Lorena (Pearce) G.; m. Barbara Ann Law, June 14, 1972; children: Jeffrey Wade, Aaron Paul. BA, U. Colo., Boulder, 1963; JD, U. Colo., 1969. Bar: Colo. 1969, U.S. Dist. Ct. Colo. 1969, U.S. Ct. Appeals (10th cir.) 1969. Staff atty. Pikes Peak Legal Services, Colorado Springs, Colo., 1969-71, dir., 1971-73; ptnr. Gaddis, Kin & Herd, P.C., Colorado Springs, 1973—. Vis. prof. U. Colo.-Colorado Springs, 1971-74; mem. Colorado Springs Estate Planning Coun., 1983—, pres., 1991. Bd. dirs. Colorado Springs Sch., 1973-96, pres., 1987-91, trustee emeritus, jud. performance commn., 1993-99; mem. Colo. Springs Cmty. Trust Bd., 1990—, chair 1999—, Pikes Peak Cmty. Found., 1997—; chmn. profl. adv. coun. Cath. Diocese of Colorado Springs, 1996-99; mem. Colo. Legal Svcs. Bd., 1999—. Mem. El Paso County Bar Assn. (probate sect. 1982—, pres. 1988), Colo. Bar Assn. (exec. council 1978), ABA, Phi Kappa Alpha. Democrat. Episcopalian. Office: 118 S Wahsatch Ave Colorado Springs CO 80903-3677

GADDIS, M. FRANCIS, mechanical and marine engineer, environmental scientist; b. Boston, July 27, 1920; s. Michael Joseph and Catherine Agnes (Lavelle) G.; m. Marie B. Leen, Nov. 22, 1946 (dec. Feb. 1979); children: Robert L., Paul L.; m. Jeanne Bowen Crites, Oct. 27, 1990. BS, U. Ala., 1945; BA, Adelphi U., 1977, MSc, cert. environ. mgmt., Adelphi U., 1979; MPhil, Columbia U., 1981, PhD, 1988. Chief marine engr. U.S. Army, Port of N.Y., 1944-45; svc. engr. Garlock Inc., Boston, 1946-47, ter. mgr. N.Y.C., 1947-61; pres., chief engr. Gaddis Engring. Co., Port Washington, N.Y., 1961—. Seals edn. workshop com. Dept. Energy, Office Naval Rsch., Am. Soc. Lubrication Engrs., ASME, 1979-80; naval arch. and marine engring. com. People to People Delegation to China, 1986, Delegation to Bicentennial Maritime Symposium, Australia, 1988, ASME Delegation to S.Am., 1989; Columbia U. del. Harwell Environ. seminar, Oxford (Eng.) U., 1982; engr. cons. Gaddis, Inc., Hilton Head Island, S.C., 1994—; People to People sci. and industry del. to Cuba, 2000. Author: Awareness of Environmental Hazards in Risk Management, 1979, Siting Criteria in Hazardous Waste Disposal, 1987, The Politics of Waste Disposal, 1989, Environmental Awareness, 1990. Recipient Disting. Alumni medal Adelphi U., 1984. Mem. ASME, Am. Soc. Naval Engrs. (Ppres. Club), Am. Soc. Tribologists and Lubrication Engrs. (emissions com. 1980-84), Nat. Assn. of Environ. Profls., Environ. Law Inst., Pacific Basin Consortium for Hazardous Waste Rsch., Fast-West Inst., Soc. Naval Architects and Marine Engrs., Assn. Environ. Profls. (Calif.), Marine Tech. Soc., N.Y. Acad. Scis., Soc. for Risk Analysis, John Henry Newman Hon. Soc., Columbia (N.Y.C.) Club, North Shore Yacht (Port Washington) Club, Adelphi U. Alumni Assn. (v.p. 1999-2003), Delta Tau Delta (MIT chpt. adviser 1946-47). Achievements include research in hydrogeological environmental considerations in toxic waste disposal facility siting, materials and systems in mechanical sealing and containment; co-development of cryogenic vapor barrier. Home: PO Box 411 Locust Valley NY 11560-0411 Office: Gaddis Engring Co PO Box 689 Port Washington NY 11050-0165

GADDIS, RICHARD WILLIAM, management educator; b. Tulsa, May 29, 1941; s. Preston Gilbert and Gladys Leona (Booton) G.; m. Janet Gail Roché, Nov. 23, 1974; 1 child, Jennifer Lee. BA, Northeastern State U., Tahlequah, Okla., 1966, MEd, 1971; EdD, U. Ark., 1988; MS in Mgmt., So. Nazarene U., Bethany, Okla., 1994; grad., Tulsa Citizens Police Acad., Broken Arrow, Okla., 1998. Bus. edn. tchr. Vinita (Okla.) High Sch., 1966-74, Oologah (Okla.) High Sch., 1974-77; bus. edn. instr. N.W. Tech. Inst., Springdale, Ark., 1977-86; asst. prof. bus./mktg. edn. SUNY, Oswego, 1988-90; asst. prof. office adminstrn. Lamar U., Beaumont, Tex., 1990-92; MBA/MSM program dir. grad. studies mgmt. So. Nazarene U., Bethany, Okla., 1992—, asst. prof. mgmt., 1992-94, assoc. prof. mgmt., 1994—2001, prof. mgmt., 2002—. Cons., lectr. in field. Contbr. articles to profl. jours. and mags. Mem. Class of XXII, Leadership Tulsa, 1995-96, Spring class Broken Arrow Citizens Police Acad., 2001. Recipient leadership tng. award Mountain-Plains Bus. Edn. Assn., 1974, Dale Carnegie pers. progress award, 1982, Golden Apple award Lamar U. Student Edn. Assn., 1991. Mem. NEA, Am. Vocat. Assn. (new profl. award 1989), Nat. Bus. Edn. Assn., Okla. Edn. Assn. (outstanding educator award 1975, outstanding univ. tchr. of yr. 1997), Okla. Bus. Edn. Assn. (adminstr. of yr. 1994), Northeastern State U. Alumni Assn. (citation of merit 1992), Mountain-Plains Bus. Edn. Assn. (Okla. rep. 1999-2002), Okla. Bus. Edn. Assn. (exec. bd. mem. 1999-2002), Alpha Phi Omega, Delta Mu Delta, Delta Sigma Pi, Kappa Delta Pi, Phi Delta Kappa, Pi Omega Pi, Rho Theta Sigma, Sigma Tau Delta, Delta Pi Epsilon. Nazarene. Home: 704 N Kalanchoe Ave Broken Arrow OK 74012-2273 Office: So Nazarene U 10159 E 11th Ste 200 Tulsa OK 74128

GADDIS ROSE, MARILYN, literature educator, translator; b. Fayette, Mo., Apr. 4, 1930; d. Merrill Elmer and Florence Georgia (Lyon) Gaddis; m. James Leo Rose, Dec. 23, 1956 (div. 1966); m. Stephen David Ross, Nov. 16, 1968; 1 child, David Gaddis Ross. BA, Central Meth. Coll., 1952; MA, U. S.C., Columbia, 1954-55; PhD, U. Mo., 1958; LHD, Ctrl. Meth. Coll., 1987. Instr. Stephens Coll., Columbia, Mo., 1958-68; assoc. prof. Ind. U., Bloomington, 1968; prof. comparative lit. SUNY, Binghamton, 1968—, disting. svc. prof., 1991—, dir. translation program, 1973—2002. Translator: (book) Axel, 1970, 1986, Eve of the Future Eden, 1981, Lui: A View of Him, 1986, Adrienne Mesurat, 1991, Volupté, The Sensual Man, 1995, Translation Horizon, 1996, Translation and Literary Criticism, 1998, Beyond the Western Tradition, 2000; editor, contbr.: book Translation Spectrum, 1981; editor: Translation Perspectives; contbr. articles to profl. jours. Fulbright fellow, U. Lyon, France, 1953—54, Humanities Rsch. Centre Sr. fellow, Australian Nat. U., 1977. Mem.: MLA (pres. N.E. sect. 1975—76, del. assembly 1974—78, 1984—87), Am. Translators Assn. (mng. editor series 1986—96, bd. dirs. 1986—88, endowed lectr. 1998—, Spl. Svc. award 1983, 1995, Alexander Gode award 1988), Am. Lit. Translators (sec.-treas. 1981—83), PEN N.Y. Home: 4 Johnson Ave Binghamton NY 13905-4312 E-mail: mgrose@binghamton.edu.

GADDY, DALE, executive; b. Asheville, N.C., Mar. 19, 1940; s. Mitchell Isaac and Dorothy Taylor G.; m. Jeannie Belk, May 27, 1962; 1 child, Taylor. BS, Appalachian State U., 1962, MA, 1963; EdD, Duke U., 1968; postgrad., U. Calif., L.A., 1969-70. Dir. rsch. Am. Assn. C.C.'s, Washington, 1970-73; v.p. Ednl. Rsch. Svc., Arlington, Va., 1973-78; dir. leadership tng. ctr. Nat. Sch. Bds. Assn., Alexandria, Va., 1978-91; dir. edn. & cert. Internat. Fabricare Inst., Silver Spring, Md., 1992-95; pres. Assn. Team, Inc., Fairfax, Va., 1995—; CEO Internat. Coun. Hotel, Restaurant & Instl. Edn., Washington, Va., 1998-2000. Adj. prof. edn. law George Mason U., Fairfax, 1975-86; adj. prof. travel. & tourism No. Va. C.C., Annandale, 1992-99; adj. prof. hospitality Va. Tech., Falls Church, 2000-01. Chair Fairfax City Sch. Bd., 1979-88 Mem. Am. Soc. Assn. Execs. (chpt. rels. sect. colun., edn. sect. coun. 1997-2000), Greater Washington Soc. Assn. Execs. (Monument award 1997). Office: Assn Team Inc PO Box 2873 Fairfax VA 22031-3513 Fax: 703-352-4478. E-mail: ateam@erols.com.

GADDY, JAMES LEOMA, chemical engineer, educator; b. Jacksonville, Fla., Aug. 16, 1932; s. Leoma Ithama and Mary Elizabeth (Edwards) Gaddy; m. Betty Maricella, Sept. 7, 1952; children: James, Teresa. BSChemE, La. Poly. U., 1955; MSChemE, U. Ark., 1968; PhDChemE, U. Tenn., 1972. Registered prof engr, Ark. Process engr. Ethyl Corp., Baton Rouge, 1955-60; project mgr., engring. supr. Ark.-La. Gas, Shreveport, La., 1960-66; assoc. prof. chem engring. U. Mo., Rolla, 1972-79, prof., dir. rsch. ctr., 1979-80; prof., head chem. engring. U. Ark., Fayetteville, 1980-88, disting. prof., 1988-91, emeritus disting. prof., 1991—. Pres Bioengineering Resources, Fayetteville, 1984—; consult to 15 orgns; teacher numerous short courses in chemical eng for indust; adminr research contracts various cos; vis. prof. Swiss Fed. Inst. Tech. Zurich, 1978. Mem ed bd: Biomass and Biofuels, Chemical Eng R&D; contbr. to numerous presentations and publs. Mem.: AAAS, AIChE (mem speakers bur), Am Soc Eng Educ, Am Chemical Soc, Omega Chi Epsilon, Alpha Chi Sigma, Tau Beta Pi (Eminent Eng 1976). Baptist. Home: 2207 Tall Oaks Dr Fayetteville AR 72703-6126 Office: Bioengring Resources 1650 Emmaus Rd Fayetteville AR 72701-7283 Personal E-mail: jlgaddy863@cs.com. Business E-Mail: jlgaddy@aol.com.

GADDY, OSCAR LEE, electrical engineering educator; b. Republic, Mo., July 18, 1932; s. Oscar Franklin and Ruth Winnie (Cowart) G.; m. Mary Margaret Vaeth, Aug. 8, 1953; children: Oscar Franklin, John Anton, William Lee. BS, U. Kans., 1957, MS, 1959; PhD, U. Ill., 1962. Rsch. asst., instr. dept. elec. engring. U. Kans., Lawrence, 1957-59; rsch. asst. dept. elec. and computer engring. U. Ill., Urbana, 1959-62, asst. prof., 1962-65, assoc. prof., 1965-69, assoc. head, 1971-84, prof. dept. elec. and computer engring., 1969-93, prof. emeritus, 1993—. Contbr. articles to profl. jours. Fellow IEEE. Avocations: skeet and trap shooting, antique firearm restoration. Home: 609 E Evergreen Ct Urbana IL 61801-5930 Office: U Ill Dept Elec & Computer Engring 1406 W Green St Urbana IL 61801-2918 E-mail: o-gaddy@uiuc.edu.

GADE, MARVIN FRANCIS, retired paper company executive; b. Clinton, Iowa, Nov. 10, 1924; s. Bernhardt Henry and Anna Mae (Jessen) G.; m. Lorraine F. McDonald, Dec. 2, 1944 (dec.); children: Michael David, Patricia Ann Gade Conn, Steven Dennis, Laura Jean Gade Walls, Mary Kay Gade Brock, Karen Lynn Gade Murphy, Jeffrey Scott; m. Carmell M. Clayton, July 16, 1995. BS in Engring., U. Iowa, 1952; postgrad. exec. program, UCLA, 1960-61. Process instrumentation engr. Standards Brands Co., Clinton, 1946-50; with Kimberly-Clark Corp. (hdqrs.), Neenah, Wis., 1952-88, sr. v.p., group exec., 1974-77, exec. v.p., 1977-88; also dir. Kimberly-Clark Corp.; pres. Kimberly Clark Health Care, Paper and Spltys. Cos., 1981-88, vice chmn. bd., 1983-88. Dir. First Bank of Childersburg, Ala. Bd. dirs. Calif. Water Quality Control Bd., 1964-67, S.C. Tech. Edn. Bd., 1968-70; bd. dirs., sec. Children's Harbor, Alexander City, Ala.; chmn. bd. adv. com. St. Jude's Hosp., Fullerton, Calif., 1962-67; trustee Fulton County Ga. Hosp. Authority, Northside Hosp., Oglethorpe U., Atlanta, Wesley Woods Hosp., Atlanta, Woodruff Art Alliance; bd. visitors Emory U., Atlanta. Served as aviator USNR, 1943-46. Home: The Brittany #802 4021 Gulf Shore Blvd N Naples FL 34103-0705 *In my lifetime of managing operations and administration I never met a "small" person - just small jobs.*

GAD-EL-HAK, MOHAMED, aerospace and mechanical engineering educator, scientist; b. Tanta, El-Gharbia, Egypt, Feb. 11, 1945; came to U.S., 1968; s. Mohamed Gadelhak and Samira (Hosni) Ibrahim; m. Dilek Karaca, July 19, 1976; children: Kamal, Yasemin. BSc in Mech. Engring. summa cum laude, Ain Shams U., Cairo, 1966; PhD in Fluid Mechanics, Johns Hopkins U., 1973. Instr. Ain Shams U., Cairo, 1966-68; postdoctoral fellow Johns Hopkins U., Balt., 1973, U. So. Calif., L.A., 1973-74; asst. prof. engring. sci. & systems U. Va., Charlottesville, 1974-76; program mgr. Flow Rsch. Co., Seattle, 1976-86; prof. aerospace & mech. engring. U. Notre Dame, Ind., 1986—2002; Inez Caudill prof. bioengring., chmn. mech. engring. Va. Commonwealth U., Richmond, 2002—. Cons. USN, Washington, 1990-91, UN, N.Y.C., 1991, many others; lectr. in field. Author: Flow Control: Passive, Active, and Reactive Flow Management, 2000; assoc. tech. editor AIAA Jour., 1988-91; assoc. editor Applied Mechanics Revs., 1988—; contbg. editor: Springer Verlag's Lecture Notes in Engineering, 1988—; reviewer Jour. Fluid Mechanics, Physics of Fluids, AIAA Jour., Jour. of Aircraft, many others; editor: Advances in Fluid Mechanics Measurements, 1989, Frontiers in Experimental Fluid Mechanics, 1989, Flow Control: Fundamentals and Practices, 1998, The CRC MEMS Handbook, 2002; contbr. numerous articles to profl. jours. Recipient Alexander von Humboldt prize, 1999; Whitehead fellow Johns Hopkins U., Balt, 1968-73; Freeman scholar, 1998; professeur invité Univ. de Grenoble, France, 1991-92; sr. guest NATO, Paris, 1991, USN Disting. Faculty fellow, 1993; professeur exceptionnel univ. de Poitiers, France, 1994; rsch. grantee USN, 1976-80, USCG, 1976-78, NASA-Ames, 1981, NASA-Langley, 1985-87, 86, ONR, 1981-85, AFOSR, 1982-85, 85, Boeing Co., 1984, NSF, 1986, 95, Flow Industries, Inc., 1986-88, Cortana Corp., 1989-90, ONR, 1991, DARPA, 1991, Bourse de Haut Niveau Ministere de la Recherche et de la Technologie, Paris, 1991-92, NATO, 1991-92, others. Fellow AIAA, Am. Acad. Mechanics, ASME, Am. Phys. Soc. Achievements include patents on method and apparatus for controlling bound vortices in the vicinity of lifting surfaces, for reducing turbulent skin friction, for controlling turbulent boundary layers, for micropumping. Office: Va Commonwealth U PO Box 843015 Richmond VA 23284-3015 E-mail: gadelhak@vcu.edu.

GADEN, ELMER LEWIS, JR., chemical engineering educator, retired; b. Bklyn., Sept. 26, 1923; s. Elmer Lewis and Gertrude Estelle (McClellan) G.; m. Jennifer Marie Soley, Mar. 28, 1964; children: David Andrew, Paul Alexander; 1 dau. by previous marriage, Barbara Joan. BS, Columbia U., 1944, MS, 1947, PhD, 1949; DEngring (hon.), Rensselaer Poly., 1987. Rsch. engr. Pfizer Inc., 1948-49; mem. faculty Columbia, 1949-74, prof. chem. engring., 1958-74, chmn. dept., 1960-69, 71-74; dean Coll. Engring. Math. and Bus. Adminstrn., U. Vt., Burlington, 1975-79; Wills Johnson prof. chem. engring. U. Va., Charlottesville, 1979-94, prof. emeritus, 1994—, chmn. dept., 1985-88. Editor: Biotech. and Bioengring. jour., 1959-83. Served with USNR, 1943-46. Mem.: AIChE, NAE, Am. Chem. Soc. Home: 3400 Rodman Dr Charlottesville VA 22901-9450 Office: U Va Dept Chemical Engineer Charlottesville VA 22903 E-mail: elg@virginia.edu.

GADOL, PETER DANIEL, writer; b. Westfield, N.J., Apr. 15, 1964; s. Norman and Sybil Rickless G.; m. Stephen Gutwillig. BA magna cum laude, Harvard U., 1986. Faculty mem. Calif. Inst. Arts, Valencia, 1996—. Author: Coyote, 1990, The Mystery Roast, 1993, Closer to the Sun, 1996, The Long Rain, 1997, Light at Dusk, 2000. Mem. PEN, Author's Guild, Associated Writing Programs. Avocations: architecture, design. E-mail: pgadol@aol.com.

GADOMSKI, ROBERT EUGENE, chemical and industrial gas company executive; b. Chgo., Mar. 24, 1947; s. Chester and Adeline (Carpinelli) G.; m. Susan Freed, Aug. 12, 1972; children: Stephen, Andrew, Elizabeth. BS, Purdue U., 1969, MS in Indsl. Adminstrn., 1970, D of Engring. (hon.), 2001, PhD (hon.), 2001; grad. advanced mgmt. program, Harvard U., fall 1990. Bus. mgr. indsl. chems. div. Air Products and Chems., Inc., Allentown, Pa., 1974-77, gen. sales mgr. indsl. chems. div., 1977-78, asst. gen. mgr. indsl. chems. div., 1978-81, mgr. chems. group mfg. div., 1981-83, gen. mgr. chems. group mfg. div., 1983-84, v.p., gen. mgr. chems. group mfg. div., 1984-86, v.p., gen. mgr. indsl. chems. div., 1986-88, v.p., gen. mgr. process systems group, 1988-90, mgmt. com., 1988—96, group v.p. process systems group, 1990-92, group v.p. chems. group, 1992-96, exec. v.p., mem. corp. exec. com., 1996—, exec. v.p. chems., Asia and Latin Am., 1998-99, exec. v.p. gases and equipment, 1999—. Chmn. March of Dimes Walkathon, Allentown, 1985; v.p. Minsi Trails coun. Boy Scouts Am., 1998—99, 2002—; bd. dirs. South Whitehall Planning Commn., Allentown, 1984—89, Lehigh Valley United Way, Allentown, 1991—94, 1999—2000, Kemerer Mus. Decorative Arts, 1991—94, St. Luke's Hosp., Bethelehem, Pa., 1994—99, Hist. Bethlehem Partnership, 1993—2002, Phila. Acad. Scis., 1999—2002, Nat. Assn. Mfg., 1999—2000. Named Disting. Alumnus, Krannert Sch. Mgmt., Purdue U., 1988, Sch. Engring., 1992. Mem. AIChE; mem. Nat. Petroleum Refiners Assn. (bd. dirs. 1986-93), Internat. Oxygen Mfrs. Assn. (bd. dirs. 2000—), Mfrs. Alliance/MAPI (trustee 2000—), Pa. Bus. Roundtable. Roman Catholic. Avocations: golf, fine dining. Office: Air Products & Chems Inc 7201 Hamilton Blvd Allentown PA 18195-1526

GADON, STEVEN FRANKLIN, lawyer; b. Roxbury, Mass., Oct. 27, 1931; s. Sydney A. and Sarah G. (Feinstein) G.; m. Barbara Kaminsky, Sept. 5, 1954; children: Richard, Susan, Amy, Beth. BS, U. Pa., 1954; LLB, Temple U., 1959; LLM, NYU, 1964. Bar: Pa. 1963; CPA, Pa. Acct. Main, Lafrentz & Co., Phila., 1956-62; ptnr. MacCoy, Evans & Lewis, Phila., 1962-66, Meltzer & Schiffrin, Phila., 1966-76, Spector, Gadon & Rosen, Phila., 1976—. Sec., bd. dirs. Simkins Industries, Inc., New Haven. Mem. Am. Assn. Attys.-CPA's, AICPA, Pa. Inst. CPA's. Jewish. Avocations: running, opera. Home: Grays Lane House 500 100 Grays Ln Haverford PA 19041-1727 Office: Spector Gadon & Rosen 1635 Market St Fl 7 Philadelphia PA 19103-2217

GADSBY, ROBIN EDWARD, chemical company executive; b. St. Leonards on Sea, Eng., Mar. 22, 1939; came to U.S., 1977, naturalized, 1988; s. John Ernest and Emily Louisa (Burt) G.; m. Olwyn Diane Bowen, Aug. 5, 1961 (div. 1981); children: Tricia Clare, Tracey Carolyn; m. Margaret Alice Fuessel, Dec. 29, 1983. MA in Natural Scis., Cambridge U., Eng., 1960, MEng, 1961; MBA, U. Chgo., 1982. CFA. Chem. engr. ICI Billingham (Eng.) div., 1961-62, corp. planner, 1962-65; plant mgr. ICI PLC Agrl. div., Heysham, Eng., 1965-67, chem. engring. mgr. Billingham, 1967-70, process tech. mgr., 1970-76, research group mgr., 1976-77; pres. Katalco Corp., Oak Brook, Ill., 1978-83; gen. mgr. Rubicon Chems. Inc., Wilmington, Del., 1984-86; pres. polyurethanes group div. ICI Ams., Inc., Wilmington, 1986-90, pres. chems. and polymers group, 1990-97. Bd. dirs., cons. Callard, Madden & Assocs., Inc., Chgo. Mem. AIChE, Am. Chemical Soc., Assn. for Investment Mgmt. and Rsch., Inst. Chem. Engrs.

(U.K. editl. bd. 1976-77), Internat. Isocynates Inst. (pres. 1990-91), Fin. Analysts Soc. Phila., Classics Country Club (Fla.), Beta Gamma Sigma. Home and Office: PO Box 630 West Chester PA 19381-0630 Fax: 610 399-9551.

GADSDEN, CHRISTOPHER HENRY, lawyer, educator; b. Bryn Mawr, Pa., Aug. 7, 1946; s. Henry White and Patricia (Parker) G.; m. Eleanore R.B. Hoeffel, July 27, 1968; children: William C., Eleanore P., Patricia C. BS, Yale U., 1968, JD, 1973. Bar: Pa. 1973, U.S. Dist. Ct. (ea. dist.) Pa. 1973. Assoc. Drinker Biddle & Reath, Phila., 1973-80, ptnr., 1980-98, mng. ptnr., 1998-2001; founding ptnr. Gadsden Schneider & Woodward LLP, King of Prussia, Pa., 2001—. Lectr. law U. Pa. Law Sch., Phila., 1986-89, 93. Author: Pennsylvania Estate Planning, 1996; contbg. author: Local Public Finance and the Fiscal Squeeze, 1977; co-editor: Administration of Estates, 1983. Mem. vestry St. Thomas Ch., Whitemarsh, Ft. Washington, Pa., 1980-82; trustee Abington (Pa.) Meml. Hosp., 1980—, chair bd. trustees, 1994-98; pres. bd. trustees Germantown Acad., Ft. Washington, 1987-90. With U.S. Army, 1968—70. Fellow Am. Coll. Trust and Estate Counsel; mem. Phila. Bar Assn. (probate and trust law sect., chair 1994), Phila. Cricket Club. Democrat. Avocations: squash, tennis, gardening. Home: 140 W Chestnut Hill Ave Philadelphia PA 19118-3702 Office: Gadsden Schneider & Woodward LLP 700 S Henderson Rd Ste 345 King Of Prussia PA 19406 E-mail: cgadsden@gsw-llp.com.

GADSDEN, JAMES, lawyer; b. Bryn Mawr, Pa., July 5, 1949; s. Charles C. and Marie Ella (Dittmann) G.; children: Hilary DuBois Nieukirk, Courtney Dittmann; m. Barbara Chase Howard, May 4, 1991. BA in Polit. Sci. with distinction, U. Rochester, 1971; JD, Columbia U., 1974. Bar: U.S. Dist. Ct. (ea. dist., so. dist.) N.Y. 1975, N.Y. 1975, U.S. Ct. Appeals (2d cir.) 1975, U.S. Ct. Appeals (3d cir.) 1999, U.S. Dist. Ct. (no. dist.) N.Y. 2001. Assoc. Carter, Ledyard & Milburn, N.Y.C., 1974-83, ptnr., 1984—. Fellow Am. Bar Found.; mem. ABA (bus. law sect., chmn. trust indentures and indenture trustees), Assn. of Bar of City of N.Y. (project fin. com. 1999—), Fed. Bar Coun., Down Town Assn. Democrat. Episcopalian. Home: 315 Mills Rd North Salem NY 10560 Office: Carter Ledyard & Milburn 2 Wall St Fl 13 New York NY 10005-2072 E-mail: gadsden@clm.com.

GADSDEN, JAMES IRVIN, ambassador; b. Charleston, S.C., Mar. 12, 1948; BA cum laude, Harvard U., 1970; MA in East Asian Studies, Stanford U., 1972; postgrad., Princeton U., 1984. Various positions to counselor for econ. affairs U.S. Embassy, Paris, 1989—93, dep. chief of mission Budapest, 1994—97; dep. asst. sec. of state for European Affairs U.S. Dept. of State, 1997—2001; spl. negotiator for agrl. biotechnology Bur. for Econ. and Bus. Affairs, Washington, 2001—01; U.S. amb. to Iceland, 2002—. Office: DOS Amb 5640 Reykjavik Pl Washington DC 20521*

GAEBE, MORRIS J. academic administrator; Chancellor Johnson and Wales U., Providence, 1990—. Office: Johnson & Wales U Office of Chancellor 8 Abbott Park Pl Providence RI 02903-3775

GAEDE, JAMES ERNEST, physician, medical educator; b. Calgary, Alta., Can., July 2, 1953; s. John Ernest and Florence Eleanor (Hilmer) G.; married, Dec. 23, 1994; children: Graham, Jason, Nikki, Mary Frances, Sydney, Camille. BA, Augustana Coll., 1975, MA, 1976; MD, U. S.D., 1980. Diplomate Am. Bd. Family Practice. Staff physician Queen of Peace, Mitchell, SD, 1983—2001, chief of staff, 1988, med. dir., 1988-89, St. Joe's Med. Assn., Howard, SD, 1988—2000, Women's Health Clinic, Mitchell, SD, 1983—2000; assoc. prof. U. of S.D. Sch. Medicine; med. dir. Desert Regional Med. Ctr., Palm Springs, Calif., 2001—. Presenter U.S. Senate, Washington, 1991. Contbr. articles to profl. jours. Bd. dirs. Dakota Weslayan U., Mitchell, 1986-89, Dakota Mental Health, Mitchell, 1988-90; mem. Commn. 2000 S.D., Sioux Falls, 1988-00; pub. health officer City of Mitchell, 1983-01. Fellow Am. Acad. Family Practice (Active Tchrs. award 1984—); mem. AMA, Calif. Acad. Family Practice, S.D. Assn. Family Practice, S.D. State Med. Assn. (del. 1983-2000, sec. 1998-99, v.p. 1999, pres. 2000), Mitchell C. of C., Mayo Alumni Assn., Doctors Mayo Soc. Avocations: sailing, music, auto restoration. Home: 2525 N Farrell Dr Palm Springs CA 92262-2601 Office: 555 Tachevah Ste 2E-101 Palm Springs CA 92262

GAEDE, JANE TAYLOR, pathologist, educator; b. Washington, July 8, 1941; d. Raleigh Colston and Margaret (Lamb) Taylor; m. William Hanks Gaede, Feb. 12, 1966; children: Geoffrey Terence, Bruce Lucas. BA, U. Miss., 1962; MD, Duke U., 1966. Diplomate Am. Bd. Pathology. Intern in surgery N.C. Bapt. Hosp., Winston-Salem, N.C., 1966-67; resident in pathology Duke Med. Ctr., Durham, N.C., 1967-71, asst. prof. pathology, 1974—, Med. U. S.C., Charleston, 1971-74; staff pathologist VA Med Ctr., Durham, 1974—. Author: Clinical Pathology for the House Officer, 1982. Fellow Am. Soc. Clin. Pathologists; mem. DAR (1st vice regent local chpt. 1992-94, regent 1996-98), N.C. Soc. Pathologists. Presbyterian. Avocations: aerobic exercise, weight training, gardening. Office: Duke Univ Med Ctr Dept Pathology PO Box 3712 Durham NC 27710-0001

GAENGLER, PETER WOLFGANG, dentist, researcher; b. Meissen, Saxony, Germany, Oct. 30, 1941; s. Wolfgang Ernst-Otto and Dorothea Friedericke (Moebius) G.; m. Sabine Gertrud Ahlborn, Nov. 6, 1970; children: Felix Peter, Beate Petra. Stomatology Diploma, Faculty of Dental Medicine, Leningrad, Russia, 1965; DrMedDent, Sch. Dental Medicine, Dresden, Germany, 1967, PhD, 1974. Diplomate in dentistry. Dentistry Community Hosp., Wittenberg, Germany, 1965-66; asst. prof. Sch. Dental Medicine, Dresden, 1966-75, prof., chmn. Erfurt, Germany, 1975-92; dean Faculty of Dental Medicine, Witten/Herdecke, Germany, 1992; bd. dirs. U. Witten/Herdecke, 1995—2002, mem. exec. bd., 2002—. Mem. FDI/WHO Joint Working Group 1/10, Geneva, 1979; v.p. for rsch. U. Witten/Herdecke, 2003—. Author: Lehrbuch der Konservierenden Zahnheilkunde, 3d edit., 1995; editor Medizin aktuell, 1975-90; mem. editl. bd. European Jour. Dental Edn., 2000—, Jour. Oral Rehab., 2001— Recipient Humboldt medal Ministry Higher Edn., Berlin, 1978; grantee in field. Mem.: Internat. Assn. for Dental Rsch. (mem. publs. com., com. on membership and recruitment 1989—93), Assn. Dental Edn. Europe (exec. com. 1997—2001), Assn. Stomatology (v.p. 1988—90, Philip-Pfaff medal 1988), Assn. Conservative Dentistry (pres. 1978—87), Hungarian Assn. Dentistry (hon. Semmelweis medal 1993), Polish Assn. Dentistry (hon.). Avocations: literature, sailing, skiing. Home: Waldweg 9 D-58313 Herdecke Germany Office: U Witten/Herdecke Faculty Dental Medicine D-58448 Witten Germany E-mail: peter.gaengler@uni-wh.de.

GAENSLER, TOMAS FRITZ, engineering executive; b. Kalmar, Sweden, Apr. 9, 1966; arrived in US, 1999; s. Reinhold Fritz and Berit Astrid Gaensler; m. Christina Eva Nilsson, Aug. 1, 1992; children: Cornelia Hanna, Amanda Linnea. MSEE, Lund U., 1990; PhD, Lund (Sweden) U., 1996. Asst. prof. Lund U., 1996—97, 1999—99; mem. tech. staff Bell Labs., Murray Hill, NJ, 1999—2001, Agere Systems, Berkeley Heights, NJ, 2001—. Cons. Bell Labs., Murray Hill, 1998—98. Author: (engineering literature) Advances in Network and Acoustic Echo Cancellation, 2001. Mem.: IEEE. Achievements include first to designed and implemented the first completely software based stereophonic handsfree communication system. Avocations: gardening, rollerblading. Office: Agere Systems Union Blvd Allentown PA 18109 E-mail: gaensler@agere.com.

GAERTNER, DONELL JOHN, retired library director; b. St. Louis, Sept. 30, 1932; s. Elmer Henry and Norine Helen (Colomb) G.; m. Darlene Oberbeck, Mar. 17, 1956; children: Karen Elaine, Keith Alan. AB in Econs., Washington U., 1954; M.L.S., U. Ill., 1955. Adminstrv. asst. St. Louis County Library, 1957-64, asst. dir., 1964-68, dir., 1968-97; ret., 1997. Past pres. bd. dirs. Emmaus Homes Inc. (for adult mentally retarded). Served to 1st lt. U.S. Army, 1955—57. Mem.: ALA, Spl. Libr. Assn., Mo. Libr. Assn. (past pres.), Order Eastern Star, Masons, Omicron Delta Gamma, Phi Beta Mu. United Ch. Of Christ. E-mail: dgaertner7@earthlink.net.

GAERTNER, GARY M., SR., judge; b. St. Louis; m. Maureen Gaertner: children: Gary M., Lisa, Mark. Student, JD, St. Louis U.; grad., Nat. Jud. Coll., U. Nev., Mo. Trial Jedges Coll., Am. Acad. Jud. Edn., U. N.H., Sch. Law U. Va., Stanford U. Laaw Sch., Harvard U. Sch. Law. Bar: Mo., Ill., U.S. Dist. Ct., U.S. Ct. Appeals, U.S. Supreme Ct. After pvt. practice; served as asst. city counselor City of St. Louis, until 1964, assoc. city counsel, 1964-97, city counselor, 1967-69; judge 22d Jud. Cir. Mo., 1969-85, including presiding judge criminal divs., juvenile judge, asst. presiding judge, and presiding judge and chief adminstrv. officer; chief judge Ct. Appeals, Ea. Dist. Mo., 1985. Past pres. Mo. Council Juvenille Ct. Judges; former chmn. juvenile subcom. Mo. Council Criminal Justice, region 5; former mem. St. Louis Commn. on Crime and Law Enforcement. Bd. dirs. Boys Town Mo.; v.p. Khoury Internat. Leagues, Policeman and Fireman's Fund of St. Louis, Shared Resource Enterprises Inc.; former dist. chmn., now dist. vice-chmn. Tomahawk dist Boy Scouts Am.; past mem. exec. bd. St. Louis Area council Boy Scouts Am. Served with USCG. Recipient awards, including Judiciary award St. Louis Grand Jury Assn., Man of Yr. award George Khoury Internat. Assn., Spl. Act. award U.S. Assn. Fed. Investigators; named an Outstanding Young St. Lousiaian, St. Louis Jaycees; diploma Jud. Ksills Am. Acad. Jud. Edn. Mem. ABA, Mo. Bar Assn., Mo. Assn. Trial Attys., Bar Assn. Met. St. Louis, Lawyers Assn. Met. St Louis. Am. Judicature Soc., Phi Delta Phi. Office: 111 N 7th St Saint Louis MO 63101-2100

GAERTNER, KENNETH C. poet, educator; b. Saginaw, Mich., Jan. 18, 1933; s. Frederick Carl and Helen M. Gaertner; m. Mary Ann Vega, Mar. 16, 1931; children: Kurt, Bonnie. Student, Bay City Jr. Coll., 1952—53. Prof. Ave Maria Coll., Ypsilanti, Mich., 2001—03. Playwright in residence Mystic Theatre, NJ, 1998—, NY, 1998—. Prodr.: (plays) Blood Money, 1975, The Old Man's Death, 1975, The Lady and God, 1975, The Moon on Snow, 1978, The Open Eye Theatre, 1978, Dog's Tooth, 1985 (Nat. One-Act Play Contest award, 1985), Seventeen Hoofbeats, 1992, Lives Over Easy, 1994, Three Hands Clapping, 1995, Dominica's Smile, 1997, Tortoise Shout, 1999, Vagrants in Love, 2001, White Stones, 2003. Sgt. USMC, 1951—54, Japan. Mem.: Dramatists Guild. Roman Catholic. Home: 211 McCotter Dr Ann Arbor MI 48103 Office: Ave Maria College 300 W Forest Ave Ypsilanti MI 48103

GAERTNER, STEFAN, human resources specialist, researcher; b. Bielefeld, Nordrhein-Westfalen, Germany, Dec. 25, 1965; Diplom Kaufmann, Universitaet of Paderborn, Germany, 1994; PhD, Ga. State U., 2000. Fin. advisor, mktg. event mgr. Sparkasse Bielefeld, Bielefeld, Germany, 1983—88; tchg./rsch. asst. Ga. State U., Atlanta, 1994—2000; cons. Mercer Human Resources Cons., N.Y.C., 2000—. Reviewer Jour. of Mgmt./Elsevier Sci. Pub., 2001—, Human Resources Mgmt. Rev. Contbr. articles. Recipient William T. Rutherford award W. T. Beebe Inst. of Pers. and Employment Relations, 2000, Waino W. Suojanen Rsch. Excellence award, Dept. Mgmt., Ga. State U., 2000. Mem.: Soc. of Indsl. and Orgnl. Psychology, Acad. of Mgmt., Phi Beta Delta. Office: Mercer Human Resources Consulting 1166 Ave of the Americas New York NY 10036-2708 Office Fax: 212-345-5708. Business E-Mail: stefan.gaertner@us.wmmercer.com.

GAFF, ALAN DALE, writer; b. Ft. Wayne, Ind., Sept. 25, 1948; s. Kenneth E. and Mona (Traxler) G.; m. Maureen Ann Oxley, Dec. 27, 1969; children: Donald Hugh, Jeffrey John. BA in History, Ind. U., 1979; MA in Am. History, Ball State U., 1980. Pres. Richmond City Greys, Ft. Wayne, 1984—, Hist. Investigations, Ft. Wayne, 1996—. Author: Brave Men's Tears, 1988, If This Is War, 1991, Our Boys, 1996, On Many A Bloody Field, 1997. Vol. Allen County Pub. Libr., Ft. Wayne, 1981—. Sgt. U.S. Army, 1969-71. Mem. DAV (life), Ind. Hist. Soc., Sons of Union Vets., State Hist. Soc. Wis., Ind. U. Alumni Assn. Avocation: golf. Home: 2812 Overlook Dr Fort Wayne IN 46808-1848 Office: US Postal Svc Centennial Sta 2525 Independence Dr Fort Wayne IN 46808-1848 E-mail: almogaff@comcast.net.

GAFF, BRIAN MICHAEL, lawyer; b. Boston, Mar. 14, 1962; s. Gilbert Gerard and Josephine Claire (Franklin) G. BSEE magna cum laude, U. Mich., 1983, MSEE, 1984; JD magna cum laude, Suffolk U., 1999. Bar: Mass. 1999, Calif. 1999, U.S. Dist. Ct. Mass. 1999, U.S. Ct. Appeals (1st cir.) 1999, U.S. Ct. Appeals (fed. cir.) 1999, U.S. Patent Office 1999, U.S. Dist. Ct. (no. dist.) Calif. 2000, U.S. Ct. Appeals (9th cir.) 1999, U.S. Supreme Ct., 2002; registered profl. engr., Mass., Calif., N.H., N.Y. Engr. GTE Communications Products Corp., Westborough, Mass., 1984; mem. tech. staff Draper Lab., Cambridge, Mass., 1984-88; engring. specialist GPT Stromberg-Carlson, Lake Mary, Fla., 1989-90; safety mgr. imaging sys. divsn. Hewlett-Packard Healthcare Solutions Group, Andover, Mass., 1990-2000; pvt. practice, 1999; assoc Testa, Hurwitz & Thibeault, LLP, Boston, 2000—. Founder, prin. Solid-State Cons., Swampscott, Mass., 1983—, SSC Constrn., Swampscott, 1991—. Mem. IEEE (sr.), NSPE, ABA, Am. Phys. Soc., Am. Vacuum Soc., Am. Intellectual Property Law Assn., Mensa, Mass. Soc. Profl. Engrs., Mass. Bar Assn., Boston Patent Law Assn., Essex County Bar Assn., Boston Bar Assn. Republican. Roman Catholic. Avocation: photography. Home: PO Box 166 Swampscott MA 01907-0266 Office: Testa Hurwitz & Thibeault LLP 125 High St Boston MA 02110-2704 E-mail: bgaff@sscco.com.

GAFFAR, ABDUL, research scientist, administrator; b. Rangoon, Burma, Dec. 10, 1940; came to U.S., 1964; s. Ismmail and Khatija (Mohamed) Darji; m. Maria C. Gaffar, May 23, 1970; 1 child, Yousuf A. MS, Brigham Young U., 1965; PhD, Ohio State U., 1967. Rsch. chemist CSIR, Karachi, 1962-63; rsch. assoc. Brigham Young U., Provo, Utah, 1964-65, Ohio State U., Columbus, 1965-67; sr. scientist Colgate Tech Ctr., Piscataway, NJ, 1967-72, rsch. mgr., 1975-80, v.p. growth tech., 1982—. Author over 100 publs. in field. Named to N.J. Inventors Hall of Fame, Bd. Dirs. Indsl. Rsch. Inst., 2001. Mem. AAAS, Am. Soc. Microbiology, Am. Chem. Soc. Achievements include over 140 patents in oral therapeutics and means of delivery to control oral and dental diseases. Home: 89 Carter Rd Princeton NJ 08540-2107 Office: Colgate Tech Ctr 909 River Rd Piscataway NJ 08854-5503

GAFFEY, VIRGINIA ANNE, retired nurse anesthetist; b. Boston, Sept. 6, 1933; d. James Hugh and Virginia (Glennon) G. Grad. collegiate nursing program, Burbank Hosp., 1955; BS in Edn., Fitchburg State Coll., Mass., 1955; cert. nurse anesthetist, Carney Hosp. Sch. Anesthesia, Boston, 1957. Cert. registered nurse anesthetist. Dir. Sch. Anesthesia, Carney Hosp., 1957-86; staff anesthetist S.E. Anesthesia Assocs., Boston, 1986-98, ret., 1998. Mem. Milton Bd. Health, 1970—2000. Recipient Helen Lamb Educators award, 1982, Louise De Marillac award Carney Hosp., 1996, Disting. Alumni award Fitchburg State Coll., 1999. Mem. Am. Assn. Nurse Anesthetists (past pres. 1969-70), Mass. Assn. Nurse Anesthetists, New Eng. Assembly Nurse Anesthetists, Milton Vis. Nurses Assn. (mem. and chmn. profl. adv. com.). Home: PO Box 11 Green Harbor MA 02041-0011

GAFFIN, JOAN VALERIE, secondary school educator; b. N.Y.C., Nov. 25, 1947; d. William John and Louise Eleanor (Liebig) Philibert; m. Ira Martin Gaffin, May 7, 1981. BS in Bus. Edn., Rider U., 1971; MA in Student Personnel Svcs., Montclair State U., 1978. Cert. coop. bus. edn. coord., bus. edn. adminstr. and coord. Bus. edn. instr., coord. Econ. Manpower Corp., N.Y.C., 1971-72; bus. edn. coord., educator Northern Valley Regional H.S., Old Tappan, N.J., 1972—; gymnastics instr. Twp. of Teaneck, NJ, 1985—2000. Adj. grad. prof. Montclair State U., Upper Montclair, N.J., 1994—. Recipient N.J. Gov.'s Outstanding Tchr. of Yr. award, 1986. Mem. NEA, Nat. Bus. Edn. Assn., N.J. Bus. Edn. Assn. (legis. com. 1990-92, bd. dirs. 1991-95, chmn. critical issues task force 1991-95, N.J. Bus. Tchr. of Yr. 1993), N.J. Edn. Assn., Eastern Bus. Edn. Assn. (Educator of Yr. 1993), N.J. Cooperative Bus. Edn. Coord.'s Assn. (Bergen sector sec. and pres., Coord. of Yr. 1993), Northeast Bergen Ind. Assn. (treas., bd. dirs. 1978—), Northern Valley Edn. Assn. (sec. 1978-80, 85-86, 91-92, Tchr. Recognition award 1990-91). Avocations: traveling, reading, cooking, exercising, antiquing. Home: 852 W Crescent Ave Allendale NJ 07401-2129 Office: Northern Valley Regional HS Central Ave Old Tappan NJ 07675

GAFFNEY, DONALD LEE, lawyer; b. Phoenix, July 7, 1952; s. Leroy H. and Myriam (Brazeal) G.; m. Debby Dunn, May 31, 1974; children: Brian, Colin, Caitlin. BA, Austin Coll., 1974; JD, U. Tex., 1977. Bar: Ariz. 1977, U.S. Ct. Appeals (9th cir.) 1979, U.S. Ct. Appeals (10th cir.) 1984, U.S. Supreme Ct. 1984. Ptnr. Streich & Lang, Phoenix, 1977-89, Snell & Wilmer, Phoenix, 1988—. Adj. prof. Ariz. State U. Law Sch., Tempe, 1983-84. Co-author: Bankruptcy, 1987; note comment and book review editor: Tex. Law Review 1976-77; contbr. to profl. jours. Mem. Gov.'s Task Force Ctrl. Ariz. Project, 1993. Austin scholar. Mem. ABA, Am. Arbitration Assn. (com. panel), Comml. Law League of Am. (bankruptcy com. 1980-84), State Bar Ariz. (chmn. bankruptcy sect., 1982-84, com. on bankruptcy rules 1979-81, uniform comml. code com. 1980—), Phi Delta Phi. Democrat. Roman Catholic. Office: Snell & Wilmer 1 Arizona Ctr Phoenix AZ 85004-0001

GAFFNEY, ELIZABETH MALLORY, editor, writer, literature educator, translator; b. N.Y.C., N.Y., Dec. 22, 1966; d. Richard Waring and Ann Walker Gaffney; m. Alexis David Boro, July 15, 1995. BA, Vassar Coll., 1988; MFA, Bklyn. Coll., 1997. Mem. editl. staff The Paris Rev., N.Y.C., 1988—93, mng. editor, 1993—95, editor-at-large, 1995—, also trustee. Writing tchr. NYU, N.Y.C., 1997—. Translator: The Arbogast Case, 2003, The Pollen Room, 1998, Invisible Woman, 2000, author short stories. Resident/fellow, MacDowell Colony, Peterborough, N.H., 1996, 1997, Blue Mountain (N.Y.) Ctr., 1999, Yaddo, Saratoga Springs, N.Y., 2000, 2001. Mem.: Phi Beta Kappa. Democrat. Avocations: hiking, kayaking, bicycling, camping. Office: The Paris Rev 541 E 72 St New York NY 10021

GAFFNEY, KAREN ELIZABETH, clinical social worker; b. Cass City, Mich., Oct. 24, 1956; d. Theron B. and Judith Ann (Dickinson) Esckilsen; m. David E. Gaffney, Dec. 29, 1990; children: Elizabeth Haley Egerer, Nathan Andrew, Megan Abigail. BA summa cum laude, Saginaw Valley State Coll., 1977; MSW, U. Mich., 1979. Cert. social worker, Mich. Clin. social worker Huron County Mental Health, Bad Axe, Mich., 1979-84; adoption worker Luth. Adoption Svc., Bay City, Mich., 1985-87; pvt. practice Bay City and Caro, Mich., 1987—. Clin. social worker Tuscola County Mental Health, Caro, 1988—, Covenant Healthcare, 2001—. Bd. dirs. natural supports program Saginaw Cath. Diocese, 1987-88; bd. dirs., sec. Caro Area United Way, 1990-92; single entry mgr. Tuscola Cmty. Mental Health, 1993-97, dir. family care ctr., 1987-2001. Office: Covenant Healthcare 1447 N Harrison Saginaw MI 48602

GAFFNEY, MARK WILLIAM, lawyer; b. Spokane, Wash., July 3, 1951; s. William Joseph and Anne Veronica (McGovern) G.; m. Jean Elizabeth O'Leary, Oct. 8, 1988. BA, U. Notre Dame, 1973; JD, George Washington U., 1976. Bar: Wash. 1976, N.Y. 1982, D.C. 1984, Conn. 1984. Law clk. antitrust divsn. U.S. Dept. Justice, Washington, 1974-76; trial atty. N.Y.C., 1976-81; assoc. Solin & Breindel, P.C., N.Y.C., 1982-83; ptnr. Chapman, Moran & Gaffney, Stamford, Conn., 1984-85; of counsel Kaplan & Kilsheimer, N.Y.C., 1985-93; corp. counsel Sta. WLNY-TV, Inc., Melville, N.Y., 1993-95. Recipient Spl. Achievement award U.S. Dept. Justice, 1978, 79. Mem.: ABA, Assn. of Bar of City of N.Y., Conn. Bar Assn., N.Y. Athletic Club. Republican. Roman Catholic. Home: 1395 Roosevelt Ave Pelham NY 10803-3605 Office: 1328 Boston Post Rd Larchmont NY 10538 E-mail: mgaffney@concentric.net.

GAFFNEY, PAUL GOLDEN, II, academic administrator, military officer; b. Attleboro, Mass., May 30, 1946; s. Paul G. and Elfrieda L. (Piepenstock) G.; m. Linda L. Myers; 1 child, Crista L. BS, U.S. Naval Acad., 1968; MS in Engring., Cath. U. Am., 1969; grad. with highest distinction, Naval War Coll., Newport, R.I., 1979; MBA, Jacksonville U., 1986, LHD (hon.), 2002, U. S.C.; degree (hon.), Jacksonville U., 2002, U.S.C., 2002, Catholic U. of Am., 2003. Commd. ensign USN, 1968, advanced through grades to vice adm., 1994, ops. officer USS Whipporwill, 1969-71, advisor Vietnamese Combat Hydrog. Survey Team, 1971-72, ocean svcs. officer Fleet Weather Cen., 1972-75, exec. asst. Office of Oceanographer Alexandria, Va., 1975-78, rsch. fellow Naval War Coll. Advanced Rsch. Newport, R.I., 1978-78, comdg. officer Oceanographic Unit 4, 1979-80, dir. Arctic and Earth Scis. Rsch. Office Naval Rsch., 1980-81; mil. asst. internat. security affairs to Asst. Sec. Def. Washington, 1981-83; comdg. office Oceanography Command Facility USN, Jacksonville, Fla., 1983-86, dir. resources Office of Oceanographer Washington, 1986-89, asst. chief, Office Chief of Naval Rsch. Arlington, Va., 1989-91, comdg. officer Naval Rsch. Lab. Washington, 1991-94, commdr. Naval Meteorology and Oceanography Command Stennis Space Ctr., Miss., 1994-97, chief naval rsch. and naval test/evaluation/tech. requirements for the Navy Staff, dep. comdt. USMC for sci. and tech. Arlington, Va., 1996-2000; pres. Nat. Def. U., Washington, 2000—03; commr. U.S. Commn. Ocean Policy, 2000—; pres. Monmouth U., West Long Branch, NJ, 2003—. Grad. rsch. asst. Cath. U. Am., Washington, 1968—. Mem. policy com. Jour. Def. Rsch., 1989-91. Acad. adv. bd. NATO Def. Coll., Rome, 2000—03, U.S. Inst. of Peace; bd. dirs. Marymount U., 2000—03, Fla. State U. Rsch. Found., Jacksonville U., 2002—03, Jacksonville (Fla.) U., 2002—03. Decorated DSM, USN, Defense DSM, Legion of Merit with three gold stars, Bronze Star with V; recipient Middendorf prize Naval War Coll., 1979. Fellow Am. Meteorol. Soc., Explorer's Club; mem. Naval Acad. Alumni Assn., Sigma Xi. Roman Catholic. Avocations: running, track and field and cross country announcing and officiating. Office: Office of the Pres Monmouth U 400 Cedar Ave West Long Branch NJ 07764-1898

GAFFNEY, RICHARD COOK, lawyer; b. Sewickley, Pa., July 14, 1931; s. John Edward and Florence Loretta (Cook) G.; m. Virginia Brady, May 15, 1954; children: Richar dCook, Charles, Kathleen, Robert, Virginia, Eileen. BS in Chem. Engring., Carnegie-Mellon U., 1953; JD, Duquesne U., 1959; exec. MBA, U. Pitts., 1982. Bar: Pa. 1960, U.S. Dist. Ct. (we. dist.) Pa. 1960, Tex. 1985. Mng. patent atty. Chevron Corp., Moraga, Calif. Mem. Patent Law Assn. Pitts. (asst. program chmn. 1981, program chmn. 1982). Mailing: 2915 Crystal Falls Dr Humble TX 77345-1303 E-mail: txgaffney@aol.com.

GAFFNEY, THOMAS, banker; b. San Francisco, Sept. 22, 1915; s. John and Hannah (Doherty) G.; m. Claire Bastian, Dec. 15, 1945; children: Bruce Edward, Bryan Keith. Cert., Am. Inst. Banking, 1940. Bank insp. Bank of Am., 1935-50; asst. cashier First Nat. Trust and Savs. Assn., Santa Barbara, Calif., 1950-51; asst. cashier, asst sec. Oakland Central Bank, Calif., 1951-53; chief insp. Transamerica Corp., San Francisco, 1953-55; v.p., auditor First Western Bank, San Francisco, 1955-61; v.p. New First Western Bank, Los Angeles, 1961-74; v.p. and auditor Lloyds Bank Calif., Los Angeles, 1974-80. Pres. Golden Gate chpt. Bank Adminstrn Inst., San Francisco, 1961, nat. bd. dirs., 1965-67, gen. chmn. conv., L.A., 1967, speaker bank convs., nationwide; chmn. crime deterrant com. Calif. Bankers Assn., 1977-79; banking cons., 1980—. Mem. Ad Hoc Com. City of L.A. to study and recommend controls on all city depts., 1977—. Mem.: Elks (bd. dir. Locker Room 67 club San Francisco 1960).

GAFFNEY, THOMAS EDWARD, physician; b. East St. Louis, Ill., Nov. 5, 1930; s. John V. and Leola (Heisner) G.; m. Edith Ann Heitholt, June 12, 1954; children— John, David, Michael. AB, U. Mo., 1951, MS, 1953; MD, U. Cin., 1957. Intern Harvard Med. Service of Boston City Hosp., 1957-58; resident medicine Mass. Gen. Hosp., 1958-59; instr. pharmacology, asst. medicine U. Cin., 1959-60; clin. assoc. Nat. Heart Inst., 1960-62; assoc. prof. pharmacology U. Cin., 1962-67, asst. prof. medicine, 1962, dir. div. clin. pharmacology, 1962-72, prof. pharmacology, 1967-72, prof. medicine, 1969-72; prof., chmn. dept. pharmacology, prof. medicine Med. U. S.C., 1972-90, disting. prof., 1986-90; vis. scientist Merck Sharp & Dohme Rsch. Labs., Rahway, N.J., 1989-93; vol. clinician Buncombe County Health Dept., 1998—. Mem. cardiovascular panel NAS Drug Efficacy Study, 1967-70; mem. pharmacology and exptl. therapeutics study sect. Nat. Heart Inst., 1967-69; mem. med. adv. bd. Coun. High Blood Pressure Rsch., 1969—; mem. Coun. on Basic Scis. of Am. Heart Assn., 1969—, mem. cardiovascular A study sect., 1972; mem. program rev. com. pharmacology and toxicology Nat. Inst. Gen. Med. Scis., 1971-75, chmn. 1973-75; mem. tech. adv. bd. S.C. Rsch. Authority, 1986-89. Mem. editorial bd. Jour. Pharmacology and Exptl. Therapeutics, 1965-77, Ann. Rev. Pharmacology and Toxicology, 1986-91. Served with USPHS, 1960-62. Recipient research career devel. award Nat. Heart Inst., 1962, 67, 72; Myrtle Wreath award for research Hadassah, 1980; NIH sr. rsch. fellow, 1989. Mem. Am. Fedn. Clin. Rsch., Am. Soc. Pharmacology and Exptl. Therapeutics, Ctrl. Soc. Clin. Rsch., Am. Soc. Clin. Investigation, Alpha Omega Alpha. Home: 348 Sugar Hollow Rd Fairview NC 28730-9560 E-mail: tegaff@worldnet.att.net.

GAFFNEY, THOMAS FRANCIS, private investor; b. Rockford, Ill., Aug. 29, 1945; s. Francis William and Catherine Zeta (Haeberle) G.; m. Donna Lee Gottfried, Apr. 17, 1971; 1 child, Cory. BA, Brown U., 1967; MBA, U. Chgo., 1969. CPA Ill. Fin. cons. Duff and Phelps, Inc., Chgo., 1969-70; dir. adminstrn. Masury-Columbia Co. subs. Alberto-Culver Co., Melrose Park, Ill., 1970-75; exec. v.p., dir. Guardian Industries Corp., Northville, Mich., 1975-87; chmn. bd. The Oxford Investment Group, Bloomfield Hills, Mich., 1985-90; chmn. bd., CEO Automotive Plastic Techs., Inc., Sterling Heights, Mich., 1990-92; chmn. Ashland Products, Inc., Chgo., 1992-95; mng. dir. Raymond James Captial, Inc., St. Petersburg, Fla., 1997—2002. Bd. dirs. Amerus Decorated chevalier de L'Orde Grand Ducal de le Couronne de Chene (Luxembourg). Mem.: AICPA. Home: 2091 Oceanview Dr Tierra Verde FL 33715-2512 E-mail: gaffneyd@aol.com.

GAFFORD, RONALD J. construction executive; B in Bldg. Constrn., Tex. A&M U., 1972; cert. Advanced Mgmt. Program, Harvard U., 1987. Devel. and constrn. ptnr. Trammel Crow Co., Atlanta; project mgr. Henry C. Beck Co., Dallas; pres. Austin Industries, Inc., Dallas, 1996—2001, pres., CEO, 2001—. Former chmn., vice chmn. Austin Comml., Inc., Austin Bridge & Road, Inc., Austin Indsl., Inc. Active mem. Dallas Together Forum, Nat. Real Estate Adv. Coun. Trust for Pub. Land; elder Preston Hollow Presbyn. Ch., 1991—; bd. dirs. Dallas Citizens Coun., Dallas Symphony Assn., Trinity Industries, Interfaith Housing Coalition, Lakehill Prep. Sch.; former bd. dirs. Assoc. Gen. Contractors of Am., Dallas chpt. and Tex. Bldg. br., Real Estate Coun., North Tex. Pub. Broadcasting, Vis. Nurses Assn., Greater Dallas C. of C. Office: Austin Industries Inc 3535 Travis St Ste 300 Dallas TX 75204-1466*

GAGAN, JAMES EPHRIAM, lawyer; b. Pawtucket, R.I., Dec. 24, 1916; s. Walter Joseph and Eva (Audette) G.; m. Claire R. Mazerolle, 1939 (div. 1947); 1 child, Barbara Ann; m. Gertrude Durgin, July 18, 1950; children— Jamie, Brian, Patricia. J.D., U. Maine, 1952. Bar: Maine 1952, U.S. Dist. Ct. Maine 1953, U.S. Tax Ct. 1953. City solicitor, corp. counsel City of Westbrook, Maine, 1960-86; ptnr. Gagan & Desmond, Westbrook, 1976-86; of counsel Desmond & Rand, Westbrook, 1986—. Mem. Maine Gov.'s Exec. Council, 1965-66. Served with USN, 1943-45, ATO. Mem. Maine Bar Assn., Cumberland Bar Assn. (pres. 1980). Democrat. Roman Catholic. Lodge: Kiwanis (pres. Westbrook 1972). Home: 6600 Sunset Way Apt 204 Saint Petersburg Beach FL 33706-2171

GAGARIN, MICHAEL, literature educator; BA, Stanford U., 1963; MA, Harvard U., 1965; PhD, Yale U., 1968. Instr. then asst. prof. classics Yale U., 1968—73; prof. classics U. Tex., Austin, 1973—, from asst. to prof. classics, 1973—, James R. Dougherty, Jr. Centennial prof. classics, 1997—. Mem.: Am. Philological Assn. (pres. 2002—03). Office: Dept of Classics Univ Texas at Austin Austin TX 78712-1181

GAGE, BEAU, artist; b. Rye, N.Y., Dec. 3, 1945; d. John Alden and Frances (Johnston) G.; m. Glenn A. Ousterhout, May 24,1980. BA, St. John's Coll., Santa Fe and Annapolis, Md., 1971; student, Internat. Ctr. Photography, N.Y.C., 1981-82, 82-83, Art Students League N.Y., 1983-87, The Sculpture Ctr. Sch., N.Y.C., 1985-87, Nat. Acad. Design, 1988-89. Staff asst. to the pres. The White House, Washington, 1972-73; key accounts mgr. Sterling Drug, Inc., Montvale, N.J., 1975-79. Works exhibited at Internat. Ctr. Photography, 1981-83, Art Students League, 1984-87, The Sculpture Ctr., 1985-87, Westbeth Gallery, N.Y.C., 1984, 86, Sotheby's Auction House, 1990, others; permanent pub. sculpture Jacksonville (Fla.) Jaguars, Inc.; permanent exhbn. Jacksonville Mus. Sci. & History. Supporter, guild mem. Martha Graham Dance Co., N.Y.C., 1989—; canopy assoc. Rainforest Alliance, 2000—; mem. adv. bd. Buglisi/Foreman Dance Co., N.Y.C., 2001—; leader Perlman Music Program, N.Y.C., 2001—. Fellow Mus. Modern Art; mem. Met. Mus. Art, Internat. Ctr. Photography, Orgn. Ind. Artists, The Nature Conservancy, Mass. Soc. Mayflower Descendants, Poets House (N.Y.C.). Avocations: astronomy, sailing, yoga. Home: 320 E 46th St Apt 34E New York NY 10017-3039 E-mail: beau7gage@aol.com.

GAGE, EDWIN C., III, (SKIP GAGE), travel and marketing services executive; b. Evanston, Ill., Nov. 1, 1940; s. Edwin Cutting and Margaret (Stackhouse) G.; m. Barbara Ann Carlson, June 26, 1965; children— Geoff, Scott, Christine, Richard BS in Bus. Adminstrn., Northwestern U., 1963, MS in Journalism, 1965. Account exec. Foote, Cone and Belding, 1965-68, dir. mktg. devel. & rsch., 1968-70; v.p. direct mktg. Carlson Mktg. Group of Carlson Cos., Mpls., 1970-75, exec. v.p., 1975-77, pres., 1977-83, also bd. dirs.; exec. v.p., COO Carlson Cos. Inc., Mpls., 1983, pres., CEO, 1984-89, pres., chief exec. officer, 1989-91; now chmn., CEO Gage Marketing Group, Mpls. Bd. dirs. Gage Mktg. Group, Carlson Holdings Inc., Carlson Real Estate, Carlson Real Estate Co., Inc., Supervalu Stores Inc., Fingerhut Cos., Kellogg adv. bd. Northwestern U., Minn. Coun. Quality, Mpls. Inst. Arts. Lt. USN. Mem. Young Pres. Orgn., Minn. Execs. Orgn. Avocations: music folk and popular, tennis, golf, hunting, fishing. Office: Gage Marketing Group 10000 Highway 55 Ste 100 Minneapolis MN 55441-6365

GAGE, FRED KELTON, lawyer; b. Mpls., June 20, 1925; s. Fred K. and Vivian L. G.; m. Dorothy Ann, Sept. 7, 1974; children: Deborah, Penelope, Amy, Lawrence. BS, U. Minn., 1948, LLB, 1950. Bar: Minn. 1950. Assoc. Wilson, Blethen & Ogle, Mankato, 1950-55; ptnr. Blethen, Gage, Krause, Blethen, Corcoran, Berkland & Peterson and predecessor firms, Mankato, 1955-90, of counsel, 1991—. Mem. State Bd. Profl. Responsibility, Minn. Supreme Ct., 1974-82, mem. legal svcs. adv. com., 1996—. Mem. Mankato Sch. Bd., 1957-66, Minn. State Coll. Bd., 1960-64; mem. Minn. Senate from 11th Legis. Dist., 1966-72; Mem. Minn. Sports Facilities Commn., 1976-84. Served with USN, 1943-46. Named Mankato Outstanding Young Man of Yr., 1956, Outstanding Man of Minn., Mankato Jr. C. of C., 1958 Fellow Am. Bar Found.; mem. ABA (assembly del. 1980-86), Minn. Bar Assn. (chmn. tax sect. 1956-58, pres. 1977-78), Order of Coif. Methodist. Office: Blethen Gage & Krause PO Box 3049 127 S 2nd St Mankato MN 56001-3658 E-mail: kgage@bglow.com.

GAGE, GEORGE H(ENRY), retired high technology company executive; b. Rochester, N.Y., Oct. 1, 1924; s. George Henry and Ethel (Morley) G.; m. Frances Irvine, Dec. 21, 1946; children: Betsey Gage La Breche, James George, Nancy Gage Mandeville. BSEE, Rensselaer Poly. Inst., 1948. Application engr. GE, Owensboro, Ky., 1948-56, comml. engr. Syracuse, N.Y., 1957-58; mgr. product planning CBS Electronics, Danvers, Mass., 1959-61; dir. planning EG&G, Inc., Bedford, Mass., 1962-75, v.p. Wellesley, Mass., 1975-83, sr. v.p., 1983-86; dir. Adams Russell Co., Inc., Waltham, Mass., 1979-89; gov. Newell Health Corp., Newton-Wellesley Hosp., 1979-87; ret. Contbg. author: Industrial Electronics Handbook, 1957, Implementation of Strategic Planning, 1982. Staff sgt. U.S. Army, 1943-46, PTO. Mem. Sigma Xi (assoc.), Tau Beta Pi, Eta Kappa Nu. Avocations: computer simulations, reading, walking. Home: 23 Fiddlers Green Lansing NY 14882-8877

GAGE, MIRIAM BETTS, retired nutritionist; b. Nelsonville, Ohio, Jan. 9, 1928; d. Charles Donald and Lillian Mary (Linscott) B.; m. Robert Averill Gowdy, Oct. 12, 1950 (div. 1977); children: Carol Jo, Robert Jr., Bruce; m. George Joel Gage, Aug. 16, 1997. BA in Home Econs., Ohio Wesleyan U., 1949; postgrad., Duke U., 1949-50, Calif. State U., L.A., 1975 76. Registered dietitian. Pvt. practice dietitian, L.A., 1977-91; cons. Nat.-in-Home Health, Van Nuys, Calif., 1984-87; clin. dietitian Lake Mead Hosp., 1991-94; pvt. practice Las Vegas, Nev., 1994-97; contract dietitian Pulse Health Svcs., Las Vegas, 1995-97; ret., 1997. Mem. Am. Diabetes Assn. (con. San Fernando Valley unit 1976-80, bd. dirs. N.W. chpt. 1977-82), Nev. Dietetic Assn. (nominating com. 1995-97), So. Nev. Dietetic Assn. (mem. chmn. 1991-92, pres. 1993-94), Cons. Nutritionists (chmn.-elect So. Calif. chpt. 1979-81), Calif. Dietetic Assn. (chmn. diabetes care practice 1979-81), Am. Heart Assn. (governing bd. N.W. chpt. 1988-89), Sierra Club, Nat. Audubon Soc. Republican. Methodist. Avocations: golfing, hiking, bird watching, camping. Home: 10813 Brinkwood Ave Las Vegas NV 89134-5248 Business E-Mail: miriamgage@ucnimc.net.

GAGE, NANCY ELIZABETH, college administrator, accountant, educator; b. Chgo., Aug. 22, 1947; d. Winfred Paul and Anne Ellen (Osbon) Rankhorn; m. Walter Howard Crane, June 14, 1969 (div. June 1977); 1 child, Patrick; m. James Lewis Gage, June 10, 1977 (div. Oct. 1981); 1 child, Laura Anne. BS, Ill. Inst. Tech., 1969; postgrad., Winona State U., 1978-80, U. Minn., 1981-82. Cert. Collegiate Mgmt. Inst.; cert. tchr. math., Wash., Mich., Ill.; Myers-Briggs Type Indicator qualified adminstr., interpreter. Tchr. math. St. Bede Acad., Eau Claire, Wis., 1977; accounts specialist U. Minn., Mpls., 1981, asst. adminstr., 1981-82, assoc. adminstr., 1982-83; grants acct. supr. Coll. of DuPage, Glen Ellyn, Ill., 1984, cash disbursements mgr., 1984-87, chief acct., 1987—. Founding mem. Ptnrs. in Edn. Coun., Coll. DuPage, 1997, chair bd/staff rels. com., 1990-92, mem. salary/benefits negotiating team, 1993-94, 98-99, pres. 1994-95, 2003-04; chmn. supervisory com. Fed. Credit Union, 1985-86, mem. project team payroll/pers. sys. implementation, 1985-87, mem. project team gen. ledger sys. implementation, 1987-89; project leader Y2K Conversion, gen. ledger sys., 1997-2000; mem. Baldrige Award Bd. Examiners, 2002—. Contbg. author math. curriculum, 1972; web developer, 1996—. Media contact coord. Common Cause, Manistique, Mich., 1975-76; bd. dirs., pres. Manistique Coop. Nursery Sch., 1974-75; mem. Bicentennial program com. Manistique Jr. Women's Group, Manistique, 1975-76, Chgo. Tchrs. Against the Vietnam War, 1969. Recipient Outstanding Svc. award Coll. of DuPage, 1987-88, 91-92; State of Ill. fellow, 1970; Ill. Inst. Tech. scholar, 1964. Mem. AAUW, Am. Soc. Profl. and Exec. Women, Am. Assn. Women in C.C.s (bd. sec. 1997-98), Classified Pers. Assn. (exec. bd. 1993-96), Cen. Assn. Coll. and Univ. Bus. Officers (2 yr. coll. com. 1990-93, drive in workshop com. 1993-97), Nat. Assn. Coll. and Univ. Bus. Officers, Manistique Ext. Homemakers Club (treas. 1974-76), Kappa Phi Delta (treas. 1967-68). Independent. Unitarian. Avocations: reading, writing, travel, social reform. Home: 2201 W Illinois Ave Aurora IL 60506 1530 Office: Coll of DuPage Fin Office 425 Fawell Blvd Glen Ellyn IL 60137-6599

GAGE, NATHANIEL LEES, psychologist, educator; b. Union City, N.J., Aug. 1, 1917; s. Hyman and Rose (Lees) Gewirtz; m. Margaret Elizabeth Burrows, June 27, 1942; children: Elizabeth, Thomas Burrows, Sarah, Anne. AB magna cum laude, U. Minn., 1938; PhD, Purdue U., 1947, LittD (hon.), 1978; PhD (hon.), U. Liège, 2001. Asst. prof. div. ednl. reference Purdue U., 1947-48; prof. edn. U. Ill., Urbana, 1948-62; prof. edn. and psychology Stanford U., 1962-87, Margaret Jacks prof. edn., 1981-87, prof. emeritus, 1987—. Sachs vis. prof. Tchrs. Coll., Columbia U., 1977; lectr. U. Hamburg, 1978, Taipei, 1989, Madrid, 1992, U. Ill., 1994, numerous others; vis. fellow Brasenose Coll., Oxford U., 1983; vis. prof. NYU, 1959, Harvard U., 1984, SUNY, Albany, 1988; mem. rsch. adv. com. Am. Coun. Edn., 1967-73, chmn., 1972-73; mem. Nat. Adv. Com. on Edn. Labs, 1966-69; cons. Internat. Inst. Ednl. Planning, Paris, 1973-74; chmn. exec. bd. Stanford Ctr. Rsch. and Devel. in Tchg., 1968-76, founding co-dir., 1965-68; also dir. program on teaching effectiveness Ctr. for Ednl. Rsch., Stanford, 1972-83; vis. scholar, chmn. planning conf. on studies in teaching Nat. Inst. Edn., 1974; chmn. project coun. internat. classroom environ. study Internat. Assn. for Evaluation of Ednl. Achievement, 1979-81; Fulbright lectr., Brazil, 1985; mem. final selection com. Spencer Found. Dissertation Yr. Fellowships, 1987, 88; participant U. S. Dept. Edn. Conf. on School-Linked Comprehensive Svcs. for Children and Families, 1994. Author: Teacher Effectiveness and Teacher Education, 1972, Scientific Basis of the Art of Teaching, 1978, Hard Gains in the Soft Sciences: The Case of Pedagogy, 1985; co-author: Educational Measurement and Evaluation, 1943, 2d edit., 1955, A Practical Introduction to Measurement and Evaluation, 1960, 2d edit., 1965, Educational Psychology, 1975, 6th edit., 1998; editor: Handbook of Research on Teaching, 1963, Mandated Evaluation of Educators, 1973, Psychology of Teaching Methods, 1976; founding editor Teaching and Teacher Education: An Internat. Jour. Rsch. and Studies, 1983-86; co-editor: Readings in the Social Psychology of Education, 1963; cons. editor Jour. Ednl. Psychology, numerous other jours. Served with USAAF, 1943-45. Recipient Creative Leadership award NYU Sch. Edn., 1980, Outstanding Writing award Am. Assn. Colls. Tchr. Edn., 1986, Disting. Alumnus award Purdue U., 1994, Rsch. and Dissemination Program award Am. Fedn. Tchrs., 2000; fellow Ctr. for Advanced Study in Behavioral Scis., 1965-66, 87-88, USPHS, 1965-66, Guggenheim fellow, 1976-77. Fellow APA (pres. divsn. ednl. psychology 1961-62, Thorndike award 1986), Am. Psychol. Soc. (charter fellow); mem. Am. Ednl. Rsch. Assn. (pres. 1963-64, Disting. Contbns. award 1988), Nat. Soc. Study Edn. (bd. dirs. 1970-80, chmn. 1972, 74, 78), Nat. Acad. Edn., Phi Beta Kappa, Sigma Xi, Phi Delta Kappa (award for meritorious contbns. to edn. 1981). Home: 85 Peter Coutts Cir Stanford CA 94305-2512 E-mail: nlgage@stanford.edu.

GAGE, PATRICK (LEONARD PATRICK GAGE), biotech/pharmaceutical consultant; b. Endicott, N.Y., May 4, 1942; s. Leonard Augustine and Mary Margaret (O'Brien) G.; m. Nancy Virginia Graffius, Aug. 7, 1965 (div. Mar. 1985); children: Darren, Cynthia; m. Evelyn Anne Devine, June 29, 1985; children: Christopher, Devin. BS, MIT, 1964; PhD, U. Chgo., 1969. NIH postdoctoral fellow Carnegie Inst., Washington, 1969-71; mem. dept. cell biology Roche Inst. Molecular Biology, 1971-80, dir. dept. molecular genetics, 1981-83, v.p. biol. R & D, 1983-84; v.p. exploratory rsch. Hoffmann-La Roche Inc., Nutley, N.J., 1984-89; exec. v.p. Genetics Inst., Inc., Cambridge, Mass., 1989-93, COO, 1993-97, pres., 1997-98, Wyeth Rsch., Collegeville, Pa., 1998—2002; sr. v.p. sci. and tech. Wyeth, 2001—02; ptnr. Flagship Venture, Cambridge, Mass. Chmn. Dublin Molecular Medicine Ctr., 2002—, Compound Therapeutics; sci. adv. bd. Perkin Elmer Inc.; life sci. adv. bd. Warburg Pincus; bd. dirs. Biotech. Inst., Neose Technologies, Inc., Protein Design Labs, Inc. Adv. bd. Life Sci. Rsch. Found., 1995—; bd. dirs. Phila. Orch. Avocations: skiing, tennis. Personal E-mail: patrickgage@comcast.net.

GAGE, ROBERT CLIFFORD, minister; b. Beverly, Mass., Nov. 20, 1941; s. George V. and Elizabeth B. (May) G.; m. Mary Neefe, June 17, 1961; children: Joanna, Jonathan, Judith, Joshua, Joy. Student, Tenn. Temple U., 1961-62; BA, Phila. Coll. of Bible, 1964; postgrad., Ea. Bapt. Theol. Sem., 1966-67, New Sch. Soc. Rsch., 1975-76; D of Religion, Newport U., 1983. Ordained to ministry Gen. Assn. Regular Bapt. Chs., 1964. Pastor Whitehall Bapt. Ch., Phila., 1964-65, Glencroft Bapt. Ch., Glenolden, Pa., 1966-68, 1st Bapt. Ch., Newfield, N.J., 1969-70, Hackensack, N.J., 1971-79, Wealthy St. Bapt. Ch., Grand Rapids, Mich., 1979-88; evangelist, 1988-91; pastor Haven Bapt. Ch., Winter Haven, Fla., 1991-2000; adminstr. Haven Christian Acad., Winter Haven, Fla., 1996-2000; pastor 1st Bapt. Ch., N.Y.C., 2000—. Radio min., 1988; dir. Sword and Shield Ministries/Rivendel Pastor's Retreat, Deposit, NY, 2003-. Author: The Birthmarks of the Christian Life, 1976, Our Life in Christ, 1978, The Pastor's Counseling Workbook, 1983, The Pre-Marriage Counseling Workbook, 1984, Discipleship Evangelism, 1985, Cultivating Spiritual Fruit, 1986, basic Discipleship, 1987, Why Me, Lord, 1988, The Unveiling, 1990; editor sword and Shield, 1969—; contbr. sermons to ch. publs.; weekly columnist Pers. Pub. Clinic, Winter Haven News Chief. Home: Apt 22B 395 South End Ave New York NY 10280 Office: 265 West 79th St New York NY 10024 E-mail: drbobgnyc@yahoo.com. *Lord Jesus Christ, the work is Thine, not ours but Thine alone, and prospered by thy power Divine, can never be overthrown.*

GAGE, TOMMY WILTON, retired pharmacologist, dentist, pharmacist, educator; b. Stamford, Tex., Oct. 6, 1935; s. Carl and Mildred (Hughes) G.; m. Loyce M. Voss, June 2, 1956; children— Sharon, Stephen, Susan, Stacey. BS, U. Tex., Austin, 1957; D.D.S., Baylor U., 1961, PhD, 1969. Gen. practice dentistry, Munday, Tex., 1963-66; mem. faculty Baylor Coll. Dentistry, Dallas, 1969—; prof. pharmacology Tex. A&M U. Sys. Health Sci. Ctr. at Baylor Coll. Dentistry, 1972—; chmn. dept. Tex. A&M U. Sys. at Baylor Coll. Dentistry, 1969-92, vice chmn. dept. oral and maxillofacial surgery and pharmacology, 1992—2000, dir. curriculum, acad. svcs., 2000—02; ret., 2002. Author papers in field, chpts. in books. Served with USAR, 1961-63. Nat. Inst. Dental Rsch. postdoctoral fellow, 1966-69; named to Baylor Coll. Dentistry Hall of Fame. Fellow Am. Coll. Dentists, Internat. Coll. Dentists; mem. ADA, Am. Soc. Pharmacology and Exptl. Therapeutics, Am. Assn. for Dental Rsch., Internat. Assn. Dental Rsch., Tex. Dental Assn. (Cooley Trophy 1976), S.W. Soc. Oral Medicine, Dallas County Dental Assn. (Dentist of Yr. 2002), Rho Chi, Omicron Kappa Upsilon. Methodist.

GAGGINI, JOHN EDMUND, lawyer; b. Chgo., Dec. 17, 1949; BA cum laude, Knox Coll., 1971; MS, Ohio U., 1972, JD magna cum laude, 1975; LLM, NYU, 1976. Bar: Ill. 1975, D.C. 1977; CPA, Ill. Law clk. to Hon. Shiro Kashiwa U.S. Ct. Claims, 1976-77; ptnr. McDermott, Will & Emery, Chgo. Adj. prof. law Chgo.-Kent Coll. Law, 1987—. Mem. ABA, Ill. State Bar Assn., Chgo. Bar Assn. (chmn. state and local tax com. 1986-87), Phi Kappa Phi, Phi Beta Kappa, Beta Alpha Psi, Phi Gamma Mu, Phi Alpha Delta. Office: McDermott Will & Emery 227 W Monroe St Ste 4700 Chicago IL 60606-5096

GAGGIOLI, RICHARD ARNOLD, mechanical engineering educator; b. Highwood, Ill., Dec. 3, 1934; s. Gustavo and Constantina Lucille (Mordini) G.; m. Anita Catherine Sage, Nov. 9, 1957; children: Catherine Anne, Michael James, Daniel Richard, Edward Thomas, Mary Esther. BME, Northwestern U., 1957, MS (NSF fellow), 1958; PhD (Gen. Electric, NSF fellow), U. Wis., 1961. Registered profl. engr., Wis., 1965. Coop. student engr. Abbott Labs. (pharms.), North Chicago, Ill., 1954-58; asst. prof. mech. engring. U. Wis., Madison, 1962-66, assoc. prof., 1966-69; prof., chmn. dept. mech. engring. Marquette U., Milw., 1969-72, prof., 1969—81, 1990—2001; dean engring. and architecture Cath. U. Am., Washington, 1981-84; prof. mech. engring. U. Mass., Lowell, 1985-89; rsch. prof. Marquette U., 2002—. Mem. U.S. Army Math. Research Ctr., Madison, 1964-66; NSF-Soc. Indsl. and Applied Math. vis. lectr., 1969-72, engring. cons., 1970—. Author: (with E.F. Obert) Thermo-dynamics, 1963; editor: Thermodynamics-Second Law Analysis, Vol. 1, 1980, Vol. 2, 1983, Analysis of Energy Systems, 1985, Computer-Aided Engineering of Energy Systems, 1986; (with M.J. Moran) Analysis and Design of Advanced Energy Systems: Fundamentals, 1987; (with G. Tsatsaronis) Fundamentals of Thermodynamics and Energy Analysis, 1990; (with G.M. Reistad) Thermodynamics and Energy Systems: Fundamentals, 1991, (with R.F. Boehm et al.) Thermodynamics and the Design of Energy Systems, 1992; hon. editor Internat. Jour. Applied Thermodynamics, 1998—; contbr. articles to profl. jours. Chmn. bd. trustees Montrose Sch., Westwood, Mass., 1987-89. Recipient Emil H. Steiger Meml. Teaching award U. Wis., 1965, Pere Marquette award for faculty excellence Marquette U., 1976, Best Paper award Am. Chem. Soc. Chem. Tech. jour. 1977; NSF postdoctoral fellow chem. engring. U. Wis., 1961-62; vis. fellow Battelle Meml. Inst., 1968-69; invited lectr., Rome, 1987, 95, Beijing 1986, 89, 97, Abu Dhabi, 1988, Zaragoza 1993, Florence, 1989, 2003, Athens, 1991, Istanbul, 1995, Bucharest, 1997, Nancy, 1997, Krakow, 1994, 98, Tokyo, 1999, others. Fellow ASME (James Harry Potter gold medal 1988, advanced energy sys. divsn. best paper award 1991, E.F. Obert best paper award 2000); mem. AIChE, Summit Edn. Assn. (sec., trustee 1993—), Sigma Xi, Pi Tau Sigma, Tau Beta Pi. Roman Catholic. Office: Marquette U Dept Mech Engring Milwaukee WI 53201-1881 Home: W2202 Wilmers Grove Rd East Troy WI 53120

GAGLIANI, WILLIAM DENNIS, school librarian; s. Gilbert Dario and Albertina Gagliani; life ptnr. Janis M. Radziun. MA, U. of Wis., Milw., 1986, BA in English and Geol. Sci., 1982. Lectr. dept. English U. Wis., Milw., 1987—88; stacks supr. Marquette U. Meml. Libr., Milw., 1988—. Author: Wolf's Trap, Thin Hung the Web, To Flutter in Memories, Icewall, Until Hell Calls Our Names (Darrell award Memphis Sci.Fiction Assn., 1999), (short stories) Kiss a Bubba Good Mornin', A Knight of Swords, Only Spectres Still Have Pity, Kneel at the Shrine, If She Promised You Heaven, Wolf's Trap, 2003, Port of Call, Lead Me Into Temptation, We Were Like Lions, Starbird, Dark Places, Underground, (e-book) Shadowplays, 2001; editor: (literary magazine) Square One. Recipient 3d prize, Sci. Fiction Writers of Earth, 1989, 2d prize, 1993, 1994. Mem.: Horror Writers Assn. (Bram Stoker award additions com. mem. 2003—). Avocations: weapons collecting, music. Home: PO Box 11921 Milwaukee WI 53211-0921 Personal E-mail: tarkusp@execpc.com

GAGLIANO, ALFONSO, Canadian government official; b. Siculiana, Italy, Jan. 25, 1942; arrived in Can., 1958; s. Vincenzo and Maria (Augello) G.; m. Ersilia Gidaro, July 3, 1965; children: Vincenzo, Maria, Immacolata. Cert. gen. acctg., George Williams U., Montreal. Sch. commr. Jérôme LeRoyer Sch. Bd., Montreal, Quebec, Can., 1977-83; pres. Jérôme-LeRoyer Sch. Commn., Montreal, 1983-84; MP St. Leonard Anjou Riding Can. Parliament, Ottawa, 1984-88, MP St. Leonard Riding, 1988-94; sec. state parliamentary affairs, dep. leader of govt. Can. Parliament House of Commons, Ottawa, 1994-96; min. of labour and dep. govt. house leader Can. Govt. House of Commons, Ottawa, 1996-97, min. pub. works and govt. svcs., 1997—; mem. parliament, 2000—. Official opposition critic for small bus., rev. Canada and Canada Post Corp., 1984-91; opposition critic for industry dept., mem. permanent com. on fin. Can. House of Commons, 1988-91; opposition critic for immigration 1990-91; chair Quebec Liberal Caucus, 1988-91; chief govt. whip, 1993-94; chair electoral commn. Liberal Party of Canad (Quebec), 1994—. Liberal Party Can. Office: Office Pub Works/Govt Svcs Place du Portage rue Laurier St QCK1A0S5 Hull QC Canada K1A OS5 E-mail: minister@pwgsc.gc.ca

GAGLIANO, CHRISTINE LOUISE, social worker; b. Pitts., Dec. 6, 1949; d. Donald Russell and Rose Annette (Rizzo) G. Student, Case Western Reserve U., 1967-68; BA in Psychology, SUNY, Stony Brook, 1975; MSW, Fla. State U., 1977. LCSW Pa., cert. Acad. Cert. Social Workers. Social worker Gannondale Sch. for Girls, Erie, Pa., 1977; family therapist Family Svcs., Erie, 1977—80; assoc. prof. social work Mercyhurst Coll., Erie, 1980—92; family therapist Gateway Rehab. Ctr., Erie, 1994. Pvt. practice, Erie, 1995—; introduced sand play therapy, Erie, 1996; developer healing workshops for social workers, 95; presenter workshops on spirituality and social work, 2001. Mem. Nat. Assn. Social Work (social policy com. Pa. chpt., 1993-94, workshop facilitator Pa. chpt., 1995-96, continuing edn. com. N.W. Pa. chpt., 1995, diplomate, qualified clin. social worker), Assn. Women in Social Work. Avocations: music, meditation. Office: 3205A W 26th St Erie PA 16506-2507

GAGLIANO, FRANK JOSEPH, playwright; b. Bklyn., Nov. 18, 1931; s. Francis Paul and Nancy (La Barbera) G.; m. Sandra Renee, Jan. 18, 1958; 1 child, Francis Enrico. BA, U. Iowa, 1954; MFA, Columbia U., 1957. Free-lance copywriter, N.Y.C., 1958-61; promotion copywriter text-film divsn. McGraw-Hill Co., N.Y.C., 1962-65; asst. prof. drama Fla. State U., 1969-72; lectr. in playwriting, dir. E. P. Conkle Workshop for Playwrights, U. Tex., Austin, 1972-75; Benedum prof. theater W.Va. U., 1976—. Disting. vis. alumni prof. U. R.I., 1975; artistic dir. Showcase of New Plays Carnegie-Mellon U., 1987—98; artistic dir. Festival of New Works U. Mich., 1999—2001. Author: (plays) Conerico Was Here to Stay, 1965, Paradise Gardens East, 1966, Night of the Dunce, 1966, Father Uxbridge Wants to Marry, 1967, The Hide-and-Seek Odyssey of Madeleine Gimple, 1968, Big Sur, 1969, The Prince of Peasantmania, 1970, The Commedia World of Lafcadio B, 1973, In the VooDoo Parlour of Marie Laveau, 1974, rev. edit. 2000, The Resurrection of Jackie Cramer, 1976, Congo Square, 1979, rev. edit., 1989, The Total Immersion of Madeleine Favorini, 1981 (1st prize Ernest Hemingway Playwriting award 1999) rev. edit., 2000, (cantata) San Ysidro, 1985, (novel) Anton's Leap, 1986, rev. edit., 1991, From the Bodoni County Songbook Anthology, 1986, (musical version), 1987, rev. edit., 1989, 90, 91, 95, My Chekhov Light, 1987, rev. edit., 1983, 92, (for German pub.) 98, Hanna-A Run on Odyssey, 1990-92, The Farewell Concert of Irene and Vernon Palazzo, 1995, And the Angels Sing (musical), 1996, Piano Bar (musical), 1998. With U.S. Army, 1954-56. Wesleyan U.-O'Neill Found. fellow, 1967; Guggenheim fellow, 1975; Rockefeller grantee, 1965, 66; Nat. Endowment for Arts grantee, 1973; Penn. Coun. Playwriting fellow, 1989. Mem. ASCAP, Dramatists Guild, New Dramatists (alumnus). Office: WVa U Creative Arts Ctr Morgantown WV 26506 E-mail: sandrico@aol.com.

GAGLIARDI, MARIO CARMELO, priest; b. Savoia di Lucania, Italy, Sept. 8, 1946; s. Michele and Maria Vittoria (Mangino) Gagliardi. PhD in Theology, Institut Catholique, Paris, 1981; PhD in Anthropology, Sorbonne, Paris, 1981; M.Polit. Sci., CUNY, Bklyn., 2001. Ordained priest Roman Cath. Ch., 1974. Priest Shrine of Our Lady of Mt. Carmel, Bklyn., 1981—; sub. priest Italian Catholic Mission, Vinterthur, Switzerland. Rep. Internat. Catholic Edn. Office at United Nations, 1982—; founder/pres. Italian Ctr. of N.Y.; exec. dir. ENCAL of N.Y., 1989—; v.p. COEMIT. Recipient Citation, Assembly of State of N.Y., 1986. Roman Catholic. Avocations: soccer, swimming, bicycling, antique coin and stamp collecting. Home: Shrine of Our Lady of Mount Carmel 275 N 8th St Brooklyn NY 11211-2102

GAGLIARDO, JOSEPH M(ICHAEL), lawyer; b. Chgo., Nov. 21, 1952; s. Joseph Anthony and Marie Vivian (Aiello) G.; m. Jennifer Ann Vozella, June 7, 1980; children: Joseph Michael Jr., Michael Anthony, John Richard. BS in Commerce, DePaul U., 1974; JD, John Marshall Law Sch., 1977. Bar: Ill. 1977, U.S. Dist. Ct. (no. dist.) Ill. 1977. Asst. corp. counsel law dept. City of Chgo., 1978-82, sr. atty. supr., 1982-83, chief asst. corp. counsel, 1983-85, dep. corp. counsel, 1985-86, first dep. corp. counsel, 1986—; ptnr. Laner, Muchin, Dombrow, Becker, Levin & Tominberg, 1988—. Editor: (annual report) Personnel and Labor Relations 1984-1985, 1985. Mem. ABA, Ill. State Bar Assn., Chgo. Bar Assn., Justinian Soc. Lawyers, Assembly Ill. State Bar Assn., Delta Mu Delta, Delta Epsilon Sigma. Office: Laner Muchin Dombrow Becker Levin Tominberg Ltd 515 N State St Ste 2800 Chicago IL 60610-4321 Fax: 312-467-9479. E-mail: jgagliardo@lmdblt.com.

GAGNE, ARMAND JOSEPH, JR., business administration and computer science educator, consultant; b. Lowell, Mass., July 21, 1936; s. Armand J. and Lillian J. (Clermont) G.; m. Beverly Ward, Dec. 19, 1970; children: Dana Andrea, Donna Angela, Deborah Ann, Denise Ann, Armand Joseph III, Charles Kenneth, Delannie Almeta, Joseph Edward, Chloe Danielle. BBA, U. S.C., 1968, MBA, 1973, PhD, 1992; PhD in Religious Studies, Christian Bible Coll., 1992; MA, U. S.C., 1996. Mgr. systems procedures Gifford-Hill Inc., Charlotte, N.C., 1970-74; contr. Automation Internat., Charlotte, 1974-75; v.p. fin. Vanply of Liberia, Monrovia, N.C., 1975-76; pres. SMS Assocs., Pink Hill, N.C., 1976-80; assoc. prof. U. S.C., Sumter, 1980—; pres., cons. Systems People Inc., Sumter, 1982—95. Seminar cons. U. Miami, Fla., 1983-84; webmaster Sumter on Line, 1997-2002, www.joegagne.com, 2002—, www.fourthgospel.com, 2000--. With USN, 1954-60, Africa. Recipient S.C. Gov.'s Prof. of yr. award,

1997-98, Outstanding Achievement award Greater Sumter C. of C., 1998, Internat. Vocat. Svc. award Sunrise Rotatary, 1998. Mem. Beta Gamma Sigma, Omicron Delta Epsilon. Republican. Baptist. Home: 1797 Wardland Rd Sumter SC 29154-7231 Office: U SC Miller Rd Sumter SC 29150-2403 E-mail: jogagne@uscsumter.edu., joegagne@joegagne.com.

GAGNE, MARY, academic administrator; Dir. Tex. Acad. Leadership in the Humanities Lamar U., Beaumont, 1998—. Recipient Blue Ribbon awards U.S. Dept. Edn., 1986-87, 90-91, Exec. Educator Best Prin. award, Nat. Tchg. award NCEA, Coca Cola Educator of Distinction award. 2000. Address: PO Box 10062 Beaumont TX 77710-0062 E-mail: gagneml@hal.lamar.edu.

GAGNIER, JOSEPH C. artist; b. Detroit, Oct. 18, 1929; s. Joseph A. Gagnier and Virginia F. De Buhl; m. Huguette M. Filion, Feb. 3, 1952 (div. 1969); children: Denise, Marcel, Michelle, Maurice, Monique, Paul. Student, U. Mich., 1957, Mich. State U., 1958. Musician Am. Fedn. Musicians, Detroit, 1954-80; mason contractor Gagnier & Assocs., St. Clair Shores, Mich., 1952-60, 85-90; landscape arch. Gagnier & Brox, Lockport, N.Y., 1960-85; profl. ski instr. Boyne Mt. Lodge, Boyne Falls, Mich., 1962-79; artist Jack Pine Studios, Roscommon, Mich., 1985—. Instr. painting, watercolor Kirtland C.C., Roscommon, 1990-91. Composer (music) Have a Merry Christmas, 1989 (Billboard Mag. award 1993). Mem. Am. Watercolor Soc. (assoc. mem.), Midwest Watercolor Soc. (life mem.), Rotary (pres. 1980-81). Avocation: writing biographical and political novels. Home: 4571 M 18 Roscommon MI 48653

GAGNON, CRAIG WILLIAM, lawyer; b. St. Cloud, Minn., Dec. 19, 1940; s. Marvin Sylvester and Signa Gunhild (Johnson) G.; children: Nicole, Jeffrey, Camille; m. Pam Peglow, Nov. 8, 1980; children: Claire, Jillian, Jane. BA, U. Minn., 1964; JD magna cum laude, William Mitchell Coll. Law, 1968. Bar: Minn. 1968, U.S. Dist. Ct. Minn. 1968, U.S. Tax Ct. 1972, U.S. Supreme Ct. 1970. Ptnr. Oppenheimer, Wolff & Donnelly, Mpls., 1968—. Chmn. bd. Equity Bank; bd. dirs. XOX Corp., First Fla. Bank. Trustee William Mitchell Coll. Law, St. Paul. 1989—, chmn. bd., 1999-2000. Named Alumnus of Notable Achievement, U. Minn. Fellow Am. Coll. Trial Lawyers; mem. Metro Breakfast Club (pres. 1993), Am. Bd. Trial Advocates (assoc.), Am. Law Inst. Avocations: hunting, fishing, golf. Home: 4807 Sunnyside Rd Edina MN 55424-1109 Office: Oppenheimer Wolff & Donnelly 45 S 7th St Ste 3400 Minneapolis MN 55402-1609 E-mail: cgagnon@oppenheimer.com.

GAGNON, EDOUARD CARDINAL, ecclesiastic; b. Port Daniel, Can., Jan. 15, 1918; Ordained priest Roman Cath. Ch., 1940, consecrated bishop 1969, elevated to cardinal 1985. Bishop, St. Paul, Canada, 1969—72; rector Can. Coll., Rome, 1972—77; v.p., sec. Vatican Com. for Family, 1973—80; titular archbishop of Guistiniana Prima, 1983; pro-pres. Pontifical Council for the Family, 1983—85, pres., 1985—90, Pontifical Com. Internat. Eucharistic Congresses, 1991—. Office: Pontifical Com Internat Eucharistic Congr Piazza San Calisto 16 00153 Rome Italy*

GAGNON, MARC, Olympic athlete; b. Chicoutimi, Que., Can., May 24, 1975; Profl. speed skater, Canada. Recipient Bronze medal relay, 1994 Olympic Games, Gold medal relay, 1998 Olympic Games, Silver medal, World Championships, 1995, 1997, Gold medal, 1993, 1994, 1996, 1998, Gold medal 5000m short track men's relay, 2002 Olympic Games. Avocations: reading, golf. Office: Speed Skating Can 2781 Lancaster Rd Ste 402 Ottawa ON K1B 1A7 Canada

GAGNON, RONALD ADELARD, library director; b. Beverly, Mass., 1956; s. Adelard Amedee and Theresa Alice Gagnon; m. Ann Margaret Morris, 1991; children: Daniel Adelard, Ellen Alice. BSBA, Salem (Mass.) State Coll., 1978; MS in Libr. and Info. Sci., Simmons Coll., Boston, 1979. Cataloger Peabody Inst., Danvers, Mass., 1979-80, head tech. svcs., 1980-85, North Shore C.C., Beverly, 1985-88; network adminstr. North of Boston Libr. Exch., Beverly, 1988-93, exec. dir., 1993—. Bd. dirs. CLSI Ea. Region Users, 1990-94; strategic planning com. Mass. Bd. Libr. Commrs., 1993-94. Contbr. articles to Library Journal, 1981-91. Bd. dirs. Danvers Hist. Soc., 1988-91; town meeting mem. Town of Danvers, 1978-82, 94—. Mem. ALA, Assn. Specialized and Coop. Libr. Agys. (interlibr. coop. and networking sect.), New Eng. Libr. Assn., Mass. Libr. Assn., Friends Peabody Inst. Roman Catholic.

GAGOSIAN, ROBERT B. chemist, educator; b. Medford, Mass., Sept. 17, 1944; m. Susan Gagosian; children: Travis, Alex. SB in Chemistry, MIT, 1966; PhD in Organic Chemistry, Columbia U., 1970; hon. degree, L.I. Univ., 2000, Northeastern U., 2000. Asst. scientist Woods Hole Oceanog. Instn., Mass., 1972-76, assoc. scientist, 1976-82, sr. scientist, 1982—, chmn. dept. chemistry, 1982-87, assoc. dir. rsch., 1987-92, sr. assoc. dir., dir. rsch., 1992-93, acting dir., 1993, pres., 2001, pres., dir., 2002—. Vis. lectr. dept. geology and geophysics Yale U., 1975, cons., lectr. in field; mem. numerous vis. coms. and rsch. panels NSF, Office Naval Rsch., univs. and rsch. orgns. in U.S. and fgn. countries; mem. corp. Bermuda Biol. Sta. for Rsch., Sea Edn. Assn. Contbr. chpts. to books, articles to profl. jours. Grantee and fellow numerous profl. and ednl. instns. including vis. scholar U. Wash., 1983, Australian Inst. Marine Scis., 1983; vis. fellow Australian Nat. U., 1983; William Evans fellow, U. Otago, Dunedin, New Zealand, 1987. Mem. Am. Chem. Soc., AAAS, Geochem. Soc. Am., Am. Geophys. Union, European Assn. Organic Geochemists, Sigma Xi. Office: Woods Hole Oceanographic Inst Fenno House MS 40A Woods Hole MA 02543

GAHAGAN, THOMAS GAIL, obstetrician, gynecologist; b. Brush Valley, Pa., Apr. 14, 1938; s. Ben D. and Zula C. (Brown) G.; m. Mary A. Miller, Dec. 23, 1960; children: David, Diane, Kevin, Keith. BA, Washington and Jefferson Coll., 1960; MD, U. Pa., Phila., 1964. Diplomate Am. Bd. Ob/Gyn. Intern U. Ky., Lexington, 1964-65, resident in ob/gyn., 1965-68; group practice Dr. Jones and Kelch P.A., Newark, Ohio, 1970-71, Naples (Fla.) Ob/Gyn., 1971-85; pvt. practice Naples, 1985-99; ret., 1999. Capt. USAF, 1968-70. Fellow ACOG, Fla. Ob-Gyn. Soc.; mem. AMA, Am. Cancer Soc. (life, bd. dirs. Collier unit 1973-93, bd. dirs. Fla. div. 1976-91, pres. 1986-87, St. George medal 1990), Fla. Med. Assn., Collier County Med. Soc. (exec. com. 1989-94, pres.-elect 1991-92, pres. 1992-93). Republican. Presbyterian. Avocations: scuba diving, flying, golf, snow skiing, fishing. E-mail: tggahagan@cs.com. *The secret to my enjoyment of life has been keeping my priorities in order.*

GAHAN, BRIAN C, petroleum engineer, researcher; b. Sandwich, Ill., Sept. 18, 1962; s. Joe Eugene and Judith Lynn Gahan; m. Cindy Ann Scholl, July 5, 1997; children: Liam Curtis, Ethan Riley, Megan Catherine. BSc, Marietta Coll., 1984; MBA, Katz Grad. Sch. of Bus., U. of Pitts., 1985; M in chem. engring., Armour Coll. of Engring. and Sci., Ill. Inst. of Tech., 2002. Technician Amerada Hess, Newburg, ND, 1982; engr. Conoco, New Orleans, 1983; petroleum engring. officer Pitts. Nat. Bank (now PNC Bank), 1985—91; prin. tech. mgr. Gas Tech. Inst., Des Plaines, Ill., 1991—. Mem.: AIAA, Laser Inst. of Am., Am. Assn. of Petroleum Geologists, Am. Inst. of Chem. Engineers (sec., Chgo. sect. 2002—03), Soc. of Petroleum Engineers (dir., Pitts. sect. 1990—91), Aircraft Owners and Pilots Assn., Am. Mensa, Inc, Pi Epsilon Tau (sec./treas 1983—84), Kappa Mu Epsilon, Lambda Chi Alpha. R-Consevative. Roman Catholic. Avocations: private pilot, history, baseball. Office: Gas Technology Institute 1700 South Mt Prospect Rd Des Plaines IL 60018 Office Fax: 847-768-0995. E-mail: brian.gahan@gastechnology.org.

GAHBAUER, REINHARD A. physician; s. Alfred and Mary G.; children: John, Alice. MD, Ludwig Maximilian U., Munich, 1969, Tech. Hochschule, 1970. Diplomate Am. Bd. Therapeutic Radiology. Radiation oncologist Cleve. Clinic Found., 1978-84; faculty Ohio State U., Columbus, 1984—, dir. radiation oncology, 1985—, prof. radiology, 1993—; chief of staff A. James Cancer Hosp., 1999-2001. Roman Catholic. Home: 812 Hard Rd Columbus OH 43235-1740 Office: Ohio State U 300 W 10th Ave Columbus OH 43210-1240

GAIBER, LAWRENCE JAY, financial company executive; b. Chgo., Mar. 20, 1960; s. Sy Bertrym and Mildred (Dickler) G. BS in Econ., U. Pa., 1982. Mgmt. intern Eisai Co. Ltd, Tokyo, 1980; dept. mgr. Anglo Am. Corp., Johannesburg, Republic of South Africa, 1982-84; pres. Sandton Fin. Group, L.A., 1984—, Swellendam Fin. Group, Studio City, Calif., 1984—, also bd. dirs. Bd. dirs. Lawrand Ltd, Satellite Telecommunication, Inst. Cellular Nutritional Immunology, Intrologater, Gaiber, Intrologater, L.A. Greetings; chmn. Mechanics Express Inc. Contbr. articles to profl. jours and mags. Mem. South Africa Found., Johannesburg, 1984—, Town Hall Calif., 1986; bd. dirs. Brentwood Arts Coun.; vice chmn. western region 1986 Pres.' dinner Rep. Nat. Com., Washington. Recipient Most Active Vol. award S. African Inst. Internat. Affairs, 1983; honoree for contbns. to aspiring entrepreneurial women Mayor Tom Bradley's Office and Nat. Network of Hispanic Women, L.A., 1986. Mem. L.A. Venture Assn., L.A. C. of C., L.A. Jr. C. of C., Van Nuys C. of C., L.A. County Rep. Lincoln Club, L.A. County Young Reps., Brentwood Rep. Club (Pres. 1984—). Clubs: Wharton Bus. Sch., Calif. Yacht. Avocation: world travel.

GAIHA, VISHNU DAS, cardiologist; b. New Delhi, May 2, 1945; MBBS, All India Inst. Med. Scis., 1968. Diplomate Am. Bd. Internal Medicine, Am. Bd. Cardiology, Am. Bd. Interventional Cardiology. Intern Albert Einstein Med. Ctr., Phila., 1969-70; resident internal medicine Northwestern U. Med. Ctr., Chgo., 1970-72; fellow cardiologist U. Mich. Hosps., Ann Arbor, 1972-74; attending physician active cons. St. Francis Hosp., Evanston, Ill., 1974—. Attending physician, cons. Swedish Covenant Hosp., Rush N. Shore Hosp., 1974—, Evanston Hosp., 2000—. Fellow Am. Coll. Cardiologists (cert.), Am. Coll. Chest Physicians. Office: 800 Austin St Ste 602 Evanston IL 60202-3446 Fax: 847-491-0949.

GAILEY, DOUGLAS MITCHELL, music educator; b. Salt Lake City, June 22, 1958; s. Myron Vern and Lois Belle Gailey; m. Jolene Dalton, July 18, 1987; children: Joshua Dalton, Justin Douglas. BA, U. Wash., 1984; MusM, U. Utah, 1986. Cert. tchr. Wash., 1991. Music educator Bingham H.S., South Jordan, Utah, 1986—91, Port Angeles H.S., Wash., 1991—. Named Rookie of Yr., Utah Music Educators Assn., 1986—87; recipient Disting. Band Dir. award, Am. Sch. Band Dirs. Assn., 1998. Mem.: North Olympic Music Educators Assn. (pres. 2003), Wash. Music Educators Assn. (assoc.; North Olympic pres. 1994—96). Non-Partisan. Avocations: fishing, backpacking, skiing. Home: 173 Alice Rd Port Angeles WA 98363 Office: Port Angeles High Sch 304 E Park Ave Port Angeles WA 98362

GAILEY, JOAN DALE, retired finance educator; b. Beaver Falls, Pa., May 10, 1940; d. Irvin D. and Elizabeth Jane (Hollander) Anderson; m. Ronald L. Gailey, Aug. 15, 1957; 1 child, Ronald. BSBA, Geneva Coll., 1975; MBA, Youngstown State U., 1980; PhD, U. Pitts., 1987. Libr. tech. Community Coll. Beaver County, Monaca, Pa., 1969-74; customer liaison, floor supr. LTV Steel, Aliquippa, Pa., 1975-79; instr. Youngstown (Ohio) State U., 1980-83, asst. prof. bus. mgmt. Kent State U., East Liverpool, Ohio, 1984-91, assoc. prof. bus. mgmt., 1992—, prof. bus. mgmt., 1998—, prof. Trumbull campus Warren, Ohio, 2001—02, prof. East Liverpool campus, 2003, ret., 2003, prof. emeritus, 2003. Cons. in bus. mgmt., 1988—; dir. Kent State East Liverpool Bus. Resource Ctr. Abstract editor Interface, 1994, 95, 96, 97, proceedings editor, 1998; co-editor: Humanities and Technology Rev., 1999—; contbr. articles to profl. jours. Mem. Rochester (Pa.) Area Planning Commn., 1989, Rochester Area Mktg. Com., 1990; tutor Adult Lit. Coun., Monaca, 1984-91; mem. adv. bd. Ret. Sr. Vol. Program, Lisbon, Ohio, 1990, vice chair, 1993-2000, facilitator Columbiana County Mini-Loan Fund, 1994-96. Recipient Kent State Teaching Devel. award, 1990, Kent State Profl. Devel. award, 1992; tchg. coun. grantee Kent State U., 1997-98, Summer award Univ. Tchg. Coun., 1999. Mem. Am. Ednl. Rsch. Assn. (editor newsletter 1993-94, program chair 1992), Nat. Assn. Indsl. Tech., Midwest MLA, Ohio Bus. Tchrs. Assn., Humanities and Tech. Assn. (exec. bd. dirs. 1997—), Assn. for Bus. Comm., Alpha Mu (Outstanding Mktg. Tchr. 1983). Office: Kent State U East Liverpool OH E-mail: jgailey@kent.edu.

GAILEY, THOMAS CHANDLER, professional football coach; b. Gainesville, Ga., Jan. 5, 1952; BS in Phys. Edn., U. Fla., 1974. Grad. asst. U. Fla., 1974-75; defensive backfield coach Troy State U., 1976-79, head coach, 1983-84; defensive backfield coach Air Force, 1979-82; asst. coach Denver Broncos, NFL, 1989-90, offensive coord., wide receivers coach, 1989-90; head coach Birmingham Fire, WFL, 1991-92, Samford U., 1993; wide receivers coach Pitts. Steelers, NFL, 1994-95, offensive coord., 1996-98; coach Dallas Cowboys, 1998-99; offensive coord. Miami Dolphins, 2000—. Office: Miami Dolphins 7500 SW 30th St Davie FL 33314-1020

GAILIUS, GILBERT KEISTUTIS, manufacturing company executive; b. Boston, June 21, 1931; s. Joseph B. and Mary K. Gailius; m. Lillian P. Romanskis, Sept. 6, 1954; children: Gregory, Laura, Louise, Gilbert, Linda, Gary. BS in Bus. Adminstrn., Suffolk U., 1958; MBA, Boston Coll., 1962. Plant controller, staff asst. corp. controller Continental Group, N.Y.C., 1954-66; v.p. fin. Foster Grant Co., Inc., Leominster, Mass., 1966-77, Midland Glass Co., Cliffwood, N.J., 1977-78, Am. Biltrite Inc., Wellesley Hills, Mass., 1978—99, v.p. strategic planning, 2001—. Also bd. dirs. Served with U.S. Army, 1952-54. Mem. Fin. Execs. Inst. Home: 1633 Sandcastle Rd Sanibel FL 33957 Office: Am Biltrite Inc 57 River St Wellesley MA 02481-2013

GAILLARD, GEORGE SIDAY, III, architect; b. Miami, Fla., Apr. 24, 1941; s. George Siday and Sarah Margaret (Crawford) G.; m. Charlalee Bailey, 1965 (div. 1969); m. Sylvia Gayle Bridgewater, July 18, 1977; 1 child, Barron Matthew. BS, Ga. Inst. Tech., 1965; postgrad., Ga. State U. Registered architect Ga., Fla. Sole propr. Fox Magnanimus, Atlanta, 1971-78, Gaillard & Assocs., Atlanta, 1978-81, 83—; mgr. design dept. Deca Inc., Miami, 1982. Sculpture exhibited in group shows at Piedmont Arts Festival, 1971, 73. Cubmaster Cub Scouts Am., Stone Mountain, Ga., 1988-89. With USMCR, 1962-68. Mem. AIA (chmn. liaison com. So. Coll. Tech. for Atlanta chpt. 1989-90), Huguenot Soc. S.C., Clan Lindsay Assn. U.S.A. Inc. (Ga. rep. 1989-95), St. Andrew's Soc. Atlanta (bd. dirs. 1996-98, interim v.p. 2002). Avocations: reading, camping, constructing and competing with blackpowder rifles.

GAILLARD, JOHN PALMER, JR., former government official, former mayor; b. Charleston, S.C., Apr. 4, 1920; s. John Palmer and Eleanor Ball (Lucas) G.; m. Lucy Huguenin Foster, July 15, 1944; children: John Palmer III, William Foster, Thomas Huguenin. LLD, The Citadel, 1975. Alderman City of Charleston, 1951-59, mayor, 1959-75; dep. asst. sec. for res. affairs Dept. Navy, Washington, 1975-77; v.p. Ruscon Corp., Charleston, S.C., 1977-86. Pres. Mcpl. Assn. S.C., 1964-65. Lt. USNR, 1941-45. Mem. C. of C., St. Andrews Soc., U.S. Conf. Mayors (adv. bd. 1969, trustee), Am. Legion, Carolina Yacht Club, Hibernian Club, Charleston Club, Elks. Episcopalian. Home: 77 Montagu St Charleston SC 29401-1238

GAILLARD, MARY KATHARINE, physics educator; b. New Brunswick, N.J., Apr. 1, 1939; d. Philip Lee and Marion Catharine (Wiedemayer) Ralph; children: Alain, Dominique, Bruno. BA, Hollins (Va.) Coll., 1960; MA, Columbia U., 1961; Dr du Troiseme Cycle, U. Paris, Orsay, France, 1964, Dr-es-Sciences d'Etat, 1968. With Ctr. Nat. Rsch. Sci., Orsay and Annecy-le-Vieux, France, 1964-84, head rsch. Orsay, 1973-80, Annecy-le-Vieux, 1979-80, dir. rsch., 1980-84; prof. physics, sr. faculty staff Lawrence Berkeley lab. U. Calif., Berkeley, 1981—. Morris Loeb lectr. Harvard U., Cambridge, Mass., 1980; Chancellor's Disting. lectr., U. Calif., Berkeley, 1981; Warner-Lambert lectr. U. Mich., Ann Arbor, 1984; vis. scientist Fermi Nat. Accelerator Lab., Batavia, Ill., 1973-74, Inst. for Advanced Studies, Santa Barbara, Calif., 1984, U. Calif., Santa Barbara, 1985; group leader L.A.P.P., Theory Group, France, 1979-81, Theory Physics div. LBL, Berkeley, 1985-87; sci. dir. Les Houches (France) Summer Sch., 1981; cons., mem. adv. panels U.S. Dept. Energy, Washington; cons. Nat. Sci. Bd., 1996-97, 2002, bd. dirs., 1997-2002. Co-editor: Weak Interactions, 1977, Gauge Theories in High Energy Physics, 1983; contr. articles to profl. jours. Recipient Thibaux prize U. Lyons (France) Acad. Art & Sci., 1977, E.O. Lawrence award, 1988, J.J. Sakurai prize for theoretical particle physics, APS, 1993; Guggenheim fellow, 1989-90. Fellow Am. Acad. Arts and Scis., Am. Philos. Soc. (mem. various coms., chairperson com. on women, J.J. Saburai prize 1993); mem. AAAS, NAS. Office: U Calif Dept Physics Berkeley CA 94720-0001

GAILLARD, THEODORE LEE, JR., writer; b. N.Y.C., Feb. 6, 1939; s. Theodore Lee and Patricia Coffin (Lindsay) G.; m. Elena Love, June 23, 1962 (div. July 1979); children: Gregory Lindsay, Jennifer Love; m. Ann Elizabeth Schwarberg, July 9, 1985. AB, Yale U., 1961; AM, Middlebury (Vt.) Coll., 1970. Asst. promotion mgr. Time-Life Internat., N.Y.C., 1961-64; history/English instr. Athens (Greece) Coll., 1964-65; tchr. English, crew coach St. Mark's Sch., Southboro, Mass., 1965-73; head upper sch., chair English dept. The Hockaday Sch., Dallas, 1973-88; dean faculty Brunswick Sch., Greenwich, Conn., 1988-89; acad. dean Lake Forest (Ill.) Acad., 1989-94; tchr. English Agnes Irwin Sch., Rosemont, Pa., 1996-97; sr. product mktg. specialist Kulick & Soffa Industries, Willow Grove, Pa., 1998; dir. comm. U. Pa. Law Sch., Phila., 1999; freelance writer Phila., 1994—. Cons. Armed Forces Jour. Internat., McLean, Va., 1996-2003; advanced placement reader in English, Ednl. Testing Svc., Princeton, N.J., 1972-81. Contbr. over 100 articles to profl. jours. and newspapers. Cpl. USMCR, 1961-67. Recipient Am. Spirit Honor medal Citizens Com. for Army, Navy and Air Force, 1962, Outstanding Tchr. award U. Chgo., 1993; English Speaking Union fellow, 1956-57. Mem. U.S. Naval Inst., Nature Conservancy, Fedn. Am. Scientists, Franklin Inn Club, Phi Beta Kappa. Episcopalian. Avocations: photography, writing, hiking, reading. Home: 755 Manatawna Ave Philadelphia PA 19128-1020

GAINER, EARL MARK, pharmacist; b. Parkersburg, W.Va., Oct. 29, 1959; s. Earl J. and Neva Lynn (Ellyson) G.; m. Drema M. Burns, Sept. 20, 1999. s. Jason Earl Gainer, Nov. 02, 2002. Student, Glenville State Coll., 1979-81; BS in Pharmacy magna cum laude, W.Va. U., 1983. Registered pharmacist, W.Va. Mgr. pharmacy dept. Rite Aid Corp., Weston, W.Va., 1984; relief pharmacist various orgns., 1985—. Singer, guitarist, songwriter: (compact disc and cassette rec.) Old Country Road, 1995, Heart & Mind, 1999. Mem. Trinity United Meth. Ch., Glenville, W.Va., 1995—. Mem. Internat. Bluegrass Music Assn., W.Va. U. Alumni Assn. (life), W.Va. U. Pharmacy Alumni Assn. (life), Golden Key, Rho Chi. Democrat. Avocations: music, sports, travel, history, antiques and collectables. Home: 18 Gables Pl Bridgeport WV 26330-9246

GAINER, JEFFERY A. writer, consultant; b. Charleston, W.Va., Oct. 27, 1958; s. Allen B. and Bethel J. G.; m. Collyer Allyson Mott, Oct. 6, 1990. BA, Marshall U., 1979. Automation specialist W.Va. Libr. Commn., Charleston, 1983-89; stockbroker Dean Witter Reynolds, New Orleans, 1989-90; software testing cons. Micro Focus, London, 1998-99; writer, mgmt. cons. ASC, Ltd., Grand Junction, Colo., 1999—; mgmt. cons. Darwin Ptnrs., Wakefield, Mass., 2000—. Contbr. articles to profl. jours. Mem.: IEEE, Mystery Writers Am., N.Y. Acad. Scis., White House Hist. Soc. Democrat. E-mail: gainerj@jeffgainer.com.

GAINER, RONALD LEE, lawyer; b. Lansing, Mich., Aug. 7, 1934; s. Asher Leroy and Gladys Irene (Harvey) G.; m. Alice Louise Sherwood, June 15, 1957; children— Gregory Sherwood, Geoffrey Scott. BA, Mich. State U., 1956; JD, U. Mich., 1959. Bar: N.Y. 1960, D.C. 1963, U.S. Supreme Ct. 1963. Atty. appellate sect., criminal div. Dept. Justice, Washington, 1963-69, dep. chief legis. and spl. projects, 1969-73, chief legis. and spl. projects, 1973-75, dir. Office of Policy and Planning, 1975-77; dep. asst. atty. gen. Office for Improvements in Adminstrn. of Justice, 1977-81, Office of Legal Policy, 1981-83, dep. assoc. atty. gen., 1984-85, assoc. dep. atty. gen., 1985-86, dep. assoc. atty. gen., 1986-89; ptnr. Gainer, Rient and Hotis (and successor Gainer and Rient), Washington, D.C., 1990—. U.S. expert mem. UN Com. on Crime Prevention and Control, 1979-92; designated mem. U.S. Sentencing Commn., 1985-88; bd. dirs., mem. adv. com. Internat. Centre Criminal Law Reform and Criminal Justice Policy, 1992—. Editorial bd.: Criminal Law Forum, 1989—. Served to capt. U.S. Ar, 1960-63. Recipient Disting. Service award U.S. Atty. Gen., 1973. Mem. Am. Law Inst., Am. Soc. Internat. Law, Internat. Soc. for Reform of Criminal Law (bd. dirs., mem. mgmt. com., 1989—), Internat. Assn. Penal Law, D.C. Bar Assn. Home: 3000 N Monroe St Arlington VA 22207-5371 Office: Gainer and Rient 3511 39th St NW #487 Washington DC 20016 E-mail: gr@us.net.

GAINES, BOYD, actor; b. Atlanta, May 11, 1953; Diploma, Julliard Sch. Performances include (stage) Spring Awakening, 1978, Oliver Oliver, 1984, The Double Bass, 1985, The Heidi Chronicles, 1988, Philadelphia, Here I Come!, 1988, She Loves Me, 1993 (Antoinette Perry award for leading actor in a musical 1994) (film) Fame, 1980, Porky's, 1982, The Sure Thing, 1985, Heartbreak Ridge, 1986, Call Me, 1988, Ray's Male Heterosexual Dance Hall, 1988, The Grass Harp, 1995, I'm Not Rappaport, 1996, (T.V.) One Day at a Time, 1981-84, Evergreen, 1985, Remington Steele, L.A. Law, 1986, Hotel, 1986, Spenser: For Hire, 1988, Pidgeon Feathers, 1988, Piece of Cake, 1990, A Woman Named Jackie, 1991. Office: Duva/Flack Assocs 200 W 57th St Ste 1008 New York NY 10019-3211

GAINES, CHERIE ADELAIDE, lawyer; b. Queens, N.Y., May 17, 1935; d. Charles Oscar and Billie (Robinson) Gaines; m. Eugene Merwyn Swann, Apr. 15, 1960 (div. Oct. 1978); children— Liana Jane, Eugene Michael, Elliott Mark. B.A., Barnard Coll., 1956; J.D., U. Pa., 1960. Bar: Calif. 1963, N.Y. 1981. Assoc. prof. law Golden Gate U., San Francisco, 1970-71; city atty. Berkeley, Calif., 1971; asst. prof. law U. San Francisco Law Sch., 1971-73; asst. regional atty. EEOC, San Francisco, 1973-79, regional atty., N.Y.C., 1979-81; dep. gen. counsel N.Y.C. Housing Authority, 1981-88; exec. dir. Bedford Stuyvesant Cmty. Legal Svcs., Bklyn., 1988-2001, The Ctr. for Jewish-Christian-Muslim Understanding, Inc., Irvington, N.Y., 2002—; practice law, San Francisco, 1963-65; chief atty. Alameda County Legal Aid Soc., Oakland, Calif., 1965-70; asst. to asst. regional adminstr. HUD, San Francisco, 1970. Founder, Phoenix Elem. Sch., Berkeley, 1969. rep. World Assembly of Youth, UN Commn. on the Status of Women, 1955; bd. dirs., treas., chmn. mgmt. com. Consumers Coop., Berkeley, 1972-76; bd. dirs. ACLU Berkeley-Albany chpt., Berkeley, 1968, San Francisco Regional Council, Berkeley, 1978. Recipient Commendation plaque Alameda Affirmative Action Com., 1971, Alameda County Human Relations Commn., 1973, Assn. Real Property Brokers, 1975. Mem. Calif. State Bar (commn. of profl. competence 1973-76, med. malpractice commn. 1972), N.Y. State Bar, Charles Houston Law Club (v.p. 1979). Episcopalian.

GAINES, ELLIOT, communications educator; b. Elizabeth, NJ, Feb. 21, 1950; s. Samuel and Martha Gaines. BA, Rutgers Univ., NJ, 1972; MA, Ohio Univ., Ohio, 1993, PhD, 1995. Prof. of comm. Ohio Univ., Athens, Ohio, 1996, Ashland Univ., Ashland, Ohio, 1996—2000, Wright State Univ., Dayton, Ohio, 2000. Author: (jour.) The Am. Jour. of Semiotics, 2001; co-author: (book) Bldg. Diverse Communities, 2001; author: (jour.) Jour. of Am. Osteo. Assoc., 1998. Grantee Internat. Study Grant, Ashland Univ./ India, 1998. Mem.: Am. Assoc. of Univ. Prof., Nat. Comm. Assoc. (vice chair 2001), Semiotic Soc. of Am. (exec. comm. 2000—02). Avocation: music. Home: 667 E Hyde Rd Yellow Springs OH 45387 Office: Wright State Univ 3640 Colonel Glenn Hwy Dayton OH 45435

GAINES, FRANCIS PENDLETON, III, judge; b. Lexington, Va., Sept. 24, 1944; s. Francis Pendleton Jr. and Dorothy Ruth (Bloomhardt) G.; m. Mary Chilton, Dec. 19, 1967 (div. Aug. 1992); children: Elizabeth Chilton, Edmund Pendleton, Andrew Cavett. Grad., Woodberry Forest Sch., Va., 1962; BA in Hist., U. Ariz., 1967; LLB, U. Va., 1969. Bar: U.S. Dist. Ct. (Ariz.) 1969, Ariz. 1969, U.S. Ct. Appeals (9th cir.) 1972, U.S. Supreme Ct. 1975. Assoc. Evans, Kitchel & Jenckes, Phoenix, 1969-75, ptnr., 1975-89, Fennemore Craig, Phoenix, 1989-99; judge Superior Ct. of Ariz., Phoenix, 1999—; assoc. presiding civil judge Maricopa County Superior Ct., 2001—, Maricopa County Complex Civil Litigation Ct., 2003—. Panel arbitrators N.Y. Stock Exch., 1984-99, NASD, 1984-99; judge pro tem Ariz. Ct. Appeals, 1994-95, Maricopa County (Ariz.) Superior Ct., 1994-99; mem. State Bar Disciplinary Hearing Com., 1991-94, chair, 1995-97; mem. nat. litig. panel U. Va. Sch. Law; mem. Ariz. Commn. on Judicial Performance Review, 2001—; lectr. and panelist CLE programs. Author: Punitive Damages-A Railroad Trial Lawyers Guide, 1985. Chmn. bd. govs. All Saints' Day Sch., Phoenix, 1990—91; sr. warden All Saints' Episcopal Ch., 1994—97, parish chancellor, 1997—99, diversity preceptor, 1999—2003; standing com. Episcopal Diocese of Ariz., 1997—2001. Recipient Outstanding Alumnus award, U. Az., 2002. Fellow: Ariz. Bar Found., Am. Bar Found.; mem.: Securities Industry Assn., Nat. Assn. Railroad Trial Coun. (exec. com. Pacific Region, v.p. 1997—98), Maricopa County Bar Assn., State Bar Ariz. (civil practice and procedure com. 2000—, professionalism course oversight com. 2001—), ABA, U. Ariz. Pres.'s Club, Univ. Club. Republican. Episcopalian. Office: Superior Ct Ariz 201 W Jefferson St Phoenix AZ 85003-2205

GAINES, IRVING DAVID, lawyer; b. Milw., Oct. 14, 1923; s. Harry and Anna (Finkelman) Ginsburg; m. Ruth Rudolph, May 22, 1947 (dec. Apr. 5, 1979); children: Jeffrey S., Howard R., Mindy S. Gaines Pearce; m. Lois Shier, Nov. 25, 1979. BA, U. Wis., Madison, 1943; JD, 1947; postgrad., U. Pa., 1943-44. Bar: Wis. 1947, Fla. 1971, U.S. Dist. Ct. (ea. dist.) Wis. 1947, U.S. Dist. Ct. (we. dist.) Wis. 1970, U.S. Dist. Ct. (so. dist.) Fla. 1972, U.S. Dist. Ct.

(mid. dist.) Fla. 1976, U.S. Ct. Appeals (7th cir.) 1954, U.S. Ct. Appeals (11th cir.) 1981, U.S. Supreme Ct. 1954. Sole practice, Milw., 1947-72; ptnr. Gaines & Saichek, S.C. (and predecessor firm), Milw., 1972-78; sr. ptnr. Gaines Law Offices, S.C., Milw., 1979—. Arbitrator N.Y. Stock Exch., 1988—, Nat. Assn. Securities Dealers, 1988—, Am. Stock Exch., 1988—; mediator Wis. Ct. of Appeals, Dist. I; interpreter Hindustani Intelligence. Contbr. articles to profl. jours. Mem. bd. visitors U. Wis. Law Sch., 1987—96, Milw. County Cir. Ct. Commn., 1997—; Hindustani intelligence interpreter. Served with U.S. Army, 1943—46. Mem.: ATLA (state committeeman 1981—83, lectr.), ABA (com. on current lit. on real property law, com. on law and medicine negligence sect., various coms. on title ins. litig. and real estate), Bar Assn. U.S. Ea. Dist. of Wis., Am. Arbitration Assn. (arbitrator 1966—, nat. panel arbitrators), Milw. Bar Assn. (exec. com. 1974—77, cts. com., past chmn. unauthorized practice of law com., econs. of law com., past chmn. negligence sect., appellate bench bar com.-civil, bench-bar com., lectr. programs, seminars), Wis. Acad. Trial Lawyers (pres. 1958—59, 1970—71, lectr.), 7th Fed. Cir. Bar Assn., State Bar Assn. Wis. (bd. govs. 1982—85, publs. com. 1982—91, past mem. com. on ethics, rsch. planning and earlier settlement coms., lectr. CLE seminars, convs.), Fla. Bar Assn. (bd. editors Fla. Bar Jour. 1972—84). Home: 7821 N Mohawk Rd Milwaukee WI 53217-3123 Office: 312 E Wisconsin Ave Ste 208 Milwaukee WI 53202-4305

GAINES, JAMES EDWIN, JR., retired librarian; b. Dalton, Ga., Feb. 21, 1938; s. James Edwin and Olivia (McCarty) Gaines; m. Sally Martin, Nov. 27, 1965 (div. May 1985); children: Thomas Martin, Robin Jeannette, Steven McCarty; m. Elizabeth Hood, July 28, 1990. AB, Emory U., 1961, MLS, 1964; PhD, Fla. State U., 1977. Tchr. English Marist Coll. H.S., Atlanta, 1961-62; grad. library asst. Emory U., Atlanta, 1962-64; asst. to head of pub. services U. Cin., 1964-65; asst. cataloger Antioch Coll., Yellow Springs, Ohio, 1965-68; dir. library Birmingham-So. Coll., Birmingham, Ala., 1968-74; head librarian Va. Mil. Inst., Lexington, 1976-93; ret., 1994. Contbr. Mem. Com. on Fgn. Rels., Charlottesville, Va., 1982—91; sec. ARC, Rockbridge County, Va., 1993—98, Rockbridge Disability Svcs. Bd., 1993—; chmn. Lexington Dem. Com., 2001—. Mem.: ALA, Va. Libr. Assn. (chmn. coll. and univ. sect. 1979—80), So. Assn. Colls. and Schs. (vis. committeeman 1979—89), Kiwanis (sec. 1985—92, 1999—2001, v.p. 2001—02, pres. 2002—03). Democrat. Presbyterian. Home: 9 Edmondson Ave Lexington VA 24450-1903 E-mail: Gainesje@vmi.edu.

GAINES, JEFFREY THOMAS, architect, urban planner; b. Inpls., Apr. 22, 1965; s. Lloyd Thomas and Susan Hadley Gaines; m. Gloria Dimech, Nov. 21, 1992; 1 child, Addison. BArch, U. Cin., 1989; M in Urban Planning, MArch, U. Mich., 1997. Arch., planner Smith, Hinchman & Grylls, Inc., Detroit, 1989-96, Albert Kahn Assocs., Inc., Detroit, 1998—. Instr. Lawrence Tech. U., Southfield, Mich., 1994, U. Mich., Ann Arbor, 1997, U. Detroit Mercy, 1997. Mem. AIA, Am. Inst. Cert. Planners, Am. Planning Assn., Mich. Soc. Planning, US Green Bldg. Coun. Home: 22637 Nona St Dearborn MI 48124-4712 Office: Albert Kahn Assocs Inc Albert Kahn Bldg 7430 2d Ave Detroit MI 48202

GAINES, JERRY LEE, retired secondary education educator; b. Seminole, Okla., Feb. 18, 1940; s. Frank Gaines and Jane M. (Crowe) Gring; m. Lorraine Louise Paulson, Oct. 7, 1961; children: Paul Martin, Mark Edwin. AA, Pasadena City Coll., 1960; BA, Calif. State U., L.A., 1964; MA, Calif. State U., Long Beach, 1969. Tchr. bus. Rolling Hills High Sch., Rolling Hills Estates, Calif., 1965-91, Palos Verdes Peninsula High Sch., Rolling Hills Estates, 1991—2002. Coord. driver edn. Palos Verdes Peninsula Unified Sch. Dist., Palos Verdes Estates, Calif., 1970-91, mentor tchr., 1984-93. Co-author driver edn. workbook; contbr. articles to traffic safety publs. Chmn. San Pedro (Calif.) Citizens Adv. Com., 1985-88; pres. South Shores Homeowners Assn., San Pedro, 1986-90, 95-96, San Pedro and Peninsula Homeowners Coalition, 1990-93; commr. City of L.A. Charter Reform Commn., 1997-99, City of L.A. Planning Commn., 2000-02; County of L.A. Workforce Investment Bd., 2002—; bd. dirs. South Bay Credit Union, 1997—. With USN, 1960-62. Mem. NEA, Calif. Tchrs. Assn., Palos Verdes Faculty Assn., Nat. Bus. Edn. Assn., Calif. Bus. Edn. Assn., Am. Driver and Traffic Safety Edn. Assn. (bd. dirs. 1982-88), Calif. Assn. Safety Edn. (pres. 1982-83, 1998-2000), Elks, Lions, Phi Delta Kappa. Avocations: travel, model railroading. Home: 2101 W 37th St San Pedro CA 90732-4707 E-mail: jgaines852@aol.com.

GAINES, JOHN STROTHER, retired educator, writer, municipal official; b. Glendale, Calif., Mar. 15, 1933; s. Jack and Mildred (Walton) G.; m. Thelma Dowling, Feb. 14, 1968 (dec. 1999); children: Jennifer Marie Kidder, Susannah Theresa McCroskey. BA in Polit. Sci., Occidental Coll., 1954; MA in Edn., Calif. State U., Northridge, 1964; EdD in Foundations, U. So. Calif., 1971. Cert. tchr., prin., supt. Vice pres. acad. affairs King Coll., Bristol, Tenn., 1979-85, prof. edn. and social scis., 1969-99, dir. tchr. edn. Pres. State of Franklin Coun. for Social Scis., 1984-85. Author: (tchrs. edition) American Government/20th Century, 1968; co-author: The Golden State, 1965, 4th edit., 2000, Government in the Golden State, 1967. Vice mayor City of Bristol, 1989-90, 91-92, 93-94, 2002-03, mayor, 1990-91, 92-93, 94-96, 99-2000; bd. dirs. Pub. Libr., Bristol, 1989-03, Tenn. Mcpl. League, 2003; chmn. Gov.'s Task Force, Bristol, 1984-86; chmn. Bristol 2000, Sch. Consolidation Commn. With U.S. Army, 1955-57, Korea. Congl. intern, Washington, 1969; Am. Fedn. Tchrs. grantee, 1970; Pew Found. sabbatical grantee, 1985; George Mason U. fellow, 1989; Nat. Endowment for Humanities fellow, 1987. Mem. Am. Pub. Power Assn. (policy mahus coun., 2003), Tenn. Coun. Social Studies (bd. dirs. 1982-92), Tenn. Assn. Colls. Tchr. Edn. (exec. bd. 1990), Sullivan County Hist. Soc. (pres. 1992-93), C. of C. (chmn. edn. com., bd. dirs.), Country Club of Bristol, Phi Delta Kappa. Republican. Baptist. Avocations: golf, travel. Home: 120 Woodside Dr Bristol TN 37620-2805

GAINES, KENDRA HOLLY, English language educator, editorial and writing consultant; b. Chgo., Dec. 6, 1946; d. Reuben B. and Frances P. Gaines; m. Kenneth C. Wolfgang, Feb. 18, 1989. BA with distinction, Mt. Holyoke Coll., 1968; MA with honor, Claremont Grad. Sch., 1971; MA, Northwestern U., 1974, PhD, 1982. Cert. life secondary and community coll. tchr., Calif., Ariz. Tchr. English, Claremont (Calif.) Collegiate Sch., 1969-72; teaching asst. Northwestern U., Evanston, Ill., 1975-78; instr. English, U. Mich., Ann Arbor, 1978-79; assoc. editor Scott, Foresman Co., Glenview, 1983-85; instr. English, sr. career tutor U. Ariz., Tucson, 1985—2002, mgr. Grad. Writing Resource website, 2002—; instr., faculty advisor Chapman U., Davis-Monthan AFB, Ariz., 1987—2002. Head Grad. Writing Inst., U. Ariz., 1996—2002; editl. cons., freelance writer, 1969—; lectr. Suzhou U., Nanjing Normal U., China, 1999; mem. adv. bd. translation studies Pima C.C.; writing cons. U. Ariz. Coll. Law; trainer S.W. Gas Corp.; writing cons., mgr. writing resource website U. Ariz., Tucson, 2002—. Contbr. articles to various publs.; writer radio scripts Holiday World of Travel, 1969—. Elected to The Imperial Russian Order of St. John of Jerusalem Ecumenical Found. (Knights of Malta), N.Y.; grantee State of Calif., 1970; Mills fellow, 1971; fellow Northwestern U., 1973-76. Mem. MLA, Nat. Coun. Tchrs. English, AAUW. Avocations: travel, photography, music, creative writing, aerobics. Home: 925 N Jerrie Ave Tucson AZ 85711-1153 Office: U Ariz Grad Coll Tucson AZ 85719 E-mail: kgaines@email.arizona.edu.

GAINES, MICHAEL JOHNSTON, parole commissioner; Grad., U. Ark., 1973, JD, 1977. Bar: Ark. 1977, U.S. Dist. Ct. Ark 1977, U.S. Supreme Ct. 1977. Pvt. practice law, 1977-78; parole hearing examiner Ark. Dept. Correction, 1978-83; criminal justice liaison and pardon and extradition counsel Gov. Bill Clinton, 1983-86; exec. dir. Ark. Supreme Ct. Com. on Profl. Conduct, 1986-89; mem. Ark. Bd. Parole, 1986-89, chmn., 1989, U.S. Parole Commn., 1994—. Mem. staff Gov. Dale Bumpers, Gov. David Pryor; mem. Bd. Correction, Gov.'s Corrections Resources Commn., Gov.'s Task Force on Crime. Mem. ABA (corrections and sentencing com., criminal justice sect.), Assn. Paroling Authorities Internat. (coun. of chairs), Am. Correctional Assn., Am. Probation and Parole Assn. Office: US Parole Commn 5550 Friendship Blvd Chevy Chase MD 20815-7256 Fax: 301-492-5307.

GAINES, ROBERT DARRYL, lawyer, food services executive; b. Kansas City, Mo., May 27, 1951; s. Ralph Robert and Betty June (Crawford) G.; m. Shanette Carrol Kirch, Aug. 14, 1977; 1 child, Ariel Kirch. BA, U. Ariz., 1972; MBA, Mich. State U., 1973; JD, U. Mo., Kansas City, 1983. Bar: Mo. 1983, Ariz. 1983. Pvt. practice law, Kansas City, 1983—; pres. Colony Lobster Pot Co., Kansas City, 1984—, Colony Pla Co., Kansas City, 1985—. Mem. ABA, Mo. Bar Assn., Ariz. Bar Assn., Kansas City Bar Assn., Nat. Restaurant Assn., Mo. Restaurant Assn., Phi Delta Phi (treas. 1982-83). Avocations: flying, racquetball. Home: 12404 Baltimore Ct Kansas City MO 64145 also: 8821 State Line Rd Kansas City MO 64114-2704 E-mail: robertgaines@cs.com.

GAINES, ROBERT PENDLETON, retired lawyer; b. Daytona Beach, Fla., Apr. 6, 1927; s. Marion Toulmin and Marion (Howie) G.; m. Doris Bolton, July 8, 1961; children: Jennifer, Amante, Edmund. BA, U. Fla., 1950, LLB, 1956. Bar: Fla. 1956, U.S. Dist. Ct. (no. dist.) Fla. 1956, U.S. Ct. Appeals (5th cir.) 1958, U.S. Ct. Appeals (11th cir.) 1982, U.S. Supreme Ct. 1988. From assoc. to ptnr. Beggs & Lane and predecessor firms, Pensacola, Fla., 1956—2002; ret., 2002. Mem. Fla. Commn. on Local Govt., Tallahassee, 1973-74. Lt. U.S. Army, 1945-47, 1950-53, Korea. Mem.: Phi Beta Kappa. Democrat. Episcopalian. Avocation: fishing. Home: 8839 Burning Tree Rd Pensacola FL 32514-5606

GAINES, ROLAND H. academic administrator; b. Tallahassee, Fla., Feb. 19, 1948; s. Willie L. and Emma L. Gaines; m. Irene Y. Jackson, Sept. 1, 1982; children: Rodney, Craig, T.J. BS, Fla. A&M U., 1968, EdM, 1970. Registrar Fla. A&M U., Tallahassee, 1968—96, assoc. v.p., 1997—2001; dir. mgmt. N.C. Ctrl. U., Durham, 2001—, interim vice chancellor, 2002—. Bd. dirs. Miracle Hill Nurs, Tallahassee, 1999—. Mem.: Nat. Assn. Student Affairs Profls., Nat. Assn. Coll. Registrars & Adminstrn. Officers, Alpha Phi Alpha (Alpha Man of Yr. 1987). Democrat. Baptist. Avocations: reading, travel, golf. Home: 22 Acornridge Ct Durham NC 27707 Office: NC Ctrl Univ 1801 Fayetteville St Durham NC 27707

GAINES, RUTH ANN, educator; BA in Drama and Speech, Clarke Coll.; MA in Dramatic Art, U. Calif., Santa Barbara. Tchr. drama East High Sch., Des Moines, 1971—. Host Classroom Connection Cable TV; former TV/radio prodr., talk show host TCI of Ctrl. Iowa, WHO; diversity facilitator Heartland Area Edn. Agy., Des Moines, 1979—; instr. speech and drama Des Moines Area C.C., 1971—. Bd. dirs. Very Spl. Arts, Hospice of Ctrl. Iowa, Westminster Ho.; former bd. dirs. YWCA of Greater Des Moines, Polk County Mental Health Assn., Drama Workshop, Des Moines Tutoring Ctr.; vice chair City Wide Strategic Plan, 1994-95; state senate candidate, 1994; racial justice coord. YWCA, 1992-93; chair Cross Cultural Rels., Des Moines Area Religious Coun., 1988-89; dir. religious edn. St. Ambrose Cathedral, 1981-83; grad. Leadership Iowa Class of 1997. Recipient Wal-Mart Tchr. of Yr., 1998, Iowa Tchr. of Yr., 1998, Angel in Adoption award, 1999, Friends of Iowa Civil Rights Commn. Tchr. of Yr. award, 2000, U. Iowa's Phyllis M. Yeager Commitment to Diversity award, 2001, I'll Make Me a World in Iowa Heritage Legacy, 2002, Des Moines Bus. Records' Woman of Influence, 2002, USA Today's All USA Tchr. Recognition 3d Team, 2002; grad. Greater Des Moines Leadership Inst., 2002; inducted into Nat. Tchr. Hall of Fame, 2003. Mem. Iowa Edn. Assn., Des Moines Edn. Assn., Delta Kappa Gamma, Phi Delta Kappa, Delta Sigma Theta, Delta Kappa Pi. Home: 3501 Oxford St Des Moines IA 50313-4562 Office: East High Sch 815 E 13th St Des Moines IA 50316-3499

GAINES, WEAVER HENDERSON, lawyer; b. Ft. Meade, S.D., Aug. 31, 1943; s. Weaver Henderson and Bertha Louise (Harris) G. AB in Philosophy, Dartmouth Coll., 1965; LLB, U. Va., 1968. Bar: N.Y. 1969, Pa. 1979, U.S. Dist. Ct. (so. dist.) N.Y. 1973, U.S. Dist. Ct. (ea. dist.) N.Y. 1975, U.S. Ct. Appeals (2d cir.) 1975. Assoc. Dewey, Ballantine, Bushby, Palmer & Wood, N.Y.C., 1970-79; sr. staff counsel INA Corp., Phila., 1979; asst. gen. counsel, sec. Thyssen-Bornemisza Inc., N.Y.C., 1979-82, v.p. strategic projects, 1982-85; v.p., dep. gen. counsel Mut. of N.Y., N.Y.C., 1985-86, sr. v.p., gen. counsel, 1986-90, exec. v.p., gen. counsel, 1990-92; pres. Unified Mgmt. Corp., 1989-90; chmn. Ixion Biotechnology, Inc., Alachua, Fla., 1993—2002, chmn. bd., 2002—. Bd. dirs. Unified Fin. Svcs., Inc., Voyetra Turtle Beach, Inc., Ixion Biotechnology, Inc., BIO Fla. Inc., Fla. Rsch. Consortium, Inc., Dance Alive!. Bd. dirs. N.Y. Lawyers for Nixon, 1972; sr. advisor Bush/Quayle '92. Capt. U.S. Army, 1968-70, Vietnam. Decorated Bronze Star. Mem. ABA, Assn. Bar City N.Y., N.Y. Athletic Club, Haile Plantation Golf and Country Club. Republican. Episcopalian. Office: Ixion Biotechnology Inc 13709 Progress Blvd Alachua FL 32615-9495 E-mail: weaver.gaines@worldnet.att.net.

GAINEY, ERNEST J., III, internet security specialist; b. Buffalo, Sept. 24, 1969; s. Ernest J. Jr. and Janice E. Gainey. Mem. internet security staff HSBC Bank USA, Buffalo, 1992—. Home: 5 Brookhaven Ln Lancaster NY 14086 Personal E-mail: ernie@moviehysteria.com.

GAINEY, KATHYRN O'REILLY, art education educator; b. Red Wing, Minn., Nov. 14, 1950; d. Wilfred and Edna (Buchholtz) O'Reilly; children: Jeb, Josh, Seth. BS in Art and Elem. Edn. cum laude, Winona State U., 1972; MS in Curriculum and Instrn., St. Cloud State U., 1978; EdD in Ednl. Leadership, U. Minn., 1996. Tchr. 3rd grade, 6th grade, then secondary art Sauk Rapids (Minn.) Sch. Dist., 1972-81, 82—; asst. prof. art edn. St. Cloud (Minn.) State U. Exch. tchr. to New Zealand, 1995; weekend host to internat. students U. Minn.; designer, implementer K-12 art curriculum Sauk Rapids Sch. Dist. 47, implementer, coord. art and acad. awards program. Artwork exhibited in juried art show; poetry included in lit. publs. Mem. Ctrl. Minn. Arts Bd., 1997—99, v.p. Recipient Excellence in Art Edn. award, 1999. Mem.: AAUW (exec. bd. 1990—96), NEA, Minn. Edn. Assn., Minn. Alliance for Arts in Edn., Art Educators of Minn. (exec. bd. 2002—), Nat. Art Edn. Assn., Kappa Pi, Phi Kappa Phi. Home: 1193 59th Ave SE Saint Cloud MN 56304-9741

GAINEY, ROBERT MICHAEL, professional hockey coach, former player; b. Peterborough, Ont., Can., Dec. 13, 1953; Hockey player Montreal Canadiens, 1973-89; coach, player Les Ecureuils, Epinal, France; head coach, gen. mgr. Minn. North Stars, NHL, 1990-96; v.p., gen. mgr. Dallas Stars, 1996—. Recipient Frank J. Selke award as Best Defensive Forward, 1977-78, 78-79, 79-80; Conn Smythe trophy as Most Valuable Player Nat. Hockey League Playoffs, 1978-79; elected to Hockey Hall of Fame, 1992.

GAINOR, THOMAS EDWARD, banker; b. St. Paul, Oct. 13, 1933; s. Joseph Paul and Teresa Cecilia (Whelan) G.; m. Janan Rose Nolan, Aug. 8, 1964; children: Mary, Michael, John, Daniel. BS, Marquette U., 1955; postgrad., Stonier Grad. Sch. Banking, Rutgers U., 1965-67, Stanford U. Exec. Program, 1977; PhD in Internat. Rels. and Diplomacy (hon.), Am. Grad. Sch. Internat. Rels. and Diplomacy, Paris, 1999. With Fed. Res. Bank of Mpls., 1958-93, asst. v.p., 1967-72, v.p., 1972-75, sr. v.p. ops., 1975-78, 1st v.p., COO, 1978-93. Bd. dirs. Am. Bancorp., 1994-96. Bd. dirs. Mpls. United Way, 1974-83, v.p., 1974-77; bd. dirs. Vis. Nurse Svc., 1967-75, pres., 1971-72; trustee Visitation Sch., 1983-89, v.p., 1985, chmn., 1986-88; mem. Commn. Archdiocesan Programs, 1983-89, chmn., 1986-87; trustee St. Joseph's Ch., 1985—; trustee St. Thomas Acad., 1989-98, chmn., 1992-98; bd. dirs. St. John Vianney Sem., 1986-2002, Cath. Charities, 1990-96; pres. Cath. Cmty. Found., 1994-2001, sec., 2002—; internat. adv. coun. Am. Grad. Sch. Internat. Rels. and Diplomacy, Paris, 1997—; bd. dirs. Total Life Care Ctrs., 1998—, v.p., 1999-2001, pres., 2002—. Served as officer USNR, 1955-58. Mem. Stanford Alumni Assn., Marquette U. Alumni Assn., Naval Res. Assn. Clubs: Six o'Clock (pres. 1982). Roman Catholic. E-mail: tjgainor@aol.com.

GAINSBURG, ROY ELLIS, publishing executive; b. Bklyn., May 1, 1932; s. Herbert Harry Gainsburg and Etta (Stein) Kornfeld; m. Vicki Bloye, July 12, 1957; children: Julie, Jeanne. AB, Brown U., 1954; LLB, Harvard U., 1957. Bar: NY 1957. From assoc. to ptnr. Szold & Brandwen, N.Y.C., 1957-87; exec. v.p. St. Martin's Press Inc., N.Y.C., 1987, pres., 1987-97, part-time v.p. adminstrn., 1997—. V.p. adminstrn. Holtzbrinck Pubs. and Tor Books; bd. dirs., exec. v.p. Macmillan Acad. Pub., Inc. Chmn. bd. dirs. The Partnership for the Homeless, N.Y.C. Democrat. Home: 157 Ralston Ave South Orange NJ 07079-2344 Office: St Martin's Press Inc 175 5th Ave New York NY 10010-7848 E-mail: roy.gainsburg@hbpub.com.

GAISER, TED JOSEPH, academic administrator, minister; b. Bluffton, Indiana, June 23, 1961; s. Noel Eugene and Grace Bernice (Klausky) Gaiser. BA history, So. CT. State U., Hamden, CT., 1986; MTS, Boston U. Sch. of Theology, 1988; MBA, Boston Coll. Carroll Sch. of Mgmt., Chestnut Hill, Mass., 1994; PhD sociology, Boston Coll. Grad. Sch. of A and S, Chestnut Hill, MA., 2000. Cert. Ordained Episcopal Diocese of Mass., 2001. Dep. dir. Corp. Design Found., Boston, 1988—90; rsch. and fin. mgr. Children's Hosp., Boston, 1990—93; grad. asst. Boston Coll., Chestnut Hill, Mass., 1993—96; sr. strategic fin. analyst, Partners Health Care, Boston, 1997; project dir. Boston Coll., Chestnut Hill, Mass., 1998, project mgr., 1999; dir. info. svc. Justice Resource Inst., Boston, 2000; dir. acad. rsch. svc. Boston Coll., Chestnut Hill, Mass., 2000—. Author: (jour. article) Soc. Sci. Computer Rev., 1997. Bd. mem. Saturday's / Sunday's Bread, Boston, 1986—99; com. mem. Brighton Main St., Brighton, Mass., 1999—; bd. mem. Supported Employment Program, Boston, 1998—. Mem.: Am. Sociological Assn. Episcopalian. Avocation: old home restoration. Home: 8 Glenmont Rd Brighten MA 02135-3113 Office: Boston Coll 140 Commonwealth Ave Chestnut Hill MA 02467 Business E-Mail: gaiser@bc.edu.

GAISFORD, WALTER DAN, surgeon; b. Salt Lake City, 1933; MD, U. So. Calif., 1958. Cert. in surgery. Intern Mich. Med. Ctr., 1958-59, resident, 1959-64; with LDS Hosp., Salt Lake City, Valley View Med. Ctr., Dixie Med. Ctr., Intermountain Surg. Ctr., Univ. Utah Med. Ctr. Assoc. clin. prof. surgery U. Utah. Fellow ACS, Am. Gastroenterol. Assn., Am. Coll. Gastroenterology; mem. Am. Soc. for Gastrointestinal Endoscopy, Soc. for Surgery of Alimentary Tract. Office: 553 Ridgecrest Cir Saint George UT 84770-5740

GAISSER, JULIA HAIG, classics educator; b. Cripple Creek, Colo., Jan. 12, 1941; d. Henry Wolseley and Gertrude Alice (Lent) Haig; m. Thomas Korff Gaisser, Dec. 29, 1964; 1 child, Thomas Wolseley. AB, Brown U., 1962; MA, Harvard U., 1966; PhD, U. Edinburgh, Scotland, 1966. Asst. prof. Newton (Mass.) Coll., 1966-69, Swarthmore (Pa.) Coll., 1970-72, Bklyn. Coll., 1973-75; assoc. prof. dept. Latin Bryn Mawr (Pa.) Coll., 1975-84, prof., 1984—. Martin Classical lectr. Oberlin Coll., 2000. Author: Catullus and his Renaissance Readers, 1993, Pierio Valeriano On the Ill Fortune of Learned Men, 1999, Catullus in English, 2001; editor Bryn Mawr Latin Commentaries, 1983—. Mem. Mid-East sel. com. Marshall Scholarships, Washington, 1975-89, chmn., 1984-89; mem. mng. com. Intercollegiate Ctr. for Classical Studies in Rome, Stanford, Calif., 1984-92, chmn., 1988-92. Decorated MBE; named Marshall scholar, U. Edinburgh, 1962—64, Phi Beta Kappa Vis. scholar, 1996—97, ACLS Travel grantee, 1985, fellow, ACLS, 1989—90, NEH sr. fellow, 1985—86, 1993—94, 1999; recipient NEH summer stipend, 1977, rsch. grantee, Am. Philos. Soc., 1980, 1993. Mem. Am. Philol. Assn. (dir. 1985-88, pres. 2000), Renaissance Soc. Am., Internat. Neo Latin Soc. Office: Bryn Mawr Coll Dept Latin Bryn Mawr PA 19010

GAITAN, FERNANDO J., JR., federal judge; b. 1948; Student, Kansas City (Kans.) C.C., 1966-67, Donnelly Coll., 1967-68, Pittsburg State U., 1968-70; JD, U. Mo., Kansas City, 1974. Atty. Southwestern Bell Telephone Co., 1974-80; judge 16th jud. cir. Jackson County Cir. Ct., 1980-86; judge Mo. Ct. Appeals (we. dist.), 1986-91; fed. judge U.S. Dist. Ct. (we. dist.) Mo., Kansas City, 1991—. Dir. Truman Libr. Inst., 2001—. Past pres. bd. dirs. De La Salle Edn. Ctr., Inc., 1985-87, active, 1983—; active Kansas City Mus., 1988—, St. Luke's Hosp., Kansas City, 1984—, NAACP, 1982—, NCCJ, 1984—. Mem. ABA, Mo. Bar Assn., Kansas City Met. Bar Assn., Lawyers' Assn., Jackson County Bar Assn., Univ. Club, Hillcrest Country Club, U. Mo. Kansas City Law Found., KCMC Child Devel. Corp., Kappa Alpha Psi. Office: US Dist Ct 7952 US Cthouse 400 E 9th St Kansas City MO 64106-2607

GAITHER, GEORGE MANNEY, marketing consultant; b. Mineola, N.Y., Sept. 21, 1930; s. Roscoe Bradley and Frances Bullitt (Williams) G.; m. Dorothy Wineman Streater, Apr. 4, 1953; children: Neal, George, Anne, Emee, Bruce. B in Journalism, U. Mo., 1952. From gen. mgr. to pres. Internat. Rsch. Assocs., Inc., N.Y.C., 1955-71; pres., founder Gaither Internat., Inc., Stamford, Conn., 1971-96; cons. GMG Cons., Winchester, Va., 1997—. Lt. U.S. Army, 1952-55, Korea. Mem. Market Rsch. Coun. Republican. Avocation: writing. Home: 2628 Windwood Dr Winchester VA 22601-6418 E-mail: gmg@visuallink.com.

GAITHER, JAMES C. lawyer; b. Oakland, Calif., Sept. 3, 1937; s. Horace Rowan Jr. and Charlotte Cameron (Castle) G.; m. Susan Good, Apr. 30, 1960; children: James Jr., Whitaker, Reed, Kendra. BA in Econs., Princeton U., 1959; JD, Stanford U., 1964. Bar: Calif. 1964, U.S. Dist. Ct. D.C. 1965, U.S. Dist. Ct. (no. dist.) Calif. 1965, U.S. Ct. Appeals (D.C. cir., 7th cir., 9th cir.), 1965, U.S. Supreme Ct. Law clk. to chief justice Earl Warren, Washington, 1964-65; spl. asst. to asst. atty. gen. John W. Douglas, Washington, 1965-66; staff asst. Pres. Lyndon B. Johnson, Washington, 1966-69; atty. Cooley Godward LLP, San Francisco, 1969-71, ptnr., 1971—, mng. ptnr., 1984-90, sr. counsel, 2000—; mng. dir. Sutter Hill Ventures, 2000. Cons. to sec. HEW, 1977, chmn. ethics adv. bd., 1977—80; bd. dirs. Levi Strauss & Co., San Francisco; bd. dir. Kineto, Milpitas, Calif.; bd. dirs. Siebel Sys., San Mateo, nVidia Corp., Santa Clara, Satmetrix, Mountain View, Calif., Hewlett Found.; with James Irvine Found.; former vice chair Carnegie Endowment for Internat. Peace; former trustee The RAND Corp. Editor: Stanford Law Rev., 1963—64. Former pres. bd. trustees, Stanford (Calif.) U.; mem. exec. com. bd. vis. Sch. Law Stanford U.; former chmn. bd. trustees Branson Sch., Ross, Calif., Ctr. for Biotech. Rsch. San Francisco; past trustee Family Svc. Agy. San Francisco, St. Stephens Parish Day Sch., Belvedere, Calif., The Scripps Rsch. Inst.; past trustee, chmn. protem Marin Cmty. Found, Marin County, Calif.; past pres. bd. trustees Marin County Day Sch., Corte Madera; past pres. bd. trustees Marin Ednl. Found., San Rafael; past treas., trustee Rosenberg Found.; past v.p., trustee, vice chmn. San Francisco Devel. Fund; past chmn. Dean's Adv. Coun. Stanford Law Sch., chmn. capital campaign; Inst. Capt. USMC, 1959-61. Recipient Disting. Pub. Svc. award HEW, 1977, Stanford Assocs. award Stanford U., 1989, 97; named Entrepreneur of Yr. Harvard Bus. Sch., 1979. Fellow Am. Acad. Arts and Scis.; mem. ABA, Calif. Bar Assn., San Francisco Bar Assn., Order of Coif, Phi Delta Phi (province 12). Democrat. Presbyterian. Avocations: tennis, hiking, camping, fishing, photography. Office: Sutter Hill Ventures 755 Page Mill Rd # A-200 Palo Alto CA 94304

GAITHER, JOHN FRANCIS, accountant, consultant; b. Louisville, Oct. 26, 1918; s. Thomas R. and Marice F. Gaither; m. Marjilee Schaeffer, Nov. 26, 1942 (dec.); children: John Francis Jr., James M.; m. Catherine W. Cox, June 18, 2002. BCS, U. Notre Dame, 1941. CPA, Ind., Ky., Ill. Controller Evansville (Ind.) div. Whirlpool Corp., 1946-56; cons. Gaither, Rutherford & Co., CPAs, 1954-93; city contr., dep. mayor City of Evansville, 1972-76. Lectr., seminar leader and cons. in health care industry, legis. contact Am. Hosp. Assn., AICPA. Author: Financial Management of Medical Laboratories; contbr. articles to profl. jours. Past pres. Buffalo Trace coun. Boy Scouts Am.; mem. adv. com. Ind. Vocat. Rehab.; past trustee Brescia U., St. Benedicts Convent; past mem. regional cmty. adv. coun. Ind. U. Med. Sch.; past chmn. community adv. coun. Evansville Ctr. Med. Edn.; past chmn. Ind. Select Com. Ednl. Fin., past chmn. Ind. Utility and Energy Regulation Adv. Commn.; vice chmn. Ind. Health Facilities Fin. Authority; dir., officer Nat. Coun. Health Facilities Fin. Authorities; past mem. Ind. Transp. Coordinating Bd.; past Gov.'s rep. Ind. Hosp. Rate Rev. Commn.; past officer YMCA, Cancer Soc., Serra Club. Officer USNR, 1941-46. Recipient various awards Boy Scouts Am., other civic groups. Mem. AICPA, Ind. Assn. CPAs, Ill. Assn. CPAs, Ky. Assn. CPAs, Evansville Assn. CPAs, Inst. Mgmt. Accts. (past pres. Evansville), Ind. Assn. Cities and Towns Controllers Div. (past pres.), Ind. Soc. Chgo. (v.p.), SAR, Soc. J. Gaither Descendants Found. (pres.), Internat. Soc. Descendants of Charlemagne, First Families of Va., Evansville Country Club, Rotary Internat. Republican. Home: 730 S Colony Rd Evansville IN 47714-0636 Office: PO Box 8408 Evansville IN 47734-8408 E-mail: johng730@aol.com.

GAITHER, JOHN FRANCIS, JR., lawyer; b. Evansville, Ind., Mar. 31, 1949; s. John F. and Marjilee G.; m. Christine Luby, Nov. 26, 1971; children: John F. III, Maria Theresa. BA in Acctg., U. Notre Dame, 1971, JD, 1974. Bar: Ind. 1974, Ill. 1975, U.S. Ct. Appeals (7th cir.) 1975, U.S. Ct. Mil. Appeals 1977. CPA, Ind. Law clk. to Hon. Wilbur F. Pell, Jr. Ct. of Appeals 7th Cir., Chgo., 1974-76; assoc. atty. Bell, Boyd & Lloyd, Chgo., 1979-82; sr. atty. Baxter Healthcare Corp., Deerfield, Ill., 1982-83, asst. sec., sr. atty., 1983-84, asst. sec., asst. gen. counsel, 1984-85; sec., assoc. gen. counsel Baxter Internat. Inc., Deerfield, 1985-87, sec., dep. gen. counsel, 1987-91; v.p. law/devel. Baxter Diagnostics Inc., Deerfield, 1991-92; v.p. law, strategic planning Baxter Global Businesses, Deerfield, 1992-93; dep. gen. counsel, v.p. strategic planning Baxter Internat. Inc., Deerfield, 1993-94, corp. v.p., corp. devel., 1994-2001; v.p., sec., gen. counsel Global Healthcare Exch., LLC, Westminster, Colo., 2001—. Editor-in-chief Notre Dame Lawyer, 1973-74; contbr. articles to profl. jours. Lt. comdr. USNR, 1976-79. Mem. ABA, Ill. Bar Assn., Ind. Bar Assn., Chgo. Bar Assn., Ind. Assn. CPAs. Avocations: sailing, skiing. also: 11000 Westmoor Cir Ste 400 Westminster CO 80021 E-mail: jgaither@ghx.com.

GAITHER, THOMAS K. communications consultant; b. June 20, 1970; BA, U. Pitts., 1993, MFA, 2000. Project mgr. William J. Green & Assocs., Pitts., 1993-98; adj. faculty U. Pitts., 1993—2000; client assoc. Burson-Marsteller, Pitts., 1998; field office coord. Inst. Shipboard Edn., 13 Countries, 1999, 2001—02; dir. pub. rels., mktg. élan comm., Pitts., 1999—2002; Park Doctoral fellow U. N.C., Chapel Hill, 2002—. Home: 109 Culbreth Park Dr Chapel Hill NC 27516-9120 E-mail: tgaither@email.unc.edu.

GAITHER, WILLIAM SAMUEL, civil engineering executive, consultant; b. Lafayette, Ind., Dec. 3, 1932; s. William Marcius and Susan Frances (Kirkpatrick) G.; m. Robin Cornwall McGraw, Aug. 1, 1959; 1 dau., Sarah Curwen. Student, Purdue U., 1950-51; BS in Civil Engring, Rose Poly. Inst., 1956; M. Sci. Engring. (Arthur Le Grand Doty fellow), Princeton, 1962, MA (Ford Found. fellow), 1963, PhD (Ford Found. fellow), 1964. Registered profl. engr., Del., Penn. Engr. Dravo Corp. (marine constrn.), Pitts., 1956-60; supt. Myer Corp., Neenah, Wis., 1960-61; supervising engr., chief engr. port and coastal devel., pipeline div. Bechtel Corp., San Francisco, 1965-67; assoc. prof. coastal engring. dept. U. Fla. at Gainesville, 1964-65; mem. faculty U. Del. at Newark, 1967-84, assoc. prof. civil engring., 1967-70, prof. civil engring., 1970; prof., dean U. Del. at Newark (Coll. Marine Studies), 1970-84, also dir. sea grant coll. program; pres., prof., trustee Drexel U., Phila., 1984-87, Weston Inst., West Chester, Pa., 1988-93; Inner City Consortium, Inc., 1993-94; owner Gaither & Assocs., Tucson, 1993—. Trustee Mut. Assurance Co., 1985-96; mem. marine bd. NRC, 1975-81; chmn. Gov.'s Oil Transp. Study Com., 1971-73; mem. Gov.'s Task Force Marine and Coastal Affairs, 1970-72, Gov.'s Coun. Sci. and Tech., Del., 1970-72; bd. dirs. Roy F. Weston, Inc., 1974-91, vice chmn., 1988-91; bd. dirs. Phila. Electric Co., 1985-89; mem. ocean affairs adv. com. U.S. Dept. State; mem. Commn. on the Future, Rose-Hulman Inst. Tech., 1991-93; mem. Cyberfab.net. LLC, 1999—. Chmn. adv. coun. dept. civil engring. Princeton U., 1973-84; bd. dirs. University City Sci. Ctr., 1984-93, Penjurdel Coun., 1984-2000, Ednl. Found. of Chester County, 1989-92; pres., dir. Soc. John Gaither Desc., Inc., 1984-87; port warden Phila. Maritime Mus., 1987-93; founding dir., sec. Internat. Consciousness Rsch. Labs., 1996—; vestryman Ch. St. Andrew and St. Monica, 1987-93, chmn. fin. com. 1991-96; bd. dirs., mem. exec. com. Phila. H.S. Acads., Inc., 1988-93; chmn. bd. govs. Environ. Tech. Acad., 1988-93, active, 1988-94; prin. sponsor Delaware Valley Sci. Fairs, 1990-93. Recipient Disting. Achievement award Rose Poly. Inst., 1975, Disting. citizenship award News Jour. Papers, Del., 1975, Norman Sollenberger award Princeton U., 1983; named to Lambda Chi Alpha Alumni Hall of Fame, 1996; named hon. citizen of Lewes, Del., 1980. Fellow: ASCE (chmn. offshore policy com. 1979—84); mem.: Nat. Water Rsch. Inst. (rsch.adv. bd. 1991—2002), Acad. Sci. Phila. (bd. dirs. 1989—92), Sea Grant Program Instns. (pres. 1973—74), Del. Acad. Scis. (pres. 1971—72), Ariz. Sr. Acad., Cosmos Club. Home and Office: 7719 S Galileo Ln Tucson AZ 85747-9605 E-mail: gaitherws@earthlink.net.

GAJARSA, ARTHUR J. circuit court judge; b. Norcia, Italy, Mar. 1, 1941; arrived in U.S., 1949; m. Melanie E. Gajarsa. BSEE, Rensselaer Polytech. Inst, 1962; JD, Georgetown U., 1967; MA in Econs., Cath. U., 1968. Bar: U.S. Patent Office 1963, DC 1968, U.S. Dist. Ct. DC 1968, U.S. Ct. Appeals (DC cir.) 1968, Conn. 1969, U.S. Supreme Ct. 1971, DC Superior Ct. 1972, U.S. Ct. Appeals (DC cir.) 1972, U.S. Ct. Appeals (9th cir.) 1974, U.S. Dist. Ct. (no. dist.) N.Y. 1980. Patent examiner U.S. Patent Office, Dept. Commerce, 1962—63; patent adviser USAF, Dept. Def., 1963—64, Cushman, Darby & Cushman, 1964—67; law clk. to Judge Joseph C. McGarraghy U.S. Dist. Ct. (D.C.), Washington, 1967—68; atty. office gen. counsel Aetna Life and Casualty Co., 1968—69; spl. counsel, asst. to commr. Indian affairs Bur. Indian Affairs, Dept. Interior, 1969—71; assoc. Duncan and Brown, 1971—72; ptnr. Gajarsa, Liss & Sterenbuch, 1972—78, Gajarsa, Liss & Conroy, 1978—80, Wender, Murase & White, 1980—86; ptnr., officer Joseph, Gajarsa, McDermott & Reiner, P.C., 1987—97; judge U.S. Ct. Appeals Fed. Cir., Washington, 1997—. Contbr. articles to profl. jours. Trustee Rensselaer Neuman Found., 1973—, Found. Improving Understanding of Arts, 1982—96, Outward Bound, 1987—96, Rensselaer Polytech. Inst., 1994—; gov. John Carroll Soc., 1992—99; regent Georgetown U., 1995—2000, bd. dirs., 2000—. Recipient Sun and Balance medal, Rensselaer Polytech. Inst., 1990, Rensselaer Key Alumni award, 1992, Albert Demers Fox award, 1999, Gigi Pieri award, Camp Hale Assn., 1992, 125th Anniversary medal, Georgetown U. Law Ctr., 1995, Order of Commendatore, Republic of Italy, 1995, Alumni Fellows award, Rensselaer Alumni Assn., 1996, Paul Dean award, Georgetown U., 1999. Mem.: Am. Judicature Assn., DC Bar Assn., Nat. Italian Am. Found. (bd. dirs. 1976—99, gen. counsel 1976—89, pres. 1989—92, vice-chair 1993—96), Fed. Cir. Bar Assn. Office: US Ct Appeals Fed Cir 717 Madison Pl NW Washington DC 20439-0002

GAJDUSEK, ROBERT ELEMER, writer, retired language educator; b. Yonkers, N.Y., Apr. 18, 1925; s. Karl Abysius and Mahtil Gajdusek; m. Juliz Lee Terry, Dec. 26, 1949 (div. Sept. 1952); 1 child, Mark Robert; m. Bettye-jo Sode, 1952 (div. Sept. 1966); m. Linda Carol Nusbaum, Oct. 20, 1966 (div. Jan. 1998); 1 child, Karl Lawrence. BA magna cuma laude, Princeton U., 1949; MA, Columbia U., 1950, postgrad., U. Calif., Berkeley, Kans. U., George Washing U., San Francisco State U. Tchg. asst. English U. Calif., Berkeley, 1950—52; instr. English Kans. U., Lawrence, 1952—54; asst. to assoc. prof. George Washington U., Washington, 1955—65; assoc. prof. Hunter Col., N.Y.C., 1965; prof. San Francisco State U., 1965—92, prof. emeritus. Author: Hemingway in His Own Country, 2002; contbr. articles. Pvt. 1st class U.S. Army, 1943—46, POW. Recipient Lifetime Achievement and Enduring Excellencein Belles Lettres and Hemingway Studies award, Nick Adams Soc., 1999; Extraordinary Achievement in Hemingway Studies award, Hemingway Soc., 1999. Avocations: travel, art. Home: 137 Granada Dr Corte Madera CA 94925 E-mail: robinegaj@aol.com.

GAJEWSKI, FERDINAND JOHN, music educator, musician, musicologist; b. Plainfield, NJ, Feb. 13, 1941; s. Ferdinand John and Mary Mitzen Gajewski. Student, Conservatoire Americain, Fontainebleau, France, 1960; S.B., Juilliard Sch. of Music, New York, NY, 1963; A.M., Harvard U., 1965, PhD, 1980. Tchg. fellow in music, tutor in music Harvard U., Cambridge, Mass., 1965—72; asst. prof. U. Tex., Austin, 1972—80; vis. prof. U. Mich., Ann Arbor. Eminent Chopinologist. Editor: (book) The Work Sheets to Chopin's Violoncello Sonata, 1988, Joseph Christoph Kessler, 24 Preludes pour le piano, 1994; contbr. articles to profl. publs. Sidney B. Heywood Meml. Fellowship (first recipient), Harvard U. Avocation: orchid cultivation. Home: 30 Westbrook Rd Westfield NJ 07090-3404 Personal E-mail: fjgajewski@aol.com.

GAJEWSKI, RONALD S. consulting and training company executive; b. Chgo., Feb. 3, 1954; s. Stanley B. and Irene M. (Onak) G.; m. D. June Easley, Nov. 22, 1980; 1 child, Mary Anne. BSEE summa cum laude, DeVry Inst., Irving, Tex., 1977; MBA summa cum laude, U. Dallas, Irving, 1981. Product mgr. Docutel Corp., Irving, 1975-82; v.p. Automated Banking, Dallas, 1983-85; asst. v.p. MTech subs. MBank, Dallas, 1986-87; dir. bus. devel. Uccel Corp., Dallas, 1987-89; dist. sales mgr. Goal Systems Internat., Dallas, 1989-90; v.p., gen. mgr. Acclivus Corp., Dallas, 1991—. Editor: (sales skills handbook) Building on the Base, 1995; mem. editl. adv. com. Sales and Mktg. Mgmt., 1996-97. Bd. dirs. Hickory Creek (Tex.) Property and Zoning Bd., 1995—. Mem. ASTD, Assn. for Svcs. Mgmt. Internat. (bd. dirs. 2003—), Instructional Systems Assn. (bd. dirs. 2003—, v.p. 2003—). Roman Catholic. Avocation: building period antique furniture reproductions. Office: Acclivus Corp 14500 Midway Rd Dallas TX 75244-3109

GAJIC, RANKA PEJOVIC, educator; b. Mostar, Bosnia-Herzegovina, Apr. 30, 1928; came to U.S., 1953; d. Radovan Ilija and Darinka Ducic Pejovic; m. Sreten Gajic, Sept. 26, 1954 (dec. Apr. 1991). Student, Belgrade (Yugoslavia) U., 1947-52; B Art Edn., Northeastern Ill. U., 1973; M Slavic Langs. and Lit., U. Ill., Chgo., 1979, ABD, 1990; MLS, Chgo. State U., 1987; PhD in Edn., Century U., 1995. Acct. Field Enterprises Ednl. Corp., Chgo., 1955-59; ins. policy writer Alexander & Co. Ins., Chgo., 1959-64; fgn. ind. travel agt. Am. Express, Chgo., 1964-69; tchr. Chgo. Pub. Schs., 1974-84, 85—; tchg. asst. U. Ill., Chgo., 1984-85. Exhibited paintings in group shows at Northeastern Ill. U., Chgo., 1976 (3d prize) Mus. Sci. and Industry, Chgo., 1976 (Hon. Mention), North River Gallery, Chgo., 1977, 79 (2d prize 1977, Hon. Mention 1979). Chgo. State U. scholar, 1986; recipient Nat. Collegiate award U.S. Achievement Acad., 1987, Am. Medal of Honor ABI, 2000, Lifetime Achievement award IBC, Cambridge, Eng., 2002, Women of Yr. award ABI, 2002. Mem. Am. Assn. for Advancement of Slavic Studies, U. Ill. Alumni Assn. (life), Mus. Contemporary Art (comm. chair North Side Affiliates chpt. 1999—), Golden Key Nat. Honor Soc. Avocations: art, literature, languages, travel. Home: 5901 N Sheridan Rd Apt 12J Chicago IL 60660-3638

GAJL-PECZALSKA, KAZIMIERA J. retired surgical pathologist, pathology educator; b. Warsaw, Nov. 15, 1925; came to U.S., 1970; d. Kazimierz Emil and Anna Janina (Gervais) Gajl; widowed; children: Kazimierz Peczalski, Andrew Peczalski. Student, Jagiellonian Univ., Cracov, Poland, 1945-47; MD, Warsaw U., Poland, 1951, PhD in Immunopathology, 1964. Diplomate Polish Bd. Pediatrics, Polish Bd. Anatomic Pathology, Am. Bd. Pathology. Attending pediatrician Children's Hosp. for Infectious Diseases, Warsaw, Poland, 1953-58, head, pathology lab., 1958-65; adj. prof. Postgrad. Med. Sch., Warsaw, Poland, 1965-70; fellow U. Minn., Mpls., 1970-72, asst. prof. dept. pathology, 1972-75, assoc. prof. dept. pathology, 1975-79, prof. dept. pathology, 1979-00, dir. immunophenotyping and flow lab., 1974-00, dir. cytology dept. pathology, 1976-95; ret., 2000. Author chpts. to book; contbr. of numerous papers to profl. jours. Fellow WHO, Paris, 1959, London, 1962, Paris, 1967, U.S. Pub. Health Svcs. fellow, 1968-69; recipient Scientific Com. award Polish Ministry of Health and Social Welfare, 1964. Mem. Am. Soc. Experimental Pathology, Am. Soc. Cytology, Internat. Acad. Pathology, British Soc. Pediatric Pathology, Polish Soc. Pathology, Polish Soc Pediatricians. Roman Catholic. Avocations: music, skiing. Office: U Minn Dept Pathology U Health Ctr PO Box 609 Minneapolis MN 55455

GALA, CANDELAS S. literature educator, language educator; b. Santander, Cantabria, Spain, Nov. 13, 1948; arrived in U.S., 1972; d. José Sánchez and Isabel Gala; children: Isabel Gala Newton, Ryan Antonia Newton. BA in Modern Philology, U. Salamanca, Spain, 1972; MA, U. Pitts., 1978, PhD, 1980. Lectr. St. Ursula's Grammar Sch., London, 1972—73, Carlow Coll., Pitts., 1973—74; tchg. asst., tchg. fellow U. Pitts., 1975—78; instr. Wake Forest U., Winston-Salem, NC, 1978—81, asst. prof., 1981—85, assoc. prof., 1985—91, full prof., 1991—, chmn. romance langs., 1996—, Wake Forest prof., 2000—. Author: Lorca: Book of Poems or the Adventures of a Quest, 1986, Lorca: Writing in a Trance Book of Poems and Diván at the Tamarit, 1992, Understanding Federico García Lorca, 1995, Collection of Critical Essays on Spanish and Latino Women Writers in the U.S., 1996; editor: Ensayos Críticos; contbr. articles to profl. jours. Mem.: MLA, Asociación Internat. de Hispanistas, Asociación de Licenciados y doctores españoles, South Atlantic MLA. Office: Wake Forest Univ Dept Romance Langs 7566 Reynolda Sta Winston Salem NC 27109

GALAHAD, ALEXANDER, writer; b. Bklyn., N.Y., Aug. 11, 1950; s. Stanley and Helen Yvette Blechor. Student, Cornell U., 1976; salesmanship degree, Dale Carnegie Course, 1978. Salesman Ormont Machine Co., Manhattan, NY, gen. mgr.; corp. bus. mgr. Sumron Corp., Atlanta; fundraiser Honcia Fordham Coun., Austin, Tex., 1981—84; salesman Galahad Prodns., Sedona, Ariz., 1986—2002, writer, pub. Trenton, NJ. Author: (book) Momular Science, 2000, Enblockenment, 2002. Scoutmaster Boy Scouts Am., Bklyn.; min. Progressive Life Ch., Trenton. Mem.: Alpha Delta Phi. Avocations: gymnastics, photography, dancing, martial arts. Home: POB 7717 Trenton NJ 08628

GALAMAGA, DONALD PETER, health and mental health systems consultant; b. Detroit, Mar. 14, 1938; s. Peter and Mary (Burnat) G.; m. Margot C. Mahoney, Jan. 2, 1965; children: Peter, Mary, Paul, Robert. AB in Econ., Coll. the Holy Cross, 1959; grad., USN Destroyer Sch., 1964; MPA, U. R.I., 1971. Commd. ensign USN, 1959, advanced through grades to capt., 1983; dir. program planning evaluation R.I. Dept. Edn., Providence, 1971-73, dep. asst. commr. edn. for budget, 1973-78; exec. dir. mgmt. and support svcs. R.I. Dept. Mental Health, Retardation and Hosps., Cranston, 1978-91, exec. dir. mental health and mgmt. svcs., 1991-93, exec. dir. divsn. integrated mental health svcs., 1993-99; orgn. and mental health sys. change cons., pub. peer rev. NIH, Washington, 1999—. Chmn. S.E. New Eng. Navy Recruiting Dist. Assistance Coun., Providence, 1975-89, Armed Forces Exec. Steering Com., Providence, 1973-75; state rep. Nat. Com. on Evaluation & Info. Sys., Washington, 1971-78; liaison panel mem. com. quality assurance and accreditation guidelines for managed care NCQA, Washington, 1997. Contbr. articles to profl. jours. Chair R.I. Mental Health Advancement Cmty. Alliance, 1999-2001; bd. dirs. Mental Health Assn. R.I., 1999—, chmn., 2001-2003; bd. dirs. Bradley Hosp., 1999—; chmn. St. Kevin Parish Coun., Warwick, R.I., 1972-82, fin. com., 1992—; budget panel subcom. chmn. United Way, Providence, 1970-75; co-dir. R.I. Allied Advocacy Group for Collaborative Care, 1999—. Recipient Creative Pub. Adminstrn. award Am. Soc. for Pub. Adminstrn., 1978, Govs. Citation, Gov. of R.I., 1980, 98, Commendation for Civic Achievement, R.I. Gen. Assembly, 1980, 98. Mem.: R.I. Coun. Cmty. Svcs. (bd. dirs. 1970—75), Nat. Assn. State Mental Health Program Dirs., Internat. Assn. Energy Engrs. (life; sr., cert., cert.), Fin. Watchdog Com. Warwick and Pub. Works Subcom., Mars Soc., Planetary Soc. Roman Catholic. Avocations: brain science research, sports memorabilia, modern jazz, reading. Home: 30 White Rock Rd Warwick RI 02889-6314

GALAMBOS, THEODORE VICTOR, civil engineer, educator; b. Budapest, Hungary, Apr. 17, 1929; s. Paul and Magdalena (Potzner) G.; m. Barbara Ann Asp, June 25, 1957; children: Paul, Ruth, Ronald, John. BSCE, U. N.D, 1953, MSCE, 1954; PhD in CE, Lehigh U., 1959; Dr. honoris causa, Tech. U., Budapest, 1982; PhD (hon.), U. N.D., 1998; DSc (hon.), U. Minn., 2001. Registered profl. engr., Pa., Minn., Mo. From asst. to assoc. prof. civil engring. Lehigh U., Bethlehem, Pa., 1959-65; prof. Washington U., St. Louis, 1965-81, head dept., 1970-78; prof. U. Minn., Mpls., 1981-96, emeritus prof., 1997—. Cons. engr. Steel Joist Inst., Myrtle Beach, S.C., 1965—; vis. prof. U.S. Mil. Acad., West Point, 1990. Author, co-author 4 books in field; editor 1 book; contbr. over 100 articles to profl. jours. Served with U.S. Army, 1954-56. Recipient T.R. Higgins award Am. Inst. Steel Constrn., 1981. Mem. ASCE (hon., Norman medal 1983, Shortridge Hardesty award 1988, E.E. Howard award 1992, OPAL award 2002), NAE, Internat. Assn. Bridge and Structural Engrs. Democrat. Baptist. Avocation: photography. Home: 4375 Wooddale Ave Minneapolis MN 55424-1060 Office: U Minn Civil Engring Dept Minneapolis MN 55455 E-mail: galam001@tc.umn.edu.

GALAN, LEONIDEZ VINDOLLO, architect; b. Poblacion, Phillipines, Aug. 8, 1948; s. Juan Garcia Galan and Maria Victoria (Vergara) Vindollo; m. Adoracion Cipriaso Galan; children: John Patrick C., Denise Victoria. BS in Architecture, Calumpit Inst., Philippines. Structural detailer Le Messuer Assoc. Engrs., St. Louis, 1968—69; arch. designer Port Authority N.Y. & N.J., 1969—85, task leader arch., 1985—. Cons. various cos.; pres. John Dendor Realty Corp.; asst. prof. arch. design N.Y. U. With U.S. Army, 1965—68, Vietnam. Mem.: Illuminating Engring. Soc., Foreign Policy Assn., Constrn. Specification Inst., Am. Inst. Architects, Lions. Roman Catholic. Avocations: tennis, bowling, swimming, dancing, boxing. Home: 179-15 Dalny Rd Jamaica Estates Jamaica NY 11432 Office: Port Authority NY & NJ One World Trade Ctr Rm 1933 New York NY 10048 Fax: 718-297-5709.

GALAN, VINCENT, anesthesiologist; b. Havana, May 31, 1960; came to the U.S., 1962; s. Manuel Vincent and Alice (Riesgo) G.; m. Maureen Elizabeth Barbas, Mar. 24, 1990; children: Marissa Marie, Annalyse Isabel. BS in Chemistry cum laude; BS in Chemistry, Berry Coll., 1980; MD, U. P.R., 1984, MD with splty. in anesthesia, 1987; MD with pain subsplty., SUNY, Bklyn., 1988; subsplty. in cardiac anesthesia, Cleve. Clinic, 1989; MD with cardiac anesthesia subsplty., Ga. State U., 1989, MBA in Fin., 1997. Diplomate Am. Bd. Anesthesia, Am. Acad. Pain Mgmt. Intern, resident Univ. P.R. Dist. Hosps., P.R., 1984-87; asst. instr. Downstate Med.-SUNY, Bklyn., 1987-88; vis. pain fellow Hermann Hosp., Houston, 1988; fellow in cardiac anesthesia Cleve. Clinic, 1989; co-dir. pain clinic So. Regional Med. Ctr., Atlanta, 1991-98, dir. pain ctr., 1998—; pres. Riverdale Anesthesia Assocs. P.C., 1998—. Pres. Operative Solutions, Inc., 1998—, Global Equity Advisors, Inc., 1998—; investment advisor, 1999—; contbg. test writer Am. Bd. Anesthesia, Hartford, Conn., 1995—. Contbr. articles to profl. jours.; abstract reviewer Pain Digest, 1995—. Mem. Am. Soc. Regional Anesthesia, Soc. Cardiovascular Anesthesiologists, Am. Acad. Pain Medicine, Am. Soc. Anesthesia, AMA, Ga. Med. Soc. Roman Catholic. Avocations: languages, history, tennis, soccer, reading.

GALANDIUK, SUSAN, colon and rectal surgeon, educator; b. N.Y.C., Mar. 6, 1957; d. Joseph and Dora (Neu) G.; m. Hiram C. Polk Jr., Dec. 22, 1991. BS cum laude, SUNY, Albany, 1976; MD summa cum laude, Julius Maximilians U., Wuerzburg, Germany, 1982. Diplomate Am. Bd. Surgery, Am. Bd. Colon and Rectal Surgery. Surg. intern Chirurgische Univ. Klinik, Julius Maximilians U., Wuerzburg, Germany, 1982-83, Cleve. Clinic Found., 1983-84, surg. resident, 1984-88; Price fellow in surg. rsch., dept. surgery U. Louisville, 1988-89, colon and rectal surgery fellow dept. surgery, 1989-90, instr. dept. surgery, 1990-91, asst. prof. dept. surgery, 1991-96, assoc. prof., 1996-2001, program dir. sect. colon and rectal surgery, 1999—, prof., 2001—; dir. Price Inst. Surg. Rsch., 2001—. Presenter in field. Editl. bd. Digestive Surgery, Mayor Clin. Procs., Diseases Colon Rectum, Archives of Surgery; contbr. Chmn. fund raising com. ARC, Louisville, 1993, 1995—97, bd. dirs., 1997—2000, chmn. bd., 2001—03; bd. mem. Fund for the Arts, 1996—2003; chair med. adv. com. Ky. chpt. Crohn's and Colitis Found. Am., Louisville, 1993—97, 1999—2003. William E. Lower Fellow Thesis prize Cleve. Clinic Found., 1986. Fellow ACS, AAUP, Am. Soc. Colon and Rectal Surgeons (mem. chmn. rsch. found. young rschrs. com. 1996—, mem. program com. 1994-96, trustee rsch. found., 2001—, membership com., 2000—); mem. AMA, Am. Med. Women's Assn., Am. Soc. Microbiology, Assn. Acad. Surgery, Assn. Women Surgeons, Collegium Internat. Chirurgiae Digestivae, Jefferson County Med. Soc., Ky. Med. Assn. (mem. cancer com.), Louisville Surg. Soc., Hiram C. Polk Jr. Surg. Soc., Ohio Valley Soc. Colon and Rectal Surgeons, Priestly Soc., Soc. Surgery of Alimentary Tract, Soc. Am. Gastrointestinal Endoscopic Surgeons, Soc. Surg. Oncology (mem. corp. rels. and issues, govt. affairs coms.), Southea. Surg. Congress (councillor 1997-99), Surg. Infection Soc., Soc. Univ. Surgeons, Am. Soc. Gastrointestinal Endoscopists, Ctrl. Surg. Assn., Western Surg. Assn., Am. Gastroent. Assn., So. Surg. Assn., Am. Gastroenterol. Assn., Am. Soc. Human Genetics, Am. Soc. Clin. Oncology, Assn. Program Dirs. in Colon & Rectal Surgery, Soc. Pelvic Surgeons, Assn. Program Dirs. in Colon and Rectal Surgery, Surg. Biol. Club I. Greek Catholic. Office: U Louisville Dept Surgery 550 S Jackson St Louisville KY 40202-1622 E-mail: S0gala01@gwise.louisville.edu.

GALANIS, JOHN WILLIAM, lawyer; b. Milw., May 9, 1937; s. William and Angeline (Koroniou) G.; m. Patricia Caro, Nov. 29, 1969; children: Lia Galanis Economou, William, Charles, John. BBA cum laude, U. Wis., 1959; JD, U. Mich., 1963; postgrad. (Ford Found. grantee), London Sch. Econs., 1964. Bar: Wis. 1965; CPA, Wis. Assoc. firm Whyte & Hirschboeck S.C., Milw., 1964-68; sr. v.p., gen. counsel, sec. MGIC Investment Corp. and Mortgage Guaranty Ins. Corp., Milw., 1968-88; ptnr. Galanis, Pollack & Jacobs, S.C., Milw., 1988—. Assoc. editor: Mich. Law Rev, 1962-63. Bd. visitors Law Sch. U. Mich., Sch. Bus. U. Wis.; past chmn. Milw. Found., bd. dirs., past pres. Milw Boys' and Girls' Club; pres. Family Svc. Milw. Recipient Disting. Svc. award Internat. Inst., Hope Chest award Nat. MS Soc., Disting. Alumni award Milw. Boys' Club, Disting. Svc. award Milw. Civic Alliance Club, 1989. Mem. ABA, Wis. Bar Assn., Milw. Bar Assn., Am. Hellenic Ednl. Progessive Assn., Order of Coif, Milw. Athletic Club, Blue Mound Golf and Country Club. Greek Orthodox. Home: 1200 Woodlawn Cir Elm Grove WI 53122-1639 Office: MGIC Pl Milwaukee WI 53201

GALANOPOULOS, KELLY, biomedical engineer; b. Athens, Greece, Jan. 4, 1952; came to U.S., 1970, naturalized, 1976; d. Panayotis and Catherine (Calas) G.; m. Dale S. Kruchten, Sept. 4, 1982; children: Catherine Roberta Kruchten, Stephanie Diane Kruchten. BA, CUNY, 1974; MS, Poly. Inst. N.Y., 1978, postgrad., 1982—, L.I. U., 1982—. Dir. bio-med. engrnig. Wyckoff Heights Hosp., Bklyn., 1980-83, Bronx Lebanon Hosp., N.Y.C., 1983-89; dir. clin. engring. Mt. Sinai Med. Ctr., N.Y.C., 1991—2002. Cons. Environ. Co., N.Y.C., 1980-85, Joint Purchasing, N.Y.C., 1980—; premier health alliance of N.Y. biomed. engring. adminstrs., 1991—; lectr. in field. Mem. Am. Soc. for Hosp. Engring. of Am. Hosp. Assn., Am. Coll. Clin. Engrs., Assn. Advancement Med. Instrumentation, IEEE, Soc. Women Engrs., N.Y. Acad. Scis. E-mail: kgalanopou@aol.com.

GALANOS, JAMES, retired fashion designer; b. Phila., Sept. 20, 1924; s. Gregory D. and Helen (Gorgoliatos) G. With Hattie Carnegie, 1944; asst. to designer Columbia Pictures Corp., Hollywood, Calif., 1946-47; trainee Robert Piguet, Paris, France, 1947-48; founder, designer Galanos Originals, L.A., 1951-99. Exhbns. include restrospectives Costume Council of Los Angeles County Mus. Art, 1974, Fashion Inst. Tech., 1976, Costume Inst. Mus. Fine Arts, Houston, 1987, Galanos Retrospective, 1951-92, 1997, Cleve. Hist. Soc., 1996, 45 yr. career retrospective Los Angeles County Mus. Art, 1997. Recipient award for distinguished service in field of fashion Neiman-Marcus, 1954; Am. Fashion Critics award Met. Mus. Art, Costume Inst., 1954; Return award, 1956; Hall of Fame, 1959; Creativity award Internat. Achievements Fair, 1956; Filene's Young Talent design award Boston, 1958; Cotton Fashion award, 1958; Lifetime Achievement award Council Fashion Designers Am., 1985; Stanley award Fashion Collectors of Dallas Hist. Soc., 1986; Otis-Parsons Design Achievement award, 1987, first Annual award for Design Excellence Costume Com. Chgo. Hist. Soc., 1992; Recognition award outstanding contbn. to the World of Fashion. Office: 1316 Sunset Plaza Dr Los Angeles CA 90069-1235

GALANT, HERBERT LEWIS, lawyer; b. N.Y.C., Oct. 16, 1928; s. Charles A. and Bertha (Rosenberg) G.; m. Fern Judith Laikin, Feb. 10, 1957; children: Peter B., John M., Amy E. BA cum laude, U. Wis., 1949; LLB magna cum laude, Harvard U., 1952; LLM, NYU, 1960. Bar: N.Y. 1955, U.S. Dist. Ct. (so. dist.) N.Y. 1956, U.S. Ct. Appeals (2d cir.) 1959. Assoc. Fried, Frank, Harris, Shriver & Jacobson, N.Y.C., 1955-61, ptnr., 1962-95, co-chair, 1992-95, of counsel, 1995—. Editor: Harvard U. Law Rev., 1950-52. Mem. Tenafly Twp. (N.J.) Bd. Ethics, 1978-88, Tenafly Twp. Planning Bd., 1997-2000. 1st lt. USAF, 1952-54. Mem. Assn. of Bar of City of N.Y., Harvard U. Club (N.Y.C.). Democrat. Jewish. Home: 150 Tekening Dr Tenafly NJ 07670-1219 Office: Fried Frank Harris Shriver & Jacobson 1 New York Plz Fl 22 New York NY 10004-1980 E-mail: herbgala@aol.com.

GALANTE, JANE HOHFELD, pianist, music historian; b. San Francisco, Feb. 14, 1924; d. Edward and Lillian (Devendorf) Hohfeld; m. Clement Galante, Dec. 26, 1956; children: Edward Elio, John Clement. AB, Vassar Coll., 1944; MA, U. Calif., Berkeley, 1949. Instr. U. Calif., Berkeley, 1948—51, Mills Coll., Oakland, Calif., 1951—54. Founder, dir. Composers' Forum of San Francisco, 1946-56. Music editor Berkeley, A Jour. Modern Culture, 1944-52; concert pianist German tours for USIS, 1952-54; Young Audience Concerts, San Francisco, 1963-70; mem. Lyra Chamber Music Ensemble, 1980-90; transl.: Darius Milhaud (Paul Collaer) including revised and edited catalog Milhaud's Compositions, 1988, Darius Milhaud: Interviews with Claude Rostand, 2002. Trustee Morrison Chamber Music Ctr., San Francisco State U., 1956—; hon. trustee San Francisco Conservatory Music, 1970-99; co-founder San Francisco Friends of Chamber Music, 1999. Decorated chevalier de l'ordre des arts et des lettres; recipient Disting. Svc. award Chamber Music Am., 1992, Pres.'s medal San Francisco State U., 1998. Mem. Am. Fedn. Musicians.

GALANTE, JORGE OSVALDO, orthopedic surgeon, educator; b. Buenos Aires, Dec. 18, 1934; arrived in U.S., 1958; m. Sofija Kabliauskas; 1 child, Charles. BA, Colegio Nacional de Buenos Aires, 1952; MD, U. Buenos Aires, 1958; DMSc, U. Goteborg, Sweden, 1967. Diplomate Am. Bd. Orthopedic Surgery. Resident in orthopaedics U. Ill., Chgo., 1960-64; assoc. investigator bioengineering lab. U. Goteborg, 1964-67; asst. prof. orthopedic surgery U. Ill. Med. Ctr., Chgo., 1967-70, assoc. prof., 1970-72; lect. in orthopedics U. Ill. Abraham Lincoln Sch. Medicine, Chgo., 1972—; adj. rsch. prof. U. Ill. Circle, Chgo., 1972—, mem. graduate faculty, 1974—; prof., chmn. dept. orthopedic surgery Rush-Presbyn.-St. Luke's Med. Ctr., Chgo., 1972-94; prof. anatomy Rush Med. Coll., Chgo., 1977—; dir. Rush Arthritis and Orthopedic Inst., 1994—. Assoc. prof. exptl. orthopedics. U. Goteborg, 1969—. Contbr. articles to profl. jours. Recipient Kappa Delta award Am. Acad. Orthopedic Surgery, 1970, Clemson (S.C.) U. award, 1975, Steindler award Orthopedic Rsch. Soc., 1990, Zimmer Award for Disting. Achievement in Orthopedic Rsch. Bristol-Myers Squibb, 1996. Office: Rush-Presbyn-St Luke's Med Ctr 1725 W Harrison Chicago IL 60612-3833

GALANTE, JOSEPH A. bishop; b. Philadelphia, Pa., July 2, 1938; BA, St. Charles Seminary, Phila.; JCD, Lateran U., Rome; MA in Spiritual Theology, U. St. Thomas, Rome. Ordained priest Roman Cath. Ch. 1964, bishop 1992. Asst. pastor Our Lady of Consolation Parish, 1964—65, St. John of the Cross, Roslyn, 1965; Bishop's sec., Diocesan Master of Ceremonies Diocese of Brownsville, Tex., 1968—72, vicar for religious, Diocesan newspaper editor 1969—72; asst. vicar for religious Archdiocese of Phila., 1972—79; residen

Good Shepherd Parish, 1972—73; defender of The Bond Archdiocesan Tribunal, Phila., 1972—74; chaplain Catholic Home for Girls, St. Vincent's Residence, 1972—81; prof. Canon Law St. Charles Seminary, 1974—77, Mary Immaculate Seminary, Northampton, Pa., 1975—78; vicar for religious Archdiocese of Phila., 1979—87; chaplain Convent of the Handmaids of the Sacred Heart, Haverford, Pa., 1981—87; undersec. Congregation for Institutes of Consecrated Life & Societies of Apostolic Life, Rome, 1987—92; aux. bishop Diocese of San Antonio, 1992—94; bishop Diocese of Beaumont, Tex., 1994—99, Diocese of Dallas, 2000—. Pres. Nat. Conf. for Vicars of Religious, 1976—80; spkr. in field. Religious affairs com. Canon Law Soc. Office: Diocese Office of Dallas PO Box 190507 Dallas TX 75219-0507*

GALANTE, JOSEPH ANTHONY, JR., computer programmer; b. Yonkers, N.Y., July 15, 1947; s. Joseph Anthony Sr. and Lavinia (Brue) G. BS in secondary edn., physics, U. Md., 1971; MS in Tech. Mgmt., Am. U., 1974; Webmaster Cert., Pa. State U., 2000. Programmer UNISYS, Green Belt, Md., 1971-76; programmer analyst N.Y. Tel., White Plains, 1976-79, Telic Corp., Darien, Conn., 1978-81; assoc. mgr. N.Y. Tel., N.Y.C., 1981-85; sr. systems specialist Telesector Resources Group, Pearl River, N.Y., 1985--. Pres. Communicators Westchester, Hasting, N.Y., 1979; chmn. by law com. Masthope Rapids Property Owners Coun., Lackawaxen, Pa., 1977-79; bd. dirs. Mast Hope Mountain Property Owners Coun., 1996—; pres. West Colang Lake Assn., 1996—; mem. Pike County Pa. Visioning Com., 1998, Land Use Task Force, 1998; mem. adv. com. Pike County Coop. Extension, 2002. Recipient Apollo 11 Team Medallion NASA, 1971, Apollo 17 Personal Contribution plaque, 1975, First Annual Bell Atlantic Leaders in Excellence award for participation in the design and devel. of the Amdahl EnView Software product, 1998; N.Y. State scholar, 1965. Mem. Masthope Rapids Assn. (bd. dirs. 1996-99), Westcolang Lake Assn. (pres. 1996-97), Masthope Rapids Property Owners Coun. (chmn. com. 1977-79), Kappa Delta Pi. Roman Catholic. Achievements include development of data conversion techniques for information interchange between UNISYS and IBM using ASCII COBOL; conversion of real time basic assembly lang. program complex from SVS to MVS. Office: NYNEX TRG 2 Blue Hill Plz Fl 4 Pearl River NY 10965-3103

GALANTER, MARC, psychiatrist, educator; b. N.Y.C., Sept. 17, 1941; s. Jacob and Ada (Simms) G. BA, Columbia U., 1963; MD, Albert Einstein Coll. Medicine, 1967. Diplomate Am. Bd. Psychiatry and Neurology with added qualifications in addiction psychiatry; cert. Am. Soc. Addiction Medicine. Intern UCLA Hosp., 1967-68; resident in psychiatry Albert Einstein Coll. Medicine-Bronx Mcpl. Hosp. Ctr., 1968-71, fellow in community psychiatry, 1972-73, clin. instr., 1972-74, dir. Drug and Alcohol Cons. Service, 1972-75, career tchr. drug abuse and alcoholism Nat. Inst. on Alcohol Abuse and Alcoholism, Nat. Inst. Drug Abuse, 1973-76, asst. prof., 1974-78, dir. div. alcoholism and drug abuse, 1975-87, assoc. prof., 1978-83, prof. dept. psychiatry, 1983-87; prof. psychiatry, dir. div. alcoholism and drug abuse NYU Sch. Med., 1987—; dir. addiction divsn., rsch. scientist Collaborating Ctr. WHO, 1987-98, dep. dir. Collaborating Ctr., 1998—. Clin. assoc. Lab. Clin. Psychopharmacology, NIMH, Washington, 1970-72; instr. psychiatry residency program St. Elizabeth's Hosp.; presenter at profl. confs. U.S., Can., Thailand, Germany, Japan, India, Kenya and Italy; chmn. Nat. Conf. on Alcohol and Drug Abuse Edn., 1977; program chmn. Internat. Conf. Med. Edn. in Alcohol and Drug Abuse, WHO and Assn. Med. Edn. and Rsch. in Substance Abuse, 1982, founder, pres., 1976-77; dir. Lab. Alcoholism and Drug Abuse WHO. Editor: Ofcl. Sci. Procs. of Nat. Coun. on Alcoholism, 1978-80, Alcohol and Drug Abuse in Medical Education, 1980, (book series) Currents in Alcoholism, 1979, 80, 81, Recent Developments in Alcoholism; mem. editl. bd. Am. Jour. Drug and Alcohol Abuse, 1978—; assoc. editor jour. Alcoholism Clin. and Exptl. Rsch., Am. Jour. of Addictions, 1979, Jour. Substance Abuse Treatment, 1995—; co-editor: Advances in the Psychosocial Treatment of Alcoholism, 1984; editor-in-chief Substance Abuse Jour., 1978—; author: Network Therapy for Alcohol and Drug and Abuse, 1993, 2nd edit., 1999, Cults: Faith, Health and Coercion, 1989, 2nd edit., 1999. Recipient Psychopharmacology award Am. Psychol. Assn., 1972; Career Tchr. award in drug abuse and alcoholism NIMN, 1973-77, Organon Tchg. awad Am. Psychiat. Assn., 1999; ann. Book award Commonwealth Fund, 1978-82, Macarthur medal Assn. Med. Edn. and Rsch., 1994. Fellow Am. Psychiat. Assn. (chmn. panel on alcoholism, nat. task force on psychiat. treatment 1983—, mem. task force on cults 1977-80, mem. com. on alcoholism, chmn. com. on addiction edn. 1992—, chmn. com. on religion 1985-90, Gold Achievement award 1993, bd. dirs. pub. group 1998--, Seymour Vastermark Edn. awrd 2002), Am. Soc. on Addiction Medicine (bd. dirs. 1986—, sec. 1995-97, pres. elect 1997-99, pres. 1999-2001); mem. AAAS, Am. Bd. Psychiatry and Neurology (vice chair com. on added qualifications in addiction psychiatry 1992-98), Rsch. Soc. on Alcoholism (sec. 1983-85), N.Y. Acad. Medicine (addiction com. 1985—), N.Y. State Task Force on Dual Psychiat. and Addictive Disorders (task force chmn. 1986-89, 93), N.Y. Psychiat. Soc., Am. Acad. Addiction Psychiatrists (v.p. 1987-89, pres. 1991-93, bd. dirs. 1986—), Nat. Inst. Alcohol Abuse and Alcoholism (Nat. Adv. Coun. 1997—). Office: Division of Alcoholism & Drug Abuse NYU School of Medicine 550 First Avenue New York NY 10016

GALANTI, RICHARD A. wholesale business executive; CFO Costco Wholesale, Issaqyah, Wash. Office: Costco Wholesale 999 Lake Dr Ste 200 Issaquah WA 98027-5367

GALASK, RUDOLPH PETER, obstetrician and gynecologist; b. Fort Dodge, Iowa, Dec. 23, 1935; s. Peter Otto and Adeline Amelia (Maranesi) G.; m. Gloria Jean Vasti, June 19, 1965 BS, Drake U., 1959; MD, U. Iowa, 1964, MS, 1967. Diplomate Am. Bd. Obstetrics and Gynecology. Research fellow in microbiology U. Iowa, Iowa City, 1965-67, resident in ob-gyn., 1967-70, asst. prof., 1970-74, asst. prof. microbiology, 1973-74, assoc. prof. obstetrics and gynecology microbiology, 1974-78, prof., 1978—, chmn. exec. com. Coll. Medicine, 1992-93, prof. dermatology, 1999—. Cons. various pharm. and diagnostic cos. Editor: Infectious Diseases in the Female Patient, 1986-89; contbr. numerous articles to profl. jours. Served to staff sgt. USNG, 1954-64 Recipient I.D.S.O.G./Ortho McNeil award for outstanding contbns. to field of infectious diseases in ob-gyn., A.P.G.O. Excellence in Tchg. award, 1997; numerous grants to study the efficacy of various antibiotics and chemotherapeutics. Fellow Am. Gynecol. and Obstet. Soc., Am. Coll. Obstetricians and Gynecologists, Infectious Disease Am.; mem. AAAS, Cen. Assn. for Obstetricians and Gynecologists, Infectious Disease Soc. for Ob-Gyn. (pres. 1982-84, founding mem.), Soc. Gynecol. Investigation (coun. 1987-90), Queens Gynecol. Soc. (hon.), Tex. Assn. Obstetricians and Gynecologists (hon.), Am. Soc. Microbiology, Izaac Walton League, Ducks Unltd. Club (sponsor), Sigma Xi. Roman Catholic. Office: Univ Iowa Hosps Dept Ob-Gyn Iowa City IA 52242 *Power is a perception that lasts a moment but respect is a legacy that lasts forever.*

GALASSI, JONATHAN WHITE, book publishing company executive; b. Seattle, Nov. 4, 1949; s. Gerard Goodwin and Dorothea Johnston (White) G.; m. Susan Grace, June 21, 1975; children: Isabel Grace, Beatrice Grace. AB, Harvard U., 1971; MA, Cambridge (Eng.) U., 1976. Editor Houghton Mifflin Co., Boston, N.Y.C., 1973-81; sr. editor Random House, Inc., N.Y.C., 1981-86; exec. editor, v.p. Farrar, Straus & Giroux, Inc., N.Y.C., 1986-87, editor in chief, sr. v.p., 1988-93, exec. v.p., editor-in-chief, 1993-99, pub., editor-in-chief, 1999—2002, pres., pub., 2002—. Author: Morning Run: Poems, 1988, North Street: Poems, 2000; editor, translator The Second Life of Art: Selected Essays of Eugenio Montale, 1982, Otherwise: Last and First Poems of E. Montale, 1986, Collected Poems of E. Montale 1920-1954, 1998; E. Montale, Posthumous Diary, 2001; editor: (poems) Paris Rev., 1978—88. Recipient Roger Klein award for editing PEN, 1984, Weidenfeld Translation prize, 1999, Premio Montale, 1999, award in lit. Am. Acad. Arts and Letters, 2000; Marshall scholar Brit. Marshall Commn., London, 1971-73; Guggenheim fellow, 1989. Fellow: Am. Acad. Arts and Sci.; mem.: Acad. Am. Poets (bd. dirs. 1990—, pres. 1994—99, chmn. 1999—2001, hon. chmn. 2002—). Office: Farrar Straus & Giroux Inc 19 Union Sq W Fl 4 New York NY 10003-3604 E-mail: jonathan.galassi@fsgbooks.com.

GALASSO, FRANCIS SALVATORE, materials scientist; b. Monson, Mass., Apr. 26, 1931; s. Paul and Rubino (Cirillo) G.; m. Lois E. Wood; children: Cynthia Egolf, Gary Galasso. BS, U. Mass., 1953; MS, U. Conn., 1957, PhD, 1960. Prin. scientist United Techs. Rsch. Ctr., East Hartford, Conn., 1974-77, sr. matreial scientist, 1977-85, mgr., 1985-91; with Galasso Tech. Assocs., Manchester, Conn., 1991—; chief materials United Techs. Rsch. Ctr., East Hartford, Conn., 1960-74. Mem. adv. bd. Chem. Rubber Co., 1971— ; cons. in space experiments NASA, Huntsville, Ala., 1971-77; vis. prof. U. Conn., Storrs, 1985—. Author 6 books; contbr. articles to profl. jours. patentee in field. Coach Manchester Little League, 1960-75, v.p., 1970-84, pres., 1984=88, mem. bd. govs. adv. com. on accreditation, 1988-90. 1st lt. USAF, 1953-55. Fellow Am. Ceramic Soc.; mem. AIME, Am. Chem. Soc., Am. Legion, Army-Navy Club, Sigma Xi. Democrat. Roman Catholic. Office: 13 Green Manor Rd Manchester CT 06040-3342 E-mail: locyngar@aol.com.

GALATIANOS, GUS A. computer executive, information systems consultant, real estate developer, educator; b. Hermoupolis, Siros, Greece, Jan. 18, 1947; came to U.S., 1973; s. Athanassios Constantine and Despina Athanassios (Stefanou) G.; m. Katerina E. Saridis, Sept. 29, 1974; children: Athanassios, Deborah. BSEE, N.Y. Inst. Tech., 1974; MSEE, Columbia U., 1977; MS in Computer Sci., Stevens Inst. Tech., 1977; PhD in Computer Sci., Poly. U., N.Y.C., 1986. Mgr. ops. Solomos Bus. Machines, Athens, Greece, 1970-73; computer cons. Univ. Computer Ctrs., N.Y.C., 1973-77; tech. dir. Computer Dynamics Corp., N.Y.C., 1977-79; assoc. prof., chmn. dept. computer sci. SUNY, Old Westbury, 1979-93, prof., 1993-2000, chmn. dept. computer sic., 1995-98; computer cons. Keane Inc., N.Y.C., 1986-98, Ins. Svcs. Office, N.Y.C., 1981-82, Computer Corp. Am., N.Y.C., 1983-84; mgr. fin. systems Singer/Electronic Systems Div., Little Falls, N.J., 1984-87. Pres. Advanced Computer Cons. Internat., N.Y.C., 1988—; pres. ACCI Properties, Inc., N.Y.C., 1988—. Author: Principles of Software Engineering, 1986, Principles of Database Systems, 1986; contbr. articles to profl. jours. Mem. Statue of Liberty Found. Inc., N.Y.C., 1984, Nat. Fedn. Blind, Balt., 1988, Rep. Presdl. Task Force, Washington, 1984—, Greater Whitestone Taxpayers Civic Assn., N.Y.C., 1984—. Served with Greek Air Force, 1965-67. Mem. IEEE, AAAS, Assn. Computing Machinery, N.Y. Acad. Scis., Am. Mgmt. Assn., Am. Assn. Artificial Intelligence, Am. Cons. League, Hellenic Univ. Club (N.Y.C.). Republican. Greek Orthodox. Avocations: music, hunting, travel, reading. Home: 17-24 Parsons Blvd Whitestone NY 11357-3041 Office: SUNY 160 Havemeyer St Brooklyn NY 11211 E-mail: accidrg@aol.com.

GALATZ, HENRY FRANCIS, lawyer; b. N.Y.C., Feb. 5, 1947; s. Julius D. and Dorothy (Kirschen) G.; children: Benjamin Chase, Brandon Kyle. BA, U. Ariz., 1970, MEd, MA with honors, 1973; JD, U. the Pacific, 1979. Bar: Ill. 1981, U.S. Ct. Appeals (7th cir.) 1981, U.S. Dist. Ct. (no. dist.) Ill. 1982, U.S. Dist. Ct. (ea. dist.) Mich. 1982, U.S. Ct. Appeals (6th cir.) 1982, U.S. Dist. Ct. (ea. dist.) Mo. 1985, U.S. Supreme Ct. 1985, U.S. Dist. Ct. Mont. 1986, U.S. Dist. Ct. (we. dist.) Tex. 1987, U.S. Dist. Ct. (no. dist.) Calif. 1992, U.S. Dist. Ct. Nebr. 1993, U.S. Dist. Ct. (no. dist.) Ohio 1997, U.S. Ct. Appeals (11th cir.) 2000; cert. coach and referee U.S. Soccer Fedn. Cons. labor rels. Phoenix Closures, Chgo., 1974-75, Galatz Elec. Corp., Las Vegas, Nev., 1975-80; labor counsel W.W. Grainger, Inc., Skokie, Ill., 1980—; pvt. practice Flossmoor, Ill., 1981—. Hearing officer Ill. State Bd. Edn., Chgo., 1982—: atty. Chgo. Legal Svcs. Found., 1983—, Ill. Inst. for Dispute Resolution, 1992—; mem. com. Employment Law Inst., Northwestern U., Evanston, Ill.; adv. coun. H-F Bus. Ptnr., 2000; mem. pres. counsel McGeorge Sch. Law, 2001-. Pres., coach Homewood-Flossmoor (Ill.) Soccer Club, 1985—, Intercollegiate Varsity Athletics (soccer and lacrosse); co-chair soccer Ill. Prairie State Games, 1992; pres. P.O.P.S. Homewood-Flossmoor H.S., 1996—; mem. bd. edn., pers. chairperson Homewood-Flossmoor H.S., 1998—, mem. improvement coun., 2001-. Recipient Judge Mason Rothwell Award, 1979, Cert. of Merit Chgo. Legal Svcs. Found., 1983. Mem. ABA, ATLA, Am. Corp. Counsel Assn. (labor and employment sect.), Ill. Bar Assn., Chgo. Bar Assn., Am. Arbitrators Assn. (arbitrator), Am. Judicature Soc., Ill. Trial Lawyers Assn., North Shore (Ill.) Labor Counsel Assn., Phi Delta Phi, Alpha Epsilon Pi. Democrat. Jewish. Avocations: soccer, lacrosse. Home: PO Box 374 Flossmoor IL 60422-0374 Office: W W Grainger Inc 100 Grainger Pkwy Lake Forest IL 60045-5201

GALATZ, NEIL GILBERT, lawyer; b. N.Y.C., Jan. 22, 1933; s. Julius D. and Dorothy (Kirschen) G.; m. Elaine Bricker, Aug. 20, 1961; children: Leesa, Lara. BA, Adelphi U., 1953; JD, Columbia U., 1956. Bar: N.Y. 1957, Nev. 1958, U.S. Dist. Ct. Nev. 1958, U.S. Ct. Appeals (9th cir.), U.S. Supreme Ct. 1976. Sr. trial dep., dist. atty. Clark County Dist. Attys. Office, Las Vegas, 1959-61; assoc. Langerman, Begam & Lewis, Phoenix, 1961-62; ptnr. Wiener, Goldwater & Galatz, Las Vegas, 1967-76; sr. ptnr. Neil G. Galatz & Assocs., Las Vegas, 1976—. Deans couns., Univ. Nev., 1995-97; spl. adv., Nev. Legis. Com., 1970-71; co-chmn., Plaintiff's Lead Counsel Com. MGM Multi-Dist. Fire Litigation, 1980-82, Hilton Fire Litigation, 1981-86; chmn. PEPCON Explosion Plaintiffs Com., 1988-92; lectr. in field. Mem. ATLA (gov. 1967-72, 76-77, 2001-03, chmn. midwinter convs. 1964, 68, 71, 73, 76, 85, student advocacy program 1973-74, legal inst. program 69, 71, citation for outstanding leadership, 1971), Internat. Acad. Trial Lawyers, Am. Bd. Trial Advocates, Western Trial Lawyers Assn. (pres. 1964-65). Internat. Soc. Barristers, Nat. Bd. Trial Advocacy, Nev. State Bar Assn. (bd. govs. 1990-00). Office: Neil G Galatz & Assocs 710 S 4th St Las Vegas NV 89101-6707 E-mail: neilgalatz@aol.com.

GALAZKA, JACEK MICHAL, publishing executive; b. Wilno, Poland, Apr. 28, 1924; s. Michal J. and Zofia Galazka; m. Jacoba J. M. Jansen, July 22, 1958. B.Com., U. Edinburgh, 1948. Dir. sales and promotion St. Martin's Press, N.Y.C., 1955-63; mgr. reference dept. Charles Scribner's Sons, N.Y.C., 1963-67, dir. mktg., 1967-74, dir. trade pub., 1974-78, exec. v.p., 1978-83, pres., 1983-85; pub. spl. interest books Macmillan Pub. Co., 1985-86, v.p., 1986; pub. The Polish Heritage Publ., 1987—, Hippocrene Books, N.Y.C., 1988—; editor, assoc. pub. New Horizon, 1998—2001. Author: 2 books; translator. With Polish Forces, 1942—45, U.K. Mem.: Pilsudski Inst. Am. (pres. 1999—). Home: 75 Warren Hill Rd PO Box 8 New York NY 10010 Office: Hippocrene Books Inc 171 Madison Ave New York NY 10016-5110

GALBIS, RICARDO, psychiatrist; b. La Habana, Cuba, Feb. 2, 1936; came to U.S., 1957; s. Ricardo and Maria Josefa (Beltran) G.; children: Maya, Ricardo Jose. BA, BS, La Salle Coll., Habana, 1953; MD, Wake Forest U., 1960. Diplomate Am. Bd Psychiatry. Resident in psychiatry U. Hosp., Paris, 1963—67; fellow Dept. Child Psychiatry Georgetown U., Washington, 1967-69; dir., co-founder Washington Free Clinic, 1968-70; psychiat. attending physician HHS, Washington, 1976-88; sr. attending psychiatrist Washington Hosp. Ctr., 1970—; exec. dir., founder ANDROMEDA, Inc., Washington, 1970—; adminstr. La Ceiba, Inc., Washington, 1989—. Cons. Pan Am. Health Orgn., Washington, 1985—; exec. bd. dirs Amigos de los Zoologicos Latinoamericanos ; mentor psychiatry and family practice cmty. programs Howard U., Georgetown U., Washington. Contbr. articles to profl. jours. Mem. ad hoc com. Access to Health Care, Washington, 1987—; COMMR. Commn. for Latino Community Devel., Washington, 1984-87. Vis. scholar French Govt., 1963-67; recipient Community Svc. award D.C. Med. Soc., 1984; named Washingtonian of Yr. Washingtonian Mag., 1985. Fellow: Washington Anthrop. Soc. (life), Am. Psychiat. Assn. (life); mem.: Medico a Medico. Democrat. Avocations: book collecting, snorkeling, canoeing. Home: 1843 S St NW Washington DC 20009-6124 Office: ANDROMEDA 1400 Decatur St NW Washington DC 20011-4376 E-mail: galbisb@aol.com., andromedatransc@aol.com.

GALBIS-REIG, DAVID, health facility administrator, physician, consultant, researcher; b. Washington, Apr. 10, 1974; s. Vicente and Josefina Galbis; m. Eva M. Vidal-Revert, Jan. 15, 1999. BS, Coll. William and Mary, 1995; MD, Va. Commonwealth U., 1999. Resident in psychiatry Va. Commonwealth U., Richmond, 1999; Spanish-English med. translator Richmond, Va., 1999—; ind. cons., 2000—; med. dir. Commonwealth Health Benefits Mgmt., Inc., Richmond, Va., 2000—. Ind. med. cons. Pfizer/Searle Pharma, Richmond, Va., 2000—01. Contbr. articles to profl. jours. Mem.: AMA, Am. Translators Assn., Am. Diabetes Assn., Am. Psychiat. Assn., Am. Coll. Occupl. and Environ. Medicine (assoc.), Phi Beta Kappa, Alpha Omega Alpha. Avocations: spending time with family and friends, soccer, reading science fiction and fantasy. Home: 2415 Fon Du Lac Rd Richmond VA 23229 Office: Commonwealth Health Benefits Mgmt 5823 Patterson Ave Richmond VA 23226

GALBRAITH, ALLAN LEE, lawyer; b. Feb. 16, 1955; s. Graeme C. and Joanne (Brack) Galbraith; m. Lorena Gail Boyd, May 28, 1982. BS in Bus., U. Idaho, 1977, JD, 1980. CPA Wash.; bar: Wash. 1980. Staff acct. Boyd Olofson & Co., C.P.A.s, Yakima, Wash., 1980—82; ptnr. Carlson Drewelow Galbraith Card & McMahon P.S., Wenatchee, Wash., 1982—92, Card & Galbraith PS, Wenatchee, 1992—97, Davis, Arneil Law Firm, LLP, Wenatchee, 1997—. Instr. bus. law Wenatchee Valley C.C.; dir., pres. Chelan-Douglas County Cmty. Action Coun., Wenatchee. Mem.: ABA, Wash. Soc. C.P.A.s, Wash. Bar Assn. (com. of bar examiners 1986—94, spl. dist. counsel profl. conduct sect. 1995—), Rotary (Wenatchee), Ctrl. Wash. Hosp. Found., Wenatchee Area C. of C.

GALBRAITH, JAMES MARSHALL, lawyer, business executive; b. Iowa City, Oct. 4, 1942; s. John Semple and Laura (Huddleston) G.; m. Margaret Rodi, Aug. 19, 1966; children: Margaret Laura, Katherine Lou, Robert James. BA, Pomona Coll., 1964; JD, Stanford U., 1967. Bar: Calif. 1968. Assoc. Gibson, Dunn & Crutcher, Los Angeles, 1967-68; ptnr. Rodi, Pollock, Pettker, Galbraith & Cahill, Los Angeles, 1968-84, of counsel, 1984—2003; pres. Bell Helmets Internat., Inc., San Marino, Calif., 1980-84; ptnr. Palm Properties Co., San Marino, Calif., 1979—2001. Pres., dir. Van de Kamp's Bakers, Inc., San Marino, Calif., 1984—87; ptnr. Huntington Hotel Assocs., San Marino, 1986—95; pres. Crestmont Fin. Svcs., Inc., 1991—, Crestmont Industries, LLC, 1996—. Author: In the Name of the People, 1977, The Money Tree, 1982, Fear of Failure, 1993, Patient Power, 1995; mem. bd. editors Stanford Law Rev., 1965-67. Trustee Pomona Coll., 1987-89, hon. trustee, 1989—; trustee, mem. exec. com. Children's Hosp. L.A., 1986-91, hon. trustee, 1991—; mem. Soc. of Fellows, Huntington Libr. Art Gallery and Bot. Gardens, 1982—; mem. Young Pres. Orgn., 1979-93. Mem. State Bar Calif., Phi Beta Kappa. Clubs: California (L.A.), Valley Hunt (Pasadena). Episcopalian. Home: 1640 Oak Grove Ave San Marino CA 91108-1109 Office: 2600 Mission St San Marino CA 91108-1676

GALBRAITH, JOHN KENNETH, retired economist; b. Iona Station, Ont., Can., Oct. 15, 1908; s. William Archibald and Catherine (Kendall) Galbraith; m. Catherine Atwater, Sept. 17, 1937; children: Alan, Peter, James. BS, U. Guelph, 1931, LLD (hon.); MS, U. Calif., 1933, PhD, 1934; postgrad., Cambridge (Eng.) U., 1937—38; LLD (hon.), Bard Coll., U. Calif.; LLD (hon.), Miami U.; LLD (hon.), U. Mass., U. Mysore, Brandeis U., U. Toronto, U. Sask., U. Mich., U. Durham, R.I. Coll., Boston Coll., Hobart and William Smith Colls., Albion Coll., Tufts U., Adelphi Suffolk Coll., Mich. State U., Louvain U., Oxford U., U. Paris, Carleton Coll., U. Vt., Queens U., Moscow State U., Harvard U., Smith Coll. London Sch. Economics, others. Rsch. fellow U. Calif., 1931—34; instr. and tutor Harvard U., 1934—39; asst. prof. econs. Princeton U., 1939—42; econ. adviser Nat. Def. Adv. Commn., 1940—41; asst. adminstr. in charge price div. OPA, 1941—42, dep. adminstr., 1942—43; mem. bd. of editors Fortune Mag., 1943—48; lectr. Harvard U., 1948—49, prof. econs., 1949—75, Paul M. Warburg prof. econs., 1959—75, ret., 1975. Hon. fellow Trinity Coll., Cambridge U.; hon. prof. U. Geneva; U.S. amb. to India, 1961—63. Author: numerous books including, American Capitalism, 1952, A Theory of Price Control, 1952, The Great Crash, 1955, The Affluent Society, 1958, The Liberal Hour, 1960, Economic Development, 1963, The Scotch, 1964, The New Industrial State, 1967, Indian Painting, 1968, Ambassador's Journal, 1969, Economics, Peace and Laughter, 1971, A China Passage, 1973, Economics and the Public Purpose, 1973, Money: Whence It Came, Where It Went, 1975, The Age of Uncertainity, 1977; author: (with Nicole Salinger) Almost Everyone's Guide to Economics, 1978; author: Annals of an Abiding Liberal, 1979, The Nature of Mass Poverty, 1979, A Life in Our Times, 1981, The Anatomy of Power, 1983, The Voice of the Poor: Essays in Economic and Political Persuasion, 1983, A View From the Stands, 1986, Economics in Perspective: A Critical History, 1987; author: (with Stanislav Menshikov) Capitalism, Communism and Coexistence, 1988; author: (novels) The Triumph, 1968, A Tenured Professor, 1990, The Culture of Contentment, 1992, A Journey Through Economic Time, 1994, A Short History of Financial Euphoria, 1993, The Good Society, 1996, Name-Dropping From F.D.R. on, 1999, The Essential Galbraith, 2001; contbr. to econ. and sci. jours. Dir. U.S. Strategic Bombing Survey, 1945, Office of Econ. Security Policy, State Dept., 1946. Recipient Medal of Freedom, 2000; fellow, Social Sci. Rsch. Coun., 1937—38. Fellow: Am. Acad. Arts and Letters (pres. 1984—87); mem.: AAAS, Ams. for Dem. Action (chmn. 1967—68), Am. Agrl. Econ. Assn., Am. Econ. Assn. (pres. 1972), Saturday, Century. Home: 30 Francis Ave Cambridge MA 02138-2010 Office: Harvard U 206 Littauer Ctr Cambridge MA 02138 Fax: 617-496-1200.*

GALBRAITH, NANETTE ELAINE GERKS, forensic and management sciences company executive; b. Chgo., June 15, 1928; d. Harold William and Maybelle Ellen (Little) Gerks; m. Oliver Galbraith III, Dec. 18, 1948; children: Craig Scott, Diane Frances. BS with high honors with distinction, San Diego State U., 1978. Diplomate Am. Bd. Forensic Document Examiners. Examiner of questioned documents San Diego County Sheriff's Dept. Crime Lab., San Diego, 1975-80; sole prop. Nanette G. Galbraith, Examiner of Questioned Documents, San Diego, 1980-82; pres., examiner of questioned documents Galbraith Forensic & Mgmt. Scis., Ltd., San Diego, 1982-97; cons., 1997—. Keynote spkr. Internat. Assn Forensic Scis., Adelaide, South Australia, 1990. Contbr. articles to profl. jours. including Jour. Forensic Scis., Forensic Sci. Internat., Internat. Jour. Forensic Document Examiners. Fellow: Am. Acad. Forensic Scis. (del. to Peoples Rep. of China 1986, USSR 1988, questioned documents sect.); mem.: Southwestern Assn. Forensic Document Examiners (charter), Am. Soc. Questioned Document Examiners (life; jour. editl. bd. 2000—), 1909 Univ. Club San Diego, Southwestern Yacht Club (life), Phi Kappa Phi. Republican. Episcopalian. E-mail: nggalbrait@aol.com.

GALBRAITH, RUTH LEGG, retired university dean, home economist; b. Lecompte, La., Nov. 5, 1923; d. Byron S. and Dora Ruth (Lindley) Legg; m. Harry W. Galbraith, June 16, 1950; 1 son, Allan Legg. BS, Purdue U., 1945, PhD, 1950. Chemist E.I. duPont de Nemours, Waynesboro, Va., 1945-46; textile chemist Gen. Electric Co., Bridgeport, Conn., 1946-47; teaching asst. Purdue U., 1947-48, research fellow, 1948-50; prof. textiles and clothing U. Tenn., Knoxville, 1950-55; asso. prof. U. Ill., Urbana, 1956-64, prof., 1964-70, chmn. textiles and clothing div., 1962-70; prof., head consumer affairs dept. Auburn (Ala.) U., 1970-73; dean Sch. Home Econs., head home econs. research, 1973-85. Mem. task force on quality of living Dept. Agr., 1967-68; mem. nat. adv. com. Flammable Fabrics Act, 1971-73; mem. U.S. Dept. Agr. Com. of Nine, 1981-83, chmn., 1983 Mem. editorial bd.: Research Jour. Home Econs., 1973-77, chmn. policy bd., 1978-80; contbr. articles to profl. jours. Recipient Disting. Alumni award Purdue U., 1970 Fellow Am. Inst. Chemists; mem. Am. Home Econs. Assn. (chmn. agy. mem. unit 1975-76, chmn. research sect. 1978-80, Outstanding Home Economist award 1984), Ala. Home Econs. Assn. (pres. 1983-84), Am. Assn. Textile Chemists and Colorists, Am. Chem. Soc., ASTM (3d v.p. com. D-13 textiles 1975-79), Assn. Adminstrs. Home Econs., Nat. Council Adminstrs. Home Econs., AAUW, Sigma Xi, Omicron Nu, Phi Kappa Phi, Delta Kappa Gamma. Home: 368 Singleton St Auburn AL 36830-6317

GALBRAITH, WILLIAM BRUCE, physician, educator; b. Romeo, Mich., Oct. 21, 1930; s. Bruce McKenzie and Helen Athelene (Stringham) G.; m. Jo Anne Fetterly Ames, June 27, 1953; children: Elise, Susan, Scott. BS, Ariz. State U., 1953; MD, George Washington U., 1957. Diplomate Am. Bd. Internal Medicine. Internship Good Samaritan Hosp., Phoenix, 1957-58; residency U. Iowa Hosps. and Clinics, Iowa City, 1958-61; instr. internal medicine U. Iowa Coll. Medicine, Iowa City, 1961-63, asst. prof., 1963-65, dir. gen. medicine tng. program, 1994-96, assoc. internal medicine, 1994-95; prof. clin. internal medicine U. Iowa, Iowa City, 1995-97, prof. emeritus, 1998—; owner Internists P.C., Cedar Rapids, Iowa, 1965-93, pres., 1986-93. Bd. dirs. Am. Bd. Internal Medicine, Phila., 1992-96. Trustee Mercy Med. Ctr., Cedar Rapids, 1997—, Meth-Wick Cmty., 1999—. Fellow ACP/ASIM (gov. for Iowa 1979-83, Laureate award 1988, master 1997); mem. Iowa Clin. Soc. Internal Medicine (Internist of Yr. 1994), Alpha Omega Alpha. Avocations: flyfishing, photography, birding. E-mail: WGalbra66@aol.com.

GALBREATH, JOSEPH C. pharmacist; b. Monmouth, Ill., Aug. 16, 1947; s. Lyle Keith Galbreath and Ada May Conard; m. Karen Sue Meyers, Jan. 3, 1981 (div. July 1996); children: Patrice Erin, Erin Alexis. BS in Pharmacy, U. Iowa, 1970. Registered pharmacist, Ill. Staff pharmacist One Stop Pharmacies, Rockford, Ill., 1970-72; pharmacy mgr. Wickwire Drug, Byron, Ill., 1972-78, Walgreens #930, Sterling, Ill., 1978-87, Walmart, Sterling, 1987-97; dir. of pharmacy Morrison (Ill.) Cmty. Hosp., 1997—. Pharmacy cons. Exceptional Care and Tng. Ctr., Sterling, 1980-86, Sterling Care Ctr., Edgewild and Colonial Acres Nursing Homes, 1980s. Mem. So. Poverty Law Ctr., ACLU, N.Y.C. With Ill. ARNG, 1970-76. Mem. Tebala Shrine Temple (life), Tebala Klownarabians (vet. mem.), Freeport Consistory Bodies, Masons (life mem. Byron lodge, chaplain 1974-78), Midwest Old Threshers and Settlers Democrat. Methodist.

Avocations: collecting polit. memorabilia, antiques, art, ephemera, travel. Home: 1308 E Lynn Blvd Apt C Sterling IL 61081-1474 Office: Morrison Cmty Hosp 303 N Jackson St Morrison IL 61270-3042

GALBUT, MARTIN RICHARD, lawyer; b. Miami Beach, Fla., June 27, 1946; s. Paul A. and Ethel (Kolnick) G.; m. Cynthia Ann Slaughter, June 4, 1972; children: Keith Richard, Lindsay Anne. BS in Speech, Northwestern U., 1968, JD cum laude, 1971. Bar: Ariz. 1972, U.S. Dist. Ct. Ariz. 1972, U.S. Ct. Appeals (9th cir.) 1972. Assoc. Brown, Vlassis & Bain PA, Phoenix, 1971-75; founder, ptnr. McLoone, Theobald & Galbut PC, Phoenix, 1975-86; of counsel Furth, Fahrner, Bluemle & Mason, 1986-89; founder Galbut & Hunter, PC, Phoenix, 1989—. Presenter guest Law Talk cable TV; former judge pro tem Maricopa County Superior Ct.; lectr. comml. real estate litigation, arbitration, mediation and intellectual property law Lorman Bus. Seminars, others. Contbr. articles to profl. jours. Chmn., Ariz. State Air Pollution Control Hearing Bd., 1984-89; active Govs. Task Force on Urban Air Quality, 1986, City Phoenix Environ. Quality Commn., 1987-88; bd. dirs. Men's Art Council Phoenix Art Mus.; bd. dirs., founder Ariz. Asthma Found. Clarion de Witt Hardy scholar, Kosmerl scholar; Russel Sage grantee. Mem. ABA, Ariz. State Bar Assn. (lectr., securities law litigation com. and sect.), Am. Arbitration Assn. (arbitrator), Nat. Assn. Securities Dealers (arbitrator, trainer and lectr.). Democrat. Jewish. Avocations: painting, collecting antiques and fine art, international travel, golf. Office: Galbut & Hunter PC 2425 E Camelback Rd Ste 1020 Phoenix AZ 85016-4216

GALDA, DWIGHT WILLIAM, financial company executive; b. Bklyn., Dec. 19, 1942; s. Fred C. and Audrey D. G.; m. Margaret L., Mar. 21, 1992; children: Cynthia A., Gregory J. BA, Widener U., 1964; postgrad., Am. U., 1965—67; MBA, Tex. Christian U., 2000; MPA, MS, U. Tex., 2002. ChFC; cert. Nat. Assn. Securities Dealers; registered Prin. and Natl. Panal Arbitration. Rep. United Svcs. Planning Assn. and Ind. Rsch. Agy., Ft. Worth, 1983-86; dist. exec. USPA and IRA, Ft. Worth, 1986-92, regional exec., 1992-96, prin., 1990-96, Carefree (Ariz.) Capital Mgmt. and Rsch., Carefree, Ariz., 1997—. Ind. cons. Dwight W. Galda Consultancy, 1985-, adf. econ. prof., Ariz. State U., 2003-; spkr. in field. Contbr. articles profl. jours.; creator U.S. Army Opposing Force Program, 1976. Lt. col. U.S. Army, 1964-82; Army attache U.S. Embassy, Cambodia, 1973-75. Recipient Pace award Dept. of Army, 1976, 77; Legion of Merit, Bronze star with V and 2 oak leaf clusters, Meritorious Svc. medal 4 oak leaf clusters, air medal with V and 4 oak leaf clusters, Vietnamese Cross of Gallantry with Silver star, Cambodian Nat. Def. Svc. medal. Fellow Assn. Investment Mgmt. and Rsch., Phoenix Soc. Investment Analysts. Episcopalian. Avocations: running, chamber music, travel. Home: 39401 N Spanish Boot Carefree AZ 85377 Office: Drawer 1168 100 Easy St Carefree AZ 85377-9600 E-mail: DGalda@CS.com.

GALDI-WEISSMAN, NATALIE ANN, secondary education educator; b. N.Y.C., Nov. 28, 1948; d. Alphonse Vincent and Jean (Banek) Galdi; m. David Allen Weissman, Feb. 7, 1987; 1 child, Adam Justin Weissman. BA, Adelphi U., 1970, MA, 1971; PhD, NYU, 1978. Tchr. Jr. High Sch. 101, N.Y.C., 1971-81, Evander Child High Sch., N.Y.C., 1981-82, South Bronx High Sch., N.Y.C., 1982—. Adj. prof. Mercy Coll., Dobbs Ferry, N.Y., 1976-88; prep. coord. South Bronx High Sch., acad. olympics coach, 1985-87, curriculum developer, 1987-90, 2000-03; tutor, 2002-03. Mem. Union Fedn. Tchr. Avocations: gardening, environmental wildlife affairs, needlepoint, knitting, dog training. E-mail: natalie797@aol.com.

GALE, ARNOLD DAVID, pediatric neurologist, consultant; b. Chgo., Nov. 2, 1949; s. Benjamin and Revelle Frances (Steinman) G.; m. Sharon Ann Stone, 1997. AB summa cum laude, Stanford U., 1971; MD, Johns Hopkins U., 1976. Diplomate Am. Bd. Pediat., Nat. Bd. Med. Examiners; med. lic., Calif. Resident in pediat. Mass. Gen. Hosp., Boston, 1976-78; postdoctoral fellow Johns Hopkins Hosp., Balt., 1978-79, resident in neurology, 1979-82; asst. prof. pediat. and neurology George Washington U. Sch. Medicine, Washington, 1982-89; dir. neurology tng. program Children's Hosp. Nat. Med. Ctr., Washington, 1982-89; clin. assoc. prof. neurology, neurological scis. and pediat. Sch. of Med. Stanford U., Stanford, Calif., 1989—; med. info. officer Muscular Dystrophy Assn., Tucson, 1992—. Cons. neurologist Vaccine Injury Program U.S. Dept. HHS, Rockville, Md., 1989—, Inst. Vaccine Saftey, Bloomberg Sch. Pub. Health Johns Hopkins U., Balt., 1998—, Anthrax Vaccine Expert Com., 1999—; mem. adv. panel FDA, Rockville, 1983—89; vis. lectr. U. Pitts. Sch. Medicine, 1981—89; clin. expert immunization com. U.S. Dept. of Health and Human Svcs., Rockville, 2003—; cons. Office Human Rsch. Protection U.S. Dept. Health and Human Svcs., 2003—; cons. Brighton Collaboration, Ctrs. for Disease Control, Atlanta, 2003—. Author: Pediatric Emergency Medicine, 1989; contbr. articles to profl. jours. Support group coord. Muscular Dystrophy Assn., San Jose, Calif., 1989—; mem. Pres.'s Com. Employment of People Disabilities, Washington, 1992—; med. adv. bd. Multiple Sclerosis Soc., Santa Clara, Calif., 1990—; v.p. Muscular Dystrophy Assn., Tucson, 1992-94, bd. dirs., 1993-96. Recipient Nat. Rehab. award, Allied Svcs., Scranton, Pa., 1994. Fellow Am. Acad. Pediat.; mem. Am. Acad. Neurology, Am. Soc. Neurol. Investigation (founding mem.), Am. Acad. Immunotherapy, Child Neurology Soc., Calif. Children's Lobby, Nat. Alumni Coun. (Johns Hopkins U.), Phi Beta Kappa, Alpha Omega Alpha. Jewish. Avocations: writing, travel. Office: 335 Elan Village Ln Unit 107 San Jose CA 95134-2540

GALE, DANIEL BAILEY, architect; b. St. Louis, Nov. 6, 1933; s. Leone Caryll and Gladys (Wotowa) G.; student Brown U., 1951-53, Ecole Des Beaux Arts, Paris, 1954-55; BArch., Washington U., 1957; m. Nancy Susan Miller, June 15, 1957; children: Caroline Hamilton, Rebecca Fletcher, Daniel Bailey With Gale & Cannon, Architects and Planners, Hellmuth, Obata & Kassabaum, Inc., Architects, St. Louis, and exec. v.p. corp. devel., dir. HOK, Inc., St. Louis, 1961-79; ptnr. Heneghan and Gale, architects and planners, Aspen, Colo., 1967-69; pres., chief exec. officer Gale Kober Assocs., San Francisco, 1979-83; pvt. practice architecture, Belvedere, Calif., 1984—; pres. Program Mgmt. Inc., Belvedere, 1984—. Recipient Henry Adams prize Washington U., 1957. Mem. AIA, Singapore Inst. Architects. Home and Office: 280 Belvedere Ave Belvedere CA 94920-2425

GALE, DIANE, music educator; b. Boston, Mass., Mar. 19, 1957; d. Charles Levine and Caroyln Ada Kaitz; m. Allen Gale, Jan. 10, 1987. BA, St. Joseph Coll., 1981; MS, C.W. Post Coll. Long Island U, 1987; student, Stony Brook U, 1988—. Piano tchr. SPTF, Suffolk County, NY, 1987—; music tchr. Solomon Schaeher Day Sch., Commache, NY, 1994—2002; adj. piano, voice NYSSMA, NY, 1998—; children's choir dir. Conglist. Ch. of Patchoque (N.Y.), 1999—; music tchr. Connetiguot Sch., Bohemar, NY, 2002—. Soprano I Long Island Symphonic Choral Assn., Bay Area Fine Arts BAFFA. Home: 33 Gabon Lane Coram NY 11727-1416

GALE, DOUGLAS MAXWELL, economics educator; b. Ottawa, Ont., Can., Mar. 27, 1950; m. Susan Elizabeth Dick, July 5, 1980. BSc, Trent U., Peterborough, Ont., 1970; MA, Carleton U., Ottawa, Ont., 1972; PhD, Cambridge (Eng.) U., 1975. Jr. rsch. fellow Cambridge U., 1975-78; lectr., reader, prof. London Sch. Econs., 1978-86; prof. econs. U. Pitts., 1986-90, Boston U., 1990-96; prof. econs., chmn. dept. NYU, N.Y.C., 1996—. Vis., assoc. prof., prof. U. Pa., 1984-88; vis. prof. MIT, Cambridge, 1989-90; mem. adv. panel NSF, 1991-92 Author: Money in Equilibrium, 1982, Money in Disequilibrium, 1983, Strategic Foundations of General Equilibrium: Dynamic Matching and Bargaining Games, 2000, Comparing Financial Systems, 2000; asst. editor Rev. Econ. Studies, 1980-83; co-editor Econ. Theory, 1990-92; assoc. editor, co-editor Econometrica, 1990-96; adv. editor Macroecon. Dynamics; assoc. editor Jour. Econ. Theory, 1986-92, 1996-2001, Rsch. in Econs., Econ. Theory. Sr. fellow Fin. Instns. Ctr., Wharton Sch., U. Pa. Fellow Econometric Soc. Office: NYU Dept Econs New York NY 10003 Fax: 212-995-3932. E-mail: douglas.gale@nyu.edu.

GALE, EDWIN JOHN, judge; b. Brattleboro, Vt., Apr. 8, 1943; s. Richard Ephriam and Florence (Mead) G.; m. Mary Elizabeth Gale; children: Karen Elizabeth, Brian Paul. BS, U.S. Naval Acad., 1965; JD, U. Santa Clara, 1972. Bar: Calif. 1972, R.I. 1979, U.S. Dist. Ct. R.I., U.S. Dist. Ct. (no. dist.) Ohio, U.S. Dist. Ct. Mass., U.S. Dist. Ct. (cen. dist.) Calif., U.S. Ct. Appeals (1st cir.). Atty. organized crime and racketeering sect. U.S. Dept. Justice, Cleve., Washington and Providence, 1972-85, chief L.A. strike force organized crime and racketeering sect., 1985-87; 1st asst. U.S. Atty.'s Office, Providence, 1987-93; U.S. atty. U.S. Dept. Justice, Providence, 1993-94; fed. bar examiner, 1995-2001; judge R.I. Superior Ct., 2001—. Fed. Bar Examiner, 1995—2000. Mem. R.I. Ho. of Dels., 1997-2001. Capt. USNR, ret. Home: 215 Kings Ridge Rd Wakefield RI 02879-2401 Office: RI Superior Ct 250 Benefit St Providence RI 02903

GALE, FOURNIER JOSEPH, III, lawyer; b. Mobile, Ala., Aug. 3, 1944; s. Fournier J. Jr. and Clara (Beckham) G.; m. Louise Smith, Aug. 7, 1965; children: Carolyn, Jeanette. BA, U. Ala., 1966, JD, 1969; postgrad., Oxford U., summer 1968. Bar: Ala. 1969. From assoc. to ptnr. Cabaniss, Johnston, Gardner, Dumas & O'Neal, Birmingham, Ala., 1969-84; ptnr. Maynard, Cooper & Gale, PC, Birmingham, 1984—. Bd. dirs. McWane, Inc., Birmingham; gen. counsel, bd. dirs. Bus. Coun. Ala., Birmingham, 1977—; bd. dirs., So. Rsch. Inst.; mem. Ala. Permanent Study Commn. on Judiciary, 1977-83; mem. Jefferson County Jud. Nominating Commn., 1993-2000; chmn. Ala. Commn. on Higher Edn., 1998-2003; spl. counsel to Gov. Don Siegelman, 1999-2002. Mem. Leadership Birmingham, 1986-87; pres. U. Ala. Law Sch. Found., 1987-89. Mem. ABA (standing com. on environ. law, standing com. on fed. judiciary), Birmingham Bar Assn. (pres. 1989), Ala. Young Lawyers Assn. (pres. 1976-77), Am. Judicature Soc. (bd. dirs. 1980-85), Jud. Conf. Ala., Am. Bar Found., Kiwanis. Roman Catholic. Home: 2937 Southwood Rd Birmingham AL 35223-1232 Office: Maynard Cooper & Gale PC 2400 Amsouth Harbert Plz Birmingham AL 35203-2600

GALE, J. DARREN, nuclear energy industry executive; b. San Antonio, Tex., Feb. 26, 1961; s. Darrel Dee and Coleen Elaine Gale; m. Marsha B. Hall, Dec. 30, 1983; children: Derek Jameson, Madeline Elizabeth. BS in Nuc. Engring., Kans. State U., 1983, MS in Nuc. Engring., 1984; MBA, Averett Coll., 1996. Technician Gen. Atomic, San Diego, 1984—86; team leader Advanced Nuc. Fuels, Richland, Wash., 1986—91; v.p. U.S. region fuel bus. unit Framatome ANP, Lynchburg, Va., 1991—. Adv. bd. dept. nuc. engring. Fla. U., Gainesville, 2000—; founding bd. dirs. Ctrl. Va. Gov.'s Sch. Sci. Tech., Lynchburg, 2002—. Mem. ch. coun., Lynchburg, 2001—03. Recipient 1st-team Acad. All-Am. Football Team, Coll. Sports Info. Dir. of Am., 1981, 1st-team Acad. All-Am. Football Team, Coll. Sports Info. Dirs. Am., 1982, Mem. Blue Key, Kans. State Chpt. Blue Key, 1981-82; scholar Leader of Tomorrow, Dane G. Hansen Found., 1979—82; Inst. Nuc. Power Ops., 1981, 1982; Student Scholar, Big Eight Athletic Conf., 1983. Mem.: Boonsboro Country Club, Phi Kappa Phi. Roman Catholic. Achievements include development of Gadolinia absorber. Avocations: golf, running, basketball, reading, travel. Home: 100 Fairfax Court Lynchburg VA 24503 Office: Framatome ANP 3315 Old Forest Rd Lynchburg VA 24506-0935 Office Fax: 434-832-2629. E-mail: darren.gale@framatome-anp.com.

GALE, JOHN A. secretary of state; b. Omaha, Nebraska, 1940; m. Carol Gale; children: David, Elaine, Steve. BA in govt. internat. relations, Carleton Coll., Northfield, Minn., 1962; JD in govt. internat. relations, Univ. Chgo. Law Sch., Northfield, Minn., 1965. Sec. state State of Nebr., 2000—; pvt. practice of law 30 yrs.; elected state chmn. Nebr. State Rep. Party, 1986; asst. U.S. atty. Lincoln, 1971; legis. asst. Wash., DC, 1968; asst. U.S. atty. Omaha, 1965. Republican. Office: NE Sec State State Capitol Ste 2300 Lincoln NE 68509

GALE, JOSEPH H. federal judge; b. Smithfield, Va., 1953; s. Robert Whitfield and Charlotte H. G. AB, Princeton U., 1976; JD, U. Va., 1980. Atty. Dewey, Ballantine, Bushby, Palmer & Wood, N.Y.C., Washington, 1980-83, Dickstein, Shapiro & Morin, Washington, 1983-84; legis. counsel Senator Daniel P. Moynihan, Washington, 1985-88; adminstrv. asst. and tax counsel Hon. Daniel P. Moynihan, Washington, 1989, chief counsel, 1990-92; chief tax counsel Senate Finance Com., Washington, 1993-94, minority chief of staff, 1995; judge U.S. Tax Ct., Washington, 1996—. Dillard fellow U. Va. Office: US Tax Court 400 2nd St NW Washington DC 20217-0002

GALE, NEIL JAN, Internet company executive, computer scientist, consultant; b. Chgo., Jan. 12, 1960; s. Jack and Adele (Field) G. AA in Computer Sci., Wright Coll., 1980; D of Bus. Mgmt. (hon.), London Inst. Applied Rsch., 1993; diploma, Academia Argentina de Diplomacia, 1994; diploma (hon.), Institut Des Affaires Internationales, Paris, 1994; D of Bus. Mgmt. (hon.), World Acad., Monchengladbach, Germany, 1994. Mgr. Gen. Fin. Co., Chgo., 1980-84; mktg. mgr. Midland Fin. Co., Chgo., 1984-85; mktg. dir. Diamond Mortgage Corp., Chgo., 1985-86; sr. fin. analyst McKay Mazda-Nissan, Evanston, Ill., 1987-88; pres., CEO, Nat. Consumer Credit Cons., Chgo., 1988—; webmaster Everything Internet (merger with Millenium Techs. Inc. 1998), Naperville, Ill., 1996-98; pres. DrGale.com, Carol Stream, Ill., 1998—. Hon. prof. bus. mgmt. Inst. des Hautes Etudes Econs. et Sociales, Brussels, 1993; hon. prof. fin. Australian Inst. Coordinated Rsch., 1994; mem. adv. coun. Internat. Biog. Ctr., Cambridge, Eng.; mem. bd. govs., Continental gov. Am. Biog. Inst., 1990—, mem. rsch. bd. advisors, 1989—; notary pub. Ill., 1986-90; bd. dirs., amb. Ill. affiliate U.S. Woman's C. of C., 2002—; bd. dirs. U.S. Dept. of Peace Coaliton, 2003—. Contbr. articles to profl. jours. First aid chmn. Walk with Israel, 1977; notary pub., Ill., 1986-90; mem. computer com. Village of Hanover Park, Ill., 1997-2000; mem. bd. advisors U.S. Women's C. of C., 2002-. Decorated Knight of Order of San Ciriaco; recipient Bus. in Urban Environment award Chgo. Bd. Edn. and Ill. Bell Tel. Co., 1978, Outstanding Achievement award Chgo. Pub. Libr., 1979. Mem. Auto Credit (hon.), Friendship Cir. Club (treas. 1976-78). Avocation: collecting antique Chicago postcards and books. Home and Office: DrGale dot com PMB 208 780 W Army Trail Rd Carol Stream IL 60188-9297 E-mail: drgale@drgale.com.

GALE, ROBERT HARRISON, JR., lawyer; b. Syracuse, Kans., Feb. 21, 1953; s. Robert H. and Avonne (Gould) G.; m. Linda C. Reitz, June 18, 1978; children: Joshua Robert, Zachary Tyler. BS, U. Kans., 1975, JD, 1978. Bar: Kans. 1978, U.S. Dist. Ct. Kans. 1978, U.S. Ct. Appeals (10th cir.) 1978. Asst. dist. atty. Johnson County, Olathe, Kans., 1978-79; Hamilton County atty. Syracuse, Kans., 1979-85, 2000—; ptnr. Gale & Gale, Syracuse, 1983-88; city atty. Syracuse, 1988—; dir. First Nat. Bank, Syracuse, 1980-82; dir., pres. S.C.A.T., Inc., Syracuse, 1982-84. Precinct committeeman Dem. Party, Johnson and Hamilton Counties, Kans.; county chmn. Dem. party; elder First Presbyn. Ch., Syracuse; pres. Sch. Bd. Unified Sch. Dist. 494. Mem. Kans. Bar Assn., Kans. County and Dist. Attys. Assn., Nat. Dist. Attys. Assn., ABA, Hamilton C. of C. (bd. dirs. 1983-84), Rotary. E-mail: rolijoza@pld.com. Home: 507 N Hamilton Syracuse KS 67878 Office: Gale & Gale 211 N Main St PO Box 906 Syracuse KS 67878-0906

GALE, ROBERT L. educational association administrator, consultant; b. St. Cloud, Minn., Jan. 13, 1927; s. John Henry and Helen (Andrews) G.; m. Barbara Carr Davis, Oct. 19, 1951; children: Jennifer Gale Dunkin, Robert L. Gale, Jr., Morgan Andrews. USN V-12 program, U.S. Naval Acad., 1944—45; BA, Carleton Coll., 1948; DHL, U. N.C., Asheville, 1989. Editor-in-chief Maco Mag. Corp., N.Y.C., 1954-57; v.p. Carleton Coll., Northfield, Minn., 1957-63; dir. recruiting Peace Corps, Washington, 1963-65; dir. pub. affairs EEOC, Washington, 1965-66; chmn., ceo Gale Assocs., Washington, 1966-74; pres. Assn. Governing Bds. Univs. and Colls., Washington, 1974-92, pres. emeritus, 1992—. Bd. trustees Carleton Coll., Northfield, 1972-2002; bd. dirs. Nat. Peace Corps Assn., Washington, BoardSource, Washington, Nat. Exec. Svcs. Corps, N.Y.C., CARE, Inc., Atlanta, 1982-96, U. Pretoria Fund. Chmn. bd. Nat. Peace Garden Monument, Washington, 1995—. With USN, 1944-45. Democrat. Episcopalian. Avocations: tennis, travel, volunteering. Home: Rt 1 Jefferson Bridge Rd Bethany Beach DE 19930-9801 E-mail: bob1barb1@aol.com.

GALE, ROBERT LEE, retired American literature educator and critic; b. Des Moines, Dec. 27, 1919; s. Erie Lee and Miriam (Fisher) G.; m. Maureen Dowd, Nov. 18, 1944; children: John Lee, James Dowd, Christine Ann. BA, Dartmouth Coll., 1942; MA, Columbia U., 1947, PhD, 1952. Lectr. Columbia U., N.Y.C., 1947-48; instr. U. Del., Newark, 1949-52; asst. prof. U. Miss., Oxford, 1952-56, assoc. prof., 1956-59; asst. prof. U. Pitts., 1959-60, assoc. prof., 1960-65, prof. Am. lit., 1965-87; ret., 1987. Fulbright prof. Inst. Univ. Orientale, Naples, Italy, 1956-58, U. Helsinki, Finland, 1975. Author: Thomas Crawford, 1964, The Caught Image: Figurative Language in Henry James, 1964, Richard Henry Dana, Jr., 1969, Francis Parkman, 1973, Plots and Characters in Mark Twain, 1973, John Hay, 1978, Luke Short, 1981, Will Henry, 1984, Louis L'Amour, 1985, rev. edit., 1992, A Henry James Encyclopedia, 1989, Matt Braun, 1990, A Nathaniel Hawthorne Encyclopedia, 1991, The Gay Nineties: A Cultural Dictionary of the 1890s in the U.S., 1992, A Cultural Encyclopedia of the American 1850s, 1993, A Herman Melville Encyclopedia, 1995, An F. Scott Fitzgerald Encyclopedia, 1998, A Sarah Orne Jewett Companion, 1999, A Dashiell Hammett Companion, 2000, An Ambrose Bierce Companion, 2001, A Lafcadio Hearn Companion, 2002, A Ross Macdonald Companion, 2002, A Mickey Spillane Companion, 2003; contbr. articles to profl. jours., chpts. to books, revs. Served with U.S. Army, 1942-46, ETO. Mem. MLA, Phi Beta Kappa. Home: 131 Techview Ter Pittsburgh PA 15213-3820

GALE, SYLVIA ELIZABETH, child protection professional; b. Nanuet, N.Y., Sept. 6, 1949; d. Maynard Elton and Marguerite F. (Goldsmith) G.; 1 child, Elizabeth R. BA, U. N.H., 1971; postgrad., Antioch Grad. Sch., 1982-83. Coord., dir. Rape and Assault Svcs., Nashua, N.H., 1976-80; investigation specialist dept. health and human svcs. N.H. Divsn. for Children, Youth & Families, Concord, 1980-98, supr. ctrl. intake, 1998-2000; supr. Nashua (N.H.) Dist. Divsn. for Children, Youth & Families, 2000—. Advisor, mem. steering com. Sexual Assault and Recovery Through Awareness and Hope (SARAH, Inc.), Derry, N.H., 1988-96; facilitator N.H. Child Fatality Rev. Com., N.H., 1991-2001; advisor Baby Steps to Recovery, Nashua, 1992-95; convenor steering com. Child Advocacy Ctr., Hillsborough, N.H., 2002—. Bd. dirs. Neighborhood Health Ctr. for Greater Nashua, 1990-96, Neighbor to Neighbor Clinic, Nashua, 1991-96, N.H. Feminist Connection, 1999-2002; vol. sponsor, bd. dirs. N.H. Parents Anonymous, 1985-88; mem. Prevent Child Abuse N.H., 1989-92, 96-99, bd. dirs., 1997-99; mem. N.H. Atty. Gen.'s Task Force on Child Abuse and Neglect, 1995—. Recipient Roger Fossum award N.H. Atty. Gen.'s Task Force on Child Abuse, 1995. Mem. Am. Profl. Soc. on Abuse Children (Pres.'s honor roll 1994), No. New Eng. Profl. Soc. on Abused Children (covening bd. dirs. 1990-98), Nat. Abortion Rights Action League, N.H. Women's Lobby, N.H. Coalition to Prevent Shaken Baby Syndrome. Home: 4 Clergy Cir Nashua NH 03063-2912 Fax: 603-889-9639. E-mail: sgale@dhhs.state.nh.us.

GALE, THOMAS MARTIN, university dean; b. Green Bay, Wis., May 16, 1926; s. Thomas Griswold and Carrie (Danz) G.; m. Mary Margaret Hardman, May 28, 1960; children— Thomas Hardman, John Martin. BA, U. Calif. at Berkeley, 1949, MA, 1950; PhD, U. Pa., 1958. Dean Coll. Arts and Scis. N.Mex. State U., 1971-91, bd. dirs. Acad. for Learning in Retirement, 1991—, ret. 1991, acting provost, 2001. With Border Books Festival, 1996-2000. Chmn. N.Mex. Humanities Coun., NEH, 1972-77; chmn. Las Cruces Am. 2000 Task Force, 1991-98; vice-chmn. N.Mex. Commn. on Higher Edn., 1997-99; pres. bd. dirs. N.Mex. State U. Found., 2001-03. With AUS, 1944-46. Social Sci. Rsch. fellow, 1952-53, 53-54; Huntington Libr. fellow, 1959; Fulbright fellow Peru, 1960; recipient N.Mex. Disting. Svc. award, 2002. Mem. Phi Beta Kappa, Phi Alpha Theta. Clubs: Rotarian. Home: 3115 Majestic Rdg Las Cruces NM 88011-4603

GALE, TRISTAN, Olympic athlete; b. Ruidoso, N.Mex., Aug. 10, 1980; Student, Salt Lake C.C. Mem. U.S. skeleton team Winter Olympic Team, Lake Placid, NY. Named Am.'s Cup champion, 2001, Am.'s Cup champion, 1st pl., Lake Placid, 2001, Calgary, 2001; recipient Gold medal, 2002 Winter Olympics, 1st pl., U.S. Olympic Team Trials, 2002, 1st, 2d, 3d pl. 1st 3 races, Nat. Team Trials, 2001. Office: US Bobsled and Skeleton Fed PO Box 828 421 Military Rd Lake Placid NY 12946-0828

GALEANO, SHARON J. institutional advancement director; b. Weymouth, Mass., June 3, 1962; d. Celeste J. Kelly; m. Mark F. Galeano, Nov. 18, 1983; children: Kira J., Kyle M., Bryce T. BA summa cum laude, U. of Balt., 1991. Sr. property mgr. Apt. Svcs., Inc., Timonium, Md., 1987—96; advancement dir. Merritt Island Christian Sch., Fla., 1997—. Mem.: Cocoa Beach C. of C. (assoc.). Avocations: travel, volunteering. Office: Merritt Island Christian Sch 140 Magnolia Ave Merritt Island FL 32952 Office Fax: 321-452-6580. Personal E-mail: sgaleano@cfl.rr.com. E-mail: sgaleano@micscougars.com.

GALEF, DAVID ADAM, British literature educator, writer; b. N.Y.C., Mar. 27, 1959; s. Harold and Winifred (Kron) G. BA, Princeton U., 1981; MA, Columbia U., 1984, PhD, 1989. Tchr. English Overseas Tng. Corp., Osaka, Japan, 1981-82; preceptor English Columbia U., N.Y.C., 1986-89; asst. prof. English U. Miss., Oxford, 1989—95, assoc. prof. English, 1995—2002, prof., 2002—, MFA program adminstr., 2001—. Summer resident Yaddo Artists Colony, Saratoga Springs, NY, 1991, 2001; spring residency Ragdale Artists Colony, Lake Forest, Ill., 2001; guest writer Montclair State U., 1996, The Writers Place, Kansas City, Mo., 1997, New Walden Writers Retreat, New Hebron, Miss., 1999. Lit. critic: The Supporting Cast: A Study of Flat and Minor Characters, 1993, Second Thoughts: A Focus on Rereading, 1998; author: Flesh, 1995, Turning Japanese, 1998, Laugh Track, 2002, (children's books), The Little Red Bicycle, 1988, Tracks, 1996; translator: Even Monkeys Fall from Trees: The Wit and Wisdom of Japanese Proverbs, 1987, Even a Stone Buddha Can Talk: More Wit and Wisdom of Japanese Proverbs, 2000 ; contbr. articles, short stories to mags. Grantee Henfield Found., 1981-82, Columbia Pres.'s scholar, 1984-86, 88-89, Miss. Faculty Rsch. Summer Support grantee, 1990, 93, 94, 2003; vis. scholar Columbia U., 1995-96; recipient Writers Exchange award Nat. Arts Club and Harvard U., 1991, Studies in Popular Culture Whatley award for best essay, 1991; Miss. Arts Coun. grantee, 1997-98. Mem. MLA, South Cen. MLA, Nat. Coun. Tchrs. English, Phi Beta Kappa. Avocation: bicycle racing. Office: U Miss Dept English University MS 38677-1848

GALELLA, JOSEPH PETER, lawyer; b. N.Y.C., Oct. 19, 1956; s. Joseph Anthony and Stella Agnes (McKee) G.; m. Elaine Fowler, Aug. 15, 1981; 1 child, Joseph George. BA, Franklin & Marshall Coll., 1978; JD, U. Miami, 1981. Bar: Fla. 1981, N.Y. 1982, U.S. Dist. Ct. (so. dist.) Fla. 1982, U.S. Ct. Appeals (11th cir.) 1982. Assoc. Karsch & Meyer, N.Y.C., 1981—82; pvt. practice Peekskill, N.Y., 1983—; office counsel Kenneth Pregno Agy., Ltd., Peekskill, 1984—; of counsel Hersh & Hersh, Peekskill, 1994—. Rep. Franklin & Marshall Coll. Alumni Admissions Program, 1979-90; bd. dirs. Peekskill Field Library, 1985—, pres. 1998—. Mem. Fla. Bar, N.Y. State Bar Assn., Westchester County Bar Assn., Peekskill Bar Assn. (pres. 1993-94), Ossing Bar Assn., Yorktown Bar Assn. Democrat. Roman Catholic. Avocations: swimming, racquetball, tennis, reading. Home: 110 Mountain View Rd Cortlandt Manor NY 10567-6238

GALER-UNTI, REGINA ANN, health educator; b. Leavenworth, Kans., Aug. 2, 1956; d. Eugene and Nancy Jean (Mitchell) Unti; m. Thomas Carlen Galer, June 3, 1978; 1 child, Caitlin Elizabeth. BS, U. Ill., 1978, PhD, 1993; MS, Ill. State U., 1983. Cert. health edn. specialist Nat. Commn. for Health Edn. Credentialing. Rsch. asst. Harlan E. Moore Heart Rsch. Found., Champaign, Ill., 1983-84; tchg. asst. U. Ill., Champaign, 1984-87, instr., 1987-91; project dir. Ctr. for Health Info., Parkland Coll., Champaign, 1993-95; vis. asst. prof. health edn. Purdue U., West Lafayette, Ind., 1995-98, asst. prof. health, 1998—. Mem. exec. bd. Champaign County Health Cre Consumers, Champaign, 1995-98. Author: Hunger and Food Assistance Policy in the United States, 1995; contbr. articles to profl. jours. Bd. dirs. Discovery Place Children's Mus., Champaign, 1994-97. Recipient Joseph A. Ross award ea. region Kiwanis, 1985, cert. of commendation Champaign County chpt. ARC, 1985-86, Tchg. for Tomorrow award Purdue U., 2000; named Faculty Mentor of Yr., Nat. Eta Sigma Gamma, 1999, Helping Students Learn Teaching Innovation award Purdue U., 2001. Mem. APHA (chmn. advocacy com. pub. health edn. and health promotion sect. 1996-2000, governing coun. 2000—), Am. Alliance for Health Edn., Nat. Assn. for Pub. Health Policy (chmn. coun. on food and nutrition policy 1996-2000), Soc. for Pub. Health Edn. (bd. dirs. 2002—). Roman Catholic. Avocation: photography. Office: Purdue U 1362 Lambert West Lafayette IN 47907-1362 E-mail: rgaler@sla.purdue.edu.

GALES, SAMUEL JOEL, retired civilian military employee, counselor; b. Dublin, Miss., June 14, 1930; s. James McNary McNeil and Alice Francis (Smith) Broadus-Gales; m. Martha Ann Jackson (div. Jan. 1978); children: Samuel II (dec.), Martha Diane Townsend, Katherine Roselein, Karlmann Von Carolyn B., Elizabeth Angelica McCain. BA, Chapman Univ., 1981, MS, 1987. Ordained Eucharist minister, Episcopal Ch., 1985; cert. tchr., Calif.; registered parliamentarian. Enlisted U.S. Army, 1948, advanced through grades to master 1st sgt., 1969, ret., 1976; tchr. Monterey (Calif.) Unified Sch. Dist., 1981-82; civilian U.S. Army Directorate of Logistics, Ft. Ord, Calif., 1982-93; collateral EEOC counselor Dept. Def., U.S. Army, 1987-93; instr. AARP Driver Safety Program, 2001—. Peer counselor, 1982-84. Active Family Svc. Agy., Monterey, 1979-85; rep. Episc. Soc. for Ministry on Aging, Carmel, Calif., 1980-86, Task

Force on Aging, Carmel, 1983-87, vestryman, 1982-85, 91-94; ombudsman Monterey County Long-Term Care Program, Calif. Dept. for the Aging, 1993-97; vol. guide Monterey Bay Aquarium Found., 1994—, vol. docent Bay Net, Ctr. for Marine Conservation, Monterey Bay Nat. Marine Sanctuary, 1997-2003. Decorated Air medal. Mem.: Am. Inst. Parliamentarians (registered parliamentarian), Am. Legion (post comdr. 1973—74), Nat. Assn. Parliamentarians (pres. 2000—01, pres. Pi Gamma unit Calif. State Assn. 2000—01), Nat. Assn. Ret. Fed. Employees (pres. chpt. 579 1999—2000), Toastmasters, Forty and Eight (chef-de-gare 1979, 1980), Comdr.'s Club Calif. (pres. Outpost 28 1981—82), Monterey Chess Club. Republican. Avocation: classical music. Home: PO Box 919 1617 Lowell St Seaside CA 93955-3811

GALESI, DEBORAH LEE, fine artist; b. Paterson, N.J., Oct. 08; d. John Michael Galesi and Ethel Marchitti; m. Samuel Corbinelli, Oct. 3, 1997. BFA, U. Colo.; pvt. student, Raymond Whyte and, Gene Scarpentoni/Art Students League, N.Y., Ben Long, Florence; Master Program, Villa Schifanoia/Inst. of, Florence. One-woman shows include: Lo Sprone, Florence, Italy, 1983, Spinetti Gallery, Florence, 1985, Benvenuti Gallery, Venice, 1986, Salaria Gallery, Spoleto, 1987, Lo Spirale, Prato, Italy, 1988, Traghetto Gallery, Venice, 1987; works exhibited at: U. Colo., Boulder, 1980, N.Y. Gallery, N.Y.C., 1981, N.J. Gallery, 1981, U. Avignon, France, 1981, Sieve Art Expo, Pontassieve, Italy, 1984, Cenacolo Gallery, Florence, 1985, Modigliani Gallery, Milan, 1990, Art Expo, Verona, 1990, Palazzo Congressi, Salsomaggiore, 1995, Palazzo, Florence, 1996, Montserrat Gallery N.Y., 1997. Vol. Natural Resource Def. Coun., Washington, Pacific Whale Found., Hawaii, Ctr. for Marine Conservation, Washington, WWF, Greenpeace. Winner competition Nat. Art Ctr., N.Y., 1978, others; recipient Stewaardess of Ctr. of Light and Harmony award, Sierra Club. Mem. Ptnrs. of Destiny. Avocations: scuba diving, music, rollerblading, chinese painting, piano. Office: PMB 523 PO Box 959 Kihei HI 96753-0959

GALEY, R. KENT, oral surgeon; b. Sewickley, Pa., Oct. 17, 1946; s. Robert Stanley and Betty Thorpe Galey; m. Karen Roche Galey, Sept. 23, 1977; children: John, Erin, Heather, Roger Kent Jr.; m. Charlene Cornell, June 14, 1969 (div. July 1977); children: Marlo, Ellen. BS in biology, Denison U., Granville, Ohio, 1968; DMD, U. Pitts., 1971. Lic. dental Pa., 1971, diplomate Am. Bd. of Oral and Maxillofacial Surgery, 1980, cert. oral and maxillofacial surgery U. Pitts., 1976. Oral and maxillofacial surgeon North Pitts. Oral Surgery Assoc. Ltd., 1976—; resident oral and maxillofacial surgery Presbyn. U. Hosp, Pitts., 1972—76. Clin. instr. dept. oral and maxillofacial surgery U. Pitts. Med. Ctr.; adj. tech. staff, clin. asst. div. oral and maxillofacial surgery Allegheny U. Hosps. Med. Coll. of Pa.; vis. prof. Parkland Meml. Hosp., Dallas; mem. U.S. Air Flight 427 Primary Identification Team, 1994; oral and maxillofacial cons. Pitts. Penguins Hockey Team; mem. Western Pa. Dental Forensic Identification Team; mem. local ethics rev. com. Am. Bd. of Oral and Maxillofacial Surgery; adv. com. Am. Bd. of Oral and Maxillofacial Surgeons; bd. mem. North Hills Passavant Hosp., Pa. Blue Shield; bd. examiner Northwestern U. Mock Bd. Rev. Course. Contbr. articles to profl. jours., chapters to books. Mem. Pub. Safety Com., Fox Chapel, Pa. Fellow: Am. Assn. of Oral and Maxillofacial Surgery (nat. pub. spokesperson, mem. strategic planning com., mem. ad hoc com. on 4 yr. curr.), Internat. Assn. of Oral and Maxillofacial Surgeons (life); mem.: Pa. Assn. of Oral and Maxillofacial Surgeons (nat. exec. com. alt. del., program com., legis. com., peer rev. com.), Western Pa. Soc. of Oral and Maxillofacial Surgeons (pres., bd. mem.), Pa. Dental Assn. (mem. pub. rel. com.), North Dental Club of Pitts. (pres., bd. mem.). Avocations: fly fishing, hiking, skiing, travel, reading. Home: 108 Hawthorne Rd Pittsburgh PA 15238 Office: North Pittsburgh Oral Surgery Assoc Ltd Ste 203 9380 McKnight Rd Pittsburgh PA 15237

GALGAN, GERALD JOSEPH, philosopher, educator; b. N.Y.C., June 12, 1942; s. Anthony and Helen Galgan. BA, Cathedral Coll., 1963; MA, Fordham U., 1966, PhD, 1971. Prof. philosophy St. Francis Coll., Bklyn., 1966—, asst. dean humanities, 2000—02. Author: The Logic of Modernity, 1982, God and Subjectivity, 1990, Interpreting the Present, 1993. Office: St Francis Coll 180 Remsen St Brooklyn NY 11201-4305 E-mail: ggalgan@stfranciscollege.edu.

GALIN, JERRY DEAN, college dean; b. Cullman, Ala., May 22, 1945; s. Herman William and Evelyn B. (McManus) G. BA, St. Bernard (Ala.) Coll., 1967; MA, U. Ala., Tuscaloosa, 1970; EdD, Nova U., 1981. Tchr. math. Morgan County Sch. Sys., Eva, Ala., 1967-74; chmn. mgmt. dept. Wallace State Coll., Hanceville, Ala., 1974-90, dean faculty devel., 1990-93, acad. dean, 1993-98. Pres. Cullman Tchrs. Credit Union, 1982-85; mem. survey team So. Assn. Colls. and Schs., 1984—; ptnr. G & G Properties, Cullman, 1989—; participant radio and TV shows. Bd. dirs., mem. fin. com. Hospice of Cullman County, Cullman, 1989-91; bd. dirs. Helen Keller Eye and Temporal Bone Bank, Florence, Ala., 1990-91, Ala. Sight Conservation Assn., Birmingham, 1990-91, Cullman County Family Recreational Complex, 1990—; pres. Cullman County Electric Coop. Operation Round-Up Commn., 1995—; chmn. Cullman County Quality Cmty. Coun., 1991-93; mem. Cullman Rural Devel. Com., 1989—; lectr. to social, civic and cmty. groups; master of ceremonies for local events. Recipient Knights of Blind award Eye and Temporal Bone Bank, 1990, 100 percent Dist. Govs. award Internat. Lions Club, 1991, Henry and Lucille Sweet award Ala. Lions Club, 1992. Mem. Ala. Econ. Devel. Orgn., Cullman Area C. of C. (pres. bd. dirs. 1993-94), Wallace State Athletic Assn. (treas. 1989—), Cullman Investment Club (pres. 1989—), Lions (numerous offices 1972—, Lion of Yr. award 1988, Melvin Jones fellow 1991). Democrat. Methodist. Avocations: coin collecting, travel. Home: 294 County Road 591 Hanceville AL 35077-8054

GALIN, TAD, SR., home business owner; b. Yurovka, Kyiv, Ukraine, Dec. 8, 1930; came to U.S., 1958, naturalized. s. Josef and Janina (Piotrowska) Przegalinski; m. Alice Soroki, May 20, 1959 (dec. Sept. 1967); m. June Ashton, June 6, 1968; children: Tad, Joseph. Lic. mortgage broker, Fla.; cert. Dietary Supplement Health Edn. Act, Am. Nutraceutical Assn. Driver's license tng. exams tchr. Lang. Sch., Cleve., 1958; with Cleaners Hanger Factory, Cleve., 1958—63; indsl. diamond specialist Felker Mfg. Co., Torrence, Calif., 1963—65; owner Lake Heating & Air Conditioning, Pontiac, Mich., 1967, Instant Credit, Flint, Mich., 1968, Remnant Market, Clarkston, Mich., 1969, Warehouse Carpet, Oxford, Mich., 1970—73; home builder Mich., 1973; owner Scientific Meditation Inst. Am., Ft. Lauderdale, 1976, Sci. of Life Ch., 1976; direct distbr. Amway Corp., Ada, Mich., 1975—86; regional v.p. A.L. Williams, Atlanta, 1988; with Nat. Safety Assocs., Memphis, 1989—; regional dir. Nat. Telephone Co., Irvine, Calif., 1991—95; co-founder, presdl. dir. Legacy for Life, Palm Bay, Fla., 1995—. Author: Stalin, Hitler & I, 2001; patentee in field. With U.S. Army, 1952-57, Korea. Avocation: classical guitar. Home: 900 Larch Cir NE Ste 104 Palm Bay FL 32905 E-mail: Tad@tadgalin.com.

GALINAT, WALTON CLARENCE, research scientist; b. Manchester, Conn., Dec. 9, 1923; m. Elizabeth Ruth Warren, 1945; children: David W., Alice R. BS with honors, U. Conn., 1949; MS, U. Wis., 1951, PhD, 1953. Asst. in genetics Conn. Agrl. Experiment Sta., 1946-50; asst. in agronomy Wis. Agrl. Experimenbt Sta., 1950-53; rsch. fellow, rsch. assoc. Bussey Inst. Harvard U., 1953-64; assoc. prof. Waltham Field Sta. U. Mass., 1964-68, prof. Suburban Experiment Sta., 1968-90, prof. emeritus plant and soil scis., 1990—. With USCG, 1943-46. Recipient Disting. Econ. Botanist award Soc. Econ. Botany, 1994; Disting. Lifetime Achievement in Sci. and Art award U. Mass., 2001. Fellow AAAS. Office: Suburban Experiment Sta U Mass 240 Beaver St Waltham MA 02452-8096 Office Fax: 781-899-6054.

GALINDO, REBECA, administrative assistant; b. Mexico City, Mex., Jan. 4, 1960; arrived in U.S., 1983; d. Jose Luiz Fernandez Altamirano and Rebaca Vales Gutuerrez; m. Ramon N. Galindo, June 27, 1980; children: Rebeca, Amelia. Tchr. aid Dade County Elem. Sch., Miami, 1988—90; adminstrv. asst. Miami-Dade C.C., 1990—94, cert. supv., 1994—98; sr. sec. Tex. Woman's U., Denton, Tex., 1999—2001; adminstrv. asst. Tex. Woman's U. Inst. Women's Health, 2001—. Spanish translator, interpreter Tex. Woman's U. Inst. Women's Health, 2001—. Vol. Tex. Woman's U. Open Ho., Denton, 2000—02, Tes. Woman's U. Sociology Girls Project, 2000, United Way, Miami, 1996—97. Office: Tex Womans U PO Box 425876 Denton TX 76209

GALINSKY, DENNIS LEE, radiation oncologist, educator; b. Des Moines, Sept. 16, 1948; s. Sam and Joyce Geraldine (Givant) G.; m. Daryl Lee Goldstein, Nov. 9, 1975; children: Dana Lauren, David Lawrence. BS, Drake U., 1970; MD, U. Iowa, 1974. Diplomate Am. Bd. Radiology. Intern U. Ariz., Tucson, 1974-75, resident in radiation oncology, 1975-77, U. Minn., Mpls., 1977-78; assoc. attending physician Evanston (Ill.) Hosp., 1978-80; dir. radiation oncology Copley Meml. Hosp., Aurora, Ill., 1980-89, U. Ill. Hosp., Chgo., 1991-93, DuPage Oncology Ctr., Winfield, Ill., 1993; assoc. prof. Rush U., Chgo., 1994—, 1994—; pvt. practice, Chgo., 1978. Clin. assoc. Northwestern U., Evanston, 1978-80; co-dir. rev. course Osler Inst., Lisle, Ill., 1991; presenter Internat. Congress Radiology, 1989, European Soc. Radiation Oncology, 1990. Contbr. articles to med. jours. Bd. dirs. Congregation Beth Shalom, Naperville, Ill., 1984-85; mem. Dist. 27 Sch. Bd., Northbrook, Ill., 1990—. Grantee NSF, 1968; recipient gold medal Am. Coll. Radiation Oncology, 2003. Fellow: Am. Coll. Radiation Oncology (vice chmn. 1991—92); mem.: AMA (del. 1996—), Chgo. Met. Area Radiation Oncology Soc. (pres. 1987—88), Beta Beta Beta. Avocations: golf, coin collecting. Office: Nuclear Oncology SC 6929 Ogden Ave Berwyn IL 60402-3649

GALINSKY, GOTTHARD KARL, classicist, educator; b. Strassburg, Alsace, Feb. 7, 1942; came to U.S., 1961, naturalized, 1971; s. Hans Karl and Edith (Margenburg) G.; m. Harriet Eileen Harris, June 29, 1986; children by previous marriage— Robert Charles, John Anthony. BA, Bowdoin Coll., 1963; MA, Princeton U., 1965, PhD, 1966. Instr. classics Princeton U., 1965-66; mem. faculty U. Tex., Austin, 1966—, prof. classics, 1972—, chmn. dept., 1974-90, Armstrong Centennial prof., 1985-91, Cailloux Centennial prof., 1991—, Disting. tchg. prof., 1999—, chmn. grad. assembly, 1977-79, chmn. faculty senate, 1981-82. Dir. summer seminars NEH, 1975, 76, 83-85, 97 2002; dir. residential seminar, 1977-78, dir. Collaborative Sch. Project, 1987-89, cons., 1976-78, 80—; classicist-in-residence Am. Acad. Rome, 1972-73, vis. scholar, 1991; mem. adv. coun. Classical Sch., 1967—, chmn., 1982-85, mem. classical jury, 1970-71; lectr. U.S.-U.K. Edn. Commn., 1973; regional chmn. Mellon Humanities Fellowships, 1982-90; nat. lectr. Phi Beta Kappa, 1989-90; vis. Mellon prof. Tulane U., 1995; vis. prof. U. Nacional de La Plata, 1997; vis. prof. Gutenberg U. Mainz, Germany, 1998, Inst. Advanced Study, Princeton, 2000, U. Tex. Inst. for the Humanities, 2001. Author: Aeneas, Sicily and Rome, 1969, Tibulli Carmina, 1971, The Herakles Theme, 1972, Perspectives of Roman Poetry, 1974, Ovid's Metamorphoses, 1975, The Interpretation of Roman Poetry, 1992, Classical and Modern Interactions, 1992, Augustan Culture, 1996; mem. editorial bd. Classical World, 1973-76, Vergilius, 1973—, Classical Jour., 1991-98, Austcr, 1996—. Mem. Leadership Austin, 1983-84. Fellow Am. Coun. Learned Socs., 1968-69, Fulbright fellow, 1972-73, Guggenheim fellow, 1972-73, NEH fellow, 1993-94; recipient Teaching Excellence award U. Tex., 1970, 76, 99, Robert W. Hamilton Author award U. Tex., 1997; Humboldt Found. sr. rsch. award, 1993, reinvitation award, 1998. Mem. Am. Philol. Assn. (Teaching Excellence award 1979, dir. 1980-83), Archaeol. Inst. Am., Classical Assn. Midwest and South (pres. 1980-81), Vergilian Soc. Am. (trustee 1972-76, v.p. 1976-77), Assn. Depts. Fgn. Langs. (exec. com. 1980-83, pres. 1983) Home: 4508 Edgemont Dr Austin TX 78731-5224 Office: U Tex Dept Classics Austin TX 78712-0308 E-mail: galinsky@mail.utexas.edu.

GALISON, PETER LOUIS, history of science educator; b. N.Y.C., May 17, 1955; m. Caroline A. Jones, 1954; two children. BA, MA, Harvard U., 1977, PhD in Physics and History of Sci., 1983; MPhil, Cambridge U., 1978. From asst. prof. to prof. philosophy and physics Stanford U., 1983-92; chmn. dept. history of sci. Harvard U., 1993-97, Mallinckrodt prof. history of sci. and physics, 1994—. Howard Found. fellow, 1985; vis. asst. prof. dept. history, Princeton U., 1985; fellow Ctr. for Advanced Study Behaviorial Sci., 1989-90, co-chmn. program history of sci., 1990-92; bd. dirs. Ctr. Philosophy and History of Sci., Boston U., 1993-96; visitor Inst. Advanced Study, 1994-95. Recipient Presidential Young Investigator award, NSF, 1986-91; named Marta Sutton Weeks faculty scholar in humanities, 1989-92; fellow John D. and Catherine T. Mac Arthur Found., 1997-2002, Max Planck prize, 1999. Fellow AAAS, Am. Acad. Arts and Scis., Am. Phys. Soc.; mem. Internat. Soc. History of Sci., History of Sci. Soc. (mem. coun. 1993-95), Sigma Xi.

GALIVAN, JOHN HENRY, biochemist, educator, public health officer, research administrator; b. Albany, N.Y., June 19, 1939; s. John Henry and Mary Hortense (Sullivan) G.; m. Nancy Lynn Stiehler, Jan. 24, 1982; children: Amanda, Brendan, Julie, Kate. BS, Union Univ., 1960; MS, SUNY, Albany, 1963; PhD, Albany Med. Coll., 1967. Postdoctoral fellow Scripps Clinic and Rsch. Found., La Jolla, Calif., 1967-70; rsch. scientist Wadsworth Labs. N.Y. State Dept. Health, Albany, 1970—, dir. pathology lab. Wadsworth Labs., 1990-92; dir. divsn. clin. scis. Wadsworth Labs State Dept. Health, Albany, 1992-94; dir. divsn. molecular medicine N.Y. State Dept. Health, Albany, 1994-98, dep. dir. oncology Wadsworth Ctr., 1994—, dir. rsch. Wadsworth Labs., 1998—; co-dir., mem. exec. leadership com. Ordway Rsch. Inst., 1998—; prof. SUNY, Albany, 1985—; sr. health rsch. svc. Wadsworth Labs., 2001—, mem. exec. coun., 1992—. From assoc. prof. to prof. biochemistry and molecular biology Albany Med. Coll., 1978—; mem. exptl. therapeutics study sect. Nat. Cancer Inst., Bethesda, Md., 1985-89, cons., 1983-97; exec. coun. U. Albany Sch. Pub. Health, 1989-91; mem. internat. sci. com. Folic Acid Symposium, Berchtesgaden, Germany, 1995-97, Washington, 2000—; mem. task force on rsch. agenda N.Y. State Dept Health, 1995-2000; mem. Internat. Clin. Chemistry Sci. Com., Basel, Switzerland, 1996-97; internat. adv. bd. Folic Acid Symposium, Washington, 2000-01. Assoc. editor Jour. Cellular Pharmacology, 1992-96; mem. editl. bd. Biofocus, 1995-99; contbr. numerous articles to profl. publs., chpt. to book. Mem. N.Y. State Legis. Com.; dir. N.Y. State Breast Cancer Tax Checkoff; mem. rsch. agenda task force N.Y. State Dept. Health; mem. ex officio com. Ctr. for Nanobiotech., Cornell U., 1998—2002. Grantee NIH, 1976—. Mem.: AAAS, NY Acad. Scis., Fedn. Am. Soc. Exptl. Biology, Am. Assn. Cancer Rsch., Caroline Seymour Assn. (v.p. 1998—), Preservation Soc. Newport, Mus. Fine Arts Boston, Sail Newport. Home: 391 State St Albany NY 12210-1207 Office: NY State Dept Health Wadsworth Ctr Empire State Plz Albany NY 12223 E-mail: galivan@wadsworth.org.

GALIZZI, MONICA, economics educator; b. Piacenza, Italy, Nov. 12, 1961; arrived in U.S., 1987; d. Giovanni and Giuliana (Vecchiotti) G.; m. Enrico Cagliero, June 25, 1994; children: Diana Anna, Erica B. BS, U. Cattolica, Milan, Italy, 1986; M in Polit. Economy, Boston U., 1990, PhD in Econs., 1994; D in Polit. Economy, U. Milan, Italy, 1990. Rsch. asst. dept. econs. Cath. U., Milan, Italy, 1986-87; instr. micro- and macro-economics, dept. econs. Boston U., 1989-92; postdoctorate rsch. fellow in econs. of labor markets U. Limburg, Maastricht, The Netherlands, 1993-94; economist Workers Compensation Rsch. Inst., Cambridge, Mass., 1994-98; adminstrv. dir. program on children Nat. Bur. Econ. Rsch., Cambridge, 1998-99; asst. prof. dept. econs. U. Mass., Lowell, 1999—. Co-author (with L. Boden): What Are the Most Important Factors Shaping Return to Work? Evidence from Wisconsin, 1996; co-author: (with Boden and T. Liu) The Workers' Story: Results from a Survey of Workers injured in Wisconsin, 1998; co-author: (with G. Gotz and T. Lin) Predictors of Multiple Workers' Compensation Claims in Wisconsin, 2000; contbr. articles to profl. jours. Mem.: Workers' Compensation Rsch. Group, European Econ. Assn., Am. Econ. Assn. Home: 76 Paul Revere Rd Lexington MA 02421-6638 Office: U Mass Lowell Dept Econs 1 University Ave Lowell MA 01854-2881 E-mail: monica_galizzi@uml.edu.

GALKIN, SAMUEL BERNARD, orthodontist; b. Newark, Feb. 9, 1933; s. Saul J. and Mollie (Kleinberg) G.; m. Gail Beth Elkin, Feb. 26, 1972; children: Scott David, Seth Paul. Student, U. Conn., 1951-54; DDS, Temple U., 1958; MS in Histology, cert. grad. orthodontics, U. Ill., 1963; cert. in craniomandibular disorders, U. Medicine and Dentistry of N.J., 1989. Diplomate Am. Bd. Orthodontics. Group practice orthodontics, Woodbridge, N.J., 1963—; staff orthodontist J.F.K. Community Hosp., Edison, N.J., 1966—, with cleft palate com., 1971—, dir. dental dept., 1979—; staff Woodbridge Health Ctr., 1967—, with dental adv. com., 1971—; dir. dept. dentistry John F. Kennedy Med. Ctr., Edison, 1979-81; staff orthodontist Perth Amboy (N.J.) Gen. Hosp., 1986—, dir. dept. dentistry, 1990—; staff orthodontist Rahway Hosp., N.J., 1986—. Asst. prof. orthodontics N.J. Coll. Medicine and Dentistry, Jersey City, 1963-73; mem. panel physicians N.J. Crippled Children Program, 1971—; dentist Woodbridge Twp. Sch., 1989—. Chmn., Woodbridge Twp. Debutante Ball, 1970; bd. dirs. Woodbridge Twp. YMCA. Lt. Dental Corps, USN, 1958-61. Mem. ADA, Mid. Atlantic Soc. Orthodontists (chmn. clinics 1969-72), N.J. Dental Soc., Middlesex County Dental Soc., Am. Soc. Dentistry for Children, Am. Assn. Orthodontists, Am. Lingual Orthodontic Assn. (charter), Am. Assn. Dental Schs., Am. Acad. Head, Neck, Facial Pain and TMJ Orthopedics, N.E. Craniomandibular Soc., N.J. Craniomandibular soc. (charter), Am. Acad. Orofacial Pain, Am. Acad. Oral Medicine, Alpha Omega (chpt. v.p. 1969—), Omicron Kappa Upsilon. Home: 3 Dorset Rd Colonia NJ 07067-3101 Office: 711 Amboy Ave Woodbridge NJ 07095-3139

GALL, BETTY BLUEBAUM, office services company executive; b. Williamson, W.Va., June 11, 1944; d. Thomas Jefferson Bluebaum and Ollie Mae (Moore) Bluebaum Walker; Charles B. Walker (stepfather); 1 child, Thomas Ethan. Ptnr., dir. Chicagoland Register, dating svc., Chgo., 1974-84; cooking instr. Elizabeth Benson Internat. Cooking Lessons, 1978-84; owner Ethnic Party People Catering, 1981-92, Phone-A-Friend Dating Svc., Chgo., 1984-90, Betty Gall Office Svcs., Chgo., 1984—; office mgr. Myers & Assocs., 1998—2000. Contbr. poetry to Nat. Libr. Poetry, 1997, 98. Mem. comm. dept. Little City Found., 1989-91. Home: 6314 N Troy St Chicago IL 60659-1414 E-mail: bettygall44@hotmail.com.

GALL, DONALD ALAN, data processing executive; b. Reddick, Ill., Sept. 13, 1934; s. Clarence Oliver and Evelyn Louise (McCumber) G.; m. Elizabeth Olmstead, June 25, 1960 (div. 1972); children: Christopher, Keith, Elizabeth; m. Kathleen Marie Insogna, Oct. 13, 1973; 1 child, Kelly Marie. BSME, U. Ill., 1956; SM, MIT, 1958, ME, 1960, ScD, 1964. Rsch. engr. GM, Detroit, 1956-57; staff engr. Dynatech Corp., Cambridge, Mass., 1959-60, mgr. ctr. systems, 1962-63; asst., assoc. prof. Carnegie-Mellon U., Pitts., 1964-69; rsch. assoc. prof. surgery and anesthesiology U. Pitts. Sch. Medicine, 1969-73; vis. fellow IBM Research Lab., Rueschlikon, Switzerland, 1970-71; pres. Omega Computer Systems, Inc., Phoenix, 1973—; CEO Omega Legal Systems, Inc., Phoenix, 1995—; bd. dirs. TTI Technologies, Inc., Omaha, 1996—. Contbr. articles to profl. jours.; inventor fuel injection system. Bd. dirs. Scottsdale Boys and Girls Club, 1982-93; mem. Scottsdale Head Honchos, 1978-87; mem. Verde Vaqueros, 1987—; mem. alumni adv. bd. dept. mech. and indsl. engring., U. Ill., 2002—. Recipient Taylor medal Internat. Conf. on Prodn. Rsch., 1970, Disting. Alumnus award dept. mech. and indsl. engring. U. Ill., 1997. Mem. ASME (life), M Tech Assn. (exec. dir., bd. dirs. 1996-98, chmn. bd. dirs. 1998-2001), Sigma Xi, Pi Tau Sigma, Tau Beta Pi, Phi Kappa Phi. Avocations: horseback riding, skiing, golf. Home: 8675 E Via de McCormick Scottsdale AZ 85258 Office: Omega Computer Sys Inc 3875 N 44th St Ste 200 Phoenix AZ 85018-5486 E-mail: dgall@omegalegal.com.

GALL, ERIC PAPINEAU, physician, educator; b. Boston, May 24, 1940; s. Edward Alfred and Phyllis Hortense (Rivard) G.; m. Katherine Theiss, Apr. 20, 1968; children: Gretchen Theiss Gall, Michael Edward. AB, U. Pa., 1962, MD, 1966. Asst. instr. U. Pa., Phila., 1970-71, post doctoral trainee, fellow, 1971-73, asst. prof. U. Ariz., Tucscon, 1973-78, assoc. prof., 1978-83, prof. internal medicine, 1983-94, prof. surgery, 1983-94, prof. family/community medicine, 1983-94, chief rheumatology allergy and immunology, 1983-93, dir. arthritis ctr., 1986-94; Herman Finch Univ. of Health Scis. prof. of medicine The Chgo. Med. Sch., North Chicago, Ill., 1994—, prof. microbiology and immunology, 1994—, chmn. dept. medicine, 1994—, chief rheumatology sect., 1994-98, assoc. dean clin. affairs, 1996-97, dir. metabolic bone unit, 1998—. Author, editor: Rheumatoid Arthritis: Illustrated Guide to Path DX and Management of Rheumatoid Arthritis, 1988, Rheumatic Disease: Rehabilitation and Management, 1984, Primary Care, 1984; editor Clin. Care in The Rhematic Diseases, 1996; contbr. numerous articles to profl. jours. Chmn. med. and scientific com. Arthritis Found., Tucson, 1979-81. Maj. M.C., U.S. Army; Vietnam. Decorated Bronze Star; recipient Addie Thomas Nat. Svc. award Arthritis Found., 1988. Fellow ACP (coun. Ill. chpt. 1995—, Laureate award 2002), Am. Coll. Rheumatology (founding chair ednl. materials com. 1986-89, bd. dirs. 1992-95, chmn. rehab. sect. 1992-95), Chgo. Inst. Medicine; mem. AMA (rep. sect. on med. schs. 1995—), Arthritis Health Professions Assn. (nat. pres. 1982-83), Am. Assn. Med. Colls., Am. Fedn. Clin. Rsch., Inst. Medicine of Chgo., Ctrl. Soc. Clin. Investigation, Arthritis Found. (nat. vice chmn. 1982-83, chmn. profl. edn. com. 1996—, chmn. ednl. materials com. 1991-96, blue ribbon com. on quality of life, trustee Greater Chgo. chpt. 1997—, exec. com. 1998—, bd. dirs. 1997—, treas. 2003—), Assn. Profs. Medicine, Ill. Med. Soc., Lake County Med. Soc. (treas. 1998-99, sec. 2000—, pres. 2002-03), Sigma Xi, Alpha Omega Alpha (counselor Chgo. Med. Sch. chpt., 1995—, regional counselor 1998—), Alpha Epsilon Delta. Avocations: photography, fishing. Office: The Chgo Med Sch Dept Medicine 3333 Green Bay Rd North Chicago IL 60064-3037 E-mail: egall@aol.com., ericgall@finchcms.edu. *Academic medicine provides the ideal opportunity to help patients, help touch and shape the lives of hundreds of students and trainees, and to add to the fund of knowledge in one's world.*

GALL, JOHN R. lawyer; b. San Francisco, 1945; BA, Miami U., 1967; JD, Ohio State U., 1970. Bar: Ohio 1971. Ptnr. Squire, Sanders & Dempsey, Columbus, Ohio. Office: Squire Sanders & Dempsey 1300 Huntington Ctr 41 S High St Columbus OH 43215-6101 E-mail: jgall@ssd.com.

GALL, JOSEPH GRAFTON, biologist, researcher, educator; b. Washington, Apr. 14, 1928; s. John Christian and Elsie (Rosenberger) G.; m. Dolores Marie Hogge, Sept. 17, 1955 (div. 1982); children: Lawrence, Barbara.; m. Diane Marie Dwyer, July 17, 1982. BS, Yale, 1949, PhD, 1952. Faculty U. Minn., 1952-63, prof., 1963; prof. biology and molecular biophysics Yale, 1963-83; staff dept. embryology Carnegie Instn., Balt., 1983—, Am. Cancer Soc. prof. developmental genetics, 1984—. Mem. cell biology study sect. NIH, 1963-67, chmn., 1972-75; chmn. bd. sci. counselors Nat. Inst. Child Health and Human Devel., NIH, 1986-90; mem. Yale Corp., 1989-95. Contbr. articles profl. jours. Recipient E.B. Wilson award Am. Soc. Cell Biology, 1983, Wilbur Cross medal Yale U., 1988, V.D. Mattia award Roche Inst. Molecular Biology, 1989, Purkinje medal Czech Acad. Scis., 1999. Mem. AAAS (Mentor award for lifetime achievement 1996), Am. Soc. Cell Biology (past pres.), Genetics Soc. Am., Nat. Acad. Scis., Am. Acad. Arts and Scis., Am. Philos. Soc., Accademia Nazionale dei Lincei, Soc. Developmental Biology (pres. 1984-85) Home: 107 Bellemore Rd Baltimore MD 21210-1314 Office: Carnegie Instn Dept Embryology 115 W University Pkwy Dept Baltimore MD 21210-3399 E-mail: gall@ciwemb.edu.

GALL, LENORE ROSALIE, educational administrator; b. Bklyn., Aug. 9, 1943; d. George W. Gall and Olive Rosalie (Weekes) Gall Bryant. AAS, NYU, 1970, cert. tng. and devel., 1975, BS in Mgmt., 1973, MA in Counselor Edn., 1977; EdM, EdD, Columbia U., 1988. Various positions Ford Found., N.Y.C., 1967-75; dep. dir. career devel. Grad. Sch. Bus., NYU, N.Y.C., 1976-79; dir. career devel. Pace Lubin Sch. Bus., N.Y.C., 1979-82, Sch. Mgmt., Yale U., New Haven, 1982-85; asst. to assoc. provost Bklyn. Coll., 1985-88, asst. to provost, 1988-91; asst. to v.p. acad. affairs Fashion Inst. Tech., 1991-94; asst. provost curriculum and instrn. N.Y.C. Tech. Coll., 1994-2000, dean students and acad. svcs., 2000—. Adj. asst. prof. LaGuardia C.C., L.I. City, N.Y., 1981-90, Sch. Continuing Edn. NYU, 1983-84; dir., sec. devel. workshop Coll. Placement Svcs., Bethlehem, Pa., 1978-81. Bd. dirs. Langston Hughes Cmty. Libr., Corona, N.Y., 1975-83, 86-92, chair, 1975-79, 82-83, 89-92, 2d v.p., 1986, 1st v.p., 1987-88, chair awards com. Dollars for Scholars, Corona, 1976-99, pres., 1999-2003; active audience devel. task force Dance Theatre of Harlem, 1992-98, hon. co-chmn., 1994-95; active alumni coun. Tchrs. Coll., Columbia U., 2000—; bd. trustees Renaissance Charter Sch., 2002, Queens (N.Y.) Borough Pub. Libr., 2003. Recipient Concerned Women of Bklyn., Inc., 1994, Edn. award Stuyvesant Heights Lions Club, Bklyn., N.Y., 1997, Edn. award Girls HS Alumni Assn., Bklyn., N.Y., 2003, Edn. award Key Women Am., Concourse Village Beach, 2003; grantee Jewish Fedn. for the Edn. of Women, 1986 87. Mem. AAUW, Assn. Black Women in Higher Edn. (exec. bd., membership chair, pres.-elect 1988, pres. 1989-93), Am. Assn. Univ. Adminstrs., Nat. Assn. Univ. Women (chaplain 1987-88, 2d v.p. 1988, 1st v.p. 1988-92, dir. N.E. sect. 1993-96, nat. 2d v.p. 1996-98, nat. first v.p. 2000-2002, nat. pres. 2002), Tchr.'s Coll./Columbia U. Alumni Coun. (chmn. nominating com. 2001-), Nat. Assn. Women in Edn., Black Faculty and Staff Assn. Bklyn. Coll. (1st vice-chair 1986-87, chair 1987-88), New Haven C. of C. (chmn. women bus. and industry conf. 1984), Nat. Coun. Negro Women Inc. (life, 1st v.p. North Queens sect. 1986-89, pres. 1989-93), Nat. Assn. Negro Bus. & Profl. Women's Club (Sojourner Truth award 1991), Phi Delta Kappa, Kappa Delta Pi, Pi Lambda Theta, Delta Sigma Theta (chmn. nominating com. Queens Alumni chpt. 2001-03, chmn. tri-com.-arts and letters, project ch., May Week 1999-2002). Mem. A.M.E. Ch. Office: NYC Coll Tech 300 Jay St Jackson Heights NY 11201-1909

GALL, MARY SHEILA, federal agency administrator; 2 children. BA, Rosary Hill Coll., 1971; MS in Edn., Old Dominion U., 1998. Staff mem. various mems. of Senate and Ho. of Reps., 1971-79; sr. legis. analyst study com. Ho. of Reps., 1980-81; dep. domestic policy adviser Office of V.P. of U.S., 1981-86; counselor to dir. U.S. Office Pers. Mgmt., 1986-89; asst. sec. human devel. svcs. HHS, Washington, 1989-91; commr. U.S. Consumer Product Safety Commn., Washington, 1991—. Chair Pres.'s Task Force on Adoption, 1987-89. Dir. rsch. George Bush for Pres. campaign, 1979-80; mem. Reagan-Bush Presdl. campaign and transition team, 1980-81; tchr. Sunday sch. Republican. Office: Us Consumer Product Safety C Washington DC 20207-0001

GALL, MEREDITH DAMIEN (MEREDITH MARK DAMIEN GALL), education educator, writer; b. New Britain, Conn., Feb. 18, 1942; s. Theodore A. and Ray (Ehrlich) G.; m. Joyce Pershing, June 12, 1968; 1 child, Jonathan. AB, EdM, Harvard U., 1963; PhD, U. Calif., Berkeley, 1968. Sr. research assoc. Far West Lab. for Ednl. Research and Devel., San Francisco, 1968-75; assoc. prof. edn. U. Oreg., Eugene, 1975-79, prof., 1980—, dept. head for tchr. edn., 2002—. Author: Handbook for Evaluating and Selecting Curriculum Materials, 1981, (with K.A. Acheson) Techniques in the Clinical Supervision of Teachers, 5th edit., 2002, (with J.P. Gall) Making the Grade, rev. 2d edit., 1993, (with W.R. Borg and J.P. Gall) Educational Research: An Introduction, 7th edit., 2002, (with J.P. Gall, D.R. Jacobsen, and T.L. Bullock) Tools for Learning: A Guide to Teaching Study Skills, 1990, (with W.R. Borg and J.P. Gall) Applying Educational Research, 4th edit., 1999; editor: (with B.A. Ward) Critical Issues in Educational Psychology, 1974; cons. editor Jour. Rsch. in Rural Edn., Forum for Reading, Jour. Exptl. Edn. USPH fellow, 1963-64. Fellow Am. Psychol. Assn.; mem. ASCD, Am. Ednl. Research Assn., Oreg. Ednl. Research Assn. (pres. 1985-86), Phi Delta Kappa (Dist. I Meritorious award 1978). Home: 4810 Mahalo Dr Eugene OR 97405-4609 Office: U Oreg Coll Edn Eugene OR 97403

GALL, ROBERT JAY, lawyer; b. Athens, Ohio, Jan. 18, 1957; s. Homer B. Jr. and Jean Elliott Gall; m. Cherie Hill, Dec. 4, 1982; 1 child, Anna Claire. AB, Miami U., 1979; JD, Coll. of William and Mary, 1982. Bar: Ohio 1982, U.S. Ct. Appeals (6th cir.) 1982, U.S. Dist. Ct. (so. dist.) Ohio 1983, U.S. Supreme Ct. 1985. Atty. Mollica, Gall, Sloan & Sillery, Athens, 1982—. Bd. dirs. Hocking Valley Bank. Former bd. dirs., vice-chair Ohio U. Coll. Osteo. Medicine, Athens, chair Sheltering Arms Hosp. Found., Athens; vice chmn. Athens County Port Authority; bd. dirs. Ohio U. Inst. Local Govt. and Rural Devel.; bd. dirs., past chair Dairy Barn Cultural Arts Ctr. Fellow Am. Coll. Trust and Estates Counsel; mem. Ohio State Bar Assn. (bd. govs. sect. for estate planning probate and trust law), Athens County Bar Assn. (past pres.), Athens Area C. of C. (bd. dirs., past chair). Office: Mollica Gall Sloan & Sillery Co LPA 35 N College St Athens OH 45701-2529 E-mail: rgall@mgss.com.

GALL, STANLEY ADOLPH, physician, immunology researcher; b. Bismarck, N.D., May 31, 1936; s. Adolph and Wilma Thelma (Nickisch) G.; m. Florence Marie Ketterling, Aug. 17, 1958; children: Stanley, Kathryn Louise, Mark Allan, Thomas Andrew. BA, U. Minn., 1958, MD, 1962. Diplomate Am. Bd. Ob-Gyn. Intern U. Oreg. Hosp., Portland, 1962-63; resident in ob-gyn U. Minn. Hosps., Mpls., 1963-66; asst. prof. ob-gyn U. Miami, Fla., 1968-73; assoc. prof. ob-gyn Duke U. Med. Ctr., Durham, N.C., 1973-78, prof., 1968—, dir. divsn. perinatal medicine; prof. ob-gyn, assoc. head dept. ob-gyn U. Ill. Coll. Medicine, 1985-89; prof. U. Louisville, 1989—, chmn. dept. ob-gyn., 1989—91. Contbr. articles to profl. jours. Capt. U.S. Army Med. Corps, 1966-68. Fellow ACOG; mem. Soc. Gynecol. Oncology, Soc. Gynecol. Investigations, Infectious Diseases Soc. Ob-Gyn, Ctrl. Assn. Obstetricians and Gynecologists, Soc. Maternal Fetal Medicine. Lutheran. Office: U Louisville Dept Ob-Gyn 550 S Jackson St Louisville KY 40202-1622

GALLAGER, ROBERT GRAY, electrical engineering educator; b. Phila., May 29, 1931; s. Jacob Boon and May (Gray) G.; m. Ruth Atwood, Oct. 19, 1957 (div. July 1981); children: Douglas, Ann, Rebecca; m. Marie Tarnowski, July 18, 1981. BEE, U. Pa., 1953; MEE, MIT, 1957, ScD, 1960. Mem. tech. staff Bell Telephone Labs., Murray Hill, N.J., 1953-54; rsch. asst. MIT, Cambridge, Mass., 1956-60, asst. prof., 1960-64, assoc. prof., 1964-67, prof., 1967—. Co-dir. Lab. Info. and Decision Systems, 1986-96; chmn. adv. com. NSF Div. on Networking and Comm. Rsch. and Infrastructure, Washington, 1989-92; mem. adv. coun. Elec. Engring. Dept., U. Pa., 1991-93; chair adv. com. Elec. Engring. Dept., The Technion, Haifa, Israel, 1999. Author: Information Theory and Reliable Communication, 1968, Discrete Stochastic Processes, 1995; co-author Data Networks, 1987, 2d edit. 1992; patentee in field. Recipient Gold medal Moore Sch., U. Pa., 1973, Harvey prize The Technion, 1999, Eduard Rhein Basic Rsch. award, 2002; Guggenheim fellow, 1978. Fellow IEEE (Baker prize 1966, Medal of Honor 1990); mem. AAAS, NAS, NAE, Infor. theory Soc. of IEEE (bd. govs. 1965-72, 79-88, pres. 1971, Shannon Award 1983). Avocations: piano, skiing. Home: 13 Strawberry Cove Gloucester MA 01930-4128 Office: MIT Dept Elec Eng/Comp Sci Rm 35-206 Cambridge MA 02139 E-mail: gallager@mit.edu.

GALLAGHER, ANNE PORTER, business executive; b. Coral Gables, Fla., Mar. 16, 1950; d. William Moring and Anne (Jewett) Porter; m. Matthew Philip Gallagher, Jr., July 31, 1976 (div. July 1998); children: Jacqueline Anne, Kevin Sharkey. BA in Edn., Stetson U., 1972. Tchr. elem. schs., Atlanta, 1972-74; sales rep. Xerox Corp., Atlanta, 1974-76, Rosslyn, Va., 1976-81, No. Telecom Inc., Vienna, Va., 1981-84, account exec., 1984-85, sales dir., 1985-91, mktg. dir., 1995-96; v.p. Fed. Pub. Sector Timeplex Fed. Sys., Inc., Fairfax, Va., 1995-96; bus. devel. dir. Informix Software, Vienna, 1996-97; sr. v.p. Tricor Industries Inc., Alexandria, Va., 1997-98; sr. v.p. fed. sys. Metromedia Fiber Network, McLean, Va., 1999—2002; sr. v.p. bus. devel. Source1 Techs., Arlington, Va., 2002—. Mem. Info. Tech. Assn. of Am., Armed Forces Comm. and Electronics Assn., Pi Beta Phi. Episcopalian. Avocations: running, working out. Home: 4643 Kirkland Pl Alexandria VA 22311-4949 Office: Source 1 Techs 2111 Wilson Blvd Ste 700 Arlington VA 22201 E-mail: AGallagher@S1tech.com.

GALLAGHER, BLANCHE MARIE, art and spirituality educator, nun; b. Waverly, Iowa, Aug. 28, 1922; d. John Joseph and Blanche Marie Gallagher. BA, Mundelein Coll., Chgo., 1944; MFA, Cath. U. Am., Washington, 1956. Tchr. Mt. Carmel Country Day Sch., Wichita, Kans., 1947-49; tchr. high sch. Holy Angels Acad., Milw., 1949-54, Xavier High Sch., St. Louis, 1954-55; prof. art and spirituality Mundelein Coll., Chgo., 1955-91, chmn. art dept., 1961-73, 78-79; prof. pastoral studies Loyola U., Chgo., 1991—. Guest prof. Grad. Theol. Union, U. Calif., Berkeley, 1988; spiritual dir. Grace Cathedral, San Francisco, 1989; adv. bd. ESEA grants, Springfield, 1968-74; adv. bd. Quest: Ctr. for Spiritual Devel., 1988-95; v.p. Pastoral Counseling Svc., 1988-94; adv. bd. N.Am. Conf. on Religion and Ecology, 1990—; rschr. Lily Found., Indpls., 1976-77, Giorgio Cini Found., Venice, 1965; presenter, leader workshops, Delhi, India, 1976, Kathmandu, Nepal, 1977, Kyoto, Japan, 1995, Colorado Springs, Colo.; keynote spkr. Christian Family Movement, Dubuque, Iowa, 1992; lectr. in field. Author: Meditations with Teilhard, 1988; one-woman exhbns. include U. Colo, Boulder, 1972, Inst. on the Future, Mt. St. Joseph Coll., Cin., 1974, U. Chgo., 1975, Parapsychology Inst., Chgo., 1977, St. Mary's Coll., Winona, Minn., 1978, Freeport (Ill.) Art Mus., 1979, Cath. Theol. Union, Chgo., 1979, Morton Coll., Chgo., 1982, Mundelein Coll., Chgo., 1982, Valparaiso (Ind.) U., 1984, St. Luke's Gallery, Chgo., 1986, North Park Coll., Chgo., 1992, Ancient Echoes Gallery, Chgo., 1992, St. Mary's U. Minn., 2003, Clarke Coll., Dubuque, Iowa, 2003. Ragdale Found. grantee, Lake Forest, Ill., 1986, 93. Mem.: Amnesty Internat. Roman Catholic. Avocations: swimming, playing bassoon. Office: Loyola U IPS 820 N Michigan Ave Chicago IL 60611

GALLAGHER, BRIAN, editor-in-chief; b. 1949; Employed The Jour. News, Westchester County, 1971—80, Gannett News Svc., Washington, 1980—83, mng. editor, 1983—86; employed USA Today, McLean, Va., 1986—91, editl. writer, 1991—99, editl. page editor, 1999—2002, exec. editor, 2002—. Office: USA Today Executive Editor 7950 Jones Branch Dr McLean VA 22102*

GALLAGHER, BRIAN JOHN, lawyer; b. Bklyn., Oct. 24, 1939; s. John Joseph and Margaret R. Gallagher; m. Mary Loughney, Sept. 10, 1966; children: Amanda, Ian. BS, Fairfield U., 1961; JD, Fordham U., 1964; postgrad., NYU Law Sch., 1969-70. Bar: N.Y. 1965, U.S. Dist. Ct. (so. dist.) N.Y. 1967, U.S. Ct. Appeals (2d cir.) 1971, U.S. Dist. Ct. (ea. dist.) N.Y. 1974, U.S. Ct. Appeals (11th cir.) 1982, U.S. Ct. Appeals (D.C. cir.) 1986. Asst. U.S. Atty. So. Dist. N.Y., 1967-71; ptnr. Kronish, Lieb, Weiner & Hellman, LLP, N.Y.C., 1976—. Mayor Village of Pelham Manor, N.Y., 1995-97, trustee, 1989-95. Mem. ABA, N.Y. State Bar Assn., Assn. Bar City N.Y., Fed. Bar Coun., Larchmont (N.Y.) Yacht Club, Williams Club, N.Y. Athletic Club. Office: 1114 Avenue Of The Americas New York NY 10036-7703 E-mail: bgallagher@klwhHp.com.

GALLAGHER, BYRON PATRICK, JR., lawyer; b. Bay City, Mich., Feb. 29, 1964; s. Byron Patrick and Ethel Jean (Gebowski) G.; m. Michelle Francis Burdick, May 21, 1994; children: Byron Patrick III, Grace Katherine. AB, Kenyon Coll., Gambier, Ohio, 1986; JD, Washington U., St. Louis, 1989. Bar: Mich. 1989, U.S. Dist. Ct. (we. dist.) Mich. 1990, U.S. Dist. Ct. (ea. dist.) Mich. 1995, U.S. Tax Ct. 2003. Ptnr. Gallagher Duby, PLC, Lansing, 1998—. Bd. dirs., initial incorporator Summit Cmty. Bank. Bd. dirs. Ingham County Social Svc. Bd., Mason, Mich., 1991-92, Ingham County Commn., Mason, 1993-97, Mich. Underground Storage Tank Fin. Assurance Authority, 1996-2002; dir. State Bldg. Authority, 2002—; Rep. cand. Mich. State Senate, 1998. Mem. Ingham County Bar Assn. (bd. dirs. 1996-99, bench bar com. 2000—), County Club of Lansing, Mich. Athletic Club. Republican. Avocations: flying, golf. Home: 951 Walbridge Dr East Lansing MI 48823 Office: Gallagher Duby PLC 2510 Kerry St Ste 210 Lansing MI 48912-3671

GALLAGHER, CYNTHIA, artist, educator; b. N.Y. BFA in Painting, Phila. U. of Arts, 1972; MFA in Painting, Queens Coll., 1974. Instr. N.Y. Inst. Tech., N.Y.C., 1974-88; adj. prof. CUNY, Queens Coll., N.Y.C., 1974—90; instr. foundations dept. Parsons Sch. Design, 1994—2001. Critic Brown U., 1994, R.I. Sch. Design, 1994, Cooper Union for Advancement of Sci. and Art, 1994; selection com. vis. artists Fashion Inst. Tech., 1992-93; graphics cons. N.Y. State Found. Arts, 1978; vis. critic NYU, N.Y.C., N.Y., 1974-75; adj. asst. prof. Phila. (Pa.) Coll. Art, 1976—, Fashion Inst. Tech., N.Y.C., N.Y., 1976—; instr. summer sch. music and art Yale U., Norfolk, Conn., 1980—. One-woman shows include 55 Mercer St., N.Y.C., 1976, 1978, Grace Borgenicht Gallery, 1981, Luise Ross Gallery, 1988, Edward Thorden Gallery, Gothenborg, Sweden, 1989, Charles More Gallery, Phila., 1990, 1991, Mary Ryan Gallery, N.Y.C., 1992, Espace Crois, Barangnon, Toulouse, France, 1993, Johnson & Johnson, New Brunswick, N.J., 1998, exhibited in group shows at Weatherspoon Mus., Greensboro, N.Y.C., 1982, Castelli Graphics, N.Y.C., 1983, Bess Culter Gallery, 1984, Parrish Art Mus., Southampton, L.I., N.Y., 1991, Tiffany's, N.Y.C., 1993, Inst. for Art and Urban Resources, Inc., L.I. City, N.Y., 1982, Nat. Mus. Women in the Arts, Washington, 1996, Montclair (NJ) Mus. Art, 1997, Represented in permanent collections Met. Mus. Art, N.Y.C., Best Inc., Citibank, 1st Nat. Bank Chgo., Home Ins. Co., Owens Corning Corp., Salomon Bros., Shearson-Lehman Am. Express, N.Y.C., San Francisco, Skadden, Arts, Slate, Meagher and Flom, Johnson, Nat. Mus. of Women in the Arts, Whitney Mus. Am. Art, Met. Mus. Art, Nat. Women's Mus., Washington, D.C.; contbr. articles to profl. jours. Mem. adv. bd., bd. dirs. YWCA Elsa Mott Ives Gallery, 1992, curator, 1993. Grantee, Creative Artists Pub. Svc. Program, 1981—82, Nat. Endowment for Arts, 1983—84, 1989—90, N.Y. Found. for Arts, 1989—90.

GALLAGHER, CYNTHIA POLANSKY, writer; b. Newton, Mass., Jan. 11, 1958; d. Aaron George and Estelle Phyllis Polansky; m. Kevin Frank Gallagher, May 5, 1991; children: Kristin Tara, Kevin Brian. BA, The George Washington U., 1980. Cert. aircraft dispatcher FAA, 1985. Aircraft dispatcher Midwest Express Airlines, Milw., 1986—87, Fed. Express, Memphis, 1987—91; adminstrv. asst. Jewish Family Svc., Memphis, 1992—96; ct. reporter Hunt Reporting, Glen Burnie, Md., 1996—2000; freelance author Crownsville, Md., 2000—. Sec. Md. Writers Assn., Arnold, Md., 2001—. Author: (novels) Far Above Rubies, 2002, (monthly column) Boxer Shorts; contbr. Chicken Soup for the Volunteer's Soul. Mem. Internat. Fund for Animal Welfare, Yarmouth, Mass., 1982—2003. Mem.: Women's Nat. Book Assn. Jewish. Avocations: crossword puzzles, knitting, racquetball, hiking, travel. Personal E-mail: author40@aol.com.

GALLAGHER, DENNIS JOSEPH, municipal official, state senator, educator; b. July 1, 1939; s. William Joseph and Ellen Philomena (Flaherty) G.; children: Meaghan Kathleen, Daniel Patrick. BA, Regis Coll., 1961; MA, Cath. U. Am., 1968; postgrad. (Eagleton fellow), Rutgers U., 1972, 86. With locals of Internat. Assn. Theatrical and Stage Employees, Denver and Washington, 1956-63; tchr. St. John's Coll. H.S., Washington, 1964-66, Heights Study Ctr., Washington, 1965-67, Regis U., Washington, 1967; mem. Colo. Ho. of Reps. from 4th Dist., 1970-74, Colo. Senate, 1974-95; councilman dist. 1, Denver, 1995—2003. Chmn. Dem. Caucus, 1982-84, Dem. Whip, 1985-87. Mem. Platte Area Reclamation Com., 1973-75; mem. Denver Anti-Crime Coun., 1976-77; trustee Denver Art Mus.; bd. dirs. Cath. Cmty. Svcs.; past mem. Colo. Commn. on Aging; past mem. Colo. State Adv. Coun. on Career Edn.; mem. Victim Assistance Law Enforcement Bd., Denver, 1984-88; bd. dirs. Denver Am. Ireland Fund. Named Gates Found. fellow Harvard U.; recipient Jacques Ellul award Media Ecology Assn., 2001. Mem.: Nat. Comm. Assn., Gerard Manley Hopkins S.J. Soc. Regis (conf. co-dir.), Western States Comm. Assn., Rocky Mountain Comm. Assn., James Joyce Reading Soc., Colo. History Group, Colo. Calligrapher's Guild, Colo. Fedn. Tchrs. (pres. local 1333 1972—74). Democrat. Catholic. Home: 5097 Meade St Denver CO 80221-1033 Office: Denver Auditor's Office 201 W Colfax Ave Sept 705 Denver CO 80202 also: 4404 Lowell Blvd Denver CO 80211-1367 Office Fax: 720-913-5253. E-mail: dennis.gallagher@ci.denver.co.us.

GALLAGHER, EDWARD ARTHUR, retired academic administrator, real estate developer; b. Ann Arbor, Mich., May 9, 1937; s. Arthur Paul and Marjorie Lillian Gallagher; m. Sylvia Mary Waterman, July 11, 1970; children: Amy Marie Woodruff, Sara Beth Zocher. BA in History, U. Mich., 1959; MA in History, U. Ill., 1961; PhD in Higher Edn. Adminstrn., U. Mich., 1968. Asst. prof. Lorain County C.C., Elyria, Ohio, 1964—67, Oakland C.C., Bloomfields Hills, Mich., 1967—68, pres. Auburn Hills Campus Elyria, 1969—74; ret., 1974; mgr. ops. Roscommon Mfg. Co., Mich., 1974—76; prof., rschr. Oakland C.C., 1976—95; owner, real estate developer Howland Lake Pines Devel. Co., LLC, Oakland County, Mich., 1993—. Contbr. Grantee, Spencer Found., 1993. Mem.: Mich. Acad. Sci., Arts and Letters (pres. 2002—), Mid-west History of Edn. Soc., History of Edn. Soc. Independent. Roman Catholic. Avocations: hiking, travel, writing history articles, jazz, classical music. Home and Office: 4875 Green Meadow Ln Rochester MI 48306*

GALLAGHER, EDWARD JOHN, II, lawyer; b. Detroit, Jan. 22, 1949; s. Edward John and Audrey (Robinson) G.; m. Diane Mary Powers, Sept. 18, 1976; children— Patrick Brian, Kerry Edward. Student St. Joseph's Coll., Rensellaer, Ind., 1966-68; BA, Western Mich. U., 1970; JD, Wayne State U., 1973. Bar: Mich. 1973, U.S. Dist. Ct. (ea. dist.) Mich. 1977, U.S. Cir. Ct. Appeals (6th cir.) 1989. Assoc. Perica, Breithart & Carmody P.C., Warren, Mich., 1973-80; chief referee Macomb County Juvenile Ct., Mt. Clemens, Mich., 1980; assoc. B.M. Freid & Assocs., P.C., Saginaw, Mich., 1980-89, ptnr., 1989—; ptnr. Freid, Gallagher, Taylor & Assocs., P.C., Saginaw, 1989—. Mem. Assn. Trial Lawyers Am., Saginaw Bar Assn., Am Arbitration Assn. (panel arbitrators), Bay County Bar Assn., Mich. Trial Lawyers Assn. Democrat. Roman Catholic. Home: 28 Center Ct Bay City MI 48708-6901 Office: Freid Gallagher Taylor & Assocs PC 604 S Jefferson St Saginaw MI 48604-1416

GALLAGHER, ELLEN, artist; b. Providence, 1965; Student, Sch. Mus. Fine Art, Boston, 1992, Skowhegan Sch. Art, 1993. One-woman shows include Akin Gallery, Boston, 1992, Mario Diacono Gallery, 1994, Mary Boone Gallery, N.Y., 1996, Anthony d'Offay Gallery, London, 1996, Gagosian Gallery, 1998, Ikon Gallery, Birmingham, 1998, Galerie Max Hetzler, Berlin, 1999, exhibited in group shows at Brandeis U., Waltham, 1993, Mus. Fine Arts, Boston, 1993, Inst. Contemporary Art, 1994, 1996, Mus. Fine Arts, 1995, Whitney Mus. Am. Art, N.Y., 1995, Whitechapel Art Gallery, London, 1996, Mario Diacono Gallery, Boston, 1997, De Beyerd Ctr. Contemporary Art, Breda, The Netherlands, 1998, others, Represented in permanent collections Mus. Modern Art, N.Y., Whitney Mus. Art, Met Mus. Art, Guggenheim Mus., Mus. Fine Art, Boston, Mus. Contemporary Art, L.A., Denver Mus. Art, Moderna Museet, Stockholm; featured in numerous articles and revs. Ann. Gund fellow, 1993, Provincetown Fine Arts Work Ctr. fellow, 1995, Joan Mitchell fellow, 1997. Office: care Mario Diacono Gallery 207 South St Boston MA 02111-2723

GALLAGHER, EUGENE BENNETT, sociologist, medical educator; b. Lancaster, Pa., Mar. 25, 1929; s. Joseph and Dorothy (Bennett) G.; m. Carol Thompson, Dec. 22, 1951 (div. July 1975); children: David Travis, Robert Thompson; m. Marilyn Milne, Aug. 20, 1977. BS, Lehigh U., 1949; MA, Harvard U., 1954, PhD, 1958. Lectr. Boston U., 1960-62; prof. U. Ky., Lexington, 1962—. Vis. prof. Bristol (Eng.) U., 1969-70, King Faisal U., Damman, Saudi Arabia, 1979-80, United Arab Emirates U., Al Ain, 1990, 97; rschr. NIH, Bethesda, Md., 1975-76. Author, editor: Infants, Mothers and Doctors, 1977, Patienthood in the Mental Hospital, 1964, Health and Health Care in Developing Countries, 1993, Global Perspectives on Health Care, 1995, Culture, Society, and Illness, 1996, Toward a Global Sociology of Health and Medicine, 2001. Fellow Am. Coun. Learned Socs., Washington, 1950; recipient Fulbright Rsch. award, 1996-97. Fellow: Am. Sociol. Assn.; mem.: Internat. Sociol. Assn. (pres. rsch. com. 1994—2002). Democrat. Avocations: piano, hiking, bicycling. Office: U Ky Dept Behavioral Sci Lexington KY 40536-0001 E-mail: ebgall@uky.edu.

GALLAGHER, GARY W(AYNE), educational services executive; b. Ponca City, Okla., May 13, 1954; s. Linden B. and Lenna J. (Greenshields) Wilson; m. Carole B. Stewart, May 1, 1979 (div. Mar. 1994); children: Heather, Danielle; m. Jani B. Viljoen, Aug. 5, 1998; children: Trevor, Derek, Stephen. BA in Polit. Sci., L.Am. Area Studies cert., Okla. State U., 1975, MS in Curriculum Studies, Supt. and Prin. Adminstrv. cert., Okla. State U., 1995, postgrad., 1995—. Tchr. Ponca City (Okla.) Pub. Schs., 1987-88; transitional sch. and work program instr. seriously emotionally disturbed children Am. Legion Children's Home, Ponca City, 1988-89; social scis. instr. Olive Pub. Schs., 1989-90; social scis. and tech. applications instr. Ponca City (Okla.) Pub. Schs., 1990-98; foundr., curriculum theorist Advanced Academics, Ponca City, Okla., 1999—2001; dir. comml. mktg. Okla. ops. Applied Techs. divsn. Sci. Rsch. Corp., 2002—. Yearbook and sch. newspaper organizer, sponsor organizer West Jr. High Parent Tchr. Student Assn., 1991; student coun. sponsor, 1991—; mem. Okla. Close-Up Exec. Com., 1992; chmn. Middle Sch. Bldg. Budget Com., 1994. Bd. dirs. Jour. Curriculum Discourse, Okla. State U., 1994—, coord. editor, 1995—. Commr. Marland Estate Commn., Fin. and Mktg. Subcoms.; coord. for ednl. activities Cherokee Strip Celebration Com., 1991-93; participant Okla. Bar Assn. Grant Writing Workshop, 1991, Okla. Bar Assn. Programs Advancing Citizenship Edn., 1991, ABA Law Related Edn. Working Conf. on Tech., Boston, 1992, Okla. Bar Assn. Advanced Grant Writing Workshop, 1993; tchr. mentor Okla. Bar Assn., PACE III Inst., 1992; tchr. coord. AT&T Learning Network, 1993; mem. State Dept. Edn. Adv./Planning Com. on Svc. Learning, 1993; chmn. fin. com. Pioneer Free-Net Steering Com., 1994—; active Ponca City Literacy Coun., Ponca City 101 Ranch Old Timers Assn., tchr. cons. Nat. Geographic Soc. Recipent Carl Albert Ctr. Bill of Rights Symposium scholarship, Nat. Bicentennial Competition of the Constn. and the Bill of Rights scholarship, 1991, 92, Gov.'s Commendation for Volunteerism, 1993, 94; named Okla. Tech. Tchr. of the Yr., Tech. and Learning Mag., 1990. Mem. ASCD, Am. Assn. Sch. Adminstrs., Nat. Assn. Secondary Sch. Prins., Nat. Assn. Elem. Sch. Prins., Internat. Internet Learning Assn., Internat. Soc. Tech. in Edn., Nat. Coun. for the Social Studies (instrnl. media/tech. com.), Am. Ednl. Rsch. Assn., Nat. Youth Leadership Coun., Okla. Alliance for Geographic Edn., Internat. Assn. Sch. Bus. Officials, Okla. Coun. for the Social Studies, Okla. Hist. Soc., Assn. Ednl. Comm. and Tech., Assn. Childhood Edn. Home: 1813 E Hartford Ave Ponca City OK 74604-2521 E-mail: gwg@cableone.net., ggallagh@scires.com.

GALLAGHER, GEORGE R. retired judge; Former sr. judge D.C. Ct. Appeals. Office: 500 Indiana Ave NW Ste 6000 Washington DC 20001-2131

GALLAGHER, GERALD RAPHAEL, venture capitalist; b. Easton, Pa., Mar. 17, 1941; s. Gerald R. and Marjorie A. G.; m. Ellen Anne Mullane, Aug. 8, 1964; children: Ann Patrice, Gerald Patrick, Megan Ann. BS in Aero. Engring., Princeton U., 1963; MBA (Exec. Club Chgo. fellow 1969), U. Chgo., 1969. Dir. strategic planning Metro-Goldwyn-Mayer, N.Y.C., 1969; v.p. Donaldson, Lufkin & Jenrette, N.Y.C., 1969-77; from v.p. to sr. v.p. planning and control Dayton Hudson Corp., Mpls., 1977-79; exec. v.p., chief adminstrv. officer subs. Mervyn's, Hayward, Calif., vice chmn., chief adminstrv. officer, 1979-85, vice chmn., chief adminstrv. office parent co., 1985-87, also dir.; gen. ptnr. Oak Investment Ptnrs., Mpls., 1987—. Bd. dirs. eStyle, Gaiam.com, Lucy Activewear, Ulta, XIOtech, Potbelly. With USN, 1963-67. With USN, 1963—67. Mem. N.Y. Soc. Security Analysts, Mpls. Club, Interlachen Country Club, Beta Gamma Sigma. Roman Catholic. Office: Oak Investment Ptnrs 4550 Wells Fargo Ctr 90 S 7th St Minneapolis MN 55402-3903 E-mail: jerry@oakvc.com.

GALLAGHER, HUBERT RANDALL, government consultant; b. Salida, Colo., Jan. 8, 1907; s. Hugh and Margaret (Dinsmore) G.; m. Luthera Wakefield, July 29, 1930; children: Hugh, Janet. AB, Stanford U., 1929; MS, Syracuse U., 1930. Instr. Syracuse (N.Y.) U., 1930-32; asst. prof. Stanford U., 1932-33; rsch. cons., later assoc. dir., coun. of state govts., 1933-50; assoc. dir. state divsn. Nat. Def. Commn., 1940-45; chmn. Internat. Bd. of Inquiry for Great Lakes Fisheries, 1940-41; office dir. Am. Mission Aid to Greece-AMAG, 1947-48; presdl. staff asst. OCDM and Office Emergency Planning (Exec. Office of Pres., White House), Washington, 1950-69. V.p. Wakefield Farm Co., 1976— ; alt. del. NATO Civil Emergency Com., 1962-64 Author: Crime Prevention, Syracuse U., 1930, Report of International Board of Inquiry for the Great Lakes Fisheries, U.S. Govt., Dept. of State, 1943; editor: The Book of the States, Coun. of State Govts., 1943-44; contbr. articles to profl. mags. Assoc. fellow Harry S. Truman Libr. Inst. Nat. and Internat. Affairs. Mem. Am. Soc. Pub. Adminstrn. (past pres. Washington 1955-56, chmn. com. emergency mgmt. disaster assistance 1983-84), Delta Tau Delta. Presbyterian. Home: 5416 Burling Rd Bethesda MD 20814-1214

GALLAGHER, JACK B(URT), composer, music educator; b. Forest Hills, N.Y., June 27, 1947; s. John Joseph and Ethel Lucille (Schaffeld) G.; m. April Lorenz, Aug. 19, 1977; children: Kelly Brooke, Ryan Timothy. BA cum laude, Hofstra U., 1969; MFA, Cornell U., 1975, D in Mus. Arts, 1982. Rotating sect. trumpeter Nat. Orchestral Assn., N.Y.C., 1968-70; tchr. instrumental, vocal music Bethpage (N.Y.) Pub. Schs., 1969-71; instr. music The Coll. of Wooster (Ohio), 1977-81, asst. prof., 1981-83, assoc. prof., 1983-91, prof., 1991—, acting chair, 1992-93. Assoc. music dir. Wooster Symphony Orch., 1984-85, music dir., 1985-86. Composer: (choral) Three Wordsworth Poems (Charles Ives Ctr. fellowship 1987), (symphonic band) The Persistence of Memory (In Memoriam: Brian Israel), 1989 (hon. mention Barlow internat. composition competition 1990), (symphonic) Symphony in One Movement: Threnody, 1991; (chamber) Exotic Dances, 1996 (nominee Pulitzer prize 1997); representative works: Toccata for Brass Quintet, 1970, Ancient Evenings and Distant Music, 1971, Sonata for Piano, 1973, Variations for Violoncello and Piano, 1973, Three Songs of Love, Joy and the Beauty of Night, 1975, Nocturne, 1976, Six Bagatelles, 1978, Invocation, 1980, Mist-Covered Mountain, 1982, To Those Who've Fail'd, 1983, Diversions Triptych, 1985, Diversions Overture, 1986, Celebration and Reflection, 1987, Heritage Music, 1988, Two Pieces for String Orchestra, 1990, Proteus Rising from the Sea, 1994, The Persistence of Memory (orch.), 1995, A Quiet Musicke, 1996, A Psalm of Life, 197/2000, Malambo, 2000.. Recipient 1st prize Va. Coll. Band Dirs. Assn., 1987, Ohio Music Tchrs. Assn. Composer of Yr., 1996; Individual Artist fellow Ohio Arts Coun., 1992, 96; grantee Meet the Composer, 1983, 88; fellow The Yaddo Corp., 1984. Mem. Soc. of Composers, Inc., Am. Music Ctr., Broadcast Music, Inc., Cleve. Composers Guild, Internat. Trumpet Guild, Pi Kappa Lambda, Sigma Alpha Iota. Avocations: films, reading. Office: The Coll of Wooster Scheide Music Ctr Wooster OH 44691 E-mail: jgallagher@wooster.edu.

GALLAGHER, JOAN FRANCES, business administration educator; b. Bridgeport, Conn., June 7, 1939; d. John J. and Margaret Rose (Suren) Nagy; m. William Hall Gallagher, Apr. 22, 1967. BSBA and SEcondary Edn., U. Bridgeport, 1966, MS in Reading Cons., 1968, cert. Mgmt. Inst. Women in Higher Edn., 1978. Cert. Mgmt. Inst. Women in Higher Edn., 1989, World Trade Inst., 1994, 6th yr. prof. cert. adminstrn. and supervision U. Bridgeport, 1978. Confidential sec. Dresser Industries, Stratford, Conn., 1955-66; tchr. West Haven (Conn.) High Sch., 1966-67, Trumbull (Conn.) High Sch., 1967-78; asst. prof. Housatonic Community Coll., Bridgeport, 1978-82, assoc. prof., 1982-86, prof. bus. adminstrn., 1987—, bus. adminstrn. chair, 1988—. Cons., dir. Office Svcs. Sch. of Word Processing, Trumbull, 1984-87; SRA cons. SRA Pubs., Chgo., 1986-87; self employed trainer, Huntington, 1986—. Speaker HCC, Fairfield County, 1980-81; facilitator Dept. of Labor Displaced Workers, Fairfield County, 1988-89. Recipient Merit award State of Conn., 1984, 88, 2000-02, Dean's award, 1984, Excellence in Tchg. award, NISOD, 1993, 99, 2000, Edn. Excellence and Disting. Svc. award State of Conn., 1991. Mem.

NAFE, Nat. Bus. Edn. Assn., Conn. Bus. Edn. Assn. (editor 1974-75, svc. award 1975), Ea. Bus. Edn. Assn., Assn. Internat. Word Processors, N.Y. Coll. Learning Skills Assn., Milford Yacht Club (editor 1988—). Roman Catholic. Avocations: boating, racquetball, fitness, cross country skiing, sewing. Home: 635 Booth Hill Rd Shelton CT 06484-3478 Office: Housatonic Community Coll 900 Lafayette Blvd Bridgeport CT 06604-2400

GALLAGHER, JOHN FRANCIS, education educator; s. John Charles Edward and Marion (McKeon) G.; m. Georgiana Frances Cole; children: Kristen Marie, John David. BA in Philosophy, Mary Immaculate Coll.; STD in Theology, U. Fribourg, Switzerland; MS in Indsl. Rels., EdD, Rutgers U. Instr. Mary Immaculate Coll., Northampton, Pa., 1962-65; asst. prof. Coll. St. Vincent De Paul, Boynton Beach, Fla., 1965-69, pres., 1966-70, assoc. prof., 1969-70; advisor instructional resources SUNY, Plattsburgh, 1970-71; dean humanities Brookdale Community Coll., Lincroft, N.J., 1971-73, v.p. acad., 1973-81; dir. Rockland Campus Iona Coll., New Rochelle, N.Y., 1981-83, dean Sch. Gen. Studies, 1983-89, provost, v.p. acad. affairs, 1989-95, prof. edn., 1995—. Mem. coll. evaluation team N.J. Dept. Higher Edn., Trenton, 1975-77, N.Y. State Edn. Dept., Albany, 1980—; coord. coll. activities to achieve accreditation by Nat. Coun. for Accreditation of Tchr. Edn., 1999—, chief instnl. rep., 1999—. Chair County Arts Festival, Monmouth County, N.J., 1972; trustee Monmouth County Arts Coun., Red Bank, N.J., 1973-76. Mem. Am. Ednl. Studies Assn., Philosophy of Edn. Soc., Soc. for History Edn., Mid. States Assn. Colls. and Scis. (coll. evaluation team 1976—), Phi Delta Kappa. Avocations: photography, classical music, tennis. Office: Iona Coll Dept Edn New Rochelle NY 10801 E-mail: jgallagher@iona.edu.

GALLAGHER, JOHN PAUL, association administrator; b. Chgo., Aug. 14, 1961; s. Wayne and Phyllis (Lehn) G. AS, Northwestern Bus. Coll., 1982; BS, DeVry Inst. Technology, Chgo., 1985. Adminstr.-treas. PREVAIL, Inc., Madison, Wis., 1991-96; exec. dir. Cordial Unltd., Inc., Madison, 1996—. Adminstrv. asst. Wis. Mental Health Consumer/Survivor Work Group, Madison, 1994-96; bd. dirs. M.C. Video Prodns., Inc. Author: How-To Aquarium Care, 2001, How-To Hair Regrowth, 2002; co-author: Stress Kit Workbook, 1996, Gaining Access: Financial Benefits for the Disabled, 1997; co-editor: The ADA, 1997, Managed Care and You, 1997; editor: State of Wisconsin Regional Areas Resource Guide, 2001. E-mail: mrjpgallagher@aol.com.

GALLAGHER, KENT GREY, theater arts educator; b. Oak Park, Ill., Nov. 9, 1933; s. Charles Joseph and Lucile Catherine Bianca (Nussle) G.; m. Sandra Rae Hamblin, Aug. 31, 1957 (div. 1975); children: Geoffrey Kent, Douglas Grey, Bradford Dean; m. Sonja Eileen Newland, Jan. 30, 1976; children: Justin Blake, Andrew Anthony. BA, Carleton Coll., Northfield, Minn., 1957; MA, Ind. U., 1960, PhD, 1962. Asst. prof., dir. theatre Ball State U., 1962-66; prof., dir. theatre Wash. State U., Pullman, 1966-76, grants adminstr., 1973-75; chmn. theatre arts Tex. Christian U., Ft. Worth, 1976—80, 1980—84, asst. to dean, grants and devel. adminstr., 1984—88; prof. No. Ill. U., DeKalb, 1980—, chair theatre arts, 1980—84. Evaluator NEH, Washington, 1976-82; cons. N. Fort Worth Devel. Corp., 1977-80, Arts V, DeKalb, 1984-86, Preserve the Egyptian Theatre Found., DeKalb, 1982-84; realtor, Geneva, Ill., 1987-88, Wayne, Ill., 1988-96; prin. Fountains of Glendale Heights Ltd., Wayne Adv. Corp., Wayne Partnership Ltd., 1992-97. Producer Walla Walla Outdoor Drama, 1969-71, Granbury Opera House, Tex., 1977-80, Ft. Worth Shakespeare in Park, 1978-80; founder, producer Ill. Stage Co., Woodstock, DeKalb, 1984; author: Foreigner in American Drama, 1966, (film) The Bariloche Connection, 1979; dir. numerous TV, film and state prodns.; contbr. articles to profl. publs. Pres. ACLU, Pullman, 1968-70, bd. dirs., 1969-71; prodn. cons. Ft. Worth Coun. Chs., 1976-80. With U.S. Army, 1953-55. Recipient Kennedy Ctr. medallion, 1980; Edwards fellow, 1961-62, Woodrow Wilson fellow, 1967; London prof. Northwest Interinstl. Coun., 1972. Mem. Am. Theatre Assn. (bd. dirs. 1968-76), Am. Coll. Theatre Festival (bd. dirs. 1972-76), Tex. Coll. Theatre Festival (bd. dirs. 1978-80), Northwest Drama Conf. (pres. 1973-74), Ill. Theatre Assn., Alpha Psi Omega. Avocation: sailing. Home: 1128 Brentwood Pl Geneva IL 60134-1628

GALLAGHER, LINDY ALLYN, banker, financial consultant; b. Kalamazoo, Sept. 27, 1954; d. Karl P. Joslow and Audrey S. Phillips; m. Thomas J. Gallagher, Nov. 29, 1975; children: James Allyn Buckley, Phillip Graham, Charles Bedloe. BS, U. Pa., 1975; MBA, Columbia U., 1982. Mem. faculty, rschr. U. Pa., Phila., 1976-80; corp. banking officer Bank of Montreal, N.Y.C., 1982-84; v.p. Citibank NA, N.Y.C., 1984-89; v.p., mgr. Chase Manhattan Bank, N.Y.C., 1989-90; pres. The Allyn Co., New Canaan, Conn., 1990-99; prin. State Street Global Advs., 1999; pvt. fin. cons., 2000—. Treas., dir. 957 Lexington Corp., 1981-87. Editor Columbia Jour. World Bus., 1980-82. Mem. Women's Nat. Rep. Club, 1986—; commr. Town of New Canaan, 1991-99; treas., sec. Young Women's League New Canaan, Inc., 1992-94; bd. dirs. Charlotte Latin Sch., 2000-. Mem. Stanwich Club, The Penn Club (N.Y.C.), The Breakers Club. Republican. Episcopalian.

GALLAGHER, LISA MARIE, music therapist; b. Massillon, Ohio, July 7, 1966; d. Gerald Joseph and Darlene L. (Loper) White; m. Edward Peter Gallagher, Sept. 10, 1994; 1 child, Megan Marie. MusB in Music Therapy, Ohio U., 1989; MA in Counseling and Human Devel., Walsh U., North Canton, Ohio, 1993. Bd. cert. music therapist, Ohio. Mental retardation profl. Echoing Ridge Residential Ctr., Canal Fulton, Ohio, 1989-92; music therapist Cleve. Music Sch. Settlement, 1992—. Mem. contg. edn. com. Certification Bd. for Music Therapists, 2000-02, sec. 2002-03, chair 2003—; numerous presentations in field. Writer, composer, prodr., performer video Music for Fun and Learning, 1995; contbr. articles to profl. jours. Organist Bible Ch., Canton, Ohio, 1985—, Sunday sch. tchr., 1995—. Mem. ACA, Am. Music Therapy Assn., Ohio Assn. for Music Therapy (treas. 1994-98, sec. 1998—2002, v.p. 2002-), Sigma Alpha Iota (v.p. program Cleve. alumnae chpt. 1997-98, 2000-02, pres. 2002-). Republican. Avocations: cross-stitching, reading, playing piano. Home: 8106 Parmenter Dr Parma OH 44129-5351 Office: Cleve Music Sch Settlement 11125 Magnolia Dr Cleveland OH 44106-1813

GALLAGHER, MICHAEL L. lawyer; b. LeMars, Iowa, Apr. 14, 1944; BA, Ariz. State U., 1966, JD, 1970. Bar: Ariz. 1970. Maj. league scout N.Y. Mets, 1967—70; atty. Snell & Wilmer, Phoenix, 1970—78, Gallagher & Kennedy, Phoenix, 1978—. Judge pro tem Maricopa County Superior Ct., 1979, Ariz. Ct. Appeals, 1985; mem. adv. bd. AMEC, Inc., Americo, U-Haul; bd. dirs. Ariz. Pub. Svc. Co., Omaha World Herald Co., Pinnacle West Capital Corp., Vincor. Chmn. gov.'s adv. com. profl. football, 1981-87, mayor's adv. com. profl. sports, 1984-91; bd. dirs. Maricopa County Sports Authority, 1989; bd. visitors law sch. Ariz. State U., 1979; dir. Valley of the Sun YMCA, chmn., 1995, Phoenix Suns Charities, 2002; trustee Peter Kiewit Found. Fellow Internat. Acad. Trial Lawyers; mem. Am. Bd. Trial Advocates (pres. Phoenix chpt. 1988). Office: Gallagher & Kennedy PA 2575 E Camelback Rd Phoenix AZ 85016-9225 E-mail: mlg@gknet.com.

GALLAGHER, MICHAEL ROBERT, consumer products company executive; b. Cedar Rapids, Iowa, Jan. 21, 1946; s. John Robert and Mabel Helen (Slaymaker) G.; m. Linda Katherine Nebb, Oct. 25, 1975; children: Megan Elizabeth, John William, Edward Michael. BS, U. Calif., Berkeley, 1967, MBA, 1968. Brand mgr. Procter & Gamble Co., Cin., 1968-72; various positions Clorox Co., Oakland, Calif., 1972-77; pres., gen. mgr. Clorox Can., Vancouver, B.C., advt. mgr. household products div., 1980-81, gen. mgr. household products div., 1982-84; pres. consumer products div. Lehn & Fink/Sterling Drug, Montvale, N.J., 1984-85; sr. v.p. Lehn & Fink Products, Montvale, N.J., 1985-87, exec. v.p., 1987-88; pres., chief exec. officer L&F Products Inc. (formerly Lehn & Fink), Montvale, N.J., 1989-95; pres., CEO Reckitt & Colman Inc., Montvale, 1995; CEO Playtex Products Inc., Westport, Conn., 1995—. Bd. dirs. Allergan, 1998—, AMN Healthcare Svcs., 2001—. Vice chmn. United Way Bergen County, N.J., 1985-87, bd. dirs., 1989-96, chmn. bd. dirs. 1993-95, chmn. Golden Ball, 1990; sports chmn. Cancer Care of Am., 1989; mem. exec. coun. Boy Scouts Am., Bergen County, 1990-95, bd. dirs. Haas Sch. Bus., U. Calif., Berkeley, 2002--; trustee St. Luke's Sch., 1998—. Mem. Soap and Detergent Assn. (bd. dirs. 1992-95), Grocery Mfrs. Assn. (bd. dirs. 1997—), Assn. Sales and Mktg. Cos. (bd. dirs. 2001—). Office: Playtex Products Inc 300 Nyala Farms Rd Westport CT 06880-6268

GALLAGHER, PATRICK TIMOTHY, emergency physician; b. Monroe, La., Oct. 1, 1955; s. Alfred David Gallagher and Mary Agnes (Rizzo) Sewell; m. Shannon Renea Ettredge, July 30, 1994; children: Sarah Elizabeth, Patrick Timothy, Jr. BS, No. La. U., 1977; MD, La. State U. Med. Ctr., 1982. Diplomate Am. Bd. Emergency Medicine. Intern Ea. Conway Meml. Hosp., Monroe, 1982-83; staff emergency physician Willis-Knighton South Hosp., Shreveport La., 1984—, dir. emergency dept., 2000—02. Fellow: Am. Acad. Emergency Medicine; mem.: AMA. Office: Willis-Knighton South Hosp 2510 Bert Kouns Industrial Loo Shreveport LA 71118-3180

GALLAGHER, PAULA MARIE, real estate appraiser; b. Omaha, Nov. 10, 1959; d. Kenneth Leroy and Phyllis Virginia (Stopak) G. Diploma, Nebr. Coll. Bus., 1979; student, Met. Tech. C.C., Omaha, 1979—81, U. Nebr., 1981—85, Coll. St. Mary, 1986—90; BS, Bellevue U., 1993. Lic. real estate appraiser and broker, Nebr. Legal sec. McCormick Cooney Mooney & Hillman P.C., Omaha, 1979; word processor Firstier Bank, Omaha, 1979-83, staff asst., 1983-84; sec. Morrissey Appraisal Svcs., Omaha, 1984; appraiser trainee Morrissay Appraisal Svcs., Omaha, 1985-88, real estate appraiser, 1988—. Residential mem. Am. Inst. Real Estate Appraisers. Mem.: Am. Bus. Women's Assn. (rec. sec. 1984—85, treas. 1988—89, Woman of Yr. award 1989), Appraisal Inst. (sr. residential appraiser), Omaha Women's C. of C. (mem. edn. com. 1990—92, mem. fin. com. 1991—2003, dir. cmty. recognition 1992, dir. edn. 1993, chmn. fin. style show 1995, pres.-elect 1996, pres. 1997, immediate past pres. 1998). Roman Catholic. Avocations: needlepoint, counted cross stitch, sewing, reading. Home: 16617 Monroe St Omaha NE 68135-2906 Office: Morrissey Appraisal Svcs 13825 P St Omaha NE 68137-2701

GALLAGHER, R. MICHAEL, academic administrator; DO, Phila. Coll. Osteo. Medicine, 1976. Bd. cert. in family practice Am. Osteo. Bd. Family Physicians, Bd. cert. in pain mgmt. Am. Acad. Pain Mgmt., Bd. cert. in headache mgmt. Nat. Bd. Cert. Headache Mgmt. Assoc. dir. Diamond Headache Ctr., Chgo.; founding dir. Univ. Headache Ctr., Moorestown, NJ; prof. family medicine, dean Sch. Osteo. Medicine U. Medicine and Dentistry of N.J. Editor Drug Therapy for Headache; co-editor: Osteopathic Medicine: A Reformation in Progress; contbr. articles to profl. med. jours. Pres. Nat. Bd. Cert. in Headache Mgmt.; sec. bd. trustees Nat. Headache Found. Fellow: Alliance of Air Guard Flight Surgeons, Coll. Physicians Phila., Am. Assn. Study of Headache, Am. Coll. Osteo. Family Physicians. Office: One Med Ctr Drive Stratford NJ 08084

GALLAGHER, RICHARD SIDNEY, lawyer; b. Minot, N.D., May 10, 1942; s. J.W.S. and Esther T. (Tappon) G.; m. Ann Rylands Larson, June 24, 1972; children: Elizabeth, Catherine. BSBA, Northwestern U., 1964; JD, Harvard U., 1967. Ptnr., chmn. dept. tax and individual planning Foley & Lardner, Milw., 1967—. Bd. dirs. Badger Meter Found., Milw. Bd. chmn. Milw. Youth Symphony Orchs., Milw., 1980-82; bd. chmn. Milw. County Performing. Arts Ctr., Milw., 1986-91; dir. Curative Rehab. Ctr., Milw., 1988-93, United Performing Arts Fund, 1991-99; pres. Donors Forum of Wis., 1997-2000. Lt. comdr., USN, 1967-69, Vietnam. Fellow Am. Coll. Tax Counsel, Am. Coll. of Trust and Estate Coun., Am. Law Inst.; mem. ABA (chmn. exempt orgns. com., sect. of taxation 1989-91, chmn. com. on adminstrn. of trusts and estates, sect. probate and trust law 1996-98). Office: Foley & Lardner US Bank Ctr 777 E Wisconsin Ave Milwaukee WI 53202

GALLAGHER, ROBERT P. bank executive; s. Robert P. Sr. and Renata Gallagher. BA in Econs., Williams Coll., 1988; MBA in Fin., NYU, 1992. Lending officer Scotiabank, N.Y.C., 1992—94; v.p. mktg. Mizuho Corp. Bank, Ltd., N.Y.C., 1994—.

GALLAGHER, SHAUN ANDREW, philosophy educator, writer; b. Phila., Oct. 3, 1948; s. John and Bridget (McBride) G.; m. Elaine DeBenedictis, May 29, 1983; children: Laura, Julia. MA, Villanova U., 1976; PhD, Bryn Mawr Coll., 1980; MA, SUNY, Buffalo, 1987. Asst. prof. Gwyneed(Pa.)-Mercy Coll., 1980-81; from asst. to assoc. prof. Canisius Coll., Buffalo, 1981-93, prof. philosophy, 1993—2003, dir. cognitive sci. program, 1996—2003; prof. and chair philosphy U. Ctrl. Fla., 2003—. Vis. scientist cognition and brain scis. Med. Rsch. Coun., Cambridge, Eng., 1994; editl. bd. The Personalist Forum, 1996—. Author: Hermeneutics and Education, 1992, The Inordinance of Time, 1998; editor: Hegel, History and Interpretation, 1996, (jour.) Phenomenology and the Cognitive Scis.; co-editor: Merleau-Ponty, Hermeneutics and Post-Modernism, 1992; : Models of the Self, 1999. Bd. dirs. Audubon Devel. Corp., Amherst, N.Y., 1988-90; chair Audubon Archtl. Com., Amherst, 1985-92; bd. dirs. Audubon Assn., Amherst, 1986-90. Fellow Whiting Found., Louvain, Belgium, 1979, NEH, 1994, 98. Mem. Am. Philos. Assn., Internat. Forum on Persons, Merleau-Ponty Soc. (bd. advisors 1989—). Avocations: irish music, british mysteries, travel. Office: Philosophy Dept Univ Ctrl Fla Buffalo NY 14208

GALLAGHER, SHERRY E. artist; b. Great Falls, Mont., Feb. 1, 1951; d. Mike and Ina (Hanson) Morris; m. Ron Gallagher, Nov. 8, 1969 (div. Sept. 1986); children: Tonya, Ronald Paul; m. Peter Northcott, Aug. 29, 1987 (div. Mar. 2002). Instr. various workshops. Exhibited in group shows at Mus. Native Am. Culture, Spokane, Wash., 1985 (Art Com. award), 1989 (Best of Show-Traditional), Gov's. Mansion Mont., 1989-90, Las Vegas Art Mus., 1992. Recipient 3d place award Safari Club Internat. Art Competition, Reno, Nev., 1992, Juror's award and Best of Show Western Art Assn., Ellensburg, Wash., 1992, Best of Show Olfield Prodns. Celebration of Western Art, Popular Vote award-profl. div. Mont. State Fair Fine Arts, 1983-85, 90, Best of Show, 1987, 89, 98. Home and Office: PO Box 3122 Great Falls MT 59403-3122

GALLAGHER, TERRENCE VINCENT, editor; b. Phila., Nov. 22, 1946; s. Harold John and Marie Elizabeth (Kershaw) G.; m. Eileen Rose Small, Dec. 26, 1971; children: Sean Terrence, Elizabeth I. BS in Journalism, Temple U., 1971. With Chilton Co., Radnor, Pa., 1971-94; asst. editor Product Design and Devel. mag, 1971-73; mng. editor Internat. Product Digest, 1973-74; editor-in-chief Instrument and Apparatus News mag., 1974-84, Hardware Age mag., 1984-94, Decorative Products World, 1989-94, Outdoor Power Equipment Mag, 1989-94, Garden Supply Retailer mag., 1989-94; editorial dir. Chilton's Home and Yard Care Group, 1989-94; chmn. editorial bd. Chilton Co., 1980-83; contbg. editor Tennis U.S.A., 1974-75; pres. Gallagher Communications, 1994—. Served to 1st lt. U.S. Army, 1966-69, Vietnam. Decorated Bronze Star with 2 V devices; Vietnamese Cross of Gallantry. Home: 141 Chaps Ln West Chester PA 19382

GALLAGHER, TESS (THERESA JEANETTE BOND), writer, poet; b. Port Angeles, Wash., July 21, 1943; d. Lesley Orfus and Georgia Marie Bond; m. Raymond Carver, June 17, 1988 (dec. Aug. 2, 1988). BA, U. Wash., 1967, MA, 1971; MFA in Creative Writing and Poetry, U. Iowa, 1974; DHL (hon.), Whitman Coll., 2000. Tchg. asst. U. Iowa, 1972-74; faculty St. Lawrence U., 1975-76, Kirkland Coll., 1976-77, U. Mont., 1978-79, U. Ariz., 1979-80, Syracuse U., 1980-90; Lois and Willard Mackey chair poetry Beloit (Wis.) Coll., 1989, Lois and Willard Mackey chair fiction, 1990; Cockefair chair disting. writer-in-residence U. Mo., Kansas City, 1994; Edward F. Arnold vis. prof. English, Whitman Coll., Walla Walla, Wash., 1996-97; poet-in-residence Bucknell U., Lewisburg, Pa., 1998. Author: (short stories) The Lover of Horses, 1987, reprint, 1992, At the Owl Woman Saloon, 1999, (poems) Instruction to the Double, 1976, reprint, 1994, Under Stars, 1978, Willingly, 1984, Amplitude: New and Selected Poems, 1987, Portable Kisses, 1992, 1996, Moon Crossing Bridge, 1992, Portable Kisses Expanded, 1994, My Black Horse: New and Selected Poems, 1995, Introduction to Call if You Need Me, 2000, Alfredo Arregnin Patterns of Dreams and Nature, 2002; contbr. short stories, poetry, and essays to publs. Hon. trustee Theodore Roethke Meml. Found.; mem. nat. adv. bd. L.A. Poetry Festival; bd. advisors Sarabande Books, Bellingham Rev. Named Lit. Lion, N.Y. Pub. Libr., 1989, 1990; recipient award for fiction, Gov. of Wash., 1987, Nancy Blankenship Pryor award, 1999, Translation award, Bloodaxe Books, 1997, Most Notable Book List, Am. Libr. Assn., 1993; NEA fellow, 1977, 1987, Lyndhurst Found. fellow, 1993, Guggenheim fellow, 1978, N.Y. State grantee, 1988. Office: care ICM Amanda Urban 40 W 57th St New York NY 10019-4001

GALLAGHER, THOMAS EDMUND, hotel executive, lawyer; AB magna cum laude, Holy Cross Coll., 1966; JD cum laude, Harvard Univ., 1969. Bar: Calif. 1970. Assoc. Gibson, Dunn and Crutcher, 1969—70, 1973—77, ptnr., 1977—92, with, 1977—79, 1979—83, 1983—87, 1988—92; legis. asst. US Senate, 1970—72; pres., CEO The Griffin Group, Inc., 1992—97; pres., CEO Resorts Internat./Griffin Gaming and Entertainment, Atlantic City, 1995—96; exec. v.p., chief adminstrv. officer, gen. counsel Hilton Hotels Corp., Beverly Hills, Calif., 1997-2000; pres. & CEO Park Place Entertainment Corp. (NYSE-PPE), Las Vegas, 2000—. Office: Park Place Entertainment Corp 3930 Howard Hughes Pky Las Vegas NV 89109

GALLAGHER, TONYA MARIE, family support specialist; b. Great Falls, Mont., Aug. 2, 1971; d. Ronald A. and Sherry E. (Morris) G. BA in Psychology, BA in Comm. Studies, U. Mont., 1994, M in Interdisciplinary Studies, 1999. Cert. family support specialist II, Mont. Project asst./resource coord VVCAP, Missoula, Mont., 1993-96; grad. asst. dept. psychology U. Mont., Missoula, 1996-97; family support specialist Western Mont. Comprehensive Devel. Ctr., Missoula, 1997—. Mem. coun. Youth in Crisis Coalition, 1995—; bd. dirs. MCAT, 1999. Vol. coord. AmeriCorps, Missoula, 1996-2000; crisis vol. YWCA Domestic Violence Assistance Program, 1992-95. Recipient Children And Youth scholarship award Am. Legion, 1993, Heisey award Mont. Cascade Coun., 1992; Mountain West Regional scholar Golden Key Nat. Honor Soc., 1994-95; Early Intervention scholar, 1994-97. Mem. AAUW, Grad. Student Assn., Psi Chi, Alpha Phi (treas. 1989). Lutheran. Avocations: stamp collecting, poetry, skiing, hiking, dance. Home: PO Box 2166 Kalispell MT 59903 Office: Western Mont Comprehensive Devel Ctr 945 4th Ave E Kalispell MT 59901

GALLAGHER, VICKI SMITH, real estate agent; b. Norfolk, Va., Dec. 6, 1950; d. James Colan and Margaret Helen (Brewer) Smith; m. Steven Robert Gallagher, Nov. 19, 1977. BS in Music Performance, Old Dominion U., 1973. Agt. GSH Residential, Chesapeake, Va., 1979-84, Realty Cons., Virginia Beach, Va., 1984-90, Leading Edge Realty, Virginia Beach, 1990—. Recipient Million Dollar Sales award, Nat. Assn. Home Builders, 1993, Humanitarian of Yr., Internat. Cat Assn. Mid-Atlantic Region, 1996, Gold award, Hampton Rds. Assn. Realtors Million Dollar Sales Club, 2001, Nat. Assn. Home Builders, 2002. Mem.: Tidewater Assn. Realtors (Million Dollar Club 1995, Million Dollar Sales Club 1996—97, Million Dollar Club 1998, Million Dollar Cir. Silver award 1999, Diamond award 1999), Va. Assn. Realtors, Tidewater Builders Assn. (Million Dollar Sales Club 1993, Silver Hammer award Millions Dollar Sales Cir. 1994, Million Dollar Cir. 1995—97, Pres.s award 1996, Million Dollar Sales Club 1998, 2001, others), Tidewater Bd. Realtors (Million Dollar Sales Club Gold award 1993, Silver award 1994, 1996, Million Dollar Sales Club Gold award 1998, others, Million Dollar Sales Club Gold award 2002), Leading Edge Realty Achievers Club (Listing Agt. of the Yr. 1996, 1997, 1998, 1999, 2000, 2001, Resale Agt. of the Yr. 2001, Resale Agent of Year 2002). Avocation: gardening. Home: 2236 Crossroad Trl Virginia Beach VA 23456-3538 Office: Leading Edge Realty Expressway Ctr 4772 Euclid Rd Ste B Virginia Beach VA 23462-3800 E-mail: ilisten@erols.com.

GALLAHER, FREDERICK BLAKE, public health specialist; b. Socorro, N.Mex., Jan. 10, 1947; s. Frederick Eugene Gallaher and Letha Evelyn Morris; m. Josephine Romy Saavedra, Aug. 1, 1981; children: Justin Blake, Patrick James. Student, U. Okla., 1973; BA in Theology, San Jose Christian Coll., 1974; MPA, U. N.Mex., 1988; MPH, Harvard U., 1995. LPN, emerg. room mgr. U. N.Mex. Hosp., Albuquerque, 1975-77, 78-79; health facility surveyor State of N.Mex. Health and Environ. Dept., Santa Fe, 1979-82, state tng. coord. emergency med. svcs., 1988-90; adminstrv. intern City of Albuquerque/Office of the Mayor, 1985-86; dir. admissions, LPN Ladera and Montebello Nursing Homes, Albuquerque, 1987-88; adminstr. Ctr. for Disaster Medicine U. N.Mex. Sch. Medicine, Albuquerque, 1990-93; dir. tng. Brewster Ambulance Co., Boston, 1993-94; spl. forces med. specialist, instr. U.S. Army, 1975-94; project mgr. Human Survival Program Harvard U., Cambridge, Mass., 1994-95; pres. High Desert Cons., Santa Fe, 1995—96; dir. Health Facility Compliance Health Dept., Santa Fe, 1996—2001; mng. dir. Gallaher Cons., 2001—02; pres. Policy and Orgnl. Consulting, Inc., Pecos, N.Mex., 2002—; CEO Pecos Valley Med. Ctr., Inc., 2003—. Presenter in field. Contbr. articles to profl. publs.; author: A Medical Handbook for Disaster and Refugee Operations, U. N.Mex., 1993. Mem. Nat. Coun. State EMS Tng. Coords. (chmn. practical exam com. 1989-90), Nat. Disaster Med. Sys., Spl. Forces Assn. (decade), Mensa, Pi Alpha Alpha.

GALLAHER, WILLIAM MARSHALL, dental laboratory technician; b. Philipsburg, Pa., June 10, 1952; s. Marshall William and Florence Marie (Millner) G. Degree in Dental Tech., Hiram G. Andrews Ctr., 1971; BS, Rutgers U., 1979. Cert. dental technician in full dentures. Dental lab. technician to pvt. practice dentist, Osceola Mill, Pa., 1971-72; dental lab. technician Profl. Dental Lab., South Amboy, N.J., 1972-79; instr. dental lab. tech. Union Tech. Inst., Neptune, N.J., 1979-84, Hiram G. Andrews Ctr., Johnstown, Pa., 1980-91; owner Gallaher's Dental Lab., Asbury Park, N.J., 1982-90; sr. dental lab. technician Denture Walk-In Ctr., Harrisburg, Pa., 1991—. Adv. bd. Union Tech. Inst., 1984-90, Hiram G. Andrews Ctr., 1991-92; founder, pres. Person Enjoying New and Innovative Software User Group, Asbury Park, 1985-90. Author instrnl. manuals. Vol. deaf svcs. Monmouth County Deaf Group, Asbury Park, 1976-77; publicity chmn. Neighbor Preservation Program, Asbury Park, 1979-82. Mem. Nat. Dental Lab. Assn., Nat. Denturist Soc., N.J. Denturist Soc., Pa. Denturist Assn., Indian Tribal Denturity Assn., Internat. Brotherhood Magicians, Internat. Magicians Soc. (life), Masons (sr. master of ceremonies 1982—). Achievements include research on low-cost denture procedures, cleft palate and post cancerous intra-oral appliances. Home: 425 Walnut St Lebanon PA 17042-1855 Office: 1700 Lincoln St Lebanon PA 17046-1545 Personal E-mail: wgallaher@aol.com.

GALLAMORE, BETTY LOU, nurse; b. Poplar Bluff, Mo., Nov. 23, 1951; d. Virgil Luther and Alta Elaine (Dickerson) Groves; m. James Dewey Gallamore, June 27, 1970 (div. 1979); 1 child, Deborah Lynn; m. Jerry L. Capes, May 28, 1988 (div. 1993). AAS, Belleville Area Coll., Ill., 1979; BSN, St. Mary Coll., Leavenworth, Kans., 1987; MS in Nursing, U. Mo., Kansas City, 1991. RN, Kans.; cert. ARNP; clin. nurse specialist in gerontology. Office nurse Mct. Orthopedics Ltd., St. Louis, 1973-81; dir. nursing Gardner (Kans.) Skilled Facility, 1982-84; staff nurse Bethany Med. Ctr., Kansas City, Kans., 1984-88; staff nurse-ICU Munson Army Hosp., Ft. Leavenworth, 1985-88; nurse coordinator VA Hosp., Leavenworth, 1988-90; staff nurse Bethany Med. Ctr., Kansas City, Kans., 1989-93, Trinity Luth. Hosp., Kansas City, Mo., 1990-95; edn. coord. Kansas City Presbyn. Manor, 1991-95; nurse Coffeyville (Kans.) Regional Med. Ctr., 1993-95, Mercy Hosp., Independence, Kans., 1993-94, traveling nurse, 1995-98; adminstrv. supr. Compton Heights Hosp., St. Louis, 1996-2000; staff nurse Woodriver Twp. Hosp., Woodriver, Ill., 1997-99, Jefferson Meml. Hosp., Crystal City, Mo., 1998-2000; staff nurse ICU/supr. Doctors Regional Med. Ctr. (Tenet Health Sys.), Poplar Bluff, Mo., 2000—; staff nurse St. Anthony's Med. Ctr., St. Louis, 2000—; staff nurse, adminstrv. supr. Forest Park Hosp., St. Louis, 2001—. Conductor workshop in field; affiliate faculty U. Mo., Kansas City, 1992—. Mem. Kans. Nurses Assn., Eagles, Nightingale Nursing Honor Soc. (fellow in nursing sci.), Sigma Theta Tau. Home: PO Box 126 Dupo IL 62239

GALLANIS, KATHRYN ANN, prosecutor; b. Evanston, Ill., June 10, 1960; d. Thomas Constantine and Helen K. (Karkazis) G.; m. Christopher Matern. BBA, So. Meth. U., 1982. Bar: Ill. 1985. Asst. states atty. Cook County States Attys. Office, Chgo., 1985-98; atty. Bruce Farrel Dorn & Assocs., 1998—. Prof. criminal justice dept. Lewis U., Romeoville, Ill., 1992—. Bd. dirs. Greek Orthodox Basketball Tournament, Glenview, Ill., 1988—, Nat. Hellenic Invitational Basketball, Chgo., 1994—, Chgo. Coun. Fgn. Rels.; life mem. Art Inst., New Trier Citizens League; mem. legis. action com. Jr. League; precinct capt. New Trier Rep. Orgn.; v.p., Chgo. Rep. Women's Network. Named one of 100 Women Making a Difference Today's Chgo. Women's Mag. Mem. ABA, Chgo. Bar Assn. (jud. evaluation com.), Womens Bar Assn., Profl. Soc. for Abused Children, So. Meth. Alumni Assn., LWV (bd. dirs.), Hellenic Am. Police Assn., Hellenic Bar Assn., Jr. League of Chgo., Chgo. Found. for Women (bd. dirs.), Delta Gamma Alumni Assn. Avocations: skiing, reading, piano, traveling. Home: 136 Melrose Ave Kenilworth IL 60043-1249 Office: Bruce Farrel Dorn & Assocs 120 N Lasalle St Chicago IL 60602-2424

GALLANT, CAROL DANIELS, not-for-profit fundraiser, consultant; d. William Russell Daniels and Caroline Neuner House; m. Allan David Gallant, July 9, 1977; children: Samuel, Ann Prevatt Irons. BS, Towson U., 1971. Cert. Assn. of Fundraising Profl., 1997. Cons. Cmty. Devel. Group, Balt., 1990—; founder, owner Sam's Bagels, Balt., 1992—; dir., tng. & info. Rural LISC, Washington, 1996—99; v.p. of devel. Devel. Tng. Inst., Balt., 1999—2002; dir., found. rels. NCB Devel. Corp., Washington, 2002—. Bd. mem. Coop. Devel. Found., Washington, 2003—. Author: Show Me The Money! A Guide To Fundraising For Community Based Organizations. Home: 2200 South Rd Baltimore MD 21209 Office: NCB Develop Corp 1725 Eye St NW Ste 600 Washington DC 20006

GALLANT, JEFFREY ANDREW, lawyer; b. Saginaw, Mich., Feb. 25, 1965; s. Thomas John and Betty Jane Gallant; m. Angelina Renee Vega, May 25, 1996. BA in Philosophy, U. Mich., 1986, JD, 1990. Bar: Mich. 1990. Trial atty. Dept. Justice, Washington, 1990-96; assoc. Feeney, Kellett, Bloomfield Hills, Mich., 1996-98; asst. U.S. atty. U.S. Dist. Ct. for Ea. Dist. Okla., Muskogee, 1998—. Candidate state rep. Rep. Orgn., Clarkston, Mich., 1996; bd. dirs. Libr. Mem. Phi Beta Kappa. Roman Catholic. Avocations: reading, volunteering. Office: US Atty Office 1200 W Okmulgee St Muskogee OK 74401-6848

GALLANT, JOEL EMANUEL, physician; b. L.A., Jan. 23, 1958; s. Alfred Joseph and Donna Jean (McVey) G. BS in Biol. Scis., U. Calif., 1979, BA in Social Ecology, 1980, MD, 1985; MPH in Internat. Health, Johns Hopkins U., 1990. Intern, resident Yale-New Haven (Conn.) Hosp., 1985-88; chief resident and instr. Yale Univ. Sch. Medicine, New Haven, 1988-89; fellow infectious diesease Johns Hopkins Univ. Sch. Medicine, Balt., 1990-92, asst. prof. medicine, 1992-97, assoc. prof. medicine, 1997—; dir. HIV clinic Johns Hopkins Hosp., Balt., 1992-2001, assoc. dir. AIDS svc., 2001—; assoc. prof. epidemiology John Hopkins Bloomberg Sch. of Pub. Health, 2003—. Mem. editl. bd. Jour. of the Gay & Lesbian Med. Assn., 1995-2002, The Hopkins HIV Report, 1996—, Johns Hopkins AIDS Svc. Website, 1997—, Thrive, 1999-2002, Moore News Quar., 2000—; contbr. articles to profl. jours. Cmty. adv. bd. Md. State AIDS Adminstrn., Balt., 1996-98, adv. com. HIV related clinical guidelines, 1995—. Recipient John C. Hume award Johns Hopkins Sch. Hygiene & Pub. Health, 1990. Fellow Am. Coll. Physicians, Infectious Disease Soc. Am., Gay and Lesbian Medical Assn., Internat. AIDS Soc., Phi Beta Kappa, Delta Omega Alpha. Avocations: sailing, bicycling, travel. Office: Johns Hopkins Univ Sch Medicine 1830 E Monument St Ste 443 Baltimore MD 21287-0003 E-mail: jgallant@jhmi.edu.

GALLANT, ROY ARTHUR, writer, education educator; b. Portland, Maine, Apr. 17, 1924; s. Edward Joseph and Lodia Belle (Dutel) Gallant; children: Jonathan Roy, James Christopher. BA, Bowdoin Coll., 1948; MS, Columbia U., 1949, postgrad., 1954—59. Reporter Retailing Daily, N.Y.C., 1949—50; writer, editor Boys' Life mag.; mng. editor Scholastic Tchr. mag., 1953—57; author-in-residence, editor Doubleday, N.Y.C., 1957—59; editl. dir. Aldus Books, Ltd., London, 1959—62; editor-in-chief Natural History Press, N.Y.C., 1962—65; dir., lectr. Southworth Planetarium U. So. Maine, 1980—2000, adj. prof. English, 1980—2001, prof. emeritus, 2001—. Mem. faculty Maine Coll. Art, 1990—93, Am. Mus. Hayden Planetarium, N.Y.C., 1972—78; earth sci. cons. Sci. and Children, 1980—89; cons. Edison Project, 1990; reviewer Am. Biol. Tchr., 1980—88; cons. editor Nature and Sci., 1965—68; cons. Pres.'s Com. for Scientists and Engrs., 1954. Author: 100 books; mem. editl. bd. Natural History mag., 1962—64; contbr. With USAAF, 1943—46, with CIC&MI, 1950—52. Recipient Outstanding Sci. Book for Children award, Nat. Sci. Tchrs. Assn., 1980, 1982, 1983, 1985, 1986, 1987, Disting. Achievement award, U. So. Maine, 1981, Publ. award, Georg. Soc. Chgo., 1980, Jr. Book award, Boys' Club Am., 1959, Nat. Mass Media award, Thomas Alva Edison Found., 1959, John Burroughs award for nature writing, 1996, Lifetime Achievement award, Maine Libr. Assn., 2001. Fellow: Royal Astron. Soc.; mem.: AAAS, Aircraft Owners and Pilots Assn., Nat. Sci. Tchrs. Assn., N.Y. Acad. Scis., Authors Guild. Home: PO Box 228 Rangeley ME 04970-0228 E-mail: rgal@megalink.net.

GALLARDO, HENRIETTA CASTELLANOS, writer; b. San Antonio, July 16, 1934; d. Francisco Garcia and Elisa Duarte (Moreno) Castellanos; m. Albert Joseph Gallardo, Aug. 19, 1965; children: Frank Cantu, Roger Cantu (dec.), Gloria Michelle. Cert., Draughn's Bus. Coll., San Antonio, 1952. Sec. Kelly Air Force Base, San Antonio, 1952-53; exec. sec. U. Tex., Dallas, 1974-82; interior decorator Plano, Tex., 1983-85; writer. Author: Tangled Web of Destiny, 1992, Marsh & Co., 1993, Everyday Heroes, 2002. Democrat. Roman Catholic. Avocations: photography, travel, reading, charity work. Home: 2212 Parkhaven Dr Plano TX 75075-2013

GALLARDO, SANDRA SILVANA, producer; b. Bronx, Jan. 13, 1947; d. Edward Francis and Grace (Mallory) G.; m. Gerald O'Connor, Jan. 21, 1968 (div. 1978); m. Billy Burrows, Sept. 21, 1985. Student, HB Studio, N.Y.C., 1964-72, CCNY, 1964-66. CEO Gallardo Studios, North Hollywood, Calif., 1980—; pres. Camellia Prodns., Studio City, Calif., 1987—. Guest spkr. IRS, Hollywood, Calif., 1990. Prodr., dir., writer The Acting Class, 1988; author: The Winning, 1998, Acting for Success, 1999 (Academic World Star); motion pictures include (co-star) Solar Crisis, The Windwalker, Death Wish II, (star) Out of the Dark, (star) The Tin Angel; movies of the week spls. and pilots include (star) Prison Stories: Women on the Inside, Calendar Girl Murders, (PBS spl., star) The People vs. Inez Garcia, (recurring) Days of Our Lives; episodic TV include (recurring) NYPD Blue, Lou Grant, (co-star) E R, (guest star) Babylon 5, (guest star) Providence, (guest star) Strong Medicine, Golden Girls, (guest star) Ressurection Blvd., (guest star) Kingpin; starred on stage in American Mosaic. Recipient Bronze Star halo So. Calif. Motion Picture Coun., 1985, Golden Eagle award Nosotros, 1989. Mem. SAG (guest spkr. 1988-96), Am. Fedn. TV Arts Scis., Am. TV Arts & Scis., Equity. Avocations: writing, paddle tennis, hiking, museums. Studio: Studio 1500 11440 N Chandler North Hollywood CA 91601 Office: Camellia Prodns # 1500 11440 N Chandler Blvd North Hollywood CA 91601 E-mail: SGalla2222@aol.com.

GALLAS, MARTIN HANS, librarian; b. Berlin, Nov. 23, 1947; came to U.S., 1953; s. Ernst Gallas and Kate Lesser; m. Myoung Ok Lee, Dec. 23, 1977; children: Monica, Matthew. AA, Springfield (Ill.) Coll., 1971; AB, U. Ill., 1973, MLS, 1974. Reference libr. Starved Rock Libr. System, Ottawa, Ill., 1979-81; libr. dir. Springfield Coll., 1974-79, Oakland City (Ind.) U., 1981-86, Ill. Coll., Jacksonville, 1986—. Translator: German POW documents for www.kriegsgefangen.de. With U.S. Army, 1965-68. Avocation: shortwave radio. Office: Ill Coll Schewe Libr 1101 W College Ave Jacksonville IL 62650-2212

GALLASPY, DIXIE, interior designer, innkeeper; b. Franklinton, La., Dec. 12, 1934; d. Fred Whithurst and Camille Gardner Yates; m. John Norman Gallaspy, June 14, 1958; children: John Whithurst, Gardener Weeks, Leland Redding. BA in Interior Design, Tex. Woman's U., 1957; floral degree, Tex. A&M Coll., 1985. Cert. interior designer, La. Dir. interior design Mullers Dept. Store, Lake Charles, La., 1958-60; draftsperson Gabriel & Reames AIA, Lake Charles, 1960-61; owner Dixie's Designs & Flowers, Bogalusa, La., 1962—; interior design dir. Gulf State Theatre, New Orleans, 1978-84, United Artists Cinemas, Dallas, 1979-80, Alfalfa Video Stores, Hammond, La., 1986-91; owner Smoky Creek Plantation Bed and Breakfast Inn, Bogalusa. Chairperson United Way of Bogalusa, 1983, Meth. Ch. Pasonage, 1972—; tchr. New Day Sunday Sch. Meth. Ch., 1972—; mem. Bogalusa Civic League, 1995—, M.A.S.H. Ladies Mardi Gras Riding Group, 1985—; vol. Rest Haven Nursing Home, 1969—; bd. dirs. Washington Parish Fair Assn., 1983-86; foun. and dir. Smoky Creek Summer Sch. for Girls, Bogolusa, 1985—. Named Woman of Yr. Bus. and Profl. Women's Club, 1977, Citizen of Yr. Bogalusa Daily News, 1983, First Queen Magic City Carnival Assn., 1981. Mem. Am. Soc. of Interior Designers (bd. dirs. La. chpt. 1975-80). Republican. Avocations: aerobic dance, organ and piano, gardening, floral arranging, reading. Home: 1737 Gaylord Dr Bogalusa LA 70427-4056 Office: Smoky Creek Plantation 1500 Youngs Rd Bogalusa LA 70427-4040 Fax: 504-735-1550.

GALLAY, ALAN, history educator; b. N.Y.C., Nov. 26, 1957; s. Harold Herman and Leona (Gittenstein) G.; m. Carol Elizabeth Coleman, Aug. 1985; 1 child, Cyrana Coleman. BA in History, U. Fla., 1978; MA in History, Georgetown U., 1981, PhD in History, 1986. Vis. asst. prof. U. Notre Dame, South Bend, Ind., 1986-87, U. Miss., Oxford, 1987-88; prof. history Western Wash. U., Bellingham, 1988—. Vis. prof. Harvard U., Cambridge, Mass., 1990-91; vis. lectr. U. Aukland, New Zealand, 1992. Author: The Formation of a Planter Elite, 1989; editor: Voices of the Old South, 1994, The Colonial Wars of North America, 1512-1763: An Encyclopedia, 1996, The Indian Slave Trade, 2002. Andrew W. Mellon Faculty fellow in the humanities Harvard U., Cambridge, 1990-91, J. William Fulbright fellow U.S. Info. Agy., Washington, 1992, NEH fellow, 1997-98; recipient Outstanding Acad. Title award Choice Mag., 2002, Bancroft prize Columbia U., 2003. Mem. Am. Hist. Assn., Orgn. Am. Historians, So. Hist. Assn., Inst. Early Am. History and Culture. Office: Dept History Western Wash Univ Bellingham WA 98225

GALLEGLY, ELTON WILLIAM, congressman; b. Huntington Park, Calif., Mar. 7, 1944; m. Janice Shrader; four children. Student, Calif. State U., L.A., 1962—63. Businessman, real estate broker, Simi Valley, Calif., from 1968; mem. Simi Valley City Coun., 1979; mayor City of Simi Valley, 1980-86; mem. 100th-108th Congresses from the 21st (now 24th) Calif. dist., 1986—; chmn. internat. rels. subcom. internat. terrorism; judiciary com.; resources com.; select com. intelligence. Mem. Congl. Human Rights Caucus, Congl. Fire Svcs. Caucus, Congl. Task Force on Tobacco and Health, Congl. Task Force on Alzheimers Disease, other congl. caucuses include Automotive, Fight and Control Methamphetamine, Friends of Animals, Wine caucus, Diabetes caucus, Fairness caucus, House Renewable Energy and Energy Efficiency caucus, Older Ams. caucus; chmn. Task Force on Urban Search and Rescue; past vice-chmn., chmn. Ventura County Assn. govts., Calif. Bd. dirs. Moorpark Coll. Found. Republican. Office: US Ho Reps 2427 Rayburn Hob Washington DC 20515-0524*

GALLEGOS, AILEEN ARROYO, financial consultant; d. Vincent Francis and Alice Hernandez Arroyo; m. Anthony Brian Gallegos, July 16, 1955; children: Amanda Silva, Alicia Silva, Maria Carmen Silva, Amanda, Adriana. BA, U. N.Mex, 1978. Waitress, cashier, mgr. Pancho's Mexican Buffet, Albuquerque, 1970—80; ops. supr., internal auditor, mktg. dir. Security Fed. Savs. & Loan, Albuquerque, 1978—86; fin. cons., v.p. Dean Witter, Albuquerque, 1986—96, UBS PaineWebber, Albuquerque, 1996—2000, RBC Dain Rauscher, Albuquerque, 2000—. Bd. dirs. Ronald McDonald Ho. Charities, Albuquerque. Mem. St. Pius H.S. Booster Club, Albuquerque; ch. choir, fin. coun. Prince of Peace Ch., Albuquerque, 2000—03. Mem.: RBC Dain Rauscher Minority Employee Assn. (chairperson 2000—03), Albuquerque C. of C. (Grad. of Leadership Albuquerque 1994), Hispano C. of C., RBC Dain Rauscher Assn. Women Fin. Cons., U. N.Mex. Alumni Assn. Avocations: singing, travel, sports, piano, violin. Office: RBC Dain Rauscher 6200 Uptown Blvd NE Ste 100 Albuquerque NM 87110 Office Fax: 505-872-5900. E-mail: aileen.gallegos@rbcdain.com.

GALLEGOS, LARRY DUAYNE, lawyer; b. Cheverly, Md., Mar. 23, 1951; s. Belarmino R. and Helen (Schlotthauer) G.; m. Claudia M. King, Oct. 1, 1994; 1 child, Will Adam. BS summa cum laude, U. Puget Sound, 1978; JD, Harvard U., 1981. Bar: Colo. 1981, U.S. Dist. Ct. Colo. 1981, U.S. Tax Ct. 1989. Assoc. Pendleton & Sabian, Denver, 1981-83, O'Connor & Hannan, Denver, 1983-86, ptnr., 1986-89, Rossi & Judd, P.C., Denver, 1989-92, Berliner Zisser Walter & Gallegos, P.C., Denver, 1992—2003, Gallegos & Assocs., P.C., 2003—. Served with U.S. Army (ARCOM), 1972-74. Mem. ABA (real property, probate and trust law sect.), Colo. Bar Assn., P.O.E.T.S., Colo. Trial Lawyers Assn., Denver Bar Assn., U.S. Golf Assn. Avocations: tennis, golf. Office: Gallegos & Assocs PC 7720 E Belleview Ave Ste B-350 Greenwood Village CO 80111 Business E-Mail: lgallegos@revealmail.com.

GALLEGOS, LOU, federal agency administrator; Student, U. Md., W.M. Highlands U. Dir. field ops. for Sen. Pete V. Domenici, 1977-84; exec. dir. Rep. Party N.Mex., 1985; state dir. N.Mex. FHA USDA, 1985-86; cabinet sec. human svcs. dept. for Gov. Garrey E. Carruthers, N.Mex., 1987-89; asst. sec. policy budget and adminstrn. Dept. Interior, Washington, 1989—2001; asst. sec. admin. USDA, 2001—. Candidate for U.S. Congress, 1984. Republican. Office: USDA Dept Admin 1400 Independence Ave SW Washington DC 20250

GALLERT, BARBARA LYNN, communications executive; b. Pasadena, Calif., June 18, 1957; d. Horst Gerhard and Annerose Gertrud Gallert. BA in History, BS in Comm. Arts, Calif. State Poly. U., Pomona, 1981; MPA, Calif. State U., San Bernardino, 1999. Linehaul dispatcher Roadway Express, Inc., Adelanto, Calif., 1982-85; cmty. rels. rep. Walnut (Calif.) Valley Water Dist., 1986-88; comm. specialist Western Mcpl. Water Dist., Riverside, Calif., 1988—. Mem. Dept. Water Resources Water Edn. Adv. Coun., Sacramento, 1988—; chair Water Edn. Adv. Coun. Western Riverside County, 1995—; presenter in field. Contbr.: Water Conservation Garden Activity Book, 1992. Dir. Greater Riverside C. of C., 1991—93; vice chair Riverside Mcpl. Mus. Bd., 1994—97; mem. Leadership So. Calif., Leadership Riverside, City of Redlands Housing Commn., 2000—03. Mem.: L.A. Conservancy. Avocations: travel, antiques, volunteer work, movies, hiking. E-mail: bgallert@wmwd.com.

GALLETTA, DENNIS F. business administration educator, consultant; b. Erie, Pa., Sept. 6, 1953; s. Frank T. and Louise M. Galletta; m. Carole S. Hostettler, May 8, 1976; children: Christy S, Lauren E. BS in accounting, Gannon Coll., 1974, MBA, 1978; PhD, U. of Minn., 1983. CPA Pa. Instr. Pa. State U., Erie, 1978—85; assoc. prof. of bus. adminstrn. U. Pitts., 1985—. Cons. in field, Pa., 1985—. (Articles & Books published) Cobol with an Emphasis on Structured Program Design, 1985; contbr. 56 articles and book chapters published; studies cited (in various news programs and bus. jour.). Fellow, Lilley Drug Co., 1986. Mem.: Assn. Info. Systems (assoc.; v.p. mem. svcs. 2000—02). Independent. Roman Catholic. Avocations: photography, personal computing, home theaters, travel. Office: U Pitts Katz Grad Sch Bus Pittsburgh PA 15260 E-mail: galletta@katz.pitt.edu.

GALLETTA, JOSEPH LEO, physician; b. Bessemer, Pa., Dec. 21, 1935; s. John and Grace (Galletta) G.; m. Teresita Suarez Soler, Feb. 19, 1961; children: John II, Angela, Eric, Christopher, Robert Francis, Michael Angelo. Student, U. Pitts., 1953-56; MD, U. Santo Tomas, Manila, 1962. Diplomate Am. Bd. Family Practice. Intern St. Elizabeth Hosp., Youngstown, Ohio, 1963-64; family practice medicine 29 Palms, Calif., 1967-77, 1977—; chief of staff 29 Palms Cmty. Hosp., 1970-71, 73-76; vice-chief of staff Hi-Desert Med. Ctr., Joshua Tree, Calif., 1976-77; chmn. dept. family practice Hemet Valley Hosp., 1981-83, med. dir. chem. dependency dept., 1985-88; med. dir. Loma Linda (Calif.) U. Behavioral Medicine Ctr. Recovery Svc., 1994-96; pres. Flexisplint, Inc. Founding mem. Hemet Hospice; former cons. Morongo Basin Mental Health Assn.; mem. adv. com. on substance abuse Riverside County, 1995—; med. dir. Addiction Medicine Specialists, Hemet Valley Recovery Svc. Established St. Anthonys Charity Clinic, Philippines, 1965; inventor Flexisplint armboards, S.E.A.R.C.H. assessment tool for addictions; developer lecture on addictions The ABC's of Addictive Behavior. Hon. mem. 29 Palms Sheriff's Search and Rescue, 1971-77; bd. dirs. 29 Palms Cmty. Hosp. Dist., Morongo Unified Sch. Dist. Served with M.C. USN, 1964-67. Fellow Am. Geriatric Soc. (founder West Coast chpt.), Am. Acad. Family Practice, Am. Soc. Addiction Medicine; mem. Calif. Med. Assn., Riverside County Med. Assn., Am. Holistic Med. Assn. (charter), Calif. Soc. Addiction Medicine (mem. exec. coun. 1995-98), Am. Acad. Family Practice, Calif. Acad. Family Practice. Roman Catholic. Home: 27691 Pochea Trl Hemet CA 92544-8180 Office: Westside Medical Pla 4020 W Florida Ave Hemet CA 92545-5279 E-mail: jgalletta@jps.net., jgallett@pe.net.

GALLI, DARRELL JOSEPH, management consultant; b. Ft. Bragg, Calif., Nov. 10, 1948; s. Joseph Germain and Esther Edith (Happajoki) G.; B.A. in Transp./Internat. Bus., San Francisco State U., 1975; BS in Computer Info. Systems, 1985; MBA Golden Gate U., 1980; m. Rondus Miller, Apr. 23, 1977 (div. 1981); 1 dau., Troyan Hulda. With Pacific Gas & Electric Co., Santa Cruz, Calif., 1972-73; with Calif. Western R.R., Ft. Bragg, 1975-77, Sheldon Oil Co., Suisun, Calif, 1978-80; mgr. House of Rondus, Suisun, 1974-79; mgmt. cons., Suisun City, 1979-82; instr. Solano Coll., 1979-81, Golden Gate U., 1981; mem. faculty U. Md. European div., Heidelberg, W.Ger., 1982-88; owner, mgr. Old Stewart House Bed and Breakfast, Fort Bragg, Calif., 1990-2002; lectr. Coll. Redwoods, Ft. Bragg, 1989-92; coord. Small Bus. Mgmt. Seminar, 1980. Author: History of Lucca. Asst. coord. Sr. Citizens Survey for Solano Coll. and Sr. Citizens Ctr., 1980; mem. Ft. Bragg City Coun., 1994-98. Served with U.S. Army, 1969-71. Lic. Calif. real estate agt. Mem. Am. Assn. M.B.A. Execs., World Trade Assn., Bay Area Elec. R.R. Assn. Democrat. Episcopalian. Club: Odd Fellows, VFW Post (comdr.). Home and Office: 150 Grove St Fort Bragg CA 95437-3226

GALLI, JOSEPH, JR., consumer products company executive; BS in Bus. Adminstrn., U. NC, 1980; MBA, Loyola Coll., Balt., 1987. With Black & Decker, 1980—99; pres. Amazon.com, 1999—2000; CEO VerticalNet, 2000—01; CEO, pres. Newell Rubbermaid Inc., 2001—. Office: Newell Ctr 29 E Stephenson St Freeport IL 61032-0943*

GALLI, STEPHEN JOSEPH, biomedical researcher; s. Joseph Marcello and Beatrice Vita Galli; m. Anne Blakeslee Stuart, Mar. 16, 1974; 1 child, David Blakeslee. BA, Harvard Coll., 1968; BMS, Dartmouth Med. Sch., Hanover, N.H., 1970; MD, Harvard Med. Sch., 1973. Diploma Nat. Bd. Med. Examiners, Mass., 1974. Instr. to full prof. pathology Harvard Med. Sch., Cambridge, 1978—99; prof. pathology, microbiology and immunology Stanford U. Sch. of Medicine, Calif., 1999—, Mary Hewitt Loveless, MD prof., 1999—, chair, dept. pathology, 1999—. Author: (over 160 jour. articles and editor 3 books) Topics in Immunology and related fields, over 100 chpts. or reviews. Mem. bd. trustees The Cambridge Sch. of Weston, Mass., 1995—2003. Recipient The Paul Kallos Meml. Lecture, Collegium Internationale Allergologicum, Austria, 1996, Sci. Achievement award, Internat. Assn. of Allergy & Clin. Immunology, 1996, Merit award, Nat. Isnt. of Health, 1995; Rsch. Fellows, Karin Gruenbaum Cancer Rsch. Found., 1971—72, Rsch. fellow, Med. Found. Boston, 1977—78. Mem.: AAAS, Accademia Nazionale dei Lincei, Assn. of Am. Physicians, Assn. of Univ. Pathologists, Collegium Internationale Allergologicum (coun. sec. 2002), Am. Soc. for Clin. Investigative Pathology (coun., v.p.-elect 2003), Am. Assn. of Immunologists. Achievements include patents for 12 medical patents. Office: Stanford Univ Sch of Medicine 300 Pasteur Dr L-235 Stanford CA 94305-5324 Office Fax: 650-725-6902.

GALLIAN, RUSSELL JOSEPH, lawyer; b. San Mateo, Calif., Apr. 24, 1948; m. Pauline G. Davis, Sept. 29, 2000; children: Lisa, Cherie, Joseph, Russell, Yvette, Jason, Ryan, Jennifer. BS, U. San Francisco, 1969, JD with honors, 1974. Bar: Calif. 1974, Utah 1975, U.S. Ct. Appeals (10th cir.) 1975, U.S. Supreme Ct. 1990; CPA, Calif. Staff acct. Arthur Andersen & Co., CPAs, San Francisco, 1969-71; treas., contr. N.Am. Reassurance Life Svc. Co., Palo Alto, Calif., 1972-74, assoc. VanCott Bagley Cornwell & McCarthy, Salt Lake City, 1975-77; sr. ptnr. Gallian & Westfall, Wilcox & Welker, St. George, Utah, 1977—. Chmn. Tooele (Utah) Planning Commn., 1978—80; atty. City of Tooele, 1978—80, Town of Ivins, Utah, 1982—2000, Town of Sprindgdale, Utah, 1987—90, Town of Virgin, 1995—2000, City of Santa Clara, 2001—; commr. Washington County, 1993—96; chmn. Washington County Econ. Devel. Coun., 1993—96; bd. dirs. Dixie Ctr., 1993—96; mem. Habitat Conservation Plan Steering Com., 1993—99; atty. Town of Rockville, 1987—. Mem. ABA, Utah State Bar Assn., Tooele County Bar Assn. (pres. 1978-79), So. Utah Bar Assn. (pres. 1986-87). Republican. Mem. Lds Ch. Office: Gallian & Westfall Wilcox & Welker LC 59 S 100 E Saint George UT 84770-3422 E-mail: carma@gwwwlaw.com.

GALLICCHIO, DAVID MICHAEL, b. Hartford, Conn., Mar. 27, 1943; s. Michael Paul and Blanche Emily (Martino) G.; m. Judith Ann Specht, Feb. 19, 1972. AS, U. New Haven, 1965; BS, Johnson State Coll., 1967; MS, So. Conn. State U., 1971, postgrad., 1979. Cert. profl. educator, Conn. Tchr. Conn. Dept. Correction, Conn. Correctional Inst. Niantic, 1967-73; prin. Unified Sch. Dist. # 1, Niantic, 1973-92; ret., 1992. Chief hostage negotiator Conn. Dept. Correction, Niantic, 1980-92; sch. dist. adminstr. Unified Sch. Dist. 1, 1993—; instr. Conn. Justice Acad., Storrs, 1980-92; assessor new tchrs. Conn. State Dept. Edn., Hartford, 1991-93; cons. Conn. Dept. Children & Families, 2000-2002; edl. cons. pvt. schs., 2003—. Contbr. articles to profl. jours. Commr. Old Saybrook (Conn.) Police Dept., 1990-94, 98—; mem., chmn. Old Saybrook Youth and Family Svcs. Commn., 1984-90; vol. Shoreline Soup Kitchen, 1998—. Avocations: boating, fishing. Home: 12 Pheasant Hill Ln Old Saybrook CT 06475-1133 Office: Conn Dept Correction Unified Sch Dist #1 24 Wolcott Hill Rd Wethersfield CT 06109-1152 E-mail: david.gallicchio@po.state.ct.us.

GALLIEN, SANDRA JEAN, social worker; b. Winchester, Mass., May 13, 1956; d. William Joseph and Shirley Ann (Ewing) Treacy. BA in Early Childhood Edn., U. Mass., 1979; Cert. Advance Study in Adminstrn., Mgmt., Harvard U., 1987; MBA in Mgmt., U. Conn., 1997; MSW, U. Conn., W. Hartford, 1998. Counselor Greater Newburyport Edn. Collaborative, Danvers, Mass., 1991-93; rsch. asst. Inst. African Am. Studies U. Conn., Storrs, 1995-98, rsch. asst. Inst. Advancement Polit. Social Work Practice W. Hartford, 1996-98; intern Conn. Women's Edn. and Legal Fund, Hartford, 1996-97, United Way, Rocky Hill, Conn., 1997—. Contbr. papers to Credit Rsch. Found., 1989. Town precinct coord. congl. campaign, Reading, Mass., 1974; mem. Coventry Dem. Town Com., 1997-99, Unitarian Universalist Soc., East Manchester, Conn., 1999—. Mem. NASW, U. Mass. Alumni Assn., U. Conn. Grad. Bus. Assn. (founder), Emily's List. Avocations: leather and wreath crafting, softball, basketball, writing. Home: 16 Vernon Ave Unit 50 Vernon Rockville CT 06066-6701 E-mail: Sandy.Gallien@ctunitedway.org.

GALLIGAN, CAROLYN M.B. artist, educator; b. Beacon, N.Y., Aug. 27, 1938; d. Joseph Arthor Bolander and Veronica Mary (Cruz) Bolander Gallio; m. David Allen Galligan, Oct. 18, 1958; children: Gregory Jay, David Scott, Nicole Anne. MS, Rochester Inst. Tech. Sch. Art and Design, 1982. Adj. art tchr. Franklin & Marshall Coll., Lancaster, Pa., 1990—, Pa. Sch. Art & Design, Lancaster, 1990—, Elizabethtown (Pa.) Coll., 1990—, Harrisburg Area C.C., Lancaster, 1990—. One-woman shows include Whitaker Ctr., Lancaster Mus., Paula Allen Gallery, N.Y.C., Md. Hall, Annapolis, among others. Grantee City of Lancaster, 1990, Puffin Found., 2000. Democrat. Home: 330 Devon Dr Lancaster PA 17603 E-mail: stras330@netzero.com.

GALLIGAN, MATTHEW G. lawyer; b. New Haven, Sept. 1, 1923; s. Matthew J. and Mary J. (Gordon) G.; m. Anne Elizabeth Reynolds, Apr. 10, 1950. BS, Fordham U., 1947; JD, Georgetown U., 1950. Bar: Conn. 1951. Sole practice, Wallingford, Conn., 1952. Asst. pros. atty. Town of Wallingford, 1953-55, town atty., 1956-57, 1960-69; counsel joint senate ho. judiciary com. Conn. Gen. Assembly, 1971; mem. adv. bd. Am. Nat. Bank, 1979. Corporator Meriden-Wallingford (Conn.) Hosp., 1975. Mem. Conn. Bar Assn., New Haven County Bar Assn., Meriden-Wallingford Bar Assn. Lodges: Elks, Rotary. Roman Catholic. Office: 300 Long Hill Rd Wallingford CT 06492-4948 Fax: 203-269-8334. E-mail: m.galligan@snet.net.

GALLIGAN, THOMAS C., JR., dean, law educator; AB, Stanford U., 1977; JD, U. Puget Sound (now Seattle U.), 1981; LLM, Columbia U., 1986. With Lane Powell Moss & Miller, Seattle; prof. law Paul Hebert Law Ctr. La. State U., Dale E. Bennett prof. law, 1997, exec. dir. La. Jud. Coll., 1996-98; dean, prof. law U. Tenn., Knoxville, 1998—, Elvin E. Overton Disting. prof. law, 2003—. Spkr. on legal topics to various groups, 1987—. Co-author: Legislation and Jurisprudence on Maritime Personal Injury Law, 1997, Louisiana Tort Law, 1996, supplemented 1997, 2000, 01, 02, Personal Injury in Admiralty, 2000, Admiralty in a Nutshell, 4th edit., 2000, Tort Law: Cases, Materials, and Problems, 3d edit., 2002, Cases and Materials on Maritime Law, 2003; contbr. articles to law revs. and acad. jours. Recipient John Minor Wisdom award for acad. excellence in legal scholarship Tulane Law Rev., 1996-97. Office: 1505 W Cumberland Ave Ste 278 Knoxville TN 37996-0001 Fax: 423-974-6595. E-mail: galligan@libra.law.uth.edu.

GALLIHER, CLARICE A. ANDREWS, secondary education educator; b. Laporte, Minn., June 28, 1922; d. Clarence Ray and Luella Anna (Leitch) Andrews; m. Ralph Galliher, June 5, 1943 (dec. Oct. 1985); children: William, Rosemary, Rosanne, Andrew. BS in Secondary Edn., St. Cloud State Coll., 1942; MS, Bemidji State U., 1967. Tchr. math. Ind. Sch. Dist. 11, Baudette, Minn., 1942-43; tchr. math. and sci. Ind. Sch. Dist. 306, Laporte, Minn., 1943-47; tchr. math. Ind. Sch. Dist. 564, Thief River Falls, Minn., 1965-79. Clk. Ind. Sch. Dist. 303 Bd. Edn., Guthrie, Minn., 1948-65; mem. sch. survey com. Hubbard county, Minn., 1961-65. Author of poems; contbr. travel articles to pubs. Mem. United Way, Thief River Falls, 1975-77, pres., 1977; mem. Bus. and Profl. Women's Club, Thief River Falls, 1973-89, pres., 1977-78, chair

Pennington County Ind. Reps., 1974; life mem. N.W. Med. Ctr. Aux., 1980—, sec., 1989-92, v.p., 1992-93, pres., 1993-94; v.p. United Meth. Women, 1987-90, pres., 1993-97; adminstrv. coun. sec. Thief River Falls United Meth. Ch., 1984-91. Named Pennington County Outstanding Sr. Citizen, 2001. Mem. AARP, AAUW (Woman of Honor 2000), NEA (life), Nat. Coun. Tchrs. Math. (life), Minn. Edn. Assn. (life), N.W. Minn. Ret. Educators (v.p. 1983-94, co-pres. 1999-2000), Ret. Educators Assn. Minn. (life), Am. Legion Aux. (life), Thief River Falls Nutrition Coun., N.W. Minn. Sr. Fedn. (sec. 1998-2003), Mensa (life), Delta Kappa Gamma Soc. Internat. (editor MN newsletter 1981-95). Avocations: travel, crafts, photography, gardening, writing.

GALLIHER, KEITH EDWIN, JR., lawyer; b. Fond du Lac, Wis., July 29, 1947; s. Keith Edwin and Dolores Mae (Hazen) G.; m. Linda Lee Dessauer, May 18, 1985; children: Patrick, Christy Lyn. B.S, U. Nev. at Las Vegas, 1970; J.D., Ariz. State U., 1974. Bar: Nev. 1974, U.S. Dist. Ct. Nev. 1974, U.S. Ct. Appeals (9th cir.) 1976, U.S. Supreme Ct. 1990. Assoc. Lionel, Sawyer & Collins., Las Vegas, 1974-75; atty. Clark County Pub. Defender, Las Vegas, 1975-76; sr. ptnr. Mills, Galliher, Lukens, Gibson, Schwartzer & Shinehouse, Las Vegas, 1976-80, Galliher & Tratos, Las Vegas, 1980-83; pres., sr. ptnr. Galliher Law Firm, Las Vegas, 1983—; instr. hotel law U. Nev.-Las Vegas, 1980; alt. mcpl. judge City Las Vegas, 1983—2000. Author: Supplement to Comparison Analysis of ABA Criminal Justice Standards to Nevada Law, 1976. State del. Democratic Party, 1976; bd. govs. March of Dimes, Las Vegas, 1978. Fellow Am. Coll. Trial Lawyers, Roscoe Pound Inst.; mem. Nat. Assn. Trial Lawyers, Nev. Trial Lawyers Assn., ABA, Nev. Bar Assn., Clark County Bar Assn., State Bar Nev. (mem. fee dispute com. 1983), Comml. Law League Am., Real Estate Securities and Syndication Inst., Nat. Coll. Criminal Def. Lawyers and Pub. Defenders. Lutheran. Home: 8609 Titleist Cir Las Vegas NV 89117-5844 Office: 1850 E Sahara Ave Ste 100 Las Vegas NV 89104-3744

GALLIMORE, MARGARET MARTIN, poet; b. Winston Salem, Mar. 20, 1947; d. Holland Henry and Dallas Cornell (Robbins) Martin; m. Elmer Harold Holden Jr., Feb. 14, 1965; children: Andrew Harold, Amy Darlene, John Alan; m. Timothy Milton Gallimore, May 9, 1986. Student, High Point (N.C.) Coll., 1988. With AT&T Network Sys., Winston-Salem, 1965-69, 73-75, prodn. operator, 1979-89; real estate salesperson Lambe-Young Real Estate Co., Kernersville, NC, 1975-79; leasing cons. Vinyard Gardens Apt./S.E. Atlantic Properties, Winston-Salem, 1994-95; comm. assoc. AT&T Phone Ctr., Winston-Salem, 1995-96; real estate salesperson Triad Piedmont Properties, Kernersville, 1996; real estate broker Winston-Salem, 1996—; asst. cmty. mgr. Lindsey Manor Apts./Steven D. Bell & Co., Kernersville, 1997; with child nutrition Winston-Salem Forsyth County Schs., 2001—03. Author poetry. Recipient Editors Choice awards (2) Nat. Libr. of Poetry, 1995, 97; named to Internat. Poetry Hall of Fame, Nat. Libr. Poetry, 1996. Mem. Internat. Soc. Poets (Disting. mem.). Home: 2534 Union Cross Rd Winston Salem NC 27107-4420

GALLINA, CHARLES ONOFRIO, nuclear scientist; b. New Brunswick, N.J., Oct. 10, 1943; s. Matthew Salvatore and Mary (Piazza) G.; m. Ellen Mary Romano, Oct. 10, 1976; children: Mary Catharine, Matthew Charles, Maria Christine. BS, Fordham U., 1965, MS, Rutgers U., 1967, PhD, 1971. Environ radiation specialist Consol. Edison N.Y., N.Y.C., 1971-72; radiation specialist AEC, Newark, 1972-73; sr. radiation specialist Nuc. Regulatory Commn., King of Prussia, Pa., 1973-76, sr. duty officer, 1973-82, investigation specialist, 1976-80, coord. emergency preparedness, 1980-82; sr. emergency preparedness engr. Tera Corp., King of Prussia, 1982; sr. radiol. engr. Hydro Nuc. Svcs., Marlton, NJ, 1982-84, dir. tech. mktg., 1984-85; mgr. bus. devel. Westinghouse Electric Corp., Moorestown, NJ, 1985-87; mgr. tech. program devel. Westinghouse Radiol. Svcs., Moorestown, NJ, 1987-89; sr. nuclear scientist Dept. Nuclear Safety State of Ill., Springfield, 1990—; pres., CEO Springfield STOPP, Inc., 1994—, IHN Comms., Inc., Springfield, 2000—. Exec. cons. Profl. Nuclear Assocs., Springfield, Ill., 1990—; mem. bd. sci. and policy advisors Am. Coun. on Sci. and Health, 1991—; spl. tech. cons. to U.S. Def. Nuclear Agy.; tech. expert in area of emergency preparedness, radiation safety environ. monitoring and reactor health physics IAEA. Tech. reviewer, contbr. Radiation Protection Management Mag., Health Physics Soc. Jour.; contbr. articles to Health Physics Soc. Jour. Pres. Providence Force Condominium Assn., 1973-77; pres., CEO STOPP (Stop Planned Parenthood) of Ill., Inc., 1993—. AEC fellow, 1968-70, USPHS fellow, 1967, fellow Fed. Water Pollution Control Assn., 1971. Mem. Am. Nuclear Soc. (vice chmn., chmn.-elect Midwest Ill. chpt. 1991-93), Delaware Valley Soc. Radiation Protections, Health Physics Soc. (charter mem. Prairie State chpt. 1990—, bd. dirs. Prairie State chpt. 1993—), Am. Coun. of Sci. and Health (bd. sci. and policy advisors 1991—). Home and Office: IHN Comm 31 Trailridge Ln Springfield IL 62704-1035 Fax: 217-547-1568. E-mail: cgallina@insightbb.com.

GALLINAT, MICHAEL PAUL, fisheries biologist; b. Flint, Mich., Nov. 1, 1962; s. Paul John Richard and Myrna Mae G.; m. Carol Ann Koshko, Sept. 8, 1989; children: Nathan Michael, Adam Andrew. BS in Fisheries and Wildlife Mgmt., Lake Superior State U., Sault Ste. Marie, Mich., 1985; MS in Fisheries Biology, Ball State U., 1987. Grad. rsch. asst. Ball State U., Muncie, Ind., 1985-87; pvt. aquatic contractor, Flushing, Mich., 1987-88; rsch. asst. U. Mich., Ann Arbor, 1988; fisheries biologist, program adminstr. Red Cliff Band of Lake Superior Chippewa, Bayfield, Wis., 1988-2000; fisheries biologist Washington Dept. Fish and Wildlife, Dayton, Wash., 2000—. Mem. Wis. Coastal Mgmt. Coun., Madison, 1991-2000, Native Peoples Fisheries Com., 1990-92; adj. mem. Lake Superior Tech. Com., 1988-2000, mem. steelhead, walleye and brook trout subcoms.; adj. faculty Envirovet Program U. Ill., 1991-95; spring chinook specialist Lower Snake River Compensation Plan Wash. Dept. Fish and Wildlife; adv. bd. Walla Walla Pks. and Recreation, 2002—; mem. BPA Captive Broodstock Tech. Oversight Com., 2001—. Mem. Am. Fisheries Soc., Sigma Xi (assoc.). Achievements include research in the biology, life history and food habits of lake trout and lake whitefish in Lake Superior; restoring Endangered Species Act (ESA) listed spring chinook salmon. Home: 104 Leonard St Walla Walla WA 99362

GALLINGER, LOIS MAE, medical technologist; b. Hibbing, Minn., Sept. 5, 1922; d. Clarence Adolph and Dorothy Mae (Stoller) Belanger; m. Ben Elton Gallinger, Sept. 1, 1956; children: Carol Elda, Gregory John. BS, U. Minn., 1946; Med. Tech. Intern, Coll. St. Scholastica, 1948-49. Cert. med. technologist. X-ray technologist Leigh Clinic, Grand Forks, N.D., 1946-47, Nicollet Clinic, Mpls., 1947-48; med. technologist Little Traverse Hosp., Petoskey, Mich., 1949-52; med. and x-ray technologist Lakeside Med. Ctr., Duluth, Minn., 1952-60; med. technologist St. Mary's Med. Ctr., Duluth, 1961-87; retired, 1987. Treas. Benedictine Health Ctr. Aux., Duluth, 1984-97, Women's Assocs. Duluth Symphony, 1986-99; cookie chmn. No. Pine Girl Scouts USA, Duluth, 1969; bd. dirs. St. Paul's Episc. Women's Club, Duluth, 1970s, greeter's chmn., 1970s, corr. sec., 1990-94, publicity chmn., 1994, asst. treas., 1997-98, treas., 1998-2002; vol. Am. Cancer Soc., 1993—, Am. Lung Assn., 1993, Am. Diabetic Assn., 1996, Am. Leukemia Assn., 1996, 98, Mothers March of Dimes, 1997. Mem. AAUW, Am. Soc. Med. Tech., Minn. Soc. Med. Tech. (regional historian 1969), Duluth Women's Club. Avocations: music, reading, playing cards, accounting, politics. Home: 364 Leicester Ave Duluth MN 55803-2203 E-mail: lggallinger@aol.com.

GALLINGER, ROBERT ARTHUR, retired military officer, writer; b. Syracuse, NY, Jan. 23, 1932; s. Charles David and Marion Anne Gallinger; m. Renate Ursula Faschon, July 10, 1953; children: Sherri Elizabeth Barry, Coleen Diane Lonas, Cathleen Roberta Petr. BBA, U. of Alaska, 1962—63; MS in Spl Studies, Telecom. Ops., George Wash. U., 1975—77, MS in Pub. Adminstrn., 1977—79. Maj. U.S. Army Signal Corps., 1965—70. Author: (novels) No Time to Die, Suffer the Fool, Deadly Encounters, A Crooked Path, Dead Light, A Debt of Honor, Whispers, Taken by Force, Escape. Advanced through ranks to major U.S. Army, ret., 1974. Decorated Three Bronze Star Medals Dept. of the Army. Mem.: Mil. Officers Assn. of Am. (life), The Am. Assn. of Ret. Persons, The VFW, Vietnam Veterans of Am. Avocations: reading, writing. Personal E-mail: majragg@aol.com.

GALLIS, CAROLE CAMPBELL, secondary education educator; b. Darby, Pa., Dec. 3, 1944; d. Jack Henry and Marion Alice (McCrea) Campbell; m. John Nicholas Gallis, June 17, 1967; children: John Christopher, Robin Noel Talbot. BS in Edn., Millersville U., 1966; MEd, Pa. State U., Great Valley, 1994. Cert. tchr. English and French, Pa. Tchr. Garden Spot H.S., New Holland, Pa., 1966-67, asst. girls basketball coach, 1966; substitute tchr. Upper Merion Area Sch. Dist., King of Prussia, Pa., 1977-84, tchr., 1984—, girls winter track coach, 1984-88. Advisor H.S. newspaper, 1994—, lit. mag., 1997—; receptionist, tchr., Phebe Anna Thome Sch., Bryn Mawr (Pa.) Coll., 1979-81; historic interpreter Mystic (Conn.) Seaport, 1976. Brownie leader, Freedom Valley Girl Scout Coun., Valley Forge, Pa., 1977-79, Brownie coord., 1979-80. Mem. NCTE, NEA, Journalism Edn. Assn., Am. Assn. Tchrs. Fgn. Lang., Pa. State Edn. Assn., Upper Merion Area Edn. Assn., Kappa Sigma Delta (pres. 1987-89), Delta Kappa Gamma. Methodist. Home: 727 Suellen Dr King Of Prussia PA 19406-1740 Office: Upper Merion Area Sch Dist 435 Crossfield Rd King Of Prussia PA 19406 E-mail: cgallis@upper-merion.k12.pa.us.

GALLIS, JOHN NICHOLAS, retired military officer, executive leadership training consultant; b. Pitts., Dec. 18, 1944; s. John Vincent Glade (dec.) and Sylvia Delores (Rizzo) Friedman (dec.); m. Carole Campbell, June 17, 1967; children: J. Christopher, Robin Noel. AS in Edn., No. Va. C.C., 1975; BS in Healthcare Adminstrn., George Washington U., 1977; MPA, Pa. State U., 1980. Enlisted USN, 1962, advanced through grades to capt., 1995; outpatient svcs. officer Submarine Med. Ctr., New London, Conn., 1974-76; patient adminstrn. officer Naval Hosp., Phila., 1977-80; officer-in-charge Naval Med. Clinic, Willow Grove, Pa., 1980-82; hosp. corpsman/dental technician rating assignment officer Bur. Naval Pers., Arlington, Va., 1982-85; dir. for adminstrn. Naval Hosp., Phila., Va., 1985-88; dir. leadership course Naval Sch. Health Scis., Bethesda, Md., 1988-91; assignment officer Med. Svc. Corps, Arlington, Va., 1991-93; exec. officer Naval Acad. Med. Clinic, Annapolis, Md., 1993-96; leadership and splty. tng. Naval Sch. Health Scis., Bethesda, 1996-98; cons., instr. Navy Medicine Ctr. Orgnl. Devel., Bethesda, 1999-2000; adj. faculty Nat. Fire Acad., Emmitsburg, Md., 2000—. Recipient Meritorious Svc. medal (3 awards), Navy Achievement medal, Navy Commendation medal (5 awards), Submarine Svc. badge. Fellow (life) Am. Coll. Healthcare Execs. Republican. Roman Catholic. Avocations: teaching, workshop. Home: 727 Suellen Dr King Of Prussia PA 19406 also: 3 Dewey Dr Annapolis MD 21401 E-mail: gallis@starpower.net.

GALLIS, PAUL EUGENE, government executive; b. Athens, Ga., Apr. 4, 1947; s. Anthony Henry and Frances Dale Gallis. AB, Davidson Coll., 1969; PhD in European History, Brown U., 1979. French tchr. Woodberry Forest (Va.) Sch., 1970—73; dep. campaign mgr. N.Y. Carter-Mondale Presdl. Campaign, N.Y.C., 1979—80; spl. asst. counselor's office Dept. of State, Washington, 1980—81; speechwriter for senator Joseph Biden U.S. Senate, Washington, 1981—84; sect. head Europe/Eurasia Congl. Rsch. Svc., Washington, 1997—. Mem.: Army-Navy Club. Office: Congressional Rsch Svc 101 Independence Ave SE Washington DC 20540-7460

GALLISON, H(AROLD) BAILEY, SR., youth agency administrator, public relations and marketing consultant; b. Orange, N.J., Apr. 6, 1924; s. Harold Hobron and Stella Camilla (Holm) G.; m. Janet Caralee Frazier, Jun. 23, 1951 (div. Jun. 1983); children: Claudia Jean, Harold Bailey II; m. Sharilyn Leone Lemkuil Gallison, Jan. 27, 1984. BA, U. Mo., 1948. Sales mgr., adminstr. Carll Mercury Dealership, La Jolla, Calif., 1952-53; exec. dir. La Jolla Town Council, 1953-63; advt. mgr. Security Pacific Bank, San Diego, 1963-70; dir. pub. rels. Mercy Hosp., San Diego, 1970-83; sr. account exec. Citadel Comm., San Diego, 1983-85; exec. dir. Community Campership Coun., San Diego, 1985—. Pres. La Jolla Civic Theatre Assn., 1973-76. With USN, 1943-46, MTO. Named Profl. of Yr., San Diego Pub. Rels. Club, 1973, Outstanding Alumni, U. Mo., 1987, Citizen of Yr., San Diego Boy Scout Coun., 1994. Mem. SAR, U.S. Navy League, Ky. Col. So. Calif. (bd. dirs. 1991-2000), U. Mo. Alumni Assn. (past bd. dirs.), Hon. Dep. Sheriff Assn., Kiwanis Club (named Kiwanian of Yr. La Jolla chpt. 1991), Am. Legion, VFW. Republican. Presbyterian. Avocations: tennis, spectator sports, walking, theatre. Office: Community Campership Coun Ste 208 7510 Clairemont Mesa Blvd San Diego CA 92111-1539

GALLIVAN, JOHN WILLIAM, publishing executive; b. Salt Lake City, June 28, 1915; s. Daniel and Frances (Wilson) G.; m. Grace Mary Ivers, June 30, 1938 (dec.); children: Gay, John W. Jr., Michael D., Timothy. BA, U. Notre Dame, 1937. With Salt Lake Tribune, 1937—, promotion mgr., 1942-48, asst. pub., 1948-60, pub., 1960-84; pres. Kearns-Tribune Corp., 1960-86, chmn. bd., 1984-99; dir., exec. com. Tele-Communications, Inc., 1989-2000. Pres. Silver King Mining Co., 1960-97. Pres. Utah Symphony, 1964-65. Mem. Sigma Delta Chi, Bohemian Club (San Francisco). Clubs: Nat. Press (Washington); Alta (Salt Lake City), Salt Lake Country (Salt Lake City), Rotary (Salt Lake City). Home and Office: 1665 White Pine Canyon Rd Park City UT 84060 Fax: 435-645-0735. E-mail: jwgallivan@earthlink.net.

GALLO, ANTHONY ERNEST, playwright, economist; b. Vandergrift, Pa., Feb. 3, 1939; s. Dominic and Sara (Raso) G.; divorced; 1 child, Thomas Augustus. BA, Coll. William and Mary, 1961; MBA, U. Pa., 1963; postgrad., U. Pitts., 1966-70. Investment analyst Pitts. Nat. Bank, 1963-66; instr. mktg. and stats. Duquesne U., Pitts., 1964-69; instr. mktg. U. Pitts., 1965-69; instr. money and banking St. Vincent Coll., Latrobe, Pa., 1966-69; asst. prof. econs. Allegheny C.C., Pitts., 1966-70; econ. cons. SBA, Washington, 1967—; bus. economist Bur. Econ. Analysis/U.S. Dept. Commerce, Washington, 1970-71; sr. economist Econ. Rsch. Svc./USDA, Washington, 1971-2000. Propr. Capitol Hill Victorian Restorations, Washington, 1970-90. Econs. editor U.S. Food Mktg. Rev., 1984-2001; contbr. 300 articles to profl. and govt. jours.; writer (plays) Eugenio, 2002, Margherita, 2002, Death at the Eastern Market, (opera librettos) Eugenio, 2003, Maiphesitos, 2003; librettist, lyricist. Mem. Capitol Hill Restoration Soc., Washington, 1972—, mem. endowment bd., 1999; mem Capitol Hill Garden Club, Washington, 1972—; commr. Vandergrift Mcpl. Authority, 1965-67; pres. Civic League, Vandergrift, 1965-70; mem. governing coun., endowment bd. Holy Rosary Ch. With U.S. Army, 1963. Named Outstanding Civic Leader, Jaycees, Vandergrift, 1967. Mem. Cosmos Club (endowment advisor 1996—2001), Arts Club Washington (endowment bd. 1996-99), John Carroll Soc., Red Circle, U.S. Food Distbn. Rsch. Soc. (bd. dirs. 1994-97), Wharton Sch. Club (bd. dirs. 1991—), Italian Cultural Soc. (bd. dirs. 1994-97), Playwright's Forum, Writers Ctr., Charter Theatre, Dramatists Guild, Am. Composers Forum, Am. Music Ctr. Roman Catholic. Avocations: reading, gardening, swimming, dancing, historic preservation, bridge. Home: PO Box 15414 Washington DC 20003-0414

GALLO, DONALD ROBERT, retired English educator; b. Paterson, N.J., June 1, 1938; s. Sergio and Thelma Mae (Lowe) G.; m. C.J. Bott, Feb. 14, 1997; 1 child, Brian Keith; 1 stepchild, Christian Perrett. BA in English, Hope Coll., 1960; MAT in English Edn., Oberlin Coll., 1961; PhD in English Edn., Syracuse U., 1968. English tchr. Bedford Jr. High Sch., Westport, Conn., 1961-65; rsch. assoc. Syracuse (N.Y.) U., 1965-67; from asst. prof. to assoc. prof. edn. U. Colo., Denver, 1968-72; reading specialist Golden Jr. High Sch., Jefferson County Pub. Schs., Colo., 1972-73; prof. English Cen. Conn. State U., New Britain, 1973-97. Instr. composition Onondaga C. C., Syracuse, 1967; vis. faculty grad. liberal studies program Wesleyan U., 1983; staff writer reading assessment Nat. Assessment Ednl. Progress, Denver, 1972-73; speaker in field; cons. to schs. and librs. Mem. editl. bd. Nat. Coun. Tchrs. English, 1985-88; compiler, editor: Speaking for Ourselves, 1990, Speaking for Ourselves, Too, 1993; editor: Connections: Short Stories by Outstanding Writers for Young Adults, 1989, Visions: Nineteen Short Stories by Outstanding Writers for Young Adults, 1987, Center Stage: One-Act Plays for Teenage Readers and Actors, 1990, Sixteen: Short Stories by Outstanding Writers for Young Adults, 1984, Books for You, 1985, Authors' Insights: Turning Teenagers into Readers and Writers, 1992, Short Circuits: Thirteen Shocking Stories by Outstanding Writers for Young Adults, 1992, Within Reach: Ten Stories, 1993, Join In: Multiethnic Short Stories by Outstanding Writers for Young Adults, 1993, Ultimate Sports: Short Stories by Outstanding Writers for Young Adults, 1995, No Easy Answers: Short Stories About Teenagers Making Tough Choices, 1997, Time Capsule: Short Stories About Teenagers Throughout the Twentieth Century, 1999, On The Fringe, 2001, Destination Unexpected, 2003; author: Presenting Richard Peck, 1989, Bookmark Reading Program, Seventh and Eighth Grade Texts and Workbooks, 1979, Heath Middle Level Literature, 1995; co-author: (with Sarah K. Herz) From Hinton to Hamlet: Building Bridges Between Young Adult Literature and the Classics, 1996; interviewer of authors for Authors4Teens.com website. Recipient Disting. Svc. award Conn. Coun. Tchrs. English, 1989, ALAN award Assembly on Lit. for Adolescents of the Nat. Coun. Tchrs. English, 1992, Cert. of Merit award Cath. Libr. Assn., 1995, Ted Hipple Svc. award NCTE, 2001. Mem. Nat. Coun. Tchrs. English, Assembly on Lit. for Adolescents, Ohio Coun. Tchrs. English Lang. Arts (named an Outstanding English Lang. Arts Educator 2003), Soc. Children's Book Writers and Illustrators, Authors Guild. Avocations: gardening, cooking, traveling, photography. Address: 34540 Sherbrook Park Dr Solon OH 44139-2046 E-mail: gallodon@aol.com.

GALLO, ERNEST, vintner; b. 1909; widowed. Co-owner, chmn. bd. dirs. E & J Gallo Winery, Modesto, Calif., 1933—. Office: E & J Gallo Winery 600 Yosemite Blvd Modesto CA 95354*

GALLO, JOAN ROSENBERG, lawyer; b. Newark, Apr. 28, 1940; BA in Psychology, Boston U.; postgrad. studies in Counseling, We. Md. Coll.; postgrad studies in Clin. Psychology, We. Grad. Sch. Psychology; JD magna cum laude, U. Santa Clara, 1975. Bar: Calif. 1975. Assoc. with Cynthia Mertens U, Santa Clara, Calif., 1975-76; sr. law clk. U.S. Dist. Ct., Calif., 1976-78; assoc. Decker and Collins, San Jose, Calif., 1978-79; from dep. city atty. to city atty. City of San Jose, 1979-2000; ptnr. Terra Law LLP, San Jose, 2000—. Mem. Psi Chi. Office: Terra Law LLP 60 S Market St Ste 200 San Jose CA 95113-2333 E-mail: jgallo@terra-law.com.

GALLO, JON JOSEPH, lawyer; b. Santa Monica, Calif., Apr. 19, 1942; s. Philip S. and Josephine (Sarazan) G.; m. Jo Ann Broome, June 13, 1964 (div. 1984); children: Valerie Ann, Donald Philip; m. Eileen Florence, July 4, 1985; 1 child, Kevin Jon. BA, Occidental Coll., 1964; JD, UCLA, 1967. Bar: Calif. 1968, U.S. Ct. Appeals (9th cir.) 1968, U.S. Tax Ct. 1969. Assoc. Greenberg, Glusker, Fields, Claman & Machtinger, L.A., 1967-75, ptnr., 1975—. Bd. dirs. USC Probate and Trust Conf., L.A., 1980—, UCLA Estate Planning Inst., chmn. 1992—. Contbr. articles to profl. jours. Fellow Am. Coll. Trust and Estate Counsel; mem. ABA (chair Generation Skipping Taxation com. 1992-95, co-chair life ins. com. 1995—), Internat. Acad. Estate and Trust Law, Assn. for Advanced Life Underwriting (assoc. mem.). Avocation: photography. Office: Greenberg Glusker Fields Claman & Machtinger LLP Ste 2100 1900 Avenue Of The Stars Los Angeles CA 90067-4502

GALLO, JOSEPH E. vintner; b. 1941; Various positions Gallo Sales Co., South San Francisco, 1962—, now pres. Office: E & J Gallo Winery 600 Yosemite Blvd Modesto CA 95354*

GALLO, ROBERT CHARLES C. research scientist; b. Waterbury, Conn., Mar. 23, 1937; s. Francis Anton Gallo, Louise Mary (Ciancuilli) Gallo; m. Mary Jane Hayes, July 1, 1961; children: Robert, Marcus, Caroline. BA, Providence Coll., 1959, DSc (hon.), 1974; MD, Jefferson Med. Coll., 1963; 15 hon. degrees from univs. in U.S., Belgium, Italy,, Argentina, Peru, Israel, Sweden. Intern, resident medicine U. Chgo., 1963-65; clin. assoc. med. br. Nat. Cancer Inst. NIH, Bethesda, Md., 1965-68, sr. investigator human tumor cell biology br., 1968-69, head sect. cellular control mechanisms, 1969-72, chief lab. tumor cell biology, 1972-93; dir., prof. medicine and microbiology Inst. Human Virology U. Md., Balt., 1993—. Adj. prof. genetics George Washington U.; adj. prof. biology Johns Hopkins U., Balt., hon. prof. biology, 1985—; hon. prof. medicine Karolinska Inst., Stockholm, 1998 ; US rep. to world com. Internat. Comparative Leukemia and Lymphoma Assn., 1981—; mem. bd. govs. Franco Am. AIDS Found., 1987, World AIDS Found., 1987. Author: (book) Virus Hunting, 1991; author: (or co-author) more than 1,100 sci. papers. With USPHS, 1965—68. Recipient Dameshek award, Am. Hematol. Soc., 1974, CIBA-GIEGY award in biomed. sci., 1977, 1988, Superior Svc. award, USPHS, 1978, Meritorious Svc. medal, 1983, Disting. Svc. medal, 1984, First F. Stohlman lecture award, Am. Soc. Hematol., 1979, Albert Lasker award for basic biomed. rsch., 1982, 1986, Abraham White award in biochem., George Washington U., 1983, First Otto Herz award for cancer rsch., Tel Aviv U., 1982, Griffuel prize, Assn. for Cancer Rsch., France, 1983, GM award in cancer rsch., 1984, Gruber prize, Am. Soc. Investigative Dermatology, 1984, Lucy Wortham prize in cancer rsch., Am. Soc. for Surg. Oncology, 1984, Gold medal, Am. Cancer Soc., 1984, Berla Internat Sci. prize, India, 1985, Hammer prize for cancer rsch., 1985, Gairdner prize for biomed. rsch., Can., 1987, spl. award, Am. Soc. Infectious Disease, 1986, Gold Plate award, Am. Acad. Achievement, 1987, Lions Humanitarian award, 1987, Japan prize in sci. and tech., 1988, Ciba Corning award, 1993, 1st Dale McFarlin award for rsch., Internat. Soc. Human Retrovirology, 1994, 1st Gustav Embden award, U. Frankfurt, 1996, Pomesa award, 1996, 1st award, Internat. Soc. Blood Transfusion, 1997, Nomura prize for AIDS and Cancer Rsch, Japan, 1998, Warren Alpert prize, Harvard U., 1998, Paul Erlich award, Germany, 1999, Hero in Medicine award, Can, 2000, Frank Annunzio sci. award, Washington, 2000, Prince Asturias prize, Spain, 2000, 1st award, Ireland C. of C. and USA, 2001, Seminal contbrns. to field of Human Retrovirology award, Internat. Soc. HTLV, 2001, award, Internat. Retrovirology Assn., 2001, World Health award, Pres. M. Gorbachev Found., 2001, Archimedes prize in sci., Italy, 2003. Mem.: NAS, Fedn. for Advanced Edn. in Scis., Am.Fedn. Clin. Rsch., Am. Soc. Microbiology, Am. Assn. Cancer Rsch., Biochem. Soc., Am. Microbiology Soc., Am. Soc. Biol. Chemists, Am. Soc. Clin.Investigation, Internat Soc. Hematology, Inst. Medicine, Royal Soc. Medicine (hon.), Royal Soc. Physicians of Scotland (hon.), Royal Soc. Medicine Belgium (sr.), Alpha Omega Alpha. Achievements include research in on viruses, AIDS and Leukemia; discovery of with co-workers of AIDS virus, discoverer of first and second human retroviruses, and Interleukin-2 (IL-2). Office: 725 W Lombard St Ste S307 Baltimore MD 21201-1009

GALLO, RUBEN, Latin American literature educator, art critic; b. Guadalajara, Jalisco, Mexico, Dec. 22, 1969; s. Ruben Gallo Ruiz and Maria Teresa Carmen Godinez Prado. PhD, Columbia U., 2000. Asst. prof. Princeton (N.J.) U., 2002—. Vis. asst. prof. Cornell U., Ithaca, NY, 2000—01. Translator: (book) Escriba subversiva. Recipient U. fellowship, Columbia U., 1995—2000, various rsch. grants for the humanities. Mem.: MLA. Home: Apt 4D 465 W 23rd St New York NY 10011 Office: Princeton U 8 Dillon Court W Princeton NJ 08544 Home Fax: 609-259-7155; Office Fax: 609-259-7155. Personal E-mail: gallo@princeton.edu. E-mail: gallo@princeton.edu.

GALLO, SERGIO ROBERTO, music educator, researcher; b. Sao Paulo, Brazil, Aug. 12, 1963; came to U.S., 1993; s. Waldomiro and Cleonice Gallo. Diplome d'excellence, Conservatoire Europeen, Paris, 1987; MM, U. Cin., 1995; DMA, U. Calif., Santa Barbara, 1998. Tchg. asst. U. Calif., Santa Barbara, 1995-97; adj. prof. piano Millikin U., Decatur, Ill., 1997-98; asst. prof. piano U. N.D., Grand Forks, 1998—, coord. cultural exch. program dept. music, 1999-2000. Performer piano recitals, 1985—. Recipient Erno Daniel Meml. prize U. Calif., 1997; grantee CD recording U. N.D., 1999. Mem. N.D. Music Tchrs. Assn., Coll. Music Soc. Roman Catholic. Avocations: travel, reading. Home: 2700 S 39th St #105 Grand Forks ND 58201 Office: U ND Dept Music Grand Forks ND 58202-7125 E-mail: sergio_gallo@und.nodak.edu.

GALLO, TONY GIOVANNI, musician, educator; s. Rocco Gallo and Jeannine Parent; m. Diane Jennifer Hrycun, July 12, 1986; children: Miranda Christina, Angela Elisa. BFA, Concordia U., Montreal, 1981—84; Diploma in Edn., McGill U., Montreal, 1984—85; MFA, York U., Toronto, 1986—89; PhD in Musicology, U. Montreal, 1992—98. Cert. tchr. Ont., 1989. Composer/performer (concert on cbc radio) Araray Zema, composer/musician (albums), (recording) Just Recieve. Ch. musician The Life Centre, Ottawa, Canada, 1989—97, Calvary Ch., Simcoe, Canada, 1997—2002, First Assemblies of God Ch., Waxahachie, Tex., 2002. Avocation: music. Office: SW Assemblies of God Univ 1200 Sycamore Waxahachie TX 75165 E-mail: tgallo@sagu.edu.

GALLO, VINCENT JOHN, financial planner; b. N.Y.C., Aug. 13, 1943; s. Nicholas and Catherine (Vitiello) G.; m. Blanche Marie Poplin, Apr. 15, 1972; children: Steven, Mark. BA, U. Dayton, 1965. Registered fin. planner; CLU; ChFC; accredited estate planner Nat. Assn. Estate Planning Couns. Mgr. methods engring. Daniel Internat. Corp., Greenville, S.C., 1971-75; exec. v.p. Am. Ind. Elec. Contractors Assn., Arlington, Tex., 1975-77; pres. Vincent J. Gallo & Assocs., Inc., Winston-Salem, N.C., 1977—. Adj. instr. Am. Coll., Bryn Mawr, Pa., 1984-86. Capt. USAF, 1966-71. Served to capt. USAF, 1966-71. Mem. Am. Soc. CLUs and Chartered Fin. Cons. (continuing edn. chmn. 1984, pres. 1988-89), Internat. Assn. Fin. Planners, Nat. Assn. Securities Dealers, Nat. Soc. Pub. Accts., N.C. Planned Giving Coun. (pres. 1997—, accredited estate planner), Winston-Salem Estate Planning Coun. (v.p.), Am. Soc. Pension

Actuaries, N.C. Soc. Accts., Mensa, Million Dollar Round Table. Avocations: tennis, reading, gourmet cooking, skiing. Home: 8800 Harwick Ct Clemmons NC 27012-9737 Office: 1400 Old mill Cir Ste C Winston Salem NC 27103-2990

GALLO, WILLIAM VICTOR, cartoonist; b. N.Y.C., Dec. 28, 1922; s. Francisco and Henrietta (Caballero) G.; m. Dolores Rodriguez, Mar. 13, 1950; children: Gregory, William. With N.Y. Daily News, 1941—, sports cartoonist, sports columnist, 1960—, assoc. sports editor, 1984—. One-man show, Spectrum Fine Arts Gallery, N.Y.C., 1981; works represented in permanent collection, Baseball Hall of Fame, Cooperstown, N.Y., Syracuse U. archives. Served with USMC, 1942-45. Named best sports cartoonist, Nat. Cartoonist Soc., 1969—73, 1984—86; named to Yonkers Hall of Fame, 1984, Westchester Hall of Fame, 1984, Boxing Hall of Fame, 2001; recipient 19 Page One awards, N.Y. Newspaper Guild, 1965—86, Elzie Segar award, 1976, Alumni Achievement award, Sch. Visual Arts, 1977, Power of Printing award, 1977. Mem. N.Y. Boxing Writers (pres.), Nat. Cartoonists Soc. (pres., Milt Caniff Lifetime Achievement award 1999), Baseball Writers, Profl. Football Writers, Turf Writers, N.Y. Press Assn., (award 1986), Soc. Silurians, Soc. Illustrators. Home: 1 Mayflower Dr Yonkers NY 10710-3801 Office: NY Daily News 450 W 33rd St New York NY 10001-2603 *Everything has to start with a dream. First the dream, and then the chasing of it. I pity the person who doesn't own a dream.*

GALLOP, JANE (JANE ANNE GALLOP), women's studies educator, writer; b. Duluth, Minn., May 4, 1952; d. Melvin Gordon and Eudice Zelda (Titch) G.; children: Max Blau Gallop, Ruby Gallop Blau. BA, Cornell U., 1972, PhD, 1976. Lectr. French Gettysburg (Pa.) Coll., 1976; asst. prof. Miami U., Oxford, Ohio, 1977-81, assoc. prof., 1981-85; prof. women's studies Rice U., Houston, 1985-87, Autrey prof., 1987-90; prof. English U. Wis., Milw., 1990-92, Disting. prof., 1992—. NEH vis. prof. Emory U., Atlanta, 1984-85; Hill vis. prof. U. Minn., Mpls., 1987; dir. seminar for coll. tchrs. NEH, Milw., 1985, 88; instr. Sch. of Criticism and Theory, Dartmouth Coll., 1991. Author: Intersections, 1981, The Daughter's Seduction, 1982, Reading Lacan, 1985, Thinking Through the Body, 1988, Around 1981, 1992, Feminist Accused of Sexual Harassment, 1997,Anecdotal Theory, 2002, Living with His Camera, 2003; editor: Pedagogy, 1995. Guggenheim fellow, 1983-84. Mem. MLA. Office: U Wis PO Box 413 Milwaukee WI 53201-0412 E-mail: jg@uwm.edu.

GALLOPOULOS, NICHOLAS EFSTRATIOS, chemical engineer; b. Athens, Apr. 5, 1936; came to U.S., 1953; s. Efstratios C. and Lucia N. (Romanides) G.; m. Mary Frances Veale, Oct. 25, 1958; children: Gregory S., Lucia Anne. BS in Chem. Engring., Tex. A&M U., 1958; MS in Chem. Engring., Pa. State U., 1959. Tech. specialist Humble Oil & Refining Co. (Exxon), Houston, 1967-68; rsch. engr. Gen. Motors Rsch. Labs., Warren, Mich., 1959-67, 68-75, asst. dept. head fuels and lubricants, 1975-85, head dept. environ. sci., 1985-89, head dept. engine rsch., 1989-99; ret., 1999. Mem. Coordinating Rsch. Coun., Atlanta, 1974-89. Author: Future Automotive Fuels, 1977; contbr. chpts. to books, articles to Sci. American, Indsl. and Engring. Chemistry. Mem. Econ. Devel. Corp., Rochester Hills, Mich., 1978-91; mem., chmn. Planning Commn., Rochester Hills, 1982-92. Fellow Soc. Automotive Engrs.; mem. Am. Chem. Soc., Internat. Soc. Indsl. Ecology, Sigma Xi. Achievements include research on the chemical mechanism of action of various lubricating oil additives, alternative fuels and their role in automotive transportation; co-founding (with R. A. Frosch) the field of Industrial Ecology. Home: 31161 Prairie Ridge Rd Libertyville IL 60048-4895

GALLOWAY, BONNIE J. investor, sociologist; b. Detroit, July 31, 1951; d. Willis Jack and Ellen Virginia (Sheppard) G.; m. Robert Charles Franklin, Jr., June 20, 1973 (dec. Apr. 1991); 1 child, Samuel Charles Franklin; m. Robert George Robinson, Feb. 20, 1993. Student, U. Vienna, 1971-72; BA, Hillsdale (Mich.) Coll., 1973; MBA, Wayne State U., 1977; PhD, Western Mich. U., 1994. Tech. rep. Ins. Co. N.Am., Detroit, 1974-76; gen. acct. Kellogg Co., Battle Creek, Mich., 1977-78; fin. analyst Upjohn Co., Kalamazoo, 1978-90; interim dir. Durant Children's Ctr., Florence, S.C., 1995; private investor self employed, Lawrenceville, N.J., 1994—. Adj. prof. Coker Coll., Francis Marion U., Florence Darlington Tech., Florence, 1995-97, Rider Coll., Lawrenceville, 1999. Bd. dirs. Portage (Ind.) Cmty. Outreach Ctr., 1983-87, United Campus Ministries/Western Mich. U., Kalamazoo, 1991-93; elder New Harvest Presbyn. Ch., Florence, 1997-98. Recipient Mayor's award of merit City of Detroit, 1977, others. Mem. Trenton Art Works, Art Mus. Princeton U., Hist. Soc. Princeton, Chi Omega Alumnae (v.p. 1999-2000). Presbyterian. Avocations: travel, reading, needlework. E-mail: Bonnie. Home: 308 Cobblestone Way Lawrenceville NJ 08648-1252

GALLOWAY, CATHERINE BLACK, publishing executive; b. Birmingham, Ala., Oct. 24, 1954; d. Robert Lee and Catherine Hicks Black; m. Michael Galloway, Aug. 25, 1984. Editl. prodn. coord. So. Med. Jour., Birmingham, Ala., 1975—2002, mng. editor, 2002—. Sec., treas. Vocat. Resources, Inc., Birmingham, 1997—2003. Mem.: Am. Med. Writers Assn. (cert. core curriculum program 1983). Office: Southern Medical Journal 35 Lakeshore Drive Birmingham AL 35209 Office Fax: 205-945-1830. E-mail: cgalloway@sma.org.

GALLOWAY, DAVID ALEXANDER, publishing company executive; b. Toronto, Ont., Can., Nov. 1, 1943; s. Robert and Dorothy Elizabeth (Kennedy) G.; m. Judy K. Clarkson, June 10, 1966; children: Andrew, Stephanie. BA, U. Toronto, 1966; MBA, Harvard U., 1968. Mktg. profl. Gen. Foods Corp., Toronto, 1968-71; ptnr. Can. Consulting Group, Toronto, 1971-80; v.p. corp. devel. Torstar Corp., Toronto, 1980-81, exec. v.p., 1981-82; pres., CEO Harlequin Enterprises, Ltd., Toronto, 1983-88, chmn., 1990-97; pres. Torstar Book Pub. and Direct Mktg. Div., Toronto, 1984-86; pres., bd. dir., CEO Torstar Corp., Toronto, 1988—. Bd. dirs. Bank of Montreal, Toronto, Corel Corp., Ottawa, Visible Genetics, Inc., Toronto. Bd. govs., faculty of adminstrv. studies York U.; trustee Hosp. for Sick Children. Mem.: Badminton & Racquet, Devil's Pulpit Golf, Caledon, Toronto. Avocations: running, golf, tennis. Home: 82 Cluny Dr Toronto ON Canada M4W 2R3 Office: Torstar Corp 1 Yonge St Toronto ON Canada M5E 1P9 Business E-Mail: dgallowstar.ca.

GALLOWAY, DAVID MALCOLM, retired education educator; b. Marlow, England, July 5, 1942; s. Malcolm Ashby and Joan Dorah (Slater) G.; m. Christina Mary King, Dec. 29, 1971; children: Patrick, Sam, Catherine. BA, U. Oxford, 1970; MSc, London U., 1972; PhD, CNAA, 1980. Chartered psychologist. Sr. ednl. psychologist Sheffield (Eng.) Local Edn. Authority, 1974-79; sr. lectr. Victoria U., Wellington, New Zealand, 1980-83; lectr. Univ. Coll., Cardiff, Wales, 1983-87; lectr., reader Lancaster U., England, 1987-91; prof. primary edn. Durham U., England, 1991—2001; ret., 2001. Author: Schools and Persistent Absentees, 1985; co-author: Schools and Disruptive Pupils, 1982, Primary School Teaching and Educational Psychology, 1991, The Assessment of Special Educational Needs: Whose Problem?, 1994, Motivating the Difficult to Teach, 1998. Chmn. Kirkby Stephen Mtn. Rescue Team, 2002—. Fellow Br. Psychol. Soc.; mem. Assn. Child Psychology & Psychiatry (chmn. 1999—2001). Avocation: beekeeping. Home: Leases, Smardale Kirkby Stephen Cumbria CA17 4HQ England Office: U Durham Sch Edn Leazes Rd Durham DH1 1TA England E-mail: d.m.galloway@durham.ac.uk., leasesgalldg@aol.com.

GALLOWAY, EILENE MARIE, space and astronautics consultant; b. Kansas City, Mo., May 4, 1906; d. Joseph Locke and Lottie Rose (Harris) Slack; m. George Barnes Galloway, Dec. 23, 1924; children: David Barnes, Jonathan Fuller. Student, Washington U., St. Louis, 1923-25; AB, Swarthmore Coll., 1928; postgrad., Am. U., 1937-38, 43; LLD (hon.), Lake Forest Coll., 1990, Swarthmore Coll., 1992. Tchr. polit. sci. Swarthmore Coll., 1928-30; editor Student Svc., Washington, 1931; staff mem. edn. div. Fed. Emergency Relief Adminstrn., 1934-35; asst. chief info. sect. div. spl. info Library of Congress, 1941-43; editor abstracts Legis. Reference Svc., 1943-51, nat. def. analyst, 1951-57, specialist in nat. def., 1957-66; sr. specialist internat. rels. (nat. security) Congl. Rsch. Svc., 1966-75, cons. internat. space activities, 1975—. Staff mem. Senate Fgn. Rels. Com., 1947; profl. staff mem. U.S. group Interparliamentary Union, 1958-66; cons. Senate Armed Svcs. Com., 1953-74, Ford Found., 1958; spl. cons. Spl. Senate Com. on Space and Astronautics, 1958; spl. cons. to Senate Com. on Aero. and Space Sci., 1958-77; cons. to Senate Com. on Commerce, Sci. and Transp., 1977-82; chmn. com. edn. and recreation Washington, 1937-38; forum leader, 1976-79; guest Soviet Acad. Sci., 1982, adult edn. U.S. Office Edn., 1938; mem. Internat. Inst. Space Law of Internat. Astronautical Fedn., 1958—, U.S. bd. dirs., v.p., 1967-79, hon. dir., 1979—, Fedn. ofcl. observer at sessions UN Com. on Peaceful Uses Outer Space and legal sub-com., 1970-94, com. for rels. with internat. orgns., 1979—; space law and sociology com. Am. Rocket Soc., 1959-62; adv. panel Office Gen. Counsel, NASA, 1971; adviser outer space del. U.S. Mission to UN Working Group on Direct Broadcast Satellites, 1973-75; observer UN Conf. Exploration and Peaceful Uses of Outer Space, Vienna, 1982; lectr. NAS, 1972, U.S. CSC, Exec. Seminar Ctr., Oak Ridge, 1973-78; ednl. counselor Purdue U., 1974; lectr. Inst. Air and Space Law McGill U., 1975, Inter Am. Def. Coll., 1977-78, U. Akron, 1984, 91; mem. panel on solar power for satellites and U.S. space policy Office Tech. Assessment, 1979-80, 82-86, cons., 1982; cons. COMSAT, 1983, FCC Commn. on U.S. Telecomm. Policy, 1983-87; spkr. internat. space law UN, N.Y.C., 1995; mem. NASA Nat. Adv. Com. on Internat. Space Sta., 1996-99, NASA Spaceflight Adv. com., 2000-03, UN seminar Space Futures and Human Security, Alpbach, Austria, 1997, chmn. Session in Internat. Astronautical Fed. Congress Concepts of Space Law, 1997; active European Space Agy. Internat. Lunar Workshop, 1994, 97; chair UN Workshop UNISPACE III Space Treaties: Strengths and Needs, Vienna, Austria, 1999. Author: Atomic Power: Issues Before Congress, 1946; author: (with Bernard Brodie) The Atomic Bomb and the Armed Services, 1947; author: History of United States Military Policy on Reserve Forces, 1775-1957, 1957, The Community of Law and Science, 1958, United Nations Ad hoc Committee on Peaceful Uses of Outer Space, 1959. Pres. Theodore Von Karman Meml. Found., 1973-84; mem. alumni council Swarthmore Coll., 1976-79; mem. organizing com., author symposium on Conditions Essential For Maintaining Outer Space for Peaceful Uses, Peace Palace, Netherlands, 1984; bd. advisers Student for Exploration and Devel. of Space, 1984—, Rockefeller Found. scholar-in-residence, Bellagio, Italy, 1976; elected to Coun. of Advanced Internat. Studies, Argentina, 1985, Uruguyan Centro de Investigacion y Difusion Aeronautica-Expacial, 1985; recipient Andrew G. Haley gold medal Internat. Inst. Space Law, 1968, Disting. Svc. award Libr. Congress, 1975, NASA Gold Medal for Pub. Svc., 1984, USAF Space Command plaque, 1984, Internat. Acad. Astronautics' Theodore Von. Karman award, 1986, Women in Aerospace Lifetime Achievment award Internat. Inst. Space Law, 1989, Leadership award NASA Johnson Space Ctr., 1997, Cologne U. Inst. Air and Space Law and German Aerospace Ctr. award, 2003; Wilton Park fellow, Eng., 1968, NASA award for contbns. to internat. space sta., 1999. Fellow: AIAA (tech. com. on legal aspects of aeros. and astronautics 1980—84, internat. activities com. 1985—, European space agy. internat. lunar workshop 1994, Pub. Svc. award and medal 2003), Internat. Acad. Astronautics (trustee emeritus, Social Scis. award 1999, Moot Ct. award 2002), Am. Astronautical Soc. (John F. Kennedy Astronautics award 1999); mem.: Nat. Aeronautic Assn. (Katharine Wright award 2003, 2003), Internat. Law Assn., Am. Soc. Internat. Law, LWV (chmn. study groups housing, welfare in D.C. 1937—38, mem. tech. com. on law and sociology task force on legal aspects 1979—), World Peace Through Law Ctr., Lamar Soc. Internat. Law, Kappa Alpha Theta, Delta Sigma Rho, Phi Beta Kappa. Episcopalian. Home and Office: 4612 29th Pl NW Washington DC 20008-2105

GALLOWAY, ETHAN CHARLES, technology development executive, former chemicals executive; b. Howell, Mich., Oct. 31, 1930; s. Almon Fred and Rose Marie (Hodkinson) G.; m. Patricia Winner, Dec. 23, 1973. BSC., Mich. State U., 1951; PhD, U. Calif., Berkeley, 1954. With Dow Chem. Co., Midland, Mich., 1954-62; dir. research plastics div. Nopco Chem. Co., North Arlington, N.J., 1962-65; successively v.p. research, exec. v.p., corp. dir. Stauffer Chem. Co., Westport, Conn., 1965-85; exec. v.p. Chesebrough-Pond's Inc., 1985-88; pres. new bus. devel. Loctite Corp., Hartford, Conn., 1988-89; pres. Edison Polymer Innovation Corp., Brecksville, Ohio, 1989-95; ret., 1995. Fellow Poly. Univ. N.Y.; mem. Indsl. Research Inst. (pres. 1978-79), Chem. Industry Inst. Toxicology (past dir.), Food Safety Council (former trustee), Council for Chem. Research (past chmn.), Conn. Acad. Sci. and Engring., Sigma Xi. Home: 6549 Thornbrook Cir Hudson OH 44236-3552

GALLOWAY, GALE LEE, oil and gas executive, rancher; b. Pearsall, Tex., Jan. 10, 1930; s. Gerald Glenn and Vida Olga (Tate) G.; m. Connie Bird, July 30, 1965; children: Georgia Gayle, Michael W., Tara Lee. BBA in Econs., Baylor U., 1952; postgrad., Tex A&I U., 1953-54, South Tex. Law Sch., 1960-63. Fin. analyst, landman, gas contracts rep., mgr. gas supply Tenneco, Houston, 1954-65; sr. v.p. Coastal States Gas, Houston, 1964-73; chmn., pres., CEO Celeron Corp., Lafayette, La., 1973-86; chmn. bd. Entex Inc., Houston, 1987-89, San Antonio, 1994—. Chmn. bd. La. Intrastate Gas, Houston, 1989, GLG Energy, Inc., Austin, Tex., 1989—, Gas Transmission Ltd., London, 1989—; dir. Goodyear Tire & Rubber, Akron, Ohio; mem. adv. com. to bd. dirs. MBank; mem. adv. com. U.S. Senator Commn. Oil and Gas; mem. Interstate Oil Compact Commn. Bd. dirs. Boy Scouts Am., La. Assn. Bus. and Industry, La. State U. Found., Baylor Coll. of Medicine, DeBakey Med. Found.; council trustees Gulf South Research Inst.; chmn. bd. regents Baylor U.; bd. regents Milsaps Coll. Officer USAF, 1952—54. Recipient Carnegie Hero medal Life Saving award, 1982, W.R. White Meritorious Svc. award, 1982, Tex. award for hist. preservation Tex. Hist. Commn., 1994, Disting. Alumni award Baylor U., Silver Beaver award, Boy Scouts Am.; named Baylor U. Hall of Fame, 1983 Mem. La. Assn. Ind. Producers and Royalty Owners (pres., bd. dirs.), Mid-Continent Oil and Gas Assn. (v.p., exec. com.), Nat. Petroleum Refiners Assn., Am. Petroleum Inst., Calif. Ind. Producers Assn., Ind. Producers Assn. Am., Interstate Natural Gas Assn. Am., Pub. Affairs Research Council, Natural Gas Men Houston, Greater Lafayette C. of C. (bd. dirs.), Natural Gas Men New Orleans, Am. Gas Assn. (bd. dirs.), Austin C. of C. Clubs: City, Petroleum; Austin Country, University (Austin). Home: 4100 Waters Edge Dr Austin TX 78731-5103 Office: PO Box 762 Pearsall TX 78061

GALLOWAY, GLADYS, artist; b. Crane, Mo., May 25, 1918; d. Thomas Lloyd Kincaid and Mae Margaret Rickman; m. William Harold Galloway, May 21, 1939 (dec.); children: Bonnie Jean, William Thomas. Cert. in tchg., Tuscola County Normal Sch., Caro, Mich., 1937. Instr. porcelain painting, 1951—; organized and directed 6 reg. porcelain art shows, 1978-80; organizer, dir. Internat. Porcelan show, Detroit, 1980; participant Brazilian porcelain Art Conf., 1982; del. porcelain artists People to People Internat., Republic of China, 1983, Italy, 1991; leader effort to get porcelain painting recognized as a fine art, U.S., 1980; tchr. hundreds of seminars, workshops, lectures, 1960—; coord., dir. summer program for Porcelain art, Delta Coll., Midland, Mich., 1984-89; guest artist Porcelain Art Exposition, Lisbon, Portugal, 1996. Author: Sparkling Tables, 1984, 7th edit., 1999, Holidays and Special Moments, 1979, 10th edit., 1999, China Painting Fun and Basics, 1975, 16th edit., 1999, Step By Step Painting, 1970, and numerous bot. study booklets; fine art porcelain painter, 1949—. Trustee People to People Intrnat., 1981-96. Named Citizen of Yr. Caro C. of C., 1977. Mem. International Porcelain Art Tchrs. (pres. 1978-80, bd. dirs. 1978-94, dir. emeritus 1994—), Mich. China Painting Tchrs. Orgn. (charter), Caro Garden Club (pres. 1966). Avocations: watercolor, porcelain and oil painting, travel, gardening, cooking, the outdoors. Home: 670 Gibbs St Caro MI 48723-1447

GALLOWAY, HUNTER HENDERSON, III, lawyer, small business owner; b. Abingdon, Va., Nov. 16, 1945; s. Hunter Henderson Jr. and Katherine Cosby (Hines) G.; m. Linda Sharlene Alley, June 20, 1971 (div. Feb. 1975); m. Deborah Lynn Brannon, Dec. 18, 1977; children: Andrew Michael, Hunter Henderson IV, Patrick B., Thomas J. BBA, U. N.C., 1968, JD, 1972. Bar: N.C. 1972, U.S. Dist. Ct. (mid. dist.) 1974, U.S. Tax Ct. 1976, U.S. Ct. Appeals (4th cir.) 1979, U.S. Supreme Ct. 1983. Assoc. Hoyle, Hoyle & Boone, Greensboro, 1972-78; sole practice Greensboro, 1978—. Tchr. U. N.C., Greensboro, 1974-82; dealer Galloway Buick Co., Greensboro, 1978—. Pres. Old North State Coun. Boy Scouts Am., 2003. Served with N.C. N.G., 1968-74. Recipient Wall Street Jour. award, U. N.C., 1968. Mem. ABA, N.C. Bar Assn., Greensboro Bar Assn., N.C. Acad. Trial Lawyers, Greensboro Mchts. Assn. (chmn. bd. dirs. 1993), Greensboro C. of C. (bd. dirs. 2001), Rotary, Bald Head Island Club, Greensboro Country Club. Democrat. Presbyterian. Avocations: trap shooting, hunting, camping. Home: 1815 Nottingham Rd Greensboro NC 27408-5612 Office: Galloway Buick Co 401 N Murrow Blvd Greensboro NC 27401-3009 E-mail: ronclarkattrap@hotmail.com.

GALLOWAY, JAMES MALCOLM, cardiologist; b. San Mateo, Calif., May 24, 1953; s. Ellison Atwell and Doris Galloway; children: Kate, Brooke, Kelly, Dillon. BS, Va. Commonwealth U., 1978; MD, Med. Coll. Va., 1982. Diplomate Am. Bd. Internal Medicine with subspecialty in cardiovascular disease. Resident in internal medicine U. Vt., Burlington, 1982-85; internist Keams Canyon (Ariz.) PHS Hosp., 1985-88; clin. dir. Whiteriver (Ariz.) PHS Hosp., 1988-90; cardiology fellow U. Ariz., Tucson, 1990-93, dir. Native Am. cardiology program, 1993—, asst. prof. clin. medicine, 1993—; dir. Ctr. for Native Am. Health, Tucson, 1996-2001, clin. asst. prof. pub. health, 1997—. Co-investigator Strong Heart Study, 1995—; prin. investigator White Mountain Heart Study, 1995—. Contbr. articles to profl. jours. Capt. USPHS, 1997—. Named Outstanding Clinician of Yr., Nat. Clin. Dirs., IHS, 1997, 2001; named one of Best Doctors in Am., 2002; recipient Salsbury award for Outstanding Contbns. to Healthcare for People of Ariz., 2001. Fellow ACP, Am. Coll. Cardiology, Am. Coll. Chest Physicians; mem. Am. Heart Assn.-Ariz. Affiliate (bd. dirs. 1993-97), Phi Kappa Phi, Alpha Omega Alpha. Office: Native Am Cardiology/Univ Ariz 1501 N Campbell Ave Tucson AZ 85724-0001 E-mail: galloway@u.arizona.edu.

GALLOWAY, JANICE, writer, editor; b. Kilwinning, Scotland, Dec. 2, 1956; d. James and Janet (McBride) G.; 1 child, James Alexander Galloway McNaught. MA, Glasgow U., 1978. Tchr. Strathclyde Regional Coun., Ayrshire, Scotland, 1980-90. Music critic. Editor (with Hamish Whyte): New Writing Scotland, 1990, 1991, 1992; author: The Trick is to Keep Breathing, 1990, Foreign Parts, 1994, Where You Find It, 1996, Clara, 2002 (Saltire book of yr., 2002), Boy Book See, 2002, +Rosengarten, 2003; librettist (with sculptor Anne Bevan): Pipelines, librettist (with composer Sally Beamish): Operas Monster. Recipient Cosmopolitan/Perrier award, 1991, E.M. Forster award in lit. Am. Acad. Arts and Letters, 1994, McVitie's prize for Scottish Writer of the Yr., 1994, Times Literary Supplement Rsch. fellow British Libr., 1999. Office: care Jonathan Cape 20 Vauxhall Bridge Rd London SW1 6RB England also: care Derek Johns AP Watt Agy 20 John St London WCIN 2DR England E-mail: djohns@apwatt.co.uk.

GALLOWAY, JOE, football player; Degree in Bus./Mktg., Ohio State U. Wide receiver Seattle Seahawks, 1995-2000, Dallas Cowboys, 2000—. Sponsor group of students at each Seattle home game Galloway Express; appeared on Wheel of Fortune with proceeds from his spins benefiting Make-A-Wish Found. Named NFL Offensive Rookie of Yr., Coll. and Pro Football Newsweekly, 1995, Consensus All-Rookie choice, 1995, AFC Offensive Player of Week, 1995, AFC Spl. Teams Player of Month, 1995; Nat. Football Found. scholar athlete; Nat. Assn. Collegiate Dirs. of Athletics scholar. Office: Dallas Cowboys 2401 E Airport Frwy Irving TX 75062

GALLOWAY, JOSEPH EDWARD, JR., retired highway engineer; b. Richmond, Va., Aug. 25, 1928; s. Joseph Edward and Elsie Catherine (Grubbs) Galloway; m. Louise Hyslop Avery, May 1, 1954; 1 child, Joseph Edward III. BS in Physics, U. Richmond, 1949. Trainee Electrical Equipment Co., Richmond, 1949-50; engr. technician Va. Dept. Hwys., Richmond, 1950-58, head phys. lab., 1958-68, asst. state materials engr., 1968-89. Pres. Va. Soc. Mentally Retarded Children, Richmond, 1977—97; mem. exec. com. Va. Nat. Guard Assn., Richmond, 1988—95, pres., 1995—96. Col. U.S. Army, 1952, col. U.S. Army, 1961—62. Named Hon. Col.-in-Chief, Va. Artillery, Adjutant-Gen., 1982—87. Fellow: ASTM (chmn. com. C-9 1988—89, Merit award 1992). Methodist. Avocations: records and audio-video tape collecting, walking. Home: 8208 Elm Dr Mechanicsville VA 23111-1314

GALLOWAY, JOSEPH LEE, JR., writer, journalist; b. Bryan, Tex., Nov. 13, 1941; s. Joseph L. and Marian D. (Dewvall) G.; m. Theresa Magdalene Null, Sept. 9, 1966 (dec. Jan. 1996); children: Lee T., Joshua J.; m. Karen Metsker McCray, Oct. 24, 1998; children: Alison, Abigail, Thomas. Grad., Refugio, Tex., 1959; DHL (hon.), St. Mary's Coll., Newburgh, N.Y., 2003. Reporter Victoria (Tex.) Advocate, 1959-61, United Press Internat., Kansas City, Mo., 1961, bureau chief Topeka, 1962-64, war correspondent, 1965-66, correspondent, 1966-68, bureau chief Jakarta, Indonesia, 1968-73, mgr. South Asia New Delhi, 1973-74, mgr. southeast Asia Singapore, 1974-75, bureau chief Moscow, 1976-80, L.A., 1980-82; west coast editor U.S.News & World Report, L.A., 1982-84; assoc. editor U.S. News, Washington, 1984-86, sr. editor, 1986-90, sr. writer, 1990—2001; spl. cons. to Sec. of State U.S. Dept. State, Washington, 2001—02; sr. mil. corr. Knight Ridder Newspapers, Washington, 2002—. Co-author: Triumph Without Victory, 1992, We Were Soldiers Once. . .and Young, 1992 (movie We Were Soldiers based on book, 2002). Dir. No Greater Love, Washington, 1990—; bd. adv. Vietnam Vets. Meml. Fund, Decorated Bronze Star with V device; recipient Nat Mag. award Am. Soc. Mag. Editors, 1991, Nat. News Media award Vet. of Fgn. Wars of U.S.A., 1992, Excellence in Arts award Vietnam Vets. Am., 1999, U.S. Infantry Assn. Order St. Maurice, 2000, U.S. Armor Assn.'s Order St. George, 2001, Denig Memorial Disting. Svc. award U.S.M.C. Combat Corr. Assn., 2001, Stanley Larsen award, 25th Div. Assn., 2002. Mem. Soc. Profl. Journalists, Overseas Press Club, 7th Cavalry Assn., 1st Cavalry Divsn. Assn., Order St. Maurice, Assn. U.S. Army (bd. advisors). Avocations: travel, gardening. Home: 809 Hillwood Ave Falls Church VA 22042 E-mail: jlgalloway2@cs.com.

GALLOWAY, JUDY A. deputy commissioner; BS in Bus. Adminstrn., Ga. State U.; postgrad., U. Colo., Denver. Program specialist Atlanta Regional Office, Dept. Health and Human Svcs.; deputy regional commr., ACF-Region VIII office Adminstrn. Children and Families, U.S. Dept. Health and Human Svcs., 1998—2000, deputy regional commr., Office of Early Childhood Programs, 2000—. Office: Denver Fed Office 1961 Stout St Denver CO 80294-3538

GALLOWAY, KENNETH FRANKLIN, engineering educator; b. Columbia, Tenn., Apr. 11, 1941; s. Benjamin F. and Carrie (Dowell) G.; m. Dorothy Elise Lamar; children: Kenneth Jr., Carole A. BA, Vanderbilt U., 1962; PhD, U. S.C., 1966. Rsch. assoc. Ind. U., Bloomington, 1966-67, asst. prof., 1967-72, assoc. prof., 1972; rsch. physicist Naval Weapons Support Ctr., Crane, Ind., 1972-74; tech. staff Nat. Bur. Standards, Gaithersurg, Md., 1974-77, chief sect., 1977-79, chief divsn., 1980-86; prof. elect. engring. U. Md., 1980-86; prof., dept. head elect. and computer engring. U. Ariz., Tucson, 1986-96; dean engring., prof. elec. engring. Vanderbilt U., Nashville, 1996—. Contbr. articles to profl. jours. Sci. and Tech. fellow U.S. Dept. Commerce, 1979-80. Fellow IEEE (gen. chmn. Nuc. and Space Radiation Effects Conf. 1985, v.p. Nuc. and Plasma Sci. Soc. 1990, chmn. radiation effects com. 1991-94, chmn. engring. rsch. and devel. policy com. 1994, gen. chmn. Internat. Electron Devices Meeting 1997), AAAS, Am. Phys. Soc.; mem. Electrochem. Soc., Am. Soc. Engring. Edn., Sigma Xi, Eta Kappa Nu, Tau Beta Pi. Office: Vanderbilt U Sch Engring VU Sta B 351826 Nashville TN 37235-1826 E-mail: kenneth.f.galloway@vanderbilt.edu.

GALLOWAY, LILLIAN CARROLL, modeling agency executive, consultant; b. Hazard, Ky., Sept. 23, 1934; d. William Zion and Clemma (Lewis) Carroll; m. Thomas Roddy Galloway, Dec. 21, 1957; children: David Junkin, Scott Thomas, Donald Lewis. Student, Cumberland Coll., 1955, Ea. U., Richmond, Ky., 1956, U. Cin., 1958, John Robert Powers Sch., Cin., 1958. Tchr. Vandalia (Ohio) Elem. Sch., 1954-56, Kenwood Elem. Sch., Louisville, 1956-57, Cin. Pub. Schs., 1957-64; founder, pres. Fairfax Model Agy., Washington, 1964-67, Cin. Model Agy. Internat., 1967—, Lillian Galloway Modeling Acad., Cin., 1971—, Children Model Agy. Internat., Cin., 1985—, Lillian Galloway Fashion Show Prodn. Co., 1998—. Cons., co-owner John Robert Powers Modeling Sch., Cin., 1957-64; pres. Student Model Bds., Cin., 1984—; dir. Career Day, Cin., 1967—. Mem. Cin. Better Bus. Bur., 1967—; trustee Knox Presbyn. Ch., Cin. Named Cin.'s Outstanding Bus. Woman, Sta. WCPO-TV, 1985, Outstanding Alumni, Cumberland Coll., 1988. Mem. DAR, Modeling Assn. Am. (chmn. convs. 1975-77), Am. Modeling Assn. Internat. (pres. 1976-77), Cin. Advertisers Club (membership and program coms., Outstanding Bus. Woman award 1985), Exec. Women Internat. (program com., chmn. bd. dirs. 1986, Woman of Achievement award 1986), Cin. C. of C., Cumberland Coll. Alumni Assn. (pres. 1982), English Speaking Union, Order Ky. Cols., Cin. Woman's Club (bd. dirs. 1992—, lecture/entertainment chmn. 1992-95), Town Club (bd. dirs. 1988—), Order Ea. Star (organist 1953—). Republican. Avocations: art, french antiques, gardening, music, travel. Home: 6027 Stirrup Rd Cincinnati OH 45244-3917 Office: 6047 Montgomery Rd Cincinnati OH 45213-1611

GALLOWAY, MARGARET ELINOR, social worker; b. Kansas City, Mo., Jan. 7, 1927; d. Roy William and Elinor Phoebe (Mapes) Brading; m. John David Galloway, Aug. 22, 1948; children: Mary Elaine, Ruth Eileen, Lois Irene,

Paula Jean, John William. BA, William Jewell Coll., 1950; MRE, Cen. Bapt. Theol. Sem., 1975; MA, U. Mo., Kansas City, 1977; MSW, U. Kans., Kansas City, 1985. Psychiat. social worker Rsch. Psychiat. Ctr., Kansas City, 1985-88; mental health clinician Jo. County Mental Health Ctr., Olathe, Kans., 1988; psychiat. social worker Truman Med. Ctr. East, Kansas City, 1988-92; mental health therapist West Cen. Mo. Mental Health Ctr., Harrisonville, Mo., 1989-94; social worker Park Lane Med. Ctr., 1992-93; psychiat. social worker Shawnee Mission Med. Ctr., 1993—. Organist Kensington Ave. Bapt. Ch., Kansas City, 1975—2000, Ruskin Heights Bapt. Ch., 2001—. Republican. Baptist. Avocations: gardening, sewing. Home: 11111 Blue Ridge Blvd Kansas City MO 64134-3202

GALLOWAY, PATRICIA DENESE, civil engineer; b. Lexington, Ky., June 14, 1957; d. Howard John and Maudine Lou (Jones) Frisby; m. Kris Richard Nielsen, Mar. 16, 1987. BS in Civil Engring., Purdue U., 1978; MBA, N.Y. Inst. Tech., 1984. Registered profl. engr. Ky., N.Y., N.J., Ariz., Wis., Wyo., Fla., Wash., Colo., Pa., Man., Can., Australia. Project engr., inspector CH2M Hill, Milw., 1978-79, master program scheduler, 1979-81; sr. cons. Nielsen-Wurster Group, N.Y.C., 1981-83, sr. engr., 1983-84, v.p., 1984-85, prin., exec. v.p., 1985-99, pres., 1999-2000, CEO and pres., 2001—. Pres. subs. cor., 1988-90; also bd. dirs.; lectr. Columbia U., U. Wis.-Madison; presenter to numerous orgns; ptnr. Unionville Vineyards, Ringoes, N.J.; pres. Unionville Aviation; gen. ptnr. Unionville Ranch, L.L.C., Wash.; chief exec. Nielson-Wurster Asia Pacific, Melbourne, Australia, 2001—; bd. dir. Civil Engring. Rsch. Found.; adv. bd. Civil Engring. Rsch. Found., 2000—, exec. com., 2001—. Contbr. articles to profl. jours. Named one of Top 10 Women in Constrn., Engring. New Record, 1986, one of Top 10 Women, Glamour Mag., 1987, 88, White House fellow regional finalist, 1990, Ky. Col., Gov. Patten, Sts. of Ky., 2002; named to Lafayette H.S. Hall of Fame, 2001; recipient Nat. Leadership Coun. Capital award, 1990, Engr. of Yr. award Mercer County Profl. Engrs., 1990, Nat. Leadership award Profl. Women in Constrn., 1995, Fed. Infrature Design award Whitehouse Commn., 1999; named Disting. Engring. Alumnus, Purdue U., 1992, Celebration of Women, Nat. Acad. Engring., 2000. Fellow ASCE (instr. constrn. claims course, bd. chair task com. on women in civil engring. 1998—2000, internat. dir., bd. dirs. 1992-95, chmn. membership com., 2001—, pres.-elect, 2003—, pres., 2004 (1st woman); mem. Am. Assn. Engring Socs., Nat. Soc. Professional Engrs., Am. Arbitration Assn., Professional Women in Construction, The Acad. Experts, UK, The Inst. Engrs., Australian Fellow, Soc. Women Engrs. (pres. Wis. chpt. 1980, pres. N.Y. chpt. 1982, Disting. New Engr. 1980), Project Mgmt. Inst. (dir. pub. bd.), Am. Assn. Cost Engrs., Am. Nuclear Soc., Garden State Wine Growers Assn. (pres. 1990-92), Somerset County C. of C. (most outstanding woman in bus. and industry 1987), Purdue Engring. Alumni Assn. (bd. dirs., 1975-2001), Toastmasters, Sigma Kappa (fin. com. 1993-97). Republican. Methodist. Avocations: scuba diving, cross-country skiing, hiking, horseback riding, wine making. Office: Nielsen-Wurster Group 345 Wall St Princeton NJ 08540-1518 Fax: 1-609-497-3412. E-mail: patnwg@aol.com.

GALLOWAY, THOMAS D. dean; B.A., Westmont Coll., Santa Barbara, 1962; M.U.P., U. of Washington, 1969, Ph.D., 1972. Research assoc., Center for Research U. of Kansas, 1972, assist. prof., Sch. of Architecture & Urban Design, 1971—74, assoc. dir. & sr. research assoc., Inst. for Soc. & Environ. Studies, 1973—75, assoc. prof., Sch. of Architecture & Urban Design, 1975—80, dir. grad. prog. in urban planning, 1974—80, assoc. dean, Sch. of Architecture & Urban Design, 1979—80; dir. & prof. Grad. Sch. of Community Planning & Urban Affairs, U. of Rhode Island, 1980—85; dir. Design Research Inst., Iowa State U., 1985—92; dean & prof. College of Design, Iowa State U., 1985—92; dean coll. architecture Ga. Inst. Tech., Atlanta, 1992—. Office: Ga Inst Technology Coll Arch 247 4th St Atlanta GA 30332-0001*

GALLOWAY, WILLIAM JEFFERSON, former foreign service officer; b. Throckmorton, Tex., Oct. 21, 1922; s. James Thomas and Ottis Virgil (Marrs) G.; m. Elizabeth Alice Cox, June 3, 1950; children— Jeff, Mary Elizabeth. BS, Tex. A&M U., 1943. Fgn. affairs officer Dept. State, 1948-50; spl. asst. to U.S. ambassador to NATO, London, Paris, 1950-53; spl. asst. to counselor Dept. State, 1953-56, 1st sec. Vienna, 1956-59, spl. asst. to dir. gen. fgn. service Washington, 1959-64; assigned Nat. War Coll., 1964-65; 1st sec., counselor polit. affairs Am. embassy, London, Eng., 1965-74; exec. asst. to under sec. state Dept. State, Washington, 1974-80, cons., 1980—. Served to capt. AUS, 1943-48. Home: The Jefferson 900 N Taylor St Apt 904 Arlington VA 22203 E-mail: wmjgallo@erols.com.

GALLOWAY, WILLIAM RODNEY, military officer; b. Warner Robins, Ga., June 21, 1966; SSgt. USAF, 1988—96; US Mil. Hist. First 5X. Republican.

GALLUP, DAVID M. lawyer; AB in French & History, Washington U., St. Louis, 1988; JD, Am. U., 1991. Bar: Md. 1992. Gen. counsel World Svc. Authority, Washington, 1992—. Sec. World Citizen Found., 1994-99; pres. World Svc. Authority, 1999—. Legal columnist World Citizen News. Mem. ABA, Md. State Bar Assn. Avocations: photography, drawing, painting, international cultural activities. Office: World Service Authority 1012 14th St NW Washington DC 20005-3406 E-mail: info@worldservice.org.

GALLUP, JANE HARRINGTON, librarian; b. Great Barrington, Mass., Jan. 4, 1949; d. William Snyder and Frances Harrington (Smith) G. BA, Boston U., 1970; MLS, Simmons Coll., Boston, 1976. Cert. tchr., Mass. Libr. Exploratory Project Econ. Alternatives, Cambridge, Mass. and Washington, 1973-76; dir. info. Ctr. Community Econ. Devel., Cambridge, Mass., 1976-80; libr. Nat. Consumer Coop. Bank, Washington, 1980-81, Golembe Assocs., Washington, 1981-89; dir. banking rsch. support svcs. Milbank, Tweed, Hadley & McCloy, Washington, 1989-93; legal asst. Bryan Cave LLP, Washington, 1994-2000, Bingham Dana LLP, Washington, 2000—01, Fried, Frank, Harris, Shriver & Jacobson, Washington, 2001—. Book reviewer Ctr. Community Econ. Devel. Newsletter, 1977-80, compiler bibliographies, 1977-80. Mem. Spl. Libraries Assn., Women in Housing and Finance. Home: 1830 Columbia Pike #G-3 Arlington VA 22204 Office: Fried Frank Harris Shriver & Jacobson Ste 800 1001 Pennsylvania Ave NW Washington DC 20004-2505 E-mail: galluja@ffhsj.com.

GALLUP, JOHN GARDINER, retired paper company executive; b. Bridgeport, Conn., Oct. 31, 1927; s. Prentiss Brownell and Evelyn (Crocker) G.; m. Paula Burgee, June 10, 1951; children: Susan, Paula, Bruce. AB, Dartmouth Coll., 1949; William Pynchon hon. degree in Humanics, Springfield Coll., 1998. Dept. mgr. J.B. White Co., Greenville, S.C., 1951, Castner Knott Dept. Store, Nashville, 1951-52; asst. store mgr. A.T. Gallup, Inc., Holyoke, Mass., 1952-55; with Strathmore Paper Co., Westfield, Mass., 1955-92, prodn. mgr., 1968-70, pres., div. mgr., 1970-92. Dir. Bank of New Eng.-West, Springfield, Mass.; chmn. Mass. Ventures, Inc. Mem. George Bush Campaign Com., 1979; chmn. Baystate Med. Center, Springfield, 1979-82; chmn. Baystate Health Systems, Inc., 1982-83; bd. dirs. Jr. Achievement Western Mass., 1979; trustee Springfield Coll., 1979-91; chmn. Valley 2,000; trustee Community Found. W. Mass., Beveridge Found; commr. Mass. Commn. Jud. Conduct; trustee St. Andrew's Ch. Longmeadow, Econ. Devel. Coun. West Mass.; dir. Willie Ross Sch. for Deaf. Served with USMC, 1945-47. Mem. Boston Paper Trade Assn. (pres. 1979), Am. Paper Inst. (exec. com. cover and text paper group 1979-91), Greater Springfield C. of C. (vice chmn. 1985-88, chmn. 1988-91, vol. econ. devel.), Visiting Nurses Assn. (bd. dirs.), Corp. fur Bus., Work and Learning (bd. dirs.), Cmty. Svc. Learning (bd. dirs.), World Affairs Coun. (bd. dirs.), Springfield Orch. Assn. (pres.), Associated Industries Mass. (hon. dir.), Century Club. Clubs: Longmeadow (Mass.) Country, Colony (Springfield). Episcopalian. Home. 64 Cambridge Cir Longmeadow MA 01106-2828 Office: 1350 Main St Ste 3 Springfield MA 01103-1627

GALLUP, PATRICIA, computer company executive; Grad., U. Conn., 1979. Chair PC Connection, Inc., Milford, Mass., 1982—, CEO, 2002—, pres., 2003—. Named Entrepreneur of Yr., Ernst & Young, 1998, 2003, N.H. High Tech. Coun., 2003; named one of Top 50 Women Bus. Owners in U.S., Working Woman, 2000—03. Office: PC Connection Inc Rt 101A 730 Milford Rd Merrimack NH 03054-4631*

GALLUS, CHARLES JOSEPH, retired journalist; b. Havre, Mont., Jan. 24, 1947; s. Raymond Charles and Anna Jo (Mack) G. BA in Polit. Sci. cum laude, Carroll Coll., 1969; MA in Polit. Sci., U. Mont., 1972. Bookkeeper's asst. Ellen Solem, CPA, Chinook, Mont., 1972; circulation asst. Havre Daily News, 1972-73, wire editor, reporter, photographer, 1973-97; ret., 1997. Mem. 2 study comms. Havre local govt., 1974-77, 84-86; mem. Hill County Dem. Ctrl. Com., Havre, 1974—. Mem. Glacier Natural History Assn., Northwinds Athletic Club, KC. Roman Catholic. Avocations: outdoor recreation, travel, reading, dancing. Home: 112 3rd St # 746 Havre MT 59501-3532

GALO, GARY A. audio-visual specialist, educator; b. Cleve., May 16, 1951; m. Ellen S. Gillespie, Nov. 8, 1975; 1 child, Michelle A. MusB in Edn., SUNY, 1973, MA in Music History and Lit., 1974. Cert. tchr. N.Y., 1974. Audio engr. Crane Sch. of Music SUNY, Potsdam, NY, 1976—. Contbr. over 170 articles and reviews to profl. jours. Mem.: Assn. for Recorded Sound Collections (co-chmn. tech. com. 1996—, rec. rev. editor 1995—), Audio Engring. Soc. Office: Crane School of Music SUNY Potsdam 44 Pierrepont Ave Potsdam NY 13676 Office Fax: 315-267-2432. E-mail: galoga@potsdam.edu.

GAL-OR, ESTHER, educator; b. Haifa, Israel, Oct. 2, 1951; d. Israel and Zipora Rubinstein; m. Mordechai Gal-Or, Oct. 25, 1975; children: Anat, Ronen, Karen. BS in Econs., Technion, Haifa, Israel, 1975, MS in Econs., 1977; PhD in Managerial Econs. & Decision Sci., Northwestern U., 1980. Asst. prof. U. Pitts., 1980-83, assoc. prof., 1985—90, prof., 1990-96, Glenn. Stinson chair competitiveness, 1996—, assoc. dean for rsch., 2002—. Vis. prof. Technion, Haifa, Israel, 1983-85, Northwestern U., Evanston, Ill., 1999. Contbr. articles to profl. jours. Recipient Pres. Disting. Rsch. award, U. Pitts., 1989, NSF awards, Agy. Health Care Policy Rsch. award. Fellow Internat. Jour. Indsl. Orgn. Office: U Pitts Katz Grad Sch Bus 368A Mervis Hall Pittsburgh PA 15260 Home: 137 Phillips Pl Pittsburgh PA 15217-1811

GALOWICH, RONALD HOWARD, real estate investment executive, venture capitalist; b. Peoria, Ill., Feb. 18, 1936; s. Louis J. and Leah (Kahn) G.; m. Eleanor Bernstein, June 16, 1957 (div. Aug., 1977); children: Jeffrey, Robert, Pamela; m. Susan E. Loggans, Sept. 11, 1977 (div. Apr. 1988); m. Linda L. Kroupa, Oct. 18, 2000. BS in Commerce and Law, U. Ill., 1957, JD, 1959. Bar: Ill. 1959, U.S. Supreme Ct. 1963. Pres. Twin Oaks-Burr Oaks Realty, Joliet, Ill., 1961-81; ptnr. Galowich & Galowich, Joliet, Ill., 1960-81; dir. real estate ops. Pritzker & Pritzker, Chgo., 1981-90; chmn. Madison Realty Group, Inc., Chgo., 1985—, Madison Group Holdings, Inc., Chgo., 1990—; founder, chmn. Initiate Sys., Inc. (formerly Madison Info. Technologies, Inc.), Chgo., 1994—. Co-founder, dir. First Health Group Corp. (formerly Health Care Compare Corp.), Downers Grove, Ill., 1982—; commr. Ill. Supreme Ct., 1968-70. Bd. visitors U. Ill. Coll. Law, 1996—, pres., 1998-2000; mem. leadership com. Cancer Inst., Rush-Presbyn. St. Lukes Med. Ctr., Chgo., 1993—; bd. dirs. Athletes Against Drugs, 1992—; bd. mgrs. Riverside Hosp. Cancer Ctr., Kankakee, Ill., 1999-2003. Fellow Am. Judicature Soc., Ill. Bar Found.; mem. ABA, Ill. Bar Assn., Urban Land Inst., Chgo. Bar Assn, YMCA (chmn. devel. com. 2002—). Jewish. Avocation: lic. airline transport pilot. Home: 1248 N Astor St Chicago IL 60610-2308 Office: Madison Group Holdings Inc 200 W Madison St Ste 2800 Chicago IL 60606-3463 E-mail: rhgalo@ix.netcom.com, rgalowich@initiatesystems.com.

GALPERIN, DELLA L. management consultant, educator; arrived in U.S., 2001; d. Samuel and Colpan Karan Galperin. BA in Psychology, McGill U., Montreal, 1990; MS in Adminstrn., Concordia U., Montreal, 1995, PhD in Adminstrn., 2002. Prof. internat. bus. Rollins Coll., Winter Park, Fla., 2001—. Cons., Montreal, 1995—2000, Winter Park, Fla., 2001—. Contbr. chapters to books, articles to profl. jours. Grantee, Fonds pour la Formation de Chercheurs et l'Aide a la Recherche, 1993, 1995, Concordia U., 1994, 1999, Bus. Literacy and Informational Tutorials: Info. Fluency Project, Associated Colls. of the South, 2002; J.W. McConnell Meml. Grad. fellow, Concordia U., 1993, 1995. Mem.: Internat. Acad. E-Business, Internat. Soc. for the Study of Work and Orgnl. Values, Acad. Internat. Bus., Acad. Mgmt., Adminstrv. Scis. Assn. (academic reviewer and program chair internat. bus. divsn. 1999—2000), Adminstrv. Scis. Assn. Can. (divsn. chair 2000—01). Office: Rollins Coll 1000 Holt Ave 2723 Winter Park FL 32789-4499 Office Fax: 407-646-1566.

GALPERIN, LEONID BORIS, petroleum engineer, chemical engineer, researcher; s. Boris Mark Galperin and Kathy Ykov Kuperman; m. Irina Zalman Faynberg, Feb. 20, 1975; 1 child, Andrew Abraham. PhD in chem. engring., Petrochemical Rsch. Inst, 1964—68. Chemical engineer, Tech. Inst., St Peterburg, Russia, 1961. Sr. rschr. Petrochemical Rsch. Inst., St. Peterburg, Russia, 1969—78; devel. specialist UOP LLC, Des Plaines, Ill., 1985—92. Sr. rschr. UOP LLC, Des Plaines, Ill., 1993—98, r & d assoc., 1999—. Mem.: Internat. Zeolite Assn. (assoc.). Achievements include 23 US patents; 5 US patents are pending; 10 European and Russian patents. Office: UOP LLC 50 East Algonquin Rd Des Plaines IL 60017-5017 Office Fax: 847-391-1274. E-mail: lbgalper@uop.com.

GALPERIN, MICHAEL Y. microbiologist; s. Yuri I. Galperin and Natalia Galperina; m. Olga Galperina, Oct. 21, 1989; children: Natalia Nikitina, Maria. PhD, Moscow State U., 1985. Staff scientist NCBI, NLM, NIH, Bethesda, Md., 1996—. Author: (textbook) Sequence-Evolution-Function. Computational Approaches in Comparative Genomics. Office: NCBI NLM Nat Insts of Health 8600 Rockville Pike Bethesda MD 20894 Office Fax: 301-435-7794. E-mail: galperin@ncbi.nlm.nih.gov.

GALSTON, ARTHUR WILLIAM, biology educator; b. N.Y.C., Apr. 21, 1920; s. Hyman and Freda (Zaks) G.; m. Dale Judith Kuntz, June 27, 1941; children: William Arthur, Beth Dale. BS, Cornell U., 1940; MS, U. Ill., 1942, PhD, 1943. Rsch. plant physiologist emergency rubber project Calif. Inst. Tech., 1943-44, sr. rsch. fellow, 1947-50, assoc. prof. biology, 1951-55; instr. Yale U., 1946-47, prof. plant physiology, 1955-65, prof. biology, 1965-72, Eaton prof. botany, 1973-90, emeritus prof., 1990, dir. div. biol. scis., 1965-66, sr. rsch. biologist, 1990—, chmn. dept. botany, 1961-62, chmn. dept. biology, 1985-88. Cons. ctrl. rsch. dept. E.I. duPont de Nemours & Co., 1956-78, Plant Resources Venture Funds, 1983-89, NASA, 1988-94; mem. divsn. biology and agr. NRC, 1963-66, 85-88, mem. com. on space biology and medicine, 1983-86; Einstein prof. Faculty Agr. Hebrew U., Jerusalem, 1980; vis. scientist Plant Breeding Inst., Cambridge, Eng., 1983; vis. fellow Wolfson Coll., Cambridge U., 1983; vis. scholar Riken Inst., Japan, 1988-89. Author: Life of the Green Plant, 1961, 3d edit. (with Peter J. Davies and Ruth L. Satter) 1980, (with James Bonner) Principles of Plant Physiology, 1952, (with Peter J. Davies) Control Mechanisms in Plant Development, 1970, Daily Life in People's China, 1973, Green Wisdom, 1981, Life Processes in Plants, 1994; editor: New Dimensions in Bioethics, 2001; mem. editorial adv. bd.: World Book Science Year, 1976-78, Pesticide Physiology and Biochemistry, 1978-88, Plant Growth Regulation, 1983-93, Chem. Engring. News, 1977-78, Environment, 1979-83; contbr. sci. articles. Served as ensign USNR, 1944-46; mil. govt. Okinawa. Guggenheim fellow Stockholm, Paris, Sheffield, Eng., 1950-51; Fulbright fellow Canberra, Australia, 1960-61; Sci. Faculty fellow NSF, London, 1967-68. Fellow AAAS (chmn. com. on meetings 1956-59, life mem.); mem. Am. Soc. Plant Physiologists (sec. 1955-57, v.p. 1957-58, pres. 1963-64), Internat. Assn. Plant Physiology (sec.-treas. 1961-67), Bot. Soc. Am. (editl. bd. 1959-61, 72-76, pres. 1967-68), Fedn. Am. Scientists (coun. 1973-76), Am. Soc. Biochemists, Molecular Biol., Am. Soc. Photobiology, Am. Inst. Biol. Scis., Am. Acad. Arts & Scis. Home: 307 Manley Heights Rd Orange CT 06477-3028 Office: Molecular Cellular & Devel Dept Biology Yale U New Haven CT 06520-8103 E-mail: arthur.galston@yale.edu.

GALSTON, WILLIAM ARTHUR, political scientist, educator; b. Bklyn., Jan. 17, 1946; s. Arthur William and Dale Judith (Kuntz) G.; m. Miriam, Sept. 15, 1968; 1 child, Ezra Moses. BA, Cornell U., 1967; MA, U. Chgo., 1969, PhD, 1973. Asst. prof. dept. govt. U. Tex., Austin, 1973-80, assoc. prof. dept. govt., 1980-82; issues dir. Mondale Pres. Campaign, Washington, 1982-84; dir. econ. and social programs Roosevelt Ctr. Am. Policy Studies, Washington, 1985-88; prof. sch. pub. affairs U. Md., College Park, 1988—; dep. asst. to pres. domestic policy The White House, Washington, 1993—95. Vis. fellow Instn. Social and Policy Studies, Yale U., 1980-81; cons. Temple for Gov. Campaign, 1982; mem. adv. bd. Ford/Aspen-Wye Rural Econ. Policy Project, 1989-92; mem. selection com. rural policy fellowships Woodrow Wilson Nat. Fellowship Found., 1989-91; cons. and spkr. in field. Author: Kant and the Problem of History, 1975, Justice and the Human Good, 1980, A Tough Row to Hoe: The 1985 Farm Bill and Beyond, 1985, Liberal Purposes, 1991 (Spitz prize 1993), Rural Development in the United States, 1995, Liberal Pluralism, 2002; editor Virtue, 1992, Philosophical Dimensions of Public Policy, 2002; mem. editl. bd. Ethics, 1991—, Nomos, 1991—; contbr. numerous articles to profl. jours. Advisor Gore for Pres. Campaign, Washington, 1988, 2000; chief speechwriter John Anderson Nat. Unity Campaign, Washington, 1980; mem. working group on bicentennial bill of rights Wilson Ctr., 1990-91. Sgt. USMC, 1969-70. Fellow Danforth Found., 1967-68, NEH, 1980-81, Woodrow Wilson Ctr., 1991-92. Mem. Am. Polit. Scis. Assn. (program chmn. normative polit. theory sect. 1992), Conf. Study Polit. Thought, Am. Soc. Polit. and Legal Philosophy (program chmn. ann. mtng. 1989), Phi Beta Kappa. Democrat. Jewish. Home: 5616 Durbin Rd Bethesda MD 20814-1014

GALT, JOHN WILLIAM, actor, writer; b. Jackson, Miss., Apr. 4, 1940; s. William Neal and Lyndel Janes (Fortenberry) G.; m. Anna Marie Kolenovsky, Dec. 14, 1965 (div. 1973); children: Joseph William, Edward Wayne; m. 2d Diane Renee Wallace, June 6, 1981; children: Christopher Wallace, Geoffrey Warren. Student, U. Md. at Munich (Germany), 1960-61; BA, Univ. Scis. Am., L.A., 1992. Owner Vox Omnia Prodns., 1999—. Toured as folksinger U.S.A. and Europe, 1960-62; voice talent on numerous radio and TV commls., Dallas, 1965-78, 80—, L.A., 1978-80; 31 film appearances as actor; looped characters in 4 movies; voice of Lyndon B. Johnson in Oliver Stone's JFK, 1992, Forrest Gump, 1994; writer film script Iceman, 1976; contbg. writer For The Love of Benji, 1977; writer screenplay Step Back From Anger, 1986, The Guardians, 1987; v.p. Tex. Ind. Feature Prodns., Inc., 1981-2003, Jackson Galt Creative Enterprise Inc, 1991-99. Co-author: What Price Paradise, 2001, The Demon King, 2001; contbg. writer The Internal Affair, 1988. With USAF, 1957-62. Recipient Dallas Citizen's Cert. Merit, 1973, Clios (28), Tellys (31), N.Y. Film Festival Silver, Addys (43), CHA Gold Spirit award; several Tops in advt. awards. Mem. NATAS (Heartland chpt.), Actor's Equity Assn., Screen Actor's Guild, AFTRA, Writers Guild of Am., Acad. for Preservation of Talking Pictures. Avocations: martial arts (2d degree black belt tae guek kwan kung fu 1993, advanced oriental broad sword combat forms, brown belt hapkiko ohtc 1989). E-mail: JohnWilliamGALT@comcast.net.

GALTERIO, LOUIS, healthcare information executive; b. N.Y.C., Apr. 20, 1951; s. Elio and Angelina (Mattina) G.; m. Elizabeth Anne Coddington, May 2, 1971; children: Jason, Heather. Student, CCNY, 1969-70, Baruch Coll., 1970-75; BS in Mgmt. summa cum laude, Mercy Coll., 1978; MBA in Fin., L.I. U., 1980. Cert. clin. therapist, diplomate Am. Bd. Hynotherapy. Asst. mgr. Mfrs. Hanover Trust, N.Y.C., 1971-82; v.p. Bankers Trust Co., N.Y.C., 1982-87; CIO Mortgage Backed Securities Clearing Corp., N.Y.C., 1987-88; sr. cons. capital markets Digital Equipment Corp., N.Y.C., 1988-90, integration exec., 1990-91; chief info. officer healthcare Health and Hosps. Corp. NYC, 1991-93; dir. clin. info. sys. Soc. of N.Y. Hosp., N.Y.C., 1993—. Mgmt. cons., neurofeedback practitioner Galterio Cons., N.Y.C., 1987—. Mem. IEEE (assoc.), Internat. Assn. Counselors and Therapists, Bankers Trust Alumni Orgn., Am. Hosp. Assn., Coll. Healthcare Info. Mgmt. Execs., Healthcare Info. and Mgmt. Systems Soc., Biofeedback Soc. Fla., Alpha Chi. Home: 2453 Nimbus Dr North Port FL 34287-5138 also: The NY Hosp 525 E 68th St # 151 New York NY 10021-4870

GALTON, STEPHEN HAROLD, lawyer; b. Tulare, Calif., Dec. 23, 1937; s. Harold Parker and Marie Rose (Tuck) G.; m. Grace Marilyn Shaw, Aug. 15, 1964; children: Mark (dec.), Bradley, Jeremy, Elisabeth. BS, U. So. Calif., 1966, JD, 1969. Bar: Calif. 1970, U.S. Ct. Appeals (9th cir.) 1973, U.S. Dist. Ct. (no. dist.) Calif. 1973, U.S. Dist. Ct. (cen. dist.) Calif. 1970, U.S. Dist. Ct. (ea. and so. dists.) Calif. 1973. Assoc. Martin & Flandrick, San Marino, Calif., 1970-71, ptnr., 1971-72; assoc. Booth, Mitchell, Strange & Smith, L.A., 1973-77, ptnr., 1978-85, Galton & Helm, L.A., 1986—. Contbr. articles to profl. jours. Mem. ABA (litigation, tort, ins. sects.), Am. Bd. Trial Advs., Calif. State Bar Assn. (del. 1974-81, chair fed. cts. com.), Wilshire Bar Assn. (pres. 1986-87), Los Angeles County Bar Assn. (trustee 1987-89). Episcopalian. Office: Galton & Helm 500 S Grand Ave Ste 1200 Los Angeles CA 90071-2624 E-mail: sgalton@galtonhelm.com., shgalton@earthlingk.net.

GALTON, VALERIE ANNE, endocrinology educator; b. Louth, Eng., May 6, 1934; came to U.S., 1959; d. Wilfrid and Eileen (Watson) Hamilton; m. Michael Galton, Aug. 26, 1956 (dec. 1968); children: Ian Andrew, Kenneth Anthony. BSc with honors, U. London, 1955, PhD, 1958., 1967-75; Research assoc. Nat. Inst. Med. Research, Mill Hill, London, 1955-58; research assoc. Med. Sch., Harvard U., Boston, 1959-61; instr., then asst. prof. Dartmouth Med. Sch., Hanover, N.H., 1961-66, assoc. prof., 1968-75, prof., 1975—. Cons. NIH, Bethesda, Md., 1973-98. Mem. editl. bd. Endocrinology, 1982-85, Am. Jour. Physiology, 1982-85, 95—; contbr. articles to profl. jours. NIH grantee, 1962—. Mem. Am. Thyroid Assn., Endocrine Soc. Home: 57 Jenkins Rd Lebanon NH 03766-2002 Office: Dartmouth Med Sch Lebanon NH 03756

GALVAN, MAX, humanities educator; b. Wanta, Aycucho, Peru, Apr. 13, 1939; arrived in USA, 1961; s. Guillermo and Benedicta (Gonzalez) Galvan; m. Monika Heimerl, Aug. 11, 1964; children: Irmgard, Elba, Rafael, Rodrigo, Maxine. PhD, Hofstra Univ., Hempstead, NY, 1985; EdD, Rutgers Univ., New Brunswick, NJ, 1984; MS, CW Post Coll. LIU, New York, NY, 1979; MA, CUNY, New York, NY, 1974. Cert. PD LIU, 1979. Tchr. PS 128, X9, Bronx, NY, 1978—80; rsch. asst. prof. Rutgers Univ., New Brunswick, NJ, 1980—83; multicultural dir. Hempstead Pub. Sch., Hempstead, NY, 1984—94; assoc. prof. Five Towns Coll., Dix Hills, NY, 1989—. SP4 U.S. Army, 1962—65. Fellow Goethe Fellowship, CUNY/ Kiel, Germany, 1979. Avocations: writing, painting, music, reading, skiing. Home: 1582 Briard St Wantagh NY 11793

GALVANI, CHRISTIANE MESCH, English as a second language educator, translator; b. Kiel, Fed. Republic Germany, Jan. 19, 1954; came to U.S., 1977; d. Edgar and Elisabeth (Depken) Mesch; m. Paul Andrew Galvani, Dec. 19, 1979; 1 child, Jacqueline. BA, U. London, 1977; MA, Rice U., 1986. Freelance translator, Houston, 1979—; instr. English, German, French Berlitz Sch. Langs., Houston, 1981-82, interpreter, translator, 1981-84, prodn. coord., 1982-84; lead ESL instr. Tex. So. U., Houston, 1989—; instr. Rice U., Houston, 1990 (summer). Translator: The Flowing Light of the Divinity, 1991. Named to Outstanding Young Women of Am., 1986 Mem. MLA, TESOL, Am. Translators Assn., Am. Lit. Translators Assn., Houston Profl. Translators Forum (dir. 1982-83), Houston Interpreter's and Translator's Assn. (sec.), Kappa Delta Pi. Avocations: music, playing the recorder, reading, piano. Home: 2926 Fairway Dr Sugar Land TX 77478-4023 Office: Tex So Univ 3100 Cleburne St Houston TX 77004-4501

GALVAO, LOUIS ALBERTO, import and export corporation executive, consultant; b. Ponta Delgada, Sao Miguel, Portugal, July 5, 1949; came to U.S., 1969; s. Jeremias B. and Margarida M. G.; m. Antonieta A. Galvao, Oct. 26, 1966 (div. 1984); children: Marlene, Vanessa. Degree in Bus. Mgmt., Indsl. & Commerce Sch., Azores, Portugal, 1968; Dr. Universal Life (hon.), Universal Life Ch., 1991. Asst. mgr. sales J.B. Galvao Imports, Azores, 1964-68; asst. supr. Union Carbide Corp., Peabody, Mass., 1969-70, Container Corp. Am., Wakefield, Mass., 1970-73; sales dir. McCulloch Oil Corp., Lake Havash City, Ariz., 1972-74; pres. Sunset Investments Corp., Phoenix, 1974—; v.p. United Universal Enterprises Corp., Phoenix, 1985—. Pres. Universal Imports, Inc., Phoenix, 1977—; dir. Global Savings & Loan Ltd., London, 1990—. Mem. Nat. Rep. Congl. Com., Washington, 1982— (cert. recognition 1981, 84, 85, Campaign Kickoff award 1984, cert. merit 1992), Rep. Presdl. Task Force, Washington, 1984— (Am. flag dedicated in his honor at Rotunda of U.S. Capital bldg. 1986, life mem., mem. presdl. electiom registry 1992), Rep. Nat. Com. (cert. recognition 1990, 92), European Movement, U.K., 1990—, Social Dem. Party, Portugal, 1990—, Washington Legal Found.; charter mem. U.S. Def. Com.; del. The Presl. Trust, Washington, 1992. Recipient award U.S. Def. Com., 1984; inducted to Rep. Nat. Hall Honor Rep. Nat. Candidate Trust, 1992. Mem. Am. Mgmt. Assn., Nat. Assn. Export Cos., Profl. Fin. Assts., Heritage Bus. Club, Senatorial Club, Universal Life Ch. Roman Catholic. Avocations: reading, traveling, biking, movies.

GALVIN, CHRISTOPHER B. electronics company executive; b. 1951; BA, Northwestern U., MBA, 1977. With Motorola, Inc., 1973—89; v.p. mktg. sales and svc. Tegal Corp., 1983; named v.p. and gen. mgr. Tegal Corp. U.S. Ops., 1984; v.p. and dir., commn., then gen. mgr., then corp. v.p. Sector's Paging

Divsn., 1985—88; sr. exec. v.p., asst. COO Motorola, Inc., Schaumberg, Ill., 1989—95, pres., COO, 1995—, CEO, 1997—. Bd. counselors Bechtel Corp.; mem. exec. com. Computer Systems Policy Project; mem. bus. coun. Am. Soc. of Corp. Executives; mem. Hong Kong Chief's Exec. Coun. of Internat. Adv.; trustee Northwestern U., Am. Enterprise Inst. Mem.: Ill. Coalition for Sci. and Tech. (dir.), Nat. Underground Railroad Freedom Ctr. (adv. bd. mem.), Am. Soc. Engring. Edn. (adv. bd. mem.). Office: Motorola Inc 1303 E Algonquin Rd Schaumburg IL 60196-1079

GALVIN, CYRIL JEROME, JR., coastal engineer; b. Jersey City, June 16, 1935; s. Cyril Jerome and Veronica Theresa (Lawlor) G. BS, St. Louis U., 1957; MS, MIT, 1959, PhD, 1963. Registered profl. engr., Md., N.J., Del. Research asst. MIT Hydrodynamics Lab., 1959-63; oceanographer Coastal Engr. Research Ctr., Washington, 1963-70, br. chief, 1970-78; prin. Cyril Galvin, Coastal Engr., Springfield, Va., 1978—. Cons. in field. Author: Littoral Processes manual, 1972; contbr. articles to profl. jours.; adv. editor Coastal Engring., 1978-94. Recipient Huber prize, ASCE, 1969, Norman medal, 1970. Mem. Am. Geophys. Union, Am. Assn. Petroleum Geologists, Soc. for Sedimentary Geology, History of Sci. Soc., History of Earth Sci. Soc. (councilor 2001-02). Roman Catholic. Office: Cyril Galvin Coastal Engr PO Box 623 Springfield VA 22150-0623

GALVIN, JOHN ROGERS, educator, retired army officer; b. Wakefield, Mass., May 13, 1929; s. John James and Mary Josephine (Logan) G.; m. Virginia Lee Brennan, June 5, 1961; children: Mary Jo, Elizabeth Ann, Kathleen Mary, Erin Elizabeth. BS, U.S. Mil. Acad., 1954; MA, Columbia U., 1962; postgrad., U. Pa., 1964-65; grad., Command and Gen. Staff Coll., 1966. Commd. 2d lt. U.S. Army, 1954, advanced through grades to gen.; mil. asst. to Supreme Allied Comdr. Europe, 1974-75; comdr. DISCOM, chief of staff 3d Infantry div., Germany, 1975-78; asst. div. comdr. 8th Infantry div., 1978-80; comdg. gen. 24th Infantry div., Ft. Stewart, Ga., 1981-83, also post comdr.; comdg. gen. VII U.S. Corps, Stuttgart, Fed. Republic Germany, 1983-85; comdr. in chief U.S. So. Command, Quarry Heights, Panama, 1985-87; supreme allied comdr. Europe, comdr.-in-chief U.S. European Command, 1987-92; ret., 1992; Olin disting. prof. nat. security studies U.S. Mil. Acad., West Point, N.Y., 1992-93; disting. vis. policy analyst The Mershon Ctr., Ohio State U., 1994-95; dean Fletcher Sch. Law and Diplomacy, Tufts U., Boston, 1995-2000; dean emeritus, 2000—. Author: The Minute Men, 1967, Air Assault, 1969, Three Men of Boston, 1976. Former bd. dirs. Wesleyan Coll. Fletcher Sch. of Law and Diplomacy fellow, 1972-73; decorated Silver Star, Legion of Merit, DFC, Bronze Star. Mem. Ctr. for Creative Leadership (past bd. govs.), Seligman (bd. dirs.), Am. Coun. on Germany (chmn. emeritus bd. dirs.), Inst. for Def. Analyses (trustee, 1995-2002). Roman Catholic. Home: 2714 Lake Jodeco Cir Jonesboro GA 30236-5329

GALVIN, KATHLEEN MALONE, communication educator; b. N.Y.C., Feb. 9, 1943; d. James Robert and Helen M. (Sullivan) G.; m. Charles A. Wilkinson, June 19,1973; children: Matthew, Katherine, Kara. BS, Fordham U., 1964; MA, Northwestern U., 1965, 80, PhD, 1968. Tchr. Evanston (Ill.) Township High Sch., 1967-72; asst. prof. Northwestern U., Evanston, 1968-73, assoc. prof., 1973-78, prof., 1978—, assoc. dean, 1988-2001. Presenter workshops in field. Author: Listening by Doing, 1986; sr. author: Family Communication, 6th edit., 2002; co-author: Person to Person, 5th edit., 1996, Basics of Speech, 3d edit., 1998; co-editor: Making Connections, 3d edit., 2002, Communication Works!, 2000; contbr. articles to profl. jours.; developer, instr. 26-video series on Family Communication (PBS Adult Satellite Sys.). Office: Northwestern U Comm Studies Dept 2299 N Campus Dr Evanston IL 60208-3545

GALVIN, MICHAEL JOHN, JR., lawyer; b. Winona, Minn., July 8, 1930; s. Michael John Sr. and Margaret Elizabeth (O'Donohue) G.; m. Frances Dennis Culligan, Sept. 7, 1957; children: Sean, Kevin, Kathleen, Nora, Mary, Margaret, Patricia. BA, U. St. Thomas, 1952; LLB, U. Minn., 1957. Bar: Minn. 1957, U.S. Dist. Ct. Minn. 1957, U.S. Supreme Ct. 1961. With sales and svc. Badger Machine Co., Winona, 1950-56; mgr. Oaks Hotel Inc., Winona, 1950-56; ptnr. Briggs & Morgan, P.A., St. Paul, 1957—. Pres. St. Paul Winter Carnival Assn., 1970; sec. St. Paul Area C. of C., 1968-71; trustee U. St. Thomas, 1978-85, Coll. St. Catherines, St. Paul, 1999—; nat. chmn. U. Minn. Law Sch. Ptnrs. in Excellence Program, 2000-01; chmn. Indianhead Coun. Boy Scouts Am., 2003—. Lt. USAF, 1952-54, USAFR, 1954-60. Named Oustanding Young Man, City St. Paul, 1964, Boss of Yr., St. Paul Jaycees, 1990; recipient Disting. Alumnus award, U. St. Thomas, 1983, Great Living St. Paulite award, St. Paul Area C. of C., 2000, Eugene and Mary Fry Cmty. award, Cretin-Derham Hall Schs., 2000, Disting. Alumnus award, U. Minn. Law Sch., 2001, Monsignor James Lavin award, U. St. Thomas, 2003. Mem. ABA (labor and employment law sect.), Minn. Bar Assn. (treas. 1991-93, pres.-elect 1993, pres. 1994-95, chair labor and employment law sect. 1984), Ramsey County Bar Assn. (exec. coun. 1965-68, 83-86, pres. 1984-85), Minn. Vol. Attys. Corp. (pres. 1993-94), Univ. Club (pres. 1962), Minn. Club (pres. 1971), St. Paul Athletic Club (pres. 1986), St. Paul Area C. of C. (bd. dirs. 1995—, chmn. 1997-98). Republican. Roman Catholic. Office: Briggs & Morgan 2200 1st St N Saint Paul MN 55109-3210 E-mail: mgalvin@briggs.com.

GALVIN, ROBERT J. lawyer; b. New Haven, Dec. 10, 1938; s. Herman I. and Freda (Helfand) Galvin; m. Susan I. Goldstein, Oct. 15, 1960 (div.); children: David B., Peter J. AB, Union Coll., Schenectady, N.Y., 1961; JD, Suffolk U., Boston, 1967. Bar: Mass. 1967, U.S. Dist. Ct. Mass. 1967, U.S. Supreme Ct. 1988. Pvt. practice, Boston, 1967-78; ptnr. Lippman & Galvin, Boston, 1978-84; of counsel Gage, Tucker & Vom Baur, Boston, 1984-86; ptnr. Davis, Malm & D'Agostine, Boston, 1986—. Lectr. Boston Ctr. Adult Edn., 1972—89, bd. dirs., v.p., 1979—, chmn. fin. com., 1985—86, pres., 1987—91; lectr. Northeastern U., Boston, 1977—78. Real estate columnist: Boston Ledger, 1981, co-author, editor: Massachusetts Condominium Law, 1988, 6th edit., 2003; contbr. book; co-author: (book) Crocker's Notes on Common Forms, 1999, 2000, 2003; contbr. articles to profl. jours. Bd. dirs., v.p. Rental Housing Assn. divsn. Greater Boston Real Estate Bd., 1974; bd. dirs. Beech Hill Found., Inc., 1989—, Thoreau Soc., Inc., 1993—, chmn. fin. com., chmn. exec. com., 1999—2000, v.p., 2001—. Recipient Walter Harding Disting. Svc. award, 2001. Fellow: Mass. Bar Found. (life; mem. Greater Boston 3 grantmaking adv. com. 1997, 1998, 1999); mem.: Cmty. Assns. Inst. (mem. atty.'s com. New Eng. chpt.), Mass. Conveyancer's Assn., Am. Arbitration Assn. (mem. comml. arbitration panel), Mass. Continuing Legal Edn. (real estate curriculum adv. com. 1983—87), Mass. Bar Assn. (coun. mem. property law sect. 1977—80, chmn. condominium com. 1979—91), Soc. Censure, Reproof and Arraingment Pub. Error, Abstract Club. Home: 344 Pond St Jamaica Plain MA 02130-2447 Office: Davis Malm & D'Agostine PC One Boston Pl Ste # 3700 Boston MA 02108 E-mail: rgalvin@davismalm.com.

GALVIN, ROBERT W. electronics executive; b. Marshfield, Wis., Oct. 9, 1922; Student, U. Notre Dame, U. Chgo.; LLD, Quincy Coll., St. Ambrose Coll., DePaul U., Ariz. State U. With Motorola, Inc., Chgo., 1940—48, exec. v.p., 1948—56, former pres., 1956, chmn. bd., 1964—90, CEO, 1964—86, chmn. exec. com., 1990—2001, also dir.; ret. from Motorola, 2003; chmn. bd. Semantech Inc., Austin, Tex. Author: America's Founding Secret: What the Scottish Enlightment Taught our Founding Fathers, 2002. Past mem. Pres.'s Commn. on Internat. Trade and Investment.; chmn. industry policy adv. com. U.S. Trade Rep.; active Pres.'s Pvt. Sector Survey; chmn. Pres.'s Adv. Coun. on Pvt. Sector Initiatives, Ill. Inst. Tech., U. Notre Dame; bd. dirs. Jr. Achievement, Chgo. With Signal Corps U.S. Army, WWII. Named Decision Maker of Yr., Chgo. Assn. Commerce and Industry-Am. Statis. Assn., 1973; recipient Nat. medal, Tech. U.S. Dept. Commerce Tech. Adminstrn., 1991, Sword of Loyola award, Loyola U., Chgo., Washington award, Western Soc. Engrs., 1984. Mem.: Nat. Bus. Hall of Fame, Electronic Industries Assn. (pres. 1966, bd. dirs., Medal of Honor 1970, Golden Omega award 1981). Office: Motorola Inc 1303 E Algonquin Rd Schaumburg IL 60196-1079

GALVIN, THOMAS JOHN, Former information science policy educator and librarian; b. Arlington, Mass., Dec. 30, 1932; s. Thomas John and Elizabeth (Rossiter) G.; m. Marie C. Schumb, Nov. 24, 1956; 1 child, Siobhan Marie Wee. AB, Columbia U., 1954; SM, Simmons Coll., Boston, 1956; PhD, Case Western Res U., 1973. Reference libr. Boston U., 1954-56; dir. Abbot Pub. Libr., Marblehead, Mass., 1956-59; asst. dir. Simmons Coll. Libr., 1959-62; assoc. dir., prof. Sch. Libr. Sci., 1962-74; dean, prof. Sch. Libr. and Info. Sci., U. Pitts., 1974-85; exec. dir. Am. Libr. Assn., Chgo., 1985-89; prof. info. sci. and policy, dir. info. sci. doctoral program SUNY at Albany, 1989-99, prof. emeritus, 1999—. Grad. fellow Case Western Res U., 1965-66; external examiner U. Ibadan, Nigeria, 1976-78; trustee Thayer Pub. Libr., Braintree, Mass., 1973-74; faculty fellow Ctr. for Tech. in Govt. SUNY, Albany. Author: Library Resource Sharing, 1977, Problems in Reference Service, 1965, Current Problems in Reference Service, 1971, The Case Method in Library Education, 1973, The On-Line Revolution in Libraries, 1978, The Structure and Governance of Library Networks, 1979, Excellence in School Media Programs, 1980, Information Technology, 1982, Priorities for Academic Libraries, 1982, Navigating the Networks, 1994, Smart IT Choices, 1996; also articles. Recipient Alumni Achievement award Simmons Coll. Sch. Libr. Sci., 1978, Disting. Alumnus award Case Western Res. U., 1979, Disting. Svc. award Pa. Libr. Assn., 1985, Ida and George Eliot prize Med. Libr. Assn., 1988, award contbr. to edn. Assn. for Libr. Info. Sci. Edn., 1993. Mem. ALA (pres. 1979-80, exec. bd., coun.; past pres. libr. edn. div., Isadore Gilbert Mudge award 1972), Assn. for Libr. and Info. Sci. Edn., Phi Beta Kappa, Beta Phi Mu. Democrat. Roman Catholic. E-mail: tgalvin@albany.edu.

GALVIN, WILLIAM C. state legislator, insurance broker; Mem. Mass. Ho. of Reps., Boston, 1991—. Democrat. Office: State House Rm 238 Boston MA 02133

GALVIN, WILLIAM FRANCIS, state official; b. Brighton, Mass., Sept. 17, 1950; m. Eileen Galvin. Degree cum laude, Boston Coll., 1972; JD, Suffolk U., 1975. Bar: Mass., Fed. Aide Gov.'s Coun., 1972; state rep. Mass. Gen. Ct., 1975-91; vice-chmn. Congl. Redistricting Com., 1981-83; chmn. Govt. Regulations Com., 1983-91; sec. of state Commonwealth of Mass., Boston, 1995—. Democrat. Office: State House, Room 337 Boston MA 02133-1000 E-mail: cis@sec.state.ma.us.*

GALVIS Y ASSMUS, PATRICIA, computer animator, educator, filmmaker; b. Cucuta, Colombia, July 20; d. Lucio Enrique Galvis and Gloria Assmus; 1 child, Ria Jocet Bailey-Galvis. BA Studio Art, Calif. State Univ., 1987; MFA, Calif. Inst. Arts, 1991. Assoc. prof. U. Mass., Amherst, 1991—. Dir. Ctr. Rsch. in Art and Tech., 1996—. Prodr., dir. : (films) Stages, 1999; producer, dir. (films) EOS, 2003; dir.: (films) Sal Vijua (Director's Award, 1994); editor: ACM SIGGRAPH Computer Graphics Quar. Fellow Lilly Tchg., Ctr. Tchg.; grantee Prodn., Interactive Entertainment Techs.

GALYA, THOMAS ANDREW, geologist; b. New Brunswick, N.J., July 11, 1947; s. Andrew Peter and Geraldine Rose Galya; m. Lanora Lucille Bucklew, Jan. 8, 1970. BS, W.Va. U., 1971; MS, U. La., Monroe, 1975; PhD, Miami U., Oxford, Ohio, 1983. Geologist Sewell Coal Co.-Pittston Co., Nettle, W.Va., 1972; chief geologist Clinchfield Coal Co.-Pittston Co., Dante, Va., 1978-82; sr. coal geologist, head coal quality group Exxon Coal Resources USA, Inc., Houston, 1982-86; staff geologist Exxon Coal and Minerals Co., Houston, 1986-89; owner, pres. Galya & Assocs., Katy, Tex., 1989; sr. geologist Occidental Petroleum-Island Creek Coal Corp., 1989-91; geologist III W.Va. Divsn. Environ. Protection, Logan, 1991-96, lead geologist statewide Office of Mining and Reclamation, 1996—2002, lead geologist statewide, 1998—2002; hydrologist Office of Surface Mining U.S. Dept. of Interior, 2002—. Tchg. asst. U. La., Monroe, 1973-75; tchg. fellow Miami U., Oxford, Ohio, 1975-77, fellow, 1977-78. Mem. Am. Inst. Profl. Geologists, Am. Assn. Petroleum Geologists, Soc. Sedimentary Geology, Geol. Soc. Am., Sigma Xi, Sigma Gamma Epsilon. Democrat. Roman Catholic. Home: 65 Dogwood Ln Madison WV 25130-1268 Office: Office of Surface Mining 1027 Virginia St E Charleston WV 25301

GALYSH, ROBERT ALAN, information technology manager; b. Cleve., Apr. 4, 1954; s. Fred Theodore and Jennie Catherine (Masiglowa) G.; m. Nanette Marie Kappus, Mar. 3, 1984; children: Joanna Marie, Matthew Glenn. BA in Econs., Cleve. State U., 1976, MA in Econs., 1982. Savs. officer Cleve. Fed. Savs., 1977-79; v.p., systems and procedures analyst Continental Fed. Savs. (formerly Cleve. Fed. Savs.), Cleve, 1979-84; data processing officer, mgr. systems and procedures Continental div. Dollar Bank FSB, Cleve, 1984-86; systems analyst Cleve. Met. Gen. Hosp., 1986-87, sr. systems analyst, 1987-90; project leader info. systems MetroHealth Sys. (formerly Cleve. Met. Gen. Hosp.), 1990-95, group mgr. info. svcs., 1995-97; project mgr. info. svcs. Fairview Health Sys., Cleve., 1997-2000; group mgr. fin. sys. Cleve. Clinic Health Sys.-Western Region, Cleve., 2000—. Mem. Nat. Warplane Mus. Mem.: Harbor Heritage Soc., Omicron Delta Epsilon. Presbyterian. Avocations: aviation history, home computing, photography, travel. Home: 26602 Sudbury Dr North Olmsted OH 44070-1844 E-mail: bgalysh@worldnet.att.net.

GAMACHE, KATHLEEN SMITH, retired psychotherapist; b. Jersey City, Sept. 13, 1936; d. Robert George and Evelyn Veronica (Kaiser) Smith; m. R. Donald Gamache, Nov. 22, 1958; children: Mariette (dec.), Nanette Campbell, Lisette Becker (dec.). BS, State Coll. N.J., 1958; MS, U. Bridgeport, 1972; postgrad., Yale U., 1986-88, Boston U., 1985. Pub. health nurse City of Jersey City, 1958-59; social worker Park City Hosp., Bridgeport, Conn., 1972-74; psychotherapist Dept. Children Youth Svcs., Bridgeport, 1979-81, City of Balt., 1958-59, Yale Behavioral Med. Clinic, New Haven, 1986-90, Fairfield Behavioral Medicine, 1989-90, Conn. Ctr. Behavioral Medicine Bio-feedback, Norwalk; ret., 1991. Part time pub. health nurse Fairfield, Conn., 1966-76. Bd. dirs. Enfield (N.H.) Shaker Mus. Recipient Best Bedside Nursing award Jersey Med. City, 1958. Mem. Soc. Behavioral Medicine. Home: 6 Simple Gifts Ln Enfield NH 03748-3557

GAMACHE, RICHARD DONALD, retired business development executive; b. Fall River, Mass., Aug. 30, 1935; s. Armand Wilfred and Imelda (Gagnon) G.; m. Kathleen Florence Smith, Nov. 22, 1958; children: Mariette (dec.), Nanette Campbell, Lisette Becker (dec.). BS, St. Peter's Coll., 1958. Account exec. Harold Shore Assocs., N.Y.C., 1965-67; v.p. Van Dyck Corp., Southport, Conn., 1967-69; pres. Shippan Corp., Stamford, Conn., 1969, INNOTECH. Corp., Trumbull, Conn., 1969-86, chmn., 1985-94; ret., 1994. Contbg. author Handbook for Creative and Innovative Managers, 1988, New Directions in Creative and Innovative Management, 1988; author: The Creativity Infusion, 1989; contbr. numerous articles to profl. jours. Formerly active Sea Island Habitat for Humanity, United Way Upper Valley, Lebanon, N.H.; active N.H. Main St. Program; pres., bd. dirs. Lower Shaker Village Bds. Avocations: music, baking, gardening. Home: 6 Simple Gifts Ln Enfield NH 03748-3557 E-mail: peperegama@aol.com.*

GAMBARDELLA, ROBERT EDWARD, retired medical social services consultant; b. New Haven, Oct. 12, 1943; s. A. Thomas and Jane (Scalese) G.; m. Lucille Cerchiaro, Apr. 18, 1970; children: Gina Marie, Andrea Christine. BA in English and Spanish, U. New Haven, 1970; MA in Counseling Psychology, Fairfield U., 1974. Cert. counselor. Health svcs. adminstr. East Haven (Conn.) Human Svcs., 1974-76; county adminstr. CMSU Mental Health/Mental Retardation Program, Danville, Pa., 1976-79; pvt. psychotherapist Benton (Pa.) Area Health Ctr., 1979-82; prison health adminstr. Basil Health Systems, Columbia, Md., 1982-84; social svcs. cons. Pub. Health Divsn., State of Del., Milford, 1984—. Mem. So. Conn. Regional Planning Bd., New Haven, 1974-76. Planning mem. Nat. Health Adv. Coun., Washington, 1993. With USAR, 1968-74. Recipient Svc. to Cmty. award East Haven Human Svcs., 1976, Svc. Appreciation award Divsn. Pub. Health, 1991. Mem. APHA, Del. Pub. Health Assn. (bd. dirs.), KC. Roman Catholic. Avocations: fishing, collecting. Home: 7 Augusta Ct Dover DE 19904-7102 E-mail: gambarlu@aol.com.

GAMBARI, IBRAHIM AGBOOLA, diplomat; b. Ilorin, Kwara State, Nigeria, Nov. 24, 1944; m. Fatima Oniyangi, 1969; 2 children. Grad., Kings Coll., Lagos, Nigeria. Lectr. Queen's Coll., NY, 1969-74; asst. prof. SUNY, Albany, 1974-77; sr. lectr. Ahmadu Bello U., Zaria, Nigeria, 1977-80, assoc. prof., 1980-83, prof., 1983-89; dir.-gen. Nigerian Inst. Internat. Affairs, 1983-84; min. for fgn. affairs Govt. of Nigeria, 1984-85; resident scholar Rockefeller Found. Bellagio (Italy) Study and Conf. Ctr., Bellagio, 1989; permanent rep. of Nigeria UN, N.Y.C., 1990—99, under-sec. gen., special advisor on Africa, 1999—. Vis. prof. Johns Hopkins U. Sch. Advanced Internat. Studies, Howard U., Washington, Georgetown U., Washington, Brookings Inst., 1986—89; hon. prof. Chugsan U., Guangzhou, China, 1985; guest scholar Wilson Ctr. Internat. Scholars Smithsonian Inst., Washington; chair Nat. Seminar Commemorate 25th Anniversary OAS, Lagos, Nigeria, 1988; trustee UN Inst. Tng. and Rsch., 1993—99; pres. exec. bd. UNICEF, 1999. Author: (book) Party Politics and Foreign Policy in Nigeria During the First Republic, 1981, Theory and Reality in Foreign Policy Making: Nigeria After the Second Republic, 1989, Political and Comparative Dimensions of Regional Integration: The Case of ECOWAS, 1991. Office: UN Dept Polit Affairs Room S-3755A New York NY 10017

GAMBARO, ERNEST UMBERTO, lawyer, consultant, engineer; b. Niagara Falls, N.Y., July 6, 1938; s. Ralph and Teresa (Nigro) G.; m. Winifred Sonya Porter, June 3, 1961 (div.); m. Monica Cuellar, Sept. 30, 1994. BA in Aeronautical Engring., Purdue U., 1960, MS with honors, 1961; JD with honors, Loyola U., L.A., 1975. Bar: Calif. 1975, U.S. Tax Ct. 1976, U.S. Supreme Ct. 1979, U.S. Ct. Appeals (9th cir.). With Aerospace Corp., El Segundo, Calif., 1962-80, counsel, 1975-80; asst. gen. counsel, asst. sec. Computer Scis. Corp., El Segundo, 1980-88; sr. v.p., gen. counsel, sec. INFONET Svcs. Corp., El Segundo, 1988-2000. Cons. bus. fin. and mgmt., 1968— ; bd. dirs. STM Wireless, Govt. Systems, Inc., Networks Telephony Corp. Newspaper columnist Europe Alfresco; contbr. articles to profl. publs. Fulbright scholar Rome U., 1961-62; recipient USAF commendation for contributions to U.S. manned space program, 1969. Mem. ABA (internat., taxation sects.), L.A. Bar Assn. (exec. com. 1976—, founder chmn. sect. law and technology 1976-78, chmn. bar reorgn. com. 1981-82), Am. Arbitration Assn. L.A. Ctr. Internat. Comml. Arbitrations (found., bd. dirs.), Internat. Law Inst. (faculty), St. Thomas More Law Soc., Phi Alpha Delta, Omicron Delta Kappa (past pres.), Tau Beta Pi, Sigma Gamma Tau (past pres.), Phi Eta Sigma. Republican. Home: PO Box 1944 Zephyr Cove NV 89448 Office: 2160 E Grand Ave El Segundo CA 90245-5024 E-mail: ernie@gambaro.com.

GAMBEE, ROBERT RANKIN, investment banker; b. N.Y.C., Aug. 26, 1942; s. Sumner and Eleanor Elizabeth (Brown) G.; m. Elizabeth Gregory Heard, 1991; children: Robert Gregory, Claire Elizabeth Fay. Grad., Phillips Exeter Acad.; AB, Princeton U., 1964; MBA, Harvard U., 1966. Assoc. corp. fin. White, Weld & Co., N.Y.C., 1966-71, v.p., 1971-73, Schroder Capital Corp. affiliate J Henry Schoder Wagg-London, N.Y.C., 1973-78, Atlantic Capital Corp. affiliate Deutsche Bank AG, Frankfurt, Germany, 1978-84; 1st v.p. Deutsche Bank Securities Inc., 1985-91, dir., 1992—. Prin. N.Y. Stock Exch., 1971—, Nat. Assn. Securities Dealers, 1971—; v.p. Apollo, Atlas, Hercules, Hermes, Mercury, Olympus, Orion, Pegasus, Taurus, Titan and Zeus Instl. Investments, Inc., 1984-92; COO, sec. Germany Fund, Inc., 1986—, The New Germany Fund, Inc., 1990—, The Future Germany Fund, Inc., 1990-95, The Ctrl. European Equity Fund, Inc., 1995—; v.p., sec. Deutsche Funds Inc., 1997-2000, Deutsche Bank Investment Mgmt. Inc., 1995—; dir. Deutsche Bank AG and Bankers Trust Co., 1999—, Deutsche Bank Securities, Inc., 2002—. Author, photographer: Nantucket Island, 1973, rev. edit., 1974, 81, paper edit., 1978, 87, 89, color edits., 1986, 88, 98, Manhattan Seascape: Waterside Views Around New York, 1975, Exeter Impressions (intro. by Nathaniel Benchley), 1980, Princeton in Color (intro by Robert F. Goheen), 1987, paperback edit., 1988, 2d rev. edit., 1993, 98, A Wall Street Christmas, 1989, rev. edit., 1990, Nantucket in Color, 1992, 94, 96, paperback edit., 1996, Wall Street-Financial Capital, 1999, Nantucket Impressions, 2001. Trustee Dwight-Englewood Sch., 1978-85, Elizabeth Morrow Sch., 1990—, Rye (N.Y.) Art Ctr., 1993—, Rye Presbyn. Ch., 1998-2001. Mem. Soc. Colonial Wars, Princeton Alumni Assn. Nantucket (v.p., sec.), Princeton Club N.Y. (gov.), Nantucket Yacht Club, Univ. Club. Republican. Presbyterian. Home: Wendover Rd Rye NY 10580 Office: Deutsche Bank Securities Inc 345 Park Ave 15th Fl New York NY 10154

GAMBERT, STEVEN ROSS, geriatrician, internist; b. N.Y.C., Aug. 22, 1949; s. Lawrence and Mildred (Engel) G.; m. Gry Magdalene Biong, Oct. 15, 1972; children: Christopher, Iselin. AB, NYU, 1971; MD, Columbia U., 1975. Diplomate Am. Bd. Internal Medicine. Assoc. prof. Med. Coll. Wis., Milw., 1979-83; assoc. dean, prof. medicine N.Y. Med. Coll., Valhalla, 1983-97; prof. medicine, vice-chmn. acad. affairs UMDNJ-NJUS, Newark, N.J., 1997-98; chair dept. medicine Sinai Hosp., Balt., 1998—; prof. medicine Johns Hopkins U., Balt., 1998—. Pres. Byram Hills Sch. Bd., North Castle, N.Y., 1994-95. Fellow ACP, Am. Geriatrics Soc., Gerontol. Soc. Am., Med. Rsch. Assn. (pres. 1993-96), Med. Bus. Assn. (pres. 1993-96). Avocations: watercolor painting, photography. Home: 220 Wendover Rd Baltimore MD 21218-1837 Office: Sinai Hospital Baltimore Dept Medicine 2401 W Belvedere Ave Baltimore MD 21215-5270 E-mail: sgambert@sinai_balt.com.

GAMBESCIA, STEPHEN FRANCIS, higher education administrator; b. Phila., Dec. 7, 1957; s. Joseph M. and Mary E. (Botto) G.; m. Susan Rice, May 8, 1982; children: Stephanie, Stephen J. BS in Sociology, St. Joseph's U., 1980; diploma in journalism and pub. rels. cum laude, Charles Morris Price Sch. Adv. and Journalism, 1984; MEd in Curriculum and Instrn., Pa. State U., 1985; PhD in Polit. Sci., Temple U., 1996; MBA, Regis U., 2003. Cert. health edn. specialist. Bookroom mgr., coach Sch. of Holy Child Jesus, Rosemont, Pa., 1980-81; health educator community health dept. St. Agnes Med. Ctr., Phila., 1981-83; coord. workplace cancer control Am. Cancer Soc., Phila., 1984-86, asst. dir. pub. edn., 1986-89, dir. corp. rels., 1990, v.p. corp. rels., 1990-92; v.p. ednl. programs and rsch. Am. Heart Assn., Phila., 1992-98; asst. to the pres. Neumann Coll., Aston, Pa., 1999, exec. dir. continuing edn., 1999-2000, chair divsn. liberal studies and continuing edn., 2000; asst. to v.p. for acad. affairs, 2000—02; asst. dean, assoc. prof. Drexel U., Phila., 2002—. Bd. govs. St. Joseph's U.; presenter in field. Assoc. editor Health Promotion Practice Jour.; contbr. articles to profl. jours. Carrie May Price Trust scholar Charles Morris Price Sch. Advt. and Journalism, 1984, NCAA Athletic scholar St. Joseph's U., 1980, Carr Alumni scholar St. Joseph's U., 1980; recipient Gov.'s Letter of Commendation, 1996. Fellow Soc. for Pub. Health Edn. (pres. Pa. chpt. 1988-89, 92-93, chmn. comms. com., nat. del. 1997-99, nat. treas. 1998-2000, chair resource devel. com., co-v.p. 2001-02); mem. APHA, Pa. Pub. Health Assn. (planning com. ann. meetings 1991, 92, 93, 98, 2001), Coalition for Tobacco Free Pa. (pres. 1993-95, chmn. bus. awards com.), Delaware Valley Healthcare Coun., Pa. State Alumni Assn. (life mem.), Phila. Coll. Physicians, St. Joseph's U. Alumni Track Club, Order Sons of Italy in Am., Men of Malvrern Retreat League (capt.). Office: Drexel U 3001 Market ST Philadelphia PA 19104- Office Fax: 215-895-2153. E-mail: Stephen.F.Gambescia@drexel.edu.

GAMBILL, JAN-MICHAEL, professional tennis player; b. Spokane, Wash., June 3, 1977; Professional tennis player, 1996—; team player Davis Cup, 1997. Office: c/o USTA 70 W Red Oak Ln White Plains NY 10604-3602

GAMBINO, RICHARD JOSEPH, materials science engineering; b. N.Y.C., May 17, 1935; BA, U. Conn., 1957; MS, Polytech Inst. N.Y., 1976. Phys. sci. U.S. Army Signal Rsch. Lab., Ft. Monmouth, NJ, 1958—60; metallurgist Pratt & Whitney Aircraft divsn. United Aircraft Corp., 1960—61; rsch. staff mem. T.J. Watson Rsch. Ctr., IBM, Yorktown Heights, NY, 1961—93; prin. rsch. sci., prof., lab. dir. SUNY, Stony Brook, 1993—. Pres. MesoScribe Technologies, Inc., 2002—. Recipient Nat. Medal of Tech., 1995. Fellow: IEEE; mem.: IEEE Magnetic Soc., Materials Rsch. Soc., Am. Vacuum Soc. (thin film divsn. bd.), Tau Beta Pi, Sigma Xi. Home: 148 Sycamore Cir Stony Brook NY 11790-3161 Office: Dept Material Scis & Engng State U NY 115 Engineering Bldg Stony Brook NY 11794-2275 E-mail: rgambino@ms.cc.sunysb.edu.

GAMBINO, S(ALVATORE) RAYMOND, medical laboratory executive, educator; b. N.Y.C., Oct. 13, 1926; s. Salvatore Benedict and Rose (Ragona) G.; m. Madeline Russo, Apr. 5, 1953; children: Catherine Rose Garroni, Stephen Raymond. BS, Antioch Coll., 1948; MD, U. Rochester, 1952. Diplomate Am. Bd. Pathology. Labs. dir. Englewood (N.J.) Hosp., 1961-68; prof. pathology Columbia U., N.Y.C., 1968-82; dir. chemistry labs. Presbyn. Hosp., N.Y.C., 1968-77; labs. dir. St. Luke's-Roosevelt Hosp., 1978-82; chief med. officer, exec. v.p. MetPath, Inc., Teterboro, N.J., 1983-94, exec. v.p., chief med. officer emeritus, 1994—. Adj. prof. pathology Columbia U., N.Y.C., 1983—; mem. Corning (N.Y.) Mgmt. Group, 1984-94; bd. dirs. Ciba-Corning, 1988-94. Co-author: Beyond Normality, 1975; editor: (newsletter) Lab Report for Physicians, 1979-98. Mem. Englewood Cliffs (N.J.) Sch. Bd., 1966-69. Served with USN, 1945-46. Mem. Am. Soc. Clin. Pathologists (editor check sample program 1968-93), Alpha Omega Alpha. Roman Catholic. Avocations: walking, writing, travel. Office: Quest Diagnostics Inc One Malcolm Ave Teterboro NJ 07608

GAMBITTA, RICHARD ANTHONY, political science educator; b. Oneida, N.Y., Aug. 28, 1946; s. Anthony Gamuel and Alice (Jones) G.; Sherry, Oct. 10, 1998; 1 child, Leon Antonio; stepson: Travis Michael Culpepper. BA, Syracuse U., 1970; MA, 1974, PhD, 1976. Assoc. prof. U. Tex., San Antonio, 1982—, discipline coord., grad. advisor of record, 1993-97, chair dept. polit. sci. and geography, 2001—, dir. Inst. Law and Pub. Affairs, 2001—. Pres. Gambitta Rsch. Assocs., San Antonio, 1986—; Fulbright sr. lectr. Chinese U. Hong Kong, 1984-85; cons. KPMG/Tex. Online, Austin, 2001—; cons., report author Tex. Dept. Transp., San Antonio, 1986-88; cons., pollster numerous polit. candidates and media, Tex., 1986—. Contbr., editor articles to profl. jours. Rsch. fellow NEH, Madison, Wis., 1979-80; Fulbright scholar, Hong Kong, 1983-85; Piper professorship Minni Stevens Piper Found., Tex., 1990. Mem. Am. Polit. Sci. Assn., ACLU, Internat. Assn. Philosophy of Law and Social Philosophy, San Antonio Dem. League. Democrat. Avocation: running. Home: 7605 Hummingbird Hill San Antonio TX 78255 Office: U Tex 6900 N Loop 1604 N San Antonio TX 78245 Fax: (210) 458-5430. E-mail: rgambitta@utsa.edu.

GAMBLE, DESIRATA, artist, poet; b. Wilkesboro, N.C. d. Robert Lee and Mary Etta Gamble; m. David Bullins, Feb. 14; 1 child, Zoe Bullins. AA with honors, Surry C.C., Dobson, N.C., 1983; BA in Psychology, U. N.C., Wilmington, 1985, BA in Studio Arts, 2001; postgrad., U. Ga., 1985—87, PhD candidate social psychology. Proofreader Joan S. Northrop, Wilmington, 1984—85; artist U. N.C., Wilmington, NC, 1996—2002; artist transp. Merle Fest, Wilkesboro, NC, 1994—2001; asst. to Merle Fest coord. David C. Bullins, 2002—03. One-woman shows include The Morning Dew, Winston-Salem, N.C., 1997—98, Claude Howell Gallery, Wilmington, 1998, The Deluxe, Wilmington, N.C., 1998—99, The Beanstalk, Boone, N.C., 1999, 2000, 2001, Daughtry's Old Books, Wilmington, NC, 2003, William Vance Nichols/Wilkes Art Gallery, 2003, Represented in permanent collections Daniel Hall, Wilkes C.C., Wilkesboro, N.C.; artist, poet: Sights of the Wind, Her White Hair Peeps and We Heard the Music for Miles, 1985 (Book award for poetry U. N.C. Wilmington); contbr. poetry to small press publs.; one-woman shows include Daughrty's Old Books, Wilmington, N.C., 2003. Mem.: Acad. Am. Poets, Southeastern Ctr. for Contemporary Art, AAUW, Ala. State Poetry Soc. Personal E-mail: gambled1@excite.com.

GAMBLE, DONALD GEOFFREY BIDMEAD, lawyer; b. Apr. 11, 1945; s. Donald Edward Gamble and Gamble Elizabeth (Binheimer); m. Dorcas Hall, Feb. 14, 1976; children: Thomas, Elizabeth, Mary, Ann, Katherine, Victoria, Margaret. BA, Haverford Coll., 1967; JD, Cath. U., Washington, 1975. Bar: D.C. 1975, Del. 1976, U.S. Tax Ct. 1975. Law clk. Hon. D.S. Smith, Washington, 1973—75; assoc. Killoran & Van Brunt, Wilmington, Del., 1975—76; atty. Du Pont Co., Wilmington, 1976—78, sr. internat. Counsel, 1984—85, mng. counsel legal dept., 1985—94, assoc. gen counsel, 1994—2000, chief internat. counsel, 2000—. Regional legal counsel Du Pont Asia Pacific, Hong Kong, 1978—82; dir. Du Pont Taiwan Ltd., Taipei, 1980—84, Du Pont Taiwan Chems. Ltd., Taipei, 1980—84, Nat. Fgn. Trade Counsel, 1990—; chmn. U.S. Industry Sector adv. com. for chems. and allied products, 1996—. Pres. Kennett Consol. Sch. Bd., 1997—2000, Cath. Ministry to the Elderly, Inc., 1985—2001; bd. dir. New Castle Civic Assn., Del., 1984. Capt. USMC, 1967—70, Vietnam. Recipient 14 Combat Decorations. Mem.: Internat. Bar Assn., Del. State Bar Assn., Army-Navy Club (Washington), Sovereign Mil. Order of Malta (knight). Republican. Roman Catholic. Home: 560 Chandlers Mill Rd Avondale PA 19311-9676 Office: Du Pont Co Legal Dept D # 7052 Wilmington DE 19898-0001

GAMBLE, DOUGLAS IRVIN, state official, educator; b. Wheeling, W.Va., Dec. 27, 1953; s. Wiley Irvin and Myrtle Stewart (Yeater) G.; m. Lois Winifred Betz, June 26, 1976; children: Rebekah Winifred, Mary Amelia, Martha Suzanne, Rachel Emma, Michael Irvin, Katrina Ruth. Student, Archtl. Assn. Sch. Architecture, London, 1975; B in Environ. Design, Miami U., Oxford, Ohio, 1976; MArch, U. Ill., 1979. Lic. asbestos worker, insp., mgmt. planner and supr. Draftsman G.T. Hardwick & Assocs., Champaign, Ill., 1976-77, Glenn G. Frazier & Assocs., Urbana, Ill., 1977-78; rsch. asst. Small Homes Coun.-Bldg. Rsch. Coun., Urbana, 1977-79; archtl. designer Carl Fischer & Assocs., Springfield, Ill., 1979-80; archtl. programmer Sarti-Huff Archtl. Group, Springfield, 1980-82, Huff Archtl. Group, Springfield, 1982-86; project mgr., accessiblity specialist Capital Devel. Bd. State of Ill., Springfield, 1986—. Instr. Parkland Coll., Champaign, 1978-79, U. Ill. Midwest Tng. Ctr., Chgo., 1987—, Lincoln Land Coll, Springfield, 1991-; pres. Family Tree Antiques, Springfield and Galena, Ill. Testifier elem. and secondary edn. com. on asbestos Ill. Senate, 1984; v.p. Faith Luth. Ch., Springfield, 1988-89; mem. subcom. on accessibility Ill. Bldg. Commn.; mem. Nat. Trust for Hist. Preservation, Nat. Fire Protection Assn. Miami U. rsch. grantee, 1975. Mem. AIA (assoc.), Constrn. Specifications Inst. (pres. Ctrl. Ill. chpt. 1990-92, membership chair North Ctrl. region 1992-93, dir. North Ctrl. region 1996-97, 2002-, mem. nat. spkrs. bur. 1988-96, Pres. cert. of appreciation Ctrl. Ill. chpt. 1988, North Ctrl. region mem. commendation award 1989, Inst. Commendation award 1990, North Ctrl. Region Dirs. Cert. award 1991), Nat. Asbestos Coun. (spkr. nat. conv. 1992), On My Own Time Art Competition, Geneal. Inst. Mid-Am., Nat. Geneal. Soc., Ill. State Geneal. Soc., Springfield Civil War Roundtable, Hon. Order Ky. Cols. Avocations: genealogy, music, antiques, photography. Home: 1425 S Whittier Ave Springfield IL 62704-3744 Office: Ill Capital Devel Bd Wm G Stratton Bldg 3d Fl 401 S Spring St Springfield IL 62706-4001 E-mail: dgamble@cdb.state.il.us.

GAMBLE, E. JAMES, lawyer, accountant; b. Duluth, Minn., June 1, 1929; s. Edward James and Modesta Caroline (Reichert) G.; m. Lois Kennedy, Apr. 3, 1954; children: John M., Martha M., Paul F. AB, U. Mich., 1950, JD, 1953. Bar: Mich. 1953, D.C. 1980; CPA, Mich. Tax acct. Ernst & Ernst, Detroit, 1957-59; assoc. Dykema, Gossett, Spencer, Goodnow & Trigg, Detroit, 1959-67; ptnr. Dykema Gossett, Detroit, 1967-94, Gamble, Rosenberger & Joswick LLP, Bloomfield Hills, 1994—. Adj. prof. law Wayne State U., Detroit, 1964-79; adj. lectr. law U. Mich., Ann Arbor, 1979-81, 93; co-reporter, prin. draftsman Uniform Principal and Income Act (1997); mem. adv. com. Restatement of the Law, 3rd, Property, Wills and Other Donative Transfers, Restatement of the Law, 3rd, Trusts; counsel Mich. State Bd. Accountancy, Lansing, 1973-77. Author: (handbook) The Revised Uniform Principal and Income Act, 1966; contbr. articles to profl. jours. Trustee Rehab. Inst., Inc., Detroit, 1961-84, chmn. bd. trustees, 1974-77; bd. dirs., sec. Jr. Achievement Southeastern Mich., 1973-86; trustee Walsh Coll. Accountancy and Bus. Adminstrn., Troy, Mich., 1975-87, Alma (Mich.) Coll., 1981-91; mem. Fin. and Estate Planning Coun. Detroit, bd. dirs., 1969-76, pres., 1975. Lt. USN, 1953-57. Recipient Bronze Leadership award Jr. Achievement, Inc., 1985 Fellow Am. Coll. Tax Counsel, Am. Coll. Trust and Estate Counsel (bd. regents 1988—, chmn. estate and gift tax com. 1989-92, pres. 1998-99), Academician, Internat. Acad. Estate and Trust Law (exec. coun. 2001—), Am. Bar Found. (life), Mich. State Bar Found.; mem. ABA (mem. spl. com. on profl. rels. with AICPA 1968-70), Mich. Bar Assn. (mem. various coms.), Detroit Bar Assn. (chmn. taxation com. 1968-74), Detroit Bar Assn. Found. (trustee, treas. 1973-79), Birmingham Athletic Club, Leland Country Club. Presbyterian.

GAMBLE, GEOFFREY, academic administrator; Degree in English, Fresno State Coll., 1965, M Linguistics, 1971; PhD Linguistics, U. Calif., Berkeley, 1975. Cert. specialist in Native Am. linguistics. Vice provost Washington State U.; provost, sr. v.p. U. Vt.; pres. Mont. State U.-Bozeman, 2000—. Office: Mont State U-Bozeman 211 Montana Hall Bozeman MT 59717-2420 Office Fax: 406-994-1893.

GAMBLE, JOSEPH GRAHAM, JR., lawyer; b. Des Moines, June 12, 1926; s. Joseph Graham and Ella Theolian (Hildreth) G.; m. Jane Elizabeth Wilkinson, Sept. 20, 1974. AB, U. Fla., 1948; LLB, U. Ala., 1950. Bar: Ala. 1950, U.S. Dist. Ct. (no. dist.) Ala. 1951, U.S. Ct. Appeals (5th cir.) 1955-81, U.S. Ct. Appeals (11th cir.) 1981, U.S. Supreme Ct. 1960. Assoc. Spain, Gillon & Young, Birmingham, Ala., 1950-60; with Liberty Nat. Life Ins. Co., Birmingham, Ala., 1960-83, asst. gen. counsel, 1973-83; sec. Torchmark Corp., Birmingham, Ala., 1980-86, asst. gen. counsel, sec., 1983-86; sole practice Birmingham, Ala., 1987—; ret., 1998. Bd. dirs. Travelers Aid Soc., Birmingham, 1976-95, Birmingham Hospitality Network, 1997—. Fellow Life Office Mgmt. Assn.; mem. ABA, Ala. Bar Assn., Birmingham Bar Assn., Phi Alpha Delta. Republican. Episcopalian. Home: 3333 Spring Valley Ct Birmingham AL 35223-2006 Office: 6 Office Park Cir Ste 318 Birmingham AL 35223-2542

GAMBLE, KATHRYN, nurse; b. Orlando, Fla., Apr. 11, 1959; d. Thomas Edward and Gertrude (Whitty) Gamble; m. Keith Devaughn Conner, May 1, 1982 (div. Aug. 1999); children: Andrew Devaughn, Kevin Devaughn. AA, Seminole C.C., 1978; BSN, U. Fla., 1980; M in Nursing, Emory U., 1988. RN, Ga.; ARNP, Fla. Pediatric nurse Henrietta Egleston Hosp. for Children, Atlanta, 1985-86; specialist in hematology/oncology U. Fla., Gainesville, 1988-91; pediatric nurse Shands Tchg. Hosp., Gainesville, Fla., 1981-85, 87-88, clin. nurse specialist pediatric oncology, 1991-93, nursing supr./educator, 1993-95, coordinated care mgr., 1995—2002, nurse mgr., 2007—. Mem. Assn. Pediatric Oncology Nurses, Oncology Nursing Soc., Internat. Transplant Nurse's Soc., Health Care Edn. Assn., Sigma Theta Tau. Democrat. Methodist. Office: Shands Teaching Hosp Dept Nursing Box 100335 1600 SW Archer Rd Dept Nursing Gainesville FL 32610-3001 E-mail: gamblk@shands.ufl.edu.

GAMBLE, LYNN HUNTER, anthropologist, educator; b. Charlotte, N.C., Jan. 31, 1949; d. Millard Gobert and Gloria Gamble; m. Chester D. King (div.); 1 child, Naomi Gamble King; m. Glenn Spencer Russell, Aug. 10, 2002. BA, U. Calif., Berkeley, 1979; PhD, U. Calif., Santa Barbara, 1991. Lectr. dept. anthropology UCLA, 1992—95, dir. Archaeological Info. Ctr., 1992—94, dir. rsch. Am. Indian Studies Ctr., 1994—96; asst. prof. dept. anthropology San Diego State U., 1997—2002, assoc. prof. dept. anthropology, 2002—. Rsch. assoc. Cotsen Inst. Archaeology, UCLA, 1992—2003, L.A. County Mus. Natural History, 1995—2003, San Diego Mus. Man, 2003. Contbr. articles to profl. jours. Grantee, Nat. Pk. Svc., Washington, 2002—03. Mem.: Soc. for Calif. Archaeology, Phi Beta Kappa. Avocation: hiking. Office: San Diego State Univ Dept Anthropology 5500 Campanile Dr San Diego CA 92182

GAMBLE, MARY G(RACE), marketing and organizational development professional; b. Evanston, Ill., Feb. 23, 1950; d. John D. and Bertha E. (Flynn) G.; m. John P. Kondrotas. BA with honors, U. Fla., 1971, MBA, 1993. Mgr. maj. market Gillette Co., Chgo., 1977-83; asst. regional sales mgr. Atlanta, 1983-85; v.p. sales and mktg. Hemochek Corp., Gainesville, Fla., 1985-89; div. mgr. Environ. Sci. & Engring., Gainesville, Fla., 1989-93; v.p., chief quality officer Hellmuth, Obata & Kassabaum, St. Louis, 1993-99, pres. Competitive Performance Sys., 1999—. Judge Fla. Quality Sterling Award. Bd. mem. Gov.'s Sterling Coun., 1989—; bd. examiners Malcolm Baldridge Nat. Quality Award. Mem. Assn. Jr. Leagues, Tampa Club, Rotary. Republican.

GAMBLE, PATRICK K. retired military officer, rail transportation executive; BA in Math., Tex. A&M U., 1967; MBA, Auburn U., 1978; Grad., Air Command and Staff Coll., Maxwell AFB, 1978; Disting. Grad., Air War Coll., Maxwell AFB, 1984. Commd. 2d lt. USAF, 1967, advanced through ranks to gen., 1998; various assignments to dep. chief of staff air/space opers. Hdqtrs. USAF/The Pentagon, Washington, 1997-98; comdr. Pacific Air Forces, Hickam AFB, 1998—2001; pres., CEO Alaska R.R. Corp., Anchorage, 2001—. Contbr. articles to profl. jours. Decorated Def. Disting. Svc. medal with one oak leaf cluster, Disting. Svc. medal with one oak leak cluster, Legion of Merit, Disting. Flying Cross, Meritorious Svc. medal with two oak leaf clusters, Air Medal with 13 oak leaf clusters, Air Force Commendation medal, Presdl. Unit citation with oak leaf cluster, Vietnam Svc. medal with three svc. stars, Republic of Vietnam Gallantry Cross with svc. star, Republic of Vietnam Gallantry Cross with Palm, NATO medal, others. Office: PO Box 107500 Anchorage AK 99510

GAMBLE, RAYMOND WESLEY, marriage and family therapist, clergyman; b. East Orange, N.J., Feb. 11, 1933; s. Kenneth Nelson and Lillian Clare (Apgar) G.; m. Margaret Gamble, Sept. 11, 1954 (div. 1964); children: Karen F., Roy B.; m. Penelope Louise Hansen, Nov. 19, 1979; 1 child, Wesley B. BA, Houghton (N.Y.) Coll., 1956; MDiv, Union Theol. Sem., Richmond, Va., 1960; postgrad., Yale U., 1967; D Ministry, Columbia Theol. Sem., Decatur, Ga., 1990. Ordained to ministry Presbyn. Ch., 1960. Student chaplain Va. State Penitentiary, 1958-60; asst. pastor Immanuel Presbyn. Ch., Lake Park, Fla., 1960-62; founder, pastor Westminster Presbyn. Ch., Palm Beach Gardens, Fla., 1962-67; exec. dir. Mental Health Assn. Palm Beach County, West Palm Beach, 1967-73; pvt. practice marriage and family therapy, West Palm Beach, Stuart, Fla., 1973—; founder, sr. pastor Palm City (Fla.) Presbyn. Ch., 1984—2003. Guest instr. Indian River Community Coll., 1978; cons., chaplain Lake Hosp., Lake Worth, Fla., 1973-75; chaplain Savannas Hosp., Port St. Lucie, Fla., 1986—; program dir., aftercare counselor narcotic addict rehab. program NIMH, West Palm Beach, 1969-73. Active numerous drug abuse rehab. programs, Palm Beach County; past mem. Com. for Mental Health Edn.; active Presbytery Tropical Fla., 1960—; past mem. ch.-coll. coun. Montreat Coll., 1988-96; past bd. dirs. Alcohol and Drug Abuse Coun. Palm Beach County, North County Drug Abuse Bd., Boca Raton (Fla.) Drug Abuse Found.; past pres. Drug Abuse Rehab. Team, Inc. Mem. Am. Assn. for Marriage and Family Therapy (clin.), Am. Assn. Christian Counselors. Avocations: sport fishing, horticulture. Home and Office: 288 NE Alice St # 101S Jensen Beach FL 34957-6006

GAMBLE, SCOTT L. civil engineer; BSc in Mech. Engring., U. Waterloo, 1981. Registered profl. engr., Ont. Project engr. Rowan Williams Davies & Irwin Inc., Guelph, Ont., Can., 1981-87, assoc., 1987-89, mgr. R&D, 1989-96, prin., 1996—, v.p. tech. devel., 1999—. Contbr. articles to profl. jours. Recipient Sir Casimir Gzowski Gold medal Can. Soc. Civil Engring., 1996. E-mail: slg@rwdi.com.*

GAMBLE, THEODORE ROBERT, JR., investment banker; b. St. Louis, Sept. 18, 1953; s. Theodore Robert and Rispah Adele (Dowse) Gamble; m. Susan Lee Stupin, Mar. 3, 1984. AB, Princeton U., 1975; MArch, Harvard U., 1977, MBA, 1979. Assoc. Morgan Stanley & Co., Inc., N.Y.C., 1979-84, v.p., 1984-86, prin., 1986-87; pres. Prescott Group Inc., N.Y.C., 1987—, mng. dir., 1999—. Transwestern Conml. Svcs., LLC, N.Y.C., 1999—2002. Mem. bus. com., mem. vis. com. Met. Mus. Art; bd. dirs., exec. v.p. Greater N.Y. coun. Boy Scouts Am.; bd. dirs. N.Y. Hist. Soc., Coll. Arms Found.; mem. vis. com. Mary Inst. St. Louis Country Day Sch.; mem. vestry St. Thomas Ch., N.Y.C.; co-chmn. adv. com. real estate devel., chmn. vis. com. Grad. Sch. Design Harvard U.; vice chancellor, bd. govs. Am. Soc. Order St. John of Jerusalem. Mem.: Young Mortgage Bankers Assn., Real Estate Bd. N.Y., Internat. Assn. Corp. Real Estate Execs., Assn. Fgn. Investors Real Estate, Nat. Assn. Real Estate Investment Trusts, Urban Land Inst. (mem. comml. and retail devel. coun., mem. internat. com.), Internat. Coun. Shopping Ctrs., Coral Beach and Tennis Club (Bermuda), City Club (Miami), Harvard Club (N.Y.C., Boston), Princeton Club (bd. govs., mem. exec. com., v.p. fin.), Doubles Club, Brook Club, Links Club, Knickerbocker Club, Univ Club, Racquet and Tennis Club, River Club. Republican. Episcopalian. Home: 860 UN Plaza New York NY 10017 Office: The Prescott Group Inc 445 Park Ave 9th Fl New York NY 10022 Office Fax: 917-322-2422. Personal E-mail: trgamblejr@msn.com. Business E-Mail: trgamblejr@prescott-group.com.

GAMBLE, THOMAS ELLSWORTH, academic administrator; b. Chgo., Nov. 14, 1941; s. Slade LeBlount and Anna Marie VanDuzer G.; m. Donna Kay Dersch, Nov. 3, 1973; children: Brendan, Shari, Oscar, Rebecca, Slade, Aubrey, David, Donna. BA in Biology, Northwestern U., 1964; MEd in Ednl. Psychology, U. Ill., 1970, PhD in Higher Ednl. Adminstrn., 1973. Asst. to dean student pers. U. Ill., Urbana-Champaign, 1968-71, asst. prof. edn., 1972, asst. dean Coll. Medicine, 1972—76, assoc. prof. Coll. Medicine Chgo., 1976—83; exec. asst. to chancellor U. Ill. Med. Ctr., Chgo., 1976-78, asst. chancellor, 1976—83; dean intercampus affairs Ill. Ea. C.C., Olney, 1983-84; dean of instrn. Wabash Valley Coll., Mt. Carmel, Ill., 1984—89, dean of coll., 1989-90; pres. Dodge City (Kans.) C.C., 1990-95, Joliet (Ill.) Jr. Coll., 1995-98; dist. pres. Brevard C.C., Cocoa, Fla., 1999—. Asst. prof. U. Ill. Coll. Edn., 1972-77; assoc. prof. U. Ill. Coll. Medicine, 1982-83; pres. Kans. Jayhawk C.C. Athletic Conf., 1993-94, Ill. N4C C.C. Athletic Conf., 1996-97. Contbr. articles to profl. jours. Bd. dirs. Kans. Newman Coll., Wichita, 1994-96, U.S. Naval Inst., 1968—, Jr. Achievement East Ctrl. Fla., Econ. Devel. Com. Fla. Space Coast, Brevard County Workforce Devel. Bd., Brevard C.C. Found.; chmn. Fla. Coun. Pres.; mem. Am. Coun. on Edn., Commn. on Adult Learning and Ednl. Credentials, 2002—; mem. policy adv. bd. Fla. Solar Energy Ctr.; mem. First Bapt. Ch. Merritt Is., Fla. Capt. USNR, 1964-87, ret. Mem. VFW (life), Am. Assn. Cmty. Colls., Am. Coun. Edn., Fla. Assn. Colls. and Univs., Fla. Assn. C.C.'s, Fla. Space Rsch. Inst., Fla. Sterling Coun., Inc. (bd. dirs.), U. Ill. Coll. Edn. Alumni Assn. (life, sr. advisor, pres. 1988-90), Rotary, Beta Beta Beta, Chi Gamma Iota, Kappa Delta Pi, Phi Delta Kappa, Phi Kappa Phi. Avocations: non-fiction reading, children, classical music, naval science. Office: Brevard CC Office of Pres 1519 Clearlake Rd Cocoa FL 32922-6598 E-mail: gamblet@brevardcc.edu.

GAMBLE, WILLIAM ARDELL, JR., interior designer, inventor; b. Kingstree, S.C., Mar. 10, 1962; s. William Ardell and Jean Terry Gamble. Student, Wofford Coll., 1980-81, Coll. of Santa Fe, 1988-90. Design dir. Santa Fe Interiors, 1988—94; CEO SpaHome, N.Y.C., 1995—, Golden Triangle Corp., N.Y.C., 1992—. Author: (biography) Water From the Moon, 2002; prodr.: (video) Fresh Faces in Fashion, 1996. Democrat. Buddhist. Avocations: mountain climbing, snow skiing, swimming, travel. Home: 785 Madison Ave 4th Fl New York NY 10021-6100

GAMBLIN, CYNTHIA MACDONALD, mathematics educator, loybbist; b. Chgo., Sept. 12, 1946; d. Robert Eugene and Janice (Billings) MacD.; m. James Bradford Gamblin, Sept. 6, 1969 (div. June 1980). BS, Washington U., St. Louis, 1969, MA in Teaching, 1971. Cert. tchr., Fla., Mo.; lic. basic ground instr. FAA. Tchr. maths. Mary Inst., St. Louis, 1969-70; exec. sec. Coalition for the Environment, St. Louis, 1971-72; office mgr. Around the World Food Corp., St. Louis, 1972-73; tchr. maths. Dunedin (Fla.) High Sch., 1973—. Mem. pub. policy com. Juvenile Welfare Bd., St. Petersburg, Fla., 1979-98, co-chmn. legis. subcom., 1989-90; advisor DHS Sailing Club, 2002—. Mem. Pinellas Classroom Tchrs. Assn. (lobbyist St. Petersburg chpt. 1979-92), Ctr. for Fla.'s Children, Jr. League of Clearwater, Phi Delta Kappa. Republican. Avocations: pilot, sailing, reading. Home: 1441 Fairway Dr Dunedin FL 34698-2270

GAMBOA, GEORGE CHARLES, retired oral surgeon, educator; b. King City, Calif., Dec. 17, 1923; s. George Angel and Martha Ann (Baker) G.; m. Winona Mae Collins, July 16, 1946; children: Cheryl Jan Gamboa Granger, Jon Charles, Judith Merlene Gamboa Hiscox. Pre-dental cert., Pacific Union Coll., 1943; DDS, U. Pacific, 1946; MS, U. Minn., 1953; AB, U. So. Calif., 1958, EdD, 1976. Diplomate Am. Bd. Oral and Maxillofacial Surgery. Fellow oral surgery Mayo Found., 1950-53; clin. prof. grad. program oral and maxillofacial surgery U. So. Calif., L.A., 1954-99; assoc. prof. Loma Linda (Calif) U., 1958-99, chmn. dept. oral surgery, 1960-63; pvt. practice oral and maxillofacial surgery San Gabriel, Calif., 1955-93. Dir. So. Calif. Acad. Oral Pathology, 1995-2002. Mem., past chmn. first aid com. West San Gabriel chpt. ARC. Fellow Am. Coll. Dentists, Am. Coll. Oral and Maxillofacial Surgeons (founding fellow), Pierre Fauchard Acad., Am. Inst. Oral Biology, Internat. Coll. Dentists, So. Calif. Acad. Oral Pathology (pres. 2001); mem. Calif. Assn. Oral and Maxillofacial Surgeons, Am. Assn. Oral and Maxillofacial Surgeons, Internat. Assn. Oral Surgeons, So. Calif. Soc. Oral and Maxillofacial Surgeons, Western Soc. Oral and Maxillofacial Surgeons, Am. Acad. Oral and Maxillofacial Radiology, Marsh Robinson Acad. Oral Surgeons, Profl. Staff Assn. L.A. County-U. So. Calif. Med. Ctr. (exec. com. 1976-99), Am. Cancer Soc. (Calif. div., profl. edn. subcom. 1977-90, pres. San Gabriel-Pomona Valley unit 1989-90), Am. Dental Assn. (sci. session chmn. sect. on anesthesiology, 1970), Calif. Dental Soc. Anesthesiology (pres. 1989-94), Calif. Dental Found. (pres. 1991-93), Calif. Dental Assn. (jud. coun. 1990-96), So. Calif. Acad. Oral Pathology (dir. 1995-2002, pres. 2000-01), San Gabriel Valley Dental Soc. (past pres.), Xi Psi Phi, Omicron Kappa Upsilon, Delta Epsilon. Seventh-Day Adventist. Home: 1102 Loganrita Ave Arcadia CA 91006-4535

GAMBOA, LUCITO G. physician, pathologist; b. Pampanga, The Philippines, Jan. 7, 1929; came to U.S., 1952; s. Serapion M. and Jacinta L. Gamboa; m. Sylvia V. Roque, Sept. 18, 1953; children: Richard, Virginia Majer, Debra Jorgensen. MS, U. Colo., 1955; MD, U. Santo Tomas, Manila, The Philippines, 1952. Diplomate Am. Bd. Pathology. Dir. pathology and clin. labs. Edgewater Hosp., Chgo., 1958-69, 80-90; dir. blood bank and sr. pathologist Little Co. of Mary Hosp., Evergreen Park, Ill., 1969-80; mem. staff Ctrl. Valley Gen. Hosp., Hanford, Calif., 1990—. Contbr. numerous articles to profl. jours. Bd. dirs. Chgo. Dist. Tennis Assn., 1973-76. Recipient Disting. Physician award Philippine Med. Soc. Chgo., 1966. Mem. Assn. Philippine Physicians in Am. (pres., founder 1972-74, Disting. Svc. award 1975), Assn. Philippine Pathologists in Am. (pres., founder 1970-72), Dove Canyon Country Club. Avocations: golf, tennis, photography, travel. Home: 18 Golf View Dr Dove Canyon CA 92679-3802 Office: Ctrl Valley Gen Hosp 1025 N Douty St Hanford CA 93230-3722 E-mail: lgamboamd@aol.com.

GAMBONE, VICTOR, JR., internist, geriatrician; b. Phila., Aug. 28, 1949; s. Victor Emmanuel and Eleanor Joyce (Porambo) G. BS, Pa. State U., 1971, MD, 1975. Diplomate Am. Bd. Quality Assurance and Utilization Rev. Physicians, Am. Bd. Internal and Geriatric Medicine; cert. med. dir. in long term care. Intern then resident in internal medicine U. S.Fla., Tampa, 1975-78, practice medicine internal medicine and geriatrics Dunedin, Fla., 1978—; med. dir. Evercare (United Health Group), Tampa, Fla., 1996—; project coord. Fla. Med. Quality Assurance, Inc., Tampa, 2000—. Med. dir. Hospice Care, Inc., Pinellas County, 1982—86, Stratford Ct. Health Ctr., Palm Harbor, Fla., 1991—, St. Mark Village, Palm Harbor, 1993—, Mease Continuing Care, Dunedin, Fla., 1993—, Mariner Health of Clearwater, 1996—, Spanish Gardens Nursing Ctr., Dunedin, 1994—98, Sylvan Health Ctr., Clearwater, 1996—2002, Manor Care Nursing Ctr., Dunedin, Fla., 1996—2001, Bayview Nursing Pavillion, Clearwater, 1996—99, Arbors of Safety Harbor, Fla., 1997—98, Mariner Health Belleair, Clearwater, 1997—98, Sabal Palms Health Care Ctr., Largo, Fla., 1997—99, Morton Plant Rehab. Ctr., 1998—2000, Drew Village Rehab. and Nursing Ctr., Clearwater, Fla., 1998—99, Oak Manor Village, Largo, 1999; chmn. dept. internal medicine Mease Health Care, Dunedin, Fla., 1989. Author: Post Operative Recall of Intra-Operative Events, 1975 (rsch. award U. Miami Med. Sch.). Fellow: ACP; mem.: AMA, Fla. Med. Assn., Fla. Geriatrics Soc., Fla. Med. Dirs. Assn. (pres. 2003—), Am. Soc. Internal Medicine, Am. Geriatrics Soc., Am. Med. Dirs. Assn. Office: Evercare 9009 Corporate Lake Dr Tampa FL 33634 E-mail: Victor.Gambone@verizon.net.

GAMBONI, CIRO ANTHONY, lawyer; b. Bklyn., Aug. 16, 1940; m. Gail Pollack, Aug. 1, 1965; children: Dina, Lee. BBA cum laude, CCNY, 1963; LLB cum laude, NYU, 1965; LLM in Taxation, Georgetown U., 1969. Bar: N.Y., U.S. Dist. Ct. (so. dist.) N.Y., U.S. Tax Ct. Ptnr. Cahill, Gordon & Reindel, N.Y.C. Mem. patron com. Lincoln Ctr. Theatre, N.Y.C. Served to capt. JAGC, U.S. Amry, 1966-69. Mem. N.Y. State Bar Assn. (tax sect.), NYU Law Review, Order of Coif, Beta Gamma Sigma, Beta Alpha Psi. Clubs: Downtown Assn., Lotos (N.Y.C.). Avocation: non-profit theater. Office: Cahill Gordon & Reindel 80 Pine St Fl 17 New York NY 10005-1790

GAMBRELL, DAVID HENRY, lawyer; b. Atlanta, Dec. 20, 1929; s. E. Smythe and Kathleen (Hagood) G.; m. Luck Coleman Flanders, Oct. 16, 1953; children: Luck Coleman, David Henry, Alice Kathleen Hagood, Mary Latimer. BS, Davidson Coll., 1949; JD cum laude, Harvard U., 1952. Bar: Ga. 1951. Pvt. practice, Atlanta, 1952-54, 56—; teaching fellow Harvard Law Sch., 1954-55; partner firm Gambrell & Stolz, LLP, 1963—. U.S. senator from Ga. to succeed Richard B. Russell Coms. on Banking and Space, 1971-72. Bd. editors: Am. Bar Assn. Jour, 1969-70. Chmn. Ga. Gov.'s Com. on Postsecondary Edn., 1978-79; bd. dirs. Nat. Legal Aid and Defender Assn., 1965-69; chmn. Dem. Party of Ga., 1970-71; trustee Ga. Legal History Found., 1996—, Lawyers Found. of Ga., 1997—; bd. dirs. Buckhead Coalition, Inc., 2003—. Mem. ABA (ho. of dels. 1975), Atlanta Bar Assn. (pres. 1965-66), State Bar Ga. (pres. 1967-68), Lawyers Club Atlanta, Ga. C. of C. (bd. dirs. 1989-92), N.C. Soc. Cin., Ga. Hist. Soc. (bd. curators 1999-2001), Met. Club (Washington), Piedmont Driving Club, Commerce Club, Capital City Club, Peachtree Golf Club, Sigma Alpha Epsilon, Omicron Delta Kappa. Democrat. Presbyterian. Home: 3205 Arden Rd NW Atlanta GA 30305-1918 Office: Gambrell & Stolz 303 Peachtree St NE Ste 4300 Atlanta GA 30308-3254 E-mail: dgambrell@gambrell.com.

GAMBRELL, JAMES BRUTON, III, lawyer, educator; b. Rochester, Minn., Jan. 17, 1926; s. James Bruton Gambrell and Martha Judson Corley; m. Helen Jeanette Roddy, Aug. 12, 1950; children: Jamey, Gretchen, James Bruton IV. BS in Mech. Engring, U. Tex., 1949; MA in Econs, Columbia U., 1950; LL.B., N.Y. U., 1957. Bar: D.C. 1957, Okla. 1958, Calif. 1961, N.Y. 1967, Tex. 1976. Mem. staff Tex. Legis. Council, Austin, 1950; instr. econs. Baylor U., Waco, Tex., 1950-51; mem. tech. staff (engr.) Bell Telephone Labs., Murray Hill, N.J., 1951-53, mem. patent staff N.Y.C., 1953-57; admitted to practice before U.S. Patent Office, 1954; asst. patent atty. Well Surveys, Inc., Tulsa, 1957-59; assoc. Townsend & Townsend, San Francisco, 1959-61; spl. asst. to commr. patents,

dir. office legis. planning U.S. Patent Office, Washington, 1961-63; ptnr. Fowler, Knobbe & Gambrell, Santa Ana, Calif., 1963-66; prof. law N.Y. U., N.Y.C., 1966-76, patent counsel, 1967-76; prof. law U. Houston, 1976-82; ptnr. Pravel, Gambrell, Hewitt, Kimball & Krieger, Houston, 1976-92, Gambrell, Wilson & Hamilton, Austin, Tex., 1993-95, Akin, Gump, Strauss, Hauer & Feld L.L.P., Austin, Tex., 1995-2000; vis. prof. law U. Tex., Austin, 2000—02. Cons. to Practicing Law Inst., N.Y.C., 1966-71, Commn. Revision Fed. Ct. Appellate System, 1974, Energy and Rsch. Adminstrn., 1976; commr. patents Patent Adv. Com., 1968-72. Author: Patent Law Perspectives, 2d edit., 6 vols., 1970-88; editor: Orange County Bar Bull., 1965-66; mem. adv. bd.: Patent, Trademark and Copyright Jour., 1972-86, 94—. Lt. (j.g.) USNR, 1943-46. Mem. ABA, Calif. Bar Assn., Tex. Bar Assn., Am. Intellectual Property Law Assn. (bd. mgrs. 1977-80), Licensing Execs. Soc., Internat. Trademark Assn., Copyright Soc., Intellectual Property Panel of Experts, Am. Arbitration Assn., Ctr. for Pub. Resources. Home: 3801 Cima Serena Dr Austin TX 78759-8229 also: PO Box 584 Hunt TX 78024 E-mail: jim@gambrell.org., gambrell@classicnet.net.

GAMBRELL, LUCK FLANDERS, corporate executive; b. Jan. 17, 1930; d. William Henry and Mattie Moring (Mitchell) Flanders; m. David Henry Gambrell, Oct. 16, 1953; children: Luck G. Davidson, David Henry, Alice Kathleen, Mary G. Rolinson. Grad., St. Mary's Coll., 1948; AB, Duke U., 1950; diplome d'etudes françaises, L'Institut de Touraine, Tours, France, 1951. Chmn. bd. LFG Co., 1960—. Mem. State Bd. Pub. Safety, 1981—90, Chpt. Nat. Cathedral, Washington, 1981—85, World Svc. Coun. YWCA, 1965—; chmn. bd. dirs. Student Aid Found., Atlanta, 1992—99; mem. Bd. Councilors The Carter Ctr., Emory U.; mem. bd. advisors Emory U., 2001—; coun. mem. Presbytery Greater Atlanta, 1988; elder First Presbyn. Ch., Atlanta; bd. dirs. Atlanta Symphony Orch., 1982—85. Named The Luck Flanders Gambrell Ctr., East Ga. Coll. in her honor, 2002. Mem.: Atlanta Jr. League, Alpha Delta Pi.

GAMBRELL, OLIN ERIC, III, municipal official; b. Anderson, S.C., Mar. 22, 1946; s. Olin E. Gambrell, Jr. and Doris V. Moore; m. Deiadra Teague Gambrell, Oct. 7, 1972; children: Heather Elizabeth, Erica Rose, Olin Eric IV. AA, Forrest Coll., Anderson, 1967, Anderson Coll., 1970; BA, U. S.C., 1972; postgrad. in bus. adminstrn., Winthrop Coll., Rock Hill, S.C., 1976-78; postgrad., Ctrl. Wesleyan Coll., 1980—81. Cert. mcpl. fin. adminstr., accredited in bus. licenses. Shift supr. Miliken Textiles, Spartanburg, S.C., 1972-74; staff mgr. Liberty Life Ins. Co., Greenville, S.C., 1974-78; regional dir. New South Life Ins., Charleston, S.C., 1978-80; town adminstr. Town of Central, S.C., 1980-88; city mgr. City of Woodruff, S.C., 1988-93; town mgr. Town of Batesburg-Leesville, SC, 1993—2001; town adminstr. Towns of Johnston and Edgefield, 2001—; cons. Gambrell Mcpl. Assocs., 2001—. Mem. Town Coun., Central, S.C., 1980-83; football ofcl. S.C., 1982-87; active Downtown Woodruff Revitalization Bd., 1988, Econ. Devel. Bd., 1988; officer Lower Piedmont Rescue Squad, 1989; active Piedmont United Way, 1989-92; deacon bd. First Bapt. Ch., 1989-92; active Piedmont Area Girl Scouts Am., 1991-94; active Spartanburg County divsn. Am. Heart Assn., 1991-93, Leadership Spartanburg, 1991, Leadership Lexington, 1995; with steering com. Spartanburg Edn. 2000, mentor program, 1991-93, Woodruff H.S. Bus. Edn. Steering Com., 1991-93; So. Bapt. Com. on Coms., 1998-99, 2001—; deacon bd. Batesburg Bapt. Ch., 1996—, treas., 1996—. Sgt. U.S. Army, 1967-69, Vietnam. Named S.C. Econ. Devel. Coll. Charleston, 1999. Mem. VFW, SCUBA, SCBLOA, Blue Ridge Underwriters Assn. (pres. 1981-82), Batesville-Leesburg C. of C., Rotary, Lions, Masons. Baptist. Avocations: family, church, community. Home: PO Box 4037 280 Crosson St Batesburg-Leesville SC 29070-1037 Office: 400 Main St Edgefield SC 29824- 130 E-mail: ogambrell@sc.rr.com.

GAMBRELL, RICHARD DONALD, JR., endocrinologist, educator; b. St. George, S.C., Oct. 28, 1931; s. Richard Donald and Nettie Anzo (Ellenburg) G.; m. Mary Caroline Stone, Dec. 22, 1956; children: Deborah Christina, Juliet Denise. BS, Furman U., 1953; MD, Med. U. S.C., 1957. Diplomate Am. Bd. Obstetrics and Gynecology, Diplomate Div. Reproductive Endocrinology. Intern Greenville Gen. Hosp., S.C., 1957-58, resident, 1961-64; commd. USAF, 1958, advanced through grades to col., chmn. dept. ob-gyn, cons. to surgeon gen. USAF Hosp., 1966-69, chief gynecologic endocrinology Wilford Hall USAF Med. Ctr. Lackland AFB, Tex., 1971-78, ret., 1978; clin. prof. ob-gyn and endocrinology Med. Coll. Ga., Augusta, 1978—2001; practice medicine specializing in reproductive endocrinology Augusta, 1978—. Fellow in endocrinology Med. Coll. Ga., 1969-71; mem. staff Westlawn Bapt. Mission Med. Clinic, San Antonio, 1972-78; assoc. clin. prof. U. Tex. Health Sci. Ctr., San Antonio, 1971-78; internat. lectr.; mem. ob-gyn. adv. panel U.S. Pharmacopeial Conv., 1986-90; mem. sci. adv. bd. Nat. Osteoporosis Found., 1988-91. Co-author: The Menopause: Indications for Estrogen Therapy, 1979, Sex Steroid Hormones and Cancer, 1984, Unwanted Hair: Its Cause and Treatment, 1985, Estrogen Replacement Therapy, 1987, Hormone Replacement Therapy, 3rd edit., 1992, 4th edit., 1995, 5th edit., 1997, Estrogen Replacement Therapy Users Guide, 1989, 2d edit., 1997; mem. editl. bd. Jour. Reproductive Medicine, 1982-85, Maturitas, 1982-99, The Female Patient, 1992—, Menopause: Jour. of the N.Am. Menopause Soc., 1995—; mem. editl. bd. Internat. Jour. Fertility, 1986-91, assoc. editor, 1988-91; contbr. articles to med. jours., chpts. to books. Deacon, Sunday sch. tchr. Baptist Ch., 1971—; mem. sci. adv. bd. Nat. Osteoporosis Found., 1988-91. Recipient Chmn.'s Best Paper in Clin. Rsch. from Tchg. Hosp. award Armed Forces Dist. Am. Coll. Ob-Gyn., 1972, 88, Host award, 1977, Chmn.'s award, 1978, Purdue-Frederick award, 1979, Outstanding Exhibit award Am. Fertility Soc., 1983, Am. Coll. Obstetricians and Gynecologists award, 1983, Thesis award South Atlantic Assn. Ob-Gyn., Winthrop award Internat. Soc. Reproductive Medicine, 1985, Chmn.'s Best Paper award Pan Am. Soc. for Fertility, 1986, Outstanding Sci. exhibit award Am. Acad. Family Physicians, 1986, 87, 92, Boston, 1994, New Orleans, 1996, Merit award ACS, 1994, Cert. of Appreciation for Sci. Exhibit, 1995, Best Doctors for Women award Good Housekeeping, 1997; named to Hall of Fame, Lloyd Meml. H.S., Erlanger, Ky., 1996. Fellow ACOG (mem. subcom. on endocrinology and infertility 1983-86, Kermit Krantz award 2000); mem. Pacific N.W. Ob-Gyn Soc. (hon.), So. Med. Assn. (2nd place Sci. Exhibit award 1992), Am. Fertility Soc., Ga. Obstetric and Gynecologic Soc., Tex. Assn. Ob-Gyn., Augusta Obstetric and Gynecologic Soc., San Antonio Ob-Gyn. Soc. (v.p. 1975-76), Chilean Soc. Ob-Gyn. (hon.), South Atlantic Assn. Obstetricians and Gynecologists (v.p. 1997-98, pres.-elect 1998-99, pres. 1999-00), Soc. Obstetricians and Gynecologists of Can. (hon.), Internat. Family Planning Rsch. Assn., Internat. Menopause Soc. (mem. exec. com. 1981-84), Internat. Soc. for Reproductive Medicine (program chmn. 1980, pres. 1986-88), Am. Assn. of Pro-Life Obs. and Gyn. (exec. bd. 1995—), Christian Med. and Dental Assn., Am. Geriat. Soc. (mem. editl. bd. 1981-83), N.Am. Menopause Soc. (Ortho-McNeil Pharm. Rsch. award 2001), Nat. Geog. Soc., Phi Chi, Alpha Epsilon Delta. Home: 3542 National Ct Augusta GA 30907-9517 Office: 903 15th St Augusta GA 30901-2607

GAMBRELL, SARAH BELK, retail executive; b. Charlotte, N.C., Apr. 12, 1918; d. William Henry and Mary (Irwin) Belk; m. Charles Glenn Gambrell (dec.); 1 child, Sarah Belk Gambrell Knight. BA, Sweet Briar Coll., 1939; D in Humanities (hon.), Erskine Coll., 1970, U. N.C., Asheville, 1986, Furman U., 1997, Johnson C. Smith U., 2003. Dir. Belk Inc., 1947—. Mem. bd. consulators Erskine Coll. and Sem.; trustee Johnson C. Smith U., Charlotte, NC, Warren Wilson Coll., Swannanoa, NC, Furman U., Greenville, SC, Charlotte Mus. of History; hon. trustee Cancer Rsch. Inst.; hon. trustee emeritus Princeton (N.J.) Theol. Sem.; mem. nat. bd., mem. asset. mgmt. and devel. com. YWCA of U.S.; asset mgmt. and devel. com. YWCA; bd. dirs. Parkinson's Disease Found., N.Y.C., N.C. Cmty. Found., Raleigh, Charlotte Philharmonic Orch., Cmty. Sch. Arts, N.C. Transp. Mus., Spencer, NC; hon. bd. dirs. YWCA, N.Y.C.; bd. dirs. YWCA of Ctrl. Carolinas. Mem. Fashion Group, Inc. (N.Y.C.), Jr. League Charlotte, Nat. Soc. Colonial Dames, DAR. Home: 300 Cherokee Rd Charlotte NC 28207-1908 Office: Belk Inc 2801 W Tyvola Rd Charlotte NC 28217-4500

GAMBRELL, THOMAS ROSS, investor, retired physician, surgeon; b. Lockhart, Tex., Mar. 17, 1934; s. Sidney Spivey and Nora Katherine (Rheinlander) G.; m. Louise Evans, Feb. 23, 1960. Student summa cum laude, U. Tex., 1953, MD, 1957. Intern Kings County Hosp., Bklyn., 1957-58; company physician Hughes Aircraft, Fullerton, Calif., 1958-65, Chrysler Corp., Anaheim, Calif., 1962-65, L.A. Angels Baseball Team, Fullerton, 1962-64; pvt. practice medicine Fullerton, 1958-91. With St. Jude Hosp., Anaheim Meml. Hosp., Fullerton Cmty. Hosp., Martin Luther Hosp.; mem. utilization rev. com. St. Mary's Convalescent Hosp., Fullerton Convalescent Hosp., Sunhaven and Fairway Convalescent Hosp.; owner Ranching (Citrus) & Comml. Devel., Ariz., Tex., N.Y., 1962-94. Author: An Ancestral History, 8 B.C. to 1986, 2001; contbr. articles to profl. jours. Organizer of care for needy elderly, North Orange County, 1962-65; sponsor numerous charity events. Fellow Am. Acad. Family Physicians; mem. AMA, Am. Geriats. Soc., Calif. Med. Assn., Tex. Med. Assn., Tex. Alumni Assn., Orange County Med. Assn., Mayflower Soc., Plantagenet Soc., Sons of Confederacy, SAR, Order Royal Descendants Living in Am. (col., listed in Living Descendants of Blood Royal), Order Crown (col.), Baronial Order Magna Carta, Order of Aesculaepius, Phi Eta Sigma, Delta Kappa Epsilon, Phi Chi. Avocations: collecting, travel, history. Office: PO Box 6067 Beverly Hills CA 90212-1067

GAMBRO, JOHN M. priest, secondary school educator; b. Chgo., Sept. 29, 1929; s. John Louis and May Frances Gambro. MA, Loyola U., Chgo., 1963; lic. in philosophy, Pontifical Faculty of Aquinas Inst., River Forest, Ill. Ordained priest Roman Cath. Ch., 1957. Tchr. Latin Fenwick H.S., Oak Park, Ill., 1957—63, chmn. dept classical langs.; tchr. Latin Bishop Lynch H.S., Dallas, 1963—78, prin., 1970—74, dean of students. Dir. of Kairos Retreats Fenwick H.S., Oak Park, 1995—2003. Mem.: Classical Assn. of Mid. West and South, The Vergilian Soc., Am. Classical League, Orders and Medals Soc. of Am., Fedn. Genealogists, Chgo. Geneal. Soc. Republican. Roman Catholic. Avocations: walking, stamp collecting, preaching. Home: 7200 Division St River Forest IL 60305-1294 Office: Fenwick HS 505 Washington Blvd Oak Park IL 60302-4095

GAMBRO, MICHAEL S. lawyer; b. N.Y.C., July 15, 1954; s. A. John and Rose A. (Grandinetti) G.; m. Joan L. Thurneyssen, Aug. 9, 1980; children: Dana E., Merrill R., Christopher J. BS summa cum laude, Tufts U., 1976; JD, Columbia U., 1980. Bar: N.Y. 1981, U.S. Dist. Ct. (so. dist.) N.Y. 1981, U.S. Dist. Ct. N.J. 1981, N.J. 1983, Calif. 1988. Assoc. Cadwalader, Wickersham & Taft, N.Y.C., 1980-86, ptnr., 1987-88, L.A., 1988-94, N.Y.C., 1994—. Harlan Fiske Stone scholar, 1978-79, 1979-80. Mem. ABA, Phi Beta Kappa, Psi Chi. Office: Cadwalader Wickersham & Taft 100 Maiden Ln New York NY 10038-4818

GAMBS, GERARD CHARLES, consulting engineer; b. Columbus, Ohio, May 2, 1918; s. Charles Raymond and Helen Mary (Casey) G.; m. Helen Mary Burns, 1942 (dec. 1971); children: Mary Helen, Gerard C. Jr.; m. Eileen Francis Goggin, July 31, 1971. B. Engring. in Mining, Ohio State U., 1940. Registered profl. engr., Ohio, Pa. Jr. mining engr. Pitts. Coal Co., 1940-42; asst. prof. Engr. Experiment Station Ohio State U., Columbus, 1946-47; asst. to v.p. Consolidation Coal Co., Library, Pa., 1947-69; bus. mgr. Gibbs & Hill, Inc., N.Y.C., 1969-70; v.p. Ford, Bacon & Davis, Inc., N.Y.C., 1970-83; consulting engr. N.Y.C., 1983—. Contbr. articles to profl. jours.; co-inventor, patentee coal treatment method and apparatus, gaseous and liquid fuels from crude oil. Bd. dirs. Tipperary Corp., Midland, Tex., 1973-86, Onan Corp., Fridley, Minn., 1971-83, Ford, Bacon &Davis, Inc., N.Y.C., 1973-83. Major Corps Engrs., U.S. Army, 1942-46. Mem. Am. Inst. Mining, Metall. and Petrol. Engrs. (sr. Mem.), Am. Soc. Mech. Engrs., Am. Nuclear Soc., Am. Coal Ash Assn. Roman Catholic. Avocations: travel, photography, writing. Home: 1725 York Ave Apt 33C New York NY 10128-7892

GAMET, DONALD MAX, appliance company executive; b. Mapleton, Kans., Feb. 21, 1916; s. Carl Adolph and Pearl May (McClanahan) G.; m. L. Pauline Fleming, Apr. 14, 1938 (dec. Dec. 1981); children: Merilyn Kay Gamet Paris, Carleton Lenoir, Kathy Lynn Gamet Stephenson; m. Marilyn Lang, Jan. 15, 1983. BBA, Ft. Hays State Coll., 1938; MBA, U. Kans., 1939, JD, 1942. CPA, Mo. Staff acct. Arthur Andersen & Co., Kansas City, Mo., 1942-46, mgr., 1946-54, ptnr., 1954-78, mng. ptnr. Kansas City office, 1956-70, vice chmn. tax practices Chgo., 1970-77, sr. ptnr., 1977-78; cons. Kansas City, 1978-84; v.p.-treas. Chgo. Pacific Corp. (merged with Maytag 1989), 1984-85, exec. v.p. fin., 1985-87, spl. cons. to chief exec. officer, 1987-89, ret., 1989. Bd. dirs. ANUHCO, Inc., Overland Park, Kans. Pres., chmn. bd. dirs. Heart Am. United Funds, Met. Kansas City, 1967-68, chmn. spl. reorgn. study com., 1980-84; mem. adv. bd. Salvation Army Kansas City, 1982-84; mem. personnel com. Village United Presbyn. Ch., 1982-84; pres., bd. dirs. Estate Planning Council Kans., 1962-63, Minority Supplier's Devel. Council Kansas City, 1983-84; bd. dirs., mem. exec. com., treas. Civic Council Kansas City, 1967-70; bd. dirs., chmn. long range planning com. Geriatic Resources Corp. Kansas City, 1982-84; bd. dirs. Metro Kansas City C. of C., 1962-70, pres., 1969-70; bd. dirs. Kansas City Indsl. Found., 1968-70, Jr. Achievement Kansas City, 1960-65. Named Boss of Yr., Met. Kansas City Jaycees, 1962; recipient Alumni Achievement award Ft. Hays State Coll., 1969. Mem. AICPA, Kansas City Club. Republican. Home: 12921 Riggs Rd Apt 102 Shawnee Mission KS 66209

GAMIN, JUDITH, poet; b. Garfield, N.J., Oct. 30, 1939; d. John S. and Marie Lillian Kovalcik; 2 children. BS, Ramapo Coll., Mahwah, N.J. Columnist, reporter Collie Shetland Sheep Dog Rev., Calif., 1970—73; assoc. editor Off Lead Obedience Mag., NY, 1972—74. Author: Diary of a Woman in Anguish, poetry to numerous lit. pubs., A Celebration in Photos, Fantasy and Verse, A Pictures and Poetry Biography, mystery short fiction.

GAMMILL, LEE MORGAN, JR., retired insurance company executive; b. N.Y.C., Mar. 25, 1934; s. Lee Morgan and Blanche (Reeves) G.; m. Jane Houchin, Apr. 2, 1960; children: Christopher Morgan, Sarah Louise. BA, Dartmouth Coll., 1956. CLU. Mgmt. trainee N.Y. Life Ins. Co., San Francisco, 1957-58, field underwriter, 1958-60, sales mgr., 1960-64, gen. mgr., 1965-71, regional supt., 1971-75, gen. mgr., 1975-86, sr. v.p., 1986-89, exec. v.p. N.Y.C., 1989-95, vice chmn. bd. dirs., 1995-98; ret., 1999. Pres. N.Y. Life and Annuity Corp., N.Y.C., 1987—; bd. dirs. N.Y. Life Securities Corp., N.Y.C., N.Y. Life Equity Corp., N.Y.C., N.Y. Life Realty Corp., N.Y.C., N.Y. Life Ins. Co.; chmn. bd. Life Ins. Mktg. and Rsch. Assn. Internat.; bd. dirs., mem. exec. com. Life Underwriters Tng. Coun. Dir. The Am. Coll.; chmn. Town Recreational Adv. Bd., Ross, Calif., 1977; trustee Ross Sch. Dist., 1978-84; trustee The Am. Coll. Mem. Gen. Agts. and Mgrs. Assn. (pres. San Francisco chpt. 1985), Nat. Assn. Life Underwriters, CLU Assn., MIll Valley Tennis Club (pres. 1972-73), Lagunitas Country Club, Pacific Union Club, Bohemian Club, The Links Club, Lyford Cay Club. Republican. Presbyterian. Avocation: tennis. Office: NY Life Ins Co 51 Madison Ave New York NY 10010-1603

GAMMON, JAMES ALAN, lawyer; b. Keokuk, Iowa, Jan. 30, 1934; s. Tench Temme and Helen Dolores Gammon; m. Joanne Mott, Aug. 31, 1957; children— Daniel, Thomas, Matthew, Kelly, Timothy. BS in Commerce cum laude, U. Notre Dame, 1956; JD, Georgetown U., 1959. Bar: D.C. 1959. Assoc. McGrath & McGrath, Washington, 1959-62; ptnr. Molnar & Gammon, Washington, 1962-72; sole practice Washington, 1972-76; ptnr. Gammon & Tierney, Washington, 1976, Gammon & Grange, Washington, 1977-89, of counsel, 1989—; pres. Gammon Media Brokers Inc., Washington, 1981-98; chmn. Gammon Media Brokers, LLC, Phoenix, 1998—; exec. v.p. Rodriguez Comm. Inc., Washington, 1999—2003, Momentum Media Capital, 2001—03. Mem. Fed. Communications Bar Assn., Christian Legal Soc., Nat. Assn. Media Brokers (pres. 1989-91). Republican. Avocation: body building. Office: 8280 Greensboro Dr Fl 7 Mc Lean VA 22102-3807 E-mail: jgammon@gmbi.com.

GAMMON, MALCOLM ERNEST, SR., surveying and engineering executive; b. Chattanooga, Tenn., Sept. 7, 1947; s. George A. and Frances Helen (Conway) G.; m. Glenna Dee Shirk, June 5, 1971; children: Malcolm Ernest Jr., Christopher Brian. BS, Miss. State U., 1970. Ops. mgr. Pyburn & Odom, Inc., Baton Rouge, 1970-84; chief exec. officer, prin. owner Hydro Cons., Inc., Baton Rouge, 1984—. Tech. contbr. (textbook) 4567 Review Questions for Surveyors, 11th edit., 1985, Elementary Surveying, 8th edit., 1989. State chmn. La. Trig Star Program, Baton Rouge, 1988-89; mem. adv. bd. La. Math. Coalition. Fellow Am. Congress on Surveying and Mapping (dir., cert. hydrographer, mem. bd. dirs. 1998-2003); mem. Am. Congress on Surveying and Mapping Hydrograher Cert. Bd.; mem. La. Soc. Profl. Surveyors (registered, pres. 1990), Miss. Assn. Profl. Surveyors (registered), Nat. Soc. Profl. Surveyors (profl. mem.), Ark. Soc. Profl. Surveyors (registered), Ala. Profl. Land Surveyors (registered). Home: 19021 Saint Clare Dr Baton Rouge LA 70810-7979 Office: Hydro Cons Inc 10275 Siegen Ln Baton Rouge LA 70810-4926

GAMMON, SAMUEL RHEA, III, association executive, former ambassador; b. Tex., Jan. 22, 1924; m. Mary Renwick. BA, Tex. A. and M. U., 1946; A.M., Princeton U., 1948, PhD, 1953. Instr. Emory U., 1952-54; joined Fgn. Service, Dept. State, 1954; served in Milan and Palermo, Italy, 1954-58; with Dept. of State, 1959-63; detailed fgn. affairs aide to Vice Pres. Lyndon Johnson, 1963; consul gen. Asmara, Ethiopia, 1964-67; counselor for polit. affairs Rome, 1967-70; detailed USIA dep. asst. dir. for W. Europe, 1970-71; exec. asst. to undersec., 1971-73; dep. exec. sec. State Dept., 1973-75; minister counselor Am. Embassy, Paris, 1975-78; ambassador to Mauritius Port Louis, 1978-80; exec. dir. Am. Hist. Assn., 1981-94. Pres. Nat. Humanities Alliance, 1986-88; bd. dirs. Consortium Social Sci. Assns., 1981-94, Truman Libr. and Inst., 1982-94, Assn. for Diplomatic Studies, 1986—. Served to Capt. AUS, 1943-46, 1950-52. Mem. Am. Fgn. Svc. Protective Assn. (bd. dirs. 1991—, pres. 1992—).

GAMPEL, ELAINE SUSAN, investment company executive, consultant; b. New Haven, Apr. 12, 1950; d. Stanley Irwin and Marion (Levine) G.; m. Alan Joseph Tedeschi, Sept. 9, 1984; children: Zachary Joseph Gampel Tedeschi, Matthew Samuel Gampel Tedeschi. BS in Spl. Edn., Boston U., 1972; MS in Counseling, So. Conn. State U., New Haven, 1975; cert. investment mgmt. analyst, Wharton Sch. Bus., 1990. Spl. edn. tchr. Ansonia (Conn.) Pub. Schs., 1972-77; v.p., investment mgmt. cons. Paine Webber Inc., Denver, 1977-89; v.p. investments Dean Witter Reynolds, Denver, 1989-93, 1st v.p. investments, sr. cons., 1993-2000, sr. v.p. investments, sr. cons., 2000—, wealth advisor, 2002—. Bd. dirs. United Cerebral Palsy of Denver, 1984-93; outside editorial bd. Denver Post, 1991-94; chair investment com. Women's Found. Colo., Denver, 1995-97; chair bd. trustees Women's Found. Colo., 2002; cmty. bd. Denver Nuggets, 1992-95. Mem. Investment Mgmt. Cons. Assn. (membership com., cert. com. 1990—), Denver Soc. Security Analysts. Avocations: tennis, running, biking. Office: Morgan Stanley 370 17th St Ste 5100 Denver CO 80202-5651

GAMPER, ALBERT R., JR., insurance executive; b. 1942; married. BA, Rutgers U.; PMD, Harvard U. With Mfrs. Hanover Trust Co., 1962—, v.p., 1971-80, sr. v.p., 1980-83, exec. v.p., 1983—, chmn. CIT group, 1987—; sector exec.v.p. Mfrs. Hanover Corp., 1985—. Office: Mfrs Hanover Corp 270 Park Ave New York NY 10017-2014 also: CIT Group Holdings Inc Ste B3 1211 Avenue Of The Americas Fl 13 New York NY 10036-8797

GAMROTH, ARTHUR PAUL, small business owner; b. Independence, Wis., Jan. 1, 1930; s. George Dominic and Frances Kathleen (Sylla) G.; m. Arline Hellen Leipski, Feb. 14, 1953; children: Shawne HCF, Bradley Paul, Todd Arthur, Timothy Curtis, Gary Mac. Diploma, Milw. Area Tech. Ctr., 1950 Mechanic Bonded Heating, Elm Grove, Wis., 1949-55; real estate salesman Anchor Realty, Waukesha, Wis., 1959-70; v.p. Ablenc, Inc., Waukesha, Wis., 1967—; pres. Energy Mgmt. of Wis., Waukesha, 1977—. Cons. E.M.O.W., Waukesha, 1977—. Designer Sophisticated Mcpl. Recycling Facility with composting capabilities; patentee biomass burner. Lobbyist RDF, Wis., 1987—. With U.S. Army, 1950-52, Korea. Recipient Spl. Recognition award U. Wis., 1986. Mem. Am. Contract Bridge League, Waukesha Bridge Club Am., Eagles. Lodges: Eagles. Republican. E-mail: ablene@yahoo.com., artgmrth1@aol.com.

GAMSKY, NEAL RICHARD, academic administrator, psychology educator; b. Menasha, Wis., Feb. 17, 1931; s. Andrew P. and Lillian G. G.; m. Irene Janet Jimos, Aug. 16, 1956; children: Elizabeth, Patricia. BS, U. Wis., 1954, MS, 1959, PhD, 1965. Counselor Appleton (Wis.) Pub. Schs., 1959—62; ednl. and counseling cons. Wis. Div. Mental Hygiene, 1967; dir. ednl svcs. Wis. Diagnostic Ctr., Madison, 1962—67; dir. rsch. pupil pers. svcs. Coop. Edn. Svc. Agy., Waupun, Wis., 1967—70; dir. student counseling ctr. Ill. State U., Normal, 1970—73, v.p. student affairs, 1973—91, prof. psychology, 1973—91. Author (with G.F. Farwell and B. Matheiu-Coughlan): The Counselor's Handbook, 1974; contbr. articles. Served with U.S. Army, 1954—56. Mem.: Am. Orhtopsychiat. Assn., Am. Coll. Pers. Assn., Am. Assn. Higher Edn., Nat. Assn. Student Pers. Adminstrs., Am. Assn. Counseling and Devel., Am. Psychol. Assn.

GAMST, FREDERICK CHARLES, social anthropologist; b. N.Y.C., May 24, 1936; s. Rangvald Julius and Aida (Durante) G.; m. Marilou Swanson, Jan. 28, 1961; 1 child, Nicole Christina. AA, Pasadena City Coll., 1959; AB, UCLA, 1961; PhD, U. Calif., Berkeley, 1967. Instr. anthropology Rice U., Houston, 1966-67, asst. prof., 1967-71, assoc. prof., 1971-75; prof. dept. anthropology U. Mass., Boston, 1975—2001, chmn. dept. anthropology, 1975-78, assoc. provost for grad. studies, 1978-83, prof. emeritus, 2001—. Cons. in social rels., human factors and ops. to R.R. industry, 1970—; acting dir. Houston Inter-Univ. African Studies Program, 1969-71, Behavioral Sci. Grad. Program, Rice U., 1974-75; mem. Joint Internat. Observer Group (for observation of Ethiopian elections), 1992; mem. com. on human factors for railroads and other fixed guideway transp. sys. Transp. Rsch. Bd., 1999—; adj. prof. anthroplogy U. Wyo., 2001—. Author: Travel and Research in Northwestern Ethiopia, 1965, The Qemant: A Pagan-Hebraic Peasantry of Ethiopia, 1969, Peasants in Complex Society, 1974, The Hoghead: An Industrial Ethnology of the Locomotive Engineer, 1980, Highballing with Flimsies: Working under Train Orders, 1990; editor: Studies in Cultural Anthropology, 1975, Letters from the United States of North America on Internal Improvements, Steam Navigation, Banking, Etc., 1990, Anthropology Quar., Golden Anniversary Spl. Issue on Indsl. Ethnology, 1977, (with Edward Norbeck) Ideas of Culture: Sources and Uses, 1976, Meanings of Work: Consideration for the Twenty-First Century, 1995, Early American Railroads: Franz Anton Ritter von Gerstner's Die Innern Communicationen (1842-1843), 2 vols., 1997, (video documentary) T-Time: The History of Mass Transit in Boston, 1984; contbr. articles and revs. to profl. publs., chpts. to books. Mem. adv. com Quincy Quarries Hist. Site, Met. Dist. Commn. Mass., 1987—2001; bd. dirs. Cheyenne Depot Found., 2002—. N.Y. State Regents scholar 1954-58, UCLA scholar 1959-60, Haynes Found. scholar 1960-61; Woodrow Wilson Nat. fellow 1961-62, Ford Found. Fgn. Area fellow 1962-63, Social Sci. Rsch. Coun. and ACLS Fgn. Area fellow 1963-66; Rice U. rsch. grantee 1967, NSF grantee 1970-72, NIMH grantee 1972-74, others. Fellow AAAS, Am. Anthrop. Assn. (Conrad Arensberg award 1995, Festschrift Session honoring life's work 2002), Soc. Applied Anthropology, Royal Anthrop. Inst. Gt. Britain and Ireland; mem. Sci. Rsch. Soc., Ry. and Locomotive Hist. Soc. (dir., editor 4 vol. Franz Anton Ritter von Gerstner project 1988—), Indsl. Rels. Rsch. Assn., Soc. for History Tech., Lexington Group in Transp. History, Ry. Fuel and Operating Officers Assn., Am. Assn. R.R. Supts., Soc. Anthrop. Work (pres. 1984-87, bd. dirs. 1987-90), Internat. Union Anthrop. and Ethnol. Scis. (chmn. curriculum com. Commn. Study of Peace 1983-86), Assn. for Study Lang. in Prehistory (bd. dirs. 1988—), Mass. Tchrs. Assn. (mem. exec. com. Faculty Staff Union 1996-2001), Cheyenne Depot Found. (bd. dirs. 2002—). Office: U Mass Dept Anthropology Harbor Campus Boston MA 02125-3393 E-mail: fcgamst@aol.com.

GAN, DEQIANG, engineer; b. Zigong, China, Jan. 29, 1966; s. Y. Tan and Y. Qu; m. Xiaolu Wang, Dec. 15, 1993; children: Annan, Julian. PhD, Xian Jiaotong U., Xian, China, 1994. Postdoc. rschr. Cornell U., Ithaca, NY, 1997—98; sr. analyst ISO New England, Inc., Holyoke, Mass., 1998—2002. Fellow Monbusho Rsch. fellowship, Ministry of Edn. Japan, 1994. Mem.: IEEE. Home: 90 Justice Dr Amherst MA 01002 Office: ISO New England Inc One Sullivan Rd Holyoke MA 01040 Personal E-mail: dgan2000@yahoo.com.

GANAPOL, BARRY DOUGLAS, nuclear engineering educator, consultant, aerospace engineer, mechanical engineer; b. San Francisco, May 15, 1944; s. Manny Myrvin and Miriam (Comar) G. BS, U. Calif., Berkeley, 1962-66, PhD, 1971; MS, Columbia U., 1967. Engr. Swiss Fed. Inst., Switzerland, 1971-72, Saclay, France, 1972-74, Argonne Nat. Lab., Chgo., 1974-76, cons., 1977-79; prof. U. Ariz., Tucson, 1976—, acting dept. head, 1995-97, interim dept. head aerospace and med. engring. dept., 2001—02, assoc. dept. head, 2003—. Cons. Los Alamos (N.Mex.) Nat. Labs., 1979-85, Sci. Application Inc., Albuquerque, 1979-82, Idaho Nat. Engring. Lab., Arcon Corp., 1989-91; vis. prof. U. Bologna, Italy, 1980-81, U. Torino, Italy, 1987, Weizmann Inst., 1989, U. Parma, Italy, 1992; X-TM staff Los Alamos Nat. Lab., 1999. Contbr. over 230 articles to profl. jours. NRC associateship NASA-Ames Rsch. Ctr., 1993-95; Meyerhoff fellow, 1989-90 Fellow Am. Nuclear Soc.; mem. IEEE, Am. Math. Assn., AAAS, Soc. Indsl. and Applied Math., Am. Soc. Elec. Engrs. (Ames Rsch. Ctr. faculty fellow 1996-97, 2000-02), Sigma Xi. Avocations: guitar, model building, country dancing. Home: 4012 E Calle Chica Tucson AZ 85711-4128 Office: U Ariz Dept Hydrology and Water Resources Dept Aerospace/Mech Engring Ame Bldg N727 Tucson AZ 85721

GANAS, PERRY SPIROS, physicist; b. Brisbane, Australia, June 20, 1937; came to U.S., 1968, naturalized, 1975; s. Arthur and Lula (Grivas) G. BS, U. Queensland, Australia, 1961; PhD, U. Sydney, 1968. Postdoctoral research asso., instr. U. Fla., 1968-70, vis. asst. research prof., 1972, vis. assoc. prof. physics, 1978, vis. assoc. research prof., 1979-80; prof. physics Calif. State U., Los Angeles, 1970—2001, emeritus prof., 2001—. Lectr. U. So. Calif., 1985-86, East L.A. Coll., 1988—; vis. prof. physics UCLA, summer 1987, 91, 92; referee Astrophys. Jour., Astron. and Astrophysics. Contbr. articles to profl. jours. Mem. AAUP, Congress of Faculty Assns., Am. Phys. Soc., Sigma Xi. Home: 11790 Radio Dr Los Angeles CA 90064-3615 Office: Calif State U Physics Dept Los Angeles CA 90032 E-mail: pganas@calstatela.edu.

GANASSI, CHIP, professional race car executive, owner; b. Pitts., May 24, 1958; m. Cara Ganassi; 1 child, Tessa. BA in Fin., Duquesne U., 1982. Exec. v.p. FRG Group, Pitts.; ptnr. Pitts. Pirates; promoter, co-mgr. Chgo. Motor Speedway; co-owner Target/Chip Ganassi Racing, 1990—. Former profl. race car driver; fastest of 9 rookies Indpls. 500, 1982; 8 top-10 finishes in 28 Indy car appearances, 86; ret., 86; co-owner Patrick Racing, 1988—89; established Reynard N.Am., Indpls., 1993. Office: c/o Target/Chip Ganassi Racing 7777 Woodland Dr Indianapolis IN 46278-1794

GANAWAY, GEORGE KENNETH, psychiatrist, psychoanalyst; b. Davenport, Iowa, Mar. 22, 1946; s. Kenneth Joseph and Elizabeth Earl (Baker) G.; m. Elzada Lawson, Dec. 27, 1969; children: Heather, Erin. BS in Clin. Psychology, Duke U., 1968; MD, Emory U., 1973; grad., Emory Psychoanalytic Inst., 2001. Diplomate Am. Bd. Psychiatry and Neurology; lic. physician, Ga. Resident in psychiatry Emory Affiliated Hosps., Atlanta, 1973-76; pvt. practice in gen. adult and adolescent psychiatry Atlanta, 1976—; regional med. advisor Social Security Disability Program, 1997—; pvt. practice psychoanalysis, 2001—; founder, program dir. Ridgeview Ctr. for Dissociative Disorders, Smyrna, Ga., 1987-96; med. cons. dissociative disorders Ridgeview Inst., 1996—; asst. prof. psychiatry Emory U. Sch. Medicine, Atlanta, 1976-80, clin. asst. prof. psychiatry, 1981—, Morehouse Sch. Medicine, Atlanta, 1990—; tchg. faculty Emory Psychoanalytic Inst., 1997—, assoc. tchg. analyst, 2002—. Psychiat. cons. Disability Adjudication br. Social Security Adminstrn., Atlanta, part-time, 1980-87, Douglas County Mental Health Clinic, Douglasville, 1977-81, South Cobb Mental Health Ctr., Austell, Ga., 1978-80, Atlanta Depression Clinic of Ctr. Metabolic Studies, 1976-77, others; ann. chmn. S.E. Regional Conf. Dissociative Disorders, 1987-96; courtesy staff Ridgeview Inst. Asst. editor Dissociation: Progress in Dissociative Disorders, 1988-98; assoc. editor Internat. Jour. Clin. and Exptl. Hypnosis, 1995-96; mem. editl. adv. bd. Insight mag.; editl. reviewer Am. Jour. Psychiatry, Child Abuse and Neglect: The Internat. Jour., Jour. Psychology and Theology, Jour. Nervous and Mental Disease, Dissociation: Progress in the Dissociative Disorders; contbr. articles to profl. jours., chpts. to textbooks of psychiatry. Sci. adv. bd. False Memory Syndrome Found., 1992—. Fellow: Am. Psychiat. Assn. (Disting. fellow), Internat. Soc. for Study of Dissociation (task force on stds. of practice 1991—96); mem.: Internat. Psychoanalytical Assn., Atlanta Psychoanalytic Soc. (chair sci. program com. 2001—03, pres.-elect 2003—), Ga. Psychiat. Physicians Assn., So. Med. Assn., Am. Psychoanalytic Assn. (pres. elect 2003—). Avocations: sailing, collecting maritime antiques. Office: D-201 5064 Roswell Rd NE Ste 201D Atlanta GA 30342-2266 E-mail: gganawa@emory.edu.

GANCZARCZYK, JERZY JOZEF, civil engineering educator, wastewater treatment consultant; b. Tarnow, Poland, May 25, 1928; emigrated to Can., 1969; s. Kazimierz G. and Franciszka (Adamczyk) Ganczarczyk; m. Elizabeth B. Sawczynska, Aug. 7, 1956; 1 dau., Magdalena-Lynn Ganczarczyk Hamilton. MA Sci. in Engring., Silesian Tech. U., Gliwice, Poland, 1950, D.Sc. in Engring., 1956; Habilitation, Warsaw Tech. U., Poland, 1962. Diplomate: registered profl. engr., Ont. Research engr. Silesian Tech. U., 1951-56, sr. lectr., 1956-63; head tech. lab. Hydroproject Cons., Gliwice, 1956-63; v.p., research prof. Water Mgmt. Research Inst., Warsaw, 1964-69; prof. civil engring. U. Toronto, 1969—. Cons. Bio-San Cons., Warsaw, 1968-69; mem. panel of experts WHO, Geneva, 1966-72; pres. J. Ganczarczyk & Assocs., Toronto, 1975— Author: Activated Sludge Treatment, 1966, 1969, 1983; inventor utilization of desulfurization slag, 1983, controlled inhibition of nitrification, 1988. Recipient award Ministry of Constrn., Warsaw, 1968; recipient Polish State award, Warsaw, 1969 Fellow Royal Soc. Health; mem. Water Environ. Fedn., Internat. Assn. Water Quality, Assn. Environ. Engring. Profs. Roman Catholic. Home: 83 Edenbridge Dr Islington ON Canada M9A 3G5 Office: U Toronto Dept Civil Engring Toronto ON Canada M5S 1A4 E-mail: ganc@civ.utoronto.ca.

GANDA, OM PRAKASH, physician, educator; b. W. Punjab, India, June 17, 1944; came to the U.S., 1971; s. U.D. and I.D. (Dhingra) G.; m. Kanchan M. Dewan, Dec. 21, 1975; children: Anjali, Kiran. MBBS, U. Rajasthan, India, 1966. Diplomate Am. Bd. Internal Medicine, Am. Bd. Endocrinology and Metabolism; cert. specialist in clin. nutrition Am. Bd. Nutrition. Resident in medicine All India Inst. Med. Scis., New Delhi, India, 1968-70, Lamuel Shattuck Hosp. and Tufts U. Sch. Medicine, 1971-72; clin. fellow in endocrinology and metabolism Boston VA Hosp., Tufts U. Sch. Medicine, 1972-73; rsch. fellow medicine E.P. Joslin Rsch. Lab. Peter Bent Brigham Hosp., Harvard Med. Sch., 1973-76; assoc. clin. prof. medicine Harvard Med. Sch., 1991—; sr. physician Joslin Diabetes Ctr.; attending physician Beth Israel-Deaconess Hosp., Boston, 1976—. Editl. bd. reviewer: Diabetes Rsch. and Clin. Practice, Diabetes, Diabetes Care, Diabetologia, Jour. Clin. Endocrinology and Metabolism, Jour. AMA, New Eng. Jour. Medicine; contbr. chpts. to books and articles to profl. jours. Fellow ACP, Royal Coll. Physicians and Surgeons of Can.; mem. Am. Diabetes Assn., Am. Fedn. Clin. Rsch., The Endocrine Soc., Am. Assn. Clin. Endocrinologists (bd. dirs.). Office: Joslin Diabetes Ctr 1 Joslin Pl Boston MA 02215-5306

GANDER, JOHN EDWARD, biochemistry educator; b. Roundup, Mont., Mar. 9, 1925; s. Loren Dwight and Blanche Lenore (Mackay) G.; m. Dorothy Alice Hoffman, Jan. 1, 1951; children: Sharon Lee, Peggy Corinne, Linda Kay. BS in Agr, Mont. State U., 1950; MS in Biochemistry, U. Minn., 1954, PhD, 1956. Asst. prof. chemistry Mont. State U., Bozeman, 1955-58; asst. prof. agrl. biochemistry Ohio State U., Columbus, 1958-62, assoc. prof., 1962-64, U. Minn., St. Paul, 1964-68, prof. biochemistry, 1968-84; prof., chmn. dept. microbiology and cell sci. U. Fla., 1984-89, prof., 1989-97, prof. emeritus, 1997—. Mem. external site visit rev. teams for Dept. Energy, USDA, NIH, 1979-93. Contbr. chpts. to books, articles to profl. jours. and encys. Served with USAAF, 1943-46. Recipient Research Career award NIH, 1966-71; research grantee USPHS, 1960-69, 74-87; research grantee NSF, 1957-75, 80-84 Mem. AAAS, Am. Soc. Biochemistry and Molecular Biology, Am. Chem. Soc., Am. Soc. Microbiology, Masons. Presbyterian. Home: 4219 Rancho Grande Pl NW Albuquerque NM 87120-5337 E-mail: jgander12@comcast.net.

GANDHI, MANISH P. microbiologist; b. Ahmedabad, Gujarat, India, Sept. 17, 1971; came to U.S., 1997; s. Prafulkumar K. and Preeti P. Gandhi; m. Tejal M. Gandhi, Oct. 26, 1996. BS, Gujarat U., Ahmedabad, 1992; cert. in Applied Microbiology, Sardar Patel U., Vallabh Vidyanagar, Gujarat, 1993; MS, Bhaynagar (Gujarat) U., 1995. Exec. microbiologist Torrent Gujarat Biotech. Ltd., Baroda, 1995; rschr., microbiologist Sardar Patel U., Vallabh Vidyanagar, 1995-97; microbiologist Leiner Health Products, Garden Grove, Calif., 1997—. Contbr.: Damaged Ecosystems and Restoration, 1998. Vol. Internat. Soc. Krishna Conciousness, Ahmedabad, 1990-92, Vallabh Vidyanagar, 1992-93. Mem. AAAS, Am. Soc. Microbiology. Avocations: reading and writing scientific articles, travel, philately, roller-skating. Home: 2255 Hawthorne Pl Tustin CA 92782-8364 Office: Leiner Health Products 7366 Orangewood Ave Garden Grove CA 92841-1412 E-mail: mgandhi@home.com.

GANDHI, OM PARKASH, electrical engineer; b. Multan, Pakistan, Sept. 23, 1934; came to U.S., 1967, naturalized, 1975; s. Gopal Das and Devi Bai (Patney) G.; m. Santosh Nayar, Oct. 28, 1963; children: Rajesh Timmy, Monica, Lena. BS with honors, Delhi U., India, 1952; MSE, U. Mich., 1957, Sc.D., 1961. Rsch. specialist Philco Corp., Blue Bell, Pa., 1960-62; asst. dir. Cen. Electronics Engring. Rsch. Inst., Pilani, Rajasthan, India, 1962-65, dep. dir., 1965-67; prof. elec. engring., rsch. prof. bioengring. U. Utah, Salt Lake City, 1967—, chmn. elec. engring., 1992-2000. Cons. U.S. Army Med. R & D Command, Washington, 1973-77; cons. to microwave and telecom. industry and govtl. health and safety orgns.; mem. Commns. B and K, Internation Union Radio Sci.; mem. study sect. on diagnostic radiology NIH, 1978-81. Author: Microwave Engineering and Applications, 1981; editor: Engineering in Medicine and Biology mag., 1987, Electromagnetic Biointeraction, 1989, Biological Effects and Medical Applications of Electromagnetic Energy, 1990; contbr. over 200 articles to profl. jours. Recipient Disting. Rsch. award U. Utah, 1979-80. Microwave Pioneer award IEEE-MTT Soc., 2001, Gov.'s medal for sci. and tech. State of Utah, 2002; grantee NSF, NIH, EPA, USAF, U.S. Army, USN, N.Y. State Dept. Health, others. Fellow IEEE (editor spl. issue Procs. IEEE 1980, co-chmn. com. on RF safety stds. 1988-97, Tech. Achievement award Utah sect. 1975, Utah Engr. of Yr. 1995), Am. Inst. for Med. and Biol. Engring.; mem. Electromagnetics Acad., Bioelectromagnetics Soc. (bd. dirs. 1979-82, 87-90, v.p., pres. 1991-94, d'Arsonval award 1995). Office: Univ Utah Dept Elec Engring 3280 Merrill Engring Salt Lake City UT 84112 Business E-Mail: gandhi@ece.utah.edu.

GANDHI, PRITESH, medical educator; b. Nairobi, Kenya, Oct. 23, 1973; s. Jitendra and Urmila Gandhi; m. Nital Gandhi, Sept. 1, 2002. PharmD, Mass. Coll. Pharmacy and Health Scis., 1997. Pharmacy State of Ill., 1997. Resident in pharmacy practice U. Ill. Coll. Pharmacy, Chgo., 1997—98; asst. prof. of pharmacy practice Mass. Coll. Pharmacy, Worcester, 1998—. Cardiovasc. pharmacotherapy specialist U. Mass. Meml. Health Care, Worcester, 1998—; adj. asst. prof. of medicine U. Mass. Med. Sch., Worcester, 2000—. Contbr. articles to profl. jours. Grantee, Wyeth and Scios Inc., 2000, 2002. Mem.: Am. Coll. Clin. Pharmacy (full mem. 1996—2002). Achievements include research in patient adherence to pharmacological therapy. Office: Mass Coll Pharmacy 19 Foster St Worcester MA 01608 E-mail: pgandhi@mcp.edu., pgandhi@mcp.edu.

GANDOLF, RAYMOND L. media correspondent; b. Norwalk, Ohio, Apr. 2, 1930; s. Raymond L. Gandolf and Rose (Brenner) Gandolf Neller; m. Blanche Haywood Cholet, Oct. 13, 1956; children— Alexandra, Jessica, Victoria, Amanda, Susanna BS in Speech, Northwestern U., 1951. Actor, 1951-62; writer, producer WCBS-TV, N.Y.C., 1963-65; writer, corr. CBS News, N.Y.C., 1965-82; corr. ABC News-Sports, N.Y.C., 1982-92, host Our World, 1986-87. Panel mem. Dictionary of Contemporary Usage, 1985 Recipient Peabody award U. Ga., 1980, Dupont award Columbia U., 1981, Emmy award, 1987. Mem. AFTRA, Writers Guild Am.

GANDOLFINI, JAMES, actor; b. Westwood, N.J., Sept. 18, 1961; Actor: (films) A Stranger Among Us, 1992, Mr. Wonderful, 1993, Italian Movie, 1993, True Romance, 1993, Angie, 1994, Terminal Velocity, 1994, Le Nouveau Monde, 1995, Crimson Tide, 1995, Get Shorty, 1995, The Juror, 1995, Night Falls on Manhattan, 1997, She's So Lovely, 1997, Perdita Durango, 1997, Fallen, 1998, The Mighty, 1998, A Civil Action, 1998, Wild Flowers, 1999, 8MM, 1999, Blow, 2000, The Mexican, 2001, The Man Who Wasn't There, 2001, The Last Castle, 2001; (TV movie) 12 Angry Men, 1997, guest appearances (TV series) Gun, 1997, (TV series) The Sopranos, 1999— (Emmy award best actor drama, 2000, 2001, 2003, Golden Globe best actor drama, 2000, Screen Actors Guild award best actor drama, 2000, 2003, TV Critics Assoc. award, 1999, 2000, 2001). Office: c/o Sanders Mgmt 2211 Corinth Ave Ste 210 Los Angeles CA 90064-1621*

GANDOLFO, LUCIAN JOHN, minister, federal official; b. Chgo., Aug. 28, 1954; s. Michael and Elda (Campi) G.; m. Lisa Mary Thornton, Aug. 24, 1985; children: Landon, Lindsay, Lauren, Lucian-Michael. AA, John Jay Coll. Criminal Justice City N.Y., 1979; AS, SUNY, Albany, 1978; BS, SUNY, Briarcliff Manor, 1980; MS, L.I. U., 1982; DD (hon.), So. Calif. Grad. Sch. Theology, 1996. Ordained to ministry, Christian Ch. of N.Am., 1996. Spl. agt. FBI, New Orleans, 1984-86, N.Y.C., 1986-95, supervisory spl. agt. Washington, 1995-97, supervisory sr. resident agt. Scranton, Pa., 1997—2002, asst. spl. agt. in charge N.Y.C., 2002—; pres. ea. dist. Christ Crusaders Christian Ch. N.Am., 1988-94; min. Italian Christian Ch., Astoria, N.Y., 1991-95, asst. pastor, 1991-94, interim pastor, 1994-95, dist. presbyter, 1996—; nat. edn. dir. Christian Ch. N.Am., 1997—; pastor Grace Full Gospel Ch. of Newark, NJ, 2001—02. Mem. Christian Ch. N. Am. (asst. dist. overseer ea. dist 2000—). E-mail: ccnaeduc@juno.com. *The greatest accomplishment in one's life is to be found in right relationship with his Creator. The Greatest honor and fulfillment a person can ever experience is to receive and obey the call of God in his (her) life.*

GANDSEY, LOUIS JOHN, petroleum and environmental consultant; b. Greybull, Wyo., May 19, 1921; s. John Wellington and Leonora (McLaughlin) G.; m. Mary Louise Alviso, Nov. 10, 1945; children: Mary M., Catherine K., John P., Michael J., Laurie A. AA, Compton Jr. Coll., 1941; BS, U. Calif., Berkeley, 1943; M in Engring., UCLA, 1958. Registered profl. engr., Calif. With Richfield Oil Corp., L.A., 1943-65, process engr., foreman, mfg. coord., 1943-61, project leader process computer control, 1961-63, light oil per. supt., 1963-64, refinery supt., 1964-65; mgr. planning Richfield div. Atlantic Richfield Co., L.A., 1966-68, mgr. evaluation products div., 1968-69, gen. mgr. supply and transp. Chgo., 1969-71, mgr. planning and mgmt. sci. N.Y.C., 1971, mgr. supply and transp. L.A., 1971-72, mgr. coordination and supply, 1972-75, mgr. domestic crude, 1975-77; v.p. refining Lunday-Thagard Oil Co., South Gate, Calif., 1977-82; petroleum cons. World Oil Corp., L.A., 1982-85; gen. petroleum cons., 1986—. Instr. chem. and petroleum tech. L.A. Harbor Coll., 1960-65; cons. on oil crops, Austria, 1991; U.S. del. in environ. affairs to Joint Inter-Govtl. Com. for Environ. Protection, USSR, 1991, asphalt tech. to Joint Inter-Govtl. Com. for Highway Design CWS, 1992; U.S. del. Econ. and Environ. Affairs, Portugal, Spain, 1994, Hist. & Econ. Affairs, Mexico, 1995, Basque Country, Spain, 1996. Contbr. articles to profl. jours. Served with C.E., AUS, 1944-45. Mem. AICE, Am. Chem. Soc., Calif. Soc. Profl. Engrs. Home: 2340 Neal Spring Rd Templeton CA 93465-8413 E-mail: marjon@tcsn.net.

GANDY, BONNIE SERGIACOMI, oncological and intravenous therapy nurse; b. Bridgeton, N.J., July 12, 1952; d. Albert A. and Jean (Goodwin) Sergiacomi; m.Robert H. Gandy, Aug. 15, 1981 (dec.); 1 child, Anthony Robert. BA, Glassboro (N.J.) State Coll., 1974; ADN, Cumberland County Coll., Vineland, N.J., 1985; BSN, U. Winston-Salem, 1999. RN, N.J., N.C., S.C., Va.; cert. tchr., N.J.; cert. oncology nurse, intravenous nurse. Staff nurse, charge nurse William B. Kessler Meml. Hosp., Hammonton, N.J., 1985-86; supr. med. outpatient unit South Jersey Hosp. System-Millville (N.J.) Div., 1986-93; dir. home care nursing Med IV Home Health Svcs., Hickory, N.C., 1994-95. IV nurse cons., IV therapist Am. Pharm. Svcs./Omnicare, Hickory, N.C., 1995—. Mem. Infusion Nurse's Soc., Oncology Nursing Soc., Phi Theta Kappa, Sigma Theta Tau Internat. E-mail: bonboni@charter.net.

GANDY, GERALD LARMON, rehabilitation counseling educator, psychologist, writer; b. Thomasville, Ga., Feb. 9, 1941; s. Larmon Brinkley and Ruby Wylene (Vickers) G.; m. Patricia Kay Haltiwanger, Jan. 22, 1966. BA, Fla. State U., 1963; MA, U. S.C., 1968, PhD, 1971. Lic. profl. counselor, Va.; lic. clin. psychologist, Va.; nat. cert. rehab. counselor; nat. cert. counselor; nat. registered psychologist; cert. profl. qualification in psychology Assn. of State and Provincial Psychology Bds. Profl. counselor U. S.C. Counseling Ctr., Columbia, 1968-70; counseling psychologist VA Regional Office, Columbia, 1970-75, chief counseling psychologist, 1974-75; ind. cons., prof. emeritus Med. Coll. Va., Va. Commonwealth U., Richmond, 1996—, prof., program dir., 1975-95. Chair nat. com. on undergrad. rehab. edn. Nat. Coun. on Rehab. Edn., 1984-89; mem. numerous state and govt. adv. coms., 1970—; cons. in field.. Author: Mental Health Rehabilitation, 1995; co-author: Rehabilitation and Disability, 1990; co-author/editor: Rehabilitation Counseling and Services, 1987, Counseling in the Rehabilitation Process, 1999; co-editor: International Rehabilitation, 1980, 89; contbr. numerous articles to profl. jours. Faculty pres. Sch. of Community and Pub. Affairs, VA Commonwealth U., 1989-93. Capt. U.S. Army, 1963-66. Recipient Disting. Svc. award Sch. of Community and Pub. Affairs, 1988, School and U. Leadership award, 1993. Fellow Internat. Acad. of Behavioral Medicine, Counseling and Psychotherapy (diplomate); mem. APA, ACA, World Fedn. for Mental Health, Phi Kappa Phi. Home and Office: Highland Springs 300 Southern Ct Richmond VA 23075-1519 E-mail: ggandy@vcu.org.

GANDY, H. CONWAY, retired judge, state official; b. Washington, Nov. 3, 1934; s. Hoke and Anne B. (Conway) G.; m. Carol Anderson, Aug. 29, 1965; children: Jennifer, Constance, Margaret. BA, Colo. State U., 1962; JD, U. Denver, 1968. Bar: Colo. 1969, U.S. Dist. Ct. Colo. 1969. Pvt. practice, Ft. Collins, Colo., 1969-81; adminstrv. law judge divsn. adminstrv. hearings State of Colo., Denver, 1981-99. Bd. dirs. Foothills-Gateway Rehab. Ctr., 1970-80, Colo. State Bd. Dental Examiners, 1976-81; Dem. candidate for Colo. Senate, 1974, dist. atty., 1976; trustee Internat. Bluegrass Music Assn. Trust Fund, 1990—; pres. Colo. chpt. Nat. Assn. Adminstrv. Law Judges, 1985-86. With USN, 1954-58. Mem. Sertoma (Centurion award 1973, Tribune award 1975, Senator award 1977, 79, sec. Honor club 1977-78, pres. Ft. Collins club 1978-79, pres. Front Range club 1988-89). Home: 724 Winchester Dr Fort Collins CO 80526-2636 E-mail: hcgcag@comcast.net.

GANDY, HORTENSE M. retired endocrinologist; b. Society Hill, S.C., Jan. 30, 1922; d. Roland and Louise (Humbert) G.; m. Flemming H. Carstensen, Dec. 31, 1971. BS, West Chester U., 1943; MS, U. Pa., 1947; MD, Howard U., 1951. From rsch. assoc. to assoc. prof. Cornell U. Med. Sch., N.Y.C., 1962-74; prof., chief medicine U. Papua New Guinea, 1975-78; Locum physician Kaiser Permanente, Honolulu, 1978—99; ret., 1999. Mem. study sect. growth and devel. NIH, 1971-73. Co-editor: Gonadotropins, 1973; contbr. articles to profl. jours. Recipient Disting. Alumni award West Chester U., 1993. Fellow ACP (laureate 1991), Royal Australasian Coll. Physicians; mem. Endocrine Soc. Avocations: orchids, needlework, reading. Home: 1645 Ala Wai Blvd Ph 3 Honolulu HI 96815-1008

GANDY, KIM ALLISON, lawyer; b. Bossier City, La., Jan. 25, 1954; d. Alfred K. and Roma Rae (Young) Gandy. GBS, La. Tech. U., 1973; JD, Loyola U., 1978. Bar: La. 1978, U.S. Dist. Ct. (ea. and we. dists.) La. 1980, U.S. Supreme Ct. 1981, U.S. Ct. Appeals (5th cir.) 1982. Mgr. South Ctrl. Bell Tel. Co., New Orleans, 1973—77; asst. dist. atty. Orleans Parish, New Orleans, 1978—79; sole practice New Orleans, 1979—. Guest lectr. in field. Treas. ERA United Coalition La., 1977—78; chmn. New Orleans del. La. Dem. Conv., 1980, 1982; vice chmn. New Orleans del., 1984; dir. Women's Lobby Network, 1980—85; founder Greater New Orleans Assn. Dem. Women, 1984. Named New Orleans Outstanding Young Career Woman, New Orleans Bus. and Profl. Women, 1980; named one of New Orleans 100 Women in Forefront, 1986; recipient Law Alumni award, Loyola U., 1976, Milton Sheen award, 1978. Mem.: ABA, Assn. Women Attys., La. Trial Lawyers Assn., La. Bar Assn., NOW (nat. dir. 1982—, exec. v.p. 1991—, Woman of Yr.). Home: 630 G St NE Washington DC 20002-4306 Office: 1826 St Claude Ave Suite 100 New Orleans LA 70116

GANDY, MAURICE EDWARD, English language educator, writer; b. Ely, Nev., Sept. 21, 1941; s. Maurice Edwin and Esther Ruth (Hutson) G.; m. Janice Kay Mitchell, Dec. 27, 1970; children: Maribeth, Megan Claire. BA in English, U. Ariz., 1966; MA in English, Ariz. State U., 1971. Instr. English Bishop State C.C., Mobile, Ala., 1979—. Adj. instr. English U. South Ala., Mobile, 1973—; sponsor and moderator creatinve writing and bus. writing seminars; contract feature writer Mobile Register, 1991—. Auithor: (poetry books) An Uncharted Inch, 1982, The Calpocalypse—A Cinovepoem, 1992; contbg. author: Literary Mobile, 2002; contbr. works to ref. publs. and poetry to anthologies. Recipient Hon. mention Writer's Digest Nat. Contest, 1988, 92. Mem. Nat. Coun. Tchrs. English, Soc. Children's Books Writers and Illustrators, Ala. Coun. Tchrs. English, Gulf Coast Assn. Creative Writing Instrs. Episcopalian. Avocation: fitness training. Home: 320 N University Blvd Mobile AL 36608 Office: Bishop State CC 351 N Broad St Mobile AL 36603-5898 E-mail: mgandy1110@aol.com.

GANEV, VENELIN IORDANOV, political scientist, educator; b. Sofia, Bulgaria, Aug. 26, 1965; s. Iordan Venelinov Ganev and Maria Georgieva Ganeva; m. Mila Mois Aroyo, Feb. 20, 1988; children: Iordan Venelinov, Martin Venelin. PhD, U. Chgo., 2000. Asst. prof. polit. sci. Miami U., Oxford, Ohio, 2001—. Office: Miami Univ Ohio 316 Harrison Hall Oxford OH 45056

GANG, VANESSA NOBLE, health facility administrator, researcher, nursing consultant; b. N.Y.C., Nov. 24, 1938; d. Edward John and Barbara Jeanne (Day) Noble; m. Seymour Gang, Sept. 17, 1970 (dec. 1976); children: Tahri, Rick. BSN, Columbia U., 1964. RN NY, cert. cmty. health, care mgmt. Rsch. asst. Sch. Medicine Harvard U., Boston, 1959-61; pub. health nurse N.Y.C. Dept. Health, 1964-68; head nurse Beth Israel Hosp., N.Y.C., 1968-71; rsch. project dir. Sch. Pub. Health Cornell U., N.Y.C., 1977-78; patient svc. mgr. Vis. Nurse Svc. N.Y., N.Y.C., 1978-80; cons. multiple home care agys. N.Y.C., 1985—98; co-founder, exec. dir. Cons. in Care, Bronx, NY, 1985—; DON Counseling Home Care Svcs., N.Y.C., 1989-91. Lectr. Columbia U., N.Y.C., 1995—, N.Y.C. Dept. Aging, 1995—96; student placement Lehman Coll., 1997; mem. faculty N.Y. Consortium Geriat. Edn. Ctrs., 1998—. Author: The Discovery Method: Clinical Interventions for Dementia, 2000. Columbia U. rsch. grantee, 1997; recipient Cmty. Svc. award N.Y.C. Bd. Edn., 1966, Sch. Nursing Disting. Alumni award Columbia U., 1998. Fellow: Am. Assn. Integrated Medicine; mem.: APHA, Nat. Assn Geriatric Care Mgrs., Gerontol. Soc. Am., Nat. Assn. Profl. Geriatric Care Mgrs., Riverdale Garden Club, Riverdale Yacht Club (bd. govs. 1983—86). Democrat. Avocation: poetry writing. Home: 405 W 263rd St Bronx NY 10471-1138 Office: Cons in Care 3725 Henry Hudson Pkwy W Bronx NY 10463-3657 E-mail: caremanagers@aol.com.

GANGAROSA, RAYMOND EUGENE, epidemiologist, electrical engineer; b. Rochester, N.Y., July 1, 1951; s. Eugene John and Rose Christine (Salamone) G. BA, Emory U., 1972; MSEE, Ga. Inst. Tech., 1976; MD, Med. Coll. Ga., 1980; M in Pub. Health, Emory U., 1991. Diplomate Am. Bd. Internal Medicine. Rsch. technician Electromagnetic Scis., Inc., Altanta, 1973-74; med. resident U. Md., Balt., 1980-81; clin. scientist Picker Internat., Cleve., 1981-88; vis. scientist Ctrs. for Disease Control, Atlanta, 1990—; doctoral candidate Emory U., Atlanta, 1990—; rsch. fellow Emory U. Ethics Ctr., 1994—; med. epidemiologist Ga. Divsn. Pub. Health, 1995-97. Coord. Instl. Rev. Bd., Cleve., 1982-84, 86-87; cons. Novel Imager Design Team, Cleve., 1987-88. Editor Picker Internat. Newsletter, 1985-87; coord. audiovisual tng. courses for magnetic resonance imaging, 1982-84; contbr. articles to profl. and law jours. Campaign dir. David Drexel for State Senate, Chapel Hill, N.C., 1972; sculptor Toys on Request, 1982—; coord. Control Alcohol, Tobacco and Drug Use, Atlanta, 1989—. Mem. AAAS, Am. Pub. Health Assn., N.Y. Acad. Scis., Soc. for Epidemiologic Rsch. Achievements include patents in magnetic resonance imaging cardiac/respiratory gating system; in integrated expert system for medical imaging scan, setup, scheduling; in reduced weight iron core magnetic resonance scanner; invented reduced weight magnet return path using correction fields, horizontal field iron core magnetic resonance scanner, litigation strategies against tobacco companies to recover health care costs, surveillance of infant mortality and child abuse, systems approach to infant mortality and addiction. E-mail: bubm@mindspring.com.

GANGLE, SANDRA SMITH, arbitrator, mediator; b. Brockton, Mass., Jan. 11, 1943; d. Milton and Irene M. (Powers) Smith; m. Eugene M. Gangle, Dec. 21, 1968; children: Melanie Jean, Jonathan Rocco. BA, Coll. New Rochelle, 1964; MA, U. Oreg.; JD, Willamette U., 1980. Bar: Oreg. 1980. Instr. French Oreg. State U., Corvallis, 1968-71, Willamette U., Salem, Oreg., 1971-74; Instr. ESL Chemeketa C.C., Salem, 1975-79; labor arbitrator Salem, 1980—; pvt. practice, 1980-86, 96—; ptnr. Depenbrock, Gangle & Greer, 1986-96. Mem. Oreg., Idaho, Wash., Mont., Calif. and Alaska Arbitration Panels; mem. NASD securities arbitration and mediation panel, mediator employment bus. and disabilities disputes; clin. prof. Portland State U., 1981-84; cons. State Oreg., 1981; land use hearings officer City of Keizer, Oreg., 1985-91; mem. mediation panel for disabilities issues Key Bridge Found., 1995—; mem. USPS Redress mediation panel, 2000 . Contbr. articles to profl. jours. Land-use chmn. Faye Wright Neighborhood Assn., Salem, 1983-84; mem. Civil Svc. Commn., Marion County Fire Dist., Salem, 1983-89; mem. U.S. Postal Svc. Expedited Arbitration Panel, 1984-91; mem. Salem Neighbor-to-Neighbor Mediation Panel, 1986-91; mem. labor arbitrator panel Fed. Mediation & Conciliation Svc., 1986—; mem. panel Prudential APCOM reviewers, 1999-2000; ct. apptd. arbitrator, mediator Marion, Polk & Yamhill Counties, 1996—; mem. Marion County Cir. Ct. Dispute Resolution Commn., 1993-95; trustee Salem Peace Plaza, 1985-97; convenor Salem Peace Roundtable, 1995; bd. dirs. Salem YWCA, 1997-2002; bd. dirs. Salem City Club, 1998-2003, pres., 2001; chair planning com. joint conf. between Oreg. Women Lawyers and Assn. Women Solicitors, 1998. NDEA fellow, 1967. Fellow Chartered Inst. Arbitrators (London); mem. Am. Arbitration Assn. (arbitrator/mediator), Assn. for Conflict Resolution (chpt. co-pres. 1993-94), Oreg. State Bar Assn. Office: Sandra Smith Gangle PC PO Box 904 Salem OR 97308 E-mail: gangle@open.org.

GANGSTAD, JOHN ERIK, lawyer; b. New Brunswick, N.J., May 16, 1948; s. Edward Otis and Ruth Margaret (Fletcher) G.; m. Cynthia Diane Coffman, July 5, 1974; children: Allison, Erik, Amy. BA, U. Tex., 1970, JD, 1974. Bar: Tex. 1974, U.S. Dist. Ct. (no. dist.) Tex. 1974. Assoc. Turner, Hitchins, McInnery, Webb & Hartnett, Dallas, 1974-76, ptnr., 1977-81, Brown McCarroll & Oaks Hartline, L.L.P., Austin, Tex., 1982-2000, Bickerstaff, Heath et al, Austin, 2000—. Partnership com. State Bar Tex., 1981-98. Bd. dirs. Found. for the Homeless, Austin, 1988—. With USNG. Mem. ABA, Tex. Bar Assn., Order of Coif. Presbyterian. Avocations: golf, reading. Home: 3106 Eaneswood Dr Austin TX 78746-6717 Office: Bickerstaff Heath et al 1700 FrostBank Plz 816 Congress Ave Ste 1700 Austin TX 78701-2443 E-mail: jgangstad@bickerstaff.com.

GANGWAL, RAKESH, airline executive; b. Calcutta, India, July 25, 1953; arrived in U.S., 1977, permanent resident; s. K. P. and C. D. Gangwal; m. Shobha Agarwal, Mar. 16, 1983. ME, Indian Inst. Tech., 1975; MBA, U. Pa., 1979. With cen. planning dept. Philips India Ltd., Calcutta, 1975-77; fin. analyst Ford Motor Co., Dearborn, Mich., 1979-80; assoc. Booz, Allen & Hamilton, Chgo., 1980-84; mgr. strategic planning United Airlines, Chgo., 1984-85, dir. flight bus. plans, 1985-86, v.p. flight adminstrn., 1986-87, v.p. revenue mgmt., 1987-94; exec. v.p. planning and devel. Air France, 1994-96; pres., CEO, U.S. Airways Group Inc., Arlington, Va., 1996—. Bd. dirs. Boise Cascade Corp.; bd. dirs. Air Transport Assn., Indian CEO High Tech Coun. Office: US Airways Group Inc 2345 Crystal Dr Arlington VA 22227-0001

GANI, JOSEPH MARK, statistics educator, administrator, researcher; b. Cairo, Dec. 15, 1924; came to U.S., 1981; s. Mark Joseph and Lucie (Israel) G.; m. Ruth Stephens, Sept. 3, 1955 (dec. Jan. 1997); children: Jonathan, Miriam, Matthew, Sarah. BSc, London U., 1947; diploma, Imperial Coll., 1948; PhD, Australian Nat. U., Canberra, 1955; DSc, London U., 1970; DSc (hon.), Sheffield U., 1989, Wollongong U., 1991. Lectr. math stats. U. Western Australia, Perth, 1953-57, sr. lectr., 1957-59, reader, 1959-60; sr. fellow Australian Nat. U., 1961-64; prof. U. Sheffield, Eng., 1965-74; chief divsn. math. and stats. Commonwealth Sci. and Indsl. Research Orgn., Canberra, 1974-81; prof. stats., chmn. dept. U. Ky., Lexington, 1981-85; prof. dept. stats. U. Calif., Santa Barbara, 1985-94; ret., 1994. Hon. vis. fellow Australian Nat. U., 1995-97, 2001—, fellow, 1998-2000; adj. prof. U. Tech. Sydney, 2001—. Author: The Condition of Science in Australian Universities, 1963; editor: Perspectives in Probability and Statistics, 1975, The Making of Statisticians, 1982, The Craft of Probabilistic Modelling, 1986, (with D.J. Daley) Epidemic Modelling: An Introduction, 1999; mng. editor: Applied Probability Jours., 1964—; advisor: Springer-Verlag Series in Statistics, 1976-95. Gov. High Storrs Sch., Sheffield, 1971-74; founder mem. South Yorkshire Family Housing Assn., Sheffield, 1972. Nuffield Found. fellow, 1956; Australian Acad. Sci. fellow, 1976, recipient Pitman medal Statis. Soc. Australia, 1994, Moyal medal of Macquarie U., 2000; named Mem. of the Order of Australia, 2000, Centenary medal, 2003. Fellow Inst. Math. Stats., Royal Statis. Soc., Am. Statis. Assn., mem. Am. Math. Soc., Internat. Statis. Inst., Australian Math. Soc. (pres. 1978-80) Office: Australian Nat U Math Scis Inst Canberra ACT 0200 Australia E-mail: gani@maths.anu.edu.au.

GANJI, JAGADEESH (JAY), cardiologist; b. Nov. 26, 1964; arrived in US, 1993; MD, JJM Med. Coll., Davanlere, India, 1988. Intern JJM Med. Coll., Davangere, 1988—89, resident in internal medicine, 1992, Chigateri Gen. Hosp., Davangere, 1989—90, St. John Hosp. and Med. Ctr., Detroit, 1994—97, cardiovascular fellow, 1997—2000, interventional cardiovascular fellow, 2000—01; cardiologist Mid Carolina Cardiology, Gastonia, NC, 2000—01, Southeastern Heart & Vascular Ctr., Greensboro, NC, 2001—. Office: Southeastern Heart & Vascular Ctr 1331 N Elm St Greensboro NC 27401 Office Fax: 336-275-0433.

GANLEY, ALBERT C. retired private school educator, writer; b. Glens Falls, N.Y., Mar. 14, 1918; s. Albert Charles and Verna Adelaide (Holland) G.; m. Barbara Ellen Thorpe, Aug. 11, 1951; children: David, Michael, Barbara. BA, Williams Coll., 1939; MA, Cornell U., 1940. Instr. in history Vestal (N.Y.) Ctrl. Sch., 1940-42, Williams Coll., Williamstown, Mass., 1946-47, Manhasset (N.Y.) H.S., 1947-64, Phillips Exeter Acad., Exeter, N.H., 1964-87, chmn. history dept., 1969-74, Cowles prof., 1982. Grader advanced placement exams Ednl. Testing Svc., Princeton, N.J., 1958-61; master tchr. Harvard U. Grad. Sch. Edn., Cambridge, Mass., summer sessions, 1959-64; vis. instr. history La Jolla (Calif.) Country Day Sch., 1978-79. Author: The Progressive Movement, 1964, Japan: A Short History, 1989; (workbook) History of a Free People, 1971; co-author: The USA Since 1945: After Hiroshima, 1993. Sgt. USAF, 1942-45, PTO. John Hay fellow, 1959-60; vis. scholar Peter House Coll., Cambridge, Eng., 1968-69. Home: 7 Riverwoods Dr Apt C109 Exeter NH 03833-4373

GANLEY, JAMES POWELL, ophthalmologist, educator; b. Altadina, Calif., Apr. 25, 1937; s. Joseph Harrington and Ruth Alice (Carr) G.; m. Anne Hay Hunter, Aug. 7, 1965; children: Anne Hay, Susan Powell, Katherine Carr, Elizabeth Pearson. BS in Biology, Mt. St. Mary's Coll., 1959; MD, Georgetown U., 1963; MPH, Johns Hopkins U., 1969, DPH, 1972. Diplomate Am. Bd. Med. Examiners, Am. Bd. Preventive Medicine (fellow), Am. Bd. Ophthalmology (fellow). Intern Washington Hosp. Ctr., 1963-64; resident in ophthalmology SUNY Upstate Med. Ctr., Syracuse, 1965-68; resident in preventive medicine Johns Hopkins U., Balt., 1969-71; sr. staff fellow Nat. Eye Inst., NIH, Bethesda, Md., 1971-74; asst. prof. ophthalmology U. Ariz. Med. Ctr., Tucson, 1974-80; assoc. prof., dept. head La. State U. Med. Ctr., Shreveport, 1980-82, asst. dean clin. affairs, 1981-87, prof., head dept., 1982-97, prof., 1998—. Mem. sci. adv. panel Onchocerciasis Control Program, WHO, Geneva, Switzerland, 1974-79; med. adv. bd. Internat. Eye Found., Bethesda, 1974-77; ophthalmic drugs adv. com. FDA, HEW, Rockville, Md., 1976-82; mem. epidemiol. and disease control study sect. NIH, 1982-86. Author: book chpts., procs.; editor: Ophthalmic Epidemiology, 1993—; editl. bd. Sightsaver, Nat. Soc. to Prevent Blindness, 1982—86, Evidence-Based Eye Care, 1999—. Bd. dirs. Northwest Lions Eye Bank, Shreveport, 1987. Lt. USN, 1964-65. Mem. Am. Coll. Preventive Medicine, Am. Acad. Ophthalmology (com. rsch. regulatory agys. and fed. sys. 1986-91, chmn. 1990-91), Internat. Soc. Geog. Ophthalmology (pres. 1982-88, treas. 1988—, exec. bd. 1988—), Am. Coll. Epidemiology, La. Assn. Blind (bd. dirs. 1980-96, 1st vice chmn., sec. exec. bd. 1989-91, chmn. bd. 1992-93), Shreveport Med. Soc. (bd. dirs. 1990-96, 2d v.p. 1993, 1st v.p. 1994, pres. 1995), Assn. Rsch. in Vision and Ophthalmology (program planning com. 1993-96, internat. mems. com. 2001—), Revs. Rsch. NIH. Republican. Roman Catholic. Avocations: tennis, swimming, sailing. Office: La State Univ Med Ctr 1501 Kings Hwy Shreveport LA 71103-3932 E-mail: jganle@lsuhsc.edu.

GANLEY, OSWALD HAROLD, university official; b. Amsterdam, The Netherlands, Jan. 28, 1929; came to U.S., 1947, naturalized, 1952; s. Eric Harold and Emily (Auerbach) G.; m. Gladys Dickens, Sept. 3, 1950; children: Robert C., Delia A. AB, Hope Coll., 1950; MS, PhD, U. Mich., 1953; MPA, Harvard U., 1965. Cert. physician asst. Rsch. asst. Walter Reed Inst., 1953-55; rsch. assoc. Merck Inst. Therapeutic Rsch., Rahway, N.J., 1955-60; asst. dir. internat. rels. Merck, Sharp and Dohme Rsch. Labs., Rahway, 1960-64; head tech. div. Bur. Internat. Sci. and Tech. Affairs, State Dept., 1965-66, head European affairs, 1966-69; sci. attaché Am. Embassy, Rome and Bucharest, 1969-73; dir. Soviet and Eastern European sci. and tech. affairs State Dept., Washington, 1973-75; diplomatic advisor to sci. adv. to pres. Washington, 1973-78; dep. asst. sec. for tech. affairs State Dept., Washington, 1975-78; rsch. assoc. John F. Kennedy Sch. Govt. Harvard U., Cambridge, Mass., 1978-80; exec. dir. Harvard Program Info. Resources Policy, 1980-94; ret., 1994. Lectr. in pub. policy Harvard U., 1980—94, Cardiology Assocs., Duke U. Med. Ctr., 1997—2001; with The Healing Place of Wake County Clinics, 2001—; prin. investigator rsch. N.C. Physicians Health Program, 2001—, bd. dirs., 2002—. Author: To Inform or to Control?, 1982, 2d edit., 1989, The Global Political Impact of VCRs, 1987; contbr. articles to sci. jours. Bd. dirs. Jaycees, 1958-60, Am. Hosp., Rome, Fulbright Commn., Ctr. Info. Policy Rsch., 1992—; dir. pub. rels. CD, Plainfield, N.J., 1962-64. Served with AUS, 1953-55, USPHS Res., 1956-84. Sci. and Pub. Policy fellow Harvard U., 1964-65 Fellow Am. Acad. Physician Assts., Am. Acad. Microbiology; mem. Am. Physiol. Soc., Am. Soc. Microbiology, Assn. Mil. Surgeons, Sigma Xi. Clubs: Circolo Catoniere Tevereremo (Rome); Cosmos; Harvard (N.Y.C.). Home: 408 N Estes Dr Chapel Hill NC 27514-7629

GANN, JOYCE ANN, obstetrician-gynecologist; b. Detroit, Apr. 14, 1937; MD, Med. Coll. Ga., 1963. Diplomate Am. Bd. Ob-Gyn. Intern Ga. Bapt. Hosp., Atlanta, 1963-64, resident in ob-gyn., 1964-67; pvt. practice Decatur, Ga. Mem. staff DeKalb Med. Ctr. (formerly DeKalb Gen. Hosp.), Decatur, Emory Eastside Hosp., Snellville, Ga. Fellow ACOG; mem. AMA, So. Med. Assn. Office: 2675 N Decatur Rd Ste 303 Decatur GA 30033-6132 also: 1700 Tree Ln Ste 250 Snellville GA 30078-6762 E-mail: jgann6070@aol.com.

GANN, PAMELA BROOKS, academic administrator; b. 1948; BA, U. N.C., 1970; JD, Duke U., 1973. Bar: Ga. 1973, N.C. 1974. Assoc. King & Spalding, Atlanta, 1973; 1975assoc. Robinson, Bradshaw & Hinson, P.A., Charlotte, 1974; asst. prof. Duke U. Sch. Law, Durham, 1975—78, assoc. prof., 1978—80, prof., 1980—99, dean, 1988—99; pres. Claremont McKenna Coll., Claremont, Calif., 1999—. Vis. asst. prof. U. Mich. Law Sch., 1977; vis. assoc. prof. U. Va., 1980 Author: (with D. Kahn) Corporate Taxation and Taxation of Partnerships and Partners, 1979, 83, 89; article editor Duke Law Jour. Mem. Am. Law Inst., Coun. Fgn. Rels., Order of Coif, Phi Beta Kappa Office: Claremont McKenna Coll Office Pres 500 E 9th St Claremont CA 91711-5903

GANNAM, MICHAEL JOSEPH, lawyer; b. Savannah, Ga., Nov. 10, 1922; s. Karam George and Annie (Abraham) G.; m. Marion Collins DeFrank, June 11, 1949; children: James, Ann, Elizabeth, Joseph. JD, U. Ga., 1948; MA, U. N.C., 1950. Bar: Ga. 1948, U.S. Dist. Ct. (so. dist.) Ga. 1950, U.S. Supreme Ct. 1971, U.S. Ct. Appeals (11th cir.) 1971. Assoc. Bouhan, Lawrence, Williams & Levy, Savannah, Ga., 1950-59; ptnr. Findley, Shea, Friedman, Gannam, Head & Buchsbaum, Savannah, Ga., 1959-70, atty. pvt. practice, 1970-81; sr. ptnr. Gannam and Gnann, Savannah, Ga., 1981—. Instr. bus. law polit. sci. and history Armstrong State Univ., 1951-62, mem. new campus planning and design com. Bd. dirs. Historic Savannah Found.; bd. dirs., legal counsel Telfair Acad. Arts & Scis.; past pres. Legal Aid Soc. Savannah; mem. Savannah-Chatham Bd. Zoning Appeals, 1961-63, Savannah Arts Com., 1982-85; chmn. Gilmer Lectr. Series Fund, 1980—; bd. dirs. Savannah Coun. World Affairs, 1983-87; pres. Savannah Bar Assn.; bd. govs. State Bar Ga., 1968-99; mem. New Chatham County Courthouse Planning and Design Com.; mem. Ga. Bicentennial Commn., 1986, 87, 88. With USAAF, PTO, 1943-46. Home: 235 E Gordon St Savannah GA 31401-5003 Office: Gannam & Gnann 130 W Bay St Savannah GA 31401-1109 E-mail: jgannam@gannam-gnann.com.

GANNON, SISTER ANN IDA, retired philosophy educator, former college administrator; b. Chgo., 1915; d. George and Hanna (Murphy) G. AB, Clarke Coll., 1941; A.M., Loyola U., Chgo., 1948, LL.D., 1970; PhD, St. Louis U., 1952; Litt.D., DePaul U., 1972; L.H.D., Lincoln Coll., 1965, Columbia Coll., 1969, Luther Coll., 1969; LHD, Augustana Coll., 1969; L.H.D., Marycrest Coll., 1972, Ursuline Coll., 1972, Spertus Coll. Judaica, 1974, Holy Cross Coll., 1974, Rosary Coll., 1975, St. Ambrose Coll., 1975, St. Leo Coll., 1976, Mt. St. Joseph Coll., 1976, Stritch Coll., 1976; LHD, Stonehill Coll., 1976, Elmhurst Coll., 1977, Manchester Coll., 1977, Marymount Coll., 1977; L.H.D., Governor's State U., 1979; LHD, Seattle U., 1981, St. Michael's Coll., 1984, Nazareth Coll., 1985, Holy Family Coll., 1986, Keller Grad. Sch. Mgmt., Our Lady of Holy Cross Coll., New Orleans, 1988. Mem. Sisters of Charity, B.V.M.; tchr. English St. Mary's High Sch., Chgo., 1941-47; residence, study abroad, 1951; chmn. philosophy dept. Mundelein Coll., 1951-57, pres., trustee, 1957—75, prof. philosophy, 1975-85, emeritus faculty, 1987—, archivist, 1986—. Contbr. articles philos. jours. Mem. adv. bd. Sec. Navy, 1975—80, Chgo. Police Bd., 1979—89; bd. dirs. Am. Coun. on Edn., 1971—75, chmn., 1974—75; nat. bd. dirs. Girl Scouts USA, 1966—74, nat. adv., 1976—85; trustee St. Louis U., 1974—87, Ursuline Coll., 1978—92, Cath. Theol. Union, 1983—89, DeVry, Inc., 1987—98, Duquesne U., 1989—91, Montay Coll., 1993—95, Mundelein Coll., 1957—75; bd. dirs. Newberry Libr., 1976—, WTTW Pub. TV, 1976—, Parkside Human Svcs. Corp., 1983—89. Recipient Laetare medal, 1975, LaSallian award, 1975, Aquinas award, 1976, Chgo. Assn. Commerce and Industry award, 1976, Hesburgh award, 1982, Woman of Distinction award Nat. Conf. Women Student Leaders, 1985, Outstanding Svc. award Coun. Ind. Colls., 1989, Woman of History award for edn. AAUW, 1989; named One of 100 Oustanding Chgo. Women, Culture in Action, 1994, Alpha Sigma Nu, 1996. Mem. Am. Cath. Philos. Assn. (exec. coun. 1953-56), Assn. Am. Colls. (bd. dirs. 1965-70, chmn. 1969-70), Religious Edn. Assn. Am. (pres. 1973, chmn. bd. 1975-78), North Cen. Assn. (commn. on colls. and univs. 1971-78, chmn. exec. bd. 1975-77, bd. dirs.), Assn. Governing Bds. Colls. and Univs. (bd. dirs. 1979-88, hon. bd. dirs. 1989-92). Home: Wright Hall 6364 N Sheridan Rd Chicago IL 60660-1726 Office: Loyola U Office Archives Sullivan Ctr 6525 N Sheridan Rd Chicago IL 60626-5344 E-mail: aganno2@luc.edu.

GANNON, JEFFREY P. trucking/relocation services executive; BE, Villanova U. V.p. internat. bus. devel. Gen. Electric Co.; pres., CEO Zenith Electronics Co.; CEO Allied Worldwide. Former pres., CEO GE Lighting Asia Pacific, GE China, GE Mex., GE Latin Am., GE USSR. Office: Allied Worldwide 215 W Diehl Rd Naperville IL 60563

GANNON, JOHN C. federal agency administrator; b. Worcester, Mass. m. Mary Ellen Gannon; children: Jonathan, Mark, Elizabeth. BA Psychology, Holy Cross Coll., 1966; MA History, Washington U., St. Louis, 1972, PhD History, 1976. Commd. ensign USN, 1967, advances through grades to capt., ret., 1990; political analyst L.Am.; with Office Econ. Rsch.; deputy dir. Office European Analysis, 1989—92, dir., 1992—97; asst. dir. analysis & prodn. CIA, Washington, 1998—. Elected Falls Church City Coun., Va., 1980—82; apptd. vice chmn., chmn. Planning Commn., 1984—88. Office: CIA Office of Dir Washington DC 20505

GANNON, JOHN SEXTON, lawyer, management consultant, arbitrator, mediator; b. East Orange, N.J., Apr. 7, 1927; s. John Joseph and Agnes (Sexton) G.; m. Diane Ditchy, Aug. 11, 1951; children: Mary Catherine, John, Lanie Elizabeth, James. BA, U. Mich., 1951; JD, Wayne State U., Detroit, 1961. Bar: Mich. 1962, Tenn. 1971, U.S. Ct. Appeals (6th cir.) 1977, U.S. Dist. Ct. (mid. dist.) Tenn. 1989; Rule 31 approved mediator Tenn. Supreme Ct. Labor negotiator, mgr. employee rels. Chrysler Corp., Highland Park, Mich., 1951-61; labor counsel, mgr. employee rels. Ex-Cell-O Corp., Highland Park, 1961-65; assoc. Constangy & Powell, Atlanta, 1966; v.p. employee rels., labor counsel Werthan Industries, Nashville, 1967-80; ptnr. Dearborn & Ewing, Nashville, 1980-90; pvt. practice Nashville, 1991—. Mem. adj. faculty Owens Sch., Vanderbilt U., Nashville, 1975—85; instr. Soc. Human Resource Mgmt. Profl. cert. program Mid. Tenn. State U., 1993—2000; pres. Employee Rels. Svcs., Nashville, 1987—; chair bd. dirs. Elk Brand Mfg. Co. Inc., Nashville, 2002—. Contbr. articles to profl. jours. Mem. Birmingham (Mich.) Bd. Zoning Appeals, 1963-66; mem. Human Rels. Commn., Nashville, 1979-89; chmn. Tenn. Citizens for Ct. Modernization, Nashville, 1979-80; chmn. Pvt. Industry Coun., Nashville, 1986-95. With USN, 1945-47. Mem. ABA, FBA (former chmn. sr. lawyers divsn. mediation and arbitration com.), Tenn. Bar Assn., Nashville Bar Assn., Nat. Orgn. Social Security Claimants Reps., Am. Arbitration Assn. (panel employment mediators and arbitrators), Univ. Club, Hillwood Country Club, Kiwanis. Home: 216 Jackson Blvd Nashville TN 37205-3300 E-mail: jg216@msn.com.

GANNON, MARC JAY, optometrist; b. Cleve., Sept. 22, 1951; s. Leonard Justin and Norma S. (Falcovich) Goldstein; m. Cheryl Denise Congress, Aug. 4, 1974; children: Jennifer, Joshua. Student, Miami U., Oxford, Ohio, 1972; OD magna cum laude, Ill. Coll. Optometry, Chgo., 1976. Cert. optometrist, Fla. Intern, then resident Naval Regional Med. Ctr., Portsmouth, Va., 1976-78; pvt. practice Ft. Lauderdale, Fla., 1978—. Pres. Oculon Vison Enhancement, Inc., Boca Raton, Fla., 1984-89, Gannon Ctr. for Low Vision, Low Vision Inst.; dir. Gannon Ctr. Low Vision. Patentee in field. Dist. exec. Lighthouse dist. Boy Scouts Am., 1980-82; pres. Kiwanis, Pompano Beach, Fla., 1981-82, Bus. Forum, Pompano Beach, 1982-83. Lt. comdre. USN, 1976-78. Mem. Am. Optometric Assn., Fla. Optometric Assn., Nat. Eye Rsch.Found., Broward County Optometric Assn., Tomb and Key Honor Soc. Avocations: sailing, scuba diving, photography. Office: 5333 N Dixie Hwy Ste 101 Oakland Park FL 33334-3453 E-mail: gannonlvi@aol.com.

GANNON, MARK STEPHEN, lawyer; b. Stuttgart, Fed. Republic Germany, Mar. 2, 1950; (parents Am. citizens); s. Vincent de Paul and Denise (Heinle) G.; m. Kathryn Ennis, Aug. 14, 1971; children: Mark Stephen II, Matthew Christopher. BA cum laude, Marquette U., 1971; JD, Emory U., 1976. Bar: Ga. 1976, U.S. Dist. Ct. (no. dist.) Ga. 1976. Assoc. Savell, Williams, Cox & Angel, Atlanta, 1976-80; ptnr. Savell & Williams, Atlanta, 1980—, mng. ptnr., 1984—. Mem. faculty Workers' Compensation Law Inst., St. Simons, Ga., 1989, 95, 98, 2000. Bd. dirs. Hillside Cottages, Inc., Atlanta, 1978-86, Briarcliff Community Sports, Inc., Atlanta, 1986-88; co-chmn. Immaculate Heart of Mary Bd. Edn., 1990-91, chmn., 1991-92. Mem.: Lawyers Club Atlanta, State Bar of Ga. (state bd. rules and mediation com. 1994—, exec. com. 1994—, Gov.'s worker's compensation adv. commn. med. comm. 2000—01, Gov.'s worker's compensation review comm. 2001—03, exec.com. 1986—91, rev. com.), Atlanta Bar Assn. (chmn. workers' compensation sect. 1989—90), Def. Rsch. Inst., Ga. Def. Lawyers Assn. Roman Catholic. Home: 1052 Clifton Rd NE Atlanta GA 30307-1228 Office: Savell & Williams 1500 The Equitable Bldg 100 Peachtree St Atlanta GA 30303-8958 E-mail: msg@savellwilliams.com.

GANNON, MARTIN JOHN, finance educator; BA in Sociology and Philosophy magna cum laude, U. Scranton, 1961; postgrad., U. Pitts., 1961—63; PhD in Indsl. Rels. and Mgmt., Columbia U., 1967. Rsch. asst. sociology U. Pitts. Grad. Sch. Pub. Health, 1962; asst. to the dir. advanced exec. programs Columbia U., 1964, asst. to prof. Sch. Bus., 1965, asst. to dir. advanced exec. tng. programs Grad. Sch. Bus., Arden House Campus, 1966, rsch. asst. Grad. Sch. Bus., 1966—67; lectr. mgmt. and orgnl. behavior U. Md. Coll. Bus. and Mgmt., College Park, 1968—69, asst. prof. mgmt., 1969—71, assoc. prof. mgmt., 1971—74, prof. mgmt., 1974—77, acting assoc. dean for acad. affairs, 1978—79; prof., chairperson faculty mgmt. and orgn. U. Md., Md. Bus. Sch., College Park, 1977—78; prof. mgmt., dir. Ctr. for Knowledge Mgmt. and Global Bus., Robert H. Smith Sch. Bus. U. Md., College Park, 1981—. John F. Kennedy Found./Fulbright prof. Thammasat U., Thailand, 1988; vis. prof. U. Kassel, Germany, 1992—96, U. Tubingen, Germany, 1996—, London Bus. Sch., 1996, U. Coll. Dublin, 1996, Bocconi (Italy) U., 1996, 98; acad. dir. Internat. Mgmt. and Compliance Tng. cert. program U. Md., Balt., 1997—; external cons. Geico Ins. Cos., 1998—; founding dir. College Park Scholars Program in Bus., Soc. and the Economy, 1998—2001; lectr. in field; cons. in field. Author: Management: An Integrated Framework, 1977, 2nd edit., 1982, Organizational Behavior, 1979, Management: Managing for Results, 1988, Spanish edit., 1995, Cultural Metaphors: Readings, Research Translations, and Commentary, 2001, Working Across Cultures: Applications and Exercises, 2001; author: (with S. J. Carroll Jr.) Ethical Dimensions of International Management, 1997; author: (with others) Strategic Management Skills, 1986, The Dynamics of Competitve Strategy, 1992, Managing Without Traditional Methods: Internation Innovations in Human Resource Management, 1996, Understanding Global Cultures: Metaphorical Journeys Through 23 Countries, 2d edit., 2001; editor: Handbook of Cross-Cultural Management, 2002; co-editor: Readings in Management, 1977; mem. editl. rev. bd.: Jour. Bus. Rsch., 1983—99, Jour. Internat. Bus. Edn., 2001; contbr. chapters to books, articles to profl. jours. Grantee, Small Bus. Adminstrn., 1985—89. Office: Univ Md 3335 Van Munching Hall College Park MD 20742-1800 Home: 30 Thomas Dr Silver Spring MD 20904

GANNON, PETER M. healthcare executive; b. Bellville, New Jersey, Apr. 6, 1973; s. Robert Ignatius and Evelyn Marion Gannon; m. Micaela Mae McLaughlin, May 11, 2002. BA, Iona Coll., New Rochelle, NY., 1995. Traffic coord. Adient, Wayne, NJ, 1996—97, acct. exec., 1997—98, sr. acct. exec., 1998—99, acct. super., 1999—2000, Torre Lazur, Parsippany, NJ, 2000; digital acct. group supr. Hyphen, Parsippany, NJ, 2001—. Author: (screenplays) Absence of Reality, 2000. Avocations: writing, travel, ice hockey, mountain biking. Home: 22 Colony Dr E West Orange NJ 07052-4615 Office: Hyphen, Inc 300 Interpace Pkwy Bldg B Parsippany NJ 07054 E-mail: peter.gannon@hyphenhealth.com.

GANNON, RICH, football player; b., Dec. 20, 1965; m. Shelley Gannon; children: Alexis, Danielle. Postgrad in criminal justice, U. Delaware. Quartback Minn. Vikings, 1987—92, Wash. Redskins, 1993, Kansas City Chiefs, 1995—98, Oakland Raiders, 1999—. Office: Oakland Raiders 1220 Harbor Bay Pky Alameda CA 94502

GANO, KENNETH REDMAN, JR., lawyer; b. Charleston, Ill., Mar. 11, 1952; s. Kenneth Redman Gano and Melba Maxine Gano Brown; m. Charlotte Amelia Carlet, May 21, 1983; children: Jacob Redman, James Alexander Greer, Benjamin Isaac. BA, Ea. Ill. U., 1977; JD, No. Ill. U., 1980. Bar: Ill. 1980, U.S. Dist. Ct. (ctrl. dist.) Ill. 1980, U.S. Dist. Ct. (so. dist.) Ill. 1989, U.S. Ct. Appeals (7th cir.) 1991. Assoc. Ron Tulin, Ltd., Charleston, 1980-82; ptnr. Newton & Gano, Charleston, 1982-84; office mgr. Gano Welding Supplies, Charleston, 1984-89; pvt. practice, 1989—. Instr. Lakeland Coll., Mattoon, Ill., 1980-82, Eastern Ill. U., Charleston, 1983. Mem.: Ill. Bar Assn. Office: 938 6th St Charleston IL 61920 Personal E-mail: triumphs@consolidated.net.

GANOE, BOB (ROBOT), model, actor; b. Louisville, Dec. 16, 1946; s. Harry Dubree and Dorothy (Clark) G. Student, U. Chgo., 1965-68. Photographer's model Bardshaw Models, Chgo., 1966-67; actor Film Inst. Amsterdam, 1968; photographer's model E.M. Jones Models Inc., Oracle, Ariz., 1980; fashion model Cosmo Model & Talent Agy., Louisville, 1998—. Appeared in (movie) American in Amsterdam, 1968; translator: Viva Surrealism (Salvador Dali); co-creator The Warhol Look, 1966-69. Social worker Bur. Pub. Assistance, Louisville, 1973; founder GIA Carangi Meml. Fund, 1999. Grantee Carnegie Found., 1964; scholar U. Chgo., 1965-68. Avocations: collecting art, antiques, jewelry, vintage clothing. Home: Ste 203 1204 Bardstown Rd Apt 203 Louisville KY 40204-1361 Office: Cosmo Model & Talent Agy 7410 New Lagrange Rd Louisville KY 40222-4871

GANOE, CHARLES STRATFORD, banker, consultant; b. Abington, Pa., July 16, 1929; s. Robert L. and Leonette (Rehfuss) G.; m. Frances-Sue Williams, Apr. 2, 1960; children: F. Hemsley, Alice N. BA, Princeton U., 1951; MBA, U. Pa., 1952. With Fidelity Bank (now Wachovia Bank), Phila., 1952—, asst. treas., 1956—60, asst. v.p., 1960—61, v.p., 1961—66, sr. v.p., 1966—69, exec. v.p., 1969—75, sr. exec. v.p., dir., 1975—79; exec. v.p. N.Y. Bank for Savs., N.Y.C., 1979—82; sr. v.p. Am. Express Internat. Banking Corp., N.Y.C., 1982—84, 1st Am. Bank of N.Y., N.Y.C., 1984—91; mng. dir. FMS Group inc., Blue Bell, Pa., 1991—94; pres. Ganoe Assocs., LLC, Princeton, NJ, 1995—. V.p. Co. for Investing Abroad (became Fidelity Internat. Corp., merged into Fidelity Internat. Bank 1972), 1963-65, pres., bd. dir., 1965-72; bd. dir., chmn. exec. com. Fidelity Internat. Bank, N.Y.C., 1970-79; mem. adv. com. Export-Import Bank U.S., 1973-74. Co-author: Offshore Lending by U.S. Commercial Banks; contbr. articles to profl. jours. Class agt. Class of 1951 Princeton U., 1954-56, treas., 1956-61, v.p., 1981-85, pres., 1985-86; bd. dirs. Phila. Coun. for Internat. Visitors, 1963-69, chmn., 1969-73; mem. Phila. Dist. Export Coun., 1966-75. Mem. Bankers Assn. for Fgn. Trade (bd. dirs. 1969—, v.p. 1971-72, exec. v.p. 1972-73, pres. 1973-74), Robert Morris Assocs. (now RMA-Risk Mgmt. Assocs.)(past pres. Phila. chpt., Duning Meml. awards 1962, 65, 68), Greater Phila. C. of C. (sec. 1960-64, treas. 1960-70, bd. dirs. 1960-73, mem. adminstrv. com.), Wharton Grad. Sch. Alumni Assn. (past pres.), Coun. Fgn. Rels., Merion Cricket Club (Haverford, Pa.), Princeton Club (N.Y.C.), Princeton (N.J.) Elm Club, Ausable Club (St. Huberts, N.Y.), Delta Psi. Home: 23 Constitution Hl W Princeton NJ 08540-6752 Office: Ganoe Assocs 475 Wall St Princeton NJ 08540-1509 E-mail: cganoe@erols.com.

GANONG, WILLIAM F(RANCIS), physiologist, physician; b. Northampton, Mass., July 6, 1924; s. William Francis and Anna (Hobbet) G.; m. Ruth Jackson, Feb. 22, 1948; children: William Francis III, Susan B., Anna H., James E. AB cum laude, Harvard U., 1945, MD magna cum laude, 1949; DSc (hon.), Med. Coll. Ohio, 1995, Ohio State U., 2003. Intern, jr. asst. resident in medicine Peter Bent Brigham Hosp., Boston, 1949-51, asst. in medicine and surgery, 1952-55; research fellow medicine and surgery Harvard U., 1952-55; asst. prof. physiology U. Calif., San Francisco, 1955-60, assoc. prof., 1960-64, prof., 1964-82, Jack D. and Deloris Lange prof., 1982-91, Lange prof. emeritus, 1991—, faculty research lectr., 1968, vice chmn. dept., 1963-68, chmn., 1970-87. Cons. Calif. Dept. Mental Hygiene. Author: Review of Medical Physiology, 21st edit., 2003, Physiology: A Study Guide, 3d edit., 1989; editor: (with L. Martini) Neuroendocrinology, vol. I, 1966, vol. II, 1967, Frontiers in Neuroendocrinology, 1969, 71, 73, 76, 78, 80, 82, 84, 86, 88, (with S. McPhee and V. Lingappa) Pathophysiology of Disease, 4th edit., 2003; editor-in-chief Neuroendocrinology, 1979-84; co-editor Frontiers in Neuroendocrinology, 1990-2002. Served with U.S. Army, 1943-46; served to capt. M.C. 1951-52. Recipient Boylston Med. Soc. prize Harvard U., 1949, A.A. Berthold medal, 1985, Lifetime Achievement award High Blood Pressure Rsch. Coun., Am. Heart Assn., 1995;

named Disting. Svc. mem. Am. Assn. Med. Colls., 1988. Fellow: AAAS; mem.: Soc. for Neurosci., Internat. Brain Rsch. Orgn., Chilean Endocrine Soc. (corr.), Endocrine Soc. (Disting. Educator award 2002), Soc. Exptl. Biology and Medicine (councillor 1989—93), Am. Soc. for Gravitational and Space Biology (bd. dirs. 1984—87), Assn. Chairmen Depts. Physiology (pres. 1976—77), Am. Physiol. Soc. (pres. 1977—78), Internat. Soc. Neuroendocrinology (hon.; v.p. 1976—80). Home: 710 Hillside Ave Albany CA 94706-1022 Office: U Calif Dept Physiology San Francisco CA 94143-0444

GANS, DENNIS JOSEPH, information technology manager, financial analyst; b. Yokohama, Japan, Sept. 7, 1949; came to U.S., 1951; s. Harry Leo and Hope Lorene (Everett) G.; m. Carolyn Johnson O'Grady, 1986; 1 child, Erik Christopher. BS in Bldg Constrn. (Engring./Mgmt.), Tex. A&M U., 1971. Project mgr. D.C.B., Inc., 1972-73, 78-79, 86-87; quality control engr. Martin Zachry, Kwajalein, Marshall Islands, 1975-76; co-owner B.G.S.Y. Enterprises, Denver, 1975; project mgr. State of Colo., 1977-78, 79-80; co-owner Denver Skatewear, 1978-80; mgr. scheduling Morrison Knudsen, Zaire, 1980-82; constrn. engr. Bechtel Internat., Jubail, Saudi Arabia, 1982; project mgr. Village at Breckenridge (Colo.) Resort, 1984-86; sr. buyer Hewlett Packard Co, Roseville, Calif., 1988-91, bus. analyst, 1991-95, sys. analyst, 1995—99, logistics specialist, 1999—2001, sys./bus. consultant, 2001—. Elem. sch. vis. scientist. Deacon, Presbyn. Ch. U.S.A.; mem. Comty. Archtl. Com. Mem. Tex. A&M U. Assn. Former Students, Sierra Club. Republican. Avocations: golf, personal computers, photography, model rocketry, astronomy. Home: 851 Sunfish St Lakeway TX 78734-4411 E-mail: gans@jps.net.

GANS, EUGENE HOWARD, cosmetic and pharmaceutical company executive, consultant; b. Dec. 17, 1929; married, 1953; 2 children. BS, Columbia U., 1951, MS, 1953; PhD, U. Wis., 1956. Lab. asst. Columbia U., 1951—53; sr. scientist group leader Hoffman-LaRoche, Inc., NJ, 1956—60; head new product devel. sect. Vick Div. R&D Labs. Richardson-Merrell, NY, 1960—64, asst. dir. devel., 1964—67, dir., 1967—71; dir. rsch. Vicks Personal Care div. Richardson-Vicks div. Proctor-Gamble, Shelton, Conn., 1972—76, v.p., dir. R&D, 1976—87; pres. Hastings Assocs., Westport, Conn., 1987—. Lincoln Techs., Westport, 1989—. Chmn. ctrl. rsch. Medicis Pharm. Co., Phoenix, 1992—; chmn. proprietary drug task group FDA, 1976—86, chmn. Consumer Health Products Assn. task group, 1996—2003; chmn. sci. adv. com. Cosmetic, Toiletry and Fragrance Assn., Washington, 1984—86. Mem.: Soc. Investigative Dermatology, Am. Acad. Dermatology, Am. Chem. Soc., Am. Pharm. Assn., Sigma Xi. Address: 5101 N Casa Blanca Dr #223 Scottsdale AZ 85253-6988 E-mail: egans48845@aol.com.

GANS, HERBERT J. sociologist, educator; b. Cologne, Germany, May 7, 1927; came to U.S., 1940, naturalized, 1945; s. Carl M. and Elise (Plaut) G.; m. Louise Gruner, Mar. 19, 1967; 1 son, David. PhB, U. Chgo., 1947, MA, 1950; PhD, U. Pa., 1957, DSc (hon.), 2003. Planner pvt. and pub. planning agys., Chgo. and Washington, 1950-53; from lectr. to assoc. prof. urban studies and planning U. Pa., 1953-64; from asso. prof. to adj. prof. sociology Tchrs. Coll., Columbia, also sr. staff scientist Center Urban Edn., 1964-69; prof. sociology and planning Mass. Inst. Tech., also Mass. Inst. Tech.-Harvard Joint Center for Urban Studies, 1969-71; prof. sociology Columbia (Ford Found. Urban chair), 1971—; Robert S. Lynd prof. sociology Columbia U., 1985— . Sr. fellow Gannett Ctr. for Media Studies, fall 1985-86, Media Studies Ctr., 1996-97; vis. scholar Russell Sage Found., 1989-90; film critic Social Policy mag., 1971-78; cons. Ford Found., HEW, Nat. Adv. Commn. Civil Disorders. Author: The Urban Villagers, 1962, 2d edit., 1982, The Levittowners, 1967, 1982, People and Plans, 1968, More Equality, 1973, Popular Culture and High Culture, 1974, rev. edit., 1999, Deciding What's News, 1979, Middle American Individualism, 1988, 1991, People, Plans and Policies, 1991, 2d edit., 1994, The War Against the Poor, 1995, 1996, Making Sense of America, 1999, Democracy and the News, 2003; co-editor: On the Making of Americans, 1979; editor: Sociology in America, 1990; adv. editor Jour. Am. Inst. Planners, 1965—75, Jour. Contemporary Ethnography, 1971—, Am. Jour. Sociology, 1972—74, Society, 1971—76, Social Policy, 1971—, Pub. Opinion Quar., 1972—86, Jour. Comm., 1974—91, Jour. Ethnic and Racial Studies, 1977—89, 1995—2003, Internat. Ency. Comm., 1984—88, The Am. Sociologist, 1991—95, Georgetown Jour. Fighting Poverty, 1992—, Critical Studies in Mass Comm., 1992—96, Rose Monograph Series, 1998—, Qualitative Sociology, 1998—2001. Bd. dirs. Ams. for Dem. Action, 1969 75, Mct. (formerly Suburban) Action Inst., 1974-85, Human Serve Inst., 1987—, Workers Def. League, 1992—, Working Today, 1995—, Rsch. Coun. Jt. Project on Equality, 1996—, Nat. Jobs for All Coalition, 1996. With AUS, 1945-46. Recipient Excelsior award SUNY, Albany, 1987, award for disting. contbn. to media and media studies Freedom Forum Media Studies Ctr., 1995; Guggenheim fellow, 1977-78, Rsch. fellow German Marshall Fund, 1984. Fellow Am. Acad. Arts and Scis.; mem. Am. Sociol. Assn. (exec. coun. 1968-71, pres. 1988, Lynd award for lifetime contbn. to rsch. cmty. and urban sociology sect. 1992, Pub. Understanding Sociology award 1999), Ea. Sociol. Soc. (pres. 1972, Merit award, 1995), Sociol. Rsch. Assn., German Sociol. Assn. (hon.). Office: Columbia U 404 Fayerweather Hall New York NY 10027 E-mail: hjg1@columbia.edu.

GANS, SAMUEL MYER, temporary employment service executive; b. June 10, 1925; s. Arthur and Goldie (Goldhirsh) G.; m. Ada S. Zuckerman, Aug. 1, 1948; children: Gary M., Jeffrey R. Grad. in acctg., Pierce Jr. Coll., 1949. Pub. acct., 1949-55; sales exec., 1955-58; franchise owner, pres., CEO Manpower, Inc., Pennsauken, N.J., 1958-86; owner Micrographic Svcs. Inc., Pennsauken, 1975—. With Allstate Svcs., Inc., County Maintenance Corp., Affiliated Personnel Svc.; owner Antique & Classic Cars Storage Garage, Inc., Voorhees, N.J.; franchise cons.; instr. motivation courses. V.p. exec. bd. United Fund Camden County; v.p., bd. dirs. So. N.J. Coun., ARC Camden County, Nat. Conf. Christians and Jews; bd. mgrs. Am. Cancer Soc. Camden County; active Boy Scouts Am., Employer Legis. Com., Camden County Bicentennial Com., Score and Ace programs, Camden, YMCA, Allied Jewish Appeal, World Affairs Coun.; mem. N.J. Gov.'s Mgmt. Commn., 1971; trustee Camden County Heart Assn., Camden County Mental Health Assn.; exec. bd., founder Big Bros. Assn. Camden County; pub. rels. com. U.S. Savs. Bonds, Camden and Trenton. With USNR, 1943-46. Mem. Nat. Assn. Temp. Svcs. (chpt. rels. com. 1973), Nat. Soc. Pub. Accts., Camden County C. of C., S. Jersy Pub. Rels. Assn. (pres. 1967), S. Jersy Mfg. Assn. (exec. bd., treas.), S. Jersey Personnel Assn. (treas.), Cherry Hill C. of C. (bd. dirs., v.p.), Better Bus. Bur. Camden County, Adminstrv. Mgmt. Soc., N.J. Assn. Temp. Svcs. (pres. 1970-72, bd. dirs.), S. Jersey Purchasing Agts. Assn., Assn. Manpower Franchise Owners, Jewish War Vets., Dolphin Beach Condo Club, Masons, Lions (pres. Camden chpt. 1972-73, Lion of the Yr. 1977), Shriners, B'Nai B'Rith. Jewish. Home: 4 N Derby Ave Ventnor City NJ 08406-2356 Office: 3801 Marlton Pike Camden NJ 08110-6312

GANS, WALTER GIDEON, lawyer; b. Trutnov, Czechoslovakia, Jan. 11, 1936; s. Frederick and Erna (Mueller) G.; m. Harriet Arlene Goldhagen, Oct. 6, 1938 (dec.); children: David Ian, Erik Anthony; m. Katherine Elizabeth Halligan, Feb. 10, 1947. BA, Bowdoin Coll., 1957; JD, NYU, 1961, LLM in Comparative Law, 1967. Bar: N.Y. 1961. Assoc. Fried, Frank, harris, Shriver & Jacobson, N.Y.C., 1961-63; internat. atty. Latex Corp., N.Y.C., 1963-67; assoc. counsel Olin Corp., New Haven and Stamford, Conn., 1967-71, counsel, 1972-75, sr. counsel internat., 1975-79; v.p., gen. counsel and sec. Siemens Corp., N.Y.C., 1979-99; spl. counsel Kaye Scholer, 2001. Active CPR Inst. for Dispute Resolution, mem. exec. com. 1995—; active European Am. Gen. Counsel Group; dir. Food and Drug Law Inst.; mem. Conf. Bd. Coun. of Chief Legal Officers; mem. lawyers com. Human Rights' Internat. Rule Coun. Fellow Coll. Comml. Arbitrators; fem. ABA (mem. antitrust, bus. law, dispute resolution, litigation, internat. law and practice sects.), Am. Arbitration Assn. (internat. panel arbitrators, corp. counsel com.), Am. Fgn. Law Assn., Am. Corp. Counsel Assn. (N.Y.C. chpt. bd. dirs.), N.Y. State Bar Assn., Assn. Bar City of N.Y. (fgn. and comparative law com. 1973-75, 82-85, com. corp. law depts. 1986-89, fed. cts. com. 1992-95, adv. com. corp. lawyers 1992-95, 125th anniversary campaign com.), Internat. Bar Assn., The Corp. Bar. Office: 425 Park Ave Ste 1836 New York NY 10022

GANSKE, J. GREG, former congressman, plastic surgeon; b. New Hampton, Iowa, Mar. 31, 1949; s. Victor Wilber and Mary Jo (O'Donnell) G.; m. Corrine Mikkelson, 1976; children: Ingrid, Briget, Karl. BA, U. Iowa, 1972, MD, 1976. Diplomate Am. Bd. Plastic Surgery, Am. Bd. Surgery. Intern U. Colo. Med. Ctr., Denver, 1976-78; resident in gen. surgery U. Oreg. Health Sci. Ctr., Portland, 1978-81, chief resident in gen. surgery, 1981-82; resident in plastic surgery Harvard Med. Sch., Boston, 1982-84; chief resident plastic surgery Brigham and Women's Hosp. and Children's Hosp., 1983-84; pvt. practice Des Moines, 1984-94; mem. U.S. Congress from 4th Iowa dist., Washington, 1994—2002; mem. energy and commerce com. Staff Iowa Luth. Hosp., Iowa Meth. Med. Ctr., Mercy Hosp. Med. Ctr., Vets. Hosp., Charter Cmty. Hosp., Des Moines Gen. Hosp. Lt. col. M.C., USAR, 1984—. Fellow ACS, Am. Soc. Plastic and Reconstructive Surgeons; mem. AMA, Am. Assn. Plastic Surgeons, Iowa Med. Soc., Polk County Med. Soc., Iowa Soc. Plastic and Reconstructive Surgeons, Am. Assn. Hand Surgery, Midwestern Assn. Plastic Surgeons, Am. Soc. for Surgery of the Hand, Iowa Acad. Surgery, Am. Cleft Palate-Craniofacial Assn. Republican. Roman Catholic.*

GANSLER, ROBERT, professional soccer coach; b. Mucsi, Hungary, July 1, 1941; came to U.S., 1952; m. Nancy Gansler; children: Robert, MIchael, Peter, Daniel. Grad., Marquette U., 1964. Head coach Kansas City Wizards/MLS, 1999—. Office: care Kansas City Wizards 706 Broadway St Ste 100 Kansas City MO 64105-2306

GANT, DONALD ROSS, investment banker; b. Long Branch, N.J., Oct. 5, 1928; s. Raymond LeRoy and Evelyn (Ross) G.; m. Jane Harriet Taylor, Sept. 12, 1953; children: Laura R., Christopher T., Sarah R., Alison A. BS, U. Pa., 1952; MBA, Harvard U., 1954. Assoc. Goldman, Sachs & Co., N.Y.C., 1954-64, ptnr., 1965-90, ltd. ptnr., 1990-99, sr. dir., 1999—. Bd. dirs. Diebold, Inc., Canton, Ohio, Stride Rite Corp., Lexington, Mass.; mem. vis. com. Harvard Bus. Sch., 1991—97. Served with U.S. Army, 1946-48. Republican. Presbyterian. Home: PO Box 83 New Vernon NJ 07976-0083 Office: Goldman Sachs & Co 85 Broad St New York NY 10004-2456 E-mail: don10285@cs.com.

GANT, LINDA GAYLE, elementary school educator; b. Mineola, Tex., Dec. 8, 1947; d. Brooks Conway and Arrie Lou (Wicker) Duncan; m. Ronald Herman Gant, July 15, 1968; children: Shannon Gant Sonoda, Shane Stuart. Lic. cosmetologist, Icenhower U. Socmetology, 1968; AAS, Eastfield Coll., 1980; BS, U. Tex., Dallas, 1983; MEd, Tex. A&M U., 1986. Cosmetologist George AFB, Victorville, Calif., 1968—69; tchr. Mesquite (Tex.) Ind. Sch. Dist., 1979—. Pub. Readers Are Leaders Co., Mesquite, 1999—, author, illustrator, 1994—, greeting card designer, 1995—; spkr. in field. Author, illustrator: children's book Readers Are Leaders, 1999. Faculty mem. McDonald Mid. Sch. PTA, 1983—92. Recipient 1st pl. award, Toastmasters Internat., 2001, 2d pl. award, 2001; scholar, Ret. Tchrs. Assn., Dallas, 1982. Mem.: Mesquite Edn. Assn., Tex. Area Artists. Avocations: drawing, reading, swimming, training dogs, needlecrafts. Home: 908 Ashland Dr Mesquite TX 75149-6002 Office: Readers Are Leaders 908 Ashland Dr Mesquite TX 75149-6002 Fax: 972-288-5806. E-mail: rlgant@airmail.net.

GANT, NORMAN FERRELL, JR., obstetrician, gynecologist; b. Wichita Falls, Tex., Feb. 16, 1939; s. Norman Ferrell and Eleanor (Taylor) Gant. BA, North Tex. State U., Denton, 1962; MD, U. Tex., 1964. Diplomate Am. Bd. Ob-Gyn. (exec. dir.). Intern Parkland Meml. Hosp., Dallas, 1964—65, resident, 1965—68; mem. faculty U. Tex. Southwestern Med. Sch., Dallas, 1968— , prof. obstetrics and gynecology, 1976—, chmn. dept., 1977—83. Bd. dirs. Am. Bd. Ob-Gyn., Inc., 1993—; v.p. Internat. Soc. for Study of Hypertension in Pregnancy, 1992—94. Co-author: Williams Obstetrics; contbr. Recipient Outstanding Alumnus award, U. North Tex., 1998. Fellow: Am. Coll. Ob-Gyn., Royal Coll. Ob-Gyn.; mem.: Inst. Medicine, Southwestern Gyn. Assembly (pres. 1993), Am. Bd. Ob-Gyn. (maternal-fetal medicine, examiner for ob-gyn. and maternal-fetal medicine bds., mem. exec. com., credentials com.), Dallas-Ft. Worth Obstet. and Gynecol. Soc., Tex. Assn. Ob-Gyns., Dallas County Med. Assns., Soc. Gynecol. Investigation (pres. 1991). Address: Am Bd Ob-Gyn 2915 Vine St Dallas TX 75204-1045 E-mail: ccash@abog.org.

GANTT, CHARLES DAVID, lawyer; b. Winston-Salem, N.C., Oct. 2, 1956; s. Charles Heman and Augusta Pharr G.; m. Charise Lowery, Aug. 11, 1979; children: Brett Daniel, Carrie Michelle. BA in Econs., U. N.C., 1978; JD, Campbell U., 1981. Bar: N.C. 1981, U.S. Dist. Ct. (we. dist.) N.C. 1981, U.S. Ct. Appeals (4th cir.) 1984, U.S. Dist. Ct. (mid. dist.) N.C. 1985, U.S. Supreme Ct. 1985. Pvt. practice, Asheville, N.C., 1981—. Spkr. in field. Mem. Buncombe County Bd. Commrs., 1996—; chmn. Land of Sky Regional Coun., 2002—; mem. Met. Sewerage Dist. Bd., 1999—. Democrat. Methodist. Avocations: hiking, camping. Office: 82 Church St Asheville NC 28801-3622 E-mail: lawyer@davidgantt.com.

GANTT, HARVEY B. former mayor; b. Charleston, S.C., Jan. 14, 1943; m. Lucinda Brawley; four children. Student, Iowa State U., 1960-62; B.Arch., Clemson U., 1965; MA, MIT, 1970. Lectr. U. N.C., Chapel Hill, 1970-72; vis. critic Clemson U., S.C., 1972-73; mem. Charlotte City Council, N.C., 1975-79; mayor pro tem City of Charlotte, 1981-83, mayor, 1983-91; chmn. Nat. Capital Planning Commn. Life mem. NAACP; bd. dirs. 100 Black Men of Charlotte, Ctrl. Piedmont Coll. Found., Am. Archtl. Found.; former bd. dirs. YMCA, Afro-Am. Cultural Ctr., Found. for the Carolinas, Charlotte C. of C., Urban League, United Negro Coll. Fund; choir mem. Friendship Bapt., former bd. trustees. Named Citizen of Yr., Charlotte chpt. NAACP, 1975, 84 Mem. AIA, Am. Planning Assn., N.C. Design Found. Avocations: tennis, reading. Office: Nat Capital Planning Commn 801 Pennsylvania Ave NW Ste 301 Washington DC 20576-0001

GANTT, JAMES RAIFORD, thoracic surgeon; b. Texarkana, Mar. 5, 1930; s. James Emmett and Nettie Ruth (Raiford) G.; m. Joan Maire Durstine, Aug. 18, 1968. BA, Baylor U., 1953; MD, Johns Hopkins U., 1957. Diplomate Am. Bd. Surgery, Am. Bd. Thoracic Surgery. Rotating intern Charity Hosp., New Orleans, 1957, resident internal medicine, 1958, resident in surgery, 1962-64, resident in thoracic surgery, 1965; NIH rsch. fellow Tulane U., New Orleans, 1959; resident in thoracic surgery Kans. U., Kansas City, 1966; pvt. practice Dallas, 1966-84, James R. GanttProfl. Assocs., 1971-84, Irving, Tex., 1978-84; chief of surgery Irving Cmty. Hosp., Irving, Tex., 1980—. Lt. USN, 1960-62. Fellow ACS; mem. AMA, So. Thoracic Assn., Am. Coll. Chest Physicians, Tex. Med. Assn. Republican. Presbyterian. Avocations: hunting, fishing. Home: 3512 Lexington Ave Dallas TX 75205-3915

GANTZ, ANN CUSHING, artist, educator; b. Dallas, Aug. 27, 1935; d. Maurice Kendrick and Margaret (Hughes) Cushing; m. Everett Ellis Gantz, Sept. 20, 1958; children: Elaine Gantz Wright, Melissa Cushing. BFA, Newcomb Coll., 1955. Tchr. Dallas Mus. of Art, 1956-65; pres. Cushing Galleries, Inc., Dallas, 1962-79; tchr. Cushing Studio Inc., Dallas, 1979—. Dir., Cushing Atelier, 1962; chair Six Operas by Six Artists Exhbn./Dallas Opera, 1996. Exhibited in group shows at Mary Nye Gallery, Dallas, Black Tulip Gallery, Lawrence Gallery, The Elms Gallery, Midland, Tex., Landmark, Tennison, Stewart, Cushing, Park Cities Galleries, Dallas, Shrednk Gallery, Denver, Hockaday Gallery, Dallas, Dallas Visual Art Ctr., 1996, McKinney Contemporary, David Dike, Valley House, Represented in permanent collections Dallas Mus., Norfolk Mus., Boston Mus., Denver Mus., New Orleans Mus., Brook Meml., Memphis. Bd. dirs. Dallas Opera, Dallas Theatre Ctr. Recipient Durrell award Dallas Mus., 1979. Mem. Tex. Fine Arts Assn. (hon.), Dallas Print and Drawing Soc. (pres. 1972-80), Tex. Printmakers (pres. 1956-70), Phi Delta Kappa, Alpha Omicron Pi. Episcopalian. Avocations: opera, theatre. Office: Cushing Studio 11333 N Central Expy Dallas TX 75243-6706

GANTZ, BRUCE JAY, otolaryngologist, educator; b. N.Y.C., May 18, 1946; m. Mary Katherine DeJong; children: Ellen Katherine, Jessica Rose, Jay Alexander. BS in Gen. Sci., U. Iowa, 1968, MD, 1974, MS in Otolaryngology, 1980; fellow neurotology, U. Zürich, Zurich, 1981-82. Asst. prof. dept otolaryngology U. Iowa Coll. Medicine, Iowa City, 1980-84, assoc. prof., 1984-87, prof., 1987—; interim head dept. otolaryngology head & neck surgery U. Iowa Hosps. & Clinics, Iowa City, 1993-95, head dept. otolaryngology head & neck surgery, 1995—. Mem. adv. bd. Deafness Research Found. Sci., 1988—. Mem. editl. bd. Am. Jour. Otology, Laryngoscope, Skull Base Surgery, Operative Techniques in Otolaryngology-Head and Neck Surgery, Anales De Otolarnolaringo-logica Mexicana, Annals Otolaryngology, Rhinology and Laryngology; contbr. articles to profl. jours. Recipient Tchr.-Investigator Devel. award Pub. Health Svc., 1981-86, Program Project award NIH, 1985—; clin. rsch. ctr. grantee NIDCD, 1990, 95. Mem. AMA, Assn. for Rsch. in Otolaryngology (pres. 1995), Deafness Rsch. Found. (state chmn. 1985—), Am. Acad. Otolaryngology-Head and Neck Surgery, Soc. Univ. Otolaryngologists, Am. Neurotology Soc. (v.p. 1994-96, pres.-elect 1996-97, pres. 1997—), Am. Otological Soc., Inst. of Medicine of NAS, Collegium Oto-Rhino-Laryngologicum Amictuae Sacrum. Office: U Iowa Hosps & Clinics 200 Hawkins Dr Iowa City IA 52242-1078

GANTZ, CARROLL MELVIN, industrial design consultant, consumer product designer; b. Sellersville, Pa., Sept. 9, 1931; s. Melvin Charles G. and Leona Alberta (Hornberger) Barner; m. Lorraine Sachs, Mar. 5, 1955; children: Erika Christine, Mitchell Allen. B.F.A., Carnegie Mellon U., 1953. Head indsl. design Hoover Co., North Canton, Ohio, 1956-72; mgr. indsl. design Black & Decker, Inc., Towson, Md., 1972-81, dir. indsl. design household products group Shelton, Conn., 1981-86; prof., head dept. design Carnegie Mellon U., Pitts., 1987—92; established Carroll Gantz Design, 1992; designer canal boat St. Helena II, Canal Fulton, Ohio, 1967-70; dir. Am. Canal Soc., York, Pa., 1974-79. Bd. dirs. Stark County Hist. Soc., 1970. Served with Security Agy. U.S. Army, 1953-56. Recipient Design award Indsl. Designers Inst., 1961, Indsl. Design Excellance award, 1995; Brashear scholar, 1949. Fellow Indsl. Designers Soc. Am. (pres. 1979-80, chmn. bd. 1981-82); mem. SAR, Omicron Delta Kappa, Tau Sigma Delta Republican. Achievements include patents for original Black & Decker Dustbuster, 1978; 28 others.

GANTZ, DAVID ALFRED, lawyer, university official; b. Columbus, Ohio, July 30, 1942; s. Harry Samuel and Edwina (Bookwalter) G.; m. Susan Beare, Aug. 26, 1967 (div. Feb. 1989); children: Stephen David, Julie Lorraine; m. Catherine Fagan, Mar. 28, 1992. AB, Harvard U., 1964; JD, Stanford U., 1967, M in Jud. Sci., 1970. Bar: Ohio 1967, D.C. 1971, U.S. Ct. Internat. Trade 1983, U.S. Ct. Appeals (9th cir.) 1972, U.S. Supreme Ct. 1972. Asst. prof. law U. Costa Rica, San Jose, 1967-69; law clk. U.S. Ct. Appeals, San Francisco, 1969-70; asst. legal advisor U.S. Dept. State, Washington, 1970-77; ptnr. Cole & Corrette, Washington, 1977-83, Oppenheimer Wolff & Donnelly, Washington, 1983-90, Reid & Priest, Washington, 1990-93, of counsel, 1993-97, Dorsey & Whitney, 1997-99; prof. law, dir. inter trade law program U. Ariz. Coll. Law, Tucson, 1993—; assoc. dir. Nat. Law Ctr. for Inter-Am. Free Trade, 1993—. Panelist U.S.-Can. Free Trade Agreement, 1989-92, Am. Arbitration Assn., 1996—, NAFTA, 1994—; judge OAS Adminstrv. Tribunal, 1987-95; adj. prof. Georgetown U. Law Ctr., 1982-93; vis. prof. law George Washington U., 2003—. Contbr. numerous articles on internat. law to profl. jours. Pres. Potomac River Sports Found., 1992-94. Mem. ABA, Am. Soc. Internat. Law, Potomac Boat Club (Washington, bd. dirs. 1986-93). Office: Ariz James E Rogers Coll Law 1201 E Speedway Blvd Tucson AZ 85721 E-mail: gantz@law.arizona.edu.

GANTZ, NANCY ROLLINS, hospital administrator, nursing administrator, consultant; b. Buffalo Center, Iowa, Mar. 7, 1949; d. Troy Gaylord and Mary (Emerson) Rollins. Diploma in nursing, Good Samaritan Hosp. and Med. Ctr., Portland, Oreg., 1973; BSBA, City U., 1986; MBA, Kennedy-Western U., 1987, PhD, 1991; postgrad. Exec. Program, Wharton Bus. Sch., 1007. Nurse ICU Good Samaritan Hosp., 1973-75; charge nurse Crestview Convalescent Hosp., Portland, 1975; dir. nursing svcs. Roderick Enterprises, Inc., Portland, 1976 78, Holgate Ctr., Portland, 1978-80, nursing cons. in field of adminstrn., 1980-84, coord. CCU; mgr. ICU/CCU Tuality Cmty. Hosp., Hillsboro, Oreg., 1984-86; head nurse ICU, cardiac surgery unit, coronary care unit Good Samaritan Hosp. & Med. Ctr., Portland, 1986-88, mgr. critical care units, 1988-92, asst. v.p. patient care svcs., 1992-93; dir. heart ctr. Deaconess Med. Ctr., Spokane, Wash., 1992-93; asst. exec. dir. Children's Cancer Ctr. King Faisal Specialist Hosp. and Rsch. Ctr., Riyadh, Saudi Arabia, 1994-96; asst. adminstr., chief nurse exec. King Fahad Nat. Children's Cancer and Rsch. Ctr., Riyadh, 1996-99; dir. pediatric intensive svcs./solid organ transplantation St. Louis Children's Hosp., 2000—02; pres. Emerson Rollins Internat. Cons. Assocs., 2002—; v.p. patient care svcs. Wishard Health Svcs., Indpls., 2002—. Mem. spkrs. bur. Nurses of Am.; mem. task force Oreg. State Health Divsn. Rules and Regulations Revisions for Long Term Health Facilities and Hosp., 1978-79; numerous internat. and nat. speaking presentations; mem. Cons. Consortium, Inc., 1997 2003; developer Cultural Appreciation through Profl. Practice and Synergy. Contbr. chpts. to books and articles to profl. jours. Recipient Wharton Fellow, U Pa. Wharton Bus. Sch., 1997. Mem.: AONE Coun. Nurse Mgrs. (bd. dirs. region 9 1991—92), AONE, ANA (cert.), AACN (chpt. cons. region 18 1978—7989, mgmt. SIC region 18 1990—92, pres. elect greater Portland chpt. 1985—86, pres. 1986 87, bd. dirs. 1985—), Geriatric Nurses Assn. Oreg. (founder, charter pres.), Am. Heart Assn., Sigma Theta Tau. Office: Tower One Ste 3000 225 East North St Indianapolis IN 46204 Fax: 775-458-0341. E-mail: rollinsgantzinternational@msn.com.

GANTZ, RICHARD ALAN, museum administrator; b. Ft. Wayne, Ind., July 28, 1946; m. Ruth Ann Kennell; 1 child, Sally Elizabeth. BS in Edn. with honors, Ball State U., 1968; MA, George Washington U., 1971; PhD, Ind. U., 1986. Social studies tchr. Ft. Wayne (Ind.) Community Schs., 1969-73; Nat. Park Svc. seasonal hist. Homestead Nat. Monument, Beatrice, Nebr., 1972; assoc. instr. Ind. U., Bloomington, 1975-76; asst. state hist. preserv. officer dept. natural resources State of Ind., 1976-90, asst. dir. divsn. mus. and memls., 1978-81, acting dir., 1982-83, dir. divsn. hist. preservation and archeology, 1981-90, acting dir. divsn. state mus. and hist. sites, 1989, dir. divsn. state mus. and hist. sites and Ind. State Mus., 1990—2001; dir. spl. projects Ind. Dept. Natural Resources, Indpls., 2001—. Mem. adj. faculty history dept. Butler U., Indpls., 1988—; mem. steering com. Dept. Commerce Heritage, Tourism and Edn., 1991-94; mem. project com. Ind. Heritage Trust, 1992-2001; chmn. Ind. Hist. Exchange Coun., 1984-91, Ind. Hist. Bridge Com., 1984-90. Contbr. articles to profl. jours. Active Ind. Main State Coun., 1985-98; sec. New Harmony State Commn., 1989-2001; mem. White River State Park Commn., 1993-2001, Ind. Gov.'s Millennium Task Force, 1998-2000, Ind. Gov.'s Residence Adv. Com., 1998—; mem. Ind. Gov.'s 2016 Task Force, 2001-; bd. dirs. Ind. Med. History Mus., 2001-, Indpls. Athletic Club Art Found., 2002--. Mem. Orgn. Am. Hists., Nat. Trust Hist. Preservation, Ind. Assn. Hists., Ind. State Mus. Soc., Assn. Ind. Mus., Midwest Mus. Conf. Office: Dept Natural Resources Exec Office 402 W Washington St Indianapolis IN 46204

GANTZ, SUZI GRAHN, special education educator; b. Chgo., May 17, 1954; d. Robert Donald and Barbara Edna (Ascher) Grahn; m. Louis Estes Gantz, July 11, 1976; children: Christopher, Joshua. BS in Edn. of Deaf and Hard of Hearing, U. Ill., 1976. Tchr. A.G. Bell Sch., Chgo., 1976-80, 88—, facilitator Edn. Connection grant, 1999-2001; sales asst. Bob Grahn & Assocs., Chgo., 1982-84; with sales dept. Isis/My Sisters Circus, Chgo., 1984 86; interpreter Glenbrook North High Sch., Northbrook, Ill., 1986-87; interpreter, aide Lake Forest (Ill.) Dist. 67, 1987-88. Mem. Northbrook Citizens for Drug and Alcohol Alliance, 1988—; cubmaster Boy Scouts Am., Northbrook, 1990-93. Mem. Ill. Tchrs. of the Hearing Impaired, A.G. Bell Soc., Coun. on Exceptional Children. Avocations: dancing, swimming. Home: 485 Laburnum Dr Northbrook IL 60062-2259 Office: AG Bell Sch 3730 N Oakley Ave Chicago IL 60618-4813

GANULIN, JUDY, public relations professional; b. Chgo., May 2, 1937; d. Alvin and Sadie (Reingold) Landis; m. James Ganulin, June 23, 1957; children: Stacy Ganulin Clark, Amy Ganulin Lowenstein. BA in Journalism, U. Calif., Berkeley, 1958. Copywriter-sec. Joe Connor Advt., Berkeley, 1958; exec. sec. Prescolite Mfg. Co., Berkeley, 1958-59; info. officer Office of Consumer Counsel, Sacramento, 1959-61; pub. rels. positions various polit. campaigns, Fresno, Calif., 1966; adminstrv. asst., editor, mktg. Valley Pubs., Fresno, 1971-80; staff asst. to county supr. Bd. Suprs., Fresno, 1980-82; field rep. Assemblyman Bruce Bronzan, Fresno, 1982-84; prin. Judy Ganulin Pub. Rels., Fresno, 1984—. Speaker new bus. workshop SBA/Svc. Corps Ret. Execs., Fresno, 1990—. Active Hadassah, Fresno, 1975—; pres. Temple Beth Israel Sisterhood, Fresno, 1976; panelist campaign workshop Nat. Women's Polit. Caucus, Fresno, 1994, 2001, publicity chmn. ctrl. Calif. chpt., 1999—2000; mem. C. of C. Art and Wine Festival Com., 1999—2000, Juvenile Justice Ctr. Task Force, 2001, Valley Women's Polit. Fund; bd. dirs. Temple Beth Israel, Fresno, 1972—75, Planned Parenthood Ctrl. Calif., Fresno, 1986—91, Empty Bowls, Sr. Companion Program. Mem. Pub. Rels. Soc. Am. (accredited pub. rels. practitioner, pres. Fresno/Ctrl. Valley chpt. 1994), Am. Mktg. Assn. (pres. ctrl. Calif. chpt. 1987-88), Calif. Press Women, Fresno Advt. Fedn., Fresno Comm. Network (v.p., pres. 1991-93), Fresno C. of C. (mem. mktg. com.

1988—), Fresno Comm. Network (formerly Pub. Rels. Roundtable) . Democrat. Avocations: traveling, reading, cooking. Office: Judy Ganulin Pub Rels 1117 W San Jose Ave Fresno CA 93711-3112 E-mail: jganulin@comcast.net.

GANZ, CHARLES, laboratory executive; Pres. En-Cas Analytical Lab., Winston-Salem, NC, 1976—. Office: En-Cas 2359 Farrington Point Dr Winston Salem NC 27107-2457

GANZ, CHARLES DAVID, lawyer; b. N.Y.C., Oct. 1, 1946; s. Harold Leonard and Mimi (Platzker) G.; m. Carol Susan Fisher, June 5, 1969; children: Jonathan, Adam, Melissa. AB, Franklin and Marshall Coll., 1968; JD, Duke U., 1972; LLM in Taxation, NYU, 1976. Bar: N.Y. 1973, U.S. Ct. Appeals (2d cir.) 1973, Ga. 1976, U.S. Dist. Ct. (so. and ea. dists.) N.Y. 1973, U.S. Ct. Appeals (11th cir) 1979, U.S. Dist. Ct. (no. dist.) Ga. 1979. Assoc. Cahill Gordon & Reindel, N.Y.C., 1972-76, Gambrell & Russell, Atlanta, 1976-77, ptnr., 1978-81, Branch, Pike & Ganz, Atlanta, 1982-95, Sutherland, Asbill & Brennan, Atlanta, 1998—. Trustee, pres. Ga. Fed. Tax Conf., 1985-87; trustee The Davis Acad., Japan Am. Soc. Ga., 1999—. Trustee Atlanta Ballet, 1980-82; trustee, pres. Am.-Israel Ednl. Inst. of the S.E., 1999—. Served to staff sgt. USAR, 1968-74. Mem. ABA, Ga. Bar Assn., N.Y. Bar Assn., Atlanta Bar Assn., Atlanta Tax Forum, The Standard Club (trustee 2003—). Jewish. Home: 160 Hidden Falls Ln NW Atlanta GA 30328-1960

GANZ, DAVID L. lawyer; b. N.Y.C., July 28, 1951; s. Daniel M. and Beverlee (Kaufman) G.; m. Barbara Bondanza, Nov. 3, 1974 (div. 1978); m. Sharon Ruth Lamnin, Oct. 30, 1981 (div. 1996); children: Scott Harry, Elyse Toby, Pamela Rebecca; m. Kathleen Ann Gotsch, Dec. 28, 1996. BS in Fgn. Svc., Georgetown U., 1973; JD, St. John's U., 1976. Bar: N.Y. 1977, D.C. 1980, N.J. 1985; cert. mediator U.S. Dist. Ct. (N.J.). Assoc. Regan, Dorsey & De Riso, Flushing, N.Y., 1977-79; ptnr. Durst & Ganz, N.Y.C., 1979-80; mng. ptnr. Ganz, Hollinger & Towe, N.Y.C., 1981-98, Ganz & Hollinger, N.Y.C., 1999—. Exec. com. Industry Coun. Tangible Assets, Washington, 1983—, bd. dirs.; pres. World Mint Coun., 1993-95; cons. in field. Author: A Critical Guide to the Anthologies of African Literature, 1973, A Legal and Legislative History of 31 USC Sec 342d-324i, 1976, The World of Coin Collecting, 1980, 3d edit., 1998, The 90 Second Lawyer, 1996, The 90 Second Lawyer's Guide to Selling Real Estate, 1997, How to Get an Instant Mortgage, 1997, Planning Your Rare Coin Retirement, 1998, Guide Commemorative Coin Values, 1999, Official Guide to America's State Quarters, 2000, rev. edit., 2002; corr. Numis. News Weekly, 1969-73, 96—, asst. editor, 1973-74, spl. corr., 1974-75, columnist, 1969-76, 96—; contbg. editor, columnist COINage Mag., 1974—; columnist Coin World, 1974-96, COINS Mag., 1973-83; contbr. articles to profl. jours. Presdl. appointee Annual Assay Commn., 1974; bd. dirs. Georgetown Libr. Assocs., Washington, 1982—, Bialystoker Home & Infirmary for the Aged, N.Y.C., 2001—, Care Plus N.J. Inc., 2003—; mem. N.Y. County Draft Bd., 1984, Bergen County, N.J., 1985—, vice chair, 1996—; mem. Citizens Commemorative Coin Adv. Com. U.S. Treas., 1993-96; sec., mem. Zoning and Adjustment Bd., Fair Lawn, N.J., 1988-92, chmn., 1993-97; elected mem. Dem. County Com. Bergen County, 1988-96, borough coun. Borough of Fair Lawn, 1998—, mayor, 1999—, Bergen County freeholder, 2003—; atty. Zoning Bd. Adjustment, Paramus, 2002-2003. Decorated Order of St. Agatha (Republic of San Marino). Fellow Am. Numis. Soc. (life); mem. Am. Numis. Assn. (life, legis. coun. 1978-81, 83-95, elected bd. govs. 1985-95, v.p. 1991-93, pres. 1993-95), Assn. of Bar of City of N.Y. (com. on state legis. 1987-90), N.Y. State Bar Assn. (mem. civil practice com., chmn. subcom. 1978-84), Profl. Numis. Guild Inc. affiliated mem. 1989—, gen. coun. 1981-92), Am. Soc. Internat. Law, Nat. Assn. Coin and Precious Metals Dealers (asoc. mem., gen. coun. 1981-85), Flushing Lawyers Club (pres. 1982-83). Democrat. Jewish. Avocation: numismatics. Office: Ganz & Hollinger PC 1394 3rd Ave New York NY 10021-0404 E-mail: davidlganz@aol.com.

GANZ, FELIX, marketing professional; b. New Brunswick, N.J., Sept. 2, 1959; s. Felice Pelligrino and Jenny (Becucci) G. BA, LaSalle U., 1983. Ops. mgr. E.R. Squibb & Sons, Princeton, N.J., 1986-88; account exec. Met. Life Ins., East Brunswick, N.J., 1988-89, Nann Agy., Inc., Metuchen, N.J., 1989-90; v.p., registered rep. Couch/Braunsdorf Ins. Group, Inc., Westfield, N.J., 1990—. Comml. arbitrator Am. Arbitration Assn., N.Y.C., 1990-2000. 1st lt. U.S. Army, 1983-86, capt. Res., 1988-99. Mem. ABA, Nat. Assn. Life Underwriters, Ind. Ins. Agts., U.S. Army Ranger Assn., Internat. Platform Assn. Avocations: flying, skydiving. Home: 11 Garnet Ct Franklin Park NJ 08823-1601 Office: Couch/Braunsdorf Ins Group 701 Martinsville Rd PO Box 888 Liberty Corner NJ 07938-0888 E-mail: fganz@couchbraundorf.com.

GANZ, HOWARD LAURENCE, lawyer; b. N.Y.C., Apr. 3, 1942; s. Myron and Beatrice (W.) Ganz; children: Beth, David. BA, Colgate U., 1963; LLB, Columbia U., 1966. Bar: N.Y. 1966, U.S. Dist. Ct. (so. dist.) N.Y. 1968, U.S. Dist. Ct. (ea. dist.) N.Y. 1969, U.S. Dist. Ct. (no. dist.) Calif. 1984, U.S. Ct. Appeals (3rd cir.) 1974, U.S. Ct. Appeals (4th cir.) 1985, U.S. Dist. Ct. (9th cir.) 1984, U.S. Dist. Ct. (D.C. cir.) 1986, U.S. Supreme Ct. 1986. Law clk. to Hon. Marvin E. Frankel U.S. Dist. Ct., N.Y.C., 1966-68; assoc., ptnr., co-chair sports law group, mem. exec. com. Proskauer Rose LLP, N.Y.C., 1968—. Articles editor: Columbia Law Rev. Named One of 100 Best Lawyers in N.Y., N.Y. Mag., 1995, One of Best Lawyers in America, 1997. Fellow Coll. Labor and Employment Lawyers; mem. Fed. Bar Coun., N.Y. State Bar Assn., N.Y. County Lawyers Assn., Assn. of Bar of City of N.Y. (chair com. on sports law 2003-). Office: Proskauer Rose LLP 1585 Broadway New York NY 10036-8299 Fax: 212-969-2900. E-mail: hganz@proskauer.com.

GANZ, MARY KEOHAN, lawyer; b. Weymouth, Mass., Nov. 17, 1954; d. Francis and Margaret (Quinn) Keohan; m. Alan H. Ganz, Sept. 7, 1980. BA magna cum laude, Emmanuel Coll., 1976; JD, Suffolk U., 1979. Bar: Mass. 1979, U.S. Dist. Ct. Mass. 1979, N.H. 1981, U.S. Dist. Ct. N.H. 1981. Pvt. practice, Seabrook, N.H., 1981—. With Anna Jaques Hosp., 2002—. Bd. dirs. My Greatest Dream Inc., Seabrook, 1985—; corporator Anna Jaques Hosp., 2002—. Mem. ABA, N.H. Bar Assn., Rockingham County Bar Assn., Seabrook Bus. and Profl. Assn. (pres. 1986-87), Seacoast Vis. Nurses Assn. (bd. dirs. 1994-2001, sec. 1997-98, v.p. 1998-99, pres. 1999-2001), Phi Delta Phi, Kappa Gamma Pi. Roman Catholic. Office: 779 Lafayette Rd Seabrook NH 03874-4215

GANZ, WILLIAM ISRAEL, radiology educator, medical director, researcher; b. Munich, Jan. 2, 1951; s. Lazar and Jean Ganz; m. Susan Rebecca Sirota, June 22, 1980; children: Tova, Debora, Harry. BA, Adelphi U., 1972; MS, MD, Albert Einstein Coll. Medicine, Medicine, 1979. Diplomate Am. Bd. Nuclear Medicine. NIH med. scientist trainee Albert Einstein Coll. Medicine, Bronx, N.Y., 1972-78, pharmacology rsch. fellow, 1978-79, NIH cardiovasc. fellow, 1979-80, resident in radiology, 1980-83; radiology/nuc. medicine fellow Barnes Hosp./Inst. Radiology, St. Louis, 1983-85; from asst. prof. to assoc. prof. U. Miami Sch. Medicine, Fla., 1985-97, coord. nuc. medicine tchg. program, 1990-97; radiation safety officer, coord. clin. nuc. medicine South Shore Hosp., 1994-97; dir. nuc. medicine Animal Rsch. Lab., 1995-97; med. dir. PET/Nuc. Medicine Ctr. and Bone Mineral Density Cts. Metabolic Imaging of Boca Raton, Fla., 1996-98; instr. radiology, nuc. medicine Mt. Sinai Med. Ctr., Miami Beach, Fla., 1998-99; staff cons. nuclear cadiology Cedars Med. Ctr., 1985—; medical dir. Imaging Ctr. and Diagnostic Testing Group, Miami, 1996—. Staff South Shore Hosp., 1994—; prof. panel Pfizer Pharms., Miami, 1986-95; guest editor Nuc. Medicine Ednl. Review, 1996—; med. dir. Diagnostic Testing Ctr. and Imaging Ctr., Atlantis, Fla., 1998—; staff physician nuclear medicine Holy Cross Hosp., Ft. Lauderdale, Fla., 1999, Clin. Neurosci. Inst. Brain Rsch. Group, 1999—; rsch. reviewer NIH, 2000—. Reviewer Jour. Nuc. Medicine, 2001—; exhibitor in field; contbr. articles to profl. jours. Recipient, RSNA cum laude award, 1990-91, NIH Svc. awards 1975-78, NSF award 1976. Mem. AMA (lectr. 2000—), Am. Coll. Nuc. Physicians, Am. Coll. Cardiology, Radiol. Soc. N.Am., Soc. Nuc. Medicine, Soc. Magnetic Resonance Imaging, Am. Soc. Orthodox Jewish Scientists. Democrat. Jewish. Home: 4333 Adams Ave Miami FL 33140-2927

GANZARAIN, RAMON CAJIAO, psychoanalyst; b. Iquique, Chile, Apr. 18, 1923; s. Eusebio Ganzarain and Maria Cajiao; m. Matilde Vidal Soto, Oct. 10, 1953; children: Ramon, Mirentxu, Alejandro. BS, St. Ignacio Coll., Santiago, Chile, 1939; MD, U. Chile, Santiago, 1947; postgrad., Chilean Psychoanalytic Inst., 1947-50, cert. tng. analyst, 1953. Assoc. prof. psychiatry U. Chile, Santiago, 1955-68, dir. dept. med. edn., 1962-68; prof. depth psychology, sch. psychology Cath. U., Santiago, 1962-68; dir. Chilean Psychoanalytic Inst., Santiago, 1967-68; tng. analyst Topeka Inst. Psychoanalysis, 1968-87; dir. group psychotherapy services The Menninger Found., Topeka, 1978-87; geog. tng. analyst Columbia U. Ctr. for Psychoanalytic Tng. and Research, Atlanta, 1987; assoc. prof. psychiatry Emory U., Atlanta, 1988—; tng. analyst Emory U. Psychoanalytic Inst., 1988—; geog. tng. analyst Fla. Psychoanalytic Inst., 2000—. Interviewed by CNN on numerous topics concerning trauma and/or the Middle East conflict. Author: Fugitives of Incest, 1988, Object Relations Group Psychotherapy, 1989; contbr. articles to profl. jours., chpts. to books. Fellow Am. Group Psychotherapy Assn.; mem. AMA, Internat. Assn. Group Psychotherapy (bd. dirs., exec. counselor 1986), Am. Group Psychotherapy Assn. (bd. dirs. 1984-87, 93-96), Internat. Psychoanalytic Assn., Am. Psychoanalytic Assn., Kans. Med. Soc., Atlanta Psychoanalytic Soc., Topeka Psychoanalytic Soc. (pres. 1985-87). Roman Catholic. Avocations: music, swimming, photography, writing, collecting antarctic stamps. Office: Emory U Psychoanalytic Inst Dept Psychiatry PO Box AF Atlanta GA 30337-0503 E-mail: rganzarain@aol.com.

GANZBURG, MIKHAIL, mathematics educator, researcher; b. Dniepropetrovsk, Ukraine, Jan. 22, 1948; s. Joseph and Gnesia Ganzburg; m. Natalia Schkolnikov, Jan. 23, 1971; 1 child, Stanislav. MS in Pure Math., Dniepropetrovsk State U., 1970, PhD, 1974. Assoc. prof. Dniepropetrovsk State U., 1981—91; vis. mem. Courant Inst. of Math. Scis. NYU, NYC, 1992—96; assoc. prof. Hampton (Va.) U., 1996—. Contbr. more than 50 articles to math. jours. Fellow, NY Acad. Scis., 1992. Mem.: Am. Math. Soc. Home: 212 Woodburn Dr Hampton VA 23664 Office: Hampton Univ Hampton VA 23668 Office Fax: 757-727-5832 (757) 727-5832. Business E-Mail: michael.ganzburg@hamptonu.edu.

GANZI, VICTOR FREDERICK, publishing executive; b. NYC, Feb. 14, 1947; s. Walter John and Gertrude (Meyer) G.; m. Patricia Frances Martin, July 10, 1971; children: Danielle Martin, Victoria Louise. BS, Fordham U., 1968; JD, Harvard U., 1971; LLM in Taxation, NYU, 1981. Bar: N.Y. 1973, U.S. Dist. Ct. (so. and ea. dists.) N.Y. 1975, U.S. Ct. Appeals (2d cir.) 1975, U.S. Tax Ct. 1975; CPA, Colo. Tax acct. Touche Ross & Co., Denver, 1971-73; assoc. Rogers & Wells, N.Y.C., 1973-78, ptnr., 1978-86, mng. ptnr., 1986-90; v.p., sec., gen. counsel Hearst Corp., N.Y.C., 1990-92, CFO, chief legal officer, sr. v.p., 1992-94, also bd. dirs., pres., CEO NYC, 2002—; exec. v.p., pres. Hearst Books/Bus. Pub. Group, 1997-98; exec. v.p., COO Heart Corp, 1998—2002. Bd. dirs. Palm Mgmt. Corp., N.Y.C., PGA Tour, Inc., ESPN, N.Y.C., IMI Sys. Inc., N.Y.C., N.Y.C. Econ. Devel. Corp., Olsten Corp.; mem. Coun. future of Law Sch., NYU Sch. Law; chmn. Hearst Argyle TV, 2003—; spkr. in field. Mem. ABA, AICPA, Colo. Soc. CPAs, Sky Club, Cherry Valley Club (Garden City, N.Y.). Office: The Hearst Corp 959 8th Ave New York NY 10019-3795

GAO, HAIYAN, science educator; d. Zhongshun Gao and Mei Chen; 1 child, Calvin Li. PhD, Calif. Inst. Tech., 1994. Rsch. assoc. U. Ill., Urbana-Champaign, 1994—96; asst. physicist Argonne (Ill.) Nat. Lab., 1996—97; asst. prof. MIT, Cambridge, Mass., 1997—2002; assoc. prof. physics Duke U., Durham, NC, 2002—. Assoc. prof. MIT, 2002. Recipient Gu Yu-Zhen Award, Tsinghua U., 1988, Ou You-Yi Award, Ou You-Yi Found., 1993, Outstanding Jr. Faculty Investigator Award, U.S. Dept. Energy, 2000. Mem.: Am. Phys. Soc. (assoc.). Achievements include research in precision measurement of neutron magnetic form factor using novel experimental technique of polarized electrons scattering from a polarized 3He nuclear target.

GAO, HONG WEN, retired chemical engineer; b. Taipei, Taiwan, Jan. 31, 1945; came to U.S., 1970; s. Don Ching and Mahn (Chen) Gao; m. Ellen Ling Tsuei, Apr. 7, 1973; children: Karen G., Judy G., Stanley G. BSChemE, Nat. Taiwan U., 1968; PhD in Chem. Engring., U. Utah, 1979. Postdoctoral rsch. assoc. U. Utah, Salt Lake City, 1979-83; sr. engr. Nat. Inst. for Petroleum and Energy Rsch., Bartlesville, Okla., 1984-93; prin. chem. engr. BDM-Okla., Inc./NIPER, Bartlesville, 1994-96, TRW/BDM Petroleum Techs., Bartlesville, Okla., 1996-98; ret., 1999. Contbr. articles to the U.S. Dept. Energy fossil energy and profl. jours. including Jour. of Rheology, Metall. Trans B, Macromolecules, Ency. of Engring. Materials, SPE Reservoir Engring., SPE Reservoir Evaluation and Engring. Fund raiser Am. Heart Assn., 1991, 94, 95. Mem. AIChE, Am. Chem. Soc., Soc. of Petroleum Engrs., Sigma Xi. Republican. Achievements include a 3-dimensional, 3-phase simulator for mobility control and permeability modification in subterranean formations, a simulator for solution mining of primary copper ore. Home: 4723 Melody Ln Bartlesville OK 74006-2725 E-mail: hgao292019@yahoo.com.

GAO, HONGJUN, mathematician; s. Mingbao Gao and Juzhen Fan. PhD, Inst. Appl. Phys. Comput. Math., Beijing, 1991—94. Assoc. prof. Nanjing Normal U., China, 2000—01, prof., 2001—. Office: Dept Math Nanjing Normal Univ Ninhai Rd 122 Jiangsu Province Nanjing 210097 China

GAO, LUJI, foreign language educator, columnist; b. Tian Jin, China, May 18, 1941; s. Shaohua and Guoqin (Yang) G.; m. Leiping (Ding), Feb. 3, 1969; children: Grace Jie, Yang. BS civil engring., Qing Hua U., Beijing, China, 1965, MS arch., 1980; M Christian ministry, Christian Witness Theol. Seminary, Calif., 2001—. Chief civil engr. First Constrn. Corp., Beijing, 1965-80; gen. mgr. Golden East Products Com., Morton Grove, Ill., 1981-82; corr. Wen Wei Po, Hong Kong, 1983-97; Mandarin Chinese instr. Coll. San Mateo, Calif., 1989—. Author: The Bronze Sword, 1981 (award Nat. Sci. Short Story Contest, Ministry of Culture, China 1981), editor-in-chief Hua Sheng TV, San Mateo, 1991-98; pres., editor-in-chief China Jour., San Francisco, 1994-95; columnist Hong Kong Econ. Jour., 1997—; contbg. articles to profl. jour. Deacon, San Francisco Mandarin Bapt. Ch., 1997-2000. Avocations: art appreciation and collection, travel, watching movies, singing. Home: 185 Santa Cruz Ave Daly City CA 94014-1051

GAO, XIUHUA, medical researcher; arrived in U.S., 2000; d. Zhenhe Gao and Shurong Pei; m. Qiguang Zhao, Feb. 26, 1959; 1 child, Yue Zhao. MB, Bejing Med. U., 1983; PhD, Tokai U., Isehara, Japan, 1993. Tchg. asst. Jilin (China) Med. Coll., 1983—88, lectr., 1988—89, 1993—94, assoc. prof., 1994—98; rsch. fellow Tokai U. Sch. Medicine, Isehara, 1998—99; postdoctoral rsch. fellow Tokai U. Sch. of Medicine, Isehara, 1999—2000; postdoctoral rsch. assoc. Baylor Coll. Medicine, Houston, 2000—02, Creighton U., Omaha, 2002—. Contbr. articles to profl. jours. Postdoctoral traineeship, Dept. Def. U.S. Army Med. Rsch. and Materiel Command Congressionally Directed Med. Rsch. Programs-Breast Cancer Rsch. Program, 2002. Mem.: Endocrine Soc., Sigma Xi. Office: Creighton Univ 2500 California Plaza Omaha NE 68178 E-mail: xiuhuagao@hotmail.com.

GAPOSCHKIN, PETER JOHN ARTHUR, programmer analyst, physicist; b. Boston, Apr. 5, 1940; s. Sergei Illarionvich and Cecilia Helena (Payne) G. Student, Boston U., 1957-58; BS, MIT, 1961; PhD, U. Calif., Berkeley, 1971. Lic. comml. radiotele. operator with radar endorsement, amateur extra class, FCC. Physicist NAVPRO, Sunnyvale, Calif., 1973-75; computer programmer Fleet Num Ocean Ctr., Monterey, Calif., 1975-79; sr. analyst Informatics, Palo Alto, Calif., 1979-80; instr. Merritt Coll., Oakland, Calif., 1980-81, San Francisco City C.C., 1981-82; programmer analyst bur. mgmt. info. systems San Francisco Pub. Utilities Commn., 1983—97; programmer analyst San Francisco Mcpl. Ry., 1997—. Mem. job acquisition com. Experience Unltd., Oakland, 1982-83. Mem. Univ. Ave. Ctr. Coun. Consumers Coop. Berkeley, 1978-86, Shattuck Ave. Ctr. Coun. Consumers Coop. Berkeley, 1987-88. Mem. AAAS, Am. Astron. Soc., Astron. Soc. Pacific, Toastmasters (area E-5 gov. 1995-96, area E-4 gov. 1996-97, dist. 4 asst. pub. rels. officer 1997-98, pub. rels. officer 1999-2000). Unitarian Universalist. Home: 1315 Dwight Way #1 Berkeley CA 94702 Office: 875 Stevenson San Francisco CA 94103 E-mail: peter_gaposchkin@ci.sf.ca.us.

GARABEDIAN, CHARLES, JR., mathematician, educator; b. Whitinsville, Mass., July 16, 1943; s. Charles and Sadie (Mandanjian) Garabedian; m. Manoushag Manougian. BS, Worcester State Coll., 1965; MEd, Framingham State Coll., 1970; PhD, U. Conn., 1981. Cert. secondary tchr. Mass. Math. tchr. Holliston (Mass.) High Sch., 1965—2001; assoc. prof. math. Framingham (Mass.) State Coll., 1971-75, 84—; math. instr. Ea. Conn. State Coll., Willimantic, 1976. Cons., math. instr. Huntington Learning Ctr., Shrewsbury, Mass., 1993—; vis. lectr. Quinsigamond C.C., Worcester, Mass., 2002—. Recipient Presdl. Disting. Tchr. award, 1991, Practitioner award, Harvard U., 1988, Disting. Tchr. award, White Ho. Commn. Presdl. Scholars, 1991, Christa Corrigan McAuliffe award, Christa McAuliffe Ctr. Edn. and Tchg. Excellence, 1996, Disting. Tchr. award, Border's Books, 2000. Mem.: Mass. Assn. Supervision and Curriculum Devel., Nat. Coun. Tchrs. Math., Nat. Assn. RR Passengers, Mass. Assn. RR Passengers, Knights of Vartan, Phi Delta Kappa. Armenian Evang. Ch. Avocations: music, photography, model railroads, cooking, reading. Home: PO Box 452 Shrewsbury MA 01545-0452

GARABEDIAN, JOSEPH ANDRE, physician; b. Lattakia, Syria, May 1, 1945; came to U.S., 1974; s. Simon and Naimah Aka Leonie (Totonjian) G.; m. Virginia Fala, June 11, 1977; children: Simone Marie, Joseph Andre, Marc Anthony. B in Sci. Session, Terra Santa Coll., Lattakia, Syria, 1962; MS, Damascus (Syria) U., 1965, MD, 1973. Resident in surgery Harasta Gen. Hosp., Damascus, 1973-74; rotating intern Mercy Cath. Med. Ctr., Darby, Pa., 1974-75; resident in surgery Sacred Heart Hosp., Norristown, Pa., 1975-77; med. house officer Montgomery Hosp., Norristown, 1977-88, emergency rm. physician, 1977-83; pvt. practice Norristown, 1978—. Med. dir. out-patient clinics Montgomery Hosp., 1988-91. Composer instrumental, orchestral and vocal works, 1958—. Bd. dirs. Armenian Sisters Acad., Radnor, Pa., 1987—93; chmn. parish coun. St. Mark's Armenian Cath. Ch., Wynnwood, Pa., 1988—92, 1999—2001; vice chmn. Armenian InterCommunal Com., Phila., 1999—2001; pres. Armenian InterCommunal Com., 2001—. Recipient Golden Lyre award Nat. Solo Piano Competition, Syria, 1961; named to Legion of Honor Chappel of the Four Chaplains, Phila., 1983, Knight of the Order of St. Gregory the Great, Holy See, The Vatican, 1992. Fellow: Am. Acad. Family Physicians; mem.: Pa. Acad. of Family Practice, Am. Acad. of Family Practice, Armenian Am. Med. and Dental Assn. Greater Phila. (v.p. 1992—94, pres. 1995—97), Montgomery County Med. Soc., Pa. Med. Soc., AMA. Armenian Catholic. Avocations: organ and piano performing, composing music, philately, coin collecting, arts. Office: 104 Egypt Rd Norristown PA 19403-3029 E-mail: drgarabedian@dnahail.com.

GARAFALO, LYNNE MARY, audiologist, speech and language pathologist; b. Boston, Apr. 29, 1954; d. Ralph Dominic and Maria Lenore (Tedeschi) G.; m. Robert Joseph Dalicandro, Mar. 22, 1975 (div. Dec. 1982); m. Edwin Joel Furman, Dec. 31, 1995. BS, Northeastern U., 1977, MS, 1992. Cert. clin. competence; lic. speech/lang. pathologist and audiologist. Speech pathologist Worcester (Mass.) Pub. Schs., 1978-90, audiologist, 1992—. Mem. traumatic brain injury team Worcester Pub. Schs., 1995—, co-founder hard of hearing program, 1995—, mem. ctrl. auditory processing com., 1998—, cochlear implant team, 2000—. Com. mem. Yankee Homecoming, Newburyport, Mass., 1992-94. Mem. Am. Speech and Hearing Assn. (ACE award 1999), Mass. Speech-Hearing Assn. Avocations: athletics, travel. Home: 8 Goulding Rd Sterling MA 01564

GARAGIOLA, JOE, JR., baseball team executive; m. Noel Garagiola; children: Meredith, Valerie, Natalie, Christopher. BA cum laude, U. Notre Dame, 1972; JD, Georgetown U., 1975. Bar: Ariz., Calif., N.Y. Gen. counsel, asst. to pres. N.Y. Yankees, N.Y.C.; ptnr. Gallagher and Kennedy, Phoenix, 1982—; chmn. bd. dirs. Phoenix Met. Sports Found., 1985-87; v.p., gen. mgr. Ariz. Diamondbacks (profl. baseball expansion team), 1995—. Vice chmn. Gov.'s Cactus League Task Force, Phoenix; mem. Mayor's profl. baseball com.; chmn. Maricopa County (Ariz.) Sports Authority, Ariz. Baseball Commn. Bd. dirs. Am. West Airlines Ednl. Found., Phoenix Meml. Hosp. Recipient Inst. Human Rels. award, Am. Jewish Com., 1998. Office: c/o Ariz Diamondbacks 401 E Jefferson St Phoenix AZ 85004-2438

GARAHAN, PETER THOMAS, software company executive; b. Queens, N.Y., Sept. 6, 1946; s. Thomas Hugh and Catherine Amelia (Slavin) G.; m. Maryam Aminzadeh, Jan. 26, 1985. BA in History and Polit. Sci, SUNY, Stony Brook, 1971; MBA, Cornell U., 1977. Real estate salesman Martin Assocs., Killington, Vt., 1972-75; asst. to pres., asst. to bd. dirs. United Nuclear Corp./UNC Resources, Falls Church, Va., 1977-79, treas., 1979-83, v.p., 1980-83; v.p., chief fin. officer Sage Systems Inc., Rockville, Md., 1984-88; exec. v.p., chief oper. officer Chartway Techs., Rockville, 1988-92; pres., chief exec. officer Med. Claims Rev. Svc., 1992-94; pres., CEO Mitchell Med., 1994-97; exec. v.p. sales and mktg. Mitchell Internat., 1995-97. Bd. dirs. Amteva Techs.; COO, dir. Amteva Techs., 1997-99; prin. The Ryegate Group, 1997—; vice chmn. Teligent, Inc., 2001—. Bd. dirs. Falls Church Jr. Achievement, 1980-83. Served with USNR, 1965-67.

GARAI, GAUTAM, engineer, researcher; b. Calcutta, W. Bengal, India, Dec. 12, 1964; s. Ramen Chandra and Usha G. B in Engring., Bengal Engring. Coll., Howrah, India, 1987; M in Engring., Jadavpur (India) U., Calcutta, 1991. Asst. systems engr. M.N. Dastur Co., Calcutta, India, 1987-88; scientist SB Saha Inst. Nuclear Physics, Calcutta, India, 1988-92, scientist SC, 1992-95, scientist SD, 1995—99, scientist SE, 1999—. Nat. scholarship Govt. India, 1981, 83. Mem.: IEEE (U.S.), Internat. Assn. Pattern Recognition (U.K.). Avocations: classical music, chess. Home: AE-236 Salt Lake City W Bengal Calcutta 700064 India Office: Saha Inst Nuclear Physics Blk -1/AF Bidhannagar W Bengal Calcutta 700064 India

GARARD, CHARLES JUSTUS, JR., language educator, writer; b. Washington, DC, Sept. 13, 1944; s. Charles Justus Garard Sr. and Jeanette Adele (Webster) Etling. BA, McKendree Coll., 1973; MA, So. Ill. U., Edwardsville, 1977; PhD, So. Ill. U., Carbondale, 1982. Adj. instr. McKendree Coll., Lebanon, Ill., 1977—81, Belleville Area Coll., Granite City, Ill., 1980—82; tchg. asst. So. Ill. U., Carbondale, Ill., 1982—86, lectr., 1986—87; adj. instr. John A. Logan Coll., Carterville, Ill., 1987—88; assoc. prof. Morris Brown Coll., Atlanta, 1988—. Writer, photographer St. Charles Jour., St. Charles, Mo., 1966—70, Tri-County Journal, Fairview Heights, Ill., 1970—71; tutor for Chinese students Cosmos Edn. Svcs., Chamblee, Ga., 1990—97, Chamblee, 2002. Author: Point of View in Fiction and Film, 1991; editor: The Enterprise Newspaper, 1976—77; contbr. articles to profl. literary publs. With USN. Grantee, McKendree Coll., 1972. Mem.: Am. Fedn. Tchrs. (sec. 1992—), Am. Assn. Univ. Profs. (sec. 1995—), Ga. Freelance Writers Assn. Avocations: writing, photography, bicycling. Home: 2040 DeKalb Ave Apt B-11 Atlanta GA 30307 Office: Morris Brown Coll G43 Martin Luther King Jr Dr NW Atlanta GA 30314

GARAUFIS, NICHOLAS G. district court judge; b. Paterson, N.J., Sept. 28, 1948; AB, Columbia Coll., 1969; JD, Columbia U., 1974. Assoc. Chadbourne & Parke, 1974-75; asst. atty. gen. N.Y. State, 1975-78; pvt. practice Queens, N.Y., 1978-86; counsel to Hon. Claire Shulman/Pres. of Borough of Queens, N.Y.C., 1986-95; chief counsel FAA, Washington, 1995-2000; judge ea. dist. U.S. Dist. Ct., Bklyn., 2000—. Office: US Dist Ct Ea Dist NY 225 Cadman Plz E Brooklyn NY 11201

GARAY, STEPHEN R. secondary school educator; b. Sewickley, Pa., July 26, 1963; s. Stephen E. and Nora Lee Garay; m. Suzanne M. Garay, Apr. 9, 1963; 2 children. MusB, Westminster Coll., 1985, MEd, 1991. Music tchr. Mercer (Pa.) Area Schs., 1985—87; music dir. Neshannock Ch., New Wilmington, Pa., 1982—; music tchr. Hermitage (Pa.) Schs., 1987—. Mem.: Hermitage Edn. Assn., Pa. Music Educators Assn. Office: Hickory High Sch 640 N Hermitage Rd Hermitage PA 16148

GARB, HOWARD NEIL, clinical psychologist, educator; b. Chgo., Jan. 27, 1955; s. Julius and Suzanne Rhoda (Weinberg) G.; m. Flora Horowitz, Sept. 20, 1981; children: Merrick, Leanna. BA in Psychology with high distinction, U. Ill., 1977, MA, 1981, PhD, 1983. Lic. psychologist Bur. Profl. and Occupl. Affairs, Pa. NIMH postdoctoral fellow Northwestern U., Evanston, Ill., 1983-84; clin. psychologist VA Health Care Sys., Pitts., 1984—2003; clin. instr. psychiatry U. Pitts., 1984-99, clin. asst. prof., 2000—02, clin. assoc. prof., 2002—03; chief Psychology Rsch. Svc. Wilford Hall Med. Ctr., Lackland AFB, Tex., 2003—. Author: Studying the Clinician, 1998; contbr. articles profl. jours., popular sci. mags. Fellow APA (divsn. 12 clin. psychology sect.); mem. Soc. for Sci. of Clin. Psychology (sect. III). Jewish. Achievements include description of the validity of judgments made by mental health professionals; description of occurrence of race bias and gender bias in clinical assessment; description of reasons why clinicians have trouble learning from clinical experience. Avoca-

tion: jazz music. Home: 3670 Hunters Cliff San Antonio TX 78230 Office: Psychology Rsch Svc Wilford Hall Med Ctr 2200 Bergquist Dr Ste 1 San Antonio TX 78236-5300 E-mail: howard.garb@lackland.af.mil.

GARBACIAK-BOBBER, JOYCE KATHERINE, news anchor; b. Chgo., July 9, 1962; d. John Anthony and Irene Helen (Mroz) Garbaciak; m. Bernard John Bobber, Apr. 8, 1989; children: Caitlin Elizabeth, Meredith Grace, Grace Carolyn. BS in Journalism, Northwestern U., 1984, MS in Journalism, 1985. Reporter, anchor WSAW-TV, Wausau, Wis., 1985-87, WTVF-TV, Nashville, 1987-88, WITI-TV, Milw., 1988—. Guest spkr. in field. Mem. Coun. of 100, Northwestern U.; vis. faculty Poynter Inst. for Journalists, 2001. Recipient various honors, Milw. Press Club, Associated Press, Wis. Broadcasters Assn., Emmy award. Mem. Radio and TV News Dirs. Assn. Office: WITI-TV 9001 N Green Bay Rd Milwaukee WI 53209-1297

GARBACZ, PATRICIA FRANCES, school social worker, therapist; b. Hamtramck, Mich., Nov. 26, 1941; d. Stanley and Frances (Harubin) G. BS, Siena Heights Coll., 1969; M. Pastoral Counseling, St. Paul U., Ottawa, Can., 1972; ThM, St. John Provincial Sem., 1983; MSW, Wayne State U., 1989. Cert. social worker Acad. Cert. Social Workers; cert. sch. social worker; lic. marriage and family therapist; cert. addictions counselor level I. Assoc. dir. vocations Archdiocese of Detroit, 1975-77; co-dir. of inst. for women Archdiocese of Lusaka (Zambia), 1977-78; pastoral minister Archdiocese of Detroit, 1979-80, assoc. dir. preformation, 1980-84; tchr., ministry coord. Bishop Borgess High Sch., Redford, Mich., 1984-86; tchr., dept. chair Aquinas High Sch., Southgate, Mich., 1986-88; therapist Community Coun. on Drug Abuse/Livonia (Mich.) Counseling, 1988-89; substance abuse therapist Oxford Inst., St. Clair Shores, Mich., 1989-91; sch. social worker Lakeshore Pub. Schs., St. Clair Shores, 1990—; therapist Macomb Child Guidance, 1989-96. Mem. NASW, Am. Assn. Marriage and Family Therapists, Mich. Assn. Sch. Social Workers. Avocations: reading, walking, piano, dulcimer, spinning and weaving.

GARBARINO, JOSEPH WILLIAM, labor arbitrator, economics and business educator; b. Medina, N.Y., Dec. 7, 1919; s. Joseph Francis and Savina M. (Volpone) G.; m. Mary Jane Godward, Sept. 18, 1948; children: Ann, Joan, Susan, Ellen. BA, Duquesne U., 1942; MA, Harvard U., 1947, PhD, 1949. Faculty U. Calif., Berkeley, 1949—, prof., 1960-88, dir. Inst. Bus. and Econ. Research, 1962-88, prof. emeritus, 1988—. Vis. lectr. Cornell U., 1959-60, UCLA, 1969, SUNY, Buffalo, 1972; Fulbright lectr. U. Glasgow, Scotland, 1969; vis. scholar U. Warwick; mem. staff Brookings Instn., 1959-60; vis. lectr. U. Minn., 1978; labor arbitrator. Author: Health Plans and Collective Bargaining, 1960, Wage Policy and Long Term Contracts, 1962, Faculty Bargaining: Change and Conflict, 1975, Faculty Bargaining in Unions in Transition. Served with U.S. Army, 1942-45, 51-53. Decorated Bronze Star. Democrat. Roman Catholic. Home: 7708 Ricardo Ct El Cerrito CA 94530-3344

GARBARINO, ROBERT PAUL, retired administrative dean, lawyer; b. Wanaque, N.J., Oct. 6, 1929; s. Attillio and Theresa (Napello) G.; m. Joyce A. Sullivan, June 29, 1957; children: Lynn, Lisa, Mark, Steven. BBA cum laude, St. Bonaventure U., 1951; JD with highest class honors, Villanova U., 1956. Bar: Pa. 1956, U.S. Dist. Ct. (ea. dist.) Pa. 1956, U.S. Ct. Appeals (3d cir.) 1962, U.S. Supreme Ct. 1962, U.S. Tax Ct. 1966, U.S. Ct. Internat. Trade 1966. Law clk. U.S. Dist. Ct. (ea. dist.) Pa., Phila., 1956-57; asst. counsel Phila. Electric Co., Phila., 1957-60, asst. gen. counsel, 1960-62; ptnr. Kania & Garbarino & predecessor firm, Phila. and Bala Cynwyd, Pa., 1962-81; assoc. dean adminstrn. Sch. Law Villanova (Pa.) U., 1981-96. Right-of-way cons. Edison Electric Inst., N.Y.C., 1960—62; trustee reorgn. Tele-Tronics Co., Phila., 1962—64; mem. bd. consultors Law Sch. Villanova U., 1967—81, mem. bd. consultors (life mem.), 1996—2003, chmn., vice chmn. bd. consultors, 1971—76; chmn. Profl. Sports Career Counseling Panel Villanova U.; mem. pres.'s adv. coun. St. Bonaventure U., NY, 1975—86, chmn., 1976—78. Contbr. articles to profl. jours.; 1st editor-in-chief Villanova U. Law Rev., 1954. Mem. community leadership seminar Fels Inst. Local and State Govt., 1961. Staff sgt. USMC, 1951-53. Mem. ABA, Phila. Bar Assn., Order of Coif. Home: 120 Ladderback Ln Devon PA 19333-1815

GARBATY, THOMAS JAY, retired English language educator; b. Jan. 10, 1930; BA, Haverford Coll., 1951; MA, U. Pa., 1954, PhD, 1957. Asst. prof. English Dept. Clemson U., 1957-60; mem faculty dept. English, U. Mich., Ann Arbor, 1960-93, prof., 1971-1993, prof. emeritus, 1993—. Vis. prof. U. Bern, Switzerland, 1970-80; TV commentator, PBS. Contbg. author Variorum Chaucer, 1970-90; asst. editor: Middle English Dictionary, 1960-61; mem. editl. bd. Genre, Envoi; editor Medieval English Lit., 1984—; contbr. to Medieval England, an Encyclopedia and Modern Language Assn. Approaches to Teaching the Canterbury Tales; reviewer, contbr. articles to profl. jours. Recipient Amoco Tchg. award, 1968, State of Mich. Tchg. Excellence award, 1990, First Biennial award U. Mich. Students with Disabilities, 1991. Mem. MLA (life, chmn. divsn. on Chaucer 1976), Medieval Acad., New Chaucer Soc., Phi Beta Kappa. Home: 2981 Hickory Ln Ann Arbor MI 48104-2840 Office: U Mich Dept English Ann Arbor MI 48109 E-mail: tgarbaty@umich.edu.

GARBER, BETTY KAHN, social worker; b. Jersey City, May 22, 1950; d. Bernard and Rita (Dorn) Kahn; m. Dale J. Garber, June 17, 1973; 1 child, Amy. AB, Washington U., St. Louis, 1971, MSW, 1973. Lic. clin. social worker, Ill.; diplomate Am. Bd. Examiners in Clin. Social Work. Social worker E. Maine Sch. Dist., Des Plaines, Ill., 1973-78, Northbrook (Ill.)/Glenview Sch. Dist., 1986—. Unit leader, asst. camp dir. Rogers Park Jewish Community Ctr., Chgo., summers, 1974, 75. Mem. sch. bd. W. Northfield Sch. Dist., Northbrook, 1983-95. Mem. NASW (bd. cert. diplomate, qualified clin. social worker, sch. social work specialist)., Acad. Cert. Social Workers. Office: Northbrook/Glenview Sch Dis 2500 Happy Hollow Rd Glenview IL 60025-1117 E-mail: bgarber@ync.net., bgarber@district30k12.il.us.

GARBER, BRUCE SAMUEL, lawyer; b. Detroit, Aug. 6, 1949; s. Jack and Freida (Fox) G.; m. Gloria Jeanne Elfond, Nov. 3, 1974; children— Jodi Gwen, Dustin Alan. B.A., U. Mich., 1971; J.D., Wayne State U., 1974. Bar: N.Mex. 1974, U.S. Dist. Ct. N.Mex. 1974, Calif. 1975, U.S. Ct. Appeals (D.C. cir.) 1975, U.S. Ct. Appeals (10th cir.) 1978, U.S. Supreme Ct., 1997. Staff atty. N.Mex. Environ. Improvement Div., Santa Fe, 1975-78, chief counsel, 1978 83; sole practice, Santa Fe, 1983-86; ptnr. Garber & Hallmark, P.C., Santa Fe, 1986—. Contbr. articles to profl. publs. Mem. N.Mex. Bar Assn., N.Mex. Supreme Ct. Specialization Bd. (chair), Calif. Bar Assn. Office: Garber & Hallmark PC 200 W Marcy St Ste 203 Santa Fe NM 87501-2036

GARBER, PAUL WILLIAM, lawyer; b. Boston, Nov. 16, 1934; s. Rubin Elias and Sarah Rose Garber. AB in Medieval History magna cum laude, Harvard Coll., 1956, JD, 1961; diploma in Command and Staff, U.S. Naval War Coll., 1967, diploma in Naval Warfare, 1970. Registered Land Court Title Examiner, 1966. Atty. Garber and Garber, Esqs., Boston, 1961-76, pres., 1976—; consul. Consulate of Chile, Boston, 1974—. Author: (with Philip C. Garber) The Political Constitution of Chile-An English Translation, 1981; contbr. articles to profl. jours. Pres. constn. chpt. Naval Res. Assoc., 1973-75, Navy Chpt. 5 Res. Officers Assn., 1979, First Region Naval Res. Assn., 1980, exec. v.p. 1971-72, Club Chileno, hon pres., 1974-80, dir. Alumni Assoc., West End House, 1963-99, Scholarship Com., 1976-99, bd. dirs. Eastern Mass. chpt. Navy League U.S., 1976-85; judge Adv. Mass. Bay Coun., NLUS, 1985-99, dir. emeritus, 1999—; trustee USS Constitution Mus., 2003—. Capt. USNR, 1956-86. Decorated Navy Commendation medal, USN; knight comdr. order Bernardo O'Higgins, Govt. Chile, 1979, grand officer, 1999. Mem.: Naval War Coll. Found. (life), Surface Warfare Assn. (life), USS Constn. Mus. (life), Navy League U.S. (life), Medieval Acad. Am. (life), USN Inst. (life), Mil. Officers Assn. Am. (life), Boston Athenaeum (life), Caleuche Club Litoral Valparaiso, Wardroom Club, Harvard Club of Boston. Avocations: gardening, reading, antiquarian rsch. Office: Consulate of Chile 1 Bernardo O'Higgins Cir Brighton MA 02135 E-mail: conchile.org@attbi.com.

GARBER, PHILIP CHARLES, lawyer; b. Boston, Nov. 16, 1934; s. Rubin E. and Sarah Rose (Schick) G. BA cum laude, Harvard U., 1956, JD, 1961. Bar: Mass. 1961, U.S. Ct. Appeals (1st cir.) 1977. Ptnr. Garber & Garber, Boston, 1961—. Title examiner Land Ct., Mass., 1966. Translator: The Political Constitution of Chile, 1980. Pres. West End House Boys Club Alumni Assn., Allston, Mass., 1982-83, Spellman Mus. Stamps & Postal History, 1993—; hon. consul, Chile, 1982. Named Comendador, Order of Bernardo O'Higgins, Republic of Chile. Mem. Harvard Club (Boston), Caleuche Club (Valparaiso). Office: Garber & Garber Esquires PC 19 Lanark Rd Boston MA 02135-7840

GARBER, ROBERT EDWARD, lawyer, insurance company executive; b. N.Y.C., Jan. 4, 1949; s. Edward Robert and Estelle (Rosenberg) G.; m. Mary Ellen Roche, Jan. 17, 1981; 1 child, Edward Thomas AB, Princeton U., 1970; JD, Columbia U., 1973. Bar: N.Y. 1974. Law clk. U.S. Dist. Ct. (so. dist.), N.Y.C., 1973-75; assoc. Debevoise, Plimpton, Lyons & Gates, N.Y.C., 1976-79; assoc. counsel, v.p. Irving Trust, N.Y.C., 1979-82, sr. v.p., 1982-87; gen. counsel Irving Bank Corp. and Irving Trust Co., N.Y.C., 1987-89; sr. v.p., dep. gen. counsel Equitable Life Assurance Soc. U.S., N.Y.C., 1989-93; sr. v.p., gen. counsel Equitable Cos., Inc. and Equitable Life Assurance Soc. U.S., 1993-94, exec. v.p., gen. counsel, 1994-99; exec. v.p., chief legal officer Equitable Life Assurance Soc. U.S., 1999—2001; exec. v.p., gen. counsel AXA Fin., Inc., 1999—2001. Served to capt. USAR, 1970-78 Home: 45 Sturgis Rd Bronxville NY 10708-5012

GARBER, SAMUEL B. lawyer, business/turnaround management consultant; b. Chgo., Aug. 16, 1934; s. Morris and Yetta G.; m. Marietta C. Bratta; children: Debra Lee, Diane Lori. JD, U. Ill., 1958; MBA, U. Chgo., 1968. Bar: Ill. 1958. Ptnr. Brown, Dashow and Langluttig, Chgo., 1960-62; corp. counsel Walgreen Co., 1962-69; v.p., gen. counsel, exec. asst. to the pres. Carlyle & Co., 1969-73; dir. legal affairs Stop & Shop Co., Inc., 1973-74; gen. counsel Goldblatt Bros., Inc., 1974-76; v.p., sec., gen. counsel, dir. Evans, Inc., 1976-99, pres., CEO, 1999-2000; prof. mgmt. DePaul U., 1975—; prin. The Garber Group, Bus. Cons. and Turnaround Management Firm, Chgo., 2000—. Adj. prof. bus. law grad. sch. bus. U. Chgo., 1993; arbitrator N.Y. Stock Exch., 1996, Chgo. Merc. Exch., 1996, Am. Stock Exch., 1997, Nat. Futures Assn., 1997; columnist Garber's Gurus Tribune Media Svcs., 1999—. With U.S. Army, 1958-60. Mem. ABA, NYSE (arbitrator 1996—), Am. Arbitration Assn. (arbitrator 1993—), Nat. Retail Fedn., Ill. Retail Mchts. Assn., Beta Gamma Sigma. Home: 2626 N Lakeview Ave Chicago IL 60614-1809 Office: DePaul U 1 E Jackson Blvd Ste 7010 Chicago IL 60604-2287 E-mail: thegarbergroup@yahoo.com.

GARBER, VICTOR, stage and film actor; b. London, Ont., Can., Mar. 16, 1949; Actor: (films) Liberace: Behind the Music, 1988, Light Sleeper, 1991, Sleepless in Seattle, 1993, Life with Mikey, 1993, Mixed Nuts, 1994, First Wives Club, 1996, Titanic, 1997, How Stella Got Her Groove Back, 1998, External Affairs, 1999, Legally Blonde, 2001, Tuck Everlasting, 2002, Home Room, 2002; (TV films) Life with Judy Garland: Me and My Shadows, 2001 (Emmy nominee); (TV series) Alias, 2001— (Emmy nominee, 2002), (TV appearances) Days and Nights of Molly Dodd, 1987, I'll Fly Away, 1991, E.N.G. intermittently, Kung Fu: The Legend Continues, 1992, Law and Order, 1990, Frasier, 1993 (Emmy nominee), Outer Limits, 1996, Invisible Child, 1999, The Music Man, 2002; (Broadway plays) Deathtrap, 1978 (Tony nominee), Sweeney Todd, 1979 (Tony nominee), Little Me, 1982 (Tony nominee), Lend Me A Tenor, 1989 (Tony nominee), revival of Damn Yankees, 1994 (Tony nominee), Art, 1998.*

GARBERDING, LARRY GILBERT, retired utilities companies executive; b. Albert City, Iowa, Oct. 29, 1938; s. Gilbert D. and Lavern Marie Garberding; m. Elizabeth Ann Hankens, Aug. 20, 1961; children: Scott Richard, Kathryn Ann, Michael John. BS, Iowa State U., 1960. CPA, Nebr. Ptnr. Arthur Andersen & Co., Chgo., 1960-71; chief fin. officer Kans.-Nebr. Natural Gas Co., Inc., Hastings, Nebr., 1971-81, Tenn. Gas Transmission, Houston, 1981-83, exec. v.p., 1983-87; pres. Tenn. Gas Mktg., Houston, 1987-88, NICOR Inc., Naperville, Ill., 1988-90; exec. v.p., chief fin. officer Detroit Edison Co., 1990—2001; ret., 2001. With U.S. Army, 1961. Mem. AICPA. Republican. Lutheran.

GARBIN, ALBENO PATRICK, sociology educator; b. Girard, Ill., June 20, 1932; s. Cipriano and Angelina (Sommavillia) G.; m. Carol Townsend Nichols, Sept. 3, 1969; children: Angela Marie, Tina Ann, A. Patrick, Carol Anne. AB, Blackburn Coll., 1956; MA, La. State U., 1959, PhD, 1963. Instr., asst. prof. sociology U. Omaha, 1961-64; asst. prof. Fla. State U., Tallahassee, 1964-66; assoc. prof., specialist occupation edn. Ohio State U., Columbus, 1966-68; prof. sociology U. Ga., Athens, 1968-97, prof. emeritus, 1997—. Served in U.S. Army, 1954-56. Recipient rsch. award Am. Personnel and Guidance Assn., 1977, Excellence in Undergrad. Tchg. award U. Ga., 1978, meritorious svc. award Ga. Soc. Assn., 1991. Mem. Am. Sociol. Assn., So. Sociol. Soc., Ga. Sociol. Assn. (v.p. (1984-85, pres.1986-87). Democrat. Roman Catholic. Avocations: gardening, photography. Home: 85 Timberland Trail Arnoldsville GA 30619-2216 Office: U Ga Dept Sociology Athens GA 30602 E-mail: algarbin@arches.uga.edu. *Hard work is a requisite, but luck can be very helpful! A loving wife and family make it all worthwhile.*

GARBRECHT, LOUIS, lawyer; b. Tulsa, Jan. 21, 1949; s. Louis and Amy (Harris) G.; m. Susan Kay Adams, July 1982; children: Kenneth, Douglas, Steven, Ursala, Heidi. BA, U. Wash., 1971; JD, U. Denver, 1975. Bar: Idaho 1975, U.S. Dist. Ct. Idaho 1975, U.S. Supreme Ct. 1980. Mng. atty. Idaho Legal Aid Svcs., Twin Falls, 1975-80; pvt. practice Twin Falls, 1980-82, Coeur D'Alene, Idaho, 1982—. Mem. Idaho State Bar (comml. law bankruptcy sect.). Democrat. Avocations: snow skiing, raquetball. Home and Office: 1400 E Sherman Ave Coeur D Alene ID 83814-4044

GARCHIK, LEAH LIEBERMAN, journalist; b. Bklyn., May 2, 1945; d. Arthur Louis and Mildred (Steinberg) Lieberman; m. Jerome Marcus Garchik, Aug. 11, 1968; children— Samuel, Jacob BA, Bklyn. Coll., 1966. Editorial asst. San Francisco Chronicle, 1972-79, writer, editor, 1979-83, editor This World, 1983-84, columnist, 1984—; also author numerous book and movie reviews, features and profiles. Author: San Francisco: the City's Sights and Secrets, 1995; panelist (radio quiz show) Mind Over Matter; contbr. articles to mags. Vice pres. Golden Gate Kindergarten Assn., San Francisco, 1978; pres. Performing Arts Workshop, San Francisco, 1977-79; bd. dirs. Home Away From Homelessness, 1994-99. Recipient 1st prize Nat. Soc. Newspaper Columnists, 1992. Mem. Deutsche Music Verein, Newspaper Guild. Democrat. Jewish. Home: 156 Baker St San Francisco CA 94117-2111 Office: San Francisco Chronicle 901 Mission St San Francisco CA 94103-2905 E-mail: lgarchik@sfchronicle.com.

GARCIA, ADOLFO RAMON, lawyer; b. Havana, Cuba, Nov. 5, 1948; came to U.S., 1961; s. Adolfo Damian and Luz I. (Garcia) G.; m. Elizabeth Ensor, July 17, 1971; children: Andrew, Laurence. AB magna cum laude, Harvard U., 1971; JD, Georgetown U., 1974. Bar: N.Y. 1975, Mass. 1981. Assoc. Cahill Gordon & Reindel, N.Y.C., 1974-79, Choate, Hall & Stewart, Boston, 1979 82; sr. ptnr. McDermott, Will & Emery, Boston, 1982—2003; ptnr., co-head internat. practice group Ropes & Gray, Boston, 2003—. Co-chmn. legal affairs com., bd. dirs. Internat. Bus. Ctr. New Eng. Inc., Boston, 1983-87; past chmn. and pres., bd. dirs. Boston Ctr. for Internat. Visitors, 1981-86; active Mass. Internat. Trade Coun., Boston, 1984-86; v.p., dir. New Eng.-Latin Am. Bus. Coun. Mem. Internat. Bar Assn., Boston Bar Assn. (co-chmn. pvt. internat. law sect. 1982-86), InterAm. Bar Assn., Essex County Club, Manchester (Mass.) Yacht Club. Republican. Home: October Hill Prides Crossing MA 01965 Office: Ropes & Gray One Internat Pl Boston MA 02110-2624 E-mail: agarcia@ropesgray.com.

GARCIA, ALEXANDER, orthopedic surgeon; b. N.Y.C., July 3, 1919; s. Alexander and Pilar (Prieto) G.; m. Helen Ann Proskey, June 12, 1943; 1 son, Alexander, III. BS, CCNY, 1940; MD, L.I. Coll. Medicine, 1943. Diplomate: Am. Bd. Orthopaedic Surgery. Intern Syracuse (N.Y.) U. Med. Center, 1944, asst. resident in gen. surgery, 1944-45, chief resident, 1945-46; resident in gen. surgery Nassau Hosp., Mineola, N.Y., 1948; asst. resident in orthopaedic surgery N.Y. Orthopaedic Hosp., N.Y.C., 1948-50, resident, jr. Annie C. Kane fellow, 1950-51, acting dir. orthopaedic service, 1976-77, hosp. dir., 1977-83, dir. emeritus, 1983—. Chief orthopaedic surg. sect. North Shore Hosp., Manhasset, N.Y., 1957-70, cons., 1970— ; mem. faculty Columbia U. Coll. Phys. and Surg., 1952—, prof. orthopaedic surgery, 1972—, chmn. dept., 1977—, Frank E. Stinchfield prof., 1978-83, Frank E. Stinchfield prof. emeritus, 1983— ; pres. med. bd. Presbyn. Hosp.-Columbia Presbyn. Med. Ctr., N.Y.C., 1979-82; cons. numerous area hosps. Editor-in-chief Orthopedic Review, 1982-89; mem. editoral bds. profl. jours. Served as officer M.C. AUS, 1946-48. Mem. Internat. Soc. Orthopaedic Surgery and Traumatology, A.C.S., AMA, Am. Acad. Orthopaedic Surgeons, Am. Assn. for Surgery of Trauma, Pan Am. Med. Assn., Assn. Bone and Joint Surgeons, Am. Orthopaedic Assn., N.Y. State Med. Soc., N.Y. Acad. Medicine, N.Y. Acad. Scis., N.Y. State Soc. Orthopaedic Surgeons, Soc. Ortopedia y Traumatologia Dominicana. Democrat.

GARCIA, ANDREW B. chemical engineer; b. Las Cruces, N.Mex., Apr. 22, 1949; s. Rudolf A. and Margaret (Rivera) G.; m. Katherine D. Montano, July 5, 1974 (dec. Aug. 1996); children: Lauren, Alexandra; m. Elaine Rose Richards, Nov. 29, 2003. BS in Chem. Engring. with honors, N.Mex. State U., Las Cruces, 1972; MBA, St. Mary's Coll., Moraga, Calif., 1979; postgrad., U. Calif., Berkeley, 1994. Registered environ. assessor; cert. hazardous materials mgr. Design engr. Gen. Electric Co., San Jose, Calif., 1972-75; chem. engr. Chevron Chem. Co., Richmond, Calif., 1975-78; supr. Chevron Corp., San Francisco, 1978-80; supply product mgr. Chevron USA Inc., Walnut Creek, Calif., 1980-89; project mgr. Chevron Land & Devel. Co., San Francisco, 1989-93; environ. project mgr. Alameda County, Oakland, Calif., 1993 95; environ. support mgr. Computer Scis. Corp., Edwards AFB, Calif., 1995-99; due diligence coordinator Greenberg Farrow Architecture, Inc., 2000; site project mgr. Knight Piesold, 2000-2001; sr. engr., project coord. MACTEC, 2001—. Park and recreation commr. City of Martinez, Calif., 1984-89; mem. citizens adv. bd. City of Martinez, 1989-91. Mem. AIChE, Project Mgmt. Inst., KC. Roman Catholic. Achievements include reputation for being expert on the site cleanup and due diligence; successful management of multimillion dollar projects. Home: 28420 Rock Canyon Dr Santa Clarita CA 91390 E-mail: garciaa1@aol.com.

GARCIA, ANDY, actor; b. Havana, Cuba, Apr. 12, 1956; Student, Fla. Internat. U.; DFA (hon.), St. John's Univ., 2000. Actor: (films) Guaguasi, 1979, Blue Skies Again, 1983, The Mean Season, 1985, 8 Million Ways to Die, 1986, The Untouchables, 1987, Stand and Deliver, 1987, American Roulette, 1988, Black Rain, 1989, Internal Affairs, 1990, The Godfather III, 1990 (Oscar nominee best supporting actor, 1999, Golden Globe nominee, 1999), Dead Again, 1991, Hero, 1992, Jennifer 8, 1992, When a Man Loves a Woman, 1994, Steal Big Steal Little, 1995, Things to Do in Denver When You're Dead, 1996, Night Falls on Manhattan, 1997, The Disappearance of Garcia Lorca, 1997, Hoodlum, 1997, Desperate Measures, 1999 (ALMA award, 1997), Lakeboat, 1999, Ocean's 11, 2001, Confidence, 2002, Blackout, 2003, Modiguami, 2003, Lazarus Child, 2003; actor, prodr.: (TV) Swing Vote, 1999, (film) Just the Ticket, 1999, The Man From Elysian Fields, 2002, The Unsaid, 2002; dir., prodr.: (films) Cachao, Like His Rhythm There Is No Other, Cachao..Goza Mi Mambo Cubano; music prodr.: (album) Cachao Master Sessions, vol. I (Grammy award 1994), Cachao Master Sessions, Vol. II (Grammy nominee 1995), Just the Ticket soundtrack, 4 songs for Steal Big, Steal Little soundtrack, Cachao-Cuba Linda, 2000(nominated for Latin Grammy, 2000, Grammy, 2001), For Love or Country: The Arturo Sandoval Story soundtrack, 2000, Cachao-Anora Si, 2003. Recipient Harvard Univ. Found. award, Star on Hollywood Walk of Fame, Hispanic Heritage award for Arts, Father of Yr. award Father's Day Coun., ALMA award, PRISM award; named Nat. Assn. of Theater Oweners Star of Yr.; nominated for Oscar and Golden Globe for Godfather III, Spirit of Hope award, 2001, Oscar de la Hoys Found. Champion award, 2000, Palm Springs Film Festival Desert Palm award, 2002, Imagen Found. Creative Achievement award, 2002, LA's BEST Focus on Family award, 2002, RP Internat. Film Artist of Vision award Office: Paradigm 200 W 57th St Ste 900 New York NY 10019

GARCIA, ANGÉLICA MARIA, elementary education educator; b. Tijuana, Mex., Mar. 22, 1963; came to U.S., 1967; d. Juan José Quijada and Paula (Magallanes) Garcia. AA, L.A. Harbor Coll., Wilmington, Calif., 1985; BA, Calif. State U., Carson, 1990, MA, 1993. Tchr. asst., tutor L.A. Harbor Coll., 1982-85; elem. tchr. asst., tutor Ambler Avenue Sch., Carson, 1985-90; bilingual elem. tchr. Hooper Avenue Elem. Sch., L.A., 1991—; mentor tchr. Hooper Avenue Elem. Sch., L.A., 1997—, mem. coordinated compliance rev. team, 1998. Jefferson cluster tchr. trainer dist. stds. L.A. Unified Sch. Dist., 1996—, tchr. trainer early literacy, 1997—; stakeholder Instrnl. Transformation Team, 1995-96; mem. pupil quality rev. team, 1995-96; co-chair local sch. leadership coun., 1998; mentor Latino Tchr. Project, U. So. Calif., 1993—; primary math. coach Hooper Ave. Sch., 2003--. Counselor Pathfinders, Carson Seventh Day Adventist Ch., 1980; treas. Carson Spanish Seventh Day Adventist Ch., 1994; pianist Harbor City Seventh Day Adventist Ch., 1995-96; mem. ednl. com. Lynwood Seventh Day Adventist Ch., 1999, ch. pianist, 2001, ch. clk., 2002. Mem. TESOL, United Tchrs. L.A. (co-chmn. 1994, chpt. chmn. 1995-98). Democrat. Avocations: playing piano, photography, reading, playing softball, drawing. Home: 320 E 181st St Carson CA 90746-1815 E-mail: angieq@earthlink.net.

GARCIA, ARIEL H. plastic surgeon; b. Iloilo, The Philippines, July 20, 1938; s. Amador D. and Pura Garcia; children: Ruel, Glenn. BS cum laude, U. of the Philippines, Manila, 1957, MD, 1961. Diplomate Am. Bd. Plastic Surgery. Attending plastic surgeon Good Samaritan Hosp., West Islip, NY, 1972—2002; assoc. attending plastic surgeon Southside Hosp., Bay Shore, NY, 1997—2002. V.p. Plastic Surg. Assocs., P.C., West Islip, 1977-97. Contbr. articles to profl. publs. Plastic surgeon team mem. med. mission Philippines Am. Group of Educators and Surgeons, Manila, 1993, San Pablo City, Philippines, 1994, Assn. of Philippine Physicians in NY, Manila, 1995, Phillipine Med. Assn. in Am., Cebu City, Phillipines, 1996. Recipient First prize Plastic Surgery Residents, NY Regional Soc. of Plastic and Reconstructive Surgeons, 1969; named Honoree for Outstanding Svc. and Commitment to the Cmty., NAACP, 1996. Fellow ACS, Am. Soc. for Laser Medicine & Surgery; mem. Am. Soc. Plastic Surgeons, Inc. Avocations: reading, travel. Office: 12712 Heacock St Ste 6 Moreno Valley CA 92553-6003

GARCIA, BONIFACIO BONNY, lawyer; b. Fresno, Calif., Oct. 27, 1956; s. Bonifacio Mata and Corinne (Miranda) G. BA magna cum laude, Loyola Marymount U., Los Angeles, 1978; J.D., Harvard U., 1981. Bar: Calif. 1981. Assoc. Fulop & Hardee, Beverly Hills, Calif., 1981-82; assoc. law firm Leff & Stephenson, Beverly Hills, Calif., 1983-84; assoc. Allen Matkins, Leck, Gamble & Mallory, Los Angeles, 1984-85; assoc. Lillick McHose & Charles, Los Angeles, 1985-88; ptnr. Tobin & Tobin, 1988—; adj. prof. history Loyola Marymount U., 1984. Author: (with others) Law and Justice, 1987. Recipient Loyola Marymount U. Pres.'s citation, 1978. Mem. Los Angeles County Bar Assn., Alpha Sigma Nu; Phi Alpha Theta. Democrat. Roman Catholic. Home: 901 E Domingo Dr San Gabriel CA 91775-2112

GARCIA, BONNIE, state official; b. N.Y.C., N.Y. m. Javier Garcia; children: Melissa, Javier. BS in Workforce Edn. and Devel., So. Ill. U. Owner consulting bus.; state assembly mem. Dist. 80 Calif. State Assembly, 2002—. Mem. edn. com.; mem. human svcs. com.; mem. local govt. com.; vice-chair jobs, econ. devel., and economy com.; mem. Coachella Valley Health Partnership, DCA Riverside County Energy Task Force Com., FISH Food Bank, Inland Empire Cmty. Devel. Corp. Republican. Mailing: Rm 4102 PO Box 942849 Sacramento CA 95814 Office: Ste B 68-700 Avenida Lalo Guerrero Cathedral City CA 92234

GARCIA, CARLOS ARTURO, medical educator; b. Mar. 20, 1935; MD, U. del Valle, Cali, Colombia, 1961. Prof. neurology and pathology La. State U., 1979-97; prof. clin. neurology, clin. prof. pathology Tulane U., New Orleans, 1997—. Author: (with L. A. Weisberg) Decision Making in Adult Neurology, 2d edit., 1993, Essentials of Clinical Neurology, 3d edit., 1996; contbr. numerous articles to profl. publs., including Neurology, Jour. Neurol. Sci., Jour. of AMA). Office: Tulane U Neurology TB 52 1440 Canal St Ste 1050 New Orleans LA 70112-2750

GARCIA, CASTELAR MEDARDO, lawyer; b. Conejos, Colo., June 3, 1942; s. Castelar M. Sr. and Anna (Vigil) G.; m. Mary Elizabeth Miller, Apr. 1, 1967; 1 child, Victoria Elisabeth. BA, Adams State Coll., 1965; JD, U. Colo., 1976. Bar: Colo. 1977, U.S. Dist. Ct. Colo. 1977, U.S. Ct. Appeals (10th cir.) 1983, U.S. Ct. Appeals (4th cir.) 1988, U.S. Supreme Ct. 1984. Human resources counselor State of Oreg., Klamath Falls, 1966-68; regional dir. Colo. Civil Rights Com., Alamosa, 1970-73; dep. dist. atty. Denver, 1977-80; chief dep. dist. atty., 1980-84; pvt. practice Alamosa, Colo., 1984—; owner Cumbres Ranch. Town atty., Manassa, Colo., 1984—; commr. Colo. Dept. Hwys., 1991, Colo. Dept. Transp., 1991—; chmn. Colo. Transp. Commn., 1996-2001. Mem. Colo. delegation to Cam Real Trade Corridor Consortium between U.S., Can. and Mex. With U.S. Army, 1968-70, Vietnam. Decorated Purple Heart. Mem.

Colo. Bar Assn., Hispanic Bar Assn., San Luis Valley Bar Assn., Caminos Antiquos Scenic By-way Assn. (founder). Republican. Roman Catholic. Home: PO Box 90 Alamosa CO 81101-0090 Office: 420B San Juan Ave Alamosa CO 81101-2554 Fax: 719-587-9209.

GARCIA, CELSO-RAMON, obstetrician, gynecologist, educator; b. N.Y.C., Oct. 31, 1921; s. Celso García y Ondina and Oliva Menèndez (del Valle) G.; m. Shirley Jean Stoddard, Oct. 14, 1950; children: Celso-Ramón Jr., Sarita Stoddard Cole. BS, Queens Coll., 1942; MD, SUNY Downstate Med. Ctr., 1945; MA (hon.), U. Pa. Intern Norwegian Hosp., Bklyn., 1945-46; resident, rsch. fellow in gynecology Cumberland Hosp., Bklyn., 1949-50; assoc. in ob-gyn. U. P.R., San Juan, 1953-54; asst. prof. ob-gyn. Sch. Medicine and Tropical Medicine, San Juan, 1954-55; co-dir. Rock Reproductive Study Ctr.; asst. obstetrician and gynecologist Boston Lying-In Hosp.; assoc. surgeon Free Hosp. for Women, Brookline, Mass., 1955-65; sr. scientist, dir. tng. program in physiology reprodn. Worcester Found. for Exptl. Biology, Shrewsbury, Mass., 1960-62; asst. surgeon, chief Infertility Clinic, Mass. Gen. Hosp.; from asst., instr. to clin. assoc. ob-gyn. Harvard Med. Sch., 1962-65; prof. obstetrics and gynecology U. Pa., Phila., 1965-92, William Shippen, Jr. prof. human reprodn., 1970-92, William Shippen, Jr. prof emeritus, 1992—, dir. infertility and reproductive endocrinology and surgery, 1987-95. Extraordinary prof. U. San Luis Potosi, Mex., 1974; rapporteur com. of experts on clin. aspects oral gestogens WHO, Geneva, 1965; mem. ad hoc adv. com. contraceptive devel., contract program Nat. Inst. Child Health and Human Devel., 1971-75; original team mem. which developed clin. application of 1st FDA approved progestagen-estrogen combinations for oral contraception (the Pill); developer, dir. 1st tng. program in physiology of reprodn. in U.S.; innovator surg. approach to infertility of women; cons. Pa. Hosp., 1973-94; asst. staff Faulkner Hosp., Jamaica Plain, Boston; courtesy staff Glover Meml. Hosp., Needham, Mass., 1962-65; adv. bd. Global Alliance for Women's Health, 1995—. Chmn. nat. med. adv. com. Planned Parenthood World Population, 1971-74; mem. nat. adv. child and human devel. coun. Nat. Inst. Child Health and Human Devel., 1981-84. With AUS, 1943-48. Recipient Carl G. Hartman award Am. Soc. Study of Sterility, 1961, Sesquicentennial award U. Mich., 1967, MD Master Tchg. award Alumni Assn. SUNY, 1989, Recognition award APGO Wyeth-Ayerst, 1993, Frank L. Babbott award SUNY, 1995, Sci. Leadership award Global Alliance Women's Health, 2000; Sidney Graves fellow in gynecology Harvard Med. Sch., 1955. Fellow: ACOG, ACS, Coll. Physicians Phila.; mem.: AMA, Boston Obstet. Soc. (emeritus), Phila. Obstet. Soc., Am. Soc. Reproduction Medicine (bd. dirs., past pres.), Soc. Reproductive Surgeons (founding pres.), Assn. Planned Parenthood Physicians (past pres.), Fedn. Columbian Socs. Ob-Gyn. (hon.), Cuban Soc. Ob-Gyn. (hon.; in exile), Am. Physiol. Soc., Am. Gynecol. and Obstet. Soc., Am. Soc. Gynecol. Surgeons, Global Alliance Women's Health (adv. bd. 1994—, rep. to U.N. Econ. and Social Coun. 1998), Alpha Omega Alpha, Sigma Xi, Masons. Democrat. Presbyterian. Home: 109 Merion Rd Merion Station PA 19066-1734 Office: 3701 Market St Philadelphia PA 19104 Business E-Mail: cgarcia@mail.obgyn.upenn.edu. E-mail: crgsr@snip.net.

GARCIA, CHRISTINE, academic administrator, educator, researcher; B Govt., U.Nex., 1961, M Polit. Sci. in Edn., 1964; PhD Polit. Sci., U. Calif., Davis, 1972. Prof. polit. sci. U. N.Mex., 1970—, asst. dir. divsn. govt. rsch., 1970—72, asst., assoc. dean Coll. Arts and Scis., 1975—80, dean coll. Arts and Scis., 1980—86, v.p. acad. affairs, 1987—90, interim provost, v.p. acad. affairs, 1993, 1998—2000, pres., 2002—. Tchr. various us.; rschr. in field. Author (editor): 10 books, 50 monographs; contbr. articles, chapters to books. Office: U NMex 115 Civic Plz Dr Taos NM 87571

GARCIA, ELISA DOLORES, lawyer; b. Bklyn., Nov. 8, 1957; d. Vincent Garcia, Jr. and Dolores Elizabeth (Canedo) Marmo; m. John Jay Hasluck, Feb. 28, 1987; children: Brooke Elisabeth, John Neville. BA, MS, SUNY, Stony Brook, 1980; JD, St. John's U., 1985. Bar: N.Y. 1986. Cons. Energy Devel. Internat., Pt. Jefferson, N.Y., 1980-83; assoc. Willkie Farr & Gallagher, N.Y.C., 1985-89; sr. counsel GAF Corp./Internat. Specialty Products, Wayne, N.J., 1989-94; regional counsel for L.Am., Philip Morris Internat., Rye Brook, N.Y., 1994-2000; exec. v.p., gen. counsel Domino's Pizza, LLC, Ann Arbor, Mich., 2000—. Mem. Glen Rock (N.J.) Planning Bd., 1992-95, chmn., 1994-95. Mem. ABA, N.Y. State Bar Assn., Mich. Bar Assn., Am. Corp. Counsel Assn. (dir. Mich. chpt.). Roman Catholic. Avocations: gardening, scuba diving. Office: Domino's Pizza LLC PO Box 997 30 Frank Lloyd Wright Dr Ann Arbor MI 48106-0997 Home: 52 Old Lyme Rd Chappaqua NY 10514-3806 E-mail: garciae@dominos.com.

GARCIA, F. CHRIS, academic administrator, political science educator, public opinion researcher; b. Albuquerque, Apr. 15, 1940; s. Flaviano P. and Crucita A. Garcia; m. Sandra D. Garcia; children: Elaine L., Tanya C. BA, U. N.Mex., 1961, MA in Govt., 1964; PhD in Polit. Sci., U. Calif., Davis, 1972. Froma asst. prof. polit. sci. to pres. U. N.Mex., Albuquerque, 1970—2002, pres., 2002—03, prof., 1978—; founder Zia Rsch. Assocs., Inc., Albuquerque, 1973-94, also chmn. bd. dirs. Cons.-evaluator North Ctrl. Assn. Higher Learning Commn., 1994—. Author: Political Socialization of Chicano Children, 1973, La Causa Politica, 1974, The Chicano Political Experience, 1977, State and Local Government in New Mexico, 1979, New Mexico Government, 1976, 81, 94, Latinos and the Political System, 1988, Latino Voices, 1992, Pursuing Power, 1997. Mem. charter rev. com. City of Albuquerque, 1999, Alburquerque Goals Commn.; bd. dirs. Nat. Hispanic Cultural Ctr., 2002—. With N.Mex. Air Nat. Guard, 1957-63. Recipient Disting. Svc. award, Am. Polit. Sci. Assn., 2001. Mem. Western Polit. Sci. Assn. (pres. 1977-78), Am. Polit. Sci. Assn. (v.p. 1994-95, exec. coun. 1984-86, sec. 1992-93, Disting. Svc. award 2001), Am. Assn. Pub. Opinion Rsch., Coun. Colls. of Arts and Sci. (bd. dirs. 1982-85), Nat. Assn. State Univs. and Land Grant Colls. (coun. acad. affairs 1987-90, exec. com. 1989), We. Social Sci. Assn. (exec. coun. 1973-76), Phi Beta Kappa, Phi Kappa Phi, Gold Key. Home: 1409 Snowdrop Pl NE Albuquerque NM 87112-6331 Office: U N Mex Polt Sci Dept Social Scis Bldg 2053 Albuquerque NM 87131-1121 E-mail: cgarcia@unm.edu.

GARCIA, GILLIAN GLENYS, economist; b. Birmingham, U.K. came to U.S., 1967; d. George Herbert and Ivy Naomi Holway; m. Richard Lorenzo Garcia, Dec. 21, 1968; children: Gina Carolyn, Andrew Richard. PhD, SUNY, Buffalo, 1974. Asst. prof. U. Calif., Berkeley, 1974-82; sr. economist Federal Res., Chgo., 1982-84, IMF, Washington, 1993—; asst. dir. U.S. GAO, Washington, 1984-89; pres. GGH Garcia Assocs. Vis. scholar Office of the Comptroller of the Currency, Washington, 1979-80, De Nederlandsche Bank, Amsterdam, 2003; nat. fellow Hoover Instn. Stanford (Calif.) U., 1980-81; disting. profl. lectr. Georgetown U., Washington, 1988-95; staff Com. Banking Housing and Urban Affairs U.S. Senate, 1989-93; vis. scholar Netherlands Ctrl. Bank, Amsterdam, 2003. Author: Mathematics for Economists and Social Scientists, 1972 Financial Deregulation and Monetary Control, 1983, Financial Reform in the '80s, 1985, The Federal Reserve: Lender of Last Resort, 1988, Bank Soundness and Macroeconomic Policy, 1996, Deposit Insurance: Actual and Good Practices, 2000. Treas. Women in Housing & Fin., Washington, 1989-90. Recipient G. Henry Wright prize U. Birmingham, Eng. Mem. Am. Econ. Assn. Avocations: running, gardening, writing. Home: 4507 Highland Green Ct Alexandria VA 22312-3132

GARCIA, GUS, former mayor; b. Zapata, TX, 1934; m. Marina Gonzalez; 3 children. BBA, U. Texas, 1959, postgrad, 1961. Cert. CPA. Coun. mem. City of Austin, Tex., 1991—2000; mayor pro-tem Austin City Coun., 1996—98; mayor Austin, Tex., 2001—03. Trustee Austin Ind. Sch. Dist. Austin CC Bd., pres. Austin Ind. Sch. Dist.; mem., chair telecom. infrastructure Austin City Coun. Com., mem. audit, finance, mem. minority & women bus. enterprise, mem. affordable housing, mem. capital area metropolitan orgn., mem. joint Austin city coun., mem. AISD bd. trustees com., mem. Tex. municipal league legis. com.; mem. Bd. Dirs. State Bar of Texas, 1986—89; co-chair Hispanic Com. for Scouting; mem. Cmty. Action Net., 1992—2000, chair, 1996—97. Recipient RECONOCIMENTO OHTLI award, Mexico's Sec. of Foreign Relations, 1996, LULAC award, 1992, Whitney M. Young, Jr. svc. award, Boy Scouts Am. Capital Area Coun., 1991, businessman of the yr., Tex. Assn. Mexican Am. Chambers Commerce, 1984, humanitarian award, Martin Luther King Assn., 1984. Mem.: Austin Chapter CPAs (pres. 1969—70, CPA of the yr. 1977), Tex. State Soc. CPAs (dir. 1969—70), Hispanic Chamber Commerce Bd. Dirs. (pres. 1982—83), Bd. Dirs. State Bar Tex., Bd. Dirs. Greater Chamber Commerce, Dropout Task Force- Greater Chamber Commerce, Tex. State Bd. Acupuncture Examiners (presiding officer 1994—97), Capital Area Planning Coun. Orgn.*

GARCIA, HENRY FRANK, supply management and project management consultant and trainer; b. San Antonio, Aug. 29, 1943; s. Henry V. and Lucia (Dominguez) G.; m. Rose Lozano, Feb. 28, 1970; children: John Henry, Rebecca. BA in Psychology, St. Mary's U., San Antonio, 1969, MA in Econs., 1974. Cert. purchasing mgr., Tex. Buyer purchasing Southwest Rsch. Inst., San Antonio, 1967-70, asst. mgr. purchasing, 1970-74, mgr. purchasing, 1974-78, asst. dir. materials mgmt., 1978-80, dir. corp. travel, 1980-87, dir. materials mgmt., 1980-87; dir. fin. and adminstrn. Ctr. for Nuc. Waste Regulatory Analyses, San Antonio, 1987—2003; ret., 2003; cons., trainer Asentrene. Instr. U. Tex., San Antonio, 1976-77; instr. materials mgmt. and econs., San Antonio Coll., 1975-83; instr. econs. St. Marys U., San Antonio, 1976-81; adj. prof. econs. Webster U., San Antonio, 1980—. Contbr. articles to profl. jours. Chmn. San Antonio Regional Minority Purchasing Council, 1983. Mem. Nat. Purchasing Inst. (pres. 1979-80, Outstanding Svc. award 1986), Nat. Assn. Purchasing Mgmt. (cert., v.p. dist. II 1987-89, Pro-D Man of Yr. award 1985, Congrove Outstanding Mem. award 1991, President's award 1994, J. Shipman Gold Medal award 1998), Purchasing Mgmt. Assn. San Antonio (pres. 1981-82, Conway L. Holmes award 1984, James H. Lieberman award 2000), Nat. Bus. Travel Assn. (v.p. 1985-86), Nat. Assn. Bus. Economists (pres. local chpt. 1978), Project Mgmt. Inst. Ipres.-elect 2003—). Democrat. Roman Catholic. Office: Asentrene PO Box 782474 San Antonio TX 78278-2474

GARCIA, JEFF, football player; b. Feb. 24, 1970; Postgrad in bus. & mktg., San Jose State U. Quartback San Francisco 49ers, 1999—, Calgary Stampede CFL, 1994—99. Office: San Francisco 49ers Ltd 4949 Centennial Blvd Santa Clara CA 95054

GARCIA, JOHN, psychologist, educator; b. Santa Rosa, Calif., June 12, 1917; married; 3 children. BA, U. Calif., Berkeley, 1948, MA, 1949, PhD, 1965. Teaching asst. U. Calif., Berkeley, 1949-51; psychologist U.S. Naval Radiol. Def. Lab., San Francisco, 1951-58; tchr. biol. sci. Oakland (Calif.) Pub. Schs., 1958-59; asst. prof. psychology Calif. State Coll., Long Beach, 1959-65; assoc. biologist, neurosurg. svc. Mass. Gen. Hosp., Boston, 1965-68; prof. psychology, chmn. psychobiology program SUNY, Stony Brook, 1968-71, chmn. dept., 1971-72; prof. U. Utah, Salt Lake City, 1972-73; prof. psychology and psychiatry UCLA, 1973-87, emeritus prof. psychology and psychiatry, 1987—. Recipient Lifetime Achievement award for neurosci., Soc. for Neurosci., 1998. Fellow Soc. Exptl. Psychologists (Howard Crosby Warren medal 1978); mem. AAAS, APA (Disting. Sci. Contbn. award 1979), Nat. Acad. Scis., Am. Psychol. Soc. (William James fellow), N.Y. Acad. Scis., Western Psychol. Assn. (pres. 1991—), Phi BEta Kappa, Sigma Xi. Address: 19442 Best Rd Mount Vernon WA 98273-8112

GARCIA, JULIA THERESA, secondary school educator; b. N.Y.C., Aug. 30, 1923; d. Ignatius Colletti-Riena and Julia Pendeleur; m. Frank Leonard Garcia, May 26, 1949 (dec. Aug. 1995); children: Julia, Frank, Annette. BA, Hunter Coll., 1951; MA, Columbia U., 1956. Cert. tchr. chemistry N.Y., asst. prin. supervision phys. scis. N.Y. Tchr. gen. sci. Alfred E. Smith Jr. H.S. Bd. Edn. N.Y.C., tchr. chemistry Alfred E. Smith H.S., asst. prin. supervision phys. scis. Alfred E. Smith H.S., prin. summer sch. Alfred E. Smith H.S. Bd. examiner sci. and math. Bd. Edn. N.Y.C., 1984—89. Active Diabetic Assn. Recipient award for dedicated svc. to children, N.Y.C. Sci. Chmn.'s Assn., 1989. Mem.: Phi Delta Kappa, N.Y.C. Acad. Sci.

GARCIA, JULIET VILLARREAL, university administrator; m. Oscar E. Garcia; two children. Grad. in Comm. and Linguistics, U. Tex. Pres. U. Tex. at Brownsville, Tex. Southmost Coll. Bd. dirs. Fed. Res. of Dallas/San Antonio br. of Tex. Commerce Bancshares Inc.; past bd. dirs. Am. Coun. Edn., chmn. bd. dirs. 1995. Bd. dirs. Carnegie Found. for Advancement of Teaching, Pub. Welfare Foun.; vice-chair adv. com. on Fin. Aid; appointed mem. White House Initiative on Ednl. Excellence for Hispanic-Ams. Named Woman of Distinction Nat. Conf. of Coll. Women Student Leaders, 1995, one of most influential Hispanics Hispanic Bus. Mag. Office: U Tex & Tex Southmost Coll Office of Pres 80 Fort Brown St Brownsville TX 78520-4956

GARCIA, JUNE MARIE, librarian; b. Bryn Mawr, Pa., Sept. 12, 1947; d. Roland Ernest and Marion Brill (Hummel) Traynor; m. Teodosio Garcia, July 17, 1928; children: Gretchen, Adrian. BA, Douglass Coll., 1969; MLS, Rutgers U., 1970. Reference libr. New Brunswick (N.J.) Pub. Libr., 1970-72, Plainfield (N.J.) Pub. Libr., 1972-75; br. mgr. Phoenix Pub. Libr., 1975-80, extension svcs. adminstr., 1980-93; dir. San Antonio Pub. Libr., 1993-99; CEO, CARL Corp., Denver, 1999-2001; v.p., chief amb. TLC/CARL, Denver, 2001—02; mng. ptnr. Dubberly Garcia Assocs., 2002—. Recipient Productivity Innovator award City of Phoenix, 1981. Mem. ALA (life, coun. 1986-90, 93-2001, pres. Pub. Libr. Assn. 1991-92, new stds. task force 1983-87, goals, guidelines and stds. com. 1986-90, chairperson 1987-90, resource allocation com. 1998-99), Freedom to Read Found. (bd. dirs.), Ariz. State Libr. Assn. (pres. 1984-85, Libr. of Yr. award 1986, Pres.'s award 1990), Beta Phi Mu. Office: 1195 S Harrison St Denver CO 80210

GARCIA, KATHERINE LEE, controller, accountant; b. Portland, Oreg., Nov. 4, 1950; d. Gerald Eugene and Dolores Lois (Erickson) Moe; m. Buddy Jesus Garcia; Nov. 19, 1977; children: Kevin, Brett, Rodd. BS cum laude, U. Nev., 1976. CPA Idaho, Nev.; cert. pub. fin. officer 2001. Retail clk. Raleys, Food King, Reno, 1968-76; sr. acct. Pieretti, Wilson and McNulty, Reno, 1976-78, Deloitte Haskins and Sells, Boise, Idaho, 1979-81, Washoe County, Reno, 1981-83, chief dep. comptr., 1983-94, comptroller, 1994—. Treas., bd. dirs. Friends of 4 (pub. TV), Boise, 1979-81; tutor RAD program, 1995-97; treas. Sierra Miners, 1998-99. Recipient Cert. of Excellence in Fin. Reporting, Govt. Fin. Officer's Assn., 1982—. Mem. AICPA, Nev. Soc. CPAs (chmn. state and local govt. com. 1992-93, 98—), Govt. Fin. Officers Assn. (mem. spl. rev. com. 1989-97, state rep.), Nev. Govt. Fin. Officers Assn. (treas. 1989-91). Republican. Avocations: jogging, sewing, biking, reading. Home: 655 Joy Lake Rd Reno NV 89511-5766 Office: Washoe County PO Box 11130 Reno NV 89520-0027 E-mail: kgarcia@mail.co.washoe.nv.us.

GARCIA, LOUIS LAWRENCE, financial executive; b. Bronx, NY, Mar. 18, 1947; s. Louis Lawrence and Hazel (Parrish) G.; m. Janice Karen Keegan, June 4, 1971; children: Michael Reid, Joanna Leigh. BBA, U. Cin., 1970; MBA, Ind. U., 1972. Asst. plant acct. mgr. Procter & Gamble, Cin., 1972-74; internal auditor, 1974-75; fin. analyst Procter & Gamble, Cin., 1975-76, supr. controls and reports, 1976-78; supr. cash and profit forecasts, 1978-79; dir. fin. planning and analysis N.Am. Van Lines divsn. PepsiCo Inc., Ft. Wayne, Ind., 1979-81, group contr., 1981-82, dir. strategic planning, 1982-83; dir. fin. analysis PepsiCo Inc., Purchase, N.Y., 1983-85; contr. Fasson Splty. divsn. Avery Dennison, Painesville, Ohio, 1985-90, dir. fin. Fasson Films divsn., 1990-94, dir. planning and analysis Ams. and Asia materials group, 1994-96, dir. fin. Mcht. divsn. N.Am., 1996-98; CFO, v.p. LBC, Inc., Lancaster, Ohio, 1998—2000, Sihl USA, Inc., San Jose, Calif., 2001—02; CFO First Alarm, Inc., Aptos, Calif., 2002—. Mem. dean's assocs. Ind. U., 1992—98. Recipient Black Achiever in Industry award Harlem (N.Y.) br. YMCA, 1984. Mem.: Fin. Exec. Networking Group. Avocations: basketball, running, tennis, golf. Home: 495 Mountain View Rd Santa Cruz CA 95065 Office: First Alarm Inc 1111 Estates Drive Aptos CA 95003 E-mail: garcia495@peoplepc.com., lgarcia@firstalarm.com.

GARCIA, LUIS CESAREO, lawyer; b. Hato Rey, P.R., Apr. 19, 1949; came to U.S., 1965; s. Cesareo and Evelina Maura Garcia; foster s. John B. and Elena Amos.; m. Kathy Jo Mims, Dec. 4, 1970; children: Joseph Amos, Evelyn Kathleen, Jeremy Adam. Student Columbus Coll., 1967-70; JD, John Marshall Law U., Atlanta, 1973; postgrad. Harvard U., 1978, 84. Bar: Ga. 1974, U.S. Dist. Ct. (mid. dist.) Ga. 1974, U.S. Ct. Appeals (11th cir.) 1983, U.S. Supreme Ct. 1977, Vt. 1991, Vt. Supreme Ct. 1991. Assoc. Keil, Riley & Fort, Columbus, Ga., 1974-75; pvt. practice, Columbus, 1975-76, 89—; sr. ptnr. Garcia & Hirsch, P.C., Columbus, 1976-79; regional mgr. Am. Family Life Assurance Co., Columbus, 1979-82, exec. v.p., chief counsel, 1982-87; sr. v.p. counsel internat. ops., 1986-88; legal counsel LMI, Inc., 1979-82; mem. legis. com. Am. Prepaid Legal Inst., Chgo., 1983-86. Bd. dirs. Better Bus. Bur. of W. Ga.-E. Ala., 1984-87; mem. bd. adv. council CETA, 1979-83; adv. bd. Ga. Pub. TV, 1979-82; chmn., bd. dirs. March of Dimes, Columbus, 1989-91. Mem. ABA, Assn. Trial Lawyers Am., Vt. Bar Assn., Ga. Bar Assn., Franklin-Grand Isle Bar Assn., Columbus Lawyers Club, Younger Lawyers Club, Sigma Delta Kappa. Episcopalian. Office: PO Box 75 85 Prim Rd 2nd Fl Colchester VT 05446-1462

GARCIA, LUIS F. social worker, photographer; b. Nogales, Ariz., Sept. 28, 1963; s. Francisco and Amanda E. Garcia; children: Vania, Fernando. BA, Our Lady of the Lake U., San Antonio, 1988. Press Photographer Am. Image Press, Wash., D.C., 1988, Profl. Photographer N.Y. Inst. of Photography, 2000, Master Photographer Internat. Freelance Photographers Assn., 2002. Social worker Sunnyvale Cmty. Svcs., Sunnyvale, Calif., 1997—2002; program mgr. Interfaith Cmty. Svcs., Escondido, Calif., 2002—. Photography calendar, China: Portraits of a Timeless land, photography, Climb Against the Odds/ Breast Cancer Fund, 2003. Cons. Breast Cancer Fund, San Francisco, 2000—03. Recipient Star award for Creativity, Leadership, and Collaboration, United Way of Silicon Valley, Vida award for Outstanding Svc., Who's Who in Photography, Recognition Press, 1998—2000. Office: Interfaith Cmty Svcs 550-B W Washington Ave Escondido CA 92025 Home Fax: 760-740-0837. Personal E-mail: lgarcia@interfaithservices.org.

GARCIA, MARC ANTHONY, diplomat; b. Bklyn., June 1962; s. Carlos Antonio and Yolande (Price) G.; m. Shequrah Rolle; 1 child, Christina Chanel. BA, Hampton Inst., 1984; postgrad., SUNY, Albany, 1986, Cen. Mich. U., 1991. Legis. aide N.Y. State Assembly, Albany, 1984-85; commd. 2d lt. U.S. Army, 1982; advanced through grades to lt. comdr. USAR; officer UN Hqrs. Secretariate, N.Y.C., 1985; program monitor N.Y. state exec. dept. USAR N.G., NY, 1985—86; spl. agt. N.Y. field office U.S. Dept. of State, N.Y.C., 1987-89, 1998—2002; attachè fgn. svc. U.S. Dept. State, Washington, 1986—. Cons. Garcia, Garcia and Peoples, Ltd., Ft. Green, N.Y., 1989—; bd. dirs. Ital Internat., Cambrie Heights, N.Y.; officer of Provost Marshall, Ft. Buchanan, P.R., 1993; observer Olympics, Seoul, Korea, 1988, Atlanta, 1996; detail agt. U.S. Presdl. Inaugural, 1988; mem. Presdl. Security Adv. Unit, Haitian govt., 1994. Author: (monograph) Caribbean Basin Initiative, 1984; contbr. articles to crime prevention series. Advocate Nat. Orgnl. for Victims Assistance, Washington, 1986—; county committeeman Kings County Com., 1984-86; assoc. Am. Mus. Natural History, Bklyn., 1985; inspector N.Y. Bd. Elections, 1984-85; catechist Archdiocese of Bklyn., 1980; Am. Security Coun. Found. Ednl. grantee Va. Army N.G., 1981, 95. Mem. NAAACP, VFW (mem.-at-large), Am. Fgn. Svc. Assn., Mil. Police Regimental Assn. (mem.-at-large), Mil. Civil Affairs Regtl. Assn. (mem.-at-large), Am. Polit. Sci. Assn., Nat. Org. Black Law Enforcement Execs. (assoc.), Assn. MBA Execs. (mem.-at-large), Joint Ctr. for Polit. Studies (assoc.), Fed. Law Enforcement Officers Assn. (spl. agt.), Res. Officer Assn. (mem.-at-large), Hampton Inst. Alumni Assn. (booster 1984-89), Blacks in Govt. Fgn. Affairs (Washington chpt.), Ft. Hamilton Officers Club, Ft. Monroe NCO Club (asst. mgr. 1982), Masons Scottish Rite, Prince Hall Affiliates, Alpha Phi Alpha Fraternity Inc. (chmn. internat. bros. affairs). Democrat. Roman Catholic. Avocation: radio telephone operator. Home: 525 FDR Ave Ste 1115 San Juan PR 00918

GARCIA, MARIA LUISA, biochemist, researcher; b. Valladolid, Spain, Oct. 9, 1953; came to U.S., 1979; d. Baldomero and Dolores (Garcia) G.; m. Gregory Kaczorowski, June 21, 1982. PhD, Autonoma U., Madrid, 1979. Sr. rsch. biochemist Merck & Co., Rahway, N.J., 1985-87, rsch. fellow, 1987-91, sr. rsch. fellow, 1991-97, sr. investigator, 1997—. Invited speaker, presenter papers in field. Contbr. numerous articles and revs. to profl. jours.; patentee in field. Mem. AAAS, Am. Soc. Biol. Chemists, Biophys. Soc., N.Y. Acad. Sci. Home: 5 Ashbrook Dr Edison NJ 08820-4318 Office: Merck Rsch Labs PO Box 2000 Rahway NJ 07065-0900 E-mail: maria_garcia@merck.com.

GARCIA, MARIETTA KAYE, elementary school educator, writer; b. San Antonio, Oct. 20, 1948; d. John Henry Wiegand Sr. and Lois Elizabeth Maynard; m. Gabriel Garcia, Nov. 28, 1975; children: Aaron Andres, Sarah Alexis. Grad. in art and edn., S.W. Tex. State U., 1972. Cert. tchr. Tex. With San Antonio Ind. Sch. Dist., 1972—79, Harlandale Ind. Sch. Dist., 1979—88, Southside Ind. Sch. Dist., 1988—2001, Bexar County Juvenille Justice Acad., 2002—. Author: All That Matters, 1994, Heart of the Hawk, 1995, Man of the Mist, 1995, Lion's Folly, 1995, Shiek and the Vixen, 1996, Lady of the Lake, 1997, Rose of Lorraine, 1998, Highlander's Maiden, 1999. Democrat. Roman Catholic. Avocations: gardening, painting.

GARCIA, MICHAEL P. federal agency administrator; b. N.Y. Grad., SUNY, Binghamton; Masters Degree, Coll. William and Mary; JD, Union U. With Cahill Gordon & Reindel, Manhattan, NY, 1989—90; law clk. N.Y. State Ct. Appeals, 1990—92; joined U.S. Attys. Office, 1992; fed. prosecutor dept. justice office U.S. Atty. So. Dist. N.Y.; asst. sec. export enforcement Dept. Commerce, Washington, 2001—. Office: Dept Commerce Export Enforcement 14th & Constitution Ave NW Washington DC 20230

GARCIA, OFELIA, dean; b. Havana, Cuba, Feb. 12, 1941; d. Ramon Garcia-Castro and Nieves (Gomez de Molina) Garcia. Student, Escuela de Bellas Artes, Havana, 1958-60; BA, Manhattanville Coll., 1969; MFA, Tufts U., 1972; postgrad., Duke U., 1973-75; D. Fine Arts (hon.), Atlanta Coll. Art, 1991. Asst. prof., art dept. chair, div. dir. humanities and fine arts Newton (Mass.) Coll., 1969-75; dir. studio art Boston Coll., Chestnut Hill, Mass., 1975-76; exec. dir. The Print Club, Phila., 1978-86; critic Pa. Acad. Fine Arts, Phila., 1982-86; pres. Atlanta Coll. Art, 1986-91, Rosemont (Pa.) Coll., 1991-96; sr. fellow Am. Coun. on Edn., 1996-97; dean, coll. arts and comm., prof. William Paterson U., 1997—. Visual arts panelist State Coun. of the Arts, Pa. and N.J., 1985-86, Ga., 1990-91; mem. vis. com. dept. art and architecture Lehigh (Pa.) U., 1990-96; bd. mgrs. Haverford Coll., 1992—. Artist exhibitions of prints and drawings; curator, juror numerous nat. and internat. or regional art exhibitions. Nat. pres. Women's Caucus for Art, 1984-86; bd. dirs. Am. Coun. on Edn., 1993-96; co-chair Mayor's Commn. for Women, City Phila., 1992-97; Arts Adv. Com. Barnes Found. Bd., 1992-95; trustee Jersey City Mus., 2000—, bd. chair, 2001--; bd. dirs. Caths. for Free Choice, 2000—. Recipient Am. Bookbuilders prize Boston Mus. Sch., 1969, Park Found. award, 1974; Kent fellow Danforth Found., 1975-80. Fellow Soc. for Values Higher Edn.; mem. Coll. Art Assn. Am. (bd. dirs. 1986-90, bd. coms. 1986-92), Commn. on Women in Higher Edn., Am. Coun. on Edn. (chair 1990-91), So. Assn. Colls. and Schs. (accreditation evaluator 1990-91), ArtTable, Inc. Roman Catholic. Office: William Paterson U 300 Pompton Rd Wayne NJ 07470-2152 E-mail: garciao@wpunj.edu.

GARCIA, OSCAR NICOLAS, computer science educator; b. Havana, Cuba, Sept. 10, 1936; s. Oscar Vicente and Leonor (Hernandez) G.; m. Diane Ford Journigan, Sept. 9, 1962; children: Flora, Virginia. BSEE, N.C. State U., 1961, MSEE, 1964; PhDEE, U. Md., 1969. Engr. IBM Corp., Endicott, N.Y., 1962-63; asst. prof. Old Dominion U., 1963-66, assoc. prof., 1969-70; research asst., instr. U. Md., 1966-69; assoc. prof. U. South Fla., Tampa, 1970-75, prof. computer sci., chmn. dept., 1975-85; prof. dept. elec. engring. and computer sci. George Washington U., Washington, 1985-95; disting. NCR prof. Wright State U., Dayton, Ohio, 1995—. Chmn. dept. computer sci. and engring. Wright State U., 1995—; dir. interactive sys. program in info., robotics and intelligent sys. divsn. Computer and Info. Sci. and Engring. Directorate, Intergovtl. Pers. Act, NSF, Washington, 1992-94; cons. and lectr. in field. Author: (with Y.T. Chien) Knowledge-Based Systems: Fundamentals and Tools, 1991. Fellow IEEE (bd. dirs. 1984-85, mem. U.S. activities bd. 1984, Profl. Leadership award 1991, Richard M. Emberson award 1994), Computer Soc. of IEEE (pres. 1981-83, awards com. chmn. 2002-03, bd. govs. 2003—, sec. bd. govs. 2003, Richard E. Merwin Disting. Svc. award 1988, Meritorious Svc. award 1991), AAAS; mem. Assn. Computing Machinery, Am. Soc. Engring. Edn., Am. Assn. Artificial Intelligence, Sigma Xi, Eta Kappa Nu, Phi Kappa Phi, Tau Beta Pi. Home: 1917 S Highgate Ct Beavercreek OH 45432-1880 Office: Russ Center Rm 303 Dept Comp Sci & Engring Wright State Univ Dayton OH 45435

GARCIA, RAFAEL JORGE, retired chemical engineer; b. Havana, Cuba, July 2, 1933; came to U.S., 1962; s. Rafael and Martha Teresa (Suarez) G.; m. Amelia Fernandez, Feb. 23, 1958; children: Amelia Maria, Rafael Jorge Jr. BA, Columbia Coll., 1954; BS in Chem. Engring., La. State U., 1957; MS in Environ. Engring., Johns Hopkins U., 1975. Registered profl. engr., Ind., Ky., La., Md.; registered environ. mgr. Chem. engr. Freeport Sulphur Co., New Orleans, 1957-58; prodn. supt. Litografia Garcia Muniz, Havana, 1958-62; chem. engr. The Am. Sugar Refining Co., Balt., 1962-63, The House of

Seagram, Balt., 1963-80, chief ecology engr. Louisville, 1981-97; cons. environ. regulatory affairs, 1998—; pres. Garcia Environ. Mem. Am. Inst. Chem. Engrs., Instrument Soc. Am., St. Matthews Lions (pres. 1986-87). Republican. Roman Catholic. Home: 912 Lake Forest Pkwy Louisville KY 40245-5126 E-mail: rj@garcia.win.net.

GARCIA, RUDOLPH, lawyer; b. Phila., June 22, 1951; s. Rudolph Sr. and Assunta Rita (Marrara) G.; m. Randi Ellen Pastor, Aug. 3, 1980; 1 child, Jonathan P. BA magna cum laude, Temple U., 1974, JD cum laude, 1977. Bar: Pa. 1977, U.S. Dist. Ct. (ea. dist.) Pa. 1977, U.S. Ct. Appeals (3d cir.) 1982, U.S. Supreme Ct. 1982. Assoc. Wright, Thistle & Gibbons, Phila., 1977-78, Saul Ewing LLP, Phila., 1978-84, ptnr., 1984—. Judge pro tem Phila. Ct. Common Pleas. Fellow: Acad. Adv.; mem.: ABA (state del. 2003—), Phila. Assn. Def. Counsel, Phila. Bar Assn. (chmn. local rules subcom. 1988—92, chmn. state civil com. 1999, bd. govs. 2000—02, vice chair fed. cts. com. 2003), Pa. Bar Assn., Justinian Soc. (bd. govs. 1999, vice-chancellor 2002—03), Phi Beta Kappa. Avocations: computers, photography, golf. Home: 235 Lloyd Ln Wynnewood PA 19096-3323 Office: Saul Ewing LLP 1500 Market St 38th Fl Philadelphia PA 19102-2186

GARCIA, SARA KRUGER, lawyer; b. San Antonio, Dec. 12, 1975, d. Daniel Yahr and Chaddle Bruckman Kruger; m. Ryan Matthew Garcia. BA cum laude, Bryn Mawr Coll., 1997; JD, U. Tex., 2000. Rsch. atty. Supr. Ct. Calif., San Jose, 2001—. Mediator, Tex., 1999—, Calif., 1999—. Recipient Peggy Guggenheim Internat. Studentship. Mem.: Nat. Order of Barristers.

GARCIA, TIERRY FERNANDEZ, otolaryngologist; b. Sorsogon, The Philippines, Dec. 20, 1919; came to U.S., 1970; MD, U. Philippines, 1942. Cert. in otolaryngology. Intern Philippine Gen. Hosp., 1941-42, resident in surgery, 1942-44; resident in otolaryngology Columbia U. Physicians & Surgeons Hosps., N.Y.C., 1948-51; fellow in gen. surgery Goldwater Meml. Hosp., 1947-48. Mem.: Am. Acad. Otolaryngology, Head and Neck Surgery, Am. Rhinologic Soc., Am. Acad. Environ. Medicine, Am. Acad. Otolaryngic Allergy.

GARCIA-BUÑUEL, LUIS, neurologist; b. Madrid, Feb. 24, 1931; came to U.S., 1955; s. Pedro Garcia and Concepcion Buñuel; m. Virginia May Hile, June 30, 1960. BA, BS, U. Zaragoza, Spain, 1949; MD, U. Zaragoza, 1955. Diplomate Am. Bd. Psychiatry and Neurology. Resident neurology Georgetown U., Washington, 1955-59; postdoctoral fellow Washington U., St. Louis, 1959-61; asst. prof. neurology Thomas Jefferson U., Phila., 1961-67; assoc. prof. U. N.Mex., Albuquerque, 1967-72, U. Oreg. Health Scis. Ctr., Portland, 1972-84; chief neurology svc. Portland VA Med. Ctr., 1972-84; pvt. practice, Phoenix, 1984—; chief staff Carl T. Hayden VA Med. Ctr., Phoenix, 1984-96. Contbr. articles to sci. jours., including Nature, Sci., Neurology, Jour. Neurol. Sci. Lt. Spanish Air Force, 1952-55. Fellow Am. Acad. Neurology (sr. mem.), Sigma Xi. Unitarian Universalist. Avocations: painting, computer art, steel-welded sculpture. Home and Office: 6301 E Pinchot Scottsdale AZ 85251-7020 Personal E-mail: lgarciabunuel@cox.net.

GARCIA-CARDEÑA, GUILLERMO, cell biologist, researcher; s. Guillermo Garcia-Gonzalez and Carmen Cardeña-Gonzalez. PhD, Yale U., 1997. Postdoctoral fellow Harvard U. Med. Sch., Boston, 1998—2002, asst. prof. pathology, 2002—. Recipient Young Investigator award in atherosclerosis rsch., Gill Heart Inst., 1998, Bristol Myers Squibb award, 1992. Mem.: N.Am. Vascular Biology Orgn., Am. Soc. Cell Biology. Office: Harvard Med Sch 221 Longwood Ave LMRC-401 Boston MA 02115 Office Fax: 617-732-5933. E-mail: ggarcia-cardena@rics.bwh.harvard.edu.

GARCIA-CASTELLON, MANUEL, literature educator; b. San Fernando, Spain, June 10, 1945, arrived in U.S., 1984; s. Domingo García-Jorquera and Carmen Castellón-Benarroch. Licenciado en teologia, Seminario Evangelico Unido, Madrid, 1971; lidenciado en filologia, U. Valencia, Spain, 1983; MA in Romance Langs., W.Va. U., 1986; PhD in Romance Langs., U. Ga., 1991. Prof. Spanish U. New Orleans, New Orleans, 1991—. Author: (poetry) Terra Pontus Astra, 1995, Guzman Poma, Pionero de la T.L., 1992, Estampas 7 Cuentos de Filipinas, 2002. Mem.: ACLU, Phi Beta Kappa. Home: 4114 Prytania St New Orleans LA 70115 Office: U New Orleans Lakefront New Orleans LA 70148

GARCIA-CORALES, GUILLERMO S. language educator; b. Santiago, Chile, July 28, 1954; arrived in U.S., 1982; s. Luis Garcia and Maria Corales; m. Alicia Gandulfo, June 6, 1973; children: Yezabel, Luz, Rodolfo. BA, U. Notre Dame, 1986, MA, 1987; PhD, U. Colo., 1992. Asst. prof. modern fgn. langs. Baylor U., Waco, Tex., 1992—97, assoc. prof., 1997—. Author: Relaciones de Poder, 1996; co-author: Poder y Crimen en la Literatura Chilena, 2002. Roman Catholic. Office: Baylor U PO Box 97391 Waco TX 76798

GARCIA DE LA RASILLA, CARMEN, language educator; arrived in U.S., 1989; PhD in History, U. Valladolid, 1990; PhD in Spanish Lit., The Johns Hopkins U., 1997. Asst. prof. Spanish St. Mary's Coll., 1998—99, U. N.H., Durham, 2001—. Vis. asst. prof. Spanish St. Mary's Coll., 1998, Bowdoin Coll., Brunswick, Maine, 1999—2000, Bard Coll., Annandale-on-the-Hudson, NY, 2000—01. Author: El Ayuntamiento de Valladolid, 1991. Fellow, U. N.H., 2003; grantee, Program Coop. Between Spanish Govt. & U.S.A., 1995, Bard Coll., 2000. Mem.: Soc. Renaissance Baroque Poetry, Modern Lang. Assn. Office: U NH 15 Libr Way Murkland Hall Durham NH 03824 Fax: 603-862-0104. E-mail: crasilla@cisunix.unh.edu.

GARCIA-FRIAS, JAVIER, engineering educator; b. Pamplona, Spain, Oct. 21, 1968; s. Lorenzo Garcia-Duran and Maria Rosario Frias-Sagardoy. Degree in elec. engring., UPM, Madrid, 1992; lic. in math., UNED, Madrid, 1995; PhD in Elec. Engring., UCLA, 1999. Rsch. assoc. Telefonica Investigacion y Desarrollo, Madrid, 1992—93, 1994—96; fellow, tchg. asst. U. Politecnica de Madrid, 1993—94; fellow, rsch. asst. UCLA, 1996—99; asst. prof. U. Del., Newark, 1999—2003, assoc. prof., 2003—. Contbr. articles to profl. jours. Recipient Premio Extraordinario de Bachillerato, Spanish Govt., 1985, Premio Nacional de Terminacion de Estudios Universitarios, 1992, Presdl. Early Career award for scientists and engrs., U.S. Govt., 2001, Career award, NSF, 2001. Mem.: IEEE. Office: U Del Dept Elec & Computer Engring Newark DE 19716 Business E-Mail: jgarcia@ee.udel.edu.

GARCIA-GODOY, CRISTIAN, historian, educator; b. Mendoza City, Argentina, June 3, 1924; came to the U.S., 1963; s. Cristián García Pontis and Renee Godoy Ponce; children: María Celina Heeter, María Inés García Robles, María Susana García Robles. Degree in law, U. Buenos Aires, 1950; diploma, U. Nacional de Cuyo, 1952; postgrad., Washington U., 1969, Cath. U., 1971. Official various banks, Argentina, 1941-62; sec. gen. Secretaria de Comercio de la Nación, Argentina, 1958-59; cabinet mem. Ministro de Economía, Río Negro, Argentina, 1959-60; pres.-organizer Banco de la Provincia de Río Negro, Argentina, 1960; internat. civil servant GS/OAS, 1962-89; prof. history Argentine Army, Washington, 1977—99. Author: Asociados Eminentes de San Martin, 1998, San Martin en el Reino Unido, 1996, Jefes Espanoles en la Formacion Militar de San Martin, 1995, Correspondencia Inedita de Tomas Godoy Cruz con su Padre Clemente Godoy y Videla, 1993, The Essential San Martin, 1993-94, Tomas Godoy Cruz: Su tiempo, su vida, su drama, 1991, Tomas Godoy Cruz, Dictamen Federalista, Introduccion y estudio, 1991, Los XII Presidentes 1850-1910, 1989, 2d edit., 1999, The San Martin Papers, 1988, Selected U.S. Supreme Court Decisions Related to Constitutional Law, 1986, San Martin y Unanue en la Liberacion del Peru, 1983, Evolucion Historica y Constitucional de la Argentina, 1982, San Martin, Selected Bibliography, 1978, Ampliación y Actualizacion 1978/96, Tribute to the Liberator General San Martin, 1978, Diario Secreto de San Martín, 2003; contbr. articles to profl. jours. Lt. Argentine Army, 1946. Decorated comdr. Order of St. Lazarus of Jerusalem; recipient Premio al Merito Historico, U.S. Belgrano Soc., 2000, Premio Educacion Premio Republica Argentina condecoracion, Palmas Sanmartinianas I.N.S. Argentina. Mem. Acad. Nat.de la Historia, Soc. Argentina de Historiadores Buenos Aires, Nat. Geneal. Soc. USA, Inst. Argentino de Ciencias Genealogicas, Inst. Bonaerense de Numismatica y Antiguedades, Acad. Nacional Sanmartiniana Buenos Aires, Junta de Estudios Historicos Mendoza, Inst. de Estudios Ibericos Buenos Aires, Inst. Urquiza de Estudios Historicos, Internat. Inst. Pub. Adminstrn. (U.K.), Acad. Polit. Sci. USA, Am. Soc. Internat. Law, Washington Fgn. Law Soc. USA, San Martin Soc. (pres.), Hermandad Ysabel la Catolica (chancellor), Instituto Urquiza de Estudios Históricos. Avocations: collecting art, rare books, maps, antiques and military decorations and historical medals. Home: 1128 Balls Hill Rd Mc Lean VA 22101-2653 Office: San Martin Soc PO Box 33 Mc Lean VA 22101-0033 E-mail: cggodoy@email.msn.com.

GARCIA-GODOY, FRANKLIN, dental educator; b. Santo Domingo, Dominican Republic, Nov. 11, 1952; s. Federico and Elizabeth Garcia-Godoy; m. Katherine Joachim; children: Franklin, Alexander. MS, DDS, Autonomous U. Santo Domingo, 1976; MS, U. Ill., Chgo., 1979. Prof., dir. clin. materials rsch. U. Tex. Health Sci. Ctr., San Antonio, 1985—2001; prof., head biomaterials rsch. Sch. Dental Medicine, Tufts U., Boston, 2001—02; prof., asst. dean clin. scis. Coll. Dental Medicine, Nova Southeastern U., Ft. Lauderdale, Fla., 2002—. Sr. clin. investigator Forsyth Inst., Boston, 2001—. Editor: Am. Jour. Dentistry, —. Recipient Leadership award, Am. Soc. Dentistry for Children, 2001. Mem.: ADA (Svc. award 1995), Internat. Assn. Dental Rsch., Hispanic Dental Assn. (founder 1991, Leadership award 2000). Office: Nova Southeastern U Coll Dental Medicine 3200 S University Dr Fort Lauderdale FL 33328 Office Fax: 954-262-1782. Business E-Mail: godoy@nova.edu. E-mail: godoy@nova.edu.

GARCIA-GREGORY, JORGE A. cardiologist; b. San Juan, P.R., July 4, 1946; s. Jose Alonso and Haydee (Gregory) Garcia; m. Vivian Ortiz, June 1, 1973; children: Jorge Alberto, Vivianna Marie, Javier, Viveca. AB, Assumption Coll., Worcester, Mass.; MD, U. P.R. Diplomate Am. Bd. Internal Medicine with subspecialty in cardiology. Intern, then resident Baylor Coll. Medicine affiliated Hosps., 1973-76; fellow in cardiology Tex. Heart Inst. St. Luke's Hosp., Houston, 1973-78; attending cardiologist Tex. Heart Inst., Houston, 1978—; attending physician St. Luke's Episcopal Hosp., Houston, 1978—; assoc. prof. Baylor Coll. Medicine, Houston, 1984—. Interventional cardiologist Tex. Heart Inst., Houston, Cardiology Cons. of Houston. Fellow ACP, Am. Coll. Cardiology, Soc. Cardiac Angiography and Interventions, Alpha Omega Alpha. Avocations: travel, physical fitness. Office: Cardiology Cons of Houston 6624 Fannin St Ste 2310 Houston TX 77030-2335

GARCIA-MELY, RAFAEL, retired education educator; b. Dec. 28, 1921; s. Rafael and Vivian (Mely) G.; m. Lucy Ortiz, Mar. 2, 1951 (div. Dec. 1968); children: Martin, Christine. BS in Social Sci., CCNY, 1946; BD, Yale U., 1949, MDiv, 1972; MA, NYU, 1951, PhD, 1959; LHD (hon.), World U., P.R., 1975. Ordained to ministry United Ch. of Christ U.S.A., 1949. Dir., cmty. coord. Brownsville Houses Cmty. Ctr. N.Y.C. Housing Authority, 1949-51; assoc. pastor, assoc. dir. Ch. of The Good Neighbor and Cmty. Ctr., N.Y.C., 1951-53; dir. New Neighbors Project Hudson Guild, N.Y.C., 1953-54; youth min. First Reformed Ch., Schenectady, N.Y., 1954-56; prof. edn. Inter-Am. U., San German, P.R., 1957-65, dean co-campus programs, 1963-65, prof. grad. edn. program metro campus, 1984-94, retired, 1994. Dep. gen sec. World Coun. Christian Edn., Geneva, 1966-68; dean of acad. affairs World U., San Juan, P.R., 1969-78; dean grad. program Internat. Inst. World U. Am., San Juan, 1978-83; adj. prof. Caribbean Residence Ctr. Dowling Coll., San Juan; dean U. of the Air, 1985-86. Editor Jour. World Christian Edn., 1966-68. Sec., bd. gov. World Univs., San Juan, 1968-83; v.p., treas. Latin Am. Evang. Coun. Christian Edn., Lima, Peru, 1968-81; bd. dirs., co-founder World Univs., Inc., San Juan, 1965-83; bd. dirs. govs. World Coun. Edn., Geneva, 1968-71; regional sec. Scholarship Commn. World Coun. Chs., Geneva, 1971-80; co-founder Fomento de la Opera, San Juan, 1977. Mem. ASCD, Am. Assn. Higher Edn., Am. Sociol. Assn., Religious Edn. Assn., Adult Edn. Assn., Phi Epsilon Chi, Phi Delta Kappa. Avocations: music, educational activities, sports. E-mail: garmely@taino.net.

GARCIA-PABON, LEONARDO, Spanish literature educator, consultant; s. Irma Pabon. PhD, U. of Minn., 1990. Assoc. prof. U. of Oreg., Eugene, 1990—. Lit. collection dir. Plural Editores, La Paz, Bolivia, 1998—. Author: (poetry) Sol de invierno. Office: Dept of Romance Langs 1233 U of Oregon Eugene OR 97403-1233 Office Fax: 9541) 346-4030. E-mail: lgarcia@oregon.uoregon.edu.

GARCIAPARRA, NOMAR (ANTHONY NOMAR GARCIAPARRA), professional baseball player; b. Whittier, Calif., July 23, 1973; Student, Ga. Tech. Shortstop Fla. St. League, Sarasota, Fla., 1994, Ea. League, Trenton, NJ, 1995, Internat. League, Pawtucket, 1996, G. C. Red Sox, 1996; shortstop, designated hitter, 2d baseman Boston Red Sox, 1996, shortstop, 1997—. Named Am. League Rookie Player of the Yr., The Sporting News, 1997, Baseball Writers' Assn. Am., 1997, Player's Choice Am. League Outstanding Rookie; recipient Thomas A. Yawkey award (team Most Valuable Player). Achievements include being a mem. of U.S. Olympic Baseball Team, 1992. Office: care Boston Red Sox Fenway Pk 4 Yawkey Way Boston MA 02215-3409

GARCIA Y CARRILLO, MARTHA XOCHITL, pharmacist; b. Austin, Tex., Dec. 7, 1919; d. Alberto Gonzalo and Guadalupe Eva (Carrillo) Garcia; m. Jerjes Jose Rodriguez, Oct. 9, 1943 (dec. 1987); children: Marie Eugenia, Jerjes Alberto, Nicanor Francisco. BS in Pharmacy, U. Tex., 1944. RPh, Tex. Retail pharmacist Ward Drug Store, Austin, Tex., 1952-57, Sommer's Drug Store, San Antonio, 1957-62, Skillern's Drug Store, Dallas, 1962-66; hosp. pharmacist Brackenridge Hosp., Austin, 1968-75; retail pharmacist Thorp Lane Pharmacy, San Marcos, Tex., 1975-77, The Pharmacy, San Marcos, 1975-79, MHMR Pharmacy, Austin, 1975-78, Ace Drug Co., Austin, 1979-82; ret. Contbg. author: The New Handbook of Texas, 1996. Recipient Citation of Achievement Tex. State Bd. Pharmacy, 1996. Mem. Am. Pharm. Assn. (emeritus mem.), Tex. Pharmacy Assn., Capitol Area Pharmacy Assn., Tex. State Hist. Assn., Ex-Students Assn. U. Tex. (life, Golden Anniversary cert. 1994). Republican. Avocations: reading, playing piano, current events, pharmacy medicine. Home: 21107 Ridgeview Rd Lago Vista TX 78645-4617

GARD, JOHN, state legislator; b. Milw., Aug. 3, 1963; m. Cathy Zeuske; 2 children. BA, U. Wis., La Crosse, 1986. Mem. from dist. 89 Wis. State Assembly, Madison, 1987—, mem. joint com. rev. adminstrv. rules, 1987-98, mem. tourism and recreation conf., 1987-98, mem. select com. welfare reform, 1987-98, chmn. assembly welfare reform com., 1987-98, co-chair joint com. on fin., mem. legis. coun., audit coms., mem. joint. com. on employment rels., spkr., 2003—. Mem. KC, Ducks Unltd., Sportsmen's Club, Lions. Office: PO Box 119 481 Aubin St Peshtigo WI 54157-1142*

GARD, JOSEPH ROBERT, cardiologist; b. Dubuque, Iowa, Oct. 4, 1944; MD, U. Iowa, 1970. Cert. internal medicine, cardiology. Intern L.A. Med. Ctr., 1970-71; resident Mayo Grad. Sch., 1971-74, resident in cardiology, 1976-78; with Bryan Meml. Hosp., Lincoln, Nebr. With U. Nebr. Med. Sch. Mem. Am. Coll. Cardiology, Am. Heart Assn., AMA, Nebr. Med. Assn., Lancaster County Med. Soc. Home: 9400 Montello Rd Lincoln NE 68520-1437 Office: 1500 S 48th St Ste 800 Lincoln NE 68506-1200

GARD, JUDY RICHARDSON, artist, educator; b. Woodward, Okla., Mar. 11, 1938; d. Russell Eugene and Bertie Easter (Bailey) Richardson; m. Robert Lee Gard, Aug. 31, 1958; children: Michael Cameron, Matthew Davis. Attended, U. Okla., 1956, 57, Volkshochschule, Wiesbaden, Germany, 1963, Am. U., 1967. Tchr. Watercolor Art Soc., Houston, 1983-90, Arrowmont Sch. Arts and Crafts, Gatlinberg, Tenn., 1992, Okla. Art Workshops, Tulsa, 1992-96. Demonstrator Elrod Elem. Sch., Houston, 1975, demonstrator, 1978—79, U. Houston, Houston, 1986; juror Soc. Layerists in Multimedia, Albuquerque, 1992, San Antonio Art League, 1992, EXPO Photog. Soc., Tulsa, 1994; critic, demonstrator Okla. Art Workshops, 1994—95. Featured artist in book, The New Spirit of Watercolor, 1989. Named Best of Show, Western Fedn. Watercolorists Tucson, 1975, Art League Houston, 1979, Tex. Watercolor Soc., 1977, 80; recipient Honor award Watercolor USA Honor Soc., 1993. Mem.: Nat. Watercolor Soc. (2d award 2001), Tex. Watercolor Soc., Am. Watercolor Soc. (Washington Sch. of Art award 1976, High Winds medal 1987). Avocations: cooking, gardening.

GARD, MICHAEL FLOYD, research engineer; b. McPherson, Kans., Nov. 14, 1949; s. Floyd Milton and Dorothy Rosalee Gard; m. Vicky Sue Vaughn, Dec. 30, 1972; children: Amanda M.C., Emily A.V. BSEE magna cum laude, Kans. State U., 1971; MSEE in Elec. and Biomed. Engring., Wash. U., St. Louis, 1972; PhDEE, So. Meth. U., 1992. Registered profl. engr., Mo., Okla.; registered patent agent. Test engr. Beech Aircraft Corp., Wichita, Kans., 1972-75; biomed. engr. VA Hosp., St. Louis, 1975-80; mgr. electonics Storz/SMR, St. Louis, 1980-81; sr. rsch. engr. Amoco Prodn. Co., Tulsa, Okla., 1981-84, ARCO Oil and Gas Co., Plano, Tex., 1984-89; sr. system devel. engr. GE Med. Systems, Milw., 1989-94; R&D engr. Subsite/The Charles Machine Works, Perry, Okla., 1994—. Adj. asst. prof. elec. engring. Okla. State U., Stillwater, 1998—. Author: EMI Control in Medical Electronics, 1979; contbr. articles to profl. jours.; patentee in field. Treas. Perry Area Habitat for Humanity, 1997-99. Recipient Mgmt. awrd GE Med. Systems, 1993. Mem. IEEE (sr., chair tech. com. environ. measurement). Avocations: amateur radio, classical music, histories and biographies. Home: PO Box 187 Perry OK 73077-0187 Office: Subsite Electronics 1950 W Fir St Perry OK 73077-5803

GARD, RICHARD ABBOTT, religious institute executive, educator; b. Vancouver, B.C., Can., May 29, 1914; parents U.S. citizens; s. Charles Ned and Clara Edna (Abbott) G.; m. Tatiana Ruzena Kristina Moravec, Nov. 1, 1952; children: Alan Moravec, Anita Nadine. BA, U. Wash., 1937; MA, U. Hawaii, 1940; postgrad., U. Pa., 1945-47; PhD, Claremont Grad. Sch., 1951; postgrad., Otani U. and Ryukoku U., Kyoto, Japan, 1953-54; DHL (hon.), Monmouth Coll., 1963. Dir. plans dept. Asia Found., San Francisco, 1954-56, spl. adviser to pres. San Francisco, Tokyo, 1956-59, cons. Buddhist affairs San Francisco, 1959-63; cultural affairs officer USIA, Washington, 1963-64; Buddhist affairs officer Dept. State, Washington, Hong Kong, 1964-69; libr. Inst. for Advanced Studies of World Religions SUNY, Stony Brook, 1971-73, dir. inst. svcs., 1971-84, pres., 1985-89. V.p. for U.S., World Fellowship of Buddhists, Bangkok, 1961-64, asst. sec. gen., 1971-75; vis. assoc. prof. Yale U., New Haven, 1959-63; adj. prof. Asian studies St. John's U., Jamaica, N.Y., 1974-78; vis. prof. Asian studies Wittenberg U., Springfield, Ohio, 1970, Grad. Inst. Oriental Humanities Hua Fan U., Taipei, Taiwan, 1994—; cons. Asian Buddhism Inst. Sino-Indian Buddhist Studies, Taipei, 1981-93, also rsch. fellow, 1993—, Inst. for Advanced Studies of World Religions, Carmel, N.Y., 1989-92, also rsch. fellow, 1993-95. Editor-in-chief series: Great Religions of Modern Man, 1961; editor, contbg. author: Buddhism, 1961; editor Buddhist Text Info., 1974-95, Buddhist Rsch. Info., 1979-84; editor-in-chief Asian Religious Studies Info., 1987-90; contbr. articles to acad., religious jours., Asia, U.S. Sec. 3 Village Men's Garden Club, Setauket, N.Y., 1980-84. Lt. col. USMCR, 1941-46, PTO. Japanese Buddhist okesa Jodo-shu, Phila., 1946, Japanese Buddhist okesa Shingon-shu, L.A., 1950; recipient Thai Buddhist Theravada award Mahamakuta Found., Bangkok, 1956, Burmese Buddhist Theravada award Shwedagon, Rangoon, 1957, Korean Buddhist Mahayana award Chogye-jong, Pom-o-sa, Republic of Korea, 1965; Rockefeller Found. Rsch. fellow U. Pa., Phila., 1946-47; Ford Found. grantee Wittenberg U., 1970. Mem. Assn. Asian Studies (pres. Mid-Atlantic region 1974-75), Tibet Soc. (bd. dirs. 1978-83, 87-89, 91-93), Internat. Assn. Buddhist Studies (bd. dirs. 1982-86, 87-94), Am. Soc. for Study Religion (exec. com. 1983-86). Buddhist. Avocations: landscape gardening, mountain hiking, chamber music. Address: PO Box 2866 Setauket NY 11733-0866

GARD, TRUDY MAY, pre-school educator, writer; b. Portsmouth, NH, Jan. 8, 1966; d. Lloyd Elmer and Eileen Marian Hanson; m. Dale Frank Gard, Oct. 3, 1998; 1 child, Kevin Dale; m. Scott Lucien Gaboury, May 10, 1986 (div. July 1997); children: Brett Lucien Gaboury, Katrina Lynn Gaboury. Cert. Nurses Asst. Missions dir. Riverside Bapt. Ch., Clinton, Maine, 1996—98; clk. Town Office, Canaan, Maine, 1996; libr. asst. Pub. Lib., 1996; receptionist Salvation Army, Waterville, 1997; indsl. stitcher Maine Expressions Dirigo Stitching, Skowhegan, 1997—99; day care provider, 1999—2001; pre-sch., kindergarten tchr. Hartland (Maine) Christian Sch., 2001—. Adv. bd. Riverside Bapt. Ch., Clinton, Maine, 1996—98, v.p. Christian edn., 1996—98, dir. children's plays, 1996—98. Author devotionals, poems, curriculum materials. Recipient cert., Am. Youth Found., 1985, cert. of merit, Foster's Daily Dem., 1985. Republican. Bapt. Avocations: guitar, singing, writing, illustration, sewing. Home: 59 Hubbard Rd Canaan ME 04924 Office: Hartland Christian School Warren Hill Road Hartland ME 04943

GARDE, ANAND MADHAV, materials scientist; b. Sangli, India, Jan. 1, 1945; came to U.S., 1968; s. Madhav Moreshwar and Malati Madhav (Javadekar) G.; m. Vandana Mukund Joshi, Jan. 22, 1972; children: Vinaya, Preeti. B in Tech., Indian Inst. Tech., Bombay, 1967; MS, Syracuse U., 1970; PhD, U. Fla., 1973. Asst. metallurgist Argonne (Ill.) Nat. Lab., 1974-79; prin. engr. Combustion Engring., Windsor, Conn., 1979-88; consulting engr. ABB Combustion Engring., Windsor, 1989-96, sr. cons. engr. Hematite, Mo., 1996—2002, Westinghouse Electric Co., 2002—. Adj. lectr. Hartford (Conn.) Grad. Ctr., 1989-98; adj prof. Rensselaer at Hartford, 1999—2002; symposium chmn. 10th Internat. Symposium on Zirconium in the Nuclear Industry, Balt., 1993. Contbr. over 43 articles, 32 tech. reports and 20 abstracts to profl. jours. Pres. India Assn. of Greater Hartford, 1982; program coord. India Festival of Sci., West Hartford, 1988-89. Recipient ASTM Schemel award, 1996; Author award Marathi Humerous Book, 2002. Mem. AIME (nuclear metallurgy com. 1984—), ASTM (B10, G1 coms. 1985—, tech. editor spl. tech. publs. 1132 & 1245, 1991, 94), Am. Soc. Metals Internat., Indian Inst. Metals. Republican. Hindu. Achievements include 10 patents for Ductile Irradiated Zirconium Alloys and Corrosion Resistant Zirconium Alloys, patents pending. Office: Westinghouse Electric Co 5801 Bluff Rd Columbia SC 29209 E-mail: anand.m.garde@us.westinghouse.com., garde1@sc.rr.com.

GARDE, JOHN CHARLES, lawyer; b. Lyndhurst, N.J., Aug. 17, 1961; s. John Charles and Jean (Shepherd) G.; m. L. Allison Ghenn, Aug. 9, 1986. BA, Drew U., 1983; JD, William and Mary, 1986. Bar: N.J. 1986, U.S. Ct. N.J. 1986, U.S. Ct. Appeals (2nd, 3rd and 7th cirs.) 1990. Law sec. to presiding judge Superior Ct Appellate div., Hackensack, N.J., 1986-87; assoc. McCarter & English, Newark, 1987-94, ptnr., 1995—. Contbr. William and Mary Law Rev. Warden St. Thomas Epis. Ch., 1987—; trustee St. Phillip's Acad., 1996-2000; trustee Diocese of Newark Episcopal Properties and Fin., 2001—, judge ecclesiastical ct., 1996-2000. Mem. ABA, N.J. State Bar Assn., Essex County Bar Assn., Order of the Coif, Phi Beta Kappa. Republican. Episcopalian. Office: McCarter & English 100 Mulberry St Newark NJ 07102-4004

GARDEBRING, SANDRA S. academic administrator; Grad., Luther Coll., Decorah, Iowa; JD, U. Minn. Dir. Region 5 U.S. EPA; commr. Minn. Pollution Control Agy., Minn. Dept. Human Svcs.; judge Minn. Ct. Appeals; assoc. justice Minn. Supreme Ct., 1991-98; v.p. U. Minn., 1998—. Chmn. bd. regional planning agy. Met. Coun. Mem. Ctr. Victims of Torture; mem. Minn. Advocates, LWV; past bd. dirs. St. Paul United Way, Camp DuNord, Project Environment Found., Clean Sites. Office: U Minn 11 Morrill Hall 100 Church St SE Minneapolis MN 55455-0110*

GARDELLA, CAROLYN M, medical researcher, director, medical educator; d. Louis George and Eileen Ann Gardella; m. Michael F Fialkow, Aug. 2, 1998; 1 child, Henry Philip Fialkow. BA, Dartmouth Coll., 1989; MD, SUNY, Stony Brook, 1995; MPH, U. Wash. Sch. Pub. Health, 2001. Lic. Wash., 1997, diplomate Am. Bd. of Obstetrics and Gynecology, 2002. Resident U. Wash., Ob-Gyn Dept., Seattle, 1995—2000; fellow, infectious diseases U. Wash., Am. Tchrs Preventive Medicine, Ctrs for Disease Control, 1999—2001; asst. prof. U. Wash. Ob-Gyn Dept., Seattle, 2001—; chief VA Puget Sound Health Care Sys., Gynecology, Seattle, 2001—. Recipient Alpha Omega Alpha Med. Honor Soc., SUNY Med. Sch., 1994, Nat. Deans' List, 1994, Janet Glascow Meml. Achievement Citation, 1995, Chief Resident award for Tchg. Excellence, U. Wash., Ob-Gyn Dept., 1999, John T. Conrad Meml. Rsch. award, 2000, Best Abstract award, Infectious Diseases Soc. for Ob-Gyn, 1999; grantee Ann. Competitive Rsch. grant, Wash. State Obstet. Soc., 1999. Fellow: ACOG; mem.: Seattle Gynecol. Soc., Infectious Diseases Soc. for Ob-Gyn. Achievements include research in infectious diseases in Ob-Gyn. Office: U Washington Med Ctr Box 356460 Seattle WA 98195-6460 Office Fax: 206-543-3915. E-mail: cgardel@u.washington.edu.

GARDELLA, FRANCIS JOHN, mathematics educator; b. S.I., Jan. 1, 1943; s. Frank C. and Margaret G. Gardella; m. Gail Gardella, Aug. 24, 1968; children: Jennifer, Derek. BS in Math., Fordham U., 1964; MA in Edn., Lehigh U., Bethlehem, Pa., 1966; MA in Math., Bklyn. Coll., 1971; EdD in Math. Edn., Rutgers U., 1974. Tchr. math. Pa. and NJ schs., 1964—73; math supr. several NJ schs., 1974—94; assoc. prof. math. edn. and math. Hunter Coll.-CUNY, 1994—, exec. dir. Ctr. for Math. Learning and Tchg., 2002—. Cons. in math., 1975—. Author: (book series) Math Problem Solver, 1999, Problems Plus, 1995, 4 other math. textbooks; co-author: Mathematical Connections, 1992. Recipient Disting. Svc. award Rutgers U. Grad. Sch. Alumni Assn., 2000, LADAS award for excellence in tchg. Hunter Coll. Sch. Edn., 2001. Mem. Nat.

Coun. Tchrs. Math., Assn. Math. Tchrs. N.J. Roman Catholic. Avocations: golf, tennis, history. Home: 30 Yorktown Rd East Brunswick NJ 08816 Office: Hunter College-CUNY 695 Park Ave New York NY 10021

GARDEN, JEROME M. physician; b. Grand Rapids, Mich., Oct. 26, 1949; m. Phyllis Garden; 5 children. BS, Roosevelt U., 1970; MS, Ill. Inst. Tech., 1974; MD, Northwestern U., 1980. Resident in internal medicine Northwestern U., Chgo., 1980-81, resident in dermatology, 1981-84, assoc. prof. dermatology, biomed. engring., pediat., 1990—; chief dermatology sect. Lakeside VA Med. Ctr., Chgo., 1984-97; med. staff Northwestern Meml. Hosp., Chgo., 1984—, Childrens Meml. Hosp., Chgo., 1990—. Contbr. chpts. to books, articles to profl. jours. Mem. Am. Acad. Dermatology, Am. Soc. Dermatologic Surgery, Am. Soc. Laser Medicine and Sugery, Chgo. Dermatol. Soc. Office: 150 E Huron St Ste 910 Chicago IL 60611-2946 E-mail: j_garden@northwestern.edu.

GARDENHIRE, RONALD CLYDE, professional athletics manager; m. Carol Kissling Gardenhire; children: Toby, Tiffany, Tara. Degree phys. edn., U. Tex. Mgr. Class A Kenosha, 1988; bench coach Minn. Twins, 1995, 1st base coach, 1996, 3d base coach, 1998, mgr., 2002—. Named Co-mgr. of Yr., So. league, 1990, Best Managerial Prospect, Baseball Am., Best Mgr., 1989; named to Carolina League All-Star team, 1979. Office: Minn Twins 34 Kirby Puckett Pl Minneapolis MN 55415 Office Fax: 612-375-7473.

GARDENIER, JOHN STARK, statistician, research ethicist, lecturer, writer; b. Portland, Maine, Apr. 10, 1937; s. John Stark and Lucia Esther (Christensen) G.; m. Margaret Elizabeth Mann, Jan. 26, 1962 (dec. 1976); children: Brenda Anne Marshall, Patricia Suzanne Depew, Linda Marie Sievering-Albrecht, Pamela Lee Antoun; m. Turkan Emine Kumbaraci, June 18, 1977; children: George Halil Bonneval, Jason Celal Stark. BA, Yale U., 1959; MS, George Washington U., 1968, DBA, 1973. Tech. staff Computer Scis. Corp., Falls Church, Va., 1968-69; sr. analyst CONSULTEC, Rockville, Md., 1969-71; ops. rsch. analyst USCG, Washington, 1971-90; survey statistician Nat. Ctr. Health Stats., Hyattsville, Md., 1990—2003; ret., 2003. Adj. assoc. prof. George Washington U., 1980-81; prof. lectr. Am. U., Washington, 1982-84; cons. in field. Comdr. USN, ret. Recipient Silver medal U.S. Dept. Transp., 1983, Dir.'s award CDC/NCHS, 2000. Mem. AAAS (profl. soc. ethics group), Am. Statis. Assn. (com. profl. ethics 1994-96, chair com. profl. ethics 1996-99, vice chair com. reps. 2002—, rep. to AAAS sect. history and philosophy of sci. 2002—), Nat. Assn. of Sci. Writers, Naval Res. Assn., Assn. Practical and Profl. Ethics. Avocations: music, jogging. Home: 1000 Salt Meadow Ln Mc Lean VA 22101-2027

GARDENIER, TURKAN KUMBARACI, statistical company executive, researcher; b. Istanbul, Turkey, Nov. 10, 1941; arrived in U.S., 1958; d. Celal and Aysel (Triandafilidu) K.; m. Harry M. Peyser, Nov. 24, 1966 (div. Aug. 1968); m. John Stark Gardenier, June 18, 1977; children: Pamela Lee, George HalilBonneval, Jason Celal Stark. AB, Vassar Coll., 1961; MA, Columbia U., 1962, PhD, 1966. Ops. rsch. scientist IIT Rsch. Inst., Chgo., 1966-68; asst. prof., chmn. Middle East Tech. U., Ankara, Turkey, 1968-70; vis. scientist Brookhaven Nat. Labs., Upton, L.I., NY, 1970-71; assoc. dir. Pfizer Pharms., N.Y.C., 1971-73; asst. prof. N.Y. State Maritime Coll., Bronx, NY, 1973-78; health scientist U.S. EPA, Washington, 1978-81; assoc. prof. Am. U., Washington, 1982-84; pres. Pragmatica Corp., Vienna, Va., 1982—. Tech. cons. Analytic Services Corp., Arlington, Va., 1982-90; expert U.S. Energy Info. Adminstrn., Washington, 1982-84; statis. expert EEO, 1990—, statis. cons. Engring. Computer Optecnomics, Annapolis, Md., 1977—; cons. C.R. Cushing Co., Marine Engring., N.Y.C., 1974-77. Organizer, pub. Symposium on Data Efficiency Design; preprocessing pub. Garden-ear Math./Stat. Series for Quantitative Literacy. Corp. mem. Am. Friends of Turkey, McLean, Va., 1983-89; com. mem. World Mut. Service Com., N.Y.C., 1982—; bd. dirs., v.p. Friends of Am. BoardSchs. in Turkey, 1986-88, Am. Turkish Assn., Washington, 1988-90, Washington parents rep. Foxcroft Sch., Middleburg, Va., 1981-84. Grantee, NSF, 1980, CENTO, 1969. Mem. Am. Statis. Assn. (audio-visual graphics com. 1979), Ops. Rsch. Soc. Am. (fin. com. 1980), Soc. Computer Simulation (assoc. editor jour. 1980-84), Soc. Risk Analysis (fin. com. 1980), AAAS (symposium organizer 1979-2003). Avocations: swimming, photography, music composition, multi-media training. Home: 1000 Salt Meadow Ln Mc Lean VA 22101-2027 Office: Pragmatica Corp 246 Maple Ave E Vienna VA 22180

GARDEZI, SYED A. medical researcher; b. Multan, Punjab, Pakistan, June 19, 1970; s. Syed Arif Raza and Sajida Gardezi; m. Anila Mushtaq; children: Mishaal, Maham. M.B.B.S., Allama Iqbal Med. Coll., Lahore, 1995. Diplomate 1997. Postdoctoral fellow M.D. Anderson Cancer Ctr., Houston, 1997—2001, Baylor Coll. Medicine, Houston, 1998—2001; pvt. practice Amarillo, Tex., 2001—. Author: Vitamin D Endocrine System Structural, Biological, Genetic and Clinical Aspects, 2000. Recipient Young Investigators award, Leo Pharms., 2000. Mem.: Am. Soc. Bone and Mineral Rsch. Home: 7905 Triumph Pl Amarillo TX 79119 Office: MD Anderson Cancer Ctr & Baylor Coll Holcombe Blvd Houston TX 77713

GARDILL, JAMES CLARK, lawyer; b. Glendale, W.Va., Sept. 29, 1946; s. James B. and Agnes T. (Clark) G.; m. Linda Ann Truban, Aug. 12, 1972; children: James Christopher, Catherine T., Rebecca Ann. Student, Wheeling Coll., 1964-65; AB, West Liberty State Coll., 1968; JD, W.Va. U., 1973. Bar: W.Va. 1973, U.S. Dist. Ct. (no. and so. dists.) W.Va. 1973, U.S. Ct. Appeals (4th cir.). Ptnr. Phillips, Gardill, Kaiser & Altmeyer, Wheeling, W.Va., 1973—; mcpl. judge City of Glendale, 1982—. Mem. W.Va. Workmen's Compensation Adv. Bd., Charleston, 1979-92 ; dir. Wesbanco Inc., Wheeling, 1982—, chmn., 1990—; dir. Wheeling Hosp., pres., 1999-2000, Easter Seal Rehab. Ctr., Wheeling, Wesbanco Bank Inc., West Va. U. Alumni Assn.; adj. lectr. Coll. Law, W.Va. U., 1998, 2002; lectr. estate planning and tax issues. Bd. dirs. Wheeling Soc. for Crippled Children. With U.S. Army, 1968-70. Mem. Estate Planning Coun., W.Va. Bar Assn., Ohio County Bar Assn. (pres. 1984-85). Democrat. Home: 408 Jefferson Ave Glen Dale WV 26038-1323 Office: Phillips Gardill Kaiser & Altmeyer 61 14th St Wheeling WV 26003-3411 E-mail: jamesgardill@PGKA.com.

GARDIN, JULIUS MARKUS, cardiologist, educator; b. Detroit, Jan. 14, 1949; s. Abram and Fania (Toba) G.; m. Susan Deanne Kelemen, Dec. 19, 1982; children: Adam Lev, Tova Michal, Margot Anne. BS with high distinction, U. Mich., 1968, MD cum laude, 1972. Diplomate Am. Bd. Internal Medicine; cert. cardiovascular diseases. Intern then resident in medicine U. Mich., Ann Arbor, 1972-75; fellow in cardiology Georgetown U., Washington, 1975-77; dir. cardiology noninvasive lab., staff cardiologist Lakeside VA Med. Ctr., Chgo., 1977-79; staff cardiologist, asst. prof. Med. Sch. Northwestern U., Chgo., 1978-79; dir. cardiology noninvasive lab. Irvine Med. Ctr. U. Calif., Orange, 1979-2000, from asst. prof. to assoc. prof. Irvine Med. Ctr., 1979-89, prof., 1989-2000, chief cardiology Irvine, 1994-99; acting chief cardiology Long Beach (Calif.) VA Med. Ctr., 1982—84; prof. Wayne State U., Detroit, 2000—; St. John Guild disting. chair, chief div. cardiology St. John Hosp. and Med. Ctr., Detroit, 2000—. Acting chief cardiology Long Beach (Calif.) VA Med. Ctr., 1982—84. Co-editor: Textbook of Two-Dimensional Echocardiography, 1983; editor: Update on Cardiovascular Diagnostics, 1982; assoc. editor Am. Jour. Cardiac Imaging, 1985-97; assoc. editor (text): Preventive Cardiology, 2000; mem. editl. bd. Archives of Internal Medicine and Chest, 1978-88, Am. Jour. Noninvasive Cardiology, 1985-95, Am. Jour. Cardiology, 1987-94, 97—, Cardiovascular Imaging, 1988—, Echocardiography, 1985—, Jour. Am. Coll. Cardiology, 1990-94, 2001— Am. Jour. Geriatric Cardiology, 1992—, Am. Jour. Sports Medicine, 1998— ; cardiovasc. area editor Jour. Clin. Ultrasound, 1989-94, Jour. Am. Soc. Echocardiography, 1992-2001; contbr. articles to profl. jours. Maj. Med. Svc. Corps USAR. Grantee Am. Heart Assn., 1980-82, 83-84, 99-2002, Nat. Heart Lung and Blood Inst., 1988—. Fellow ACP, Am. Coll. Cardiology (physician workforce adv., health care reform and echocardiography coms., 1993-99), Am. Heart Assn. (fellow coun. clin. cardiology, coun. epidemiology and prevention, coun. cardiovascular radiology, mem. ACC/AHA/ACP-ASIM com. to update guidelines for mgmt. of patients with chronic stable angina 1998-99, 2001-02), Soc. Geriatric Cardiology (v.p. 1990-92, pres. 1992-93, disting. fellow 2003); mem. Internat. Cardiac Doppler Soc. (sec., bd. dirs., chmn. Pan-Am. sect. 1984—, v.p. 1988-90, pres. 1990-92), Am. Soc. Echocardiography (bd. dirs., treas. 1989-91, v.p. 1991-93, pres. 1993-95, chmn. nomenclature and stds. 1991-95, chmn. task force on standardized echo report 1999-2002, co-chmn. writing group on vascular imaging, guidelines for arterial ultrasound testing writing group 2001), U. Mich. Med. Ctr. Alumni Assn. (bd. govs. 1979-81), Phi Beta Kappa, Alpha Omega Alpha, Phi Delta Epsilon. Jewish. Office: St John Hosp and Med Ctr PBII Ste 470 22201 Moross Rd Detroit MI 48236 E-mail: julius.gardin@stjohn.org.

GARDINER, E. NICHOLAS P. executive search executive; b. Boston, June 19, 1939; s. John Pennington and Juliana (Geszty) G.; m. Judith Beck, Jan. 19, 1975 (div. Sept. 1981); m. Sigrid Becker Bron, Mar. 19, 1987; stepchildren: Christian Bron, Eric Edouard Bron. BA, Yale U., 1961; PMD, Harvard Bus. Sch., 1971. Gen. mgr. W.R. Grace & Co., N.Y.C., 1965-70, Envases Sanmarti div. W.R. Grace & Co., Lima, Peru, 1967-70; dir. corp. devel., N.Y. Internat. Basic Economy Corp., 1970-72, v.p., N.Y., 1974-78; v.p. Cen. Nat. Corp., 1973, Boyden Assocs., N.Y.C., 1979-80, ptnr., 1980-83, sr. v.p., 1982-83; pres., chief exec. officer Haley Internat. Inc., N.Y.C., 1984-87; mng. dir. Gardiner Stone Hunter Internat. Inc., N.Y.C., 1987-92; exec. Paul Ray & Co., N.Y.C., 1992-93; pres. Eric Salmon & Ptnrs. Inc., N.Y.C., 1993-95, Gardiner Internat., N.Y.C., 1995—, Gardiner, Townsend & Assocs., N.Y.C., 1998—2002. Dir. Radio Free Europe/Radio Liberty Fund.; dir. Am. Coun. on Germany, French-Am. Found. Served to 1st lt. USMCR, 1961-64. Mem. Inst. Francais des Rels. Internat., Royal Inst. Internat. Affairs, The Brook, Racquet and Tennis Club, Jesters Club, Polo Club (Paris). Republican. Episcopalian. Home: One White Pine Rd Sterlington NY 10974-2650 Office: Gardiner Internat 645 5th Ave 18th Flr New York NY 10022-6018

GARDINER, HOBART CLIVE, petroleum company executive; b. Boston, Jan. 12, 1929; m. Patricia Williams, Oct. 14, 1950. BA, Yale U., 1950; postgrad., U. Central Caracas, Venezuela. Various mgmt. positions Esso Standard Oil Co. S.A., Havana, Cuba, 1954, Panama City, Panama, 1954, San Salvador, El Salvador, 1954-56, Guatemala City, Guatemala, 1956, country mgr. San Jose, Costa Rica, 1956-57, Tegucigalpa, Honduras, Brit. Honduras, 1957-60; asst. employee rels. mgr. Esso Interamerica Inc., Coral Gables, Fla., 1960; pres., gen. mgr. Esso Standard Oil Co., S.A., San Juan, P.R., 1960-62; v.p. Internat. Petroleum Co. Ltd., Bogota, Colombia, 1962-64, ops. mgr. Talara, Peru, 1964-66; pres. Esso Std. Oil (Chile), Santiago, 1966-69; L.Am. area advisor Standard Oil Co. N.J., N.Y.C., 1969-71; v.p. Esso Standard Oil Co. C.Am., Panama, San Salvador, El Salvador, 1971-74; gen. mgr. Esso Chile, Uruguay and Paraguay, Montevideo, Uruguay, 1974-77; pub. affairs program mgr. Exxon Corp., N.Y.C., 1977-79; asst. gen. mgr. Esso Caribbean, Coral Gables, Fla., 1979-81; v.p. fin. and adminstrn. Internat. Exec. Svc. Corps., Stamford, Conn., 1982-84, v.p. L.Am. and Caribbean, 1984-90, exec. v.p., 1990-93, pres., CEO, 1993—. Trustee Internat. Devel. Conf. Adv. coun. Save the Children. With U.S. Marine Corps., 1950-52. Mem. Country Club of Fairfield, Met. Club Washington, D.C. Episcopalian. Office: IESC PO Box 10005 333 Ludlow St Stamford CT 06904-2005

GARDINER, JOHN ANDREW, political science educator; b. Niagara Falls, N.Y., July 10, 1937; s. William Cecil and Anne Charlotte (Hicks) G.; m. Jane Enstrom, Nov. 6, 1993; children: Margaret, Allison, Barrett. BA, Princeton U., 1959; MA, Yale U., 1962; LLB, Harvard U., 1963, PhD, 1966. Bar: Mass. 1963. Asst. prof. U. Wis., Madison, 1965-68; assoc. prof. SUNY, Stony Brook, 1968-69; chief rsch. planning Nat. Inst. Justice, Washington, 1969-71, dir. rsch. ops., 1971-73, asst. dir., 1973-74; prof. polit. sci. U. Ill., Chgo., 1974—, head dept. polit. sci., 1974-76, dir. office social sci. rsch., 1987—2002, acting assoc. dean Liberal Arts and Scis., 1991—92, 2000—02. Author: Fraud Control Game, 1984, Decisions for Sale, 1978, Politics of Corruption, 1970, Traffic and the Police 1969; contbr. articles to profl. jours. V.p. Ill. Citizens for Better Care, Chgo., 1988—90; rsch. dir. Chgo. Ethics Project, 1986—88. Rsch. fellow Am. Judicature Soc., 1985-86. Mem. Phi Beta Kappa. Office: U Ill Pol Sci M/C 276 1007 W Harrison St Chicago IL 60607-7137 E-mail: gracelan@uic.edu.

GARDINER, JOHN JACOB, leadership educator, writer, philosopher, speaker; b. Tel Aviv, Feb. 6, 1946; came to U.S., 1952; s. Leon and Zipora Zucker; m. Joanna Meredith Winslow, 1967 (div. 1998); children: James, Katharine. BA, U. Fla., 1967, PhD, 1973; postgrad., U. Oreg., 1978, Stanford U., 1983. Tchr., dept. chair Keystone Heights (Fla.) Sch., 1968-72; instr., asst. to v.p. acad. affairs U. Fla., Gainesville, 1973-75; asst. prof. edn. The Citadel, Charleston, S.C., 1975-77; prof., dept. chair Okla. State U., Stillwater, 1979-91, Seattle U., 1991—. Assoc. in edn. Harvard U., 1985; vis. asst. prof. Fla. State U., Tallahassee, 1977-78, U. Oreg., Eugene, 1978-79; chair bd. Pacific N.W. Postdoctoral Inst., Seattle, 1995-99; bd. dirs. Internat. Leadership Assn., Conflict Resolution Inst., Human Connection Inst., Ctr. for Advanced Study of Leadership, U. Md., College Park; co-founder All Russia Leadership Devel. Ctr., Novosibirsk, 1999-2000; mem. exec. com. Internat. Leadership Assn., 2001-03. Co-author: UNESCO Guide, 1991, Insights on Leadership, 1998, Building Leadership Bridges, 2003. Recipient Svc. to State award Gov. and Ho. of Reps., 1991; fellow W. K. Kellogg Found., 1972-73; grantee James McGregor Burns Leadership Acad. Ctr. for Advanced Study of Leadership, 1998. Mem. Am. Coun. Edn. (bd. dirs. Nat. Leadership Group 1985-96), Assn. Study of Higher Edn. (bd. dirs. 1983-85), Am. Ednl. Rsch. Assn. (bd. dirs. divsn. J 1983-85), Vashon Island Rotary Club (pres. 2000-01, dist. 5030 gov. 2003—, permanent fund chair dist. 5030, 1996-2002). Avocations: walking, reading, gardening, public speaking. Office: Seattle U 413 Loyola Hall Broadway and Madison Seattle WA 98122

GARDINER, JUDITH KEGAN, English language and women's studies educator; b. Chgo., Dec. 17, 1941; d. Albert and Esther (Oswianza) Kegan; divorced; children: Viveca, Carita. BA, Radcliffe Coll., 1962; MA, Columbia U., 1964, PhD, 1968. Prof. English, gender and women's studies U. Ill., Chgo., 1969—, acting dir. women's studies, 1989, 91, interim dir. Ctr. for Rsch. on Women and Gender, 2002—. Author: Rhys Stead Lessing, 1989; editor: Provoking Agents, 1995, Masculinity Studies and Feminist Theories, 2002; editor Feminist Studies, 1989—; also articles. Organizer Newberry Libr. Feminist Lit. Criticism Group, Chgo., 1985-95. Fellow NEH, 1988. Office: U Ill Dept English M/C 162 601 S Morgan St Chicago IL 60607-7120 E-mail: gardiner@uic.edu.

GARDINER, LESTER RAYMOND, JR., lawyer; b. Salt Lake City, Aug. 20, 1931; s. Lester Raymond and Sarah Lucille (Kener) G.; m. Janet Ruth Thatcher, Apr. 11, 1955; children: Allison Gardiner Bigelow, John Alfred, Annette Gardiner Weed, Leslie Gardiner Crandall, Robert Thatcher, Lisa Gardiner West, James Raymond, Elizabeth Gardiner Smith, David William, Sarah Janet Boyden. BS with honors, U. Utah, 1954; JD, U. Mich., 1959. Bar: Utah 1959, U.S. Dist. Ct. Utah 1959, U.S. Ct. Appeals (10th cir.) 1960. Law clk. U.S. Dist. Ct., 1959; assoc. then ptnr. Van Cott, Bagley, Cornwall & McCarthy, Salt Lake City, 1960-67; ptnr. Gardiner & Johnson, Salt Lake City, 1967-72, Christensen, Gardiner, Jensen & Evans, 1972-78, Fox, Edwards, Gardiner & Brown, Salt Lake City, 1978-87, Chapman & Cutler, 1987-89, Gardiner & Hintze, 1990-92; CEO and pres. Snowbird Ski and Summer Resort, Snowbird Corp., 1993-97; prin., mgmt. cons. Ray Gardiner Assocs., 1998—. Reporter, mem. Utah Sup. Ct. Com. on Adoption of Uniform Rules of Evidence, 1970-73, mem. com. on revision of criminal code, 1975-78; master of the bench Am. Inn of Ct. I, 1980-90; mem. com. bar examiners Utah State Bar, 1973; instr. bus. law U. Utah, 1965-66; adj. prof. law Brigham Young U., 1984-85. Mem. Republican State Central Com. Utah, 1967-72, mem. exec. com. Utah Rep. Party, 1975-78, chmn. state convs., 1980, 81; mem. Salt Lake City Bd. Edn., 1971-72; bd. dirs. Salt Lake City Pub. Library, 1974-75; trustee Utah Sports Found., 1987-91; bd. dirs. and exec. com. Salt Lake City Visitors and Conv. Bur., 1988-91, 93-98. Served to 1st lt. USAF, 1954-56. Mem. Utah State Bar Assn. Mem. Lds Ch. Office: Ray Gardiner Assocs 93 Laurel St Salt Lake City UT 84103-4349

GARDINER, PAMELA NAN, performing arts company executive; m. David Edward Miller, 1974 (div. 1988); m. Anton Labuschagne, 1988 (div. 1999). BA, U. Wis.; MA, Columbia U.; JD, Case Western Res. U. Bar: Ohio, Wis., Fla. Trust officer Cleve. Trust Co., 1975-78; asst. dean acad. affairs Coll. Letters and Sci. U. Wis., 1978-84; exec. dir. Madison Festival of the Lakes, 1984-88, Miami (Fla.) City Ballet, 1988—. Bd. dirs. Performing Arts Ctr. Found., Miami Beach Prodn. Industry Coun. Office: Miami City Ballet 2200 Liberty Ave Miami Beach FL 33139-1641

GARDINER, STEVE E. secondary school educator, writer; b. Denison, Tex., Apr. 17, 1954; s. Wallace and Lavone Gardiner; m. Peggy K. Peach, June 7, 1981; children: Greta, Romney, Denby. BS, Chadron (Nebr.) State Coll., 1977; MEd, Mont. State U., 2000. English tchr. Campbell County H.S., Gillette, Wyo., 1977—81, Colegio Roosevelt, Lima, Peru, 1981—82, Jackson Hole (Wyo.) H.S., 1985—95, Billings (Mont.) Sr. H.S., 1995—. Author: Devils Tower: A Climber's Guide, 1986, Why I Climb: Personal Insights of Top Climbers, 1990, Under the Midnight Sun, 2002; contbr. articles to profl. jours. Fellow, NEH, 1989, 1991, 1995. Mem.: NEA, Journalism Edn. Assn. Democrat. Avocations: travel, mountain climbing, backpacking. Office: Billings Sr HS 425 Grand Ave Billings MT 59102

GARDINER, T(HOMAS) MICHAEL, artist; b. Seattle, Feb. 5, 1946; s. Thomas Scott Gardiner and Carolyn Virginia (Harmer) Bolin; m. Kelly Michelle Floyd, Mar. 7, 1981 (div. Dec. 1983); m. Diana Phyllis Shurtlieff Rainwater, Sept. 26, 1986; children: Rita Em, Nigel Gus. BA in Philosophy, Sulpician Sem. N.W., Kenmore, Wash., 1969; student, Cornish Inst. Arts, 1971-73. Seaman Tidewater Barge, Camas, Wash., 1969; pari-mutuel clk. Longacres Racetrack, Renton, Wash., 1969-92; dock worker Sealand, Inc., Seattle, 1970. Tchr. Coyote Jr. H.S., Seattle, 1989-95, Sch. Visual Concepts, Seattle, 1990-95; tchr., vis. artist Ctrl. Wash. U., Ellensburg, 1991; installer fine art Artech, Seattle, Wash., 1999—. Represented in permanent collections Microsoft Corp., Stoel Rives LLP, Stokes Lawrence PS, Seattle Water Dept., Nordstrom, Seattle City Light, Mus. of N.W. Art, LaConner, Wash., Sultan (Wash.) Sch. Dist., King County Portable Works Collection, SAFECO Ins. Co., Seattle, City of Portland Collection, 1988, Highline Sch. Dist., Seattle, U. Wash. Med. Ctr.; commns. include ARTp Metro Art Project, Seattle, interior painting Villa del Lupo restaurant, Vancouver, B.C., Can.; illustrations included in The New Yorker Mag., Am. Illustration 13, The Seattle Times. Recipient Best Design award Print Mag., 1985; Nat. Endowment for Arts Fellowship grantee, 1989. Democrat. Roman Catholic. Home and Office: 3023 NW 63rd St Seattle WA 98107-2566 E-mail: gardiner@speakeasy.org.

GARDINER, WILLIAM DOUGLAS HAIG, bank executive, director; b. Chatham, Ont., Can., Apr. 21, 1917; s. William Henry and Elsie May (Armstrong) G.; m. Jean Elizabeth Blatchford, Sept. 5, 1945; children: Donald W. B., Campbell D., Gregory F. Grad., Kennedy Collegiate Sch., Windsor, Ont. Asst. gen. mgr. Royal Bank of Can., Montreal, 1961-64, Vancouver, 1964-67, v.p., dist. gen. mgr., 1967-73, dep. chmn., exec. v.p., 1973-77, vice chmn., dir., 1977-80; pres. W.D.H.G. Fin. Assocs. Ltd., Vancouver. Served to lt. comdr. RCNVR. Decorated Order of Canada. Mem.: Shaughnessy Golf Club. Presbyterian. Home: 3115 W 49th Ave Vancouver BC Canada V6N 3T3

GARDINER, WILLIAM RALPH, electrical engineer, consultant; b. Washington, July 26, 1931; s. William Ralph and Mary Imogene (Perrie) G.; m. Eloise Lee, Dec. 24, 1959; children: Robin Claire, Melissa Ellise; m. Susan Alice Dodson. BSEE, Thomas U., 1977; PhD, Am. State U., 1998. Enlisted USAF, 1950, advanced through grades to tech. sgt., 1961, resigned, 1963; owner Electronic Comm. Co., Perry, Fla., 1963-75; enlisted USN, 1975, advanced through grades to master chief petty officer, 1985, ret., 1989; aerospace cons. E.I. Dupont, Wilmington, Del., 1989-92; tchr. Charles County C.C., La Plata, Md., 1992-93; drug and alcohol counselor Va. Dept. Corrections, Haynesville, Va., 1993-96. Mem. Royal Soc. St. George, SAR, Am. Legion (post comdr. 1998-2000), Assn. Naval Aviation, Fleet Res. Assn., Air Force Assn., U.S. Naval Inst. Republican. Anglican. Achievements include development of the USN FA-18 aircraft; assisted in the inauguration of wire/cable maintenance training for NASA space shuttle program; produced video for aircraft electricians use for armed forces and industry. Avocation: aviation. Home and Office: 314 Chilton Rd Zacata VA 22581-9999 E-mail: trampus314@aol.com.

GARDINO, VINCENT ANTHONY, broadcasting executive; b. N.Y.C., Sept. 19, 1953; s. Anthony John and Carmelina Mary (Boglia) Gardino. BA magna cum laude in History, St. Francis Coll. V.p. N.Y. sales mgr., dir. spl. programming and sales Metro Radio Sales, N.Y.C., 1976-79; acct. exec. WABC-AM Radio, N.Y.C., 1979-81; dir. ABC Radio Network, N.Y.C., 1981-85, ABC Direction and Entertainment Radio Networks, 1981-85; pres., COO Selcom Radio, N.Y.C., 1985—; v.p., gen. sales mgr. Sta. WOR-AM, N.Y.C., 1985-95; v.p. ea. sales CNBC, 1995-98; exec. dir. corp. underwriting sales Sta. WNYC-FM, Sta. WNYC-AM, 1998—. Cons. DEI, Inc., 2001—; adj. assoc. prof. comm./arts St. Francis Coll., NY, 2003—. Mem. Mus. Broadcasting, Internat. Radio and TV Soc., Famija Piemonteisa (bd. dirs.) NYU Med. Ctr. (Kaplan Cancer Ctr., bd. dirs.), St. Francis Coll. Alumni Assn. (bd. dirs.), N.Y. Athletic Club, Columbus Citizens Found., Inc. Roman Catholic. Avocations: tennis, golf, skiing, historical autograph collecting. Office: WNYC AM/FM 1 Centre St New York NY 10007-1602 E-mail: Vgardino@wnyc.org.

GARDNER, ANNE LANCASTER, judge; b. Corpus Christi, Tex., Aug. 19, 1942; d. Jack Quinn and DeWitte (Benton) Lancaster; m. Terry Gardner; 1 child, Travis Gregory. BA, U. Tex., 1964, LLB, 1966. Bar: Tex. 1966. Asst. dir. CLE State Bar Tex., 1966-67; law clk. to U.S. Dist. Ct. judge, 1967-71; ptnr. Simon, Peebles, Haskell, Gardner & Betty, Ft. Worth, 1971-85, McLean, Sanders, Price, Head & Ellis, P.C., Ft. Worth, 1985-88, Shannon, Gracey, Ratliff & Miller, Ft. Worth, 1988-2000, chair appeals sect.; justice Ct. of Appeals (2d dist.) Tex., 2000—. Mem. adv. commn. State Bd. Legal Specialization Appellate Civil Law, chair, 1993-94; mem. Tex. Supreme Ct. adv. com., 1993-98; chmn. merit selection Panel for U.S. Magistrate Judges, no. dist. Tex., 1995. Editor legal jours. Fellow Tex. Bar Found. (life); mem. ABA, Tarrant County Bar Assn. (dir., v.p., pres.-elect 1993, pres. 1994), Tex. Assn. Def. Counsel (bd. dirs.).

GARDNER, ARNOLD BURTON, lawyer; b. N.Y.C., Jan. 3, 1930; s. Harry P. and Ruth G. (Gutfreund) G.; m. Sue Shaffer, Aug. 24, 1952; children—Jonathan H., Diane R. BA summa cum laude, U. Buffalo, 1950; LL.B., Harvard U., 1953. Bar: N.Y. State bar 1954. Assoc. firm Kavinoky & Cook (and predecessor), Buffalo, 1953-58, ptnr., 1958—, sr. ptnr., 1977—. Mem. Buffalo Bd. Edn., 1969-74, pres., 1971-72; mem. nat. bd. govs. Am. Jewish Com., 1972-95, nat. v.p., 1986-89; chmn. N.Y. State Edn. Dept. Task Force on Tchr. Edn. and Certification, 1975-77; trustee SUNY, 1980-99, vice chmn., 1991-95; bd. govs. Hebrew Union Coll., Jewish Inst. Religion, Cin., 1981-87; trustee N.Y. State Archives, 1994—; mem. N.Y. State Bd. Regents, 1999—. With U.S. Army, 1954-56. Recipient Community Service award NCCJ, 1974, 88, Lawyer of Yr. U. Buffalo Sch. of Law, 1994. Mem. N.Y. State Bar Assn., Erie County Bar Assn., Am. Law Inst. Clubs: Buffalo. Home: 89 Middlesex Rd Buffalo NY 14216-3617 Office: Kavinoky & Cook 120 Delaware Ave Rm 600 Buffalo NY 14202-2793 E-mail: agardner@kavinokycook.com.

GARDNER, BRIAN E. lawyer; b. Des Moines, July 13, 1952; s. Lawrence E. and Sarah I. (Hill) G.; m. Rondi L. Veland, Aug. 7, 1976; children: Meredith Anne, Stephanie Lynn, John Clinton. BS, Iowa State U., 1974; JD, U. Iowa, 1978. Bar: Iowa 1978, Mo. 1978, Kans. 1979, U.S. Ct. Appeals (10th cir.) 1980, U.S. Dist. Ct. Kans. 1979, U.S. Dist. Ct. (we. dist.) Mo. 1978. Assoc. Morrison, Hecker, Curtis, Kuder & Parrish, Kansas City, Mo., 1978-80, Parker & Handsaker, Nevada, Iowa, 1980-81, Morrison, Hecker, Curtis, Kuder & Parrish, Overland Park, Kans., 1981-83; ptnr. Morrison & Hecker, Kansas City, Mo., 1983—2002, mng. ptnr., 1990—93, 1996—2002; city atty. Mission Hills, Kans., 1992—; co-mng. ptnr. Stinson Morrison Hecker LLP, Kansas City, 2002—. Bd. dirs. Overland Park Conv. and Visitors Bur., 1985-97, chmn., 1988-90; dir., mem. exec. com. Johnson County C.C. Found., Overland Park, 1990—, pres., 1997-98; bd. dirs. KCPT, 1993-99, 2000—, chmn., 1997-98; active Kansas City Area Devel. Coun., 1992—, Civic Coun. Greater Kansas City, 1998—. Mem. Kans. Bar Assn., Kans. Assn. Def. Counsel, Kansas City Met. Bar Assn., Mo. Bar Assn., Johnson County Bar Assn., Blue Hills Country Club, Cardinal Key, Phi Beta Kappa. Lutheran. Avocation: golf. Office: Stinson Morrison Hecker LLP 2600 Grand Blvd Kansas City MO 64108-4606

GARDNER, BRUCE ELWYN, lawyer; b. N.Y.C., Jan. 28, 1953; s. Parker and Mary P. (Pinkston) G. BA, UCLA, 1975; JD, Syracuse U., 1978; LLM in Taxation, Georgetown U., 1987. Bar: Ill. 1981, U.S. Dist. Ct. (no. dist.) Ill. 1981, U.S. Ct. Appeals (5th cir.) 1981, U.S. Dist. Ct. (so. dist.) Tex. 1982, U.S. Ct. Appeals (7th cir.) 1982, U.S. Ct. Appeals (9th cir.) 1983, U.S. Claims Ct. 1983, U.S. Ct. Mil. Appeals 1983, U.S. Supreme Ct. 1985, Tex. 1988, D.C. 1990. Estate tax atty. IRS, Chgo., 1979-80; appeals officer Ill. Dept. Revenue, Chgo., 1980-81, hearing officer, 1981-82; agt. IRS, Houston, 1982-84, tax law specialist Washington, 1984-86, appeals officer Houston, 1986-87, atty. Washington, 1987-91, sr. trial atty. Sacramento, 1991-94; atty., dept. fin. and revenue D.C. Ct., 1995-96; asst. gen. counsel Office of Chief Fin. Officer, D.C. Govt., 1995-96; atty. The Gardner Kane Firm, P.C., 1994—; asst. gen. counsel United

Negro Coll. Fund, 1999—. Named one of Outstanding Young Men Am., U.S. Jaycees, 1983, 84, 85, 86, 90; recipient Spl. Achievement award IRS, 1986, 90. Mem. ABA. Avocations: tennis, racquetball, music, travel. Office: IRS 1111 Constitution Ave NW Washington DC 20224-0001 also: PO Box 6183 Washington DC 20044-6183

GARDNER, BRUCE LYNN, agricultural economist; b. Solon Mills, Ill., Aug. 31, 1942; s. Robert W. and Jeannette (Hopper) G.; m. Mary Agacinski, Sept. 5, 1964. BS, U. Ill., 1964; PhD, U. Chgo., 1968. Asst. prof. econs. N.C. State U., Raleigh, 1968-75; sr. staff economist Pres. Council of Econ. Advisers, Washington, 1975-77; prof. Tex. A&M U., College Station, 1977-80, U. Md., College Park, Md., from 1981; asst. sec. U.S. Dept. Agriculture, Washington, 1989—. Author: Optimal Stockpiling of Grain, 1979 (Outstanding Research award Am. Assn. Agrl. Econs. 1980), The Governing of Agriculture, 1981, The Economics of Agricultural Policies, 1987. Fellow Am. Assn. Agrl. Econs. (bd. dirs. 1984-87).

GARDNER, CARLA DENEEN, social worker; b. St. Louis, Mo., July 27, 1964; m. Bruce Elliott Gardner. BSW, U. Mo., 1986, MSW, St. Louis U., 1990. Lic. clin. social worker 1992. Program specialist Magdala Found., St. Louis, 1986—87; social worker intern VA Med. Ctr., St. Louis, 1989—90; social worker Christian Hosp. Northeast, St. Louis, 1990—93; childrens casemgr. Dept. Mental Health, St.Louis, 1993—97; social worker Pattonville Sch. Dist., St. Ann, 1997—. Grief support group facilitator Christian Hosp. Northeast, St. Louis, 1992—93. Scholar, U. Mo., 1982—86, Acad. scholar, St. Louis U., Sch. Social Work, 1989—90. Mem.: Sch. Social Work Assn. Mo. (treas. 2001). Pentecostal. Home: 7823 Ellington Dr Normandy MO 63121 Office: Pattonville Sch Dist 11097 St Charles Rock Rd Saint Ann MO 63074 Business E-Mail: cgardner@psdr3.org.

GARDNER, CAROL ELAINE, elementary school educator; b. Savannah, Ga., Dec. 12, 1958; d. Marshall Lee and Carol Elaine (Brown) Williams; m. Jacky Lee Gardner, Sept. 29, 1979; children: Brian Alexander, Brandon Lee, Brent Matthew. BE, Cameron U., Lawton, Okla., 1979. Cert. elem. tchr., Okla. Tchr. grade 4 Swinney Elem. Sch., Lawton, 1980, tchr. grade 1, 1980—. Lawton Sch. Dist curriculum adv. bd., 1990-91; rep. Profl. Planning Devel. Coun., 1992—, chmn. fin. com., 1996-97; mem. Bldg. Leadership Team, 1991—; mentoring tchr. Cameron U., 1995-2002; mem. Dist. Ednl. Instrn. Coun., 2002—. Chair youth program Lawton Pub. Sch. Recipient Environ. award, Pub. Svc. Co. Okla., 1996. Mem. NEA, Lawton Area Reading Coun., Profl. Sci. Curriculum Alignment Coun. Jehovah'S Witness. Avocations: reading, biking, hiking, coin collecting. Home: 2306 NW 72nd St Lawton OK 73505-1007

GARDNER, CLYDE EDWARD, healthcare executive, consultant, educator; b. Steubenville, Ohio, Oct. 8, 1931; s. Peter D. and Louella Mary (Gillespie) G.; m. Patricia Jackson, Oct. 4, 1953 (div. Dec. 1977); 1 child, Bruce Stephen. BA, San Francisco State U., 1969, MS, 1971. Adminstr. Gardner Convalescent Hosp., Napa, Calif., 1955-68; exec. dir. Haight Ashbury Free Med. Clinic, San Francisco, 1970-71; lectr. San Francisco State U., 1969-71; dir. planning and rsch. divsn. N. Country Com. on Area Wide Health Planning, Canton, N.Y., 1971-77; prof. Gov.'s State U., University Park, Ill., 1977-83; sr. ptnr. Health Care Cons., Park Forest, Ill., 1983-86; exec. dir. Mahoning Shenango Area Health Edn. Network, Youngstown, Ohio, 1986-90; pres., CEO Mahoning Edn. and Tng. Network, Youngstown, Ohio, 1990-92, Health Sci. Assocs., Tucson, 1992—. Adj. prof. SUNY, Canton, 1975-76, Youngstown State U., 1987-90; bus. rep. Apollo Coll., 1994-95; rschr. FMR Rsch.; artist in residence Gardner Studio, 1994-2002; lectr. San Francisco State U., 1969-71. Author: Data Book for Health and Institutional Planning, 1981; author of numerous pub. health planning, health edn. studies and funded pvt., state and fed. health care grants, 1971-90. Pres. Found. I Ctr. for Human Devel., Harvey, Ill., 1978-83, U. Profls. of Ill., Chgo., 1982-83; bd. dirs. Blue Cross/Blue Shield Drug and Alcohol Benefit Study, Chgo., 1980-83; coord. pub. rels. and resource devel. VISTA; vol. Habitat for Humanity, Vista Leadership Corp, Tucson, 1997-98 Recipient Recognition award Ill. Dangerous Drugs Commn., 1980, 81, Outstanding Svc. award U. Profls. Ill., 1983-84, Outstanding Svc. award Ill. Fedn. Tchrs., 1983. Mem. Disabled Artist Assn. (bd. dirs., chair resource devel. com. 1992-93). Democrat. Avocations: painting, writing.

GARDNER, DALE RAY, lawyer; b. Broken Arrow, Okla., May 8, 1946; s. Edward Dale and Dahlia Faye (McKeen) G.; m. Phyllis Ann Weinschrott, Dec. 27, 1969. BA in History, So. Ill. U., 1968; MA in History, St. Mary's U., San Antonio, 1975; JD, Tulsa U., 1979. Bar: Okla. 1979, Colo. 1986, Tex. 1991, U.S. Ct. Mil. Appeals 1988, U.S. Ct. Claims 1989, U.S. Dist. Ct. (no. dist.) Okla. 1981, U.S. Dist. Ct. Colo. 1986, U.S. Dist. Ct. (so. dist.) Tex. 1992, U.S. Ct. Appeals (10th cir.) 1986, U.S. Dist. Ct. (ea. dist.) Okla. 2003. Pvt. practice, Sapulpa, Okla., 1979-80, 94—; asst. dist. atty. child support enforcement unit 24th Dist. Oklahoma, Sapulpa, 1980-86, 94-95; pvt. practice Aurora, Colo., 1986-91, Houston, 1991-94; mng. atty. Hyatt Legal Svcs., Aurora, 1988-89; city atty. City of Sapulpa, Okla., 1996-99. Author: Immigration Act of 1965: The Preliminary Results, 1974, Teapot Dome: Civil Legal Cases that Closed the Scandal, 1989. Mem. Child Support Enforcement, Sapulpa, 1980-86, 94-96; trustee United Way, Sapulpa, 1985, 95, subchair for attys. campaign, 2000, 2002; Domestic Violence Counsel, Sapulpa, 1985; chmn. bd. trustees, elder, deacon 1st Presbyn. Ch., Sapulpa, 1985. Capt. U.S. Army, 1969-75, Vietnam., lt. col Res., judge adv., ret. Mem. Okla. Bar Assn., Tex. Bar Assn., Creek County Bar (pres. 2003), Gold Coat Club (pres.), Sertoma (pres. Sapulpa 1985, pres. Collumbine 1988, 90, Sertoman of Yr. 1985), Rotary Internat. Democrat. Avocations: fishing, post card collecting. Home: 1533 Terrill Cir Sapulpa OK 74066-2567 Office: 7 S Park St Sapulpa OK 74066-4219 E-mail: ltcja@sbcglobal.net.

GARDNER, DAVID CHAMBERS, adult education educator, psychologist, business executive, author; b. Charlotte, N.C., Mar. 22, 1934; s. James Raymond and Jessica Mary (Chambers) Bumgardner m. Grace Joely Beatty, 1984; children: Joshua Avery, Jessica Sarah. BA, Northeastern U., 1960; MEd, Boston U., 1970, EdD, 1974; PhD, Columbia Pacific U., 1984. Diplomate Am. Bd. Med. Psychotherapists. Mgr. market devel. N.J. Zinc Co., N.Y.C., 1961-66, COMINCO, Ltd., Montreal, Que., Can., 1966-68; dir. Alumni Ann. Giving Program, Northeastern U., Boston, 1968-69; dir. career and spl. edn. Stoneham (Mass.) Pub. Schs., Boston, 1970-72; assoc. prof. divsn. instructional devel. and adminstrn. Boston U., 1974—, prof. emeritus, 1999—; sr. ptnr. Gardner Beatty Group, 1990—; chmn. bd. CyberHelp, Inc., 1995—; v.p. for edn. and mktg. Kaleidoscope Software, Inc., 1997-98; exec. v.p. ISMChina, Ltd., Rancho La Costa, Calif., 1998—; prin. The Human Factors Rsch. Group, Foster City, Calif., 2001—; dir. human factors rsch. Titoma, Inc., Taipei, Taiwan, 2003—. Coord. program career vocat. tng. for handicapped, Boston U., 1974-82, chmn. dept. career and bus. edn., 1974-79, also dir. fed. grants, 1975-77, 77-79; co-founder Am. Tng. and Rsch. Assocs., Inc., chmn. bd., 1979-83, pres., chief exec. officer, 1984—; dir. La Costa Inst. Lifestyle Mgmt., 1986-87. Author: Careers and Disabilities: A Career Approach, 1978; co-author: (with Grace Joely Beatty) Dissertation Proposal Guidebook: How to Prepare a Research Proposal and Get It Accepted, 1980, Career and Vocational Education for the Mildly Learning Handicapped and Disadvantaged, 1984, Stop Stress and Aging Now, 1985, Never Be Tired Again, 1990; co-author: The Visual Learning Guide Series, 1992, 93, 94, 95, 96, 97, Internet for Windows: America Online Edition, 1995, Cruising America Online for Windows, 1995, Windows 95: The Visual Learning Guide, 1995, Quicken 5 for Windows, 1995, The Visual Learning Guide, 1995, Excel for Windows 95: The Visual Learning Guide, 1995, Word for Windows 95, The Visual Learning Guide, 1995, Windows NT 4.0 Visual Desk Reference, 1997, Discover Netscape Communicator, 1997, Discover Internet Explorer, 1997, A Visual Guide to Installing Linux-Mandrake 7.1 onto a Windows Machine, Visual Desk Reference, 2000, A Visual Guide to Installing Linux Red Hat 6.2 on a Windows Machine, 2000, How to Import from China, 2000; editor Career Edn. Quar., 1975-81; contbr. articles to profl. jours. With AUS, 1954-56. U.S. Office Edn. fellow Boston U., 1970, U.S. Office Edn.-Univ. Boston rsch. fellow, 1974. Fellow Am. Assn. Mental Deficiency (Ann. Profl. Tchr. and Rsch. award Region X 1979); mem. Nat. Assn. Career Edn. (bd. dirs., past pres.), Coun. for Exceptional Children, Ea. Ednl. Rsch. Assn. (founding dir.), Am. Vocat. Assn., Phi Delta Kappa, Delta Pi Epsilon.

GARDNER, DAVID JOHN, communications executive, recording engineer; b. Binghamton, N.Y., Jan. 8, 1953; s. Daniel Sparrow and Anne Mae (Worthing) G.; m. Nancy Tipton Peacock, 1992; 1 child, Deborah Anne. AA, Broome Community Coll., Binghamton, 1973; BA, Hofstra U., 1975. Prodn. control analyst IBM, Systems Mfg. Div., Endicott, N.Y., 1971-73; rec. engr. Eye-Full Films, San Francisco, 1972-78; gen. mgr. J.K. Theater Corp., Binghamton, 1975-77; rec. engr. The Image Works, Binghamton, 1977-80; audio/video engr. Sta. WBNG, Binghamton, 1977-78; media technician Nat. Sci. Found., Washington, 1978-79; tech. ops. RCA Americom Svcs., Inc., Princeton, N.J., 1980-84, supr. ops., 1984-86; mgr. network ops. ctr. GE Americom, Inc., Princeton, 1986-90, mgr. Vernon Valley tech. ops., 1990-92, mgr., customer svcs. and ops., 1992-95; dir. media svcs. Orion Atlantic, Rockville, MD, 1995-99; dir. mktg. svcs. Loral Skynet, Bedminster, NJ, 1999—. Owner, pres., rec. engr. Ind. Sound, Binghamton, 1963—; co-founder, COB, bd. dirs. New Orleans Rec. Co., 1980—, Street Rhythm Prodns., Street Rhythm Records, Bklyn., 1980—. Mem. Soc. Broadcast Engrs., Soc. Motion Picture and TV Engrs. Lodges: Order of DeMolay. Episcopalian. Avocations: tennis, basketball, audio/video recording. Office: Loral Skynet 500 Hills Dr Bedminster NJ 07921-1538 Home: PO Box 205 Springtown PA 18081-0205

GARDNER, DONALD E. toxicologist, consultant; b. Council Bluffs, Iowa, Nov. 1, 1931; s. Charles and Clara Gardner; m. Elly K. Gardner, June 2, 1960; children: Stephanie, Susan, Stephen, Stuart. BS, Creighton U., 1955, MS, 1958; PhD, U. Cin., 1971. Cert. toxicologist Acad. Toxicol. Scis. Rsch. immunologistU.S. Biol. Labs. Ft. Detrick, Frederick, Md., 1960—62; scientist dir. USPHS, Research Triangle Park, NC, 1964—82; rsch. microbiologist, dep. chief Exptl. Biology Lab. Nat. Ctr. for Air Pollution Control and U.S. EPA, Research Triangle Park, NC, 1964—75; dir. inhalation toxicology divsn. U.S. EPA, Research Triangle Park, NC, 1980—82; v.p., chief scientist ManTech Internat., Research Triangle Park, NC, 1982—94; pres., toxicology cons. Inhalation Toxicology Assocs., Inc., Raleigh, NC, 1994—. Mem. NRC, Nat. Acad. Sci., 1988—2002, co-chair com. on toxicology, 1995—97; mem. task force com. World Health Orgn.; expert in field; pres., v.p., bd. dirs. Acad. Toxicol. Sci., 1998—2000; adj. prof. N.C. State U., Duke U., 1975—95, U. Mass., Amherst, 1994—. Founding editor Jour. Inhalation Toxicology, 1988—; editor: Toxicology of the Lung, 1988—, 1993—, Target Organ Toxicology Series (15 vols.), 1992—, New Perspectives: Toxicology and the Environment, 1999—. Named to Alumni Hall of Fame, Abraham Lincoln H.S., Council Bluffs, Iowa, 2001; recipient Outstanding Pub. Svc. award, NASA, Univ. Alumni Merit award, Creighton U., 1980. Mem.: Nat. Soc. Toxicology (nominating com. 1981, program com. 1984—87, N.C. chpt. pres. and v.p. 1989—92), Soc. Toxicology, Nat. Acad. Scis. (life). Avocations: travel, fishing, photography, reading. Home: PO Box 97605 Raleigh NC 27624 Office: Inhalation Toxicology Assocs PO box 97624 Raleigh NC 27624

GARDNER, DONALD GENE, management consultant, educator; b. Sept. 11, 1955; s. Walter Garland and Donna Marie (Metcalf) G.; m. Karen Elaine Daugs, May 29, 1983. BS Carroll Coll., 1977, PhD Purdue U., 1981. Asst. prof. mgmt. U. Colo., Colorado Springs, 1981—85, assoc. prof., 1985—90, full prof., 1990—. Asst. rsch. prof. U. Wis., Madison, 1984—86; vis. prof. Australian Grad. Sch. Mgmt., 1996; establishment chair mgmt. James Cook U., Australia, 2000—02; cons. in field. Contbr. articles on work motivation and stress. David Ross fellow, Purdue U., 1980. Mem.: APA (Hon. Mention Dissertation 1982), Acad. Mgmt. (Best Dissertation award 1982). Lutheran. Office: Coll Bus Univ Colo Colorado Springs CO 80933-7150

GARDNER, DONNA RAE (DIEHL), education educator; b. Johnstown, Pa., Sept. 25, 1954; d. G. Edwin and Hilda M. (Batley) D.; m. William W. Gardner. BS in Edn., Geneva Coll., 1976; MEd, U. Pitts., 1984; EdD, U. Ga., 1997. Cert. tchr., Pa. Substitute 2d and 3d grade tchr. Portage (Pa.) Elem./Mid. Sch., 1976-77, 3d grade tchr., 1977-86, 2d grade tchr., 1986-87; assoc. prof. Toccoa Falls (Ga.) Coll., 1987—. Chair Curriculum Rev. Com. for Accelerated Christian Edn.; spkr. in field. Editor (newsletter) Chalk Talk, Pew Pal; contbr. revs., articles to profl. publs., and ch. newsletter. Mem. choir First Alliance Ch., Toccoa, 1989-92, 96—; storyteller Stephens County Schs., Toccoa. Grantee U. Ga., 1991-92, Ga.'s Educators Profl. Devel. Mem. Internat. Reading Assn., Nat. Coun. Tchrs. English, Ga. Assn. Colls. Tchr. Edn., Ga. Assn. Ind. Colls. Tchr. Edn. Office: Toccoa Falls Coll PO Box 875 Toccoa Falls GA 30598

GARDNER, EDWARD TYTUS, III, company executive; b. Dayton, Ohio, July 1, 1949; s. Edward Tytus Jr. and Elizabeth (Paxton) G.; m. Margaret L. workman, Dec. 27, 1984; children: Lindsay Elizabeth, Christopher Workman, Edward Earnshaw. BS, Denison U., Granville, Ohio, 1973; MS, Ohio U., 1975, PhD, 1978. Asst. prof. W.Va. State Coll., Institute, 1978-82; chmn., CEO Cambridge Ednl., South Charleston, W.Va., 1982-2000; CEO Jaguar Ednl., Charleston, W.Va., 2002—. Pres., co-founder Systems Software Assocs., Inc., 1982-90; adj. asst. prof. W.Va. State Coll., 1978-81; instr. Ohio U., Athens, 1972-78. Contbr. articles to profl. jours. Office: Jaguar Ednl PO Box 389 Charleston WV 25322-0389

GARDNER, ELIZABETH ANN HUNT, artist, poet, genealogist; b. Chgo., Aug. 8, 1916; d. William Luther and Elizabeth (Miller) Hunt; m. Vernon Everett Gardner, Mar. 25, 1950. Student, Wilson Tchrs. Coll., Washington, 1934-35. Art instr. Studio 6624, Falls Church, Va., 1968—. Vol. arts tchr. Anderson Orthopedic Hosp., Arlington, Va., 1958-66; flower judge, Alexandria, Va., 1965. Author and photographer: Accidental Surprises in Art, Spotlight on Little Mountain Garden Gems, Collection of Poetry on Current Themes Hand Illuminated; photographer numerous color photographs; exhbn. Smithsonian Inst., Washington; one-woman show at Bowie Art Ctr., 1997; oil paintings, watercolors, brass rubbings included in area exhbns.; presenter recitation of original compositions. Mem. Washington Figure Skating Club, North Star Astronomy Club (Asheville, N.C.), Nat. Audubon Soc., Cornell Lab. Ornithology, Nat. Wildlife Fedn., Shillelaghs the Travel Club. Unitarian Universalist. Avocation: ornithology.

GARDNER, ELLA HAINES, artist; b. Montfort, Wis. d. Robert Daniel and Gena Helena (Helgeson) Haines; m. Russell Robert Gardner, June 1, 1937; children: Russell R., Wayne, Keith. One-woman show include Bank of Granton, Wis., 1977—, Marshfield (Wis.) Living Ctr., 1985—, First Nat. Bank, Neillsville, Wis., 1982—84, Dept. Industry, Labor and Human Rels., Madison, Wis., 1987, Marshfield Libr., 1990, 1991, 2001, The Mabel Tainter Meml. Mus., Menomonie, Wis., 1996, McMillan Meml. Gallery, Wisconsin Rapids, Wis., 1997, Lucille Tack Ctr. for the Arts Mus., Spencer, Wis., 1998, Marshfield Pub. Libr., 2001, 2002, 2-woman shows, Jail Mus., Neillsville, 1985, exhibited in group shows at Rahr West Mus., Manitowoc, Wis., 1982, gov.'s Office, Madison, 1983, 1988—89, King (Wis.) Treatment Ctr., 1983, Tuffs Mus., Neillsville, 1983, Silverman Gallery, Spring Green, Wis., 1989, New Visions Gallery, Marshfield, 1989, 1990, 2002—03, Art for Faith, Janesville, 1990, Wis. Ctr., Madison, 1997, Porter Bulls Gallery, Meml. Union, 1998, Ctrl. Wis. Triennial, 2002—03, numerous pvt. collections; author: A Celebration of Life, 1998. Charter mem. Nat. Mus. Women in the Arts. Recipient K & M Kuemmerlin award, 1986, Grumbacher Bronze award, 1987, Northwood Art Assn. award, 1987, Traveling Show award, 1987, 97-98, Obermiller Edn. award, 1993, Ctrl. Wis. State Fair award, 1973-99, 2002, State exhibit award 1998, 99, 2002, Kenneth Kummerlein Meml. award, 1998, Creative Souls Art Guild award, 1999. Mem.: Wis. Women in the Arts (Centerfold award for logo for Wis. Regional Artist Assn. 2001), Wis. Regional Artists Assn. (Meml. award 1988, Contour award 1978, 1981, 1984, 1985, 1986, 1987, 1988, 1991, 1993), Park on the Avenue. Avocations: sewing, gardening. Home: 610 E 6th St Marshfield WI 54449

GARDNER, EMERSON N., JR., military officer; b. Chestertown, Md., Oct. 16, 1951; Grad. cum laude, Duke U., 1973; grad., Basic Sch., Def. Lang. Inst., Command and Staff Coll., Armed Forces Staff Coll., Norwegian Def. Coll. Commd. 2d lt. USMC, 1972, advanced through grades to maj. gen., 2003, helicopter pilot; White Ho. liaison officer, presdl. helicopter commd. pilot, 1980-85; commdg. officer 26th MEU, 1996-98; staff officer 9th Marine Amphibious Brigade, Okinawa, Japan, 1986-87; asst. chief of staff for ops. and logistics Allied Forces No. Europe, Kolsas, Norway and High Wycombe, England, 1993-95, High Wycombe, Eng., 1994-95; asst. dep. chief of staff aviation USMC, 1998-2000, dep. comdr. Marine Forces Atlantic, 2000—02, dir. ops. U.S. Pacific Command, 2002—. Decorated Def. Superior Svc. medal., Legion of Merit with Gold star, Def. Meritorious Svc. medal, Air medal; Olmsted scholar, 1978, Germany. E-mail: egardner@hq.pacom.mil.

GARDNER, ERIC RAYMOND, lawyer; b. Derry, N.H., Nov. 13, 1946; s. William Rudolph and Lois Brooks (Wilson) G.; m. Kathleen Linda Chertok, June 14, 1969 (div. Mar. 1985); children: Matthew Eric, Thomas Martin; m. Melissa Rae Hastings, Oct. 21, 1988. BA in Polit. Sci., U. N.H., 1969; JD, Boston U., 1972. Bar: N.H. 1972, Mass. 1972, U.S. Dist. Ct. N.H. 1987, U.S. Supreme Ct. 1979. Law clk. N.H. Supreme Ct., Concord, 1972-73; assoc. Goodnow, Arwe, Ayer & Prigge, Keene, N.H., 1973-76; ptnr. Goodnow, Arwe, Ayer, Prigge & Gardner, Keene, N.H., 1977-81; pvt. practice Keene, N.H., 1981—. Appointee N.H. Supreme Ct. Profl. Conduct Com., Concord, 1984-93; sr. counsel Am. Coll. Barristers. Editor Boston U. Law Rev., 1971-72. Clk., dir. Monodnock United Way, Keene, 1975-80; dir. Keene Family YMCA, 1974-82; chair Cheshire County Crimestoppers, Inc., 1997-98. Fellow N.H. Bar Found.; mem. ABA, ATLA, Am. Bd. Trial Advocates, Nat. Bd. Trial Advocacy, N.H. Trial Lawyers Assn., Million Dollar Advocates Forum, Greater Keene C. of C. (clk., dir. 1975-80). Avocations: flying, golf, tennis, skiing, travel. Office: PO Box C 372 West St Keene NH 03431-2455

GARDNER, EVERETTE SHAW, JR., information sciences educator, consultant, author; b. Osceola, Ark., Oct. 3, 1944; s. Everette Shaw and Evelyn (Fletcher) G.; m. Mary Ann Sihelnik, May 28, 1966; children: Cynthia Anne, Stacey Diane. BBA, Memphis State U., 1966; MBA, U. N.C., 1974, PhD, 1978. Commd. ensign USN, 1966, advanced through grades to comdr., 1980, ret., 1986; assoc. prof. U. Houston, 1987-88, chmn. dept. of decision and info. scis., 1988-95, prof., 1989—, dir. Ctr. Global Mfg., 1991—. Bd. dirs., pres. Gardner Rsch., Inc., Sugar Land, Tex., 1987—; cons. NASA Johnson Space Ctr., Houston, 1988-89, Shell Oil Co., Houston, Continental Airlines, Houston, 1993—, Continental Micronesia, Guam, Delta Airlines, Atlanta, 1997-2000, Hawaiian Airlines, Honolulu, 2000—, Texaco, Houston, Pennzoil, Houston, Arthur Andersen, Houston, Exxon Co. USA, Houston, Compaq Computers, Houston, Frito-Lay, Dallas, Southwestern Bell, Houston, Centel Comm., Houston, Sys. Evolution, Houston, Tenneco, Houston, Spring Comm., L.A., Alamo Water Refiners, San Antonio, Houston Livestock Show and Rodeo, Oil and Gas Consultants Inc., Tulsa, 1996-99, Telecheck Svcs. Inc., Houston, 1997-99, Randalls Food Markets, Inc., Houston, 1997-99, Trees Inc., Houston, 1999-2000, Tex. Industries, Inc., Houston, 2001—. Co-author: Quantitative Approaches to Management, 1993; author: (software) Autocast: Business Forecasting System, 1992, The Spreadsheet Forecaster, 1994, The Spreadsheet Quality Manager, 1993; assoc. editor Internat. Jour. of Forecasting, 1985-97, Mgmt. Sci., 1987-91, Interfaces, 1987-92; contbr. articles to profl. jours.; columnist Lotus mag., 1986-92. Bd. dirs. Women's Home Houston, 1992-97; mem. Republican Nat. Com. Mem. NRA, La. Shooting Assn., Tex. State Rifle Assn., Internat. Inst. Forecasters (pres. 1990-92, dir. 1987-94), Inst. for Ops. Rsch. and Mgmt. Scis., Operational Rsch. Soc., U.S. Naval Inst., Am. Prodn. and Inventory Control Soc. (bd. dirs. Houston chpt. 1997-98), Ret. Officers Assn., Sons. of Confederate Vets., Mus. of Confederacy Richmond Va., Confederate Meml. Hall New Orleans. Presbyterian. Avocations: competitive pistol shooting, tennis, gardening, civil war history. Office: U Houston 4800 Calhoun Rd Houston TX 77204-6282 E-mail: FGardner@uh.edu.

GARDNER, GEOFFREY, writer, English educator; b. Chgo., Mar. 23, 1943; s. Alan and Marion Gardner; m. Frieda Gardner, Sept. 16, 1966 (div. Oct. 1985); 1 child, Kate; m. Christin Payack, Dec. 1, 1986. BA in English, NYU, 1964; postgrad., Columbia U., 1965-67, U. Minn., 1970-72; MA in Philosophy, New Sch., N.Y.C., 1971. Lectr. Bklyn. Coll., N.Y.C., 1966-67, CUNY, 1967-69; instr. N.Y. Inst. Tech., N.Y.C., 1968-70; dir. interlibrary loan Hamline U., St. Paul, 1974-81; lectr. Tufts U., Medford, Mass., 1984—. Lit. executor Estate of George Dennison, 1987—. Editor: The Ark, 1976-84, For Rexroth: A Festschrift, 1980, Swords that Shall not Strike: Poems of Protest and Rebellion by Kenneth Rexroth, 1999; translator: The Horses of Time: Poems of Jules Supervielle, 1985; co-editor: Temple, 1994, An Existing Better World: Notes on the Bread and Puppet Theater, 1999. Bd. dirs. Minn. Tenants Union, Mpls., 1979-81, Southside Family Sch., 1979-81; co-chair steering com. Cambridge (Mass.) Tenants Union, 1987-91. Small Press Editor's grantee Coordinating Coun. Lit. Mags., 1976-80, Editor's grantee NEA, 1979, Translation grantee NEA, 1987. Mem. Poetry Soc. Am., Acad. Am. Poets. Home: 461 Gilsum Rd Sullivan NH 03445 Office: Tufts U English Dept 210 East Hall Medford MA 02155

GARDNER, GRACE JOELY, author, consultant; b. Lynn, Mass., 1947; d. Joseph B. and Shirley E. (Phillips) B.; m. David C. Gardner, Mar. 24, 1984. BA, Simmons Coll., 1968; MEd, Boston U., 1972, EdD, 1979; PhD, Columbia Pacific U., 1984. Diplomate Am. Bd. Med. Psychotherapists (fellow); lic. psychologist, Mass. Tchr. Braintree (Mass.) H.S., 1968—70; asst. prof. Quincy (Mass.) Jr. Coll., 1971—77; sr. rsch. assoc. Boston U., 1977—79; owner, mgr. Gardner Beatty Group, Rancho La Costa, Calif., 1979—; v.p. CyberHelp, Inc., Carlsbad, Calif., 1995—; pres. Self-Test Labs., Inc., 1999—; dir. human experience rsch. Rare Medium, Inc., 2001—. Dir. human factors rsch. France Telecom R&D, 2001—. Author (with David C. Gardner) over 45 books, including Access for Windows 95, ACT 2.0 for Windows, Cruising American On-line (2.0 and 2.5), Cruising CompuServe, Cruising Microsoft Netowrk, Excel 5 for Mac: The Visual Learning Guide, Excel 5 for Windows; The Visual Learning Guide, Internet for Windows: The Visual Learning Guide (AOL 2.0 and 2.5 edits, Microsoft 95 edit.), Lotus 123 for Windows: The Visual Learning Guide (v4), Powerpoint for Windows 95: The Visual Learning Guide, Quicken 5 for Windows: The Visual Learning Guide, Windows 95: The Visual Learning Guide, WinFaxPro: The Visual Learning Guide (7.0), Wordd 7 for Windows 95: The Visual Learning Guide, WordPerfect 6 for DOS: The Visual Learning Guide, Works for Windows 95: The Visual Learning Guide, Dissertation Proposal Guidebook: How to write a research proposal and get it accepted, 1979, Career and Vocational Education, 1984, Stop Stress and Aging Now, 1986, Never Be Tired Again!, 1989 (Book-of-Month Club selection), Discover Internet Explorer, 1997, Discover Netscape Communicator, 1997, Windows NT 4.0 Workstation: Visual Desk Reference, 1997, Visual Guide to Installing Mandrae7-1 on a Windows Machine, 2000.

GARDNER, GWENDOLYN SMITH, retail executive; b. Bristol, Va., Mar. 2, 1948; d. Julian B. and Margaret Smith; m. Clyde Eugene Gardner Jr., July 20, 1968; children: Jennifer Ellen, Julie Anne. Student, U. N.C., Charlotte, 1966-67, King's Bus. Coll., 1967-68, Ctrl. Piedmont C.C., 1969. Cert. store profl. Asst. bookstore mgr., textbook mgr. Ctrl. Piedmont C.C., Charlotte, 1969-90; bookstore mgr. Davidson (N.C.) Coll., 1990—. Mem. Nat. Assn. Coll. Stores (tchr., facilitator, Stanford, Calif., 1990-91, nominating and cert. coms., 1991, chair cert. com. 1993, 94, store evaluator 1993, trustee 1996-99, Pres.' award 1994, pres. 2002—, fin. and budget com. 2002—), Coll. Stores Assn. N.C. (pres. 1990, S.E. regional com. 1994-95, course materials com. 1995-96, bd. liaison S.E. regional com., cert., assessment and evaluation 1998-99, ann. meeting com. chair 1999—). E-mail: gwgardner@davidson.edu.

GARDNER, HOWARD ALAN, travel company executive, writer, editor; b. Rockford, Ill., June 24, 1920; s. Ellis Ralph and Leanor (Roseman) Gardner; m. Marjorie Ruth Klein, Sept. 29, 1945; children: Jill, Jeffrey. BA, U. Mich., 1941. With advt. dept. Chgo. Tribune, 1941-43; mgr. promotion dept. Esquire mag., 1943-46; advt. mgr. Mrs. Klein's Food Products Co., 1946-48; pres. Sales-Aide Svc. Co., 1948-56, Gardner & Stein, 1956-59, Gardner, Stein & Frank, Inc., Chgo., 1959-83, Fun-derful World, Chgo., 1983—. Mem.: Connoisseurs Internat., Nat. Geog. Soc., Am. Geog. Soc., Confrerie de la Chaine des Rotisseurs, Travel Industry Assn. Am., Mid-Am. Club, Internat. Club, Carlton Club, Travelers' Century Club, Phi Beta Kappa. Home: 100 E Bellevue Pl Chicago IL 60611-1157 Office: Fun-derful World 100 E Bellevue Pl Chicago IL 60611-1157

GARDNER, HOWARD EARL, writer; b. Scranton, Pa., July 11, 1943; s. Ralph and Hilde (Weilheimer) G.; m. Ellen Winner; children: Kerith, Jay, Andrew, Benjamin. AB summa cum laude, Harvard U., 1965, PhD, 1971; hon. degree, Curry Coll., 1992, New Eng. Conservatory of Music, 1993, Ind. U., 1995, Moravian Coll., 1996, Cleve. Inst. of Music, 1996, Salem State Coll., 1996, L.I. U., 1997, Macalester Coll., 1997, Tel-Aviv U., 1998, Princeton U., 1998, Pa. State U., 1998, Ithaca Coll., 1999, Conn. Coll., 1999, McGill U., 1999, U. Hartford, 2000, Mass. Sch. Profl. Psychology, 2000, Nat. U. Ireland, 2001, U. Toronto, 2001; MA, Wheaton Coll., 2002. Lectr. edn. Harvard U., Cambridge, Mass., 1971-86, co-dir. Project Zero, 1972-2000, prof. edn., 1986-98—, Hobbs prof. cognition and edn.; 1998—, affiliated prof. psychology, 1987—. Prof. neurology Boston U. Sch. Medicine, 1984-87, adj. prof. neurol-

ogy, 1987—; rsch. psychologist Boston VA Med. Ctr., 1978-93. Author: The Shattered Mind, 1975, Art, Mind and Brain, 1982, Frames of Mind, 1983 (Best Book award Am. Psychol. Assn. 1984), The Mind's New Science, 1985 (William James award 1988), To Open Minds, 1989, The Unschooled Mind, 1991, Multiple Intelligences, 1993, Creating Minds, 1993, Leading Minds, 1995, Extraordinary Minds, 1997, The Disciplined Mind, 1999, Intelligence Reframed, 1999, (with M. Csikszentmihalyi and W. Damon) Good Work, 2001. Recipient Grawemeyer award in edn., 1990, Disting. Svc. medal Columbia U. Tchr.'s Coll., 1994, Pa. Gov.'s award in humanities, 1994, McGovern award Smithsonian Inst., 1998, Walker prize Boston Mus. of Sci., 1999, Samuel T. Orton award Internat. Dyslexia Assn., 1999, medal of the Pres. of Italy, 2001; MacArthur Prize fellow, 1981, Guggenheim Found. fellow, 2000; rsch. grantee numerous govtl. and pvt. founds. Fellow AAAS; mem. Am. Acad. Arts and Scis., Nat. Acad. Edn. (v.p.), Phi Beta Kappa. Office: Harvard U Grad Sch Edn Larsen Hall Cambridge MA 02138

GARDNER, HOWARD GARRY, pediatrician, educator; b. Gary, Ind., Oct. 5, 1943; s. Oscar and Anita (Arenson) G.; m. Judith (Geen), June 21, 1986; children: Molly, Joseph. BA, Ind. U., 1965, MD, 1968. Intern, resident St. Louis U., 1969-73; pvt. practice Hinsdale (Ill.) Pediatrics, 1973-79, DuPage Pediatrics, Darien, Ill., 1979—; attending staff Hinsdale Hosp., 1973—, chmn. dept. pediatrics, 2000—02; courtesy staff Childrens Meml. Hosp., Chgo., 1988—. Clin. prof. dept. pediatrics Loyola U. Sch. of Medicine, Maywood, 1983-2002; chmn. dept. pediatrics Hinsdale Hosp., 1983-85, 2000-02; med. adv. bd. YMCA of the USA, Chgo., 1989—. Mem. editl. bd. Pediatric News, 1990—; contbr. articles to profl. jours. Co-chmn. med. adv. bd. DuPage Easter Seal Ctr., Villa Park, Ill.; past, founding mem. bd. dirs. Loyola Ronald McDonald House; co-founder, past pres. Ill. Child Passenger Safety Assn.; mem. med. adv. bd. Pathways Awareness Found.; officer, steering com. DuPage Interagy. Coun. on Early Intervention. Lt. USN, 1969-71. Recipient Outstanding Clin. Tchr. award Loyola Med. Sch., 1978, Tchr. of Yr. Hinsdale Hosp. Family Practice Residency, 1981, Chgo. Caring Physician's award Met. Chgo. Health Care Coun., 1987, Buckle Up Am.! award Ill. Coalition for Safety Belt Use, 1991, Parent and Child Edn. Soc. 20th Anniversary Achievement award, 1992, Outstanding Vol. award West Suburban United Way, 1999, Carol Sanicki Crystal Heart award Easter Seals, DuPage, 2002. Fellow Am. Acad. Pediat. (past pres. Ill. chpt., past mem. nat. nominating com., instnl. rev. bd., com. on injury and poison prevention, Pisani Pediatrician of Yr. award 1986); mem. Chgo. Pediat. Soc. (past pres., Archibald Hoyne Pediatrician of Yr. 1994), Ill. Maternal and Child Health Coalition (bd. dirs., pres., 2000-2002, Advocacy award 1996), DuPage County Med. Soc. (bd. dirs.). Democrat. Jewish. Avocations: reading, skiing, photography. Office: DuPage Pediatrics 1306 Plainfield Rd Darien IL 60561-5038

GARDNER, J. STEPHEN, lawyer; b. Dayton, Ohio, May 10, 1944; s. David L. and Mary (Webb) Gardner; m. Sandra Ellen Ott, Dec. 23, 1967; children: Stephen, Truett, P.J. BA in Math., U. Fla., 1966, JD, 1969. Bar: Fla. 1969, U.S. Dist Ct. (mid. dist.) Fla. 1971. Co-founder, ptnr. Ott & Gardner, Tampa, Fla., 1971-72, Bucklew, Ramsey, Ott & Gardner, Tampa, 1972-75; ptnr. Trinkle & Redman, Brandon, 1976-81; co-founder, shareholder Bush, Ross, Gardner, Warren & Rudy, P.A., Tampa, 1981—. Mem. adv. bd. SouthTrust Bank, 1986, South Hillsborough Cmty. Bank, 1988-92. Past chmn. Tampa Downtown Partnership; past pres. Davis Islands Civic Assn.; bd. dirs. Young Life Tampa, 1972, 88; bd. dirs. F.L.O.A.T., Inc., 1986-87, v.p. 1987; mem. Leadership Tampa Class of 1980; mem. bd. counelors U. Tampa, 1976-84; chmn. pastor-parish com. Hyde Park United Meth. Ch., 1982, chmn. ch. and society com., 1975, chmn. budget raisning com., 1984, lay leader, 1985, Sunday sch. supt., 1986-87, Sunday sch. tchr., 1973-86, mem. adminstrv. bd., 1974-87, chmn., 1976, co-chmn. capital campaign com., 1997, chmn. bd. trustees, 2000. 1st lt. U.S. Army, 1969-71, Vietnam; capt. USAR, 1972-75. Decorated Bronze star with oak leaf cluster. Mem. AMA, Fla. Bar Assn. (probate rules com. 1985-87), Hillsborough County Bar Assn., Tampa Tennis Assn. (past pres.), Ye Mystic Krewe Gasparilla, Tampa Yacht and Country Club (past commodore), Exch. Club (past pres. Tampa), Univ. Club Tampa (past pres.). Methodist. Office: Bush Ross Gardner Warren & Rudy PA PO Box 3913 Tampa FL 33601-3913

GARDNER, JAMES, recreational management executive; b. Ridgeland, S.C., May 27, 1953; s. Shirley Mae Gardner; m. Cathy Brantley, Dec. 27, 1986; 1 child, Jasmine Charese. BA, St. Augustine's Coll., 1975. Parks and recreation dir. Jasper County Coun., Ridgeland, 1992—. Dist. dir. Am. Youth Basketball Tour, 1999; bd. dirs. U. S.C., New River Campus; bd. trustees East Coast Greenway Alliance, 2003. S.C. state chmn. East Coast Greenway, 2001; mem. Town of Ridgeland Planning Commn., 2001; pres., dir. Low Country Amateur Athletics, Inc., 1993; pres. Southeastern Pro-Am Basketball Assn. Home: PO Box 399 Ridgeland SC 29936-0399 E-mail: jazzys@hargray.com., jgardner@jaspercountysc.org.

GARDNER, JAMES RICHARD, pharmaceutical company executive; b. Wellsville, N.Y., Nov. 18, 1944; s. James Myers and Adelaide (Stockman) G.; m. Linda Marie Cuomo, Oct. 14, 1967; children: Alexandra K., Mindy M. BS in Engring., U.S. Mil. Acad., 1966; M in Pub. Adminstrn., Princeton U., 1968, PhD, 1977; MBA, L.I. U., 1977; grad., U.S. Army War Coll., 1989. Commd. 2d lt. U.S. Army, 1966, advanced through grades to maj., 1976, resigned, 1977; staff asst. Office of U.S. Atty. Gen., 1973; asst. prof. U.S. Mil. Acad., West Point, N.Y., 1974-77; dir. agrl. planning Pfizer, Inc., N.Y.C., 1977-81, dir. corp. strategic planning, 1981-89, sr. dir. corp. strategic planning, 1989-94, v.p. corp. investor rels., 1994—. V.p. Pfizer Found., N.Y.C., 1985-99; mem. faculty U.S. Army Command Gen. Staff Coll., 1986-92; mem. adv. coun. Ctr. Internat. Studies, Princeton U., 1987—; mem. adv. coun. Dept. Astrophysical Scis. Princeton U., 1992-99; head USAR polit. and mil. affairs div. Dept. Army, 1989-92; mem. adv. coun. Coll. Sci. Pa. State U., 1999—; mem. adv. bd. The Neuropathy Assn., 2000–. Author: (with others) American National Security, 1981, Business Competitor Intelligence, 1984; editor: Handbook of Strategic Planning, 1986; contbr. articles to profl. jours. Strategic planning com. United Way of Tri-State, N.Y.C., 1984-87; dir. adminstrn. Pfizer Inc. United Way campaign, N.Y.C., 1985-87; bd. dirs. Greater N.Y. couns. Boy Scouts Am., 1988-2000; N.Y.C. chmn. Nat. Eagle Scout Assn., 1989-92. Col. USAR, 1988-93. Decorated Bronze Stars (3), Air medals, Rep. Vietnam Gallantry Cross with Silver Star, Army Ranger; Recipient George Washington medal The Freedoms Found., Valley Forge, Pa., 1970; recipient Silver Beaver award Boy Scouts Am., 1991, Disting. Eagle award, 1992. Mem. Planning Forum (pres. N.Y.C. chpt. 1985-86), N.Am. Soc. Corp. Planning (nat. v.p. 1984-85), West Point Soc. N.Y. (bd. dirs. 1984-91, v.p. 1986-88, pres. 1988-90), Nat. Investor Rels. Inst. (bd. dirs. N.Y.C. chpt. 1995-97), U.S. Mil. Acad. Assn. Grads. (strategic planning com. 1992-96), Phi Kappa Phi. Republican. Roman Catholic. Avocations: youth activities, woodworking, astronomy, outdoor sports. Home: 40 Brundige Dr Goldens Bridge NY 10526-1416 Office: Pfizer Inc 235 E 42nd St New York NY 10017-5755

GARDNER, JANET PAXTON, journalist, film/video producer; b. Dayton, Ohio, Sept. 6, 1940; d. Edward Tytus and Mary Elizabeth (Paxton) G.; m. George Karl Debreczeny, Sept. 10, 1964 (div. Feb. 1970); 1 child, Karl Philip; m. George Edward Bradshaw Morren, Jr., Nov. 6, 1980. BFA in Art and Architecture, Cooper Union, 1965; MFA in Film Prodn., NYU, 1971; postgrad., Columbia U., 1976. Film editor, assoc. prodr. Sta. WRC-TV, NBC, Washington, 1972; asst. film editor NBC News, N.Y.C., 1973-74; newswriter, field prodr. NewsCenter4 NBC, N.Y.C., 1974-75; freelance film editor CBS News, N.Y.C., 1976-79; staff reporter, feature writer The Plain Dealer, Cleve., 1979-81; edn. columnist, editor Glamour mag., N.Y.C., 1981-82; staff writer Asbury Park Press, Neptune, N.J., 1985-86; press officer UN, 1989; owner, mgr. prodr. The Gardner Documentary Group, N.Y.C., 1991—. Mem. adj. faculty journalism Univ. Coll., Rutgers U., Newark, 1988-92, Montclair State Coll., Upper Montclair, N.J., 1992; mem. L.A. Times pub.-prof. exch. program, 1989. Prodr., dir., writer documentary videos The United Nations: It's More Than You Think, 1991, Vietnam: Land of the Ascending Dragon, 1993, Children of the Night & Starting Over, 1994, A World Beneath The War, 1996, Dancing Through Death: The Monkey Magic & Madness of Cambodia, 1999, Precious Cargo: Vietnamese Adoptees Come of Age, 2001, Siberian Dream, 2003; editor CBS News documentary film The Black Robes, 1978; prodr. Preparing To Give Birth, 1977, Choices in Childbirth, 1977, (film) Inside Ladies Home Jour., 1970; contbr. to NY Times, Phila. Inquirer, Boston Globe, Newsday, The Nation, Glamour, Working Women, New Woman, Diversion, Health Week, Indochina Newsletter, NJ Monthly, also others. Co-chair peace and social order com. Religious Soc. of Friends, Princeton, N.J., 1994; participant U.S.-Indochina Reconciliation Project Del. to Vietnam, 1987, to Cambodia, 1990. Nominee Emmy award Outstanding Hist. Programming, NATAS, 1997; recipient spl. citation, Edn. Writers Assn., 1983, 2d place award for news reporting, N.J. Press Women, 1990, 1st place award for newspaper feature writing, 1990, cert. of merit, Media & Methods mag., 1992, Lowell Thomas award for video on Vietnam, Soc. Am. Travel Writers Found., 1993, Bronze Apple award, Nat. Edn. Film and Video Festival, 1993, Golden Eagle award, CINE, 1994, 1999, 2001, Spl. Jury award, 2001, Silver Apple award, Nat. Edn. Film and Video Festival, 1997, Best Feature Reporting TV award, Soc. Profl. Journalists N.Y. chpt. Deadline Club, 1998, 2001, Bronze medallion (nat. award), Sigma Delta Chi, Best Feature Reporting TV award, Soc. Profl. Journalists N.Y. chpt., 2001, award, Chgo. Internat. Film Festival, 2002; fellow Woolrich writing fellow, Columbia U. Sch. Gen. Studies, 1976. Mem. Soc. Profl. Journalists (juror nat. mag. awards 1985, scholastic press awards 1986, chief juror editl. writing awards 1988), Investigative Reporters and Editors, Internat. Documentary Assn., North Jersey Press Club (2d place award for bus. feature writing 1990, 1st place award 1991, 1st place award for best documentary 1992, 2d place award for feature photography 1993), N.Y. Women in Film and TV. Avocation: travel. Home: 180 Riverside Dr Apt 2D New York NY 10024 Office: Ste 2420 330 W 42d St New York NY 10036-6902

GARDNER, JANETTE LYNN, critical care nurse, educator; b. Easton, Pa., Nov. 20, 1955; d. William H. and Sylvia J. (Fritts) Weller; m. Richard D. Gardner, Jan. 26, 1980; children: Kristen, Daniel, Stephanie. Diploma in nursing, Abington (Pa.) Meml. Hosp., 1977; BS, St. Joseph's Coll., North Windham, Maine, 1989. RN, Pa.; cert. in chemotherapy, BCLS, ACLS, trauma nursing. Critical care educator Easton Hosp., 1980-89, preceptor, staff nurse surg. ICU, 1989-94; ECU nurse, 1994—. Mem. sexual assault nurse examiners Easton Hosp. Contbr. articles to profl. journs. Mem. Pa. Nurses Assn., Lehigh Valley Profl. Educators. Address: 170 Anderson Rd Asbury NJ 08802

GARDNER, JERRY LEE, financial consultant; b. Long Beach, Calif., Sept. 8, 1943; s. Don Gerard and Carol (Sorenson) G.; m. Rita Frandsen, May 29, 1969; children: Marc Don, Edward David, Victor John, Denise, Joyce, John Mackay, Michael Christopher. BA, Brigham Young U., 1971; MA, Calif. State U., Sacramento, 1973; postgrad., U. Calif., Davis, 1990-99. Account exec. duPont Glore Forgan & Co., Sacramento, 1973-74, E.F. Hutton & Co., Sacramento, 1974-84; sr. investment advisor Am. Savs., Sacramento, 1984-89; fin. cons. The Golden 1 Credit Union, Sacramento, 1989—. Mem. Leaders Coun., Mass. Fin. Svcs., Boston, 1993-2003; mem. Commerce Club, Franklin Templeton Group, San Mateo, Calif., 1993-98; v.p. LDS Bus. Assocs., 1992-94. Mem. Valley Choral Soc., 2000—03; living history reinactor Old Sacramento Living History Assn., 2000—03. With U.S. Army, 1965—68, Vietnam. Recipient MVP award, Fin. Network Investment Corp., 1994—95, Century Club, 1996—2000, Amb. Club, 2001, Gov.'s award, 2002. Mem. Fin. Planning Assn., BYU Mgmt. Soc. (bd. dirs. 1990—), Valley Choral Soc., United Families Internat., LDS Ch. Avocations: travel, history of california, violin, guitar. Office: The Golden 1 Credit Union 6507 4th Ave Sacramento CA 95817-2611

GARDNER, JOAN, medical, surgical nurse; b. Ft. Worth, Oct. 5, 1950; d. Bert and Pearl (Sandgarten) G. BS in Edn., U. Tex., 1972, BS in Communication, 1976; diploma, Brackenridge Hosp., 1982. RN, Tex. Trust asst. Austin (Tex.) Nat. Bank; tchr. English and reading Columbus (Tex.) Ind. Schs.; staff orthopedics nurse Seton Med. Ctr., Austin, 1982-83, staff nurse gyn. surgery and post partum, 1983-84, staff nurse post partum, 1984-85, staff nurse gyn. surgery and ear, nose, throat, and eye, 1986, charge nurse gen. surgery, 1988-92, staff nurse short-term surgery, 1992-99; radiology charge nurse South Austin Hosp., 1999—. Home: 6301 Niederwald Strasse Kyle TX 78640 Office: 901 W Ben White Blvd Austin TX 78704

GARDNER, JOEL ROBERT, writer, historian; b. N.Y.C., May 12, 1942; s. Stephen H. and Diana (Schneider) G.; m. Holly Alpine Phelps, July 7, 1980. BA, Tulane U., 1962; MA, UCLA, 1966. Assoc. editor The Riverdale (N.Y.) Press, 1966-68; oral historian UCLA Oral History Program, 1971-80, La. State Archives, 1980-82; asst. dir. La. Divsn. of the Arts, 1983-85; dir. Perkins Ctr. for the Arts, 1985-87; pres. Gardner Assocs., Cherry Hill, N.J., 1987—. Cons. The Pew Charitable Trusts, 1988-94, Robert Wood Johnson Found., 1991—, John D. and Catherine T. MacArthur Found., 1994—. Author: Oral History for Louisiana, 1980, 75 Years of Good Taste: A History of the Tasty Baking Company, 1990, A History of the Pew Charitable Trusts, 1991, (with others) In the Company of Writers, 1991, Neighbor Caring for Neighbor, 1996; editor: Built in Louisiana, 1985, Oral History and the Law, 1985. Bd. dirs. N.J. Com. for the Humanities, 1991-94, sec., 1993-94; pres. Trenton Cmty. Mus. Sch., 1999—. Mem. Oral History Assn. (bd. dirs. 1982-83), Oral History for Middle Atlantic Region (v.p. 1991-92, pres. 1992-93), Rotary (Garden State club 1998—). Democrat. Jewish. Office: 210 E Miami Ave Cherry Hill NJ 08034

GARDNER, JOEL SYLVANUS, tempest products company executive; b. New Bern, N.C., Aug. 12, 1942; s. John and Josephine R. (Tilghman) m. Jessie Hall Gardner, Aug. 18, 1963; children: John H., Jeremy L. BS in Textiles, N.C. State U., 1970; Diploma in Law, LaSalle Ext. U., Chgo., 1979; MBA, Va. Poly. Inst., 1976; D in Mgmt., Calif. U., Petaluma, 1990. Mgr. contracts Foster Assocs., Washington, 1973-75, Hazleton Labs., Vienna, Va., 1975-77; mgr. contracts and bus. devel. Dynamac Corp., Rockville, Md., 1977-79; procurement mgr. Sperry Corp., Reston, Va., 1977-81; asst. to pres. PE Systems, Alexandria, Va., 1981-84; pvt. cons. Alexandria, Va., 1984-85; pres. Quality Tempest Products, Fairfax, Va., 1985-88; owner, pres. TEPs, McLean, Va., 1988—. Bd. advisors Westco Inc., Silver Spring, Md., 1986, 87. Mem. Nat. Contract Mgmt. Assn. (cert.). Adventist. Avocations: boating, flying. Home: 635 Frederick St SW Vienna VA 22180-6360

GARDNER, JOHN HOWLAND, III, neurologist; b. New Haven, Conn., Oct. 1, 1931; s. John Howland Jr. and Ruth (Huntley) G.; m. Anne Kates Larkin, Apr. 23, 1960; children: Elizabeth Larkin Gardner Milgram, Helen Douglass Gardner. Student, Harvard U., 1949-52; MD, Yale, 1956. Diplomate Am. Bd. Psychiatry and Neurology. Intern Stanford, 1956-57; asst. to assoc. resident in medicine Strong Mem. Hosp., Rochester, N.Y., 1957-59; resident in neurology Boston City Hosp., 1959-61; resident in neuropathology Strong Mem. Hosp., Rochester, N.Y., 1961-62; officer in charge in neurology USAF Hosp. Keesler AFB, Biloxi, Miss., 1962-64; asst. prof. Case Western Res. U. Sch. Med., Cleve., 1965-67; asst. clin. prof. Case Western Res. U. Sch. Medicine, Cleve., 1967-83, assoc. clin. prof., 1983-98, emeritus assoc. prof. neurology, 1998—; chief of neurology St. Luke's Hosp., Cleve., 1967-85; neurologist U. Suburban Health Care Ctr., Cleve., 1975-96. Pres. Greater Cleveland Chpt. Epilepsy Fdn. Am., 1973-75; chmn. Mediation Comm. Acad. Med. Cleveland, 1982-84. Vestryman, St. Paul's Episcopal Church, Cleveland Hts., 1980-82. Capt. USAF, 1962-64. Decorated Commendation Medal, USAF. Fellow Am. Acad. Neurology; mem. AMA, Acad. Med. Cleveland, Ohio State Med. Assn., Yale Alumni Assn. (v.p. Cleve. 1988—). Republican. Avocations: skeet shooting, photography, hunting, music, sailing.

GARDNER, JOSEPH LAWRENCE, editor, writer; b. Willmar, Minn., Jan. 26, 1933; s. Elmer Joseph and Margaret Eleanor (Archer) G.; m. Sadako Miyasaka, Feb. 25, 1967; children: Miya Elise, Justin Lawrence. Student, U. Portland, Oreg., 1951-52; BA summa cum laude, U. Oreg., 1955; MA (Woodrow Wilson fellow), U. Wis., 1956. Researcher, writer, asst. editor, mng. editor Am. Heritage Books div. Am. Heritage Pub. Co., Inc., N.Y.C., 1959-65; editor Am. Heritage Jr. Library and Horizon Caravel Books, 1965-68; mng. editor Newsweek Books div. Newsweek Inc., N.Y.C., 1968-70, editor, 1971-76; sr. staff editor Reader's Digest Gen. Books, N.Y.C., 1976-81, group editor gen. reference, 1982-84; dir. internat. book pub. Reader's Digest Assn., Inc., 1984-88; pres., editorial dir. Gardner Assocs., 1989—. Author: Labor on the March, 1969, Departing Glory, Theodore Roosevelt as Ex-President, 1973; editor: Newsweek Condensed Books and book series, including Wonders of Man, Milestones of History, The Founding Fathers, World of Culture, 1971-76, The World's Last Mysteries, 1978, Reader's Digest Wide World Atlas, 1979, Reader's Digest Atlas of the Bible, 1981, Eat Better, Live Better, 1982, Mysteries of the Ancient Americas, 1986, Reader's Digest Atlas of the World, 1987, Great Mysteries of the Past, 1991, The Story of Jesus, 1993, Who's Who in the Bible, 1994, Complete Guide to the Bible, 1998; contbg. editor Through Indian Eyes, 1996. Bd. dirs. Friends of Scarsdale Library, 1976-81, v.p., 1979-81; trustee Scarsdale Adult Sch., 1978-84, treas., 1981-83; trustee Scarsdale Pub. Library, 1983-84, 86-91, pres., 1989-91. Served with AUS, 1956-58. Mem. PEN, Phi Beta Kappa, Sigma Delta Chi, Phi Kappa Psi. Home and Office: 10 E End Ave Apt 15C New York NY 10021-1122 E-mail: jlgardner@worldnet.att.net.

GARDNER, KERRY ANN, librarian; b. Honolulu, May 19, 1955; d. Byron Patton and Claire Gardner. BA in Polit. Sci. magna cum laude, Temple U., 1976; MA in L.Am. Studies, U. Ariz., 1983, MLS, 1990. Documents libr. FMC Corp., Chgo., 1977-78; grad. rsch. asst. U. Ariz., Tucson, 1983-86; rsch. cons. Tucson, 1983-92; libr. asst. I Phoenix Pub. Libr., 1988-89; project mgr. U. Ariz., 1990-92; mgr. faculty resource libr. U. Ariz. Ctr. English as 2d Lang., 1989-90, 91-92; pub. svcs. libr. Bryan Wildenthal Meml. Libr., Sul Ross State U., Alpine, Tex., 1992-95; libr. dir. Am. U., Dubai, United Arab Emirates, 1995-96; literacy libr. Sterling Mcpl. Libr., Baytown, Tex., 1996-98; libr. Valle Verde campus, El Paso C.C., 1998—; co-head libr. Valle Verde campus, El Paso C.C., 2001—02. Indexer Hispanic Am. Periodicals Index, 1995; maintain GPO Access Web site, 1998—. Contbr. articles to profl. publs. Tchr. English Literacy Vols. Am., 1991-92, 96-98. Named Libr. of Yr., Border Regional Libr. Assn., 2001; grad. scholar, U. Ariz., 1976—77, 1981—82. Mem.: NEA, SALALM (marinalized peoples and ideas subcom. acquisitions com. 1995—98, elec. resources com. 1995—98), ALA, Tex. Faculty Assn., Tex. C.C. Tex. Assn., Assn. Borderlands Scholars, Border Regional Libr. Assn. (chair publicity com. 1999—2002, chair. Libr. of the Yr. com. 2002—03), Assn. Coll. and Rsch. Librs., Tex. Libr. Assn. (legis. com. coll. and univ. librs. divsn. 1993—94), Beta Phi Mu. Avocations: travel, birding. Office: El Paso C C Valle Verde Campus PO Box 20500 El Paso TX 79998-0500

GARDNER, LENANN MCGOOKEY, management consultant; d. James Lester McGookey; m. Ken Reidy, Mar. 24, 2001; 1 child, Lindsay Erica McGookey Gunther. MBA, Harvard U., 1976. V.p. mktg. MNC Fin., Balt., 1990—91; pres. LM Gardner Mgmt. Consulting, Inc., Albuquerque, 1992—. Dir. of mktg., advt. and strategic planning Blue Cross Blue Shield, Balt., 1988—89. Chair devel. com. Cuidando Los Ninos, Albuquerque, 2003. Mem.: Am. Mktg. Assn. (Profl. Svcs. Marketer of the Yr. 1996), Harvard Club. Office: LM Gardner Mgmt Consulting Inc #308 11024 Montgomery NE Albuquerque NM 87111 Office Fax: 505-828-1777. Personal E-mail: lenann@youcansell.com. E-mail: lenann@youcansell.com.

GARDNER, LIZ See WEDDINGTON, ELIZABETH GARDNER

GARDNER, MARTIN RALPH, law educator; b. Salt Lake City, Nov. 3, 1944; s. Ralph John and Elaine (Ward) G.; children: Joshua, Erin, Bryn, Linsey, Jacob. BS, U. Utah, 1969, JD, 1972. Bar: Utah 1972, Nebr. 1979. Instr. law U. Ind., Bloomington, 1972-73; asst. prof. law U. Ala., Tuscaloosa, 1973-77, U. Nebr., Lincoln, 1977-78, assoc. prof. law, 1978-80, prof. law, 1980—. Contbr. articles to profl. publs. Served with USNG, 1962—. Home: 7100 Old Post Rd Unit 8 Lincoln NE 68506-2940

GARDNER, MEREDITH LEE, communication consultant; b. Providence, Nov. 25, 1941; d. Leo and Gertrude Gloria (Ketover) Gleklen; m. Daniel Ezra Mahni, May 28, 1971 (div. 1980). A.A., Colby Sawyer Coll., New London, N.H., 1961; B.A., NYU, 1963; M.A. in Devel. Psychology, Columbia U., 1965; Phd. in Behavioral Psychology, Commonwealth Open U., Office Student Activities, Hunter Coll., N.Y.C., 1965-66; dir. Internat. Office, Boston Coll., Chestnut Hill, Mass., 1966-72; dir. ret. sr. vol. program Commonwealth of Mass., Boston, 1972-74, dir. Office Citizen Participation, 1974-76; research assoc. Hadley Lockwood, N.Y.C., 1976-78; assoc. Gilbert Tweed Assocs., N.Y.C., 1978-80; sr. assoc. MBA Mgmt., Inc., 1980-81; pres. Too Young To Retire, N.Y.C., 1981-87; v.p. sales Halliday/Herrmann and Maverick, 1987-89; pres., cons. The Strategic Edge, 1989—; motivational speaker interpersonal comm., team bldg. and conflict resolution, 1989—; spkr. change mgmt., interpersonal com. team bldg. and conflict resolution, 1989—. Author: My Friend Frank, 1985. Bd. dirs. exec. forum NYU. Mem. Internat. Enneagram Assn., World Bus. Acad., Orgn. Devel. Network, Metro. N.Y. Assn. Applied Psychology, Nat. Acad. T.V. Arts and Scis. Assn. Quality and Participation (bd. dirs. N.Y. Metro chpt.), Toastmasters Internat. (disting.), DTM (divsn. lt. gov. 1990). Avocations: sailing; bicycling; flea market hunting; dancing; talking with older people.

GARDNER, MURRAY BRIGGS, pathologist, educator; b. Lafayette, Ind., Oct. 5, 1929; s. Max William and Margaret (Briggs) G.; m. Alice E. Danielson, June 20, 1961; children: Suzanna, Martin, Danielson, Andrew. BA, U. Calif., Berkeley, 1951; MD, U. Calif., San Francisco, 1954. Intern Moffitt Hosp., San Francisco, 1954-55; resident in gen. practice Sonoma County Hosp., Santa Rosa, Calif., 1957-59; resident in pathology U. Calif. hosps., San Francisco, 1959-63; faculty U. So. Calif. Sch. Medicine, Los Angeles, 1963-81, prof. pathology, 1973-81, U. Calif., Davis Sch. Medicine, 1981—, chmn. dept. pathology, 1982-90. Contbr. chpts. to books, numerous articles in field to profl. jours. Served to lt. M.C. USNR, 1957-59. NIH grantee, 1968— Fellow AAAS; mem. Coll. Am. Pathologists, Internat. Acad. Pathology. Home: 8313 Maxwell Ln Dixon CA 95620-9662 Office: Ctr of Comparative Medicine U Calif Davis Davis CA 95616 E-mail: mbgardner@ucdavis.edu.

GARDNER, NANCY AUGUSTINE, researcher; b. Washington, Oct. 11, 1965; d. Reginald Cooper and Juno Yolanda Augustine; m. Mark Wayne Gardner, May 22, 1994. BA in Econs., George Washington U., 1987; M of Planning, U. Va., 1990; MA in Econs., Georgetown U., 2000; postgrad., George Washington U., 2001—. Planner County of Stafford, Va., 1990-94; planner II County of Prince William, Va., 1994-96; county planner III County of Henrico, Richmond, Va., 1996-99. Harold Howe II fellow, Am. Youth Policy Forum, 2003—. Mem. Am. Planning Assn. (bd. dirs. Nat. Capital area chpt. 2000-2002), Mensa. E-mail: ngardner@gwu.edu.

GARDNER, PETER JAGLOM, lawyer, publisher; b. NYC, 1958; s. Ralph David and Natalie (Jaglom) G.; m. Victoire Taittinger, 1984; children: Evan, Emma, Nadya, Parker. BA, Middlebury (Vt.) Coll., 1980; JD, M in Environ. Law magna cum laude, Vt. Law Sch., 1999; M in Intellectual Property Law, Franklin Pierce Law Ctr., 2002. Pres. Transatlantic Comml. Svcs. Corp., 1985-90; pub. Northern Centinel, Kinderhook, NY, 1991—98; pres., CEO Centinel Co., 1991—. Rsch. fellow Vt. Law Sch., 2002—; vis. scholar Tuck Sch., Dartmouth Coll., 2002—. Mem. editl. bd. N.H. Bar Jour., 2002—; contbr. articles to profl. jours. Trustee Ford Sayre Meml. Ski. Coun.; bd. overseers Hitchcock Found., 2003—. Mem.: Howe Libr. Corp., Am. Intellectual Property Law Assn., Licensing Execs. Soc. (USA and Can. chpts.), Frank Rowe Kenison Inn of Ct. (treas. 1999—2001), Vt. Bar Assn., N.Y. Bar Assn., N.H. Bar Assn. (sec. intellectual property law sect. 2002—, vice-chair 2003—), ABA, Overseas Press Club. Office: Stebbins Bradley Harvey & Miller PA 41 S Park St Hanover NH 03755-2109

GARDNER, R. SCOTT, lawyer; b. Sedalia, Mo., May 15, 1958; s. Robert S. Gardner and Susan Mitchell Gardner-Callis; m. Judy K. Gardner, June 4, 1988; children: Theodore Scott, Meredith Glyn, Madeline Jane. BSBA, U. Mo., 1980; AD, Vanderbilt U., 1983. Assoc. Margolin & Kirwan, Kansas City, 1983-84; assoc. ptnr. Martin, Gibson & Gardner, Sedalia, Mo., 1984-87; ptnr. Gardner, Gardner & Gardner LLP, Sedalia, Mo., 1987—. Mem. Sedalia Rotary Club (gear editor 1994-98), Granite Lodge # 272 (master 1994-95, 98-99), Rotary Club of Pettis County (charter, pres. 2001-02). Republican. Episcopalian. Avocations: reading, model railroading, computers. Home: 1705 Hickory Ln Sedalia MO 65301-8998 Address: 416 S Ohio Ave Sedalia MO 65301-4410

GARDNER, RALPH DAVID, advertising executive; b. N.Y.C., Apr. 16, 1923; s. Benjamin and Myra (Berman) G.; m. Nellie Jaglom, Apr. 9, 1952; children: Ralph David, John Jaglom (dec.), Peter Jaglom, James Jaglom. Diploma in journalism, NYU, 1942; diploma in mil. adminstrn., Colo. State Coll., 1943. With N.Y. Times, Paris, 1942-55, copy boy, city desk, fgn. corr., started internat. edit., 1949, bur. mgr. for Germany and Austria, Frankfurt, 1950, resigned, 1955; pres. Ralph D. Gardner Advt., N.Y.C., 1955—. Dir. Gardner Internat. Corp.; Quality Irish Food Export (Dublin) Ltd.; dir. various other U.S. and fgn. corps.; writer, book reviewer, lectr., bibliographer 19th Century Am. lit.; Mary C. Richardson lectr. SUNY-Geneseo, 1974; vis. prof. U. Wyo., Baylor U., others; mem. faculty Georgetown U. Writers Conf., 1976, 80; Hess research fellow U.

Minn., 1979; book reviewer, host Ralph Gardner's Bookshelf, WVNJ-N.Y., other radio stas., 1974-87. Author: Horatio Alger, or The American Hero Era, 1964, 78, 90, Road to Success: The Bibliography of the Works of Horatio Alger, 1971, Introduction to Silas Snobden's Office Boy, 1973, Introduction to Cast Upon the Breakers, 1974, History of Street & Smith, in Publishers for Mass Entertainment in 19th Century America, 1980, Introduction to a Fancy of Hers, 1981, The Disagreeable Woman, 1981 (English-Speaking Union selection 1981), Struggling Upward, 1984, Writers Talk to Ralph D. Gardner, 1989, others; contbr. to: N.Y. Times Book Rev., Sat. Eve. Post, No. Centinel, 1st Printings of Am. Authors, vol. 5, 1987, Children's Lit. Rev., Vol. 87, 2003; syndicated newspaper columnist Maturity News Svc., 1987—. Mem.-at-large Greater N.Y. council Boy Scouts Am., 1950-60; bd. dirs. Fresh Air Council, 1964-66; mem. hon. exec. com. Nat. Citizens for Public Libraries. Served as newswriter with Air Corps and Inf. AUS, 1943-46, ETO.; field Corr. Yank Mag. Recipient award for lit. Horatio Alger Soc., 1964, 72, 81, 85, 91; spl. citation scroll Horatio Alger Assn. Disting. Ams., 1978 Mem. Manuscript Soc., Bibliog. Soc. Am., Childrens Lit. Assn., Friends of Princeton U. Libr., Syracuse U. Libr. Assocs. (hon.), Brandeis U. Bibliophiles (hon.), Overseas Press Club of Am. (chmn. best book on fgn. affairs awards com., bd. govs. 1987-88, 92-94, v.p. 1988-92), Frankfurt Press Club, Nat. Book Critics Cir., Soc. Silurians, PEN, Grolier Club, Baker St. Irregulars, Alpha Epsilon Pi. Home: Apt 5N 135 Central Park W New York NY 10023-2413

GARDNER, RAYMOND ALAN, webmaster, writer; b. Schenectady, N.Y., Feb. 28, 1943; s. George and Alice S. Gardner; children: Eva, John, Craig. AAS in Computer Info. Sys., Schenectady County C.C., 2000; AAS in Telecomm. Mgmt., C.C. of the Air ForceC., 1999; AAS in Electronics Tech., USN, 1965. Divsn. mgr. Sears Roebuck & Co., Albany, NY, 1970—78; gen. mgr. DG Petroleum Equipment Distbr., Schenectady, NY, 1978—93; web and database developer R Gardner Enterprises, Schenectady, NY, 1994—2000; web developer USAF, Randolph AFB, San Antonio, Tex., 2000—02. Author: (Book) The Cause of Liberty, 1997. Vol. St Jude Children's Hosp. Telethon, Schenectady, 1997—2000; database developer N.Y. State Emergency Mgmt. Office, Albany, NY, 1999—2000; Bd. dirs. Highlands at Woodlake Homeowners Assn., 2002. TSgt. (E-6) NY Air N.G., 1994—2002. Decorated Air Force Commendation medal with oak leaf cluster; recipient Svc. to Civil Authorities award, State of N.Y., 2000, Mil. Outstanding Vol. Svc. medal, 2002. Mem.: San Antonio Living History Assn. (webmaster 2001, v.p. 2002). Episcopalian. Avocations: golf, gardening, walking, art. Home: 5004 Crestwood Hill Dr San Antonio TX 78244 Office: R Gardner Enterprises 5004 Crestwood Hill Dr San Antonio TX 78244 Personal E-mail: rgardnertx@prodigy.net. Business E-Mail: rgardnertx@prodigy.net.

GARDNER, RENEE VANESSA, pediatric hematologist/oncologist, researcher; d. Robert Frank Gardner. MD, Harvard U., 1975. Lic. pediats. Am. Bd. of Pediat. Resident, hematology/oncology fellow Children's Hosp. of Buffalo and Roswell Pk. Meml. Cancer Inst., Buffalo, 1975—81; assoc. prof. pediats. Children's Hosp. of New Orleans, 1993—. Mem. Children's Oncology Group, Arcadia, Calif., 1993—2002. Paintings/charcoals. Mem. Make-a-Wish, New Orleans, 2002. Recipient Am. Cancer Soc. Jr. Faculty Clin. fellowship, 1978—80, Am. Cancer Soc. Clin. fellowship, 1984—86. Mem.: Am. Soc. of Pediat. Hematology/Oncology, Am. Soc. Hematology. Achievements include research in hematopoietic, alternative medicine. Avocations: reading, drawing/painting, piano, symphony, travel.

GARDNER, RICHARD HARTWELL, retired oil industry executive; b. Cambridge, Mass., Oct. 9, 1934; s. Richard Hosmer and Marjorie Georgine Gardner; m. Helen Carolyn McIntyre, Oct. 11, 1957; children: Pamela, Hartwell. AB, Colgate U., 1956; MBA, Harvard U., 1961. Treas. Mobil Latin Am. Inc., N.Y.C., 1964-66; asst. treas. Mobil Internat., 1966-68; treas. Mobil Europe Inc., London, 1968-70; treas. N.Am. divsn. Mobil Oil Corp., N.Y.C., 1970-72, dep. treas., 1972-73, treas., 1974-95, Mobil Corp., 1976-95; retired, 1995. Dir. Pioneer Natural Resources, Inc., Irving, Tex.; chmn. Oil Investment Corp. Ltd., Hamilton, Bermuda. Chmn. Acts 29 Ministries, Atlanta. 1st lt. USAF, 1956—59. Mem. Am. Petroleum Inst., Fin. Execs. Inst. (chmn. 1986-87). Democrat.

GARDNER, RICHARD KENT, retired librarian, educator, consultant; b. New Bedford, Mass., Dec. 7, 1928; s. Francis and Millicent Annetta (Kent) G. AB cum laude, Middlebury Coll., Vt., 1950; Dipl. Litt., U. Paris, 1954; MS in Library Sci., Western Res. U., 1955; PhD, Case Western Res. U., 1968. Asst. librarian Case Inst. Tech., 1955-57; library adviser Mich. State U. adv. group pub. adminstrn. to Govt. South Vietnam, 1957-58; librarian, assoc. prof. Marietta Coll., Ohio, 1959-63; founding editor Choice: Books for Coll. Libraries, Middletown, Conn., 1963-66, editor, 1972-77; lectr., then assoc. prof. Case Western Res. U. Sch. Library Sci., 1966-69; prof. agrege Ecole de Bibliotheconomie, U. Montreal, 1969-70, prof. titulaire, 1970-72, 82-93, dir., 1970-72, 82-87; prof. Grad. Sch. Library and Info. Sci. UCLA, 1977-82; ret., 1993. Internat. libr. edn. cons., 1966-93. Author: Cataloging and Classification of Books, with the Vietnamese Decimal Classification, 1958, rev. edit., 1966, Opening Day Collection, 1965, rev. edit., 1974, Education for Librarianship in France: An Historical Survey, 1968, Library Collections: Their Origin, Selection, and Development, 1981 (Blackwell award 1982), Education of Library and Information Professionals: Present and Future Prospects, 1987; also articles. Mem. Forest Press com. Lake Placid Ednl. Found., 1972-87; trustee Russell Library, Middletown, 1975-77. Served with AUS, 1951-53 Mem. ALA, Ohio Library Assn. (exec. bd. 1962-63), Can. Library Assn., Assn. Coll. and Research Libraries, Music Library Assn., Ohio Coll. Assn. (v.p. librarians sect. 1962-63, pres. 1963), Corp. des Bibliothecaires professionals du Que. (adminstrv. council 1970-72), Tudor Singers Montreal (v.p. 1970-72), Assn. internat. des ecoles des scis. de l'information Home: 13610 Shaker Blvd Apt 403 Cleveland OH 44120-1551 E-mail: rkgardn@en.com.

GARDNER, RICHARD NEWTON, diplomat, lawyer, educator; b. N.Y.C., July 9, 1927; s. Samuel I. and Ethel (Elias) G.; m. Danielle Luzzatto, June 10, 1956; children: Nina Jessica, Anthony Laurence. AB magna cum laude, Harvard U., 1948; JD, Yale U., 1951; PhD, Oxford U., 1954. Bar: N.Y. 1952. Corr. UP, 1946-47, AP, 1948; teaching fellow internat. legal studies Harvard Law Sch., 1953-54; with Coudert Bros., N.Y.C., 1954-57; assoc. prof. law Columbia U., 1957-60, prof., 1960-61, 65-66, Henry L. Moses prof. law and internat. orgn., 1967-77, 81—; of counsel Morgan, Lewis & Bockius, 1997—; U.S. amb. to Italy Am. Embassy, Rome, Italy, 1977-81, U.S. amb. to Spain Madrid, 1993-97. Dep. asst. sec. state internat. orgns. Dept. State, 1961-65; vis. prof. U. Istanbul, 1958, U. Rome, 1967-68; dep. U.S. rep. UN Com. on Peaceful Uses of Outer Space, 1962-65; U.S. alt. del. 19th UN Gen. Assembly; sr. adviser U.S. del. to 20th and 21st UN Gen. Assemblies; U.S. alt. del. 55th UN Gen. Assembly; rapporteur UN Com. Experts on Econ. Restructuring, 1975; mem. Pres.'s Commn. on Internat. Trade and Investment Policy, 1970-71, U.S. Adv. Com. on Law of Sea, 1971-76; cons. to sec.-gen. UN Conf. on Human Environment, 1972, UN Conf. Environment and Devel., 1992; mem. pres.'s adv. com. Trade Policy and Negotiations, 1998—. Author: Sterling-Dollar Diplomacy, 1956, New Directions in U.S. Foreign Economic Policy, 1959, In Pursuit of World Order, 1964, Blueprint for Peace, 1966, (with Max F. Millikan) The Global Partnership: International Agencies and Economic Development, 1968; note editor: Yale Law Jour, 1950-51. Bd. dirs. Ditchley Found., Salzburg Seminar. Served with AUS, 1945-46. Recipient Detur prize for disting. scholarship Harvard U., 1948, Arthur S. Flemming award, 1963; Harvard Club scholar, 1944, Rhodes scholar, 1951-53. Mem. ABA, UN Assn. (dir.), Assn. Bar City N.Y., Council Fgn. Relations, Am. Acad. Arts and Scis., Am. Philosophical Soc., Phi Beta Kappa, Order of Coif, Century Assn, Met. Club. Clubs: Century Assn. (N.Y.C.); Met. (Washington). Office: Columbia U Sch Law 435 W 116th St New York NY 10027-7297

GARDNER, ROBERT, financial services executive; b. Dec. 19, 1949; s. Sam and Edythe (Berman) G.; m. Barbara Paccione, Apr. 21, 1975; children: Theodore Mathew, Jessica Andrea. BA in Philosophy, Hunter Coll., 1978. Account exec. Merrill Lynch & Co., N.Y.C., 1977-80; v.p. Lehman Bros., N.Y.C., 1980-89; v.p. investments Prudential Securities, N.Y.C., 1989-97, 1st v.p., retirement planning advisor, 1998—. Mem. Internat. Assn. Fin. Planning. Avocations: golf, reading. Office: Prudential Securities Inc PO Box 4355 Manhasset NY 11030-4355

GARDNER, ROBIN PIERCE, engineering educator; b. Charlotte, N.C., Aug. 17, 1934; s. Robin Brem and Margaret (Pierce) G.; m. Linda Jean Gardner, Oct. 21, 1976. B.Ch.E., N.C. State U., 1956, MS, 1958; PhD, Pa. State U., 1961. Scientist Oak Ridge Inst. Nuclear Studies, 1961-63; research engr., asst. dir. measurement and controls lab. Research Triangle Inst., Research Triangle Park, N.C., 1963-67; research prof. nuclear engring. and chem. engring., dir. Center Engring. Applications of Radioisotopes, N.C. State U., 1967—. Cons. Oak Ridge Inst. Nuclear Studies, Research Triangle Inst., Oak Ridge Nat. Lab., Internat. Atomic Energy Agy., NASA, AEC, TVA, Alcoa. Author: (with Ralph L. Ely, Jr.), Radioisotope Measurement Applications in Engineering, 1967; regional editor Applied Radiation and Isotopes, Jour. Fine Particle Soc.; contbr. articles to sci. jours. Served to 1st lt. AUS, 1956. Recipient Alcoa Found. Disting. Rsch. award N.C. State U. Sch. Engring., 1986, Alumni Disting. Grad. Professorship award, 1996, R.J. Reynolds award for excellence in tchg. and rsch., 1998; Centennial fellow Coll. Earth and Mineral Scis., Pa. State U., 1996. Fellow Am. Nuc. Soc. (Radiation Industry award isotopes and radiation divsn. 1984), Am. Nuc. Soc., Am. Soc. Engring. Edn. (Glenn Murphy award for Outstanding Nuc. Engring. 2003), Sigma Xi, Phi Kappa Phi, Phi Lambda Upsilon. Home: 3005 Randolph Dr Raleigh NC 27609 6941 Office: NC State U Ctr Engring Applications of Radioisotope Dept Nuclear Engring Raleigh NC 27695-0001 E-mail: gardner@ncsu.edu.

GARDNER, RULON E. Olympic athlete; b. Afton, Wyo., Aug. 16, 1971; s. Reed and Virginia Gardner. Grad., Ricks Coll., 1991; BS in Phys. Edn., U. Nebr., 1996. Began competing in wrestling, 1991; Nat. Jr. Coll. Athletic Assn. champion, 1991; Nat. Jr. Coll. Athletic Assn. 4th place, 1993; Nat. Champion, Greco-Roman, 1995, 1997; World Cup Champion, Greco-Roman; Sr. Greco-Roman champion, Belt Series winner, 1997, 1998, 2001; Greco-Roman World Championships 5th place, 1997; Vantaa Cup champion, Finland, 1998; Pan-Am. Champion, 1998; Winter Classic champion, 1999; Olympic champion, 2000; World Wrestling Championships Gold medallist, 2001. Named AP Male Athlete of Yr., 6th place, 2000, USA Wrestling Greco-Roman Wrestler of Yr., 2000, Flag Bearer, Closing Ceremonies, Olympics, Sydney, 2000, USA Wrestling Man of Yr., 2001, USOC Sportsman of Yr., 2001; named one of Top 100 Most Powerful in sports, Sporting News, 2000; named to Ricks Coll. Athletic Hall of Fame, 2001, Wyo. Sports Hall of Fame, Athlete of Yr., 2001; recipient Best Original Score award, USA Today's Sports, 2000, Arete award, U.S. Olympic Spirit award, 2001, ESPY award for Male U.S. Olympic Athlete of Yr., 2001, Jesse Owens award, 2001, USOC Citizenship through Sports Alliance award, 2001.*

GARDNER, RUSSELL MENESE, lawyer; b. High Point, N.C., July 14, 1920; s. Joseph Hayes and Clara Emma-Lee (Flynn) G.; m. Joyce Thresher, Mar. 7, 1946; children: Winthrop G., Page Stansbury, June Thresher. AB, Duke U., 1942, JD, 1948. Bar: Fla. 1948, U.S. Ct. Appeals (5th cir.) 1949, U.S. Tax Ct. 1949, U.S. Supreme Ct. 1985. Ptnr. McCune, Hiaasen, Crum, Gardner & Duke and predecessor firms, Ft. Lauderdale, Fla., 1948-90, Gunster, Yoakley, & Stewart, 1990—. Bd. govs. Shepard Broad Law Ctr. Nova S.E. U. Trustee Mus. of Art, Inc., Ft. Lauderdale, pres., 1964-67; bd. dirs. Stranahan House, Inc., 1981—, pres., 1983-85; bd. dirs. Ft. Lauderdale Hist. Soc., 1962—, pres. 1975-85, pres. emeritus, 1985—; mem. estate planning council Duke U. Sch. Law; bd. dirs., vice chmn. Broward Performing Arts Found., Inc., 1985—. Served to lt. USNR, 1943-49. Fellow Am. Coll. Trust and Estate Counsel; mem. ABA (real property, probate, trust sect.), Am. Judicature Soc., Fla. Bar Assn. (probate, guardianship rules com. 1978-2002, probate law com.), Broward County Bar Assn. (estate planning council), Coral Ridge Country Club, Lauderdale Yacht Club, Tower Club. Republican. Presbyterian. Office: PO Box 14636 Fort Lauderdale FL 33302-4636 E-mail: rgardner@gunster.com.

GARDNER, SANDI B. biology educator; b. Chicago Heights, Ill., June 24, 1959; d. Robert S. and Lenore M. (D'Arcy) Bushor; m. Daniel E. Gardner, Apr. 16, 1988 (div. 1997); 1 child, C(atherine) J. BS in Phys. Edn./Recreation, U. Ill., Chgo., 1981; MS in Environ. Biology, Govs. State U., University Park, Ill., 1988; postgrad., Ill. Inst. Tech., Chgo., 1993-95; PhD, Walden U., Mpls., 1997. Profl. scout Wau Bon Girl Scout Coun., Fond Du Lac, Wis., 1981-82; pre-sch. tchr. Anita M. Stone Ctr., Flossmoor, Ill., 1982-84, Alsip (Ill.) Pre-Sch., 1984-85; tchg. asst. Govs. State U., 1986-89; park ranger Ind. Dunes Nat. Lakeshore, Porter, 1986-92; prof. biology South Suburban Coll., South Holland, Ill., 1990-96. Adj. prof. Ind. U.-N.W., Gary, 1990—92, Govs. State U., 1989—93; mem. spl. populations adv. bd. South Suburban Mental Health, South Holland, 1992—94; staff develop./curriculum specialist Purdue U., 1995—96, adj. faculty, 1996; prof. biology Triton Coll., River Grove, Ill., 1996—, chair sci. dept., 2001—, adv. pre-profl. orgn., 2002; cons. Taylor U., Ft. Wayne, Ind., 1999—2001; workshop presenter, cons. in field. Author: Relationship Between Computer Anxiety and Computer Use, 1996, WebWeaver Environmental Science Online, 2001, Lab Manual Genetics, 2002; co-author: Case Studies for Anatomy and Physiology, 1992, Lab Manual for General Biology, 1994, 1999, 2001, Teachers/Student Guide to Virtual Biology Laboratory CD-ROM, 1997, WebWeaver Study Guide, 1998. Leader, vol., trainer Calumet coun. Girl Scouts U.S., Highland, Ind., 1981-84, 93—; vol. Lincoln Park Zoo, 1986-88, Brookfield Zoo, 1996-2000; coach AYSO Soccer, River Forest, Ill., bd. dirs. 1999; adv. Phi Theta Kappa Triton Coll, River Grove, Ill., 1996-2000; vol. mentor West Lake Hosp., 2002; vol. Amb. Walden U., 2002; co-chair accreditation com. NCA, 20003—. Recipient Spl. Achievement award Nat. Park Svc., 1988; Hand-On Sci. for Tchrs. award EPA, 1992; grantee R&D Triton, 1998—, On-line Biology, 1999, Plastination, 1999, HECA, 1999-2000, On-Line Tutoring Ctr., 2000-01. Mem. Nat. Sci. Tchrs. Assn., Nat. Assn. Biology Tchrs., Ill. Assn. C.C. Biology Tchrs. (pres. 1999-2001), Phi Delta Kappa (v.p. membership 1999—). Home: PO Box 5922 River Forest IL 60305 Office: Triton Coll 2000 N 5th Ave River Grove IL 60171-1907 E-mail: sbgardner@aol.com.

GARDNER, SANDRA LEE, nurse, outreach consultant; b. Louisville, Dec. 1, 1946; d. Jane Marie (Schwab) Gardner. Nursing diploma, Sts. Mary and Elizabeth Hosp., Louisville, 1967; BSN magna cum laude, Spalding Coll., 1973; MS, U. Colo., 1975, Pediatric Nurse Practitioner, 1978. RN. Premature coordinator Meth. Evang. Hosp., Louisville, 1967-71; charge nurse Children's Hosp., Louisville, 1971-73, staff/charge nurse Denver, 1973-74, perinatal outreach coord., 1974-76; asst. prof. U. Colo. Sch. Nursing, 1976-79; co-founder, vice chmn. bd. dirs. Denver Birth Ctr., 1977-79; dir., cons. Profl. Outreach Consultation, Aurora, Colo., 1980—. Founding mem. Colo. Perinatal Car Council, Denver, 1975—; founding dir. Neonatal Nursing Edn. Found., Aurora, 1982— Co-editor: Handbook of Neonatal Intensive Care, 1985, 1989, 1993, 1998, 2002 (Am. Jour. Nursing Book of Yr. award, 2002), Legal Aspects of Maternal-Child Nursing Practice, 1997. Foster parent educator Dept. Social Svcs., 1976-78; in pub. edn. KVOD Radio/Channel 2, Denver, 1978; nursing supr. 9 Health Fair, Denver, 1980. Recipient Gerald L. Hencemann award March of Dimes, Denver, 1978. Mem. ANA (Book of Yr. 1986, 89), Nat. Neonatal Nurses Assn. Democrat. Avocations: downhill skiing, hiking, biking, gardening, reading, travel. Home: 12095 E Kentucky Ave Aurora CO 80012-3233 E-mail: gardnerslconsult@aol.com.

GARDNER, SETH FREDERICK, music educator; b. Messhoppen, Pa., Dec. 18, 1953; m. Mary Joan Bowman, July 19, 1953. Bachelor Music, Ithaca Coll., Ithaca, NY, 1971—75. H.s. music tchr. Lackawanna Trail Junior-Senior H.S., Factoryville, Pa., 1976—77; bassist First Encounter, Honesdale, Pa., 1977—78; music tchr. Haverford Sch. Dist., Havertown, Pa., 1979—; bassist Easy St., Perkesie, Pa., 1981—, Tom Rudolph Orch., Wallingford, Pa., 2001—. Clinician Pa. Music Educators Assn., Harrisburg, Pa., 1998, Harrisburg, 2003, performance judge, 2000—, Music Showcase Festivals, Harrisburg, Pa., 2001—. Mem.: Am. Choral Directors Assn., Pa. Music Educators Assn., Music Educators Nat. Conf. Methodist. Achievements include Orchestra and choir performances State Music Educators Convention; Choir performances Music Educators Eastern Conference; Choir performance Music Educators National Conference. Avocations: antique automobiles, road bicycling. Office: Haverford Township Middle School 1701 E Darby Road Havertown PA 19083

GARDNER, SHERYL PAIGE, gynecologist; b. Bremerton, Wash., Jan. 24, 1945; d. Edwin Gerald and Dorothy Elizabeth (Herman) G.; m. James Alva Beat, June 20, 1986. BA in Biology, U. Oreg., 1967, MD cum laude, 1971. Diplomate Am. Bd. Ob-Gyn. Intern L.A. County Harbor Gen. Hosp., Torrance, Calif., 1971-72, resident in ob-gyn., 1972-75; physician Group Health Assn., Washington, 1975-87; pvt. practice Mililani, Hawaii, 1987—. Med. staff sec. Wahiawa (Hawaii) Gen. Hosp., 1994-95. Mem. Am. Coll. Ob-Gyn., Am. Soc. Colposcopy and Cervical Pathology, Hawaii Med. Assn., N.Am. Menopause Soc., Sigma Kappa, Alpha Omega Alpha. Democrat. Avocation: supporter numerous environ., peace and social concern groups. Office: 95-1249 Meheula Pkwy Ste B10A Mililani HI 96789-1763

GARDNER, STEPHEN DAVID, lawyer, law educator; b. Newark, Dec. 3, 1939; s. Henry and Florence (Temeles) G.; m. Mary Francis Voce, Sept. 19, 1973; children: Benjamin Voce-Gardner, Daniel Voce-Gardner. BA, U. Fla., 1961, LLB, 1964; LLM in Taxation, NYU, 1965. Bar: Fla. 1964, N.Y. 1967, U.S. Supreme Ct. 1980. Assoc. Maguire Voorhis & Wells, Orlando, Fla., 1965-66; assoc. prof. law NYU Sch. Law, N.Y.C., 1966-68, adj. prof. law, 1969—; assoc. Hughes Hubbard & Reed, N.Y.C., 1968-71; ptnr. Kronish Lieb Weiner & Hellman, N.Y.C., 1971—, mng. ptnr., 1980-99. Dir. Safra Nat. Bank, N.Y.C., 1987—, David Schwartz Found., N.Y.C., 1980—. Contbr. articles and revs. to profl. jours. Sgt., USAR, 1969-72. Mem. N.Y. State Bar Assn., Fla. Bar, Assn. Bar of City of New York, Tax Club of N.Y., Order of Coif. Jewish. Avocations: skiing, swimming, gardening. Office: Kronish Lieb Weiner & Hellman 1114 Ave of Americas New York NY 10036

GARDNER, STEVEN, health insurance specialist; b. Springfield, Mo., Nov. 8, 1950; s. Arthur Daniel and Elizabeth Irene Gardner; life ptnr. Kenny Kightlinger. Corp. tng. specialist BlueCross and BlueShield of Mo., Springfield, 1996—2002; instrnl. designer WellPoint Health Networks, Springfield, 2002—. Mem. Ozarks Literacy Coun., Springfield, 2000—01. Sgt. e-5 U.S. Army, 1970—76. Fellow, Acad. for Healthcare Mgmt., 2002. Democrat. Mem. Disciples Of Christ. Avocations: travel, wine, computers, reading. Office: WellPoint Health Networks 3534 East Sunshine Springfield MO 65804 E-mail: steve.gardner@wellpoint.com.

GARDNER, SUE SHAFFER, lawyer; b. Buffalo, Jan. 19, 1931; d. Harvey Jay Shaffer and Freda (Ballotin) Harris; m. Arnold B. Gardner, Aug. 24, 1952; children: Jonathan H., Diane R. BA, Smith Coll., Northampton, Mass., 1952; JD, SUNY, Buffalo, 1976. Bar: N.Y. 1977, U.S. Dist. Ct. (we. dist.) N.Y. 1977. Assoc. Kavinoky & Cook, Buffalo, 1976-81, ptnr., 1981—. Chmn. tax and legal com. Found. for Jewish Philanthropies, Buffalo, 1981-84; mem. dean's adv. com. SUNY Law Sch., Buffalo, 1995—. Bd. dirs. City of Buffalo Landmark and Preservation Bd., 1985—89, chair, 1986; bd. mgrs. Buffalo and Erie County Hist. Soc., 1988—2000; bd. dirs. SUNY-Buffalo Law Sch. Alumni Assn., 1984—86, ARC, Buffalo, 1978—94, chairperson, 1984, mem. eastern ops. adv. coun. Washington, 1985—86, chmn. ea. ops. adv. coun., 1985—86; bd. dirs. Cmty. Found. of Greater Buffalo, NY, 1999—, vice chair, 2003; bd. mem. Western N.Y. Women's Fund, 1999—, chair bd., 2003. Recipient Leadership award YWCA, Buffalo, 1987, ann. citation NCCJ, Buffalo, 1988, Disting. Alumni award SUNY-Buffalo, 1989, Outstanding Women award, 1992, Citizen of Yr. award YMCA, 1991, Red Jacket award Buffalo and Erie County Hist. Soc., 2001. Fellow Am. Coll. Estate and Trust Counsel; mem. N.Y. State Bar Assn., N.Y. State Women's Bar Assn., Estate Analysts Western N.Y., N.Y. State Interest in Lawyers Accounts Fund (bd. dirs. 1991—), Erie County Bar Assn. (chmn. surrogate's ct. com. 1987-89, bd. dirs. 1989-93), Am. Jewish Com. (nat. legal com. 1988-99). Home: 89 Middlesex Rd Buffalo NY 14216 3617 Office: Kavinoky & Cook 120 Delaware Ave Ste 600 Buffalo NY 14202-2793

GARDNER, THOMAS NEVILLE, communications educator; b. New Orleans, La, July 7, 1946; s. Edward Neville and Margaret Agnes (Guess) G.; m. Karen Levine, Mar. 12, 1994; m. Jennifer N. Johnston, Dec. 22, 1979 (div. Aug. 1990); children: Sarah Rose Johnston-Gardner, Koby Leor Gardner-Levine. BA in Sociology, U. Va., 1971; MA in Journalism, U. Ga., 1981; MPA, Harvard U., 1985. Chmn. So. Student Organizing Com, Nashville, 1967-69; rsch. dir. Va. Rsch. Inst., Charlottesville, Va., 1971-73; media specialist Atlanta Jr. Coll., Ga., 1975-77; teaching asst. journalism U. Ga., Athens, Ga., 1977-79; reporter, columnist Montgomery Advertiser, Ala., 1980-83; pub. rels. dir. Ala. State Employees Assn., Montgomery, Ala., 1983-84; dir. comm. Union Concerned Scientists, Cambridge, Mass., 1985-87; pub. affairs officer Harvard U. Div. Sch., Cambridge, Mass., 1987-88; sr. editor Harvard Inst. Internat. Devel., Cambridge, Mass., 1988-92; pres., comm./edit. cons. Thomas N. Gardner & Assoc., Cambridge and Amherst, Mass., 1992—. Tchg. asst. comm. dept. U. Mass., Amherst, 1993—96; mng. dir. Media Edn. Found., 1996—2001; asst. prof. comm. Westfield State Coll., 2001—. Author: Rah's Hidden Treasure, 1992, SSOC: A Brief History of the Southern Student Organizing Committee, 2002; contbr.: We Won't Go, 1967; mng. editor: Reforming Economic Systems in Developing Countries, 1991. Bd. dirs. Men's Resource Ctr. of We. Mass. Recipient 1st Prize Photography So. Regional Coun., Atlanta, 1978, Govt. Reporting award Ala. State Employees Assn., Montgomery, 1982. Mem. Soc. Profl. Journalists, Nat. Comm. Assn. Office: Westfield State Coll Dept Comm Westfield MA 01086-1630

GARDNER, TIMOTHY JOSEPH, surgeon, educator; b. Phila., Dec. 6, 1938; s. Joseph Thomas and Elva (Flynn) G.; m. Nina Hooton, July 4, 1964; children: Julie, Joseph, Emily, Nicholas. BA, Georgetown Coll., 1962; MD, Georgetown U., 1966. Intern Johns Hopkins Hosp., Balt., 1966-67, asst. resident in surgery, 1967-68, 71-74, rsch. fellow cardiac surg. lab., 1970-71, chief resident, 1974-75, chief resident in cardiac surgery, 1975-76, asst. prof., 1976-80, assoc. prof., 1980-86; prof. Johns Hopkins U. Sch. Medicine, 1986-93, Hosp. U. Pa., Phila., 1993—, chief divsn. cardiothoracic surgery, 1993—. Speaker in field; vis. prof. Royal Australasian Coll. Surgeons, Hobart, Tasmania, 1994, Royal Prince Alfred Hosp., Sydney, 1989, U. Kans. Sch. Medicine, 1984, Children's Hosp. Phila., 1981. Contbr. articles to profl. jours.; guest editl. reviewer: Jour. Thoracic and Cardiovascular Surgery, 1981-83, Circulation, 1983-91; book reviewer: Annals Thoracic Surgery, 1985-89. With U.S. Army, 1968-70. Fellow ACS, Am. Coll. Cardiology; mem. Am. Surg. Assn., Assn. for Acad. Surgery, Balt. City Med. Soc., Med. and Chirurgical Faculty Md., So. Thoracic Surg. Assn., Soc. Thoracic Surgeons, Soc. Univ. Surgeons, Am. Assn. for Thoracic Surgery, So. Surg. Assn., Am. Surg. Assn., Am. Heart Assn. (mem. coun. on cardiovasc. surgery). Home: PO Box 18 Chatham PA 19318-0018 Office: Hosp U Pa 3400 Spruce St Philadelphia PA 19104-4206

GARDNER, TRUDI YORK, lawyer, insurance company executive; b. Portland, Oreg., Mar. 19, 1947; d. Harry and Martha (Gevurtz) York; m. Alan Joel Gardner, Dec. 19, 1971; children: Jordan Casey, Andrew Ryan. BA, UCLA, 1969; MS, Portland State U., 1971; postgrad. N.Y. Law Sch., 1975-76; JD Lewis and Clark Law Sch., 1977. Bar: Washington 1978, U.S. Dist. Ct. (we. dist.) Wash. 1979; cert. tchr. Calif., Oreg. Law clk. U.S. Atty.'s Office (so. dist.) N.Y.C., 1976, to law firm, Portland, Oreg., 1977; fin. relations specialist Puget Sound Power & Light Co., Bellevue, Wash., 1978-79; asst. atty. gen. Dept. Labor and Industries, State of Wash., Seattle, 1979-80; sole practice, Bellevue, 1980-81; regional atty. for Mont., Idaho, Wash., Oreg, Utah and Wyo., Ins. Corp. of Am., Houston, 1981-84, regional v.p., 1984-87; sr. legis. counsel Indsl. Indemnity Corp., San Francisco, 1990—; curriculum cons. Portland (Oreg.) Pub. Schs., 1972. Assoc. editor: Multnomah Lawyer, Multnomah County Bar Assn., Portland, 1973. Contbr. articles, cover stories to Sunday supplement of The Oregonian, San Francisco Examiner and Chgo. Tribune, radio scripts for Am. Heritage Assn. to Sta. KWJJ; contbr. short stories to mags. Mem. King County United Way Conf. Panel for Developmentally Disabled, Seattle, 1978-79. Mem. Wash. State Bar Assn. (pub. relations com. 1978-81), Seattle-King County Bar Assn., Portland City Club, Seattle Mcpl. League, Pi Sigma Alpha, Pi Lambda Theta. Clubs: Women's Univ.; Bellevue Athletic. Home and Office: 215 Tiburon Ct Walnut Creek CA 94597-3437

GARDNER, WANDA JOYCE, harpist, business owner, home educator; b. Whittier, Calif., Sept. 18, 1950; d. Kenneth Moore and Audrey Louise (Dillinger) G.; m. Bruce Alan Myron, 1990; children: William Kenneth, Thomas Andrew. Student, Music Acad. of the West, 1967-68; BFA, UCLA, 1972. Harpist Am. Youth Symphony, UCLA Symphony, San Gabriel Symphony, Rio Hondo Symphony, COTA Symphony, Burbank Symphony, others, 1965-72; instr. harp, Los Angeles, 1967-72; solo harpist Clebanoff Strings U.S. tour, 1970, Dome of the Sea Restaurant, Las Vegas, 1978-79; freelance harpist, Portland, Oreg., 1979—; bookkeeper, 1979-90; home educator to sons, 1995—. Owner Wanda's Collectibles, 1999—. Mem. Am. Harp Soc., Am. Fedn. Musicians, Am. String Tchrs. Assn. E-mail: wjoycem@ipinc.net.

GARDNER, WILFORD ROBERT, physicist, educator; b. Logan, Utah, Oct. 19, 1925; s. Robert and Nellie (Barker) G.; m. Marjorie Louise Cole, June 9, 1949; children: Patricia, Robert, Caroline. BS, Utah State U., 1949; MS, Iowa State U., 1951, PhD, 1953; DSc (hon.), Ohio State U., 2002. Physicist U.S. Salinity Lab., Riverside, Calif., 1953-66; prof. U. Wis., Madison, 1966-80; physicist, prof., head dept. soil and water sci. U. Ariz., Tucson, 1980-87; dean coll. natural resources U. Calif., Berkeley, 1987-94; dean emeritus, 1994—; adj. prof. Utah State U., 1995—. Author: Soil Physics, 1972. Served with U.S. Army, 1943-46. Recipient Hon. Faculty award, U. Ghent, Belgium, 1972, Centennial Alumnus award, Utah State U., 1986; fellow, NSF sr. fellow, 1959, Fulbright fellow, 1971—72. Fellow: AAAS, Am. Soc. Agronomy; mem.: NAS, Soil Sci. Soc. Am. (pres. 1990, Rsch. award 1962), Internat. Union Soil Sci. (hon.), Internat. Soil Sci. Soc. (pres. physics commn. 1968—74).

GARDNER, WILLIAM LANSING, III, business educator; b. Woodbury, NJ, Oct. 3, 1956; s. Ralph Graves Gardner, Elizabeth Moore Gardner; m. Marilyn Melvin Melvin (div. May 31, 2000); children: William Lansing Gardner IV, Scott Reilly. Bachelors of Science, Susquehanna University, Selinsgrove, Pennsylvania, 1974—78; Masters of Business Administration, Florida State University, Tallahassee, FLorida, 1978—80; Doctor of Business Administration, Florda State University, Tallahassee, Florida, 1980—84. Assistant Professor of Management Southern Illinois University at Carbondale, Carbondale, IL, 1984—89; Hearin-Hess Assistant Professor of Management University of Mississippi, University, MS, 1989—91, Hearin-Hess Associate Professor of Management, 1991—98, Management Area Coordinator, 1998—2000, Interim Associate Dean for Faculty and Research, 2000—01, Michael S. Starnes Professor of Management, 1998—2002, School of Business Administration Graduate Coordinator, 2001—02. Editorial Review Board Academy of Management Journal, Briarcliff Manor, NY, 2000—02, Leadership Quarterly, 2000—02; Co-Organizer Leadership Quarterly/Ole Miss Bi-Annual Leadership Symposium, University, MS, 2000—02. Author: (Journal Article) Academy of Management Review, 1982, 1985, 1987, 1998, (Journal Author) Academy of Management Journal, 1988, Leadership Quarterly, 1999, (Journal Article), 2000 (Best Paper, 2000), Journal of Management, 1988, 1986, Organizational Dynamics, 1990, 1992, Journal of Management Studies, Journal of Social Psychology, 2000, Sex Roles, 1983. Mem.: Beta Gamma Sigma, Sigma Iota Epsilon, Southern Management Association (Track Chair, Organizational Behavior/Conflict Management/Org Cognition 1995—95), Southern Management Association (Board Member 1997—2000, Best Reviewer, Organizational Behavior/Organizational Theory/Organizational Development Track 2000), Academy of Management. Avocation: Music Collector, Audiophile, Sports Enthusiast, Travel. Office: University of Mississippi PO Box 1848 University MS 38677-1848 Office Fax: (662)915-7968. Business E-Mail: bgardner@bus.olemiss.edu.

GARDNER, WILLIAM MICHAEL, state official; b. Manchester, N.H., Oct. 26, 1948; s. William George and Mildred Irene (Claus) G.; m. Kathleen Gordon, May 21, 1978; children: William Gordon, Kathleen Meghan. BA, U. N.H., 1970; diploma, London Sch. Econs., 1972; ME, U. N.C., Greensboro, 1973; MPA, Harvard U., 1985. Mem. N.H. Ho. of Reps., Concord, 1973-76; sec. state State of N.H., Concord, 1976—. Chmn. N.H. Mcpl. Records Bd., 1978—; pres. Nat. Assn. Secs. State, 1998—99. Editor: Towns Against Tyranny: Hills Borough County New Hampshire During the American Revolution 1775-83, 1976, New Hampshire: The State That Made Us a Nation, 1989. Mem. exec. com. Hillsborough County, N.H., 1973-74; chmn. Manchester Del., 1974-75; trustee Belanger-Gardner Found., Bishop's U., Can., 1985—. Democrat. Roman Catholic. Office: Office Sec State 107 N Main St State Ho Rm 204 Concord NH 03301-3222

GARDNER, WOODFORD LLOYD, JR., lawyer; b. Pryor, Okla., Feb. 4, 1945; s. Woodford Lloyd Sr. and Capitola Overstreet (Arterburn) G.; m. Sandra Kaye Bishop, Aug. 7, 1966; children: Allison Wood, John Bishop. BS, Western Ky. U., 1967; JD, U. Ky., 1969. Bar: Ky. 1969, U.S. Dist. Ct. (ea. dist.) Ky. 1969, U.S. Dist. Ct. (we. dist.) Ky. 1979. Law clk. to presiding justice U.S. Dist. Ct. (ea. dist.) Ky., Lexington, 1969; ptnr. Redford, Redford & Gardner, Glasgow, Ky., 1971-91, Richardson, Gardner, Barrickman & Alexander, Glasgow, Ky., 1992—; commr. Glasgow Water Co., 2000—. Bd. dirs. South Ctrl. Bank of Barren County, Inc., Nat. Park Concessions, Inc., Mammoth Cave, Ky., chmn. bd, pres., 2001; judge, exec. Barren County, Glasgow, 1982-94; atty. Commonwealth of Ky., 1975-76. Mng. editor Ky. Law Jour., 1968-69; co-editor: Barren County Heritage; contbr. articles to profl. jours. With U.S. Army, 1969-71. Recipient Ernie award Glasgow-Barren County C. of C., 1988. Mem. Ky. Bar Assn. (ho. of dels. 1978-85), Barren County Bar Assn. (pres. 1978-79). Office: Richardson Gardner Barrickman & Alexander 117 E Washington St Ste 1 Glasgow KY 42141-2696

GARDOCKI, CHRISTOPHER, professional football player; b. Stone Mountain, Ga., Feb. 7, 1970; m. Sally Gardocki; 1 child, Christopher. Student, Clemson U. Punter Chgo. Bears, 1991-94, Indpls. Colts, 1995-98, Cleve. Browns, 1999—. Co-creator game NFL Trivia Blitz. Named to Pro Bowl, 1996. Office: Cleve Browns 1085 W 3rd St Cleveland OH 44114-1001 also: Cleveland Browns 76 Lou Groxa Blvd Berea OH 44017

GARDOM, GARDE BASIL, lieutenant governor of British Columbia; b. Banff, Alta., Can., July 17, 1924; s. Basil and Gabrielle Gwladys (Bell) G.; m. Theresa Helen Eileen Mackenzie, Feb. 11, 1956; children: Kim Gardom Allen, Karen Gardom MacDonald, Edward, Brione Gardom MacDonald, Brita Gardom McLaughlin. BA, LLB, U. B.C., Vancouver, 1949. Bar: called to bar 1949. With Campbell, Brazier & Co., 1949; sr. partner Gardom & Co., Vancouver, 1960-75; apptd. Queen's Counsel, 1975; mem. B.C. Legis. Assembly for Vancouver-Point Grey, B.C., 1966-87; atty. gen. B.C., 1975-79; min. intergovtl. rels., 1979-86; policy cons. Office of Premier, 1986-87; agt. gen. for B.C. London, 1987-92; mem. Premier's Econ. Adv. Coun., 1988-91; apptd. lt.-gov. B.C., 1995—. Dir. Crown Life Ins. Co., 1993-95. Named to B.C. Sports Hall of Fame, 1995; named Freeman of City of London, 1992; hon. col. British Columbia Regiment. Mem. Can. Bar Assn., B.C. Law Soc., Vancouver Lawn Tennis and Badminton Club, Union Club of B.C., Royal Overseas Club, Phi Delta Theta. Anglican. Office: Govt House 1401 Rockland Ave Victoria BC Canada V8S 1V9

GARDUNIO, JOSEPH, landscaping company executive; b. Chgo., Feb. 12, 1955; m. Marta Salas; children: Joey, Ricky, Alex, Selena. Pres. Unico Landscaping Inc., 1991—. Office: Unico Landscaping Inc 5119 S Hoyne Ave Chicago IL 60609-5513

GARELICK, MARTIN, retired transportation executive; b. Rochester, N.Y., May 18, 1924; s. Samuel and Esther (Gerber) G.; m. Betty J. Mann, Jan. 18, 1951. BSC.E., Purdue U., 1947. With Milw. Rd. R.R., 1947-78, asst. v.p. mktg. devel. and planning, 1973-76, v.p. ops., 1976-78; exec. v.p., chief operating officer AMTRAK, Washington, 1978-80; v.p. Wyer, Dick & Co., Chgo., 1980-82; v.p., gen. mgr. N.J. Transit Rail Ops., Newark, 1982-84; dir. Kyle Rys., Inc., Scottsdale, Ariz., 1979-97; ret., 1997. Served with U.S. Army, 1943-46. Mem. Am. Soc. Traffic and Logistics, Am. Assn. R.R. Supts., Tau Epsilon Phi. Jewish. Home: 20876 Del Luna Dr Boca Raton FL 33433-1788 E-mail: garelick@worldnet.att.net.

GAREY, DONALD LEE, pipeline and oil company executive; b. Ft. Worth, Sept. 9, 1931; s. Leo James and Jessie (McNatt) G.; m. Elizabeth Patricia Martin, Aug. 1, 1953; children: Deborah Anne, Elizabeth Laird. BS in Geol. Engring., Tex. A&M U., 1953. Registered profl. engr., Tex. Reservoir geologist Gulf Oil Corp., 1953-54, sr. geologist, 1956-65; v.p., mng. dir. Indsl. Devel. Corp. Lea County, Hobbs, N.Mex., 1965-72, dir., 1972-86, pres., 1978-86; v.p., dir. Minerals, Inc., Hobbs, N.Mex., 1966-72, pres., dir., 1972-86, CEO, 1978-82; mng. dir. Hobbs Indsl. Found. Corp., 1965-72, dir., 1965-76; v.p. Llano, Inc., 1972-74, exec. v.p., COO, 1974-75, pres., 1975-86, CEO, also dir., 1978-82; pres., CEO Pollution Control, Inc., 1969-81. Pres. NMESCO Fuels, Inc., 1982-86; chmn., pres., CEO Estacado, Inc., 1986—, Natgas Inc., 1987—; pres. Llano Co2, Inc., 1984-86; cons. geologist, geol. engr., Hobbs, 1965-72. Chmn. Hobbs Manpower Devel. Tng. Adv. Com., 1965-72; mem. Hobbs Adv. Com. for Mental Health, 1965-67; chmn. N.Mex. Mapping Adv. Com., 1968-69; mem. Hobbs adv. bd. Salvation Army, 1967-78, chmn., 1970-72; mem. exec. bd. Conquistador coun. Boy Scouts Am., Hobbs, 1965-75; vice chmn. N.Mex. Gov's Com. for Econ. Devel., 1968-70; bd. regents Coll. Southwest, 1982-85. Capt. USAF, 1954-56. Mem. AIPG, AAPG, SPE of AIME. Home: 315 E Alto Dr Hobbs NM 88240-3905 Office: Broadmoor Tower PO Box 5587 Hobbs NM 88241-5587

GAREY, FRANCIS BENJAMIN, retired merchant banker; b. Richmond, Va., Aug. 29, 1934; s. Francis Milton and Artrice Dungan Garey; m. Jo Ann McLelland, Dec. 28, 1957 (div. July 21, 1986); children: Francis Benjamin Garey, Jr., Susan Morrison Greenburg. Diploma, U. Okla., 1971; BA, U. Richmond, 1959; MS in Banking, Rutgers U., 1978. Cert. fin. analyst Dun & Bradstreet, 1967. Intelligence officer, analyst CIA, Langley, Va., 1959—65; asst. v.p., mgr. credit dept. Bank Va., Richmond, Va., 1969—74, v.p. Roanoke, 1976—78, Crestar Bank, Richmond, Va., 1974—76; sr. v.p. Sovran Bank, Richmond, Va., 1978—85; rep. leasing and fin. svcs. United Leasing, Fin. Group Va., 1985—91; sr. officer Southside Bank, Urbanna, Va., 1991—95; owner Finishing Touches. Author: (novels) Assassination by Decree, 2001. Team capt. United Way Greater Richmond, 1981—82; budget rev. com. City of Richmond, 1977. With U.S. Army, 1954—57. Mem.: Middlesex County C. of C. (dir. 1992—95, treas. 1992—95), Pi Sigma Alpha, Phi Delta Theta. Episcopalian. Avocations: writing, reading, gardening, fine cuisine. Home: Mill Forest - PO Box 112 Urbanna VA 23175 Personal E-mail: forest@crosslink.net.

GAREY, MARK EDWARD, secondary school educator, band director; b. Savannah, Tenn., Apr. 6, 1962; s. James M. and Flora B. Garey; m. Daphne Luttrell, June 21, 1986; 1 child, McKenzie Leigh. BMus Edn., Middle Tenn. State U, 1984; EdM in Adminstrn. and Supervision, Middle Tenn. State I, 1991. Band dir. Freedom Mid. Sch., Franklin, Tenn., 1984—; asst. band dir. Centennial H.S., Franklin, Tenn., 1996—. Mem.: Tenn. Music Educators Assn. (registration chmn. 1997—), MTSBOA (pres. elect 2003—05, exec. bd. 2003—09, pres. 2005—07, past pres. 2007—09), Mid. Tenn. Sch. Band and Orch. Assn. (exec. bd. 1994—96, 2003—, pres.-elect 2003—), Music Educators Nat. Conf., Tenn. Bandmasters Assn., Phi Beta Mu. Republican. Meth. Avocations: spectator sports, gardening, numismatics, philately. Office: Freedom Mid Sch Band 750 Hwy 96 W Franklin TN 37064

GAREY, PATRICIA MARTIN, artist; b. State College, Miss., Nov. 11, 1932; d. Verey G. Martin and Eva Myrtle Jones; m. Donald L. Garey, Aug. 1, 1953; children: Deborah Anne Garey Furst, Elizabeth Laird Garey Jones. BS in Costume Design, Tex. Women's U., 1953; MFA, Tex. Tech. U., 1973; postgrad. in art history, Two-Dimensional Studio Art, 1970-73. Prodn. mgr. Con Advt. Agy., Roswell, N.Mex., 1958-63; art instr. Coll. of Southwest, Hobbs, N.Mex., 1967-69, 72-73, prof. art history, art appreciation, 1974-76; studio artist Hobbs, 1976—; prof. art/painting and drawing N.Mex. Jr. Coll., 1997-98. Instr. Cloudcroft Artists Sch., N.Mex., 1991; prof. drawing, painting N.Mex. Jr. Coll.; prof. art hist. Coll. of Southwest, 1999—2001; rep., drawing instr. Villa Maria Ctr. for the Arts, Perugia, Italy, 1996; apptd. N.Mex. Arts Commn., 1999; artist-in-residence N.Mex. Art Commn., Santa Fe, 1975—76. Artist (one-woman shows) Sand Hills Mus., Kermit, Tex., 1968, N.Mex. Jr. Coll., Hobbs, 1969, 1985, Coll. of SW, 1974, 1979, Sangre de Cristo Arts Ctr., Puebl, 1979, U. Tex. of Permian Basin, Odessa, 1980, N.Mex. Jr. Coll., (represented by) Beverly Gordon Gallery, Dallas, Sylvia Ullman Am. Crafts, Cleve., Design Today, Lubbock, Tex., El-Dor Galleries Old-Town, Albuquerque, Front Room Gallery, Dallas, Tex. Art Gallery, Galeria de la Paloma, Santa Fe, (exhibitions) Roswell Mus. Art, Four Women Artists of Hobbs, N.Mex., 1966, Lubbock Mcpl. Garden and Arts Ctr., 1966, Laguna Gloria Art Mus., 1968—, Southeastern N.Mex. Small Painting Exhibit, 1975 (2d pl., 1966, 2d pl. Graphics, 2d pl. Sculpture, 2d pl. Acrylics, 1st pl. Ceramics, 1st pl. Drawing, 2d pl. Painting), Americas Gallery, Taos, 1974, Blair Gallery, Santa Fe, 1976, Mus. Fine Arts, 1976, Tex. Tech. U. Grad. Show, 1977, Little Rock Art Ctr., Ark., 1978, Hills Gallery, Santa Fe, 1979, Llano Estacado Art Assn., Dallas Mus. Fine Art, 1986, 1987, 1988, 1990, Beaux Arts Ball Art Auction, 1990, Okla. City Mus. Art nat. drawing competition, Little Rock Art Ctr., El Paso Sun Carnival, Tex., Govs. Gallery, State Capitol, Santa Fe, 1997, L.E.A.A., Hobbs, N.Mex., 1999 (Best of Show, 1st pl. watercolor), (permanent collections) Home Scis. Dept., Tex. Tech. U., The Round House/State Capitol, Santa Fe, Villa Maria Ctr. for the Arts, Raimondi Collection, Perugia, Italy, docent Meadows Mus. of Art So. Meth. U., Dallas, 1990, Govs. Invitiational, Govs. Gallery, 1996, 35 Clay Workers of N.Mex., artist (exhibitions) Southeastern N.Mex. Small Painting Exhibit, 1976, 1987, 1988, 1990, (permanent collections) State Capitol, Santa Fe, N.Mex. Jr. Coll. Arts commr. State of N.Mex., 1999—2002, N.Mex. Arts Commn., 1999—2003; artistic bd. S.W. Symphony, Hobbs, 1987—99; Bd. dirs. The Bridge Breast Ctr., Dallas, 1992—93, Llano Estacado Art Assn. Recipient Best of Show award for mixed media Llano Estacado Art Assn. Regional Show, Hobbs, N.Mex., 1996, Best of Show award for ceramics, 1999, 1st pl. award for watercolor, 1999. Mem. Delta Phi Delta, Chi Omega. Democrat. Methodist. Avocations: swimming (mem. Sr. Olympics N.Mex. Nat. Swim Team 1997), southern cooking, piano, classical music, book collecting. Studio: 315 E Alto Dr Hobbs NM 88240-3905 also: Piney Woods Cloudcroft NM 88350

GARFIAS, LUIS FRANCISCO, chemical engineering researcher; b. Macuspana, Tabasco, Mex., Mar. 20, 1968; s. Francisco and Carmen (Mesias) G., children: Louise and Francisco Degree in Chem. Engring., Autonomus U. Yucatan Merida, Merida, Mex., 1991; M in Corrosion Sci. and Engring., U. Manchester Inst. Sci. Tech., Eng., 1993; DPhil in Materials Sci., Oxford (Eng.) U., 1996. Registered profl. engr., Merida. Engr. asst. Engr. devel. corp., Coatzacoalcos Ver, Mex., 1985; rsch. asst. Cinvestav-Ipn U. Merida, 1989-92; postdoctoral rschr. in chem. engring. U. Minn., Mpls., 1996-98; rschr. Bell Labs. Lucent Tech., Murray Hill, NJ, 1998—. Tchr. physics Peninsular Coll., Merida, 1989—. Editor Turbine mag., 1987-88; contbr. articles to profl. jour.; inventor in field. Mem. Chem. Engr. Inst., Nat. Assoc. of Corrosion Engr., Electrochemical Soc. and Am. Chem. Soc., Mexican Physics Soc., Mex. Inst. Chem. Engr. (pres. student sect. 1989-90). Roman Catholic. Avocations: basketball, football, soccer, tennis. Office: Lucent Techs Bell Labs Reliability Dept Rm 1T-206 600 Mountain Ave Murray Hill NJ 07974

GARFIELD, ERNEST, bank consultant; b. Colorado River, Ariz., July 14, 1932; s. Emil and Carmen (Ybarra) G.; m. Betty Ann Redden, Apr. 18, 1953; children: Laural, Jeffery Alan. BS, U. Ariz., 1975; B of Internat. Mgmt., Am. Grad. Sch., Phoenix, 1975, M of Internat. Mgmt., 1976. Owner Garfield Ins. Agy., Tucson, 1962-70; senator State of Ariz., Phoenix, 1967-68, dep. treas., 1970-71, treas., 1971-74; commr. Ariz. Corp. Commn., Phoenix, 1974-79; chmn. United Bancorp Systems, Inc., Phoenix, 1979—, Interstate Bank Developers, Inc., Scottsdale, 1994—. Chmn. The White House Conf. on Energy, Com. on Energy Policy of Nat. Assn. Regulatory Utility Commn.; pres. Western Conf. Pub. Svc. Commns.; mem. Ad Hoc Com. on Regulatory Reform, Electric and Nuclear Energy Com. Mem. Ariz. Kidney Found., Multiple Sclerosis Soc., Rep. Senatorial Inner Circle, 1989; mem. Pres. Bush Task Force, 1989; mem. adv. bd. St. Joseph's Hosp., Phoenix; mem. establishment com. Pima County Jr. Coll., Tucson; mem. orgn. com. Pima County Halfway House, Tucson; chmn. Ariz. Gov. Commn. on Rape Prevention, 1988, Nat. Commn. on Rape Prevention, 1990—; commr. Ariz. Gov. Commn. on Violence Against Women, 1993-2003; active Ariz. Gov.'s Sexual Assault Task Force; dir. Ariz. Sexual Assault Network; bd. dirs. Ariz. Cactus-Pine coun. Girl Scouts U.S.; mem. Men Against Violence Network. With U.S. Army, 1952-55. Recipient Outstanding Young Men Ariz. award, Press Club award; named to U.S. Arty. Hall of Fame, 1999. Mem.: Thunderbird Internat. Banking Inst. (mem. adv. coun. 1990—), Ariz.-Mex. C. of C. Republican. Roman Catholic. Avocation: graphology. Home and Office: 8442 N 72nd Pl Scottsdale AZ 85258-2762 E-mail: egarfield@qwest.net.

GARFIELD, EUGENE, information scientist, author, publisher; b. N.Y.C., Sept. 16, 1925; s. Ernest and Edith (Wolf) Garofano; m. Faye Byron, 1945 (div.); 1 child, Stefan; m. Winifred Koziolek, 1955 (div.); children: Laura, Joshua, Thea; m. Catheryne Stout, 1983; 1 child, Alexander Merton. BS, Columbia U., 1949, MS, 1954; PhD, U. Pa., 1961, Vrije U., Brussels, 1988; DHL (hon.), SUNY, Albany, 1990; DL (hon.), Thomas Jefferson U., 1991; MD (hon.), Universita Di Roma Tor Vergata, 1994, Charles U., Prague, 1995. Rsch. chemist Evans R&D Corp., 1949-50; chemist Columbia U., 1950-51; mem. staff machine index project Johns Hopkins U., 1951-53; pres. Eugene Garfield Assocs., Phila., 1954-60; chmn., founder Inst. Sci. Info., Phila., 1960-93, chmn. emeritus, 1994—; pub., owner The Scientist, 1986—. Adj. prof. info. sci. U. Pa., 1974—, mem. libr. bd. overseers; coun. mem. Rockefeller U., 1978—. Creator sci. info. svc. Current Contents, 1956; bi-weekly columnist Current Comments in Current Contents, 1956—, Commentary in The Scientist, 1986—; author: Essays of an Information Scientist, 15 vols., 1962-93 (Book of Yr. Am. Soc. Info. Sci. 1977), Citation Indexing: Its Theory and Application in Science, Technology and Humanities, 1979, Transliterated Dictionary of the Russian Language, 1979; cons. editor Scientometrics; mem. editorial bd. Jour. Info. Sci.; bd. dirs. Ann Revs. Inc.; developer Sci. Citation Index, 1961—, Index Chemicus, 1960—; contbr. articles to profl. jours. With AUS, 1943-45. Recipient John Price Wetherill medal Franklin Inst., 1984, Derek de Solla Price Meml. medal, 1984, John Scott award City of Phila., 1986; first Grolier Soc. fellow, 1953-54. Fellow AAAS (chmn. sect. T), Inst. Info. Scientists London (hon.); mem. Info. Industry Assn. (past chmn. bd., past pres., Hall of Fame award), Nat. Assn. Sci. Writers, Chem. Notation Assn. (award 1980), Soc. Scholarly Pub., Spl. Libraries Assn., Authors League Am., Med. Library Assn., Am. Soc. Info. Sci. (award of merit 1975, past pres. Delaware Valley chpt.), Am. Chem. Soc. (Skolnick award div. chem. info. 1977, Patterson-Crane award 1983), Drug Info. Assn., Fedn. Am. Scientists. Achievements include patents in field. Address: The Scientist 3600 Market St Ste 450 Philadelphia PA 19104-2648 Office: Inst Sci Info 3501 Market St Philadelphia PA 19104-3302

GARFIELD, JOAN BARBARA, statistics educator; b. Milw., May 4, 1950; d. Sol L. and Amy L. (Nusbaum) Garfield; m. Michael G. Luxenberg, Aug. 17, 1980; children: Harlan Ross and Rebecca Ellen (twins). Student, U. Chgo., 1968; BS, U. Wis., 1972; MA, U. Minn., 1978, PhD, 1981. Prof. ednl. psychology Coll. Edn., U. Minn., Mpls., 1995—, Disting. tchg. prof. stats., 1995—. Mem. Nat. Rsch. Coun.'s Applied and Theoretical Stats., 1996-99. Co-editor books on assessment and tech. in stats. edn. Fellow Am. Statis. Assn. (newsletter co-editor 1994-2000, chair sect. on statis. edn. 2003-04); mem. Am. Ednl. Rsch. Assn., Nat. Coun. Tchrs. Math., Internat. Assn. for Statis. Edn. (v.p. 1997—), Internat. Statis. Inst. Jewish. Office: U Minn Dept Edn Psychology 315 Burton Hall Minneapolis MN 55455

GARFIELD, LEONARD, museum director; Archtl. hist. State of Wash., preservation programs coord.; with King County Office Cultural Resources; exec. dir. Mus. History and Industry, Seattle, 1998—. Office: MOHAI 2700 24th Ave E Seattle WA 98112-2031

GARFIELD, LESLIE JEROME, real estate executive; b. N.Y.C., Mar. 23, 1932; s. Jack and Anne (Weinert) G.; m. Johanna Rosengarten, Sept. 28, 1960; children: Clare Louisa, Jed Herbert, Cory Alexander. BA, U. Wis., Madison, 1953; MA, Harvard U., 1956; MBA, Columbia U., 1958. V.p. Pease & Elliman, Inc., N.Y.C., 1965—68, William A. White & Sons, Inc., N.Y.C., 1968—78; pres. Leslie J. Garfield & Co., Inc., N.Y.C., 1978—. Co-chmn. Internat. Print Ctr. Chmn. bd. dirs. N.Y. Youth Symphony, 1986—, pres. bd. dirs., 1975-86, bd. dirs. Carnegie Hill Neighbors, N.Y.C., 1985—; coun. Elvehjem Mus. Art Com. prints and illustrated books Mus. Modern Art; bd. overseers Mus. Fine Arts, Boston. Mem. Real Estate Bd. N.Y. (chmn. sales brokers com. 1985-86), Century Assn., Nat. Arts Club, Grolier Club. Avocation: collecting 20th century works on paper. Office: 654 Madison Ave New York NY 10021-8404

GARFIELD, ROBERT EDWARD, journalist; b. Phila., Pa., June 20, 1955; s. Samuel M. Garfield and Nancy G. Rowen; m. Carla Patricia Cain, Dec. 16, 1977; children: Kathryn Sarah, Allison Patricia, Ida Rose; m. Milena Trobozic, Mar. 11, 2001. BA, Pa. State U., 1977. Reporter Reading Times, Pa., 1977-81, Wilmington News-Jour., Del., 1981-82; columnist USA Today, Washington, 1982-85, Crain News Svc. and Advt. Age, Washington, 1985—; corr. Nat. Pub. Radio, 1986—. Analyst ABC News, 1999—; co-host On the Media, Nat. Pub. Radio, 1999—. Host Ad Age Reports program Fin. News Network, 1989-91; polit. advt. analyst CBS This Morning, 1992; contbg. writer Washington Post Mag., 1985-97; corr. Here and Now, Sta. WETA-TV, 1995; contbg. editor Civilization Mag., 1996-98; contbg. columnist U.S.A. Today, 1995-98; corr. CNBC "Power Lunch", 1996-99, Adam Smith's Money Game, 1998; author: Waking Up Screaming from the American Dream, 1997, And Now a Few Words from Me, 2003. Recipient Keystone award Pa. Newspaper Pubs. Assn., 1981, Best of Gannett award Gannett Co. Inc., 1982, journalism award Saatchi & Saatchi/Compton Advt., 1984, 85, award Am. Soc. Bus. Press Editors, 1994, Neal award Am. Bus. Press, 1996, Internat. Radio award NY Festivals, 2003, RTNDA Edward R. Murrow award, 2003, Arthur Rowse award Nat. Press Club, 2003. Mem. Nat. Press Club. Jewish.

GARFIELD, SOL LOUIS, retired psychologist; b. Chgo., Jan. 8, 1918; s. Julius and Rebecca (Friedman) G.; m. Amy Louise Nusbaum, Dec. 25, 1945; children: Ann, Joan, Stanley, David. BS, Northwestern U., 1938, MA, 1939, PhD, 1942. Diplomate Am. Bd. Profl. Psychology. Chief clin. psychology VA Hosp., Mendota, Wis., 1946-47; assoc. prof. psychology U. Conn., Storrs, 1947-49; chief clin. psychology VA Mental Hygiene Clinic, Milw., 1949-51; chief clin. psychology tng. VA Hosp., Downey, Ill., 1951-57; prof. med. psychology dept. psychiatry U. Nebr., Omaha, 1957-63; prof. psychology, dir. clin. psychology Columbia U., N.Y.C., 1964-70, Washington U., St. Louis, 1970-86, prof. emeritus, 1986—2002; ret., 2002. Cons. in field.; mem. com. clin. drug evaluation NIH, Washington, 1960-63; mem. adv. com. rsch. on depression NIMH, Washington, 1978-88. Author: Clinical Psychology, 1957, 3d edit., 1983, Psychotherapy—An Eclectic Approach, 1980, 2d edit., 1995; co-editor: Handbook of Psychotherapy and Behavior Change, 1971, 4th edit., 1994; editor Jour. Cons. and Clin. Psychology, 1979-84. 2d lt. U.S. Arny, 1942-46. Fellow APA (coun. reps. 1955-58, 60-63, 65-67, 75-78, Disting. Prof. Contbn. to Knowledge award 1979, pres. divsn. clin. psychology 1964-65), AAAS, Soc. Psychotherapy Rsch. (pres. 1976-78, Disting. Rsch. award 1989). Avocations: tennis, reading. Home: 1890 E 107th St Apt 808 Cleveland OH 44106

GARFIELD-WOODBRIDGE, NANCY, writer; b. N.Y.C. d. Solomon and Betty Silbowitz; m. George Charles Woodbridge, Apr. 20, 1980; children from previous marriage: Maurice Garfield, Joshua Garfield. BA in Lit., Bennington Coll., 1955; MS in Edn., Hofstra U., 1972, postgrad., 1973. Cert. tchr. K-8, English 7-9 N.Y. Editl. asst. Wenner Gren Found. Anthropol. Rsch., N.Y.C., 1952—55; picture editor Forbes Mag., N.Y.C., 1955—56; editor-in-chief The Gifted Child Mag., N.Y.C., 1957—58; v.p. Info. Retrieval Systems, Great Neck, NY, 1958—72; rsch. assoc. to v.p. and editor N.Y. Inst. Tech., Westbury, 1972—73; dir. spl. projects Girl Scouts of USA, N.Y.C., 1973—2000; children's author, 2000—. Spkr. v.p.'s task force on youth employment, Little Rock, 1979, gov.'s conf. on juvenile justice, Baton Rouge; presenter Edn. Commn. for the States, Denver, 1979. Author: The Tuesday Elephant, 1968, The Dancing Monkey, 1970, Juvenile Justice, 1981; contbr. articles to profl. jours. and mags. Vol. Kennedy Kenya Airlift Program, N.Y.C., 1962, Biafran Refugee Campaign, N.Y.-London, 1967; fundraiser Sara's Ctr. Very Spl. Arts Festival, L.I. to Washington. Scholar Breadloaf Writers Conf., Vt., 1967. Mem.: Acad. Am. Poets, The Author's Guild, Milford Fine Arts Coun., Soc. Children's Book Writers and Illustrators. Avocations: travel, reading, opera, painting, photography.

GARFIN, LOUIS, retired actuary; b. Mason City, Iowa, June 7, 1917; s. Sam and Etta (Larner) G.; m. Clarice Fagen, Apr. 11, 1943; children: Eugene Arthur, Erica. Student, Mason City Jr. Coll., 1934-36; BA, State U. Iowa, 1938, MS, 1939, PhD, 1942. Instr. USAAF, Scott Field, Ill., 1942-43; instr. math. Ill. Inst. Tech., Chgo., 1943, U. Minn., 1943-44; actuary Oreg. Ins. Dept., Salem, 1946-52; assoc. actuary Pacific Mut. Life Ins. Co., Los Angeles, 1952-62, actuary, 1962-64, v.p., chief actuary, 1964-82, cons. actuary, 1982-90; ret., 1990. Bd. dirs. Calif. Health Decisions, 1989-95, chairperson, 1993-94, Laguna Beach Cmty. Clinic, 1989-93; treas. Laguna Canyon Found., 1990-99, Mykonos Village, 1999—. Fellow Soc. Actuaries; mem. Am. Acad. Actuaries (v.p. 1976-78), Internat. Congress Actuaries (dir. 1977-80), Actuarial Club Pacific States (pres. 1967-68), Los Angeles Actuarial Club (pres. 1959-60), Am. Math. Soc., Phi Beta Kappa, Sigma Xi. Home: 4013 Arcadia Way Oceanside CA 92056-5139 E-mail: lgarfin@aol.com.

GARFIN, STEVEN R. orthopedic surgeon; b. Mpls., June 12, 1946; s. Rudolph and Beatrice G.; m. Susan L. Kaner, June 22, 1969; children: Jessica M., Cory E. BA in Math. cum laude, U. Minn., 1968, MD, 1972. Diplomate Am. Bd. Orthop. Surgery. Intern U. Calif., San Diego, 1972-73, resident in orthop. surgery, 1975-79; fellow disorders of the spine Pa. Hosp., Phila., 1980-81; from asst. prof. to assoc. prof. U. Calif., San Diego, 1980-89, prof. orthop., 1989—, chair, 1997—. Patient care com. U. Calif., San Diego, clin. adv. com., coun. of chairs, 1996—, oversight com., chmn. patient care com., 1996-97, VA deans

com., clin. svc. chief, strategic planning task force, thornton adv. group, 1997. Lt. comdr. USPHS, 1973-75. Rsch. grantee Orthop. Rsch. and Edn. Found., 1984, 88, 97, VA, 1989-90, N.Am. Spine Soc., 1994-95, Instl. grant Bristol-Meyers Squibb/Zimmer, 1997. Fellow: Am. Acad. Orthop. Surgeons; mem.: AC Orthop. Soc., AC Orthop. Assn., Cervical Spine Rsch. Soc. (Outstanding Cervical Spine Rsch. award 1989, 1992, pres. 1996), Western Orthop. Assn., Spine Study Group, Orthop. Rsch. Soc. (Young Investigator Recognition award 1993), N.Am. Spine Soc. (exec. com. 1985, ad hoc com. on nomneclature and coding 1986—90, chmn. diagnostic and therpeutic com. 1992, pres. 1997, sec. 1993—94, AcroMed Rsch. award 1988– 89, Wiltse award 2000, Outstanding Poster award 2000), Internat. Soc. Study Lumbar Spine (Volvo award 1996, 1983), Rsch. Soc., Little Orthop. Club, Wilson-Bost Interurban Orthop. Club, Alpha Omega Alpha. Jewish. Office: Univ Calif 200 W Arbor Dr MC8894 San Diego CA 92103 E-mail: sgarfin@ucsd.edu.

GARFINKEL, BARRY HERBERT, lawyer; b. Bklyn., June 19, 1928; s. Abraham and Shirley (Siegel) G.; m. Gloria Lorenz, Feb. 16, 1969; children—David, James, Paul. BSS, CCNY, 1950; LLB, Yale U., 1955. Bar: N.Y. State 1955, U.S. Supreme Ct. 1959. Law clk. to Hon. Edward Weinfeld U.S. Dist. Ct., N.Y.C., 1955-56; assoc. Skadden, Arps, Slate, Meagher & Flom, N.Y.C., 1956-61, ptnr., 1961-2000, of counsel, 2000—. Trustee, chmn. Practising Law Inst., Law Ctr. Found. of N.Y. U. Sch. Law Aperture Found., program com. 2d. Cir. Jud. Conf. Mng. editor: Yale Law Jour. Bd. dirs., former dir. Jewish Mus., Legal Aid Soc.; former trustee N.Y. Community Trust; pres. coun. Mus. City of N.Y.; chmn. lawyers' div., spl. gifts campaign United Jewish Appeal/Fedn. Jewish Philanthropies, 1979-81; mem. print com. Whitney Mus., Com. on Rsch. Libraries N.Y. Pub. Lib. Recipient Torch of Learning award Am. Friends of Hebrew U., 1983, Brandeis Distingsh. Community Svc. award Brandeis U., 1985. Fellow: Am. Bar Found., Coll. of Commercial Arbitrators, Am. Coll. Trial Lawyers; mem.: ABA, Am. Law Inst., N.Y. State Bar Assn., Assn. of Bar of City of N.Y. (exec. com., judiciary com., past chmn. fed. cts. com.), Am. Arbitration Assn., Yale (N.Y.C.), Yale Club (N.Y.C.). Home: 211 Central Park W New York NY 10024-6020 Office: Skadden Arps Slate Meagher & Flom 4 Times Sq Fl 24 New York NY 10036-6595

GARFINKEL, HARMON MARK, retired specialty chemicals company executive; b. Bklyn., May 20, 1933; s. Samuel and Elsie (Schwartz) G.; m. Lorraine Plawsky, Mar. 4, 1956; children: Elyse, Michelle. BA, Bklyn. Coll., 1957; PhD, Iowa State U., 1960; postgrad. program for mgmt. devel., Harvard U. Bus. Sch., 1973. Dir. bio-organic tech. Corning Inc., N.Y., 1973-74, dir. applied chemistry and biology, 1974-75, dir. biomed. and chem. tech., 1975-78, dir. research, 1978-85; v.p. R&D Engelhard Corp., Edison, N.J., 1985-95, cons., 1995—. Instr. math. Elmira Coll., 1964. Patents and publs. in field. Mem. AAAS. Am. Chem. Soc., Am. Phys. Soc., Am. Inst. Chemists, Am. Ceramics Soc. Republican. Jewish. Home: 3836 Outlook Ct Jupiter FL 33477-1309 E-mail: Harmgarf@aol.com.

GARFINKEL, HERBERT, political science educator, university official; b. N.Y.C., June 16, 1920; s. Julius Louis and Gertrude (Goldstone) G.; m. Evelyn Epstein, Sept. 3, 1940; children— Laura, Paul. MA, U. Chgo., 1950, PhD, 1956. Instr. polit. sci. Ill. Inst. Tech., 1948-51; research asst. Nat. Opinion Research Ctr., U. Chgo., 1950-51; instr. Mich. State U., 1951-53; asst. prof. Dartmouth, 1953-59; faculty Mich. State U., East Lansing, 1959—, prof. polit. sci., 1964-73; dean James Madison Coll., 1966-73; provost, vice chancellor acad. affairs U. Nebr., Omaha, 1973-78, interim chancellor, 1977-78; v.p. acad. affairs and prof. polit. sci. U. Louisville, 1978-85, v.p. emeritus, prof. emeritus, 1985— NATO prof. Inst. Social Studies, The Hague, Netherlands, 1965-66 Author: When Negroes March, 1959, 2d edit., 1969, (co-author) The Democratic Republic, 1966, 2d edit., 1970, The Constitution and The Legislature, 1961; contbr. articles to profl. jours. Served as officer U.S. Mcht. Marine, 1943-45. Ctr. for Advanced Study Behavioral Scis. fellow, 1958-59; research fellow Social Sci. Research Council, 1960-61 Mem. Am. Polit. Sci. Assn. Home: 4204 N Timber Cir Peoria IL 61614-7864 Office: U Louisville Dept Of Political Sci Louisville KY 40292-0001 E-mail: heg1021@aol.com.

GARFINKEL, LAWRENCE SAUL, academic administrator, educator, television producer; b. N.Y.C., Mar. 9, 1932; s. Benjamin and Rose (Rochkind) G.; m. Adrienne Rederer, June 26, 1960; children: Andrew, Rodger, Craig. BS in Art Edn., NYU, 1953, MA in Higher Edn., 1955, postgrad. in Edn. Comm., 1975. Tchr., supr. art, prin. high schs. West Hempstead Pub. Schs., N.Y., 1954-56, dir. related arts, 1957-69, dir. cmty. rels., 1961-71; prof. edn. adminstrn. and comm., dir. instrnl. comm. program Hofstra U., Hempstead, N.Y., 1969-76; dir. summer television & media insts.; dir. gifted programs Sachem Pub. Schs., Lake Ronkonkoma, N.Y., 1978-79; dir. ednl. comm. Coll. Dentistry, Kriser Dental Ctr., NYU, 1979-91, ret.; adj. prof. dept. speech Baruch Coll., CUNY, 1980-91, Adelphi U., Stern Coll.-Yeshiva U., St. Johns U., Temple U., N.Y. Inst. Tech.; adj. prof. dept. media arts C.W. Post-L.I. U., 1991—. Adj. assoc. prof. art dept. Nassau C.C.; cons. bd. regents N.Y. State Edn. Dept., Ctr. Urban Edn., N.Y.C. Pub.: Restorative Dentistry, 1985; illustrator: Classroom Television, 1970; illustrator N.Y. Times, John Huston Prodns., Century Theatres, Nat. Audio Visual Assn., and numerous publs.; editl. cartoonist Merrick Life; asst. prodr. WPIX-TV, programming Dumont Network; pub. Garson Assocs.; contbr. articles to profl. jours. Coord. youth edn. Mothers Against Drunk Driving, Long Island Area, 1997-99; bd. dirs. Hist. Soc. Merricks, 1983— pres., 2001-; bd. dirs. Higher Edn. Assn. TV, 1972; v.p. Health Equities, N.Y.C.; oral historian Bi Centennial Commn., 1975. Nominee, Woodrow Wilson Found.; named alt., Fulbright award; recipient Grad. Arch award medal, NYU, scholarship masters NYU, numerous awards, Nat. Com. Sch. Pub. Rels.; grad. tchg. fellow, NYU. Mem. N.Y. Acad. Sci., L.I. Art Tchrs. Assn. (pres. 1967-68), Nat. Com. Art Edn. (co-pres. 1967). Avocations: illustrating, lecturing on communications theory, arts, visual literacy, teaching. Home and Office: Garson Assocs 172 Babylon Tpke Merrick NY 11566-4407

GARFINKEL, LEE, advertising agency executive; married; 2 children. BA, CUNY. From copywriter to exec. v.p., exec. creative dir. Levine, Huntley, Schmidt & Beaver; exec. v.p., sr. creative dir., also dir. BBDO; chief creative officer, chmn. Lowe, Lintas & Ptnrs., N.Y.C., 1992—. Stand-up comedian and musician. Named 1986 East Coast All-Star Team as Best TV Copywriter, Adweek, Creative Dir. of Yr. on 1994 Nat. Creative All-Star Team; selected ann. Forty Under Forty feature Crain's New York Bus.; named one of top three creative dirs. as well as number one copywriter in U.S., Winners mag., 1989; inducted in Am. advt. Fedn. Hall of achievement. Mem. One Club for Art and Copy (bd. dirs., pres. 1992-95). Avocations: song writing, collecting guitars, animated art, cars. Office: Lowe Lintas & Ptnrs 1 Dagitammarskjold Plaza New York NY 10017

GARFINKEL, PATRICIA GAIL, speech writer, policy analyst, poet; b. N.Y.C., Feb. 15, 1938; d. Wynn E. Walker and Rose Davis; divorced; children: Jon A. Garfinkel, Jef Adam Garfinkel. BA, NYU, 1959; studied poetry with Poct Henry Taylor, Va., 1972-75. Speech writer U.S. Ho. of Reps. Com. on Sci., Washington, 1976-94; speechwriter Nat. Sci. Found., Arlington, Va., 1995—. Author (books of poetry): Ram's Horn, 1980, From the Red Eye of Jupiter, 1990 (award), Making the Skeleton Dance, 2000. Poetry posted in pub. places, N.Y.C., including 2000 buses. Avocations: sketching, painting. Home: 900 N Stuart St Apt 1001 Arlington VA 22203-4107 E-mail: pgarfink@nsf.gov.

GARFINKLE, ELAINE MYRA, writer; b. Canton, Ohio, July 24, 1936; d. Clifford and Dora Adelman Margolis; m. Jack George Garfinkle, Dec. 27, 1959; 1 child, Marcia Lizabeth. Grad. H.S., Canton. Gen. mgr., editor, pub. Stark Jewish News, Inc., Canton, 1970—83; owner, writer, rschr. Canton Writing Svc., 1978—90; pres., treas. Marce Pubs., Inc., Canton, 1979—83; owner, rschr. Leo Rsch. unlimited, Canton, 1979—83; cmty. rels. supr. Goodwill Rehab., Canton, 1984—87; advt. exec. Cmty. Newspapers, Massillon, Ohio, 1987—91. Historian, pub., compiler, author Through the Years, the Informal History of the Canton Area Jewish Community 1870-2003, 58 vols. Trustee Cleve. Jewish Genealogy Soc.; advocate for spl. edn., sr. adult and consumer product affairs; mem., supporter Stark County Hist. Soc., McKinley Mus.; vol. and program presenter Canton Jewish Cmty. Ctr. Mem.: Friends of Ctr. Jewish History, Ohio Libr., Friends North Canton, Am. Friends Hebrew U., YIVO Inst. Jewish Rsch., Am. Jewish Hist. Soc., Canton Jewish Cmty. Fedn. (edn. com. mem., Outstanding Svc. award 1996—2002), Internat. Jewish Women (life; past pres., treas.), Am. Heart Assn. (cmty. rels. com. 1992—96, Outstanding Svc. award 1992—96), Am. Sephardi Fedn., Leo Baeck Inst., Hadassah (former edn. com. mem.), Shaaray Torah Sisterhood (former social action chmn.). Jewish. Avocations: photography, practical psychology, music, reading, studying Jewish history.

GARFINKLE, ROBERT ALLEN, writer, astronomer; b. Alameda, Calif., July 1, 1947; s. Wilfred and Wilma (Carlow) G.; m. Kathleen Mary, June 25, 1972; children: Kimberlee Suzanne, Annmarie. BA in History, Calif. State U., Hayward, 1975, BA in English Lit., 1994. Auto mechanic various cos., Fremont, Calif., 1967-79; engring. writer Westinghouse Electric Corp., Sunnyvale, Calif., 1981-91; sr. engring. writer Northrop Grumman Corp., Sunnyvale, 1995-2000; sr. tech. writer ESS Tech., Fremont, Calif., 2000—02. Author: Star-Hopping: Your Visa to Viewing the Universe, 1995; co-author: Advanced Skywatching, 1997; contbr. articles to mags. Pres. bd. Union San. Dist., Fremont, 1984-89; mem. coun. City of Union City, Calif., 1989-97. Fellow Royal Astron. Soc. London; mem. AAAS, Brit. Astron. Assn., Royal Astron. Soc. Can., San Jose Astron. Assn., Assn. Lunar and Planetary Observers, East Bay Astron. Soc. E-mail: ragarf@earthlink.net.

GARFUNKEL, ALAN J. lawyer; b. Savannah, Ga., Oct. 26, 1947; s. Sylvan Adler Garfunkel and Eve D. (Darmstadter) Goldmann; m. Lori A. Corsun, June 27, 1993; children: S. Jonathan, Michael J., Danielle A., Joshua B. AB, NYU, 1968, LL.M. in Taxation, 1975; JD, Columbia U., 1972. Bar: N.Y. 1972, U.S. Dist. Ct. (so. and ea. dists.) N.Y. 1974, U.S. Ct. Appeals (2d cir.) 1975, U.S. Tax Ct. 1975. Sr. trial atty. Office of Chief Counsel, IRS, N.Y.C., 1972-77; assoc. firm Proskauer Rose Geotz & Mendelsohn, N.Y.C., 1977-80; atty. pvt. practice, N.Y.C., 1980—. Served with USAR, 1969-74. Mem. N.Y. State Bar Assn. (tax sect.), New York County Lawyers Assn., Bar Assn. of City of N.Y., Omicron Delta Epsilon. Home: 63 Lincoln Rd Scarsdale NY 10583-7533 Office: 477 Madison Ave New York NY 10022-5802 E-mail: ajgnyclaw@aol.com.

GARG, DEVENDRA, financial executive; b. Mathura, India, Feb. 14, 1948; came to U.S., 1972; s. Lalta Prasad and Sushila (Elhence) G.; m. Manju Gupta, May 8, 1973; children: Sumeet, Preeti. BSc, U. Allahabad, India, 1967; BE, ME, Indian Inst. Sci., Bangalore, 1970, 72; MBA, Rensselaer Poly. Inst., Troy, N.Y., 1977. Product analyst Comten/Univac, Hartford, Conn., 1973-77; audit specialist, then mgr. region audit Xerox Corp., Rochester, N.Y., 1977-85, mgr. cost devel. and control, strategic fin. analysis Webster, N.Y., 1985-87, mgr. planning and analysis Reprographics Bus. Unit, 1987-89, mgr. bus. analysis, 1989-90, mgr. fin. planning and systems devel., 1990-92, contr. worldwide mfg., 1992-95, v.p. fin. ops. U.S. customer ops. Rochester, 1995-96, v.p. fin. prodn. sys., 1997-2000, v.p. fin. worldwide bus. svcs. Webster, 2000—01, v.p., CFO documentation sys. and solution group, 2001—02, v.p., CFO bus. group ops., 2003—. Adj. faculty St. John Fisher Coll., Rochester, 1988-91. Mem. budget steering com. Rochester Sch. Bd., 1989-91; treas. Sch. Indian Culture, Rochester, 1990-91; bd. dirs. United Way of Rochester, 1994—. Avocations: travel, reading, geopolitical structures. Home: 7 Roxbury Ln Pittsford NY 14534-4202 Office: Xerox Corp 70 Linden Oaks Dr Rochester NY 14625 E-mail: devgarg@msn.com.

GARG, SANDEEP, oncologist; s. J.K. and Vinod Garg; m. Manisha Singhi, Jan. 3, 1995; 1 child, Aarush. B Medicine, B Surgery, Jawaharlal Nehru Med. Coll., Ajmer, India, 1993; MD, JLN Med. Coll. and associated Hosps., Ajmer, India, 1996. Diplomate Medical Oncology Am. Bd. of Medicine, 2002, Am. Bd. Internal Medicine, 2000. Cons. oncologist North Oakland Med. Ctr., Pontiac, Mich., 2002—; cons. oncologists St Joseph Mercy Oakland Hosp., Pontiac, Mich., 2002—. Author: Am. Jour. of Hematology, NEJM, Internat. Jour. of Cardiology; reviewer Jour. of Med. Sci. Monitor; contbr. Mem.: AACR (assoc.), ASCO (assoc.), ACP-ASIM (assoc.).

GARG, UDAY RAMAKANT, financial analyst; b. Mumbai, India, Jan. 12, 1979; s. Ramakant and Prema Garg. BS in Fin., Wharton Bus. Sch., 2000. Analyst Deutsche Bank Alex. Brown, N.Y.C., 2000—02; assoc. Portico Capital, Greenwich, Conn., 2002—. Co-founder Agribution, Phila., 1999—2000. Avocation: tennis. Home: 10 E 29th St Apt 41H New York NY 10016 Office: Portico Capital LLC 537 Steamboat Rd Ste 300 Greenwich CT 06830 Personal E-mail: udayrgarg@hotmail.com. E-mail: uday@porticocapital.com.

GARG, VIJAY KUMAR, telecommunications engineer; b. Jahangirabad, India, July 7, 1938; arrived in U.S., 1965; s. Reoti S. and Prem V. (Mittal) G.; m. Pushpa Bansal, May 11, 1961; children: Nina Taneja, Meena Dorr, Ravi K. Garg. BS, Banaras U., Varanasi, India, 1960; MS, U. Calif., Berkeley, 1966; PhD, Ill. Inst. Tech., 1973. Registered profl. structral engr., Ill., profl. engr., Ill. Asst. prof. engring. U. Jodhpur, India, 1960-65; structural engr. Chgo. Bridge, Oakbrook, Ill., 1967-69; devel. engr. GMC, Lagrange, Ill., 1969-76; mgr. dynamic rsch. AAR, Chgo., 1976-84; assoc. prof. engring. U. Maine, Orono, 1984-85; dist. mem. tech. staff Bell Labs Lucent Techs., Naperville, Ill., 1985-2000, Motorola Inc., Arlington Heights, Ill., 1997; prof. elec. and computer engring. U. Ill., Chgo., 1999—. Vis. prof. elec. and comm. engring. U. Ill., Urbana, 1996-97; adj. prof. engring. Ill. Inst. Tech., Chgo., 1976-84. Author: Wireless and Personal Communications System, 1996, Applications of CDMA in Wireless Communications, 1997, Dynamics of Railway Vehicle System, 1984, Advanced Dynamics, 1984, Principles and Applications of GSM, 1999, CDMA IS-95 and CDMA 2000, 2000, Wireless Network Evolution-2G to 3G, 2002. Recipient NSF travel grants India, 1984, China, 1985. Fellow ASME, ASCE; mem. IEEE (sr.). Democrat. Hindu. Avocations: gardening, travel, reading, music. Home: 146 Somerset Rd Hinsdale IL 60527-5429 Office: 851 S Morgan St Chicago IL 60605-4220 E-mail: vgarg@ece.uic.edu., garg.v@attbi.com.

GARGANO, FRANCINE ANN, lawyer; b. Plainfield, N.J., Feb. 10, 1957; d. Rosalie Janice Gargano. BA Seton Hall U., 1980; JD cum laude, Detroit Coll. of Law, 1983. Bar: N.J. 1983, U.S. Supreme Ct. 1986. Sole practice, North Plainfield, N.J., 1983—; dir. YWCA Legal Clinic, Plainfield, 1983—; Union County coordinator Haitian Pro Bono Projects, ABA, Plainfield, 1983—. Rsch. asst. prof. Detroit Coll. Law, Detroit, 1980-83. Author: Homosexual Marriages Are Not Possible. Trustee Plainfield Area YWCA, 1983-84; bd. dirs. Haitian Advancement Assn., Elizabeth, N.J., 1983-84; mem. N. Plainfield Bd. Adjustment; mem. Historic Preservation commn., Youth Svcs. commn., Mcpl. Alliance. Recipient Internat. Legal Scholar award Detroit Coll. Law Internat. Law Soc., 1980-82, Jessup Internat. Law Competition award, 1982, H. Rakol Scholarship award Detroit Bar Assn., 1982, Vol. of Yr. Congl. award, 1995. Mem. ABA, Union County Bar Assn., N.J. Bar Assn., Plainfield Bar Assn., Am. Immigration Lawyers Assn., Detroit Coll. Law Internat. Law Soc. (pres. 1980-82), Vicinage 13 Women's Bar Assn. (pres.), Somerset County Bar Assn. (chmn. ADR com.). Democrat. Roman Catholic.. Office: 5J Mountain Blvd Warren NJ 07059-5699 E-mail: garganof@webtv.net.

GARGIULO, ANDREA W. lawyer; b. Hartford, Conn., Apr. 26, 1946; d. Charles M. and Irma S. (Rubin) Weiner; m. Richard A. Gargiulo, Nov. 26, 1975; 1 child, John K. BA, Smith Coll., 1968; JD cum laude, Suffolk U., 1972. Bar: Mass. 1972, U.S. Dist. Ct. Mass. 1975, U.S. Ct. Appeals (11th cir.) 1981, U.S. Supreme Ct. 1983. Asst. dist. atty. Middlesex County, Mass., 1972-75; chmn. Boston Fin. Commn., 1975-77; counsel Gargiulo, Rudnick, & Gargiulo, Boston, 1976—. Chmn. Boston Licensing Bd., 1977-89; lectr. Northeastern U. Coll. Criminal Justice, Boston, 1978, 80; bd. dirs. Arbella Mut. Ins. Co.; host (TV show) Women Today, 1994-96. Mem. Mass. Ethics Commn., 1985-88; mem. bd. overseers Children's Hosp., Boston, 1983-99; chmn. Mass. Bd. Bar Overseers, 1996. Mem. Beacon Hill Garden Club, Harvard Mus. Assn., Wianno Yacht Club, St. Botolph Club. Avocations: sailing, theatre, book collecting. Home: 13 W Cedar St Boston MA 02108-1211 Office: Gargiulo Rudnick & Gargiulo 66 Long Wharf Boston MA 02110-3605

GARGIULO, ANTONIO ROSARIO, reproductive endocrinologist, researcher, clinician; b. Naples, Italy, June 13, 1964; s. Antonio and Anna Maria (Esposito) G.; m. Elisabetta de Siena, July 10, 1993; children: Anna Violetta, Rossella Marina, Antonio Mauro. MD, U. Naples, 1989. Resident in ob-gyn. U. Tex., Houston, 1992-96; fellow in reproductive endocrinology Harvard Med. Sch./Brigham & Women's Hosp., Boston, 1996-98, instr. ob-gyn. and reproductive biology, 1998—. Rsch. grantee Am. Soc. Reproductive Medicine, 1999-2000. Mem. Am. Soc. for Reproductive Medicine, European Soc. for Human Reproduction and Embriology. Avocations: nature photography, equitation, guitar playing. Office: Brigham and Women's Hosp 75 Francis St Boston MA 02115-6106

GARIBALDI, MARIE LOUISE, former state supreme court justice; b. Jersey City, Nov. 26, 1934; d. Louis J. and Marie (Serventi) G. BA, Conn. Coll., 1956; LLB, Columbia U., 1959; LLM in Tax. Law, NYU, 1963. Atty. Office of Regional Counsel, IRS, N.Y.C., 1960-66; assoc. McCarter & English, Newark, 1966-69; ptnr. Riker, Danzig, Scherer, Hyland & Pernutti, Newark, 1969-82; assoc. justice N.J. Supreme Court, Newark, 1982-2000. Contbr. articles to profl. jours. Trustee St. Peter's Coll.; co-chmn. Thomas Kean's campaign for Gov. of N.J., 1981, mem. transition team, 1981; mem. Gov. Byrne's Commn. on Dept. of Commerce, 1981. Recipient Disting. Alumni award NYU Law Alumni of N.J., 1982; recipient Disting. Alumni award Columbia U., 1982 Fellow Am. Bar Found.; mem. N.J. Bar Assn. (pres. 1982), Columbia U. Sch. Law Alumni Assn. (bd. dirs.) Roman Catholic.

GARIBALDI, RYAN SKIP, mathematician, educator; BS, Purdue U., 1992; PhD, U. Calif. San Diego, La Jolla, 1998. Postdoctoral staff Swiss Fed. Inst. Tech. (ETH), Zurich, Switzerland, 1998—99; asst. prof. UCLA, 1999—2002; asst. prof. dept. math. Emory U., Atlanta, 2002—. Mem.: Math. Assn. Am., Am. Math. Soc. Office: Emory Univ Dept Math Atlanta GA 30322

GARIMELLA, SATYA V. cardiologist; b. Hyderabad, India, Mar. 26, 1967; s. Ramakrishna Garimella; m. Chandrika Kanugovi Garimella, June 1, 1990; children: Manasa, Madhulika B., Ashrith A. M.B.B.S., Osmania Med. Coll., Hyderabad, 1990; MD, St. Francis Hosp., 1996. Diplomate Am. Bd. Internal Medicine, Am. Bd. Cardiology. Resident in internal medicine St. Francis Hosp., Evanston, Ill., 1993—96, fellow in cardiology, 1996—97, U. Louisville Hosp., 1997—99; electrophysiology fellow Vanderbilt U., Nashville, 1999—2000; cardiology cons. Mountain Comprehensive Health Corp., Whitesburg, Ky., 2000—. Contbr. Recipient Best Resident award, St. Francis Hosp., 1996. Mem.: Am. Coll. Cardiology (assoc.). Hindu. Avocations: reading, tennis, swimming. Home: 102 Cowan St Whitesburg KY 41858 Office: Mountain Comprehensive Health Corp 226 Medical Plaza Ln Whitesburg KY 41858

GARING, IONE DAVIS, civic worker, club woman; b. Huntsville, Ala., Jan. 8, 1930; d. Drury McNary and Ione (Thompson) Davis; m. John Seymour Garing, Apr. 26, 1952; children: John Davis, Susan Carolyn. BSc in Edn. cum laude, Ohio State U., 1951. Tchr. Columbus (Ohio) Pub. Schs., 1952-54, Upper Arlington Pub. Sch., Columbus, 1957-58; libr. Newton (Mass.) Libr., 1955; interviewer audits and surveys Elmo Roper, Boston, 1956. Mem. adv. com. Sch. Com. on Spl. Edn., Lexington, Mass., 1979-80; mem. adv. bd. Cary Meml. Libr., Lexington, 1989—. Active numerous civic orgns., including mem. Town Meeting, Lexington, 1980-2002; mem. Lexington 2020 Vision Study, 2001; mem. exec. bd. Lexington Dem. Com., 1987-89, mem., 1986—; del. Mass. Dem. Convs., 1986, 88, 90, 92, 94, 96, 98, 2000, 2002, mem. exec. bd. Friends Coun. on Aging, 1986, PTA's, 1965-79; vol. Meals on Wheels, 1985-89; pres. United Meth. Women, Lexington, 1973-75; bd. dirs. Meth. Weekday Sch., 1971-80; co-organizer 1st town-wide hazardous waste collection in U.S., Lexington, 1983; vol. Lexington Hist. Soc., 1978—; co-founder, chmn. Friends of Cary Meml. Libr. Orgn., 1990-97, bd. dirs., 1990—; founding mem., treas., Precint 8 Residents Assn., 1996-03. Mem. LWV (pres. Lexington 1983-85), AAUW (Mass. long range planning com.), DAR (vice regent 1977-80, Mass. chmn. scholarships and loan com. 1980-83), Florence Crittenton League, Outlook Club (pres. 1985-87, chmn. scholarships com. 1990-2002), Lexington Field and Garden Club (2d vice-pres. 2000-2002), North Shore Rock and Mineral Club (Peabody, Mass.), Brookline Bird Club, Minute Man Nat. Pk. Assn., Alpha Chi Omega. Avocations: conservation, gardening, bird watching, genealogy, travel. Home: 157 Cedar St Lexington MA 02421-6507

GARINGER, LOUIS DANIEL, religion educator; b. Johnson City, Tenn.; s. Merrion X. and Hilda (Gasteiger) G.; m. Joanne Mazna, June 21, 1958. AB, U. Tenn., 1947, JD, 1949; MA in Govt, Harvard, 1957. Staff writer Christian Sci. Monitor Youth Forums, Boston, 1949-51; teaching fellow, tutor govt. Harvard, 1955-58; assoc. dir. Salzburg Seminar in Am. Studies, 1958-60; editorial writer Christian Sci. Monitor, 1965-67, religious affairs editor, 1967-71; research, 1971-72; assoc. prof. polit. sci. and religion Principia Coll., Elsah, Ill., 1973-86; dir. Found. Bibl. Research, Charlestown, N.H., 1987-88. Vis. scholar Boston U. Sch. Theology, 1980, Grad. Theol. Union, Berkeley, Calif. Contbr. articles to profl. jours. Served with AUS, 1951-53. Recipient Religious Pub. Relations Council merit award, 1969; William E. Leidt award for religious reporting, 1970 Mem. Scarabbean, Pi Kappa Phi, Phi Kappa Phi, Phi Eta Sigma, Sigma Delta Pi, Phi Alpha Eta. Home: 105 Spaulding Hill Rd West Chesterfield NH 03466-3120 E-mail: countrystars@juno.com. *Unless religion means a deep and heartfelt love for God and man expressed in very concrete and practical ways, unless it cuts to the very core of our being and radically changes our lives, it is worth little or nothing.*

GARIOLO, RICHARD, psychotherapist; b. NYC, June 10, 1949; s. Salvatore Joseph and Assunta Gariolo; m. Jean Tolhurst, June 5, 1982. BS in econ., Fordham U., 1971; MBA in acctg., Rutgers U., 1974; MS in counseling, Iona Coll., 1995. Lic. professional counselor NJ. Fin. exam. US Sec. and Ex. Comm, NYC, 1974—78; auditor US Dept. of Labor, Boston, 1978—83; internal auditor US Dept. of Army, West Point, NY, 1983—84; fin. examiner Nat. Credit Union Admin., New City, NY, 1984—86; fin. mgr. Vancorf Fed. Credit Union, NYC, 1991—92; counselor Straight & Narrow, Paterson, NJ, 1994—99, Pvt. Practice, Emerson, NJ, 1999—. Contbr. articles various profl. jours. First Lt U.S. Army, 1971—78. Mem.: Am. Counseling Assn. Office: Richard Gariolo 16 Chestnut St Ste 1W Emerson NJ 07630 Office Fax: 201-967-9466.

GARLAND, CEDRIC FRANK, epidemiologist, educator; b. La Jolla, Calif., Nov. 10, 1946; s. Cedric and Eva (Caldwell) Garagliano. BA, U. So. Calif., 1967; MPH, UCLA, 1970, DrPH, 1974. Asst. prof. Johns Hopkins U., Balt., 1974-81; prof. Sch. Medicine U. Calif., La Jolla, 1981—. Contbr. chpts. to books, articles to profl. jours. Recipient Aristotle award for acad. excellence UCLA, 1974, Golden Apple award for Tchg. Excellence Johns Hopkins U., 1980, Environ. Health Coalition Disting. Svc. award, 1984, NIH Rsch. Career award, 1982. Fellow Am. Coll. Epidemiology; mem. Physicians for Social Responsibility (chmn. info. resources 1982—), Soc. Epidemiol. Rsch., Sierra Club (chmn. Save Our Shore 1982—, Disting. Achievement award 1984). Roman Catholic. Achievements include work with Dr. Frank Garland and Dr. Edward Gorham who together played a role in establishing the association between deficiency of vitamin D and calcium, and risk of intestinal, breast, and ovarian cancer; this group also played a role in establishing that ultraviolet A is a cause of human melanoma. Office: U Calif Dept 0631C Dept Family & Preventive Medicine 9500 Gilman Dr La Jolla CA 92093-0631

GARLAND, G(ARFIELD) GARRETT, sales executive, golf professional; b. Lakewood, Ohio, Dec. 17, 1946; s. Garfield George and Lois Marie (Calavan) G.; m. Debra Ann Threlkel; children, Brandon Palmer, Blake Hamilton. BA, U. Colo., 1974. Broker Marcus & Millichap, Newport Beach, Calif., 1982-84; v.p. Pacific Coast Fed., Encino, Calif., 1984-85; dir. of acquisitions Prudential Investment Fund, L.A., 1985-86; v.p. A.S.A.I., L.A. and Tokyo, 1986-89; divisional mgr. Lojack Corp., L.A., 1984—2002; pres. Collegiate Scholarship Svcs. of Am., 1991-92, BBG Enterprises, 2000—. Cons. Centinela Hosp. Fitness Inst. Mem. Pres.'s Coun. on Competitiveness, 1992, Childhelp USA. Capt. U.S. Army, 1967-71. Mem. VFW, PGA of Am., L.I.F.E. Found., Am. Legion, World Affairs Coun., Internat. Platform Assn., U.S. Ski Team, Natural Historic Preservation Trust. Avocations: golf, reading. Home: 17638 Raymer St Northridge CA 91325-3113 Office: 17638 Raymer St Northridge CA 91325-3113

GARLAND, HOWARD, psychology educator; b. Bklyn., June 22, 1946; s. Murray and Norma (Luft) G.; m. Eileen Mary Cohen, Aug. 21, 1968; children: Eric Lee, Adam Marc. BA, Bklyn. coll., 1968; MS, Cornell U., 1971, PhD, 1972. Asst. prof. Upsala Coll., East Orange, N.J., 1972-74; prof. U. Tex., Arlington, 1974-88; vis. prof. U. Ill., Champaign, 1985-86; prof., chair U. Del.,

Newark, 1988—. Contbr. over 30 articles to profl. jours. Mem. Internat. Assn. Applied Psychology, Am. Psychol. Soc., Soc. I/O Psychology, Acad. Mgt. Home: 9 Falling Tree Ct Newark DE 19711-7462 Office: U Del 118 Lerner Hall Newark DE 19716

GARLAND, HOWARD, mathematician, educator; b. Detroit, Oct. 27, 1937; s. Max and Sylvia M. Garland; m. Sylvia F. Garland, June 25, 1961; children: Miriam, Libby. BS, U. Chgo., 1957; PhD, U. Calif., Berkeley, 1964. Instr. Yale U., New Haven, Conn., 1964-65; asst. Inst. for Advanced Study, Princeton, N.J., 1965-66; asst. prof. Yale U., New Haven, 1966-69, chair dept. math., 1995-98, Einar Hille chair prof., 1996—; assoc. prof. Cornell U., Ithaca, N.Y., 1969-71; prof. Columbia U., N.Y.C., 1971-72, SUNY, Stony Brook, 1972-73, Yale U., New Haven, 1973—. Co-chair organizing com. for program in Lie Theory, Math. Scis. Rsch. Inst., Berkeley, 1983-84. Contbr. rsch. articles to profl. jours. Mem. Am. Math. Soc. E-mail: hgarland@math.yale.edu.

GARLAND, JAMES WILSON, JR., retired physics educator; b. Washington, Aug. 1, 1933; s. James Wilson and May M. (Midgett) G.; m. Katherine Elizabeth Landgraf, Dec. 27, 1958; children— Caroline Elizabeth, Margaret Lee. Student, Oberlin Coll., 1954; MS, U. Chgo., 1958, PhD, 1963. Acting asst. prof. U. Calif., Berkeley, 1963-66, asst. prof., 1966-67; assoc. prof. physics U. Ill., Chgo., 1967-69, prof., 1969-94; retired, 1994. Vis. prof. Cambridge U., Eng., 1965; cons. Argonne Nat. Lab., Westinghouse, Gould, Standard Oil. Contbr. articles to profl. jours. Vol. tutoring program. With U.S. Army, 1954-56. Sloan Found. fellow, 1964-66. Democrat. Presbyterian. Home: 2889 Tramway Pl NE Albuquerque NM 87122-2277 E-mail: jkgarland@hubwest.com.

GARLAND, LARETTA MATTHEWS, nursing educator; b. Jacksonville, Fla. d. Wilburn L. and Clyde-Marian (Chamberlin) Matthews; m. John B. Garland, Mar. 2, 1946; children: John Barnard, Brien Freeling, Amy-Gwin. Diploma, Fla. State Sch. Nursing, 1942; BSN, Emory U., 1950, MA, 1953; BA in Edn., U. Fla., 1951; cert. cardiovascular nurse specialty, Tex. Med. Ctr., 1965; EdD, U. Ga., 1975; postgrad. in counseling and guidance, Ga. State U., 1969; grad. cert. in gerontology, 1981. Cert. nat. counselor. Office and staff nurse, Lakeland, Fla., 1942, 45; nurse ARC, Buffalo, 1956; asst. prof. nursing Med. Coll. Ga., 1965-67; instr. Emory U., 1952-54, assoc. prof., 1967-71, prof., 1972-86, prof. emeritus, 1987—. Ednl. psychologist, dir. gerontol. nurse practitioner program, 1978-80, asst. to dean, 1983-86. Author: (with Carol Bush) Coping Behavior and Nursing, 1982; contbr. articles to profl. jours. With Nurse Corps, U.S. Army, 1942-45. Decorated 2 Bronze Stars; recipient Outstanding Tchg. award Emory U. Sch. Nursing Grad. Srs., 1977, Appreciation award So. Region Constituent Leagues, Nat. League for Nursing award, 1987, Mabel Korsell award of appreciation Ga. League Nursing, 1987, Spl. Recognition award Ga. Nurses Assn., 1988, 90, Nurse of Yr. award, 1992, Appreciation award Ga. Assn. Nursing Students, 1990, Van de Vrede award Ga. League Nursing, 1993; HEW fellow, 1967-68. Mem. APA, AACD, ANA, Ga. Assn. Nursing Students (hon.), Nat. League Nursing, Bs. and Profl. Women, China Burma India VA Assn. (mem. nat. bd. 1993—), 14th Air Force Asssn. (Flying Tigers), Hump Pilots Assn., Ormond Beach Womens Club, Ormond Beach Hist. Trust, Nat. Assn. Women Vet. (steering com.), Women in Mil. Svc. Meml. Found. (charter), ARC Nurses, Panhellenic Assn., Hist. Trust, Alpha Chi Omega, Sigma Theta Tau, Kappa Delta Pi, Alpha Kappa Delta, Omicron Delta Kappa. Office: Emory U Nell Hodgson Woodruff Sch Atlanta GA 30322-0001

GARLAND, MERRICK BRIAN, federal judge; b. Chgo., Nov. 13, 1952; AB summa cum laude, Harvard U., 1974, JD magna cum laude, 1977. Bar: D.C. 1979, U.S. Dist. Ct. D.C. 1980, U.S. Ct. Appeals (D.C. and 9th cirs.) 1980, U.S. Ct. Appeals (4th cir.) 1983, U.S. Ct. Appeals (10th cir.) 1996, U.S. Supreme Ct. 1983. Law clk. to judge U.S. Ct. Appeals (2d cir.), N.Y.C., 1977—78; law clk. to justice U.S. Supreme Ct., Washington, 1978—79; spl. asst. to atty. gen. U.S. Dept. Justice, Washington, 1979—81; from assoc. to ptnr. Arnold & Porter, Washington, 1981—89; assoc. ind. counsel U.S. Dept. Justice, Washington, 1987—88, asst. U.S. atty., 1989—92; ptnr. Arnold & Porter, Washington, 1992—93; dep. asst. atty. gen., criminal divsn. Dept. Justice, Washington, 1993—94, prin. assoc. dep. atty. gen., 1994—97; judge U.S. Ct. Appeals, Washington, 1997—. Lectr. Harvard U. Law Sch., 1985—86. Author: Deregulation and Jud. Rev., Harvard Law Rev., 1985, Antitrust and State Action, Yale Law Jour., 1987, Antitrust and Federalism, Yale Law Jour., 1987. Mem.: Phi Beta Kappa. Office: US Court of Appeals 333 Constitution Ave NW Washington DC 20001-2802

GARLAND, RICHARD ROGER, lawyer; b. Princeton, Ill., Aug. 20, 1958; s. Louis Roger and Irene Marie (Tonozzi) G. BA in Polit. Sci. summa cum laude, U. S. Fla., 1979; JD with honors, U. Fla., 1982. Bar: Fla. 1982, U.S. Dist. Ct. (mid. dist.) Fla. 1983, U.S. Ct. Appeals (11th cir.) 1987, U.S. Supreme Ct. 1988, U.S. Ct. Appeals (fed. cir.) 1995; Fla. Bar cert. in appellate practice, 1995. Instr., supr. appellate advocacy U. Fla., Gainesville, 1981-82; assoc. Dickinson, O'Riorden, Gibbons, Quale, Shields & Carlton, Venice, Fla., 1983-85, Sarasota, Fla., 1986-90; ptnr., sr. atty. Dickinson & Gibbons, Sarasota, Fla., 1991—. Pres. parish coun. San Pedro Cath. Ch., North Port, Fla., 1986-92; mem. Sarasota County Libr. Adv. Bd., 1999-2001. Mem. ABA, Fla. Bar Assn., Sarasota County Bar Assn. (editor newsletter 1991-93, bd. dirs. 1994-96, treas. 1996-97, sec. 1997-98, v.p. 1998-99, pres.-elect 1999-2000, pres. 2000-01), Judge John M. Scheb Am. Inn of Ct. (treas. 1998-99, counselor 1999-2000, pres.-elect 2000-01, pres. 2001-02, master), U. South Fla. Alumni Assn., Sarasota County Gator Club (bd. dirs. 2001-02, v.p. 2002-03), Phi Kappa Phi, Pi Sigma Alpha. Democrat. Roman Catholic. Office: Dickinson & Gibbons PA 1750 Ringling Blvd Sarasota FL 34236-6836 E-mail: rgarland@dglawyers.com.

GARLAND, SYLVIA DILLOF, lawyer; b. N.Y.C., June 4, 1919; d. Morris and Frieda (Gassner) Dillof; m. Albert Garland, May 4, 1942; children: Margaret Garland, Paul B. BA, Bklyn. Coll., 1939; JD cum laude, N.Y. Law Sch., 1960. Bar: N.Y. 1960, U.S. Ct. Appeals (2d cir.) 1965, U.S. Ct. Claims 1965, U.S. Supreme Ct. 1967, U.S. Customs Ct. 1972, U.S. Ct. Appeals (5th cir.), 1979. Assoc. Borden, Skidell, Fleck and Steindler, Jamaica, N.Y., 1960-61, Fields, Zimmerman, Skodnick & Segall, Jamaica, 1961-65, Marshall, Brater, Greene, Allison & Tucker, N.Y.C., 1965-68; law sec. to N.Y. Supreme Ct. justice Suffolk County, 1968-70; ptnr. Hofheimer, Gartlir & Gross, N.Y.C., 1970—. Asst. adj. prof. N.Y. Law Sch., 1974-79; mem. com. on character and fitness N.Y. State Supreme Ct., 1st Jud. Dept., 1985—, vice chmn., 1991—. Author: Workman's Compensation, 1957, Labor Law, 1959, Wills, 1962; contbg. author: Guardians and Custodians, 1970; editor-in-chief Law Rev. Jour., N.Y. Law Forum, 1959-60 (svc. award 1960); contbr. articles to mag. Trustee N.Y. Law Sch., 1979-90, trustee emeritus, 1991—; pres. Oakland chpt. B'nai Brith, Bayside, N.Y., 1955-57. Recipient Disting. Alumnus award N.Y. Law Sch., 1978, Judge Charles W. Froessel award N.Y. Law Sch., 1997. Mem. ABA (litigation sect., family law sect.), N.Y. State Bar Assn. (family law sect.), Queen's County Bar Assn. (sec. civil practice 1960-79), N.Y. Law Sch. Alumni Assn. (pres. 1976-77), N.Y. Law Forum Alumni Assn. (pres. 1963-65). Jewish. Home: 425 E 58th St New York NY 10022-2300

GARLAND, WILLIAM JAMES, engineering physics educator; b. St. John's, Nfld., Can., July 26, 1948; B in Engring. Physics, McMaster U., Hamilton, Ont., Can., 1970, M in Engring. Physics, 1971, PhD in Chem. Engring., 1975. Registered profl. engr., Ont. Design engr. Ont. Hydro, Toronto, Can., 1975-79; design specialist Atomic Energy of Can. Ltd., Mississauga, Ont., 1979-83; assoc. prof. McMaster U., 1983-97, chmn. dept. engring. physics, 1988-94, prof., 1997—; dir. McMaster Nuclear Reactor, 1994-95. Cons. System Analytics, Burlington, Ont., 1982—. Mem. Am. Nuclear Soc., Can. Nuclear Soc., Assn. Profl. Engrs. Ont. Office: McMaster U Dept Engring Physics 1280 Main St W Hamilton ON Canada L8S 4L7 E-mail: garlandw@mcmaster.ca.

GARLATHY, FRANK BRYAN, minister; b. Johnstown, Pa., May 6, 1946; s. Frank and Helen Rebecca (Casriel) G.; m. Mary Kay Campbell, July 27, 1968; children: Joshua, Elizabeth. BA in Philosophy cum laude, Otterbein Coll., 1967; MDiv, United Theol. Sem., Dayton, Ohio, 1970; D Ministry, Grad. Theol. Found., Notre Dame, Ind., 1988. Ordained to ministry United Meth. Ch., 1970. Pastor Christy Park United Meth. Ch., McKeesport, Pa., 1970-71, Fayette City (Pa.) United Meth. Ch., 1972-79, Riverview United Meth. Ch., Beaver Falls, Pa., 1979-83; assoc. dir. McKeesport Neighborhood Ministry, 1971-72, Trinity United Meth. Ch., Indiana, Pa., 1983-91; First United Meth. Ch., Erie, Pa., 1991-95, pastor Vandergrift, Pa., 1995-99, Rochester, Pa., 1999—. Chaplain Beaver County Jail, Beaver, Ind., 1981-83, Ind. Borough Police Dept., 1990-91; mission amb. Western Pa. Conf., Pitts., 1985-86; pres. Ind. Area Coun. Chs., 1985-87, United Campus Ministry, Ind., 1990-91. Composer, performer (record album) Sweet Release, 1978, Spirit, 1991; radio talk show host Sta. WLKK, Erie, Pa., 1993-95. Mem. Belle Vernon (Pa.) Area Sch. Bd., 1977—79; v.p. Christians United in Beaver County, 2003—. Mem. Am. Acad. Religion, Bibl. Archaeology Soc., Quiz and Quill. Home: 345 Jefferson St Rochester PA 15074-2003 Office: 341 Jefferson St Rochester PA 15074-2003 E-mail: garlox@msn.com. *Our lives are a series of choices based upon the words "open" and "closed." We can extend an open hand or a closed fist. We can cultivate an open mind or a closed rationality. God gives us many choices.*

GARLICK, MICHAEL, lawyer, franchise consultant; b. N.Y.C., Oct. 20, 1944; s. Nathan S. and Gertrude (Finkel) G.; m. Judith Ann Schaufeld, May 12, 1977; children: Nathan S., Max Aaron, Jacob Abraham. B.A., Lehigh U., 1966; J.D., NYU, 1969. Bar: N.Y. 1970, Fla. 1971, Calif. 1973, D.C. 1974, Tex. 1995, Co. 1995, U.S. Dist. Ct. (so. dist.) Fla. Gen. counsel Internat. House of Pancakes Fla., Miami, 1970-74, cons., 1983— ; sr. ptnr. Garlick, Cohn, Darrow & Hollander, Miami, 1974-79; gen. counsel Internat. Adv. Group, Inc., Miami, 1980—; Editor Lawletter, 1981-83. Served with U.S. Army, 1969. Mem. Forum Com. on Franchising, ABA, Dade County Bar Assn. North Miami Beach Karate (pres. 1970-80), Tai Chi Chaun Assn. (pres. 1983—), Phi Beta Kappa, Beta Alpha Psi. Office: 1515 N Federal Hwy Boca Raton FL 33432-1911

GARLING, CAROL ELIZABETH, real estate executive and developer; b. Detroit, Sept. 23, 1939; d. Elmer Daniel and Elizabeth Aldene (Kish) Champagne; m. Fred C. Garling, Mar. 7, 1963 (dec. Nov. 1972). BS, U. Detroit, 1960, degree in criminology, 1972. Lic. real estate broker. Land developer, builder Garling Bldg. Co., Dearborn, 1962-73; specialist indsl. security Cen. Security, Inc. and Garling Security Services, Dearborn, 1973-79; owner, realtor, broker Carol Garling Realty, Inc., Dearborn, 1976-80; broker, realtor Embassy Realty, Inc., Ft. Lauderdale, Fla., 1981—; land developer Garling Bldg. and Devel., Raleigh, N.C., 1986-98; exec. Garling Realty, Scottsdale, Ariz., 1992—; designated broker. Mem. Ft. Lauderdale Bd. Realtors, Scottsdale, Ariz. Bd Realtors, Plum Hollow Colf Club (Southfield Mich., life mem.). First woman lic. in indsl. security field.

GARLOFF, SAMUEL JOHN, psychiatrist; b. Erie, Pa., Nov. 14, 1947; BS, Mansfield (Pa.) State Coll., 1969; MS, Johns Hopkins U., 1974; DO, Phila. Coll. Osteo. Medicine, 1978. Flexible intern Walter Reed Army Med. Ctr., Washington, 1978-79; resident in psychiatry Dwight David Eisenhower Army Med. Ctr., Ft. Gordon, Ga., 1981-84; officer in charge USA Health Care Clinic, Rock Island, Ill., 1980-81; divsn. psychiatrist Ft. Hood, Tex., 1984-86; pvt. practice, Pottsville, Pa., 1986-93; med. dir. counseling ctr. Good Samaritan Regional Med. Ctr., Pottsville, 1988-96, asst. med. dir., 1988-91, med. dir., 1991-94, v.p. med. affairs, 1994-97; med. dir. regional devel. Behavioral Health Ctrs., Pottsville, 1998-99; med. dir. partial hospitalization program Miners Meml. Med. Ctr., Coaldale, Pa., 1999-2001; psychiatrist Access Svcs., Orwigsburg, Pa., 1999—. Clin. cons. III Corps Drug and Alcohol Program, Ft. Hood, Tex., 1984-86; psychiat. cons. Turning Point, Pottsville, Pa., 1986-88, med. dir., 1988-91; psychiat. cons. Luzerne County MH/MR, Hazleton, Pa., 1987-88, Operation Plus Adolescent Partial Hospitalization Program, Pottsville, 1987-95. Chmn. spl. gifts com. St. Joseph Ctr. for Spl. Learning, Pottsville, 1989; bd. dirs. Good Samaritan Found., Pottsville, 1989-95, sec. 1993-95; bd. dirs. Schuylkill unit Am. Cancer Soc., 1990-91, St. Joseph's Ctr. Spl. Learning Devel. Bd., 1990-93, Mansfield Univ. Found., 1991-2002, AIDSNET, 1991-92; chair physician divsn. Schuykill United Way, Pottsville, 1994-98, e-physician online adv. bd., 2000—. Maj. M.C., U.S. Army, 1978-86. Recipient Achievement award for cmty. outreach/edn. Hosp. Assn. Pa., 1993. Fellow Am. Coll. Med. Quality (bd. cert., treas. Pa. chpt. 1993-95, sec. 1995-97, v.p. 1997-99, pres. 1999—, columnist 1996—, Disting. fellow award 1996), Am. Acad. Pain Mgmt. (bd. cert.); mem. Am. Osteo. Assn., Am. Coll. Neuropsychiatrists, Internat. Assn. Med. Specialists, Nat. Coalition Physicians Against Family Violence, Pa. Osteo. Med. Assn. (vice chmn. dist. 11 1997-98, trustee 1998—), Pa. C. of C., Schuylkill County C. of C., N.E. Pa. Regional Health Care Coalition (physician adv. com. 1998—). Home: 1759 Tall Oaks Rd Orwigsburg PA 17961-9543 Office: PO Box 254 Orwigsburg PA 17961-0254 E-mail: garloff2@pottsville.infi.net.

GARLOUGH, WILLIAM GLENN, marketing executive; b. Syracuse, N.Y., Mar. 27, 1924; s. Henry James and Gladys (Killam) G.; m. Charlotte M. Tanzer, June 15, 1947; children: Jennifer, William, Robert. BEE, Clarkson U., 1949. With Knowlton Bros., Watertown, N.Y., 1949-67, mgr. mfg. svcs., 1966-67; v.p. planning, equipment systems divsn. Vare Corp., Englewood Cliffs, N.J., 1967-69; mgr. mktg. Valley Mould divsn. Microdot Inc., Hubbard, Ohio, 1969-70; dir. corp. devel. Microdot Inc., Greenwich, Conn., 1970-73, v.p. corp. devel., 1973-76, v.p. adminstrn., 1976-77, v.p. corp. devel., 1977-78; v.p. corp. devel. Am. Bldg. Maintenance Industries, San Francisco, 1979-83; pres. The Change Agts., Inc., Walnut Creek, Calif., 1983—; bd. dirs. My Chef Inc.; mem. citizens adv. com. to Watertown Bd. Edn., 1957. Bd. dirs. Watertown Cmty. Chest, 1958-61; ruling elder Presbyn. Ch. With USMCR, 1942-46. Mem. Am. Mgmt. Assn., Inst. Mgmt. Cons. (cert.), Bldg. Svc. Contractors Assn., Internat. Sanitary Supply Assn., Mensa, Am. Mktg. Assn., TAPPI, Assn. Corp. Growth (pres. San Francisco chpt. 1984-85, v.p. chpts. west 1985-88), Lincoln League (pres. 1958), Marine's Meml. Club, Am. Contract Bridge League (life master), Clarkson Alumni Assn. (Watertown sect. pres. 1955), No. N.Y. Contract Club (pres. 1959), No. N.Y. Transp. Club, Tau Beta Pi. Office: The Change Agts Inc 2557 Via Verde Walnut Creek CA 94598-3451

GARMAN, DAVID KLINE, federal agency administrator; b. Greensboro, N.C., May 29, 1957; s. Jack Donald and Jane (Holtzclaw) G. BA in Pub. Policy, Duke U., 1979; student, Johns Hopkins U., 1995—. Legis. aide Senator Stone U.S. Senate, Washington, 1980-81, legis. asst. Senator Murkowski, 1981-85, chief of adminstrn., exec. asst., 1986-90, profl. staff mem. intelligence com., 1991-92, spl. projects dir. Sen. Murkowski, 1993-94, profl. staff subcom. energy R & D, 1995—2001; asst. secy., energy efficiency & renewable energy U.S. Dept. Energy, Washington, 2001—. Republican. Office: US Dept Energy Energy Efficiency & Renewable Energy 1000 Independance Ave SW Washington DC 20585-0001

GARMAN, RITA B. judge; b. Aurora, Ill., Nov. 19, 1943; m. Gill Garman; children: Sara Ellen, Andrew Gill. BS in econs., U. Ill., 1965; JD with distinction, U. Iowa, 1968. Asst. state atty. Vermilion County, 1969—73; pvt. practice Sebat, Swanson, Banks, Lessen & Garman, 1973; assoc. cir. judge, 1974—86; cir. judge Fifth Jud. Cir., 1986—95, presiding cir. judge, 1987—95; judge Fourth Dist. Appellate Ct., 1996—2001; Supreme Ct. justice Ill. State Supreme Ct., 2001—. Mem.: Ill. Judge's Assn., Vermilion County Bar Assn., Iowa Bar Assn., Ill. State Bar Assn. Office: 3607 N Vermilion Ste 1 Danville IL 61832

GARMAN, STEPHEN LOUIS, city manager; b. Hutchinson, Kans. s. Sherman Ross and Freda Mae Garman; m. Donna Kay Garman (div.); children: Sean, Heidi, Christian; m. Paige Garman, Nov. 14, 1999. BS, Oklahoma City U., 1966; MA, U. Okla., 1969. Asst. city mgr. City of Oklahoma City, 1970-74; city mgr. City of Westminster, Colo., 1974-78, City of Pensacola, Fla., 1978-86; pres. Govt. Credit Corp., Pensacola, 1986-99; city mgr. City of Decatur, Ill., 1999—. Mem.: Ill. City Mgrs. Assn., Internat. City Mgrs. Assn., Decatur C. of C. (bd. dirs.), Decatur Club. Avocations: scuba diving, reading. Home: 1989 W Macon Decatur IL 62522 Office: City of Decatur 1 Gary Anderson Plz Decatur IL 62523

GARMEL, MARION BESS SIMON, retired journalist; b. El Paso, Tex., Oct. 15, 1936; d. Marcus and Frieda (Alfman) Simon; m. Raymond Lewis Garmel, Nov. 28, 1965 (dec. Feb. 1986); 1 child, Cynthia Rogers; 1 stepchild, Christine Blum. Student, U. Tex., El Paso, 1954-55; BJ, U. Tex., Austin, 1958. Exec. sec. Nat. Student Assn., Phila., 1958-59, pub. rels. dir., 1960-61; sec. World Assembly Youth, Paris, Brussels, 1959-60; dictationist Wall Street Jour., Washington, 1961; libr., staff writer Nat. Observer, Silver Spring, Md., 1961-70; art critic Indpls. News, 1971-91, editor Free Time sect., 1975-91, critic radio and TV, 1991-95; theater critic Indpls. Star and News, 1995-99; television critic Indpls. News, 1995-99; theater critic Indpls. Star, 1999—2002, ret., 2002. Mem. Nat. Fedn. Press Women (1st Place Critics award 1974), Ind. Soc. Profl. Journalists (1st place criticism 2002), Hadassah Women's Zionist Orgn. Am. (life), Women's Press Club Ind. (1st Place Critics award 1995, 2002). Jewish. Avocation: tennis. Home: 226 E 45th St Indianapolis IN 46205-1712 E-mail: mgarmel@earthlink.net.

GARMENT, LEONARD, lawyer, author; b. Bklyn., May 11, 1924; s. John and Jennie Eckert G.; m. Grace Albert Garment, June 20, 1951 (dec. 1976); children: Ann Rebecca, Sara, Paul; m. Suzanne Rose Weaver, Jan. 1, 1980. LLB, Bklyn. Law Sch., 1949. Mem. Mudge Stern Williams & Tucker, N.Y.C., 1949-69; counsel, asst. Pres. Richard Nixon, Washington, 1969-74; asst. Pres. Gerald Ford, Washington, 1974; counselor UN amb. Daniel P. Moynihan & William Scranton, N.Y.C., 1975-77; U.S. rep. Commn. on Human Rights of UN Econ. and Social Coun., N.Y.C., 1975-77; mem. Dickstein Shapiro Morin & Oshinsky, Washington, 1980-93, Mudge Rose Guthrie Alexander & Ferdon, Washington, 1993-95; of counsel Verner Liipfert Bernhard McPherson & Hand, Washington, 1998—. Author: In Search of Deep Throat: The Greatest Political Mystery of our Time, 2000, Crazy Rhythm: My Journey from Brooklyn, Jazz, and Wall Street to Nixon's White House, Watergate and Beyond..., 1997. Trustee, pres. Jazz Mus. in Harlem, N.Y., 2000—; co-dir. The Willis Conover Jazz Preservation Found., Inc., Washington, 1996—; mem. Corp. of Yaddo, Saratoga Springs, 1990—. Pvt. U.S. Army, 1944. Mem. ABA, D.C. Bar Assn., Assn. of N.Y. Bar Assn., The Century Assn. Jewish. Avocation: musician. Office: Jazz Museum in Harlem 104 E 126th St New York NY 10035 Fax: 202-371-6279. E-mail: lgarment@jazzmuseuminharlem.org.

GARMER, WILLIAM ROBERT, lawyer; b. Balt., May 8, 1946; s. William M. and Grace (DeLane) G.; 1 child, Lindsey DeLane; m. Kimberly Nichols. BA, U. Ky., 1968, JD, 1975. Bar: Ky. 1975, U.S. Dist. Ct. (ea. and we. dists.) Ky. 1977, U.S. Ct. Appeals (6th cir.) 1980, U.S. Supreme Ct. 1979. Law clk. to chief judge U.S. Dist. Ct. (ea. dist.) Ky., Lexington, 1975-76; assoc. prof. law litigation skills U. Ky. Law Sch., Lexington, 1981—; ptnr. Savage, Garmer, Elliott & O'Brien, PLLC, Lexington, 1984—. Casenote editor St. Mary's Law Jour., 1974; contbr. articles to profl. jour. Elder Presbyn. Ch. With USAF, 1969-73. Fellow: Am. Coll. Trial Lawyers; mem.: ATLA (bd. govs. 1996—, chair coun. state pres. 1995), ABA, Ky. Acad. Trial Attys. (bd. govs. 1984—89, treas. 1990, sec. 1991, v.p. 1992, pres. 1994, named Ky. Trial Lawyer of Yr. 1998), Fayette County Bar Assn., Ky. Bar Assn. (com. on specialization and cert. 1982—, litigation com. 1989—), Phi Delta Phi (named One of Best Lawyers in Am. 1989—). Democrat. Office: Savage Garmer Elliot & O'Brien PLLC 141 N Broadway St Lexington KY 40507-1230 E-mail: bgarmer@sgelaw.com.

GARMISE, DAVID BRUCE, otolaryngologist, educator; b. N.Y.C., Mar. 1, 1935; AB in History, U. N.C., 1956, MD, 1960. Intern Beth Israel Hosp., N.Y.C., 1960-61; resident gen. surgery Bronx VA Hosp., 1961-62, resident ear, nose and throat, 1962-65; pvt. practice Ruhway, N.J., 1967-92; chief Ear Nose and Throat dept. The Rahway Hosp., 1969-92; med. dir. Hospice for the Low County, Hilton Head Island, SC, 1993—2001; ret. Assoc. clin. prof. NJCMD-Rutgers, 1972-92. Capt. U.S. Army, 1965-67. Fellow Am. Acad. Otolaryngology-Head and Neck Surgery. Home and Office: 104 Lancy Ct New Bern NC 28562-8968

GARMON, LANCE C. psychology educator; b. Hugoton, Kans., Dec. 23, 1967; BA, Washburn U., 1990; PhD, Ohio State U., 1999. Asst. prof. Ohio State U., Newark, 1999—. Office: Ohio State Univ 1179 University Dr Newark OH 43055

GARMONG, ROBERT ALLEN, philosophy educator; b. Akron, Ohio, Mar. 10, 1969; s. John Richard and Janis Rowley Garmong. BA in Econs. and Polit. Sci., U. Chgo., 1991; PhD in Philosophy, U. Tex., 2002. Adj. prof. Pace U., Pleasantville, NY, 1995—96, S.W. Tex. State U., San Marcos, 1997—99, Huston-Tillotsen Coll., Austin, Tex., 1999—2000; asst. instr. U. Tex., Austin, 2001—. Mem.: Am. Philos. Assn. Office: U Tex 316 Waggener Hall Austin TX 78712

GARN, STANLEY MARION, physical anthropologist, educator; b. New London, Conn., Oct. 27, 1922; s. Harry and Sadie Edith (Cohen) G.; m. Priscilla Crozier, Apr. 8, 1950; children: Barbara, William David. AB, Harvard U., 1942, AM, 1947, PhD, 1948. Rsch. assoc. chem. engring. Chem. Warfare Svc. Devel. Lab. MIT, 1942-44; tech. editor Polaroid Co., 1944-46; cons. applied anthropology, 1946-47; rsch. fellow cardiology Mass. Gen. Hosp., Boston, 1946-52; instr. anthropology Harvard U., 1948-52; anthropologist Forsyth Dental Infirmary, Boston, 1947-52; dir. Forsyth face size project Army Chem. Corps, 1950-52; chmn. dept. growth and genetics Fels Rsch. Inst., Yellow Springs, Ohio, 1952-68; fellow Ctr. Human Growth and Devel. U. Mich., Ann Arbor, also prof. nutrition and anthropology, 1968-92, prof. emeritus, 1993—. Raymond Pearl lectr. Human Biol. Coun., 1992—; E.B.D. Neuhauser lectr. Soc. Pediatric Radiology, 1981. Author: Human Races, 1970, Gain and Loss of Cortical Bone, 1970; also contbr. over 1000 articles to profl. jours.; editorial bds. numerous jours. Recipient Disitng. Svc. award, U. Mich., Charles Darwin Lifetime Achievement award, Am. Assn. Phys. Anthropologists, 1994, Franz Boas award, Human Biol. Coun., 2002. Fellow AAAS, Am. Acad. Pediatrics (hon. assoc.), Am. Anthropol. Assn., Am. Acad. Arts and Scis., Human Biology Coun., Am. Soc. Clin. Nutrition, Am. Soc. Nutrition Scis.; mem. NAS, Am. Assn. Phys. Anthropologists, Internat. Assn. Dental Rsch., Internat. Orgn. Study Human Devel., Am. Soc. Naturalists, Internat. Assn. Human Biologists (coun.). Office: U Mich Ctr Human Growth & Devel 300 N Ingalls St Ann Arbor MI 48109-2007 Home: 1200 Earhart Rd #223 Ann Arbor MI 48105-2566

GARNAR, MARTIN LUTHER, librarian; b. Huntington, N.Y., Oct. 22, 1971; s. Richard Luther and Joan Doreen Garnar; life ptnr. Edward Dennis Scholz, June 25, 1994. M of Libr. and Info. Svcs., U. Denver, 2000; MA in History, SUNY at Binghamton, 1995, BA in History and Geography, 1993. Reference libr. Dayton Meml. Libr. Regis U., Denver, 1999—. Chair, intellectual freedom com. Colo. Assn. of Libraries, Wheat Ridge, Colo., 2000—. Contbr. Mem.: ALA (chair, Eli M. Oboler book award com. 2002—), Phi Beta Kappa. Democrat. Unitarian Universalist. Home: 4563 Beach Ct Denver CO 80211 Office: Regis University Mail Stop D-20 3333 Regis Blvd Denver CO 80221-1099 Office Fax: 303-964-5497. E-mail: mgarnar@regis.edu.

GARNER, ALBERT HEADDEN, investment banker; b. Memphis, Dec. 17, 1955; s. Jesse B. Jr. and Noella (Headden) Garner; m. Wanatha Porter, July 2, 1977; children: Cyrus Dalton, Shelby Harris, Pleasant Noel. BS in Engring., Princeton U., 1977. Assoc. Devel. and Resources Corp., N.Y.C., 1977-79, Lazard Freres & Co., N.Y.C., 1979-83, v.p., 1984-88; gen. ptnr. Lazard Freres & Co. LLC, N.Y.C., 1989-95, mng. dir., 1995—. Elder 1st Presbyn. Ch., N.Y.C.; bd. dirs. Prospect Park Alliance. Home: 1510 Albemarle Rd Brooklyn NY 11226-4506 Office: Lazard Freres & Co LLC 30 Rockefeller Plz Fl 59 New York NY 10112-5900

GARNER, BRYAN ANDREW, law educator, consultant, writer; b. Lubbock, Tex., Nov. 17, 1958; s. Gary Thomas and Mariellen (Griffin) G.; m. Pan Anurugsa, May 26, 1984; children: Caroline Beatrix, Alexandra Bess. BA, U. Tex., 1980, JD, 1984; LLD (hon.), Thomas M. Cooley Law Sch., 2000. Bar: Tex. 1984, U.S. Ct. Appeals (5th cir.) 1985, U.S. Dist. Ct. (no. dist.) Tex. 1986. Law clk. to judge U.S. Ct. Appeals (5th cir.), Austin, Tex., 1984-85; assoc. Carrington, Coleman, Sloman & Blumenthal, Dallas, 1985-88; dir. Tex./Oxford Ctr. for Legal Lexicography U. Tex. Sch. Law, Austin, 1988-90; adj. prof. law So. Meth. U., Dallas, 1990—. Vis. assoc. prof. law U. Tex., 1988—90; pres. LawProse, Inc., 1990—; vis. scholar U. Salzburg, 1995, 98, U. Glasgow, 1996, U. Cambridge, England, 1997; chmn. plain-lang. com. State Bar Tex., 1989—95; lectr. in field; cons. in field. Author: A Dictionary of Modern Legal Usage, 1987, A Dictionary of Modern Legal Usage, 2d edit., 1995, The Elements of Legal Style, 1991, Guidelines for Drafting and Editing Court Rules, 1996, A Dictionary of Modern American Usage, 1998, Securities Disclosure in Plain English, 1999, The Winning Bried, 1999, Legal Writing in Plain English, 2001, The Redbook: A Manual on Legal Style, 2002; editor: Scribes Jour. Legal Writing, 1989—2000, Tex, Our Texas, 1984, Black's Law Dictionary, 1996, Black's Law Dictionary, 7th edit., 1999, A Handbook of Basic Law Terms, 1999; A Handbook of Business Law Terms, 1999; editor: A Handbook of Family Law Terms, 2001; mem. editl. bd.: Tex. Law Rev., 1984; contbr. articles to profl. jours. Recipient Henry C. Lind award, Assn. Reporters

Judicial Decisions, 1994, Clarity award, State Bar Mich, 1997, Outstanding Young Tex. Ex. award, 1998. Fellow: Tex. Bar Found.; mem.: ABA, Tex. Bar Assn. (chmn. plain lang. com. 1990—), Am. Law Inst. (commn. on bylaws & coun. rules 1993—94), Scribes (exec. bd. 1990—2001, pres. 1997—98), Dictionary Soc. N.Am., Am. Dialect Soc., Philos. Soc. Tex., Friars (abbot 1981—84), Bent Tree Country Club, Phi Beta Kappa. Republican. Avocation: golf. Home: 6478 Lakehurst Ave Dallas TX 75230-5131

GARNER, CARLENE ANN, fundraising consultant; b. Dec. 17, 1945; d. Carl A. and Ruth E. (Mathison) Timblin; m. Adelbert L. Garner, Feb. 17, 1964; children: Bruce A., Brent A. BA, U. Puget Sound, 1983. Adminstrv. dir. Balletacoma, 1984-87; exec. dir. Tacoma Symphony, 1987-95; prin. New Horizon Cons., Tacoma, 1995-98; co-owner Stewardship Devel., 1998—. Cons. Wash. PAVE, Tacoma, 1983-84. Treas. Coalition for the Devel. of the Arts, 1992-94; pres. Wilson High Sch. PTA, Tacoma, 1983-85; chmn. Tacoma Sch. Vol. Adv. Bd., 1985-87; pres. Emmanuel Luth. Ch., Tacoma, 1984-86, chmn. future steering com., 1987-93; sec.-treas. Tacoma-Narrows Conf., 1987-98; vice chmn. Tacoma Luth. Home, 1996-98; pub. mem. Wash. State Bd. Pharmacy, 1993-98. Mem. N.W. Devel. Officers Assn. (chair Tacoma/Pierce County com. 1994-96), Jr. Women's Club Tacoma (pres. 1975-76, pres. Peninsula dist. 1984-86), Gen. Fedn. Women's Club-Wash. State (treas. 1988-90, 3d v.p. 1990-92, 2d v.p. 1992-94, 1st v.p. 1994-96, pres. 1996-98, Clubwoman of Yr. 1977, Outstanding FREE chmn. Gen. Fedn. 1982), Commencement Bay Woman's Club (pres. 1990-92), Gen. Fedn. of Women's Club (bd. dirs., chair nat. conv. 1995, state pres. 1996-98, chair cmty. improvement program 1998-2000, treas. 2000—02, recording sec. 2002-). Lutheran. E-mail: cagarner@mindspring.com.

GARNER, CHARLES WILLIAM, educational administration educator, consultant; b. Pine Grove Mills, Pa., Apr. 18, 1939; s. Adam Krumrine and Blanche Ella (Gearhart) G.; m. Karyl J. Packer, Sept. 8, 1962; children: Ronald Adam, Juliet Paige. Student, U.S. Navy Electronics Airborne Sonar Sch., 1959; BS in Bus. Edn., Pa. State U., 1965, MEd in Higher Edn. Adminstrn., 1968, EdD in Vocat. Indsl. Edn., 1974. Cert. govt. fin. mgr. Adminstrv. asst. dept. psychology Pa. State U., 1965-75; asst. prof., site adminstr. March AFB, Calif. for So. Ill. U., 1975-77; asst. prof., coordinator Ft. Knox Ctr.- U. Louisville, 1977-78; assoc. prof., acting vice dean Rutgers U., Camden, N.J., 1978-79, assoc. prof. urban edn., chmn. dept. edn. Univ. Coll. New Brunswick, N.J., 1978-81, assoc. prof. vocat. tech. edn. Grad. Sch. Edn., 1981—, chmn. dept. vocat. tech. edn., 1982-85, assoc. prof. edn. adminstrn., 1985—, exec. dir. Vocat. Edn. Resource Ctr., 1983-88, dir. continuing edn., 1987-89, program chair edn. adminstrn., 1990-96; cons. CWG Assocs., McElhattan, Pa., 1989—; pres. Penn State Auto Repair, Inc., Williamsport, Pa., 1997-2000. Author: Accounting and Budgeting in Public and Nonprofit Organizations: A Manager's Guide, 1991, Financial Management of School Districts in New Jersey: For School Leaders, 1996, Education Finance for School Leaders: Strategic Planning and Administration, 2004; contbr. articles to profl. jours.; co-editor: Occupational Edn. Forum, 1979-85; editl. reader Jour. Indsl. Tchr. Edn., 1981; producer, host talk show pilot for pub. TV, 1979; producer, host: TV tape series Rutgers U.: Current Issues in Vocat. Edn., 1979; editor edn. sect. Pub. Budgeting and Financial Management, 1995. Bd. dirs., treas. Cerebral Palsy League of Union County, N.J., 1996-99. With USN, 1959-62. Grantee N.J. Dept. Edn. Divsn. Vocat. Edn., 1978-88; grantee HEW, 1979-80. Mem.: AAUP, DAV (life), Nat. Soc. for Study of Edn., Spl. Needs Pers. (exec. coun. 1980—81, pres. 1981—82), Assn. Govt. Accts., Am. Edn. Rsch. Assn., Non-Commd. Officers Assn. (life), Elks (exalted ruler 1972—73), Epsilon Pi Tau (trustee 1983—88), Omicron Tau Theta, Phi Delta Kappa. Home: PO Box 456 Mc Elhattan PA 17748 Office: Rutgers U Dept Ednl Theory Admin New Brunswick NJ 08903 E-mail: wgarner@rci.rutgers.edu. *Our influence in life is determined by the good deeds we do rather than by the emotions that we feel.*

GARNER, DORIS TRAGANZA, educator; b. Phila., Oct. 13, 1934; d. Charles Thomas and Elizabeth Marie (Blatteau) Traganza; m. Joseph Anthony DeMatteo, Apr. 12, 1958 (dec. Aug. 1968); children: Maria Louise, Carol Ann, Nicholas Joseph, Elizabeth Joan, Charles Traganza, Ann Seton; m. Doyle Daniel Garner, July 11, 1970 (div. Feb. 1989); 1 child: Jean Estelle. Student in piano with, Leo Ornstein, Phila., 1948—54; BA in Psychology cum laude, U. Pa., 1955; postgrad., Temple U., 1955-59; MS in Ednl. Adminstrn., SUNY, Albany, 1978, PhD in Ednl. Adminstrn. and Higher Edn., 1983. Cert. tchr., N.Y. Elem. tchr. Phila. Sch. Dist., 1955-59; asst. to asst. dean grad. studies SUNY, Albany, 1977-78, asst. to asst. v.p. acad. affairs, 1979; curriculum rsch. assoc. John Jay Coll., CUNY, N.Y.C., 1979; asst. in higher edn. doctoral office N.Y. State Edn. Dept., Albany, 1979-84, coord. program rev. master's programs, 1985-87, assoc. in higher edn. coll./univ. evaluation, 1987-89, asst. to dep. commr. higher edn. and professions, 1989-95, divsn. dir. coll./univ. evaluation, 1995-96, staff dir. N.Y. State Regents Task Force on Tchg., 1996-98, supr. acad. program rev., 1998—2002; supr. higher edn. N.Y. State Edn. Dept., 2002—; conf. panelist on preparing tchrs. to use technology, 2002. Featured spkr. CUNY conf. on tchr. edn. reform, 2000, NYACTE/NYSATE conf. on tchr. edn., 2001, plenary spkr., 2003; expert witness for plaintiffs, Campaign for Fiscal Equity v. N.Y. State, 1999; invited participant Inaugural Portfolio Conf., Annenberg Inst. for Sch. Reform, Boston, 1998; chair session on state policy Am. Assn. Colls. for Tchr. Edn., New Orleans, 1988; plenary session panelist on tchg. reform Edn. Conf. of Empire State Reports, 1998; presenter in field. Editor (manuscript) Regents College: The Early Years by D.J. Nolan, 1998. Mem. Shaker H.S. Theater Support, Latham, N.Y., 1988-89; pianist at non-profit functions, Albany, N.Y., 1992-94; cmty. theater actor Stagecrafters, Phila., 1951. Avocations: grandchildren and children, reading on social and political issues, piano, plays, concerts, nature.

GARNER, DOUGLAS, music educator; s. Don and Katie Garner. BS in Music Edn., Pa. State U., 1997. Cert. K-12 music, chorus, band, orch. Music educator, choral dir. Mifflin County Sch. Dist., Lewistown, Pa., 1997—. Mem.: Pa. Music Educators Assn., Am. Choral Dirs. Assn. Office: Indian Valley Mid Sch 125 Kish Rd Reedsville PA 17084

GARNER, FRADLEY HAMILTON, freelance writer, editor, narrator; b. Potsdam, N.Y., June 20, 1926; s. L. Hamilton and Geneva Van Bergen Garner; children: Luke, Glen, Nicholas. Pregrad, 24th Corps U., Seoul Korea, 1946; BS in Psychology, St. Lawrence U., Canton, N.Y., 1950; MA in Cultural Anthropology, Colgate U., Hamilton, N.Y., 1970; postgrad., SUNY, Potsdam, 1950, Northwestern U., Evanston, Ill., 1951. Divsnl. pub. rels. mgr. Pfizer, Inc., N.Y.C., 1955-60. Author: Environment Denmark, 1972, Walt Disney's Donald Duck's Fritidsbok, 1976, Greenland: Arctic Denmark, 1977, Jakobshavn/Ilulissat: A Town in Greenland, 1977, Walt Disney's The Haunted Hotel, 1978; co-founder, editor Scoot mag., 1955; assoc. editor Family Health mag., 1969; internat. editor, columnist Ecology Today, 1971-72, Environment mag., 1973-77; editor: TMI World, 1988; chief translator, copy editor: Danish Music Rev., 1994-95, Katalog, the Danish Jour. Photography and Video; appeared in film The Prince of Jutland, 1994; country editor, writer Insight Guide Denmark, 2000—; covered Denmark's dogsled patrol Sirius in No. Greenland for Internat. Edits. Reader's Digest; Nordic-Tanganyika project in Dar es Salaam, Tanzania for Scanorama mag.; Denmark contbr. DownBeat, Jersey Jazz, 2000-; contbr. numerous articles to profl. jours. and gen. mags.; narrator over 500 indsl., sci. and gen. documentary films and videos; bassist Copenhagen Symphony Orch., 1995-. Bd. dirs. HOF Internat. Edn. Program, 2000—. Named Denmark amateur Runner of Yr., (Aarets Eremitageløber), 1995. Mem. Fgn. Press Assn. in Denmark. Home: Ordruphøjvej 32 DK-2920 Charlottenlund Denmark Fax: +45-3964-1315 . E-mail: fradgar@get2net.dk.

GARNER, HARVEY LOUIS, computer scientist, consultant, electrical engineering educator; b. Lake, Colo., Dec. 23, 1926; s. Homa and Violet (Thuelin) G.; m. Yvonne Lillian King, Aug. 7, 1949; children-Susan Ann, Harvey Thomas. BS, U. Denver, 1949, MS, 1951; PhD, U. Mich., 1958. Engr. with devel. MIDAC and MIDSAC computers U. Mich., 1951-55, instr. elec. engring., 1955-58, asst. prof., 1958-60, assoc. prof., 1960-63, prof., 1963-70; dir. Information Systems Lab., 1960-64, Systems Engring. Lab., 1964-66, acting chmn. dept. communications scis., 1965-67, prof. computer and communications scis., 1967-70; prof. elec. engring. Moore Sch. Elec. Engring., 1970-86, dir., 1970-76, Microelectronics and Computer Tech. Corp., Austin, 1984-88; cons. in system design and computer arithmetic, 1988—. Gen. chmn. 1st Nat. Computer Conf. and Exhbn., N.Y.C., 1973; gen. chmn. Islands Applications Conf., Tokyo, Japan, 1972 Contbr. articles to profl. jours. Served with USNR, 1945-46. Fellow IEEE; mem. Assn. Computing Machinery (apptd. nat. lectr. 1965), AAAS, Am. Assn. Artificial Intelligence, Sigma Xi, Eta Kappa Nu, Sigma Pi Sigma. Home and Office: 7400 Rockberry Cv Austin TX 78750-7920

GARNER, JAY MONTGOMERY, former career officer; b. Arcadia, Fla., Apr. 15, 1938; s. James Harley and Consuello Adelaide (Pooser) G.; m. Mary Connie Kreigh, Dec 30, 1958; 1 child, Lori Lee Gibson. BA, Fla. State U., 1962; MA, Shippensburg U., 1983; attended, Air Defense Artillery Sch., Marine Corps. Command and Staff Coll., US Army War Coll., US Army Air Defense Sch., Ft. Bliss, Tex., 1962, Defense Lang. Inst., SW br., Ft. Bliss, 1966-67, Air Defense Artillery Officer Advanced Course, US Army Air Defense Sch., 1969, Vietnam Tng. Ctr. Fgn. Svc. Inst., Dept. State, Washington, 1970-71, Marine Corps. Command and Staff Coll., Quantico, Va., 1974-75, US Army War Coll. Carlisle Barracks, Pa., 1982-83. With Fla. Nat. Guard; enlisted USMC; commd. 2d lt. US Army, 1962, advanced through grades to lt. gen., 1994, asst. platoon leader to platoon leader to exec. officer, Battery C, 3d Missile Battalion, 7th Artillery, US Army Europe, 1962-64, inactive Army Nat. Guard, 1964 65, ops. officer 53d Artillery Brigade, 1965-66, asst. subsector advisor, later dep. dist. sr. advisor adv. team 38, military assistance command, 1967-68, comdr. Battery B, 5th Battalion, 7th Artillery, US Army Air Defense Commd., 1968, chief, programs br., logistics divsn., office mil. assistance, US Army Southern Commd. Ft. Amador, Canal Zone, 1969-70, dist. sr. advisor, adv. team 36, military assistance commd., 1971-72, S-3, then plans, tng. officer, reserve component study, later S-3, 1st Battalion, 3d Air Defense Artillery, 101st Airborne Divsn. (Airmobile), 1972-74, staff officer, firepower divsn., requirements directorate, later asst. exec. officer, office dept. chief staff ops. Washington, 1975-78, comdr. 1st Basic Combat Tng. Battalion, tng. and doctrine command, 1978-79, comdr. 2d Battalion, 59th Air Defense Artillery, 1st Armored Division, US Army Europe, 1979-81, comdr. 108th Air Defense Artillery Brigade, 32d Army Air Defense Command, US Army Europe, 1984-86, dir. force requirements (combat support systems) office of dep. chief of staff ops. and plans, 1986-88, dep. commdg. gen. US Army Air Defense Artillery Ctr., asst. commandant US Army Air Defense Artillery Sch. Ft. Bliss, 1988-90, dep. commdg. gen. V Corps. US Army Europe, 7th Army, 1990-91, commdg. gen. joint task force BRAVO, 1991, asst. dep. chief staff ops. and plans force devel. Office of Dep. Chief of Staff Ops. and Plans, 1992-94; commdg. gen. U.S. Army Space and Strategic Def. Command, 1994-96; asst. vice chief of staff U.S. Army, 1996-97; ret., 1997; dir. Office of Reconstruction and Humanitarian Assistance, 2003. Pres. SY Tech. (now SYColeman Corp.), 1997—2003. Decorated DSM with oak leaf cluster, Def. Superior Svc. Medal with oak leaf cluster, Legion of Merit with 4 oak leaf clusters, Bronze Star, Air medal, Meritorious Svc. Medal, Joint Svc. Commendation Medal, Army Commendation Medal, Combat Infantryman Badge, Parachutist Badge, Army Staff Identification Badge. Democrat. Episcopalian. Avocations: health, fitness.*

GARNER, JIM D. state official; b. Coffeyville, Kans., June 14, 1963; s. Wayne W. and Carol L. Garner. AA with honors, Coffeyville C.C., 1983; BA in History with distinction, U. Kans., 1985, JD, 1988. Bar: Kans. 1988, U.S. Dist. Ct. Kans. 1988, U.S. Ct. Appeals (10th cir.) 1990, U.S. Supreme Ct. 2003. Jud. clk. for Dale E. Saffels U.S. Dist. Judge, Kans., 1988-90; atty. Hall, Levy, Lively, DeVore, Belot and Bell, Coffeyville, 1990-92; pvt. practice Coffeyville, 1992—; mem. Kans. Ho. of Reps., 1991—2003, minority leader, 1999—2003; sec. Kans. Dept. Human Resources, 2003—. Mem. assembly on fed. issues Nat. Conf. of State Legislatures; mem. Program for Emerging Polit. Leaders, Darden Sch. of Bus., U. Va., 1994, Bowhay Inst. for Legis. Leadership Devel., Coun. of State Govts., U. Wis., 1995. Active cmty. co-chair, City of Coffeyville's Youth Focus Task Force, 1998; adv. com. Youth and Bus. Tng. Program; bd. dirs. Hospice Care Inc., Coffeyville, 1993-97, Pioneer chpt. ARC, 1998—; mem. task force Coffeyville C.C. Honors Program, 1998—; leadership Coffeyville Class of 1995; mem. legis. adv. bd. Dem. Leadership Coun., 1999-2002; mem. bd. govs. U. Kans. Law Sch., 2000-02. Mem. Kans. Bar Assn., Order of Coif, Phi Alpha Theta, Phi Kappa Phi, Lions, Rotary. Home: 902A Lewark St Coffeyville KS 67337-3108 Office: PO Box 538 114 W 9th St Coffeyville KS 67337-5810

GARNER, JO ANN STARKEY, retired elementary and special education educator; b. Ft. Hamilton, N.Y., Dec. 25, 1934; d. Joseph Wheeler and Irene Dorothy (Vogt) Starkey; m. James Gayle Garner, Mar. 2, 1957; children: Mary Vivian Pine, Margaret Susan Gillis, Kathryn Lynn. BA in History, Govt., Law, U. Tex., Austin, 1956; postgrad., Trinity U., 1973. Cert. deaf edn. and elem. tchr., Tex. Kindergarten tchr. Platenstrasse Internat. Sch., Frankfurt, Fed. Republic Germany, 1964-66; tchr. of deaf Sunshine Cottage Sch. for Deaf, San Antonio, 1966-2000; ret., 2000. Speech cons. Trinity U., 1978, cooperating tchr., 1978-87; fiesta coord. Sunshine Cottage. Active San Antonio Fiesta Commn., Poweshiek County Iowa Geneal. Soc.; chmn. book com. San Antonio Geneal. and Hist. Soc. Mem. Tex. (charter) and Nat. Alexander Graham Bell Assn., Tex. State Geneal. and Hist. Soc., Rep. Nat. Com., German-Texan Heritage Soc., Pioneers of Ind., Olde Mecklenburg Geneal. Soc. N.C., Pioneers of Ill., Ill. Geneal. Soc., Madison County (Ill.) Geneal. Soc., Tex. Pioneers, Alpha Delta Pi. Republican. Mem. Catholic Episcopal Ch. Avocations: writing, painting, history, genealogical research, science. Home: 2027 Edgehill Dr San Antonio TX 78209-2023

GARNER, JULIE LOWREY, occupational therapist; b. Paris, Tex., Aug. 6, 1953; d. John Robert and Rachel (Garner) Lowrey; m. Kenneth Wayne Garner, Jan. 29, 1983. BS, U. Tex., Galveston, 1975; MS, Tex. Woman's U., 1982; MEd, Tex. A&M U., Commerce, 2001. Cert. occupational therapist, Tex.; cert. to administer and interpret So. Calif. Sensory Integration Tests Sensory Integration Internat., neurodevel. treatment approach to cerebral palsy. Occupational therapist Presbyn. Hosp. Dallas, 1976-77; occupational therapist region X Ednl. Svc. Ctr., Richardson, Tex., 1977; occupational therapist Duncanville (Tex.) Ind. Sch. Dist., 1977-81, 89-90, Grand Prairie (Tex.) Ind. Sch. Dist., 1978-81, U. Tex., Dallas, 1981-83, Lewisville (Tex.) Ind. Sch. Dist., 1983-85, Collin County Coop. Spl. Svcs., Wylie, Tex., 1983-89, Commerce (Tex.) Ind. Sch. Dist., 1990-97, M.J. Care, Gunter, Tex., 1997-99. Bd. dirs. United Cerebral Palsy Assn. Dallas, 1980-84. Recipient Hurdle Cert. of Honor Soroptimist Internat., Dallas, 1976. Mem. Am. Occuptl. Therapy Assn. Methodist. Avocations: sewing, arts and crafts, computers. Home: 1313 Flameleaf Dr Allen TX 75002-4424

GARNER, JUNE BROWN, journalist; b. Detroit, July 19, 1923; d. Simpson and Vela (Wilkerson) Malone; m. Warren C. Garner, June 28, 1961; 1 dau., Sylvia G. Mustonen. Student, Wayne State U., 1941. Columnist, classified advt. mgr. Mich. Chronicle, Detroit, 1945-74; columnist Detroit News, 1974-87, Mich. Chronicle, 1990-92; CFO Warren Garner Realty, Southfield, Mich., 1992-96; reading tchr. North Tazewell (Va.) Elem. Sch., 1996—. Author: June Brown's Guide to Let's Read, 1981, June Brown's Tool Kit, 2000. Founder The Let's Read Summer Sch., 1980—. Recipient Best Column awards Detroit Press Club, 1971, 72, Nat. Newspaper Pubs. Assn., 1968, 69, Sch. Bell award Mich. Edn., Assn., 1989, Am. Promise award, 1999, Tazewell County Pub. Sch. award, 1998. Mem. S.W. Va. Reading Coun. Methodist. Home: 107 Vernon Ave Tazewell VA 24651-1432 E-mail: june_garner@hotmail.com.

GARNER, MARY COX, not-for-profit developer; b. Memphis, Tenn., Nov. 12, 1937; d. Allen Cox, Jr. and Hortense Beare Cox; m. Sanford Garner, Jr., Apr. 30, 1960; children: Sanford III, James Allen, Robert Reiney. BA in Religion and English, Randolph Macon Women's Coll., 1959; MA in Clin. Psychology, Goddard Coll., 1975; JD, George Mason Law Sch., 1980; LLM in Internat. Law with highest honors, George Washington U., 1985. Bar: D.C. 1982. Tchr. grades 3-5 Arlington Pub. Sch., Memphis, 1959—61; counselor, therapist Georgetown U., Washington, 1975—80; advisor U.S. Trade Rep., Washington, 1985—87; with office of gen. counsel Arms Control Disarmament Agy., Washington, 1987—89; v.p. Hope Inc. Found., Washington, 1989—. Adv. bd. Inst. for Mental Health, Washington, 1980—, Found. for Conscious Evolution, Santa Barbara, Calif., 1999—. Founder Coop. Cir. United Religions Initiative, Washington, 1996—. Mem.: Soc. Am. Poets, Am. Soc. Internat. Law, Writer's Ctr. Episcopalian. Avocations: writing, reading, mentoring, walking, teaching. Home: 3316 R St NW Washington DC 20007 Office: Hope Inc 3316 R St NW Washington DC 20007

GARNER, PAUL TRANTHAM, auditor; b. Cameron, Tex., May 25, 1951; s. W.H. and Dorothy L. (Gohmert) G.; m. Tatyana Tokareva; children: Paul Christopher, Gregory Trantham, Michael Nickolas. BBA, U. Tex., 1973; MS in Bus. Adminstrn., U. No. Colo., 1980. Cert. systems profl. Engr. Tex. Instruments, Inc., Austin, 1980; mgr. performance audit divsn. State of Tex. Auditor's Office, Austin, 1980-95; dir. data svcs. Tex. Workers Compensation Commn., Austin, 1995-98; info. tech. cons. Audit Force, Inc., Dallas, 1998-2000; asst. city auditor City of Dallas. Asst. city auditor City of Dallas; mem. faculty Austin C.C., 1982; seminar lectr. in field. Mem. Bergstrom-Austin Community Coun. Lt. col. U.S. Army, 1973-99. U.S. Army ednl. scholar, 1969. Mem. Assn. for Systems Mgmt. (pres.), Am. Evaluation Assn., Legis. Prog. Evaluation Soc., Tex. Assn. State Sys. for Computing and Comms. (treas.), Austin Endowment Soc. (bd. dirs.), Austin Bus. Club., Rotary. Avocations: numismatics, scuba diving. Home: 2108 Bishop Dr Flower Mound TX 75028-2142 Office: City Auditor's Office 1500 Marilla 2FN Dallas TX 75201

GARNER, PHIL, former professional baseball manager; b. Jefferson City, Tenn., Apr. 30, 1949; m. Carol; children: Eric, Bethany, Ty. BS, U. Tenn., Knoxville, 1973. Profl. baseball player Oakland Athletics, 1973-76, Pitts. Pirates, 1977-81, Houston Astros, 1981-87, L.A. Dodgers, 1987, San Francisco Giants, 1988; coach Houston Astros, 1989-91; mgr. Milw. Brewers, 1991-99, Detroit Tigers, 1999—2002. Named to All-Star team, 1976, 80, 81. Office: Detroit Tigers 2100 Woodward Ave Detroit MI 48201-3474

GARNER, RICHARD KEITH, classicist, educator; b. Tahlequah, Okla., Mar. 6, 1953; s. Willard Eugene Garner and Marianne (Aingworth) Gifford. BA in Slavic Lang./Lit. summa cum laude, Princeton U., 1975; MA in Slavic Langs. & Lits., Harvard U., 1976; MA, U. Chgo., 1980, PhD in Classics, 1983. Jr. fellow Harvard Soc. Fellows, Cambridge, Mass., 1980-83; asst. prof. Yale U., New Haven, 1983-88, assoc. prof., 1988-93, Olin faculty fellow, 1993-94; dean Hons. Coll. Adelphi U., Garden City, N.Y., 1994—. Dir. grad. studies classics dept. Yale U., 1990-91, head of instrn. for classical langs. Summer Lang. Inst., 1991-93, mem. Yale U. com. on fgn. lang. instrn., 1992-93, exec. com., 1990-91, exec. com. on programs in humanities, 1989-90, ad hoc com. on teaching in Yale Coll., 1988 89, teaching & learning com., 1986. Author: Law and Society in Classical Athens, 1987, From Homer to Tragedy: The Art of Allusion in Greek Poetry, 1990; contbr. articles and revs. to profl. jours. Humanities fellow U. Chgo., 1976-79; recipient Yale Coll.-Sidonie Miskimin Clauss prize for teaching excellence in humanities, 1986, Sarai Ribicoff award for encouragement of teaching, 1986, Heyman prize for jr. faculty rsch., 1986, William Clyde DeVane medal for disting. scholarship & teaching Yale Coll., 1992; Morse fellow, 1987-88; NEH summer rsch. stipend grantee, 1990; elected Loeb lectr., 1994. Mem. Am. Philological Assn. Home: 429 Terrace Ave Garden City NY 11530-5427 also: 45 Brompton Rd Garden City NY 11530 E-mail: garner@adelphi.edu.

GARNER, ROBERT EDWARD LEE, lawyer; b. Bowling Green, Ky., Sept. 26, 1946; s. Alto Luther and Katie Mae (Sanders) G.; m. Suzanne Marie Searles, Aug. 22, 1981; children: Jessica Marie, Abigail Lee. BA, U. Ala., Tuscaloosa, 1968; JD, Harvard U., 1971. Bar: Ga. 1971, U.S. Dist. Ct. (no. dist.) Ga. 1974, U.S. Ct. Appeals (5th cir.) 1974, U.S. Ct. Appeals (11th cir.) 1981, Ala. 1982, U.S. Ct. Appeals (4th cir.) 1991, S.C. 1992. Assoc. Gambrell, Russell & Forbes, Atlanta, 1972-76, ptnr., 1976-80, Haskell, Slaughter & Young and predecessors, Birmingham, Ala., 1981-88, mng. ptnr., 1986-87, of counsel, 1988-90; gen. counsel, sec. Builders Transport, Inc., 1988-90; ptnr. Nelson, Mullins, Riley & Scarborough, Atlanta and Columbia, S.C., 1991-96; mem. Haskell Slaughter Young & Rediker, LLC, Birmingham, 1996—, mng. ptnr., 2000—02. 1st lt. JAGC, USAF, 1971-72. Mem. ABA (com. on fed. regulation of securities, subcom. on disclosure matters and continuous reporting, ad hoc com. on pub. co. info. practices), State Bar Ga., Ala. State Bar, Birmingham Bar, S.C. Bar, U. Ala. Alumni Assn., Harvard U. Alumni Assn., Am. Soc. Corp. Secs. (mem. tech. com.), Phi Alpha Theta, Pi Sigma Alpha. Republican. Home: 284 Kings Crest Ln Pelham AL 35124-2846 Office: Haskell Slaughter Young & Rediker LLC 2001 Park Pl North Ste 1400 Birmingham AL 35203-2618 E-mail: relg@hsy.com.

GARNER, STEVEN C. emergency physician; m. Anne Garner; 2 children. Grad., Chgo. Med. Sch. Diplomate Am. Bd. Radiology, Am. Bd. Emergency Physicians. Chief med. officer St. Vincent Hosp. & Med. Ctr., NY; sr. v.p. St. Vincent Cath. Med. Ctrs.; intern Brookdale Med. Ctr., Bklyn.; asst. prof. radiology N.Y. Med. Coll. Cons. N.Y.P.D; cons. U.S. customs dept. N.Y. JFK Internat. Airport; fellow Am. Acad. of Emergency Physicians. Mem.: Am. Coll. of Radiology (nat. emergency radiology com.), Am. Heart Assn. (edn. com.). Office: 88-25 153 Rd St Jamaica NY 11432

GARNETT, GRIFFIN TAYLOR, lawyer, writer; b. Washington, Aug. 15, 1914; s. Griffin Taylor and Susie Lee (Crump) G.; m. Harriet Waddy Brooke, Sept. 21, 1938; children: Griffin Taylor III, Thomas Brooke. BA, U. Richmond, 1936; LLB, Nat. U. Law Sch., 1940. Bar: Va. 1940, D.C. 1945. Asst. clk. U.S. Dist. Ct., Washington, 1939-41; ptnr. Radigan & Garnett PC, Arlington, Va., 1995—2002. Bd. dirs. Fairfax County Nat. Bank, Va., 1949-60. Author: (short stories) Pleasant Living, 1993, (novel) The Sandscrapers, 1995, Taboo Avenged, 1997, Sam's Legacy, 2003. Past mem. retirement bd., Arlington, Va., publ utilities commn. Sr. lt. U.S. Navy, 1943-46, SW Pacific. Mem. Va. Bar Assn., Arlington Bar Assn. (pres. 1960), Arlington Hosp. Assn. (gen. coun. 1950-60), Washington Golf & Country Club (pres. 1971). Republican. Episcopalian. Avocations: golfing, cruising, reading, creative writing, music. Home: 900 N Taylor St # 904-020 Arlington VA 22203 Office: Radigan & Garnett PC 2009 N 14th St Ste 408 Arlington VA 22201

GARNETT, KEVIN, professional basketball player; Profl. basketball player Minnesota Timberwolves, 1995—. Named to All-NBA Third Team, 1998-99, NBA Player of Week, USA Basketball Sr. Nat. Team, 1999, All-Rookie Second Team, 1995-96. Office: Minnestoa Timberwolves 600 1st Ave N Minneapolis MN 55403-1400

GARNETT, STANLEY IREDALE, II, lawyer, utility company executive; b. Petersburg, Va., Aug. 11, 1943; s. Stanley Arthur and Edith (Keirstead) G.; m. Beverly Jackson; children: Matthew S.A., Andrew F.W., Christie, Alfred. BA, Colby Coll., 1965; MBA, U. Pa., 1967; JD, NYU, 1973. Bar: N.Y. 1974. Sr. fin. analyst Standard Oil Co. of N.J., N.Y.C., 1967-70; assoc. Milbank, Tweed, Hadley & McCloy, N.Y.C., 1973-81; v.p.-legal and regulatory Allegheny Power Sys., Inc., N.Y.C., 1981-90, v.p. fin., 1990-94, sr. v.p. fin., 1994-95; sr. advisor Putnam, Hayes & Bartlett, 1996-97, 98 00; exec. v.p. Fla. Progress Corp., St. Petersburg, 1997-98; ptnr. PA Consulting Group, 2000—. Bd. dirs. Bay Corp Holdings, Inc. Vice chmn. Episcopal Ch. Bldg. Fund; trustee, sec. ICB Internat. Ctr. for Disabled. Joseph P. Wharton scholar, 1965-67. Mem. ABA, N.Y. State Bar Assn. Republican. Episcopalian. Home: 2504 Sunset Way Pass A Grille Beach FL 33706 E-mail: stan.garnett@paconsulting.com.

GARNICK, JERRY JACK, periodontist, educator; b. Bklyn., Dec. 31, 1932; s. Harry and Dora (Borenstein) G.; m. Bernice Alpert, June 30, 1957; children: Nettie Noma Albrecht, Murray Richard, Ilene Lenore Goldman. MS, U. Mich., 1959, DDS, 1957. Diplomate Am. Bd. Periodontology. Assoc. prof., dept. periodontics U. Conn., 1971-74, acting head dept. periodontics, 1973-74; assoc. prof. Med. Coll. Ga., Augusta, 1974-77, prof. periodontics, 1977-98, dir. grad. studies, 1974-91, prof. grad. studies, 1980-98, acting chair dept. periodontics, 1987-91, chair, 1991-98, prof. emeritus, 1998—. Assoc. head clin. periodontology Eastman Dental Ctr., Rochester, NY, 1966-71, assoc. in periodontics, 1964-66, rsch. assoc., 1961-64. Contbr. articles to profl. jours. Chmn. B'nai B'rith, Rochester, NY, 1965, Walton Way Temple, 1981-85; pres. AYS Synagogue, Augusta, 1997-98. Fellow Am. Coll. Dentistry; mem. Am. Acad. Periodontology, Internat. Assn. Dental Rsch., Am. Assn. Dental Sch., Conn. State Dental Assn., Ga. Dental Assn., So. Acad. Periodontology. Avocations: tennis, walking. E-mail: garnick@adelphia.net.

GARNIER, JEAN-PIERRE, pharmaceutical executive; married; three children. PhD in Pharmacology, U. Louis Pasteur, France, 1972; MBA, Stanford U., 1974. Various positions to pres. U.S. Pharms. Products Divsn. Schering-Plough Corp., 1975-89, 89-90; pres. Smithkline Beecham, Phila., 1990-93, pres. N.Am. pharm., 1993—94, chmn. pharms., 1994—95, COO, 1995—2000, CEO, 2000—; also bd. dirs. Trustee Eisenhower Exch. Fellowships, Inc.; former bd

dirs. Phila. Mus. of Art, Mass. Eye and Ear Hosp., others. Decorated Chevalier de la Legion d'Honneur, 1997; recipient Communicator of Yr. award Internat. Assn. Bus. Communicators, 1993. Mem. Am. Soc. French Legion of Honor, United Technologies Corp. (bd. dirs.), The Acad. of Natural Scis. (emeritus trustee), Am. Found. for Pharm. Edn. (past bd. dirs.), French/Am. C. of C., others. Avocations: fluent in several langs.; competitive tennis and paddle playing, squash, golf, wind surfing. Office: GlaxoSmithKline Box 7929 One Franklin Plz Philadelphia PA 19101

GARNIER, OLIVIER PIERRE, economist; b. Lyon, Rhone, France, Sept. 16, 1959; came to U.S., 1990; s. Pierre Henri and Odette (Reveyron) G.; m. Françoise Marie Bel, Oct. 1, 1983; children: Albane, Constance, Leonore. Grad., Ecole Poly., Paris, 1981; postgrad., Ecole Nat. Stats. l'Adminstrn. Economique, Paris, 1981-83, U. Paris, 1983. Economist Nat. Inst. for Stats. and Econ. Studies, Paris, 1983-85, chief of staff, 1988-90; sr. economist Ministry of Econs. and Fin., Paris, 1985-87; vis. economist Fed. Res. Bd. of Govs., Washington, 1990-92; chief econ. advisor to treasury dir. J.C. Trichet, Paris, 1993-94; chief. econ. advisor Min. Fin., Paris, 1994-97; head strategy and rsch. SG Asset Mgmt., Paris, 1998—. Asst. prof. U. Paris, Sorbonne, 1983-85; assoc. prof. Ecole Nat. Stats. l'Adminstrn. Econs., Paris, 1985-88, Paris Bus. Sch., 1985-87. Contbg. author: Le Travail: Marchés, Régles, Conventions, 1986, Economic Policies for the 1990s, 1992. Served with French Army, 1978-81. Mem. Am. Econ. Assn., Société d Economie Politique. Avocations: tennis, skiing, golf. Home: 12 Rue Ernest André 78110 Le Vesinet France Office: SG Asset Mgmt 2 Place de la Coupole 92708 Paris La Defense Cedex France E-mail: olivier.garnier@sgam.com.

GARNIEZ, NANCY CABALLERO, pianist, educator; b. Chgo., Sept. 3, 1937; d. Archibald E. and Sofia (Torres) Caballero; m. Bernard Garniez, July 29, 1959 (div. 1983); children: Rachelle, Jacob. BA, Oberlin (Ohio) Coll., 1958; postgrad., Hochschule fur Musik, Frankfurt, Ger., 1958-59, Mannes Coll. Music, N.Y.C., 1959-63. Tchr. piano, chamber music, chamber music pedagogy Mannes Coll. Music, N.Y.C., 1972—; founding mem. Alaria Chamber Ensemble, Inc., N.Y.C., 1983—; coord. chamber music Mannes Coll. Music, N.Y.C., 1985—; piano soloist N.Y.C., 1990—. Author: What Might It Mean? An Uncommon Glossary of Musical Terms and Concepts for the Stuck Bored, and Curious, 1999; pianist, recorded: The Lovely Milleress (Schubert), 1978, Haydn/Bartok, 2003. Fulbright scholar, 1958. Home: 949 W End Ave Apt 11C New York NY 10025-3586 E-mail: nancygarniez@erols.com.

GARNISS, JOAN BREWSTER, musician, educator; b. Bangor, Maine, Aug. 10, 1940; d. William Ayer Brewster and Constance Miriam (Witham) Page; adopted d. Woodrow Evans Page; m. Howard Freeman Garniss, Aug. 26, 1962; children: Gretchen, Jonathan. MusB, Boston U., 1962, MusM, 1991. cert. music tchr., Music Tchr. Nat. Assn. Pvt. practice, Dover-Foxcroft, Maine, 1954-58, Hingham, Mass., 1963-65, Waltham, Mass., 1974—. Musician: (albums) En blanc et noir, 2001, Duo Con Anima, 1987, (accompanist) Wintersauce Chorale, 1984—86. Co-founder, pres. Waltham Band Parents, 1979-82, Waltham Music Festival, 1994-97; pres. Friends Waltham Pub. Libr., 1980-83 (bd. dir. 1980-89, 1995—); trustee Waltham Pub. Libr., 1986—, co-chmn. fundraising com., 1995-96; dir. children's choir, All Saints Ch., 1963-66; vol. Boston Pub. Sch., 1969-73; active City Coun. Citizens Com. Transp., Waltham, 1977. Mass. Cultural Affairs Coun. grantee, 1988-89. Mem. UUA/MA N.E. Dist. (human rels. chmn. 1967-70), LWV (v.p. 1979-83, pres. 1983-85, sec. 1997-2003, bd. dir., 2003—, Outstanding Mem. award, 1995), Music Tchrs. Nat. Assn.(rep. East Divsn. Cmty. Outreach, 1995-97,) Ind. Music Tchr. Forum oversight com., 1997-99, Mass. Music Tchrs. Assn. (v.p. 1987-91, pres.-elect 1991-93, pres. 1993-97, immediate past pres. 1997-99), New England Piano Tchr. Assn. (co-chmn. junior recitals com. 1982-88, student master class 1988-90, dir. 1988-90, chair Ensemble Festival, 2000—;), Mass. Libr. Trustees Assn., Lexington Music Club, Mu Phi Epsilon, Pi Kappa Lambda. Avocations: needlework, travel, reading, grandchildren.

GAROFALO, DONALD R. window manufacturing executive; b. St. Paul; With Andersen Corp., 1965—93, v.p. bus. planning and devel., 1993—95, sr. v.p., bus. planning and devel., 1995—96, exec. v.p., COO, 1996—98, CEO, pres., 1998—. Office: Andersen Corp 100 4th Ave N Bayport MN 55003-1096

GAROFALO, DOUGLAS, architectural firm executive, educator; b. Schenectady, N.Y., 1958; B in Architecture, Notre Dame, 1981; Masters, Yale U., 1987. Assoc. prof. U. of Ill. Chgo. Sch. of Architecture. Facilitator design lab. Archeworks. Recipient Young Arch. award, Archtl. League of N.Y., 1991; fellow, Am. Inst. of Architecture, 2003; grantee Skidmore, Owings & Merrill Found. Traveling Fellowship, 1987. Mem.: AIA (Young Arch. award 1995, Design award 1992). Office: Garofalo Archs 3752 N Ashland Ave Chicago IL 60613 Fax: 773-975-2069. E-mail: doug@a-node.net.*

GARON, PHILIP STEPHEN, lawyer; b. Duluth, Minn., Nov. 11, 1947; s. Lawrence and Helen (Cohen) G.; m. Phyllis Sue Ansel, Mar. 22, 1970; children: Edward B., Sara B. BA summa cum laude, U. Minn., 1969, JD summa cum laude, 1972. Bar: Minn. 1972, D.C. 1973, U.S. Dist. Ct. Minn. 1974. Assoc. Covington & Burling, Washington, 1972-74, Faegre & Benson, Mpls., 1974-79, ptnr., 1980—. Mem. mgmt. com. Faegre & Benson, 1992—, chmn., 2001—. Co-author: Minnesota Corporation Law & Practice, 1996 (Burton award for legal writing 2001). Bd. dirs. Herzl Camp, Webster, Wis., 1985-91, Beth El Synagogue, Mpls., 1989-99, v.p., 1993-96; bd. vis. U. Minn. Law Sch., 2003-. Mem. Minn. Bar Assn. (pres. exec. coun. bus. law sect. 1996-97). Avocations: tennis, reading, bridge. Office: Faegre & Benson 2200 Wells Fargo Ctr 90 S 7th St Ste 2200 Minneapolis MN 55402-3901

GARON, RICHARD JOSEPH, JR., political organization worker; b. Bronxville, N.Y., Sept. 9, 1948; s. Richard Joseph Sr. and Jeane Helen (Schlemmer) G.; m. Karen Barclay, Jan. 15, 1972; children: Cynthia Beth, Timothy Michael. BA, Hartwick Coll., 1972; MA, NYU, 1975, PhD, 1983. Legis. asst. U.S. rep. Benjamin A. Gilman, Washington, 1977-79, adminstrv. asst. U.S. rep., 1985-89; staff cons. House Com. on Fgn. Affairs, Washington, 1983-85; staff asst. House Com. on Post Office & Civil Svc., Washington, 1979-83, dep. minority staff dir., 1989-92; Rep. chief of staff House Com. on Fgn. Affairs, Washington, 1993-95; chief of staff House Com. on Internat. Rels., Washington, 1995—2001; writer, 2001—. NYU scholar, 1976-77. Republican. Episcopalian. Home: 11526 Gunner Ct Woodbridge VA 22192-5745

GARONZIK, SARA ELLEN, stage producer; b. Phila., Jan. 12, 1951; d. Milton and Bernice (Kohn) G. BA in Spanish cum laude, Temple U., 1972. Producing artistic dir. Phila. Theatre Co., 1982—. Bd. dirs. Arts and Bus. Coun. Greater Phila., Artreach, Phila. Theatre Co., Theatre Alliance Greater Phila. Recipient prize Sigma Delta Pi, 1972, award of Honor, Alumnae Assn. Girls H.S., 1997. Office: Phila Theatre Co 230 S 15th St Philadelphia PA 19102 Business E-Mail: sgaronzik@phillytheatreco.com.

GAROSSHEN, PAULETTE SHARON, writer; b. Aschnutt, Mass., July 31, 1951; children: Charolotte Sharon Romagnano, Sonya Lynn, Nicholas J. Grad. h.s. Author (self publisher): Book I.

GARPOW, JAMES EDWARD, retired financial executive; b. Detroit, July 30, 1944; s. Roy Joseph and Jeanne Beechner (Brader) G.; m. Elizabeth Marie Conte, Aug. 30, 1969; children: Barbara Jean, Susan Marie. BBA, U. Mich., 1968. CPA, Mich. Audit mgr. Ernst & Young, Detroit, 1966-73; mgr. corp. acctg. Fed. Mogul Corp., Detroit, 1973-79; corp. contr. LOF Plastics, Inc., Detroit, 1979-80; treas., CFO, KMS Industries, Inc., Ann Arbor, Mich., 1980-83; asst. sec., corp. contr. Simpson Industries, Inc., Mich., 1983—, treas., 1995-99; ret., 1999. Mem. AICPA, Mich. Assn. CPA, Fin. Execs. Internat., Beta Alpha Psi, Alpha Kappa Psi. E-mail: jgarpow@attbi.com.

GARR, CARL ROBERT, manufacturing company executive; b. Olean, N.Y., Apr. 4, 1927; s. Frederick H.J. and Mary Magdalene (Zimmerman) G.; m. Arlene Crawford, Dec. 20, 1947 (dec. Aug. 2000); children: Christine Garr Weber, Anne Garr Shields, Elizabeth Garr Reese; m. Emily B., May 22, 2002. BS in Physics, Kent State U., 1950; MS in Physics, Case Inst. Tech., 1953, PhD in Metall. Engring, 1957. Supr. engring. Bettis plant Westinghouse Co., 1956-58; supt. tech. services, nuclear fuel ops. Olin Mathieson Chem. Corp., 1958-62; dir. engring. and research Albuquerque divsn. ACF Industries Inc., N.Y.C., 1962-68, v.p. research and devel., 1968-70; v.p. ACF Industries, Inc., N.Y.C., 1976-82; pres., chief exec. officer Polymer Corp. subs. ACF Industries, Inc., Reading, Pa., 1970-76, 1984-86, chmn., 1987—; pres., chief exec. officer Empire Steel Castings, Inc., Reading, 1982-84; v.p. Chesebrough-Pond's Inc., 1984-86; chief exec. officer, chmn. bd. Bank of Pa., Reading, 1988-92; vice-chmn. Dauphin Deposit Corp., 1988-92. Served with USN, 1944-46. Mem. Am. Soc. Metals, Sigma Xi, The Boulders Club (Carefree, Ariz.). Home: PO Box 2962 Carefree AZ 85377-1210

GARR, DANIEL FRANK, restaurateur; b. Chgo., Sept. 4, 1950; s. Daniel Jacob and Sophie Evelen (Kurranty) G.; m. Dawn Marie Ciciora, May 7, 1983. AA, No. Ill. U., 1970; cert. recording engr., Inst. Audio Research, 1974. V.p. Garbaczewski Corp., Chgo., 1979-89, pres., 1989—2002; treas., CEO Gemtech Packaging Inc., Chgo., 1990—92. Pres. Fantasy Food Corp., Chgo., 1985-93; v.p. Dynamic Design Products, 1990; pres. Proline Tools, Md., 1998—. Bd. dirs. Am. Cancer Soc., 1993. Republican. Roman Catholic. Avocations: music, racquetball, photography. Home: 13713 Cavecreek Ct Lockport IL 60441-8653 Office: Chesdan's Pizzeria and Grille 15764 S Bell Rd Homer Glen IL 60441

GARRA, RAYMOND HAMILTON, II, marketing executive; b. Apr. 2, 1934; s. Raymond Hamilton and Dorothy (Gardner) Garra; m. Sandra Beatrice Pheasant, Dec. 27, 1962 (div. May 1970); children: Therese Helene, Raymond Hamilton III. Gen. mgr. fine paper divsn. Noland Paper Co., Inc., Buena Park, Calif., 1959—67; v.p. sales Western Lithograph Co., Inc., L.A., 1971—73; pres. World Sports Mktg., Inc., Miss Calif. Teen-ager, Inc., 1974—79, Westaire Properties, Inc., Westaire Travel and Tours, 1975—93, Teragar Mktg., 1994—, Gamra Graphics, Inc., 1996—. Exec. bd. U. Calif., Irvine Sports Assocs.; founder Internat. Divers Festivals, 1979, West Coast Challenge Cup Yacht Regatta, 1983; participant (swimming) Nat. Sr. Olympics, 1995, 1997, 2001; mem. Rep. State Ctrl. Com., 1966—67. With USCGR, 1956—59, lt. comdr. Res. Flotilla Comdr., USCG Aux., 1990. Recipient Sports Family of Yr. award, 1975. Mem.: Balboa Bay, Bahia Cornithian Yacht, Buena Park C. of C. (sec. 1967), Mensa (founder Orange County soc. 1964), Navy League (Greater Palm Springs coun. 2003), Nat. Coronado 25 Assn. (pres. 1969—70, Yachtsman of Yr. award 1971), Desert Legionaires, Shriners (pres. El Bandito club 1992), Phi Kappa Psi (pres. Orange County Alumni Assn. 1994—2002). Home: 82361 Crosby Dr Indio CA 92201

GARRARD, JOHN, JR., bank executive, city councilman; b. Flora, Miss., Apr. 8, 1926; s. John and Annie (Hales) G.; m. Fonda Solomon, June 2, 1946; children: John Michael, David Solomon. BA, Millsaps Coll., 1949. Tchr. Escambia County High Sch., Atmore, Ala., 1949-53; pres., CEO First Nat. Bank, Atmore, 1953-86, vice chair bd., 1986—; city councilman City of Atmore, 1996—. Coord., treas. Atmore Men's Club Share Program and Meals on Wheels; tutor Escambia County H.S.; mem. Ala. Children's Policy Coun. for Escambia County; chmn. bd. emeritus Atmore Pub. Libr., 1962—; fin. chmn. Atmore YMCA, 1994—99. Recipient Half Century Club plaque, Ala. Bankers Assn., 2003. Mem. Atmore Hist. Soc. (treas. 1994—), Atmore Rotary (treas., pres. 1962-95, Citizen of Yr. 1981), Atmore C. of C. (past pres.), 10 Gallon Club ARC, YMCA's Men-in-Action Prison Ministry, Am. Legion, VFW. Democrat. Methodist. Avocations: coin collecting, depression glass, blue willow, antiques, collecting junk. Home: 303 E Pine St Atmore AL 36502-3620

GARRARD, JOHN GORDON, educator; b. London, Aug. 28, 1934; came to U.S., 1962, naturalized, 1977; s. John Harold and Ella Veronica (Rudman) G.; m. Carol Elizabeth Hamersen, Oct. 27, 1979; children: Michelle Elizabeth, Alison Veronica; children by previousmarriage: Richard Gordon, Alexander John. BA, Oxford U., 1958; MA, Columbia U., 1963; cert., Russian Inst., 1964, PhD, 1966. Lectr. in Russian lang. and lit. Carleton U., Ottawa, Ont., Can., 1958-62; asst. prof. Russian lit. Dartmouth Coll., Hanover, N.H., 1964-69, assoc. prof., 1969-71; vis. assoc. prof. Ind. U., Bloomington, 1970-71; prof. Russian lit. U. Va., Charlottesville, 1971—, chmn. dept. Slavic langs. and lit., 1971-76, dir. Ctr. for Russian and East European Studies, 1972-83. Cons. Nat. Endowment for Humanities-Nat. Humanities Ctr., 1977; dir. Summer Seminar for Coll. Tchrs. NEH, 1976, 77 Editor: Vladimir Tendryakov: Three Novellas, 1967, The Eighteenth Century in Russia, 1973, The Russian Novel from Pushkin to Pasternak, 1983; author: Mixail Culkov: An Introduction to His Prose and Verse, 1970, Mikhail Lermontov, 1982; editorial bd.: Slavic Rev., 1978-80; contbr. articles to profl. jours. Served with Brit. Army, 1952-54. St. Antony's Coll., Oxford Assoc. fellow, 1967-68; sr. research fellow Russian Inst., Columbia U., 1975; scholar-in-residence Bellagio, 1976; sr. scholar exchanges USSR Acad. Sci., 1980 Mem. So. Conf. Slavic Studies (pres. 1979-80), MLA (nominating com. 1979-81, adv. com. publs. 1975-79), Am. Assn. Advancement of Slavic Studies, Assn. Internationale des Langues et Litteratures Slaves (treas. 1972—)

GARREANS, LEONARD LANSFORD, protective services official, criminal justice professional; b. Glenwood, Iowa, Mar. 25, 1942; s. Ernest Lyle and Kathryn Hermine (Seeger) G.; m. Wanda Marian Ackley, Aug. 24, 1963; children: Kirk Anthony, Debra Renee, David Lance, Diana Jasmine. BSE summa cum laude, John Brown U., 1973; MSE, State Coll. Ark., 1974; postgrad., U. Ark., 1978-79; PhD, Internat. U., Independence, Mo., 1984. Cert. secondary tchr., guidance counselor, jailer, notary pub. Tex., intoxilyzer operator; lic. police instr. Draftsman Pacific Pumping Co., Oakland, Calif., 1963; chem. operator Allied Chem. Corp., El Segundo, Calif., 1963-69; asst. swimming coach John Brown U., Siloam Springs, Ark., 1972-73; grad. asst. State Coll. Ark., Conway, 1973-74; tchr./coach, dir. athletics The Alliance Acad., Quito, Ecuador, 1974-78; teaching asst. U. Okla. Summer Inst. Linguistics, Norman, 1979-81; dir. guidance and counseling Lomalinda High Sch. Summer Inst. Linguistics, Colombia, 1981-87; internat. trainer, cons. Summer Inst. Linguistics, Dallas, 1987-89, pers. devel. officer, 1989-93; cmty. supervision officer Dallas County, State of Tex., Dallas, 1993-95; literacy proctor Dallas County Cmty. Supervision and Corrections Dept., 1999—; detention officer, tng. officer, acting supr. Richardson (Tex.) Police Dept., 1995—. Internat. dir. of intercultural comm. course Summer Inst. Linguistics, Dallas, 1988-89. Vol. probation officer Benton County (Ark.) Juvenile Youth Authority, 1970-72; mem. Jaycees, 1970. With USMC, 1960-63. Mem. Am. Assn. Ret. Persons. Republican. Evangelical. Avocations: hiking, camping, reading, motorcycling. Home: 7346 Cave Dr Dallas TX 75249-1303 Office: Richardson Police Dept 140 N Greenville Ave Richardson TX 75081-6006 *Nothing in life is more important than one's relationship to God. Anything I may have accomplished in this life has been the direct result of God working through me. To God be the glory!*

GARRELICK, JOEL MARC, acoustical scientist, consultant; b. N.Y.C., May 20, 1941; s. Samuel J. Garrelick and Phyllis Weidenbaum; m. Renee Brosell, Dec. 22, 1963; children: Kevin, Jenine, Daniel. BCE, CCNY, 1963, ME, 1965; PhD, CUNY, 1969. Lectr. CCNY, 1968-69; scientist Cambridge (Mass.) Acoustical Assocs., 1969-75, corp. scientist, 1976-97; sr. corp. scientist Cambridge Acoustical Assocs./Anteon Corp., 1998—2002; prin. scientist Applied Phys. Sci. Inc., 2002—. Contbr. articles to profl. jours. Fellow Acoustical Soc. Am.; mem. ASME. Office: CAA Inc 84 Sherman St Cambridge MA 02140-3261 E-mail: jgarrelick@aphysci.com.

GARREN, SANFORD M. secondary school educator; s. Roy L. and Judith Garren; m. Juliet L. Garren, July 9, 1994. BME, Lee U., Cleve., Tenn., 1992; MusM, U. Tenn. Knoxville, 1994. Tchr. Bradley Ctrl. High Sch., Cleve., Tenn. Home: 278 Quail Run Trace Cleveland TN 37312

GARRETSON, DONALD EVERETT, retired manufacturing company executive; b. Elizabeth, N.J., Nov. 22, 1921; s. James W. and Helen (Crane) G.; m. Adele F. Anderson, Sept. 17, 1949; children— James Robert, Katherine Crane, Donald Everett, Peter Andrew, Andrea Drew. AB in Commerce, Washington and Lee U., 1943; MBA, Harvard U., 1947; student, Northwestern U., 1942, 48; PhD (hon.), Macalester Coll., 1985. With Arthur Andersen & Co. (C.P.A.'s), Chgo., 1947-50; with Minn. Mining & Mfg. Co., St. Paul, 1950-88, asst. treas., 1963-67, treas., 1967-77, v.p., 1972-77, v.p. fin., chief fin. officer, 1977-82; corp. v.p., pres. 3M Found., 1982-85; cons. 3M Community Svc. Program, 1985-88. Bd. dirs. Delta Dental Plan Minn.; past mem. acctg. coun. of Conf. Bd. and Machinery and Allied Products Inst.; past chmn. Internal Auditors of Midwest. Dir., past pres. Liberty Plaza Corp., St. Paul; past dir. First Mchts. State Bank, St. Paul; past chmn. bd. trustees Macalester Coll., St. Paul, now hon. trustee; past bd. dirs. Minn. Orchestral Assn.; bd. dirs. St. Paul Chamber Orch.; past pres., chmn. fund drive, lifetime dir. various coms., past regional chmn. St. Paul United Way; nat. bd. dirs. Jr. Achievement, hon. dir.; past chmn. Jr. Achievement of Upper Midwest, hon. dir.; chmn., past pres. Minn. Landmarks, Inc.; dir. Mairs and Power Growth and Balanced Funds., 1984—; cons. J&B Wholesale, Inc.; dir., past chmn. Minn. Pvt. Coll. Fund; hon. trustee Minn. Ind. Sch. Fund; endowment investment com. Sci. Mus. Minn.; past chmn. bd., dir. Presbyn. Homes of Minn., 1989—. Served to lt. USNR, 1943-46. Mem.: Skyline Country Club, Pool and Yacht Club, Lilydale Tennis Club. Presbyterian (elder). Home: 1146 Ivy Hill Dr Saint Paul MN 55118-1829

GARRETSON, JUDITH ANNE, education educator; d. James L. and Luxie A. Garretson. BA in Mktg. and Econs., Pitts. State U., 1990, MBA, 1992; PhD in Bus. and Mktg., U. Ark., 2000. Grad. asst., rschr. Pitts. (Kans.) State U., 1990—91; acct. mgr. US Awards, Inc., Pitts., 1991—92; instr. mktg. Buena Vista U., Storm Lake, Iowa, 1992—96; lectr. mktg. U. Ark., Fayetteville, 1996—2000; asst. prof. mktg. La. State U., Baton Rouge, 2000—. Mem. Deans Adv. Bd., 1997—2000. Contbr. articles to profl. jours. Mem.: Soc. for Consumer Psychology, Am. Acad. Advt., Assn. for Consumer Rsch. Office: La State Univ Coll Bus 3119C CEBA Baton Rouge LA 70803 Office Fax: 225-578-6539.

GARRETT, BRAD, actor, comedian; b. Woodland Hills, Calif., Apr. 14, 1960; Actor in films including: Suicide Kings, 1997, A Bug's Life (voice), 1998, Eight Men Out, 1988, George B, 1998, Postal Worker, 1998, Sweet and Lowdown, 1999, An Extremely Goofy Movie (voice), 2000, Facade, 2000, Stuart Little 2, 2002, The Country Bears (voice), 2002, Finding Nemo (voice), 2003; TV films include: Club Land, 2001, Bleacher Bums, 2002, Gleason, 2002, Legend of the Lost Tribe, 2002; TV series include: The Transformers, 1986, First Impressions, 1988, Eck! the Cat, 1992, Biker Mice From Mars, 1993, 2 Stupid Dogs, 1993, Pursuit of Happiness, 1995, Project G.e.e.K.e.R., 1996, Everybody Loves Raymond, 1996- (Emmy award best sup. actor comedy series, 2002, 2003), Toonsylvania, 1998, Hollywood Squares; TV guest appearances include: Seinfeld, 1990, Superman, 1996, Roseanne, 1988, The King of Queens, 1998, Batman: The Animated Series, 1992; appeared on Broadway in Chicago, 2002. Office: Metropolitan Talent Agy 4526 Wilshire Blvd Los Angeles CA 90010-3801*

GARRETT, C. LYNN, researcher, business consultant; b. Corpus Christi, Tex., Aug. 6, 1962; d. Billie Doyle and Ruth L. (Conklin) Grundy; m. James Glass, Aug. 18, 1979; children: Joshua Curran, Leah Michelle. BA in Psychology, Calif. State U., San Bernardino, 1992, MS in Indsl./Orgnl. Psychology, 1994. Orgnl. cons. Bethesda (Md.) Tri-Star Navy Hosp. Family Treatment Program, 1995-96, Betty Ford Ctr., Rancho Mirage, Calif., 1996-97; staff adminstr. GTE Telephone Ops., Irving, Tex., 1995-96, staff mgr. bus. market segmentation, 1996-97, specialist market rsch., 1997—; statis. analysist dept. mkt. scis. Verizon, Irving, 2000; mgr. consumer rsch. and analysis The Totterdale Group, Irving, 2001—. CEO, owner, founder Garrett Evaluation and Measurement Corp., 1997—. Co-author, editor customer opinion report; author: Developing a Measure of Co-Dependent Behavioral Intentions, 1994. Mem. APA (assoc.). Avocations: family activities, reading, biking, boating, water skiing. Office: 604 Trees Dr Cedar Hill TX 75104-5081 E-mail: lgarrett@totterdalegroup.com.

GARRETT, CHARLES GEOFFREY BLYTHE, physicist, consultant; b. Ashford, Kent, Eng., Sept. 15, 1925; came to U.S., 1950, naturalized, 1989; s. Charles Alfred Blythe and Laura Mary (Lotinga) G. BA in Natural Scis., Trinity Coll., Cambridge U., Eng., 1946; MA in Natural Scis., PhD in Physics, Cambridge U., 1950. Instr. physics Harvard U., 1950-52; mem. tech. staff Bell Labs., Murray Hill, N.J., 1952-54, supr., 1955-56, dept. head, 1960-69; dir. AT&T Bell Labs., Murray Hill-Morristown, N.J., 1969-87. Chmn. Gordon Conf. on non-linear optics, 1964 Author: Magnetic Cooling, 1954, Gas Lasers, 1963; contbr. articles to profl. jours.; patentee in field Named knight of Sovereign Order St. John of Jerusalem (Orthodox) Fellow: IEEE (life), Am. Phys. Soc.; mem.: Guild of Carillonneurs in N.Am. Episcopalian. Avocations: piano, harpsichord, carillon, restoring 18th century houses and older Rolls-Royce cars. Home: 7 Fithian Ln East Hampton NY 11937-2605

GARRETT, CHARLES LEROY, JR., pathologist; b. Simpsonville, S.C., May 7, 1940; s. Charles Leroy Sr. and Iva Marie (Brown) G.; m. Susan Olga Spann, June 5, 1962 (dec. Oct. 1963); m. Mazie Antoinette Franklin, Dec. 26, 1964; 1 child, Edith Louise. BS, Wofford Coll., 1961; MD, Med. U. S.C., 1966. Diplomate Am. Bd. Pathology. Resident in pathology Med. U. S.C., Charleston, 1966-69, asst. prof. pathology, 1970-72; fellow in legal medicine Med. Coll. Va., Richmond, 1969-70; dep. chief med. examiner Dade County, Miami, Fla., 1972-74; pathologist Richland Meml. Hosp., Columbia, S.C., 1974-76; dir. labs. Onslow Meml. Hosp., Jacksonville, N.C., 1976-. Lt. comdr. USN, 1967-73. Fellow Coll. Am. Pathologists, Am. Soc. Clin. Pathologists, Am. Acad. Forensic Scientists, Fedn. State Med. Bds.; mem. AMA (del. 1995—), Nat. Assn. Med. Examiners (bd. dirs. 1981-86), N.C. Med. Soc. (pres. 1997-98), N.C. Med. Bd. (pres.-elect 2003), N.C. Path. Soc. (pres.-elect 2003), Masons, Alpha Omega Alpha. Republican. Episcopalian. Avocation: ornithology. Home: 132 Dockside Dr Jacksonville NC 28546-9768 Office: Onslow Meml Hosp 317 Western Blvd Jacksonville NC 28546-6379

GARRETT, DWAYNE EVERETT, veterinary clinic executive; Office: Wentzville Veterinary 602 E Pearce Blvd Wentzville MO 63385-1538

GARRETT, GEORGE PALMER, JR., creative writing and English language educator, writer; b. Orlando, Fla., June 11, 1929; s. George Palmer and Rosalie (Toomer) G.; m. Susan Parrish Jackson, June 14, 1952; children: William, George, Rosalie. Grad., Hill Sch., 1947; AB, Princeton U., 1952, MA, 1956, PhD, 1985; DLitt (hon.), U. South, 1995. Asst. prof. English Wesleyan U.; writer-in-residence, resident fellow in creative writing Princeton U., 1964-65; former assoc. prof. U. Va.; prof. English Hollins Coll. Va., 1967-71; prof. U. S.C., Columbia, 1971-73, Princeton U., 1974-78, U. Mich., 1979-80, 83-84; Hoyns prof. creative writing U. Va., Charlottesville, 1984—2001; prof. Bennington Coll., 1980; Coal Royalty chair U. Ala., 1994. Author The Reverend Ghost: Poems (Poets of Today IV), 1957, King of the Mountain, 1958, The Sleeping Gypsy and Other Poems, 1958, The Finished Man, 1959, Which Ones Are the Enemy, 1961; (poems) Abraham's Knife, 1961, In the Briar Patch, 1961; (plays) Sir Slob and the Princess, 1962, Cold Ground Was My Bed Last Night, 1964; (screenplays) The Young Lovers, 1964, The Playground, 1965, Do, Lord, Remember Me, 1965, For a Bitter Season, 1967, A Wreath for Garibaldi, 1969, Death of the Fox, 1971, The Magic Striptease, 1973, Welcome to the Medicine Show, Postcards/Flashcards/Snapshots, 1978, To Recollect a Cloud of Ghosts: Christmas in England 1602-03, 1979, Luck's Shining Child: Poems, 1981, The Succession: A Novel of Elizabeth and James, 1983, The Collected Poems of George Garrett, 1984, James Jones, 1984, An Evening Performance: New and Selected Short Stories, 1985, Poison Pen, 1986, Understanding Mary Lee Settle, 1988, Entered from the Sun, 1990, The Sorrows of Fat City, 1992, Whistling in the Dark, 1992, My Silk Purse and Yours, 1992, The Old Army Game, 1994, The King of Babylon Shall Not Come Against You, 1996, Days of Our Lives Lie in Fragments, 1998, Bad Man Blues, 1998, Going to See the Elephant, 2001; editor The Girl in the Black Raincoat, 1966, The Sounder Few, 1971, Film Scripts I-IV, 1971, Craft So Hard to Learn, 1973, The Writer's Voice, 1973, Intro V, 1974, Intro 6: Life As We Know It, 1974, Intro 7: All of Us and None of You, 1975, Botteghe Obscure Reader, 1975, Intro 8: The Liar's Craft, 1977, Intro 9: Close to Home, 1978, Eric Clapton's Lover, 1990, The Wedding Cake in the Middle of the Road, 1992, Elvis in Oz, 1992, That's What I Like (About the South), 1993, The Yellow Shoe Poets, 1999. Served in occupation of Trieste, Austria and Germany. Recipient Rome prize Am. Acad. Arts and Letters, 1958-59, Sewanee Rev. fellow poetry, 1958-59, Am. Acad. and Inst. of Letters award, 1985, T.S. Eliot award Ingersoll Found., 1990, Pen/Malamud award, 1990, Hollins Coll. medal, 1992, U. Va. Pres.'s Report award, 1992, Aiken-Taylor award, 1999, Gov.'s award Commonwealth of Va., 2000; named Cultural Laureate of Va., 1986; Ford Found. grantee in drama, 1960, Nat. Found Arts grantee, 1966; Guggenheim fellow, 1974, resident fellow Bellagio Ctr., 2000. Fellow: Am. Acad. in Rome; mem.: PEN, MLA, Fellowship So. Writers (vice chancellor 1988, chancellor 1993—97), Poetry Soc. Am., Writers Guild Am. East, Authors League. Democrat. Episcopalian. Home: 1845 Wayside Pl Charlottesville VA 22903-1630 Office: Univ Va Dept English Charlottesville VA 22903 E-mail: gpg@virginia.edu.

GARRETT, GERALD R. sociology educator, criminologist, consultant; b. Mt. Vernon, Wash. s. Kenneth J. and Pearl Odessa (Wells) G. AB in Sociology, Whitman Coll., 1962; MA in Sociology, Wash. State U., 1966, PhD, 1970. Instr. sociology U. Wis., Whitewater, 1966-67; asst. prof. sociology Carroll Coll., Waukesha, Wis., 1967-68; rsch. assoc. Columbia U., N.Y.C., 1968-70; from asst. prof. to prof. U. Mass., Boston, 1970—2002, prof. emeritus, 2003—, dir. criminal justice, 1995—2002, assoc. chair dept. sociology, 1998—2000, chair, 2000—01. Vis. prof. U. Md. Europe, Heidelberg, Germany, 1975-76, Boston U. Overseas Grad. Programs, Heidelberg, 1978-84, Wash. State U., Pullman, 1977, 78, Spokane, 1994, 96, 99; vis. scholar Nat. Inst. Alcohol Abuse and Alcoholism, Rockville, Md., 1987; cons. Nat. Ctr. Substance Abuse Treatment, Rockville, 1990-2000; active Nat. Task Force on Higher Edn. and Criminal Justice, Washington, 1974-76. Co-author: Women Alone, 1976, Manny: A Criminal Addict's Story, 1977, Responding to the Homeless, 1992, Crime, Justice, and Society, 2d edit., 1996; co-prodr., co-author (video and book): Working with the Homeless, 1990; guest editor Criminal Justice Policy Rev., 1989. Mem. cert. com. Mass. Criminal Justice Tng. Coun., Waltham, 1988-95; mem. coll. adv. com. Mass. Coun. on Compulsive Gambling, Boston, 1994-96; bd. dirs. Mass. Halfway Houses, Inc., Boston, 1993-98; mem. Higher Edn. Ctr. for Alcohol and Other Drug Abuse Prevention, 1996-2001, nat. adv. bd. Addiction Tech. Transfer Ctr., K.C., steering com. New England Addiction Tech. Transfer Ctr., Brown U., R.I. Fellow Nat. Inst. Mental Health, 1968-70. Mem. Am. Soc. Criminology (life), Acad. Criminal Justice Scis. (life), Internat. Coalition of Addiction Studies Edn. (life, bd. dirs. 1993-98, pres. 1995-96), Ea. Sociol. Soc. (co-chair program, co-chair conf. 1982, 83, 91), Soc. for the Study Social Problems (program co-chair 1981), N.E. Assn. Criminal Justice Scis. (exec. bd. 1996-2000, pres. 1998-99), Addiction Tech. Transfer Ctrs. (mem. nat. adv. com, practice com. 1998—), New Eng. Addiction Tech. Transfer Ctr. (steering com. 1998—). Office: U Mass Dept Sociology 100 Morrissey Blvd Boston MA 02125-3393

GARRETT, JAMES LEO, JR., theology educator; b. Waco, Tex., Nov. 25, 1925; s. James Leo and Grace Hasseltine (Jenkins) G.; m. Myrta Ann Latimer, Aug. 31, 1948; children: James Leo III, Robert Thomas, Paul Latimer. BA, Baylor U., 1945; BD, Southwestern Bapt. Theol. Sem., 1948, ThD, 1954; ThM, Princeton Theol. Sem., 1949; PhD, Harvard U., 1966; postgrad., Oxford U., 1968—69, St. John's U., 1977, Trinity Evang. Div. Sch., 1989. Ordained to ministry Baptist Ch., 1945. Pastor Bapt. chs. in Tex., 1946-48, 50-51; successively instr., asst. prof., assoc. prof., prof. theology, disting. prof., disting. prof. emeritus Southwestern Bapt. Theol. Sem., Ft. Worth, 1949-59, 79—, assoc. dean for PhD degree, 1981-84; prof. Christian theology So. Bapt. Theol. Sem., Louisville, 1959-73; dir. J.M. Dawson Studies in Ch.-State, prof. religion Baylor U., Waco, Tex., 1973-79, Simon M. and Ethel Bunn prof. Ch.-State Studies, 1975-79. Interim pastor Bapt. chs. in Tex., D.C., Ind. and Ky.; guest prof. Hong Kong Bapt. Theol. Sem., 1988; coord. 1st Conf. on Concept of Believers' Ch., 1967; chmn. Study Commn. on Coop. Christianity, Bapt. World Alliance, 1968-75; sec. Study Commn. on Human Rights, 1980-85; co-chmn. Study and Rsch. Divsn., 1995-99; theol. lectr. Wake Forest, N.C., Torreon, Mex., Cali, Colombia, Recife, Brazil, Montevideo, Uruguay, Oradea, Romania, Dallas, Yalta and Odessa, Ukraine. Author: The Nature of the Church According to the Radical Continental Reformation, 1957, Baptist Church Discipline, 1962, Evangelism for Discipleship, 1964, Baptists and Roman Catholicism, 1965, Reinhold Niebuhr on Roman Catholicism, 1972, Living Stones: The Centennial History of Broadway Baptist Church, Fort Worth, Texas, 1882-1982, 2 vols., 1984—85, Systematic Theology Vol. 1, 1990, Vol. 2, 1995, 2d edit. Vol. 1, 2000, Vol. 2, 2001; co-author: Are Southern Baptists "Evangelicals"?, 1983; co-editor: The Teacher's Yoke: Studies in Memory of Henry Trantham, 1964; editor: The Concept of the Believers' Church, 1970, Baptist Relations with Other Christians, 1974, Calvin and the Reformed Tradition, 1980, We Baptists, 1999, The Legacy of Southwestern, 2002, Southwestern Jour. Theology, 1958—59, Jour. of Ch. and State, 1973—79. Mem. Am. Soc. Ch. History, Bapt. Hist. and Heritage Soc., Conf. on Faith and History, Nat. Assn. Bapt. Profs. Religion. Home: 5525 Full Moon Dr Fort Worth TX 76132-2309 Office: PO Box 22117 Fort Worth TX 76122-0117

GARRETT, JAMES WILLIAM, computer company executive; b. Corpus Christi, Tex., Dec. 5, 1946; s. George Perce and Beulah Belle (Kerrel) G.; m. Barbara Merle Moore, July 1, 1972; 1 child, Eva Christine. BS, Ohio State U., 1969. Commd. 2d lt. USAF, 1969, advanced through grades to major, 1980, ret., 1988; dir. maintenance Techno-Scis. Inc., Lanham, Md., 1988-97; owner Southwest Tech. Solutions, Del Rio, Tex., 1998—. Sec./treas. Val Verde Airlines, Del Rio, Tex., 1989-91. Pres. Buena Vista PTO, 1990-91; dir. Val Verde Citizens Aligned for Responsibility in Govt. Master Mason; mem. Lions. Office: SW Tech Solutions 150 Freedom Way Del Rio TX 78843-5234 E-mail: bgarrett2@earthlink.net.

GARRETT, JOSEPH EDWARD, aerospace engineer; b. Hendersonville, NC, Mar. 4, 1943; s. Kenneth Pace and Anna Lou (Lytle) G.; m. Aurelia Jane Pryor, Aug. 7, 1971. BS in Aerospace Engring., N.C. State U., 1966; MS in Aerospace Engring., Ga. Inst. Tech., 1978. Registered profl. engr., Ga. Basic and fatigue loads assoc. aircraft engr. LASC-Ga. (formerly Lockheed-Ga.), Marietta, 1966-67, basic and fatigue loads structures engr., 1967-75, fatigue and fracture mechanics sr. structures engr., 1975-80, company planning, 1980-82, fracture mechanics structures engr., 1982-91, advanced structures sr. engr., 1991-96, fatigue and fracture mechanics sr. structures engr., 1996—2003, aero. engr., 2003—. Loaned exec. United Way, Atlanta, 1984, Cobb County chmn. for Individual Gifts, Marietta, 1985, chmn. Cobb County Adv. Com., Marietta, 1987-88, bd. dirs., Atlanta, 1987-88. AIAA assoc. fellow (dir. Region II 1990-96, Mem. of Yr. Atlanta sect. 1986, Booster of Yr. 1988, 92, 94, 95, Sustained Svc. award 1999); mem. Inst. Cert. Mgrs. Lockheed Ga. Mgmt. Assn. (v.p. mem. achievement 1988-89, v.p. adminstrn. 1989-90, Booster of Month 1980, 1st Lockheed-Ga. Cert. Mgr. of Yr. 1989). Republican. Baptist. Avocations: landscaping, woodworking. Home: Ste A9-342 3595 Canton Rd Marietta GA 30066-2658 Office: LASC-Ga Dept 6 E5M Zone 0441 86 S Cobb Dr Marietta GA 30063-0441 E-mail: joe.e.garrett@lmco.com., joeflash@flash.net.

GARRETT, KATHRYN ANN BYERS (KITTY GARRETT), legislative clerk; b. Antlers, Okla., July 10, 1930; d. Stansell Harper and Vena Clifford (Crawford) Byers; m. William Donald Garrett, Jan. 13, 1955 (dec. June 1992); children: William Mark, Amy Kathryn, Ann Elizabeth Garrett Jenni. Student, Okla. A&M U., 1948-50. Sec. Garform Industries, Wagoner, Okla., 1951-52; sec. to exec. sec. Okla. Edn. Assn., Oklahoma City, 1952-55; sec. revenue and taxation com. Ho. Reps., State of Okla., Oklahoma City, 1969-76, bill clk./ins. clk., 1976-84, asst. chief clk./jour. clk., 1985-93; ret., 1994. Mem. Okla. Heritage Assn., Gamma Book Club, Salvation Army Women's Aux. Republican. Avocations: china painting, bridge, reading, travel. Home: 1429 Wilburn Dr Oklahoma City OK 73127-3253 E-mail: kittygar@prodigy.net.

GARRETT, LEE (HOMER SIMMONS HOLCOMB), retired broadcaster; b. Roanoke, Va., Sept. 29, 1925; s. Homer Simmons and Dorothy (Pollard) H.; m. Charlotte Wade Holcomb, Feb. 28, 1953; childre: David Lee Holcomb, Sharon Kay Holcomb Thompson. Student, Shenandoah Coll., Dayton, Va., 1946-47. Announcer Sta. WSVA, Harrisonburg, Va., 1946-47; program dir. Sta. WROV, Roanoke, 1948-53; announcer, reporter, news anchor, mgr. community svcs., commentator Sta. WSLS-TV, Roanoke, 1953-87. Mem. Roanoke County Bd. Suprs., 1986-89, vice chmn., 1987, chmn., 1988-89; vice chmn. Roanoke County Social Svcs. Bd., 1986-87, mem., 1987-89; mem. Va. Aviation Bd., 1990-94; vice chmn. Roanoke Regional Airport Commn., 1988-89; mem. Roanoke County Ext. Leadership Coun., Va. Poly. Inst. and State U., 1992—. with USAAF, 1943-45; bd. dirs. Va. Aeronaut. Hist. Soc., Richmond, 1998—, Youth Haven Sanctuary, 2000—; mem. ctr. com. Roanoke County Dem. Party. 2d lt. USAF, 1952-53, Korea; lt. col. USAFR ret. Recipient Coll. medallion Va. Western C.C., 1966, Pres.'s award Ferrum (Va.) Coll., 1970. Mem. AARP, Nat. Assn. Desktop Pubs., mem. Ret. Officers Assn. (pres. 1993-94, 97, pres. 1999, bd. dirs. 2000—), Mil. Order World Wars (comdr. 1992-94), Am. Legion, Nat. D-Day Meml. Found. (chmn. 1992-94), Quiet Birdmen, Airforce Assn., League Older Ams., Silver Falcons Assn. (USAF), Air Force Fellowship ROA Wing (v.p. dirs.), Mil. Officers Assn. Am., Hunting Hills Country Club, Rotary, Optimists (pres. 1995-98, bd. dirs. 1998-2002), Roanoke Businessmens Club (pres. elect), Masons, Kazim Shrine Club (dir. staff), Cotillion Club, 300 Club, VIP Club. Baptist. Avocations: computing, amateur radio, woodcrafting, painting in oils. Home: 4501 Tanglewood Ln Roanoke VA 24018-2455

GARRETT, LELAND EARL, nephrologist, educator; b. Spartanburg, S.C., Jan. 8, 1949; s. Leland Earl and Mary Lillian (Butler) G.; m. Sarah Anne Pryor, Aug. 13, 1970 (div. 1978); 1 child, Katherine; m. Nancy Jean Swenson, May 3, 1980; children: Christopher, Jennifer. BS, N.C. State U., 1971; MD, Med. U. S.C., 1976. Commd. 2d lt. USAF, 1971, advanced through grades to lt. col., 1985, ret., 1991; intern Wilford Hall, USAF Med. Ctr., 1976-77; resident USAF Med. Ctr., 1977-79; fellowship Duke U. Med. Ctr., 1979-81; pvt. practice Wake Nephrology Assocs., Raleigh, N.C., 1991—. Clin. prof. medicine U. N.C., Chapel Hill, 1998—. Contbr. articles to profl. jours. Chair-elect Urban Ministries, 2000—01, chmn., 2001—02; mem. adv. chmn. N.C. affiliate Nat. Kidney Found., Charlotte, 1994—2001; med. dir. Open Door Clinic, 1996—98; chmn. Carolina Renal Care, 2000—02; pres. med. staff Raleigh Cmty. Hosp., 2000—02; data chair, bd. dirs. Southeastern Kidney Coun., Raleigh, 1993—97, 1998—, treas., 2000—01, chmn., 2002—; bd. dirs. South Tex. Organ Bank, San Antonio, 1984—86, Urban Ministries, 1997—, treas., 1998—2000; bd. dirs. Carolina Renal Care, 1999—2002. Named Physician of Yr. N.C. affiliate Nat. Kidney Found., 1995. Fellow ACP, Am. Soc. Nephrology, Internat. Soc. Nephrology. Lutheran. Avocation: medical informatics. Office: Wake Nephrology Assocs 3604 Bush St Raleigh NC 27609-7511

GARRETT, MARK WILLIAM, research engineer; b. Phillipsburg, N.J., June 11, 1960; s. Curtis William and Julia May Garrett; m. Llyn Kiyo Kawasaki, May. 20, 1989. BS, Columbia U., 1982, MS, 1984, PhD, 1993. Rsch. mgr. Telcordia Techs., Inc., Morristown, N.J., 1984—. Contbr. articles to profl. jours. Mem. IEEE (sr.). Office: Bellcore 445 South St Morristown NJ 07960-6438

GARRETT, MARSHALL LEE, JR., anesthesiologist, educator; b. Sacramento, 1951; m. Carol E. Kolbo, June 21, 1986; children: Mackenzie Lee, Lane Christian, William James. BA cum laude, U. of the South, 1972; MD, Creighton U., 1978. Diplomate Am. Bd. Anesthesiology. Intern St. Mary Med. Ctr., Long Beach, Calif., 1978—79; resident anesthesiology U. Fla., Gainesville, 1979-81; chief fellow cardiothoracic anesthesiology Clevel. Clin. Found., 1988-89; anesthesiologist Cypress Fairbanks Med. Ctr., Houston. Assoc. prof. U. Calif. Med. Ctr., Davis, Thomas Jefferson U., Phila. Mem. Am. Soc. Anesthesiologists, Soc. Cardiothoracic Anesthesiologists, Tex. Med. Assn., Phi Beta Kappa.

GARRETT, PAUL JAMES, financial planner; b. Chgo., Aug. 18, 1962; children: Tristan Paul, Annie. Registered rep. Inland Securities, Oak Brook, Ill., 1988-91; v.p. New Eng. Securities, Chgo., 1991-96; v.p., prin. Oak Brook Securities Corp., Oak Brook Terrace, Ill., 1996-2001; prin. Garrett Consulting, Glen Ellyn, Ill., 2001—. Republican. Avocation: musician. Office: Garrett Consulting Corp Ste C-114 800 Roosevelt Rd Glen Ellyn IL 60137

GARRETT, REGINALD HOOKER, biology educator, researcher; b. Roanoke, Va., Sept. 24, 1939; s. William Walker and Lelia Elizabeth (Blankenship) G.; m. Linda Joan Harrison, Mar. 15, 1958 (div.); children: Jeffrey David, Randal Harrison, Robert Martin; m. Catherine Leigh Touchton, June 12, 1989 (div.). BS, Johns Hopkins U., 1964, PhD, 1968. Asst. prof. biology U. Va., 1968-73, assoc. prof., 1973-82, prof., 1982—. Guest prof. U. Paul Sabatier, France, 2003; cons. in field. Author textbooks; contbr. articles to profl. jours. NIH fellow, 1964-68; Fulbright Hays fellow, 1975-76; Thomas Jefferson vis. fellow, 1983; grantee NIH, NSF Mem. Am. Soc. Biochemistry and Molecular Biology, Am. Soc. Microbiology, Am. Soc. Plant Physiology, Soc. Gen. Physiology, Sigma Xi, Phi Lambda Upsilon, Phi Sigma Office: U Va Dept Biology Gilmer Hall Charlottesville VA 22904

GARRETT, RICHARD G. lawyer; b. N.Y.C., Oct. 16, 1948; BA magna cum laude, Emory U., 1970, JD, 1973. Bar: Ga. 1973, Fla 1979; U.S. Dist. Ct. (no. dist.) Ga. 1973, (so. dist.) Fla. 1979, U.S. Dist. Ct. (so. dist. trial bar) Fla. 1979; U.S. Ct. Appeals (5th cir.) 1974; U.S. Ct. Appeals (9th. cir., 11 cir.) 1981; U.S. Supreme Ct. 1981. Program dir., instr. rsch., writing and advocacy Emory U. Sch. Law, 1972-73; gen. counsel Greenberg, Traurig, Miami, Fla., prin. shareholder, 1978—. Past chmn. litigation dept., exec. com. bd. dirs. Greenberg, Traurig, Miami. Editor Emory Law Journal, 1972-73. Recipient 1st place and Best Brief award Region V Nat. Moot Ct. Competition, 1972. Mem. ABA, The Fla. Bar Assn., State Bar Ga., Omicron Delta Kappa, Order of the Barristers. Office: Greenberg Traurig 1221 Brickell Ave Miami FL 33131-3224

GARRETT, ROBERT, financial advisory executive; b. Morristown, N.J., Feb. 27, 1937; s. Harrison and Grace Dodge (Rea) G.; m. Jacqueline E. Marlas, July 10, 1965; children: Robert Jr., Johnson. AB, Princeton U., 1959; MBA, Harvard U., 1965. V.p. Smith, Barney & Co., N.Y.C., 1965-69, Robert Garrett & Sons, N.Y.C. and Balt., 1969-71; 1st v.p. Smith, Barney, Harris Upham & Co., N.Y.C., 1972-78; sr. v.p. Smith, Barney Real Estate Corp., N.Y.C., 1978-84; exec. v.p. Security Capital Corp., N.Y.C., 1978-85; pres. Robert Garrett & Sons Inc., N.Y.C., 1986—. Pres. AdMedia Ptnrs. Inc., 1990—; bd. dirs. Mickelberry Corp.; chmn. bd. dirs. Penn Virginia Corp. Trustee Near East Found., Cleveland H. Dodge Found., Abell Found., N.Y. Bot. Garden, Adirondack Mus. With AUS, 1959-63. Mem. Univ. Club of N.Y., Nantucket Yacht Club, Piping Rock Club (L.I.), River Club of N.Y., Knickerbocker Club of N.Y. Republican. Episcopalian. Home: 800 Park Ave New York NY 10021-2760 Office: 444 Madison Ave New York NY 10022-6903

GARRETT, ROBERTA KAMPSCHULTE, nurse; b. Amityville, N.Y., Aug. 15, 1947; d. Robert Henry and Gertrude Ann (Schweitzer) Kampschulte; m. Paul R. Garrett Jr., Nov. 26, 1977; children: Samantha Kristine, Kelly Nicole. BS, U. Fla., 1969. RN, Fla.; cert. in oncology nursing. Staff nurse Valley Hosp., Ridgewood, N.J., 1969-70; asst. head nurse Broward Gen. Hosp., Ft. Lauderdale, Fla., 1970-71; CCU nurse Grady Meml. Hosp., Atlanta, 1972-77; nurse to pvt. physician Orlando, Fla., 1977-94; case mgmt. Fla. Healthcare Sys., Orlando, 1996—. Owner 2 Tropical Smoothie stores, Fla., 1999—2002; area developer Tampa/St. Petersburg Tropical Smoothie, 1999—2003. Republican. Lutheran. Avocation: jogging.

GARRETT, ROBIN SCOTT, public information officer; b. Sparta, NC, Jan. 24, 1965; d. Milton William Scott, Peggie Adams Scott; m. William Earle Garrett; 1 child, Nicolas. BS Mgmt. and Mktg., Univ. SC, 2003. Medical Clerk WJBD VA Medical Center, Columbia, SC, 1986—86; Sec./Steno. WJBD VA Med. Ctr., Columbia, SC, 1986—91, Civilian Pay Technician, 1991—95, Lead Civilian Pay Technician, 1995—97, Fiscal Admin. Sup., 1997—2000. VALUE (VA Leadership Upward Expectations) Graduate Dept of Veterans Affairs, Atlanta, 1999—2000; developed new strategy on budgeting salaries VA Med. Ctr., Columbia, SC, 2000; conducted feasibility study on establishing an adult day care facility WJBD VA Med. Ctr., Columbia, SC, 1999; prepared strategic mgmt. plans Edward Jones Investments, Columbia, SC, 2002, Ashley Fetner Fine Art Photography, Columbia, SC, 2002. Notary Pub. State of SC, Columbia, SC, 1996—2006. Named Fed. Woman of Yr., 1995; recipient CPCU Mem. Scholarship, Lanville Mengedoht, 2003. Mem.: National Society of Collegiate Scholars (life), Golden Key National Honor Society (life), Beta Gamma Sigma (life), Phi Beta Kappa (life). Baptist. Avocation: photography, travel, hiking, reading, music. Home: 101 Fox Run Dr Hopkins SC 29061-9231 Personal E-mail: rgarrett@sc.rr.com.

GARRETT, SCOTT, congressman; b. Englewood, N.J., July 9, 1959; BA, Montclair State U.; JD, Rutgers U. Congressman 5th Dist. N.J. U.S. Ho. Reps., 2003—; mem. N.J. Gen. Assembly, majority leader, chmn. banking and ins. com., mem. agr. com., mem. edn. com. Republican. Office: 1641 Longworth House Office Bldg Washington DC 20515*

GARRETT, SHIRLEY GENE, nuclear medicine technologist; b. Evanston, Ill., Apr. 19, 1944; d. Nathan and Emma Louise (Uecker) G. AA, Oakton C.C., 1977; AS in Nuc. Medicine, Triton Coll., 1980; BA, Northea. Ill. U., 1983; MA, Govs. State U., University Park, Ill., 1985. Cert. nuclear medicine technologist. Nuc. medicine technologist Chgo. Osteo. Hosp., 1980-88, Little Co. of Mary Hosp., Evergreen Park, Ill., 1989; nuclear medicine technologist Lutheran Gen. Hosp., Lincoln Park, Ill., 1989; nuc. medicine technologist Mt. Sinai Hosp., Chgo., 1990-92; technologist nuc. medicine Swedish Covenant Hosp., Chgo., 1992-93; pres. Providence Hosp. of Cook County, Chgo., 1994—. Contbr. articles to profl. jours. Vol. Ravenswood Hosp., Chgo., 1986-2000, Mt. Sinai Hosp., 1990-92, Congl. Health Ministry, Ch. of St. Lukes. Mem. Soc. Nuc. Medicine (mem. bylaws com. technologist sect. Ctrl. chpt. 1982-83, 85-86, 92-2000, mem. continuing edn. com. 1986-87, chmn. nominating com. 1987-88, 92-93, mem. edn. com. 1988-89, pres.-elect 1989-90, mem. bd. govs. 1990-92, 97-2000, pres. 1991-92, chmn. bylaws com. 1992-93, bd. govs. ctrl. chpt. 1997-2000), Assoc. and Tech. Affiliates Chgo. Area (coord. edn. 1981-84, mem. adv. bd. 1983-84, 87-88, 96-97, pres. 1985-87, chmn. nominating com. 1987-89). Lutheran.

GARRETT, STEVEN LURIE, physicist; b. LA, Apr. 3, 1949; s. Fred Ellis and Vivian Dorothy (Lurie) Garrett. BS in Physics, UCLA, 1970, MS in Physics, 1972, PhD in Physics, 1977. Asst. prof. Naval Postgrad. Sch., Monterey, Calif., 1981-85, assoc. prof., 1985-88, prof., 1988-95; United Techs. prof. of Acoustics Pa. State Univ., State College, Pa., 1995—. Rosen prof. Technion, Haifa, Israel, 1985; cons. in field, Monterey, Calif., 1982—. Contbr. Fellow, Miller Inst. Basic Rsch. in Sci., 1978—81. Fellow: Acoustical Soc. Am. (Hunt fellow 1978, Silver Medal in Phys. Acoustics and Engring. Acoustics 1993); mem.: Soc. Audio Engrs., Am. Soc. Engring. Edn., Sigma Xi. Achievements include patents in field. Home: PO Box 10271 State College PA 16805-0271 Office: Grad Program in Acoustics PO Box 30 State College PA 16804-0030 Business E-Mail: sxg185@psu.edu.

GARRETT, SUSAN, state senator; b. Lake Forest, Ill., Feb. 11, 1950; m. Scott Garrett; children: Brett, Liz. BA Polit. Sci., Lake Forest Coll. State Senator US Senate, Dist. #29, Ill., 2003; State Rep. House of Rep., Ill., 1998—2002. Legis. assignment Comm. on Ed.; mem. Health & Human Svc.; vice-chairperson Trans.; mem. HHS-BDD subcommittee; sub-chairperson Health & Human Svc. Health Care; mem. Health and Human Svc. Subcommittee on Behavioral and Devel.. Disabilities. Mem.: Market Square 2000 (Bd. of Dir.), Susan Garrett Marketing Assoc. (founder). Democrat. Episcopalian. Office: Capitol M118 Capitol Bldg Springfield IL 62706 also: District 425 Sheridan Rd Highwood IL 60040*

GARRETT, THEODORE LOUIS, lawyer; b. New Britain, Conn., Sept. 4, 1943; s. Louis and Sylvia (Greenberg) G.; m. Bonnie Garrett, Nov. 27, 1968; children— Brandon, Natalie. BA, Yale U., 1965; JD, Columbia U., 1968. Bar: N.Y. 1968, D.C. 1971, U.S. Supreme Ct. 1973. Law clk. to Judge J. Joseph Smith U.S. Ct. Appeals for 2d Circuit, 1968-69; spl. asst. to asst. atty. gen. William H. Rehnquist Dept. Justice, Washington, 1969-70; law clk. to Chief Justice Warren E. Burger U.S. Supreme Ct., 1970-71; assoc. Covington & Burling, Washington, 1971-76, ptnr., 1976—. Editor, prin. author: Corporate Counsel Environmental Law Guide, 1993; author: Environmental Law and the Eleventh Amendment, 2000; co-author: Clean Air Act Desk Book, 1991; contbg. author: A Practical Guide to Environmental Law, 1987, Liability for Hazardous Waste Sites Under CERCLA, 1988, Practice Under the New Federal Sentencing Guidelines, 4th edit., 2001, Environmental Dispute Handbook, 1991, Environmental Litigation, 1991, 2d edit., 1999; editor, contbg. author: The Environmental Law Manual, 1992, RCRA Policy Documents, 1993, RCRA Practice Manual, 1994; contbr. articles to profl. jours. Named One of 100 Influential Lawyers in Nat. Law Jour., 1994. Mem. ABA (chair sect. environ., energy and resources, mem. exec. com. 1995-2001, exec. bd. Environ. Lawyer, adv. bd. ABA Jour., contbg. author Trends, mem. task force on superfund reform, liaison standing com. on environ.law, mem. exec. com. 1995-2002), D.C. Bar Assn. (steering com. environment, energy and natural resources sect., 1991-97, co-chair 1992-94, chair coun. on sects, 94-95). Home: 6604 Broxburn Dr Bethesda MD 20817-4710 Office: Covington & Burling 1201 Pennsylvania Ave NW PO Box 7566 Washington DC 20044-7566 E-mail: tgarrett@cov.com.

GARRETT, THOMAS MONROE, chemist; b. San Francisco, Mar. 10, 1961; s. Walter Norman and Sally Ann (Sharpless) G.; m. Karen Lynn Garcia, June 7, 1987; children: Andrew Henry, Alexander Monroe. BS with hons., Stanford U., 1983; PhD, U. Calif., Berkeley, 1988. Postdoctoral fellow U. Louis Pasteur, Strasbourg, France, 1988-90; part owner, v.p., dir. rsch. MCP Industries, Inc., Corona, Calif., 1990—; pres. Athletic Polymer Sys., Inc., Corona, 2000—. Contbr. articles to profl. jours.; patentee in field. Recipient Bourse Chateubriand, France. Fellow Am. Inst. Chemists; mem. Am. Chem. Soc., N.Am. Soc. Trenchless Tech., L.A. Soc. Coatings Technology, Rotary, Phi Lambda Upsilon, Sigma Xi. Republican. Episcopalian. Achievements include co-discovery of first perfect trigonal prismatic iron (III) complex; strongest bidentate iron chelating agts.; self-assembling pentameric silver (I) complex; a process to make sand bounce like a superball; co-developer first U.S.-made clay microtunneling pipe; invented smart materials for redistribution of .5 kiloton construction forces. Office: MCP Industries Inc PO Box 1839 Corona CA 92878

GARRETT, THOMAS W. career officer; b. Jan. 2, 1947; Commd. officer U.S. Army, advanced through grades to maj. gen., commdg. gen. Total Army Pers. Command, 1997—. Office: PERSCOM Hoffman II Bldg 200 Stovall St Ste 7n22 Alexandria VA 22332-0400

GARRETT, WILBUR (BILL GARRETT), magazine editor; b. Kansas City, Mo., Sept. 4, 1930; s. Clay Dean and Cecil Zora (Melton) G.; m. Lucille Hall, Dec. 26, 1950; children: Michael Dean, Kenneth Lewis. BJ, U. Mo., 1954; LittD (hon.), U. Miami. With Nat. Geog. mag., 1954-90, editor, 1980-90; faculty photojournalism workshop U. Mo., 1963, 64, 69, 70, 73, 74, 75, 77, 78, 79, 80, 94; editor Cosmos Jour., 1995-98; designer photog. exhbn. U.S. Pavilion, N.Y. World's Fair, 1965; designer-producer Nat. Geog. Soc. exhbns. 23d, 24th, 25th Picture of Year Competition; mem. XIX Olympiad Cultural Com.; bd. dirs. Congentrix Energy, Inc., Nat. Geographic Soc., 1980-90, rsch. and exploration com., 1981-90; bd. advisors Corbis Prodns., Inc. Ptnrs. for Livable Cmtys.; bd. govs. The Nature Conservancy, 1988-98, Am. Land Conservancy; bd. dirs. Heritage USA; trustee W. Eugene Smith Meml. Fund.; founder, pres. La Ruta Maya Conservation Found., 1990. With USNR, 1946-52. Decorated Order of the Quetzal (Guatemala). Recipient Newhouse citation U. Syracuse, 1963, Rotondi award, Italy, 1998, Mag. Photographer of Year award, 1968, Disting. Service in Journalism award U. Mo., 1978, Nat. mag. awards for excellence, 1984, 89, 90, 91; leadership medal UN Environ. Programme, Chevron Environ. award 1990, La Pluma Plata Pres. of Mex., 1990. Mem. Cosmos Club (Washington). Home and Office: 209 Seneca Rd Great Falls VA 22066-1108

GARRETT, WILLIAM WALTON, retired law educator; b. Birmingham, Ala., Aug. 13, 1926; s. H. Bascom and Josephine (Pattillo) G.; m. Marion Huey, July 31, 1950; children: Susan Garrett Hodgson, William W. Garrett Jr. A.C.E., Oreg. State U., 1946; BBA, U. Ala., 1950; LLB, Birmingham Law Sch., 1954; JD, Cumberland Law Sch., 1961; LLM, Yale U., 1962. Merchant WW Garrett & Son, Birmingham, 1950-60; atty. in pvt. practice Birmingham, 1954-61; prof. law U. Memphis, Tenn., 1962-85, ret., 1985. Author: Tennessee Divorce Alimony and Child Custody, 2002; editor Tenn. Family Law Letter, 1985—. Sunday sch. tchr. First United Meth. Ch., Waynesville, N.C., 1987—; project dir. Haywood Habitat for Humanity, 1995—. With U.S. Army, 1943-46. Democrat. Avocations: librarian, swimming, volunteering. Home: PO Box 911 1873 Lakeshore Dr Lake Junaluska NC 28745-8700

GARRETTO, LEONARD ANTHONY, JR., insurance company executive; b. N.Y.C., Apr. 13, 1925; s. Leonard and Evenia (Egidio) G.; m. Theresa Cennamo, Aug. 6, 1949; children: Deborah, Mark, Michael, Paula, David. BEE, Manhattan Coll., 1951. Engr. Gen. Precision Lab. Inc., Pleasantville, N.Y., 1951-53, project adminstr., 1953-55, project mgr., 1955-58, subcontracts mgr., 1958-59; adminstrv. engr. Sperry Sys. Mgmt. divsn. Sperry Rand Corp., Great Neck, N.Y., 1959-61, mgmt. svcs. adminstr., 1961-63, mgmt. svcs. mgr., 1963-65, fin. planning mgr., 1965-66, planning mgr., 1966-68, dir. adminstrn., 1968; agt. First Investors Corp., N.Y.C., 1966-69, dist. mgr., 1969-70; gen. mgr. David Gracer Co., N.Y.C., 1970-72; v.p. regional sales Somerset Capital Corp., N.Y.C., 1972-75; regional dir. Wis. Nat. Life Ins. Co., Oshkosh, 1975-77, regional sales v.p. Englewood Cliffs, N.J., 1977-84, sr. regional sales v.p., 1984-86, area sales v.p. Stroudsberg, Pa., 1986-93, ret., 1993; owner Ter-Len-Co Benefits, Bushkill, Pa., 1993—. With U.S. Army, 1943-45, ETO. Democrat. Roman Catholic. Home: 94 Saw Creek Est Bushkill PA 18324-9403

GARRIGAN, RICHARD THOMAS, finance educator, consultant, editor; b. Cleve., Mar. 4, 1938; s. Walter John and Priscilla Marie (Hill) G.; m. Kristine Ottesen, Dec. 26, 1962; 1 child, Matthew Osborne. BS summa cum laude, Ohio State U., 1961, MA, 1963; MS, U. Wis., 1966, PhD, 1973. Asst. prof. fin. U. Wis., Whitewater, 1974-76, assoc. prof., 1976-77; v.p. rsch. Real Estate Rsch. Corp., Chgo., 1975-76; presdl. exch. exec. Fed. Home Loan Bank Bd.,

Washington, 1977-78; assoc. prof. DePaul U., Chgo., 1978-83, prof., 1983—. Mem. Midwestern regional adv. bd. Fed. Nat. Mortgage Assn., 1993-96; mem. adv. bd. Bell Fed. Bank, Chgo., 1996-98; bd. dirs. Fed. Home Loan Bank Chgo., 1983-86. Co-editor: The Handbook of Mortgage Banking, 1985, Real Estate Investment Trusts, Structure, Analysis and Strategy, 1998; editor Dow Jones-Irwin Series in Real Estate, 1987-90; contbr. articles to profl. jours. Served with U.S. Army, 1955-58. Alfred P. Sloan scholar, 1959-61; recipient Excellence award Haskins and Sells, 1960, Achievement award Pres.'s of U.S. Commn. on Exec. Exchange, 1978; fellow Mershon Nat. Security, Ohio State U., 1961-62, urban studies Ford Found., 1964-65, bus. Ford Found., 1965-66. Mem. Am. Real Estate Soc., Am. Real Estate and Urban Econs. Assn., Bldg. Owners and Mgrs. Assn. of Chgo. (adv. bd. 1994-98), Sphinx, Univ. Club Chgo., Lambda Alpha Internat. (Ely chpt. sec. 1984, v.p. 1985, pres. 1986), Beta Gamma Sigma, Phi Kappa Phi, Phi Eta Sigma. Home: 10002 Meadowdale Cir Spring Grove IL 60081-8687 Office: DePaul U Fin Dept 1 E Jackson Blvd Chicago IL 60604-2201

GARRIGAN, WILLIAM HENRY, III, firefighter, paramedic; b. Evergreen Park, Ill., Apr. 5, 1954; s. William Henry Jr. and Mary Jane (O'Connell) G.; m. Melissa Ann Vaughan, Aug. 2, 1980; children: William, Vaughan, Amanda. AA, Coll. of DuPage, Glen Ellyn, Ill., 1975; grad. paramedic tng., Loyola Med. Ctr., Maywood, Ill., 1976; student, No. Ill. U., 1976-77; BS, So. Ill. U., 1987. Cert. instr. CPR, Am. Heart Assn.; adv. cert. fire fighter III; cert. fire apparatus engr.; cert. fire svc. instr. I. Firefighter/paramedic North Palos (Ill.) Fire Dept., 1977-78, Oak Brook (Ill.) Fire Dept., 1979—, asst. coord. emergency med. svcs., 1983-87, coord. emergency med. svcs., 1987-97. Mem. edn. com. for paramedic edn. Village of Downers Grove, Ill., 1990—; mem. safety com. Village of Oak Brook, 1987—; mem. ambulance report com. Good Samaritan Hosp., Downers Grove, 1988—. ACLs provider Heart Assn. South Cook County, Ill., 1986—; com. mem., advancement chmn. Troop 699, Boy Scouts of Am., Palos Park, Ill., AYSO coach, 1994, active Quigley South High Sch. Alumni Assn., 1972—; trainer, coach Palos Panthers Soccer Club, 1999. Recipient acknowledgement of contbn. Dept. Pub. Health, State of Ill., 1987, recognition and appreciation of dedication and svc. Village of Oak Brook, 1989. Mem. Nat. Assn. EMTs, Ill. Profl. Firefighters Assn., North Palos Firemen's Assn. (pres. 1982-84, Outstanding Svc. award 1988), Profl. Assn. Specialty Divers, Dive Rescue Inc. Internat., Phi Kappa Sigma Alumni Assn. Republican. Roman Catholic. Avocations: golf, water skiing, scuba diving, swimming. Office: Oak Brook Fire Dept 1212 Oak Brook Rd Oak Brook IL 60523-4003

GARRIGLE, WILLIAM ALOYSIUS, lawyer; b. Camden, N.J., Aug. 6, 1941; s. John Michael and Catherine Agnes (Ebeling) G.; m. Jeannette R. Regan, Aug. 15, 1965 (div.); children: Maeve Regan, Emily Way; m. Rosalind Chadwick, Feb. 17, 1984; 1 child, Susan Chadwick. BS, LaSalle U., 1963; LLB, Boston Coll., 1966. Bar: N.J. 1966, U.S. Dist. Ct. N.J., U.S. Ct. Appeals (3rd cir.) 1973, U.S. Supreme Ct., 1973; cert. civil trial atty., N.J.; cert. civil trial adv., Nat. Bd. Trial Advocacy; diplomate Am. Bd. Profl. Liability Attys. Assoc. Taylor, Bischoff, Neutze & Williams, Camden, 1966-67, Moss & Powell, Camden, 1967-70; ptnr. Garrigle and Palm, Cherry Hill, N.J., 1970—. Sr. counsel Am. Coll. Barristers. With USAR, 1959-67. Mem. ABA, N.J. State Bar Assn., Burlington County Bar Assn., Camden County Bar Assn., Internat. Assn. Def. Counsel, Def. Rsch. Inst., N.J. Def. Assn., Am. Bd. Trial Advs. (diplomate; pres. South Jersey chpt. 2001), Fedn. of Ins. and Corp. Counsel, Trial Attys. N.J., Camden County Inn of Ct. (master of the bench, chmn. 1989-96, treas. 1996—), Tavistock Country Club. Home: 223 E Main St Moorestown NJ 08057-2905 Office: Garrigle and Palm 1415 Route 70 E Ste 204 Cherry Hill NJ 08034-2237 E-mail: garrigle@aol.com.

GARRIGUS, UPSON STANLEY, animal science and international agriculture educator; b. Willimantic, Conn., July 2, 1917; s. Harry Lucien and Bertha May (Patterson) B.; m. Olive Tyler, July 2, 1942; children— Beth Ellen, Mark Tyler BS with high honors, U. Conn., 1940; MS, U. Ill., 1942, PhD, 1948; cert., Washington and Lee U., 1943, Sorbonne, 1944. Asst. U. Conn., Storrs, 1936-40; grad. asst. U. Ill., Urbana-Champaign, 1940-42, 46-48, asst. prof., then assoc. prof., 1948-55, prof., 1955—, head Sheep divsn., 1949-64, head Runinant divsn., 1964-70, prof. animal sci., internat. agr., assoc. head dept. animal sci., 1972-87, prof. emeritus, 1987—. Mem. Am. Dehydrator's Rsch. Coun., 1958-70; mem. Nutrient Requirements of Sheep Com., NRC, 1953-75, Non-protein Nitrogen Utilization Com., NRC, 1970-76; cons. UN Devel. Program, Jugoslavia, 1976, Midwest Univs., Consortium Internat. Activities Higher Edn., Indonesia, 1980, AID, Thailand, 1981, U. New Eng., Australia, Higher Edn. Indonesia, 1989. Contbr. numerous articles to profl. jours. Active Cmty. United Ch. of Christ; bd. dirs. Univ. YMCA, Champaign, Ill., 1956-62, 64-70; chmn. Baily Scholarships, 1972-76. Lt. maj. U.S. Army, 1942-46. Decorated Bronze Star. Recipient Nat. Block and Bridle Merit trophy, 1940; Service award Eastern States Exposition, 1959; Disting. Service award YMCA, 1970, 77; Animal Sci. Teaching and Counseling award U. Ill., 1980; Nat. Feed Ingredients Assn. travel fellow, 1971; outstanding alumni award Coll. Agriculture & Natural Resources U. Conn., 1996. Fellow AAAS, Am. Soc. Animal Sci. (Jean Claude Bouffault Meml. award in internat. animal agriculture 1994); mem. Soc. Exptl. Biology and Medicine, Am. Inst. Nutrition, Am. Inst. Biol. Sci., Coun. Agr. Sci. and Tech., Am. Registry Profl. Animal Scientists, Sigma Xi, Phi Kappa Phi, Phi Sigma, Gamma Sigma Delta. Home: 811 W William St Champaign IL 61820-5832 Office: 186 Animal Scis Lab 1207 W Gregory Dr Urbana IL 61801-4733 E-mail: garrigus@uiuc.edu.

GARRIOTT, LOIS JEAN, clinical social worker, educator; b. Avon Park, Fla., Mar. 22, 1944; d. John Arnold and Katherine Faith (Morton) G.; m. Bertram Paul Martin, Mar. 9, 1963 (div. Dec. 1978); children: Heidi, Ivy, Kurt, Aaron. AA, Macomb County Community Coll., Warren, Mich., 1969; BA in Psychology, U. Mich., Dearborn, 1974; MSW in Group Work, Wayne State U., 1978. Family therapist Cath. Social Svcs., Port Huron, Mich., 1978-79; specialist St. Clair County Community Mental Health, Algonac and Marine City, Mich., 1979-80, clinician, 1980-85, clin. supr., 1985-88; clinician Ctr. for Personal Growth, Port Huron, Mich., 1986-99, Macomb Family Svcs., Richmond, Mich., 1999—; pvt. practice Roseville, Mich., 1988—. Adj. lectr. Wayne State U., Detroit, 1987-89, mem. faculty, 1990—. Mem. Acad. Cert. Social Workers (diplomate). Avocations: crocheting, cake decorating, making quilts. Office: Wayne State U Thompson Home Rm 418 Detroit MI 48202

GARRIOTT, OWEN KAY, astronaut, scientist; b. Enid, Okla., Nov. 22, 1930; m. Evelyn Long; children by previous marriage: Randall O., Robert K., Richard A., Linda S. BSEE, U. Okla., 1953; MS, Stanford U., 1957, PhD, 1960; DSc (hon.), Phillips U., Enid, 1973. NSF fellow Cambridge (Eng.) U., Radio Research Sta., Slough, Eng., 1960-61; asst. and assoc. prof. elec. engring. Stanford U., 1961-65; astronaut, scientist Johnson Space Ctr. NASA, Houston, 1965-86, sci. pilot Skylab-3, 1973, dep. dir. Sci. and Applications Directorate, 1974-76, dir. Sci. and Applications Directorate, 1976, asst. dir. for space and life scis., 77-78, mission specialist on first Spacelab flight, 1983, project scientist Space Sta. Program, 1984-86; v.p. Space Programs Teledyne Brown Engring., Huntsville, Ala., 1988-93; co-founder Enid (Okla.) Arts and Scis. Found., 1993; adj. prof. lab. for structural biology U. Ala. in Huntsville. Served with USN, 1953-56. Recipient Disting. Svc. medal NASA, 1973, Gold medal City of Chgo., 1974, Robert J. Collier trophy, 1974, V.M. Komarov diploma Fedn. Aeronautique Internationale, 1974, Robert H. Goddard Meml. trophy, 1975; inducted into Okla. Hall of Fame, 1980, U.S. Astronaut Hall of Fame, 1997, Okla. Mil. Hall of Fame, 2000. Fellow Am. Astronautical Soc., AIAA (assoc.); mem. IEEE, Am. Geophys. Union, Assn. Space Explorers (dir., treas.), Internat. Acad. Astronautics, Astronaut Scholarship Found. (v.p. and vice-chmn. bd. dirs.), Sigma Xi, Tau Beta Pi.

GARRIS, WILLIAM RALPH, criminal justice educator; b. Lancaster, S.C., Mar. 21, 1950; s. Dixon Jerome and Ann (Williamson) G.; m. Rhonda Morgan, Dec. 2, 1978; 1 child, Andrea Blake. BA in Govtl. and Internat. Studies, U. S.C., BA in Social and Behavioral Sci., 1973, MA in Criminal Justice, 1987. Prof. criminal justice, adminstr. U. S.C., Lancaster. Mem. adv. bd. dirs. First Citizens Bank, Gt. Falls, S.C.; summary ct. judge. Co-author: Faces of Violence in America, 1996. Summary ct. judge State of S.C., Chester County, 1995—. Lt. col. S.C. Nat. Gurard, 1970-95; bd. dirs. Gov.'s Cmty. Youth Coun., 1999. Mem. Rotary Club (pres. Lancaster chpt. 2003—). Avocations: jogging, kayaking. Office: Univ SC PO Box 889 Lancaster SC 29721

GARRISH, THEODORE JOHN, publishing executive; b. Detroit, Jan. 6, 1943; s. Theodore and Adella Beatrice (Kimball) Garrish; m. Joy Ann Ziegler, Aug. 4, 1967 (div. 1979); children: Theodore John, Amelia Sutter. AB, U. Mich., 1964; JD cum laude, Wayne State U., 1968. Bar: Mich. 1969, DC 1972. Trial atty. U.S. Dept. Justice, Washington, 1969-72; pub. opinion analyst Com. for Reelection of Pres., Washington, 1972; chief advt. substantiation FTC, Washington, 1973-74; asst. spl. counsel to Pres. Washington, 1974; asst. to sec. U.S. Dept. Interior, Washington, 1976, legis. counsel, 1981-82; gen. counsel Consumer Product Safety Commn., Washington, 1976-78; ptnr. Deane, Snowdon, Shutler, Garrish & Gherardi, Washington, 1978-81; gen. counsel Dept. Energy, Washington, 1983-85, asst. sec., 1985-89; fed. insp. Alaska Natural Gas Transp. Sys., 1986-89; Wash. counsel Flanagan Group, 1989-91; pres. Brewery Mgmt. Co., 1989-94, Kent Island Investment Co., 1989-91, chmn., 1991-94; mng. ptnr. Wild Gooose Brewery, 1989-91, dir., 1994-98; v.p. Hospitality Assocs., Washington, 2002—. Mem. U.S. Adminstrv. Conf., Washington, 1976—78, Washington, 1983—85, Pres.'s Commn. Catastrophic Nuc. Accidents, 1988—90; sr. v.p. Am. Nuc. Energy Coun., 1991—94; v.p. Nuc. Energy Inst., 1994—2000; energy program mgr. Bechtel Nat., Inc., 2001—03; dep. dir. Office Civilian Radioactive Waste Mgmt., Dept. Energy, Washington, 2003—. Advisor Nat. Policy Forum, 1994—96; dir. Nat. Energy Resources Orgn., 1987—2001, counsel, 2001—03; asst. to group dir. Pres. Inaugural Com., 1973, dep. exec. dir., 1981; mem. adv. com. human concerns Rep. Nat. Com., 1979; del. Mich. Rep. Conv., 1966. Mem.: DC Bar Assn., Mich. Bar Assn., Fed. Bar Assn., Alpha Delta Phi. Congregationalist. Home: 103 Chesapeake Ave Annapolis MD 21403-3305 Office: 1000 Independence Ave SW Washington DC 20585 also: Dept Energy Office Civilian Radioactive Waste Mgmt 5A-085 Forrestal Bldg Washington DC 20585 E-mail: tedco2000@hotmail.com.

GARRISON, ARLENE ALLEN, engineering executive, engineering educator; BA in Liberal Arts, U. Tenn., 1975, PhD in Analytical Chemistry, 1981, BSEE, 1988. Instr. analytical chemistry, grad. rsch. asst. U. Tenn., Knoxville, 1975-81, rsch. assoc., 1981, sr. electonic design engr. dept. chemistry, 1985-89, rsch. asst. prof. dept. chemistry, 1989—; dir. measurement and control engring. ctr. Coll. Engring. U. Tenn., Knoxville; licensing exec. U. Tenn., Knoxville, 1998-99, dir. industry programs and tech. transfer, 1999-2000, asst. v.p., 2000—. Mem. NRC bd. assessment for Nat. Inst. Standards and Tech., Panel for Chem. Sci. and Tech., 1996-2001; mem. chemistry dept. alumni steering com. U. Tenn. Knoxville, 1994—; participant in NATO Advanced Study Inst. on Analytical Applications of Fourier transform infrared to Molecular and Biolog. Systems, Florence, Italy, 1980; organizer insl. spectroscopy symposium Internat. Conf. on Raman Spectroscopy, Hong Kong; co-chair Soc. Photo-Optical Instrumentation Engrs. conf. on optical methods for chem. process control, 1994; sci. bd. Iternat. Forum Process Analytical Chemistry, 1993—; presenter in field. Contbr. over 29 articles to profl. jours. Chair bd. trustees Fountain City United Meth. Ch., 1991-94; sec. Wesley Found. Bd., 1992-93; bd. dirs. Appalachian Sci. Fair, 1993-2003, WATTec, 1994-96, Discovery Ctr., 1995-98; mem. Pub. Bldg. Authority, 1995-2003, chair, 2000-02. Recipient Chancellors Citation for extraordinay cmty. svc., 1993. Mem. Soc. for Applied Spectroscopy (Meggars award 1982), Soc. of Photo Instrumentation Engrs., Coblentz Soc. (bd. mgrs. 1989-92, pres. 1997-98), Am. Chem. Soc. (sec. East Tenn. sect. 1988-90, chair-elect 1991, chair 1992, steering com. divsns. chem. edn. and analytical chemistry, chair Williams Wright award com. 1991, 92). Phi Beta Kappa, Phi Kappa Phi, Alpha Lambda Delta. Office: U Tenn Office Rsch and Info Tech 409 Andy Holt Tower Knoxville TN 37996-0147 Business E-Mail: garrison@tennessee.edu.

GARRISON, BETTY BERNHARDT, retired mathematics educator; b. Danbury, Ohio, July 1, 1932; d. Philip Arthur and Reva Esther (Meter) Bernhardt; m. Robert Edward Kvarda, Sept. 28, 1957 (div. 1964); m. John Dresser Garrison, Jan. 17, 1968; 1 child, John Christopher. BA, BS, Bowling Green State U., 1954; MA, Ohio State U., 1956; PhD, Oreg. State U., 1962. Teaching asst. Ohio State U., Columbus, 1954-56; instr. Ohio U., Athens, 1956-57, San Diego State Coll., 1957-59; teaching asst. Oreg. State U., Corvallis, 1959-62; asst. prof. San Diego State U., 1962-66, assoc. prof., 1966-69, prof., 1969-96. Reviewer of articles and books, 1963-97; contbr. articles to profl. jours. NSF fellow, 1960-61, 61-62. Home: 5607 Yerba Anita Dr San Diego CA 92115-1027

GARRISON, CHARLES EUGENE, retired automotive executive; b. New London, Conn., Apr. 9, 1943; s. Charles Westel and Thelma Rae (Coleman) G.; m. Trudy Elisabeth Thorburn, Aug. 26, 1967 (div.); children: Matthew Charles, Mark Andrew; m. Beverley Halcyone Watkins, Apr. 19, 1991. BA, Mich. State U., 1965, MBA, 1966. Supr. service garage and motor pool Mich. State U., East Lansing, 1972, mgr. automotive services dept., 1972-2001, ret., 2001. Co-owner The Latest Scoop, 1980—; fleet mgmt. instr. various agys., 1985—; cons. in field, 1985—. Elder Holt Presbyn. Ch., 1975-77, mem. various coms., 1977-85; divsn. coord. United Way, 1972-73; mem. East Lansing Mass Transit com., 1972-75; judge Ingham County Fair, 1977-80. Capt. USAF, 1967-72. Recipient Vol. Achievement award United Way, 1984, 85, Cost Reduction Incentive award Nat. Assn. Coll. and Univ. Bus. Officers, Gov. Mich. Energy Mgmt. award, 1988, Spl. Energy Innovation award U.S. Dept. of Energy, 1990. Mem. Nat. Assn. Fleet Adminstrs., Big Ten Transp. Assn., U. Club. Mich. State U. (bd. dirs., pres. 1986-94), Kiwanis (sec. 1995-97, Internat. Diamond Single Svc. award 1982, Mich. dist. Disting. Pres. award 1982, Outstanding Bull. Editor 1983, Disting. Sec. award 1997). Lodges: Kiwanis (Internat. Diamond Single Service award 1982, Mich. dist. Disting. Pres. award 1982, Outstanding Bulletin Editor 1983). Avocations: golf, bowling, bridge, spectator sports. Home: 3730 Lott Ave Holt MI 48842-9414 E-mail: garriso9@msu.edu., cegarris@pplant.msu.edu.

GARRISON, DAVID LACEY, JR., oil company executive; b. Houston, July 12, 1945; s. David Lacey and Marie Bel (Gardiner) G.; m. Pamela Jean Reid Adger, Mar. 7, 1970 (div. July 1975); 1 child, James Gardiner; m. Robin Childers, Apr. 2, 1977; children: Robert Adam, Susan Alexandra. LLD, La Academia Mexicana, Mexico City, 1991. Landman Chapman Oil Co., Houston, 1978; ptnr. J.A. Bel et al, Lake Charles, La., 1964—; pres. Garrison Oil Co., Houston, 1979-84, Lakeside Exploration Corp., Houston, 1984—. V.p., bd. mem. Lacassane Co., Inc., Lake Charles, 1990—. La. commr. of Indian Affairs, Baton Rouge, 1972—75; vice-chmn. Sam Houston Area coun. Boy Scouts Am., 1995—, bd. dirs. So. Region, 1999—; bd. dirs. Nat. Cath. Com. on Scouting, 1997—2001. Decorated Knight Comdr. Pontificial Order St. Gregory the Gt. (Vatican City), Knight Comdr. with Star Equestrian Order of the Holy Sepulchre, Knight Grand Cross with Gold Star Sacred Military Constantinian Order of St. George, Knight Sovereign Mil. Order of Malta (Rome), Knight of Justice Most Venerable Order of St. John (U.K.). Roman Catholic. Avocations: hunting, fishing. Home: 3731 Olympia Dr Houston TX 77019-3029 Office: Garrison Properties 3939 Essex Ln Ste 100 Houston TX 77027-5190 E-mail: dlgarrison@houston.rr.com.

GARRISON, ELIZABETH JANE, artist; b. Elmira, N.Y., Feb. 11, 1952; BFA, Ringling Sch. Art and Design, 1973; postgrad., Mansfield U., 1976-78; MS, Fla. State U., 1980. Exhibits include Mus. Contemporary Art, The Netherlands, Mus. Fine Arts, St. Petersburg, Fla., Renwick Gallery, The Smithsonian Inst., Washington, and others; represented in permanent collections Yale U. Art Gallery, New Haven, Conn., Kunstgewerbe Mus., Berlin, Honolulu Acad. Arts. Nat. Endowment Arts fellows, 1981, 88; Saltonstall Found. grantee, 1996. Home: 317 Elm St Ithaca NY 14850-3018

GARRISON, GENE KIRBY, artist, writer, photographer; b. Clayton, Del., Aug. 11, 1925; d. Leighton Bradley and Adelaide (Stevens) Kirby; m. Elbert Wingate Garrison; children: Robert Kirby, David Andrew. AA, Phoenix Coll., 1964. Founder Desert Artists, Inc. Author: Widow... or Widow-to-Be?, 1991, reissued as Widowhood Happens, 2002, Javelina, Have-uh-WHAT?, 2003; co-author: From Thunder to Breakfast, 1978, 2002; exhibits include Desert Artists, Inc., Cave Creek, Ariz., 1983-99, es Posible Gallery, Scottsdale, Ariz., 1992-98, Imagine Gallery, Scottsdale, 1988-2000; co-author: From Thunder To Breakfast, 2003; articles writer Carefree Enterprise, 1973-93; freelance writer, 1972—; freelance photographer, 1972—. Literary arts com. Foothills Cmty. Found., Carefree, Ariz., 1994-97; historian Desert Foothills Cmty. Theater, Carefree, 1975-95; active Sedona (Ariz.) Arts Ctr., Oak Creek Canyon Camera Club, Sedona; tutor Sedona Literacy Ctr. Mem.: Soc. Layerists in Multi-Media, Profl. Writers of Prescott, Sedona (Ariz.) Writers. Avocations: theater, travel. Home: 495 Rodeo Rd Sedona AZ 86336-3369

GARRISON, GENEVA, retired administrative assistant; b. Bowling Green, Ky., Feb. 14, 1933; d. Claude Harrison and Helen (Bohannon) Garrison; m. Marion Murphey Dare, Jr., Aug. 1955 (div. Mar. 1972); 1 child, Marcus Glenn. AAS, U. Louisville, 1975, BLS summa cum laude, 1977. Tchr. behavior disorders, learning disabilities, mentally handicapped Jefferson County Schs., Louisville, 1974—77; coord. parent edn. project U. Louisville, 1977—79; exec. sec. to dir. AHES Western Ky. U., Bowling Green, 1980, sec., asst. to dir. devel., 1980—84, exec. sec. to exec. v.p. adminstrv. affairs, 1984—87, sec. to pres., 1987—89; ret., 1989. Part-time crisis counselor LifeSkills Inc., Bowling Green, 1993—96. Author: (poetry) to profl. jours. Recipient Omicron Delta Kappa Outstanding Grad. Sr. award, U. Louisville, 1978. Mem.: AAUW, DAR, Warren County Ret. Tchrs. Assn., Ky. Ret. Tchrs. Assn., Oak Ridge Camera Club, So. Appalachian Nature Photography Club, Internat. Soc. Poets, Phi Kappa Phi (scholar 1978). Avocations: photography, nature walks, book collecting, fashion . Home: 733 Newman Way Bowling Green KY 42104-3810

GARRISON, GUY GRADY, librarian, educator; b. Akron, Ohio, Dec. 17, 1927; s. Grady and Emma (Dodson) G.; m. Joanne Ruth Sergeant, Mar. 22, 1964; 1 dau., Anne Olivia. BA, Baldwin-Wallace Coll., 1950; MS, Columbia U., 1954; PhD, U. Ill., 1960. Mem. staff Oak Park (Ill.) Pub. Library, 1954-58; head reader services Kansas City (Mo.) Pub. Library, 1960-62; prof., dir. library research center Grad. Sch. Library Sci., U. Ill., 1962-68; prof., dean Coll. Info. Studies, Drexel U., 1968-87, Alice B. Kroeger prof., 1987-91, dean emeritus, prof. emeritus, 1992—. Contbr. articles to profl. jours. Served with AUS, 1950-52. Mem. ALA, Assn. for Library and Info. Sci. Edn., Beta Phi Mu. Home: 731 Limehouse Rd Wayne PA 19087-2856 E-mail: guy.garrison@drexel.edu.

GARRISON, JOHN RAYMOND, organization executive; b. Bridgeton, NJ, Jan. 30, 1938; s. Raymond Wilson and Clara Ella (Moore) G.; m. Sally Anne Woodruff, Sept. 10, 1960; children: Glenn Thomas Wilson, Matthew Moore. AB, Harvard U., 1960; MPA (scholastic award), NYU, 1964. Adminstrv. asst. N.Y. State Banking Dept., 1962-63; planner N.J. Dept. Econ. Devel. and Conservation, 1963-64; sr. planner N.Y. State Office Regional Devel., 1964-66; mem. staff Gov. N.Y. State Exec. Chamber, 1966-71; program sec. Office of Lt. Gov., N.Y. State, 1971-73; dep. commr. adminstrn. N.Y. State Health Dept., 1973-75; exec. v.p. Hosp. Assn. N.Y. State, 1975-78; CEO Nat. Easter Seal Soc., 1978—90, Am. Lung Assn., N.Y.C., 1990—2001, Cherish Our Children Internat., Shiloh, NJ, 2001—; pres. J.R. Garrison and Assocs., 2001—. Bd. dirs. Internat. Union Against TB and Lung Disease, 1996—, World No Tobacco Day, 1999—; Nat. Bd. on Respiratory Care, 2003. Mem.: Harvard Club (NYC). Office: JR Garrison and Assocs PO Box 209 Shiloh NJ 08353

GARRISON, KATHLEEN MARIE, social worker; b. Gt. Falls, Mont., Aug. 18, 1954; d. Harry W. and Frances V. (Gallagher) Keith; m. Robert M. Garrison, Mar. 29, 1980; children: Marie Michelle, Lisa Celeste. BA, U. Mont., 1977, postgrad., 1979-80, Western Wyo. Coll., 1986-87. Habilitation aide Boulder River Sch. and Hosp., Boulder, Mont., 1977-78; program implementer Ivy Arts, Missoula, 1978-79; exec. dir. Vol. Info. & Referral Svc., Rock Springs, Wyo., 1980-84; caseworker for S.W. Wyo., Cath. Social Svcs., Rock Springs, 1991-96. Rep. Western Welcome Svc., 1994-96. Founding mem., bd. pres., bd. treas Children's Discovery Found., Rock Springs, 1992—98; vol., aux. coord. Meml. Hosp. of Sweetwater County, 1995—2001; program coord. Sweetwater Family Resource Ctr., 2001—; mem. Rock Springs Area Cmty. Found., 1997—; founding mem. Noteworthy Ball; bd. dirs., treas. S.W. Counseling Svc., Rock Springs, 1992—99. Home: 1017 Ford Cir Rock Springs WY 82901-4442

GARRISON, MAURICE ALLEN MARTIN, missionary, minister; b. Margie, Minn., Sept. 4, 1924; s. Edward Richard and Malvina Anna (Brown) G.; 1 foster child, Simeon Ben. BS(med.), U. Minn., 1946, BA cum laude, 1947; STB, Gen. Theol. Sem., N.Y.C., 1952, STM, 1954; grad., Macalester Coll., St. Paul, 1943. Ordained priest, Episc. Ch., 1953. Lectr. St. Andrew's Sem., Manila, The Philippines, 1953-57; founder St. Mary's Sem., Odibo, Namibia, 1962-66; lectr. St. John's Sem., Lusaka, Zambia, 1967; prin. Codrington Coll., Barbados, 1969-70; lectr. Trinity Coll., Legon, Ghana, 1979-85, St. Paul's Theol. Coll., Limuru, Kenya, 1985-87, St. Mark's Theol. Coll., Dar es Salaam, Tanzania, 1987-89, 92-94; apptd. missionary Episc. Ch. U.S.A., 1953-57, 80-90, ret., 1990. Curate Trinity Ch., N.Y.C., 1957-61, 72-73; parish priest Resurrection Ch., N.Y.C., 1970-71, Church House, Khartoum, Sudan, 1981, St. Matthew Ch., Addis Ababa, Ethiopia, 1985; chaplain Bklyn. House of Detention, 1968-75; asst. priest Transfiguration Ch., N.Y.C., 1990, 99-2002, St. Mary the Virgin Ch., N.Y.C., 1998-2002. V.p. Am. Indian Cmty. House, N.Y.C., 1975; bd. edn. Sch. Dist. 9, N.Y.C., 1975; asst. priest St. Mary the Virgin, 1993-2001, Ch. of the Transfiguration, 1995—. With U.S. Army, 1943-46. Canonry award Diocese of Kumasi, 1979; named Sr. Episc. Missionary, World Mission Com. Episcopal Ch. Ctr., 1990. Home: 102 Washington Ave Brooklyn NY 11205

GARRISON, PAUL CORNELL, retired office products company executive; b. Marietta, Ohio, June 18, 1935; s. William John and Alice Ray (Wilson) G.; m. Carole Virginia Whinery, July 3, 1960; children: Kristin, Holly, Craig, Kelee. Student, Ohio State U., 1953, Marietta Coll., 1958. V.p. Garrison Brewer Co., Marietta, 1955-64, pres., 1965-93; dir. of design Garrison Brewer Co. Div. of Stationers, Inc., 1992-93; asst. v.p. Barry R. Ankney, Inc., Marietta and Akron, Ohio, 1996—2002; assoc. Am. Family Life Assurance Co., Columbus, Ga., 2002—. V.p. Innerspace Interiors, Inc., Marietta, 1979-2002. Pres. Eve, Marietta, 1982-85, YMCA, 1974-76; chmn. Marietta Com., 1986, United Way Campaign, 1986. With U.S. Army, 1957-61. Republican. Presbyterian.

GARRISON, ROBERT FREDERICK, astronomer, educator; b. Aurora, Ill., May 9, 1936; s. Robert W. and Dorothy I. (Rydquist) G.; m. Ada V. Mighell, June 7, 1957 (div. 1980); children— Forest L., Alexandra, David C. BA in Math., Earlham Coll., 1960; Postgrad., U. Wis., 1961-62; PhD in Astronomy and Astrophysics, U. Chgo., 1966. Research assoc. Mt. Wilson and Palomar Obs., Pasadena, Calif., 1966-68; asst. prof. U. Toronto, Ont., Can., 1968-74, assoc. prof., 1974-78, prof. astronomy, 1978—2001, prof. emeritus, 2001—, assoc. dir. D. Dunlap Obs.; dir. U. Toronto So. Obs., Chile, 1970-98. Bronowski lectr., 1987; Sigma Xi lectr., 1988—90. Editor: The MK Process and Stellar Classification, 1984; co-editor: The MK Process at Fifty Years: A Powerful Tool for Astrophysical Insight, 1994; contbr. articles to profl. jours. Bd. dirs. Bruce Trail Assn., 1975—76. With USMC, 1954—56. Recipient Dean's award Lifetime Achievement as Outstanding Tchr., 2001, Queens Golden Jubilee medal, 2003. Mem.: Royal Can. Inst. (v.p. 1991—93, pres. 1993—94), Internat. Astron. Union (pres. com. 45 on stellar classifications 1985—88), Royal Astron Soc. Can. (v.p. 1996—2000, pres. 2000—02), Am. Assn. Variable Star Observers, Astron. Soc. Pacific, Am. Astron Soc. (Shapley lectr. 1985—), Can. Astron. Soc. (coun. 1978—81), U. Chgo. Club Can. (v.p. schs. 1982—88, pres. 1988—90). Office: David Dunlap Obs 123 Hillsview Dr Richmond Hill ON Canada L4C 1T3 E-mail: garrison@astrolutoronto.ca.

GARRISON, TRUITT B. architect; b. Lubbock, Tex., Apr. 6, 1936; s. Miles Elisha and Iva J. (Greenway) G.; m. Joyce Ann Ward, June 27, 1959; children: Todd Michael, Craig Mitchell. BArch, Tex. Tech U., 1962; postgrad., Grad. Sch. Design Exec. Program, Harvard U., 1971. Registered architect, 42 states. With Welton Becket & Assocs., Houston, 1962-63; sr. v.p. Caudill Rowlett Scott, Houston, 1963—, also dir.; sr. v.p., dir. ops. Internat. Group CRS Sirrine, 1963-97, cons., 1997—. Bd. dirs. Global Group; exec. v.p., gen. mgr. archtl. svcs. divsn. CRSS Architects, Inc., 1988, pres., 1990, exec. v.p., 1992-94; exec. v.p. CRSS Inc. Peace Shield Divsn., 1994-96, cons., 1997-99; mem. bd. Houston Architecture Found., 1992-96. Pres. bd. Epernay Homeowners Assn., 1978—; sec. bd. Happy Hill Farm Acad., 1999—; chmn. bd. dirs. HHF&A, 2001—02; mem. fin. com. Celebrate Arch., 1994—96, 1998; mem. De Cordova City Coun., 2000; alderman City of DeCordova, 2000—; bd. dirs. St. Lukes Meth. Ch., 1970—71, Epernay Homeowners Assn., 1977—86, DeCordova Bend Estates Homeowners Assn., 1999—2000, Happy Hill Farm Acad. With U.S. Army, 1958—59. Named Officer of Yr. Caudill Rowlett Scott, 1980 Fellow: AIA; mem.: Nat. Coun. Archtl. Registration Bds., Tex. Soc. Architects, DeCordova Bend Estates Country Club (bd. dirs., pres. 1999—). Home and Office: 4917 Rio Vista Dr Granbury TX 76049-5172

GARRISON, WALTER R. corporate executive; b. St. Louis, July 7, 1926; s. Walter Raymond and Esther Elizabeth (Kohlhepp) G.; m. Rose Faye Wilson, Aug. 10, 1946 (dec.); children: Bruce, Susan Garrison, Mark, Pamela Garrison Phelan, C. Jeffrey; m. Jayne Bacon, Apr. 15, 1973; stepchildren: James (dec.),

Jack. BSA.E., U. Kans., 1948, MSA.E., 1950; DBA (hon.), Spring Garden Coll., 1986. Registered profl. engr., Pa., N.J., Fla., Ill. Structural engr. Boeing Airplane Co., Seattle, 1950-53, cons. engr., 1953-56; staff engr. CDI Corp. and predecessor Comprehensive Designers, Inc., Phila., 1956-58, v.p., 1958-61, pres., chmn. bd., 1961—. Dir., chmn. bd.; mem. World Affairs Coun., Phila., 1983, World Pres.' Orgn., 1985. Chmn. bd. trustees Pa. Inst. Tech., Media, 1953—; mem. Upper Providence Twp. Environ. Adv. Coun., 1977-82, Pa. Bd. Pvt. Schs., 1965-71; mem. adv. bd. Sol C. Snider Entrepreneurial Ctr. Wharton Sch., U. Pa., 1987-94. Recipient Disting. Engring. Svcs. award, U. Kans., 1990, Good Scout award Boy Scouts Am., 1995, Legend CEO of the Year award, 1996, 1st recipient of World Affairs Coun. Annual Atlas award, 1998, Disting. Svc. Citation, U. Kans., 2001. Mem. ASME (industry adv. bd. 1987-98), NSPE, Phila. Pres. Orgn. (past chmn., bd. dirs.), Young Pres.' Orgn., Tau Beta Pi, Sigma Tau, Union League Club. Republican. Presbyterian. Home: 238 Sycamore Mills Rd Media PA 19063-2028 Office: CDI Corp 800 Manchester Ave Media PA 19063-4036

GARRISON, WILLIAM LLOYD, cemetery executive; b. Ridgway, Pa., Dec. 26, 1939; s. Lloyd and Mary Rebecca (Morrow) G.; m. Mary Jo Florio, May 30, 1964 (div. Mar. 2002); children: David, Mark. BA in Psychology, Ohio Wesleyan U., 1962; postgrad., Garrett Theol. Sem., 1962-63, U. Pa., 1963-64; MSW, Fla. State U., 1967; MS in Mgmt., Case Western Res. U., 1976. Caseworker Mpls. Ct. Chgo., 1963-64, United Cerebral Palsy Assn., Phila., 1964-65; psychiat. social worker Bellefaire, Shaker Heights, Ohio, 1967-74; dir. pers. and tng. Ctr. Human Services, Cleve., 1974-81, dir. resource devel., 1981-83; exec. dir. Cleve. Soc. for the Blind, 1983-85, Cleve. Eye Bank, 1983-85; exec. v.p. Lake View Cemetery Assn., Cleve., 1985-87, pres., CEO, 1987—; v.p. Lake View Cemetery Found., Cleve., 1988—. Adj. prof. Sch. Applied Social Sci., Case Western Res. U., 1974-80; v.p. E.A. Mabry Inc., Akron, Ohio, 1970-2001; chmn. agri-bus. adv. com. Cleve. Pub. Schs., 1990—, bus. adv. directorate, 1991-97. Dist. cub scout chmn. Boy Scouts Am., 1979-81, dist. chmn., 1981-84, scoutmaster, 1983-87, mem. coun. exec. bd., 1981—, asst. coun. commr., 1984-87, v.p. Boy Scouting, 1987-89, scoutmaster to world jamboree in Australia, 1988, coun. commr., 1989-92, cubmaster, 1997-2003, area v.p., 1992-95, area pres., 1995-97, area chmn. 19th World Jamboree, Chile 1997, region exec. com. 1995-97, nom. com. 1997—, mem. nat. coun., 1989—, nat. cub scout leader tng. chmn., 1998-99, nat. cub scout com. vice chmn., 1999—, v.p. Cub Scouting, 2003—; mem. pers. com. Lake Erie coun. Girl Scouts U.S., 1982-89; mem. Big Bros., Cleve., 1968-73; pres. Mayfield Heights Homeowners Assn., 1974-84, Cuyahoga County Reach Out Counseling Svcs., trustee, 1977-95, pres., 1991-95; bd. dirs. Garfield Meml. United Meth. Ch., 1979-81, vice chair pastor/parish rels. com., 1999-2000; mem. del. assembly United Way Svcs. of Cleve., 1987-95; trustee Alta House Cmty. Ctr., 1994-2000, Ctr. for Families and Children, 1995-2002; co-founder, v.p. East Cleveland Parks Assn., 1998—, pres., 2002—; co-chair civic divsn. United Way Campaign, 1999-2001; founder, pres. East Cleveland Twp. Cemetery Found., 2001—. Recipient Dist. award Merit Boy Scouts Am., 1980, Silver Beaver award, 1984, Silver Antelope award, 1994, 4-Way Test award, Rotary Club Cleve., 2000, honorable mention No. Ohio LIVE Award of Achievement, 1994, 2002; Menninger Found fellow. Mem. NASW, Acad. Cert. Social Workers, Soc. Human Resource Mgmt., Pers. Accreditation Inst., Internat. Cemetery and Funeral Assn. (cert. cemetery exec. 1997, membership com. 1993-2000, strategic planning com. 1994-96, hist. cemetery adv. com. 1994-, dir. 2003-), Ohio Assn. Cemetery Supts. and Ofcls. (exec. bd. 1992-97, v.p. 1993, pres.-elect 1994, pres. 1995-96), Greater Cleve. Cemetery Assn. (pres. 1987-90), Nat. Eagle Scout Assn., Greater Cleve. Pers. Coun., Social Agys. Employees Union (pres. 1970 73), Greater Cleve. Growth Assn., St. Luke's Hosp. Assn., Cleve. U. Cir. Inc., Am. Soc. Assn. Execs., Assn. Fundraising Profls., Cleve. Restoration Soc., Ohio Assn. Hist. Socs. and Museums, N.E. Ohio Intermus. Coun., Ohio Hist. Soc., Am. Field Svc., Cleve. Playhouse Club, Rotary (trustee Cleve. club 1993-96, v.p. 1996, pres. 1997-98, del. 88th Rotary Internat. conv. Glasgow, Scotland, 89th Indpls.), Cleve. Rotary Found. (trustee 1997-99, v.p. 1999-2000, pres. 2000-01), Hist. Cemetery Alliance (co-founder), Internat. Fellowship of Scouting Rotarians, Univ. Club, Delta Tau Delta, Phi Mu Alpha. Office: Lake View Cemetery Assn 12316 Euclid Ave Cleveland OH 44106-4313

GARRISON, WILLIAM LOUIS, civil engineering educator; b. Nashville, Apr. 20, 1924; s. Sidney Clarence and Sara (Elisabeth) McMurry; s. Marcia Fordyce Stanley, Aug. 31, 1938; children: Sara, Ann, Helen, Deborah, James, Jane, John. BS, Peabody Coll., 1946, MS, 1947; PhD, Northwestern U., 1950. From asst. prof. to prof. dept. geography U. Wash., Seattle, 1950-60; prof. dept. geography, civil engring. Northwestern U., Evanston, Ill., 1960-67, dir. transp. ctr., 1965-67; dir. ctr. for urban studies U. Ill., Chgo., 1967-69; Weidlein Prof. Environ. Engring. U. Pitts., 1969-73; dir. Inst. for Transp. Studies U. Calif., Berkeley, 1973-81, prof. civil engring., 1981—. Cons. U.S. Bur. Pub. Rds., Washington, 1960-68; bd. govs. Regional Sci. Research Inst., Phila., 1964—; adv. com. on econs. NSF, Washington, 1958-63; panel on values of social sci. research Nat. Sci. Bd., Washington, 1963-64. Author: Geographical Impact of Highway Improvements, 1960, Tomorrow's Transportation, 2000; author, editor Jour. Transp. Tech., 1985; editor: Quantitative Geography, 1969; articles in field. Served to capt. USAF, 1943-46. Recipient Disting. award U. Coun. of Transp. Rsch. Ctrs., 1999. Mem. Transp. Research Bd. (chmn. 1972-73, Roy C. Crum award 1973), Regional Sci. Assn. (pres. 1960), ASCE, Assn. Am. Geographers (Outstanding research award 1958), AAAS. Home: 10 Rancho Diablo Dr Lafayette CA 94549-2722 Office: U Calif Dept Civil Engring Berkeley CA 94720-0001 E-mail: garrison@newton.berkeley.edu.

GARRISON-FINDERUP, IVADELLE DALTON, writer, educator; b. San Pedro, Calif., Oct. 4, 1915; d. William Douglas and Olive May (Covington) Dalton; m. Fred Marion Garrison, Aug. 8, 1932 (dec. Nov. 1984); children: Douglas Lee, Vernon Russell, Nancy Jane; m. Elmer Pedersen Finderup, Apr. 8, 1994 (dec. Oct. 1997). BA, Calif. State U., Fresno, 1964; postgrad., U. Oreg., 1965, U. San Francisco, 1968. Cert. secondary tchr., Calif. Tchr. Tranquillity (Calif.) H.S., 1964-78, West Hills Coll., Coalinga, Calif., 1970-74. Lectr. in field. Author: Roots and Branches of Our Garrison Family Tree, 1988, Roots and Branches of Our Dalton Family Tree, 1989, The History of James' Fresno Ranch, 1990, 3d edit., 1993, There is a Peacock on the Roof, 1993; (with Vernon R. Garrison) William Douglas Dalton, a Biography, 1995, Sam (The Cat That Thought He Was a Boy), 1997, Amanda and Her Feathered Friends, 1997, Freddy Goes on a Trailer Outing, 1998, David Learns to Count, 1998, Laura and the Lizard: a fairy tale, 2001. Mem. DAR (sec. 1987-89, regent 1989-91, regent Fresno chpt. 1999-2001, scholarship chmn. 2002, nat. recognition for excellence in cmty. svc. Cert. of Award 1995), Nat. Trust for Hist. Preservation, Frazier Clan N.Am., Fresno City and County Hist. Soc. (life), Fresno Archaeology Soc. (sec. 1994), Children of the Am. Revolution (life patriot, sr. pres. 1991-97), Westerners Internat., Fresno Gem and Mineral Soc., Thora # 11 Dannebrog, Friends of the Libr. (Fresno), Chaffee Zoolog. Gardens of Fresno, Archaeological Inst. Am. (San Joaquin Valley chpt., charter mem.), Fresno County Archaeological Soc. Fresno Met. Mus., Baker Hist. Mus. (life), Fresno Gem and Mineral Soc. Republican. Lutheran. Avocations: quilting, knitting. Office: Garrison Libr 3427 Circle Ct E Fresno CA 93703-2403

GARRISON-JACKSON, ZINA, retired tennis player; b. Houston, Nov. 16, 1963; m. Willard Jackson. Mem. U.S. Olympic tennis team, 1988 (Bronze Medal in Singles and Gold Medal in Doubles - with Pam Shriver). Winner tournaments including Wimbledon Jr. Singles, 1981, U.S. Open Jr. Singles, 1981, U.S. Open Doubles Title (with Mary Joe Fernandez), 1993, Can. Doubles, 1986, 87, Birmingham, 1990; finalist Wimbledon, 1990. Office: c/o USTA 70 W Red Oak Ln White Plains NY 10604-3602 also: c/o Advantage International 1751 Pinnacle Dr Ste 1500 Mc Lean VA 22102-3833

GARRITANO, JOSEPH A. information scientist; B n Mgmt. Info. Sys., Pace U., 1998, MS in Info. Sys., 2003. Sr. programmer analyst Prudential Securities, N.Y.C., 2000—01; project leader Prudential Fin., N.Y.C., 2001—. Mem. 62nd Precinct Cmty. Coun., Bklyn., 2001—02. Mem.: Assn. for Computing Machinery, Project Mgmt. Inst., Delta Kappa Epsilon Nu Zeta Alumni Assn. (pres. 1999—2002). Home: Po Box 1035 New York NY 10272-1035 Personal E-mail: jgarritano@acm.org.

GARRITY, JUNE H. communications director, executive secretary; b. Bingham Canyon, Utah, June 15, 1929; d. John Werner Holmes and Helga Vera Forsnes; m. William Denn Garrity, June 20, 1954 (dec. June 5, 1970); 1 child, John William. BA in Journalism, U. Nev., 1951. Editor comm. dept. EDO Western Corp., Salt Lake City, 1976—81; media/pub. rels. dir. LIBRA Corp., Salt Lake City, 1981—89; legal sec. DeLyle H. Condie, Esq., 1995—99; sec. to Dr. John Anjewierden divsn. cmty. edn. Salt Lake C.C., 1997—99; part-time office mgr. Law Offices of David Paul White, Murray, Utah, 1999—. Writer, designer, editor. oceanographic publ. The Flying Fish, monthly newsletter EDO ECHO, bimonthly newsletter The LIBRA Scale, writer, asst. editor: employee publ. Kennescope; contbr. poetry and articles to anthologies and mags. Recipient Gold Medal award, State Advt. Fedn. Mem.: Internat. Assn. Bus. Communicators (Award of Excellence), DANAE, PEO, Daus. of the Nile, Order of Ea. Star (grand officer for State of Utah, Worthy Matron), Gamma Phi Beta (pres., local alumnae mem.). Avocations: travel, golf, skiing, photography. Home: 6271 S 530 E Murray UT 84107

GARRITY, RODMAN FOX, psychologist, educator; b. Los Angeles, June 10, 1922; s. Lawrence Hitchcock and Margery Fox (Pugh) G.; m. Juanita Daphne Mullan, Mar. 5, 1948; children: Diana Daphne, Ronald Fox. Student, Los Angeles City Coll., 1946-47; BA, Calif. State U., Los Angeles, 1950; MA, So. Meth. U., Dallas, 1955; Ed.D., U. So. Calif., 1963. Tchr. elem. sch. Palmdale (Calif.) Sch. Dist., 1952-54; psychologist, prin. Redondo Beach (Calif.) City Schs., 1954-60; asst. dir. ednl. placement lectr., ednl. adviser U. So. Calif., 1960-62; asso. prof., coordinator credentials programs Calif. State Poly. U., Pomona, 1962-66, chmn. social sci. dept., 1966-68, dir. tchr. preparation center, 1968-71, coordinator grad. program, 1971-73, prof. tchr. preparation center, 1968—, coordinator spl. edn. programs, 1979—. Cons. psychologist, lectr. in field. Pres. Redondo Beach Coordinating Council, 1958-60; mem. univ. rep. Calif. Faculty Assns., 1974-76. Served with Engr. Combat Bn. AUS, 1942-45. Mem. Prins. Assn. Redondo Beach (chmn. 1958-60), Nat. Congress Parents and Tchrs. (hon. life), Am. Psychol. Assn., Calif. Tchrs. Assn. Democrat. Office: Calif State U Dept Special Edn Pomona CA 91768 *Empathetic reaching out to others transcends the obvious importance of achievement and intellectual ability. This has been a basic guide for my endeavors in the helping professions.*

GARRITY, THOMAS JOHN, pharmaceutical executive; b. Connellsville, Pa., Feb. 19, 1949; s. John Peter and Helen (Russo) G.; m. Susan Lucille Maddox, Sept. 10, 1977; children: Stephen Thomas, Laura Christine. SB in Aeros. and Astronautics, MIT, 1970; MBA, U. Chgo., 1974. Various positions Eli Lilly & Co., Indpls., 1978-86, European area dir. Elanco divsn. London, 1986-90, dir. fin. planning Indpls., 1990-92, dir. pub. policy, 1992-94; CFO PCS Health, Scottsdale, Ariz., 1994—2000; exec. v.p. Advance PCS, Scottsdale, 2000—01. Vice pres. Zionsville (Ind.) Planning Commn., 1984-86; trustee Orchard Country Day Sch., 1991-95, Ariz. Sci. Ctr., 1999-2002. Mem.: Ariz. C. of C. (bd. dirs. 1996—2001).

GARRITY, VINCENT FRANCIS, JR., lawyer; b. Phila., July 26, 1937; s. Vincent Francis and Anne (Glenn) G.; m. Maryellen O'Brien, May 8, 1965; children: Vincent III, Ellen, Christopher, Elisa. AB cum laude, Coll. of Holy Cross, Worcester, Mass., 1959; LLB, Harvard U., 1962. Bar: Pa. 1963, U.S. Dist. Ct. (ea. dist.) Pa. 1963. Assoc. Duane, Morris & Heckscher, Phila., 1963-70; ptnr. Duane, Morris LLP, Phila., 1970—2002, co-chmn. bus. law dept., 1981—94, of counsel, 2003—. Lectr., U. Pa. Law Sch., 2000, 02, 03; disting. practitioner in residence Cornell Law Sch., 2001; adj. prof. Temple U. Sch. Law, 1996—; presenter, panelist in field. Contbr. numerous articles to profl. jours. With USAR, 1962—68. Fellow Am. Bar Found.; mem. ABA (com. on corp laws bus. law sect. 1983-89, participant in preparation Model Bus. Corp. Act, vice chmn. 1991-95, chmn. 1995-98, com. on negotiated acquisitions), Pa. Bar Assn. (chmn. sect. corp. banking and bus. law 1981-83, vice chmn. Title 15 task force on 1988 Pa. Bus. Corp. Law 1983—, Spl. Achievement award 1982), Am. Law Inst. (elected), Merion Golf Club (Ardmore, Pa.), Union League Phila. Roman Catholic. Home: 118 Derwen Rd Bala Cynwyd PA 19004-2710 E-mail: garrity@duanemorris.com.

GARRO, BARBARA, artist, writer; b. Camden, NJ, Feb. 3, 1943; d. Dominic and Mildred Barbara (Homiak) G.; m. James Edward Stephano, Nov. 28, 1964 (div. 1975); children: Victoria Lynne, Karen Marie. BS, SUNY, Albany, 1993, MA, 1996. CPCU. Sales, mktg. asst. Publickers Distillers Products, Inc., Phila., 1961-62; paralegal LaBrum & Doak/ Rawle & Henderson/Miller, Pincus & Greenberg, Phila., 1962-67; bus. owner Retail Sundries Store, Phila., 1967-72; various positions with pub. conglomerates, 1972-78; free-lance writer, 1978—; tax cons. Safeguard Scientifics, Inc., King of Prussia, Pa., 1980, corp. ins. adminstr., 1980-85; dir. risk mgmt. Comcast Corp., Bala Cynwyd, Pa., 1985-87; v.p. risk and ins. mgmt. svcs. UK&W Tech. Resources, Ltd., Albany, N.Y., 1987-89; CEO Electric Envisions, Inc., Saratoga Springs, N.Y., 1989—. Speaker, workshop facilitator on personality understanding, emotional intelligence and Enneagram staging; art tchr. Character Architectural Tech., trainer Newspaper columnist Corp Talk, 1986-2001, Ins. Tips, 1990-2001, Comm. Lines, 1993-2001, Bus. Talk, 1994-2001, Book Review, 1997-2002; writer, prodr., star performer syndicated pub. TV show Mother Goose & Gander; author: Grow Yourself A Life You'll Love; feature songwriter (with Margy Ward) Magic Night Music CD. Chaplain Saratoga County Jail, NY, 2000—; prayer line vol. Peale Ctr. for Chirstian Living., Pawling, NY, 2000—; Adv. bd. Upper Merion CATV, King of Prussia, Pa., 1987. Mem. Soc. CPCU, Am. Watercolor Soc., Upper Hudson Valley Watercolor Soc., Internat. Women's Writing Guild, Internat. Enneagram Assn., Inst. Noetic Scis. Republican. Roman Catholic. Avocations: exploring human and animal nature, antique collecting and restoring, student of life and love, music, theater. Office: Electric Envisions Inc 205 Regent St Ste 900 Saratoga Springs NY 12866-3319

GARRO, SUSAN ANN, adult nurse practitioner; b. Lynchburg, Va., May 12, 1944; children: Lisa, Tony, Pilar. BSN, Cath. U. of Am., 1984, MSN, 1995. RN, S.C.; cert. adult nurse practitioner. Adult nurse practitioner Dr. R.D. Gibbs, Moncks Corner, S.C., 1996-98, Ralph H. Johnson VA Med. Ctr., Charleston, S.C., 1998—; clin. faculty adult nurse practitioner program Med. U. of S.C. Sch. of Nursing, Charleston, 1997-2000. Guardian ad litem State of S.C. Office of Gov., Charleston, 1996—. Mem.: ANA, Am. Coll. Nurse Practitioners, S.C. Nurses Assn. and Advanced Practice Coun. (mem.-at-large 2001—03), Am. Acad. Nurse Practitioners, Low Country Advanced Practice Nurses (pres. 1998—2001), Sigma Theta Tau. Home: 22 Short St Charleston SC 29401-1908 Office: VA Med Ctr 109 Bee St Charleston SC 29401-5703 E-mail: suegarro@aol.com.

GARROTT, CARL LEE, foreign language educator; b. Indpls., Dec. 4, 1948; s. George Richard and Rosie (Diggs) G. BA, Ky. State U., 1970; MA, Tenn. State U., 1974; EdS, Western Ky. U., 1977; EdD, U. Ky., 1985; postgrad., U. Guadalajara (Mex.), 1999— 2000, Inst. de Filologia Hispanica, 1990, 91, 93, Monteverde Inst., Costa Rica, 2002—03. Instr. Cath. High Sch., Frankfort, Ky., 1969-70, Christian County Schs., Hopkinsville, Ky., 1974-81; prof. Chowan Coll., Murfreesboro, N.C., 1984-95; assoc. prof. Hampton U., 1995-98; prof. Va. State U., 1998—. Author: (monograph) The Thinking Man in France, 1977, (book) José Martí Poesía, Cuentos, Teatro, 2001, A Systematic Approach to Teaching Intonation Patterns in French, 2003; contbr. articles to profl. jours. Donor Sci. Enrichment Scholarship, Hertford County, 1984-91, 93; founder African-Am. Forum, Franklin, Southampton, 1987—. Sgt. U.S. Army, 1971-73. Woodrow Wilson Found. fellow, 1970, U. Ky. fellow, 1970-71, 81-84; grantee Ford Found., Starr Found., Va. Found. Humanities; faculty rsch. grantee Hampton U. Mem. MLA, Am. Assn. Tchrs. Spanish and Portuguese, Am. Assn. Tchrs. French, N.E. Conf. on the Tchg. Fgn. Langs., Am. Assn. for Applied Linguistics, Coll. Lang. Assn., Afro-Latin Am. Rsch. Assn., County Alliance for Sci., Cmty. Concert Assn., Alpha Phi Alpha, Alpha Mu Gamma. Democrat. Baptist. Avocation: shortwave radios. Office: Va State Univ Dept Langs and Lit Petersburg VA 23806 E-mail: cgarrott@vsu.edu.

GARROW, DAVID JEFFRIES, historian, author; b. New Bedford, Mass., May 11, 1953; s. Walter and Barbara Mae (Fassett) G. BA, Wesleyan U., Middletown, Conn., 1975; MA, Duke U., 1978, PhD, 1981. Instr. polit. sci. Duke U., Durham, N.C., 1978-79; vis. mem. Sch. Social Sci., Inst. Advanced Study, Princeton, N.J., 1979-80; asst. prof. polit. sci. U. N.C., Chapel Hill, 1980-84; assoc. prof. polit. sci. City Coll. N.Y., CUNY Grad. Ctr., 1984-87, prof., 1987-91. Vis. fellow Joint Ctr. Polit. Studies, Washington, 1984; sr. advisor Eyes on the Prize: Am.'s Civil Rights Yrs., PBS TV documentary broadcast, 1985-90; bd. dirs. Martin Luther King Jr. Papers Project, King Ctr., Atlanta; fellow 20th Century Fund, 1991-93; James Pinckney Harrison vis. prof. history Coll. William and Mary, 1994-95; disting. historian in residence Am. U., 1995-96, disting. Presdl. prof., Emory U., 1997—. Author: Protest at Selma: Martin Luther King and the Voting Rights Act of 1965, 1978 (Chastain award 1979), The FBI and Martin Luther King, Jr.: From "Solo" to Memphis, 1981, Bearing the Cross: Martin Luther King, Jr. and the Southern Christian Leadership Conference, 1986 (Pulitzer Prize for Biography 1987, Robert F. Kennedy book award 1987), Liberty and Sexuality: The Right to Privacy and the Making of Roe v. Wade, 1994; editor: The Montgomery Bus Boycott and the Women Who Started It: The Memoir of JoAnn Gibson Robinson, 1987; co-editor: The Eyes on the Prize Civil Rights Reader, 1987, 91, The Forgotten Memoir of John Knox, 2002; contbr. articles to publs. and profl. jours. Recipient NEH grant, 1984-85, Ford Found. grant, 1979-80, Lyndon B. Johnson Found. grant, 1979-80, Eisenhower World Affairs Inst. grant, 1985-86. Phi Beta Kappa. Democrat. Avocations: bicycling, hiking. Home and Office: Emory U Law Sch Atlanta GA 30322-2770

GARROW, ROBERT JOSEPH, JR., mathematician, educator; b. Buffalo, Dec. 24, 1929; s. Robert Joseph and Lillian (Andrews) Garrow; m. Mary Lou Laughlin, Aug. 8, 1961 (div. Sept. 1974); children: Sandra, Scott, R. Todd; m. Carrie Eileen Parker, Mar. 20, 1998. BS in Math., Ohio State U., 1961; MS in Math., Xavier U., 1969. Prof. math. Franklin U., Columbus, 1961—92, head basketball coach, 1962—70, chmn. dept. math., 1970—90; prof. Columbus State U., 1983—90; part-time prof. Urbann U., Columbus, 1985—95; founder, pres., chmn. bd. Montessori Acad., Columbus, 1972—92, Montessori Child Devel. Ctr., Columbus, 1975—86. Pres. Franklin Ednl. Svcs., Inc., Columbus, 1961—63; instr. math. Ohio State U., 1960—61; weights engr. N.Am. Aviation, Columbus, 1957—60; owner propane gas bus., Columbus, 1954—56. Contbr. articles. Sgt. USAF, 1950—54. Recipient Award for Outstanding Tchrs. in a Univ., Ohio Ho. of Reps., 1990. Mem.: SIAM, Am. Soc. for Engring. Edn., Am. Math. Assn., Am. Math. Soc. Mailing: PO Box 123 9605 E Bayshore Rd Lakeside Marblehead OH 43440

GARROWAY, NEIL WARREN, internist, endocrinologist, geriatrician; b. Bklyn., Dec. 26, 1945; s. Solomon and Doris (Palley) G.; m. Cynthia Moeller, May 28, 1972; children: Nathan, Joshua, Jordan. AB, Cornell U., 1966; MD, SUNY, Buffalo, 1970. Intern Barnes Hosp., 1970-72; resident in medicine Vanderbilt U. Hosp., 1972-73, resident in endocrinology, 1973-75; med. dir. N.E. Med. Ctr., Rochester, N.Y., 1975-80, dir. ambulatory svcs. The Genesee Hosp., Rochester, 1981-94, sr. v.p. med. affairs, 1994-99; pvt. practice Rochester, 1975—; med. dir. Ind. Living for Srs., 1999-2000; assoc. clin. prof. endocrinology U. Rochester Med. Ctr., 2000—. Med. dir. Rochester (N.Y.) Primary Care Network, 1987-96. Avocation: tennis. Office: U Rochester Med Ctr Endocrine Divsn 601 Elmwood Ave Box 693 Rochester NY 14642 E-mail: neil_garroway@urmc.rochester.edu.

GARRUTO, JOHN ANTHONY, cosmetics executive; b. Johnson City, N.Y., June 18, 1952; children: James, Christopher, Catherine, Gabrielle. BS in Chemistry, SUNY, Binghamton, 1974; AAS in Bus. Adminstrn., Broome Coll., 1976. Rsch. chemist Lander Co. Inc., Binghamton, 1974-77, rsch. dir. St. Louis, 1977-79, Olde Worlde Products, High Point, N.C., 1979-81; v.p. rsch. and devel. LaCosta Products Internat., Carlsbad, Calif., 1981-89; chief ops. officer Randall Products Internat., Carlsbad, 1989-91; pres. Dermasearch Internat., 1991-92; chief tech. officer Innovative Bioscis. Corp., Oceanside, Calif., 1992-95; v.p. rsch. Garden Botanika, Oceanside, Calif., 1995-99; pres., founder Free Radical Tech., 1999—. Cons. Trans-Atlantic Mktg., Binghamton, 1975-78; instr. cosmetic sci UCLA, 1991—, UCLA Ext.; lectr. to cosmetic industry. Patentee in field. Mem. AAS, Soc. Cosmetic Chemists (newsletter editor 1980-81, publicity chmn. 1984—, edn. chmn. 1987, employment chmn. 1994—, chmn. elect 1999-2000, chmn. 2000, nat. elections com. 2001—), Inst. for Food Technologists (sec. beauty industry west), Pacific Tech. Exch., Fedn. Am. Scientists, N.Y. Acad. Scis., Cosmetic, Toiletry and Fragrance Assn. (sci. adv. com.).

GARRUTO, RALPH MICHAEL, research anthropologist, educator, biologist, neuroscientist; b. Binghamton, N.Y., Nov. 20, 1943; s. Ralph Anthony and Josephine Janet (DiMartino) G.; children: Jessica Anne, Jason Michael, John Ralph. BS, Pa. State U., 1966, MA, 1969, PhD, 1973. Postdoctoral fellow NIH, Bethesda, Md., 1972-73, staff, then sr. staff fellow, 1973-78, from rsch. biologist to supervisory rsch. biologist, 1978—2003; adj. prof. med. genetics Coll. Medicine U. South Ala., Mobile, 1982—; adj. sr. scientist biol. anthropology Pa. State U., University Park, 1985; rsch. prof. biomedical anthropology neuroscis. SUNY, Binghamton, 1997, assoc. dir. Inst. Biomed. Tech., 2000—, dir. biomed. anthropology program, 2002—; adj. clin. prof. pathology Upstate Med. U., Syracuse, 1998—. Participant anthropol. and biomed. fieldwork, Asia, Pacific Islands, L.Am., 1969—; mem., NIH rep. U.S. Nat. Com. U.S. Man and the Biosphere Program, 1993-95; founding mem. bd. trustees Nat. Mus. Health and Medicine Found., Washington, 1989-91; exec. sec. Commn. on Aging and the Aged, Zagreb, Yugoslavia, 1985-89; cons. WHO, 1987; chair selection com. Paul T. Baker Disting. lectr. in human biology and anthropology Pa. State U., 1986-98; adj. clin. prof. pathology SUNY Upstate Med. U., Syracuse; Wellcome Found. lectr., vis. prof. U. Mich., Dearborn, 2001. Co-editor: Biological Anthropology and Aging: Perspectives on Human Variation over the Lifespan, 1994, Dermatoglyphics: Science in Transition, 1991; contbr. articles on neurodegenerative disorders, neurosci. and aging to profl. jours.; patentee bil. agts. Recipient Commendation for Rsch., Guam Legislature, 1987, Spl. Achievement award, 1990, Merit award NIH, 1991, Dir.'s award, 1993; Wenner-Gren Found. leadership grantee, 1986, grantee, 1993-95; Alumni fellow Pa. State U., 1987. Fellow AAAS, Am. Coll. Epidemiology, Am. Dermatoglyphics Assn. (sec.-treas. 1981-82, pres. 1987-89, disting. achievement award 1995), Human Biology Assn. (pres./pres.-elect 1993-96, exec. com. 1991-93), Internat. Assn. of Human Biologists (pres. 1999-2002, Gorjanović-Krambergeri medal 1999-2000), Internat. Genetic Epidemiology Soc. (founding fellow), NAS, Third World Acad. Scis. (assoc.); mem. Soc. for Neurosci., World Fedn. Neurology (rsch. com. on neuroepidemiology). Avocations: field trialing, environmental projects. E-mail: rgarruto@binghamton.edu.

GARRY, JAMES B. historian, naturalist, storyteller, writer; b. Taylor, Tex., Apr. 28, 1947; s. Mahon Barker and Grace (Dellinger) G. BS, U. Mich., 1970, MS, 1975. Part-time wilderness guide, naturalist Triangle X Ranch, Moose, Wyo., 1969-75; community organizer, media cons., tchr. Hobart St. Project, Detroit, 1974-75; media specialist, lobbyist Powder River Basin Resource Coun., Sheridan, Wyo., 1975-76; pvt. practice media and polit. cons. Big Horn, Wyo., 1976-78; video and film artist-in-residence Wyo. Coun. on the Arts/Sheridan Coll., Sheridan, 1978-80; mem. staff Great Plains Lore and Natural History, Big Horn, 1980—. Storyteller Buffalo Bill Hist. Ctr., Cody, Wyo., 1980—; tchr. Yellowstone (Wyo.) Inst., summers 1986—; tour study leader, rsch. collaborator Smithsonian Instn., Washington, 1984—. Co-author: Writing About Wildlife, 1974; author, editor: Buck: Stories by Lloyd Buck Bender, 1984, This Ol' Drought Ain't Broke Us Yet But We're All Bent Pretty Bad, 1992, The First Liar Never Has a Chance: Curly, Jack and Bill (and Other Characters of the Hills, Brush and Plains), 1994; storyteller in field. 2d lt. U.S. Army, 1970. Recipient Spl. Heritage award Old West Trail Found., 1983; named one of Individual Humanist of Yr., Wyo. Coun. for Humanities, 1986. Democrat. Roman Catholic. Avocation: nature. Home: PO Box 2165 Cody WY 82414-2165 Office: Great Plains Lore & Natural History PO Box 2165 Cody WY 82414-2165

GARSCADDEN, ALAN, physicist; b. Glasgow, Scotland, June 10, 1937; came to U.S., 1962; s. Andrew and Sarah Florence (Black) G.; m. Avril Margaret Thompson Garscadden, Jan. 24, 1962; children: A. Graeme, A.K. Neil, A.K. Gael, A.E. Hilary. BS (hon.), Queens U., Belfast, Ireland, 1958; PhD in Physics, 1962. Rsch. physicist Aerospace Rsch. Labs, Wright-Patterson AFB, 1962-73; lab. dir., 1973-75; rsch. physicist Aero Propulsion and Power Divsn., 1975-91; chief scientist Aero Propulsion Directorate, 1991-94, Wright Lab., 1995-97, Propulsion Directorate/Air Force Rsch. Lab., Wright-Patterson AFB, 1997—, Edwards AFB, Calif., 1997—. Adj. prof. physics Air Force Inst. Tech., Wright Patterson AFB, 1969—; bd. dirs. Von Karman Inst., Brussels; trustee Ohio Aerospace Inst., 1996-98. Contbr. articles to profl. jours. Commr. Planning Commn., Village of Yellow Springs, 1985-96. Recipient Disting. Svc. medal USAF, 1998; fellow Air Force Rsch. Lab. Fellow IEEE, AIAA, Am. Phys. Soc. (Will Allis prize 2002), Inst. Physics (U.K.). Avocation: history of colonial science. Office: AFRL/PR Air Force Rsch lab 1950 5th St Wright Patterson Afb OH 45433-7251

GARSH, THOMAS BURTON, publisher; b. New Rochelle, N.Y., Dec. 12, 1931; s. Harry and Matilda (Smith) G.; m. Beatrice J. Schmidt; children: Carol Jean, Thomas Burton, Janice Lynn. BS, U. Md., 1955. Edn. rep. McGraw Hill Book Co., N.Y.C., 1959-68; mktg. mgr. D.C. Heath & Co., Boston, 1969-71; dir. mktg. Economy Co., Oklahoma City, 1971-72; sr. v.p. Macmillan Pub. Co., N.Y.C., 1972-78; pres. Am. Book Co., N.Y.C., 1978-81; founder, pres., dir. Am. Ednl. Computer, Inc., Palo Alto, Calif., 1981-86. Founder, chmn., chief exec. officer OmnyEd Corp., Palo Alto, 1987-91; pres. Silver Burdett & Ginn divsn. of Simon and Schuster, 1991-92; dir. Fifty Plus Fitness Assn., Palo Alto, Calif. Publ. Homes and Land of Santa Clara, 1998—. Mem. county council Boy Scouts Am., 1963-65; mem. ch. council on Interracial Affairs, 1966-68, pres., 1967; vice-chmn. Madison County Democratic Party, 1967. Mem. Assn. Am. Pubs., Profl. Bookman's Assn., Omicron Delta Kappa, Sigma Alpha Epsilon. Clubs: Cazenovia Country (founder). Home: 401 Old Spanish Trl Portola Valley CA 94028

GARSHNEK, VICTORIA, physiologist, research educator; b. L.A., July 19, 1957; d. Nicholas and Nadia (Bolotov) G. BS in Biomed. Chemistry, Oral Roberts U., 1979; MS in Physiology, U. Oreg., 1982, PhD in Physiology, 1985. Rsch. technician Sch. Medicine Oral Roberts U., Tulsa, 1979-80; naval aerospace physiologist Naval Aerospace Med. Inst., Pensacola, Fla., 1981-84; space biomed. analyst Gen. Electric/NASA Hdqrs., Washington, 1985-87; sr. rsch. scientist George Washington U./NASA Hdqrs., Washington, 1987-91; asst. rsch. prof. Inst. Space Policy George Washington U., Washington, 1989-91; scientist prin. advanced planning Lockheed Engring. & Scis. Co., Moffett Field, Calif., 1991-94; sr. environ. scientist Oceanit Labs., Honolulu, 1994-96; dir. telemedicine rsch. Pacific E-Health Innovation Ctr., Tripler Army Med. Ctr., Hawaii, 1996-2000; rsch. scientist Ctr. of Excellence for Disaster Mgmt., Tripler Army Med. Ctr., 2000—; telemedicine rsch. coord. U. Hawaii Sch. Medicine, Honolulu, 2003—. Editorial cons. for space physiology and medicine 2d edit. NASA Hdqrs./Lea & Febiger Books, Washington, 1985—; editorial and tech. cons. Time-Life Books: Voyage Through the Universe Series, 1989—; mem. editorial bd. US/USSR Publs., Washington, 1989—. Co-editor: Working in Earth Orbit & Beyond, 1989; contbr. articles to profl. jours. Instr., counselor sch. without walls program NASA Hdqrs., 1988, 89. Lt. (j.g.) USN, 1981-84. Recipient NASA Hdqrs. Cosmos Achievement award 1989, 91. Fellow Explorers Club; mem. AIAA, Aerospace Med. Assn. (assoc. fellow, chmn. planning subcom. of edn. and tng. com. 1989-91), Medispace Assn. (hon.). Republican. Greek Orthodox. Achievements include developed method to measure bone blood flow in rodents during simulated weightlessness. Office: Ctr of Excellence for Disaster Mgmt 1 Jarrett White Rd Tripler Army Medical Center HI 96859

GARSON, ARNOLD HUGH, publishing executive; b. Lincoln, Nebr., May 29, 1941; s. Sam B. and Celia (Stine) Garson; m. Marilyn Grace Baird, Aug. 15, 1964; children: Scott Arnold, Christopher Baird, Gillian Grace, Megan Jane. BA, U. Nebr., 1964; MS, UCLA, 1965. Reporter Omaha World-Herald, 1965-69, Des Moines Tribune, 1969-72, city editor, 1972-75; reporter Des Moines Register, 1975-83, mng. editor, 1983-88; editor San Bernardino (Calif.) County Sun, 1988-96; pub., pres. Sioux Falls (S.D.) Argus Leader, 1996—; v.p. Gannett Pacific Newspaper Group, 2000—. Pres. S.D. Symphony Orch.; mem. adv. bd. Neuharth Ctr. U. S.D. Recipient Pub. Svc. Reporting award, Am. Polit. Sci. Assn., 1969, Mng. Editors Sweepstakes award, Iowa AP, 1976, John Hancock award for excellence in bus. and fin. journalism, 1979, Calif.-Nev. AP award for column writing, 1995. Mem.: S.D. Newspaper Assn. (past pres.). Jewish. Home: 5 S Riverview Hts Sioux Falls SD 57105-0252 Office: Sioux Falls Argus Leader PO Box 5034 Sioux Falls SD 57117-5034

GARSON, ARTHUR, JR., dean, medical educator; b. N.Y.C., N.Y. m. Suzan Garson; 2 children. Grad., Princeton U., 1970; MD, Duke U., 1974; fellow pediat. cardiology, Baylor Coll. Medicine, 1979; MPH, U. Tex., Houston, 1992. V.p. Tex. Children's Hosp.; chief pediat. cardiology Baylor Coll. Medicine, 1988, sr. v.p., dean acad. ops., 1995; assoc. vice chancellor health affairs Duke U., 1992; dean, v.p. U. Va. Sch. Medicine, 2002—. Pres. Am. Coll. Cardiology, 2000—01; mem. White House Adv. Panel on Health Sys. Improvement. Mem.: Assn. Acad. Health Ctrs., U. Hosps. Consortium, Assn. Am. Med. Colls., Health Sys. Improvement (White Ho. adv. panel), Quality Nat. Adv. Coun., Agy. Healthcare Rsch., Am. Coll. Cardiology (pres. 2000—01, mem. bd. trustees, mem. gov. rels., mem. quality of care). Office: U Va Health Sys PO Box 800851 Charlottesville VA 22908 E-mail: garson@virginia.edu.

GARSTANG, ROY HENRY, astrophysicist, educator; b. Southport, Eng., Sept. 18, 1925; came to U.S., 1964; s. Percy Brocklehurst and Eunice (Gledhill) G.; m. Ann Clemence Hawk, Aug. 11, 1959; children: Jennifer Katherine, Susan Veronica. BA, U. Cambridge, 1946, MA, 1950, PhD, 1954, Sc.D., 1983. Research assoc. U. Chgo., 1951-52; lectr. astronomy U. Coll., London, 1952-60; reader astronomy U. London, 1960-64, asst. dir. Obs., 1959-64; prof. astrophysics U. Colo., Boulder, 1964-94, chair faculty assembly, 1988-89, prof. emeritus, 1994—; chmn. Joint Inst. for Lab. Astrophysics, 1966-67. Cons. Nat. Bur. Standards, 1964—73, Internat. Comm. Illumination, 1990—; v.p. commn. 14 Internat. Astron. Union, 1970—73, pres., 1973—76; Erskine vis. fellow U. Canterbury, New Zealand, 1971; vis. prof. U. Calif., Santa Cruz, 1971. Editor: Observatory, 1953-60; Contbr. numerous articles to tech. jours. Recipient Excellence in Svc. award, U. Colo., 1990. Fellow Am. Phys. Soc., AAAS, Optical Soc. Am., Brit. Inst. Physics, Royal Astron. Soc.; mem. Am. Astron. Soc., Royal Soc. Scis. Liege (Belgium). Achievements include rsch. on atomic physics and astrophys. applications; calculation of atomic transition probabilities, atomic spectra in very high magnetic fields and magnetic white dwarf stars; modelling of light pollution. Home: 830 8th St Boulder CO 80302-7409 Office: U Colo Boulder CO 80309-0440 E-mail: garstang@earthlink.net. *It is a privilege to help others to learn about the wonderful universe in which we live.*

GARSTEN, JOEL JAY, gastroenterologist; b. N.Y.C., Jan. 10, 1948; s. Richard Maxwell and Gertrude Ann (Perlberg) G.; m. Marion Susan Moscovitz, July 10, 1971; children: Bryan David, Lauren Roberta. BA in Biology, CUNY, 1968; MD, Georgetown U., 1973. Resident in internal medicine Cornell-Coop. Hosps. Program, N.Y.C., 1973-76; fellow gastroenterology Yale Affiliated Gastroenterology Program, New Haven and Waterbury, Conn., 1976-78; gastroenterologist Gastroenterology Assocs. of Waterbury, 1978-90; physican, mng. ptnr. Digestive Disease Ctr. of Conn., 1990—; dir. sect. of gastroenterology Waterbury Hosp. Health Ctr., 1990—; assoc. dir. Yale Affiliated GI fellowship program Waterbury Hosp. and Hosp. of St. Raphael, New Haven and Waterbury, 1990-2000; clin. instr. internal medicine Yale U. Sch. Medicine, New Haven, 1978, asst. clin. prof., 1981, assoc. clin. prof., 1987—. Med. dir. Liberty Health Plan, Naugatuck, Conn., 1987-89, Physicians Health Plan, Trumbull, Conn., 1989-90, med. adv. bd., 1990-92. Contbr. articles to profl. jours. Med. adv. chmn. Crohn's and Colitis Found., WTBY Satelite, Waterbury, 1990—; resource speaker Waterbury Celiac Group, Thomaston, Conn., 1990—, Am. Cancer Soc., 1991—; prin. investigator multiple drug trials. Fellow ACP; mem. Am. Soc. for Liver Disease, Conn. Soc. Internal Medicine (pres. sect. gastroenterology 1996-98), Am. Soc. Internal Medicine, Am. Gastroenterology Assn., Am. Soc. Parenteral and Enteral Nutrition, others. Achievements include introduction of home parenteral nutrition of sclerotherapy, esophageal stenting, percutaneous gastrostomy, other endoscopic techniques to Waterbury; prin. investigator in drug rsch. trials (chosen for Best Drs. in the N.E.). Home: 47 Harvest Ct Cheshire CT 06410-1844 Office: Digestive Disease Ctr Conn 60 Westwood Ave Waterbury CT 06708-2460

GARSTKA, JOHN EDWARD, interior design educator; b. Holyoke, Mass., Dec. 28, 1940; s. Edward Joseph and Viola (Delage) G.; m. Caron Paula McKane, June 30, 1972; children: John Paul, Caron. BFA in Interior Architecture, R.I. Sch. Design, 1962; MS, U. Mass., 1975; PhD, U. Tex., 1994. Designer R.J. Hubert, AIA, South Hadley, Mass., 1962-68, Bernard Vinick Assocs., Hartford, Conn., 1968-69; tchr. Palmer (Mass.) High Sch., 1969-75; instr. interior design Tex. Tech. U., Lubbock, 1975-78, U. Ky., Lexington, 1978-81, Southwest Tex. State U., San Marcos, 1982—. Design cons. P.K. Design Assocs., Lexington, 1980-81; cons., San Marcos, 1982—. Mem. Am. Soc. Interior Designers (profl.), Interior Design Educators Council (treas. 1983-84, co-editor I.D.E.C. Bibliography 1983), Am. Soc. Archtl. Historians. Home: 302 Blueridge Trl Austin TX 78746-5409

GART, HERBERT STEVEN, communications executive, producer; b. Phila., June 11, 1937; s. Jack and Celia (Miller) G.; m. Lillian Allen Jay, Aug. 12, 1969; 1 child, Heather Joy. Student, Temple U., 1955-59. Pres. BSM Prodns., Inc., N.Y.C., 1965-70, Herbert S. Gart Mgmt., Inc., N.Y.C., 1963-84, Whitfeld Music, Inc., N.Y.C., 1965-90, The Rainbow Collection, Ltd., N.Y.C., 1971—. Personal mgr.: (1963—) Bill Cosby, Buffy Sainte-Marie, Jose Feliciano, Jesse Colin Young, The Youngbloods (Gold Record award Rec. Industry Assn. Am. and RCA Records 1968), Don McLean (5 Platinum Record awards Rec. Industry Assn. Am. and United Artists 1972), Andy Breckman (3 Emmy awards 1982, 85), Peter Tork (The Monkees), Ed Begley Jr. (several Emmy nominations), Jack Bruce (Cream), Felix Pappalardi (Mountain), Tim Hauser (Manhattan Transfer), Tommy West (Jim Croce), The Persuasions, Headsoup, Alix Dobson (feminist leader) Roger Davidson, Roxy Dawn, Ashley Cleveland, (record prodn.) (1965—) Janis Ian (Gold Record award Rec. Industry Assn. Am. and Columbia Records 1975, 9 nominations for and 3 Grammy awards won Nat. Acad. Rec. Arts and Scis. 1975), Dick Feller, Roy Buchanan, Charlie Daniels, Mississippi John Hurt, Felix Pappalardi, Roger Davidson. Office: The Rainbow Collection Ltd PO Box 300 Solebury PA 18963-0300 E-mail: yes@therainbow.com.

GART, MURRAY JOSEPH, journalist, consultant; b. Boston, Nov. 9, 1924; s. John and Frieda (Fisher) G.; m. Jeanne Brooks, Feb. 26, 1950; children: Mitchell Brooks, Marcia Anne. BA in Econs, Northeastern U., 1949, LHD (hon.), 1970. Reporter Honolulu Star-Bull., 1949-50; editor Weekly Ind. Record, Cape May County, N.J., 1950-51; reporter, city editor Wichita Beacon, 1951-53; reporter, news editor Wichita Eagle, 1953-55; bur. chief Time-Life mag. News Svc., Toronto, Can., 1955-57, Boston, 1957-59; chief Midwest corr. Time mag., 1959-61, bur. chief, 1961-64, London, 1964-66; asst. mng. editor Fortune mag., N.Y.C., 1966-69; chief of corrs. Time-Life News Svc., 1969-78; asst. mng. editor Time mag., 1972-78; editor The Washington Star, 1978-81; sr. editor Time Inc., 1981-82; assoc. Johns Hopkins Fgn. Policy Inst., Washington, 1982-84; cons. Time, Inc., 1982-89. Dir. Mid. East Inst., 1988—, Am. Near Ea. Refugee Aid, 1993—, bd. dirs. Washington Inst. Fgn. Affairs; Geopolitics of Energy, 1985-94, Editor: Cosmos Jour., 1992-95. Served with AUS, 1943-46. Recipient Best Mag. Fgn. Affairs Reporting award, Overseas Press Club, 1988. Mem. Coun. on Fgn. Rels., Cosmos Club, Northeastern U. Corp. Home: 2120 Connecticut Ave NW Washington DC 20008-1729 E-mail: mgart@att.net.

GARTENBERG, SEYMOUR LEE, retired recording company executive; b. N.Y.C., May 27, 1931; s. Morris and Anna (Banner) G.; m. Anna Stassi, Feb. 18, 1956 (dec. Feb. 3, 1998); children: Leslie, Karen, Mark; m. Phyllis H. Hecker, Mar. 14, 1999. BBA cum laude, CCNY, 1952, LHD (hon.), 1996. Asst. contr. Finlay Straus, Inc., N.Y.C., 1950-56; contr. Tappin's Inc., Newark, 1956; sr. v.p. Columbia House divsn. CBS, N.Y.C., 1956-65; v.p. fin. Columbia Records divsn. CBS, N.Y.C., 1965-67; exec. v.p. Columbia House divsn. CBS, N.Y.C., 1967-73; pres. CBS Toys Divsn., Cranbury, N.J., 1973-78; v.p. CBS/Columbia Group, N.Y.C., 1978—; sr. group v.p. CBS Records Group, 1979-87; exec. v.p. CBS Records Inc., 1987-91; ret., 1991. Mem. Inst. of Mgmt. Accts., Am. Mgmt. Assn., Mill Island Civic Assn.

GARTH, BRYANT GEOFFREY, law educator, foundation executive; b. San Diego, Dec. 9, 1949; s. William and Patricia (Feild) G.; m. Gwendolyn Sessions; children: Heather, Andrew, Daniela. BA magna cum laude, Yale U., 1972; JD, Stanford U., 1975; PhD, European U. Inst., Florence, Italy, 1979. Bar: Calif. 1975, Ind. 1988. Law clk. to judge U.S. Dist. Ct. (no. dist.) Calif., San Francisco, 1978-79; asst. prof. Ind. U., Bloomington, 1979-82, assoc. prof., 1982-85, prof., 1985-92, dean Law Sch., 1986-90; dir. Am. Bar Found., Chgo., 1990—. Cons. Ont. Law Reform Commn., 1984-85, 94, World Bank Argentina Project, 1993-94, World Bank Ecuador Project, 2003; vis. assoc. prof. U. Mich., Ann Arbor, 1983-84; bd. dirs. Internat. Human Rights Law Inst.; mem. bd. visitors Stanford U. Law Sch., 1993-2000. Author: Neighborhood Law Firms for the Poor, 1980; co-editor: Access to Justice: A World Survey, 1978, Access to Justice: Emerging Issues and Perspectives, 1979, Dealing in Virtue, 1996, Internationalization of Palace Wars, 2002; contbr. articles to profl. jours. V.p. H.G. & K.F. Montgomery Found. Rsch. grantee NSF, 1982, 91, 92, 95, 99, 2001, Nat. Inst. Dispute Resolution, 1985, Ind. Supreme Ct., 1989, Italian Coun. Rsch., 1989, Keck, 1995, MacArthur, 1997. Mem.: Law and Soc. Assn., Am. Law Inst. Democrat. Office: Am Bar Found 750 N Lake Shore Dr Chicago IL 60611-4403 E-mail: bggarth@abfn.org.

GARTH, LEONARD I. judge; b. Bklyn., Apr. 7, 1921; s. Frank A. and Anne F. Goldstein; m. Sarah Miriam Kaufman, Sept. 6, 1942; 1 child, Tobie Gail Garth Meisel. BA, Columbia U., 1942; postgrad., Nat. Inst. Pub. Affairs, 1942—43; LLB, Harvard U., 1952. Bar: N.J. 1952. Mem. firm Cole, Berman & Garth (and predecessors), Paterson, NJ, 1952—70; judge U.S. Dist. Ct. for Dist. N.J., Newark, 1970—73; U.S. cir. judge Ct. Appeals for 3d Cir., 1973—; lectr. Inst. Continuing Legal Edn.; lectr., coadj. mem. faculty Rutgers U. Law Sch., 1978—98, Seton Hall Law Sch., 1980—95. Mem. N.J. Bd. Bar Examiners, 1964—68; mem. com. on revision gen. and admiralty rules Fed. Dist. Ct. N.J.; former mem. com. on fin. disclosure Jud. Conf. U.S.; adv. bd. Fed. Cts. Study Com. Pres.; trustee Harvard Law Sch. Assn. N.J., 1958—63; adv. bd. Law and Soc. Major of Ramapo Coll. 1st lt. U.S. Army, 1943—46. Mem.: FBA, ABA (N.J. fellows, appellate judges conf.), Am. Law Inst., Passaic County (N.J.) Bar Assn. (pres. 1967—68). Office: Ct Appeals ML King Jr Fed Bldg 50 Walnut St Rm 5040 Newark NJ 07102-3506 also: 20613 US Courthouse Philadelphia PA 19106 E-mail: chambers_of_judge_leonard_garth@ca3.uscourts.gov.

GARTH-LEWIS, KIMBERLEY, state official, political scientist; b. Sacramento, Calif. children: Shavaugn, Veronica. BS, U. San Francisco, 1981; MPA, Golden Gate U., 1986, DPA, 1992. Cert. lifetime credential for pub. adminstrn. and colls. Rschr. in neurology U. Calif.-San Francisco Med. Ctr., 1978—81; ins. investigator ExpiFax Svc., Calif. and Nev., 1982—85; exec. asst. U.S. Embassy, London, 1985—86, Dept. Def. Dependent Sch., England, 1986—87; cons. Calif. Legislature, Sacramento, 1988—92; lobbyist Calif. Correctional Peace Officers Assn., Sacramento, 1992—95; prof. Calif. State U., 1993—95, U. San Francisco, San Francisco, 1992—; criminal justice specialist Office of Gov. of Calif., 1999—2002; cons. Dept. of Edn., Calif., 2002—. Cons., owner KAGL & Affiliates, Inc., Sacramento, 1995—; chmn. welfare reform Human Svcs. Coord. Coun., Sacramento, 1999; cons. Bur. Justice Correctional, 1999—; bd. dirs. Calif. Criminal Justice Inst., 2002. Bd. dirs. NAFE, Calif., 1990—92. Recipient Calif. Resolution, Calif. State Legislature, 1990, Outstanding Woman's award, YWCA, 1999. Avocations: reading, running. Home: PO Box 293402 Sacramento CA 95828 Fax: 916-689-2797. E-mail: KAGL@hotmail.com.

GARTHOFF, RAYMOND LEONARD, diplomat, diplomatic historian; b. Cairo, Mar. 26, 1929; parents Am. citizens; s. Arnold Alexander and Margaret Louise (Frank) G.; m. Vera Alexandrovna Vasilieva, Sept. 16, 1950; 1 child, Alexander Raymond. AB, Princeton U., 1948; MA, Yale U., 1949, PhD, 1951. Rsch. staff RAND Corp., Washington, 1950-57; estimates officer CIA, Washington, 1957-61; with U.S. Dept. of State, Washington, 1961-79, ambassador, 1977-79; sr. fellow Brookings Instn., Washington, 1980-94. Author: Detente and Confrontation, 1985, rev. edit., 1994, Deterrence and Revolution in Soviet Military Doctrine, 1990, The Great Transition, 1994, Reflections on the Cuban Missile Crisis, 1987, rev. edit. 1989, A Journey through the Cold War, 2001, 11 other books; editor, co-author 80 books; contbr. over 100 articles to profl. jours. Recipient Arthur S. Flemming award Jaycees, 1965, Superior Honor award Dept. of State, 1965, Disting. Honor award, 1972, Wilbur L. Cross medal Yale U., 1992. Mem. Coun. Fgn. Rels., Am. Assn. for Advancement of Slavic Studies, Soc. for Historians of Am. Fgn. Rels., Internat. Inst. for Strategic Studies, Acad. Polit. Sci., Assn. Diplomatic Studies. Home: 1901 Wyoming Ave NW Apt 14 Washington DC 20009

GARTHWAITE, GENE RALPH, historian, educator; b. Mt. Hope, Wis., July 15, 1933; s. Ralph Albert and Merle I. (Quarne) G.; div.; children: R. Andrew, Alexander, Martin. BA, St. Olaf Coll., 1955; postgrad., U Chgo., 1958-59; PhD, U. Calif., 1969; MA, Dartmouth Coll., 1987. From instr. to prof. history Dartmouth Coll., Hanover, N.H., 1968-98, chair Asian studies, 1980-92, chair history dept., 1992-96, Jane & Raphael Bernstein prof. in Asian studies, 1998—. Author: Khans and Shahs, 1983; contbr. articles to profl. jours. Capt. USAF, 1955-58. Grantee Social Sci. Rsch. Coun., NEH, 1979-80, 91-93. Mem. Middle East Studies Assn. (dir. 1968—), Soc. Iranian Studies (exec. sec. 1969—), Phi Beta Kappa. Democrat. Episcopalian. Avocation: gardening. Office: Dartmouth Coll Dept History Hanover NH 03755

GARTLAND, ALICE JOHNSON, artist; b. Phila., Jan. 27, 1922; d. Nelson Vincent Johnson and Alice Marie McDonald; m. Henry Joseph Gartland, Apr. 15, 1944; children: Kevin Henry, Michael Henry, Sean Henry. Student, Mary Washington Coll., 1945-46, George Washington U., 1950, Santa Fe C.C., 1971-72, Fla. C.C. With U.S. Govt., Petersburg, Va., 1942—44, Phila., 1940—44; tchr. Fla. C.C., Jacksonville, 1989-90; writer, columnist Art Scene Beaches Leader Newspaper, Jacksonville, 1991—. Paintings exhibited St. Augustine Art Assn., 1994, Beaches Fine Arts Guild, 1990 (1st Prize), Gainesville Fine Arts Guild, 1980, Art League, Washington, 1975, 84, Fla. Capitol, Tallahassee, 2001. Pres., founder Beaches Art Found., Jacksonville, 1990; pres. Beaches Arts Ctr., Jacksonville; bd. dirs., 1st v.p. Beaches Area Hist. Soc., Jacksonville, 1995-2000; bd. dirs., chmn. cultural adv. bd. City of Atlantic Beach, Fla., 1995-2000; apptd. by mayor Cultural Coun. City of Jacksonville, 2002—; bd. dirs. Beaches Fine Arts Coun., Jacksonville Beach, Fla., City Grants Com., Jacksonville, 1991, 92. Recipient Monetary award Jacksonville Comty. Found., 1994. Mem. Nat. Soc. Arts and Letters. Republican. Roman Catholic. Avocations: reading, gardening, painting. Home: 1140 Seminole Rd Atlantic Beach FL 32233-5505

GARTLAND, JOHN JOSEPH, physician, writer; b. Phila., Nov. 16, 1918; s. John Joseph and Jane Madelyn (Lafferty) G.; m. Madelyn T. Duffy, Jan. 5, 1944; children: Lynn, Barbara, John Jr., Patricia, Mary Ellen. AB, Princeton U., 1941; MD, Jefferson Med. Coll., 1944. Diplomate Am. Bd. of Orthopaedic Surgery. Chief orthopaedic surgery Meth. Hosp., Phila., 1960-68, Lankenau Hosp., Phila., 1968-70; James Edward prof., chmn. dept. of orthopaedic surgery Jefferson Med. Coll., Thomas Jefferson U., Phila., 1970-85, dir. office departmental rev. Jefferson Med. Coll., 1986-89, univ. med. editor, 1990—. Author: Fundamentals of Orthopaedics, 1965, 4th edit., 1986, Medical Writing and Communicating, 1993; contbr. numerous articles to profl. jours. Trustee Thomas Jefferson U., 1996-2002. Served to capt. U.S. Army, 1945-47. NIH grantee, 1971-74. Fellow Am. Acad. Orthopaedic Surgeons (pres. 1979-80), Am. Orthopaedic Assn.; mem. Coun. Med. Splty. Socs. (pres. elect 1987, pres. 1990), Overbrook Golf Club (Bryn Mawr, Pa.), Alpha Omega Alpha, Sigma Xi. Democrat. Roman Catholic. Avocations: tennis, writing. Office: Thomas Jefferson U 1710 Edison Bldg 130 S 9th St Philadelphia PA 19107

GARTLAND, WILLIAM JOSEPH, JR., research institute administrator; b. N.Y.C., Apr. 15, 1941; s. William Joseph and Mary (Klik) G.; m. Margaret Louise Wenstadt, June 20, 1981. BS, Holy Cross Coll., 1962; MA, Princeton U., 1964, PhD, 1967. Asst. rsch. scientist NYU Med. Ctr., N.Y.C., 1967-69; postgrad. rsch. biologist U. Calif., San Diego, 1969-70; grants assoc. div. rsch. grants NIH, Bethesda, Md., 1970-71; program adminstr. genetics program Nat. Inst. Gen. Med. Scis., 1971-76; exec. sec. Recombinant DNA Adv. Com., 1975-88; dir. Office Recombinant DNA Activities, 1976-88; U.S. rep. European Sci. Found. Liaison Com. on Recombinant DNA Rsch., 1976-81; NIH rep. Recombinant DNA Com. of USDA, 1978-88; asst. dir. for preclin. scis. AIDS program Nat. Inst. Allergy and Infectious Diseases, NIH, Bethesda, Md., 1988-89; chief resources and ctrs. br. AIDS div. Nat. Inst. Allergy and Infectious Diseases, NIH, Bethesda, Md., 1989—. Mem. exec. recombinant DNA com. NIH, 1976-88; U.S. head U.S.-Japan Coop. Program for Recombinant DNA Rsch., 1982-88; U.S. head AIDS panel U.S.-Japan Coop. Med. Sci. Program, 1988—; mem. faculty CSC exec. seminar program and advanced study program Brookings Instn. Co-author articles in field. Recipient Dirs. award NIH, 1978, spl. recognition award USPHS, 1988. Mem. AAAS, Am. Soc. Human Genetics, Am. Soc. Microbiology Clubs: Sierra, Washington Ski. Home: 12300 Morning Light Ter Gaithersburg MD 20878-2090 Office: 45 Center Dr Msc 6402 Bethesda MD 20892-0001

GARTNER, ALAN P. municipal official; b. N.Y.C., Apr. 4, 1935; s. Harold J. and Mary T.; children: Jonathan, Rachel, Daniel. BA, Antioch Coll., 1956; MA, Harvard U., 1960; PhD, Union Grad. Sch., 1973. Tchr. Newton (Mass.) H.S., 1961—65; cmty. rels. dir. Congress of Racial Equality, 1965-66; exec. dir. Econ. Opportunity Coun. of Suffolk County, 1966-68; dir. New Careers Tng. Lab., N.Y.C., 1968-81; prof. Queens Coll., 1972-76, Grad. Sch., CUNY, 1976—81, dir. Ctr. for Advanced Study in Edn. Grad. Sch., 1978-81, dir. Office of Sponsored Rsch., 1983-92, dean Rsch. and Univ. Progs., 1992-98, prof., 1983—2002; dir. policy rsch. Office of Mayor, City of NY, 2002—; exec. dir. N.Y.C. Charter Revision Commn., 2003—. Exec. dir. divsn. spl. edn. N.Y.C. Pub. Schs., 1981-83; exec. dir. N.Y.C. Districting Commn., 1990-92; pub. Social Policy mag., N.Y.C., 1971-93; exec. dir. task force on N.Y.C. Cmty. Sch. Bd. Governance, 1998; exec. dir. Charter Revision Commn., 2003—. Author: Paraprofessionals and Their Performance, 1971, The Preparation of Human Services Professionals, 1976; co-author: Children Teach Children, 1971, The Service Society and Consumer Vanguard, 1974, Self Help in the Human Services, 1977, Help: A Working Guide to Self-Help Groups, 1979, Supporting Families With a Child With Disabilities, 1991, Inclusion and School Reform, 1997, Inclussion: A Service, Not a Place, 2002; co-editor: After Deschooling, What?, 1973, Public Service Employment, 1973, What Nixon is Doing to Us, 1973, The New Assault on Equality, 1974, What Reagan is Doing to Us, 1982, The Self-Help Revolution, 1985, Beyond Reagan, 1985, Images of the Disabled/Disabling Images, 1987, Caring for America's Children, 1989, Beyond Separate Education, 1989, Inclusion and School Reform, 1997. Bd. dirs. N.Y. Civil Liberties Union, 1973—2002; bd. dirs. Antioch Coll., 1974-75; treas. Congress Racial Equality, N.Y.C., 1962-64, chairperson, Boston, 1960-64. Ford Found. fellow, 1956-58; Florina Lasker fellow, 1961-62; Poynter fellow, 1976 Office: Office of Mayor City Hall New York NY 10007 E-mail: agartner@cityhall.nyc.gov.

GARTNER, DANIEL LEE, computer information executive; b. Newark, Ohio, Jan. 24, 1945; s. Harold Jerome and Hazel Marie (Wright) G.; m. Holly L. Hanbaum, July 31, 1993; 1 child, Sarah Marie. Student, Ohio State U., 1967-74; BA, Park Coll., 1978; MS, USAF Inst. Tech., 1982. Computer programmer USAF, Newark AFB, 1974-78, computer systems analyst, 1978-82, chief info. ctr., 1981-82, chief customer support div., 1988-92, chief office staff support, 1992-95; adj. prof. logistics and computers Park Coll., Newark, 1986-91. Cons. pvt. sector, Newark, 1983—. Designer 1st broadband local area network, 1st info. ctr. Air Force Logistics Command. Adv. Boy Scouts Am., Newark AFB, 1984-86; active Big Bros. and Big Sister, Newark AFB, 1986; bd. dirs. Newark YMCA, Licking County Planning Commn.; 1st chmn. Licking Park Dist., 1990-91. Mem. Newark C. of C. (mem. leadership tomorrow 1986). Avocation: computers. Home: 1500 Londondale Pkwy Newark OH 43055-1696 Office: Gartner Consulting 1500 Londondale Pkwy Newark OH 43055 E-mail: dlgartner@hotmail.com.

GARTNER, HAROLD HENRY, III, lawyer; b. L.A., June 23, 1948; s. Harold Henry Jr. and Frances Mildred (Evans) Gartner; m. Denise Helene Young, June 7, 1975 (div. 2003); children: Patrick Christopher, Matthew Alexander. Student, Pasadena City Coll., 1966-67, George Williams Coll., 1967-68, Calif. State U., Los Angeles, 1969; JD cum laude, Loyola U., Los Angeles, 1972. Bar: Calif. 1972, U.S. Dist. Ct. (cen. dist.) Calif. 1973, U.S. Ct. Appeals (9th cir.) 1973. Assoc. Hitt, Murray & Caffray, Long Beach, Calif., 1972; dep. city atty. City of L.A., 1972-73; assoc. Patterson, Ritner & Lockwood, L.A., 1973-79; mng. ptnr. all offices Patterson, Ritner, Lockwood, Gartner & Jurich, L.A., Ventura, Bakersfield, and San Bernardino, Calif., 1991—. Instr. law Ventura Coll., 1981. Recipient Am. Jurisprudence award Trusts and Equity, 1971. Mem. ABA, Am. Bd. Trial Advocates, Calif. Bar Assn., Ventura County Bar Assn., Nat. Assn. Def. Counsel, Assn. Am. Bd. Trial Advocates, So. Calif. Def. Counsel, Ventura County Trial Lawyers Assn. Clubs: Pacific Corinthian Yacht. Republican. Avocations: sailing, scuba diving, flying. Home: 272 Camino Toluca Camarillo CA 93010 Office: Patterson Ritner Lockwood Gartner & Jurich 260 Maple Ct Ste 231 Ventura CA 93003-3570 E-mail: hgartner@dock.net.

GARTNER, JESSIE LEE, family nurse practitioner; b. St. Paul, Kans., Feb. 7, 1940; d. Herbert Lee and Lela V. (Shouse) Moore; m. Billy C. Couey, June 18, 1960 (dec. Feb. 1981); m. Gary E. Gartner, Dec. 10, 1988. AAS with honors, Coffeyville C.C., 1986; ADN with honors, Labette County C.C., 1987; postgrad., Oxford U., 1991; BSN, Mo. So. State Coll., 1992; MSN, U. Mo., Kansas City, 1996. Cert. emergency nurse. Clk.-typist Pittsburg (Kans.) State U., 1957-62, Jayhawk Distbrs., Independence, Kans., 1962-64; office mgr., asst.

compt. Starcraft Corp., Independence, 1964-74; bookkeeper, parts sales rep. O'Malley Equipment, Independence, 1975-77; sec. Guaranty Performance, Independence, 1977-78; sec., bookkeeper Independence C.C., 1978-81; paramedic Coffeyville (Kans.) Regional Med. Ctr., 1981-87; clin. nurse St. John Regional Med. Ctr., Joplin, Mo., 1987-96, APN, 1997—. CPR instr. Coffeyville Regional Med. Ctr., 1984-87; TNCC instr. St. John Regional Med. Ctr., 1991-96; vol. asst. Kans. Bd. of Emergency Medicine, Coffeyville, 1981-87; mem. fact-finding tour of nurse practitioners to China. Vol. Nat. Multiple Sclerosis Found., Joplin, 1989-91, Over 60 Olympics, Joplin, 1990, Spl. Olympics State Bowling Tournament, 1993. Mem. Emergency Nurses Assn. (cert., mem. trauma com., treas. 1994-96), Advanced Practice Nurse Orgn. (pres. 1997-98), Nursing Honor Soc., Order Ea. Star (past matron, Grand Chpt. Page award 1962, 91, chmn. state nursing com. 1994, 2000), St. Johns Hundred Club. Avocations: bowling, handwork, reading. Home: 415 S Connor Ave Joplin MO 64801-2927 Office: St John Med Ctr 2550 Lusk Dr Neosho MO 64850-8855

GARTNER, JOSEPH CHARLES, business systems administrator; b. Detroit, Feb. 3, 1945; s. Joseph Owen and Frances Alice (Harrington) G.; m. Marilyn Jean Kern, June 26, 1971; children: Stephanie, Jonathan, Jamie Lynn. Student, U. Mich., 1963 66; BSE, Marquette U., 1968; MBA, U. Rochester, 1979. Cert. systems profl. Constrn. engr. B.A.S.F., Wyandotte, Mich., 1966-67; systems engr. IBM Corp., Milw., 1968-70; mgr. mgmt. info. systems Borg Warner Corp., Toledo, Ohio, 1970-73; dir. info. systems Donnelly Corp., Holland, Mich., 1973-75; mgr. fin. systems Bausch & Lomb, Rochester, N.Y., 1975-82, mgr. EDP audit, 1982-85; mgr. bus. systems Wegmans Food Markets Inc., Rochester, 1985-97; group mgr. bus. sys. The Penn Traffic Co., Syracuse, N.Y., 1997—. Trustee Fairport (N.Y.) Pub. Libr., 1992—. Mem. Assn. for Systems Mgmt. (internat. dir. 1984-87, Disting. Svc. award 1988), KC (grand knight 1985-87), Genesee Valley Dist. PTA (legis. chmn. 1985—). Home: 3139 Fox Rd Syracuse NY 13215-9744 Office: The Penn Traffic Co PO Box 4737 1200 State Fair Blvd Syracuse NY 13221-4737 E-mail: gartnerjc@aol.com., jgartner@penntraffic.com.

GARTNER, LAWRENCE MITCHEL, pediatrician, medical college educator; b. Bklyn., Apr. 24, 1933; s. Samuel and Bertha (Brimberg) G.; m. Carol Sue Blicker, Aug. 12, 1956; children— Alex David, Madeline Hallie. AB, Columbia U., 1954; MD, Johns Hopkins U., 1958. Intern pediatrics Johns Hopkins Hosp., 1958-59; resident pediatrics Albert Einstein Coll. Medicine, 1959-60, chief resident, 1960-61, instr. pediatrics, 1962-64, asst. prof., 1964-69, assoc. prof., 1969-74, prof., 1974-80, dir. divsn. neonatology, 1967-80, dir. divsn. pediatric hepatology, 1967-80; dir. clin. research unit Rose F. Kennedy Ctr., 1972-80; attending physician Hosp. of Albert Einstein Coll. Medicine, 1967-80; prof. dept. pediatrics U. Chgo. Pritzker Sch. Medicine, 1980-98, prof. dept. obstetrics and gynecology, 1995-98, prof. emeritus pediatrics and obstetrics and gynecology, 1998—; chmn. dept. pediatrics, med. dir. Wyler Children's Hosp., U. Chgo. Med. Ctr., 1980-93. Chmn. Physician's Breastfeeding Network of Ill., 1993-98. Contbr. articles to med. jours. and textbooks. Pediatrician-of-the-Yr. award Ill. chpt. Am. Acad. Pediatrics, 1995; recipient award NIH, 1967-74; Appleton Century Crofts prize, 1956; Mosby book award, 1958. Mem. AAAS, Am. Pediatric Soc. (chmn. coun. 1989-90), Soc. Pediatric Rsch., Perinatal Rsch. Soc., Am. Assn. Study Liver Disease, Chgo. Pediatric Soc. (editor 1990-91, treas. 1992-93, sec. 1993-94, v.p. 1994-95, pres. 1995-96), Am. Acad. Pediatrics (chair breastfeeding workgroup 1994-2000, chair exec. com. sect. on breastfeeding 2000—), N.Am. Soc. Pediatric Gastroenterology (pres. 1974-75), The Milk Club (chmn. 1994-96), Acad. Breastfeeding Medicine (founding bd. dirs. 1994-95, editor newsletter 1995-2000, v.p. 1997-98, pres., 1998-99), LaLeche League Internat., Phi Beta Kappa, Alpha Omega Alpha. E-mail: gart@midway.uchicago.edu.

GARTNER, MICHAEL GAY, editor, television executive, baseball executive; b. Des Moines, Oct. 25, 1938; s. Carl David and Mary Marguerite (Gay) Gartner; m. Barbara Jean McCoy, May 25, 1968; children: Melissa, Christopher (dec.), Michael. BA, Carleton Coll., 1960; JD, NYU, 1969; LittD (hon.), Simpson Coll., 1984; LLD (hon.), James Madison U., 1989; LittD (hon.), Grand View Coll., 1990, Iowa Wesleyan Coll., 1997; LLD (hon.), Drake U., 2001. Bar: NY, Iowa. With Wall St. Jour., N.Y.C., 1960—74, page one editor, 1970—74; exec. editor Des Moines Register and Tribune, 1974—76, editor, 1976—82, editl. chmn., 1982—85, v.p., 1975—76, exec. v.p., 1977, pres., COO, 1978—85; editor Courier-Jour. and Louisville Times, 1986—87; gen. news exec. Gannett Co., 1987—88; pres. NBC News, 1988—93; editor, co-owner Ames (Iowa) Daily Tribune, 1986—99; chmn., majority-owner Iowa Cubs, 1999—; chmn., co-owner New West Newspapers, 2000—. Trustee Freedom Forum Newseum, Washington; dir. People for the Am. Way, Wells Fargo Banks of Iowa Inc.; commentator Iowa Pub. Radio; hon. trustee Simpson Coll.; mem. Pulitzer Prize Bd., 1982—92, chmn., 1991—92. Recipient Pulitzer prize for editl. writing, 1997; fellow, Harvard U. Inst. Politics, 1994. Mem.: Am. Soc. Newspaper Editors (pres. 1986—87), Assn. Bar City N.Y., Iowa Bar Assn., ABA, Garden of Gods Club, Wakonda Club. Home: 5315 Waterbury Rd Des Moines IA 50312-1923 also: 366 W 11th St New York NY 10014-6225 Office: 350 SW 1st St Des Moines IA 50309-4631 E-mail: mggartner@aol.com.

GARTON, CHARLES, classics educator; b. Leeds, Eng., Aug. 13, 1926; came to U.S., 1965; s. John Charles and Mary Garton; m. Hilary Joan Smithers, Jan. 9, 1960; children: Hugh James Lauriston, Christopher John. BA, Cambridge (Eng.) U., 1949, MA, 1953; postgrad., U. Basle, Switzerland, 1949, Brit. Sch. at Rome, 1950. Asst. lectr. classics U. Hull, Eng., 1951-53; lectr. classics U. Newcastle-upon-Tyne, 1953-65; assoc. prof. classics SUNY, Buffalo, 1965-72, prof. classics, 1972-91, prof. emeritus, 1991—. Author: Personal Aspects of the Roman Theater, 1972, Lincoln School: A Summary Honours Board, 1988; editor and trans. John Carlisle's Orationes et Declamationes, 1972, The Metrical Life of Saint Hugh, 1986, co-editor and trans. Theophylact, On Predestined Terms of Life, 1978, Germanos, On Predestined Terms of Life, 1979, Robert Froriep: Aspects of the Tongue, 1982; editor: Arethusa, 1968—71, Arethusa Monographs, 1985—91; assoc. editor : Arethusa, 1974—85; contbr. numerous articles to profl. jours. Sub-lt. Bris. Royal Navy, 1946. Person scholar U. Cambridge, 1949, Charles Oldham scholar, 1949-50. Mem. Lincoln Record Soc., Classical Assn. of Eng. and Wales (mem. coun. 1956-57). Home: 568 Seabrook Dr Williamsville NY 14221

GARTON, ROBERT DEAN, state legislator; b. Chariton, Iowa, Aug. 18, 1933; s. Jesse Glenn and Ruth Irene (Wright) G.; m. Barbara Hicks, June 17, 1955; children: Bradford, Brenda. BS, Iowa State U., 1955; MS, Cornell U., 1959. Pers. rep. Cummins Engine Co., Columbus, Ind., 1959-61; owner Garton Assocs. Mgmt. Cons., Columbus, 1961-96; dean profl. devel. Ivy Tech. State Coll., Columbus, 1996—; mem. Ind. Senate, Indpls., 1970—, minority caucus chmn., 1976-78, majority caucus chmn., 1978-80, pres. pro tempore, 1980—. Bd. dir. Rural Water Sys. Mem. exec. com. Nat. Conf. State Legislatures, 1989-92; chmn. Mid-West Conf. State Legislatures, Coun. State Govts., 1984-85, mem. gov. bd., 1985—; chmn. Ind. Civil Rights Commn., 1969-70; mem. exec. com. Nat. Fedn. Young Reps., 1966; trustee Franklin Coll., 1998—; bd. dirs. Independent Colls. of Ind., State Legis. Leaders Found., 2003. With USMCR, 1955-57. Co-recipient Legislator of the Yr. award, Ind. Civil Liberties Union, 2000, William M. Bulger Excellence in State Legis. Leadership award, 1999; named Hon. Citizen, Iowa, 1962, Tenn., 1977, winner internat. speech contest, Toastmasters, 1962, Small Bus. Champion, Ind. Small Bus. Coun., 1997, Pub. Servant of the Yr., Ind. Assn. Rehab. Facilities, 2000; named one of 5 Outstanding Young Men in Ind., 1968; recipient Man of Yr., Ind. Rep. Mayor's Assn., 1991, Disting. Svc. award, Jr. C. of C. of Columbus, 1968, Guardian Small Bus. award, Nat. Fedn. for Ind. Bus., 1990, 1993, 1994, Lee Atwater Leadership award, Nat. Rep. Legislator Assn., 1991, Outstanding Pub. Svc. award, Podiatric Assn., 1993, United Sr. Action Legis. Leadership award, 1994, Outstanding Govt. Leader award, Apt. Assn. Ind., 1998, Freedom of Road award, ABATE of Ind., 2000, Senator of Yr. award, Ind. Primary Health Care Assn., 2001, Friend of Edn. award, N. Ctrl. Bus. Edn. Assn., 2001, Disting. Pub. Svc. award, Am. Legion, 2001, Pub. Sector award, Benjamin Harrison Medallion, 2001, Benjamin Harrison medallion, 2001, Friend of Autism award, 2001. Mem. Rotary, Beta Theta Pi. Office: Ivy Tech State Coll PO Box 1111 Columbus IN 47202-1111 E-mail: gprice@iga.state.in.us.

GARTON, THOMAS WILLIAM, lawyer; b. Ft. Dodge, Iowa, Jan. 19, 1947; s. H. Boyd and Ruth A. (Porter) G.; m. Marcia K. Hoover, June 21, 1969; children: Geoffrey, Matthew. BA, Carleton Coll., 1969; JD magna cum laude, U. Minn., 1974. Assoc. Fredrikson & Byron, PA, Mpls., 1974-80, shareholder, 1980—, chmn. corp. practice group. Adj. prof. William Mitchell Coll. Law, St. Paul, Minn., 1977-80, U. Minn. Law Sch., Mpls., 1980; bd. dirs. RS/Eden Programs; presenter continuing legal edn. seminars on tax, mergers and acquisitions, and bus. planning, 1977—. With U.S. Army, 1969-71. Mem. ABA (tax sect.), Minn. Bar Assn. (dir. tax coun. 1987-89). Office: Fredrikson & Byron PA 4000 Pillsbury Ctr 200 S Sixth St Minneapolis MN 55402-1425 E-mail: tgarton@fredlaw.com.

GARTZ, PAUL EBNER, architect, systems engineer; b. Chgo., July 17, 1946; s. Friedrich Samuel and Lillian Louise (Koroschetz) G. BSEE, Ill. Inst. Tech., 1969; MSEE, Stanford U., 1970. Engring. co-op Western Electric, Chgo., 1965-69; mem. tech. staff Bell Telephone Labs., Whippany, N.J., 1969-74; sales mgr. Evelyn Wood Reading Dynamics, N.Y.C., 1975-78; owner Gartz Design, Montclair, N.J., 1976-79; mktg. rep. United Computing Systems, Seattle, 1979; assoc. tech. fellow Boeing, Seattle, 1980—. Bd. dirs. Walla Walla (Wash.) Coll. of Engring.; chmn. bd., pres. SDF, Inc., L.A.; educator Seattle U., 1987—, Walla Walla Coll., 1989, U. Wash., 1992—. Contbr. articles to profl. publs. Recipient Nat. Hist. Preservation award Nat. Hist. Preservation Soc., N.J., 1980. Mem. AIAA (mem. Digital Avionics Tech. com.), IEEE (pres.-elect, sr. mem., exec. v.p. bd. govs. Aerospace Electronic Sys. Soc., disting. lectr. to India 1997, Harry Rowe Mimno award 1987, chmn. 17th Digital Avionics Systems Conf. 1998), Sys. Devel. Forum (bd. dirs. 1987-95), Internat. Coun. Sys. Engring. (tech. bd. dirs.). Achievements include advances in systems engring., scis., methods and tools on aerospace and computing software systems; rsch. in state-of-the-art application of general systems theory to man-made systems, human engring. and mgmt. orgnl. structures, bus. analysis. Home: 9912 Arrowsmith Ave S Seattle WA 98118-5907 Office: The Boeing Co MC 9U-KF PO Box 3707 Seattle WA 98124-2207 E-mail: paul.e.gartz@boeing.com.

GARTZ, ROLF FRITZ, foundation administrator; b. Bonn, Germany, Dec. 23, 1940; s. Fritz and Hildegard (Rhein) G.; m. Christel Anneliese Overgahr gen. Willebrand, Aug. 7, 1970; 1 child, Stephan. *From 1964-69, Rolf Gartz pursued studies in physics, atomphysics, chemistry, biochemistry, biology, and cell biology at Bonn and Cologne University in Germany.* Student, Bonn and Cologne U., Germany, 1964—69; DSc in Cell Biology, Bonn U., 1969; Doctorate (hon.), State U. Social Scis., Moscow, 2000. Civil servant, govt. dir., Germany, 1970-90; mng. chmn. Eduard Rhein Found., Hamburg, Germany, 1990—. Bd. dirs. Prof. Rhein Found., Koenigswinter, Germany, 1987—; academician Internat. Informatization Acad., 2000. *The Eduard Rhein Foundation intends to confer annual awards averaging 150.00 Euro. Thus, the Eduard Rhein Award is the largest technology award of its kind in Europe.* Decorated Cross of the Order of Merit Fed. Republic of Germany; recipient Sputnick medal Russian Fedn. Cosmonautics, 2000, Highest Order of Merit, Internat. Informatization Acad., 2001. Mem. AAAS, N.Y. Acad. Scis., Assn. German Natural Scientists and Physicians, German Soc. Cell Biology, European Cell Biology Orgn., Max Planck Soc. for Advancement of Sci., Fedn. Biochemical Soc., Internat. Union Biochemistry and Molecular Biology. Avocations: hunting, riding. Home and Office: Eduard Rhein Found Alex V Humboldt Ste 6 D-56727 Mayen Germany

GARVER, DAVID L. psychiatrist; b. Feb. 3, 1939; BA, Oberlin Coll., 1960; MD, Case Western Res. U., 1965. Intern Cleve. Met. Gen. Hosp., 1966; resident U. Colo. Med. Ctr., 1971; rsch. fellow Ill. State Psychiat. Inst., 1972; instr. psychiatry U. Chgo., 1972-78; prof. psychiatry, pharmacology and cell biophysics U. Cin. Coll. Medicine, 1978-88; prof. psychiatry U. Ala., Birmingham, 1989-91, Southwestern Med. Ctr., Dallas, 1991-99, U. Louisville, 1999—. Vis. prof. psychiatry Washington U., St. Louis, 1989. Contbr. articles to profl. jours. Chmn. VA Merit Rev. Bd. for Mental Health and Behavioral Sci., Washington, 1992-93; chmn. NIMH Program Projects and Clin. Rsch. Ctrs., Washington, 1987-88. Office: Univ of Louisville Dept Psychiatry/Behav Sci 500 S Preston St Louisville KY 40202-1702 E-mail: garverdl@msn.com.

GARVER, FREDERICK MERRILL, industrial engineering executive; b. Indpls., Mar. 25, 1945; s. Clyde Louis and Elizabeth Kemp (Finch) G.; m. Ruth Sikkema, Nov. 8, 1969. BS, Western Mich. U., 1967; postgrad., Grand Valley State U., 1976-77; MS, Western Mich. U., 1990, Cert. mfg. engr. Methods analyst Boeing Co., Seattle, 1968-69; indsl. engr. Wolverine World Wide, Inc., Rockford, Mich., 1969-72; mgr. indsl. engring. Leigh Products Inc., Coopersville, Mich., 1972-77; dir. indsl. engring. Integrated Metal Techs., Spring Lake, Mich., 1977-79; mgr. mfg. engring. Haworth Inc., Holland, Mich., 1979-88, Hart & Cooley, Inc., Holland, 1988-92; mfg. engr. Trumark Inc., Lansing, Mich., 1992-94; sr. adv. process engr. Walker Mfg. Inc., Grass Lake, Mich., 1994-97; sr. mfg. engr. Pridgeon and Clay Inc., Grand Rapids, Mich., 1997—. Mem. Inst. Indsl. Engrs. (sr.), Soc. Mfg. Engrs. (sr., ad hoc govt. relations com.), Chem. Coaters Assn., Assn. Bus. Advocating Tariff Equity, Assn. Finishing Processes, Precision Metal Forming Assn. Western Mich. (dir.-at-large 2000—), Jaycees (treas. Ithaca, Mich. chpt. 1971). Forming Assn. We. Mich. (vice chmn., 2003-). Republican. Avocations: computers, skiing, tennis. Home: 9466 Tannis Rd Clarksville MI 48815-9727 Office: Pridgeon and Clay Inc 50 Cottage Grove SW Grand Rapids MI 49507-1685 E-mail: fgarver@pridgeonandclay.com.

GARVER, NEWTON, philosophy educator; b. Buffalo, Apr. 24, 1928; s. John N. Jr. and Dorothy M. (Lamy) G.; m. Anneliese L. Sprecher, Apr., 1957; children: Julia Amy, Cecily Cay, Geoffrey, Miriam. AB, Swarthmore Coll., 1951; BPhil, Oxford U., Eng., 1954; PhD, Cornell U., 1965. Tchr. English Nat. Coll., Choueifat, Lebanon, 1954-56; instr. philosophy Cornell U., Ithaca, N.Y., 1956-57; lectr. philosophy U. Minn., Mpls., 1958-61, U. Buffalo, 1961-66; assoc. prof. philosophy SUNY, Buffalo, 1966-71, prof. philosophy, 1971—, disting. svc. prof., 1991—. Author: Jesus, Jefferson, and the Task of Friends, 1983; (with S.C. Lee) Derrida and Wittgenstein, 1994, This Complicated Form of Life, 1994; (with E.H. Reitan) Nonviolence and Community, 1995; co-editor: (with P. Hare) Naturalism and Rationality, 1986; (with J.B. Brady) Justice, Law and Violence, 1989. Workshop trainer Alternatives to Violence Project, N.Y. State Prisons, 1990—2002; pres. Bolivian Quaker Edn. Fund, 2002—; bd. dirs. Syracuse, 1992—95, Quaker Bolivia Link, 2000—. Mem.: Am. Philos. Assn. (parliamentarian). Mem. Soc. Of Friends. Avocations: languages, mushrooms, travel. Home: 11253 Boston Rd East Concord NY 14055 Office: SUNY 109 Park Hall Buffalo NY 14260-4100

GARVER, ROBERT VERNON, research physicist; b. Mpls., June 2, 1932; s. Walter Burdette and Daveda Margaret (Hansen) G.; m. Shirley Marie Phillips, June 15, 1957; children: Debra, Douglas, Daniel, Mary, Jennifer. BS, U. Md., 1956; M.E.A., George Washington U., 1968. Physicist Harry Diamond Labs., Washington, 1956-69, supervisory physicist Adelphi, Md., 1969-89. Program mgr. Army High Power Microwave Hardening Tech., 1982-89; cons. Weinschel Engring., Gaithersburg, Md., 1970-75; chmn. electromagnetic effects subcom. DoD VHSIC Qualification Com., 1981-89; pvt. cons., 1989-95; sr. engr. Xeta Internat. Corp., Crystal City, Va., 1990-95; cons. Envisioneering, Inc., Dahlgren, Va., 2000—, Developer of Loop Flight Tech., The Gerver Product Co., 2000-. Author: Microwave Diode Control Devices, 1976; inventor Microwave Diode Switch; patentee in field. Elder Presbyn. Ch., Germantown, Md., 1975. Served with U.S. Army, 1953-54. Fellow: IEEE (editor Jour. Solid State Cirs. 1969—73, mem. nat. adminstrv. com. profl. group microwave theory and techniques); mem.: Toastmasters. Republican. Home and Office: 2393 Bear Den Rd Frederick MD 21701-9328

GARVER, THOMAS HASKELL, curator, art consultant, writer; b. Duluth, Minn., Jan. 23, 1934; s. Harvie Adair and Margaret Hope (Foght) G.; m. Natasha Nicholson, Apr. 13, 1974. BA, Haverford Coll., 1956; MA, U. Minn., 1965. Asst. to dir. Krannert Art Mus., U. Ill., Urbana, 1960-62; asst. dir. fine arts dept. Seattle World's Fair, 1962, Rose Art Mus., Brandeis U., Waltham, Mass., 1962-68; dir. Newport Harbor Art Mus. (now Orange County Mus. Art), Calif., 1968-72, 77-80; curator exhbns. Fine Arts Mus. of San Francisco, 1972-77; dir. Madison (Wis.) Art Ctr., 1980-87; asst. prof. Calif. State U., 1970-71, 79-80. Curator art collection Rayovac Corp., Madison, 1985-2001; organizing curator O. Winston Link Mus., Roanoke, Va., 2001—. Author: Twelve Photographers of the American Social Landscape, 1967, Just Before the War: Urban America from 1935-41, 1968, The Paintings of George Tooker, 1985, rev. edit., 1992, The Last Steam Railroad in America: Photographs by O. Winston Link, 1995; exhbn. catalogues including Robert Rauschenberg, 1969, Tom Wesselmann, 1971, Reginald Marsh, 1972, Joseph Raffael, Paintings From the California Years, 1977, George Herms, 1978, 83, Nathan Oliveira, 1984, George Tooker, Paintings, 1983-87, 88, Mind and Beast: Contemporary Artists and the Animal Kingdom, 1992, Flora: Contemporary Artists and the World of Flowers, 1995, Trains that Passed in the Night: The Railroad Photographs of O. Winston Link, 1998, WATER: Contemporary Artists Who Use Water as a Theme in Their Art, Gibbes Mus. of Art, Charleston, S.C., 1999 Trustee U.S.S. Mass. Meml. Commn., Fall River, 1965-68; trustee South Coast Repertory Co., Costa Mesa, Calif., 1970-72; trustee Wis. Citizens for Arts, 1985-87; mem. Newport Beach Art Commn., 1978-79; mem. steering com. Archives Am. Art, San Francisco, 1977-80; mem. Madison Com. for Arts, 1984-87. Mem. Western Assn. Art Mus. (pres. 1970-71, trustee 1970-73), Art Mus. Assn. Am. (pres. 1979-82, trustee 1979-85). Home and Office: 1962 Atwood Ave Madison WI 53704-5221 E-mail: thgart@aol.com.

GARVEY, DANIEL EDWARD, foundation administrator, educator, academic administrator; b. Westfield, Mass., Apr. 25, 1950; s. John Henry and Ruth Marie (Long) G.; m. Barbara Nelson, Apr. 28, 1973; children: Kathryn, Connor. BA in Sociology, Worcester State Coll., 1973; MA in Social Change, Cambridge Goddard Coll., 1974; PhD in Edn., U. Colo., 1990. Dir. Upward Bound U. N.H., Durham, 1974-79, assoc. dean students, 1979-88, adj. assoc. prof., 1988—; exec. dir. Assn. for Exptl. Edn., Boulder, Colo., 1988-91; v.p. Am. Youth Found., Ossipee, N.H., 1991—; pres. Prescott Coll., 2001—. Adj. assoc. prof. Moscow State U.; cons. in field. Guest editor Multi-Cultural Issues in Edn., 1992; author Management Development Directory, 1989; contbr. articles to profl. jours.; editorial reviewer Assn. for Exptl. Edn. Coach Youth Soccer, South Berwick, Maine. Avocations: music, woodworking. Office: Prescott Coll Office of Pres 220 Grove Ave Prescott AZ 86301

GARVEY, EDWARD PATRICK, repairman; b. San Jose, Calif., Sept. 5, 1965; s. Louis Jerome and Dorothea Margaret Garvey. AA in Electronics Tech., Columbia Basin Coll., 1987; AA in Radioactive and Hazardous Materials, N.Mex State U., 1990. Laborer Little Caesar's Pizza, Richland, Wash., 1991—92; tv/microwave repairman At Home Electronics, Kennewick, Wash., 1992—. Mem.: Toastmasters Internat. (assoc.; sgt. at arms 2002—02, Competent Toastmaster 1995). Independent. Achievements include design of timing lights for my toasmasters club. Avocations: sweepstakes, camcorder filming, electronics experiments, writing, song parodies. Home: 1102 C Goethals Richland WA 99352 Office: At Home Electronics 313 E 1st Kennewick WA 99336 Personal E-mail: punforever@hotmail.com.

GARVEY, JANE ROBERTS, lawyer; b. N.Y.C., Oct. 21, 1919; d. George Alexander and Helen Hickson (Hernon) Roberts; m. Francis Bernard Garvey, June 1, 1946; children: Ellen, Jane, Francis B. Jr. BA, Coll. New Rochelle (N.Y.), 1938; LLB, Columbia U., 1941. Bar: N.Y. 1942, U.S. Bd. Immigration Appeals 1957, U.S. Immigration and Naturalization Svc. 1957, U.S. Supreme Ct. 1958. Jr. assoc. Wikes, Riddel, Bloomer, Jacobi & Maguire, N.Y.C., 1942-44; assoc. Jackson, Nash, Brophy, Barringer & Brooks, N.Y.C., 1944-46; ptnr. Francis B. Garvey Esq., Babylon, N.Y., 1946—. Gov., internat. dir. Zonta Internat., Chgo., 1982-86; dir. planned giving Am. Heart Assn., 1984-87. Recipient spl. commendation USN, 1946, hon. commendation Suffolk County (N.Y.) Legislature, 1983, Angela Merici award for achievement in profl. and civic activities, Ursula Lauris citation for Disting. Svc. to Coll. of New Rochelle, 1978; named Hon. Big Sister of Yr., Big Sister/Big Bros., Washington, 1977, named to LAdy Comdr. Equestrian Order of the Holy Sepulchre granted by Pope John XXIII, named Woman of Yr., Zonta Internat., Suffolk County, 1991. Mem. ABA, N.Y. Bar Assn., Babylon Yacht Club, Southward Ho Golf Club (hon.), Zonta Internat. Found. (pres. 1998-2000). Republican. Roman Catholic. Avocations: sailing, travel. Home: 64 W Islip Rd West Islip NY 11795-4536 Office: Francis B Garvey PO Box 788 Babylon NY 11702-0788

GARVEY, JEFFREY MATTHEW, medical librarian, educator; b. N.Y.C., Sept. 7, 1950; s. James W. and Mary Lou (Hendren) G.; m. Elaine Perry, Sept. 2, 1974; children: James W., Robert P., Todd M. BA, Colgate U., 1972; MLS, Syracuse U., 1974. Dir. libr. svcs. Samaritan Med. Ctr., Watertown, N.Y., 1974—. Libr. cons. various orgns., 1980—. Bd. dirs. Watertown Family YMCA, 1997—, chmn. fin. devel. com., 2000—. Recipient award for outstanding svc. in librarianship North Country Regional Centennial Commn., N.Y. Libr. Assn., 1990, 7th Ann. award for excellence in libr. svc. North Country Reference and Rsch. Resources Coun., 1997. Mem.: Nat. Network Librs. of Medicine (regional adv. com. Mid. Atlantic Region 2002—), Med. Libr. Assn. (pres. elect Upstate N.Y.-Ont. chpt.). Home: 24189 County Route 159 Watertown NY 13601-5702 Office: Samaritan Med Ctr 830 Washington St Watertown NY 13601-4099 E-mail: jgarvey@northnet.org.

GARVEY, JOANNE MARIE, lawyer; b. Oakland, Calif., Apr. 23, 1935; d. James M. and Marian A. (Dean) G. AB with honors, U. Calif., Berkeley, 1956, MA, 1957, JD, 1961. Bar: Calif. bar 1962. Assoc. firm Cavaletto, Webster, Mullen & McCaughey, Santa Barbara, Calif., 1961-63, Jordan, Keeler & Seligman, San Francisco, 1963-67, ptnr., 1968-88, Heller, Ehrman, White & McAuliffe, 1988—. Bd. dirs. Mexican-Am. Legal Def. and Ednl. Fund; chmn. Law in a Free Soc., Continuing Edn. of Bar; mem. bd. councillors U. So. Calif. Law Center. Recipient Paul Veazy award YMCA, 1973, Internat. Women's Yr. award Queen's Bench, 1975, honors Advs. for Women, 1978, CRLA award, Boalt Hall Citation award, 1998, Judge Lowell Jensen Cmty. Svc. award, 2001, Margaret Brent award, 2003. Fellow Am. Bar Found.; mem. ABA (gov., state del., chmn. SCLAID, chmn. delivery of legal svcs.), Calif. State Bar (v.p., gov., tax sect., del., Jud Klein award, Joanne Garvey award), San Francisco Bar Assn. (pres., pres. Barristers), Am. Law Inst., Calif. Women Lawyers (founder), Order of Coif, Phi Beta Kappa. Democrat. Roman Catholic. Home: 16 Kensington Ct Kensington CA 94707-1010 Office: 333 Bush St San Francisco CA 94104-2806 E-mail: jgarvey@hewm.com.

GARVEY, JOHN BURWELL, lawyer; b. Fort Knox, Ky., Sept. 29, 1952; s. Dale Martin and Sancha Mary (Kilbourn) G.; m. Cotton M. Cleveland, July 13, 1996; children: Emerald, Noelle, Coral, James, David, Teak. AB cum laude, Harvard U., 1974; JD cum laude, Suffolk U., 1978. Bar: Kans. 1978, U.S. Dist. Ct. Kans. 1979, N.H. 1981, U.S. Dist. Ct. N.H. 1981, U.S. Supreme Ct. 1984, Mass. 1985. Assoc. Sulloway & Hollis, Concord, N.H., 1981-85, ptnr., 1986—, chair trial dept., 2002—. Adj. prof. evidence Franklin Pierce Law Ctr., Concord, N.H., 1986-88, 2000—; with Leadership N.H. 1993; vice chair Ausbon Sargent Land Preservation Trust, 2002—. Lt. USNR, 1978-81. Recipient Bill of Rights award N.H. Civil Liberties Union, 1997. Mem. ABA, ATLA, N.H. Trial Lawyers Assn., N.H. Bar Assn. (chmn. com. coop. cts. 1997-2000), Maritime Law Assn., New London Outling Club (pres. 2002—). Avocations: song writing, sailing, jogging, little league coaching, baseball. Office: Sulloway & Hollis 9 Capitol St PO Box 1256 Concord NH 03302-1256 E-mail: jgarvey@sulloway.com.

GARVEY, PAT, vocalist, composer, actor, novelist; b. Jamestown, N.D., Dec. 12, 1931; s. James Everett and Irene Mae Garvey. BA in Drama, San Jose State U., 1958. Guitarist Neighbors, 1962, Pat and Victoria, 1963—72. Composer popular songs including The Lovin' of the Game, Fugacity (Today is the First Day of the Rest of My Life), Tryin' to Hold the Wind Up With a Sail, Traitor from Decatur, A Robin Knows a Burning Flame, Where Were You When I Needed You, Two More Nights in This Old Tavern, That Which I Should Have Spoken Out, My Praying Mantis Pal, The Irish Soldado, Chemicals, I Met Her at the Laudramat, Mexico Mexico; playwright: Tamaloo, The Major and The Mayor, Bon Voyage, Miss Tischhauser, Queen of the Yukon; editor: Tradewinds, The Solid Muldoon; albums include Mr. & Mrs. Garvey, The Black Ball Line, The Lovin' of the Game, No Spring Chicken, Press One if You Love Me, Dear Karen, The Moon is a Streetlamp on Sheffield Avenue, actor in plays at univ. and local theatres, author numerous poems; author: (novels) The Music Detective. With USAF, 1950—53. Home: PO Box 1641 Mount Juliet TN 37121

GARVEY, RICHARD ANTHONY, lawyer; b. N.Y.C., Jan. 10, 1950; s. James Joseph Garvey and Janet Mary (Mooney) Rowse. AB, Boston Coll., 1972; JD, Harvard U., 1975. Bar: N.Y. 1976. Assoc. Simpson Thacher & Bartlett, N.Y.C., 1975-82, ptnr., 1982-93, 97—. Mem. ABA, N.Y. State Bar Assn., Assn. Bar City N.Y., Phi Beta Kappa. Address: c/o Simpson Thacher & Bartlett 425 Lexington Ave New York NY 10017 E-mail: rgarvey@stblaw.com.

GARVEY, RICHARD CONRAD, journalist; b. Northampton, Mass., May 23, 1923; s. Michael Edward and Lucy Lillian (Bradford) G.; m. Anne Elizabeth Vanasse, May 18, 1957 (dec. Jan. 1988); children: Philip, John, Mary, Margaret; m. Allison McCrillis Lockwood, Dec. 29, 1990. Student, U. Mass., 1941-43, LHD (hon.), 1974; D of Humanics (hon.), Springfield Coll., 1982; LLD (hon.), Our Lady of Elms Coll., 1982. Reporter Daily Hampshire Gazette, Northampton, 1943-44, Springfield (Mass.) Daily News, 1944-50, asst. mng. editor, 1950-66, editor, 1966-87; assoc. pub. Springfield Union-News, Sunday Rep., 1987-2000. Author: Oliver Smith, Esq., 1948, (with others) The Northampton Book, 1954, St. Mary's of Haydenville, 1968, History of Springfield College, 1985, Bringing Home the News: 175 Years of the Springfield Newspapers, 1999; contbr. articles to World Book Ency., 1977—. Trustee Forbes Libr., Northampton, 1952-57, 2000—; chmn. bd. dirs. Springfield Coll., 1979-81, Mercy Hosp., Springfield, 1980-82. Decorated Knight-Comdr. of Holy Sepulchre; recipient Grenville Clark award World Federalists, 1962, Humanitarian award NCCJ, 1989. Mem. Rotary (pres. 1984-85, Paul Harris award 1985). Roman Catholic. Home: 19 Washington Ave Northampton MA 01060-2822

GARVEY, SHEILA HICKEY, theater educator; b. Erie, Pa., Dec. 23, 1949; d. Robert Francis and Mary Virginia (Sullivan) H.; children: Sean Timothy, Darragh Burgess. BS, Emerson Coll., 1971; MA, Northwestern U., 1973; PhD, NYU, 1984; grad., The Circle in the Square, N.Y.C., 1975. Preceptor NYU, N.Y.C., 1978-80; sabbatical replacement Rutgers U., Camden, N.J., 1980-81; asst. prof. Dickinson Coll., Carlisle, Pa., 1981-88; full prof. So. Conn. State U., New Haven, 1988—. Editor: Jason Robards Remembered, 2002; contbr. articles to profl. jours. Scholar JFK Ctr. Performing Arts, Am. Coll. Theatre Festival, 1993; Rsch. grantee Dickinson Coll., 1987-88, So. Conn. State U., 1988-90, 92, 94, 98, 2003, Faculty Devel. grant, 1988-90, 92, 94, 97; Dana fellow Dickinson Coll., 1987. Mem. New Eng. Theatre Conf. (bd. dirs., coll. divsn. 1992-95, chair coll. and univ. com. 1991-95, life mem. Coll. Fellows), Eugene O'Neill Soc. (pres. 2000-02, v.p. 2001—), Conn. Critics' Cir., Conn. Critics Cir. (bd. dirs.). Roman Catholic. Home: 273 Knob Hill Dr Hamden CT 06518-2737 Office: So Conn State U 501 Crescent St New Haven CT 06515-1330

GARVICK, KENNETH RYAN, broadcast engineer, announcer, educator; b. Akron, Ohio, Apr. 11, 1945; s. Kenneth Rodger and Dorothy Lillian (Lincks) G. Diploma, DeVry Inst. Tech., Chgo., 1966, Cleve. Inst., 1970, 81. Cert. electronic technician. Electrical Repairman RCA Consumer Electronics, Indpls., 1966-70; compilation technician Howard W. Sams & Co., Indpls., 1970-73; broadcast engr. Sta. WIBC/WNAP Fairbanks Broadcasting, Indpls., 1973; announcer, engr. Stas. WHYT-AM, WNON-FM, 1974-76; transmitter engr. Sta. WISH-TV, Indpls., 1976-79; electronics instr. Arsenal Tech. High Sch., Indpls., 1979-82; announcer, engr. Stas. WSVL AM/FM, 1979-81; instr. various schs., Ohio, 1987—; announcer, engr. Sta. WMAN-AM, 1994-95. Author: Gerberich Descendants from York, PA, 1987; contbr. articles to profl. jours. With Signal Corps U.S. Army, 1966-72, Vietnam. Mem. Soc. Broadcast Engrs., Arsenal Tech., Radio Club (sec. 1979-82). Republican. Avocations: film history, amateur radio, bicycling. Address: PO Box 88 Shauck OH 43349-0088

GARVIN, ANDREW PAUL, information company executive, author, consultant; b. N.Y.C., July 24, 1945; s. Gene G. and Nora (Sheldon) London; m. 2d Linda Gail Bernstein, Oct. 1, 1983; children: Kira, Jeffrey. BA, Yale U., 1967; MS, Columbia U., 1968. Corr. Newsweek mag., N.Y.C., 1967-68; v.p. Four Elements, Inc., N.Y.C., 1968-69; co-founder, pres. FIND SVP, Inc., N.Y.C., 1970—, Info. Clearing House, Inc., N.Y.C., 1970—. Author: How to Win With Information, 1983, The Art of Being Well Informed, 1996. Chmn. Nat. Info. Conf. and Expn., Washington, 1979. Mem. Info. Industry Assn. (dir. 1979-82 Product of Yr. award 1974), Assn. Info. Mgrs. (dir. 1978-82), Am. Mktg. Assn., Am. Mgmt. Assn., Spl. Libraries Assn., St. Elmo Soc. (treas. 1974-81), Young Pres.' Orgn. Home: 401 E 89th St New York NY 10128 Office: FIND SVP 625 Avenue Of The Americas New York NY 10011-2095

GARVIN, C(LARENCE) ALEXANDER, JR., economics educator; b. Clarksville, Tenn., Sept. 1, 1921; s. Clarence Alexander and Lena (Medcalf) G.; m. Alice Esther Hand, Sept. 4, 1970. BA in English, U. Tenn., 1942, PhD in Econs., 1973; MA in Internat. Rels., U. Chgo., 1948; MA in Math., U. Pitts., 1983. Adj. instr. mktg. Austin Peay State U., Clarksville, 1960-61; lab. instr. acctg. Vanderbilt U., Nashville, 1964-65; grad. teaching asst. in econs. U. Tenn., Knoxville, 1966-69; assoc. prof. econs. Indiana U. Pa., 1969-75, prof., 1975—; ptnr., gen. mgr. Garvin Furniture Co., Clarksville, 1948-62; mem. senate Indiana U. Pa., 1976-78, chmn. senate subcom. for faculty rsch., 1976-80. Vis. fellow Sch. Econs. and Social Studies, U. East Anglia, Norwich, Eng., 1979-80; vis. prof. Am. U. in Cairo, 1984-86; presenter in field. Contbr. articles to profl. jours. Bd. dirs. Indiana U. Pa. Found., chmn. investment com., 1978-81; vestryman Trinity Episcopal Ch., Clarksville, 1961-62; vestryman Christ Episcopal Ch., Indiana, 1975-78, sr. warden, 1977-78, del. to dist. and diocesan conv., 1978-82; trustee Episcopal Diocese Pitts., 1978-81; vestryman St. Peter's Episcopal Ch., Blairsville, Pa., 1987-90, jr. warden, 1989-90, sr. warden, 1991—; Episcopal lay reader and minister, 1977—. Lt. USNR, 1942-46. Scholar Vanderbilt U., 1964-65. Mem. AAUP (pres. Indiana chpt. 1975-76), Am. Econ. Assn., Am. Math. Assn., Royal Econ. Assn., We. Econ. Assn., Ea. Econ. Assn. (area rep. 1974-78) Atlantic Econ. Assn. (exec. com. 1990—, chair disting. speaker adv. bd. 1992—), Pa. Econs. Assn. (bd. dirs., sec.-treas. 1973-78), Omicron Delta Epsilon, Beta Gamma Sigma. Home: 293 N 7th St Indiana PA 15701-1809 Office: Indiana U Pa Dept Econs Indiana PA 15701

GARVIN, FLORENCE WARD, management consultant; b. Ft. Sam Houston, Tex., Oct. 6, 1928; d. Edward Joseph and Florence Emily (Bock) Ward; m. Sheldon R. Rappaport, Mar. 2, 1950 (div. July 1969); children: Bruce Ward, Lisa Lynn; m. Stefan J. Garvin, Oct. 3, 1981. BA, Our Lady of Lake U., San Antonio, 1949; postgrad., Trinity U., San Antonio, 1949-50. Co-founder, asst. to pres. Pathway Sch., Norristown, Pa., 1961-68; adminstrv. dir. Neurosurg. Clinic for Children, Media, Pa., 1968-70; v.p. for devel. Vanguard Schs., Haverford, Pa., 1970-72; asst. to pres. Elwyn (Pa.) Inst., 1972-75; pvt. practice Media, 1976-78; cons. employee rels. dept. E.I. DuPont de Nemours & Co., Inc., Wilmington, Del., 1978-85, sr. bus. assoc. internat. dept., 1985-89, mgr. bus. rels. devel., 1989-90, mgr. internat. human resources devel. human resources dept., 1990-94. Dir. spl. project Gabriella and Paul Rosenbaum Found., 1997—2001; mng. dir. Rose Tree media Ednl. Found., 2000—01; cons. Del. County Office of Adult Svcs., 2003—. Charter mem. and bd. dirs. Montgomery County Mental Health Clinics, 1956-72; bd. dirs. Phila. United Fund, 1969-72; bd. mgrs., sec. Garrett-Williamson Found., 1973-81; bd. dirs. Mary Campbell Ctr., Wilmington, 1978-81; trustee Wilmington Coll., 1979—, Curtis Inst. Music, 1985-92; mem. devel. com. Mercy Haverford Hosp., 1994-95; mem. policy coun. Del. County Head Start, 1994-96; pres. bd. dirs. AIDS Task Force/Phila. Cmty. Health Alternatives, 1994-96; bd. dirs. Pacific Rim Bus. Coun., 1994-96, Nationalities Svc. Ctr., 1996-98, Green Cir. Program, 1996-98; bd. dirs. East Side Charter Sch., Wilmington, Del., 1996-98; pres. bd. dirs. Delaware County AIDS Network, 1999-2002. Home: 2 Yarmouth Ln Media PA 19063-4327

GARVIN, GLENN, journalist, writer; b. Fort Campbell, Ky., Jan. 14, 1954; s. Arthur R. and Estelle Hutter Garvin. BA, Stanford U., Stanford, CA, 1971—75. Reporter/film critic Delta Democrat-Times, Greenville, Miss., 1975-76; investigative reporter Austin American-Statesman, Austin, Tex., 1976—79; editor in chief Inquiry mag., San Francisco, Calif., 1979—82; reporter Wash. Times, Washington, 1982—86, fgn. corr. San Jose, Costa Rica, 1986—88; editor, fgn. desk Miami Herald, Miami, Fla., 1993—96, fgn. corr. Managua, Nicaragua, 1996—2001, tv critic Miami, Fla., 2002—. Author: Everybody Had His Own Gringo: The CIA and the Contras, 1992; co-author (with Ana Rodriguez): Diary of a Survivor: Nineteen Years In A Cuban Women's Prison, 1995. V.p. Stanford Alumni Assn., Austin, Tex., 1978—79, Miami, Fla., 1994—96. Recipient Investigative reporting, Miss. Press Assn., 1977, Newsfeatures, Tex. AP Mng. Editors, 1978, newswriting, 1979, Freedom of Info., AP, 1978, newswriting, Fla. Press Assn., 1994, Jane M. Harrah Media award, ABA, San Francisco chpt., 1982, Sports Writing, Md/Va/Del. Press Assn., 1983, Feature Writing, 1984, Sportswriting, Washington Sigma Delta Chi, 1983, Newswriting, 1985, Edwin M. Hood award, Nat. Press Club, 1988, Consumer Writing, Western Press Assn., 1994, H.L. Mencken award, Free Press Assn., 1984. Home: 1314 Pizarro Coral Gables FL 33134 Office: Miami Herald 1 Herald Plaza Miami FL Personal E-mail: ggarvin@herald.com.

GARWOOD, JOHN DELVERT, former college administrator; b. Carroll, Nebr., Mar. 20, 1915; s. Harvey and Forrest (Hill) G.; m. Kathleen Marie Schnoor, Aug. 6, 1943; children: Jan Dierks, Shelley Hill. AB, Wayne (Nebr.) State Coll., 1936; Ph.M., U. Wis., 1940; postgrad., U. La., 1940-41, U. So. Calif., 1947; PhD in Econs. U. Colo., 1951. Supt. schs., Lindsay, Nebr., 1936-38; teaching fellow U. La., 1940-41, U. Colo., 1949-51; instr. Morning-side Coll., Sioux City, 1941- 42; prof. econs. Ft. Hays (Kans.) State U., 1947-49, 51-62, dean faculty, 1962-79, v.p. for acad. affairs, 1979-80. Author: Back to the Basics, 1978. Mem. exec. com. Kans. Council Econ. Edn.; 1961— ; pres. Smoky Hill Pub. TV Corp., 1977-79, Danforth asso., 1957— . Served with AUS, 1942-46. Recipient Disting. Service award Ft. Hays State U., 1982 Mem. NEA, Kans. Tchrs. Assn. (pres. 1969-70), Am. Econ. Assn., Phi Kappa Phi, Sigma Phi Sigma, Pi Gamma Mu, Phi Delta Kappa, Lambda Delta Lambda, Kappa Mu Epsilon. Lutheran. Home: 1193 Leisure World Mesa AZ 85206-3068

GARWOOD, ROBERT ASHLEY, JR., systems engineer; b. Cordele, Ga., Sept. 11, 1955; s. Robert Ashley Sr. and Mary Ann (Meng) G.; m. Christine Allison Haire, Aug. 31, 1981. BA, LaGrange Coll., 1978. Rep. sales Met. Life Ins. Co., Atlanta, 1978-79; assoc. ptnr. Stephen D. Jones & Assocs., Roswell, Ga., 1979-80; supr. Six Flags Over Ga., Atlanta, 1979-86; asst. mgr. Wolf Camera, Kennesaw, Ga., 1986; asst. mgr. data base Days Inn Corp., Atlanta, 1986-92; comm. analyst The Emory Clinic, Atlanta, 1992-97; owner So. Visions-Comm. Cons., Norcross, Ga., 1997—; mgr. U.S. Advanced Networks, Inc. Network Mgmt. Ctr., Norcross, 1998—2001; sys. engr. Stellent, Inc., 2001—. Pastor United Meth. Ch., West Ga., 1975-79. Mem.: Pi Tau Chi. Democrat. Avocations: writing, sports, philosophy. Home and Office: 3276 Harmon Ridge Ct Buford GA 30519-6986

GARWOOD, VICTOR PAUL, retired speech communication educator, audiology; b. Detroit, Sept. 13, 1917; s. Paul J. and Helen (Garwood) Schultz; m. Dorothy Anne Olson, Mar. 13, 1942; children: Don Paul, Martha Hill Garwood Steelmon. BA, U. Mich., 1939, MS, 1948, PhD, 1952. Teaching fellow, head exam. div. Speech-Hearing Clinic, U. Mich., 1946-50; instr., asst. prof., assoc. prof., prof. dept. speech U. So. Calif., Los Angeles, 1950-67, prof., chmn. grad. program in communication disorders, 1967-71; on leave as sr. ednl. audiologist Los Angeles Unified Sch. Dist., 1972-76; prof. speech communication, prof. sci. and tech., and otolaryngology, 1964-87; prof. emeritus, 1988—; cons. audiology Childrens Hosp., Los Angeles; cons. audiology and speech pathology Medi-Cal Benefits div. Dept. Health Services, State of Calif., 1970-87, com. on employees with disabilities, 1979-86. Mem. profl. adv. com. on speech and hearing Welfare Planning Coun., L.A., 1966-68; mem. hearing aid dispensers examining com. Bd. Mem. Quality Assurance State Calif., 1971-79, chmn., 1977-79; mem. adv. bd. Hope for Hearing Rsch. Found. UCLA; reviewer register SERS U.S. Dept. Edn., 1993; mem. Health and Long Term Care Commn., Area Agy. and Aging Adv. Coun., L.A. County, 1995—; co-chair 6th Internat. Conf. on Retirement in Colls. & Univs., 1998. Contbr. articles to profl. jours. Postdoctoral fellow NIH, 1957-58; Spl. Research fellow NIH, 1960-63 Fellow Am. Speech and Hearing Assn. (life), Calif. Acad. of Audiology, Am. Acad. of Audiology; life mem. Am. Psychol. Assn., Western Psychol. Assn., Psychonomic Soc., Acoustical Soc. Am., Acad. Rehab. Audiology, Calif. Speech and Hearing Assn. (trustee Found. 1989-91, Honors award 1983), Calif. Speech Pathologists and Audiologists in Pvt. Practice (appreciation award 1987), So. Calif. Communication Group (bd. dirs. 1986-88); mem. AAUP (chmn. comm. 1995—), Retired Faculty Assn. U. So. Calif. (historian 1988-90, pres. 1990-92, treas. 1993-95, Emeriti coun., spkr. 1990—), Sigma Xi. Home: 1240 Chautauqua Blvd Pacific Palisades CA 90272-2603

GARWOOD, WILLIAM EVERETT, chemist researcher; b. Kirkwood, N.J., Oct. 25, 1919; s. Everett and Ethel Mary (Horner) G.; m. Betty Marie Spangberg, June 19, 1946; children: John Ernest, Christine Louise, Deborah Ann. BA in Chemistry, U. N.C., 1942; postgrad., Temple U., 1947-54. Rsch. scientist Mobil R & D Corp., Paulsboro, N.J., 1942-87; cons. Mobil Tech. Co., Paulsboro, 1987-99, Exxon Mobil, 2000—. Vis. scientist U. Ill., 1969; adj. prof. Rowan U. of N.J., 1990—. Co-author: Shape Selective Catalysis in Industrial Applications, 1989, 2d edit., 1996; 117 patents in field; contbr. 30 articles to profl. jours. With USN, 1944-46. Mem. Am. Chem. Soc. (chmn. South Jersey sect. 1960), Phila. Catalysis Club, Rotary. Republican. Methodist. Avocations: violin, building harpsichords, jogging, swimming.

GARWOOD, WILLIAM LOCKHART, judge; b. Houston, Tex., Oct. 29, 1931; s. Wilmer St. John and Ellen Burdine (Clayton) Garwood; m. Merle Castlyn Haffler, Aug. 12, 1955; children: William Lockhart, Mary Elliott. BA, Princeton U., 1952; LLB with honors, U. Tex., 1955. Bar: Tex. 1955, U.S. Supreme Ct. 1959. Law clk. to judge U.S. Ct. Appeals (5th cir.), 1955—56; mem. Graves, Dougherty, Hearon, Moody & Garwood (and predecessor firms), Austin, Tex., 1959—79, 1981; justice Supreme Ct. Tex., Austin, 1979—80; judge U.S. Ct. Appeals (5th cir.), 1981—97, sr. judge, 1997—; dir. Anderson, Clayton & Co., 1976—79, 1981, exec. com., 1977—79, 1981. Mem. adv. com. on appellate rules U.S. Cts., 1994—2001, chair, 1997—2001. Pres. Child and Family Svc. of Austin, 1970—71, St. Andrew's Episcopal Sch., Austin, 1972; bd. dirs. Cmty. Coun. Austin and Travis County, 1968—72, Human Opportunities Corp. Austin and Travis County, 1966—70, Mental Health and Mental Retardation Ctr. Austin and Travis County, 1966—69, United Fund Austin and Travis County, 1971—73; mem. adv. bd. Salvation Army Austin, 1972—. With U.S. Army, 1956—59. Fellow: Tex. Bar Found. (life); mem.: Tex. Law Rev. Assn. (pres. 1990—91, dir. 1986—96), Am. Law Inst. (life), Chancellors, Phi Delta Phi, Order of Coif. Episcopalian. Office: US Ct Appeals Homer Thornberry Jud Bldg 903 San Jacinto Blvd Austin TX 78701-2451

GARY, JONATHAN MARK, academic administrator; b. Dallas, July 13, 1971; s. Alvin Lynn and Judy Bergstrom Gary; m. Emily Greer, Aug. 10, 2002. MusB in Piano Performance in Piano Performance, Ouachita Bapt. U., Arkadelphia, Ark., 1993; MusM i in Piano Performance and Pedagogy, Baylor U., Waco, Tex., 2000; Performance Cert., Stanislawa Moniuski Music Acad., Gdansk, Poland, 1995. Professional Kindermusik Educator Kindermusik Internat., NC, 1999. Dir. fine arts inst. and after sch. program EOAC Waco Charter Sch., 1995—2000; asst. dir. U. Mary-Hardin Baylor Conservatory, Belton, Tex., 2000—. Asst. music dir. organist Lakewood Christian Ch., Waco, 2002—. Dir. ops. Christian Cultural Awareness Assistance League, Houston, 2000—03. Scholar, Baylor U., 1996—99. Mem.: Tex. Music Tchrs. Assn., Cen. Tex. Music Tchrs. Assn. (chair sonata festival 2000—03), Nat. Guild Piano Tchrs. Coll. Musicians, Music Tchrs. Nat. Assn. (Star award 2000), Phi Mu Alpha Sinfonia (pres. 1992—93). Avocations: travel, gardening, piano, organ, weightlifting. Office: Univ Mary Hardin-Baylor Box 8012 900 Coll St Belton TX 76513

GARY, JULIA THOMAS, retired minister; b. Henderson, N.C., May 31, 1929; d. Richard Collins and Julia Branch (Thomas) G. BA, Randolph-Macon Woman's Coll., 1951; MA, Mt. Holyoke Coll., 1953; PhD in Chemistry, Emory U., 1958; MDiv cum laude, Candler Sch. Theology, 1986. Ordained to Meth. Ch. as deacon, 1986, as elder 1989. Instr. Mt. Holyoke Coll., South Hadley, Mass., 1953-54, Randolph-Macon Woman's Coll., Lynchburg, Va., 1954-55; from asst. prof. to prof. chemistry Agnes Scott Coll., Decatur, Ga., 1957-84, dean, 1969-84; pastor-in-charge St. Matthew United Meth. Ch., East Point, Ga., 1987-92. Bd. dirs. Global Health Action, Inc., Atlanta, treas., 1991-97, v.p., 1997—; chmn. coord. coun. Decatur Area Emergency Assistance Ministry, 1995-96. Contbr. articles to profl. jours. Recipient Alumnae Achievement award Randolph-Macon Woman's Coll., 1990. Mem.: Sigma Xi, Phi Beta Kappa. Avocations: music, gardening. Home: 117 Bruton St Decatur GA 30030-3767 E-mail: REVJTG@aol.com.

GARY, RICHARD DAVID, lawyer; b. Richmond, Va., Apr. 25, 1949; s. Morton Nathan and Blanche (Rudy) G.; m. Linda Levene, Aug. 6, 1972; children: Brent Ryan, Lauren Renee. AB in Econs., U. N.C., 1971; JD, U. Va., 1974. Bar: Va. 1974. From assoc. to ptnr. Hunton & Williams, Richmond, 1974—. Guest lectr. law Coll. William and Mary, Williamsburg, 1983-90. Pres. Beth Sholom Home Cen. Va., Richmond, 1989-91; chmn. Beth Sholom Home Va., 1991-92. Recipient Disting. Svc. award Beth Sholom Home Cen. Va., 1984. Mem. ABA (pub. utilities sect. council mem.), Va. State Bar (chmn. adminstrn. law sect. 1982-83), Va. Bar Assn., Richmond Bar Assn., Fed. Com. Bar Assn., Fed. Energy Bar Assn. Avocation: sports. Office: Hunton & Williams Riverfront Plz East Twr PO Box 1535 Richmond VA 23219-1535 Home: 121 Countryside Ln Richmond VA 23229-7336 E-mail: rgary@hunton.com.

GARY, THOMAS, lawyer; b. Englewood, NJ, Apr. 29, 1950; s. Alfred and Gloria Gary; m. Deborahann Theresa Berko (div.); 1 child, Jordan Ian; m. Olga C. Puerto, Nov. 23, 1994. BA, Oberlin Coll., 1972; JD, Emory U., 1975; LLM in Taxation, U. Miami, 1984, MBA, 1997. Bar: Pa. 1975, Mo. 1980, US Supreme Ct. 1980, Fla. 1983, US Dist. Ct. (so. dist.) Fla. 1986, US Dist. Ct. (no. dist.) Fla. 2002, US Ct. Appeals (11th cir.) 1986. Law clk. to Hon. Caleb R. Layton III, Wilmington, Del., 1975-76; assoc. in contract litigation White and Williams, Phila., 1976-78; assoc. in comml. litigation Morgan, Lewis & Bockius, Phila., 1978-80; ptnr. in labor litig. Elliot, Kaiser & Freeman, Kans. City, Mo., 1980-82; assoc. in contract and comml. litig. Thomas Gary & Assoc., P.A., Coral Gables, Fla., 1985-99; sr. asst. atty. gen. antitrust sect. State of Fla., Tallahassee, 1999—. Bd. editors The Matrimonial Strategist, 1998-99. Mem. oversight com. Put Something Back, 1996-99; mem. Coral Gables City/HS Rels. Com., 1995-99. Mem. ABA, Tallahassee Bar Assn. Home: 1384 White Star Ln Tallahassee FL 32312-7520 Office: Office of Atty Gen PL-01 The Capitol Tallahassee FL 32399-1050 E-mail: tom_gary@oag.state.fl.us.

GARYPIE, RUDOLPH RENWICK, library director; b. Massapequa, N.Y., May 21, 1932; s. Rudolph Seigfried and Muriel Anderson Garypie; m. Barbara Mathilda Phillips, July 13, 1963; children: Robert, Catherine. BA, Hamilton Coll., 1954; MLS, U. Mich., 1956. Cert. Libr. of Mich. Profl. asst. Wayne (Mich.) Libr., 1956-62; libr. dir. Ingham County Libr., Mason, Mich., 1962-67, Sioux City (Iowa) Pub. Libr., 1967-69, Genesee Dist. Libr., Flint, Mich., 1969-76, Oxford (Mich.) Pub. Libr., 1976-84, Garfield County Libr., New Castle, Colo., 1984-90, Marshall (Mich.) Dist. Libr., 1990—. Judge Am. Film Festival, N.Y.C., 1961-62. Organizer regional libr. coop. sys. Capital Libr. Coop., Lansing, Mich., 1965, Siouxland Libr. Coop., Sioux City, 1968, Marshall Dist. Libr., 1995; founder, pres. Garfield County Literacy, Glenwood Springs, Colo., 1984-90; pres., treas. Calhoun County Literacy, Battle Creek, Mich., 1992-2001. Mem. ALA (life), Pub. Libr. Assn., Mich. Libr. Assn., Detroit Suburban Librs. Roundtable, Rotary Club (Paul Harris fellow 1998). Unitarian Universalist. Avocation: camping. Home: 411 W Michigan Ave Marshall MI 49068-1473 Office: Marshall Dist Libr 124 W Green St Marshall MI 49068-1536 E-mail: rgarypie@monroe.lib.mi.us.

GARZA, ADOLPH ARANDA, broadcast engineer, consultant; b. San Angelo Tex., Aug. 21, 1959; s. James Lara and Alice Bernal (Aranda) G. Student, U. Tex., 1977-81, Angelo State U., summer 1979. Busboy, waiter San Angelo Country Club, Tex., 1978-80; chief bartender Bentwood Country Club, San Angelo, Tex., 1980-84; asst. baker Furrs Bakery, San Angelo, Tex., 1984; night club owner Gasoline Alley/The Longhorn, San Angelo, Tex., 1984-86; from asst. to engr. to facilities chief KXQZ/KIXY-FM, San Angelo, Tex., 1984-88; chief engr. Stas. KAYJ/KIXY-FM, San Angelo, Tex., 1988—, KWFR-FM, San Angelo, Tex., 1995—. Cons. Glenn B. Callison Broadcast Consulting, Dallas, 1986—. U. Tex. scholar, 1977. Mem. Internat. Platform Assn. Clubs: Tapatio Springs Country. Democrat. Roman Catholic. Avocations: golfing, boxing, bartending, stereo equipment installation. Office: Foster Comm Co 2824 Sherwood Way San Angelo TX 76901-3514

GARZA, ALVARO, physician; b. Monterrey, Nuevo Leon, Mex., June 11, 1949; came to U.S., 1957; s. Alvaro and Petra Garza; m. Aurora Licudine, Oct. 1, 1984; children: Edolfo, Evante. BA, U. Calif., San Diego, 1971; MD, U. Calif., San Francisco, 1975; MPH, Calif. State U., San Diego, 1983. Diplomate Am. Bd. Pediatrics. Intern in pediats. U.Calif., San Diego, 1975-76, resident in pediats., 1976-78; fellow in ambulatory pediats. U. Calif., San. Diego, 1978—80; pvt. practice pediatrician Chula Vista, Calif., 1980-84; med. epidemiologist Ctrs. Disease Control, Atlanta, 1984-86, Pan Am. Health Orgn., Mexico City, 1986-89; chief non-infectious disease San Francisco Dept. Health, 1990-93; pub. health med. officer Calif. Dept. Health Svcs., Emeryville, 1993-96; pub. health officer Stanislaus County Health Svcs., Modesto, Calif., 1996-99; chief Calif. Office Binat. Border Health, Calif. Dept. Health Svcs, San Diego, 1999—2002; health and policy rsch. dir. Latino Ctr. for Med. Edn. and Rsch., U. Calif. San Francisco-Fresno, 2003—. Asst. clin. prof. pediat. U. Calif., San Francisco, 1994-98; mem.child lead poisoning prvention adv. com. Ctrs. Disease Control and Prevention, Atlanta, 1996-98. Contbr. articles to profl. jours. Fellow Am. Acad. Pediat.; mem. APHA, U.S.-Mex. Border Health Assn. Avocations: running, dancing, bicycling, hiking. Office: 550 E Shaw Ave Ste 210 Fresno CA 93710-7702

GARZA, ANTONIO O. ambassador; BBA, U. Tex., Austin, 1980; JD, So. Meth. U., 1983. Formerly of counsel Garza & Garza, Brownsville, Tex.; judge Cameron County Ct., Tex., 1988—94; sec. state State of Tex., 1995-97; atty. Bracewell & Patterson, LLP, 1997—98; commr. Tex. R.R., 1998—2001; amb. to Mex., 2002—. Dir. parks adv. bd. Tex. Parks and Wildlife Commn.; past mem. State Job Tng. Coord. Coun., Census Complete Count Com., U.S. Marshall Selection Com.; conferee jud. conf., U.S. Ct. Appeals (5th cir.), 1986.; mem. presdl. del. Fed. Elections, El Salvador, 1991; mem. del. to Poland/Hungary, Am. COun. Young Polit. Leaders, 1993. Past dir. United Way So. Cameron County; past pres. Rio Grande Valley Big Bros./Big Sisters; dir. Brownsville Adult Lit. Coun. Cameron County; active H.O.S.T. program Brownsville Ind. Sch. Dist.; coach soccer and jr. varsity basketball. Names One of Five Outstanding Young Texans Exes, 1989, One of Five Outstanding Young Texans, 1990. Office: US Embassy Paseo de la Reforma 305 06500 Colonia Cuauhtemoc Mexico*

GARZA, ED, mayor; b. San Antonio; Student in bus. adminstrn., U. Tex., Austin; B in Landscape Architecture, MS in Land Devel., Tex. A&M U. With various planning, devel., real estate fin., landscape architecture, and architecture firms; dir. land planning and devel. Internat. Waterfront Group, San Antonio; elected dist. 7 rep. San Antonio City Coun.; elected mayor City of San Antonio, 2001. Mem. San Antonio Trees Bd.; past bd. dirs. Jefferson Neighborhood Assn., Woodlawn Lake Neighborhood Assn.; bd. dirs. Hispanic Elected Local Ofcls., 1998—, Nat. League of Cities, 2000—. Named one of 40 Under 40 Rising Stars, San Antonio Bus. Jour., 1996. Office: City Hall PO Box 839966 San Antonio TX 78203-3966*

GARZA, EMILIO M(ILLER), federal judge; b. San Antonio, Tex., Aug. 1, 1947; s. Antonio Peña and Dionisia (Miller) Garza. BA, U. Notre Dame, 1969, MA, 1970; JD, U. Tex., 1976. Assoc. Clemens, Spencer, Welmaker & Finck, San Antonio, 1976—82, ptnr., 1982—87; dist. judge 225th Dist. Ct., Bexar County, San Antonio, 1987—88; U.S. dist. judge U.S. Dist. Ct. (we. dist.) Tex., San Antonio, 1988—91; U.S. cir. judge U.S. Ct. Appeals (5th cir.), San Antonio, 1991—. Adv. coun. U. Tex. San Antonio Coll. Fine Arts and Humanities, 1992—98; adv. bd. Phoenix Inst., 1992—; bd. advisors Hispanic Law Jour. U. Tex. at Austin Sch. Law, 1992—96; adv. com. Notre Dame Law Sch., 1998—; bd. dirs. Symphony Soc. San Antonio, 1987—89; mem. Century Club San Antonio, 1987—88. Capt. USMC, 1970—79, active duty USMC, 1970—73. Mem.: San Antonio Bar Assn., State Bar Tex. Office: 8200 I-10 W Ste 501 San Antonio TX 78230 also: US Ct Appeals 600 Camp St New Orleans LA 70130*

GARZA, REYNALDO G. federal judge; b. Brownsville, Tex., July 7, 1915; s. Ygnacio and Zoila (Guerra) Garza; m. Bertha Champion, June 9, 1943; children: Reynaldo G., David C., Ygnacio Daniel, Bertha Victoria, Monica Bernadette. AA, Brownsville Jr. Coll., 1935; BA, U. Tex., 1937; LLB, U. Tex. Sch. of Law, 1939; LLD (hon.), U. St. Edwards, Austin, Tex., 1965. Bar: Tex. 1939. Sole practice, 1939—42, 1946—50; prinr. Sharpe, Cunningham & Garza, 1950—60, Cunningham, Garza & Yznaga, 1960—61; judge U.S. Dist. Ct. Tex., Brownsville, 1961—74, chief judge, 1974—79; circuit judge U.S. Ct. Appeals (5th cir.), Brownsville, Tex., 1979—82, sr. judge, 1982—. Treas. Cameron County Child Welfare Bd., 1950—52; mem. Tex. Good Neighbor Commn., 1957—61; commr. City of Brownsville, 1947—49; trustee Brownsville Ind. Sch. Dist., 1941—42. Served with USAF, 1942—45. Decorated knight Order St. Gregory the Great, Pius XII; recipient Pro Ecclesia et Pontifice medal, Pope Pius XII, 1952. Mem.: State Bar of Tex., Cameron County Bar Assn. Office: US Ct Appeals 600 E Harrison St Brownsville TX 78520-7114

GARZA, ROBERTO JESUS, retired education educator; b. Hargill, Tex., Apr. 10, 1934; s. Andres and Nazaria (De La Fuente) G.; m. Idolina Alaniz, Aug. 24, 1957; children: Roberto Jesus Jr., Sylvia Lynn. BA in Psychology, Tex. A&I Coll., 1959. MA in Spanish, 1964; EdD in Curriculum and Instrn., Higher Edn., Okla. State U., 1975. High sch. tchr. and counselor, Tex., Ill., Wyo., 1959-64;

instr., chmn. dept. St. Joseph (Mo.) Jr. Coll., 1964-65; teaching asst. U. Wash., Seattle, 1965-66; instr., chmn. dept. S.W. Tex. Jr. Coll., Uvalde, 1966-68; prof. Spanish Sul Ross State U., Alpine, Tex., 1968-70; adminstr. Office of Equal Opportunity, Edinburg, Tex., 1970-71; NEH rsch. fellow U. Notre Dame, Ind., 1972-73; prof., chmn. dept. higher edn. U. Tex., Brownsville, 1973-96; ret., 1996. Cons. migrant edn. S.W. Lab., Austin, 1966-67; psychometrist Peace Corps, San Marcos, Tex., 1965; counselor Job Corps, San Marcos, 1966; higher edn. tchr. edn. evaluator Tex. Edn. Agy., Austin, 1980-85; mem. Tex. Edn. Agy. Accreditation Team, 1979—; journalism scholarship com. KGBT-TV and KRGV-TV, 1979—; mem. So. Assn. Schs. and Colls. Accreditation Team, 1990—; cons. U.S. Dept. Edn., 1993—. Author, editor Contemporary Chicano Theatre: An Anthology, 1975. Trustee, v.p., pres. Brownsville Ind. Sch. Dist., 1985-87; mem. Cameron County Appraisal Dist., Brownsville, 1985-87, Tex. Ho. Reps. Resolution #521, 1987; assoc. dir. Reynaldo Garza Law Sch., Edinburg, 1985-87. With U.S. Army, 1954-56. Recipient recognition/appreciation award Brownsville Ind. Sch. Dist., 1987; grantee NDEA, 1963, John Hay Whitney Found., 1970-71; NEH fellow Notre Dame U., 1972-73. Mem. AAUP, So. Assn. of Colls. and Schs., Tex. Assn. Coll. Tchrs., Am. Assn. for Higher Edn., Smithsonian Assocs., Phi Delta Kappa. Democrat. Roman Catholic. Home: 2 Alvarado Ave Rancho Viejo TX 78575-9501

GARZA, THOMAS JESUS, language educator; b. Refugio, Tex., Aug. 20, 1958; s. Tomas Contreras and Rosie Madrigal Garza; m. Elizabeth Merle Richmond, Jan. 9, 1993. BA, Haverford Coll., 1980; MA, Bryn Mawr, 1981; EdD, Harvard U., 1987. Lang. tng. supr. Fgn. Svc. Inst., Rosslyn, Va., 1987-90; assoc. prof. U. Tex., Austin, 1990—, dir. Ctr. for Russian, East European & Eurasian Studies, 2002—. Author: (textbook) Breakthrough! American English for Speakers of Russian, 1995 (books) Fundamentals of Russian Verbal Conjugation, 1995, (chpts.) The Russian Context, 2001, The Learning and Teaching of Slavic Languages and Cultures, 2000, Curriculum and Content, 1991. Tchr. edn. grantee NEH, 1992-95; Mellon fellow Nat. Fgn. Lang. Ctr., 1988, Fulbright-Hays Doctoral Dissertation fellow Internat. Rsch. Exch. Bd., 1986-87, Larsen doctoral rsch. fellow Harvard Grad. Sch. Edn., 1985-87, Harvard U. Minority Prize fellow, 1983-85, Danforth fellow, 1980-84; named to Acad. Disting. Tchrs., U. Tex., 2003. Mem. MLA (exec. com. on tchg. langs. 1998-2002), Am. Coun. Tchrs. Russian (bd. dirs. 1998-2004), Am. Assn. Tchrs. of Slavic and East European Langs. (chair pedagogy 1993-98), Am. Coun. on Tchg. of Fgn. Langs., Am. Comparative Lit., Phi Beta Kappa. Avocations: films, cooking, travel. Office: U Tex Dept Slavic Langs/Lits Austin TX 78712 Office Fax: 512-471-6710. E-mail: tjgarza@mail.utexas.edu.

GARZA, XAVIER, artist, writer; b. McAllen, Tex., Oct. 14, 1968; s. Margarito and Amalia Garza; m. Irma Isabel Rodriguez, Sept. 27, 1964. BFA, U. Tex., 1994. Cert. tchr. Tex. Art tchr. Donna (Tex.) Ind. Sch. Dist., 1994—2000, Northside Ind. Sch. Dist., San Antonio, 2000—01, 2001—. Artist, writer, performance artist San Benito (Tex.) Sch. Dist., 1998—2001. Masked Marvels, 2000. Mentor San Benito Ind. Sch. Dist., 1998—2000. Home: 5903 Danny Kaye Apt 1204 San Antonio TX 78240 Office: Northside Ind Sch Dist 1725 Richland Hills Dr San Antonio TX 78251 Personal E-mail: xaviergarza@hotmail.com.

GARZA-LOZANO, NEREYDA, language educator; b. Matamoros, Mexico, June 20, 1961; arrived in U.S., 1984; d. Ignacio Garza and Ninfa Lozano; children: Aideé Karina Lara-Garza, Lizabeth Viridiana Lara-Garza. BS in Social Sci., Matamoros, 1980; AA in Liberal Arts, Fresno City Coll., 1994; BA in Spanish, Calif. State U., Fresno, 1995, MA in Spanish, 1997. Elem. sch. tchr. Miguel Hidalgo Sch., Ebano, Mexico, 1980—84; part-time Spanish instr. Calif. State U., Fresno, Calif., 1997—99; full time Spanish instr. Fresno City Coll., 1999—. Sec. CVFLA, Fresno, 2001—02; presenter in field. Contbr. articles to profl. jours. Coord. cultural activities Fresno City Coll., 1999—, coord. Cinco de Mayo activities, 2001—03; coord. Latin Film Festival Arte Am., Fresno, 2003. Grantee Mexican Am. Studies, NEH, 1999, Fulbright, Chile, 2000; McNair scholar, Calif. State U. Fresno, 1997. Mem.: Latino Faculty Assn. (v.p. 2002—03), Calif. Lang. Tchrs. Assn., Am. Assn. Tchrs. Spanish and Portuguese, Phi Kappa Phi. Republican. Roman Catholic. Avocations: hiking, camping, films, travel. Office: State Ctr CC 1101 E University Ave Fresno CA 93741

GARZI, JOHN JOSEPH, maintenance engineer; b. Mt. Vernon, N.Y., Oct. 1, 1942; s. John and Alberta (Galbina) Garzi; m. Dorothy Loretta Fleissner, July 10, 1961 (div. Feb. 1972); children: John Michael, Katherine Jane; m. Carol Isabella Castelli, Nov. 30, 1991. Grad. high sch., Mt. Vernon, N.Y. Stock rm. foreman, material cutter Precision Circuits, Inc., New Rochelle, N.Y., 1965-66; ship painter USCG Yard, Curtis Bay, Md., 1966-67; salesman Coca-Cola Bottling Co., Balt., 1967-80; owner Kemo-Sabe Trading, Severna Park, Md., 1978-86; ceramic tile installer The Tile Shop, Gulford, Conn., 1987-91; maintenance engr. Richmond County Savs. Bank, S.I., N.Y., 1992—. Motion picture movie extra Quiz Show, City Hall, Eddie. Candidate Rep. County Councilman, Anne Arundel County, Md., 1982. With USCG, 1960-65. Mem. Disabled Am. Vets. (life). Republican. Roman Catholic. Avocations: jewelry making, home improvement. Home: 158 Armstrong Ave Staten Island NY 10308-3103 Office: Richmond County Savs Bank 1214 Castleton Ave Staten Island NY 10310-1799

GARZIONE, JOHN EDWARD, physical therapist; b. Newburgh, N.Y., Jan. 3, 1950; s. John Edward and Della Elizabeth (Gentila) G.; m. Anita Louise Hirschman, Sept. 21, 1974; children: Adriana, Katrina. AAS, Orange County C.C., Middletown, N.Y., 1970; BS, Ithaca Coll., 1973. Mem. staff phys. therapy Chenango Meml. Hosp., Norwich, N.Y., 1973-74; sr. phys. therapist N.Y. State Vets. Home, Oxford, N.Y., 1974-86; CEO Chenango Therapeutics, Norwich, 1975—; lic. examiner N.Y. State, 1976-86; cons. phys. therapy Broome Devel. Ctr., Binghamton, N.Y., 1985—, Upstate Home for Children, Milford, N.Y., 1986-88, Hospice Chenango County, Norwich, 1991—. Adj. instr. Czenovia Coll., 1982-87, Ithaca Coll., 1993-94; clin. instr. EMPI Corp., 1996—; cons. BlueCross/Blue Shield, Utica, 1998-2001, YMCA, Norwich, N.Y., 2000; guest lectr. electrotherapy Utica Coll., 2000; presenter in field. Contbr. articles to profl. jours. Bd. dirs. STRIDE, 2000-2003. Mem. Am. Phys. Therapy Assn. (sec. pain mgmt. spl. interest group 1996-2001, v.p. 2001-2003), Am. Coll. Sports Medicine, Am. Acad. Pain Mgmt. (clin. assoc., Continuing Edn. Excellence award 1996, 99, 2000, 01, 02), N.Y. Acad. Scis., Lions (v.p. 1990). Home: PO Box 451 Sherburne NY 13460-0451 Office: Chenango Therapeutics Country Club Rd Norwich NY 13815-1613 E-mail: jgarzione@juno.com.

GARZON, AMALIA, Spanish educator, translator; b. Guayaquil, Ecuador, July 10, 1957; arrived in U.S., 1983; d. Luis E. Garzon and Nelly G. Morante; m. David D. Ramsower; children: Alexander, Angela, Philippe. AA, Del Mar Coll., 1990; BA cum laude, Tex. A&M U., 1991, MA, 1995; ABD, Ariz. State U., 2002. Cert. transl. Ariz. Supr. fgn. langs. lab. Del Mar Coll., Corpus Christi, Tex.; adj. instr. Spanish Maricopa C.C., Mesa and Chandler, Ariz.; tchg. assoc. Spanish Ariz. State U., Tempe. Bilingual examiner Ariz. State U., Tempe; bilingual writer, transl. Evans Newton Inc., Scottsdale. Recipient Regent's scholarship, Ariz. State U., 1997—2003. Mem.: MLA, ACTFL. Office: Ariz State U Main Campus Tempe AZ 85287-0202

GASBARRO, PASCO, JR., lawyer; b. Providence, Apr. 3, 1944; s. Pasco and Helen (Casali) G.; m. Mary Alyce McNamara, May 30, 1967; children: Pasco, John A., Christopher E. AB, Brown U., Providence, 1966; JD, Boston U., 1969. Bar: R.I. 1969, U.S. Dist. Ct. R.I. 1971, Mass. 1972, U.S. Dist. Ct. Mass. 1974. Law clk. R.I. Supreme Ct., Providence, 1969-70; atty. R.I. Legal Svcs., Providence, 1970-71, New Eng. Elec., Westborough, Mass., 1971-76; counsel Narragansett Elec. Co., Providence, 1976-79; asst. gen. counsel New Eng. Elec., Westborough, 1979-83; ptnr. Hinckley, Allen & Snyder LLP, Providence, Boston, Concord, NH, 1983—. Del. White House Conf. on Small Bus., 1995; mem. adv. bd., Advanced Technol. Mfg. Ctr. Former chmn. adv. coun. R.I. Small Bus. Devel. Ctr.; mem. adv. bd. Advanced Tech. and Mfg. Ctr. Mem. ABA, R.I. Bar Assn., Brown Club of R.I. Office: Hinckley Allen & Snyder LLP 1500 Fleet Ctr Providence RI 02903-2319

GASCOIGNE, NICHOLAS ROBERT JOHN, immunologist, researcher; b. London, Eng., Jan. 13, 1958; came to U.S., 1983; s. Robert John and Elisabeth Gascoigne; m. Stephanie Bremond, Aug. 30, 1986; children: Francesca Elisabeth, Harry Nicholas. BSc, U. Wales, Aberystwyth, 1980; PhD, U. London, 1983. Postdoctoral fellow Sch. Medicine Stanford (Calif.) U., 1983-87; asst. prof. The Scripps Rsch. Inst., La Jolla, Calif., 1987-92, assoc. prof., 1993-97, assoc. prof. tenured, 1997—. Mem. study section com. ad hoc NIH, Bethesda, Md., 1993, 97, 99; mem. sci. study com. Am. Heart Assn., Dallas, 1994-98; mem. sci. rev. com. Concern Found., Beverly Hills, Calif., 1997—. Contbr. articles to profl. jours. including Nature, Sci., Immunity, and Immunology Today; assoc. editor Jour. Immunology, 1995-01. Grantee NIH, 1988 —; spl. fellow Leukemia Soc. Am., 1985 87, scholar, 1989-94; fellow Cancer Rsch. Inst., 1983-85. Mem. Am. Assn. Immunologists (com. 1988—, minority affairs com. 1992-00), Brit. Soc. Immunologists, AAAS. Office: The Scripps Rsch Inst 10550 N Torrey Pines Rd La Jolla CA 92037-1000

GASCOINE-MOLINA, JILL VIOLA, actress, writer; b. London, Apr. 11, 1937; d. Francis Gascoine and Irene Ethel Greenwood; m. William Keith, Mar. 18, 1965 (div. June 1973); children: Sean William, Adam Francis; m. Alfred Molina, Mar. 1, 1985. Student, Theatre Sch., London. Actress theater, TV, films, London. Author: Addicted, 1994, Lilian, 1996, Just Like A Woman, 1997. Named Best Actress on TV, TV Times Mag. Viewers Vote, 1983, 1984. Avocation: designing gardens.

GASICH, WELKO ELTON, retired aerospace executive, management consultant; b. Cupertino, Calif., Mar. 28, 1922; s. Elija J. and Catherine (Paviso) Gasich; m. Patricia Ann Gudgel, Dec. 28, 1973; 1 child, Mark David. AB cum laude in Mech. Engring. (Bacon scholar), Stanford U., 1943, MS in Mech. Engring., 1947, cert. in fin. and econs. (Sloan exec. fellow), 1967; Aero. Engr., Calif. Inst. Tech., 1948. Aerodynamicist Douglas Aircraft Co., 1943-44, supr. aeroelastics, 1947-51; chief aero design Rand Corp., 1951-53; chief preliminary design aircraft divsn. Northrop Corp., Los Angeles, 1953-56, dir. advanced systems, 1956-61, v.p., asst. gen. mgr. tech., 1961-66, corp. v.p., gen. mgr. Northrop Ventura divsn., 1967-71, corp. v.p., gen. mgr. aircraft divsn., 1971-76, corp. v.p., group exec. aircraft group, 1976-79, sr. v.p. advanced projects, 1979-85, exec. v.p. programs, 1985-88, ret., 1988; aerospace cons. Encino, Calif., 1988—. Author: (book) 40 Years of Ferrari V-12 Engines, 1990. Chmn. adv. coun. Stanford Sch. Engring., 1981—83; past. mem. adv. coun. Stanford Grad. Sch. Bus.; chmn. United Way, 1964; chmn. Scout-O-Rama, L.A. coun. Boy Scouts Am., 1964, chmn. explorer scout exec. com., 1963—64. Served to lt. USN, 1944—46. Fellow: AIAA, Soc. Automotive Engrs.; mem.: NAE, Navy League, Stanford Grad. Sch. Bus. Alumni Assn. (pres. 1971), Bel Air Country Club, Conquistadores del Cielo Club. Republican. Achievements include patents in field. Office: 10900 Chalon Rd Los Angeles CA 90077

GASIORKIEWICZ, EUGENE ANTHONY, lawyer; b. Milw., Jan. 7, 1950; s. Eugene Constantine and Loretta Ann (Kasprzak) G.; m. Iana Jamieson, Jan. 12, 1980; children: Suzanne A., Alexei E. AB, Regis Coll., 1971; JD, U. Miss., 1974. Bar: Wis. 1974, U.S. Supreme Ct. 1986. Law clk. to presiding justice Miss. Supreme Ct., Jackson, 1974-75; assoc. Schoone, McManus & Hanson SC, Racine, Wis., 1975-79; ptnr. Hanson & Gasiorkiewicz SC, Racine, Wis., 1979-90; pres., shareholder Hanson, Gasiorkiewicz & Weber, SC, Racine, 1990-96, Hanson & Gasiorkiewicz, SC, Racine, 1997—. Lectr. labor law U. Wis., Racine, 1975-76, worker's comp., State Bar Wis., 1984-86, med. malpractice, Wis. Acad. Trial Lawyers, 1986. Mcpl. judge Village of Wind Point, Wis., 1983-85; moot ct. instr., The Prairie Sch., Racine, 1986-87. Named one of Best Lawyers in Am., Consumer Guide, 2001. Mem. State Bar Wis. (spl. ethics com. regarding trust accts. 1988-89), Assn. Trial Lawyers Am., Am. Arbitration Assn., Wis. Acad. Trial Lawyers (bd. dirs. 1999—), Nat. Bd. Trial Advocacy (cert. civil trial advocate), Racine County Bar Assn. (liaison local physicians and attys. 1990—). Roman Catholic. Avocation: tennis. Home: 3929 S Brook Rd Franksville WI 53126-9303 Office: Hanson & Gasiorkiewicz SC 2932 Northwestern Ave Racine WI 53404-2249 E-mail: info@lawracine.com.

GASKELL, IVAN GEORGE ALEXANDER DE WEND, art museum curator; b. Weston-super-Mare, Somerset, U.K., Feb. 26, 1955; came to U.S., 1991. s. William George Keith de Wend and Johanna Catharina (van Leeuwen) G.; m. Jane Susan Whitehead, May 9, 1981; 1 child, Alexander Leo Ralph de Wend. Attended, Worcester Coll., Oxford, 1973-76, Courtauld Inst. Art, London, 1976-80; MA in Modern History, Oxford U.; MA in History of Western Art, London U.; PhD in History of Art, Cambridge U. Rsch. fellow, acad. curatorial asst. Warburg Inst. London U., 1980-83; fellow Wolfson Coll. Cambridge U., 1983-91, mem. faculty architecture, history of art, 1983-91; sr. lectr. fine arts Harvard U., Cambridge, Mass., 1991—, head dept. paintings and sculpture Fogg Art Mus., 1991—, Margaret S. Winthrop curator of paintings, 1991—, sr. lectr. history, 2002—; 8. Presenter papers at numerous internat. confs., 1978—; chair seminars in field; lectr. Royal Acad., Nat. Gallery, London, Courtauld Inst. Art, 1982—. Author: The Thyssen-Bornemisza Collection: Dutch and Flemish Painting, 1990, Vermeer's Wager: Speculations on Art History, Theory and Art Museums, 2000; co-editor: The Language of Art History, 1991, Landscape, Natural Beauty and the Arts, 1993, Explanation and Value in the Arts, 1993, Nietzsche, Philosophy and The Arts, 1998, Vermeer Studies, 1998, Sketches in Clay for Projects by Gianlorenzo Bernini, 1999, Performance and Authenticity in the Arts, 1999, Politics, Aesthetics and The Arts, 2000; joint gen. editor: Cambridge Studies in Philosophy and the Arts, 1988-2000; contbr. articles, revs. to profl. jours. Mem. Coll. Art Assn., Am. Soc. for Aesthetics. Avocation: sight-seeing. Office: Harvard U Fogg Art Mus 32 Quincy St Cambridge MA 02138-3845 E-mail: gaskell@fas.harvard.edu.

GASKILL, HERBERT LEO, accountant, engineer; b. Seattle, July 1, 1923; s. Leo Dell and Vesta Rathbone (Dahlen) G.; m. Margaret Helen Jenkins, Mar. 1, 1944 (div.); children: Margaret V., Herbert Leo; m. Opal Jordan, June 13, 1992; 1 child, Ann. BS, MSChE, U. Wash., 1949, MBA, 1976. CPA, Wash. Asst. prof. and exec. officer dental materials Sch. Dentistry, U. Wash., 1950-56; ops. analyst The Boeing Co., Seattle, 1958-71, mktg. cons. govt. programs, 1972-74; pvt. practice acctg. Seattle, 1976-80; hazardous waste mgr. Boeing Co., Seattle, 1980-86; project mgr. Western Processing Remediation, 1986-95; ret., 1995. Contbr. articles to profl. jours. Active Seattle Art Mus., Pacific N.W. Aviation Hist. Found. Lt. (j.g.) USNR, 1941-46. TAPPI fellow, 1956, U. Wash. Engring. Exptl. Sta. fellow, 1957. Mem. Wash. Soc. CPAs. Home: 1236 NE 92nd St Seattle WA 98115-3135

GASKIN, FELICIA, biochemist, educator; b. Carlisle, Pa., Jan. 17, 1943; d. Joseph A. and Wanda J. (Rakowski) G.; m. Shu Man Fu, Nov. 29, 1969; children: Kai-Ming, Kai-Mei. AB in Chemistry, Dickinson Coll., Carlisle, Pa., 1965; MA in Organic Chemistry, Bryn Mawr Coll., 1967; PhD in Biochemistry, U. Calif., San Francisco, 1969. Postdoctoral fellow Stanford U., Palo Alto, Calif., 1969-71; rsch. assoc. Rockefeller U., N.Y.C., 1971-72, Columbia U., N.Y.C., 1972-74; asst. prof., then assoc. prof. Albert Einstein Coll. Medicine, N.Y.C., 1974-82; prof. Sch. Medicine U. Okla., Oklahoma City, 1982-88, U. Va., Charlottesville, 1988—. Mem. Okla. Med. Rsch. Found., 1982-88. Contbr. articles to profl. jours. Recipient rsch. career devel. award NIH, 1975-80; Nat. Inst. Neurol. Diseases and Stroke spl. fellow, 1972-74. Mem. AAAS, Am. Soc. Biochemistry and Molecular Biology, Am. Soc. for Cell Biology, Soc. Neurosci. Office: U Va Sch Medicine Box 800203 Charlottesville VA 22908-0001

GASKINS-CLARK, PATRICIA RENAE, dietitian; b. Ft. Sill, Okla., July 24, 1959; d. Jay Frank and Iwana (Robinson) Gaskins; m. Gene Martin Clark, June 6, 1986; children: Taylor Renae, Kyle Gene. BS, Cameron U., 1982; MS, Cen. State U., 1986. Cert. consumer scientist; registered dietitian. Nutrition specialist William E. Davis & Sons, Inc., Oklahoma City, 1985-87; dietitian intern Okla. Teaching Hosps., Oklahoma City, 1987; clin. dietitian Grady Meml. Hosp., Chickasha, Okla., 1987-89; chief clin. dietitian Presbyn. Hosp., Oklahoma City, 1989-90; mgr. food and nutrition svcs. Norman (Okla.) Regional Hosp., 1990—. Cheer coach Moore Raiders. Mem. Am. Dietetic Assn., Cameron U. Alumni Assn., Oklahoma City Dist. Dietetic Assn., Okla. Dietetic Assn., Cen. State U. Alumni Assn., Phi Upsilon Omicron. Republican. Baptist. Avocations: reading, jazzercise, weight lifting. Office: Norman Regional Hosp 901 N Porter Ave Norman OK 73071-6482 E-mail: pattyc@nrh-ok.com.

GASKINS-DAINIS, INA R. retired real estate agent; b. Nashville, Ga., Dec. 14, 1920; d. David D. Gaskins and Ailsa Jane Hughes; m. Alphonse P. Dainis, June 12, 1947; children: Michael L., Karen, Andrew P., Robert E., Gregory M., David A. Diploma Cecil's Bus. Coll., 1942. Bookkeeper Haverty's, Asheville, NC, 1942—44; asst. bookkeeper, sec. Dr. William J. Turbyfill, 1944—47; bookkeeper Asplund, Jenkinstown, Pa., 1970—72; sales clk. John Wanamaker, 1972—77; sales Wickert Real Estate, Spring House, Pa., 1980—89. Author: (geneology) The Gascoignes of Eng. and Am., 2001. Mem.: DAR. Home: 1222 Brittany Pt Estates Lansdale PA 19446

GASLOW, PAM, writer, artist; BFA, George Washington U., 1992. Author: Girls Are Weird; exhibitions include Mary O. Fritchie Outdoor Art Show and Exhbn., Westhampton, N.Y., 2002 (first place mixed media). Republican. Personal E-mail: poodlette@aol.com.

GASNER, DONN ALLAN, music educator; b. Madison, Wis., Mar. 24, 1958; s. Allan Arnold and Dorothy Mae Gasner; m. Renee Phyllis Fillingsness, June 30, 1984; children: Jocelyn, Olivia. MusB, U. Wis., Whitewater, 1981. Cert. instrumental music and vocal music edn. K-12. Elem. band dir./H.S. marching band dir. Ft. Atkinson Pub. Schs., Wis., 1981—84; dir. of bands Horicon H.S., Wis., 1984—. Chmn. North Ctrl. Assn. Sch. improvement team Horicon H.S., 1997—2000; percussion instr. Wis. Sch. Music Assn. State Honors Band, Madison, 1985; guest condr. summer band camp U. Wis., Whitewater, 1982. Dir.: (plays) Oliver, 1992, West Side Story, 1996, Seven Brides For Seven Brothers, 2000; actor, dir.: (plays) Fiddler on the Roof, 2002. Fellow Kohl Tchr. fellow, WEAC/DPI, 1989. Mem.: NEA, Horicon Edn. Assn. (pres. 1995—96), Wis. Edn. Assn., Nat. Band Assn. (bd. dirs. Wis. chpt. 1982—86), Wis. Sch. Music Assn. (guest clinician 1981—2002, mem. coun., Master Adjudicator 2003, Will Schmid scholar 2001). Home: 718 Neitzel St Horicon WI 53032 Office: Horicon HS 841 Gray St Horicon WI 53032 Personal E-mail: dagasner@charter.net. E-mail: dgasner@horicon.k12.wi.us.

GASNER, WALTER GILBERT, retired dermatologist; b. N.Y.C., May 6, 1912; s. Charles and Gussie Gasner; m. Shirley M. Friedman, Dec. 31, 1937; children: Douglas, Jane, John, Mary. MD, Med. Coll. S.C., 1936; postgrad., NYU Med. Sch., 1945-48. Diplomate in dermatology and syhilology. Assoc. prof. Albert Einstein Med. Sch., Bronx, N.Y., 1955-75; chief of dermatology Grasslands Hosp., Westchester County, N.Y., 1955-75. Contbr. articles to med. jours. Lt. col. USAF, 1936-64. Fellow ACP; mem. Nat. Ski Patrol. Avocations: skiing, fishing. Home: Harbor Pond Farm Block Island RI 02807-0391

GASPAR, ANNA LOUISE, retired elementary school educator, consultant; b. Chgo., May 12, 1935; d. Miklos and Klotild (Weiss) G. *Father, Miklos Gaspar, born in Kaba, Hungary in 1885, was a member of Hungarian Art Institute and exhibited at Gallery of Arts and National Salon of Budapest. A war painter during World War I for the Hungarian Government and the Imperial and Royal Press, he came to the US in 1921 and was recognized as a mural painter of historical subjects and as an ecclesiastical artist. He died in 1946. Photographs, original letters and prizes are on file at the Archives of American Art, Smithsonian Inst. in Wash. D.C. Mother, Klotild (Weiss), born in Sombor, Hungary in 1900, lived in Chicago from 1932-57. She edited and typed masters theses and doctoral dissertations for college and university graduate students.* BS in Edn., Northwestern U., 1957. Cert. elem. tchr., Calif. Tchr. 6th grade Pacific Palisades Elem. Sch., L.A., 1957-58; tchr. 1st grade Eastman Street Elem. Sch., L.A., 1959, Glassell Park, L.A., 1959-62, Stoner Ave. Elem. Sch., L.A., 1962-67; 2nd-4th grade tchr. Brentwood Elem. Sch., L.A., 1967-78; tchr. 4th and 5th grades Brockton Avenue Elem. Sch., L.A., 1978-90; vol., established Swakopmund Tchrs. Resource Ctr., Peace Corps, Namibia, 1991-93; tchr. English, Atlantic Sr. Primary Sch., Swakopmund, Namibia, 1992; career info. cons. Peace Corps., 1991—; substitute tchr. Hebrew Acad./Pre-Primary, Las Vegas, 1994-2000. Mem. Elderhostel Programs: Alaska, 2000, Victoria BC, 2000, Hungary, 2001, Banff Ctr. Can. 2002, Mpls., 2002, San Francisco, 2002, Phoenix Valley, 2003, Santa Fe, 2003, Taos, N.Mex., 2003, Albuquerque, 2003; mem. Bet Knesset Bamidbar Temple. Mem.: Calif. State Ret. Tchrs. Assn., So. Nev. Peace Corps Assn., Peace Corps, Northwestern U. Alumni Assn. Democrat. Jewish. Avocations: world travel, playing piano, art, collecting costume dolls, folk music. Home: 2700 Hope Forest Dr Las Vegas NV 89134-7322

GASPAR, MAX R. surgeon; b. Sioux City, Iowa, May 10, 1915; s. Edgar Mathias and Mabel Agnes (Teefey) G.; m. Virginia Hunter, June 2, 1938 (div. Nov. 1968); children: Karen, Thomas, James, Susan, Mary Ann; m. Lia Sylvia Rista, Jan., 25, 1969. BA, Morningside Coll., 1936; BS, U. S.D., 1938; MD, U. So. Calif., 1941. Diplomate Am. Bd. Surgery, Am. Bd. Surgery with Spl. Competence in Vascular Surgery. Instr. in surgery U. So. Calif., L.A., 1947-48, Coll. Med. Evangelists, L.A., 1948-50, UCLA, 1950-53; asst. clin. prof. surgery Coll. Med. Evangelists, 1953-55, asst. prof. surgery, 1955-59; assoc. clin. prof. surgery Loma Linda U., 1959-63, clin. prof. surgery, 1963-66, U. So. Calif., 1966-90, emeritus prof. surgery, 1990—. Chief surgery L.A. County/UCLA Harbor Gen. Hosp., 1958; attending surgeon L.A. County/U. So. Calif. Gen. Hosp., 1955-91, consulting surgeon, 1991—; dir. vascular surgery Loma Linda U., 1956-66. Author: (textbook) Peripheral Arterial Disease, 1981; contbr. numerous articles to profl. jours. and chpts. to books. Dir. Cath. Welfare Bd., Long Beach, Calif., 1960-62, Am. Heart Assn., Long Beach, 1964-65, Am. Cancer Soc., Long Beach, 1967-70; trustee St. Mary's Found., Long Beach, 1985-94. Lt. USN, 1943-46. Recipient Alumnus of Yr. award U. So. Calif., 1979, Disting. Svc. medal L.A. County/U. So. Calif. Med. Ctr., 1983. Fellow Am. Coll. Surgeons; mem. Am. Surg. Assn., Soc. for Clin. Vascular Surgery (pres. 1979-81), Soc. Internat. de Chirurgie, Soc. for Vascular Surgery. Republican. Roman Catholic. Avocations: tennis, flying, fly fishing, scuba diving, western history. Office: 1780 St John Rd Seal Beach CA 90740

GASPARRINI-ETHERIDGE, CLAUDIA, publishing company executive, scientist, writer; b. Genova, Italy, Apr. 25, 1941; arrived in US, 1984; d. Corrado and Tina (Pizzuti) G.; m. James K. Etheridge, Oct. 15, 1998. D in Earth Scis., U. Rome, 1965; cert. in English, U. Cambridge, Eng., 1965, Pitman Inst., London, 1965. Sr. tech. U. Toronto, Can., 1966-67, rsch. asst., 1967-70, rsch. assoc., 1970-72; phys. scientist II Geol. Survey Can., Ottawa, 1973; rsch. scientist Nat. Inst. for Metallurgy (now Mintek), Johannesburg, 1974-75; ind. cons. Toronto, 1976; pres., owner Minmet Sci. Limited, Toronto, 1977—, Jacksonville, Fla., 1982-86, Tucson, 1986—2000, The Space Eagle Pub. Co., Inc., Toronto, Tucson, 1986—, 1987—; writer, pub., 1989—. Adviser Chinese chpt. Internat. Precious Metals Inst., 1996—2000; guest lectr. U. Heidelberg, 1990, 91, Inst. Precious Metals, Kunming, China, 1984, U. Padua, U. Florence, 1995; presenter in field. Author: Gold and Other Precious Metals-The Lure and the Trap, 1989, How to Get the Most Out of the Legal System Without Spending a Fortune, 1990, Gold and Other Precious Metals-From Ore to Market, 1993, Murder of the Mind-The Practice of Subtle Discrimination, 1993, Murder of the Mind-The Practice of Subtle Discrimination, rev. 2d edit., 1996, When You Make the Two One, 1994, When You Make the Two One, rev. 2d edit., 1996; author: (as Gloria J. Duv) How to Run a Successful Mail Order Business by Defrauding the Public, 1995; author: Deceit-The Fad of the Nineties, 1997, Gold and Other Precious Metals-Occurrence, Extration, Applications, 2000, From Darkness to Light, 2001, Mechanics-Doctors, Does the Quality of Their Assistance Justify the Fees?, 2002, Subtle Discrimination, 2003, The Enemy Within, 2003; mem. bd. editors: Chinese mag. Gold Sci. and Tech., 1996—2000; contbr. Scientist Sci. by Mail Program, Boston Mus. Sci., 1991-92; mem. rsch. bd. advisors Am. Biog. Inst., Raleigh, N.C., 1990—; hon. mem. Internat. Biog. Ctr. Adv. Coun., Cambridge, Eng., 1992—. Recipient Cert. Appreciation Outstanding Svc. Internat. Precious Metals Inst., 1994; named hon. mem. organizing com. Internat. Conf. on Precious Metals, Kosice, Slovakia, 1995. Avocations: classical music, computers and computer applications, collecting books, crystals, precious and semi-precious stones. Home and Office: 7990 E Snyder Rd Apt 4108 Tucson AZ 85750-9007 Office: Minmet Sci Ltd/ The Space Eagle Pub Co Inc 1210 Sheppard Ave E # 200 North York ON Canada M2K 1E3 also: Via Ugo de Carolis 62 00136 Rome 00136 Italy

GASPARRO, MADELINE, banker; b. Jersey City, Oct. 5, 1928; d. Donato and Anna (D'Urso) D'Achille; m. Dominick J. Gasparro, Apr. 30, 1949; children: Dorothy, Joseph, Donato, Frank. Grad. high sch., Jersey City. Cert. Staloysius Eucharistic Min. 2003. Salesperson credit dept. and employee sales J.C. Penney, Parlin, N.J.; head teller Amboy Madison Nat. Bank, Old Bridge, N.J., bank mgr., br. mgr., 1983-97; ret., 1997. Chpt. chmn. South Amboy Hosp., mem. fin. com.; eucharist minister St. Bernadette Ch. of Parlin. Mem. NAFE, Nat. Assn. Bank Women (past hostess), Fin. Women Internat. (chmn. membership Raritan Bay group 1990-91, v.p. 1991-92, pres. 1992-93), Altar Rosary Soc. (past pres.). Address: 12 Baltusrol Dr Jackson NJ 08527-3991 E-mail: domgas@aol.com.

GASPER, GEORGE, JR., mathematics educator; b. Hamtramck, Mich., Oct. 10, 1939; s. George Gregory and Anastasia Gasper; m. Brigitta Gasper, July 1, 1967; children: Karen, Kenneth. BS, Mich. Technol. U., 1962; MA, Wayne State U., 1964, PhD, 1967. Predoctoral traineeship NASA, 1966-67; vis. lectr. U. Wis., Madison, 1967-68; postdoctoral fellow U. Toronto, Ont., Can.,

1968-69, vis. asst. prof., 1969-70; asst. prof. math. Northwestern U., Evanston, Ill., 1970-73, assoc. prof., 1973-77, prof., 1977—. Co-author: Basic Hypergeometric Series, 1990; assoc. editor Jour. Math. Analysis and Applications, 1985-95, The Ramanujan Jour., 1995—. Fellow Alfred P. Sloan Found., 1973-75. Mem. Am. Math. Soc., Soc. Indsl. and Applied Math. (assoc. editor Jour. Math. Analysis 1984-85, vice chair activity group on orthogonal polynomials and spl. functions 1993-95). Office: Northwestern U Dept Math Lunt Bldg Evanston IL 60208-0001

GASPER, JO ANN, consulting firm executive; b. Providence, Sept. 25, 1946; d. Joseph Siegleman and Jeanne Van Matre Shoaf; m. Louis Clement Gasper, Sept. 21, 1974; children: Stephen Gregory, Jeanne Marie, Monica Elizabeth, Michelle Bernadette (dec.), Phyllis Anastasia, Clare Genevieve. BA, U. Dallas, 1967, MBA, 1969. Adminstrv. asst. U. Dallas, 1964-68; asst. dir. adminstrn. Britian Convalescent Ctr., Irving, Tex., 1964-68; pres. Medicare Ctrs., Inc., Dallas, 1968-69; bus. mgr., treas. U. Plano, Tex., 1969-72; ins. agt. John Hancock Ins. Co., Dallas, 1972-73; systems analyst Tex. Instrument, Richardson, 1973-75; pvt. practice acctg., bus. cons. McLean, Va., 1976-81; editor, pub. Congl. News for Women and the Family, McLean, Va., 1978-81, Register Report, McLean, Va., 1980-81; dep. asst. sec. for social services policy HHS, Washington, 1981-85; exec. dir. White House Conf. on Agys., HHS, Washington, 1982-85; dep. asst. sec. for population affairs HHS, Washington, 1985-87; policy advisor to under sec. U.S. Dept. Edn., Washington, 1987-88, cons.; pres. Franklin Pk. Assocs., 1989—; exec. dir. Nat. Assn. for Abstinence Edn., 1989-94; mgr. TSR, 1995-98. Tchr. Grapevine-Colleyville Ind. Sch. Dist., 1998—. Co-chmn. St. John's Refugee Resettlement Commn., Va., 1977; bd. dirs., treas. Coun. Inter-Am. Security, Washington, 1978-80; active Fairfax County Citizens Coalition for Quality Child Care, Va., 1979-80; del. White House Conf. on Families, Va., 1979-80; mem. U.S. adv. Inter-Am. Commn. on Women, OAS, 1982-85; U.S. del. XVI Pan Am. Child Congress, Washington, 1984; mem. nat. family policy adv. bd. Reagan-Bush Campaign, 1980; mem. City of Colleyville Planning and Zoning Comm., 2000-02. Recipient Eagle Forum award, 1979, Wanderer Found. award, 1980, Bronze medal HHS, 1982; named Outstanding Conservative Woman, Conservative Digest, 1980-81 Mem. Exec. Women in Gov. (treas. 1985, sec. 1986) Roman Catholic.

GASPER, RUTH EILEEN, real estate executive; b. Valparaiso, Ind., July 16, 1934; d. Reuben John and Effie (Wesner) Tenpas; m. Ralph L. Gasper, May 25, 1957. Student, Purdue U., 1952-56; BA, Govs. State U., 1982. Analyst computer sys. Leo Burnett Advt., Chgo., 1958-69; nat. adminstr. registrars Sports Car Club Am., Denver, 1977-79; pres. Ainslie Inc., Fla., 1982—. Mem. North River Commn. Housing Com., Chgo., 1982-83, fin. com. Mayor's Task Force on Homelessness City of Chgo. Area coord. Concerned Action party, Lansing, Ill., 1977; chief race registrar Ind. N.W. Region Sports Car Club Am., 1969-80; co-founder, Single Rm. Operators Assn., 1987-98. Mem. Dolphin Beach Club Condo Assn., Fantasy Island II Condo Assn. (sec.). Avocations: sports car racing, classical music.

GASPERINI, ELIZABETH CARMELA (LISA GASPERINI), marketing consultant, graphic designer; b. Newark, Sept. 26, 1961; d. Enrico Caesar and Wanda Claudia (Stanziale) G. BFA, Caldwell (N.J.) Coll., 1983. Advt. specialist J.C. Penney Corp., Wayne, N.J., 1982-83; asst. prodn. mgr. Internat. Postal Mktg. Corp., Montville, N.J., 1983-84; art dir. Healy, Dixcy & Forbes, W. Caldwell, N.J., 1984-86; sr. mktg. specialist Am. Varityper Corp., E. Hanover, N.J., 1986-88; product promotion mgr. Brother Internat. Corp., Somerset, N.J., 1988-90; mktg. specialist Ishida USA Inc., Lincoln Park, N.J., 1990-92; mktg. promotions mgr. Nat. Electronic Info. Corp., Secaucus, N.J., 1992-95; self-employed mktg. cons. Towaco, N.J., 1995-96; mgr. mktg. svcs. AmeriHeath Ins. Co. N.J., Iselin, N.J., 1996-98; mktg. cons. Towaco, N.J., 1998—; mgr. client segment mktg. Merck-Medco Managed Care LLC, 2000—. Telemktg. specialist Sears, Roebuck & Co., Fairfield, N.J., 1984-96; owner, cons. Gasperini Graphics, Towaco, N.J., 1984—; art cons. Italico Pubs., Livingston, N.J., 1982-92. Mem. N.J. Art Assn., N.J. Italian-Am. Assn. (cons. 1982-92). Republican. Roman Catholic. Avocations: photographer, painter, pianist, crafts designer, unique and antique jewelry collector. Home and Office: 10 Willard Ln Towaco NJ 07082-1517

GASPERONI, ELLEN JEAN LIAS, interior designer; b. Rural Valley, Pa.; d. Dale S. and Ruth (Harris) Lias; student Youngstown U., 1952-54, John Carrol U., 1953-54, Westminster Coll., 1951-52; grad. Am. Inst. Banking; m. Emil Gasperoni, May 28, 1955; children: Sam, Emil, Jean Ellen. Mem. Coeurde Coeur Heart Assn., Orlando Opera Guild, Orlando Symphony Guild. Mem. Jr. Bus. Women's Club (dir. 1962-64), Sweetwater Country Club (Longwood, Fla.); Lake Toxaway Golf and Country Club (N.C.). Presbyterian. Home: 1126 Brownshire Ct Longwood FL 32779-2209 also: 92 Cold Mountain Rd Lake Toxaway NC 28747-9630

GASPERONI, EMIL, SR., realtor, developer; b. Hillsville, Pa., Nov. 13, 1926; s. Attico and Rose Mary (Sarnicola) G.; m. Ellen Jean Lias, May 28, 1955; children: Samuel Dale, Emil Attico, Jean Ellen. Diploma in real estate, U. Pitts., 1957. Owner, pres. Gasperoni Real Estate, New Castle, Pa., 1956-63, Ft. Lauderdale, Fla., 1965-86, Gasperoni Internat. Group, Longwood, Fla., 1986—. Founder, chmn. bd. Fill-R-Up Auto Wash Systems Inc., Ft. Lauderdale, 1967-72. With U.S. Army, 1945-46, ETO. Mem. Nat. Inst. Real Estate Brokers, Fla. Assn. Mortgage Brokers, Sweetwater Country Club, Lake Toxaway Country Club (N.C.). Home: 1126 Brownshire Ct Longwood FL 32779 Office: 931 Wekiva Springs Rd Longwood FL 32779-2501 E-mail: gasperoni@commercialrealtyfla.com.

GASQUE, HARRISON (ALLARD HARRISON GASQUE), optical supply company executive; b. Richmond, Va., Oct. 10, 1958; s. Thomas Nelson and Susan (Folline) G.; m. Diane Cynthia Phillips, Nov. 14, 1992; 1 child, Folline Elaine. Grad., Columbia Sch. Broadcasting, Washington, 1982; attending, Ashworth Coll. Disc jockey Sta. WKDK-AM, Newberry, SC, 1981—83, WEEL-AM, Washington, 1983-85; announcer, disc jockey Sta. WWGO-FM, Columbia, 1986-87; announcer Sta. WNOK-AM, Columbia, 1987-88, Sta. WODE-AM, Columbia, 1989-90, Sta. WYYS-FM, Columbia, 1991, Sta. WSCQ-FM, Columbia, 1991-94; v.p. transp. Palmetto Optical Supply, 1986—. Mem. Coun. of Conservative Citizens. Recipient Presdl. Order of Merit award, 1991. Mem.: SCV (life; media officer Lt. Gen. Wade Hampton Camp 273), 1st Tuesday Rep. Club, Alpha Epsilon Rho, Phi Kappa Psi. Avocations: singing, coin, stamp and record collecting, tennis, basketball, football. Home: 3728 Linbrook Dr Columbia SC 29204-4438 E-mail: hgasque@sc.rr.com.

GASQUE, THOMAS JAMES, retired English educator; b. Florence, SC, Sept. 6, 1937; s. Thomas Jefferson and Margaret Olive (Reaves) G.; m. Alice Marie Tealey, May 31, 1969; 1 child, Susanna Rachel White. AB, Wofford Coll., 1959; MA, Emory U., 1962; PhD, U. Tenn., 1970. Instr. Clemson (S.C.) U., 1961-62, Columbia (S.C.) Coll., 1962-63; tchg. asst. U. Tenn., Knoxville, 1963-68; asst. prof. U. S.D., Vermillion, 1968-72, assoc. prof., 1972-88, prof., 1988—2003, chmn. dept. English, 1971-76; ret., 2003. Editor: Anthology of Humanities Essays, 1997; contbr. articles to profl. jours. Lt. Infantry, 1960. Fulbright Rsch. and Tchg. grantee German Fulbright Commn., Oldenburg, Germany, 1988-89. Mem. MLA, Am. Name Soc. (bd. advisors 1986-88, v.p. 1999-2000, pres. 2001-02, editor Names: A Journal of Onomastics 1988-92), New Chaucer Soc. Home: 119 N Yale St Vermillion SD 57069-2720 E-mail: tgasque@usd.edu.

GASS, GERTRUDE ZEMON, psychologist, researcher; b. Detroit; d. David Solomon and Mary (Goldman) Zemon; m. H. Harvey Gass, June 19, 1938; children: Susan, Roger. BA, U. Mich., 1937, MSW, 1943, PhD, 1957. Lic. clin. psychologist, Mich. Mem. faculty Merrill-Palmer Inst., Detroit, 1958-69, lectr., 1967; mem. faculty Advanced Behavioral Sci. Ctr., Grosse Pointe, Mich., 1969-72; pvt. practice clin. psychology Birmingham, Mich., 1972—. Adj. prof. psychology U. Detroit, 1969-75; cons. Continuum Ctr. Oakland U., Rochester, Mich., 1961-77, Traveler's Aid, Detroit, 1959-75; pres. Shapero Sch. Nursing, Detroit, 1967-72, cons. 1958-78; psychol. cons. Physician's Ins. Co. of Mich., 1988—, mgmt. Mich. Bell Telephone, 1979-82. Mem. Adv. Com Sch. Needs, 1954-56; trustee Sinai Hosp. Detroit, 1972-99; bd. dirs. Tribute Fund United Cmty. Svcs., 1955-67. Fellow Am. Assn. Marriage-Family, Am. Orthopsychiatric Assn. (v.p. 1975-76), Mich. Psychol. Assn.; mem. Am. Psychol. Assn., Psychologists Task Force (v.p. 1977-84), Mich. Inter-Profl. Assn. (pres. 1976-78), Mich. Assn. Marriage Counselors (1979-80, pres. 1979-80), Mental Health Adv. Svc., Blue Cross and Blue Shield of Mich., Phi Kappa Phi, Pi Lambda Theta. Home and Office: 6155 E Longview Dr East Lansing MI 48823

GASS, MANUS M. accountant, business executive; b. Montreal, Que., Can., June 28, 1928; came to U.S., 1948, naturalized, 1953; s. Maurice and Bertha (Silverberg) G.; m. Estella L. Gass; children: Thomas Evan, Winifred Caitlyn. Student, McGill U., 1945-48; BBA cum laude, CCNY, 1953. CPA, N.Y. Pres., dir. Buitoni Foods Corp., South Hackensack, N.J., 1966-86; chief exec. officer Stavola Constrn. Inc., Tinton Falls, N.J., 1989—. Dir. Buitoni Perugina Inc., N.Y.C., Perugina Chocolates & Confections Inc., Little Ferry, N.J.; acct. Am. Jewish Tercentenary Com., 1953-54 Chmn. River Edge-Oradell United Jewish Appeal, 1964-65, 67-76; mem. Shade Tree Commn., River Edge, 1987—; bd. govs. Hackensack Med. Center. Mem. Am. Inst. C.P.A.s, N.Y. State Soc. C.P.A.s, Fin. Execs. Inst. Home: 184 Woodland Ave River Edge NJ 07661-2321

GASS, SAUL IRVING, educator; b. Chelsea, Mass., Feb. 28, 1926; s. Louis and Bertha Gass; m. Gertrude Gass, June 30, 1946; children: Ronald S., Joyce A. BS in Edn., MA in Math., Boston U., 1949; PhD in Engring. Sci., U. Calif., Berkeley, 1965. Mathematician USAF, 1949-55; applied sci. rep. IBM, Washington, 1955-58; dir. ops. rsch. CEIR, Inc., Arlington, Va., 1959; mgr. project mercury IBM Fed. Systems, Gaithersburg, Md., 1960-63, mgr. civil programs, 1965-69; sr. v.p. World Systems Lab., Bethesda, Md., 1969-70; v.p. Mathematica, Inc., Bethesda, 1970-75; prof. U. Md., College Park, 1975—2001, prof. emeritus, 2001—. Cons. Nat. Inst. Std. and Tech., Gaithersburg, 1976—. Author: Linear Programming, 1958, Illustrated Guide to Linear Programming, 1970, Decision Making, Models and Algorithms, 1985; editor: Encyclopedia of Operations Research and Management Science, 1996. Pres. Ops. Rsch. Soc. Am., 1976. With U.S. Army, 1944-46. Fulbright scholar Fulbright Commn., 1995-96, Fulbright Sr. specialist, 2002; recipient Steinhardt Meml. award Ctr. of Naval Analysis, 1996, Kimball award Ops. Rsch. Soc. of Am., 1991. Fellow Inst. for Ops. Rsch. and the Mgmt. Scis. (Expository Writing award 1997); mem. Assn. for Computing Machinery (coun. mem. 1960-62), Math. Assn. of Am., Soc. for Indsl. and Applied Math., Math. Programming Soc.

GASS, WILLIAM H. writer, educator; b. Fargo, N.D., July 30, 1924; s. William Bernard and Claire (Sorensen) G.; m. Mary Patricia O'Kelly, 1952 (div.); children: Richard, Robert, Susan; m. Mary Alice Henderson, 1969; children: Elizabeth, Catherine. AB, Kenyon Coll., 1947, LHD (hon.), 1973, 85; PhD, Cornell U., 1953. Instr. philosophy Coll. of Wooster, Ohio, 1950-54; asst. prof. Purdue U., Lafayette, 1954-60, assoc. prof., 1960-66, prof. philosophy, 1966-69, Washington U., St. Louis, 1969-79, David May Disting. Univ. prof. in humanities, 1979-99; dir. Internat. Writers Center, 1990—2001. Vis. lectr. U. Ill., 1958-59; mem. Rockefeller Commn. on Humanities, 1978-80; mem. literature panel Nat. Endowment for the Arts, 1979-82. Author: Omensetter's Luck, 1966, In the Heart of the Heart of the Country, 1968, Willie Masters' Lonesome Wife, 1968, Fiction and the Figures of Life, 1970, On Being Blue, 1974, The World Within the Word, 1978, The Habitations of the Word: Essays, 1984, The Tunnel, 1995, Finding a Form, 1996, Cartesian Sonata, 1998, Reading Rilke, 1999, Tests of Time, 2002; contbr. to periodicals including N.Y. Rev. of Books, N.Y. Times Book Rev., New Republic, TriQuar., Salmagundi, others. Office: 6304 Westminster Pl Saint Louis MO 63130

GASSEL, PHILIP MICHAEL, lawyer; b. Chgo., June 5, 1947; s. Arnold and Claire (Segal) G.; m. Mollyann Pollak, Aug. 29, 1971; children: Miriam, Harry, Naomi. BS, Northwestern U., 1968; JD, Columbia U., 1972. Bar: N.Y. 1973, U.S. Dist. Ct. (ea. and so. dists.) N.Y. 1974, U.S. Ct. Appeal (2nd cir.) 1975, U.S. Supreme Ct. 1976. Sr. atty. N.Y.C. Dept. Consumer Affairs, 1972-74, Legal Svcs. for the Elderly, N.Y.C., 1974-79; assoc. Epstein Becker & Green P.C., N.Y.C., 1979-84, ptnr., 1984—. Trustee Lincoln Square Synagogue, N.Y.C., 1978—. Mem. Am. Health Lawyers Assn., N.Y. State Bar Assn. Office: Epstein Becker & Green PC 250 Park Ave Fl 14 New York NY 10177-0001 E-mail: pgassel@ebglaw.com.

GASSER, WILBERT, JR., (WILBERT WARNER GASSER JR.), retired banker; b. Marquette, Mich., Apr. 5, 1923; s. Wilbert Warner and Mildred (Carpenter) G.; m. Mary C. Kratz, Dec. 6, 1952; 1 child, Wilbert Warner III. Student, Purdue U., 1941-42; BS in Bus., Ind. U., 1948. With Gary (Ind.) Nat. Bank (name changed later to Gainer Bank), 1948-92, v.p., 1953-63, chmn. bd., 1964-92, ret. Pres. Gary YMCA, 1960-62; treas. Gary Urban League, 1960-65, N.W. Ind. Heart Assn., 1961-64; bd. dirs., treas. Meth. Hosp., Gary. With USAAF, 1943-46. Mem. Gary C. of C. (v.p. 1961), Kiwanis (treas. Gary club 1963—). Presbyterian. Home: 149 Shore Dr Ogden Dunes IN 46368-1015

GASSERE, EUGENE ARTHUR, lawyer, business executive; b. Beaumont, Tex., Oct. 20, 1930; s. Victor Eugene and Althea June (Haight) G.; m. Mary Alice Engelhard, Aug. 4, 1956; children— Paul, John, Anne. BS, U. Wis., 1952, JD, 1956; postgrad., Oxford U., 1956-57. Bar: Wis. bar 1956. Asst. counsel Wurlitzer Co., Chgo., 1958-61, Campbell Soup Co., Camden, N.J., 1961-65; asst. to pres. Thilmany Pulp & Paper Co., Kaukauna, Wis., 1966-68; with Skyline Corp., Elkhart, Ind., 1968-92, v.p., gen. counsel, asst. sec., 1973-92, ret., 1992—. Pres., bd. dirs. Elkhart Urban League, 1972-73, Elkhart Symphony, 1975-76, Elkhart Concert Club, 1976-77. Served with U.S. Army, 1952-54. Mem. Wis. Bar Assn., Phi Mu Alpha. Home: PO Box 165 Mindoro WI 54644-0165 Office: Skyline Corp 2520 Bypass Rd Elkhart IN 46514-1584 E-mail: pelt2ridge@aol.com.

GASSMAN, MERRILL LOREN, biological sciences educator, consultant; b. Chgo., Feb. 10, 1943; s. Alfred Gassman and Elvina (Chessen) Levin; m. Beverly Sue Sacks, Sept. 3, 1967; children— Debra Eileen, Sharyl Jorene, Aaron Howard. S.B. in Biology, U. Chgo., 1960-64, S.M. in Botany, 1964-65, Ph.D. in Botany, 1965-67. Predoctoral fellow NASA, U. Chgo., 1964-67; postdoctoral fellow USPHS, Rockefeller U., 1967-68; guest investigator Rockefeller U., N.Y.C., 1967-68; research scientist Internat. Minerals, Libertyville, Ill., 1968-69; asst. prof. U. Ill., Chgo., 1969-75, assoc. prof., 1975-82, prof. biological sciences, 1982—2000, prof. emeritus, 2000; film cons. Coronet Films, Inc., Deerfield, Ill.; cons. textbook Wm. C. Brown Pub., Dubuque, Iowa, Scott, Foresman Co., Glenview, Ill. Contbr. chpts. to books and articles to reference jours. NSF grantee, 1972-87. Mem. Am. Soc. Plant Biology, Am. Soc. for Biochemistry and Molecular Biology. Office: U Ill Dept Biol Scis 845 W Taylor St Rm 3262 Chicago IL 60607 E-mail: mgassman@uic.edu.

GAST, RICHARD SHAEFFER, lawyer; b. Pueblo, Colo., Aug. 1, 1956; s. Robert Shaeffer and Ann (Day) G.; m. Beverly Paterson, Aug. 22, 1981; children: Charles Edward, Robert Shaeffer. BA, Stanford U., 1978; JD, U. Colo., 1981. Bar: Colo. 1981, U.S. Dist. Ct. Colo. 1981. Assoc. March, Myatt, Korb, Carroll & Brandes, Ft. Collins, Colo., 1981-85; shareholder, officer, dir. March & Myatt, P.C., Ft. Collins, Colo., 1985-97, Myatt Brandes & Gast PC, Ft. Collins, 1998—. Bd. dirs. Elk Falls Ranch Co., Legacy Land Trust; mem. Jud. Performance Commn., 1992-94. Contbg. editor U. Colo. Law Rev., 1980-81. Organizer local fundraising Am. Cancer Soc., Ft. Collins, 1985-86; mem. Larimer County Land Use Plan Citizens' Rev. Com., Ft. Collins, 1986; mem. choices 95 com., Ft. Collins, 1988; dir. Colo. Lawyers Trust Account Found., 1990-96, chair, grants com., 1990-96, pres., 1995-96; bd. dirs. Ft. Collins Area United Way, 1991-98, pres., 1996-97; bd. dirs. Neighbor to Neighbor, Inc., 1988-91, Legacy Land Trust, 2001—; hearing officer Poudre Sch. Dist., 1995-97. Mem. ABA (corps., bus. and banking law sect.), Colo. Bar Assn. (mem. exec. coun. young lawyers divsn. 1988-91, chmn. 1990-91, bd. govs. 1990-91, 97-98, v.p. 1997-98, exec. coun. 1997-98, budget com. 1997-2000, real estate sect. coun. 1998—, chair 2003—, bd. govs. 1990-91, 97-98, long-range planning com. 2000-01, joint mgmt. com. 2001—, chair 2003-04, Outstanding Young Lawyer 1987), Larimer County Bar Assn. (chmn. legal aid program 1986, chmn.-elect young lawyers sect. 1986-87, chmn. 1987-88), Ft. Collins C. of C. (legis. affairs commn. 1988-92). Democrat. Episcopalian. Avocations: skiing, running, soccer, backpacking, mountain biking. Home: 1129 Oakmont Ct Fort Collins CO 80525-2855 Office: Myatt Brandes & Gast PC 323 S College Ave Ste 1 Fort Collins CO 80524-2845 E-mail: rgast@verinet.com.

GASTEYER, CARLIN EVANS, museum administrator, museum studies educator; b. Jackson, Mich., Mar. 30, 1917; d. Frank Howard and Marian (Spencer) Evans; m. Harry A. Gasteyer, Jan. 8, 1944; 1 dau., Nancy Catherine. Student, Barnard Coll., 1934-35; BA, CUNY, 1983. Clk. First Nat. City Bank, 1939-42; statistician Bell Tel. Labs., 1942—45; dir. asst. S.I. Mus., 1956-61; bus. mgr. Mus. City N.Y., 1961-63; asst. dir., 1967-70; mus. adminstr., 1963-66; asst. dir. Monmouth (N.J.) Mus., 1966-67; vice dir. adminstr. Bklyn. Mus., 1970-74; dir. planning Snug Harbor Cultural Ctr., S.I., NY, 1975—79; cable tv cons., 1980—2003. Adj. lectr. mus. studies Coll. S.I. CUNY, 1985-94, asst. higher edn. officer, 1995. Active Girl Scouts; co-founder, pres. Jr. Mus. Guild, S.I. Mus., 1956-58; mem. N.Y.C. Local Sch. Bd. 54, 1960-61. Mem. Am. Assn. Mus., Mus. Coun. N.Y.C. Home: Eatontown, NJ. Died Feb. 26, 2003.

GASTIL, RAYMOND WESLEY, urban designer; b. Cambridge, Mass., Nov. 21, 1958; s. Raymond Duncan and Jeannette Carr Gastil. BA in Comparative Lit., Yale U., 1980; MArch, Princeton U., 1991. Dir. regional design program Regional Plan Assn. N.Y., N.J., and Conn., N.Y.C., 1991-95; exec. dir. Projects Pub. Architecture Van Alen Inst., N.Y.C., 1995—. Mem. dept. architecture adv. com. Parsons Sch. Design, N.Y.C., 1996—; vis. lectr. Pratt Inst., Bklyn., 1997, U. Pa., Phila., 2000; panelist N.Y. Coun. Arts, N.Y.C., 2000-02. Author: Beyond the Edge: New York's New Waterfront, 2002, (with Robert A. M. Stern) Modern Classicism, 1988; contbg. author: The Italian Garden: Art, Design, and Culture, 1996, New York, 2001; contbg. writer Blueprint Mag., 1987-90. Mentor N.J. Inst. Tech., Newark, 1997-98; mem. steering com. Pier 40 Cmty. Design, N.Y.C., 1999; mem. adv. bd. U. Va. Sch. Architecture, 2002—. Fellow Inst. Urban Design; mem. AIA (assoc.; mem. oculus publ. com. N.Y. chpt. 1999-2000). Office: Van Alen Inst 30 W 22d St New York NY 10010 E-mail: rgastil@vanalen.org.

GASTIL, RUSSELL GORDON, geologist, educator; b. San Diego, June 25, 1928; s. Russell Chester and Frances (Duncan) G.; m. Emily Janet Manly, Sept. 13, 1958; children— Garth Manly, Mary Margaret, George Christopher, John Webster. A.B, U. Calif. at Berkeley, 1950, PhD, 1954. With Shell Oil Co., 1954, Canadian Javelin Co., 1956-58; lectr. U. Calif. at Los Angeles, 1958-59; faculty San Diego State U., 1959—, prof. geology, 1965—, chmn. dept., 1969-72. Publisher: We Can Save San Diego, 1975; Contbr. papers to profl. lit. Democratic candidate U.S. Ho. of Reps., 1976; mem. Calif. Dem. Central Com., 1977-78; coordinator 41st Congl. dist. Common Cause, 1977; pres. Grossmont-Mt. Helix Improvement Assn., 1978-80; mem. San Diego County Air Pollution Hearing Bd., 1977-80; trustee Friends com. on legislation edn. com., 1994-01. Recipient 2002 Dibblee medalist for outstanding geologic field mapping. Fellow Geol. Soc. Am. (vice chmn. Cordilleran sect. 1967, gen. chmn. ann. meeting San Diego 1991); mem. Soc. Econ. Mineralogists and Paleontologists, Am. Geophys. Union. Home: 9435 Alto Dr La Mesa CA 91941-4226 Office: San Diego State U Dept Geol Scis San Diego CA 92182 Personal E-mail: jgastil@home.com.

GASTL, EUGENE FRANCIS, lawyer; b. Shawnee, Kans., Apr. 28, 1932; s. Bert J. and Bessie C. (Bell) G.; m. Deanna J. Cordon, June 7, 1959 (div. May 1978); children: Philip E., Catherine L., David B., Brenda M.; m. Arline Blackwood, June 15, 1979. BA, U. Kans., 1954, LLB, 1956, JD, 1968. Bar: Kans. 1956, U.S. Dist. Ct. Kans. 1956. Sole practice, Shawnee, 1959—. State rep. Kans. Legislature, Topeka, 1961-65, 71-79, senator, 1965-69. Served to specialist grade 3 U.S. Army, 1956-58. Mem. ABA, Kans. Bar Assn., Johnson County Bar Assn., Assn. Trial Lawyers Am., Shawnee C. of C. (v.p. 1965-67). Lodges: Optimist (bd. dirs. 1961-63). Democrat. Methodist. Avocation: reading. Home: 5420 Bluejacket St Shawnee Mission KS 66203-1924 Office: 5811 Nieman Rd Shawnee Mission KS 66203-2855

GASTLE, TIMOTHY ANTHONY, music educator; b. Buffalo, N.Y., Dec. 16, 1968; s. Paul R. and Grace L. Gastle. MusB, SUNY, Buffalo, NY, 1992, BA in Vocal Performance, 1995; MusM, SUNY, Fredonia, NY, 1998. Cert. music educator N.Y., 1998. Theatrical vocal music dir. and vocal coach St. Francis HS, Athol Springs, NY, 1992—; HS choral dir. Iroquois Ctrl. H.S., Elma, NY, 1995—. Music min. Saints Peter & Paul Ch., Hamburg, NY, 1992—, ensemble dir., 1992—; chmn. of music com. Buffalo (N.Y.) Diocesan Liturgical Commn., 1999—. Dir.: (plays). Chmn. bd. dirs. Buffalo (N.Y.) Diocesan Liturgical Commn., 2001—03. Mem.: Am. Choral Director's Assn., Ch. Musicians Guild of Buffalo, Erie County Music Educator's Assn., Music Educator's Nat. Conf., N.Y. State Sch. Music Assn. (adjudicator 1996—, Gold with Distinction award 2002). Avocations: reading, travel, skiing, gardening, cooking. Office: Iroquois High School 2111 Girdle Rd Elma NY 14059 Office Fax: 716-652-9305. E-mail: tim_gastle@iroquois.wnyric.org.

GASTMANN, ALBERT LODEWIJK, retired political science and language educator, writer; b. Arnhem, The Netherlands, Oct. 28, 1919; s. Lodewijk A. Gastmann and Petronella M. Uhlenbeck. BA, Columbia Coll., 1949; MA, Columbia U., 1953, PhD, 1963. Clerical officer Netherlands Embassy, Chungking, China, 1943—46; tchr. Abraham Lincoln Am. Sch., Lima, 1950—53; instr. modern langs. Trinity Coll., Hartford, 1954—57, asst., assoc. prof. polit. scis., 1957—75; prof., lectr. Law Sch. Netherlands Antilles, Curacao, 1975—79; prof. Trinity Coll., Hartford, 1975—91, ret., 1991. Author: The Politics of Surinam and The Netherlands Antilles, 1968 (German Honor Soc. Delta Phi Alpha award), Urbanization Planning and Development in Caribbean, 1989, (with Scott MacDonald) Mitterand's Headache, 1984, A History of Credit and Power in the Western World, 2001; contbr. articles to profl. jours., chpts. to books. Served Netherlands Navy 1941-43. With Netherlands Armed Svcs., 1940—43. Mem. Caribbean Studies Assn. U.S. (founding mem.), Pi Gamma Mu, Delta Phi Alpha. Home: 244 Avery Heights Hartford CT 06106-4092 Office: Trinity Coll Polit Sci 300 Summit St Hartford CT 06106

GASTON, EDWIN WILLMER, JR., retired English language educator; b. Nacogdoches, Tex., Feb. 22, 1925; s. Edwin Willmer and Fannie (Meisenheimer) G.; m. Martha Middlebrook, Feb. 16, 1946; children: John E. F., Thomas M., Weldon K. BS, Stephen F. Austin State U., 1947, MA, 1951; PhD, Tex. Tech U., 1959. Editor various mags. and newspapers, 1947-50; radio broadcaster, 1947-50; dir. publs., asst. prof. English and journalism Stephen F. Austin State U., Nacogdoches, 1950-53, assoc. prof., 1955-64, prof., 1965-86, chmn. dept. English, 1965-69, dean Grad. Sch., 1976-81, v.p. for acad. affairs, 1981-86, prof. emeritus, 1986—. Instr. Tex. Tech U., 1953-55. Author: The Early Novel of the Southwest, 1961, A Manual of Style, 1961, Conrad Richter, 1965, (updated ed. 1989), Eugene Manlove Rhodes, 1967; editor: (with others) Southwestern American Literature: A Bibliography, 1980; contbr. articles to anthologies, encys., profl. jours. Served as cpl. USMC, 1942-46, PTO. Recipient Disting. Prof. award Stephen F. Austin State U., 1969, U. Helsinki, 1965, Disting. Svc. award Assn. Coll. Honor Socs., 2000; Fulbright scholar U. Helsinki, 1964-65. Mem. MLA (south cen. region), Nat. Coun. Tchrs. English, Southwestern Am. Lit. Assn., Western Am. Lit. Assn., Tex. Folklore Soc. (treas. 1970-96, past pres.), Alpha Chi (pres. 1967-79, pres. emeritus 1979—, Disting Alumnus award 1999). Avocations: reading, travel. Home: 709 Bostwick St Nacogdoches TX 75965-2416

GASTON, JOSEPH, minister, education; arrived in U.S., 1986; s. Denizard and Marie T. Gaston; m. Marie Yanick Eugene, Dec. 26, 1981; children: Mardochee, Nathaniel, Eunice, Timothee. BS in Econs., State U. Haiti, Port-au-Prince, 1982; MA in Christian Edn., So. Bapt. Theol. Sem., Louisville, 1997; PhD in Ch. Edn. and Leadership, So. Bapt. Theol. Sem., 2003. Economist, analyst Econ. Dept. Haiti, Port-au-Prince, 1981—83; tchr. various h.s., Haiti and U.S., 1980—95; minister, prof. various, 1979—2001; leadership trainer Haitian Ministries USA, 1995—; leadership devel. dir. Fla. Bapt. Conv., Jacksonville, 2002—. Chair Nat. Christian Leadership, 2002. Mem.: AAUP, N.Am. Christian Edn. Assn. Baptist. Office: Florida Baptist Conv 1230 Hendricks Ave Jacksonville FL 33065

GASTON, MARGARET ANNE, retired business educator; b. Regina, Sask., Can., Aug. 28, 1930; Came to U.S., 1948. d. William Julius and Mary Josephine (Collins) Grogan; m. Robert F. Gaston, 1955 (dec. Mar. 1970); 1 child, Robert. BA in Bus. Edn., Cen. Wash. U., 1959; MEd, Western Wash. U., 1972; postgrad., Boston U., 1984. Cert. tchr. K-12, cert. vocat. tchr., Wash. Bus. educator Manson (Wash.) Sch. Dist., 1956-59; instr. K-12 Eastmont Sch. Dist., East Wenatchee, Wash., 1959-63; instr., chmn. dept. bus. Skagit Valley Coll. Whidbey Campus, Oak Harbor, Wash., 1970-90. Part-time instr. bus. edn. Wenatchee Valley Coll., 1959-65. Contbr. articles to profl. jours. Fellow Western Wash. U., Bellingham, 1968-69. Mem. AAUW, NEA, Wash. Edn. Assn., Bus. and Profl. Women, Delta Pi Epsilon, Beta Sigma Phi. Home: 20 Little Mountain Estates 2610 E Section St Mount Vernon WA 98274-6100

GASTON, MARILYN HUGHES, health facility administrator; b. Cin. children: Amy Marie, Damon Allen. AB in Zoology, Miami U., Oxford, Ohio, 1960; MD, U. Cin., 1964. Diplomate Am. Bd. Pediats. Intern Phila. Gen. Hosp., 1964—65; resident in pediat. Childrens Hosp. Med. Ctr., Cin., 1965—67, asst. dir. out-patient dept., 1967—68, Convalescent Hosp. for Children, Cin., 1968—69; med. dir. Lincoln Heights (Ohio) Health Ctr., 1969—72; dir. Sickle Cell screening clinic Cin. Health Dept., 1972—76; med. expert Nat. Heart, Lung & Blood Inst./NIH, Bethesda, 1976—79; commd. 2d lt. USPHS, 1979—89; dir. divsn. medicine Bur. Health Professions, Rockville, Md., 1989—90; dir., asst. surgeon gen., assoc. adminstr. for bureau Bur. Primary Health Care, Rockville, Md., 1990—2002; chief medical officer National Minority Health Month, 2002—. Instr. pediats. U. Cin. Coll. Medicine, 1967—68, asst. clin. prof. divsn. cmty. pediats., 1968—70, asst. prof. pediats., 1970—76, assoc. prof. pediats., 1976—77; asst. clin. prof. pediats. Cin. Tech. Coll., 1974—76, Howard U. Coll. Medicine, 1978—91, Uniformed Svcs. U. the Health Scis., 1987—; attending pediatrician Children's Hosp. Med. Ctr., 1969—76, attending pediatrician and clinician, 1969—76, dir. med. staff, 1969—76; attending pediatrician Bethesda Hosp., 1974—76; pediatrician Hosp. Albert Schweitzer Deschapelles, Haiti, 1967; presenter, lectr., spkr. in field. Author: AL Bibliography: Comprehensive Sickle Cell Centers, 1977; co-author (with C.L. Calhoun), 1981; author: Management and Therapy of Sickle Cell Disease, 1984, 1988, Prime Time: The African American Woman's Complete Guide to Midlife Health and Wellness, 2003; author: (with others) Newborn Screening for Sickle Cell Disease and Other Hemoglobinopathies, 1989; contbr. articles. Co-chair Nat. Sickle Cell Dirs., 1974; med. advisor Sickle Cell Awareness Group, 1971—77, State Crippled Children's Svcs., 1975—77; bd. trustees Child Health Assn., 1974—77; bd. dirs. U. Cin. Found., 1989—, George Washington U. Life Scis., 1993—, U. Md. Ctr. for Minority Rsch. External Adv. Bd., 1993—, Komen Found. for Breast Cancer, Wellesley Ctr. for Women, Nat. Black Woman's Health Project. Named Woman of the Yr. in Medicine, Harriet Tubman Black Women's Dem., 1976; named one of Outstanding Young Women in Am., 1973, Outstanding Black Women in Cin., 1974; named to Ohio Women's Hall of Fame, 1990; recipient Phyllis Wheatley award, State of Ohio, 1975, Hildrus A. Poindexter award, Pub. Health Svcs., 1990, State of Ohio Gov.'s award, 1987, Disting. Alumnae award, U. Cin., 1989, Pub. Health award, D.C. Health Care for the Homless Project, Inc., Nathan Davis award, AMA. Mem.: APHA, AAAS, Inst. of Medicine/NAS, N.Y. Acad. Scis., Am. Med. Women's Assn., Am. Pediat. Soc., Am. Soc. Hematology, Nat. Med. Assn. (Living Legend award), Nat. Assn. Med. Minority Educators, Am. Acad. Pediats., Alpha Kappa Alpha, Sigma Delta Epsilon. Office: Nat Minority Health Month 1101 Pennsylvania Ave, NW, Ste 820 Washington DC 20004

GASTON, PAUL E. former professional basketball team executive; m. Dana Halsey; children: John and Peter (twins), Sarah. BA, MA, Brown U. Staff in fin. advertising and pub. rels., London; pres Brookwood Investments, N.Y.C.; chmn. of the bd. Boston Celtics Ltd., 1992—2002.

GASTON, PAUL LEE, academic administrator, language educator; b. Hattiesburg, Miss., Aug. 23, 1943; s. Paul Lee and Ruth (Gooch) Gaston; m. Eileen Margaret Higgins, June 29, 1968; children: Elizabeth, Tyler Lee. BA, S.E. La. U., 1965; MA, U. Va., 1966, PhD, 1970. Ordained min. Episc. Ch., 1990. Prof. English So. Ill. U., Edwardsville, 1969-88, assoc. v.p., 1984-88; dean Coll. Arts and Scis. U. Tenn., Chattanooga, 1988-93; provost, exec. v.p. No. Ky. U., Highland Heights, 1993-99, provost Kent (Ohio) State U., 1999—. Author: W. D. Snodgrass, 1978, Concordance Conrad, Arrow of Gold, 1980; contbr. articles to profl. jours. Bd. dirs. Ohio Learning Network, Ohio Lik. Mem.: Nat. Assn. State U. and Land Grant Colls., Assn. Specialized and Profl. Accreditors, Phi Beta Kappa. Democrat. Avocations: softball, hiking, calligraphy. Office: Kent State U Office of Provost PO Box 5190 Kent OH 44242-0001 E-mail: pgaston@kent.edu.

GASTWIRTH, DONALD EDWARD, lawyer, literary agent; b. N.Y.C., Aug. 7, 1944; s. Paul and Tillie (Scheinert) G. BA, Yale U., 1966, JD, 1974. Bar: Conn. 1979, U.S. Dist. Ct. Conn. 1981. Mem. advt. staf New Yorker mag., N.Y.C., 1967-68; v.p. Reader's Press, New Haven, 1968-74, dir., 1968-75; exec. v.p. Mainstream TV Studio, New Haven, 1974-77, dir., 1974-79; pres. Quasar Assocs., New Haven, 1979-89; account exec. Bache Halsey Stuart Shields Inc., New Haven, 1977-79; ptnr. Gastwirth, McMillan & Still, New Haven, 1981-84; pres. Don Gastwirth & Assocs. Literary Agy., New Haven, 1984—. Adj. prof. law Thomas Jefferson Sch. Law, 1996-99; lectr. in field; advisor fund raising, mem. benefit com. John Steinbeck Lit. Project, 1986-94; assoc. fellow Trumbull Coll., Yale U. Assoc. prodr. Yankee Fishing (TV series, 1995-98); contbr. to Nat. Rev., Wall St. Jour., New Haven Register; mem. bd. advisors Yale Lit. Mag., 1987-94, Touchstone Mag., 1990-95, 98-99. Trustee Yale Ctr. for Parliamentary History, 1995-2002. Mem.: PEN Writers Assn., ABA, Writers Guild Am., Berzelius Soc., Lambs Club, Yale Club (N.Y.), Elizabethan Club. Home and Office: 265 College St New Haven CT 06510-2420

GASTWIRTH, GLENN BARRY, medical association administrator; b. N.Y.C., Sept. 18, 1946; s. Milton and Janette (Wasserman) G.; m. Joy Ann Binstock, Nov. 29, 1969; children: Sara Beth, Bradley Aaron. BA, Ohio State U., 1968; postgrad., NYU, 1968-69; Dr.Podiatric Medicine, N.Y. Coll. Podiatric Medicine, N.Y.C., 1974. Diplomate Am. Bd. Podiatric Surgery. Pvt. practice podiatry, Southgate, Mich., 1975-86, Tri-County Family Podiatrists, Pontiac, Mich., 1979-86; dir. sci. affairs Am. Podiatric Med. Assn., Bethesda, Md., 1986-92, dep. exec. dir., 1992—98; editor-in-chief Jour. Am. Podiatric Med. Assn., 1989-91; exec. editor, 1991—; exec. dir. Am. Podiatric Med. Assn., Bethesda, Md., 1998—. Pres. Cold Spring Sch. PTA, Potomac, Md., 1988-90; bd. dirs. Nat. Coun. on the Aging, 1996—; chair del. coun. Nat. Voluntary Orgns. for Ind. Living for the Aging. NIH fellow, 1968-69; N.Y.C. Dept. Pub. Health fellow, 1970. Fellow Am. Coll. Foot Surgeons, Am. Coll. Podiatric Med. Rev. (sec. 1990—); mem. Mich. Podiatric Med. Assn. (pres. 1981-82, Legion of Merit 1982), Am. Pub. Health Assn. (sect. council mem. 1972-74), Am. Diabetes Assn., Am. Podiatric Med. Assn. (ho. of dels. 1973-74, 80-86, Disting. Svc. citation 1996). Avocations: running, writing. Office: Am Podiatric Med Assn 9312 Old Georgetown Rd Bethesda MD 20814-1646

GASTWIRTH, STUART LAWRENCE, lawyer; b. N.Y.C., Feb. 26, 1939; s. Jack Keith and Lillian (Gurchinsky) G.; m. Norma Blechman, June 13, 1965; children: Andrew Evan, David Eric, Jason Marc. BA, Hofstra U., 1959; JD, Cornell U., 1962. Bar: N.Y. 1963. Assoc. Cole & Deitz, N.Y.C., 1962-67; atty. Central State Bank, N.Y.C., 1967-69; ptnr. Semon & Gastwirth, Jericho, NY, 1969-75; sole practice Jericho, 1975-81; ptnr. Gastwirth, Mirsky & Stein LLP, Manhasset, Southampton, NY, 1997—. Chmn. Adult Edn. Adv. Com., Great Neck, 1982; mem. exec. com. PTA North H.S., Great Neck, 1983—85, pres., 1984—87, corr. sec., 1992, 1993, 2d v.p., 1994, 1st v.p., 1995, pres., 1998—2000; pres. bd. dirs. Kings Point Civic Assn., 1998—2000. Mem. Nassau County Bar Assn., N.Y. State Bar Assn., Bank Lawyers Conf. of N.Y., Exchange Club of North Shore (pres. 1972-73, L.I., N.Y.), Great Neck Cmty. Fund. Jewish. Home: 49 Fairway Dr Manhasset NY 11030-3906 E-mail: gaslaw@aol.com.

GAT, URI, engineer, scientist; b. Jerusalem, June 28, 1936; came to U.S., 1969; s. Werner Hagelberg and Lore Jeanny (Kastor) Goldschmidt; m. Ruth Tasse, July 24, 1961; children: Erann, Irit. BSc, Technion, IIT, Haifa, Israel, 1963; Dr in Engring., RWTH, Aachen, Fed. Republic of Germany, 1969. Registered profl. engr., Ky. Fighter pilot, jet instr. Israeli Air Force, Israel, 1954-63; scientist, project coord. Kenforschungsanlage, Juelich, Germany, 1963-69; asst. prof. U. Ky., Lexington, 1969-74; scientist, program mgr. Oak Ridge (Tenn.) Nat. Lab., 1974—2000; nuc. engring. cons., 2000—. Adj. prof. nuc. engring. U. Tenn., Knoxville, 1986-98; metric coord. U. Ky., Lexington, 1971-74; mem. U.S.-Russian Team on safeguarding nuc. materials, 1996-2000, cons., 2000-. Contbr. articles to profl. jours. Vice chmn. ACLU, Oak Ridge. Capt. Israeli Air Force, 1954-63. Mem. ASTM (acting chmn., vice chmn. Internat. System Units), Am. Nuclear Soc., U.S. Metric Assn., Sigma Xi. Achievements include patents for design of Molten Salt Nuclear Reactors, for design of closed flow without pump.

GATANAS, HARRY D. career officer; b. Bklyn., Mar. 21, 1947; Commd. officer U.S. Army, advanced through grades to brig. gen.; commdg. officer White Sands Missile Range White Sands (N.Mex.) Missile Range, 1998-99; comdg. gen. Army Test and Evaluation Command, Alexandria, Va, 1999—. Office: OPTEC 4501 Ford Ave Ste 820 Alexandria VA 22302-1435

GATCH, JERALD V. music educator; b. Baton Rouge, La., Jan. 4, 1963; m. Sidney Marie Adickes, Dec. 29, 1987; children: Katherine Victoria, Alexander Bull. MusB in Edn., U. of S.C., 1985, MusM, 1987. Freelance musician, SC, 1985—; dir. of bands Lexington (S.C.) HS, 1993—. Condr. S.C. Philharm. Youth Orch., Columbia, 2002—; choir dir. Lexington (S.C.) United Meth. Ch., 1993—. Recipient Legion of Honor, John Philip Sousa Found., 2001. Mem.: S.C. Band Dirs. Assn. (chmn.various coms. 1991), Am. Sch. Band Dirs. Assn., Nat. Band Assn. (corr. Citation Excellence 1996, 1998, 2000, 2001, 2002, Cert. of Merit 2002), Phi Beta Mu. Republican. Avocations: golf, fishing, skiing. Office: Lexington High School Bands 2463 Augusta Highway Lexington SC 29072 Office Fax: 803-359-8726. E-mail: jgatch@lexington1.net.

GATCH, MILTON MCCORMICK, JR., library administrator, clergyman, educator; b. Cin., Nov. 22, 1932; s. Milton McCormick and Mary (Curry) G.; m. Ione Georganna White, Aug. 25, 1956; children: Ione Waite, Lucinda McCormick, George Crosby White. AB, Haverford Coll., 1953; student, U. Cin. Sch. Law, 1953-55; BD, Episc. Theol. Sch., Cambridge, Mass., 1960; MA, Yale U., 1961, PhD, 1963. Ordained priest Episc. Ch., 1961. Chaplain Wooster Sch., Danbury, Conn., 1963-64; chaplain, chair humanities dept. Shimer Coll., Mt. Carroll, Ill., 1964-67; assoc. prof. English No. Ill. U., DeKalb, 1967-68; prof. English U. Mo., Columbia, 1968-78, chair dept., 1971-74; prof. ch. history Union Theol. Sem., N.Y.C., 1978-98, acad. dean and provost, 1978-89, dir. Burke Libr., 1990-98, emeritus, 1998—. Mem. coun. Coll. of Preachers, 1992-98; vis. fellow Emmanuel Coll., Cambridge, 1991; Bonhöffer vis. prof. Humboldt U., Berlin, 1998. Author: Death: Meaning and Mortality in Christian Thought and Contemporary Culture, 1969, Loyalties and Traditions: Man and His World in Old English Literature, 1971, Preaching and Theology in Anglo-Saxon England, 1977, So Precious a Foundation: The Library of Leander van Ess, 1996, The Yeats Family and the Book, 2000, Eschatology and Christian Nurture, 2000; contbr. numerous articles on antiquarian, medieval subjects. With U.S. Army, 1955-57. NEH sr. fellow, 1974-75. Fellow Soc. of Antiquaries London, Medieval Acad. Am. (del. to Am. Coun. Learned Socs. 1981-93); mem. Internat. Soc. Anglo-Saxonists (founding, mem. adv. bd. 1980-85), Am. Coun. Learned Socs. (bd. dirs. 1992-93), Early English Text Soc., Bibliog. Soc., Bibliog. Soc. Am., Am. Printing History Assn. (trustee 1995-99), Yale Libr. Assocs. (trustee 1999—), Century Assn., Grolier Club. Democrat. Avocations: book collecting, gardening, photography. E-mail: mac@miltongatch.us.

GATELY, MARK DONOHUE, lawyer; b. Balt., Jan. 6, 1952; s. Bernard Patrick and Margret (Donohue) G.; m. Rosemary Connolly, Dec. 27, 1986; children: Maeve Donohue, Harry John Connolly, Fiona Anne McCourt. BA, U. Md., 1974, JD, 1977. Bar: Md. 1977, U.S. Dist. Ct. Md. 1978, U.S. Ct. Appeals (4th cir.) 1978, U.S. Ct. Appeals (D.C. cir.) 1981, D.C. 1982, U.S. Supreme Ct. 1994, U.S. Ct. Appeals (3d cir.) 1988, U.S. Dist. Ct. (D.C. cir.) 1991, U.S. Ct. Appeals (7th cir.) 1993. Law clk. to Hon. C. Stanley Blair U.S. Dist. Ct. Md., Balt., 1977-78; asst. atty. gen. Office Md. Atty. Gen., Balt., 1980-81; assoc. Miles & Stockbridge, Balt., 1978-84, ptnr., 1984-2000, chair litigation dept., 1992-2000; ptnr. Hogan & Hartson, 2000—. Fellow Am. Coll. Trial Lawyers, Internat. Acad. Trial Lawyers, Am. Bd. Trial Advs.; mem. Order of Colf. Office: Hogan & Hartson LLP 111 S Calvert St Ste 1600 Baltimore MD 21202 E-mail: mdgately@hhlaw.com.

GATER, CHRIS, advertising executive; With Christian Brann Ltd., 1977-94; CEO, vice chmn. Brann Worldwide (formerly Christian Brann Ltd.), Deerfield, Ill., 1994-97, CEO, 1997—2000, chmn., 1997—. Office: Brann Worldwide 540 Lake Cook Rd Ste 150 Deerfield IL 60015-5604

GATES, AUDREY CASTINE, city government administrator; b. Napoleonville, La., Dec. 9, 1937; d. Lawrence Curtis and Ethel (Ray) Castine; m. George M. Gates III, Nov. 22, 1959; children: George M. IV, Geoffrey L. BA in Fgn. Langs., Dillard U., 1958. Tchr. Orleans Parish Sch. Bd., New Orleans, 1959-69; asst. dir. consumer affairs City of New Orleans, 1972-85, dir. residential parking, 1985-89; prin. analyst New Orleans City Coun., 1989-94, dir. rsch., 1994—. Fellow Loyola Inst. Politics, Metro. Area Com.; mem. Palm Air Civic Assn. Mem. Govt. Rsch. Assn., Delta Sigma Theta. Office: 1300 Perdido St Rm Le2 New Orleans LA 70112-2125

GATES, BILL (WILLIAM HENRY GATES III), software company executive; b. Seattle, Wash., Oct. 28, 1955; s. William H. and Mary M. (Maxwell) G.; m. Melinda French, January 1, 1994; 3 children Grad. high sch., Seattle, 1973; student, Harvard U., 1973-75. Founder, chmn. bd. Microsoft Corp., Redmond, Wash., 1976—, CEO, 1976—99, chief software architect, 1999—. Bd. dirs. ICOS. Author: The Future, 1994, The Road Ahead, 1995, Business at the Speed of Thought, 1999. Recipient Howard Vollum award, Reed Coll., Portland, Oreg., 1984, Nat. medal Tech. U.S. Dept. Commerce Tech. Adminstrn., 1992; named CEO of Yr., Chief Executive mag., 1994. Office: Microsoft Corp 1 Microsoft Way Redmond WA 98052-8300

GATES, BRUCE CLARK, chemical engineer, educator; b. Richmond, Calif., July 5, 1940; s. George Laurence and Frances Genevieve (Wilson) G.; m. Jutta M. Reichert, July 17, 1967; children: Robert Clark, Andrea Margarete. BS, U. Calif., Berkeley, 1961; PhD in Chem. Engring., U. Wash., 1966. Rsch. engr. Chevron Rsch. Co., Richmond, Calif., 1967-69; from asst. prof. to assoc. prof. U. Del., Newark, 1969-77, prof. chem. engring., 1977-85, H. Rodney Sharp prof., 1985-92, assoc. dir. Ctr. Catalytic Sci. & Tech., 1977-81, dir. Catalytic Ctr. Sci. & Tech., 1981-88; prof. chem. engring. U. Calif., Davis, 1992—. Author: Catalytic Chemistry, 1992; co-author: Chemistry of Catalytic Processes, 1979; co-editor: Metal Clusters in Catalysis, 1986, Surface Organometallic Chemistry, 1988, Advances in Catalysis, 1996—. Fulbright Rsch. grantee Inst. Phys. Chemistry U. Munich, 1966-67, 75-76, 83-84, 90-91; recipient Sr. Rsch. award Humboldt Found., U. Munich, 1998, Sr. Humboldt Found. fellow Inst. Phys. Chemistry, U. Munich, 1998-99, 2002 Mem.: Catalysis Soc. N.Am. (bd. dirs. 1997—), Am. Chem. Soc. (Del. sect. award 1985, Petroleum Chemistry award 1993), AIChE (Alpha Chi Sigma award 1989, William H. Walker award 1995, R.H. Wilhelm award 2002). Achievements include research in catalysis, surface chemistry and reaction kinetics, chemical reaction engineering, petroleum and petrochemical proccesses, catalysis by solid acids, zeolites, soluble and supported transition-metal complexes and clusters, catalytic hydroprocessing. Office: U Calif Dept Chem Engring & Materials Sci Davis CA 95616 E-mail: bcgates@ucdavis.edu.

GATES, CHARLES CASSIUS, rubber company executive; b. Morrison, Colo., May 27, 1921; s. Charles Cassius and Hazel LaDora (Rhoads) Gates; m. June Scowcroft Swaner, Nov. 26, 1943 (dec. Dec. 2000); children: Diane, John Swaner. Student, MIT, 1939-41; BS, Stanford U., 1943; DEng (hon.), Mich. Tech. U., 1975, Colo. Sch. Mines, 1985. With Copolymer Corp., Baton Rouge, 1943-46, Gates Rubber Co., Denver, 1946-96, v.p., 1951-58, exec. v.p., 1958-61, chmn. bd., 1961-96, CEO; chmn. bd. Gates Corp., Denver, 1982-96, CEO, 1982-96, also bd. dirs., pres., 1994-96; chmn. Cody Res., LP, Denver, 1996—, Gates Capital Mgmt., LLC, Denver, 1996—. Trustee Gates Found., Calif. Inst. Tech., Pasadena, Denver Art Mus. Found., Graland Country Day Sch. Found. Named Mgmt. Man of the Yr., Nat. Mgmt. Assn., 1965, Citizen of the West, March of Dimes, 1987; named to Colo. Bus. Hall of Fame, 1998; recipient Cmty. Leadership and Svc. award, Nat. Jewish Hosp., 1974. Mem.: Conf. Bd. (dir.), Shikar-Safari Internat., Wigwam Club, Castle Pines Golf Club, Augusta Nat. Golf Club, Country Club Colo., Old Baldy Club, Club Ltd., Boone and Crockett Club, Waialae Country Club, Outrigger Canoe Club, Denver Country Club, Roundup Riders Rockies, Conquistadores del Cielo. Office: Cody Resources LP 3575 Cherry Creek N Dr Denver CO 80209-3601

GATES, CHARLES WOODLEY, SR., city official; b. Dayton, Ohio, Jan. 14, 1943; s. Theodore and Nellie M. (Black) G.; m. Nina J. Wright, Sept. 27, 1969; children: Charles W. Jr., Stephanie L. BSBA, U. Dayton, 1965. Acct. NCR Corp., Dayton, 1966-68, asst. sect. head mktg. and acctg., 1968-70; asst. contr. Montgomery County Community Action Agy., Dayton, 1970; airport compt. City of Dayton, 1970-75, supt. airport adminstrn., 1975-89; dir. aviation City of Austin, Tex., 1989-98, dir. aviation fin. and adminstrn., 1998—. Sec. West Area YMCA, Dayton, 1979-89; bd. dirs. Dayton Area YMCA, 1985-89, Austin Area Urban League, 1992—. Recipient nat. achiever's award Airport Minority Adv. Coun., 1991, Outstanding Black in Govt. award BOSS, 1991; named Outstanding Man of Yr. AME Ch., Ctrl. Tex. Annual Conf., 1998. Mem. Am. Assn. Airport Execs., Airport Operators Coun. Internat. (econ. com. 1974—). Office: Austin Dept Aviation 3600 Presidential Blvd Austin TX 78719-2363

GATES, GREGORY ANSEL, lawyer; b. Cortland, N.Y., Sept. 25, 1953; s. Herbert Ansel and Mary (O'Connor) G.; m. Margaret Anne Schell, Aug. 9, 1975; children: Ryan Mary, Connor Ansel. BA, SUNY, Oswego, 1975; JD, Albany Law Sch. Union U., 1978. Bar: N.Y. 1979, U.S. Dist. Ct. (no. dist.) N.Y. 1979, U.S. Dist. Ct. (no. dist.) Calif. 1985, U.S. Ct. Appeals (2d cir.) 1993, U.S. Supreme Ct. 1994. Assoc. Levene Gouldin and Thompson, Binghamton, N.Y., 1979-84, ptnr., 1984-85, Hickey, Sheehan and Gates, Binghamton, N.Y., 1985—. Mem. Continuing Edn. Adv. Com., Binghamton, 1982-87. Commn. of Elections Broome County Gov., Binghamton, 1984-97, town justice, 1997—; pres. Broome County Magistrates Assn., 2002-; dir. Broome Sports Found., 1987--; counsel Broome County Democratic Com., 1984-87. Mem. ABA, N.Y. Bar Assn., Assn. Trial Lawyers Am., Broome County Bar Assn. (dir. 1988-91). Democrat. Roman Catholic. Avocations: hockey, golf, travel. Office: Hickey Sheehan and Gates PO Box 2124 Binghamton NY 13902-2124

GATES, JAMES DAVID, retired association executive, consultant; b. East Cleveland, Ohio, July 9, 1927; s. James Adelbert and Margaretta (Voigt) G.; m. Carol Marie Schreiber, June 9, 1956; children: David, Keith, Robert. AB, Hiram (Ohio) Coll., 1951; MA, Columbia, 1956; EdD, George Washington U., 1975. Tchr. Maple Heights (Ohio) City Schs., 1951-61; profl. asst. Nat. Council Tchrs. Math., Reston, Va., 1961-63, exec. sec., 1963-76, exec. dir., 1976-95. Mem. faculty U. Va., 1963-66, George Washington U., 1966-75; assoc. dir. Math. Scis. Edn. Bd., Ctr. for Sci., Math., and Engring. Edn., Nat. Rsch. Coun., 1997-99. Mem. Va. Coalition Math. and Sci.; bd. dirs. MathCounts Found.; sec.-treas. Jr. Engring. Tech. Soc. Served with AUS, 1945-46. Fellow AAAS; mem. NEA, ASCD, Nat. Coun. Suprs. Math., Nat. Coun. Tchrs. Math., Math. Assn. Am., Assn. State Suprs. Math., Benjamin Banneker Assn., Assn. Math. Tchr. Educators, Am. Math. Assn. Two-Yr. Colls., Rotary. Home: 11303 Fieldstone Ln Reston VA 20191-3905 E-mail: jamgate@aol.com.

GATES, JAY RODNEY, museum director; b. Kansas City, Mo., Nov. 21, 1945; s. William Russell and Kathleen (Keys) G.; m. Susan Gates, Apr. 4, 1981; 1 child, Douglas. MA, Inst. European Studies, Vienna, Austria, 1967; BA in Art History, Coll. of Wooster, 1968; MA in Art History, U. Rochester, 1970. Instr. art history, mus. curator Coll. of Wooster, Ohio, 1971-73; asst. curator dept. art history and edn. Cleve. Mus. Art, 1973-76; curator edn. St. Louis Art Mus., 1976-78; dir. Brooks Meml. Art Gallery, Memphis, 1978-81; asst. dir., curator Am. art Nelson-Atkins Mus. Art, Kansas City, Kans., 1981-83; prof. art history, dir. Spencer Mus. Art, U. Kans., Lawrence, 1983-87; dir. Seattle Mus. Art, 1987-93, Dallas Mus. Art, 1993-98, The Phillips Collection, Washington, 1998—. Adj. instr. art history Case Western REs. U., Cleve., 1973-76. Past trustee Mus. African-Am. Culture, Dallas, Am. Fedn. Arts, N.Y.C. Mem. Assn. Art Mus. Dirs. (past trustee and treas.). Office: The Phillips Collection 1600 21st St NW Washington DC 20009

GATES, JEFFREY RALPH, research scientist, epidemiologist; s. Ralph Elwin and Beverly Lorraine Gates; m. Caroline Elisabeth Porchet; children: Rachael, Stephanie, Jason. D of Health Sci., Loma Linda (Calif.) U., 1988. Cert. nutritionist N.Y. Sr. clin. data specialist Dupont-Merck Pharma, Geneva, 1990—93; rsch. assoc. III Cornell U., Ithaca, NY, 1993—96; preventive care specialist/cons. International sites, 1996—2001; clin. rsch. dir. Battle Creek (Mich.) Lifestyle Health Ctr., 2001—. Preventive care specialist / cons. La Lega Vita e Salute, Rome, 1999—2001, Guam SDA Clinic, Tamuning, GM, Weimar (Calif.) Inst. Singer: Living to 120 and Beyond; contbr. articles to profl. jours. Missionary sci. tchr. Gitwe Coll., Rwanda, 1979—81. Mem.: N.Y. Acad. Sci. Green Party. 7th Day Adventist. Achievements include research in anti-tumor botanical extract formulations / protocols. Avocations: hiking, foreign languages, biblical escatology, music composing, herbalism. Office: Battle Creek Lifestyle Health Ctr 101 N 20th St Battle Creek MI 49015

GATES, KEITH R. music educator; b. Johnstown, Pa., Sept. 29, 1948; s. Richard Eugene and Tina Gates. MusB, Juilliard Sch., 1970, MusM, 1973. Assoc. prof. McNeese State U., Lake Charles, La., 1983—. Music instr., composer Gov's. Program for Gifted Children, Lake Charles, La., 1986—2003; organist Temple Sinai, Lake Charles, 1990—2003; pianist, dir. Bethel Presbyn. Ch., Lake Charles, 1984—2003. Composer: (Operas) The Christmas Coin, 2001, Tom Sawyer, 1986, The Hollow, 1988, Evangeline, 1996, various symphonies, concertos and chamber music. Recipient Newly Published Music award, Nat. Flute Assn., 1992; grantee La. Artist fellowship, La. Divsn. of Arts, 1988—98. Home: 504 Moss St Lake Charles LA 70601 Office: McNeese State U Lake Charles LA 70609 E-mail: krg@mail.mcneese.edu.

GATES, LESLIE CARLISLE, sociology educator; b. Bonn, Germany, Mar. 7, 1968; B.A. in History, Princeton U., Princeton, N.J., 1986—90; PhD in Sociology, U. Ariz., Tucson, Arizona, 1994—2001. Asst. prof. sociology Binghamton U., NY, 2001—. Recipient Women's Leadership Award, Friends Princeton U. Women's Ctr., 2003. Mem.: Latin Am. Studies Assn., Am. Sociol. Assn. Office: Dept Sociology Binghamton U Binghamton NY 13905

GATES, LISA, private chef, caterer; b. Washington, July 11, 1955; d. Chester Robert and Peggy Jean (Dalton) Gates; m. Sergio Vivoli, Nov. 3, 1978 (div. Nov. 1984); m. Mitchell Cohen, Sept. 21, 1987 (div. Febr. 1995). AA, Fleming Coll., Florence, Italy, 1974. Dir. The Am. Sch. in Switzerland, Lugano, 1974-80; counter person Bar Gelateria Vivoli, Florence, 1978-80; costumer, choreographer, scene designer English Theatre of Florence, 1978; tchr. Dance Sch. Theatre, Florence, 1978-81; sec., treas. Vivoli Da Firenze, Inc., L.A., 1981-82; event coord. Calif. Catering Co., Beverly Hills, Calif., 1983; chef, sales rep. St. Germain To Go, West Hollywood, Calif., 1984; chef, cons. Posh Affair Catering Co., L.A., 1984-87; owner, chef, party planner Lisa Gates-Vivoli Catering, L.A., 1985—; catering mgr. Maple Drive Restaurant, Beverly Hills, 1990-91; pvt. chef, 1991—2001, 2001—. Mem. Mus. Contemporary Art, L.A., L.A. County Mus. Art, L.A. Music Ctr. Unified Fund. Recipient Outstanding Achievement in Art award Bank of Am., Miraleste, Calif., 1972. Mem. Am. Inst. Wine and Food, Roundtable for Women in Foodsvc., Women Chefs and Restaurateurs. Democrat. Avocations: dance, dining, music. Home and Office: 1227 N Orange Grove Ave West Hollywood CA 90046-5311

GATES, MAHLON EUGENE, applied research executive, former government official, former army officer; b. Tyrone, Pa., Aug. 21, 1919; s. Samuel Clayton and Elsie (Nieweg) G.; m. Esther Boone Campbell, July 4, 1972; children by previous marriage: Pamela Townley, Lawrence Alan. BS, U.S. Mil. Acad., 1942; MS, U. Ill., 1948; postgrad., Command and Gen. Staff Coll., 1957, Army War Coll., 1962, Harvard U., 1965. Commd. 2d lt. U.S. Army, 1942, advanced through grades to brig. gen., 1966; area engr. Iran, Gulf Dist., 1960-61; chief, engr. br., officer Personnel Directorate, Dept. Army, 1963-64; gen. staff Dept. Army, 1964-66; comdg. gen. Cam Ranh Bay, Vietnam, 1966-67; dir. constrn., 1967; dir. research, devel. and engring. Army Materiel Command, Washington, 1971; ret., 1972; mgr. Nev. ops. office AEC now Dept. Energy, Las Vegas, 1972-82; sr. v.p. S.W. Rsch. Inst., San Antonio, 1982-89, ret., 1989. Leader U.S. sci. team to N.W. Territories during recovery ops. for crashed nuclear-powered Russian satellite, 1978. Past pres. Boulder Dam Area council Boy Scouts Am.; past chmn. adv. bd. Clark County C.C. Decorated D.S.M., Legion of Merit, Bronze Star, Air medal; Army Distinguished Service Order 1st class Govt. Vietnam; Meritorious Service award; named Meritorious Exec. ERDA. Home: 1 Towers Park Ln Apt 2011 San Antonio TX 78209-6439 E-mail: ink1942@aol.com. *Cherish the past; do not worship it.*

GATES, MARSHALL DEMOTTE, JR., chemistry educator; b. Boyne City, Mich., Sept. 25, 1915; s. Marshall DeMotte and Virginia (Orton) G.; m. Martha Louise Meyer, Sept. 9, 1941; children: Christopher David, Catharine Louise, Marshall DeMotte III, Virginia Alice. BS, Rice Inst., 1936, MS, 1938; PhD, Harvard, 1941; D.Sc. (hon.), MacMurray Coll., 1963. Asst. prof. chemistry Bryn Mawr Coll., 1941-43; vis. prof. Harvard, 1946; assoc. prof., 1947-49; Max Tishler lectr., 1953; tech. aid NDRC, 1943-46; lectr. chemistry U. Rochester,

1949-52, part-time prof., 1952-60, prof., 1960-68, Charles Frederick Houghton prof. chemistry, 1968-81, prof. emeritus, 1981—. Welch Found. lectr., 1960; adv. bd. Chem. Abstracts Services, 1974-76; vis. prof. Dartmouth Coll., 1982, 84, 85, 86; charter fellow Coll. Problems Drug Dependence, 1992—. Mem. com. on drug addiction and narcotics, divsn. med. scis. NRC, 1956-70, also com. on organic nomenclature divsn. of chemistry; mem. Pres.'s Com. on Nat. Medal of Sci., 1968-70. Recipient Edward Peck Curtis award for excellence in undergrad. teaching, 1967; Armed Services cert. of appreciation, 1946; Disting. Alumnus award Rice U., 1986 Fellow Am. Acad. Arts and Scis., N.Y. Acad. Scis.; mem. Am. Chem. Soc. (editor Jour. 1963-69), Nat. Acad. Scis. Achievements include first synthesis of morphine, 1952. Office: U Rochester Chemistry Dept Rochester NY 14627

GATES, MARTINA MARIE, food products company executive; b. Mpls., Mar. 19, 1957; d. John Thomas and Colette Clara (Luetmer) G. BSBA in Mktg. Mgmt. cum laude, U. St. Thomas, 1984, MBA in Mktg., 1987. Tchrs. asst. Mpls. Area Vocat. Tech. Inst., Mpls., 1978-79; sec., regional sales mgr. Internat. Multifoods, Mpls., 1979, sec. bakery mix, mktg. mgr., 1979-80, sec., v.p. sales and new bus. devel., 1980, customer svc. rep. regional accounts, 1980-81, customer svc. rep. nat. accounts, 1981-82, credit coordinator indsl. foods divsn., 1982-85, asst. credit mgr. consumer foods divsn., 1985, advt./sales promotion mgr. indsl. foods divsn., 1985-86, asst. credit mgr. fast food and restaurant divsn., 1986-87, dir. devel. USA and Can. franchise area, 1987-89; dir. franchise devel. FIRSTAFF, Inc., Mpls., 1989-90; dir. adminstrn. Robert Half Internat., Inc., Mpls., 1990-94; dir. client svcs. The NPD Group, Inc., Chgo., 1994—. Vol. seamstress Guthrie Theater Costume Shop, Mpls., 1975—; alumni mem. New Coll. Student Adv. Council St. Thomas, St. Paul, 1984—; vol. Mpls. Aquatennial, 1987. Mem. Streeterville Orgn. of Active Residents, Omicron Delta Epsilon. Avocations: golf, fine arts, needlework, tennis, skiing.

GATES, MILO SEDGWICK, retired construction company executive; b. Omaha, Apr. 25, 1923; s. Milo Talmage and Virginia (Offutt) G.; m. Anne Phleger, Oct. 14, 1950 (dec. Apr. 1987); children: Elena Motlow, Susan Gates Suman, Virginia Lewis, Anne Symington, Milo T.; m. Robin Templeton Quist, June 18, 1988; stepchildren: Robert L. Quist, Catherine Brisbin, Sarah Mazzocco. Student, Calif. Inst. Tech., 1943-44, BS, Stanford U., 1944, MBA 1948. With Swinerton & Walberg Co., San Francisco, 1955—, pres., 1976—, chmn., 1988-96, ret. Bd. dirs., trustee Children's Hosp. San Francisco; trustee Grace Cathedral, San Francisco; bd. dirs. Calif. Acad. Scis. Lt. (j.g.), USNR, 1944-46. Mem. Pacific-Union Club, Bohemian Club. Republican. Home: 7 Vineyard Hill Rd Woodside CA 94062-2531

GATES, RICHARD DANIEL, retired manufacturing company executive; b. Trenton, Mo., Mar. 27, 1942; s. Daniel G. and Effie Wright (Johnson) G.; m. Jean Gates, Jan. 26, 1966; 1 child, Daniel Wright. BS, U. Mo., 1964; M.C.S., Rollins Coll., Winter Park, Fla., 1968; postgrad., Harvard U., 1976. Mgmt. assoc. Western Electric Co., N.Y.C., 1964-66; bus. mgmt. adminstr. Martin Marietta Aerospace Co., Orlando, Fla., 1966-68, chief indsl. engring., 1968-69; fin. analyst Martin Marietta Co., N.Y.C., 1969-70, sr. acct., 1970-71; controller Dragon Cement Co., divsn. Martin Marietta Co., 1971-72, N.E. divsn. Martin Marietta Aggregates Co., 1972-73; asst. controller, then asst. treas. Rubbermaid, Inc., Wooster, Ohio, 1973-79, treas., 1979-80, v.p., treas., 1980-91, sr. v.p. bus. devel., investor rels. and corp. communications, 1991-98; ret., 1998. Pres. The Rubbermaid Found., Wooster. Mem. Wooster City Fin. Task Force, All Am. City Com.; chmn. Wooster Growth Assn.; active local Cub Scouts.; adviser Art Center, chmn. maj. indsl. capital campaign Boy Scouts Camp; trustee, chmn. Wayne Ctr. Arts; mem. parents' com. St. Paul's Sch., Wesleyan U. Mem. Nat. Assn. Corporate Treas., Main St. Wooster Inc. (bd. trustees), Beta Gamma Sigma, Omicron Delta Kappa. Clubs: Harvard Bus. Sch. Wooster Country (bd. dirs.). Home: Apt 5317 2805 Oak Trlal Ct Arlington TX 76016-4307

GATES, ROBERTA PECORARO, nursing educator; b. Elmira, N.Y., May 22, 1948; d. Patrick George and Verle Elizabeth (Warriner) Pecoraro; m. William Franklin Gates III, May 20, 1972; 1 child, William Franklin IV. BSN, U. Ariz., 1970; MSN in Family Nursing, U. Ala., Huntsville, 1981. Cert. clin. specialist in med.-surg. nursing; bd. cert. Advanced practice nurse; cert. lactation counselor. Charge nurse St. Mary's Hosp. and Mental Health Ctr., Tucson, 1970-72; asst. head nurse Torrance (Calif.) Meml. Hosp., 1973-74; dist. nurse Sierra Sands Sch. Dist., Ridgecrest, Calif., 1974-76; instr. Albany (Ga.) Jr. Coll., 1978-80, John C. Calhoun Coll., Decatur, Ala., 1981-83; learning resources coord. Albany State Coll., 1984-85; asst. prof. Sinclair C.C., Dayton, Ohio, 1990-91, Darton Coll., Albany, 1986-89, 92—. Bd. dirs. Network Trust, Albany; cons. Cmty. Health Inst., Albany, 1993, Early County Bd. Edn., Blakely, Ga., 1994, Ga. State U., 1996—, Ga. Interagy. Coordinating Coun., 1997—; mem. Dist. Health Perinatal Bd., 2002; mem. Breastfeeding Task Force, 2002; cons. Project SCEIs, Ga. State U., 1996—. Author: A Model for Adolescent Health Promotion in the Dougherty County Community, 1993. Mem. Ga. Coun. Prevention of Child Abuse, Albany, 1988, 93; mem. Albany Mus. Art, 1993—; mem. Cmty. Ptnrs. Health Care Initiative, Dayton, 1990-91; bd. dirs. March of Dimes, Albany, 1986-89; mem. Albany-Dougherty 2000, DOCO Alternative Adv. Bd., State Consortium Early Intervention, Babies Can't Wait, 1995. Recipient NISOD award tchg. excellence, 2002; Named to Outstanding Young Women of Am., 1983. Mem. Ga. Higher Edn. Consortium, Sigma Theta Tau, Phi Kappa Phi. Avocations: gardening, walking, boating, reading. Office: Darton Coll 2400 Gillionville Rd Albany GA 31707-3023

GATES, SHEREE HUNT, counseling administrator, educator, writer; b. Buford, Ga., Oct. 3, 1958; d. Erwin Albion and Betty Joyce (Herndon) Hunt; m. Roger Lee Gates Jr., Jan. 29, 1960; children: Roger L. III, Christopher A. BS, U. Md., 1984; MEd, Boston U., 1985; EdD, U. Ga., 1992. Cert. tchr., sch. counselor. Placement dir., dir. student svcs. Phillips Jr. Coll., Augusta, Ga., 1985-86; client svcs. coord., battered women counselor Safe Homes, Augusta, 1986-87; tchr. Richmond County Bd. Edn., Augusta, 1987-89; sch. counselor Redcliffe Elem. Sch., Aiken, S.C., 1989-91; tchr. Barton Chapel Elem. Sch., Augusta, Ga., 1991-93; instr. English, U. Izmir, Turkey, 1993-95; tchr. E. Vaughan Elem. Sch., Woodbridge, Va., 1995-98; counseling dir. AG Wright Mid. Sch., Stafford, Va., 1998—2001, SHAPE Am. Elem. Sch., Belgium, 2001—. Dodea educator, 2001—. With U.S. Army, 1979-83. Mem.: ASCD, ACA, Ednl. Leadership Assn., Phi Delta Kappa, Alpha Sigma Lambda. Democrat. Avocations: photography, travel, painting, quilting, scrapbooking. Office: Shape Am Elem Sch Shape Belgium

GATES, STEPHEN FRYE, lawyer, oil industry executive; b. Clearwater, Fla., May 20, 1946; s. Orris Allison and Olga Betty (Frye) Gates; m. Laura Daignault, June 10, 1972. BA in Econ., Yale U., 1968; JD, MBA, Harvard U., 1972. Bar: Fla. 1972, Mass. 1973, Ill. 1977, Colo. 1986. Assoc. Choate, Hall and Stewart, Boston, 1973-77; atty. Amoco Corp., Chgo., 1977-82, gen. atty., 1982-86; regional atty. Amoco Prodn. Co., Denver, 1987-88; asst. treas. Amoco Corp., Chgo., 1988-91, assoc. gen. counsel, corp. sec., 1991-92; v.p. Amoco Chem. Co., 1993-95; v.p., gen. counsel Amoco Corp., Chgo., 1995-98; exec. v.p., group chief of staff BP Amoco, London, 1999-2000; sr. v.p., gen. counsel, sec. FMC Corp., Chgo., 2000—01; ptnr. Mayer, Brown, Rowe,and Maw, Chgo., 2002—03; sr. v.p., gen. counsel Conoco Phillips, Houston, 2003—. Bd. dirs. Nat. Legal Ctr. Pub. Interest, Washington, 1999—. Trustee Newberry Libr., Chgo., 1998—, Appleseed Found., 2003—; mem. adv. coun. Chgo. Schweitzer Urban Fellows Program, 1996—2000; mem. adv. bd. Chgo. Vol. Legal Svcs. Found., 1996—98; mem. Chgo. Crime Commn., 2000—, bd. dirs., 2000—03. Knox fellow, 1972—73. Fellow: Am. Bar Found., Royal Soc. Arts (London); mem.: ABA, Yale Club, Chgo. Club, Univ. Club. Office: Conoco/Phillips 600 N Dairy Ashford Houston TX 77252 E-mail: steve.gates@concophillips.com.

GATES, STEVEN LEON, physician; b. Newton, Kans., Aug. 13, 1954; s. Leon Martin and Mary Lorine (Adams) G.; m. Paula Ellen Banwart, Jan. 1, 1977; children: Stephanie, Scott, Jeffrey. DO summa cum laude, S.W. Okla. State U., 1976; DO, Okla. State U., 1986. Lic. pharmacist, Okla.; cert. internal medicine with cert. of added qualifications in geriatrics. Intern Osteopathic Med. Ctr. Tex., Ft. Worth, 1986-87; resident in internal medicine Dallas/Ft. Worth Med. Ctr., Grand Prairie, Tex., 1987-90; pharmacist M & D Star Drug Store, Okmulgee, Okla., 1976-80; pharmacist, mgr. Wal-Mart Pharmacy Divsn., Okmulgee, Okla., 1980-82; chief med. resident Ready Care Minor Emergency Ctr., Bedford, Tex., 1987-90; jail physician Tarrant County Sheriff's Dept., Ft. Worth, 1989-90; pvt. practice internal medicine Grand Prairie, Tex., 1990-97, Cleburne, Tex., 1997—. Internal medicine physician and minor emergency physician Ready Care Med. Clinic, Bedford, Tex., 1990-91; dir. med. edn. Dallas/Ft. Worth Med. Ctr.-Grand Prairie, 1991-96; clin. asst. prof. dept. medicine Tex. Coll. Osteopathic Medicine, Ft. Worth, 1990— Fellow Am. Bd. Internal Medicine: mem. Am. Coll. Osteopathic Internists (bd. cert.), Am. Osteopathic Assn., Tex. Osteopathic Med. Assn., Tex. Med. Assn., Tarrant County Med. Soc., Sigma Sigma Phi. Republican. Avocations: sporting events, reading, yard work. Home: 601 Rockdale Rd Cleburne TX 76033-4551

GATES, SUSAN INEZ, magazine publisher; b. San Francisco, Jan. 14, 1956; d. Milo Sedgewick and Anne (Phelger) G. BA in English/French magna cum laude, U. Colo., 1978; MS in Journalism, Columbia U., 1983. With GEO Mag., N.Y.C., 1978-79, New York Mag., N.Y.C., 1981-82, Ladd Assocs., N.Y.C., 1983-85, McNamee Cons., N.Y.C., 1986-88; founding pub. BUZZ mag., L.A., 1989-97; co-chmn. Mind Over Media, L.A., 1997—. Contbg. writer San Francisco Chronicle and Examiner Book Rev., 1983-86. So. Calif. adv. bd. Natural Resources Def. Coun., L.A., 1989-96. Mem. Advt. Club of L.A. (bd. dirs. 1995-98), Phi Beta Kappa. E-mail: sgates@cncdsl.com.

GATES, THEODORE ALLAN, JR., database administrator; b. Washington, May 24, 1933; s. Theodore Allan and Margaret (Camp) G.;m. Anne Bissell, Sept. 8, 1955; children: Virginia Anne, Nancy Bissell, Theodore Allan III (dec.), Margaret Kenyon. Student, U. Md., 1951-53, 56-57, 68-69. Mem. staff Arthur D. Little Sys., Burlington, Mass., 1976-77, Corp. Tech. Planning, Portsmouth, N.H., 1977-78; project mgr. Honeywell Info. Sys., Phoenix, 1978-81, tech. mgr. Seattle, 1981-83; mgr. data and software engring. ISC Sys. Corp., Spokane, Wash., 1983-90; project mgr. Boeing Computer Svcs., Seattle, 1990—96, The Boeing Co., Bellevue, Wash., 1996—. With U.S. Army, 1953-56, Korea. Recipient Superior Performance award Census Bur., 1958. Mem. Air Force Assn., U.S. Naval Inst., Smithsonian Assocs., Internat. Oracle Users Group, Mus. of Flight, Commodores Club (Boston), Masons, Shriners. Lutheran. Avocations: photography, sailing, music. Home: 3208 168th Pl SE Bellevue WA 98008-5730 Office: Boeing Co M/S 67-EE PO Box 3707 Seattle WA 98124-2207

GATES, THOMAS EDWARD, civil engineer, waste management administrator; b. Tachikawa AFB, Japan, June 25, 1953; came to U.S., 1954; s. Harold Charles and Masako (Endo) G. BS, Kans. State U., 1979, MS, 1981; JD (hon.) Seattle U., 2001. Registered profl. engr., Wash., Kans., Alaska. State insp. Riley County Pub. Works, Manhattan, Kans., 1977-78, field supr., 1978, cons., 1979; grad. rsch. asst. Kans. State U., Manhattan, 1979-81; engr. Battelle Pacific N.W. Labs., Richland, Wash., 1981-83, rsch. engr., 1983-85, sr. rsch. engr., 1985-86; mgr. waste package projects BWIP, 1986-88; mgr. Seattle Univ. Sch. Law, 1988—2001; acting mgr. support projects BWIP, 1988; mgr. for def. programs Westinghouse Hanford Co., Richland, 1988-89, staff mgr. engring. and devel. divs., 1990, mgr. tech. assessment and application, 1990-91, mgr. tech. demonstration program ops., 1991-94; mgr. Sonalysts, Inc., Kennewick, Wash., 1994-97, PLG, Inc., Richland, 1997-98; cons., 1999—. Cons. Elec. Power Rsch. Inst., Washington, Atomic Energy of Can., Ltd. Rsch. Co., Ottawa, Can.; lead judge Wash. State Sci. Talent Search, Richland, 1985-90; chmn. Wash. State Solid Waste Adv. Com., 1996-98. Contbr. 7 articles to profl. jours., 14 tech. reports; session works, obtaining accelerated data on concrete degradation, 1981, concrete durability and degradation processes, 1986, Wash. state air transp. com., 1993-94. Councilman City of Richland, 1988-93, mayor, 1990; mem. Phys. Planning Com., Richland, 1982-87, chmn., 1984-87; instr. Christian catechism doctrine Christ The King Ch., Richland, 1981-82; bd. dirs. Salvation Army Adv. Coun., Richland, 1987-89, chmn., 1988-89; bd. dirs. Benton-Franklin Cmty. Action Com., Pasco, Wash., 1992-93, vice chmn. program com., 1988-89; mem. bd. March of Dimes, Junction City, Kans., 1976-80, chmn. bd., 1979-80; chmn. dept. campaign United Way, Richland, 1984; bd. dirs. Assn. Wash. Cities, 1990-93, mem. resolution com., 1989-91, mem. legis. com., 1989-92, mem. energy adv. com., 1990-93, mem. local govt. adv. com., 1990-93, mem. mcpl. rsch. coun., 1991-93; mem. Benton County Solid Waste Adv. Com., 1990-98, chmn., 1990-98; mem. hazardous materials mgmt. tech. adv. com. Columbia Basin Coll., 1990-95, chmn., 1991-95. Mem. ASCE (tech. coun. on computer practices pub. com. 1986-96), Am. Concrete Inst. (tech. com. on computers 1983—, com. on radioactive and hazardous waste mgmt. 1983—2002, com. on student activities 1984—, com. on concrete nuclear structures subcoms. 1 and 4 1996—, Harry F. Thomson scholar 1980), Kiwanis Club of Richland (disting. pres. 1995-96), KC (Sir Knight of Yr. 1992). Roman Catholic. Avocations: gardening, woodworking, reading. Home: 33207 11th Ave SW Federal Way WA 98023-5325

GATEWOOD, BARBARA J. medical legal consultant, lawyer; b. Akron, Ohio, June 4, 1954; d. Nicholas and Olive (Jones) Rusyn; m. Paul D. Gatewood, Aug. 7, 1987; children: Elizabeth Anne, Joseph Paul. RN, Akron City Hosp., 1975; BA, U. Akron, 1985, JD, 1988. RN, Ohio; bar: Ohio 1989. Asst. head nurse/surg. nurse Akron City Hosp.; staff nurse Canton (Ohio) Aultman Hosp.; med. legal cons. Akron; pres. Gatewood Assocs. Inc., Naples, Fla. Bd. dirs. Child Guidance Ctrs., Friends of Children's Hosp. Aux., Akron City Hosps. Mem. ABA, Am. Soc. Law and Medicine, Ohio Bar Assn., Cleve. Bar Assn., Akron Bar Assn., Akron City Hosp. Sch. Nursing Alumni Assn., Summit County Med. Soc. Aux., U. Akron Sch. Law Alumni Assn., Soc. of Law and Medicine, Akron Woman's City Club, Phi Alpha Delta.

GATEWOOD, DOUG, state representative; b. Columbus, Kans., Nov. 16, 1955; m. Crystal Gatewood; children: Amber, Beau. AA, Pitts. State U., 1975. Owner Custom Automotive Interiors; mem. Kans. Ho. of Reps., 1999—. Bd. dirs. Columbus Indsl. Devel. Corp. Mem. City Coun.; mayor Columbus. Mem.: Columbus C. of C. (past bd. dirs.), Lions. Democrat. Baptist. Office: 302-S State Capitol 300 SW 10th Ave Topeka KS 66612 Address: PO Box 306 Columbus KS 66725*

GATEWOOD, ROBERT PAYNE, financial planning executive, retired; b. Nebr., Mar. 4, 1923; s. Robert Harvey and Bess (Payne) G.; m. Marilyn Wengert, June 6, 1946; children: Robert, Lottie, Traber, Cy, Marilyn, Bess, John, Anthony, Judemarie, Anne, Tressa, Joseph, Ruth. BS, U.S. Naval Acad., 1946; postgrad., La. State U., 1974. CLU. Estate planner J.D. Marsh & Assocs., 1950-56; pres. estate planning Fin. Corp. Am., 1956-61; pres. Robert P. Gatewood & Co., 1961-99; owner, operator SEG Cellular Telephone Co. Internat. lectr. Contbr. articles to profl. jours. With USN, 1946—50. Recipient Bernard L. Wilner Meml. award. Mem. D.C. Assn. Life Underwriters (pres. 1965-66), Assn. Advanced Life Underwriting Million Dollar Round Table, Am. Soc. CLUs & Chartered Fin. Cons. (pres. 1975-76), Washington D.C. Estate Planning Coun., East Coast Estate Planning Coun., Fla. Assn. CLUs and ChFCs, Palm Beach Assn. Life Underwriters, 25 Million Dollar Internat. Forum (founder), Knights Malta. Republican. Home: 6 Loggerhead Ln Manalapan FL 33462 E-mail: wengate@bellsouth.net.

GATEWOOD, WILLARD BADGETT, JR., retired historian; b. Pelham, N.C., Feb. 23, 1931; s. Willard Badgett and Bessie Lee (Pryor) G.; m. Mary Lu Brown, Aug. 9, 1958; children: Willard Badgett III, Elizabeth Ellis. BA, Duke U., 1953, MA, 1954, PhD, 1957. Asst. prof. history East Tenn. State U., 1957-58, East Carolina U., 1958-60; assoc. prof. N.C. Wesleyan Coll., 1960-64; prof. U. Ga., 1964-70; Alumni Disting. prof. history U. Ark., 1970-98, ret., 1998, provost and chancellor, 1984-85. Author: Theodore Roosevelt and the Art of Controversy, 1970, Smoked Yankees, 1971, Black Americans and the White Man's Burden, 1975, Slave and Freeman, 1979, Free Men of Color, 1982, Aristocrats of Color, 1990, Arkansas Delta, 1993; mem. bd. editors Ga. Rev., 1968-70, Jour. Negro History, 1972-74, Ark. Hist. Quar., 1992-94. Bd. dirs. Winthrop Rockefeller Found., 1990-96. Recipient Parks Excellence in Teaching award Phi Alpha Theta, 1970, Michael Rsch. award, 1967; Outstanding Teaching award Omicron Delta Kappa, 1979, rsch. award U. Ark. Alumni Assn., 1980, Gingles award Ark. Hist. Assn., 1982, Chancellor's medal, 1994, Ledbetter prize, 1994; Truman Libr. fellow, 1963; Acad. Arts and Scis. grantee, 1962. Mem. So. Hist. Assn. (pres. 1986-87), Ark. Hist. Assn., Orgn. Am. Historians, Phi Beta Kappa. Presbyterian. E-mail: wgatewood@cox-internet.com.

GATHRIGHT, JOHN BYRON, JR., colon and rectal surgeon, educator; b. Oxford, Miss., Sept. 29, 1933; s. J. Byron Sr. and Connie (Love) G.; m. Barbara Cooper, Sept. 19, 1959; children: John Byron III, Lin, John Miles, Peter C. BS, U. Miss., 1955; MD, Northwestern U., 1957. Diplomate Am. Bd. Colon and Rectal Surgery (pres. 1989-90), Am. Bd. Surgery. Intern Charity Hosp., New Orleans, 1957-58, resident in gen. surgery, 1958-62; fellow in colon & rectal surgery Alton Ochsner Med. Found., New Orleans, 1962-63; mem. staff So. Bapt. Hosp., New Orleans, 1963-69, Ochsner Found. Hosp., New Orleans, 1969-97, chmn. colon and rectal surgery dept.; clin. prof. surgery Tulane U., New Orleans, 1991—. Vis. surgeon So. La. Med. Ctr., Houma, 1977-97; trustee, exec. com., bd. dirs. Alton Ochsner Med. Found., 1980-97. Assoc. editor Diseases of the Colon and Rectum, 1977-93, Perspectives in Colon and Rectal Surgery, 1987-97, Colon and Rectal Surgery Outlook, 1987-97; mem. bd. editors Current Concepts in Gastroenterology, 1980-89. Fellow ACS (grad. edn. com. 1981-89, Am. Soc. Colon and Rectal Surgeons (pres. 1989-90), Soc. Coloproctology of Eng. and Ireland (hon.), Internat. Soc. Univ. Colon and Rectal Surgeons (sec. 1990-2002), Mex. Soc. Colon and Rectal Surgeons (hon.). Republican. Presbyterian. Avocations: boating, photography. E-mail: jbeegee2@cox.net.

GATI, WILLIAM EUGENE, architect, designer and planner; b. Apr. 10, 1959; s. John and Edith Gati. Student, The Juilliard Sch. of Music, 1965-77; BS in Architecture, CCNY, 1980, BArch cum laude, 1982; MS in Urban Planning, CUNY, 1985. Registered architect, N.Y., N.J. Freelance designer, N.Y.C., 1978-83; designer Urban Living, Inc., N.Y.C., 1983-84, Robert L. Henry, Architect, N.Y.C., 1984-86, Glass & Assocs., N.Y.C., 1986-87; prin. architect William E. Gati, RA, AIA, N.Y.C., 1987—; prin. Architecture Studio, N.Y.C., 1991—; writer Home Editor Resident Publs., 1995-97. Prof. architecture N.Y. Inst. Tech., Old Westbury, 1985-89; instr. religious architecture Cooper Union, N.Y.C., 1989; instr. architecture St. John's U., N.Y.C., 1995—; curator Fundamentals of Architecture, N.Y. Inst. Tech., 1987; bd. dir. Queen's (N.Y.) Design Ctr.; lectr. in field. Archtl. designs include offices for Here's Life, N.Y.C., alterations to Calvary Bapt. Ch., N.Y.C., El Eden Ch., Bklyn., Living Word Christian Ctr., N.Y.C., All Saints Ch., Queens, N.Y.C., Dr. Aviles Med. Ctr., Queens, Tampellini Residence, Queens, Beninen Residence, Queens, Khafi Residence, Queens, expansion for Flushing Christian Sch., Queens, N.Y., Faith Assembly Ch., Queens, P.S. 68 annex, Queens, Perkovich Residence, Queens, Kaufman Residence, L.I., Cardinal Residence, Mas, Lindas Natural Kitchen, Queens, Resurrection Ch., Bklyn., Dr. Peter Chin's Med. Offices, Queens, Dr. Peter Murowski's Med. Offices, Queens, Dr. Larry Weinstein med. offices, Quantum Feet Store, Queens, Greenberg Residence, Queens, Parson Residence, Queens; author: Solar Energy Techniques, 1979 (AIA Recognition 1979), Frank L. Wright, 1981, Theory of Modern Architecture, 1981, Boston's Pub. Space, 1985, Vacant Lots, Architectural League N.Y.C., 1987; contbg. illustrator Jonathan Friedman Creations in Space, Fundamentals of Architecture. Chmn. religious architecture com., organized series: Places for Worship, N.Y.C. 1990; planning bd. Kew Gardens; dir. Queens Design Ctr. Recipient Design award, Queens County Builder's Assn., 2002, Builders award, 2002. Mem. AIA (mem. religious arch. com. N.Y.C., v.p. Queens chpt., head coms., bd. dirs. N.Y. State chpt.), Mcpl. Art Soc. (assoc.), Archtl. League (assoc.), CCNY Alumni Assn. (v.p. 1983-92), N.Y. Arts Group, Christian Architects Fellowship (pres.). Avocations: photography, chess, piano, art. Office: 11231 84th Ave Jamaica NY 11418-1321 E-mail: wgati@williamgati.com.

GATIPON, BETTY BECKER, medical educator, consultant; b. New Orleans, Sept. 8, 1931; d. Elmore Paul and Theresa Caroline (Sendker) Becker; m. William B. Gatipon, Nov. 22, 1952 (dec. 1986); children: Suzanne, Ann Gatipon Sved, Lynn Gatipon Pashley. BS magna cum laude, Ursuline Coll., New Orleans, 1952; MEd, La. State U., 1975, PhD, 1983. Tchr. Diocese of Baton Rouge, 1960-74, edn. cons. to sch. bd., 1974-78; dir. Right to Read program Capital Area Consortium/Washington Parish Sch. Bd., Franklington, La., 1978-80; dir. basic skills edn. Capital Area Consortium/Ascension Parish Sch. Bd., Donaldsonville, La., 1980-82; instr. Coll. Edn. La. State U., Baton Rouge, 1982-84; evaluation cons. La. Dept. Edn., Baton Rouge, 1984-85; dir. basic skills edn. Capital Area Basic Skills/East Feliciana Parish Sch. Bd., Clinton, La., 1985-86; program coord. La. Bd. Elem. and Secondary Edn., New Orleans, 1987-89; dir. divsn. of med. edn., dept. family medicine Sch. Medicine La. State U. Med. Ctr., New Orleans, 1989—. Evaluator East Feliciana Parish Schs., 1982-86; presenter math. methods workshops Ascension Parish Schs., 1980-84. Author curriculum materials, conf. papers; contbr. articles to edn. jours. Curatorial asst. La. State Mus., New Orleans, 1987—; soprano St. Louis Cathedral Concert Choir, New Orleans, 1988—; chmn. Symphony Store, New Orleans Symphony, 1990—; lector St. Francis Xavier Ch. Mem. Am. Ednl. Rsch. Assn., Assn. Am. Med. Colls., Midsouth Ednl. Rsch. Assn., La. Ednl. Rsch. Assn., Soc. Tchrs. Family Medicine, New Orleans Film and Video Buffs, Phi Kappa Phi, Phi Delta Kappa. Roman Catholic. Avocations: music, aerobic walking, classic movies. Home: 105 10th St New Orleans LA 70124-1258 Office: LA State U Med Ctr Sch Medicine 1542 Tulane Ave New Orleans LA 70112-2825

GATISON, KAREN ANN, private school educator; b. Bridgeport, Conn., Apr. 1, 1953; d. Harold George and Teresa Mary Russer; children: Jonathan Isaiah, Denise Nicole. AS in Office Tech. and Mgmt., Ctrl. Fla. C.C., Ocala, 1992, AA in Bus. Mgmt., 1994; BA in Bus. Mgmt., St. Leo Coll., 1996. Tchr. Cambridge Acad., Ocala, Fla., 1996—. Bd. dirs. Help Agy. Forest, Silver Springs, Md. Mem.: NAFE, Nat. Bus. Edn. Assn., Nat. Women's History Project, Nat. Coun. Tchrs. Math., Phi Beta Lambda (profl. divsn. 1995—, historian 1993—94, Most Valuable Mem. 1994). Home: 2702 NE 22d Ct Ocala FL 34470-3850 Office: Cambridge Acad 3855 SE Lake Weir Rd Ocala FL 34480-9152 E-mail: karen@cambridgeacademy.com.

GATJE, ROBERT FREDERICK, architect; b. Bklyn., Nov. 27, 1927; s. Frederick Christopher and Erna Henrietta (Kelting) G.; m. Barbara Mansfield Wright, Oct. 20, 1956 (div. Aug. 1981); children: Alexandra Lord, Marianna Gatje Perrier, Margot Gatje Small. B.Arch., Cornell U., 1951; Fulbright scholar, Archtl. Assn. Sch. Architecture, London, 1951-52. Architect Gatje, Papachristou Smith (formerly Marcel Breuer Assocs.), N.Y.C., 1953-56, assoc., 1956-87, ptnr., 1965-87, dir. Paris office, 1964-66; ptnr. Richard Meier and Ptnrs., N.Y.C., 1987-95. Architect: Broward County Main Library, 1980; co-architect: IBM France Research Center, 1962, Ski Town, Flaine, France, 1969, IBM Mfg. Center, Boca Raton, Fla., 1969, Armstrong Rubber Co. Hdqrs, New Haven, 1969, Baldegg (Switzerland) Convent, 1972, Mundipharma GmbH Hdqrs, Limburg, Ger., 1975; author: Marcel Breuer, A Memoir, 2000. Trustee Deep Springs Coll., Calif., 1974-82, N.Y. Hall of Sci., 1985-96, N.Y. Found. for Arch., 1994-96; pres. Telluride Assn., 1953-55; bd. dirs. Franklin and Eleanor Roosevelt Inst. With C.E., AUS, 1946-47. Telluride scholar, 1947-51; Skidmore, Owings and Merrill scholar, 1950-51; recipient Clifton Beckwith Brown medal Cornell U. Coll. Architecture, 1951, Charles Goodwin Sands medal, 1951 Fellow AIA (pres. N.Y. chpt. 1975-76, Sch. medal 1951);l mem. Ordre des Architectes Francais, Century Assn., Am. Arbitration Assn. Democrat. Home: 1040 5th Ave Apt 6A New York NY 10028-0137 E-mail: bobgatje@earthlink.net.

GATLIN, KAREN CHRISTENSEN, English language educator, retired; b. Iowa City, Iowa, Feb. 18, 1943; d. Carl Archibald and Esther Agnes (Bradley) Christensen; m. John Charles Gatlin, Apr. 4, 1964 (div. Sept. 1976); children: Britt Jonene, Shawna Lynne. BS in Secondary Edn., N.E. Mo. State U., 1964; MA in Multicultural Edn., U. N.Mex., 1989. Cert. secondary English tchr., reading K-12, French. Tchr. 8th grade English Ernie Pyle Jr. H.S., Albuquerque, 1964-69; tchr. 7th grade English Truman Mid. Sch., Albuquerque, 1974-81; tchr. 6th/7th grade English and 8th grade French Madison Mid. Sch., Albuquerque, 1981-87; clin. supr. student tchg. U. N.Mex., Albuquerque, 1987-89; French instr. U. N.Mex. Continuing Edn., Albuquerque, 1988-93; tchr. English Sandia H.S., Albuquerque, 1989-96, ret., 1996. Mem. profl. stds. com. A.F.T.-APS, Albuquerque, 1989-90; mem. restructuring com. APS-Sandia H.S., Albuquerque, 1989-90; participant United World Coll. Restructuring Symposium, Las Vegas, 1990; tour leader, counselor E.F. Inst. for Cultural Exch., France, Gt. Britain and Germany, 1985, 90, 95, 96; guest spkr. multi-cultural tchr. edn. Auburn U., Montgomery, Ala., 1989. Mem. LWV, Albuquerque Tchrs. Fedn., Delta Kappa Gamma, Phi Delta Kappa, Kappa Delta Pi (v.p. 1964). Avocations: travel, art, writing. Home: 5801 Cubero Dr NE Albuquerque NM 87109-3870 E-mail: kgatlin718@aol.com.

GATLIN, TONY FRANKLIN, electrical engineer; b. Sheffield, Ala., Oct. 2, 1959; s. Winford Franklin and Clara Florence (Chapman) G.; m. Anita Ellen Sanders, May 26, 1984; 1 child, Anna Beth. BEE, Auburn (Ala.) U., 1981, MS in Elec. Engring., 1983; PhD. Elec. Engring., U. Ala., Huntsville, 2001.

Registered profl. engr., Ala. Elec. engr., 1981-83, Missile and Space Intelligence Ctr., Huntsville, Ala., 1983—. Mem. IEEE. Mem. Ch. of Christ. Home: 802 Meadowview St Athens AL 35611-4734

GATONS, ANNA-MARIE KILMADE, government official; b. Albany, N.Y., Oct. 21, 1946; d. Daniel Joseph Jr. and Tomasina (Fallone) Kilmade; m. Robert A. McCarthy, Sept. 3, 1967 (div. Apr. 1990); children: Daniel Kilmade McCarthy, Kevin Michael McCarthy; m. Paul K. Gatons, July 28, 1991. BA, Coll. of St. Rose, 1970. Staff support positions HUD, Washington, 1976-79, mgmt. analyst, 1979-81, staff budget analyst, 1981-83, chief of the budget and legislation coord. br., 1983-91, dir. exec. secretariat, 1992-95; dir. exec. secretariat for atty. gen. Dept. of Justice, Washington, 1995—2001; corr. mgmt. officer Office of Asst. Atty. Gen. for Adminstrn., Washington, 2001—02; dir., exec. sec. Immigration and Naturalization Svc., Washington, 2002—03; dir., exec. secretariat U.S. Immigration and Customs Enforcement, Dept. Homeland Security, Washington, 2003—. Mem. St. Rose Alumni Assn. Roman Catholic. Avocations: reading, needlework, decorating. Home: 7705 Huntsman Blvd Springfield VA 22153-3912 Office: US Immigration and Customs Enforcement Exec Secrt Rm 7045 Dept of Homeland Sec 425 I St NW Washington DC 20530

GATOS, HARRY CONSTANTINE, engineering educator; b. Greece, Dec. 27, 1921; came to U.S., 1946, naturalized, 1955. s. Constantine B. and Paraskevi (Merintzos) G.; m. Dawn Spiropoulos, July 15, 1950 (div. 1980); children: Pamela Dawn, Niki Ann, Constantine Harry; m. Ronna M. Galipeau, Apr. 10, 1988. Diploma in chemistry, U. Athens, Greece, 1945; MA in Chemistry, Ind. U., 1948; PhD, MIT, 1950; DSc, Ind. U., 1983. Instr. U. Athens, 1943-46; mem. research staff MIT, 1948-52; from sect. leader to divsn. head solid state divsn. Lincoln Lab., 1955-64; prof. materials sci. and elec. engring. MIT, Cambridge, 1962-90, prof. emeritus, 1990—. Research engr. E.I. duPont de Nemours & Co., Inc., 1952-55; Cons. to industry, govt., 1962— Editor-in-chief Surface Sci.; contbr. 350 articles to profl. jours. Trustee Longy Sch. Music, Cambridge, Mass. Decorated golden cross Order of Merit Poland; recipient medal for exceptional sci. achievement NASA, 1974; Solid State Sci. and Tech. award Electrochem. Soc., 1975, Acheson medal Electrochem. Soc., 1982, Harry C. Gatos Disting. Lecture and Prize, 1991, Gallium Arsenide award, 1992, Welker Gold medal, 1992. Fellow AAAS; mem. Electrochem. Soc. (hon. mem., pres. 1967-68), Materials Research Soc. (pres. 1972-75), Am. Phys. Soc., Am. Inst. Metall. Engrs., Nat. Acad. Engring., Am. Acad. Arts and Scis., Acad. Athens (corr.), Cambridge Soc. for Early Music (trustee) Home: 83 Cambridge Pkwy Unit W301 Cambridge MA 02142-1241 Office: MIT Dept of Materials S&E Cambridge MA 02139

GATSKI, THOMAS BERNARD, research scientist; b. Hazleton, Pa., Aug. 30, 1948; s. Thomas August and Agnes (Hovan) G.; m. Rosann Marcinkus, June 20, 1970; 1 child, Megan Marie. BS, Pa. State U., 1970, MS, 1972, PhD, 1976. Postdoctoral assoc. Brown U., Providence, 1975 77; rsch. scientist NASA Langley Rsch. Ctr., Hampton, Va., 1977-85, sr. rsch. scientist, 1985—. Co-editor: Studies in Turbulence, 1991, Instabilities and Turbulence in Engineering Flows, 1993, Transition, Turbulence and Combustion, 1994; editor Theoretical and Computational Fluid Dynamics, 1991—; contbr. articles to profl. jours. Bd. pres. United Way Greater Williamsburg, Va., 1990-97. Mem. Rotary Internat. (program chair 1994-95 Williamsburg chpt., pres. 1997-98). Avocation: golf. Office: NASA-Langley Rsch Ctr Ms 128 Hampton VA 23681-0001 E-mail: gatski@widomaker.com.

GATTO, JOHN TAYLOR, educational consultant, writer, speaker; b. Monongahela, Pa., Dec. 15, 1935; s. Andrew Michael Mario and Frances Virginia (Zimmer) G.; m. Janet MacAdam, Dec. 29, 1961; children: Briseis Lucrezia, Raven Taylor. BS, Columbia U., 1959; MA, Hunter Coll., 1971; postgrad., Cornell U., 1954, 55, 86, U. Pitts., 1956, Yeshiva U., 1963, Calif. State U., 1984, Lehman Coll., 1987, Reed Coll., 1990. Cert. secondary tchr., N.Y. Copywriter Ted Bates Advt., N.Y.C., 1960-61; screenwriter Lotus Prodns., N.Y.C., 1961-62; instr. in English N.Y.C. Bd. Edn., 1962-71; lectr. Queens Coll., N.Y.C., 1971-76; dir. The Lab Sch., N.Y.C., 1976-91; pres. Oxford Ednl. Cons., Oxford, N.Y., 1991—. Songwriter (ASCAP listed), N.Y.C., 1967-72; ednl. cons. Bd. Higher Edn., N.Y.C., 1971-76; script cons. Marvel Comics, DC Comics, N.Y.C., 1972-73; sr. staff designer Huckleberry Designs, N.Y.C., 1976—; pres. Lava MT Records; adv. bd., Nat. Coalition Alternative Cmty. Schs., 1998—, Nat. TV Turnoff Week, 1999. Author: One Flew Over the Cuckoo's Nest: A Critical Study, 1975, Howard Phillips Lovecraft: A Critical Study, 1976, The Adventures of Snider, the CIA Spider, 1979, Are You My Father? An Odyssey Across the Barren Land of Adoption and Homelessness, 1990, Dumbing Us Down: The Hidden Curriculum of Compulsory Schooling, 1991, The Exhausted School, 1992, A Different Kind of Teacher, 2001, The Underground History of American Education, 2002, The Fourth Purpose: An Investigation of Modern Schooling, 2003; contbr. articles to jours. and newspapers; composer Ballads of Sorrow and Sadness, 1968, Iphigenia in Aulis, 1969; recordings include Richard Nixon's Checkers Speech, 1976, Two Attacks on the Media, 1977, The Rats in the Walls, 1978, The Haunter of the Dark, 1979; author (filmscript) The Fourth Purpose, 2000. Founder The I.S. 44 Market, sch. fundraiser, N.Y.C.; dist. leader N.Y. Conservative Party, 1973—, state Committeeman, 1978—; candidate N.Y. State Senate, Albany, 1986, 88, 90; candidate for pres. Manhattan Borough, N.Y.C., 1989; mem. adv. bd. TV-Free Am., 1995—; sec. edn. Libertarian Party Shadow Cabinet, 1993—. Nominee Pres.'s Vol. Action award, 1984; recipient Citizen of the Week award Assn. for a Better N.Y., 1986, 1st prize Nat. Writing Contest Geraldine Dodge Found. and Tchrs. Coll., Columbia U., 1990, Spectrum Medal World Soc. Achievement of Human Potential, 1993, Alexis de Tocqueville award, 1998; named N.Y.C. Tchr. of Yr., Coun. Chief State Sch. Officers and Nat. Assn. Secondary Sch. Prins., 1989, N.Y. State Senate Resolution, 1990, N.Y. Alliance for Pub. Edn., 1991, N.Y. State Tchr. of Yr., Encyclopedia Brittanica, 1990, N.Y. State Edn. Dept., 1991; NEH grantee, 1983, 86, 90; N.Y. Tchr. Consortium grantee, 1984; Coun. for Basic Edn. Ind. Study fellow, 1984; Lehman Coll. fellow, 1987; Mario Salvadori fellow Inst. for the Built Environment, CUNY, 1989, Snowbird fellow Met. Life Ins. Co., 1990; commendations from Pres. Ford, Pres. Carter, Pres. Reagan, N.Y. Gov. Cuomo, N.Y. Mayors Koch and Dinkins. Fellow Scholars Cir., Chenango Upland Pistol Club (pres. 1975-2003), Marshall Chess Club, Audubon Soc., U.S. Mycol. Soc., Scottish Heritage Assn., Working Press of the Nation. Roman Catholic. Avocations: pistol-hunting, mycology, chess, ancient religions, graphoanalysis. Office: 235 W 76th St New York NY 10023-8210 Home: PO Box 562 Oxford NY 13830-0562 Fax: 212-721-6124.

GATTO, JOSEPH DANIEL, investment banker; b. Italy, Feb. 25, 1956; came to U.S., 1956; s. Philip and Gilda Gatto; m. Susan Elizabeth Rehm, May 9, 1987; children: Philip, Catherine, Peter, Elizabeth. AB magna cum laude, Princeton U., 1978; JD cum laude, MBA, U. Pa., 1984. Bar: N.Y. 1985. Assoc. Goldman, Sachs & Co., N.Y.C., 1984-87, v.p., 1987-90, group head strategic devel., 1990-94, gen. ptnr., 1994—, chmn. global consumer banking, 2001—. Mem. adv. coun. Woodrow Wilson Sch. Pub. and Internat. Affairs Princeton U.; mem. adv. bd. Wharton Dirs. Inst.; trustee Brunswick Sch.; lectr. World Econ. Forum. Editor-in-chief Jour. Corp. Law and Securities Regulation, 1984. Mem. Maritime Ctr. Mem. World Wildlife Fund, Aubudon Soc., Wharton Club. Roman Catholic. Avocations: golf, skiing, cooking, reading. Office: Goldman Sachs & Co 85 Broad St New York NY 10004-2456

GATTO, LOUIS CONSTANTINE, educational association administrator; b. Chgo., July 4, 1927; s. Louis S. and Marie (Bacigalupo) Gatto; m. Kathleen M. Paquette, July 7, 1951 (dec.); children: Christine Gatto Glasgow, Beth Gatto Roberts, Mark, Gregory, Janine, Sandra Gatto Minniear; m. Marilyn R. Bennett, Feb. 9, 1991 (dec.). Student, Amherst Coll., 1945-46; BA, St. Mary's Coll., Minn., 1950; postgrad., U. Minn., 1950-51; MA, DePaul U., 1956; PhD, Loyola U., Chgo., 1965; LittD (hon.), Marian Coll., Indpls., 1989; LHD (hon.), Martin U., Indpls., 1996. Speech asst. St. Mary's Coll., 1949-50; staff artist TV Times, Mpls., 1950-51; chmn. dept. English Zion-Benton H.S., Ill., 1951-56; tchr. New Trier H.S., Winnetka, Ill., 1956-57; instr. English St. Josephs Coll., Rensselaer, Ind., 1957-58, asst. prof., 1958-63, assoc. prof. Medieval and Renaissance lit., 1963-66, prof., 1966-71, asst. acad. dean, dir. summer session, 1967, acad. dean, 1968, v.p. acad. affairs, 1969-71; pres., prof. English Marian Coll., Indpls., 1971-89; dir. spl. projects, cons. svc. Independent Colls. of Ind., 1989—; amb. Independent Colls. Ind. Found., 1989—91; dir. Ind. Compact, 1989-99, West Point liaison officer, 1990—, dir. Operation Expanded Horizons, 1992—. Mem. Ind. N.W. Consortium Pvt. and Pub. Instns., 1968—71; selection com. Ind. Fulbright Found., 1968—70; mem. cmty. adv. coun. Indpls. Pub. Schs., 1976—77; mem. policy adv. coun. parent/child devel. project Bank St. Coll. Edn., 1976—79; mem. Hist. Landmarks Found. Ind., 1973—89; mem. long range devel. plan adv. com. Ind. Vocat. Tech. Coll., 1985—86; mem. adv. com. Alcohol Safety Action Project, 1972—75; mem. exec. com. adv. bd. Ctr. Econ. Edn., Ind. U.-Purdue U., Indpls., 1978—89; mem. exec. com. Ind. Conf. Higher Edn., 1973—75, 1978—81, 1987—89, pres., 1979—80; chmn. Consortium Urban Edn., 1974—75, pres., 1975—89; dir. spl. projects Ind. Conf. Higher Edn., 1992—94, exec. sec., 1994—. Contbr. articles to profl. jours. Vice chair Hamilton County ARC, 1999; bd. dirs., treas. Associated Colls. Ind., 1976—78, v.p., 1984—86; mem. Benjamin Harrison Meml. Commn., 1987—91; mem. adv. bd. Sta. WYFI; mem. gov.'s commn. Hoosier Celebration, 1988; Ind. lobbyist Ind. Higher Edn., 1989—90; chmn. Ind. Ameritech. Partnership Awards Program, 1990—95; asst. dir. Ednl. Facilities Auth., 1991—93, exec. dir., 1994—; with Army War Coll., 1974; mem. Senator Lugar's merit selection com. West Point, 1995—; mem. adv. com. 21st century scholars program State Student Assistance Commn., 1998—2002; mem. adv. com. Ind. Coun. Quality Tchg. Student Learning, 2000—02; bd. dirs. Greater Indpls. Progress Com., ARC, Hosp. Audiences Inpls., 1974—76, Ind. Higher Edn. Telecom. Sys., 1987—95, Hamilton County ARC, Ind. Colls. and Univs. Ind., chmn., 1979—80, 1986—88. With AUS, 1945—46, with Ill. N.G., 1946—50. Recipient Sagamor of the Wabash award, State of Ind., 1980, 1989, Outstanding Svc. award, Ind. Health Careers, 1983, Cir. award, Ind. Coalition Blacks in Higher Edn., 1986, Outstanding Contbns. award, Army Career And Alumni Assn., 1994; fellow ACE, 1966—67. Mem.: Nat. Assn. Higher Ednl. Facilities Authorities (v.p. 2001—02, pres. 2003—), Ind. Conf. Higher Edn. (Dedicated Svc. award 1994), Am. Coun. Edn. (Ind. coord. fellow program 1999—), Friends of West Point Membership, West Point Soc. Ind., Heslar Naval Armory Club (life), Alpha Phi Omega. Home: 24 Apple Tree Cir Fishers IN 46038-1110 E-mail: iefa@msn.com.

GATWOOD, DIANNE N. music educator; b. Evansville, Ind., Aug. 25, 1946; d. Herve Joseph Normand and Clyta Mae Hart; m. Dwight Dean Gatwood, Jr., Dec. 26, 1971; children: David Alan. MusB, Brescia Coll., 1967; MusM, M in Music Edn., Peabody Coll., 1969. Cert. tchr., Ky., Tenn., Ohio. Instr. U. Tenn., Martin, 1973-74; assoc. prof. Dyersburg (Tenn.) State C.C., 1973-87; asst. prof. Lambuth Coll., Jackson, Tenn., 1977-81, Bethel Coll., McKenzie, Tenn., 1979-80; instr. Weakley County Schs., Dresden, Tenn., 1985-86; assoc. prof. Union U., Jackson, 1988—; dir. fine arts U. Sch. Jackson, 1990-91. Condr. Dyersburg (Tenn.) Choral Soc., 1981-87; soloist, clinician Tenn. Gov.'s Sch. Humanities, Martin, 1993-97; pres. West Tenn. Music Tchrs. Assn., Jackson, 1994-95. Author: Singing: A Manual for Singers, 1990. Faculty advisor Sigma Alpha Iota, Union U., 1992-99. NDEA grad. fellow Peabody Coll., Nashville, 1967. Mem. Internat. Soc. for Music Edn., Nat. Assn. Tchrs. Singing, Music Educators Nat. Conf. (clinician so. divsn. conf. 1997), Music Tchrs. Nat. Assn., Martin Area Music Tchrs. Assn. (pres. 1995-97), So. Bapt. Ch. Music Conf., Kappa Delta Pi, Pi Kappa Lamda (charter). Avocations: walking, biking, raising plants. Home: 109 S Dodd Dr Martin TN 38237-2302 Office: Union Univ 1050 Union University Dr Jackson TN 38305-3697

GAUBERT, RONALD JOSEPH, gas and oil industry executive, management consultant, real estate broker; b. Lafayette, La., Dec. 1, 1946; s. Harold E. and Cecile (Mouton) G.; m. Linda Bock; children: Ellen, Brad. BS, U. So. La., Lafayette, 1973. Controller Lafayette Drug Co., 1973-76; treas. Mar-Low Corp., Lafayette, 1976-78; pres. Ron J. Gaubert & Assoc., Lafayette, 1978—, Lanscor Devel. Corp., Lafayette, 1978—, Energy R&D Corp., 1994—; CEO, Stonehenge Corp., 1986—. Chmn. Venture Capital Forum, Lafayette. Pres. adv. bd. Cathedral Carmel Parents Booster Assn., Lafayette, 1985-86, mem. sch. bd., 1985-86, pres. Parish Council, Holy Cross Ch.; fin. chmn. St. Thomas More H.S., 1997-99, Leadership Lafayette, 1999—; bd. dirs. La. Open. Served with U.S. Army, 1966-69. Mem. Petroleum Inds., La. Assn. Ind. Prodrs. and Royalty Owners, Krewe of Gabriel. Republican. Roman Catholic. Office: PO Box 53152 Lafayette LA 70505-3152

GAUCH, EUGENE WILLIAM, JR., retired air force officer; b. Newark, Dec. 6, 1922; s. Eugene William and Wilhelmina Katrina (Beiswenger) G.; m. Beryl Merle Walker, Jan. 15, 1947 (dec. Oct. 1995); children: Kathryn A. (Mrs. Jerry T. Stansfield), Tracey L. Enlisted as pvt. USAAF, 1942; advanced through grades to brig. gen. USAF, 1972; assigned Okinawa, World War II and Korean War; tng. and standardization officer SAC, Offutt AFB, Neb., 1955-59; ops. staff officer 72 Bombardment Wing, Ramey AFB, P.R., 1959-63; asst. exec. sec. to air staff bd. Office Vice Chief Staff Air Force, Washington, 1963-67; asst. chief staff, exec. to comdr. 7th Air Force, Vietnam, 1967-68; faculty Nat. War Coll., 1969; exec. to comdr. Hdqrs. Tactical Air Command, Langley AFB, Va., 1969-70, chief staff, 1970-72; comdr. 834th Air Div., Little Rock AFB, 1972-74; dir. automated mobility requirements DSC/Plans and Ops., Hdqrs. USAF, Washington, 1974—75; ret. USAF, 1975. Decorated Legion of Merit with 3 oak leaf clusters, D.F.C., Air medal with 4 oak leaf clusters, Air Force Commendation medal. Home: 628 Owl Way Sarasota FL 34236-1928

GAUCHER, JANE HEYCK, retail executive; b. Houston, Feb. 11, 1936; d. Theodore Richard and Gertrude Paine (Daly) Heyck; m. Donald Holman Gaucher, June 15, 1957 (dec.); children: Susan Heyck Merrill, Beverly Jane. AB cum laude, Brown U., Providence, 1957. Mgr. Bride and Groom Registry Berings, Houston, 1990-99; asst. mgr. Pavillon Christofle, Houston, 1999—2002; mktg. rep. dinnerRings, 2002—. Pres. Antique Study Group, Houston, 1974-75. Bd. dirs. Jr. League Houston, 1963, sustaining bd., 1990-93; mem. Kinkaid Sch. Alumni Bd., Houston, 1995-98, Mus. So. History Bd., 2000-. Avocations: tennis, running, golfing, mah jongg, bridge. Home: 1905B Potomac Dr Houston TX 77057-2921

GAUDET, JEAN ANN, retired librarian, educator; b. Oakland, Calif., Dec. 28, 1949; d. Edwin Joseph and Teresa Maureen (McDonnell) G. BS, Madison Coll., Harrisonburg, Va., 1971; MLS, George Peabody Coll. for Tchrs, Nashville, 1973. Libr., gifted edn. tchr. Prince William County Schs., Manassas, Va., 1971—2003, ret., 2003. Chmn. PSHS Site-Based Mgmt. Com., Dumfries, Va., 1989-92, 98-2001; chmn. Cmty. Choir, Woodbridge, Va., 1983-85; citizen ambassador People to People, Russia and Poland, 1992, China, 1993, 2000, Australia, 1994. Named Prince William Assn. for Edn. of Gifted Tchr. of Yr., 1998. Mem. ALA, Va. Edn. Media Assn., Va. Assn. for Edn. of Gifted, Delta Kappa Gamma (sec. 1994—), Beta Phi Mu, Alpha Beta Alpha. Home: 16820 Francis West Ln Dumfries VA 22026-2110 E-mail: gaudetja@cs.com.

GAUDI, BERNARD SCOTT, astronomer, researcher; b. Beruit, Lebanon, Feb. 19, 1974; s. Bernard Scott and Theresa Marie Gaudi. BS, Mich. State U., 1991—95; MSc, The Ohio State U., 1995—97, PhD, 2000. Hubble fellow Inst. for Advanced Study, Princeton, NJ, 2000—. Contbr. articles to profl. jours. Hubble fellowship, Space Telescope Sci. Inst., 2000—. Mem.: Am. Astron. Soc. Atheist. Office: Institute for Advanced Study Einstein Drive Princeton NJ 08540 E-mail: gaudi@sns.ias.edu.

GAUDIANI, CLAIRE LYNN, retired academic administrator; b. Venice, Fla., Nov. 10, 1944; d. Vincent Augustus and Vera (Rossano) Gaudiani; m. David Graham Burnett; children: David Graham, Maria. BA, Conn. Coll., 1966; MA in French and Italian, Ind. U., 1969, PhD in French and Italian, 1975; PhD (hon.), Purdue U., 1989, Whitman Coll., 1989. Asst. prof. Purdue U., W. Lafayette, Ind., 1977—80, Emory U., Atlanta, 1980—81; sr. fellow in romance langs., acting assoc. dir. Joseph H. Lauder Inst. Mgmt. and Internat. Studies U. Pa., Phila., 1981—88; pres. Conn. Coll., New London, 1988—2001; sr. rsch. scholar Yale Law Sch., 2001—. Mem. commn. internat. edn. Am. Coun. Edn.; bd. dirs. So. NEw ENg. Telephone Co.; cons. Dana Found., Exxon Found., Rockefeller Found. Author: The Cabaret Peotry of Theophile de Viau: Texts and Traditions, 1980, Teaching Writing in the Foreign Language Curriculum, 1981; co-author (with Carol Herron and others): Strategies for Development of Foreign Language and Literature Programs, 1984; contbr. articles to profl. jours.; author: The Greater Good: How Philanthropy Saves American Capitalism, 2003. Chair assessment task force United Way, New London, 1988; hon. chair Summer Music Fund, 1988; trustee Hazen Found.; bd. dirs. Eugene O'Neill Theatre Ctr. Recipient Coll. medal, Conn. Coll., 1987; fellow rsch. fellow, Nat. Humanities Ctr., 1980—81, Am. Coun. Learned Socs., 1976—77. Mem.: MLA (adv. com. fgn. lang. programs 1988—), Conn. World Trade Assn. (bd. dirs.), Am. Assn. Higher Edn. (bd. dirs. 1988—), Phi Beta Kappa. Roman Catholic. Office: Yale Law School P O Box 208215 New Haven CT 06520

GAUDIERI, ALEXANDER V. J. museum director; b. 1940; divorced; 1 child. BA, Ohio State U., 1962; diploma, Sorbonne U. Paris, 1962; postgrad., Colgate U., 1963; MBA in Internat. Fin., Am. Grad. Sch. Internat. Commerce, 1965; MA, NYU, 1976. With Sotheby Parke Bernet, 1972—; internat. banking officer Marine Midland Bank, N.Y.C., 1965-71; dir. Telfair Acad. Arts and Scis., Savannah, Ga., 1977-83; dir. Montreal (Can.) Mus. Fine Arts, 1983—88. Adj. prof. mus. studies program Grad. Sch. Arts and Scis., NYU; dir. Samuel F.B. Morse hist. site Locust Grove, Poughkeepsie, N.Y., 1995-96. Interim dir., pres. capital campaign Armory Art Ctr., 2002—; mem. bd. sponsors Attingham Park Program, Eng.; bd. dirs. Young Concert Artists, N.Y.C. Barton Kyle Yount scholar. Mem. Assn. Art Mus. Dirs., Am. Assn. Mus. (accreditation commn.), Brit. Nat. Trust, Soc. Archtl. Historians. Office: PO Box 3 Palm Beach FL 33480

GAUDREAU, GAYLE GLANERT, computer resource educator; b. Hartford, Conn., June 10, 1944; d. Edward Eugene and Evelyn Ruth (Manning) Glanert; m. George C. Gaudreau, Nov. 15, 1974; children: Christopher, Matthew, Nathan. BS in Bus. Edn., Ctrl. Conn. State U., New Britain, 1969, MS in Edn., 1974; postgrad., U. Conn. Cert. tchr. bus. edn., coord. coop. work experience, Conn. Group leader Pratt & Whitney Aircraft, East Hartford, Conn., 1964-67; coord. bus. edn. Wethersfield H.S., 1969-92; computer resource tchr. Wethersfield (Conn.) Bd. Edn., 1992—. Part-time instr. Manchester (Conn.) C.C., 1973-74; mem. adv. bd. State of Conn. Bus. Edn., 1992; mem. adv. bd. bus. edn. Ctrl. Conn. State U., 1993—; cooperating tchr. State of Conn.; mem. Wethersfield Technology Com., 1993—. Named Disting. Educator, Wethersfield Bd. Edn.; recipient edn. alumni award Ctrl. Conn. State U. Sch. Bus., 1996. Mem. USTA (capt. sr. team), Conn. Educators Computer Assn., Conn. Bus. Educators' Assn., Am. Fedn. Tchrs., Wethersfield Fedn. Tchrs., Phi Delta Kappa, Pi Lambda Theta, Delta Pi Epsilon. Avocations: tennis, cooking, hiking, boating. Home: 1 Falcon Ln Glastonbury CT 06033-2731 Office: Wethersfield HS 411 Wolcott Hill Rd Wethersfield CT 06109-2981 E-mail: GayleG8198@aol.com.

GAUDREAU, RUSSELL A., JR., lawyer, educator; b. Weymouth, Mass., Feb. 25, 1943; s. Russell A. and Jean (Sandwell) G.; m. Elizabeth Flanagan, Dec. 26, 1966; children: Russell A. III, Seth F. BA, U. Mass., Amherst, 1965; JD cum laude, Suffolk U., 1968; LLM in Taxation, NYU, 1969. Law clk. to Hon. Harold R. Tyler, Jr., U.S. Dist Ct. (so. dist.) N.Y., 1969-70; assoc. Ropes & Gray, Boston, 1970-79, mng. ptnr. Washington, 1990-94, ptnr. Boston, 1979—. Adj. prof. law Bentley Coll., 1978-80; adj. prof. law Boston U. Law Sch., 1980—; adj. prof. law Georgetown U. Law Ctr., 1991—; frequent spkr. in field. Editor-in-Chief Suffolk U. Law Rev. Bd. dirs. Parents' and Children's Svcs., Handel and Haydn Soc. Fellow: Am. Coll. Employee Benefits Counsel; mem.: ABA (tax. sect., com. employee benefits), Boston Bar Assn., The Group, Inc., D.C. ERISA and Tax Discussion Groups, D.C. Bar Assn., New Eng. Benefits Coun. (dir.). Office: Ropes & Gray One International Pl Boston MA 02110

GAUDY, EDWARD, landscape architect, consultant; b. Buenos Aires, Dec. 27, 1927; came to U.S., 1957; s. Fernando and Elena (Duval) G.; m. Celia Nora Valls. Grad. in Landscape Arch., U. Buenos Aires, 1952. Lic. landscape arch., N.Y., Mass., Conn., N.J., Pa., Coun. Landscape Archtl. Registration Bds. Jr. landscape arch. Clarke & Rapuano, L.A.'s, N.Y.C., 1958-63; assoc. landscape arch. Zion & Breen, L.A.'s, N.Y.C., 1963-70; prin. Edward Gaudy, Environ. Design, South Nyack, N.Y., 1970-79; ptnr. Gaudy-Hadley Assocs., Nyack, 1979-89; prin. E.G.A. Site and Land Planning, Nyack, 1989—. Cons. playgrounds devel. Nyack Village. Designer waterfront projects: Haverstraw Marina, Clermont Condos Marina, Nyack, N.Y.; contbr. articles to profl. jours. Mem. Planning Bd., South Nyack, 1974. Mem. Am. Soc. Landscape Archs. (N.Y. chpt. v.p. 1972-73), Rotary Internat. (sr., Paul Harris fellow 1978). Avocations: sailing, swimming, oil painting. Office: EGA Site and Land Planning 42 Main St Nyack NY 10960-3204 E-mail: v.ega@verizon.net.

GAUEN, PATRICK EMIL, newspaper correspondent; b. St. Louis, July 15, 1950; s. Louis Otto and Wilma Ellen (Rogers) G.; m. Patti Lynn Seib, Dec. 8, 1972 (div. 1992); children: Bethany, Heather; m. Karen Earhart, July 11, 1992; 1 stepchild, Christopher Stephenson. Student, So. Ill. U., 1968-70. Reporter, photographer Collinsville (Ill.) Herald, 1969-72, news editor, 1972-78; reporter St. Louis Globe-Democrat, 1978-84, mng. editor, 1984-85; reporter Ill. affairs St. Louis Post-Dispatch, 1985-89, polit. corr., 1989—, pub. safety team leader, 2000—; faculty univ. coll. Washington U., St. Louis, 1991—2001. Pub. safety reporting team leader St. Louis Post Dispatch, 2000. Recipient Outstanding Med. News Series award Ill. State Med. Soc., 1970, Best Feature Story award Suburban Newspapers Am., 1971, Best News Story award Suburban Newspapers Am., 1973, Best Spot News Story award UPI Editors Ill., 1972, Best Pub. Svc. Reporting award Ill. Press Assn., 1974, Best Feature Story award, 1975, Bar-News Media award Bar Assn. Met. St. Louis, 1987, Bob Hardy award Southern Ill. Chiefs of Police and Southwestern Law Enforcement, 1996, Terry Hughes award St. Louis chpt. Newspaper Guild, 1996, Liberty Bell award Madison County Bar Assn., 1999. Mem. Mid-Am. Press Inst. (bd. dirs. 1985—), Press Club Met. St. Louis (bd. dirs. 1985—), Sigma Delta Chi (bd. dirs. St. Louis chpt. 1985—, chpt. pres. 1985-86, 86-87). Avocations: reading, photography. Home: 30 Meadowlark Ln Highland IL 62249-3000 Office: St Louis Post Dispatch 900 N Tucker St Saint Louis MO 63101 E-mail: pgauen@post-dispatch.com.

GAUER, LINETTE-JEAN CRETE, accountant; b. Newark, Oct. 19, 1940; d. Harry John Gauer and Dorothy Jean Hill; m. Jerome Thomas Filipek, Jan. 30, 1960 (div. July 1986); children: John Thomas Filipek, Lynda-Jean Reichl. B in Liberal Studies, St. Edwards U., 1984. Staff acct. Garland Shelton CPA, Austin, Tex., 1981—83; bookkeeper, office mgr. Schroeder-Brooke Designers, Austin, 1983—84; staff acct. Robert West CPA, Austin, 1984—87; acctg. clk. Econo-Lube 'n Tune, Newport, Calif., 1991—92; staff acct. Glasser & Mermelstein CPAs, Santa Ana, Calif., 1992—93; bookkeeper, office mgr. Big Bros./Big Sisters Bucks County, Jamison, Pa., 1993—94; acctg. mgr. Bucks County Hist. Soc. Mercer Mus., Doylestown, Pa., 1994—. Contbr. articles to profl. jours.; singer: The Love Notes; Mercer Museum Audio Guide and various public svc. announcements. Mem. educating the cmty. com. Bucks County Coun. on Alcohol and Drug Dependence, Doylestown, 1997—; demonstrator Swedish weaving Scandinavian Festival at Waterloo Village, Stanhope, NJ; deacon Doylestown Presbyn. Ch. Mem.: AAUW (former rec. sec. 1994, auditor). Avocations: sewing, smocking, beading, writing, voice talent. Home: 74 Colonial Heritage Pk Doylestown PA 18901-2237 Office: Bucks County Hist Soc/Mercer Mus 84 S Pine St Doylestown PA 18901-4999 E-mail: opalflamingo@yahoo.com

GAUFF, SUSAN TYRRELL, marketing and human resources executive; b. Hackensack, N.J., Oct. 19, 1946; d. Donald Eugene and Henrietta Dorothy (Benson) Tyrrell; m. James Anthony Gauff, Apr. 13, 1973; children: James Timothy, Janet Gauff Anthos, David Phillip. Student, Centenary Coll., 1967. Coord. market rsch. Warner-Lambert, Morris Plains, N.J., 1967-69; coord. pub. rels. Western Union Corp., N.Y.C., 1969-73; pvt. cons. practice in communications Princeton, N.J., 1973-75; asst. mgr. advt. Electronic Assocs., Inc., West Long Branch, N.J., 1975-79; dir. communications Mohawk Data Scis., Parsippany, N.J., 1979-83, Franklin Computer Corp., Pennsauken, N.J., 1983-84; dir. advt. and sales promotion Racal-Milgo, Miami, Fla., 1984-86; dir. corp. communications Siemens Info. Systems, Boca Raton, Fla., 1986-90; dir. mktg. communications Siemens Pvt. Communications Systems and Rolm Systems, Santa Clara, Calif., 1990-91; sr. dir. market and corp. communications Siemens Rolm Comm. Inc., Santa Clara, Calif., 1991-95; v.p. comm. Lexmark Internat., Inc., Lexington, Ky., 1995-97; sr. v.p. people and comm. Sarnoff Corp., Princeton, NJ, 1997—2002; mng. prin. The Growth Solutions Group, Princeton, NJ, 2002—. Mem. bus. adv. bd. Rider U. Named one of Outstanding Young Women of Am., 1971, Marketer of Yr., Advt. Age, 1995; recipient Tribute to Women in Industry award, 1993, Delaware Valley Human Resources Dept. of Yr., 2000. Mem. Bus. Mktg. Assn. (cert., chpt. pres. 1988-89, internat. v.p. media rels. com. 1989-90, internat. sec. 1990-92, internat. treas. 1994-95), Assn. Nat. Advertisers, Pub. Rels. Soc. Am., N.J. State C. of C., N.J. Tech. Coun., NJ 300, Soc. for Human Resources Mgmt., N.J. Human Resources Planning Group, Cherry Valley Country Club (bd. dirs. 2002—). Avocation: golf. Home: 6 Moselem Springs Ct Skillman NJ 08542 E-mail: sgauff@rcn.com.

GAUGER, MICHELE ROBERTA, photographer, studio administrator, corporate executive; b. Elkhorn, Wis., Feb. 28, 1949; d. Robert F. and Christiane J. (Guiffaut) Marszalek; m. Richard C. Gauger, May 3, 1969 (div.). Student, U. Wis., Superior, 1967-69, U. Wis., Whitewater, 1978-80, Winona Sch. Profl. Photography, Chgo., 1984-91; MA in Photography, 1994. Wedding photographer Fossum Studio, Elkhorn, 1973-78; owner Photography by Michele, Whitewater, 1978-81; pres., photographer, mgr. Michele Inc. Wis., Whitewater, 1981—, Foxes Reg., 1987. Instr. Whitewater Experience (Sch.), 1997—2003, Yucatan Experience, 2003; spkr. in field; lectr. in field. Contbr. articles to profl. jours.; exhibitions include Chinese Nat. Gallery, Beijing, 1987, 1988 (2d pl. award, 1988), 1989 (Bronze medal, 1989), 1991, 1994, 1995, 1996 (Bill Stockwell Lifetime Achievement award, 1995). Mem. Nat. Arbor Found., Nebr., 1984—. Named to Wis. Ct. Honor, 1991, 1996; recipient 1st pl. Wedding Photography award, Internat. Wedding Photography, 1983, 1984, 1987, 1988, 1989, 1991, 1996, 2s pl. award, 1985, 1996, Grand award, 1988. Mem.: N.Am. Hunters Assn., Winona Sch. Profl. Photography Alumni Assn., Wedding & Portrait Photo Internat. Photographers Assn. (Lifetime Achievement award 2003), Profl. Photographers Am. (Nat. Loan Collectional 1984, Epcot Exhibit 1996), Whitewater C. of C., Whitewater Sportsman Club (chmn. bd. dirs. 2001—02). Republican. Roman Catholic. Avocations: world travel, big game hunting, horseback riding, cooking. Home and Office: Michele Inc N7240 Sand Pyramid Rd Whitewater WI 53190-4479

GAUGHAN, DENISE MARIE, epidemiologist; b. N.Y.C., Dec. 29, 1967; d. Edward and Marjorie Anne Gaughan. MPH, Yale U., 1999. Rsch. assoc. Yale U., New Haven, 1997—99; epidemiologist Harvard U., Boston, 1999—. Roman Catholic. Avocation: swimming. Office: Harvard Univ 655 Huntington Ave Boston MA 02115 Personal E-mail: dmdgaughan@aol.com. E-mail: gaughan@sdac.harvard.edu.

GAUGHAN, EUGENE FRANCIS, retired accountant; b. Aug. 31, 1945; s. Eugene Francis and Ruth Mae (Webster) Gaughan; m. Arlene Barber, July 8, 1972 (dec. May 1981); m. Margaret Duffy, Jan. 2, 1983. AB, Coll. Holy Cross, 1967; MBA, Rutgers U., 1968; postgrad., Duke U., 1989; MME, INSEAD, France, 1990; JD, Seton Hall U., 2003. CPA N.Y., N.J., Conn., Fla. Staff acct. Price Waterhouse LLP, N.Y.C., 1968-70, sr. acct., 1970-72, mgr., 1972—78, sr. mgr., 1978-79, ptnr., 1979-98, PricewaterhouseCoopers, N.Y.C., 1998-99, World Firm Coun. Ptnrs., N.Y.C., 1987-90. Mem. supr. bd. Price Waterhouse Ea. Europe, 1991—97; trustee Lenox Hill Hosp.; bd. dirs. Manhattan Eye, Ear and Throat Hosp. Mem.: AICPA, Am. Acctg. Assn., N.Y. State Soc. CPAs (bd. dirs. 1986—89), Am. Health Lawyers Assn., N.J. State Bar Assn., N.Y. State Bar Assn., Doonbeg Golf Club, Laurel Links Golf and Country Club, KC. Roman Catholic. Home: Apt 7B 164 E 72nd St New York NY 10021-4363 also: PO Box 1675 Quogue NY 11959-1675 E-mail: efgmd@aol.com.

GAUGHAN, PATRICIA ANNE, judge; b. Cleve., Oct. 21, 1953; d. John James and Alma Marie (Friedmann) G.; m. Roger Andrew Andrachik, Apr. 24, 1987; children: Brett Gaughan, Kathryn Gaughan. BA, St. Mary's Coll., 1975; JD, U. Notre Dame, 1978. Bar: Ohio 1978, Ind. 1978. Asst. county pros. Cuyahoga County Pros. Office, Cleve., 1978-83, 84-87; asst. U.S. atty. U.S. Atty.'s Office, Cleve., 1983-84; assoc. Reid, Johnson, Downes, Andrachik & Webster, Cleve., 1984-87; judge Common Pleas Ct. Cuyahoga County, Cleve., 1987-96, exec. com., 1993-96; judge U.S. Dist. Ct. (no. dist.) Ohio, Eastern divsn., 1996—. Adj. prof. trial advocacy Cleve. Marshall Coll. of Law, 1983-87; mem. rules adv. com. Supreme Ct. of Ohio, Columbus, 1991-97; mem. paralegal studies adv. bd. Notre Dame Coll., Cleve., 1991—. Bd. dirs. Nat. Conf. Met. Cts., 1993—, Newburgh House of Hope, Cleve., 1994-96, Conflict Resolution Ctr., Cleve., 1995-98; mem. children's trust fund bd. Cuyahoga County Commrs., Cleve., 1984-92; v.p. Leukemia Soc., Lymphoma Soc. Mem. Ohio State Bar Assn., Ohio Jud. Conf. Assn., Cleve. Bar Assn. (trustee 1994-97), Cuyahoga County Bar Assn., Fed. Judges Assn., Fed. Cir. Bar Assn., Am. Judicature Soc., Common Pleas Ct. Judges Assn., Harold H. Burton Inn of Ct. (master of the bench 1991-96), Kappa Gamma Pi. Office: US Dist Ct 201 Superior Ave E Ste 202 Cleveland OH 44114-1201

GAU-KRUEGER, SUSAN MARIE, social worker; b. Wausau, Wis., Mar. 2, 1952; d. Michael Edward and Laura Theresa (Heil) Gau; m. Robert E. Krueger, Jr., May 23, 1987; children: Isaac Alexander, Ethan William. BS in Social Welfare and Polit. Sci., U. Wis., Eau Claire, 1973; MSW, U. Iowa, 1982. Lic. clin. social worker, Va.; lic. clin. social worker, Wis., 1995. Sch. social worker Gt. River Area Edn. Agy. 16, Burlington, Iowa, 1983; therapist Rappahannock Community Svcs. Bd., Fredericksburg, Va., 1984; infant specialist Alexandria (Va.) Community Svcs. Bd., 1984; family therapist Sch. for Contemporary Edn., Springfield, Va., 1984-85; spl. edn. guidance counselor Leary Sch., Alexandria, 1984-85; mental retardation specialist Rappahannock-Rapidan Community Svcs. Bd., Warrenton, Va., 1985-87, child specialist, 1987—94; pvt. practice psychotherapy Va., 1994—95; pvt. practice, 1995—. Sch. social worker Rappahannock Pub. Schs., 1994-95; childcare adv. bd., 1996-2002, aquatic adv. bd., 1999-2000, YMCA; co-chmn. pack adv. com. Boy Scouts Am., 1999-. Vol. South and North divs. Milwaukee County Hosp., Milw., 1974-77; den leader Boy Scouts Am., Wausau, 1977-78; bd. dirs. United Cerebral Palsy, Wausau, 1980-81. Mem. NASW, Am. Assn. Marriage and Family Therapy. Avocations: swimming, skiing, biking, handicrafts. Office: Alliance Couns Profls 2600 Stewart Ave Ste 270 Wausau WI 54401-1404 also: Melonas Counseling Ste 4 2801 E Main St Merrill WI 54452

GAUL, STUART CRAWFORD, lawyer; b. Olympia, Wash., Oct. 23, 1925; s. Adolph Carl Adam and Alice Mary (Crawford) G.; m. Joan Katherine Boffa, Oct. 5, 1963; children: Stuart Jr., Christopher P. BA, Reed Coll., 1948; LLB, Harvard U., 1951. Bar: N.Y. 1952, Wash. 1952, U.S. Dist. Ct. (so. dist.) N.Y. 1952, U.S. Customs Ct. 1961, Pa. 1977, U.S. Dist. Ct. (we. dist.) Pa. 1979, U.S. Supreme Ct. 1987. Assoc. White & Case, N.Y.C., 1951-56; sr. gen. atty. USX Corp., N.Y.C. and Pitts., 1956-86; asst. gen. counsel Aristech Chem. Corp., Pitts., 1986-90; of counsel Thorp, Reed, Armstrong, Pitts., 1991—2003. Sgt. U.S. Army, 1944-46, PTO. Democrat. Presbyterian.

GAULIN, JEAN, gas industry executive; b. Montreal, July 9, 1942; s. Paul and Bertha (Lariviere) Gaulin; m. Andrée LeBoeuf; children: Marie-Claude, Philippe, Mathieu. Student, St. Jean Royal Mil. Coll.; chem. engr., BSc., Ecole Polytechnique Montreal U., 1967. Dir. Que. Refinery of Canadian Ultramar Ltd., 1976—79; v.p. Golden Eagle Can., Montreal, 1977—79; v.p. supply and refining Ultramar Can. Inc., Toronto, 1979—80, pres., 1985—89, Nouveler Inc., Montreal, 1980—82; pres., COO Gaz Métropolitain, Inc., Montreal, 1982—85; CEO Ultramar PLC/Am. Ultramar, Ltd., 1989—92; chmn. bd., CEO Ultramar Corp., Greenwich, Conn., 1992—96; vice-chmn., pres., COO Ultramar Diamond Shamrock, San Antonio, 1996, corp. vice-chmn., pres., COO, 1997—99, CEO, 1999—. Bd. dirs. Scepter Resources Ltd., Ultramar PLC London, Quebec Tel., Ultramar Can., Inc. Bd. dirs. Internat. Ctr. for Rsch. and Studies in Mgmt., Montreal, 1982—, Found. de l'Universite du Quebec a Montreal, 1982—, Inst. de Cardiologie de Montreal, 1983—; pres. Telethon for Quebec Soc. Disabled Children, 1986. With Can. Navy, 1958—62. Mem.: Ordre des Ingénieurs du Que, Am. Gas Assn., Can. Gas Assn. (dir. 1982—), St. Denis Club. Office: Ultramar Diamond Shamrock Inc 6000 N Loop 1604 W San Antonio TX 78249

GAULKE, MARY FLORENCE, library administrator; b. Johnson City, Tenn., Sept. 24, 1923; d. Gustus Thomas and Mary Belle (Bennett) Erickson; m. James Wymond Crowley, Dec. 1, 1939; 1 son, Grady Gaulke (name legally changed); m. 22nd, Bud Gaulke, sept. 1, 1945 (dec. Jan. 1978); m. 3rd, Richard Lewis McNaughton, Mar. 21, 1983 (div. 1995). BS in Home Econs., Oreg. State U., 1963; MS in L.S., U. Oreg., 1968; Phd in Spl. Edn., 1970. Cert. std. pers. supr., std. handicapped learner, Oreg. Head dep. home econs. Riddle Sch. Dist. (Oreg.), 1963-66; libr., cons. Douglas County Intermediate Edn. Dist., Roseburg, Oreg., 1966-67; head resident, head counselor Prometheus Project So. Oreg. coll.ect, Ashland, summers 1966-68; supr. librs. Medford Sch. Dist. (Oreg.), 1970-73; instr. psychology So.Oreg. Coll., Ashland, 1970-73; libr. supr. Roseburg Sch. Dist., 1974-91; resident psychologist Black Oaks Boys Sch., Medford, 1970-75. Mem. Oreg. Gov.'s Coun. Librs., 1979. Author: Vo-Ed Course for Junior High, 1965; Library Handbook, 9167, Instructions for Preparation of Cards for All materials Cataloged for Libraries, 1971, Handbook for Training Library aides, 1972. Coord. Laubach Lit. Workshops for High Sch. Tutors, Medford, 1972. Fellow Internat. Biog. Assn. (life); mem. ALA, So Oreg. Libr. Fedn. (sec. 1971-73), Oreg. Libr. Assn., Pacific N.W. Libr. Assn., Am. Biog. Inst. (lifetime dep. gov. 1987—), Internat. Biog. Ctr. (hon., adv. coun. 1990), Delta Kappa Gamma (pres. 1980-82), Delta Kappa Gamma (pres. 1980-82), Phi Delta Kappa (historian, rsch. rep.). Democrat. Methodist. Office: 119 Orchard Ln Ashland OR 97520-9627 also: 15003 Birch St Long Beach WA 98631 also: 2604 Tower St Titusville FL 32796 Fax: 360-642-7093. E-mail: gg@willapabay.org.

GAULL, ERIK SAMUEL, municipal official; b. Atlanta, ., Oct. 3, 1961; s. Judith Kline Rosenthal, Gerald Edward Gaull, Michael Rosenthal (Stepfather); m. Karen Linwood Severy. AB, Columbia U., N.Y.C., 1985; MPP, Georgetown U., Washington, 1995; MBA, Georgetown U., 1998. Registered paramedic 1987. Editor Dem. Study Group, US Ho. of Reps., Washington, 1987—89; legis. dir. Office of Congressman Alan Wheat (D-MO), Washington, 1989—90; ops. mgr. N.Mex. Dept. Health, Santa Fe, 1990—93; sr. program mgr. TriData Corp., Arlington, Va., 1993—98, dir. local govt. studies, 1998—2000; dir. Operational Improvements Divsn., Office of the Dep. Mayor, Washington, 2000—. Adj. asst. prof. dept. emergency medicine George Washington U., Washington, 1998—; adj. faculty Nat. Fire Acad., Emmitsburg, Md., 1996—; editl. adv. bd. mem. Emergency Med. Svcs. Mag., Van Nuys, Calif., 1993—; edit. rev. bd. Prehosp. and Disaster Medicine, Madison, Wis., 1997—. Contbg. editor Emergency Care (6e), 1993. Pres. Palisades Citizens Assn., Washington, 2001—. Recipient Police and Fire-Rescue Svc. Meritorious award, Montgomery County, Md., 1991, "Erik Gaull Day" in the City of New York, Pres. of the Coun. of the City of New York, 1985; scholar Ben Franklin Mem. Medal scholar, Internat. Assn. of Fire Chiefs, 1994, 1997. Office: Office of the Deputy Mayor 1350 Pennsylvania Ave NW Washington DC 20004

GAULT, JEFFREY WAYNE, information technology executive; b. Kansas City, Mo., Sept. 10, 1948; s. Wayne Clark and Phyllis Gault; m. Rose Godefroy, Mar. 21, 1974; children: Jacqueline Hickenbottom, John C., Claire J. BS, U.S. Mil. Acad., 1970; MPA, U. Okla., 1977; MA in German Lang. and Lit., Middlebury Coll., 1979; MA in Nat. Security and Strategic Studies, U.S. Naval War Coll., 1991. Commd. 2d lt. U.S. Army, 1970, advanced through grades to col.; comdr. 4th Battalion, 1st AD Artillery, Neubruecke, Germany, 1987—89; dep. comdr. 11th Air Def. Brigade, Riyadh, Saudi Arabia, 1990—91; dir. dept. tactics U.S. Air Def. Sch., Ft. Bliss, Tex., 1991—94; comdr. U.S. Army Forces, Dhahran, Saudi Arabia, 1993—94, U.S. Army Garrison, Ft. Bliss, 1994—96; chief of staff U.S. Army, Ft. Bliss, 1996—99, ret., 1999; program mgr., sr. cons. Computer Sci. Corp., Arlington, Va., 1999—2002; exec. Boeing Co., 2002—. State dir. Vets. for Earley for Gov., Richmond, Va., 2001; county chmn., mem. state steering com. Vets. for George Bush, Farifax County, Va., 2000; bd. dirs. El Paso (Tex.) Sch. Dist. Fund, El Paso, 1996—99, Yucca Coun. Boy Scouts Am., El Paso, 1995—99, Greater El Paso C. of C., El Paso, 1996—99. Decorated Cross of Honor Govt. of Germany; recipient Mayor's award for civic leadership, Office of Mayor, El Paso, 1999. Mem.: VFW, DAV. Republican. Presbyterian. Home: 7430 Spring Summit Rd Springfield VA 22150 Office: Boeing Corp 1421 Jefferson Davis Hwy Arlington VA 22202

GAULT, ROSETTE FORD, artist, writer, composer, inventor; b. N.Y.C., 1951; BA in Comm., U. Colo., 1975; MFA in Ceramics, U. Puget Sound, 1978. Acting dir. Pottery N.W., Seattle, 1986; instr. ceramics Oreg. Coll. Arts and Crafts, Portland, 1993-94. Artist-in-residence Banff (Can.) Centre for Arts, 1990-91, 98, 99, 2002; spkr. in field. Author: Paperclay for Ceramic Sculptors, 1993, 3d edit., 2003, Paper Clay, 1998, 2d edit., 2003; exhibited in numerous group shows; patentee in field; contbr. articles to profl. jours. Mem. Wash. Potters Assn. (sec. 1988-89), N.W. Designer Craftsmen, Coll. Art Assn. Office: New Century Arts Inc PO Box 9060 Seattle WA 98109-0060

GAULTNEY, JOHN ORTON, life insurance agent, consultant; b. Pulaski, Tenn., Nov. 7, 1915; s. Bert Hood and Grace (Orton) G.; m. Elizabethine Mullette, Mar. 30, 1941; children: Elizabethine G. McClure, John Mullette, Walker Orton, Harlow Denny. Student, Am. Inst. Banking, 1936; diploma, Life Ins. Agy. Mgmt. Assn., 1948, Little Rock Jr. Coll., 1950; Mgmt. C.L.U. diploma, 1952; grad. sales mgmt. and mktg., Rutgers U., 1957. CLU. With N.Y. Life Ins. Co., 1935—, regional v.p., 1956-64, v.p. N.Y.C., 1964-67, v.p. in charge group sales, 1967-68, v.p. mktg., 1969-80, agt., 1980—; life ins. cons., 1981—. V.p. N.Y. Life Variable Contracts Corp., 1969-80; hon. dir. Bank of Frankewing (Tenn.), 1984— Elder Presbyn. Ch., 1952; chmn. Downtown YMCA, Atlanta, 1963-65; mem. Bd. Zoning Appeals, Bronxville, N.Y., 1970-80; mem. Nashville YMCA, 1981—; mem. pub. rels. com. Nat. Coun. YMCAs, 1965-80; mem. internat. world svc. com. YMCA, 1968-80; chmn. Vanderbilt YMCA, N.Y.C., 1974-76, bd. dirs., 1966-76; bd. dirs. Memphis YMCA, 1939-40, Little Rock YMCA, 1941-55, Atlanta YMCA, 1959-65, chmn. downtown, 1962-63; bd. dirs. Greater N.Y. YMCA, 1975-80, chmn. fund drive, 1972; dir. Internat. Assn. Y's Men's Clubs, 1936-42. Capt. inf. AUS, 1942-45, MTO. Decorated Silver Star, Bronze Star with 3 clusters, Purple Heart with 2 clusters.; recipient Devereux C. Josephs award N.Y. Life Ins. Co., 1954, Cross of Mil. Svc., UDC, 1973; named Ark. Traveler, 1955; hon. citizen Tenn., 1956; Tenn. Amb., 1981-87; Ky. col., 1963; inducted into Tenn. Ins. Hall of Fame, 2001. Mem. Am. Soc. CLUs, Tenn. Soc. CLUs, Ark. Soc. CLUs (pres. 1950-51), Nat. Assn. Life Underwriters, Heritage Found., Carnton Assn. (bd. dirs. 1981-90, pres. 1987-88), N.Y. So. Soc. (trustee 1965-80), Williamson County Hist. Soc. (pres. 1983-85), Brentwood Hist. Trust, Giles County Hist. Soc., 361st Inf. Assn. World War II (pres. 1967-70), Mass. Soc. of the Cin., SAR (N.Y. state dir. 1970-80), Soc. Colonial Wars, Descendants of Colonial Clergy, Tenn. Sons of Revolution, Assn. Preservation Tenn. Antiquities (trustee 1984-93), Tenn. Soc. in N.Y. (pres. 1971-74, trustee 1980-85), Newcomen Soc. in Am., English Speaking Union, Capital City Club (Atlanta), Nashville City Club, Victory Svcs. Club (London), Nat. Sojourners (pres. 2000-2001), Heroes of '76 (comdr. 1993-94), Sovereign Mil. Order of the Temple of Jerusalem, Rotary, Masons, Shriners, Jesters. Home: 6109 Johnson Chapel Rd Brentwood TN 37027-5720 Office: NY Life Ins Co Bank of America Plaza 17th Fl Nashville TN 37219-1606 E-mail: tjgaultney@webtv.net.

GAUNAURD, GUILLERMO C. physicist, engineer, researcher; b. Havana, Cuba, July 19, 1940; arrived in U.S., 1961; s. Celestino Carlos and Ana Marie (Herrera) G.; m. Marlene Jane Johnson, June 10, 1967. AB in Math., Cath. U. Am., Washington, 1964; BSME, Cath. U. Am., 1966, MS, 1967, PhD, 1971. Cons. engr. Ocean Systems Inc. (div. Union Carbide), Arlington, Va., 1966-68; sr. cons. engr. Litton Industries Inc., College Park, Md., 1968-71; rsch. physicist, sci. and tech. materials dept. Naval Surface Warfare Ctr., White Oak and Carderock Divsns., West Bethesda, Md., 1971-2000; sr. physicist, directorate sensors and electron devices Army Rsch. Lab., Adelphi, Md., 2001—. Lectr. U. Md. Sch. Engring., College Park, 1983-92, Cath. U. Am. Sch. Engring., Washington, 1974-78. Contbr. over 400 articles to profl. jours., chpts. to books and conf. procs.; patentee in field. Mem. Randolph Hills Civic Com., Rockville, Md., 1971—. Recipient various publ. awards and sci. excellence medals; grantee Office Naval Rsch., 1967—; Fellow Nat. Defense Edn. Act, 1967-70. Fellow ASME, IEEE (editor IEEE Jour. Oceanic Engring. 1987—, assoc. editor IEEE Jour. Ultrasonics, Ferroelectrics and Frequency Control 1992—), Acoustical Soc. Am. (various offices, assoc. editor Linear Acoustics 2002—), Washington Acad. Scis.; mem. AIAA, Philos. Soc. Washington, Optical Soc. Am., Internat. Union Math. Physics, Am. Acad. Mechanics, Washington Soc. Engrs., N.Y. Acad. Scis., Sigma Xi, Tau Beta Pi. Avocations: photography, classical music. Home: 4807 Macon Rd Rockville MD 20852-2348 Office: Army Rsch Lab Code AMSRL-SE-RU Microwaves Br 2800 Powder Mill Rd Adelphi MD 20783-1197 Fax: 301-394-4690. E-mail: ggaunaurd@arl.army.mil., electron20@aol.com.

GAUNCE, MICHAEL PAUL, insurance company executive; b. Paris, Ky., Oct. 17, 1949; s. Paul D. and Mary E. (Gardner) G.; m. Annette Beauchamp. BA, U. Ky., 1971. Cert. Life Underwriters Tng. Coun. Agt., mgr. Equitable Life of N.Y., Lexington, Ky., 1972-74; agt., regional mgr. Assn. Ins. Marketers, Inc., Indpls., Cin., South Bend, Ind., 1974-77; pres., chmn. Ins. Corp. Am., Indpls., 1977—. Chmn. bd. Argent Ins. Corp., Indpls., Alternative Healthcare Marketers, Inc., Indpls.; dir., past chmn. Brokers Ins. Corp., Indpls.; dir. Brokers Ins. Corp. Tenn., Nashville, Brokers Ins. Agy., Atlanta; dir., Brokers Ins. Corp., Ky., Agy. Mgmt. Corp., Indpls.; cons. adv. bd. Blue Cross/Blue Shield, Indpls., 1982-89; mem. adv. bd. Acordia, Inc., Indpls., 1996-98; mem. adv. group Trustmakr Ins. Co., 2000. Active Rep. Nat. Com. Mem. Ind. Assn. Employee Benefit cons. (pres. 1984-88), Elks, Greenwood C. of C., Franklin C. of C., Seymour C. of C. Republican. Avocations: fishing, swimming, reading, investments, travel. Office: Ins Corp Am 5140 Commerce Cir Indianapolis IN 46237-9744

GAUNT, JANET LOIS, arbitrator, mediator; b. Lawrence, Mass., Aug. 23, 1947; d. Donald Walter and Lois (Neuhart) Bacon; children: Cory C., Andrew D. BA, Oberlin Coll., 1969; JD, Wash. U., St. Louis, 1974. Bar: Wash. 1974, U.S. Dist. Ct. (we. dist.) Wash. 1974, U.S. Ct. Appeals (9th cir.) 1978. Assoc. Davis, Wright, Todd, Riese & Jones, Seattle, 1974-80; arbitrator/mediator Seattle, 1981—. Dir. Seattle King County Labor Law Sect., 1976-77; mem. Pacific Coast Labor Law Planning Com., 1977-83; com. vice chmn. Wash. State Task Force on Gender and Justice on the Cts., 1987-89; chmn. Wash. Pub. Employment Rels. Commn., Olympia, 1989-96. Author, editor: Alternative Dispute Resolution, 1989; author: Public Sector Labor Mediation and Arbitration, Arbitration and Mediation in Washington, 2d edit., 1995. Recipient Pass the Torch award, Wash. Women Lawyers, 1999. Mem. Nat. Acad. Arbitrators (dir. rsch. and edn. found. 1991-96, bd. govs. 1998-2001, v.p. 2002—), Am. Arbitration Assn., Wash. State Bar Assn., Wash. Women Lawyers (state co-pres. 1986). E-mail: j.gaunt@comcast.net.

GAUS, CLIFTON R. healthcare executive; MHA, U. Mich.; ScD, Johns Hopkins U. Mem. faculty Johns Hopkins U. Sch. Pub. Health, Balt., Georgetown U. Med. Sch., Washington; assoc. adminstr. policy, planning and rsch. Health Care Financing Adminstrn.; former adminstr. Agy Health Care Policy amd Rsch. HHS; sr. v.p. for R & D, Kaiser Permanente, Oakland, Calif.; exec. vice pres., chief admin. ofcr. Well Point Health Networks, Inc., Thousand Oaks, Calif. Co-founder, past pres., bd. dirs. Assn. Health Svcs. Rsch. Office: Well Point Health Networks Inc One Well Point Way Thousand Oaks CA 91362

GAUS, DAVID SHEERIN, publisher; b. Indpls., Aug. 4, 1943; s. Arthur Richard and Laura Sheerin Gaus. BA in Zoology, U. Chgo., 1964; MA in Biology Northwestern U., 1965. Chmn., CEO D.S. Gaus Corp., Indpls., 1983—. Pub., writer (newsletter) Sci-Notes, 1981—. Vol. Peace Corps, 1965-67. Avocations: physical fitness, walking, cooking. Home and Office: 5345 E Washington St Apt 36 Indianapolis IN 46219-6442 E-mail: gausdavids@yahoo.com.

GAUSS, JOHN A. federal agency assistant secretary, retired naval officer; b. Salem, Mass. BS in Engring. and Physics, Cornell U., 1969; M of Philosophy, Naval Postgrad. Sch., 1976, PhD in Electronics Engring. Commd. ensign USN, 1969, advanced through ranks to rear adm.; various assignments to comdr. Def. Info. Systems Agy., Arlington, Va., 1994-97; dir. Allied & Fleet Requirements Divsn. Space, Info. Warfare Command & Control Directorate, Washington, 1997—2001; asst. secy. and chief info. officer for info. and tech. U.S. Dept. Veterans Affairs, Washington, 2001—. Decorated Def. Disting. Svc. medal, Legion of Merit (3 times), Meritorious Svc. medal, Navy Achievement medal. Office: US Dept Veterans Affairs Info and Tech 810 Vermont Ave NW Washington DC 20420 Office Fax: 202-273-8800.

GAUSS, KARL FREDERIK, internist, educator, geriatrician; b. Elmira, N.Y., July 19, 1956; s. Louis H. and Agnes L. (Yacubic) G.; m. Paula A. Tuite, Aug. 14, 1982; children: Erich Louis, Kurt William, Elsa Katarina. BS in Biology summa cum laude, SUNY, Geneseo, 1981; MD with honors, SUNY, Syracuse, 1985. Diplomate Am. Bd. Internal Medicine, Am. Bd. Geriat. Resident in internal medicine SUNY Health Sci. Ctr., Syracuse, 1985—88, asst. clin. instr. dept. internal medicine, 1988—95, clin. asst. prof., 1995—; pvt. practice Cortland, NY, 1988—; med. dir. Cortland Meml. Nursing Facility, Cortland, 1997—; chmn. dept. geriat. Cortland Meml. Hosp., Cortland, 2001—, chmn. dept. medicine, 2002—; chmn. dept. geriat., 2002—. Pres. PHI Aeromed. Cons., Inc., Cortland, 1989-95; attending physician, mem. med. staff Cortland Meml. Hosp., 1988—, chmn. dept. internal medicine, 1989-93; dir., staff physician Moravia (N.Y.), Health Ctr., 1992-93; cons. physician Tully (N.Y.) Hill Drug and Alcohol Rehab. Ctr., 1990-92; aviation med. examiner Cortland County, 1988—; profl. and sci. presenter in field. Exhibited photography in group shows Everson Art Mus., Syracuse, 1986, N.Y. State Fair, Syracuse, 1992. Fellow ACP; mem. Am. Geriat. Soc., Flying Physicians Assn. (bd. dirs. 1994), N.Y. State Med. Soc. (Cortland county del. 1988—), Cortland County Med. Soc. (pres. 1992—), Aircraft Owners and Pilots Assn, Harley Owners Group, Porsche Club of Am. Republican. Avocations: sailing, flying, high performance driving, motorcycling. Office: Cortland Internist Assocs 6 Euclid Ave Ste H Cortland NY 13045-1291

GAUSTAD, EDWIN SCOTT, historian, educator; b. Rowley, Iowa, Nov. 14, 1923; s. Sverre and Norma (McEachron) G.; m. Helen Virginia Morgan, Dec. 19, 1946; children— Susan, Glen Scott, Peggy Lynn. BA, Baylor U., 1947; MA, Brown U., 1948, PhD, 1951. Instr. Brown U., 1951-52, Am. Council Learned Socs. scholar in residence, 1952-53; dean Shorter Coll., 1953-57; prof. humanities U. Redlands, 1957-65; assoc. prof. history U. Calif., Riverside, 1965-67, prof., 1968-89, prof. emeritus, 1989; prof. Princeton (N.J.) Theol. Sem., 1991-92, Auburn U., 1993, Vis. prof. Baylor U., 1976, U. Calif., Santa Barbara, 1986, U. Richmond, 1987. Author: The Great Awakening in New England, 1957, New Historical Atlas of Religion in America, new edit., (with P.L. Barlow), 2001, Religious History of America, revised edit., (with Leigh E. Schmidt), 2002, Dissent in American Religion, 1973, Baptist Piety: The Last Will and Testimony of Obadiah Holmes, 1978, George Berkeley in America, 1979, Faith of Our Fathers, 1987, Liberty of Conscience: Roger Williams in America, 1991, Revival, Revolution, and Religion in Early Virginia, 1994, Sworn on the Altar of God: A Religious Biography of Thomas Jefferson, 1996, Church and State in America, 1998, 2d edit., 2003, Memoirs of the Spirit, 1999, Roger Williams: Prophet of Liberty, 2001. Served to 1st lt. USAAC, 1943-45. Decorated Air medal; Am. Council Learned Socs. grantee, 1952-53, 72-73; Am. Philos. Soc. grantee, 1972-73 Mem. Am. Soc. Ch. History (pres.), Orgn. Am. Historians, Phi Beta Kappa. Democrat. Baptist. Home: 599 Vista De La Ciudad Santa Fe NM 87501-6300 E-mail: egaustad@aol.com.

GAUTHIER, ABBIE GAIL, administrative assistant, writer; b. Lafayette, La., Apr. 1, 1961; d. Ray Gene Monceaux and JoAnn Perry; m. Samuel Gayle Gauthier, Dec. 30, 1978; 1 child, Dustin Cole. Student, McNeese State U. Babysitter, house cleaning, Egan, La., 1975—77; office clk. Iota High Sch., 1978—79; bookkeeper, purchasing agt. Acadia Savs. & Loan, Crowley, 1979—90; teller Bank Commerce & Evangeline, 1991—92; substitute tchr. Acadia Parish Sch. Bd., 1993—94; processing clk., sec. H&R Block/1st Presbyn. Ch., 1994—; para-educator Acadia Parish Sch. Bd., 1994—2002; adminstrv. asst. Farm Bur., Jennings, 2003—. Author: Pierre The Cajun Frog. Tchr. St. Michael's Cath. Ch., Egan, 1987—89. Avocations: writing, reading, cooking.

GAUTHIER, BERNARD GUSTAVE, pediatric nephrologist, educator; b. Paris, May 2, 1934; came to U.S., 1970; s. Gustave and Odette (Bernadoy) G.; m. Jellie Bosma, Dec. 22, 1964; children: Philippe, Jean-Paul. MB, BS, U. Sydney, Australia, 1962. Diplomate Am. Bd. Pediatrics, Am. Bd. Pediatric Nephrology. Intern Bankstown Dist. Hosp., Sydney, 1962-63; intern in pediatrics Royal Alexandra Hosp. for Children, Sydney, 1964; resident Prince of Wales Children's Hosp., Sydney, 1965-68; fellow in pediatric nephrology SUNY Health Scis. Ctr., Bklyn., 1970-72; staff pediatrician Prince of Wales Children's Hosp., Sydney, 1968-70; nephrologist SUNY Health Scis. Ctr., Bklyn., 1972-73, chief pediatric nephrology, 1973-75, asst. prof. pediatrics, 1973-75, asst. prof. Stony Brook, 1975-89; chief pediatric nephrology Schneider Children's Hosp. North Shore L.I. Jewish Health Sys., New Hyde Park, NY, 1975-94, pediatric nephrologist, 1995—; asst. prof. pediatrics, Albert Einstein Coll. Medicine, Bronx, N.Y., 1989-90, assoc. prof. pediatrics, 1990-95, prof. pediatrics, 1995—; chief emeritus Schneider Children's Hosp., 2000—. Cons. Institutional Rev. Bd. N.Y., N.Y.C., 1992—. Author: (with others) Nephrology and Urology for Pediatricians, 1982; editor Pediatric Nephrology Update, 1987-97, Children's Hosp. Quarterly, 1989-2000, Pediatric Nephrology, 1998. Fellow Royal Australasian Coll. Physicians. Avocations: music (cello), reading, travel. Home: 45 Mason Dr Manhasset NY 11030-2006 E-mail: gauthier@lij.edu., Bernardg@optonline.net.

GAUTHIER, CELESTE ANNE, lawyer; b. New Orleans, Oct. 25, 1969; d. Wendell Haynes and Anne (Barrios) G.; 1 child, Trenton Michael; m. Michael F. Balluff, Jan. 1, 2000. BA in Sociology, U. New Orleans, 1992; JD, Loyola U., New Orleans, 1995. Bar: La. 1996, U.S. Dist. Ct. (ea. dist.) La. 1996, U.S. Ct. Appeals (5th cir.) 1996. Law clk. Gauthier & Murphy, Metairie, La., 1992-95; law clk. to Hon. Judge Burns 24th Jud. Dist. Ct., Gretna, La., 1996, law clk. to Hon. Judge Sullivan, 1997-98; assoc. Gauthier, Downing, LaBarre, Dean & Sulzer, Metairie, La., 1998—, The Gauthier Law Firm, Metairie. Advocate Jeff 25, Jefferson, La., 1997—. Mem. Young Dems. Am., 1995—, St. Catherine of Siena Parish, Metairie, 1994—. Mem.: ABA, ATLA, Young Leadership Coun., La. Trial Lawyers Assn. (chair People's Law Sch. spring 1999, coun. dirs. 2001—03, ho. of dels. 24th jud. dist. 2003—), New Orleans Bar Assn., Jefferson Bar Assn. (treas. young lawyers sect. 1998—99, chair 2000—01, ho. of dels. 24th jud. dist. 2003—), La. State Bar Assn. (young lawyers dist. 2 rep. 1998—2002), La. Bar Found., Fed. Bar Assn., Country Day Parents Assn. (young leadership coun. 1998—2002, Jefferson chamber 1998—, Jefferson young leaders 2001—). Democrat. Roman Catholic. Avocations: spending time with my son, skiing, reading, walking, culinary interests. Office: Gauthier Downing LaBarre Dean Sulzer 3500 N Hullen St Metairie LA 70002-3420 E-mail: celeste@gauthier-downing.com.

GAUTHIER, DOREEN ANN, librarian; b. Davenport, Iowa, July 18, 1941; d. Clifford H. and Dorothy H. Wildman; m. William E. Gauthier, July 18, 1989. BA, Midland Coll., Fremont. Nebr., 1972; grad. cert., U. Omaha, 1972; MA, U. South Fla., 1996. Children's libr. Keene Meml. Libr., Fremont, Nebr., 1967-77; circulation libr. Pompano Beach (Fla.) Libr., 1978-79; libr. dir. Lighthouse Point (Fla.) Libr., 1979—. Dir. Fla. Pub. Libr. Assn., Lakeland, 1992—98. Mem. ALA, Fla. Libr. Assn., Broward County Libr. Assn. Episcopalian. Home: 1990 NE 32nd Ct # 44 Lighthouse Point FL 33064-7684 Office: Lighthouse Point Library 2200 NE 38th St Ste A Lighthouse Point FL 33064-3913

GAUTHIER, SERGE GASTON, neurologist; b. Montreal, Que., Can., Sept. 18, 1950; s. Gaston and Suzanne (Tremblay) G.; m. Louise Gauthier; children: Eric, Judith. BA, Coll. Ste-Marie, 1969; MD, U. Montreal, 1973; neurology, McGill U., 1977. Fellow Med. Rsch. Coun. Can., 1976-78; staff Montreal Neurol. Hosp. and Inst., 1978-86; dir. McGill Ctr. for Studies in Aging, Verdun, 1987-97, dir. Alzheimer unit, 1997—. Contbr. articles on treatment of Alzheimer's disease to med. jours. Office: McGill U Ctr Studies Aging 6825 Blvd La Salle Verdun QC Canada H4H 1R3 E-mail: serge.gauthier@mcgill.ca.

GAUTIER, DICK, actor, writer; b. Los Angeles, Oct. 30, 1937; s. Aldoma Napoloeon and Marie Antionette Gautier; children: Christine, Rand, Denise. Student pub. schs., Los Angeles. Comedian, hungry i, San Francisco; appeared in N.Y.C. supper clubs including Blue Angel, Bonsoir, Coconut Grove; starred on Broadway as Conrad Birdie in Bye Bye Birdie, 1960-62 (Tony award and Most Promising Actor nominee); appeared in motion pictures including Billy Jack Goes to Washington, Divorce, American Style, Ensign Pulver, Manchu Eagle, Fun with Dick and Jane; played Hymie in series Get Smart; starred in TV series Mr. Terrific, CBS, It's Your Bet, NBC, Can You Top This?, Here We Go Again, ABC; starred as Robin Hood in TV series When Things Were Rotten, ABC, 1975; author: The Art of Caricature, 1985, The Creative Cartoonist, 1988, The Career Cartoonist, 1992, Actors as Artists, 1992, Drawing and Cartooning 1001 Faces, A Child's Garden of Weirdness, 3 books art instrn., 1992, Musicians as Artists, 1994; (screenplay) Uncle Sam; contbg. writer to numerous TV situation comedies; composer numerous songs. Active in Thalians Charity. Served with Spl. Services br. USN. Mem. Actors Equity Assn., AFTRA, Screen Actors Guild, ASCAP, Am. Guild Variety Artists. Office: 11333 Moorpark St Studio City CA 91602 2618 E-mail: DICK@DICKGAUTIER.com.

GAUTIER, GARY, writer; b. New Orleans, Nov. 20, 1956; s. Camille Gautier; 1 child, Rachael. MA, U. Tex., 1985; PhD, U. Colo., 1993. Instr. U. Colo., Boulder, 1987—98, La. State U., Baton Rouge, 1998—99, U. New Orleans, New Orleans, 1999—2000; sr. tech. writer Penta Corp., New Orleans, 2001—. Dir. Statewide Outreach Essay Contest, Colo., 1997—98. Author: (children's book) Spaghetti and Peas, Landed Patriarchy in Fielding's Novels; editor: A Practical Guide to Hazardous Waste Management, Administration and Compliance. Vol. Whittier Elem., Boulder, Colo., 1996—97, Gentilly Ter. Elem. Sch., New Orleans, 2000; grader La. State Lit. Rally, Baton Rouge, 1999. Recipient Juvenile Fiction Julia Collier award, Deep South Writers Conf., 1996. Mem.: Audubon Nature Inst. Avocations: marathon runner, theater, travel. Home: 4314 Toulouse St New Orleans LA 70119 Personal E-mail: ggautier1@cox.net.

GAUVEY, RALPH EDWARD, educational consultant; b. Greenville, Ohio, Mar. 3, 1929; s. Ralph A. and Irene Gauvey; m. Frances Jean Horswell, Sept. 18, 1949; children: Ralph Jr., Debra Lou, John. PhD, Ohio State U., 1961. Pres. Urbana (Ohio) U., 1953-63, Roger Williams U., Bristol, R.I., 1963-80; dean, prof. N.Y. Inst. Tech., Old Westbury, 1980-97; cons. Thomas H. Langevin Assocs., Lady Lake, Fla., 1996—. Author: Foundations of Education, 1986, Off Campus Learning, 1988, Liberal Arts-The Keystone, 1990. Chmn. Gov.'s Commn. on Ednl. TV, R.I. Com. for Humanities. Home: 3910 Santa Clara Fort Myers FL 33903 E-mail: emailx379@cs.com.

GAUVEY, SUSAN KATHRYN, judge; b. Van Wert, Ohio, Mar. 1, 1948; d. Richard David and Asta Walburga (Frericks) G.; m. David E. Kern, May 10, 1975; children: Megan E. Gauvey-Kern, Kevin C. Gauvey-Kern, Elizabeth H. Gauvey-Kern. Student, Georgetown U., 1968-69; BA cum laude Polit. Sci., Rosary Coll, River Forest, Ill., 1970; JD, Northwestern U., 1973; postgrad. Mental Hygiene, Johns Hopkins U., 1976-77. Bar: Wash. 1974, Md. 1975. Law clerk to fed. dist. ct. judge We. Dist. Ct., Seattle, Wash., 1973-74; staff atty. Mental Health Law Project Legal Aid Bur., Balt., 1975-77, chief Mental Health Law Project, 1977-79; asst. atty. gen. Dept. Health and Mental Hygiene Office of Atty. Gen., Balt., 1979-81, asst. atty. gen. Civil Divsn., 1981-86, prin. counsel trial litigation, 1984-86; with litigation divsn. Venable, Baetjer and Howard L.L.P., Balt., 1986-96; magistrate judge U.S. Dist. Ct. for Md., Balt., 1996—. Contbr. articles to profl. jours. Chair bd. dirs. Marian House for Women. Mem. Nat. Assn. Women Judges, Wranglers Law Club, Lawyers' Roundtable. Democrat. Office: US Courthouse 101 W Lombard St Baltimore MD 21201-2605

GAVALAS, ALEXANDER BEARY, artist; b. Limerick, Ireland, Jan. 6, 1945; came to U.S., 1946; s. Emmanuel Zenon and Mary (Beary) G. Diploma, Sch. Art & Design, N.Y.C., 1963; student Guilmant Organ Sch., 1970, Kerpel Sch. Dental Tech., 1972; BA, Coll. New Rochelle, 1995. Cert. 20th Century Hudson River Artist. One man shows at Krasl Art Ctr., St. Joseph Mich., 1980, The Tweed Mus. Art, U. Minn., Duluth, 1980, Fine Arts Center of Clinton, Ill., 1980, Western Ill. U. Library Gallery, Macomb, 1981, Ft. Wayne Mus. Art, Ind., 1982, Mary Crest Coll., Eberdt Art Gallery, Davenport, Iowa, 1982, Arnot Art Mus., Elmira, N.Y., 1982, Queens Coll. Art Ctr., Flushing, N.Y., 1983; exhibited in group shows Taft Hotel, N.Y.C., 1964, J. Walter Thompson Art Gallery, N.Y.C., 1964, Hudson River Mus., Yonkers, N.Y., 1974-75, Far Gallery, N.Y.C., 1976-79, Eric Galleires, N.Y.C., 1981-82, Served as Art Juror for NYC Scholastic Art Awds., Scholastic, Inc., NYC, 1999. Contbr. articles to profl. jours. Juror N.Y.C. Scholastic Art award, 1999. Honorable mention Congl. record 88th congress for cultural contbr. to Life or Nation, 1964, award for work on spl. file Smithsonian Inst. from Harry Rand. Address: 65 Horton St Malverne NY 11565-1512 E-mail: classics3@optonline.net.

GAVANDE, SAMPAT ANAND, agricultural engineer, soil scientist; b. Nasik, India, Mar. 1, 1936; came to U.S., 1960; s. Ananda Bala and Saraja G. Gavande; m. Shaila Sawant, Feb. 25, 1968; children: Neil, Vikram. MS in Agrl. Engring., Kans. State U., 1962; PhD in Soils, Irrigation and Drainage, Utah State U., 1966. Registered profl. engr., Tex.; cert. profl. soil scientist; cert. profl. agronomist. Tech. officer FAO, UN, Turrialba, Costa Rica, 1966-69, Chapingo, Mex., 1969-72, Saltillo, Mex., 1973-77, chief tech. advisor Rome and Asuncion, Paraguay, 1987-89; sr. scientist/engr. Radian Corp., Austin, Tex., 1977-82; hydrologist/sr. engr. Tex. Water Commn., Austin, 1983-87; chief tech. support br. Tex. Dept. Health, Austin, 1989-92; team leader Tex. Natural Resources Commn., Austin, 1992—. Cons. soil/water FAO, UN, Kenya, 1985, watershed cons., Chile, 1987, India, 1989, watershed mgmt. cons., Iran, 1989, Indonesia, 1990. Author: (textbook in Spanish lang.) Soil Physics and Its Applications, 1972; contbr. over 60 articles to tech. publs., 1968-77. Mem. Rep. Presdl. Task Force, Austin and Washington, 1989-91; bd. dirs. India Community Ctr., Inc., Austin, 1991—. Mem. ASTM, Am. Soc. Agrl. Engrs., Am. Soc. Soil Sci., Am. Soc. Agronomy. Achievements include design of cost-effective, renovative tillage, drainage land reclamation, solid and liquid waste management, soil and water conservation systems for arid, semi-arid and humid areas. Home and Office: c/o TNRCC 4501 Upvalley Ct Austin TX 78731-3666 E-mail: sam.gavande@worldnet.att.net.

GAVELIS, JONAS RIMVYDAS, dentist, educator; b. Boston, Jan. 11, 1950; s. Mykolas and Janina Gavelis; m. Bonnie Sylvester; children: Gregory, Nikolas. BS, U. Mass., Amherst, 1971; DMD, U. Conn., 1975. Resident in dentistry Cabrini Health Care Ctr., N.Y.C., 1975-76; fellow in prosthetic dentistry Sch. Dental Medicine Harvard U., Boston, 1976-78; asst. prof., 1982—; instr., 1978-79; asst. prof. Sch. Dental Medicine U. Conn., Farmington, 1979-82; practice dentistry specializing in prosthodontics Harvard Cmty. Health Plan, Boston, 1982-92, Rockport, Mass., 1991—. Contbr. articles on prosthetic dentistry to profl. jours. Fellow Acad. Gen. Dentistry (Vernon S. Johnson award 1981); mem. ADA, N.E. Prosthodontic Soc. (past pres.), Harvard Odontol. Soc. (pres.-elect), Am. Acad. Crown and Bridge Prosthodontics, Am. Coll. Prosthodontists, New Eng. Aquarium Dive (Boston), Cape Ann Sportsman's Club, Rotary, Omicron Kappa Upsilon. Roman Catholic. Home: 1238 Washington St Gloucester MA 01930-1056 Office: 227 Main St Rockport MA 01966-2024

GAVENCAK, JOHN RICHARD, pediatrician, allergist; b. Bklyn, June 21, 1949; m. Madeline Gavncak Aug. 12, 1972. BA, NYU, 1970; MD, N.Y. Med. Coll., Valhalla, 1974. Diplomate Am. Bd. Pediatrics, Am. Bd. Allergy and Immunology. Resident in pediats. Met. Hosp., N.Y.C., 1974-76, fellow in allergy and immunology, 1976-78; pvt. practice allergist East Rockaway, N.Y., 1976—. Fellow Am. Coll. Pediatrics, Am. Coll. Allergy and Immunology.; mem. N.Y. Allergy Soc., Long Island Allergy Soc. Avocations: fishing, gardening, boating. Office: John R Gavencak MD 53-42 Francis Lewis Blvd Bayside NY 11364 also: 400 E Atlantic Ave East Rockaway NY 11518

GAVERAS, HARRY, architect; b. N.Y.C., Feb. 9, 1971; s. Christos and Kyriaki Gaveras. BArch, Cooper Union U., 1993; MArch in Urban Design, Harvard U., 1997. Draftsman, project mgr. Alison Spear Arch., N.Y.C., 1993-95; mem. sr. design staff Karlsberger Arch., N.Y.C., 1998; project arch. Moser/Martocchio A&D, N.Y.C., 1999; pres. Propylaea Arch. Atelier, N.Y.C., 2000—. Co founder Founds. Design Internat., N.Y.C., 1993-97. Orpheus Assn. traveling grantee, 1992. Mem. Harvard Club N.Y.C. Avocations: painting, writing fiction, travel. Office: Propylaea Arch Atelier 330 Wadsworth Ave # 3D New York NY 10040 E-mail: gaveras@aol.com.

GAVEY, JAMES EDWARD, investment company executive; b. Buffalo, June 6, 1942; s. George W. and Clara E. (Hanley) G.; m. Joan M. Moran, June 6, 1964; children: Philip W., Peter J., John P. BS, LeMoyne Coll., 1964; MBA, Columbia U., 1965. Acct. Peat, Marwick, Mitchell & Co., Buffalo, 1960-64; bus. cons. Arthur Andersen & Co., N.Y.C., 1965-73; pres. Gavey & Co., Inc., N.Y.C., 1973-87; founder, 1988—; pres. Island Investment Realty, Marco Island, Fla., 1990—. Contbr. articles to profl. jours. Chmn. com. United Fund, Bronxville, N.Y., 1970—; commr. Tuckahoe (N.Y.) Housing Authority, 1974-76, chmn., 1976-81, capt. N.Y. ann. fund Fordham Prep. Sch., 1980-83. Recipient various achievement awards. Mem. AICPA, N.Y. State Soc. CPAs, Fla. Soc. CPAs, Nat. Assn. Rev. Appraisers, Internat. Inst. Valuers, Nat. Apt. Assn., Nat. Assn. Home Builders, Internat. Platform Assn., Newcomen Soc. N.Am., Rotary, Union League, Cooperstown Country Club. Republican. Roman Catholic. Home and Office: 218 Main St Cooperstown NY 13326 E-mail: Jim@Gavey.com.

GAVIAN, PETER WOOD, investment banker; b. Brewster, Mass., Dec. 8, 1932; s. Sarkis Peter and Ruth Millicent (Wood) G.; children: Sarah, Deborah Gavian Costolloe, Margaret Elizabeth. BA, Yale U., 1954; MBA, Harvard U., 1959. Chartered fin. analyst; USCG master's lic. Assoc. McKinsey & Co., N.Y.C., 1959-61; sec./treas. Greater Washington Investors, 1961-64, 70-71; v.p. fin. NUS Corp., Washington, 1965-66; asst. to group v.p. internat. Carborundum Co., Niagara Falls, N.Y., 1966-68; pvt. investment banker Washington, 1968—; pres. Corp. Fin. of Washington, Inc., 1976—. Expert witness in bus. valuation, 1980—; lectr. Am. U., Washington, 1978-80; trustee Calvert Group Funds, Bethesda, Md., 1980—; dir. Am. Civil Liberties Union Va., 1993-95. Contbr. articles to profl. jours. Vol. varsity sailing coach U.S. Naval Acad., 1981-89. Lt. USN, 1954-57. Mem. Washington Soc. Investment Analysts (pres. 1978-79), Am. Soc. Appraisers (pres. Washington chpt. 1998-99), Assn. Investment Mgmt. and Rsch. Avocation: sailboat racing. Home: 12 Spa Creek Landing Annapolis MD 21403 E-mail: peter.gavian@verizon.net.

GAVIN, DELANE MICHAEL, television writer, producer, director; b. Pierre, S.D., Oct. 6, 1935; s. Daniel Everett and Evelyn Agnes (Michaelson) G.; m. Paula Ethel Handelman, Feb. 22, 1969. BA in Journalism, San Francisco State U., 1962; MA in Journalism, UCLA, 1971; MBA in Organizational Behavior, U. So. Calif., 1982. With San Francisco Examiner, 1961-62; corr. AP, San Francisco, Reno and Las Vegas, Nev., 1962-64; reporter Las Vegas Rev.-Jour. Sun, 1964-65; editor suburban sect. Los Angeles Times, 1965-66; writer, producer news Sta. KNXT-TV, Hollywood, Calif., 1966-68; writer, reporter, dir., producer news Sta. KNBC-TV, Burbank, Calif., 1968-76; documentary writer, producer, dir. NBC-News, N.Y.C., 1976-78; med. producer KABC-TV, Hollywood, 1978—99. Instr. journalism U. So. Calif., 1978-90; sr. lectr. Calif. State U., Northridge, 1994-95. Served with USNR, 1955-57. Recipient Christopher award for directing Sta. NBC News TV The Christophers, 1973, for producing, 1976, Golden Mike award Radio and TV Assn., 1968, 69, 70, 72, 74, 75. Mem. Acad. TV Arts and Scis. (bd. govs. 1976-80, 82-86, 88-92, Emmy award 1968, 69, 70, 72, 73, 74), Dirs. Guild Am., Writers Guild Am., AFTRA, Nat. Assn. Broadcast Employees and Technicians, Wire Service Guild, Am. Newspaper Guild, Greater L.A. Press Club (bd. dirs. 1999—), Sigma Delta Chi. Home: 16635 Nanberry Rd Encino CA 91436-3209 E-mail: mikegavin35@aol.com.

GAVIN, DONALD GLENN, b. Newark, Oct. 12, 1942; s. Louis Brooks and Elizabeth (Nievert) Gavin; m. Irene Dunn, Nov. 25, 1965; children: Andrew Scott, Mitchell Bryant. BS in Econs., U. Pa., 1964, JD, 1967; LLM, George Washington U., 1972. Bar: Pa. 1967, D.C. 1972, Va. 1973. Law clk. Ct. Common Pleas, Phila., 1967—68; assoc. to ptnr. Lewis, Mitchell & Moore, Washington and Vienna, Va., 1972—74; founding ptnr. Wickwire, Gavin & Gibbs, P.C., Washington, L.A. and Vienna, 1974—. Lectr. in field. Contbr. articles to profl. jours. To capt. JAG U.S. Army, 1968—72. Mem.: ABA (mem. coun. pub. contract law sect., chmn. fed. grant legis., policies and remedies com., past chmn. grant coordination com., past chmn. environ. law com.), Phila. Bar Assn., Va. State Bar Assn., D.C. Ct. Claims Com., Fed. Bar Assn. Office: Wickwire Gavin International Gateway 8100 Boone Blvd Ste 700 Vienna VA 22182-7732

GAVIN, HENRI PHILIPPE, engineering educator, researcher; b. Lausanne, Switzerland, May 14, 1964; came to U.S., 1966; s. Paul Henri and Eleanor Bell (Ingram) G.; m. Robin Magee, Aug. 26, 1989. BS in Engring., Princeton U., 1986; MS in Engring., U. Mich., 1988, PhD, 1994. Lab. technician Princeton (N.J.) U., 1986-87, 89-91; rsch. asst. U. Mich., Ann Arbor, 1992-94, rsch. fellow, 1994-95; asst. prof. Duke U., Durham, NC, 1995—2002, assoc. prof., 2002—. Proposal reviewer NSF, Arlington, Va., 1996—. Career grantee NSF, 1995, Jr. Faculty Enhancement grantee Oak Ridge Assoc. U., 1996. Mem. ASCE (assoc.), Soc. Exptl. Mech., Sigma Xi (assoc.). Office: Duke U Dept Environ Engring Box 90287 Durham NC 27708

GAVIN, JAMES JOHN, JR., diversified company executive; b. Phila., July 18, 1922; s. James John and Mary E (Ludlow) G.; m. Zita C. Kabeschat, Aug. 23, 1952; children— William, James, Kevin, Steven, Peter. BS in Econs, U. Pa., 1949. Sr. acct. Peat, Marwick, Mitchell & Co., Phila., 1949-53; chief acct. Indian Head Mills, Inc. (name changed to Indian Head Inc.), N.Y.C., 1953, asst. treas., 1953-56, contr., 1956-61, treas., v.p., 1961-66, v.p. fin., 1966-68; v.p. fin., contr. Borg-Warner Corp., Chgo., 1968-75, sr. v.p. fin., 1975-85, vice-chmn., 1985-87. Served with USNR, 1943-46. Mem. Delta Sigma Pi, Beta Alpha Psi, Beta Gamma Sigma. Home: 161 Thorntree Ln Winnetka IL 60093-3731

GAVIN, JOAN ELAINE, special education educator; b. Onalaska, Wis., July 26, 1950; d. Vernon and Helen Ruth Weinberg; m. A.M. Gavin, June 13, 1986; stepchildren: John Edward, Daniel James, Mark Ambrose, Scott Michael. BS in Elem. Edn., U. Wis., La Crosse, 1973, MS in Spl. Edn., ED/LD, 1975. Cert. 1-8 elem. tchr., tchr. emotionally disturbed and learning disabled, Wis.; cert. crisis prevention intervention; cert. CPR. Tchr. emotionally disturbed and learning disabilities De Soto (Wis.) Area Schs., 1975-79; tchr. elem. emotionally disturbed coop. program Elroy-Kendall-Wilton Schs., Elroy, Wis., 1979-84, Wilton, Wis., 1984-86, Kendall, Wis., 1986-93, elem. tchr. Elroy, 1993-2000, Ithaca Schs., 2000—01; spl. edn. ED/LD tchr. Wonewoc (Wis.) Ctr. Schs., 2001—. Mem. dist.-wide insvc. com. Elroy-Kendall-Wilton Schs., 1986-2000, facilitator AODA program, mem. CORE com. AODA, 1994-2000, chairperson dist. wide insvc. com. 1997-2000. Developer, bd. dirs., treas. Kinship of Elroy, Inc., 1980-89; pres., coord. County-Wide Kinship, Kinship, Inc., 1984-94; active Kids for Kids. Honor scholar, 1968; grantee NSF Sci. Enhancement Project, U. Wis., 1985, 86, 88, 89, 90. Mem. Am. Legion Aux., U. Wis.-LaCrosse Alumni Assn. Avocations: collecting coins, stamps, antiques, depression and carnival dishes. E-mail: gavijoa@wc.k12.wi.us.

GAVIN, MARY ELLEN, consultant; b. Chgo. d. Francis Edward and Agnes Mary (Rolder) Des Enfants; m. William Francis Gavin; children: Michael James, Terence Francis. MBA, U. Palmers Green, Eng., 1999. Lic. pvt. investigator. Analyst A.C. Nielsen, Chgo.; asst. br. mgr. Borg-Warner Fin. Svc., Chgo.; asst. leasing mgr. Borg-Warner Leasing, Chgo., midwest leasing mgr.; v.p. Gen. Equipment Leasing, Chgo.; leasing mgr. Pitney Bowes Credit Corp., Chgo.; ind. rep. Gen. Elec. Mobile Radio & Tele., Chgo.; pres. Gavin Communications, Annapolis, Md.; owner Gavin & Assocs., Chantilly, Va. Adult edn. tchr. Fairfax County, 1996—, Nova C.C., 2000—. Author: And Still We Celebrate, 2001, We Celebrate the Macabre, 2002; editor: Post War Letter Messages From the Heart, 1997. Teaching asst. St. Timothy Sch., Chantilly, 1997-98. Mem.: The Writers of Chantilly (founder), Nat. Assn. Writers, Women in Mgmt., Wash. Ind. Writers, Internat. Women's Writing Guild, Associated Writing Program George Mason Univ., Nat. Writers Assn. Republican. Roman Catholic. Home and Office: 15227 Louis Mill Dr Chantilly VA 20151-1315 E-mail: megavin@erols.com.

GAVIN, MARY JANE, medical and surgical nurse; b. Prairie Du Chien, Wis., Sept. 1, 1941; d. Frank Grant and Mary Elizabeth Wolf; m. Alfred William Gavin, Nov. 9, 1963; children: Catherine Heidi Elizabeth, Carl Alfred Eric. Student, North Cen. Coll., Naperville, Ill., 1959-61; BS, RN, U. Wis., 1964; postgrad., Deepmuscle Tng. Ltd., 1980; postgrad. in deep muscle therapy. RN, Wis. Staff nurse U. Wis. Hosps., Madison; RN home response VA, Milw. Unit chair Badger Girls State, 1991—; mem. Wis. Am. Legion Aux.; mem. task force for handicapped Eastside Wis. Evang. Luth. Ch., Madison, 1993. U. Wis. scholar. Mem. Monona Grove Am. Legion Aux. (pres. Unit 429 1990—). Home: 702 Fairmont Ave Madison WI 53714-1424

GAVIN, ROBERT MICHAEL, JR., education consultant; b. Coatesville, Pa., Aug. 16, 1940; s. Robert Michael and Helen Regina (Finnegan) G.; m. Charlotte Marie Dugan, June 2, 1962; children— Anne, Patricia, Robert, Charles, Sean. BA, St. John's U., Collegeville, Minn., 1962; PhD, Iowa State U., 1966; DSc (hon.), Haverford Coll., 1986, St. John's U., 1996. Mem. faculty Haverford (Pa.) Coll., 1966-84, prof. chemistry, 1975-84, dir. computing, 1979-80, provost, dean faculty, 1980-84, interim pres., 1996-97; pres. Macalester Coll., St. Paul, 1984-96, Cran Brook Ednl. Cmty., Bloomfield Hills, Mich., 1997—2001; ret., 2001. Bd. dirs. Hartford Funds, SCT Corp., St. John's U., Minn. Author papers in field. Pres. Haverford Twp. Sch. Bd., 1975. Recipient Dreyfus Tchr.-Scholar award, 1973; NSF fellow, 1969-70 Democrat. Roman Catholic. Home: 751 Judd St Marine On Saint Croix MN 55047

GAVIRIA TRUJILLO, CESAR, international organization administrator, former president of Colombia, economist; b. Pereira, Colombia, Mar. 31, 1947; m. Ana Milena Muñoz Gómez; children: Simón, María Paz. BA in Econs., U. de Los Andes, Bogota; JD (hon.), U. Libre de Colombia, 1990; Degree (hon.), Northeastern U., 2002. Chief of planning Dept. of Risaralda, 1969; mem. council Pereira, 1970-74; asst. to chief Nat. Planning Dept., 1971-72; dir. Transformadores T.P.L., SA, 1972-73; mem. Ho. of Reps., 1974-90; mayor, 1975-76; dep. min. of devel. Republic of Colombia, Bogota, 1978-79; pres., third commn. Ho. of Reps., 1980-81, pres., 1983-84; adj. dir. Liberal Party, 1986; min. of fin. and pub. credit Republic of Colombia, Bogota, 1986-87, min. of interior, 1987-89, pres., 1990-94; sec. gen. Orgn. Am. States, 1994—. La Intervención del Estado en la Economía, Aspectos Políticos del Plan de Integración Nacional, Deuda Pública Latinoamericana; columnist El Tiempo. Recipient W. Averell Harriman Democracy award, 2002, Nat. Dem. Inst. Democracy award, 2002. Office: OAS Office of Secretary General 17th St and Constitution Ave NW Washington DC 20006

GAVRAS, CONSTANTIN See COSTA-GAVRAS

GAVRILOV, LEONID A. gerontologist; b. Sverdlovsk, Russia, Aug. 28, 1954; s. Anatoly M. and Ludmila L. G.; m. Natalia S. Tuchnina, Mar. 26, 1954; 1 child, Anna. PhD, Moscow State U., 1980. Profl. chemist, geneticist. Prin. rsch. scientist Moscow State U., 1980-97; rsch. assoc. NORC/U. Chgo., 1997—. Bd. mem. Experimental Gerontology, J. Anti-Aging Med., The Scientific World J. Author: The Biology of Life Span, 1991; referee: sci. jours. Recipient Ind. Scientist award Nat. Inst. on Aging, 2001. Mem. Gerontol. Soc. Am., Population Assn. Am., Internat. Union for the Scientific Study of Population. Office: Center on Aging NORC/Univ Chicago 1155 E 60th St Chicago IL 60637 E-mail: lagavril@midway.uchicago.edu.

GAVRITY, JOHN DECKER, insurance company executive; b. S.I., N.Y., Oct. 26, 1940; s. John S. and Eleanor R. (Decker) G.; m. Camille Appello, April 16, 1998; children: John, Joseph. BS, Wagner Coll., 1963. From staff to assoc. actuary U.S. Life, N.Y.C., 1963-74; from actuary to exec. v.p., fin. actuary USLIFE Corp., N.Y.C., 1975-97, exec. v.p., chief actuary, 1997-98, ret., 1998. Fellow Soc. Actuaries; mem. Am. Acad. Actuaries Republican. Roman Catholic. Home: 688 New Dorp Ln Staten Island NY 10306-4933

GAW, JAMES RICHARD, corporate executive; b. Bklyn., Sept. 2, 1943; s. James A. and Catharine (Clough) G.; m. Lorraine Osenbruk, July 21, 1973; children: Sean James, Joshua Timothy, Desiree Ann. BA, L.I. U., 1965; MA, St. John's U., 1967. Cert. Health Cons. Underwriter Royal-Globe Ins. Co., N.Y.C., 1969-70; rep. Blue Cross/Greater N.Y., N.Y.C., 1970-75; mktg. specialist Community Health Plan, Albany, N.Y., 1975-78; dir., mktg. support Blue Cross/Northeastern N.Y., Albany, 1978-82, sr. advisor to pres., 1982-84, dir. program svcs. Empire Blue Cross/Shield, N.Y.C., 1984-89, dir. records mgmt., 1989-90; dir. adminstrn. and facilities svcs., 1990-99; dir. corp. devel. Support Svcs. Alliance, Schoharie, N.Y., 1999-2001; v.p. ins. svcs. Support Svcs. Alliance, Inc., 2001—. N.Y. state project dir. Blue Cross Assn., Chgo., 1979-83; preceptor Union U., Schenectady, N.Y., 1980-82. V.p. Cath. Charities, Albany, 1983-88; gov. Adirondack Mountain Club, Inc., Glen Falls, N.Y., 1980-83; mem. Nat. Com. on Alcohol & Drugs, Chgo., Washington, 1980-82; pres. Schoharie Family & Community Svcs., Cobleskill, N.Y., 1976-78; coord. Health Info. Sharing Project, Albany, 1979-81. With USMC, 1967-69, Vietnam. Recipient Svc. Award Recognition Schoharie Family and Cmty. Svcs., 1988, Energy Conservation awrd Silverlight/Am. Energy Care, 1994; grantee Nat. Inst. Drug Abuse, 1981-83. Mem. Internat. Facilities Mgmt. Assn., Assn. Records Mgmt. and Administr., Bldg. Owners and Mgrs. Assn., Am. Inst. Arch. (affiliate), Schoharie County C. of C. (bd. dirs., treas. 2000—). Roman Catholic. Avocations: hiking, camping, photography, furniture design, bagpiping.

GAWF, JOHN LEE, foreign service officer; b. Salida, Colo., July 22, 1922; s. John and Gertrude (Bondurant) G.; m. Elizabeth Laflin, Dec. 31, 1950; children: Mary Anne, Katherine, Matilda, Anthony, Margaret, John Alan. BS, U.S. Naval Acad., 1945; MS, George Washington U., 1969. Instr. U. Colo., 1947-48; elec. engr. Bechtel Corp., San Francisco, 1948-50, TVA, Knoxville, Tenn., 1950-52; vice consul Fgn. Service, State Dept., Guadalajara, Mexico, 1954-56; policy info. officer Washington, 1956-57; internat. relations officer, 1957; officer-in-charge El Salvadoran affairs, 1958-59, Honduran affairs, 1958-60; consul Genoa, Italy, 1960-63; 1st sec. Am. Embassy, Caracas, Venezuela, 1963-65; 1st sec. Am. Embassy Ottawa, Ont., Can., 1965-68; detailed to Nat. War Coll., Washington, 1968-69, congl. relations officer, 1969-70; internat. relations officer Naples, Italy, 1970-74; consul gen. Belize City, Belize, 1974-78;

counselor Am. Embassy, Rome, 1978-82, minister counselor, 1981-83; detailed to Stanford U. Ctr. for Internat. Security and Arms Control, 1983-84; detailed to Armed Forces Staff Coll., 1984-87; cons. in field, 1987—. Served to lt. comdr. USNR, 1945-47, 52-54.

GAWRONSKI, ELIZABETH ANN, retired army officer; b. Panama City, Fla., Oct. 11, 1943; d. Myron Harvey Belyeu Sr. and Irene (Sewell) Belyeu Coates; m. Kenneth E. Gawronski Sr., Sept. 16, 1972; 1 child, Kenneth Edward Jr. BS in Edn., Fla. State U., 1965; MA in Edn., U. Ala., 1974, EdS, 1975. Commd. 2d lt. USAR, 1965, advanced through grades to lt. col., 1986; comdr. Women's Army Corps, Aberdeen Proving Ground, Md.; asst. to chief-of-staff U.S. Army Missile Command, Redstone Arsenal, Ala.; officer-in-charge, instr. Women's Army Corps Sch., Ft. McClellan, Ala.; ops. officer 3392d USAR Sch., Huntsville, Ala.; occupl. specialty instr. 1163d USAR Sch., Bronx, N.Y.; pers. mgmt. staff Adjutant Gen. Corps; staff officer LOGEX, Ft. Lee, Va., pers. staff officer Camp Pickett, Va.; postal staff officer Mil. Postal Svc. Agy., Alexandria, Va.; inspector gen. U.S. Army Missile Sch., Redstone Arsenal, sr. staff officer, various positions, 1988-94; comdg. officer 184th IMA Detachment, Redstone Arsenal, 1994-96; ret., 1996. Exhibitions include Signature 2000, Signature 2001, Limelight Series, 2002, Monte Sano Art Show, 2003. Vol. Huntsville City Schs., 1988-96, Boy Scouts Am., Huntsville, 1993-95, Huntsville Art League, 1997. Decorated Meritorious Svc. medal. Mem.: Watercolor Soc. Am., Internat. Soc. Exptl. Artists, Art League Madison, Watercolor Soc. Ala., Res. Officers' Assn. (life), Phi Delta Kappa, Kappa Delta Pi. Methodist. Home: 8044 Lauderdale Rd SW Huntsville AL 35802-2916

GAY, CARL LLOYD, lawyer; b. Seattle, Nov. 11, 1950; s. James and Elizabeth Anne (Rogers) G.; m. Robin Ann Winston, Aug. 23, 1975; children: Patrick, Joel, Alexander, Samuel, Nora. Student, U. of Puget Sound, 1969-70; BS in Forestry cum laude, Wash. State U., 1974; JD, Willamette U., 1979. Bar: Wash. 1979, U.S. Dist. Ct. (we. dist.) Wash. 1979. With Taylor & Taylor, 1979-82, Taylor, Taylor & Gay, 1982-85; prin. Greenaway & Gay, Port Angeles, Wash., 1985-91, Greenaway, Gay & Tassie, Port Angeles, 1991-96, Greenaway, Gay & Angier, Port Angeles, 1996—2001, Greenaway, Gay & Tulloch, 2002—. Judge pro tem Clallam County, Port Angeles, 1981-85; commr. superior Ct., 1985-91; judge Juvenile Ct., 1983-87, instr. Guardian Ad Litem Program, Port Angeles, 1985—, Peoples Law Sch., 1989—. Bd. dirs. Cmty. Concert Assn., Port Angeles, 1982—85, 1994—, pres., 1984—85, 1988—89, 1999—2000; bd. dirs. Am. Heart Assn., 1987—, Clallam County YMCA, 1987—2002, exec. com., 1995—; adv. com. Salvation Army, Port Angeles, 1982—; subdivsn. chmn., bd. dirs. United Way Clallam County, 1987—; bd. dirs., pres. Friends of Libr., Port Angeles, 1983—91; trustee Fisher Cove, 1988—; advisor youth in govt. program YMCA, 1986—; chmn. long-range planning com. Port Angeles Sch. Dist.; bd. govs. Peninsula Coll. Found., 2000—; advisor United Meth. Youth Coun., 1987—, trustee, 1989—; pres. Holy Trinity Luth. Ch., 2001—. Named Clallam County Citizen of Yr., 1987; recipient Disting. Svc. award, Clallam County Pro Bono Lawyers, 1998, YMCA, 1992. Mem.: ATLA, ABA (real property, probate and trust and gen. practice sects.), Wash. State Trial Lawyers Assn., Superior Ct. Judges Assn. (com.), Nat. Coun. Juvenile and Family Ct. Judges, Clallam County Bar Assn. (pres. 1995), Wash. Bar Assn. (real property, probate, elder law and trust sects.), Kiwanis (local bd. dirs. 1982—84, pres. 1986—87, Kiwanian of Yr. 1983—84). Lutheran. Avocations: backpacking, cross country skiing, raquetball, sailing. Home: 3220 Mcdougal St Port Angeles WA 98362-6738 Office: Greenaway Gay & Tulloch 829 E 8th St Ste A Port Angeles WA 98362-6452 E-mail: clgay@tenforward.com.

GAY, CHARLES W., JR., academic administrator; b. Tulsa, June 30, 1937; s. Charles W. Sr. and Juanita T. (Reeder) G.; m. Sarah E. Frost Smith, Sept. 8, 1953 (div. June 1967); children: Timothy L., Patrick N.; m. Louise M. Kiser, Dec. 22; stepchildren: Beth L., Richard E. Macatee. BS in Forest Mgmt., Okla. State U., 1962, MS in Range and Livestock Mgmt., 1964. Range rsch. asst. Santa Rita Explt. Range/U.S. Forest Svc., Tucson, 1962; range mgmt. extension specialist to assoc. prof. N.Mex. State U., 1964-68, chief of party livestock devel. project in Paraguay, 1969-72; gen. mgr. agr. divsn. Collier Cobb and Assocs./Hudson Farms and Farm Svcs., Pike Road, Ala., 1973-79; v.p. Gay Sales and Svcs., Inc., Tulsa, 1979-83; assoc. chief of party, adj. prof. on range mgmt. project Utah State U., Rabat, Morocco, 1983-86, rsch. asst. prof. of range sci. Logan, 1986-87, acting dept. head range scie., 1987-88, asst. to dean for adminstrv. affairs, ext. program leader, 1989—2001, asst. dean extension & adminstrn., 2001, assoc. v.p. for university extension. Invited lectr. Bank of Am. Symposium, 1978, Global Natural Resources Monitoring and Assessments Conf., Venice, Italy, 1989, Icelandic Soil Conservation Svc., Iceland, 1989; invited vis. scientist N.W. Plateau Inst. of Biology, Haibei Alpine Rsch. Sta., China, 1992; co-chmn. U.S. Range Mgmt. Task Force/USDA and Mex.'s Dept. Agr. and Water Resources. Editorial bd., assoc. editor: Arid Soil Rsch. and Rehab. jour.; contbr. articles to profl. jours. Pres. bd. dirs. Nora Eccles Harrison Mus. Art, 1994-97; bd. dirs. USU Cmty. Credit Union, 1991-97, Utah Festival Opera Co., 1995-99; trustee, past dir. Devel. for the Logan Chamber Music Soc., 1988-89; chmn. joint com. for Mendon Ward, Boy Scouts Am., 1989-90; Dem. Party chmn., Mendon, 1990—; mem. Kiwanis Youth Devel. Com., Logan; bd. advisors Stokes Nature Ctr., Logan, Utah, 2000. Recipient Phillips Petroleum Grad. Rsch. scholarship, Ala. Coop. Extension Leadership award 1978, Goodyear award for land stewardship and resource conservation, 1998, Disting. Svc. award Epsilon Sigma Phi, 2000, Internat. Svc. award, 2002. Mem. N.Y. Acad. Scis., Soc. Range Mgmt. (sec., chmn. internat. affairs com., others), Soc. Am. Foresters (chair range ecology work group), Am. Mgmt. Assn., Soc. Internat. Devel. (mentor), Utah Soc. Environ. Edn., Intermountain Assn. Environ. Edn., Assn. of Natural Resources Ext. Profls. (pres. 2001), Joint Coun. Ext. Profls. Avocations: sailing, classical music and theatre, lit., tennis, gardening. Office: Utah State Univ Ext 4900 Old Main Hill Logan UT 84322-4900 E-mail: chuckg@ext.usu.edu.

GAY, DAVID EDWARD RYAN, economist; b. Bryan, Tex., Sept. 19, 1945; s. John Gordon and Emma Louise (Ryan) G.; B.A., Tex. A&M U., 1968; Ph.D. (NDEA fellow), 1973; postdoctoral Kans. U., 1974, U. Chgo., 1979, U. Miami, 1980. Asst. prof. econs. U. Ark., Fayetteville, 1973-77, assoc. prof., 1977-83, prof., 1983—; vis. scholar U. Glasgow (Scotland), 1975, Hoover Instn. Stanford U., 1975; vis. assoc. prof. DePaul U., 1979; vis. assoc. prof. U. Colo., 1980, Tex. A&M U., 1980-81; vis. prof. Brigham Young U., 1983-84, Justus-Liebig U., Giessen, Germany, 1993; vis. prof. Higher Sch. Econ, Moscow, 1993, Pvt. Inst. Internat. Bus. Studies, Munich, 1994, Consort Internat. Bus. Studies, Italy; rsch. fellow Internat. Ctr. Econs., Turin, Italy, 1994, 96-97, 2002; co-dir. UA Tchr. and Faculty Support Ctr., 1999-2002. Bd. dirs. N.W. Ark. Community Concerts, 1975-76, Tex. A&M Opera and Performing Arts Soc., 1972-73; bd. govs. Ark. Union, 1977-79, Tex. A&M Commn. on Visual Arts, 1982—; Outstanding Econ. Grad., coll. Lib. Arts, Tex. A&M U., 1995, Recipient Disting. Achievement in Svc., Tchg., Svc. Ark. Alumni Assn., 1996. Mem. Am. Econ. Assn., Am. Fin. Assn. (life), Assn. Pvt. Enterprise Edn. (mem. exec. com. 1993-97, 2000–, pres.1995-96), Eastern Econ. Assn. (founding, life), Pub. Choice Soc., Royal Econ. Soc. (life), So. Econ. Assn. (life), Southwestern Econs. Assn. (pres. 1981-82), Southwestern Soc. Economists (v.p. 1986-87, pres. 1988-89, Outstanding Educator award 2002), Southwestern Social Sci. Assn. (exec. coun. 1981-83, 85—, sec. 1985-86, v.p. 1986-87, pres. 1988-89, membership dir. 1991–), Western Econ. Assn. (life), Western Social Sci. Assn. (exec. coun., pres. 1983-84, appreciation award 1985, 1990, 30th anniversary appreciation award 1988), Mid-South Acad. Econs. and Fin. (exec. council, pres. 1986-87), Missouri Valley Econ. Assn. (dir., exec. com. 1984-86, 93-95, pres. 1992-93), Southwestern Fedn. Administrn. Disciplines (v.p. 1989-90, pres. 1990-91, mem. exec. coun. 1991-96), Mont Pelerin Soc., Assn. for Arid Land Studies (v.p. 1987-89, pres. elect 1989-90, pres. 1990-91, 2002-2003), Sigma Xi, Beta Gamma Sigma (chpt. sec. 1985-89, outstanding UA honor soc. 1988, 2d place nat. award 1989, 1997-2002, 1st place 1990), Alpha Kappa Psi (adviser 1977-79), Phi Kappa Phi, Omicron Delta Epsilon (advisor 1986—), Phi Beta Delta (chpt. pres. 1991-93, internat. pres-elect 2001-02, internat. pres. 2002-2003). Republican. Methodist. Mem. editorial bd. Ark. Bus. and Econ. Rev., 1976-98, Bus. and Econ. Perspectives, 1984-91, Social Sci. Quar., 1982-99, dep. editor, 1984-93, Jour. Bus. Strategies, 1987-1993, Social Science Jour., 1987-2000; contbr. articles to profl. jours.

GAY, DOUGLAS MACKENZIE, pharmacologist; b. Ilion, NY, May 7, 1959; s. Raymond Edward and Alice (Fean) G.; m. Carol Ann Houser Gay, June 2, 1984; children: Elizabeth Ann, Stephanie Marie, Rebecca Danielle. BS in Pharmacy, Albany (N.Y.) Coll. of Pharmacy, 1982. Grad. intern Fay's Inc., Liverpool, N.Y., 1982-83, staff pharmacist Dewitt, N.Y., 1983, Mohawk Valley Gen. Hosp., Ilion, N.Y., 1983-85, Fay's Inc. # 127, Utica, N.Y., 1985-87, supervising Pharmacist, 1987-93, Fay's Inc. # 35, Ilion, N.Y., 1993-96, Eckerd Inc. # 5081, Ilion, N.Y., 1996—. Fay's Drugs Spkrs. group, Fay's Inc., Ilion, N.Y., 1992-96; peer rev. cons. Eckerd Drugs, 1999—; judge Eckerd Drugs Quiz Show, 1993—, Exec. bd. Gen. Herkimer coun. Boy Scouts Am., Revolutionary Trails coun., 2002—. Mem. Am. Pharm. Assn., Elks (chaplain Ilion lodge 1995-96, esquire 1996-97, loyal knight 1997-98, leading knight, 1998-99, exalted ruler 1999-2000, trustee 2000—, chmn. drug awareness N.Y. State ctrl. dist. 1995—). Avocations: camping, travel, snowmobiling, reading, photography. Home: PO Box 326 Ilion NY 13357-0326 Office: Eckerd Drugs # 5081 45 Central Plz Ilion NY 13357-1701

GAY, E(MIL) LAURENCE, lawyer; b. Bridgeport, Conn., Aug. 10, 1923; s. Emil Daniel and Helen Lillian (Mihalich) Gulyassy; m. Harriet A. Ripley, Aug. 2, 1952; children: Noel L., Peter C., Marguerite S., Georgette A. BA, Yale U., 1946; JD magna cum laude, Harvard U., 1949. Bar: N.Y. 1950, Conn. 1960, Calif. 1981, Hawaii 1988. Assoc. Root, Ballantine, Harlan, Bushby & Palmer, N.Y.C., 1949—52; mem. legal staff U.S. High Commr. Germany, Bad Godesberg, 1952—53; law sec., presiding justice appellate div. 1st dept. N.Y. Supreme Ct., N.Y.C., 1953—54; assoc. Debevoise, Plimpton & McLean, N.Y.C., 1954—58; v.p., sec.-treas., gen. counsel Hewitt-Robins, Inc., Stamford, Conn., 1958—65; pres. Litton Gt. Lakes Corp., N.Y.C., 1965—67; sr. v.p. fin. AMFAC, Inc., Honolulu, 1967—73, vice chmn., 1974—78; fin. cons. Burlingame, Calif., 1979-82; of counsel Pettit & Martin, San Francisco, 1982—88, Goodsill, Anderson, Quinn & Stifel, Honolulu, 1988—. Editor: Harvard Law Rev., 1948—49. Pres. Honolulu Symphony Soc., 1974—78; officer, dir. numerous arts and ednl. orgns.; bd. dirs. Loyola Marymount U., 1977—80, San Francisco Chamber Soloists, 1981—86, Honolulu Chamber Music Series, 1988—. 1st lt. U.S. Army, 1943—46. Mem.: ABA, Hawaii State Bar Assn. (vice chair bus. law soc. 1997—98), Phi Beta Kappa. Republican. Roman Catholic. Avocations: music, literature. Home: 1159 Maunawili Rd Kailua HI 96734-4641 Office: Goodsill Anderson Quinn & Stifel 1099 Alakea St #1800 Honolulu HI 96814 Office Fax: 808-547-5880.

GAY, ESMOND PHELPS, lawyer; b. New Orleans, Sept. 15, 1952; s. Charles Fenner and Harriott (Phelps) G.; m. Marian Enochs, June 6, 1981; children: Jacqueline Elinor, Marian Phelps. AB, Princeton (N.J.) U., 1975, JD, Tulane U., 1979. Bar: La. 1979, U.S. Dist. Ct. (ea. dist.) La. 1979, U.S. Ct. Appeals (5th cir.) 1986. Assoc. Christovich & Kearney, New Orleans, 1979-84, ptnr., 1985—. Mem. Met. Area Com., New Orleans, 1989—; elected participant Met. Leadership Forum, New Orleans, 1988. Mem. ABA, State Bar Tex., Internat. Bar Assn., Fed. Bar Assn., La. Bar Assn. (Ho. of Dels., pres. 2000-01), New Orleans Bar Assn. (bd. dirs. 1997-99), Fed. Ins. and Corp. Counsel (chmn. maritime law com.), La. Assn. Def. Counsel (bd. dirs. 2003—), Def. Rsch. Inst. Home: 237 Hector Ave Metairie LA 70005-4117 Office: Christovich & Kearney 601 Poydras St Ste 2300 New Orleans LA 70130-6078

GAY, FRANCES MARION WELBORN, private school educator; b. Charleston, SC, Feb. 18, 1956; d. Melvin Floyd and Frances Helen (Looper) G.; m. Douglas Herring Westbrook, Mar. 29, 1997; 1 child, Douglas Herring Westbrook Jr. BA in English, Hollins Coll., 1979; MAT in English, The Citadel, Charleston, 1989. Cert. tchr. grades 5-12, S.C. Tchr. English, grades 7-8 Charleston Day Sch., 1986-87; tchr. grades 3-4 St. Paul's Acad., Ravenel, S.C., 1987-88; dir. devel. Charleston Day Sch., 1988-89, dir. devel. and admissions, 1989-92; tchr. science, grade 5 Ashley Hall, Charleston, 1992-95, tchr. Lang. Arts, grade 6, 1992—. Faculty adv. Cerberus mag., 2001—. V.p. women of the ch. French Huguerot Ch., 1997—99. Named one of Outstanding Young Women of Am., 1991; recipient Ashley Hall Spiral dedication, 2001. Mem. DAR, Hollins Alumnae Club of Charleston (pres. 1983-93), Garden Club of Charleston, Jr. League of Charleston (chmn. violence on view 1989, corrs. sec. 1992), Huguenot Soc. of S.C. (ch. docent 1985-86), English Speaking Union, Friends of the Confederate Home and Coll., Nat. Soc. Colonial Dames of the 17th Century, The Scottish Soc. of Charleston. Avocations: sewing, piano, target shooting, gardening, white-water rafting. Office: Ashley Hall 172 Rutledge Ave Charleston SC 29403-5877

GAY, JOHN MARION, federal agency administrator, organization-personnel analyst; b. Sept. 23, 1936; s. John Henry and LolaBell (Collins) Gay; m. Rebecca Jane Gay; children: John Marion II, Dierdre, Michael, Michelle(dec.), Steven, Christina. BA, Tex. So. U., 1956; MSW, U. Richmond, 1968; BS, Fla. Meml. Coll., 1976; MBA, Nova U., 1977. Cert. tchr. Fla. Compensation analyst SE Banks, N.A., Miami, Fla., 1976—78; personnel job analyst Kaiser Transit Group, Miami, 1978—80; tribal adminstr. Miccosukee Indians, Everglades Nat. Park, Fla., 1980—81; tchr. Broward County Schs., Fort Lauderdale, Fla., 1981—83, Dade County Schs., Miami, 1983—84; from postal employee to postal inspector US Postal Svc., North Miami Beach, Fla., 1984—96; postal inspection svc. detail US Postal Svc. DHQ, North Miami Beach, 1996—2003; ret. Corp. coord. United Negro Coll. Fund, Dade County, Fla., 1977; bd. govs. Tuskegee Airmen's Nat. Mus. With USAF, 1956—59. Recipient Honor award, Alpha Kappa Mu, 1974, award, Fla. Meml. Coll. Alumni Assn., 1978; scholar Max Fleischmann, United Negro Coll. Fund, 1975. Fellow: NEA; mem.: Nat. Assn. Postal Suprs., Tuskegee Airmen, Inc. Democrat. Avocations: bowling, tennis, writing. Home: 450 NW 87th Rd Apt 103 Plantation FL 33324-6585

GAY, MARILYN FANELLI MARTIN, television producer, writer, talk show hostess, journalist; b. San Francisco, July 16, 1925; d. Louis and Gertrude (Dondero) Fanelli; m. William Thomas Martin, Jan. 11, 1953 (div. 1956); m. Mel Raymond Gay, May 3, 1963. Student, U. Calif., Berkeley, 1943-46, U. Oreg., 1946. Pres., CEO Marilyn Gay Pub. Rels., 1975—94. Prodr./dir. Young Set Playhouse, Radio KRE, Berkeley, 1944-45; prodr., hostess, writer; (TV) In God We Trust--KTLA-TV, L.A., Protestant Ch. Fedn., 1954-55, A Woman's World, NBC-TV outlet, Las Vegas, 1956; (radio) Party with the Stars, KBIG, L.A., 1958; writer Passing Parade Films ABC-TV Network, 1958, Tel. Time; asst. editor Gen. Practice mag., L.A., 1961; prodr., hostess, writer The Marilyn Gay Show, Group W Cable, Valley Cable, Cox Cable, Century Cable, King Cable, Cablevision, Simmons Cable, Century Cable, Verdugo Hills TV, Jones Intercable, Am. Cable, Copley Colony Cable, AOL Time Warner, 1982—; nat. dir. spl. features, coord. radio and TV, Invest in America Nationwide Campaign, 1957; contbg. by-lined feature writer Los Angeles Times, 1957. Recipient Outstanding Good Citizen award DAR, 1943, Commemorative medal of Honor Hallmark, 1985; named to Hall of Fame of personalities of Am., 1985. Mem. Writers Guild Am.-West (founding mem.), Internat. Platform Assn., U. Calif. Alumni Assn., Alpha Delta Pi. Mem. Ch. of Religious Science. Address: 1243 S Petit Ave # 245 Ventura CA 93004

GAY, PAMELA DIANE, dance critic, historian, educator; b. Dayton, Ohio, Dec. 1, 1945; d. Richard Lewis and Patricia Rose (Jacques) G. BA, U. Calif., Berkeley, 1977; MA, Hunter Coll., 1989; PhD in French, La. State U., 1998. Interpreter Arts Am., Washington, 1985-86; vis. scholar in dance history U. Calgary, Alta., Alberta, 1980; lectr. Univ. Franche-Comté, Besancon, France, 1992-93; instr. La. State U., Baton Rouge, La., 1995-2000; asst. prof. French, Ala. State U., Montgomery, 2000—. Dir. Arts Seminars Internat., San Francisco, 1982-85; adv. Lagniappe Studies Unlimited, La. State U., 1993-99; liaison La. State U. in Paris, 1993. Contbr. International Dictionary of Ballet, 1994; author: (jour.) Pensée Libre, 1998; contbg. editor The Phoenix, Dance Scope, Les Saisons de la Danse. Active Nat. Alliance Mentally Ill, 1998. Mem. Eighteenth Century Soc., Modern Lang. Assn., Rousseau Assn. Anglican. E-mail: pdgaywhite@aol.com.

GAY, PETER, history educator, author; b. Berlin, June 20, 1923; came to U.S., 1941, naturalized, 1946; s. Morris Peter and Helga (Kohnke) G.; m. Ruth Slotkin, May 30, 1959; stepchildren: Sarah Khedouri, Sophie Glazer Cohen, Elizabeth Glazer. BA, U. Denver, 1946; MA, Columbia U., 1947, PhD, 1951; LHD (hon.), U. Denver, 1970, U. Md., 1979, Hebrew Union Coll., Cin., 1983, Clark U., 1985, Suffolk U., Boston, 1987, Tufts U., 1988, U. Ill., 2003. Faculty Columbia U., N.Y.C., 1947-69, prof. history, 1962-69, William R. Shepherd prof. history, 1967-69; prof. comparative European intellectual history Yale U., New Haven, 1969—, Durfee prof. history, 1970-84, Sterling prof., 1984-93, Sterling prof. emeritus, 1993—; dir. Ctr. for Scholars and Writers N.Y. Pub. Libr., 1997—. Dir. Ctr. Scholars and Writers N.Y. Pub. Libr. Author: The Dilemma of Democratic Socialism: Eduard Bernstein's Challenge to Marx, 1952, Voltaire's Politics: The Poet as Realist, 1959, The Party of Humanity: Essays in the French Enlightenment, 1964, A Loss of Mastery: Puritan Historians in Colonial America, 1966, The Enlightenment: An Interpretation, vol. I, The Rise of Modern Paganism, 1966, Weimar Culture: The Outsider as Insider, 1968, The Enlightenment, vol. II, The Science of Freedom, 1969, The Bridge of Criticism: Dialogues on the Enlightenment, 1970; author: (with R.K. Webb) Modern Europe, 1973; author: Style in History, 1974, Art and Act, 1976, Freud, Jews, and Other Germans, 1978, Education of the Senses, 1984, Freud for Historians, 1985, The Tender Passion, 1986, A Godless Jew: Freud, Atheism, and the Making of Psychoanalysis, 1987, Freud: A Life for Our Time, 1988, A Freud Reader, 1989, Reading Freud: Explorations and Entertainments, 1990, The Cultivation of Hatred, 1993, The Naked Heart, 1995, Pleasure Wars, 1998, My German Question: Growing Up in Nazi Berlin, 1998, Mozart, 1999, Schnitzler's Century: The Making of Middle-Class Culture, 1815-1914, 2001, Savage Reprisals, Bleak House, Madame Bovary, 2002. Fellow Am. Coun. Learned Soc., 1959-60, Ctr. Advanced Study Behavioral Scis., 1963-64; Guggenheim fellow, 1967-68, 77-78; Overseas fellow Churchill Coll., Cambridge, 1970-71; Rockefeller Found. fellow, 1979-80; Wissenschaftskolleg zu Berlin, 1984; recipient First Amsterdam prize in Hist. Sci., 1991. Mem. Am. Philos. Soc., Am. Inst. Arts and Letters (gold medal in history 1996), Ctr. for Scholars and Writers (dir.), N.Y. Pub. Libr., Phi Beta Kappa. Home: Apt 15A 760 W End Ave New York NY 10025-5524

GAY, ROBERT DERRIL, public agency director; b. Savannah, Ga., June 23, 1939; s. Roscoe Degomar and Mollie Ann (Jones) G. BA, Oglethorpe U., 1962; MA, Emory U., 1966, PhD, 1984. Dep. dir. Divsn.. Mental Health and Mental Retardation Ga. Dept. Human Resources, Atlanta, 1975-77, asst. commr., 1977-78, dir. Divsn. Mental Health and Mental Retardation, 1978-81; dep. dir. DeKalb County Health Dept., Decatur, Ga., 1981-94; dir. DeKalb Community Mental Health, Mental Retardation and Substance Abuse Svc. Bd., Decatur, 1994—. Vis. instr. Oglethorpe U., 1966, 67, 85-94, Emory U. Sch. Nursing, 1970; mem. Ga. Gov.'s Coun. on Devel. Disabilities, 1978-81, Ga. Gov.'s Coun. on Mental Health and Mental Retardation, 1978-81, DeKalb County Coun. on Devel. Disabilities, 1981—. Bd. dirs. St. Joseph's Mercy Care Svcs., 1994-2000. Mem. Am. Sociol. Assn. So. Sociol. Soc., Ga. Sociol. Assn., Nat. Assn. State Mental Health Program Dirs. (bd. dirs. 1986-92, pres. 1990-91), Atlanta Mercy Mobile Health Program (bd. dirs. 1987-94, chair 1991-94). Home: 2295 Dunwoody Xing Apt I Atlanta GA 30338-7332 Office: DeKalb Community Svc Bd PO Box 1648 Decatur GA 30031-1648

GAY, SARAH ELIZABETH, lawyer; b. Cambridge, Mass., May 24, 1950; d. Frank Smith and Jane (Spencer) Fussner; m. Kirk D. Gay; 1 child, John Russell. BA, Harvard/Radcliffe, 1972; JD, U. Oreg., 1975. Bar: Alaska 1976, U.S. Dist. Ct. Alaska 1976, U.S. Ct. Appeals (9th cir.) 1976, U.S. Supreme Ct. 1980. Assoc. Ely, Guess & Rudd, Anchorage, 1975-77; asst. atty. gen. natural resources sect. State of Alaska, Anchorage, 1977-88, asst. atty. gen. oil spill sect., 1989-91, sect. supr. natural resources sect., 1991-93; corp. counsel Alaska Safari, Inc., Alaska's Valhalla Lodge, Inc., Anchorage, 1993—; pvt. practice Anchorage, 1993—. Workshop leader U. Oreg. Law Sch., Eugene, 1989; chmn. Anchorage Mcpl. Airports Adv. Com., 1990-93; food safety adv. com. Dept. Environ. Conservation, State Alaska, 2000—. Mng. bd. editor U. Oreg. Law Rev., Eugene, 1975. Citizens' adv. bd. Land Conservation & Devel. Bd., Salem, Oreg., 1975. Mem. Alaska Bar Assn. Law Examiners, Phi Delta Phi. Avocations: commercial pilot, sport fish lodge operator. Address: Valhalla Lodge Nondalton AK 99640 Fax: 907-243-6095. E-mail: sarah@valhallalodge.com.

GAY, SPENCER BRADLEY, radiologist, educator; b. Washington, June 12, 1948; s. Lendall Croxton and Claudine (Moss) G.; m. Debie Farris (div. Sept. 1982); 1 child, Colin Bradley; m. Marit Corinne Anderson; children: Chelsea Britt, Kristen Corinne. BS, U. Miami, Fla., 1973; MD, U. Va., 1983. Dir. Full Circle Farm, Somerset, Va., 1974-78; pres. Cen. Va. Title Agy., Orange, 1977-79; resident in radiology U. Va. Health Scis. Ctr., Charlottesville, 1983-87, fellow in radiology, 1987-88, asst. prof., 1988-94, assoc. prof., 1994-2000, prof., 2000—. Mem. Med. Soc. Va., Am. Roentgen Ray Soc., Radiol. Soc. N.Am. Episcopalian. Avocations: windsurfing, woodcarving, music. Office: U Va Health Sci Ctr PO Box 800170 Charlottesville VA 22902-0170 E-mail: sbg2d@virginia.edu.

GAY, WILLIAM ARTHUR, JR., thoracic surgeon; b. Richmond, Va., Jan. 16, 1936; s. William Arthur and Marion Harriette (Taylor) G.; m. Frances Louise Adkins, Dec. 17, 1960; children— William Taylor, Mason Arthur. BA, Va. Mil. Inst., 1957; MD, Duke U., 1961. Intern Duke U. Med. Ctr., Durham, NC, 1961—63, resident in surgery, 1965—71; asst. prof. surgery Cornell U. Med. Coll., N.Y.C., 1971—74, assoc. prof., 1974—78; cardiothoracic surgeon-in-chief N.Y. Hosp., 1976—84; prof., chmn. dept. surgery U. Utah Sch. Medicine, 1984—92; v.p. for health scis. U. Utah, 1990—91; chmn. Am. Bd. Thoracic Surgery, 1995—97; thoracic surgeon Barnes Hosp., St. Louis. Prof. surgery Sch. Medicine Washington U., St. Louis. Contbr. With USPHS, 1963—65. Recipient Career Scientist award, Irma T. Hirschl Charitable Trust, 1972. Mem. ACS, Soc. Vascular Surgery, Soc. Thoracic Surgery, Am. Assn. Thoracic Surgery (treas. 1989-94), Am. Surg. Assn., Soc. Univ. Surgeons (treas. 1977-80) Office: 1 Barnes Hospital Plz Saint Louis MO 63110-1036 E-mail: gayw@msnotes.wustl.edu.

GAY, WILLIAM C. philosophy educator; b. Clearwater, Fla., Apr. 25, 1949; s. Oscar Merchant and Gaye (Sanderson) G.; m. Carol Fern Stewart, June 12, 1971; 1 child, Heather Elyse. BA in Philosophy, Carson-Newman Coll., 1971; PhD in Philosophy, Boston Coll., 1976. Lectr. Brandeis U., Waltham, Mass., 1976-78; vis. asst. prof. Amherst (Mass.) Coll., 1978-79; asst. prof. Ind./Purdue U. of Ft. Wayne, 1979-80, U. N.C., Charlotte, 1980-86, assoc. prof. philosophy, 1986-96, prof. philosophy, 1996—, chair, 1993-2001. Author: (with Michael Pearson) The Nuclear Arms Race, 1987, (with T.A. Alekseeva) Capitalism with a Human Face, 1996; editor: (with T.A. Alekseeva) On the Eve of the 21st Century, 1994; (with I.I. Mazour and A.N. Chumekou) Global Studies Encyclopedia, 2003; editor Concerned Philosophers for Peace newsletter, 1987-2002; assoc. editor Philosophy & Social Criticism, 1978-86, bd. cons. editors, 1987—; editor spl. series Contemporary Russian Philosophy, Philosophy of Peace; contbr. articles to profl. jours., chpts. to books. Mem. Am. Philos. Assn., Concerned Philosophers for Peace, Phi Beta Delta. Avocations: swimming, hiking, cooking. Home: 8805 Crosstimbers Dr Charlotte NC 28215-9771 Office: Univ of NC Dept Philosophy Charlotte NC 28223 Fax: 704 687 2172. E-mail: wcgay@email.uncc.edu.

GAY, WILLIAM INGALLS, veterinarian, health science administrator; b. Sussex, N.J., Jan. 25, 1926; s. William David and Dorothy Julia (Ingalls) G.; m. Millicent Ruth Chapman, June 10, 1948. DVM, Cornell U., 1950; grad., Fed. Exec. Inst., 1972. Diplomate Am. Coll. Lab. Animal Medicine. Pvt. practice vet. medicine, Richmond Hill, N.Y., 1950-52; chief animal hosp. sect. lab. aids br. divsn. research services NIH, Bethesda, Md., 1954-63, asst. chief lab. aids br. divsn. research services, 1962-63, asst. chief animal resources br. divsn. research facilities and resources, 1964-65; program dir. comparative medicine Nat. Inst. Gen. Med. Scis., NIH, 1966-67, program adminstr. radiology and physiology tng. programs, 1966, chief research grants br., 1967-70, acting assoc. dir., 1970; assoc. dir. extramural programs Nat. Inst. Allergy and Infectious Diseases, NIH, 1970-80, dir. animal resources program, divsn. research resources, 1981-88; cons. ROW Svcs., Rockville, Md., 1989-98; pvt. practice Bethesda, Md., 1999—. Mem. com. on primates Inst. Lab. Animal Resources, NRC, 1961-63, chmn. subcom. on cat standards, 1963-64, mem. standards com., 1965-66; program chmn. Internat. Symposium on Lab. Animals, 1969 Author numerous papers on expt. surgery and lab. animal research.; editor: Methods of Animal Experimentation, 7 vols. Mem. sci. adv. bd. Mark L. Morris Found., 1966-71, trustee, 1971-84; mem. grants adv. council The Seeing Eye, 1971-74. Served as lt. Vet. Corps, AUS, Walter Reed, 1952-54. Recipient Superior Service cert. HEW, 1975, NIH Dir's. award, 1983, Superior Service award USPHS, 1987. Mem. AVMA (sec.-treas. D.C. chpt. 1957-58, v.p. 1962, pres. 1963), AAAS, Am. Assn. Lab. Animal Sci. (dir. 1961-69, program chmn. 1962-64, exec. bd. 1963, 66, nat. pres. 1968, chmn. awards com. 1969, Griffin award 1971, pres. Washington br. 1962, chair Gala 2000 com.), NIH Alumni Assn. (bd. dirs. 1994, v.p. 1995-98, pres. 1999-2002), Phi Zeta, Cosmos Club.

GAYDOS, JOEL CARL, physician; b. Edenborn, Pa., Apr. 7, 1942; s. Joseph and Ann G.; m. Charlotte Ann Klaus, June 5, 1965; children: Kathryn, Joseph, Steven, Jennifer. AB, W.Va. U., 1964, MD, 1968; MPH in Epidemiology, U. Pitts., 1972. Diplomate Nat. Bd. Med. Examiners, Am. Bd. Preventive Medi-

cine. Intern Walter Reed Gen. Hosp., Washington, 1968-69, resident in gen. preventive medicine, 1972-74; commd. 2d lt. U.S. Army, 1964, advanced through grades to col.; mil. physician Med. Corps, 1968-97; dir. occupl. and environ. health U.S. Army Environ. Hygiene Agy., Aberdeen Proving Ground, Md., 1983-85; occupl. health cons., chief preventive medicine cons. divsn. Dept. of the Army Office of the Surgeon Gen., Falls Church, Va., 1985-89; assoc. prof., assoc. dean acting Uniformed Svcs. U. of the Health Scis., Bethesda, Md., 1989-93; dir. clin. preventive medicine U.S. Army Ctr. for Health Promotion and Preventive Medicine, Aberdeen Proving Ground, Md., 1994-97; dir. pub. health practices Dept. of Def. Global Emerging Infections Surveillance & Response Sys., 1997—; sr. scientist Henry M. Jackson Found., Rockville, Md., 1997—. Adj. prof. Uniformed Svcs. U. Health Scis., 1999—, George Washington U., Washington, 2000—. Contbr. numerous articles to profl. jours., chpts. to books. Decorated Def. Superior Svc. medal, Legion of Merit. Fellow Am. Coll. Preventive Medicine, Am. Coll. Occupational & Environ. Medicine; mem. AMA, Soc. for Epidemiologic Rsch., Assn. Tchrs. Preventive Medicine, Am. Soc. Tropical Medicine & Hygiene, Assn. Mil. Surgeons of U.S. Office: Walter Reed Arm Inst of Rsch Divsn Preventive Medicine 503 Robert Grant Ave Silver Spring MD 20910-7500

GAYDOS, MARY, writer, researcher, actress; b. Marblehead, Ohio, Feb. 13, 1936; d. George Joseph Gaydos and Dorothy Marian Vargosick Saunders. BFA, Ohio U., 1958; MLS, Queens Coll., 1972. Narrator various art programs, cable TV, 1992—. Actress off-broadway, cinema, TV, 1958-70; writer, moderator (radio series) Fgn. Film Industry, 1970-71; prodr. Milliken Fabric's Fashion Show, 1978; book rev. critic MD Med. Newsmag., N.Y.C., 1973-76; stage mgr. Women in the Performing Arts Festival at Lincoln Ctr., 1977; narrator (film) The Art and Architecture of Belgrade and Kosovo (honoree World Lang. Inst., N.Y.C, 2001); narrator dedication of Nikola Tesla Meml. sponsored by Hons. R. Giuliani and G. Pataki, N.Y.C., 2001.; host of Broadway's 47th Ann. Drama Desk awards, 2002, 48th Ann. Drama Desk awards, 2003, 26th Ann. Medieval Festival, Cloisters Mus./Met. Mus. Art, 2003. Fundraiser for non-profit orgns. including Skowhegan Sch. of Art and Design, The Spanish Inst., Legal Aid Soc., Nat. Energy Found., Archdiocese of N.Y.'s Inner-City Scholarship Fund, 1979-87. Named honoree, World Lang. Inst., 2001; recipient Mayor's Merit award, Hon. Ed T. Koch, N.Y.C., 1989. Mem. Actors Equity Assn., Screen Actors Guild, C.G. Jung Found., Am. Teilhard Assn. for the Future of Man, Am. Soc. of Psychical Rsch. Home: 101 W 85th St Apt 6-12 New York NY 10024-4487 E-mail: mmgaydos@hotmail.com.

GAYER, ELLIOTT, lawyer; b. Bklyn., June 29, 1951; s. Frank Wolf and Amelia Charlotte (Luftig) Gayer; m. Belle Linda Tuchinsky, June 30, 1972; 1 child, Sheridan. BS in law, JD, Western State U., San Diego. Bar: Ga. 1980, Calif. 1980, U.S. Dist. Ct. (so. dist.), Calif. 1980, U.S. Dist. Ct. (cen. dist.), Calif. 1982, U.S. Cir. Ct. Appeals 1982. Atty. Am. Tax & Law Ctr., San Diego, 1980—82; ptnr. Repici & Gayer, Newport Beach, Calif., 1982—; atty. Fine Artists Guild, Newport Beach, Calif., 1983—. Mem.: Calif. Attys. Criminal Justice, Calif. Trial Lawyers Assn. Democrat. Jewish. Home: General Delivery New York NY 10001-9999

GAYLE, GIBSON, JR., lawyer; b. Waco, Tex., Oct. 15, 1926; s. Gibson and Elsie (Little) G.; m. Martha Jane Wood, May 29, 1948; children: Sally Ann, Alice, Gibson III, Jane, Philip. AB, LLB, Baylor U., 1950; D Human Medicine (hon.), Baylor Coll. Medicine, 1991. Bar: Tex. 1950. Since practiced in, Houston; sr. ptnr., chmn. exec. com. Fulbright & Jaworski., 1979-92; adj. prof. U. Tex. Law Sch. Instr. U. Houston Law Sch., 1951-55. Bd. editors: Am. Bar Assn. Jour, 1967-72. Trustee M.D. Anderson Found., bd. govs. Harris County Ctr. for Retarded, 1956-76; Tex. Med. Ctr. Inc., Leon Jaworski Found.; bd. dirs., pres. Am. Bar Endowment, 1970-80; chmn. Baylor Coll. Medicine, 1982-91, trustee, 1977—. 2d lt. F.A. AUS, 1945-47. Fellow Am. Bar Found. (dir. 1978-79), Tex. Bar Found. (chmn. 1968-69); mem. ABA (chmn. jr. bar conf. 1959-60, ho. of dels. 1960-62, 63—, sec. 1963-67), Houston Bar Assn., State Bar Tex. (dir. 1966-69, pres. 1976-77), Houston C. of C. (dir. 1979-87) Home: 11727 Broken Bough Cir Houston TX 77024-5115 Office: Fulbright & Jaworski LLP 1301 Mckinney St Ste 5100 Houston TX 77010-3031

GAYLE, HELENE D. public health physician; b. Buffalo; BS in Psychology cum laude, Columbia U., 1976; MD, U. Pa., 1981; MPH, John Hopkins U., 1981. Diplomate Am. Bd. Pediats. Intern then resident in pediats. Children's Hosp. Nat. Med. Ctr., Washington, 1981-84; epidemic intelligence svc. officer br. epidemiology divsn. nutrition Ctr. Health Promotion and Edn., 1984-86; preventive medicine resident divsn. evaluation and rsch. office internat. health program Ctrs. Disease Control Ga. State Dept. Health, 1986-87; med. epidemiologist pediats. and family studies sect., AIDS program Ctrs. Disease Control, 1987-89, acting spl. asst. minority HIV policy coordination office dep. dir. (HIV), 1988-89, asst. chief sci., 1989-90, chief internat. activity divsn. HIV/AIDS, 1990 92, assoc. dir. Washington, 1994-96; agy. AIDS coord., chief divsn. HIV-AIDS Agy. Intl. Devel., Washington, 1992-94; dir. Nat. Ctr. HIV, Sexually Transmitted Diseases and Tb Prevention Ctrs. Disease Control, Atlanta, 1995—. Lectr. Sch. Medicine Morehouse U., 1987—92; lectr. masters in pub. health program Emory U., Atlanta, 1989, 90, clin. asst. prof. cmty. medicine, 1996—; cons. WHO, others; bd. dir. Africa Am. inst. Global Health Coun., Internat. Ctr. Rsch. in Women; dir. HIV/AIDS and Tb program Bill & Melinda Gates Found., 2001—. Contbr. articles to profl. jours. Adm. USPHS. Merit scholar, 1981; recipient Henrietta and Jacob Lowenburg prize, 1981, Model Excellence award Colgate-Palmolive Co., 1992. Mem. AAS, AMA, APHA, Am. Coll. Epidemiology, Internat. AIDS Soc., Soc. Against AIDS in Africa, Inst. Medicine, Coun. Fgn. Rels. Mailing: PO Box 23350 Seattle WA 98102 E-mail: heleneg@gatesfoundation.org.

GAYLE, MARGOT, preservationist, writer; b. Kansas City, Mo., May 14, 1908; d. David Bunn and Edith Mildred (Cheatham) McCoy; widowed; children: Carol, Gretchen Gayle Ellsworth. BA, U. Mich., 1930; MS, Emory U., 1933. Dir. Civil Def. Vol. Office, Washington, 1943—45; script writer CBS, N.Y.C., 1945-48; dir. pub. rels. N.Y.C. Dept. Commerce and Pub. Events, 1953—56; dep. dir. pub. info. N.Y.C. Planning Commn., 1956-58; columnist N.Y. Daily News, N.Y.C., 1976-92. Mem. Art Commn. of City of N.Y., 1981—84. Author: Cast Iron Architecture in New York: A Photographic Survey, 1974; co-author (with Michele Cohen): Metal in America's Historic Buildings, 1980, The Art Commission and the Municipal Art Society Guide to Manhattan's Outdoor Sculpture, 1988; (with Carol Gayle) Cast-Iron Architecture in America: The Significance of James Bogardus, 1998; contbr. articles to profl. jours., introductions to books. Co-founder Victorian Soc. Am., N.Y.C., 1966; Dem. state committeewoman, dist. leader, Manhattan, 1953-61; co-chair Com. to Restore Hist. Yorkville Clock, 1999. Recipient Nat. Trust for Hist. Preservation award, 1980, Doris Freedman award City of N.Y., 1986, N.Y. State Honor award, 1988, Henry-Russell Hitchcock award Victorian Soc. in Am., 1989, Lucy Moses award Landmarks Conservancy, 1990, George Lewis award AIA, 1993, Robert Ponte award Am. Planning Assn., 1994, Preservation award Met. Hist. Structures Assn., 1995, Assoc. of the Art Commn., 1995, Pioneer Preservation award Met. Hist. Structures Assn., 1999, Lifetime Achievement award N.Y. State Hist. Preservation, 2000, Spl. Recognition award N.Y.C. Art Commn., 2001. Mem. Friends of Cast Iron Architecture (founder, pres.), Mcpl. Art Soc. N.Y. (Jacqueline Kennedy Onassis medal for preservation of the Soho cast iron hist. dist. 1997), Victorian Soc. Am. (met. chpt. Lifetime Achievement award 1997, Book award 1999), Fine Arts Fedn. N.Y. (pres.), Women's City Club, Soc. Indsl. Archaeology (Gen. Tools Lifetime Achievement award 1997), Preservation League N.Y. State (Lifetime Achievement award 1999), Victorian Soc. in Am. (Pres. award 1999), Friends of the Upper East Side Hist. Dists. (Ralph Menapace award 2000), Secial Recognition award, Art Commn. of N.Y.C., 2001.

GAYLES, JOSEPH NATHAN, JR., administrator, fund raising consultant; b. Birmingham, Ala. s. Joseph Nathan Webster and Ernestine Gayles; children: Jonathan, Monica. AB summa cum laude, Dillard U., 1958, LL.D. (hon.), 1983; PhD, Brown U., 1963; postgrad., Oreg. State U., 1962-63, U. Uppsala, Sweden, 1965; D.Sc (hon.), Morehouse Sch. Medicine, 2000. Asst. prof. chemistry Oreg. State U., 1962-63; Woodrow Wilson teaching asso., asst. prof. chemistry Morehouse Coll., 1963-66, assoc. prof. chemistry, 1969-71, founding dir. med. edn. project, 1971-75; dir. Sch. Medicine, 1975-77, prof., 1971-77; pres. Talladega (Ala.) Coll., 1977-83; v.p., research prof. medicine Morehouse Sch. Medicine, Atlanta, 1983-97; chmn., CEO Jon-Mon and Assocs., Inc., Fund Raising Cons., 1983—; cons. v.p. Clark Atlanta U., 1996-98; v.p. advancement Sojourner Douglass Coll., 2002—. Staff scientist, project dir. IBM Research Lab., San Jose, Calif., 1966-69 Contbr. articles to profl. jours. Bd. dirs. Woodrow Wilson Nat. Fellowship Found., 1978-98, Rotary Internat., 1991—, Found. Ctr. Bd., 1994-96; bd. overseers Sch. Medicine, Morehouse Coll., 1977-81; bd. dirs. Donoho Sch., Anniston, Ala., 1979-83, Camp Cosby, YMCA, 1978-80, Met. Atlanta Coun. on Alcohol and Drug Abuse, 1972-74, Coun. for Internat. Exchange Scholars, 1979-83; exec. bd. North Ctrl. Ga. Health Sys. Agy., 1975-77; mem. Indsl. Devel. Com., Talladega, 1979-83; mem. exec. bd. Choccolocco coun. Boy Scouts Am., 1980-83; mem. Gov.'s Commn. on Future of Ala. in Yr. 2000, 1982-83; trustee Morehouse Coll., 1976-77, Talladega Coll., 1977-83, Morehouse Med. Coll., 1981-83; mem. nat. adv. coun. divsn. rsch. resources NIH, 1980-85; pres. Ala. Ctr. for Higher Edn., 1980-83; bd. visitors MIT, 1981-88. Woodrow Wilson fellow, 1958-59; Dreyfus Found. Tchr.-scholar, 1972; recipient Tchr. of Yr. award Morehouse Coll., 1976; Alumnus of Yr. award Dillard U., 1977; Presdl. Leadership award Morehouse Sch. Medicine, 1986 Mem. Am. Phys. Soc., Am. Chem. Soc., Am. Assn. Polit. and Social Scientists, Nat. Assn. Equal Opportunity in Higher Edn. (bd. dirs. 1979-82), Sigma Xi, Phi Beta Kappa, Alpha Phi Alpha. Office: Jon Mon Assoc Inc 1515 Austin Rd SW Atlanta GA 30331-2205

GAYLIN, NED L. psychology educator; b. Cleve., May 2, 1935; s. Harry C. and Fay I. G.; m. Rita Atran, June 30, 1957; children: Hilarie C., Ann E., Jed J., Daniel S. BA, U. Chgo., 1956, MA, 1961, PhD, 1965. Counselor Bellefaire Children's Home, Cleve., 1953, Sonja Shankman Orthogenic Sch., Chgo., 1954-56; group worker, supr. Jewish Community Ctrs. Chgo., 1957-60; grad. rsch. asst. Com. Human Devel., U. Chgo., 1959-60; intern Inst. Juvenile Rsch., Chgo., 1960-61, staff psychologist, 1965-68; intern Counseling and Psychotherapy Rsch. Ctr., U. Chgo., 1961-63; grad. teaching asst. dept. psychology U. Chgo., 1961-63; psychol. cons. State Ill., Rockford, 1961-64; psychotherapist, cons. Counseling and Psychotherapy Rsch. Ctr., U. Chgo., 1963-65, psychol. cons., lectr., 1965; lectr. dept. social sci. S.E. Jr. Coll., Chgo., 1965-66; psychol. cons. Peace Corps, No. Ill. U., DeKalb, 1966-68; chief psychologist S.W. Suburban Mental Health Assn., LaGrange, Ill., 1966-68; psychol. cons. Virginia Frank Child Devel. Ctr., Chgo., 1966-68; child clin. rsch. psychologist NIMH, Bethesda, Md., 1968-70; lectr., cons. Washington Sch. Psychiatry, 1968-72; chmn. dept. family and community devel. Coll. Human Ecology U. Md., College Park, 1970-77, prof., dir. family therapy tng. Coll. Health and Human Performance, 1977—2003, prof. emeritus, 2003—. Mem. rsch. com. Md. Community Coordinated Child Care, 1970-75. Author: Family, Self, and Psychotherapy, 2001; contbr. articles in field to profl. jours. USPHS grantee, 1961-63; U. Chgo. fellow and scholar, 1954-56, 58-60; State Ill. edn. and tng. grantee, 1963-65 Mem. APA, Nat. Coun. on Family Rels., Am. Assn. Marriage and Family Therapy, Groves Conf. on the Family, Assn. for Devel. of Person-Centered Approach, Sigma Xi. Home: 4617 Norwood Dr Chevy Chase MD 20815-5348 Office: Univ Md 1204 Marie Mount Hall College Park MD 20742-7515 E-mail: ng3@umail.umd.edu.

GAYLIN, WILLARD, physician, educator; b. Cleve., Feb. 23, 1925; s. Harry C. and Fay (Baumgard) Gaylin; m. Betty Schofer, June 15, 1947; children: Joan Deborah, Ellen Andrea. AB, Harvard U., 1947; MD, Western Res. U., 1951. Lic. psychiatrist N.Y. Intern Cleve. City Hosp., 1951—52; resident psychiatry Bronx VA Hosp., 1952—54; faculty Columbia Psychoanalytic Sch., 1956—, clin. prof. psychiatry, 1972—; adj. prof. psychiatry Union Theol. Sem.; adj. prof psychiatry and law Columbia Sch. Law, 1970; founder The Hastings Ctr., Briarcliff Manor, NY, 1970—, chmn. bd., 1970—96. Author: The Meaning of Despair, 1968, In The Service of Their Country: War Resisters in Prison, 1970, Partial Justice. A Study of Bias in Sentencing, 1974, Caring, 1976; author: (with others) Doing Good: The Limits of Benevolence, 1978; author: Feelings: Our Vital Signs, 1979, The Killing of Bonnie Garland: A Question of Justice, 1982, The Rage Within: Anger in Modern Life, 1984, Rediscovering Love, 1986, Adam and Eve and Pinocchio, 1990, The Male Ego, 1992, The Perversion of Autonomy, 1996, Talk Is Not Enough: How Psychotherapy Really Works, 2000, Hatred: The Psychological Descent into Violence, 2003; contbr. articles to profl. jours. Bd. dirs. Helsinki Watch., Nat. Bd. Planned Parenthood. Served with USNR, 1943—45. Recipient George E. Daniels medal of Merit for contbns. to psychoanalytic medicine, 1973, Elizabeth Cutter Morrow lectureship, Smith Coll., 1970; fellow Chubb, Yale U., 1972. Fellow: Am. Psychiat. Assn.; mem.: N.Y. Psychiat. Soc., Am. Psychoanalytic Assn., Inst. Medicine NAS. Fax: 914 478-8212. E-mail: willgaylin@aol.com.

GAYLOR, DONALD HUGHES, surgeon, educator; b. Bklyn., Apr. 17, 1926; s. Norman Hunter and Frances (Hughes) G.; m. Joan Winifred Power, Apr. 3, 1948; children: David, Christopher, Steven, Susan, Timothy. AB, U. Rochester, 1946, MD, 1949. Diplomate Am. Bd. Surgery, Am. Bd. Thoracic Surgery. Commd. lt. (j.g.) USN, 1949, advanced through grades to capt. M.C., 1966; intern U.S. Naval Hosp., Phila., 1949-50; student flight surgeon Sch. Aviation Medicine, Pensacola, Fla., 1950-51; flight surgeon U.S. Naval Sta., Trinidad, B.W.I., 1951-53; resident gen. surgery U.S. Naval Hosp., St. Albans, N.Y., 1953-57; postgrad. fellow surgery Royal Victoria Hosp., McGill U., Montreal, Can., 1957; resident thoracic surgery U.S. Naval Hosp., St. Albans, N.Y., 1957-59; resident cardiovascular surgery St. Francis Hosp., Roslyn, N.Y., 1958; staff thoracic surgeon U.S. Naval Hosp., Portsmouth, Va., 1959-64; surgeon U.S.S. Enterprise, 1964; staff thoracic surgeon U.S. Naval Hosp., Nat. Naval Med. Ctr., Bethesda, Md., 1964-65, chief thoracic and cardiovascular surgery, 1965-68; chief surgery, exec. officer U.S.S. Repose, 1968-69; exec. officer Naval Med. Sch., Bethesda, Md., 1969-72; ret., 1972; clin. assoc. surgery U. Pa. Sch. Medicine, 1976-90; prof. clin. surgery Hahnemann U. Sch. Medicine, 1986-96. Chief surgery Allentown (Pa.) Hosp., 1972-90, Sacred Heart Hosp., 1973-76, Lehigh Valley Hosp. Ctr., 1974-90. Contbr. articles to profl. jours. Fellow ACS; mem. AMA, Am. Thoracic Soc., Am. Trauma Soc. (pres. Pa. divsn. 1979-83, treas. 1985-91), Soc. Thoracic Surgeons (founding), Pa. Assn. for Thoracic Surgery, Assn. Mil. Surgeons U.S., Am. Trauma Soc. (founding mem.). Roman Catholic. Home and Office: 3761 Devonshire Rd Allentown PA 18103-9628

GAYLOR, JAMES LEROY, biomedical research educator; b. Waterloo, Iowa, Oct. 1, 1934; s. David P. and Lena (Livingston) G.; m. Marilyn Louise Gibson, Mar. 25, 1956; children: Douglas, Ann, Robert, Kenneth. BS, Iowa State U., 1956; MS, U. Wis., 1958, PhD, 1960. From asst. prof. to prof. biochemistry Cornell U., Ithaca, N.Y., 1960-77, chmn. biochemistry, molecular and cell biology sect., 1970-76; prof., head dept. biochemistry U. Mo., Columbia, 1977-80; assoc. dir. life scis. rsch. E.I. duPont Cen. Rsch., Wilmington, Del., 1981-83, dir. health sci. rsch., 1984-85; dir. biol. rsch. E.I. duPont Pharms., Wilmington, Del., 1986-87; v.p. sci. and technology Johnson & Johnson, New Brunswick, NJ, 1987-97; adj. prof. biochemistry Emory U. Sch. Medicine, 1997-01. Vis. prof. U. Ill., summer, 1964-65; sabbatical leave U. Oreg. Sch. Medicine, 1966-67, U. Osaka, Japan, 1973-74; vis. lectr. La Molina, Peru, summer 1962; nutrition cons. Pew Found., Phila., 1986-92; mem. bd. sci. counselors div. cancer prevention Nat. Cancer Inst., NIH, Bethesda, Md., 1987-91. Contbr. over 150 rsch. articles to profl. jours.; mem. editl. bd.: Jour. Biol. Chemistry, 1970-76, Biochimica Biophysica Acta, 1971-81, Jour. of Lipid Rsch., 1972-87, assoc. editor, 1983-87. NIH fellow, 1958-60, Spl. fellow, 1966-67, Guggenheim fellow, 1973-74. Fellow: Am. Heart Assn. (emeritus); mem.: Am. Chem. Soc. Achievements include patents for specific synthetic inhibitors of cholesterol synthesis; research on biosynthesis of cholesterol and other membrane-bound enzymes including inborn errors of cholesterol synthesis. Home: 14125 Bounty Ave Corpus Christi TX 78418

GAYLORD, EDSON I. manufacturing company executive; Chmn., pres. Ingersoll Milling Machine Co., Rockford, Ill. Recipient M. Eugene Merchant Mfg. medal ASME/SME, 1991. Died Apr. 2000.

GAYNES, BRUCE IRA, optometrist, pharmacist, educator; b. Chgo., Feb. 25, 1954; s. Milton and Blanche Gaynes; m. Sara Michelle Levsky, Oct. 6, 1990; children: Jeffrey Steven, Matthew Norman. O.D., Illinois Coll. Optometry, 1983; M.S., Ind. U., 1989; PharmD, U. Ill., Chgo., 1996. Asst. prof. Rush Coll. Medicine, Chgo., 1996—. Bd. dirs. Am. Found. for Blind, Chgo., 2001—. Fellow: Am. Acad. Optometry; mem.: Am. Coll. Clin. Pharmacology. Achievements include research in assessing methods to reduce medication errors. Avocation: travel. Office: Rush Eye Ctr 1725 W Harrison Chicago IL 60612 Office Fax: 312-563-2718. E-mail: bgaynes@rush.edu.

GAYNOR, JOSEPH, chemical engineer, technical-management consultant; b. N.Y.C., Nov. 15, 1925; s. Morris and Rebecca (Schnapper) G.; m. Elaine Bauer, Aug. 19, 1951; children: Barbara Lynne, Martin Scott, Paul David, Andrew Douglas. B in Chem. Engring., Poly. Inst., 1950; MS, Case Western Res. U., 1952, PhD, 1955. Rsch. asst. Case Inst., Cleve., 1952-55; with Gen. Engring. Labs. GE, Schenectady, N.Y., 1955-66, mgr. R & D sect., 1962-66; group v.p. rsch. Bell & Howell Co., 1966-72; mgr. comml. devel. group, mem. pres.' office Horizons Rsch., Inc., Cleve., 1972-73; pres. Innovative Tech. Assocs., Ventura, Calif., 1973—; mem. nat. materials adv. bd. com. NAS; chmn. conf. com. 2d internat. conf. on bus. graphics, 1979; program chmn. 1st internat. congress on advances in non-impact printing techs., 1981; mem. adv. com. 2d internat. congress on advances in non-impact printing techs., 1984; chmn. publs. com. 3rd internat. congress on advances in non-impact printing techs., 1986; chmn. internat. conf. on hard copy media, materials and processes, 1990. Editor: Electronic Imaging, 1991, Procs. Advances in Non-Impact Printing Technologies, Vol. I, 1983, Vol. II, 1988, 3 spl. issues Jour. Imaging Tech., Proc. Hard Copy Materials Media and Processes Internat. Conf., 1990; delivered invited keynote address NIP-17 Digital Printing Techs. Internat. Conf., 2001; patentee in field. Served with U.S. Army, 1944-46. Fellow AAAS, AIChE, Imaging Sci. and Tech. Soc. (sr., gen. chmn. 2nd internat. conf. on electrophotography 1973, chmn. bus. graphics tech. sect. 1976—, chmn. edn. com. L.A. chpt. 1978—), Am. Soc. Photobiology, Sigma Xi, Tau Beta Pi, Phi Lambda Upsilon, Alpha Chi Sigma. Home: 108 La Brea St Oxnard CA 93035-3928 Office: Innovative Tech Assocs 3639 Harbor Blvd Ste 203E Ventura CA 93001-4255

GAYNOR, MARK LESLIE, clinical social worker; b. N.Y.C., July 9, 1950; s. Jules and Shirley (Rosenberg) G. BA in Sociology, CCNY, 1973; MSW, Columbia U., 1975; postgrad., New Hope Guild Tng. Program. Cert. social worker, N.Y., Conn.; lic. clin.social worker, Conn.; bd. cert. diplomate in social work. Treatment coord. dept. child and adolescent psychiatry Kings County Downstate Med. Ctr., N.Y., 1975-76; group therapist Epilepsy Found. Nassau County, Hempstead, N.Y., 1975-76; sr. social worker, clin. mgr. partial hospitalization Yale Psychiat. Inst., New Haven, 1977-80; pvt. practice New Haven, 1977—. Therapist Student Counselling Ctr., Conn. Coll., New London, 1980-81; cons. Chapel Haven, New Haven, 1978-79, 83—, New Haven Halfway House, 1980-83; dir.devel. Mental Health Care Assocs., 1991-95; cons. for practice and orgn. devel., 1995—; presenter at profl. confs. Mem. NASW, Conn. Soc. Clin. Social Workers (past bd. dirs.). Office: 418 Orange St New Haven CT 06511-6405

GAYNOR, MARTIN SCOTT, economist; b. Cleve., May 30, 1955; s. Joseph and Elaine (Bauer) G.; m. Ellen Laura Garrett Vegh, Nov. 22, 1984; children: Shoshana Ruth, Noah Eli, Gabriel Ari. BA, U. Calif., San Diego, 1977; MA, Northwestern U., 1979, PhD, 1983. Asst. prof. Va. Polytech. Inst. and State U., Blacksburg, 1981-82; instr. Rutgers U., Newark, 1982-83; asst. prof. U. Tex., Arlington, 1983-86; sr. economist Ctr. for Health Econs. Rsch., Needham, Mass., 1986-88; asst. prof. Johns Hopkins U., Balt., 1988-94, assoc. prof., 1995-95, Carnegie Mellon U., Pitts., 1995-98, E.J. Barone prof., 1998—. Vis. asst. prof. SUNY, Binghamton, 1985-86; rsch. assoc. Nat. Bur. Econ. Rsch., Cambridge, Mass., 1983—; vis. Inst. Econs., Hungarian Acad. Scis., Budapest, 1991. Contbr. articles to profl. jours. Mem. Am. Econs. Assn., Econometric Soc. Democrat. Jewish. Avocations: backpacking, hiking. Office: Heinz Sch Carnegie Mellon U Pittsburgh PA 15213-3890 E-mail: mgaynor@cmu.edu.

GAYNOR, SUZANNE MARIE, health care executive, researcher; b. Jan. 10, 1941; d. Howard Aloyousis and Irene Marie (Dunn) Gaynor; m. John Michael Hayes, May 26, 1962 (div. 1982); children: Marguerite Hayes, Jennifer Hayes, Christopher Hayes. Diploma in nursing, Fitzgerald-Mercy Sch. Nursing, 1961; BS, Marymount U. Va., 1977, MBA, 1981; DrPH, U. Mich., 1991. RN Pa., Va. Svc. coord. Upjohn Health Care, Washington, 1972—74, tng. coord., 1974—75; health intern U.S. Senate, Washington, 1977; health analyst Am. Blood Commn., Arlington, Va., 1977—79, dir. regionalization program, 1979—83, cons., 1983; dir. regional svcs. Greater NY Blood Program, N.Y.C., 1983—89; mem. faculty Mt. Sinai Sch. Medicine, 1989—; mem. interacy. tech. com. Working Group on Blood Resources and Blood Substitutes Dept. HHS, 1981—83; mem. subcom. on blood supply and blood svcs. Com. on Pub. Health N.Y. Acad. Medicine, 1984—; mem. Glood Bank Task Force Region II, Regional Comprehensive Hemophilia Treatment Ctrs. Co-founder, chmn. East Harlem Asthma Working Group, Inc., N.Y.C., 1996—; mem. East Harlem Asthma Working Group, Inc. Housing Subcom., N.Y.C., 1998—; co-founder, chmn. CUES Asthma Working Group, N.Y.C., 2000—; mem. Manhattan Consortium for Children with Spl. Health Car Needs, N.Y.C., 2000—; mem. asthma working group Ctr. for Urban Epidemiol. Studies NY Acad. Medicine, 1996—; mem. com. on environ. N.Y.C. Asthma Partnership, 2001—, mem. steering com., 2000—02, chmn. com. on the environ., 2001—02; mem. pediat/child health subcom. East Harlem Cmty. Health Com., 1995—2002. Contbr. articles to profl.jours. Discussion leader Jr. Great Books, Arlington, 1974—75; bd. dirs. LWV, 1973—76, mem. bd. dirs., study com., membership com., 1971—76. Recipient Plaque for Recognition of Svc., Am. Blood Commn., 1983—83, Healthy Housing award, Indoor Environ. Health and Tech. Conf., 2003; grantee, NHLBI,SBIR, 2003—; PEW fellow, U. Mich. Grad. Sch. Pub. Health, 1986—91, Health Homes Demonstration grant, HUD, 2003—, Healthy Homes, Healthy Families grant, EPA, 2002—. Mem.: Assn. Tchrs. Preventive Medicine, APHA, NOW, NAFE, Assn. for Health Svcs. Rsch., Coun. Cmty. Blood Ctrs. (membership com.), Am. Assn. Blood Banks (dist. adv. group), Internat. AIDS Soc., Am. Soc. Law and Medicine, Delta Sigma Epsilon. Roman Catholic. Avocations: reading, travel, music, theater. Office: Mt Sinai Sch Medicine 1 Gustave L Levy Pl Box 1043 New York NY 10029

GAYVORONSKY, LUDMILA, artist, educator; b. Kharkov, Ukraine, Dec. 4, 1939; came to the U.S., 1980; d. Pavel Nikanorovich Nikitin and M. Eva Lazarevna Skibityanskaya; m. Alexander Vitalievich Eremenko, June 9, 1996; 1 child, Gleb. Diploma in Meteorology, Hydrometeorol. Inst., Odessa, Ukraine, 1961; PhD in Geography, World Meteorol. Ctr., Moscow, 1965; BFA, Acad. Fine Art, Moscow, 1968. Engr.-climatologist Climatol. Obs., Samara, Russia, 1961-62; engr.-agrometeorologist World Meteorol. Ctr., Moscow, 1965-66; editor Inst. Tech. Info., Moscow, 1966-68, chief editor, 1969-79; instr. fine art Sts. Cosmas & Damian Human Svcs. Ctr., S.I., N.Y., 1983-93; prof. fine art Lebanon (N.H.) Coll., 1997—. Artist stage art constrn. for Childrens Week, Lincoln Ctr., N.Y.C., 1990, wall mural for Sinergia, Inc., N.Y.C., 1992-93, wall mural Town of Newport, N.H., 1998, backdrop panel Dicken's Fair, 1997. Recipient Gold medal Festival of Art, Moscow, 1968, Jurors prize distinction Spring Art Competition, Moscow, 1969, medal of honor Ukrainian Inst. Am., N.Y.C., 1988, cert. of appreciation USCG, Governors Island, N.Y., 1989, Jurors prize discinction Sunapee (N.H.) Art Fair, 1999; named acad. knight Acad. Verbano, Italy, 1999. Mem. World Phenomenological Inst. (artist in-residence 1997—), N.H. Art Assn., Acad. Fine Arts, Acad. Verbano (Italy). Mem. Orthodox Ch. of Am. Home: 26 Church St Newport NH 03773-1908 E-mail: ludmila.gayvoronsky@verizon.net.

GAZAWAY, BARBARA ANN, music educator, art educator; b. Lebanon, Pa., Jan. 7, 1942; d. Ammon Mark Brubaker and Margaret (Lesher) Dierwechter; m. Hal Prentiss Gazaway; children: Farideh Dunford, Ramin Dunford, Ammon Dunford, Lavada Kahumoku, Rene Dunford. *Barbara and her sisters, Linda, Nancy, Jean, and Joan entertained extensively throughout Pennsylvania, over a five year period, singing ballads, sacred, folk and barber shop. They appeared on local TV and radio programs, churches, and Civic organizations. In the summers they entertained at the 4-H State Convention, in the Poconos, where they sang for Fred Waring at his resort. They also spent a summer on Martha's Vineyard Island entertaining the guests at The Harbor View. Barbara worked at the Mt Gretna Inn for two summers as a baker and entertained the guests after meals playing selections on the piano, and singing with her sisters. She has five children: Farideh, who started her own clothing line of extreme sports apparel and children's sports clothes, Ramin, an Alaskan State Trooper, Ammon, a student at BYU, Idaho, with plans to become a physical therapist, Lavada, a music student and Russian language major, and Rene, Jr., currently on a Vancouver, Canada mission. Barbara and her husband, Hal, have five grandchildren.* BS in Music Edn., West Chester State U., 1963; cert. in elem. edn., Brigham Young U., 1979. Cert. Multiple Subject Tchg. Credential 1984, type A tchg. cert. 1990. Elem. music tchr. Oxford (Pa.) Sch. Dist., 1963—65; elem. classroom tchr. Lebanon (Pa.) Sch. Dist., 1965—67; elem. music tchr. U.S. Dept. Edn., European Area, Bad Kreuznach, Germany, 1968—70, elem. classroom tchr. Darmstadt, Germany, 1972—74, elem. music tchr. Alconbury,

England, 1974—75; instrumental music instr. Lebanon (Pa.) Cath. H.S., 1976—78, h.s. music tchr., 1976—77; music instr. Brigham Young U., Provo, Utah, 1978—79; elem. vocal music tchr. Bennett Valley Union, Santa Rosa, Calif., 1987—89; elem. vocal music instr. Anchorage Sch. Dist., 1990—2000; pvt. practice, 2001—. Owner, dir. Millcreek Nursery Sch., Newmanstown, 1975—76; instr. Homestay Am. Japanese Exch. Program, Santa Rosa, Calif., 1987; show pianist Marquee Theater, Santa Rosa, Calif., 1985—85; governess, Stuttgart, Germany, 1967—68; opermädchen Internat. Student Info. Svc., Mautern, Austria, 1967; singer, waitress The Harbor View, Martha's Vineyard Is., Mass., 1964; singer, baker, pianist The Inn, Mt Gretna, Pa., 1963; active Experiment in Internat. Living Home Stay Program, Switzerland, 1962; gasthaus worker Am. Student Info. Svc., Feldkirch, Austria, 1965; pres. Internat. Reading Assn. Campus Chpt. *While teaching in Germany, Barbara received recognition for her efforts to sustain a program for underachieving second graders. In Darmstadt Elementary School, Barbara, along with another teacher again received recognition for introducing the open school concept in their classrooms. After teaching seven years in Germany for the US Department Of Education, European Area, Barbara returned to her home state, Pennsylvania. There she developed and operated a pre-school program for preschoolers at a local church. The program is still in operation. While attending Brigham Young University, Barbara taught elementary education majors as an Assistant Professor in Music Education. In 1978, she was elected President of the International Reading Association, BYU student chapter. That year the chapter made three quilts with a reading theme to present to the International Reading Association President.* Singer: Sister Quartet, 1956—64. Family Coun. sec. Anchorage Pioneer Home, 2001—02; sec. Alpine Condominium Assn., Anchorage, 2001—02; chair Beautification Com., Anchorage, 2001—02; co-chair County Rep. Com., Santa Rosa, 1984—84; co-chair mission com. Trinity Christian Reformed Ch., Anchorage, 2001—02, co-facilitator divorce recovery program, 1999—; praise and worship team Anchorage First Free Methodist Ch. Mem.: NEA, Internat. Reading Assn. (pres.), Music Educators Nat. Conv. First Free Meth. Avocations: travel, hiking, reading, gardening, cooking. Personal E-mail: gazaway_barbara@hotmail.com.

GAZELL, JAMES ALBERT, public administration educator; b. Chgo., Mar. 17, 1942; s. Albert James and Ann Marion (Bloch) G. BA in Polit. Sci. with honors, Roosevelt U., 1963, MA in Polit. Sci., 1966; PhD in Govt., So. Ill. U., 1968. Instr. Roosevelt U., Chgo., 1965, 67, So. Ill. U., Carbondale, 1966-68, asst. prof. San Diego State U., 1968-72, assoc. prof., 1972-75, prof., 1975—. Cons. County San Diego, 1973, Ernst and Ernst, Detroit, 1973, Wadsworth Pub. Co., 1995, McGraw-Hill Pub. Co., 1997. Author books; contbr. articles to profl. jours.; assoc. editor Encyclopedia of Public Administration and Public Policy, 1999; mem. editl. bd. Internat. Jour. Pub. Adminstrn., Internat. Jour. Orgnl. Theory and Behavior. Mem. ACLU, Am. Soc. Pub. Adminstrn., Nat. Ctr. for State Cts., Nat. Assn. Ct. Mgmt., Nat. Assn. for Ct. Mgmt. Home: 4319 Hilldale Rd San Diego CA 92116-2135 Office: San Diego State U 5500 Campanile Dr San Diego CA 92182-0002 E-mail: jgazell@mail.sdsu.edu.

GAZZANIGA, ANTONETTE J. secondary school educator; b. Lawrence, Mass., Feb. 6, 1945; d. Anthony George and Lena (LaSpina) Calderone; m. Angelo L. Gazzaniga Jr., Aug. 6, 1966 (dec. Feb. 1993); 1 child, David. BA, Merrimack Coll., 1966; MEd, Mass. State Coll., North Adams, 1972; adminstrn. cert., Fordham U., 1990. Cert. tchr., supr., Mass., N.Y., N.J. English and applied art instr., supr. McCann Tech. Sch., North Adams, Mass., 1969-79; English instr., chair dept. J.S. Burke H.S., Goshen, N.Y., 1979-85; English instr. Goshen H.S., 1985—. Adj. instr. humanities Marist Coll., Poughkeepsie, N.Y., 1993—; cons. to corp. execs. on Am. culture and idiom Minolta Advanced Tech., Inc., Goshen, 1994-99; presenter in field. Mem. ASCD, N.Y. State Tchrs. Assn., Nat. Coun. Tchrs. English, Goshen Tchrs. Assn., Delta Kappa Gamma (sec. 1995—). Roman Catholic. Avocations: needlework, gardening, computer. Home: 36 Pine Hill Rd Highland Mills NY 10930-3422 E-mail: ntuckt@warwick.net.

GAZZETTA, MORENO AUGUSTO, engineer; b. Zurich, Switzerland, July 7, 1962; s. Giobatta and Velia Anna Gazzetta; divorced; children: Timo, Nadine, Ramon, Dominic. Diploma in elec. engring., ETH, Zurich, 1985. Engr. RCA, Zurich, 1986-89, Oerlikon-Contraves, Zurich, 1990—. Mem. IEEE, Sportfischer Verein Rumlang (treas. 1992—), Handharmonika Club Zurich Albisrieden (mem. elite orch., musician, Silver medal). Avocations: family, fly fishing, fly tying, playing accordion, composing and arranging music. Office: Oerlikon-Contraves AG Birchstr 155 8050 Zurich Switzerland E-mail: m.a.gazzetta@ieee.org., m.a.gazzetta@computer.org.

GDANITZ, ROBERT J. research scientist, educator; b. Cologne, Germany, July 15, 1962; arrived in U.S., 2000; s. Johannes P. Gdanitz, Erika E. (Horenkohl) Knight. Diploma in chemistry, U. Cologne, 1986; PhD in theoretical chemistry, 1988, habilitation in theoretical physics, 1997, privatdozent in theoretical physics, 1999. Sci. cons. Ciba-Geigy, Basel, Switzerland, 1989—91; postdoctoral staff U. Vienna, 1991—94, U. Kassel, Germany, 1994—98; privatdozent U. Braunschweig, Germany, 1998—2000; asst. rsch. prof. U. Utah, Salt Lake City, 2000—, N.C. A&T State U., Greensboro, 2002—. Contbr. articles to profl. jours. Achievements include invention of the averaged coupled-pair functional; development of method to predict molecular crystal structures; explicity correlated (r12) multi-reference configuration interaction to accurately solve the electronic Schrödinger equation of small atoms and molecules. Office: NC A&T State U Dept Phys Rm 101 Marteena Hall Greensboro NC 27411 Office Fax: 336-256-0815. Business E-Mail: gdanitz@ncat.edu.

GE, JISHENG, pharmaceutical researcher; s. Lai Ge and Bo Wang; m. Xiaobing Zhu, Mar. 22, 1989; children: Victor, Michel. PhD, Iowa State U., 1996. Postdoctoral rsch. scientist Monsanto Co., St. Louis, 1996—99; sr. rsch. scientist KV Pharm. Co., St. Louis, 2000—. Contbr. articles to profl. jours. Mem.: Am. Assn. of Pharm. Soc., Am. Chem. Soc. Achievements include patents for Us 6407042; Us 6130186; Us 6093681. Office: KV Pharm Co 8054 Litzsinger Rd Saint Louis MO 63144 Office Fax: 314-645-1687. E-mail: jge@kvph.com.

GE, PINGHUA, research scientist; s. XinHong Ge and YuYing Cheng; m. Yunling Man, Sept. 18, 1990; children: Liang Danny, Yang Tommy. BS, ZhongShan U., GuangZhou, China, 1984; MS, Beijing Normal U., 1990, Kans. State U., 1997; PhD, U. Del., 1999. Chemistry lectr. NanTong (China) Med. Coll., 1984—87; rsch. engr. Nat. Pharm. R & D Ctr., Beijing, 1990—92; postdoctoral rsch. fellow U. S.C., Columbia, 1998—2000, U. Ill., Urbana. Mem.: AAAS, Biophysics Soc., Am. Chem. Soc. Achievements include research in Synthesis And Coordination Chemistry Of Sulfur-Rich Transition Metal Chelates, Poly(Methylthiomethyl)Borate, Artificial Models For Mimicing Active Sites Of Sulfur-Containuing Metalloenzyme Sites; Synthesis Of Highly Conjugated Rigid Polyphenyleneethylene Polymers, Synthesis Of Macrocyclic Molecules By Using Alkyne Metathesis Methods; Antanna Fluorescent Dyes For Lanthanides, New Lanthanide Chelates For Fluorescence Labeling Of Biomolecules. Office: Univ Ill Dept Physics 1110 W Green St Urbana IL 61801

GE, XIANPING, computer scientist; b. Fushun, China, Jan. 5, 1973; ME, Shanghai Jiao Tong U., 1987—94; PhD, U. of Calif. at Irvine, 1997—2002. PhD fellowship, IBM, 2001.

GEAKE, RAYMOND ROBERT, psychologist; b. Detroit, Oct. 26, 1936; s. Harry Nevill and Phyllis Rae (Fox) G.; m. Carol Lynne Rens, June 9, 1962; children: Roger Rens, Tamara Lynne, William Rens. BS in Spl. Edn., U. Mich., 1958, MA in Guidance and Counseling, 1959, PhD in Edn. and Psychology, 1963. Coord. child devel. rsch. Edison Inst., Dearborn, Mich., 1962-66; dir. psychology dept. Plymouth (Mich.) State Home and Tng. Sch., Mich. Dept. Mental Health, 1966-69; pvt. practice ednl. psychology Northville, Mich., 1969-72; mem. Mich. Ho. of Reps., 1973-76, Mich. Senate, 1977-98. Adj. asst. prof. edn./psychology dept. Madonna Coll., Livonia, Mich., 1984-86. Co-author: Visual Tracking, A Self-instruction Workbook for Perceptual Skills in Reading, 1962. Trustee-at-large Schoolcraft C.C., 1969-72, chmn. bd. trustees, 1971-72; vice chmn. nat. adv. com. on mental health and illness of elderly HEW, 1976-77; vice chmn. human svcs. com., assembly fed. issues Nat. Conf. State Legislatures, 1994-95. Recipient Recognition award Found. for Improvement of Justice, 1993. Fellow Mich. Psychol. Assn.; mem. NEA (life), APA, Rotary. Republican.

GEALT, ADELHEID MARIA, museum director; b. Munich, May 29, 1946; came to U.S., 1950; d. Gustav Konrad and Ella Sophie (Daeschlein) Medicus; m. Barry Allen Gealt, Mar. 15, 1969. BA, Ohio State U., 1968; MA, Ind. U., 1973, PhD, 1979. Registrar Ind. U. Art Mus., Bloomington, 1972-76, curator Western art, 1976—, acting/interim dir., 1987-89, dir., 1989—. Adj. assoc. prof. H.R. Hope Sch. Fine Arts, Ind. U., Bloomington, 1985—89, assoc. scholar, 1986, assoc. prof., 1989—; mem. nat. adv. coun. Valparaiso U. Art Mus.; commr. Indiana Arts Commn., 1997—2001. Author: Looking at Art, 1983, Domenico Tiepolo The Punchinello Drawings, 1986; co-author: Art of the Western World, 1989, Painting of the Golden Age: A Biographical Dictionary of Seventeenth-Century European Painters, 1993, Domeinco Tiepolo: Master Draftsman, 1996, Giandomenico Teipolo, Disegni dal mondo, 1996; contbg. author Critic's Choice, 1999. Grantee Nat. Endowment for Arts, 1982, 83, Am. Philos. Soc., 1985, NEH, 1985, Samuel H. Kress Found., 1999-2000. Mem. Assn. Art Mus. Dirs. Office: Ind U Art Mus 7th St Bloomington IN 47405-3024

GEALT, MICHAEL A. environmental microbiologist, educator; b. Phila., Nov. 27, 1948; s. Edward Leonard Gealt and Lillian Rose Brenner; m. Maryjanet McNamara, Jan. 2, 1981; 1 child; m. Antonia Malandrucco, May 12, 1967 (div. 1977); 2 children. BA, Temple U., 1970; PhD, Rutgers U., 1974. Rsch. assoc. Med. Sch. Rutgers U., Piscataway, N.J., 1974-76; postdoct. assoc. Inst. Cancer Rsch., Phila., 1976-78; asst. prof. biol. scis. Drexel U., Phila., 1978-84; assoc. prof., 1984-90; prof., 1990-2000; dir. Sch. Environ. Sci., Engring. and Policy, 1994-2000; dean Sch. Engring., Math. and Sci. Purdue U. Calument, Hammond, Ind., 2000—, prof. biology, 2000—. Contbr. articles to profl. jours. Grantee EPA, 1983, 85, 89, NSF, 1981, 94, 97, USAF, 2002. Mem. AAAS, Am. Soc. Microbiology (chair environ. and applied micro divsn. 1995), Am. Soc. Cell Biology, Assn. Environ. Engrs. & Science Profs., Am. Assn. Higher Educ., Am. Soc. Engring. Educ., Sigma Chi. Avocations: motorcycles, photography. Office: Purdue U Calumet Sch Engring Math and Sci 2200 169th St Hammond IN 46323-2068

GEAR, CHARLES WILLIAM, computer scientist; b. London, Feb. 1, 1935; came to U.S., 1962, naturalized, 1977; s. Charles James and Margaret (Dumbleton) G.; m. Sharon Sue Smith, Jan. 25, 1958 (div. Oct. 1970); children— Kathlyn Jo, Christopher William Gilpin; m. Ann Lee Morgan, Nov. 19, 1976 BA, Cambridge U., 1956, MA, 1960; MS, U. Ill., Urbana, 1957, PhD, 1960; D (hon.), Royal Inst. Tech., Stockholm, 1987. Engr. IBM, Hursley, Eng., 1960-62; prof. dept. computer sci. U. Ill. Urbana, 1962-90, head dept., 1985-90; v.p. NEC Rsch. Inst., Princeton, N.J., 1990-92, pres., 1992-2000, pres. emeritus, 2000—. Vis. prof. Stanford U., Calif., 1969-70, Yale U., New Haven, 1976 Author: Computer Organization and Programming, 1969, 74, 80, 85, Numerical Initial Value Problems, 1971, Introduction to Computer Science, 1973, Introduction to Computers, Programming and Applications, 1978; Pascal Programming, 1983; Computer Applications and Algorithms, 1986. Recipient Fulbright award, 1956, Forsythe award Spl. Interest Group for Numerical Analysis, 1979, Alumni Honor award Engring. Coll., U. Ill., 1992, Alumni Achievement award U. Ill., 2001, Outstanding Civilian Svc. medal Dept. of Army, 2002. Fellow AAAS, IEEE, Am. Acad. Arts and Scis., Assn. Computing Machinery (coun. 1976-78); mem. Nat. Acad. Engring., Soc. Indsl. and Applied Math. (coun. 1980-85, pres. 1987-88). Office: NEC Rsch Inst 4 Independence Way Ste 4 Princeton NJ 08540-6685 E-mail: cwg@research.nj.nec.com.

GEARHART, JOHN WESLEY, III, musician, educator; b. Hampton, Va., Apr. 3, 1950; s. John Wesley Jr. and Carolyn (Scott) G.; m. Laurie Brasfield, June 10, 1972; children: Jennifer B., Courtney S. Student, Guilford Coll., 1968-69; BA, Coll. William & Mary, 1972; MusM, Temple U., 1975; postgrad., Westminster Choir Coll. Organist First Presbyn. Ch., Hampton, Va., 1965-68, First Bapt. Ch., Greensboro, N.C., 1968-69; asst. organist/choirmaster Bruton Parish Ch., Williamsburg, Va., 1969-73; asst. organist John Wanamaker Store, Phila., 1973-78; organist/choirmaster Grace Presbyn. Ch., Jenkintown, Pa., 1973-78; recording artist, harpsichordist Independence Hall, Phila., 1974-78; organist/choirmaster St. Paul's Episc. Ch., Mobile, Ala., 1978-93; harpist Biloxi Symphony, 1990-93, Port City Symphony, 1990-93; dir. music St. John the Divine Episcopal Ch., 1993—. Lectr., recitalist Colonial Williamsburg Found., 1971-73; lectr. Coll. William & Mary, 1972-73; faculty mem. Spring Hill Coll., 1980-93; cons. 1973-93. Contbr. articles to profl. jours.; composer 48 Hymn Descants, 1980; performed for 12 segments The Protestant Hour (nat. radio broadcasts) 1987-88. Treas., chmn. fin. Mobile Theatre Guild, Inc., 1980-85; mem. bd. Mobile Student Symphony, 1991-93; treas. Mobile chpt. Am. Guild Eng. Handbell Ringers, 1987-93; dir. 70-voice St. Paul's Comty. Choral Soc., Mobile, 1985-93; founder/dir. 20-voice Mobile Vocal Arts Ensemble, 1979-93; del. 4th Internat. Congress Organists, Cambridge, Eng., 1988. Ala. State Arts Coun. Individual fellow, 1990. Mem. Am. Guild Organists (dean 1980-82, treas. Mobile chpt. 1983-88, 92-93, chmn. region VI conv. Mobile 1991), Am. Harp Soc. (pres. Gulf Coast chpt. 1992-94), Assn. Anglican Musicians, Organ Hist. Soc., Phi Mu Alpha. Republican. Episcopalian. Avocations: gardening, cooking, playing harp, travel, collecting paperweights. Home: 12511 Woodthorpe Ln Houston TX 77024-4110 Office: St John The Divine Episcopal Ch 2450 River Oaks Blvd Houston TX 77019-5826

GEARHEART, MARK EDWIN, lawyer; b. Wichita, Kans., July 20, 1955; BS, U. No. Colo., 1977; JD, U. Calif., San Francisco, 1980. Bar: Calif. 1980, U.S. Dist. Ct. (no. dist.) Calif. 1980; cert. specialist in workers compensation, Calif. Assoc. Ury and Goldstein, Vallejo, Calif., 1980-83; mng. atty. Boxer, Ury & Gearheart, Pleasant Hill, Calif., 1983-92; pvt. practice, Pleasant Hill, 1992-93; ptnr. Gearheart & Otis, Pleasant Hill, 1993—. Mem. ATLA, ABA, Nat. Workplace Injury Litigation Group, Calif. Applicants Attys. Assn. (pres. Walnut Creek chpt. 1998—). Democrat. Office: Gearheart & Otis 367 Civic Dr Ste 17 Pleasant Hill CA 94523-1935

GEARHISER, CHARLES JOSEF, lawyer; b. Dyersburg, Tenn., Aug. 14, 1938; s. Charles Josef Gearhiser and Mary Josephine (Plant) Wickham; m. Joy Edwards; children: Charles J. III, Laura, Christy. BS, Austin Peay State U., 1960; LLB, U. Tenn., 1961. Bar: Tenn. Assoc. Strang, Fletcher, Carriger & Walker, Chattanooga, 1961-63; law clk. to presiding justice U.S. Dist. Ct. (ea. dist.) Tenn., Chattanooga, 1963-64; asst. U.S. atty. Dept. Justice, Chattanooga, 1964-66; ptnr. Stophel, Caldwell & Heggie, Chattanooga, 1966-74, Gearhiser, Peters, Lockaby & Tallant and predecessor firms, Chattanooga, 1974—. U.S. commnr., 1966-73; U.S. magistrate U.S. Dist. Ct. (ea. dist.) Tenn., 1973-78, Chattanooga. Chmn. bd. dirs. S.E. Tenn. Legal Services, Chattanooga, 1978-81. Fellow Am. Coll. Trial Lawyers, Tenn. Bar Found.; mem. ABA, Tenn. Bar Assn. (bd. govs. 1992, 1994, 1999), pres-elect, 1999-2001, pres. 2001-2002, Chattanooga Bar Assn. (sec., treas 1972-73, pres. 1973-74), Assn. Trial Lawyers Am., Tenn. Trial Lawyers Assn., Chattanooga Trial Lawyers Assn., Nat. Inst. Trial Advocacy (civil trial adv. 1981), Am. Bd. Trial Advs. (charter mem. Tenn. chpt.), Order of Coif. Democrat. Methodist. Home: 12 N Crest Rd Chattanooga TN 37404-1827 Office: Gearhiser Peters Lockaby & Tallant 320 McCallie Ave Chattanooga TN 37402-2018

GEARY, BARBARA ANN, recital and concert pianist, music educator; b. Chgo., July 2, 1935; d. Edmond Francis and Helen Mary (Brophy) G. BA in French, St. Mary's Coll., Notre Dame, Ind., 1957; postgrad., Middlebury Coll., 1958; MusM in Piano, Ind. U., 1961; postgrad., U. Paris, 1966-67, 69-70. Grad. asst. Ind. U., 1962-63; prof. piano Ohio U., 1963-69; mem. piano faculty U. N.C., 1970; prof. piano Okla. State U., 1973-78. Debut piano recital Wigmore Hall, London, 1972; touring pianist in U.S., 1971—, in western Europe, 1972, 76-83, 91-92; producer-performer narrated concerts Gottschalk Gala, Lisztomania, From Paris With Love, Fiesta Hispanica, Gottschalk to Gershwin: The Ragtime Connection, Piano Concerts for Kids; lecture-recitals in French on French piano music.; performed in festivals in U.S., France, on QE2. Activist for Eviron. Sustainability. Recipient scholarship French govt., 1970. Mem. Am. Liszt Soc., Coll. Music Soc., Gottschalk Soc. Internat. (founding mem.). Roman Catholic. Avocations: French and German langs., playing chamber music. Home and Office: 2545 S Birmingham Pl Tulsa OK 74114-3225 E-mail: bgearypiano@alumni.indiana.edu.

GEARY, DANIEL PATRICK, postal service worker; b. St. Louis, May 2, 1963; s. John James and Kathleen Mary (Hogan) G. ASBA, Lewis and Clark C.C., Godfrey, Ill., 1983; B Liberal Studies, St. Louis U., 1990. Laborer U.S. Postal Svc., St. Louis, 1991—. Roman Catholic. Avocations: reading, television, radio. Home: 913 Alpine Ridge Dr Ballwin MO 63021-7627 Office: US Postal Svc 1720 Market St Saint Louis MO 63155-0001

GEARY, DAVID CYRIL, psychology educator; b. Providence, June 7, 1957; s. Cyril Geary and Shirley Irene Files; m. Leslie Lynne Reller, Aug. 21, 1982; children: Corie, Nicholas. BS, U. Santa Clara, 1979; MS, Calif. State U., Hayward, 1981; PhD, U. Calif., Riverside, 1986. Vis. asst. prof. U. Tex., El Paso, 1986-87; asst. prof. psychology U. Mo., Rolla, 1987-89, prof. psychology Columbia, 1989—, Middlebush prof. psychol. sci., 2000—, chmn. psychol. sci., 2002—. Author: Children's Mathematical Development, 1994; Male, Female: The Evolution of Human Sex Differences, 1998; contbr. articles to profl. jours. Guest Voice of Am., NPR, 1992, 95, 97; contbr. Math. Framework for Calif. Pub. Schs., Calif. Dept. Edn., 1999. Recipient Excellence in Rsch. in Intelligence award MENSA Edn. and Rsch. Found., 1992; grantee NIH, 1994-98, 2001—. Mem. AAAS, Am. Psychol. Soc., Psychonomic Soc., Human Behavior and Evolution Soc. Avocation: black belt karate. Office: U Mo Dept Psychology 210 Mcalester Hall Columbia MO 65211-2500 Fax: 573-882-7710. E-mail: GearyD@Missouri.edu.

GEARY, DAVID PATRICK, criminal justice educator, consultant, writer; b. Milw., May 20, 1928; s. Cornelius John and Madeline (Cushway) G.; m. Mary Ann Delavan, June 19, 1954; children: Patrick, John, Daniel, Peter. BS, LaVerne U., L.A., 1971; MPA, U. So. Calif., 1972; PhD, Marquette U., 1979; postgrad., U. Mich., 1980. Cert. life teaching credential, Calif. Police officer City of Greendale, Wis., 1950-55; chief police City of Hales Corners, Wis., 1955-61, City of Salem, Oreg., 1961-65, City of Ventura, Calif., 1965-72; assoc. prof. criminal justice U. Wis., Milw., 1972-76, U. South Fla., Tampa, 1976-79, U. Nev., Reno, 1979-82, Va. Commonwealth U., Richmond, 1982—, pres. faculty senate, 1989. Mem. vis. faculty Ventura Coll., 1966-72, Carthage Coll., Kenosha, Wis., 1974; cons. Commn. on Accreditation for Law Enforcement Agys., Fairfax, Va., 1990; cons. to Va. State Police, 1994, Richmond Va. Police, 1996—; cons. to city atty. and police dept. City of Dallas, 1990; cons. to atty. gen. City of Birmingham, 1991; cons. to postal insp. U.S. Postal Svc., Washington, 1992; cons. to City of Richmond, 1996—. Author: How To Deliver Death News, 1981; editor: Community Relations, 1976; also articles. Gen. chmn. Arts in Justice, Anderson Gallery, Richmond, 1989. With U.S. Maritime Svc., 1944-46. Named Outstanding Young Man, U.S. Jaycees, Hales Corners, 1965; rsch. fellow U.S. Govt. Law Enforcement Assistance Adminstrn., 1976. Mem. AAUP (pres. Va. Commonwealth U. chpt. 1987, 94), Va. Assn. Criminal Justice Educators (pres. 1985-87), Va. Internat. Human Rights and Responsibilities Found., Inc. (founder 1998). Home: 7678 Yarmouth Dr Richmond VA 23225-2145 Office: Va Commonwealth U 816 W Franklin St # 2017 Richmond VA 23284-9030 *Don't let the barbarians get you. Don't let them injure your body, but more important don't let them get into your head and make you one of them.*

GEARY, JAMES MARTIN, writer, communications executive; b. New London, Conn., Jan. 3, 1952; s. Joseph Theodore and Martha Mary Geary. Co-dir. Cath. Peace Fellowship, Washington, 1971—72; hosp. attendant Marshall Hale Hosp., San Francisco, 1974—77; dir. client svcs. Shanti Project, Berkeley, Calif., 1978—81, exec. dir. San Francisco, 1982—88; trainer Outreach Inc., Daytona Beach, Fla., 1991—95; author, motivational spkr. Ormond Beach, Fla., 1996—. Exec. prodr. video series Shanti Project, San Francisco, 1982—88, Calif. Dept. Health, 1983. Contbg. author (book) Gifts for the Living, 1988; author: (book) Delicate Courage, 2002. Recipient Outstanding Cmty. Svc. award, Bay Area Physicians for Human Rights, 1984, Humanitarian award, AIDS Atlanta, 1986, medal, U. Calif.-San Francisco, 1988. Democrat. Avocations: tennis, bridge, spiritual studies, after-death communication. Home: 205 Lynnhurst Dr Ormond Beach FL 32176-3712

GEARY, MARIE JOSEPHINE, art association administrator; b. Boston, Dec. 1, 1933; d. Vincent and Maryanne (DeAngelo) Bianco; m. John Francis Geary, Oct. 11, 1959; 1 child, John Francis Jr. Grad., Medford H.S., 1951. Registrar grad./postgrad. div. Tufts U. Sch. Dental Medicine, Boston, 1951-60; reporter, arts editor Chelmsford (Mass.) Newsweekly, 1970-82; owner, mgr. Village Sq. Art Gallery, Chelmsford, 1976-80; founder, owner A Way With Words, Chelmsford, 1980—; founder, dir. Eastcoast Quilters Alliance, Westford, Mass., 1988—. Mktg. cons. Westford Regency Inn, 1991; cons. to arts orgns. for seminar planning, curator exhibits, 1999—. Contbr. articles to profl. mags. Pub. rels. dir. New England Quilt Mus., Lowell, 1986-88; founder, pres. Chelmsford Art Soc., 1970-75; founder, bd. dirs. Chelmsford Cultural Coun., 1980-84; founder, dir. pub. rels. Chelmsford Crafters, Inc., 1976-80; publicity dir. Chelmsford Town 4th of July Celebration, 1971-74; founder Women in Bus. Conf., 1994. Mem. Am. Quilting Soc., Chelmsford Quilters (pres. 1985-89, 99-2003), New Eng. Quilters Guild (Compass editor 1985-88), Chelmsford Book Discussion Soc., Quilters Connection (Quiltations editor 1992-93, v.p. 1994-95, pres. 1995-96), Middlesex Women's Network, Women in Bus. (formed 1993, coord. 1st conf. 1994), Enterprising Women. Republican. Roman Catholic. Avocations: art, antiques, reading, economics, marketing trends. Home: 38 Amble Rd Chelmsford MA 01824-1968 Office: Eastcoast Quilters Alliance PO Box 711 Westford MA 01886-0021 E-mail: eqaquilter@aol.com.

GEARY, MICHAEL PHILIP, lawyer; b. Harvey, Ill., Dec. 19, 1954; s. John Thomas and Patricia Ann (Carpenter) G. BA, Georgetown U., 1977; JD, St. Mary's U., San Antonio, 1980. Bar: Tex. 1980, D.C. 1986, Ohio 1989. Asst. legis. counsel Office of Legis. Counsel, U.S. Senate, Washington, 1980-90; pvt. practice Westlake, Ohio, 1990-94; exec. dir. Ashtabula County Legal Aid Corp., Jefferson, Ohio, 1994-2000, McNair & Geary Co., LPA, Jefferson, Ohio, 2000—. Trustee Contact-Ashtabula County, 1995-96, Ashtabula County Cmty. Housing Devel. Orgn., Inc., 1998-2000, United Way of Ashtabula County, 2003—; mem. Leadership Ashtabula County, Jefferson, 1994—. Mem. Ohio State Bar Assn., Ashtabula County Bar Assn. Republican. Roman Catholic. Office: McNair & Geary Co LPA 35 W Jefferson St Jefferson OH 44047-1027

GEARY, PATRICK JOSEPH, security administrator, writer; b. Milw., Mar. 6, 1957; s. David Patrick and Mary Ann (Delavan) G. BS, Va. Commonwealth U., 1984; MA, U. Richmond, 1987, U.S. Naval War Coll., 2000. Operations security cert. profl. Tech. publs. writer Dept. Def. Security Inst., Richmond, Va., 1987-88; ops. security officer David Taylor Naval Rsch. Ctr., Bethesda, Md., 1988-91, Space and Naval Warfare Sys. Command, Arlington, Va., 1991-92; divsn. head office of security Naval Sea Sys. Command, Arlington, Va., 1992—2002; dir. Office of Security and Continuity Planning Dept. of Treasury, Washington, 2002—03. Pres. Ybor City Jaycees, Tampa, Fla., 1979, Reno Jaycees, 1980-81; regional/dist. dir. Nev. Jaycees, Reno, 1981-83; co-campaign mgr. state assembly Rep. Party of Nev., Reno, 1982; senator Jaycees Internat., Coral Gables, Fla., 1983, life mem.; active West End Jaycees Richmond, 1983-98. Decorated superior civilian svc. medal Dept. Navy, 1995; recipient Charles Kulp meml. award U.S. Jaycees, 1981, Nat. Interagy. award for individual achievment in ops., 1998; Albright grad. fellow U. Richmond, 1985. Mem. NRA, KC, Nat. Def. Indsl. Assn. (life), Ops. Security Profls. Soc. (life, charter, nat. bd. dirs. 1995-, pres. 2000-2003), Nat. Assn. Parliamentarians, Nat. Mil. Intelligence Assn. (life), U.S. Naval War Coll. found. (alumni life), Va. Commonwealth U. Alumni Assn. (life), Pi Sigma Alpha, Alpha Phi Sigma. Roman Catholic. Avocations: water skiing, basketball, football, parliamentary procedure, pistol shooting. Home: 816 Cresthill Rd Fredericksburg VA 22405-1614

GEARY, RANDOLPH LEE, vascular surgeon, educator; b. 1959; BS, U. Idaho, 1982; MD, U. Wash., 1986. Resident in surgery U. Wash., Seattle, 1986-91, resident in vascular surgery, 1992-94; rsch. fellow Am. Heart Assn., Seattle, 1991-92; asst. prof. surgery Wake Forest U., Winston-Salem, N.C., 1994-99, assoc. prof. surgery, 1999—; attending surgeon N.C. Bapt. Hosp., Winston-Salem, 1994—. Prin. investigator rsch. grants NIH, 1998—. Contbr. articles to profl. jours. Mem.: Am. Soc. Investigational Pathology, Am. Assn. for Vascular Surgery, Soc. Vascular Surgery, So. Assn. Vascular Surgery, Soc. Univ. Surgeons, Assn. Acad. Surgery. Office: Wake Forest U Sch Medicine Medical Center Blvd Winston Salem NC 27157-0001

GEARY, ROBERT FRANCIS, JR., English educator; b. Boston, May 4, 1944; s. Robert Francis and Anne Theresa (Glynn) G.; m. Anna Rose Perrone, Dec. 18, 1971; children: Teresa, Maria. BA, Boston Coll., 1966; MA in English, U. Va., 1967, PhD in English, 1971. From asst. prof. to prof. English James Madison U., Harrisonburg, Va., 1971-85, prof., 1985—, head dept., 1981-90. Author: The Supernatural in Gothic Fiction, 1992. Grantee NEH, 1975, 79, James Madison U., 1991, 92, 94. Mem. Internat. Assn. Fantastic in Arts (divsn.

head sci. fiction 1996-97, treas. 2002—), S. Atlantic MLA, Phi Beta Kappa. Avocation: detective and horror fiction. Home: 1440 Crawford Ave Harrisonburg VA 22801-2905 Office: Dept English James Madison U Harrisonburg VA 22807-0001

GEBAIDE, STEPHEN ELLIOT, retired mathematics and computer science educator; b. Bklyn., Oct. 28, 1946; s. David and Ruth (Kaplan) G. BS, Bklyn. Coll., 1968; MS, Pratt Inst., 1975. Tchr. math., computer sci., coach math/computer teams Robert H. Goddard Jr. High Sch., Ozone Park, NY, 1968—2002, mentor tchr.; ret., 2002, adj. asst. prof. computer info. systems Fiorello H. LaGuardia C.C., Long Island City, NY, 1984—. Math. team coach and advisor, computer team coach and advisor, mentor tchr., math. curriculum devel., computer sci. curriculum devel. Robert H. Goddard Jr. High Sch., Ozone Park; microcomputer instr. for sch. dist. pers. Cmty. Sch. Dist. 27, Ozone Park. Recipient 1st place team award N.Y.C. Interscholastic Math. League, 1981, NSPE, 1988. Mem. United Fedn. Tchrs., Assn. Computer Educators, Assn. Tchrs. Math. N.Y.C., Nat. Coun. Tchrs. Math., Assn. Math. Tchrs. N.Y. State, Mensa. Jewish. Avocations: logical puzzles, physical fitness, volleyball. Home: 67-15 Dartmouth St Forest Hills NY 11375-4024

GEBARSKI, STEPHEN S. neuroradiologist, educator; b. Milw., July 15, 1952; BS, Marquette U., 1974; MD, U. Wis., 1978. Diplomate Am. Bd. Radiology. Neuroradiology fellow U. Mich., Ann Arbor, 1981-83, asst. prof. radiology, 1983-87, assoc. prof., 1987-95, prof. radiology, 1996—. Mem. grant rev. panel Mich. Health Care, Edn. and Rsch. Found., Detroit, 1995—; mem. operating subcom. Gen. Clin. Rsch. Ctr., Ann Arbor, 1995—. Author: Principals of Spinal Surgery, 1996, Neurological Surgery, 1995, Otolaryngology-Head and Neck Surgery, 1993; author (manuscripts) Periodicals: Radiology, AJNR, 1982-96; editl. bd. Radiology, 1991—. Gov. Mich. League, Ann Arbor, 1995—; mem. U. Mich. Faculty Senate, 1992—. Recipient Cert. of Spl. Distinction, Radiology Jour., 1986-90. Mem. Radiol. Soc. N.Am. (chmn. meeting notes com. 1993—), F.J. Hodges Soc., Am. Soc. Neuroradiology (sr.), Am. Roentgen Ray Soc., Phi Beta Kappa, Alpha Omega Alpha. Office: Univ of Mich Hosps Dept Radiology 1500 E Medical Center Dr Ann Arbor MI 48109-0630

GEBAUER, AUGUST WILLIAM, editor, writer; b. Little Rock, Apr. 7, 1940; s. August William and Mary Elizabeth (Lee) G. AB, Hendrix Coll., 1962; MA, Tulane U., 1964, PhD, 1975; MLS, George Peabody U., 1978. Instr. English U. New Orleans, 1965-69; instr. English, libr. Memphis State U., 1969-74, 76-79; tech. writer Williams-Fenix & Scisson, New Orleans, 1979-81, OAO Corp., New Orleans, 1981-84, Walk, Haydel & Assocs., New Orleans, 1984-85; tech. editor Systematic Mgmt. Svcs., New Orleans, 1985-89, Tucker & Assocs., New Orleans, 1990-97, Critique, Inc., New Orleans, 1997—; English instr. Delgado C.C., New Orleans, 1997-98. Mem.: MLA, Wilderness Soc., Sierra Club. Home: 838 Lowerline St Apt 14 New Orleans LA 70118-5161 E-mail: billgebauer@msn.com.

GEBAUER, KURT MANFRED, management executive; b. Paterson, N.J., Dec. 12, 1951; s. Werner and Edna Julie (Harris) G.; . Cheryl Lawton, Oct. 24, 1981. BA, Bucknell U., 1974. Gen. mgr. Sta. WUDO, Lewisburg, Pa., 1973-74; v.p. New Sound Assocs., Lewisburg, 1974-75; ops. mgr. Sta. WCRV, Washington, N.J., 1975-76; pres. WTS Corp., Rockaway, N.J., 1976—. Product mgr. BestWare, Inc., 1994-95, dir. internat. ops., 1995-96, mng. dir. MYOB (now MYOB US, Inc.) product line, 1996-99; internet & e strategist MYOB Global Technology, 1999—; personal and bus. mgr. Light, 1980-82; N. Am. tour mgr. Cleo Laine/John Dankworth, 1980-82, bus. and concert mgr., 1983-93; East Coast tour mgr. Henry Mancini, 1980-86; cons. Warren Broadcasting Co. (WFMV-FM), Blairstown, N.J., 1977-79, Cam Kay, Inc., 1979-84 1st Nat. Bank of Hope, N.J., 1986-88; dir. Sonoma-Hope, Inc., 1984—, Keynight Pty. Ltd., 1988-93, Consolidated Libr. Assocs., Inc., 1989-96, Distinctive Artists Mgmt., Inc., 1990-95. Sound. designer A Little Night Music, Mich. Opera Theater, 1983, Lady in Waiting, Houston Ballet, 1984, The Merry Widow, Mich. Opera Theater, 1984; prodr. DRG album Cleo at Carnegie: The 10th Anniversary Album, 1986 (Grammy award for best female jazz vocalist 1995), RCA Victor album Woman to Woman, 1989, Blues and Sentimental, 1993, Golden Records albums: Cleo Laine Live in Manhattan, 2001, Quintessential Cleo, 2001. Mem. Pi Delta Epsilon. Office: WTS Inc 10 Bank St Ste 55 Rockaway NJ 07866-3428

GEBAUER, PHYLLIS VICTORIA FELTSKOG, writer, educator; b. Chgo., Ill., Oct. 17, 1928; d. Gustave Moritz Emmanuel and Ethel Wilhelmina Feltskog; m. Frederick August Gebauer, Dec. 2, 1950 (dec. Apr. 1998). BS in Spanish, Northwestern U., 1950; MA in Spanish, U. Houston, 1966. Procedures coord. Boeing, Renton, Wash., 1957—60; spanish tchr. Bellevue Sch. Dist., Bellevue, Wash., 1963—64; tchr. Lennox Sch. Dist., Lennox, Calif., 1966—67, San Dieguito Dist., Cardiff, Calif., 1967—68; spanish tchr. Highline Sch. Dist., Seattle, 1969—70; filmmaker Gebauer Prodns., Santa Barbara, Calif., 1970—74; freelance writer, 1974—; instr. writers program U. Calif., L.A., 1989—. Workshop leader Santa Barbara Writer's Conf., Santa Barbara, 1980—, So. Calif. Writer's Conf., San Diego, 1989—93, San Diego State U. Writer's Conf., San Diego, 1995—. Author: The Pagan Blessing, 1979; contbr. articles to profl. jours., stories to mags. Named Outstanding Tchr., UCLA Ext., 1992; recipient Bronze plaque, Columbus Ohio Film Festival, 1974. Mem.: Dorothy L. Sayers Soc., Pen Ctr. U.S.A. West (exec. v.p. 1984—87), Sigma Delta Pi, Phi Sigma Iota, Phi Beta Kappa. Democrat. Unitarian Universalist. Avocations: swimming, reading, movie going.

GEBBIA, ROBERT JAMES, tax executive; b. New Castle, Pa., Nov. 29, 1947; s. Joseph A. and Helen M. (Staransky) G.; m. Eileen A. Zuk, Oct. 2, 1971; children: Jamie, Christopher, Maria. BS, Youngstown State U., 1969; MBA, Canisius Coll., 1979. CPA Va. Tax law specialist IRS, Washington, 1972-74, IRS agt. Detroit and Buffalo, 1974-77; tax supr. Peat, Marwick, Mitchell, Buffalo, 1977-79; tax mgr. Coopers & Lybrand, Pitts., 1979-81; tax dir. UNC Resources, Falls Church, Va., 1981-85; sr. tax mgr. Occidental Petroleum, Tulsa, 1985-88; dir. taxes Carpenter Tech., Reading, Pa., 1988—. Instr. Albright Coll., Reading, 1989—; treas. Carpenter Tech. Fed. Pac, Carpenter Tech. Pa. Pac. Treas. Carpenter Tech. Pa./Fed. PAC. With U.S. Army, 1970-71, Vietnam. Decorated Bronze Star, Army Commendation medals (2). Mem. Mfrs. Alliance for Productivity and Innovation, Pa. Chamber of Bus. and Industry, Tax Execs. Inst., Nat. Assn. Corp. Treasurers, Berks County C. of C. Roman Catholic. Avocation: tennis. Home: 217 Logan Ave Wyomissing PA 19610-2655 Office: Carpenter Tech 1047 N Park Rd Wyomissing PA 19610 E-mail: rgebbia@cartech.com.

GEBBIE, KRISTINE MOORE, health science educator, health official; b. Sioux City, Iowa, June 26, 1943; d. Thomas Carson and Gladys Irene (Stewart) Moore; m. Lester N. Wright; children: Anna, Sharon, Eric. BSN, St. Olaf Coll., 1965; MSN, UCLA, 1968; DPH, U. Mich., 1995. Project dir. USPHS Tng. Grant, St. Louis, 1972—77; coord. nursing St. Louis U., 1974—76, asst. dir. nursing, 1976—78, clin. prof., 1977—78; adminstr. Oreg. Health Div., Portland, 1978—89; sec. Wash. State Dept. Health, Olympia, 1989—93; coord. Nat. AIDS Policy, Washington, 1993—94; assoc. prof. Sch. Nursing Columbia U., 1994—; assoc. prof. Oreg. Health Scis. U. Portland, 1980—90. Chair secretarial panel on evaluation of epidemiologic rsch. activities U.S. Dept. Energy, 1989—90; mem. Presdl. Commn. on Human Imunodeficiency Virus Epidemic, 1987—88. Author (with Deloughery and Neuman): Consultation and Community Orgn., 1971; author: (with Deloughery) Political Dynamics: Impact on Nurses, 1975; author: (with Scheer) Creative Teaching in Clinical Nursing, 1976. Bd. dirs. Lusth. Family Svcs. Oreg. and S.W. Wash., 1979—84, Oreg. Psychoanalytic Found.1, 1983—87. Recipient Disting. Alumna award, St. Olaf Coll., 1979; scholar Disting. scholar, Am. Nurses Found., 1989. Fellow: Am. Acad. Nursing; mem.: Am. Soc. Pub. Adminstrn. (Adminstrn. award II 1983), N.Am. Nursing Diagnosis Assn. (treas. 1983—84), Inst. Medicine, Am. Pub. Health Assn. (exec. bd.), Assn. State and Territorial Health Ofcls. (pres. 1984—85, exec. com. 1980—87, McCormick award 1988). Office: Columbia U Sch Nursing 630 W 168th St New York NY 10032-3702

GEBERTH, FRANCES WHITE, painter; b. Mt. Vernon, N.Y., May 9, 1925; d. Milo J. and Frances Bame White; m. William J. Geberth, June 27, 1948; children: Elizabeth, Deborah. Student, Parsons Sch. Design, 1946-48. Pub.'s asst. Moore-Robbins Pub., N.Y.C., 1943-45; display advt. Macy Newspapers, White Plains, N.Y., 1945-46; propr. Summer Gallery, Harwich Port, Mass., 1985-87, Fo'cas'le House Gallery, Harwich Port, Mass., 1987—. Illustrator: A Quest for Good Eating, 1994, To Always Persevere, 1995. Chair Arts Lottery Coun., Harwich, 1984-90; mem. Archtl. Adv. Bd., Harwich, 1990-94. Mem. Guild Harwich Artists, Harwich Hist. Soc. (mus. chair 1996-98, 2001—, pres. 1999-2000, newsletter editor 2002—), Questers (sec. chpt. 950 2000—), Gen. Soc. Mayflower Descs., Creative Arts Ctr. Avocation: antique costume identification and preservation. Home and Office: Fo'cas'le House Gallery 35 Wendys Way Harwich MA 02645-2507 E-mail: fgeberth@capecod.net.

GEBHARDT, SUZANNE MARIE, insurance company executive; b. Wausau, Wis., Mar. 31, 1958; d. Marvin J. and Janet S. (Reinhold) Huebner; m. Robert B. Gebhardt, Apr. 4, 2003. BBA in Risk Mgmt. and Ins., U. Wis., 1980. CLU, CPCU. Individual life product analyst Wausau (Wis.) Ins. Cos., 1981-82, individual life product coord., 1982-85, dir. individual life products, 1985-87, casualty mktg. specialist, 1987-91, market devel. coord., 1991-94, dir. market R&D, 1994-97, dir. mktg., prodr. svcs., 1997-99; mgr. comml. mkts. ops. Liberty Mut. Ins. Group, Wausau, 1999—2001; strategic initiatives and planning coord. Church Mut. Ins. Co., Merrill, Wis., 2001—02, mgr. orgn. devel. and strategic initiatives, 2003—. Instr. Wausau Ins. Cos. and North Cen. Tech. Coll., Wausau, 1989-94. Loaned exec. United Way, 1997. Mem. Am. Soc. CLUs, CPCU Soc., U. Wis. Bus. Alumni, Wausau Country Club (ladies golf chmn. 1992, 99, treas. 1997). Office: Church Mutual Ins Co 3000 Schuster Ln Merrill WI 54452

GEBO, SUSAN CLAIRE, consulting nutritionist; b. Bristol, Conn., June 22, 1954; d. Ernest Edward and Lena Clara (Jullian) G.; m. Joseph Louis Vasile, Oct. 10, 1987. BS, Cornell U., 1976; MPH, U. Mich., 1980. Registered dietitian. Pub. health nutritionist Navajo & Apache County Health Dept., Holbrook and St. Johns, Ariz., 1976-77; coord., WIC nutritionist Miss. State Bd. Health, Tupelo, 1977-78; asst. state WIC nutrition coord. Conn. Dept. Health Svcs., Hartford, 1978-79; nutritionist Cmty. Health Svcs., Hartford, 1981-84; pvt. practice West Hartford, Conn., 1983—; faculty, nutritionist U. Conn. Family Medicine Residency Program, Hartford, 1985—; nutritionist Wesleyan U. Student Health Svcs., Middletown, Conn., 1988—. Adj. faculty U. Hartford, West Hartford, 1981-88, So. Conn. State U., New Haven, 1985-2002, Albertus Magnus Coll., 1991-2000, St. Joseph Coll., West Hartford, 1992—, Manchester C.C., 1994—; fellow Nat. Nutrition Consortium, Washington, 1980. Author: What's Left to Eat?, 1992; writer (video) The Diet Interview: A Guide for Paraprofessionals, 1980, featured in video Culinary Hearts Kitchen Course, Am. Heart Assn., 1988, panenelist (PBS-TV spl.) Women's Hearts at Risk, 1996, featured nutrition expert (PBS-TV series) 3 episodes America's Walking, 2003. Bd. dirs. Am. Heart Assn., Hartford, chmn. program com. greater Hartford br., 1989-91; mem. com. State Communications, 1991-94, media spokesperson, 1991— (Outstanding program award 1990, Outstanding HeartGuide Spokeswoman 1990, Time, Feeling, and Focus award, 1992). Mem. AAUP, Am. Pub. Health Assn., Am. Dietetic Assn., Conn. Dietetic Assn. (co-chmn. pub. rels. com. 1991-93, mem. media spokesperson com. 1993-98, Registered Dietitian of Yr., 1994, del. 1996-99). Avocations: walking, photography, gardening. Office: 854 Farmington Ave West Hartford CT 06119-1587 E-mail: sgebo1@prodigy.net.

GECHT, MARTIN LOUIS, physician, bank executive; b. Chgo., July 12, 1920; s. Max and Sarah (Rolnick) G.; m. Francey Ann Heytow; children: Lauren Paula Gecht Kramer, Susan Ellen Gecht Rieser, Robert David. BA, U. So. Calif., 1941; MD, U. Health Sci./Chgo. Med. Sch., 1945; DHL (hon.), U. Health Scis., 2000. Intern Brookdale Med. Center, N.Y.C., 1944-45; resident in dermatology Cook County Hosp., 1955-58; gen. practice medicine, 1946-59; practice medicine specializing in dermatology, 1959-99; organized Allport Med. Group, 1948, now pres. Chmn. bd. Albany Bank & Trust Co. N.A., 1976—. Trustee, mem. exec., fin. coms., chmn. audit com. Finch U. Health Sci./Chgo. Med. Sch.; participant numerous activities Jewish Fedn. Chgo.; Chgo. Com. Weizmann Inst. Sci., internat. bd. dirs.; mem. adv. com. on prints and drawings, life trustee Art Inst. Chgo.; bd. dirs. Lyric Opera of Chgo.; bd. trustees Chgo. Symphony Orch. Recipient Disting. Service award Anti-Defamation League, B'nai B'rith, 1975, 83. Mem. Am. Bankers Assn., Ill. Bankers Assn., AMA, Ill. Med. Soc., Chgo. Med. Soc. Councilors, Am. Acad. Dermatology (life), Soc. Indsl. Medicine and Surgery. Clubs: Metropolitan, Standard, High Ridge (Palm Beach, Fla.). Jewish. Home: 1110 N Lake Shore Dr Apt 37 Chicago IL 60611-1054 Office: Albany Bank & Trust Co NA 3400 W Lawrence Ave Chicago IL 60625-5188

GECKIL, ILHAN KUBILAY, economist, consultant; b. Elazig, Turkey, July 22, 1975; s. Ali and Hacere Bilhan Geckil; life ptnr. Onur Yavuz. BA in economics, Koc U., Istanbul, Turkey, 1999; MA in economics, Mich. State U., 2001. Tchg. asst. Mich. State U., 1999—2000; economist/cons. Anderson Econ. Group LLC, Lansing, Mich., 2000—. Scholarship, Vehbi Koc Found., 1994—99, Tchg. assistantship, Mich. State U., 1999—2000. Mem.: Nat. Assn. of Bus. Economics. Libertarian. Office: Anderson Economic Group 615 W Ionia St Lansing MI 48933 Personal E-mail: ilhankubilaygeckil@yahoo.com. E-mail: igeckil@andersoneconomicgroup.com.

GECKLE, GEORGE LEO, III, retired English language educator; b. Danbury, Conn., Dec. 2, 1939; s. George Leo and Dorothy Marion (Hill) G.; m. Justine Virginia Carroll, Aug. 19, 1961 (dec. Nov. 26, 2002); children: George, Richard. AB, Middlebury Coll., 1961; MA, U. Va., 1962, PhD, 1965. Asst. prof. English U. Wis., Madison, 1965-68, U. S.C., Columbia, 1968-70, assoc. prof. English, 1970-74; prof. English U S.C., Columbia, 1974—2002; dir. honors program U. S.C., Columbia, 1970-73, dir. English grad. studies, 1974-76, 77-78, chmn. English dept., 1978-87. Author: John Marston's Drama, 1980, Tamburlaine and Edward II: Text and Performance, 1988; editor: Twentieth Century Interpretations of Measure for Measure, 1970, Measure for Measure, Shakespeare: The Critical Tradition, 2001. Fulbright grantee sr. prof. category U. Bamberg, Fed. Republic Germany, 1984-85; recipient 1st Jo Ann Boydston Essay prize Assn. for Documentary Editing, 1995. Mem. MLA, South Atlantic MLA, Shakespeare Assn. Am., Southeastern Renaissance Conf. (pres. 1985-86). Home: 5925 Timle Ln Columbia SC 29206-1629 Office: U South Carolina Dept English Humanities Bldg Columbia SC 29208-0001

GECKLE, KATHERINE L. interior designer; b. Watertown, Mass., Mar. 9, 1945; d. Paul Emile and Alice Dolores Landry; m. Robert Alan Geckle, July 22, 1967; chilren: Sarah Nicole Findley, Robert Alan Jr. BA, Middlebury Coll., 1967. Design cons. Lexington Gardens, Newtown, Conn., 1983-86; interior designer Ethan Allen Inc., Danbury, Conn., 1986-91; spl. edn. tutor Newtown (Conn.) Sch. Sys., 1993-96. Interior designer, planner C.H. Booth Libr. PTO officer, vol. Newtown Sch. Sys., 1974-84; v.p., chmn. long-range planning C.H. Booth Libr. Bd. Trustees, Newtown, 1992-2000; mem. Newtown Friends of the Libr., 1994—. Named Libr. Trustee of Yr. Assn. Conn. Libr. Bds., Inc., 1996. Republican. Roman Catholic. Avocations: reading, needlework. Home: 33 Poverty Hollow Rd Newtown CT 06470

GECKLE, ROBERT ALAN, manufacturing company executive; b. Newtown, Conn., July 12, 1944; s. George Leo and Dorothy Marion (Hill) G.; m. Katherine Bernarda Landry, July 22, 1967; children: Sarah Nicole, Robert Alan Jr. BA in Econs., Middlebury Coll., 1967; MBA in Mktg., U. Pa., 1969. Sales mgr. Branson Cleaning Equipment Co., Stamford, Conn., 1969-71, product mgr. Shelton, Conn., 1971-73, dir. mktg., 1973-75, gen. mgr., 1975-78, pres., 1978-86, Branson Ultrasonics Corp., Danbury, Conn., 1987-94; pres., CEO Scan-Code, Inc., Rocky Hill, Conn., 1994-97; pres. Fluid and Power Systems Group, Textron, Providence, 1997—2002; adv. dir. Investcorp Internat., 2002—. Bd. dirs. Neptune Techs. Group, SI Corp., Playpower Corp. Contbr. articles on ultrasonics to profl. jours.; patentee in field. Bd. dirs. Danbury Health Systems, 1988—; mem. Pres.'s Club, 1988—. Mem. Conn. Bus. Industry Assn. (bd. dirs. 1991, exec. com., 1992), Ridgewood Country Club, Danbury C. of C. Republican. Roman Catholic. Avocations: golf, gardening. Office: Investcorp Internat 280 Park Ave New York NY 10017

GECKLER, RICHARD DELPH, metal products company executive, retired; b. Toledo, Nov. 4, 1918; s. Maurice T. and Edith (Payne) G.; m. Elaine Mary Campbell, June 27, 1965; 1 child, Elaine Demian; 1 child by previous marriage, Carole Faye (Mrs. Gene Hendrix). AB, DePauw U., 1939. Chem. engr. Standard Oil Co., Ind., 1939-45; with Aerojet-Gen. Corp., Calif., 1945-68, v.p., mgr. solid rocket plant, Sacramento, 1956-63, corp. v.p., El Monte, 1963-68; chmn. bd., chief exec. Aerojet Delft Corp., 1968-69; exec. v.p. Anellux Systems Corp., El Segundo, Calif., 1970-71; pres. Marquardt Co., 1972-73, Pitter Metal Products, Inc., 1972-89, J.L. Mallard Co., 1972-89, Geckler Industries, Inc., 1972—2003; ret., 2003. Asst. dir. strategic weapons Office Sec. Def., 1964-66 Recipient Meritorious Pub. Service citation Navy Dept., 1961 Fellow Am. Inst. Aeros. and Astronautics; mem. Am. Chem. Soc., Am. Math. Soc., Am. Assn. of Artificial Intelligence, The Athenaeum, Phi Beta Kappa. Home: 7450 Olivetas Ave # D316 La Jolla CA 92037-4902 E-mail: geckler@cts.com.

GEDA, YONAS ENDALE, neuropsychiatrist, researcher; s. Endale Geda Wakenie and Almaz Genemie Korbie; m. Tigist W. Tsegaye, Oct. 7, 1994; children: Ezra, Abigail. MD, Haile Selassie/Addis Ababa U., Ethiopia, 1991. Diplomate Am. Bd. Neurology and Psychiatry. Gen. med. practitioner Armed Forces Gen. Hosp., Addis Ababa, 1991—93; intern in internal medicine Wright State U., Dayton, Ohio, 1995—96; resident in psychiatry Mayo Clinic, Rochester, Minn., 1996—2000, fellow in behavioral neurology, 2000—01, neuropsychiatrist, 2001—. Recipient merit award, Laughlin Found., 1999, Mayo Brothers Dist. Fellowship Award. Ethiopian Orthodox Christian. Office: Mayo Clinic 200 1st St SW Rochester MN 55905 Office Fax: 507-284-4158. Business E-Mail: geda.yonas@mayo.edu.

GEDDES, BARBARA SHERYL, communications executive, consultant; b. Poughkeepsie, NY, May 27, 1944; d. Samuel Pierson and Dorothy Charlotte (Graham) Brush; m. James Morrow Geddes, Feb. 24, 1968 (div. Dec. 1980); 1 child, Elisabeth. BA, Skidmore Coll., 1968. Project leader Four-Phase Systems, Cupertino, Calif., 1976—77, Fairchild Co., San Jose, Calif., 1979—80; mgr. tech. publs. Mohawk Data Scis., Los Gatos, Calif., 1977—79; project mgr. Advanced Micro Computers, Santa Clara, Calif., 1980—81; mgr. tech. publs. Sytek Inc., Mountain View, Calif., 1981—83; v.p. comms. sys. Strategic Inc., Cupertino, 1983—86; pres., mng. ptnr. Computer and Telecomms. Profl. Svcs., Mountain View, Calif., 1986—89; v.p. corp. mktg., sec. First Pacific Networks, Sunnyvale, Calif., 1988—94; pres. Auration, Inc., Palo Alto, 1994—; v.p. mktg., corp. sec. Tachyon Semiconductor Corp., San Jose, 1999—. Cons. H-P, Varian, Aydin Energy, Chemelex, also others, 1972—; v.p. Conf. Recorders, Santa Clara, 1975—77; advisor Tele-PC, Morgan Hill, Calif., 1983—88. Editor: Mathematics/Science Library, 7 vols., 1971; contbr. numerous articles to profl. jours. Advisor Los Altos Hills Planning Commn., Calif., 1978—79; mem. Santa Clara County Adoptions Adv. Bd., 1971—73, Las Cumbres Archtl. Control Commn., Los Gatos, 1983. Named N.Y. State Regents merit scholar, 1962. Mem.: Women in Comms. (pres. San Jose 1983—84), Bus. and Profl. Advt. Assn., Nat. Soc. for Performance and Instrn., Assn. for Computing Machinery (editor 1970—72). Democrat. Home: 10072 Senate Way Cupertino CA 95014-5710 Personal E-mail: sherry@netmagic.net.

GEDDES, LANELLE EVELYN, nurse, physiologist; b. Houston, Sept. 15, 1935; d. Carl Otto and Evelyn Bertha (Frank) Nerger; m. Leslie Alexander Geddes, Aug. 3, 1962. BSN, U. Houston, 1957, PhD, 1970. Staff nurse Houston Ind. Sch. Dist., 1957-62; instr. to asst. prof. physiology Baylor U. Coll. Medicine, 1972-75; asst. prof. nursing Tex. Women's U., 1972-75; prof., head Purdue U. Sch. Nursing, Lafayette, Ind., 1975-91. Contbr. chpts. to books, articles to med. jours. Recipient tchg. awards. Mem. Am. Nurses Assn., Am. Assn. Critical-Care Nurses, AAAS, N.Y. Acad. Scis., Phi Kappa Phi, Sigma Theta Tau, Iota Sigma Pi. Lutheran. Office: Purdue Univ West Sch Nursing Lafayette IN 47907

GEDDES, LESLIE ALEXANDER, bioengineer, physiologist, educator; b. Scotland, May 24, 1921; s. Alexander and Helen (Humphrey) G.; m. Irene P. Bloomer; 1 child, James Alexander; m. La Nelle E. Nerger, Aug. 3, 1962. BEE, MEngring., SeD (hon.), McGill U.; PhD in Physiology, Baylor U. Med. Coll. Demonstrator in elec. engring. McGill U., 1945, research asst. dept. neurology, 1945-52; cons. elec. engring. to various indsl. firms Que., Can.; biophysicist dept. physiology Baylor Med. Coll., Houston, asst. prof. physiology, 1956-61, assoc. prof., 1961-65, prof., 1965-74; dir. Lab. of Biophysics, Tex. Inst. Rehab. and Research, Houston, 1961-65; prof. physiology Coll. Vet. Medicine, Tex. A. and M. U., College Station, 1965-74, prof. biomed. engring., 1969-74; Showalter Disting. prof. bioengring. and elec. engring. Purdue U., West Lafayette, Ind., 1974-91, Showalter Disting. prof. emeritus, 1991—. Cons. NASA Manned Spacecraft Center, Houston, 1962-64, USAF, Sch. Aerospace Medicine, Brooks AFB, 1958-65; expert witness, 1981—. Author: 22 books; cons. editor: Med. and Biol. Engring., 1969—, Med. Research Engring., 1964-74, Med. Electronics and Data, 1969—; mem. editorial bd.: Jour. Electrocardiology, 1968—, med. instr., 1974—; contbr. over 750 articles to bioengring. Mem. Soc. Free Space Floaters, 1961. With Can. Army OTC. Fellow: IEEE (Leadership award, Edison medal, IEEE 3d Millennium award, World of Difference award, Lee De Forest award 2001), AAAS, Royal Soc. Medicine, Am. Inst. for Med. and Biol. Engring., Am. Coll. Cardiology, Nat. Acad. Forensic Engrs., Australasian Coll. Physicists in Biology and Medicine; mem.: NAE, NSPE, Am. Physiol. Soc., Assn. for Advancement Med. Instrumentation (Leadership award), Biomed. Engring. Soc., Tex. Soc. Profl. Engrs., Radio Club Am., Phi Zeta, Tau Beta Pi, Sigma Xi. Achievements include patents for Holder 23 U.S. patents. Home: 400 N River Rd Apt 701 West Lafayette IN 47906-3131 Office: Purdue U POTR Bldg West Lafayette IN 47907-1296 E-mail: geddes@ecn.purdue.edu.

GEDDES, ROBERT L. state legislator; b. Preston, Idaho, Nov. 14, 1955; m. Tammy Geddes; children: Megan, Emily, Lizabeth, Robert W., Jess. Student, Ricks Coll.; BS in Geology, Utah State U. Geologist; environ. specialist, 1985—; mem. Idaho Senate, Dist. 32, Boise, 1996—, pres. pro tem., 2003—. Vice chair local govt. and tax. com., mem. agrl. affairs, resources and environment, and state affairs coms.; assoc. bd. mem. Caribou County Soil Conservation Dist. Past chair Caribou County Rep. com. Mem. Am. Inst. Mining (past chair Snake River sect.). Republican. Office: State Capitol PO Box 83720 Boise ID 83720-3720*

GEDDIE, ROWLAND HILL, III, lawyer; b. Tuscaloosa, Ala., Jan. 7, 1954; s. Rowland Hill Jr. and Mary Martha (McGaughy) G.; m. Peggy O'Neal Emmons, Aug. 13, 1977; children: Mary Catherine, Virginia Jane. BA, U. Miss., 1976, JD, 1978. Bar: Miss. 1978, U.S. Dist. Ct. (no. dist.) Miss. 1978, Tex. 1979, Mo. 1995. Assoc. Baker & Botts, Houston, 1978-87; assoc. gen. counsel Lower Colo. River Authority, Austin, Tex., 1987-88; sr. counsel Houston Industries Inc./Houston Lighting & Power Co., 1988-92; contract atty. Tandy Corp./TE Electronics Inc., Ft. Worth, 1993; v.p., gen. counsel, sec. O'Sullivan Industries Holdings Inc., Lamar, Mo., 1993—. Treas. Southgate Civic Club, Houston, 1991-92; mem. Barton Co. C. of C. (dir. 2003-04). Presdl. scholar U.S. Govt., Washington, 1972. Mem.: Am. Corp. Counsel Assn., Lamar Swim Team Assn., Inc. (pres. 2000—02), Lamar Rotary Club (v.p. 2001—02, pres. 2002—03). Methodist. Avocations: personal computers, cycling, scuba diving, swimming. Home: 1503 Gulf St Lamar MO 64759-1830 Office: O'Sullivan Industries Inc 1900 Gulf St Lamar MO 64759-1899 E-mail: rowland.geddie@osullivan.com.

GEDDIE, THOMAS EDWIN, retired small business owner; b. Oct. 7, 1930; s. Nolen Dawson and Fannie (Troublefield) G.; m. Minnie Maxine Smith, Feb. 18, 1968, children: Susan, Tommy, Sherry. BS in Agr., Okla. State U., 1951; postgrad., Tex. A&M U., 1951. Owner, oper. Thomas E. Geddie Assocs., Athens, 1955—96; ret., 1996; pvt. investor. With U.S. Army, 1952—54. Mem.: Masons (32 deg.). Presbyterian. Home: 901 Clifford St Athens TX 75751-2959 Office: 314 N Faulk St Athens TX 75751-2030

GEDDY, VERNON MEREDITH, JR., lawyer; b. Norfolk, Va., Apr. 12, 1926; s. Vernon Meredith and Carrie Cole (Lane) G.; m. Marie Lewis Sibley, Dec. 22, 1949; children: Anne Lewis Geddy Cross, Vernon M. Geddy III AB cum laude, Princeton U., 1949; LL.B., U. Va., 1952. Bar: Va. Ptnr. Geddy & Harris (and predecessor firms), Williamsburg, Va., 1952-80; ptnr. McGuire, Woods, Battle & Boothe (and predecessor firms), Williamsburg, Va., 1980-91, Geddy, Harris & Geddy (and predecessor firms), Williamsburg, 1991-99, Geddy, Harris, Franck & Hickman, L.L.P., Williamsburg, 1999—. Former dir. United Va. Bankshares, Nat. Ctr. for State Cts. Mem. Williamsburg City Coun., Va., 1968-80; trustee Colonial Williamsburg Found., 1981-95, Va. Hist. Soc., Richmond, 1981-88, 93-99, Va. Mus. Fine Arts, 1982-91; bd. dirs. Williamsburg Cmty. Hosp., 1969-85, WHRO, Pub. Telecoms. for Hampton Roads, Jamestown-Yorktown Found.; chmn. Williamsburg Cmty. Health Found. Sgt. USAAF, 1944-46, PTO. Named to Raven Soc. Fellow Am. Bar Found. (award 1976); mem. ABA, Va. Bar Assn. (pres. 1972-73), Va. State Bar, Williamsburg

Bar Assn. (pres. 1975-93), Omicron Delta Kappa, Commonwealth Club. Episcopalian. Office: Geddy Harris Franck & Hickman LLP PO Box 379 1177 Jamestown Rd Williamsburg VA 23185

GEDEON, LUCINDA HEYEL, museum director; b. Port Chester, N.Y., Oct. 13, 1947; d. Philip H. and Isabel (Oldham) H.; m. Francis A. Sprout, Feb. 8, 1987. BA, Calif. State U., Long Beach, 1978; MA, UCLA, 1981, PhD, 1990. Asst. curator Grunwald Ctr. UCLA, 1978-81, asst. dir. Grunwald Ctr., 1981-83, acting dir. Grunwald Ctr., 1983-85; chief curator Ariz. State U. Art Museum, Tempe, 1985-91; dir. Neuberger Mus. SUNY, Purchase, 1991—. Author: (exhbn. catalogues) Tamarind: Los Angeles to Albuquerque, 1985, Fiber Concepts, 1989 (book) The Art of Leonard Lehrer, 1986; gen. editor: Melvin Edwards Sculpture: A Thirty Year Retrospective, 1993, Shared Beginnings Separate Passages: A Retrospective of the Work of Carol Anthony and Elaine Anthony, 1996, June Wayne; A Retrospective, 1997, Elizabeth Catlett Sculpture: A Fifty-Year Retrospective, 1998, Marisol, 2001, Toshiko Takaezu, 2001, Grace Hartigan, 2001; contbr. articles to profl. jours. Chairperson Tempe Mcpl. Arts Commn., 1989-90; bd. dirs. Balboa Art Conservation Ctr., San Diego, 1986-91, Arttable, N.Y., 1995-98, Westchester Arts Coun., 1998—. Recipient Individual Arts award Westchester Arts Coun., 2002, Chancellor's award Excellence, SUNY, 2002; Edward A. Dickson History of Art fellow UCLA, 1984, Afro-Am. Studies fellow, 1984. Mem. Am. Assn. Mus., Assn. Art Mus. Dirs. Office: Neuberger Mus Art SUNY at Purchase 735 Anderson Hill Rd Purchase NY 10577-1402 E-mail: lucinda.gedeon@purchase.edu.

GEDER, LASZLO, neurologist, educator; b. Debrecen, Hungary, Aug. 11, 1932; came to U.S., 1974, naturalized, 1982; s. Joseph and Irene (Kardoss) G.; m. Julianna Toth, Sept. 22, 1956; children: Judith, Martha, Laszlo. MD, U. Debrecen, 1956, PhD, 1969. Assoc. prof. dept. microbiology Med. Sch., U. Debrecen, 1956-72; rsch. assoc. Children's Hosp., Cin., 1964-65; Welcome rsch. fellow dept. virology Med. Sch., U. Birmingham, Eng., 1970-71; acting head dept. microbiology Ahmadu Bello U., Zaria, Nigeria, 1972-74; assoc. prof. dept. microbiology Pa. State U., Coll. Medicine, Hershey, 1974-80; physician in neurology, dept. medicine Milton S. Hershey Med. Ctr., 1980-85, prof. neurology dept., 1985—. Dir. adult rehab. U. Hosp. Rehab. Ctr., 1988—; mem. Nat. Prostatic Cancer Project. Contbr. numerous articles on viral oncology and Neurorehab. to profl. jours. Mem. AAAS, Am. Soc. Microbiology, Am. Acad. Neurology, N.Y. Acad. Scis., Sigma Xi. Home: 3860 Colebrook Rd Elizabethtown PA 17022-9075 Office: Pa State U Milton S Hershey Med Ctr Div Neurology Hershey PA 17033 E-mail: lgeder@aol.com.

GEDEVANISHVILI, SHALVA, materials scientist, researcher; b. Tbilisi, Georgia, Feb. 15, 1964; s. Vsevolod and Eliso Gedevanishvili; m. Lela Kometiani, Feb. 28, 1993; children: Alexander, Anna. BS, Tbilisi Tech. U., 1986; PhD in Metall. Engring., Inst. Metallurgy, Tbilisi, 1990. Rsch. scientist Inst. Metallurgy, Tbilisi, 1990—93; post doctoral rschr. U. Calif., Davis, 1993—96; rsch. assoc. Pa. State U., State College, 1996—99, Philip Moris USA, Richmond, Va., 1999—2001; rsch. scientist Chrysalis Techs. Inc., Richmond, Va., 2001—02, Philip Morris USA, Richmond, Va., 2002—. Contbr. articles to profl. jours. Recipient Innovations in Real Materials award, Internat. Union Materials Rsch. Socs., 1998, 1st pl., Internat. Metallographic Soc., 2000. Mem.: Am. Soc. Metals Internat., Materials Rsch. Soc., Am. Ceramic Soc. Achievements include four Russian patents, three US patent, one US patents pending; research in materials synthesis, development of inorganic advanced materials. Avocations: photography, travel.

GEDIMAN, HELEN K. psychologist; b. Bklyn., Mar. 23, 1931; d. Louis B. and Minnie Mabel Kornfeld; m. Lewis M. Gediman, Dec. 26, 1960 (div. Oct. 1977); 1 child, Paul Henry. AB, Harvard U., 1952, EdM, 1954; AM, Boston U., 1953; PhD, NYU, 1959. Postdoc. fellow in psychology Albert Einstein Coll. Med., N.Y.C., 1959—61, asst. clin. prof. psychology in psychiatry, 1972—85; chief psychologist Tappan Zee Mental Health Ctr., North Tarrytown, NY, 1960—64; pvt. practice N.Y.C., 1961—; rsch. assoc., NIMH fellow in psychology NYU Grad. Sch. Arts and Scis., N.Y.C., 1964—72; faculty, tng. and supervising analyst NY Freudian Soc., N.Y.C., 1972—. Adj. clin. prof. psychology NYU Postdoctoral Program in Psychoanalysis and Psychotherapy, N.Y.C., 1972—. Author: Fantasies of Love and Death in Life and Art, 1995; co-author: The Many Faces of Decit, 1996; contbr. articles to profl. jours. Mem.: NY Freudian Soc. (mem.-at-large 1993—97, bd. dirs. 1994—2000, rec. sec. 1997—99, pres.'s adv. bd. dirs. 2001—), Internat. Psychoanaltic Assn., Am. Psychoanalytic Assn., Am. Psychol. Assn. (bd. dirs. sect. 1 divsn. psychoanalysis 1999—, mem.-at-large divsn. 39 sect. I 1999—). Avocations: theater, music, travel, reading, needlework. Home: 50 E 89th St # 30E New York NY 10128 Office: 55 E 87th St # 1B New York NY 10128-1043 E-mail: helengediman@aol.com.

GEDJEYAN, HOVANNES JOHN, real estate broker; b. Yerevan, Armenia, June 20, 1956; arrived in U.S., 1976; s. Minas Mike and Zvart Joyce Gedjeyan; m. Gaiane D. Astvatsatrian, Apr. 22, 1983; children: Minas Mike, Zvart Joyce. Import/export The Milinger Co., Valencia, Calif., 1989—; life ins. broker Dept. Ins., Glendale, Calif., 1986—, Santa Monica, 1987—; real estate broker Dept. Real Estate, Glendale, 1988—. Mem.: Awesome A Shrine Club (1st v.p.), Al Malaikah Temple (nobel), Scottish Rite, Masons. Republican. Avocations: painting, travel, hunting, swimming. Home: 222 Monterey Rd #1206 Glendale CA 91207 Office: Magic Realty 409 S Glendale Ave #200 Glendale CA 91205

GEDROC, MARIA, artist; b. Chgo., Nov. 4, 1967; BFA, No. Ill. U., 1989; M of Art Adminstrn., Art Inst. Chgo., 1995. Graphic designer, painter, 1990—. Exhibited in numerous individual and group art shows; works pub. in Chgo. Art Scene, 1999. Vol. numerous art orgns.

GEE, CHUCK YIM, dean; b. San Francisco, Aug. 28, 1933; s. Don Yow Elsie (Lee) G. AA, City Coll. of San Francisco, 1953; BSBA, U. Denver, 1957; MA, Mich. State U., 1958; PhD (hon.), China Acad. Chin. Cultural U., 1972; D of Pub. Svc. (hon.), U. Denver, 1991. Assoc. dir. Sch. of Hotel and Restaurant Adminstn. U. Denver, 1958-68; cons. East West Ctr., Honolulu, 1968-74; assoc. dean and prof. Sch. of Travel Industry Mgmt. U. Hawaii, 1968-75, dean and prof. Sch. Travel Industry Mgmt., 1976-99, interim dean Coll. Bus. Adminstrn., 1998-99, dean emeritus, 2000—. Vis. prof. Sch Bus. and Commerce, Oreg. State U., 1975; hon. prof. Nankai U., Tianjin, China, 1987—, Shanghai Inst. Tourism, 1994—, Dept. Tourism Huaqiao U., Xiamen, China, 1995—; cons. Internat. Sci. and Tech. Inst., Washington, 1986-90; trustee Pacific Asia Travel Assn. Found., San Francisco; chmn. Govs. Tourism Tng. Coun., Honolulu, 1989-92, chmn., 1992-96, chmn. industry coun. PATA, 1994-96, PATA Human Resource Devel. Coun., 1996-99, chmn. PATA Coun. on Ednl. Devel. and Certification, 2000-02; mem. State Workforce Devel. Coun., 1997-98, Pacific Asia Travel Assn. Human Resource Devel. Coun, 1996-98; acad. Inst. Cert. Travel Agts., Wellesley, Mass., 1989—; mem. Coun. on Hotel, Restaurant and Edn., 1967-2000, Honolulu Commn. on Fgn. Rels., 1979-98; mem. Pacific Asian Affairs Coun.; sr. acad. adv. China Tourism Assn. Cons., Inc., 1993—; adv. World Tourism Orgn. Internat. Tourism Edn. and Tng. Ctr., 1991-2000; external examiner sch. accountancy and bus. Nanyang Tech. U., Singapore, 1996-98; bd. dirs. ProjectonNet.com. Author: Resort Devel. and Mgmt., 1988, 2d edit., The Story of PATA, 2d edit., co-editor, 2001; co-author: The Travel Industry, 1988, 3d edit., 1997, Profl. Travel Agency Mgmt., 1990, Internat. Hotels: Devel. and Mgmt., 1994; editor: Internat. Tourism: A Global Perspective, 1997; founding dir., Hong Kong, China, Hawaii Chamber of Commerce, 1998-; mem. adv. bd. Asian Hotelier mag., 1997-99, Get2Hawaii.com, 2001—. Bd. dir. Hawaii Visitors Bur., 1993-95, Kaukini Med. Ctr., Honolulu, 1986-95, KMC, 1996-, Travel and Tourism Adv. Bd., US Dept. Commerce, Washington, 1982-90, Pacific Rim Found., Honolulu, 1987-93, Cmty. Entrepreneurs, Hawaii Dept. Edn., 1997—; vice-chmn. Tourism Policy Adv. Coun., Dept. Bus. and Econ. Devel., Honolulu, 1978-92; chmn. Kaukini Geriat. Care, Inc., bd. dir., 1992-95; trustee Pata Found., 1984-95, Kuakini Health System, 1988-2003; consulting com. Beijing Inst. Tourism, 1992—; v.p. Hawaii Vision 2020, 1992-93; mem. Mayor's Task Force on Waikiki Master Plan, 1992-93; devel. bd. Miss Hawaii Scholarship Pageant, 1993-; workforce devel. coun. Hawaii Dept. of Labor and Indsl. Rels., 1996-98; bd. dir., Cmty. Enterprises, Hawaii Dept. Edn., 1997—, Hong Kong Hawaii C. of C., 1999—. Served US Army, 1953-55. Recipient NOAH award Acad. Tourism Orgns., 1987, Gov.'s Proclamation honors State of Hawaii, 1998,1999,2003; named Mayor's Proclamation, 2003; named State Mgr. of Yr., State of Hawaii, 1995; named one of 100 Who Made a Difference in Hawaii during 20th Century, Star Bull., 1999. Mem. Acad. for Study of Tourism (emeritus), Pacific Asia Travel Assn. (hon. life Hawaii chpt., bd. dirs. 1993-96, chmn. industry coun. 1994-96, 50th Anniversary Hall of Honors, 2001, Grand award 1991, Life award 1990, Presdl. award 1986), Travel Industry Am. (Travel Industry Hall of Leaders award 1988), China Tourism Assn. (award of excellence 1992), China-Hawaii C. of C. (founding dir. 1998), Hong Kong-China-Hawaii C. of C. (bd. dirs. 1999—), Golden Key. Office: U Hawaii Sch Travel Industry Mgmt 2560 Campus Rd Honolulu HI 96822-2217 E-mail: cgee@hawaii.edu.

GEE, ELWOOD GORDON, academic administrator; b. Vernal, Utah, Feb. 2, 1944; s. Elwood A. and Vera (Showalter) Gee; m. Elizabeth Dutson, Aug. 26, 1968 (dec. Dec. 1991); 1 child, Rebekah; m. Constance Bumgarner, Nov. 26, 1994. BA, U. Utah, 1968; JD, Columbia U., 1971, EdD, 1972. Asst. dean U. Utah, Salt Lake City, 1973—74; jud. fellow U.S. Supreme Ct., Washington, 1974—75; assoc. dean Brigham Young U., Provo, Utah, 1975—79; dean W.Va. U., Morgantown, 1979—81, pres., 1981—85, U. Colo., 1985—90, Ohio State U., Columbus, 1990—97, Brown U., Providence, 1998—2000; chancellor Vanderbilt U., Nashville, 2000—. Author: Education Law and Public Schools, 1975, Law and Public Education, 1980, Violence, Values and Justice in American Education, 1982, Fair Employment Practice, 1982. Fellow, W.K. Kellogg, 1971—72, Mellon fellow, 1977—78. Mem.: ABA, Adminstrv. Conf. U.S., Phi Kappa Phi, Phi Delta Kappa. Mem. Lds Ch. Office: Vanderbilt U Chancellors Office 211 Kirkland Hall Nashville TN 37240 E-mail: gordon.gee@vanderbilt.edu.

GEE, ROBERT LEROY, agriculturist, dairy farmer; b. Oakport Twp., Moorhead, Minn., May 25, 1926; s. Milton William and Hertha Elizabeth (Paschke) G.; m. Mae Valentine Erickson, June 18, 1953 BS in Agronomy, N.D. State U., 1951, postgrad., 1955, Colo. A&M U., 1954. Farm labor controller Minn. Extension Service, Clay County, 1944-45, county 4-H agt., 1951-57; rural mail carrier U.S. Postal Service, Moorhead, Minn., 1946-47; breeder registered shorthorn cattle and registered southdown sheep Moorhead, Minn., 1950-63; owner, operator Gee Dairy Farm (Oak Grove Farm), Moorhead, Minn., 1957—. Asst. prof. status U. Minn., 1951-57; bd. dirs. Red River Valley Fair, West Fargo, N.D., 1960-86, Minn. Dairy Promotion Bd., St. Paul, 1968-69; bd. dirs. Red River Valley Devel. Assn., Crookston, Minn., 1973—, v.p., 1992—; bd. dirs. Red River Milk Producers Pool, Minn., N.D., 1963-78, treas., 1968-78; bd. dirs. Cass Clay Creamery Inc., Fargo, N.D., 1969-96, chmn. bd., 1982-85, 92-95, v.p., 1990-91; bd. dirs. U.S. Meat Animal Rsch. Ctr., Clay Ctr., Nebr., 1970; mem. Nat. Dairy Promotion Bd., Washington, 1984-88. Treas. Oakport Twp., 1974-82, supr., 1986-2002, v.p., 1987-2002; mem. Clay County Planning and Zoning Commn., 1991-2000, vice chmn., 1992-96, chmn., 1996-2000; mem. Clay County Bd. Adjustment, 1995-2000, chmn., 1996-2000. With USN, 1945-46. Recipient Grand Champion Farm Flock award Man. Expn., 1960, Clay County's Outstanding Agriculturist award, 1996; named Clay County King Agassiz, Red River Valley Winter Shows, 1966, Grand Champion forage exhibit Red River Valley Winter Shows, 1979, 82; co-recipient Clay County Dairy Farm Family of Yr. award Red River Valley Dairymen's Assn., 1979. Mem. Minn. Milk Producers Assn. (bd. dirs. 1977-88, 93-97, sec. 1972-78, treas. 1977-87), Minn. Assn. Coops. (bd. dirs. 1984-96), State Coop. Assn. (dairy council 1975-96), Am. Farm Bur. Fedn., Nat. Farmers Union, Kragnes Farmers Elevator Assn., Red River Valley Livestock Assn., Am. Shorthorn Breeders Assn., Am. Southdown Breeders Assn., Holstein-Friesian Assn. Am. Republican. Mem. United Ch. of Christ. Club: Agassiz (v.p. 1979-81, pres. 1981-82) (Moorhead) Avocations: hunting, fishing, skiing. Home and Office: 8595 2nd St N Moorhead MN 56560-7103

GEE, ROBERT NEIL, law librarian; b. Miami, Okla., June 22, 1956; s. Robert Sanford and Nancy Ann (Neil) G. AA, Tulsa Jr. Coll., 1976; BA, U. Okla., 1978, JD, 1981; LLM, George Washington U., 1984. Bar: Okla. 1981, U.S. Suprem Ct. 1986, D.C. 1989. Legal reference specialist Library of Congress, Washington, 1984-94; chief law libr. pub. svcs. Law Libr. of Congress, Washington, 1994—. Mem. ABA (recipient Silver Key cert. 1981), Fed. Bar Assn., Okla. Bar Assn., Am. Judicature Soc., D.C. Bar Assn., Phi Delta Phi. Avocations: reading, bowling, travel, current events.

GEE, SHARON LYNN, funeral director, educator; b. Berea, Ohio, Jan. 11, 1963; d. Donald Edward Gee and Janet Lee Floyd. Cert. in mortuary sci., Wayne State U., 1986, BS Psychology, 1987. Mortuary sci. lic. Mich., Nat. Bd. Cert. Funeral Dir. Mgr., funeral dir. Pixley Funeral Home, Keego Harbor, Mich., 1996—; lectr. instr. dept. mortuary sci. Wayne State U., Detroit, 1996—2003, asst. prof. embalming, 2003—. Recipient Residential Beautification award, City of Royal Oak, Mich., 1993. Mem.: West Bloomfield C. of C., Tri City Bus. Assn., Mich. Embalmers Soc. (pres. 2000—), Mich. Funeral Dirs. Assn., Nat. Funeral Dirs. Assn. (pursuit of excellence achievement award 1997—), Optimist Internat., Keego Harbor Chpt. (Keego Harbor chpt.), A-Dock Sailing Club. Avocations: sailing, circa 1910 home renovation and restoration. Office: Pixley Funeral Home Godhardt-Tomlinson Chapel 2904 Orchard Lake Rd Keego Harbor MI 48320 Office Fax: 248-681-2147. Business E-Mail: ad7158@wayne.edu.

GEE, SHARRI A. physician; b. Bryan, Ohio, Feb. 10, 1968; d. Ronnie R. Rohrs and Sharon A. Beck; m. Jeffrey Michael Gee, July 23, 1994; children: Jeffrey Allen, Jessica Lynn. AD, Northwest State C.C., 2002. Cert. nursing asst., Ohio. Nurse Harborside Healthcare NWO, Bryan, Ohio, 1985—2002. Author: poetry. Methodist. Avocations: poetry, inline skating, sketching, tennis.

GEE, WILLIAM, surgeon; b. Riverhead, N.Y., Nov. 4, 1931; s. John Eccleston and Agnes Katherine (Shea) G.; m. Beverly Joan Furrow, Aug. 11, 1956 (dec. Jan. 1995); children: Catherine, William, Michael, Patricia, Susan. Student, CUNY, Bklyn., 1955-57; MD, SUNY, Bklyn., 1961. Intern Naval Hosp., St. Albans, N.Y., 1961-62, resident, 1963-67; instr. surgery U. Calif., San Francisco, 1972-73; asst. prof. surgery George Washington U., Washington, 1974-77; med. dir. vascular lab. Lehigh Valley Hosp., Allentown, Pa., 1977-2000; prof. clin. surgery Pa. State U., Hershey, Pa., 1995—. Adj. prof. surgery Med. Coll. Pa./Hahnemann U., Phila., 1986—. Contbr. articles to profl. jours., chpts. to books; inventor in field. Capt. USN, 1951-55, 60-77. Vascular Surgery fellow U. Calif., San Francisco, 1972-73. Mem. Am. Coll. Surgeons, Am. Heart Assn., Ea. Vascular Soc., Delaware Valley Vascular Soc., Chesapeake Vascular Soc., Am. Assn. Vascular Surgery, Soc. Vascular Surgery, Soc. Mil. Vascular Surgeons. Avocation: computers. Fax: (610) 966-9301.

GEEKER, NICHOLAS PETER, lawyer, judge; b. Pensacola, Fla., Dec. 15, 1944; BA in English, La. Poly. Inst., 1966; JD, Fla. State U., 1969. Bar: Fla. 1969, U.S. Dist. Ct. 1970, US. Supreme Ct., 1980. Assoc. firm Merritt & Jackson, Pensacola, 1969; law clk. U.S. Dist. Judge D.L. Middlebrooks, Tallahassee, 1970-73; asst. state atty. Fla. 1st Jud. Circuit, 1973; asst. U.S. atty. No. Dist. Fla., 1973-76, U.S. atty., 1976-82; sole practice Pensacola, Fla., 1982-85; circuit judge Fla. 1st Jud. Circuit, 1985—. Mem. Fed.-State Joint Com. on Law Enforcement. Mem. Fla. Bar Assn., Fla. Trial Lawyers Assn. (editor Newsletter 1975), Phi Delta Phi. Office: 190 Government St Pensacola FL 32501-5773

GEEL, CHRISTOPH W. orthopedic trauma surgeon; b. July 8, 1948; m. Maja Schneider, Nov. 30, 1974; children: Bettina, Felix. Diploma of Medicine, U. Basel, Switzerland, 1974, postgrad., 1975-79. Oberarzt dept. gen. surgery and trauma U. Basel, 1974-79; oberarzt dept. anesthesia U. St. Gallen, Switzerland, 1979-89; oberarzt. dept. gen. surgery and trauma U. Chur, Switzerland, 1979-87; asst. prof. dept. orthopedics Syracuse (N.Y.) U., 1987-92, assoc. prof., 1992-97, prof., 1997—. Maj. Swiss Army, 1974—. Fellow ACS; mem. Orthopedic Trauma Assn., Swiss Bd. Surgery, Internat. Assn. Surgery of Trauma. Office: Dept Orthopedics 550 Harrison St Ste 100 Syracuse NY 13202-3096

GEENTIENS, GASTON PETRUS, JR., former construction management consultant company executive; b. Garfield, N.J., Apr. 6, 1935; s. Gaston Petrus and Margaret (Piros) G.; m. Barbara Ann Chamberlin, Oct. 14, 1960; children: Mercedes Frith, Faith Piros. BSCE, The Citadel, 1956. Registered profl. engr., 15 states. Plant engr. Western Elec. Co., Inc., Kearny, N.J., 1956-58, owner's rep. N.Y.C., 1960-64; v.p. Gentyne Motors, Inc., Passaic, N.J., 1958-60; project engr. Ethyl Corp., Baton Rouge, La., 1964-65; mgr. Timothy McCarthy Constrn. Co., Atlanta, 1965; asst. to v.p. A.R. Abrams, Inc. and Columbia Engring., Inc., Atlanta, 1965-66; supr. engring. and constn. Litton Industries, N.Y.C., 1966-71; pres. G.P. Geentiens Jr., Inc., Charleston, S.C., 1971-82; gen. ptnr. Engineered Enterprises Co., Charleston, 1973-76; dir. Cayman Broadcasting Assocs., Cayman Islands, B.W.I., 1977-82. Mem. Ramapo (N.Y.) Republican Com., 1961-64. Served to 1st lt. C.E., AUS, 1956-58. Mem. ASCE, Tau Beta Pi. Home: 1219 Pembrooke Dr Charleston SC 29407-7748

GEER, JACK CHARLES, retired pathology educator; b. Galesburg, Ill., Sept. 19, 1927; s. John Charles and Ruth Helen (McGee) G.; m. Sara Kathleen Williamson, Feb. 16, 1951; children: Charles Robert, Richard John, John Michael, Cynthia Jane, Michael James. BS, La. State U., 1950, MD, 1956. Rsch. asst. prof. La. State U., Baton Rouge, 1954-66; prof. U. Tex., San Antonio, 1966-67; prof., chmn. Ohio State U., Columbus, 1967-72; assoc. pathologist Davidson Labs., Columbus, 1972-75; prof. pathology U. Ala., Birmingham, 1975-90, prof. emeritus, 1990—, chmn. dept., 1975-88. Cons. nutrition study sect. Nat. Heart, Lung and Blood Inst., Bethesda, Md., 1965-69, cons., chmn. pathology study sect., 1976-80; mem. rsch. com. Am. Heart Assn., 1968-82, pres. Ala. affiliate, 1983-84. Author: Smooth Muscle Cells in Atherosclerosis, 1972; mem. editorial bd.: Jour. Exptl. and Molecular Pathology, 1967—, Am. Jour. Pathology, 1969-80; contbr. articles to profl. jours. Mem. Ala. region ARC Blood Svcs., 1979-90. With USN, 1945-47, ATO. USPHS research career devel. award, 1959-66; recipient Disitng. Faculty citation La. State U., 1964, Disting. Service award Am. Heart Assn., 1972-75, Outstanding Vol. Achievement award ARC, 1981; named to ALumni Hall of Distinction La. State U., 1982. Fellow Coll. Am. Pathologists; mem. AMA, Am. Registry Pathology (exec. mem., pres. 1985-87). Home: 3744 Wimbleton Dr Birmingham AL 35223-2730

GEER, JAMES FRANCIS, mathematics educator; b. Syracuse, N.Y., Oct. 3, 1940; s. Francis Bion and Dorothy (Wilder) G.; m. Linda Sundquist, Sept. 18, 1965; children: Jim, Bill, Wendy, Jennifer. BA in Math., Harpur Coll., 1962; MA in Math., U. Va., 1964; PhD in Math., NYU, 1967. Staff mathematician IBM Corp., Endicott, N.Y., 1967-69; from asst. prof. math to prof. math. SUNY, Binghamton, 1969—. Cons. IBM Corp., Gen. Electric, NASA, 1970—. Rsch. grantee NSF, Office Naval Rsch., NASA, others. Mem. Soc. Indsl and Applied Math., Am. Acad. Mechanics. Methodist. Home: 247 Old Newark Valley Rd Endicott NY 13760 Office: SUNY Watson Sch Engring Binghamton NY 13902

GEER, JOHN FARR, retired religious organization administrator; b. N.Y.C., Oct. 15, 1930; s. William Montague and Edith Jaffray (Farr) G.; m. Carolyn Boston, June 25, 1954; children: Jennifer, Evelyn, John Farr. BA, Princeton U., 1952; LLB, Columbia U., 1957. Bar: N.Y. State 1957. Asso. firm Sullivan & Cromwell, N.Y.C., 1957-65, Whitman & Ransom (and predecessor firms), N.Y.C., 1965-67, ptnr., 1967-73; v.p., gen. counsel, sec. Am. Standard Inc., N.Y.C., 1973-89, ret., 1989; sr. v.p., gen. counsel, sec. The Church Pension Fund, N.Y.C., 1991-97. Trustee Protestant Episcopal Soc. for Promoting Religion and Learning in State N.Y., 1960-82, treas., 1968-82; trustee Gen. Theol. Sem., 1980-95, vice chmn. bd. trustees, 1986-95; mem. Corp. for Relief Widows and Children of Protestant Episcopal Clergymen in State of N.Y., 1960—, treas., 1967-98. 1st lt. F.A. AUS, 1952-54, Korea. Mem. Phi Delta Phi. Clubs: Princeton (N.Y.C.). Episcopalian. Home: 151 Central Park W New York NY 10023-1514

GEER, RONALD LAMAR, mechanical engineering consultant, retired oil company executive; b. West Palm Beach, Fla., Sept. 2, 1926; s. Marion Wood and Bertha (Lightfoot) G.; m. Geneva Yvonne Chappell, Dec. 24, 1951; children— Ronald Lamar, Mark Randall. B.M.E., Ga. Inst. Tech., 1951. With Shell Oil Co., 1951—, sr. staff mech. engr., head office, 1969-71, cons. mech. engr., 1971-86. Mem. various govt., univ. adv. coms. Contbr. articles on petroleum drilling and prodn. to profl. jours.; patentee petroleum drilling and prodn. equipment; mem. Shell Oil Co. team recognized in Offshore Tech. Conf. Disting. Achievement award to co., 1971, for individuals, 1984. Recipient Robert Earll McConnell award Am. Inst. Mech. Engrs., 1995; named to Offshore Energy Ctr. Pioneer Engring Tech. Hall of Fame, 1999, Offshore Energy Ctr. Industry Pioneer Hall of Fame, 2002. Mem. Nat. Acad. Engring., NRC (marine bd.), Nat. Security Indsl. Assn. (petroleum panel, research and engring. adv. com.), ASME (hon.), Marine Tech. Soc., Am. Petroleum Inst., Model-A Ford Club Am., Classic T-Bird Club Internat., Thistle Class Assn., Pi Tau Sigma. Republican. Home: 14723 Oak Bend Dr Houston TX 77079-6418 also: 430 Covered Bridge Ln # 135 Sky Valley GA 30537-2593

GEERTZ, CLIFFORD JAMES, anthropology educator; b. San Francisco, Aug. 23, 1926; s. Clifford James and Lois (Brieger) G.; m. Hildred Storey, Oct. 30, 1948 (div. 1981); children: Erika, Benjamin; m. Karen Blu, 1987. AB, Antioch Coll., 1950; PhD, Harvard U., 1956, LL.D. (hon.), 1974; L.H.D. (hon.), No. Mich. U., 1975, U. Chgo., 1979, Bates Coll., 1980, Knox Coll., 1982, Brandeis U., 1984, Swarthmore Coll., 1984, New Sch. for Social Research, Yale U., 1987, Williams Coll., 1991, Princeton U., 1995, Cambridge (Eng.) U., 1997; L.H.D. (hon.), Colby Coll., 2003. From asst. prof. to prof. dept. anthropology U. Chgo., 1960-70; prof. dept. social sci. Inst. for Advanced Study, Princeton, N.J., 1970—, Harold F. Linder prof. social sci., 1982-2000, prof. emeritus, 2000—; Eastman prof. Oxford U., 1978-79. Author: The Religion of Java, 1960, Peddlers and Princes, 1963, The Social History of an Indonesian Town, 1965, Islam Observed, 1968, The Interpretation of Cultures, 1973, (with H. Geertz) Kinship in Bali, 1975, (with L. Rosen and H. Geertz) Meaning and Order in Moroccan Society, 1979, Negara: The Theatre State in Nineteenth-Century Bali, 1980, Local Knowledge, 1983, Works and Lives, 1988, After the Fact, 1995, Available Light, 2000. Served with USNR, 1943-45. Nat. Acad. Scis. fellow, 1973—; recipient Asian Cultural prize, 1992, Bintang Jasa Utama, Govt. of Indonesia, 2002; recipient award Republic of Indonesia. Fellow AAAS, Am. Philos. Soc., Am. Acad. Arts and Scis., Brit. Acad. (corr.); mem. Am. Anthrop. Assn., Assn. for Asian Studies, Middle East Studies Assn. Office: Inst for Advanced Study Princeton NJ 08540 E-mail: geertz@ias.edu.

GEERTZ, HILDRED STOREY, anthropology educator; b. N.Y.C., Feb. 12, 1927; d. Walter Rendell and Helen (Anderson) Storey; m. Clifford Geertz, 1948 (div. 1979); children: Erika, Benjamin. BA, Antioch Coll., Yellow Springs, Ohio, 1948; PhD, Radcliffe Coll., 1956. Lectr. U. Chgo., 1963-68; from assoc. prof. to prof. anthropology Princeton (N.J.) U., 1970-98; ret., 1998. Chmn. dept. anthropology Princeton U., 1972-77, 86, 88-89. Author: The Javanese Family, 1961, (with Clifford Geertz) Kinship in Bali, 1974, Images of Power: Balinese Paintings Made for Gregory Bateson and Margaret Mead, 1994, (with Geertz and Lawrence Rosen) Meaning and Order in Moroccan Society, 1979; editor: State and Society in Bali, 1992.

GEESEMAN, ROBERT GEORGE, lawyer; b. Shreveport, La., Oct. 23, 1944; s. George Robert and Cora (Hamilton) Glasgow; m. Rosemary Monahan, Aug. 19, 1967; 1 child, Regan Glasgow. BA, Yale U., 1966; JD, U. Mich., 1969. Bar: Pa. 1969, U.S. Dist. Ct. (we. dist.) Pa. 1969, U.S. Supreme Ct. 1973, U.S. Tax Ct. 1979. Assoc. Blaxter, O'Neill, Houston & Nash, Pitts., 1969-75; ptnr. Lynch, Lynch, Carr & Kabala, Pitts., 1975-81, Lynch, Kabala & Geeseman, Pitts., 1981, Kabala & Geeseman, Pitts., 1981—2002; spl. counsel Fox, Rothschild, O'Brien & Frankel, L.L.P., Pitts., 2002—. Lectr. tax law and employee benefits. Mem.: ABA (mem. closely held bus. com. sect. taxation, bd. editors Withdrawal Retirement and Disputes, bd. editors What You and Your Firm Should Know), Pitts. Inst. Legal Medicine, Allegheny County Bar Assn., Pa. Bar Assn., John's Island Country (Vero Beach, Fla.), Rosslyn Farms Country Club, Rivers Club, Mory's Club (New Haven), Phi Delta Phi. Address: Fox Rothschild O'Brien and Frankel LLP 625 Liberty Ave Fl 29 Pittsburgh PA 15222-3110

GEFFE, PHILIP REINHOLD, electrical engineer, consultant; b. Napa, Calif., Oct. 22, 1920; s. Eugene Carl and Mary Rebecca (Woliston) G.; m. Barbara Ann Wean; children: Bethann, Philip, Timur. Student, Calif. Inst. Tech., 1947-49. Chief filter engr. Triad Transformer Corp., Venice, Calif., 1952-56; dir. engring. Hycor, Inc., Sylmar, Calif., 1957-60; sr. staff engr. Axel Electronics Inc., Jamaica, N.Y., 1962-65; fellow engr. Westinghouse Electric Corp., Balt., 1965-74; staff engr. Lynch Communication Systems, Inc., Reno, 1974-80, Scientific-Atlanta, Inc., Atlanta, 1980-85, K&L Microwave, Inc., Salisbury, Md., 1985-87; ind. cons., 1988—; sr. engr. PULSE divsn. Technitrol, San Diego, 1997—; ret., 2003. Cons. in field, 2001—02. Author: Simplified Modern Filter Design, 1963; contbr. articles to profl. jours.; patentee in field. Master

U.S. Chess Fedn. New Windsor, N.Y., 1968 Fellow IEEE; mem. AAAS Address: 28789 Calle De La Paz Murrieta CA 92563-5790 Office: Svc Sta and Mini Mart Sales Inc POB 1113 Murrieta CA 92564-1113

GEFFEN, DAVID, recording company executive, producer; b. Bklyn., Feb. 21, 1943; s. Abraham and Batya (Volovskaya) Geffen. Student, CUNY. Agt. with William Morris, N.Y.C., 1964—68, Ashley Famous, 1968; exec. v.p., agt. Creative Mgmt. Assocs., 1969; founder (with Laura Nyro) and pres. Tuna Fish Pub. Co.; pres. Asylum Records, 1970—73, Geffen-Roberts, Inc., 1970—71, Elektra-Asylum Records, 1973—76; founder and pres. Geffen Records, L.A., 1980—89, chmn.; head Geffen Film Co.; vice-chmn. Warner Bros. Pictures, 1974, v.p., 1975; exec. asst. to chmn. Warner Comm., 1977; co-founder Dreamworks SKG, Universal City, 1995—. Mem. faculty Yale U., 1978; apptd. Regent U. Calif., Govt. Calif., 1980—87. Prodr.: (films) Personal Best, 1982, Risky Business, 1983, After Hours, 1985, Lost in America, 1985, Little Shop of Horrors, 1986, Beetlejuice, 1988, Men Don't Leave, 1990, Interview with the Vampire, 1994; co-prodr.: (plays) Master Harold...and the Boys, 1982, Cats, 1982, Good, 1982, Dreamgirls, 1983, Social Security, 1986, Madam Butterfly, 1988 (9 Tony award, Best Play), (musical) Miss Saigon. Bds. dirs. Los Angeles County Art Mus. Avocation: collecting modern art. Office: Dreamworks SKG 100 Universal City Plz Bldg 477 Universal City CA 91608

GEFFKEN, MEG COMSTOCK, secondary education educator; b. Lansdowne, Pa., Mar. 11, 1940; d. Reynolds Vincent and Anne (Manley) Comstock; m. John Frederic Geffken, Mar. 5, 1965; children: John, Tiffany, Richard, Anne, Sara, James, Shannon. BA, Coll. Misericordia, 1961; MA, Northwestern U., 1962. Cert. tchr., Pa. Instr. English Mt. Aloysius Jr. Coll., Cresson, Pa., 1962-64, Sacred Heart Acad., San Francisco, 1964-65, Armstrong State Coll., Savannah, Ga., 1966-68, Newman Coll., Aston, Pa., 1970-72; chairperson English dept. Benton (Pa.) Area Sch. Dist., 1975-85; tchr. advanced placement English N.W. Sch. Dist., Shickshinny, Pa., 1985—. Adj. Pa. Coll. Tech., Williamsport, Pa., 1985-2002; cons. advancement placement English lit. Coll. Bds., 1995-2000, reader advanced placement exams., 1996—; mem. scholarship selection com. Atlantic Fed. Credit Union, N.J., 1998—. Committeeperson Republican Grand Old Party, Sugarloaf Twp., 1980-90, 97—. Mem.: Pa. State Edn. Assn. (regional co-chair comm. com. 1992—, newspaper editor The Charge 1998—2001), Luzerne County Reading Coun. (treas. 1994—95, exec. coun. 1995—2000, pres. 1995—98), Phi Delta Kappa (v.p. 1996—, Educator of Yr. 2000). Republican. Roman Catholic. Avocations: traveling, rading, geneology, performing oral interpretation of biographies of famous american women. Home: 377 Stevens Hill Rd Benton PA 17814 Office: NW Area Sch Dist 243 Thorne Hill Rd Shickshinny PA 18655

GEFKE, HENRY JEROME, lawyer; b. Milw., Aug. 4, 1930; s. Jerome Henry and Frances (Daley) G.; m. Caroline Ann Lawrence, June 25, 1955 (div. Jan. 1968); children: Brian Lawrence, David Jerome; m. Mary Clare Nuss, Aug. 28, 1976; children: Lynn Marie, James Scott. BS, Marquette U., 1952, LL.B., 1954; postgrad., Ohio State U., 1955-56. Bar: Wis. 1954, Tax Ct. U.S 1969; C.P.A., Wis. Accountant-auditor John G. Conley & Co. (C.P.A.s), Milw., 1956-59; with J.I. Case Co., Racine, Wis., 1959-68, corp. sec., asst. gen. counsel, 1965-68; assoc. Maier & Mulcahy, S.C., Milw., 1968-69; prin. Mulcahy, Gefke & Wherry, S.C., Milw., 1969-73; individual practice law Milw., 1973—. Corp. officer, dir. various bus. corps. Pres., bd. dirs. Big Bros., Greater Racine, 1965-67; trustee Racine County Instns., 1960-63; bd. dirs., sec., legal counsel Racine Transitional Care, Inc., 1973-76; bd. dirs., legal counsel Our Home Found., Milw., 1979-82; bd. dirs. Racine County Mental Health Assn., 1963-67, Alliance for Mentally Ill Milw. County, 1986-88; bd. dirs., sec., legal counsel Glendale Econ. Devel. Corp., 1996 ; bd. dirs. Glendale Bus. Coun., 1996-97; bd. dirs. Glendale Assn. of Commerce, Inc., 1997—, treas., 1998-2000, pres. 2000-02. Mem. Wis. Bar Assn., Milw. Bar Assn., Wis. Inst. CPA's, Delta Sigma Pi, Delta Theta Phi. Home: 5521 N Lydell Ave Glendale WI 53217-5042 Office: 400 W Silver Spring Dr Milwaukee WI 53217-5053 E-mail: hjgjdcpa@aol.com.

GEFREH, PAUL THOMAS, lawyer; b. Scranton, Pa., Apr. 17, 1953; s. Adam and Florence (Ksiazek) G.; m. Nanette Neudeck, July 16, 1983; children: Mark, Tasha. BA, N.D. State U., 1974; JD, U. Neb., 1977. Bar: Colo. 1977, U.S. Dist. Ct. Colo. 1977, U.S. Ct. Appeals (10th cir.) 1987. Computer programmer U.S. Dept Transp., Washington, 1974-75; ptnr. Lebel & Gefreh, Colorado Springs, Colo., 1977-78; assoc. Murray, Baker & Wendelken, Colorado Springs, 1978-81, Hendricks & Hendricks P.C., Colorado Springs, 1981-84; sole practice Colorado Springs, 1984—; dir. Ent Fed. Credit Union, 1997—. Trustee U.S. Bankruptcy Ct., Denver, 1984—. Officer Pikes Peak Children's Advs., Colorado Springs, 1978-84; leader advisor, Boy Scouts Am. Mem. ABA, Colo. Bar Assn., El Paso Bar Assn., Colorado Springs Jaycees (officer 1978-84). Roman Catholic. Avocations: hiking, gardening. Office: 2125 N Academy Blvd Colorado Springs CO 80909-1507 Office Fax: 719-597-4534. E-mail: Paul.Gefreh@PSINET.com.

GEGELMANN, SHARON FAY, piano teacher; b. Dickinson, N.D., Mar. 11, 1958; d. Jacob and Marjorie Jeanette (Hoff) G.; m. Mark D. Schields, Aug. 30, 1986; children: Rachel, Rebekah, Luke. BS, Moorhead State U., 1981; postgrad., U. of Mary, 1995. CPA, N.D. Dep. auditor Dunn County, Dickinson, N.D., 1981-82; piano tchr., 1982—; sr. acct. ANG Coal Gasification Co., Dickinson, 1983-89; acct. Reichert Fisher & Co., Dickinson, 1990-91. Libr. Hope Christian Acad., Dickinson, 1997—; troop leader Girl Scouts, Dickinson, 1997-99. Mem. Music Tchrs. Nat. Assn. (sec.-treas. 1999-2001), Dakota Western Auto Club (treas. 1997-98), St. Cecilia Music Club, Theodore Roosevelt Amateur Radio Club.

GEGGEL, ROBERT LESLIE, pediatric cardiologist; b. N.Y.C., Mar. 25, 1952; s. Carl Richard and Elizabeth Tilly (Gutmann) G.; m. Karen Brown, May 14, 1983; children: Amelia, Ezra. BS, Yale Coll., New Haven, 1974; MD, U. Pa., Phila., 1978. Diplomate Am. Bd. Pediatrics, Am. Bd. Pediatric Cardiology. Intern Children's Hosp., Boston, 1978-79, resident, 1979-81, fellow, 1981-84; asst. prof. pediat. Tufts U. Sch. Medicine, Boston, 1984-90, assoc. prof., 1990-97; assoc. chief pediat. cardiology New Eng. Med. Ctr., Boston, 1995-97; assoc. prof. pediat. Harvard Med. Sch., Boston, 1998—; sr. assoc. cardiology Children's Hosp., Boston, 1998—. Contbr. articles to profl. jours. Fellow Am. Coll. Cardiology, Soc. Cardiac Angiography; mem. AMA, Mass. Med. Soc. Office: Childrens Hosp 300 Longwood Ave Boston MA 02115-5737

GEH, HANS-PETER, retired library director, consultant; b. Frankfurt am Main, Germany, Feb. 11, 1934; s. Peter and Maria Geh; m. Roswitha Dieterich, Aug. 31, 1968. MA, U. Bristol, Eng., 1963; PhD, U. Frankfurt am Main, 1963. Subject specialist City and Univ. Libr., Frankfurt am Main, 1962—69; dir. Libr. Sch., Frankfurt am Main, 1967—69, Stuttgart, Germany, 1970—80, Württemberg State Libr., Stuttgart, 1970—97, prof., 2003—. Cons. UNESCO, 1971—; chmn. libr. assns. and lit. socs., Germany, 1965—. Author: Insular Policy in England before the Tudors, 1964; co-editor jours., 1965—; also articles. Trustee Biblioteca Alexandrina, Egypt. Decorated Order of Merit (Germany). Mem. Internat. Fedn. Libr. Assns. and Instns. (pres. 1985-91); European Found. for Libr. Coop. (pres. 1991-95); hon. mem. numerous internat. libr. assns. Avocation: travel. Home: Hebbergstrasse 76/1 70794 Filderstadt Germany Office: Württemberg State Libr Konrad-Adenauer-Strasse 8 70049 Stuttgart Germany E-mail: gehhp@t-online.de.

GEHA, ALEXANDER SALIM, cardiothoracic surgeon, educator; b. Beirut, June 18, 1936; came to U.S., 1963; s. Salim M. and Alice I. (Hayek) G.; m. Diane L. Redalen, Nov. 25, 1967; children— Samia, Rula, Nada BS in Biology, Am. U. Beirut, 1955, MD, 1959; MS in Surgery and Physiology, U. Minn.-Rochester, 1967; MS (privatum), Yale U., 1978. Asst. prof. U. Vt., Burlington, 1967-69; asst. prof. Washington U., St. Louis, 1969-73, assoc. prof., 1973-75, Yale U., New Haven, 1975-78, prof., chief cardiothoracic surgery, 1978-86, Case Western Res. U. and U. Hosp. of Cleve., 1986-98; Jay L. Ankeney prof. cardiothoracic surgery Case We. Reserve U., 1994-98; pres. Univ. Cardiothoracic Surgeons, Inc., Cleve., 1986—; prof., chief cardiothoracic surgery U. Ill., Chgo., 1998—; chief cardiothoracic surgery Mt. Sinai Hosp. Med. Ctr., Chgo., 2000—. Cons. VA Hosp., West Haven, Conn., 1975-86, VA Hosp., Cleve., 1986-98, Westside VA Hosp., Chgo., 1998—, Cleve. Met. Health Med. Ctr., 1986-98, Mt. Sinai Med. Ctr., Cleve., 1990-98, Waterbury Hosp., 1976-86, Sharon Hosp., 1981-86, Michael Reese Hosp., 2002—; mem. study sect. Nat. Heart Lung and Blood Inst., 1981-85. Editor: Glenn's Thoracic and Cardiovascular Surgery, 4th edit. 1983, 5th edit. 1991, 6th edit. 1996; editor Basic Surgery, 1984. Bd. dirs. New Haven Heart Assn., 1981-85 Mem. AMA, Assn. Clin. Cardiac Surgery (chmn. membership com. 1978-80, sec.-treas. 1980-83, pres. 1988), Am. Heart Assn. (bd. dirs. 1981-85. councils on basic sci., cardiovascular surgery), Am. Coll. Chest Physicians (steering com. 1980-84), Am. Assn. Thoracic Surgery, Am. Coll. Cardiology, ACS (chmn. coordinating com. on edn. in thoracic surgery, chmn. 1992-95), Am. Lung Assn., Am. Physiol. Soc., Am. Surg. Assn., Assn. Acad. Surgery, Central Surg. Assn., European Assn. Cardiothoracic Surgery, Internat. Soc. Heart and Lung Transplantation, Internat. Soc. Cardiovascular Surgery, Lebanese Order Physicians, New Eng. Surg. Soc., Pan Am. Med. Assn., Halsted Soc., Soc. Thoracic Surgeons (govt. rels. com., manpower com., program com., edn. and resources com.), Soc. for Vascular Surgery, Soc. Univ. Surgeons, Chgo. Surg. Soc., also others. Home: 854 W Fullerton Ave Chicago IL 60614-2413 Office: ILL Chgo 840 S Wood St Chicago IL 60612-7317 E-mail: ageha@uic.edu.

GEHLERT, SALLY OYLER, dental hygienist, consultant; b. Cin., Feb. 12, 1949; d. Ralph Thomas and Inez R. (Morgan) Oyler; m. Robert Gehlert; 1 child, Chloe. AS, U. Cin., 1971, M in Ednl. Adminstrn., 1976; BS in Allied Health Edn., U. Ky., 1974. Registered dental hygienist, Ohio. Dental hygienist, Cin., 1971—; dental cons. Proctor & Gamble Corp., Cin., 1985-95, John O. Butler Co., Chgo., 1990—, Cin., 1985—. Adv. bd. John O. Butler Co., Chgo.; cons. in field. Edit. adv. Journal of Dental Hygiene, 1993; author ednl. programs for dental profls. Mem. Am. Dental Hygienist Assn., Ohio Dental Hygienist Assn., Cin. Dental Hygienist Assn. Home: 2476 Walnutview Ct Cincinnati OH 45230-2455 E-mail: sallygehlert@fuse.net.

GEHLMANN, SHEILA CATHLEEN, psychologist, research analyst; b. Lorain, Ohio, Mar. 25, 1958; d. Donald Eugene and Barbara Ann Gehlmann. BSBA and Psychology, Aquinas Coll., 1986; MS in Applied Indsl./Orgnl. Psychology, Stevens Inst. Tech., 1991. Grad. intern selection and testing divsn. AT&T, Morristown, N.J., 1989-90; projects mgr. Stevens Inst. Tech., Hoboken, N.J., 1988-90; test and measurement specialist Dept. Pers. City of New York, 1990-91; rsch. analyst APA, Washington, 1991-97; rsch. cons. Denver, 1997—; pres. Healthy Work, Castle Rock, Colo., 1998—; consulting practice, 1998. Author: (with others) Stress and Well Being at Work: Assessments and Interventions for Occupational Mental Health, 1992; assoc. editor Jour. Psychol. Practice, 1995—. Vol. Sta. WCTC Cable Channel 9, Wyoming, Mich., 1980-85; participant K-9 walk, Muscular Dystrophy Assn., Fairfax, Va., 1993-94. Named one of Outstanding Women of Am., 1988. Mem. APA (assoc.), NAFE, Soc. Indsl. Orgnl. Psychology, N.Am. Assn. Masters in Psychology, Am. Psychol. Soc., Mid-Atlantic Camaro Club, Colo. Camaro Club. Avocations: photography, camping, cross-country skiing, needlepoint, tennis. Also: 10 Lowell Dr Castle Rock CO 80104-2084

GEHM, DENISE CHARLENE, ballerina, arts administrator; b. Miami, Fla., Dec. 14, 1951; d. Charles William and Verna Mae (Wiley) Gehm; m. Gary Edward MacDougal, June 15, 1992. BA cum laude, NYU, 1994; MA, Columbia U., 1998; studied ballet with, George Milenoff, Thomas Armour. Soloist ballerina Harkness Ballet, N.Y.C., 1970-71, Nat. Ballet Washington, 1971-73; prin. ballerina Chgo. Ballet, 1974, Ballet de Caracas, Venezuela, 1975; featured ballerina Joffrey Ballet, N.Y.C., 1976-91. Appeared in Broadway plays : West Side Story, 1979; Phamtom of the Opera, 1988; with Rudolf Nureyev in : Nijinsky's L'Apres-Midi d'Un Faune, 1979; prin. dancer : Homage to Diaghilev, Broadway and State Theatre N.Y., 1979; featured roles include : Joffrey's Nutcracker; Arpino's Suite St.-Saens; Cranko's Taming of the Shrew; Ashton's Midsummer Night's Dream; Robbin's N.Y. Export Opus Jazz. Bd. dirs. Lincoln Ctr. Inst.; dir. Fund for Dance, 1994. Recipient Founders Day award NYU, 1994, Disting. Alumni award NYU Gallatin Sch., 1998; Harkness House for Ballet Arts scholar, 1969. Episcopalian.

GEHMAN, TERRY LEE, music industry professional; b. Ephrata, Pa., June 10, 1947; s. Richard M. G. and Pauline E. (Eberly) G.; m. Joyce Elaine Hornberger, Aug. 25, 1968; children: Angela Renee, Lisa Marie. BS in Music Edn., Lebanon Valley Coll., 1969; masters equivalent, West Chester U., 1972. Band dir. Conestoga Valley Sch. Dist., Lancaster, Pa., 1969—2002; personal mgr., musician Younger Bros. Band, Lancaster, 1969-86, Shucks, Lancaster, 1986-93; pres., talent producer, fair cons. Anjoli Prodns., Leola, Pa., 1984—. Writer, producer (record albums) Younger Brothers, 1980, Back Porch Singin', 1982; writer (record album) Younger Brothers Band, 1984; producer (record albums) Alive & Kickin, 1987, I Love To Dance, 1990, Mile Marker Ten, 1990, Careless Moon, 1990; producer, dir. (video) I Love To Dance, 1990, (tv spl.) Xmas With the Younger Brothers, 1984. Celebrity spokesman Am. Cancer Soc., Lancaster, 1984-86. Mem. Country Music Assn., Acad. Country Music, Pa. Assn. County Fairs, Internat. Country Music Buyers Assn., Am. Fedn. Musicians, Pa. Music Educators Assn., Music Educators Nat. Conf., NEA, Pa. State Educators Assn., Rajah Temple, Shriners, Phi Mu Alpha Sinfonia. Avocations: travel, photography. Office: Anjoli Prodns 24 Center Square Rd Leola PA 17540-9724

GEHR, LYNNE CONNOLLY, anesthesiologist; b. Parkersburg, W.Va., May 10, 1955; d. Ira and Evelyn Virginia Connolly; m. Todd William Benjamin Gehr; children: Meghan, Elizabeth. BS, U. Ariz., 1976; MD, W.Va. U., 1981. Diplomate Am. Bd. Anesthesiology with subspecialty in critical care medicine 1986. Anesthesiologist McGuire Clinic, Richmond, Va., 1985—87; anesthesiogist Med. Coll. Va., Richmond, Va., 1987—. Dir. simulation Med. Coll. Va., Richmond, 1999—2002, dir. anesthesiology resident ICU edn., 2000—02, dir. anesthesiology resident lecture series and anatomy lab experience, 2000—, clin. dir. and cons. MITAC telemedicine project, 2001—03. Contbr. articles to profl. jours. Bd. dirs. Goochland Count Fellowship, Goochland Courthouse, 2001. Recipient Cmty. Svc. Assoc. award, VCU, 1996; grantee Found. Anesthesia Edn. and Rsch. grantee, Internat. Anesthesia Rsch. Soc., 1992, AD Williams grantee, MCV/VCU, 1990, 2001. Fellow: Am. Coll. of Chest Physicians; mem.: Va. Soc. of Anesthesiologists, Va. Soc. of Medicine, Soc. of Cardiothoracic Anesthesiologists, Soc. Tech. in Anesthesia, Soc. of Critical Care, Internat. Anesthesia Rsch. Soc., Am. Soc. of Anesthesiologists (anesthesiologist overseas tchg. program mem. 1998), Deep Creek Lake Yatch Club, Fishing Bay Yacht Club, Deep Run Hunt Club, Alpha Lambda Delta, Phi Beta Kappa. Home: 1249 Turkey Trot Rd Manakin Sabot VA 23103 Office: MCV/VCU 9th and Marshall Sts Richmond VA 23298 E-mail: tgehr@hsc.vcu.edu.

GEHRES, JAMES, retired lawyer; b. Akron, Ohio, July 19, 1932; s. Edwin Jacob and Cleora Mary (Yoakam) G.; m. Eleanor Agnew Mount, July 23, 1960. BS in Acctg., U. Utah, 1954; MBA, U. Calif.-Berkeley, 1959; JD, U. Denver, 1970, LLM in Taxation, 1977. Bar: Colo. 1970, U.S. Dist. Ct. Colo. 1970, U.S. Tax Ct. 1970, U.S. Supreme Ct. 1973, U.S. Ct. Appeals (10th cir.) 1978, U.S. Ct. Claims 1992. Atty. IRS, Denver, 1965-80, atty. chief counsel;s office, 1980—2002; ret., 2002. Contbr. articles to profl. jours. Treas., dir. Colo. Fourteeners Initiative. With USAF, 1955-58, capt. Res. ret. Mem. ABA, Colo. Bar Assn., AICPA, Colo. Soc. CPAs, Am. Assn. Atty.-CPAs, Am. Judicature Soc., Order of St. Ives, The Explorers Club, Am. Alpine Club, Colo. Mountain Club, Colo. Mountain Club Found. (bd. dirs., pres.), Beta Gamma Sigma, Beta Alpha Psi. Democrat. Office: 935 Pennsylvania St Denver CO 80203-3145

GEHRICKE, JEAN-GUIDO, psychologist, researcher; s. Horst and Militta Gehricke; m. Gina E. Latter, Dec. 24, 1998. BA, Freie U., Berlin, 1988, MA, 1992, PhD, 1998. Rsch. assoc. UCLA, 1995 -99; profl. rschr. U. Calif., Irvine, 1999—2001; asst. rsch. prof. Univ. of Calif., Irvine, 2001—. Author: (novels) Facial activity, emotion, and social context in depression, 1998; contbr. articles to profl. jours. Grantee grant, German Acad. Exch. Soc., 1994, Transdisciplinary Tobacco Use Rsch. Ctr., 2002. Mem.: Soc. for Rsch. on Nicotine and Tobacco, Soc. Psychophysiological Rsch., Soc. Behavioral Med., Am. Psychosomatic Soc. Avocations: astronomy, painting. Office: U Calif 3340 Social Ecology II Irvine CA 92697 Business E-Mail: jgehrick@uci.edu.

GEHRIG, EDWARD HARRY, electrical engineer, consultant; b. Portland, Oreg., Oct. 31, 1925; s. Henry Oscar and Selma Victoria (Charf) G.; m. May 20, 1950; children: Cynth Ann, Nanette Lou, Timothy Alexander. BA in Physics, Reed Coll., 1948; BSEE, Stanford U., 1949; MSEE, Oreg. State U., 1951. Registered profl. engr., Oreg. Physicist AEC, 1950-52; head system planning Bonneville Power Adminstrn., Portland, 1963-72, chief transmission design, 1972-76, chief R & D, 1976-81; ind. cons. Lake Oswego, Oreg., 1982—. Participant Electric Power Rsch. Inst. and GE Project UHV; designer, distbr. for Lindal Cedar Homes, Seattle, 1987—. Patentee in field; contbr. articles to profl. jours. Chmn. Lake Grove Zoning Bd., Lake Oswego, Oreg., 1962-64; elder First Presbyn. Ch., Portland; coach basketball, soccer, Lake Grove. Sgt. U.S. Army, 1944-46, ETO. Recipient Meritorious Svc. award Dept. of Interior, 1979. Fellow IEEE. Democrat. Avocations: woodcraft, golf. Home: PO Box 2062 Lake Oswego OR 97035

GEHRING, DAVID AUSTIN, physician, cardiologist, administrator; b. Bryn Mawr, Pa., Dec. 6, 1930; s. Harry Rittenhouse and Anne Gardiner (Bozarth) G.; m. Joan Helen Lotz, June 7, 1953 (div. Aug. 1982); children: David, Paul, Peter, Sue, Barbara, Eric; m. Victoria Marie Damiano, Sept. 2, 1982 (dec. May 2000); children: Theresa, Judy Lynne, Michael Austin; m. Rose Y. Barron, May 5, 2001. BA magna cum laude, U. Pitts., 1952, MD, 1956; grad., Naples Sch. of Real Estate, Fla., 2000. Diplomate Am. Bd. Internal Medicine; cert. geriatric medicine. Commd. USN, 1956, advanced through grades to lt. comdr., intern, then resident in internal medicine U.S. Naval Hosp., 1956-60, mem. staff internal medicine U.S. Naval Hosp., 1960-61, chief internal medicine heart sta. U.S. Naval Hosp. Annapolis, Md., 1961-63, resigned, 1963, cardiologist K.G.E. Med. Group, Woodbury, NJ, 1963—82; cardiologist, pres. Hobbs Cardiology, P.A., Hobbs, N.Mex., 1982-86; med. dir. Polk (Pa.) Ctr., 1986-91; physician, chief grade VA Med. Ctr., Coatesville, Pa., 1991-97, assoc. chief of staff for ambulatory care, 1993-96, chief med. svc., 1995-96, chief primary care and chief of staff, 1995-96, chief of staff, 1995-96, cardiologist, 1996-97; assoc. med. dir. for correctional med. svcs. South Jersey, 1997-98; site med. dir. South Woodstate Prison, 1997-98; clin. dir. Del. Hosp. Chronically Ill, 1998-99; clin. dir. long term care pub. health divsn. State of Del., 1998-99; physician VA Clinic, Naples, Fla., 2002—. Clin. dir. Del. Hosp. for Cronically Ill, Smyrna, 1998—99; v.p. Regent Park Villas II Assoc., Inc., Naples, Fla., 1999—2000, pres., 2000—01; realtor VIP Lodge McKee Realtors, 2000—01, VIP Lodge McKee, 2000—01; sect. chief VA Med. Ctr., Salisbury, NC, 2001—02, occupl. health physician, 2002, mem. ethics com., 2001—02, mem. hosp. disaster com., 2002, chair small pox com., 02; testing cardiologist Anthropometrics United Med. Group, Cherry Hill, NJ, 1974—82; clin. asst. prof. medicine Temple U. Hosp., Phila., 1975—82; adj. asst. prof. medicine Jefferson Meml. Coll., 1981—82; chief cardiac rehab. unit Lea Regional Hosp., Hobbs, 1982—86; chief med. svcs. 829th Sta. Hosp., USAR, Lubbock, Tex., 1984—86; cons. cardiology, Oil City, Pa., 1986—91; staff Franklin (Pa.) Regional Med. Ctr., 1986—90, Oil City Area Health Ctr., 1986—91; teaching staff St. Joseph Hosp., Lancaster, Pa., 1991—97; clin. preceptor U. Pa. Sch. Nursing, 1993—96; cons. Southeastern Vets. Ctr., Spring City, Pa., 1997—98, Providence Med. Ctr., Media, 1997—98; others; assoc. med. dir. Correctional Med. Svcs. South Jersey, 1997—98; mem. adult protective svcs. coun. State of Del., 1998—99; mem. profl. devel. com. Naples Area Bd. Realtors, 2000—01, mem. complaint rev. com., 2000—01; chair pharmacy and therapeutics com. Dept. Health and Social Svcs., State of Del., 1998—99; mem. pharmacy and therapeutics com. for VISN 6 dept. Vet. Affairs, 2001—02; cons. in field. Author: EKG Workbook, 1972, EKG Workbook I, 1978; contbr. articles to profl. jours. Project dir. 23 Greater Del. Valley Reg. Med. Program, Pa., 1971—75; mem. ACLS Inst. and affiliated faculty Pa. Heart Assn., 1986—98, bd. dirs. N.W. chpt., 1988—90; bd. dirs. Inst. Christianna Hosp., Del., 1998—99; bd. dirs. adv. com., chmn. personnel com. med. health, rehab., drugs and alcohol Venango County, Franklin Purl, Pa., 1986—90, pres., 1988—89; mem. Health Care Adv. Com. to Congressman William F. Clinger, Jr., 23d Dist., 1989—91, Naples Mus. Art, 2000—; patron Philharmonic Ctr. for Arts, 1998—, Carolina Opera, 2001—03; lector St. Joseph Ch., Oil City, 1987—91, eucharistic min., 1990—92, 1992—93, Sacred Heart Ch., Mt. Ephraim, 1994—99, lector, 1998—99. Lt. col. USAR, 1983—90. Recipient Outstanding Svc. award Am. Cancer Soc. N.J., 1967, Benjamin Berkowitz award N.J. Heart Assn., 1975, Nat. Def. Svc. medal, 1975, USAR Components Achievement medal, 1988, Letter of Commendation USAR, 1988, 90, Pres.'s medal of Merit, Rep. Task Force, 1984Letter of Commendation Sec. of Vets. Affairs, 1994; Cert. of Appreciation, Sec. of State N.Mex., 1982, Venango County Commrs., 1987, 88, 89, 90, Polk Ctr. award of Merit, 1991, Spl. Contbn. award and Mgr. of Yr. award VAMC Coatesville, 1996, Spl. Contbn. award, VA Med. Ctr., Salisbury, NC, 2002. Fellow ACP (life, Recognition awards 1967-70), Am. Coll. Cardiology, Am. Coll. Chest Physicians, Coll. Physicians of Phila., Am. Coll. Clin. Pharmacology; mem. AMA, Am. Geriatrics Soc., St. Jude Soc., Holy Name Soc., Assn. Miraculous Medal (promoter 1987—), Venango County Med. Soc. (pres. 1989-91), Assn. Mil. Surgeons, Am. Coll. Physician Execs., Am. Legion, Elks, KC. Republican. Roman Catholic. Avocations: stamp collecting, reading, walking, swimming, opera. Home: 2347 Butterfly Palm Dr Naples FL 34119 Office: VA Primary Care Clinic Ste 101 2685 Horseshoe Dr S Naples FL 34109 Fax: 239-659-0526. E-mail: daustin30@aol.com.

GEHRING, DONALD D. education educator; b. Trenton, N.J., Oct. 9, 1937; s. Philip F. and Elsie E. (Jackson) G.; m. Bettie Groover, Aug. 6, 1960; children: Lisa Anderson, David. BS, Ga. Inst. Tech., 1960; MEd, Emory U., 1966; EdD, U. Ga., 1971. Asst. to dean men Emory U., Atlanta, 1962-66; dir. housing West Ga. Coll., Carrollton, 1966-69; dean student devel. Mars Hill (N.C.) Coll., 1971-78; prof. higher edn. U. Louisville, 1978-91; prof. Bowling Green State U., 1991-2000. Tchr. People's Republic China, El Salvador Editor Coll. Student Affairs Jour.; contbr. numerous articles to profl. jours. Founder Assn. Student Jud. Affairs. Lt. USN, 1960-62. Recipient S. Earl Thompson award Assn. Coll. and Univ. Housing Officers, Outstanding Tchr. Sch. Edn. award. Mem. Nat. Assn. Student Pers. Adminstrn. (Outstanding Contbr. to Lit. or Rsch. award, Excellence as Grad. Faculty Mem. award), Am. Coll. Pers. Assn. (sr. scholar), Assn. Student Jud. Affairs (Disting. Svc. award), Am. Assn. for Higher Edn., So. Assn. for Coll. Student Affairs (past pres., Melvene Hardee and H. Howard Davis awards). E-mail: dgehrin1@earthlink.net.

GEHRING, FREDERICK WILLIAM, mathematician, educator; b. Ann Arbor, Mich., Aug. 7, 1925; s. Carl E. and Hester McNeal (Reed) G.; m. Lois Caroline Bigger, Aug. 29, 1953; children: Kalle Burgess, Peter Motz. BSE in Elec. Engring., U. Mich., 1946, MA in Math, 1949; PhD (Fulbright fellow) in Math, Cambridge U., Eng., 1952, ScD, 1976; PhD (hon.), U. Helsinki, Finland, 1977, U. Jyväskylä, 1990, Norwegian U. Sci. & Technology, 1997. Benjamin Peirce instr. Harvard U., Cambridge, Mass., 1952-55; instr. math. U. Mich., Ann Arbor, 1955-56, asst. prof., 1956-59, assoc. prof., 1959-62, prof., 1962-96, T.H. Hildebrandt prof. math., 1984-96, prof. emeritus, 1996, chmn. dept. math., 1973-75, 77-84, disting. univ. prof., 1987—; hon. prof. Hunan U., Changsha, People's Republic of China, 1987. Vis. prof. Harvard U., 1964-65, Stanford U., 1964, U. Minn., 1971, Inst. Mittag-Leffler, Sweden, 1972, Mittag-Leffler, Sweden, 1990; Lars Onsager prof. Norwegian Tech. Hochschule, Norway, 1995; chair program in Geo Function Theory, Math. Scis. Rsch. Inst., Berkeley, 1986. Editor Duke Math. Jour., 1963-80, D. Van Nostrand Pub. Co., 1963-70, North Holland Pub. Co., 1970-94, Springer-Verlag, 1974-2002; editl. bd. Procs. Am. Math. Soc., 1962-65, Ind. U. Math. Jour., 1967-75, Math. Revs., 1969-75, Bull. Am. Math. Soc., 1979-85, Complex Variables, 1981—, Mich. Math. Jour., 1989, Annales Academiae Scientiarum Fennicae, 1996—, Conformal Geometry and Dynamics, 1997—, Computational Methods and Function Theory, 2001—; contbr. numerous articles on rsch. in pure math. to sci. jours. With USNR, 1943-46. Decorated comdr. Finnish White Rose; NSF fellow, 1959-60, Fulbright fellow, 1958-59; Guggenheim fellow, 1958-59; Sci. Rsch. Coun. sr. fellow, 1981; Humboldt fellow, 1981-84; U. Auckland Found. fellow, 1985; Finnish Acad. fellow U. Helsinki, 1989. Mem. NAS, Am. Acad. Arts and Scis., Assn. Women in Math., Math. Assn. Am., Am. Math. Soc. (coun. 1969-75, 80-83, trustee 1983-93, mem. editl. bd. 1997-98), Inst. for Math. and Its Applications (gov. 1981-84), Swiss Math. Soc., Finnish Math. Soc., London Math. Soc., European Math. Soc., Finnish Acad. Sci., German Math. soc., Royal Norwegian Soc. Scis. and Letters. Home: 2139 Melrose Ave Ann Arbor MI 48104-4067

GEHRING, RONALD KENT, lawyer; b. Ft. Wayne, Ind., Feb. 5, 1941; s. Ronald G. and Beverly M. (Failor) G.; m. Teresa L. Eyer, June 18, 1966; children: Gregory D., Douglas K., Suzanne C. AB, Ind. U., 1963, JD, 1967. Bar: Ind. 1967, U.S. Dist. Ct. (no. and so. dists.) Ind. 1967, U.S. Ct. Appeals (7th cir.) 1975. Assoc. Peters, McHie, Enslen & Hand, Hammond, Ind., 1967-70; ptnr. Tourkow, Danehy, Crell, Hood & Gehring, Ft. Wayne, 1971-79, Grossman, Boeglin & Gehring and predecessor, Ft. Wayne, 1980-84; pvt. practice, Ft. Wayne, 1984—. Panelist Ind. Collection Law Seminar, 1982-83; atty. Ind. Dist. Luth. Ch. Bd. dirs. Concordia Cemetery Assn., 1982-83, Luth. Assn. Broadcasting, Inc. Mem. ABA, Ind. Trial Lawyers, Comml. Law League, Ind. Bar Assn., Allen County Bar Assn., Phi Delta Phi. Office: 202 W Berry St Ste 321 Fort Wayne IN 46802-2242

GEHRING, WALTER JAKOB, biology and genetics educator; b. Zurich, Switzerland, Mar. 20, 1939; s. Jakob and Marcelle (Rebmann) G.; m. Elisabeth Lott, Jan. 31, 1964; children: Stephan, Thomas. Diploma in Zoology, U. Zurich, 1963, PhD, 1965. Rsch. assoc. U. Zurich, 1963-67; postdoctoral fellow Yale U., New Haven, Conn., 1967-69, assoc. prof., 1969-72; prof. U. Basel, Switzerland, 1972—. Assoc. editor: Jour. Exptl. Zoology, Mechanisms of Devel., Trends in Genetics, Growth & Differentiation. Recipient Otto Nägeli prize Zurich, 1982, Warren Triennial Harvard Med. Sch., Cambridge, Mass., 1986, Dr. Albert Wander prize City of Bern, Switzerland, 1986, Charles Léopold Mayer prize Inst. of France, Paris, 1986, Louis Jeantet prize for medicine City of Geneva, 1987, Prix d'Honneur, Moet Hennessy Louis Vuitton, 1993, Newcomb Cleve. prize AAAS, 1994-1995, Otto Warburg-medaille, 1996, Paul Wintrebert prize U. Pierre and Marie Curie, 1996, March of Dimes prize Devel. Biology, 1997, Karl von Frisch prize German Zool. Soc., 2000, Kyoto prize Inamori Found., 2000, Preis der Alfred Vogt Stiftung zur Förderung der Augenheilkunde, Zürich, 2001, Premio Balzan, Fondazione Internat. Premio E. Balzan. Mem. AAAS, NAS, European Molecular Biology Orgn., European Devel. Biology Orgn., Deutsche Akademie der Naturforscher Leopoldina, Academia Europaea, Genetics Soc. Am., Internat. Soc. for Developmental Biology, Swiss Soc. for Cell Biology, Molecular Biology and Genetics, Am. Soc. for Developmental Biology, Human Genome Orgn., Royal Soc. London (fgn.), Acad. Scis. (fgn.), Sigma Xi. Avocations: birdwatching, photography. Home: Hochfeldstrasse 32 CH-4106 Therwil Switzerland Office: U Basel Biozentrum Klingelbergstrasse 70 CH-4056 Basel Switzerland E-mail: walter.gehring@unibas.ch.

GEHRINGER, RICHARD GEORGE, publishing executive; b. Newark, Oct. 31, 1949; s. George John and Constance Mary (Volz) G.; m. Phyllis Jean Salerno, Nov. 13, 1977; children: Alexandra Rane, Skyler George. BS, U. S.C., 1972; MBA, St. John's U., Jamaica, N.Y., 1976. Cert. cash mgr., treasury profl. Mgmt. trainee Avdel Corp., Teterboro, N.J., 1972-74; purchasing analyst Resistoflex Corp., Roseland, N.J., 1974-76; staff acct. McGraw-Hill Pub. Co., Hightstown, N.J., 1976-78; fin. analyst corp. real estate McGraw-Hill, Inc., N.Y.C., 1978-79; bus. mgr., corp. real estate McGraw-Hill Inc., N.Y.C., 1979-80; asst. contr. McGraw-Hill Book Co., N.Y.C., 1980-81; contr. Oxford U. Press Inc., Fair Lawn, N.J., 1981-86, v.p., CFO N.Y.C., 1986—90, Cary, NC, 1990—95, sr. v.p., CFO N.Y.C., 1995—. Fin. advisor Pi Kappa Alpha, Columbia U., N.Y.C., 1988-89; bd. dirs. Fin. Execs. Inst., Di[illegible] Pen & Inc., Books Alive!. Mem. Fin. Execs. Inst., Inst. Mgmt. Accts., Treasury Mgmt. Assn., Bldg. Owners' and Mgrs.' Assn. of Greater N.Y., N.C. Citizens for Bus. and Industry, Raleigh C. of C., Assn. for Financial Planners Republican. Roman Catholic. Home: 120 Overleigh Rd Bernardsville NJ 07924-1510 Office: Oxford U Press Inc 198 Madison Ave New York NY 10016-4341 E-mail: richard.gehringerr@oup-usa.org.

GEHRKE, KAREN MARIE, retired accountant; b. Gaylord, Minn., Apr. 12, 1940; d. Stanley Henry and Frieda Marie (Hammel) Ostermann; m. Orville Raymond Gehrke, Oct. 21, 1961 (div. Aug. 1994); children: Kimberly, Karla, Kent. Grad. high sch., Gaylord, 1958. Inspector Fingerhut Mfg., Gaylord, 1959-60; rewinder 3M, Hutchinson, Minn., 1960-61, packer, 1971-72; sec. Boehmke Ins. Agy., Gaylord, 1961-63, Law Office of H.A. Knobel, Gaylord, 1964-68; teller First State Fed. Savs. and Loan, Hutchinson, 1969; sec. Wally's Tire Shop, Hutchinson, 1970, Lyle R. Jensen, CPA, Hutchinson, 1974-84; owner Karen M. Gehrke L.P.A., Hutchinson, 1984—2001; ret., 2001. Mem. Nat. Assn. Female Execs., Nat. Soc. Pub. Accts., Minn. Assn. Pub. Accts., Hutchinson Area C. of C.

GEHRLEIN, WILLIAM VINCENT, business education educator; b. Erie, Pa., June 8, 1946; s. Vincent Francis and Eunice Mae (Knauff) G.; m. Sheila Eileen Lawson, Nov. 25, 1973 (div. May 1991); m. Barbara Elaine Eller, June 29, 2001. BS in Physics, Gannon Coll., 1968; MS in Physics, Pa. State U., 1972, PhD in Bus. Adminstrn., 1975. Postdoctoral fellow Pa. State U., State College, Pa., 1975-77; asst. prof. Clarkson Coll., Potsdam, N.Y., 1977-78; assoc. prof. U. Del., Newark, 1978-81, prof. of bus. adminstrn., 1981-2001. Mem. editl. bd.: Social Choice and Welfare; guest editor: Spl. Issue of Annals of Opers. Rsch., 1990, 97; contbr. numerous articles to profl. jours.; mem. bd. assoc. editors Inst. of Indsl. Engrs., 1985. With U.S. Army, 1968-70. Fellow Ctr. for Advanced Study, U. Del., 1988; grantee NSF, 1978. Mem. Internat. Soc. for Social Choice and Welfare (exec. coun.), Opers. Rsch. Soc. of Am. Avocations: running, fishing, genealogy. Office: Dept Bus Adminstrn Univ Del Newark DE 19716

GEHRY, FRANK OWEN, architect; b. Toronto, Ont., Can., Feb. 28, 1929; arrived in U.S., 1947; s. Irving and Thelma (Caplan) Gehry; m. Berta Aguilera, Sept. 11, 1975; children: Alejandro, Samuel;children: Leslie, Brina. BArch, U. So. Calif., 1954; postgrad., Harvard U., 1956—57. Registered profl. architect, Calif. Designer Victor Gruen Assocs., LA, 1953—54, planning, design and project dir., 1958—61; project designer, planner Pereira & Luckman, LA, 1957—58; prin. Frank O. Gehry & Assocs., Santa Monica, Calif., 1962—. Prin. works include Loyola Law Sch., LA, 1978—92, Temporary Contemporary Mus., 1983, Calif. Aerospace Mus., 1984, Frances Goldwyn Regional Br. Libr., Hollywood, Calif., 1986, U.C.I. Info. and Computer Sci./Engring. Rsch. Lab. and Engring Ctr., Irvine, Calif., 1986—88, Vitra Internat. Mfg. Facility and Design Mus., Weil am Rhein, Germany, 1989, Chiat/Day Hdqs., Venice, Calif., 1991, Am. Ctr., Paris, 1994, Advanced Tech. Labs. Bldg., Iowa City, 1992, U. Toledo Ctr. for Visual Arts, 1992, Walt Disney Concert Hall, LA, 1993, Frederick R. Weisman Art Mus., Mpls., 1993, Vitra Internat. Hdqs., Basel, Switzerland, 1994, Disney Ice, Anaheim, Calif., 1995, EMR Communication and Tech. Ctr., Bad Oeynhausen, Germany, 1995, Team Disneyland Adminstrn. Bldg., Anaheim, 1996, Nationale-Nederlanden Bldg., Prague, Czech Republic, 1996, Guggenheim Mus., Bilbao, Spain, 1997, Experience Music Project, Seattle, 2000, Weatherhead Sch. Mgmt., Cleve., 2002. Trustee Hereditary Disease Found., Santa Monica, Calif., 1970—. Recipient Arnold W. Brunner Meml. prize in architecture, 1983, Eliot Noyes Design chair, Harvard U., 1983, Charlotte Davenport Professorship in architecture, Yale U., 1982, 1985, 1987—89, Pritzker Architecture prize, 1989, Wolf prize in art, 1992, Praemium Imperiale, 1992, Dorothy and Lilian Gish award, 1994, Nat. Medal of Arts, 1998. Office: Frank O Gehry & Assocs 1520B Cloverfield Blvd Santa Monica CA 90404-3502

GEIB, KARLMANN, legal administrator; Pres. Superior Ct. Office: Fed Ct of Justice Herrenstr 45A Karlsruhe Germany Fax: 721-159-830.

GEIDUSCHEK, E(RNEST) PETER, biophysics and molecular biology educator; b. Vienna, Apr. 11, 1928; came to U.S., 1945, naturalized, 1946; s. Sigmund and Frieda (Tauber) G.; m. Joyce Barbara Brous; 2 children BA, Columbia U., 1948; A.M., Harvard U., 1950, PhD, 1952. Instr. chemistry Yale U., New Haven, 1952-53, 55-57; asst. prof. chemistry U. Mich., Ann Arbor, 1957-59; asst. prof. biophysics U. Chgo., 1959-62, assoc. prof., 1962-64, prof., 1964-70; prof. biology U. Calif., San Diego, 1970-94, rsch. prof., 1994—, chmn. dept., 1981-83, 94. Cons. USPHS, 1963-69, NIH, 1991-94, 98-2003. Editl. bd. Biophys. Jour., 1967-69, Ann. Revs. Biophysics and Bioengring., 1971-74, Virology, 1972—, Sci., 1977-84, Seminars in Virology, 1990-98, Ency. Virology, 1990-2000. Served with U.S. Army, 1953-55 Recipient rsch. award Am. Postgrad. Med. Assn., 1962, USPHS, 1962, Order of Merit of Italian Republic; Guggenheim fellow, 1964-65. Fellow AAAS, Am. Acad. Microbiology; mem. NAS, Am. Acad. Arts and Scis., Am. Soc. Biochemistry and Molecular Biology (pub. affairs com. 1988-90), Am. Soc. Microbiology, Am. Soc. Virology (coun. 1985-87). Office: U Calif at San Diego Divsn Biol Scis Ctr Molecular Genetics La Jolla CA 92093-0634

GEIER, CONSTANCE B. education educator; b. Apr. 19, 1952; d. Morris John and Patricia Venoy Kurle; 2 children. BS in Edn., No. State U., 1974, MS in Edn., 1991; EdD in Ednl. Psychology, U. S.D., 1997. Assoc. prof. No. State U., Aberdeen, SD, 1991—. Office: No State Univ 1200 S Jay Aberdeen SD 57401 E-mail: geierc@northern.edu.

GEIER, PHILIP HENRY, JR., advertising executive; b. Pontiac, Mich., Feb. 22, 1935; s. Philip Henry and Jane (Gillen) G.; m. Faith Power, children: Hope Geier Smith, Johanna Geier. BA, Colgate U., 1957; MS, Columbia U., 1958. With McCann-Erickson, Inc., Cleve., 1958-60, N.Y.C., 1960-68; chmn. McCann-Erickson Internat. U.K. Co., London, 1969-73; exec. v.p. McCann-Erickson Europe, 1973-75; vice chmn. internat. ops. McCann Worldwide, London, 1973-75; vice chmn. internat. Interpublic Group of Cos., Inc., N.Y.C., 1975-77, pres., chief operating officer, 1977-80, chmn., chief exec. officer, 1980—2001, pres., 1985—2000. Bd. dirs. Woolworth Corp., Fiduciary Trust Corp. Dir. Sch. of Am. Ballet, Internat. Tennis Hall of Fame; bd. overseers Meml. Sloan-Kettering Cancer Ctr., Columbia U. Bus. Sch.; trustee Whitney Mus. of Am. Art; trustee MU of Delta Kappa Epsilon Found. Mem.: Doubles (N.Y.C.); River (N.Y.C.); Sloane (London); Hurlingham (London). Office: Interpublic Group Cos Inc Ste 400 1271 Avenue Of The Americas Fl 44 New York NY 10020-1459*

GEIER, PHILIP OTTO, III, academic administrator; b. Cin., 1948; s. Philip O. Jr. and Susanne (Ernst) G.; m. Amy Yeager, Dec. 27, 1975; children: Katherine, Elizabeth, Christopher. BA in Am. Civilization with honors, Williams Coll., 1970; attended, U. Paris, 1973; MA in History, Syracuse U., 1975, PhD in Am. Studies and History, 1980. Instr. history and Am. studies Dickinson Coll., Carlisle, Pa., 1976-77; Fulbright lectr. U. Paris-Sorbonne, 1977-78; interim exec. dir. French-Am. Found., N.Y.C., 1978-79; assoc. dir. Am. Farm Sch., Thessaloniki, Greece, 1979-82; v.p. external affairs World Learning, Brattleboro, Vt., 1982-93; pres., dir. Armand Hammer United World Coll., Montezuma, N.Mex., 1993—. Bd. dirs. Fulbright Prize Com., Washington, Pine Manor Coll., Info. Markets Corp.; chair social Svcs. and Internat. Exch. Commn. 2d U.S.-USSR Emerging Leaders Summit, Moscow and Sochi, 1990, del. to 1st Commn., Phila., 1988; mem. Coun. Fgn. Rels., Pacific Coun. on Internat. Policy, L.A. 2d lt. Supply Corps, USN, 1970-72, Vietnam. Fulbright award Fed. Republic of Germany, 1988. Avocations: international relations, outdoor recreation. Office: United World Coll PO Box 248 Montezuma NM 87731-0248

GEIER, SHARON LEE, special education educator; b. Dayton, Ohio, Nov. 21, 1943; d. Robert Stanley Murphy and Mary Frances (Ross) Briggs; m. Arthur M. Geier, Jan 23, 1965; children: Arthur William, Bradford Robert. BA, Wilmington (Ohio) Coll., 1965; cert. spl. edn., Wright State U., 1976; MS in Edn., U. Dayton, 1995. Cert. elem. tchr., Ohio, edn. handicapped. Tchr. 1st grade Fairborn (Ohio) City Schs., 1965-66, Kettering (Ohio) City Schs., 1967-71, Xenia (Ohio) City Schs., 1975-81, tchr. 3rd grade, 1981-82, tchr. learning disabled, 1982—. Tchr. specifically learning disabled Camp Progress Centerville (Ohio) Schs., summers, 1977, 78; coord. MicroSoc. Program, 1995-2000, 2002-03. Founder, pres. Twig 6 Children's Med. Ctr. Aux., Dayton, 1971-73, chmn. Jr. Aux., 1972-74, Recipient Doer award Miami Valley Regional Ctr. and Dayton Area Citizens for Spl. Edn., 1988; Martha Holden Jennings scholar, 1980-81; named Spl. Educator of Yr., Spl. Edn. dept. Cen. State U., 1993. Mem. AAUW, ASCD, Coun. Exceptional Children (Outstanding Chpt. Pres. Ohio Fedn. 1989, pres. Greene County chpt. 1987-89, treas. Ohio divsn. learning disabilities 1989-91, pres. 1991-93, treas. Greene County chpt. 1999—), Ohio Fedn. Coun. for Exceptional Children (liaison S.W. region 1989-94, liaison chmn. 1992-93, 93-94, sec. 1994-97, v.p. 1997-98, pres. elect 1998-99, pres. 1999-2000, past pres. 2000-01), Green Key Honor Soc. Republican. Avocations: reading, music, painting, plants, aerobics. Home: 1134 Napa Rdg Centerville OH 45458-6017 E-mail: sgeier89@aol.com.

GEIGER, ALBERT J., JR., radiologist, retired; b. Elberton, Ga., 1929; s. Albert James and Sara Frances (Asbury) G.; m. Laura Marvine Gillespie, June 10, 1956; children: Albert J. III, Laura E. Geiger Hornsby, Suzanne C. Geiger Ballenger. AB, Princeton U., 1951; MD, Emory U., 1955. Bd. cert. radiology, 1965; diplomate Am. Bd. Radiology. Intern Grady Meml. Hosp., Atlanta, 1955-56; resident in radiology Emory U. Hosp., Atlanta, 1958-61; rsch. fellow USPHS Nat. Cancer Inst., Atlanta, 1959-60; staff St. Anthony's Hosp., St. Petersburg, Fla. Adv. bd. St. Petersburg (Fla.) Jr. Coll. Sch. Radiologic Tech., 1990-95. Mem. AMA, Fla. Med. Assn., Fla. Radiology Soc., Radiol. Soc. N.Am., So. Med. Assn., Pinellas County Med. Soc. (bd. govs. 1984-87, Achievement award 1982), St. Anthony's Hosp. Med. Alumni, Rotary Club St. Petersburg (pres. 1970-71). Republican. Methodist.

GEIGER, GORDON HAROLD, engineer; b. Chgo., Apr. 21, 1937; BE, Yale U., 1959; MS, Northwestern U., Evanston, Ill., 1961; PhD, Northwestern U., 1964. Registered engr., Ariz. Prof., dept. head U. Ariz., Tucson, 1973—80; sr. cons. Inland Steel Co., Indiana Harbor, Iowa, 1980—82; v.p., tech. dir. Chase Manhattan Bank, N.Y.C., 1982—83; exec. v.p. North Star Steel, Wayzata, Minn., 1988—93; sr. v.p. Cargill, Inc., Wayzata, Minn., 1988—93; CEO Qualitech Steel Corp., Pittsboro, Ind., 1994—99; dir., prof. engring. mgmt. program U. Ariz., Tucson, 2000—. Fellow: Am. Soc. for Metals Internat. (pres. 2001—02).

GEIGER, H. JACK, medical educator; b. Nov. 11, 1925; m. Nicole Schupf. Student, U. Wis., 1943, U. Chgo., 1947—50; MD, Case Western Res. U., 1958; M in Sci. Hygiene, Harvard U., 1960; ScD (hon.), SUNY, Purchase, 1992. Intern Boston City Hosp. Harvard U., 1958—59, asst. resident in medicine, 1962—63, sr. resident in medine, 1963—64, clin. asst. in medicine, 1964—65; postdoctoral rsch. fellow social sci. and medicine Harvard U., 1959—61, instr. preventive medicine, 1961—62; asst. prof. pub. health, 1964—65; assoc. prof. Tufts U. Sch. Medicine, 1965—66, prof., 1966—71, chmn. dept. cmty. health and social medicine, 1969—71; dir. health ctrs. Columbia Point, Boston, Mound Bayou, Miss., 1965—71; project co-dir. SUNY, Stonybrook, 1971—73, prof., chmn. dept. cmty. medicine, 1971—77; Henry J. Kaiser sr. fellow Stanford U., 1983—84; Arthur C. Logan prof. chmn. cmty. health/social medicine CUNY Med. Sch., 1978—97. Prof. emeritus CUNY Med. Sch., 1987—97; vis. prof. medicine Harvard U., 1972—73. Mem. editl. bd.: Am. Jour Pub. Health; contbr. articles to profl. jours. Recipient Disting. Svc. award, Miss. Assn. Community Health for Poor, 1973, Nat. Health Achievement award in cmty. health, Blue Cross and Blue Shield Assns. N.Am., 1979, Disting. Pub. Svc. award, Nat. Assn. Cmty. Health Ctrs., 1981, Mass. League Cmty. Health Ctrs, 1986, Robert H. Felix Disting. Svc. award, St. Louis U. Sch. Medicine, 1986, Founders award, Miss. Delta Health Ctr., 1990, Disting. Alumnus award of merit, Harvard U. Sch. Pub. Health, 1992. Fellow: APHA (1st Ann. Excellence award 1972), AAAS (Inst. Medicine Mission to South Africa 1989, organizer conf. on health care for post-apartheid South Africa 1990), Scientists Inst. Pub. Info.; mem.: Herman Biggs Soc., Soc. Health and Human Value, Soc. Advancement of Ambulatory Care, Physicians for Social Responsibility (founding mem.), Com. on Health in South Africa (nat. pres.), Physicians for Human Rights (expert med. cons. to UN Human Rights Ctr. to Yugoslavia 1992, leader human rights missions to Yugoslavia 1993, founding mem., pres., West Bank and Gaza Strip 1988, 1990, numerous others), Inst. Medicine NAS (sr.), Assn. Health Svcs. Rsch. (Iraq and Kurdistan 1991), Assn. Behavioral Scis. and Med. Edn., Assn. Tchrs. Preventive Medicine, Internat. Epidemiol. Assn., Am. Coll. Preventive Medicine. Office: CCNY Sch Medicine New York NY 10031

GEIGER, JOHN GRIGSBY, editor, writer, reporter; b. Ithaca, N.Y., Jan. 20, 1960; s. Kenneth Warren and Shirley Frances (Gilchrist) G.; m. Marina Jimenez, Oct. 15, 1999. BA, U. Alberta, 1981. Weekly columnist Edmonton Sun, 1981-83, reporter, 1983-86, Edmonton Jour., 1986-87, columnist, 1987-95, edtl. writer, 1995-98; dep. nat. editor Nat. Post, 1998-99, acting nat. editor, 1999-2000, fgn. editor-UN, 2000, rev. editor, 2000—. Co-author: Frozen in Time: The Fate of the Franklin Expedition, 1987 (best seller in U.K., Germany, Canada), Dead Silence, 1993 (best seller Canada), (children's book) Buried in Ice, 1992; editor: Empire of the Bay, 1989. Recipient Edward Dunlop award of excellence, Edward Dunlop Found., 1984. Episcopalian. Office: Nat Post 300-1450 Don Mills Rd Toronto ON Canada M3B 3R5 Fax: 416-442-2212. E-mail: jgeiger@nationalpost.com.

GEIGER, LOREN DENNIS, classical musician; b. Buffalo, Jan. 23, 1946; s. Carroll Chester and Edith Lucile (Swedenborg) G.; m. Elaine Louise Sivers, Aug. 21, 1976; children: Rebecca, Sarah, Diana. MusB, U. Rochester, 1968, MusM, 1970. Cert. educator, N.Y. Band dir. Orchard Pk. (N.Y.) Cen. Schs., 1969—. Orch. libr. Clarence (N.Y.) Orch., 1996—, Orchard Park (N.Y.) Symphony, 1998—; tubist Niagara Falls (N.Y.) Philharm., 1970-73, Orchard Park Symphony, 1973—, Amherst Symphony, Snyder, N.Y., 1974—, Clarence Summer Orch., 1974—; condr. 20th Century Band, Buffalo, 1984-91. Editor: Boombah Herald, 1973-98; arranger numerous mus. selections. Committeeman Orch. Park Symphony Music, 1976-84, 94—; active Music Educators Nat. Conf. Mem. Am. Fedn. Musicians, N.Y. State Sch. Music Assn., Circus Windjammers Unltd. (charter), Internat. Mil. Music Soc. (charter), Pi Kappa Lambda. Avocation: composition. Home: 15 Park Blvd Lancaster NY 14086-2510 Office: Orchard Park Cen Sch 60 S Lincoln Ave Orchard Park NY 14127-2664

GEIGER, MARK WATSON, management educator; b. Grand Forks, N.D., Aug. 22, 1949; s. Louis George and Helen Marjorie (Watson) G.; children: Harley, Uintah, Klaus. BA, Carleton Coll., 1971; MBA, U. Pa., 1975; MA, U. Mo., 2000. CPA, N.Y. Bldg. contractor Spiral Remodeling, Phila., 1976-78; EDP project mgr. Ariz. State Govt., Phoenix, 1978-81; mgr. internal audit Gulf & Western Industries, N.Y.C., 1981-85; v.p. spl. projects Kidder, Peabody & Co., Inc., N.Y.C., 1986-90; v.p., chief adminstrv. officer Analytical Bio-Chemistry Labs., Inc., Columbia, Mo., 1990-92; ind. mgmt. cons. Columbia, 1992-94; asst. prof. fin. William Woods U., Fulton, Mo., 1994—. Rsch. grantee William Woods U., 1994, Mo. State Hist. Soc., 1997, 2001. Mem. AICPA, Mensa, SAR, Am. Hist. Assn., So. Hist. Assn., Mo. Hist. Soc., Phi Alpha Theta. Avocations: creative writing, long-distance swimming, target shooting, horseback riding. Home: 1508 Hickam Dr Columbia MO 65202

GEIGER, RICHARD BERNARD, engineer, retired federal agency administrator; b. Huron County, Mich., May 4, 1936; s. Clement T. and Elizabeth A. (Volmering) G.; m. Norma J. Edwards, Sept. 6, 1958; children: Brenda, Jeffrey, Lisa, Paula, Pamela. AAS, St. Clair C.C., Port Huron, Mich., 1961; BS in Civil Engring., George Washington U., 1972; M in Urban Affairs, Va. Poly. Inst. & State U., 1980. Registered profl. engr., Mich., D.C. Engring. technician Bur. Pub. Rds., Gatlinburg, Tenn., 1958-63, hwy. engr. Arlington, Va., 1964-67; planning engr. Fed. Hwy. Adminstrn., Arlington, 1967-73, environ. engr., 1973-77, Washington, 1977-80, hwy. engr., 1980-89; asst. chief, divsn. transp. Bur. Indian Affairs, Washington, 1989-91, chief, divsn. transp., 1991-94, ret., 1994. Mem. Nat. Rsch. Coun. (Transp. Rsch. Bd.), Washington, 1989—. V.p. Ch. Share Com., Annandale, Va., 1990-91. With U.S. Army, 1954-56. Recipient Svc. award Am. Assn. State Hwy. and Transp. Ofcls., 1983, Superior Achievement award Fed. Hwy. Adminstrn., 1986. Mem. ASCE (life, Outstanding Student award 1971), NSPE (life), Nat. Assn. County Engrs., Order of the Engr. (life), Am. Legion (life), Disabled Am. Vets. (life). Avocations: tennis, bowling, walking. Home: 6903 Fern Ln Annandale VA 22003-1909

GEIGER, RICHARD STUART, lawyer; b. Dallas, Feb. 21, 1936; s. Gilbert A. and Letitia (Wells) G.; m. Phyllis Scott McGee, June 4, 1954; children— R. Scott, Angela G., Margaret L., P. Claire, Amy S. LL.B., So. Meth. U., 1962. Bar: Tex. 1962, U.S. Ct. Appeals (5th cir.) 1969, U.S. Supreme Ct. 1968. Sole practice, Dallas, 1962-75; ptnr. Thompson, Coe, Cousins & Irons, Dallas, 1975—. Editor in chief Tex. Ins. Law Reporter. Mem. Tex. Ho. of Reps., 1972-76. Democrat. Episcopalian. Clubs: Austin, Crescent (Dallas). E-mail: rgeiger@thompsoncoe.com. Office: Plaza of the Americas 700 N Pearl St 25th Fl Dallas TX 75201

GEIGERMAN, CLARICE FURCHGOTT, writer, consultant; b. Charleston, S.C., Sept. 24, 1916; d. Melvin and Doreta (Brown) Furchgott; m. Henry D. Geigerman, Jr., July 4, 1941 (dec. Nov. 1967); children: Henry D. III, Robert M.; m. Bruce Franklin Woodruff, Jr., Dec. 11, 1982. A in Bus., Draughon Sch. Commerce, 1935; student, U. Ga., 1935-36, Am. Inst. Banking, 1936-41, Ga. Inst. Real Estate, 1972. Dir. payroll and pers. Atlanta Ordnance Dept., 1935-41, 45-46; freelance writer Atlanta Press Club, 1964—; pvt. practice as pub. rels. cons. Atlanta, 1970—; ins. agent Am. Family Life, Atlanta, 1970—; real estate agent Ackerman & Co., Atlanta, 1972—; freelance actress Women-In-Film, Atlanta, 1974—. Writer TV Digest, 1961-62; writer, contbg. editor Arts Mag., 1962-63; author, editor newsletter, mag. Atlanta Music Club, 1973; columnist Jewish Georgian, 1989—, Buckhead Weekly, 1995—; appeared in motion picture Driving Miss Daisy, 1991. Pres. Atlanta Civic Ballet, 1962-64, So. Regional Opera, Atlanta, 1968-75; mem. Atlanta Funds Rev. Bd., 1973-75; v.p. Atlanta Playhouse Theatre, pres., bd. dirs.; 1st v.p. Met. Atlanta Better Films, 1992-96, pres., 1997—; active Salvation Army, Atlanta History Ctr., Atlanta Bot. Garden, High Mus., Art English Speaking Union; bd. dirs. Active Votors, 1965-75; bd. dirs., v.p. Atlanta Symphony, 1966-68; bd. dirs. Alliance Theatre Guild; v.p. Atlanta chpt. Freedoms Found. Named Hon. Lt. Col. on Gov.'s Staff, Gov. Zell Miller, 1994-97. Mem. NAFE, NATAS, Atlanta Ballet Assn., World Assn. Women Journalists, Pub. Rels. Soc. Am., Nat. Trust for Hist. Preservations. Democrat. Jewish. Home and Office: 620 Peachtree St NE Atlanta GA 30308-2313

GEIKEN, ALAN RICHARD, contractor; b. Toledo, Aug. 24, 1923; s. Martin Herman and Herta Regina G. BS in Engring., Iowa State U., 1950. Engr., sec. Hot Spot Detector, Inc., Des Moines, 1950-53, sales engr., asst. gen. mgr., 1953-60; pres., owner Alan Geiken Inc., Sacramento, 1960—. Cons. on grain storage. Served with USAAF, 1943-45. Mem. Am. Soc. Agrl. Engrs., Coun. for Agrl. Sci. and Tech., Grain Elevator and Processing Soc., Sacramento Engrs. Club. Lutheran. Developed electronic system to maintain healthful condition of stored grain and bulk foods. Address: PO Box 214505 Sacramento CA 95821-0505

GEIL, MARK D. education educator; BS, NC State U., 1989—93; PhD, Ohio State U., 1993—97. Asst. prof. Sch. of Applied Physiology, Ga. Tech, Atlanta, 1997—. Grad. fellowship, NSF, 1994—97, Rsch. grant, US Olympic Com., 1997—98. Mem.: Gait and Clin. Movement Analysis Soc. (comm. com. 2002—03), Am. Soc. of Biomechanics. Bapt. Office: Georgia Inst of Tech 281 Ferst Dr Atlanta GA 30332-0356

GEIL, WILMA JEAN, librarian; b. Pitts., May 24, 1939; d. George Andrew and Elfrieda (Hemker) G. BA, Swarthmore Coll., 1961; MLS, U. Ill., 1964, MusM, 1967. Assoc. music librarian U. Ill., Urbana, 1963—2001; ret., 2001. Co-author: Resources of American Music History, 1981; contbr. articles to profl. jours. Mem. Music Libr. Assn. (bd. dirs. 1983-85, rec. sec. 1988-90), Soc. Am. Music (sec. 1975-83, spl. issues coord. Am. Music 1983-89, bd. dirs. 1997-1999, Disting. Svc. award 2003). Home: 60 N Kuakini St No 1 B Honolulu HI 96817

GEILIKMAN, MIKHAIL BORIS, research scientist, educator; b. Saratov, Russia, July 18, 1945; arrived in U.S., 1997; s. Boris Toviy Geilikman and Natalia Dolotova; m. Elena D. Temkina, Feb. 17, 1982; 1 child, Boris Michael. MS, Moscow Engring. Phys. Inst., 1962; PhD, USSR Acad. Sci., 1968. Rschr. Inst. Exptl. Mineralogy USSR Acad. Sci., Chernogolovka, Russia, 1971—85; sr. rschr. Internat. Inst. Earthquake Prediction Theory and Math. Geophysics, Moscow, 1985—92; rsch. prof. U. Waterloo, Waterloo, Canada, 1992—97; prin. engring. scientist Shell Internat. Exploration and Prodn., Houston, 1997—. Vis. prof. U. Alta., Edmonton, Alta., Canada, 1990—91; cons. Alta. Rsch. Coun., 1991—92. Grantee, Imperial Oil - Esso, 1996—97. Mem.: N.Y. Acad. Scis., Soc. Petroleum Engrs., Am. Geophys. Union. Office: Shell Internat Exploration PO Box 4704 Houston TX 77210-4704

GEILING, LOUISE ELIZABETH, elementary school educator, secondary school educator; b. New Milford, N.J., Aug. 25, 1934; d. Samuel and Susan Lagrotteria; m. Jacob V. Geiling, Apr. 17, 1960 (dec. Apr. 1998); children: Janet Darvin, Lois Nagie. BS, Montclair State U., N.J., 1955; MA, Montclair State U., 1959; postgrad., William Paterson Coll., Monmouth Coll. Cert. tchr. K-8, tchr. 9-12 in social studies, geography, guidance counselor. Tchr. 4th grade Roosevelt Sch., River Edge, NJ, 1955—56; tchr, reading specialist, guidance counselor Bergenfield Jr./Sr. H.S., NJ, 1956—60; tchr. learning disabilities, elem. and mem. child study team River Vale Schs., 1971—81, tchr. gifted and talented, 1981—85, elem. tchr., 1985—94; substitute tchr. grades K-8 Waldwick Bd. Edn. and Allendale Bd. Edn., NJ, 1994—2001. Contbr. CCD tchr. Assumption Parish, Emerson, NJ, 1962—64; tchr. CCD St. Elizabeth Parish, Wyckoff, NJ; leader Girl Scouts U.S., Park Ridge, NJ, 1971—73. Recipient A+ Tchr. award, Students of River Vale, 1990. Mem.: AAUW (charter, v.p. 1962—64), Jr. Women's Club (v.p. 1965—67). Roman Catholic. Avocations: piano, bridge, writing, sports. Home: 181 Mabie Ct Mahwah NJ 07430

GEIS, JEROME ARTHUR, lawyer, legal educator; b. Shakopee, Minn., May 28, 1946; s. Arthur Adam and Emma Mary (Boegemann) G.; m. Beth Marie Bruger, Aug. 11, 1979; children: Jennifer, Jason, Joan, Janice. BA in History, Govt. magna cum laude, St. John's U., Collegeville, Minn., 1968; JD cum laude, U. Notre Dame, 1973; LLM in Taxation, NYU, 1975. Bar: Minn. 1973, U.S. Dist. Ct. Minn. 1973, U.S. Tax Ct. 1973, U.S. Ct. Appeals (8th cir.) 1973. Law clk. Minn. Supreme Ct., St. Paul, 1973-74; assoc. Dudley & Smith, St. Paul, 1975-76, Briggs & Morgan P.A., St. Paul, 1976-79, chief tax dept., 1983-95. Adj. prof. tax law William Mitchell Coll. of Law, St. Paul, 1976-83. Columnist Minn. Law Jour., 1986-89, Bench & Bar, 1990—; editl. cons.: Sales

and Use Tax Alert; former reviewer Summary Reporter: Finance and Commerce, Minnesota State Bar Assn.; corr. State Tax Notes. Bd. dirs. Western Townhouse Assn., West St. Paul, 1979, St. Matthews Cath. Ch., West St. Paul, 1981; adv. bd. Minn. Inst. of Legal Edn., 1984—. Served to specialist 4th class U.S. Army, 1969-71. Fellow Am. Coll. Tax Counsel; mem. ABA, Am. Law Inst., Tax Inst. Am. (chmn. sales and use tax commn. 1988-90), Nat. Tax Assn., Am. Judicature Soc., Minn. Bar Assn. (bd. dirs. tax coun. sect. 1984-93, 94-97, 99—, chmn. 1990-91), Ramsey County Bar Assn., Minn. Taxpayers Assn. (bd. dirs. 1988—), Inst. Property Taxation, Supreme Ct. Hist. Soc., Nat. Assn. State Bar Tax Sects. (exec. com. 1993—), Citizens League, Minn. Club (bd. dirs. 1997-2000), KC, Kiwanis (bd. dirs. 2000-02). Home: 1116 Dodd Rd Saint Paul MN 55118-1821 Office: Briggs & Morgan PA 2200 1st St N Saint Paul MN 55109-3210 E-mail: JGeis@Briggs.com.

GEIS, JOHN P. military career officer; b. Jonesboro, Ark., Jan. 31, 1947; Commd. officer U.S. Army, advanced through grades to brig. gen.; comdg. gen. U.S. Army Armament Rsch., Devel. and Engring. Ctr., Dover, N.J., 1998—; comdr. U.S. Army Simulation, Tng. and Instrumentation Command, Orlando, Fla., 1999—. Office: USA/STRICOM 12350 Research Pkwy Orlando FL 32826-3261

GEIS, TARJA PELTO, educational coordinator, consultant, counselor, teacher, professor; m. John J. Geis; children: Jeffrey, Steven. BS in Edn. and Art, Towson U., 1967, MEd in Elem. Edn., 1970; EdD in Edn., Nova Southeastern U., 1986. Nat. bd. cert. tchr., 2002. Tchr. Balt. County, Balt., 1967-70, Prince George's County, Bowie, Md., 1970-73, Dade County, Miami, Fla., 1979-84, ednl. specialist fed. programs, 1984-85, tchr., chairperson, 1985-89; co-originator, saturn coord. Dr. Gilbert L. Porter Elem., Miami, 1990-96; counselor Kendale Lakes, Miami, 1995—, advanced acads. educator, 1997—. Adj. prof. Barry U., 1996—; presenter South Fla. Thinking Skills Conf., 2001, M-DCPS Advanced Acad. Conf., 2001—02. Editor: Chapter I Connection newsletter, 1984, Leo-T Times newsletter, 1987, Phi Delta Kappa newsletter, 1987. Validator NAEYC, Dade Reading Coun., 1999—; chair Restructuring Pub. Edn. Internat. Conf., Miami, 1990; mem. Lindgren Lakeowner Assn., Miami; svc. Feeding the Needy, Miami, 1990—. Named Tchr. of the Yr., South Area Dade County Pub. Schs., 1987, 2002, Fla. Master Tchr., Dept. Edn. Fla., 1988; grantee, Found. Excellence, 1986, 1988, 1989, 1991, 2001—02; DRC Literacy grantee, 2001—02. Mem.: NAEYC, Nat. Bd. Professionalization of Tchg. Stds., Internat. Reading Assn. (assoc. supervision and curriculum devel.), Fla. Reading Assn. (presenter 39th Conf. 2001), Phi Delta Kappa (pres. U. Miami chpt. 1991—92, Svc. Key award 1994, Travel scholarship 1997—98). Avocations: art and design, writing, travel, Reiki master, master hypnotherapist. Home: 12764 SW 112th Ter Miami FL 33186-4721

GEISEL, CAMERON MEADE, JR., investment professional; b. Harrisburg, Pa., Oct. 7, 1937; s. Cameron Meade and Dorothy Mae G.; m. Martha L. Frohring, Sept. 3, 1977 (dec.); children: Melissa Ellen, Gregory Stuart, Andrew Frohring, Martha Bliss; m. Saskia Hessler, Sept. 8, 1991. BA, Bucknell U., Lewisburg, Pa., 1960; grad. Sch. Credit and Fin. Mgmt., Harvard U., 1970; Advanced Mgmt Program, Harvard Bus. Sch., 1985. With Phila. Nat. Bank, 1961-86, asst. v.p., then v.p., 1965-77, sr. v.p., 1977-86. Bd. dirs. Hessler Properties, Inc. Trustee Lankenau Hosp. Found., Fox Chase Cancer Ctr., Cardigan Mountain Sch. Corp.; chmn. adv. bd. mgrs. Morris Arboretum. 2d lt. inf. U.S. Army, 1960-61. Mem. U.S. Coun. Internat. Bus. (trustee, exec. com.), Merion Golf Club, Merion Cricket Club, Phila. Club, Racquet Club (Phila.), Royal Ashdown Forest Golf Cloub, Royal and Ancient Golf Club of St. Andrews, Honourable Co. of Edinburgh Golfers, Loblolly Pines Golf Club. Republican. Episcopalian. Home: 1411 Youngsford Rd Gladwyne PA 19035-1232

GEISEL, HAROLD WALTER, diplomat; b. Chgo., May 11, 1947; s. Gustav and Stefi Geisel; m. Susan L. Gordon, Oct. 2, 1983; children: Jacqueline Julie, Katherine Louise. BA in History, Johns Hopkins U., 1968; MBA, U. Va., 1970. Commd. fgn. service officer Dept. State, 1970, adminstrv. officer, 1973-75; 1st sec. Am. embassy, Bern, Switzerland, 1975-78, Bamako, Mali, 1978-80; adminstrv. officer Dept. State, Washington, 1980-82; consul gen. U.S. consulate gen., Durban, South Africa, 1982-85; mem. NATO Def. Coll., Rome, 1985-86; adminstrv. counsellor Am. Embassy, Rome, 1986-88, adminstrv. minister-counsellor Bonn, 1988-92, adminstrv. minister-counselor Moscow, 1992-93; exec. asst. to under-sec. Dept. State, Washington, 1993-94, deputy inspector gen., 1994-95, dep. asst. sec. for info. mgmt., 1995-96, amb. to Mauritius, Seychelles, and Comoros, 1996-99, sr. negotiator, 1999-2000; acting dep. asst. sec. logistics mgmt. Dept. State A/LM, Washington, 2001—; head U.S. Dels. to U.S.-Chinese COCA Negotiations, 2002. Jewish. E-mail: hwgeisel@mindspring.com.

GEISELHART, LORENE ANNETTA, English language educator; b. Rake, Iowa, June 28, 1929; d. Charles Tobias and Altha May (Mills) Knutson; m. James Willis Geiselhart, June 1, 1947 (div. 1971); children: Nancy Joyce, Larry Paul, Richard Ray, Kathleen Ann. Cert., Luther Coll., 1949; BA, U. No. Iowa, 1965, MA, 1989; postgrad., U. Iowa, 1990—. Pub. sch. tchr., Postville, Iowa, 1947-48; adminstrv. asst. to county supt. schs. Decorah, Iowa, 1948-49; pub. sch. tchr. Galesville and Trempealeau, Wis., 1949-51, Iowa Braille and Sight-Saving Sch., Vinton, 1959-70, South Winneshiek Community Sch., Ossian, Iowa, 1970-94; instr. English to univ. students Nanchong Inst. Edn., Sichuan, China, 1995-96. Student tchr. supr. Luth. Coll., Decorah, 1971-94. Sec. Calmar (Iowa) Improvement Assn., 1987-92; active Calmar Luth. Ch. Coun., 1975-80, 89-91, mem. choir, 1975-80, pres. Ch. Circle, 1975-77, 88-92. Mem. AAUW (pres. 1969-70, 96-2000, sec. 1990-92), NEA, Iowa Reading Coun., Iowa State Edn. Assn., NE Iowa Rosemaling Assn. (sec. 1991-94), Delta Kappa Gamma (pres. Beta Eta chpt. 1978-81, state fellowship com. 1982-84, grantee 1988). Democrat. Avocations: rosemaling, golf, bridge, painting, reading.

GEISENDORFER, JAMES VERNON, religious writer, researcher; b. Brewster, Minn., Apr. 22, 1929; s. Victor H. and Anne B. (Johnson) G.; m. Esther Lillian Walker, Sept. 23, 1949; children: Jane, Karen, Lois. Student, Augustana Coll., 1950-51, Augsburg Coll., 1951-54, Orthodox Luth. Sem., 1954-55; BA, U. Minn., 1960; LLD, Burton Coll. and Sem., 1961. Grain buyer Pillsbury Mills, Inc., Worthington, Minn., 1947-48; acct. Boote Hatcheries, Worthington, 1949-50; night supr. Strutwear, Inc., Mpls., 1951-52; dispatcher Chgo. and North Western Ry., 1953-54; office mgr. Froedtert Malt Corp., Mpls., 1955-56, Nat. Automotive Parts Assn., 1957-60; sr. creative writer Brown & Bigelow, St. Paul, 1960-72; religious rschr., writer, 1972—. Rsch. cons. Inst. for the Study of Am. Religion; mem. panel of reference Chelston Bible Coll., New Milton, Eng. Author: (with J. Gordon Melton) A Directory of Religious Bodies in the United States, 1977, Religion in America, 1983, Religion USA, 1989; mem. editl. bd. Biog. Dictionary Am. Cult and Sect Leaders; contbr. articles to books and jours.; cons. editor Directory of Religious Organizations in the United States, 1977. Recipient Amicus Poloniae medal Polish Ministry of Culture and Edn., 1969. Mem. AAAS, Am. Acad. Religion, Acad. Ind. Scholars, Wis. Evang. Luth. Synod Hist. Inst., Augustana Hist. Soc., Royal Anthrop. Inst., Ea. Territorial Hist. Soc. (charter), Medieval Acad. Am., Renaissance Soc. Am., George Eliot Fellowship, Wis. Acad. Scis., Arts and Letters, Aristotelian Soc., Hegel Soc. Am., Sixteenth Century Studies Conf., Am. Cath. Philos. Assn., N.Am. Conf. on British Studies, Internat. Soc. for Comparative Study of Civilizations, Collingwood Soc., Internat. Assn. Greek Philosophy, Brit. Soc. Philosophy Religion, Inst. Interdisciplinary Rsch., Inst. for Advanced Studies in Culture, Canon Law Soc. Am. Lutheran. Address: 1001 Shawano Ave Green Bay WI 54303-3020

GEISENDORFER, NANCY KAY, mathematics educator; b. Greeley, Colo., Apr. 9, 1970; d. Bernard and Lyn Stadler; m. Grant Geisendorfer; children: Garrett, Graham. AA, Northeastern Jr. Coll., Sterling, Colo., 1990; BA, U. No. Colo., 1992. Tchr. math. Lester Arnold H.S., Commerce City, Colo., 1996—2001; tchr. John Mall High, Walsenburg, Colo., 2001—02, Conrad Ball Middle Sch., Loveland, Colo., 2003—. Author: Beaver Creek Adventures. Mem. Colo. Tchr. Assn. (rep. 1994—), PTA (sec. 1998—). Avocations: writing, rock collecting, hiking. Home: 1533 E 21st Loveland CO 80538

GEISER, ELIZABETH ABLE, publishing company executive; b. Phillipsburg, N.J., Apr. 28, 1925; d. George W. and Margaret I. (Ross) G. AB magna cum laude, Hood Coll., 1947. Promotion mgr. coll. dept. Macmillan Co., N.Y.C., 1947-54; promotion mgr. R.R. Bowker, N.Y.C., 1954-60, sales mgr., 1960-67, dir. mktg., 1967-70, v.p., 1970-73, sr. v.p., 1973-75, sr. v.p., pub. book divsn.; adj. prof., dir. U. Denver Pub. Inst., 1976—; sr. v.p. Gale Rsch. Co., 1976-91, cons., 1991—. Cons. Excerpta Medica, Elsevier, 1976-82; lectr. pub. procedures Radcliffe Coll., 1966-75; lectr. schs. libr. sci. U. Wash., U. So. Calif.; panel mem. TV series Living Library, 1970 Editor: The Business of Book Publishing, 1985; contbr. Manual of Bookselling, 1969. Trustee Hood Coll., 1993-99. Inducted into Publishing Hall of Fame, 1988. Mem. Assn. Am. Pubs. (exec. coun. prof. and scholarly pub. divsn. 1989-91, adv. coun. Frankfurt book fair 1971, sch. and libr. promotion and mktg. com. 1972-76, bd. dirs. 1982-85), ALA (pres. exhibits roundtable 1968-70, bd. dirs. exhibits roundtable 1968). Presbyterian. Home: 3329 E Bayaud Ave Denver CO 80209 Office: Pub Inst 335 E 51st St Apt 5E New York NY 10022-6765

GEISER, MARJORIE EILEEN, dietitian, life coach; b. Kodiak, Alaska, June 5, 1954; d. Don and Janet (Levine) Carothers; m. Don E. Geiser, Mar. 22, 1979; 1 child, Cassandra. BS in Nutrition and Dietetics, Loma Linda (Calif.) U., 1990. Registered dietitian, Med. Exercise Specialist, Cert. Personal Trainer. Clin. dietitian Riverside (Calif.) Gen. Hosp., 1990-96; owner MEG Fitness, Running Springs, Calif., 1996—. Nutrition cons. Wash. State Potatoe Commn., 2002—; cons., dietitian Sanofi-Synthe Lab, 2002—03. Author newspaper column Mountain News, 1997. Mem. Am. Dietetic Assn., Nat. Strength and Conditioning Assn. (exec. com., 2002—, sec. 2003—), Am. Coun. on Exercise, Calif. Dietetic Assn. Avocations: weight training, gardening, reading.

GEISER, ROBERT NEIL, computer scientist; b. Cleve., Jan. 20, 1961; s. Roger Neal and Betty Lou (Keiner) G.; m. Laura Jane Burkholder, June 18, 1983; children: Jessika Christen, Benjamin, Matthew. BS in Acctg., AS in Data Processing, U. Akron, 1982. CPA, Ohio; cert. data processor, Ohio. Acct., programmer G&S Titanium, Inc., Wooster, Ohio, 1979-83, cons., 1983-93; computer specialist, acct. Hall, Kistler & Co., Canton, Ohio, 1983-88; owner Computer Productivity Assistance, Wooster, 1988—. MIS dir. G&S Titanium, Inc., 1993—. Group leader Appalachia Service Project Home Repair, various locations, 1984-87; mem. Grace Brethren. Mem. AICPA, Ohio Soc. CPAs (chmn. local computers in practice 1987-88, mem. statewide computers in practice panel 1987-95), Nat. Assn. Accts. (Mem. of Yr. award 1984-85), Assn. of the Inst. for Cert. of Computer Profls. Republican. Avocations: backpacking, boy scout leader, web page design, reading and studying the bible. Home: 9520 E Moreland Rd Apple Creek OH 44606-9448 Office: G&S Titanium Inc 1550 Spruce St Wooster OH 44691-4600

GEISER, THOMAS CHRISTOPHER, lawyer; b. Bern, Switzerland, Aug. 13, 1950; came to U.S., 1952; s. Henry Abraham and Pia Margaret (Tschudin) G.; m. Catherine Barlow Yeakle, Oct. 20, 1973 (div. Mar. 1983); m. Donna Lea Schweers, Jan. 3, 1987; 1 child, Kelsey Schweers. BA, U. Redlands, Calif., 1972; JD, U. Calif., San Francisco, 1977. Bar: Calif. 1978. Atty. Internat. Bur. Fiscal Documentation, Amsterdam, The Netherlands, 1977-78; assoc., ptnr. Hanson, Bridgett, Marcus, Vlahos & Stromberg, San Francisco, 1979-85; ptnr. Epstein, Becker, Stromberg & Green, San Francisco, 1985-90, Brobeck, Phleger & Harrison, San Francisco, 1990-93; sr. v.p., gen. counsel, sec. WellPoint Health Networks Inc., Woodland Hills, Calif., 1993-96, exec. v.p., gen. counsel, sec., 1996—. Mem. Am. Health Lawyers Assn., Calif. Soc. Health Care Attys., Order of Coif. Office: WellPoint Health Networks Inc 1 Wellpoint Way Thousand Oaks CA 91362-3893

GEISER, WILLIAM FRANCIS, education educator; b. N.Y.C., Feb. 23, 1944; s. Joseph Francis and Catherine Rose Geiser; m. Joanne Bortz, Oct. 4, 1969; children: Kirsten, Eric. BA, CUNY, 1971, MS, 1973; EdD, St. John's U., N.Y., 1998. Cert. tchr. math., social studies, common brs., N.Y. Facilities asst. engring. N.Y. Tel., N.Y.C., 1969-71; tchr. Baldwin (N.Y.) Pub. Schs., 1971-73, North Rockland Schs., Garnerville, N.Y., 1973-99; asst. prof. Mt. St. Mary Coll., Newburgh, N.Y., 1999—. Chmn. divsn. edn. Mt. St. Mary Coll., 2000-01. Pres. Cornwall (N.Y.) Cmty. Theater, 1983; mem. zoning bd. appeals Village of Cornwall on Hudson, N.Y., 1992—. With U.S. Army, 1962-65. Mem. ASCD, Am. Ednl. Rsch. Assn., Nat. Coun. Math. Tchrs., N.Y. State Math. Tchrs., Phi Delta Kappa. Avocations: cross country skiing, hiking, acting. Home: 20 Washington St Cornwall On Hudson NY 12520-1606 Office: Mt St Mary Coll Powell Ave Newburgh NY 12550-1238

GEISERT, WAYNE FREDERICK, educational consultant, retired administrator; b. Elmo, Kans., Dec. 20, 1921; s. Frederick Jacob and Martha E. (Lauer) G.; m. Ellen Maurine Gish, July 2, 1944; children: Gregory Wayne, Bradley Kent, Todd Wilfred. AB, McPherson Coll., Kans., 1944; PhD in Econs, Northwestern U., 1951; LLD (hon.), Manchester Coll., 1987; HHD (hon.), James Madison U., 1992; LHD (hon.), Bridgewater Coll., 1994, McPherson Coll., 1994. Instr. Hamilton (Kans.) High Sch., 1946-48; part-time instr. Kendall Coll., Evanston, Ill., 1948-50; grad. asst. Northwestern U., 1950-51; from assoc. prof. to prof. and head dept. econs. and bus. Manchester Coll., North Manchester, Ind., 1951-57; dean coll. McPherson Coll., 1957-64; pres. Bridgewater (Va.) Coll., 1964-94, pres. emeritus, 1994—; chmn. bd. First Va. Bank/Planters, Bridgewater, 1988-94; vice chmn. bd. First Va. Bank of the Shenandoah Valley, 1994-95. Cons. in ednl. field; pres. Assn. Va. Colls., 1970-71; exec. com. Church-related Colls. and Univs. in the South, 1973-74. Bd. dirs. Univ. Center in Va., 1964-78; pres. Council Ind. Colls. in Va., 1984-85; bd. dirs. Shenandoah Valley Ednl. TV, chmn. bd., 1979-84; bd. dirs. Va. Found. Ind. Colls., v.p., 1974-76, pres., 1976-78; moderator Ch. of Brethren, 1973-74, chmn. rev. and evaluation com., 1975-77, mem. gen. bd., 1977-82, vice chmn., 1977-78, chmn. gen. services commn., 1979-82, chmn. pension bd., 1979-82; chmn. United Way campaign, 1979-80; ednl. del. Dalian U. Fgn. Langs., Peoples Republic China, 1985, 90, 94; organizer, host for travel tours abroad; vol. fund raiser to various orgns. Served with USNR, 1944-46, PTO. Recipient Alumni Citation of Merit, McPherson Coll., 1974, Profl. Educator of Yr. award James Madison U., 1983; Geisert Hall named in his honor by Bridgewater Coll., 1990; named Meritorious Alumnus, Chapman (Kans.) H.S., 1994. Mem. Am. Econ. Assn., Harrisonburg-Rockingham County C. of C. (bd. dirs. 1977-82, pres. 1980-81), Rotary, Omicron Delta Kappa, Pi Kappa Delta, Alpha Psi Omega, Lambda Soc. Home: 1492 Cumberland Dr Harrisonburg VA 22801-8608 Office: Bridgewater Coll Office of the Pres Emeritus Bridgewater VA 22812

GEISINGER, KURT FRANCIS, university administrator, psychometrician; b. Danville, Pa., Jan. 11, 1951; s. Karl William and Florence Eva (Graber) G.; m. Janet Frances Carlson, Sept. 22, 1984. AB with honors, Davidson Coll., 1972; MS, U. Ga., 1974; PhD, Pa. State U., 1977. Instr. Pa. State U., University Park, 1975-76; dir., rsch. svcs. Bartell Assocs., State College, Pa., 1976-77; asst. prof. to prof. and chmn. dept. psychology Fordham U., Bronx, N.Y., 1977-92; prof. psychology, dean of arts and scis. SUNY, Oswego, 1992-97; acad. v.p., prof. psychology LeMoyne Coll., 1997—2001; v.p. acad. affairs U. St. Thomas, Houston, 2001—. Mem. tech. adv. com. on Grad. Record Exam., Ednl. Testing Svc., Princeton, N.J., 1995-2003, chair, 2000-03, vis. rsch. assoc., 1976, bd. dirs., 2001—; mem. SAT com. Coll. Bd., 2001-03; cons. expert witness N.Y.C. Depts. Law and Pers., 1981-92, Fox and Fox Counsellors at Law, N.Y.C., 1986-98; cons. Assessment Alternatives, Florham Park, N.J., 1987-92; co-chair Joint Com. on Testing Practices, 1993-97. Cons. editor Ednl. Rsch. Quar., Coll. Bd. Rev., Internat. Jour. Testing. Fellow APA (Com. on Psychol. Testing and Assessment 1998-2000), Am. Psychol. Soc.; mem. Am. Ednl. Rsch. Assn., Nat. Coun. on Measurement in Edn., Northeastern Ednl. Rsch. Assn. (newsletter editor 1988-91, pres. 1986-89, bd. dirs. 1984-86), Phi Kappa Phi (Fordham U. chpt. pres. 1984-86), Psi Chi, Sigma Xi, Alpha Sigma Mu. Democrat. Lutheran. Avocations: swimming, softball, golf, computer activities. Home: 3935 Indian Point Missouri City TX 77459 Office: Office VP Acad Affairs Univ St Thomas 3800 Montrose Blvd Houston TX 77006 E-mail: kurtgeis1@aol.com.

GEISLER, HANS EMANUEL, gynecologic oncologist; b. Ratibor, Germany, Apr. 5, 1935; came to U.S., 1938; s. Harry and Marianne C. (Barthel) G.; m. Margaret Ann Colglazier; children: Dorothy Marianne, Kathleen Marie, Stephan Harry, Suzanne Joan, John Patrick. AB with hons., Xavier U., 1955; MD, Loyola U., Chgo., 1959. Cert. Am. Bd. Ob-Gyn., Gynecologic Oncology. Pvt. practice, Indpls., 1965—. Asst. prof. ob-gyn. Ind. U. Med. Ctr., Indpls., 1967—84, dir. gynecol. tumor svc., 1967—70; dir. gynecol. oncology Meth. Hosp., Indpls., 1970—72; dir. gynecol. oncology div. St. Vincent Hosp., Indpls., 1972—; clin. assoc. prof. ob-gyn. Ind. U. Med. Ctr., Indpls., 1984—90; dir. gynecol. oncology Meth. Hosp., Indpls., 1985—91; chmn. cancer com. St. Vincent Hosp., Indpls., 1985—, dir. oncology program, 1985—88; clin. prof. ob-gyn. Ind. U. Med. Ctr., Indpls., 1990—; assoc. Ed. Eur. J. Gyn. Onc., 2000—; chmn. dept. hematology/oncology St. Vincent Hosp., 2002—. Assoc. editor European Jour. Gynecol. Oncology, 2000; contbr. articles to profl. jours. Mem. Marion County Cancer Soc., Indpls.; profl. edn. com. Am. Cancer Soc., Indpls., Fire Merit Bd., Indpls., Com. to Select Police Chief, Indpls., 1975; pres. St. Luke Parish Coun., 1988—90; active Archdiocesan Pastoral Coun., 1991—94; bd. dirs. Culture of Life Found.; pres. bd. dirs. Seraphim Cancer Rsch. Found. Decorated knight Equestrian Order of Holy Sepulchre of Jerusalem; recipient Respect Life award Indpls. Right to Life, 1998; named Disting. Physician, St. Vincent Hosp. and Health Ctrs., 1996. Fellow ACOG, ACS; mem. AMA, Ind. Med. Soc., Indpls. Med. Soc., Soc. Gynecol. Oncologists, Cen. Assn. Ob-Gyn., Continental Gynecol. Soc. (pres.), Soc. Meml. Gynecol. Oncologists (pres.), Am. Assn. Pro-Life Ob-Gyn. (bd. dir.), Am. Assn. for Med. Ethics, European Soc. Gynecol. Oncologists, Internat. Soc. Gynecol. Oncologists, pres., Ind. Gynecologic Oncology, LLC, 2003. Republican. Roman Catholic. Avocations: golf, walking. Home: 362 Millridge Dr Indianapolis IN 46290-1116 Office: 8301 Harcourt Rd Ste 201 Indianapolis IN 46260

GEISLER, NATHAN DAVID, financial consultant; b. Kokand, Russia, Jan. 22, 1946; s. Leon and Esther (Korn) G.; m. Susan D. Starsky, 1982; 1 child, Jonathan Starsky Geisler. BA, Ohio State U., 1968; JD, U. Toledo, 1970. Asst. v.p. Merrill Lynch Pierce Fenner & Smith, Toledo, 1973-89, 1st v.p., 1989—. Home: 2600 Forestvale Rd Toledo OH 43615-2251 Office: 333 N Summit St Toledo OH 43604-2617

GEISLER, THOMAS MILTON, JR., lawyer; b. Orange, N.J., Jan. 16, 1943; s. Thomas M. and Helen K. (Thomas) G.; m. Sarah Ann Farrell Geisler, Aug. 6, 1977; children: Sarah C., Ann. C. AB in Math. (cum laude), Harvard Coll., Cambridge, Mass., 1965; JD, Harvard Law Sch., Cambridge, Mass., 1968. Bar: NJ, NY, Conn., U.S. Dist. Ct. (2d cir.), U.S. Supreme Ct. Asst., base legal officer U.S. Naval Submarine Base, New London, Conn., 1969-71; appellate def. counsel Naval Appellate Review Activity, Washington, 1971-72; assoc. Shearman & Sterling, N.Y.C., 1973-80, ptnr., 1980-91; pvt. practice N.Y.C., 1991-96, New Haven, Conn., 1994—. Dir., bd. dirs. Friends of Harvard Law Record, Cambridge, Mass., 1997—. Author: Am. Jur. Proof of Facts 3d, 1995, 1996, 1998, 1999, 2001; editor: Trial Practice Newsletter, 1986—2001. Lt., USNR, 1969-72. Recipient Litigation Star ABA Litigation Sect., 1997, Navy Achievement award USN, Washington, 1971. Mem. ABA (trial practice com.), Conn. Bar Assn., Harvard Club of So. Conn., Harvard Club of N.Y.C., Quinnipiack Club, Madison Beach Club. Presbyterian. Avocations: tennis, squash, theater, concerts. Office: 205 Church St Ste 508 New Haven CT 06510 E-mail: T1827@aol.com.

GEISMAR, RICHARD LEE, communications executive; b. Paterson, N.J., Aug. 22, 1927; s. Sylvan and Marjorie (Leeser) G.; m. Patricia Willard, Nov. 27, 1954; children: John, Elisabeth, Nancy. B in Mgmt. Engring., Rensselaer Poly. Inst., 1949; MBA, Harvard, 1951. With DuMont TV Network, 1951-55, Metromedia, Inc. (and predecessors), N.Y.C., 1955-69, also bd. dirs.; pres., dir. Reeves Telecom Corp., 1969-70; comm. cons. BGW Assocs., Inc., 1970-84; chmn. Broad St. Comm. Corp., 1971-84; pres. Broad St. Ventures, 1984-98; chmn. Broad St. TV, 1989-96. Bd. dirs., treas. Greenwich chpt. ARC, mem. state svc. coun, 1992-96; bd. dirs., treas. Greenwich Adult Day Ctr., Inc., 1997—. Served with USNR, 1945-46. Mem. Riverside Yacht Club, Sigma Xi. Republican. Congregationalist. Home: 18 Hidden Brook Rd Riverside CT 06878 E-mail: daddick37@aol.com.

GEISMAR, THOMAS H. graphic designer; b. Glen Ridge, N.J., July 16, 1931; s. Arthur D. and Adeline (Caro) G.; m. Joan Hyams, Nov. 9, 1958; children: Peter, Kathryn, Pamela. BA, Brown U., 1953; MFA, Yale U., 1955; DFA (hon.), Corcoran Sch. of Art, Washington, 1995. Founder Brownjohn, Chermayeff & Geismar, N.Y.C., 1957; founder Chermayeff & Geismar Assocs., N.Y.C., 1960, prin., 1960-90; pres. Chermayeff & Geismar Inc., 1991—; prin. Cambridge Seven Assocs. (Architects), 1963-99; founder, partner MetaForm, Inc., N.Y.C., 1980-90. Lectr. Chmn. com. signs and symbols Dept. Transp.; mem. council Yale U. Author: Spiritually Moving: A Collection of American Folk Art Sculpture, 1998, TM: Trademarks Designed by Chermayeff & Geismar, 2000. Mem. Pres. coun. Carnegie Mellon U., Pitts. Served with U.S. Army, 1955-57. Recipient 1st Internat. Design award, Osaka, Japan, 1983, 1st Presdl. Design award Pres. Reagan, 1985, Yale Arts award, 1985; named to Hall of Fame, N.Y. Art Dirs.' Club, 1998; selected as one of 100 Alumni with Greatest Impact on the 20th Century, Brown Univ., 2000. Mem. Am. Inst. Graphic Arts (Gold medal 1979), Alliance Graphique Internationale, Phi Beta Kappa. Office: Chermayeff & Geismar Inc 15 E 26th St Fl 12 New York NY 10010-1596

GEISMER, ALAN STEARN, JR., lawyer; b. Cleve., June 23, 1948; s. Alan S. and Barbara (Peck) G.; m. Susan Dangel, Oct. 17, 1976; children: Lily, Sarah. AB magna cum laude, Harvard U., 1970, JD, 1975; cert., Cambridge U., 1972. Bar: Mass. 1975, U.S. Dist. Ct. Mass. 1975, U.S. Ct. Appeals (1st cir.) 1979. Assoc. Dangel & Smith, Boston, 1975-77, Mason & Martin, Boston, 1977-79, Goldstein & Manello, Boston, 1979-80; ptnr. Berlin, Clarey & Green, Boston, 1980-86, Kassler & Feuer P.C., Boston, 1986-99, Lane, Altman & Owens, LLP, Boston, 1999-2001, Sugarman, Rogers Barshak & Cohen P.C., Boston, 2001—. Bd. dirs. Concert Dance Co., Boston, 1981-91, pres., 1985-91; bd. dirs. Jewish Family and Children's Svc., Boston, 1986—, clk., 1989-90, v.p., 1990-93, pres. 1993-96; bd. dirs. Dance Umbrella, Boston, 1991-95; bd. dirs. World Music, Boston, 1995—; bd. dirs. Vol. Lawyers for the Arts, 1994—, clk., 1997-2002, pres., 2002—; bd. dirs. Assn. Jewish Family and Children's Agy., 1996-2002; bd. trustees Pro Arte Chamber Orch., 2001—. Knox fellowship Harvard Coll., 1970. Fellow Am. Acad. Matrimonial Lawyers (bd. mgrs. Mass. chpt. 1995-98, 2001—); mem. ABA, Boston Bar Assn., Longwood Cricket Club (Chestnut Hill, Mass.), Badminton & Tennis Club. Democrat. Avocations: skiing, bicycling, kayaking, tennis, hiking, biking. Home: 61 Lexington Ave Cambridge MA 02138-3320 Office: Sugarman Rogers Barshak & Cohen PC 101 Merrimac St Boston MA 02114-4737 E-mail: geismer@srbc.com.

GEISSBUHLER, STEPHAN, graphic designer; b. Zofingen, Kanton Aargau, Switzerland, Oct. 21, 1942; came to U.S., 1967; s. Theodor and Ruth (Schneider) G.; m. Elissa Beth Feuerman, June 26, 1983; children by previous marriage: Marc Phillip, Christopher Luke; children: Alexander Charles, Benjamin Adam. MA, Sch. Design Basel, 1964. Designer J.R. Geigy A.G., Basel, Switzerland, 1964-67; assoc. prof., dept. chmn. Phila. Coll. Art, 1967-73; design cons. Murphy-Levy-Wurman Architects, Phila., 1968-71; designer/assoc. Anspach-Grossman-Portugal, Inc., N.Y.C., 1973-75; assoc. ptnr Chermayeff & Geismar, Inc., N.Y.C., 1973-79, ptnr., 1979—. Mem. Faculty for Improvement of Fed. Graphics, Washington, 1976—; vis. lectr. in field Served with Swiss Army, 1962-67. Recipient nat. prize for applied art Fed. Govt. Switzerland, 1966, 67, Gold medal N.Y. Art Dirs. Club, 1984; recipient others Mem. Am. Inst. Graphic Arts (v.p., dir. 1980-83, pres. N.Y. chpt. 1984-86), Am. Ctr. for Design, Group for Environ. Edn., Alliance Graphique Internat. (pres. U.S. membership 1993—), N.Y. Art Dirs. Club. Methodist. Office: Chermayeff & Geismar Inc 15 E 26th St Fl 12 New York NY 10010-1596 E-mail: steffg@cgnyc.com.

GEISSELMANN, FRIEDRICH, librarian; b. Göppingen, Germany, Aug. 14, 1943; m. Dagmar Geisselmann; 1 child, Agnes. PhD, U. Tübingen, Germany, 1972; Bibliotheksassesor, Bibliotheksschule, Frankfurt, 1973. Head of cataloging dept. Univ. Libr., Augsburg, Germany, 1975-89, dir. Regensburg, Germany, 1990—. Mem. IFLA, Deutscher Bibliotheksverband (chair). E-mail: Friedrich.Geisselmann@bibliothek.uni-regensburg.de.

GEISSER, JOHN EDWARD, legislative representative; b. Worcester, Mass., Oct. 5, 1970; s. John M. and Phyllis E. G. BA in Politics, St. Anselm Coll., Manchester, N.H., 1992; MA in Polit. Sci., U. R.I., Kingston, 1993. Legis. analyst Williams & Jensen, P.C., Washington, 1995-97; legis. asst. Congressional Cons., Washington, 1997-98; legis. analyst Acad. Managed Care Pharmacy, Alexandria, Va., 1998-00, dir govt. rels., 2000-01; sr. pub. policy analyst

Pharm. Rsch. and Mfrs. of Am., Washington, 2001—03, dir. state policy, 2003—. Mem.: Am. Polit. Sci. Assn. Avocations: political campaign, reading, hiking, skiing. Home: 909 E St SE # 4 Washington DC 20003 E-mail: jgeisser@phrma.org.

GEISSER, SEYMOUR, statistics educator; b. Bronx, N.Y., Oct. 5, 1929; s. Leon and Rose (Kielmanowicz) G.; m. Mary Lee George, Jan. 30, 1955 (div. Apr. 21, 1977); children— Mindy Sharon, Dan Levi, Georgia Lynn, Adam Dov.; m. Anne S. Flaxman, Mar. 21, 1982. BA, CCNY, 1950; MA, U. N.C., 1952, PhD, 1955. Mathematician NIMH, Bethesda, Md., 1955-61; chief biometry sect. Nat. Inst. Arthritis and Metabolic Diseases, Bethesda, 1961-65; prof. stats. SUNY-Buffalo, 1965-70, chmn., 1965-70; prof. Sch. Stats. U. Minn., 1971—, dir., 1971—2001. Professorial lectr. George Washington U., 1960-65; vis. asso. prof. Iowa State U., Ames, 1960; vis. prof. U. Wis., Madison, 1964, U. Tel-Aviv (Israel), 1971, U. Waterloo (Can.), 1972, Stanford U., 1976, 88, Carnegie-Mellon U., Pitts., 1976, U. Orange Free State, Bloemfontein, South Africa, 1978, 93, Harvard U. Sch. Public Health, 1981, U. Chgo., 1985, U. Warwick, Coventry, Eng., 1986, Univ. Modena, Italy, 1996, Nat. Chiao Tung Univ., Tawain, 1998; mem. biometric and epidemiological methodology adv. com. FDA, 1976-78, mem. arthritis adv. com., 1978-84; mem. NIH Biometry and Epidemiology Study sect. 1974-76; com. on Nat. Stats., 1984-87; chmn. Nat. Acad. Panel on Occupational and Health Stats., 1985-86; expert witness on forensic statistics; Lady Davis vis. prof. Hebrew U. Jerusalem, 1991, 94, 99. Author: Predictive Inference, 1993; assoc. editor Jour. Am. Statis. Assn., 1968-70, 86-88; editor: Bayesian and Likelihood Methods in Statistics and Econometrics, 1989, Statistics in Genetics, 1999, Diagnosis and Prediction, 1999; contbr. articles to sci. jours. Bd. dirs. Savage Trust, 1978—2000; bd. of trustees Nat. Inst. of Statistical Sci., 1999—2001. Scholar Merck Rsch. Lab., 2002—03. Fellow Inst. Math. Stats. (mem. coun. 1978-80), Royal Statis. Soc., Am. Statis. Assn. (bd. dirs. 1964-65); mem. Biometric Soc., Math. Assn. Am., Internat. Statis. Inst., Psychometric Soc., Can. Statis. Soc., Sigma Xi. Home: 1770 Summit Ave Saint Paul MN 55105-1834

GEISSINGER, FREDERICK WALLACE, finance company executive; b. Huntingdon, Pa., Oct. 3, 1945; s. Harry Lloyd and Elizabeth Gertrude Geissinger; m. Anne Beth Lawrence, Feb. 14, 1970; children: Amy Elizabeth, Jacqueline Marie. AB, Dartmouth Coll., 1967; MBA, U. Chgo., 1969. Lic. in securities and real estate, N.Y.C. Corp. banking officer Chase Manhattan Bank, N.Y.C., 1969-74, dir. corp. planning, 1974-76, asst. gen. mgr. Tokyo, 1976-80, chief staff Western Hemisphere N.Y.C., 1980-83, budget dir., 1983-86, sr. v.p. real estate, 1986-90; exec. v.p. Daiwa Securities Am. Inc., N.Y.C., 1990-92; prin. Geissinger and Assocs., N.Y.C., 1993; CEO Am. Gen. Land Devel. Inc., Houston, 1994-95, Am. Gen. Mortgage and Land Devel. Inc., 1995; chmn., CEO Am. Gen. Finance, Evansville, Ind., 1995—; vice chmn., group exec. Am. Gen. Corp., Houston, 1998—. Trustee Pelham (N.Y.) Bd. Edn., 1983-86. Mem. Urban Land Inst. (coun. 1986—), Real Estate Bd. N.Y., Pelham Country club (bd. govs. 1987-92, pres. 1990-92). Republican. Presbyterian. Avocations: skiing, golf, tennis, coaching girls soccer, classical music.

GEISSINGER-ROBERTSON, RUTH FABRY, retired obstetrician, gynecologist; b. N.Y.C., Apr. 23, 1916; BA, Hunter Coll., N.Y.C., 1935; MD, U. Mich., 1939. Diplomate Am. Bd. Ob-Gyn. Intern U. Mich. Hosp., Ann Arbor, 1939; resident Lawrence Hosp., Bronxville, N.Y., 1941, Woman's Hosp., N.Y.C., 1942-43, Lincoln Hosp., N.Y.C., 1944; attending obstetrician and gynecologist N. Westchester Hosp. Ctr., Mt. Kisco, N.Y., 1947-85, mem. hon. staff, 1986—. Home: 41 Timber Rdg Mount Kisco NY 10549-3623 E-mail: ruthrobertson@mymailstation.com.

GEIST, GEORGE F. state legislator; b. Pottsville, Pa., June 18, 1955; BA cum laude, Ursinus Coll.; JD, Rutgers U. Sch. Law. Assembly mem. dist. 4 N.J. State Assembly. Atty. Chmn. Camden County Rep. Com., 1983-91. Office: c/o Secretary of the General Assembly State House, CN-098 Trenton NJ 08625*

GEIST, KATHE STERNBACH, art history, cinema and English educator, writer; b. Lansing, Mich., Mar. 6, 1948; d. Robert John and Margaret Antoinette Geist; m. Steven Sternbach, Feb. 14, 1991. BA, U. Mich., 1970, PhD, 1981. Prof. Ill. State U., Normal, 1983-88, Koryo Coll., Nagoya, Japan, 1991-93, Bentley Coll., Waltham, Mass., 1993-97, Mass. Coll. of Pharmacy and Health Scis., Boston, 2001—02, Showa Boston Inst., 2003. Panel chair Soc. for Cinema Studies, New Orleans, 1986, Coll. Art Assn., Houston, 1988; editor Asian Cinema Studies Soc., 1986-88; consumer advocate. Author: Cinema of Wim Wenders, 1988; contbr. chpts. to books and articles to profl. jours. Mem. exec. bd. Friends of the Muddy River, 1997—; coord. Brookline Artists Open Studios, 1997-2002.

GEISTFELD, JAMES GORDON, veterinarian; b. St. James, Minn., Oct. 11, 1947; s. Victor Edgar and Viola Otille (Becker) G.; m. Barbara Jean Lane, July 22, 1972; children: Matthew James, Erin Michal. BA, St. Olaf Coll., Northfield, Minn., 1969; DVM, U. Minn., 1973; MBA, U. Evansville, 1983. Diplomate Am. Coll. Lab. Animal Medicine. Epidemiologist Ctrs. for Disease Control, Atlanta, 1973—75; postdoctoral fellow Bowman Gray Sch. Medicine, Winston-Salem, NC, 1976—77; staff veterinarian Mead Johnson Rsch. Ctr., Evansville, Ind., 1977—82; sr. rsch. scientist Bristol-Myers Co., Evansville, Ind., 1982—87; dir. lab. animal medicine and surgery Rorer Pharm. Co., Ft. Washington, Pa., 1988—90; v.p. TNT Genetics Svcs., Albany, NY, 1995—97; dir. lab. animal medicine, v.p. Taconic Ventures, Inc., Germantown, NY, 1990—2001; exec. dir. Taconic Farms, Inc., Germantown, 2002—03, v.p. sci. affairs, 2003—. Cons. Ind. State U., Terre Haute, 1982-87, U. Evansville, 1983-87, OrienTreich Found., Cold Spring-on-Hudson, N.Y., 1992—, SUNY, Albany, 1997—; adj. prof. U. Pa., Phila., 1989-90; mem. expert coms. NIH/ILAR; dir. Mutant Mouse Regional Resource Ctr., NIH; bd. dirs. La Mesa Group, McKinney, Tex., Chilmark Music Inc., Southaven, Miss. Contbr. articles to profl. jours. Mem. ch. coun. 3d Luth. Ch., Rhinebeck, N.Y., 1992-96; trustee Friends of Clermont, Germantown, 1994-96; mem. C.L. Davis Found. Recipient Hole-In-The-Shoe award, USPHS, 1975; fellow, NIH, 1975—77. Mem. AVMA, Am. Soc. Lab. Animal Practitioners, Am. Coll. Lab. Animal Medicine, Am. Assn. for Lab. Animal Sci., Am. Assn. Ind. Vets., Am. Gnotobiotic Soc., Internat. Soc. for Gnotobiology, Global Alliance Lab. Animal Standardization Coun., Am. Soc. Microbiology, Rip Van Winkle Hiking Club (leader 1991-94), Catskill 3500 Hiking Club, Sigma Xi. Lutheran. Achievements include design of a new dog run, new animal research facilities; first to report a new mouse bacterial pathogen-group B type V streptococcus; discovery of several new animal models for human disease research. Home: 288 Linden Ave Red Hook NY 12571-1032 Office: Taconic Inc 273 Hover Ave Germantown NY 12526-5320 E-mail: jgei@taconic.com.

GEISTFELD, RONALD ELWOOD, retired dental educator; b. St. James, Minn., Nov. 9, 1933; s. Victor E. and Viola (Becker) G.; m. Lois N. Tolzman Wilkens, June 15, 1955 (div. June 1974); m. Annette L. Swenson, Jan. 14, 1977; children: Shari, Mark, Steven, Ann, Leah, Erik. AA, Bethany Jr. Coll., 1952; BS, U. Minn., 1954, DDS, 1957. Pvt. practice dentistry, Northfield, Minn., 1959-72; clin. asst. prof. dentistry U. Minn. Sch. Dentistry, Mpls., 1969-72, assoc. prof., 1972-82, chmn. dept. operative dentistry, 1978-87, prof., 1982-97, prof. emeritus, 1997; dir. quality programs Pentegra Dental Group, Inc., 1998-2000. Dental cons. Hennepin County Med. Ctr., Mpls., 1975-96, VA Hosp., Mpls., 1977-96, VA Hosp., St. Cloud, Minn., 1978-96, Human Performance and Informatics Inst., Atama, Japan, 1990-95, K-9 Dental Sys. Quidnunc Australia Pty. Ltd., 1994-95, Metro Dental Group, Mpls., 1995-2000, The Dentists Ins. Co., 1995-99, VGM Expert Systems, 1996-98, Met. Life Ins. Co., 1996—, Pentegra Ltd., 1997-2000; mem. resource faculty for Bush faculty devel. program on excellence and diversity in teaching U. Minn., 1993-94; founder Global Network for Systematic Healthcare, 2003. Pres. PTA, Northfield, 1965, Arts Guild, Northfield, 1968; bd. dirs., chairperson Rice County Health and Sanitation Bd., Faribault, Minn., 1966-74; bd. dirs. Northfield Bd. Edn., 1969-74; pres. Roseville Luth. Ch., 1987-88. Capt. U.S. Army, 1957-59. Am. Coll. Dentists fellow, 1972; recipient Prof. of Yr. award Century Club, 1996-97. Mem. Am. Dental Assn. (chairperson operative dentistry sect. 1979-80, curriculum cons. 1981-88, grants and spl. projects request evaluator 1988-92, Am. fund for Dental Health, edit. review bd. JADA 1992-96), Minn. Dental Assn. (ethics com. 1969-76, chairperson sci. and ann. sessions com. 1984-86, spkr. house del. 1992-96, del. to ADA 1992-96, bd. dirs. 1992-96), Mpls. Dist. Dental Soc. (program chairperson 1978-79, peer rev. com. 1988-92, bd. dirs. 1979-80, 87-89, MDA del. 1989-92), Minn. Acad. Restorative Dentistry (pres. 1979-80), Minn. Acad. Gnathological Rsch. (pres. 1986-87), Am. Assn. Dental Schs. (chairperson operative dentistry sect. 1984-85, edit. rev. bd. 1984-88), Acad. Operative Dentistry (exec. council 1978-81, rsch. com. 1987-89), Am. Acad. Gold Foil Operators, Northfield C. of C. (treas. and chairperson 1968-70), Delta Sigma Delta, Omicron Kappa Upsilon (Theta chpt.). Lodges: Rotary (pres. Northfield 1972-73). E-mail: RAGeist@aol.com.

GEITHNER, PAUL HERMAN, JR., retired banker; b. Phila., June 7, 1930; s. Paul Herman and Henriette Antonine (Schuck) G.; m. Irmgard Hagedorn, Sept. 6, 1956; children: Christina, Amy, Paul. BA cum laude, Amherst Coll., 1952; MBA with distinction, U. Pa., 1957. Sec.-treas. Ellicott Machine Co., Balt., 1964-68. Successively v.p., sr. v.p., exec. asst to the chmn., First Va. Banks, Inc., Falls Church, 1968-85, pres., chief adminstrv. officer, 1985-95, also bd. dirs., vice chmn., 1986-95; pres. First Va. Life Ins. Co., 1974-96; bd. trustees Bridgewater Coll., Va., 1988—. Bd. dirs. Fairfax Symphony Orch., Va., 1988—, pres., 1991—92; bd. dirs. Va. Coll. Fund, 1987—91; trustee Va. Banker Sch. Bank Mgmt., 1988—92; sec.-treas. Fairfax Symphony Orch. Found., 1999—. Lt. USNR, 1952—55. Mem. Va. Bankers Assn. (pres. 1992-93). Home: 4290 Highlands Bridge Rd Sarasota FL 34235 Office: 1st Va Banks Inc 6400 Arlington Blvd Falls Church VA 22042-2336

GEJDENSON, SAM, former congressman; b. Eschwege, Fed. Republic of Germany, May 20, 1948; children: Mia, Ari. AS, Mitchell Coll., 1968; BA, U. Conn., 1970. Mem. Conn. State Ho. of Reps., 1974-78; coal broker, 1978-79; legis. liaison Conn. Office Policy and Mgmt., Hartford, 1979-80; mem. U.S. Congress from 2d Conn. dist., Washington, 1981-2001; owner & founder Sam Gejdenson Internat., 2001—. Democrat. Office: Sam Gejdenson International 84 Johnson Point Rd Branford CT 06405

GEJMAN, PABLO VICTOR, physician, scientist; b. Buenos Aires, July 13, 1954; came to U.S., 1986; s. Marcos and Elena (Korenstein) G.; m. Alicia Mabel Anijovich, Feb. 12, 1985; children: Ilan, Ron S., Maya G. MD, U. Buenos Aires, 1979. Rsch. asst. U. Buenos Aires, 1975-78; resident Hadassah U. Hosp. Dept. Psychiatry, Jerusalem, 1983-86; clin. assoc. NIH, Nat. Inst. Mental Health, Bethesda, Md., 1986-92, chief unit molecular clin. investigation, 1992—, pres. Internat. Assoc., 1995-97. Faculty mem. U. Fed. Minas Gerais, Belo Horizonte, Brazil, 1991; hon. mem. fgn. corr. Argentina Assn. Biol. Psychiatry, Buenos Aires, 1992; adj. grad. asst. prof. dept. genetics and human genetics Howard U., Washington, 1992-94; mem. med. adv. bd. Am. Friends of Sarah Herzog Meml. Hosp., Ezrath Nashim, Jerusalem, 1993-97; vis. prof. psychiatry U. Laval Robert Giffard, Quebec, Can., 1995-97; prof. U. Chgo., 1998—; chief genetics of schizophrenia rsch. program U. Chgo., 1998—. Mem. editl. bd. Psychiat. Genetics, 1994—, sect. editor; contbr. articles to profl. jours. Med. Rsch. fellow U. Buenos Aires, 1979-81, Consejo Nacional de Investigación Científica y Técnica, Buenos Aires, 1981-82, Hadassah Hosp., Dept. Endocrinology, 1983-84; Internat. Fogarty fellow, 1986; recipient Endocrinology prize Found. Argentina de Endocrinología, Buenos Aires, 1980, J.M. Davies Investigator award Nat. Alliance for Mentally Ill, 1999, Disting. Investigator award Nat. Alliance for Rsch. in Schizophrenia and Affective Disorders, 2000. Fellow Am. Psychopathological Assn.; mem. AAAS, Am. Soc. Human Genetics. Home: 1695 Lake Cook Road #230 Highland Park IL 60635 Office: ENH & Northwestern Univ ENH Rsch Inst 1001 Univ Pl Evanston IL 60201

GEKAS, GEORGE WILLIAM, former congressman; b. Harrisburg, Pa., Apr. 14, 1930; m. Evangeline Charas, 1971 BA, Dickinson Coll., 1952, JD, 1958. Bar: Pa. 1959. Asst. dist. atty. Dauphin County, Pa., 1960-66; mem. Pa. Ho. of Reps. from 103d dist., Harrisburg, 1966-74, Pa. Senate from 15th dist., Harrisburg, 1977-82, 98th-106th Congresses from 17th Pa. dist., 1983—2002; mem. judiciary com.; chmn. house judiciary subcom. comml. and adminstrv. law. Republican.*

GEKELMAN, DIANA, dentist, dental educator, researcher; d. Edward and Margareta Gekelman; m. Jean-Sebastien Elkaim. DDS, U. Sao Paulo, Brazil, 1993, specialization in endodontics, 1997, MS, 2000. Post-doctoral fellow lasers in dentistry U. Calif., San Francisco, 2000—02, asst. clin. prof. divsn. endodontics, 2002—. Presenter in field; spkr. nat. and internat. confs. Sci. reviewer (articles); contbr. articles to profl. jours. Grantee, FAPESP (Sao Paulo Found. Rsch.), 1999—2000, FDCTO, 2000, Lares Rsch., 2001—02. Mem.: ADA, San Francisco Dental Soc., Calif. Dental Assn., Am. Assn. Endodontists, Am. Assn. Dental Rsch., Soc. Photo-Optical Instrumentation Engrs., Acad. Laser Dentistry, Internat. Assn. Dental Rsch. Office: University of California San Francisco Sch Dentistry 707 Parnassus Ave San Francisco CA 94143-0758

GELA, GEORGE, electrical engineering researcher; b. Przemysl, Poland, Jan. 24, 1950; came to Can., 1965, came to U.S., 1984; s. Bogdan and Stefania (Olejnik) G.; m. Joanne Lillian Babyn, June 19, 1976; children: Natalka, Oksana. BASc, U. Toronto, Ont., Can., 1973; MASc, U. Toronto, 1975, PhD, 1980. Registered profl. engr., Ont. Rsch., teaching asst. U. Toronto, 1973-80; project leader Trench Electric Co., Toronto, 1980-83; asst. prof. elec. engring. Ohio State U., Columbus, 1984-90; sr. rsch. engr. EPRI-Lenox, 1990—. Cons. Trench Electric, Toronto, 1978-79, Panex, Newark, Ohio, 1987-88, Edison Welding Inst., Columbus, 1988-90, Ont. Hydro, Toronto, 1988. Contbr. numerous articles to sci. jours. Nat. Rsch. Coun. Can. fellow, 1980-82, 82-83. Mem.: IEEE (sr.; officer exec. com., past chmn. corona and field effects subcom., past chmn. tech. working group of ESMOL, Outstanding Engr. Region 1 2000), Internat. Chmn. IEC/TC78 Live Working, Conf. Internat. Grands Reseaux a Haute Tension, Power Engring. Soc. Ukrainian Catholic. Avocations: sports, chess, stamp collecting, photography. Office: EPRIsolutions-Lenox 115 E New Lenox Rd Lenox MA 01240-2245 E-mail: geogela@epri.com.

GELATT, CHARLES DANIEL, manufacturing company executive; b. La Crosse, Wis., Jan. 4, 1918; s. Philo Madison and Clara (Johnson) G.; m. Jane Leicht, Mar. 6, 1942 (div. 1972); children: Sarah Jane Gelatt Gephart, Charles D., Philip Madison; m. Paula Jo Evans, Aug. 22, 1973 (div. 1978); m. Sue Anne Jimieson, Dec. 11, 1983. BA, MA, U. Wis., 1939. V.p. Gelatt Corp., La Crosse, 1940-52, pres., 1952-95, chmn., 1995—99; pres. No. Engraving Corp., Sparta, Wis., 1958-67, chmn., 1967-96, chmn. emeritus, 1996—; pres. N.E. Co. Ltd., 2000—. Trustee Northwestern Mut. Life Ins. Co., Milw., 1960-88, mem. exec. com., 1961-77; chmn. North Ctrl. Trust Co., La. Crosse, 1989-93; mem. bd. regents U. Wis., 1947-74, pres. bd. regents, 1955-57, v.p., 1964-68, pres., 1968-69; mem. Wis. Coordinating Com. for Higher Edn., 1955-59, 64-69, chmn., 1956; chmn. Assn. Governing Bds. Univs. and Colls., Washington, 1971-72; trustee Carroll Coll., Waukesha, Wis., 1971-79, Viterbo U., La. Crosse, 1972-2002; trustee Gundersen Found., La Crosse, 1973-95. Mem. Phi Beta Kappa. Home: 9133 Collins Ave Miami FL 33154 Office: PO Box 1087 La Crosse WI 54602-1087

GELATT, JAMES PRENTICE, nonprofit management consultant; b. Endicott, N.Y., July 11, 1944; s. Howard and Harriette Marie (Prentice) G.; m. Cathy Lynn Clutter, Oct. 15, 1977; children: Charles Prentice, Leslie Paige. BA, St. Lawrence U., 1966; MA, Colgate U., 1969; PhD, U. So. Calif., L.A., 1980. Teaching cert., N.Y. Dir. planning and devel. Human Resources Ctr., Albertson, N.Y., 1968-75; conf. coord. White House Conf. on Handicapped Individuals, Washington, 1975-77; dir. spl. projects Kennedy Inst. Johns Hopkins U., Balt., 1977-79; sr. policy assoc. Ctr. for Studies in Social Policy, Washington, 1979-81; dir. planning, sponsored programs Am. Speech-Lang.-Hearing Assn., Rockville, Md., 1981-95. Mem. adj. faculty grad. sch. U. Md. Author: Planning for Excellence, 1989, Managing Nonprofit Organizations in the 21st Century, 1992; project adminstr. IMPACT, 1988 (Excellence in Edn. award 1989); contbr. articles to profl. jours. Founder, Assn. Found. Group, Rockville, 1987—; mem. commn. on edn. St. Paul's United Meth. Ch., Kensington, Md., 1989-91, chair staff parish rels. com., 2001—. HHS grantee, 1981-89. Mem. Am. Soc. Assn. Execs. (Future Leaders award 1988), Greater Washington Soc. Assn. Execs (strategic planning com., chair found. edn. com. 1990), Nat. Soc. Fundraising Execs, (bd. dirs. Washington chpt. 1990—, pres. 1995), World Future Soc. Avocations: jogging, piano. Home and Office: 11512 Regency Dr Potomac MD 20854-3733

GELB, ALVIN MEYER, physician; b. Stamford, Conn., May 4, 1930; s. Jacob and Rose Gelb; m. Ronda Shainmark, Mar. 7, 1954; children: Jeffrey, Janet, Daniel, Michael. AB, NYU, 1950, MD, 1954. Diplomate Am. Bd. Medicine, Am. Bd. Gastroent. Intern Cin. Gen. Hosp., Conn., 1954-55; residency in internal med. Mt. Sinai Hosp., NYC, 1955—56, resident, 1958—59, fellow in gastroent., 1959—61, instr., asst., assoc. attending physician, 1961-70; chief of medicine French-Polyclinic Hosp., NYC, 1970-75; chief of gastroent. Beth Israel Hosp., NYC, 1975—2002. Editor, author: Clinical Gastroent. in the Elderly, 1996. Capt. US Army, 1956-58, Korea. Fellow Mt. Sinai Hosp., NY, 1959-61. Fellow ACP; mem. Am. Gastroenterol. Assn., Am. Coll. Gastroent., Am. Soc. Gastroent. Endoscopy, NY Gastroenterol. Assn. (pres.), NY Acad. Gastroenterology (pres.), Am. Soc. Gastroent. and Endoscopy, NY Soc. Gastroent. Endoscopy. Democrat. Jewish. Avocations: music, opera, reading, theatre, history. E-mail: agelb@bethisraelny.org.

GELB, ARTHUR, electrical and systems engineering executive; b. N.Y.C., Sept. 20, 1937; m. Linda Lewis; children: Ronald, Caren, Laurie. BEE, CUNY, 1958; MS in Applied Math., Harvard U., 1959; ScD in Systems Engring., MIT, 1961. Engr. Aviation Gas Turbine div. Westinghouse Electric Corp., Kansas City, Mo., 1956, Am. Dist. Telegraph Co., N.Y.C., 1957-58, Draper Lab., Cambridge, Mass., 1959; dept. mgr. Dynamics Research Corp., Stoneham, Mass., 1961-66; pres., chief exec. officer TASC (The Analytic Sciences Corp.), Reading, Mass., 1966-93, chmn., 1993-94, sr. chmn., 1994; pres. Four Sigma Corp., Woburn, Mass., 1995—. Chmn. adv. bd. Ctr. for Tech., Policy and Indsl. Devel., MIT, 1987-97; mem. MIT Corp., 1996—; mem. Lincoln Lab. Adv. Bd. Co-author: Multiple-Input Describing Fns., 1968, Applied Optimal Estimation, 1974; contbr. articles to profl. jours. Bd. dirs. Massport, Boston, 1977-85; bd. regents Higher Edn., Mass., 1989-90; mem. Higher Edn. Coord. Coun., Mass., 1990-95. Named Outstanding Young Engr. CUNY, 1969. Fellow AIAA, IEEE (bd. editors Control Systems Mag. 1981-91), AAAS; mem. Mensa. Avocations: music, tennis, golf, microcomputing, math. Office: Four Sigma Corp 61 Holton St Woburn MA 01801-5263

GELB, BRUCE STUART, city commissioner, consultant; b. N.Y.C., Feb. 24, 1927; s. Lawrence M. and Joan Friedman (Hewett) G.; m. Lueza Denise Thirkield, June 6, 1953; children: John T., Joan H., Richard E., M. Constance. BA, Yale U., 1950; MBA, Harvard U., 1953. With Clairol Inc., 1950—51, 1957—61, v.p. mktg., 1961-65, exec. v.p., pres., 1965-76; brand mgr. Procter & Gamble, 1953-57; with Bristol-Myers Co., N.Y.C., 1957-89, sr. v.p., 1977-85, exec. v. p., 1981-84, pres. consumer products group, 1985-89; dir., vice-chmn. Bristol Myers, 1985-89; dir. USIA, Washington, 1989-91; amb. to Belgium Brussels, 1991-93; N.Y.C. commr. UN Consular Corps and Internat. Bus., N.Y.C., 1994-97; with UN Devel. Corp., 1994—2003. Sr. cons. Bristol Myers Squibb, 1997-2001. Life trustee Choate Rosemary Hall Sch.; mem. Pres.'s Arts and Humanities Com., 1989-91; trustee John F. Kennedy Ctr. for Performing Arts, 1989-91, Howard U., 1987-89; vice-chair Madison Sq. Boys and Girls Club; trustee Woodrow Wilson Ctr., pres. Woodrow Wilson Coun., 2003. Office: 150 E 52nd St Fl 12 New York NY 10022-6017 E-mail: jojoricos@aol.com.

GELB, GEORGE EDWARD, lawyer; b. Miami, Fla., June 23, 1946; s. Monroe and Violet (Abelson) G.; m. Kathryn Mary Peterson, Dec. 21, 1973; children— Christine Mary, Joseph Edward. B.A., U. Miami, 1968; J.D., U. Del., 1975; LL.M., NYU, 1978. Bar: Fla. 1977, N.J. 1977, Pa. 1977, U.S. Dist. Ct. (so. dist.) Fla. 1977, U.S. Ct. Appeals (5th cir.) 1977, U.S. Ct. Appeals (11th cir.) 1981, U.S. Supreme Ct. 1983. Asst. atty. gen. Del. Atty. Gen.'s Office, Wilmington, 1975-76; pres., atty. George E. Gelb, P.A., Miami, Fla., 1978— . Chmn., Wilmington Young Republicans, atty. City of Wilmington Rep. Com., asst. counsel Del. Rep. State Com., 1975-76. Roman Catholic. Club: Coral Gables Country. Office: George E Gelb P A 19 W Flagler St Ste 1116 Miami FL 33130-4410

GELB, HAROLD SEYMOUR, industrial company executive, investor; b. N.Y.C., Apr. 26, 1920; s. Daniel and Fanny (Gelb) G.; m. Sylvia M. Miller, Sept. 24, 1942; children: Richard, Alan. BBA, CCNY, 1941. CPA, N.Y. With S.D. Leidesdorf & Co. (CPAs), N.Y.C., 1943-78, mng. partner, 1969-78; sr. ptnr. Ernst & Young, N.Y.C., 1978-82; chmn. United Indsl. Corp., N.Y.C., 1995. Past vice chmn. Citizens Budget Commn., N.Y.C., now trustee emeritus; past chmn. N.Y. State Bd. Pub. Accountancy; mem. bd. arbitrators Am. Arbitration Assn. Pres. Bronx-Lebanon Hosp. Ctr., 1977; bd. dirs., v.p. S.D. Leidesdorf Found., 1969-80; trustee Accts. Found., 1973-80, Adelphi U., 1997—; bd. overseers Albert Einstein Med. Coll., 1977-79; bd. dirs., sec. Benjamin Cardozo Law Sch., 1977-89; mem. Gov.'s Task Force, Bus. Alliance with Edn., Mayor's Com. on Taxi Regulatory Issues, 1981-82. Recipient Disting. Cmty. Svc. award Brandeis U., 1978 Mem. AICPA (coun. 1970-76), N.Y. State Soc. CPAs (past v.p., bd. dirs.), Metropolis Country Club (White Plains), Town Club (Scarsdale), Econ. Club (N.Y.). Home: 181 Fox Meadow Rd Scarsdale NY 10583-2334 Office: 570 Lexington Ave New York NY 10022-6837 E-mail: hgelb@unitedindustrial.com.

GELB, JOSEPH DONALD, lawyer; b. Wilkes-Barre, Pa., Dec. 13, 1923; s. Edward and Esther (Fierman) G.; m. Anne Mirman, July 3, 1955; children: Adam, Roger. Student, Pa. State Coll., 1943; BS, U. Scranton, 1950; LLB, George Washington U., 1952. Bar: D.C. 1954, Md. 1963, U.S. Supreme Ct. 1972. Adjudicator War Claims Commn., 1952-54; pvt. practice Washington and Md., 1954-69; ptnr. Gelb & Pitsenberger, Washington, 1969-74; prin. Joseph D. Gelb Chartered, Washington, 1974-80, Gelb, Abelson & Siegel, P.C., Washington, 1980-82, Gelb & Siegel, P.C., Washington, 1982-85, Joseph D. Gelb, Chartered, Washington, 1985-93, Gelb & Gelb, P.C., Washington, 1994—. Served with USAAF, 1943-46 Mem. Md. Bar Assn., D.C. Bar Assn., Bethesda Country Club, B'nai B'rith, Masons. Home: 9620 Annlee Ter Bethesda MD 20817-1410 also: 525 N Ocean Blvd Pompano Beach FL 33062-4640 Office: Gelb & Gelb PC 1120 Connecticut Ave NW Washington DC 20036-3902 E-mail: lawyers@gelbandgelb.com.

GELB, JUDITH ANNE, lawyer; b. N.Y.C., Apr. 5, 1935; d. Joseph and Sarah (Stein) G.; m. Howard S. Vogel, June 30, 1962; 1 child, Michael S. BA, Bklyn. Coll., 1955; JD, Columbia U., 1958. Bar: N.Y. 1959, U.S. Dist. Ct. (so. and ea. dists.) N.Y. 1960, U.S. Ct. Appeals (2d cir.) 1960, U.S. Ct. Mil. Appeals 1962. Asst. to editor N.Y. Law Jour., N.Y.C., 1958-59; confidential asst. to U.S. atty. ea dist. N.Y., Bklyn., 1959-61; assoc. Whitman & Ransom, N.Y.C., 1961-70, ptnr., 1971-93, Whitman Breed Abbott & Morgan LLP, N.Y.C., 1993-2000, Winston & Strawn LLP, N.Y.C., 2000—. Mem.: ABA (individual rights sect., real property and trust law sect.), Assn. Bar City N.Y., N.Y. State Dist. Attys. Assn., N.Y. State Bar Assn. (trusts and estates com.), Fed. Bar Coun., Columbia Law Sch. Alumni Assn. (bd. dirs.), Princeton Club. Home: 169 E 69th St New York NY 10021-5163 Office: Winston & Strawn LLP 200 Park Ave New York NY 10166-0005 E-mail: jgelb@winston.com.

GELB, LESLIE HOWARD, organization president, lecturer; b. New Rochelle, N.Y., Mar. 4, 1937; s. Max and Dorothy (Klein) G.; m. Judith Cohen, Aug. 2, 1959; children: Adam, Caroline, Alison. AB magna cum laude in Govt. and cum laude in Philosophy, Tufts U., 1959; MA, Harvard U., 1961, PhD, 1964. Teaching fellow govt. and social scis., non-resident tutor Winthrop House, Harvard U., 1962-64, assoc. def. studies program, 1963-64; asst. prof. govt. Wesleyan U., Middletown, Conn., 1964-65; exec. asst. to U.S. Senator Jacob K. Javits, 1966-67; dep. dir. policy planning staff Dept. Def., Washington, 1967-68, dir., 1968, acting dep. asst. sec. def. for policy planning and arms control staff, 1968-69; dir. sec. def. Vietnam task force, 1967-68; sr. fellow Brookings Instn., Washington, 1969-73; corr. N.Y. Times, Washington, 1973-77; dir. bur. politico-mil. affairs Dept. State, Washington, 1977-79; sr. assoc. Carnegie Endowment for Internat. Peace, 1979-81; chmn. Carnegie Endowment Panel on Future U.S. Security and Arms Control, 1980-81; nat. security corr. N.Y. Times, 1981-86, dep. editorial page editor, op-editorial page editor, 1986-90, fgn. affairs columnist, 1991-93; pres. Coun. Fgn. Rels., 1993—2003, pres. emeritus, sr. fellow bd, 2003—. Bd. dirs. certain funds advised by Salomon Bros. Asset Mgmt., certain registered investment cos. advised by subs. of CIBC Oppenheimer Corp., britannica.com, The Nixon Ctr.; mem. The Trilateral Commn., 1993-2000; chmn. adv. bd. Emerging Europe Pvt. Equity Fund III. Author: The Irony of Vietnam: The System Worked, 1979, Anglo-American Relations, 1945-49, 1988; co-author: Our Own Worst Enemy: The Unmaking of American Foreign Policy, 1984; contbr. numerous articles to mags.; sr. cons. and producer "The Crisis Game," 1983 (Emmy, DuPont, Hood awards); sr. editor postwar history of U.S. "45/85," 1985 Trustee emeritus Tufts U., Carnegie Endowment for Internat. Peace; mem. adv. bd. Sch. Internat. and Pub. Affairs, Columbia U., 1997-2001; bd. dirs. James A. Baker III Inst. Pub. Policy; adv. mem. Ctr. Press, Politics and Pub. Policy, Harvard U. John F. Kennedy Sch. Govt., 1991-2001.

Recipient Woodrow Wilson award, 1980, Page One award in explanatory journalism, 1985, Nat. Father of Yr. award U.S. Nat. Com. on Fathers and Mothers of Yr. Awards, 1993; mem. N.Y. Times Pulitzer Prize Winning Team, 1985. Fellow AAAS; mem. Internat. Inst. Strategic Studies, Coun. Fgn. Rels. Home: 150 E 69th St New York NY 10021-5704 Office: Coun Fgn Rels 58 E 68th St New York NY 10021-5953

GELB, RICHARD MARK, lawyer; b. N.Y.C., June 12, 1947; s. Harold Seymour and Sylvia Mildred (Miller) G.; m. Gail Kleven, July 29, 1973; 1 child, Daniel Kleven. BA, NYU, 1969; JD, Boston Coll., 1973. Bar: Mass. 1973, N.Y. 1975, D.C. 1975, U.S. Dist. Ct. (so. and ea. dists.) N.Y. 1975, U.S. Ct. Appeals (2d cir.) 1975, U.S. Dist. Ct. Conn. 1977, U.S. Ct. Appeals (1st cir.) 1978, U.S. Dist. Ct. Mass. 1978, U.S. Supreme Ct. 1980. Assoc. Proskauer Rose, LLP, N.Y.C., 1975-77; ptnr. Gelb & Gelb LLP, Boston, 1987—. Contbr. articles to profl. publs. Mem. Mass. Bar Assn. (ethics com. 1991-96, civil litig. coun. 1994-96, chmn. bus. litig. com. 1992-94, assoc. editor Mass. Law Rev. 1982-87), Am. Inn of Ct. Found. (trustee 1994-98), Boston Inn of Ct. (co-pres. 1993-94), Boston Coll. Law Sch. Intellectual Property Am. Inns of Ct. (pres. 1998-2000, treas. 2001-02), Boston Coll. Law Sch. Alumni Coun. (v.p. comms. 2001-03), Suffolk U. Law Sch. Litig. Am. Inn Ct. (co-pres. 2002—), Pi Sigma Alpha. Democrat. Jewish. Home: 60 Pine Hill Rd Swampscott MA 01907-2240 Office: Gelb & Gelb LLP 20 Custom House St Ste 1030 Boston MA 02110-3559

GELBARD, ROBERT SIDNEY, ambassador; b. N.Y.C., Mar. 6, 1944; s. Charles and Ruth (Fisher) G.; m. Alene Marie Hanola, July 27, 1968; 1 child, Alexandra Pauline. AB, Colby Coll., 1964; MPA, Harvard U., 1979; JD (hon.), Villanova U., 1998, Colby Coll., 2002. Vol. Peace Corps, Bolivia, 1964-66; joined Fgn. Svc., Dept. State, 1967; staff asst. sr. seminar in Fgn. Policy, Fgn. Svc. Fgn. Svcs., Dept. State, 1967-68; assoc. dir. Peace Corps, The Philippines, 1968-70; vice consul U.S. Consulate, Porto Alegre, Brazil, 1970-71, prin. officer, 1971-72; internat. economist Office Devel. Fin., Bur. Econ. and Bus. Affairs, Washington, 1973-75, Office Regional Polit. Econ. Affairs, Bur. European Can. Affairs, Dept. State, Washington, 1976-78; first sec. Am. Embassy, Paris, 1978-82; dep. dir. Office Western European Affairs, Bur. European and Can. Affairs, Washington, 1982-84; dir. Office So. African Affairs, Bur. African Affairs, Washington, 1984-85; dep. asst. sec. Bur. Inter-Am. Affairs, Dept. State, Washington, 1985-88; amb. to Bolivia La Paz, 1988-91; prin. dep. asst. sec. Bur. Inter-Am. Affairs, Dept. State, 1991-93; asst. sec. of state Internat. Narcotics and Law Enforcement Affairs, Washington, 1993-97; spl. rep. of pres. and sec. state for The Balkans, 1997-99; U.S. amb. to Indonesia and East Timor, 1999—2001; sr. v.p. internat. affairs and govt. rels. ICN Pharm., Inc., 2002; internat. bus. cons., 2003—. Chmn. bd. Kosovo Airways. Mem.: Bolivian-Am. C. of C. (bd. dirs.), Am. Acad. Diplomacy, Am. Fgn. Svc. Assn. Home: 3712 Huntington St NW Washington DC 20015

GELBART, LARRY, writer, producer; b. Chgo., Feb. 25, 1928; s. Harry and Frieda (Sturner) G.; m. Pat Marshall, Nov. 25, 1956; children: Gary, Paul, Adam, Becky. LittD (hon.), Union Coll., Schnectady, N.Y., 1986; LHD (hon.), Hofstra U., 1999. Writer: for radio series The Eddie Cantor Show, 1946, Maxwell House Coffee Time with Danny Thomas, 1946, Duffy's Tavern, 1946, Command Performance, 1946-47, Jack Carson, 1947-48, The Jack Paar Show, 1949, The Joan Davis Show, 1949, The Bob Hope Show, 1949-52; for ballet, Peter and the Wolf, 1992; for theatre My L.A., 1950, The Conquering Hero, 1960, A Funny Thing Happened on the Way to the Forum, 1962 (Tony award with Burt Shevelove best musical play 1963), Sly Fox, 1976, One, Two, Three, Four, Five, 1988, City of Angels, 1989 (Drama Desk award best book of musical 1989, Tony award best musical, best book of musical 1990, Best New Musical citation NY Drama Critics Circle 1990, Outer Critics Circle award outstanding Broadway musical, contbn. to comedy award 1990, Edgar Allan Poe award best mystery play 1990), Mastergate, 1989 (Outer Critics Circle award contbn. to comedy 1990), (co-author) Jerome Robbins' Broadway, 1989; for films The Notorious Landlady, 1962, The Thrill of It All, 1963, (also co-producer) The Wrong Box, 1966, Not With My Wife You Don't, 1966, The Chastity Belt, 1968, A Fine Pair, 1969, Oh, God, 1977 (Acad. award nomination best screenplay material from another medium 1977, Edgar Allan Poe award, Mystery Writers Am. award, Writers Guild award), Movie, Movie, 1978 (Writers Guild award, Christopher award), Neighbors, 1981, Tootsie, 1982 (Acad. Award nomination best screenplay written directly for screen 1982, LA Film Critics award, NY Film Critics award, Nat. Soc. Film Critics award), (also exec. producer) Blame It on Rio, 1984, Bedazzled, 2000; writer, prodr., co-prodr. TV shows M*A*S*H, 1972-76 (Emmy award nomination outstanding writing comedy 1972, 75, Writers Guild Am. award 1972, 74, Emmy award outstanding comedy series 1973, Emmy award nominations outstanding comedy series 1974, 75, George Foster Peabody award 1975, Humanitas award), Roll Out!, 1973-74, Karen, 1975, United States, 1980, After M*A*S*H, 1983-84 (Emmy award nomination outstanding directing comedy series 1983); TV adaptation Mastergate, 1992; writer, exec. prodr. HBO film Barbarians at the Gate, 1993 (Outstanding Made-for-TV-Movie Emmy award, Best Made-for-TV-Motion Picture award The Am. TV Awards, Program of Yr., The TV Critics Assn., Cable Ace award, Writing in a Movie or Miniseries), Weapons of Mass Distraction, 1997; Best Teleplay awd., PEN Ctr. USA West, writer TV shows The All-Star Revue, 1950-53, The Red Buttons Show, 1952-55, Honestly, Celeste!, 1954, The Patrice Munsel Show, 1954-62, Caesar's Hour, 1955-57 (Emmy award nominations best comedy writing 1955, 56, 57), The Pat Boone Chevy Showroom, 1957-60, The Danny Kaye Show, 1963 (Emmy award nomination outstanding writing comedy or variety show 1963), The Marty Feldman Comedy Machine, 1972, (TV movie) And Starring Pancho Villa as Himself, 2003, Like Jazz, A New Kind of Musicial, 2003; author: Laughing Matters, 1998. Served with AUS, 1945-46. Recipient Lee Strasberg Lifetime Achievement in Arts and Sci. award, 1990, William S. Paley award for excellence in TV, Anti-Defamation League, 2001, citation for disting. svc., AMA, 2001. Mem. Dramatists Guild, Writers Guild Am. (award 1972, 74), ASCAP, Dir. Guild Am. Address: 807 N Alpine Dr Beverly Hills CA 90210-2901

GELBEIN, JAY JOEL, accountant; b. Bklyn., Sept. 11, 1949; s. Leo and Sara (Eskolsky) G.; m. Marilyn Stern, Dec. 8, 1974; children: Moshe, Avi, Danielle. BS, Bklyn. Coll., 1972; MS with distinction, L.I. U., 1978. CPA, N.Y.; cert. fin. planner; registered investment advisor. Appellate conferee IRS, N.Y.C., 1971-79; tech. mgr. AICPA, N.Y.C., 1979-81; pvt. practice acctg. and tax cons. Staten Island, N.Y., 1979—. Prof. bus. Kingsborough C.C., Bklyn., 1981—; nat. tax lectr. Author: Tax-wise Investing for High Income Taxpayers, 1992, 2d edit., 1993; contbr. to The Practical Accountant, 1991; co-author: Accounting Demonstration Problems Workbook. Mem. AICPA, N.Y. State Soc. CPAs (mem. profl. svc. corp. com.), Inst. Cert. Fin. Planners. Home and Office: 13 President St Staten Island NY 10314-4119

GELBER, DON JEFFREY, lawyer; b. L.A., Mar. 10, 1940; s. Oscar and Betty Sheila (Chernitsky) G.; m. Jessica Jeasun Song, May 15, 1967; children: Victoria, Jonathan, Rebecca, Robert. Student UCLA, 1957-58, Reed Coll., 1958-59; AB, Stanford U., 1961, JD, 1963. Bar: Calif. 1964, Hawaii 1964, U.S. Dist. Ct. (cen. and no. dists. Calif.) 1964, U.S. Dist. Ct. Hawaii 1964, U.S. Ct. Appeals (9th cir.) 1964, U.S. Supreme Ct. 1991. Assoc. Greenstein, Yamane & Cowan, Honolulu, 1964-67; reporter Penal Law Revision Project, Hawaii Jud. Council, Honolulu, 1967-69; assoc. H. William Burgess, Honolulu, 1969-72; ptnr. Burgess & Gelber, Honolulu, 1972-73; prin. Law Offices of Don Jeffrey Gelber, Honolulu, 1974-77; pres. Gelber & Wagner, Honolulu, 1978-83, Gelber & Gelber, Honolulu, 1984-89, Gelber, Gelber, Ingersoll, Klevansky & Faris, Honolulu, 1990-2002, Gelber, Gelber, Ingersoll & Klevansky, 2002--; legal counsel Hawaii State Senate Judiciary Com., 1965; adminstrv. asst. to majority floor leader Hawaii State Senate, 1966, legal counsel Edn. Com., 1967, 68; majority counsel Hawaii Ho. of Reps., 1974; spl. counsel Hawaii State Senate, 1983. Contbr. articles to legal publs. Mem. State Bar Calif., ABA (sect. bus. law), Am. Bankruptcy Inst., Hawaii State Bar Assn. (sect. bankruptcy law, bd. dirs. 1991-93, pres. 1993). Clubs: Pacific, Plaza (Honolulu). Office: Gelber Gelber Ingersoll & Klevansky 745 Fort Street Mall Ste 1400 Honolulu HI 96813-3877

GELBER, LINDA CECILE, lawyer, banker; b. Hackensack, N.J., Oct. 30, 1950; d. Melvin W. and Beverly E. (Gilman) Gelber. B.A., Ind. U., 1972, M.B.A., 1974, J.D., 1978; cert. fin. svcs. counselor, Am. Bankers Assn. Nat. Grad. Trust Sch., 1983. Bar: Ind. 1978, U.S. Dist. Ct. (so. dist.) Ind. 1978, U.S. Supreme Ct. 1983, N.J. 1988, U.S. Dist. Ct. N.J. 1988. Program analyst Ind. Legis. Svcs. Agy., Indpls., 1978-80; v.p., trust officer First Nat. Bank, Kokomo, Ind., 1980-85, asst. v.p. Mchts. Nat. Bank, Indpls., 1985-87, Midlantic Nat. Bank, Edison and Englewood, N.J., 1987-90; pvt. con. N.J., N.Y., 1990—; part-time instr. Indiana U., Kokomo, 1981-82, Ball State U., Muncie, Ind., 1979-80. Bd. dirs. United Way, Kokomo, 1983-85, div. chmn. fund raising campaign, 1983; mem. Estate Planning Coun. Indpls. Mem. ABA, Am. Inst. Banking (v.p. 1983-85), Howard County (Ind.) Bar Assn. (sec.-treas. 1981), Indiana State Bar Assn., N.J. State Bar Assn., Bergen County Bar Assn. Club: Altrusa (Kokomo). Office: Midlantic Nat Bank 1 Engle St Englewood NJ 07631-2910

GELBER, LOUISE C(ARP), lawyer; m. Milton Gelber (dec.); children: Jack, Bruce, Julie McCoy. BA, JD, U. Calif., 1944. Bar: Calif. 1945, U.S. Dist. Ct. (so. dist.) Calif. 1945, U.S. Supreme Ct. 1965. Pvt. practice; commr. Calif. Bd Examiners for Nursing Home Adminstrs.; adminstr. Calif. Dept. Consumer Affairs. Speaker local drug rehab. hosp.; mem. Vis. Nurses Bd.; commr. Calif. Adv. Cost Control to State Govt.; mem. temporary judge panel L.A. County; settlement officer dispute resolution svc. Pasadena Superior Ct. Mem. editorial staff U. Calif. Law Rev. Calif. nominee for State Assembly, 1992; judge pro tem Rio Hondo Mcpl. Ct.; pro bono Bd. Legal Aid; v.p. local PTA; mem., invocator Arcadia Coord. Coun.; bd. dirs. Foothill Apt. Assn., People-For People; active ARC, Community Chest, United Way, Boy Scouts Am., Girl Scouts U.S. Mem. ABA, Calif. Bar Assn., Foothill Bar ASsn., L.A. County Bar ASsn., Pomona Valley Bar Assn., Citrus Bar Assn., Arcadia C. of C. (legis. com.), So. Calif. Women Lawyers (treas.), Pasadena C. of C., Bus. and Profl. Women Lawyers (past state legis. chmn., state legis. adv.), Order of Eastern Star, LWV, Sierra. Home and Office: 1225 Rancho Rd Arcadia CA 91006-2241 E-mail: french.court@verizon.net.

GELBER, PHILIP MICHAEL, cardiologist; b. N.Y.C., June 14, 1946; s. Gabriel and Jeanne Gloria (Wagner) G.; m. Patricia A. Meyers, Sept. 16, 1972; children: Jacob, Toby, Jen. AB, U. Chgo., 1967, MD, 1971. Resident Montefiore Hosp., Bronx, 1971-73, NYU-Bellevue, N.Y.C., 1973-74; pres. Cardiovascular Cons. L.I., New Hyde Park, N.Y., 1976—. Contbr. articles to profl. jours. Mem. vis. com. U. Chgo., 1995. Cardiology fellow NYU-Bellevue, 1974-76. Mem. Am. Coll. Cardiology (com. info. tech. 1991—). Office: Cardiovascular Cons 3003 New Hyde Park Rd New Hyde Park NY 11042-1214

GELBKE, CLAUS-KONRAD, nuclear physics educator; b. Celle, Germany, May 31, 1947; came to the U.S., 1976; s. Heinz and Gertraud Gelbke; m. Brigitte Zabeschek, Apr. 6, 1973; children: Susanne, Martin. Diploma für physik, U. Heidelberg, Germany, 1970, doctor rerum naturalium, 1973. Wissenschaftlicher asst. Max-Planck-Inst für Kernphysik, Heidelberg, 1973-76; physicist Lawrence Berkeley (Calif.) Lab., 1976-77; assoc. prof. physics Mich. State U., East Lansing, 1977-81, prof. physics, 1981-87, assoc. dir. nuclear sci. Nat. Superconducting Cyclotron Lab., 1987-90, disting. prof., 1990—, dir. Nat. Superconducting Cyclotron Lab., 1992—. Summer visitor Brookhaven Nat. Lab., Upton, N.Y., 1974, U. Washington, Seattle, 1975. Alfred P. Sloan fellow, 1979-83; Scholarship Studienstiftung des Deutschen Volkes, 1971-72; Humboldt Rsch. award U.S. Scis. Fellow Am. Physical Soc. Office: Mich State U Cyclotron Lab S Shaw Ln East Lansing MI 48824 E-mail: gelbke@nscl.msu.edu.

GELBOIN, HARRY VICTOR, biochemistry educator, researcher; b. Chgo., Dec. 21, 1929; s. Herman and Eva (Jurkowsky) Gelboin; m. Stella Bezansky, June 19, 1951; m. Marlena Maisels, Apr. 1, 1962; children: Michele Ida, Lisa Rebecca, Sharon Anna, Tamara Rachel. BA in Chemistry, U. Ill., 1951; MS in Biochemistry and Oncology, U. Wis., 1956, PhD in Biochemistry and Oncology, 1958; DSc (hon.), U. Inonu, Malatya, Turkey, 1999. Devel. chemist U.S. Rubber Co., Chgo., 1952-54; rsch. asst. McArdle Meml. Lab. for Cancer Rsch., U. Wis., 1954-58; biochemist lab. cellular pharmacology NIMH, 1958-60, biochemist lab. clin. sci., 1960-61; supervisory biochemist chemistry sect., diagnostic rsch. br. Nat. Cancer Inst., 1962-64, head chemistry sect., carcinogenesis studies br., 1964-66, chief lab. molecular carcinogenesis, div. cancer etiology, 1966—; adj. prof. Georgetown U., 1974-78. Vis. prof. Hebrew U., Jerusalem, 1985-86; Keynote speaker Carcinogenesis, Gordon Res. Conf., 1965; Franz Bielschowsky Meml. lectr., Dunedin, New Zealand, 1966; Smith Kline French hon. lectr. U. Fla., 1974, U. Mich., 1976; hon. lectr. Israel Cancer Soc. and U. Tel Aviv, Israel, 1983; Keynote lectr. Internat. Conf. Carcinogenesis, Alghero, Italy, 1986; Nakasone hon. lectr. Japan Found. Promotion Sci., Tokyo, Osako, 1989; keynote speaker U.S. organizer and co-chmn. Princess Takamatsu Cancer Symposium, Tokyo, 1990; plenary lectr. Glinos Found., Athens, 1996; mem. bd. dirs. Internat. Soc. Polycyclic Aromatic Com.; also speaker numerous domestic lectures and in 25 foreign countries. Editor 8 profl. books; assoc. editor Cancer Rsch., 1968-79, 83-87, mem. editl. adv. bd., 1965-67; assoc. editor Biochem. Toxicology, 1984—; mem. editl. bd. Chemico-Biol. Interactions, 1969-75, Archives Biochemistry and Biophysics, 1969-76, Life Scis., 1976, Environ. Health Scis., 1976-78; contbr. and co-contbr. over 420 sci. papers to med. publs.; editor/co-editor 10 books, 8 patents. Recipient Superior Svc. award NIH, 1970, Claude Bernard award U. Montreal, 1970, New Horizons award Radiol. Soc. N.Am., 1970, Merit awards Sr. Sci. Svc. NIH, 1983, 85, EEO award NIH, 1989 Fellow: Amer. Coll. Clin. Pharmacol.; mem.: Internat. Soc. for Study Xenobiotics, Internat. Soc. for Preventive Oncology, Am. Soc. for Pharmacology and Exptl. Therapeutics, Am. Soc. Biol. Chemists, Am. Cancer Soc. (adv. com. on carcinogenesis, mem. coun. 1975—), Am. Assn. for Cancer Rsch., AAAS. Achievements include research in on molecular mechanism chem. carcinogenesis, metabolism and activation of drugs and environ. agts., toxicology of xenobiotics, specific inhibitory monoclonal antibodies to human P450; devel. activation for chem. binding to DNA used in Ames Mutation detection sys. Personal E-mail: HGG@helix.nih.gov .

GELBURD, DIANE ELIZABETH, conservationist; b. N.Y.C., Sept. 28, 1952; d. Irving and Margaret Beryl (Thorbes) G. BA, George Washington U., 1974, MA, 1978; PhD, Am. U., 1988. Archeologist, anthropologist Smithsonian Instn., George Washington U., Dobe, Botswana, 1976; archeologist Bur. Reclamation, Washington, 1977, Nat. Park Svc., Washington, 1977-79, assoc. anthropologist, 1979-80; nat. cultural resources specialist Soil Conservation Svcs., Washington, 1980-88, asst. dir. econ. and social scis. divsn., 1988-91, nat. rsch. coord., 1991-92, assoc. dep. chief for programs, 1992-95; regional conservationist for East Natural Resources Conservation Svcs., Beltsville, Md., 1995-98; dir. ecol. scis. divsn. Natural Resources Conservation Svc., Washington, 1998—. Co-chmn. White House Interagy. Ecosys. Initiative, 1994-96. Contbr. articles to profl. jours. CPR instr. ARC, Arlington, Va., 1983-86; mem. steering com. Fed. Preservation Forum, 1989-90; mentor fellowship program Coun. for Basic Edn., 1991-93. Recipient Achievement award Bur. Reclamation, Washington, 1977, Fred H. Nothman Hon. Mention award, 1988, Cert. of Appreciation, Soil Conservation Svc., 1988, Disting. Svc. award USDA, 1986, Spl. Commendation award Soil Conservation Svc. Am., 1986, Recognition award Soil Conservation Svc., 1986, Cert. of Merit, 1987, 88, 89, 91; tchg. fellow George Washington U., 1975-77, Am. U. fellow, 1986-87, Grad. Acad. Excellence award, 1988; named Mgr. of Yr., NHQ, 1991, U.S. Presdl. Productivity and Quality Improvement award, 1991, SES Performance awards, 1995, 98, 2000-02, named to Matawan Regional H.S. Hall of Fame; named Super Supr. of Yr. Assn. for People with Disabilities in Agr., 1999. Mem. Am. Soc. Conservation Archeology (exec. com. 1988-90), Am. Anthrop. Assn., Am. Women in Sci., George Wright Soc. (local chpt. treas. 1982), Soil and Water Conservation Soc. (program com. 1992, vice chmn. human resources divsn. 1985-86, chmn. 1986-87, local chpt. sec. 1984, v.p. 1985, pres. 1987), Soc. Am. Archeology (exec. com. fed. archaeology 1979-84, pub. edn. com. 1990-93, save the past for the future 1988-91, profl. rels. com. 1990-93, assoc. editor book reviews Am. Antiquity 1989-93), Exec. Women Govt. (treas. 1998-99, pres. 1999-2000), Sr. Exec. Assn. (bd. dirs. 2002--), Phi Kappa Phi. Lutheran. Office: US Dept Agr Natural Resources Cons Svcs PO Box 2890 Washington DC 20013-2890 E-mail: diane.gelburd@usda.gov.

GELCA, RAZVAN, education educator; b. Timisoara, Timis, Romania, Feb. 28, 1967; s. Gheorghe and Olimpia Tatiana Gelca. PhD, U. Iowa, Iowa City, Iowa, 1997. Rschr. Inst. of Math. of the Romanian Acad., Bucharest, Romania, 1990—91; asst. prof. U. Mich., Ann Arbor, Mich., 1997—2000, Tex. Tech U., Lubbock, Tex., 2000—. Coach of the us internat. math. olympiad team Am. Math. Competitions, Lincoln, Nebr., 1997—2002; asst. editor Math. Mag., 2000—; mem. of us math. olympiad adv. panel Am. Math. Competitions, Lincoln, Nebr., 1997—; assoc. editor Revista Matematica din Timisoara, Timisoara, Romania, 1985—89. Author: (mathematics problem book) Mathematical Olympiad Challenges; contbr. scientific papers to profl. jour. Recipient Gold Medal, Internat. Math. Olympiad, 1985, Diploma of Merit in Math., Romanian Ministry of Edn., 1989, First Prize, Balkan Math. Olympiad, 1985, Romanian Math. Olympiad, 1985, Romanian Nat. Student Competition, 1986, First prize, 1987, D.C. Spriestersbach Dissertation Award, U. Iowa, 1998, Romanian Nat. Fellowship, U. Timisoara, 1987 and 1988; grantee Rackham Summer Grant, U. Mich., 1999, Reseach Enhancement Fund, Tex. Tech U., 2000 and 2001. Home: 2908 21st St Lubbock TX 79410 Office: Dept Math and Stat Tex Tech Univ Lubbock TX 79410 Personal E-mail: rgelca@math.ttu.edu. E-mail: rgelca@math.ttu.edu.

GELDER, DONALD CLIFFORD BARNARD, artist; b. Naples, N.Y., Apr. 17, 1933; s. Clifford Barnard and Ruby Alberta (Davis) G.; m. Sandra Lea Boyles Smith, June 9, 1962 (div. 1980); children: Sheril Lea, Andrea Beth, Victoria Lynn, Kristina Carol; m. Nancy Figuracion Gelder, Jan. 14, 1983; children: Ryan, Mary Alejandra Louise, William Alfred II. Diploma, Buffalo Fine Arts Acad., 1953. Stained glass designer Willet Studios, Phila., 1962-66, Frone Stained Glass Studio, Buffalo, 1966-68, United Archtl. Svcs., Buffalo, 1968-75, The Judson Studios, L.A., 1975-82, Luxfer Studios, Toronto, Ont., Can., 1983-84, Gelder Studios, Naples, 1984—. Art lectr. Am. Sci. Glassblowers Soc., Phila., 1964, Depew (N.Y.) Mid. Sch., 1967. Freelance portrait painter. With U.S. Army, 1954-56. Recipient Gold Key award Scholastic Mags., 1949, Mural Commendation award Col. Howard Smigelow, 1955, Fannie Benjamin award Meml. Art Gallery, 1956, First Pl. award in crafts St. John's Ch., 1970. Mem. Am. Soc. Portrait Artists, Brit. Soc. Master Glass Painters, Portrait Soc. Am., Am. Portrait Soc. Republican. Baptist. Avocations: genealogy, piano music. Home: Hill Grove House 8205 West Hollow Rd Naples NY 14512 Studio: Gelder Studios 7 Main St Naples NY 14512 E-mail: GelArt66@aol.com.

GELDER, JOHN WILLIAM, lawyer; b. Buffalo, Aug. 7, 1933; s. Ray Horace and Grace Catherine (Kelly) G.; m. Martha J. Kindleberger, June 12, 1953; William R., Mark S., Cathryn J. Gelder Brooks, Carolyn G. Gelder Bird BBA, U. Mich., 1956, JD with distinction, 1959. Bar: Mich. 1960, D.C. 1981, U.S. Supreme Ct. 1982. Assoc. Miller, Canfield, Paddock and Stone, P.L.C., Detroit, 1959-68, mng. ptnr., 1975-81, 90-93, ptnr., 1968-93, prin., 1994—. Bd. dirs. Tecumseh Products Co., 1989—. Asst. editor Mich. Law Rev., 1958, 59 Trustee, officer Herrick Found., Detroit, 1989—. Mem. State Bar Mich. (coun. mem. bus. law sect. 1984-90), Order of Coif, Bloomfield Hills Country Club. Home: 30845 River Crossing St Bingham Farms MI 48025-4656 Office: Miller Canfield Paddock & Stone PLC 840 W Long Lake Rd Ste 200 Troy MI 48098-6358 E-mail: gelder@millercanfield.com.

GELDON, FRED WOLMAN, lawyer; b. NYC, July 18, 1946; s. Earl R. and Ruth Judith (Abrahams) G.; m. Anne Wolman, June 2, 1974; children: Todd Wolman, Elise Wolman. AB magna cum laude, Princeton U., 1968; MA in Physics, U. Calif., Berkeley, 1970; JD magna cum laude, Harvard U., 1973. Bar: Calif. 1973, D.C. 1974, U.S. Dist. Ct. D.C. 1974, U.S. Ct. Appeals (D.C. cir.) 1974, U.S. Supreme Ct. 1978, U.S. Ct. Claims 1981, Md. 1984, U.S. Ct. Appeals (4th cir.) 1984. Law clk. to hon. William Bryant U.S. Dist. Ct. (D.C. dist.), Washington, 1973-74; from assoc. to ptnr. Leva, Hawes, Symington, Martin & Oppenheimer, Washington, 1974-83; asst. dir. torts br. civil div. U.S. Dept. Justice, Washington, 1983-85; ptnr. Janis, Schuelke & Wechsler, Washington, 1985-87; dep. gen. counsel Electronic Data Sys. Corp., Herndon, Va., 1987-89, gen. counsel govt. sys. group, 1989—, dir. govt. strategic bus. unit support, 1994—; gen. counsel EDS Fed., 1999—. Adj. prof. computer sci. George Mason U.; instr. ESI-Internat. Fed. Publ. Contbr. articles to profl. jours. Pres. Potomac Springs Civic Assn., Rockville Md., 1983-84, 88-89, 99-2002. Mem. ABA (pub. contracts law com., subcom. on ethics), Fed. Cir. Bar Assn. (vice chmn. govt. contracts appeals com. 1986), Sigma Xi, Phi Beta Kappa. Democrat. Jewish. Avocations: music, computers, stamp collecting, scuba diving. Office: Electronic Data Systems 13600 Eds Dr Herndon VA 20171-3225

GELEHRTER, THOMAS DAVID, medical and genetics educator, physician; b. Liberec, Czechoslovakia, Mar. 11, 1936; married 1959; 2 children. BA, Oberlin Coll., 1957; MA, U. Oxford, Eng., 1959; MD, Harvard U., 1963. Intern, then asst. resident in internal medicine Mass. Gen. Hosp., Boston, 1963-65; rsch. assoc. in molecular biology NIAMD NIH, Bethesda, Md., 1965-69; fellow in med. genetics U. Wash., 1969-70; asst. prof. human genetics, internal medicine and pediatrics Sch. Medicine Yale U., 1970-73, assoc. prof., 1973-74, U. Mich., Ann Arbor, 1974-76, prof. internal medicine and human genetics, 1976-87, dir. divsn. med. genetics, 1977-87, chmn. dept. human genetics, prof. human genetics and internal medicine, 1987—. Josiah Macy, Jr. Found. faculty scholar and vis. scientist Imperial Cancer Rsch. Fund Labs., London, 1979-80; vis. fellow Inst. Molecular Medicine; Keeley vis. fellow Wadham Coll., U. Oxford, Wellcome Rsch. Travel grantee, 1995. Mem. editl. bd. Jour. Biol. Chemistry, 1995-2000. Trustee Oberlin Coll., 1970-75; mem. adv. com. NIH Recontinant DNA, 2002—. Rhodes scholar, 1957-59. Fellow AAAS, Am. Coll. Med. Genetics; mem. Am. Soc. Human Genetics (bd. dirs. 1994-96), Am. Soc. Clin. Investigation, Am. Soc. Biochemistry and Molecular Biology, Assn. Am. Physicians. Office: 1241 Catherine St PO Box 0618 Ann Arbor MI 48109-0618 E-mail: tdgum@umich.edu.

GELENBE, SAMI EROL, computer scientist, educator; b. Istanbul, Turkey, Aug. 22, 1945; arrived in France, 1972; s. Ali Yusuf and Maria (Sacchet) G.; m. Deniz Arman, June 8, 1968; 1 child, Pamir. BSEE, Mid. East Tech. U., Turkey, 1966; MSEE, Poly. Inst. Bklyn., 1968, PhD in Elec. Enring., 1969; DSc, U. Paris, 1973; D of Engring. honoris causa (hon.), U. Rome, 1996. Asst. prof. U. Mich., Ann Arbor, 1970-72; prof. U. Liege, Belgium, 1972-79, U. Paris, 1979—. Sci. dir. Inria, Rocquencourt, France, 1973—82; sci. advisor Sec. State, Paris, 1984—86; chaired prof. Duke U., 1993—98; assoc. dean engring. U. Ctrl. Fla., 1998—2003, univ. chaired prof., 2001—03; chair tech. adv. bd. U.S. Army Simulation and Tng. Command, 1999—2003; Dennis Gabor chair Imperial Coll., London, 2003. Author: (books transl. into Japanese and Korean) Analysis and Synthesis of Computer Systems, 1980, 1980, Introduction aux reseaux de files d' attente, 1982, Multiprocessor Performance, 1988, Concurrency Control in Distributed Databases, 1989, Introduction to Networks of Queues, 1999; mem. editl. bd.: Acta Info., 1978—, Performance Evaluation, 1979—, IEEE Transactions on Software Engring, 1979—92, Computer Comms., 1999—, Telecomm Systems, 1993—, Simulation Practice and Theory, 1996—, Computer Jour., Annales des Telecommunications, 2002—, Computational Mgmt. Sci., 2002—, Recherche Opérationnelle, 1994—; contbr. articles to profl. jours. Decorated chevalier and officer Order of Merit France,, chevalier Palmes Academiques, France; recipient Silver Core award, IFIP, 1980, Sci. award, Parlar Found., Turkey, 1994, French Acad. Sci. award, Grand Prix France Telecom, 1996; fellow, Fulbright Found., 1966, Gordon McKay fellow, Harvard U., 1974. Fellow: ACM (Meritorious Svc. award 1989, Meritorious Svc. award of IEEE Computer Soc. 1992), IEEE, IEE; mem.: Eta Kappa Nu, Epsilon Pi Upsilon, Sigma Xi. Avocations: history, bike riding. E-mail: erol@cs.ucf.edu.

GELFAND, ISRAEL MOSEEVICH, mathematician, biologist; b. Ukraine, Russia, Sept. 2, 1913; came to U.S., 1990; m. Tanya Alexeevskaya, 1979; children: Sergey, Vladimir, Tanya. DSc, Moscow State U., 1935; degree (hon.), U. Oxford, Eng., 1973, Harvard U., 1976, U. Paris VI-VII, 1974, U. Uppsala, 1977, Scuola Norm. Sup., Pisa, 1985, Kyoto U., 1989, NYU, 1992, U. Pa., 1990. Prof. math. Rutgers U., New Brunswick, N.J., 1990—. Contbr. more than 600 books and papers in math., biology, and math. edn. Fellow MacArthur Found., 1994; recipient Wolf prize, 1978, Achieve, Wigner medal, 1979, Kyoto prize Inamory Found., 1989. Mem. Nat. Acad. Sci. (life), Acad. Sci., Royal Soc. Sweden, Royal Soc. (Eng.), Japan Acad. Sci., Acad. Sci. (Paris), Royal Irish Acad., Accademia dei Lincei. Achievements include development of theory of commutative normed rings; research in fields of biology and medicine, including development of general principles of organization of control in complex systems; research in C*-algebras, representations theory, integral geometry, inverse problems, nonlinear differential equations, modern theory of hypergeometric functions, and noncommutative algebra.

GELFAND, IVAN, investment advisor; b. Cleve., Mar. 29, 1927; s. Samuel and Sarah (Kruglin) G.; m. Suzanne Frank, Sept. 23, 1956; children: Dennis Scott, Andrew Steven. BS, Miami U., Oxford, Ohio, 1950; postgrad., Case Western Res. U., 1951; grad., Columbia U. Bank Mgmt. Program, 1968; certs., Am. Inst.

Banking, 1952-57. Acct. Cen. Nat. Bank Cleve., 1950-53, v.p., mgr. bank and corp. investments, 1957-75; chief acct. Stars & Stripes newspaper, Darmstadt, Germany, 1953-55; account exec. Merrill, Lynch, Pierce, Fenner & Smith, Inc., Cleve., 1955-57; chmn., CEO Gelfand, Quinn & Assos., Inc., Cleve., 1975-83; v.p., mng. dir. Prudential-Bache Securities, Inc., 1983-85; pres. Lindow, Gelfand and Quinn, Inc., 1976-83; co-editor Gelfand-Quinn/Liquidity Portfolio Mgr. Newsletter, 1978-81, Gelfand-Quinn Analysis/Money Market Techniques, 1981-84; money market columnist Nat. Thrift News, 1976-78, guest money market columnist, 1982-85; pres. Ivan Gelfand & Assocs., Inc., 1985-90; sr. v.p. Prescott, Ball & Turben, Inc., 1986-88; v.p., dir. fixed income investments Roulston & Co., 1988-90; chief exec. officer Gelfand Ptnrs. Asset Mgmt., Cleve., 1990-97; chmn. Maxus Investment Group, Inc., 1997—, Gelfand Maxus Asset Mgmt., 1997—. Instr. investments adult divsn. Cleve. Bd. Edn., 1956-58, Am. Inst. Banking, 1958-68; talk show host Sta. WERE, Cleve., 1993-95, station financial analyst, 1997—; lectr. econs., fin. instn. portfolio mgmt., cash mgmt., 1972—; guest lectr., spkr. nat. and local TV and radio stas.; fin. advisor, commentator ABC/TV Sta. WEWS Channel 5, Cleve., 1996-97. Mem. investment com. United Torch Cleve., 1972-74; study-rev. team capt. Lake Erie Regional Transp. Authority, 1973-77; trustee Mt. Sinai Med. Ctr., Cleve., 1983-92, 93-96, treas., 1986-89, chmn. investment com., 1989-92; trustee Cleve. Coll. Jewish Studies, 1988-93, Ret. Sr. Vol. Program, 1996—, v.p. 1999—, chmn. investment com., 1998—; mem. bond com. Jewish Cmty. Fedn., Cleve., 1979-91, fin. com., 1981-85, trustee, 1986-89, 90-92; mem. Cuyahoga County Rep. Fin. Com., 1978-82, exec. com. Cuyahoga County Rep. Orgn., 1982—; trustee Nat. Multiple Sclerosis Soc., Cleve. Ctr. No. Ohio Reg., 1991-96, Laurelwood Hosp., Cleve., 1994-97. With AUS, 1945-47. Mem. Nat. Assn. Bus. Econs., Cleve. Soc. Security Analysts, Les Politiques, Oakwood Club, Union Club, Cleve. Econ. Club (pres. 1991-92), Thursday Econ. Club, Masons. Home: 2900 Alvord Pl Cleveland OH 44124-4702 Office: Maxos Investment Group Inc Erieview Tower 1301 E 9th St Ste 36 Cleveland OH 44114-1800

GELFAND, JANELLE ANN, music critic; b. Oakland, Calif., Jan. 24, 1951; d. David E. and Ruth J. (Ainsworth) Magnuson; m. Michael J. Gelfand, Mar. 24, 1973; children: Rebecca, Karin. BA, Stanford U., 1973, MusM, U. Cin., 1976, PhD, 1999. Rotating instr. U. Cin. Coll. Conservatory Music, 1991-92; classical music critic The Cin. Enquirer, 1993—. Author: (tchr. guides) Cincinnati Symphony Orchestra Children's Concerts, 1986-89; editor Music Rsch. Forum, 1993-94; contbr. articles to profl. jours. Bd. dirs. Friends of Women's Studies, U. Cin., 1997-2003. Recipient Corbett award for grad. rsch. Ohio Fedn. Music Clubs, 1996; named Wyoming Citizen of Yr., City of Wyoming, Ohio, 1993. Mem. Music Critics Assn. N.Am., Soc. Profl. Journalists, Ohio Newspaper Woman's Assn. Office: The Cincinnati Enquirer Cincinnati OH 45202

GELFAND, JEFFREY ALAN, physician, educator; b. N.Y.C., Sept. 13, 1946; s. Michael R. and Doris (Eichmann) G. BS, U. Pa., 1967; MD, Tufts U., 1971. Bd. cert. internal medicine, 1976, infectious diseases, 1980, allergy and immunology, 1981. Intern Johns Hopkins Hosp., Balt., 1971-72, resident, 1972-73, chief resident, 1976-77; rsch. fellow NIH, Bethesda, Md., 1973-76; asst. prof. Tufts Univ. Sch. Medicine, Boston, 1977-82, assoc. prof., 1982-90, prof., 1991—; vice chmn. dept. medicine New Eng. Med. Ctr., Boston, 1991, acting chmn., 1994-95, chmn. dept. medicine, physician-in-chief, 1995-98, dr. v.p. rsch. & technology, 1998—; dean rsch. Tufts U. Sch. Medicine, Boston, 1998-99; sr. attending physician Mass. Gen. Hosp., Boston, 1999—. Dean rsch. Tufts U. Sch. Medicine, Boston, 1998-99. Contbr. articles to profl. jours. Lt. commdr. USPHS, 1973-76. Office: Mass General Hosp 55 Fruit St Boston MA 02114-2696 E-mail: jgelfand@partners.org

GELFAND, JOEL MITCHELL, dermatologist, researcher; s. Martin and Rita Gelfand; m. Chiara Baxt Gelfand. BS, Tufts U., 1993; MD, Harvard U., Boston, 1998; MSCE, U. Pa., 2003. Diplomate Am. Bd. Dermatology. Med. intern Mt. Sinai Hosp., N.Y.C., 1998—99; resident in dermatology U. Pa., Phila., 1999—2002, instr. dermatology, 2002—03, asst. prof. dermatology, 2003—. Mem.: Soc. Investigative Dermatology (bd. dirs. 2001—03). Office: Hosp U Pa 3600 Spruce St - 2 Maloney Building Philadelphia PA 19104

GELFAND, LAWRENCE EMERSON, historian, educator; b. Cleve., June 20, 1926; s. Maurice Hirsch and Rachel S. (Shapiro) G.; m. Miriam J. Ifland, June 14, 1953; children: Julia M., Daniel B., Ronald S. BA, Western Res. U., 1949, MA, 1950; PhD, U. Wash., 1958. Asst. prof. history U. Hawaii, 1956-58; acting asst. prof. history U. Wash., 1958-59; asst. prof. history U. Wyo., 1959-62, U. Iowa, Iowa City, 1962-64, assoc. prof., 1964-66, prof., 1966-94, chmn. history dept., 1989-92; prof. emeritus, 1994—; vis. prof. U. Oreg., summer 1966, U. Mont., summer 1970, U. Wash., 1974. Mary Ball Washington prof. Am. History, Univ. Coll., Dublin, Ireland, 1987-88. Author: The Inquiry: American Preparations for Peace 1917-1919, 1963; contbg. editor: The Treaty of Versailles: A Reassessment after 75 Years, 1999; editor: A Diplomat Looks Back (Memoirs of Lewis Einstein), 1968; Essays on the History of American Foreign Relations, 1972; Herbert Hoover: The Great War and Its Aftermath 1914-1923, 1979; contbr. chapters to books. Bd. curators State Hist. Soc. Iowa, 1970-72; mem. adv. bd. Nat. Archives for Region VI, 1968-74; chmn. Ctr. for Study Recent History of U.S., Iowa City, 1981-91; mem. rsch. and book prize com. Hoover Presdl. Libr., 1996-99. Served with AUS, 1944-46. Decorated Purple Heart; Am. Council Learned Socs. grantee in Korean studies, summer 1951; Rockefeller Found. grantee, 1964-65. Mem. Am. Hist. Assn., Orgn. Am. Historians, Soc. for Historians of Am. Fgn. Relations (v.p. 1981, pres. 1982) Home: 1437 Oakcrest St Iowa City IA 52246-1622

GELFAND, MICHAEL JOSEPH, radiology educator; b. Detroit, Mar. 4, 1945; s. Jacob and Mildred (Weine) G.; m. Janelle Ann Magnuson, Mar. 24, 1973; children: Rebecca Ann, Karin Janelle. BA, U. Mich., 1966; MD, Stanford U., 1971. Diplomate Am. Bd. Pediatrics, Am. Bd. Nuclear Medicine. Intern Children's Hosp., Cin., 1973-74, resident in pediatrics, 1974-75; resident in nuclear medicine U. Cin., 1975-77, asst. prof. pediatrics, 1978-90, assoc. prof. pediatrics, 1990-95, prof. pediatrics, 1995—, asst. prof. radiology, 1977-83, assoc. prof., 1983-90, prof. radiology, 1990—. Asst. attending radiologist Children's Hosp. Cin., 1978-79, attending radiologist, 1979—. Editor: Effective Use of Computers in Nuclear Medicine (Gelfand M.J., Thomas S.R.), 1998, Pediatric Nuclear Imaging, 1994 (Miller J.H., Gelfand M.J.); contbr. chpts. to books, articles to med. jours. Served with USPHS, 1971-73. Mem. Soc. Nuclear Medicine (treas. 1993-96, fin. chmn. 1996-2000, v.p. 2001-02, pres. 2002--), Soc. Pediatric Radiology, Radiologic Soc. N.Am, Am. Coll. Radiology, Am. Coll. of Nuclear Physicians, Ohio State Radiol. Soc. Office: Childrens Hosp Cincinnati OH 45229-3039

GELFAND, NEAL, oil company executive; b. Bronx, N.Y., Nov. 8, 1944; s. Daniel and Faye (Frank) G.; m. Jane Auerbach, Sept. 11, 1982; children: Alexandra, Laura. BS in Psychology, CCNY, 1965; MS in Indsl. Psychology, Western Mich. U., 1967; PhD in Organizational Psychology, U. Houston, 1972. Ptnr. Hay Assocs., N.Y.C., 1972-80; sr. v.p. human resources Amerada Hess Corp., N.Y.C., 1980—. Mem. APA, N.Y. Acad. Scis. Office: Amerada Hess Corp 1185 Ave Of The Americas New York NY 10036-2601

GELFMAN, PETER TRUSTMAN, lawyer; b. New Rochelle, N.Y., Oct. 3, 1963; s. Robert William and Phyllis (Trustman) G.; m. Marguerite Gabrielle Dreifuss, Sept. 6, 1992; children: Justine Caroline, Max Sokoloff. AB magna cum laude, Harvard Coll., 1986; JD, Yale U., 1989. Bar: N.Y. 1989, D.C. 1990, U.S. Dist. Ct. (so. and ea. dists.) N.Y. 1990, U.S. Ct. Appeals (2d cir.) 1991. Assoc. Cravath, Swaine & Moore, N.Y.C., 1989-91; asst. U.S. Atty. U.S. Dist. Ct. (so. dist.), N.Y.C., 1992-96; sr. atty. Westvaco Corp., N.Y.C., 1996-99; sr. assoc. gen. counsel Sequa Corp., N.Y.C., 1999—. Mem. Town Village Civic Club, Scarsdale, N.Y., 1998—, co-chair edn. com., 1999-2001, 1st v.p., 2001-02, pres., 2002-03; bd. edn. Mt. Pleasant Cottage UFSD, Pleasantville, N.Y., 1999—; bd. ethics Scarsdale (N.Y.) Village, 1999—; mem. legis. adv. com. Scarsdale (N.Y.) Bd. Edn., 2000-02; selection com. Scarsdale Bowl, 2001-03. Mem. ABA, Am. Corp. Counsel Assn., Assn. Bar City of N.Y., Harvard Club N.Y.C. Office: Sequa Corp 200 Park Ave Fl 44 New York NY 10166-0005

GELFMAN, ROBERT WILLIAM, lawyer; b. N.Y.C., Jan. 22, 1932; s. Irving and Lillian (Meltzer) G.; m. Phyllis Trustman, Dec. 18, 1955; children: Lisa Jane (Mrs. Gary S. Matthews), Peter Trustman. BS, U. Pa., 1953; LL.B., Harvard U., 1956. Bar: N.Y. 1956, Mass. 1956. Sr. counsel Paul, Hastings, Janofsky & Walker, LLP, N.Y.C. Dir. Graycor, Inc.; trustee Independence Savs. Bank; adj. prof. Columbia U. Grad. Sch. Bus. Adminstrn.; past chmn. bd. dirs. Arrow Lock Corp.; mem. panel disting. neutrals CPR Inst. for Dispute Resolution. Former trustee, v.p. Jewish Bd. Guardians; past chmn. bd. Hawthorne Cedar Knolls Sch., past pres. bd. edn. Served to capt. USAF, 1957-60. Mem. Am. Law Inst., Am. Arbitration Assn. (mem. maj. real estate dispute panel of arbitrators), ABA, Assn. Bar City N.Y., N.Y. County Lawyers Assn. Clubs: Harvard (N.Y.C.); Metropolis Country (White Plains, N.Y.). Jewish. Home: 18 West Ln Greenwich CT 06831-2632 Office: Paul Hastings Janofsky & Walker LLP 75 E 55th St New York NY 10022-3205

GELFOND, RICHARD L. film company executive; BA in Polit. Sci., SUNY, Stony Brook, 1976; JD, Northwestern U. Law clk. to Hon. Max Rosenn U.S. Ct. Appeals (3d cir.); atty. Drexel Burnham Lambert Inc., mng. dir., 1990; vice-chmn. IMAX Corp., Ont., Canada, 1994—96, co-chmn., co-CEO, 1996—. Bd. trustees Stony Brook Found., chair, 2001—; bd. dirs. Brookhaven Sci Assocs. Office: IMAX Corp 2525 Speakman Dr Mississauga ON Canada L5K 1B1

GELHAUS, ROBERT JOSEPH, lawyer, publisher; b. Missoula, Mont., Oct. 17, 1941; s. Francis Joseph and Bonnie Una (Mundhenk) G. AB magna cum laude, Harvard Coll., 1963; LlB, Stanford U., 1968. Bar: Calif. 1970, U.S. Dist. Ct., U.S. Ct. Appeals 1970. Assoc. firm Howard, Prim, Rice, Nemerovski, Canady & Pollak, San Francisco, 1970-74; sole practice San Francisco, 1974—. Editor in chief Harcourt Brace Jovanovich Legal & Profl. Publs., Inc., 1974-78; pres. Robert J. Gelhaus, A Profl. Corp., 1978—; instr. econs. U. Wash., 1964-65; instr. law Stanford Law Sch., 1968-69; cons. FCC, 1968-69; asst. Calif. Law Revision Commn., 1967-68. Author (with James C. Oldham): Summary of Labor Law, 12th edit., 1972. Mem. Calif. Bar Assn., Harvard Club San Francisco, Order Coif, Omicron Delta Epsilon. Home: 1756 Broadway San Francisco CA 94109-2458

GELINAS, MARC ADRIEN, healthcare administrator; b. Springfield, Mass., Aug. 25, 1947; s. Marcel Joseph and Jeanette G.; m. Mary Lillian Smith, Mar. 3, 1984; 1 child, Alexander Joseph Marcel. BS in Zoology, U. Mass., 1969; Cert. in Phys. Therapy Duke U. Med. Ctr., 1970; MHA, Duke U., 1978; D (hon.) Hamburgerology, McDonald's Hamburger U., Oak Brook, Il., 1988. Acting dir. patient svcs. div. U. Mass. Health Ctr., Amherst, 1975-76, mgr. clin. support svcs., 1976; adminstr. Health Care Systems, Inc., Durham, N.C., 1978; dir. gen. support svcs. Burlington County Meml. Hosp., Mt. Holly, N.J., 1978-80; v.p. facilities and program devel. Nexus Healthcare Corp., Mt. Holly, 1980-82; adminstr. Burlington Geriatric Ctrs., Inc., Mt. Holly, 1982-84; regional v.p. northeast Vol. Hosps. of Am., Inc., Irving, Tex., 1984-86, v.p. bus. devel., 1986-88; pres., owner LSG Bus. Devel. Group, Colleyville, Tex., 1988-93; v.p. strategic devel. Harris Meth. Health System, Ft. Worth, 1993-95; v.p. product mgmt. Harris Meth. Health Plan, Arlington, Tex., 1995-97; pres. Bus. Directions, Inc., Southlake, Tex., 1997—. Mem. Planning and Zoning Commn., Colleyville, 1987-89; com. mem. Woodland Hills Homeowners Assn., Colleyville, 1986-87; scoutmaster Boy Scouts Am., 1995-97, cubmaster pack 575, 1996-97; pres. Parent Tchr. Club, St. Vincent's Sch., 1995-97. 1st lt. U.S. Army, 1970-71; capt. USAR, 1971-76. Fellow Am. Coll. Healthcare Execs.; mem. Am. Hosp. Assn. Democrat. Episcopalian. Avocation: Karate. Office: Business Directions Inc 1710 Egret Ln Southlake TX 76092-5800

GELINAS, ROBERT ALBERT, lawyer; b. Springfield, Mass., May 28, 1930; s. Albert Edward and Alvena Loretta Gelinas; m. Judith Ann Marcure, Jan. 30, 1954; children: Lyn Ann, William, John, Michele. BS, St. Michael's Coll., 1951; LLB, Boston U., 1953. Bar: Mass. 1953, U.S. Dist. Ct. Mass. 1959, U.S. Ct. Appeals (1st cir.) 1965. Ptnr. Bulkley, Richardson and Gelinas LLP, Springfield, Mass., 1957—. Spl. asst. atty. gen., Mass., 1964-70; mem. faculty trial advocacy program Mass. CLE; trustee Holyoke C.C., 1992-2002, chmn. bd. trustees, 1999-2001. Mem. Mass. Rep. Com., 1964-72; chmn. profl. unit United Way, Springfield, 1996; mem. com. Nat. Conf. Chicopee Cmty. Ctr., past pres. Recipient Tree of Life award Jewish Nat. Fund, 1997. Mem. ATLA, Mass. Acad. Trial Attys., Mass. Bar Assn., Hampden County Bar Assn. (exec. com., medico-legal com. 1992—). Roman Catholic. Avocation: outdoor activities. Office: Bulkley Richardson and Gelinas LLP 1500 Main St Ste 2700 Springfield MA 01115-0001 E-mail: rgelinas@bulkley.com.

GELL, MAURICE, engineering executive, educator; b. Bklyn., Dec. 1, 1937; s. Hyman and Bessie (Leventhal) G.; m. Joan Hoffman, May 29, 1960; children: Carol, David. BS, Columbia U., 1961; PhD, Yale U., 1965. Rsch. assoc. Pratt & Whitney, North Haven, Conn., 1966-69, sr. rsch. assoc. Middletown, East Hartford, Conn., 1969-81, asst. mgr. East Hartford, 1981-86, mgr., 1986-93; prof.-in-residence dept. of metallurgy and materials engring. U. Conn., Storrs, 1993—. Mem. vis. com. Carnegie-Mellon U., Pitts., 1986—. Co-editor: Superalloys, 1980, 1984; contbr. articles to profl. jours. NSF postdoctoral fellow; recipient George Mead medal UTC, 1980, 91, Leadership award, 1989. Fellow Am. Soc. Metals Internat. (chmn. awards nominating com. 1990, engring. materials achievement award 1986); mem. The Metall. Soc. Achievements include ten patents in superalloy development; development of single crystal superalloy turbine airfoils and ceramic thermal barrier coatings for gas turbine engines. Home: 27 Franklin Cir Newington CT 06111-5222 Office: U Conn Dept Metallurgy & Materials Engring 99 N Eagleville Rd Storrs Mansfield CT 06268-1712

GELLER, ESTHER (BAILEY GELLER), artist; b. Boston, Oct. 26, 1921; d. Harry and Fannie (Geller) G.; m. Harold Shapero, Sept. 21, 1945; 1 child, Hannah. Diploma, Sch. Boston Mus. Fine Arts, 1943. Tchr. Boston Mus. Sch., 1943, Boris Mirski Sch., 1945-49. Art cons. Leonard Morse Hosp., Natick, Mass. One-woman shows at Boris Mirski Art Gallery, Boston, 1945-46, 49, 52, 61, Addison Gallery Am. Art, Children's Art Centre, Andover, Mass., 1953-55, Mayo Gallery, Provincetown, Mass., 1958, Marion (Mass.) Art Centre, 1966, St. Mark's Sch., Southboro, Mass., 1969, Decenter Gallery, Copenhagen, 1969, Regis Coll., Weston, Mass., 1970, Am. Acad. Gallery, Rome, 1971, Newton (Mass.) Libr., 1973, Newton Art Centre, 1978, Artworks of Wayne, Providence, 1979, Stonehill Coll., Easton, Mass., 1986; 2-person show at The Ctr. for Arts in Natick, 2001; exhibited in group shows at San Francisco Mus., Va. Mus. Art, Chgo. Art Inst., Worcester Art Mus., U. Ill., Smith Coll., Inst. Contemporary Art, DeCordova Mus., USIA traveling show, USIS circulating exhbn., Far East, Boston Mus., Regis Coll., 1984, Danforth Mus. Art, 1995, Boston Ctr. for Arts, 1997, Firehouse Artists Show, Natick, 1998, Univ. Place, Cambridge, 1999, Mass. State House, Boston, 2000, Boston U. Art Gallery, 2002, Visionary Decade Thorne-Sagendorph Art Gallery, Keene, N.H., 2003. Cabot fellow, 1949; Studios Am. Acad. fellow, 1949-50, 70-71, 75; MacDowell Colony-Yaddo fellow, 1945, 67, 69 Mem. Boston Visual Arts Union, Arts Wayland Assn. Home: 9 Russell Cir Natick MA 01760-1223 Studio: 5 Summer St Natick MA 01760-4511

GELLER, HAROLD ARTHUR, earth and space sciences executive, educator; b. Bklyn., June 14, 1954; s. Morris and Minnie (Kaplan) G. BS, SUNY, Albany, 1983; MA, George Mason U., 1992, postgrad. cert. in C.C. Edn., 2002. Rsch. asst. SUNY at Downstate Med., Bklyn., 1972-74; rsch. asst. CUNY at Bklyn. Coll., 1974-75; engring. aide FBI, Washington, 1977-78; lab. supr. ENSCO Inc., Springfield, Va., 1978-80; assoc. engr. Def. Systems Inc., McLean, Va., 1980-83; staff scientist/systems engr. Sci. Applications Internat. Corp., McLean, 1983-87; systems engr. Grumman Aerospace, Reston, Va., 1987-88, Sci. Applications Internat. Corp., McLean, 1988-90; rsch. asst. Naval Rsch. Lab., George Mason U., 1990-91; project mgr. Rsch. and Data Systems Corp., Greenbelt, Md., 1991-92; dep. dir. Washington ops. Consortium Internat. Earth Sci. Info. Network, Washington, 1992-96; instr. physics and astronomy George Mason U., 1993—; sr. sys. engr. Sci. Applications Internat. Corp., McLean, Va., 1996-99. Computer cons., Burke, Va., 1986—87. Commonwealth fellow, 1992-93. Mem.: Astronomical League (media relations officer 2000-01), Asn. Community Col. Educ. (v.p. 2000-01), Potomac Geophys. Soc. (1st v.p. 1994-95, 2000-01, pres. 1995-96, 2001-02), Am. Geophys. Union, Am. Astron. Soc., AAAS, AIAA (chmn. corp. liason com. 1989-90, chmn. pub. affairs com. 1990-91). Democrat. Jewish. Office: George Mason U Dept Physics 4400 University Dr Fairfax VA 22030-4444 E-mail: hgeller@gmu.edu.

GELLER, JANICE GRACE, nurse; b. Auburn, Ga., Feb. 25, 1938; d. Erby Ralph and Jewell Grace (Maughon) Clack; m. Joseph Jerome Geller, Dec. 23, 1973; 1 child, Elizabeth Joanne. Student, LaGrange Coll., 1955-57; BS in Nursing, Emory U., 1960; MS, Rutgers U., 1962. Nat. cert. group psychotherapist; cert. clin. nurse specialist. Psychiat. staff nurse dept. psychiatry Emory U., Atlanta, 1960; nurse educator Ill. State Psychiat. Inst., Chgo., 1961; clin. specialist in mental retardation nursing Northville, Mich., 1962; faculty Coll. Nursing Rutgers U., Newark, 1962-63, faculty Advanced Program in Psychiat. Nursing, 1964-66; faculty Coll. Nursing U. Mich., Ann Arbor, 1963-64; faculty, Teheran (Iran) Coll. for Women, 1967-69; clin. specialist psychiat. nursing Roosevelt Hosp., N.Y.C., 1969-70; faculty, guest lectr. Columbia U., N.Y.C., 1969-70; supr. Dept. Psychiat. Nursing Mt. Sinai Hosp., N.Y.C., 1970-72; pvt. practice psychotherapy N.Y.C., 1972-77, Ridgewood, N.J., 1977-96. Faculty, curriculum coord. in psychiat. nursing William Alanson White Inst. Psychiatry, Psychoanalysis and Psychology, N.Y.C., 1974-84; mem. U.S. del. of Community and Mental Health Nurses to People's Republic of China, 1983. Contbr. articles to profl. jours.; editorial bd. Perspectives in Psychiat. Care, 1971-74, 78-84; author: (with Anita Marie Werner) Instruments for Study of Nurse-Patient Interaction, 1964. Mem. Bergen County Rep. Com., 1989. Recipient 10th Anniversary award Outstanding Clin. Specialist in psychiat.-mental health nursing in N.J., Soc. Cert. Clin. Specialists, 1982; Fed. Govt. grantee as career tchr. in psychiat. nursing, Rutgers U., 1962-63; cert. psychiat. nurse and clin. specialist, N.J., N.Y. Mem. AAAS, ANA (various certs.), N.C. Nurses Assn., Soc. Cert. Clin. Specialists in Psychiat. Nursing (chmn.), Coun. Specialists in Psychiat./Mental Health Nursing, Am. Group Psychotherapy Assn. (cert. group psychotherapist), Am. Assn. Mental Deficiency, World Fedn. Mental Health, Sigma Theta Tau. Address: 307 Chatterson Dr Raleigh NC 27615-3137 Fax: (919) 518-0495.

GELLER, JEFFREY LAWRENCE, financier; b. N.Y.C., Sept. 23, 1953; s. Jerome Charles Geller and Harriet (Rogers) Blum; m. Karina Musheli, Nov. 22, 1990. BA, Columbia U., 1975, MBA, 1979. Sr. fin. analyst W.R. Grace & Co., N.Y.C., 1979-83, asst. to the pres., 1983; v.p. Bank of Am., N.Y.C., 1984-86; exec. v.p. Union Holdings, Inc., N.Y.C., 1986-91; pres., CEO Geller Ptnrs., Inc., N.Y.C., 1991—, also bd. dirs.; pres. Std. Capital Holdings L.L.C., N.Y.C., 1996—; vice chmn., bd. dirs. RS Holdings Group. Inc., 1999—; mng. dir. Fortrend Internat LLC, 2001—. V.p. Idle Wild Foods, Inc., Liberal, Kans., 1986-91, ZG Holding Corp., N.Y.C., 1986-91, also bd. dirs.; exec. v.p. Acorn Internat. Ltd., N.Y.C., 1993-94, also bd. dirs.; bd. dirs. Deran Holding Co., Inc., Soprigest Corp. Fin. Ltd. Co-author: President's Private Sector Survey on Cost Control, 1983. Mem. com. Am. Cancer Soc., N.Y.C., 1982-86, Friends of Lenox Hosp., N.Y.C., 1985—, Children's Village, Dobbs Ferry, N.Y., 1985-87, Save Venice, Inc., N.Y.C., 1987—. Mem. Columbia Club, Rockefeller Club, Le Club. Avocations: tennis, riding. Office: Geller Partners Inc 750 Lexington Ave 30th Fl New York NY 10022

GELLER, KENNETH ALLEN, otolaryngologist; b. Bklyn., Feb. 5, 1948; MD, U. So. Calif., 1972. Cert. in otolaryngology. Intern L.A. County-U. So. Calif. Med. Ctr., L.A., 1972-73; resident in gen. surgery Wadsworth VA Hosp., L.A., 1973-75; resident in otolaryngology UCLA Health Scis. Ctr., L.A., 1975-78; active Childrens Hosp., L.A., 1978—; courtesy Glendale Meml. Hosp., 1983—, Tarzana Hosp., 1984—, Huntington Meml. Hosp., 1993—. Assoc. clin. prof. U. So. Calif. Mem. ACS, Am. Acad. Otolaryngology-Head and Neck Surgery, Am. Acad. Pediatrics, Am. Bronco-Esophagological Assn., Am. Soc. Pediat. Otolaryngology. Office: Childrens Hosp Divsn Otolaryngology # 58 4650 Sunset Blvd Los Angeles CA 90027-6062 E-mail: kgeller@chla.usc.edu.

GELLER, KENNETH STEVEN, lawyer; b. N.Y.C., Sept. 22, 1947; s. Edward and Sylvia R. (Tannenbaum) G.; m. Judith B. Ratner, Sept. 9, 1990; children: Eric Jonathan, Lisa Beth. BA magna cum laude, CCNY, 1968; JD magna cum laude, Harvard U., 1971. Bar: N.Y. 1972, U.S. Dist. Ct. (so. and ea. dists.) N.Y. 1972, U.S. Ct. Appeals (2d cir.) 1972, U.S. Ct. Appeals (D.C. cir.) 1974, U.S. Supreme Ct. 1975, U.S. Ct. Appeals (10th cir.) 1976, D.C. 1986, U.S. Ct. Appeals (6th cir.) 1987, U.S. Ct. Appeals (4th cir.) 1987, U.S. Ct. Appeals (9th cir.) 1988, U.S. Ct. Appeals (5th and 11th cirs.) 1990, U.S. Dist. Ct. D.C. 1991, U.S. Ct. Appeals (3rd and 7th cirs.) 1991, U.S. Ct. Appeals (Armed Forces) 1995, U.S. Ct. Appeals (8th cir.) 1996, U.S. Ct. Appeals (fed. cir.) 1999. Law clk. U.S. Ct. Appeals (2d cir.), 1971-72; assoc. Nickerson, Kramer, Lowenstein, Nessen & Kamin, N.Y.C., 1972-73; asst. spl. prosecutor Watergate Spl. Prosecution Force, Washington, 1973-75; asst. to solicitor gen. Dept. Justice, Washington, 1975-79, dep. solicitor gen., 1979-86; ptnr. Mayer, Brown, Rowe & Maw LLP (formerly Mayer, Brown & Platt), Washington, 1986—, mng. ptnr., 1995—. Mem. adv. bd. State and Local Legal Ctrs., 1986-92; mem. adv. com. on rules U.S. Ct. Appeals for Armed Forces, 1994—; mem. adv. com. on procedures Ct. Appeals D.C. Cir., 2000—. Co-author: (Stern, Gressman, Shapiro & Geller) Supreme Court Practice, 8th edit., 2002; contbg. author: Business and Commercial Litigation in Federal Courts, 1998; contbr. articles to profl. jours. Mem. vis. com. Harvard U. Law Sch.; trustee, chmn. publs. com. Supreme Ct. Hist. Soc. Recipient Younger Fed. Lawyer award FBA, 1981, Presdl. Disting. Exec. award. Office: Mayer Brown Rowe & Maw LLP 1909 K St NW Washington DC 20006-1152 E-mail: kgeller@mayerbrown.com.

GELLER, MARGARET JOAN, astrophysicist, educator; b. Ithaca, N.Y., Dec. 8, 1947; d. Seymour and Sarah Geller. AB, U. Calif., Bekeley, 1970; MA, Princeton U., 1972, PhD, 1975; DSc (hon.), Conn. Coll., 1995, Gustavus Adolphus Coll., 1997, U. Mass., Dartmouth, 2000. Rsch. assoc. Harvard Coll. Obs., Cambridge, Mass., 1978-80; asst. prof. Harvard U., Cambridge, 1980-83; astrophysicist Smithsonian Astrophys. Obs., Cambridge, 1983—. Goodspeed-Richardo lectr. U. Pa., 1992; Brickwedde disting. lectr. JHU, 1993; Hogg lectr. Royal Astro. Soc. Can., 1993; Bethe lectr. Cornell U., 1996; Hilldale lectr. U. Wis., 1999. Contbr. articles to profl. jours.; mem. editl. bd. Sci., 1991—94. Named Libr. Lion, N.Y. Pub. Libr., 1997; recipient Newcomb-Cleve. prize, 1989—90, Klopsteg award, Am. Assn. Physics Tchrs., 1996, ADION medal, 2002; fellow, MacArthur Found., 1990—95. Fellow: AAAS, APS; mem.: NAS (coun. mem. 2000—), Assoc. Univs. Rsch. in Astronomy (dir.-at-large), Am. Astron Soc. (councillor), Am. Acad. Art and Scis. (coun. mem.), Internat. Astron Union, Phi Beta Kappa (senator 1998—99). Office: Smithsonian Astrophys Obs 60 Garden St Cambridge MA 02138-1516

GELLER, MARVIN ALAN, meteorology educator, researcher; b. Boston, Mar. 19, 1943; s. James and Saide (Schlager) G.; m. Lynda Louise Grafinger, June 16, 1968; children: Stephanie, Steven. BS in Applied Math., MIT, 1964, PhD in Meteorology, 1969. From asst. prof. to prof. U. Ill., Champaign-Urbana, 1969-77; prof. U. Miami, Fla., 1977-80; rsch. scientist NASA Goddard Space Flight Ctr., Greenbelt, Md., 1980-84, chief Lab. for Atmospheres, 1984-89; prof., head Inst. for Terrestrial and Planetary Atmospheres SUNY, Stony Brook, 1989-2000, dean, dir. Marine Scis. Rsch. Ctr., 1998—2002, prof. atmospheric scis., 2002—. Contbr. articles to profl. jours. Fellow Am. Meteorol. Soc.; mem. Sci. Com. Solar-Terrestrial Physics (pres. 2000--), Am. Geophys. Union (pres. atmospheric scis. sect. 2000-02), Nat. Assn. U.S. Nat. Acads. Democrat. Jewish. Avocations: golf, music. Home: 145 Oakwood Rd Port Jefferson NY 11777-1423 Office: SUNY-Stony Brook Msrc Stony Brook NY 11794-5000

GELLER, NORMAN HARVEY, music arranger, conductor; b. Pitts., Dec. 30, 1934; s. Jack and Rose (Block) G. Student, John Carroll U., 1953-55, Cleve. Conservatory Music, 1952-53. Music dir., pianist RCA Records, N.Y.C. and Los Angeles; arranger, condr., orchestrator NBC-TV, N.Y.C.; music dir. The Great Radio City Spectacular, Las Vegas, 1995-2000. Music dir., arranger numerous performers including Lena Horne, 1990-93, Vic Damone 1977-96, Diahann Carroll, 1985-96, Ed Ames, 1967-73, Ed McMahon, 1976-77, John Gary, 1968-69, Phil Ford and Mimi Hines, 1972-77, Joe Williams, 1973, Ethel Merman, 1964, Peter Nero, 1965-66, Paul Lynde, 1976-77, Monty Hall, 1976, Ray Bolger, 1962-63, Kay Armen, 1963-68, Allen and Rossi, Dick Haymes, 1971-72, Rip Taylor, 1972, Susan Anton, 1995—; music dir. Playboy Clubs, 1961-62, Thunderbird Hotel, 1973, Sands Hotel, 1981-82, (TV series) The New Original Amateur Hour, 1992-93; condr. natl. co. "I Do, I Do," 1969-70, Gene Kelly's Salute to Broadway nat. tour, 1976. Mem. Nat. Acad. Rec. Arts and Scis. Clubs: Friars (N.Y.C.). E-mail: normgeller@earthlink.net.

GELLER, ROBERT JAMES, advertising agency executive; b. N.Y.C., May 5, 1937; s. Jerome and Pearl (Klein) G.; m. Lois Dee Fromkin, June 9, 1968; children: Richard Evan, Stephen Laurence. BS, CCNY, 1958. Account exec. Furman, Feiner & Co., N.Y.C., 1958-62; media supr. Interpublic Group of Cos., N.Y.C., 1962-64; asst. media dir. Foote, Cone & Belding, N.Y.C., 1964-69; pres.

Adforce, Inc., N.Y.C., 1970-92, Robert J. Geller & Assocs., Inc., N.Y.C., 1993—; pres., CEO Reel Am., Inc., N.Y.C., 2000—; mng. dir. Charter Media, 2002—. Contbr. numerous articles to profl. jours. Pres. Robert J. and Lois F. Geller Found. Mem. Assn. Nat. Advertisers (mem. mgmt. policy com. 1980-92, corp. membership com. 1990-92), Am. Advt. Fedn. (bd. dirs. 1988—, mem. corp. membership com. 1989—, plans rev. com. 1990—, asst. sec. 1992—), Advt. Club N.Y.C. Republican. Home: 155 E 76th St New York NY 10021-2810 also: Parsonage Ln Sagaponack NY 11962 Office: Robert J Geller & Assocs Inc 708 Third Ave 29th Fl New York NY 10017 E-mail: rjgeller@mindspring.com.

GELLER, RONALD GENE, biomedical researcher, consultant; b. Peoria, Ill., Jan. 15, 1943; s. Harold H. and Rose G.; m. Lois S. Geller, Sept. 5, 1971; children: Andrea, Steven, Lauren. BS in Zoology, U. Wis., 1964, PhD in Physiology, 1969. Spl. research fellow Nat. Heart Inst. NIH, Bethesda, Md., 1969-71, sr. staff fellow Nat. Heart, Lung and Blood Inst., 1971-72, grants assoc., 1972-73, asst. chief, chief hypertension and kidney diseases br. Nat. Heart, Lung and Blood Inst., 1973-78, assoc. dir. extramural and collaborative programs Nat. Eye Inst., 1978-86, acting dir. divsn. program analysis Office Program Planning and Eval., 1986, dir. divsn. program analysis, 1987-89, dir. divsn. extramural affairs Nat. Heart, Lung and Blood Inst., 1989-99; dir. Office of Extramural Programs, Office of Dir., NIH, 1999—2002; sr. assoc. Health Rsch. Assocs., Gaithersburg, Md., 2002—. Instr. Found. for Advanced Edn. in Sci.; USPHS trainee, 1966-67 Contbr. articles to profl. jours. Wis. Heart Assn. fellow, 1967-69 Mem. Am. Heart Assn. (med. adv. bd. coun. for high blood pressure rsch. 1972), Am. Physiol. Soc. Home and Office: 14960 Dufief Dr North Potomac MD 20878-2593

GELLER, SANDRA R. continuing legal education administrator; b. N.Y.C., Feb. 1, 1949; BA magna cum laude, Dowling Coll., Oakdale, N.Y., 1971; JD, Hofstra U., 1975. Bar: N.Y. 1976, U.S. Tax Ct. 1976, U.S. Dist. Ct. (so. and ea. dist.) N.Y. 1976. Assoc. dir. Practising Law Inst., N.Y.C. Mem. ABA (Am. Law Inst./Am. Law Network subcom. 1990—), Assn. Bar of City of N.Y., N.Y. County Lawyers Assn., N.Y. State Bar Assn. Office: Practising Law Inst 810 7th Ave Fl 26 New York NY 10019-5818

GELLER, SEYMOUR, retired educator, researcher; b. N.Y.C., Mar. 28, 1921; m. Sarah Levine, Aug. 23, 1942 (dec.); children: Margaret J., Susan C. BA, Cornell U., 1941, PhD, 1949. Rsch. chemist E.I. du Pont de Nemours Co., Waynesboro, Va., 1950-52; mem. tech. staff Bell Telephone Labs., Murray Hill, N.J., 1952-64; group leader Rockwell Internat. Sci. Ctr., Thousand Oaks, Calif., 1964-71; prof. dept. elec. and computer engring. U. Colo., Boulder, 1971-90, prof. emeritus, 1990—, faculty fellow, 1977-78, 85-86, Croft Rsch. prof. Coll. Engring. and Applied Sci., fall 1980, rsch. lectr., 1985. Lectr. Enrico Fermi Internat. Sch. Physics, Varenna on Lake Como, Italy, 1977. Contbr. over 200 papers to profl. publs.; two papers on garnets Citation Classics; holder 7 patents on ferrimagnetic garnets. 1st lt. U.S. Army, 1943-46, PTO. Recipient Creativity award NSF, 1983; duPont postdoctoral fellow Cornell U., 1949-50. Fellow IEEE, Am. Phys. Soc., Mineral. Soc. Am.; mem. Sigma Xi, Phi Kappa Phi. Jewish. Achievements include substantial number of discoveries in work on ferrimagnetic garnets; discovery and prediction of superconductivity in non-transition metal compounds with sodium chloride and related type structure; determination of crystal structures of substantial number double-salt halogenide solid electrolytes and structural features which account for conductivity in highly conducting ionic solids. Avocation: Am. Indian artifacts. E-mail: dseygel.worldnet.att.net.

GELLER, STEPHEN ARTHUR, pathologist, educator; b. Bklyn., Apr. 26, 1939; s. Sam John and Alice (Podber) G.; m. Kate Eleanor DeJong, June 24, 1962; children: David Phillip, Jennifer Lee. BA, Bklyn. Coll., 1959; MD, Howard U., 1964. Diplomate Am. Bd. Pathology, Nat. Bd. Med. Examiners. Intern Lenox Hill Hosp., N.Y.C., 1964-65; resident in pathology Mt. Sinai Hosp., N.Y.C., 1965-69; chief lab. Naval Hosp., Beaufort, S.C., 1969-71; asst. prof. pathology Mt. Sinai Med. Ctr., N.Y.C., 1971-75, assoc. prof., 1975-78, prof., 1978-84; chmn. dept. pathology Cedars-Sinai Med. Ctr., L.A., 1984—; prof. pathology UCLA, 1984—. Co-author: Histopathology, 1989, Biopsy Interpretation of the Liver, 2003; contbr. articles to profl. jours. Recipient Excellence in Teaching award CUNY, 1974. Fellow Coll. Am. Pathologists, Am. Soc. Clin. Pathologists; mem. Am. Assn. Study of Liver Diseases, Hans Popper Hepatopathology Soc., Calif. Soc. Pathologists (sec. 1989-91, v.p. 1991-93, pres. 1994-96), L.A. Soc. Pathologists (v.p. 1989-91, pres. 1992), N.Y. Pathol. Soc., Alpha Omega Alpha. Democrat. Jewish. Avocations: music, photography, writing fiction. Office: Cedars Sinai Med Ctr 8700 Beverly Blvd Los Angeles CA 90048-1865 E mail: geller@cshs.org.

GELLER, WILLIAM ALAN, criminal justice researcher, police and public safety consultant; b. Bklyn., June 4, 1950; s. Maurice and Shirley F.E. (Scherker) G.; m. Julia Marie Arment, Oct. 1, 1978. BA, SUNY, Buffalo, 1972; JD, U. Chgo., 1975. Bar: Ill. 1975, U.S. Dist. Ct. (no. dist.) Ill. 1975. Law clk. to Hon. Walter V. Schaefer Ill. Supreme Ct., Chgo., 1975-76; exec. dir. Chgo. Law Enforcement Study Group, 1976-81; project dir. Am. Bar Found., Chgo., 1981-86; spl. counsel Chgo. Park Dist., 1986-88; assoc. dir. Police Exec. Rsch. Forum, 1987-97; dir. Geller & Assocs. Consulting, Wilmette, Ill., 1997—. Mem. Pres. Clinton's Transition Team (U.S. Dept. Justice search team mem.), 1992-93; mem. staff Office Presdl. Pers., Washington, 1993; commr. Wilmette Fire and Police Commn., 1985-88; cons. Local Initiatives Support Corp., 1995—, Nat. Inst. Justice, U.S. Dept. Justice, Washington, 1980—, Office of Cmty. Oriented Policing Svcs., U.S. Dept. Justice, 1994-2002, dep. atty. gen., 1993-94, civil rights divsn., 2001, fellow, 1999-2001, N.Y.C. Police Dept., 1985-88, 93, FBI, Washington, 1986—, Police Found., 1986-92, N.Y.C. Met. Transp. Authority, 1991, Boston Police Dept., 2002-, Des Moines Police Dept., 2002, Detroit Police Dept., 2003-, Albuquerque Police Dept., 1997, Charlotte-Mecklenburg Police Dept., 1998, Seattle Police Dept., 1998, Fed. Signal Corp., 1990, Chgo. Police Bd., 1991-95, St. Louis Police Dept., 1991-97, Office of the Mayor, Washington, 1992-93, St. Louis, 1997-2001, Boulware & Assocs., 1992—, U.S. Info. Agy., 1999, Burkhalter & Assocs., 1992-95, Wash. Post, 1998, Harvard U. Office Gen. Counsel, 1995, Ill. Criminal Justice Info. Authority, 1993; mem. rsch. adv. com. Chgo. Police Dept., 1983-86; mem. Cook County Sheriff's adv. com. on internal affairs, 1986; mem. exec. com. Chgo. Ethics Project. Author: Split-Second Decisions: Shootings Of and By Chicago Police, 1981, Deadly Force: What We Know..A Practitioner's Desk Reference on Police-Involved Shootings in the United States, 1991, Police Violence: Understanding and Controlling Police Abuse of Force, 1996, And Justice For All, 1995, Managing Police Innovation, 1995; also many articles to profl. jours., mags., and newspapers; editor: Police Leadership in America: Crisis and Opportunity, 1985, Local Government Police Management, 1991, 2003; script cons. (TV show) L.A. Law, 1991; mem. expert adv. panel RAND Corp., 2002-03. Co-chmn. Citizens for Safety Vests, Chgo., 1982-83; mem. adv. bd. March of Dimes Met. Chgo., 1983; bd. dirs. John Howard Assn., Chgo., 1978—99, Bus. and Profl. People for Pub. Interest, 1988—, Travel Light Theatre, Chgo., 1980-82; mem. adv. bd. Yale U. Nat. Ctr. Children Exposed to Violence, 2000—; mem. priority grants com. United Way Met. Chgo., 1990-92; mem. task force on criminal justice studies, Clark-Atlanta U., 1991-95; mgr. Harvard Exec. Session on Drugs and Cmty. Policing, Cambridge, Mass., 1990-92. Recipient Richard J. Daley Police medal of honor, City of Chgo., 1983, commendation N.Y.C. Police Commr., 1986, commendation St. Louis Police Chief, 1997; grantee Nat. Inst. Justice, 1980, 84, 88, 90, 91, Chgo. Bar Found., 1980, Chgo. Cmty. Trust, 1976-80, 84, 85, Charles Stewart Mott Found., 1990, Edna McConnell Clark Found., 1998. Mem. ABA (com. on stds. for criminal justice 1983-86, prison and jail problems com. 1985-86), Internat. Assn. Chiefs Police, Police Exec. Rsch. Forum, NOBLE, am. Soc. Criminology, Acad. Criminal Justice Scis. Home and Office: 2116 Thornwood Ave Wilmette IL 60091-1452 E-mail: wageller@aol.com.

GELLERT, EDWARD BRADFORD, advertising agency executive; b. Meadowbrook, Pa., Sept. 8, 1924; s. N. Henry and Edna Louise (Smith) G.; m. Audrey Marie Bethilde Freese, Dec. 18, 1948; children: Audrey M.F. Gellert Taylor, E. Bradford III, Christina M.H.E. BA, Yale U., 1945W, PBK, 1946-48; student Law, NYU, 1950-51, studies in advt. effectiveness, 1949-50; French, Berlitz Sch., 1967; student, N.Y. Inst. Fin., N.Y.C., 1972; student creative writing course, U. Conn., 1960, real estate broker's lic., 1971. From trainee to new product mgr. Vick Chem. Co., N.Y.C., 1948-55; account exec. Compton Advt., N.Y.C., 1956-60; v.p., acct supr. Young and Rubican Adv. Agy., N.Y.C., 1960-67; v.p. mktg., dir. Church & Dwight, 1967—69; pres. Gellert & Jackson Acquisitons and Mergers, N.Y.C., 1969-74; sales and mktg. dir. The Gellert Co., Boise, Idaho, 1975-79; pres., owner CIPRA Advt., Boise, 1979—. Bd. dirs. Healthwise, Boise, Idaho, 1993—. Author, illustrator, publisher: You're Not Too Old to Win at Tennis, 1984 (1988 selected by U.S. Dept. Info. 1 of 200 Sports Books for exhibit in 100 internat. cities). 2d lt. Army Air Corps, 1943-45. Recipient Harvard Club award, 1941; Bronze award Am. Legion, 1939. Mem. Boise C. of C., Nat. Fedn. Ind. Bus., Nat. Eagle Scout Assn. (life), Screen Actors Guild (life), Am. Fedn. TV and Radio Artists (life), U.S. Tennis Assn. (life), Yale Club N.Y.C., Boise Racquet and Swim Club. Republican. Episcopalian. Avocations: tennis, creative writing, art, yard work. Home and Office: Cipra Advt 314 E Curling Dr Boise ID 83702-1629

GELLERT, EDWARD BRADFORD, III, b. Norwalk, Conn., Aug. 19, 1954; s. Edward Bradford and Audrey Marie (Freese) G.; m. Juliet Pendleton Kostritsky, Dec. 21, 1980. BA, Yale U., 1976; MArch, Columbia U., 1979; cert. Real Estate Inst., NYU, 1983; cert., Nat. Coun. Archtl. Registration Bds. Registered arch., N.Y. Rsch. asst. Regional Plan Assn., N.Y.C., 1977-78, arch. Urban Devel. Authority, Colombo, Sri Lanka, 1979-80, Mullen Palandrani, N.Y.C., 1980 81, Cossutta & Assocs., N.Y.C., 1981-83; project arch. Smotrich & Platt, N.Y.C., 1983-84, Teare Herman Gibans, Inc., Cleve., 1984-85, Dalton, Dalton, Newport/URS, Cleve., 1986-87, Richard L. Bowen Arch., 1987-90, Michael Benjamin Arch., Cleve., 1990-2000, The Austin Co., 2000—02, URS Corp., 2002—; sr. project arch. URS, 2002—. Prin. works include Keuffner residence, Darien, Conn., 1982-83, Bronzeville Crescent Townhouse, Chgo., Dayton Hope Urban Planning Study, Dayton, Shorbey Club, Bratenahl, Ohio, Ohio Wesleyan Campus Ctr., Delaware, Ohio, Renaissance Village Townhouses, Cleve., Carl B. Stokes Social Svcs. Mall, Cleve., Spaces Gallery, Cleve., Costello Residence, Chesterton, Ind., Salomon-Weiss Residence, Erie, Pa.; contbg. author: Cousteau Almanac of the Environment, 1981. S.I. Advance; The Buffalo News N.Y.; Shaw High Sch. Ea. Clevland. Bd. dirs. Christ Episcopal Ch., Shaker Heights, 1996-99, Interfaith Hospitality Network, 1999—; mem. rev. com. Shaker Sq. Hist. Dist., 1993-2000; mem. Shaker Heights Archtl. Bd. Rev., 1993—; spkr. Hope conf. Ohio HUD, Columbus, 1993-95. Columbia U. Grad. Sch. Arch. and Planning William Kinne Fellows fellow, 1979; recipient 2d prize for fiction Atlantic Monthly, 1972. Democrat. Episcopalian. Home: 3330 Maynard Rd Cleveland OH 44122-3436 Office: URS Corp 800 W St Clair Ave Cleveland OH 44113

GELLERT, GEORGE GEZA, food importing company executive; b. N.Y.C., Apr. 15, 1938; s. Imre and Martha (Tessler) G.; m. Barbara Rubin, July 21, 1963; children— Andrew, Amy, Thomas. BS, Cornell U., 1960, MBA, 1962, LL.B., 1963. Bar: N.Y. State bar 1963. Atty. SEC, Washington, 1963-64; v.p., exec. v.p., pres. Atalanta Corp., N.Y.C., 1966—, chmn. bd., 1978—. Chmn. U.S.-Rumanian Econ. Council; bd. dirs. Am. Importers Meat Products Group. Trustee Cornell U., 1995-99, mem. Cornell U. Council. Served to 1st lt. Office Staff Judge AUS, 1964-66. Decorated Army Commendation medal; recipient Outstanding Alumni award Cornell U., 2000, Ellis Island Nat. Medal of Honor, 2001, Ernst & Young Master Entrepreneur of the Yr. award, 2001. Mem. Am. Importers Assn. (dir., exec. com. meat product group), Am. Assn. Exporters and Importers (bd. dirs.), Met. Pres.'s Orgn. Home: PO Box 213 New Vernon NJ 07976 Office: Atalanta Corp Atalanta Plz Elizabeth NJ 07206 E-mail: ggellert@atalanta1.com.

GELLERT, JAY M. health and medical products executive; BA, Stanford U. Sr. v.p., COO Calif. Healthcare System, 1985-88; pres., CEO Bay Pacific Health Corp., 1988-91; dir. Shattuck Hammond Ptnrs. Inc.; pres., COO Health Systems Internat. Inc., Health Net, Inc. (formerly Found. Health Systems Inc.), 1998, pres., CEO, 1999—. Office: Health Net Inc 21650 Oxnard St Woodland Hills CA 91367-4901

GELLERT, MICHAEL ERWIN, investment banker; b. Prague, Czechoslovakia, June 15, 1931; s. Oswald Rudolf and Grete (Petschek) G.; m. Mary Crombie, Jan. 11, 1969; children: John Matthew, Catherine Ann. BA, Harvard U., 1953; MBA, U. Pa., 1955. Exec. dir. Drexel Burnham Lambert and predecessor co., NYC, 1958-89; gen. ptnr. Windcrest Ptnr., NYC, 1967—. Bd. dirs. Devon Energy Corp., Oklahoma City, High Speed Access Corp., Denver, Humana Inc., Louisville, Six Flags, Inc., Oklahoma City, Seacor Smit, NYC, Smith Barney World Funds, NY, Travelers Series Fund, Inc., NYC. Chmn. bd. trustees Caramoor Ctr. for Mus. and Arts, Katonah, NY, Carnegie Instn. Washington; vice chmn. bd. trustees New Sch. U., NYC. With U.S. Army, 1955-57. Fellow: AAAS; mem.: Harvard Club (NYC), Am. Acad. Arts and Sci. (trustee), The Field Club (Greenwich), Penn Club (NYC), Burning Tree Country Club (Greenwich, Conn.). Office: Windcrest Ptnrs 122 E 42nd St New York NY 10168-0002

GELLES, RICHARD JAMES, sociology and psychology educator, academic administrator; b. Newton, Mass., July 7, 1946; s. Sidney S. and Clara (Goldberg) G.; m. Judy S. Isacoff, July 4, 1971; children: Jason Charles, David Philip. AB, Bates Coll., 1968; MA, U. Rochester, 1971; PhD, U. N.H., 1973. Asst. prof. sociology U. R.I., Kingston, 1973-76, assoc. prof., 1976-81, prof., 1982-98, dean Coll. Arts and Scis., 1984-90; Joanne and Raymond Welsh chair child welfare/family violence Sch. of Social Work, U. Pa., 1998—, dean, 2002—. Cons. Children's Hosp. Med. Ctr., Boston, 1973—; lectr. Harvard Med. Sch., Boston, 1979-88, 95—; rsch. dir. Louis Harris and Assocs., N.Y.C., 1981-82, cons., 1982-86; cons. Sage Pubs., Newbury Park, Calif., 1986—. Author: (books) The Violent Home, 1974, Family Violence, 1979; co-author: Behind Closed Doors: Violence in the American Family, 1980, Intimate Violence, 1988, The Book of David, 1996. Mem. Am. Sociol. Assn. (chair family sect. 1985-86, recipient Disting. Contributions to Teaching award Sect. on Undergrad. Edn. 1979), Nat. Council Family Relations (chair rsch. and theory sect. 1989-91, v.p. publs. 1996-98). Jewish. Avocations: tennis, golf. Office: Sch of Social Work U Pa 3701 Locust Walk Philadelphia PA 19104-6214 Business E-Mail: gelles@ssw.upenn.edu.

GELLHORN, ALFRED, physician, educator; b. St. Louis, June 4, 1913; s. George and Edna (Fischel) Gellhorn; m. Olga Frederick, Aug. 4, 1939; children: Martha, Anne, Christina, Maria, Edna. Student, Amherst Coll., 1930—32, DSc (hon.), 1969; MD, Washington U., St. Louis, 1937; DSc (hon.), CCNY, 1979, SUNY, 1984, Albany Med. Coll., 1986, U. Pa., 1992. Diplomate Am. Bd. Internal Medicine. Gen. surg. tng. Barnes Hosp., St. Louis, 1937—39; gynecology trainee Passavant Meml. Hosp., Chgo., 1939—40; fellow Carnegie Instn. of Washington, Balt., 1940—43; instr., later asst. prof. physiology Coll. Physicians and Surgeons, Columbia U., N.Y.C., 1943—45, asst., then assoc. prof. pharmacology, 1945—48, assoc. prof. clin. cancer research dept. medicine, 1948—52, assoc. prof. medicine, 1952—58, prof. medicine, 1958—68; prof. medicine and pharmacology, dean Sch. Medicine, also dir. Med. Ctr. U. Pa., Phila., 1968—73; dir. Ctr. Biomed. Edn., City Coll., v.p. for health affairs CUNY, 1974—79, emeritus, 1979—; dir. med. affairs N.Y. State Dept. Health, Albany, 1983—96; rsch. dir., cons. diamond fund fell. prgm. Aaron Diamond Post Doctoral Rsch. Fell. Prgm., 1996—. Cons. Commonwealth Fund, NY, 1979—80, Aaron Diamond Found., 1987—; vis. prof. Harvard Sch. Pub. Health, 1980—83; physician Francis Delafield Hosp., N.Y.C., 1949—52, chief med. svc., 1952—68; vis. prof. medicine Albert Einstein Med. Sch.; dir. Inst. Cancer Rsch., Columbia; bd. regents Nat. Libr. Medicine. Mem.: ACP, Am. Soc. Biol. Chemistry, Inst. Medicine, Am. Soc. Pharm. and Exptl. Therapeutics, Am. Assn. Cancer Rsch. (pres. 1962—63), N.Y. County Med. Soc., Assn. Am. Physicians, Soc. for Clin. Investigation, Coll. Physicians Phila. Office: 5 Penn Plaza Rm 301 New York NY 10001 E-mail: axg08@health.state.ny.us.

GELLHORN, ERNEST ALBERT EUGENE, lawyer; b. Oak Park, Ill., Mar. 30, 1935; s. Ernst and Hilde Betty (Obermeier) G.; m. Jaquelin Ann Silker, Feb. 1, 1958; children: Thomas Ernest, Ann Lois. BA cum laude, U. Minn., 1956, LLB magna cum laude, 1962. Bar: Ohio 1962, Va. 1975, Ariz. 1976, D.C. 1986, Calif. 1990. Assoc. Jones, Day, Reavis & Pogue, Cleve., Washington, L.A., 1962-66; prof. law Duke U. Law Sch., 1966-70, U. Va. Law Sch., 1970-75; dean Coll. Law, Ariz. State U., Tempe, 1975-78, U. Wash. Law Sch., Seattle, 1978-79; T. Munford Boyd prof. U. Va. Law Sch., Charlottesville, 1979-82; dean, Galen J. Roush prof. Case Western Res. U. Sch. Law, Cleve., 1982-86; ptnr. Jones, Day, Reavis & Pogue, L.A., Washington, 1986-94; George Mason U. Found. prof. law, 1995—. Sr. counsel Commn. CIA Activities Within U.S., 1975. Co-author: Antitrust Law and Economics, 4th edit., 1994, Administrative Law and Process, 4th edit., 1997, The Administrative Process, 4th edit., 1993. Lt. USNR, 1956-59. Mem. ABA, Ariz. Bar Assn., Va. Bar Assn., Ohio Bar Assn., D.C. Bar Assn., Calif. Bar Assn., Phi Beta Kappa, Order of Coif. Home: 2907 Normanstone Ln NW Washington DC 20008-2725 E-mail: gellhorn@pipeline.com.

GELLIN, GERALD ALAN, dermatologist; b. Bklyn., May 24, 1934; m. Lucille E. Gellin. AB, U. Pa., 1954; MD, NYU, 1958. Diplomate Am. Bd. Dermatology. Chief sect. dermatology VA Hosp., Bklyn., 1964-67; clin. prof. U. Calif. Med. Ctr., San Francisco, 1969—. Chief dermatology divsn. VA Hosp., Bklyn., 1963-67, San Francisco Gen. Hosp., 1969-73, Calif. Pacific Med. Ctr., 1986—. Contbr. articles to profl. jours. With USPHS, 1967-69. Fellow ACP. Office: 3838 California St San Francisco CA 94118-1522

GELLINEAU, ANTONIO CORTES, system software specialist; b. Mt. Vernon, N.Y., May 20, 1952; BSEE, MIT, 1974, MSEE and Computer Sci., 1976; MA in Computer Sci., U. Tex., Austin, 1986. Tech. staff Bell Telephone Labs., Raritan River, N.J., 1974-76, TRW, Redondo Beach, Calif., 1976-80; sr. scientific programmer, analyst Magnavox Govt. and Indsl. Electronics Co., Ft. Wayne, Ind., 1980-82; project engr. Schlumberger Oil Well Svcs., Austin, 1982-86; staff specialist Data Gen., Westboro, Mass., 1987-89; sr. devel. engr. missile systems divsn. Raytheon, Tewksbury, Mass., 1990-97, Huntsville, Ala., 1998-2000; prin. engr. Thales Aviation Engring., Silver Spring, Md., 2000—03; prin. software engr. Raytheon Co., Portsmouth, RI, 2003—. Tchr. U. Mass., 1990-98, Fitchburg State Coll., 1990-98. Avocation: chess. Office: Thales Aviation Engring 22605 Gateway Center Dr Clarksburg MD 20871-2001

GELLINEK, CHRISTIAN JOHANN, German educator; b. Potsdam, Prussia, Germany, May 11, 1930; came to U.S., 1961; s. Christian M. and Margaretha C. (Lorenzen) G.; m. Janis Little (div.); m. Josepha E. Schellekens, Sept. 5, 1975; children: Else M., Saskia K., Torsten C.M., Jens P.C. BA, U. Toronto, Ont., 1959, M.Edn., 1961; MA, Yale U., 1963, PhD, 1964; dr.phil.habil., Basel (Switzerland) U., 1974. Head of classics Pickering Coll., Newmarket, Ont., Can., 1959-61; jr. faculty Yale U., New Haven, 1961-71; prof. German U. Fla., Gainesville, 1971-87; rsch. assoc. Inst. Comparative City Rsch., Muenster, Germany, 1988-94, Inst. Social Econs., St. John's, Nfld., Can., 1994-95, Nicolas Brown Inst., Providence, 1995-96, Inst. German History of Law, Muenster, 1996-98; guest prof. U. South Fla., Tampa, 1998-99; guest prof. German Brigham Young U., Provo, Utah, 1998—. Author 20 books including: Literature, History, Ethnology: Hugo Grotius, 1983, Stadtkultur, 1990, Philipp Scheidemann Cologne, 1994, Those Damned Dutch, 1996, Northwest Germany in Northeast America, 1997, Christus in Amerika, 1999; co-author (with H.W. Kelling) Avenues Towards Mormonism, 2001. Fulbright grantee, 1980-81, 85, 91. Mem. MLA. Calvinist. Avocations: walking, swimming. E-mail: gellinek@yahoo.com.

GELLIS, WILLARD LEON, poet, English educator; b. N.Y.C., N.Y.C., June 9, 1936; s. Harold and Edna Alperin G.; m. Jill Brody Gellis, Jun 15, 1965 (div. 1970); 1 child, Jenny B.; m. Shirley Routten, Aug. 21, 1981. AB in Lit. Art, Hofstra Coll., 1958; MA in Lit., U. Md., 1961; PhD in Lit., NYU, 1972. Cert. English tchr., N.Y. Univ. prof. Lockhaven (Pa.) Coll., 1965-66; univ. prof. Calumet campus Purdue U., Hammond, Ind., 1966-70; English tchr. spl. edn. N.Y.C. Pub. Schs., 1977-86; vis. tchr. SUNY, Farmingdale, 1988-89. Host Ideas and Images Pub. Access TV, Hamptons, The Abiding Voice. Author 30 books including Tramping Dirtyside, 2000, Fire Rat, 1998 (Best Fiction 1996); (CD) No Grease on the Gump (Spoken Word), 1996, Under Algol, 2001, My Back Against the Wall, 2003. Poet Sch. of Cultural Arts. With USAR, 1954-58.

GELLMAN, GLORIA GAE SEEBURGER SCHICK, marketing professional; b. La Grange, Ill., Oct. 5, 1947; d. Robert Fred and Gloria Virginia (McQuiston) Seeburger; m. Peter Slate Schick, Sept. 25, 1978 (dec. 1980); 2 children; m. Irwin Frederick, Gellman, Sept. 9, 1989; 3 children. BA magna cum laude, Purdue U., 1969; student, Lee Strasberg Actors Studio; postgrad., UCLA, U. Calif.-Irvine. Mem. mktg. staff Seemac, Inc. (formerly R.F. Seeburger Co.); v.p. V.I.P. Properties, Inc., Newport Beach, Calif., pres. Glamglo Prodns. Host radio show Orange County Art Bytes, Sneak Previews from the Orange County Performing Arts Ctr.; prodr. corp. videos; co-prodr. PBS TV series Bus. Beyond Borders; exec. prodr. PBS documentary Treasures of Tibet. Profl. actress, singer, artist, writer; TV and radio talk show hostess, Indpls.; performer radio and TV comml.s.; feature writer arts and entertainment column H mag., The Grand Taw mag.; co-prodr. Fullerton: Then and Now (PBS); exec. prodr. (video) Paris Air Show, 2003, Treasure of Tibet, PBS. Mem. Orange County Philharm. Soc., bd. dirs. women's com.; mem. Orange County Master Chorale, Orange County Performing Arts Ctr., v.p., treas. Crescendo chpt. OCPAC Ctr. Stars, 1st v.p. membership; bd. dirs. Newport Harbor (Calif.) Art Mus., v.p. membership, mem. acquisition coun.; bd. dirs., mem. founders soc. Opera Pacific, mem. exec. com. bd. dirs.; patron Big Bros./Big Sisters Starlight Found.; mem. Visionaries Newport Harbor Mus., Designing Women of Art Inst. Soc. Calif.; past pres. Opera Pacific Guild Alliance; past pres. Spyglass Hill Philharm. Com.; v.p. Pacific Symphony Orch. League, chair endowment sect., spl. events chair; bd. dirs. Pacific Symphony Orch., v.p. cmty. affairs, vice chair vol. devel.; mem. UCI Found. of U. Calif. Irvine Bd., mem. devel. com., honors com., pub. affairs and advocacy com.; mem. social scis. dean's adv. coun. U. Calif., Irvine; chmn. adv. coun. Cold War Studies Ctr., Chapman U.; chmn. numerous small and large fundraisers; mem. com. Red Cross; mem. Fashionables of Chapman U.; bd. dirs. Sta. KOCE PBS TV; founder UCI Humanities Assocs. Recipient Lauds and Laurels award U. Calif., Irvine, 1994, Gellman Courtyard Sculpture honoring contbn. to Sch. of Humanities, U. Calif., Irvine, Most Outstanding Vol. award Pacific Symphony, 2002, Most Outstanding Vol. award Pacific Symphony Orch. League, 2002. Mem. AAUW, AFTRA, SAG, Internat. Platform Assn., Actors Equity, U. Calif.-Irvine Chancellor's Club, U. Calif.-Irvine Humanities Assocs. (founder, pres., bd. dirs.), Mensa, Orange County Mental Health Assn., Seneca Network, Balboa Bay Club, U. Club, Club 39, Islanders, Covergirls, Pacific Symphony Super Club (founder), Pacific Symphony "Symphony 100" (pres., founder), Alpha Lambda Delta, Delta Rho Kappa. Republican. Home: PO Box 1993 Newport Beach CA 92659 0993

GELLMAN, ISAIAH, environmental consultant; b. Akron, Ohio, Feb. 19, 1928; s. Meyer and Pearl (Milker) F.; m. Lola Malkis, Dec. 27, 1947; children: Paula, Judith. B in Chem. Engring., CCNY, 1947; MS, Rutgers U., 1950, PhD, 1952. Rsch. assoc. Rutgers U., 1948-52; process engr. Abbott Labs., 1952-56; with Nat. Coun. Paper Industry for Air and Stream Improvement Inc., N.Y.C., 1956—, tech. dir., 1969-77, exec. v.p., 1977-87, pres., 1987-95; environ. cons. Gellman Assocs., N.Y.C., 1995—. Lectr. Johns Hopkins U., 1961-65 NIH fellow, 1948-52 Fellow TAPPI; mem. Sigma Xi.

GELL-MANN, MURRAY, theoretical physicist, educator; b. N.Y.C., Sept. 15, 1929; s. Arthur and Pauline (Reichstein) Gell-Mann; m. J. Margaret Dow, Apr. 19, 1955 (dec. 1981); children: Elizabeth, Nicholas; m. Marcia Southwick, June 20, 1992; 1 stepchild, Nicholas Levis. BS, Yale U., 1948; PhD, Mass. Inst. Tech., 1951; ScD (hon.), Yale U., 1959, U. Chgo., 1967, U. Ill., 1968, Wesleyan U., 1968, U. Turin, Italy, 1969, U. Utah, 1970, Columbia U., 1977, Cambridge U., 1980; D (hon.), Oxford (Eng.) U., 1992, So. Ill. U., 1993, U. Fla., 1994, So. Meth. U., 1999. Mem. Inst. for Advanced Study, 1951; instr. U. Chgo., 1952—53, asst. prof., 1953—54, assoc. prof., 1954, Calif. Inst. Tech., Pasadena, 1955—56, prof., 1956—67, R.A. Millikan prof. physics, 1967—93, R.A. Millikan prof. emeritus, 1993—; disting. fellow Santa Fe Inst., 1993—, co-chmn. sci. bd., 1985-2000; mem. Inst. for Advanced Study, 1955, 1967—68. Vis. prof. MIT, spring, 1963, CERN, Geneva, 1971—72, Geneva, 1979—80, U. N.Mex., 1995—; vis. assoc. prof. Columbia U., 1954; overseas fellow Churchill Coll., 1966; mem. Pres.'s Sci. Adv. Com., 1969—72, Pres.'s Com. of Advisors on Sci. and Tech., 1994—2001; mem. sci. and grants com. Leakey Found., 1977—80; chmn. bd. trustees Aspen Ctr. for Physics, 1973—79; founding trustee Santa Fe Inst., 1982, chmn. bd. trustees, 1982—85, co-chmn. sci. bd., 1993—2000; prof., disting. fellow, 1993—; cons. Inst. Def. Analysis, Arlington, Va., 1961—70, Rand Corp., Santa Monica, Calif., 1956; mem. physics panel NASA, 1964, Coun. Fgn. Rels., 1975—, Los Alamos (N.Mex.) Sci. Lab., 1956—, Lab. fellow, 1982—; mem. adv. bd. Network Physics, 1999—. Author (with Y. Ne'eman): Eightfold Way, 1964; author: The Quark and the Jaguar, 1994. Citizen regent Smithsonian Instn., 1974—88; trustee Wildlife Conservation Soc., 1994—; bd. dirs. J.D. and C.T. MacArthur Found., 1979—2002, Calif. Nature Conservancy, 1984—93, Aero Vironment, Inc., 1971—; chmn Lovelace Insts., 1993—95. Named to UN Environ. Program Roll of Honor for

Environ. Achievement, 1988; recipient Dannie Heineman prize, Am. Phys. Soc., 1959, E. O. Lawrence Meml. award, AEC, 1966, Franklin medal, 1967, Carty medal, NAS, 1968, Rsch. Corp. award, 1969, Nobel prize in Physics, 1969, Erice prize, 1990; fellow NSF postdoctoral, vis. prof., Coll. de France and U. Paris, 1959—60. Fellow: Am. Phys. Soc.; mem.: AAAS, NAS, Russian Acad. Scis. (fgn.), Indian Acad. Scis. (fgn.), Pakistan Acad. Scis. (fgn.), Royal Soc. London (fgn.), French Phys. Soc. (hon.), Conservation Internat. (sci. adv. com. 1993), Am. Philos. Soc., Coun. on Fgn. Rels., Am. Acad. Arts and Scis. (v.p. 1970—76, chmn. We. ctr. 1970—76), Athenaeum (Pasadena), Explorers Club (N.Y.C.), Century Assn., Cosmos Club (Washington). Address: Santa Fe Institute 1399 Hyde Park Rd Santa Fe NM 87501-8943

GELM, RICHARD JOSEPH, political scientist, educator; b. Mpls., Dec. 26, 1962; s. Richard Henry and June Catherine Gelm. BA in Polit. Sci., U. Calif., San Diego, 1984; MA in Polit. Sci., U. Calif., Davis, 1986, PhD in Polit. Sci., 1991. Instr. San Jose (Calif.) State U., 1990-91; asst. prof. U. La Verne, Calif., 1991-96, assoc. prof., 1996—2002, chair dept. history & polit. sci., 1997—, prof., 2002—. Author: Review of Politics, 1993, Politics & Religious Authority, 1994. Campaign cons., So. Calif., 1996, 2000. Mem. AAUP (pres. chpt. 1997-99), Polit. Sci. Assn., Am. Assn. Higher Edn., Western Polit. Sci. Assn. Democrat. Roman Catholic. Avocations: travel, baseball, photography. Office: U La Verne 1950 3d St La Verne CA 91750 E-mail: gelmr@ulv.edu.

GELMAN, BARRY, pediatrician, educator; b. Flushing, N.Y., July 24, 1963; s. Seymour and Beverly Vivian Gelman; m. Donna Ruth Herskowitz, June 2, 1991. BS, U. Miami, 1984; MD, U. Fla., 1988. Diplomate Nat. Bd. Med. Examiners, Am. Bd. Pediatrics, Pediatric Critical Care Medicine; lic., Fla., N.Y. Resident in pediatrics North Shore U. Hosp., Cornell U. Med. Coll., Manhasset, N.Y., 1988-91; fellow in pediatric critical care medicine U. Miami/Jackson Meml. Med. Ctr., Miami, Fla., 1991-94; asst. prof. clin. pediatrics U. Miami Sch. Medicine, 1994-2001, assoc. prof. clin. pediatrics, 2001—. Dir. pediat. residency tng. Jackson Meml. Hosp., Miami, Fla., 2002—. Fellow Am. Acad. Pediatrics; mem. Soc. Critical Care Medicine, Phi Beta Kappa (Delta chpt.). Office: Univ Miami Sch Medicine PO Box 016960 (R-131) Miami FL 33101 E-mail: b.gelman@miami.edu.

GELMAN, LARRY, actor, film director; b. Bklyn., Nov. 3, 1930; s. Frank and Dorothy Gelman. Student, CCNY, 1954-55. Actor: (TV series) The Odd Couple, Bob Newhart Show, Maude, Mary Tyler Moore Show, Eight is Enough, Kojak, Raid on Entebbe, Triangle Factory Fire, Barney Miller, Simon and Simon, Night Court, Amazing Stories, Hill St. Blues, Remington Steele, Our House, Cagney and Lacey, Scarecrow and Mrs. King, Grand Slam, Jake and the Fat Man, In the Heat of the Night, Doogie Howser, M.D., On Our Own, Kirk, Weird Science, Home Improvement, Touched by an Angel; (films) Funny Girl, Super Dad, O'Hara's Wife, Dreamscape, Double Exposure, Mr. Saturday Night, A Different Approach (Motion Picture Acad. award nominee, 1979); (plays) Einstein: The Man Behind the Genius. Pres. Nat. Jewish Theater So. Calif. With USMC, 1951—53. Mem.: AFTRA, SAG, Acad. TV Arts and Scis. (nominee award for outstanding single performance by a supporting actor in comedy or drama series 1977—78), Acad. Motion Picture Arts and Scis., Actors Equity Assn., Am. Guild Variety Artists. Jewish.

GELMAN, LEONID MOISEEVICH, scientist, vibroacoustician, educator; b. Kiev, Ukraine, Apr. 15, 1949; s. Moisey Morduh-Leybovich and Mariya Grigorevna (Dubinskaya) G.; 1 child, Anna. *Mother Mariya, physician, born November 6, 1922 (deceased 1985), MS with honors, Kiev Medical Institute, was head of hospital cardio laboratory, physician of high category. Father Moisey, engineer, born January 20, 1915 (deceased 1994), MS with honors, Leningrad Civil Aviation Institute, was chief engineer of building company. Daughter Anna, economist, financier, born Kiev, Ukraine, June 23, 1975, BS with honors, Business Administration, 1996, Tech. U. Ukraine, MA Economics, Finance, 1998, Binghamton U., NY. Business analyst MKI Frustum, White Plains, NY. AIESEC (International Student Organization in Business, Economics) alumnus. Recipient Muskie Graduate Fellowship USIA.* MS with honors, Nat. Tech. U. Ukraine, 1972; PhD, Acoustical Inst., Moscow, 1987, DSc, 1993. Academician Russian Acad. Natural Scis., Ukrainian Acad. Scis. of Nat. Progress, Acad. Scis. of Applied Radioelectronics of Belarus, Russia, Ukraine; prof., sr. rsch. officer Cranfield U., England; with STI -Tech, Rochester, 2000, Model Shop, Cin., 2000, Argonne Nat. Lab., Argonne, 2000. Vis. lectr. Cleve. U., 1996, Boston U., 1997, Wayne U., Detroit, 1997, U. Mich., Ann Arbor, 1997, CUNY, 1998, U. Le Mans, France, 1998, Zhitomir U. Engring. Tech., 1998, Tel-Aviv U., 1999; vis. prof. Technion, Israel, 1999, U. S.C., 2000, 01, Enitechnologie, Italy, 2001-02; mem. coun. conferment DSc, PhD, Nat. Tech. U. Ukraine, prin. investigator, chief designer grants contracts, mil. oriented rsch. developer, 1972-92. *Original significant scientific contribution in vibroacoustical recognition: diagnostics of complex systems (turbomachinary, reciprocating machinery, gearboxes); underwater recognition, in lead roles for distinguished Universities. Internationally recognized awards for excellence from US, UK, Italy and Israel. World-renowned leader in vibroacoustical machinery diagnostics. Full University Professor since 1996. Member of journal editorial boards and scientific committees of international conferences, and author of numerous papers in refereed journals; reviewer for journals with distinguished reputations. Accounts of his activity is included in "500 Great Minds of the Early 21st century" BWW, USA, 2002.* Contbr. more than 100 articles to profl. jours.; holder 17 patents. Recipient award U.S. Internat. Sci. Found., awards U.S. Civilian R&D Found., award U.S. MacArthur Found., award Israel Lady Davis Fellowship Trust, U.K. Dept. Trade and Industry; Italian Landau-Volta fellowship, U. S.C. fellowship; grantee U.S. NRC, U.S. Nat. Acad. Scis., U.K. Royal Soc. Mem. Acoustical Soc. Am. (award), Acoustical Soc. Japan, Russian Acoustical Soc., Ukrainian Soc. Nondestructive Testing, London Inst. EE, Internat. Inst. Acoustics Vibration, N.Y. Acad. Scis., U.K. Inst. Diagnostic Engr., Brit. Inst. NDT. Avocations: modern literature, sports, dancing. Office: Cranfield U Sch of Enging AMAC Cranfield Bedfordshire MK 43 0AL England Home: Flat 10 14 St Andrews Rd Bedford MK40 2LJ England Fax: 44 (0) 1234 750195. E-mail: gelmanlm@yahoo.com., L.Gelman@cranfield.ac.uk.

GELMAN, SANDOR M. lawyer; b. Pitts., Aug. 26, 1938; s. Harold Milton and Elsie (Markus) G.; m. Judith Ilene Meyers, Feb. 16, 1969; children: Jascha David, Gabriel Elliot. BBA, U. Mich., 1960, JD, 1963. Bar: Mich. 1964, U.S. Dist. Ct. (ea. dist.) Mich. 1964. Assoc., Bellinson & Doctoroff, Detroit, 1963-64, Goldman & Grabow, Detroit, 1964-65; legal advisor, prosecutor Oakland County, Pontiac, Mich., 1965-68; ptnr. Gelman & Baumkel, Troy, Mich., 1968— . Pres. Oakland Family Services, Pontiac, Mich., 1980-82. Mem. ABA, Am. Trial Lawyers Assn., State Bar Mich. (mem. family law council 1981-87, chmn. advt., certification and specialization com. 1980-86), Oakland County Bar Assn. (pres. 1984-85, bd. dirs. 1975-85), Detroit Bar Assn. Democrat. Jewish. Lodges: Kiwanis, B'nai B'rith. Home: 6745 Woodside Trl West Bloomfield MI 48322-3914

GELMAN, STEPHEN, writer, editor; b. N.Y.C., Mar. 15, 1934; s. Abraham and Sydelle Gelman; m. Rita Golden, Dec. 11, 1960 (div. July 1986); children: Mitchell, Jan; m. Deborah Watson Mason, Oct. 7, 1995. BA, Bklyn. Coll., 1955; MS, Columbia U., 1957. Mng. editor Sport Mag., N.Y.C., 1958—66; assoc. editor, sr. editor, article editor Life Mag., N.Y.C., 1966—72; founding editor New Times Mag., N.Y.C., 1973—74; cons. editor various mags. including New West Mag., TV Guide, Viking-Penguin Books, Time Inc., L.A., 1974—86; v.p. Book of the Mo. Club, N.Y.C., 1986—88; cons. editor Time Inc., N.Y.C., 1988—99; sr. exec. editor George Mag., N.Y.C., 1999—2001; cons. editor Reader's Digest, Pleasantville, NY, 2001—. Author: 18 books; contbr. Office: S Gelman Enterprises Inc 64 E 86th St New York NY 10028

GELMANN, EDWARD PAUL, oncologist, educator; b. N.Y.C., May 31, 1950; m. Connie Sommers; children: Lauren R., Elyssa R., Emily B, Jonathan S. BS magna cum laude, Yale U., 1972; MD, Stanford U., 1976. Diplomate Nat. Bd. Med. Examiners, Am. Bd. Internal Medicine. Intern then resident U. Chgo. Hosps., 1976-78; med. staf fellow Nat. Cancer Inst., Bethesda, Md., 1979-83, sr. investigator, 1983-88; adj. assoc. prof. microbiology Georgetown U., Washington, 1986-88, prof. medicine and cell biology, 1988—, chief med. oncology divsn., 1988-93, chief hematology/oncology divsn., 1993-95, vice chair Dept. Medicine, 1997-98. Dir. urologic oncology program Lombardi Cancer Rsch. Ctr., 1990-93, dir. prostate cancer program, 1993—. Mem. editorial bd. jour. Blood, 1985-90; ad hoc reviewer jours.; contbr. 150 articles to profl. jours. Sr. surgeon USPHS, 1978-88. Grantee Nat. Cancer Inst., 1990—. Fellow ACP; mem. AAAS, Am. Soc. Clin. Investigation, Am. Assn. Cancer Rsch., Am. Soc. Clin. Oncology. Office: Georgetown U 3800 Reservoir Rd NW Washington DC 20007-2196

GELOOO, NADIM AHMAD, cardiologist; b. Karashi, Pakistan, July 17, 1966; arrived in U.S., 1974; s. Hashim and Noor Bano Geloo; m. Bina Feroz Ali, May 1, 1994 (div. May 1994). BS in Biology magna cum laude, Va. Commonwealth U., 1989; MD, Med. Coll. Va., 1994. Diplomate Am. Bd. Internal Medicine, Am. Coll. Cardiovascular Disease. Asst. prof. East Carolina U., Greenville, NC, 2001—02; interventional cardiologist Prince William Cardiology Assocs., Manassas, Va., 2002—. Contbr. articles to profl. jours. Mem.: Soc. Cardiac Angiography and Intervention, Am. Coll. Cardiology, Alpha Kappa Lambda. Islam. Achievements include demonstration of safety of edenosine pharmacologic stress testing in patients with end stage renal disease and in patients with resting bradycardia. Avocation: skiing. Office: Prince William Cardiology 8596-B Sudley Rd Manassas VA 20110 E-mail: ngeloo@aol.com.

GELOS, R. GASTON, economist; b. Montevideo, Uruguay, Jan. 8, 1969; arrived in U.S., 1994; s. Rafael Pedro Gelos, Sigrid Martha Gelos; m. Elisabeth Stefanie Melczer; children: Nicholas, Felicia. Diplom-Volkswirt, U. Bonn, Germany, 1994; PhD, Yale U., 1998. Staff member Dep. Fgn. Min. H. Schaefer, Bonn, Germany, 1989—94; economist Internat. Monetary Fund, Washington, 1998—. Contbr. articles to profl. jours. Mem. exec. bd. Youth of Free Dem. Party, Bonn, Germany, 1990—91; mem. fed. econ. com. Free Dem. Party, Germany, 1992—94. Scholar, Nat. German Scholarship Found., 1989—94, 1996—98. Mem.: Deutsche Gesellschaft fuer Auswaertige Politik, European Econ. Assn., Am. Econ. Assn. Office: Internat Monetary Fund 700 19th St NW Washington DC 20431

GELOSO-BARONE, ROSALIA A. lawyer; b. Rye, N.Y., Apr. 21, 1962; d. Vincent M. and Patricia (Checca) G. BA in Journalism with honors, Boston Coll., 1984; JD cum laude, Pace U., 1988. Bar: N.Y. 1988, Conn. 1988, U.S. Dist. Ct. (so. and ea. dists.) N.Y. 1988. Project asst. Fin. Acctg. Standards Bd., Stamford, Conn., 1984-85; legal asst. Merrill Lynch Realty, Inc., Stamford, 1985-86, U.S. Attorney's Office, N.Y.C., 1987-88; legal asst./staff atty. Westchester County Attorney's Office, White Plains, N.Y., 1988-92; sr. staff atty. U.S. Dist. Ct. (so. dist.) N.Y., 1995-98; law lectr. bus. dept and legal assistant program Norwalk (Conn.) C.C., 1998—. Adj. prof. bus. law Norwalk C.C., Berkeley Coll., Katherine Gibbs Sch., U. Conn., 1992-95. Alumni admissions counselor Boston Coll., Fairfield County, Conn., 1984—. Recipient Merit Scholarship Pace Law Sch., 1986-88. Mem. ABA, N.Y. State Bar Assn., Conn. Bar Assn.

GELPI, ALBERT JOSEPH, English educator, literary critic; b. New Orleans, July 19, 1931; s. Albert Joseph and Alice Marie (Delaup) G.; m. Barbara Charlesworth, June 14, 1965; children: Christopher Francis Cecil, Adrienne Catherine Ardelle. AB, Loyola U., New Orleans, 1951; MA, Tulane U., 1956; PhD, Harvard U., 1962. Asst. prof. Harvard U., 1962-68; assoc. prof. Stanford U., 1968-74, prof. Am. lit., 1974-99, Wm. Robertson Coe prof. Am. lit., 1978-99, Coe prof. emeritus, 1999—, chmn. Am. studies program, 1980-83, 94-97, assoc. dean grad. study and research, 1980-85, chmn. English dept., 1985-88. Author: Emily Dickinson: The Mind of the Poet, 1965, The Tenth Muse: The Psyche of the American Poet, 1975, A Coherent Splendor: The American Poetic Renaissance 1910-1950, 1987; editor: The Poet in America: 1650 to the Present, 1974, (with Barbara Charlesworth Gelpi) Adrienne Rich's Poetry, 1975, Wallace Stevens: The Poetics of Modernism, 1985, (with Barbara Charlesworth Gelpi) Adrienne Rich's Poetry and Prose, 1993, Denise Levertov: Selected Criticism, 1993, The Blood of the Poet: Selected Poems of William Everson, 1994; editor Cambridge Studies in American Literature and Culture, 1981-91, Living in Time: The Poetry of C. Day Lewis, 1998, The Wild God of the World: An Anthology of Robinson Jeffers, 2003, Wild God of Eros: A William Everson Reader, 2003, (with Robert J. Bertholf) The Letters of Robert Duncan and Denise Levertov, 2003. Served with U.S. Army, 1951-53. Guggenheim fellow, 1977-78 Mem. MLA, Am. Lit. Assn. Democrat. Roman Catholic. Home: 870 Tolman Dr Palo Alto CA 94305-1026 Office: Stanford U Dept English Stanford CA 94305

GELPI, ARMAND PHILIPPE, internist; b. Denver, Aug. 27, 1925; BS, U. Calif., Berkeley, 1946; MD, U. Calif., San Francisco, 1949. Diplomate Am. Bd. Internal Medicine. Intern Santa Clara Valley Med. Ctr., San Jose, Calif., 1949-50; asst. resident U. Calif. Med. Ctr., San Francisco, 1952-53, San Francisco Gen. Hosp., 1953-54; chief resident Santa Clara Valley Med. Ctr., 1954-55; staff physician VA Med. Ctr., Fresno, Calif., 1955-58, fellow hematology/oncology San Francisco, 1957-58; pvt. practice San Leandro, Calif., 1958-59; chief medicine Arabian Am. Oil Co., Dhahran, Saudi Arabia, 1959-68; trainee, immunology Stanford U., Palo Alto, Calif., 1967-68; med. dir. Charles E. Drew Health Ctr., East Palo Alto, Calif., 1968-70; assoc. med. dir. student health Stanford U., 1970-78, 79-81; physician specialist Stanford U. Med. Ctr., 1978-79, 81-83; staff physician NASA/Ames Rsch. Ctr., Mountain View, Calif., 1983-97; prof. emeritus Stanford U., 1987—. Attending physician Chaboya Clinic, San Jose, 1983-86, Dept. Veterans Affairs, Palo Alto, 1986-94. Vol. Sonoma Valley Sch. Dist., 1994—. Lt. med. corps USN, 1950-52. E-mail: apgelpi@vom.com.

GELPI, DONALD LOUIS, theology studies educator; b. New Orleans, May 30, 1934; s. Albert Joseph Gelpi and Alice Marie Delaup. MA in Philosophy cum laude, degree in Philosophy, St. Louis U., 1958, degree in Theology, 1965; PhD, Fordham U., 1970. Ordained priest Roman Cath. Ch., 1964. Asst. prof. philosophy Loyola U., New Orleans, 1969—73; co-founder, co-dir. Inst. Spirituality and Worship Jesuit Sch. Theology, Berkeley, Calif., 1973—77, prof. hist. and systematic theology, 1973—99, prof. emeritus, 1999—. Bellarmine lectr. Xavier U., Cin., 1979, lectr. theology Beckman Ch., 2001; Luce fellow Grad. Theol. Union, Berkeley, 1993—94; co-founder, participant John Courtney Murray Group, Berkeley, 1979—. Author: Varieties of Transcendental Experience, 2000, The Gracing of Human Experience, 2001, The Firstborn of Many: A Christology for Converting Christians, 2001. Active Bread for the World, Berkeley, 1988—. Recipient Luce Found. fellowship, 1993—94. Mem.: Cath. Theol. Soc. Am., Jesuit Philos. Assn., Nature Conservancy. Democrat. Roman Catholic. Avocations: backpacking, hiking, oil pastels, ukelele. Home and Office: Jesuit Sch Theology at Berkeley 1735 Le Roy Ave Berkeley CA 94709-1003 Fax: 510-841-8536.

GELTMAN, EDWARD ALAN, lawyer; b. Newark, Apr. 14, 1946; s. Donald and Muriel G.; m. Elizabeth Ann Glass, Jan. 2, 1989; children: Andrew, Jeffrey, Rachel. BA with honors, Franklin & Marshall Coll., 1968; JD with honors, George Washington U., 1971. Bar: D.C. 1971, U.S. Ct. Appeals (D.C. cir.) 1971, U.S. Supreme Ct. 1980. Trial atty. FTC, Washington, 1971-73; assoc., then ptnr. Nicholson & Carter, Washington, 1973-79; ptnr. Squire, Sanders & Dempsey, Washington, 1979—. Contbr. articles to profl. jours. Mem. ABA (antitrust sect.), Order of Coif. Office: Squire Sanders & Dempsey 1201 Pennsylvania Ave NW Washington DC 20004-2491

GELTMAN, EDWARD MARK, cardiologist, educator; b. Oceanport, N.J., Feb. 22, 1946; s. Irving Robert and Goldie (Bazoll) G.; m. Nancy Milner, Aug. 25, 1968; 1 child, Joshua Aaron. BS, MIT, 1967; MD, NYU, 1971. Diplomate Am. Bd. Internal Medicine, Am. Bd. Cardiovasc. Disease. Intern Bellevue Hosp., N.Y.C., 1971-72, resident in internal medicine, 1972-74; fellow in clin. cardiology Washington U., Barnes Hosp., St. Louis, 1976-78, instr. medicine, 1978-79, asst. prof., 1979-84, assoc. prof., 1984-92, prof., 1992—, dir. heart failure and transplant program, 1994—. Steering com., chmn. ancillary studies, publs. com. SAVE Study (Bristol-Myers Squibb), Princeton, N.J., 1987-92; steering com. MACH-1 Study, Roche, 1995-98; lectr. in field. Reviewer of 16 med. jours.; contbr. over 100 articles to profl. jours. and chpts. to books. Pres. St. Louis chpt. Am. Heart Assn., 1987-88, also bd. dirs., pres. Mo. affiliate, 1992-94, bd. dirs, exec com. coun. on clin cardiology 1990-92. Maj. M.C., USAF, 1974-76. Fellow ACP, Am. Coll. Cardiology (regional councilor Mo. chpt. 1993-2001). Avocations: photography, golf, rowing. Home: 15 Crosswinds Dr Olivette MO 63132-4303 Office: Washington Univ Sch of Medicine Campus Box 8086 660 S Euclid Ave Saint Louis MO 63110-1010 E-mail: egeltman@lm.wustl.edu.

GELTZER, ROBERT LAWRENCE, lawyer, arbitrator, mediator, former retail executive; b. N.Y.C., Jan. 27, 1945; s. Edward and Grace Theresa (DeFeo) G.; m. Elise Anne Lewis, Nov. 11, 1972; 1 child, Joshua Alexander. BA Biochemistry and Polit. Sci., Queens Coll., N.Y.C., 1965; JD, George Washington U. Law Sch., 1968; postgrad., CCNY. Bar: N.Y., 1969, U.S. Dist. Ct. (so. and ea. dists.), U.S. Ct. Appeals (2nd cir.), U.S. Supreme Ct., U.S. Ct. Mil. Appeals. Ptnr. Tendler, Biggins & Geltzer, N.Y.C., 1990—2002; sole practitioner, 2002—. Appointments include: Private Law Practice, 1968-71; Assoc. Atty. for Legal and Governmental Affairs for Allied Stores Corp., 1971-74; Sr. Atty. for J.C. Penney, 1974-84; Northeastern Regional Counsel, 1984-88; counsel firm Meyer, Suozzi, English & Klein, 1988-89. Admitted to N.Y. State Bar, 1969; U.S. Dist. Cts. Appeal (so. and ea. dists.) (2d cir.), 1974; U.S. Supreme Ct., 1976. Dir., Credit Specialist Program at Adelphi Univ., 1976-78; mem. ABA Bd. Govs., 1988-91, bd. program com., 1988-90, bd. ops. com., 1990-91, liaison commn. on mentally disabled, 1988-89, liaison standing com. on specialization, 1989-91, spl. com. on youth edn., 1988-91, spl. com. on pub. understanding about the law, 1988-91; House of Delegates, 1980-86, 88-93, 94-97; chair Task Force on Providing Mem. Benefits for Disabled Lawyers, 1991-93; mem. standing com. on pub. edn. about law, 1992-98; mem. Law Day Task Force, 1994-97, Nat. Conf. on Lawyers and Corp. fiduciaries, 1986-87; Standing Com. on Legal Drafting, 1979-82; Spl. Com. on Youth Edn. for Citizenship, 1982-86; chmn. Tellers Com., 1982-83; Conf. of Section Chairs, chair fiscal com., 1986-88; Annual Meeting Host Coms., mem. (1986), vice-chair, (1993); Coordinating Group on Bioethics and the Law, (1991-96); liaison to Standing Com. on Scope and Correlation of Work, 1988-91, mem. Standing Com., 1991-96, chair, 1994-95; corp. Com. of Resource Devel. coun., 1987-92; Sci. and Tech. Sect. (coun. mem. 1981-84, 91-93) sec., 1984-85, vice chair, 1985-86, chair-elect, 1986-87, chair, 1987-88; chair Nat. Conf. on Birth, Death & Law, 1987-88; Corp., Banking and Bus. Law Sect. (co-chmn. Corporate Counsel Com., mem. Consumer Fin. Svc. Commn., Long-Range Planning Com., Issues Affecting the Profession Com., Comml. Arbitration Com., 1992—), Bus. Bankruptcy Com., (1992—), Consumer Bankruptcy Com., (1992—); Individual Rights and Responsibilities Sect. (vice-chmn. Equal Protection of the Laws, mem. 1st Amendment Rights Com., 1992-97), Rights of the Elderly Com., (1992-97), Rights of Children Com., (1992-97); Economics of Law Practice Sect. (mem.); Family Law Sect. (mem.); Judicial Adminstrn. Div. (Exec. Com., Lawyers' Conf.; chair Membership Com., Jud. Compensation Com.; Litigation sect., 1st co-chair com. on corp. counsel, mem. class action com., liaison with ABA com.); co-chair Nat. Conf. on the Role of the Lawyer in the 1980s (1979-81). New York State Bar Assn. House of Delegates (1981-97); Exec. Com. At-Large Mem., (1992-95), state bar del., 1995-97, liaison to atty. and community com. juvenile justice commn., solo and small firm practitioners commn. and judicial evaluation commn.; Founder and 1st Chmn. Corp. Counsel Sect. (1981-83); chair Commn. to Provide Legal Svcs. to Middle Income Consumers (1995—); chair Unlawful Practice of Law Com. (1990-92), chair Solo and Small Firm Practitioner Task Force (1991-96); mem. Action Unit #5 pertaining to Regulatory Reform (1980-83); mem. Law Simplification Task Force (1982-88), chair Pub. Rels. Com., 1983-86; mem. AIDS and the Law Com. (1988-91); recipient Corp. Counsel of Yr. award (1989). Assn. of the Bar of the City of N.Y.: del. to N.Y. State Bar House of Delegates, 1988-92, mem. Profl. and Jud. Ethics Com. (1982-83); Sci. and Law Com. (1985-88); Children and the Law Com. (1985-88); N.Y. County Lawyers' Assn.: mem., bd. dirs. (1982-88); chmn. spl. projects com., 1992-96; mem. 75th Anniversary Steering Com. (1982-84); mem. Federal Legislation, State Legislation, Trade Regulation, and Alcoholism in the Profession committees; mem. Am. Law Inst.; life fellow Am. Bar Found. (fellow, vice chair N.Y. fellows, 1988-91, chair, 1991-96); fellow N.Y. Bar Found., ABA Young Lawyers' Div. (fellow, bd. dirs.); life mem., dir. N.Y. state chair (1979-82) of Am. Judicature Soc. Adjunct prof., Pace College. Mem. Am. Soc. for Polit. and Legal Philosophy; Am. Soc. for Legal History: General Com., Conf. on Personal Finance Law; speaker at various state and local bar assns. (Ark., Calif., Colo., Conn., Ill., Mich., N.J., N.Y., Pa., Va., W.Va. and various programs of practicing law instns. and ABA Nat. Insts.). Pro Bono General counsel for Nat. Kidney Found. (1981-91). Co-first male mem. of Nat. Assn. Women Lawyers. Bd. dirs. Fund for Justice and Edn. (1988-91), Community Action for Legal Svcs. (1988-90). Mem. Vol. Lawyers for the Arts. Past chancellor commander, past spl. dep. grand chancellor Knights of Pythias. Mem. American Jewish Com., Masons, Phi Epsilon Phi, Phi Delta Phi, George Washington U. Law Sch. Alumni Assn. Contbr. to various profl. jours. in areas of fed. and state consumer credit legislation, regulation, litigation and compliance, class action litigation, law firm mgmt., consumer, comml., gen. practice and state civil litigation issues affecting the legal profession. Fellow Am. Bar Found.; mem. Congregation Temple Emanu-El; mem. legal com., bicentennial com. Am. Jewish Com.; mem. Jewish Welfare Bd.; chair JC Penney Legal Dept.'s Ann. Blood Dr., 1979, 83; mem. Vol. Lawyers for the Arts; pro bono gen. counsel, chair legal com. Nat. Kidney Found. 1981-91. Mem. ABA (bd. govs. rep. N.Y. State 1988-91; mem. ho. of dels. 1980-86, 88-93, 95—; vice chmn. tellers com. 1981-82; chmn. 1982-83, bd. dirs. Am. Bar Retirement Assn. 1988-91, Nat. Jud. Coll. 1988-91, Fund. Justice and Edn. 1988-91; bd. govs. liaison standing com. on scope and correlation of work 1988-91, 91-96; spl. com. on youth edn. for citizenship 1982-86, mem. standing com. 82-86; commn. on public understanding about the law 1989-91; mem. steering com. on unmet legal needs of children 1996-97 ; chair task force on member benefits for disabled lawyers 1991-93; mem. standing com. on pub. edn. 1992-95; mem. law day working group 1994-95; chmn. fiscal com. conf. of sect. chairs 1987-89, Nat. Conf. on Birth, Death and Law, 1987-88, ann. meeting host coms. 1986, vice chair, 1993, coordinating group on bioethics and the law 1991-95; chmn. subcom. on liaison with state and local bars 1983-86; mem. young lawyers divsn., corp., banking and bus. law sect., litigation sect., sci. and tech. sect., gen. practice sect., individual rights and responsabilities sect., numerous other sects. and coms.), Am. Law Inst., Am. Judicature Soc. (life, mem. mem bership com. 1979-80, chair N.Y. State 1989-94), N.Y. State Bar Assn. (founder 1981, first chair corp. counsel sect. 1981-83, Corp. Counsel of Yr. award 1989; mem. at large exec. com. 1992-95, liaison, ho. of dels. 1981-87, 88-93, 95-97; mem. spl. com. alternat dispute resolution 1993—, numerous other coms., sects.), Assn. Bar City of N.Y., N.Y. County Lawyers' Assn., Fed. Bar Assn. Home: 115 E 87th St New York NY 10128

GELTZER, SHEILA SIMON, public relations executive; b. N.Y.C. d. Sidney E. and Bertie (Rome) Simon; m. Howard E. Geltzer, Sept. 10, 1967; children: Jeremy Niles, Gabriel Lewis. BA, Queens Coll., 1961. With Philip Lesly Co., N.Y.C., 1962-63, Benjamin Co., N.Y.C., 1963-68; ptnr. Simon and Geltzer, Inc., N.Y.C., 1968-74, Ries and Geltzer, N.Y.C., 1974-79; pres. Geltzer and Co., Inc., N.Y.C., 1979—2000; mng. dir., exec. prin. Publicis Dialog, N.Y.C., 2000—. Mem. Pub. Relations Soc. Am. (counselors acad.), Women in Communications, Women in Pub. Relations, Nat. Council of Women. Office: Publicis Dialog 498 West End Ave New York NY 10024

GELZER, DAVID GEORG, English educator, missionary; b. Vevey, Vaud, Switzerland, Oct. 7, 1919; came to U.S., 1937; s. Heinrich Gelzer and Charlotte Elisabeth Lüdecke; m. Elisabeth Genilla Bennett, June 12, 1949; children: Charlotte, Rebekah, Miriam (dec.), Christian, Stuart. BA, U. Dubuque, 1941, B. in Div., 1943; PhD, Yale U., 1952; D. Humane Letters (hon.), Wilson Coll., Chambsburg, Pa., 1972; D. Div. (hon.), Tainan (Taiwan) Theol. Sem., 1994. Ordained to ministry Presbyn. Ch., 1943. Prof. religion, German Albertson Coll., Caldwell, Idaho, 1946-50; prof. religion, German, Coll. Evangélique de Libamba, Makak, Cameroon, 1952-61; prof. history theology and ecumenics Faculté Théologie Protestante, Yaoundé, Cameroon, 1960-75, dean, 1960-69; prof. theology, ch. history Tainan Theol. Sem., 1975-84; lectr., ecumenics Yale Div. Sch., New Haven, Conn., 1982; lectr. ecumenics McCormick Theol. Sem., Chgo., 1984; prof. theology, ecumenics Talua Ministry Training Ctr., Luganville, Vanuatu, 1985-88, acting prin., 1985-87. English lang. editor Taiwan Ch. News, 1980-84. Pres. Canterbury Cleric, Phila., 1992—95, sec., 1995—99, mem. governing bd. Stony Point Center, NY; election judge Swarthmore (Pa.) We. Dist., 1994—2001; treas., bd. dirs. Swarthmore Sr. Citizen Assn., 1997—2000. Recipient Alumnus Distinction award U. Dubuque, 1949, 20th Century Achievement award Internat. Biog. Ctr.; decorated Chevalier de la Légion d'Honneur, Republic of Cameroon, 1971. Internat. Assn. Mission Studies. Democrat. Presbyterian. Avocations: classical music, reading, swimming. Home and Office: 912 Harvard Ave Swarthmore PA 19081-2208

GEMELL, NICHOLAS I. retired radiologist; b. Kaunas, Lithuania, 1921; s. Nicholas Simon Gemelitzki; m. Karen Elinor Moroni, Sept. 3, 1964; children: Julie Helene, Kathryn Lynn. MD, U. Munich, 1950. Diplomate Am. Bd.

Radiology. Intern St. Francis Hosp., Poughkeepsie, N.Y., 1951-52; resident in radiology Mt. Sinai Hosp., Chgo., 1954-55, Ohio State U. Hosp., Columbus, 1956-57; asst. chief, dept. radiology Michael Reese Hosp. and Med. Ctr., Chgo., 1958-63, consulting radiologist, 1965-74; consulting radiologist, med. dept. Amoco Oil Company, 1975-77; consulting forensic radiologist Med. Examiner's Office, County of Cook and City of Chgo., 1975-77; radiologist Sherman Hosp., Elgin, Ill., 1978-89. Mem. Health Planning Agy. Task force, Kane, Lake and McHenry counties, Ill., 1975-77; chief staff McHenry (Ill.) Hosp., 1975-77, chief radiology, 1964-77. Mem. AMA, Am. Coll. Radiology, Radiolog. Soc. N.Am.

GEMELLO, JOHN MICHAEL, economics educator, consultant, academic administrator; b. Palo Alto, Calif., Feb. 3, 1946; s. Mario John and Kathryn Marie (Volarvich) G.; m. Linda Marino, Sept. 17, 1966; children: Matthew, Gina. BA, U. Santa Clara, 1967; PhD, Stanford U., 1975. Asst. prof. econs. U. Toronto, Canada, 1972—75, San Francisco State U., 1976—82, assoc. prof., 1982—86, prof., 1986—90, chmn. dept. econs., 1986—90, assoc. v.p. for acad. resources, 1990—2002, interim v.p., acad. affairs, 2002—03, provost, v.p. academic affairs, 2003—. Nat. lectr. Nova U., Ft. Lauderdale, Fla., 1977-84; cons. Calif. State Teaching Commn. on Teaching Profession, 1985, Inst. Rsch. on Ednl. Fin. and Governance, Stanford U., 1981-82. Mem. planning commn. City of Millbrae, Calif., 1979-83. Capt. USAR, 1973-75. Mem. Am. Econ. Assn., Western Econ. Assn., Western Regional Sci. Assn. Democrat. Roman Catholic. Office: San Francisco State U 1600 Holloway Ave San Francisco CA 94132-1722 E-mail: jgemello@sfsu.edu.

GEMERY, HENRY ALBERT, economics educator; b. Shelton, Conn., Sept. 5, 1930; s. John and Mary (Benco) G.; m. Pamela Joyce Malcolm, Aug. 30, 1958; children: John Malcolm, Pamela Ann. BS, So. Conn. State Coll., 1952; MBA, Harvard U., 1958; PhD, U. Pa., 1967; MA hon., Colby Coll., 1977. Asst. dir. admissions Colby Coll., Waterville, Maine, 1958-61, from instr. to Pugh Family prof. econs., 1961—2001, emeritus, 2001—. Assoc. Charles Warren Ctr., Harvard U., 1989-90. Contbg. author, co-editor: The Uncommon Market, 1979, Science Technology and Environment, 1994; author: monograph Emigration from the British Isles, 1980, European Emigration to North America, 1984. Served to 1st lt., C.E. U.S. Army, 1953-56. NDEA fellow U. Pa., 1963-65; NIH postdoctoral fellow U. Pa., 1968-69; Charles Warren fellow Harvard U., 1982-83 Mem. Am. Econs. Assn., Cliometric Soc., Econ. History Assn., Internat. Union for Sci. Study of Population Home: 1185 Pond Rd Sidney ME 04330-2015 Office: Colby Coll Mayflower Hill Waterville ME 04901 E-mail: hagemery@colby.edu.

GEMIGNANI, JOSEPH ADOLPH, lawyer; b. Hancock, Mich., Apr. 17, 1932; s. Baldo A. and Yolanda M.; m. Barbara A. Thomson, Sept. 5, 1953; children: Joseph, Jon. BSME, Mich. Technological U., 1953; JD, U. Mich., 1958. Bar: Wis. 1959, Mich. 1960, U.S. Dist. Ct. (ea. and we. dists.) Wis., U.S. Ct. Appeals (7th cir.), U.S. Ct. Appeals (fed. cir.). In-house counsel McGraw Edison Co., Milw., 1958-60; ptnr. Michael, Best & Friedrich, Milw., 1960—. 1st lt. USAF, 1953-55. Home: 616 E Day Ave Milwaukee WI 53217-4841 Office: Michael Best & Friedrich 100 E Wisconsin Ave Ste 3300 Milwaukee WI 53202-4108

GEMIGNANI, MICHAEL CAESAR, clergyman, retired educator; b. Balt., Feb. 23, 1938; s. Hugo J. and Dorothy G.; m. Carol A. Federico, June 30, 1962 (dec.); children: Stephen, Susan; m. Nilda B. Keller, May 18, 1985. BA, U. Rochester, 1962; MS, U. Notre Dame, 1964, PhD, 1965; JD, Ind. U., 1980. Bar: Ind. 1980, U.S. Dist. Ct. Ind. 1980, Maine 1987, U.S. Dist. Ct. Maine 1987, Tex. 1990; ordained to ministry Episcopal Ch., 1973. Asst. prof. math. SUNY, Buffalo, 1965-68; assoc. prof. Smith Coll., 1968-72; prof., chmn. dept. math. scis. Ind. U.-Purdue U., Indpls., 1972-81; dean Coll. Scis. and Humanities Ball State U., Muncie, Ind., 1981-86; dean Coll. Arts and Scis. U. Maine, Orono, 1986-88; sr. v.p., provost U. Houston-Clear Lake, 1988-91, prof. math. and computer sci., 1991-92; rector St. Paul's Episcopal Ch., Freeport, Tex., 1991—. Vicar St. Francis Episcopal Ch., Zionsville, Ind., 1974-79; pres. Met. Indpls. Campus Ministry, 1975-76, bd. dirs., 1974-81; mem. adv. bd. Ind. Office Campus Ministry, 1973-86, pres., 1983-85; chair divsn. spiritual formation Episcopal Diocese of Tex., 1997—. Author: books including Elementary Topology, 1967, 2d rev. edit., 1972, Introductory Real Analysis, 1970, Law and the Computer, 1981, Computer Law, 1985, Legal Guide for EDP Managers, 1989, To Know God: Small Group Exercises in Spiritual Formation, 2001, Spiritual Formation for Pastors Tending the Fire Within, 2002; composer; rsch., publs. in math. Mem. ABA, AAAS, Am. Math. Soc. (chmn. N.E. sect. 1970-71, chmn. Ind. sect. 1975-76), Scribes, Sigma Xi, Kappa Sigma. E-mail: mgmign@mastnet.net.

GEMMELL-AKALIS, BONNI JEAN, psychotherapist; b. Lansing, Mich., Mar. 11, 1950; d. James Stewart Gemmell and Alpha Alice (Hackenberg) Vanden Bosch; m. Gary Alfred Eddy, Jan. 1, 2001; 1 stepchild, Patrick Eddy;children: Scott Aaron, Ty Alexander, Zachary Alan. BS, Ctrl. Mich. U., 1972, MA, 1974. Ltd. lic. psychologist, Mich.; cert. social worker, Mich. Clin. psychologist, sr. mental health therapist Lincoln Ctr. for Emotionally Disturbed Children & Youth, Lansing, 1974-77; outpatient psychologist Grand Rapids (Mich.) Child Guidance Clinic, 1978-81; pvt. practice Grand Rapids Psychiat. Svcs., 1981-88, 96—, Associated Therapists, Inc., Grand Rapids, 1988-96, pres., 1989-90. Grad. fellow Ctrl. Mich. U., 1972-73. Mem. Mich. Psychoanalytic Coun., Mich. Women Psychologists, Mich. Assn. Profl. Psychologists, Am. Group Psychotherapy Assn. (founder nat. registry 1996), Grand Rapids Area Psychology Assn., Psi Chi. Home: 632 Duxbury Ct SE Grand Rapids MI 49546-9605 Office: 1025 Spaulding Ave SE Ste B Grand Rapids MI 49546-3703

GEMMETT, ROBERT J. university dean, English language educator; b. Schenectady, Mar. 11, 1936; s. A James and Dorothy M. (MacFarlane) G.; m. Kendra B. Baxter, Jan 24, 1964; children: Stephen, Scott, David, Kerry. BA cum laude, Siena Coll., 1959; MA, U. Mass., 1962; PhD, Syracuse U., 1967. Instr. Clarkson U., N.Y., 1964-65; assoc. prof. English SUNY, Brockport, 1965-70, prof., 1970-92, 97—, chmn. dept., 1975-79, dean humanities, 1979-82, dean letters and scis., 1982-92; prof. English, provost, v.p. for acad. affairs SUNY Coll., Buffalo, 1992-97. Author: Poets and Men of Letters, 1975, William Beckford, 1977, Beckford's Fonthill: The Rise of Romantic Icon, 2003; editor: Biographical Memoirs of Extraordinary Painters, 1969, Dreams, Waking Thoughts and Incidents, 1971, The Consummate Collector, 2000. 2d lt. U.S. Army, 1959. Recipient Chancellor's Excellence in Teaching award SUNY, 1975; fellow, rsch. grantee SUNY, 1967-69, 84-85. Office: SUNY Dept English Brockport NY 14220 E-mail: rgemmett@brockport.edu.

GEMMING, MARY FRANCES, college educator, writer, astrologer; b. Elmira, N.Y., June 3, 1941; d. Walter and Antoinette Grybos; m. Curtiss Gemming, Dec. 30, 1981. AAS in Bus. Adminstrn., Corning (N.Y.) C.C., 1966; PhD, U. Metaphysics, Studio City, Calif., 1998; BSBA, Rochester Inst. Tech., 1984. Adminstrv. asst. Gannett Newspapers, Rochester, N.Y., 1968-79; cost analyst Eastman Kodak Co., Rochester, 1979-92; tchr. Sch. Bd. Manatee County, Bradenton, Fla., 1993—. Part-time tchr. Bd. Continuing Edn., Fairport, N.Y., 1977-91. Author: Mystical Secrets of the Stars, 1999, Discovering Treasures of Peace, 2000. Recipient Wall St. Jour. award, Corning C.C., 1966. Mem. Assn. for Rsch. and Enlightenment, Am. Fedn. Astrologers, Rochester Astrological Assn. (pres. 1980-82). Avocations: yoga, swimming.

GEMS, GERALD ROBERT, physical education educator; b. Chgo., Mar. 21, 1947; s. Gerald Julius and Frances Ann (Di Benedetto) Gems; m. Deborah Lynn Coy, June 25, 1977 (div. Oct. 1, 1996); children: Brooke Allison, Sean Christopher. AA, Mayfair Jr. Coll., Chgo., 1975; BA, Northeastern Ill. U., 1977; MS, U. Ariz., 1980; PhD, U. Md., 1989. Mem. work study program Mayfair Coll., Chgo., 1973—75, Northeastern Ill. U., Chgo., 1975—77; grad. tchg. asst. phys. edn. dept. U. Ariz., Tucson, 1977—78; athletic dir., tchr. phys. edn., head phys. edn. dept., intramural dir. Carol Morgan Sch., Santo Domingo, Dominican Republic, 1978—79; athletic dir., tchr. Webb Schs., Claremont, Calif., 1979—85; grad. tchg. asst. phys. edn. dept. U. Md., College Park, 1985—88; prof. North Ctrl. Coll., Naperville, Ill., 1988—. Cons. Chgo. Hist. Soc., 1999—2000, 2002; presenter in field; cons. in field. Author: Windy City Wars: Labor, Leisure, and Sport in the Making of Chicago, 1997, For Pride, Profit, and Patriarchy: Football and the Incorporation of American Cultural Values, 2000; editor, compiler: Sports in North America: A Documentary History, vol. 5 1880-1900, 1995, book revs. co-editor: Jour. Sport History, 1996—2000, 2002—, book revs. editor:, 2000—01, mem. editl. adv. bd.: ABC-CLIO, 2001, mem. editl. bd.: Football Studies Jour., 2001—; contbr. chapters to books, articles to profl. jours. Mem. accreditation team Ill. State Bd. Edn., Springfield, 1990, 1992, 1995; Roads scholar, lectr. Ill. Humanities Coun., Chgo., 1999—2003. Cpl. USMC, 1966—68. Mem.: Chgo. Hist. Soc., Nat. Assn. for Ethnic Studies, Profl. Football Rschrs. Assn., Curriculum and Instrn. Acad., Nat. Assn. for Girls' and Women's Sport, Sport Philosophy Acad., Sport Art Acad., Sport Sociology Acad., Internat. Soc. for the History Phys. Edn. and Sport, Nat. Assn. Sport and Phys. Edn., Am. Alliance for Health, Phys. Edn., Recreation and Dance, Orgn. Am. Historians, N.Am. Soc. for Sport History (pres.-elect 2001—02, pres. 2003—, disting. lectr. com. 1995—97), Nat. Geog. Soc. Avocations: reading, travel, sports. Office: North Ctrl Coll 30 N Brainard Naperville IL 60566

GEN, MARTIN, corporate executive; b. Feb. 14, 1926; s. Max and Gussie (Bluestone) G.; m. Sara Tobin; children: Gilda Gen Paul, Sam Gen. Student, Syracuse U., 1946-50; BA, Pace U., 1950. Lic. pvt. detective. V.p., treas. Merlin, Inc., North Bergen, N.J., 1950-73; pres. Washmasters, Inc., North Bergen, 1950-73; pres., exec. dir., CEO Expert Investigation and Protective Industries, Inc., Kenilworth, N.J., 1974—. Pres. InterGlobal Trading, Kenilworth, N.J.; pres., exec. dir. EIP Inc., Kenilworth, N.J., 1973-74; pres. Expert Investigation. Bd. dirs. Jewish Nat. Fund, Teaneck, N.J., 1986—, YMHA, Union, N.J., 1970, Fedn. Union County, N.J., 1970, Jewish Ednl. Ctr., Elizabeth, N.J., 1960. Served with USN, 1943-46, ETO, PTO. Named Man of Yr., YMHA, Bnai Brith. Mem. Am. Soc. Indsl. Security, Club 100. Home and Office: PO Box 195 Kenilworth NJ 07033-0195

GENACK, AZRIEL Z. physicist, educator; b. New York, NY, Dec. 8, 1942; s. Isaac and Rose Genack; m. Ahuva Swiatycki, Mar. 30, 1966; children: Yakov, Yitzi, Daniel, Avi, Elie. BS, Columbia Coll., New York, NY, 1960—64, PhD, 1964—73. Rsch. assoc. City Coll. of CUNY, New York, NY, 1973—75, IBM Rsch. Lab., San Jose, Calif., 1975—77; sr. staff physicist Exxon, Linden, NJ, 1977—84, Annandale, NJ, 1977—84; dist. prof. Queens Coll. of CUNY, Flushing, NY, 1984—; cto Chiral Photonics, Clifton, NJ, 1999—. Author articles on photon localization in liquid crystals; contbr. articles to profl. publs. Recipient Best paper, Hewlett Packard, 1999; fellow fellowship, Am. Phys. Soc., 1993, sr. Fulbright fellow, Technion /Israel, 1999. Achievements include discovery of innovative meas. for photon localzn. in various frequency range intensity, dwell times and probability distribution; Expl. lasing in liq. crys. and Raman scatng; development of laser frequency swchng. and ac.-opt. tomography. Office: Queens Coll of CUNY Dept of Physics 65-30 Kissena Blvd Flushing NY 11367

GENARO, DONALD MICHAEL, industrial designer; b. Hoboken, N.J., Feb. 22, 1932; s. Gustav G. and Margaret (DeMave) G.; m. Margaret Hermes, June 23, 1956; children: Susan, Karen. BID, Pratt Inst., 1957. Archtl. designer F.W. Fisher-Architects, N.J. and N.Y., 1951-52; indsl. designer Henry Dreyfuss Assocs., N.Y.C., 1957-63, assoc., 1963-68, ptnr., 1968-82, sr. ptnr., 1982-94; ret., 1994. Cons. AT&T, Bell Labs., John Deere, Polaroid, and various others; lectr. on design, 1962—. Designer of Trimline Phone; holder over 200 patents; contbr. numerous articles to profl. jours. Trustee, chmn., bd. dirs. Pascack Valley Hosp.; bd. dirs. Well Care Group, Inc. Represented in permanent collection at Mus. of Modern Art and Cooper-Hewitt (Smithsonian) Museum; recipient Contemporary Achievement award Pratt Inst., 1970, Best Product Design 1983 Time Mag., several design awards from Indsl. Designers Soc. of Am. and Indsl. Design Mag.; named one of 25 Best Designed Products Fortune Mag., 1977. Mem. Indsl. Designers Soc. Am.

GENBERG, IRA, lawyer; b. Newark, July 27, 1947; s. Jack and Ann (Lerman) G.; m. Rosemary Lawlor, Jan. 15, 1981; children: Jack Michael, Anne Rebecca. AB magna cum laude, Rutgers U., 1969; JD, U. Pa., 1972. Bar: Ga. 1972, D.C. 1978. Assoc. Haas, Holland, Levison & Gibert, Atlanta, 1972-75; ptnr. Stokes, Shapiro, Fussell & Genberg, Atlanta, 1975-87; ptnr., head litigation sect. Smith, Gambrell & Russell LLP, Atlanta, 1987—. Spkr. Seminar on Constrn. Litigation, Atlanta, 1985, Seminar on Constrn. Law, Atlanta, 1986; co-chmn. Seminar on Trying A Complex Constrn. Case, 1994. Contbr. articles to Constrn. Bus. Review Mag. Mem. ABA, Ga. Bar Assn., Atlanta Bar Assn., D.C. Bar Assn. Office: Smith Gambrell & Russell LLP 1230 Peachtree St NE Atlanta GA 30309-3592

GENCO, ROBERT JOSEPH, immunologist, periodontist, educator, scientist; b. Silver Creek, N.Y., Oct. 31, 1938; s. Joseph A. and Santa G. (Barone) Genco; m. Sandra Clarke, Sept. 14, 1957; children: Deborah Genco Powell, Robert M., Julie Clarke Alford. DDS cum laude, SUNY, 1963; PhD, U. Pa., 1967. Asst. prof. dept. oral biology Sch. Dental Medicine SUNY, Buffalo, 1967—69, assoc. prof., 1969—72, prof., 1972—, chmn. dept. oral biology, 1977—, Disting. Univ. Prof., 1990—. Editor: Jour. Periodontology, 1988—. Recipient Gold medal, ADA, 1991. Fellow: AAAS (chmn. dental sect 1980); mem.: Am. Assn. Immunology, Am. Acad. Periodontology, Internat. Assn. Dental Rschrs. (pres. 1991—92), Inst. Medicine, Am. Assn. Dental Rschrs. Avocations: music, sports. Office: SUNY at Buffalo Periodontal Disease Rsch Ctr 135 Foster Hall 3435 Main St Buffalo NY 14214

GENDELL, GERALD STANLEIGH, retired public affairs executive; b. Stamford, Conn., June 14, 1929; s. Irving and Henrietta (Lund) G.; m. s. Marion F. Belvin, July 28, 1952; children: Carin Gaye, Danna Joyce, Adrian Leigh, Jeffrey Lund, David Blake, Marc Steven, Bradley Howard. BS, NYU, 1949. With Procter & Gamble Co., Cin., 1954-91, dir. community affairs and contbns., 1976-80, mgr. external affairs divsn., 1980, mgr. pub. affairs div., 1981—91, also pres., trustee Procter & Gamble Fund. Trustee Glen Manor Home, 1978-80, Queen City Housing Corp., Cin., 1981-89, Cin. Local Initiative Support Corp., The Spire Found., Jewish Fedn. So. Ariz.; vice chmn. bd. trustees Jewish Hosp. of Cin.; bd. dirs., trustee Nat. Coun. on Econ. Edn., 1985-91; mem. met. adv. coun. U. Cin.; mem. adv. coun. George Mason U. Sch. Law, 1988-91; mem. Cin. Mayor's Com. on Econ. Devel.; chmn. Found. for Pub. Affairs; mem. bd. overseers Hebrew Union Coll.; pres. Jewish Cmty. Found. of So. Ariz.; bd. dirs. Jewish Fedn. of So. Ariz., Ariz. Jewish Post. 1st lt. U.S. Army, 1950-53. Mem. Pub. Affairs Coun. Am. (bd. dirs. 1981-91, chmn. 1988-89), Greater Cin. C. of C. (vice chmn., mem. exec. com. 1981-87), Conf. Bd., Bankers Club (bd. govs. 1988-93).

GENDELMAN, HOWARD ELIOT, biomedical researcher, physician; b. Phila., Mar. 18, 1954; s. Seymour and Soffia (Raphael) G.; m. Bonnie Rae Bloch, June 15, 1980; children: Lesley, Sierra, Adam. BS, Muhlenberg Coll., 1975; MD, Pa. State U., 1979. Rsch. assoc. Pa. State U., Hershey, 1978-79; resident in internal medicine Montefiore Hosp. Ctr. Albert Einstein Coll. Medicine, Bronx, N.Y., 1979-82; clin. and rsch. fellow depts. neurology and medicine Johns Hopkins U. Med. Sch., Balt., 1982-85, asst. prof. divsn. infectious diseases, 1985-89; staff physician in infectious diseases Walter Reed Army Inst. Rsch., Washington, 1987-93; spl. expert sect. biochem. virology Lab. Molecular Microbiology/NIH, Bethesda, Md., 1985-87; prin scientist Henry M. Jacksoun Found. Advance. Mil. Med. Uniformed Svcs. Univ. Health Sci. Ctr., 1988-92, rsch. assoc., prof. dept. pathology, 1990-92; chief lab. viral pathogenesis U. Nebr. Med. Ctr., Omaha, 1993-97, David T. Purtilo Disting. chair. pathology and microbiology, 1997—; dir. Ctr. for Neurovirology and Neurodegenerative Disorders, Omaha, 1997—. Lectr. dept. infectious diseases The Johns Hopkins U. Sch. Pub. Health, Balt., 1985-92; cons. Glax Wellcome, Research Triangle Park, N.C., 1987, Schering-Plough, Kenilworth, N.J., Applied Biotechs., Beltsville, Md., 1990, Viragen, 1990, others. Editl. reviewer Jour. Histochemistry and Cytochemistry, Jour. Virology, Am. Jour. Pathology, Jour. Clin. Investigation, New Eng. Jour. Medicine, Jour. Neuroimmunology, AIDS, Jour. Immunology, Gastroenterology, Lab. Investigation, Jour. Infectious Disease, Revs. of Infectious Disease Sci.; sect. editor Jour. Leukocyte Biology; assoc. editor Jour. Neurovirology; mem. editl bd. JAMA, Jour. Neurotoxicology, HIV Revs., Jour. Neuroimmunology; contbr. articles to New Eng. Jour. Medicine, Sci., Jour. Immunology, Jour. Virology, Jour. Exptl. Medicine, others. Lt. col. USAR, 1984-97. Recipient Disting Alumnus award, Pa. State U., 1999, Jacob Javitz Neurosci. award, NINDS, 2001; fellow, Carter Wallace, 1987—93; grantee NIH, Amfar; scholar, J. William Fulbright Found., 2000. Mem. ACP, AMA, Am. Soc. Virology, Am. Soc. Microbiology, Reticuloendothelial Soc. Achievements include discovery of rsch. in glial (microglia and astroglia) cells in the neurodegenerative mechanisms of HIV dementia and other neurodegenerative disorders. Home: 125 S 127th St Omaha NE 68154 Office: Univ Nebr Med Ctr 600 S 42nd St Omaha NE 68198-1002 also: 985125 Nebr Med Ctr Omaha NE 68198-5215 E-mail: hegendel@unmc.edu.

GENDRON, MICHÈLE MARGUERITE MADELEINE, librarian; b. Paris, Mar. 15, 1947; came to U.S., 1950; d. Gerard Joachim and Denise Marie Louise (Le Morvan) G. BA, Orlinda Pierce Coll. for Women, Athens, Greece, 1969; MS, U. Ill., 1971. Libr. Free Libr. Phila., 1971-75, head, Kingsessing Br., 1975-76, head, Ramonita G. de Rodriguez Br., 1976-91, curator spl. collections ctrl. children's dept., 1991-92, head, lit. dept., 1992—. Cons. devel. Hist. Children's Lit. Collection Montgomery County-Norristown (Pa.) Pub. Libr., 1993-94; organizing mem. Pa. Libr. Assn.'s 1st Conf. Svcs. to Youth, Harrisburg, Pa., 1987-89, Women's Network's 1st Conf. on P.R. Woman in Phila., 1981. Author: (bibliographies) Booklist, 1983; contbr. bibliographies Destination World, 1979, Stories to Share, 1985. Trustee Legal Svcs. Fund Dist. Coun. 47 of Am. Fedn. State, County and Mcpl. Employees, 1985-95, mem. exec. bd. Local 2186, 1996—. Recipient Charles Scribner award Scribner Pub., 1976, Nat. Security Forum, Air War Coll., 1985. Mem. ALA (Assn. Libr. Svcs. Children, Mildred Batchelder award selection com. 1979-81, 85-87, internat. rels. com. 1981-85, chair 1984-85, libr. instrn. round table 1991-93), Pub. Libr. Assn. (mktg. to pub. librs. 1991—, svcs. to multicultural populations 1991, sec. exec. com. mktg. pub. libr. svcs. sect. 1995-96), Alliance Francaise de Phila., Franklin Inn Club, Beta Phi Mu. Roman Catholic. Office: Free Libr of Phila Lit Dept 1901 Vine St Philadelphia PA 19103-1116

GENDZWILL, JOYCE ANNETTE, retired health officer; b. Milw., Aug. 8, 1927; d. Felix Vincent and Antoinette Marie (Borske) G.; m. Lauren E. Trombley, June 13, 1952 (div. Jan. 1960); children: Regan Eve Trombley Kovacich, Eugene Vincent, Paul Quentin. BS, U. Mich., 1949, MD, 1952, MPH, 1961. Cert. pub. mgr., Ala. Internship USPHS, Detroit, Cleve., 1952-53; dir. extern edn. Beyer Meml. Hosp., Ypsilanti, Mich., 1953-54; resident in radiology St. Luke's Hosp., Denver, 1954-55; health officer Dickinson-Iron Dist. Health Dept., Stambaugh, Mich., 1959-76; dir. bur. local health svc. Ala. Dept. Pub. Health, Montgomery, Ala., 1976-81, asst. state health officer, 1981-91; ret., 1991. Mem. AMA, So. Med. Assn., Mensa, Phi Beta Kappa, Delta Omega, Phi Kappa Phi. Home: 6580 Thorman Rd Port Charlotte FL 33981-5579

GENEGO, WILLIAM JOSEPH, lawyer; b. Albany, Mar. 27, 1950; s. William Joseph and Olga Alice (Sultan) G. BS in Bus. and Pub. Adminstrn. magna cum laude, NYU, 1972; JD, Yale U., 1975; LLM, Georgetown U., 1977. Bar: D.C. 1975, Calif. 1982, U.S. Supreme Ct. 1984, other dist. and appellate cts. Spl. asst. state's atty. Cir. and Dist. Cts. Montgomery County, Md., 1975-77; staff atty. legal intern program Georgetown U. Law Ctr., Washington, 1975-77, adj. prof., dep. dir. legal intern program, 1977-79; cons., vis. supervising atty. Yale Legal Svcs. Orgn., Law Sch. Yale U., New Haven, 1977; with Baker & Fine, Cambridge, Mass., 1980-81; asst. clin. prof. Law Ctr. U. So. Calif., L.A., 1981-83, assoc. clin. prof., 1983-86, clin. prof., 1986-89, adj. prof., 1990-92; vis. prof. law Boston U., 1990, UCLA, 1991-92; pvt. practice Law Offices of William J. Genego, Santa Monica, Calif., 1990-2000; ptnr. Nasatir, Hirsch, Podberesky & Genego, Santa Monica, 2000—. Mem. practitioners' adv. group U.S. Sentencing Commn., 1989—; presenter in field. Mem. adv. bd. Criminal Practice Manual, Bur. Nat. Affairs, 1987-2000; editor Yale Law Jour., 1974-75; contbr. articles to legal publs. Bd. dirs. Nat. Network for Right to Counsel, 1986-88. Recipient Ann. Humanitarian award inmate rep. com. Fed. Correctional Instn., Danbury, Conn., 1974. Mem. NACDL (chairperson com. on rules of practice and procedure 1991—, Pres.'s award 1988), ABA (mem. ad hoc com. on U.S. Sentencing Commn. 1986—, chairperson competency com. sect. criminal justice 1983-85), Nat. Legal Aid and Defender Assn. (chairperson def. counsel competency com. 1984-87), Calif. Pub. Defenders Assn., Calif. Attys. for Criminal Justice. Office: Main St Law Bldg 2115 Main St Santa Monica CA 90405-2215

GENEL, MYRON, pediatrician, educator; b. York, Pa., Jan. 6, 1936; s. Victor and Florence (Mowitz) G.; m. Phyllis Norma Berkman, Aug. 25, 1968; children: Elizabeth, Jennifer, Abby. Grad., Moravian Coll., 1957; MD, U. Pa., 1961; MA (hon.), Yale U., 1983; DSc (hon.), Moravian Coll., 1995. Diplomate Am. Bd. Pediat. Intern Mt. Sinai Hosp., N.Y.C., 1961-62; resident in pediat. Children's Hosp. Phila., 1962-64; trainee pediat. endocrinology Johns Hopkins Hosp., Balt., 1966-67; instr. pediat. U. Pa. Sch. Medicine, 1967-69, assoc. in pediat., 1969-71; trainee in genetics, inherited metabolic diseases Children's Hosp. Phila., 1967-69, assoc. physician, 1969-71; attending physician Yale-New Haven Hosp., 1971—; faculty Yale U. Sch. Medicine, New Haven, 1971—, dir. pediat. endocrinology, 1971-85, program dir. Children's Clin. Rsch. Ctr., 1971-86, prof., 1981—, assoc. dean, 1985—, dir. Office Govt. and Cmty. Affairs, 1985—. Genetic adv. bd. State of Conn., 1979—82, 1994—; cons. subcom. investigations, oversight com. sci. and tech. U.S. Ho. of Reps., 1982—84; mem. adv. bd. New Eng. Congenital Hypothyroidism Collaborative; cons. Hosp. St. Raphael, Milford Hosp., Norwalk Hosp., Stamford Hosp., Danbury Hosp., Greenwich Hosp.; chmn. transplant adv. com. Office of Commr. Conn. Dept. Income Maintenance, 1984—92; health policy fellowship bd. Inst. Medicine, 1989—95; clin. rsch. roundtable Inst. Medicine Nat. Rsch. Coun., 2000—. Contbr. articles to profl. jours. Bd. dirs. Rsch. America!, 1997—2000. Capt. USAR, 1964—66. Robert Wood Johnson Health Policy fellow Inst. Medicine NAS, Washington, 1982-83; recipient ann. award Conn. Campaign Against Cooley's Anemia, 1979, Ann. Comenius Alumni award Moravian Coll., 1990, Abraham Jacobi Meml. award Am. Acad. Pediat. and AMA, 1999. Fellow: AAAS; mem.: AMA (med. schs. sec. 1985—, coun. on sci. affairs 1994—2001, task force on fin. grad. med. edn. 1995, alt. del. governing coun., med. schs. sec. 1995—98, task force on privacy and confidentiality 1998—99, del. 1998—2002, chair 2003—), APHA, Assn. Patient Oriented Rsch., N.Y. Acad. Medicine, Conn. Acad. Sci. and Engring. (coun. 2000—), Soc. Pediat. Rsch. (Disting. Svc. award 2003), Endocrine Soc. (rsch. initiative com. 1995—99, legis. affairs com. 2002—), Conn. United for Rsch. Excellence (chmn. steering com. 1989—90, pres. 1990—93, chmn. bd. dirs. 1993—94), Conn. Endocrine Soc., Nat. Assn. Biomed. Rsch. (bd. dirs. 1990—93, exec. com. 1991—93), Assn. Program Dirs. (pres.-elect 1980—81, pres. 1981—82), New Haven County Med. Assn. (bd. govs. 1990—2002), Assn. Am. Med. Colls. (adminstrv. bd. coun. acad. socs. 1987—92, chmn.-elect coun. acad. socs. 1989—91, exec. coun. 1989—92, adv. panel on rsch. 1999—2003), Am. Soc. Bone and Mineral Rsch., Am. Pediat. Soc., Am. Fedn. Med. Rsch., Am. Diabetes Assn. (co-recipient Jonathan May award 1979), Am. Coll. Preventive Medicine, Am. Coll. Nutrition, Am. Assn. Clin. Endocrinologists, Am. Acad. Pediat. (task force organ transplants, com. on fed. govt. affairs), Sigma Xi. Jewish. Office: Yale Sch of Med PO Box 208000 New Haven CT 06520-8000 Home: 30 Richard Sweet Dr Woodbridge CT 06525-1126 E-mail: myron.genel@yale.edu.

GENESI, SUSAN PETROVICH, educator, consultant; b. Philipsburg, Pa., Mar. 24, 1957; d. Richard and Margaret (Ohs) Petrovich; 1 child, Lindsay Margaret. BS in Elem. Edn., Pa. State U., 1981, cert. ednl. adminstrn., 1998, MA in Edn. Adminstrn., 1999; PA Superintend Ency Letter of Eligibility, 2002. Cert. elem. tchr., Pa.; cert. kindergarten tchr., Pa.; cert. instrnl. tech. specialist; cert. grant specialist. Adminstr. Philipsburg-Osceola Area Sch. Dist., Pa., 1981—, prin., 1998. Commr. Pa. Profl. Stds. and Practices Commn., Harrisburg, Pa., 1995—; mem. content validation panel for early adolescence English Nat. Bd. for Profl. Tchg. Stds., Atlanta, 1997; workshop presenter on topics of coop. learning; presenter Keystone State Reading Assn., Hershey, Pa., 1995, 96; coop. tchr. Pa. State U., State College, 1994—; mem. various coms. throughout the sch. dist. Contbr. articles to profl. jours. Mem. Philipsburg Bicentennial Com., 1996-97; organizer Philipsburg Elem. Philipsburg Days, 1994. Mem. ASCD, NEA, Pa. State Edn. Assn., Philipsburg-Osceola Area Edn. Assn. (com. 1981—), Phi Delta Kappa. Republican. Presbyterian. Avocations: traveling and shopping with daughter, computer technology, exploring new trends in education and technology, relaxing at the beach. Office: North Lincoln Elem Sch/ Wallaceton Boggs Elem Sch 200 Short St Philipsburg PA 16866-2640 E-mail: sxg23@psu.edu.

GENEST, JACQUES, physician, clinical scientist, administrator; b. Montreal, Que., Can., May 29, 1919; s. Rosario and Annette (Girouard) G.; m. Estelle Deschamps, Oct. 3, 1953; children: Paul, Suzanne, Jacques, Marie, Helene. BA, Coll. Jean de Brebeuf, Montreal, 1937; MD, U. Montreal, 1942; LLD (hon.), Queen's U., 1966, U. Toronto, Can., 1970; DSc (hon.), Laval (Can.) U., 1973,

Sherbrooke U., 1974, Meml. U. Nfld., 1978, McGill (Can.) U., 1979, U. Ottawa, 1980, St. Francis Xavier U., 1983, SUNY, Buffalo, 1984, Rockefeller U., 1986, Concordia U., Montreal, 1986, Chinese Acad. Med. Scis., 1987, U. Montpelier, France, 1989. Summer student Harvard Med. Sch., Boston, 1938, 39; resident in medicine and pathology Hôtel-Dieu Hosp., Montreal, 1942-45, cons. physician in nephrology, endocrinology and internal medicine, 1952-91; rsch. fellow Johns Hopkins Hosp., Balt., 1945-48, Harvard Sch. Chemistry, Boston, 1948, Rockefeller Hosp. Med. Rsch., N.Y.C., 1948-51; prof. medicine U. Montreal, 1965-96; prof. exptl. medicine McGill U., Montreal, 1960-98; founder, 1st dir. Clin. Rsch. Inst. Montreal, 1965-84, adviser, 1984-94. Bd. dirs. Merck & Co., Rahway, N.J., Montreal Trust. Editor: (with Erich Koiw) Hypertension, 1972; (with Erich Koiw and Otto Kuchel) Hypertension: Physiopathology and Treatment, 1977, 83; (with Marc Cantin, Otto Kuchel, Pavel Hamet) 2d edit., 1983; author: One Ideal, One Life, 1998. Decorated companion Order of Can., grand officer Ordre Nat. du Que.; recipient award Gairdner Found., 1963, Archambault medal Can. Assn. for Advancement Sci., 1965, Marie-Victorin Sci. prize Govt. of Que., 1977, Royal Bank award, 1980, Isaac Walton Killam award, 1986, Armand Frappier prize Govt. of Que., 1996, Patronat du Quebec prize, 1998, Grand Montrealais prize, 2000, FCAR award Govt. Que., 2001,Purkynje medal Czech Acad. Sci., 2002; named to Can. Med. Hall of Fame, 1994. Master ACP; fellow Royal Coll. Physicians and Surgeons Can. (James H. Graham award of merit 1993), Royal Soc. Can. (Flavelle medal and award 1968); mem. Assn. Am. Physicians, Am. Clin. and Climatol. Assn., Am. Heart Assn. (Stouffer prize 1969, Disting. Scientist award), Peripatetic Club. Roman Catholic. Home: 5955 Wilderton Ave PH-L6 Montreal QC Canada H3S 2V1 Office: Inst de REcherches Cliniques Montreal QC Canada H2W 1R7 E-mail: jacgensr@sympatico.ca.

GENÉT, BARBARA ANN, accountant, travel counselor; b. N.Y.C., Oct. 14, 1935; d. Arthur Samuel and Louise Margaret (Scheider) G. Profl. cert. in acctg., U. Calif., La Jolla, 1995, student, 1996—; BS of Acctg., U. Phoenix, 2001; MBA, Keller Grad. Sch. Mgmt., 2003. Asst. to chmn. bd., asst. v.p. pub. rels. Brink's Inc., Chgo., 1976-78; co-owner, pres. Ask Mr. Foster, Chgo., 1982-90; with Profl. Cmty. Mgmt., Laguna Hills, Calif., 1990-92; travel counselor E.J. Brown & Assocs., San Diego, 1992-94; tchr.'s asst. U. Calif-San Diego, La Jolla, 1996—. Rep. Becker CPA-CMA Rev., San Diego, 1995— Becker scholar, 1995, scholar Marks CPA Rev., 1996. Mem. Am. Soc. Woman Accts., Inst. Mgmt. Accts., Inst. Cert. Travel Agts., Order Ea. Star, Ladies of Shrine N. Am. Zonta Internat. of La Jolla (treas. 1998-2000). E-mail: barbaragenet@cox.net.

GENETSKI, ROBERT JAMES, economist; b. N.Y.C., Dec. 26, 1942; s. Alex and Helen Genetski. BS, Ea. Ill. U., 1964; MA, NYU, 1968, PhD, 1972. Tchr. English St. Procopius Acad., Lisle, Ill., 1965-66; research analyst Nat. Econ. Research Assn., N.Y.C., 1967-68; lectr. econs. NYU, N.Y.C., 1969-70; econ. analyst Morgan Guaranty Trust Co., N.Y.C., 1969-71; sr. v.p., economist Harris Trust & Savs. Bank, Chgo., 1971-88; pres. Stotler Econs., Chgo., 1988-90; sr. v.p., chief economist The Chgo. Corp., 1990-91; pres. Robert Genetski & Assocs., 1991—; sr. mng. dir. Chgo. Capital, 1995-2000. Lectr. econs. NYU, 1969-70, U. Chgo., 1973; vis. prof. Wheaton (Ill.) Coll., 1986; mem. census adv. com. U.S. Dept. Commerce, 1983-86; bd. dirs. Fin. Security Corp., Suburban Fed. Savs. Bank. Author: (with Beryl Sprinkel) Winning with Money, 1977, Taking the Voodoo out of Economics, 1986, 88, A Nation of Millionaires, 1997. Chmn. ednl. com. Sch. Bd. Dist. 25, West Chicago, Ill., 1973-79; bd. dirs. Ctrl. DuPage Health Svcs., 1988-94. Mem. Am. Statis. Assn., Am. Econ. Assn. (fin. com. 1983—), Nat. Assn. Bus. Economists (editor Newsletter 1978), Western Econ. Assn., Am. Bankers Assn. (econ. adv. com. 1980-83), U.S. C. of C. (econ. adv. com. 1985—) Office: 195 N Harbor Dr Ste 4903 Chicago IL 60601 E-mail: rgenetski@earthlink.net.

GENETT-SCHRADER, ANN G. public relations executive; b. Glendale, Calif., Apr. 22, 1945; d. James Charles Genett, Gladys Miller Genett; m. John Charles Schrader. BA cum laude, U. Houston, 1967. Tchr. English, journalism Coll. of Bahamas, Nassau, The Bahamas, 1976—79; publs. editor Am. Airlines, Inc., Ft. Worth, 1979—90; corr. supr. Mary Kay Cosmetics, Dallas, 1997—2000; mgr. mktg. commn. Carter BloodCare, Bedford, 2000—02; media rels. mgr. Carter & Burgess, Inc., Ft. Worth, 2002—. Comm. cons., Bedford, 1994—97. Author: Careers: Women in Aviation, 1975. HEB leadership class of 2001 Hurst/Euless/Bedford C. of C., Bedford, 2001—01; mem. Bedford Beautification Commn., 2001; tutor, mentor Adopt-a-School, 2001. Named Best Airline Newspaper, Airline Editors Forum of the Air Transport Assn, 1981, 1982. Mem.: Soc. Profl. Journalists, Pub. Rels. Soc. Am. (treas. 2003). Avocations: marathons, gardening, travel, photography. Office: Carter & Burgess Inc 777 Main St Fort Worth TX 76012 Office Fax: 817-735-2890. Business E-Mail: Genett-SchraderAG@c-b.com.

GENG, CHUAN-DONG, research scientist; b. Fuling, Chongqing, China, May 7, 1972; s. Shoumin Geng and Yiqun Liu; m. Ping Xia, Ping, Sept. 18, 1998; 1 child, Nerissa. BS, Sichuan U., Chengdu, China, 1994; PhD, Shanghai Inst. Biochemistry, China, 1999. Rsch. assoc. LSU Health Sci. Ctr., New Orleans, 1999—. Mem.: Endocrine Soc., Am. Soc. for Biochemistry and Molecular Biology, Sigma Xi. Achievements include research in hGR expression regulation and Leukemia; discovery of functional novel hGR mRNA splice variances and GRE in 1A promoter; Identified genes linked to alphid resistant phenotype in cotton; development of Develop Disease Resistant Cotton And Tobacco Using Biotechnology Engineering Technique. Office: Boichemistry/LSU Health Sci Ctr 1901perdido St New Orleans LA 70112 E-mail: cgeng@lsuhsc.edu.

GENGE, WILLIAM HARRISON, advertising executive, writer; b. Warren, Pa., May 7, 1923; s. Valleau Francis and Beatrice (Badger) G.; m. Beverly Ann Milway, June 23, 1945 (dec. May 1991); children: Deborah Ann, William Dean. BA, U. Pitts., 1948; grad., Internat. Mktg. Inst., Harvard U., 1967. Writer Bull. Index, Pitts., 1947-48; editor Gulf Oil Corp., 1948-53; with Ketchum Communications, Inc., 1953—98, sr. v.p., 1965-68, exec. v.p., 1968-70, pres., 1970-79, chmn., 1979-93, also dir.; pres. Civique, Inc., Pitts., 1993—. Nat. vice-chmn. The Children's Health, Edn. and Fitness Found.; bd. dirs. Fed. Home Loan Bank. Chmn. bd. visitors U. Pitts. Press., U. Pitts. Grad. Sch. Bus., Pitts. Opera Theatre, City Theatre; Bd. dirs. Pitts. Symphony; Chatham Coll.; Pitts. Youth Symphony; U. Pitts. 1st lt. USAF, 1942—46, prisoner of war, 1944—45. Decorated Purple Heart. Mem. Pitts. Golf Club, Fox Chapel Golf Club, Duquesne Club, Rolling Rock Club, Phi Gamma Delta. Republican. Presbyterian (elder). Avocations: tennis, sailing, golf, reading, writing. Home: 5045 5th Ave Pittsburgh PA 15232-2130 *Whatever degree of achievement I've attained is due to unflagging optimism, perseverance and effort, a Christian outlook at least 50% of the time, and recognition that no man can do it alone. You need friends and supporters all along the way.*

GENGLER, SUE WONG, health educator, evaluation consultant, speaker, trainer; b. Hong Kong, Apr. 6, 1959; came to U.S., 1966; d. Tin Ho and Yuet Kum (Chan) Wong; m. Clayton J. Gengler, 1995. BS, UCLA, 1981; MPH, Loma Linda (Calif.) U., 1990; DrPH, Loma Linda U., 1995. Cert. health edn. specialist. Asst. to the dir. Project Asia Campus Crusade for Christ, San Bernardino, Calif., 1982-83, Campus Crusade for Christ-Internat. Pers., San Bernardino, 1983-90; health educator San Bernardino County Pub. Health, 1990-92; community lab. instr., rsch. asst. dept. health promotion and edn. Loma Linda (Calif.) U. Sch. Pub. Health, 1992-95; behaviorist/educator Anaheim Hills Med. Group/St. Jude Heritage Med. Group, Anaheim, Calif., 1995-96; direct svcs. dir. Alternatives to Domestic Violence, Riverside, Calif., 1997—2001; evaluation cons., domestic violence sect. Maternal and Child Health br. Calif. Dept. Health Svcs., 1999—2001; health edn. mgr. Inland Empire Health Plan, San Bernadino, Calif., 2001—. Mem. Minority Health Coalition, San Bernardino, 1990-92, Com. for the Culturally Diverse, San Bernardino, 1990-92; vol. Am. Cancer Soc.; chair Gt. Am. Smokeout, Inland Empire, 1991; bd. dirs. Family Svcs. Agy., San Bernardino, 1994-96. Selma Andrews scholar Loma Linda U., 1994; named Outstanding Young Woman of Yr., 1983, Hulda Crooke Scholar, Loma Linda U., 1989; recipient Am. Cancer Soc. Rose award, 1991 (Calif.), Gaspar award, 1991 (nat.), Chief's award of Excellence Corona Police Dept. Mem. APHA, Nat. Coun. for Internat. Health, Soc. Pub. Health Edn. Avocations: travel, reading, volleyball, calligraphy, music. E-mail: gengler-s@iehp.org.

GENGOR, VIRGINIA ANDERSON, financial planning executive, educator; b. Lyons, N.Y., May 2, 1927; d. Axel Jennings and Marie Margaret (Mack) Anderson; m. Peter Gengor, Mar. 2, 1952 (dec.); children: Peter Randall, Daniel Neal, Susan Leigh. AB, Wheaton Coll., 1949; MA, U. No. Colo., 1975, MA, 1977. Cert. fin. planner Coll. Fin. Planning. Chief hosp. intake svc. County of San Diego, 1966-77; chief Kearny Mesa Dist. Office, 1977-79, Dept. Children of Ct., 1979-81, chief child protection svcs., 1981-82; registered rep. Am. Pacific Securities, San Diego, 1982-85; registered tax preparer State of Calif., 1982—; registered rep. (prin.) Sentra Securities, 1985—; assoc. Pollock & Assocs., San Diego, 1985—86; pres. Gengor Fin. Advisors, 1986—. Cons. instr. Nat. Ctr. for Fin. Edn., San Diego, 1986-88; instr. San Diego Community Coll., 1985-88. Mem. allocations panel United Way, San Diego, 1976-79; children's cir. Child Abuse Prevention Found., 1989—; chmn. com. Child Abuse Coord. Coun., San Diego, 1979-83; pres. Friends of Casa de la Esperanza, San Diego, 1980-85, bd. dirs., 1980—; 1st v.p. The Big Sis. League, San Diego, 1985-86, pres., 1987-89. Mem. NAFE, AAUW (bd. dirs.), Inst. Cert. Fin. Planners, Fin. Planning Assn., Inland Soc. Tax Cons., Nat. Assn. Securities Dealers (registered prin.), Nat. Ctr. Fin. Edn., Am. Bus. Women's Assn., Navy League, Freedoms Found. of Valley Forge, Internat. Platform Assn. Presbyterian. Avocations: community service, travel, reading. Home: 6462 Spear St San Diego CA 92120-2929 Office: Gengor Fin Advisors 4950 Waring Rd Ste 7 San Diego CA 92120-2700 E-mail: vgengor@cox.net.

GENIA, JAMES MICHAEL, lawyer; b. Chgo., Sept. 16, 1964; s. Anthony Leo and Anne Louise (Hawley) Genia. BA, Augsburg Coll., 1987; JD, William Mitchell Coll. Law, 1990. Bar: Minn. 1990, U.S. Dist. Ct. Minn. 1992, U.S. Ct. Appeals (8th cir.) 1994, U.S. Supreme Ct. 1999. Jud. law clk. State of Minn., Duluth, 1990-92; dep. solicitor gen. Mille Lacs Band of Ojibwe Indians, Onamia, Minn., 1992-93, solicitor gen., 1993-99; atty. Lockridge Grindal Nauen, Mpls., 1999—2002, ptnr., 2002—. Bd. dirs. Woodlands Nat. Bank., chmn. bd. dirs.; vice chmn. bd. dirs. Anishinabe O. I. C.; lectr. Am. Indian sovereignty and treaty rights various univs., continuing edn. seminars, civic groups, 1992—; adj. prof. St. Cloud State U., 1999—. Actor: (plays) Mille Lacs Cmty. Theater, 1996—. Bd. dirs. Johnson Inst. Found., 1998—. Named Atty. of the Yr., Minn. Lawyer Newspaper, 1999; named one of Top 100 All-Time Grads., William Mitchell Coll. Law, 2000. Mem.: ATLA, Minn. State Bar, Minn. Am. Indian Bar Assn., Fed. Bar Assn., Am. Indian C. of C. (bd. dirs. 2001—), William Mitchell Coll. Law Alumni Assn. (bd. dirs. 1996—99). Avocations: softball, golf, jogging, reading, acting. Office: Lockridge Grindal Nauen 100 Washington Ave S Ste 2200 Minneapolis MN 55401-2179 E-mail: jmgenia@locklaw.com.

GENIESSE, ROBERT JOHN, lawyer; b. Appleton, Wis., Sept. 16, 1929; s. Arthur John and Rhoda (Miller) G.; m. Jane Elizabeth Fletcher, June 10, 1961; children: Julia Forrest, Thomas Guy. BA magna cum laude, Williams Coll., 1951; LLB cum laude, Harvard U., 1957. Bar: N.Y. 1958, D.C. 1982. Assoc. Debevoise and Plimpton, N.Y.C., 1957-61, 64-66, ptnr., 1966-94; asst. U.S. atty. So. Dist. N.Y., 1962-63, chief appellate atty., 1963-64. Editor Harvard Law Rev., 1955-57. Bd. dirs. Legal Action Ctr., N.Y., 1973-78, Environ. Def. Fund, 1974-82; trustee Williams Coll., 1974-87; trustee World Monuments Fund, 1993—, sec., gen. counsel, 1995—; trustee Nat. Bldg. Mus., 1994-2000; trustee Sterling and Francine Clark Art Inst., Williamstown, Mass., 1974-2001, pres., 1987-98; trustee Ringling Mus. Art, Sarasota, Fla., 2001—. 1st lt. Inf. U.S. Army, 1952-54. Mem. N.Y. State Bar Assn., D.C. Bar Assn., Soc. Alumni of Williams Coll. (pres. 1973-74), Phi Beta Kappa. Home: PO Box 516 Boca Grande FL 33921-0516 also; 2101 Connecticut Ave NW Apt 61 Washington DC 20008-1757 Office: Devevoise & Plimpton 555 13th St NW Ste 1100E Washington DC 20004-1163

GENINI, RONALD WALTER, history educator, historian; b. Oakland, Calif., Dec. 5, 1946; s. William Angelo and Irma Lea (Gays) G.; m. Roberta Mae Tucker, Dec. 20, 1969; children: Thomas, Justin, Nicholas. BA, U. San Francisco, 1968, MA, 1969. Cert. secondary edn. tchr., Calif.; adminstrv. svcs. credential. Tchr. Ctrl. Unified Sch. Dist., Fresno, Calif., 1970—. Judge State History Day, Sacramento, 1986-94; mem. U.S. history exam. devel. team Golden State, San Diego, 1989-93; securer placement of state-registered landmarks; guest appearance History Channel program "UFO Hotspots," Jan. 2003. Author: Romualdo Pacheco, 1985, Darn Right It's Butch, 1994, Theda Bara, 1996; contbr. articles to profl. jours.; cited as authority on Theda Bara by Ency. Brit. Online Am. Women in History, 1999, also on Romualdo Pacheco by Biog. Directory of Am. Congress. Bd. dirs. Fresno Area 6 Neighborhood Coun., 1973-74, Fresno City and County Hist. Soc., 1975-78, St. Anthony's sch. bd., Fresno, 1980-84; mem. Good Company Players, Fresno, 2000—. Named one of Outstanding Young Educators Am., Fresno Jaycees, 1978; recipient recognition for Tchr. Cares award Calif. State Assembly and Fresno City Coun., 1996. Mem. Calif. Hist. Soc. Democrat. Avocations: writing history 19th century Calif. and early Hollywood, motion picture scriptwriter, commercial acting. Home: 1486 W Menlo Ave Fresno CA 93711-1305 Office: Ctrl HS 2045 N Dickenson Ave Fresno CA 93722-9643 E-mail: rgenini@hotmail.com.

GENIS, ALICE SINGER, psychologist; b. Vilnius, Lithuania, June 8, 1926; d. Nahum Singer and Miriam Singer (Smith) Galerkin; widowed; children: naomi Genis-Mazin, Robert Genis. Esq., Ludwig Maximillian U., Munich, 1950; BA, Pace U., 1974; MA, Mercy Coll., Dobbs Ferry, N.Y., 1978, Coll. of New Rochelle, 1983. Cert. sch. psychologist. Lab. tech. Queens Gen. Hosp., N.Y.C., 1952-55; with Daycare Ctr. Presbyn. Ch., Peekskill, N.Y., 1972-73; psychologist Mental Health Clinic, Peekskill, 1978-80; asst. sch. psychology Pines Bridge Sch., Yorktown, N.Y., 1980-82; biofeedback therapist Med. Cmty. Ctr., Cortland, N.Y., 1985-94; sch. psychologist BOCES, Yorktown, N.Y., 1983-85. Presenter in field. Contbr. articles to profl. jours. Vol. Hosp. Aux., Peekskill, 1962-98; com. Heart Fund Ball, Westchester, 1970s, 80s; pres. Norchester Hadassam, Peekskill, 1983-85, 88-91; mem. The Field Libr., Peekskill. Named Woman of Merit, Westchester Hadassh, White Plaines, N.Y., 1996; recipient New Life award Israel Bonds, Peekskill, 1979, Presl. awards Norchester Hadassah, 1985, 91. Mem. Nat. Assn. Sch. Psychologists, Biofeedback and Psychophysiology Performing Ctr. for the Arts. Avocations: music, piano, swimming, gardening, travel. Home: 1 Birchwood Ln Cortlandt Manor NY 10567-6709

GENKIN, BARRY HOWARD, lawyer; b. Philadelphia, Aug. 8, 1949; s. Paul and Pearl (Rosenfeld) G.; m. Marian (Block), Aug. 15, 1975; children: Matthew Todd, Kimberly Beth. BS(hon.), Pa. State U., 1971; JD (hon.), U. Balt., 1974; LLM in taxation, Georgetown U., 1977. Bar: Pa., 1975; Wash., 1977; N.Y., 1995. Spl. counsel divsn. corp. fin. SEC, Washington, 1975-78; ptnr. Blank and Rome, LLP, Phila., 1979-93, firm officer, fin. ptnr., exec. com., co-chmn. corp. dept., dist. com., mgmt. com., chmn. budget com. Pres. bd. dirs. Smeal Bus. Sch., Pa. State U., pres., 2003-2005; lectr. various orgn. Contbr. U. Balt. Law Rev., 1991—; lectr. various orgn. Mem. ABA; Pa. Bar Assn.; Savs. Insts.; Pa. Savs. League; N.J. Savs. League.; Meadowlands Country Club; Heuisler Honor Soc.; Omicron Delta Kappa. Home: 544 Howe Rd Merion Station PA 19066-1129 Office: Blank & Rome LLP One Logan Sq Philadelphia PA 19103

GENKIN, GENNADY, physicist; b. Gomel, Belorussia, USSR, May 19, 1934; s. Mark Genkin and Vera Korb; m. Mara Fainstein, June 29, 1956; children: Leonid, Alla. MS in Physics, State U. of Gorky, USSR, 1959, PhD in Physics, 1965; DSc, State U. of Kazan, USSR, 1976; Prof. Physics, Highest Attestation Commn., USSR, 1990. Rschr. Radiophys. Inst., Gorky, 1959-61, sr. rschr., 1961-76; leading rschr. Inst. of Applied Physics/Acad. of Sci., Nizhny, Novgorod, Russia, 1976-95. Vis. scholar dept. of physics and astronomy Northwestern U., Evanston, Ill., 1996—. Contbr. articles to profl. jours. Office: Northwestern U Phys and Astron 2145 Sheridan Rd Evanston IL 60208-0834 E-mail: gena@pluto.phys.nwu.edu.

GENKINS, GABRIEL, physician; b. Berlin, Mar. 20, 1928; came to U.S., 1940, naturalized, 1945; s. Arkady and Tamara (Schlesinger) G.; children: Karen Lee Genkins Fairbank, Steven M., Amy E. BS, NYU, 1949, MD, 1952. Diplomate Am. Bd. Internal Medicine, Diplomate Am. Bd. Cardiology. Intern, resident Mt. Sinai Hosp., N.Y.C., 1952-57; practice medicine specializing in cardiology N.Y.C.; clin. prof. medicine Mt. Sinai Med. Ctr., N.Y.C., 1973—, chief myasthenia gravis clinic and rsch. labs., 1972—; attending physician in cardiology Mt. Sinai Hosp., N.Y.C., 1973—; v.p. bd. dirs. Myasthenia Gravis Found., 1973—, mem. nat. med. adv. bd., 1956—. Contbr. articles to profl. jours., chpts. to books Served with airborne inf., U.S. Army, 1945-46 Democrat. Office: 30 E 60th St New York NY 10022-1008

GENN, NANCY, artist; b. San Francisco; d. Morley P. and Ruth W. Thompson; m. Vernon Chathburton Genn; children: Cynthia, Sarah, Peter. Student, San Francisco Art Inst., U. Calif., Berkeley. Lectr. on art and papermaking Am. Ctrs. in Osaka, Japan, Nagoya, Japan, Kyoto, Japan, 1979-80; guest lectr. various univs. and art mus. in U.S., 1975—; vis. artist Am. Acad. in Rome, 1989, 94, 2001. One woman shows of sculpture, paintings include, De Young Mus., San Francisco, 1955, 63, Gumps Gallery, San Francisco, 1955, 57, 59, San Francisco Mus. Art, 1961, U. Calif., Santa Cruz, 1966-68, Richmond (Calif.) Art Center, 1970, Oakland (Calif.) Mus., 1971, Linda/Farris Gallery, Seattle, 1974, 76, 78, 81, Los Angeles Inst. Contemporary Art, 1976, Susan Caldwell Gallery, N.Y.C., 1976, 77, 79, 81, Nina Freudenheim Gallery, Buffalo, 1977, 81, Annely Juda Fine Art, London, 1978, Inoue Gallery, Tokyo, 1980, Toni Birckhead Gallery, Cin., 1982, Kala Inst. Gallery, Berkeley, Calif., 1983, Ivory/Kimpton Gallery, San Francisco, 1984, 86, Eve Mannes Gallery, Atlanta, 1985, Richard Iri Gallery, L.A., 1990, Harcourts Modern and Contemporary Art, San Francisco, 1991, 93, 96, Am. Assn. Advancement of Sci., Washington, 1994, Anne Reed Gallery, Ketchum, Id., 1995, Michael Petronko Gallery, N.Y., 1997, Mills Coll. Art Mus., Oakland, Calif., 1999, Takada Gallery, San Francisco, 1999, 2000, 2003, Ulivi Gallery, Prato, Italy, 2002, Fresno Art Mus., Calif., 2003, Bolinas Mus., Calif., 2003; group exhbns. include San Francisco Mus. Art, 1971, Aldrich Mus., Ridgefield, Conn., 1972-73, Santa Barbara (Calif.) Mus., 1974, 75, Oakland (Calif.) Mus. Art, 1975, Susan Caldwell, Inc., N.Y.C., 1974, 75, Mus. Modern Art, N.Y.C., 1976, traveling exhbn. Arts Coun. Gt. Britain, 1983-84, Inst. Contemporary Arts, Boston, 1977, J.J.Brookings Gallery, San Francisco, 1997, Portland (Oreg.) Art Mus., 1997—, Takada Gallery, San Francisco, 1999, 2000; represented in permanent collections Mus. Modern Art, N.Y.C., Albright-Knox Art Gallery, Buffalo, Libr. of Congress, Washington, Nat. Mus. for Am. Art, Washington, L.A. County Mus. Art, Art Mus. U. Calif., Berkeley, McCrory Corp., N.Y.C., Mus. Art, Auckland, N.Z., Aldrich Mus., Ridgefield, Conn., (collection) Bklyn. Mus., (collection) U. Tex., El Paso, Internat. Ctr. Aesthetic Rsch., Torino, Italy, Cin. Art Mus., San Francisco Mus. Modern Art, Oakland Art Mus., L.A. County Mus., City of San Francisco Hall of Justice, Harris Bank, Chgo., Chase Manhattan Bank, N.Y.C., Modern Art Gallery of Ascoli Piceno, Italy, Mills Coll. Art Mus., Oakland, Calif., Mills Coll. of Art, Oakland, Calif., Leighton Gallery, Blue Hill, Maine, various mfg. cos., also numerous pvt. collections; commd. works include, Bronze lectern and 5 bronze sculptures for chancel table, 1st Unitarian Ch., Berkeley, Calif., 1961, 64, bronze fountain, Cowell Coll., U. Calif., Santa Cruz, bronze menorah, Temple Beth Am, Los Altos Hills, Calif., 1981, 17, murals and 2 bronze fountain sculptures, Sterling Vineyards, Calistoga, Calif., 1972, 73, fountain sculpture, Expo 1974, Spokane, Wash.; vis. artist Am. Acad., Rome 1989. U.S./Japan Creative Arts fellow, 1978-79; recipient Ellen Branston award, 1952; Phelan award De Young Mus., 1963; honor award HUD, 1968 Home: 1515 La Loma Ave Berkeley CA 94708-2033

GENNETT, TIMOTHY, academic administrator; b. Richmond, Ind., July 25, 1951; s. Henry and Barbara Milda (Collignon) G.; m. Sharon Gail Cox, Mar. 5, 1976. BS in Chemistry, Purdue U., 1973, MS in Indsl. Adminstrn., 1974, MSEd, 1984. Lic. amateur radio operator. Sales engr. Gulf Oil Corp., San Antonio, 1975-77; asst. mgr. residence halls Purdue U., West Lafayette, Ind., 1977-82, mgr. residence halls, 1982-90, asst. dir. residence halls, 1990-95, dir. facilities housing and food svcs., 1995—2003. Bd. dirs. Gennett Graphics, Lafayette, Ind.; presenter in field. Contbr. articles to profl. jours. Damage assessement coord. ARC, Tippecanoe County, Ind., 1998-2000. Named Vol. of Yr. Disaster Svsc. ARC, 1996 Mem. Assn. Higher Edn. Cable TV Adminstrs. (bd. dirs. 2000—), Tippecanoe Amateur Radio Assn. (sec. 1995-97), Soc. Cable TV Engrs. Office: Purdue U 105 Smalley Ctr West Lafayette IN 47906-4205

GENOVA, DIANE MELISANO, lawyer; b. Aug. 8, 1948; d. Joseph Louis and Ines (Fiumana) Melisano; m. Joseph Steven Genova, Jan. 15, 1983; children: Anthony Robert, Matthew Edward. AB, Barnard Coll., 1970; postgrad., Harvard U., 1970-71; JD, Columbia U., 1975. Assoc. Milbank, Tweed, Hadley & McCloy, N.Y.C., 1975-80; v.p., asst. resident counsel Morgan Guaranty Trust Co. N.Y., N.Y.C., 1981-90, mng. dir., assoc. gen. counsel, 1990-2000, J.P. Morgan Chase & Co., N.Y.C., 2001—. Harlan Fiske Stone scholar, 1972-75. Mem. Assn. of Bar of City of N.Y., N.Y. State Bar Assn., Internat. Swaps and Derivatives Assn. (bd. dirs. 1999—). Roman Catholic. Office: J P Morgan Chase & Co 270 Park Ave New York NY 10022 E-mail: genova_diane@jpmorgan.com.

GENOVA, PAMELA A. French literature educator; b. Chgo., Nov. 11, 0961; d. Anthony Charles and Veronica Barton Genova. BA, U. Kans., 1983; MA, U. Ill., 1986, PhD, 1991. Asst. prof. French U. Okla., Norman, 1991—97, assoc. prof. French, 1997—, assoc. dean, 1999—. Sr. cons. editor World Lit. Today, Norman, 2001—. Author: (book) Symbolist Journals: A Culture of Correspondence, 2002, André Gide dens le abyriathe de lamytholexhalité, 1995; contbr. ACLS fellow, 1997—98, Am. Philos. Soc. fellow, 1997, NEH fellow, 1997. Mem.: South Central MLA (exec. com. 1999—2001), Nature Conservancy, Sierra Club. Avocations: gardening, hiking, travel, birdwatching. Office: Univ of Oklahoma 633 Elm St Norman OK 73019

GENOVESE, EDGAR NICHOLAS, humanities educator; b. Balt., Sept. 18, 1942; s. E.N. and Elizabeth (Hlobick) G.; m. Janice Kay Hodapp, July 8, 1969; children: Domenica Rose, Charles Anthony. AB, Xavier U., 1964; PhD, Ohio State U., 1970. Instr. Kenwood Sr. High Sch., Essex, Md., 1964-66; prof. classics and humanities San Diego State U., 1970—2003, prof. emeritus, 2003—. Dept. classics and humanities chair, San Diego State U.; steering com. mem., Calif. Humanities Project, Davis, 1986-90. Contbr. articles to profl. jours. Mem. AAUP, Am. Philol. Assn., Golden Key, Phi Kappa Phi, Mortar Bd., Phi Beta Kappa. Office: San Diego State U 5300 Campanile Dr San Diego CA 92115-8143

GENOWAYS, HUGH HOWARD, systematic biologist, educator; b. Scottsbluff, Nebr., Dec. 24, 1940; s. Theodore Thompson and Sarah Louise (Beales) G.; m. Joyce Elaine Cox, July 28, 1963; children: Margaret Louise, Theodore Howard. AB, Hastings Coll., 1963; postgrad., U. Western Australia, 1964; PhD, U. Kans., 1971. Curator Mus. of Tex. Tech U., Lubbock, 1972-76, lectr. Mus. Sci. Program, 1974-76; curator Carnegie Mus. Natural History, Pitts., 1976-86; dir. U. Nebr. State Mus., Lincoln, 1986-94; chair mus. studies program U. Nebr., 1989—95, 1997—, prof. state mus., 1986—2003, prof. mus. studies, 1989—, prof. natural resource scis., 1997—2003, prof. phase d retirement program, 2003—. Author, editor:(with Michael A. Mares) Mammalian Biology in South America, 1982, (with Marion A. Burgwin) Natural History of the Dog, 1984; (with Mary R. Dawson) contbns. in Vertebrate Paleontology, 1984, Species of Special Concern in Pennsylvania, 1985, Current Mammalogy, 1987, 90, Biology of the Heteromyidae, 1993, Storage of Natural History Collections: A Preventive Conservation Approach, 1996, (with Robert J. Baker) Mammalogy: A Memorial Volume Honoring Dr. J. Knox Jones, Jr., 1996, (with Ted Genoways) A Perfect Picture of Hell: Eyewitness Accounts by Civil War Prisoners from the 12th Iowa, 2001, (with Lynne M. Ireland) Museum Administration: An Introduction; editor: Collections: A Journal for Museum and Archive Professionals, 2003--. Packmaster Allegheny Trails coun. Boy Scouts Am., 1981-83, asst. scoutmaster, 1983-86. Grantee Fulbright Found., 1964, NSF, 1977-86, R.K. Mellon Found., 1981-86, Smithsonian Fgn. Currency Program, 1983-84, Inst. Mus. Svcs., 1989-96. Mem. Am. Soc. Mammalogists (pres. 1984-86, C. Hart Merriam award 1987, editor Spl. Pubs. 1995-96, historian 1997—, elected hon. mem. 2002), Internat. Theriological Congress (steering com. 1985—), Southwestern Assn. Naturalists (pres. 1984-85, trustee 2003--), Am. Assn. Mus., Nebr. Mus. Assn. (pres. 1990-92, 1st Hugh H. Genoways Achievement award 1994, sec. 1997-2000), Assn. Systematics Collections (bd. dirs. 1993-94), Nat. Inst. for Conservation Cultural Property (bd. dirs. 1993-94), Sociedad Argentina para Estudio Mamiferos, Lincoln Attractions and Mus. Assn. (chair 1987-94), Soc. Systematic Biologists, Rotary (bd. dirs. Lincoln N.E. club 1990-92). Office: U Nebr-Lincoln State Mus W436 Nebraska Hall Lincoln NE 68588-0514

GENRICH, MARK L. foundation administrator; b. Buffalo, Aug. 28, 1943; m. Allison Forbes, 1967; children: Audrey, Liza, Colby. BA, Bucknell U., 1966. Editl. writer Palladium-Item, Richmond, Ind., 1970; writing exec. Bruce Eberle & Assocs., Inc., Vienna, Va., 1975-77; dep. editor editl. pgs. Phoenix Gazette, 1977-96; editl. writer, columnist The Ariz. Republic, Phoenix, 1996-98; dir. Warne Ctr. Goldwater Inst., Phoenix, 1998-2000; pub. rels. dir. Quest Comm. Internat., Inc., 2000—02; dir. Ariz. Affairs, 2002—. Participant U.S. Army War

Coll., Carlisle, Pa., U.S. Naval War Coll., Newport, R.I.; participant arms control, disarmament programs including Space & Arms talks, Geneva; chmn. New Tech. Com., Journalism in Edn. Com.; mem. various coms. Creator, host cable TV program focus on polit. figures; regional editor The Masthead. Grantee European Cmty. Visitor Programme, 1993; recipient highest honors editl. writing, newspaper design Ariz., Western Region; highest honor Maricopa County Bar Assn.; Hoover Inst. media fellow, 1985. Mem. Nat. Conf. Editl. Writers (bd. dirs., included vol. Editl. Excellence), First Amendment Cong. (bd. dirs.), Soc. Profl. Journalists/Sigma Delta Chi, ABA (com. prisons, sentencing). Avocations: coaching competitive soccer, tennis, photography, riding. Home: 130 W Pine Valley Dr Phoenix AZ 85023-5283 Office: Qwest Comm Internat Inc 4041 N Central Ave 11th Fl Phoenix AZ 85012

GENS, RALPH SAMUEL, electrical engineering consultant; b. Berlin, Nov. 25, 1924; s. Alexander and Renata Gens; m. Ida L. Mattson; children: Marilyn R., David A. BS in Elec. Engring., Oreg. State U., 1949. Registered profl. engr., Oreg. Engr. Bonneville Power Adminstrn., Portland, Oreg., 1949-80, chief, system engr., 1966-74, mgr. planning, research and devel., 1974-77, chief engr., asst. adminstr. for engring and constrn., 1977-80; cons. Portland, 1980—. Advisor NSF, 1971-76; mem. adv. com. Project UHV, 1968-79; mem. Electricity Commn. of Papua, New Guinea, 1981-88; chmn. energy rsch. adv. bd. U.S. Dept. Energy, 1984-85, mem., 1985-89; chmn. planning coordination com. of Western Systems Coordinating Coun., 1975-76. Contbr. articles to profl. jours.; patentee in field. Served as sgt. U.S. Army, 1943-46, PTO. Recipient Disting. Service award Dept. Interior, 1978. Fellow IEEE (chmn. surge protective devices com. 1971, chmn. Portland sect. 1968, William M. Harbishaw award 1984, Centennial medal 1984, medal for engring. excellence 2003); mem. NAE, Internat. Conf. Large High Voltage Electric Systems (U.S. v.p. 1979-80, chmn. study com. system analysis and technique 1986-92, Atwood award 1990, Internat. honorary mem., 1992), Electric Power Rsch. Inst. (rsch. adv. com. 1977-80), Tau Beta Pi, Sigma Tau, Eta Kappa Nu, Pi Mu Epsilon.

GENSHEIMER, CYNTHIA FRANCIS, economics educator; b. Bloomington, Ind., Feb. 16, 1953; d. Norman C. and Beverly Francis; m. Joseph M. Gensheimer, Dec. 27, 1975; children: Michael Francis, Lydia Jane, Juliana Ruth. BA, U. Rochester, 1974; PhD, UCLA, 1979. Prin. analyst Congl. Budget Office, Washington, 1978-83; vis. asst. prof. Vassar Coll., Poughkekepsic, NY, 1989—94. Author: Raising Funds For Your Child's School: Over 600 Great Ideas for Parents and Teachers, 1993. UCLA Found. fellow, 1974-77. Mem. Am. Econ. Assn., Nat. Tax Assn., Phi Beta Kappa. Home: 2503 W 70th Ter Shawnee Mission KS 66208-2743

GENSHEIMER, ELIZABETH LUCILLE, software specialist; b. Louisville, Jan. 25, 1955; d. Theodore Rudolph and Florence Virginia (Nieder) G. BS in Computer Sci., U. Louisville, 1976, postgrad., 1977-78; MS in Applied Cognition and Neurosci., U. Tex., Dallas, 2002. Weapons analyst CIA, Washington, 1975-76; engr. software Tex. Instruments, Dallas, 1978-81, No. Telecom, Inc., Richardson, Tex., 1981-83; mem. sci. staff Bell No. Rsch., Richardson, 1983-88, magnet mgr. univ. interrels. program U. Southwestern La., 1986-88, mgr. product test Meridian Data Network Sys., 1988-89; mgr. devel. software test Convex Computer Corp., Richardson, Tex., 1989-93; software cons. Ft. Worth Tech. Cons., 1993-95; software devel. and verification Hewlett-Packard Co. (Compaq Computer/Tandem Telecom), 1995—; owner faire.net. Cons. webpage design. Mem. Nature Conservancy, Nat. Geog. Soc., North Tex. Water Garden Soc. (bd. dirs. 1997-2000), Whale Watch Soc. Avocations: hiking, photography, renaissance faires, tennis, horseback riding. Home: PO Box 796005 Dallas TX 75379-6005 E-mail: gensie@cirr.com., renfaireJunkie@faire.net.

GENSLER, GARY, federal agency administrator; b. Balt. m. Francesca Danieli; children: Anna, Lee, Isabel. BS in Econs., U. Pa., 1978, MBA, 1979. With mergers and acquistion dept. The Goldman Sachs Group, L.P., 1979-84, supr. advisor media cos., 1984-88, ptnr., 1988, with fixed income divsn., with ops. tech. and fin. divsn., 1994, co-head fin., 1995—; asst. sec. treasury for fin. markets Dept. Treasury, Washington, 1997-99, undersec. domestic fin., 1999—. Nat. trustee Balt. Mus. Art. Office: Dept Treasury 15th And Pennsylvania Ave Washington DC 20220-0001

GENSLER, PHILIP, JR., investment counselor; b. New Orleans, Mar. 7, 1936; s. Philip and Louise (Tusson) G.; m. Elizabeth Turner Pratt, Nov. 27, 1957; chdren: Philip Gensler III, David Scott, Nina Pratt. BA, Tulane U., 1957. Sales mgr. Quaid Fence Co., New Orleans, 1959-61; acct. exec. Merrill Lynch, New Orleans, 1961-73; exec. v.p., sec. Waters, Parkerson & Co., New Orleans, 1973—. Chmn., pres. Met. Crime Commn., New Orleans, 1983-84; gen. chmn. Times Picayune Doll & Toy Fund, New Orleans, 1983-84; bd. dirs. Better Bus. Bur., New Orleans, 1998—. Col. U.S. Army Res., 1959-90, ret. Mem. Fin. Analysts of New Orleans (pres. 1980-81), New Orleans Country Club, Beau Chene Country Club, Tchefuncte Country Club. Republican. Roman Catholic. Avocation: golf. Home: 303 Glorias Pl Mandeville LA 70471-1612 Office: Waters Parkerson & Co Inc 228 Saint Charles Ave Ste 512 New Orleans LA 70130-2682 E-mail: pgensler@wpcoinc.com.

GENT, ALAN NEVILLE, physicist, educator; b. Leicester, Eng., Nov. 11, 1927; came to U.S., 1961, naturalized, 1972; s. Harry Neville and Gladys (Hoyle) G.; m. Jean Margaret Wolstenholme, Sept. 1, 1949; children: Martin Paul Neville, Patrick Michael, Andrew John; m. Ginger Lee, Sept. 4, 1997. BS, U. London, 1946, BS in Physics, 1949, PhD in Sci., 1955; DHC, U. Haute-Alsace, France, 1997; DSc (hon.), De Montfort U., Eng., 1998. Lab. asst. John Bull Rubber Co., Leicester, Eng., 1944-45; research physicist Brit. (now Malaysian) Rubber Producers' Research Assn., 1949-61; prof. polymer physics U. Akron, Ohio, 1961-88, Dr. Harold A. Morton prof. polymer physics and polymer engring., 1988-94; prof. emeritus, 1994—; dean grad. studies and research U. Akron, 1978-86. Vis. prof. dept. materials Queen Mary Coll., U. London, 1969-70; vis. prof. dept. chem. engring. McGill U., 1983; Hill vis. prof. U. Minn., 1985; cons. Goodyear Tire & Rubber Co., 1963-2002, Gen. Motors, 1973-87. Contbr. articles to profl. publs. Served with Brit. Army, 1947-49. Recipient Mobay award, Cellular Plastics divsn. Soc. of Plastics Industry, 1963, Colwyn medal Plastics and Rubber Inst. Gt. Brit., 1978, Adhesives award Com. F-11, ASTM, 1979, Internat. Rsch. award Soc. Plastics Engrs., 1980, Whitby award Rubber Chem. divsn. Am. Chem. Soc., 1987, Pub. Svc. medal NASA, 1988, Charles Goodyear medal Rubber Chem. divsn. Am. Chem. Soc., 1990; installed Ohio Sci. Tech. and Industry Hall of Fame, 1993. Mem. NAE, Soc. of Rheology (pres. 1981-83, Bingham medal 1975), Adhesion Soc. (pres. 1978-80, 3M award 1987, Pres.'s award 1997), Am. Phys. Soc. (chmn. divsn. high polymer physics 1977-78, High Polymer Physics prize 1996). Democrat. Office: U Akron Inst Polymer Science Akron OH 44325-3909 E-mail: gent@uakron.edu.

GENTER, JOHN ROBERT, grocery industry executive; b. Huntsville, Ala., Oct. 16, 1957; s. John C. and Madge (McDaniel) G.; m. Margaret F. MacNaughton, Sept. 5, 1981; children: John Thomas, Lois Katharine. BS in Mktg. and Bus. cum laude, U. Ala., 1980. Sales rep. Food divsn. Procter & Gamble, Cin., 1980-81, dist. field rep., 1981, unit mgr., 1982-84; divsn. trade devel. mgr., regional mgr. Frito-Lay, Inc., Dallas, 1984-85; field mktg. mgr. vintage divsn. E&J Gallo Winery, Modesto (Calif.), Tampa, 1985, state mgr., 1986, divsn. mgr., 1986-91, region mgr. chain div., 1992-95; dir. mktg. Purity Wholesale Grocers, Boca Raton, Fla., 1995-96; bus. mgr. Acosta Sales Co., Tampa, 1996-97; divsn. mgr. Sutter Home Winery, Tampa, 1998-99, gen. sales mgr. South, 1999—2000, trainer sales mgmt., 1999-2000; S.E. regional sales mgr. Banfi Vintners, Old Brookville, NY, 2000—03; East Coast mgr. PuraFilter, Las Vegas, Nev., 2003—. Trainer Sales Mgmt. Tng. Sch. Procter & Gamble, Cin., 1982-83, Sales Devel. Program Frito-Lay, Dallas, 1984-85. Author: (with others) E&J Gallo Field Marketing Manual, 1986. Mem. vestry St. John's Ch., Tampa, 1998-2001, active Father's Ministry, chmn. Every Mem.; youth soccer, basketball coach YMCA; trustee Patrons of St. John's Sch.; mem. St. John's Sch. Bd., 2003—. Recipient Coach of Yr. award Tampa Tribune. Mem. U. Ala. Alumni Assn., Soc. de Vinum Honoratus, Beta Gamma Sigma. Republican. Episcopalian. Home and Office: 559 Ladrone Ave Tampa FL 33606-4036 E-mail: jrgenter@aol.com.

GENTILCORE, EILEEN MARIE BELSITO, elementary school principal; b. Glen Cove, N.Y. d. Samuel Francis and Nellie Theresa (McKenna) Belsito; m. James Matthew Gentilcore, Aug. 4, 1951; children: Kevin, John, Scott. BS in Edn., SUNY, Potsdam; MS in Edn., Hofstra U., 1968, profl. diploma, 1976, EdD, 1979. Tchr., first grade Sea Cliff, N.Y., 1951-52; founder, pre-K Germany Officers Sch., Munich, 1952-53; tchr., first grade Peekskill (N.Y.) Schs., 1953-54; tchr., second grade Syosset, N.Y., 1954-55, reading cons., 1970-84, head tchr., 1974-84, prin., 1985-96; ret., 1996. Bicentennial adv. bd. Syosset Community, 1976; adv. bd. mem. Telicare, Uniondale, N.Y., 1978-80; cons. in field. Author: Developmental Learning, 1979. Organizer med. team to Honduras, 1998; mem. Nassau County Graffiti Task Force, 1994—. N.Y. State PTA fellow, 1971, 72, 73, Hofstra fellow, 1971; recipient Jenkins award N.Y. State PTA, 1968, Hon. Life, 1976, Pius X award Rockville Ctr. Diocese, 1985, Disting. Svc. award, N.Y. State PTA Dist., 1996, Teddy Roosevelt Achievement award, 1999, Award for outstanding svc. Rotary Internat., 1999, Abe Gordon Rotary Internat. V.P. Outstanding Svc. award, 2000, R.I. Internat. Achievment award, 2000. Citation for meritorious svc., R.I. Internat. Found., 2002, Rotary Internat. Svc. Above Self award, 2003, Zone 32 Disting. Past Dist. Gov. award, Barcelona, Spain, 2002; named Woman of Distinction, N.Y. State Senate, 1998, Woman of Distinction, Syosset-Woodbury Rep. Club and Senator Carl Marcellino, 1999; grantee Karla Project, 1998, honoree Gift of Life Inc., 1999, Internat. Task Force for Children at Risk, Rotary Internat. Literary Task Force Coord. Zone 32. (2003-04). Mem.: Syosset Prins. (pres. 1992), Rotary (pres. Syosset-Woodbury 1993—95, gov. aide 1995, Gift of Life pres. 1996—97, vocat. dir. dist. 7250 1996—97, med. mission to Honduras 1997, 1st woman dist. gov. dist. 7250 1998—99, Children at Risk Task Force 2000—, conf. chair Zone 32 2000—, coord. RI literacy task force zone 32 2003—, chair RI centennial com. dist 7250 2003—, med. mission to Russia 1995 dist. 7250, coord. Internat. Children at Risk task force, v.p., coord. Internat. Avoidable Blindness task force 2002—, launched Operation Mitch, Honduras, N.Y. State Senate Woman of Distinction 1998, Internat. Achievement award 1999, Meritorious Svc. citation 2002, Disting. Past Dist. Coord. citation 2002, Internat. Global award 2002, Paul Harris fellow, Svc. Above Self award 2003), Kappa Delta Pi, Alpha Sigma Omicron. Roman Catholic. Avocations: swimming, writing, reading, gardening. Fax: 516-921-0206.

GENTILE, ANTHONY, coal company executive; b. Aguila, Italy, Nov. 1, 1920; s. Gregorio and Antonieta (Duronio) G.; m. Nina Angela Discipio, Mar. 4, 1943; children: Robert Henry, Anita Marie, Rita Ann, Thomas Gregory. Student, Youngstown Coll., 1939-42; LH (hon.), U. Steubenville, 1977; DHL (hon.), 1988. Co-owner Pike Inn-Restaurant, Bloomingdale, OH, 1946-52; asst. to owner Huberta Coal Co., Steubenville, OH, 1952-55; gen. mgr. Half Moon Coal Co., Weirton, W.Va., 1955-57, Ohio River Collieries Co., Columbus, OH, 1957-59, pres., 1959—, Lafferty Coal Mining Co., Eastern Ohio Coal Co., 1959—; vice pres. Big Mountain Coals Inc., Prente, WV, 1962—. Chmn. bd., 1962—; pres. Bither Mining Co. W.Va.; v.p. N & G Constrn., Bannock Land Co.; chmn., pres. Bannock Coal Co., Lafferty, Ohio, 1985-88, chmn., 1988—; chmn. bd. dirs. Mining and Reclamation Council Am., Washington; bd. dirs. Union Bank, Stuebenville. Mem. 1st Ohio Trade Commn. to Europe, 1965; mem. adv. bd. St. John Med. Ctr., Steubenville; trustee Coll. Steubenville, Ohio Valley Hosp., past chmn., Steubenville. Served to 1st lt. AUS, 1942-45, capt. Decorated Purple Heart, Silver Star; recipient Citizen of Yr. awd. Wintersville, C. of C., 1976, Conservation award for Ohio River Collieries Gov. Ohio., 1977, Humanitarian award Jeffersonian Lodge, Jefferson County, Ohio, 1977, Visionary award Jefferson County, 1999, Macedonia Visionary award AHA, 1999, Commodore award Gov. of Ohio, 1965; honoree Ohio Cancer Rsch. Assocs., 2000; inductee Upper Ohio Valley Lou Holtz Hall of Fame, 2000. Mem. Am. Mining Congress (mem. adv. council coal divsn. 1965). Home: 4 Normandy Dr Wintersville OH 43953-3800 Office: Ohio River Collieries Co PO Box 128 Bannock OH 43972-0128

GENTILE, JOSEPH F. lawyer, educator; b. San Pedro, Calif., Jan. 15, 1934; s. Ernest B. and Icy Otie (Martin) Gentile; m. Joanna Beck, Mar. 17, 2001; children: Kim Yvonne, Kevin James, Kelly Michele, Kristien Elyse, Kerri Nicole. BA cum laude, San Jose State U., 1955; JD, U. La Verne, 1966; cert. in indsl. rels., UCLA, 1959; teaching credential, Calif. C.C., 1972; M.Pub. Adminstrn., U. So. Calif., 1976. Bar: Calif. 1967, U.S. Supreme Ct. 1972. Mem. indsl. relations staff Kaiser Steel Corp., Fontana Works, 1957-62; labor relations counsel Calif. Trucking Assn., Burlingame, Calif., 1964-68; acting dir. indsl. relations, labor relations counsel McDonnell Douglas Corp., Santa Monica, Calif., 1968-70; sr. partner Nelson, Kirshman, Goldstein, Gentile & Rexon, Los Angeles, 1970-76; individual practice, 1976—; Evening instr. bus. econs., indsl. relations U. Calif., 1969-94; evening instr. personnel and indsl. relations San Bernardino Valley Coll., 1969-72; evening instr. transp. Mt. San Antonio Coll., 1972-74; lectr. labor law Loyola U., 1973-74; lectr. Grad. Sch. Pub. Adminstrn., U. So. Calif., 1976-80; adj. prof. law Pepperdine U., 1981—; chmn. Employee Relations Commn., Los Angeles County, 1979—. Mem. arbitration panel Fed. Mediation and Conciliation Service, Calif. Counciliation Service; mem. employee rels. bd. L.A. City, 2000—. Contbr. articles to profl. jours. Served with AUS, 1955-57. Mem. ABA, Calif. Bar Assn., Los Angeles County Bar Assn. (past chmn. exec. com. labor law sect.), Am. Arbitration Assn. (chmn. regional adv. coun., arbitration panel, nat. bd. dirs. 1985-91), Phi Sigma Alpha, Phi Alpha Delta. Office: PO Box 570398 Tarzana CA 91357-0398

GENTILE, ROBERT DALE, optometrist, consultant; b. Pottsville, Pa., Oct. 24, 1946; s. Joseph and Evelyn Marie (Warfield) Gentile; m. Patricia Diane Fernsler, June 20, 1969; 1 child, Heather Ly Luxon. BA in Sci., Pa. State U., 1968; BS in Optometry, Pa. Coll. of Optometry, Phila., 1974, OD, 1977; MA in Human Resources, Webster U., 1985. Bd. cert. Am. Acad. Optometry. Advanced through ranks to lt. col. AUS, 1968-94; chief optometry 9th Gen. Dispensary, Aschaffenburg, Germany, 1977-80; optometrist Brook Army Med. Ctr., Ft. Sam Houston, Tex., 1980-82; chief eye sect., medicine and surgery divsn. Acad. Health Scis., Ft. Sam Houston, 1982-84; chief optometry Dunham Army Health Clinic, Carlisle Barracks, Pa., 1984-88, Med. Dept. Activity, Berlin, 1988-91, 121st Evacuation Hosp., Seoul, Republic of Korea, 1991-93; optometry cons. 18th Med. Command, Seoul, 1991-93; chief optometry Raymond W. Bliss Army Cmty. Hosp., Ft. Huachuca, Ariz., 1993-94; optometrist Naval Hosp., Camp Pendleton, Calif., 1994-96. Cons. New Vision Internat., Escondido, Calif., 1996—; adj. prof. U. Houston Coll. Optometry, 1980-84, Pa. Coll. Optometry, 1980-84, New England Coll. Optometry, Boston, 1980-84. Decorated Legion of Merit, Meritorious Svc. medal with 3 Oak Leaf Clusters, Army Commendation medal with 4 Oak Leaf Clusters. Fellow Am. Acad. Optometry; mem. Am. Optometric Assn., Armed Forces Optometric Assn., Calif. Optometric Assn., Berlin Internat. Med. Soc., 38th Parallel Med. Soc., Silver Caduceus Soc. of Korea. Avocations: golf, gymnastics, table tennis, nutrition, exercise. Home and Office: 2241 Canyon View Gln Escondido CA 92026-5020

GENTINE, LEE MICHAEL, marketing professional; b. Plymouth, Wis., Feb. 18, 1952; s. Leonard ALvin and Dolores Ann (Becker) G.; m. Debra Ann Suemnicht, Dec. 29, 1973; children: Amanda, Joshua, Jonathan. BBA, U. Notre Dame, 1974; MBA, DePaul U., 1977. Acct. Hurdman & Cranston, Chgo., 1974-75; sales rep. Sargento Cheese Inc., Plymouth, 1975-78, mktg. mgr., 1978-81, sr. v.p. mktg., 1981-84, exec. v.p. mktg., 1984-89, pres. consumer products divsn., 1989-97. Mem. adv. bd. Kaytee Products Inc., Chilton, Wis., 1994-98; mng. ptnr. Dairyland Investors Group, L.L.P., 1997—; bd. dirs. Sargento Foods Inc. Bd. dirs. Plymouth Softball Assn., 1980—; pres. Plymouth Indsl. Devel. Corp., 1981-85, Parish Coun., 1989-90; chmn. Plymouth Advancement Com., 1992-96, pres., 1992-2002; mem. adv. bd. St. Nicholas Hosp., 1998—; pres. Quit Qui Oc Athletic Alliance, Inc., 1999—; vice chmn. Elkhart Lake Tourism Commn., 1998—. Named One of 100 Best and Brightest Advt. Execs., Advt. Age, 1986. Mem. Am. Mktg. Assn., Sheboygan County C. of C. (bd. dirs. 1987-89), Beta Gamma Sigma. Roman Catholic. Avocations: softball, golf, home rehabilitation. Office: Dairyland Investors Group LLP 601 Eastern Ave Plymouth WI 53073-1913

GENTLE, JAMES EDWARD, computer software executive; b. Statesville, N.C., May 31, 1943; s. Wint Farley and Vertie Mae (Pardue) Gentle, Wint Farley and Vertie Mae (Pardue) Gentle; m. Joyce Ellen Lodge, June 26, 1966 (dec. Sept. 1988); m. Maria Engracia Quijano, June 26, 1992. BS, U. N.C., 1966; MA, La. State U., 1969; MCS, Tex. A&M U., 1973, PhD, 1974. Assoc. prof. Iowa State U., 1974—79; dir. rsch. and design IMSL, Inc., Houston, 1979—92; prof.. George Mason U., Fairfax, Va., 1992—. Program dir. stats. and probability program in math. and phys. scis. NSF, 1996—; adj. prof. Rice U. Author (with others): (book) Statistical Computing, 1980; author: Elements of Computational Statistics, 2002, Random Number Generation and Monte Carlo Methods, 2003; editor: (book) Procs. 15th Symposium on the Interface, 1983, Current Index to Statistics, 1980—85, Random Number Generation and Monte Carlo Methods, 1998, Numerical Linear Algebra for Applications in Statistics, 1998, Elements of Computational Statistics, 2002; contbr. Recipient H.O. Hartley award, Tex. A&M U., 1981; fellow sr. rsch. fellow, U.S. Bur. Labor Stats., 1993—95. Fellow: Royal Statis. Soc., Am. Statis. Assn. (dir.); mem.: Internat. Statis. Inst., Am. Fedn. Info. Processing Socs. (bd. dirs.), Internat. Assn. Statis. Computing, Assn. Computing Machinery. Home: 6051 Burkewood Way Burke VA 22015-3021 Office: George Mason Univ Fairfax VA 22030

GENTLE, KENNETH WILLIAM, physicist; b. Oak Park, Ill., Oct. 27, 1940; s. William and Cathryn Mary (Spence) G. BS, MIT, 1962, PhD, 1966. Asst. prof. dept. physics U. Tex., Austin, 1966-69, assoc. prof., 1970-75, prof. physics, 1976—, chair dept. physics, 1997-2001. Sloan fellow, 1973-75 Fellow Am. Phys. Soc. Home: 212 Buckeye Trl Austin TX 78746-1420 Office: Univ Tex Dept Physics Austin TX 78712

GENTNER, PAUL LEFOE, architect, consultant; b. Seattle, Feb. 24, 1944; s. Edward George and Opal Eloise (Davis) G.; m. Glenda Frank Hoy, May 25, 1975; 1 stepchild, Robert Michael Hurd. AA in Architecture, Anne Arundel C.C., Arnold, Md., 1970; BS in Engring., Century U., 1984. Registered arch., Md., Tex., Va. Project rep. RTKL Assocs., Inc., Balt., 1970-73; staff architect James R. Grieves Assocs., Balt., 1973-77; sr. engr. Morrison-Knudsen (MKSAC), Columbia, Md., 1977-79, staff engr., 1979-81; planning mgr. Morrison-Knudsen Internat. Inc., Barranquilla, Colombia, S.Am., 1981-86; staff architect RTKL Assocs., Inc., Balt., 1986-92; specifications writer Sverdrup Cpr., Arlington, Va., 1992-93; mgr. specifications Daniel, Mann, Johnson, & Mendenhall, Balt., 1993-95, Arlington, Va., 1995-96; cons. Marriott Internat., Washington, 1996-98; with arch. and constrn. design mgmt. Marriott Internat. Corp., Washington, 1998—. With USNR, 1965-68, Vietnam; Persian Gulf, 1990-91. Mem. AIA, Constrn. Specifications Inst. (cert. constrn. specifier, bd. dirs. Balt. chpt. 1991-92, 1st v.p. 1993-94, pres. 1994-95), Soc. Am. Mil. Engrs., Bricklayers (local # 1). Home: 2028 Park Ave Baltimore MD 21217-4816 Office: Marriott Internat Dept 70/104 13 Marriott Dr Washington DC 20058 E-mail: pgentarch@aol.com., paul.gentner@marriott.com.

GENTRY, ALBERTA ELIZABETH, elementary education educator; b. Richter, Kans., Feb. 18, 1925; d. John Charles and Dessie Lorena (Duvall) Briles; m. Kenneth Neil Gentry, June 1, 1947; children: Michal Neil, Alan Dale, Elisa Ann. BE, Emporia (Kans.) Tchrs. Coll., 1975. Cert. tchr., Kans. Tchr. Chippewa Rural Sch., Ottawa, Kans., 1943-44; prin., tchr. Pomona (Kans.) Grade Sch., 1944-47, tchr., 1960-61, Silverlake Rural Sch., Pomona, 1947-48, Hawkins Rural Sch., Ottawa, 1948-49, Davy Rural Sch., Ottawa, 1950-53, Eugene Field Sch., Ottawa, 1953-54, Centropolis Grade Sch., Ottawa, 1964, Appanoose Elem. Sch., Pomona, 1964-90, ret., 1990. Trainer student tchr., 1985-86. Author: Proven Ideas for Classroom Teachers, 1988. Project leader, supporter 4-H, Franklin County, Kans., 1963-67; den mother Boy Scouts Am., Ottawa, 1955-66; dir. Bible sch., tchr. Trinity Meth. Ch., Ottawa, 1955-70, supt., 1955-66, mem. choir, 1947—. Named to Kans. Tchrs. Hall of Fame, 1991. Mem. NEA, Kans. Tchrs. Assn., Kans. Edn. Assn., Alpha Delta Kappa (sec. 1988-90). Republican. Methodist. Avocations: bird watching, arts and crafts, family genealogy, flower gardening, music. Home: PO Box 2 Pomona KS 66076-0002

GENTRY, BERN LEON, SR., minority consulting company executive; b. Goldsboro, N.C., Sept. 9, 1941; s. Theodore Alfonso and Ruth Ester (Taylor) G.; m. Jane A. Price, Nov. 11, 1965; children: Michelle Lorraine, Bern Leon. Student, Rutgers U., 1959-61, Temple U., 1961-63, Cornell U., 1966-67, U. Okla., 1971. Tax acct. IRS, Phila., 1965-66; collection mgr., credit mgr., appliance store mgr., soft goods mdse. mgr. Sears, Roebuck & Co., Phila., 1966-71; program mgr., dir. nat. urban affairs U.S. Jr. C. of C., 1971-73, cons., 1973—; pres. Together, Inc., Tulsa, 1973—. Contbr. articles to profl. jours. Mem. nat. adv. bd. Boys Clubs Am., 1971— ; mem. nat. Black alliance for grad. level edn. U. Mich.; past pres., bd. dirs. Tulsa Econ. Opportunity Task Force; pres. Community Service Agy.; bd. dirs. Jr. Achievement. Recipient award of accomplishment Sears Staff Sch., 1967; award of appreciation Black Peoples Unity Movement Econ. Devel. Corp., 1971; George Washington Honor medal Freedoms Found., 1974, 76; Keys to cities of Roanoke, Va.; Keys to cities of Baton Rouge, La.; Keys to cities of New Orleans; named Outstanding Young Man Camden, 1970; Outstanding Chpt. Pres. N.J. Jaycees; Outstanding Jaycee. Mem. Nat. Urban League, NAACP, Am. Mgmt. Assn., Nat. Assn. Human Rights Workers, Assn. Black Found. Execs., Nat. Assn. Pub. Relations Execs., Nat. Civil Service League, Nat. Assn. Community Devel., Nat. Assn. Vol. Services Coordinator, Camden Jaycees (pres. 1970-71), Tulsa Met. C. of C. Office: Together Inc PO Box 52528 802 E 6th St Tulsa OK 74120-3610

GENTRY, DAVID RAYMOND, textile engineer; b. Easley, S.C., Sept. 26, 1933; s. Thomas Herbert and Rosalie (Howard) G.; m. Mary Lynn White, June 5, 1955; children: David R. Jr., Mary Diane Gentry Windsor. BS, Clemson Coll., 1955; MS, Inst. Textile Tech., Charlottesville, Va., 1957; PhD, Clemson U., 1972. Rsch. engr. WestPoint (Ga.) Mfg. Co., 1957-60; asst. prof. Clemson (S.C.) U., 1960-67; mgr. testing and evaluation Phillips Fibers Corp., Greenville, S.C., 1967-73; assoc. prof. Ga. Inst. Tech., Atlanta, 1973-78; sr. devel. engr. Amoco Fabrics & Fibers Co., Atlanta, 1978-80, mgr. fibers devel., 1980-84, dir. fibers devel., 1985-90, rsch. assoc., 1990-92, sr. rsch. assoc., 1992-99; pres. Gentry and Assocs. Textile Consultants, 2000—. Fellow NSF, 1966, Sirrine Found., 1965-67, Inst. Textile Tech., 1955-57. Mem. ASTM (sec. com. D-13 textiles 1974-80), Am. Assn. Textile Technologists (sec. Piedmont chpt. 1963-65), The Fiber Soc., The Textile Inst. (assoc.), Phi Psi (sec., pres. Iota chpt. 1953-55, faculty adviser 1961-65), Phi Kappa Phi. Home: 3456 Embry Cir Atlanta GA 30341-5612 E-mail: drgentry@attbi.com.

GENTRY, DONALD WILLIAM, engineering executive, mining engineer; b. St. Louis, Jan. 18, 1943; s. William Henry and Roberta Elizabeth (Bardelmeier) G.; m. Sheila Carol Schuepbach, Aug. 21, 1965; children: Tara Cassandre, Chad Ryan. BSE., U. Ill., 1965; MS, U. Nev., 1967; PhD, U. Ariz., 1972, DEng (hon.), 2002. Asst. prof. mining engring. Colo. Sch. Mines, Golden, 1972-74, assoc. prof., 1974-77, asst. to dean faculty, assoc. prof., 1977-78, asst. to dean faculty, 1978-79, prof. mining engring., 1978-83, dean undergrad. studies, 1983-84, dean engring. and undergrad. studies, 1990-95, head dept. mining engring., 1995-98, prof. mining-engring., 1998—; pres., CEO, bd. dirs. PolyMet Mining Corp., Golden, 1998—2003; pres., CEO Terra Nova Resources, Golden, 2003—. Contbr. articles to profl. jours. Mem. Soc. Mining Engrs. of AIME (pres. 1993), AIME (dir. Colo. sect. 1982-83, Krumb lectr. 1987, pres. 1996, Mineral Industry Edn. award 1991, Daniel C. Jackling award 1998), Nat. Acad. Engring. (elected 1996). Republican. Lutheran. Home: 6590 Ridgeview Dr Morrison CO 80465-2700

GENTRY, JAMES ROBERT, education educator; b. Evanston, Ill., Nov. 15, 1945; s. Lonnie W Gentry and Goldie Lee Brumback-Gentry; m. Barbara June Wolfer, Nov. 29, 1968; children: Robin June Black, Dale James. AA in social sci., Citrus Coll., 1964; BS in social sci., Calif. State Poly. U., 1966; MA in hist., Calif. State U. at LA, 1968; PhD in hist., U. of Utah, 1985. Instr. of history Cascade Coll., Portland, Oreg., 1968—69; prof. of history Coll. of So. Idaho, 1969—, chair of social sci. and edn. dept., 1997—. Contbr. articles to jours. Mem. Twin Falls County Hist. Preservation Commn., Idaho, 1987—2003. Mem.: Idaho Assn. of Colleges of Tchr. Edn. (corr.), Am. Hist. Assn. (corr.), Phi Alpha Theta (corr.). Am. Bapt. Achievements include assisted in development and implementation of a J.A. & Kathryn Albertson grant under the Recreating Idaho colleges and schools of education initiative. Avocations: walking, movies, reading, canoeing. Home: 675 Alturas Dr N Twin Falls ID 83301-4334 Office: College Of Southern Idaho 315 Falls Ave Twin Falls ID 83301 Office Fax: 208-736-4743. E-mail: jgentry@csi.edu.

GENTRY, JAMES WILLIAM, retired state official; b. Danville, Ill., Aug. 14, 1926; s. Carl Lloyd and Leone (Isham) G.; m. Dorothie Shirley Hechtlinger, Mar. 18, 1967; 1 stepdau., Susan Mushkin. AB, Fresno State Coll., 1948; MJ, U. Calif., Berkeley, 1956. Field rep. Congressman B.W. Gearhart, Fresno, Calif., 1948, Assemblyman Wm. W. Hansen, Fresno, 1950, sec., 1953-56; exec. asst. Calif. Pharm. Assn., L.A., 1956-69; asst. adminstr., dir. pub. info. So. Calif. Comprehensive Health Planning Coun., 1969-71, acting adminstr., 1971-72, exec. sec., 1972-73, Calif. Adv. Health Coun., 1973-85, fed. cons., 1986-88.

Editor, pub. Calif. Pharmacy Jour., L.A., 1956-69; pub. rels. dir. PAID Prescriptions, 1963-64; dir. pub. info. Comprehensive Health Planning coun., L.A. County, 1969; fed. cons. Calif. Health Care Commn., 1973-75; acting pub. info. officer Calif. Office Statewide Health Planning and Devel., 1978-79, interim dir., 1983; mem. L.A. Civil Svc. Police Interview Bd., 1967-72, Calif. Health Planning Law Revision Commn.; asst. sgt.-at-arms Calif. State Assembly, 1950; exec. sec. Calif. Assembly Interim Com. on Livestock and Dairies, 1954-56; mem. adv. bd. Am. Security Coun.; former mem. Calif. Bldg. Safety Bd. Editor: Better Health, 1963-67, Orientation Conf. Comprehensive Health Planning, 1969, commentary, 1969-71, Program and Funding, 1972, Substance Abuse, 1972; editl. adv. Pharm. Svcs. for Nursing Homes: A Procedural manual, 1966. Mem. Fresno County Rep. Ctrl. Com., 1950; charter mem. Rep. Presdl. Task Force. Served to col. AUS, 1949-85, Korea, 1950-53. Decorated Legion of Merit, Bronze Star medal, Commendation Ribon with metal Pendant; recipient pub. awards Western Soc. Bus. Publs. Assn., 1964-67. Mem. Am. Assn. Comprehensive Health Planning, Pub. Rels. Soc. Am., Allied Drug Travelers So. Calif., L.A. Press Club, Mil. Police Assn., Mil. Officers Assn. Am., Res. Officers Assn. (life), Assn. US Army, US Senatorial Club, The Victory Svcs. Club of London, Pi Gamma Mu, Phi Alpha Delta, Sigma Delta Chi. Home: 1603 Patriots Colony Dr Williamsburg VA 23188-1341

GENTRY, MARGARET BURTON, retired elementary school teacher; b. Iva, SC, Oct. 19, 1939; d. Emory Goss and Olivia (Copeland) Burton; m. Aubrey Lee Gentry, July 5, 1981 (dec. Apr. 1991). AA, Anderson (S.C.) Coll., 1962; BS, East Tenn. U., 1964; Cert. Grad. Study, U. Ga., 1969-72; postgrad., Clemson U., 1969-72. Cert. tchr., Ga.; cert. poll mgr., 2002. Salesperson Browns Five and Ten Store, Iva, 1958-61; adminstrv. asst. SC Hwy. Dept., Anderson, 1962; spl. asst. to prof. govt. and history East Tenn. State U., Johnson City, 1962-64; tchr. grade 4 DeKalb County, Decatur, Ga., 1964-71; adminstrv. asst. Poinsettia Heat and Treat Co., Anderson, 1965; tchr. grade 4 Elbert County, Elberton, Ga., 1971-99; ret., 1999. Researcher for pictorial history of Iva Reviva Civic and Cmty. Devel., 1998-99; pres. Willing Workers Class, Iva, 1998—; del. Saluda Bapt. Assn., Iva, 1999—; cert. nat. poll mgr. for presdl. and local elections, 2000-. work scholar Anderson Coll., 1960-62; named. Girls Aux. Queen Union Bapt. Ch., Iva, 1955. Mem. NEA, Ga. Assn. Edn. (rep. plant facility 1970-80, Gift/Letter of Appreciation 1999, cert. poll mgr. 2002), Ga. Retired Tchr., SC Retired Tchr., Elbert County Assn. Edn., Anderson County Ret. Educators Assn., Tartan Cross Soc. Republican. Baptist. Avocations: travel, sewing, genealogy, music, gardening. Home: 311 W Jackson St PO Box 474 Iva SC 29655-0474

GENTRY, MARSHALL BRUCE, English educator; b. Little Rock, July 28, 1953; s. Robert Bruce and Daisy Belle (Stockwell) G.; m. Alice Ruth Friman, Sept. 24, 1989. BA in English and Journalism with high honors, U. Ark., 1975; MA in English, U. Chgo., 1976; PhD in English, U. Tex., 1984. Instr., teaching asst. U. Tex., Austin, 1976-82; vis. asst. instr. English Tex. A&M U., College Station, 1983-84, vis. asst. prof., 1984-85; asst. prof. U. Indpls., 1985-91, assoc. prof., 1991-98, prof., 1998—2003, chair dept. English, 1997—2003; prof. Ga. Coll. & State Univ., 2003—. Author: Flannery O'Connor's Religion of the Grotesque, 1986; co-editor: Conversations with Raymond Carver, 1990, The Practice and Theory of Ethics, 1996; editor The Flying Island mag., 1999-2002, Flannery O'Connor Review, 2003—; contbr. articles to profl. jours. Mem. AAUP (chpt. pres. 1989-91), MLA, Midwest MLA, South Cen. MLA, South Atlantic MLA, Soc. Study So. Lit., Soc. Study Midwestern Lit., Coll. English Assn., Ind. Coll. English Assn. (co-pres. 1989-90, v.p. 2002, 03), Flannery O'Connor Soc., Phi Beta Kappa, Phi Kappa Phi. Office: Ga Coll & State Univ Dept English Campus Box 44 Milledgeville GA 31061-3697 E-mail: bruce.gentry@gcsu.edu.

GENTRY, NANCY O'PRY, medical/surgical nurse; b. Columbus, Ga., Nov. 23, 1953; d. Julian R. Sr. and Patricia A. (Carroll) O'Pry; m. Leland R. Gentry, Dec. 3, 1976; children: Erin Moore, Corey Leland. Diploma, Charity Hosp. Sch. Nursing, New Orleans, 1974; BSN, Incarnate Word Coll., San Antonio, 1985; MPH, U. N.C., 1988. Cert. nephrology nurse, ACLS, PALS, health promotion dir. Commd. 2d lt. USAF, 1975, advanced through grades to lt. col., charge nurse hemodialysis unit, charge nurse med.-surg. unit Bergstrom AFB, Tex., charge nurse renal dialysis unit Lackland AFB, Tex., charge nurse nephrology and oncology clinics Keesler AFB, Miss., health promotion mgr.; retired, 1995; sr. sys. analyst J.R. O'Pry Cons., Inc.; clin. bus. analyst IntraNexus, Inc. Mil. cons. nephrology/dialysis USAF Surgeon Gen. Contbr. articles to profl. jours. Recipient excellence in creative writing award, peer award for clin. excellence, 1985, Life Saver award Am. Cancer Soc., 1993, Pub. Edn. Life Saver award, 1994; Spirit of Keesler award Air Force Assn. Mem. APHA, Am. Nephrology Nurses Assn. (Clin. Practice award 1990), Am. Heart Assn. (bd. dirs.), Am. Cancer Soc. (v.p. profl. activities)., Sigma Theta Tau. Home: 671 N Haven Dr Biloxi MS 39532-4323

GENTRY, ROBERT VANCE, physicist, researcher, writer; b. Chattanooga, July 9, 1933; s. Vance Ault and Sara Frances (Northington) G.; m. Patricia Ann Gentry, Jan. 20, 1953; children: Patricia Lynn, Michael Vance, David Wayne. BS in Physics, U. Fla., 1955, MS, 1956; D.Sc. (hon.), Columbia Union Coll., Takoma Park, Md., 1977. Nuclear engr. Gen. Dynamics Co., Ft. Worth, 1956-58; sr. engr. Martin Co., Orlando, Fla., 1958-59; instr. math. U. Fla., Gainesville, 1959-61, Walla Walla (Wash.) Coll., 1961-62; instr. physics Ga. Inst. Tech., 1962-64; research physicist Archeol. Research Found., Atlanta, 1965-66; mem. faculty Columbia Union Coll., 1966-84, assoc. prof. physics, 1977-84; cons. physicist, 1984-86; research physicist Earth Sci. Assocs., Knoxville, Tenn., 1986—. Guest scientist chemistry div. Oak Ridge Nat. Lab., 1969-82, 89; hon. asst. res. prof. physics U. Tenn.-Knoxville, 1982-83. Author: Creation's Tiny Mystery, 1986, 2d edit., 1988, 3d edit., 1992; chief rschr. (video) Fingerprints of Creation (Telly award 1993), The Young Age of the Earth, 1994; contbr. articles to profl. jours. Fellow NSF, 1962, grantee, 1971-77; grantee NASA, 1970-72 Mem. AAAS, Am. Phys. Soc., Am. Geophys. Union, N.Y. Acad. Scis., Sigma Xi (assoc.). Seventh-day Adventist. Achievements include discovery of polonium radioactive halos in granites, a new model of the universe to explain the Hubble redshift relation and the 2.7K Cosmic Blackbody Radiation without the use of spacetime expansion. Home: PO Box 12067 Knoxville TN 37912-0067 E-mail: esa@halos.com. *To recognize that success in any field is not the result of chance or destiny but instead the reward of faithfully developing those talents endowed by the Creator provides the highest possible incentive for achieving that station in life for which each individual is uniquely fitted.*

GENTRY, VERNESSA DIANA, principal, consultant; b. Longview, Tex., July 19, 1959; d. Clarence and Helen Marie Carr; m. William Abbott Gentry, Aug. 23, 1980; children: William Bryan, Ashely Briana. AA, Tyler Jr. Coll., Tyler, Tex., 1979; BEd, Stephen F. Austin Coll., 1980, MEd, 1987, mid-mgmt. cert., 1994. Reading tchr. Mid. Sch., Longview, 1981-84, lang. arts tchr., 1984-86, sci. tchr., 1986-94, asst. prin. Henderson, 1994-96; prin. Tatum (Tex.) Mid. Sch., 1996-2000, Forest Park Mid. Sch., Longview, Tex., 2000—. Cons. Edn. Leadership, 1997. Mem. Tex. Middle Sch. Assn. (dir. region 5 1995—, region 7 prin. of yr. award 1999), Delta Sigma Theta (outstanding educator award 1996). Avocations: reading, antique shopping, shopping at the mall. Home: RR 21 Box 91 Longview TX 75603-9428 Office: 1515 Lake Dr Longview TX 75601-4816 E-mail: vgentry@lisd.org.

GENUIT, DAVID WALTER, podiatrist; b. Stockton, Calif., May 12, 1949; s. Walter Morales and Betty Alice (Behney) G. BS in Biology, U. Calif., Davis, 1971; BS in Med. Sci., Calif. Coll. Podiatric Medicine, 1973, D in Podiatric Medicine, 1975. Diplomate Am. Bd. Podiatric Surgery, Nat. Bd. Podiatry Examiners, Am. Acad. Pain Mgmt., Am. Bd. Forensic Examiners, Am. Assn. Police Surgeons; cert. therapist; registered hypnotherapist; cert. hypnotherapist. Practice medicine specializing in podiatry, Bremerton, Wash., 1975—; pvt. practice hypnotherapy, 1990—. Clin. instr. Edmonds (Wash.) Community Coll., 1979-84, Bremerton Naval Hosp., 1981—, Olympic Coll., Bremerton, 1987—. Contbr. articles to profl. jours. Med. Explorer Search and Rescue, Bremerton, 1981—; mem. Nat. Assn. for Search and Rescue, 1980—. Fellow Am. Acad. Podiatric Sports Medicine; mem. Am. Podiatric Med. Assn., Wash. State Podiatric Med. Assn. Office: PO Box 895 Seabeck WA 98380

GENUNG, DAN BALDWIN, minister, writer; b. Prescott, Ariz., July 23, 1915; s. Dan Baldwin and Kathleen Ulrich Genung; m. Frances Ulrich Genung, Oct. 1, 1942; children: David Dan, Linda Joy McKown, Carol Dale Wilson, Bruce Michael. BA, U. Ariz., 1938; MA, U. Chgo., 1940, degree, 1941, postgrad., 1952—53. Founding pastor All Peoples Christian Ch. and Ctr., L.A., 1942—56; pastor Oceanside (Calif.) First Christian Ch., 1957—64, Foothill Christian Ch., LaCrescenta, Calif., 1967—70, Mt. Hollywood Congregational Ch., L.A., 1970—84. Bd. dirs. L.A. Urban League; chmn. bd. YMCA, Verdugo Hills, Calif.; pres. Disciplined Order of Christ. Author: Death in His Saddlebags, 1992, A Street Called Love, 1999; contbr. articles. Mem.: Kiwanis (pres. 1981—82), Rotary (pres. 1963—64). Home: 614 W 8th St Claremont CA 91711

GENZ, PATRICIA ANN, English language and literature educator; b. N.Y.C., July 3, 1946; d. John Joseph and Amy (Maltbie) Hayes; m. Michael Andrew Genz, July 8, 1972; children: Andrew, Daniel. BA in English, Mercy Coll., Dobbs Ferry, N.Y., 1969; MAT in English, Yale U., 1970. Tchr. Hamden (Conn.) H.S., 1969-74; vice prin., tchr. Calverton Sch., Huntingtown, Md., 1975-76; dir. planning and cmty. rels. Charles County C.C., La Plata, Md., 1986-89; mng. editor Times Crescent newspaper, La Plata, 1989-90; prof. English lang. and lit. Coll. So. Md., La Plata, 1992—. Reviewer for divsn. policy analysis Am. Coun. on Edn., Washington, 1994-95; presenter at regional confs. Mem. exec. coun. Scholars program Charles County Bd. Edn., 1992-94. Recipient Faculty award Women on Campus Student Orgn., 1995, Faculty Excellence award Faculty SEnate, 1995. Mem. MLA, Nat. Coun. Tchrs. English, Assn. Faculties for Advancement of C.C. Tchg. Office: Coll Sthn Md 8730 Mitchell Rd La Plata MD 20646-2867

GEOFFREY, IQBAL (MOHAMMED JAWAID IQBAL JAFREE), artist, educator, lawyer; b. Chiniot, Pakistan, Jan. 1, 1939; s. Syed Iqbal Hussain and Shahzadi Mumtazjehan Shah; m. Regina Wai-ling Cheng, 1967 (div. 1978); children: Syed Husyein Haider, Shahzadi Zohra Elinoi Cheng-Jafree; m. Ceyyeda Farzawna Nuccwe, Mar. 3, 1988. BA with distinction, Govt. Coll., Lahore, 1957; LLB summa cum laude, Punjab U., Lahore, 1959; trained under Chief Justice of Pakistan, Malik Mohammed Akram, 1959-60, trained under A.K. Brohi, 1966—67; LLM with honors, Harvard U., 1966; A.I.C.E.A., London, 1961, A.M.B.I.M., 1969; PhD, Read U., 1970; also LLD; MA with highest honors, U. Ill., Springfield, 1973; cert. in postgrad. bus. adminstrn., Bradford U., 1976. Bar: Pakistan 1959, U.S. Supreme Ct. 1975, Pakistan Supreme Ct., 1996. Ptnr., chair firm Geoffrey & Khitran (internat. lawyers), 1960—; gen. counsel Pakistan Inst. Human Rights, 1960—; human rights officer UN, 1966-67; chief acct. Brit. Lion Films, London, 1968-69; asst. atty. gen. State of Ill., 1972-73; gen. counsel The Shahzadi Mumtaz Jehan Trust, 1972—; chief acct. Embassy of Kuwait, London, 1974-75. Gen. counsel Asian-Am. Cmty. Legal Aid Clinic, 1972-; mem. bd. govs. Hunerkada Coll. of Art, Islamabad, 1991—; drafted Art. 164 of the Pakistan Law of Evidence, Establishment of Office of Ombudsman Order, Pakistan, 1983; spl. advisor to the Pres. of Pakistan, 1980-84; examiner Pub. Internat. Law Punjab U., 1969-70; prof. St. Mary's Coll., 1967-68, CWS U., 1970-71, Cleve. State U., 1971-72; disting. univ. vis. prof. Hunerkada Coll. Art, Lahore Law Coll. and Silver Jubilee U. prof. Read U. Law Ctr.; presenter, lectr., art critic, conceptual art, fine arts, urban affairs and aesthetics; founder Am. U. Pakistan, 1970; evaluator Global Law Sch. Program NYU, 2001—. Author: Qose-Qizah, 1957, Justice is the Absence of Dictatorial Prerogative, 1965, Human Rights in Pakistan, Harvard 1966, A Critical Study of Moral Dilemmas, Iconographical Confusions and Complicated Politics of XX Century Art Harvard U., 1967, The Concept of Human Rights in Islam (foreword by ICJ Mr. Justice Richard R. Baxter), 1980 Art Embodies Cerebral Legerdemain of Accelerated Communal Soul; co-author: ABA: BLI Recognition and Enforcement of Money Judgments, 1994, International Agency and Distribution Law, 1996 ; editor: PU Law Rev., 1958-59; grad. editor: Harvard Art Rev., 1965-66; one-man shows include Hyde Park, London, 1960-62, Galerie de Seine, Alfred Brod Galleries, 1962, New Vision Centre, 1963, Drian Gallery, 1965, London, Ward-Nasse, Boston, Hull (Eng.) U., Birmingham (Eng.) U., Queens U., Arts Coun. No. Ireland, Los Angeles Mcpl. Art Gallery, Pakistan Arts Council, Lahore, Grand Central Moderns, N.Y.C., Green Ross Gallery, Henri Gallery, Washington, St. Mary's Coll., Ind., Franklin Coll., Miami Mus. Modern Art, Herbert Johnson Art Mus. Cornell U., Everson Art Mus., Syracuse, N.Y., Indus Gallery, Karachi, 1988, Hayward Gallery, London, 1989-90, The Embassy of France, Islamabad, 1992, 2000, Victoria Miro Gallery, 1992-93, Royal Coll. Art, 1993, The Lavatory, NI, 1993—, The Southall Graveyards, Middlesex, 1993—, The Highbury Cemetery, London, 1994—, Nat. Art Gallery, Pakistan, 1994, 2001, H.W. Janson Gallery Modern Art, 1994, 2002, Lahore Art Gallery, 1993, 95, 98-99, 2001, Shakir Ali Mus. Art, Lahore, 1996, Golden Jubilee, Sua Sponte Artfest, Tate Gallery, Britain, 2000—, Nat. Gallery, London, 1998—; Durriya Kazi/AN Gallery, Karachi, 1998, Sadiq Pub. Sch., 1999, Croweaters Gallery, Lahore, 1999, Canvas Gallery, Karachi, 2001, Alliance Francaise Gallery, Islamabad, 2000, Tate Modern Sua Sponte show, 2000-2001, Dickinson State U. Mus. and Art Gallery (curated by Sharon Linnehan), 2002; group shows include biennnials, Paris, Sao Paolo, Brazil, N.Y.C., Montreal, Tokyo World Fairs, Ljubljana, Yugoslavia, Arts Council Gt. Britain touring exhibits, Hayward Gallery, London, The Asia House, London, 2000—, others include six sculptures, 3-D paintings, 18 canvases primal, ethereal art works Brunei Gallery U. London SOAS, 2000, other 60 artwork pieces; represented in permanent collections Herbert Johnson Mus. Cornell U., Philips Collection, Washington, Boston Mus. Fine Arts, Pasadena Mus. Art, Arts Council Gt. Britain, Tate Gallery, London, Eng., Brit. Mus., London, Chase Manhattan Bank, N.Y.C., Boston Safe Deposit and Trust Co., St. James's Palace, Worcester Art Mus., U. Mass., Smith Coll., Lord Baden-Powell House, London, U. London, Royal Norwegian Festival, 2002, also pvt. collections; pioneer Conceptual Art. Recipient The Albairuni Prize, Central Model High Sch., Lahore, 1953, Paris Biennial award, 1965, pub. radio tribute by Pakistan Pres., Sir Ayub Khan, 1964, Lauréat de la Biennale de Paris award André Malraux Min. Culture, Sir Philip Hendy and Lord Goodman Bursary award Arts Coun. Gt. Britain, 1968, Disting. Comty. Svc. award L.A.W., 1970, Outstanding Citizenship award Citizenship Coun. Met. Chgo., 1979, Sir Herbert Read medal, 1992, State of Wash. Cen. Wash. State U. award for creativity, 1970, King Hussein Human Rights Medal, 2002, Millennium Human Rights award Lahore High Ct. Bar Assn., 2002; Aug. 14 designated Syed Iqbal Jafree Day by Gov. Thompson, Ill., 1977, Iqbal Geoffrey Day-Jan. 20 Gov. Edgar, Ill., 1992; Huntington Hartford II and John D. Rockefeller III fellow, 1962-65, Queen Elizabeth II fellow Bradford U. Mgmt. Ctr., 1975-76, Fay B. Kent fellow Alpha Chi Omega, 1963, 65; named as Young Virtuoso Time Mag., 1953, Disting. Lord William Gaunt, The Times, London, 1962, Much More Than a Genius Sir Jeffrey Jowell; designated a living legend Govt. Pakistan, 1994; featured in Oxford Companion to the Twentieth Century Art. Fellow Royal Soc. Arts, London, 1961. Home: 416 S Warson Rd Saint Louis MO 63124-1212 Office: Geoffrey & Khitran 1 Mozang Rd, I Geoffrey Sq Lahore 54000 Pakistan also: 36 Oaklands Rd London W7 England Fax: 92-42-636-9430. E-mail: iqbaljafree@hotmail.com. *An artist empowers your dreams, endeavoring to quash the otherness while ameliorating virtual chasms that segregate ideas. Easier said than done! Inevitable that any catalyst distresses status quo. Dissent is the ascent of art. Art sustainsinquisition of truth. It is neo-wisdom along new mores. Very simply, art is the chip on the shoulder of the bridge between now and zen. An artist implements what you did not expect from art. The bottom line (take it for a ride) remains that only art can make a difference. Else know-thing.*

GEOFFRION, ARTHUR MINOT, management scientist; b. N.Y.C., Sept. 19, 1937; s. Arthur Joseph and Dorothy Arline (Senter) G.; m. Helen Mathilda Hamer, Dec. 22, 1962; children: Susan, Deborah. BME, Cornell U., 1960, M Indsl. Engring., 1961; PhD, Stanford U., 1965. Asst. prof. in ops.rsch. UCLA, 1965-67, assoc. prof., 1968-70, prof. Grad. Sch. Mgmt., 1971-97; chair in mgmt. James A. Collins, 1998—. Dir. Insight, Inc., Manassas, Va. Author: Perspectives on Optimization, 1972; contbr. chpts. to books and articles to profl. jours. Recipient System Sci. prize NATO, Brussels, 1976, Harold Larnder Meml. prize Can. Operational Rsch. Soc., 2002; Ford Found. faculty rsch. fellow, 1967-68; rsch. grantee NSF, 1968-91, Ford Found., 1969-72, Office Naval Rsch., 1972-90; fellow Internat. Acad. Mgmt., 1996. Mem. NAE, Inst. Mgmt. Scis. (pres. 1981-82, Disting. Svc. medal 1992), Ops. Rsch. Soc. Am., Inst. for Ops. Rsch. and Mgmt. Scis. (pres. 1997, George E. Kimball medal 2000, fellow 2002), Omega Rho (hon. mem. 1991). Achievements include research on optimization theory (parametric concave programming, integer programming, multi-criterion optimization, large-scale, decomposition, duality theory), optimization applications (to logistics, prodn., fin.), aggregation, foundations of modeling, analytical methods for e-business. Home: 322 24th St Santa Monica CA 90402-2518 Office: The Anderson Sch at UCLA Box 951481 Los Angeles CA 90095-1481

GEOFFROY, CHARLES HENRY, retired business executive; b. Longford, Ireland, Sept. 24, 1926; came to U.S., 1927, naturalized, 1945; s. Francis Louis and Kathleen Elizabeth (Fetherston) G.; m. Alida Baird McClenahan, Apr. 24, 1954; children: Evan Lloyd, Mark Lee, Douglas Baird. BA, Haverford Coll., 1949; postgrad., U. Pa., 1950. With GM Ins. Corp., Phila., 1950-51; mgr. rsch. dept. Ward Wheelock Co., Phila., 1951-54; assoc. rsch. dir., account exec. Lennen & Newell, Inc., N.Y.C., 1954-59; account exec. Young & Rubicam, Inc., N.Y.C., 1959-64, v.p. L.A., 1965-67; pres., mng. dir. Young & Rubicam, Ltd., Toronto, Ont., Can., 1968-74; pres., dir. J.K. Gill Co. Ltd., Portland, Oreg., 1974-80; pres., chief operating officer Grantree Corp., Portland, 1980-83; pres. Rathcline Corp., Portland, 1984-86; chmn. Wide Travel Internat., Portland, 1986-94, ret., 1994. With AUS, 1945-46. Fellow Inst. Can. Advt.; mem. Portland Execs. Assn., Waverley Country Club, Arlington Club, Huguenot Soc. Great Britain and Ireland, Rotary. E-mail: cgeoff8520@aol.com.

GEOFFROY, GREGORY L. academic administrator, educator; b. Honolulu, July 8, 1946; s. Glenn Gaylord and Lucille Lavaughn (Lewis) G.; m. Kathleen Carothers, Apr. 17, 1971; children: Susan, Janet, David, Michael. BS in Chemistry, U. Louisville, 1968; PhD in Chemistry, Calif. Inst. Tech., 1974. Asst. prof. dept. chemistry Pa. State U., University Park, 1974-78, assoc. prof. dept. chemistry, 1978-82, prof. dept. chemistry, 1982-88, head dept. chemistry, 1988-89, dean Eberly Coll. Sci., 1989-97; provost, sr. v.p. acad. affairs U. Md., 1997; pres. Iowa State U., 2001—. Bd. dirs. Assn. Advancement Res. Astro., Washington; cons. Union Carbide Corp., South Charleston, W.Va., 1984-95, ARCO Chem., Newtown Square, Pa., 1988-92. Author: Organometallic Photochemistry, 1979; contbr. articles to profl. jours. Recipient Tchr.-Scholar award Camille & Henry Dreyfus Found., 1978, fellowship John Simon Guggenheim Found., 1982. Fellow AAAS; mem. Am. Chem. Soc. (chair inorganic chemistry divsn. 1990). Avocations: mountain biking, skiing. Office: 1750 Beardshear Hall Ames IA 50011

GEOGHEGAN, WILLIAM DAVIDSON, religion educator, minister; b. Wilmington, Del., July 16, 1922; s. Presley Downs and Mildred Alphaeus (Davidson) G.; m. Sarah Elizabeth Phelps, Oct. 5, 1946; children: Grace, Andrew, Emily, William Davidson II. BA, Yale U., 1943; postgrad., Harvard U., 1943-44; MDiv, Drew U., 1945; PhD, Columbia U., 1951. Ordained to ministry United Meth. Ch. as deacon, 1947, as elder, 1948. Pastor United Meth. Ch., Christiana, Del., 1947-50, chaplain, asst. prof. religion U. Rochester, N.Y., 1950-54; asst. prof. religion Bowdoin Coll., Brunswick, Maine, 1954-62, assoc. prof., 1962-66, prof., 1966-90, prof. emeritus, 1991—, chmn. dept. religion, 1954-79, 81-85, spring 1988. Vis. scholar Columbia U. and Union Theol. Sem., 1964-65; founder, chair Bowdoin Coll. Jung Seminar, 1980—; founder Dept. Religion Bowdoin Coll., Brunswick, Maine. Recipient Alumni award Bowdoin Coll. Alumni Assn., 1981. Mem. AAUP, Am. Acad. Religion, Hegel Soc. Am., Internat. Soc. for Neoplatonic Studies, Soc. Christian Philosophers, Town and Coll. Club, Phi Beta Kappa, Zeta Psi. Address: Bowdoin Coll 8400 College Sta Brunswick ME 04011-8484 Home: PO Box 336 10 Burroughs Ln Wolfeboro NH 03894-4917

GEO-KARIS, ADELINE JAY, state legislator; b. Tegeas, Greece, Mar. 29, 1918; Student, Northwestern U.; LLB, DePaul U. Bar: Ill. Founder Adeline J. Geo-Karis and Assocs., Zion, Ill.; former mcpl., legis. atty. Mundelein, Ill., Vernon Hills, Ill., Libertyville Twp., Ill., Twp. Long Grove (Ill.) Sch. Dist. Justice of peace; former asst. state's atty.; mem. Ill. Ho. of Reps., 1973-79; mem. Ill. Senate, 1979—, asst. majority leader, 1992—; former mayor City of Zion, Ill. Served to lt. comdr. USNR, Res. ret. Recipient Americanism medal DAR; named Woman of Yr. Daughters of Penelope, Outstanding Legislator Ill. Fedn. Ind. Colls. and Univs., 1975-78, Legis. award Ill. Assn. Park Dists., 1976; Sponsor Guilty but Mentally Ill law. Greek Orthodox. Office: Ill State Senate State Capitol Springfield IL 62706-0001*

GEORGAKAKOS, KONSTANTINE PETER, research hydrologist; b. Athens, Greece, Sept. 12, 1954; came to U.S., 1977; MS, MIT, 1980, ScD, 1982. Postdoctoral rschr. NOAA-Nat. Rsch. Coun., Silver Spring, Md., 1982-85, rsch. hydrologist Office Hydrology, 1985; asst. prof. CEE U. Iowa, Iowa City, 1986-89, assoc. prof., 1989-94; dir., sr. rsch. hydrologist Hydrologic Rsch. Ctr., San Diego, 1994—; full rsch. hydrologist IV Inst. Oceanography U. Calif., San Diego, 1994—. Cons. Food & Agriculture Orgn. UN, Rome, 1995—; sci. rev. panelist Nat. Oceanography Atmosphere Adminstrn., Silver Spring, 1996; reviewer NSF, NOAA, NASA, Washington, 1986—. Editor Jour. Applied Meteorology, 1995, Jour. Hydrology, 1996; contbr. articles to profl. jours. Coach Little League Soccer Club Del Mar, San Diego, 1994—. Rsch. associateship Nat. Rsch. Coun., Washington, 1982; recipient Presdl. Young Investigator award NSF, Washington, 1987. Mem. ASCE (assoc. editor 1996—), Am. Geophys. Union (chair hydrology 1991-93), Am. Meteor. Soc. (chair hydrology sect. 1991-93, elected expert on the WMO Commn. Hydrology Working Group on Applications). Achievements include development of flash flood prediction system used nationally by U.S. Nat. Weather Svc., elucidated dynamics and scaling of rainfall and soil water, role of soil water in development of future land surface hydrologic response; performed integrated impact assessments of climate variability and temperature change; developed operational system for rain estimation from satellite multispectral data. Office: Hydrologic Rsch Ctr 12780 High Bluff Dr Ste 250 San Diego CA 92130-3017 E-mail: kgeorgakakos@hrc-lab.org.

GEORGAKOPOULOS, ANASTASIOS, molecular biology; b. Athens, Greece, Jan. 31, 1965; s. Elias and Aikaterinh (Anagnostopoulou) G. BS, U. Athens, Greece, 1988, PhD, 1997. Lab. asst. U. Athens, Greece, 1983-84, 84-85; rsch. coord. Greek Ministry Health, Athens, 1984; asst. rschr. Greek Anticancer Inst., Athens, 1985-86; lab. rschr. Nat. Hellenic Rsch. Found., Athens, 1989-90, postdoctoral fellow, 1997; postdoctoral fellow dept neurobiology and psychiatry Mt. Sinai Sch. Medicine, N.Y.C., 1997-2000, instr. dept. neurobiology and psychiatry, 2000—03, asst. prof., 2003—. Computer specialist NHRE/IBRB, Athens, 1990—; cons. in field of computer graphics, Athens, 1989—. Co-author: Study for the Greek Ministry of Health, 1984. With Greek Med. Corps, 1994-96. Mem. AAAS, N.Y. Acad. Scis., Mensa. Avocations: music, drawing, photography, exercising. Office: Mt Sinai Sch Medicine Dept Psychiatry One Gustave L Levy Pl New York NY 10029

GEORGALAS, ROBERT NICHOLAS, English language educator; b. N.Y.C., Nov. 11, 1951; s. Nicholas and Dora (Patisso) G.; m. Joanne Louise Pepe, Sept. 5, 1981. BA, Lehman Coll., 1972; MA, CCNY, 1974; MFA, Columbia Coll., Chgo., 1997. Mktg. coord. Am. Express Co., N.Y.C., 1978-79; media supr. Wunderman Ricotta & Kline, N.Y.C., 1979-82, Needham Harper & Steers, N.Y.C., 1982-84; v.p., media dir. J. Walter Thompson Direct, N.Y.C., 1984-88, Leo Burnett USA, Chgo., 1988-91; prof. English Coll. of DuPage, Glen Ellyn, Ill., 1991—. Adj. assoc. prof. English Marymount Manhattan Coll., N.Y.C., 1979-88; voting judge Echo Awards, N.Y.C., 1987. Contbr. fiction to mags. Recipient Gold Effie award Am. Mktg. Assn., 1983, 91. Mem. NEA, MLA, Nat. Coun. Tchrs. English. Avocations: writing, swimming, traveling, theater, cinema. Home: 360 E Randolph St Chicago IL 60601-5069 Office: Coll of DuPage 425 Fawell Blvd Glen Ellyn IL 60137-6784 E-mail: georgala@cdnet.cod.edu.

GEORGANAS, NICOLAS D. electrical engineering educator; b. Athens, Greece, June 15, 1943; s. Demetrios N. and Athanasia (Kotsovou) G.; m. Jacynthe Savard, June 17, 1972; children: Nikita, Emmanuel. Diploma in Engring., Nat. Tech. U. Athens, 1966; PhD summa cum laude, U. Ottawa, Ont., Can., 1970. Registered profl. engr., Ont. Lectr., elec. engring. U. Ottawa, 1970-71, asst. prof., 1971-76, assoc. prof., 1976-80, prof., 1980—, chmn., 1981-84, dean engring., 1986-93. Vis. prof. IBM, LaGaude, France, 1977-78, INRIA/Bull-Transac, Paris, 1984-85, Bell-No. Rsch., Ottawa, 1993-94, CRC, Ottawa, 1997. Author: Queueing Networks—Exact Computational Algorithms: A Unified Theory by Decomposition and Aggregation, 1989; contbr. over 100 articles to profl. jours., more than 200 conf. articles. Fellow IEEE, Can. Acad. Engring., Royal Soc. Can., Engring. Inst. (Killam prize). Home: 1915 Montereau Ave Gloucester ON Canada Office: U Ottawa Faculty Engring SITE 161 Pasteur St Ottawa ON Canada K1N 6N5 E-mail: n.georganas@ieee.org.

GEORGANTZIS, NIKOLAOS, economist; b. Athens, Greece, Sept. 6, 1962; arrived in Spain, 1993; s. Dimitrios and Aekaterine Georgantzis; m. Aurora Garcia-Gallego, Aug. 27, 1993; children: Dimitris, Irina. BA in Econs., Pireus (Greece) U., 1986; MPhil in Econs., Swansea (U.K., Wales) U., 1989; MA in

Econs., European U. Inst., Florence, Italy, 1990, PhD in Econs., 1993. Trainee EU Commn., Brussels, 1992; prof. U. Jaume I, Castellon, Spain, 1993-98, tenured prof., 1998—, dir. grad. studies, 1994—99, dir. Laboratori d'Economia Exptl. Fellow rschr. Lineex, Valencia, 1998—, IMOP, Athens, 1999. Author, editor: Spatial Economics and Ecosystems, 2000; contbr. articles to profl. jours., chpt. to book. Rsch. rep. European U. Inst., 1991-92. Recipient Post-Madrid Conf. prize IFREE/Tinker Found., 1999; grantee IKY, Greece, 1989, European U. Inst., Italy, 1992. Achievements include experimental economics work dedicated to the study of learning in oligopolistic markets and valuation of ecological products. Home: 50 Avda Ferrandis Salvador 12100 Grao-Castellon Spain Office: U Jaume I Campus Riu Sec 12071 Castellon Spain

GEORGE, ALEXANDER ANDREW, lawyer; b. Missoula, Mont., Apr. 26, 1938; s. Andrew Miltiadin and Eleni (Efstathiou) G.; m. Penelope Mitchell, Sept. 29, 1968; children: Andrew A., Stephen A. BBA honors, U. Mont., 1960, JD, 1962; postgrad., John Marshall U., 1964-66. Bar: Mont. 1962, U.s. Ct. Mil. Appeals 1964, U.S. Tax Ct. 1970. Sole practice, Missoula, 1966—. Mem. adv. com. U. Mont. Tax Inst., 1973-76; adj. lectr. U. Montana Law Sch. Corp. Taxation. Pres. Missoula Civic Symphony, 1973; nat. dir. Assn. Urban and Cmty. Symphony Orch., 1974, Mont. Eye Endowment Found.; pres. Greek Orthodox Ch., 1978, 91. Served to capt. JAG U.S. Army, 1962-66. Recipient Jaycee Disting. Svc. award, 1973. Mem.: Mont. Soc. CPA, Mont. Law Found. (treas. 1986—92), Western Mont. Bar Assn. (pres. 1971, lifetime achievement award 1998), State Bar Mont. (pres. 1981), Glacier-Waterton Internat. Peace Pk. Assn. (bd. dirs. 1999—2002), Ahepa (pres. 1967, state gov. 1968), Rotary (pres. 1972, state chmn. found. 1977, membership com. chmn. 1978), Sigma Nu (alumni trustee 1966—71), Alpha Kappa Psi, Phi Delta Phi. Home: 4 Greenbrier Ct Missoula MT 59802-3342 Office: 210 N Higgins Ave Ste 234 Missoula MT 59802-4497

GEORGE, ALEXANDER LAWRENCE, political scientist, educator; b. Chgo., May 31, 1920; s. John and Mary (Sargis) G.; m. Juliette Lombard, Apr. 20, 1948; children: Lee Lawrence, Mary Lombard. AM, U. Chgo., 1941, PhD, 1958; DHL (hon.), U. San Diego, 1987; PhD (hon.), U. Lund, Sweden, 1994. Rsch. analyst OSS, 1944-45; dep. chief rsch. br. Info. Control divsn. Office Mil. Govt. for Germany, 1945-48; specialist study of decision-making and internat. rels. RAND Corp., Santa Monica, Calif., 1948-68, head dept. social sci., 1961-63; prof. polit. sci. and internat. rels. Stanford (Calif.) U., 1968—. Lectr. U. Chgo., 1950, Am. U., 1952—56; chmn. com. on Conflict Rrsolution NRC/NAS, 1995—2000. Author: (with Juliette L. George) Woodrow Wilson and Colonel House: A Personality Study, 1956, Propaganda Analysis, 1959, The Chinese Communist Army in Action, 1967; (with others) The Limits of Coercive Diplomacy, 1971; (with Richard Smoke) Deterrence in American Foreign Policy: Theory and Practice, 1974 (Bancroft prize for Deterrence in Am. Fgn. Policy 1975), Towards A More Soundly Based Foreign Policy: Making Better Use of Information, 1976, Presidential Decisionmaking in Foreign Policy, 1980, Managing U.S.-Soviet Rivalry, 1983; (with Gordon Craig) Force and Statecraft, 1983, 3rd edit., 1995; editor: (with others) U.S.-Soviet Security Cooperation: Achievements, Failures, Lessons, 1988, Avoiding War: Problems of Crisis Management, 1991, Forceful Persuasion, 1992, Bridging the Gap: Theory and Practice of Foreign Policy, 1993; (with William E. Simons) The Limits of Coercive Diplomacy, 2d. edit., 1994; (with Juliette L. George) Presidential Personality and Performance, 1998. Mem. Carnegie Commn. on Preventing Deadly Conflict, 1993-97. Fellow Ctr. Advanced Study Behavioral Scis., 1956-57, 76-77, NIMH, 1972-73, MacArthur Prize, 1983-88, Disting. fellow U. S. Inst. Peace, 1990-91, 91-92; Founds. Fund for Rsch. in Psychiatry grantee, 1960, NSF rsch. grantee, 1971-73, 75-77; recipient award for behavioral rsch. relevant to prevention of nuclear war NAS, 1997, Johan Skytte prize in polit. sci., Uppsala U., Swden, 1998; Carnegie Corp. grantee, 1999. Mem. Am. Acad. Arts and Scis., Coun. on Fgn. Rels., Am. Polit. Sci. Assn., Internat. Studies Assn. (pres. 1973-74), Am. Philos. Soc., Phi Beta Kappa. Home: 944 Lathrop Pl Stanford CA 94305-1060 E-mail: algeorge@stanford.edu.

GEORGE, ALFRED L., JR., medical educator, researcher; b. Batavia, NY, June 14, 1956; BA in Chemistry, Coll. of Wooster, Ohio, 1978; MD, U. Rochester, 1982. Diplomate Am. Bd. Internal Medicine, Am. Bd. Nephrology. Intern and resident in internal medicine Vanderbilt U. Hosps., Nashville, 1982—86; chief resident in medicine St. Thomas Hosp., Nashville, 1985—86; instr. medicine Vanderbilt U. Sch. Medicine, Nashville, 1985—86, asst. prof. dept. medicine nephrology and pharmacology, 1992—95; assoc. prof. medicine and pharmacology Vanderbilt U., Nashville, 1995—; postdoctoral fellow in clin. nephrology renal-elctrolyte sectl dept. medicine Hosp. of U. Pa., Phila., 1986—87; rsch. fellow dept. medicine and dept. biochemistry and biophysics U. Pa., Phila., 1988—91, rsch. assoc. dept. medicine and Inst. Neurol. Scis., 1991—92. Vis. postdoctoral fellow Inst. Suisse de Recherches Experimentales sur le Cancer, Lausanne, Switzerland, 1987—88. Mem. editl. bd.: Am. Jour. Physiology, 1996—, jour. reviewer: Neuron, —, Nature Genetics, —, Jour. Membrane Biology, —; Jour. Biol. Chemistry, —; jour. reviewer: Kidney Internat., —, Jour. Physiology, —. Mem.: AAAS, Biophys. Soc., Am. Heart Assn. (mem. coun. on kidney disease, established investigator award 1996), Am. Soc. Nephrology. Office: Vanderbilt U Med Ctr 21st And Garland Ave Bldg Ii Nashville TN 37232-0001

GEORGE, ARTHUR CHARLES, lawyer; b. Boston, Dec. 9, 1954; s. Charles Arthur and Diana Kanavos George; m. Soteria Liousas, May 22, 1983; children: Charles Arthur, Peter Arthur, Elizabeth Diana. BSBA, Boston U., 1976; JD, New Eng. Sch. Law, 1979. Bar: Mass. 1980, U.S. Dist. Ct. Mass. 1981, U.S. Ct. Appeals (1st cir.) 1981. Lawyer Arthur C. George, Esq., Randolph, Mass., 1980-86; ptnr. George & George, Stoughton, 1987—. Town counsel Town of Holbrook, Mass., 1986—; mem. Rep. Town Com., Holbrook, 1988—, chmn., 1990-2000; co-leader Adventurer's 4-H Club, Holbrook, 1988—; trustee Bridgewater State Coll., 1999—. Recipient Cert. of Appreciation, Mass. Chpt. Black Rep. Coun., citation Mass. State Senate, 1995, Salute to Excellence award U. Mass. Ext. and Mass. 4-H Found., 1998, Lucem Diffundo Plate award Mayor of New Bedford, 2001. Mem. Mass. Bar Assn., Bar Assn. Norfolk County (former coun. mem.), Ripon Soc. (nat. sec. 1992-94), Holbrook Sportsmen's Club. Avocations: research and policy, political speechwriting, chess, baseball. Office: 1st Fl 10 Cabot Pl Fl 1 Stoughton MA 02072-4600

GEORGE, BOYD LEE, consumer products company executive; b. 1942; BBA, U. Notre Dame, 1963; LLB, U. Va., 1966. With Merchants Distbrs., Inc., 1969-72, v.p., 1972-76, pres., COO, 1976-83, chmn. bd., 1983—; chmn., CEO Alex Lee, Hickory, N.C., 1992—. Capt. USMC, 1966-69. Office: Alex Lee PO Box 800 120 4th St Dr Hickory NC 28603*

GEORGE, CECELIA G. photographer, writer, artist, musician; BA, Fresno (Calif.) State U., 1964. Concert, profl. violinist Pasadena, Fresno and Monterey Symphonies, Calif., 1958—92; interior designer, 1987– 2000; model, 1990—98. Color design cons., coord., 1964—95; inspirational spkr., 1980—2002. Author: Against My Will, 1998; contbr. poetry to jours. Mem. arts coun. for Robinson Jeffers Tor House Monterey Peninsula Arts Coun., Carmel, 1994—96; pres. Youth Orch., Monterey, Calif., 1985—90; mem. Tchrs. Edn. Bd., Monterey, 1986—89; bd. dirs. Chataquia Dance Club, Pacific Grove, Calif., 1999—2002. Democrat. Avocations: gardening, design, dancing, music, swimming. Fax: 831-372-7254.

GEORGE, DAVID SANDERSON, Spanish language educator, writer; b. Mpls., Minn., Feb. 8, 1942; s. William Allen and LaVerne Helen Eloise George; m. Beatriz de Arruda Zonis, May 26, 1985; 1 child, Alexander Sanderson. PhD, U. Minn., 1981. Asst. prof. Spanish Middlebury (Vt.) Coll., 1978—85; prof. Spanish Lake Forest (Ill.) Coll., 1985—. Area studies presenter Cendant Intercultural, Chgo., 1991—; vis. scholar U. of Chgo. Ctr. for Latin Am. Studies, 1996—2001. Author: (drama criticism) Flash & Crash Days: Brazilian Theatre in the Post-Dictatorship Period; contbr. literary reference, drama criticism; author: (play) À Mão Armada, (drama criticism) The Modern Brazilian Stage; translator: (short stories) Scent of Love, (novel) Early Mourning; author: (drama criticism) Grupo Macunaíma: Carnavalização e Mito; translator: (novel) Village of the Ghost Bells, (short stories) Bag of Stories; contbr. book of travel essays. Recipient fellowship for coll. tchrs., NEH, 1987—88, summer stipends, 1993, Oskar Nobling Medal for contbns. to rsch. on Brazilian lit., Sociedade Brasileira de Língua e Literatura, 1998, fellowship for coll. tchrs., NEH, 1995, summer stipends, 2002; grantee summer seminars, 1989, 1994. Mem.: MLA, Latin Am. Studies Assn., Brazilian Studies Assn. Liberal. Avocations: reading, travel, bicycling. Office: Lake Forest Coll 555 N Sheridan Rd Lake Forest IL 60045 Personal E-mail: george@lfc.edu.

GEORGE, DEINABO DABIBI, writer, computer specialist, educator; b Boston, Jan. 31, 1970; s. Orlando and Carol (Gibbons) G. Student, Tuskegee U., 1988, Bronx Cmty. Coll., 1989 90; BA in Black Studies, CCNY, 1993. Tchr. phys. edn. Intermediate Sch. 306, Bronx, 1994-95; sr. network/user support technician NYU, N.Y.C., 2000—. Pres., owner Black Odyssey Enterprises, Inc., Bronx, 1995—; adj. prof. Marymount Manhattan Coll., 1997-98. Author: (lit. anthology) Death Standard, 1993, Recitations from the Prophet, 1998. Mem. Black Alumni Assn. City Coll., Alumni Assn. City Coll. Avocations: working out, collecting comic books and related memorabilia, writing poetry, computer technology. Home and Office: Black Odyssey Enterprises Inc 1992 Morris Ave Bronx NY 10453-4829 Fax: 718-299-5843. E-mail: deinabo.george@verizon.net.

GEORGE, DEVERAL D. editor, journalist, advertising consultant; b. Dallas, Nov. 23, 1939; s. Jack Weldon and Lleen Lelia (Humc) G. Student, U. Tex., 1958-61; BA, North Tex. State U., 1964; P.BA, U. Houston, 1974. Copywriter advt. agys., Houston, Dallas, 1964-70; free lance journalist, 1970-73, 75-76; copy and creative dir. Schey Advt., Houston, 1973, Bruce Advt., Houston, 1973-75; editor-in-chief, v.p. Bus. and Energy Internat., Houston, 1976-80; editor Ultra mag., 1980-81; freelance journalist Houston, 1981-83, 84-85; editor Saudi Bus. Mag.; cons. Saudi Research and Mktg. Inc., Houston, Washington, and Jeddah, Saudi Arabia, 1983-84; writer, advt. cons. Dale Carnegie & Assocs., Garden City (N.Y.) and Houston, 1985-90; mng. editor internat. Offshore Mag., Houston, 1991-97; editor Schlumberger Oilfield Rev., 1997-98, Oil and Gas Online, Vertical Net, Horsham, Pa., 1998-2001, Houston, 1998-2001; owner, mng. editor Oil and Gas Internat., Houston, 2001—. Author: Cathedrals of Mexico, and Other Poems, 1963, The Erratic Pilgramage, 1973, The Whole World Cookbook, 1976, The Offshore Atlas, 1995; screenplays: The Monument, 1980, Armageddon, 1981; television series Treasure Hunt, 1984; editor: Worldwide Directory of Petroleum Ministries and National Oil Companies, 1995; mem. editl. bd. Xi'an Petroleum Inst., China. Del., Democratic Conv., 1972; mem. Houston Outdoor Group. Mem. ACLU, Am. Assn. Petroleum Geologists, Soc. Exploration Geophysicists, Geophys. Soc. Houston, Soc. Internat. Devel., N.Am. Congress on Latin Am., Amnesty Internat., Internat. Platform Assn., Ctr. for Study of Dem. Instns., Asia Soc., World Expeditionary Assn., Soc. Profl. Journalists-Sigma Delta Chi, Houston Press Club. Clubs: Houston Press. Home: 8310 Braesdale Ln Houston TX 77071 1228 Office: PO Box 710046 Houston TX 77071-1030

GEORGE, DONALD RICHARD, retired principal; b. Coffeyville, Kans., Oct. 1, 1926; s. Murl C. and Georgia M. (Leib) G.; m. Zepha Lowry, June 5, 1949; children: Donna L. Kellison, David L., Mary M. Tribby. BS in Edn., Pitts. State U., 1960; MS in Edn., Emporia State U., 1965. Tchr., asst. prin. Hugoton (Kans.) Elem. Sch., 1954-75; prin. Nelson Elem. Sch., Haysville, Kans., 1975-80, W.D. Munson Primary Sch., Mulvane, Kans., 1980-93, ret., 1993. IDEA Kettering Found. fellow, 1978-83. Mem. Nat. Assn. Elem. Sch. Prins., Kans. Assn. Elem. Sch. Prins., United Sch. Adminstrs. Kans., Lions, Phi Delta Kappa. Mem. Ch. of God. Avocations: farming, golf, woodworking. Home: 713 Tristan Dr Mulvane KS 67110-1212

GEORGE, DONALD WARNER, online columnist and editor, freelance writer; b. Middlebury, Conn., June 24, 1953; s. Lloyd Foster and Vivian (Minor) G.; m. Kuniko Ninomiya, Apr. 24, 1982; children: Jennifer Ayako, Jeremy Naoki. BA, Princeton U., 1975; MA, Hollins (Va.) Coll., 1977. Tchg. fellow Athens (Greece) Coll., 1975-76, Internat. Christian U., Tokyo, 1977-79; TV talk show host Japan Broadcasting Corp., Tokyo, 1977-79; freelance writer, 1980-81; travel writer San Francisco Examiner, 1981-82, sr. editor Calif. Living mag., 1982-85, sr. editor Image mag., 1985-87, travel editor, 1987-95; cyber columnist, Global Network Navigator American Online, Berkeley, Calif., 1995-96; editor Salon Wanderlust Online Travel Mag., 1997-2000; global travel editor Lonely Planet Publs., 2001—. Recipient gold award Pacific Asia Travel Assn., 1987-94, 2002. Mem. Soc. Am. Travel Writers (Lowell Thomas award 1987-94, 2002). Office: Lonely Planet 150 Linden St Oakland CA 94607 E-mail: dgeorge@lonelyplanet.com.

GEORGE, DUANE M. editor; b. Rome, N.Y., Jan. 15, 1969; s. Jesus C. George, Monica R. George. BA, U. Guam, 1991. Mng. editor Latte Mag., Tamuning, 1998—2000; editl. editor Pacific Daily News, Hagatna, 2000—. Mem.: Soc. Profl. Journalists (bd. dirs. 2000 –01, pres. Micronesia chpt. 1999—2000, bd. dirs. 1997—99, Best News Story 1998, 1999, Best Column/Editl. 1998). Avocation: web graphics design. Office: Pacific Daily News Box DN Agana GU 96932 Office Fax: 671-477-3079. Business E-Mail: dgeorge@guampdn.com.

GEORGE, EDDIE, professional football player; b. Sept. 24, 1973; Student, Fork Union Mil. Acad. Running back Tenn. Oilers (now called Tenn. Titans), 1996—. Named NFL Rookie of Yr., 1996, first alternate to Pro Bowl; recipient Heisman Trophy. Achievements include placed third AFC rushing and in total yards from scrimmage. Office: Tennessee Titans 460 Great Circle Rd Nashville TN 37228-1404

GEORGE, EMERY EDWARD, foreign language and studies educator, writer; b. Budapest, Hungary, May 8, 1933; came to U.S., 1946, naturalized, 1954; AB, U. Mich., 1955, MA, 1959; postgrad., Fed. Rep. Germany, 1961-62; PhD, U. Mich., 1964. Instr. U. Ill., Champaign-Urbana, 1964-65, asst. prof. German, 1965-66, U. Mich., Ann Arbor, 1966-69, assoc. prof., 1969-75, prof., 1975-88, prof. emeritus, 1988—, faculty program in comparative lit., 1969—, faculty program Center for Russian and East European Studies, 1975—. Author: Hölderlin's Ars Poetica, 1973, Mountainwild: Poems, 1974, Black Jesus, 1974, A Gift of Nerve: Poems, 1966-77, 1978, Kate's Death, 1980, The Poetry of Miklos Radnoti: A Comparative Study, 1986, The Boy and the Monarch, 1987, Voiceprints, 1987; (essay) The Allegory of Spandau, 1990 (Kenyon Rev. 2d ann. nonfiction award 1991), Hölderlin and the Golden Chain of Homer, 1992, Blackbird: Poems on the World and Work of Franz Kafka, 1993, Valse Triste: Songs and Ballads, 1997, Hölderlin's Hymn Der Einzige, 1999, Compass Card: One Hundred Villanelles, 2000, Iphigenie in Manhattan: A Play in Five Acts, 2001, Iphigenie in Czestochowa: A Play in Five Acts, 2001, Orest: A Play in Five Acts, 2001, Iphigenie in Auschwitz: A Play in Five Acts, 2001; editor: Friedrich Hölderlin: An Early Modern, 1972, (with L.T. Frank) Husbanding the Golden Grain, 1973, Contemporary East European Poetry: An Anthology, 1983, expanded, 1993, (with D. E. Sattler) Friedrich Hölderlin, Homburger Folioheft (Frankfurter Hölderlin-Ausgabe, Supplement III), 1986, 93; also transls.; contbr. poetry, non-fiction prose, transls., articles, revs. to scholarly jours., lit. publs.; founding editor Mich. Germanic Studies; assoc. editor Russian Lit. Triquar.; mem. editl. bd. advisors Germano-Slavica, 1973-77; editl. bd. Mich. Monographs in the Humanities, 1979—, (yearbook) Cross Currents, 1986—. Served with M.I. U.S. Army, 1957-58. Recipient Avery and Jule Hopwood award in poetry U. Mich., 1960; Ottendorfer Meml. fellow, 1961; Am. Council Learned Socs. Publs. award, 1964; Rackham Publ. award U. Mich., 1973, 80; Hungarian PEN Research and Travel grant, 1979; IREX Exchange fellow to Hungary, 1981, Deutsche Forschungsgemeinschaft research and travel grantee, 1986. Fellow: Internat. Acad. Poets; mem.: MLA, Assn. Literary Scholars and Critics, Hungarian Writers Assn., Hungarian Acad. Scis., Shelley Soc. NY, Poetry Soc. Am., Holderlin-Gesellschaft. Home: 16 Buckingham Ave Trenton NJ 08618-3312 E-mail: eegeorge@hotmail.com. *Listen carefully to language, to words; try to write each day. Make no separation between writing and scholarship, between old and new literature. Monitor the eternal present. Try to achieve newness, a sense of experiment from within.*

GEORGE, ERNEST THORNTON, III, financial consultant; b. Charleston, S.C., Dec. 29, 1950; s. Ernest Thornton and Betty (Long) T.; m. Frances Thomson, Sept. 30, 1977; children: Ernest Thornton IV, Andrew Neal, Katherine Frances. Student, U. Miss., 1969-71; BS in Mktg., Miss. State U., 1973. CFP; CLU; registered investment advisor. Product cons. Mfrs. Life Ins. Co.; registered prin., 1977—; rep., br. mgr. Raymond James Fin. Svcs., Starkville, Miss., 1989—; owner, prin. Investment Mgmt. Group Inc., Starkville, 1982—, Wealth Mgmt. Group, Inc. Founding mem. bd. dirs. First Citizens Nat. Bank of Starkville; guest lectr. Miss. State U.; Dalbar rated adv. Co-author: Business Strategies, 2002; mem. editl. bd.: Fin. Svcs. Advisor; contbr. articles to profl. jours. Bd. dirs. exec. bd. Pushmataha area coun. Boy Scouts Am., Republican party; past pres. Men of Ch., Presbyn. Ch., chmn. bd. deacons, elder, men's Sunday Sch. tchr.; bd. dirs. Oktibbeha County Libr., past pres.; bd. dirs. Starkville Acad.; mem. stds. com. Miss. Pub. Libr.; bd. dirs. North Miss. chpt. Nat. Com. on Planned Giving, past pres. Recipient Silver Beaver award. Mem. Nat. Assn. Christian Fin. Advisors, East Miss. Life Underwriters Assn. (past pres.), Soc. Fin. Svcs. Profls. (bd. dirs. Miss. chpt.), Miss. Estate Planning Coun., Fin. Planning Assn.(bd. dirs. Miss. chpt.), Oktibbeha County C. of C. (exec. bd.), Rotary (bd. dirs. Starkville, Paul Harris fellow), Sigma Chi, Pi Sigma Epsilon. Home: 1672 Valley Hill Cir Starkville MS 39759-9748 Office: Raymond James Fin Svcs 102 S Jackson St PO Box 963 Starkville MS 39760-0963

GEORGE, FRANCIS, archbishop; b. Chgo., Jan. 16, 1937; Cert. ordained priest Roman Cath. Ch., 1963. Provincial ctrl. region Oblates of Mary Immaculate, 1973—74, vicar gen., 1974—86; bishop Diocese of Yakima, Wash., 1990—96; archbishop Archdiocese of Portland, Oreg., 1996—97, Archdiocese of Chgo., 1997—98, cardinal, 1998—. Chancellor Cath. Ch. Ext. U. St. Mary of Lake, 1997; mem. Congregation Divine Worship, Discipline of Sacraments, Congregation for Oriental Chs., 2001—, Congregation Insts., Consecrated Life, Socs. Apostolic Life, Pontifical Commn. for Cultural Heritage of Ch., 1999—, Pontifical Coun. Cor Unum, 1998, Congregation Evangelization of Peoples. Mem.: Coll. Cardinals. Roman Catholic. Office: Archdiocese of Chgo Pastoral Ctr PO Box 1979 Chicago IL 60690-1979

GEORGE, FRANK RICHARD, science and technoloty officer; b. Oakland, Calif., Dec. 30, 1953; s. Frank Louis and Josephine Marie (Fonzeno) G.; m. Mary Cecelia Ritz, June 29, 1980; children: Matthew, Lindsay. BS, U. Calif. Davis, 1975; MA, Calif. State U., Sacramento, 1978; PhD, U. Colo., 1981. Rsch. neurophysiologist dept. neurology U. Calif., Irvine, 1981-82; rsch. assoc. dept. genetics and cell biology Dight Labs., and Dept. Psychiatry U. Minn., 1982-85; rsch. asst. prof. dept. pharmacology and toxicology U. Md., Balt., 1985-91; from staff fellow to sr. fellow NIH/Nat. Inst. Drug Abuse, Balt., 1985-91; faculty mem./coord. preclinical rsch. Ctr. Alcoholism, Substance Abuse and Addictions, Albuquerque, 1991-94; ptnr. Sci. Svcs., Ariz. and N.Mex., 1991—; chmn. bd./exec. v.p., chief sci. officer Amethyst Techs. Inc., Scottsdale, Ariz., 1995—; founder, chief sci. tech. officer Regenesis Biomed., Scottsdale, Ariz., 1997—. Ad hoc cons. mem. NIH, Bethesda, 1989-2002; sr. cons. Sci. Svcs., Albuquerque, 1991-97. Editor: (book) Behavioral and Biochemical Issues in Substance Abuse, 1991; author Genetic Approaches to Substance Abuse Mechanisms; contbr. over 85 articles to profl. jours. Coach Nat. Little League Baseball, Scottsdale, Ariz., 1996-2001. Grantee Nat. Inst. of Health, 1983—, recipient New Investigator Rsch. award, 1983. Mem. Coll. on Problems of Drug Dependence, Am. Coll. Neuropsychopharmacology, Internat. Soc. for Biomed. Rsch. on Alcoholism. Democrat. Roman Catholic. Avocations: alpine skiing, scuba diving, youth programs, musician. Office: Regenesis Biomedical 1435 N Hayden Rd Scottsdale AZ 85257-3773 E-mail: george@regenesisbiomedical.com.

GEORGE, FRANK WADE, small business owner, antiquarian book dealer; b. Austin, Tex., Aug. 22, 1918; s. Frank Wade and Rosa Scott (Slaughter) W.; m. Marjorie Ann Miller, Dec. 27, 1948 (div. Jan. 1955); children: Frank Wade III, Gregory Scott, Barbara Lee; m. Martha Jeanne Wagner, Feb. 8, 1964 (dec. 1996); m. Wenona Thoma, 1996. Student, Tex. Sch. Fine Arts, 1936-41, Mexico City Coll., 1947; BJ, U. Tex., 1948. Office mgr. Tex. Sch. Fine Arts, 1936-41; mgr. Austin Symphony Orch., 1946-48, Erie (Pa.) Philharmonic Orch., 1948-49, Birmingham (Ala.) Symphony Orch., 1949-50, Ala. Pops Orch., Birmingham, 1955-62, Town and Gown Theatre, Birmingham, 1962-65; pres. Birmingham Opera Co., 1973-75; asst. cashier First Nat. Bank of Birmingham, Birmingham, 1950-80; Owner Books! By George, Birmingham, 1981—. Co-founder Margo George Fashion Prodns., 1951, Hanna Antiques, 1981; participant Antiquarian Book Seminar, U. Denver, 1986. Pres. Rockwood Plantation Condominium Assn., 2001—; treas. Greater Birmingham Arts Alliance, 1971—75, Birmingham Opera Guild, 1971—74, So. Regional Opera, 1981—84; trustee Birmingham Symphony Assn., 1973—75; chmn. artist hospitality Arts Hall of Fame, Birmingham, 1974; judge nat. coun. auditions Met. Opera Assn., 1981; docent Birmingham Mus. Art, 1980—82. Mem. Gideons Internat. (pres. 1980-83), Allegro Mus. Club (v.p. 1993-94), Ala. Symphonic Assn. (dir. speakers bur. 1995), Rockwood Plantation Condominium Assn. (pres. 2001—), Avocations: lay preaching, public speaking, reading, writing, travel. Home: 1851 Rockwood Rd Birmingham AL 35216-1425 Office: Books! By George 2424 7th Ave S Birmingham AL 35233-3318

GEORGE, GARY MARK, pastor, church administrator; b. Dover, Ohio, Feb. 10, 1957; s. L. Mark and Gaynalee Ethel (Stonebraker) G.; m. Lorraine Renee Baab, July 30, 1980; children: G. Mark, Michael Wayne. BS cum laude, Asbury Coll., 1979; MDiv, Ashland (Ohio) Theol. Sem.; DMin, Asbury Theol. Sem., 1998. Ordained elder United Methodist Ch. Dir. youth ministry Scott Meml. United Meth. Ch., Cadiz, Ohio, 1979-80; pastor Dellroy (Ohio) United Meth. Ch., 1980-83; assoc. pastor Dueber United Meth. Ch., Canton, 1983-86; pastor Mt. Zion United Meth. Ch., Canton, 1986-91; sr. pastor Christ United Meth. Ch., Newcomerstown, Ohio, 1991-99; dist. supt. Steubenville dist. United Meth. Ch. Mem. Bd. Ordained Ministry, North Canton, 1992-99; chmn. Cambridge (Ohio) Dist. Com. for Ordained Ministry, 1992-99; mem. Bd. Ch. & Soc., North Canton, 1990-92. Treas. Newcomerstown Acad. Boosters, 1993-95; adv. bd. Gordon DeMarco Found., Newc omerstown, 1994-96; mem. Appalachian Devel. Com., 2000—; elected mem. United Meth. Ch. Gen. Conf., 2000, 2004, North Ctrl. Jurisdictional Conf., 2000, 2004. Mem. Newcomerstown Ministerial Assn. (pres. 1994-95, treas. 1996-98), Urban Mission Ministries (bd. dirs. 1999—), Conf. Coun. on Fin. and Adminstrn. (bd. laity 1999-2001, bd. pensions 2001-02), Phi Alpha Theta. Avocations: american history, politics, personal computing, sports. Office: United Meth Ch 352 Canton Rd Wintersville OH 43953-3904 E-mail: garygeorga@1st.net.

GEORGE, GERALD WILLIAM, author, administrator; b. Caldwell, Kans., Aug. 4, 1938; s. Chester Dale and Mildred M. (Jolitz) G.; m. Patricia Rae Woolsey, Sept. 23, 1961 (div. 1989); children: Brian William, Roxane Elizabeth; m. Carol Maryan Bell, Sept. 18, 1993. BA, U. Wichita, 1960; MA, Yale U., 1962. Instr. Bethany Coll., Lindsborg, Kans., 1962; reporter Salina (Kans.) Jour., 1962-64; staff writer The Nat. Observer, Washington, 1964-67; editorial assoc. Woodrow Wilson Nat. Fellowship Found., Princeton, N.J., 1967-68; spl. asst. to chmn. NEH, Washington, 1969-70; free-lance writer Washington, The Netherlands, 1971-73; mng. editor book series Am. Assn. State and Local History, Nashville, 1973-78, dir., 1978-87, mem. steering com. endowment campaign, 1999—; free-lance writer, cons. to hist. orgns. Arlington, Va., 1987-90; exec. dir. Nat. Hist. Publs. and Records Commn., 1990-94; program devel. officer Coun. on Libr. Resources, Washington, 1995; exec. dir. Nat. Hist. Publs. and Records Commn., Washington, 1995-97; dir. commns. Nat. Archives and Records Adminstrn., College Park, Md., 1997-2000; spl. projects assoc. Coun. on Libr. and Info. Resources, Washington, 2000—. Author: Visiting History, Arguments Over Museums and Historic Sites, 1990, Imitations of Indonesia and Other Poems, 1997; co-author: Starting Right: A Basic Guide to Museum Planning, 1986; mng. editor: The States and the Nation; mem. editl. bd.: Ency. of the Am. West; contbr. articles to profl. jours. and mags. Recipient Woodrow Wilson fellow, 1960-61. Mem. Am. Assn. State and Local History, Nat. Trust Hist. Preservation, Soc. Am. Archivists, Hist. Soc. of Washington, Kans. State Hist. Soc., Scenic Am. Office: Coun on Libr and Info Resources Ste 500 1755 Massachusetts Ave NW Washington DC 20036 E-mail: maryangeorge@msn.com.

GEORGE, GRANT, information technology executive; BA in German, Calif. State U., Fullerton. Test engr., test mgr. Tandem Computers; prin., owner Coop. Solutions Inc.; with Taligent; corp. v.p. Microsoft, Redmond, Wash., 1994—. Office: One Microsoft Way Redmond WA 98052-6399

GEORGE, JAMES EDWARD, accountant; b. Mt. George, Ark., May 22, 1943; s. Opal W. Sr. and Mildred M. (Dacus) G.; m. Corliss Ann Johnson, Sept. 3, 1965; children: J. Mark, Ty C., Ryan E. BA in Acctg., U. Ark., Little Rock, 1967; MS in Logistics, Air Force Inst. Tech., 1979; grad., Air Command and Staff Coll. of USAF, 1987, USAF Air War Coll., 1992. CPA, Ark. Commd. 2d lt. USAF, 1967, advanced through grades to capt.; commdr. Field Tng. Detachment, Mt. Clemens, Mich., Kadena AFB, Japan and Kunsan AFB, Korea, 1967-73; supr. maintenance Field Maintenance Squadron, Craig AFB, Ala.,

1973-75; flightline br. chief Royal AFB, Bentwater, Eng., 1976-77; officer in charge quality control Tactical Fighter Wing, Royal AFB, Bentwater, 1977-78; left active duty USAFR, 1978, advanced through grades to lt. col., 1988, ret., 1994; pub. utility auditor Ark. Pub. Svc. Commn., Little Rock, 1979-98; exec. dir. Ark. State Bd. Pub. Accountancy, Little Rock, 1998—2003. Lectr. pub. utility income taxes and depreciation 12th and 13th ann. ea. utility rate seminar Nat. Assn. Regulatory Utility Commrs., 1984, 85; adj. faculty U. Ark., Fayetteville; mem. acctg. adv. coun. U. Ark., Little Rock, 2002--. Bd. dirs. Brockington Rd. Ch. of the Nazarene, 1989—94, 1998—2002. Mem. Ark. Soc. CPA's (pres. Ctrl. Ark. chpt. 1992-93, 95-96, chmn. membership com. 1991-93, bd. dirs. 1994-97, mem. exec. com. 1996-97, chmn. public rels. com. 1997-2003, Outstanding Ark. CPA in Industry and Bus. award 1995), Toastmasters (pres. Uptown chpt. 1985, Able Toastmaster award 1988), Officers Club (bd. dirs. Kadena AFB 1971-72). Home: 5015 Lakeview North Little Rock AR 72116

GEORGE, JAMES NOEL, hematologist, oncologist, educator; b. Columbus, Ohio, Sept. 23, 1938; BA, MD, Ohio State U., 1962. Diplomate Am. Bd. Internal Medicine subspecialty in hematology, lic. Okla. Bd. Med. Licensure and Supervision, Tex. State Bd. Med. Examiners, Ohio State Med. Bd. Intern, resident dept. medicine Vanderbilt U. Sch. Medicine, Nashville, 1962—63, 1966—67; resident in medicine, hematology fellow, chief resident med. Strong Meml. Hosp., U. Rochester (N.Y.) Sch. Medicine, 1967—70; rsch. hematologist Walter Reed Army Inst. Rsch., Washington, 1963—66; from asst. prof. to assoc. prof. dept. med. divsn. hematol. U. Tex. Health Sci. Ctr., San Antonio, 1970—81, prof. dept. medicine divsn. hematology, 1981—89; rsch. assoc. Theodor Kocher Inst., Berne, Switzerland, 1975—76; prof. dept. medicine, chief hematology-oncology sect. U. Okla. Health Sci. Ctr., Oklahoma City, 1990—99; staff physician Okla. Blood Inst., Oklahoma City, 1994—. Vis. prof. dept. physiol. chemistry U. Wis., Madison, 1987—88; prof. associe U. Paris VII, Hopital Lariboisiere, 1988—89; mem. transfusion com. Bexar County Hosp., 1970—87; chmn. hematology peer rev. panel NASA Life Scis. Space Flight Experiment Program, 1978; mem. NIH Hematology Study Sect. I, 1986—94; mem. adv. bd. Gladstone Found. Labs. for Cardiovasc. Rsch., U. Calif., San Francisco, 1991; bd. trustees Gorgas Sci. Found., Inc., Brownsville, Tex., 1992—. Mem.editl. bd.: Blood, 1985—90. Mem. oncology task force Midwest City Regional Hosp., 1995—. Capt. M.C. U.S. Army, 1963—66. Recipient 1st Ann. Lyndon B. Johnson award, Tex. affiliate Am. Heart Assn., 1976. Fellow: ACP; mem.: So. Soc. for Clin. Investigation, Ctrl. Soc. Clin. Rsch., Am. Soc. Hematology (com. on ednl. affairs and tng. 1986—89, sci. subcom. on platelets 1986—89, com. on publs. 1991—, chmn. edn. program on platelets 1993, 1994, ad hoc com. on practice guidelines 1994—, chmn. subcom. on platelets 1995, nominating com. 1995, chmn. edn. program on platelets 1996), Am. Soc. Clin. Investigation, Am. Heart Assn. (thrombosis coun.), Am. Fedn. for Clin. Rsch., Alpha Omega Alpha (councilor Tex. Epsilon chpt. 1978—81). Office: U of Okla Health Scis Ctr Dept Medicine Hemat-Onc Sec PO Box 26901 Oklahoma City OK 73190-0001

GEORGE, JEAN CRAIGHEAD, author, illustrator; b. Washington, July 2, 1919; d. Frank Cooper and Carolyn (Johnson) Craighead; m. John L. George, Jan. 28, 1944 (div. Jan. 1964); children: Twig George Pittenger, John Craighead, Thomas Lothar. BA, Pa. State U., 1941. Reporter Washington Post, 1943-44; artist Pageant mag., 1945; reporter United Features, 1945-46; roving editor Reader's Digest, 1966-80; continuing edn. tchr. Chappaqua, N.Y., 1960-68. Author, illustrator: My Side of the Mountain, 1959, Summer of the Falcon, 1962, Gull Number 737, 1964, The Thirteen Moons, 1967-69, Coyote in Manhattan, 1968, River Rats, Inc., 1968, Who Really Killed Cock Robin, 1972, Julie of the Wolves, 1972, American Walk Book, 1978, Cry of the Crow, 1980, Journey Inward, 1982, The Talking Earth, 1983, One Day in the Alpine Tundra, 1984, How to Talk to Your Animals, 1985, One Day in the Prairie, 1986, Water Sky, 1987, (mus.) One Day in the Woods, 1988, The Shark Beneath the Reef, 1989, On the Far Side of the Mountain, 1990, One Day in the Tropical Rain Forest, 1990, The Missing 'Gator of Gumbo Limbo, 1992, The Fire Bug Connection, 1993, The First Thanksgiving, 1993, Dear Rebecca, Winter Is Here, 1993, Animals Who Have Won Our Hearts, 1994, Julie, 1994, To Climb a Waterfall, 1995, Acorn Pancakes & Dandelion Salad, 1995, There's an Owl in the Shower, 1995, Everglades, 1995, The Case of the Missing Cutthroat Trout, 1996, The Tarantula in My Purse, 1996, Look to the North, A Wolf Pup Diary, 1997, Julie's Wolf Pack, 1997, Arctic Son, 1997, Rhino Romp, 1998, Giraffe Trouble, 1998, Dear Katie, the Volcano Is a Girl, 1998, Survival Filmstrips, 1984, (film) My Side of the Mountain, 1965, Nature Filmstrips, 1978-80, One Day in the Woods Musical for Children (music by Chris Kubie), 1997, Elephant Walk, 1998, Gorilla Gang, 1999, Morning, Noon and Night, 1999, Frightful's Mountain, 1999, Snow Bear, 1999, How to Talk to Your Dog, 2000, How to Talk to Your Cat, 2000, Nutik, the Wolf Pup, 2001, Nutik & Amaoq Play Ball, 2001, Tree Castle Island, 2002, Cliff Hanger, 2002, Frightful's Daughter, 2002, Fire Storm, 2003. Recipient Aurianne award, 1957, Newbery Honor Book award, 1961, medal, 1973, Hans Christian Andersen Honor List award, 1964, Pa. State Woman of Yr. award, 1968, World Book award, 1971, Kerlan award, 1982, U. So. Miss. award, 1986, Washington Irving award, 1991, 92, Knickerbocker award, 1991, Washington Post Children's Book Guild award, 1998, Empire State award, 1998, runner-up Lamplighter award, 2002, Regina medal Cath. Libr. Assn. Address: 20 William St Chappaqua NY 10514-3114

GEORGE, JOEY F. computer science educator; s. John Nathaniel and Lalage Loree George; m. Karen Gardner, June 23, 1979; children: Evan Ann, Caitlin Jennifer. BA, Stanford U., 1979; MEd, Converse Coll., 1980; PhD, U. Calif., Irvine, 1986. Prof. U. Ariz., Tucson, 1986—93, Fla. State U., Tallahassee, 1993—98, 1999—, La. State U., Baton Rouge, 1998—99. Co-chair 2001 Internat. Conf. on Info. Systems, New Orleans, 1999—2001; chair MIS dept. Coll. Bus. Fla. State U., Tallahassee, 1995—98. Author: (textbooks) Modern Systems Analysis & Design, 3d edit., Essentials of Systems Analysis & Design; contbr. articles to profl. jours.; assoc. editor MIS Quar. Jour., Mpls., 1992—97, Info. Sys. Rsch. Jour., 1995—2000. Elder Fellowship Presbyn. Ch., Tallahassee, 1993—2002. Grantee, NSF, 1991—93, Air Force Office of Sci. Rsch., 2001—. Mem.: Assn. for Info. Sys. (chair ICIS exec. 2001—03), Assn. for Computing Machinery. Avocations: hiking, reading.

GEORGE, JOEY RUSSELL, lawyer; b. Bklyn., Oct. 8, 1963; s. Jonas and Celeste Dorothy (Russell) G. BA, Howard U., 1985; JD, Harvard U., 1988. Bar: N.Y. 1989, Conn. 1989, U.S. Dist. Ct. (so. and ea. dists.) N.Y. 1989, U.S. Supreme Ct. 1992. Asst. prosecutor Queens County Dist. Atty., Kew Gardens, N.Y., 1988-90; asst. gen. counsel Exec. Office of the Pres., Office Mgmt. and Budget, Washington, 1990-91; assoc. dir. for policy The White House, Washington, 1991-93; pvt. practice, 1993—94; chief staff, chief counsel com. govt. reform subcom. on govt. efficiency, fin. mgmt. and intergovtl. rels. U.S. Ho. Reps., Washington, 1995—2002; inspector gen. U.S. Corp. for Nat. and Cmty. Svc., Washington, 2002—. Trustee Howard U., Washington, 1984-85; big brother Big Bros. Am. Cambridge, Mass., 1986-96; bd. advisers City Harvest, 1993-95. Mem. ABA (vice chmn. govt. ops. com., adminstrv. law sect. 1997-99), Ripon Soc. (pres. Harvard chpt. 1986-87, nat. v.p. 1987-88, bd. dirs. ednl. fund 1989-97, pres. ednl. fund 1993-97), Harvard Club, Univ. Club, Rotary Club of Washington D.C., Phi Beta Kappa, Pi Sigma Alpha, Phi Alpha Theta. Republican. Episcopalian. Office: Ste 830 1201 New York Ave NW Washington DC 20252

GEORGE, JOHN ANTHONY, health corporation executive; b. New Kensington, Pa., July 11, 1948; s. Moses and Veronica (Raymond) G.; m. Leah Diane Vota, Oct. 30, 1971 (div. 1992); children: Jessica, Cara, John, Ethan; m. Carolyn D. Dozier, Sept. 22, 2000. BS, Duquesne U., Pitts., 1970; MBA, U. Pitts., 1973; MS in Taxation, Robert Morris Coll., Pitts. CFP. Asst. adminstr. mental health and mental retardation program Western Psychiat. Inst. and Clinic, Pitts., 1971-72; adminstrv. dir. Latrobe (Pa.) Area Hosp., 1973-76; asst. dir. Presbyn. U. Hosp., Pitts., 1976-80; owner, prin. George-Anstey Food Distributing Corp., Pitts., 1978-81; mgmt. cons. Arthur Young & Co., Pitts., 1980-82; exec. dir. Ea. Allegheny County Health Corp., 1982-85; pres. Alpha Health Network, 1985-88; pres., bd. dirs. Intergroup Svc. Corp., 1988—; mng. ptnr. Med. Benefit Svc., 1991—. Bd. mgrs. Health Coalition Ptnrs.; lectr. in field. Contbr. articles to profl. jours. Bd. dirs. Southwestern Pa. chpt. ARC. Mem. Am. Coll. Health Care Execs., Am. Assn. Prepared Provider Orgns. Roman Catholic. Home: 5121 Ellsworth Ave Pittsburgh PA 15232-1419 Office: 401 Shady Ave Suite A207 Pittsburgh PA 15206-4450 E-mail: jgeorge@igs-ppo.com.

GEORGE, JOHN MARTIN, JR., lawyer; b. Normal, Ill., Dec. 17, 1947; s. John and Ada George; m. Judy Ann Watts; children: Sarah, Michael. AB with high honors, U. Ill., 1970, AM, 1971; PhD, Columbia U., 1976; JD cum laude, Harvard U., 1982. Bar: Mass. 1982, U.S. Dist. Ct. Mass. 1983, Ill. 1984, U.S. Dist. Ct. (no. dist.) Ill. 1984, U.S. Ct. Appeals (11th cir.) 1987, U.S. Ct. Appeals (9th cir.) 1988, U.S. Ct. Appeals (7th cir.) 1992, U.S. Ct. Appeals (3d cir.) 2000. Assoc. Hill & Barlow, Boston, 1982-84, Sidley & Austin (now Sidley, Austin, Brown & Wood), Chgo., 1984-89, ptnr., 1989—. Editor Harvard U. Law Rev., 1980-82. Sr. warden Trinity Ch., 1998-2000. Mem. ABA, Chgo. Bar Assn., Mid-Day Club, Phi Beta Kappa. Democrat. Episcopalian. Office: Sidley Austin Brown & Wood Bank One Plz Chicago IL 60603-2003 E-mail: jgeorge@sidley.com.

GEORGE, JOYCE JACKSON, lawyer, judge emeritus; b. Akron, Ohio, May 4, 1936; d. Ray and Verna (Popadich) Jackson; children: Michael Eliot, Michelle René. BA, U. Akron, 1962, JD, 1966; postgrad., Nat. Jud. Coll., Reno, 1976, NYU, 1983; LLM, U. Va., 1986. Bar: Ohio 1966, U.S. Dist. Ct. (no. dist.) Ohio 1966, U.S. Ct. Appeals (6th cir.) 1968, U.S. Supreme Ct. 1968. Tchr. Akron Bd. Edn., 1962-66; asst. dir. law City of Akron, 1966-69, pub. utilities advisor, 1969-70, asst. dir. law, 1970-73; pvt. practice Akron, 1973-76; referee Akron Mcpl. Ct., 1975, judge, 1976-83, 9th dist. Ct. Appeals, Akron, 1983-89, Peninsula, Ohio, 1989; U.S. atty. No. Dist., Ohio, 1989-93; v.p. adminstrn. Telxon Corp., Akron, 1993-96; pres. Ind. Bus. Info. Svcs., Inc., Akron, 1996—. Tchr., lectr. Ohio Jud. Coll., Nat. Jud. Coll.; cons. in field. Author: Judicial Opinion Writing Handbook, 1981, 3d edit., 1993, 4th edit., 1998, Referee's Report Writing Handbook, 1992; contbr. articles to profl. publs. Recipient Outstanding Woman of Yr. award Akron Bus. and Profl. Women's Club, 1982; Alumni Honor award U. Akron, 1983, Alumni award U. Akron Sch. Law, 1991; Dept. Treasury award, 1992; named Woman of Yr. in politics and govt. Summit County, Ohio, 1983. Mem.: ABA, Akron Bar Assn., Ohio Bar Assn. Fax: 330-668-2910.

GEORGE, KATIE, lawyer; b. Chillicothe, Ohio, Sept. 4, 1953; d. Harry Paul and Tina Lillian George; m. Nov. 25, 1972 (div. Nov. 1983); 1 child, Alison; m. Timothy John Nusser, June 30, 1985. BBA, U. Toledo, 1983, JD, 1986, MBA, 1989. Bar: Ohio 1987, U.S. Dist. Ct. (no. dist.) Ohio 1993, Fla. 1994. Law clk. Allotta, Singer & Farley, Co. LPA, Toledo, 1985-86; mgmt. specialist Dept. Pub. Utilities City of Toledo, 1987-91, acting commr. Dept. Health, 1992-93, acting mgr. Dept. Pub. Safety, 1991-94; pvt. practice Toledo, 1987-96, Pensacola, Fla., 1996—; asst. dist. legal counsel State of Fla., 1996-97, chief legal counsel, 1997—. Part-time instr. U. Toledo, 1987-88, U. West Fla., 1997. Bd. dirs. Toledo BlockWatch, 1993, Ohio Pub. Employers Labor Rels. Assn., 1991-92; mem. Missing and Exploited Children Comprehensive Action Program, 1997-99. Mem. Fla. Bar Assn., Escambia Santa Rosa Bar Assn. Avocations: gardening, photography, scuba diving. Office: 160 Governmental Ctr Ste 601 Pensacola FL 32502-5734

GEORGE, KENNETH MARTIN, anthropology educator; b. Glen Ridge, N.J., Dec. 25, 1950; AB in English, Tufts U., 1975; AM in Folklore, U. N.C., 1978; MA in Anthropology, U. Mich., 1980, PhD in Anthropology, 1989. Vis. asst. prof. dept. anthropology Tuland U., New Orleans, 1989, U. S.C., Columbia, 1990; asst. prof. anthropology Harvard U., Cambridge, Mass., 1990—, Allston Burr sr. tutor, 1992. Contbr. articles to profl. publs. Fellow Wenner-Gren Found., 1981, Social Sci. Rsch. Coun., 1981, Fulbright Found., 1982, Aga Khan Trust for Culture, 1992. Mem. Am. Anthropology Assn., Soc. for Cultural Anthropology, Am. Ethnological Soc., Am. Folklore Soc., Soc. for Linguistic Anthropology. Office: Harvard U Dept Anthropology William James Hall Rm 350 Cambridge MA 02138

GEORGE, LARRY DARNELL, dean, educator; b. Los Angeles, Calif., Jan. 15, 1957; s. Leonard and Lillie Mae George; m. Beverly Janet Gafford, Dec. 22, 1979 (div. June 15, 1984); 1 child, Jason Anthony. BS Civil Engring., U. Calif., Davis, 1979; MDiv in Systematic Theology, Spring Valley Bible Coll. and Sem., 1983; MDiv in Bibl. Studies, San Francisco Theol. Sem., 1990; MA in Religion/NT, Vanderbilt U., 1994, PhD in Religion/NT, 1997. Design engr. Chevron, USA, Richmond, Calif., 1979—86; Christian edn. dir. Prog. Bapt. Ch., Berkeley, Calif., 1986—90; grad. writing asst. Vanderbilt U., Nashville, 1990—97; asst. dean, prof. Am. Bapt. Coll., Nashville, 1997—99; acad. dean, and asst. prof. Payne Theol. Sem., Wilberforce, Ohio, 1999—. Pres. World Christian Outreach, Oakland, Calif., 1986—90; chmn. of the bd. Math, Engring., Sci. Achievement, Richmond, Calif., 1983—86; pres. Black Engring. Assn., Davis, Calif., 1977—79. Author: (book) Reading the Tapestry; editor: What Does it Mean to be Black and Christian?. Mem. NAACP, Nashville, Tenn., 1997—79; v.p. UJIMA, Davis, Calif., 1978. Mem.: Soc. of Bibl. Lit. (com. 1989—2002), Friends for Payne (ex-official 1999—2002), Alpha Phi Alpha (v.p. 1977—79). Democrat. Baptist. Avocations: chess, swimming, skiing. Home: 406 Forest Avenue Dayton OH 45405 Office: Payne Theological Seminary 1230 Wilberforce-Clifton Road Wilberforce OH 45405 Office Fax: 937-331-2401. E-mail: ldgeorge@email.msn.com.

GEORGE, LARRY WAYNE, lawyer; b. Cin., Oct. 31, 1954; BS in Civil Engring., Va. Poly. Inst. and State U., 1979; JD, W.Va. U., 1982. Bar: W.Va. 1982, U.S. Ct. Appeals (4th cir.) 1983, D.C. 1992, Va. 1993. Assoc. Baer & Colburn, L.C., Huntington, W.Va., 1982-85; pvt. practice Charleston, W.Va., 1985-89; dep. dir. W.Va. Dept. Natural Resources, Charleston, 1989-90; commr. W.Va. Dept. Energy, Charleston, 1990; atty. Larry W. George Law Offices, 1991—. Majority counsel W.Va. Senate, 1984-85. Mem. W.Va. Water Resources Bd., 1978-82; mem. nat. coal coun. U.S. Dept. Energy, 1985-89; mem. coun. on energy and environment Nat. Govs. Assn., 1989-91; chmn. Environ. Transition com. for Gov.-elect Cecil Underwood, 1996-97; chmn. econ. com. Govs. Mining Task Force, 1998. Mem. ABA, W.Va. State Bar (com. on environ. law 1986—, com. on bus., banking and corp. law 1996—), ASCE (energy, environ. and water resources divs.), W.Va. Land & Mineral Owners Coun. (treas.-sec. 2000—), Energy & Mineral Law Found., W.Va. Highlands Conservancy (pres. 1983-86). Home: 3 Birch Tree Ln Charleston WV 25314-2275 Office: Ste 201 200 Association Dr Charleston WV 25311 E-mail: lgeorge@george-wvlaw.com.

GEORGE, LILA GENE PLOWE KENNEDY, music educator; b. Sioux City, Iowa, Sept. 25, 1918; d. Eugene Preston Plowe and Lila Mazo Pickel; m. Richard Painter George; children: Eugenia, Richard Jr. BA in English and French, U. Okla., 1939, MusB in Theory, 1940; postgrad., Northwestern U., 1950, Columbia U., 1963—65; pvt. piano study with Egon Petri, Silvio Scionti & Edward Steuermann; pvt. composition study with Nadia Boulanger, Fontainebleau, France, 1971—78. Pvt. piano tchr., Oklahoma City, 1938—42, Talara, Peru, 1947—54, Houston, 1954—60, 1970—, Pelham Manor, NY, 1960—65. Soloist Oklahoma City Little Symphony, 1939, Houston Symphony, 1957; judge piano competitions Nat. Guild Piano Tchrs., Tex. State Music Tchrs. Mem.: Houston Tuesday Musical Club (pres. 1960), European Piano Tchrs. Assn., Am. Music Ctr. (composer). Republican. Episcopalian. Avocation: genealogy. Home: 701 N Rusk Wharton TX 77488

GEORGE, LINDA SHUMAKER, writer, educator; b. Lenoir, N.C., Sept. 24, 1949; d. Thomas Craig and Mary Poole Shumaker; m. Richard George, Feb. 14, 1986; 1 child, Alexander Thomas Oscar. BA, NYU, 1971; MA, Harvard U., 1975, PhD, 1980. V.p. internat. divsn. Mfrs. Hanover Trust Co., N.Y.C., 1981-87; adj. asst. prof. dept. history Drew U., Madison, N.J., 1989-91; vis. scholar Hagop Kevorkian Ctr. for Near Ea. Studies NYU, 1992-93; lectr. in Mid. Ea. langs. and civilizations Columbia U., N.Y.C., 1992-94; freelance writer, 1992—. Author: The Golden Age of Islam, 1998, Letters from the Homefront: World War I, 2001, Around the World in 800, 2002; editor: Far Brook Bull., 1995—2001. Charles McConn scholar NYU, 1967-68; fellow Ctr. for Arabic Study Abroad, Cairo, 1973-74; Radcliffe grantee for grad. women Harvard U., 1980, summer seminar for coll. tchrs. grantee NEH, 1991. Mem. The Authors Guild, Am. Rsch. Ctr. in Egypt (fellow 1977-78), Mid. East Studies Assn., Soc. Children's Book Writers and Illustrators. Avocations: opera, ice hockey.

GEORGE, MARIE IVANKA, humanities educator; b. Oakland, Calif., June 13, 1958; d. Richard J. and Breda I. George. BA, Thomas Aquinas Coll., Santa Paula, CA, 1979; MA, LAVAL U., Quebec City, Canada, 1982, PhD, 1987; BA, Queens Coll., Flushing, NY, 2000, MA, 2002. Asst. prof. philosophy St. John's U., Jamaica, NY, 1989—94, assoc. prof. philosophy, 1994—. Editor: (book) Faith, Scholarship & Culture in the 21st Century; contbr. chapters to books. Dir. R.C.I.A. Mary's Nativity, Flushing, NY, 1991—2002. Recipient Awards For Papers In Humility Theology, John M. Templeton Found., 1994, 1996; grantee Two Grants For Course On Sci. & Religion, 1997, 2000. Mem.: Soc. Aristotelian Studies, Soc. Ancient Greek Philosophy, Am. Cath. Philos. Assn. Roman Catholic. Avocations: hiking, cycling, classical music. Office: Dr Marie George Saint John's University 8000 Utopia Parkway Jamaica NY 11439 Office Fax: 718-990-1907. E-mail: georgem@stjohns.edu.

GEORGE, MARILYN L. music educator, musician; b. Pipestone, Minn., Dec. 5, 1941; d. Wellington Ernest and Lily Esther Sack Hertel; m. Stanley Paul George; children: Deborah, Diane, Linnea. BA in Music, U. Minn., 1964; M in Sacred Music, Bob Jones U., 1967; postgrad., U. North Colo., 1976-78. Faculty Bob Jones U., 1967-75; tchr. Pvt. Acad., N.J., 1975-76; faculty U. S.D., 1977-78, U. No. Colo., 1978-80, Earlham Coll., Richmond, Ind., 1980-83, Oral Roberts U., Tulsa, Okla., 1983—2000, Valley Christian Schs., San Jose, Calif., 2000—. Cellist Ind. Arts Trio, Richmond, 1980—83, Dayton (Ohio) Philharm., 1980—83, Tulsa Philharm. Orch., 1984—87, 1994—97, 1999; prin. cellist Okla. Sinfonia, Tulsa, 1983—2000, Tulsa Ballet Orch., 0199—2000; cellist Trio Cantabile, Tulsa, 1990—97; cellist in piano quartet Tulsa Fest, 1997—98; cello instr. Nat. Music Camp, Interlochen, Mich., 1969—74, Interlochen, 1975—76; founder, dir. Suzuki program Oral Roberts U., Tulsa, 1984—2000, S. Valley Suzuki String Acad., Gilroy, Calif., 2000—; cello workshop presenter Calif. Music Edn. Conf.-Bay Area, San Jose State U., 2002—03; cello clinician Children Friendship Concert Tour to Eng., 2001, Suzuki Inst., Salt Lake City, 2001, Oreg. Suzuki Inst., 2003. Cellist benefit concert Okla. Sinfonia, Pawnee, Okla., 1999; mem., tchr., musician United Meth. Ch., Tulsa, 1990—2000; musician prayer breakfast Nat. Day of Prayer, Civic Conv. Ctr., Tulsa, 1999; mem., musician First Presbyn. Ch., Hollister, Calif., 2000—. Recipeint A Best Choice for Music Instrn. award Tulsa Kids Parent Picks, 1998. Mem. Am. Fedn. Musicians, Music Tchrs. Nat. Assn., Suzuki Assn. Ams., Suzuki Assn. Greater Tulsa (founder, pres. 1987-97). Avocations: reading, walking, cooking, traveling. Home: 1630 Valley Oaks Dr Gilroy CA 95020

GEORGE, MARY GAE, music educator; b. Seattle, May 4, 1930; d. Howard Ruskin and Gwynnyefred A. E. (Craig) Gaetz; m. David Thorp, June 14, 1952 (div. Mar. 1955); 1 child, Jennifer Gae Fellows; m. Jon P. George, Aug. 31, 1965 (dec. Jan. 1982). MusB, Yale U., 1952. Cert. music tchr., Md., Fla., Utah. Instr. Montgomery Coll., Rockville, Md., 1960-65, Contemporary Sch. Music, Rockville, 1971-81; pres. Artistry at the Piano, Inc., Orange City, Fla., 1982—; founder, dir. Artistry Alliance, Orange City, 1983—; pres., exec. editor Artistry Press Internat., Orange City, 1990—; pres., prodr. Artistry Prodns., Orange City, 1991—; co-dir. GreyWolf Performing Arts Inst., Orange City, 1993—. Com. mem. pedagogy cert. programs Nat. Conf. on Piano Pedagogy, 1984—; founder, dir. Artistry Ensemble Festival Stetson U., DeLand, Fla., 1985-88; guest lectr. European Piano Tchrs. Assn. Internat. Conv., Eng., 1987-89, MTNA Symposium on Computer Assisted Music Instn., Wichita, Kans. and Salt Lake City, 1988-89 Mpls, Wash. DC 2000-2001; founder, dir. Nat. Conf. on Pedagogy and Performance, 1989; chmn. Ind. Music Tchrs. Forum for State of Fla., 1989-92; cons. The New Sch. for Music Study, Princeton U. Author: The Art of Movement, 1992; co-author: Artistry at the Piano, 1982, Formingreforming, 1991. Mem. Music Tchrs. Nat. Assn., Fla. State Music Tchrs. Assn. (bd. dirs. 1986-92), Md. State Music Tchrs. Assn., Utah Music Teachers Assn., Kindermusik Tchrs. Assn. Avocation: desk top publishing. Home and Office: Greywolf Performing Arts Inst 10830 S 1000 E Sandy UT 84094-5928 E-mail: mg@greywolf-artistry.com.

GEORGE, MARY WIEDENBECK, reference librarian, educator; b. Ann Arbor, Mich., Jan. 23, 1948; d. Marcellus L. and Jane Kathryn (Young) Wiedenbeck; m. Emery Edward George, May 9, 1969. AB, U. Mich., 1969, AMLS, 1970, AM, 1975. Reference libr. U. Mich., Ann Arbor, 1970-80; head gen. and humanities reference divsn. Princeton (N.J.) U. Libr., 1980-2000, user edn. coord., 2000—01; interim dir. slide and photograph collections dept. art and archeology Princeton U., 2001—02, acting interlibr. svcs., libr., 2002, libr. instrn. coord., sr. rschr., 2002—. Adj. asst. prof. Coll. Info. Sci. and Tech., Drexel U., Phila., 1982-92, 96-2002; adv. bd. Bibliography Revision project MLA, N.Y.C., 1978-80; part-time lectr. dept. library and info. sci. Rutgers U., 2001-02; part-time lectr. writing program Princeton U., 2002; speaker in field. Co-author: Learning the Library, 1982; co-editor Rsch. Strategies, 1983-90; contbr. chpt. to book. Adv. bd. Dictionary of the History of Ideas, 2003—. Recipient Hopwood award in writing U. Mich., 1969, Disting. Alumna award, 1987. Mem. ALA (Shera award for rsch. 1989). Office: Firestone Libr Princeton U One Washington Rd Princeton NJ 08544 E-mail: mwgeorge@princeton.edu.

GEORGE, MELVIN DOUGLAS, retired university president; b. Washington, Feb. 13, 1936; s. Douglas Elmer and Catherine Evelyn (McNelly) G.; m. Meta Jane Barghusen, Aug. 17, 1958; children— Elizabeth Anne, Margaret Susan BA, Northwestern U., 1956; PhD, Princeton U., 1959. From asst. to assoc. prof. math. U. Mo., Columbia, 1960-67, prof., assoc. dean, 1967-70, v.p. acad. affairs, 1975-85; dean Coll. Arts and Scis. U. Nebr., Lincoln, 1970-75; pres. St. Olaf Coll., Northfield, Minn., 1985-94, pres. emeritus, 1994—; v.p. instnl. rels. U. Minn., Mpls., 1994-96; prof. math. emeritus U. Mo., Columbia, 1996—, interim pres., 1996-97, pres. emeritus, 1997—. Contbr. articles to profl. jours. Recipient Robert W. Martin award for Acad. Freedom, Mo. conf. AAUP, 1985 Mem. Am. Math. Soc., Math. Assn. Am. Lutheran. Avocations: music; swimming. Home: 1509 W Rollins Rd Columbia MO 65203-2378

GEORGE, MICHAEL JOSEPH, lawyer; b. Great Falls, Mont., Sept. 12, 1961; s. Mitchell A. and Marie C. George; m. Sydne Kolstad, July 20, 1996. BSBA, U. Mont., 1983, JD, 1986. Bar: Mont. 1986, U.S. Dist. Ct. Mont. 1986, U.S. Ct. Appeals (9th cir.) 1988. Assoc. Hoyt & Blewett, Great Falls, Mont., 1986-96; ptnr. Lucero & George, LLP, Great Falls, 1997—. Bd. dirs. Charlie's Friends of CM Russell Mus., Great Falls, 1992-96, Big Bros. and Big Sisters of Great Falls, 1998-2003, pres., 2001-02, U. Mont. Grizzly Athletic Assn., Great Falls, 2003—. Mem. ATLA, Mont. Trial Lawyers Assn., State Bar Mont., Cascade County Bar Assn. Office: Lucero & George LLP PO Box 3505 615 Second Ave N Ste 200 Great Falls MT 59403-3505

GEORGE, NASHWA E. accountant, educator; b. Cairo; came to U.S., 1976; d. Nazif Atia and Enayat Wardan (Ghabrial) Soukar; m. Souwar George, Aug. 23, 1980; children: Meena, Sarah, Christine. B.Commerce, Cairo U., 1967, MS, 1973; MBA, CUNY, 1984, PhD, 1988. Asst. prof. econs. Cairo U., 1967-76, Hunter Coll.-CUNY, 1985—99, Montclair State U., Upper Montclair, NJ, 1999—. Mem. N.Y. CPA Soc., Inst. Mgmt. Acctg., Am. Acctg. Assn. Avocations: reading, travel. Office: Montclair State U 1 Normal Ave Montclair NJ 07043

GEORGE, PETER JAMES, economist, educator; b. Toronto, Sept. 12, 1941; s. Ralph Langlois and Kathleen May (Larder) G.; m. Gwendolyn Jean Scharf, Oct. 19, 1962 (dec. Mar. 1997); children— Michael James, Katherine Jane; m. Allison Mary Barrett, July 31, 1998. BA with honors, U. Toronto, 1962, MA, 1963, PhD, 1967; DU (hon.), U. Ottawa, 1995; D Hon. C. (hon.), Lviv Nat. Poly U., 2001; DLitt (hon.), Nipissing U., 2002. Lectr. McMaster U., 1965-67, asst. prof., 1967-71, assoc. prof., 1971-80, prof. econs., 1980—, assoc. dean grad. studies, 1974-79, dean social scis., 1980-89, pres., vice chancellor, 1995—; spl. lectr. U. Toronto, 1967; vis. lectr. U. Cambridge, 1974; economist Govt. of Ont., 1963; project mgr. Tanzania Tourist Corp., 1970-71; pres. Coun. Ont. Univs., Toronto, 1991-95; hon. prof. Beijing U. Sci. and Tech., 1998. Author: Government Subsidies and the Construction of the Canadian Pacific Railway, 1981, The Emergence of Industrial America: Strategic Factors in American Economic Growth Since 1870, 1982; Appointed to Ont. Coun. on Univ. Affairs, 1987-91. Decorated Order of Can., 1999; recipient commemorative medal 125th Anniversary Confedn. of Can., 1993; recipient The Queen's Golden Jubilee medal, 2002. Mem. Can. Econs. Assn., Can. Hist. Assn., Am. Econ. Assn., Econ. History Assn., Econ. History Soc. Office: McMaster U Office Pres GH-238 1280 Main St W Hamilton ON Canada L8S 4L8 E-mail: presdnt@mcmaster.ca., pgeorge@mcmaster.ca.

GEORGE, PETER T. orthodontist, consultant; b. Akron, Ohio, 1929; s. Tony and Paraskeva (Ogrenova) G.; children: Barton Herrin, Tryan Franklin. BS, Kent State U., 1952; DDS, Ohio State U., 1956; Cert. in Orthodontics, Columbia U., 1962. Diplomate Am. Bd. Orthodontics. Pvt. practice orthodontics, Honolulu, 1962—2000. Cleft palate cons. Hawaii Bur. Crippled Children,

1963-90; asst. prof. Med. Sci. Editor Hawaii State Dental Jour., 1965-67. Mem. Hawaii Gov.'s Phys. Fitness Com., 1962-68; mem. Honolulu Mayor's Health Coun., 1967-72; mem. med. com. Internat. Weightlifting Fedn., 1980-84; chmn. bd. govs. Hall of Fame of Hawaii, 1984; bd. dirs. Honolulu Opera Theatre, 1986-91; chmn. bd. Hawaii Internat. Sports Found., 1988-91; U.S. Weightlifting coach, USSR, 1979, asst. coach Olympic Weightlifting team, 1980. Served to Capt. Dental Corps, U.S. Army, 1956-60. Silver medallist weightlifting, London, 1948; Olympic Gold medalist in weightlifting, Helsinki, 1952, Melbourne, 1956; six times world champion; recipient Disting. Service award Hawaiian AAU, 1968; Gold medal Internat. Weightlifting Fedn., 1976; named to Helms Hall of Fame, 1966; named to 100 Gold Olympians, 1996. Fellow Am. Coll. Dentistry, Internat. Coll. Dentistry; mem. Hawaii Amateur Athletic Union (pres. 1964-65), U.S. Olympians (pres. Hawaii chpt. 1963-67, 80-2000), Am. Assn. Orthodontists, Honolulu Dental Soc. (pres. 1967-68), Hawaii Dentists Assn. (pres. 1976), Hawaii Soc. Orthodontists (pres. 1972). Achievements include invention of first dental appliance to prevent sleep apnea; jetlogger, an anti jet lag instrument. Home and Office: 1649 Kalakaua Ave Ste 204 Honolulu HI 96826-2494 E-mail: ptgeorge@pacinfo.net.

GEORGE, RICHARD LEE, oil industry executive; b. Colo., May 16, 1950; s. Albert H. and Betty Lou (McDill) G.; m. Julie G. White, June 4, 1972; children: Zachary Ryan, Matthew Shane, Emily Christine. BS in Engring., Colo. State U., 1973; JD, U. Houston, 1977; grad. program for mgmt. devel., Harvard Bus. Sch., 1984. Bar: Tex. 1978; registered profl. engr., Tex. Dep. mng. dir. Sun Oil Britain, London, 1982-86, dist. mgr. Aberdeen, Scotland, 1986-87; v.p. Internat. E. and P. Sun Exploration & Prodn., Dallas, 1987-88; mng. dir. Sun Internat. Exploration & Prodn., London, 1988-91; pres., COO Suncor, Inc., North York, Canada, 1991, pres., CEO, 1991-93, chmn., pres., CEO, 1993-94; pres., CEO Suncor Energy Inc., Calgary, Canada. Bd. dirs. Dofasco Inc., Enbridge Inc., GlobalSantaFe Internat., Inc.; chair Canadian Coun. Chief Execs. Active Can. Inst. for Advanced Rsch. Office: Suncor Energy Inc 112-4th Ave SW Box 38 Calgary AB Canada T2P 2V5

GEORGE, RICHARD NEILL, retired lawyer; b. Watertown, N.Y., Apr. 6, 1933; s. Wendell Dow and Frances Laura (Small) G.; m. Patricia Harman Jackson, June 21, 1958; children: Frances Harman, Richard Neill, Mary Elizabeth AB, Yale U., 1955; JD, Cornell U., 1962. Bar: N.Y. 1962. Assoc. Nixon Peabody, LLP (formerly Nixon, Hargave, Devans & Doyle), Rochester, N.Y., 1962-70, ptnr., 1970-2000, ret., 2000. Committeeman, Brighton Town Republican Com., Rochester, 1966-78; ruling elder Twelve Corners Presbyn. Ch., Rochester, 1977-79, 84-87; mem. permanent jud. commn. Presbytery of Genesee Valley, 1988-94, moderator. Capt. USAF, 1956-59. Mem. ABA, N.Y. State Bar Assn., Monroe County Bar Assn., Fed. Energy Bar Assn., Exeter Alumni Assn. of Rochester (pres. 1970—), Country Club of Rochester, Yale Club (N.Y.C.), Amelia Island Club. Republican. Avocations: golf, reading. Home: 14 Oakfield Way Pittsford NY 14534-1888

GEORGE, ROBERT PETER, political philosopher, lawyer; b. Morgantown, W.Va., July 10, 1955; s. Joseph Michael and Catherine Victoria (Sellaro) G.; m. Cindy Schrom, Dec. 11, 1982; children: David, Rachel. BA, Swarthmore Coll., 1977; MTS, JD, Harvard U., 1981; PhD, Oxford U., 1986; DChE (hon.), U. Steubenville, 2000; LLD (hon.), Spring Arbor U., 2001; LHD (hon.), Inst. for Psychol. Scis., 2002; LLD (hon.), Gonzaga U., 2002; ScD (hon.), Hillsdale Coll., 2003. Bar: Pa. 1987, N.J. 1987, U.S. Dist. Ct. N.J. 1987, U.S. Ct. Appeals (4th cir.) 1991, U.S. Supreme Ct. 1990. Lectr. New Coll. Oxford U., Eng., 1982-85, vis. fellow, 1988; from asst. prof. to prof. Princeton (N.J.) U., 1986-99, McCormick prof. jurisprudence, 1999—, dir. James Madison Program in Am. Ideals and Instns., 2000—; of counsel Robinson & McElwee, Charleston, W.Va., 1990—. Dir. Mellon Law Seminar, Princeton U., 1986-88, faculty parliamentarian, 1987—, mem. exec. com. Program in Law and Pub. Affairs, 1998—; chmn. vis. examiners Swarthmore (Pa.) Coll., 1988, 92; mem. acad. adv. bd. Judiciary Leadership Devel. Coun., 1990—; presdl. apt. U.S. Commn. Civil Rights, 1993-98; mem. Pres.'s Coun. on Bioethics, 2002; Royden B. Davis vis. prof. Georgetown U., 1994; Harold Gill Reuschlein disting. vis. prof. Villanova U., 2002; Jack Rudin and John Driscoll disting. vis. prof. Iona Coll., 2002; faculty assoc. U. Ctr. for Human Values, 1999—; bd. govs. Ave Maria Law Sch., Ann Arbor, Mich., 1999—; internat. adv. bd. Ctr. for the Study of Constitutionalism, U. London; adv. bd. mem. Program in Human Rights and Medicine, U. Minn., 1999—, Of the People Found.; bd. dirs. Inst. for Am. Values, 1999—, Ethikon Inst., 2000—, Ethics and Pub. Policy Ctr., 2000—, Inst. on Religion and Democracy, 2001--, Family Rsch. Coun., 2002--; internat. adv. bd. Notre Dame Ctr. for Ethics and Culture; mem. dir.'s adv. group U. Pa. Ctr. for Rsch. on Religion and Urban Civil Soc., 2002--; mem. adv. coun. Faith and Reason Inst., 2001— mem. internat. sci. com. Persona y Derecho; mem. adv. bd. The Bioethics Project, 2001—; U.S. rep. to 20th anniversary Comité Consultatif d'Ethique, Paris, 2003. Author: Making Men Moral: Civil Liberties and Public Morality, 1993, In Defense of Natural Law, 1999, The Clash of Orthodoxies: Law, Morality, and Religion in Crisis, 2001; editor: Natural Law Theory, 1992, The Autonomy of Law: Essays on Legal Positivism, 1996, Natural Law, Liberalism and Morality, 1996, Natural Law and Moral Inquiry: Ethics, Metaphysics and Politics in the Work of Germain Grisez, 1998, Great Cases in Constitutional Law, 2000, Natural Law and Public Reason, 2000, Constitutional Politics: Essays on constitution Making, Maintenance and Change, 2001, Natural Law, 2003; mem. editl. bd. Am. Jour. Jurisprudence, 1990—; mem. editl. adv. bd. First Things, 1996—; series editor New Forum Books of Princeton U. Press, 1996—; mem. bd. cons. editors Academic Questions, 1997—; assoc. editor Touchstone Mag., 2001—; contbr. articles to profl. jours. Chmn. Federalist Soc. Religious Liberties Practice Group, 1996-99. Recipient Justice Tom C. Clark award, 1990, ABA Silver Gavel award, 1991, Paul Bator award Federalist Soc., 1994, Outstanding Prof. award Templeton Found., 1997, Cardinal Wright award Fellowship of Cath. Schs., 1999, David W. Peck medal for eminence in law Wabash Coll., 1999, John Lancaster Spalding Medal Diocese of Peoria, 2001, Richard M. Weaver award for scholarship Ingersoll Found., 2002, St. Thomas More award Mass. Pro-Life Legal Def. Fund, 2002; U.S. Supreme Ct. Jud. fellow, 1989, Frank Knox fellow Harvard U., 1981; grantee Howard Found., 1988, Bradley Found., 1994, Pew Found., 1997-98. Fellow Wilberforce Forum (sr.); mem. Nat. Assn. Scholars (bd. dirs. 1996—), Am. Pub. Philosophy Inst. (bd. dirs.), Coun. on Fgn. Rels., Philosophy Edn. Soc. (bd. dirs.), Sudan Relief and Rescue (bd. dirs.), Paul Ramsey Colloquium of Inst. on Religion and Pub. Life, Johnson and Chesterton Club, Cosmos Club, Phi Beta Kappa. Avocations: fishing, literature, bluegrass banjo, guitar, folk music. Home: 371 Prospect Ave Princeton NJ 08540-4078 Office: Princeton U 244 Corwin Hall Princeton NJ 08544-1169 E-mail: rgeorge@princeton.edu.

GEORGE, RONALD M. state supreme court chief justice; b. L.A., Mar. 11, 1940; AB, Princeton U., 1961; JD, Stanford U., 1964. Bar: Calif. 1965. Dep. atty. gen. Calif. Dept. Justice, 1965-72; judge L.A. Mcpl. Ct., L.A. County, 1972-77, Superior Ct. Calif., L.A. County, 1977-87, supervising judge criminal divsn., 1983-84; assoc. justice 2d dist., divsn. 4 Calif. Ct. Appeal, L.A., 1987-91; assoc. justice Calif. Supreme Ct., San Francisco, 1991-96, chief justice, 1996—. Mem. Calif. Judges Assn. (pres. 1982-83), Conf. Chief Justices (pres.). Avocations: hiking, skiing, running. Office: Calif Supreme Court 350 Mcallister St Fl 5 San Francisco CA 94102-4797

GEORGE, RUSSELL LLOYD, lawyer, former state legislator; b. Rifle, Colo., May 28, 1946; s. Walter Mallory and Eleanora (Michel) G.; m. Neal Ellen Moore, Nov. 24, 1972; children: Russell, Charles, Thomas, Andrew. BS in Econs., Colo. State U., 1968; JD, Harvard Law Sch., 1971. Bar: Colo. Shareholder Stuver & George, P.C., Rifle, 1976—; dir. Co. Div. Wildlife, Denver, 2000—. State rep. dist. 57 Colo. Gen. Assembly, 1993—., speaker of the House, Colo Gen.Assembly. Fellow Colo. Bar Found.; mem. Colo. Bar Assn., Rotary Internat., Masonic Lodge. Republican. Methodist. Home: 1300 E 7th St Rifle CO 81650-2123 Office: 6060 Broadway Denver CO 80216

GEORGE, SARAH B. museum director; Dir. Utah Mus. of Natural History and Hansen Planetarium, Salt Lake City. Office: Utah Mus Natural History U Utah 1390 E Pres Cir Salt Lake City UT 84112

GEORGE, STEPHAN (STEVE) ANTHONY, web site designer; b. Waterloo, Iowa, Sept. 20, 1946; s. Leon Eugene and Marie Weires George; m. Cheryl Ann Pisano, Jan. 21, 1950; m. Lucille Donohue Lynch, June 7, 1969 (div. May 31, 1987). AB in biology/philosphy, Bellarmine U., Louisville, KY, 1965—69; MA in plant sci., Ind. U., Bloomington, Ind., 1969—76; MA in counseling - depth psychol., Pacifica Grad. Inst., Carpenteria, CA, 1998—2000. Field svc. engr. Hewlett-Packard Co., Indianapolis, Ind., 1977—77, Am. bus. devel. mgr. Atlanta, 1995—97, Phoenix, 1997—98; pres. AZNetwork On-The-Web, L.L.C., Phoenix, 1998—; grief counselor Hospice of the Valley, Phoenix, 2000—; product support engr. Hewlett-Packard Co., Avondale, Pa., 1977—78, tng. specialist, 1978—79, European product mgr. Waldbronn, Germany, 1980—82, North Am. product mgr. Palo Alto, Calif., 1982—84, mktg. specialist Santa Clara, Calif., 1984—87, internat. mktg. specialist Victoria, Hong Kong, 1987—90, applications engring. cons. Atlanta, 1990—91, edn. ctr. mgr., 1991—95. Plenary lectr. Royal Dutch Acad. of Sci., Amsterdam, Netherlands, 1981; consulting editor LC/GC Mag., Springfield, Oreg., 1981—99; NSF fellow Ind. U., Bloomington, Ind., 1969—71. Editor (author): (scientific book) Diode Array Detection in HPLC; author: (scientific article) Metal Finishing, Proceedings 2nd Beijing Conference, (poetry) The Msounds (National Library of Poetry), Loving Brings Infinity (American Poetry Anthology), Moments Inbetween (National Library of Poetry), (scientific article) Proceedings National Academy of Science, American Laboratory, Industrial Research and Development, Chromatographia, Science, (scientific ariticle) American Laboratory, (scientific article) Liquid Chromatography and HPLC Magazine, American Laboratory. Mem.: Am. Acad. of Bereavement. Independent. Avocations: computers, travel, reading. Personal E-mail: steve.george@pobox.com. E-mail: sgeorge@aznetwork.com.

GEORGE, STEPHEN CARL, reinsurance executive, educator, medical and life consultant, expert witness, expert witness; b. Miami, Fla., July 11, 1959; s. Joseph P. and Beatrice P. George; 3 children. BS in MIS, Fla. State U., 1983; MBA in Health Adminstrn., U. Miami, 1986. Provider rels. spec. Travelers Health Network, Phila., 1987-89; prin. Tyler & Co., Atlanta, 1989-93; risk mgmt. cons. John Alden - Provider Group, Miami, 1994; pres. Provider Risk, Inc., Miami, 1995—. Spkr. U. Miami, 1995-97; adj. prof. Nova U. Southeastern, 1996—; speaker in field. Contbr. articles to profl. jours. Vol. Habitat for Humanity, Miami, Fla., 1995—, innkeeper Covenet House.; del. U. So. Calif.-L.A.—People to People Amb. Programs, Moscow and St. Petersburg and Tallinn, Estonia A.A. Green scholar. Mem. Am. Coll. of Health Care Execs. (regents adv. coun. 1995-97), Toastmasters Internat. (CTM), South Fla. Exec. Forum, Alpha Kappa Psi. Avocations: family, water sports, scouting. Office: Provider Risk Inc 9761 SW 123rd St Miami FL 33176-4929 E-mail: reinsurance@providerrisk.com.

GEORGE, THOMAS, artist; b. N.Y.C., July 1, 1918; s. Rube and Irma (Seeman) Goldberg; m. Lavergne Burton, July 16, 1951; children John R., Geoffrey T. BA, Dartmouth Coll., 1940. One-man shows include Feragil Gallery, N.Y.C., 1951, 53, Korman Gallery, N.Y.C., 1954, Dartmouth Coll., 1965, Contemporaries Gallery, N.Y.C., 1956, Bridgestone Mus., Tokyo, 1957, Betty Parsons Gallery, N.Y.C., 1959, 63, 65, 66, 68, 70, 72, 74, 76, 78, 81, Reid Gallery, London, 1962, 64, Del. Mus., 1971, 76, Henie-Onstad Art Mus., Oslo, 1971, Princeton U. Art Mus., 1975, Dartmouth Coll., 1979, 90, Nat. Gallery, Oslo, 1980, Maxwell Davidson Gallery, N.Y.C., 1983, 85, 88, 90, Riis Gallery, Oslo, 1982, 84, 86, 88, 90, Hood Art Mus., Dartmouth Coll,1990, Snyder Fine Art, N.Y.C., 1991, Snyder Fine Art, N.Y.C., 1991, 93, 96, Julian Hartnoll Gallery, London, 1993, Williams Gallery, Princeton, 1997, 99, Mercer County (NJ) Coll., 2002; retrospective exhbn. N.J. State Mus., 1987; group exhbns. include Met. Mus. Art, N.Y.C., Am. Fedn. Arts, Mus. Modern Art, N.Y.C., Whitney Mus. Ann., N.Y.C., Carnegie Internat., Pitts., Pa. Acad., Japan Internat. Biennial Art, Tokyo, White House, Lausanne (Switzerland) Mus.; represented in permanent collections Whitney Mus., Mus. Modern Art, N.Y.C., Bklyn. Mus., Tate Gallery, London, Nat. Coll. Fine Arts at Smithsonian Instn., Washington, Chase Manhattan Coll., N.Y.C., Library of Congress, Bridgestone Mus., Hood Art Mus., Dartmouth Coll., Lausanne Mus. Art, Mus. Fine Arts, Houston, U. Calif. Art Mus., Berkeley, Santa Barbara Mus. Fine Arts, Okla. Art Ctr., U. Calif. Mus., Santa Clara, Yale U. Art Gallery, Flint (Mich.) Inst., N.J. State Mus., Rose Art Mus., Brandeis U., Heine-Onstad Art Mus., San Francisco Mus. Art, Del. Art Mus., Nat. Gallery, Oslo, Princeton Art Mus., Inst. Advanced Study, Princeton, many corp. collections; fellow, Edward MacDowell Colony, vis. artist, U. Tex., 1978, artist-in-residence, Dartmouth Coll., 1979 (Recipient purchase prize Bklyn. Mus. 1955, Ford Found. 1961, Whitney Mus. Ann. Am. Painting 1962, N.J. State Mus. 1971, Purchase prize N.J. State Mus. 1971, Olympic games Poster/Print Commn. 1974) Served with USNR, 1942-45. Recipient Presdl. medal Dartmouth Coll., 1991; Princeton Arts Coun. award, 1992, 2000; Rockefeller Found. grantee, 1957. Address: 1087 The Great Rd Princeton NJ 08540-4801 *A good artist must work hard all his life. He must know his craft and, most important of all, he must feel deeply about something in life.*

GEORGE, THOMAS FREDERICK, academic administrator; b. Phila., Mar. 18, 1947; s. Emmanuel John and Veronica Mather (Hansel) G.; m. Barbara Carol Harbach, Apr. 25, 1970. BA in Chemistry and Math., Gettysburg (Pa.) Coll., 1967; MS in Chemistry, Yale U., 1968, PhD, 1970. Rsch. assoc. MIT, 1970; postdoctoral fellow U. Calif., Berkeley, 1971; mem. faculty U. Rochester, N.Y., 1972-85, prof. chemistry, 1977-85; dean Faculty Natural Sci. and Math., prof. chemistry and physics SUNY-Buffalo, 1985-91; provost, acad. v.p., prof. chemistry and physics Wash. State U., Pullman, 1991-96; chancellor, prof. chemistry and physics U. Wis., Stevens Point, 1996—2003; chancellor U. Missouri, St. Louis, 2003—; Disting. vis. lectr. dept. chemistry U. Tex., Austin, 1978; lectr. NATO Advanced Study Inst., Cambridge, Eng., 1979; Disting. speaker dept. chemistry U. Utah, 1980; Disting. lectr. Air Force Weapons Lab., Kirtland AFB, N.Mex., 1980; mem. com. recommendations U.S. Army Basic Sci. Research, 1978-81; lectr. NATO Summer Sch. on Interfaces under Photon Irradiation, Maratea, Italy, 1986; organizer NSF workshop on theoretical aspects of laser radiation and its interaction with atomic and molecular systems Rochester, N.Y., 1977; vice chmn. 6th Internat. Conf. Molecular Energy Transfer, Rodez, France, 1979; chmn. Gordon Rsch. Conf. Molecular Energy Transfer, Wolfeboro, N.H., 1981. Adj. rsch. prof. physics Korea U., Seoul, 1994-99, vis. prof. physics, 1994-2003; Dow lectr. polymer sci. U. Detroit Mercy, 1996; mem. program com. Internat. Conf. on Lasers, San Francisco, 1981-83, ACS Symposium on Recent Advances in Surface Sci., Rochester sect., 1982, Internat. Laser Sci. Conf., Dallas, 1985, external rev. com. for chemistry Gettysburg Coll., 1984, awards com. ACS Procter and Gamble student prizes in chemistry, 1982-83, Free-electron Laser peer rev. panel Am. Inst. Biol. Sci. Med., alt., bd. trustees alt. Calspan-UB Rsch. Ctr., 1989-91; organiser APS Symposium on Laser-Induced Molecular Excitation/Photofragmentation, N.Y., 1987; co-organizer ACS Symposium on Phys. Chemistry High-Temp. Supercondrs., L.A., 1988; co-organizer MRS Symposium on High-Temperature Superconductors, Alfred, N.Y., 1988; chmn. SPIE Symposium on Photochemistry in Thin Films, L.A., 1989; mem. internat. program adv. com. Internat. Sch. Lasers and Applications, Sayanogorsk, East Siberia, USSR, 1989; lectr. on chemistry at cutting edge Smithsonian Instn./Am. Chem. Soc., Washington, 1990; Musselman lectr. Gettysburg Coll., 1999; mem. internat. adv. com. Xth Vavilov Conf. Nonlinear Optics, Novosibirsk, USSR, 1990; Am. coord. NSF Info. Exchange Seminar for U.S.-Japan Program of Cooperation in Photoconversion and Photosynthesis, Honolulu, 1990; mem. program com. Optical Soc. Am. Topical Meeting on Radiative Processes and Dephasing in Semiconductors, Coeur d'Alene, Idaho, 1998; mem. sci. com. Sixth Brijuni Internat. Conf. on Interdisciplinary Topics in Physics and Chemistry, Brijuni Isles, Croatia, 1998; mem. super-regional steering com. Wis. Econ. Summit, 2000; mem. exec. bd. N.Y. State Inst. on Superconductivity, 1990-91; mem. ONT/ASEE rev. panel for Engring. Edn. postdoctoral fellowship program, 1990; mem. rev panel rsch. experiences for undergrads of sci. and tech. rsch. ctrs., NSF, 1989, mem. rev. panel grad. res. traineeships NSF, 1992; cons., lectr. in field. Co-author: (with Blackwell) Notes in Classical and Quantum Physics, 1990, (with Kluwer) Fundamentals in Chemical Physics, 1998; also over 600 papers in field; mem. editl. bd. Molecular Physics, 1984-90, Jour. Cluster Sci., 1989-97; mem. adv. bd. Jour. Phys. Chemistry, 1980-84; mem. adv. editl. bd. Chem. Physics Letters, 1979-81, Chem. Materials, 1989; mem. editl. bd. Jour. Quantum Nonlinear Phenomena (Soviet jour), 1991-96, Nova Jour. Theoretical Physics, 1996-97; editor-at-large Marcel Dekker, 1989; editor: Photochemistry in Thin Films, 1989; co-editor Internat. Jour. Theoretical Physics, Group Theory, and Nonlinear Optics, 1999—; co-editor: Chemistry of High-Temperature Superconductors, Vol. I, 1987, vol. II, 1988, ACS Symposium Series, Computational Studies of New Materials, 1999, Optics of Nanostructural Materials, 2001, Modern Topics in Chemical Physics, 2001; feature editor Jour. of Optical Soc. of Am., Spectrochimica Acta, Optical Engring. Tchr., scholar Camille and Henry Dreyfus Found., 1975-85; bd. mgrs. Buffalo Mus. Sci., 1986-92; mem. exec. bd. N.Y. State Inst. on Superconductivity, 1990-91; mem. canvassing com. ACS; mem. external rev. com. for chemistry Gettysburg Coll., 1984; mem. NEASC site visit team Boston U., ten-yr. accreditation, 1989; bd. dirs. Wash. State Inst. for Pub. Policy, 1991-96; trustee Wash. State U. Found., 1991-96; bd. dirs. Wash. Tech. Ctr., 1992-96; mem. exec. com. Northwest Acad. Forum, 1992-96, chmn. 1994-95; mem. rev. panel Grad. Rsch. Traineeships, NSF, 1992, mem. rev. panel for sci. and tech. ctr. proposals, 1998, rev. panel for preproposals for sci. and tech. ctrs., 1998; mem. Project 435 Dist. Leadership Coun., Wis. Assn. Biomed. Rsch. and Edn./Research America!, 1997; mem. Commn. on the Future of Gettysburg Coll., 1997-98; bd. dirs. Portage County Bus. Coun., 1998—, Stevens Point Area YMCA, 1998—, sec.-treas., 2002-2004; bd. dirs. United Way Portage County, Wis., 1997—, chmn. 1999 campaign, pres., 2002-2004; bd. dirs. Tech. Alliance State Wash., 1996, U. Wis.-Stevens Point Found., 1996—, Paper Sci. Found., 1996—; bd. trustees/dirs. (alt.) Assoc. Western Univs., 1993-96; bd. dirs. alt. Joint Ctr. Higher Edn., Spokane, 1996; mem steering com. Ctr. for Advanced Tech. in Healthcare Instruments and Devices, 1988-90; with Midwestern Higher Edn. Commn., 1999—; exploring chair Mushkodany Dist. Wis. Samoset Coun. Boy Scouts Am., 1998, finance chair, 1999, pres.-elect, 2001; bd. dirs. St. Michael's Hosp., Stevens Point, Wis., 1999-2000, Midwestern Higher Edn. Commn., 1999—, Distributed Learning Workshop, Midwestern Higher Edn. Commn., 1999-, Wis. Ctr. Acad. Talented Youth, 2001-; bd. trustees WiSys Tech. Found., 2000-; bd. commnrs. Acad. Advanced Distributed Learning Lab. (UW-US Dept. Def.), 2001; adv. coun. Ednl. Directories Unlimited, 2001—; mem. adv. bd. New Economy Workforce Coalition, Wausau, 2001; bd. dirs. Marathon County Ptnrs. in Edn., 2002. Sloan fellow, 1976-80, postdoctoral fellow, 1990, Guggenheim fellow, 1983-84; recipient Disting. Alumni award Gettysburg Coll., 1987. Fellow AAAS, Soc. Photo-Optical Instrumentation Engrs., Am. Phys. Soc., N.Y. Acad. Scis., Inst. Superconductivity (steering com. 1987-91); mem. Am. Chem. Soc. (exec. com. phys. div. 1979-82, 85-89, 94-97, vice chmn. 1985-86, chmn.-elect 1986-87, chmn. 1987-88), Am. Assn. State Colls. and Univs. (acad. affairs subcom. on sci. edn. rsch. and tng., coun. state reps.), Wis. Assn. for Biomed. Rsch. and Edn., European Phys. Soc., Royal Soc. Chemistry (Marlow medal and prize 1979), Phi Beta Kappa, Sigma Xi (exec. com. U. Rochester 1984-85, faculty scholar award 1999). Democrat. Lutheran. Office: U Missouri-St Louis 8001 Natural Bridge Rd Saint Louis MO 63121-4499 E-mail: tgeorge@umsl.edu.*

GEORGE, W. PEYTON, lawyer; b. Ada, Okla., Oct. 2, 1936; s. William Peyton and Jodie (Kite) G.; m. Nancy Whorton, Aug. 14, 1966; 1 child, Richard Peyton. BS, U. Ctrl. Okla., 1961; grad., FBI Acad., 1962; JD, Am. U., 1969; postgrad., Army War Coll., 1981. Bar: Va. 1969, D.C. 1970, Okla. 1986. Oil field worker, Okla. and Tex., 1954-59; officer Oklahoma City Police Dept., 1959-62; agt. FBI, Va., N.J., D.C., 1962-69; congl. liaison for sec. Agr. USDA, Washington, 1969-73; ptnr. W. Peyton George, P.C., Washington, 1973-81, Miles & Stockbridge, Washington, 1981-90, Lathrop & Gage, L.C., Washington, 1990—2001, New Capitol Solutions, Santa Fe, 2001– . Col. USAR, 1957-91. Decorated Legion of Merit, Meritorious Svc. medal with oak leaf cluster. Mem. Masons (32 deg.), Shriner. Republican. Office: New Capitol Solutions 907 Old Santa Fe Trail Santa Fe NM 87505 Business E-Mail: peyton@newcapitolsolutions.com.

GEORGE, WALTER EUGENE, JR., architect; b. Wichita Falls, Tex., Oct. 28, 1922; s. Walter Eugene and Mamie Alta (Evans) G.; m. Mary Carolyn Hollers Jutson, May 20, 1980. B.Arch., U. Tex., 1949; M.Arch., Harvard U., 1950. Designer Wiltshire and Fisher (architects), Dallas, 1950-51; partner Pendley, George and Bowman (architects and engrs.), Austin, 1952-57; asst., then assoc. prof. architecture U. Tex., 1956-62; prof. architecture, chmn. dept. U. Kans., 1962-67; dean Coll. Architecture, U. Houston, 1967-69; practice of architecture Austin, 1969-71, 74—; resident architect Colonial Williamsburg, Va., 1971-73; sr. lectr. engring. U. Tex., Austin, 1975-96, San Antonio Conservation Soc. prof. architecture San Antonio, 1997—. Served as pilot USAAF, 1943-46, ETO. Decorated Air medal with oak leaf cluster, Purple Heart; recipient 2d award 1st ann. Southwestern furniture competition, Dallas Mus. Fine Arts. Mem.: AIA (Mont San Michele and Chartres award 1949), Tex. Soc. Archs. (Edward J. Romieniec award for outstanding archtl. educator 2001), Soc. Archtl. Historians, Archaeol. Inst. Am., Tau Sigma Delta. Episcopalian. Office: PO Box 4426 Austin TX 78765-4426

GEORGE, WILLIAM DOUGLAS, JR., retired consumer products company executive; b. Chgo., Nov. 21, 1932; s. William D. and Kathryn (McWhinney) G.; m. Elinor A. Elsing, June 20, 1964; children: David W., Douglas E., Stephen J. BA, Depauw U., 1954; MBA, Harvard U., 1959. With Gen. Mills, Mpls., 1959-70; dir. corp. devel. Brown Group, Inc., St. Louis, 1970-74, v.p., 1974-81; exec. v.p. S.C. Johnson & Son, Inc., Racine, Wis., 1981-89, pres., COO worldwide consumer products, 1990-92; pres., CEO SC Johnson and Son, 1993-97, ret., 1997. Bd. dirs. Arvin Inds., Inc., Ralcorp Holdings, Inc., Reilly Industries. Trustee Carthage Coll. With U.S. Army, 1955-57.

GEORGE, WILLIAM WALLACE, manufacturing company executive; b. Muskegon, Mich., Sept. 14, 1942; s. Wallace Edwin and Kathryn Jean (Dinkeloo) G.; m. Ann Tonnlier Pilgram, Sept. 6, 1969; children: Jeffrey, Jonathan. BS in Indsl. Engring. with honors, Ga. Inst. Tech., 1964; MBA with high distinction, Harvard U., 1966. Asst. to asst. sec. Dept. Def., Washington, 1966-68; spl. civilian asst. to sec. Navy, Washington, 1968-69; with Litton Industries, 1969-78, dir. long-range planning, 1969-70, v.p., 1976—; with Litton Microwave Cooking Products, 1970-78, v.p., 1970-71, exec. v.p., 1971-73, pres., 1973-78; v.p. corp. devel. Honeywell, Mpls., 1978-80, exec. v.p., 1983-87; pres. Honeywell Europe (S.A.), 1980-82, Indsl. Automation, 1987, Space and Aviation Systems, Mpls., 1988-89; pres., chief oper. officer Medtronic Inc., Mpls., 1989-91, pres., CEO, 1989-96, chmn., CEO, 1996—2002. Bd. dirs. Dayton-Hudson, Imation. Bd. dirs. Minn. Symphony Orch., 1976-80, United Way, 1976-79, 96—, nat. chmn., Belgium, 1982-83, campaign chair, 1997; bd. dirs., pres., treas. Guthrie Theater, 1977-84; vice-chmn. United Theol. Sem., 1977-80, Abbott-Northwestern Hosp., 1984—, vice-chair, 1989-91, chair, 1991-93, Health Span, 1989-94; trustee Macalaster Coll., 1987-93, Allin Health Sys., 1994—, vice-chair, 1997—, Mlps. Inst. Arts, 1993—, chmn. Minn. Thunder Pro Soccer, 1994—. Recipient Meritorious Civilian Service Award Sec. Navy, 1969 Mem. Sigma Chi (Internat. Balfour award 1964, trustee 1971-77, Disting. Alumni award Harvard U., 1997). Clubs: Minneapolis, Minikahda. Episcopalian. Home: 2284 W Lake Of The Isles Pky Minneapolis MN 55405-2434 Office: George Family Found 1818 Oliver Ave S Minneapolis MN 55405

GEORGE-LEPKOWSKI, SUE ANN, retired echocardiographic technologist; b. Altoona, Pa., Sept. 17, 1948; d. Charles Frederick and E. Anita (Haller) G.; m. Walter Lepkowski. AS, BS in Agronomy, Pa. State U., 1968, 70, MEd in Agronomy, Biol. Scis., Edn., 1972; PhD, Columbia & Columbia Pacific U., 1980; DS, Columbia Pacific U., 1981. Internship echocardiology West Pa. Hosp., Pitts., 1979-80; echocardiography tech. Bronson Meth. Hosp., Kalamazoo, 1981-82; echocardiographic technologist Nalle Clinic, Charlotte, 1983-85; tech. dir. Carolina Cardiology, Asheville, N.C., 1985-86; chief echocardiographic technologist Candler Gen. Hosp., Savannah, Ga., 1986-88; echocardiography, clin. specialist, technical spl. edn. specialist, chief technologist Self Meml. Hosp., Greenwood, S.C., 1988-97; clin. specialist, educator, echocardiographic technologist Anderson Area Med. Ctr., Anmed, 1997-99, sr. technologist, 1997-99; imaging specialist, clin. specialist adult and pediat. echo Carolina Imaging Ctr., 199-2000; ret., 2000; part time teacher TriCounty Tech. Coll., 2000—. Tchr. Tri County Tech. Coll., 2002; journalist, cons., rschr., lectr. in field. Author: My Readheaded Angel, 1999, On Duty, 1999; contbr. over 90 articles to profl. jours.; co-author: Clinical 2-D Echocardiography; clarinetist Mood Indigo. Past mem. choir, Carolina Mountain Brass, Gospell Quartet; percussionist, clarinetist Images; past edn. chmn. Greenwood Lupus Group, past pres.; former edn. chmn. S.C. Lupus Found.; team leader Fibromyalgia Syndrome; vol. in veterinary ultrasound; mission work in pediat. echo Recipient ACP award, Berkeley-Whittinger award for rsch. and acad. excellence, various citations. Mem. Am. Soc. Ultrasonic Tech. Specialists, Am. Assn. Physician Assts., Am. Inst. Ultrasonic Medicine (sr.), Soc. Diagnostic Med. Sonographers, Am. Registry Diagnostic Med. Sonographers (registered diagnostic cardiac sonographer adult, pediatric echocardiographer), Altoona/Pa. State U. Alumni Assn., Columbia Pacific U. Alumni Assn., Altoona H.S. Alumni Assn., IPTAY, S.C. Ultrasound Soc., N.C. Ultrasound Soc., Am. Soc. Echocardiography, Pa.

State Carolina Club, USGA, PGA, LPGA, Soc. Pediatric Echocardiography, Phi Epsilon Phi, Am. Assn. Physician Asst. Mem. Dutch Reformed Ch. Avocations: music, hiking, aerobics, animals, golf. Home: 113 Greenforest Dr Anderson SC 29625-4903

GEORGES, PAUL GORDON, artist, educator; b. Portland, Oreg., June 15, 1923; s. Thomas Theseus and Daisy G.; m. Lisette Blumenfeld, Jan. 23, 1950; children: Paulette, Yvette. Student, U. Oreg., Jr. Cert., 1946—47; student, Fernand Leger U., Paris. Prof. fine arts Brandeis U., Waltham, Mass., 1977-85, prof. emeritus, 1985; founding mem., chmn. bd. Artist Choice Mus.; represented by Salander-O'Reilly Gallery, N.Y.C. Vis. artist U. Pa., Phila., Queens Coll., Bklyn., Boston U., Yale U., Dartmouth U. One-man shows include Reed Coll., 1948, 56, Tibor De Nagy Gallery, 1955, 57, Zabriskie Gallery, N.Y.C., 1959, Great Jones Gallery, 1960, 61, Allan Frumkin Gallery, N.Y.C. and Chgo., 1962-64, 66, 68, Fischbach, N.Y.C., 1974, 76, Rose Art Mus., Brandeis U., 1981, Zolla Lieberman Gallery, Chgo., 1982, More Gallery, Pa., 1983, 91, 2002, Anne Plumb Gallery, N.Y.C., 1984, 86, 88, 91, Vered Gallery, East Hampton, N.Y., 1989, 91, 96, Greenville (N.C.) Mus., 1989, Salander-O'Reilly Gallery, N.Y.C., 1992, 94, 96, 98, 2000, 03, Galerie Darthea Speyer, Paris, 1995, Sordoni Art Gallery, Wilkes U., Wilkes-Barre, Pa., 1995, Retrospective Ctr. for Figurative Painting, N.Y.C., 2000; exhibited in group shows at PS I Mus., L.I. City, 1991, Am. Acad., 1991, 99, Art Inst. Chgo., 1999, Ctr. for Figurative Paiting, Inc., 2000; represented in permanent collections Whitney Mus., Va. Mus. Fine Arts, Frances and Sydney Lewis Collection, Corcoran Art Collection, Hirshorn Mus., Mus. of Modern Art, Neuberger Mus., Portland Art Mus., Guildhall Mus., Henry Justin Collection, N.Y.C., Art Inst. Chgo. Recipient Hallmark award, Carol Beck Gold medal, award Longview Found., Hassam Purchase award, Am. Acad., 1990, Arthur and Esther Gottlieb Found., 1992, Pollock/Krasner award, 1993, Bernard Altman prize Nat. Acad., 1981, Andrew Carnegie prize, 1982; grantee CAPS; Pacific Theatre WWII 1943-45, Purple Heart, Bronze Star. Mem. NAD, Am. Acad. Inst. Arts Letters (Art award 1986), Nat. Acad. (Ranger Purchase award 1986) Office: care Salander-O'Reilly Galleries 20 E 79th St New York NY 10021-0106

GEORGES, PETER JOHN, lawyer; b. Wilmington, Del., Sept. 8, 1940; s. John Peter and Olga Demetrius (Kazitoris) G. BS in Chemistry, U. Del., 1962; JD, John Marshall Law Sch., 1970; LLM in Patent and Trade Regulations, George Washington U., 1973. Bar: Ill. 1970, U.S. Ct. Appeals (fed. cir.) 1972, D.C. 1973, U.S. Supreme Ct. 1973, Del. 1977. Chemist engring. labs Bell & Howell Co., Chgo., 1966; patent coordinator Armour & Co., Chgo., 1967; patent agt., atty. UOP Inc., Chgo., 1968-71, Washington counsel Arlington, Va., 1972-77; ptnr. Kile, Gholz, Bernstein & Georges, Arlington, 1977-78; assoc., then ptnr. Law Office Sidney W. Russell, Arlington, 1978-83; mng. officer Breneman & Georges (and predecessor law firms), Alexandria, 1983—; founding ptnr. Lenastri Properties and Joanastri Properties, Alexandria, Va. Served to 1st lt. USMC, 1963-65, Vietnam. Mem. ABA, Ill. Bar Assn., D.C. Bar Assn., Del. Bar Assn., Fed. Cir. Bar Assn., Assn. Trial Lawyers Am., Am. Intellectual Property Law Assn., Am. Hellenic Lawyers Soc. Home: 1637 13th St NW Washington DC 20009-4302 Office: Breneman & Georges 3150 Commonwealth Ave Alexandria VA 22305-2712

GEORGES, RICHARD MARTIN, lawyer, educator; b. St. Louis, Nov. 17, 1947; s. Martin Mahlon Georges and Josephine (Cipolla) Rice. AB cum laude, Loyola U., New Orleans, 1969; JD cum laude, Stetson Coll. Law, 1972. Bar: 1972, U.S. Dist. Ct. (mid. dist.) Fla. 1973, U.S. Ct. Appeals (11th cir.) 1981, U.S. Supreme Ct. 1982. Ptnr. Kieffer & Georges, St. Petersburg, Fla., 1973-80, Kieffer, Georges & Ranter, St. Petersburg, Fla., 1980-85; pvt. practice St. Petersburg, Fla., 1985—. Adj. prof. Fla. Inst. Tech., Melbourne, 1977-86, Stetson Coll. Law, 1985-90, 2000-2002, Eckerd Coll., St. Petersburg, 1986-89; mem. Fla. Cts. Tech. Comm., 1998—. Contbg. author: Florida Law of Trusts, 1983, author: Future Lawyer column on legal tech.. Arbitrator United Steelworkers Union, Continental Can Co., 1975-80; hearing examiner City of St. Petersburg, 1982—; me. citizen's adv. com. Pinellas County Met. Planning Orgn., 1986-87; exec. committeeman Pinellas County Rep. Party, Clearwater, Fla., 1981-82. 1st lt. U.S. Army, 1972. Recipient Rafael Steinhardt award Stetson Coll. Law, 1972, Clint Green award, 1972. Mem. ABA, Fla. Bar, St. Petersburg Bar Assn. (chmn. computer com.), Fla. Camera Club Coun. (pres. 1985), Suncoast Camera (Clearwater, v.p. 1982-84, pres. 1985), Phi Alpha Delta. Roman Catholic. Office: PO Box 14545 Saint Petersburg FL 33733 E-mail: futurelawyer@futurelawyer.com.

GEORGES, ROBERT AUGUSTUS, emeritus educator, researcher, writer; b. Sewickley, Pa., May 1, 1933; s. John Thomas and Pauline Pantzis G.; m. Mary Virginia Ruth, Aug. 11, 1956; 1 child, Jonathan Gregory. BS, Ind. U. of Pa., 1954; MA, U. Pa., 1961; PhD, Indiana U., 1964. Tchr. Bound Brook (N.J.) High Sch., 1954-56, Southern Regional High Sch., Manahawkin, N.J., 1958-60; asst. prof. U. Kans., Lawrence, 1963-66, UCLA, 1966-70, assoc. prof., 1970-76, prof., 1976-94; prof. emeritus, 1994—. Vice chmn. Folklore and Mythology Program UCLA, 1966-82, chmn. 1983-86. Author: Greek-American Folk Beliefs and Narratives, 1980; co-author: People Studying People: The Human Element in Fieldwork, 1980, American and Canadian Immigrant and Ethnic Folkore: An Annotated Bibliography; co-author: Folkloristics: An Introduction, 1996; editor: Studies on Mythology, 1968; translator: Two Studies on Modern Greek, Folklore by Stilpon P. Kyriakides, 1968; contbr. numerous articles to folklore periodicals. With U.S. Army, 1956-58. NDEA fellow, 1962-63, Guggenheim fellow, 1969-70. Fellow Am. Folklore Soc.; mem. Calif. Folklore Soc. Home: 906 Fiske St Pacific Palisades CA 90272-3841 E-mail: rgeorges@ucla.edu.

GEORGESCO, VICTOR, printing company executive; b. Bucharest, Romania, Mar. 17, 1948; came to U.S., 1978; s. Paul D. and Maria C. (Bender) G. BS, Poly. U., Bucharest, 1968. Overseas br. mgr. Metal Import Export, Bucharest, 1968-77; asst. mgr. Otto Botner GMBH, Duesseldorf, West Germany, 1977-78; purchasing agt. Trico Industries, Torrance, Calif., 1978-86; exec. v.p. ops. Beverly Ctr. Printing Co., L.A., 1986—. Mem. Purchasing Mgmt. Assn. (L.A. chpt.). Office: 8104 W 3rd St Los Angeles CA 90048-4309

GEORGESCU, PETER ANDREW, advertising executive; b. Bucharest, Romania, Mar. 9, 1939; came to U.S., 1954, naturalized, 1954; s. V.C. Rica and Lygia (Bocu) G.; m. Barbara Anne Armstrong, Aug. 21, 1965; 1 son, Peter Andrew. AB cum laude, Princeton U., 1961; MBA, Stanford U., 1963. With Young & Rubicam, Inc., N.Y.C., 1963—, dir. mktg., 1977-79, exec. v.p. Cen. Region, dir., 1979-82; pres. Young & Rubicam Internat., N.Y.C., 1982-86, Young & Rubicam Advt., N.Y.C., 1986—; pres., CEO Young & Rubicam Inc., from 1994; CEO, chmn. bd. dirs. Young & Rubicam Inc, to 1999, chmn. emeritus, 2000—. Bd. dirs. Briggs & Stratton, Inc. Mem. Coun. on Fgn. Rels., Am. Assn. Advt. Agencies (bd. dirs.), Internat. Advt. Assn., Inc. (bd. dirs.), Links Club, River Club, Racquet Club, Casino Club, Brooks Club. Office: Young & Rubicam Inc 285 Madison Ave New York NY 10017-6486

GEORGIADIS, GREGORY MINAS, orthopedist, educator; b. Urbana, Ill., Feb. 27, 1959; s. Minas Prodromos and Vassiliki Evangelia Georgiadis; m. Catherine Patricia Girod, July 8, 1977; children: Andrew, Catherine, Stephen. BS in Chemistry, Ind. U., 1980, MD, 1984. Diplomate Am. Acad. Orthop. Surgery. Intern surgery, resident orthop. surgery Wayne State U., Detroit, 1984—89; fellow orthop. trauma Case We. Res. U., Cleve., 1989—90; asst. prof. Orthop. Wayne State U., Detroit, 1990—94, Med. Coll. Ohio, Toledo, 1994—99, assoc. prof. Orthop., 1999—. Contbr. chapters to books, articles to profl. jours. Fellow: ACS, Am. Acad. Orthop. Surgery; mem.: Orthop. Trauma Assn. (Edwin G. Bovill award 1991), Alpha Omega Alpha, Phi Beta Kappa. Republican. Greek Orthodox. Avocations: travel, reading, movies. Office: Med Coll Ohio Dept Orthop Surgery 3065 Arlington Ave Toledo OH 43614

GEORGIADIS, JOHN G. mechanical engineer, educator; b. Filiates, Epirus, Greece, Sept. 14, 1959; m. Hilary Georgiadis; 1 child, Alexis V. Dipl. Mech. Engring., Nat. Tech. U. of Athens, Greece, 1982; PhD, UCLA, 1987. Asst. /assoc. prof. Duke U., Durham, NC; prof. of mech. engring. and bioengring. U. of Ill., Urbana, Ill., 1992—. Desalination thrust leader NSF Sci. & Tech. Ctr. of Adv. Materials for Purif. of Water with Systems (CAMPWS), Urbana, Ill. Assoc. tech. editor (original research) ASME Jour. Heat Transfer. Recipient Presdl. Young Investigator award, NSF, 1991—95, Assoc., Centre Nat. de Recherche Scientifique (France), 1999; grantee Sci. and Tech. Ctr. grantee, NSF, 2002—. Achievements include first to quantified measurement error in MRI velocimetry. Office: University of Illinois /Urbana-Champaign 1206 West Green 140 MEB Urbana IL 61801 Office Fax: 217-333-1942. E-mail: georgia @ uiuc.edu.

GEORGIEV, GOSHKO ATANASOV, agrometeorologist, researcher; b. Sofia, Bulgaria, May 29, 1959; came to U.S., 1996; s. Atanas Dimitrov and Maria Georgieva (Nenova) G.; m. Raynichka Tonuva Toncheva Georgieva, Nov. 4, 1984; 1 child, Maria Goshkova Georgieva. MS, Hydrometeorlogical Inst., Odessa, Ukraine, 1983; PhD, Hydromet Ctr. of Russia, Moscow, 1990. Grad. asst. Nat. Inst. Meteorology and Hydrology, Sofia, Bulgaria, 1983-86; vis. scientist Hydromet Ctr. Russia, Moscow, 1986-90; asst. prof. NIMH-BAS, Sofia, Bulgaria, 1990-96, head agromet forecasting, 1995-96; postdoctoral assoc. U. Ga. Coll. Agr. and Environ. Sci., Griffin, Ga., 1996-99; sr. scientist Earth Satellite Corp., Rockville, Md., 1999—. Cons. ACT-Sofia Ltd., Bulgaria, 1992-95; cons., developer Hardware Design Ltd., 1995-96, Pyramid Computers Inc., 1997-99; web designer/developer Bulgarian DC Soc., 2000—. Contbr. articles to profl. jours. Avocations: soccer, tennis, software. Office: Earth Satellite Corp 6011 Executive Blvd Ste 400 Rockville MD 20852-3804 E-mail: goshko@earthsat.com.

GEORGIEVA, ANNA VLADIMIROVA, mathematician; b. Varna, Bulgaria, Feb. 10, 1970; arrived in U.S., 1989; d. Vladimir Georgiev Georgiev and Snijina Vassileva Georgieva. BS, Denison U., 1992; MA, Duke U., 1994, PhD, 1998. Postdoctoral fellow CIIT Ctrs. Health Rsch., Research Triangle Park, NC, 1998—99; vis. asst. prof. math. N.J. Inst. Tech., Newark, 2000—01; modeling scientist, fellow Novartis Pharma, East Hanover, NJ, 2001—. Adjunct prof. New Jersey Inst. Tech., 2001—. Contbr. articles to profl. jours. Mem.: Assn. Women in Math., Soc. Indsl. Applied Math., Am. Assn. Pharm. Scientists. Avocations: reading, swimming, movies. Office: 4051423 1 Health Plz East Hanover NJ 07936

GEORGIOU, RUTH SCHWAB, retired social worker; b. Milford, Del., June 9, 1922; d. Lafayette and Ola (Moody) Burlingame; m. Matheos Georgiou, July 16, 1960 (dec. Sept. 1984); children: Eleni Georgiou Strawn, Diana Georgiou LaRue, Theodora Evtychia. BA in Liberal Arts with honors, U. Mich., 1943; MS in Social Adminstrn., U. Pitts., 1945. Cert. social worker, N.Y. Child welfare officer Unitarian Svc. Com., Germany, 1947-48; dir. Camp Bluebird Jewish Bd. of Guardians, N.Y.C., 1949; asst. dir. Girls Club of Bklyn. Bklyn. Hebrew Orphan Asylum, 1949-52; asst. dir. Suburban Agy., Hempstead, N.Y., 1954-57; co-dir. Suburban Homemaking & Maternity Agy., Hempstead, 1957-61; med. social worker Glen Oaks (N.Y.) Nursing Home, 1967-68; sr. care worker N.Y. Dept. Health-Social Svcs. Dept., Mineola, 1968-69; social work supr. Tampa (Fla.) Lighthouse for the Blind, 1976-78; med. social worker Global Home Health Svcs., Pinellas and Pasco, Fla., 1979-89; ret., 1989. Social work cons. Spanish Gardens Nursing Home, Dunedin, Fla., 1980-82, St. Mark's Village, Palm Harbor, Fla., 1982-83; mem. adv. bd. Med. Pers. Pool, New Port Richey, 1986-98; tutor elem. edn. Pinellas Sch. Support Team, 1999—. Author: (manual) Homemaker's Manual, 1956. Co-chmn. sr. care of Planned Approach to Community Health, New Port Richey, 1988-89; pres. Community Svc. Coun. West Pasco, New Port Richey, 1985-86, bd. dirs., 1985-91. Recipient cert. of appreciation Cmty. Svc. Coun. West Pasco, 1986, 91. Mem. NASW (membership chmn. Pasco subunit Fla. chpt. 1991-99, chmn. membership Tampa Bay unit 1992-97, Social Worker of Yr. award 1991, Ret. Social Worker of Yr. award 97), Acad. Cert. Social Workers; life mem. Cmty. Svc. Coun. West Pasco. Avocation: bible studies. Home: 300 S Walton Ave Apt 53 Tarpon Springs FL 34689-6011

GEORGOPOULOS, MARIA, architect, artist, inventor; b. Moussata, Cefalonia, Greece, Apr. 2, 1949; came to U.S., 1973; d. Vassilios and Joulia Georgopoulos; 1 child, Demetrios. BArch, Nat. Poly. Sch. Greece, Athens, 1972; MS, Columbia U., 1976. Registered architect, N.Y., Greece. Project mgr. Architects Design Group, N.Y.C., 1976—79, Griswold, Heckel & Kelly, N.Y.C., 1979—80; project dir. Lehman Bros., Kuhn Loeb Inc., N.Y.C., 1980—85; v.p. L.F. Rothschild Inc., N.Y.C., 1985—89; corp. art collection archivist, dir. facilities mgmt. The Dreyfus Corp., N.Y.C., 1989—. Mem. AIA, Greek Inst. Architects, Douglaston (N.Y.) Club. Home: 14 Melrose Ln Douglaston NY 11363-1221 Office: The Dreyfus Corp 200 Park Ave New York NY 10166-0099

GEPFERT, ALAN HARRY, management consultant, business educator, author; b. Cleve., Sept. 24, 1930; s. Joseph Harry and Freda Natalia (Schleicher) G.; m. Mary Caroline Austin, Aug. 26, 1959; 1 child: Grace Mary Cooper. BS in Engring. Adminstrn., MS in Ops. Rsch., Case Western Res. U., 1953, postgrad., 1953-56. Instr. Case Western Res. U., Cleve., 1953-58, mem. ops. rsch. cons., 1953-58; dir. statis. rsch. Chgo. and North Western Rlwy., 1958-62; cons. McKinsey & Co., Inc., N.Y.C., 1962-70; exec. Mobil Oil, N.Y.C., 1970-86; prin. Strategic Systems Solutions, New London, NH, 1986—. Instr. Colby-Sawyer Coll., New London, 1992-97, N.H. Tech. Coll., 1992-97, stone sculptor, New London, 2000—. Author (with others) The Arts of Top Management, 1971, Turnaround Management, 1972, Strategic Planning For MIS, 1977; cons. editor Modern Railroads mag., 1959-70; contbr. articles to profl. jours. Trustee 1st Bapt. Ch., White Plains, N.Y., 1969-70; deacon 1st Bapt. Ch., New London, N.H., 1999-2001, dir. Pegasus Therapeutic Riding, Darien, Conn., 1985-88, Masonic Charity Found., Wallingford, Conn., 1989-93, New London Hosp., 1990-92. Mem.: Inst. for Ops. Rsch. and Mgmt. Scis. (chmn. fin. com. 1964—65, vice chmn. coll. on info. sys. 1981—82, acad. practitioner com. 1989—91, chmn. edn. com. 1992—97), Shriners (sec. 1994—96), Masons (32 deg., dist. edn. officer Grand Lodge of N.H. 1998—2000, dist. grand lectr. 2000—01, dist. dep. grand master 2002—), Sigma Xi, Tau Beta Pi. Republican. Avocations: mineralogy, paleontology, geology, piano. Home and Office: Strat Sys Solutions 236 Little Sunapee Rd New London NH 03257-5105 E-mail: ahgepfert@adelphia.net.

GEPFORD, BARBARA BEEBE, retired nutrition educator; b. Buffalo, N.Y., Sept. 2, 1930; d. Kenneth Hildreth and Martha Bell (Griswold) Beebe; m. William George Gepford, Dec. 28, 1952; children: David, Scott, Joanna, Andrea. BS in Home Econs. Edn., Iowa State U., 1952. Nutrition instr. Sidon Girl's Sch., Lebanon, 1953-56; instr. textiles and clothing Beirut Univ. Coll., Lebanon, 1955-56, 62-63; nutrition cons. Hong Kong Coun. of Social Svcs., 1967-71; commd. fraternal worker Presbyn. U.S.A., Lebanon, Hong Kong, 1953-71; mgr. Lila's Fabric Store, Cambridge, Ohio, 1973-74. Overseas missionary advisor to Assembly Coun. of Presbyn. Ch., U.S.A., 1971-72. Elder Presbyn. Ch., New Concord, Ohio, 1974-79, mem. com. on Ministry, Detroit, 1987-94; pres. Presbyn. Women of Littlefield Ch., 1987-89; vice-moderator Presbyn. Women of Presbytery of Detroit, 1985-87, moderator, 1997-99; synod of covenant women's rep. Churchwide Coordinating Team of Presbyn. Women, 1999-2002; chair Presbyn. Women Triann. Global Exch. to Africa, 2002-03; advisor YWCA Head Start Program, Dearborn, Mich., 1988-91; bd. dirs. YWCA, 1985-96, pres., 1993-95. Named Ohio Mother of the Yr., Am. Mothers Com., New Concord, 1978. Mem., AAUW (bd. dirs. 87-89, internat. rels. area rep.). Democrat. Avocations: reading, gardening, sewing, knitting. Home: 9421 Westwind Dr Livonia MI 48150-4530 E-mail: barbbgepford@msn.com, wiamfrd@msn.com.

GEPFORD, WILLIAM GEORGE, minister; b. Kansas City, Mo., Jan. 12, 1927; s. Herbert John and Anna Ruth (Minckemeyer) G.; m. Barbara Joan Beebe, Dec. 28, 1952; children: David Proctor, Scott Allen, Joanna Lynn, Andrea Laine. BS in Elec. Engring., Colo. State U., 1949; MDiv., McCormick Sem., 1953; MEd, U. Colo., 1957; DSc in Theology, San Francisco Sem., 1973. Ordained to ministry Presbyn. Ch. (U.S.A.), 1953. Edn. missionary Presbyn. Ch., Lebanon, 1953-63; dean students Am. U., Beirut, 1961-63; asst. min. First Presbyn. Ch., Boulder, Colo., 1963-65; missionary, student min. Presbyn. Ch., Hong Kong, 1965-71; chaplain, student life dir. Muskingum Coll., New Concord, Ohio, 1972-79; dir. Am./Arab Ministry Presbytery of Detroit, Mich., 1979—. Dean of students Am. Univ. Beirut, Lebanon, 1961-63; dir. student ctr. YMCA (Chinese), Hong Kong, 1965-71; acting assoc. dean of students, Muskingum Coll., New Concord, 1977-78; mem. gen. assembly, adv. study com. on Islam, N.Y., 1983-86; bd. dirs. Interfaith Activities, Presbytery of Detroit; founder Muslim/Christian Dialogue Group, 1985; adv. bd. Arab Community Ctr. of Econ. and Social Svcs., Dearborn, 1983—; mem. Am. Arab Anti-Discrimination com., adv. com., Detroit, 1984—, others; cons. Interfaith Ministries, Presbytery of Detroit, 1992—; bd. mem. McGehee Interfaith Loan Fund Bd. Dirs., 2001—. Mem. adv. bd. ACCESS, Dearborn, Mich., 1985—; clergy participant Interfaith Round Table of Detroit, 1985—; bd. dirs. Human Svcs., Inc., Dearborn; mem. citizens adv. bd. WTVS Ch. 56 PBS, Detroit, 1986-89; bd. dirs. Freedom House, Detroit; mem. Mich. Coalition Human Rights, 1999—, Met. Christian Coun., 1996—; mem. planning com. Detroit 300 Celebration. With USN, 1945-46. Mem. McCormick Sem. Alumni Assn. (pres.-elect 1991-93), Kiwanis (pres. Dearborn 1986-87), Phi Delta Kappa. Democrat. Home: 9421 Westwind Dr Livonia MI 48150-4530 E-mail: wiamfrd@msn.com.

GEPHARDT, DONALD LOUIS, university official; b. St. Louis, Mar. 27, 1937; s. Louis Andrew and Loreen Estelle (Cassell) G.; m. Zenaida Otero Gephardt, June 10, 2000; children from previous marriage: Lisa Diane, Francis Joseph. B Music Edn., Drake U., 1959; BS, Juilliard Sch., 1961, MS, 1962; EdD, Washington U., St. Louis, 1978. Clarinet instr. Henry Street Settlement Music Sch., N.Y.C., 1961-64; music tchr. Wantagh (N.Y.) Elem. Schs., 1962-67; music tchr., band and orch. dir. W.C. Mepham High Sch., Bellmore, N.Y., 1967-70; assoc. prof. music, band and jazz ensemble conductor Nassau C.C., Garden City, N.Y., 1970-83, chmn. music dept., 1977-83, dean instrn., 1984-90; dean Coll. Fine and Performing Arts, Rowan U., Glassboro, N.J., 1990—, acting exec. v.p., provost, 1994-95. Clarinetist Des Moines Symphony Orch., 1956-59, Aspen (Colo.) Festival Orchestra, 1959-60, Henry Schuman's Wind Ensemble Workshop, 1965-69, L.I. Symphony Orch., 1970-82; clarinetist Seuffert Band, 1962-90, Great Neck (N.Y.) Symphony, 1967-80; contbr. articles to profl. jours. Bd. dirs. L.I. Symphony, 1980-82; surrogate speaker Richard Gephardt for Pres., 1987-88. Mem. Music Educators Nat. Conf. (chpt. advisor 1970-83, 2-yr. coll. chmn. Ea. divsn. 1982-83), N.Y. State Sch. Music Assn. (chmn. rsch. 1982-84), N.J. Music Educators Assn., Alliance for Arts Edn. N.J. (past pres.), Nassau Music Educators Assn. (rec. sec. 1968-69, 1st v.p. 1969-70, pres. 1970-71), Coll. Music Soc., Internat. Coun. of Fine Arts Deans (pres.-elect 2001-02, pres. 2003—), Young Audiences of N.J. (bd. dirs.), Arts Edn. Partnership (steering com.), Phi Mu Alpha Sinfonia. Democrat. Avocations: cooking, reading. Office: Rowan U NJ Coll Fine-Performing Arts Glassboro NJ 08028

GEPHARDT, RICHARD ANDREW, congressman; b. St. Louis, Jan. 31, 1941; s. Louis Andrew and Loreen Estelle (Cassell) G.; m. Jane Ann Byrnes, Aug. 13, 1966; children: Matthew, Christine, Katherine. BS, Northwestern U., 1962, JD, U. Mich., 1965. Bar: Mo. 1965. Ptnr. Thompson & Mitchell, St. Louis, 1965-76; alderman 14th ward City of St. Louis, 1971-76; mem. U.S. Congress from 3d Mo. dist., 1979—; Dem. leader, mem. house dem. policy com.; minority leader, 1994—2002; 2004 pres. candidate. Dem. committeeman 14th ward, St. Louis, 1968-71; pres. Children's Hematology Rsch. Assn., St. Louis Children's Hosp., 1973-76; candidate for Dem. nomination for Pres. of U.S., 1987-88. Mem. Mo. Bar Assn., St. Louis Bar Assn., Am. Legion, Young Lawyer's Soc. (chmn. 1972-73), Kiwanis. Clubs: Mid-Town (St. Louis). Democrat. Office: US Ho of Reps 1236 Longworth House Office Bldg Washington DC 20515-0001 also: 11140 S Towne Sq Rm 201 Saint Louis MO 63123*

GEPHART, MICHELE MARIE, elementary education educator; b. Buffalo, Sept. 16, 1969; d. Michael Raymond and Nancy Marie (Young) M.; m. Joseph Donald Gephart, July 15, 1989. AA, Villa Maria Coll., 1989; BEd, Daemen Coll., 1992; M in Reading Edn., Canisius Coll., 1995. Tchr. Queen of Martyrs Sch., Cheektowaga, N.Y., 1992, Our Lady of Czestchowa Sch., Cheektowaga, 1992-98, St. Bernard's, Buffalo, 1999—2001, St. Benedict's, Amherst, NY, 2001—02; reading tchr. Buffalo Pub. Schs., 2002—. Avocations: ceramics, sports. Home: 9453 E Eden Rd Eden NY 14057

GEPPERT, JOHN GUSTAVE, JR., lawyer; b. DuBois, Pa., July 1, 1956; s. John Gustave and Patricia C. (Greenland) G.; m. Karen M. Platt, Jan. 30, 1988. BBA, U. Notre Dame, 1978; JD, Seton Hall U., 1983. Bar: N.J. 1983, U.S. Dist. Ct. N.J. 1983, U.S. Ct. Appeals (3d cir.) 1984. Law clk. to judge U.S. Ct. Appeals for 3d Cir., Newark, 1983-84; assoc. Pitney, Hardin, Kipp & Szuch, Morristown, N.J., 1984-86, Wiley, Malehorn & Sirota, Morristown, 1986-88, ptnr., 1988—. Editor-in-chief Seton Hall Law Rev., 1982-83. Active Rockaway Twp. (N.J.) City Coun., 1980-83, Rockaway Twp. Planning Bd., 1982; trustee N.J. Tchrs. Pension and Annuity Fund, Trenton, 1981-83; pres., bd. dirs. Literacy Vols. Am., Morris County, 1997-99; bd. dirs. United Way Morris County, 1997—. Mem. ABA, N.J. Bar Assn., Morris County Bar Assn., Lions (bd. dirs. Rockaway 1983-88). Republican. Avocations: sports, travel, reading. Office: Wiley Malehorn & Sirota 250 Madison Ave Morristown NJ 07960-6108 E-mail: jgeppert@wmands.com.

GERA, RALUCCA MIHAELA, mathematician, educator; b. Romania, July 7, 1977; d. Petru and Stephanie Muntean; m. Florin Adrian Gera, Apr. 27, 1976. Grad., Western Mich. U., 2000, M in Math., 2002. Tchg. asst. Western Mich. U., Kalamazoo. Contbr. articles to profl. jours. Pres. Pi Mu Epsilon, Kalamazoo, 1999—2000. Mem.: MAA. Achievements include research in domination in stratified graphs and other Graph theory research topics. Personal E-mail: ralucca.gera@wmich.edu.

GERACI, RICHARD V. military officer, government agency administrator; BS in Mgmt., Park Coll.; M.Mgmt., Webster U.; MS in Systems Mgmt., Fla. Inst. Tech.; MA in Nat. Security Affairs and Strategic Studies, U.S. Naval War Coll. Commd. 2d lt. U.S. Army, 1975—, advanced through grades to brig. gen.; platoon leader, battery exec. officer, asst. ops. officer 3d Battalion 32nd Army Air Def. Command, Germany; Patriot plans and future war plans officer, G3 32d AADCOM; battalion ops. officer 1st Bn. 7th ADA (PATRIOT; brigade ops. officer and dep. brigade comdr. 94th ADA Brigade; battalion ops. officer 3d Battalion 1st ADA, Tng. Brigade, Ft. Bliss, Tex.; garrison ops., plans, tng., mobilization officer Installation Support Activity, U.S. Army, Aberdeen Proving Grounds, Md.; dep. commdg. gen. Army Space Command and Ops., U.S. Army Space and Missile Def. Command, Colorado Springs, Colo. Decorated Legion of Merit, Meritorious Svc. medal, silver and 2 bronze oak leaf clusters, Army Commendation medal with 2 oak leaf clusters, Army Achievement medal with 1 oak leaf cluster, S.W. Asia Svc. medal, Saudi-Kuwaiti Liberation medal, Kuwaiti Liberation medal. Office: Army Space Command 1670 N Newport Rd Attn: SMDC-ZD Colorado Springs CO 80916-2749

GERAGHTY, PATRICK JAMES, organ recovery manager; b. Evanston, Ill., June 23, 1971; s. Martin Patrick and Maureen (Ganey) G.; m. Diana Lee Stanton, June 17, 1995; children: Mary Katherine, Colleen Ashley. BS, George Washington U., 1993. Nationally registered emergency med. technician-paramedic, cert. procurement transplant coord. Paramedic/firefighter Bethesda (Md.)/Chevy Chase Rescue Squad, 1991—, sgt., ALS svcs. coord., 1994-96; organ recovery coord. Washington Regional Transplant Consortium, Falls Church, Va., 1993-96; transplant coord. Lifenet Transplant Svcs., Richmond, Va., 1996-2000; mgr. organ recovery Lifenet, Richmond, 2000—03; dir. organ recovery svcs. Doner Network Am., Phoenix, 2003—. Rep. EMS Com., Montgomery County, Md., 1993-96. Office: Done Network Am 201 W Cooledge Phoenix AZ 85013

GERALD, BARRY, radiology educator, neuroradiologist; b. Greenville, Miss., Feb. 10, 1934; s. Louis Elmo and Eula (Mitchell) G.; m. Marjorie Brown, Aug. 6, 1955; children: Lucy Gerald Cook, Lee, Paul. Student, U. Miss., Oxford, 1951-54; MD, U. Miss., Jackson, 1958. Diplomate Am. Bd. Radiology. Intern Hermann Hosp., Houston, 1958-59, resident in radiology, 1959-62; fellow in pediatric radiology Children's Hosp. Med. Ctr., Cin., 1962-64; mem. faculty dept. radiology U. Ark., Little Rock, 1964-65, 67-69; dir. radiology dept. Children's Hosp. Med. Ctr., Oakland, Calif., 1965-66; mem. faculty dept. radiology U. Tenn. Coll. Medicine, Memphis, 1969—, prof., chmn. dept., 1979-95; fellow in neuroradiology Tufts-New Eng. Med. Ctr., Boston, 1971-72. Dir. radiology dept. Le Bonheur Children's Hosp., Memphis, 1983-88, 1991-2002; acting dir. radiology dept. St. Jude Children's Rsch. Hosp., Memphis, 1985-87; trainee Nat. Cancer Inst., 1960-62. Contbr. articles to med. jours., chpts. to books. Fellow Am. Coll. Radiology; mem. Am. Soc. Neuroradiology, Soc. for Pediatric Radiology, Radiol. Soc. N.Am. (councillor 1980-85), Am. Roentgen Ray Soc., Southeastern Neuroradiologic Soc. (founder, pres. 1977-78), So. Radiologic Conf. (pres. 1975-76). Avocations: tennis, american history. Home: 694 Clanlo Dr Memphis TN 38104-5067 Office: U Tenn Dept Radiology 800 Madison Ave Memphis TN 38103-3400 E-mail: bgerald@utmem.edu.

GERALD, MICHAEL CHARLES, pharmacy educator; b. N.Y.C., Nov. 20, 1939; s. Tobias Gerson and Ruby Rose (Weinstock) G.; m. Gloria Elaine Gruber, Jan. 31, 1965; children— Marc Jonathan, Melissa Suzanne, B.S. in Pharmacy, Fordham U., 1961; Ph.D., Ind. U., 1968. Registered pharmacist, N.Y. Postdoctoral fellow USPHS, U. Chgo., 1968-69; asst. prof. Coll. Pharmacy Ohio State U., Columbus, 1969-74, assoc. prof., 1974-80, prof., 1980-93, prof. and assoc. dean., 1984-93; dean, prof. Sch. Pharmacy U. Conn., Storrs, 1993-02; prof., 2002—. cons. WHO, Geneva, 1983-84; mem. adv. panel U.S. Pharmacopeia Com. Revision, Washington, 1980-85. Author: Pharmacology: An Introduction to Drugs, 2d edit. 1981, Nursing Pharmacology and Therapeutics, 2d edit. 1988, The Poisonous Pen of Agatha Christie, 1993; (co-author) The Nurse's Guide to Drug Therapy: Drug Profiles for Patient Care, 1984, Editor: Instruction in Pharmacology: New Approaches and New Faces, 1979. Mem. FDA Drug Abuse Adv. Com., 1993—. Served to 1st lt. USAF, 1963-65. USPHS fellow Ind. U., 1965-68; Gustavus A. Pfeiffer Meml. Research fellow Am. Found. Pharm. Edn., 1983-84. Fellow Acad. Pharm. Scis. (sect. sec. 1975-77, sect. v.p. 1978-79). (sect. sec. 1975-77, sect. v.p. 1978-79); mem. Am. Assn. Colls. of Pharmacy (bd. dirs. 1980-82), Am. Soc. Pharmacology and Exptl. Therapeutics, N.Y. Acad. Scis., Soc. Neurosciences. Avocations: photography, reading, music, walking E-mail: michael.gerald@uconn.edu.

GERALDSON, RAYMOND I., JR., lawyer; b. Racine, Wis., Oct. 19, 1940; s. Raymond I. Sr. and Evelyn (Thorpe) G.; m. Melinda Paine, June 13, 1964; children: Amy Geraldson-Bhote, Raymond I. III. BA, DePauw U., 1962; JD, Northwestern U., 1965. Bar: Ill. 1965, D.C. 1966, U.S. Dist. Ct. (no. dist.) Ill. 1967. Ptnr. Pattishall, McAuliffe, Newbury, Hilliard & Geraldson, Washington, 1965-67, Chgo., 1967—. Adj. prof. John Marshall Law Sch. 1978—; lectr. in field. Contbr. articles on trademark law to profl. jours. Trustee Kendall Coll., 1985—, chmn., 1990-2000. Mem. ABA, Ill. State Bar Assn. (coun. sect. intellectual property law 1978-82, chmn. 1980-81), Chgo. Bar Assn., 7th Cir., Intellectual Property Law Assn. Chgo. (bd. dirs. 1984-86, 92-93, pres. 1991-92), Internat. Trademark Assn. (bd. dirs. 1985-87), Am. Intellectual Property Law Assn., Lawyers for Creative Arts (hons. coun. 1994—, bd. dirs. 1974-94, pres. 1976-78), Lawyers Club Chgo., Econ. Club Chgo., Sunset Ridge Country Club, Union League Club of Chgo., Chi. Office: Pattishall McAuliffe Newbury Hilliard & Geraldson 311 S Wacker Dr Ste 5000 Chicago IL 60606-6631

GERARD, DONALD GORDON, physician; b. Hart, Mich., July 26, 1930; s. John Allen Gerard and Doris Evelyn Gray; m. Donna Mae Walters, Aug. 27, 1955; children: Philip, Rebecca, John, Dorothy, James, Elizabeth. AS, Grand Rapids (Mich.) C.C., 1950; BS, Calvin Coll., 1955; MD, Wayne State Coll., 1959. Diplomate Am. Bd. Family Practice. Intern Butterworth Hosp., Grand Rapids, 1959-60; pvt. practice Lowell, Mich., 1960-94; med. dir. Lowell Med. Ctr., 1975-94; chief dept. family practice Butterworth Hosp., 1982-89, chmn. utilization rev. com., 1990-94; pres. West Mich. Acad. of Family Practice, 1989-91; med. dir. Cornerstone Coll. Health Svc., Grand Rapids, 1994-99; team physician Lowell Area Schs., 1963—. Chmn. Look Com., City of Lowell, 1995—. Mem. Lowell Area Sch. Bd., 1963-72. 1st lt. U.S. Army, 1951-53. Mem. AMA, Am. Acad. Family Physicians. Avocations: reading, church-related activities, lang. study. Home: 2360 Gee Dr Lowell MI 49331-9505 E-mail: dggerard@sprynet.com.

GERARD, GARY, neurologist; b. N.Y.C., Apr. 16, 1949; s. Victor and Sylvia G.; m. Pauline Judd; 1 child, Michael. BA, NYU, 1971; MD, Hahnemann U., 1975. Diplomate Am. Bd. Neurology and Psychiatry. Intern medicine Brookdale Med. Ctr., Bklyn., 1975-76; resident in diagnostic radiology Mt. Sinai Med. Ctr., N.Y.C., 1976-78; resident in neurology L.I. Jewish Med. Ctr., New Hyde Park, NY, 1978-81; chief of neurology Winthrop U. Hosp., Mineola, NY, 1984-89; assoc. prof. neurology and radiology, dir. cerebrovascular lab. Med. Coll. Ohio, Toledo, 1990-94, vice chmn. neurology, 1991-94; med. dir. Neurology Ctr. Ohio, Toledo, 1994—, dir., 1994-96. Contbr. chpts. to books; guest editor jour. Seminars in Neurology, 1986. Bd. dirs. Ohio Rsch. Ctr., Toledo, 1994-97. Recipient Robert J. Tidrick award Med. Coll. Ohio, 1991. Fellow Am. Heart Assn. (stroke coun.); mem. Am. Acad. Neurology (neuroimaging com. 1985-90), Am. Pain Soc., Am. Acad. Pain Mgmt., Am. Assn. Study of Headache, Am. Soc. Neurorehab., Nat. Headache Found., Am. Soc. Neuroimaging (bd. dirs. 1984-90). E-mail: ggerard3@ix.netcom.com.

GERARD, JAMES WILSON, publishing consultant; b. Chgo., May 16, 1935; s. Ralph Waldo and Margaret (Wilson) G. Student, U. Vt., 1955, Roosevelt U., 1955-59. Ptnr UNIPUB, N.Y.C., 1962-77; pres. Brookfield (Vt.) Pub. Co., 1977—. Bd. dirs. Renouf Pub. Co., Ltd. Mem. Am. Assn. Scholarly Pub., Les Ambassadeurs Club. Democrat. Home: 333 E 34th St New York NY 10016-4977 Office: Brookfield Mktg Inc 1517 Sagebrush Rd Palm Springs CA 92264 E-mail: jgerard@ashgate.com., jgerard@dc.rr.com.

GERARD, JULES BERNARD, law educator; b. St. Louis, May 20, 1929; s. John Baptist and Faith Vera (Clinton) G.; m. Camilla Roma Smith, Aug. 8, 1953; children— Lisa, Karen Julia Student, Iowa State Coll., 1947-49; AB, Washington U., St. Louis, 1957, JD, 1958. Bar: N.Y. 1959, U.S. Supreme Ct. 1979. Assoc. Donovan, Leisure, Newton & Irvine, N.Y.C., 1958-60; asst. prof. law U. Mo., Columbia, 1960-62; asst. prof., assoc. prof. law Washington U., 1962-67, prof., 1967-99, prof. emeritus, 1999—. Author: Local Regulation of Adult Businesses, 1992, Proposed Washington D.C. Amendment, 1979, (with others) Sum and Substance Constitutional Law, 1976, (with others) Federal Land Use Law, 1986; editor: 100 Years of 14th Amendment, 1973; editor-in-chief Washington U. Law Quar., 1958; contbr. articles to profl. jours., chpts. to books. Mem. Mo. Adv. com. U.S. Commn. on Civil Rights, 1987-92. Served to 1st lt. USAF, 1950-54 Mem. ABA Republican. Avocations: collecting scrimshaw and antique photographica, photography. Home: 1564 Yarmouth Point Dr Chesterfield MO 63017-5639 Office: PO Box 1120 Saint Louis MO 63188-1120 E-mail: gerard@law.wustl.edu.

GERARD, LEO W. trade association administrator; b. Sudbury, Ont., 1947; LLD(hon.), Laurentian U., 1994; attended, Canadian Labour Congress Labour Coll. Dir. Dist. 6, Ont., Canada, 1985, 1989; chmn. Steelworkers Health and Welfare Fund; with Heartland Labor Capital Funds; nat. dir. Can., 1991; sec.-treas. United Steelworkers Am. USWA, chief steward; internat. sec.-treas. United Steelworkers Am. USWA, 1997, United Steelworkers Am. USWA, 1993, internat. pres., 1993—. Staff rep. Canadian Labour Congress Labour Coll., 1977. Contbr. articles to profl. pubs. Office: United Steelworkers Am 5 Gateway Ctr Pittsburgh PA 15222

GERARD, ROY DUPUY, oil company executive, retired; b. New Orleans, Sept. 14, 1931; s. Lester Charles and Helene (Dupuy) G.; m. Minnie Harper, May 17, 1958; children: Roy Dupuy Jr., Nannette Gerard Helmcamp, Carl, Denise Ingram. BSChemE, La. State U., 1953, MSChemE, 1958. Registered profl. engr., La. Chemist, technologist various plants Shell Chem. Co., Houston, La., N.Y., 1958-69; dept. head Shell Devel. Co., Emeryville, Calif., 1969-71, dir. indsl. chems. and petrochems. Houston, 1973-75, mgr. chem. R & D, 1975-77, gen. mgr. Westhollow rsch., 1982-90; pres. Saudi Petrochem. Co., Al Jubail, Saudi Arabia, 1980-82; mgr. logistics econs., supply and econs. and mktg. Shell Oil Co., Houston, 1971-73, gen. mgr. engring. products, 1977-80, v.p. health, safety and environ., 1990-92, ret., 1992; pvt. investor, stocks, bonds, etc., 1992—. Mem., vice chmn. coun. environ. affairs Conf. Bd., 1991—; mem., chmn. chem. engring. vis. com. U. Tex., Austin, 1985-87; mem. chem. engring. vis. com. La. State U., Baton Rouge, 1987-90, mem. dean's adv. com., 1990-2001; mem. chem. engring. vis. com. Tex. A&M U., College Station, 1989, U. Tenn., Knoxville, 1989 1st lt. C.E., U.S. Army, 1954-56. Mem. AICE, Coun. for Chem. Rsch. (chmn. 1991—), Am. Indsl. Health Coun. (bd. dirs., exec. com. 1990—), Am. Petroleum Inst. (health and environ. gen. com. 1990—), Raveneaux Country Club (Spring, Tex.). Republican. Roman Catholic. Avocations: fishing, golf, woodworking. E-mail: rgerard914@aol.com.

GERARD, WHITNEY IAN, lawyer; b. N.Y.C., Oct. 31, 1934; s. Harold Todd and Beatrice Roma (Meyer) G.; m. Marion Lehane, Apr. 1, 1966; children: Ian Alexandre, Stefan Meredith. AB, Princeton U., 1956; JD, Harvard U., 1963. Bar: N.Y. 1964. Wine exporter Alexis Lichine et Cie, Bordeaux, France, 1956-58; wine cons. S.S. Pierce Co., Boston, 1960-75; assoc., then ptnr. Alexander and Green, N.Y.C., 1963-84; ptnr., chmn. internat. practice comm. Chadbourne and Parke LLP, N.Y.C., 1984—. Bd. dirs. U. Cape Town Fund, Inc., N.Y.C., Dreyfus Liquid Assets, Inc., The Dreyfus Fund, Inc., Dreyfus Worldwide Dollar Money Market Fund, Inc., Dreyfus Lifetime Portfolios, Inc., Dreyfus Short Intermediate Mcpl. Bond Fund, Dreyfus Short Intermediate Govt. Fund. and other Dreyfus funds. 1st lt. USAF, 1958-60. Mem. ABA, N.Y. State Bar Assn., Internat. Bar Assn., Univ. Club, Ancient Order of Beefeaters (Chief Warder 1965-90). Democrat. Avocations: classical music, ballet, theater, mountain hiking, literature. Home: 940 Park Ave New York NY 10028-0311 also: 102 W Center Rd West Stockbridge MA 01266-9378 Office: Chadbourne & Parke LLP 30 Rockefeller Plz New York NY 10112-0129

GERARD, WILLIAM BLAKE, literature educator; s. William Joseph Gerard and Eileen Caffery Iaizzo; m. Carol Rosen; children: Samuel Amedeo, Joseph Harry. BA, Fla. Atlantic U., 1996, MA, 1997; PhD, U. Fla., 2002. Pub., editor Rubber Chicken Mag., Longwood, Fla., 1992—94; prof. dept. English and philosophy Auburn U., Montgomery, Ala. Office: Auburn Univ Montgomery Dept English and Philosophy PO Box 244023 Montgomery AL 36124 Personal E-mail: wbgerard@knology.net.

GERARD-SHARP, MONICA FLEUR, communications executive; b. London, Oct. 4, 1951; came to U.S., 1975; d. John Hugh Gerard-Sharp and Doreen May (Kearney) Dewhurst; m. Ali Edward Wambold, Nov. 21, 1981; children: Marina, Daniela, Dominica. BA in Philosophy and Lit. with honors, U. Warwick, Eng., 1973; MBA in Fin., Mktg. and Internat. Bus., Columbia U., 1980. Editor Inst. Chem. Engrs., London, 1973-74; sub-editor TV Times, London, 1974-75; press officer, editor UN, N.Y.C., 1975-78; bus. mgr. Time-Life Video, N.Y.C., 1980-81; mgr. fin. analysis Time-Life Films, N.Y.C., 1981; v.p. T.V.I.S., N.Y.C., 1982-83; dir. strategy and devel. HBO, ATC, N.Y.C., 1984-85; asst. treas., officer Time Inc., N.Y.C., 1985—87; pub. Travel Today and other mags. Fairchild Pubs. subs. Capital Cities/ABC, N.Y.C., 1987-88; dir. video programming Fairchild Pubs., Capital Cities/ABC, N.Y.C., 1988-89; pub. Entrée and Home Fashions Mags., N.Y.C., 1988-90; pres. Monali Inc., N.Y.C., 1991—. Cons. UN Bus. Council, N.Y.C., 1979; bd. rep. U.S.A. Network, N.Y.C., 1983-85. Editor: Everyone's United Nations, 1977; contbg. editor Asia Pacific Forum, 1976-77; contbr. articles to profl. jours. and mags., 1973-78. Treas. Help the Aged, Eng.; nat. devel. bd. Chances for Children, 1995-, pres. 2001-; adv. bd. Am. Mus. Natural History, 1998—; pres. bd. Am. Friends of Royal Ct. Theatre, 1998-2000. Bronfman fellow, 1979-80. Mem. Nat. Acad. Cable Programming, Am. Film Inst., Beta Gamma Sigma. Roman Catholic. Avocations: antiques, photography, wildlife. Home: Deer Park 128 Sunset Hill Rd Pleasant Valley NY 12569 Office: Monali Inc 26 E 80th St New York NY 10021-0110

GERATHY, E. CARROLL, former insurance executive, real estate developer; b. Long Island City, N.Y., June 25, 1915; s. Joseph Hewson and Emma E. (Donady) G.; m. Julia F. Gill, Sept. 7, 1942; children: Nancy, John; m. Joyce K. Baker, Dec. 31, 1972; children: Stephen Baker, Nancy Baker; m. Betty Ann Durkin, Jan. 27, 1984. MBA, U. Chgo., 1962. C.L.U. With McKesson & Robbins, Inc., 1933-48; with Prudential Ins. Co. Am., 1948-78, sr. v.p., 1964-78; project dir. Hilton Hawaiian Village, Hilton Hotels Corp., 1979-81, Third Newark Gateway Urban Renewal Assn., 1981-91. Mem. N.J. C. of C., Canoe Brook Country Club (N.J.). Home: 42 Knob Hill Dr Summit NJ 07901-3051

GERBA, CHARLES PETER, microbiologist, educator; b. Blue Island, Ill., Sept. 10, 1945; s. Peter and Virginia (Roulo) G.; m. Peggy Louise Scheitlin, June 6, 1970; children: Peter, Phillip. BS in Microbiology, Ariz. State U., 1969; PhD in Microbiology, U. Miami, 1973. Postdoctoral fellow Baylor Coll. Medicine, Houston, 1973-74, asst. prof. microbiology, 1974-81; assoc. prof. U. Ariz., Tucson, 1981-85, prof., 1985—. Cons. EPA, Tucson, 1980—, World Health Orgn., Pan Am. Health Orgn., 1989—; advisor CRC Press, Boca Raton, Fla., 1981—. Editor: Methods in Environmental Virology, 1982, Groundwater Pollution Microbiology, 1984, Phage Ecology, 1987, Pollution Sci., 1996; contbr. numerous articles to profl. and sci. jours. Mem. Pima County Bd. Health, 1986-92; mem. sci. adv. bd. EPA, 1987-95. Recipient McKee medal Water Environ. Fedn., 1996; named Outstanding Research Scientist U. Ariz., 1984, 92, Outstanding Rsch. Team, 1994. Fellow AAAS (environ. sci. and engring.), Am. Acad. Microbiology, Am. Soc. Microbiology (divsn. chmn. 1982-83, 87-88, pres. Ariz. chpt. 1984-85, councilor 1985-88); mem. Internat. Assn. Water Pollution Rsch. (sr. del. 1985-91), Am. Water Works Assn. (A.P. Black award 1997), Water Quality Assn. (Hom. Mem. award 1998). Achievements include research in environmental microbiology, colloid transport in ground water, wastewater reuse and risk assessment. Home: 1980 W Paseo Monserrat Tucson AZ 85704-1329 Office: U Ariz Dept Microbiol & Immunol Wat Tucson AZ 85721-0001 E-mail: gerba@ag.arizona.edu.

GERBEHY, CHRISTINE PETRIC, medical, surgical, and mental health nurse; b. Jersey City, Mar. 21, 1952; d. Miro and Eileen M. (Schmidt) Petric; m. Steven John Gerbehy; children: Rachel Lauren, Emily Rose. AAS, Bergen Community Coll., Paramus, N.J., 1978; BSN with honors, Felician Coll., Lodi, N.J., 1988. With med. and surg. dept. Bergen Pine County Hosp., Paramus, 1978-88, staff nurse, psychiatry, 1988-98, Bergen Regional Med. Ctr., Paramus, 1998—. Mem. ANA, Sigma Theta Tau (Mu Theta chpt.).

GERBER, DAVID A. lawyer; b. N.Y.C., Dec. 4, 1944; AB, U. Rochester, 1966; PhD, U. Tex., 1970; JD, UCLA, 1977. Bar: Calif. 1977, U.S. Dist. Ct. (ctrl. dist.) Calif. 1978, U.S. Dist. Ct. (no., ea. and so. dists.) Calif. 1982, U.S. Ct. Appeals (9th cir.) 1978, U.S. Ct. Appeals (1st cir.) 1981, U.S. Ct. Appeals (3d cir.) 1985, U.S. Ct. Appeals (7th cir.) 2001, U.S. Supreme Ct. 1986. Litig. atty. Loeb & Loeb, L.A., 1977-93, Nordman, Cormany, Hair & Compton, Oxnard, Calif., 1993-95, D. Gerber Law Offices, Channel Islands Harbor, Calif., 1995—. Contbr. articles to profl. jours. Trustee L.A. Copyrigt Soc., 1991-94. Mem. State Bar Calif. (exec. com. of intellectual property sect. 1988-91). Office: 3600 Harbor Blvd Ste 226 Oxnard CA 93035-4184 E-mail: dgerberlaw@aol.com.

GERBER, DAVID JOSEPH, legal educator, lawyer; b. St. Louis, Aug. 14, 1945; s. Joseph Harding and Elvera Louise (Duesenberg) G.; m. Ulla-britt Junemark, Aug. 16, 1981; children: Eric David, Marcus David. BA, Trinity Coll., 1967; MA, Yale U., 1969; JD, U. Chgo., 1972. Bar: N.Y. 1973. Assoc. Casey, Lane & Mittendorf, N.Y.C., 1972-75; asst. to dirs. Inst. Fgn. Law, U. Freiburg, Germany, 1975-76; legal adv. Peltzer and Riesenkampff, Frankfurt, Germany, 1977-78; prof. law Chgo.-Kent Coll. Law, Ill. Inst. Tech., 1982—. Vis. prof. U. Stockholm, Sweden, 1979, U. Freiburg, 1991, 2002, Northwestern U., 1999, Washington U., 2000, U. Uppsala, Sweden, 2001, U. Pa., 2001. Author: Law and Competition in Twentieth Century Europe, 1998, 2d edit., 2002; mem. editl. bd.: Am. Jour. Comparative Law, Jour. Internat. Econ. Law, Jour. Competition Law. Mem. ABA, Internat. Acad. Comparative Law. Office: Ill Inst Tech Kent Coll Law 565 W Adams St Chicago IL 60661-3613 E-mail: dgerber@kentlaw.edu.

GERBER, DOUGLAS EARL, classics educator; b. North Bay, Ont., Can., Sept. 14, 1933; s. Earl Jacob and Bertha (Cox) G.; m. Joan Isobel Warner, Nov. 22, 1986; 1 dau., Allison S. BA, U. Western Ont. (Can.), London, 1955, MA, 1956; PhD, U. Toronto, 1959. Lectr. Greek U. Toronto, 1958-59; mem. faculty dept. classics U. Western Ont., London, 1959-99, assoc. prof., 1964-69, prof., 1969-99, chmn. dept., 1969-97, vice provost for acad. affairs, 1984-86, W.S. Fox chair of classics. Author: A Bibliography of Pindar, 1513-1966, 1969, Euterpe: An Anthology of Early Greek Lyric, Elegiac and Iambic Poetry, 1970, Emendations in Pindar, 1513-1972, 1976, Pindar's Olympian One: A Commentary, 1982, Lexicon in Bacchylidem, 1984, Greek Iambic Poetry, 1999, Greek Elegiac Poetry, 1999, A Commentary on Pindar Olympian Nine, 2002; editor Greek Poetry and Philosophy; Studies in Honor of Leonard Woodbury, 1984, A Companion to the Greek Lyric Poets, 1997. Mem. Classical Assn. Canada (treas. 1960-62, pres. 1988-90), Am. Philol. Assn. (editor trans. 1974-82), Classical Assn. Middle West and South, Classical Assn. (Gt. Britain). Home: 2 Grosvenor St London ON Canada N6A 1Y4 Office: U Western Ont Dept Classics London ON Canada N6A 3K7 E-mail: degerber@uwo.ca.

GERBER, EDWARD F. lawyer, educator; b. Houston, Oct. 10, 1932; s. Edward F. and Lucille (Beaver) G.; m. Eileen Healy, Sept. 1, 1956; children: Gretchen, Eric, Nils. BS, Syracuse U., 1957, LLB, 1960, JD, 1968. Bar: N.Y. 1960, U.S. Dist. Ct. (no. dist.) N.Y. 1960. Pvt. practice law, Syracuse, N.Y., 1960-64; first asst. dist. atty. Onondaga County, Syracuse, N.Y., 1964-67, spl. prosecutor, 1976; pvt. practice law Syracuse, N.Y., 1977—; ret. Lectr. Coll. of Law Syracuse U., 1968—; counsel Onondaga County Sheriff, 1978-94, N.Y. State Police Benevolent Assn., 1983—, N.Y. State Police Investigators Assn.; faculty Criminal Law Services Syracuse U. Trial Practice Sessions. Bd. dirs. Onandaga County Young Rep. Club, 1964-66. With USN, 1951-54. Named one of Best Lawyers in Am., 1989. Fellow Am. Coll. Trial Lawyers; mem. Upstate Trial Lawyers Assn. (pres. 1978-79), Onandaga County Bar Assn. (dir. 1969-71), Onandaga Bar Found. (pres. 1983). Home: 21 Drumlins Ter Syracuse NY 13224-2217 Office: 614 James St Ste 100 Syracuse NY 13203-2220 Fax: (315) 472-8299. E-mail: efgesq@yahoo.com.

GERBER, FRANCES JOYCE, early childhood educator; b. Bklyn. d. Albert E. and Stella Emsellem; m. Gary A. Gerber, June 10, 1962; children: Steven W., Stacy E. BS in Edn., U. Bridgeport, 1963, MS in Early Childhood Edn., 1986, Ed.D. Educational Leadership, 1999. Dir., head tchr. Saugatuck Nursery Sch., Westport, Conn., 1969—71; coord. Early Childhood Edn. Saugatuck Child Care Svc., Westport, 1972—76; dir., head tchr. Emmanuel Nursery Sch., Weston, Conn., 1979—84, Housatonic C.C., Bridgeport, Conn., 1985—90, coord. Early Childhood Edn., 1990—. Resource coord. Early Childhood Edn. Capitol Region Edn. Coun., Hartford, Conn., 1986—2000; prof. Early Childhood Edn. Housatonic C.C. Lab Sch., Bridgeport, 1997—; ednl. cons. Nursery Schs. and Headstart, Fairfield County, Conn., 1985—; v.p. Mid-Fairfield AEYC Chapt., 1992—93, pres., 1994—96. Named Woman of Substance, Conn. Post Newspaper, 2001; recipient Excellence in Tchg. award, Nat. Inst. for Staff and Orgn. Devel., 1992, 1998. Mem.: Assn. for Edn. Young Children, Conn. Assn. for Edn. Young Children (v.p. 1996—98, pres. 1994—96, v.p. 1992—93), Nat. Coun. for Profl. Recognition (coun. rep.), Nat. Assn. for Edn. Young Children (nat. validator), Mid-Fairfield AEYC Chapt., Phi Kappa Phi. Avocations: sailing, cooking, gardening, music, herbs. Home: 15 White Birch Ridge Weston CT 06883 Office: Housatonic Cmty Coll 900 Lafayette Blvd Bridgeport CT 06604*

GERBER, GWENDOLYN LORETTA, psychologist, educator; b. Calgary, Alta., Can. came to U.S., 1958; d. Ernest and Alma (Tesky) G. AB, UCLA, 1961, MA, 1964, PhD, 1967; cert. in psychoanalysis, NYU, 1970. Lic. psychologist, N.Y. Clin. psychologist Hillside Hosp., Glen Oaks, N.Y., 1970-73; asst. prof. psychology John Jay Coll. of Criminal Justice CUNY, N.Y.C., 1973-77, assoc. prof. psychology, 1977-90, prof., 1991—; pvt. practice in psychotherapy N.Y.C., 1970—. Contbr. chpts. to books and numerous articles to profl. jours. USPHS fellow, 1962-63, 66-67, NIMH fellow, 1967-69; CUNY grantee, 1989-92, 99-2000, 45 Found. grantee, 1991-96. Fellow: APA (bd. dirs. sect. III 1988—92, liaison divsn. 35 1989—, bd. dirs. sect. III 1994—95, bd. dirs. divsn. 39 1997—2004), N.Y. Acad. Scis. (chair psychology com. 1992—94); mem.: N.Y. State Psychol. Assn. (pres. acad. divsn. 1989—90, coun. rep. 1991—96, 2003—05, William Wundt award 1993, Disting. svc. award 1996, Kurt Lewin award 1999), Phi Beta Kappa, Psi Chi, Chi Delta Pi. Office: John Jay Coll CUNY 445 W 59th St New York NY 10019-1104

GERBER, JOEL, federal judge; b. Chgo., July 16, 1940; s. Peter H. and Marcia L. (Weber) G.; m. Judith R. Smilgoff, Aug. 18, 1963; children— Jay Lawrence, Jeffrey Mark, Jon Victor BSBA, Roosevelt U., Chgo., 1962; JD, DePaul U., Chgo., 1965; LL.M., Boston U., 1968. Bar: Ill. 1965, Ga. 1974. Trial atty. IRS, Boston, 1965-72, staff asst. to regional counsel Atlanta, 1972-76, dist. counsel Nashville, 1976-80, dep. chief counsel Washington, 1980-83, acting chief counsel, 1983-84; judge U.S. Tax Ct., Washington, 1984—; gen. counsel ATF Credit Union, Boston, 1968-70; lectr. Vanderbilt U. Sch. Law, Nashville, 1976-80. Lectr. U. Miami Grad. Law Sch., 1986-90. Recipient awards U.S. Treasury Dept., 1979, 81, 82; Presdl. Meritorious Exec. Rank award, 1983. Office: US Tax Ct 400 2nd St NW Rm 432 Washington DC 20217-0002

GERBER, LAWRENCE, lawyer; b. Chgo., Oct. 2, 1940; BBA, Loyola U. Chgo., 1962; JD, Northwestern U., 1965. CPA Ill.; bar: Ill. 1965. Ptnr. McDermott, Will & Emery, Chgo., mng. ptnr., 1991—. Author: Hospital Restructuring: Why, When and How, 1983. Mem.: Ill. Assn. Hosp. Attys., Am. Acad. Hosp. Attys. Office: McDermott Will & Emery 227 W Monroe St Ste 4400 Chicago IL 60606-5096

GERBER, MICHAEL ALLEN, pediatrician; b. Chgo., Jan. 13, 1948; s. Robert and Shirley Gerber; m. Rita Estrin, May 25, 1974; children: Andrew, Rachel. AB, Cornell U., 1970; MD, Yale U., 1974. Diplomate Am. Bd. Pediatrics, Am. Bd. Pediatric Infectious Diseases. Intern in pediats. U. Wis. Hosp., Madison, 1974-75; resident in pediats. U. Rochester, N.Y., 1975-77; fellow in pediatric infectious diseases U. Minn., Mpls., 1977-79; mem. faculty U. Conn. Sch. Medicine, Farmington, 1979-98; med. officer NIH, Bethesda, 1998-2001; mem. faculty Children's Hosp. Med. Ctr. Cin., 2001—. Office: Childrens Hosp Med Ctr Div Infectious Diseases 3333 Burnet Ave Cincinnati OH 45229 E-mail: michael.gerber@chmcc.org.

GERBER, MICHAEL LEWIS, cardiac surgeon; b. Pitts., Mar. 25, 1938; s. Max H. and Fay F. Gerber; m. Barbara Schulman, Feb. 23, 1963; children: Michael L., Laurel E., Andrew D. BS, U. Pitts., 1959, MD, 1963, JD, 1990; LLM, Georgetown U., 1992. Diplomate Am. Bd. Surgery, Am. Bd. Thoracic Surgery. Intern Ind. U. Med. Ctr., 1963-64; resident U. Pitts. Med. Ctr., 1964-68, Allegheny Gen. Hosp., 1968-69; resident in plastic surgery Eastern Va. Med. Coll., 1993-94, U. Mass. Med. Ctr., Worcester, 1994-95; clin. instr. surgery U. Pitts. With USAR, 1963-69. Mem. ACS, Soc. Thoracic Surgeons, AMA, Am. Coll. Chest Physicians, Pan-Pacific Surg. Assn., Am. Heart Assn., Am. Assn. for Thoracic Surgery, Pitts. Thoracic Surg. Soc. (past pres.). Republican. Home: 1535 El Paso Real La Jolla CA 92037-6303 E-mail: mlgerber@san.rr.com.

GERBER, NATALIE ELLEN, editor; m. Rob Lash, Feb. 22, 1998. PhD, U. Calif., Berkeley, 2002. Asst. festival dir. Geraldine R. Dodge Poetry Festivals, Morristown, NJ, 1994—2000; asst. to U.S. poet laureate Robert Hass Berkeley, Calif., 1995—97; asst. to Czeslaw Milosz, 1999—2000; editl. assoc. Barnes & Noble U., N.Y.C., 2002—. Co-founding dir. Lunch Poems Reading Series, Berkeley, 1996—2000. Recipient Ruth R. Lily Poetry prize, Boston U., 1991, NY Dance Critics' Cir. award, N.Y. Dance Critics Cir., 1993; fellow, U. Calif. Chancellor's Office, Berkeley, 2000—01. Mem.: MLA.

GERBER, ROBERT EVAN, judge; b. N.Y.C., Feb. 12, 1947; s. Milton M. and Miriam (Simon) G. BS with high honors, Rutgers U., 1967; JD magna cum laude, Columbia U., 1970. Bar: N.Y. 1971, U.S. Dist. Ct. (so. and ea. dists.) N.Y. 1972, U.S. Ct. Appeals (2d cir.) 1973, U.S. Ct. Appeals (9th cir.) 1974, U.S. Ct. Appeals (10th cir.) 1975, U.S. Ct. Appeals (11th cir.) 1983, U.S. Supreme Ct. 1983, U.S. Ct. Appeals (5th cir.) 1987, U.S. Ct. Appeals (6th cir.) 1989, U.S. Ct. Appeals (3d cir.) 1997. Assoc. Fried, Frank, Harris, Shriver & Jacobson, N.Y.C., 1970-71, 72-78, ptnr., 1978-2000; judge U.S. Bankruptcy Ct. (so. dist.) N.Y., N.Y.C., 2000—. Served to 1st lt. USAF, 1971-72. James Kent scholar, 1970, Harlan Fiske Stone scholar, 1969. Mem. ABA, Assn. Bar City N.Y. (sec. spl. com. on energy 1974-79), Fed. Bar Coun., Am. Bankruptcy Inst., Tau Beta Pi. Office: US Bankruptcy Ct US Custom House One Bowling Green New York NY 10004

GERBER, ROGER ALAN, lawyer, business consultant; b. Bklyn., Jan. 27, 1939; s. Edward and Anne (Rothstein) G.; m. Jane E. Satlow, Sept. 20, 1964; children: Dina Huebner, Deborah Tor, Tamar Gerber. BA magna cum laude (Rufus Choate scholar), Dartmouth Coll., 1959; JD, Harvard U., 1962. Bar: N.Y. 1963. Real estate atty. ABC, Inc., 1965-68; assoc. Kaye, Scholer, Fierman, Hays & Handler, other law firms, 1968-75; v.p., gen. counsel ISS Internat. Service System, Inc., N.Y.C., 1975-83; v.p., sec., gen. counsel Meyers Parking System, Inc., N.Y.C., 1975-89, sr. exec. v.p., chief oper. officer, 1989-95, also bd. dirs., 1981-91; pres. Meyers Realty Co., N.Y.C., 1982-95. Arbitrator Am. Arbitration Assn., 1973—; bd. dirs. Nat. Parking Assn., 1991-92; mem. adv. bd. Mid. East Forum, 1995—; bd. dirs. Jewish Inst. for Nat. Security Affairs, 1995—. Treas. Scarsdale (N.Y.) Democratic Com., 1977-83; v.p., exec. com. Bd. Jewish Edn., Greater N.Y., 1977—; bd. trustees PEF-Israel Endowment Fund, 1997—; bd. dirs. Conf. Jewish Social Studies, 1975-93, Jewish Conciliation Bd., N.Y.; class agt. Dartmouth Coll. Mem. N.Y. State Bar Assn., Phi Beta Kappa. Clubs: Harvard (N.Y.C.). Home: 26 Sage Ter Scarsdale NY 10583-2045 E-mail: RG26@aol.com.

GERBER, RUDOLPH JOSEPH, lawyer, educator; b. St. Louis, Oct. 25, 1938; s. Rudolph Vogt and Isable Helen (Bauer) G.; children: Jennifer, Kristin, Joseph. MA in Comparative Lit., Columbia U., N.Y.C., 1964; PhD with grand

distinction, U. Louvain, Belgium, 1966; JD, Notre Dame U., 1971; LLM, U. Va., 1986; Anglo-Am. law cert., Cambridge (Eng.) U., 1992, Oxford (Eng.) U., 1994. Bar: Ariz. 1972, Calif. 1987. Asst. prof. philosophy St. Louis U., 1966-67, U. Notre Dame, Ind., 1967-71; legal counsel bd. suprs. County of Maricopa, Phoenix, 1972-74, pub. defender, 1972-76, atty., 1976-79, judge superior ct., 1979—, assoc. chief presiding judge, 1985-88; judge Ariz. Ct. Appeals, Phoenix, 1988—2001; assoc. Shugart, Thomson, Kilroy, Goodwin Raup, 2001—. Prof. Western Internat. U., 1983-2000; law and justice prof. Ariz. State U., Tempe, 2001--; legal editor Kennikat Press, N.Y.C., 1985-88; del. Nat. Conf. State Cts.; mem. faculty Nat. Jud. Coll. Author: Contemporary Punishment, 1972, Contemporary Issues in Criminal Justice, 1976, Criminal Law of Arizona, 1979, 2d edit., 1993, The Insanity Defense, 1984, Lawyers, Courts and Corrections, 1989, The Grand Canyon Railroad, 1990, 2d edit., 1994; contbr. articles to profl. jours. mem. editl. bd. Am. Jour. Jurisprudence. Minority counsel Ariz. Senate, Phoenix, 1977-78. Fulbright fellow, Belgium, 1964-66. Mem. Ariz. Bar Assn., Calif. Bar Assn. Democrat. Roman Catholic. Avocations: swimming, hiking, skiing, gardening, tennis. Home: 15807 N 15th Way Phoenix AZ 85022-3250 Office: Ariz Ct Appeals State Capital Phoenix AZ 85007 also: Sugart Thomson et al 3636 N Central #1200 Phoenix AZ 85012 E-mail: RudyJGerber@aol.com.

GERBER, WILLIAM NORMAN, motion picture executive; b. Las Vegas, Apr. 30, 1957; s. Roy Herbert and Constance Doris Gerber. West coast dir. Nemporer Records, L.A., 1978—79; exec. v.p. Lookout Mgmt., L.A., 1979—84; prin. owner Gerber/Rodkin Co., L.A., 1985—86; v.p. theatrical prodn. divsn. Warner Bros., Inc., Burbank, Calif., 1986—98, co-pres. worldwide theatrical prodn., 1998; prodr. Gerber Pictures, 1998—. Office: Gerber Pictures 9465 Wilshire Blvd Beverly Hills CA 90212-2612 Fax: 310-385-5881.

GERBERDING, JULIE LOUISE, federal agency administrator; BA in chemistry and biology, MD, Case Western Reserve U., Cleve.; MPH, U. Calif., Berkeley, 1990. Intern and resident in internal medicine U. Calif., San Francisco, fellow in clin. pharmacology and infectious diseases; acting deputy dir. Nat. Ctr. for Infectious Diseases; assoc. clin. prof. medicine Emory U.; assoc. prof. medicine, epidemiology and biostatistics U. Calif., San Francisco; dir., divsn. healthcare quality promotion CDC, dir., 2002—. Dir., Prevention Epicenter U. Calif., San Francisco; mem., bd. scientific counselors CDC, mem., HIV adv. com., mem., scientific program com.; mem. Nat. Conf. Human Retroviruses; cons. NIH, AMA, Occupational Safety and Health Adminstrn., Nat. AIDS Commn., U.S. Congress, and WHO. Edtl. bd. Annals of Internal Medicine, assoc. editor Am. Jour. Medicine, contbr. to profl. publs. and textbooks. Fellow: Infectious Diseases Soc. Am. (chair and co-chair com. profl. devel. and diversity, mem. nominations com., co-chair. annual program com.); mem.: Soc. for Healthcare Epidemiology Am. (mem. AIDS/Tuberculosis com., bd. acad. counselor), Am. Soc. Clin. Investigation, Alpha Omega Alpha, Phi Beta Kappa. Office: 1600 Clifton Rd NE 214 Atlanta GA 30333*

GERBERDING, MILES CARSTON, lawyer; b. Decatur, Ind, Oct. 25, 1930; s. Arnold H. and Luella E. (Lapp) G.; m. Ruth H. Hostrup, Aug. 20, 1955 (dec. Mar. 1992); children: Karla M. Smith, Greta E. Cowart, Kent E., Brian K.; m. Joan W. Fackler, Jan. 2, 1993; stepchildren: Stephen W. Fackler, Deborah E. Holbrook. BS, Ind. U., 1954, JD, 1956. Bar: Ind. 1956, US Dist. Ct. (so. and no. dists.) Ind. 1956, Mich. 1984. Ptnr. Nieter & Smith, Ft. Wayne, Ind., 1956-58, Barrett, Barrett & McNagny, Ft. Wayne, 1958-85, Barnes & Thornburg, Ft. Wayne, 1985-97; pvt. practice Frankfort, Mich., 1998—. Lectr., writer Ind. Continuing Legal Edn. Forum. Contbr. articles to profl. jour. Pres. Luth. Assn. Elem. Edn., 1968-69; vice chmn., mem. Ind. Supreme Ct. Commn. on Continuing Legal Edn., sec.; bd. dirs. Big Bros., Ft. Wayne, Jr. Achievement, Ft. Wayne, United Way Allen County; pres. Concordia Ednl. Found., Greater Ft. Wayne C. of C. Found.; chmn. bd. visitors Ind. U. Sch. Law, Bloomington, 1984-85, mem. 1979-94; vice chmn. United Way of Allen County Campaign, 1990-92, chmn., 1992-93, dir., 1992-98; trustee Boys and Girls Club Ft. Wayne; sec. Willoughby Rotary Found., 1999—. With USMC, 1950-52. Decorated UN medal, Korean Svc. medal with star; recipient Christus Magister award Luth. Edn. Assn., 1971, Disting Svc. award Ind. U. Sch. Law, 1999; named Grad. of Yr., Concordia Alumni Assn., 1993. Fellow: Mich. Bar Found., Ind. Bar Found. (dir.), Am. Coll. Trust and Estate Counsel, Am. Coll. Tax Counsel, Am. Bar Found.; mem.: VFW, ABA (rep. Nat. Conf. Lawyers and CPAs 1980—86, nominating com., ho. dels. credentials com., chmn. Ind. del. 1985—94, ho. dels. mem. com., vice-chmn. com. on state and local bars-sr. lawyers divsn., med. profl. liability com., coordinating com. on outreach, marital deduction com. taxation sect., standing com. on bar svc., com. on pub. understanding about law), Korean War Vets. Assn., Nat. Conf. Bar Pres. (exec. coun. 1983—86), Ind. CLE Forum (pres. 1978—79), Am. Judicature Soc., Allen County Bar Found. (former bd. dir., sec.), Lawyer-Pilot Bar Assn., Allen County Bar Assn. (dir.), Benzie County Bar Assn. (pres. 1999—2000), State Bar Mich. (treas. Sr. Lawyers 1999—2000, chmn.-elect 2000—01, chmn. 2001—02, com. on mandatory CLE, com. on quality profl. life), Ind. Bar Assn. (pres. 1979—80, del. ABA 1979—94), Am. Legion, Benzie Area Hist. Soc. (dir.), TerraLex (former co-vice chmn. N.Am., dir. 1993—96), Frankfort Rotary Club, Arcadia Lions Club. Republican. Lutheran. Home: 17726 N Ridgewood PO Box 6 Arcadia MI 49613-0006 Office: PO Box 272 Frankfort MI 49635-0272 also: PO Box 118 Arcadia MI 49613-0118 E-mail: mcgerb@bignetnorth.net.

GERBERDING, WILLIAM PASSAVANT, retired university president; b. Fargo, N.D., Sept. 9, 1929; s. William Passavant and Esther Elizabeth Ann (Habighorst) G.; m. Ruth Alice Albrecht, Mar. 25, 1952; children: David Michael, Steven Henry, Elizabeth Ann, John Martin. BA, Macalester Coll., 1951; MA, U. Chgo., 1956, PhD, 1959. Congl. fellow Am. Polit. Sci. Assn., Washington, 1958-59; instr. Colgate U., Hamilton, N.Y., 1959-60; research asst. Senator E.J. McCarthy, Washington, 1960-61; staff Rep. Frank Thompson, Jr., Washington, 1961; faculty UCLA, 1961-72, prof., chmn. dept. polit. sci., 1970-72; dean faculty, v.p. for acad. affairs Occidental Coll., Los Angeles, 1972-75; exec. vice chancellor UCLA, 1975-77; chancellor U. Ill., Urbana-Champaign, 1978-79; pres. U. Wash., Seattle, 1979-95. Cons. Dept. Def., 1962, Calif. Assembly, 1965. Author: United States Foreign Policy: Perspectives and Analysis, 1966; co-editor, contbg. author: The Radical Left: The Abuse of Discontent, 1970. Trustee Macalester Coll., 1980—83, 1996—2001, Gates Cambridge Trust, U. Cambridge, England, 2000—. With USN, 1951—55. Recipient Distinguished Teaching award U. Calif., Los Angeles, 1966; Ford Found. grantee, 1967-68 Office: Univ Wash PO Box 352800 Seattle WA 98195-2800

GERBERDING COWART, GRETA ELAINE, lawyer; b. Ft. Wayne, Ind., Aug. 17, 1960; d.Ruth (Hostrup) G., stepmother Joanie Wyatt Gerberding; m. T. David Cowart, Aug. 12, 1995. BS with high distinction, Ind. U., 1982; JD cum laude, 1985. Bar: Ind. 1985, U.S. Dist. Ct. (so. dist.) Ind., CPA, Ind., CEBS. Sr. tax cons. Ernst & Whinney, Indpls., 1985-87; assoc. Klineman, Rose, Wolf and Wallack P.C., Indpls., 1987-89, Hall Render Killian Heath & Lyman P.C., Indpls., 1989-95; ptnr. Haynes and Boone, L.L.P., Dallas, 1996—. Presenter at seminars. Author: (with G.P. Gooch) Trust and Estate Income Tax Reporting and Planning, 1985; contbr. chpt. to books, articles to profl. jour. including Jour. Deferred Compensation, 403(b) Answer Book, Benefits Law Jour. Chmn. hospitality area Virginia Slims Tennis Tournament, Indpls., 1987-89; vol. Jello Tennis Classic Tennis Tournament, Indpls., 1990-91; coord. Hospitality and Ball Kids, 1990, Jr. Jamboree GTE Tennis Tournament, Indpls., 1990; vol. Ctr. for Exploration The Children's Mus., Indpls., 1991-94; com. on funding Vision 2002 Luth. Camp Assn., Inc., 1993-94; bd. dir., 1997—, chmn., 2001, Arcadia Found.; women's retreat com. King of Glory Luth. Ch., 1997—, fin. com., 2000—; bd. dir. Brianwood Retreat Ctr., 1998-2001. Glen Peters fellow Ind. U., 1984. Fellow Ind. Bar Found.; mem. ABA (com. marital deduction legis. real property and probate sect. 1986-87, tax section, gen. income tax com. 1987-89, employee benefits com. 1988—, subcom. health plan design and state regulation 1993—, health care task force 1994—, chmn. COBRA subcom. 1997-2002, vice chair employee benefits com. 2002—), Ind. Bar Assn. (acct.-lawyers com. 1986-89, co-chmn. com. on legis. 1988-92, coun. tax sect. 1988-96, sec.-treas. 1991-92, vice-chmn. tax sect. 1992-93, chair elect 1993-94, chair 1994-95), Indpls. Bar Assn., Indpls. Jaycees (treas. 4th Festival 1987 monthly dinner meetings 1988), West Indy Racquet Club (USTA Volvo Tennis Team 1986-87, RCA tounament credentials com. 1993-94), Indpls. Racquet Club (USTA Volvo tennis team 1988-91, 96). Avocations: tennis, golf, skiing, swimming, artwork. Office: Haynes and Boone LLP 901 Main St Ste 3100 Dallas TX 75202-3789

GERBERG, JUDITH LEVINE, human resource company executive; b. NYC, Mar. 21, 1940; d. Murray Joseph and Pearl (Berens) Levine; 1 child, Lilia Anya Berens. BS in Comparative Lit., Columbia U., 1963, postgrad. in organizational devel., 1989; MA in Psychology and Art, NYU. Registered art therapist; cert. clin. mental health counselor; nat. cert. counselor, career mgmt. profl. Program dir. Women's Selling Game, N.Y.C., 1979-84; mem. faculty Parsons Sch. Design, N.Y.C., 1979-85; pres. Gerberg & Co., N.Y.C., 1984—. Orgnl. devel. mgmt., leadership devel., valuing diversity, team bldg., comm. skills, stress mgmt.; founder Powerhouse, 1st outplacement for creative profls.; mem. N.Y. steering com. Women's Study in Religion Program Harvard Div. Sch.; pres. Career Counselors Consortium, 2000--. Co-author: The New York Women's Directory, 1973; contbr. articles and book revs. to various publ. Chmn. pub. rels. Profl. Women's Caucus, 1972; facilitator NYC Contr.'s Women's Econ. Task Force, 1994-95; mem. Harvard Divinity Sch.: Women in Religion Leadership Conf. NY State scholar. Mem. Am. Art Therapy Assn. (life, bd. dir. 1980-84), NY Art Therapy Assn. (founding v.p. 1975), The Forum at Stephen Wise (co-chmn. 1986-87), Fin. Women's Assn., Women's Venture Fund., Internat. Assn. Career Mgmt. Profl. (co-chair future focus com.), Career Counselors Consortium (pres. 2000-). Office: 250 W 57th St Ste 2315 New York NY 10107-2315 Fax: 212-315-2324. E-mail: gerbeg@gerberg.com.

GERBERICH, SUSAN GOODWIN, epidemiologist, educator; b. Cortland, N.Y. d. Arthur George and Elizabeth Pratt Goodwin; m. William Warren Gerberich; children: Bradley Kent, Brian Keith, Beth Clarice. BS summa cum laude, U. Minn., 1975, MS, 1978, PhD, 1980. Prof. U. Minn., Mpls., 1983—; dir. Regional Injury Prevention Rsch. Ctr., Mpls., 1987—, Ctr. for Violence Prevention and Control, Mpls., 1994—. Pres. Gerberich, Inc., Shorewood, Minn., 1985—; cons. Injury Prevention/Epidemiology, 1985—; cons. Nat. Inst. for Occupl. Safety and Health and Ctrs. for Disease Control. Contbr. articles to profl. jours. Trauma adv. com. Minn. Dept. of Health, Mpls., 1999—, mem. Brain and Spinal Cord adv. com., 1993—. Named to Blue Ribbon Panel Nat. Inst. for Occpl. Safety and Health, Washington, 1990-93, 96, Ctr. for Disease Control, Atlanta, 1986-91. Mem. APHA (gov. coun. 1994-96,98-2003), Injury Control and Emergency Health Svcs., Soc. for Epidemiol. Rsch. Avocations: tennis, golf, sailing, rollerblading. Office: EOH/SPH/U Minn/MMC 807 420 Delaware St SE Rm 1156 Minneapolis MN 55455-0374 E-mail: gerbe001@umn.edu.

GERBIE, ALBERT BERNARD, obstetrician, gynecologist, educator; b. Toledo, Nov. 20, 1927; s. Louis and Fay (Green) G.; m. Barbara Hirsch, June 29, 1952; children: Gail Diane, Stephen Ralph. MD, George Washington U., 1951. Intern Michael Reese Hosp., Chgo., 1951-52; preceptorship in Ob-Gyn under Drs. R.A. Reis, J.L. Baer, E.J. DeCosta, Chgo., 1952-55; practice medicine specializing in Ob-Gyn Chgo., 1955—; mem. faculty Northwestern U. Med. Sch., Chgo., 1952—, prof. Ob-Gyn, 1972—, dir. continuing grad. edn., 1975—. Mem. staff Northwestern Meml. Hosp., 1955—; chief divsn. ob-gyn. Children's Meml. Hosp.; v.p., dir. Am. Bd. Ob-Gyn, 1976—, chmn. 1988—, pres. 1990, historian, 1998; chmn. liaison com. for ob-gyn., 1989; rep. Am. Bd. Med. Specialties; bd. dirs. Chgo. Maternity Ctr. Author textbooks; assoc. editor Surgery, Gynecology, and Obstetrics, Am. Jour. Ob-Gyn.; editor ACOG Current Jour. Rev.; contbr. chpts. to books, articles to profl. jours. Served with U.S. Army, 1946-47. Mem. ACS (bd. govs.), ACOG (chmn. learning resources commn.), AMA, Am. Gynecol. Soc., Am. Assn. Obstetricians and Gynecologists, Am. Gynecol. and Obstet. Soc., Am. Bd. Med. Specialties, Am. Coll. Sports Medicine, Ctrl. Assn. Ob-Gyn, Soc. Human Genetics, Southwestern Ob-Gyn. Soc., Chgo. Gynecol. Assn. (pres. 1977-78), Skokie Valley Figure Skating Club, (pres. 2003). Office: Ste 900 251 E Huron St Chicago IL 60611-4814

GERBNER, GEORGE, communications educator, university dean emeritus; b. Budapest, Hungary, Aug. 8, 1919; came to U.S., 1939, naturalized, 1944; s. Arpad and Margaret (Muranyi) G.; m. Ilona Kutas, Oct. 8, 1946; children: John C., Thomas J. Student, U. Budapest, 1937-38, UCLA, 1940-41; BA, U. Calif.-Berkeley, 1943; MS, U. So. Calif., 1951, PhD, 1955; LHD (hon.), LaSalle Coll., Phila., 1980, Emerson Coll., 1989, Worcester State Coll., 1992. Reporter, asst. fin. editor The Chronicle, San Francisco, 1942-43; engaged in free-lance publicity, 1947-48; instr. Pasadena (Calif.) Jr. Coll., 1948-51, El Camino Coll., Los Angeles, 1951-56; asst. prof., then assoc. prof. U. Ill., Urbana, 1956-64; prof. communications Annenberg Sch. Communications, U. Pa., 1964—, dean, 1964-89, dean emeritus, 1989—; Bell Atlantic Prof. of Telecomms. Temple U., Phila. Founder, dir. Cultural Indicators Project, 1968—; founder, pres. Cultural Environment Movement, 1993—; vis. prof. Temple U., Phila., 1997—, U. Budapest, 1993, Salesian U., Rome, 1992; Disting. vis. prof. Am. U., Washington, 1995, 96; vis. lectr. U. Athens, 1996, Am. U., 1995-96, Temple U., 1997, Villanova U., 1997-2000. Author numerous articles and books in field.; editor Jour. of Communication, 1974-91; chmn. editorial bd. Internat. Ency. of Communications. 1st lt. inf., AUS, 1943-46, ETO. Decorated Bronze Star; grantee U.S. Office Edn., 1959, NSF, 1962, 80, 83, NIMH, 1958, 71-82, Internat. Sociol. Assn., 1963, UNESCO, 1963, 83, 85, Nat. Commn. Causes and Prevention Violence, 1969, Surgeon Gen.'s Sci. Adv. Com., 1970, White House Office Telecomm. Policy, 1977, U.S. Adminstrn. on Aging, 1978, AMA, 1979, Com. on Religious Rsch., 1983, Nat. Inst. Drug Abuse, 1985-86, W. Alton Jones Found., 1987-88, Hoso Bunka (Japan) Found., 1990-91, U.S. Commn. on Civil Rights, 1991, Nat. Cable TV Assn., 1992, SAG, AFTRA, 1992-93, Turner Broadcasting Sys., 1993, AARP, 1994, Ark. Trust, 1994, Ctr. for Substance Abuse Prevention, 1994, Robert Wood Johnson Found., 1995-97, Sloan Found., 1997, SAG, 1999-2001; recipient Excellence in Media award Internat. TV Assn., 1992. Fellow Internat. Communication Assn.; mem. Am. Sociol. Assn., Internat. Assn. Mass Communication Research (hon. life), Assn. Edn. Journalism (Paul J. Deutschman award for excellence in rsch. 1996). Home: 234 Golfview Rd Ardmore PA 19003-1002 E-mail: ggerbner@comcast.net. *Here's to the success of our hopeless endeavor.*

GERDE, CARLYLE NOYES (CY GERDE), lawyer; b. Long Beach, Calif., Oct. 22, 1946; m. Priscilla A. Murphy, July 4, 1976. BA in Am. Studies, Purdue U., 1967; JD, Ind. U., 1970. Bar: Ind. 1971, U.S. Supreme Ct. 1976, U.S. Tax Ct. 1980. Ptnr. Hanna Gerde & Russell; Lafayette, Ind., 1972-86; registered lobbyist Ind. Twp. Assn., 1975-86; spl. counsel Nat. Assn. Towns and Twps., Washington, 1976-86. Adj. prof. indsl. engring. Purdue U., 1972-96; participant White House Conf. Rural Policy, 1978, White House Conf. on Block Grants, 1981, White House Conf. on Liability Ins., 1986; mem. Ind. Gen. Assembly Study Commn. Bd. of govs. Tippecanoe County Hist. Assn., Lafayette, 1976-00, Ams. for Nuclear Energy, Washington (co-founder, v.p. 1977-00); pres. Battle Ground (Ind.) Hist. Corp., 1986; del. State of Ind. GOP Conventions. Mem. Ind. State Bar Assn., Tippecanoe County Bar Assn., Nat. Assn. Town and Twp. Attys. (co-founder, v.p. 1985-88), Am. Agrl. Lawyers Assn., Lafayette Country Club, Skyline Club, Columbia Club. Office: Hanna & Gerde PO Box 1098 Lafayette IN 47902-1098 E-mail: gerde@hannagerde.com.

GERDEMANN, JAMES WESSEL, plant pathologist, educator; b. Warrenton, Mo., Nov. 13, 1921; s. Carl Edward and Cora Wilhelmina (Wessel) G.; m. Janice Mae Olbrich, July 2, 1949; children— Stephen, Dale, Glenn. BA, U. Mo., 1945, MA, 1946; PhD, U. Calif., Berkeley, 1948. Teaching asst. U. Mo., Columbia, 1945-46; research asst. U. Calif., Berkeley, 1946-48; prof. plant pathology U. Ill., Urbana, 1948-81, prof. emeritus, 1981—. Author: Taxonomy of the Endogonaceae, 1974; condr. research in field; contbr. writings to publs. Recipient Ruth Allen award, 1977, Funk award, 1977, excellence in undergrad. teaching award U. Ill., 1976 Fellow Am. Phytopathol. Soc.; mem. Am. Mycol. Soc. Home: PO Box 391 Yachats OR 97498-0391

GERDES, DAVID ALAN, lawyer; b. Aberdeen, S.D., Aug. 10, 1942; s. Cyril Fredrick and Lorraine Mary (Boyle) G.; m. Karen Ann Hassinger, Aug. 3, 1968; children: Amy Renee, James David. BS, No. State Coll., Aberdeen, 1965; JD cum laude, U. S.D., 1968. Bar: S.D. 1968, U.S. Dist. Ct. S.D., 1968, U.S. Ct. Appeals (8th cir.) 1973, U.S. Supreme Ct. 1973. Assoc. Martens, Goldsmith, May, Porter & Adam, Pierre, S.D., 1968-73; ptnr. successor firm May, Adam, Gerdes & Thompson, Pierre, 1973—. Chmn. disciplinary bd. S.D. Bar, 1980-81, mem. fed. practice com. U.S. Dist. Ct., S.D., 1986-91, 94—; mem. fed. adv. com. U.S. Ct. Appeals (8th cir.), 1989-93; bd. dirs. U.S.D. Law Sch. Found., 1973-84, pres., 1979-84. Mng. editor U. S.D. Law Rev., 1967—68; author: Physician's Guide to South Dakota Law, 1982. Chmn. Hughes County Rep. Ctrl. Com., 1979-81; del. Rep. State Conv., co-chair platform com., 1988, 90; state ctrl. committeeman, 1985-91. Served to lt. Signal Corps, AUS, 1965-68. Mem. ABA, Nat. Coun. Bar Pres., Internat. Assn. Def. Counsel, Assn. Def. Trial Attys., Am. Judicature Soc., Am. Bd. Trial Advocates, State Bar S.D. (chmn. professionalism com. 1989-90, pres. 1992-93), Pierre Area C. of C. (pres. 1980-81), S.D. C. of C. (bd. dirs. 1998—), Lawyer-Pilots Bar Assn., Def. Rsch. Inst., Am. Soc. Med. Assn. Counsel, Kiwanis, Elks. Republican. Methodist. Office: May Adam Gerdes & Thompson PO Box 160 503 S Pierre St Pierre SD 57501-0160

GERDES, MICHELLE ANN, designer; b. Trenton, N.J., Sept. 23, 1961; d. Paul and Kathryn (Sinchock) Kaniuka; m. Christopher John Gerdes, Apr. 5, 1986; children: Andrew Paul, Alexander Robert. BA magna cum laude, Kean Coll. N.J., 1983. Asst. art dir. Medecommunications (divsn. Med. Econs. Co.), Oradell, N.J., 1983-84; sr. designer mag. Med. Econs. Co., Oradell, 1984-85, asst. art dir. mag., 1985-86; asst. art dir. Butterfly Originals, Mt. Laurel, N.J., 1986-87; design coord. J.B. Lippincott Co., Phila., 1987-88; asst. art dir. TV Guide, Radnor, Pa., 1988-91; freelance art dir. Sewell, N.J., 1991-92; advt. designer Current Science, Phila., 1992-95; freelance art director, designer Norristown, Pa., 1995-96; asst. art dir. Lapidary Jour. Primedia, Inc., Devon, Pa., 1996—. Recipient Cert. of Excellence award Art Dirs. Club of N.J., 1986, Merit award, 1987. Roman Catholic. Avocations: travel, photography, crafts, exercise training. Home and Office: 2816 Breckenridge Blvd Norristown PA 19403-1200

GERDES, NEIL WAYNE, library director, educator; b. Moline, Ill., Oct. 19, 1943; s. John Edward and Della Marie (Ferguson) G. AB, U. Ill., 1965; BD, Harvard U., 1968; MA, Columbia U., 1971; MA in Libr. Sci., U. Chgo., 1975; DMin, U. St. Mary of the Lake, 1994. Ordained to ministry Unitarian Universalist Assn., 1975. Copy chief Little, Brown, 1968-69; instr. Tuskegee Inst., 1969-71; libr. asst. Augustana Coll., 1972-73; editl. asst. Library Quar., 1973-74; libr., prof. Meadville Theol. Sch., Chgo., 1973—; libr. program dir. Chgo. Cluster Theol. Schs., 1977-80; dir. Hammond Libr., 1980—; prof. Chgo. Theol Sem., 1980—. Affiliated minister 1st Unitarian Church, Chgo., 2002—. Mem. exec. bd. Sem. Coop. Bookstore, Chgo., 1982-2002, Ctr. for Religion and Psychotherapy, Chgo., 1984-97, Ind. Voters of Ill., 1986-89, Hyde Park-Kenwood Cmty. Orgn., Chgo., 1988-89; pres. Hyde Park-Kenwood Interfaith Coun., 1986-90, Inst. for Spiritual Leadership, 2000—; chair libr. coun. Assn. Chgo. Theol. Sch., 1984-88, 96-98; trustee Civitas Dei Found., 1994—; mem. alumni coun. Harvard Divinity Sch., 1999—, sec., 2001—. Mem. ALA, Am. Theol. Library Assn., Chgo. Area Theol. Library Assn., Unitarian Universalist Mins. Assn. (sec., treas. nat. body 1990-94), Assn. Liberal Religious Scholars (sec., treas. 1975—), Phi Beta Kappa Office: Chgo Theol Sem Hammond Libr 5757 S University Ave Chicago IL 60637-1507

GERDES, RALPH DONALD, fire safety consultant; b. Cin., Aug. 11, 1951; s. Paul Donald and Jo Ann Dorothy (Meyer) G. BArch, Ill. Inst. Tech., 1975. Registered architect, Ill. Architect Schiller & Frank, Wheeling, Ill., 1976; sr. assoc. Rolf Jensen & Assocs., Inc., Chgo., 1976-84; pres. Ralph Gerdes & Assocs., Inc., Indpls., 1984-88, chmn., 1988—; gen. mgr. Ralph Gerdes Cons., LLC. Lectr. Purdue U., Ind. U., Ill. Inst. Tech., Butler U., Ball State U.; bd. dirs. Ind. Fire Svcs. Inst. Co-author: Planning and Designing the Office Environment, 1981. Recipient Joel Polsky prize Am. Soc. Interior Designers, 1983. Mem.: AIA (bldg. performance and regulations com., liaison to Nat. Fire Protection Agy., liaison to Internat. Code Coun.), ASHRAE, Archs. and Engrs. Bldg. Ofcls. (bd. dirs. 1994—, Ind. code devel. com.), Ind. Fire Safety Assn. (bd. dirs. 1986—92, 1994—95, pres. 1989—91), Internat. Code Coun., Nat. Fire Protection Assn. (tech. coms.), Soc. Fire Protection Engring. (assoc.; exec. com. Ind. chpt. 1992—, pres. 1995—96), Indpls. Soc., Maple Creek Country Club. Roman Catholic. Home: 556 Lockerbie Cir N Indianapolis IN 46202-3600 Office: 5510 S East St Ste E Indianapolis IN 46227

GERDING, THOMAS GRAHAM, medical products company executive; b. Evanston, Ill., Feb. 11, 1930; s. Louis Henry and Helen Frances (Graham) G.; m. Beverly Ann Starnes, June 18, 1955; children: Mark, David, Gail, Gene Ann. Student, U. Notre Dame, 1948-49; BS in Pharmacy, Purdue U., 1952, MS, 1954, PhD, 1960, D (hon.), 2002. From instr. to asst. prof. Purdue U., West Lafayette, Ind., 1956-61; dir. product devel. Pitman-Moore divsn. Dow Chem., Indpls., 1962-64; tech. dir. new products Glenbrook Labs., N.Y.C., 1964-66; dir. product devel. Sterling-Winthrop Rsch. Inst., Rensselaer, N.Y., 1966-70; v.p. rsch. and devel. Calgon Consumer Products, Rahway, N.J., 1970-77; v.p., dir. rsch. and devel., quality assurance, consumer affairs, engring. Johnson & Johnson Products Inc., New Brunswick, N.J., 1977-88; pres. Thomas G. Gerding, Inc., Georgetown, Tex., 1988-96; dir. Drug Dynamics Inst. U. Tex., Austin, 1988-95; pres. Newform Devel. Labs., Inc., Georgetown, Tex., 1993—. Deans adv. coun. Purdue U. Sch. Pharmacy, 1996—2001, U. Tex. Coll. Pharmacy, 2002—. Sgt. U.S. Army Med. Svc. Corp, 1954-56. Recipient Disting. Alumni award, Purdue U., 1984, Best Friend award, U. Tex., 2002. Mem.: Am. Assn. Pharm. Scientists, Am. Chem. Soc., U. Tex. Club, Berry Creek Country Club, Union League Club (Chgo.). Republican. Achievements include research in pharmaceutics, wound care and unique drug delivery systems; 6 patents. Home: 340 Shell Spur Georgetown TX 78628 Office: Newform Devel Labs Inc PO Box 52 Georgetown TX 78627-0052

GERDNER, LINDA ANN, nursing researcher, educator; b. Burlington, Iowa, Sept. 17, 1955; d. Richard Paul and Edna Marie Gerdner. AA, Southeastern C.C., 1975, ADN, 1977; BSN, Iowa Wesleyan Coll., 1980; MA, U. Iowa, 1992, PhD, 1998. RN, Iowa, Ark., Minn. Staff devel. coord. Elm View Care Ctr., Burlington, Iowa, 1985—88, DON, 1988—89; tchg./rsch. asst. U. Iowa Coll. Nursing, Iowa City, 1989-92; nursing faculty Grand View Coll., Des Moines, 1992-93; project dir. Nat. Caregiver Tng. Project, U. Iowa Coll. Nursing, 1992-97, predoctoral fellow, 1996-98; postdoctoral fellow/faculty dept. psychiatry U. Ark. Med. Scis., VA Med. Ctr., Little Rock, 1998—2000; asst. prof. U. Minnesota Sch. Nursing, 2001—. Presenter in field; cons. Alverno Health Facility, Clinton, Iowa, 1997—. Mem. referee panel Clin. Nursing Rsch., 1997—, Western Jour. Nursing Rsch., 1998—, Jour. Gerontol. Nursing, 1999—, Internat. Jour. Geriatric Psychiatry, 2000—, Internat. Psychogeriatrics, 2002—, Alzheimer's Disease and Related Disorders, 2002—, Nursing Research, 2003—; contbr. chapters to books, articles to profl. jours. Recipient AARP Andrus Found. grad. fellowship in gerontology Assn. Gerontology in Higher Edn., 1996-97, Rsch. award Am. Soc. Aging, 1999. Mem.: ANA, Coun. Nursing and Anthropology, Am. Assn. Geriatric Psychiatry, Midwest Nursing Rsch. Soc. (Outstanding Poster award 1993), Mid-Am. Contress on Aging (Best Grad. Paper award 1994), Am. Geriatric Soc., Internat. Psychogeriatric Assn. (task force on behavioral and psychol. symptoms of dementia 1999—, scientific advisory com. 2001, IPA/Bayer Rsch. award 1999), Sigma Theta Tau (Best of Image award 1997). Avocations: reading, traveling, walking, music, photography. Home: 1160 Cushing Cir Apt 318 Saint Paul MN 55108 Office: Weaver-Densford Hall 308 Harvard St SE Minneapolis MN 55455-0353 E-mail: gerdn001@umn.edu.

GERDT, BARRY LEE, music educator; b. Alton, Ill., Oct. 9, 1952; s. Clarence H. and Martha A. Gerdt; m. Gail Lee Sheridan, June 14, 1975; children: Jason Samuel, Joel David. BA Sacred Music, Bob Jones U., 1970—74; MA Sacred Music, Pensacola Christian Coll., 1985—89. Music dir. Oak Forest Christian Acad., Ill., 1975—78; music tchr. Miss. Valley Christian Sch., Alton, Ill., 1978—85; music pastor Eagledale Bapt. Ch. and Sch., Indpls., 1985—93; music dir. Northland Bapt. Bible Coll., Dunbar, Wis., 1993—; band dir. Faith Bapt. Sch., 1994—. Principle horn Alton Civic Orch., Ill., 1984—85; adjudicator/guest condr. Colo. Assn. of Christian Schools, Longmont, 2002; guest condr. Hawaii Assn. of Christian Schools. Musician: (sacred choral arrangements) One Needful Thing, (sacred choral) The Blessing of the Lord, I Will Go. Recipient Dedication of Yearbook, Northland Bapt. Bible Coll., 2002. Mem.: Am. Choral Directors Assn., Music Educators Nat. Conf., Calligraphy Guild of Ind. (sec. of bd. 1990—93). Republican. Baptist. Achievements include first to Started and developed instrumental programs in all of the schools I have served in. Avocations: woodworking, calligraphy. Home: W10791 Hwy 8 Dunbar WI 54119 Office: Northland Baptist Bible College W10085 Pike Plains Rd Dunbar WI 54119 Office Fax: 715-324-6133. Personal E-mail: bgerdt@nbbc.edu. E-mail: bgerdt@nbbc.edu.

GERDTS, WILLIAM HENRY, art history educator; b. Jersey City, N.J., Jan. 18, 1929; s. William Henry and Suzanne (Zanowick) G.; m. Elaine Evans, Apr. 4, 1953 (div. 1962); 1 child, Jeffrey Evans Dee; m. Abigail Booth, July 23, 1976. BA, Amherst Coll., 1949; MA, Harvard U., 1950, PhD, 1966; LHD (hon.),

Amherst Coll., 1992; DFA (hon.), Syracuse U., 1996. Resident dir. Hist. Myers House, curator Norfolk (Va.) Mus., 1953-54; curator paintings and sculpture Newark (N.J.) Mus., 1954-66; prof. art history U. Md., College Park, 1966-69; v.p. Coe Kerr Gallery, N.Y.C., 1969-71; prof. art history CUNY, 1971-99, prof. emeritus, 1999—, acting exec. officer art history PhD program, 1977-79, exec. officer, 1979-85. Vis. lectr. Johns Hopkins U., Balt., 1969-71; adj. prof. Rutgers U., New Brunswick, N.J., 1975, Washington U., St. Louis, 1977; mem. adv. bd. Archives Am. Art, Smithsonian Instn., N.Y.C., 1981—. Author: American Still-Life Painting, 1971, American Neo-Classic Sculpture: The Marble Resurrection, 1973, The Great American Nude: A History in Art, 1974, A Man of Genius: The Art of Washington Allston, 1979, Masters of the Humble Truth: Masterpieces of American Still Life, 1801-1930, 1981, American Impressionism, 1984, rev., 2001, The Art of Henry Inman, 1987; (with James L. Yarnall) The National Museum of American Art's Index to American Art Exhibition Catalogues From the Beginning through the 1876 Centennial Year, 6 vols., 1986, Art Across America: Regional Painting in America through 1920, 3 vols., 1990, others. Summer Rsch. grantee U. Md., 1968, Mellon Found., 1974; Guggenheim Found. fellow, 1980, Am. Philos. Soc. fellow, 1980. Office: CUNY Grad Ctr 365 5th Ave New York NY 10016-4334

GERDY, HARRY, lawyer; b. Chgo., Nov. 19., 1935; s. Abraham and Frances (Koerner) G.; m. Marianne B. Burke, 1970. B.S. in Commerce, Roosevelt U., 1957; J.D., DePaul U., 1966. Bar: Ill. 1966, U.S. Dist. Ct. (no. dist.) Ill. 1967. Spl. agt. Criminal Investigation div. IRS, Chgo., 1961-67; atty. Law Offices of Merwin Auslander, Chgo., 1967-69; chief counsel Ill. Dept. Gen. Services, Chgo., 1969-73; pvt. practice law, Chgo., 1973-75; regional counsel U.S. Gen. Services Adminstrn., Chgo., 1975—. Mem. bus. adv. council Jones Comml. High Sch., Chgo., 1976-79; adv. council Nat. Assn. State Purchasing Ofcls., Washington, 1974. Mem. ABA, Ill. Bar Assn., Fed. Bar Assn. (dir. 1976-79). Home: 2318 N Lakewood Ave Chicago IL 60614-3149 Office: GSA Regional Counsel 230 S Dearborn St Ste 3820 Chicago IL 60604-1562

GERE, JAMES MONROE, civil engineering educator; b. Syracuse, N.Y., June 14, 1925; s. William S. and Carol (Hixson) G.; m. Janice M. Platt, June 1, 1946; children— Susan M., William P., David S. BS, Rensselaer Poly. Inst., 1949, MS, 1951; PhD, Stanford, 1954. Registered profl. engr., Calif., N.Y. Instr. Rensselaer Poly. Inst., 1949-51; faculty Stanford U., 1954—; prof. civil engring., 1962—; assoc. dean Sch. Engring., 1960-67, exec. head dept. civil engring., 1967-72. Cons. and lectr. in field, 1954— Author 7 textbooks in field, also tech. papers. Served with USAAF, 1943-46, ETO. Fellow ASCE; mem. Am. Soc. Engring. Edn., Earthquake Engring. Research Inst., Sigma Xi, Tau Beta Pi.

GERE, RICHARD, actor; b. Phila., Aug. 31, 1949; m. Cindy Crawford, 1991 (div.); m. Carey Lowell, 2002; 1 child, Homer James Jigme. Attended, U. Mass. Played trumpet, piano, guitar and bass and composed music with various musical groups, acting appearances with Provincetown Playhouse in Great God Brown, Camino Real, Rosencrantz and Guildenstern are Dead; off-Broadway prodn. Killer's Head, Richard Farina: Long Time Coming and Long Time Gone, Back Bog Beast Bait; in Broadway prodn. Taming of the Shrew; London and Broadway prodns. Midsummer Night's Dream; Broadway prodns. Habeas Corpus, Bent; on Broadway Soon, Grease; appeared in and composed music for Volpone at Seattle Repertory Theatre; film debut in Report to the Commissioner, 1975; other films include Baby Blue Marine, 1976, Looking for Mr. Goodbar, 1977, Days of Heaven, 1978, Blood Brothers, 1978, Yanks, 1979, American Gigolo, 1980, An Officer and a Gentleman, 1982, Breathless, 1983, Beyond the Limit, 1983, The Cotton Club, 1984, King David, 1985, Power, 1986, No Mercy, 1986, Miles from Home, 1988, Internal Affairs, 1990, Pretty Woman, 1990, Rhapsody in August, 1991, Final Analysis, (also exec. prodr.) 1992, Sommersby, 1993, Mr. Jones, 1993, Intersection, 1994, First Knight, 1995, Primal Fear, 1996, Red Corner, 1997, The Jackal, 1997, An Alan Smithee Film: Burn Hollywood Burn, 1998, Runaway Bride, 1999, Autumn in New York, 2000, Dr. T and the Women, 2000, The Mothman Prophecies, 2002, Unfaithful, 2002, Chicago, 2002; TV movie Strike Force, 1975, And the Band Played On, HBO, 1993 (Emmy nomination, Supporting Actor - Special, 1994), AFI's 100 Years...100 Movies, 1998; author: Pilgrim Photo Collection, 1998; exec. prodr. (films) Final Analysis, 1992, Mr. Jones, 1993, Sommersby, 1993; TV guest appearance Kojak, 1973.*

GEREAU, MARY CONDON, political corporate executive; b. Winterset, Iowa, Oct. 10, 1916; d. David Joseph and Sarah Rose (Stack) Condon; m. Gerald Robert Gereau, Jan. 14, 1961. Student, Mt. Mercy Jr. Coll., 1935-37; BA, U. Iowa, 1939, MA, 1941. Program dir. ARC, India, 1943-45; dean of students Eastern Mont. Coll., 1946-48; supt. pub. instrn. State of Mont., 1948-56; sr. legis. cons. NEA, 1967-73; dir. legis. Nat. Treasury Employees Union, 1973-76; legis. asst. to Senator Melcher Mont., 1976-86; pres. Woman's Party Corp., 1991—. Co-chmn. Truman Commerative Com., 1994—. Contbr. articles on state govt. and edn. to profl. jours. Nat. chmn. Equal Rights Ratification Coun.; pres. Coun. Chief State Sch. Officers, 1956; exec. bd. Rural Edn. Assn., 1953—56; mem. campaign staff Kennedy, Johnson, Humphrey, Jackson; v.p. Nat. Women's Party, 1984—91; mem. Westmoreland Dem. com.; bd. dir. Coun. Chief State Sch. Officers, 1953—56. Named Conservationist of Yr. Mont. Conservation Coun., 1952, Roll Call Cong. Staffer of Yr., 1985; recipient Disting. Svc. State Sch. Officers, 1956, medal of honor Vet. Feminists of Am., 2000. Mem. U.S. Congress Burro Club (pres. 1983-84), Mont. State Soc. of Wash. E-mail: grg1@3n.net.

GEREBEN, ISTVAN BELA, retired oceanographer, retired acoustical engineer; b. Sopron, Hungary, Jan. 17, 1933; s. Jozsef Gereben and Iren Dold; m. Erzsebet Terez Gombas, Feb. 7, 1936; children: Erzsebet Czifra, Balazs, Geza, Agnes Schafer. MS in Engring., Tech. U. of Sopron, Hungary, 1956. Geophysicist Office of Geodesy and Geophysics, Budapest, Hungary, 1956; rsch. asst. Lamont Geol. Obs., Palisades, NY, 1959—62; rsch. engr. Westinghouse Electric Co., Balt., 1962—66; sr. engr. Hydrospace Rsch. Corp., Rockville, Md., 1966—70; divsn. mgr. TRACOR, Inc., Rockville, 1970—72; tech. mgr. TRW Inc. Sys. Divsn., McLane, Va., 1972—96; cons. engr. Marine Acoustics Inc., Arlington, Va., 1996—98. Editor: Defiant Voices. Co-chmn. Hungarian Freedom Fighters' Fedn. U.S.A., Washington, 1962—92; dir. Freedom Fedn., Washington, 1975—93; dir. nat. rep. com. Heritage Groups, Washington, 1972—90; exec. sec. coord. com. Hungarian Organizations in N.Am., Washington, 1972—90. Recipient Hungarian Freedom award, Hungarian Freedom Fighters' Fedn. U.S.A., 1981, Imre Nagy Meml. Plaque, Pres. of the Hungarian Republic, 1996, Knight's Cross of the Order of Merit, Republic of Hungary, 2003. Mem.: U.S. Naval Inst., Am. Geophys. Union. Achievements include development of measurement systems supporting the U.S. Navy's submarine silencing program; low freqency active and passive sonar systems; research in the impact of U.S. Navy sonar systems on marine life, authored impact studies for several sonar operational areas. Avocations: travel, reading, classical music, human rights. Home: 2762 Meadow Forest Drive Duluth GA 30097 Personal E-mail: gerebenib@aol.com.

GEREIGHTY, ANDREA SAUNDERS, polling company executive, poet; b. New Orleans, July 20, 1938; d. Andrew Jackson and Jeanne Teresa (Martin) Saunders; m. Dennis Anthony Gereighty Jr., May 19, 1959 (wid.); children: Deni Ann, David Dennis, Peggy T. Cert., Exeter Coll., Oxford, Eng., 1972; BA, U. New Orleans, 1974, MA in English with distinction, 1978. Cotton analyst Anderson-Clayton, Metairie, La., 1956; records retrieval profl. Shell Oil Co., New Orleans, 1956-60; census coord. St. Vincent De Paul Ch., New Orleans, 1960-65; bldg. funds dir. St. Francis Xavier Ch., Metairie, 1965-70; tchr. spl. edn. Deckbar Elem. Sch., Jefferson, La., 1966-70; tchr. English Chalmette (La.) H.S., 1971-73; assoc. prof. English dept. U. New Orleans, 1973-75; tchr. secondary edn. Berlin-Am. H.S., 1980-81; owner, founder, CEO New Orleans Field Svcs. Assocs., 1974—. Guest speaker Delgado Coll., New Orleans, 1989; guest presenter Rabouin Vo-Tech., New Orleans, 1980; lectr., guest presenter poetry at New Sarpy Sch., 1994-95; guest presenter St. Mark's Episcopal Ch., Latter Libr., N.O. Pub. Libr., others. Author: (public opinon polls book) Asking Q's, 1980; (poetry) Illusions and Other Realities, 1974, Restless for Cool Weather, 1990, Season of the Crane, 1994; publ., editor Desire Street, 1997—; author numerous poems. Recipient Coda award Poets and Writers, 1983, Poetry award of honor Nat. League Am. Pen Women, 1973, Deep South Writers, 1984, 88, 90, 92, 94, 95, 96, 97, 98, 99, 2d place award Nuyarikin Poet's Cafe, N.Y.C., Ellipsis Poetry prize, 1983, 85, 87, 90, other poetry awards. Mem. Am. Mktg. Assn., Mktg. Rsch. Assn., Nat. Geneal. Soc., Jefferson Geneal. Soc., Geneaol. Soc. of New Orleans, New Orleans Poetry Forum (dir. 1990—), New Orleans Track Club. Democrat. Roman Catholic. Avocations: writing poetry, jogging, genealogy, dogs, camping. Office: New Orleans Field Svcs 257 Bonnabel Blvd Rear Office Metairie LA 70005-3738

GEREN, GERALD S. lawyer; b. Chgo., Nov. 10, 1939; s. Ben and Sara (Block) G.; m. Phyllis Freeman, Feb. 11, 1962; children: Suzanne, Gregory, Bradley. BSMetE, Ill. Inst. Tech., 1961; JD, DePaul U., 1966. Bar: Ill. Supreme Ct. 1966, U.S. Ct. Customs and Patent Appeals 1967, U.S. Patent and Trademark Office 1967, U.S. Dist Ct. (no. dist.) Ill. 1969, U.S. Supreme Ct. 1972, U.S. Ct. Appeals (7th cir.) 1972, U.S. Ct. Appeals (fed. cir.) 1982. Engr. Internat. Harvester, Chgo., 1961-64; atty. Corning Glass Works, Corning, N.Y., 1966-69; assoc. Silverman & Cass, Chgo., 1969-70, Siegal & Geren, Chgo., 1970-71, ptnr. Epton, Mullin & Druth, Chgo., 1971-84, Hill, Steadman & Simpson, Chgo., 1984-94, Gerald S. Geren Ltd., Chgo., 1994-96, Lee, Mann, Smith, McWilliams, Sweeney & Ohlson, 1997—2002, Barnes & Thornburg, 2003—. Contbr. articles to Indsl. Rsch. and Devel., Design News mags. Pres. Chgo. High Tech. Assn., 1981-86, v.p., 1986-87; mem. strategic planning com. Econ. Devel. Commn., Chgo., 1986-91; mem. Ill. Ctr. for Indsl. Tech., 1984-90, Ill. Mfg. Tech. Network, Chgo., 1986-91; mem. pres.' coun., rsch. coun., alumni bd. Ill. Inst. Tech., 1991—, The Leukemia Soc. Am. (Ill. chpt. bd. mem. 1988-90). Mem. ABA, Ill. Bar Assn., Chgo. Bar Assn., Patent Law Assn. Chgo., Am. Intellectual Property Law Assn., Execs. Club, Chgo. Econ. Club, Comml. Club Chgo. (small bus. com. 1985—), Met. Club Chgo. Office: Lee Mann Smith McWilliams Sweeney & Ohlson 209 S La Salle St Ste 410 Chicago IL 60604-1203

GEREN, PETE (PRESTON GEREN), former congressman; b. Ft. Worth, Jan. 29, 1952; m. Beckie Ray; 3 children. Student, Ga. Inst. tech.; BA, U. Tex., 1974, JD, 1978. Atty. pvt. practice, 1978-83; exec. asst. Sen. Lloyd Bentsen, 1983-85; mem. 101st-104th Congresses from Tex. 12th dist., Washington, 1989-96; sr. v.p. Pub. Strategies, Inc., Ft. Worth, 1997-98, atty., 1997-99, Ft. Worth, 1999—. Office: 500 Throckmorton St Ste 1400 Fort Worth TX 76102-3712

GERETY, PETER LEO, archbishop; b. Shelton, Conn., July 19, 1912; s. Peter Leo and Charlotte (Daly) Gerety. Student, St. Thomas Sem., Bloomfield, Conn., 1934, Sem. St. Sulpice, Paris, 1939. Ordained priest Roman Catholic Ch., 1939. Asst. pastor, New Haven, 1939—42; dir. Blessed Martin de Porres Interracial Ctr., 1942—56; pastor New Haven, 1956—66; coadjutor bishop Portland, Maine, 1966—; apostolic adminstr., 1967—; bishop, 1969—74; archbishop of Newark, 1974—86; archbishop emeritus, 1986—. Roman Catholic. Address: St John Vianney Residence 60 Home Ave Rutherford NJ 07070-1760

GERETY, ROBERT JOHN, microbiologist, pharmaceutical company executive, pediatrician, vaccinologist; b. Jersey City, Oct. 16, 1939; s. James Leo and Helen (Beck) G.; m. Joan Imelda Grant, Feb. 3, 1967; children: Andrew, Kathleen, Nancy. BA with spl. honors, Rutgers U., 1962; MA, Stanford U., 1966, PhD, 1971; MD, George Washington U., 1970. Diplomate Nat. Bd. Med. Examiners. Rsch. assoc. dept. med. microbiology Stanford (Calif.) U. Med. Sch., 1969-70; intern in pediatrics Stanford U. Hosp., 1970-71, resident, 1974-75; staff assoc. Lab. Viral Immunology, NIH, Bethesda, Md., 1971-72; staff assoc. Bur. Biologics, FDA, Bethesda, 1972-73, dir. hepatitis br., 1973-84, assoc. dir. medicine and sci., chief infectious diseases br., 1984-85; exec. dir. virus & cell biology Merck Rsch. Labs., West Point, Pa., 1985-89, chief clin. evaluation of vaccines and antiviral drugs, 1985-89; v.p. devel. ops. Biogen, Inc., Cambridge, Mass., 1989-93; v.p. pharm. ops. Immulogic Pharm. Corp., Waltham, Mass., 1993-94, CEO, pres. and dir., 1994-96; v.p. devel. and regulatory affairs ORAVAX, Cambridge, Mass., 1997-99; exec. v.p. corp. devel. Cell Gate Inc., Sunnyvale, Calif., 1999-2000; v.p. regulatory affairs and clin. ops. Inhale Therapeutic Sys., San Carlos, Calif., 2000—02; v.p., head proprietary products group Nektar Pharms., San Carlos, 2002—. Adj. prof. medicine Jefferson Med. Sch., Phila., 1985; Plenary lectr. Internat. Symposium on Viral Hepatitis and Liver Disease, London, 1987; mem. U.S. Army Med. R&D Adv. Bd., 1987; mem. AIDS subcom. Nat. Inst. Allergy and Infectious Diseases, 1988; mem. Nat. Vaccine Adv. Com., 1990-92, sci. bd. Oravax, Cambridge, Mass., 1991-94, numerous others; participant confs., symposia and workshops. Editor: Non-A, Non-B Hepatitis, 1981, Hepatitis A, 1984, Hepatitis B, 1985; mem. editl. bd. Biols., 1990-94; contbr. over 200 articles to sci. jours. Med. dir. USPHS, 1970-85. Recipient commendation medal USPHS, 1975, Outstanding Svc. medal, 1982, Disting. Svc. medal, 1985; Patriotic Svc. award U.S. Dept. Treasury, 1983; Henry Rutgers fellow, 1961-62, fellow NIH, 1962-65, Calif. Tb and Health Assn., 1964-67, U.S. Health Professions scholar and microbiology fellow, 1966-70. Fellow Infectious Disease Soc. Am.; mem. AMA, Am. Soc. for Microbiology, Am. Acad. Pediatrics, Am. Assn. Immunologists, William Beaumont Soc., Henry Rutgers Soc., Internat. assn. for Biol. Standards, Internat. Soc. Interferon Rsch. Achievements include development and/or approval of vaccine against Hepatitis A and Hepatitis B, pediatric vaccines including Hemophilus Influenza B, and Biogen's beta interferon product to treat multiple sclerosis (Avonex); patents for Inactivation of Non-A, Non-B Hepatitis Agent; Hepatitis B Immune Globulin used to Inactivate Hepatitis B Virus in Injectable Biological Products; Detection of Non-A, Non-B Hepatitis Associated Antigen; Heat Treatment of a Non-A, Non-B Hepatitis Agent to Prepare a Vaccine; Hepatitis B Core Antigen Vaccine; Hepatitis B Core Antigen Vaccine Made by Recombinant DNA; Purified Antigen from Non-A, Non-B Hepatitis Causing Factor: Screening Test for Reverse Transcriptase Containing Viruses in human blood. Home: 1850 Sand Hill Rd Apt 10 Palo Alto CA 94304-2144 E-mail: rgerety@ca.nektar.com.

GERETY, TOM, academic administrator, lawyer, educator, philosopher; b. NYC, July 22, 1946; m. Adelia Moore, Oct. 7, 1972; children: Finn, Carrick, Amias, Rowan. BA, Yale U., 1969, MPhil, 1974, JD, PhD, Yale U., 1976; MA, Amherst Coll., 1995; LLD (hon.), Williams Coll., 1995; LHD, Doshisha U., 1996; LLD (hon.), Wesleyan U., 2001. Tchr. Peru project Joint Ctr. Urban Studies Harvard-MIT, Lima, 1966—67; bilingual tchr. Boston Pub. Schs., 1970—71; assoc. lectr. philosophy, master's asst. Morse Coll. Yale U., New Haven, 1972—74; asst. prof., fellow Ctr. Profl. Ethics Chgo. Kent Coll. Law, Ill. Inst. Tech., 1976—78; prof. law U. Pitts., 1978—86; dean, Nippert prof. Coll. Law U. Cin., 1986—89; pres., prof. philosophy Trinity Coll., Hartford, Conn., 1989—94, Amherst (Mass.) Coll., 1994—2003; exec. dir., Brennan prof. Brennan Ctr. for Justice, NYC, 2003—. Vis. asst. prof. Ind. U. Sch. Law, Bloomington, 1977—78; vis. prof. constl. law and jurisprudence Stanford U. Sch. Law, 1983—84; occasional appellate litigation in constl. law ACLU, 1981—; chair New Engl. Small Coll. Athletic Conf., 1991—92, 2000—01; chair bd. dirs. Consortium on Financing Higher Edn., 1993—95; testimony before the Senate Judiciary Com., Subcom. on Constitution on various proposed amendments. Writer, cons., on-air corr., fundraiser Visions of the Constitution, Nat. Endowment for Humanities TV series in constl. law, 1985—88, commentaries in various media Washington Post, Boston Globe, Chgo. Tribune, Christian Sci. Monitor, L.A. Times, MacNeil Lehrer Report, Nat. Pub. Radio; contbr. articles. Bd. mem. Internat. Rescue Com., 1989—, Save the Children U.S., Conn. State Bd. Edn., 1992—94. Fellow Kent fellow, Danforth Found., 1972—76, Woodrow Wilson fellow, 1983. Office: Brennan Ctr for Justice 12th Fl 161 Avenue of the Americas New York NY 10013

GERGECEFF-COOPER, LORRAINE, artist, consultant; b. Ill. d. Harry Robert and Grace Johnson; m. George William Gergeceff (dec. 1984); m. John Cooper, Jr., May 30, 1992 (dec. 2002); children: Jill Gergeceff Lohnes, Jon Rice Gergeceff. Cert., Internat. Sommerakad., Salzburg, Austria, 1962, Sch. Landscape Painting, Dordogne, France, 1973; BS, So. Ill. U., 1953; MFA, U. Guanajuato, San Miguel Allende, Mex., 1970. Tchr., gallery dir. Ursuline Acad., Oakland, Mo., 1962-70; instr. McKendree Coll., Lebanon, Mo.; artist Forum Creative Dynamics, St. Louis, 1995, Unique Paintings, Webster Groves, Mo., 1997-98; owner LorPaint Gallery, Webster Groves, 1998—. Cons. JDR 3 Through Awareness Classroom Environment; founder, dir. Ursuline Art Gallery, Oakland, Mo. Author: Careers in Art, Self Designed Fabrics; one woman shows at Kinsella Gallery, Long Art Gallery, Ursuline Art Gallery, Notre Dame Coll., University City Libr., St. Louis U.; group shows include St. Louis Art Mus., Art Mus. St. Louis, Bellas Artes, Cuernavaca, Mex., Mus. Arts and Scis., Mo. Hist. Soc., Spete Kukla Gallery, Samos, Greece, Internat. Acad. Fine Arts, Salzburg, Austria, Highland Gallery, Atlanta, St. Louis Artists' Guild, 2002, Galeria Osman, Mex., Creative Art Gallery, St. Louis, 2001, 02, Centro Cultural El Nigromante, San Miguel de Allende, Mex., Art Expo '96, Webster Groves, Mo., Nat. Mus. Women in the Arts, Mo. Water Colo Assn., St. Peter's Cultural Art Ctr., 2001, 02, Oil and Acrylic Nat. Exhbn., 2001, Collector's Choice, St. Louis, 2002, CJ Mggs Art Gallery, 2002, Oil and Acrylic Nat. Exhibit, 2002. Backer Repertory Theater, Webster Groves, Mo., 1996—. Best of Show Kinsella Gallery, Long Art Gallery, Ursuline Art Gallery; recipient prize St. Louis Artists' Guild, 1969, 71, 75; named Outstanding Secondary Educator, 1971. Mem. St. Louis Art Mus., Chgo. Art Inst., Guild of Opera Theater, Art St. Louis, St. Lousi Artists' Guild (spl. events, prize 1969, 71, 75), St. Louis Watercolor Soc. (signature), Soc. Multi Media Layerists. Avocations: travel, sailing, reading. Address: LorPaint Gallery 16 N Gore Ave Ste 201 Webster Groves MO 63119-2315 E-mail: lorpaint@aol.com.

GERHARD, LEE CLARENCE, geologist, educator; b. Albion, N.Y., May 30, 1937; s. Carl Clarence and Helen Mary (Lahmer) G.; m. Darcy LaFollette, July 22, 1964; 1 dau., Tracy Leigh. BS, Syracuse U., 1958; MS, U. Kans., 1961, PhD, 1964. Exploration geologist, region stratigrapher Sinclair Oil & Gas Co., Midland, Tex. and Roswell, N.Mex., 1964-66; asst. prof. geology U. So. Colo., Pueblo, 1966-69, assoc. prof., 1969-72; assoc. prof., asst. dir. West Indies Lab. Fairleigh Dickinson U., Rutherford, N.J., 1972-75; asst. geologist State of N.D., Grand Forks, 1975-77, geologist, 1977-81; prof., chmn. dept. geology U. N.D., Grand Forks, 1977-81; mgr. Rocky Mountain div. Supron Energy Corp., Denver, 1981-82; owner, pres. Gerhard & Assocs., Englewood, Colo., 1982-87; prof. petroleum geology Colo. Sch. Mines, Denver, 1982—, Getty prof., 1984-87; state geologist, dir. geol. survey State of Kans., Lawrence, 1987-99, prin. geologist, 1999—; founder, co-dir. Energy Rsch. Ctr., U. Kans., 1990-94. Presdl. appointee Nat. Adv. Com. on Oceans and Atmosphere, 1984-87. Contbr. articles to profl. jours. Served to 1st lt. U.S. Army, 1958-60. Danforth fellow, 1970-72; named to Kans. Oil and Gas Hall of Fame, 2002. Fellow Geol. Soc. Am.; mem. Am. Assn. Petroleum Geologists (hon. mem., Disting. Svc. award 1989, Journalism award 1996, pres. divsn. environ. geosci. 1994-95, hon. mem. divsn. environ. geoscis. 1998, v.p., Pub. Outreach award 1999, 2003), Am. Inst. Profl. Geologists, Rocky Mountain Assn. Geologists, Colo. Sci. Soc., Kans. Geol. Soc. (hon.), Sigma Xi, Sigma Gamma Epsilon. Home: 1628 Alvamar Dr Lawrence KS 66047-1714 Office: Kans Geol Survey 1930 Constant Ave Lawrence KS 66047-3724 E-mail: leeg@sunflower.com.

GERHARDT, CAROL ASHBY, visual artist; b. Wabash, Ind., Aug. 10, 1946; d. Dale Martin Ashby and Helen Irene Harper; 4 children from previous marriage. BS, U. Houston, 1986, postgrad., 1994—96. Exec. dir. Penguin Photography Studio, Houston, 1986—87, photographer, 1987—90; photojournalism faculty North Harris County Coll., Houston, 1990—92; art faculty Houston Ind. Sch. Dist., 1992—2003. Exhibitions include UN/UNIFEM, Marias do Mundo, Brazil, 2001, Diverse Works Art Space, Houston, 1996.

GERHARDT, FRITZ, ecologist, educator, researcher; b. Lynchburg, Va., Sept. 25, 1961; s. Earl Alvin and Sally Flournoy Gerhardt; m. Amy Kristin Acker, July 21, 2001. BA, Grinnell Coll., 1983; MFS, Harvard U., 1993. Biol. technician U. S. Fish & Wildlife Svc., Anchorage, 1987—91; rsch. and tchg. asst. Harvard U., Cambridge, 1991—94, Dartmouth Coll., Hanover, NH, 1994—97; field biologist, prin. Langlois Mountain Inst., Strafford, Vt., 1997—99; rsch and tchg. asst. U. Colo., Boulder, 1999—. Tchg. asst. Oreg. Inst. Marine Biology, Charleston, 1998; vis. instr. Middlebury Coll., Vt., 1998. Fellow, Dartmouth Coll., 1994—97, U. Colo., 2001; scholar, Harvard U., 1991—93. Mem.: Soc. Conservation Biology, Ecol. Soc. Am., Am. Inst. Biol. Sci. Achievements include research in factors structuring natural communities, including the effects of physiography, natural and human disturbances, and global change on the structure and composition of plant communities. Avocations: travel, woodworking, gardening.

GERHARDT, LESTER A. engineering educator, dean; b. Bronx, N.Y., Jan. 28, 1940; s. David and Mary G.; m. Karen Rita Zimmerman, Sept. 2, 1961; children: Brian, Douglas. BEE, CUNY, 1961; MSEE, SUNY, Buffalo, 1964, PhD, 1969; Doctorate (hon.), Danish Tech. U., 2000. Engr., asst. dir rsch. Bell Aerospace, Buffalo, 1961-70; assoc. prof. Rensselaer Polytechnic Inst., Troy, N.Y., 1970-74, prof., 1974—, chmn. elect., computer and systems engring. dept., 1975-86, dir. CIM Program, 1986-91, assoc. dean engring., 1991—. Acting dir. Ctr. for the Mfg. Productivity, 1991-92, founding dir., 1979-80, dir. Ctr. for indsl. Innovation, 1993—; nat. del. NATO, 1980—, chair Rsch. Collaborative Grants Programme; mem. AFSB com. on Robotics and Artificial Intelligence, 1986-89, mem. com. Tactical Communications Nat. Acad. Scis.; mem. adv. bd. N.Y. Gov. Carey's Panel on Telecommunications, NSF, chair. adv. bd.; active internat. cons. to industry, the gov't, and other Universities. Recipient Inventor of Yr. award N.Y. State Intellectual Property Law Assn., 1997, Rsch. adminstrn. award Engring. Rsch. Coun., 2002. Fellow: ASEE (chmn. engring. rsch. coun. 1996—98, bd. dirs. 1996—98, inaugural award for rsch. adminstrn. engring. rsch. coun. 2002), IEEE. Avocations: sailing, photography, tennis. Office: Rensselaer Poly Inst Deans Office Sch Engring JEC 3002 Troy NY 12180

GERHARDT, PHILIPP, microbiologist, educator; b. Milw., Dec. 30, 1921; s. Philipp W. and Agnes (Daigh) G.; m. Vera Mary Armstrong, Feb. 24, 1945; children: Ellen Daigh, Stephen Philipp, Doris Mary. PhB with honors, U. Wis., 1943, MS, 1947, PhD, 1949. Diplomate: Am. Bd. Med. Microbiology. Faculty microbiology Oreg. State U., 1949-51, Med. Sch., U. Mich., Ann Arbor, 1953-65; prof., chmn. dept. microbiology and pub. health Colls. Natural Sci., Human Medicine, Osteo. Medicine, Vet. Medicine and Agr. Exptl. Sta. Mich. State U., East Lansing, 1965-75, prof., assoc. dean for research and grad. study Coll. Osteo. Medicine, 1975-87, prof. dept. microbiology and pub. health, 1987-91, prof. emeritus, 1992—. Adj. sr. sci. Mich. Biotech. Inst., 1985-92 ; dir. Ribi Immuno Chem Research Inc., 1985-99; cons. various univs. and corps. Editor in chief: Manual of Methods for General Bacteriology, 1981, Methods for General and Molecular Bacteriology, 1993. With AUS, 1943-46, 51-52. Wis. Alumni Rsch. Found, fellow, 1946-47; NIH rsch. fellow, 1947-49; recipient Disting. Faculty award Mich. State U., 1982, Pasteur award Ill. Soc. Microbiology, 1993. Fellow AAAS, Am. Acad. Microbiology (charter, bd. govs. 1970-76); mem. Am. Soc. Microbiology (hon., sec. 1961-67, v.p. 1973-74, pres. 1974-75, coun. and coun. policy com. 1961-67, 74-76), Brit. Soc. Gen. Microbiology, Internat. Union Microbiol. Socs. (v.p. 1978-82, pres. 1982-86, exec. bd. 1978-90), Internat. Coun. Sci. Unions (steering com. internat. bioscis. network 1985-91, pres. com. biotech. 1987-89), Polish Med. Soc. (hon.), Phi Beta Kappa, Sigma Xi. Achievements include rsch. and publs. on microbial endospores, permeability, fermentations. Home: 529 Woodland Dr East Lansing MI 48823-3273 Office: Mich State Univ Dept Microbiol/Molecular Gene East Lansing MI 48824-3273

GERHART, EUGENE CLIFTON, lawyer; b. Bklyn., Apr. 7, 1912; s. Herman Eugene and Mary Elizabeth (Hamilton) G.; m. Mary Richardson Schreiber, Mar. 30, 1939; children: Catherine Gerhart Landon, Virginia Gerhart Mason. AB, Princeton U., 1934; LLB, Harvard U., 1937. Bar: N.J. 1938, N.Y. 1945. Practiced in, Newark, 1938-43, Binghamton, N.Y., 1946—; counsel firm Coughlin & Gerhart, Binghamton; sec. to Judge Manley O. Hudson, Secretariat/League of Nations, Geneva, 1934; lectr. bus. law U. Newark, 1942-43, Triple Cities Coll., 1946-48, Harpur Coll., Endicott, N.Y., 1953-55; lectr. indsl. and labor relations Cornell U., Ithaca, N.Y., 1946; dir., gen. counsel Columbian Mut. Life Ins. Co., 1949-83, acting pres., 1969-70, chmn. bd., 1970-82. Mem. coun. SUNY, Cortland, 1967-77, chmn., 1971-77; mem. Select Task Force on Ct. Reorgn. N.Y. State Senate; mem. jud. nominating com. 3d Jud. Dept., State of N.Y.; mem. N.Y. Unified Ct. Sys. Judicial Records Disposition and Archives Devel. Com. Author: American Liberty and Natural Law, America's Advocate: Robert H. Jackson, Robert H. Jackson: Lawyer's Judge, 2003, Arthur T. Vanderbilt: The Compleat Counsellor, Quote It!, Quote It II, The Lawyer's Treasury, Quote It Completely!, 1998, World Reference Guide to more than 5500 Memorable Quotations from Law and Literature, 1998; spl. contbg. author: Law Office Econs. and Mgmt, 1962— ; mem. editl. bd. Quar. Report of Conf. on Personal Fin. Law, 1965; contbr. articles to legal, other publs. Chmn. Harpur Forum SUNY, Binghamton, 1983-84. Lt. USNR, 1943-46. Fellow Am. Bar Found., Am. Coll. Probate Counsel, N.Y. State Bar Found.; mem. ABA (editor Jour. 1946-67, Ross Essay award 1946), Internat. Assn. Ins. Counsel, Assn. Life Ins. Counsel, Am. Judicature Soc., Am. Law Inst., N.Y. State Bar Assn. (editor-in-chief jour. 1961-97, editor-in-chief emeritus 1997—, Disting. Svc. award 1998), Assn. Bar City N.Y., Broome County Bar Assn. (pres. 1961-62, Lifetime Achievement award 1995), Selden Soc., Broome County Princeton Alumni Assn., Harvard Law Sch. Assn. Upstate

N.Y. (pres. 1955-57), Scribes (pres., dir. 1966-67), St. Andrew's Soc. Clubs: Rotary (pres. 1969-70), Cosmos, Oteyokwa Lake (pres. 1971-73), Nassau, Harvard of N.Y, Princeton of N.Y. Republican. Home: 34 W End Ave Binghamton NY 13905-4026 Office: 20 Hawley St Binghamton NY 13901-3216

GERHART, GLENNA LEE, pharmacist; b. Houston, June 11, 1954; d. Henry Edwin and Gloria Mae (Mrnustik) G. BS in Pharmacy, U. Houston, 1977. Registered pharmacist, Tex. Staff pharmacist Meml. City Med. Ctr., Houston, 1977-84; asst. dir. pharmacy Meml. Hosp.-Meml. City Med. Ctr., Houston, 1984-98; pharmacy supr. Meml. Hermann-Meml. City Hosp. Pharmacy, Houston, 1998—; staff pharmacist Christus St. Catherine Health and Wellness Ctr., 2000—02. Active Humane Soc. U.S. Mem.: Pharm. and Therapeutics Soc., Houston-Galveston Area Soc. Hosp. Pharmacists, Tex. Soc. Health-Sys. Pharmacists, Tex. Pharm. Assn., Am. Soc. Hosp. Pharmacists, Am. Pharm. Assn., Nat. Birman Fanciers, Houston SPCA, U. Houston Alumni Orgn. (life), Humane Soc. U.S., Plumeria Soc. Am., Greentrails Ladies Club, Nat. Cougar Club, Houston Cat Club, Slavonic Benevolent Order of Tex., Kappa Epsilon. Republican. Methodist. Avocations: reading, gardening, running, raising cats. Home: 19811 Cardiff Park Ln Houston TX 77094-3031 Office: Memorial Hermann-Memorial City Hosp 920 Frostwood Dr Houston TX 77024-2312 E-mail: glenna_gerhart@mhhs.org., glennacat@aol.com.

GERHART, JAMES BASIL, physics educator; b. Pasadena, Calif., Dec. 15, 1928; s. Ray and Marion (van Deusen) G.; m. Genevra Joy Thomesen, June 21, 1958; children: James Edward, Sara Elizabeth. BS, Calif. Inst. Tech., 1950; MA, Princeton, 1952, PhD, 1954. Instr. physics Princeton, 1954-56; asst. prof. physics U. Wash., Seattle, 1956-61, assoc. prof., 1961-65, prof., 1965-98, prof. emeritus, 1998—. Exec. officer Pacific Northwest Assn. for Coll. Physics, 1972-94, bd. dirs., 1965-99, chmn., 1970-72; governing bd. Am. Inst. Physics, 1973-76, 78-81. Recipient Disting. Teaching award U. Wash. Regents and Alumni Assn., 1982, Ann. Gerhart lectr. 1997. Fellow Am. Phys. Soc, AAAS; mem. Am. Assn. Physics Tchrs. (sec. 1971-77, v.p. 1977, pres.-elect 1978, pres. 1979, Millikan medal 1985). Home: 2134 E Interlaken Blvd Seattle WA 98112-3433 E-mail: gerhart@dirac.phys.u.wahington.edu.

GERHART, STEVEN GEORGE, lawyer; b. Osage, Iowa, July 9, 1948; s. Grant George and Marjory Justine (Heckel) G.; m. Victoria Rae Cobb, Nov. 24, 1973; children: Sarah Jean, Melissa Rae, Nathaniel Scott, Abigail J. BA, U. Iowa, 1970, JD, 1973; postgrad. N.Am. Bapt. Sem., Sioux Falls, S.D., 1992—. Bar: Iowa 1973, Ill. 1975, N.D. 1982; postgrad. N.Am. Bapt. Sem., 1992—. Atty., FPC, Washington, 1973-75, People's Gas Co., Chgo., 1975-76; asst. gen. atty. Iowa Electric Light & Power Co., Cedar Rapids, Iowa, 1976-82; gen. counsel, sec. Montana-Dakota Utilities Co. (now MDU Resources Group Inc), Bismarck, N.D., 1982-87; legal com. Midwest Gas Assn., Mpls., 1977-87, Edison Electric Inst., Washington, 1983-87, Am. Gas Assn., Arlington, Va., 1983-87; legal counsel Profl. Christian Counseling Ctr., Inc., Bismarck, N.D., 1987-91, resigned; bd. dirs. Steer, Inc., Liberty House, Inc.; now v.p. adminstrv. law Sioux City Brick and Tile Co. Mem. elder-deacon bd. Century Baptist Ch., Bismarck, 1984-90. Mem. ABA, N.D. Bar Assn. Home: 2400 Oxford Cir Sioux City IA 51106-0578 Office: Sioux City Brick and Tile Co PO Box 807 Sioux City IA 51102

GERICKE, PAUL WILLIAM, minister, educator; b. St. Louis, Apr. 8, 1924; s. Orville Herman and Irma Rose (Reinhart) G.; m. Jean Fisher, Feb. 18, 1953; 1 child, Michael Paul. BSEE, Washington U., St. Louis, 1949; BD, So. Bapt. Theol. Sem., 1960; ThD, New Orleans Bapt. Theol. Sem., 1964; MA, U. New Orleans, 1972. Ordained to ministry So. Bapt. Conv., 1952. Instr. electronics USAF, 1949; calibration engr. Emerson Electric Co., St. Louis, 1950; asst. pastor Calvary Bapt. Ch., St. Louis, 1951-53, Forest Ave. Bapt. Ch., Kansas City, Mo., 1954; pastor First Bapt. Ch., Marceline, Mo., 1955-56, New Hope Bapt. Ch., St. Louis, 1957, Summit Park Bapt. Ch., Louisville, 1959-60, Logtown (Miss.) Bapt. Ch., 1960-64; asst. prof., dir. libr. svcs. New Orleans Bapt. Theol. Sem., 1965-73, assoc. prof., dir. libr., 1973-91, assoc. prof. comms., dir. Comm. Ctr., 1991-92, dir. rsch. and planning, 1992-93, prof. comms. N. Ga. Campus, 1993, acad. counselor, 1993—, dir. of libr., 1993—99, prof. comms. emeritus, 1999—. Mgr. Sta. WSBN-FM, New Orleans, 1979-85, chmn., 1985-92; bd. dirs. religious access channel REACH, New Orleans, 1985-93. Author: The Preaching of Robert G. Lee, 1967, The Ministers Filing System, 1971, Sermon Building, 1973, Crucial Experiences in the Life of D.L. Moody, 1978, Pastor's Library, 1986, Great Preachers of the Church, 1996. Served with AC USNR, 1942-46. Mem. Am. Radio Relay League, Theta Xi. Republican. Avocation: amateur radio. Home: 482 Sletten Dr Lawrenceville GA 30045 *My life has been completely changed by a personal encounter with Jesus Christ in 1951. Through faith in Him as Savior and Lord, I received a new life, a new sense of values, a new purpose in life, and a new hope both for this life and the life to come. My purpose now is to seek first the kingdom of God and all the other things I need will be given unto me.*

GERINGER, JAMES E. former governor; b. Wheatland, Wyo., Apr. 24, 1944; m. Sherri Geringer; children: Jen, Val, Rob, Meri, Beckie. BS in Mechanical Engring., Kans. State U., 1967. Commd. officer USAF; with contract administration Mo. Basin Power Project's Laramie River Sta., 1977-79; elected mem. Wyo. Legislature, 1982; farm owner, 1977—; gov. State of Wyo., 1994—2002. Participant in various space devel. programs, Calif., devel. variety Air Force and NASA space boosters including launches of reconnaissance satellites, the NASA Viking Mars lander, an upper stage booster for the space shuttle and the Global Positioning Satellite System; chief of computer programming at a ground receiving station for early warning satellites. Mem. Nat. Fedn. Ind. Bus., Am. Legion, Farm Bur., Farmer's Union, Rotary, Lions, Ducks Unlimited, Pheasants Forever, C. of C. Republican. Lutheran. Office: 10248 Hexton Ct Littleton CO 80124-9769*

GERINGER, JOHN MICHAEL, economist, educator; b. Indpls., Nov. 13, 1958; s. R.J. and J.A. Geringer BS, Ind. U., 1980; MBA, U. Wash., 1983, PhD, 1986. Vis. asst. prof. Portland (Oreg.) State U., 1983-84; asst. prof. So. Meth. U., Dallas, 1985-87, U. Western Ont., London, 1987-92; prof. Calif. Poly. U., San Luis Obispo, 1992—. Vis. prof. Helsinki Sch. Econs. & Bus. Adminstrn., 1993—, Bond U., Gold Coast, Australia, 1996—, Monterey (Calif.) Inst. Internat. Studies, 1996—2000. Author: Joint Venture Partner Selection, 1989; co-author: Business Policy, 1992, International Business, 8th edit., 2002. Recipient decade award Acad. Internat. Bus., 1999. Mem. Acad. Mgmt., Strategic Mgmt. Soc., Licensing Execs. Soc., Western Acad. Mgmt., Assn. Japanese Bus. Studies. Office: Cal Poly Coll Business San Luis Obispo CA 93407

GERJUOY, EDWARD, physicist, lawyer; b. Bklyn., May 19, 1918; s. Abraham and Clara (Hirsch) G.; m. Clark Jacqueline Reid, Aug. 26, 1940; children: Neil, David Leif. BS cum laude, CCNY, 1937; MA, U. Calif., Berkeley, 1940, PhD, 1942; JD magna cum laude, U. Pitts., 1977. Bar: Calif. 1977, Pa. 1978. Assoc. dir. sonar analysis group Divsn. War Research, Columbia, 1942-46; mem. faculty U. So. Calif., Los Angeles, 1946-51; vis. assoc. prof. N.Y. U., 1951-52; mem. faculty U. Pitts., 1952-58, 64-82, prof. physics, 1964-82, prof. emeritus, 1982—; mem. Pa. Environ. Hearing Bd., 1982-86, cons. hearing examiner, 1987-89; of counsel Rose, Schmidt, Hasley & DiSalle, Pitts., 1987-2001. Mem. rsch. staff Gen. Atomic div. Gen. Dynamics Corp., San Diego, 1958-62; dir. plasma and space applied physics RCA Labs., Princeton, N.J., 1962-64; cons. Westinghouse Rsch. Labs., 1952-58; mem. adv. com. health physics divsn. Oak Ridge Nat. Labs., 1967-71, chmn. com., 1971-74; assoc. Tucker Arensberg Very & Ferguson, Pitts., 1978-80; vis. fellow Joint Inst. Lab. Physics, U. Colo., Boulder, 1970; vis. sci. USSR Acad. Sci. Lebedev Inst., Moscow, 1972; hearing examiner Pa. Environ. Hearing Bd., 1980-81; vis. scholar Stanford Math. Dept., 1987; cons. EPA, 1977-81,; cons. atty. Reed, Smith, Shaw & McClay, Pitts., 1993--; adj. prof. U. Pitts. Law Sch., 2000. Author: (with A. Yaspan) Reverberation, in series The Physics of Sound in the Sea, 1968; editor: Physics Text Series, 1960-62, Jour. Comments on Atomic and Molecular Physics, 1971-74, Jurimetrics Jour. of Law Sci. and Tech., 1980-87; contbr. chpts. and numerous articles to tech. and legal lit. Bd. dirs. Pitts. ACLU, 1975-80, 92-95, vice-chmn., chair-elect, chair Am. Phys. Soc. Forum on Physics and Soc., 1994-97; bd. dirs. Pitts. Group Against Smog and Pollution, 2002—. Fellow AAAS, Am. Phys. Soc. (panel on pub. affairs 1976-79, 94-96, chmn. 1981, governing coun. 2000—, audit com. 2002-), Inst. Physics, Phys. Soc. (Eng.); mem. ABA (chmn. phys. scis. com., sect. sci. and tech. 1976-77, coun. sci. and tech. 1977-80, 84, 87-91), Phi Beta Kappa, Sigma Xi, Order of Coif. Achievements include first predictions of interference in Zeeman Effect allowing magnetic dipole and electric quadrupole transitions, and (with others) of beats between photons of different frequencies; first derivation of transition rates in many-particle collisions from a purely time-independent formalism; first development (with others) of routine procedure for constructing variational estimates of very wide class of quantities. Home: 400 Richland Ln Pittsburgh PA 15208-2732 Office: Univ Pitts Dept Physics 100 Allen Hall Pittsburgh PA 15260 E-mail: gerjuoy@pitt.edu. *I have tried to avoid overspecialization, while not letting myself descend into dilettantism. I believe I have succeeded in these endeavors. The last phase of my career, embarking on a law degree at age 56, earning the degree and passing the bar at 59, and then being employed full time as a judge in environmental disputes, probably is an extreme example of career restlessness. I am not sorry to have strayed from a straight line career path, and it has kept me feeling young in my so-called golden years. Nevertheless— and this is more a comment about the present world than about me— I do not believe I would advise young men today to be guided by me.*

GERJUOY, HERBERT GEORGE, educator, psychologist, consultant, poet; b. Bklyn., Apr. 22, 1929; s. Abraham and Clara (Hirshkowitz) G.; m. Irma Lewis Rossman, May 6, 1952 (div. 1965); children: Judith Hope, Amy Beth; m. Carol Judith Arenberg, Dec. 30, 1966; children: Berenice Tamar, Ilana Martha. AB magna cum laude, U. So. Calif., 1949; MA, State U. Iowa, 1952, PhD, 1953. Cert. psychologist, Ohio. Rsch. assoc. in psychology State U. Iowa, Iowa City, 1953—54; instr. psychology Ind. U., Bloomington, 1954—57; assoc. prof. psychology U. Toledo, 1957—62; rsch. psychologist Ednl. Testing Svc., Princeton, NJ, 1962—67; sr. staff scientist HumRRO, Alexandria, Va., 1967—70; prof. pub. adminstrn. SUNY, Albany, NY, 1970—75; sr. staff scientist The Futures Group, Glastonbury, Conn., 1975—79; pres. Program Strategics, Inc., West Hartford, Conn., 1979—85; asst. prof. computer sci., soc. sci., psychology Three Rivers C.C., Norwich, Conn., 1987—99; asst. prof. computer info. sys., adj. instr. psychology Tunxis C.C., Farmington, Conn., 1999—2001, coord. computer info. sys., 1999—2001, adj. instr. computer info. sys., 2001; adj. instr. pub. adminstrn Marist Coll., Poughkeepsie, NY, 1999—2002; adj. prof. econs. Tunxis C.C., Farmington, Conn., 2003—. Pres. Bravo Corp., West Hartford, 1988-91; editor The Red Fox Rev., Norwich, 1992-99; sr. rsch. assoc. Ark. Inst., Little Rock, 1994; adj. lectr. math. & computer sci. Eastern Conn. State U., 1997-99. Editor: Rehabilitation: Pathways. . ., 1962, Population, Education, and Social Welfare in Sub-Saharan Africa, 1995, (newsletter) Kol Kehilah (Voice of the Congregation), Hartford, 2002—; co-author: Life-Extending Technologies, 1980, Youth Crime in Arkansas, 1994. Chief observer Ground Observer Corps, so. Ind., 1956-57; cons. Schenectady Narcotics Info. Ctr., 1974-75; mem. edtl. bd. Future Rsch. Qtrly., 1984—. Recipient Outstanding Contbn. award Am. Acad. Rehab. Therapy, 1962. Mem.: AAAS, NY Acad. of Arts and Sci., Conn. Acad. of Arts and Scis., Stratford Writers Group, Sigma Xi. Democrat. Jewish. Avocations: foundations of mathematics, writing, music. Home: 8 Lexington Rd West Hartford CT 06119-1747 E-mail: elemhg@comcast.net.

GERKEN, WALTER BLAND, insurance company executive; b. N.Y.C., Aug. 14, 1922; s. Walter Adam and Virginia (Bland) G.; m. Darlene Stolt, Sept. 6, 1952; children: Walter C., Ellen M., Beth L., Daniel J., Andrew P., David A. BA, Wesleyan U., 1948; MPA, Maxwell Sch. Citizenship and Pub. Affairs, Syracuse, 1958. Supr. budget and adminstrv. analysis, Wis., Madison, 1950-54; mgr. investments Northwestern Mut. Life Ins. Co., Milw., 1954-67; v.p. finance Pacific Mut. Life Ins. Co., L.A., 1967-69, exec. v.p., 1969-72, pres., 1972-75, chmn. bd., 1975-87, chmn. exec. com. Los Angeles, 1987-95, also dir.; ret. sr. advisor Boston Consulting Group. Bd. dirs. Mullin Cons., Inc.; vice-chmn. Global Fin. Group, 2000—. Bd. dirs. Keck Found.; trustee emeritus Occidental Coll. L.A., Wesleyan U., Middletown, Conn.; bd. dirs. Nature Conservancy Calif.; mem. Calif. Citizens Budget Com., Calif. Commn. Campaign Fin. Reform, Calif. Commn. on Higher Edn.; bd. dirs., former chair Exec. Svc. Corps. So. Calif.; v.p. Orange County Cmty. Found.; mem. adv. bd. The Maxwell Sch. Citizenship and Pub. Affairs, Syracuse U. Decorated D.F.C., Air medal. Mem. Calif. Club, Dairymen's Country Club (Boulder Junction, Wis.), Automobile Club So. Calif. (bd. dirs.), Pauma Valley Country Club, Edison Internat., Times Mirror Co. Office: Pimco Advisors LP 800 Newport Center Dr Newport Beach CA 92660-6309 E-mail: wgerken@pimcoadvisors.com.

GERLACH, DOUGLAS ELDON, financial writer, Internet developer; b. Columbus, Ohio, May 19, 1963; s. Eldon Chloral and Judith Ann (Benadum) G.; 1 child. BA, Bennington (Vt.) Coll., 1985. Sr. editor, co-creator website Nat. Assn. of Investors Corp., 1995—; founder, editor-in-chief Investorama.com, N.Y.C., 1995-2000; internet bus. analyst First Albany Corp., N.Y.C., 1997-98; sr. editor Armchair Millionaire.com, New York, NY, 1998—. Cons. editor Mutual Funds mag., 2000—. Actor: Investor's Web Guide, 1997; author: Complete Idiot's Guide to Online Investing, 1998, 2d edit., 2000, The Armchair Millionaire, 2001, Investment Clubs for Dummies, 2001; contbr. articles to mags. Recipient Disting. Svc. award Investment Edn. Inst., 1996. Mem. Nat. Writers Union, Computer Press Assn., Pioneer On-Line Investment Club (pres. 1994—), Am. Assn. of Individual Investors (life), Nat. Assn. of Investor Corp. Computer Group (bd. dirs. 1995—), Mensa.

GERLACH, FRANKLIN THEODORE, lawyer; b. Portsmouth, Ohio, Apr. 11, 1935; s. Albert T. and Nora Alice (Hayes) G.; m. Cynthia Ann Koehler, Aug. 1, 1958; children: Valarie, Philipp. BBA, U. Cin., 1958; MPA, Syracuse U., 1959; JD, U. Cin., 1961. Bar: Ohio 1961, U.S. Dist. Ct. (so. dist.) Ohio 1969, U.S. Supreme Ct. 1971. Dir. purchasing, planning and renewal City of Portsmouth, 1961-62, city mgr., 1962-66, mayor, 1990-97; asst. dir. Ohio U., Portsmouth, 1966-68; sole practitioner law Portsmouth, 1968—. Solicitor Village New Boston, Ohio, 1968-70; trustee Ohio Acad. Trial Lawyers, Columbus, 1984-85. Recipient Outstanding Young Man of Ohio award Portsmouth Jaycees, 1968, Ohio Jaycees, 1969. Mem. Scioto County Bar Assn. (pres. 1986). Democrat. Avocation: antiques. Home: 1221 20th St Portsmouth OH 45662-2924 Office: 814 7th St Portsmouth OH 45662-4128 E-mail: lawyergg@zoomnet.net.

GERLACH, JAMES WILLIAM, congressman; b. Ellwood City, Pa., Feb. 25, 1955; s. Jack Allen and Helen (Fitzgerald) G.; m. Karen Devanna, 1980; children: Katie, Jimmy, Robby. BA, Dickinson Coll., 1977, JD, 1980. Bar: Pa. Pvt. practice, Downingtown, Pa.; mem. Pa. Ho. of Reps., Dist. 44, Harrisburg, 1991-94; legis. aide Pa. Senate, Harrisburg, 1978-80; mem. Pa. Senate, Dist. 44, Harrisburg, 1995—2002, 108th Congress, 6th Dist., 2003—; mem. small bus. com., transportation com. Mem. Chester County Agr. Devel. Coun. Named Guardian of Small Bus., Nat. Fedn. Ind. Bus. Mem. Pa. Bar Assn., Lions (bd. dirs. Downingtown), Sigma Chi. Republican. Home: 1230 Pottstown Pike Ste 4 Glenmoore PA 19343-9533 Office: Senate Box 203044 168 Capitol Bldg Harrisburg PA 17120*

GERLACH, MURNEY, administrator, educator, historian; b. June 5, 1950; m. Shirl Creighton, 1984; children: Chris, Brendan, Julia, Gregory. BA in Govt., Lake Forest (Ill.) Coll., 1972; MA in European History, San Diego State U., 1976; DPhil in Brit. and Am. History, New Coll., Oxford (Eng.) U., 1983. Profl. tennis instr., San Diego, 1970-80; tutor in politics and history Oriel and Exeter Colls., Oxford U., 1979-80; univ. archivist, thesis reviewer San Diego State U., 1983-86, univ. archivist and historian, 1986-88; asst. to v.p. for univ. rels. U. San Diego, 1988-89, spl. asst. to the pres., 1989-91; asst. to pres., asst. sec. of corp. Brown U., Providence, 1992-97; assoc. dean Coll. Arts and Scis., Roger Williams U., Bristol, R.I., 1998-99; dir. R.I. Hist. Soc., Providence, 1999—. Asst. prof., lectr. in history Bryant Coll., Roger Williams U., Brown U., U. San Diego, San Diego State U., 1982—; sec., Farview Inc., 1992-97. Author: British Liberalism and the United States: Political and Social Thought in the Late Victorian Age, 2001. Sec. bd. fellows, sec. adv. and exec. com. Brown U., 1992-97; pres. bd. dirs. Coronado (Calif.) Hist. Assn., 1992; chair County of San Diego Christopher Columbus Quincentenary Jubilee Commn., 1990-92; bd. dirs. San Diego Hist. Soc., 1987-92, Heritage-Harbor Corp., 1999—; bd. advisors San Diego Naval Hist. Assn., 2001—. Mem. Am. Assn. Museums (museums and cmty. nat. task force 2000—), Am. Hist. Assn., Nat. Coun. for Pub. History, Brown Faculty Club, Vincents Club (Oxford, Eng.), Am. Assn. State and Local History, New Eng. Mus. Assn., Nat. Trust for Hist. Preservation, Nat. Coun. for History Edn., U. Oxford Soc., San Diego Hist. Soc. Office: RI Hist Soc 110 Benevolent St Providence RI 02906-3152 E-mail: mgerlach@rihs.org.

GERLACH, THURLO THOMPSON, electrical engineer; b. Sparta, Ill., Oct. 30, 1916; s. Kenneth Frederick and Golda M. (Thompson) G.; m. Ellen Marie Kuhn, July 14, 1946. BEE, Tri-State U., 1937; grad., Air Force Command and Staff, 1952. Registered profl. engr., Ill., Mont. Dist. engr. Ill. Power Co., Centralia, 1937-40, area engr. Sparta, 1940-41, Granite City, Ill., 1946-48; engr. U.S. Bur. Standards, Washington, 1948-50, Fed. Power Commn., Washington, 1953-56, Bur. of Reclamation, Billings, Mont., 1950-51, 56-77; cons. Billings, 1977—. Del. heavy engr. constrn. program Citizen Amb. Program, Peoples Republic of China, 1990, USSR, 1991, Panama, 1996. Active People to People Internat., Kansas City, Mo., 1989—. Major USAF, 1941-46, 51-53. Mem. NSPE, IEEE, U.S. Com. Large Dams, Elks, Masons. Methodist. Achievements include participation in development, construction and operation of Missouri River Basin power system. Home and Office: 533 Park Ln Billings MT 59102-1018

GERLANC, GLENN MARC, lawyer; b. N.Y.C., Jan. 25, 1950; BA, Harvard U., 1972; JD, Hofstra U., 1977; LLM, NYU, 1987. Bar: N.J. 1977, N.Y. 1989. Asst. prosecutor Bergen County Prosecutor's Office, Hackensack, N.J., 1977-80; assoc. atty. Beattie & Padovano, Montvale, N.J., 1980-81; atty. pvt. practice, Hackensack, 1981-90; ptnr. Parisi, Gerlanc & Greenfield P.A., Hackensack, 1991-93, Parisi & Gerlanc P.A., 1993—. Mem. ATLA, N.J. Bar Assn., Bergen County Bar Assn., Million Dollar Advs. Forum. Office: Parisi & Gerlanc PA 190 Moore St Hackensack NJ 07601-7418

GERLING, JOSEPH ANTHONY, lawyer; b. Dayton, Ohio, Feb. 25, 1952; s. Clarence Anthony and Betty Jane (Blue) G.; m. Janet Mary Cox, July 6, 1974; children: Anthony, Andrew, Christopher. BCE, U. Notre Dame, 1974; JD, Ohio State U., 1977. Bar: Ohiho 1977. Rsch. scientist Battelle Meml. Inst., Columbus, Ohio, 1974-77; assoc. Lurie Gifford & Davis, Columbus, 1977-78, Lane Alton & Horst, Columbus, 1978—. Mem. Columbus Bar. Assn. (pres. 1987-88), Athletic Club Columbus. Avocations: sports, basketball, softball, photography. Home: 2278 Viburnum Ln Columbus OH 43235-4266 Office: Lane Alton & Horst 175 S Third St Columbus OH 43215-5152 E-mail: jgerling@lah4law.com.

GERLITS, FRANCIS JOSEPH, lawyer; b. Chgo., Mar. 29, 1931; s. John T. and May (Cameron) G.; m. Suzanne Long, June 20, 1953; children: Kathleen, Karen, Mary Cameron, Francis Jr. Ph.B., U. Notre Dame, 1953; JD, U. Chgo., 1958. Bar: Ill. 1958. Ptnr. Kirkland & Ellis, Chgo., 1964-95, of counsel, 1995; gen. counsel Internat. Harvester Co. (now Navistar Internat. Corp.), Chgo., 1985-90. Mem. ABA, Order of Coif, Tavern Club, Chicago Club Office: Kirkland & Ellis 200 E Randolph St Fl 54 Chicago IL 60601-6636

GERLITZ, CURTIS NEAL, business executive; b. Jan. 26, 1944; s. Gustav Albert and Elna G.; m. Audrey Jean D'Almaine, Oct. 6, 1973. BSBA, U. Minn., 1966; MBA, No. Ill. U., 1990. Purchasing agt. I. S. Berlin Press, Chgo., 1973-75; asst. purchasing agt. Daubert Chem. Co., Oak Brook, Ill., 1975-78; purchasing mgr. IBG Internat., Wheeling, Ill., 1978-86; dir. purchasing Advance Process Supply Co., Chgo., 1986-91; pres. Selectech, Mount Prospect, Ill., 1991—. Decorated Purple Heart. Mem. Nat. Assn. Purchasing Mgmt., Purchasing Assn. Chgo., Mfrs. Agts. Nat. Assn., United Assn. Mgrs. Reps. (mem. nat. bd. advisors 1994-96), Beta Gamma Sigma, Sigma Iota Epsilon. Home: 404 S Helena Ave Mount Prospect IL 60056-2854 Office: Selectech Internat Inc 119 S Emerson St Ste 142 Mount Prospect IL 60056

GERLITZ, FRANK EDWARD, engineer; b. Phila., May 31, 1948; s. Frank Edward and LaNieta Vivian (Souden) G. BS, Bucknell U., 1970, U. Wis., 1973, MS, 1977, PhD, 1990. Biomed. engr. Otto Hiller Co., Madison, Wis., 1973-78, U. Wis., Madison, 1973-84, Madison Area Tech. Coll., 1975-76, Ray-O-Vac, Madison, 1978-81, AEC, Inc., Elk Grove Village, Ill., 1984-88; faculty engring. U. Mich., Ann Arbor, 1989—, Washtenaw Coll., Ann Arbor, 1991—, Ea. Mich. U., Ypsilanti, 1994—. Mem. Am. Soc. Engring. Edn., SME, SPE. Home: 2312 Prairie St Ann Arbor MI 48105-1444 Office: Washtenaw Coll 4800 W Huron River Dr Ann Arbor MI 48103-9418 E-mail: gerlitz@wccnet.org.

GERLOFF, GARY MARTIN, writer; b. Hayward, Calif., Nov. 22, 1967; s. Ray Claude (dec.) and Doris Elaine (dec.) Gerloff; m. Jill Marie Wimer, May 9, 1968; 1 child, Stephen Ray. Diploma Minor in Music, Calif. State U., 1989, BS in Phys. Edn., 1997. Cert. Police Officer Stds. & Trng., Calif., 1991, Police Officer Stds. & Trng., Idaho, 1999. Dep. sheriff LA Sheriff's Dept., 1991—94; health, fitness coord. YMCA, Boise, 1997—99; trooper Idaho State Police, Boise, 1999—2002; freelance writer Clovis, Calif., 2002—. Musician: (musical recording) Los Hooligans Traditions (Rec. Contract, 1997). Conservative. Lutheran. Avocations: writing, landscaping, instrumental music, exercise, reading. Personal E-mail: gerloffmk@attbi.com.

GERLT, WAYNE CHRISTOPHER, lawyer; b. Hartford, Conn., Mar. 7, 1948; m. Elaine Della Barnarda, Feb. 27, 1970; 3 children. BA, U. Conn., 1970; JD, Capital U., 1975. Bar: Ohio 1975, Conn. 1976, U.S. Dist. Ct. Conn. 1976, U.S. Supreme Ct. 1979. Sole practice, South Windsor, Conn., 1984—. Mem. ABA, Conn. Bar Assn., Order of Curia. Roman Catholic. Home: 2620 Ellington Rd South Windsor CT 06074-2207 Office: 435 Buckland Rd PO Box 1132 South Windsor CT 06074-1132

GERMAIN, REGINA, lawyer; b. Bath, Maine, Mar. 19, 1961; d. Peter Daniel and Regina Germain. BSFS, Georgetown U., 1983; JD, U. Pitts., 1989; LLM, Georgetown U. Law Ctr., 2003. Bar: Pa. 1989, U.S. Supreme Ct. 1997. Sr. legal counselor UN's High Commr. for Refugees, Washington, 1995-2001; tchg. fellow Ctr. Applied Legal Studies, Georgetown U. Law Ctr., 2001—03. Author: AILA's Asylum Primer: A Practical Guide to U.S. Asylum Law and Procedure, 3d edit., 2003. Office: 722 Thayer Ave Silver Spring MD 20910

GERMAN, FRANK WILLIAM, broadcaster; b. Haverhill, Mass., Apr. 22, 1921; s. Frank William German and Jane Rose Amirault; m. Mary W. Gibbs, June 12, 1948 (dec. Sept. 1999); children: Paul, Thomas, Ann, Kay. BA, Emerson Coll., 1950. Radio announcer WIXHR, Cambridge, Mass., 1946-48, WBMS, Boston, 1948-50; sales WELL, Battle Creek, Mich., 1950-52; radio announcer WJWL, Georgetown, Del., 1952-54, WOND, Pleasantville, N.J., 1954-56; program dir. WJWL, Georgetown, 1956-58; ops. mgr. WBEE, Harvey, Ill., 1958-86; ret. Elected Tinley Park Village Clk., 1969—; sec. Sch. Dist. 228, Midlothian, Ill., 1990. Staff sgt. U.S. Army, 1942-46. Mem. Internat. Inst. (dir. 1984-88), Mspl. Clk. Ill. (pres. 1978), S & W Cook County Clks. (pres. 1971—). Independent. Roman Catholic. Avocation: photography. Home: 16835 New England Ave Tinley Park IL 60477 Office: Village of Tinley Park 16250 Oak Park Ave Tinley Park IL 60477

GERMAN, G. MICHAEL, lawyer; b. Gary, Ind., June 15, 1952; s. George N. and Mary Ann G. Student, Wabash Coll., Crawfordsville, Ind., 1970-72; BA, U. Ill., 1976; JD, U. San Francisco, 1981. Bar: Calif. 1982, U.S. Ct. Appeals (9th cir.) 1983, U.S. Supreme Ct. 1988, U.S. Ct. Appeals (D.C. cir.) 1990, U.S. Dist. Ct. (no., so., ea. and cen. dists.) Calif. 1982, U.S. Dist. Ct. (no. dist.) Ind. 1983. Assoc. Acret & Perrochet, San Francisco, 1979-84; ptnr. German & Siggins, San Francisco, 1984-86; pvt. practice San Francisco, 1987—2000; dep. atty. gen. Calif. Dept Justice, San Francisco, 2000—03, San Diego, 2003—. Pres. bd. Dolores Plaza Condo Assn., San Francisco, 1984-86; v.p., treas., pres. Log Cabin Club of San Francisco, gen. counsel Log Cabin of Calif., 1995—; gen. counsel San Francisco County Rep. Ctrl. Com., 1996-2003. With USN, 1972-75. Mem.: Maritime Law Assn. U.S. (proctor in admiralty 1984—), League Am. Bicyclists (legal advisor 1989—2000), Olympic Club, Sigma Chi. Roman Catholic. Avocations: swimming, cycling. Office: Calif Dept Justice 110 West A St Ste 1110 San Diego CA 92101

GERMAN, JEFFREY ALLEN, physician; b. Lake Charles, La., Sept. 23, 1966; m. Carrie Michael Newton, Aug. 11, 1990; 1 child, Allison Michelle. MD, La. State U. Health Sciences Ctr., 1992. Board Certified Am. Acad. of Family Practice, 1995. Chief resident Dept. of Family Medicine LSUHSC-S, Shreveport, La., 1994—95, physician instr., 1995—97, asst. prof., 1997—2002, assoc.

prof., 2003—. Music compact disc, Worth It All. Ordained deacon Brookwood Bapt. Ch., Shreveport, La., 1999—2003, sunday sch. tchr., 1995—2003; active mem. Samaritan Counseling Ctr., Shreveport, La., 1998—2001; ann. short term med. missionary Mexican Indian Tng. Ctr., Cordoba, Mexico, 1995—2003. Mem.: Am. Acad. of Family Physicians, Alpha Omega Alpha (faculty councilor 1999—2003). Avocations: triathlons, flyfishing, playing acoustic guitar. Office: LSUHSC-Shreveport 1501 Kings Hwy Shreveport LA 71103

GERMAN, JUNE RESNICK, lawyer; b. N.Y.C., Feb. 24, 1946; d. Irving and Stella (Weintraub) Resnick; m. Harold Jacob German, May 31, 1974; children: Beth Melissa, Heather Alice, Bret. BA, U. Pa., 1965; JD, NYU, 1968. Bar: N.Y. 1968, U.S. Dist. Ct. (ea. and so. dists.) N.Y. 1974, U.S. Ct. Appeals (2d cir.) 1973, U.S. Supreme Ct. 1973. Atty., sr. atty., supervising atty. Mental Health Info. Svc., N.Y.C., 1968-77; atty., advisor Course in Human Behavior Mems. of N.Y. State Judiciary, Nassau and Suffolk County, 1980; pvt. practice Huntington, N.Y., 1985—. *June Resnick German brought several test cases which guaranteed rights to mentally disabled persons in the civil and criminal justice system, including a landmark case which established that, in New York State, civil involuntary patients have (a) a right to treatment, (b) a right to be treated in a facility that is least restrictive of their liberty, and (c) a right not to be transferred to a correctional facility. She has written several articles pertaining to the rights of the mentally disabled and has prepared amicus curiae briefs to the United States Supreme Court in the fields of mental health and environmental law.She has successfully represented the "Mi Casa" orphanage, an organization caring for 500 Guatemalan children, in litigation to recover funds wrongfully seized by the United States.* Contbg. author: Bioethics and Human Rights, 1978, Mental Illness, Due Process and the Acquitted Defendant, 1979; contbr. chpts. to books, articles to profl. jours. Chmn. Citizen's Ad Hoc Com. Constrn. of the Dix Hills Water Adminstrn. Bldg., Huntington, N.Y., 1985-90; mem. Citizens Adv. Com. for Dix Hills Water Dist., Huntington, 1992—; dir. House Beautiful Assn. at Dix Hills, 1986—, Citizens for a Livable Environment and Recycling, Huntington, 1989-93; active Suffolk County (N.Y.) Dem. Com., 1986—, Deer Park Avenue Task Force, Town of Huntington, 1997-98, Dix Hills Revitalization Com., 1999-2000. Mem. Suffolk County Bar Assn. Jewish. Avocations: tennis, hiking, travel. Office: 150 Main St Huntington NY 11743-6908

GERMAN, LEWIS, fire and rescue chief, consultant; b. Washington, Aug. 13, 1948; s. Al L and Harriet Charlotte German; m. Penelope S. Sullivan (dec.); life ptnr. Mary A. Hunter. Fire & rescue dep. chief Bethesda-Chevy Chase (Md.) Rescue Squad, 1997—99, fire & rescue chief, 1999—2001. Fire/rescue assistant chief Bethesda Chevy Chase (Md) Rescue Squad, 1990—97. Vol. Bethesda-Chevy Chase Rescue Squad, Md., 1966—2001. Mem.: Bethesda Chevy Chase Rescue Squad (life; Chief 1999—2001). Avocations: cooking, travel, outdoors. Home: 6123 Swansea Street Bethesda MD 20817 also: 6400 Brisa Del Mar El Paso TX 79912 Personal E-mail: lgerman@erols.com. E-mail: lgerman@sbcglobal.net.

GERMAN, MONICA ANN, small business owner; b. Delphos, Ohio, Jan. 7, 1935; d. Leo John and Catherine M. Allemeier; m. Carl John German, July 30, 1955; children: Barbara Brewster, James, Francis. Cert. life. ins. agt. Ohio. Sales person Avon, Delphos, 1967—70; head infirmary St. John's Grade Sch., Delphos, 1973—76; clk. Century Ho. Wares, Lima, Ohio, 1979—85; life ins. agt. A. L. Williams, Lima, 1985—87; dir. Sunrider Internat., Delphos, 1987—. Author: (autobiography) Thankful for the Little Things, 1995, Faith Got Me Through, 1991. Vol. record keeper St. John's Ch., Delphos, 1979—82. Conservative. Roman Catholic. Avocations: travel, fishing, reading, music, photography. Personal E-mail: german@wcoil.com.

GERMAN, RANDALL MICHAEL, materials engineering educator, consultant; b. Bainbridge, Md., Nov. 12, 1946; s. Eugene Knox and Helen (Schrufer) G.; m. Carol Jean Hosmer, Dec. 21, 1968; children: Eric, Garth. BS in Materials Sci., San Jose State U., 1968; MS in Metall. Engring., Ohio State U., 1971; PhD in Materials Sci., U. Calif., Davis, 1975; cert. mgmt. devel., Hartford Grad. Ctr., 1979. Materials scientist Battelle Columbus Labs., Columbus, Ohio, 1968-69; tech. staff Sandia Nat. Lab., Livermore, Calif., 1969-77; dir. R&D Mott Metall. Corp., Farmington, Conn., 1977-78; dir. rsch. J.M. Ney Co., Bloomfield, Conn., 1978-80; Hunt prof. Rensselaer Poly. Inst., Troy, N.Y., 1980-91; Brush chair prof. materials Pa. State U., University Park, 1991—. Founder Six Cos., Inc., Troy, 1989—, Xform; dir. PIM Symposium, 1990—. Author: Powder Metallurgy Science, 1984, 2d edit., 1994, Liquid Phase Sintering, 1985, Powder Packing Characteristics, 1989, Injection Molding, 1990, Sintering Theory and Practice, 1996, Injection Molding of Metals and Ceramics, 1997, Powder Metallurgy of Iron and Steel, 1998, PIM Design and Applications, 2003; contbr. numerous articles to profl. jours.; patentee in field. Named Hon. Prof. N.E. U. Tech., 1985, Disting. Alumni U. Calif., 1990, Penn State Engring. Soc. Outstanding and Premiere Rschr. award, 1995. Fellow ASM Internat. (chmn. Geissler award 1983), Am. Powder Metallurgy (spkr., organizer, bd. dirs.); mem. Minerals, Metals, Materials Soc. (chmn. 1983-85), Am. Ceramic Soc., Materials Rsch. Soc., Alpha Sigma Mu (hon.). Avocation: bicycling. Home: 1145 Outer Dr State College PA 16801-8240 E-mail: rmg4@psu.edu., cisp@psu.edu.

GERMAN, WILLIAM, newspaper editor; b. N.Y.C., Jan. 4, 1919; s. Sam and Celia (Norack) G.; m. Gertrude Pasenkoff, Oct. 12, 1940 (dec. 1998); children: David, Ellen, Stephen. BA, Bklyn. Coll., 1939; MS, Columbia U., 1940; Nieman fellow, Harvard U., 1950. Mng. editor KQED, Newspaper of the Air, 1968; editor Chronicle Fgn. Service, 1960-77; reporter, asst. fgn., news, mng., exec. editor, editor San Francisco Chronicle, 1940-2000, editor emeritus, 2000—. Lectr. U. Calif., Berkeley, 1946-47, 68-70 Editor: San Francisco Chronicle Reader, 1962. Bd. trustees World Affairs Coun. Served with AUS, 1943-45. Mem. AP Mng. Editors Assn., Am. Soc. Newspaper Editors, Commonwealth Club of Calif. (pres. 1995). Home: 150 Lovell Ave Mill Valley CA 94941-1883 Office: San Francisco Chronicle 901 Mission St San Francisco CA 94103-2905 E-mail: wgerman@sfchronicle.com.

GERMANN, RICHARD P(AUL), consultant, pharmaceutical company chemist, executive; b. Ithaca, N.Y., Apr. 3, 1918; s. Frank E.E. and Martha Minna Marie (Knechtel) G.; m. Malinda Jane Plietz, Dec. 11, 1942; 1 child, Cheranne Lee. Student, U. N.Mex., 1938-39; BA, U. Colo., 1939, postgrad., 1940-41, Western Res. U., 1941-43, Brown U., 1954. Chief analytical chemist Taylor Refining Co., Corpus Christi, 1943-44; rsch. devel. chemist Calco Chem. divsn. Am. Cyanamid Co., 1944-52; devel. chemist charge pilot plant Alrose Chem. Co. divsn. Geigy Chem. Corp., 1952-55; new product devel. chemist, rsch. divsn. W.R. Grace & Co., Clarksville, Md., 1955-60; chief chemist soap-cosmetic divsn. G.H. Packwood Mfg. Co., St. Louis, 1960-61; coord., promoter chem. product devel. Abbott Labs., North Chicago, Ill., 1961-71; internat. chem. cons. to mgmt., 1971-73; pres. Germann Internat. Ltd., 1973-82, Ramtek Internat. Ltd., 1973-2000. Real estate broker, 1972-90; cons. major Japanese chem. cos., 1971-85; cons. dept. chemistry Bowling Green (Ohio) State U., 1988. Author: The Technical Man of the Sea of Change, 1965, Decontamination of Plant Wastes--An Overview, 1969, Science's Ultimate Challenge--The Re-evaluation of Ancient Occult Knowledge, 1978, Science and Innovation, 1993; patentee in U.S. and fgn. countries on sulfonamides, vitamins, detergent-softeners and biocides. Rep. Am. Inst. Chemists to Joint Com. on Employment Practices, 1969-72; vestryman St. Paul's Episc. Ch., Norwalk, Ohio, 1978-81, chmn. adminstrn. and long-range planning comm., 1980-81, The Ch. of Light, Friends of the Norwalk Pub. Libr., 1996-97, pres., 1997-99; trustee Svcs. for the Aging, Inc., 1982-94, treas., 1992-93, pres., 1994; mem. nutritional coun. Ohio Dist. Five Area Agy. on Aging, 1983-84; sr. adv. Ohio Assn. Ctrs. for Sr. Citizens, Inc., 1982-90; bd. dirs. Christie Lane Industries, 1981—, chmn., 1988-94; mem. com. Huron County Disaster Svcs. Agy., 1987-89, sec. Fellow AAAS, Am. Inst. Chemists (chmn. com. employment rels. 1969-72), Chem. Soc. (London); mem. Am. Chem. Soc. (councilor 1971-73, chmn. membership com. chem. mktg. and econs. divsn. 1966-68, chmn. program com. 1968-69, del. at large for local sects. 1970-71, chmn. 1972-73, chmn. Chgo. program com. 1966-67, chmn. Chgo. endowment com. 1967-68, dir. Chgo. sect. 1968-72, chmn. awards com. 1972-73, sec. chem. mktg. and econs. group Chgo. sect. 1964-66, chmn. 1967-68), Am. Numastic, Internat. Sci. Found., Sci. Rsch. Soc. Am., Comml. Chem. Devel. Assn. (chmn. program com. Chgo. conv. 1966, mem. fin. com. 1966-67, ad hoc com. of Comml. Chem. Devel. Assn. and Chem. Market Rsch. Assn. 1968-69, co-chmn. pub. rels. Denver conv. 1968, chmn. membership com. 1969-70, mem. directory com. 1967-68, employment com. 1969-70), Nat. Security Indsl. Assn. (com. rep. ocean sci. tech. com., maintenance adv. com., tng. ad. com. 1962-70), Midwest Planning Assn., Am. Assn. Textile Chemists and Colorists, Am. Pharm. Assn., Midwest Chem. Mktg. Assn., Am. Mgmt. Assn., N.Y. Acad. Scis., Internat. Platform Assn., Am. Meteorol. Soc., Water Pollution Control Fedn., Lake County Bd. Realtors, World Future Soc., Midwest Planning Assn., Am. Fedn. Astrologers, Washington Astrological Assn. (v.p. 1959-60), Ancient Astronaut Soc., Am. Philatelic Soc., Am. Numismatic Assn., Am. Rose Soc., AARP (pres. Huron county Firelands chpt. #4110 1986-88, chmn. legis. com. 1988-90, active project vote, pres. 1997-98, bd. dirs. 1998—), Friends Norwalk Pub. Libr. (sec. 1997-98, pres. 1998-2000), Chemists Club (N.Y.C., Chgo.), Torch Club, Toastmasters, Lions (sec. Allview, Md. 1956-57), Kiwanis, Masons, (32nd degree, Knights Templar, Rotary, Gamma Delta (pres. Cleve. chapt. 1941-42), Sigma Xi, Alpha Chi Sigma (chmn. profl. activities com. 1968-70, pres. Chgo. chpt. 1968-70). Home and Office: 394 Cleveland Rd #11H Norwalk OH 44857-8500 *Total knowledge, whether it be in business, science, history, or religion, is a mirage. That which we believe to be true today will be subject to continuous modification throughout all eternity as understanding of the universe continues to expand. This belief has made my life an adventure in which I have attempted to find the many "reasons why" which determine the way we think and live. It is obvious that all the fields in question are interrelated in many ways. History shows that dogma in any discipline or a lack of knowledge of the past has always inhibited or prevented man's spiritual, scientific or material growth. The incorrect beliefs thus perpetuated become the cross we bear that prevents us in no small part from living our lives to the fullest during our short stay here on earth. Since I believe that there is a hidden reason for everything that happens during our lifetime, logic tells me that in the eons to come each soul will continue its adventures through many rebirths both here on this earth and on earths in many distant galaxies far out in the universe as God allows us to increase our knowledge of the real reason for our existence.*

GERMANO, WILLIAM PAUL, publisher; b. Yonkers, N.Y., Oct. 10, 1950; s. William Peter and Edna Mary (Gilmore) G.; m. Diane Grace Gibbons, July 21, 1973; 1 child, Christian. BA in English, Columbia U., 1972; PhD in English, Ind. U., 1981. Editor Columbia U. Press, N.Y.C., 1980-83, editor in chief, 1983-85; v.p., editorial dir. Routledge, Chapman and Hall Inc., N.Y.C., 1986-92, Routledge, Inc., N.Y.C., 1992-96, v.p., dir. pub. humanities, 1996—. Author: Getting It Published: A Guide for Scholars and Anyone Else Serious About Serious Books, 2001. Mem. MLA, PEN, The English Inst. Home: 33 Riverside Dr New York NY 10023-8012 Office: Routledge 29 W 35th St New York NY 10001-2291 E-mail: wgermano@taylorandfrancis.com.

GERMANOWSKI, JANET, women's health and medical surgical nurse, educator, researcher; b. Augusta, Ga., Oct. 29, 1943; d. Leonard and Marion (Davis) Volkin; m. Peter J. Germanowski, Dec. 28, 1970; children: Peter, Lauren. BSN, U. Pitts., 1965, MSN, 1990, postgrad., 1999. Cert. clin. rsch. coord. Rsch. assoc. HealthAmerica, Pitts.; project coord. Aminoguanidine Drug Trial, U. Pitts.; project nurse cholesterol lowering intervention program U. Pitts.; head nurse, office mgr. dept. ob-gyn. Magee Women's Hosp., Pitts., 1971-86; acting clin. instr. U. Pitts. Sch. Nursing, 1989, grad. student asst., 1987-90; project nurse cholesterol lowering intervention program U. Pitts., 1990-94; project coord. Aminoguanidine Drug Trial, U. Pitts., 1994-95; rsch. assoc. HealthAmerica, Pitts., 1995-97; head nurse, office mgr. dept. ob-gyn. Magee Women's Hosp., Pitts.; grad. student asst. U. Pitts. Sch. Nursing, sr. clin. rsch. coord. nTouch Rsch., Pitts., 1997—. Contbr. articles to profl. jours. Mem. ANA, NAACOG, Pa. Nurses Assn., Sigma Theta Tau. Home and Office: 54 Ridgecrest Dr Pittsburgh PA 15235-4548

GERMANY, DANIEL MONROE, aerospace engineer; b. Lake Village, Ark., Sept. 14, 1937; s. Jones Harry and Sara (Farrar) G.; m. Edie Germany; children: Cheryl Germany, Danel Germany, Dianne Germany, Randall Robertson, Rick Robertson, Vaughn Loiuse. BSM.E., Miss. State U., 1959. Aerospace systems engr. NASA Marshall Space Flight Center, Huntsville, Ala., 1960-78; tech. exec. asst. to assoc. adminstr. of shuttle transp. systems NASA Hdqrs., Washington, 1978-79, dir. orbiter programs, 1979-81; asst. mgr. Orbiter Project Office Johnson Space Ctr., Houston, 1982, mgr. Flight Equipment Project Office, 1983-85, dep. mgr. Space Sta. Project Office, 1985-86, dep. mgr. Orbiter and GFE Projects Office, 1987-90, mgr. Orbiter and GFE Projects Office, 1990-95; ind. aerospace cons., 1995-97; program dir. Honeywell Aerospace, Houston, 1997—2002. Aerospace cons., 2002—. Republican.

GERMINARIO, LOUIS THOMAS, materials scientist; b. Molfetta, Apuglia, Italy, Sept. 27, 1947; came to U.S., 1956; s. Diego and Angela Germinario; m. Violet Joan Maas, May 19, 1984; children: Stephanie, Victoria. BA, Gettysburg (Pa.) Coll., 1970; MS, Cath. U. Am., 1972, PhD, 1973. Staff scientist, cons. EMV Assocs. Microanalysis Lab., Rockville, Md., 1972-73; postdoctoral rsch. assoc. Ariz. State U., Tempe, 1973-75; NIH fellow Johns Hopkins U., Balt., 1975-78; sr. rsch. assoc. Case Western Res. U., Cleve., 1978-81; rsch. chemist Eastman Chem. Co., Kingsport, Tenn., 1981-86, sr. rsch. chemist, 1986-91, prin. rsch. chemist, 1991-95, rsch. assoc., 1995—2002, sr. rsch. assoc., 2002—. Session chmn. IUPAC Internat. Symposium on Macromolecules, Akron, 1995. Contbr. articles to profl. jours. Grantee Sigma Xi, 1972, Biophys. Soc., 1978. Mem. Am. Chem. Soc., Electron Microscopy Soc. Am. (session chmn. 1975), N.Y. Acad. Sci., Microscopy Soc. Am. (session chmn. 1995), Sigma Xi, Beta Beta Beta. Achievements include new concepts in catalysis design via mixed metal oxide polyester catalysis, polymer structure-property behavior; heterogeneous catalyst characterization; patents on improved photostability and weatherability of polyesters, methods for reducing peel defects on adhesive bonded plastics, nanostructured coatings for improved gas barrier properties of shaped plastic articles, methods to produce polyester containers with reduced coefficient of friction, improved clarity and reduced mold plate-out, photocurable coatings for polyester articles. Office: Eastman Chemical Co Eastman Rd Kingsport TN 37662-5150 E-mail: germ@eastman.com.

GERMROTH, PETER, biologist, educator; b. Frankfurt, Hessen, Germany, Dec. 15, 1958; came to US, 1998; m. Jennifer R. Langford, Aug. 7, 1998. Dr. phil. nat., Goethe U., Frankfurt, 1990. Tchg. cert. Hessen, Germany. Researcher Max Planck Inst. Brain Rsch., Frankfurt, 1987-90; tchr. Goethe Sch., Frankfurt, 1993-98; tchr. biology North Shore Country Day Sch., Winnetka, Ill., 1999-2001. Adj. lectr. Pensacola (Fla.) J. Coll., 1999, 2001—02, Okaloosa Walton C.C., Niceville, 1999, Niceville, 2001—02; lectr. Hillsborough C.C., 2002—. Editor, translator: Spectrum Akademischer Verlag, 1988-98, The Forebrain in Non-Mammals, 1990; mem. editl. bd., contbr. Neuropsychology, German edit., 1993; contbr. articles to profl. jours. Bd. dirs., pub. rels. officer Hessischer Philologen Verband, Wiesbaden, Germany, 1992-98. Mem.: Nat. Sci. Tchrs. Assn., Human Anatomical and Phys. Soc., Soc. German Physicians and Scientists. Avocations: reading, writing, scuba diving. Office: Hillsborough Community Coll Dale Mabry Campus 4001 Tampa Bay Blvd Tampa FL 33614

GERN, JAMES E. physician, researcher; b. Milwaukee, Wis. MD, U. of South Fla., 1978—81. Lic. allergist/immunologist Am. Bd. of Allergy and Immunology, 1991. Assoc. prof. of pediat. U. of Wis., 1992—. Fellow: Am. Acad. of Allergy, Asthma, and Immunology. Office: University of Wisconsin Hosp K4/918 CSC 600 Highland Ave Madison WI 53792-9988

GERNAND, BRADLEY ELTON, library manager, archivist; b. Hugo, Okla., Aug. 29, 1964; s. Charles D. Jr. and Mary Ellen (Akins) G. BA, U. Okla., 1985, MA, 1987, postgrad., 1987—. Archivist Western History Collections, Norman, Okla., 1982-89, Nat. Archives of U.S., Washington, 1989—91, Libr. of Congress, Washington, 1991—2001; libr. mgr. Inst. for Def. Analyses, Alexandria, Va., 2001—. Lachenmeyer Media fellow U. Okla., 1985-87. Independent. Baptist. Avocations: photography, reading, history. Office: Inst for Def Analyses 4850 Mark Center Dr Alexandria VA 22311-1882

GERNER, EDWARD WILLIAM, medical educator; b. N.Y.C., Nov. 8, 1940; s. David and Anne (Robbins) G.; m. Judith E. Delbaum, June 5, 1983; 1 child, Danielle. BA magna cum laude, Clark U., 1961; MD, NYU, 1965. Diplomate Am. Bd. Ophthalmology, Am. Bd. Neurology. Intern Presbyn. U. Pitts. Hosp., 1965-66; resident Hosp. U. Pa., Phila., 1967-69; instr. dept. neurology U. Pa. Sch. Medicine, Phila., 1967-69, instr. dept. ophthalmology, 1972-74; attending neurologist Tulane U. Sch. Medicine, New Orleans, 1969-71; asst. surgeon Wills Eye Hosp., Phila., 1981-88, assoc. surgeon, 1988—; asst. prof. dept. neurology T. Jefferson U. Sch. Medicine, Phila., 1978-88, asst. prof. dept. ophthalmology, 1982-88, assoc. prof., 1988—. Bd. dirs. Pa. Physicians Healthcare Plan, Harrisburg. Contbr. chpts. to books and articles to profl. jours. Lt. comdr. USPHS, 1969-72. N.Y. State Regent scholar N.Y. State Bd. Regents, 1957-61; Jones fellow Mayo Clinic, Rochester, Minn., 1965. Fellow Am. Acad. Ophthalmology, Am. Acad. Neurology; mem. Royal Soc. Medicine (affiliate), Phi Beta Kappa. Avocations: photography, gardening. Office: 1015 Chestnut St # 1125 Philadelphia PA 19107-5127

GERNERT, JEFFREY JARED, clinical psychologist; b. Takoma Park, Md., Dec. 15, 1961; s. Earl Clifford and Darlene (Grant) Gernert. BA, U. Pa., 1987; MPhil, George Washington U., 1993, PhD, 1995. Lic. psychologist, D.C., Md. Psychology intern St. Elizabeth's Hosp., Washington, 1993-94, postdoctoral fellow, 1994-96; clin. psychologist Comprehensive Geriatric Svcs., Towson, Md., 1996-2000; pvt. practice, 2000—. Contbr. articles to profl. jours. Mem.: APA. Home: 1916 17th St NW Apt 508 Washington DC 20009-6205 E-mail: jgernert@hotmail.com.

GERNON, CLARKE JOSEPH, SR., mechanical and forensic engineering consultant; b. New Orleans, Dec. 27, 1944; s. Edward James and Mary Emma (Harvey) G.; 1 child, Clarke Joseph Jr. BSME, La. State U., 1969, MS in Engring. Mechanics, 1971. Registered profl. engr., La., Tenn., S.C. Mech. engr. Barnard and Burk, Inc., Baton Rouge, 1969-72; project engr. Lurgi-Knost, Inc., Baton Rouge, 1972-73; project mgr. The Rust Engring. Co., Baton Rouge, 1973-78, Imes and Assocs., Inc., Baton Rouge, 1978-86; mech. engr. and owner Futuretech Design, Baton Rouge, 1986—. Patentee in field. Vice chmn. Dixie Elec. Adv. Bd.; founding chmn. Capital Resource Conservation and Devel. Coun., Inc.; major supporter A Child's Wish; mem. Aero-space Task Force of MetroVision Partnership of New Orleans; incorporator and bd. dirs. Plantation Estates Civic Assn., Inc.; past pres. and bd. dirs. La. Miss. Christmas Tree Assn.; bd. dirs. Nat. Christmas Tree Assn., treas.; mem. quarantine adv. com. La. Dept. Agr. for Christmas Trees. Mem. ASME, Am. Welding Soc., So. Bldg. Code Congress Internat., Nat. Fire Protection Assn., Am. Acad. Forensic Scis. Roman Catholic. Avocations: model railroading, tropical fish, ornamental iron work. Office: Futuretech Design PO Box 896 Pearl River LA 70452-0896 E-mail: cjg@cgernon.com.

GERNSTEIN, STANLEY B. lawyer; b. Los Angeles, Apr. 20, 1941; s. Julius and Bess (Belle) Gernstein; m. Jane Ellen Hirschfield, June 9, 1963; children: Mark, Paul, Julie. Student, Brandeis U, 1958—62; BA, U. Chgo., 1964; PhD polit. sci., Harvard U., 1970; JD, Rutgers U., 1970. Bar: Ohio 1974, Mich. 1974, US Dist. Ct. (ea. dist.)/Mich. 1974. Asst. prof. polit. sci. U. Calif.-Davis, 1967—70, Livingston Coll., Rutgers U., 1970—73; asst. prof. law U. Toledo, Ohio, 1973—74; assoc. prof., 1974—77; ptnr. Henigman, Miller, Schwartz & Cohn, Detroit, 1972—78; judge US Bankruptcy Ct., Eas. Dist. Mich., 1982—84; adj. prof. law U. Detroit, 1982—, Wayne State U. Fellow Nat. Def. Grad. fellow, 1962—64, Thompson fellow, U. Chgo., 1964—67. Mem.: Detroit Bar Assn., Mich. Bar Assn., Fed. Bar Assn. Office: Room 102 A Fed Bldg 600 Church St Rm 102 Flint MI 48502-1214

GERO, ANTHONY GEORGE, securities and commodities trader; b. London, May 31, 1936; came to U.S., 1947; s. Stephen Gero and Ilona (Braun) Von Rieger; m. Joan Selinger, Nov. 20, 1969 (div. 1980); m. Gale Gendason, Feb. 14, 1989; 1 child, Danielle Joy. BS, NYU, 1959; cert., Investment Bankers Inst. U. Pa., 1965. Reporter USIS Chilean Eartquake Relief/Am. Embassy, 1959-60; ptnr. Goodbody & Co., 1960-64, Charles Plohn & Co., N.Y.C., 1964-67; v.p., dir. Internat. First Hanover Corp., N.Y.C., 1967-69; v.p. Drexel Burnham & Co., N.Y.C., 1971-80; 1st v.p. Prudential Securities, N.Y.C., 1981—2003; sr. v.p. Legg Mason Wood Walker Inc., NYC, 2003—. Mem. U.S. Dept. Commerce, Nat. Def. Exec. Res., 1989—; bd. dirs. Commodity Clearing Corp.; arbitrator Nat. Assn. Securities Dealers, N.Y. Stock Exch., 1992—. Author: Precious Metals, 1985. Dir., treas. children's fund Commodities Exch. Ctr., N.Y.C., 1980—; chmn. NYMEX Charitable Trust, N.Y.C., 1990-95; dir. Futures Options for Kids, 1995—. Recipient Cert., Holocaust Meml., 1991. Mem. Internat. Precious Metals Inst. (dir. 2000—), N.Y. Produce Exch., N.Y. Merc. Exch. (bd. dirs., treas. N.Y.C. chpt. 1974—), Commodity Exch. (bd. dirs. 1995), N.Y. Coffee, Sugar and Cocoa Exch., N.Y. Cotton Exch. (bd. dirs. 1995), Commodity Floor Brokers and Traders Assn. (chmn. 1990—), Investment Brokers Assn., Westchester County Policy Revolver Age, Westchester County Sheriff's Assn., N.Y. Police Res. Assn., Securities Industry Assn. (swaps and derivatives commn.), Police Res. Assn. N.Y.C., N.Y. State Troopers Alumni Assn. Republican. Avocations: photography, amateur radio, chess. Home: 180 East End Ave New York NY 10128-7763 Office: Legg Mason Inc 58th Fl One Chase Manhattan Plz New York NY 10005

GEROGEDES, KIMBERLY, historian, educator; d. J. Georgedes and J. Smith-Call. BA, U. Utah, 1983; MA, U. Colo, 1985; PhD, U. Wis., 1995. Asst. prof. history Franciscan U., Steubenville, Ohio, 1994—99, assoc. prof. history, 1999—, chair dept. history, 1999—. Cons. Christian History Project, 2000—02. Assoc. editor: Fides Quaerens Intellectum, 2000—; contbr. articles to profl. publs. Sec. Hist. Landmarks Commn., Steubenville, 2001—03. Fellow, Inst. European History, Mainz, Germany, 1989—91, Marie Christine Kohler fellow, U. Wis., 1990—94; grantee Summer Rsch. grantee, Franciscan U., 2000, Fgn. Travel award, U. Wis., 1988, 1990. Mem.: Soc. Cath. Social Scientists, Fellowship Cath. Scholars, Am. Soc. Ch. History, Medieval Acad. Am., Delta Kappa Gamma. Republican. Roman Catholic. Avocations: drawing, painting, martial arts. Office: Franciscan U 1235 Univ Blvd Steubenville OH 43952-1763 Office Fax: 740-283-6401. E-mail: kgeorgedes@franciscan.edu.

GEROLD, CHARLES MCADOW, real estate broker; b. Chgo., Feb. 21, 1927; s. Charles Augustus and Ethel McAdow Gerold; m. Adriana Youssif, June 15, 1967; children: Michael, James, Eric, Laura. BA, U. Wash., 1949, MA, 1954; PhD, Columbia Pacific U., 1983. Lic. securities dealer 1983, real estate broker 1974. Mng. editor Go Newspapers, Seattle, 1949—52; editor El Segundo (Calif.) Herald, 1953; asst. to pres. Internat. Rels. Inst., N.Y.C., 1955—56; farm labor svc. GS7-GS12 U.S. Dept. Labor, Washington, 1956—61; computer programmer Space Techs. Lab., L.A., 1967—68; asst. to pres. Advanced Mgmt. Systems, Santa Ana, Calif., 1968—69; chief of ops. Fair Practice and Tng. Clinic, L.A., 1969—70; dir. pers. Queen of Angels Hosp., L.A., 1970—71; adminstr. Bay Gen. Hosp., Chula Vista, Calif., 1971—73; pres.'s staff U. Calif., Berkeley, 1974—76; founder, pres. Health Care Mgmt. Search, Lafayette, Calif., 1976—83; stockbroker Merrill Lynch, Walnut Creek, Calif., 1983—84; real estate broker Gerold Real Estate, Moraga, Calif., 1984—. Tchr. English to Mex. adults Am. English Inst., Mexico City, 1953—54; tchr. electronic data processing El Camino Coll., Torrance, Calif., 1960—61; tchr. computers in mgmt., pers. adminstrn., etc. U. So. Calif., L.A., 1961—67; tchr. pers. adminstrn. Calif. State U., San Diego, 1972—73; tchr. U. So Calif. Grad. Program, Honolulu, Japan, Spain, France and Germany, 1965—67. Author (as Charles Perdu): (play) Dust, 1957 (Alden award, 1957), Echoes of Valor, 1993; Idylls Hymns Dirges, 2002. Pvt. USMC, 1945—46, Pacific. Fellow Inst. World Affairs, 1955—56. Home: 17 Woodford Dr Moraga CA 94556

GERON, CHRISTOPHER DOUGLAS, ecologist, environmental scientist, researcher; b. Springfield, Ohio, Dec. 11, 1961; s. Douglas Norman and Judith Carol Geron; m. Marie Lynn Miranda, July 28, 1990; children: Thompson Christopher, Elizabeth Mariel, Joy Viviana. MS, NC State U, Raleigh, NC, 1984—86; BS, Ohio State U, Columbus, OH, 1980—84. Sr. environ. sci. U.S. EPA, Rsch. Triangle Pk., NC, 1989—. Commr. Parkwood. Athletic Assn., Durham, NC, 2000—02. Recipient Superior Team Performance, Particulate matter team, U.S. EPA, Air & Waste Mgmt. Assn., 1990—2002. Achievements include research in Developed models and exptl. data on the contbn. of ecol. processes to chem. composition of the atmosphere. This info. has been used to devel. air pollution control strategies. Avocations: coach, outdoor, travel. Home: 451 Chatham Glen Dr Durham NC 27713 Office: US Environ Protection Agy 109 TW Alexander Dr MD E305-02 Research Triangle Park NC 27711 Home Fax: 919-541-7885; Office Fax: 919-541-7885. Personal E-mail: geron.chris@epa.gov. E-mail: geron.chris@epa.gov.

GERONEMUS, DIANN FOX, social work consultant; b. Chgo., July 4, 1947; d. Herbert J. and Edith (Robbins) Fox; 1 dau., Heather Eileen. BA with high honors, Mich. State U., 1969; MSW, U. Ill., 1971. Diplomate Am. Bd. Clin. Social Work; lic. clin. social worker, marriage and family therapist, Fla.; cert. case mgr.; bd. cert. diplomate clin. social work. Social worker neurology, neurosurgery and medicine Hosp. of Albert Einstein Coll. Medicine, 1971-74;

prin. social worker ob-gyn. and newborn infant svc. Rush-Presbyn.-St. Luke's Med. Ctr., 1974-75; social worker neurology, adminstr. Multiple Sclerosis Treatment Ctr., St. Barnabas Hosp., Bronx, N.Y., 1975-77, socio-med. rschr. dept. neurology and psychiatry, 1977-79, dir. social svc., 1979-80. Field work instr. Fordham U. Grad. Sch. Social Service, 1979-80; preceptor, social work program Fla. Atlantic U., Fla. Internat. U.; mem. edn. com., med. adv. bd., program cons. Nat. Multiple Sclerosis Soc., 1980-83, area service cons., 1983-86; pvt. practice psychotherapy; social work cons.; cons. in gerontology, rehab. and supervision, social worker, home health, geriatric care mgr., 1980—. Contbr. articles to profl. jours. Mem. Ombudsman Coun., 1992-94, vice chmn., 1993-94; sec. bd. dirs. South Fla. chpt. NMSS Broward Meals on Wheels; sec. bd. dirs. Homebound Program; sec., chmn. com. Nat. Multiple Sclerosis Soc. Grantee Nat. Multiple Sclerosis Soc., 1977-79. Mem. NASW, Acad. Cert. Social Workers, Am. Orthopsychiat. Assn. Jewish. Home: 833 NW 81st Way Fort Lauderdale FL 33324-1216

GERRA, MARTIN J(EROME), JR., economist, educator; b. N.Y.C., May 14, 1927; s. Martin Jerome and Margaret (Landi) G.; m. Anita Little, June 14, 1949; children: Ellen Gerra Conner, Martin J. III. BS, Georgetown U., 1949; MA, Cath. U., 1954. Economist U.S. Bur. Labor Statis., Washington, 1949-51; mgr. demand analysis USDA, Washington, 1952-61; lectr. polit. economy Johns Hopkins U., 1960—61; staff economist Lockheed Aircraft Corp., Marietta, Ga., 1962-64; mgr. internat. econs. IBM Corp., Armonk, N.Y., 1964-88; prof. econs. N.C. State U., Raleigh, 1989-91. Adj. prof. Coll. Notre Dame of Md., 1991-2000; assoc. Centre for Econ. and Bus. Rsch., London, 1991—; spl. asst. to pres. Gallandet U., 1974-75. Bd. dirs. Westchester Svcs. for Hearing Impaired, N.Y.C., 1977-81. Social Sci. Rsch. Coun. fellow, 1956, Johnston fellow in polit. Economy, Johns Hopkins U., 1958-59. Mem. Am. Econ. Assn. Home: 3505 Calvend Ln Kensington MD 20895-3110

GERRARD, JOHN M. state supreme court justice; b. Schuyler, Nebr., Nov. 2, 1953; BS, Nebr. Wesleyan U., 1976; MPA, U. Ariz., 1977; JD, U. of Pacific, 1981. Pvt. practice, Norfolk, 1981-95; city atty. City of Battle Creek, Nebr., 1982-95; justice Nebr. Supreme Ct., Lincoln, 1995—. Office: Nebr Supreme Ct 2219 State Capitol Lincoln NE 68509-8000 also: PO Box 98910 Lincoln NE 68509*

GERRARD, KEITH, lawyer; b. Malden, Mass., Feb. 8, 1935; s. William Francis and Mary Ethel (Compton) G.; Linda Jane Fay, Apr. 16, 1974; children by previous marriage: Jessica, Elizabeth; stepchildren: Elizabeth Perera, Jonathan Perera. AB, Harvard U., 1956, LLB, 1963. Bar: Wash. 1963. Assoc., Perkins Coie, Seattle, 1963-70, ptrn., 1970—. Served to 1st lt. USAF, 1956-59. Fellow Am. Coll. Trial Lawyers; mem. ABA, Wash. State Bar Assn., Seattle-King County Bar Assn., Rainier Club (Seattle). Office: Perkins Coie 1201 3rd Ave Fl 40 Seattle WA 98101-3029

GERRAS, STEPHEN JOSEPH, military officer, psychologist; b. Reading, Pa., June 23, 1960; s. Charles Stephen and Anne Christina Gerras; m. Ann Catherine Kelliher, Oct. 12, 1991; children: Joshua Stephen, Zachary Charles. PhD., Pa. State U., State Coll., Pa., 1992; BS, West Point Acad., West Point, NY, 1982; M Strategic Studies, U.S. Army War Coll., Carlisle Barracks, PA, 2002; MS, Pa. State U., State Coll., Pa., 1991. Bn. comdr. 24th Transp. Bn., Fort Eustis, Va., 1998—2001; liaison officer to Turkish mil. Office of Def. Cooperation, Ankara, Turkey, 2002—. Mem., army chief of staff strategic leadership task force U. S. Army War Coll., Carlisle Barracks, Pa., 2001—02. Author article to profl. jours. Lt. col. U.S. Army, 1982—2003. Recipient Douglas MacArthur Leadership Award, U.S. Army Command and Gen. Staff Coll., 1996. Mem.: Soc. of Indsl. and Orgnl. Psychologists. Avocations: travel, weightlifting, reading. Home Fax: 90-312-418-5661. Personal E-mail: stevegerras@hotmail.com.

GERRATT, BRADLEY SCOTT, public administrator; b. Norwood, Mass., Apr. 21, 1953; s. Irving and Lucille (Levine) Gerratt; m. Susan Lathrop Powers, Oct. 11, 1981; children: Nathan Powers, Aaron Powers. BA, Clark U., 1975; MA, MBA, U. Chgo., 1979. Gov.'s fellow Ill. Dept. Pub. Aid, Springfield, summer 1978; budget analyst Mass. Dept. Social Svcs., Boston, 1979-81, adminstrv. svcs. mgr., 1981-84; CFO City of Boston, Neighborhood Devel. and Employment Agy., 1984-85; dir. adminstrn. and fin. Pub. Facilities Dept. City of Boston, 1985-88; dep. dir. John F. Kennedy Libr., Boston, 1988-94, dir., 1994-2000; dir. adminstrn. and fin. Boston Pvt. Industry Coun., 2000—02; dep. dir. Dept. of Traffic, Parking and Transp. City of Cambridge, Mass., 2002—. Office: Dept Traffic Parking and Transp 238 Broadway Cambridge MA 02139

GERRETSEN, GILBERT WYNAND (GIL GERRETSEN), marketing mentor; b. Rotterdam, The Netherlands, May 8, 1955; arrived in Can., 1957, Can. citizen, 1960; arrived in U.S., 1980, naturalized, 1983; s. Everhardus Hubertus and Johanna (Boers) G.; m. Susan Boggs, June 27, 1980. B of Commerce, U. Calgary, Alberta, Canada, 1976. Group ins. adminstr., asst. supr. group acctg. Great-West Life Assurance, Winnipeg, Canada, 1978-80; supr. policyholder svc. Founders Life Ins., Tampa, Fla., 1980-81; cons. specialist group ins. William M. Mercer, Inc., Tampa, Fla., 1981-82; exec. dir. Junior Achievement, Greenville, S.C., 1982-85; pres. Jr. Achievement So. Ariz., Tucson, 1985-88; sr. dir. devel. Junior Achievement, Seattle, 1988-90; sr. dir. mktg. Washington Special Olympics, Seattle, 1990-92; chief mktg. officer ALM Internat., Greenville, 1992-94. Founder, pres. BizTrek Internat., Greenville, 1994—. Pub. (newsletter) BizTrek Mktg. Minute. Bd. dirs. Jr. Achievement, 1995-99, Greenville Humane Soc., 1996-97, S.C. Soc. for Prevention of Cruelty to Animals, 1996-97, Child Evangelism Fellowship, 1996, C. of C. Small Bus. Coun., 1996-99, Clemson U. Small Bus. Devel. Coun., 1996-2003, Greenville Chamber Edn. Com., 1996-99, CEO Roundtable, 1995-2000, Downtown Greenville Christian Businessmen's Com.; bd. dirs. Greenville Work Tng. Ctr., 1995-1999, chmn., 1997-99. Avocations: biblical studies, model railroading, oil painting. Office: 710 E McBee Ave Greenville SC 29601-3027 E-mail: WW@BizTrek.com.

GERRINGER, ELIZABETH (THE MARCHIONESS DE ROE DEVON), writer, lawyer; b. Edmund, Wis., Jan. 7, 1934; d. Clyde Elroy and Matilda Evangeline Knapp; m. Roe (Don Davis) Devon Gerringer-Busenbark, Sept. 30, 1968 (dec. Dec. 1972). Student, Madison Bus. Coll., 1952, San Francisco State Coll., 1953-54, Vivian Rich Sch. Fashion Design, 1955, Dale Carnegie Sch., 1956, Arthur Murray Dance Studio, 1956, Biscayne Acad. Music, 1957, L.A. City Coll., 1960-62, Santa Monica (Calif.) Jr. Coll., 1963; JD, U. Calif., San Francisco, 1973; postgrad., Wharton Sch., U. Pa., 1977, London Art Coll., 1979; PhD, U. Cambridge, 1979; student, Goethe Inst., 1985. Bar: Calif., 1965. Ordained to ministry, 1978. Atty. Dometrik's JIT-MAP, San Francisco, 1973—. Cons. in field; pres., tchr. Environ Improvement, Originals by Elizabeth. Actress Actors Workshop San Francisco, 1959, 65, Theatre of Arts Beverly Hills, Calif., 1963, also radio; artist, poet, singer, songwriter, playwright, dress designer; author: The Cardinal, 1947, Explorations in Worship, 1965, The Magic of Scents, 1967, New Highways, 1967, The Grace of Romance, 1968, Happening-Impact-Mald, 1971, Seven Day Rainbow, 1972, The Day of the Lone Survivor, 1972, Zachary's Adversaries, 1974, Fifteen from Iowa, 1977, Bart's White Elephant, 1976, Skid Row Minister, 1978, Points in Time, 1979, Special Appointment-A Clown in Town, 1979, Happenings, 1980, Candles, 1980, The Stranger in the Train, 1983, Votes from the Closet, 1984, Wait for Me, 1984, The Stairway, 1984, The River is a Rock, 1985, Happenings Revisited, 1986, Comparative Religion in the United States, 1986, Lumber in the Skies, 1986, The Fifth Season, 1987, Summer Thoughts, 1987, Crimes of the Heart, 1987, Toast Thoughts, 1988, The Contrast of Russian Literature Through the Eyes of an American Artist, 1988, A Thousand Points of Light, 1989, The Face in The Mirror, 1989, Sea Gulls, 1990, Voices on the Hill, 1991, It's Tough to Get a Matched Set, 1991, Equality, 1991, Miss Geranium, 1991, Forest Voices, 1991, Golden Threads, 1991, Castles in the Air, 1991, The Cave, 1991, Angels, 1991, Real, 1991, An Appeal to Reason, 1992, We Knew, 1992, Like It Is, 1992, Politicians Anonymous, 1993, Wheels Within Wheels, 1994, A Tree for All Seasons, 1995, The Visitor, 1995, Time Frames, 1996, Save the Dance, 1998, Flowers For My Grandfather, 1999, Last Day at Mission Rock, 1999, Waiting for the Train, 1999, The Influence of Rural Life Upon Culture, 1999, The Crowd, 2001, Without Saying Goodbye, 2002, The Moon's Agreement, 2003. Steering com. Explorations in Worship. Address: 1008 10th St #275 Sacramento CA 95814-3502 Fax: 916-442-3735.

GERRISH, BRIAN ALBERT, theologian, educator; b. London, Aug. 14, 1931; s. Albert and Doris (King) G.; children from previous marriage: Carolyn, Paul; m. Dawn Ann De Vries, Aug. 3, 1990; 1 child, Heather. BA, Queens' Coll., Cambridge, Eng., 1952, MA, 1956; cert., Westminster Coll., Cambridge, 1955; S.T.M., Union Theol. Sem., N.Y.C., 1956; PhD, Columbia U., 1958; D.D. (hon.), U. St. Andrews, Scotland, 1984. Ordained to ministry Presbyn. Ch., 1957. Asst. pastor West End Presbyn. Ch., N.Y.C., 1956-58; tutor philosophy of religion Union Theol. Sem., N.Y.C., 1957-58; instr. ch. history McCormick Theol. Sem., Chgo., 1958-59, asst. prof., 1959-63, assoc. prof., 1963-65; assoc. prof. hist. theology U. Chgo., 1965-68, prof., 1968-85, John Nuveen prof., 1985-96, John Nuveen prof. emeritus, 1996—. Disting. Svc. prof. theology Union Theol. Sem., Va., 1996—2002; Cunningham lectr. U. Edinburgh, Scotland, 1990. Author: Grace and Reason: A Study in the Theology of Luther, 1962 (Japanese transl. 1974), reprinted, 1979, Tradition and the Modern World: Reformed Theology in the Nineteenth Century, 1978, The Old Protestantism and the New: Essays on the Reformation Heritage, 1982, A Prince of the Church: Schleiermacher and the Beginnings of Modern Theology, 1984, 2001, Korean transl., 1988, Grace and Gratitude: The Eucharistic Theology of John Calvin, 1993, 2002, Continuing the Reformation: Essays on Modern Religious Thought, 1993, Saving and Secular Faith: An Invitation to Systematic Theology, 1999, The Pilgrim Road: Sermons on Christian Life, 2000; editor: The Faith of Christendom: A Source Book of Creeds and Confessions, 1963, Reformers in Profile, 1967, Reformatio Perennis: Essays on Calvin and the Reformation in Honor of Ford Lewis Battles, 1981, Reformed Theology for the Third Christian Millennium: The 2001 Sprunt Lectures, 2003; co-editor: Jour. Religion, 1972-85; contbr. articles to profl. jours. Am. Assn. Theol. Schs. faculty fellow, 1961; Guggenheim fellow, 1970; Nat. Endowment Humanities fellow, 1980 Fellow Am. Acad. of Arts and Scis.; mem. Am. Soc. Church History (pres. 1979), Am. Theol. Soc. (Midwest divsn. pres. 1973-74). Home: 9142 Sycamore Hill Pl Mechanicsville VA 23116-5806

GERRITSEN, HENDRIK JURJEN, physics educator, researcher; b. The Hague, The Netherlands, Jan. 19, 1927; came to U.S., 1957; s. Hendrik Pieter and Augusta (Koopmans) G.; m. Lida Buitelaar, June 13, 1955 (div. 1968); children: Robert, Steven, Albert, Leon; m. Heide Robertson Hoppe, Dec. 28, 1978, (div. 2002); m. Maria Emilio, Jan. 17, 2003. AB in Physics and Chemistry, U. Leiden, 1948; PhD in Physics, 1955. Scientist RCA Labs., Zurich, Switzerland, 1955-57, Princeton, N.J., 1957-67; lectr. electrophysics Chalmers U., Sweden, 1961-62; prof. physics Brown U., Providence, 1967-97, prof. emeritus, prof. rsch., 1997—; prof. physics U. Utrecht, Netherlands, 1974, U. Karlsruhe, W. Germany, 1981-82; cons. Polaroid Corp., Cambridge, Mass., 1968-70; prin. investigator U.S. Bur. Mines, Brewster, Pa., 1970-76, Honeywell, Mpls., 1980-87, NSF, Dept. Energy and AERG., 1968-98; cons. Krieger Corp., Providence, 1986-89. Dir. Ladd Observatory, Providence, 1985-89. Contbr. sci. articles to profl. jours., 1968—; patentee. Vis. IREX scholar, Baltic Republics. Fulbright grantee Rostock, Germany, 1995, 96. Mem. Fedn. Am. Scientists, Union of Concerned Scientists, Profl. Photographers Soc. Am. (hon.), Am. Optical Soc., Celestial Observers (hon.), Sigma Xi. Office: Brown U Physics Dept Hope/George St Providence RI 02912 E-mail: gerritsen@physics.brown.edu.

GERRITY, J(AMES) FRANK, II, building materials company executive; b. Newton, Mass., Dec. 3, 1918; s. Joe Warren and Margaret (McKee) G.; m. Ruth Mathes, Jan. 30, 1943; children: Margot Gerrity Finley, James F. III, Peter, Ruth Gerrity Timme, Betsey Gerrity Lamson. AB, Harvard U., 1939, MBA, 1943. Salesman Gerrity Co., Boston, 1946-49, pres., 1949-79, chmn., 1979—, pres. Newton, Mass., 1994—. Trustee York Health Found.; treas. Mass. Eye and Ear Infirmary, Boston, 1980—; chmn. bd. dirs. Jackson Lab., Bar Harbor, Maine, 1975-79; pres. York Hosp., Maine, 1980—; trustee Episcopal Diocese Boston, 1978-82, Dumaine's Trust, York Hist. Landmarks; vestryman Ch. of the Redeemer; hon. consul Iceland, 1969—. Lt. (sr. grade) USNR, 1943-46. Mem. The Country Club (Brookline, Mass.), Harvard U. Club (Boston). Republican. Home: 59 Cramond Rd Chestnut Hill MA 02467-2830 Office: Gerrity Co 90 Oak St Newton MA 02464-1439

GERRY, DALE FRANCIS, defense adviser, legislative administrator; b. Bangor, Maine, Apr. 18, 1950; s. Richard Woodman and Corrine (Paddock) G.; m. Dale Marie Ahearn, Dec. 22, 1976. BA, U. Maine, 1972. Dist. rep. Congressman William S. Cohen, Bangor, 1972-76, spl. asst., 1976-77, senate campaign coord. Portland, Maine, 1977-78; legis. asst. mil./communications/transp./maritime affairs Senator William S. Cohen, Washington, 1979-94; sr. def. advisor Sens. William S. Cohen and Olympia J. Snowe, Washington, 1994-97; hon. dep. asst. sec. Mine and Undersea Warfare, USN, Washington, 1997-2001; lobbyis Strategic Mktg. Innovations, Inc., Washington, 2001—. Cons. polit. candidates. Bd. dirs. Maine State Ballet, Bangor, 1976-79. Recipient Disting. Pub. Svc. award, Dept. of Navy. Republican. Roman Catholic. Avocations: scuba diving, politics, music, theater, gardening. Home: 4708 Tecumseh St College Park MD 20740-2156 Office: SMI Inc 1020 19th St NW Washington DC 20036 Fax: (202) 467-5469. E-mail: Dale@StrategicMI.com.

GERRY, DEBRA PRUE, psychotherapist, recording artist, writer; b. Oct. 9, 1951; d. C.O. and Sarah E. Rawl; m. Norman Bernard Gerry, Apr. 10, 1981 (div. 1998); 1 child, Gisele Psyche Victoria. BS, Ga. So. U., 1972; MEd, Armstrong State U., 1974; PhD, U. Ga., 1989. Cert. Ariz. Bd. Behavioral Health Examiners. Spl. edn. tchr. Chatham County Bd. Edn., Savannah, Ga., 1972-74; edn. and learning disabilities resource educator Duval County Bd. Edn., Jacksonville, Fla., 1974-77; ednl. resource counselor spl. programs adminstr. Broward County Bd. Edn., Ft. Lauderdale, Fla., 1977-81; pvt. practice Scottsdale, Ariz., 1990—. Contbr. author coll. textbooks; contbr. articles to profl. jours.; prodr. musical album Welcome to this World. Vol., fundraiser, psychol. cons., group leader Valley AIDS Orgns., Phoenix, 1990-96; fundraiser Hosp. Health Edn. Programs, Scottsdale, 1992-93; mem. com. for women's issues Plz. Club, Phoenix, 1992-93; pres. Laissez Les Bon Temps Rouler, Wrigley Club, Phoenix, 1993-96; mem. bd. Sojourner' Ctr., 1996, exec. bd., 1997-98, v.p., 1999; exec. bd. Breast Found., Inc., Phoenix, 1997-98; appointee Ariz. Supreme Ct., Foster Care Rev. Bd., Phoenix, 1996-2001. Recipient Rudy award Shanti Orgn., 1991. Mem. APA, NOW, ACA, Internat. Soc. Poets (disting., Poet of Merit award 1996), Nat. Assn. Women Bus. Owners, Assn. for Multicultural Coun., Assn. for Specialists in Group Work, Mensa, Phi Delta Kappa, Kappa Delta Epsilon, Sigma Omega Phi, Kappa Delta Pi. Avocations: ballroom dancing, playing musical instruments, singing, travel, air sports. E-mail: dgerryphd@aol.com.

GERRY, JOSEPH JOHN, bishop; b. Millinocket, Maine, Sept. 12, 1928; s. Bernard Eugene and Blanche Agnes (McManemon) G.. AB summa cum laude, St. Anselm's Coll., Manchester, N.H., 1950; postgrad., St. Anselm's Sem., 1954; MA, U. Toronto, 1955; PhD, Fordham U., 1959; LLD, Benedictine Coll., 1986, St. Anselm Coll., 1986; DD, St. Joseph's Coll., Windham, Maine, 1990. Joined Order of St. Benedict, Roman Catholic Ch., 1948, ordained priest Roman Cath. Ch., 1954. Asst. dean studies St. Anselm's Coll., 1958—59, dean studies, 1971—72, chancellor, 1972—86; consecrated bishop, 1986; auxiliary bishop, 1986—89; bishop Portland, Maine, 1989—. Roman Catholic. Home: 199 Western Promenade Portland ME 04102-3514 Office: 510 Ocean Ave Portland ME 04103-4936

GERSCH, CHARLES FRANT, lawyer; b. N.Y.C., Oct. 30, 1942; BA, NYU, 1964; MA, New Sch. for Social Rsch., 1969; JD, U. Puget Sound, 1986. Bar: Wash. 1987, U.S. Dist. Ct. (we. dist.) Wash. 1988. Vol. VISTA Housing Code Enforcement, South Bronx, N.Y., 1967-68; editorial rsch. mgr. Fawcett Pubs., N.Y.C., 1969-71; instr. sociology William Woods Coll., 1972-74, Chapman Coll., 1974-81; vol. law clk. Thurston County Wash. Superior Ct., 1986; pvt. practice Tacoma, 1988—. Mem. Wash. State Bar Assn., Tacoma/Pierce County Bar Assn.

GERSH, BERNARD J. cardiologist, researcher, educator; b. Johannesburg, Oct. 2, 1941; came to U.S., 1978; s. Maurice and Revee Gersh; m. Alison D. Brunette, 1967 (div. 1973); children: Brunette, Jonathan, Amanda; m. Ann Gersh, Oct. 28, 1977; children: Kate and Sarah (twins); 1 stepchild, Brione. MB BChir, U. Cape Town, South Africa, 1965; DPhil, Oxford (Eng.) U., 1970. Cons. Mayo Clinic, Rochester, Minn., 1978-93, 98—; prof. medicine Mayo Med. Sch., Rochester, 1985-93, 93-98, 98—; W. Proctor Harvey tchr. Georgetown U. Med. Ctr., Washington, 1993-98, chief divsn. cardiology, 1993-98, prof. medicine. Sr. specialist, sr. lectr. Groote Schuur Hosp. and U. Cape Town, 1973-78 Editor/author 8 books; contbr. 400 articles to profl. jours. Past chmn. coun. clin. cardiology Am. Heart Assn., 1995-98. Rhodes scholar, 1965. Fellow Royal Coll. Physicians, Am. Coll. Cardiology (trustee 1995-2000); mem. Assn. Univ. Cardiologists, Am. Clin. and Climatol. Soc., Cosmos Club (Washington), Vincent's Club (Oxford U.), Western Province Cricket Club, Marylebone Cricket Club (London). Home: 2501 Institute Rd SW Rochester MN 55902-1156 Office: Mayo Clinic Cardiovasc Diseases 200 1st St SW Rochester MN 55905-0002 E-mail: gersh.bernard@mayo.edu.

GERSH, DARREN, television correspondent; BA in English cum laude, Yale U., 1984. Prodr. documentary Roosevelt Ctr., Washington; news prodr. Sta. WJXT-TV, Jacksonville, Fla., 1987-88; assoc. prodr. Money Politics, Sta. WJLA-TV, Washington; Wash. bur. chief Nightly Bus. Report, Washington. Office: NBR 1325 G St NW Ste 1005 Washington DC 20005-3126*

GERSHENGORN, MARVIN C, research scientist, director; MD, NYU. Prof. Weill Med. Coll. of Cornell U., NYC, 1983—2001; sci. dir. Niddk, Nih, Bethesda, Md., 2001—. Office: Niddk Nih 9000 Rockville Pike Bethesda MD 20892

GERSHENGORN, MARVIN CARL, physician, scientist, educator; b. N.Y.C. MD, NYU, 1971. Diplomate Am. Bd. Internal Medicine. Intern Strong Meml. Hosp., Rochester, N.Y., 1971-72, asst. resident in medicine, 1972-73; asst. prof. medicine NYU Sch. Med., 1976-80, assoc. prof., 1980-83; prof. medicine Cornell U. Med Coll., N.Y.C., 1983-2001; Abby Rockefeller Mauze disting. prof. Weill Med. Coll. Cornell U.; sci. dir. divsn. Intramural Rsch. Nat. Inst. Diabetes & Digestive & Kidney Diseases, NIH, 2001—. Office: NIH Nat Inst Diabetes & Digestive & Kidney Diseases Bldg 10 Rm 9N222 Bethesda MD 20892-1818

GERSHKOFF, IRA, architectural firm executive, consultant; b. Havehill, Mass., Oct. 23, 1951; s. Stanley S. and Phyllis K. Gershkoff; m. Pamela C. Cass, Apr. 8, 1979; children: Amy, Brian. BS, Mass. Inst. Tech., Cambridge, Mass., 1973; MS, Mass.Inst. Tech., Cambridge, Mass., 1974. Mgr. Am. Airlines, Ft. Worth, 1982—89; mgr. corp. R & D United Airlines, Elk Grove, Ill., 1989—91; mng. dir. Am. Airlines, Ft. Worth, 1991—94; v.p. Sabre, Southlake, Tex., 1994—2000; v.p. CIO Polar Air Cargo, Long Beach, Calif., 2000—01; ptnr. Tatum CIO Ptnrs., L.A., 2002, pres. G & I Architectures, Palos Verdes, Calif., 2002—. Chmn. AGIFORS Crew Mgmt. Study Group, Chgo., 1984—91, bd. mem. AMR Mgmt. Assn., Ft. Worth, 1994—98. Author: The Boston Driver's Handbook, 1982. Mem.: Inst. for Ops Rsch. and Mgmt. Sci. Achievements include patents pending for Adaptive Aircraft Assignment, 1999.

GERSHMAN, ALEXEI, electrical engineer, researcher; b. Nizhny Novgorod, Russia, Oct. 10, 1962; arrived in Germany, 1995, Can., 1999; s. Boris N. Gershman and Emma F. Krupnova; m. Olga L. Jarakhtina, Nov. 24, 1990; 1 child, Ekatherina. Diploma in elec. engring., Gorky (Russia) State U., 1984, PhD in Elec. Engring., 1990. Cert. in radiophysics and electronics. Jr. rschr. Inst. Radiotechnics, Gorky, 1984-87; rsch. scientist Inst. Radiophysics, Gorky, 1987-89, Inst. Applied Physics, Nizhny Novgorod, 1989-95, sr. rsch. scientist, 1995-99; assoc. prof. McMaster U., Hamilton, Canada, 1999—2002, full prof., 2002—. Guest scientist Swiss Fed. Inst. Tech. (EPFL), Lausanne, 1994—95, Ruhr U., Bochum, Germany, 1995—97, sci. rschr., 1997—99. Contbr. over 170 articles to profl. publs.; mem. editl. bd.: EURASIP Jour. Wireless Comm. Networking. Recipient Young Scientist award, Union Radio Sci. Internat., Kyoto, 1993, Premier Rsch. Excellence award, Ont., Can., 2000, Wolfgang Paul award, Alexander von Humboldt Found., Germany, 2001, Disting. Young Scientist fellow, Pres. Russia, 1994, Young Explorers prize, Can. Inst. for Advanced Rsch., 2002; fellow Swiss Acad. Tech. Sci. fellow, 1994, Alexander von Humboldt Found. fellow, 1995; grantee, Internat. Sci. Found., N.Y.C., Internat. Assn. (INTAS), Brussels, Russian Found. Basic Rsch., Moscow, 1993—97, German Rsch. Found., Branco Weiss Found., Zurich, Nat. Scis. and Engring. Rsch. Coun. Can. Mem. IEEE (sr., assoc. editor IEEE Transactions on Signal Processing 1999—, mem. sensor array and mutichannel processing tech. com. IEEE signal processing soc., 1999—). Avocations: history of science, table tennis, travel. Office: McMaster U Comm Rsch Lab Dept Elec and Computer Engring Hamilton ON Canada L8S 4K1 E-mail: gershman@ieee.org.

GERSHON, BERNARD, broadcast executive; Sr. v.p. ABC News.com, N.Y.C. Office: ABC News dot com D 7 W 66th St 3rd Fl New York NY 10023-6390

GERSHON, RICHARD A. commmunications educator; b. Apr. 20, 1952; s. Phillip and Sylvia Gershon; m. Casey, Aug. 25, 1978; 1 child, Matthew. BA in English, Goddard Coll., Plainfield, Vt., 1974; MEd in Edn., U. Vt., 1980; PhD in Mass Communication, Ohio U., 1986. Instr. English and Mass Communication Rice Meml. High Sch., Burlington, Vt., 1976-81; sr. bus. editor Telecom. Mag., Dedham, Mass., 1984-86; asst. prof. telecommunications SUNY, New Paltz, 1986-89; prof. telecommunications Western Mich. U., Kalamazoo, 1989—. Chair Policy and Planning Task Force for Greater Kalamazoo Telecity Project. Author: Transnational Media Corporation: Global Markets and Free Market Competition, 1997, Telecommunications Management: Industry Structures and Planning Strategies, 2001 (Nat. Cable TVs Mus.'s Book of Yr. award); contbr. articles to profl. jours. Mem. Broadcast Edn. Assn. (chair elect for internat. div.). Office: Western Mich U Dept Comm Kalamazoo MI 49008 E-mail: Richard.Gershon@wmich.edu.

GERSHON, WILLIAM I. marketing and communications executive, writer, voiceover actor; b. Chgo., 1934; s. Irving and Ruth Gershon; m. Matilda May Gershon, 1957. Grad., Wright Jr. Coll., Chgo., 1954; BA in Speech and English, Roosevelt U., 1956. Classical music dir., announcer Sta. WNIB-FM, Chgo., 1955-57; writer H. Epstein Advt., Chgo., 1956-59; asst. to copy chief Walgreen Co., Deerfield, Ill., 1959-61; advt. mgr. Lyon & Healy, Inc., Chgo., 1961-63; writer/account mgr. Garfield-Linn & Co., Chgo., 1963-78, v.p., 1978-82; sr. writer Abelson-Taylor, Inc., Chgo., 1983-84; owner Bill Gershon Mktg. Communications, Skokie, Ill., 1982—. Creator name Expocenter for Chgo.'s Apparel Ctr. Expn. Hall; voiceover actor American Heritage Voices From the Front (The Civil War, World War I), children's book narrations, sales tng. and employee tng. modules, radio and TV commls., indsl. narrations. Mem. Independent Writers of Chgo. Office: Bill Gershon Mktg Comm 9828 Crawford Ave Skokie IL 60076-1107

GERSIN, KEITH STEVEN, surgeon; b. Boston, Oct. 14, 1964; s. Alvin and Joyce Saundra Gersin. BA cum laude, Boston U., 1986; MD, Georgetown U., 1991. Diplomate Am. Bd. Surgery. Resident in gen. surgery Berkshire Med. Ctr., Pittsfield, Mass., 1991-97; gen. surgeon Berkshire Med. Ctr., Pittsfield, Mass., 1998-2000; endoscopic surgery fellow The Cleve. Clinic Found., 1997-98. Contbr. articles to profl. jours. Recipient Disting. Leadership award Internat. Directory Disting. Leadership, 1998. Fellow ACS; mem. Am. Soc. Gastrointestinal Endoscopy, Soc. Am. Gastrointestinal Endoscopic Surgeons. Office: U Cin Med Ctr Dept Surgery 231 Bethesda Ave Dept S Cincinnati OH 45267-0001

GERSKE, JANET FAY, lawyer; b. Nov. 14, 1950; d. Bernard G. Gerske and L. Fay (Knight) Capron. BS, Northwestern U., 1971; JD, U. Mich., 1978. Bar: Ill. 1978, U.S. Dist. Ct. (no. dist.) Ill. 1978. Pvt. practice, Chgo., 1978—80, 1984—2002; assoc. Jerome H. Torshen Ltd., Chgo., 1980—84. Chpt. chair Ind. Voters Ill./Ind. Precinct Orgn., Chgo., 1982—83; co-chmn. Ill. Women's Agenda Com., 1985—88, fin. officer, 1987—88; dir. Chgo. Abused Women Coalition, 1986—90, sec., treas., 1988—90; co-chair legal status of women com. Young Lawyers sect. Chgo. Bar Assn., 1984—85; co-chair rights of women com. Ill. Women's Bar Assn., 1985—86, dir., 1988—90. Democrat. Home: 850 W Oakdale Ave Chicago IL 60657-5122

GERSON, DONALD FRANKLIN, pharmaceutical executive; b. Kansas City, Mo., Oct. 22, 1946; s. Nathaniel C. and Sareen R. (Epstein) G.; m. Mavis Gail Meadows, May 12, 1979; children: Benjamin Asa, Alexander Roald, Jonas Elliott. BSc, U. Western Ont., London, Can., 1968; PhD, McGill U., Montreal, Que., Can., 1972. Mem. Basel (Switzerland) Inst. for Immunology, 1979-82; mgr. process devel. Genex Corp., Gaithersburg, Md., 1982-83; head biotech. Alta. Rsch. Coun., Edmonton, Can., 1983-87; asst. v.p. mfg. Connaught Labs., Toronto, Ont., 1987-92; v.p. R & D Apotex Fermentation, Inc., Winnipeg, Man.,

Can., 1992-94; mng. dir. Wyeth-Lederle Vaccines, Pearl River, N.Y., 1994-2000; v.p. mfg. Acambis, Inc., Cambridge, Mass., 2000—. Contbr. or co-contbr. chpts. to books, articles to publs. including Jour. Cell Physiology, Biotechnol. Bioengring., Devels. in Indsl. Microbiology, Plant Physiology, Applied Environ. Microbiology, European Jour. Applied Microbiology, Process Biochemistry, Can. Jour. Microbiology, Jour. Fermentation Tech., Sci., Agts. and Actions, Jour. Chem. Tech. and Biotech., Drug Info. Jour., others. Mem. Cosmos Club (Washington). Achievements include U.S. patents for process for production of lovastatin using coniothyrium fuckelli; U.S. and Canadian patents for hydrocarbon extraction agents and microbiological processes for their production, for microbiological production of novel biosurfactants, for measuring degree of mixing in turbulent liquid; European patent application for controlled dose dropper construction. Office: Internat AIDS Vaccine Initiative 110 William St 27th Fl New York NY 10038-3901 E-mail: dgerson@iavi.org.

GERSON, DONALD JEROME, computer scientist, consultant; b. N.Y.C., Apr. 26, 1934; s. Irwin I. Gerson and Helen Sacks; m. Barbara A. Jaques, Aug. 21, 1960 (dec. Oct. 1998); 1 child, Laura Melissa; m. Emma Sue Gaines, June 24, 2000. BA in Meteorology, N.Y.U., 1956; MS in Computer Sci., U. Md., 1975. Oceanographer Naval Oceanographic Office, Suitland, Md., 1956-78, Defense Mapping Agy., Bethesda, Md., 1978-83; imagery scientist CIA, Langley, Va., 1983-97; prin., owner Gerson Imaging Solutions, LLC, Silver Spring, Md., 1997—. Instr. George Washington U., Washington, 1983-88, U.S. rep. working group on sea ice World Meteorological Org., Geneva, 1975-77. Co-author: Processes in Marine Remote Sensing, 1982, Radius, Image Understanding for Imagery Intelligence, 1997; contbr. articles to profl. jours. Recipient Goldsborough award for best tech. paper of yr., 1983, Intelligence Commendation medal CIA, 1997. Fellow: Royal Geog. Soc. (Eng.), Explorers Club (Wash. chpt. chmn. 1986—88); mem.: IEEE, Am. Soc. Media Photographers, Applied Imagery Pattern Recognition Com. (chmn. 1975—), Cosmos Club, Sigma Xi. Avocations: photography, racewalking, recreational vehicle camping, hiking, book collecting. E-mail: donald@GersonImagingSolutions.com.

GERSON, ELLIOT FRANCIS, foundation administrator; b. New Haven, July 15, 1952; s. Louis Lieb and Elizabeth (Shanley) G; children: Emily, Hilary, Alexander, Marissa, Jillian; m. Amy Shapiro, May 23, 1993. AB summa cum laude, Harvard Coll., 1974; BA with first class honors, Oxford U. (Eng.), 1976, MA, 1981; JD, Yale U., 1979. Bar: Conn. 1981, D.C. 1982, U.S. Dist. Ct. Conn. 1982, U.S. Ct. Appeals (D.C. cir.) 1982, U.S. Supreme Ct. 1985. Law clk. to judge U.S. Ct. Appeals, Washington, 1979; staff asst. to sec. Dept. Def. The Pentagon, Washington, 1979-80; law clk. to Justice Stewart U.S. Supreme Ct., Washington, 1980-81; assoc. Verner, Liipfert, Bernhard & McPherson, Washington, Hartford, Conn., 1981-83; dep. atty. gen. State of Conn., Hartford, 1983-86; v.p. Travelers Corp., Hartford, 1986-90, sr. v.p., 1990-93; pres. Travelers Ins. Co., 1993-95; exec. v.p. MetraHealth Cos., Inc., 1995-96, United Healthcare, 1996; pres. ETC, Inc., 1996—97, CEO, 1997-99, Lifescape, LLC, 1999-2000; pres. FHC Health Sys., Inc., 2000—03, ValueOptions, Inc., 2001—03; policy dir., nat. fin. chair Joseph I. Lieberman for Pres., Inc., Vienna, Va., 2003—. Dir. Bazelon Ctr. Mental Health Law, 1997—. Editor: Conn. Law Tribune, 1986-88. Mem. Sec. State's Adv. Com. Internat. Law, Washington, 1984-86; mem. Gov.'s. Commn. Design Environ. Policy for Conn., 1969; dir. Eastern Conn. Develop. Coun. Inc., 1981-86, Hartford State Co., 1985-95, pres., 1990-93, Hartford Ballet, 1986-88, Greater Hartford Arts Coun., 1986-90, 94-95; mem. Conn. Humanities Coun., 1987-90; dir. Conn. Civil Liberties Union, 1987 89, Conn. Women's Ednl. and Legal Fund, 1987-91; staff mem. commn. Critical Choices Ams., 1973-74; mem. Council Fgn. Relations Inc., N.Y.C., 1981-86, 98—, Yale Law Sch. Com. Pub. Interest Law, New Haven, 1983-85; elector Wadsworth Atheneum, Hartford, 1983-93; sec. Conn. Rhodes Scholar Selection Com., 1982-94; asst. Am. sec. Rhodes Scholarship Trust, 1976-79, Am. sec., Eng., 1998—; treas. Am. South African Scholarship Assn., Inc., 1986-94; trustee Conn. Pub. Broadcasting, 1988-92, Conn. Histo. Soc., 1993-95, The Shakespeare Theatre, Washington, 1996—; trustee Hartford Courant Fedn., 1988-95, pres., 1992-94. Rhodes scholar 1974; recipient Sec. Def. Meritorious Civilian Service medal, 1980. Mem. Conn. Bar Assn. (long range planning com. 1984-87), Spee Club (pres. 1973-74, Cambridge, Mass.), Cosmos Club (Washington), River Bend Golf Club (Great Falls, Va.), Phi Beta Kappa. Democrat. Home: 480 River Bend Rd Great Falls VA 22066-4016 Office: 8229 Boone Blvd Ste 240 Vienna VA 22182 E-mail: amsec@rhodesscholar.org.

GERSON, GARY STANFORD, rabbi; b. Ypsilanti, Mich., June 17, 1945; s. Bernard and Ruth Edith (Levin) G.; m. Carol Roberts, Oct. 12, 1969; children: Jordana, Jessica. BA magna cum laude, Western Mich. U., 1967; MA in Religion, Temple U., 1976; grad., Reconstructionist Rabbinical Coll., 1976; MA in Psychology, Temple U., 1977; Dr. Ministry, Chgo. Theol. Seminary, 1984; cert., Phila. Child Guidance Clin. Ordained rabbi, 1976. Rsch. fellow U. Pa., 1969, teaching asst., 1972, Temple U., Phila., 1974-75; rabbi Temple Brith Achim, King of Prussia, Pa., 1974-78; asst. rabbi Temple Beth Israel, Chgo., 1978-79; rabbi Oak Park (Ill.) Temple B'nai Abraham Zion, 1979—. Psychologist Benjamin Rush Ctr. for Mental Health and Mental Retardation Svcs., Phila., 1977-78. Contbr. articles to profl. jours. Mem. adv. bd. Ctr. for Jewish-Christian Studies, Chgo., 1985—, Nat. Abortion rights Action League, Ill., 1985—, Ctr. for Ch.-State Studies, Chgo., 1986—, Cmty. Response, 1989—; chmn. Religious Coalition for Abortion Rights policy coun., 1984-88; active Justice Campaign, 1985; bd. dirs. ACLU, Ill., 1999—; bd. dirs. Jewish Fedn. Met. Chgo., 1995-96; exec. bd. Anti-Defamation League; bd. dirs. Ctr. for Religion and Psychotherapy of Chgo., 2002-03. Fulbright grantee, 1967, Hebrew U. fellow, 1969-70, Dropsie U. fellow, 1970-71. Mem. Chgo. Assn. Reform Rabbis (v.p. 1987-91, pres. 1991-93), Cen. Conf. Am. Rabbis (exec. bd. 1991-93), Chgo. Bd. Rabbis (exec. com. 1983-90), Union Am. Hebrew Congregations (exec. com. Gt. Lakes region 1991-93), Olin-Sang-Ruby Union Inst. (bd. govs. 1990, chmn. rabbinic adv. com.), United Jewish Appeal (rabbinic cabinet 1980—), Oak Park-River Forest Comty. of Congregations (v.p. 1994-96, pres. 1996-98), Fulbright Assn., Omicron Delta Kappa. Avocations: hiking, travel, classical, folk and irish music, opera. Office: Oak Park Temple Bnai Abraham Zion 1235 N Harlem Ave Oak Park IL 60302-1397

GERSON, IRWIN CONRAD, advertising executive; b. NYC, Mar. 18, 1930; s. Leon and Charlotte (Steinhause) G.; m. Lenore Greenblatt, Nov. 29, 1953; children: Jill Beth, Matthew Ted. BS, Fordham U., 1953; MBA, NYU, 1959; DHL, Albany Coll. Pharmacy, 1992, L.I. U., 2001. Ter. mgr. Wyeth Labs. divsn. Am. Home Products, 1956-58; account exec., supr. William Douglas McAdams, Inc., NYC, 1958-66, v.p., 1966-68, sr. v.p., 1969-70, exec. v.p., 1971-74, pres., 1974-86, chmn. bd., 1987-96, Lowe McAdams Healthcare, NYC, 1996-98, chmn. emeritus, 1999-2000. Instr. sales mgmt. Columbia Coll. Pharm. Sci., 1967-77; bd. dir. ANDRX Corp., Enzo Biochem. Inc.; bd. advisors Lifelong Learning Soc., Fla. Atlantic U., 2000—. Editorial adv. bd.: US Jour. Drug and Alcohol Dependence, 1977-83. Trustee, bd. dirs. Chemotherapy Found., 1971-86; bd. dir. Nutritional Rsch. Found., 1977-85, Am. Found. for Pharm. Edn., 1996-2003, Conn. Grand Opera, 1983-93, Stamford Chamber Orch., 1985-93; mem. coun. overseers Arnold and Marie Schwartz Coll. Pharmacy and Health Sci., LI U., 1986-90, chmn., 1990-99; bd. trustees Bus. Publs. Audit of Circulation, 1988-95, vice chmn., 1992-93, chmn., 1993-94; bd. trustees LI U., 1989-99; trustee Albany Coll. Pharmacy, Union U., 1993-97. With AUS, 1954-56. Named to Med. Advt. Hall of Fame, 1999. Mem. Am. Assn. Advt. Agys. (bd. govs. NY coun. 1991-95, ea. region 1995-98), Pharm. Advt. Coun. (bd. dirs. 1974-84, treas. 1976-77, v.p. 1979-81), Alpha Zeta Omega. Home: 189 Spyglass Ln Jupiter FL 33477-4090

GERSON, MARTIN LYONS, secondary school educator; b. Morristown, Tenn., Sept. 12, 1961; s. Allan Jerome and Bernice (Misner) G. BS, Purdue U., 1984; MA for Tchrs., Ga. State U., 1986, cert. ednl. specialist, 1994. Cert. secondary math. tchr., Ga. Tchr. math. Cross Keys H.S., Atlanta, 1984—97; tchr. S. Gwinnett H.S., Snellville, Ga., 1997—2003, Peachtree Ridge H.S., 2003—. Instr. math. Ga. State U., Atlanta, 1988-90, Dekalb Coll., Atlanta, 1990-96. Named Tchr. of Month math. students Cross Keys High Sch., 1989, South Gwinnett H.S., 2001, HERO Club, Cross Keys H.S., 1990, Tchr. of Yr. faculty Cross Keys H.S., 1990, West Dekalb Rotary Club, Atlanta, 1991. Mem. Nat. Coun. Tchrs. Math., Ga. Coun. Tchrs. Math., B'nai B'rith. Jewish. Avocations: bowling, collecting bobbleheads, hats and crystal figures. Home: 1196 Mandalay Ct SW Lilburn GA 30047-4227 Office: Peachtree Ridge HS 1555 Old Peachtree Rd Suwanee GA 30024 E-mail: marty_gerson@gwinnett.k12.ga.us.

GERSON, MYRON CRAIG, cardiologist, researcher; b. Cleve., Oct. 27, 1947; s. Gerald and Estelle Anita Gerson; m. Joanne Steiner, June 21, 1969; children: Craig Alan, Linda Deborah. BA in Med. Scis., U. Wis., 1969; MD, Ind. U., Indpls., 1972. Diplomate Am. Bd. Internal Medicine. Intern in internal medicine Ind. U. Sch. Medicine, Indpls., 1972-73; resident Ind. U. Hosp., 1972-75, fellow in cardiology, 1977-79; prof. medicine and radiology, dir. cardiac exercise lab., assoc. dir. divsn. cardiology U. Cin., 1979—. Editor: Cardiac Nuc. Medicine, 3d edit., 1997; editl. adv. bd. Jour. Nuc. Cardiology, 1993-95, editl. bd., 1996—; editl. bd. Am. Heart Jour., 1997—; contbr. articles to profl. jours. V.p. Ohio Cardiac Coun., Columbus, 1987-90. Maj. USAF, 1975-77. NIH grantee, 1989-92. Fellow Am. Coll. Cardiology (trustee Ohio chpt. 1994-96), Am. Heart Assn. (coun. clin. cardiology, coun. rep. Ohio 1989-92, grantee 1980-87, 92-94, 97—); mem. Am. Soc. Nuclear Cardiology (founder, mem. exec. coun.). Avocation: bicycling. Office: U Cin Divsn Cardiology PO Box 670542 Cincinnati OH 45267-0001

GERSON, RALPH JOSEPH, corporate executive; b. Detroit, Nov. 30, 1949; s. Byron Hayden and Dorothy Mary (Davidson) G.; m. Erica Ann Ward, May 20, 1979. BA, Yale U., 1971; MSc, London Sch. Econs., 1972; JD, U. Mich., 1975. Bar: Mich. 1975, D.C. 1976, U.S. Dist. Ct. D.C. 1976, U.S. Ct. Appeals (D.C. cir.) 1976. Counsel Dem. Nat. Com., Washington, 1975-77; spl. asst. U.S. Spl. Trade Rep., Washington, 1978-79; counselor to spl. Middle East negotiator Office of Pres., Washington, 1979-80; ptnr. Akin, Gump, Strauss, Hauer and Feld, Washington, 1981-83, 85-87; dir. Mich. Dept. Commerce, Lansing, 1983-84; exec. v.p. Guardian Industries Corp., Auburn Hills, Mich., 1988-93, also bd. dirs., 1988—; pres., CEO Guardian Internat. Corp., 1993—. Bd. dirs. Pistons-Palace Found., U.S. Spain Coun., Nat. Endowment for Democracy; chmn. Hungarian-U.S. Bus. Coun.; trustee Henry Ford Mus., Detroit Symphony Orch. Hall, Citizens Rsch. Coun.; mem. U.S. Adv. Com. for Trade Policy and Negotiations. Mem. ABA, D.C. Bar Assn., Mich. Bar Assn., Coun. Fgn. Rels., World Pres. Orgn., Royal Automobile Club, Franklin Hills Country Club, Bloomfield Open Hunt Club, Yale Club of NYC. Office: Guardian Industries Corp 2300 Harmon Rd Auburn Hills MI 48326-1714

GERSON, STUART MICHAEL, lawyer; b. N.Y.C., Jan. 16, 1944; s. James and Ethel (Cherney) G.; m. Pamela Somers, July 28, 1979; children: James Barker, Somers Elizabeth, Lindsey Dakota. BA in Polit. Sci., Pa. State U., 1964; JD, Georgetown U., 1967. Bar: D.C. 1968, N.Y. 1999, U.S. Supreme Ct. 1974, U.S. Ct. Appeals (DC cir.) 1972, U.S. Ct. Appeals (5th cir.) 1972, 81, U.S. Ct. Appeals (9th cir.) 1978, U.S. Ct. Appeals (2d cir.) 1979, U.S. Ct. Appeals (11th cir.) 1981, U.S. Ct. Appeals (6th cir.) 1982, U.S. Ct. Appeals (4th cir.) 1984, U.S. Ct. Appeals (3d cir.) 1985, U.S. Ct. Appeals (8th cir.) 1986, U.S. Ct. Appeals (1st, 7th, 10th, fed. cirs.) 1989. Asst. U.S. atty. City of Washington, 1972-75; assoc., then ptnr. Reed Smith Shaw & McClay, Washington, 1975-80; pvt. practice; ptnr. in charge litigation Epstein, Becker & Green, Washington, N.Y.C., 1980-89; adj. prof. of law Georgetown U., 1991; asst. atty. gen. in charge civil div. U.S. Dept. Justice, Washington, 1989-93; acting Atty. Gen. U.S., 1993; atty. and head of litigation Epstein, Becker & Green, P.C., Washington and N.Y.C. Bd. dirs. Counsel for Ct. Excellence; mem. bd. legal advisors Heritage Found, Washington Legal Found., Nat. Legal Ctr. for the Pub. Interest. Contbr. articles to profl. jours. Gen. counsel Nat. Rep. Senatorial Com., Washington, 1985-86; sr. advisor presdl. campaign George Bush, 1988; leader transition team Office Pres. Elect, 1988; advisor Transition Office Pres. Elect, 2000. Capt. USAF, 1967-72. Decorated Meritorious Svc. Medal. Fellow Am. Bar Found.; mem. ABA, D.C. Bar Assn. (steering com. litigation 1985-93), The Barristers (pres.), Am. Health Lawyers Assn., Am. Inns of Ct., Metro. Club, Lawyers Club. Episcopalian. Avocations: competitive running, national track and field official, sailing, reading history. Office: Epstein Becker & Green PC 1227 25th St NW Ste 700 Washington DC 20037-1175 also: 250 Park Ave New York NY 10177-0001

GERSONI-EDELMAN, DIANE CLAIRE, author, editor; b. Apr. 16, 1947; d. James Arthur and Edna Bernice (Krinski) Gersoni; m. James Neil Edelman, Oct. 5, 1975; children: Michael Lawrence, Sara Anne. Asst. editor, then assoc. editor Sch. Libr. Jour. Book Rev., 1968—72; freelance writer, 1972—74, 1977—; writer, editor Scholastic Mags., Inc., N.Y.C., 1974—77. Cons., spkr. in field. Author: Sexism and Youth, 1974, Work-Wise: Learning About the World of Work from Books, 1980; contbr. articles and book revs. to anthologies, newspapers and mags.

GERSONY, WELTON MARK, physician, pediatric cardiologist, educator; b. Syracuse, N.Y., Nov. 19, 1931; s. Irving and Ann (Cohen) G.; m. Susan; children: Neal, Anne, Richard, Deborah. AB, Syracuse U., 1954; MD, SUNY, Syracuse, 1958. Diplomate Am. Bd. Pediatrics, Sub Bd. Pediatric Cardiology. Intern Cleve. Met. Gen. Hosp., 1958-59, resident in pediatrics, 1959-61, Babies and Childrens Hosp., Cleve., 1959-61; fellow in cardiology Harvard U., 1963-65; asst. prof. pediatrics U. Tex., Dallas, 1965-68, Columbia U., 1968-71, assoc. prof., 1971-74, prof., 1974—, Alexander S. Nadas prof., 2000—. Adj. prof. Cornell U., 1998—, prof., 2000—; dir. div. pediatric cardiology Columbia-Presbyn Med. Ctr., Columbia-Cornell Pediatric Cardiovasc. Ctr., 1999—; pres. faculty practice orgn., Coll. of Physicians and Surgeons, Columbia U.; vis. dir. pediatric cardiology Gt. Ormond St. Hosp. Sick Children, London, 1984-85; organizer 2d World Congress Pediatric Cardiology, N.Y.C., 1985; chmn. steering com. World Congress Pediatric Cardiology and Cardiac Surgery, 1989-97; mem. Sub.-bd. Pediatric Cardiology, 1976-83, chmn., 1981-83, com. ofcl. examiners, 1983-90; cons. in drug evaluation AMA, 1985—; cons. Extramural Affairs div. Nat. Heart Lung and Blood Inst., 1988—; James Overall vis. prof. pediatrics Vanderbilt U., 1991; lectr. Brit. Heart Found., 1991, Toby Keenan Meml. Symposium U. Md., 1994; Gladys Fashena lectr. Southwestern Med. Ctr. Dallas, 1994; Jerome D. Solomon Meml. lectr. Nat. Ctr. Advanced Med. Edn., Chgo., 1994, 98; mem. adv. bd. Congress of Pediat. Cardiology Internat., 1998—; Chameides lectr. U. Conn., 1999; Kangos Meml. lectr. Robert W. Johnson, 2000; Plenary lectr. 10th Asian Congress of Pediats., Taipei, 2000, World Congress of Pediatric Cardiology and Pediatric Surgery, Toronto, 2001; Flyer lectr. Harvard U., 2001; Zuberbueller lectr. U. Pitts, 2002; Raskind lectr. U. Pa., 2003; prin. investigator NIH grants, Natural History of Congenital Heart Defects, 1977, 93, Indonethacin Closure of Patent Ductus Arteviocus, 1983, Pediat. Heart Network, NIY/NHCBI, 2002—/ Author: Nelson's Textbook of Pediatrics, 1983, 3d edit., 1991, Congenital Heart Disease in The Adult, 2001; assoc. editor: The American Heart Association Consultant, 2001; mem. editl. bd. Pediatric Cardiology, 1978-90, Jour. of Pediatrics, 1986-93, Jour. Am. Coll. Cardiology, 1990-94, Cardiology in the Young, 1990, Progress in Pediatric Cardiology, 1991—; editl. bd. Circulation, 1993-96, cons. editor, 1996—; internat. adv. bd. Japanese Circulation Jour., 1996—; contbr. revs. to profl. jours., chpts. to books. Mem. internat. com., bd. dirs. Internat Cardiology Found., 1993—; mem. program com. Internat. Kawasaki Disease Chmn. Cardiology Symposium, 1989, 1992, 1995, 1998, 2001. Capt. M.C. U.S. Army, 1961—63. Falkner fellow U. Sydney, Australia, 1983; NIH grantee, 1977, 82, 83, 2002. Fellow Am. Coll. Cardiology, Am. Acad. Pediatrics; mem. AMA (accreditation coun. for grad. med. edn. 1994—), Soc. Pediatric Rsch., Am. Pediatric Soc., Am. Heart Assn. (pres. coun. cardiovascular disease in the young 1988-90, T. Duckett Jones lectr. 1998), Am. Fedn. Clin. Rsch., Harvey Soc., Assn. European Paediatric Cardiologists (corr.), Internat. Soc. for Adult Congenital Heart Disease, Am. Contract Bridge League (life master). Achievements include research on cardiovascular disease in infants, children and adults, natural history of congenital heart disease in children; patent ductus arteriosus in premature infants; persistence of the fetal circulation. Office: Columbia U 630 W 168th St New York NY 10032-3795

GERSOVITZ, JEREMY, lawyer; b. Montreal, Que., Can., July 28, 1956; came to U.S., 1984; s. Benjamin and Sarah Valerie Gersovitz; 1 child, Alexander Samuel. BA in Polit. Sci., Columbia Coll., 1980; MS in Journalism, Northwestern U., Chgo., 1985; JD, U. Mont., 1992. Bar: Mont. 1992, U.S. Dist. Ct. Mont. 1992. Law clk. to Judge T.C. Honzel, 1st Jud. Dist., Helena, Mont., 1992-94; pvt. practice Townsend, Mont., 1994-95; part-time pub. defender Broadwater County, Townsend, Mont., 1994-95; pvt. practice Helena, 1995-97; part-time pub. defender Lewis & Clark County, Helena, 1995-97, pub. defender, 1997—. Mem. bd. editors The Mont. Lawyer., 1996—. Mem. ABA, State Bar Mont., 1st Jud. Dist. Bar Assn. Jewish. Home and Office: 532 N Warren St Helena MT 59601-4014

GERST, PAUL HOWARD, physician; b. Sept. 24, 1927; s. David and Hilde (Werbel) G.; m. Elizabeth Carlsen, Aug. 3, 1957; children— Steven R., Jeffrey C., Andrew L. AB, Columbia U., 1948, MD, 1952. Diplomate: Am. Bd. Surgery, Am. Bd. Thoracic Surgery. Intern Columbia Presbyn. Med. Center, N.Y.C., 1952-53, resident, 1956-62, mem. staff, 1962—; instr. physiology U. Pa., 1955-56; practice medicine specializing in surgery N.Y.C., 1962—; asst. clin. prof. surgery Columbia U., 1964-72; prof. surgery Albert Einstein Coll. Medicine, 1972—. Dir. surgery Bronx-Lebanon Hosp. Center, N.Y.C., 1964— Contbr. articles to profl. jours. Served to 1st lt. U.S. Army, 1953-55. USPHS postdoctoral fellow, 1955-56; Recipient Research Career Devel. award, 1964-65 Fellow A.C.S.; mem. Am. Physiol. Soc., N.Y. Soc. for Thoracic Surgery, N.Y. Surg. Soc., N.Y. Soc. for Cardiovascular Surgery, Am. Heart Assn. Home: 141 Tekening Dr Tenafly NJ 07670-1218 Office: Bronx Lebanon Hosp Ctr 1650 Grand Concourse Bronx NY 10457 7606

GERSTEIN, DAVID BROWN, hardware manufacturing company executive, professional basketball team executive; b. N.Y.C., Jan. 30, 1936; s. Frank and May G.; m. Jane Ellen Bender, May 4, 1963; children: Mark, James. Student, Columbia U., 1951-54, postgrad., 1954-58; BS, Seton Hall U., 1959. With Thermwell Products Co., Paterson, N.J., 1958—, sales mgr., 1965-68, v.p., 1968-74, pres., 1974—. Prin. owner N. J. Nets NBA franchise, 1978—; v.p. Lever Mfg. Co., Paterson; pres. Woodlowe Realty, Paterson, Wait Assocs., Paterson, Dim Assocs., Mahwah, N.J. Chmn. adv. council energy and conservation State of N.J.; co-chmn. athletic program Seton Hall U. Office: Thermwell Products Co Inc 420 Rte 17 S Mahwah NJ 07430

GERSTEIN, JOE WILLIE, lawyer; b. Atlanta, July 29, 1927; s. Arthur and Tena (Hartman) G.; m. Doris Renate Florsheim, May 20, 1956 (dec. 2000); children: Ellen Claire Gerstein Crooke, Kim Carol Gerstein Wainer; m. Sheila Brooks Kamensky. Oct. 20, 2001. AB, Duke U., 1949, JD, 1952. Bar: Ga. 1953, U.S. Tax Ct., U.S. Ct. Appeals (fed. cir.) 1965, U.S. Supreme Ct. 1967. Sr. ptnr. Gerstein, Carter & Chestnut and predecessor firm Gerstein & Carter, Atlanta and Doraville, Ga., 1957-76; sole practice Doraville, 1976—. Former city atty. Doraville; lectr. on taxes, wills, trust and estates at various civic, profl. and ch. orgns.; bd. dirs. Atlanta Estate Planning Council. Contbg. editor Duke U. Law Rev. Past dir. Social Service Fedn. Atlanta. Served with USN, 1944-47. Fellow Am. Coll. Trust and Estate Counsel; mem. ABA, Ga. Bar Assn., Atlanta Bar Assn., Decatur-DeKalb Bar Assn., Met. Atlanta Council Rotary Club Pres. (past chmn.), Comml. Law League Am. (past nat. recording sec.), Atlanta Tax Forum, Big Canoe Men's Golf Assn. (golf com.), Zeta Beta Tau (v.p. AU chpt.), Phi Delta Phi. Clubs: Standard (Atlanta) (legal and golf coms.). Lodges: Rotary (North DeKalb past pres.), Masons (past offices), B'nai B'rith (Gate City past v.p.). Jewish. Office: 6485 Peachtree Industrial Blvd Doraville GA 30360-2112 Home: 1073 Tennyson Pl NE Atlanta GA 30319-1924

GERSTEIN, MARK BENDER, biophysicist, bioinformatician; b. N.Y.C., Feb. 23, 1966; s. David Brown and Jane Ellen (Bender) G. AB in Physics/History summa cum laude, Harvard U., 1989; PhD, Cambridge U., 1992. Damon Runyon fellow Stanford (Calif.) U., 1994—96; asst. prof. to tenured assoc. prof. molecular biophysics and biochemistry, computer sci. dept. Yale U., New Haven, 1997—, Al Williams assoc prof. biomed. informatics, molecular piophysics and biochemistry, computer sci., 2003—, co-dir. computational biology and bioinformatics program, 2003—. Contbr. articles to sci. jours. Mem. Phi Beta Kappa.

GERSTEIN, MARK DOUGLAS, lawyer; b. Chgo., Nov. 16, 1959; s. Robert Henry and Helene Roberta Gerstein; m. Julia Sara Wolf, Apr. 13, 1986; children: Allison Ruth, Evan Benjamin. BA, U. Mich., 1981; JD, U. Chgo., 1984. Bar: Ill., U.S. Dist. Ct. (no. dist.) Ill. Ptnr., assoc. Katten Muchin & Zavis, Chgo., 1984-96; equity ptnr. Latham & Watkins, Chgo., 1996—, equity ptnr., global co-chair mergers and acquisitions group, 1999—. Dir. Assocs. Ravinia Festival, Chgo., 1996-2000, Youth Guidance, Chgo., 1995—. Mem. Chgo. Bar Assn. (chmn. com. on corp. control 1998-99), Standard Club. Avocations: sailing, cycling. Office: Latham & Watkins 233 S Wacker Dr Ste 5800 Chicago IL 60606-6362 E-mail: mark.gerstein@lw.com.

GERSTENBERGER, DONNA LORINE, humanities educator; b. Wichita Falls, Tex., Dec. 26, 1929; d. Donald Fayette and Mabel G. AB, Whitman Coll., 1951; MA, U. Okla., 1952, PhD, 1958. Asst. prof. English U. Colo., Boulder, 1958-60; prof. U. Wash., 1960-96, prof. emeritus, 1996—, chmn. undergrad. studies, 1971-74, assoc. dean Coll. Arts and Scis., dir. Coll. Honors and Office Undergrad. Studies, 1974-76, chmn. dept. English, 1976-83, vice chmn. faculty senate, 1984-85, chmn. faculty senate, 1985-86. Cons. in field; bd. dirs. Am. Lit. Classics; mem. grants-in-aid com. Am. Coun. Learned Socs.; chmn. region VII, Mellon Fellowships in Humanities, 1982-92; mem. adv. com. Grad. Record Exams, 1990-93, Coun. Internat. Exch. of Scholars, 1992-95. Author: J.M. Synge, 1964, 2d edition, 1988, The American Novel: A Checklist of Twentieth Century Criticism, vols. I and II, 1970, Directory of Periodicals, 1974, The Complex Configuration: Modern Verse Drama, 1973, Iris Murdoch, 1974, Richard Hugo, 1983; editor: Microcosm, 1969, Swallow Series in Bibliography, 1974—; assoc. editor: Abstracts of English Studies, 1958-68; founder, editor jour. Seattle Rev., 1983-96. Bd. dirs. N.W. Chamber Orch., Seattle, 1975-78, Wash. Friends Humanities, 1991—; trustee Wash. Commn. Humanities, 1985-91, pres., 1988-90; mem. vis. com. Lehigh U., 1987-92; pres. Am. Commn. for Irish Studies/West, 1989-91. Grantee Am. Council Learned Socs., 1962, 88, Am. Philos. Soc., 1963 Mem. MLA, Am. Com. Irish Studies. Office: U Wash Box 354330 Dept English Seattle WA 98195-4330

GERSTENBERGER, VALERIE, media coordinator; b. Amherst, Ohio, Sept. 7, 1913; d. Frank Abraham Eppley and Ethel Elizabeth Dute; m. William Jacob Jenkins, Aug. 13, 1944 (div. May 1964); m. Henry Louis Gerstenberger, Nov. 8, 1984 (dec. Aug. 2001). BA, Baldwin-Wallace Coll., 1936; MA, Kent State U., 1963; postgrad., U. Iowa, 1938—39. Asst. drama dir. Baldwin-Wallace Coll., Berea, Ohio, 1936—38; English/speech tchr. St. Elmo (Ill.) H.S., 1940—42, Clearview H.S., Lorain, Ohio, 1942—57; speech tchr. Kent State U., Elyria, Ohio, 1963—66, Cleve. State U., Lakewood, Ohio, 1966—70; media coord. Amherst (Ohio) Pub. Schs., 1957—80; drama dir. Amherst (Ohio) Pub. H.S., 1957—60, 1975—78. Mem./pres. Amherst Pub. Libr. Bd., 1963—92; cons. for libr. expansion Am. Pub. Libr., 1972—73; costume designer various orgns. Various civic positions and contbns. including founding of Community Theater, local edn. programs and cataloging documents for Amherst Hist. Soc. Named to Gallery of Success, Amherst (Ohio) HS, 1987, Ohio Cmty. Theatre Assn. Hall of Fame, 2003; recipient Merit award, Baldwin Wallace Coll., 1986; Paul Harris fellow, Rotary Internat., 1983. Mem.: Amherst Hist. Soc., Phi Mu. Republican. Congregationalist. Home: 439 Shupe Ave Amherst OH 44001

GERSTING, JUDITH LEE, computer scientist, educator, computer scientist, researcher; b. Springfield, Vt., Aug. 20, 1940; d. Harold H. and Dorothy V. (Kinney) MacKenzie; m. John M. Gersting, Jr., Aug. 17, 1962; children: Adam, Jason. BS, Stetson U., 1962; MA, Ariz. State U., 1964, PhD, 1969. Assoc. prof. computer sci. U. Ctrl. Fla., Orlando, 1980-81; asst. prof. Ind. U.-Purdue U., Indpls., 1970-73, assoc. prof., 1974-79, prof., 1981-93, U. Hawaii, Hilo, 1994—. Staff scientist Indpls. Ctr. Advanced Rsch., 1982—84. Author: Mathematical Structures for Computer Science, 1996, 2003; contbr. articles to sci. jours. Mem.: Assn. Computing Machinery. Avocations: youth soccer, reading. Office: U Hawaii 200 W Kawili St Hilo HI 96720-4075 E-mail: gersting@hawaii.edu.

GERSTMAN, BUDDY BURT, health science educator; b. Bklyn., May 30, 1954; s. Joseph and Bernadine Joyce (Barnett) G.; m. Maureen Linda Gerstman, May 23, 1985; children: Emily, Deborah, Efrem, Jordan. BA, SUNY, Binghamton, 1976; DVM, Cornell U., 1980; MPH, U. Calif., Berkeley, 1984; PhD, U. Calif., Davis, 1989. Pvt. practice as veterinarian, No. Calif., 1980-85; epidemiologist FDA, Rockville, Md., 1985-90; prof. pub. health San Jose (Calif.) State U., 1990—. Author: Epidemiological Text, 1998; contbr. articles to sci. jours. Mem. APHA, Internat. Soc. Pharmacoepidemiology, Soc. for Epidemiologic Rsch.

GERSTMAN, GEORGE HENRY, lawyer; b. N.Y.C., July 25, 1939; m. Rozanne Millman, Dec. 24, 1960; children: Heidi Ann, Gary Daniel. BSEE, U. Ill., 1960; JD with honors, George Washington U., 1963. Bar: Ill. 1964, U.S. Dist. Ct. (no. dist.) Ill. 1964, U.S. Patent Office 1964, U.S. Supreme Ct. 1971, U.S. Ct. Appeals (7th cir.) 1971, U.S. Ct. Appeals (2d cir.) 1980, U.S. Ct. Appeals (Fed. cir.) 1982. Patent examiner U.S. Patent Office, Washington, 1960-63; assoc. Dressler, Goldsmith et al, Chgo., 1963-70; ptnr. Lettvin & Gerstman, Chgo., 1970-75, Gerstman, Ellis & McMillin, Ltd., Chgo., 1976-99, Seyfarth Shaw, Chgo., 2000—. Asst. patent editor George Washington Law Rev., 1962-63. Govt. appeal agt. Selective Svc. System, Evanston, Ill., 1967-73; mem. Northbrook (Ill.) Bd. Zoning Appeals, 1971-90. Mem.: Standard Club (Chgo.), Order of Coif, Patent Law Assn. Chgo., Am. Intellectual Property Law Assn., Chgo. Bar Assn., ABA. Avocations: art, boating. Home: 219 Sheridan Rd Kenilworth IL 60043-1216 Office: Seyfarth Shaw 55 E Monroe St Ste 4200 Chicago IL 60603-5863

GERSTMAN, HUBERT LOUIS, healthcare risk manager, speech and language pathologist, audiologist, otolaryngology educator; b. Buffalo, Feb. 20, 1934; s. Sidney and Lillian (Ruben) G.; m. Nanci Rebeckah Wintrub, June 7, 1959; children: Evana Rachel, Gavriella, Joshua Michael. BS, SUNY, Geneseo, 1955; MEd, Pa. State U., 1960, EdD, 1962. Clinician Pa. State U., University Park, 1960-62; psychologist St. Elizabeth Hosp., Washington, 1962-63; asst. prof. speech U. Akron, Ohio, 1963-65; instr. Tufts Sch. Dental Medicine, Boston, 1967-87; assoc. prof. Tufts Sch. Medicine, Boston, 1965-87; chief speech, hearing and lang. ctr. New Eng. Med. Ctr. Hosp., Boston, 1965-87; assoc. prof. surgery SUNY, Stony Brook, 1989-93; risk. mgr., ins. investment Seattle, 1993—. Cons. in field; pres. Acoustic Corp. Am., Boston, 1971-78, Gerstman Cons., Natick, Mass., 1965-87; adj. prof. Emerson Coll., Boston, 1971-87. Contbr. chpts. to books. Chmn. adv. bd. Boston Vis. Nurse Assn., 1978-87; advisor Mass. Dept. Pub. Welfare, 1969-76, Model Cities Program, 1968-73; organizer Citizens for Humphrey, 1968; pres. Bellevue Cmty. Band, 1999-2000. With U.S. Army, 1955-57. Recipient 1st Gerstman award Mass. Hearing Soc., 1976. Fellow Am. Speech Lang. Hearing Assn. (various bds. and coms., chair profl. svcs. bd. 1986-87); mem. Assn. Service Programs (pres. 1981-87), Nat. Alliance Stuttering (pres. 1987-88), Acoustic Soc. Am., Am. Cleft Palate Assn., B'nai B'rith. Jewish. Avocations: theatrical producing, magic, tuba. Home and Office: 11234 NE 146th St Kirkland WA 98034-1012

GERSTNER, JONATHAN NEIL, religious studies educator; b. Latrobe, Pa., Aug. 5, 1957; s. John H. and Edna Rachel Gerstner; m. Kathleen Jipping, June 20, 1987; children: Sarah Elizabeth, Jerusha Joy, Monica Kaye, Nathanael John, Micaia Eden. BA, Mich. State U., 1979; MA, U. Chgo., 1980, PhD, 1985. Ordained to ministry, Reformed Ch. in Am. Asst. prof. systematic and practical theology Payne Theol. Sem., Wilberforce, Ohio, 1986-89, acting acad. dean, 1988-89; exec. sec. Reformed Ch. in Can., Cambridge, Ont., 1989-94; prof. ch. history and apologetics Knox Theol. Sem., Ft. Lauderdale, Fla., 1994—98; prof. systematic theology and apologetics Knox Theol Sem., 1999; adj. prof. Ottawa Theol. Hall, Ottawa, Canada, 1997—2002, Sch. of Pastoral Studies, Rio de Janeiro, 1999—; dean and prof. of systematic theology and apologetics New Geneva Theol. Sem., Balt., 2001—02; corp. trainer MCI, Hunt Valley, Md., 2002—. Mem. governing bd. Can. Coun. Ch., Toronto, Ont., Canada, 1989—94, Evang. Fellowship Can., Willowdale, Ont., Canada, 1989—94; bd. dir. Ligonier Ministries Can., Guelph, Ont., Canada, 1992—2002; radio program host, 1998—2002; sr. pastor Inverness Presbyn. Ch., Balt., 2000—02. Author: The Thousand Generation Covenant: Dutch Reformed Covenant Theology and Group Identity in Colonial South Africa, 1652-1814, 1991; (with others) Trust and Obey, 1996, Christianity in the History of South Africa, 1997, Onward Christian Soldiers, 1999. Grad. fellow Rotary Internat., 1983. Mem. Am. Acad. Religion, Am. Soc. Ch. History, Phi Beta Kappa, Phi Kappa Phi.

GERSTNER, LOUIS VINCENT, JR., computer company executive; b. Mineola, N.Y., Mar. 1, 1942; s. Louis Vincent and Marjorie (Rutan) G.; m. Elizabeth Robins Link, Nov. 30, 1968; children: Louis, Elizabeth. BA in Engring., Dartmouth Coll., 1963; MBA, Harvard U., 1965; DBA (hon.), Boston Coll., 1994; LLD (hon.), Wake Forest U., 1997, Brown U., 1997; D of Engring. (hon.), Rensselaer Poly. Inst., 1999; LLD (hon.), Notre Dame U., 2001. Dir. McKinsey & Co., N.Y.C., 1965-78; exec. v.p. Am. Express Co., N.Y.C., 1978-81, vice-chmn. bd., 1981-83, chmn. exec. com., 1983-85, pres., 1985-89, chmn., CEO travel related svcs., 1985-89; chmn., CEO RJR Nabisco Inc., N.Y.C., 1989-93; chmn. bd., CEO IBM, Armonk, NY, 1993—2002, also dir., chmn. bd., 2002, ret., 2002; chmn. The Carlyle Group, 2003—. Bd. dirs. Bristol-Myers Squibb Co.; mem. Pres.'s Nat. Security Telecom. Adv. Com., 1994-97, Adv. Com. for Trade Policy and Negotiations, 1995-2002; chmn. Computer Sys. Policy Project, 1999-2001; adv. bd. DaimerChrysler, 2001—, Sony Corp., 2002—. Author: Who Says Elephants Can't Dance: Inside IBM's Historic Turnaround, 2002; co-author: Reinventing Education: Entrepreneurship in America's Public School, 1994. Bd. dirs. Meml. Sloan Kettering Hosp., 1978-89, 98—, vice-chmn., 2000—, United Negro Coll. Fund, 1987-91, Lincoln Ctr. for Performing Arts, 1984-2002, N.Y. Times, 1986-97, AT&T, 1987-93, Caterpillar, 1984-89, Coun. Fgn. Rels.; trustee Joint Coun. on Econ. Edn., 1975-87, chmn. 1983-85; active Bus. Roundtable, 1991-98, The Bus. Coun., 1992; vice-chmn., bd. dirs. New Am. Schs. Devel. Corp., 1991-98; trustee N.Y. Pub. Libr., 1991-96; bd. regents Smithsonian Instn., 1996-99; co-chmn. Achieve, 1996-2002, chmn. emeritus, 2003—; chmn. The Teaching Commn., 2003— Recipient Cleveland E. Dodge Medal for disting. svc. to edn. Tchrs. Coll., Columbia U., Disting. Svc. to Sci. and Edn. award Am. Mus. Natural History, Award for Excellence in Bus., Engring. and Tech., John M. Olin Sch. of Washington U., 1999; named Knight of British Empire, 2001. Fellow Am. Acad. Arts and Scis., Am.-China Soc., Nat. Acad. Engring. Office: IBM Corp 20 Old Post Rd Armonk NY 10504-1709

GERSTNER, MARY JANE, nurse; b. Rochester, N.Y., June 27, 1953; d. Thomas J. and Jane E. Gerstner. Diploma, St. Joseph's Hosp. Health Ctr. Sch. Nursing, 1974; BSN, Nazareth Coll., 1982. Cert. RN N.Y. Staff nurse oper. rm. U. Rochester Med. Ctr./Strong Meml. Hosp., 1974-79, staff nurse ob.-gyn. unit, 1981-83, 84-86; staff nurse oper. rm. St. Mary's Hosp., Rochester, 1983-84, Genesee Hosp., Rochester, 1985-95; nurse 1st asst. Genesee Valley Plastic Surgery, Canandaigua, N.Y., 1995; staff nurse oper. rm. U. of Rochester (N.Y.) Med. Ctr., 1996-00, nurse 1st asst., 2000—. Mem.: ARC, Genesee Valley Nurses Assn., Assn. Peri-Operative RNs, Sigma Theta Tau.

GERSTNER, ROBERT WILLIAM, structural engineering educator, consultant; b. Chgo., Nov. 10, 1934; s. Robert Berty and Martha (Tuchelt) G.; m. Elizabeth Willard, Feb. 8, 1958; children: Charles Willard, William Mark. BS, Northwestern U., 1956, MS, 1957, PhD, 1960. Registered structural and profl. engr., Ill. Instr. Northwestern U., Evanston, Ill., 1957-59, research fellow, 1959-60; asst. prof. U. Ill., Chgo., 1960-63, assoc. prof., 1963-69, prof. structural engring., architecture, 1969-92, prof. emeritus, 1992—. Structural engr. cons., 1959—; mem. State of Ill. Structural Engring. Bd., 1992-94. Contbr. articles to profl. jours. Pres. Riverside Improvement Assn., 1973-77, 79-82. Mem. AAUP, ACLU, ASCE, Am. Soc. Engring. Edn., Structural Engrs. Assn. Ill. (bd. dirs. 1986-89, 92-94, sec. 1989-91, pres. 1991-92). Home: 2628 W Agatite Ave Chicago IL 60625-3011

GERT, BERNARD, philosopher, educator; b. Cin., Oct. 16, 1934; s. Max and Celia (Yarnovsky) G.; m. Esther Libbye Rosenstein, Aug. 3, 1958; children: Heather Joy, Joshua Noah. BA, U. Cin., 1956; PhD, Cornell U., 1962. Instr. philosophy Dartmouth Coll., Hanover, NH, 1959-62, asst. prof. philosophy, 1962-66, assoc. prof., 1966-70, prof., 1970—, chmn. dept. philosophy, 1971—74, 1979—81, 1998—2001, Stone prof. intellectual and moral philosophy, 1981-92, 1998—, Eunice and Julian Cohen prof. ethics and human values, 1992-98. Vis. assoc. prof. philosophy Johns Hopkins U., Balt., 1967-68; vis. prof. philosophy Edinburgh U., fall 1974, Hebrew U. Jerusalem, 1985-86, Nacional U. de la Plata and U. Buenos Aires, Argentina, fall 1995; adj. prof. psychiatry Dartmouth Med. Sch., 1976—. Author: The Moral Rules: A New Rational Foundation for Morality, 1970, 1973, 1975, German edit. 1983, Morality: A New Justification of the Moral Rules, 1988, Morality: Its Nature and Justification, 1998; co-author: Philosophy in Medicine: Conceptual and Ethical Issues in Medicine and Psychiatry, 1982, Japanese edit. 1984; first author: Morality and the New Genetics: A Guide for Students and Health Care Providers, 1996, Bioethics: A Return to Fundamentals, 1997; editor: Hobbes' Man and Citizen, 1972, reprinted with revisions, 1991, Rationality, Rules, and Ideals: Critical Essays on Bernard Gert's Moral Theory, 2002; contbr. chpts. to books, articles to profl. jours. NEH fellow, 1969-70, Hastings Ctr. fellow, 1986--; recipient NSF-NEH Sustained Devel. award, 1980-84, Fulbright lectureship, Israel, 1985-86, Argentina, fall 1995; prin. investigator NIH, 1990-93. Fellow Nat. Humanities Ctr. 2001-2002; mem. Am. Philos. Assn., Am. Soc. Polit. and Legal Philosophy, Soc. Ethics Across the Curriculim, Assn. Practical and Profl. Ethics. Avocations: squash, poker. Home: 8 Bridgman Rd Hanover NH 03755-1302 Office: Dartmouth Coll Dept Philosophy Hanover NH 03755 E-mail: bernard.gert@dartmouth.edu.

GERTENBACH, ROBERT FREDERICK, medical research organization executive, accountant, lawyer; b. N.Y.C., Feb. 26, 1923; s. Charles and Margaret (Klag) G.; m. Arlene Turney (div. 1968); m. Carol Jean Roberts, Aug. 20, 1977; children: Stephen, Gail. BBA, CCNY, 1947; JD, Fordham U., 1952. Bar: N.Y. 1952; CPA, N.J., N.Y. Acct. Orens, Reiner, Weissbarth, N.Y.C., 1947-50, Price Waterhouse & Co., N.Y.C., 1950; asst. gen. counsel Thomas J. Lipton Inc., Englewood Cliffs, N.J., 1950-68; asst. to pres. Eastwood-Nealley Inc., Belleville, N.J., 1968-69; sr. product mgr. CPC Internat., Englewood Cliffs, 1970-73; v.p. Council of Better Bus. Burs., Inc., N.Y.C., 1973-80; pres. Council for Tobacco Research-U.S.A., Inc., N.Y.C., 1984-92, ret., 1992. Served to 1st lt. USAAF, 1943-45, PTO. Mem. ABA. Avocations: reading, walking.

GERTH, DONALD ROGERS, university president; b. Chgo., Dec. 4, 1928; s. George C. and Madeleine (Canavan) G.; m. Beverly J. Hollman, Oct. 15, 1955; children: Annette, Deborah. BA, U. Chgo., 1947, AM, 1951, PhD, 1963. Field rep. S.E. Asia World Univ. Svc., 1950; asst. to pres. Shimer Coll., 1951; Admissions counselor U. Chgo., 1956-58; assoc. dean students, admissions and records, mem. dept. polit. sci. San Francisco St. U., San Francisco, 1958-63; assoc. dean instnl. relations and student affairs Calif. State Univ., 1963-64; chmn. commn. on extended edn. Calif. State Univs. and Colls., 1977-82; dean of students Calif. State U., Chico, 1964-68, prof. polit. sci., 1964-76, assoc. v.p. for acad. affairs, dir. internat. programs, 1969-70, v.p. acad. affairs, 1970-76; co-dir. Danforth Found. Research Project, 1968-69; coordinator Inst. Local Govt. and Public Service, 1968-70; pres., prof. pub. policy and adminstrn. Calif. State U., Dominguez Hills, 1976-84, prof. emeritus, 1984—2003. Past chair Accrediting Commn. for Sr. Colls. and Univs. of Western Coll. Assn.; chmn. admissions coun. Calif. State U.; bd. dirs. Ombudsman Found., L.A., 1968-71; com. continuing edn. Calif. Coordinating Coun. for Higher Edn., 1963-64; lectr. U. Philippines, 1953-54, Claremont Grad. Sch. and Univ. Ctr., 1965-69; chair Sacramento World Trade Ctr.; chmn. Calif. State U. Inst., No. Calif. World Trade Ctr. Co-author: The Learning Society, 1969; author, editor: An Invisible Giant, 1971; contbg. editor Education for the Public Service, 1970, Papers on the Ombudsman in Higher Education, 1979. Mem. pers. commn. Chico Unified Sch. Dist., 1969-76, chmn., 1971-74; adv. com. on justice pgorams Butte Coll., 1970-76; mem. Varsity Scouting Coun., 1980-84; chmn. United Way campaign Calif. State Univs., L.A. County, 1981-82; bd. dirs. Sacramento Area United Way, campaign chmn., 1991-92, exec. com., 1991-96, vice chmn., 1992-94, chmn.-elect, 1994-95, chmn., 1995-96; mem. bd. dirs. South Bay Hosp. Found., 1979-82; mem. The Cultural Commn., L.A., 1981-84; mem. com. govtl. rels. Am. Coun. Edn. Capt. USAF, 1952-56. Mem. Internat. Assn. Univ. Pres. (pres. 1996-99), Am. Polit. Sci. Assn., Am. Soc. Pub. Adminstrn., Soc. Coll. and Univ. Planning, Western Govtl. Rsch. Assn., World Affairs Coun. No. Calif., Assn. Pub. Adminstrn. Edn. (chmn. 1973-74), Western Polit. Sci. Assn., Am. Assn. State Colls. and Univs. (bd. dirs.), Calif. State C. of C. (edn. com.), Assn. Governing Bds. of Univs. and Colls., Calif. State U. Inst. (chmn. bd. dirs.), UN Ednl., Sci. and Cultural Orgn. (mem. adv. com.), UN Univ. Coun., World Trade Ctr. Sacramento, (chmn.), Sacramento Club (bd. dirs.), Comstock Club. Democrat. Episcopalian. Avocations: tennis, skiing, reading. Home: 7132 Secret Garden Loop Roseville CA 95747-8339 Office: Calif State U 2000 State Univ Drive East Rm 3022 Sacramento CA 95819

GERTIS, NEILL ALLAN, writer; b. Buffalo, Mar. 24, 1943; s. Alfred Charles and Gertrude Charlotte (Hurst) G.; m. Gail C. Morgan, Oct. 3, 1966 (div. Aug. 1982); m. Alma Ann Sullivan, Sept. 15, 1984; children: Charlotte Ann, Joseph Alfred, Daniel Andrew, Martin Alexander. Community planner Alaska State Housing Authority, Anchorage, 1968-72, libr. dir., 1968-72; real estate appraiser Gertis Assocs., Buffalo, 1972-76; ops. mgr. Chem. Equipment Labs., Phila., 1979-83; tech. writer Gen. Dynamics, Groton, Conn., 1983-84; sr. tech. writer communication products MTS Systems Corp., Mpls., 1984-94, mgr. tech. tng., 1994-97; supr. tech. publs. Rockwell Automation, Mpls., 1997—. Author: Student Housing Demand in Anchorage, 1972; editor: Guide to Periodical Holdings in the Anchorage Area, 1970, Storm Drainage for Chester Creek, Anchorage, 1969; editor Engring. Graphics, Anchorage, 1968-72. Served with U.S. Army, 1965-69. Mem. Alaska Library Assn. Republican. Avocations: computers, antiques, restoration, writing, reading. Home: 1157 Tyler St S Shakopee MN 55379-2070

GERTJEJANSEN, DOYLE, artist, educator; b. Tracy, Minn., Sept. 1, 1948; BA, Mankato State U., 1969; MFA, U. Minn., 1971. Instr. fine arts U. New Orleans, 1971-75, grad. coun., 1986-91, prof. fine arts, 1988—, chmn. dept. fine arts, 1995-97. Panelist Insts. and the ARtist Optima Studio, New Orleans, 1982; visual arts com. New Orleans Contemporary Arts Ctr., 1983—86; dir. Sculpture Front U. New Orleans, 1984—86, project dir. for traveling exhbn. So. Folk Images Univ. Senate, 1984, permanent art collection com., 1984—87; task force on pub. sculpture Downtown Devel. Dist. and Arts Coun. New Orleans, 1985; mem. downtown pub. art com. Arts Coun. New Orleans, 1986, mem. percent for art com., 1987—89, bd. dirs., 1988—89, mem. art-works artists steering com.; bd. dirs. New Orleans Contemporary Arts Ctr., 1996—99; chair visual arts com. N.D. Contemporary Arts Ctr., 1997—99. One-man shows include Augusta Coll. Fine Arts Gallery, Sioux Falls, S.D., 1968, Coffman Gallery U. Minn., Mpls., 1971, U. No. Ala., Florence, 1975, La. Crafts Coun., New Orleans, 1980, Arthur Roger Gallery, 1981, 1983, 1985, New Orleans Ctr. Performing Arts, 1984, Susan Abeline Gallery, Zurich, Switzerland, 1986, Galerie Simonne Stern Ltd., Atlanta, 1989, Galerie Simonne Stern, New Orleans, 1987, 1989, 1990, 1993, 1996, Conkling Gallery Mankato (Minn.) State U., 1989, exhibited in group shows at Galerie Simonne Stern, New Orleans, 1994, 1995, 1999, New Orleans Ctr. Contemporary Art, 1995, La. Arts and Sci. Ctr., Baton Rouge, 1995, Contemporary Arts Ctr., New Orleans, 1995, Positive Space Gallery, 1996, 1996, Delfina Studio Trust, London, 1996, Ctr. Contemporary Art, Winston-Salem, N.C., 1997, U. West Fla., 1997, D.C. Arts Ctr., Washington, 1998, Gunma Print Artists Assn., Maebshi City, Japan, 1999, numerous others, Represented in permanent collections Adams & Reese, New Orleans, Ariz. State U., Ark. Art Ctr., Hotel Intercontinental, New Orleans, Middleberg, Riddle & Gianna Attys., New Orleans Mus. Art, Pan Am. Life, New Orleans, Premier Bank, Baton Rouge, Scudder, Stevens and Clark, Boston, State St. Rsch. and Mgmt. Co., TJM Corp., New Orleans, Westminster, Corp., other pvt. collections. Recipient Artist of Yr. award, New Orleans Contemporary Arts Ctr. Century Club, 1993, South Ctrl. Artists award, Phi Kappa Phi, 1996; DeBois Faculty fellow, U. New Orleans Coll. Urban and Pub. Affairs, 1992, regional fellow, NEA/So. Arts Fedn., 1996, fellow, La. Divsn. Arts, 1998. Office: c/o Galerie Simonne Stern 518 Julia St New Orleans LA 70130-3624

GERTLER, JANOS JOHN, electrical engineer, educator; b. Vienna, Sept. 9, 1936; came to U.S., 1981; s. Mor and Marta (Ungar) Gertler; m. Judit Andai, July 29, 1965; 1 child, Nicholas Balazs; m. Eva Anna Vas, Dec. 30, 2000. Diploma in engring., Tech. U., Budapest, Hungary, 1959; Candidate of Sci., Hungaraian Acad. Scis., Budapest, 1967, DSc, 1980. Rsch. assoc. Power Systems Rsch. Inst., Budapest, 1959-65; asst. prof. Tech. U., Budapest, 1965-67; postdoctoral fellow U. Toronto, Ont., Can., 1967-68; sr. rsch. assoc. Automation Rsch. Inst., Budapest, 1968-70, dep. dir., 1971-81; vis. prof., assoc. dean engring. Poly. Inst. N.Y., Bklyn., 1984-85; prof. George Mason U., Fairfax, Va., 1985—. Assoc. vis. prof. Case Western Res. U., Cleve., 1977, vis. prof., 1982-84; cons. Bailey Controls, Cleve., 1983-84, GM, Warren, Mich., 1989-96; plenary spkr. internat. confs., 1974, 86, 91, 92, 93, 94, 95, 00. Author: Fault Detection and Diagnosis, 1998; series editor Internat. Fedn. Automatic Control Procs., 1984-96; editor Ann. Revs. in Control, 1996—; contbr. articles to profl. jours. Fellow IEEE; mem. Hungarian Nat. Acad. Scis. (fgn. mem.), Internat. Fedn. Automatic Control (chmn. publ. bd. 1993-96, 96-99, advisor for life, 1999—). Achievements include rsch. in the theory and application of model-based diagnosis in engineering systems; development of generalized parity relation method; application to car engines. Office: George Mason U Elec Engring Dept Fairfax VA 22030

GERTLER, MENARD M. physician, educator; b. Saskatoon, Sask., Can., May 19, 1921; arrived in U.S., 1947, naturalized, 1953; s. Frank and Clara (Handelman) G.; m. Anna Paull, Sept. 4, 1943; children: Barbara Lynn, Stephanie Jocelyn, Jonathan Paull. BA, U. Sask., Saskatoon, 1940; MD, McGill U., Montreal, 1943, MS, 1946, DSc (hon.), 1999, NYU, 1960. Intern Royal Victoria Hosp., Montreal, Que., Can., 1943-44; resident Mass. Gen. Hosp., Boston, 1947-50; also research fellow in medicine Mass. Gen. Hosp., Harvard Med. Sch., 1947-50; dir. cardiology Francis Delafield divsn. Columbia Presbyn. Med. Ctr., N.Y.C., 1950-54; spl. research fellow NIH, NYU Dept. Biochemistry, 1954-56; prof. Sch. Medicine, dir. cardiovascular research Rusk Inst. NYU Med. Ctr., 1958-71; sr. med. examiner FAA, 1975; dir. Washington Fed. Savs. & Loan Assn., 1972-83; adj. prof. medicine McGill U., 1996—; clin. prof. medicine N.Y. Hosp.-Cornell Med. Ctr., attending physician. Prof. medicine Weill Med. Sch., Cornell U.; attending physician N.Y. Hosp./Presbyn. Hosp., 1998—; med. dir. Sinclair Oil Corp., 1958-68; internat. cons. cardiovascular diseases, social and rehab. svcs. HEW, Washington, 1968-92. Author: Coronary Heart Disease in Young Adults, 1954, Coronary Heart Disease, 1974; Contbr. articles to profl. jours. Pres. Friends of McGill U., 1983-2001; mem. dean's com. McGill U. Med. Sch. With M.C., Royal Can. Army, 1940-43. Recipient Founders Day award NYU, 1959, medal of honor McGill U., 1993, award of merit McGill U., 1993. Mem. Gallatin Assocs. NYU, Cosmos Club (Washington), Harvard Club (Boston), Univ. Club. Home and Office: 1000 Park Ave Apt 2C New York NY 10028-0934

GERTRUDE, KATY See WILHELM, KATE

GERTZ, DAVID LEE, homebuilding company executive; b. Denver, July 30, 1950; s. Ben Harry and Clara (Cohen) G.; m. Bonnie Lee Schulein, June 2, 1973; children: Joshua, Eva. BS, U. Colo., 1972; MBA, U. Colo., Denver, 1993. Real estate broker Crown Realty, Denver, 1972-73; pres. Sunshine Plumbing Co., Lakewood, Colo., 1974-76, Sunshine Diversified, Inc., Lakewood, 1976—, Sunshine Master Builders, Ltd., Lakewood, 1990—. Sec.-treas. Wight Lateral Ditch Co., Lakewood, 1987-91. Builder Taylor Made semi-custom homes. Cub master Boy Scouts Am., Lakewood, 1989-91, asst. scout master, 1991-94; chmn. Parade of Homes com., 1999-2000. Scholar, Evans Scholars, U. Colo., 1968-72. Mem.: Home Aid Denver (bd. dirs., pres.), Colo. Assn. Home Builders (bd. dirs., legis. com., accessability com.). Avocations: skiing, golf. Office: Sunshine Master Builders 7120 E Orchard Rd Englewood CO 80111 E-mail: dlgertz@sunshinemb.com., sunshin256@aol.com.

GERTZ, MORIE ABRAHAM, physician; b. Chgo., Aug. 7, 1952; s. Nathan and Hannah (Tischler) G.; m. Marcia Graifman, Dec. 7, 1975; children: Jaimee, Jessica. BA with highest distinction, Northwestern U., 1972; MD cum laude, Loyola Med. Sch., 1975. Diplomate Am. Coll. Physicians. Intern St. Joseph Hosp., Chgo., 1976; resident Presbyn.-St. Lukes Med. Sch., Chgo., 1976-79; fellow Mayo Clinic, Rochester, Minn., 1979-82, cons. hematology, 1983—, sect. head hematology, 1994-97; chmn. divsn. hematology Mayo Med. Sch., Rochester, 1997—, prof. medicine, 1995—; disting. clinician Mayo Clinic, Rochester, 2002—. Vis. physician Boston U. Med. Sch., 1982-83. Contbr. articles to profl. jours. including New Eng. Jour. Medicine, Bone Marrow Trans., Jour. of Neurol. Psychology, Hepatology. Head Indian Princess YMCA, Rochester, 1993. Fellow ACP; mem. Ctrl. Soc. Clin. Rsch., Am. Soc. Clin. Oncology, Am. Soc. Hematology, Sigma Xi (pres. 1997), Phi Beta Kappa, Alpha Omega Alpha. Avocations: bridge, computers. Office: Mayo Clinic 200 1st St SW Rochester MN 55905-0002

GERTZ, THEODORE GERSON, lawyer; b. Chgo., Sept. 8, 1936; s. Elmer and Ceretta (Samuels) G.; m. Suzanne C., June 19, 1960; children: Craig M., Candace C., Scott W. BA, U. Chgo., 1958; JD, Northwestern U., 1962. Bar: Ill. 1962, U.S. Dist. Ct. (no. dist.) Ill. 1962. Assoc. Marks, Marks & Kaplan, Chgo., 1962-64, Lowitz, Vihons & Stone, Chgo., 1964-66, ptnr., 1966-71, Pretzel & Stouffer, Chgo., 1971-94, Shefsky, Froelich, Chgo., 1995—. Gen. counsel Hull House Assn., Chgo., 1977—, Blind Svc. Assn., Chgo., 1987—, Lawyers for the Creative Arts, Citizens Against Suburban Sprawl, Mettawa, Ill., 1995—. Author: A Guide to Estate Planning, Illinois Advance Estate Planning. Dir., treas. Mettawa Open Lands, 1987—; former trustee Village of Mettawa, 1994—, Pub. Interest Law Initiative, Chgo; bd. mem., Lawyers for the Creative Arts, 2002—. With U.S. Army, 1962-64. Fellow Ill. Bar Found., Ill. Bar Assn., Chgo. Bar Assn., Law Club. Democrat. Jewish. Avocations: reading, nature, working out, dancing, traveling. Home: 950 Benson Ln Libertyville IL 60048-2406 Office: Shefsky and Froelich 444 N Michigan Ave Ste 2600B Chicago IL 60611-3998

GERUE, GERALD G. management consultant; b. Beloit, Wis., Jan. 30, 1951; s. George William and Helen GeRue; m. Marjorie A. Mack; children: Carin A., Brett T.;1 child, George William. AAS in Acctg., Rock Valley Coll., 1976; BS in Mgmt. and Comm., Concordia U. Wis., 1997, MBA in Fin., 2001. Mgr. Purchasing Quigley-Smart Inc., Beloit, Wis., 1970—95; mgr. Office and Acctg. Rockford Area C. of C., Ill., 1996; mgr. Office and Sales Palmer's Beloit Nurseries, South Beloit, Ill., 1996; lead pub. svc. rep. State of Ill., Rockford, 1996—99; mgr. Purchasing Jensen's Plumbing and Heating, Woodstock, Ill., 1997—99; gen. mgr. Control and Climate Distbrs., Rockford, 1999—. Owner GeRue Tax Svc., South Beloit, 1975—90; adj. faculty Upper Iowa U., Janesville, 1997—, Concordia U., Madison, Wis., 1997—, Blackhawk Tech. Coll., Beloit, 1997—. Chair, bd. dirs. Mid Town Dist., Rockford, 2000—; mayor City of South Beloit, 1995—99. Mem.: AAUP. Avocations: golf, antiques, reading, travel, Trap Shooting, Civil War History. Home: 12818 Stamford Ln Roscoe IL 61073 Office: Control and Climate Dist 635 7th St Rockford IL 61104*

GERVAIS, SISTER GENEROSE, hospital consultant; b. Currie, Minn., Sept. 18, 1919; d. Philip Frederick and Elizabeth Eleanor (Sandgathe) G. BS, Stout State U., Menomonie, Wis., 1945; M. Hosp. Adminstrn., U. Minn., 1954. Joined Sisters of St. Francis, Roman Catholic Ch., 1938; adminstrv. dietitian St. Marys Hosp., Rochester, Minn., 1948-50, adminstrv. asst., 1951-52, asst. adminstr., 1954-63, assoc. adminstr., 1963-71, hosp. adminstr., 1971-81, exec. dir., 1981-85, bd. trustees, 1968-86; hosp. cons., 1985-90. Cons. dietitian Mercy Hosp., Portsmouth, Ohio, 1950-51; bd. dirs. 1st Nat. Bank, Rochester, 1974-78, Fed. Res. Bank Mpls., 1978-86, St. Francis Med. Ctr., LaCrosse, Wis., 1979-87, S.E. Minn. Health Systems Agy., 1978-83, S.E. Minn. Health Coun., 1983-87, Unity Home Health Svcs., Inc., LaCrosse, 1994-95; v.p., sec. Family Health Ctr. LaCrosse, Inc., 1985-91, pres., 1991-93; mem. residency adv. bd. St. Francis-Mayo Family Practice, 1993-95; mem. v.p., bd. dirs. Caledonia Health Care Ctr., 1986-90; bd. dirs. Franciscan Health System, LaCrosse, 1987-94, mem., treas., bd. dirs. Franciscan Cmty. Programs 1985-94. Bd. dirs. United Way of Olmstead County, 1968-73, Sr. Citizens Svcs. Inc., Rochester, Minn., 1988-94, Diocese of Winona Found., 1991-2000, Madonna Towers, Rochester, 1987—, chair, 1991-97, Olmstead County Hist. Soc., 1994-97, Regina Med. Ctr., Hastings, Minn., 1996-02, Madonna Meadows, 2002; pres. Poverello Found., Rochester, 1983—; bd. adv. Winona State U. Rochester Ctr., 1985-93; mem. fin. coun. Diocese of Winona, 1986-91; mem. Franciscan Skemp Healthcare Cmty. Bd., LaCrosse, 1995—. Decorated Lady of Equestrian Order of Holy Sepulchre, 1989; recipient Alumni Disting. Service award U. Wis.-Stout, 1978, Teresa of Avila award Coll. of St. Teresa, 1980, Outstanding Achievement award Rochester chpt. U. Minn. Alumni Assn., 1981, Women of Achievement in Area of Bus. award YWCA, 1985, Pro Ecclesiae et Pontifice medal, 1985, Service to Mankind award Sertoma 700 Club, 1987, Mayor's Medal of Honor City of Rochester, 1990, The Athena award, 1994, Outstanding Alumni award Coll. Human Devel., U. Wis.-Stout, 2001; named Boss of Yr., Rochester Jaycees, 1980, named in her honor Sister Generose Gervais Bldg. St. Marys Hosp., 1991; Paul Harris fellow Nat. Rotary Club, 1998. Mem. Cath. Health Assn. U.S. (trustee 1979, vice chair 1981-82, chair 1982-83, speaker membership assembly 1983-84), Am. Coll. Hosp. Adminstrs., Am. Hosp. Assn., Minn. Hosp. Assn., Minn. Conf. Cath. Health Facilities (past dir.), Rochester Area C. of C. Republican. Address: 1216 2nd St SW Rochester MN 55902-1906

GERVAIS, PAUL NELSON, foundation administrator, psychotherapist, public relations executive, author; b. Augusta, Maine, June 28, 1947; s. Adrien and Phyllis (Sullivan) G. B in Bible and Doctrine/Ministerial Studies, Berean Coll., 1975; M, U. Maine, 1987; M in Marriage and Family Therapy, Coll. Clin. Family Sci., 1988; cert. in Constl. Law, U. Maine, 1969; Dr., N.Am. Biblical Sem., Buffalo, 1987; M. in Marriage and Family, San Antonio Theol. Sem., 1988; PhD in Psychology, San Antonio Theol. Sem., St. Paul, 1989; PhD in

Marriage and Family Therapy, Minn. Grad. Sch., 1990. Cert. behavioral analyst, clin. supr., registered clin. therapist, lic. marriage and family therapist, clin. profl. counselor, profl. counselor, pastoral counselor Maine. Reporter No. New Eng. divsn. News dept. NBC Radio divsn., N.Y.C., 1966-70; dir. pub. rels. Kennebec Valley Med. Ctr., Augusta, 1970-73, Penobscot Bay Med. Ctr., Rockport, Maine, 1973-74; pres., chmn. bd. dirs. Ministry of Miracles Evangelistic Assn., Maine, 1975—; staff clinician Augusta Police Dept. News dir. Maine Broadcasting Sys., Augusta, 1966—70; advisor, assoc. dir. pub. rels. State VA Svcs., Maine, 1969—70; family counselor Gracelawn Meml. Park, Auburn, Maine, assoc. dir., 1987; pres., CEO Motivational Resources; behavioral scientist Augusta Police Dept. Pioneered one of first radio and TV health edn. programs from which proceeded other nat. and internat. programs in field; mental health columnist Maine Sunday Paper; internat. network TV guest. Active Rep. Nat. Com., Washington, 1987, Dole for Pres. exploratory Com., 1987—, also adv. com., 1987, steering com. Campaign Am., 1987-88; mem. Presdl. Task Force, Washington, 1989, Rep. Senatorial Inner Circle, 1989—, U.S. Senatorial Club, Washington, 1989-90, Nat. Rep. Senatorial Com., Washington, 1990; CEO Gracelawn Meml. Park, Auburn, Maine, 1988—; spl. advisor, dep. Kennebec County Sheriff's Office, also dep. sheriff. Recipient vice-presdl. Citation Office of U.S. V.P. Hubert Humphrey, 1968, Malcolm T. MacEachern Citation Am. Health Congress, 1973; cert. in pub. rels. Chgo. chpt. Am. Hosp. Assn.; Presdl. Medal of Merit Pres. George Bush, 1989. Fellow Profl. Assn. Christian Counselors and Therapists; mem. AACD, Am. Acad. Family Therapists (exec. dir.), Acad. for Eating Disorders, Nat. Assn. Anorexia Nervosa and Associated Disorders, Publicity Club Boston (disting. bell ringer award 1974), Nat. Christian Counselors Assn. (mem. licensing bd., chmn. legal com.), Am. Mental Health Counselors Assn., Maine Network Associated Profl. Practitioners, Maine Assn. for Counseling and Devel., Mensa. Baptist. Home and Office: Am Acad Profl Family Therapists 16 Julianne Ln Augusta ME 04330-6251

GERVAY, JOSEPH EDMUND, chemist, researcher, retired research scientist; b. Budapest, Hungary, Dec. 29, 1931; arrived in U.S., 1966; s. Joseph Edmund Gervay Sr. and Elisabeth Hajdu; m. Helen Yvonne Hedri, June 11, 1956; 1 child, Michael Steven. BSc with honors, U. Montreal, Can., 1961; MSc, PhD, U. B.C., Vancouver, Can., 1965. Rsch. chemist E.I. du Pont de Nemours & Co., Parlin, NJ, 1965—74, sr. rsch. chemist, 1975—84, rsch. assoc. Wilmington, Del., 1984—89, sr. rsch. assoc., 1990—93; ret., 1993. Cons., advisor, bd. mem. Ultrafine Techs., Inc., Wilmington, Del., 1996—. Contbr. articles to profl. jours. Mem.: NRA (sr.), Am. Chem. Soc. (sr.), Dupont Country Club. Achievements include patents in field. Avocations: tennis, sailing, bicycling, politics, reading.

GERWICK, BEN CLIFFORD, JR., construction engineer, educator; b. Berkeley, Calif., Feb. 22, 1919; s. Ben Clifford and Bernice (Contrap) Gerwick; m. Martelle Louise Beverly, July 28, 1941 (dec. Jan. 1995); children: Beverly Brian, Virginia Wallace, Ben Clifford III, William; m. Ellen Chaney Lynch, May 18, 1996. BS, U. Calif., 1940. With Ben C. Gerwick, Inc., San Francisco, 1946—, pres., 1952-88, chmn., 1988-2000, hon. chmn., sr. tech. cons., 2000—; exec. v.p. Santa Fe-Pomeroy, Inc., 1968-71; prof. civil engring. U. Calif., Berkeley, 1971-89, prof. emeritus, 1989—. Sponsoring mgr. Richmond-San Rafael Bridge substructure, 1953—56, San Mateo-Hayward Bridge, 1964—66; lectr. constrn. engring. Stanford U., 1962—68; cons. major bridge and marine constrn. projects; cons. engr. ocean structures and overwater bridges, also offshore structures and bridges U.S., North Sea, Arctic Ocean, Japan, Australia, Indonesia, Arabian Gulf, China, Europe, Can., S.E. Asia, S.Am.; mem. Arctic Rsch. Commn., 1990—95. Author: (book) Russian-English Dictionary of Prestressed Concrete and Concrete Construction, 1966, Construction of Prestressed Concrete Structures, 1971, Construction of Prestressed Concrete Structures, 2d edit., 1996, Construction and Engineering Marketing for Major Project Services, 1981, Construction of Marine and Offshore Structures, 1986, Construction of Marine and Offshore Structures, 2d edit., 2000; contbr. articles to profl. jours. Chmn. marine bd. Nat. Rsch. Coun., 1978—80. With USN, 1940—46, comdr. USNR, ret. Named one of Top Engrs. in Past 125 Yrs., Engring. News Record, 2000; recipient Goldern Beaver award, Beavers Constrn. Soc., 1974, Mörsch medal, Deutsche Beton Verein, Weisbaden, Germany, 1978, Blakely Smith Ocean Engring. medal, Soc. Naval Archs. and Marine Engrs., 1981, Lockheed Ocean Engring. award, Marine Tech. Soc., 1982, Citation, U. Calif., Berkeley, 1989, Internat. award, Japan Soc. Civil Engring., 2001. Fellow: ASCE (hon. Karp award 1976, G. Brooks Earnest award 1980, Peurifoy award 1989, Pres.'s award 1989, Disting. Constructor award 2000, Ralph B. Peck Lectr. award 2001, Outstanding Lifetime Achievement award 2001), Norwegian Concrete Soc. (Holand award 2002, Ivar Holand award 2002), Am. Segmented Bridge Inst., Nat. Acad. Constrn., Internat. Assn. Bridge and Structural Engrs., Deep Founds. Inst. (Disting. Svc. award 1996), Am. Concrete Inst. (hon.; dir. 1960, Turner award 1974, Corbetta award 1981, Franklin Inst. Brown award 1984, Offshore Tech. Rsch.Ctr. Honors award 1992); mem.: NAE, Nat. Acad. Engrs., Prestressed Concret Inst. (hon.; pres. 1957—58), Fédn. Internat. Procontrainte (pres. 1974—78, now hon. pres., Freyssinet medal 1982), World Trade Club (San Francisco), Claremont Country Club (Oakland), Bohemian Club (San Francisco). Congregationalist. Home: 5727 Country Club Dr Oakland CA 94618-1717 Office: Ben C Gerwick Inc 20 California St Fl 4 San Francisco CA 94111-2607 E-mail: bcg@gerwick.com.

GERWIN, LESLIE ELLEN, lawyer, public affairs and community relations executive; b. L.A., May 18, 1950; d. Nathan and Beverly Adele (Wilson) G.; m. Bruce Robert Leslie, July 3, 1978; 1 child, Jonathan Gerwin Leslie. BA, Prescott Coll., 1972; JD, Antioch Sch. Law, 1975; MPH, Tulane U., 1988. Bar: D.C. 1975, N.Y. 1981, U.S. Dist. Ct. D.C. 1977, U.S. Dist. Ct. (so. dist.) N.Y. 1980. Staff asst. U.S. Congress, Washington, 1970-72; cons. Congl. Subcom., Washington, 1972-73; instr. U. Miami Law Sch., Coral Gables, Fla., 1975-76; assoc. prof. law Yeshiva U., N.Y.C., 1976-86; vis. assoc. prof. law Tulane Law Sch., New Orleans, 1983-84; pub. policy cons. New Orleans, 1987—; pres. Ariadne Cons., New Orleans, 1994—; dir. devel. and community rels. Planned Parenthood La., Inc., New Orleans, 1989-90; legal advisor La. Coalition for Reproductive Freedom, 1990-92; exec. v.p. Met. Area Com., New Orleans, 1992-94; exec. dir. Met. Area Com. Edn. Fund, New Orleans, 1992-94. Bd. dirs. Inst. for Phys. Fitness Rsch., N.Y.C., 1982-86, Challenge/Discovery, Crested Butte, Colo., 1977-80; cons. FDA, Washington, 1977-78, U. Judaism, L.A., 1974-75; mem. Met. Area Com. Leadership Forum, New Orleans, 1988; adj. asst. prof. La. State U. Sch. Medicine, 1996—, La. State U. Med. Sch., Dept. of Public Health and Preventive Medicine. Contbr. articles to profl. jours. Mem. Ind. Dem. Jud. Screening Panel, N.Y.C., 1980; bd. dirs. New Orleans Food Bank for Emergencies, 1987-89; profl. adv. com. MAZON-A Jewish Response to Hunger, L.A., 1986-89; bd. dirs. Second Harvesters Food Bank Greater New Orleans, 1989-94, La. State LWV, 1990-91, Anti-Defamation League, New Orleans, 1989-95, Jewish Endowment Found., 1987-93; trustee Jewish Fedn. Greater New Orleans, 1989-95, 97-99, mem. exec. com., 1997-99; trustee Emergency Food and Shelter Program, S.E. La., 1988—; v.p. Tulane U. B'nai B'rith Hillel Found., 1987-90; steering com. Citizens for Pers. Freedom, 1989-91; steering com. Metro 2000, 1989-90; sec. New Orleans sect. Nat. Coun. Jewish Women, 1990-91, state pub. affairs chmn., 1992-96; bd. Contemporary Arts Ctr., 1993-97; chair, bd. advocates Planned Parenthood La., 1995—; v.p. Edn. Tikvat Shalom Conservative Congregation, 1995-97, chair New Orleans Israel Bonds, 1996-98; mem. Cmty. Rels. Com., 1986-99, vice chair, 1995-97, chair 1997-99; adminstr. Area Tng. Ctr., USTA, New Orleans, 1996-2001; v.p. ritual Shir Chadosh Conservative Congregation, 2002—. Fellow Inst. of Politics, 1990-91; scholar Xerox Found., 1972-75; Decorated Order of Barristers; named One of Ten Outstanding Young Women of Am., 1987; recipient Herbert J. Garon Young Leadership award Jewish Fedn. Greater New Orleans, 1990; named YWCA Role Model, 1992. Mem. ABA, N.Y. Bar Assn., N.Y. Acad. Scis., Am. Pub. Health Assn., D.C. Bar Assn., Nat. Moot Ct. Honor Soc., Pub. Health Honor Soc., Calif. State Dem. Club (Key Svc. award 1988), Delta Omega.

GERY, JOHN ROY OCTAVIUS, secondary school educator, poet; b. Reading, Pa, June 2, 1953; s. Malcolm R. Dougherty and Eugenie Gunesh (Guran) Gery, Addison H. Gery, Jr. (Stepfather). BA in English with honors, Princeton U., 1975; MA in English, U. Chgo., 1976; MA in Creative Writing, Stanford U., 1978. Lectr. English San Jose State U., 1977-79; lectr. Stanford U., 1977-79; from instr. to assoc. prof. U. New Orleans, 1979—95, prof. English, creative writing, 1995-2000, rsch. prof., 2000—, dir. creative writing, 1986—90, 1996. Vis. assoc. prof. U. Iowa, Iowa City, 1991, Iowa City, 93; dir. Philol. Assn. La., Lafayette, New Orleans, 1986—88, Ezra Pound Ctr. Lit., Brunnenburg Castle, Italy, 1990—; resident poet Cummington Cmty. Arts, 1993, Bucknell U., 2001, 03; bd. dir. New Orleans Poetry Jour. Press. Author: (poems) Charlemagne: A Song of Gestures, 1983, The Enemies of Leisure, 1995, Nuc. Annihilation and Contemporary Am. Poetry, 1996, various poems; co-translator: For the House of Torkom, 1999; author: (poems) American Ghost: Selected Poems, 1999, Davenport's Version, 2003, A Gallery of Ghosts, 2004. Treas. Educators Social Responsibility, New Orleans, 1982—90; co-chair polit. action New Orleans Progressive Alliance, 1986—90. Recipient Deep South Poetry awards, Deep South Writers Conf., 1984, 1987, Critics' Choice award for poetry, 1995—96, European award, Cir. Franz Kafka, 2000; Poetry fellow, Wesleyan U. Writers Conf., 1989, Creative Writing fellow, Nat. Endowment Arts, 1992—93, Artist fellow, La. Divsn. Arts, 2002. Mem.: MLA, Gulf Coast Assn. Creative Writing Tchr. (2d v.p. 1996—98), La. State Poetry Soc., Assoc. Writing Programs, Poets & Writers. Democrat. Avocations: jazz piano, travel, baseball, films, art. Office: U New Orleans Dept English Lakefront New Orleans LA 70148-2315 E-mail: jgery@uno.edu.

GERYK, LAURA A. language educator; b. Westfield, Mass., Aug. 15, 1963; d. Florian F. and Carol A. Geryk. MA pending, U. of Kans., Lawrence, KS, 1997—2003; BA, U. of Mass., Amherst, Mass., 1988—90. Tchr. Chicopee MA Pub. Schools, Chicopee, Mass., 1999—, RC Diocese of Springfield, Springfield, Mass., 1991—97. Mentor tchr./cons. Chicopee Pub. Sch., Chicopee, Mass., 2000—; mentor tchr. RC Diocese of Springfield, Springfield, Mass., 1995. Mem.: Modern Lang. Assoc. (MLA), Psi Chi Soc. (life). Home: 24 Ina Street Springfield MA 01109 Personal E-mail: lgeryk@aol.com.

GESELL, THOMAS FREDERICK, physicist, educator; b. East Cleveland, Ohio, Apr. 28, 1940; s. Carl Frederick and Clara Elizabeth Gesell; m. Diane Corinne Wilson, June 12, 1964; children: Thomas, Barbara Gibson, Eric. BS in Physics, San Diego State U., 1965; MS in Physics, U. Tenn., 1968, PhD in Physics, 1971. Asst. prof. health physics U. Tex. Sch. of Pub. Health, Environ. Scis. Discipline, Houston, 1971—75, assoc. prof., chair, 1975—81; chief, dosimetry br. Radiol. and Environ. Sciences Lab. U.S. Dept. Energy, Idaho Falls, 1981—87, dep. asst. mgr. Idaho Ops. Office, 1987—88, dir. Radiol. and Environ. Sciences Lab., 1988—91; prof. Idaho State U., Pocatello, 1991—. Mem. sci. adv. bd. U.S. EPA, Washington, 1996—2002. Author: (book) Environmental Radioactivity, 1997; editor: Environmental Exposure: Facts vs. Fiction, 2000. Fellow: Health Physics Soc. (dir. 2001—); mem.: Nat. Coun. Radiation Protection and Measurements (v.p., dir.). Office: Idaho State U Dept Physics Campus Box 8106 Pocatello ID 83209 Office Fax: 208-282-4649. Business E-Mail: gesell@physics.isu.edu.

GESHELL, RICHARD STEVEN, lawyer; b. Colorado Springs, Colo., Aug. 6, 1943; s. Peter Steven and Ann Elizabeth (Irwin) G.; m. Carol Ann Reed, Sept. 6, 1965; 1 child, Carmen Marie. BA in Chemistry, Ariz. State U., 1965; JD, U. Nebr., 1968. Bar: Nebr. 1968, U.S. Dist. Ct. Nebr. 1968, Hawaii 1983, U.S. Dist. Ct. Hawaii 1983, U.S. Ct. Appeals (9th cir.) 1984, U.S. Supreme Ct. 1986. With Robak and Geshell, Columbus, Nebr., 1968-83; ptnr. R. Steven Geshell, Honolulu, 1983—. Lawyer; b. Colorado Springs, Colo., Aug. 6, 1943; s. Peter Steven and Ann Elizabeth (Irwin) G.; m. Carol Ann Reed, Sept. 6, 1965; 1 child, Carmen Marie. BA in Chemistry, Ariz. State U., 1965; JD, U. Nebr., 1968. Bar: Nebr. 1968, U.S. Dist. Ct. Nebr. 1968, Hawaii 1983, U.S. Dist. Ct. Hawaii 1983, U.S. Ct. Appeals (9th cir.) 1984, U.S. Supreme Ct. 1986. Mem. Robak and Geshell, Columbus, Nebr., 1968-83; ptnr. R. Steven Geshell, Honolulu, 1983—. Served to capt. USAR, 1974-83. Mem. Hawaii Bar Assn., Blue Key (pres. 1964-65), Elks (chief forum 1984, trustee), Phi Sigma Kappa. Republican. Capt. USAR, 1974-83. Mem. Hawaii Bar Assn., Blue Key (pres. 1964-65), Elks (chief forum 1984, trustee), Phi Sigma Kappa. Republican. Home: 1155 Kaluanui Rd Honolulu HI 96825-1357 Office: Ste #116 6600 Kalanianaole Hwy Honolulu HI 96825 E-mail: geshell@lava.net.

GESKE, ALVIN JAY, lawyer; b. Whitefish, Mont., Apr. 17, 1942; s. Alvin Emil and Ada Jay (Best) G.; m. Cheryl S. Glaze, Aug. 10, 1968; children: David, Daniel. BA in Econs. with high honors, So. Meth. U., 1964; JD with honors, U. Chgo., 1967; LLM in Taxation with high honors, George Washington U., 1974. Bar: Tex. 1967, D.C. 1972, U.S. Ct. Appeals (4th cir.) 1984, U.S. Tax Ct. 1982, U.S. Ct. Claims 1992. Atty. Jackson, Walker, Winstead, Cantwell & Miller, Dallas, 1967-68; from atty. to asst. br. chief legis. and regulation divsn. Office Chief Counsel IRS, Washington, 1970-74; atty. Childs, Fortenbach, Beck & Guyton, Houston, 1974-75; legis. atty. Joint Com. on Taxation U.S. Congress, Washington, 1975-78, asst. legis. counsel, 1978-81; atty. Davis & McLeod, Washington, 1981-83, Richard P. Sills PC, Washington, 1983-85, Stein, Sills & Brodsky PC, Washington, 1985-87, Wickham & Geske, Washington, 1987, Sills & Brodsky PC, Washington, 1988-93, Holland & Knight, Washington, 1993—. Contbr. articles to profl. jours. With U.S. Army, 1968-70. Mem. ABA (past chmn. com. on agr. sect. taxation), Order of Coif, Phi Beta Kappa, Phi Delta Phi. Office: Holland & Knight 2099 Pennsylvania Ave NW Washington DC 20006 E-mail: ageske@hklaw.com.

GESMER, ELLEN FRANCES, lawyer; b. Boston, Sept. 6, 1950; d. Henry and Bessie (Nathanson) Gesmer; m. Alan Stuart Hyde, May 23, 1976; children: Toby Matthew Hyde, Laura Zoe Hyde. BA summa cum laude, Radcliffe Coll., 1972; JD, Yale U., 1976. Bar: Mass. 1977, N.Y. 1979, Mich. 1983. Law clk. to Hon. Joseph L. Tauro, Boston, 1976—77; dir. litig. Bed-Stuy Cmty. Legal Svcs., Bklyn., 1977—83; clin. asst. prof. U. Mich. Law Sch., Ann Arbor, 1983—84; assoc. Teitelbaum & Hiller, P.C., N.Y.C., 1985—87; ptnr. Gulielmetti & Gesmer, P.C., N.Y.C., 1987—. Mem. legal adv. com. Sanctuary for Families, 2002—. Pub. mem. Rent Guidelines Bd., 1990—92; bd. dirs. Hispanic Housing Coalition, 1982—83, Legal Svcs. Alumni Assn., 1985—90, Keystone Dance Found., Inc., 1993—98. Mem.: Women's Bar Assn. (family law com. 1997—, com. jud. 1998—99), Crime Victims Bar Assn., Assn. City Bar NY (com. on rights of crime victims 1990—93, com. profl. responsibility 1998—2001, com. on profl. discipline 2001—), Am. Arbitration Assn. (comml. panel mem.), Women's Bar Assn. State NY (statewide com. domestic violence 2002—, rep. N.Y.C. chpt.). Office: Gulielmetti & Gesmer PC 401 Broadway Ste 1901 New York NY 10013-3005 E-mail: egesmer@gulges.com.

GESN, PAUL RANDALL, social psychologist, researcher; b. Shreveport, La., July 15, 1969; s. Paul Anthony and Karen Eileen Gesn; life ptnr. Joe Briseno, Apr. 25, 1967. PhD, U. Tex., Arlington, 1992—97. Postdoctoral fellow U. Toledo, 1997—99; rsch. scientist Tex. Health Quality Alliance, Austin, 1999—2001; testing and assessment analyst Tex. Edn. Agy., Austin, 1999—2001, rsch. specialist, 2002—. Contbr. articles to jour. Mem.: APA, Am. Psychol. Soc. Democrat-Npl. Roman Catholic. Avocations: piano, music theory. Office: Texas Edn Agency 1701 N Congress Ave Austin TX 78701 Personal E-mail: pgesn@netscape.net. E-mail: pgesn@tea.state.tx.us.

GESSAMAN, DONALD EUGENE, government executive, federal official, consultant; b. Dayton, Ohio, Nov. 11, 1939; s. Stanley Loran and Alma Elizabeth (Tevis) G.; m. Jane Alexander Giles, Oct. 16, 1965; 1 child, William Arthur. BS in Indsl. Mgmt., U. Cin., 1964; MS in Indsl. Engring., Stanford U., 1972. Exec. trainee Office of Sec. of Def., Washington, 1966; with nat security divsn., dep. divsn. chief Office Mgmt. and Budget, Exec. Office of Pres., Washington, 1967-90, dep. assoc. dir., 1990-95; cons. EOP Group, Inc., Washington, 1995—. Office: EOP Group Inc 819 7th St NW Washington DC 20001-3762

GESSEL, DAVID CLYDE, lawyer, consultant; b. Salt Lake City, June 9, 1959; s. Clyde David and Mary Louise (Gardner) G.; m. Diana Marie Allen, Nov. 10, 1987; children: Michael Allen, Megan Elizabeth, James David, Matthew Allen. BS in Polit. Sci. cum laude, U. Utah, 1983; MA in Polit. Sci. and Pub. Policy, Rutgers U., 1986; JD, U. Va., 1991. Bar: Utah 1991; cert. assn. exec. Legis. asst., legis. dir. Congressman Ron Packard, Washington, 1986-88; atty. Jones, Waldo, Holbrook and McDonough, Salt Lake City, 1991-94; v.p. govt. rels. and legal affairs Utah Hosps. and Health Sys. Assn., Salt Lake City, 1994—. Exec. editor Va. Environ. Law Jour., 1990-91. Rep. LDS Ch., Australia, 1978-80. Recipient Elbert D. Thomas award U. Utah, Salt Lake City, 1983; Eagleton fellow Eagleton Inst. Politics of Rutgers U., New Brunswick, N.J., 1985-86. Mem. Am. Soc. Assn. Execs., Am. Health Lawyers Assn., Utah Bar Assn., Phi Delta Phi. Avocations: travel, history, golf, politics. Office: Utah Hosps and Health Sys Assn 2180 S 1300 E Ste 440 Salt Lake City UT 84106-2856

GEST, HOWARD, microbiologist, educator; b. London, Oct. 15, 1921; m. Janet Olin, Sept. 8, 1941 (dec. 1994); children: Theodore Olin, Michael Henry, Donald Evan; m. Virginia Davies Ollis, Jan. 6, 1998. BA in Bacteriology, UCLA, 1942; postgrad. in biology (Univ. fellow), Vanderbilt U., 1942; PhD in Microbiology (Am. Cancer Soc. fellow), Washington U., St. Louis, 1949. Rsch. asst. Metall. Lab. (Manhattan Project) U. Chgo., 1943; from jr. to assoc. chemist Clinton Labs. (Manhattan Project), Oak Ridge, 1943-46; Instr. microbiology Western Res. U. Sch. Medicine, 1949-51, asst. prof. microbiology, 1951-53, asso. prof., 1953-59; USPHS spl. research fellow in biology Calif. Inst. Tech., 1956-57; prof. Henry Shaw Sch. Botany, Washington U., 1959-64, dept. zoology, 1964-66; prof. Ind. U., Bloomington, 1966-78, disting. prof. microbiology, 1978—, disting. prof. emeritus microbiology, 1987—, adj. prof. history and philosophy of sci., 1983—, chmn. dept. microbiology, 1966-70, disting. faculty rsch. lectr., 1987. NSF sr. postdoctoral fellow Nat. Inst. Med. Rsch., London, 1965—66, Guggenheim fellow Imperial Coll., London, U. Stockholm, U. Tokyo; vis. prof. dept. biophysics and biochemistry U. Tokyo and Japan Soc. Promotion Sci., 1970; mem. study sect. bacteriology and mycology NIH, 1966—68, chmn. study sect. microbial chemistry, 1968—69, mem. study sect. microbial physiology and genetics, 1988—90; mem. com. microbiol. problems of man in extended space flight Nat. Acad. Scis.-NRC, 1967—69; Guggenheim fellow Imperial Coll., London, UCLA, 1979—80; 1st H.D. Peck lectr. U. Ga., 1994; Cummings lectr. Bucknell U., 1997. Fellow: AAAS, Am. Acad. Microbiology; mem.: Am. Acad. Arts and Scis., Am. Soc. Microbiology (hon.). Office: Ind U Dept Biology Bloomington IN 47405

GEST, HOWARD DAVID, lawyer; b. Bergenfield, N.J., Jan. 24, 1952; m. Lucy Acevedo; 1 child, Aaron. AB in Econs., U. Calif., Berkeley, 1974; JD, Hastings Coll., 1977. Bar: Calif. 1977. Staff atty. U.S. Ct. Appeals (9th cir.), San Francisco, 1977-78; asst. U.S. atty. Cen. Dist. Calif., L.A., 1978-83; ptnr. Sidley & Austin, L.A., 1983-99, Burhenn & Gest, L.A., 2000—. Office: Burhenn & Gest LLP Ste 2200 624 S Grand Ave Los Angeles CA 90017 E-mail: hgest@burhenngest.com.

GEST, KATHRYN WATERS, public affairs professional; b. Boston, Mar. 20, 1947; d. Mendal and Anna Waters; m. Theodore O. Gest, May 28, 1972; 1 child, David Mendal. BS, Northwestern U., 1969; MS, Columbia U., 1970. Reporter The Patriot-Ledger, Quincy, Mass., 1968; writer Europe desk Voice of Am., Washington, 1969; reporter St. Louis Globe Democrat, 1970-77, Congl. Quar., Washington, 1977-78, news editor, 1978-80, asst. mng. editor, 1980-83, mng. editor, 1983-87; St. Louis corr. Time Mag., 1975-77, The Christian Sci. Monitor, 1976-77; press sec. to Sen. William S. Cohen, Washington, 1987-96; chmn., U.S. del. Internat. Labor Orgn. Tripartite Meeting on Conditions of Employment and Work of Journalists, Geneva, 1990; exec. v.p., dir. internat. issues Powell Tate, 1996—. Election observer Nat. Dem. Inst., Albania, 1996. Recipient award for investigative reporting Inland Daily Press Assn., 1975 Mem. bd., Nat. Press Found. Soc. Profl. Journalists, Women's Fgn. Policy Group, Internat. Women's Media Fund, Nat. Press Club. Office: Powell Tate 700 13th St NW Ste 1000 Washington DC 20005-6618 E-mail: kgest@webershandwrck.com.

GESTELAND, RAYMOND F. geneticist; b. Madison, Wis., Apr. 2, 1938; s. Elmer Raymond and Bernice Jeanette (Elver) G.; m. Harriett McDonough, April 18, 1960; children: Becky, Christopher, Katherine, Per. BS in Chemistry, U. Wis., 1960, MS in Biochemistry, 1961; PhD in Biochemistry, Harvard U., 1965. Asst. dir., sr. staff investigator Cold Spring Harbor (N.Y.) Lab, 1967-78; asst. prof., assoc. prof. SUNY, Stony Brook, 1967—78; investigator Howard Hughes Med. Inst., Bethesda, Md., 1978—98; prof. biology U. Utah, Salt Lake City, 1978—, disting. prof. human genetics, 1984—, chmn. human genetics, 1984-2000, v.p. for rsch., 2000—. Adj. prof. bioengring. U. Utah, Salt Lake City, 1989—; dir. Utah Ctr. Human Genome Rsch., Salt Lake City, 1989—2000. Office: U Utah Dept Human Genetics 15 N 2030 E Salt Lake City UT 84112-5330

GESTON, MARK SYMINGTON, lawyer; b. Atlantic City, N.J., June 20, 1946; s. John Charles and Mary Tobiatha (Simmington) G.; m. Gayle Francis Howard, June 12, 1971 (div. Aug. 1972); m. Marijke Havinga, Aug. 14, 1976; children: Camille LaCroix, Robert L. LaCroix, Emily S. Geston. AB in History (with honors), Kenyon Coll., 1968; JD, NYU, 1971. Bar: Idaho, U.S. Ct. Appeals (9th cir.). With Eberle & Berlin, Boise, Idaho, 1971—. Author: Lords of the Starship, 1967, Out of the Mouth of the Dragon, 1969, The Day Star, 1972, The Seige of Wonder, 1975, Mirror to the Sky, 1992, The Stronghold If, 1973; contbr. stories to Amazing Stories, Fantasy and Sci. Fiction. Recipient prize for achievement in lit., Kenyon Coll., 1968; named Root-Tilden fellow NYU, 1968-71. Mem. Idaho State Bar Assn., Phi Beta Kappa. Avocation: writing. Office: Stoel Rives LLP 101 S Capitol Blvd Boise ID 83702

GESUALDI, LOUIS J. social sciences educator; b. Stamford, Conn., May 22, 1955; s. John and Catherine Pelli Gesualdi. BS in biology, BA in anthropology, U. Conn., 1978; MA in Sociology, St. John's U., 1980; PhD in Sociology, Fordham U., 1988. Tchr. Immaculata HS, N.Y.C., 1980—82; adj. instr. Cathedral Coll., Queens, NY, 1983—86; instr. St. John's U., Sociology Dept., Jamaica, NY, 1986—90, asst. prof., 1990—92, assoc. prof., 1992—2003. Author: The Italian Immigrants of Connecticut, 1997, (articles) various publications, 1997—2000. Mem. Human Rights Coun. of Queens, 1988—90. Recipient Assoc. Calandra scholar, Calandra Italian Am. Inst., 1998—2003, Hibernian Rsch. award, Cushwa Ctr. Notre Dame U., 1994. Mem.: Acad. of Criminal Justice, Am. Sociological Assn., Am. Italian Hist. Assoc. Office: St John's U 8000 Utopia Pkwy Jamaica NY 11439 E-mail: gesualdl@stjohns.edu.

GETANEH, MISGANAW, physicist, educator; b. Wogeda, Gonder, Ethiopia, Sept. 22, 1953; s. Getaneh Nigatu and Tiringo Tigabu; m. Eleni Kassa Bitewilgn, June 24, 1994; children: Saba, Selam. BS in Physics, Addis Ababa U., 1982; MS in Physics, Temple U., 1992, PhD in Physics, 1996. Registered profl. engr., Ethiopian Airlines, Ethiopia, 1979. Aviation mechanic Ethiopian Airlines, Addis Ababa, Ethiopia, 1979—82; grad. asst. Bahir Dar (Ethiopia) Teachers Coll., 1982—84; lectr. Addis Ababa (Ethiopia) U., 1984—88; tchg./rsch. asst. Temple U., Phila., 1988—96; asst. prof. of physics Physics Dept. Lincoln (Pa.) U., 1996—. Contbr. articles to profl. jours. Named Individual Chess Champion Of Addis Ababa Ethiopia, Provisional Ethiopian Chess Fedn., 1980; fellow, USN, 2000—02. Mem.: Nat. Soc. Of Black Physicists, America Phys. Soc. Ethiopian Orthodox Church. Avocations: chess, reading. Home: 521 B Oakdale Road Newark DE 19713 Office: Physics Department Lincoln University 1570 Old Baltimore Pike Lincoln University PA Office Fax: 610-932-1054. Personal E-mail: mgetaneh@aol.com. E-mail: mgetaneh@lu.lincoln.edu.

GETCHELL, CHARLES WILLARD, JR., lawyer, publisher; b. L.A., May 29, 1929; s. Charles Willard and Katharine (Fitch) G.; m. Angela Winthrop, Sept. 16, 1961; children: Katharine Chisholm, Emily Erskine, Sarah Fields. AB, Stanford U., 1951, JD, 1954. Bar: Calif. 1955, Mass. 1979, U.S. Dist. Ct. (no. dist.) Calif. 1960, Mass. 1983, U.S. Ct. Appeals, 9th cir. 1960, U.S. Supreme Ct. 1985. Atty. Air Materiel Force, Chateauroux, France, 1958-59; asst. U.S. atty. No. Dist. Calif., San Francisco, 1960-61; asst. mgr. Citibank, N.Y.C., Brussels, 1961-68; v.p. Wood Struthers & Winthrop, N.Y.C., Brussels, 1969-77; ptnr. Gray, Wendell, Chalmers & Dahlen, Boston, 1981-87; pub. The Ipswich (Mass.) Press, 1980—. Pres. Yorkham Timber Co., Inc., 1986-2000; bd. dirs. Sabre Trust (UK); chmn. Sabre Europe (Belgium); sec. Sabre Found., 1995—; sr. fellow Salzburg Seminar, 1997—. Translator: European Monetary Unity: For Whose Benefit? (Pascal Salin), 1980; contbr. occasional essays, verse. Mem. steering com. Bilderberg Meetings, The Hague, 1980—85; trustee Shore Country Day Sch., 1978—84; bd. dirs. Salzburg Seminar, 1985—89. Lt. j.g. USNR, 1955—58. Mem. Belgian Am. Ednl. Found.; fellow Mass. Hist. Soc., Tavern Club. Republican. Office: Ipswich Press PO Box 291 Ipswich MA 01938-0291

GETCHELL, SYLVIA FITTS, librarian; b. Dover, N.H., July 3, 1925; d. Perley Irving and Marguerite Elizabeth (Marden) F.; m. L. Forbes Getchell, July 17, 1948; children: Ann Marden, Faith Perley, Edward Fitts, William Forbes. BA in History magna cum laude, U. N.H., 1947; BS in Libr. Sci., Simmons Coll., 1948. Profl. cataloger Libr. Columbia U., N.Y.C., 1948-51, U. N.H., Durham, 1951-52; sch. libr. Newmarket (N.H.) Pub. Schs., 1970-85; curator Stone Sch. Mus., Newmarket, 1966—. Author: Marden Family Genealogy, 1974, Tide Turns on the Lamprey: History of Newmarket, N.H., 1984, Fitts

Families: A Genealogy, 1989; co-editor: Piscataqua Pioneers, Selected Biographies of Early Settlers in Northern New England, 2000. Libr. Am. Independence Mus., Exeter, N.H., 1990—, bd. govs., 1992-99; bd. dirs. Newmarket Hist. Soc., 1966—, past pres.; curator Stone Sch. Mus., 1966—; bd.dirs. Piscataqua Pioneers, Portsmouth, N.H., 1969—, past pres.; 18th century re-enactor 1st Newmarket Colonial Militia, 1973—; former chair ann. fund drive local chpt. ARC; past collector, Sun. sch. tchr. Newmarket Cmty. Ch.; former treas. Aux. of N.H. Dental Soc.; mem. N.H. Hist. Soc. Mem. DAR (mem. and past sec. N.H. attic commn. 1994-2000, N.H. state historian 2000—), New Eng. Hist. Geneal. Soc., Newmarket Women's Club (past treas.), Huguenot Soc. N.H., Soc. Daus. Colonial Wars. Republican. Avocations: genealogy, oil painting, needlework, travel. Home: 51 N Main St Newmarket NH 03857-1216

GETCHES, DAVID HARDING, law educator, state environmental executive, lawyer; b. Abington, Pa., Aug. 17, 1942; s. George Winslow Getches and Ruth Erskine (Harding) Fossette; m. Ann Marks, June 26, 1964; children: Matthew, Catherine, Elizabeth. AB, Occidental Coll., 1964; JD, U. So. Calif., 1967. Bar: Calif. 1968, U.S. Supreme Ct. 1971, D.C. 1972, Colo. 1973. Assoc. Luce, Forward, Hamilton & Scripps, San Diego, 1967-69; directing atty. Calif. Indian Legal Services, Escondido, 1969-70; founding dir. Native Am. Rights Fund, Boulder, Colo., 1970-76; ptnr. Getches & Greene, Boulder, 1976-78; prof. U. Colo. Sch. Law, Boulder, 1978—, dean, 2003—; exec. dir. Colo. Dept. Natural Resources, Denver, 1983-87. Ptnr. MB Land Co., Centro Bldg. Devel. Co. Author: Water Law in a Nutshell, 1997; co-author: Cases and Materials on Federal Indian Law, 1998, Water Resources Management, 1993, 5th edit., 2002; contbr. articles to profl. jours. Bd. trustees Grand Canyon Trust. Mem. Colo. Bar Assn., D.C. Bar, Calif. Bar, Wilderness Soc. (governing coun.), Defenders of Wildlife (bd. dirs.). Democrat. Home: 627 Pine St Boulder CO 80302-4739 Office: U Colo Sch Law Boulder CO 80309-0401 E-mail: getches@colorado.edu.

GETER, RODNEY KEITH, plastic surgeon; b. Baton Rouge, La., Nov. 13, 1946; s. Arglous William and Jewel Alma (Rudolph) G. BA in Chemistry with honors, U. Mo., 1975, MD, 1979. Resident in gen. surgery U. Mo., Columbia, 1979-83, fellow in microvascular surgery, 1983-84, resident in plastic surgery, 1984-86; pvt. practice Springfield (Mo.) Clinic, 1986—. Chmn. dept. surgery St. John's Regional Health Ctr., Springfield, 1992-94, chmn. two hosp. coms., 1994-97; v.p. med. staff St. John's Hosp., 1996-97, chmn. plastic surgery dept., 2000-02. Contbr. articles to profl. jours. Pres. Springfield Music Found., 1989—; leader troop 210 Boy Scouts Am., Springfield, 1995-98. Sgt. Spl. Forces, U.S. Army, 1968-71, Vietnam. Mem. Am. Soc. Plastic and Reconstructive Surgeons, Greene County Med. Soc., Mo. State Med. Assn., Phi Beta Kappa, Phi Lambda Upsilon. Avocations: playing keyboard in band, fishing, backpacking. Office: Springfield Clinic 3231 S National Ave Springfield MO 65807-7396

GETIS, ARTHUR, geography educator; b. Phila., July 6, 1934; s. Samuel J. and Sophie Getis; m. Judith M. Marckwardt, July 23, 1961; children: Hilary Hope Tarazi, Victoria Lynn, Anne Patterson Tibbetts. BS, Pa. State U., 1956, MS, 1958; PhD, U. Wash., 1961. Asst. instr. geography U. Wash., 1960-61; asst. prof. Mich. State U., 1961-63; faculty Rutgers U., New Brunswick, N.J., 1963-77, prof. geography, 1969-77, dir. grad. programs in geography, 1970-73, chmn. New Brunswick geography dept., 1971-73; prof. geography U. Ill., Urbana-Champaign, 1977-90, San Diego State U., 1990—, doctoral program coord., 1990-92, Stephen/Mary Birch Found. Endowed Chair of Geog. Studies, 1992—, Albert W. Johnson Univ. Rsch. Lectureship, 1995; head dept. U. Ill., 1977-83, dir. Sch. Social Scis., 1983-84; centennial fellow Pa. State U., 1996; A. Robinson lectr. Ohio State U., 1999. Vis. lectr. Bristol U., Eng., 1966-67, UCLA, summers 1968, 74, U. B.C., 1969; vis. prof. Princeton U., 1971-74; vis. disting. prof. San Diego State U., 1989; mem. Regional Sci. Research Group, Harvard U., 1970; panelist NSF, 1981-83 Author: (with B. Boots) Models of Spatial Processes, 1978, Point Pattern Analysis, 1988, (with J. Getis and J.D. Fellmann) Geography, 1981, Human Geography, 7th edit., 2001, Introduction to Geography, 8th edit., 2002, (edited with J. Getis) The United States and Canada, 1995, 2d edit., 2001, The Tyranny of Data, 1996, (edited with M.M. Fischer) Recent Developments in Spatial Analysis, 1997; co-editor Jour. Geographical Systems, 1992—; contbg. editor, assoc. editor: Jour. Geography, 1972-74; mem. editl. bd. Nat. Geog. Rsch., 1984-90, Rsch. and Exploration, 1991-95, Geog. Analysis, 1991—. Papers in Regional Sci., 1999-02, Annals of Regional Sci., 1999—; contbr. articles to profl. jours. Mem. Urbana Zoning Bd. Appeals, 1980-84; co-pres. Univ. High Sch. Parent-Faculty Orgn., 1982-83; bd. dirs. Univ. Consortium for Geog. Info. Scis., 1997—, pres.-elect, 2000-02, pres., 2002-03. Rutgers U. faculty fellow, 1970; East-West Center sr. fellow, 1974; NSF grantee, 1983-85, 1992-94, 99—, NIH grantee, 1999—; recipient Walter Isard award N.Am. Regional Sci. Coun., 1997. Mem. Assn. Am. Geographers (grantee 1964-65, vis. scientist 1970-72, chair math. models and quantitative methods splty. group 1991-92, recipient award for disting. scholarship, 2002), Western Regional Sci. Assn. (bd. dirs. 1992-97, pres. 1998-99), Regional Sci. Assn. (pres. N.E. sect. 1973-74, bd. dirs. 1998—), Internat. Inst. Brit. Geographers, Internat. Geog. Union (sec. commn. math. models 1988-96), Sigma Xi. Home: 5135 Jumilla St San Diego CA 92124-1503 Office: San Diego State U Dept Geography San Diego CA 92182

GETMANENKO, NATALIYA I. Russian educator, researcher; d. Ivan T. Mikhailenko and Klavdia I. Morozova; m. Val P. Getmanenko, Aug. 18, 1982; 1 child, Stanislav. EdM, State Pedagogical Sch., Kherson, Ukraine, 1980; EdD, State Pedagogical U, Moskow, Russia, 1992; PhD in Russian Lang. Edn., Fed. Ministry of Profl. Edn., Moskow, Russia, 1998. H.s. tchr. Russian lang. and lit., Kherson, Ukraine, 1980—88; tutor Russian lang. and culture Kyiv, Ukraine, 1992—93; prof. Russian lang. State Pedagogical U., Moscow, 1994—2001; prof. Russian lang. and culture Brigham Young U., Provo, Utah, 2001—. Author: Teaching Students The Norms of Russian, 1997; contbr. articles to profl. jours. Mem.: Russian Univ. Faculty Assn. (assoc.), Assn. Tchrs. of Slavic and East European Langs. (assoc.). Avocations: classic art, classic ballet, history of architecture, history of arts, movies. Office: Brigham Young Univ 4094 Jesse Knight Humanities Provo UT 84602

GETNICK, NEIL VICTOR, lawyer; b. Bklyn., Oct. 28, 1953; s. Irving Murray and Zita (Ellman) G.; m. Margaret Joan Finerty, May 21, 1978. BA in Govt. magna cum laude, Cornell U., 1975, JD, 1978. Bar: N.Y. 1979, U.S. Dist. Ct. (so. and ea. dists.) N.Y. 1983. Asst. dist. atty. trial divsn. N.Y. County, N.Y.C., 1978-81, asst. dist. atty. frauds bur., 1981-82; ptnr. Getnick & Getnick, N.Y., 1983—. Mem. Criminal Justice Act panel U.S. Dist. Ct. for So. Dist. N.Y., N.Y.C., 1984-89. Editor-in-chief: Civil Prosecution News, 1994-96. Recipient Pub. Citizenship award N.Y. Pub. Interest Rsch. Group, 1977. Mem. ABA (litigation and criminal law sects.), N.Y. State Bar Assn. (exec. com. comml. and fed. litigation sect., chair com. on civil prosecution), Assn. of Bar of City of N.Y., N.Y. County Lawyers Assn., Internat. Assn. Ind. Pvt. Sector Inspectors Gen. (pres. 1994—), Internat. Assn. of Ind. Pvt. Sector Inspectors Gen. (pres. 1994—). Office: Getnick & Getnick Rockefeller Ctr 620 5th Ave 4th Flr New York NY 10020-2457

GETNICK, RICHARD ALAN, ophthalmologist; b. Bklyn., Jan. 31, 1943; s. George Sherry and Helen Schrier Getnick; m. Paula Beth Hamar, Aug. 19, 1967; children: Pamela Ellen, Geoffrey Scott, Emily Lynn. AB magna cum laude, Princeton U., 1964; MD, Yale U., 1968. Diplomate Nat. Bd. Medical Examiners, Am. Bd. Ophthalmology. Intern Case Western Res. U., 1968-69; staff assoc. NIH, Inst. Allergy & Infectious Disease, 1969-71; resident in ophthalmology Wills Eye Hosp., Phila., 1971-74; pvt. practice Waterbury, Conn., 1974-80; ophthalmologist Eye Assocs. Waterbury, 1980-87, OptiCare, Waterbury, 1988—. Asst. clin. prof. surgery U. Conn. Med. Ctr., John Dempsey Hosp., Farmington, 1978—; attending surgeon St. Mary's Hosp., Waterbury, 1977—, Waterbury Hosp., 1977—. Contbr. articles to profl. jours. Fellow ACS, Am. Acad. Ophthalmology; mem. New Eng. Opthalmol. Soc., Conn. Soc. Eye Physicians, New Haven County Med. Assn., Waterbury Med. Assn., Wills Eye Hosp. Soc., Princeton Club Cen. Conn., Phi Beta Kappa. Avocations: downhill skiing, water skiing, travel. Office: OptiCare 87 Grandview Ave Ste 1 Waterbury CT 06708-2563 E-mail: rgetnick@opticare.net.

GETS, LISPBETH ELLA, ret. educational administrator; b. Jhelum, Pakistan, Mar. 18, 1931; came to U.S., 1952, naturalized, 1955; d. Henry Ellis and Constance Selina (Bodell) Glenn; m. Terence Mathew Gets, Jan. 19, 1952; children: Erik Charles, Alison Beth, Hugh Malcolm, Adrienne Lea. AA, Santa Fe Community Coll., 1973-74; BA with high honors U. Fla., 1976, postgrad., 1977-89, MS, edml. specialist cert., 1989. Cert. adminstr., supr., Fla. Editorial asst. John Trundell Pub., London, 1950-52; exec. secretarial positions, various cos., Chgo., Ft. Smith, Ark. and Jamestown, N.Y., 1952-58; tchr. spl. edn. Buchholz High Sch., Gainesville, Fla., 1976-81; asst. prin. Sidney Lanier Sch., Gainesville, 1981-83, 1987-2003, ret. 2003; prin. Monarch Ctr. for Exceptional Students, Gainesville, 1983-87 . Named Tchr. of Yr. Gatorland chpt. Coun. for Exceptional Children, 1981. Mem. Council Exceptional Children (chpt. pres. 1983—), Fla. Assn. Exceptional Sch. Adminstrs. (state chmn. 1988-90), Phi Delta Kappa. Democrat. Episcopalian. Home: 4601 NW 13th Ave Gainesville FL 32605-4534

GETSKE, KATHRINE, psychiatric social worker; b. Memphis, Jan. 19, 1937; d. Noble Owen and Annie Lou (Robertson) Fowler; m. Raymond Nicholas Getske, Nov. 27, 1965; children: Philip David, Raymond Nicholas Jr., Barbara Lynn, Virginia Kathrine. BS cum laude, Memphis State U., 1960; MA, Presbyn. Sch. Christian Edn., Richmond, Va., 1962; MSW, U. Tenn., 1989. Lic. cert. social worker, Tenn.; cert. dir. Christian edn. Dir. Christian edn. 1st Presbyn. Ch., Auburn, Ala., 1962-64; social worker ARC, Memphis, 1964-65, Dept. Human Svcs., Memphis, 1985-86; vol. coord. Johnson Aux. to the Regional Med. Ctr., Memphis, 1986-87; psychiat. social worker Memphis Mental Health Inst., 1990-91; med. and psychiat. social worker St. Joseph Hosp., Memphis, 1991-94; therapist Delta Med. Ctr., Memphis, 1999—, Magnolia Counseling Assocs., Batesville, Miss., 2000—. Pres. Johnson Aux. to Regional Med. Ctr., Memphis, 1985-86; mem. Dixon Gallery, Brooks Mus. League; elder Balmoral Presbyn. Ch.; del. to Cuba, People to People Amb. Program, 2001. Mem. AAUW (pres. Memphis chpt. 1976-78, legis. chair 1990-91, named grant honoree 1985), Acad. Cert. Social Workers, Whitehaven Garden Club (sec., treas.), Kennedy Book Club, Beethoven Club (bd. dirs.), Roseleigh Garden Club. Republican. Avocations: travel, bridge, reading. Home: 7607 Shady Rose Cv Memphis TN 38119-9109

GETTEN, THOMAS FRANK, lawyer; b. Akron, Ohio, Oct. 11, 1947; s. Frederick Bush and Edna (Vandever) Getten; m. Nancy Hobson, Aug. 16, 1972; children: Elisabeth, Douglas, Tad. BS in Petroleum Enging., La. State U., 1970, JD, 1974. Bar: La. 1974. Petroleum engr. Standard Oil Calif., L.A. and New Orleans, 1970—71; shareholder Liskow & Lewis, New Orleans, 1974—95; ptnr. Nesser, King & LeBlanc, New Orleans, 1996; gen. counsel Forcenergy, Inc., Miami, 1997—2001; ptnr. King, LeBlanc & Bland, New Orleans, 2001—. Mem.: ABA, La. Bankers Assn. (coun. com.), New Orleans Bar Assn., La. Bar Assn., Order of the Coif, Tau Beta Pi. Republican. Episcopalian. Office: King LeBlanc & Bland LLP 201 St Charles Ave Ste 3800 New Orleans LA 70170 Business E-Mail: tgetten@klb-law.com.

GETTIER, EDMUND LEE, III, philosophy educator; b. Balt., Oct. 31, 1927; s. Edmund Lee Jr. and Clara Frances (Schuele) G.; m. Astrid Elizabeth Pfeiffer, Mar. 1957 (div. 1965); children: Evan E. (dec.), Elizabeth L., Edmund L. IV, Sheila A., David B.; m. Lucia Milda Mingela, July 8, 1966; children: Daina N., Jonathan M. BA, Johns Hopkins U., 1949; PhD, Cornell U., 1961. Instr. to asst. prof. Wayne State U., Detroit, 1957-67; assoc. prof. to full prof. U. Mass., Amherst, 1967—2001, prof. emeritus, 2001—. With U.S. Army, 1953-55. Mellon Post Doctoral Fellow, U. Pitts., 1964-65. Home: 77 Weatherwood Rd Amherst MA 01002-9802 Office: U Mass Dept Philosophy Amherst MA 01003 E-mail: gettier@philos.umass.edu.

GETTIG, MARTIN WINTHROP, retired mechanical engineer; b. South Bend, Ind., Nov. 8, 1939; s. Joseph H. and Esther (Scheppele) G.; m. Nancy Caroline Buchannan, June 25, 1960 (dec. 1965). Student, Pa. State U., 1957-60, 89—. Process engr. Gettig Tech. Inc., Spring Mills, Pa., 1960-88. Inventor ultralight non-solid state miniature ignition systems for model aircraft employing small two cycle spark ignition engines. Staff sgt. Pa. N.G., 1961-67. Mem. NRA, Model Engine Collectors Assn., Soc. Antique Modelers and Model Airplanes, Acad. Model Awronautics, Univ. Club Pa. State U., Delta Phi. Republican. Lutheran. Home: PO Box 85 Boalsburg PA 16827-0085

GETTING, IVAN ALEXANDER, physicist, former aerospace company executive; b. N.Y.C., Jan. 18, 1912; s. Milan and Harriet (Almasy) G.; m. Dorothea Louise Gracy, Oct. 2, 1937 (dec. Sept. 1976); children: Nancy Louise Secker, Ivan Craig, Peter Alexander; m. Helen Avery, Jan. 9, 1977. SB, MIT, 1933; DPhil, Oxford U., 1935; DSc (hon.), Northeastern U., 1954, U. So. Calif., 1986. Jr. fellow Harvard U., Cambridge, Mass., 1935-40; mem. staff, head divsn. 8 radiation lab. MIT, Cambridge, 1940-45, assoc. prof. elec. engring., 1945-46, prof., 1946-50; asst. for devel. planning, dep. chief of staff USAF, Washington, 1950-51; v.p. engring and research Raytheon Corp., Waltham, Mass., 1951-60; pres., chief exec. officer The Aerospace Corp., El Segundo, Calif., 1960-77. Cons. USAF, USN, U.S. Army, NRC, Dept. Def., others, 1945—. Contbr. articles to profl. jours.; patentee in field. Dir. Los Angeles World Affairs Council, 1961—. Fellow: IEEE, IEEE (hon.; pres. 1978), Am. Inst. Physics; mem.: Nat. Acad. Engring. (Draper award 2003), Am. Acad. Arts and Scis., Cosmos Club, L.A. Yacht Club.

GETTLER, BENJAMIN, lawyer, manufacturing company executive; b. Louisville, Ky., Sept. 16, 1925; s. Herbert and Gertrude (Cohen) G.; m. Deliaan Angel, Mar. 1972; children: Jorian, Thomas, Gail, John, Benjamin. BA in Econs. with high honors U. Cin., 1945; JD (Frankfurter scholar), Harvard U., 1948. Bar: Ohio 1949, U.S. Supreme Ct. 1955. Ptnr. Brown & Gettler, Cin., 1951—73, Gettler, Katz & Buckley, Cin., 1973—87; chmn. bd. Am. Controlled Industries Inc., Cin., 1973—86; chmn. bd. dirs., pres. Colorpac Inc., Franklin, Ohio, 1973—86; chmn. bd., pres. Vulcan Internat. Corp., Wilmington, Del., 1988—, Vulcan Corp., Clarksville, Tenn., 1988—; chmn. exec. com. Valley Industries, Inc., Cin., 1973—86; vice chmn. bd. Cin. Southern R.R., 1987—91; chmn. bd. Trusthouse, Inc., Cin., 1987—. Chmn. bd. dirs. ACI Internat., Inc., Cin., 1990—; spl. counsel U. Cin., 1975-77, trustee, 1994-2003, vice chmn. bd., 1999-2000, chmn., 2000-2002; bd. dirs. PNC Bank, Ohio, 1988-96. Chmn. bd. Jewish Inst. Nat. Security Affairs, 1994-98, chmn. policy com., 1998—; chmn. Cin. Bonds for Israel, 1969; chmn. Nat. Israel Commn., Nat. Jewish Cmty. Rels. Adv. Coun., 1981-82; mem. Ohio, Ky. and Ind. Mass Transit Policy Com., 1970-75; pres. Cin. Jewish Cmty. Rels. Coun., 1978-80; trustee Jewish Hosp. Cin., 1978-92, chmn., 1991-92; chmn. Midwest Hosp. Sys., Inc., 1987-90, 92-93; pres. Jewish Found. Cin., 1995-99, chmn., 1999-2002; trustee Health Alliance Greater Cin., 1995-96, 2000-2001; chmn. Cin. Coalition for Reagan, 1980; co-chmn. Hamilton County Reagan Bush Campaign Ohio, 1984; chmn. Rep. Fin. Com., Hamilton County, 1991-92; mem. Hamilton County Rep. Policy Com., 1990—; trustee Rockwern Found., 1998—, Southwest Ohio Regional Transit Authority, 2003—. Capt. U.S. Army, 1955-56. Mem. ABA, Cin. Bar Assn., Shoe Last Mfrs. Assn. (pres. 1984-85), Footwear Industries Am. (bd. dirs. 1989-2000), Phi Beta Kappa, Omicron Delta Kappa. Clubs: Coldstream Country, Harvard. Office: Vulcan Corp 30 Garfield Pl Ste 1040 Cincinnati OH 45202-4322

GETTNER, ALAN FREDERICK, lawyer; b. N.Y.C., Dec. 25, 1941; s. Victor Salomon and Henriette Seldner (Herrmann) G.; m. Monah Lawrence, Jan. 19, 1969. BA, Yale U., 1963; MA, U. Chgo., 1964; PhD, Columbia U., 1971, JD, 1979. Bar: N.Y. 1980. Assoc. Debevoise & Plimpton, N.Y.C. and Paris, 1979-84, Holtzmann, Wise & Shepard, N.Y.C., 1984-85, ptnr., 1986-95, mem. exec. com., 1992-94; ptnr. Patterson, Belknap, Webb & Tyler, LLP, N.Y.C., 1995—, chmn. bus. devel. com., 2000—03. Mem. ABA (sect. on bus. law, com. on opinions), Assn. Bar City N.Y., Internat. Bar Assn., Internat. Law Assn., The Lotos Club. Office: Patterson Belknap Webb & Tyler LLP 1133 Ave Americas New York NY 10036-6710 E-mail: agettner@pbwt.com.

GETTO, ERNEST JOHN, lawyer; b. Dubois, Pa., May 24, 1944; s. Ernest F. and Olga (Gagliardi) G.; m. Judith Payne, Aug. 19, 1967; children: Matthew Payne, Christopher Ernest, Sarah Elizabeth. BA, Cornell U., 1966; JD, Vanderbilt U., 1969. Bar: N.Y. 1970, Calif. 1973. Assoc. Simpson Thacher & Bartlett, N.Y.C., 1969-73; from assoc. to ptnr. Kadison, Pfaelzer, Woodard, Quinn & Rossi, Los Angeles, 1973-80; ptnr. Latham & Watkins, L.A., 1980—. Lectr. in field. Contbr. articles to profl. jours. Bd. dirs. Calif. Pediatric Ctr., Los Angeles, 1977—. Mem. ABA, Calif. Bar Assn., L.A. Bar Assn., N.Y. State Bar Assn., Jonathan Club, Wilshire Country Club. Republican. Roman Catholic. Office: Latham & Watkins 505 Montgomery St San Francisco CA 94111 Home: 1904 Broadway St San Francisco CA 94109

GETTS, NINO, studio owner; b. White Plains, N.Y., Nov. 12, 1944; s. William and Mary L. (Riccardi) G.; m. Karen Larish, Feb. 6, 1976 (div. June 1984). Student, SUNY Purchase, 1992-95. V.p. Chess Media Unlimited, Inc., Mamaroneck, N.Y., 1995—. Composer numerous musical compositions. Avocations: winemaking, stamp collecting, coin collecting. Home: 7 Lincoln Pl Ossining NY 10562-5212

GETTY, GERALD WINKLER, lawyer; b. Chgo., June 17, 1911; s. Oliver and Pearl (Winkler) G.; m. Helen Brennan, Oct. 2, 1938 (dec. 1966); children: Michael, Muriel, Marie; m. Gracia Gibbs, June 3, 1967. JD, DePaul U., 1938, JD (hon.), 1972. Bar: Ill. 1938, Ind. 1938, U.S. Supreme Ct. 1960. Lawyer U.S. Govt., Chgo., 1938-42; pub. defender Cook County, Chgo., 1942-72; ptnr. Getty and Getty, Dolton, Ill., 1972-83; prin. Gerald W. Getty and Assocs., Dolton, 1983—. Author: Public Defender, 1972, Theory of Condominium and Cooperative Apartment Law, 1993. Mem. Elks. Home and Office: 4033 Lake Getty Ln Irons MI 49644

GETTYS, THOMAS WIGINGTON, medical researcher; BS in Biology, Lander Coll., 1978; PhD in Nutrition, Clemson U., 1984. Grad. rsch. asst. animal sci. dept. Coll. Agr. Clemson (S.C.) U., 1979—84; rsch. assoc. Howard Hughes Med. Inst., Dept. Molecular Physiology and Biophysics Vanderbilt U. Sch. of Medicine, Nashville, 1985—87; rsch. assoc. divsn. gastroenterology, dept. medicine Duke U. Med. Ctr., Durham, NC, 1987—90, rsch. asst. prof. divsn. gastroenterology, dept. medicine, 1990—, rsch. asst. prof. dept. cell biology, 1992—93; assoc. prof. medicine Med. U. S.C., Charleston, 1993—, assoc. prof. biochemistry and molecular biology, 1995—, prof. medicine, 2000—. Contbr. articles to profl. jours., chapters to books. Recipient Rsch. award, Am. Diabetes Assn., 1996; fellow predoctoral rsch., Clemson U., 1981—82; grantee, NIH, 1990, 1994, 1996, 1998, USDA, 1997, 2000. Mem.: Am. Soc. Biochemistry and Molecular Biology, Sigma Xi. Office: Pennington Biomed Rsch Ctr 6400 Perkins Rd Baton Rouge LA 70808

GETZ, BERT ATWATER, investment company executive; b. Chgo., May 7, 1937; s. George Fulmer Jr. and Olive Cox (Atwater) G.; m. Sandra Maclean, July 17, 1958; children: Lynn Getz, George F., Bert A. Jr. BSBA, U. Mich., 1959. V.p. Globe Corp., Scottsdale, Ariz., 1960-74, pres., bd. dirs., 1974—, CEO, 1992—. Bd. dirs. Bank of Am., Ill., Dean Foods Co., Franklin Park, Ill., Mayo Found., Rochester, Ameritas Life Ins. Corp., Lincoln. Bd. dirs. Western Golf Assn., Golf, Ill., Ind. U. Found., Bloomington; chmn. bd. govs. Merit Club, Libertyville, Ill.; trustee Lawrenceville (N.J.) Sch., 1972—, pres. bd. dirs. 1984-90, trustee emeritus, 1990; trustee Ariz. Cmty. Found., Phoenix, 1978—, chmn. bd. dirs., 1981-89, chmn. emeritus, 1989. Mem. Phoenix Thunderbirds, Paradise Valley Country Club, John Gardiners Tennis Ranch, Merit Club, Sigma Chi, Theta Theta. Republican. Episcopalian. Avocations: tennis, golf. Home: 6335 W Highway 120 Libertyville IL 60048-9788 Office: Globe Corp 6730 N Scottsdale Rd Ste 250 Scottsdale AZ 85253-4416

GETZ, JAMES EDWARD, legal association administrator; b. Shelbyville, Ill., June 8, 1950; s. William Forrest and Betty Jean (Mitchell) G.; m. Rita Genevieve Boyd, June 16, 1973; children: Christopher Brandon, Sarah Lynne. BS in Edn., Eastern Ill. U., 1972, MA, 1974. Grad. asst. Political Sci. Dept. Eastern Ill. U., Charleston, 1972-73; tchr. Plano (Ill.) Community Schs., 1973-74; conservation police officer Ill. Dept. Natural Resources, Office Law Enforcement, Springfield, Ill., 1974-77, region IV Ops. supr.; region IV comdr. Ill. Dept. Conservation Div. Law Enforcement, Springfield, 1980-82; deputy chief Ill. Dept. Natural Resource, Office Law Enforcement, 1982-86, region II comdr., 1986-90; Lake Mich. enforcement ops. comdr. Ill. Dept. Natural Resources divsn. Law Enforcement, Springfield, 1990—. Boating law adminstr. State Ill., 1984-86; chmn. several coms. Nat. Assn. State Boating Law Adminstrs.; mem Nat. Boating Safety Adv. Coun. U.S. Coast Guard; pres. Conservation Police Lodge #146, Fraternal Order Police, 1993-96. Author: Illinois Public Act 84-515, 1985; Illinois Public Act 85-147, 1987. Mem. Nat. Marine Mfr. Assn. Boat Cert. Com., Gt. Lakes Fisheries Commn. Law Enforcement Com. (vice chmn. 1986-90, chmn. 1990-92), Am. Boat & Yacht Coun. (bd. dirs. 1992-99). Avocations: boating, history, genealogy, civil war reenacting. Home: 1709 N Orleans St Mchenry IL 60050-3885 Office: Ill Dept Natural Resources 701 N Point Dr Winthrop Harbor IL 60096-1371 E-mail: jgetz@dnrmail.state.il.us.

GETZ, LOWELL VERNON, financial advisor; b. Schenectady, NY, Feb. 28, 1932; s. Leon and Harriet Esther (Friedman) G.; m. Judith Ruth Schwartz, Oct. 14, 1956; children: Marshall, Andrew. BS in Econs., U. Pa., 1953; MBA, Harvard Univ., 1955. Treas. R. Dixon Speas Assocs., Inc., Manhasset, NY, 1969-72, Coverdale & Colpitts, Inc., N.Y.C., 1972-74; fin. mgr. Bovay Engrs., Inc., Houston, 1974-79; sec., treas. Rice Center, Houston, 1979-82. Guest lectr. U. Houston, 1980-81, Harvard Grad. Sch. of Design, 1985—; Univ. of Wisconsin, Madison, 1998; overseas instr. Tongji U., Shanghai, People's Republic of China, 1990, Shanghai Mcpl. Constrn. Commn., 1992, Assn. Consulting Engrs., London, 1995 and 1998; condr. seminars in field. Author: Financial Management and Project Control for ConsultingEngineers, 1983; Financial Management for the Design Professional, 1984, Business Management in the Smaller Design Firm, 1986, Managing Ownership Transition in Design Firms, 1987, Mergers, Acquisitions, and Sales, 1987; co-author: Ownership Transition, Options and Strategies, 1996; contbg. editor: Valuation Survey of Design Firms, 1991-97, Insider's Guide to Cashing in on your Equity in an A/E/P or Environment Consulting Firm, 1993, Financial Management for Design Firms, 1997, (with others) Architect's Handbook of Professional Practice, 1993, (with others) Valuing Professional Practices and Licenses, 1998-00; contbr. articles to profl. pubs. Served as lt. USNR, 1955-58. Mem. Profl Svcs. Mgmt. Assn. (pres. 1988, treas. 1981-82, bd. dirs. 1979-88, 86-88), Tex. Soc. CPAs (chmn. mgmt. adv. svcs. com. Houston chpt. 1982-83), Am. Inst. CPAs (mem. various mgmt. adv. svcs. subcoms. 1981-87, Cert. of Ednl. Achievement in Bus. Valuation, accredited in bus. valuations), Am. Soc. Appraisers (sr.), Inst. Mgmt. Cons. (cert.). Home: PO Box 19159 Houston TX 77224-9159 Office: 820 Gessner Rd Ste 265 Houston TX 77024-4258

GETZ, MARY E. medical/surgical nurse; b. North Towanda, Pa., July 16, 1947; d. Leo T. and Ruth (Goodrich) Squires; m. Robert R. Getz, Dec. 23, 1971; children: Jesse T., Megan K. Diploma, Jefferson Hosp., Phila., 1968; BSN, Mansfield U. of Pa., 2001. RN, Pa.; cert. ACLS, med./surg. nurse. Staff nurse Meml. Hosp. Inc., Towanda, Pa., 1968—. Mem. ANA, Pa. State Nurses Assn., Jefferson Nurses Alumni Assn., Acad. of Med.-Surg. Nurses (mem. ethics com., mem. performance improvement for med./surg. advance directives com.). Home: RR 2 Box 2368 Dushore PA 18614-9301 E-mail: rmgetz@epix.net.

GETZ, MELISSA B. secondary education educator; b. Balt., May 26, 1969; d. Stanley (adoptive father) and Kathy Getz. BS, Va. Poly. Inst. and State U., 1991; MS, U. Calif., Davis, 1994; tchg. cert., Calif. State U., Sacramento, 1995. Tchr. Berkeley (Calif.) H.S., 1995-96; sci. tchr. Tennyson H.S., Hayward, Calif., 1996—. Cluster leader, East Bay (Calif.) Biotech. Edn. Partnership, 1999-2002; girls tennis coach, Tennyson H.S., 1997-99, Sci. Explorations Club advisor, 2000-01. Bd. dirs. Bridgewater Homeowners Assn., Albany, Calif., 1999—. Mem. ASCD, Nat. Assn. Biology Tchrs. (life), Assn. Women in Sci. (Sacramento Valley and East Bay chpts.), Nat. Sci. Tchrs. Assn., Calif. Sci. Tchrs. Assn., Phi Beta Kappa. Home: 545 Pierce St # 1208 Albany CA 94706 Office: Tennyson H S 27035 Whitman St Hayward CA 94544 E-mail: ntropi@aol.com.

GETZ, MORTON ERNEST, medical facility director, gastroenterologist; b. Bklyn., May 22, 1930; s. Jacob Michael and Regina (Kohn) G.; m. Carol Washer, Aug. 12, 1956; children: Jacob Michael, Deborah Etta. AB, Emory U., 1950; MS, Purdue U., 1952; MD, Wake Forest U., 1956. Intern Jackson Meml. Hosp., Miami, Fla., 1956-57, resident in medicine, 1957-58; sr. surgeon NIH, Atlanta and Bethesda, Md., 1958-60; chief resident in medicine Jackson Meml. Hosp., 1960; NIH fellow in gastroenterology U. Miami, 1960-61; pvt. practice internal medicine and gastroenterology Coral Gables, Fla. Mem. courtesy staff South Miami Hosp., Bapt. Hosp., Drs. Hosp.; attending physician Cedars Med. Ctr. Contbr. articles to profl. jours. With USPHS, 1958-60. Mem. AMA, Am. Soc. Internal Medicine, Internat. Hospice Physicians, Am. Assn. Hospice and Palliative Medicine, Nat. Coun. Hospice Profls., Miami Fla. Gastroenterologic Soc., Dade County Soc. Internal Medicine, So. Med. Assn., Fla. Med. Assn.,

Dade County Med. Assn., Ind. Acad. Scis., N.C. Acad. Sci., Phi Rho Sigma. Democrat. Jewish. Avocations: art collecting, fishing. Office: Douglas Gardens Hospice 5200 NE 2d Ave Miami FL 33137 E-mail: mgetz@MJHHA.org., megetz@worldnet.att.net.

GETZ, ROBERT LEE, newspaper columnist; b. Francesville, Ind., Oct. 1, 1943; s. Benjamin Jacob and Helen Juanita (Thomas) G.; m. Lisa Gale Schneller, Sept. 11, 1972 (div. June 1988); children: Chase H., Page L., Tracy M.; m. Jeannie McCoy, Mar. 17, 1994 (div. June 2000). Student, Andrews U., 1962. Reporter Logansport Pharos-Tribune, Ind., 1964; sports editor Rochester Sentinel, Rochester, 1965; sports writer, columnist Bloomington Herald-Telephone, Bloomington, 1967-70; sports editor Boca Raton News, Fla., 1972-74, columnist, feature writer, 1973-74; columnist Wichita Eagle, Kans., 1975—2003. Author: A Bookful of Bob Getz, 1992. With U.S. Army, 1965-67. Avocations: tennis, basketball.

GETZ, WAYNE MARCUS, biomathematician, researcher, educator; b. Johannesburg, Republic of South Africa, Apr. 26, 1950; came to U.S., 1979; m. Jennifer Bryna Gonski, Feb. 15, 1972; children: Stacey Lynn, Trevor Russell. BSc with honors, U. Witwatersrand, South Africa, 1972, PhD, 1976; DSc, U. Cape Town, South Africa, 1995. Rsch. scientist Coun. for Sci. and Indsl. Rsch., Pretoria, South Africa, 1974-79; biomathematician U. Calif., Berkeley, 1979—, prof. entomology, 1987-93, prof. environ. scis., 1993—, chair divsn. insect biology, 1995—2000, Berkeley chancellor's prof., 1998—2001. Extraordinary prof. U. Pretoria, South Africa, 2003—, fellow Mammal Rsch. Inst.; cons. Nat. Marine Fisheries Svc., 1980—89. Author: (with R. Haight) Population Harvesting: Demographic Models of Fish, Forest, and Animal Resources, 1989; editor Oxford U. Press book series Biol. Resource Mgmt., 1983-97; mem. editl. bd. Ecol. Applications, 1994-96, Annales Zoologica Fennici; contbr. articles to profl. jours. Rsch. grantee NSF, NIH, James S. McDonnell Found., Whitehall Found., Alfred P. Sloan Found., Def. Advanced Rsch. Programs Adminstrn.; Alexander von Humboldt U.S. Sr. Scientist awardee, 1993. Fellow AAAS, Calif. Acad. Scis., Stellanbosch Inst. for Advanced Studies; mem. Soc. Am. Naturalist, Internat. Soc. for Ecol. Modelling, Ecology Soc. Am., Resource Modelling Assn. (pres. 1995-96, bd. dirs. 1992-98), Soc. for Math. Biology. Office: Univ Calif Dep Env Sci Policy Mgmt Berkeley CA 94720-0001

GETZOFF, WILLIAM MOREY, lawyer; b. Chgo., Mar. 2, 1947; s. Byron M. and Mabel A. (Chapman) G.; m. JoAnne D. Goclan, Oct. 27, 1974; children—David, Claire. B.A., Oberlin Coll. (Ohio), 1968; J.D., U. Ill., 1972. Bar: Ill. 1972, U.S. Dist. Ct. (no. dist.) Ill. 1972, U.S. Ct. Appeals (7th cir.) 1972, U.S. Tax Ct. 1973. Ptnr. Getzoff & Getzoff, Chgo., 1972—. Mem. Chgo. Bar Assn., Ill. State Bar Assn. Home: 1515 Colfax St Evanston IL 60201-2320 Office: Getzoff & Getzoff 150 S Wacker Dr Ste 650 Chicago IL 60606-4197

GEUSIC, JOSEPH EDWARD EDWARD, physicist; b. Nesquehoning, Pa., Nov. 21, 1931; s. Joseph John and Mary Martha (Kosch) Geusic; m. Irene Jean Hosak, July 18, 1953; children: Patricia, Mark, Michael, Mary Ellen, Robert, Joseph. BS in Physics, Lehigh U., 1953; MS in Physics, Ohio State U., 1955, PhD in Physics, 1958. Rsch. assoc. physics dept. Ohio State U., Columbus, 1955-58; mem. tech. staff AT&T Bell Labs., Murray Hill, N.J., 1958-62, supr. solid state laser group, 1962-66, head solid state optical device dept., 1966-70, head magnetics dept., 1970-84, head semiconductor laser dept., 1984-94; pres. Geusic Info. Svcs., Inc., 1996—. Adj. fellow Micron Tech, Advanced Research Inst. Contbr. articles to profl. publs. Recipient R. W. Wood prize, Optical Soc. Am., 1993, Clinton J. Davisson Patent award trophy, AT&T, 1993. Fellow: IEEE (Quantum Electronics award 1992); mem.: Am. Inst. Physics, Sigma Xi. Achievements include first report of paramagnetic spectra of Cr 3+ in Ruby; invention of Nd/YAG laser, barium sodium niobate nonlinear optical material; first demonstration of continuous operating optical parametric oscillator; development of semiconductor lasers for terrestrial and undersea lightwave communication systems, magnetic bubble materials and devices; 55 patents in field. Home: 261 Lorraine Dr Berkeley Heights NJ 07922-2341 E-mail: josephgeusic@micron.com.

GEVERS, MARCIA BONITA, lawyer, lecturer, mediator, consultant; b. Mpls., Oct. 11, 1946; d. Sam and Bessie (Gottlieb) Fleisher; m. Michael A. Gevers, Sept. 13, 1970; children: Sarah Nichole, David Seth. BA, Nat. Coll. Edn., 1968; MA, N.E. Ill. U., 1973; JD, DePaul U., 1980. Bar: Ill. 1980, U.S. Dist. Ct. (no. dist.) Ill. 1980, U.S. Supreme Ct. 1985. Tchr. The Harris Sch., Chgo. Bd. Edn., N. Suburban Spl. Edn. Dist., Highland Park, Ill., 1968-73; legis. asst., campaign mgr. Ill. State Rep., Dolton, 1974-79; sole practice Park Forest, Dolton, Ill., 1980-83; ptnr. Getty and Gevers, Dolton, 1983-87; pvt. practice Marica B. Gevers & Assocs., Flossmoor, Ill., 1987—. Adj. prof. Gov.'s State U., University Park, 1986-87. Contbr. articles to profl. jours.; producer, host cable TV show, The Law and You, 1982-83. Bd. dirs. Park Forest Zoning Bd. Appeals, Fair Housing Rev. Bd., Housing Bd. Appeals, EEO Rev. Bd., 1975-88; pres. bd. dirs. South Suburban Cmty. Hebrew Day Sch., Olympia Fields, Ill., 1982-86; bd. dirs. Congregation Beth Sholom Ch., Park Forest, 1980-82, Congregation Beth Sholom Ch., Park Forest, 1980-82, Anita M. Stone Jewish Cmty. Ctr., 1996—; pres. Ill. Women's Polit. Caucus; mem. steering com. Nat. Women's Polit. Caucus, Washington; pres., founder Metro South Women's Polit. Caucus, Chgo. suburbs; alt. del. Dem. Nat. Conv., N.Y.C., 1980. Mem. ABA (family law sect.,juvenile, stepfamilies and pub. rels. coms.), Ill. State Bar Assn., Chgo. Bar Assn. (matrimonial law com., Guardian Ad Litem subcom.), Acad. Family Mediators, Am. Arbitration Assn. (arbitrator), Lodges: Hadassah, B'nai B'rith Women. Office: Marcia B Gevers & Assocs 19710 Governors Hwy Flossmoor IL 60422-2040

GEVIRTZ, CLIFFORD MARK, anesthesiologist; b. N.Y.C., Apr. 18, 1956; MD, Tulane U., 1981. Diplomate Am. Bd. Anesthesiology subspeciality bd. pain mgmt. Intern, rotating Montefiore Med. Ctr., Bronx, N.Y., 1981-82; resident in surgery Albert Einstein Coll. Medicine, Bronx, N.Y., 1982-83, resident in anesthesia, 1983-85; fellow in anesthesiology Mass. Gen. Hosp., Boston, 1985-86; instr. in anesthesiology NYU Med. Ctr., N.Y.C., 1986-87; asst. prof. Albert Einstein Coll. Medicine, 1987-95; anesthesiologist Bronx Mcpl. Hosp., 1987-94, Montefiore Med. Ctr., Bronx, 1990-94, Jack Weiler Hosp., Bronx, N.Y., 1987-94, Metro Hosp. Ctr., 1994-99; assoc. prof. N.Y. Med. Coll., 1994-99; chief of anesthesiology Bronx VA Hosp., 1999—; pain mgmt. coord. Vets. Integrated Svc. Network 3; clin. assoc. prof. Mt. Sinai Sch. Medicine, 1999—. Adj. assoc. prof. N.Y. Coll. Podiatric Medicine, 1995—. Editor: Topics in Pain Management, 2003—. Mem. AMA, Am. Soc. Anesthesiologists. Office: Bronx VA Hosp Dept Anes 130 W Kingsbridge Rd Bronx NY 10468-3904 E-mail: clifford.gevirtz@med.va.gov.

GEWARTOWSKI, JAMES WALTER, retired electrical engineer; b. Chgo., Nov. 10, 1930; s. Joseph Walter and Irene Dorothy (Dziekanowski) G.; m. Marion Ruth Wakeman, June 23, 1956; children: Marion, Diane, Patricia, John, Karen. BS in Elec. Engring., Ill. Inst. Tech., 1952; S.M., MIT, 1953; PhD, Stanford U., 1958. Research asst. Stanford Electronics Lab., Calif., 1954-57; supr. microwave sources AT&T Bell Labs., Inc, Murray Hill, N.J., 1957-71, supr. high bit rate optical data link group Allentown, Pa., 1971-88, supr. SL optical relay/receiver group Breinigsville, Pa., 1988-89, ret. Co-author: Principles of Electron Tubes, 1965, Fundamentals of Electron Tubes, 1969; contbg. author: Microwave Semiconductor Devices and Their Circuit Applications, 1969; contbr. articles to profl. jours. Fellow IEEE (Browder J. Thompson Meml. prize 1960); mem. Sigma Xi, Tau Beta Pi, Eta Kappa Nu, Serra Internat. Republican. Roman Catholic. Home: 2908 Edgemont Dr Allentown PA 18103-5410

GEWEKE, JOHN FREDERICK, economics educator; b. Washington, May 11, 1948; s. Robert William and Winnifred Lois (Quies) G.; m. Lynne Marie Osborn, Aug. 22, 1970; children: Andrew Robert, Alan Reid. BS, Mich. State U., 1970; PhD, U. Minn., 1975. Asst. prof. U. Wis., Madison, 1975-79, assoc. prof., 1979-82, prof., 1982-83, Duke U., Durham, N.C., 1983-86, William R. Kenan Jr. prof., 1986-90, dir. Inst. Stats. and Decision Scis., 1987-90; prof. U. Minn., Mpls., 1990—. Editor Jour. Bus. and Econs. Stats., 1989-92; co-editor Jour. Applied Econometrics, 1993—; assoc. editor Econometrica, 1984-88, 95—. Rsch. fellow Sloan Found., N.Y.C., 1982. Fellow Econometric Soc., Am. Stats. Assn.; mem. Am. Econ. Assn., Internat. Soc. for Bayesian Analysis (pres. 1999). Office: U of IA Dept Econs Iowa City IA 52242

GEWERTZ, BRUCE LABE, surgeon, educator; b. Phila., Aug. 27, 1949; s. Milton and Shirley (Charen) G.; children: Samantha, Barton, Alexis; m. Diane Weiss, Aug. 31, 1997. BS, Pa. State U., State Coll., 1968; MD, Jefferson Med. Coll., Phila., 1972. Diplomate Am. Bd. Surgery. Surg. resident U. Mich., Ann Arbor, 1972-77; asst. prof. U. Tex., Dallas, 1977-81; assoc. prof. U. Chgo., 1981-87, prof. surgery, 1988—, faculty dean med. edn., 1989-92, Dallas Phemister prof., chmn. dept. surgery, 1992—. Teaching scholar Am. Heart Assn., Dallas, 1980-83; pres. Assn. Surg. Edn., 1983-84. Author: Atlas of Vascular Surgery, 1989, Surgery of the Aorta and its Branches, 2000; editor Jour. Surg. Rsch., 1987—; patentee removable vascular filter. Recipient Jobst award Coller Surg. Soc., 1975, Coller award Mich. chpt. Am. Coll. Surgeons, 1975, Outstanding Sci. Alumnus award Pa. State U., 2003. Mem. Soc. Vascular Surgery, Midwestern Vascular Soc. (pres. 1993, 94-95), Soc. Clin. Surgery, Soc. Univ. Surgeons, Chgo. Surg. Soc. (treas. 1989-92, pres.-elect 2003), Am. Surg. Assn., Point O'Woods Club (Benton Harbor, Mich.). Office: U Chgo MC 5029 5841 S Maryland Ave Chicago IL 60637-1463

GEWIRTZ, LEONARD BENJAMIN, rabbi; b. N.Y.C., Jan. 25, 1918; s. Henry (dec. May 22, 2003) and Leah Peshe (Greenberg) G.; m. Gladys Sarah Kerstein, Nov. 21, 1948; children: Isaac Meir, Joseph Jacob. BS cum laude, CCNY, 1941; grad., Hebrew Theol. Coll., 1945; postgrad., Dropsie Coll., 1952. Ordained rabbi, 1945. Supply rabbi Beth Shalom Congregation, Danville, Ill., 1943-45; rabbi Congregation Oir Chodosh, Chgo., 1945-47, Congregation Adas Kodesh Shel Emeth, Wilmington, Del., 1947-88; rabbi emeritus, from 1988. Dir. campus activities Hillel U. Del., Newark, 1960-63; instr. Gratz Hebrew High Sch., Wilmington, 1971-83; founder, speaker WDEL weekly radio program Rabbi Speaks, 1950—. Author: Authentic Jew and His Judaism, 1961, Authentic Jewish Living, 1977, Jewish Spirituality: Hope and Redemption, 1985, A Jewish Voice, 1998; contbr. articles religious jours. Pres. Del. Citizens Conf. Social Work, Wilmington, 1954-56; bd. govs. Del. Mental Health Assn., 1967-71, Jewish Community Ctr. Recipient Heritage award Israel Bonds, 1992, Reunification award, 1992; Sanctuary of Synagogue Rabbi Leonard B. Gewirtz named in his honor, 1994, Mezuza award for Cmty. Svc. State of Israel Bonds, 1997. Mem. ACLU, Pacem En Terris, Rabbinic Assn. Del. (pres. 1967-69, 75-77, 80-82), Rabbinical Coun. Am. (chmn. social actions 1966-68, exec. com. 1960-64), Phila. Bd. Rabbis (40 Yr. Continuous Svc. award 1984), Jewish Fedn. (bd. govs.), B'nai Brith (cert. honor). Home: Wilmington, Del. Died May 22, 2003.

GEWIRTZ, MINDY L. organizational and human relations consultant; b. N.Y.C., Mar. 19, 1951; d. Martin and Miriam (Altman) Lebovicz; m. Gershon C. Gewirtz, Sept. 7, 1971; children: Yussy, Henoch, Sora Leah, Adina, Doniel. MPS, N.Y. Inst. Tech., 1977; MSW, SUNY, Albany, 1981; PhD in Orgnl. Sociology, Boston U., 1995. Lic. ind. clin. social worker; diplomate Am. Bd. Clin. Social Workers. Project coord. Ringel Inst. Gerontology SUNY-Albany, 1980-82; coord. sr. adult dept. Jewish Family Svcs., Albany, 1983-84; dir. eldercare connection long distance caregiving svc. Jewish Family and Children's Svc., Boston, 1984-93; prin. GLS, Inc., Boston, 1988—; postgrad. fellow orgnl. devel. & human resources cons. Boston Inst. Psychotherapy, 1990. Adj. asst. prof. Boston U. Sch. Social Work; cons. Ibis Cons. Group, Cambridge, 1990—; orgn. and mgmt. cons. Boston Digital Equipment Corp., Boston, 1988-92; orgnl. cons. Malden Mills, Lawrence, Mass., 1992-99; presdl. adviser Am. Type Cutter Collection, 2002. Co-author: Sustaining Top Leadership: Promise and Pitfalls in Collaborative Work Systems, 2002; assoc. author: Human Dilemmas in Work Organizations, 1994; contbr. articles to profl. jours. and publs. Mem. Boston Work and Family Forum, New England Human Resources Assn., Greater Boston Orgnl. Devel. Network. Recipient Max Siporin Social Work fellow. Mem. NASW, ACSW (bd. cert. diplomate), Am. Assn. Bus. Women (career advancement fellow), Phi Beta Kappa. Home: 23 Browne St Brookline MA 02446-3804

GEWIRTZ, PAUL D. lawyer, legal educator; b. May 12, 1947; s. Herman and Matilda (Miller) Gewirtz; m. Zoë Baird, June 8, 1986; children: Julian, Alec. AB summa cum laude, Columbia U., 1967; JD, Yale U., 1970. Bar: D.C. 1973, U.S. Supreme Ct. 1976. Law clk. to Hon. Marvin E. Frankel U.S. Dist. Ct (so. dist.) N.Y., 1970—71; law clk. to Justice Thurgood Marshal U.S. Supreme Ct., Washington, 1971—72; assoc. Wilmer, Cutler & Pickering, Washington, 1972—73; atty. Ctr. Law and Social Policy, Washington, 1973—76; assoc. prof. then prof. Yale Law Sch., New Haven, 1976—, Potter Stewart prof. Law, 1992—, dir. The China Ctr., 1999—. Dir. Global Constitutionalism Project, 1996—; spl. rep. the Presdl. Rule of Law Initiative US Dept. of State, 1997—98; US rep. European Commn. on Democracy through Law, 1996—2000. Author: Law's Stories, 1996, The Case Law Sys. in Am., 1989; contbr. numerous articles to profl. jours. Mem.: Am. Law Inst., Coun. on Fgn. Rels. Office: Yale U Law Sch PO Box 208215 New Haven CT 06520-8215 E-mail: paul.gewirtz@yale.edu.

GEWIRTZ-FRIEDMAN, GERRY, editor; b. N.Y.C., Dec. 22, 1920; d. Max and Minnie (Weiss) G.; m. Eugene W. Friedman, Nov. 11, 1945; children: John Henry, Robert James. BA, Vassar Coll., 1941. Editor Package Store Mgmt., 1942-44, Jewelry Mag., 1945-53; freelance editor promotion dept. McCall's Mag., Esquire, 1953-56; free-lance fashion and gifts editor Jewelers Circular Keystone, N.Y.C., 1955-71; editor, pub. The Fashionables, 1971-74, The Forecast, 1974—, Nat. Jeweler, Ann. Fashion Guide, 1976-80; editor, assoc. pub. Exec. Jeweler, 1980-83; editor The Fashion Source (formerly Internat. Fashion Index), N.Y.C., 1984—; freelance editor and mktg. specialist, 1995—. Ptnr. Gary Gewirtz-Editl. and Mktg.; free-lance editl. wrtier, 1995—. Corr. Internat. Mktg. News. Mem. exec. com. Inner City Council of Cardinal Cooke, N.Y.; chairperson women's task force United Jewish Appeal Fedn.; former bd. govs. Israel Bonds; former trustee Israel Cancer Research Fund, Central Synagogue; bd. dirs. Double Image Theater; former pres. women's aux. Brandeis U. Honored guest Am. Jewish Com., 1978; Israel Cancer Research Fund, 1978-81; recipient Disting. Community Service award Brandeis U., 1987; named to Jewelry Hall Fame, 1988. Mem. N.Y. Fashion Group, Nat. Home Fashions League (former pres.), Women's Jewelry Assn. (pres. 1983-87, named editor who has contbd. most to jewelry industry 1984, free lance editor). Home: 45 Sutton Pl S New York NY 10022-2444

GEWITZ, MICHAEL HAROLD, pediatrician; b. Jan. 20, 1949; m. Judith Lipshutz, May 12, 1973; children: Emily, Andrew. BA, Yale U., 1970; MD, Hahnemann U., 1974. Intern Children's Hosp. Phila., Phila., 1974-75, resident, 1975-76, Hosp. Sick Children, London, 1976-77; fellow Yale New Haven Hosp., 1977-79; dir. noninvasive cardiology Children's Hosp. Phila., 1979-83; asst. prof. pediat. Sch. Medicine U. Pa., Phila., 1979-83; chief pediat. cardiology N.Y. Med. Coll. and Westchester Med. Ctr., 1983-91; dir. dept. pediat., chief pediat. cardiology Children's Hosp. Westchester, Valhalla, N.Y., 1991—; prof., vice chair dept. pediat. N.Y. Med. Coll., Valhalla, N.Y., 1992—; pres. med. staff Westch Med. Ctr., 1998—. Mem. exec. com. Coun. on Cardiovasc. Disease in the Young, Am. Heart Assn., 1999—; mem. com. on rheumatic fever, endocarditis and Kawasaki disease Am. Heart Assn., 1995—, vice chair, 2001—. Editor: (book) Primary Pediatric Cardiology, 1995; assoc. editor: (journal) Heart Diseases, 1999—. Fellow Am. Acad. Pediatrics, Am. Coll. Cardiology, N.Y. Acad. Medicine; mem. Pediat. Acad. Soc., Am. Coll. Phys. Execs.

GEX, LUCIEN MARION, III, (BEAU GEX), legislative staff member; b. New Orleans, Oct. 5, 1959; s. Lucien Marion Jr. and Nancy (Gould) G. BS, U. So. Miss., 1982. Registered appraiser. Claims adjuster Allstate Ins., Biloxi, Miss., 1985-89; dist. chief of staff Congressman Gene Taylor, Gulfport, Miss., 1989—. Appraiser Lucien M. Gex III Appraisals, Long Beach, Miss., 1999—. Mem. adv. bd. U. So. Miss., Hattiesburg, 2000—, St. Stanislaus H.S., 1999—. Mem. World Trade Club, Bay Waveland Yacht Club (dir.), Kappa Alpha. Roman Catholic. Home: 129 Markham Dr Long Beach MS 39560 Office: Congressman Gene Taylor 2424 14th St Gulfport MS 39501 E-mail: beaugex@mindspring.com.

GEYER, ALAN FRANCIS, theology educator, politics educator; b. Dover, N.J., Aug. 3, 1931; s. Curtis Bayley and Ada Lucile (Wehrly) G.; m. Joanne Shirley Goodnow, Mar. 28, 1953 (div. 1984); children: Nancy Kathryn, Peter Lincoln, David Curtis, Philip Marshall; m. Barbara Graham Green, Apr. 20, 1985; children: Christopher Donald Green Geyer, Elisabeth Frances Green Geyer. BA, Ohio Wesleyan U., 1952; STB, Boston U., 1955, PhD, 1961; DLitt (hon.), Ohio Wesleyan, 1970. Asst. prof. polit. sci. Lycoming Coll., Williamsport, PA., 1957-58; pastor Trinity Meth. Ch., Newark, 1958-60; asst. prof., assoc. prof. polit. sci. Mary Baldwin Coll., Staunton, Va., 1960-65; dir. internat. rels. United Ch. Christ, N.Y.C., 1965-68; editor The Christian Century The Christian Century Found., Chgo., 1968-72; Dag Hammarskjöld prof. peace studies Colgate U., Hamilton, N.Y., 1972-77; exec. dir. Ch. Ctr. Theology and Pub. Policy, Washington, 1977-87; prof. polit. ethics and ecumenics Wesley Theol. Seminary, Washington, 1987-96. Resident ethicist Washington Nat. Cathedral, 1994-96; ecumenist Washington Nat. Cathedral, 1997-2000; governing bd. Nat. Coun. Chs., N.Y., 1982-84; cons. United Meth. Coun. Bishops, 1984-86; adv. World Coun. Chs., Geneva, 1968, 83; sr. scholar Ch's. Ctr. for Theology and Pub. Policy, Washington, 1987—; canon ethicist Washington Nat. Cathedral, 2000—. Author: Piety and Politics, 1963, The Idea of Disarmament, 1982, Christianity and the Superpowers, 1990, Ideology in America: Challenges to Faith, 1997; co-author: Lines in the Sand: Justice and the Gulf War, 1992; editl. bd.: Disarmament Times, 1980 97. Bd. trustees Ohio Wesleyan U., Del., Ohio, 1970-73; mem. Nat. Com. U.S.-China Rels., 1966—. Fellow Soc. Values in Higher Edn.; mem. Am. Polit. Sci. Assn., Soc. Christian Ethics (pres. 1984 85), Internat. Inst. Strategic Studies, U.N. Assn., Arms Control Assn. Democrat. Methodist. Avocations: composing music, cartography, astronomy, model trains, sports. Home and Office: 5014 Smallwood Dr Bethesda MD 20816-2830

GEYER, DENNIS LYNN, university administrator and registrar; b. Bay City, Mich., Feb. 17, 1950; s. Walter R. and Bettie Jane (Powers) G.; m. Karen Sue Bickel, Sept. 5, 1970; children: Sarah Denise, Zachary Dennis. Student, Northwestern Luth. Coll., 1967-68; BA, Mich. State U., 1971, MA, 1976. Tchr., coach Aurora (Colo.) Jr. High Sch., 1972-74; asst. to the registrar Lansing (Mich.) C.C., 1974-77; counselor Adams County Sch. Dist. # 14, Commerce City, Colo., 1977-78; registrar, asst. dir. student svcs. U. Colo. Health Sci. Ctr., Denver, 1978-88; univ. registrar, NCAA compliance officer, instnl. rsch. rep. Humboldt State U., Arcata, Calif., 1988-98, dir. admissions and records, 1996-98; univ. registrar SUNY, Stony Brook, 1998-2001, George Washington U., Washington, 2001—. Co-author: A Guidebook for Student Services, 1977. Mem. Jaycees, Bay City, 1971-73; mem. Luth. Ch. of Arcata, pres., 1993-96, chair edn. com., 1990-93, mem. campus ministry bd., 1993-98, co-chair pastoral search com., 1996-97; mem. Lord of Life Luth. Ch., sec., 1983-87, pres., 1987-88; mem. Promise Keepers, 1994-98; mem. Messiah Luth. Ch., campus ministry bd., 1999-2002, v.p. Ch. Coun., 2001-03, Campus Min. Bd. Mem. Am. Assn. Collegiate Registrars and Admissions Officers (chair distance edn. com. 1999-2001, chair local phys. arrangements com. ann. meeting 2003), Nat. Collegiate Athletic Assn. (instn. compliance officer 1990-98, oversight com., student info. lead), Calif. Assn. Instl. Rsch., SUNY Registrar's Assn., Mid. States Assn. Collegiate Registrars and Officers of Admission. Avocation: traveling. Home: 79 Quaker Path Stony Brook NY 11790-1334 E-mail: dgeyer@gwu.edu.

GEYER, GEORGIE ANNE, syndicated columnist, educator, author, biographer, TV commentator; b. Chgo., Apr. 2, 1935; d. Robert George and Georgie Hazel (Gervens) G. BS, Northwestern U., 1956, LHD (hon.), 1993; postgrad., U. Vienna, Austria, 1956-57; LittD (hon.), Lake Forest Coll., 1980, Coll. Mt. St. Joseph, 1986, Notre Dame, 1986, Wilson Coll., 1987, Linfield Coll., 1987, St. Mary-of-the Woods Coll., 1989, U. Indpls., 1991, Colby-Sawyer Coll., 1992, Franklin Coll., 1992, Cabrini Coll., 1994; LHD (hon.), Northwestern U., 1984, U. S.C., 1991, Rockhurst (Jesuit) Coll., Kansas City, 1992, Spring Hill Coll., 1993, Lebanon Valley Coll., 1994, Hofstra U., 1995, Loyola U., Chgo., 1996, Westminster Coll., 1996, Govs. State U., 1997, Notre Dame Coll., 1999, Knox Coll., 1999. Reporter Southtown Economist, Chgo., 1958; soc. reporter Chgo. Daily News, 1959-60, gen. assignment reporter, 1960-64, corr. Lat. Am., Ctrl. Am., Soviet Union, Middle East, Europe, 1964-75, roving fgn. corr. and columnist, 1967-75; syndicated columnist Los Angeles Times Syndicate, 1975-80, Universal Press Syndicate, 1981—; Lyle M. Spencer prof. journalism Syracuse U., 1977. Regular news commentator PBS' Washington Week in Review; questioner on Presdl. debate, Oct., 1984; steering com. Aspen Inst. Latin Am. Governance Project, 1981-82; commentator on the BBC; regular panelist Voice of America; sent by Internat. Communication Agy. on 3 worldwide speaking tours on Am. journalism: Nigeria, Zambia, Tanzania and Somalia, 1979, Philippines and Indonesia, 1981, Iceland, Norway, Belgium and Portugal, 1982; rep. Fulbright scholar program 40th anniversary, New Zealand, 1987; commencement speaker various colls., univs. including U. S.Carolina, Rockhurst Coll., St. Mary's Notre Dame; sr. fellow Annenburg Washington, 1992-93; columnist on fgn. policy, internat. affairs The Chgo. Tribune, The Wash. Times, Universal de Caracas, The Dallas Morning News, Diario las Americas, The Denver Post, others; speaker, lectr. in field. Author: The New Latins, 1970, The New 100 Years War, 1972, The Young Russians, 1976; (autobiography) Buying the Night Flight, (Weintal prize citation Sch. Fgn. Svc. Georgetown U. 1984, Chgo. Found. for Lit. award 1984), 1983, reissued, 1996, Guerilla Prince, The Untold Story of Fidel Castro, 1991, Waiting for Winter to End, An Extraordinary Journey Through South Central Asia, 1994, Americans No More: The Death of Citizenship, 1996; subjects of interviews include Prince Sihanouk of Cambodia, Yassar Arafat, Anwar Sadat, King Hussein of Jordan, Pres. Khaddafy of Libya, the Ayatollah Khomeini, Sultan Qaboos of Oman, Pres. Juan Peron of Argentina, Pres. Siad Barre of Somalia, Prime Minister Mauno Koivisto of Finland, Anastasio Somoza, Jerzy Urban, Janusz Onyszkiewicz, Prime Minister Edward Seaga of Jamaica, Pres. Ronald Reagan, Pres. George Bush, others; discovered and had first interview with second most-wanted Nazi, Walter Rauff in Tierra del Fuego, Chile, 1966; found Dominican pres. Juan Bosch in hiding in P.R. during Dominican revolution, 1965; held by Palestinians as Israeli spy, 1973; imprisoned in Angola for writing about revolutionary government, 1976; contbr. chpts. to books, articles numerous pubs. Active Orgn. for S.W. Community Chgo., 1960-64; trustee Am. U., Washington, 1981-86; Coun. Fgn. Rels. Recipient 1st prize Am. Newspaper Guild, 1962; 2d prize Ill. Press Editors Assn., 1962; award for best writing on Latin Am. Overseas Press Club, 1967; Merit award Northwestern U., 1968; Nat. Headliner award Theta Sigma Phi, 1968; Maria Moors Cabot award Columbia U., 1970; Hannah Solomon award Nat. Council Jewish Women, 1973; Ill. Spl. Events Commn. Woman's award, 1975; Northwestern U. Alumni award, 1991; Fulbright scholar U. Vienna, 1956-57; Woodrow Wilson fellow Rollins Coll., Winter Park, Fla., 1982; Presdl. Citation award Am. Univ., 1985; Disting. fellow Mortar Bd. Nat. Sr. Honor Soc., Am. U., 1982, Stewart Alsop award Assn. Former Intelligence Officers, 2000; Sr. fellow Annenberg Washington Program, Washington, 1982-83; fellow Soc. Prof. Journalists, 1992; named Outstanding Illinoisian, Ill. State Assn., 2001; named to Hall of Fame of Soc. of Profl. Journalists, 2001. Mem.: Chgo. Coun. Fgn. Rels. (bd. dirs.), Washington Inst., Women's Inst. for Freedom of Press, Internat. Soc. Polit. Psychology, Internat. Inst. Strategic Studies, Inst. Internat. Edn. (bd. dirs.), Women in Comm., Soc. Profl. Journalists, Cosmos Club (1st women mem.), Gridiron Club. Home and Office: The Plaza 800 25th St NW Washington DC 20037-2207 Home Fax: 202-333-3198; Office Fax: 816-932-6658. *I have never compromised seriously on any ethical or moral principle, and I truly believe that the women of my generation can bring a new and cleansing element to American public life. Whatever I have accomplished I could not have done without profoundly analyzing myself; but I also find that in professional life the old injunction to "Know Thyself" reaches women more than men. It has been a constant struggle, often with little personal approval or backing, which I feel also adds to a woman's inner strength.*

GEYER, HAROLD CARL, artist, writer; b. Cold Spring, N.Y., Aug. 16, 1905; s. Harold Carl and Mary Brindsmaid (de Camp) G.; m. Ina Helen Doane, July 29, 1943. BA, Yale U., 1926, B.F.A., 1930. Exhibited one-man shows, Aux Arcades, Troyes, France, 1984, group shows, Library of Congress, Soc. Am. Etchers, NAD, N.Y.C.; represented permanent collections, Library of Congress, Bibliotheque, Paris; (featured etchings) Ombres Et Lumieres de Troyes, 1989; author, artist: All Men Have Loved Thee, 1941, The Long Way Home, 1949. Recipient 3d Purchase prize Library of Congress, 1945 Mem. NAD, Soc. Am. Graphic Artists Home: RR 1 Chilmark MA 02535-9801

GEYER, MICHAEL, history educator; PhD, Albert Ludwigs U., Freiburg, Germany. Prof. history U. Chgo., 1986—. Recipient Guggenheim fellowship, 2003. Office: U Chgo Dept History 1126 E 59th St Chicago IL 60637*

GEYMAN, JOHN PAYNE, physician, educator; b. Santa Barbara, Calif., Feb. 9, 1931; s. Milton John and Betsy (Payne) Geyman; m. Eugenia Clark Deichler, June 9, 1956; children: John Matthew, James Caleb, William Sabin. AB in

Geology, Princeton U., 1952; MD, U. Calif., San Francisco, 1960. Diplomate Am. Bd. Family Practice. Intern Los Angeles County Gen. Hosp., 1960—61; resident in gen. practice Sonoma County Hosp., Santa Rosa, Calif., 1961—63; pvt. practice specializing in family practice Mt. Shasta, Calif., 1963—69; dir. family practice residency program Community Hosp. Sonoma County, Santa Rosa, 1969—71; assoc. prof. family practice, chmn. divsn. family practice U. Utah, 1971—72; prof., vice chmn. dept. family practice U. Calif., Davis, 1972—77; prof., chmn. dept. family medicine U. Wash., 1977—90, prof. family medicine, 1990—93; prof. family medicine emeritus, 1993—. Author: The Modern Family Doctor and Changing Medical Practice, 1971, Family Practice: Foundation of Changing Health Care, 1980, 1985, Flight as a Lifetime Passion: Adventures, Misadventures and Lessons, 2000, Falling Through the Safety Net: Americans Confront the Perils of Health Insurance, 2003; editor: Content of Family Practice, 1976, Family Practice in the Medical School, 1977, Research in Family Practice, 1978, Preventive Medicine in Family Practice, 1979, Profile of the Residency Trained Family Physician in the U.S. 1970—79, Funding of Patient Care, Education and Research in Family Practice, 1981, The Content of Family Practice: Current Status and Future Trends, 1982; editor Archives of Family Practice, 1980, 1981, 1982, founding editor Jour. Family Practice, 1973—90, editor Jour. Am. Bd. Family Practice, 1990—2003; co-editor: Behavioral Science in Family Practice, 1980, Evidence-Based Clinical Practice: Concepts and Approaches, 2000, Textbook of Rural Medicine, 2000, Health Care in America: Can Our Ailing System Be Healed?, 2002; editor: Family Practice: An International Perspective in Developed Countries, 1983. Served to lt. (j.g.) USN, 1952—55, PTO. Recipient Gold-Headed Cane award, U. Calif. Sch. Medicine, 1960, Alumnus of Yr. award, 1998. Mem.: Inst. Medicine NAS, Soc. Tchrs. Family Medicine, Am. Acad. Family Physicians. Unitarian Universalist. Home: 53 Avian Ridge Ln Friday Harbor WA 98250-8895 Office: Univ Wash Sch Medicine Dept Family Medicine PO Box 354696 Seattle WA 98195-4696

GEYSER, LYNNE M. lawyer, writer; b. Queens, N.Y., Mar. 28, 1938; d. Henry and Shirley Dannenberg; m. Lewis P. Geyser, 1956 (div. 1974); 1 child, Russell D. Geyser. BA, Queens Coll., 1960; JD, UCLA, 1968. Bar: Calif. 1969. Atty. Zagon, Schiff, Hirsch & Levine, Beverly Hills, Calif., 1969-70; atty., registered legis. advocate Beverly Hills, Malibu, Calif., 1973-75, atty. Freshman, Marantz, Comsky & Deutsch, Beverly Hills, Malibu, Calif., 1971-74; prof. law Glendale (Calif.) U. Law, 1974-76, U. Iowa Sch. Law, Iowa City, 1976-77, Pepperdine U., Malibu, 1977-78; pvt. practice Newport Beach, Calif., 1978-81, San Clemente, 1978—. Part-time prof. law Western State Law Sch., Fullerton, Calif., 1978; cons. atty. The Irvine Co., Newport Beach, 1981-86, Std. Mgmt. Co., L.A., 1987-88; instr. Saddleback Coll., Mission Viejo, Calif., early 1990's; lectr., instr. Calif. Assn. Realtors Grad. Realty Inst., 1972-78, U. So. Calif. brokers tng. courses, L.A., 1978-80, UCLA real estate and corp. courses for paralegals, 1973-76; creator and lectr. course on disclosure for licensees, L.A., San Diego and Orange Counties, Calif., 1978-81; faculty advisor, rev. advisor Glendale U. Coll. Law, 1975-76. Chief articles editor UCLA Law Rev., 1967; adv. bd. The Rsch. Jour., 1976; contbr. poetry and short stories to jours. Mem. exec. bd. L.A. County Art Mus. Contemporary Art Coun., L.A., 1971-73; bd. trustees Westwood (L.A.) Art Assn., 1974; bd. govs. La Costa Beach Homeowners Assn., Malibu, 1975; pres. Dana Point (Calif.) Coastal Arts Coun., 1989-90; teaching participant Jr. Achievement, Newport Beach, 1985. Recipient 6 Am. Jurisprudence awards, 1966-68, 2 West Hornbook awards, 1967; nom. Douglas Law Clk. UCLA Law Sch., 1967. Fellow The Legal Inst.; mem. AALS (chair-elect environ. law sect. 1977), San Clemente Sunrise Rotary, Order of Coif. Avocations: world travel, fine arts, writing, computers, performing arts, graphics. Office: PO Box 4715 San Clemente CA 92674-4715

GHABBOUR, ELHAM A. research scientist, educator; arrived in U.S., 1993; d. Afifi A. Ghabbour and S. Abo-zid. BS, Alexandria U., Egypt, 1982, MS, 1988, PhD, 1995. Postdoctoral rsch. fellow Northeastern U., Boston, 1996—98, staff scientist, 1999—2001, sr. rsch. scientist, 2002—. Co-editor: Barnett Inst. Gazette; contbr. articles to profl. jours.; editor: Humic Substances: Structures, Properties and Uses, 1998, Understanding Humic Substances: Advanced Methods, Properties and Applications, 1999, Humic Substances: Versatile Components of Plants, Soil and Water, 2000, Humic Substances: Structures, Models and Functions, 2001, Humic Substances: Nature's Most Versatile Materials. Recipient Advanced Rsch. award, Barnett Inst., 1998, Innovation Rsch. award, 2000; grantee, USDA NRICGP, 2002. Mem.: AAUP, Soil Sci. Soc. Am., Internat. XAFS Soc., Internat. Humic Substances Soc. (founder, nat. coord. Egyptian chpt. 1996—), Royal Soc. Chemistry, Am. Chem. Soc., Internat. Soil Sci. Soc., Environ. Friends Soc., Phi Beta Delta (pres. NU chpt. 2002—), Sigma Xi. Office: Northeastern U Dept Chemistry Boston MA 02115-5000

GHAFOURIFAR, PEDRAM, pharmacologist; b. Tehran, Iran, Dec. 23, 1965; s. Ahmad and Sorour (Ghashghai) G.; m. Zahra Ramezani, Feb. 17, 1987; children: Parnian, Parham. PharmD, U. Tehran, 1990, PhD, 1995. Postdoctoral fellow Swiss Fed. Inst. of Tech., Zurich, Switzerland, 1996-2000; rsch. asst. prof. U. Mass. Med. Sch., Worcester, 2000—01; asst. prof. pharmacology La. State U., Shreveport, 2001—. Hon. rsch. fellow Wolfson Inst. for Biomed. Rsch., U. Coll. London, 1999-2000; prin. rsch. fellow Univ. Coll. London, 1999-2000; invited vis. scientist Dana-Farber Cancer Inst., Harvard Med. Sch., Boston, 1999-2000. Author: Methods in Enzymology, 1998, 2002, Endocytobiology, 1999, Mitocondrial Ubiquinone, 2000; editor: Antioxidants and Redox Signaling, 2003; contbr. articles to profl. jours. Recipient The New Century award of the Europe 500, 2000. Mem.: AAAS, Fedn. Am. Soc. for Exptl. Biology, Am. Soc. Pharmacology and Exptl. Therapy, Nat. Orgn. Outstanding Talents, The Cell Death Soc., Nitric Oxide Soc., Oxygen Soc., Iranian Pharm. Soc., Swiss Tissue Culture Soc., Soc. Physiology and Pharmacology, N.Y. Acad. Scis. Home: 9900 Wildoak Dr Shreveport LA 71106 Office: 1501 Kings Hwy Shreveport LA 71103-4228 E-mail: pghafo@LSUHSC.edu., pedramgf@yahoo.com.

GHANDHI, SORAB KHUSHRO, electrical engineering educator; b. Allahabad, India, Jan. 1, 1928; came to U.S., 1947, naturalized, 1960; s. Khushro S. and Dina (Amroliwalla) G.; m. Cecilia M. Ghandhi; children: Khushro, Rustom, Behram. B.Sc. in Elec. and Mech. Engring, Benares (India) Hindu U., 1947; MS, U. Ill., 1948, PhD, 1951. Mem. electronics lab. Gen. Electric Co., 1951-60; mgr. electronic components and functions lab., research divsn. Philco Corp., 1960-63; prof. elec. engring. Rensselaer Poly. Inst., Troy, N.Y., 1963—, chmn. electrophysics and electronic engring. divsn., 1968-75, prof. electrophysics, elec., computer and systems engring. dept., 1975-92, active emeritus prof., 1992—. Cons. to industry, 1963— Co-author: (with R.F. Shea editor) Principles of Transistor Circuits, 1953, Transistor Circuit Engineering, 1957, Amplifier Handbook, 1966; author: The Theory and Practice of Microelectronics, 1968, Semiconductor Power Devices, 1977, VLSI Fabrication Principles: Silicon and Gallium Arsenide, 1983, 2d edit., 1994; editor Solid State Electronics, 1993-98. J.N. Tata fellow, 1947-51. Fellow IEEE; mem. Electrochem. Soc., Am. Standards Assn., Sigma Xi, Eta Kappa Nu, Pi Mu Epsilon, Phi Kappa Pi. Address: 2716 Cita Ave Escondido CA 92029-5816 Fax: (760) 746-0660. E-mail: ghandhi@ieee.org.

GHARIB, HOSSEIN, medical educator; b. Tehran, Feb. 2, 1940; came to U.S., 1958; s. Mohammad and Zahra Gharib; m. Zahra Gharib, Feb. 4, 1948; children: Mohammad, Yasamin, Mahmood. BS, Ohio State U., 1962; MD, U. Mich., 1966. Intern Phila. Gen. Hosp., 1966-67; resident Mayo Clinic, Rochester, Minn., 1967-69, fellow, 1969-72; prof. Mayo Med. Sch., Rochester, 1994—. Fellow ACP, Am. Coll. Endocrinology (trustee 1999-2000, 2003—); mem. AMA, Am. Assn. Clin. Endocrinologists (bd. dirs., v.p. 2000-01, pres, 2002), Endocrine Soc., Am. Thyroid Assn. (Paul Starr award 2002), Iranian Acad. Med. Sci. (hon.), Romanian Endocrine Soc., Assn. Medici Endocrinology. Office: Mayo Clinic Rochester MN 55905-0001 E-mail: gharib.hossein@mayo.edu.

GHARIB, SUSIE, television newscaster; b. N.Y.C., Nov. 27, 1950; d. Ali and Homa (Razzaghmanesh) G.; m. Fereydoun Nazem, Jan. 20, 1973; children: Alexander, Taraneh. BA magna cum laude, Case Western Res. U., 1972; M in Internat. Affairs, Columbia U., 1974. Reporter Cleve. Plain Dealer, 1972-73; assoc. editor Fortune Mag., N.Y.C., 1974-83; anchor, reporter Bus. Times/ESPN, N.Y.C., 1983-85; bus. reporter ABC News, N.Y.C., 1986-87; anchor Fin. News Network, N.Y.C., 1989-90, CNBC Network, Ft. Lee, N.J., 1993-98, Nightly Bus. Report, N.Y.C., 1998—. Moderator/host Xerox Corp., Stanford, Conn., 1989-95, KPMG Peat Marwick, N.Y.C., 1992-95; cons. Adam Smith's Money World/PBS, N.Y.C., 1987. Bd. dirs. First Fortis, Inc., 1991-2000, Ice Theatre of N.Y., 1988-90. Mem. Fgn. Policy Assn., N.Y. Fin. Writers Assn., Overseas Press Club, Econ. Club N.Y., Phi Beta Kappa, Sigma Delta Chi. Democrat. Avocations: figure skating, tennis, classical piano. Home: 44 E 73rd St New York NY 10021-4173

GHAUSI, MOHAMMED SHUAIB, electrical engineering educator, university dean; b. Kabul, Afghanistan, Feb. 16, 1930; came to U.S., 1951, naturalized, 1963; s. Mohammed Omar and Homaira G.; m. Marilyn Buchwold, June 12, 1961; children: Nadjya, Simine. BS summa cum laude, U. Calif., Berkeley, 1956, MS, 1957, PhD, 1960. Prof. elec. engring. NYU, 1960-72; head elec. scis. sect. NSF, Washington, 1972-74; prof., chmn. elec. engring. dept. Wayne State U., Detroit, 1974-77; John F. Dodge prof. Oakland U., Rochester, Mich., 1978-83, dean Sch. Engring. and Computer Sci., 1978-83; dean Coll. Engring., U. Calif., Davis, 1983-96, interim vice chancellor rsch., vice provost, dean grad., 1996-97. Mem. adv. panel NSF, 1989. Author, co-author: Principles and Design of Linear Active Circuits, 1965, Introduction to Distributed-Parameter Networks, 1968, Electronic Circuits, 1971, Modern Filter Design: Active RC and Switched Capacitor, 1981, Electronic Devices and Circuits: Discrete and Integrated, 1985, Design of Analog Filters, 1990, Introduction to Electronic Circuit Design, 2003, also numerous articles.; cons. editor Van Nostrand Rinehold Pub. Co., 1968-71. Mem. disting. alumni rev. panel Elec. Engring. and Computer Sci. programs U. Calif., Berkeley, 1973; mem. external bd. visitors U. Pa., 1974. Recipient Outstanding Alumnus award in Elec. Engring. and Computer Sci., U. Calif., 1998. Fellow IEEE (chmn. edn. medal com. 1990-92, Centennial medal, Alexander von Humboldt prize 1983, circuits and systems soc. edn. award); mem. Circuits and System Soc. (v.p. 1970-72, pres. 1976), N.Y. Acad. Scis., Engring. Soc. Detroit, Sigma Xi, Phi Beta Kappa, Tau Beta Pi, Eta Kappa Nu. Office: U Calif Office of Dean Coll Engring Davis CA 95616 E-mail: msghausi@uc.davis.edu.

GHAYOUR, KAVEH, aeronautical engineer; b. Tehran, Tehran, Iran, Jan. 1, 1968; s. Hossein Ghayour and Mahin Zehtab Tabrizi; m. Mahsa Memarzadeh, Aug. 26, 1973; 1 child, Mina Caroline. PhD, Old Dominion U., Norfolk, VA, 1990—99. Author: (research in computational fluid dynamics) Optimal Control of Aeroacoustic Noise Generated by Cylinder Vortex Interaction. Recipient WS Atkinz Prize, Atkinz Cons. Firm, 1993. Mem.: AIAA. Office: Rice U 6100 Main St Houston TX 77005 Personal E-mail: kghayour@yahoo.com. E-mail: kaveh@rice.edu.

GHAZANFAR, SHAIKH MOHAMMED, economics educator, researcher, author; b. Jullundar, Brit. India, Apr. 1, 1937; came to U.S., 1958; s. Shaikh Mehboob and Farhat (Elahi) Bakhsh; m. Rukhsana Sharif, Aug. 16, 1965; children: Farah, Asif, Kashif. BA with honors, Wash. State U., 1962, MA, 1964, PhD in Econs., 1968. Instr. econs. Wash. State U., Pullman, 1962-64, rsch. economist, 1964, teaching asst., 1965-67, instr., 1967-68; asst. prof. U. Idaho, Moscow, 1968-72, assoc. prof., 1972-77, prof., 1977—2002, head dept., 1979-81; head, 1993—2001; coord. internat. studies program U. Idaho, Moscow, 1989—93, prof. emeritus, 2002—. Adj. faculty U. Idaho, 2002-03; vis. prof. U. Punjab, Lahore, Pakistan, fall 1974-75, U. Md., College Park, spring 1974-75, King Abdulaziz U., Jeddah, Saudi Arabia, 1983-866; mem. budget forecast Idaho Legis., 1974-93. Author: Medieval Islamic Economic Thought: Filling the Great Gap in European Economics, 2003; contbr. more than 50 articles to profl. jours., 150 publ. for conf. presentations. Mem. Latah County Task Force on Human Rights, 1988-92. Mem. Nat. Tax. Assn., Mid.-Ea. Studies Assn., Amnesty Internat., History of Econs. Soc. Office: U Idaho Dept Econs Moscow ID 83843

GHAZARBEKIAN, SAHAK, retired civil servant, consultant; b. Meshed, Iran, Mar. 1, 1928; came to U.S., 1964; s. Vartan Ghazarbekian and Satenik Abrahamian; m. Bonnie J. Bakke (dec. Nov. 1988); m. Sonia Etmekjian. BS in Physics, U. Tehran, 1952; BA in Pub. Adminstrn., Am. U., Beirut, 1956; grad. diploma PA, Internat. Inst. Social Studies, The Hague, The Netherlands, 1962; postgrad., Princeton U., 1965. Adminstrv. officer U.S. Ops. Mission, Tehran, 1952-54; assoc. pub. adminstrn. advisor Joint U.S./Iran Govt., Tehran, 1954-58; dep. dir. Plan Orgn. Iran, Tehran, 1958-63, chief mgmt. bur., 1963-65; dir. gen. Office of Prime Min., Tehran, 1965-69; chief pub. adminstrn. sect. UN Econ. and Social Commn. for Asia and the Pacific, Bangkok, 1969-74, chief projects ops. office, 1974-77. Chief program coord. and monitoring office UN Asia and Pacific Commn., Bangkok, 1977-80; chief joint planning sect. UN Hdqs., N.Y.C., 1980-88; cons. in field, N.Y.C., 1988—. Contbr. articles to profl. jours. Mem. Ea. Regional Orgn. for Pub. Adminstrn., Manila, 1968-80. Recipient Svc. Citation of Distinction, Shah of Iran, 1967, 68, Order of Homayoun, Shah of Iran, 1968; Parvin fellow Woodrow Wilson Sch., Princeton U., 1964-65. Avocations: travel, history study, lecturing, translating. Home: 5 Archway Pl Forest Hills Flushing NY 11375-5255

GHERARDI, GHERARDO JOSEPH, pathologist; b. Lucca, Italy, July 1, 1921; came to U.S., 1933; s. Mario E. and Maria (Gilli) G.; m. Celeste Tranfaglia, Sept. 16, 1957; children: Roberta, Ronald, Mark, Peter. BA, Princeton U., 1942; MD, Columbia U., 1945. Diplomate Am. Bd. Pathology. Pathologist in charge, assoc. prof. pathology Tufts N.E. Med. Ctr., Boston, 1954-70; assoc. prof. pathology Tufts Med. Sch., 1954-70; sr. pathologist Farmingham (Mass.) Union Hosp., 1970-93; assoc. prof. pathology Boston U. Sch. Medicine, 1970—. Capt. AUS, 1945-48. Fellow Coll. Am. Pathologists; mem. N.E. Soc. Pathologists (past pres.).

GHERTY, JOHN E. food products and agricultural products company executive; b. 1944; married. BBA, U. Wis., 1965, JD, 1968, MA, 1970. Lawyer corp. law dept. Land O' Lakes Inc., Arden Hills, Minn., 1970-79, asst. to pres., 1979-81, group v.p., 1981-89, pres., CEO, 1989—. Bd. dirs. CF Industries, Long Grove, Ill., Minn. Life Ins., St. Paul. Bd. dirs. Grad. Inst. Coop. Leadership, Greater Twin Cities United Way. Mem.: 4-H Found. (bd. dirs.), Minn. Bus. Partnership (bd. dirs.), Nat. Coun. Farmer Coops. (bd. dirs., chmn.). Office: Land O'Lakes PO Box 64101 Saint Paul MN 55164-0101 also: 4001 Lexington Ave N Saint Paul MN 55126-2934

GHETTI, BERNARDINO FRANCESCO, neuropathologist, neurobiology researcher; b. Pisa, Italy, Mar. 28, 1941; s. Getulio and Iris (Mugnetti) G.; m. Caterina Genovese, Oct. 8, 1966; children— Chiara, Simone. MD cum laude, U. Pisa, 1966, specialist in mental and nervous diseases, 1969. Lic. physician, Italy; cert. Edn. Council for Fgn. Med. Grads.; diplomate Am. Bd. Pathology. Postdoctoral fellow U. Pisa, 1966-70; research fellow in neuropathology Albert Einstein Coll. Medicine, Bronx, N.Y., 1970-73, resident, clin. fellow in pathology, 1973-75, resident in neuropathology, 1975-76; asst. prof. pathology Ind. U., Indpls., 1976-77, asst. prof. pathology and psychiatry, 1977-78, assoc. prof. pathology and psychiatry, 1978-83, prof. pathology and psychiatry, 1983—91, assoc. dir. program in med. neurobiology, 1983—2000, assoc. dir. divsn. neuropathology, 1989-93, prof. pathology, psychiatry, med. and molecular genetics, 1991-97, dir. Alzheimer Disease Ctr., 1991—, dir. divsn. neuropathology, 1993—, Disting. prof. pathology and lab. medicine, psychiatry, med. and molecular genetics, neurology, 1997—. Mem. Nat. Inst. Neurol. Disorders and Stroke rev. com. NIH, 1985-89; mem. NIH Reviewers Res., 1989-93. Contbr. articles and abstracts to profl. jours. Mem. Alzheimer's disease rsch. scientific rev. com. Am. Health Assistance Found., 1998—. Recipient Potamkin Prize, 1999. Mem. Internat. Soc. Neuropathology (v.p. 2000-03), Am. Acad. Neurology, Am. Neurol. Assn., Am. Assn. Neuropathologists (pres. 1996-97), Soc. Neurosci., Assn. Research in Nervous and Mental Diseases, Internat. Brain Research Orgn., Am. Soc. Cell Biology, Italian Soc. Psychiatry, Italian Soc. Neurology, Sigma Xi Roman Catholic. Home: 1124 Frederick Dr S Indianapolis IN 46260-3421 Office: Ind U 635 Barnhill Dr Rm 138 Indianapolis IN 46202-5126 E-mail: bghetti@inpui.edu.

GHEZ, ANDREA MIA, astronomy and physics educator; b. N.Y.C., June 16, 1965; d. Gilbert and Susanne (Gayton) G.; m. Tom La Tourette, May 1, 1993; 1 child, Evan LaTourette-Ghez. BS, MIT, 1987; MS, Calif. Inst. Tech., 1989, PhD, 1993. Hubble postdoctoral fellow U. Ariz., Tucson, 1992-93; vis. rsch. scholar Inst. Astronomy, Cambridge, England, 1994; asst. prof. physics and astronomy UCLA, 1994-97, assoc. prof. physics and astronomy, 1997—. Recipient Young Investigator award NSF, 1994, Fullam Dudley award, 1995; fellow Pacific Telesis, 1991, Sloan fellow, 1996, Packard fellow, 1996, Pierce prize, 1998, Maria Goeppert-Meyer award, Am. Phys. Soc., 1999. Mem. Am. Astron. Soc., AAUW (Anne Jump Cannon award 1994), Phi Beta Kappa. Achievements include discovery of formation of young low mass stars in multiple star systems, production of the first diffraction-limited image with the keck 10-m telescope (the largest telescope in the world), and measurement of stellar motions which indicate the presence of a supermassive black hole at the center of our own galaxy. Home: 224 Barlock Ave Los Angeles CA 90049 Office: UCLA Dept Astronomy 405 Hilgard Ave Los Angeles CA 90095-1562

GHIARDI, JAMES DOMENIC, lawyer, educator; b. Gwinn, Mich., Nov. 10, 1918; s. John B. and Margaret M. (Trosello) G.; m. Phyllis A. Lindmeier, Sept. 5, 1945; children— Catherine, Jeanne, Mary. PhB, Marquette U., 1940, LLB, 1942, JD, 1968. Bar: Wis. bar 1942. Prof. law Marquette U. Law Sch., Milw., 1946-89, prof. law emeritus, 1990—; research dir. Def. Research Inst., Milw., 1962-72; of counsel firm Kluwin, Dunphy, Hankin & McNulty, Milw., 1972-87. Author: Personal Injury Damages, Wisconsin, 1964, Punitive Damages, Vol. I, 1981, Vol. II, 1985; contbr. articles to profl. jours. Served to capt. Med. Adminstrv. Br. U.S. Army, 1942-45. Recipient award for teaching excellence Marquette U. Faculty, 1971, Edward A. Uhrig Found., 1971, Alumni of Yr. award Marquette U. Law Sch., 1971, Charles L. Goldberg award for outstanding pub. svc. Wis. Law Found., 1986, Charles C. Pinckney award for legal scholarship and svc. to the legal profession N.Y. Def. Bar Assn., 1986. Fellow Am. Bar Found.; mem. ABA (mem. ho. of dels. 1967-80, Disting. Prof. Torts and Ins. Law award Torts and Ins. Practice sect. 1989), Milw. Bar Assn. (Lifetime Achievement award 1993), State Bar Wis. (gov., mem. exec. com. 1962-72, pres. 1970-71), Am. Law Ins., Wis. Bar Found., Am. Legion. Office: Sensenbrenner Hall Marquette U Law Sch PO Box 1881 Milwaukee WI 53201-1881

GHIGNA, CHARLES, poet; m. Debra Ghigna; children: Chip, Julie. Author numerous poems. Recipient Book-of-the-Month Club selection, Scholastic Sch. Book Club selection, Parents' Choice Book award, Helen Keller Lit. award, Ala. Libr. Assn. Book award.

GHIL, MICHAEL, atmospheric scientist, geophysicist; b. Budapest, Hungary, June 10, 1944; s. Louis and Ilona V. (Dobo) Cernat; m. Michèle J. Denizot, July 8, 1982; children: Emmanuel A., Mirella J. BSc cum laude, Technion-Israel Inst. Tech., Haifa, Israel, 1966, MSc in Mech. Engring., 1971; MS, NYU, 1973, PhD in Math., 1975. Rsch. asst. to instr. Technion-Israel Inst. Tech., Haifa, 1966-71; rsch. assoc. NASA Goddard Inst. Space Studies, N.Y.C., 1975-76; rsch. asst. prof. math. Courant Inst. Math. Scis., N.Y.C., 1976-79, rsch. assoc. prof. atmos. sci., 1979-82, rsch. prof., 1982-86; prof. atmos. sci. and geophysics UCLA, 1985—. Chmn. dept. atmospheric scis., UCLA, 1988-92; dir. Climate Dynamics Ctr., UCLA, 1986-92, Inst. Geophys. Planet Phys. UCLA, 1992—; disting. vis. scientist Jet Propulsion Lab, Calif. Inst. Tech./NASA, Pasadena, Calif., 1988—; Condorcet chair Ecole Normale Supérieure, Paris, 1995; Elf-Aquitaine/CNRS chair Acad. Scis., Paris, 1996, Collège de France, Paris, 1997. Author: Topics in GFD: Atmospheric Dynamics, Dynamo Theory and Climate Dynamics, 1987; editor: Turbulence and Predictability in Geophysical Fluid Dynamics and Climate Dynamics, 1985, Dynamic Meteorology: Data Assimilation Methods, 1981, Natural Climate Variability on Decade-to-Century Time Scales, 1995, Data Assimilation in Meteorology and Oceanography: Theory and Practice, 1997. Mem. adv. bd. Calif. Space Inst., San Diego, 1986-90; chmn. sci. adv. coun. Climate Sys. Modeling Program, Boulder, Colo., 1988—; bd. dirs. New Sun Found. Geneva, 1994-99, bd. govs. Weizmann Inst. Sci. Rehovot, Israel, 1995-2000. Fellow Am. Meteorol. Soc. (profl. com. 1989-92), Am. Geophys. Union, mem. Nat. Rsch. Coun. (climate rsch. com. 1989-98), Soc. for Indsl. and Applied Math., Roy Astron. Soc. (assoc., hon.), Acad. Europaea (fgn.), Sigma Xi. Democrat. Jewish. Avocations: hiking, climbing, squash, skiing, swimming, arts, literature, music, languages. Office: UCLA Inst Geophys Planet Phys 405 Hilgard Ave Los Angeles CA 90095-9000

GHILARDUCCI, M. TERESA, economist, educator; b. Roseville, Calif., July 22, 1957; d. Harry Enrico and Marion (Phillips) G.; m. William Andrew O'Rourke, July 9, 1986; 1 child, Joseph Ghilarducci O'Rourke. BA, U. Calif., Berkeley, 1978, PhD, 1984. Rsch. asst. Inst. Indsl. Rels., Berkeley, 1982-84; prof. econs. U. Notre Dame, Ind., 1984—. Adv. bd. Pension Benefit Guaranty Corp., Washington, 1995-2002; cons. in field. Author: Labor's Capital: The Economics and Politics of Private Pensions, 1992, Portable Pensions for Casual Labor Markets, 1995. Trustee Ind. Pub. Employees Retirement Fund, Indpls., 1997-2002. Mem. Am. Econs. Assn. Democrat. Roman Catholic. Avocation: reading. Office: U Notre Dame Dept Econs Notre Dame IN 46556 E-mail: ghilarducci.1@nd.edu.

GHIORSE, WILLIAM CUSHING, microbiology educator, editor; b. Quincy, Mass., Dec. 3, 1940; s. John Thaxter and Ruth Alice (Winkler) G.; m. Rosemary Joyce Green (div. 1981); children: Christopher, Charlotte; m. Margaret Anne Searle, June 4, 1988. BA, U. Vt., 1963; MS, Rensselaer Polytech. U., 1969, PhD, 1973. Electron microscopist N.Y. State Dept. Health, Albany, 1964-73; postdoctoral rschr. Cornell U., Ithaca, N.Y., 1973-76, asst. prof., 1978-84, assoc. prof., 1984-90, prof., 1990—; Alexander Humboldt fellow Kiel (Germany) U., 1976-78. Mem. adv. bd. plant biotech. dept. Rutgers U., 1992-2000; mem. adv. bd. astrobiology NASA, 2000-02. Co-editor-in-chief Geomicrobiology Jour., 1995—; contbr. articles to profl. jours. including Applied and Environ. Microbiology, Jour. Bacteriology, Geomicrobiology, among others. Mem. AAAS, Am. Soc. Microbiology, Am. Geophys. Union, Am. Acad. Microbiology. Avocations: astronomy, gardening, geology. Office: Cornell U Dept Microbiology Wing Hall Ithaca NY 14853 E-mail: wcg1@cornell.edu.

GHISELIN, BREWSTER, author, English language educator emeritus; b. Webster Groves, Mo., June 13, 1903; s. Horace and Eleanor (Weeks) G.; m. Olive F. Franks, June 7, 1929; children: Jon Brewster, Michael Tenant. AB, UCLA, 1927; MA, U. Calif.-Berkeley, 1928, student, 1931-33, Oxford U., Eng., 1928-29; LHD, U. Utah, 1994. Asst. in English U. Calif., Berkeley, 1931-33; instr. English U. Utah, 1929-31, 34-38, lectr., 1938-39, asst. prof., 1939-46, assoc. prof., 1946-50, prof., 1950-71, prof. emeritus, 1971, Disting. Rsch. prof., 1967-68. Dir. Writers' Conf., 1947-66; poetry editor Rocky Mt. Rev., 1937-46; assoc. editor Western Rev., 1946-49; lectr. creativity, cons. Inst. Personality Assessment and Research, U. Calif., Berkeley, 1957-58; editorial adv. bd. Concerning Poetry, 1968— Author: Against the Circle, 1946, The Creative Process, 1952, new paperback edit., 1985, 95, The Nets, 1955, Writing, 1959, Country of the Minotaur, 1970, (with others) The Form Discovered: Essays on the Achievement of Andrew Lytle, 1973, Light, 1978, Windrose: Poems, 1929-1979, 1980, (with others) Contemporary Authors, 1989; (poems) Flame, 1991. Bd. advisors Silver Mountain Found. Ford Found. fellow, 1952-53; recipient award Nat. Inst. Arts and Letters, 1970; Blumenthal-Leviton-Blonder prize Poetry mag., 1973; Levinson prize, 1978; William Carlos Williams award Poetry Soc. Am., 1981; Gov.'s award for arts Utah Arts Council, 1982; LHD hc, U of Utah, 1994. Mem. MLA, Utah Acad. Scis., Arts and Letters (Charles Redd award), Phi Beta Kappa, Phi Kappa Phi. Home: 1115 Jefferson Way Laguna Beach CA 92651-3022 *To be human is to be a user of the basic resources of society, those modes and forms of vision and action that by determining the character and quality of men's experience shape everything men do and are.*

GHORMLEY, LUTHER WAYNE, surgeon; b. Abilene, Texas, 1926; MD, U. Tenn. Med. Sch., Memphis, 1947. Diplomate Am. Bd. Surgery. Intern Mpls. Gen. Hosp., 1948-49; resident St. Louis City Hosp., 1949-50, Okla. City VA Hosp., 1950-53; pvt. practice Osler Clinic, Blackwell, Okla., 1953—. Hosp. appt. Blackwell, Okla. Regional Med. Ctr. Fellow Internat. Coll. Surgeons; mem. AMA; Alpha Omega Alpha. Office: Osler Clinic 115 W Bridge Ave Blackwell OK 74631-2800

GHOSH, ALOK, pharmaceutical executive; s. Benoy and Maya Ghosh; m. Alpana Ghosh; 1 child, Soham. MPharm, Jadavpur U., Calcutta, India, 1978. Officer develop. Bengal Immunity, Calcutta, India, 1978—84; mgr. formulation develop. Lupin Lab. Ltd., Bombay, 1984—88; mgr., Quality Assurance Astra AB, Bangalore, India, 1988—93; dir. corp. quality assurance Ranbaxy Lab Ltd., New Delhi, 1993—2001; v.p. ops. Ronbaxy Phar. Inc., North Brunswick, NJ, 2001—. Office: Ranbaxy Pharm Inc 1385 Livingston Ave North Brunswick NJ 08902 E-mail: alok.ghosh@ranbaxy.com.

GHOSH, ASISH, control engineer; b. Calcutta, India, Sept. 2, 1935; came to U.S., 1978; s. Sudhangsu Kumar and Lotika (Roy) G.; m. Aparna, Sept. 20, 1968; children: Annapurna, Ashapurna. BSc, Delhi (India) U., 1954; diploma in advanced studies, Cambridge (Eng.) U., 1968. Chartered engr., U. K. Rsch. scientist Imperial Chem. Industries, Runcorn, Eng., 1968-74; sys. engr. Foxboro Can. Inc., Montreal, Que., 1974-80; project engr. Foxboro (Mass.) Co., 1980-82, sr. engr., 1982-87, prin. engr., 1987-88, cons., 1989-94, product mgr., 1994-95; v.p. ARC Adv. Group, Dedham, Mass., 1995—; vice chmn. World Batch Forum, 1999—2000, trustee, 2002—. Co-author: Batch Process Automation, 1987; also articles. Mem. Instrument Soc. Am. (life sr.), Inst. Elec. Engrs. (U.K.). Achievements include pioneering work in automating fluid batch manufacturing processes. Home: 3 Gannett Way Hopedale MA 01747 Office: ARC Adv Group Three Allied Dr Dedham MA 02026 E-mail: ghosh.a@comcast.net.

GHOSH, BHASKAR KUMAR, statistics educator, researcher; b. Dibrugarh, India, Feb. 10, 1936; came to U.S., 1961; s. Saroj Kumar and Usha Rani (Bose) G.; m. Hedwig Graf, 1960; children: Monica, Anita, Rebecca. BSc, Calcutta U., 1955; PhD, London U., 1959. Statistician Atomic Power Constrn., London, 1959-60; asst. prof. U. London, 1960-61, Lehigh U., Bethlehem, Pa., 1961-63, assoc. prof., 1963-68, prof., 1968—. Vis. prof. MIT, Cambridge, Mass., 1968, Va. Tech., Blacksburg, 1978-80, U. Munster, Germany, 1986-87. Author: Sequential Tests of Statistical Hypotheses, 1970; editor: Handbook of Sequential Analysis, 1991; editor: Sequential Analysis, 1982-95. Recipient U.S. Sr. Rsch. Scientist award Alexander von Humboldt Found., 1986-87, 92. Fellow Royal Statis. Soc., Inst. Math. Statistics. Home: 1440 E University Ave Bethlehem PA 18015-4718 Office: Lehigh U Dept Math 14 E Packer Ave Bethlehem PA 18015-3175

GHOSH, NARENDRA NATH, research scientist; b. Bankura, West- Bengal, India, Apr. 8, 1970; s. Nanda Dulal and Purnima Ghosh; m. Swayang Probha Biswas, Mar. 8, 1980. MSc in Chemistry, Indian Inst. Tech., Kharagpur, 1992—94, PhD in Chemistry, 1998. Rsch. scholar Indian Inst. Tech., Kharagpur, India, 1994—98; postdoctoral rschr. U. Del., Newark, 1998—2000; faculty dept. chemistry Birla Inst. Tech. and Sci., Pilani, India, 2000—02; postdoctoral rschr. U. Tenn., Knoxville, 2002—. Chair Conf. on Materials for the New Millennium, India, 2000. Achievements include research in nanomaterials, mesoporous solids, polymer and inorganic chemistry. Home: 1611 Laurel Ave Knoxville TN 37916 Office: Dept Chemistry Circle Dr Knoxville TN 37996 Personal E-mail: naren70@yahoo.com. E-mail: ghosh@novell.chem.utk.edu.

GHOSH, PARTHA S. management consultant; b. Calcutta, W. Bengal, India, May 8, 1951; s. Radha Kishore and Phul Rani (Dey) G.; m. Akiko Tamura, Sept. 24, 1980; children: Arun, Pradeep. BS in Chem. Engring., Indian Inst. Technology, Kharagpur, India, 1971; MS in Chem. Engring., MIT, 1976, MS in Bus. Adminstrn., 1977. Devel. engr. Union Carbide, Calcutta, 1971-74; assoc. McKinsey & Co., N.Y., 1977-82, prin., 1983-89; CEO Partha S. Ghosh & Assocs., Tokyo and Boston, 1989—; sr. advisor Monitor Group. Chmn. Global Online, Tokyo, 1994-96, Creavision, Calcutta, 1997— Contbr. numerous articles to profl. jours. and newspapers; spkr. in field. Internat. fellow Rotary Club, Evanston, Ill., 1975. Mem. AICE, Am. Chem. Soc. Avocations: social work, cmty. svc. Home: 110 Mattison Dr Concord MA 01742-4146 E-mail: ParthaSG@aol.com.

GHOSH, RAJA, engineering educator; b. Calcutta, West Bengal, India, Oct. 8, 1966; s. Ranendra Nath and Rupali G.; m. Sutapa Dutta, Apr. 20, 1999. BS, Jadavpur U., Calcutta, 1990; MTech, 1992; DPhil, U. Oxford, 1999. R&D exec. SunPharma, Baroda, India, 1992-93; inst. fellow Indian Inst. Tech. Delhi, New Delhi, 1993-94; rsch. fellow Jadavpur U., Calcutta, 1994-95; dept. lectr. U. Oxford, 1998—2002; asst. prof. McMaster U., Hamilton, Canada, 2002—. Author: Protein Bioseparation Using Ultrafiltration: Theory, Applications and New Developments, 2003; reviewer Jour. Membrane Sci., Biotech. and Bioengring., Chem. Engring. Sci., Jour. Chromatography, others; contbr. articles to profl. jours. Dept. Biotechnology schlar Govt. of India, 1990-92, Commonwealht scholar Assn. Commonwealth Univs., 1995-98. Mem. AIChE. Achievements include development of of carrier phase ultrafiltration; pulsed injection ultrafiltration and supported multi-liquid membrane. Avocation: history of science and technology. Office: McMaster U Dept Chem Engring 1280 Main St W Hamilton ON Canada L8S 4L7 E-mail: rghosh@mcmaster.ca.

GHOSH, SAMBHUNATH (SAM GHOSH), civil engineering educator, environmental engineer; BS, U. Calcutta; MS, U. Ill.; PhD, Ga. Inst. Tech. Engr. Wiedeman & Singleton, Atlanta, 1963—65; mgr. bioengring. rsch. Gas Technology Inst., Chgo., 1971—85; prof. civil engring. U. Utah, Salt Lake City, 1985—2000; prof. civil, agrl. and geol. engring. N.Mex State U., Las Cruces, 2000—01; pres. EnviroEnergetics, 1988—. Recipient Ill. Energy award, 1985, Utah Gov.'s award for energy innovation, 1986, John Ericsson award and Gold medal in Renewable Energy U.S. Dept. Energy, 1994, George Bradley Gascoigne medal, Water Environment Fedn., 1996, Thomas R. Camp medal, Water Environment Fedn., Alexandria, Va., 2001. Home: 1281 E Federal Heights Dr Salt Lake City UT 84103-4325 E-mail: ghoshsambhunath@hotmail.com.

GHOSH, SANJIB KUMAR, retired science educator, consultant; b. Calcutta, India, Sept. 9, 1925; arrived in U.S., 1960; s. Sasanka Kumar and Suniti Bala Ghosh; m. Tapati Bose, Aug. 16, 1951; children: Sanjoy (Ron), Sujoy (Raja). BSc with honors, Calcutta U., 1945; degree in photogrammetric engring., Internat. Tng. Ctr., Delft, The Netherlands, 1957; PhD, Ohio State U., 1964. Cert. photogrammetrist Am. Soc. Photogrammetry and Remote Sensing. Surveyor Survey of India, 1946—60; from asst. instr. to assoc. prof. Ohio State U., Columbus, 1960—80; prof. Laval U., Canada, 1980—91; prof. emeritus Laval U. and Ohio State U., 1992—. Vis. prof., Japan, Nigeria, Brazil, India, 1975—90; cons. UN, N.Y.C., 1981—. Author: 5 books; contbr. chapters to books; inventor in field. Named finalist, Can. Award of Excellence, invention category, 1986; recipient cert. Commendation, Ohio Ho. of Reps., 1978; fellow, UN, 1956—57; grantee, Am. Soc. Photogrammetry and Remote Sensing, 1970—95. Fellow: Am. Congress on Surveying and Mapping (life), Geog. Soc. India (life); mem.: Internat. Soc. Photogrammetry and Remote Sensing (various offices), Am. Soc. Photogrammmetry and Remote Sensing (various offices). Achievements include patents for stereo-radiographic brain surgery outfit; invention of new method of determining latitude and azimuth with any unknown star; calibration of lunar orbiter IV system for NASA. Avocations: photography, reading. Home: 6344 Thorncrest Dr Galloway OH 43119-8824 Fax: 614-870-8538. E-mail: ghosh@copper.net.

GHOSH, SATYENDRA KUMAR, structural engineer, educator; b. Berhampore, W. Bengal, India, Sept. 17, 1945; came to U.S., 1975; s. Santosh Kumar and Sadhana (Bose) G.; m. Sumita Majumdar, July 4, 1973; children: Elka, Sourish. BE, U. Calcutta, India, 1966; MA in Sci., U. Waterloo, (Ont., Can.), 1969, PhD, 1972. Structural engr. Kuljian Corp., Calcutta, India, 1966-67; rsch. and teaching asst. U. Waterloo, 1967-69; 70-72, postdoctoral fellow, 1973, rsch. assoc., 1973, adj. prof., 1973-74; rsch. and teaching asst. U. Pitts., 1969-70; structural engr. Portland Cement Assn., Skokie, Ill., 1974-75, sr. structural engr., 1975-80, prin. structural engr., 1980-83, program mgr. engineered structures, 1988; dir. engineered structures and codes, 1989-98; pres. S.K. Ghosh Assocs., Inc., Northbrook, Ill., 1998—; assoc. prof. civil engring. U. Ill.-Chgo., 1984-87, adj. prof. of civil engring., 1988—; cons. Portland Cement Assn., Skokie, Ill., 1984-87; ptnr. Elan Assocs., Waterloo, 1972-73; vis. lectr. dept. Materials Engring. U. Ill., Chgo., 1980, 82, 83; prin. FIntel Ghosh Inc., Chgo., 1984-87. Treas. Ill. chpt. Assn. of Indians in Am., 1981-82, v.p., 1983-84. Recipient U. Calcutta Gold medal, 1966. Fellow Inst. of Engrs. India (Engring. Congress prize 1982), Am. Concrete Inst. (Structural Rsch. award 1992), Precast/Prestressed Concrete Inst. (Charles Zollman award 1998); mem. ASCE, Earthquake Engring. Rsch. Inst. (pres. Ill. chpt. 1998—). Contbr. articles in field to profl. jours. Home: 1811 E Cree Ln Mount Prospect IL 60056-1819 Office: SK Ghosh Assocs Inc 1856 Walters Ave Northbrook IL 60062

GHOSH, SUJIT KUMAR, statistics educator, researcher; b. Barrackpore, India, Jan. 8, 1970; came to the U.S., 1993; s. Ajit Kumar and Sabita Ghosh; m. Swagata Sarkar, June 27, 1997. B of Stats. with honors, Indian Statis. Inst., Calcutta, 1990, M of Stats., 1992; PhD, U. Conn., 1996. Assoc. prof. N.C. State U., Raleigh, 1996—. Cons. Ctr. for Real Estate, U. Conn., Storrs, 1995. Contbr. articles to profl. jours. Recipient Travel award NSF, 1995, 2000, grant NSF, 1998-99, 2000—. Mem. Am. Statis. Assn., Internat. Statis. Assn., Cmty. of Sci., Internat. Soc. Bayesian Analysis, Sigma Xi (v.p. N.C. chpt.), Office: NC State Univ 2501 Founders Dr Raleigh NC 27695-8203 Fax: 919-515-1169. E-mail: sujitg@netzero.net., sghosh@stat.ncsu.edu.

GHOSHAL, NANI GOPAL, veterinarian, educator; b. Dacca, India, Dec. 1, 1934; arrived in U.S., 1963; s. Priya Kanta and Kiron Bala (Thakurta) Ghoshal; m. Chhanda Banerjee, Jan. 24, 1971; 1 child, Nupur. G.V.Sc.; B.V.C., India, 1955; DTVM, U. Edinburgh, 1961; D in Med. Vet., Tieraertzliche Hochschule Hannover, Fed. Republic Germany, 1962; PhD, Iowa State U., 1966. Vet. asst. surgeon West Bengal State Govt., India, 1955-56; instr. Bengal Vet. Coll., U. Calcutta, 1955-56; rsch. asst. M.P. Govt. Coll. Vet. Sci. and Animal Husbandry, Mhow, India, 1956-59; rsch. officer ICAR, India, 1963; instr. Iowa State U., Ames, 1963-66, asst. prof., 1967-70, assoc. prof., 1970-74, prof. vet. gross anatomy, 1974—. Chmn. Internat. Vet. Medicine Com., 1967—79; cons. Morocco-Minn. project U. Minn. Internat. Agrl. Programs, AID, 1983—88; adj. prof. Inst. Agronomique et Veterinaire, Hassan II, Rabat, Morocco, 1984—88. Co-author, editor: book Getty's Anatomy of Domestic Animals, 5th edit., 1975; author (with Tankred Koch, Peter Popesko): Venous Drainage of Domestic Animals, 1981; contbr. chapters to books, articles to profl. jours. Recipient German Acad. Exch. Svc. award, Govt. Fed. Republic of Germany, Bonn, 1961—62, Norden Disting. Tchr. award, 1978, Dr. William O. Reece award for Outstanding Advising, Coll. Vet. Medicine, 1997; various scholarships and grants. Fellow: Royal Zool. Soc. Scotland (life); mem.: AAAS, Iowa Vet. Med. Assn., N.Y. Acad. Scis., Pan Am. Assn. Anatomy, Am. Assn. Anatomists, Am. Assn. Vet. Anatomists, World Assn. Vet. Anatomists, Sigma Xi, Phi Kappa Phi, Gamma Sigma Delta, Phi Zeta. Home: 1310 Glendale Ave Ames IA 50010-5526 Office: Iowa State U Coll Vet Medicine 2086 Dept Biomed Scis Ames IA 50011-1250 E-mail: nghoshal@iastate.edu.

GHRIST, JOHN RUSSELL, audio/visual technician; b. Hammond, Ind., Feb. 6, 1949; s. Glenn H. and Marjorie (Fancher) G.; divorced; children: Timothy, Thomas, Peter, James, Bonnie. BS, Ind. U., 1997. Lic. radiotelephone operator, amateur radio. Religious music host WYCA, Hammond, Ind., 1967-71; news reporter WJOB, Hammond, 1971-73; music show host WFLM, Crown Point, Ind., 1979-85, WTAS, Beecher, Ill., 1982-86; radio traffic reporter WLTH, Gary, Ind., 1985-88, Shadow Traffic Network (WLS/WMAQ), Chgo., 1985-87; audio-visual technician ET IV Ill. Dept. Transp., Schaumburg, 1985—; music show host Sta. WFXW, Geneva, Ill., 1985-89; engring.-tech. 4, audio visual tech. Ill. Dept. Transp., 1983—. Program host Musical Memories, Elgin Hour and Jazz Casual, Sta. WEPS-FM Elgin H.S., Ill., 1997—2001, Midwest Ballroom, Sta. WDCB, Coll. of DuPage, Ill., 2001—; announcer radioentertainment.com, Crown Point, Ind., 2001—. Author: (books) Valley Voices, 1997, Jct. 20: The Story of Udina, 1996, Radioville, The Town That Never Was, 1996, Billy Sunday - The Dundee Prophet, 1995, Plato Center Memories, 1998, Twice Around the Bases, 2001. Lindbergh School Compilation, 2003. Cmty. activist, Elgin, 1996—. Recipient award "Ill. Reaches Out", State of Ill., Springfield, 1994, Ind. Bell Pioneers Com. Svc. award Bell Telephone Co., Crown Point, 1987, Com. Svc. award USDA Soil Conservation, Crown Point, 1979, others; inducted into Elgin Hist. Soc. Heritage Hall of Fame, 1997, Elgin Sports Hall of Fame Found., 2001; recipient Elgin Sch. Cmty. Svc. award, 1998, Mayor's Heritage Commn. award, 1998, Caring Hearts award, Vol. Ctr. of N.W. Suburban Chgo./United Way, 2003. Mem.: Nat. Ballroom and Entertainment Assn. (Broadcast Excellence award 2001), Valley AM Radio Assn. (assoc.), Udina Hist. Soc. Nazarene. Avocations: softball pitcher, collector of old records, astronomer, historian, writer. Office: PO Box 1073 Dundee IL 60118 E-mail: johnrussell_radio16@yahoo.com.

GHYMN, ESTHER MIKYUNG, English educator, writer; b. Seoul; d. Yong Shik and Kyung hee (Park) Kim; m. Kyung-Il Ed Ghymn; children: Jennifer, Eugene. MA, U. Hawaii; MAT, U. Pitts.; PhD, U. Nev., Reno, 1990. Lectr. English, U. Nev., Reno, 1993—, ESL coord., 1996—, mem. ethnic studies bd., 1998—. Author: The Shapes and Styles of Asian American Prose Fiction, 1990, Images of Asian American Women Writers, 1995; editor APANN News, Asian Am. Studies: Identity, Images, Issues Past and Present, 2000. Bd. dirs. Asian Americans No. Nev., 1992-95, Multicultural Office, Truckee Meadows C.C., Reno, 1994-96, mem. steering com. Access to Success, 1996; mem. affirmative action adv. bd. U. Nev., Reno, 1998, Ethnic Studies Bd., 1997—, women's studies bd., 1998—, chair liaison com., 1998—, chair lang. com., 1999—, chair ethnic studies bd., mem. steering com. Global and Cross-Cultural Ctr.; series editor Peter Lang Pub. Mem. Phi Beta Delta. Avocations: teaching, writing, reading, travel. E-mail: emg@admin.unr.edu.

GIACABETTI, THOMAS, musician, educator; b. Phila., Apr. 10, 1951; s. Thomas and Isabella Giacabetti; m. Patricia Irene Uetz, Oct. 8, 1977; children: Powell, Dallas, Caitlin. Prof. Temple U., Phila., 1979—; tchr. music Camden Cath. H.S., Cherry Hill, NJ, 1985—90; prof. Bucks County C.C., Newtown, Pa., 1986—91, Stockton State Coll., Pomono, NJ, 1986—97, U. Arts, Phila., 1990—, co-chair dept. guitar, 2002—; prof. Rowan U., Glassboro, NJ, 1997—. Dir. Fusion Ensemble, Temple U., Phila., 1983—; equipment evaluator Jazz Timer, 2003. Avocations: tennis, computers. Home: 112 Laureba Ave Stratford NJ 08084

GIACCHI, JUDITH ADAIR, elementary education educator; b. Rochester, N.Y., Dec. 8, 1947; d. William Robert Peters and L. Virginia (Coulter) Peters Sweet; m. Alphonse Robert Giacchi, Aug. 8, 1970; children: Christina Marie, Anthony Robert. BS, SUNY, Buffalo, 1969. Permanent cert. tchr., N.Y. Data processing control clk. Neisner Bros., Inc., Rochester, 1969-70; tchr. Syracuse (N.Y.) City Sch. Dist., 1970—. Tchr. insvcs. and workshops Syracuse sch. dists., 1972—; master tchr. Syracuse U., 1983—; chmn. bldg. level team, 1988—98; collaborative Field Team Rep., mem., 1988—; trainer, ednl. rsch. and dissemination thinking math I, II and III, 2001—; rep. N.Y. State Tchrs. Retirement Sys. convs. and N.Y. State United Tchrs. convs., 1987—89. Contbr. articles to profl. publs. Corr. sec., rec. sec., legis. chmn. Nate Perry Sch. PTA, Liverpool, N.Y., 1983-95; troop aide Girl Scouts U.S.A., Liverpool, 1982-86; rep., mem. strategy com. Syracuse Labor Coun., 1995-97; mem. Union Cities Planning Com., 1997. Recipient award N.Y. State Legislature, 1994, various minigrants. Mem. N.Y. State United Tchrs. Fedn. (rep. convs. 1990-92), Ctrl. N.Y. Romance Writers Group, Onondaga County Tchrs. Assn. (award 1989), Syracuse Tchrs. Assn. (various coms., chief bldg. rep. 1984-2000). Avocations: reading, writing, needlecrafts, music, computers. Office: Porter Magnet Sch Tech & Career Exploration 512 Emerson Ave Syracuse NY 13204

GIACCONI, RICCARDO, astrophysicist, educator; b. Genoa, Italy, Oct. 6, 1931; arrived in U.S., 1956, naturalized, 1967; s. Antonio and Elsa (Canni) Giacconi; m. Mirella Manaira, Feb. 15, 1957; children: Guia Giacconi Trutter, Anna Lee, Marc A. PhD, U. Milan, Italy, 1954; ScD (hon.), U. Chgo., 1983; laurea honoris causa in astronomy, U. Padua, 1984; ScD (hon.), Warsaw U., 1996; laurea honoris causa in physics, U. Rome, 1998; Dr Tech. and Sci. (hon.), U. Uppsala, 2000. Asst. prof. physics U. Milan, 1954—56; rsch. assoc. Ind. U., 1956—58, Princeton U., 1958—59; exec. v.p., dir. Am. Sci. & Engring. Co., Cambridge, Mass., 1959—73; prof. astronomy Harvard U.; also assoc. dir. high energy astrophysics divsn. Center Astrophysics, Smithsonian Astrophys. Obs./Harvard Coll. Obs., Cambridge, 1973—81; dir. Space Telescope Sci. Inst., Balt., 1981—92; prof. astrophysics Johns Hopkins U., 1981—99, U. Milan, Italy, 1991—99; dir.-gen. European So. Obs., Garching, Germany, 1993—99; pres. Assoc. Univs., Inc., Washington, 1999—; rsch. prof. Johns Hopkins U., 1999—. Richtmeyer meml. lectr. Am. Assn. Physics Tchrs., 1975; mem. space sci. adv. com. NASA, 1978—79, mem. adv. com. innovation study, 1979—; mem. NASA Astrophysics Coun., mem. adv. com. innovation study astronomy adv. com., 1979—; mem. high energy astronomy survey panel Nat. Acad. Scis., 1979—80, mem. Space Sci. Studies Bd., 1980—84, 1989—; mem. adv. com. Max-Planck Inst. für Physik und Astrophysik; chmn. bd. dirs. Instituto Guido Donegani, Gruppo Montedison, 1987—89; mem. vis. com. to divsn. of phys. scis. U. Chgo., U. Padua; chmn. ISC E-1 (galactic and extragalactic astrophysics) Com. on Space Rsch. (COSPAR), 1982—93; Russell lectr. Co-editor: X-ray Astronomy, 1974, The X-Ray Universe, 1985, author numerous articles and papers in field.; inventor x-ray telescope, discoverer of x-ray stars. Decorated Targhe d'Oro della Regione Puglia, Cavaliere di Gran Croce dell'Ordine al Merito della Repubblica Italianna; recipient Röntgen prize in astrophysics, Physikalish-Medizinische Gesellschaft, Wurzburg, Germany, 1971, Exceptional Sci. Achievement medal, NASA, 1971, 1980, Disting. Pub. Svc. award, 1972, 2003, Space Sci. award, AIAA, 1976, Elliot Cresson medal, Franklin Inst., 1980, Gold medal, Royal Astron. Soc., 1982, A. Cressy Morrison award, N.Y. Acad. Sci., 1982, Bruce medal, 1987, Heinneman award, 1987, Wolf Prize in Physics, 1987, Nobel prize in physics, 2002; fellow, Fulbright, 1956—58. Mem.: Am. Philos. Soc., Royal Astron. Soc., Max-Planck Soc. (ext. mem.), Academia Nazionale dei Lincei (fgn.), Md. Acad. Sci. (sci. coun. 1982—), Internat. Astron. Union, Am. Acad. Arts and Scis., Italian Phys. Soc. (Como prize 1967), Am. Astron. Soc. (Henry Norris Russell lectr. 1981, Darwin lectr. Royal Soc. 1993, chmn. high energy astrophysics divsn., Helen B. Warner award 1966), NAS (rep. 1979—82), AAAS, Cosmos Club (Washington). Office: Associated Univs Inc 1400 16th St NW Ste 730 Washington DC 20036-2252

GIACOLETTO, LAWRENCE JOSEPH, electronics engineering educator, researcher, consultant; b. Clinton, Ind., Nov. 14, 1916; s. Pete and Antonia (Savio) G.; m. Maxine Lorraine Dicks, May 31, 1941; 1 child, Carol Giacoletto. BSEE, Rose-Hulman Inst. Tech., 1938; MS in Physics, State U. Iowa, 1939; PhDEE, U. Mich., 1952. Rsch. engr. RCA Labs., Princeton, N.J., 1946-56; rsch. mgr. sci. lab. Ford Motor Co., Dearborn, Mich., 1956-61; prof. elec. engring. Mich. State U., East Lansing, 1961-87, prof. emeritus, 1987—; owner CoRes Inst., Okemos, Mich., 1965—. Author: Differential Amplifiers, 1970; editor: Electronics Designers' Handbook, 1977; patentee in field. Ret. Lt. col. USA, 1976 Fellow IEEE (bd. dirs. 1964-65), AAAS (del. 1977-79), University Club (Lansing, Mich.), Sigma Xi. Independent. Roman Catholic. Home: 4465 Wausau Rd Okemos MI 48864-2741 Office: CoRes Inst 4465 Wausau Rd Okemos MI 48864-2741 E-mail: giacolet@pilot.msu.edu.

GIADROSICH, DONALD LOUIS, research scientist, retired electrical engineer; b. Oceans Springs, Miss., Apr. 5, 1932; s. Edward and Ella May Giadrosich; m. Diana Davidson, Jan. 20, 1956; children: Kirk, Dana, Keith, Kevin(dec.). BSEE, Miss. State U., 1957; MS in Sys. Analysis and Econs., U. Md., 1967. Sr. electronics engr. Hughes Aircraft Co., Culver City, Calif., 1959—64; dir. advanced rsch. and tech. U.S. Naval Weapons Sys. Analysis Office, Washington, 1964—66; dir. ctrl. sys. analysis group Joint Chiefs of Staff, Sandia Base, N.Mex., 1966—67; chief scientist, chief ops. analysis Air Force Ctr., Eglin AFB, Fla., 1994, USAF Tactical Fighter Weapons Ctr., Nellis AFB, Nev., 1976—80; chief operational applications USAF Tactical Air Warfare Ctr., Eglin AFB, Fla., 1967—76; dir. ops. analysis Hdqrs. USAF Europe, Ramstain AB, Germany, 1980—82; ret., 1994. Tech. advisor USAF Sci. Adv. Bd., Washington, 1982—94; mem. tech. adv. bd. Dept. Def. Joint Testing, Washington, 1982—94; mem. study group on live fire testing F-22 NRC, Washington, 1995. Author: Operations Research Analysis in Test and Evaluation, 1995; contbr. more than 30 articles to profl. publs. Coach Little League and other youth activities, Destin, Fla., 1967—76. Recipient Gen. Lewis H. Brereton award in Aerospace, Air Force Assn., 1986, Presdl. Rank award, Office of Pers. Mgmt., Washington, 1986, 1991. Mem.: Inst. Ops. Rsch. and Mgmt. Scis., Am. Legion. Achievements include contributions in modeling and simulation, electronic combat, intelligence synthesis, large scale military exercises, aircraft missile and weapons systems, armament and avilnics, range systems. Home: 3811 Indian Trail Destin FL 32541

GIAEVER, IVAR, physicist; b. Bergen, Norway, Apr. 5, 1929, arrived in U.S., 1957, naturalized, 1963; s. John A. and Gudrun (Skaarud) Giaever; m. Inger Skramstad, Nov. 8, 1952; children: John, Anne Kari, Guri, Trine. Siv. Ing., Norwegian Inst. Tech., Trondheim, 1952; PhD (hon.), Rensselaer Poly. Inst., 1964, Union College, 1974; PhD U. of Oslo (hon.), 1976; PhD (hon.), Michigan Tech. U., 1976, Worcester Polytechnic Inst., 1977, Norwegian Inst. of Tech., 1985, Clarkson U., 1985, SUNY, 1985. Patent examiner Norwegian Patent Office, Oslo, 1953—54; mech. engr. Can. Gen. Electric Co., Peterborough, Canada, 1954—56; applied mathematician Gen. Electric Co., Schenectady, 1956—58, physicist Research and Devel. Ctr., 1958—88; Inst. prof. Rensselaer Poly. Inst., Troy, NY, 1988—; also prof. U. Oslo, 1988—. Served with Norwegian Army, 1952—53. Recipient Nobel prize for Physics, 1973; fellow Guggenheim, 1970. Fellow: Am. Phys. Soc. (Oliver E. Buckley prize 1965), mem.: NAS, IEEE, Korean Acad. of Sci., Swedish Acad. of Engring., Norwegian Acad. Tech., Norwegian Acad. Sci., Am. Acad. Arts and Scis., Nat. Acad. Engring. (V.K. Zworykin award 1974), Norwegian Profl. Engrs. Office: Rensselaer Poly Ins Physics Dept 110 8th St Troy NY 12180-3522*

GIAIMO, JOSEPH OCTAVIUS, lawyer; b. July 12, 1934; married; children: James, Cynthia, Jennifer. BBA, St. John's U., 1959, LLB, 1961; Hon, 1986. Assoc. Havens, Wandless, Stitt and Tighe, N.Y.C., 1961-64; asst. legis. rep. Office of Mayor, N.Y.C., 1964-66; ptnr. Adams & Giaimo, N.Y.C., 1966-70, Giaimo & Kaufman, N.Y.C., 1970-71, Manton & Giaimo, N.Y.C., 1972-76; sole practice N.Y.C., 1976-82; ptnr. Giaimo & Vreeburg, N.Y.C., 1982—. Asst. counsel to various N.Y. state assemblymen, 1966-77; legis. asst. Ins. com., 1978-80; counsel to com. on govtl. employees, 1981-84. Contbg. editor St. John's U. Law Rev., 1959-60, research editor, 1961. Mem. N.Y. State Mental Health Services Council, 1984-89. Served with USN. Mem. St. John's U. Sch. Law Alumni Assn. (bd. dirs., pres.), St. John's Alumni Fedn. (bd. dirs.). Home: 113 Warwick Ave Flushing NY 11363-1037 E-mail: jogktg@aol.com.

GIALAMAS, GUS G. orthopedic surgeon; b. Chgo., Jan. 11, 1954; s. George Gust and Alexandra (Speropoulos) G.; m. Lyle Leah Duncan, Mar. 3, 1979; children: George Constantine, Leslie Anne, Patricia Elena. BS in Natural Sci., Pepperdine U., 1979; MD, Chgo. Med. Sch., 1986. Diplomate Am. Bd. Orthopaedic Surgery, Nat. Bd. Med. Examiners. Rschr. Harrington Arthritis Rsch. Ctr., Phoenix, 1985-86; intern in gen. surgery U. Calif., San Francisco, 1986-88, orthopaedic resident, 1986-92, chief resident, orthopaedic surgery, 1992; attending orthopaedic surgeon Seaview Orthopaedic Med. Group, San Clemente, Calif., 1992—; chief of staff San Clemente (Calif.) Hosp., 2003—. Chief sect. of orthopaedics San Clemente Hosp. and Med. Ctr., 1993—, chmn. dept. surgery, 1998—, chief of staff, 2003—. Bd. dirs. Boys and Girls Club, San Clemente, Calif., 1995—; vol. orthopaedic surgeon, Operation Rainbow/Cen. Am., 1990—; team physician San Clemente H.S., 1992—. Fellow Am. Acad. Orthopaedic Surgeons; mem. Western Orthopaedic Assn. (bd. dirs. 1994—), Abbott Orthopaedic Soc. Avocations: golf, softball coach. Office: Seaview Orthopaedic Med Gr 653 Camino De Los Mares Ste 109 San Clemente CA 92673-2808

GIALLANZA, CHARLES PHILIP, lawyer; b. Hornell, N.Y., Nov. 18, 1950; s. Charles Joseph Jr. and Rena Eugena (Foster) G.; children: Charles Edward, Juleah Marie. AS in Aerospace Sci., U. Albuquerque, 1977; BA in Polit. Sci. and English, U. South Fla., 1979; JD, John Marshall Law Sch., 1982. Bar: Ga. 1983, U.S. Dist. Ct. (no. dist., Atlanta divsn.) Ga. 1983; cert. air traffic contr. FAA. With USAF, 1971-79; air traffic contr. USAF Res., McDill AFB, Tampa, Fla., 1977—79, Dobbins AFB, 1980-81, USN Res., Dobbins AFB; assoc. James B. Pilcher, P.C., Atlanta, 1982-83; pvt. practice Snellville, Ga., 1983—. Advocate assisting Cubans detained in Atlanta prison, 1985, 86; capt. Ga. Def. Force, 1985-86. Recipient photography awards USAF, 1975. Mem. Ga. Bar Assn., Atlanta Bar Assn., Gwinnet Bar Assn. (law day com. 1987-88, Pro Bono Project award for outstanding svc. to citizens of Gwinnett County and the legal cmty. 2000). Avocations: cross-training, running, weightlifting. Office: 3881 Stone Mountain Hwy Ste 5 Snellville GA 30039-3978 Fax: 770-978-4450. E-mail: Charles@GiallanzaLaw.com.

GIALLOMBARDO, LESLIE, publishing executive; Adv. dir. The Desert Sun, Palm Springs, Calif., The Idaho Statesman, Boise; v.p. adv. The Tennessean, 1995, sr. v.p. mktg., 1999, pres., pub., 2002—. Mgmt. positions Reno (NE) Gazette-Jour., Statesman Jour., Salem, Oreg. Named seven time winner Pres.'s Ring. Office: 1100 Broadway Nashville TN 37203 E-mail: lgiallom@tennessean.com.*

GIALLORENZI, THOMAS GAETANO, optical engineer; b. N.Y.C., Feb. 28, 1943; s. Amedeo and Eleanor (Spica) G.; m. Margaret Mary Marrin, Sept. 6, 1966; children: Thomas R., Kathy. BS in Engring. Physics, Cornell U., 1965, MS in Engring. Physics, 1966, PhD, 1969. Tech. staff Gen. Tel. & Electronics Lab., Bayside, N.Y., 1969-70; sect. head, optical techniques br. Naval Rsch. Lab., Washington, 1970-76, head optical techniques br., 1976-79, supt. optical scis. divsn., 1979—. Lectr. in field and at profl. soc. confs. Editor Jour. Lightwave Tech., 1983-88; contbr. over 80 articles to profl. jours.; over 30 patents in field. Mem. adv. bd. U. Va., 1986-92. Recipient Applied Sci. award Rsch. Soc. Am., 1973, Meritorious Civilian Svc. award USN, 1978, Conrad

award USN, 1985, Disting. Exec. Rank award Pres. of U.S., 1990, 98, Meritorious Exec. Rank award Pres. of U.S., 1984, Disting. Civilian Svc. award Dept. Def., 1987. Fellow IEEE (assoc. editor Procs. 1990-95, Lightwave Comms. 1989-92, Harry Diamond award 1986, John Tyndell award 1990), IEEE Laser and ElectroOptics Soc. (pres. 1996), Optical Soc. Am. (editor Jour. Lightwave Tech. 1983-89, assoc. editor Applied Optics 1991-94); mem. Nat. Acad. Engring., U.S. Naval League (Albert Michelson award 1995, USN Rodger Easton award Office of Naval Rsch. 1998). Home: 8704 Side Saddle Rd Springfield VA 22152-2731 Office: Naval Rsch Lab Optical Scis Divsn Washington DC 20375-0001

GIAMBALVO, VINCENT, management consultant; b. Bklyn., Nov. 10, 1942; s. Frank and Anna (Pepey) G.; m. Rose Marie Esposito, Sept. 8, 1968; 1 child, Gina Marie. BA, Hunter Coll., 1966; MA, Northeastern U., 1970, PhD, 1973. Rsch. assoc. Northeastern U., Boston, 1972; asst. prof. behavioral sci. SUNY, N.Y.C., 1973-77; tng. specialist ADP Network Svcs., Ann Arbor, Mich., 1978-80; mgr. human resource devel. ADT Security Systems, Parsippany, N.J., 1981-88; dir. tng. and devel. Duro-Test Corp., Fairfield, N.J., 1989-93, dir. human resources, 1993-97, human resource cons., 1997-98; v.p. tng. and career devel. Great Atlantic and Pacific Tea Co., Montvale, N.J., 1998-99; mgmt. cons., 2000—. Instr. Am. Soc. Tng. and Devel. cert. program Kean Coll., 1982-85; nat. and internat. sales and mktg. cons. Biofeedtrac Inc., Bklyn., 1984-92. Contbr. articles on edn. and vision sci. to profl. jours. With USNR, 1964-71. NDEA Title IV fellow, 1968-71. Mem. ASTD (sec. Ann Arbor chpt. 1978-79, pres. 1980, leadership devel. coord. North N.J. chpt. 1989-90, pres.-elect 1991, pres. 1992), Am. Mgmt. Assn. Democrat. Roman Catholic. Home: 21 Eldor Ave New City NY 10956-1433 Fax: (845) 634-2426. E-mail: RoseVin@aol.com.

GIAMBASTIANI, EDMUND P., JR., military officer, federal agency administrator; b. Canastota, N.Y., May 4, 1948; Grad. with leadership distinction, US Naval Acad., 1970. Commd. ensign USN, 1970, advanced through grades to admiral, various assignments including weapons officer, USS Puffer, 1971-75, enlisted program mgr., staff Navy Recruiting Command Hdqrs., 1975-78, flag aide to dep. comdr., 1975-78, engr. officer, USS Francis Scott Key, 1978-82, comdr. Submarine NR-1, 1982-85, mem. staff of Asst. Chief Naval Ops. for undersea warfare, 1985-86, spl. asst. to dep. dir. for intelligence, CIA, comdr. USS Richard B. Russell, 1987-90, fellow Chief Naval Ops. Strategic Studies Group, 1991, comdr. Submarine Devel. Squadron 12, 1991-93, jt. task group comdr., spl. warfare exercise, dir. strategy and concepts Naval Doctrine Command, currently dir. submarine warfare divsn. Washington, 1996-98, comdr. Submarine Force, U.S. Atlantic Fleet Norfolk, Va., 1998—2000, dep. chief of naval ops. for resources, warfare req. and assessments, 2000—01; sr. mil. assist. to sec. of def., 2001—02; comdr. U.S. Joint Forces Command, Norfolk, Va., 2002—. Decorated Legion of Merit with 3 gold stars, DSM with 2 gold stars.*

GIAMBRA, JOEL ANTHONY, county executive; m. Michelle Giambra; children: Gabriella, Nicholas, Dominic, Joel Anthony. Student, Bryant & Stratton Bus. Inst., 1973; AAS in Bus. Adminstrn., Erie C.C., 1978. Legis. asst. Erie County Legis., Buffalo, 1975-76, cmty. aide, mem. citizens adv. com., 1976; sgt.-at-arms Buffalo Common Coun., 1976-77; dir. field ops. western N.Y. Carter/Mondale Re-Election Com., Buffalo, 1980; monitor/evaluator Divsn. Employment & Tng., Buffalo, 1982-90; comptroller City of Buffalo, 1990-2000; Erie County exec. Buffalo, N.Y., 2000—. Bd. dirs. Buffalo Fine Arts Acad.; mem. Loaned Exec. Club, United Way Buffalo & Erie County. Recipient Bus. First 40 under 40 award, 1995, Erie C.C. Found. Disting. Alumni award, Be-A-Friend Big Brother/Big Sister Program Dir.'s award, Disting. Svc. to Preservation award Landmark Soc. Niagara Frontier, 1984, Appreciation award Preservation Coalition Erie County, 1984, Man of Yr. award YMCA, 1998, Donald A. Miller Cmty. Svc. award, 2000, Man of Yr. award Buffalo Renaissance Found., 2000, Italian-Am. Achievement award Good Govt. Club, 2000, Abraham Lincoln Leadership award, 2000, Paul Harris Fellow Rotary Found. Rotary Internat., 2001, Erie Cmty. Coll. Light of Leadership award, 2002, Frank E. Van Lare award, N.Y. Water Environ. Assn., 2002, Buffalo award, Buffalo Niagara Assn. of Realtors, 2002; named Buffalo News Outstanding Citizen, 2001. Mem. NCCJ, N.Y. State Fin. Officers Assn. (bd. govs. 1992), West Side Bus. & Taxpayers' Assn. (Man of Yr. 1984), Forest Dist. Civic Assn., Jr. C. of C., Kiwanis Club Buffalo, Leadership Buffalo (adv. bd.), Romulus Club. Office: Erie County 95 Franklin St Buffalo NY 14202-3925 E-mail: giambraj@bflo.co.erie.ny.us.

GIAMMARTINO, FRANK ARNOLD, chiropractor; b. Bronx, N.Y., Dec. 8, 1930; s. Carmine Donato and Linda Maria Giammartino; m. Lydia Di Russo, Sept. 5, 1963. BS in Pre-Med., Coll. of the City of N.Y., 1955; DC, Lincoln Coll. of Chiropractic, 1959. Cert. doctor of chiropractic N.Y., 1959. Pvt. practice, N.Y.C., 1960—; diagnostic electromyography Neurological Assoc., Westchester, NY, 1984—. Rschr. Einstein Coll. Medicine, 1961—66. 1st lt. Med. Svc. U.S. Army, 1953—55. Fellow: N.Y. Chemists Club; mem.: Am. Chiropractic Assn., N.Y. Acad. Sci. Republican. Roman Catholic. Avocations: piano, boating, golf. Office: 170 Parkway South Mount Vernon NY 10552-2337

GIAMMO, SALVATORE JOSEPH, public relations executive; b. Denver, Oct. 19, 1944; s. Ernest (Stepfather) and Annette Pecsok; m. Dawn Louise Harrison, Sept. 2, 1967; children: Kevin, Todd, Joseph, Jeffrey. BA in Journalism, Kent State U., 1967; MA in Comms., U. No. Colo., 1978. Commd. 2d lt. USAF, 1967, advanced through grades to col., 1991, pub. affairs officer, 1967-94; ret., 1994; sr. pub. affairs rep. Jacobs Engring. Group Inc., Albuquerque, 1994-97; dir. pub. affairs U. N.Mex. Health Scis. Ctr., Albuquerque, 1997—. Mem. curriculum com. Leadership Albuquerque, 1999—2000. Decorated Legion Merit, . Fellow: Pub. Rels. Soc. Am.; mem.: Air Force Assn. (life), Air Force Pub. Affairs Alumni Assn. (life). Republican. Roman Catholic. Avocations: music, travel. Office: UNM Health Scis Ctr Office of Pub Affairs 1007 Stanford NE Ste 170 Albuquerque NM 87131 Fax: (505) 272-3680. E-mail: sgiammo@salud.unm.edu.

GIAMPIETRO, PHILIP FRANCIS, clinical geneticist, pediatrics educator; b. Springfield Gardens, N.Y., Oct. 29, 1956; s. Frank Nicholas and Amelia (D'onofrio) G.; m. Adeline Marie Kaam; children: Jennifer, Grace. BS in Biol. Scis., SUNY, Stony Brook, 1978, MD, 1986; PhD in Biomedical Scis., CUNY, 1983. Intern Univ. Hosp., Stony Brook, 1986-87; resident L.I. Jewish Hosp., New Hyde Park, N.Y., 1987-89; fellow in clin. genetics N.Y. Hosp./Cornell U. Med. Coll., N.Y.C., 1989-92, asst. prof. pediatrics, 1992—. Mem. Am. Coll. Med. Genetics, Am. Acad. Pediatrics, Am. Soc. Human Genetics. Office: NY Hosp Divsn Human Genetics 525 E 68th St # 150 New York NY 10021-4885

GIAMPIETRO, WAYNE BRUCE, lawyer; b. Chgo., Jan. 20, 1942; s. Joseph Anthony and Jeannette Marie (Zeller) G.; m. Mary E. Fordeck, June 15, 1963; children: Joseph, Anthony, Marcus. BA, Purdue U., 1963; JD, Northwestern U., 1966. Bar: Ill. 1966, U.S. Dist. Ct. (no. dist.) Ill. 1966, U.S. Ct. Appeals (7th cir.) 1967, U.S. Tax Ct. 1977, U.S. Supreme Ct. 1971. Assoc. Elmer Gertz, Chgo., 1966-73; mem. firm Gertz & Giampietro, Chgo., 1974-75; pvt. practice, 1975-76; ptnr. Poltrock & Giampietro, 1976-87, Witwer, Burlage, Poltrock & Giampietro, 1987-94, Witwer, Poltrock & Giampietro, Chgo., 1995—2002, Stitt, Klein, Daday, Aretos & Giampietro LLC, Arlington Heights, Ill., 2003—. Former cons. atty. Looking Glass divsn. Traveler's Aid Soc. Contbr. articles to profl. jours. Pres. Chgo. 47th Ward Young Republicans, 1968; bd. dirs. Ravenswood Conservation Commn. Lutheran. Avocation: stamp collecting. Home: 23 Windsor Dr Lincolnshire IL 60069-3410 Office: Stitt Klein Daday Aretos & Giampietro LLC 121 S Wilke Ste 500 Arlington Heights IL 60005 Business E-Mail: wgiampietro@skdaglaw.com.

GIANARIS, NICHOLAS VASIL, economics educator; b. Dafne, Greece, Nov. 23, 1929; came to U.S., 1960; s. Vasilis H. and Demetra (Spyropoulos) N.; m. Magda Theodorou, July 1, 1963; children: Bill, Mike. BS, Grad. Sch. Econs. and Bus., Athens, Greece, 1955; LLB, U. Athens, 1958; MA, NYU, 1962, Phd with honors, 1968. Statistician, researcher Port of Piraeus Authority, Greece, 1955-60; statistician NYU, N.Y.C., 1961-62; law cons. Ebasco, N.Y.C., 1966-67; prof. Fordham U., N.Y.C., 1965—. Author: Economic Development: Thought and Problems, 1978, The Economies of the Balkan Countries, 1982, Greece and Yugoslavia: An Economic Comparison, 1984, Greece and Turkey: Economic and Geopolitical Perspectives, 1988, Contemporary Public Finance, 1989, The European Community and the United States, 1991, Contemporary Economic Systems: A Regional and Country Approach, 1993, The European Economic Community, Eastern Europe and Russia, 1994, Modern Capitalism: Privatization, Employee Ownership and Industrial Democracy, 1996, Geopolitical and Economic Changes in the Balkan Countries, 1996, Greece and the European Union, 1997, The North American Free Trade Agreement and the European Union, 1998, Globalization: A Financial Approach, 2001; contbr. articles to profl. jours. Home: 21-70 42nd St Astoria NY 11105-1404 Office: Fordham U Lincoln Ctr New York NY 10023

GIANCOTTI, FILIPPO GIUSTO, cell and molecular biologist; b. Rome, Mar. 25, 1958; MD, U. Torino, Italy, 1981, PhD, 1987. Diplomate Italian Bd. Hematology/Oncology. Intern and resident dept. hematology U. Torino Sch. Medicine, 1979—83; sr. rsch. fellow La Jolla (Calif.) Cancer Rsch. Found., 1987—91; asst. prof. Sch. Medicine, NYU, 1991—96, assoc. prof., 1996; assoc. prof. Sch. Medicine Cornell U., N.Y.C., 1996—2000, prof. Sch. Medicine, 2000—; assoc. mem. Sloan-Kettering Inst. Meml. Sloan-Kettering Cancer Ctr., 1996—2000, mem., 2000—. Cons. NIH, 1994—. Contbr. articles to profl. jours. including, Cell, European Molecular Biology Orgn. Jour., Jour. of Cell Biology. Recipient Lucille P. Markey Charitable Trust award, 1992—96, Established Investigatorship award, Am. Heart Assn., 1996—; fellow Sr. postdoctoral fellow, European Molecular Biology Orgn., 1987—89, postdoctoral, European Orgn. for Rsch. and Treatment Cancer and Nat. Cancer Inst., 1987—89, Am. Cancer Soc., 1989—90, Arthritis Found., 1990—93, Whitehead Presdl., 1992—93. Mem.: ASCB, AAAS. Achievements include patent on novel fibronectin receptor. Office: Cellular Biochemistry/Biophysics Program Box 216/1275 York Ave Meml Sloan-Kettering Cancer New York NY 10021

GIANFRANCISCO, JAMES ANTHONY, colon and rectal surgeon; b. Chgo., Jan. 1, 1951; m. Nancy Jayne Gianfrancisco. BS, Northwestern U., 1972, MD, 1973. Diplomate Am. Bd. Surgery, Am. Bd. Colon and Rectal Surgery. Pres. medical staff Palos Cmty. Hosp., Palos Hts., Ill., 1998—2000. Fellow Am. Coll. Surgeons, Am. Soc. Colon and Rectal Surgeons; mem. Am. Soc. for Gastrointestinal Endoscopy, Chgo. Surgical Soc., Chgo. Soc. Colon and Rectal Surgeons (sect., treas. 1981—). Avocations: running, biking. Office: 9050 W 81st St Justice IL 60458-1350

GIANITSOS, ANESTIS NICHOLAS, surgeon; b. Chios, Greece, Aug. 31, 1961; came to U.S., 1966; s. Dimitrios and Soultani (Zannikos) G.; m. Laurie S. Hallmark, children: Alexia Soultani, Dimitri Jacob. BA summa cum laude, Boston U., 1983, MD, 1987. Physician U. Wis. Hosp., Madison, 1987-92; pres. Tricorp Informational Svcs., Williams Bay, Wis., 1989-93; staff urologist Riverview Clinic, Janesville, Wis., 1992-98; pres. Geneva Mktg. Sys., Lake Geneva, Wis., 1996—; med. dir. Men's Health Ctr. Mercy Health Sys., So. Wis., No. Ill., 1998—; staff urologist Mercy Regional Urology Ctr., Janesville, 1998—. Cons. Rural Wis. Hosp. Coop., Sauk City, 1989-93; staff urology Mercy Health Sys., Janesville, 1998—; med. dir. So. Wis. chpt. US TOO, 1993—. Mem. editl. bd. Men's Total Health Digest, 2001—; contbr. articles to profl. jours. Commonwealth scholar, Augustus Howe Buck scholar. Fellow Internat. Coll. Surgeons; mem. Am. Assn. Clin. Urologists, Am. Urologic Assn., Wis. Med. Soc., Pelvic Health Consortium, Inc. Republican. Greek Orthodox. Avocations: photography, travel, baseball, investing, rare wine. Home: 1237 Geneva National Ave W Lake Geneva WI 53147-5009 Office: Mercy Men's Health Ctr 1000 Mineral Point Ave Janesville WI 53545-2940 E-mail: lshang@elknet.net., ngianitsos@mhsjvl.org.

GIANLORENZI, NONA ELENA, painter, art dealer, educator; b. Virginia, Minn., July 20, 1939; d. Teto Nicholas and Lena Dora (Zini) Gianlorenzi; m. George Michael Devlin, July 20, 1966 (dec. Feb. 1990); children: Gian Loren Kjellesvig Waering, Helena Nicole Devlin Seidel. BA, Bklyn. Coll./CUNY. Painter self employed, N.Y.C., 1960—; asst. dir. Am. Art Gallery, N.Y.C., 1961-67; owner, dir. Asage Art Gallery, N.Y.C., 1977-88; pvt. art dealer Art Space Inc., Bklyn., 1989—. Tchr. art and aesthetics St. Francis Sch. Deaf, Bklyn., 1968-71, Mt. Carmel, Queens, N.Y., 1968-71, Charles Borromeo Sch., Bklyn., 1968-71. Ford fellow, 1992-94, Loy fellow, 1992-94; Art Studio scholar, 1961. Address: 415 Rugby Rd Brooklyn NY 11226-5611

GIANNAMORE, DAVID MICHAEL, electronics engineer; b. Steubenville, Ohio, May 25, 1956; s. Robert Anthony and Marjorie Irene (Smith) G.; m. Tracy Lynn Rayburn, Apr. 3, 1982; children: Cynthia Marie, Robert Joseph. AAS in Electronic Engring., Jefferson County Tech. Inst., 1977. Video tech. Sta. WSTV-TV, Steubenville, 1977; svc. tech. TCI of Ohio, Steubenville, 1978-80; cable splicer Gen. Telephone Ohio, Cadiz, 1980-81; customer svc. rep. Ohio Power Co., Steubenville, 1981-84; svc. engr. Warner Amex, Columbus, Ohio, 1985-86; tng. instr. Liebert Global Svcs., Worthington, Ohio, 1986-90, tng. instr., supr., 1990-93, project mgr., 1993-95, quality mgr., 1995—. Mem. Am. Soc. for Quality (cert. quality mgr., cert. quality auditor), Assn. for Svc. Mgmt. Internat. Avocations: family activities, Karate, sports, music. Office: Liebert Global Svcs 610 Executive Campus Dr Westerville OH 43082-8871 E-mail: dave.giannamore@liebert.com.

GIANNAROS, DEMETRIOS SPIROS, economist, educator, politician; b. Karlovasi, Samos, Greece, Oct. 4, 1949; came to U.S., 1964; s. Spiridon Demetrios and Irene (Kiriakou) G.; m. Elizabeth Sampson, June 5, 1977; children: Edward, Spiros Jason. BA in Econs., U. Mass., 1972; MA in Econ. Devel., Boston U., 1976, MAPE in Polit. Econ., 1977, PhD in Econs., 1981. Mgr. Samos Imex Corp., Boston, 1974—77; asst. prof. econs. Suffolk U., Boston, 1977—79; prof. U. Hartford, West Hartford, Conn., 1980—, dir. internat. programs, 1993—94, dir. exec. MPA program, 1986—88, assoc. to sr. v.p., dir. internat. studies, 1988—91; mem. Bd. Edn., Farmington, Conn., 1993—95; dir. U.S. Consortium for Mgmt. Edn. in Ctrl. and Ea. Europe, 1993—98; vice chmn. fin. com. Conn. Gen. Assembly, 1995—98; state rep., mem. edn. com., fin. revenue and bonding coms. Conn., 1995—; chmn. energy & tech. com., 1999—2002; chmn. edn. com., 2003—. Mem. Conn. Internat. Trade Coun., 1995-96; spl. asst. to pres. George Washington U., Washington, 1988-89; cons. to pub. and pvt. orgns., 1977—; bd. advisors Fatshoe.com, 2000—. Bd. dirs. Coll. Southea. Europe, 1992-97. NSF grantee, 1983-84, U. Hartford Coffin grantee, 1983-8, Mellon Found. grantee, 1991-92; Am. Coun. on Edn. fellow, 1988-89. Fellow Am. Coun. on Edn. (mem. exec. bd. coun.); mem. Am. Hellenic Ednl. and Progressive Assn., Am. Econ. Assn., Internat. Econ. Assn., N.E. Bus. and Econs. Assn. (pres. 1990-92, bd. dirs. 1989-95), Exchange Club, Helicon Soc. (pres., bd. dirs. 1975-78), Hellenic Soc., Paideia, World Affairs Coun., World Hellenic Interparliamentary Union (alt. pres. 1998-2002, pres. 2002—). Greek Orthodox. Avocations: travel, water sports, museums, political activities, nature. Home: 56 Basswood Rd Farmington CT 06032-1142 Office: U Hartford Econs Dept 200 Bloomfield Ave Hartford CT 06117-1545

GIANNASCOLI, B. GREG, musician, entrepreneur; b. Philadelphia, Oct. 25, 1965; s. Brian F. and Patricia A. (Musi) Giannascoli; m. Yukyung Kim Giannascoli, Oct. 28, 2000. MusB, Rowan U., Glassboro, NJ., 1988; MusM, Va. Commonwealth U., Richmond, VA., 1991. Solo percussion artist, Piscataway, NJ; tchr. New Jersey City U., Jersey City; prin. percussion Riverside Symphonia, Lambertville, NJ; sect. percussion Princeton Symphony, Princeton, NJ, Philly Pops with Peter Nero, Phila.; owner and dir. Giannascoli Sch. of Mus., Piscataway. Solo recording Concertino, 1995, Velocoties, 1999, duo recording Recollections of the Inland Sea, 2001. Recipient Artist Intern. Comp., New York, NY., 2001—02, Patrons of Wisdom, Toronto, Can., 1997. Mem.: Am. Fedn. Mus. #204 and #77, Mus. Tchr. Nat. Assn., NRA. Republican. Roman Catholic. Avocations: exercise, gardening, fishing, cats and fish, shooting.

GIANNETTI, LOUIS DANIEL, film educator, film critic; b. Natick, Mass., Apr. 1, 1937; s. John and Vincenza (Zappitelli) G.; m. Justine Ann Gallagher, Sept. 7, 1963 (div. 1980); children: Christina, Francesca. BA, Boston U., 1959; MA, U. Iowa, 1961, PhD, 1967. Asst. prof. English Emory U., Atlanta, 1966-70; prof. English and film Case Western Res. U., Cleve., 1970—2001, prof. emeritus English and film, 2002—. Author: Understanding Movies, 1972, rev. 9th edit., 2002, Godard and Others, 1975, Masters of the American Cinema, 1981, (with S. Eyman) Flashback, 1986, 4th rev. edit., 2000. Democrat. Office: Case Western Res U Dept English Euclid Ave Cleveland OH 44106-2706

GIANNETTI, STEPHEN P. publishing executive; Ea. regional mgr. Reader's Digest; advt. dir. Prevention, 1993—96, assoc. pub., 1996—98, publisher, 1998—2000; v.p., pub. Nat. Geog. Mag., N.Y.C., 2000—; group pub. Nat. Geog. Mags., 2002—. Office: National Geographic 711 Fifth Ave New York NY 10022*

GIANNI, GASTON LOUIS, JR., federal agency administrator; b. Steubenville, Ohio, Aug. 12, 1942; m. Sue Jones; 3 children. BS in Acctg., Franciscan U. Steubenville, 1964; postgrad., Pa. State U., 1980, Harvard U., 1989. Various positions to sr. exec. Gen. Actg. Office; inspector gen. Fed. Deposit Ins. Corp., 1996—. Mem., past chair audit com., vice chair Pres.'s Coun. on Integrity and Efficiency. With D.C. Nat. Guard, 1964-70. Mem. Inst. Mgmt. Accts., Assn. Govt. Accts., Inst. Internal Auditors, Cert. Govt. Auditing Profls. Office: Fed Deposit Ins Co Office Inspector Gen 801 17th St NW Washington DC 20434-0002

GIANNI, KEITH BRIAN MICHAEL, internist; b. NYC, Sept. 17, 1942; s. Carmello Vito and Clara (Buccolieri) Giannitrapani; children: Ellen, Christian, David, Rachel; m. Amanda Lane (Jones). BA, Stanford U., 1965, MD, 1968. Diplomate Am. Bd. Internal Medicine. Intern U. Utah Hosp., Salt Lake City, 1968-69, chief med. resident in internal medicine, 1969-71; chief dept. medicine Bassett Army Hosp., Ft. Wainright, Alaska, 1973-74; chmn. dept. medicine Fairbanks (Alaska) Meml. Hosp., 1974, chief of staff, 1975-76, 91, 1994-95; pvt. practice in internal medicine Fairbanks, 1974—. Maj. U.S. Army, 1971-74. Fellow ACP. Avocations: flying, sailing, computers, art, skating. Office: 1222 Well St Ste 1 Fairbanks AK 99701 E-mail: gianni@alaska.net.

GIANNINI, MATTHEW CARLO, lawyer, educator; b. Youngstown, Ohio, July 12, 1950; s. Matthew and Graziella (Nistri) G. BS, Youngstown State U., 1973, postgrad., 1973-75; JD, U. Dayton, 1978. Bar: Ohio 1978, U.S. Dist. Ct. (no. dist.) Ohio 1978, U.S. Supreme Ct. 1982. Assoc. D'Apolito, Infante, Huberman and Gentile, Youngstown, 1978-84; ptnr. D'Apoloito, Infante and Giannini, Youngstown, 1984—; asst. prof. forensic psychiatry Northeastern Ohio U. Coll. Medicine, 1981-84, assoc. prof. forensic psychiatry, 1984—. Agt. Safeco Title Ins. Co., 1978—; sr. cons. forensic medicine Fair Oaks Psychiatry Hosp., Summit, N.J., 1979—; instr. Paralegal Inst. Ohio, 1980—; instr. comml. law Youngstown State U., 1980—. Author: (with A.J. Giannini and A.E. Slaby) Physicians Guide to Overdose and Detoxification, 1984; contbr. numerous articles to profl. jours., chpts. to books. Mem. ABA, Am. Inst. Biol. Scis., Ohio Bar Assn. Republican. Roman Catholic. Avocations: tennis, golf. Home: 7284 Yellow Creek Dr Poland OH 44514-2647 Office: 1040 S Commons Pl Ste 200 Youngstown OH 44514

GIANNINI, VALERIO LOUIS, investment banker; b. NYC, Feb. 7, 1938; s. Gabriel M. and Luisa M. (Casazza) G.; m. Linda Martin, Oct. 6, 1979; children: Martin Louis, Alexander Elliot, Charles Gabriel. BSE, Princeton U., 1959. With Kidder Peabody & Co., NYC, 1961-64; sr. cons. IIT Rsch. Inst., Chgo., 1964-66; sec. Giannini-Voltex, LA, 1966-68; pres. V.L. Giannini & Co., LA, 1968-76; chmn. Namco Chems., Inc., 1975; dir. White House ops., Washington, 1977-78; dep. spl. asst. to Pres. for adminstrn. White House, 1979-80; dep. asst. sec. Dept. Commerce, Washington, 1980-81; prin. Cumberland Investment Group, NYC, 1981-87; pres. Numex Corp., 1986-87; CEO, Geneva Bus. Network, Inc., Irvine, Calif., 1987-90. Founder Eurosearch Ptnr., Newport Beach, Calif., 1990; prin. Newcap Ptnr., 1995; bd. dir. Dudek & Assoc., Pro-Dex, Inc.; adj. prof. Argyros Sch. Bus., Chapman U., 2001. Pres. Lido Jr. Sailing Found., 2000—. Lt. USNR, 1959-61. Mem. N.Y. Yacht Club, Newport Harbor Yacht Club. Office: 2082 Michelson Dr Ste 450 Irvine CA 92612-1204

GIANNINY, OMER ALLAN, JR., retired humanities educator; b. Charlottesville, Va., Dec. 5, 1925; s. Omer Allen and Frances Belle (Bussenger) G.; m. Jean Claire Post, July 31, 1948; children: Donald Hagen, James Emory, Peter Arnold, Robert Matthew, Gary Lee. BME, U. Va., Charlottesville, 1947; MEd, U. Va., 1958, EdD, 1967; postgrad., Rutgers U., 1947-48. Registered profl. engr., Va. Refinery engr. Esso Std. Oil Co., Linden, N.J., 1947-51; rsch. engr. U. Va., Charlottesville, 1953-56, asst. prof. Sch. Engring., 1955-65, 67-71, lectr., 1965-67, assoc. prof. humanities Sch. Engring., 1971-82, prof. humanities Sch. Engring., 1982-93, chmn., 1979-80, 90-93, prof. emeritus, 1993—. Ednl. cons. Newport News Shipbuilding, Va., 1962, Inst. Textile Tech., Charlottesville, 1984-2001. Co-author: Thomas Jefferson's Rotunda Restored, 1981. Served to lt. USNR, 1942-46, 51-53. Mem. Am. Soc. Engring. Edn. (dir. 1980-82), Soc. History Tech. (group chmn. 1983-85), The Raven Soc., Phi Beta Kappa, Tau Beta Pi, Phi Delta Kappa. United Methodist. Home: 1711 King Mountain Rd Charlottesville VA 22901-3047 E-mail: agianniny@earthlink.net.

GIANNOBILE, WILLIAM VICTOR, periodontist, educator; b. Chgo., Jan. 2, 1965; s. Vick Anthony and Janice Lorraine (Parduhn) G.; m. Angela Renee Rotar, May 19, 1990. BS in Chemistry, U. Mo., Rolla, 1987; MS in Oral Biology, DDS in Dental Surgery, U. Mo., Kansas City, 1991; PhD in Oral Biology, Harvard U., 1996. cert. periodontist, Mass. Fellow in periodontology Harvard U., Boston, 1991-96, instr., 1996-98; mem. staff Forsyth Dental Ctr., Boston, 1996-98; asst. prof. dentistry U. Mich., Ann Arbor, 1998—2002, assoc. prof. dentistry, 2002—. Patentee in field. Recipient Miyahara Clin. Rsch. award Acad. Dental Internat., 1997, Dentist-Scientist award NIH, 1991-96; fellow NIH, 1988. Mem. Am. Assn. Dental Rsch., Am. Acad. Periodontology (Balint Orban prize 1995, Young Investigator award 1996), Am. Dental Assn. Roman Catholic. Office: University Michigan 1011 N University Ave Ann Arbor MI 48109-1078

GIANNOPOULOU, ATHINA, physician, surgeon; b. Xanthi, Greece, May 12, 1962; came to U.S., 1990; d. Alexandros and Pipina (Papanikas) Giannopoulou; m. Nick Kanopoulos, Feb. 28, 1992; 1 child, Tasos Kanopoulos. MD with honors, U. Thessaloniki, Greece, 1987. Diplomate Am. Bd. Plastic and Reconstructive Surgery. Resident in gen. surgery Theagenio Med. Ctr., Thessaloniki, 1987-90; rsch. fellow Duke U. Hosp., Durham, N.C., 1991-92; resident in gen. surgery U. N.C. Hosps., Chapel Hill, 1992-96, resident in plastic surgery, 1996-98; fellow aesthetic and oculoplastic surgery Paces Plastic Surgery, Atlanta, 1998-99; pvt. practice Faces Plastic Surgery, Chapel Hill, N.C., 1999—. Contbr. articles to profl. jours. Avocations: skiing, swimming, gourmet cooking, fashion design. Home: 3723 Dairy Pond Pl Durham NC 27705 Office: 1515 W NC Hwy 54 Ste 130 Durham NC 27707 E-mail: facesps@aol.com.

GIANNOTTA, STEVEN LOUIS, neurosurgery educator; b. Detroit, Apr. 4, 1947; s. Louis D. and Betty Jane (Root) G.; m. Sharon Danielak, June 13, 1970; children: Brent, Nicole, Robyn. Student, U. Detroit, 1965-68; MD, U. Mich., 1972. Diplomate Am. Bd. Neurol. Surgeons. Surg. intern U. Mich., Ann Arbor, 1972-73, neurosurg. resident, 1973-78; asst. prof. neurosurgery UCLA, 1978-80, U. So. Calif., Sch. Medicine, L.A., 1980-83, assoc. prof. neurosurgery, 1983-89, prof. neurosurgery, 1989—. Bd. dirs. Am. Bd. Neurol. Surgery, 1995—2001, sec., 1999—2000, chmn., 2000—01. Fellow ACS, Am. Heart Assn. (stroke coun., rsch. grantee 1980, 84), So. Calif. Neurol. Soc. (pres. 1993-94), Congress Neurol. Surgeons (sec. 1986-89, v.p. 1993) Soc. Clin. Neuroscis. (L.A. pres. 1992-93), Am. Assn. Neurol. Surgeons (bd. dirs. 2001-). Democrat. Roman Catholic. Avocations: golf, skiing, sports cars. Office: Dept Neurosurgery Ste 5046 1200 N State St Los Angeles CA 90033-1029

GIANNOUKAKIS, NICK, educator; arrived in U.S., 1997; s. George Giannoukakis and Panagiota Kolotouros; m. Koula Kaskavaltzis, May 7, 2000. BSc, McGill U., Montreal, Que., Can., 1991, PhD, 1997. Apolytirion Byzantine Music Conservatory, Athens, Greece, 1990. Post-doctoral rsch. fellow U. Pitts., 1997—2000, asst. prof., 2000—. Cons. Gryffon Investment, Montreal, 1995—97. Composer: (digital recording) Byzantine Soundscapes Part 1 and 2; dir.: (music workshop and choir) Byzantine Choir of the Greek Orthodox Diocese of Pittsburgh; contbr. articles to profl. jours. Protopsaltis (master cantor) Greek Orthodox Diocese Pitts. Grantee, NIH, 2000—; Doctoral fellow, Telethon of Stars, Montreal, 1995—96, Fonds pour la formation de Chercheurs et l'Aide a la Recherche-Fonds de la Recherche en Santé du Quebec, 1996—97, Post-Doctoral fellow, 1997—2000, Juvenile Diabetes Found. Internat., 1997—2000. Mem.: Am. Hellenic Ednl. Progressive Assn. (adv. 1997—2002, gov. 1998—2002), Am. Soc. Byzantine Music and Hymnology (founder and dir. 2000—02), European Soc. for Gene Therapy, Am. Diabetes Assn., Amercian Soc. for Gene Therapy. Greek Orthodox. Achievements include

patents pending for gene therapy to prevent beta cell apoptosis; Oligonucleotide modification of dendritic cells for tolerance induction. Avocations: medieval religious music, history of medicine, history. Office: Univ Pitts 3460 Fifth Ave Pittsburgh PA 15213 Office Fax: 412-692-8131. E-mail: ngiann1@pitt.edu.

GIANOULAKIS, JOHN LOUIS, lawyer; b. St. Louis, Nov. 22, 1938; s. Louis John and Marie (Pappas) G.; m. Louise Marotta, Jan. 1961 (dec. 1970); children: Christopher Louis, Kia Louise, Candlin Hamilton Dobbs; m. Dora Rodliff Deady, Sept. 2, 1972. AB, Wash. U., 1960; JD, Harvard U., 1963. Bar: Mo. 1963, U.S. Dist. Ct. (ea. dist.) Mo. 1963, U.S. Ct. Appeals (8th cir.) 1974, U.S. Supreme Ct. 1975, U.S. Ct. Appeals (7th cir.) 1982, U.S. Ct. Appeals (6th cir.) 1987. From assoc. to ptnr. Thompson, Walther & Shewmaker, St. Louis, 1963-70; ptnr. Kohn, Shands & Gianoulakis, St. Louis, 1971-73, Kohn, Shands, Elbert, Gianoulakis & Giljum, LLP, St. Louis, 1973—. Mem., pres. bd. dirs. Legal Svcs. of Ea. Mo., Inc., St. Louis, 1972-81; mem. bar com. 22d Jud. Cir., St. Louis, 1977-85. V.p., pres. University City (Mo.) Sch. Bd., 1970-76; vice-chair Washington U. Alumni Bd. Govs., 2000-01, exec. vice-chair, 2001-2002, chair 2002-03; bd. trustees Washington U., 2001-03. Recipient Arts and Scis. Disting. Alumnus award Washington U., 2000. Fellow: Am. Coll. Trial Lawyers; mem.: ABA, Bar Assn. Met. St. Louis, Mo. Bar Assn., Spanish Lake Cmty. Assn. (dir. 1999—), Mo. Bluffs Assn. (pres. 1999—2001), Noon Day Club, Norwood Hills Country Club. Democrat. Home: 44 Clearview Park Saint Louis MO 63138-3302 Office: Kohn Shands Elbert Gianoulakis & Giljum LLP One US Bank Plz 24th Fl Saint Louis MO 63101 E-mail: jgianoulakis@ksegg.com.

GIANTURCO, DELIO E. management consultant, educator, author; b. Washington, Sept. 28, 1940; s. Elio and Valentine (McGillycuddy) G.; m. Mary Elizabeth Jordan, Jan. 31, 1961; children: Lisa, Grace, Mark. BS in Fgn. Trade, Georgetown U., 1963; MA, George Washington U., 1967. Staff asst. to Robert J. Corbett of Pa. U.S. Ho. of Reps., Washington, 1960-62, legis. asst. to Robert L.F. Sikes of Fla., 1962-63; sr. v.p. guarantees, ins. and exporter credits, treas., comptroller, exec. v.p., vice chmn., 1st v.p., dir. Export-Import Bank, Washington, 1963-77; pres. First Washington Assocs., 1978—. Dir. Fgn. Credit Ins. Assn., N.Y.C., 1971-76; adj. prof. George Mason U., 1995—. Office: First Washington Assocs 1501 Lee Hwy Ste 102 Arlington VA 22209-1147 E-mail: fwa@mindspring.com.

GIAQUINTO, JANE SCHNEIDER, finance executive; d. Harold and Mary Schneider; m. Joseph Giaquinto. Student, U. Mich., Ann Arbor, 1979-81; B Gen. Studies, U. Cin., 1983; MBA, Xavier U., Cin., 1986. Rsch. analyst Western Southern Life, Cin., 1983-85, investment analyst, 1985-87, sr. investment analyst, 1987-88; sr. analyst MBIA Ins. Corp., Armonk, N.Y., 1989-90, asst. v.p., 1990-92, v.p., 1992-98; corp. utility analyst cons. N.Y.C., 1998—2000; v.p. Merrill Lynch, 2000—. Moderator NYSSA Career Chat, N.Y.C., 1999; moderator Edison Elec. Inst. Ann. Fin. Com. Meeting, N.Y.C., 1997, 99, Orlando, 1999, mem. planning com., 1997, 99; co-chair and facilitator MBWC Program, N.Y.C., 1999; mem. planning com. WHHS N.Y. Region Alumni, N.Y.C., U.C. N.Y. Women's Com., N.Y.C.; mem. planning com. Am. Gas Assn. Fin. Forum, Scottsdale, Ariz., 1997; panelist Edison Elec. Inst. Fin. Conf., Palm Desert, Calif., 1996. Exec. com. mem. MBIA Invitational, Westchester County, N.Y., 1998; tutor, Time to Read, Armonk, 1992-98; fundraising coord. Back to Sch. Clothes for Kids, Armonk, 1993-95; program chair, Meet Profl. Women Program, Cin. Bus. and Profl. Women, 1986-87. Mem. Mcpl. Bond Women's Club (co-chair, facilitator program 1999), Wall St. Utility Group, Fin. Women's Assn. (mem. Wall St. Exch. Summer Network). E-mail: jane_s_giaquinto@ml.com., jgiaquinte@na2.us.ml.com.

GIARDINA, DAVID VINCENT, music educator; b. Richmond, Va., July 11, 1952; s. David D. and Charlotte J. Giardina; m. Lynette J. Giardina, Sept. 7, 1985. BA, St. Anselm Coll., Manchester, N.H., 1974. Adj. faculty Trinity Coll., Hartford, Conn., 1988—; guitar instr. Manchester C.., 1989—; music instr. St. Joseph Coll., West Hartford, Conn., 1990—; guitar instr. Hartford Conservatory, 1991—; music instr. Leomis Chaffee Sch., Windsor, Conn., 1996—; founder, dir. Fiesta del Norte, 1988—. Composer: nd Landscapes, 2000. Mem. adv. com. Conn. Commn. on the Arts, Hartford, 1998. Recipient Arts Appreciation award, m O'Neill, Conn., 1987. Mem.: Conn. Classical Guitar Soc. (founder). Avocations: astronomy, canoeing, skiing, bicycling, hiking. Home: 146 Naubuc Ave East Hartford CT 06118

GIARDINA, ELSA GRACE VONNA, cardiologist, educator; b. Newark, Aug. 1, 1941; d. John and Elsa (Freda) G.; m. Alan L. Saroff, June 1, 1974; 1 child, John Saroff. AB, Bryn Mawr Coll., 1961; MD, N.Y. Med. Coll., 1965. Diplomate Am. Bd. Internal Medicine, Am. Bd. Cardiology; cert. internal medicine, cardiovascular disease. Resident Roosevelt Hosp., N.Y.C., 1965-69; cardiology resident Columbia Presbyn. Med. Ctr., N.Y.C., 1969-71, NIH cardiovascular pharmology fellow, 1971-72; asst. prof. medicine Columbia U., N.Y.C., 1972-79, assoc. prof. medicne, 1980-87, prof. medicine, 1987—. Mem. cardiorenal adv. com. Food & Drug Adminstrn., Rockville, Md., 1984-88; mem. pharmacology study sect. NIH, Bethesda, Md., 1989-93; dir. Ctr. for Women's Health, Columbia-Presbyn. Med. Ctr., N.Y.C., 1994—. Contbr. articles to profl. jours. Fellow Am. Coll. Physicians, Am. Coll. Cardiology. Office: Columbia U 630 W 168th St New York NY 10032-3795

GIAVIS, THEODORE DEMETRIOS, commercial illustrator, artist; b. Lowell, Mass., Feb. 24, 1920; s. Demetrios Harry and Nicoletta (Karas) G.; m. Theano Theofanus, May 11, 1958; 1 child, Andrew. BFA, Mass. Coll. Art, Boston, 1942; postgrad., Franklin Inst. Photography, 1950-51. Freelance comml. advt. artist, Boston, 1946-47; staff artist Sunday Mag. sect. Boston Post, 1947-53, art dir. Sunday Mag., 1953-54; comml. advt. artist Rahl Studios, N.Y.C., 1955-75; freelance comml. advt. artist Westport, Conn., 1975-85; fine artist, 1985—. Staff sgt. USAF, Guam, 1943-46. Recipient 1st place New Canaan (Conn.) Arts Show, 1971, 72, 23d New Eng. Show at Silvermine (Conn.), Anya Magnus award, 1991. Mem. Milford Fine Arts Coun. (Anya Maganus award 1991). Greek Orthodox. Avocations: tennis, bowling. Home: 2220 Pinnacle Cir S Palm Harbor FL 34684-1761

GIBALA, RONALD, metallurgical engineering educator; b. New Castle, Pa., Oct. 3, 1938; s. Steve Anthony and June Rose (Frank) G.; m. Janice Claire Grichor; children: Maryellen, Janice, David, Kristine. BS, Carnegie Inst. Tech., 1960; MS, U. Ill., 1962, PhD, 1964. Engring. technician Crane Co., New Castle, Pa., 1956-59; engr. U.S. Steel Rsch. Labs., Monroeville, Pa., 1960; rsch. asst. U. Ill., Urbana, 1960-64; asst. prof. metallurgy Case Western Res. U., Cleve., 1964-69, assoc. prof., 1969-76, prof. metallurgy and materials sci. and macromolecular sci., 1976-84, co-dir. materials rsch. lab., 1981-84; dir. metallurgy program NSF, 1982-83; prof., chmn. dept. materials sci. and engring. U. Mich., Ann Arbor, 1984-94, L.H. and F.E. Van Vlack prof. materials sci. and engring., 1998—. Dir. electron microbeam analysis lab. U. Mich., Ann Arbor, 2002—. Contbr. articles to profl. jours.; editor: Hydrogen Embrittlement and Stress Corrosion Cracking, 1984. Pres. Woodhaven Hills Homeowners Assn., 1989-91. Recipient Alfred Noble prize ASCE, 1969, NASA Materials Sci. Divsn. Paper award, 1992; named Outstanding Young Mem. Cleve. chpt. Am. Soc. Metals, 1971; Tech. Achievement award Cleve. Tech. Socs. Council, 1972; vis. research fellow C.E.N.G. Labs., Grenoble, 1973-74, Matthias fellow Los Alamos Nat. Lab., 1991-92, Disting. Merit award U. Ill., 1998; vis. scientist Sandia Nat. Labs., 1998-99. Fellow TMS/AIME (dir. 1981-87), Am. Soc. Metals (chpt. chmn. 1975-76); mem. AAAS, Materials Research Soc. (councillor 1995-97, v.p. 1998, pres. 1999), Am. Ceramic Soc., Sigma Xi, Tau Beta Pi, Alpha Sigma Mu. Clubs: Suburban Ski (pres. 1981-82). Democrat. Home: 1543 Stonehaven St Ann Arbor MI 48104-4149 Office: U Mich Dept Materials Sci Engring Ann Arbor MI 48109-2136

GIBALDI, JOSEPH, publishing executive; b. Bklyn., Aug. 20, 1942; s. Ignatius G. and Angela Peritore; m. Anita, Aug. 15, 1962; children; Laura G. Pise, Joseph M. BA in English, CCNY, 1965, MA in English, 1967; PhD in Comparative Lit., NYU, 1973. Tchr. English Bklyn. Tech. H.S., 1965-70; instr. English Bklyn. Coll., 1970-73; asst. prof. comparative lit. U. Ga., 1973-76; dir. book acquisitions Modern Lang. Assn., N.Y.C., 1976—. Adj. prof. humanities New Sch. U., N.Y.C., 1985—, NYU, 1994—. Author: MLA Handbook for Writers of Research Papers, 1977, 6th edit., 2003, MLA Style Manual, 1985, 2nd edit., 1998, Introduction to Scholarship, 1981, 2nd edit., 1992, Interrrelations of Literature, 1982, others; contbr. articles to profl. jours. NYU fellow, 1972, Duke U. fellow, 1976. Mem. Am. Comparative Lit. Assn., Modern Lang. Assn. Avocation: opera. Office: Modern Lang Assn 26 Broadway 3d Fl New York NY 10004-1789 E-mail: jgibaldi@mla.org.

GIBANS, JAMES DAVID, architect; b. Akron, Ohio, Feb. 10, 1930; s. Myer Jacob and Sylva (Hirsch) G.; m. Nina Freedlander, July 16, 1955; children: David Myer, Jonathan Samuel, Amy, Elisabeth. BA, Yale U., 1951, BArch, MArch, Yale U., 1954. Architect George K. Raad & Assocs. et al, San Francisco, 1958-63; project architect Ward and Schneider, Cleve., 1964-68; sr. assoc. William A. Gould and Assocs., Cleve., 1968-74, Don M. Hisaka and Assoc., Cleve., 1974-76; pvt. practice architecture Cleve., 1976-81; v.p. Teare Herman & Gibans, Inc., Cleve., 1981-89; v.p., treas. Herman Galvin Gibans, Inc., Cleve., 1989-91, HGG, Inc., Cleve., 1991-94, Herman Gibans Fodor, Inc., 1994—2000, v.p., 1994—. Faculty Edn. for Aesthetic Awareness Cleve. State U., 1977—79. Mem. Cleve. Landmarks Commn., 1993—; trustee, mem. exec. com., 1st v.p. Cleve. Chamber Music Soc., 1970—78; mem. adv. bd. Environ. Resource Ctr. Cleve. Pub. Libr., 1973—76; mem. design rev. com. Shaker Sq. Hist. Dist., 1991—93; bd. dirs. Cleve. Soc. Contemporary Art, 1985—86, Friends of Shaker Sq., 1994—96, Shaker Sq. Area Devel. Corp., 1996—, v.p., 1996—97, treas., 1997—2001, pres., 2001—03; trustee Clev. Found. for Arch., 1999—, chair focus com., 1999—2001, pres., 2001—03. Served with U.S. Army, 1955—57. Fulbright grantee, 1954-55. Fellow AIA (sec. Cleve. chpt. 1972-74, bd. dirs. 1984-86, treas. 1989, v.p. 1990, pres. 1991); mem. Architects Soc. Ohio (trustee 1975-76, bd. dirs. 1985-88), Cleve. City Club, Fulbright Assn. (bd. dirs. N.E. Ohio chpt. 1995-99, treas. 1998-99), N.E. Ohio Jazz Soc. (bd. dirs. 1991-96, v.p. 1993-95, pres. 1995-96), Rowfant Club (chair bldgs. and furnishings com. 2002—). Democrat. Jewish. Avocations: music, art, jogging, cross-country skiing. Home: 13800 Shaker Blvd Cleveland OH 44120-1585 Office: Herman Gibans Fodor Inc 1304 W 6th St Cleveland OH 44113-1304 E-mail: jgibans@hgfarchitects.com.

GIBARA, SAMIR G. tire manufacturing executive; b. Cairo, Egypt, Apr. 23, 1939; B in bus. adminstrn., Cairo U., 1960; M in internat. bus. and fin., Harvard U., 1964; attended, Kellogg Grad. Sch. Mgmt. Exec. Program, Northwestern U., 1985. Mgmt. trainee Goodyear Tire & Rubber Co., Akron, Ohio, 1964, v.p. European region, v.p. French operations, v.p., strategic planning and bus. devel., acting v.p., fin., chief fin. officer, 1992, exec. v.p., N. Am. tire oper., 1994, pres., COO, chmn., 1996—2003, ret., CEO, 1996—2002, mem. bd. dir., 1995—; head Goodyear Morocco; pres. Goodyear Canada; v.p. mktg. Internat. Harvester. Adv. Internat. Trade Ctr., Brussels; econ. adv. Moroccan Govt. Delegation to the U.S.; v.p., bd. mem. Am. C. of C., France; vis. prof., bus. univ. throughout Europe and U.S.; bd. dirs. Internat. Paper Co., Sumitomo Rubber Indus., Kobe, Japan, 1999—2003; exec. com. Rubber Mfr. Assn., mem. bus. coun., mem. bus. roundtable, mem. exec. mgmt. assn.; mem. Ohio Roundtable, Akron Reg. Devel. Bd.; bd. trustees Summa Health Sys., Cleveland Symphony Orchestra; past chmn. Summit County United Way Campaign, Ohio. Named Bus. Person Yr., France-Am. C. of C., Luxembourg C. of C., hon. alumnus, Univ. Akron; recipient knighted, French Order Nat. Merit, inducted, Am. Acad. Achievement. Office: Goodyear Tire & Rubber Co 1144 E Market St Akron OH 44316-0002

GIBB, MATTHEW DEWOLFE, physician; b. Bklyn., Nov. 7, 1957; s. Frederic Stephen and Patricia Ann (Mattson) G. AB, Dartmouth Coll., 1979; MD, St. Louis U., 1983. Diplomate Am. Bd. Med. Examiners; diplomate in internal medicine, interventional cardiology and cardiovascular diseases Am. Bd. Internal Medicine. Intern Naval Hosp., Portsmouth, Va., 1983-84, resident San Diego, 1987-89, fellow in cardiology, 1989-92; fellow in interventional cardiology U. Calif., San Diego, 1991-92; chmn. divsn. cardiology, dir. cardiac catheterization lab. Naval Hosp., Oakland, Calif., 1992-94; dir. invasive/interventional cardiology, dir. med. ICU Carle Clinic Assn./Carle Found. Hosp., Urbana, Ill., 1994—, also cardiologist, dir. cardiac catheterization labs., head cardiology divsn., 2000—. Clin. instr. medicine U. Calif., San Diego, 1991—92; clin. asst. prof. medicine U. Ill. Coll. Medicine, Urbana, 1995—; vice chmn. bd. govs. Carle Clinic Assn., 2001—02, chmn. bd. govs., 2003—; lectr. in field. Comdr. USN, 1983-92. Fellow ACP, Am. Coll. Cardiology; mem. AMA, Ill. State Med. Soc., Champaign County Med. Soc. Avocations: flying, antique collecing, fine wines. Office: Carle Clinic Assn 602 W University Ave Urbana IL 61801-2594

GIBB, ROBERTA LOUISE, lawyer, artist; b. Cambridge, Mass., Nov. 2, 1942; d. Thomas Robinson Pieri and Jean Knox Gibb. BS, U. Calif., La Jolla, 1969; JD, New Eng. Sch. Law, 1982; student in Epislemology and Colorusium, MIT, 1972—85. Bar: Mass. 1978. Legal aide Mass. State Legis., 1973; practice law Mass., 1980—. Author: To Boston With Love, 1980, The Art of Inflation, 1981, The Art of Economics, 1982; co-prodr.: (documentary film) Lovins on the Soft Path; contbr. articles to profl. jours.; Exhibited in group shows at Geraci Galleries, Rockport, Mass., 1996—, Rockport Art Assn. Gallery, 1996—, Represented in permanent collections, Nat. Art Mus. Art, Indpls.; prodr.: (TV documentary) Where the Spirit Leads, 1980—, 2000; executor 5 murals, sculptor Albert Einstein, Pres. Carter, Pres. Johnson, Pres. Reagan, Mother Theresa, Eleanor Roosevelt, The Marathon, Fire Dancers, Birth, Olympia, The Family, The Left Handed Squash Player, Basketball, Germain Gliddin, numerous others. Bd. dir. Essex County Environ. and Conservation, Rockport, Mass., 1980-85. Women winner Boston Marathon, 1966, 67, 68, 1st woman to run Boston Marathon, 1966; inducted into Road Runners of Am. Hall of Fame, 1982 Mem.: Inst. Study of Natural Sys. (founder, pres. 1976—), Rockport Art Assn., Nat. Sculpture Soc., Mass. Bar, Boston Athletic Assn., U.S. Assn. Club Rome, Coll. Club, Club Rome (sec. bd. dirs. 1999—). E-mail: bobbigibb@aol.com.

GIBB, ROBIN, vocalist, songwriter; b. Douglas, Isle of Man, Eng., Dec. 22, 1949; s. Hugh and Barbara G.; m. Molly Hullis, Dec. 4, 1968 (div. July 1985); m. Dwina Murphy, July 31, 1986; 1 child, Robin John; children from previous marriage: Spencer, Melissa. Performed in: (with bros. Barry and Maurice as group) amateur shows The Blue Cats, Manchester, in 1950's; formed: (with bros.) The Bee Gees, 1958, disbanded, 1969, reunited, 1971; appeared in (with bros.) local clubs, Brisbane, Australia; released: (with bros.) 1st single record Three Kisses of Love, Australia, 1963; appeared on (with bros.) own weekly TV show, Australia, in 1960's; returned to (with bros.) Eng., 1967, signed with (with bros.) NEMS Enterprises; made (with bros.) 1st U.S. TV appearance on Am. Bandstand, 1967; rec. group for Robert Stigwood Orgn.; composer (with bros.): music and lyrics for film Saturday Night Fever, 1977 (40 million copies sold/biggest selling sound track); appeared in movie Sgt. Pepper's Lonely Hearts Club Band, 1978; albums include Bee Gees First, 1967, Horizontal, 1968, Idea, 1968, Rare, Precious and Beautiful, Vol. I, 1968, Odessa, 1970, Best of the Bee Gees, 1969, Rare, Precious and Beautiful, Vols. I, II, III, 1970, Two Years On, 1972, Trafalser, To Whom It May Concern, 1973, Life in a Tin Can, 1974, Best of Bee Gees, Vols. I, II, 1973, Mr. Natural, 1974, Main Course, 1976, Children of the World, 1976, Bee Gees Gold Vol. I, 1976, Odessa, 1976, Here At Last...Bee Gees...Live, 1977, Saturday Night Fever (biggest selling soundtrack of all time), 1977, Sgt. Pepper's Lonely Hearts Club Band, 1978, Spirits Having Flown, 1978, Bee Gees Greatest Hits, 1979, (solo) Robins Reign, Secret Agent, 1983, E.S.P., 1989 (Platinum album), High Civilization, 1991, Size Isn't Everything, 1994, (solo) How Old are You?, 1999, Walls Have Eyes, Children of the World, 1976, Living Eyes, 1982, Secret Agent (solo), 1986, One, 1989, The Very Best of the Bee Gees, 1990, Tales from the Brothers Gibb-A History in Song 1967-90, 1990, High Civilization, 1991, Size Isn't Everything, 1993, Still Waters, 1997, Bee Gees: One Night Only, 1998, This is Where I Came In, 2001, (solo) Robin Gibb, 2002; writer songs (with bros.) Guilty, Heartbreaker, Islands in the Stream, and numerous others; charity performances include UNICEF, UN Show, 1978, N.Y. Police Athletic League, Madison Sq. Garden, 1979, Free Nelson Mandela Concert, Wembly Stadium, Eng., 1990, Hurricane Relief, Joe Robbie Stadium, Miami, 1992. Recipient Ivor Novello awards, 1968-69, 76-77, 77-78, Six (6) Grammy awards, numerous Gold and Platinum albums and singles RIAA, numerous gold and platinum albums and singles worldwide; inducted into Songwriters Hall of Fame, 1994, Rock 'n Roll Hall of Fame, 1997; Internat. Artists award at Am. Music Awards, outstanding contribution to British Music at The Brit Awards, London, Lifetime Achievement award at World Music Awards, 1998-99. Office: Middle Ear 1801 Bay Rd Miami Beach FL 33139-1415

GIBBES, WILLIAM HOLMAN, lawyer; b. Hartsville, S.C., Feb. 25, 1930; s. Ernest Lawrence and Nancy (Watson) G.; m. Frances Hagood, May 1, 1954; children: Richard H., William H. Jr., Lynn. BS, U. S.C., 1952, LLB, 1953. Bar: S.C. 1953, U.S. Ct. Mil. Appeals 1954, U.S. Dist. Ct. S.C. 1956, U.S. Supreme Ct. 1959, U.S. Ct. Appeals (4th cir.) 1965. Asst. atty. gen., Columbia, S.C., 1957-62; ptnr. Berry & Gibbes, Columbia, 1962-68, Berry, Lightsey, Gibbes, Columbia, 1968-72; mem. Gibbes Law Firm, P.A., Columbia, 1972—; house of dels. S.C. Bar, 1994-96. Chief judge U.S. Army Legal Svcs. Agy., 1980-83. Author: Control of Highway Access - Its Prospects and Problems, Legal Dimensions of Community Health Planning, 1969, Manual for Fee Appraisors, 1960; contbr. articles to S.C. Law Review, Law Rev. Digest, 1960. Chmn. bd. dirs. U. S.C. YMCA, 1956-60. Brig. gen. JAGC, USAR 1980-83. Recipient Legion of Merit, U.S. Army, 1983. Mem. ABA (mil. laws com. 1984-90, meml. com.), S.C. Bar Assn. (exec. com. 1961-62), Am. Bd. Trial Advocates (sec.-treas. 1994-95, pres.-elect 1995-96, pres. 1996-97), Judge Advs. Assn. (pres. 1982-83), Richland County Bar Assn., S.C. Credit Ins. Assn. (gen. counsel 1963-94), Tarantella Club, Caprician Club, Summit Club, Doonbeg (Ireland) Golf Club, Forest Lake Country Club, Kiawah Island Club, Kappa Sigma Kappa, Omicron Delta Kappa, founding mem. Doonberg Golf Club, Cnty. Clare Ireland, 2002. Episcopalian. Home: 35 Avian Tr Columbia SC 29206-4965 E-mail: gibbesbill@msn.com.

GIBBONS, CELIA VICTORIA TOWNSEND (MRS. JOHN SHELDON), editor, publisher; b. Fargo, N.D. d. Harry Alton and Helen (Haag) Townsend; m. John Sheldon Gibbons, May 1, 1935; children: Mary Vee, John Townsend. Student, U. Minn., 1930-33. Advt. mgr. Hotel Nicollet, Mpls., 1933-37; contbg. editor children's mags., 1935—; ptnr. Youth assocs. Co., Mpls., 1942-65; pub. art dir. Mines and Escholier mags., 1954-65; founder Bull. Bd. Pictures, Inc., Mpls., 1954, pres., 1954—. Founder Periodical Litho Art Co., Mpls., 1962, pres., 1962-65; artist Cath. Boy mag., 1938; artist, designer book Palaces That Went To Sea, 1990; chief photographer Cath. Miss mag., 1955; cons., contbg. editor Nereus Pub. Co., 1998-. Mem. Women's aux. Mpls. Symphony Orch.; mem. Ft. Lauderdale (Fla.) Art Mus.; Rep. chairwoman Golden Valley, Minn., 1950; alt. del. Hennepin County Rep. Conv., 1962. Mem. Mpls. Inst. Arts, Internat. Inst., St. Paul Arts and Sci., Art Guild Boca Raton, Woman's Club, Minikahda Club, Deerfield Beach Women's Club. Home: 1416 Alpine Pass Tyrol Hills Minneapolis MN 55416 Office: 1057 Hillsboro Mile Hillsboro Beach FL 33062

GIBBONS, DONA ALDEN COE, electrical engineer; b. Springfield, Mass., Mar. 9, 1975; s. Arthur Coe and Virginia Elaine Fife Gibbons. BEE, B in Computer Engring., Coop. Edn. BEE, Coop. Edn. Bachelor of Software Engring., Auburn U., 2000. Cert. profl. Comptia Network, 03. Thinkpad product specialist, server qas analyst IBM Personal Sys. Group, Research Triangle Park, NC, 1996—98; goverment contract U. S. Army - Ft. Benning, Columbus, Ga., 1999—2002; network specialist - instl. support earmy Troy State U. - SE Regions, Columbus, Ga. Mem.: ASCD, IEEE, Assn. for Computing Machinery, Auburn Alumni Assn. Home: 1081 Lee Rd 439 Salem AL 36874 Office: Troy State Univ - Southeast Region 506 Manchester Expressway Suite B-15 Columbus GA 31904 Office Fax: 706-660-9146. Personal E-mail: gibboda@netscape.net. E-mail: gibbonsd@troyst.edu.

GIBBONS, EDWARD FRANCIS, psychobiologist; b. Bronx, N.Y., Dec. 25, 1949; s. Edward Francis and Mary Theresa (Westervelt) G. BS, SUNY, Stony Brook, 1977, PhD, 1986. Dir. ctr. for sci. and tech. Briarcliffe Coll., Woodbury, NY, 1992—96, asst. prof. liberal arts and scis. dept. Patchogue, NY, 1993—2000, assoc. prof. liberal arts and scis. dept., 2000—, chair liberal arts and scis. dept., 2001—, acting asst. dean acad. affairs, 2001—02, asst. dean acad. affairs, 2002—. Series editor: SUNY Press Series on Endangered Species, 1986-95, Naturalistic Environments in Capitivity for Animal Behavior Research, 1994, Conservation of Endangered Species in Captivity: An Interdisciplinary Approach, 1995; contbr. articles to profl. jours. Sgt. USAF, 1970-74. Grantee Inst. Mus. Svcs., 1988-90, N.Y. State Dept. Edn., 1993-95. Mem. AAAS, N.Y. Acad. Scis., Soc. Behavioral Medicine, L.I. Soc. Women in Sci. and Tech. (bd. dirs., founder), Soc. for Conservation Biology, Soc. History of Tech., Sigma Xi. Roman Catholic. Home: 2409 Saddle Rock Rd Holbrook NY 11741 Office: Briarcliffe Coll 10 Lake St Patchogue NY 11772-2506 E-mail: edgibbons@aol.com.

GIBBONS, JAMES ARTHUR, congressman; b. Reno, Dec. 16, 1944; s. Leonard A. and Matilda (Hancock) G.; m. T. Dawn Sanders-Snelling, June 21, 1986; children: Christopher, Jennifer, James A. Jr. BS in Geology, U. Nev., Reno, 1967, MS in Mining Geology, 1973; JD, Southwestern U., 1979. Bar: Nev. 1982, U.S. Dist. Ct. Nev. 1982. Hydrologist U.S. Fed. Water Master, Reno, 1963-67; geologist Union Carbide Co., Reno, 1972-75; comml. pilot Western Airlines, Inc., L.A., 1979-88; pilot Delta Airlines, Salt Lake City, 1988-96; sr. land mgr., atty. Homestake Mining Co., Reno, 1980-82; pvt. practice Reno, 1982—; mem. U.S. Congress from Nev. 2nd dist., 1997—; mem. house resource com., armed svcs. com., homeland sec. com. Environ. atty. Alaskan Wilderness Soc., Anchorage, 1982-83; mem. Congressional Com. on Nat. Security, 1997—, Resources, 1997—, Intelligence, 1997—, Vets. Affair, 1999—. Contbr. articles to profl. pubs. Mem. Nev. Coun. on Econ. Edn., 1986; mem. Nev. State Assembly, 1988-94. Lt. col. Nev. Air Nat. Guard, Persian Gulf, 1990-91; with USAF, 1967-72. Decorated DFC. Mem. Assn. Trial Lawyers of Am., Nev. Trial Lawyers Assn., Rocky Mt. Mineral Law Found., Comml Law League Am., Am. Inst. Mining Engrs., Nev. Landman's Assn. (chmn. 1981-82, cons. atty. 1982-83). Republican. Avocation: flying. Office: US Ho Reps 100 Cannon Ho Office Bldg Washington DC 20515-0001 E-mail: mail.gibbons@mail.house.gov.*

GIBBONS, JOHN HOWARD HOWARD (JACK GIBBONS), government official, physicist; b. Harrisonburg, Va., Jan. 15, 1929; s. Howard K. and Jessie Diana (Conrad) G.; m. Mary Ann Hobart, May 21, 1955; children: Virginia Neil, Diana Conrad, Mary Marshall. BS in Math. and Chemistry, Randolph-Macon Coll., 1949, ScD (hon.), 1977; PhD in Physics, Duke U., 1954, ScD (hon.), 1997; PhD in Humane Letters and Sci. (hon.), Ill. Inst. Tech., 1994; PhD in Sci. (hon.), Mt. Sinai Med. Sch., 1995; ScD (hon.), U. Delaware, 1996, U. Md., 1997. Physicist and group leader nuclear geophysics Oak Ridge Nat. Lab., 1954-69, dir. environ. program, 1969-73; dir. Energy Conservation Office, Fed. Energy Adminstrn., Washington, 1973-74; prof. physics, dir. Energy, Environ. and Resources Center, U. Tenn., Knoxville, 1974-79; dir. Office of Tech. Assessment, U.S. Congress, 1979-92; asst. to Pres. for sci. and tech. Exec. Office of the Pres., Washington, 1993-98; dir. of sci. and tech. policy Exec. Office of Pres., Washington, 1993-98; Karl T. Compton lectr. MIT, 1998-99; sr. fellow NAE, 1999-2000; sr. advisor U.S. Dept. State, 1999-2000. Energy and resources com. Aspen Inst., 1979—92; mem. adv. com. Stanford U. Sch. Engring., 1984—87, Electric Power Rsch. Inst., 1986—92; mem. Carnegie Corp. Sci., Tech. and Govt. Task Force on Long Term Goals and Priorities, 1990—92; bd. dirs. bd. dirs. Supercritical Combustion Tech. Interstate Gen. LP, Dynamac Corp., Gibbons Surg. Corp.; mem. com. advisors Nat. Renewable Energy Lab., 1998—; pres. Resource Strategies, 1998—; bd. dirs. Black Rock Forest Consortium, George and Marta Brown Found.; mem. internat. adv. bd. Com. on Internat. Programs, Nat. Academics, 2001—; mem. spl. fields and interdisciplinary engring. peer com. Nat. Academics, 2001—. Author: This Gifted Age: Science and Technology at the Millennium, 1997; contbr. articles to profl. jours. Chmn. bd. assocs. Randolph-Macon Coll., Ashland, Va., 1980-83, trustee, 1977-79; bd. dirs. World Resources Inst., 1998—. Decorated comdr. Ordre des Palmes Academiques (France), officer's cross Order of Merit (Germany); recipient Disting. Svc. award Fed. Energy Adminstrn., 1974, Pub. Svc. award Fedn. Am. Scientists, 1990, Disting. Alumni award James Madison U., 1993, Life Achievement in Sci. award Commonwealth of Va., 1995, First Seymour Cray High Performance Computing Industry Recognition award, 1997, Disting. Svc. medal NASA, 1998. Fellow: NSF (Disting. Pub. Svc. award 1998), AAAS (bd. dirs. 1988—90, Philip Hauge Abelson prize 1993), Am. Assn. Engring. Socs. (chmn.'s award 1998), Am. Phys. Soc. (Leo Szilard award for physics in pub. interest 1991), Assn. for Women in Sci.; mem.: NAE (Arthur Bueche award 1998), Am. Assn. Engring. Socs., Am. Philos. Soc., N.Y. Acad. Scis. (bd. govs. 1998—, trustee 1998—), Coun. Fgn. Rels., Cosmos Club, Sigma Pi Sigma (John P. McGovern Sci. and Soc. award and medal 1997), Pi Mu Epsilon, Omicron Delta Kappa, Pi Gamma Mu, Phi Beta Kappa, Sigma Xi (pres. 2000—01). Episcopal. Avocations: hiking, farming, conservation, non-governmental organizations (ngo's). Home: PO Box 497 The Plains VA 20198 E-mail: jackgibbons@erols.com. *My formal training in physics, backed by a liberal arts education, enabled me to drink deeply from the sweet spring of basic research for many years. When I took leave from disciplinary research and became immersed in analysis of socio-technical issues, it was a most discom-*

forting step. But having taken it, the new challenges were not only enlivening, but also surprisingly susceptible to the problem-solving approaches I had learned in science. The lessons: (1)Training in physics is an effective instrument to learn how to solve many kinds of problems; (2)A change in professional direction about every decade or so is a great tonic; (3)Attacking issues from fresh perspectives is a natural ingredient of creativity.

GIBBONS, JOHN MARTIN, JR., physician, educator; b. N.Y.C., Feb. 25, 1933; s. John Martin and Mary Frances (Darr) G.; m. Mary Therese Peyser, Dec. 26, 1955; children: Catherine Way, Mary Sloan, John M. III, Fredericka Kerr, Myles. AB, Holy Cross Coll., 1954; MD, Georgetown U., 1958. Diplomate Am. Bd. Ob-Gyn., Am. Bd. Maternal and Fetal Medicine. Intern and resident ob-gyn Saint Vincent's Hosp., N.Y.C., 1958—63; from asst. to assoc. prof. ob-gyn. U. Conn., Farmington, 1970—78, prof. ob-gyn., 1978—. Chief dept. ob-gyn. Fordham Hosp., N.Y.C., 1968-70; dir. dept. ob-gyn. Saint Francis Hosp. and Med. Ctr., Hartford, Conn., 1970-93, sr. v.p. for med. affairs, 1993-99; mem. adv. coun. Nat. Inst. Child Hhealth and Human Devel., 2001—. Mem. Capital Area Health Consortium Bd., 1978-2000 ; mem. exec. com. Combined Hosps. Fund, 1978-82, Mt. Sinai Hosp. Bd., 1990-95; mem. Bristol Hosp. Bd.; mem. Hartford Ballet Bd., 1978-83, hon. mem., 1983-95, v.p., 1993-95, pres., 1995-97; mem. Hartford Stage Bd., 1999—; mem. Med. Delivery Sys., Inc., 1985-88, Greater Hartford Arts Coun., 1988-92, 95-97; corporator Wadsworth Atheneum, 1987-97; overseer Bushnell Meml. Hall, 1990—. Capt. USAR, 1963-68. Fellow ACOG (dist. treas. 1987-91, dist. vice chmn. 1991-94, nat. fin. com. 1992-00, dist. chmn. 1994-97, nat. treas. 1997-00, pres.-elect 2002-03, pres. 2003—), ACS, Soc. Maternal-Fetal Medicine, Obstet. Soc. Boston; mem. Conn. State Med. Soc. (sec. ob-gyn., vice chmn. 1979-82, chmn. 1982-85), Hartford Med. Soc., Hartford Golf Club, Harvard Club of N.Y.C., Lotos Club (N.Y.C.). Office: Saint Francis Hosp Med Ctr 114 Woodland St Hartford CT 06105-1208 E-mail: jgibbons@stfranciscare.org.

GIBBONS, JOSEPH HARRISON, engineering educator, farmer; b. Turbeville, S.C., Sept. 4, 1934; s. James Harry and Roxie Lanie Gibbons; m. Geneva F. Gibbons, June 10, 1956; children: Karen, Lisa. BS in Chem. Engring., U. S.C., 1956; MS in Chem. Engring., U. Pitts., 1958, PhD in Chem. Engring 1961. Registered profl. engr., S.C. Chem. engr. Du Pont, Aiken, SC, 1955, Westinghouse, Pitts., 1956—63; assoc. prof. U. S.C., Columbia, 1963—74, prof., 1974—, chair chem. engring. dept., 1977—93, assoc. dean, 1991—2001, dean, 1999—2000. Named Engr. of Yr., S.C. Soc. Prof. Engrs., Columbia, 1993. Fellow: AIChE; mem.: NSPE, Am. Soc. for Engring. Edn., Am. Chem. Soc., Tau Beta Pi, Phi Beta Kappa. Baptist. Avocations: fishing, woodworking, classic cars. Home: 6300 Macon Rd Columbia SC 29209 Office: U SC Columbia SC 29208-0001

GIBBONS, JULIA SMITH, federal judge; d. John Floyd and Julia Jackson (Abernathy) Smith; m. William Lockhart Gibbons, Aug. 11, 1973; children: Rebecca Carey, William Lockhart Jr. BA, Vanderbilt U., 1972; JD, U. Va., 1975. Bar: Tenn. 1975. Law clk. to judge U.S. Ct. Appeals, 1975-76; assoc. Farris, Hancock, Gilman, Branan, Lanier & Hellen, Memphis, 1976-79; legal advisor Gov. Lamar Alexander, Nashville, 1979-81; judge 15th Jud. Cir., Memphis, 1981-83, U.S. Dist. Ct. (we. dist.) Tenn., Memphis, 1983—2002, chief judge, 1994-2000; judge U.S. Ct. Appeals (6th cir.), Memphis, 2002—. Fellow: Memphis and Shelby County Bar Found., Tenn. Bar Found., Am. Bar Found.; mem.: Memphis Bar Assn., Phi Beta Kappa, Order of Coif. Presbyterian. Office: US Ct Appeals 1157 Federal Bldg 167 N Main St Memphis TN 38103-1816

GIBBONS, MILES JOSEPH, JR., foundation administrator; b. Scranton, Pa., June 25, 1935; s. Miles J. and Claire (Kennedy) G.; m. Carole Forker; children: Miles D., Elisabeth D. BA, Dickinson Coll., Carlisle, Pa., 1957; JD, Georgetown U., 1964; postgrad., Harvard U., 1996. Cost acct. U.S. Steel, Johnstown, Pa., 1957-60; acct. RCA Svc. Co., Alexandria, Va., 1961-64; atty. Keating, Waterval and Johnson, Falls Church, Va., 1964-65; staff atty. AMP Inc., Harrisburg, Pa., 1965-68; counsel to minority leader Ho. of Reps. Commonwealth of Pa., Harrisburg, 1968-70; assoc. atty. Morgan, Lewis and Bockius, Harrisburg, 1968-71, ptnr., 1971-81, of counsel, 1981-84; exec. dir. The Helen F. Whitaker Fund, Mechanicsburg, Pa., 1984—, The Franklin H. and Ruth L. Wells Found., Machanicsburg, 1983—; CEO, pres. The Whitaker Found., Rosslyn, Va. and Mechanicsburg, Pa., 1981-2000. Mem. sch. bd. Northern York County Sch. Dist., Dillsburg, Pa., 1984-88; chair problem solving com. United Way of Capital Region, Harrisburg, 1990-91; bd. dirs. United Way of Pa., 1994-95; bd. dirs. South Ctrl. Pa. Housing Devel. Found., Harrisburg, 1990-95, mem. exec. com., 1991-95; bd. dirs. Coun. for Pub. Edn., Harrisburg, 1989-92, The Fredricksen Found., Mechanicsburg, Pa., 1990—; mem. adv. bd. Milton S. Hershey Med. Sch., 1992-98; vol. Big Bros./Big Sisters, Harrisburg, 1990-95; co-chair Found. Exec. Rountable, Harrisburg, 1989-99; bd. dirs. Capital Campaign Review Com., Harrisburg, 1989—, chair, 1992—. Recipient Pub. Svc. award Messiah Coll., 1997, Founder's Day award Lebanon Valley Coll., 1999. Mem. Rotary Club Harrisburg (pres. 1988-89, Community Svc. award 1990). Office: The Helen F Whitaker Fund 4718 Old Gettysburg Rd Mechanicsburg PA 17055-4378 E-mail: mgibbons@whitaker.org.

GIBBONS, REX VINCENT, geologist; b. Lumsden, Nfld., Can., Feb. 12, 1946; s. Clayton Manuel and Nita Mildred (Vincent) G.; m. Marjorie Stagg, May 20, 1966; children: Kim, Emily, Vince. BA in Edn., BSc, Meml. U. of Nfld., 1967, MSc in Geology, 1969; PhD in Geology, Calif. Inst. Tech., 1974. Registered profl. geologist, Nfld. Rsch. scientist NASA/Johnson Space Ctr., Houston, 1974-76; sr. geologist Nfld. Dept. Mines & Energy, St. John's, 1976-89; mem. Ho. of Assembly, St. John's West, Nfld., 1989-97, minister of mines and energy, 1989-94, 96-97, minister of natural resources, 1994-96; exec. v.p., sr. geosci. cons. Jacques Whitford Environment Ltd., Nfld. Geosci. Ltd., St. John's, 1997—. Bd. dirs. Newfoundland Power, Donner Minerals Ltd. Contbr. numerous articles to profl. jours.; assoc. editor Geosci. Canada, 1980-85. Mem. Avalon Consol. Sch. Bd., St. John's, 1982-89, chmn., 1986-89; bd. mgmt. St. James United Ch., 1983-87; bd. regents Meml. U. of Nfld., 1978-81; bd. dirs. Nfld. Lung Health Found., Nfld. Sci. Ctr., Nfld. Ocean Industries, 1998-2001, St. John's Bd. Trade, 1998-2000. Nat. Rsch. Coun. Can. grad. bursary, 1968-69; Nfld. Govt. grad. fellow, 1967-68, Centenary scholar, 1966-67. Mem.: Assn. Profl. Engrs. and Geoscientists of Nfld., Can. Inst. Mining, Metallurgy & Petroleum (councillor, nat. v.p. 1982—87, nat. pres. 2001—02). Liberal. Avocations: fly fishing, curling, canoeing, hunting, genealogy. Home: 34 Spratt Pl St John's NF Canada A1E 4M2 Office: Jacques Whitford Environ 607 Torbay Rd St John's NF Canada A1A 4Y6 E-mail: rex@roadrunner.nf.net.

GIBBONS, ROBERT D. biostatistics educator; b. Chgo., June 28, 1955; s. Sidney W. and Rozlyn Gibbons; m. Carol Homa, Sept. 16, 1979; children: Julie, Jason. BA, U. Denver, 1976; PhD, U. Chgo., 1981. Asst. prof. biostats. U. Ill., Chgo., 1981-85, assoc. prof., 1985-93, prof., 1993—; dir. Ctr. Health Stats., U. Ill., 2000—. Mem. health sci. policy bd. NAS-Inst. Medicine, Washington, 1999—, mem. com. on efficacy and safety of hypnotic halcion, 1998, mem. com. on solid organ transplantation, 1999; reviewer health svcs. rsch. internal rev. group NIH, 1992-95; mem. com. on organ transplantation Inst. Medicine, 1999; testifier on allocation organs for transplantation U.S. Congress, 1999. Author: Statistical Methods for Groundwater Monitoring, 1994, Statistical Methods for Detection and Quantification of Environmental Contamination, 2000; contbr. articles to sci. jours., including Jour. Am. Statis. Assn., Sci. Recipient young investigator award Office Naval Rsch., 1985, rsch. scientist award NIH, 1995, 20th Century Disting. Svc. award Lukacs Symposium, 1999. Mem.: Inst. Medicine. Avocations: skiing, tennis. Office: U Ill at Chgo 1601 W Taylor St Chicago IL 60612-4310 Fax: 312-996-2113. E-mail: rdgib@uic.edu

GIBBONS, ROBERT JOHN, lawyer; b. Bklyn., Dec. 3, 1944; s. David Thomas and Virginia Marie G.; m. Judith Ann Borst, Nov. 23, 1968; children: Robert, Sharon, Suzanne. BA, St. John's U., Jamaica, N.Y., 1966; JD, Fordham U., 1969. Bar: N.Y. 1970. Assoc. Mudge, Rose, Guthrie, Alexander & Ferdon, N.Y.C., 1969-76; ptnr. Wood, Dawson et al, N.Y.C., 1976-77, Debevoise & Plimpton, N.Y.C., 1977—. Trustee New Canaan County Sch., Conn., 1983-91, pres. bd. trustees, 1988-91; bd. dirs. New Canaan Baseball Inc., 1982-88, New Canaan Field Club; mem. Utilities Commn. Town of New Canaan, 1986-90. Mem. ABA, N.Y. State Bar Assn., Assn. of Bar of City of N.Y. Home: 221 Michigan Rd New Canaan CT 06840-2223 Office: Debevoise & Plimpton 919 3rd Ave Fl 23 New York NY 10022-6225

GIBBONS, ROBERT PHILIP, management consultant, director; m. Mary Jane M. Jamieson, June 12, 1965; children: Laura Ann, Robert John. BSME, Stevens Inst. Tech., 1955; MS in Indsl. Mgmt., Purdue U., 1959. Ptnr. Touche Ross Co., N.Y.C., 1959—74; v.p., gen. mgr. Carborundum Co., Niagara Falls, NY, 1975—78; ptnr. Main Hurdman, N.Y.C., 1978—84, Zolfo, Cooper & Co., N.Y.C., 1984—86, Gibbons, Quintero & Co., N.Y.C., 1986—90, Gibbons & Co., Tenafly, NJ, 1990—. Apptd. trustee U.S. Trustee and U.S. Bankruptcy Ct. Contbr. Bd. dirs., chmn. audit com., compensation com. Weldotron Corp., 1974—91. With U.S. Army, 1956—58. Mem.: Turnaround Mgmt. Assn., Am. Bankruptcy Inst., Inst. Mgmt. Cons. (cert.), Am. Prodn. and Inventory Control Soc. (cert.). Office: Gibbons & Company 46 Knoll Rd Tenafly NJ 07670-1050

GIBBONS, SAM MELVILLE, business executive, former congressman; b. Tampa, Fla., Jan. 20, 1920; s. Gunby and Jessie Kirk (Cralle) G.; m. Martha Hanley, Sept. 14, 1946; children: Clifford, Mark, Timothy. JD, U. Fla., 1947. Bar: Fla. 1947. Mem. Fla. Ho. of Reps., 1952-58, Fla. Senate, 1958-62, 88th-104th Congresses from 7th (now 11th) Fla. dist., 1962-96; ranking minority mem. ways and means com. U.S. Ho. Reps, chmn. ways and means com., 1994-95, mem. joint taxation com., 1996—; chmn. Gibbons & Co., Washington, 1996—. Founder, 1st pres. U.S. Fla. Found., 1958. Served to maj. AUS, 1941-45, ETO. Decorated Bronze Star; named Outstanding Young Man Tampa Jr. C. of C., 1954; recipient President's award Tampa C. of C., 1955; featured in Tom Brokaw book The Greatest Generation and Steve Ambrose's "D" Day. Mem. Tampa Bar Assn. (dir.), Hillsborough Bar Assn. (dir.), Greater Tampa C. of C. (dir.) Democrat. Presbyterian (deacon). Office: Gibbons and Co 1455 Pennsylvania Ave NW Washington DC 20004-1008*

GIBBONS, WILLIAM JOHN, lawyer; b. Chgo., Jan. 22, 1947; s. Edward and Lottie (Gasiorek) G.; children: Maximilian Clay, Bartholomew David, Ariel Katherine. BA, Northwestern U., 1968, JD, 1972. Bar: Ill. 1972, U.S. Dist. Ct. (no. dist.) Ill. 1972, U.S. Ct. Appeals (9th cir.) 1980, U.S. Supreme Ct. 1982, U.S. Ct. Appeals (7th cir.) 1984, U.S. Ct. Appeals (3d cir.) 2002. Assoc. Kirkland and Ellis, Chgo., 1972-76; ptnr. Hedlund, Hunter and Lynch, Chgo., 1976-82, Latham and Watkins, Chgo., 1982—, mng. ptnr. Chgo. office, 1995-2000. Served with USAR, 1968-74. Mem.: ABA, Chgo. Coun. Lawyers, Seventh Cir. Bar Assn., Chgo. Bar Assn. (chair class action com. 1994—95), Riverpark Club (Chgo.). Home: 1515 S PRairie # 913 Chicago IL 60605-3024 Office: Latham & Watkins Sears Tower Ste 5800 Chicago IL 60606-6306

GIBBONS, WILLIAM REGINALD, JR., poet, novelist, translator, editor; b. Houston, Jan. 7, 1947; s. William Reginald and Elizabeth (Lubowski) G.; m. Virginia Margaret Harris, June 8, 1968 (div. July 1982); m. Cornelia Maude Spelman, Aug. 18, 1983. AB, Princeton U., 1969; MA, Stanford U., 1971, PhD, 1974. Instr. Spanish Rutgers U., Brunswick, N.J., 1975-76; lectr. creative writing Princeton U., 1976-80, Columbia U., N.Y.C., 1980-81; prof. English Northwestern U., Evanston, Ill., 1981—, editor TriQuarterly, 1981-97; prof. MFA Program for Writers Warren Wilson Coll., 1989—. Author: Roofs Voices Roads, 1979 (Quar. Rev. prize), The Ruined Motel, 1981, Saints, 1986, Maybe It Was So, 1991, Five Pears or Peaches, 1991, William Goyen: A Study of the Short Fiction, 1991, Sweetbitter, 1994, Sparrow: New and Selected Poems, 1997, Homage to Longshot O'Leary, 1999, It's Time, 2002; translator: Selected Poems of Luis Cernuda, 1978, Guillén on Guillén, 1979, Euripides' Bakkhai, 2001, (with Charles Segal) Sophokles' Antigone, 2003; editor: The Poet's Work, 1979; (with G. Graff) Criticism in the University, 1985, The Writer in Our World, 1986, Fiction of the Eighties, 1990, Thomas McGrath: Life and the Poem, 1991, New Writing from Mexico, 1992. Woodrow Wilson fellow Stanford U., 1969-70; Fulbright fellow Spain, 1971-72; Guggenheim fellow, 1983-84; NEA fellow, 1984; Ill. Arts Coun. fellow, 1988; recipient Translation prize Denver Quar., 1977, Short Story award Tex. Inst. Letters, 1986, Carl Sandburg award, 1992, Anisfield-Wolf Book award, 1995, Jesse Jones award Tex. Inst. Letters, 1995, Ill. Arts Coun. Lit. awards, 1996, 97, Balcones Poetry prize, 1998, Best Book of Poems award Tex. Inst. Letters, 2002, others. Mem. PEN Am. Ctr., Poetry Soc. Am. (John Masefield Meml. award 1991), Associated Writing Programs (bd. dirs. 1984-87), The Guild Complex (bd. dirs. 1989—). Office: Northwestern U Dept English Univ Hall 215 Evanston IL 60208-0001 E-mail: rgibbons@northwestern.edu.

GIBBS, ANTONY (TONY GIBBS), film editor; Editor: (films) The Loneliness of the Long Distance Runner, 1962, A Taste of Honey, 1962, Tom Jones, 1963, The Luck of Ginger Coffey, 1964, The Knack...And How to Get It, 1965, The Loved One, 1965, Petulia, 1968, Performance, 1970, Walkabout, 1971, (with Robert Lawrence) Fiddler on the Roof, 1971, Jesus Christ Superstar, 1973, Rollerball, 1975, The Sailor Who Fell from Grace with the Sea, 1976, A Bridge Too Far, 1977, (with Graeme Clifford) F.I.S.T., 1978, Yesterday's Hero, 1979, (with George Trirogoff) Butch and Sundance: The Early Days, 1979, (with Anne V. Coates and Stanley Warnow) Ragtime, 1981, The Dogs of War, 1981, Bad Boys, 1983, Dune, 1984, Agnes of God, 1985, Tai-Pan, 1986, Russkies, 1987, Stealing Home, 1988, (with Lou Lombardo) In Country, 1989, The Runner, 1990, The Taking of Beverly Hills, 1992, The Man Without a Face, 1993, Don Juan DeMarco, 1995, Ronin, 1998, Reindeer Games, 2000, (TV movies) Devlin, 1992, A Case for Life, 1996, Crime of the Century, 1996, George Wallace, 1997, James Dean, 2001. Office: 15691 Royal Ridge Rd Sherman Oaks CA 91403-4208 E-mail: SeymourPrd@aol.com.

GIBBS, BEATRICE ESTHER, librarian; b. Malden, Mass., Oct. 16, 1918; d. Joseph S. and Della N. (Rainen) G.; m. Howard Konowitch (dec. 1976); children: Paula, Bonnie, Marian, Ben. BA, Tufts U., 1969; MA, Rowan State U., 1972. Tchr. Mid. Twp., Cape May Courthouse, N.J., 1964-75; libr., head children svcs. Cape May County Libr., Cape May Courthouse, 1975-84; libr. Montgomery County Libr., Bethesda, Md., 1985—. Appeared weekly WCMC TV program, 1976-84; dir. Children's Resource Ctr., 1994-96. Columnist: (book rev.) Gazette. Pres. PTA, Wildwood, N.J., 1964-70; leader Girl Scouts Am., Wildwood, 1964-70; dir. Coop Nursery, Wildwood, 1966-70. With USN, 1942-45. Mem. ALA, NCJW, Cape May County Art League (v.p. 1960-65), Cape May County Hist. Soc. (sec. 1965-68), Montgomery Libr. Staff Assn., Women in the Arts Mus., Tufts Alumni Assn., Internat. Reading Assn., Internat. Board Books for Young Children (del.), Am. Legion, Primetimers. Avocations: travel, photography, museums, music, art. Home: 8100 Connecticut Ave Apt 523 Chevy Chase MD 20815 Office: Montgomery County Library 5501 Massachusetts Ave Bethesda MD 20816-1932

GIBBS, CARROLL ROBERT, historian, writer; b. Washington, June 13, 1949; s. Carroll Robert Gibbs and Dora Reynolds; m. Bettie Jean Robinson, June 8, 1997. BJ, Howard U., 1986. Author: Black Georgetown Remembered, 1991, Black Explorers, 1992, Black Inventors: From Africa to America, 1995, Black, Copper & Bright: D.C.'s Black Civil War Regiment, 2002; contbr. articles to newspapers and mags. Hist. cons./cmty. scholar D.C. Cmty. Humanities Coun., 1991—. With U.S. Army, 1967-70. Recipient Man of the Yr. Cmty. Svc. award Seat Pleasant Met. Area Bus. & Profl. Women, 1987, Outstanding Leadership award D.C. Black History Celebration Com., 1999, award Mid. States Coun. Social Studies, 1999. Mem. Company Mil. Historians. Avocations: fencing, cycling.

GIBBS, CHARLES CLARENCE, anesthesiologist; b. Syracuse, N.Y., Jan. 17, 1951; MD, SUNY, Syracuse, 1977. Diplomate Am. Bd. Anesthesiology. Intern SUNY Upstate Med. Ctr., Syracuse, 1977-78, resident in anesthesiology, 1978-80; fellow in anesthesiology VA Med. Ctr., Syracuse, 1980-81; pvt. practice Adirondack Anesthesia Svcs. PC, Saranac Lake, N.Y., 1985—. Fellow Am. Coll. Anesthesiologists; mem. AMA, Am. Soc. Anesthesiology, Med. Soc. State of N.Y., N.Y. State Soc. Anesthesiologists. Home: Villa dell' Arcobaleno Rainbow Lake NY 12976-0098 Office: Adirondack Anesthesia Svcs PC PO Box 890 Saranac Lake NY 12983-0890

GIBBS, CHRISTOPHER HOWARD, musicologist, educator; b. N.Y.C., Feb. 20, 1958; s. Howard Glenn and Janet Gibbs; m. Helena Sedlackova, Sept. 27, 1993 BA, Haverford Coll., 1980; MPhil, Columbia U., 1987, PhD, 1992. Vis. asst. prof. music Haverford (Pa.) Coll., 1992—93; asst. prof. music Buffalo (N.Y.) U., 1993—2001, assoc. prof., 2001—03; Ottaway prof. music Bard Coll., Annandale-on Hudson, NY, 2002—; co-artistic dir. Bard Music Festival, 2000—; program annotator The Phila. Orch. Lectr., Carnegie Hall, Lincoln Ctr., Cleve. Symphony, N.Y. Philharm., Phila. Orch.; music critic Chautauquan Daily, 1994—; musicol. dir. Schubertiade, 92d St. Y, N.Y.C., 1995-97, musicol. adviser, Schubert Festival, Carnegie Hall, 1997. Author: The Life of Schubert, 2000; editor: The Cambridge Companion to Schubert, 1997; contbr. articles to profl. jours., anthologies, and ref. works, including New Grove Dictionary of Music and Musicians, revised edit.; author program notes, Phila. Orch., 2000—, Carnegie Hall, Great Performers at Lincoln Ctr., 92d St. Y, other instns. and record cos.; participant NPR and Pub. Radio Internat. broadcasts. Mem. bd. trustees, Chautauqua (N.Y.) Instn., 1998—; artistic co-dir. Bard Music Festival, Recipient ASCAP Deems Taylor award, 1998; fellow Am. Coun. Learned Socs., 1999-2000. Mem. Am. Musicol. Soc., Internat. Franz Schubert Inst. (N.Am. sec. 1998—). Home: 442 E 20th St New York NY 10009 Office: Bard Coll Music Dept Annandale On Hudson NY 12504 E-mail: Gibbs@Bard.edu.

GIBBS, DAVID GEORGE, retired food processing company executive; b. Vancouver, B.C., Can., May 5, 1925; s. Albert Edward and Florence (Bedford) G.; m. Lenore Joyce De Geer, Oct. 7, 1949; 1 dau., Susan Caroline. Grad. high sch.; MBA, Simon Fraser U., 1975. C.G.A., Can. Audit clk. Price Waterhouse (chartered accountants), 1943-46; with Kelly Douglas Co. Ltd., Vancouver, 1946-89, controller, 1965-89, v.p., 1975-89. Elected bd. dirs., elected pres. Western Lettuce Now Inc., 1996. Treas. Burrard Yacht Club, Coalition to Eliminate Abuse of Srs., D.K.G.D. Enterprises Ltd. Named Ky. col., 1968 Mem. Fin. Execs. Inst., B.C. Hot House Growers Assn. (bd. dirs. 1998-2002). Clubs: Capilano Lions (charter pres. 1977), Masons. Home: 956 Belgrave St North Vancouver BC Canada V7R 1Z2

GIBBS, DAVID N(EIL), history and political science educator; b. New Brunswick, NJ, June 1, 1958; s. Bernard and Sybil (Nemet) G. BA, George Washington U., 1979; MA, Georgetown U., 1983; PhD, MIT, 1989. MacArthur Fellow U. Wis., Madison, 1989-90; asst. prof. polit. sci. U. Ariz., Tucson, 1990—96, assoc. prof., 1996—. Udal fellow, 1998. Mem. Ctr. Middle East Studies, U. Ariz., 1990—. Author: The Political Economy of Third World Intervention, 1991; contbr. articles to profl. jours. and newspapers. Home: 105 E 17th St Tucson AZ 85701-0027 Office: Univ Ariz 215 Social Scis Tucson AZ 85721-0027 E-mail: dgibbs@arizona.edu.

GIBBS, DENIS LAUREL, radiologist; b. Wayne, Mich., Mar. 6, 1945; s. Laurel Pierce and Alwyn Marie (Larson) G.; m. Paula Kay Lynn, Sept. 6, 1974 (div. Aug. 1988); children: Jeremy Paul, Matthew Ryan, Kevin Christopher, Denis Patrick; m. Kathleen Marie DeLaFuente, July 9, 1989; 1 child, Andrew Zachery. BS, Andrews U., Berrien Springs, Mich., 1967, postgrad., 1967-69; DO, Kansas City Coll. Osteopathic Medicine, 1974. Diplomate Am. Bd. Radiology. Intern, radiology resident Doctors' Hosps., Columbus, Ohio, 1974-78, staff radiologist, 1978; chmn. dept. radiology Rocky Mountain Hosp., Denver, 1978-88, vice chief of staff, 1982, chief of staff, 1983, 84; chmn. dept. radiology Colo. Plain Med. Ctr. Regional Trauma Ctr., Ft. Morgan, 1988—2002, vice chief of staff, 1992—93; staff radiologist, VICE CHMN. DEPT. Lakeland Med. Ctr., Niles, Mich., 2002—, radiologist, vice chair of dept., 2002—. Med., legal cons., Colo., 1979—, Calif., 1979—, Fla., 1979—; consulting radiologist East Morgan Hosp., Luth. Health Sys., Brush, Colo., 1988—2002; CEO IRS Radiology Cons., P.C., Ft. Morgan, 1988—2002, Interstate Radiology Services, Henderson, Nev., 2002—; v.p. Niles Imaging Physicians, Mich., 2002—. Med. reviewer Post Grad. Medicine. Mem. Am. Osteopathic Assn., Am. Osteopathic Coll. Radiology, Am. Roentgen Ray Soc., Nat. Assn. Seventh-Day Adventist Osteopaths, Colo. Med. Soc., Soc. Nuclear Medicine Physicians. Republican. Avocations: snorkeling, skin diving, racquetball, sports car enthusiast and owner, travel. Office: PO Box 820 Niles MI 49120

GIBBS, FREDERICK WINFIELD, lawyer, communications company executive; b. Buffalo, Mar. 22, 1932; s. Walter L. M. and Elizabeth Mari (Georgi) G.; m. Josephine Janice Jarvis, Dec. 20, 1954; children: Michael, Mathew, Robyn. BA cum laude, Alfred U., 1954; JD with Tax honors, Rutgers U., 1989. Bar: Pa. 1989, N.J. 1989, U.S. Dist. Ct. N.J. 1989. With N.Y. Tel. Co., 1954-65, ITT, 1965-86; mng. dir. ITT Standard Electrica, S.A., 1971-75; chief exec. officer ITT Standard Electrica, Brazil, 1975-77; exec. dir. ops. ITT Communications Ops. Group ITT Communications Ops. Group, 1977; corp. v.p. ITT, 1977-80; pres. U.S. Tel. and Tel. Corp., 1977-79, exec. dir., sr. group exec., 1980-86; dir. System 12, ITT, 1979-80; exec. v.p. ITT, 1980-86, ITT Telecommunications Corp., 1983-86; pvt. practice law Pemberton, N.J., 1989-95; founding ptnr. Gibbs & Gregory Attys. at Law, Pemberton, 1995—. Cons. ITT, 1986-89, The World Bank/IFC, 1989—; pres. Mulberry Hill Enterprises, 1989—; bd. dirs. ACT Mfg.. Eion Mfg. Trustee Alfred U., 1981—; trustee Whitesbog Found., 1996—, pres. bd. trustees, 2000—; mem. planning bd. Barnegat Light, N.J., 1992-2002; elected Borough Coun., Barnegat Light, 1992, re-elected, 1995, 98; bd. dirs. Burlington County Red Cross, 1999—, Our Gang Players, Inc. Named Hon. Citizen of Rio de Janeiro, 1973; inducted to Alfred Univ. Athletic Hall of Fame, 1993. Mem. ABA, N.J. Bar Assn., Pa. Bar Assn., Burlington County Bar Assn., Barnegat Light Taxpayers Assn. (v.p. 1989-90, pres. 1990-92), Rotary Internat. (bd. dirs. Pemberton club 1996-97, v.p. 1997-98, pres. 1999-00, Pemberton Rotarian of Yr. 1996-97). Home: 12 E 17th Street Rd Barnegat Light NJ 08006

GIBBS, HOPE KATZ, journalist; b. Phila., July 8, 1964; d. Joel S. and Bobbi A. (Brownstien) K.; m. Michael Gibbs, 1995; children: Anna Paige, Dylan. Studied abroad, Tel Aviv U., 1983-84; BA in Comms., U. Pa., 1986; postgrad., George Washington U., 1988-91. Cert. massage therapist. Staff writer Dominion Post, Morgantown, W.Va., 1986-87; asst. editor Miami (Fla.) Herald, 1987-88; editor Adler Pub. Co., Washington, 1988-89; assoc. editor New Miami mag., 1989-91; publs. specialist George Washington U., Washington, 1991—; freelance writer Washington, 1993—. Comms. specialist Fairfax (Va.) City Schs., 2002; founder, pres. Grand Handmade Gifts, Inc., 2001—. Author: The Erotic Edge, 1995; journalist; author short stories, poetry; contbr. to Washington Post, USA Today, several nat. mags. Founder The Writing's on the Wall. Democrat. Jewish. Avocations: writing children's books, travel. Home: 13908 Stonefield Ln Clifton VA 20124-2553

GIBBS, HOWARD CEDRIC, civil engineer; b. Tuskeegee, Ala., Nov. 27, 1950; s. Lindbergh Howard and Mary Elizabeth (Edwards) G.; m. Patricia Ann Alexander, May 10, 1979; children: James Howard, Jonathan Charles. BSCE, U. of D.C., 1979; MS, George Washington U., 1996. Registered profl. engr. Tech. asst. Potomac Electric Power Co., Washington, 1972-79, civil engr., 1979-83, sr. civil engr., 1983—. Mem. Washington Bldg. Code Adv. Com., 1981—; mem. Washington Bd. Registration Profl. Engrs., 1997—, vice chmn., 2002—; pres. D.C. Coun. Engring. and Archtl. Socs., 2002—. Judge Carmody Hills Sch. Sci. Fair, Prince George's County, Md., 1990-93, St. Peter's Interparish Sch., Washington, 1990; den leader Cub Scouts Am., Washington, 1990. Mem. NSPE, ASCE (Outstanding Grad. 1979), Nat. Fire Protection Assn., Alpha Phi Alpha. Democrat. Baptist. Office: Potomac Electric Power Co 1900 Pennsylvania Ave NW Washington DC 20068-0002 E-mail: hcgibbs@pepco.com.

GIBBS, JAMES ALANSON, geologist; b. Wichita Falls, Tex., June 18, 1935; s. James Ford and Clovis (Robinson) G.; m. Judith Walker, June 18, 1966; children: Ford W., John A. BS, U. Okla., 1957, MS, 1962. Cert. profl. geologist. Geologist Calif. Co., New Orleans, 1961-63, Lafayette, La., 1963-64; cons. geologist, oil prodr. Dallas, 1964—. Chmn. Five States Energy Co., 1984—. Author: Finding Work as a Petroleum Geologist: Hints to the Jobseeker, 1984, Becoming an Independent Geologist: Thriving in Good Times and Bad, 1999. Trustee Inst. for Study Earth and Man, So. Meth. U. Lt. USNR, 1957-59. Recipient Regents award U. Okla., 1996. Mem. AAAS, Am. Geol. Inst. (trustee, William B. Heroy Disting. Svc. award 1994), Geol. Soc. Am., Dallas Geol. Soc. (pres. 1975-76, hon. mem. 1986), Am. Assn. Petroleum Geologists (sec. 1983-85, pres. 1990-91, found. trustee 1998—, Disting. Svc. award 1987, hon. mem. 1995), Am. Inst. Profl. Geol., Ind. Petroleum Assn. Am., Nat. Petroleum Coun., Houston Geol. Soc., West Tex. Geol. Soc., Soc. Ind. Profl. Earth Scientists (past chmn. Dallas chpt., hon. mem. 1999), Dallas Country Club, Dallas Petroleum Club, Explorers Club, Sigma Xi, Sigma Gamma Epsilon, Phi Delta Theta. Republican. Methodist. Home: 3514 Caruth Blvd Dallas TX 75225-5001 Office: 4925 Greenville Ave Ste 1220 Dallas TX 75206-4015 E-mail: jagibbs@fivestates.com.

GIBBS, JAMES HOWARD, broadcast executive; b. Dover, Ohio, Jan. 3, 1929; s. Howard James and Berniece Ruth (Spahr) Gibbs; m. Bettye Jean Porter, Nov. 10, 1956 (dec. June 7, 2003); children: Charles Kenneth(dec.), Tammy Ann. Grad. H.S., Dover, 1947. Announcer KWED Radio, Sequin, Tex.,

1947-48; owner KIVY Radio, Crockett, Tex., 1948—; news dir. Sta. WFAA-TV, Dallas, 1956-57. Home: 111 Valley Ln Crockett TX 75835-1325 Office: KIVY Radio 403 S 5th St Crockett TX 75835-2128 E-mail: jhgibbs@pcstx.net.

GIBBS, JAMIE, landscape architect, interior designer; b. D, Aug. 24; s. Irvin Lee and Glenna Lillian (Reid) G. BS in Landscape Architecture, BSA, MSA, Purdue U., 1977; MA in Historic Preservation, Columbia U., 1981. Cert. landscape architect; registered interior designer. Prin. designer Ind. Dept. Natural Resources, Indpls., 1977-78, Stoeppelwerth and Assocs., Indpls., 1978-79; dir. Bronx (N.Y.) Frontier Devel. Corp., 1979-81; owner, prin. designer Jamie Gibbs and Assocs., N.Y.C., 1979—. Adj. prof. Parsons Sch. Design, 1988—; cons. Tapestria divsn. of Hunter Douglas, 2001—02. Author: Landscape It Yourself, 1988, (booklet) All About Roses, 1990; mem. editl. bd. Window Fashions, 1994-02, Fine Furniture Internat. 1995-98; contbr. articles to popular mags., profl. jours.; major projects include residential and resort design in U.S., P.R., St. Maarten, Moscow, Rio de Janeiro, Jamaica, Hilton Head, N.C.; designer The Jamie Gibbs Vintage Collection selection of trims and fabrics, 2002. Bd. dirs. Coalition to Save City and Suburban Homes, N.Y.C., CityLore, N.Y.C., Civitas, 1992—, N.Y. Coun. on Alcoholism, 1997-2000; bd. dirs., assocs. com. Fedn. Protestant Welfare Agys., N.Y.C., 1987-2000; bd. dirs. Grosvenor Neighborhood House, N.Y.C., 1990-97; adv. bd. N.Y. Found. for Sr. Citizens, N.Y.C., 1988-97, Counseling in Schs., Inc., N.Y.C., 1982-92, Hudson River Park Alliance, 1998—. Recipient various certs. of appreciation; Design scholar Columbia U., 1980. Mem. Am. Soc. Landscape Designers, Am. Soc. Interior Designers, Assn. Profl. Landscape Designers, Allied Bd. Trade., Internat. Furniture and Design Assn. Republican. Episcopalian. Avocation: collecting 18th and 19th high style furniture and decorative objects. Office: Jamie Gibbs and Assocs 340 E 93rd St New York NY 10128-5547 Fax: 212-369-6332. E-mail: jamiegibbsassocs.@aol.com.

GIBBS, JUNE NESBITT, state legislator; b. Newton, Mass., June 13, 1922; d. Samuel Frederick and Lulu (Glazier) Nesbitt; m. Donald T. Gibbs, Dec. 8, 1945 (dec. 2001); 1 child, Elizabeth. BA in Math., Wellesley Coll., 1943; MA in Math., Boston U., 1947; postgrad. computer sci., U. R.I., 1981-84. Mem. from R.I. Rep. Nat. Com., 1969-80, sec., 1977-80; mem. R.I. Senate, Dist. 48, Providence, 1985—2003, R.I. Senate, Dist 12, 2003—. Mem. dcf. adv. com. Women in Svcs., 1970-72, vice chmn., 1972 Mem. Middletown Town Coun., 1974-80, 82-84, pres., 1978-80. Lt. (j.g.) USNR, 1943-46. Avocation: windsurfing. Home: 163 Riverview Ave Middletown RI 02842-5324 Office: Senate Minority Office State House Providence RI 02903 *To help restore faith in our government every elected official must constantly seek to do all he can for the people he serves and continually guard against doing anything which is self-serving or takes personal advantage of his office in any way.*

GIBBS, LAWRENCE BLAIR, lawyer; b. Hutchinson, Kans., Aug. 31, 1938; married; 2 children. BA, Yale U., 1960; JD, U. Tex., 1963. Assoc., then ptnr. Branscomb, Gary, Thomasson & Hall, Corpus Christi, Tex., 1963-72; dep. chief counsel IRS, Washington, 1972-73, acting chief counsel, 1973, asst. commr., 1973-75; ptnr. Johnson and Swanson, Dallas, 1976-86; commr. IRS, Washington, 1986-89; ptnr. Johnson & Gibbs, Washington and Dallas, 1989-94; mem. Miller & Chevalier, Washington, 1994—. Bd. advisors Taxation Mergers & Acquisitions. Trustee So. Fed. Tax Inst. Mem. ABA (vice chmn. adminstrn. sect. taxation 1991-92), FBA, State Bar Tex. (chmn. taxation sect. 1978-86), D.C. Bar Assn., Am. Law Inst., Communities Found. Tex. Adv. Bd., Am. Coll. Trust and Estate Counsel (bd. regents 1990-96). Office: Miller & Chevalier 655 15th St NW Ste 900 Washington DC 20005-5799 E-mail: lgibbs@milchev.com.

GIBBS, L(IPPMAN) MARTIN, lawyer; b. N.Y.C., Feb. 27, 1938; s. Harold and Shirley (Marks) G.; m. Dona Lynn Fagg, May 2, 1968; 1 child, Bradford M. BA, Brown U., 1959; JD, Columbia U., 1962. Bar: N.Y. 1963. Atty. various orgns., 1963-69; from assoc. to ptnr. Finley, Kumble, Wagner, Heine & Underberg, N.Y.C., 1969—87; ptnr. Clifford Chance US LLP, N.Y.C., 1987—. Bd. dirs. First Republic Bank, San Francisco. Regional dir. United Fund Drive of Rye, N.Y., 1979; trustee South St. Seaport Mus., 1995—. With USAR, 1962-68. Mem. ABA, Assn. Bar City N.Y. Avocations: sailing, golf. Office: Clifford Chance US LLP 200 Park Ave New York NY 10166-0005 E-mail: martin.gibbs@cliffordchance.com.

GIBBS, MARGARET SMITH, psycholgy educator; b. Emmetsburg, Iowa, Sept. 24, 1941; d. Hubert Smith and Lorna (Staley) G.; m. Richard Bennett, May 30, 1975. BA, Brandeis U., 1963; PhD, Harvard U., 1970. Diplomate Am. Bd. Profl. Psychology. Psychologist counseling ctr. Hofstra U., Hempstead, N.Y., 1966-71; prof. psychology Fairleigh Dickinson U., Teaneck, N.J., 1971—, acting dean Coll. Liberal Arts, 1992, dir. PhD program clin. psychology, 1989—95, 1998—2001, acting provost Teaneck-Hackensack campus, 1997-98; psychotherapist pvt. practice, N.Y., N.J., 1972—. Cons. various legal firms, 1978—. Co-editor: Community Psychology, 1980, Psychopathology in Childhood, 1982, Community Psychology and Mental Health, 1992; contbr. articles to profl. jours. Bd. dirs. Orange Environ., Goshen, N.Y., 1980—. Mem. APA. Avocation: tennis. Office: Fairleigh Dickinson U River Rd Teaneck NJ 07666

GIBBS, MARTIN, biologist, educator; b. Philadelphia, Penn., Nov. 11, 1922; s. Samuel and Rose (Sugarman) G.; m. Svanhild Karen Kvale, Oct. 11, 1950; children: Janet Helene, Laura Jean, Steven Joseph, Michael Seland, Robert Kvale. BS, Phila. Coll. Pharmacy, 1943; PhD, U. Ill., 1947. Scientist Brookhaven Nat. Lab., 1947-56; prof. biochemistry Cornell U., 1957-64; Abraham S. and Gertrude Berg prof. biology, chmn. dept. Brandeis U., Waltham, Mass., 1965-93. Cons. NSF, 1961-64, 69-72, NIH, 1966-69, Cosmos Club, 1984; mem. corp. Marine Biol. Lab., Woods Hole, Mass., 1970, RESA lectr., 1969; NATO cons. fellowship bd., 1968-70; mem. Coun. Internat. Exch. of Scholars, 1976-82; chmn. adv. com. selection Fulbright Scholars for Eastern Europe; adj. prof. Bot. Inst., U. Munster, Fed. Republic of Germany, 1978, 80, 87; adj. prof. dept. botany U. Calif., Riverside, 1979-89. Author: Structure and Function of Chloroplasts, Crop Productivity-Research Imperative, Revisited, Hungarian-USA Binational Symposium on Photosynthesis; editor in chief Plant Physiology, 1963-92; assoc. editor: Physiologie Vegetale, 1966-76, Ann. Rev. Plant Physiology, 1966-71. Recipient Charles Reid Barnes award, 1984, Adolph E. Gude award, 1993, Martin Gibbs medal, 1993, U. Ill. Achievement award, 1996; Alexander von Humboldt fellow, 1987. Mem. NAS, AAUP, Am. Soc. Plant Physiologists (Barnes, Gude, Gibbs medal), Russian Soc. Plant Physiologists (hon. life mem.), Am. Acad. Arts and Scis., Am. Soc. Biochem. Molec. Biology, Can. Soc. Plant Physiologists (hon. life mem.), Acad. Scis. France. Home: 32 Slocum Rd Lexington MA 02421-5622 E-mail: mgibbs8912@aol.com.

GIBBS, MARY L. writer, writers' services provider; b. Farmington Hills, Mich., May 2, 1973; d. Morris Whitehead and Elizabeth Sotnik, Thomas Sotnik (Stepfather); m. Gregory W. Gibbs; children: Johnathon, Bethany. Adminstrv. asst. Mobile Edn., Redford, Mich., 1994—96; receptionist Document Svcs., Livonia, Mich., 1996. Tchr.'s asst. The Learning Tree, Livonia, 1996—97; owner Gibbs Ink, Redford, 2001—. Author: (book) Secrets of the Maiden, 2000, Sensible Savings: Money Savers and Makers on the Web, 2002; actor: (Olympic fencing demonstrations) Michigan Renaissance Festival, 2000; editor: (newsletter) The Notebook and Pen, 2001. Founder Writer's Support Network, Redford, 2001—02; color guard coach Redford Union H.S., 2002—. Recipient 1st Pl. award, Writer's Arena monthly contest, 2000. Mem.: Writer's Arena Writing Group (owner 2001—02), Internat. Thespian Soc., Knights of Iron Stage Combat Team, Schoolcraft Coll. Fencing Club (pres. 2000—01, Ladies' Club Champion 1999). Avocations: reading, writing, swing dancing, theater, fencing. Office: Writer's Support Network/Gibbs Ink PO Box 40653 Detroit MI 48239 Business E-Mail: MarytheAuthor@aol.com.

GIBBS, NANCY PATRICIA, lawyer; b. Vancouver, B.C., Can., Dec. 22, 1946; d. Richard Braidreth and Ann Dorothy (Marriott) G.; m. Frank Weber Hughes, Aug. 28, 1971 (div.); 1 dau., Adrianne Elizabeth Hughes. BA in Chemistry, U. Wash., 1968, JD, 1971. Bar: Wash. 1971, U.S. Dist. Ct. (we. dist.) Wash. 1971, U.S. Ct. Appeals (9th cir.) 1972, U.S. Supreme Ct. 1980. Assoc. Davis, Wright, Todd, Riese & Jones, Seattle, 1971-76, ptnr., 1977— . commr. on salaries of state elected officials Washington State Commn., 1987—. Trustee, Seattle Aquarium Soc., 1982-83, 2d v.p., 1983-84; trustee Northwest Chamber Orchestra, 1985-88, mem. exec. com. 1986-87, treas. 1987-88; mem. adv. bd. Sr. Rights Assistance Project, 1978-80, Evergreen Legal Services Corp., 1980-81. Named Newsmaker of Future, Seattle C. of C./Time Mag., 1978; Cathedral fellow Cathedral Assocs., 1983-84. Mem. Seattle-King County Bar Assn. (treas. 1977-79, trustee 1979-82, 2d v.p. 1983-84, 1st v.p. 1984-85, pres. 1985-86), Seattle King County Bar Found. (trustee 1979-82, pres. 1981-82), U. Wash. Law Sch. Alumni Assn. (trustee 1978-82, treas. 1982-83, v.p. 1983-84, pres. 1984-85), Assn. Immigration and Nationality Lawyers, Fed. Bar Assn., ABA (mem. Nat. Met. Bar Leaders Caucus 1985—, mem. exec. com. 1986—), Wash. Bar Assn. (chmn. law related edn. com. 1980-82, disciplinary proceeding hearing officer, 1981—), Phi Alpha Delta. Episcopalian. Club: Wash. Athletic (Seattle); Sand Point Country. Bd. dirs. The Public Defender, 1987—; contbr. articles to profl. jours. Office: Century Sq Century Sq Ste 2600 Seattle WA 98101

GIBBS, NELSON F. federal agency administrator; CPA Calif. Cons. gen. mgmt. and fin. sys. cons. Deloitte & Touche, L.A., 1962—70, audit ptnr., 1971—81, dir. audit ops., 1982—85, lead client svc. ptnr., 1986—87, sr. ptnr. Tokyo, 1988—91; corp. contr. Northrop Grumman Corp., L.A., 1991—99; exec. dir. cost acctg. stds. bd. Office Mgmt. and Budget, Washington, 1999—2001; asst. sec. of USAF for installations, environment, and logistics Dept. of Def., Washington, 2001—. Officer U.S. Army, 1959—62. Office: Asst Sec of USAF 1670 Air Force Pentagon Washington DC 20330-1670

GIBBS, PATRICIA HELLMAN, physician; b. Boston, Oct. 22, 1958; d. Frederick Warren and Patricia Christina (Sander) H.; m. Richard D. Gibbs, Dec. 22, 1984; children: Ruth, Samuel, Matthew, Kate, Frank. BA summa cum laude, Williams Coll., 1982; MD, Yale U., 1987. Diplomate Am. Bd. Family Practice. Intern, resident in family practice U. Wash., Seattle, 1987-90; ptnr. Tricia Gibbs, MD and Richard Gibbs, MD, San Francisco, 1990-95; co-founder, med. dir. San Francisco Free Clinic, 1993—. Supervising physician San Francisco Ballet, 1990-95. Co-author: Medical and Orthopedic Issues of Active and Athletic Women-Skiing, 1993, Spine Care-Dance, 1993. Founder Sugar Bowl Acad., 1999. Women's scholar Williams Coll., 1982, Class of '25 Athlete scholar, 1982; named Family Physician of Yr., Calif. Acad. Family Physicians, 1998. Mem. AMA, Am. Acad. Family Physicians, Phi Beta Kappa, Sigma Xi. Avocations: distance running, ski racing, computers. Office: San Francisco Free Clinic 4900 California St San Francisco CA 94118-1115 E-mail: pgibbs@sttc.org.

GIBBS, SARAH PREBLE, biologist, educator; b. Boston, May 25, 1930; d. Winthrop Harold and Edith Dorothea (Hill) Bowker; m. Robert H. Gibbs, June 9, 1951 (div. 1962); 1 dau., Elizabeth Dorothea; m. Ronald J. Poole, Feb. 2, 1963 (div. 1980); 1 son, Christopher Harold. AB, Cornell U., 1952, MS, 1954; PhD, Harvard U., 1962. Research assoc. Inst. Animal Genetics Edinburgh U., 1963-65; asst. prof. botany McGill U., Montreal, Que., Can., 1966-69, assoc. prof. biology, 1969-74, prof., 1974-98, Macdonald prof. bot., 1998, Macdonald emeritus prof., 1999—. Recipient Darbaker prize, Bot. Soc. Am., 1975, Gilbert Morgan Smith medal, NAS, 2003; fellow, NSF, 1958—61, NIH, 1961—63. Fellow: AAAS, Royal Soc. Can.; mem.: Can. Assn. Univ. Tchrs., Phycol. Soc. Am. (award of excellence 1999), Am. Soc. Cell Biology, Can. Soc. Cellular and Molecular Biology (pres. 1972—73), Phi Kappa Phi, Sigma Xi, Phi Beta Kappa. Home: 70 Henley Ave Montreal QC Canada H3P 1V3 Office: McGill U Dept Biology 1205 Avenue Docteur Penfield Montreal QC Canada H3A 1B1 E-mail: chezgibbs@aol.com.

GIBBS, SYDNEY ROYSTON, health facility administrator; b. West Plains, Mo., June 15, 1934; s. Wallace Pemberton and Leila Mary (Royston) G.; m. Clarice Ellen Smith, Dec. 28, 1958; children: Sydney Royston Jr., Julie Gibbs Erwin. BS with honors, U. Ala., 1955; MD, U. Tenn., 1958. Diplomate Am. Bd. Surgery. Intern U. Tenn. Hosps., Knoxville, 1959; pvt. practice Roberta, Ga., 1960; jr. asst. surgery resident U. Ala. Hosps., Birmingham, 1961; ptnr. Drs. Clinic and Hosp., Bessemer, Ala., 1963-66; jr. surgery resident Lloyd Noland Hosp., Birmingham, 1967-68, sr. surgery resident, 1969; pvt. practice Bessemer, 1970-88; med. dir. ACIPCO Health Svcs., Birmingham, 1989—. Pres. med. staff Bessemer Carraway Med. Ctr., 1982-83, mem. bd. trustees, 1982-83, chief of surgery, 1974-75. Contbr. articles to profl. jours. Witness on employer mandate/health security act U.S. Ho. of Reps., 1994; active deacon bd. Shades Mountain Bapt. Ch., 1980; med. missionary Antigua, West Indies, 1975, 78. Major U.S. Army, 1962. Fellow ACS, Southeastern Coll. Surgeons; mem. Am. Coll. Physician Execs., Birmingham Acad. Medicine. Avocations: woodworking, travel. Office: ACIPCO Health Svcs 2930 16th St N Birmingham AL 35207-4806 E-mail: sydney@wwisp.com.

GIBBS, TYSON, chairman anthropology department; b. Knoxville, Tenn., Feb. 22, 1951; s. Lemuel and Alma Gibbs; m. Sheilla Janifer. BA, Dartmouth Coll., 1973; MA, U. Fla., 1977, PhD, 1979. Cert. Gerontology 1979. Asst. prof. U. S.C. Sch. Medicine, Columbia, 1980—83; dir. ctr. on aging Meharry Med. Coll., Nashville, 1983—87, W. Ga. U., Carrollton, Ga., 1992—93; dir. geriat. programs Emory U., Atlanta, 1993—94; asst. to assoc. prof. U. N. Tex., Denton, 1995—, chmn. anthropology dept., 1999—. Expert Nat. Cancer Inst., Rockville, Md., 1988—90, cons., Bethesda, 1993; vis. prof. Ga. State U., Atlanta, 1990—91; dir. Applied Culture Anthropology Rsch. Ctr., Denton, 1999—; dir. rsch. Dept. Family Med. Tex. Osteopathic Med. Sch., Fort Worth, 1999—2000; cons. Ednl. Testing Svc., Princeton, NJ, 1999—. Nat. Park Svc., Atlanta, 2000—. Author: (book) Black Collectibles Sold in America, 1986 (Outstanding Svc., McNair Scholars Program, 2001), Encyclopedia of Black Dolls, 1987, 200 Years of Tennessee Decorative Arts, 1990, A Guide To Ethnic Health Collections in the United States, 1996 (S.C. Children's Scholar, 1982), Guide to Resources on Ethnic Studies in Minority Populations, 2001 (Whitney Young Scholar, 1980). Steering com. mem. Nat. Inst. Aging, Bethesda, 1986—88; task force mem. Office of Sec. Health and Human Svcs., Washington, 1989—90; mem. Gov.'s Subcommittee on Primary Prevention, Columbia, SC, 1980—82, Task Force on Health Edn., Columbia, SC, 1980—83; bd. mem. RSVP, Denton, Tex., 1996—98. Mem.: Am. Anthropology Assn. Office: Dept Anthropoology U N Tex Box 310409 Denton TX 76203 Office Fax: 940-369-7833. Business E-Mail: tgibbs@scs.unt.edu.

GIBBY, MABEL ENID KUNCE, psychologist; b. St. Louis, Mar. 30, 1926; d. Ralph Waldo and Mabel Enid (Warren) Kunce; student Washington U., St. Louis, 1943-44, postgrad., 1955-56; B.A., Park Coll., 1945; M.A., McCormick Theol. Sem., 1947; postgrad. Columbia U., 1948, U. Kansas City, 1949, George Washington U., 1953; M.Ed., U. Mo., 1951, Ed.D., 1952; m. John Francis Gibby, Aug. 27, 1948; children— Janet Marie (Mrs. Kim Williams), Harold Steven, Helen Elizabeth, Diane Louise (Mrs. Roderick Rohrich), John Andrew, Keith Sherridan, Daniel Jay. Dir. religious edn. Westport Presbyn. Ch. Kansas City, Mo., 1947-49; tchr. elementary schs., Kansas City, 1949-50; high sch. counselor Arlington (Va.) Pub. Schs., 1952-54; counselor adult counseling services Washington U., 1955-56; counseling psychologist Coral Gables (Fla.) VA Hosp., 1956—; counseling psychologist Miami (Fla.) VA Hosp., 1956—, chief counseling psychology sect., 1982-86; sr. psychologist Office Disability Determination Fla. Hdqrs., 1987-94. Sec. bd. dirs. Fla. Vocat. Rehab. Found. Recipient Meritorious Service citation Fla. C. of C., 1965, President's Com. on Employment of Handicapped, 1965; commendation for meritorious service Com. on Employment of Physically Handicapped Dade County, 1965, named Outstanding Rehab. Profl., 1966, 81; named Profl. Fed. Employee of Year, Greater Miami Fed. Exec. Council, 1966; Outstanding Fed. Service award Greater Miami Fed. Exec. Council, 1966; Fed. Woman's award U.S. Civil Service Commn., 1968, Community Headliner award Theta Sigma Phi, 1968, Outstanding Alumni award Park Coll., 1968, Freedom award The Chosen Few, Korean War Vets. Assn., 1986; certificate of appreciation Bur. Customs, U.S. Treasury Dept., 1969, Fla. Dept. Health and Rehab. Services, 1970. Mem. Am., Dade County (past sec.) psychol. assns., Nat., Fla. (past dir. Dade County chpt.) rehab. assns., Nat. Rehab. Counseling Assn. (past sec.). Patentee in field. Home: 7107 Aberdeen Ave Dallas TX 75230-5406

GIBERT, CHARLENE WEST, gifted education educator; b. Ft. Worth; m. Wayne Gibert, 1975; 1 child, Christine. MusB, Tex. Tech U., 1964; MEd, U. Houston, 1978, EdD, 1991. Cert. tchr., profl. counselor, Tex. Elem. tchr. music Lubbock (Tex.) Ind. Sch. Dist., 1965-68; jr. high sch. tchr. lang. arts Clear Creek Ind. Sch. Dist., Houston, 1968-79, tchr. gifted and talented edn. Spring Br. Ind. Sch. Dist., 1981—. Cons. gifted and talented field. Editor, contbr: Biographical Dictionary of Gifted Education, 1988; also articles. Mem. First Presbyn. Ch., Houston. Mem. Nat. Assn. for Gifted Children, Tex. Assn. for Gifted and Talented, T Avocations: music, travel. Home: 1926 Abby Aldrich Ln Katy TX 77449-2817

GIBERT, STEPHEN P. government educator, defense consultant; b. North Augusta, S.C., July 16, 1924; s. Paul C. and Helen B. Gibert; m. Cynthia L. Livingstone, June 8, 1968; children: Stephen Jr., Julia, Clare, Christopher, Jennifer. BA, Wofford Coll., 1948; MA, Harvard U., 1952; PhD, Johns Hopkins U., 1958. Prof. govt. Georgetown U., Washington, 1958—. Vis. prof., cons. U. Rangoon, Burma, 1961-62; dir. MS in fgn. svc. program Georgetown U., 1964-68, dir. nat. security studies program, 1977-2000; co-dir. village rsch. project in Thailand, U.S. Dept. Def. and Royal Thai Govt., Bangkok, 1971. Author: Soviet Images of America, 1977, (in Japanese) The America That Can Say No, 1994; author, editor: Security in Northeast Asia: Approaching the Pacific Century, 1988; co-author: Arms for the Third World: Soviet Military Diplomacy, 1969, East Asia in American Foreign Policy, 1990; co-editor: America and Island China: A Documentary History, 1989; mem. bd. editors Asian Perspective, Orbis, Comparative Strategy, Studies in Global Security, National Security Studies Quar. Mem. Gov. Reagan's Def. Adv. Group; active Reagan presdl. campaign, 1980. Sgt. U.S. Army Air Corps, 1944-46, PTO. Mem. Internat. Inst. Strategic Studies (life), Cosmos Club (life). Episcopalian. Avocations: tennis, classical music. Office: Georgetown U 35th and O Sts NW Washington DC 20057 Home Fax: (202) 687-5858; Office Fax: (202) 687-5175. E-mail: giberts@georgetown.edu.

GIBLETT, ELOISE ROSALIE, hematologist, educator; b. Tacoma, Wash., Jan. 17, 1921; d. William Richard and Rose (Godfrey) Giblett. BS, U. Wash., 1942, MS, 1947, MD with honors, 1951. Mem. faculty U. Wash. Sch. Medicine, 1957—, research prof., 1967—87, emeritus research prof., 1987—. Assoc. dir., head immunogenetics Puget Sound Blood Ctr., 1957—79, exec. dir., 1979—87, emeritus exec. dir., 1987—; former mem. several rsch. coms. NIH. Author: Genetic Markers in Human Blood, 1969; mem. editl. bd. numerous jours. including: Blood, Am. Jour. Human Genetics, Transfusion, Vox Sanguinis; contbr. over 200 articles to profl. jours. Recipient fellowships, grants Emily Cooley, Karl Landsteiner, Philip Levine and Alexander Wiener immunohematology awards, disting. alumna award, U. Wash. Sch. Medicine, 1987. Fellow. AAAS; mem.: NAS, Assn. Am. Physicians, Western Assn. Physicians, Am. Fedn. Clin. Rsch., Internat. Soc. Hematologists, Brit. Soc. Immunology, Am. Assn. Immunologists, Am. Soc. Hematology, Am. Soc. Human Genetics (pres. 1973), Alpha Omega Alpha, Sigma Xi. Home: 6533 53rd Ave NE Seattle WA 98115-7748 Office: Puget Sound Blood Ctr 921 Terry Ave Seattle WA 98104-1256

GIBLETT, PHYLIS LEE WALZ, middle school educator; b. Denver, July 17, 1945; d. Henry and Leah (Pabst) Walz; m. Giblett, May 31, 1975; children: Leann Ruth, Douglas Henry, John Peter. BSBA, U. Denver, 1967; MBA, 1969. Tchr. bus., publications tchr. Aurora South Mid. Sch., Colo., 2003; info. specialist, 1996—2003; tchr. Aurora Pub. Sch., 1967—80, 1982—86, 1988—96; tchr., on leave, 1980—82; chmn. bus. dept., 1972—79; evening tchr. S.E. Met. Bd. Coop Svc., 1967—68; post secondary/adult classes Aurora Pub. Sch., 1972—75, C.C. Denver, North Campus, 1973; tchr. Aurora Pub. Sch. Adult Edn., 1983—84. Named Miss Future Bus. Tchr. Mem.: Century Elem. Sch. PTA (reflections chmn. 1987—89, mem 1988 89, reflections chmn. 1990—93), Aurora Dist. Tech. Com. (mem. 1975—79), Mentor com. (facilitator 1991—92, exploratory tchr. facilitator 1992—96), Aurora Edn. Assn., NEA, Colo. Vocat. Assn., Colo. Educators for/About Bus., Colo. Bus. Edn. Assn. (pres. 1976—77), Aurora Coun. PTA (treas. 1987—89), Colo. Curriculum Specialist Com. (mem. 1976—77), Future Bus. Leaders Am. (adviser chpt. 1976—78), South Mid. Sch. (mem. dist. tech. com.), Program Cadre (steering com. shared decision making 1990—96, zero tolerance com. 1992—94, mem. 1995—97, tech. cadre facilitator 1996—), Aurora Pub. Sch. Sys. (tech. com. 1991—, dist. tech. trainer 1992—), Nat. Mountain-Plains (participant leadership conf. 1977), Delta Pi Epsilon (pres.-elect Eta chpt. 1978, pres. 1980—81), Phi Beta Lambda of Colo. (mem. 1965). Republican. Luth.

GIBLIN, CLAIRE L. artist; b. Bklyn., Dec. 26, 1947; d. Giacomo and Bella D. (Mercaldo) Callegari; m. William J. Giblin, Sr., July 22, 1995; children: Clinton J. Green III, William J. Giblin, Jr., John. Student, Lebanon Valley Coll., F&M Coll. Recipient Grand prize/Best of Show, Hanover Arts Commn., Va., 1996, Nat. Grand prize, Nat. Acad. of Fine Arts, 2000, hon. mention award Highland Cultural Ctr., N.Y., 1997, Crabbie award Art Calendar Mag., 1997, Silver award Fed. Trust, Phila., 1997, Judges award, 1997, 2d pl. Lititz Outdoor Art Show, 1999, Judges award L.C.A.A. Art Assn., 1999, 2d pl. award York Art Assn., 1999, 3d pl. Landis Woods, 2000, 2001, Lansdale, 2001, Judges Choice award Mt. Gretna, Pa., 2002, Grumbacher Gold medallion, 2002. Mem. N.Y. Artists Equity, Phila. Art Alliance, Phila. Tri-State Artists Equity, Internat. Registry Artists and Artwork, Lancaster Mus. Art, Harrisburg Art Assn., Nat. Assn. Painters in Casein and Acrylic, Woodmere Art Mus. Home: 22 Laurelgate Pl Millersville PA 17551-2110

GIBLIN, JAMES CROSS, author, editor; b. Cleve., July 8, 1933; s. Edward Kelley and Anna Belle (Cross) G. BA, Case Western Res. U., 1954; MA, Columbia U., 1955. Asst. editor Criterion Books, N.Y.C., 1959-62; editor Lothrop, Lee & Shepard Co., N.Y.C., 1962-67; editor in chief Clarion Books, N.Y.C., 1967-79, pub., 1979-89, contbg. editor, 1989—. Author: The Scarecrow Book, 1980, The Skyscraper Book, 1981, Chimney Sweeps: Yesterday and Today, 1982 (Am. Book award 1983, Golden Kite award 1983), Fireworks, Picnics and Flags: The Story of the Fourth of July Symbols, 1983, Walls: Defenses Throughout History, 1984 (Golden Kite award 1985), The Truth About Santa Claus, 1985 (Boston Globe-Horn Book Nonfiction Honor Book award 1986), Milk: The Fight for Purity, 1986, From Hand to Mouth, 1987, Let There Be Light: A Book About Windows, 1988 (Golden Kite award 1989), Writing Books for Young People, 1990, The Riddle of the Rosetta Stone: Key to Ancient Egypt, 1990, The Truth About Unicorns, 1991, Edith Wilson: The Woman Who Ran the United States, 1992, George Washington: A Picture Book Biography, 1992, Be Seated: A Book About Chairs, 1993, Thomas Jefferson: A Picture Book Biography, 1994, When Plague Strikes: The Black Death, Smallpox, AIDs, 1995, The Dwarf, the Giant and the Unicorn: A Tale of King Arthur, 1996, Charles A. Lindbergh: A Human Hero, 1997 (Orbis Pictus Honor Book award 1998), The Mystery of the Mammoth Bones, and How it Was Solved, 1999, The Amazing Life of Benjamin Franklin, 2000 (Orbis Pictus Honor Book award 2001), The Century That Was: Reflections on the Last One Hundred Years, 2000, Fireworks, Picnics and Flags: The Story of the Fourth of July Symbols, rev. edit., 2001, The Life and Death of Adolf Hitler, 2002 (Robert F. Sibert Informational Book award 2003); also numerous articles and short stories. Mem. Authors Guild, Soc. Children's Book Writers and Illustrators (bd. dirs.). Avocations: traveling, museum exhibits, movies, plays, walking. Home: 200 E 24th St Apt 1606 New York NY 10010-3919 *Having written books for both children and adults, I find the juvenile field more stimulating and exciting because of the responsibility the children's writer has to his or her impressionable young readers. If the writer gives them solid, truthful, imaginatively treated books, he or she is contributing in a very real sense to their education and development.*

GIBLIN, JEAN-ELLEN DORSEY, university administrator, economics educator; b. Annapolis, Md., Apr. 23, 1941; d. E. Thomas and Eleanor Louise (Miller) Dorsey; 1 child, Eleanor Louise. BS in Bus. Econs. with high honors, U. R.I., 1965; MA in Econs., Columbia U., 1966; PhD in Econs., New Sch. Social Rsch., 1976. Instr. econs. Fairleigh-Dickinson U., Madison, N.J., 1968-70; prof. econs. Fashion Inst. Tech., SUNY, N.Y.C., 1970—, curriculum dir. Title VI Internat. Edn. Grant, 1985-86, coord. internat. trade option, 1986-90, acting dean bus. and tech. divsn., 1989-91, acting v.p. acad. affairs, 1990-92, v.p. acad. affairs, 1992-97. Cons. Haldi Assocs. and Gillis, Haldi & Clark, mgmt. and econ. cons., N.Y.C., 1977-87, Lutine Corp., N.Y.C., 1983; cons., rsch. assoc. Ctr. Econ. Planning, N.Y., 1973-76. Contbr. articles to profl. jours. Mem. AAUP, Assn. SUNY Community and Tech. Coll. Acad. Officers., Am. Econs. Assn. (mem. nat. conv. com. 1977, 82, 85, chmn. exhibits 1982, 85), Downtown Economists Luncheon Group of N.Y.C. (program chmn. 1983-84), Ea. Econs. Assn., Met. Econs. Assn. N.Y. (pres. 1980-81, exec. bd. mem. 1981-85, nominating com. 1989), N.Y. Acad. Sci. (econs. sect.), N.Y. Assn. Bus. Economists, Women's Econ. Round Table, Omicron Delta Epsilon (life), Phi Kappa Phi (life). Office: Fashion Inst Tech SUNY 227 W 27th St New York NY 10001-5992

GIBLIN, LOUIS, lawyer; b. Omaha, Neb., Nov. 1, 1944; s. Richard and Mary (Mahoney) G.; m. Janis Schoblocher, May 20, 1977; 1 child, Marijo. AB, Creighton U., 1966; MBA, U. Chgo., 1968; cert. in investment mgmt.,

Princeton U., 1986; MS, Northwestern U., 1998; JD, Chgo.-Kent Coll. of Law; cert. in employment law, Chgo.-Kent Coll. Law. Cert.: (mediation law). Asst. v.p. No. Trust. Co., Chgo., 1968-73; v.p. MGIC Investment Corp., Milw., 1973-85; 1st v.p. Smith Barney Harris Upham and Co., Milw., 1985-93. Chmn. fin. analyst seminar Northwestern U., Evanston, Ill., 1990; adj. faculty U. Wis., Milw., 1985—; adviser Financiers U. Wis., Milw., 1986-2002; sr. exam. grader Inst. CFAs, 1986—; fin. svcs. vol., corp. cons. Skoda Koncern, Czech Republic, 1993-2001. Founder Joint Univ./Soc. Scholarship program, CFA exam, 1988; trustee St. Stephen's Ch., Milw., 1989-99; chmn. investment com., mem. fin. com. & ops. com. United Way, Milw., 1989-2002; mem. Oak Creek (Wis.) Housing Authority, City of Oak Creek Cost Reduction Com., Oak Creek Econ. Devel. Authority; mem. Creighton U. Alumni Senate, 1991-99; mem. adv. com. Creighton U.; bd. dirs. Creighton U. Alumni, 1993. Pulitzer Prize nominee, 1985. Mem. Internat. Soc. Fin. Analysts (charter), Internat. Inst. Forecasters, N.Y. Soc. Security Analysts, Nat. Assn. Bus. Economists, Nat. Options and Futures Soc. (bd. dirs. 1986-93), Deutsch-Amerikanischer Nat. Kongress, North Atlantic Cultural Exch. League, Internat. Inst. Am. Host, Milw. Investment Analysts Soc. (bd. dirs. 1988-99), Fin. Analysts Fedn. (bd. dirs.), Milw. Investment Analysts Soc. (pres. 1989-90), Mensa. Home: 7468 S Logan Ave Oak Creek WI 53154-2234

GIBLIN, PATRICK DAVID, retired banker; b. St. Louis, July 24, 1932; s. Patrick Joseph and Ann Jane (Gill) G.; children: Mary Clare, Christopher, Gregory. BBA, Manhattan Coll., 1954; MBA, St. John's U., Jamaica, N.Y., 1965. Staff auditor KPMG Peat Marwick, N.Y.C., 1956-59; chief plant acct. div. Am. Machine & Foundry, Bklyn., 1959-63; with CBS, N.Y.C., 1963-73, controller electronic video rec. div., 1968-73, dir. corp. acctg., 1967-68; vice chmn., chief fin. officer CRESTAR Fin. Corp., Richmond, 1973-95; ret., 1995. Served with U.S. Army, 1954-56. Mem. Delta Mu Delta. Roman Catholic. Home: 18217 Mainsail Pointe Dr Cornelius NC 28031-5199

GIBLIN, THOMAS PATRICK, labor union administrator, political organization administrator; b. East Orange, N.J., Jan. 15, 1947; s. John Joseph and Theresa Elizabeth (Moran) G.; m. Mary Katherine Hughes, June 20, 1970; children: Thomas P. Jr., Noreen M., Edward M., Patrick F., Anne T. BA, Seton Hall U., 1969. Pres. Internat. Union of Oper. Engrs. Local 68, West Caldwell, N.J., 1975—; freeholder Essex County, Newark, 1977-78, 82-89, surrogate, 1990-93; chmn. Dem. Party State of N.J., 1993—2001; Dem. Chmn. Essex Co., Newark, 1993—2002. Candidate from 25th legis. dist. N.J. Assembly, 1973; treas. Essex County Dem. Com., Newark, N.J., 1979-82; alt. del. Dem. Nat. Conv., San Francisco, 1984, Atlanta, 1988, del. Chgo., 1996, LA, 2000; commr. N.J. Real Estate Commn., Trenton, 1979-82; lay adv. bd. St. Vincent Acad., 1984—; chmn. bd. trustees St. Barnabas Burn Found., 1989-93, United Way Essex, 1976-82, 89-95; bd. dirs. Essex unit Assn. Retarded Citizens, 1986-96; trustee North Jersey Blood Ctr., 1991—. Named Man of Yr. United Cerebral Palsy, 1980; recipient Cert. of Merit, U.S. Dept. of Labor, 1979, Community Svc. award Frontiers Internat., 1985, Humanitarian award, N.J. Blood Ctr., 1988. Mem. N.J. Ins. Underwriting Assn. (bd. dirs. 1982-90). Democratic. Roman Catholic. Avocations: reading, swimming, traveling. Home: 40 Montague Pl Montclair NJ 07042-2820 Office: PO Box 534 West Caldwell NJ 07007

GIBNEY, FRANK BRAY, publisher, editor, writer, foundation executive; b. Scranton, Pa., Sept. 21, 1924; s. Joseph James and Edna May (Wetter) G.; m. Harriet Harvey, Dec. 10, 1948 (div. 1957); children: Alex, Margot; m. Harriet C. Suydam, Dec. 14, 1957 (div. 1971); children: Frank, James, Thomas; m. Hiroko Doi, Oct. 5, 1972; children: Elise, Josephine. BA, Yale U., 1945; DLitt (hon.), Kyung Hee U., Seoul, Korea, 1974. Corr., assoc. editor Time mag., N.Y.C., Tokyo and London, 1947-54; sr. editor Newsweek, N.Y.C., 1954-57; staff writer, editorial writer Life mag., N.Y.C., 1957-61; pub., pres. SHOW mag., N.Y.C., 1961-64; pres. Ency. Brit. (Japan), Tokyo, 1965-69, TBS-Brit., Tokyo, 1969-75, vice chmn., 1976-99; v.p. Ency. Brit., Inc., Chgo., 1975-79; vice chmn., bd. editors Ency. Brit., Chgo., 1978—; pres. Pacific Basin Inst., Pomona Coll., Claremont, Calif., 1979—. Prof. Pomona Coll., 1997—; bd. dirs. U.S. Com. for Pacific Econ. Cooperation, 1988—, v.p., 1993-95; cons. com. on space and aeros. U.S. Ho. of Reps., Washington, 1957-59; vice chmn. Japan-U.S. Friendship Commn., 1984-90, U.S.-Japan Com. Edn. and Cultural Interchange, 1984-90. Author: Five Gentlemen of Japan, 1953, The Frozen Revolution, 1959, (with Peter Deriabin) The Secret World, 1960, The Operators, 1961, The Khrushchev Pattern, 1961, The Reluctant Space Farers, 1965, Japan: The Fragile Super-Power, 1975, 3rd edit., 1996, Miracle by Design, 1983, The Pacific Century, 1992, Korea's Quiet Revolution, 1993; co-author: The Battle for Okinawa, 1995; editor: The Penkovskiy Papers, 1965, Senso, 1995, Unlocking The Bureaucrats' Kingdom, 1998, The Nanjing Massacre, 1999. Served to lt. USNR, 1942-46. Decorated Order of the Rising Sun 3d Class Japan, Order of Sacred Treasure 2d Class Japan. Mem. Council on Fgn. Relations, Tokyo Fgn. Corr. Club, Japan-Am. Soc., Japan Soc. Clubs: Century Assn., Yale (N.Y.C.); Tokyo; Tavern, The Arts (Chgo.). Roman Catholic. Home: 1901 E Las Tunas Rd Santa Barbara CA 93103-1745 E-mail: fgibney@silcom.com.

GIBOR, AHARON, biologist, educator; Office: Dept Biology U Calif Santa Barbara CA 93106

GIBRAN, KAHLIL, sculptor; b. Boston, Nov. 29, 1922; s. Nicholas and Rose (Gibran) G.; m. Jean English, July 1, 1957; children: Timothy; by previous marriage, Nicole. Student, Boston Mus. Sch., 1940-43. Exhibited widely as painter, 1949-52, life sized steel sculpture, 1953—, one person show bronzes, Cambridge Art Assn., 1977, Charlottesville, Va., 1993; exhbn.: Boston Arts Festival, 1985, Santa Fe, 1993, The Jean and Kahlil Gibran Collection, Danforth Mus. Art, Framingham, Mass., 2002-03; ann. exhbn. Bologna-Landi Gallery, East Hampton, L.I., N.Y., Denenberg Fine Arts, San Francisco, 1997, Contemporary Sculpture Chesterwood, 1997, St. Botolph Club, 1998, Art of the Spirit Forest Hills Cemetery, 1998, Copley Soc., 2001; included in Forum 49 Retrospective, Provincetown Art Assn., 1999; exhibited lifesize bronze Into the Millennium, Boston, 1999, commd. bronze plaque of Kahlil Gibran, Copley Sq., Boston, 1977, Judge Francis Ford, Fed. Ct. House, Boston, 1977, Judge Anthony Julian, Fed. Ct. House, Boston, Elliot Norton medal, Boston, 1983, bronze figure of Kahlil Gibran, Worcester State Coll., 1987, West Canton Street Child, Hayes Pk., Boston, 1992, Processional Cross All Soul's Episcopal Ch., San Diego, 1993, bronze plaque composer Amy Beach, 28 Commonwealth Ave., Boston; inventor Gibran Tripod, Mus. Modern Art collection; sculpture and painting show Copley Soc., 1994; represented in permanent collections Pa. Acad., Tenn. Fine Arts Ctr., Norfolk (Va.) Mus., Chrysler Mus., William Rockhill Gallery, Swope Gallery, Brockton Fine Arts Ctr.; author: Sculpture--Kahlil Gibran, 1970, (with wife Jean Gibran) Introduction to Lazarus and His Beloved, 1973, Kahlil Gibran, His Life and World, 1974, rev. edit., 1991; author: (monograph) Observations on the Reasons for the Cremona Tone, 1993. Pres. Kahlil Gibran Scholarship Fund, Boston, 1974. Recipient George Widener award Pa. Acad., 1958; Guggenheim fellow, 1959-61; award Nat. Inst. Arts and Letters, 1961; Grand prize Boston Arts Festival, 1964; John Gregory award sculpture, 1965; Gold medal Sacred Art Show, Trieste, Italy, 1966 Address: 160 W Canton St Boston MA 02118-1216

GIBSON, ANNEMARIE, writer, editor; b. Linz, Austria, Oct. 6, 1947; d. Marion Alfred and Maria Anna (Ostermann) Green; m. Stephen Rawlings Gibson, Mar. 2, 1968; children: Stephanie Anne, Timothy Michael. AA, Cecil C.C., 1984; BA, Towson (Md.) State U., 1993. Editl. asst. US Army Environ. Hygiene Agy., Aberdeen Proving Ground, 1979-84, writer, editor, 1984-90; pub. affairs specialist US Army Ctr. for Health Promotion and Preventive Medicine, Aberdeen Proving Ground, 1990-95, supervisory tech. writer, editor, 1995-99, tech. writer, editor, mgr., 1999—, acting pub. affairs officer, 2003—, pub. affairs officer, co-lateral duty, 2003. Editl. adv. bd. US Army Ctr. for Health Promotion and Preventive Medicine, Aberdeen Proving Ground, 1990—, spkr. bur., 1993—, facilitator 1992—, mentor 1996—. Pres. Cecil County Ladies Aux. Md. State Firemen's Assn., Elkton, Md., 1995-98; sec. Ladies Aux. Water Witch Fire Co. Port Deposit, Md., 1985—. Mem. Federally Employed Women (life, sec. 1991—), US Army Environ. Hygiene Agy. (life). Office: US Army Ctr Health Promotion/ Preventive Medicine 5158 Black Hawk Rd Aberdeen Proving Ground MD 21010-5403 Fax: 410-436-1039. E-mail: annemarie.gibson@apg.amedd.army.mil.

GIBSON, BARRY JOSEPH, magazine editor; b. Boston, Feb. 6, 1951; s. Joseph Wray and Marjorie Mitchell (Jacobs) G.; m. Jean Harley Reese, Oct. 11, 1980; 1 child, Michael Reese BA, U. Miami, 1973. Assoc. editor Salt Water Sportsman, Boston, 1977-81; assoc. boating editor Outdoor Life, N.Y.C., 1981-82; editor Directory for Boats, Accessories and Fishing Tackle, Boston, 1981-83, Salt Water Sportsman, Boston, 1981—, v.p., 1981-88. Adviser Internat. Commn. for Conservation Atlantic Tuna, Washington, 1986-89; mem. New Eng. Fishery Mgmt. Coun., 1987-96, chmn., 1992; cons. sport fishing industry. Contbr. numerous articles to profl. jours. Charter boat capt., Boothbay Harbor, Maine, 1971— Recipient Mako Outdoor Writer Yr., Mako Marine Inc., 1982 Mem. Outdoor Writers Assn. Am., New England Outdoor Writers Assn. (excellence in writing award 1982), Northeast Charterboat Capts. Assn. (founding mem. 1988—), Atlantic Sportfishing Assn. (bd. dirs. Natick, Mass. 1988-90). Clubs: Boothbay Harbor Tuna (pres. 1979). Avocation: sport fishing. Office: Salt Water Sportsman Inc 263 Summer St Boston MA 02210-1506

GIBSON, BEATRICE ANN, retired systems analyst, artist; b. Canton, Ohio, Feb. 4, 1926; d. Paul Cummins Gibson and Luella Mae (Clements) Gibson Ward. Student, Cleve. Sch. Art, 1941-44, Carnegie Mellon U., 1945-47; BA, U. Chgo., 1951; postgrad., Northwestern U., 1955-57, Oxbow Summer Sch., 1957-59, Sch. Art Inst. Chgo., 1956-60; ind. study, Italy, Greece, Spain, France, England, 1960-61, France, Netherlands, England, 1987; postgrad., EBA Sch. Art, San Francisco, 1988. Procedure analyst U.S. Steel Corp., Chgo., 1955-61; methods analyst Continental Ins. Cos., San Francisco, 1962-64; forms, methods analyst Ins. & Securities Inc., San Francisco, 1964-74; sr. systems analyst Calif. State Automobile Assn., San Francisco, 1974-91; ret., 1991. Mem., editor, officer San Francisco Ins. Women's Assn., 1962-68. One-woman exhibits include Diablo Valley Coll., Pleasant Hill, Calif., 1983, EBA Sch. Art, San Francisco, 1991; group exhbns. include Old Town Art Fair, Chgo., 1955, Navy Pier Exhbn., 1956, Laguna Beach (Calif.) Gallery, 1963, San Francisco Civic Ctr. Exhbn., 1964, Hayward (Calif.) Art Show, 1983, EBA Sch. Art, 1988-93. Recipient Recognition award Calif. State Automobile Assn., 1991. Mem. Assn. Systems Mgmt. (emeritus, editor, sec. 1968—, v.p. 1973-74, pres. San Francisco chpt. 1975-76, Disting. Svc. Merit award 1978, Achievement award 1985).

GIBSON, BENJAMIN FRANKLIN, physicist; b. Madisonville, Tex., Sept. 3, 1938; s. Mitchell Osler and Christine (Bennett) G.; m. Margaret Alice Ferguson, July 20, 1968; children: James M., Michael W., Stuart W. BA, Rice U., 1961; PhD, Stanford U., 1966. Postdoctoral fellow Lawrence Livermore (Calif.) Nat. Lab., 1966-68; rsch. assoc. NAS, Nat. Bur. Stds., Gaithersburg, Md., 1968-70, CUNY, Bklyn., 1970-72; group leader, T-5 Los Alamos (N.Mex.) Nat. Lab., 1982-86, staff mem., 1972—; detailee Dept. of Energy Divsn. Nuclear Physics, 1980-81. Program adv. com. MIT Bates Electron Accelerator, Boston, 1985-89, 98—; mem. subatomic physics grant selection com. Can. Natural Scis. and Engring. Rsch. Coun., 1994-96, theory rev. panel NSF, 1997, 98. Co-editor: Three-body Force in the Three-Nucleon System, 1986, Procs. of LAMPF Workshop on pi K Physics, 1991, New Vistas in Physics with High-Energy Pion Beams, 1993, Properties and Interactions of Hyperons, 1994, Baryons '95, 1996, 20 Years of Meson Factory Physics: Accomplishments and Prospects, 1997; assoc. editor Phys. Review C, 1988-02, editor, 2002--, mem. editl. bd., 1978-79, 87-88; mem. editl. bd. FEW Body Sys., 1986—; contbr. articles to profl. jours. Recipient Sr. Scientist Rsch. award Alexander von Humboldt Found., 1992; Japan Soc. Promotion of Sci. rsch. fellow Tohoku U., 1984; vis. fellow U. Melbourne, Australia, 1986, Flinders U., Adelaide, Australia, 1987, Murdoch fellow Inst. for Nuclear Theory, U. Wash., Seattle, 1992. Fellow Am. Phys. Soc., Few-Body Sys. Topical Group (vice chmn. 1990-92, chmn. 1992-93, divsn. nuclear physics (sec.-treas. 1995—). Achievements include patents in field of epithermal-neutron well logging. Office: T-16 MS-B283 Los Alamos NM 87545-0001 E-mail: bfgibson@lanl.gov.

GIBSON, CATHY, administrative assistant; b. Bpston, June 25, 1950; d. Hillard Gibson and Catherine Short; m. Albert William, Jan. 9, 1987 (div. July 1996); children: James, Dana. Student, Roxbury C.C. Past office tech. Roxbury C.C., Boston. Mem. League of Women Voters, Transition of Body Mus., 2003. Baptist. Avocations: cooking, swimming, scrabble. Home: 162 W Springfield St Apt C Boston MA 02118

GIBSON, CHARLES DEWOLF, broadcast journalist; b. Evanston, Ill., Mar. 9, 1943; s. Burdett and Georgiana (Law) G.; m. Arlene Joy Gibson, July 20, 1968; children: Jessica Law, Katherine Burdett. AB, Princeton U., 1965. Corr. RKO Radio, Washington, 1966; anchorman Sta.-WLVA-TV, Lynchburg, Va., 1967-69, Sta.-WMAL-TV (now WJLA-TV), Washington, 1970-73; corr. TVN, Inc., Washington, 1974-75, ABC News, Washington, 1975-80, Capitol Hill corr., 1981-87; co-host Good Morning Am. ABC TV, N.Y.C., 1987-98, 99—; co-host 20/20, 1999—. Nat. journalism fellow NEH, U. Mich., 1973-74. Office: Good Morning America 147 Columbus Ave New York NY 10023-5900*

GIBSON, CHRISTINA RENEE, radiation therapist; b. Greensboro, N.C., Aug. 28, 1964; d. Milton Irvin and Rebecca (Vernon) Gibson; m. Paul Stephen Fryar, Feb. 4, 1999; 1 child, Paige. Student, Moses Cone Hosp., Greensboro, 1986, Roanoke (Va.) Meml. Hosp., 1988; BS in Biology, Greensboro Coll., 1993; MPH, U. N.C.-G, 2001. Cert. in radiation therapy and radiography. Staff radiographer Moses Cone Hosp., 1986-87, staff radiation therapist, 1988-90; clin. instr. radiation therapy Forsyth Tech. C.C., Winston-Salem, N.C., 1989-91, 93-95, chair dept. radiation therapy, 1995—. Locum tenens radiation therapist Pro-Med, Atlanta, 1991-93. Mem. Am. Soc. Radiologic Technologists (1st pl. sci. exhibit award 1995), N.C. Soc. Radiologic Technologists (bd. dirs. 1998-99, awards). Avocations: swimming, walking, making scrapbooks. Office: Forsyth Tech CC 2100 Silas Creek Pkwy Winston Salem NC 27103-5197 E-mail: cgibson@forsyth.cc.nc.us.

GIBSON, CHRISTOPHER PATRICK, military career officer; b. Rockville Center, N.Y., May 13, 1964; s. Robert Francis and Barbara Ann G.; m. Mary Joanne Gerardi, Oct. 12, 1996; children: Kathleen, Margaret, Connor. BA, Siena Coll., 1986; MPA, Cornell U., 1995, PhD, 1998. Commd. 2d lt. U.S. Army, 1986, advanced through grades to lt. col., 2002. White House intern V.P. Al Gore's Reinventing Govt. Initiative, Washington, 1993-94; spkr. in field. Master ceremonies Hermandad, Inc., L.I., 1995. Decorated Bronze Star, Legion of Merit; recipient Disting. Hon. Grad. (Marshall award) Commd. and Gen. Staff Coll., 2000; Congl. fellow for rep. Jerry Lewis, 2002-03. Fellow Inter-Univ. Sem. Armed Forces and Society; mem. Am. Legion, Ctr. Study Presidency. Roman Catholic. Avocations: N.Y. Mets and N.Y. Jets, Irish music, chess. Home: 1626 30th St NW Washington DC 20007

GIBSON, CLAUDE LOUIS, English educator; b. Okmulgee, Okla., Nov. 27, 1940; s. Wayne Wishard and Leona Jean Gibson; m. Linda Kay Farha, June 20, 1960 (div. Feb. 1984); children: Patrick Neal, Michael David, Laura Caroline; m. Joanna Barnett, Jan. 9, 1986. BA, U. Ark., 1964, MA, 1965, PhD, 1976. Prof. English Tex. A&M U., College Station, 1976—, dir. freshman English, 1980-84, dir. undergrad. studies, 1994—. Mng. editor Coll. English Assn. Publs., 1977-80; assoc. Inst. for Ednl. Inquiry, Seattle, 1997—. Guest editor, contbr. spl. issue CEA Critic, 1981; contbr. articles, revs. to profl. jours.; author abstracts, monograph in field. Fellow Acad. for Edn. Devel., 2000, Richardson fellow, 1998-2000. Mem. MLA, Coll. English Assn., Nat. Coun. Tchrs. English, South Ctrl. MLA, Tex. Assn. Coll. Tchrs. (chpt. pres. 1986-87). Home: 1603 Laura Ln College Station TX 77840 Office: Tex A&M U Dept English College Station TX 77843 E-mail: cgibson@tamu.edu.

GIBSON, COLVIN DONALD, human resources specialist; b. N.Y.C., Nov. 10, 1945; s. Beatrice White; m. Ann T. Tucker, June 15, 1985; 1 child: Rachel C. BA in History, Va. State Coll., 1968. Various positions Exxon Mobil Corp., Tex., La., 1971-88, coord. hdqrs. employee rels., 1991—97, advisor compensation and exec. programs, 1998—2000; sect. supr. Exxon U.S.A., Houston, 1984-88, benefits advisor, 1988; sr. cons. HR Staff Resources and Assocs. Inc., Irving, 2001—. Chmn. scouting com. Wheeler Ave. Bapt. Ch., Houston, 1978-86, scoutmaster, asst. scoutmaster; bd. dirs. Salvation Army, Irving, 1992—; vice chmn. Irving Cmty. Devel. Corp., former pres. Irving Black Arts Coun.; vice rector bd. dirs. Norfolk State U. Capt. U.S. Army, 1968-70. Mem. Nat. Soc. Stock Profls., Nat. Alumni Assn. Norfolk State U. (pres. 1983-87, dist. alumnus 1990), Rotary. Baptist. Avocations: travel, tennis, visual and performing arts. Home: 2110 Texas Ash Dr Irving TX 75063-3464

GIBSON, DAVID FREDERIC, foundation executive, engineering educator; b. West Newton, Mass, Jan. 10, 1942; s. Lionel C. and Dorothy (MacAfee) G.; m. Rebecca Harper, Aug. 24, 1963; children: Karen, Kathleen. BS in Indsl. Engring., Purdue U., 1963, MS in Indsl. Engring., 1964, PhD in Indsl. Engring., 1969. Registered profl. engr., Mont. Indsl. engr. USN, Forest Park, Ill., 1963; rsch. asst. Purdue U., West Lafayette, Ind., 1963-64, instr., 1968; asst. prof. Mont. State U., Bozeman, 1969-72; dean Arkansas Tech., Russellville, 1971-72; from assoc. prof. to prof. Mont. State U., Bozeman, 1972—, asst. dean of engring., 1977-83, dean of engring., 1983—2000; pres., exec. dir. Mont. State U. Found., 2001—. Contbr. articles to profl. jour. Accreditation visitor Accrediting Bd. for Engring. and Tech., Balt., 1987-96, mem. engring. accreditation com., 1991-96; mem. Mont. Bd. Profl. Engr. and Land Surveyors, Helena, 1983-97, chmn. Grantee in field. Mem. Am. Soc. for Engring. Edn., Inst. Indsl. Engring., Nat. Soc. Profl. Engr. (v.p., chmn. profl. engr. in edn.), Nat. Coun. Engr. Examiners. Lutheran. Home: 2409 Springcreek Dr Bozeman MT 59715-6036

GIBSON, DAVID MARK, biochemist, educator; b. Kokomo, Ind., Aug. 7, 1923; s. Carl Banta and Marie (Loop) Gibson; m. Margaret Lockhart, June 2, 1951 (dec. Apr. 1992); children: Carl L., John L., Shauna Gibson Kopp, Heather Gibson Garrison, Mark C.; m. Wilda Lee Preston, July 7, 2001. AB, Wabash Coll., 1944; MD, Harvard, 1948. Intern Northwestern U. Med. Sch., 1948-49; research assoc. biochemistry U. Ill., Urbana, 1950-53; rsch. assoc., asst. prof. Inst. Enzyme Rsch. U. Wis., 1953-55, 55-58; assoc. prof. biochemistry Ind. U. Sch. Medicine, Indpls., 1958-61, prof., 1961—, Grace M. Showalter prof., 1974-92, prof. emeritus, 1992—, chmn., 1967-88. Established investigator Am. Heart Assn., 1957—62; vis. prof. U. Padua, Italy, 1964—65, U. Utrecht, Netherlands, 1975. Author: (textbook) Metabolic Regulation in Mammals, 2002. Recipient Career Devel. award, NIH, 1962—67. Mem.: AAAS, Biochem. Soc. (Eng.), Am. Diabetes Assn., Am. Soc. Biol. Chemists, Am. Soc. Cell Biology, Sigma Xi. Achievements include research in biochemical mechanisms and control fatty acid synthesis and cholesterol synthesis. Home: 1745 Graham Rd Mansfield OH 44904-9744

GIBSON, DENISE DAWN, social worker, educator; b. Akron, Ohio, Feb. 4, 1951; d. Clarence O. and Lucille I. (Bloom) G. BA in Psychology, U. Akron, 1976; MS in Social Work, Case Western Res. U., 1978; PhD in Cultural Found., Kent State U., 2002. Cert. social worker; lic. social worker, Ohio. Clin. social worker Kevin Coleman Mental Health Ctr., Kent, Ohio, 1978-81; supr. parent therapy Youth Residential Svcs., Akron, 1981-84; supr. Transitional Living Ctr. Western Res. Human Svcs., Akron, 1984-86, dir. case mgmt., 1986-88; pvt. practice Kent, 1979-90; adj. instr. behavioral scis., asst. dir. student support Northeastern Ohio U., Rootstown, 1988-93, student personal advisor, 1994—, coord. student advising, 1997—. Mem. faculty U. Akron, 1984-88, 2001; mem. adj. faculty behavioral scis., Northeastern Ohio U. Coll. Medicine, 1988—; faculty Ursuline Coll. 2002; trustee, pres. Coleman Profl. Svcs., Kent, 2002. Chair Portage County AIDS Task Force, Kent, 1990-93; mem. Portage County Leadership Class of 1994. Mem. NASW, Am. Ednl. Studies Assn. Home: 1928 Middleton Rd Hudson OH 44236-1304 Office: NEOUCOM PO Box 95 Rootstown OH 44272-0095 E-mail: ddg@neoucom.edu.

GIBSON, DIANNA R. financial consultant; b. Indpls., Nov. 7, 1950; d. Armour J. and Dorothy E. (Rough) Keller; m. Thomas Gibson III; children: Jennifer, Adrian. BA, Earlham Coll., 1972; MPA, N.Mex. State Univ., 1981. Libr. asst. N.Mex. State Univ., Las Cruces, 1976-78, ops. supr., 1978-83, asst. dir. pers., 1983-99; fin. advisor AIG VALIC, 1999—. Presenter in field. Planning com. Gov.'s Conf. for Women, N.Mex., 1987; bd. dirs. Am. Heart Assn., Las Cruces, 1983-89; mem. ad hoc com. N.Mex. Ednl. Retirement Bd., 1994; active State of N.Mex. Workers Compensation Panel, 1992. Recipient Pres. award for Svc. N.Mex. State Univ., 1982. Mem.: AAUW (coll. liaison 1986—99, editor 1999, Gold Circle mem., Gold Star status 2000), Coll. and Univ. Pers. Assn. (sec., vice chair, chair 1983—99, Roadrunners award 1994), Phi Kappa Phi. Home: PO Box 2314 Mesilla Park NM 88047-2314 Office: PO Box 2314 Mesilla Park NM 88047

GIBSON, ELISABETH JANE, retired principal; b. Salina, Kans., Apr. 28, 1937; d. Cloyce Wesley and Margaret Mae (Yost) Kasson; m. William Douglas Miles, Jr., Aug. 20, 1959 (div.); m. Harry Benton Gibson Jr., July 1, 1970. AB, Colo. State Coll., 1954-57; MA, San Francisco State Coll., 1967-68; EdD, U. No. Colo., 1978; postgrad., U. Denver, 1982. Cert. tchr., prin., Colo. Tchr. elem. schs., Santa Paula, Calif., 1957—58, Salina, Kans., 1958—63, Goose Bay, 1963—64, Jefferson County, Colo., 1965—66, Topeka, 1966—67; diagnostic tchr. Ctrl. Kans. Diagnostic Remedial Edn. Ctr., Salina, 1968—70; instr. Loretta Heights Coll., Denver, 1970—72; co-owner Ednl. Cons. Enterprises, Inc., Greeley, Colo., 1974—77; resource coord. region VIII Resource Access Project Head Star Mile High Consortium, Denver, 1976—77; exec. dir. Colo. Fedn. Coun. Exceptional Children, Denver, 1976—77; asst. prof. Met. State Coll., Denver, 1979; dir. spl. edn. N.E. Colo. Bd. Coop. Edn. Svcs., Haxtun, Colo., 1979—82; prin. elem. jr. h.s. Elizabeth, Colo., 1982—84; prin., spl. projects coord. Summit County Schs., Frisco, Colo., 1985—92; prin. Frisco Elem. Sch., 1985—91; ret., 2002. Cons. Mont. Dept. Edn., 1978-79, Love Pub. Co., 1976-78, Colo. Dept. Inst., 1974-75, Colo. Dept. Edn., 1984-85, mem. proposal reading com., 1987—; pres. Found. Exceptional Children, 1980-81; pres. bd. dirs. N.E. Colo. Svcs. Handicapped, 1981-82; bd. dirs. Dept. Ednl. Specialists, Colo. Assn. Sch. Execs., 1982-84; mem. Colo. Title IV Adv. Coun., 1980-82; mem. Mellon Found. grant steering com. Dolo. Dept. Edn., 1984-85; mem. Colo. Dept. Edn. Data Acquisition Reporting and Utilization Com., 1983, Denver City County Commn. for Disabled, 1978-81; chmn. regional edn. com. 1970 White House Conf. Children and Youth; bd. dirs. Advs. for Victims of Assault, 1986-91; mem. adv. bd. Alpine Counseling Ctr., 1986-92; mem. placement alternatives commn. Dept. Social Svcs., 1986—; mem. adv. com. Colo. North Ctrl. Assn., 1988-91; sec. Child Care Resource and Referral Agy., 1992—; mem. Child Care Task Force Summit County, 1989-92; mem. tchr. cert. task force Colo. State Bd. Edn., 1990-91; chmn. Summit County Interagy. Coord. Coun., 1989-93. Co-author: (with H. Padzensky) Goal Guide: A minicourse in writing goals and behavioral objectives for special education, 1975, Assaying Student Behavior: A minicourse in student assessment techniques, 1974; contbr. articles to profl. jours. Recipient Vol. award Colo. Child Care Assn., 1992, Ann. Svc. award Colo. Fedn. Coun. Exceptional Children, 1981; San Francisco State Coll. fellow, 1967-68; named Vol. of Season, Hospice of Metro Denver, 2003. Mem. ASCD, Nat. Assn. Elem. Sch. Prins., Colo. Assn. Retarded Citizens, North Ctrl. Assn. (state adv. com. 1988-91), Order Ea. Star, Kappa Delta Pi, Pi Lambda Theta, Phi Delta Kappa. Republican. Methodist. Home: 4505 S Yosemite St Unit 114 Denver CO 80237-2520 E-mail: ejgibson@netzero.net.

GIBSON, EMMITT E. career officer; b. Feb. 7, 1944; Commd. officer U.S. Army, advanced through grades to maj. gen., commdg. gen. Aviation and Missile, 1997-98, dep. dir. resources and requirements, 1998—. Office: FSRAD J-8 9000 Defense Pentagon Rm 1e962 Washington DC 20318-0001

GIBSON, ERNEST WILLARD, III, retired state supreme court justice; b. Brattleboro, Vt., Sept. 23, 1927; s. Ernest William and Dorothy Pearl (Switzer) G.; m. Charlotte Elaine Hungerford, Sept. 10, 1960; children: Margaret, Mary, John. BA, Yale U., 1951; LLB, Harvard U., 1956. Bar: Vt. State's atty. Windham County, Vt., 1957-61; mem. Vt. Ho. of Reps., 1961-63, chmn. judiciary com., 1963; chmn. Vt. Pub. Svc. Bd., 1963-72; judge Vt. Superior Ct., 1972-83; assoc. justice Vt. Supreme Ct., 1983-97, ret., 1997. Chancellor Episcopal Diocese Vt., 1977-98, trustee, 1972-99, pres. bd. trustees, 1991-99, dep. to gen. conv., 1976-94. Served in U.S. Army, 1945-46, 51-53, Major Army Nat. Guard, 1956-71. Mem. Vt. Bar Assn. Avocations: bridge, tennis. Home: 11 Baldwin St Montpelier VT 05602-2110

GIBSON, EVERETT KAY, JR., space scientist, geochemist; b. Seagraves, Tex., May 13, 1940; s. Everett Kay and Lillie Gertrude (Ivey) G.; m. Mary Morgan Shott, Oct. 13, 1973; 1 son, Bradford Pierce Gibson. BS, Tex. Tech U., Lubbock, 1963, MS, 1965; PhD, Ariz. State U., 1969. Instr. Tex. Tech. U., 1963-65; postdoctoral research assoc. NASA Johnson Space Center, Houston, 1969-70, space scientist, geochemist, 1970-91; sr. scientist NASA-Johnson Space Ctr., 1991—; vis. program mgr. NSF, Washington, 1979; mission sci. advisor Apollo 14; test dir. Lunar Receiving Lab. NASA, 1971, prin. investigator Lunar Sample Analysis Program, 1971-90, mem. Lunar Sample Analysis Planning Team, 1974-77, prin. investigator Planetary Geology Program, 1978-

86, prin. investigator Mars Data Analysis Program, 1979-84, prin. investigation Exobiology Program, 1983—. Mem. U.S. Antarctic Meteorite Search Team, 1979-80; adj. prof. geology U. Houston, 1975-90; sr. Leverhulme vis. fellow Open U., Milton Keynes, Eng., 1984-85; cons. The Economist (London), BBC, London; interdiscipline scientist Mars Express/Beagle 2 Mission to Mars, European Space Agy., 2001—. Assoc. editor 5th, 6th, 7th, 8th, 9th and 12th Proc. Lunar and Planetary Sci. Conf., 1974-81; assoc. editor: Chondrules and Their Origins, 1983; contbr. articles to sci. jours. Bd. dirs. Clear Creek Basin Authority, Harris County, Tex., 1974-75; col. Commemorative Air Force, 1983—, life mem., 1987, aircraft sponsor, 1988, exec. officer, 1990-2002; exec. bd. Wings Over Houston Air Show, 1990—. Recipient award for lunar sci. team participation NASA Johnson Space Ctr., 1974, Manned Flight Awareness award, 1993, Laurel Space award Aviation Week and Space Tech., 1972, 97; recipient Exceptional Sci. Achievement medal NASA, 1997, Disting. Achievement award Ariz. State U., 1980, Silver Magnolia award Commemorative Air Force, 1993, 99, Ariz. State U. Hall of Fame award, 1998, Scientist of Yr. award Tex. Acad. of Sci., 2000. Fellow Meteoritical Soc. (sec. 1974-80, councilor 1987-90); mem. Am. Chem. Soc., Internat. Soc. for Study of Origin of Life, AAAS, Am. Geophys. Union, Sigma Xi, Phi Lambda Upsilon. Baptist. Home: 1015 Trowbridge Dr Houston TX 77062-2726 Office: NOW SR Astromaterials Rsch Office Nasa Johnson Space Ctr 2101 Nasa Rd 1 Houston TX 77058 E-mail: ekgmars@aol.com.

GIBSON, FLORENCE ANDERSON, talking book company executive, narrator; b. San Francisco, Feb. 7, 1924; m. V.H. Carlos Gibson, Aug. 30, 1947; children: Nancy Derwent, Christopher Carlos, Katherine Wayne Bolland, Diana Corona. Student, Finch Jr. Coll., N.Y.C., 1941-42; BA in Dramatic Lit., U. Calif., Berkeley, 1944; student, Neighborhood Playhouse, N.Y.C., 1944-45. Radio actress, San Francisco, 1944, 46, 47; chmn. Washington com. Am. Field Svc., 1958-60, 62-65, founder, chmn. Peruvian Com., 1960-62; treas., distbn. mgr. Living Garden and Concern 1975 calendars, 1971-75; sec. exec. com Fgn. Student Svc. Coun., 1973-76; narrator Talking Books Libr. of Congress div. for Blind and Physically Handicapped, 1975-96; narrator Recorded Books, Inc., 1979; founder, pres. Audio Book Contractors, Inc., 1982—. Narrator numerous unabridged books on cassettes. Actress, appearing in Blithe Spirit, 1945, Ah, Wilderness, 1946, Traffic Ct. TV series, others, recorded more than 1000 books on cassettes. Bd. dirs. Fgn. Student Svc. Coun., Concern, Inc., Rec. for the Blind, Children's Theater of Washington; vol. in occupational therapy Children's Hosp., Washington, 1949-50; vol. lobbyist student exch. program Am. Field Svc. Recipient 3 Parents' Choice awards, 1983, 84, 86, Audiophile Earphone award, 1999; named Best Female Narrator, Book World, 1989; selected as A Notable Children's Recording, ALA, 1983, 87, 88, 89. Home: 4626 Garfield St NW Washington DC 20007-1025 Office: Audio Book Contractors Inc PO Box 40115 Washington DC 20016-0115 E-mail: flogibsonabc@aol.com.

GIBSON, FRANCES ERNST, music educator; b. San Antonio, Dec. 7, 1925; d. Joseph Omer Ernst and Olga Catherine Ochs; m. Edwin Wray Gibson, Sr. MusB summa cum laude, Our Lady of the Lake U., 1947; MusM, U. Tex., 1970. Faculty piano dept. Our Lady of the Lake U., San Antonio, 1947—51; pvt. music tchr. Fredericksburg, Tex., 1951. Piano accompanist Point Theater, Ingram, Tex., 1958; ch. organist St. Mary's Cath. Ch., Fredericksburg, 1965-70; participant Internat. Piano Workshops, 1979-91. Co-author: Music Lovers' Cookbook, 1992; performer Tex. Sch. of the Air, Austin, 1947, 125th Ann. Celebration, Fredericksburg, 1972. Free concert arranger Fredericksburg Music Club, Inc., 1987—; chmn. Concert Series, 1987—. Recipient Outstanding Alumni award Our Lady of the Lake U., San Antonio, 1997. Mem. Nat. Guild Piano Tchrs. (local chmn. 1952-93, adjudicator 1975-92), Music Tchrs. Nat. Assn., Fredericksburg Music Club, Inc. (bd. mem., program chair, pres. 1989-93), Frank van der Stucken Internat. Music Festival (bd. mem., program chmn. 1991-94, performer 1991, artistic dir.), Sigma Alpha Iota (Sword of Honor 1943), Sigma Alpha Iota Alumnae (pres. 1950-51), Alpha Chi, Delta Kappa Gamma Catholic Daughters. Roman Catholic. Avocations: reading, traveling, gourmet cooking. Home: 809 W Travis St Fredericksburg TX 78624-2524

GIBSON, GEORGE EDWARD, JR., civil engineering educator, consultant, researcher; b. Meridian, Miss., June 12, 1958; s. George Edward Sr. and Doris Jean (Griffin) G.; m. Roberta Gail Howard, Dec. 17, 1983; children: Stacey Kathryn, Gaines Sullivan. BSCE with honors, Auburn U., 1980; MBA in Engring. Mgmt., U. Dallas, 1987; PhD in Civil Engring., Auburn U., 1990. Registered profl. engr., Tex. Mfg. supr. Tex. Instruments, Inc., Dallas, 1984-88; grad. teaching asst. Auburn (Ala.) U., 1988-89, grad. rsch. asst., 1989-90; vis. asst. prof. N.C. State U., Raleigh, 1990-91; prof. U. Tex., Austin, 1991—, assoc. chmn. archtl. engring., 2000—. Cons. Bus. Roundtable, N.Y.C., 1991, Miller Bldg. Corp., Wilmington, N.C., 1991, Arrowsmith Tchs., Austin, 1992-93, DuPont Co., Wilmington, Del., 1993-94, Union Carbide Corp., Danbury, Conn., 1994-95, Hudson Engring. Corp., Houston, 1994, Electricidad de Caracus, Venezuela, 1994, Tex. Dept. Transp., Austin, 1995, Gen. Electric, Atlanta, 1996, NASA, 1997-2001, Smithsonian Instn., Washington, 2001-02, 3M, St. Paul, 2000-, Gen. Svcs. Adminstrn., Washington, 2001-02, Norsk Hydro, Oslo, 2000, U.S. Dept. State, Washington, 2002—; mem. pre-project planning task force Constrn. Industry Inst., 1991-94, front end planning rsch. team, 1994-97, pre-project planning edn. team, 1996, implementation strategy com. 1997-2002, PDRI for bldg. projects rsch. team, 1998-2000; risk assessment for internat. projects rsch. team Constrn. Industry Inst., 2001-. Contbr. articles to profl. jours. Mem. adminstrv. bd. Bethany United Meth. Ch., Austin, 1992-94; bd. trustees Wesley Found. of Austin, 1993-98. Capt. Corps of Engrs. U.S. Army, 1980—84. Recipient scholarship ROTC, 1976-80, Dept. Civil Engring. Tchg. Excellence award Lockheed Aircraft Co., 1994, Lockheed - Martin award, 1996, Rschr. of Yr. Construction Industry Inst., 1996, Instr. of Yr. Constrn. Industry Inst., 1998. Mem. ASCE, NSPE (Edn. Excellence award 2002), Tau Beta Pi (faculty advisor 1995-2000), Phi Kappa Phi. Avocations: photography, fishing, hunting, golf. Home: 9805 Cinnabar Trl Austin TX 78726-2423 Office: Univ Tex Dept Civil Engring ECJ 5 208 Austin TX 78712-1076

GIBSON, JAMES B. mayor; b. Las Vegas, 1948; BA, Brigham Young U., 1972; JD, Calif. Western, 1975. Gen. counsel Am. Pacific Corp.; ptnr. Rooker and Gibson Law Firm; now mayor City of Henderson, Nev., 1997—. Bd. dirs. Las Vegas (Nev.) Monorail; bd. dir. Las Vegas (Nev.) Convention and Visitors Authority; mem. City of Henderson (Nev.) Redevelopment Agy.; alternate So. Nev. Water Authority; mem. regional trans. com. City of Henderson. Recipient Good Scout award, Boulder Dam Area Coun., 2002, Humanitarian award, Nat. Jewish Med. and Rsch. Ctr., 2002. Mem.: Hendersn C. of C. (named Outstanding Mem. 1994). Office: City Hall 240 S Water St Rm 203 Henderson NV 89015-7296 E-mail: jbg@ci.henderson.nv.us.*

GIBSON, JAMES ELLIOT, architect; b. McMinnville, Oreg, Aug. 14, 1922; s. James H. and Julia Etta (Cummins) G.; m. Clara June Bosson, Dec. 19, 1948 (dec. Sept. 1967), children: Graeme E.B., Randolph U., James B.P.; m. Suzan Bailliere Brand Brown, Jan. 1, 1980 (dec. June 1998); children: John W. Brown, Natalie T. Brown, Frank D. Brown, Susannah Brown Kavanaugh. BS in Music, U. Oreg., 1944; BArch, U. Mich., 1950. Registered architect, Mich., Fla., SC, Ohio; cert. NCARB. Architect Harley, Ellington & Day, Inc., Detroit, 1950-69, James E. Gibson, Architects & Assoc., Inc., Vero Beach, Fla., 1969-83, Gibson & Silkworth, Architects & Assoc., Inc., Vero Beach, 1983-97; arch. Gibson & Assoc., Architects, Inc., Vero Beach, 1997—. Pres. Vero Beach Concert Assn., 1971-79, 81-83, pres. Treas. Coast Opera Assn., Vero Beach, 1979-81; bd. dir. Atlantic Classical Orch., Vero Beach, 1992-03, pres. 1998-2003, 1998—; bd. dir., mem. adv. bd. Riverside Theatre, Vero Beach; mem. adv. bd. Ctr. for the Arts, Vero Beach. Staff sgt. US Army, 1942-46, ETO. Recipient Bus. in the Arts award, 1986, Aurora Grand award Assoc. Gen. Contractors, 1985. Mem. AIA, John's Island Club (Vero Beach), Carolina Yacht Club (Charleston, SC). Avocations: musical performance, antiques collecting, sculpture, historical preservation. Office: Gibson & Assocs Architects 606 Azalea Ln Vero Beach FL 32963-1832

GIBSON, JANNETTE POE, educator, consultant; b. Lubbock, Tex., Oct. 29, 1948; d. Hugh Miller and Norma Grace (Harrison) Poe; m. William Carroll Gibson, June 30, 1967; children: Darin L., Arminda L. Gibson Peery, Victoria L. Gibson Dixon. BS, East Tex. State U., 1971, MEd, 1981; postgrad., Tex. A&M U., Commerce, 1992—. Tchr. Como (Tex.)-Pickton Ind. Sch. Dist., 1971-77; tchr., cons. Diosese of Dallas, Diocese of Tyler, Tex., 1982-87; tchr., supr. Hyder Migrant Ctr., Dateland, Ariz., 1987-88; tchr., adult ESL edn. dir. Ariz. Western U., Hyder Campus, 1988-89; tchr. Sulphur Springs (Tex.) Ind. Sch. Dist., 1989-98; cons., presenter Multicultural/Migrant Edn., 1987—; edn. diagnostician Sulphur Springs ISD Spl. Edn. Dept., 1998—. Cons. ESL edn. and early childhood edn. and child devel. U.S. Dept. Edn., 1988-89; profl. adv. com. Sulphur Springs Ind. Sch. Dist., 1990, 92, 96; doctoral adv. bd. East Tex. State U., 1993-96; regional adv. com. migrant edn. Region VIII Svc., 1994-97, advisor Tex. Edn. Agy. assessments of ESL/LEP children, 1997-98; cons. for devel. of culture and lang. bias-free assessments to sch. dists. in Tex.; presenter in fields of migrant edn. and ESL; private cons. assessment in sch. dists., Tex. Mem. AAUW, NEA, Tex. State Tchrs. Assn., TAMU Doctoral Students Assn., TESOL, Classroom Tchrs. Assn. Tex., Tex. Ednl. Diagnosticians Assn., N.E. Tex. Assn. Ednl. Diagnosticians, Mensa, Alpha Chi, Phi Beta Kappa, Kappa Delta Pi. Democrat. Methodist. Avocations: reading, gardening. Home: 1707 Houston St Sulphur Springs TX 75482-2319 Office: 411 College St Sulphur Springs TX 75482-2809

GIBSON, JERRY LEIGH, oil company executive; b. El Dorado, Ark., Jan. 24, 1930; s. Oscar Edward and Ruth (Coleman) G.; m. Alma Gail Peoples, Apr. 11, 1953; children: Sallie Gail, Gregory Leigh. BBA with honors, U. North Tex., 1951; MBA, So. Meth. U., 1956. With Exxon Mobil, 1952-59, 60-66, asst. to asst. comptr.; mgmt. cons. KPMG CPAs LLP, 1959; v.p., sec., treas. Riviana Foods Inc., Houston, 1966-69; pres., treas., chief exec. officer Intermedco Inc., Houston, 1969-73; pres., chief exec. officer Automated Fin. Svcs., Houston, 1973-75; v.p. fin. A-Z Internat. Tool Co., Houston, 1975-80; pres., chief exec. officer, owner JHJ Drilling Co., Houston, 1980-85; pres., chief exec. officer Kellywood Corp., Houston, 1986—. Tchr. acctg. So. Meth. U., 1956-57. With USAF, 1950-52. Home and Office: 6801 Auckland Ct Austin TX 78749-4136 E-mail: jerrylg1@earthlink.net.

GIBSON, JOHN, news anchor, correspondent; B film sch., UCLA. Reporter Hollywood Reporter, L.A., 1969-72, various locations, Calif., 1974-77; bur. chief, anchor Weekend Mag., Sta. KCRA-TV, San Francisco, 1979-89; anchor, corr. In Am., 1989-92; corr. NBC News, Burbank, Calif., 1992-94; West Coast corr. NBC News Channel, 1994—2000; anchor News Chat and InterNight, Playback MSNBC, N.Y.C.; host, The Big Story with John Gibson Fox News, New York, NY, 2000—. Office: Fox News Channel 1211 Ave of the Americas New York NY 10036*

GIBSON, JOHN ERIC, judge; b. Montreal, Que., Can., Sept. 25, 1958; arrived in U.S., 1960; s. John Conrad Gibson and Jeon Tappan Shaw; m. Cecily Ann-Marie Nagel. BA, Wash. State U., 1982; MA, U. Wash., 1987, JD, 1990. Bar: Wash. 1990, Quinault Nation 1991. Tribal atty. Quinault Indian Tribe, Taholah, Wash., 1990—97; instr. Ctrl. Wash. U., Ellensburg, Wash., 1990—97; tribal judge N.W. Inter Tribal Ct., Wash., 1997—. Mem.: Crime Victims Bar Assn. Avocations: climbing, skiing, golf, backgammon, chess. Home: 2715 50th SW Seattle WA 98116 Office: 2701 California Ave SW # 66 Seattle WA 98116 Office Fax: 206-938-0258. Business E-Mail: seattlelawyer@hotmail.com.

GIBSON, JOHN PHILLIPS, pathologist, toxicologist; b. Pittsburg, Kans., Sept. 18, 1930; s. Laurence Milburn and Muriel Phillips Gibson; m. Mary Louise Heath Gibson; children: Brian Heath, Susan Phillips. BS, Kans. State U., 1953, DVM, MS, Kans. State U., 1959; PhD, Ohio State U., 1964. Diplomate Am. Coll. Vet. Pathologists, 1964, Am. Bd. Toxicology, 1981. Instr. vet. bacteriology Purdue U., West Lafayette, Ind., 1959—60; rsch. assoc. Ohio State U., Columbus, Ohio, 1960—64; toxicologist William S. Merrell Co., Cin., 1964—70; dept. head pathology & toxicology Merrell Dow Pharmaceuticals Inc., Cin., 1970—90; dir. drug safety Marion Merrell Dow Inc., Cin., 1990—93; cons. toxicology, pathology and drug safety Cin., 1994—. Adv. bd. Cincinnati Drug & Poison Info. Ctr., Cincinnati, Ohio, 1991—2000; instl. review bd. Hill Top Rsch., Cincinnati, Ohio, 1994—. 1st lt. Army Arty., 1953—55, Korea. Mem.: Am. Vet. Med. Assn., Soc. Toxicologic Pathology, Soc. Toxicology, Am. Coll. Vet. Pathologists. Home: 550 Woodbrook Ln Cincinnati OH 45215-2513

GIBSON, JOHN ROBERT, federal judge; b. Springfield, Mo., Dec. 20, 1925; s. Harry B. and Edna (Kerr) G.; m. Mary Elizabeth Vaughn, Sept. 20, 1952 (dec. Aug. 1985); children: Jeanne, John Robert; m. Diane Allen Larrison, Oct. 1, 1986; stepchildren: Holly, Catherine. AB, U. Mo., 1949, JD, 1952. Bar: Mo. 1952. Assoc. Morrison, Hecker, Curtis, Kuder & Parrish, Kansas City, Mo., 1952-58, ptnr., 1958 81; judge U.S. Dist. Ct. (we. dist.) Mo., 1981-82, U.S. Ct. Appeals (8th cir.), Kansas City, 1982-94, sr. judge, 1994—. Mem. Mo. Press-Bar Commn., 1979-81; mem. com. on adminstrn. of magistrate sys. Jud. Conf. U.S., 1987-91, mem. security and facilities com., 1995-2001. Vice chmn. Jackson County Charter Transition Com., 1971-72; mem. Jackson County Charter Commn., 1970; v.p. Police Commrs. Bd., Kansas City, 1973-77. Served with AUS, 1944-46. With U.S. Army, 1944—46. Recipient Citation of Merit award U. Mo. at Columbia Sch. of Law, 1994. Fellow Am. Bar Found.; mem. ABA, Mo. State Bar (gov. 1972-79, pres. 1977-78; Pres.' award 1974, Smithson award 1984), Kansas City Bar Assn. (pres. 1970-71), Lawyers Assn. Kansas City (Charles Evan Whittaker award 1980), Fed. Judges Assn. (bd. dirs. 1991-97), Phi Beta Kappa, Omicron Delta Kappa. Presbyterian. Office: US Ct Appeals 8th Cir 400 E 9th St Ste 1040 Kansas City MO 64106-2695*

GIBSON, JOHN ROBERT, software engineer; b. Murfreesboro, Tenn., Dec. 24, 1948; s. Donald Cotis Gibson and Sara Elizabeth Garner; m. Corinne de Marie Pallatto, Sept. 2, 1978 (div. July 1989). BSEE, U. Ala., 1973. Commd. 2d lt. USAF, 1973, advanced through grades to capt., 1977, resigned, 1983; computer programmer/analyst Computer Scis. Corp., Colorado Springs, Colo., Ridgecrest, Calif., 1984-90; sci. computer programmer Boeing Computer Support Svcs., Ridgecrest, 1990-91; computer engr. USAF, Edwards AFB, Calif., 1993-95; software tester EER Sys., Inc., Ridgecrest, 1996-97; software engr. EDO Tech. Svcs. Ops., Edwards AFB, 1997—2001; embedded programming AOA Inc., Westlake Village, Calif., 2002—. Contbr. articles to profl. jours. Candidate for Calif. State Senate, Antelope Valley Libertarian Party, 2000, treas., 2000-02. Mem. Calif. Checker Assn. (pres. 1999-2003). Avocations: anime, checkers, coins, history, skiing. Home: 563 Hampshire Rd Apt 171G Westlake Village CA 91361-2228 E-mail: j_gibson@aoa-gps.com.

GIBSON, JOHN WHEAT, lawyer; b. Waco, Tex., June 27, 1946; s. John Wheat and Dorothy (Carpenter) G.; m. Melanie McGarrahan Gibson; children: Madeleine, Ruth, Abigail, Jack. BA, U. Tex., 1969, MA, 1976; cert., Casa Nicaraguense, 1986; JD, Baylor U., 1986. Bar: Tex. 1986, U.S. Dist. Ct. (no. dist.) Tex. 1987, U.S. Ct. Appeals (5th cir.) 1988, U.S. Supreme Ct., 2000. Copy editor Waco Tribune Herald, 1976-78; editor Clifton (Tex.) Record, 1978; instr. Temple (Tex.) Jr. Coll., 1978-82, Ea. Ill. U., Charleston, 1982-83; paralegal McLennan County Jail, Waco, 1985-86; staff atty. Proyecto Adelante, Dallas, 1986-87; assoc. Natkin & Flores-Saldivar, Ft. Worth, 1987; pvt. practice law Dallas, 1988—; ponente Primera Jornada Internacional de Juristas, San Salvador, El Salvador, 1990. Reporter Sta. KWTX, Waco, 1981-82. Cons. Com. in Solidarity with People El Salvador, 1986-88, adviser, 1988; cons. Cooperativo Refugiados Centroamericanos, 1986-88, Centro Social Hispanico, 1997-99; bd. dirs. Am.-Arab Anti-Defamation Com., 1998-2000. Recipient Friend of Youth award Optimist Club, Temple, 1980, Adviser of Yr. award Tex. Intercollegiate Press Assn., 1980. Mem. Tex. Bar Assn., Nat. Lawyers Guild (co-chair Tex.-Okla. region 2001-02), Tex. Trial Lawyers Assn. (pres. student chpt. spring 1985), Am. Immigration Lawyers Assn., ACLU. Green Party. Episcopalian. Avocations: bicycling, camping. Office: 701 Commerce St Ste 110 Dallas TX 75202-4521

GIBSON, JOSEPH LEE, lawyer, lecturer; b. Lufkin, Tex., Mar. 12, 1940; s. Mitchell Osler and W. Christine (Bennett) Gibson; m. Bethanna Bunn, May 27, 1983; 1 child, Mark Corbett. BA, Baylor U., 1962; LLB, Harvard U., 1965. Bar: Tex. 1965, D.C. 1967. Legis. counsel Maritime Adminstrn., Washington, 1965-66; counsel govt. activities subcom. U.S. Ho. of Reps., Washington, 1966-68; assoc. Kirkland & Ellis, and predecessor, Washington, 1968-69; ptnr. Gibson, Branham & Farmer, Washington, 1969-73; counsel Montgomery Ward & Co., Washington, 1974-78; gen. counsel Credit Union Nat. Assn., Washington, 1978-79; counsel Diplomat Nat. Bank, Washington, 1979-80, also dir.; asst. solicitor Econ. Regulatory Adminstrn., Dept. Energy, Washington, 1980—; lectr. on equal employment in broadcasting, 1971-77, on consumer credit, privacy, electronic fund transfers, 1975—; atty. for mem. Nat. Commn. on Electronic Fund Transfers, Washington, 1976-78. Mem. various campaign and conv. staffs Democratic Party, Young Democrats, Tex. and Washington, 1965-80. Recipient Disting. Service award Maritime Adminstrn., 1966, Disting. Service award Dept. Energy, 1983. Methodist. Address: 966 Towlston Rd Mc Lean VA 22102-1026 Office: Dept Energy Econ Regulatory Adminstrn 1000 Independence Ave SW Washington DC 20585-0001

GIBSON, JOSEPH WHITTON, JR., retired chemical company executive; b. Norristown, Pa., Feb. 24, 1922; s. Joseph Whitton and Nellie (Dear) G.; m. Norma Jean Stewart, Sept. 21, 1946; children: Joseph Whitton, Winn S. Gobeil, Philip B. BS, Worcester Poly. Inst., 1944; postgrad., Princeton U., 1944, MIT, 1945. With E. I. duPont de Nemours & Co., Wilmington, Del., 1946-91, sr. research engr., 1961-79, sr. tech. specialist printing systems, imaging systems, 1979-91. Mem. pantyhose sizing com. Nat. Assn. Hosiery Mfrs., 1969-71. Contbr. articles to profl. jours. Treas. Mayfield Civic Assn.; v.p. Brandywine Babe Ruth; treas. Shellcrest Swim Club; IRS VITA vol., 1995—; vol. LPGA/AJGA, 1997—, US Census 2000, 1999—. Served to lt. USNR, 1944-46. Recipient Joseph W. Gibson Jr. award tech. excellence established duPont, 1992, Internat. Man of Yr. award Internat. Biog. Centre, Cambridge, Eng., Dateline Recognition award Chem. Heritage Found., Phila., Dupont Lavoisier award, 2000. Mem. Am. Assn. Textile Chemists and Colorists (mem. history and archives com. 1994—, Olney medal 1979), Am. Chem. Soc., Fiber Soc. (hon.), Internat. Platform Assn., Planetary Soc., Sigma Xi, Tau Beta Pi. Republican. Episcopalian. Achievements include the invention of thermosol dyeing, sparkle hosiery, synthetic leather, fish swimway, printing plates. Home: 1215 Hillside Blvd Wilmington DE 19803-4211

GIBSON, JUDITH W. clinical therapist; b. Syracuse, N.Y., Apr. 27, 1942; d. Nathan Whitney and Helen-Alycia (Fancher) Watson; m. Robert Glenn Gibson, Aug. 1964 (dec. Oct. 1966); 1 child, Heidi. BA in English, Syracuse U., 1978, MA in Religion, 1985, MSW, 1987. LCSW Acad. Cert. Social Workers. Bookkeeper Stickley Furniture, Fayetteville, N.Y., 1965-67; adminstrv. asst. Agway Inc., Dewitt, N.Y., 1967-82; asst. dir. housing Syracuse U., 1983-87; dir. preventive svcs. The Salvation Army, Syracuse, 1990—2002; clinician Psychol. Health Care PLLC, Syracuse, 2002—. Mem. NASW, Sexual Abuse Study Team. Roman Catholic. Avocations: reading, arts, travel. Home: 9 Carriage House E # A Manlius NY 13104-2355

GIBSON, LAWRENCE EDWARD, dermatologist; b. Rochester, Minn., Oct. 21, 1955; s. Smith Hison and Lucille (Holmes) G.; m. Rokea Adel El-Azhary, Apr. 5, 1995; children: Sarah Elizabeth, Dylan Sharif Myers, Matthew Edward. BA, Carson-Newman Coll., Jefferson City, Tenn., 1976; MD, U. Louisville, 1980. Diplomate Am. Bd. Dermatology; lic. physician Minn., Ariz., Fla. Intern Mayo Clinic, Rochester, Minn., resident in dermatology, 1982-85; staff St. Mary's Hosp., Rochester, Minn., 1986—, Meth. Hosp., Rochester, Minn., 1986—; fellow in dermatopathology Mayo Clinic/Mayo Grad. Sch., Rochester, Minn., 1985-86; cons., asst. prof. Mayo Clinic and Mayo Med. Sch., Rochester, 1986-98, prof. dermatology, 1998—. Nancy Middleton Smith lectr. U. Louisville, 1997, David Weedon lectr., 2002. Contbr. chpts. to books.; editor-in-chief: Internat. Jour. Dermatology, 2001—. Vol., coach Rochester Youth Soccer, 1996, 99. Fellow Am. Acad. Dermatology; mem. Internat. Soc. Dermatology (dir. dermatopathology internat. workshops 1997-99), Am. Soc. Dermatopathology. Avocations: travel, fitness, woodworking, sailing. Office: Mayo Clinic 200 1st St SW Rochester MN 55905-0002

GIBSON, MARGARET FERGUSON, poet, educator; b. Phila., Feb. 17, 1944; d. John Spears and Mattie Leigh (Doyle) Ferguson; m. Ross Shackelford Gibson Jr., Aug. 27, 1966 (div. 1971); m. David W. McKain, Dec. 27, 1975; stepchildren: Joshua, Megan. BA, Hollins Coll., 1966; MA, U. Va., 1967. Instr. Madison Coll., Va., 1967-68, Va. Commonwealth U., 1968-70; asst. prof. George Mason U., Va., 1970-75; vis. prof. U. Conn., 1976-77, lectr., 1977-84; writer in residence Phillips Acad./Andover, Mass., 1984-87; vis. prof., MFA program Va. Commonwealth U., 1988-89, U. Mass., 1991-92; asst. prof. Ea. Conn. State U., 1989-91; vis. prof. U. Conn., 1992—. Author: Signs, 1979, Long Walks in the Afternoon, 1982 (Lamont Selection 1982), Memories of the Future, 1986 (co-winner Melville Cane award 1986-87), Out in the Open, 1989, The Vigil, 1993 (finalist Nat. Book award in poetry 1993), Earth Elegy, New and Selected Poems, 1997, Icon and Evidence, 2001, Autumn Grasses, 2003; contbr. poetry to anthologies including Ardis Anthology of New Am. Poetry, Contemporary New Eng. Poetry, Fifty Years of American Poets; contbr. to mags. including Ga. Rev., Prairie Schooner, Minn. Rev., Mich. Quar. Rev., Gettysburg Rev., Iowa Rev., Shenandoah. Woodrow Wilson grantee, 1966, Nat. Endowment for Arts grantee, 1985, Individual artist grantee Conn. Commn. on Arts, 1976, 88; Lila Wallace teaching fellow Woodrow Wilson Found., 1994—. Mem. Phi Beta Kappa. Democrat. Buddhist. Avocations: environment, hiking, gardening. Address: 152 Watson Rd Preston CT 06365-8837 E-mail: margibson@juno.com.

GIBSON, MCGUIRE, archaeologist, educator; b. Bushwood, Md., Nov. 6, 1938; s. Thomas Laurie and Essie Mae (Owens) Gibson. BA, Fordham U., 1959; MA, U. Chgo., 1964, PhD, 1968. Asst. prof. anthropology U. Ill., Chgo., 1968-71; asst. prof. U. Ariz., Tucson, 1971-72; from asst. prof. to assoc. prof. U. Chgo., 1972—81, prof., 1981—. Ann. prof. Am. Schs. Oriental Rsch., Baghdad, Iraq, 1969—70; dir. Nippur Expdn., Iraq, 1972—, Dhamar Expdn., Yemen, 1978—98, Hamoukar Expdn., Syria, 1999—; chmn. Coun. Am. Overseas Rsch. Ctrs., 1984—88, treas., 1988—92, mem. exec. com., 1995—. Author: (book) The City and Area of Kish, 1972; editor: Irrigation's Impact on Society, 1974, Seals and Sealing in the Ancient Near East, 1977, The Organization of Power: Aspects of Bureaucracy in the Ancient Near East, 1987, Uch Tepe II, 1990, Nippur III, 1993; author, editor: book Excavations in Nippur, 12th Season, 1978, Uch Tepe I, 1981. Mem. UNESCO Fac-Finding Mission to Iraq; mem. arts com. Union League Civic and Arts Found., Chgo., 1984—86; mem. adv. bd. Chgo. Humanities Festival, 2003—. Recipient Yemeni Arch. Svc. award, 1998; grantee, Am. Numismatic Soc., 1966, Am. Philos. Soc., 1969, Nat. Geog. Soc., 1978, 1989, NSF, 1994, NEH, 1995—98. Fellow: Deutsche Orient-Gesellchaft, Royal Anthrop. Inst., Brit. Sch. Archaeology Iraq; mem.: AAAS, Civil War Landscapes Assn., Am. Assn. Rsch. Baghdad, Mid. E. Studies Assn., Am. Inst. Yemeni Studies, Am. Anthrop. Assn., Am. Inst. Archaeology, Quadrangle Club, Sigma Xi. Democrat. Avocations: architectural restoration, study of oriental rugs. Office: U Chgo Oriental Inst 1155 E 58th St Chicago IL 60637-1540 E-mail: m-gibson@uchicago.edu.

GIBSON, MEL, actor, film director, producer; b. Peekskill, N.Y., Jan. 3, 1956; emigrated to Australia, 1968; s. Hutton and Anne Gibson. Grad., Nat. Inst. Dramatic Art, Sydney, Australia, 1977. Founder Icon Prodns. Works include: (films) Summer City, 1977, Mad Max, 1979, Tim, 1979, Attack Force Z, Gallipoli, 1981, The Road Warrior (Mad Max II), 1982, The Year of Living Dangerously, 1983, The Bounty, 1984, The River, 1984, Mrs. Soffel, 1984, Mad Max Beyond Thunderdome, 1985, Lethal Weapon, 1987, Tequila Sunrise, 1988, Lethal Weapon II, 1988, Bird on a Wire, 1989, Hamlet, 1990, Air America, 1990, Lethal Weapon III, 1992, Forever Young, 1992, Maverick, 1994, Pocahontas, 1995 (voice only), Father's Day, 1997, Conspiracy Theory, 1997, Lethal Weapon 4, 1998, The Million Dollar Hotel, 1999, Payback, 1999; actor, dir.: The Man Without a Face, 1993; actor, dir., prodr.: Braveheart, 1995 (Golden Globe award for best dir. of film 1996, Acad. award for best dir. 1996, Acad. award for best picture of yr. 1996, Outstanding Directorial Achievement in Motion Picture award nominee Dir. Guild Am. 1996, Oscar award for Best Dir.), Ransom, 1996, (voice) Chicken Run, 2000, The Patriot, 2000, What Women Want, 2000, Signs, 2002, We Were Soldiers, 2003, The Singing Detective (also prodr.), 2003, prodr. writer, dir. The Passion, 2004; performed with Nimrod Theatre Co. in plays including Death of a Salesman, Romeo and Juliet, with South Australian Theatre Co., from 1978, appeared in plays including Oedipus, Henry IV, Cedoona; work in TV series includes The Sullivans, The Oracle (Australia); exec. prodr. (TV) The Three Stooges, 2000. Favorite Movie Actor, People's Choice award, 1997. Roman Catholic. Office: ICONS Productions Producers Bldg # 3 4000 Warner Blvd Rm 17 Burbank CA 91522-0001

GIBSON, MELVIN ROY, pharmacology educator; b. St. Paul, Nebr., June 11, 1920; s. John and Jennie Irene (Harvey) G. BS, U. Nebr., 1942, MS, 1947, DSc (hon.), 1985; PhD, U. Ill., 1949. Asst. prof. pharmacognosy Wash. State U., Pullman, 1949-52, assoc. prof., 1952-55, prof., 1955-85, prof. emeritus, 1985—. Editor: Am. Jour. Pharm. Edn, 1956-61; editorial bd., co-author: Remington's Pharm. Sci, 1970, 75, 80, 85; editor, co-author: Studies of a Pharm. Curriculum, 1967; author over 100 articles. Served as arty. officer AUS,

1942-46. Decorated Bronze star, Purple Heart; sr. vis. fellow Orgn. for Econ. Cooperation and Devel., Royal Pharm. Inst. (now part of Uppsala U.), Stockholm, Sweden and U. Leiden (Holland), 1962; recipient Rufus A. Lyman award, 1972, Wash. State U. Faculty Library award, 1984, Disting. Alumnus award U. Nebr., 1999; named Wash. State U. Faculty Mem. of Yr., 1985. Fellow AAAS; assoc. fellow Am. Coll. Apothecaries; mem. AAUP, VFW (life), N.Y. Acad. Scis., Am. Pharm. Assn., Am. Soc. Pharmacognosy (pres. 1964-65), Am. Assn. Coll. Pharmacy (exec. com. 1961-63, bd. dirs. 1977-79, chmn. coun. faculties 1975-76, pres. 1979-80, Disting. Educator award 1984), U.S. Pharmacopeia (revision com. 1970-75), Am. Found. Pharm. Edn. (hon. life, bd. dirs. 1980-85, exec. com. 1981-85, vice chmn. 1982-85), Am. Inst. History of Pharmacy (sponsor), U. Nebr. Chancellor's Club, U. Nebr. Pres. Club, Sigma Xi, Phi Kappa Phi, Omicron Delta Kappa, Rho Chi, Spokane Club, Kappa Psi (Nat. Svc. citation 1961). Democrat. Presbyterian. Home: 707 W 6th Ave Apt 41 Spokane WA 99204-2813

GIBSON, MICHAEL, artist; b. Atlanta, 1962; BFA, U. Ga., 1989. Exhibitions include include U. Ga. Main Gallery, Athens, 1988—89, exhibitions include N.B.H.V. Internat., Hamburg, Germany, 1989, exhibited in group shows at Athens Art Space, Atlanta, 1990, exhibitions include Art Space, 1991, Swan Coach House, 1991, Lowe Gallery, Atlanta, 1992—93, Contemporary Internat. Mus. Art, 1992, Lowe Gallery, L.A., 1993, Chassie Post, N.Y., 1994—95, Chassie Post Gallery, Atlanta, 1994—95, Caesarea Gallery, Boca Raton, Fla., 1994, Nexus Contemporary Arts Ctr., 1995, New Mus. Contemporary Art, N.Y.C., 1995, Consult Art, Atlanta, 1997, So. Ctr. Contemporary Art, Winston-Salem, 1997, Fay Gold Gallery, Atlanta, 1997, Art Walk, 1998, Columbus Mus., 1998, Miss. Mus. Art, 1998, Mobile Mus. Art, 1998, Cummer Mus. Art, 1998, Represented in permanent collections N.B.H.V., Hamburg, Hunter Mus., Chattanooga, Peter Gabriel, London, exhibitions include others; featured numerous publs. and catalogues. Office: care Fay Gold Gallery 764 Miami Cir NE Atlanta GA 30324-5908 Fax: 404 365-8633.

GIBSON, MILTON EUGENE, cardiologist; b. Laporte, Ind., July 11, 1939; s. Maurice Wayne and Mary Leola Gibson; m. Gloria Jean Birky, Aug. 12, 1961; children: Kevin Scott, Bradley Mark. BA, Valparaiso U., 1961; MD, Ind. U., 1965. Diplomate Am. Bd. Internal Medicine, Am. Bd. Cardiovasc. Disease, Am. Bd. Interventional Cardiology. Rotating intern Meml. Hosp. of South Bend, 1965—66; resident in internal medicine Meth. Hosp. Grad. Med. Ctr. 1968—70, fellow in cardiology, 1970—72; cardiologist Cardiology Assocs., Inc., South Bend, Ind., 1972-88, pres., 1984-88; cardiologist, pres. The Heart Group, South Bend, 1988—. Chmn. cardiac cath com. Meml. Hosp., South Bend, 1973-90, St. Joseph's Med. Ctr., South Bend, 1999-2001; chmn. dept. medicine Meml. Hosp., South Bend, 1976-79; asst. clin. prof. medicine Ind. U., Indpls., 1980—. Author: Heart Sounds and Murmurs, 1973; contbr. articles to profl. jours. Pres. Am. Heart Assn., Indpls., 1977, pres. St. Joseph County chpt., 1975; bd. dirs. Vis. Nurse Assn., South Bend, 1984; mem. adv. bd. South Bend Pops Orch., 1978. Capt. U.S. Army, 1966-68, Vietnam. Decorated Bronze Star; recipient Man of Yr. award St. Joseph County Heart Assn., 1976. Fellow Am. Coll. Cardiology, Am. Coll. Chest Physicians, Coun. Critical Cardiology, Am. Heart Assn.; mem. ACP.

GIBSON, ORPHA RAY, educator; b. Blue Eye, Mo., Feb. 20, 1934; s. Claude Bertrum and Sylvia Jane Hudson G.; m. Nancy Lou Lawson, Dec. 23, 1962; children: Gregory Ray, Nancy Ann, Bethany Jane. BS, Southwest Mo. State U., 1961; MEd, U. Ark., 1964, EdD, 1968. Tchr., coach Blue Eye Pub. Schs., 1960-61, Bradleyville (Mo.) Pub. Schs., 1961-62, Waynesville (Mo.) Pub. Schs., 1962-66; assoc. prof. Southwest Bapt. U., Bolivar, Mo., 1967-71; supt. schs. Pleasant Hope (Mo.) Pub. Schs., 1971-72, Cabool (Mo.) Pub. Schs., 1972-73; prof., dir. tchr. edn. Coll. of the Ozarks, Point Lookout, Mo., 1973-97, prof. edn. emeritus, 1997—. Coun. of faculty athletics rep. Nat. Assn. of Intercollegiate Athletics, Tulsa, 1989-95, faculty athletics rep., Tulsa, 1973-97; coach State Championship Basketball Team, Bradleyville, Mo., 1962. Sec. Sch. Bd. of Edn., Blue Eye, 1974-95; deacon First Bapt. Ch., Blue Eye, 1986—. With U.S. Army, 1956-58, Japan. Named to Hall of Fame Nat. Assn. Intercollegiate Athletics, Tulsa, 1997, Coll. of the Ozarks, Point Lookout, 1997. Mem.: Kappa Delta Pi, Phi Delta Kappa. Baptist. Achievements include coaching Missouri State Class S basketball championship team from Bradleyville in 1962. Avocations: spectator sports, reading, horseback riding, family activities, travel.

GIBSON, PAMELA, business development consultant, audio director; b. Springville, N.Y., Nov. 3, 1950; d. Donald Wesley and Arveda Patricia Gibson; 1 child, Simon James Swist. Student, Stephens Coll., 1967-68. Owner Tiger Eye Recorders, N.Y.C., 1968-85; audio dir. NBC, N.Y.C., 1969-84; computer engr., account exec. Microage Corp., Houston, 1985-93; computer network engring. bus. devel. exec. KPMG Cons., N.Y.C., 2000—. Cons. Legal Aid Soc., N.Y.C.; networking cons. Cisco Systems, 1999, IBM, 1988-99. Audio dir. Today Show, 1969-76, Late Night with David Letterman, 1979-84. Bd. dirs. Houston Youth Symphony and Ballet, 1990-92. Named one of 100 Yrs. Houston's Pioneer Women and Today's Leaders, City of Houston, 1993; recipient Cisco Internet Commerce award of excellence, 1999, Networking award/Pub. Spkg. award, 1990. Avocations: gardening, watercolors, landscape and floral design. Office: pamelagibson@KPMG dot com 105 W Creek Ave Cutchogue NY 11935-2434

GIBSON, PATRICE VANDEGRIFT, anthropologist, educator; d. Roger Dale and Florence Macrae Vandegrift; m. Chris Gibson, Dec. 31, 1977; children: Jedediah, Lucas. BA, UCLA, 1971, MA, 1973, PhD, 1981. Cert. C.C. tchr. Prof. of anthropology Am. River Coll., Sacramento, 1990—; co coordinator chimpanzoo program Jane Goodall Inst., Tucson, 1986—. Coord. learning communities for student success Am. River Coll., Sacramento, 1999—2003, co-dir. ctr. for tchg. and learning, 1996—99, Sacramento, 2003—04. Mem.: Soc. for Anthropology in Cmty. Colleges, Am. Anthrop. Assn. Avocations: travel, cooking. Office: American River Coll 4700 College Oak Dr Sacramento CA 95841 Office Fax: 916-484-8519. E-mail: gibsonp@arc.losrios.edu.

GIBSON, PATRICIA, family educator; b. Troy, Ala., Feb. 27, 1950; d. Amos Tellis, Iredell Flowers; children: Amirah, Hassan, AlQadr Jones, Malik Jones, Tamena Jones, AlDuha Jones, Bayyinah Jones, Kasim Jones. Student, Roxbury C.C., Boston, 1984—87. Cert. early childhood edn., human services. Med. asst.; early childhood presch. tchr.; case mgr.; counselor/outreach worker; advocate; family educator. Mem. parent counsel Headstart, 1980—90; mem. Boston Parent Coun., 1986—90; missionary Grace Ch. of All Nations, Boston, 1990—, songstress. Recipient Award for poetry, Internat. Poetry Soc., 2001. Avocations: walking, writing, singing, aerobics, arts and crafts.

GIBSON, PAUL RAYMOND, international trade and investment development executive; b. Cathay, Calif., Apr. 10, 1924; s. Otto and Louella (Vestal) G.; m. Janice Elizabeth Carter, dec. 19, 1952; children: Scott C., Paula S. BS in Fgn. Svc., Georgetown U., 1956. With U.S. Govt. Marshall Plan, Heidelberg, Germany, 1948-52; export mgr. Asia, Philip Morris Co., San Francisco, 1952-54; founder, v.p., gen. mgr. McGregor and Werner Internat. Corp., Washington, 1954-62; v.p., dir. McGregor and Werner Corp., 1955-62; v.p. fin. Parsons & Whittemore, Inc., N.Y.C., 1962-65; founder, pres. Paul R. Gibson & Assocs., Washington, 1965-70; mng. dir. Black Clawson Pacific Co., Sydney, Australia, 1970-72; pres. Envirotech Asia Pacific, Sydney, 1972-75, Envirotech Internat., Menlo Park, Calif., 1975-80; founder, pres. INTERACT, San Francisco, 1980-91; pres. The Manchester Group, Ltd., Washington, 1987-89; pres., mng. assoc. Projects Internat. Assocs., Inc., Washington, 1991—; pres. Projects Internat., Inc., 1996—, Sustainable Project Mgmt. USA, 1994—. Mem. Pacific Basin Econ. Coun., 1975—, vice chmn. policy and planning U.S. sect., 1976-91, chmn. Vietnam Task Force, 1998-2000; mem., trustee San Francisco World Affairs Coun., 1980-91; mem. World Affairs Coun., Washington, 1998—. Served to sgt. USMC, 1941-45. Mem. U.S. C. of C. (chmn. Asia-Pacific coun. Am. C. of C. 1973-74, mem. adv. com. 1975—), Dirs. Cir., Mus. Natural History Smithsonian Instn., Confrerie des Chevaliers du Tastevin (chevalier, sous commanderie de Washington 1992-2002), Rural Health Internat. (co-chmn. 2002—), Am. Nat. Club (Sydney). Home: 2631 Golfside Ct Naples FL 34110 Office: Projects Internat Inc 1800 K St NW Ste 1000 Washington DC 20006-2202 E-mail: prgpii@cs.com.

GIBSON, RALPH H(OLMES), photographer; b. Jan. 16, 1939; Student in photography, U.S. Navy, 1956-60, San Francisco Art Inst., 1960-61; DFA (hon.), U. Md., 1991, Ohio Wesleyan U., 1997. Lectr. at numerous schs., museums. Exhibited photography in one-man shows including Madison (Wis.) Arts Ctr., 1975, Hoesch Mus., Duren, W. Ger., 1975, Castelli Graphics, N.Y.C., 1976, 80, 82, 91, Balt. Mus. Art, 1976, Van Reekum Galerji Mus., Apeldoorn, Netherlands, 1977, Swedish Mus. Photography, 1977, Mus. Modern Art, Oxford, Eng., 1977, Photographers Gallery, Melbourne, Australia, 1977, Robert Self Gallery, London, 1978, Mus. Modern Art, Brisbane, Australia, 1978, I.C.A. Mus. Art, Richmond, Va., 1979, Canon Gallery, Geneva, 1979, Grapestake Gallery, San Francisco, 1979, Kunstmuseum, Dusseldorf, Fed. Republic Germany, 1980, Night Gallery, London, 1980, Mus. Folkwang, Essen, Fed. Republic Germany, 1981, Mattingly Baker Gallery, Dallas, 1981, Sprengel Mus., Hanover, W. Ger., 1981, Cantieri Navali, La Giudeca, Venice, Italy, 1981, F.I.A.C., Paris, 1982, Olympus Gallery, London, 1892, Centre Georges Pompidou, Paris, 1982, Shadai Gallery, Tokyo, 1982, Sun Valley Ctr. for the Arts, Idaho, 1983, Seattle Art Mus., 1983, Weston Gallery, Carmel, Calif., 1984, Consejo Argentino de Fotografia, Buenos Aires, Argentina, 1985, Bouwfonds Hovelaken, The Netherlands, 1985, Castelli Uptown, N.Y.C., 1985, Galerie Agathe Gaillard, Paris, 1985, Leo Castelli Gallery, N.Y.C., 1985, 87, Ministry of Culture Hall, Marrakech, Morocco, 1986, Nat. Exhibit Hall, Moabane, Swaziland, 1986, Musee Carnavalet, Paris, 1986, Hellenic Ctr. Photography, Athens, 1987, Mus. Fine Arts, Alexandria, Egypt, 1987, Museo Archivi Alinari, Florence, Italy, 1987, Circulo de Bellas Artes, Madrid, 1987, Internat. Ctr. Photography, N.Y.C., 1987, Villa Medici, Rome, 1987, Mpls. Inst. Arts, 1988, Bibliotheque Nationale, Paris, 1988, Moderna Museet, Fotografiska Museet, Stockholm, 1989, Arts Club Chgo,, 1989, Albin O. Kuhn Libr. and Gallery, U. Md., Balt., 1990, Musee Nicephore Niepce, Chalon Sue Soane, France, 1990, Princessehof Mus., Leuwarden, Holland, 1991, Okla. City Art Mus., 1991, Espace Photo Paris Audiovisuel, 1991, Photography House, Prague, 1992, Kunstverein Emmerich, Haus imm Park, 1996—, High Museum of Art, Atlanta, GA., 1997, MMK, Frankfurt, Germany, 1998, Maison Européenne De La Photographie, Paris, 1999; Greenville Cnty. Museum of Art, Greenville, Whitney Museum of American Art- N.Y.C., Ger., 1992, Boca Mus. Art, Boca Raton, Fla., 1993, 94, Butler Mus. Am. Art, Ohio, 1994, Frankfurt Kunstverein, 1996, Internat. Ctr. Photography 5-yr. world wide travelling exhbn., Villa Medici, Rome, 1986—, Mus. Carnavalet, Paris, 1986—, Leo Castelli Gallery, N.Y., Galerie Eric Van de Weghe, Brussels, Expo 1991, ICAC/Weston Gallery, Tokyo, others; exhibited in numerous group shows, including, Mus. Modern Art, N.Y.C., 1978, Hayden Gallery, MIT, Cambridge, 1978, Bologna Art Fair, Italy, 1978, Walker Art Center, Liverpool, Eng., 1978, Cleve. Mus. Art, 1978, Musée Marseilles, 1980, Addison Gallery of Art, Phillips Acad., Andover, Mass., 1981, Mus. Folkwang, Essen, 1981, San Francisco Mus. of Modern Art, 1982, 84, 85, Met. Mus. Art, N.Y.C., 1982, Whitney Mus. Art, N.Y.C., 1983, Houston Ctr. for Photography, 1983, Mus. Art, Phila., 1983, Denver Art Mus., 1984, Nat. Mus. Art, Washington, 1984, Sesnon Gallery, U. Calif.-Santa Cruz, 1984, Mus. of Modern Art, Paris, 1984, Pace-McGill Gallery, N.Y.C., 1985, Barbican Art Gallery, London, 1985, Bronx Mus., N.Y.C., 1985, Kunsterin, Stuttgart, Fed. Republic Germany, 1985, Musee Cantonal, Lausanne, Switzerland, 1985, Lehigh U., Pa., 1985, Gallery Hirondelle, N.Y.C., 1986, Villa Medici, Rome, numerous others; represented in permanent collections, including Nat. Gallery Ottawa, Ont., Can., Whitney Mus. Am. Art, Bibliotheque National de France, Paris, Mus. Modern Art, N.Y.C., Internat. Mus. Photography, George Eastman House, Rochester, N.Y., Fogg Art Mus., Boston, Met. Mus. Art, N.Y.C., Australian Nat. Gallery, Canberra, Nat. Gallery Victoria, Australia, Art Gallery South Australia, Victoria and Albert Mus., London, Mus. Modern Art, Brisbane, Fotografiska Museet, Moderna Museet, Stockholm, Sweden, Musee Reattu, Arles, France, G. Ray Hawkins Gallery, Los Angeles, Mus. Fine Arts, Alexandria, Egypt, Mus. Art, Athens, Greece; author: Apropos de Mary Jane, 1990, Chiaroscuro, 1990; author, illustrator: The Strip, 1966, The Hawk, 1968, The American Civil Liberties Union Calendar, 1969, The Somnambulist, 1970, Deja-vu, 1973, Days at Sea, 1975, Syntax, 1983, Tropism, 1987, Archive-Early Work, 1988; navarin editor: In-Situ, 1988, Les Cahiers des La Photographie, 1988, L'Histoire de France, 1991, Deux ex Machina, Taschen edits., 1999, Ex Libris Powerhouse edits., 2000. Decorated comdr. Ordre Arts et Lettres (France); recipient Leica medal of excellence award, 1988, grand medal City of Arles, France, 1994, Silver Plumb award Design Trust for Pub. Space, 2000; fellowship grantee Nat. Endowment for Arts, 1973, 75, 86-87, creative artists pub. svc. grantee N.Y. State. Coun. Arts, 1977, grantee Eastman Kodak Co., 1989, Murray and Isabella Rayburn Found., 1994; Guggenheim fellow, 1985-86. Address: 331 W Broadway New York NY 10013-2265 *Photography is a way for measuring my perception-I trust my photographs and study them intensely. After working over forty years, I realize that the years of struggle are over. Now begin the years of struggle.*

GIBSON, REGINALD WALKER, federal judge; b. Lynchburg, Va., July 31, 1927; s. McCoy and Julia Ann (Butler) G.; 1 child, Reginald S. BS, Va. Union U., 1952; postgrad., Wharton Grad. Sch. Bus. Adminstrn., U. Pa., 1952-53; LL.B., Howard U., 1956. Bar: DC 1957, Ill. 1972. Agt. IRS, Washington, 1957-61; trial atty. tax div. US Dept. Justice, Washington, 1961-71; sr. tax atty. Internat. Harvester Co., Chgo., 1971-76, gen. tax atty., 1976-82; judge US Ct. of Fed. Claims, Washington, 1982-95; sr. judge US Ct. Fed. Claims, Washington, 1995—. Mem. bus. adbv. council Chgo. Urban League, 1974-82. Served with AUS, 1946-47. Recipient cert. award U.S. Dept. Justice Atty. Gen., 1969, recipient spl. commendation U.S. Dept. Justice Atty. Gen., 1970, Wall St. Jour. award, 1952, Am. Jurisprudence award, 1956; named Alumni of Yr. Howard U. Sch. Law, 1984. Mem. DC Bar Assn., Chgo. Bar Assn., Fed. Bar Assn., Nat. Bar Assn., Claims Ct. Bar Assn., J. Edgar Murdock Am. Inn of Ct. (taxation com.). Clubs: Nat. Lawyers (Washington). Baptist. Office: 717 Madison Pl NW Washington DC 20439-0002

GIBSON, REX HILTON, lawyer; b. Galveston, Tex., May 17, 1963; BBA, Southern Meth. U., 1985, JD, 1988. Bar: Tex. 1988, U.S. Tax Ct. 1989, U.S. Ct. Claims 1992. Tax assoc. Exxon Co., U.S.A., Houston, 1988, tax atty., 1988-92, sr. tax atty., 1992, Exxon Co., Internat., Florham Park, N.J., 1992-95, Exxon Ventures (CIS) Inc., Houston, 1995-99; tax counsel ExxonMobil Internat. Ltd., London, 2000—01, ExxonMobil Devel. Co., Houston, 2001—; bd. dirs. Internat. Tax and Investment Ctr., 2002—; mem. tax. com. Petroleum Adv. Forum, 2000—; vice chair Cspian Mirad Taxation Com., 2003—. Mem. ABA (taxation sect., natural resources com. 1995—, environ. taxes com. 1990—), State Bar Tex. (taxation sect., oil, gas & minerals law sect. 1989—), Houston Bar Assn. (taxation sect. 1995—), Houston Livestock Show and Rodeo Assn., Beta Alpha Psi. Avocations: snow skiing, hiking, fishing, golf. Office: Exxon-Mobil Devel Co Ste 1670 17001 Northchase Dr Houston TX 77060 E-mail: rex.h.gibson@exxonmobil.com.

GIBSON, ROBERT MYLES, neurosurgeon, consultant; b. Dunragit, Scotland, May 5, 1927; s. Robert and Mary (Harvey) G.; m. Ena Millar; children: Alastair, Stroma. MBChB, Glasgow U., 1949, MD, 1952; MS, McGill U., Can., 1952. Accredited neurol. surgeon. Cons. neurosurgery and health dept. U. Leeds (Eng.), 1960-92; chmn. faculty Pre-Hosp. Care, 1995—. Treas. Gen. Med. Coun. U.K., 1992—. Contbr. articles to profl. jours. Hon. brigadier Royal Army Med. Corps, 1962-92. Decorated officer Order Brit. Empire; hon. neurosurgeon Brit. Army, 1962-94. Fellow Royal Coll. Surgeons (v.p. Edinburgh 1986-89). Office: 27 Clarendon Rd Leeds LS2 9NZ England

GIBSON, SAMUEL NORRIS, educational organization executive, retired clergy; b. Troy, Ala., Sept. 2, 1926; s. Clarence Samuel Gibson and Annie Pearl Clark; m. Ellen Ruth Waldo, June 19, 1948 (div. Aug. 1972); children: Richard Waldo, Christopher Samuel; m. Ella Marie Booth, Oct. 28, 1972; stepchildren: Curtis David Schurman, Darryl John Schurman. BS in Architecture, Ga. Inst. Tech., 1947; BD, Yale U., 1951, STM, 1955; PhD, U. Pitts., 1980. Cert. ednl. planner Am. Inst. Cert. Ednl. Planners. Exec. dir. Pa. State U. Christian Assn., State College, 1956-64; rsch. dir. Study of the Methodist Campus Ministry, Nashville, 1964-66; exec. minister Univ. and City Ministries, Pitts., 1967-72; pres. Alternative Learning Lab., Pitts., 1971-77; exec. dir. East End Coop. Ministry, Pitts., 1978-82, United Meth. Ch. Union, Pitts., 1982-88; regional dir. Internat. Edn. Forum, Bay Shore, N.Y., 1989-97; pres. ASA Internat., Inc., Pitts., 1997—. Co-founder Youth Learning Ctr., 1971. Author: Public Policy in Alabama Higher Education, 1980, (booklet) The Windows of Calvary, 1989; editor: (booklets) You and the Communist Challenge, 1960, Riverfront Development Study, 1990. Trustee Otterbein Coll., Westerville, Ohio, 1984-89; pres. The Univ. Sch., Pitts., 1981-88; chair ch. coun. Calvary Meth. Ch., Pitts., 1991-99; mem. exec. com. Nat. Campus Ministry Assn., 1967-70; co-founder, treas. The Dollar Energy Fund, Pitts., 1983-92; candidate Senate of Commonwealth of Pa., Pitts., 1975; mem., chair Allegheny Historic Preservation Soc., Pitts., 1989—; mem. steering com. Mayor's Commn. on Families, Pitts., 1986-90; alumni pres. Leadership Pitts., 1986—. With USNR, 1943-46. Area studies fellow Ford Found., 1953-54, campus ministry fellow Danforth Found., 1972-73, Paul Harris fellow Rotary Internat. Found., 1993. Mem. Ind. Ednl. Counselors Assn., Rotary (pres. Pitts. East chpt. 1984, 2001), Longue Vue Club, Shannopin Country Club. Democrat. Avocations: folk songs, church architecture, genealogy, book collecting, gardening. Home: 29 Newgate Rd Pittsburgh PA 15202 Office: ASA Internat 7119 Church Ave Ben Avon PA 15202 E-mail: asassc@aol.com.

GIBSON, SCOTT RUSSELL, nurse; b. New Castle, Pa., Feb. 5, 1956; s. Earle A. and Barbara (Gormley) G.; m. Michele Moshier, May 10, 1980; children: Kathleen, Andrew, Benjamin, Noah. BSN with honors, Indiana U. Pa., 1989, MA in Adult Edn./ Comm. Tech., 2001; postgrad., RN Anesthetist Sch., Altoona, 1992-94. Cert. transplant technician, U.S. Navy Sch.; cert. emergency nurse 1989. Staff nurse Ind. (Pa.) Hosp., 1989-96; regional faculty BLS program Am. Heart Assn., 1989—; faculty instr. Ind. Vocat. Tech. LPN Sch., 1990-92; with infusion dept. Diamond Drugs, Inc., 1996-2000; staff nurse Ind. U. Pa., 2000—; asst. dir. Pechan Health Ctr., Ind., Pa., 2002—. Am. Heart Assn.-Cmty. Tng. Ctr. co-ord., 1995—. Mem. Am. Heart Assn., 1979, ARC, 1974. With USN, 1979-86. Mem. Emergency Nurses Assn.

GIBSON, SHERE CAPPARELLA, foreign language educator; b. Norristown, Pa., Sept. 4, 1956; d. Anthony and Patsy (Robbins) Capparella. BA in Spanish and French, Rosemont (Pa.) Coll., 1978; BA in Mktg., Ursinus Coll., 1991; student, Institut Internat. D'Enseignement de la Langue Française, France, 1992, Escuela de Idiomas, Spain, 1992; MEd in Multicultural Edn., Eastern Coll., 1993; ballet student, Novak and Kovalska; Spanish flamenco/castanet student, José Greco; dance student, Harrisburg Dance Conservatory; postgrad., Clayton Coll. of Natural Health, 2001—. Cert. in French/Spanish. Salesperson Spectrum Communications Corp., Norristown, 1977-79, sales and mktg. mgr., 1986-87; asst. sales and adminstrv. asst. Tettex Instruments, Inc., Fairview Village, Pa., 1979-83; owner, instr. Shere's World of Dance and Fine Arts, Jeffersonville, Pa., 1982-88; multilingual adminstrv. asst. Syntex Dental Products, Inc., Valley Forge, 1984-86; v.p. Captrium Devel. Corp., Exton, Pa., 1987-89; cons. Mary Kay Cosmetics, 1988-96; sales mgr. Spectrum Communications, 1989-92; tchr. Spanish and French Middletown (Pa.) Area Sch. Dist., 1992-94; adj. prof. Spanish Messiah Coll., Grantham, Pa., 1996—; market rsch. analyst Capital Health Sys., Harrisburg, Pa., 1995; Spanish and French tchr. Elizabethtown (Pa.) Area Sch. Dist., 1996-97; Spanish, French, and German tchr. The Milton Hershey Sch., 1997-98; tng. cons., 1999—; tech. recruiting specialist SHS Staffing Solutions, Harrisburg, Pa., 2000—01; trainer/curr. developer Capital Region Health Sys., 2002—; world lang. tchr. Milton Hershey Sch., 2002, world lang. chair, mem. multicultural com., mem., 2002—. V.p. La Bella Modeling Agy., Collegeville, Pa., 1979-82; choreographer and dance instr. La Bella Sch. Performance, Collegeville, 1979-82. Judge state and nat. pageants Miss Am. Scholarship, Jr. Miss. Nat. Teen and Pre-Teen, All-Am. Talent, Ofcl. Little Miss Am., Little Miss Diamond, Talent Olympics, Talent Unltd., 1979—; producer, choreographer Miss Montgomery County Pageant, Plymouth Meeting, Pa., 1985; co-producer, choreographer Miss Del. Valley Pageant, Horsham, Pa., 1983-84; confraternity Christian Doctrine kindergarten tchr. Visitation Parish, 1987-88; adult leadership acad., Milton Hershey Sch., 2003. Recipient award Internat. Leaders in Achievement, 1989, Community Leaders of Am., 1989, Internat. Woman of Yr., 199-2000. Mem. Am. Soc. Tng. and Devel., Am. Holistic Health Assn., Am. Naturopathic and Holistic Assn., Nat. Integrative Medicine Coun., Am. Coun. Tchrs. Fgn. Langs., Am. Assn. Tchrs. French, Pa. State MLA, Pa. State Edn. Assn., Christian Children's Fund, Am. Assn. Tchrs. Spanish, Kappa Delta Pi. Roman Catholic. Avocations: health and fitness, travel, ballroom, tap, jazz and modern dance. Home: 4700 Cumberland St Harrisburg PA 17111-2725

GIBSON, THOMAS RICHARD, automobile import company executive; b. 1942; s. Gilbert G. and Mary Ellen (Wilbraham) G.; m. Sophie Harned, Oct. 14, 1967; children: Mattehw B., Katherine A., Caroline Q. AB, DePauw U., 1964; MBA, Harvard U., 1967. Various sales mgmt. positions Ford Motor Co., Dearborn, Mich., 1967-80; dir. mktg. ops. Chrysler Corp., Highland Pk., Mich., 1980-81; sr. v.p., sales and mktg. Subaru of Am., Cherry Hill, N.J., 1981-84; exec. v.p. ops., 1984-86; pres., COO, 1986-92; chmn. Asbury Automotive Group, 1994—, CEO, 1994-99, acting CEO, 2001—02. Bd. dirs. Children's Hosp. Phila., 1986-89, Glassobry (N.J.) State Coll., 1985-89; trustee U.S. Ski Team, 1990-95. Served with USMC, 1964-65. Mem. DePauw U. Alumni Assn. (bd. dirs. 1987, trustee 1992-96). Avocations: tennis, golf, paddle tennis. Office: Asbury Automotive Group 300 Barr Harbor Dr Ste 710 Conshohocken PA 19428 Office Fax: 610-260-9650.*

GIBSON, WALKER, retired English language educator, poet, writer; b. Jacksonville, Fla., Jan. 19, 1919; s. William Walker Sr. and Helen (Jones) G.; m. Nancy Close, 1942; children: David R., Susan M., William Walker. III, John S. BA, Yale U., 1940; MA, U. Iowa, 1946. Rsch. asst. writers workshop U. Iowa, 1945-46; instr. English Amherst (Mass.) Coll., 1946-48, asst. prof., 1948-54, assoc. prof., 1954-57; assoc. prof., dir. freshman English Washington Square Coll. NYU, N.Y.C., 1957-61, prof., 1961-67; prof. English U. Mass., Amherst, 1967-87, dir. freshman English, 1967-70, dir. rhetoric program, 1970-72, dir. undergrad. studies in English, 1974-76, prof. emeritus, 1984. Lectr. Yale Summer Music Sch., 1948-56; dir. NYU Summer Inst. for Secondary Tchrs. English, 1962, NDEA Summer Inst. for Secondary Tchrs. English, NYU, 1965, Summer Seminars for Coll Tchrs, NEH, 1973-75; prof. summer intern teaching program Smith Coll., 1963, 64, 66, 67; vis. prof. Swarthmore Coll., 1965-66; prof. NDEA Summer Inst. at Mass., 1968, Bread Loaf Sch. English, Middlebury Coll., 1976, 77. Author: (verse) The Reckless Spenders, 1954 Come As You Are, 1957, (texts) Seeing and Writing: Fifteen Exercises in Composing Experience, 1959, Tough Sweet & Stuffy, 1966, Persona: A Style Study for Readers and Writers, 1969, (antholgy text) Poems in Progress, 1963; co-author: The Macmillan Handbook of English, 1960, 2nd edit, 1965; contbg. author: Traditions of Inquiry, 1985, The Legacy of Language, 1987, others; editor: Limits of Language, 1962, New Students in Two-Year Colleges, 1979; co-editor: The Play of Language, 1971; prose and verse published in The New Yorker, Story, Atlantic, Harpers, Saturday Review, The Nation, Furioso, Carleton Miscellany, Mass. Review, N.Y. Times Mag., others, reprinted in anthologies and texts; book reviews in N.Y. Times Book Review, Coll. English, Poetry, Nation, others; acad. articles in Victorian Studies, Modern Language Notes, N.Y.U. Law Review, Coll. Composition and Comm., ADE Bulletin, Coll. English, English Jour., The Quarterly Review of Doublespeak, Rhetoric Review, Chronicle of Higher Edn., others; contbns. to TV and film include Sunrise Semester, CBS-TV, full-year course Modern Literature: British and American, 1962-63, semester course Studies in Style, 1966-67, film The Speaking Voice and the Teaching of Composition, 1963, videotapes on dramatic role-playing in student writing, 1971, 84. 1st lt. U.S. Army Air Corps, 1941-45. Ford Found. fellow 1955-56; John Simon Guggenheim Found. fellow, 1963-64; grantee NEH, 1973-77. Mem. MLA (selection com. for scholar's libr. 1968-71, del. assembly 1976-77, exec. com. divsn. on tchg. of writing 1976-80, chmn. divsn. 1979), Nat. coun. Tchrs. English (commn. on curriculum 1962-65, chmn. coll. sect. 1969-71, pres. elect and pres. coun. 1971-73, com. pub. doublespeak 1972-90, chmn. emeritus assembly 1986-87, Disting. Lectr. award 1969, Disting. Svc. award 1988), CCCC (exec. com. 1966-69), 5 Coll. Learning in Retirement (pres. 1990-91). Avocations: reading, writing. Home: 38 Lessey St Amherst MA 01002-2118

GIBSON, WILLIAM FORD, author; b. Conway, S.C., Mar. 17, 1948; s. William Ford and Otey (Williams) G.; m. Deborah Thompson, June 1972; children: Graeme Ford, Claire Thompson. BA, U. B.C., 1977. Author: (novels) Neuromancer, 1984 (Hugo award World Sci. Fiction Soc. 1985, Philip K. Dick award Phila. Sci. Fiction Soc. 1985, Nebula award Sci. Fiction Writers Am. 1985, Porgie award West Coast Rev. of Books 1985), Count Zero, 1986, Mona Lisa Overdrive, 1988, (with Bruce Sterling) The Difference Engine, 1990, Virtual Light, 1993, Pattern Recognition, 2003; (short story collections) Burning Chrome, 1986; text to accompany performance art by Robert Longo: Dream Jumbo, 1989; story: (film) Johnny Mnemonic, 1995. Office: c/o Ace Books 1268 London Rd London SW16 4ER England*

GIBSON, WILLIAM LEE, financial consultant; b. Newark, Dec. 1, 1949; S. Joseph Wilton Gibson and Margaret (Reynolds) Gibson Leavens; stepson William Barry Leavens, Jr.; m. Lorraine Wrightson Besch, July 10, 1982. BA in chemistry, Bucknell U., 1972; postgrad., Harvard Bus. Sch., 1977; MBA, NYU,

1987, Sch. of Advanced Fin. Mgmt., 1995. With Bur. Solid Waste Mgmt EPA, Cin., 1970-71; chemist Dow Chem. Co., Midland, Mich., 1972-75; mktg. cons. Westvaco, Charleston, S.C., 1976; sales rep. Diamond Shamrock Co., Cleve., 19777-79; market devel. specialist strategic planing and ventures operation GE, Pittsfield, Mass., 1979-81; mktg. programs mgr. Allied-Signal Corp., Morristown, N.J., 1981-86, mgr. tech. and bus. devel., 1986-91, sr. sales mgr., 1991-93; v.p. Merrill Lynch, Short Hills, N.J., 1994—. Former pres., trustee Hartford Family Found; v.p. Leavens Found. Trustee N.J. Symphony Orch.; treas. Coun. N.J. Grantmakers. Mem. Harvard Bus. Sch. Club N.Y., Harvard Club N.Y. Home: 8 Lone Oak Rd Basking Ridge NJ 07920-1613 Office: 51 John F Kennedy Pky Short Hills NJ 07078-2702

GIBSON, WILLIAM S. corporation executive, lawyer. B.S., U. Ill., 1954, J.D., 1959. Bar: Ill. 1959. Asst. dir. Ill. Dept. Ins., 1969-71; v.p. govt. affairs Am. Ins. Assn., 1971-77; v.p., assoc. gen. counsel Continental Ins. Co., 1977-78, v.p., gen. counsel, 1978-79, corporate v.p., gen. counsel Continental Corp./Continental Ins. Cos., N.Y.C., 1979-82, v.p., dir. govt. and pub. affairs, 1982— . Office: Continental Corp/Continental Ins Cos 180 Maiden Ln New York NY 10038-4925

GIBSON, WILLIAM SHEPARD, insurance company executive; b. Bklyn., Jan. 2, 1933; s. William S. and Mary (Keeney) G.; m. Charmaine Wallett, May 26, 1967; children: Susan, Joshua/1 stepdau., Tracy; children by previous marriage: William, Gregory. BS in Acctg., U. Ill., 1954, JD, 1959. Counsel Am. Ins. Assn., Chgo., 1963-69; asst. dir. ins. State of Ill., Chgo., 1969-71; v.p. midwest Am. Ins. Assn., Chgo., 1971-77; v.p., gen. counsel Continental Ins., N.Y.C., 1977-82; v.p. govt. affairs Continental Corp., N.Y.C., 1982-95; dep. supt. N.Y. Ins., N.Y.C., 1995-97; v.p. Peterson Worldwide, N.Y.C., 1997—2001; pres., CEO Interboro Mut. Ind. Ins. Co., 2002—. Chmn. bd. N.J. Auto Ins. Assn., Newark, 1983-89; chmn. Continental PAC, 1981-95; mem. N.Y. Motor Vehicle Indemnity Corp. Bd. dirs. Lower Manhattan Cultural Coun. Served with U.S. Army, 1954-56. Mem. ABA, Ill. State Bar Assn., N.Y. Bar Assn., Internat. Assn. Ins. Counsel, N.Y. Med. Malpractice Ins. Assn. Congregationalist. Home: 80 Warren St Apt 67 New York NY 10007-1039 Office: 155 Mineola Blvd Mineola NY 11501

GIDDENS, DON PEYTON, engineering educator, researcher; b. Augusta, Ga., Oct. 24, 1940; BS in Engring., Ga. Inst. Tech., 1963, MS in Aerospace Engring., 1965, PhD, 1967. Assoc. aircraft engr. Lockheed-Ga. Co., Atlanta, 1963; mem. tech. staff Aerospace Corp., San Bernardino, Calif., 1966-67; asst. prof. Ga. Inst. Tech., Atlanta, 1968-70, assoc. prof., 1970-77, prof., 1977-82, Regents prof., 1982-92, dir. Sch. Aerospace Engring., 1988-92; dean engring. Johns Hopkins U., Balt., 1992-97; prof., chmn. dept. biomed. engring. Ga. Inst. Tech./Emory Med. Sch., Atlanta, 1997—. Mem. sci. adv. com. Whitaker Found. Contbr. numerous articles to profl. jours. Fellow ASME, Am. Inst. Med. Biol. Engrs.; mem. AAAS, Am. Heart Assn., Biomed. Engring. Soc., Natl. Acad. Engrg., Soc. Sigma Xi (nat. lectr. 1983-87). Avocation: whitewater canoeing. Office: Ga Inst Tech GT/Emory Dept Biomed Engr Atlanta GA 30332-0535

GIDDENS-JONES, EMILY JANE, architectural and interior designer, consultant; b. Jackson, Miss, Sept. 18, 1924; d. Jasper Franklin and Erma Jane (Simmons) Giddens; m. William Everard Jones, Nov. 10, 1947 (div. July 1967). BA, Belhaven Coll., 1946; postgrad., Phila. Mus. Coll. Art, 1964. Dir. design Office Supply Co., Jackson, 1954-58; dir. design and prodn. Designers Fore Ltd., NYC, 1969-75, John F. Saladino, Inc., NYC, 1975-79; pres., CEO, owner Cross Quadrate Design, NYC, 1972—. Assoc. prof. interior design Post Coll., Waterbury, Conn., 1978 79; cons. Flexcon, Inc., Spencer, Mass., 1985-89. Contbr. articles to profl. jours. Sec. bd. dir. Cornwall (Conn.) Extras for Kids, 1993-2001; interior designer Cornwall town offices, 1996—. Honors Scholar Belhaven Coll., 1942-46. Mem. Chi Delta. Presbyterian. Avocations: reading, writing, music, composing, painting. Home: 49 Popple Swamp Rd Cornwall Bridge CT 06754-1137 Office: Cross Quadrate Design 138 E 38th St New York NY 10016-2646

GIDDINGS, CLIFFORD FREDERICK, retired corporate executive; b. East Dorset, Vt., May 28, 1936; s. Frederick Daniel and Natalie (Abbott) G. BA, U. Vt., 1958; MA, U. Wis., 1961; postgrad., Sorbonne U., Paris, 1958, U. Chgo., 1963-65. French master Lake Forest (Ill.) Acad., 1961-63; asst. head reference dept. The Newberry Library, Chgo., 1964-68, assoc. head reference dept., 1972-74; dir. library services Scott, Foresman and Co., Glenview, Ill., 1968-71; asst. mgr. Albert E. Barrett, Inc., Trenton, N.J., 1975-80, exec. v.p., 1980-97, ret. Fulbright scholar U.S. Dept. State, Grenoble, France, 1958-59. Mem. Associated Gen. Contractors of N.J., N.J. Asphalt Pavement Assn., Nat. Asphalt Pavement Assn., Utility and Transp. Contractors Assn. N.J., Fulbright Assn. Episcopalian. Avocations: classical discography, Am. antique furniture, philately. Home: 66 Line Rd Princeton Junction NJ 08550-3402

GIDDINGS, HELEN, personnel management executive; b. Dallas, Apr. 21, 1942; d. Arthur and Catherine (Warren) Ferguson; m. Donald Giddings; children: Lizette, Lisa, Stanley. BA in Bus., U. Tex., 1968. Tng. dir. Sears, Roebuck, Dallas, 1975-77; personnel mgr. Sears, Roebuck & Co., Dallas, 1977-81, dir. community affairs for 11 states, 1979-81; pres. Select Personnel, Dallas, 1981-86; exec. dir. Leadership Dallas, 1985-86; state rep. dist. 109 State of Tex., 1982-86. Trustee Dallas Alliance, 1981—, exec. dir., 1987. Gov. Dallas Symphony, 1980—; elected mem. Dallas Assembly, 1981—; mem. Dist. 6 State Bar Grievance Com.; bd. dirs. Dallas Theatre Ctr., 1984—; exec. dir. Leadership Dallas, 1984, state rep., 1992. Recipient Woman of Yr. award Committee of 100, Dallas, 1980, Achieving Against the Odds award East Oak Cliff-Dallas Ind. Sch. Dist., 1981. Mem. Dallas Black C. of C. (pres. 1981-82), Dallas Hist. Soc. (sec. 1983—, vice-chair), Zeta Phi Beta (Woman of Yr. award 1984), Alpha Phi Alpha (Community Service award 1987). Methodist. Avocations: public speaking, the arts.

GIDDINGS, LUCILLE CASSELL, nurse; b. Jan. 30, 1947; d. Curtis Emmitt and Rose (Lucente) Cassell; m. William Alfred Giddings, Apr. 2, 1977. RN, St. Clare's Hosp., N.Y.C., 1969; BA, Coll. Mt. St. Vincent, Bronx, N.Y., 1979; MPA, NYU, 1982. Diplomate cert. healthcare exec. Am. Coll. Healthcare Execs. Staff nurse various hosps., N.Y., 1969-71; elem. sch. nurse Pt. Chester-Rye Town Bd. Edn., 1971-82; dir. interdepartmental svcs. Our Lady of Mercy Hosp. Med. Ctr., Bronx, 1982-83, dir. admissions, 1984-86, asst. adminstr., 1986-87, v.p. med. support svcs., 1987-89; dir. patient registration Greenwich (Conn.) Hosp. Assn., 1989-91, asst. v.p. patient support svcs., 1991, v.p. ambulatory care, 1991-96; health svcs. mgmt. cons. New Dimensions in Leadership, Inc., 1983-84; pres., CEO Nantucket Cottage Hosp., 1996—. Chmn. Pt. Chester br. ARC, 1978; mem. cmty. adv. bd. Jr. League of Greenwich; mem. first selectman's com. for people with spl. needs, domestic abuse com. Town of Greenwich; mem. needs assessment com., planning com. United Way of Greenwich; Citizen Amb. Program del. to China, 1992. Recipient Rev. Mother Jean Marie award, 1969, Shepard award United Way, 1992, Bravo award YWCA, 1992. Mem. NYU Alumni Assn., Coll. Mt. St. Vincent Alumni Assn. Home: 28 Vesper Ln Nantucket MA 02554-4343 Office: 57 Prospect St Nantucket MA 02554-2799 E-mail: lgiddings@ackhosp.org.

GIDDON, DONALD B(ERNARD), psychologist, educator; b. Newark, May 1, 1930; s. William and Ruth (Franklin) G.; m. Phoebe L. Rothman, Aug. 28, 1955; children: David, Kenneth, Joanna, James. AB, Brown U., 1952; MA, Boston U., 1953; D.MD, Harvard U., 1959; PhD in Psychology, Brandeis U., 1961. Lectr. psychology Brandeis U., 1954-71, 82-84, lectr. physical edn., 1985-89; prof., chmn. dental ecology Harvard U., 1972-75, vis. prof., 1976-89, lectr., 1989-98, clin. prof. growth and devel., 1999—, lectr. health services adminstrn. Sch. Pub. Health, 1972-75, asst. dean adminstrn. Sch. Dental Medicine, 1973-75; assoc. staff New Eng. Med. Center, 1964-73; assoc. prof., chmn. dept. social dentistry Tufts U., Boston, 1964-67, prof., chmn. dept. social dentistry, 1967-72, asst. dean, 1967-69, assoc. dean, 1969-71; dean NYU Dental Ctr., 1975-78, prof. behavioral sci. and community health, 1976—; prof. psychology Grad. Sch. Arts and Scis., prof. anesthesiology NYU Med. Center, 1976-80; prof. Faculty of Medicine, U. Groningen, The Netherlands, 1980-81. Cons. Astra Pharm. Products, Inc., 1960—; cons. dept. medicine and surgery VA, 1966-69, med. rsch. cons., 1988-90, Peter Bent Brigham Hosp., 1975-76, Meml. Sloan-Kettering Cancer Ctr., 1976-78; vis. staff physician (surgery) NYU Med. Ctr., 1976—, Brookdale Hosp. Med. Ctr., 1977—, Goldwater Meml. Hosp., 1977-80; cons. psychologist dept. anesthesiology Brigham and Women's Hosp., 1979—; vis. prof. U. Gothenburg, Sweden, 1971, Royal Dental Coll., Aarhus, Denmark, 1972, U. Pa., 1972; vis. prof. medicine McGill Med. U., 1981-83; vis. prof. psychology Mass. Coll. Pharmacy and Allied Health Scis., 1984-89; clin. prof. Brown U., 1989—; clin. prof. psychology U. Ill., Chgo., 1994—; founding dir. Rsch. Inst., Royal Victoria Hosp., Montreal, Can., 1981-82, mem. NIH study section 2000-. Contbr. articles to profl. jours. Bd. dirs. Mass. Health Coun., 1965-70, pres., 1968-69; pres. Hamilton sch. PTA, Newton Lower Falls, Mass., 1963-64; trustee Emerson Coll., 1991-2000, Berkshire Opera, 1996—; mem. Com. on Univ. Resources, bd. overseers Harvard U., 1991—, NIH study sect., 2000—. Named Fulbright scholar, 1971. Fellow AAAS, APA, Acad. Behavioral Med. Rsch., Am. Pub. Health Assn., Am. Coll. Dentists, Internat. Coll. Dentists, Internat. Coll. Psychosomatic Medicine, Royal Soc. Medicine; mem. AAUP, Am. Statis. Assn., Internat. Assn. Study Pain, Am. Psychosomatic Soc., Am. Coll. Sports Medicine, Am. Dental Soc. Anesthesiology (assoc. editor 1965-72, chmn. ethics com. 1979-81), Behavioral Sci. in Dental Rsch. (pres. 1976-77), Internat. Assn. Dental Rsch. (pres. Boston sect. 1965-66), Am. Pain Soc. (dir. 1977-79), Soc. Behavioral Med., Soc. Psychophys. Rsch., Soc. Clin. and Experimental Hypnosis, Sigma Xi. Office: 277 Linden St Wellesley MA 02482-5900 E-mail: donald_giddon@hms.harvard.edu.

GIDEL, ROBERT HUGH, real estate investor; b. Ft. Dodge, Iowa, Sept. 19, 1951; s. Wayne D. and Mary A. (Ziegler) G.; m. Linda Carol Lombardo, Oct. 23, 1976; children: Jill, Allison, Robert. BSBA, U. Fla., 1973. Comml. loan officer Century Bank, St. Petersburg, Fla., 1975-77; asst. v.p. N.Y. Life, Washington, 1977-81; exec. v.p. Heller Real Estate Fin. Co., Chgo., 1981-86; pres., mng. dir., bd dirs. Alex Brown Realty Advisors, Balt., 1986-90; mng. dir., bd. dirs. Alex Brown Kleinwort Benson Realty Advisors, Balt., 1990-93; pres., bd. dirs. Brazos Ptnrs. L.P., Dallas, 1993-99. Pres., COO, bd. dirs. Paragon-Group Inc., 1996-97; CEO, bd. dirs. Meridian Realty Trust VIII, 1997-98; mng. ptnr., bd. dirs. Liberty Ptnrs., 1997—; bd. dirs. Fortress Registered Investment Trust, Fortress Investment Fund II, Developers Diversified Realty Corp., Am. Indsl. Properties,1997-2001, Lone Star Opportunity Fund I, II,III, and IV, Brazos Fund, Pinnacle Holdings, U.S. Restaurant Properties; exec. dir. U. Fla. Ctr. Real Estate Studies. Contbr. articles to profl. publs. Fellow Homer Hoyt Inst. Mem. Nat. Coun. Real Estate Investment Fiduciaries, Pension Real Estate Assn., Assn. Fgn. Investors in Real Estate, Nat. Assn. Real Estate Investment Trusts, L'Hirondelle Club (Balt.), Bent Tree Country Club (Dallas), University Park (Fla.) Country Club, Haile Plantation (Gainesville, Fla.). Republican. Roman Catholic. Home: 7343 Barclay Ct University Park FL 34201-2340 Office: Liberty Ptnrs 677 N Washington Blvd Sarasota FL 34236 E-mail: RGidel@aol.com.

GIDEON, FRANCIS C., JR., career officer; BS in Engring. Scis., USAF Acad., 1966; grad., Squadron Officer Sch., 1970, Indsl. Coll. Armed Forces, 1971; MS in Sys. Mgmt., Air Force Inst. Tech., 1974; grad., Air Command and Staff Coll., 1979, Air War Coll., 1981; exec. devel. program, U. Pitts., 1988; grad., Def. Sys. Mgmt. Coll., 1990. Cert. program mgmt. level II, test and evaluation level III. Commd. 2d lt. USAF, 1966, advanced through grades to maj. gen., 1994; pilot tng., 1966-67; pilot F-100, 1968-69; pilot F-100, F-4 RAF Lakerhealth, England, 1969-73; pilot Air Force Inst. Tech., 1973-74; F-4 test pilot 6512th Test Squadron, Edwards AFB, Calif., 1975-76; test pilot, ops. officer A-10 Joint Test Force, Edwards AFB, 1976-80; chief devel. plans aircraft divsn. Air Force Sys. Command, Andrews AFB, Md., 1981; dep. dir. Devel. Plans Tactical Sys. Directorate, Andrews AFB, 1982-84; chief F 15 projects and test divsn. F-15 Sys. Program Office, Wright-Patterson AFB, Ohio, 1984-85; dir. Fighter Attack Sys. Program Office, Wright-Patterson AFB, 1985-86, Strike Sys. Program Office, Wright-Patterson AFB, 1986-87; comdr. 4950th Test Wing, Wright-Patterson AFB, 1987-88, Fgn. Aerospace Sci. and Tech. Ctr., Wright-Patterson AFB, 1988-92; vice comdr. Sacramento Air Logistics Ctr., McClellan AFB, Calif., 1992-93; dir. of ops. Hdqs. Air Force Materiel Command, Wright-Patterson AFB, 1993-97; chief of safety USAF, comdr. Hdqs. Air Force Safety Ctr., Kirtland AFB, N.Mex., 1997—. Decorated Disting. Svc. medal, Legion of Merit with oak leaf cluster, D.F.C. Office: HQ USAF/SE 9700 G Ave SE Ste 240 Kirtland Afb NM 87117-5670

GIDEON, KENNETH WAYNE, lawyer; b. Lubbock, Tex., July 25, 1946; s. Melton Jean and Mary B. (Lanham) G.; m. Carol Almack, June 2, 1968; children: Christopher Lynn, Kevin Almack, Timothy Charles, Emily Susan BA, Harvard U., 1968; JD, Yale U., 1971. Bar: Tex. 1971, U.S. Tax Ct. 1971, U.S. Ct. Claims 1972, U.S. Supreme Ct. 1981, D.C. 1984. Assoc. Fulbright & Jaworski, Houston, 1971-78, ptnr., 1978-81, Washington, 1983-86; chief counsel IRS, Washington, 1981-83; ptnr. Fried, Frank, Harris, Shriver & Jacobson, Washington, 1986-89, 92-93; asst. sec. tax policy Dept. Treasury, Washington, 1989-92; ptnr. Wilmer, Cutler & Pickering, Washington, 1994-2000, Skadden, Arps, Slate, Meagher & Flom, 2000—. Mem. Spring Valley (Tex.) City Coun., 1978-79. Capt. U.S. Army, 1971-72. Fellow Am. Bar Found., Am. Coll. Tax Counsel (regent 1999—); mem. ABA (vice chair govt. rels. 1995-97, mem. coun. 1987-89, sect. taxation), Am. Law Inst., Orgn. Econ. Cooperation and Devel. (Paris, vice chmn. com. on fiscal affairs 1990-92). Office: Skadden Arps Slate Meagher & Flom 1440 New York Ave NW Washington DC 20005-2111

GIDEON, RICHARD WALTER, broadcasting management consultant; b. Phila., Nov. 23, 1928; s. Walter Richard and Amelia Molly (Ebinger) G.; m. Yolanda Elena Josefe, Jan. 12, 1957 (dec. Jan. 1995); children: Richard E. and Michael J. (twins). BS in Econs., U. Pa., 1952. Statis clk. Triangle Pubs. Inc., Phila., 1952-55, rsch. mgr., 1955-62; asst. dir. media rsch. Young & Rubicam, N.Y.C., 1962-63; with John Blair & Co., N.Y.C., 1963-75, dir. rsch., 1967-75, v.p., 1969-75, dir. sales strategy, 1973-75; pres. Dick Gideon Enterprises, Palm Beach Gardens, Fla., 1975-92; prin. Verus Info. Corp., Medford, N.J., 1985-92. Editor: Statistical Trends in Broadcasting, 1970—77. Dist. leader Westchester County Republican Com., 1974-76; mem. adv. com. to N.Y. Assemblyman Gordon Burrows, 1974-76. With USMC, 1946-48, USMCR, 1948-50, USAFR, 1952-64. Mem. Broadcast Pioneers Phila., Navy League U.S., Sigma Phi Epsilon. Home: 8 Nightingale Dr Hamilton NJ 08690-3572 E-mail: papiuno@worldnet.att.net.

GIDEON-HAWKE, PAMELA LAWRENCE, fine arts small business owner; b. N.Y.C., Aug. 23, 1945; d. Lawrence Ian Verry and Lily S. (Stein) Gordon; m. Jarrett Redstone, June 27, 1964; 1 child, Justin Craig Hawke. Grad. high sch., Manhattan. Owner Gideon Gallery Ltd., L.A. and Las Vegas, 1975—. Pres. San Fernando Valley West Point Parents Club, 1990-93; mem. Rep. Congl. com. on tax reform, Rep. Congl. com. for small bus., State of Calif. Named Friend of Design Industry Designers West Mag., 1987, Bus. Woman of the Yr. for Calif., Rep. Congl. Com.; Knighted, Dame of Grace, Lady Pamela Gideon-Hawke, by order of St. John, Knights of Malta, 1999. Mem. Am. Soc. Interior Designers (publicist), Internat. Soc. Interior Designers (trade liaison 1986-88), Network Exec. Women in Hosp. (pres. Las Vegas chpt., pres. L.A. chpt. 2002--), Internat. Furnishings and Design Assn. (pres.). Avocations: ice-skating, fashion design, writing, cooking, law enforcement. Office: Gideon Gallery Ltd 8121 Lake Hills Dr Las Vegas NV 89128-7089 also: 8748 Melrose Ave Los Angeles CA 90069-5015

GIEBEL, MIRIAM CATHERINE, librarian, genealogist; b. Williamsburg, Iowa, Oct. 10, 1934; d. John Timothy and Helen Gertrude (Wright) Donahoe; m. William Herbert Giebel, Sept. 30, 1967; 1 child, Sara Ann Giebel Ward. BS, Marquette U., Milw., 1956; MS in Library Science, Rosary Coll., River Forest, Ill., 1960; cert. in paralegal, Roosevelt U., Chgo., 1992; cert. in family history rsch., Brigham Young U., 1992. Asst. acquisitions dept. Marquette U. Libr., Milw., 1956-58; tech. svcs. libr. Chicago Heights (Ill.) Pub. Libr., 1959-63, ext., reference libr., 1974-99, vol. coord./webmaster, 1999-2000, webmaster, 2000—01, geneal. rschr., 2002—; libr. Little Co. Mary Nursing, Evergreen Park, Ill., 1963-64; asst. libr. hdqrs. ALA, Chgo., 1964-67. Mem.: DAR (chpt. registrar 1994—2001), Fedn. Bus. Profl. Women (state libr. chair 1994—96), Daus. Union Vets. 1861-1865, Daus. Colonial Wars, Dames Ct. Honor, Ill. Cameo Soc. of DAR (state v.p. 1996—99, state pres. 1999—2001), U.S. Daus. of 1812 (chpt. pres. 1991—97, Ill. state registrar 1994—97, Ill. state pres. 1997—99, nat. chair lineage and geneal. records 1997—2000, hon. state pres. life, chpt. registrar 1997—), Soc. Ind. Pioneers (life). Roman Catholic. Avocations: reading, personal genealogical research, Web surfing. E-mail: MirGiebel@aol.com.

GIEBELS, SHARON J. human services manager; b. Chgo., Aug. 21, 1946; d. George A. and Margaret C. (Hilgers) Joosten; m. Gary F. Giebels, Oct. 1, 1966; children: Marci Viola, Mindy Jean. BS, SUNY, Albany, 1996; MS in Health Svcs. Adminstrn., Nova Southeastern U., 1998. Cert. retirement housing profl. Am. Assn. Homes and Svcs. for the Aging. Dir. village svcs. Gulf Coast Village, Cape Coral, Fla., 1988-96, dir. rsch. and edn., 1996-98; assoc. exec. dir. Cypress Cove, Ft. Myers, Fla., 1998—. Instr. Fla. Dept. Elder Affairs, 1998—; mem. adv. bd. Fla. Gulf Coast Univ. Ctr. for Positive Aging, 2001—; team mem. Gerontology Process Mgmt., Ft. Myers, 1998—; bd. mem. Dr. Piper Ctr., Ft. Myers, 1999—, pers. com. chmn. 1999—; internat. spkr. in field; Alzheimer's rschr. Sec. Cape Coral Civic Assn., 1992. Mem. Am. Med. Dirs. Assn. (spkrs. bur.), Am. Geriatrics Soc. (spkrs. bur.), Sigma Beta Delta. Roman Catholic. Avocations: music, sailing, writing, traveling. Office: Cypress Cove 10200 Fort Myers FL 33908 E-mail: giebels@yahoo.com.

GIEDT, BRUCE ALAN, paper company executive; b. Fargo, N.D., May 7, 1937; s. Alexander and Alice Mildred (Rognaldson) G.; m. Suzanna Tae Abbott, Apr. 30, 1963; children: Alex, Jeffrey, Marybeth; m. 2d, Gail Ann Platt. BA, U. Wash., 1959; MBA, Harvard U., 1965. From regional sales mgr. to v.p. service products bus. units Crown Zellerbach Corp., San Francisco, 1965—; pres. Champion Paper Distbrs., Inc., Riverside, Calif., 1981-87, Pioneer Packaging, Phoenix, 1987—, Woodale, Ill., 1997—. Author: The Future of Commercial Arbitration, 1965. V.p. exec. com. Keep Riverside AHead, econ. devel. com., bd. dirs.; exec. com. mem. Riverside C. of C., devel. com. Served to Capt. USAF, 1959-63. Evans scholar Western Golf Assn., 1967. Mem. Am. Paper Inst. (past com. chmn.). Lodges: Elks. Republican. Lutheran. Home: 704 Foothills East cir Payson AZ 85541 Office: 730 E University Dr Phoenix AZ 85034-6509

GIEL, JAMES ARTHUR, JR., employee benefits manager; b. Pitts., Aug. 29, 1952; s. James and Suan Helen (Barry) G.; m. Sharyl Dawn Unrath, Apr. 22, 1978; children: James Arthur III, Maggie Anne. BA, Westminster Coll., New Wilmington, Pa., 1974; MA in Pers. Administrn. and Indsl. Rels., St. Francis Coll., Loretto, Pa., 1987. Tchr. Shaler Area Schs., Glenshaw, Pa., 1974—77; group ins. underwriter Equitable Life Assurance Soc., N.Y.C., 1977—79; pension clk. Allegheny Ludlum Industries, Inc., Pitts., 1979—80; benefits adminstr. Allegheny Internat., Pitts., 1980—86; mgr., asst. v.p. employee benefits Union Nat. Corp., Pitts., 1986—89; v.p., dir. employee benefits Integra Fin. Corp., Pitts., 1989—96; mgr. employee benefits Armco Inc., Pitts., 1996—99; mgr. employee benefits and relocation Heinz N.Am., Pitts., 1999—2001; cons. Todd Orgn. Pitts., 2001—02; mgr. employee benefits and HRIS ANH Refractories Co., Pitts., 2002. Dir. Strawberry Way Child Ctr., Pitts., 1985 92; Rep. committeeman Allegheny County, Glenshaw, 1992-97; elder Elfinwild Presbyn. Ch., Glenshaw, 1986—, deacon, 1980-86; bd dirs. Shaler Twp.-Shaler Oaks, 1994-96; mem. strategic planning com. Shaler Area Sch. Dist., 1994-96, sch. bd. dir., 1997—, pres. 1999-2001, trustee, 2003—; dir. Bread of Life Food Pantry, 2003—; mem. com. Allegheny Policy Coun., 1995-96. Mem. Human Resource Info. Specialist Soc., Workers in Employee Benefits, Pitts. Human Resources Assn., Tristate Compensation Assn., Pitts. Bus. Group on Health (exec. com. 1997), Human Resources Sys. Profls., Travelers Aid Soc. Pitts. (bd. dirs. 1994—, sec. bd. dirs. 1998—), Westminster Coll. Alumni Assn. (alumni coord. 1988—), Towers Perrin Roundtable, Elfinwild Lions (pres. 1984), Shaler Soccer Club (treas. 1993-95, pres. 1995-97, bd. dirs. 1997-2002, Shaler Area Soccer Boosters 1997-2001, pres. 1998, 99, 2000, 01), Rivers Club. Avocations: coaching soccer and baseball, music, civic activities. Office: ANH Refractories Co 400 Fairway Dr Moon Township PA 15108 Personal E-mail: gielwest@attbi.com.

GIELEN, UWE PETER, psychology educator; b. Berlin, Aug. 15, 1940; s. Alfred and Ursula (Hackemesser) G. MA in Psychology, Wake Forest U., 1968; PhD in Social Psychology, Harvard U., 1976. Asst. prof. psychology York Coll./CUNY, NYC, 1977-80; assoc. prof. St. Francis Coll., Bklyn., 1980-87, chmn. dept. psychology, 1980-90, prof., 1987—, exec. dir. Inst. for Internat. and Cross-Cultural Psychology, 1998—. Co-author: The Kohlberg Legacy for the Helping Professions, 1991; sr. editor: Psychology in International Perspective, 1992, The Family and Family Therapy in Internat. Perspective, 1998, International Approaches to the Family and Family Therapy, 1999; co-editor; Cross-cultural Topics in Psychology, 1994, 2001, Advancing Psychology and Its Applications: International Perspectives, 1994, Psychology in the Arab Countries, 1998, International Perspectives on Human Development, 2000, Migration: Immigration and Emigration in International Perspective, 2003, It's All About Relationships, 2002; founding editor World Psychology, 1995-97; editor-in-chief Internat. Jour. Group Tensions, 1997-2002; mem. editl. bd. Moral Edn. Forum, 1988-95, Internat. Psychologist, 1996-2000, Internat. Jour. Health Promotion and Edn., 2001--; contbr. articles to profl. jours. Del. to UN Internat. Coun. Psychologists, NY, 1985-92. Rsch. grantee H.F. Guggenheim Found., NY, 1986-88, Pacific Cultural Found., Taipei, Taiwan, 1986-87. Fellow APA, Am. Psychol. Soc.; mem. Internat. Assn. Cross-cultural Psychology, Internat. Coun. Psychologists (pres.-elect 1993-94, pres. 1994-95, exec. bd.), NY Psychol. Assn. (Kurt Lewin award 1993, Wilhelm Wundt award 1999), NY Acad. Sci. (vice-chmn. adv. bd. psychology sect. 1998-2000, chmn. 2000-02), Bklyn. Psychol. Assoc., Soc. Cross-Cultural Rsch. (pres.-elect 1997-98, pres. 1998-99, exec. bd. dir.). Office: St Francis Coll Psychology Dept 180 Remsen St Brooklyn NY 11201-4305 E-mail: ugielen@hotmail.com.

GIENAPP, HELEN FISCHER, jewelry company owner; b. Saginaw, Mich., Oct. 9, 1921; d. John Frederick and Dorothea (Schleicher) Fischer; m. Walter Lawrence Gienapp, Oct. 10, 1942; children: Karen Lynne, Roger Alan, David Paul, Marcia Lou, Richard Kevin. Grad. h.s., Saginaw. Adminstrv. asst. Muskegon (Mich.) Devel. Corp., 1961-66; exec. asst. to pres. Greater Detroit C. of C., 1966-80; owner Internat. Jewelry, Ferndale, Mich., 1990—. Mem. Ferndale Woodward Dream Cruise Com., 2000—; pres. Internat. Luth. Women's Missionary League, St. Louis, 1979—83; bd. dirs. Hist. Trinity, Inc., Detroit, 1990—; dir. English dist. Luth. ch.-Mo. Synod, Farmington, Mich., 1988—97, Mission Opportunities Short Term Ministries, Ann Arbor, 1995—; area coord. Am. Bible Soc.; mem. bd. dirs. Coun. of Luth. Women, 2001—, Luth. Ctr. Assocs., 2002—; mission advocate Luth. Ch.-Mo. Synod, 1998—2000; bd. dirs. Ferndale Youth Assistance Bd., 1998—. Named Luth. Woman of Yr., Mich. Dist. of Luth. Ch.-Mo. Synod, 1983, Mich. Vol. of Yr., Am. Bible Soc., 1998. Mem. Internat. Assn. Adminstrv. Profls., Women's Econ. Club Detroit. Home: 371 Channing St Ferndale MI 48220-2555

GIENAPP, WILLIAM EUGENE, history educator; b. Denton, Tex., Feb. 27, 1944; s. William Herman and June Beatrice (Wade) G.; m. Erica Lee Kilian, Aug. 24, 1968; children: William Kenneth, Jonathan Eric. BA, U. Calif., Berkeley, 1967, PhD, 1980; MA, Yale U., 1969. Acting. instr. U. Calif., Berkeley, 1979-80; asst. prof. U. Wyo., Laramie, 1980-85, assoc. prof., 1985-89; prof. Harvard U., Cambridge, Mass., 1989—. Chmn. Lincoln Prize Jury, 1997, Avery Craven Award Com., 1998; bd. advisors Lincoln Forum, Lincoln Studies Ctr., Knox Coll., 1997-2002; mem. adv. bd. Hist. Soc., 1998-2000; mem. adv. com. Abraham Lincoln Bicentennial Commn. Author: Origins of the Republican Party, 1987 (Avery Craven award, 1988); co-author: Nation of Nations, 1990, 2d edit., 1993, 3rd edit., 1997, 4th edit., 2000, Why the War Came, 1996, Nation of Nations: Concise Narrative, 1995, 3d edit., 2001, Civil War and Reconstruction, 2001, Abraham Lincoln and Civil War America, 2002, This Fiery Trial: The Speeches and Writings of Abraham Lincoln, 2002; mem. editl. bd. Presidential Papers of Abraham Lincoln. Mem. Civil War Soc., So. Hist. Assn., Hist. Soc., Soc. Hists. Early Republic, Soc. Am. Baseball Rsch. Office: Harvard U Dept History Cambridge MA 02138 E-mail: wgienapp@fas.harvard.edu.

GIER, KARAN HANCOCK, psychologist; b. Sedalia, Mo., Dec. 7, 1947; d. Ioda Clyde and Loma (Campbell) Hancock; m. Thomas Robert Gier, Sept. 28, 1968. BA in Edn., U. Mo., Kansas City, 1971; MA in Edn., Webster U., 1974; MA in Counseling Psychology, Western Colo. U., 1981; MEd in Guidance and Counseling, U. Alaska, 1981; PhD in Edn., Pacific Western U., 1989. Nat. cert. counselor. Instr. grades 5-8 Kansas City-St. Joseph Archdiocese, 1969-73; ednl. cons. Pan-Ednl. Inst., Kansas City, 1973-75; instr., counselor Bethel (Alaska) Regional HS, 1975-80; ednl. program coord. Western Regional Resource Ctr., Anchorage, 1980-81; counselor U. Alaska, Anchorage, 1982-83; coll. prep. instr. Alaska Native Found., Anchorage, 1982; counselor USAF, Anchorage, 1985-86; prof. U. Alaska, Anchorage, 1982—; dir. Omni Counseling Svcs., Anchorage, 1984—; prof. Chapman Coll., Anchorage, 1988—93. Workshop

facilitator over 100 workshops. Co-author: (book) Coping with College, 1984, Helping Others Learn, 1985, The Tutor Training Handbook, 1996; editor, co-author: book A Student's Guide, 1983, contbg. author: developmental Yup'ik lang. program, 1981; contbr. articles to profl. jours. Mem. Ctr. Environ. Edn., Beta Sigma Phi, Bethel, Alaska, 1976—81. Recipient 3d pl. color photo award, Yukon-Kuskokwim State Fair, 1978, Notable Achievement award, USAF, 1986, Meritorious Svc. award, Anchorage C.C., 1984—88. Mem.: AACD, Nat. Rehab. Counselors, Nat. Rehab. Assn., Alaska Career Devel. Assn., Alaska Assn. Counseling and Devel. (pres.-elect 1989—90), Coll. Reading and Learning Assn. (editor newsletter peer tutor spl. interest group 1988—95, bd. dirs. Alaska state coord, internat. tutor program, Robert Griffin Long and Outstanding Svc. award, Cert. of Appreciation 1986—93, Spl. Recognition award 1994—95), Wolf Song Alaska, Human Soc. U.S. Wolf Haven Am. Avocations: travel, wolf preservation, photography, music, acting. Home and Office: 8102 Harvest Cir Anchorage AK 99502-4682

GIERAS, JACEK FRANCISZEK, electrical engineering educator, scientist; b. Maleniec, Voivodship Piotrkow Tryb, Poland, Apr. 2, 1947; s. Stanislaw Gieras and Zofia Rychlewska-Gieras; m. Janina Omilianczyk, Sept. 25, 1975; children: Izabella Anna, Karolina Maria, Michael Benjamin. MSEE, Tech. U., Lodz, 1971; PhD, Tech. U., Poznan, Poland, 1975, DSc, 1980. Project engr. Factory of Loudspeakers Tonsil, Wrzesnia, Poland, 1971; lectr. Tech. U. Poznan, 1971-73, sr. lectr., 1973-75, asst. prof., 1975-77, Acad. Technology and Agr., Bydgoszcz, Poland, 1977-81, assoc. prof., dean, 1981-83, assoc. prof., head of dept., 1985-87, prof., 1987—. Vis. assoc. prof. Queen's U., Kingston, Ont., Can., 1983-85; prof. U. Cape Town, 1989-98; vis. prof. endowed chair in transp. sys. engring. U. Tokyo, 1996; guest prof. Chungbuk Nat. U., Korea, 1996-97; scientist United Technologies Rsch. Ctr., East Hartford, Conn., 1998—. Author: Special Purpose Electric Machines, 1983, Linear Induction Motors, 1990, Linear Induction Drives, 1994; (with M. Dabrowski) Induction Machines with Solid Rotors, 1977, Handbook of Electric Motors (edited by W.H. Middendorf and R.H. Engelmann), 1995; (with M. Wing) Permanent Magnet Motor Technology: Design and Applications, 1996, 2d edit., 2002; (with Z. Piech) Linear Synchronous Motor, 1999; contbr. articles to profl. jours. Recipient Silver medal Polish Assn. of Elec. Engring., Poland, 1979; fellow Polish Ministry of Edn., 1976, 81, NSERC of Can., 1983, Italian Ministry of Sci. and Tech. Rsch., 1994, Merit awards U. Cape Town, 1995, 96, 97, 98. Fellow N.Y. Acad. Scis., IEEE; mem. Internat. Acad. Electrotech. Scis. Roman Catholic. Avocations: railways, music, overseas travel, home improvement. Address: United Tech Rsch Ctr Mail Stop 129-15 411 Silver Ln Hartford CT 06118-1127 also: Univ Cape Town Dept Elec Engring Rondebosch 7700 South Africa E-mail: gierasjf@utrc.utc.com.

GIERTZ, J. FRED, economics educator; b. Wichita, Kans., Jan. 18, 1943; s. Joe L. and Frieda J. (Hamblin) G.; m. Donna Hyland, Sept. 13, 1969; children: Seth H., Gabrielle H. BA, Wichita U., 1964; MA, Northwestern U., 1966, PhD, 1970. Instr. econs. Miami U., Oxford, Ohio, 1968-70, asst. prof., 1970-73, asso. prof., 1973-78, prof., 1978-80; prof. econs. Inst. Govt. and Pub. Affairs U. Ill., Urbana, 1980—, acting dir., 1993-94; exec. dir. Nat. Tax Assn., 2000—. Rsch. dir. Ill. Tax Reform Commn., 1982-83; dir. Ameritech fellowship program U. Ill., 1987-93; adviser Transition Team of Ill. Gov. Jim Edgar, 1990-91; trustee State Univs. Retirement System, 1995—; cons. in field. Mem. editl. bd.: Quarterly Rev. Econs. and Bus, 1979-88; contbr. articles in field to profl. jours. Mem. athletic bd. U. Ill., 1998-2002. Mem. Midwest Econs. Assn. (v.p. 1978-79), Am. Econ. Assn., Ill. Econ. Assn. (pres. 1986-87), Pub. Choice Soc., Nat. Tax Assn., Univ. Club Chgo., Champaign Country Club. Home: 601 Park Lane Dr Champaign IL 61820-7630 Office: U Ill Inst Govt Pub Affairs 1007 W Nevada St Urbana IL 61801-3812 E-mail: jgiertz@uiuc.edu.

GIERYN, THOMAS FREDRICK, sociologist, educator; b. Rochester, N.Y., July 8, 1950; s. Fred V. and Betty (Sprau) Gieryn; m. Carolynne Dawson, Aug. 25, 1973; children: Nathaniel Thomas, Patrick Dawson, Samuel William. BA magna cum laude, Kalamazoo Coll., Mich., 1972; PhD in Sociology, Columbia U., N.Y.C., 1979. Rudy prof. sociology Ind. U., Bloomington, 1978—. Hansmann fellow Inst. for Advanced Study, Princeton, NJ, 1996—97; vis. assoc. prof. Cornell U., Ithaca, NY, 1988—89; mem. adv. bd. Nat. Mus. Am. History, Smithsonian Instn., Washington, 1990—94; cons. Random House/McGraw-Hill, N.Y.C., 1981—95. Author: (book) Cultural Boundaries of Science, 1999; contbr. articles to profl. jours. Recipient Pres.'s award, Ind. U., 1994. Fellow: AAAS; mem.: History of Sci. Soc., Soc. for Social Studies of Sci. (coun. mem. 1982—84), Am. Sociol. Assn. (sect. chair 1999—2000, Merton Book prize 1999), Phi Beta Kappa. Avocations: street maps, horticulture. Home: 2603 Spicewood Ln Bloomington IN 47401 Office: Indiana Univ Dept Sociology Ballantine 754 Bloomington IN 47405

GIESBRECHT, MARTIN GERHARD, retired economics educator, clarinetist; b. Newark, Aug. 25, 1933; s. Theodore Gerhard and Martha Margarete (Thurm) G.; m. Patricia Maxine Berlin, July 4, 1957 (dec. Sept. 2000); children: Lisa, Martin F., Theodore K. BA, Rutgers U., 1955; Dr. Oec. Publ., U. Munich, 1958; diploma internat. bus., German-Am. C. of C., 1991. Asst. prof. econs. Wilmington (Ohio) Coll., 1958-63, assoc. prof. econs., 1963-75, prof. econs., 1975-87, No. Ky. U., Highland Heights, 1987—98, prof. emeritus, 1998—. Mem. bd. dirs. Econs. Assocs., Villa Hills, Ky.; mem. spkrs. bur. WMKV-FM, Cin., 2002—; econ. commentator, WNKU, 1989—, WMKV, 1997—. Author: The Evolution of Economic Society, 1972, Using Economics, 1976, Space Settlements, 1977, The Wealth of People, 1978, A Guide to Everyday Economic Statistics, 1990, 6th edit., 2003, A Guide to Everyday Economic Thinking, 1997. Chmn. Ohioans for the Merit Selection of Judges, Clinton County, 1979. Fellow Ford Found., Ind. U., 1964, Gen. Electric Found., U. Chgo., 1966, NSF, Miami U., 1971, NASA-Am. Soc. Engring. Edn., Stanford U., 1975; Danforth Found. assoc. Wilmington Coll., 1969-82; recipient award Am. Heart Assn., Clinton County, 1977, Excellence award Soc. Profl. Journalists, 1993, award of distinction The Communicator, 2001. Mem. Am. Econs. Assn., Ohioana Libr. Assn., Cin. Musicians Assn., Ea. Econ. Assn., Midwest Econ. Assn., Ky. Econ. Assn. (trustee 1989-92, 96—), Ohio Assn. Economists (pres. 1977-78), Ohio Acad. Sci., Amyotrophic Lateral Sclerosis Assn. (bd. dirs. Ky. chpt. 2001—). Avocation: jazz clarinetist. Home: 2501 Kingston Ct Covington KY 41017-3760

GIESE, HEINER, lawyer, real estate investor; b. Passau, Germany, Apr. 16, 1944; came to U.S., 1950, naturalized, 1957; s. Heinz Emil and Wilma Maria (Dunner) G.; m. Barbara Ann Kent, June 28, 1969; children: Anna, Peter. BS in Internat. Affairs, Georgetown U., 1966; JD, U. Wis., 1969. Bar: Wis. 1969, U.S. Dist. Ct. (ea. and we. dists.) Wis. 1969, U.S. Ct. Appeals (7th cir.) 1974, U.S. Supreme Ct. 1974. Law clk. U.S. Dist. Ct., Madison, 1969-70; assoc. Cannon, McLaughlin, Herbon & Staudenmeier, Milw., 1969-74; ptnr. Levin & Giese, Milw., 1974-85, Giese & Weden Law Offices, Milw., 1985—. Bd. dirs. German Fest Milw., 1981-84, legal counsel, 1981—; bd. dirs. German Lang. and Sch. Soc., 1976—, pres., 1982—; bd. dirs. Goethe House, Milw., 1982—, sec., 1997—; Wis. gov.'s rep. Presdl. Commn. for German-Am. Tricentennial, 1983. Recipient Outstanding Young Lawyer award, 1979, Order of Merit, Fed. Republic Germany, 1993, Citizen of Yr., Milwaukee Legal Auxiliary, 1992. Mem. ABA (young lawyers divsn., regional vice chmn. membership com. 1979-81), Wis. Bar Assn., Milw. Bar Assn. (chmn. lawyer referral svc. 1980-83, 91-93, bd. dirs. 1993-96), Milw. Young Lawyers Assn. (pres. 1978-79), Milw. Apt. Assn., Wis. State Bar. Democrat. Lutheran. Home: 2022 N 72nd St Wauwatosa WI 53213-1828 Office: Giese & Weden 1216 N Prospect Ave Milwaukee WI 53202-3014

GIESE, ROBERT JAMES, minister; b. Eau Claire, Wis., Apr. 7, 1950; s. Walter H. and Doris B. (Kuhn) G.; m. Jo Ann P. Zutz, June 19, 1971; 1 child, Rachel. BS in Zoology, U. Wis., 1972; MDiv, Christ Sem.-Seminex, St. Louis, 1978; D Ministry in Pastoral Care and Counseling, Luth. Sch. Theology, Chgo., 1990. Ordained to ministry Evang. Luth. Ch. Am., 1979. Min. Christian Ministry in Nat. Pks., NYC, 1974-77; chaplain Bear Creek Boys Ranch, Lodi, Calif., 1978-79; pastor Trinity Luth. Ch., Rolling Meadows, Ill., 1979—. Exec. cons. Stephen Ministries, St. Louis, 1974-82; sec. Chgo.-Milw. Conf. Evang. Luth. Ch. Am., Chgo., 1983-85, v.p., 1985-86; youth adv. Luth. Social Svc., Chgo., 1987-88. Contbr. articles to profl. jour. Bd. dir. The Bridge Youth Svc., Palatine, Ill., 1983-87; pres., bd. dir. Racetrack Ministries, Arlington Heights, Ill., 1990-94, 2000—, v.p., 1994-2000; dean N.W. Conf. Chgo. Metro Synod ELCA, 1992-96, mem. nominating com. 1999-2001; mem. steering com. Rolling Meadows Tomorrow, 1995-99; mem. Rolling Meadows Bd. Ethics, 1997—2002, mem. sr. citizens' com., 1999—2002, mem. sr. housing com., 2003—. Mem. AACC, Assn. of Personality Type. Home: 3203 Meadow Dr Rolling Meadows IL 60008-2728 Office: Trinity Luth Ch 3201 Meadow Dr Rolling Meadows IL 60008-2798 E-mail: rjgiese@msn.com. *I believe that the more I am able to know and accept myself for who I am as God knows and accepts me for who I am through Christ, the more I will be enabled to know and accept those with whom I am called to minister.*

GIESE, WILLIAM HERBERT, tax accountant; b. Boston, Jan. 19, 1944; s. Robert Ewald and Harriet (Blaney) G.; m. Elaine Rabe, May 26, 1973; children: Amy Theiss, Katherine Clark, Lauren Stearns. BA, Amherst Coll., 1966; MBA, U. Pa., 1968. CPA. Staff acct. Price Waterhouse, Phila., 1968-70, sr. acct., 1970-73, mgr., 1973-79, ptnr., 1979-95; pres. William H. Giese, Ltd., Ardmore, Pa., 1995-97, Tax Counselors of Bryn Mawr, Inc., Pa., 1997-2000; ptnr. Tax Counsellors of Bryn Mawr, LLC, 2001—. Spkr. Wharton Tax Conf. Phila., 1988; bd. dirs. Verion, Inc., Exton, Pa. Treas. Dunwoody Home and Village, Newtown Square, Pa., 1988—2000; past pres. North Ardmore Civic Assn., Phila., Squash Racquets Assn., Bala Cynwyd; fin. chmn. U.S. Amateur Golf Tournament, 1989; past treas. U.S. Squash Racquets Assn., Bala Cynwyd; Bd. dirs. Dunwoody Home and Village, Newtown Square, Pa., 1998—2000; bd. dirs. Lankenau Found., Phila., 1990—2001. Mem. AICPA, Pa. Inst. CPA's, Merion Golf Club (Ardmore, Pa.), Merion Cricket Club (Haverford, Pa.), Phila. Racquet Club. Republican. Presbyterian. Avocations: squash, golf, tennis. Home: 133 Edgewood Rd Ardmore PA 19003-2507 Office: 101 S Bryn Mawr Ave Ste 360 Bryn Mawr PA 19010

GIESECKE, ADOLPH HARTUNG, anesthesiologist, educator; b. Oklahoma City, Apr. 19, 1932; s. Adolph H. and Goldia (Lynn) G.; m. Veronica Morel, June 11, 1954; children: Carl E., Suzanne G., Noel M., Hans E. MD, U. Tex. Med. Br., Galveston, 1957. Diplomate Am. Bd. Anesthesiology. Intern William Beaumont Army Hosp., El Paso, Tex., 1957-58; resident U. Tex., Dallas, 1960-63, from asst. prof. to prof. anesthesiology, 1963-81, chmn. anesthesiology, 1981-92; Fulbright lectr. Johannes Gutenberg U., Mainz, Germany, 1970-71. Lay reader Episcopal Ch., Irving, Tex., 1968—. Capt. USAR, 1957-60. McLaughlin Scholar, 1955. Mem. Am. Soc. Anesthesiology, So. Soc. Anesthesiology (pres. 1972), Internat. Trauma Anesthesia and Critical Care Soc. (pres. 1992-95), Japan Soc. Anesthesiologist (hon.), Tex. Med. Assn. (del. 1992-94), Wood Libr. Mus. (bd. trustees 1990-99), U. Tex. Med. Br. Alumni Assn. (Disting. Ashbel Smith Alumnus award 1989), Alpha Omega Alpha. Republican. Episcopalian. Avocations: tennis, gardening. Office: U Tex Southwestern Med Sch 5322 Harry Hines Blvd Dallas TX 75390-9068 E-mail: adopph.giesecke@utsouthwestern.edu.

GIESEN, JOHN WILLIAM, advertising executive; b. St. Paul, Apr. 5, 1928; s. William J. and Salome Anna (Shopnitz) G.; m. Mary Lou Gilbertson, May 20, 1950; children: Cynthia, John, Lee Ann, Gregory, David, Laurie. Student, St. Thomas Coll., 1948-50, U. Minn., 1950-52, St. Paul Sch. Assoc. Arts, 1951-53. Advt. rep. St. Paul Dispatch-Pioneer Press, 1950-54; advt. mgr. Bruce Pub. Co., St. Paul, 1954-56; nat. advt. mgr. Duluth Herald News Tribune, 1956-60; account exec. N.W. Ayer & Son, Inc., Chgo., 1960-64, acct. supr., 1964-66; account exec. Leo Burnett, Inc., Chgo., 1966-68, v.p. account supr., 1968-74; exec. v.p. Barickman Advt., Denver, 1974-77, chmn. exec. com., 1977-82; pres. Doyle Dane Bernbach Advt., Denver, 1982-86, DDB Needham Worldwide, Denver, 1986-88, chmn., 1988-89; pres., chief exec. officer The Advt. Consortium, Inc., Denver, 1989-94; pres., CEO The Giesen Group, Inc., Denver, 1994—. Chmn. Sts. Faith-Hope Charity Elem. Sch. Bd., Winnetka, Ill., 1972-74, Rocky Mountain Council 4 A's, 1985; hon. bd. Colorado Spl. Olympics, 1988. With U.S. Army, 1946-48, res. 1949-60. Mem.: Denver Advt. Fedn. (dir. 1980—82), Rotary. Republican. Roman Catholic. Home and Office: 6186 E Princeton Ave Englewood CO 80111-1035 E-mail: jwgiesen@concentric.net.

GIESEN, RICHARD ALLYN, business executive; b. Evanston, Ill., Oct. 7, 1929; s. Elmer J. and Ethyl (Lillig) G.; m. Jeannine St. Bernard, Jan. 31, 1953; children: Richard Allyn, Laurie J., Mark S. BS, Northwestern U., 1951. Research analyst new bus. and research depts. Glore, Forgan & Co., Chgo., 1951-57; asst. to pres. Gen. Dynamics Corp., N.Y.C., 1957-60, asst. treas., 1960-61, asst. v.p. ops. and contracts, 1961-63; fin. cons. IBM Corp., 1963, exec. asst. to sr. v.p., 1964-65; treas. subs. Sci. Research Assocs., Inc., Chgo., 1965-66, v.p. fin. and adminstrn., 1966-67, exec. v.p., chief operating officer, 1967-68, pres., chief exec. officer, 1968-80; pres., chief exec. officer, chmn. exec. com., dir. Field Enterprises, Inc., Chgo., 1980-83; pres. RLM Investments, 1983-93; chmn., pres., CEO Am. Appraisal Assocs., Inc., 1984-93; chmn., CEO Continental Glass & Plastic, Inc., Chgo., 1988—, Continere Corp., 1988—. Bd. trustees Asia House Funds, 1994-98. Bd. trustees Asia House Fund, 1994-98; mem. bus. adv. coun. Chgo. Urban League, 1968-83; prin. Chgo. United, 1980-83; mem. adv. coun. Technol. Inst., Northwestern U.; mem. pres.'s coun. Nat. Coll. Edn., Evanston, Ill., 1977-86; bd. dirs. Am. Cancer Soc.; mem. adv. coun. J.L. Kellogg Grad. Sch. Mgmt., Northwestern U.; dir. Jr. Achievement Chgo., 1993-2002; trustee Chgo. Edn. TV Assn., 1975-81, Inst. Internat. Edn., 1971—, chmn. midwest adv. bd., 1997-2003. Mem. Chief Execs. Orgn., Webhannet Golf Club, Chgo. Club, Shoreacres (Lake Bluff, Ill) Club, Milw. Club, Alpha Tau Omega, Beta Gamma Sigma. Clubs: Chicago, Shoreacres (Lake Bluff, Ill.), Milw. Office: Continental Glass & Plastic 841 W Cermak Rd Chicago IL 60608-4582 Fax: 312-666-7501. E-mail: richard.giesen@cgppkg.com.

GIESS, EDWARD AUGUST, crystal growth scientist; b. Mineola, N.Y., Sept. 12, 1929; s. Edward Ernest and Ruth Giess; m. Rosemary Giess, Aug. 15, 1953; 3 children. BS in Ceramic Engring., SUNY, 1951, MS in Ceramic Technology, 1952, PhD in Ceramics, 1958. Rsch. engr. Titanox Divsn. Nat. Lead Co., Sayreville, N.J., 1952-55; IBM rsch. staff mem. T.J. Watson Rsch. Ctr., Yorktown Heights, 1958-92; adj. prof. dept. electrical engring. U. N.C., Charlotte, 1992-97. Editor procs., 1984, 89; author: (with others) Handbook for Crystal Growth North Holland, 1994; contbr. numerous articles to profl. publs. Mem. Town Planning Bd., Somers, N.Y., 1976-85, North Salem, 1991-92; mem. vestry ch. bd. St. Patrick Episcopal Ch., Mooresville, 1994. Fellow AIChe, Am. Ceramic Soc. (chair electronics divsn. ferroelectrics subcom. 1968-70, chair ednl. com., 1972-74); mem. Am. Assn. Crystal Growth (v.p. 1981-84, exec. com. 1975—, symposium chair 1984—, chair crystal growth conf. 1982), Materials Rsch. Soc., Lambda Chi. Achievements include 6 patents; research in rotating disk method for growing magnetic garnet (bubble) films by liquid phase epitaxy; algorithm for sintering/densification of cordierite type glass ceramic powders used for integrated circuit semiconductor chip carriers, substrates for cuprate superconducing oxide films. E-mail address. Home: 513 Fearrington Post Pittsboro NC 27312-8568 E-mail: giessea@mindspring.com.

GIESSELMANN, MICHAEL, engineering educator; b. Basel, Switzerland, Oct. 1956; s. Guenter and Hedwig Giesselmann. D of Elec. Engring., Tech. U. Darmstadt, Germany, 1986. Lic. profl. engr., Tex. Assoc. prof. Texas Tech. U., Lubbock, 1992—2002, prof., 1992—. Chmn. bd. Pulsed Power Inc., 2001—. Author: (book chpt.) Computer Simulation of Power Electronics and Motor Drives, 2001. Mem.: NSPE, IEEE (sr.; treas. South Plains sect. 1992—94, chair 2003 Pulsed Power Conf. 2001—), Tex. Soc. Profl. Engrs. Avocation: piloting. Office: Texas Tech U ECE Dept Mail Stop 3102 Lubbock TX 79409 Business E-Mail: Michael.Giesselmann@ttu.edu.

GIESSER, BARBARA SUSAN, neurologist, educator; b. Bronx, N.Y., Jan. 21, 1953; d. David and Evelyn (Cohen) G.; m. Philip D. Kanof, June 17, 1979; children: David, Marisa. BS, U. Miami, 1972; MS, U. Tex., Houston, 1974; MD, U. Tex., San Antonio, 1978. Diplomate Am. Bd. Psychiatry and Neurology. Intern Montefiore Hosp., Bronx, 1978-79; resident Bronx Mcpl. Hosp. Ctr. (Albert Einstein Coll. Medicine), 1979-82; asst. prof. neurology Albert Einstein Coll. Medicine, Bronx, 1983-91; med. dir. Gimbel MS Comprehensive Care Ctr., Teaneck, N.J., 1985-90, Rehab. Inst. of Tucson, 1991-95; assoc. prof. clin. neurology Ariz. Health Scis. Ctr., Tucson, 1993—2002; assoc. clin. prof. neurology UCLA, 2002—. Author: Neurology Specialty Board Review, 3d edit., 1986, 4th edit., 1996; contbr. articles to profl. publs. Dean's Tchr. scholar Ariz. Health Scis. Ctr., 1995. Fellow Am. Acad. Neurology (undergrad. edn. subcom. 1999—, Tchr. Recongnition award 2002); mem. Nat. Multiple Sclerosis Soc. (rsch. grant 1989, 97, 2003, mem. profl. adv. com. Desert S.W. chpt. 1994-2000, bd. dirs. 1994-2000, counselor Am. Acad. Neurology sect. on Multiple Sclerosis 1997-99, nat. chair client edn. com. 1999-2003, mem. med. adv. bd. 1999-2002). Office: UCLA Sch Medicine Neurology Reed Neurologic Rsch Ctr 710 Westwood Plz Los Angeles CA 90095

GIEVERS, KAREN A. lawyer; b. Culver City, Calif., Apr. 27, 1949; d. Ernest Conrad and Josephine Theresa (Passolt) Prevost; m. Joseph R. Gievers, Nov. 16, 1968 (dec. Feb. 1987); children: Daniel Steven, Donna Ann; m. Frank J. Bach, Nov. 23, 1997. AA, Miami Dade C.C., 1974; BA, Fla. Internat. U., 1975; JD cum laude, U. Miami, 1978. Bar: Fla. 1978, U.S. Dist. Ct. (so. dist.) Fla. 1978, U.S. Dist. Ct. (mid. and no. dist.) Fla. 1979, U.S. Ct. Appeals (5th cir.) 1979, U.S. Ct. Appeals (11th cir.) 1981, U.S. Ct. Claims 1980, U.S. Supreme Ct. 1982; cert. civil trial atty Fla. Bd. Legal Specialties, 1985, Nat. Bd. Trial Advocacy, 1992. Assoc. Sams, Anderson, Gerstein & Ward, P.A., Miami, 1978, Anderson, Moss, Russo & Gievers, P.A., Miami, 1979-83; ptnr., 1983—87; pvt. practice Karen A. Gievers, P.A., 1987—. Bd. editors: So. Dist. Digest, 1981-85. Lectr. FACT, Miami, 1984; pres. Operation SafeDrive, 1987—; mem. MADD, 1986; bd. trustees We Will Rebuild, 1992-93; candidate treas., ins. commr. State of Fla., 1994, candidate sec. state, 1998. Mem. Fla. Bar Assn. (mem. trial lawyers exec. coun. 1985-88, editor trial lawyers sect. 1984, vice-chmn. evidence com. 1985-88, chmn. 1988-89), Am. Bd. Trial Advocates (pres. elect Fla. 2002), Acad. Fla. Trial Lawyers (chmn. pub. com. 1984-86, bd. dirs. 1985-87, treas. 1988-89, sec. 1987-88, pres. elect 1989-90, pres. 1990-91, recipient Pres.'s award 1986, 90), Assn. Trial Lawyers Am., Dade County Bar Assn. (bd. dirs. 1981-84, 85-87, treas. 1987-88, sec. 1988-89, 2nd v.p. 1989-90, 1st v.p. 1990-91, pres.-elect 1991-92, pres. 1992-93), Dade County Trial Lawyers Assn. (sec. 1984, treas. 1985, pres. 1987), Fed. Bar Assn., Fla. Assn. Women Lawyers, Children's Advocacy Found. (pres., dir. 2000), Zool. Soc. Fla., Fla. Consumer Fedn. (bd. dirs. 1985-87), Lions Internat., Gray Panthers, Banker's, Gov.'s. Democrat. Office: 524 E College Ave Tallahassee FL 32301-2529

GIFFEN, DANIEL HARRIS, lawyer, educator; b. Zanesville, Ohio, Feb. 11, 1938; s. Harris MacArtor and Anne Louise (Crawford) G.; m. Jane Louise Cayford, Nov. 23, 1963 (div. 1970); children: Sarah Louise, Thomas Harris; m. Linda Eastin, Aug. 19, 1972. AB, Coll. of William and Mary, 1960; MA, U. Pa., 1962, MA, 1967; testamur, U. Exeter, Eng., 1971; JD, Case Western Res. U., 1973. Bar: Ohio 1973. Corp. asst. U. Pa. Lippincott Libr., Phila., 1961-63; assoc. curator La. State Mus., New Orleans, 1963-64; sec. N.H. Hist. Soc., Concord, 1964-69; asst. dir. Syracuse (N.Y.) U. Arents Rsch. Libr., 1969-70; pvt. practice Cleve., 1973-99; asst. prof. law Cleve. State U., 1976-79; asst. prof. Kent (Ohio) State U., 1980-98, prof. emeritus, 1998—. Editor Walter Drane Co., Cleve., 1974-76; lectr. Monadnock C.C., Peterborough, N.H., 1968-69; vis. scholar London Libr., 1991-92. Author: Adventures in Vermont, 1969, Adventures in Maine, 1969, New Hampshire Colony, 1970; contbr. articles to profl. jours. Hon. life mem. Pres.'s Coun., Coll. William and Mary, 1980. Recipient Kenyon English Prize scholarship, 1956; fellow Heritage Found., 1959-60, Nat. Trust, 1959-61, 67, 73. Fellow Saltire Soc. (Scotland); mem. ABA, Ohio Bar Assn., Am. Soc. Interior Design, Am. Assn. Mus., Am. Assn. State and Local Historians, Nat. Trust, Soc. Archtl. Historians, Masons, Shriners. Episcopalian. Home: 6058 Mad River Rd Centerville OH 45459-1508

GIFFEN, LOIS KEY, artist, psychosynthesis counselor; b. Hollis, Okla., Dec. 18, 1932; d. Andrew Finley and Audra Agnes (Griffith) Key; m. Robert Edward Giffen, June 26, 1954; children: John Andrew, Mark Alexander. BA, U. Chgo., 1951; diploma, Inst. Psychosynthesis, London, 1988. Artist, 1945—; social group worker Neighbourhood Clubs, Oklahoma City, Okla., 1956-59; tchr. Unity of the Keys, Key West, Fla., 1994—. Workshop facilitator Fla. Coalition for Peace and Justice, 1990; organizer for tchg. student mediators in elem. schs. Peace Edn. and Awareness Ctr., Santa Barbara, 1992-93; mentor Take Stock in Children Program; tchr. art program for children Fla. Keys Land and Sea Trust. Editor: The London Bridge Mag., 1981—84, The CCL Cookbook, 1986; one-man shows include Gippsland Regional Art Ctr., Sale, Victoria, Australia, 1973, Anjuian Angkatan Pelakis Semalaysia, Kuala Lumpur, 1976, Am. Consulate-USIS, Benghazi, Libya, 1962, Fla. Keys Art Guild Gallery on Pigeon Key, Marathon, Artists in Paradise, Big Pine Key, Fla., exhibitions include Art in the Pk., Ft. Zachary Taylor, 2001—03, Ft. Zachary Taylor State Parks Key Women Arts, 2003, Key West Mus. Art and History. V.p., mem. bd. dirs. Internat. Women's Club, Benghazi, Libya, 1960-65; mem. bd. dirs. Gippsland Regional Art Ctr., Sale, Victoria, Australia, 1971-73; com. chmn., mem. bd. dirs. Am. Women's Club, London, 1981-88; mem. bd. dirs. Commonwealth Countries League, London, 1982-88, Welcome to London Internat. Club, London, 1983-88; mem. Univ. Women's Club, London, 1985-88; adv. bd. Fla. Keys Coun. of the Arts, Inc.; vol. Practical Acad. Cultural Edn. program for teenage girls at risk. Mem. Assn. for Transpersonal Psychology, Assn. for the Advancement of Psychosynthesis, Bus. and Profl. Women's Club, Fla. Keys Art Guild, Lower Keys Artists Network, Marathon Sailing Club, Marathon Yacht Club. Democrat. Mem. Unity Ch. Avocations: sailing, swimming, reading, astrology, gardening. Home: 2000 Manor Ln Marathon FL 33050

GIFFIN, GORDON D. former ambassador, lawyer; b. Springfield, Mass. m. Patti Alfred; 1 child, Kelley. BA, Duke U., 1971; JD, Emory U., 1974. Bar: Ga. 1974, DC 1979. Dir. legis. affairs, chief counsel to Senator Sam Nunn U.S. Senate, 1974-79; assoc. Hansell and Post, Atlanta, 1979-86; sr. ptnr. Long, Aldridge & Norman, Atlanta and Washington, until 1997; amb. to Can., Am. Embassy, Ottawa, Canada, 1997—2001. Former adj. prof. law Emory U. Sch. Law, Atlanta; bd. dirs. Overseas Pvt. Investment Corp., 1993-97. Treas. Senator Sam Nunn Campaign Com., 20 yrs.; with Senator Nunn and Gov. Clinton founder Dem. Leadership Coun., 1984, mem. bd., 1984-96; mem. com. to host Dem. Nat. Conv., Atlanta, 1988, chmn. site selection com., Chgo., 1996, gen. counsel, 1992, 96; presdl. elector, Ga., 1992, 96; chmn. Ga. Clinton primary campaign, 1992, Clinton-Gore Gen. Election Campaign, 1992; dep. dir. pers. White House Transition Team, 1992; sr. advisor on south, also chmn. Clinton-Gore effort in Ga., Clinton Reelection Campaign, 1996; active Atlanta Olympic Games Com., 1996; former mem. bd. dirs. Ga. C. of C., Trees Atlanta Found., Atlanta Hist. Soc., Atlanta Ballet. Named One of 100 Most Influential Georgians, Ga. Trend mag., 3 times. Democrat. Office: Dept State Am Ambassador To Canada Washington DC 20521-0001

GIFFIN, MARGARET ETHEL (PEGGY GIFFIN), management consultant; b. Cleve., Aug. 27, 1949; d. Arch Kenneth and Jeanne (Eggleton) G.; m. Robert Alan Wyman, Aug. 20, 1988; 1 child, Samantha Jean. BA in Psychology, U. Pacific, Stockton, Calif., 1971; MA in Psychology, Calif. State U., Long Beach, 1973; PhD in Quantitative Psychology, U. So. Calif., 1984. Psychometrician Auto Club So. Calif., L.A., 1973-74; cons. Psychol. Svcs., Inc., Glendale, Calif., 1975-76, mgr., 1977-78, dir., 1979-94; rschr. Social Sci. Rsch. Inst., U. So. Calif., L.A., 1981; dir. Giffin Consulting Svcs., L.A., 1994—. Instr. Calif. State U., Long Beach, 1989-90; mem. tech. adv. com. on testing Calif. Fair Employment and Housing Commn., 1974-80, mem. steering com., 1978-80. Mem. APA, Soc. Indsl. Organizational Psychology, Pers. Testing Coun. So. Calif. (pres. 1980, exec. dir. 1982, 88, bd. dirs. 1980-92). Home and Office: 260 S Highland Ave Los Angeles CA 90036-3027 E-mail: peggygiffin@cs.com.

GIFFIN, MARJIE G. writer; b. Columbia City, Ind., Nov. 22, 1951; d. Robert Edwards and Harriett (Brown) Gates; m. Kenneth Neal Giffin, May 17, 1975; children: Christopher, Matthew, Elisabeth Anne. AB in Lit. magna cum laude, Ind. U., 1974; MA in Lit., Butler U., 1982. Cert. tchr., Ind., 1974, gifted and talented edn., 2000. Advt. writer Curtis Pub. Co., Indpls., 1974-75; pub. rels. dir. Dept. Parks and Recreation, Indpls., 1975-76; comms. dir. Acad. Pub. Svc., Indpls., 1976-78; editor Wayne Twp. Sch. Dist., Indpls., 1983-88; assoc. faculty Ind. U./Purdue U., Indpls., 1992-94; freelance writer Indpls., 1978—; rschr./writer W.B. Brown historical Project, 2001. Mem. grad. sch. arts/scis. alumni bd. Ind. U., 1976-78; bd. dirs. Indpls. Pub. Libr., 1985-86; adv. bd. Ind. U. arts/scis. newsletter, 1977-78. Author: Water Runs Downhill, 1981, If Tables Could Talk, 1988, A Walk Through Time, 1989. Indpls. Zoo, Indpls. Children's Mus.; bd. dirs. Marion County Welfare Bd., 1981-82, Sycamore Sch. Assn., 1998-2001. Honoree Girls, Inc., Indpls. Forum Series, 1991. Honoree Ind. Authors Day, 1990. Mem. Ind. Hist. Soc., Hist. Landmarks found., Acad. Am. Poets, Kappa Alpha Theta. Republican. Roman Catholic. Avocations: water sports, poetry, reading, history, writing. E-mail: mggiffin@aol.com.

GIFFIN, SANDRA LEE, nursing administrator; b. Tacoma, July 16, 1957; d. Clayton Eugene and Carol Lee (Fisher) Peterson; m. Herbert Kent Giffin, May 6, 1989. Diploma, Tacoma Gen. Hosp. Sch. Nursing, 1978; BSN magna cum laude, Pacific Luth. U., 1980; MS, Oreg. Health Scis. U., 1994. Cert. in nursing

adminstrn. Staff nurse Mary Bridge Children's Hosp., 1978-81, evening nurse supr., infection control nurse, 1981-83, asst. med./surg. nurse mgr., 1983-84, med./surg. nurse mgr., 1984-89; dept. dir. Oreg. Poison Ctr. Oreg. Health Scis. U., Portland, 1989—, instr., Sch. Nursing, 1994—, dept. dir. nurse cons. program, 1995-2000, interim dir. physician cons. program, 2000. Presenter in field. Author/presenter abstracts in field. Sec. Rocky Butte Neighborhood Assn., 1996; sec. bd. dirs. Make A Wish Found. Oreg., 1989-96; mem. adv. bd. Oreg. Safe Kids Coalition; active Oreg. Interagy. Hazardous Comm. Coun., Oreg. Sch. Health Edn. Coalition. Grantee Agy. for Toxic Substances and Disease Registry/Am. Assn. Poison Control Ctrs., 1992, Oreg. State Health Divsn., 1993-94. Mem. Am. Acad. Ambulatory Care Nursing, Am. Assn. Poison Control Ctrs., N.W. Orgn. Nursing Execs. (apptd. mem. commn. on health care policy 2000). Avocations: skiing, reading, bicycling, travel, cooking. Office: Oreg Poison Ctr 3181 SW Sam Jackson Park Rd Portland OR 97201-3011

GIFFIN, WALTER CHARLES, retired industrial engineer, educator, consultant; b. Walhonding, Ohio, Apr. 22, 1936; s. Charles Maurice and Florence Ruth (Davis) G.; m. Beverly Ann Neff, Sept. 1, 1956; children— Steven, Rebecca B. Indsl. Engring., MS, Ohio State U., 1960, PhD, 1964. Registered profl. engr., Ohio. Research engr. Gen. Motors Research Labs., Warren, Mich., 1960-61; research assoc. systems research group Ohio State U., Columbus, 1961-62, instr. indsl. and systems engring., 1962-64, asst. prof., 1964-68, assoc. prof., 1968-71, prof., 1971-87, prof. emeritus, 1987—; prof. engring. U. So. Colo., Pueblo, 1987-92; ret., 1992—. Cons. in field Author: Introduction to Operations Engineering, 1971; Transform Techniques for Probability Modeling, 1975; Queueing: Basic Theory and Applications, 1978 NASA Research grantee, 1978-83 Mem.: Exptl. Aircraft Assn. (Oshkosh, Wis. and Pueblo, Colo.). Home: 419 Fairway S Dr W Pueblo CO 81007

GIFFORD, BARRY COLBY, writer; b. Chgo., Oct. 18, 1946; s. Adolph Edward Stein and Dorothy Marjorie Colby; m. Mary Louise Gifford, Oct. 23, 1970; children: Phoebe, Asa Colby. Author: Wild at Heart, 1990 (Palme d'Or award), Night People, 1992 (Premio Brancati, Italy), The Phantom Father, 1997 (Book of Yr. N.Y. Times), Wyoming, 2000 (Book of Yr. L.A. Times), The Rooster Trapped in the Reptile Room: A Barry Gifford Reader, 2003. Recipient Syndicated Fiction award PEN, N.YT., 1984, Maxwell Perkins award PEN West, L.A., 1983. Office: 833 Bancroft Way Berkeley CA 94710

GIFFORD, CARLA J. education educator; b. Spangler, Pennsylvania, July 19, 1956; d. William Carlton and Joann F. (Farrell) Rummel; m. Steven E. Gifford, Jan. 18, 1995; children: Rebecca Lynn, Mark Daniel. BS edn., Peru St. Coll., Peru, NE., 1995; libr. media specialist, U. Nebr., Omaha, Nebr., 1996—97. Cert. K-12 IA. and NE., 1995. Libr. media specialist St. James Seton Sch., Omaha, 1995—96, George Little Rock Sch., George, Iowa, 1997—2000; instr. N.W. IA. Cmty. Coll., Sheldon, Iowa, 1998—. Web devel. cons. Her Realm, Melvin, Iowa, 2000—01. Mem. Women's Aux. Am. Legion, Melvin, Iowa. Mem.: NEA. Avocations: violinist, pianist, tutoring children, tng. horses. Home: 5944 250th St Melvin IA 51350 Office: NW IA Cmty Coll Bus Divsn 603 W Park St Sheldon IA 51201-1060 Business E-Mail: GiffFylz@iowatelecom.net

GIFFORD, CHARLES KILVERT, banker; b. Providence, Nov. 8, 1942; s. Clarence H. and Priscilla (Kilvert) G.; m. Anne Dewing, Oct. 3, 1964; children: Ramsay, Charles, John, Jessica BA, Princeton U., 1964. With Chase Manhattan Bank, N.Y.C., 1964-66; with BankBoston, 1966—, loan officer, 1967, asst. v.p., 1970, v.p., 1973, first v.p., 1978, sr. v.p., 1979, exec. v.p., 1981; vice-chmn. BankBoston and First Nat. Bank of Boston, 1987, pres., 1989, chmn., CEO, 1995—99; pres., COO FleetBoston Fin. Corp., Boston, 1999—2001, pres., CEO, 2001—. Bd. dirs. Mass. Mut. Life Ins. co., NSTAR Corp. Trustee New Eng. Aquarium, Boston, 1982, Dana Farber Cancer Ctr., Boston, Sta. WGBH, Make-A-Wish Found., Northeastern U., Junior Achievement; bd. dirs. Boston Pvt. Ind. Coun., Assn. Res. City Bankers; chmn. success by 6 leadership coun. United Way, mem. exec. com.; chmn. Boston Plan for Excellence in Pub. Schs. Mem. Greater Boston C. of C. (chmn.). Office: FleetBoston Financial Corp 100 Federal St Boston MA 02110-2003

GIFFORD, DALE L. human resources executive; b. May 30, 1950; BA, U. Wis., 1971. With Hewitt Assocs. LLC, Lincolnshire, Ill., 1972—, CEO, 1992—, chmn., 2002—. Office: Hewitt Associates 100 Half Day Rd Lincolnshire IL 60069-3242*

GIFFORD, DONALD GEORGE, legal educator; b. Medina, Ohio, July 26, 1952; s. George W. and Ruth Ann (Reed) G.; m. Nancy Ray Aten, Mar. 24, 1973; children: Rebecca, Caroline. BA, Wooster Coll., 1973; JD, Harvard U., 1976. Bar: Ohio 1976, Fla. 1984. Assoc. Gallagher, Sharp, Fulton, Norman & Mollison, Cleve., 1976-77; ptnr. Noble & Gifford, Millersburg, Ohio, 1977-79; asst. prof. law U. Toledo, 1979-82, assoc. prof. law, 1982-84; prof. U. Fla., Gainesville, 1984-89; assoc. dir. academic task force for rev. ins. and tort systems Fla. Gov.'s Office, Gainesville, 1986-88; dean, prof. law W.Va. U., Morgantown, 1989-92; prof. law U. Md., Balt., 1992—, dean, 1992-99. Contbr. articles to profl. jours.; author 3 books. Chmn. Gov.'s Lead Paint Poisoning Commn., Md., 1992-94; vice chair Md. Alt. Dispute Resolution Task Force, 1997-2000. Mem. Ohio Bar Assn., The Fla. Bar. Am. Law Inst. Office: U Maryland Sch Law 500 W Baltimore St Baltimore MD 21201-1602 E-mail: dgifford@law.umaryland.edu.

GIFFORD, ERNEST MILTON, biologist, educator; b. Riverside, Calif., Jan. 17, 1920; s. Ernest Milton and Mildred Wade (Campbell) G.; m. Jean Duncan, July 15, 1942; 1 child, Jeanette AB, U. Calif., Berkeley, 1942, PhD, 1950; grad., U.S. Army Command and Gen. Staff Sch., 1965. Asst. prof. botany, asst. botanist expt. sta. U. Calif.-Davis, 1950-56, assoc. prof. botany, assoc. botanist, 1957-61, prof. botany, botanist, 1962-87, prof. emeritus, 1988—, chmn. dept. botany and agrl. botany, 1963-67, 74-78. Author: (with A. S. Foster) Morphology and Evolution of Vascular Plants, 3d edit., 1989, (with T. L. Rost) Mechanisms and control of Cell Division, 1977; editor in chief Am. Jour. Botany, 1975-79; advisor to editor Ency. Brit.; contbr. articles on anatomy, ultrastructure and morphogenesis of higher plants to profl. jours. Served to maj. U.S. Army, 1942-46; ETO; to col. USAR, 1946-73. Decorated Bronze Star medal; named disting. contbr. Ency. Brit., 1964; NRC fellow Harvard U., 1956; Fulbright research scholar, France, 1966; John Simon Guggenheim Found. fellow, France, 1966; NATO sr. postdoctoral fellow, France, 1974; recipient Acad. Senate Disting. Teaching award U. Calif.-Davis, 1986. Mem. Bot. Soc. Am. (v.p. 1981, pres. 1982, merit award 1981), Internat. Soc. Plant Morphologists (v.p. 1980-84), Am. Inst. Biol. Scis., Sigma Xi. Office: U Calif Divsn Biol Scis Sect Plant Biology Davis CA 95616-8536

GIFFORD, FEREUZA, retired military officer; b. Keene, NH, May 24, 1917; d. John Amos and Leafie Mitchell Gifford; m. John Joseph Pydynkowski Jr., June 1936 (div. June 1941); 1 child, Patricia Mitchell Pydynkowski. Grad., Nat. Maritime Union, 1974; AS in Geology, City Coll. of San Francisco, 1981; AB, Maritime Acad., Piney Point, Md., 1992. Turbo-supercharger tester GE Lynn (Mass.) Riverworks, 1942—43; civilian recruit USN, Boston, Vallejo, Calif., 1943—45; stewardess for convoy SS Fermina, 1947, M.T. Ottawa, San Francisco, 1956, SS United States, N.Y.C., 1960—73, SS Santa Rosa, 1974. Author: (poetry) The Falling Rain, 2000 (Editor's Choice award Internat. Libr. of Poetry) Mem.: VFW, Air Force Assn. Achievements include invention of safety handles, Gifford's Lizards, rescuing disabled submarines. Home: 330 Clementina St Apt 621 San Francisco CA 94103-4126

GIFFORD, FRANKLIN ANDREW, JR., meteorologist, consultant; b. Union City, N.J., May 7, 1922; s. F.A. and Hazel (Sheehan) G.; m. Eleanor Mary Frith, Aug. 7, 1943; children: Michael J., Robert K. BS, NYU, 1947; MS, Pa. State U., 1954, PhD, 1955. Area chief meteorologist Northwest Airlines, N.Y.C., 1945-50; rsch. meteorologist U.S. Weather Bur. (NOAA), Washington, 1950-55; dir. Atmospheric Turbulence Diffusion Lab. NOAA, Oak Ridge, Tenn., 1955-80. Cons. Los Alamos Nat. Lab., 1980—, U.S. NRC Adv. Com. on Reactor Safety, Washington, 1958-82; cons. Internat. Atomic Energy Agy., Vienna, 1966-82; mem. U.S.-USSR Bilateral Working Group on Air Pollution, 1974-75. Author: Meteorology and Atomic Energy, 1968; contbr. over 140 articles to profl. jours. Capt. USAF, 1943-45, ETO. Recipient Gold medal U.S. Dept. Commerce, 1963. Fellow AAAS, Am. Meteorol. Soc. (Contbn. to Applied Meteorology award 1990). Home: 109 Gorgas Ln Oak Ridge TN 37830-5417 E-mail: fagifford@aol.com.

GIFFORD, GERALD FREDERIC, retired science educator; b. Chanute, Kans., Oct. 24, 1939; s. Gerald Leo and Marion Lou (Browne) Gifford; m. Cinda Jean Lowman, June 26, 1982. Student, Kans. U., 1957-60; BS in Range Mgmt., Utah State U., 1962, MS in Watershed Mgmt., 1964, PhD in Watershed Sci., 1968. Asst. prof. watershed sci. Utah State U., Logan, 1967-72, assoc. prof., 1972-80, prof., 1980-84, chmn. watershed sci. unit, 1967-84, dir. Inst. Land Reclamation, 1982-84; head range, wildlife and forestry U. Nev., Reno, 1984-92, chmn. environ. and resource sci. dept., 1992—94, prof. hydrology and natural resource mgmt., 1994—2000, ret., 2000. Exch. scientist NSF, Canberra, Australia, 1974; cons. Smithsonian Inst., Nat. Pk. Svc., Office Tech. Assessment, Tex. Tech U., U. Minn., Bur. Land Mgmt. AMAX Coal Co., Nat. Commn. Water Quality, 1967—. Author: (book) Rangeland Hydrology, 1981; assoc. editor: Jour. Range Mgmt., 1982—87, 1991—95, Arid Soil Rsch. and Rehab., 1985—90; contbr. scientific papers to profl. pubs. Mem.: Soil and Water Conservation Soc., Am. Water Resources Assn. Avocations: racquetball, antiques, garage sales. Home: 3880 Squaw Valley Cir Reno NV 89509-5663 E-mail: fredandcinda@aol.com.

GIFFORD, HEIDI, writer, editor; b. New Haven, Jan. 28, 1961; d. Prosser and Dee Dee (O'Sullivan) Gifford; m. George Melas, July 15, 1995; children: Luke, Lily. BA in English Lit., Yale U., 1983; MPA in Internat. Econs., Columbia U., 1991. Edtl. asst. Yale U. Press, New Haven, 1985, asst. to the dir. Gov.'s Office of Fed. Rels., Boston, 1987-89; asst. dir. internat. trade and econs. Coun. on Fgn. Rels., N.Y.C., 1991-94; elections analyst Nightly News with Tom Brokaw/NBC News, N.Y.C., 1995-96; writer and editor Comms. Devel., N.Y.C., 1997—. Assoc. USIA Fgn. Press Ctr., N.Y.C., 1990-91. Mem. Inst. of World Affairs. Episcopalian. Avocations: crew, marathon running. E-mail: heidigiff@earthlink.net.

GIFFORD, JOHN F. computer company executive; Founded AMD, Sunnyvale, Calif., 1969, Maxim Integrated Products, Sunnyvale, 1983, chmn., pres., CEO, 1992—. Office: Maxim Integrated Products 120 San Gabriel Dr Sunnyvale CA 94086-5150

GIFFORD, JOHN IRVING, retired agricultural equipment company executive; b. Lockport, N.Y., July 23, 1930; s. John Jacob and Carrie (McAdam) G.; m. Sara Jane Bauer, Jan. 28, 1955; children: John Hutchins, James Scott. BS, Purdue U., 1952, MS, 1956. Sales trainee Am. Nat. Foods, Inc., L.A., 1956; economist Deere & Co., Moline, Ill., 1956-65, pers. adminstr., 1965-70, mgr. data svcs., 1970-96; stats. cons. to cos. and trade assns., 1996—. Mem. USDA Agrl. Stats. adv. com., 1997—. Bd. dirs., Rock Island (Ill.) sect. Easter Seal Found., 1981-87; v.p. coun., St. John Luth. Ch., Rock Island, 1981-82; pres., Rock Island Little League, 1981-82; v.p. Babe Ruth Baseball, Rock Island, 1983; mem. agrl. census adv. com. U.S. Dept. Commerce, 1997-98; mem. adv. com. stats. USDA, 1999—. 1st lt. U.S. Army, 1952-54, Korea. Recipient Leadership recognition Equipment Mfrs. Inst. Mem. Nat. Assn. Bus. Econs., Equipment Mfrs. Assn., Farm and Indsl. Equipment Inst., Constrn. Industry Mfrs. Assn., Outdoor Power Equipment Inst., Engine Mfrs. Assn., Internat. Farm Tractor Com., Internat. Harvesting Equipment Com. (chmn. statistics com. 1994-95), Rock Island (Ill.) Noon Kiwanis Club. Avocations: reading, golf. E-mail: gifford@revealed.net.

GIFFORD, NANCY (MUMTAZ), artist, poet; b. Youngstown, Ohio, Feb. 24, 1948; d. John S. Baytos and Helen E. Yochman; m. Michael B. Gifford, Feb. 24, 1995; children: Harriet, Ben, Emma, Kristopher. Degree, Kent (Ohio) State U., 1970; student, Fashion Inst. of Am., 1970—71, The Film Sch., Half Moon Bay, Calif., 1975—76. One-woman shows include Argon Gallery, Venice, Calif., 1984, Merging One Gallery, Santa Monica, Calif., 1986, 1987, Carminel Gallery, N.Y.C., 1988, Schreiber/Cutler Gallery, 1988, L.A. County Mus. of Art, 1991, exhibited in group shows at Craft & Folk Art Mus., L.A., 1984, Bowers Mus., 1987, Carnegie Art Mus., 1987 (1st pl. award), Riverside (Calif.) Art Mus., 1988, Mus. of the Hudson Highlands, N.Y., 1989, Mus. of N.Mex., Santa Fe, 1990, Corcoran Gallery, 1990, Naples (Fla.) Art Mus., 2001, HW Gallery, Naples, Fla., 2002; author: (haiku poetry and drawings) The War Room, 2001, Modern Haiku, 2003. Patron, bd. dirs. Naples Art Assn., 1999—; patron Naples Art Mus., 1997—, Haiku Soc. of Am., 2002, Mus. of Contemporary Art, Miami, 2003. Recipient award of excellence, Scarsdale (N.Y.) Art Soc., 1987, Juror's award, Fine Arts of Burbank, Calif., 1987, award of excellence, Gallery 54, N.Y.C., 1988, award of merit, von Liebig Art Ctr., 2003. Avocations: swimming, hiking, yoga. Home: 568 9th St S Ste 354 Naples FL 34102 E-mail: nangifford@home.com.

GIFFORD, NELSON SAGE, financial company executive; b. Newton, Mass., May 3, 1930; s. Gordon Babcock and Hariette Rose (Dooley) G.; m. Elizabeth B. Brow, Nov. 12, 1955; children: Susan Helen, Ian Christopher, Diane Brow. AB, Tufts Coll., 1952; HHD (hon.), U. Mass., 1989; PhD (hon.), Tufts U., 1996. With Dennison Mfg. Co., Framingham, Mass., 1954-90, mem. acctg. staff, 1954-63, controller, 1964-65, gen. mgr., 1965-67, v.p., 1967-72, pres., 1972-86, chmn., 1986-90; vice chmn. Avery Dennison Corp., Boston, 1990-91; prin. Fleetwing Capital, Boston, 1992—. Bd. dirs. Nypro Inc., Clinton, Mass., MDT Group, Westford, Mass.; mng. dir. Ptnr.'s Fund, Boston. Past bd. dirs. New Eng. Colls. Fund, Reed and Barton, Taunton, Mass., John Hancock Fin. Svcs., Boston, J.M. Huber Corp., Edison, N.J.; corp. mem. Newton Wellesley Hosp., Mass. Gen. Hosp.; past chmn. Wellesley Pers. Bd.; past trustee Woods Hole Oceanographic Inst., Mass., 1984-90; chmn. bd. trustees Tufts U., 1986-95. Lt. comdr. USNR, 1952-60. Mem. Silvanus Packard Soc., Mass. Bus. Roundtable (bd. dirs., vice chmn. 1982-88), Assoc. Industries Mass. (bd. dirs. 1976-86), Kittansett Club, Brae Burn Country Club, Beverly Yacht Club. Soc. Tufts Followes. Home: 14 Windsor Rd Wellesley MA 02481-6134 Office: Fleetwing Capital 75 Federal St Boston MA 02110-1913 E-mail: giffordn@msn.com.

GIFFORD, PORTER WILLIAM, retired construction materials manufacturing company executive; b. Dallas, Dec. 14, 1918; s. Porter William and Evelyn Victoria (Bonorden) G.; m. Elizabeth Butte, Jan. 19, 1946 (dec.); children: Porter William III, Sharon Elizabeth, Geoffrey Butte; m. Kay Williams Manley, Mar. 22, 1997. BSME, Cornell U., 1941. With Gifford-Hill & Co., Inc., Dallas, 1941-86, pres., 1958-69, chmn. bd. dirs., 1969-71; pres. Qdot Corp., Dallas, 1974-78, Aerological Rsch. Systems, Inc., Dallas, 1991-99. Trustee Found. Econ. Edn., Internat. Linguistics Ctr., Dallas, Future of Freedom Found., Fairfax, Va. Maj. USAAC, 1941-46. Decorated Bronze Star. Mem. Tau Beta Pi, Delta Kappa Epsilon. Home: 9106 Esplanade Dr Dallas TX 75220-7800

GIFFORD, PROSSER, library administrator; b. NYC, May 16, 1929; s. John Archer and Barbara (Prosser) G.; m. Shirley Mireille O'Sullivan, June 26, 1954; children: Barbara, Paula, Heidi. BA, Yale U., 1951, PhD, 1964; BA, Oxford (Eng.) U., 1953, MA, 1958; LLB, Harvard U., 1956; MA, Amherst Coll., 1969, LHD, 1980; LLD, Doshisha U., Kyoto, Japan, 1979. Bar: DC 1956. Asst. to pres. Swarthmore Coll., 1956-58; asst. prof. history Yale, 1964-66; dir. 5 yr. B.A. program, 1965-66; dean faculty Amherst Coll., 1967-79, assoc. prof. history, 1967-69, prof. history, 1969-79; dep. dir. Woodrow Wilson Internat. Ctr. for Scholars, Washington, 1975-76, 80-87, acting dir., 1987-88; dir. scholarly programs Libr. Congress, 1990—. Chmn. Merton Coll. Charitable Corp., 1991—; Sir Thomas Bodley fellow Merton Coll., 2001. Co-editor, contbr.: Britian and Germany in Africa, 1967, France and Britain in Africa, 1971, Transfer of Power in Africa, 1982, Decolonization and African Independence, 1988, Creating French Culture, 1995, Democracy and the Rule of Law, 2001. Trustee, Hotchkiss Sch., 1971-81, Concord Acad., 1972-78; chmn. bd. trustees Woods Hole Marine Biol. Lab., 1978-90. Rhodes scholar, 1951-53; Fgn. Area fellow No. Rhodesia, 1963-64 Mem. Assn. Yale Alumni (gov. 1972-77), Woods Hole Oceanographic Inst. (mem. corp.), Internat. House of Japan, India Internat. Ctr., Century Club, Cosmos Club, Elizabethan Club, Woods Hole Golf and Tennis Club, Quisset Yacht Club. Home: 540 N St SW Apt 903S Washington DC 20024-4557 also: 59 Penzance Rd Woods Hole MA 02543-0005 E-mail: pgif@loc.gov, prossgiff@worldnet.att.net.

GIFFORD, RAY WALLACE, JR., retired physician, educator; b. Westerville, Ohio, Aug. 13, 1923; s. Ray Wallace and Alma Marie (Wagoner) G.; m. Frances Anne Moore, Jan. 13, 1973; 1 son, George; children by previous marriage: Peggy, Cynthia, Susan. BS, Otterbein Coll., 1944, ScD (hon.), 1986; MD, Ohio State U., 1947; M.Sc., U. Minn., 1952. Diplomate: Am. Bd. Internal Medicine. Intern Colo. Gen. Hosp., Denver, 1947-48; fellow in internal medicine Mayo Clinic, Rochester, Minn., 1949-52; practice medicine specializing in hypertension and nephrology; asst. prof. medicine, cons. sect. medicine Mayo Clinic, Mayo Found., Rochester, 1953-61; staff mem. dept. hypertension and nephrology Cleve. Clinic Found., 1961-67, head dept. hypertension and nephrology, 1967-85, sr. physician dept. hypertension and nephrology, 1986-93, acting chmn. dept. hypertension and nephrology, 1991-92, cons. dept. hypertension and nephrology, 1994-99, bd. govs., 1973-78, vice chmn., 1977-78, vice chmn. div. medicine, 1978-93, chmn. regional health affairs, 1986-93, 94-98; prof. internal medicine Ohio State U. Coll. Medicine, Columbus, Ohio, 1993—2000. Asst. attending physician U.S. Congress, 1954-56; chmn. hypertension task force Intersoc. Commn. on Heart Disease Resources, 1979-81; mem. nat. high blood pressure coordinating com. Nat. Heart, Lung and Blood Inst., 1978—; mem. 2d, 3d, 4th, 6th and 7th, and chmn. 5th joint nat. cons. on detection, evaluation and treatment of high blood pressure, 1979-80, 83-84, 87-88, 91-92, 96-97, 2003; mem. Congl. Commn. on Drug Approval Process, 1981-82; mem. adv. com. to dir. NIH, 1982-86; mem. Joint Commn. on Accreditation of Healthcare Orgns., 1989-90; mem. Forum on Drug Devel., Inst. Medicine, 1990-94. Author (with William Manger): Pheochromocytoma, 1977, 1996, 100 Questions and Answers About Hypertension, 2001; editl. bd.: Stroke Jour., 1971—74, Am. Jour. Cardiology, 1973—78, mem. editl. bd.: Geriatrics, 1974—2002, Hypertension Rsch., 1994—99, Jour. Cardiovascular Risk, 1994—98, Jour. Geriatric Cardiology, 1994—98; contbr. numerous papers. Mem. Rochester City Coun., 1960-61, Rep. precinct committeeman, Cleveland Heights, Ohio, 1966-70. Lt. comdr. M.C., USNR, 1954-56. Recipient Alumni Achievement award Ohio State U., 1962, Alumni Medalist award, 1989; Disting. Sci. Achievement award Otterbein Coll., 1970, Spl. Achievement award, 1992; individual achievement award high blood pressure edn. programs Nat. Heart, Lung and Blood Inst., 1989, Bristol Myers lifetime achievement award Am. Heart Assn., 1992; spl. achievement award Cleve. Clinic Alumni Assn., 1994; Ray W. Gifford, Jr. endowed chair in hypertension established at Cleve. Clinic, 1994; named to Cleve. Med. Hall of Fame, 1997. Fellow ACP (master), Am. Coll. Cardiology (bd. trustees 1969-70, gov. Ohio chpt. 1970-73), Am. Coll. Chest Physicians (chmn. com. on hypertension 1970-72, Simon Rodbard Meml. award 1982); mem. AMA (coun. on sci. affairs 1976-85, vice chmn. 1981-83, chmn. 1983-85, trustee 1986-90), Am. Heart Assn. (bd. dirs. 1969-72, chmn. stroke coun. 1970-72), Am. Soc. Clin. Pharmacology and Therapeutics (pres. 1976-77, Oscar B. Hunter Meml. award in Therapeutics 1979, Henry W. Elliott award Disting. Svc. 1995), Ctrl. Soc. Clin. Rsch., Internat. Soc. Hypertension, Interstate Postgrad. Med. Assn. (pres. 1976-77), Interam. Soc. Hypertension, Coun. on Geriatric Cardiology (bd. dirs. 1989-92), Ohio State U. Alumni Assn. (bd. dirs. 1990-95). Methodist. Home: 15522 E Cactus Dr Fountain Hills AZ 85268

GIFFORD, WILLIAM C. lawyer, educator; b. Aurora, Ill., Sept. 18, 1941; AB, Dartmouth Coll., 1963; LLB, Harvard U., 1966 Bar: Ill. 1966, D.C. 1968, N.Y. 1976, Paris 1994. Assoc., ptnr. Ivins, Phillips & Barker, Washington, 1967-74; assoc. prof. Cornell Law Sch., 1974-78; counsel, ptnr. Wilmer, Cutler & Pickering, 1978-83; ptnr. Davis Polk & Wardwell, N.Y.C., 1983-98, sr. counsel, 1998—. Vis. lectr. Yale Law Sch., 2003. Author: International Tax Planning, 1974, 2d edit., 1979; (with E.A. Owens) International Aspects of U.S. Income Taxation, 1982. Office: Davis Polk & Wardwell 450 Lexington Ave New York NY 10017-3911 E-mail: gifford@dpw.com.

GIFFUNI, FLORA B. artist, educator; b. Naples, Italy, Oct. 26, 1919; widowed, 1990; children: Joann Sher, Vincent, Catherine. BFA, NYU, 1945; MFA, Columbia U., 1948. Art tchr. Immaculate Conception Sch., N.Y.C., 1952-62; interior designer NSID, N.Y.C., 1962-72; pres., founder Pastel Soc. of Am., N.Y.C., 1973-95, chmn., 1995—. Contbr. articles to profl. jours. Mem. Pastel Soc. West Coast (adv. 1985-93), Northwestern Pastel Soc., Catherine Wolfe Art Club (editor 1968-72), Nat. Art Club (chmn. 1993—), Columbus Club, Salmagundi Club, Allied Artists of Am. Home: 15 Gramercy Park S New York NY 10003-1705 Office: Pastel Soc of Am 15 Gramercy Park S New York NY 10003-1705

GIFT, DAVID AYRES, academic administrator; s. Robert Ayres and Katherine (Weil) G.; m. Debra Ruth Meyka, Sept. 7, 1974; children: Jason Ayres, Ryan Michael. MS, Mgmt., MIT, Cambridge, MA, 1992—93; MS, Computer Sci., Mich. State U., East Lansing, MI, 1975—80, BS, Physics, 1971—75. Specialist/instr./programmer Dept. of Radiology, Mich. State U., East Lansing, Mich., 1976—91, specialist and asst. chairperson, 1991—98; asst. v.p. for integrative mgmt. Mich. State U., East Lansing, Mich., 1998—2001, vice provost, libraries, computing and tech., 2001—. Cons. Sec. Nuclear Medicine, Cin., 1980—83, Commonwealth of Australia, 1984—85, GE Co, Milw., 1987; dir. and sec. Mid-Michigan MRI, Inc., Lansing, 1988—2001; cons. McLaren Gen. Hosp., Flint, Mich., 1989—90, Am. Osteo. Coll. Radiology, 1991; dir. U. Rehab. Alliance, Inc., Lansing, Mich., 1994—2001, Radiation Oncology Alliance, Inc., Lansing, Mich., 1996—2001, Merit Network, Inc., Ann Arbor, Mich., 2001—, Gt. Lakes Cancer Inst., Inc., East Lansing, Mich., 2001—01; Cons. Mich. Atty. Gen., 1996. Contbr. to profl. publs. Chmn. bd. trustees, Univ. Luth. Ch., East Lansing, 1986-88. Mem.: AASS, Nat. Consortium for Continuous Improvement in Higher Edn. (exec. coun. 2001—03). Office: Michigan State University 400 Computer Center East Lansing MI 48824

GIFT, GERALD BRENTON, biology educator; b. Chambersburg, Pa., Aug. 30, 1949; s. Melvin Robert and Evelyn Irene G.; m. Barbara Ann, Aug. 4, 1984. BS, Shippensburg U., 1971; MS, U. Maine, 1988. Biology tchr., sci. dept. chmn. Mercersburg (Pa.) Acad., 1971—. Pres. Tuscarora Wildlife Edn. Project, Mercersburg, 1990—. Named Wal-Mart Tchr. of Yr., 1995. Mem. Am. Soc. Mammalogists, Pa. Acad. Scis., Pa. Wildlife Fedn., Wildlife Soc. Pa. Avocations: gardening, reading, softball. Home: 248 N Main St Mercersburg PA 17236-1746 Office: Mercersburg Acad 300 E Seminary St Mercersburg PA 17236-1551 E-mail: giftb@desupernet.net.

GIGER, ANDREAS, education educator; b. Zurich, Switzerland, Sept. 2, 1965; arrived in U.S., 1990; s. Urs Giger and Gilberte Giger-Tétaz. PhD, Ind. U., 1999. Cert. licensed Phil. I U. Zurich, 1989. Assoc. dir. Ctr. for History of Music Theory and Lit., Ind. U., Bloomington, 1998—2000; asst. prof. La. State U., 2000—. Editor: Am. Musicological Soc. Newsletter, 2002—, (book) Music in the Mirror: Reflections on the History of Music Theory and Literature for the 21st Century, 2002. Mem.: Am. Inst. for Verdi Studies, Am. Musicological Soc. Home: 3363 Hundred Oaks Ave Baton Rouge LA 70808

GIGER, MARYELLEN LISSAK, medical physicist; d. Frank and Margaret Lissak; m. Charles Giger; children: Megan, Jennifer, Charlie, Eric. BS summa cum laude, Ill. Benedictine Coll., 1978; MSc, U. Exeter, Eng., 1979; PhD, U. Chgo., 1985. Asst. prof. U. Chgo., 1986—91, assoc. prof., 1991—2000, prof., 2000—. Dir. advanced imaging program Cancer Rsch. Ctr. U. Chgo., 1994—, dir. grad. programs in med. physics, 1998—; presenter in field. Author: (manuscript in investigative radiology) Computerized Detection of Pulmonary Nodules in Computed Tomography Images (Stauffer Award, 1995), (manuscript in medical physics) Multifractal Radiographic Analysis of Osteoporosis (Sylvia Sorkin Greenfield Award, 1995); contbr. chapters to books, articles to profl. jours. Leader Girl Scouts, Elmhurst, Ill., 1994—2001. Recipient President's Scholarship award, Ill. Benedictine Coll., 1975, 1976, 1977, Rev. Shonka, O.S.B. Scholarship Award in Physics, 1977, First Pl. award Young Investigators' Symposium, Am. Assn. Physicists in Medicine, 1985, Jr. Faculty Rsch. award, Am. Cancer Soc., 1988, Faculty Rsch. award, 1991; grantee, Wendy Will Case Cancer Fund, 1989, NIH, Nat. Cancer Inst., 1989—95, 1999—2001, 2000—, 2001—, U.S. Army, DOD, 1993—96, 1996—2000, 1998—2001, 1999—2002; Rotary Internat. fellow, Rotary, 1978—79, Louis Block Rsch. grantee, U. Chgo., 1986, Am. Cancer Soc. Instl. grantee, 1986. Fellow: AIMBE, Am. Assn. Physicists in Medicine; mem.: IEEE, Soc. for Computer Applications in Radiology, Assn. Univ. Radiologists, Internat. Soc. for Optical Enging. Achievements include first to in computer-aided diagnosis research; patents for computer-aided diagnosis for breast and lung cancer detection and diagnosis; assessment of breast cancer risk and assessment of osteoporosis. Office: U Chgo 5841 S Maryland Ave Chicago IL 60637 Office Fax: 773-702-0371. E-mail: m-giger@uchicago.edu.

GIGER, URS, veterinarian; b. Zurich, Switzerland, Apr. 21, 1953; arrived in U.S., 1981; s. Max and Susanne Giger; m. Therese C. Giger, Jan. 15, 1981; 1 child, David Brian. DVM, U. Zurich, 1977, doctoral thesis, 1979, Privatdozent, 1990; MS, U. Pa., Phila., 1991. Diplomate Am. Coll. Vet. Internal Medicine, European Coll. Vet. Internal Medicine, FVH. Postgrad. rschr. extpl. medicine and biology U. Hosp., Zurich, 1978-81; postdoctoral fellow U. Fla., Gainesville,

1981-82, resident in internal medicine, 1982-84; instr. in medicine U. Pa., Phila., 1984-85, asst. prof. medicine, 1985-87, asst. prof. in med. genetics, 1987-91, assoc. prof., 1991-95, prof. medicine, chief sect. med. genetics, 1995—, Charlotte Newton Sheppard prof., 1995—. Dir. transfusion medicine U. Pa.; dir. Josephine Deubler Genetic Disease Testing Lab. U. Pa., Faculty U. Zurich joint appt., 1990—. Contbr. more than 200 publs. Recipient Transfusion Medicine award, NIH, 1989, Internat. Sci. Lifetime Achievement award, World Small Animal Vet. Assn., 2002. Mem. Am. Assn. Vet. Medicine, Am. Soc. Hematology, Am. Coll. Vet. Internal Medicine, European Coll. Vet. Internal Medicine, Am. Soc. Vet. Clin. Pathology, Assn. Vet. Hematology and Transfusion Medicine, Internat. Soc. Animal Genetics. Avocations: horse back riding, sailing, windsurfing, scuba diving, swimming. Office: U Pa Vet Sch 3850 Spruce St Philadelphia PA 19104-6010

GIGES, BURTON, psychiatrist, educator, consultant; b. N.Y.C., Dec. 7, 1924; s. Elias and Jenny Giges; m. Ilka Ruth Giges, Aug. 15, 1954; children: Elinor Bashe, Julie Silver. BS magna cum laude, CCNY, 1946; MD, NYU, 1948. Diplomate Am. Bd. Psychiatry. Rsch. fellow U.S. Army Rsch. and Grad. Sch., Washington, 1950-52, Rockefeller Inst., N.Y.C., 1952-53; pvt. practice in medicine, 1953—57; resident in psychiatry, 1957—60; pvt. practice in psychiatry, 1960—; dir. Cmty. Mental Health Bd., Westchester County, N.Y., 1965-71; asst. clin. prof. dept. psychiatry Albert Einstein Coll. Medicine, Bronx, N.Y., 1965-82; pvt. practice in sport psychology, 1990—; clin. prof. dept. psychology Springfield (Mass.) Coll., 1994—. Cons. sport psychology USA Track and Field, 1995—, Westchester Track Club, 1990—, Met. Athletics Congress, N.Y.C., 1993-97. Contbr. articles to profl. jours., chpts. to books; mem. editl. bd. The Sport Psychologist, Champaign, Ill., 1999—. Bd. dirs. Gestalt Ctr., L.I., NY, 1980—98. Pvt. U.S. Army, 1944, Mason Gen. Hosp., Brentwood, NY, capt. U.S. Army, 1950—52, Walter Reed Hosp., Washington. Fellow Am. Psychiat. Assn.; mem. Assn. for Advancement of Applied Sport Psychology (cert. cons.), Westchester Psychiat. Soc. (chmn. pub. health and program coms., exec. coun.), Alpha Omega Alpha, Phi Beta Kappa. Avocation: exercise. Home and Office: 250 Broadfield Rd New Rochelle NY 10804

GIGGLEMAN, GENE FELTON, academic administrator, veterinarian; b. Dallas, Aug. 23, 1953; s. Gene Felton Giggleman and Linda Jean Long; m. Katherine Ann Lowe, May 31, 1975; children: Kristin Lane, Cynthia Lauren. DVM, Tex. A&M U., 1981. Prof. anat. sci. Parker Coll. Chiropractic, Dallas, 1992—, dean Ctr. Basic Sci., 1994—2000, dean acad. affairs, 2000—. Veterinarian In Home Vet. Care, Grapevine, Tex., 1990—. Worship team mem. Carroll Bapt. Ch., Southlake, Tex., 1996—2003. Cable Scholarship, Tex. A&M U., 1981. Mem.: Tex. Vet. Med. Assn. Conservative-R. Baptist. Avocations: herpetology, motorcycling. Home: 2105 Brentcove Dr Grapevine TX 76051 Office: Parker Coll Chiropractic 2500 Walnut Hill Ln Dallas TX 75229-5668 Home Fax: 800-999-6552; Office Fax: 214-902-3418. E-mail: ggiglman@parkercc.edu.

GIGLI, IRMA, physician, educator, academic administrator; b. Cordoba, Argentina, Dec. 22, 1931; d. Irineo and Esperanza Francisca (Pons de Gigli) Gigli; m. Hans J. Muller-Eberhard, June 29, 1985. BA, Liceo Nacional Manuel Belgrano, Cordoba, 1950; MD, Universidad Nacional de Cordoba, 1957. Intern Cook County Hosp., Chgo., 1957—58, resident in dermatology, 1958—60; fellow in dermatology NYU, 1960—61; mem. faculty Harvard Med. Sch., 1967—75, asso. prof. dermatology, 1972—75; chief dermatology service Peter Bent Brigham Hosp., Robert B. Brigham Hosp., 1971—75; prof. dermatology and exptl. medicine N.Y. U. Med. Center, N.Y.C., 1976—82, mem. Irvington Houst Inst., mem. faculty N.Y. Grad. Sch. Med. Scis., dir. Asthma and Allergic Disease Center for Immunodermatology Studies, 1980—91; prof. medicine, chief div. dermatology U. Calif.-San Diego, 1983—95; prof. medicine and dermatology, vice chair medicine for sci. U. Tex. Health Sci. Ctr., Houston, 1995—; assoc. dir. Inst. Molecular Medicine for Prevention Human Diseases U. Tex., Houston, 1998—2003, dep. dir., 2003—, Walter and Mary Mischer prof. molecular medicine, 1998—; dir. Rsch. Ctr. Immunology and Autoimmune Diseases, 1995—. Mem. Nat. Inst. of Allergy and Infectious Diseases Coun., 1978—79, bd. sci. counselors, 1997—; chmn. study sect. Allergy and Immunology Inst., NIH, 1978—83; mem. Guggenheim Found. Western Hemisphere and Phillippines Com. of Selection; adv. bd. NIH Fogarty Internat. Ctr., 1984—97. Recipient Rsch. award, Am. Cancer Soc., 1970—72, NIH, 1972—76; grantee, Guggenheim Found., 1974—75. Mem.: Am. Acad. Arts and Scis., Henry Kunkel Soc. (councilor 1999—), PEW Latin Am. Fellows Program in Biomed. Scis. (nat. adv. com. 1998—), Inst. Medicine/NAS, Am. Dermatol. Assn., Assn. Am. Physicians, Am. Acad. Allergy, Am. Acad. Dermatology, Am. Assn. Immunologists, Am. Soc. Clin. Investigation, Soc. Investigative Dermatology (hon.; pres. 1990—91, Stephen Rothman Meml. award 1996). Office: U Tex Health Sci Ctr Inst Molecular Medicine 2121 W Holcombe Blvd Houston TX 77030-3303

GIGLIO, JAMES NICHOLAS, humanities educator, writer; b. Akron, Ohio, Mar. 28, 1939; s. Frank Maris Giglio and Mary Matthew Naturale; m. Frances Theresa Jendrisak, June 19, 1965; children: Peter Jason, Anthony Matthew. BA, Kent State U., Ohio, 1961, MA, 1964; PhD, Ohio State U., 1968. Asst. prof. history SW Mo. State U., Springfield, 1968—73, assoc. prof. history, 1973—78, prof. history, 1978—2000, disting. prof. history, 2000—. Exam and table leader Advance Placement (AP) in U.S. History readings, Princeton, NJ, 1977—; editl. bd. mem. Presdl. Studies Quar., N.Y.C., 1992—99; evaluator manuscripts for various publs. Author: (book) H.M. Daugherty and the Politics of Expediency, 1978, (scholarly book) Truman In Cartoon and Caricature, 1984, The Presidency of John F. Kennedy, 1991, John F. Kennedy: A Bibliography, 1995, Musial: From Stash to Stan the Man, 2001, (book) Debating the Kennedy Presidency, 2003, many scholarly articles and reviews. Mem. apptd. by gov. State Hist. Records Bd., Jefferson City, Mo., 1985—87; past mem. task force of Mo. hist. records bd. Mo. State Archives, Jefferson City, Mo. Lt. U.S. Army, 1962—63, capt. USAR. Recipient Inducted into Mo. Writers Hall of Fame, 1997; grantee Rsch. grant, Truman Libr. Inst., 1978, 1982, Fellowship, Nat. Endowment for the Humanities, 1983, John F. Kennedy Libr. Found., 1991. Mem.: The Soc. for Am. Baseball Rsch., Orgn. of Am. Historians. Democrat. Roman Catholic. Achievements include Founder of Mid-Am. Conf. on history, a regional conf. that draws nat. Avocations: golf, fishing. Home: 1300 South Virginia Ave Springfield MO 65807 Office: Southwest Mo State U 90 S National Ave Springfield MO 65804 Home Fax: 417-836-5523. Personal E-mail: jng890f@smsu.edu.

GIGLIO, WILLIAM VITO, secondary education educator; b. Elizabeth, N.J., Oct. 23, 1946; s. Vito William and Ann (Tobac) G.; m. Carol Lynn Faulkner, July 4, 1970; children: W. Scott, Robert M. BSBA, Seton Hall U., 1968, MA in Secondary Bus. Edn., 1970; prins. and suprs. certs., Montclair State U., 1978. Bus. edn. tchr., coach Middlesex (N.J.) H.S., 1968-72, Mt. Olive H.S., Mt. Olive Township, 1972-74, Ridge H.S., Basking Ridge, N.J., 1974—. Chmn. cmty. rels. com. Strategic Planning for Twp. Sch. Bd., Basking Ridge, 1996-97. Baseball coach Am. Legion, Somerset-Hunterdon County, 1991-96; mem. Bernards Twp. Youth Sports Coun.; coach Ctrl. Jersey Baseball League, 1997. Named Somerset County Baseball Coach of Yr., Newark Star-Ledger, 1995, Somerset County H.S. Baseball Coach of Yr., 2000, N.J. State Baseball Coach of Yr., 2000, Cen. Jersey Baseball Coach of Yr., Courier-News, 2000; recipient Group II State Champions Coaches award N.J. Scholastic Baseball Coaches Assn., 2000, 02; named to Union County Baseball Assn. Hall of Fame, 2003. Mem. NEA, N.J. State Interscholastic Atletic Assn., Baseball Coaches Assn., Nat. Fedn. High Sch. Coaches Assn., N.J. Edn. Assn., Somerset County Edn. Assn., Bernards Twp. Edn. Assn., Babe Ruth Baseball, N.J. Scholastic Coaches Assn. Roman Catholic. Home: 70 Harrison Brook Dr Basking Ridge NJ 07920-2415 Office: South Finley Ave Basking Ridge NJ 07920 E-mail: giglio2@erols.com.

GIGUIERE, MICHELE LOUISE, lawyer; b. Spokane, Feb. 11, 1944; d. Karl Earl and Mildred Elaine (Phillips) G. BA, U. Pacific, 1965; MS, U. So. Calif., 1969; JD, Lincoln Law Sch., 1980. Bar: Calif. 1980. Exec. trainee J.W. Robinson Co., L.A., 1965-66; tchr. Novato (Calif.) Unified Sch. Dist., 1967-78; asst. dept. mgr. Emporium, San Rafael, Calif., 1970—74; atty. pvt. practice, Fair Oaks and Sacramento, Calif., 1980—. Mem. State Bar Calif., Sacramento County Bar Assn., Calif. Women Lawyers, Women Lawyers Sacramento. Democrat. Presbyterian. Office: 4811 Chippendale Dr Ste 702 Sacramento CA 95841-2554 E-mail: michelegiguiere@msn.com.

GIJON, JOSÉ ENRIQUE, special education educator; b. El Paso, Tex., June 14, 1966; s. José Enrique and Irma Martinez Gijon; m. Luz Maria Loya, Feb. 6, 1993; children: Emilio José, Eduardo José, Daniela Isabel. BS, Univ. Tex., El Paso, Tex., 1998, MEd, 2003—. Cert. tchg. in elem. edn. and special edn. Tchr. El Paso Sch. Dist., Tex., 1995—. Cath. Avocations: golf, soccer. Office: Alta Vista Elem Sch 1000 N Grama El Paso TX 79902

GIKAS, PAUL WILLIAM, medical educator; b. Lansing, Mich., July 23, 1928; s. John and Minnie (Neumann) G.; m. Lois Suzanne Haglund, Dec. 27, 1952; children— Sandra Jane, Sarah Elizabeth, Paula Suzanne. AB, U. Mich., 1950, MD, 1954. Diplomate: Am. Bd. Pathology. Chief lab. service VA Hosp., Ann Arbor, Mich., 1960-68; mem. faculty U. Mich. Med. Sch., Ann Arbor, 1959—, assoc. prof. pathology, 1966-69, prof., 1969-95, prof. emeritus, 1995—, faculty rep. to Big Ten Intercollegiate Conf., Nat. Collegiate Athletic Assn., 1982-88, asst. dean for admissions, 1990-97. Cons. Armed Forces Inst. Pathology, 1966-74 Author: The Accident Problem, 1976, Uropathology, 1976, Forensic Aspects of the Highway Crash, 1983; co-editor: The Prevention of Highway Injury, 1967. Mem. adv. com. traffic safety HEW, 1966-68; mem. Gov. Mich. Spl. Commn. Traffic Safety Mich., 1964; chmn. bd. dirs. Pub. Citizen, Inc., 1971-2002; co-trustee Center Study Responsive Law, Washington, 1969-71. Served to capt. M.C. AUS, 1956-58. Recipient Auto Safety award Med. Tribune, 1966-67, Distinguished Service award U. Mich., 1965, Disting. Svc. award U. Mich. Med. Ctr. Alumni Soc., 1998. Fellow Coll. Am. Pathologists, U.S. and Can. Acad. Pathology, Alpha Omega Alpha, Nu Sigma Nu. Lutheran. Achievements include rsch. with preservation of blood for transfusion by freezing and rsch. in pathogenesis of injury in highway crashes. Home: 1900 Mershon Dr Ann Arbor MI 48103-5939

GIL, DAVID GEORG, social policy educator; b. Vienna, Mar. 16, 1924; came to U.S., 1953; s. Oskar and Helene (Weiss) Engel; m. Eva Aviva Breslauer, Aug. 2, 1947; children: Daniel W. and Gideon R. (twins). BA, Hebrew U., 1957; MSW, U. Pa., Phila., 1958, DSW, 1963. Lic. social worker, Mass., ind. clin. social worker. Farmworker, laborer, 1939—43; counselor, tchr. Home for Dependent, Neglected and Delinquent Children, Tel-Mond, Palestine, 1943-45; probation officer Dept. Social Welfare, Palestine and Israel, 1945-53; fellow UN, Phila., 1953-54; asst. dir. Youth Probation Svc., Jerusalem, 1955-57; family counselor Jewish Family Svc., Phila., 1957-59; supr., rsch. assoc. Assn. Jewish Children, Phila., 1959-63; rsch. dir. Soc. to Prevent Cruelty to Children, Boston, 1963-64; from asst. to prof. social policy Brandeis U., Waltham, Mass., 1964—. Dir. Ctr. for Social Change, Heller Grad. Sch., Brandeis U., Waltham, 1984—, Kenneth L. Pray lectr. U. Pa., Phila., 1991; vis. prof. George Washington U. Sch. of Social Work, 1975-2002. Author: Violence Against Children, 1970, Unravelling Social Policy, 1973, 76, 81, 90, 92, The Challenge of Social Equality, 1976, Beyond the Jungle, 1979, Confronting Injustice and Oppression, 1998; editor: Child Abuse and Violence, 1979; co-editor: Toward Social and Economic Justice, 1985, The Future of Work, 1987; chair faculty senate Brandeis U., 1989-92. Rep. bd. trustees Brandeis U., 1990-94; co-chair Socialist Party, 1995-99; mem. exec. com. Nat. Jobs for All Coalition, 1997—. Rsch. grantee U.S. Children's Bur., Washington, 1965-73, project grantee Levinson Found., Boston, 1983, 85. Mem. NASW (del. assembly 1987-90, Social Worker of Yr. award 2000), NASW Mass., Assn. Humanist Sociology (pres. 1981), Am. Orthopsychiat. Assn. (bd. mem. 1990-93). E-mail: gil@brandeis.edu.

GILBERT, ALAN JAY, lawyer; b. Newark, Oct. 11, 1951; s. Stanley David and June Helene (Gordon) G. Sc.B. magna cum laude, Brown U., 1973; J.D. magna cum laude, U. Mich., 1977. Bar: Colo. 1977, U.S. Dist. Ct. Colo. 1977, U.S. Ct. Appeals (10th cir.) 1977, U.S. Ct. Appeals (9th cir.) 1978, U.S. Ct. Appeals (D.C. cir.) 1979, solicitor gen., State of Colo., Environ. engr. U.S. EPA, State of Rhode Island, Providence, 1973-74; mem. firm Sherman & Howard, Denver, 1977-1999; adj. prof. Sch. Bus. Adminstrn., lectr. Law Sch., U. Denver, 1984-92. Mem. editl. adv. bd. Environ. Law Reporter, 1994—1999. Trustee at large, Rocky Mt. Mineral Law Found., 1991-93, 95. Mem. ABA (vice chair natural resources sect.). Office: Colorado Dept of Law 1525 Sherman St Denver CO 80203-3665 Home: 1425 Cherryville Rd Greenwood Vlg CO 80121-1223

GILBERT, ARMIDA JENNINGS, American literature educator; b. Sumter, S.C., July 10, 1953; d. Joseph Gatliff and Katherine Armida (Jennings) G. BS, U. S.C., 1976, MA, 1986, PhD, 1989. Vis. asst. prof. U. S.C., Columbia, 1989-90; asst. prof. Kent (Ohio) State U., 1990-97, Auburn (Ala.) U., 1998-99, E. Ga. Coll., Statesboro, 1999—. Contg. author: The Historical Guide to Ralph Waldo Emerson, 2000, The Emerson Dilemma, 2000; asst. editor Bibliography of U.S. Literature, 1989, Contemporary Authors, 1986-87; editl. asst. Studies in the American Renaissance, 1985-89; contbr. articles to profl. jours. Advisor U. S.C. Alliance for Peace, 1988-90; interviewee for film women's studies U. S.C., 1989; reader Kent State U. Press, Longman Press, Prose Studies, others. Travel to Collections grant Nat. Endowment for the Humanities, 1992. Mem. MLA, Ralph Waldo Emerson Soc. (adv. bd. 1996—, founding mem.), Philolog. Assn. of the Carolinas (organizer spl. sessions 1991-95), Sigma Tau Delta (advisor 1993-94). Office: E Ga Coll Dept Humanities 1709 Chandler Rd Statesboro GA 30458-4950

GILBERT, ARTHUR CHARLES, aerospace engineer, consulting engineer; b. N.Y.C., Sept. 23, 1926; s. Phillip Saul and Annie (Taishoff) G.; children: Pamela Stephanie Gilbert Remis, Randi Ilene Gilbert Cutler. B Aero. Engring., NYU, 1946, M Aero. Engring., 1947, ScD in Engring., 1956. Registered profl. engr., N.Y., Mich., D.C., Washington. Rsch. engr., sr. exec. aerospace manufacturer various orgns., 1947-68; cons. CIA, 1964-68; v.p., mng. ptnr. Systems Technology Lab., Inc., 1968-70; mem. sci. staff divsn. sci. and tech. CIA, 1968-70; founder, bd. dirs. Auto-Train Corp., 1969-79; chief scientist Chief Naval Ops. Exec. Panel, 1970-75; v.p., dir. engring. R & D Data Solutions Corp., 1975-77; v.p. Unified Industries, 1977-78; with OAO Corp., 1978-81; pres. Arthur C. Gilbert, SCD, PE, Boston, 1981—. Consulting engr. in field; USN-asst. sec. Navy R&D, Washington, 1988—90; vis. prof. USN War Coll., Newport. Mem. Spitfire Soc. U.K., Cosmos Club Washington. Achievements include 2 patents for high speed machinery, helicopter propulsion systems; contributing to numerous articles and books on helicopters, high speed, rotating structures, acoustics, vibration and photo-elasticity. Home and Office: Arthur C Gilbert SCD PE 330 Beacon St Apt B23 Boston MA 02116-1106 E-mail: drArthur4@aol.com.

GILBERT, BEN WILLIAM, retired newspaper editor; b. N.Y.C., Feb. 10, 1918; s. Harry and Tessie (Wertheimer) Goldberg; m. Maurine Coffee, Mar. 11, 1941 (dec.); children: Ian R. Gilbert, Amy G. Mann. B of Social Sci., CCNY, 1937; MA in Journalism, U. Mo., 1939. Reporter St. Louis (Mo.) Star Times, 1940-41, Washington Post, Washington, 1941-45, city editor, day mng. editor, assoc. editor, 1945-70; on-air editor newsroom Sta. WETA-TV, Washington, 1970-71; gen. asst. to mayor Washington City Govt., 1972, planning dir., 1972-78. Cons. various orgns., Washington, 1979-84; mem. Nat. Capital Planning Commn., Washington, 1973-78. Author, editor: Ten Blocks From White House, 1968, Lifting the Veil From the 'Secret City': The Washington Post and the Racial Revolution, 1993. Mem. ethics com. Group Health Wash., Tacoma, 1985—, Landmarks Preservation Commn., 1985—, chair, 1986-91; bd. dirs. Pennsylvania Ave. Devel. Corp., Washington, 1974-78; steering com. Tacoma Cultural Plan, 1992-93; mem. Pub. Art working Group, Tacoma, 1993—; mem. adv. group on comprehensive plans Pierce County Citizens, 1993-94; mem. Group Health Med. Ctr. Coun., Tacom, 1985-86, 99—; vice-chair Self Help for Hard of Hearing People, Tacoma, 1999-2000, chair, 2000-2001. Recipient TV Emmy award D.C. TV Assn., 1970, State Historic Preservation award Wash. State Office Hist. Preservation, 1995, Disting. Citizen award Tacoma Mcpl. League, 1995, Silver Gavel award ABA, 1969. Mem. Am. Inst. Cert. Planners, City Club Tacoma (vol. editor newsletter, rsch. reports, bd. dirs.), City Club Tacoma (bd. dirs. 1986—), Phi Beta Kappa, Kappa Tau Alpha. Democrat. Avocations: photography, public affairs, reading, writing. Home and Office: 421 N 6th St Tacoma WA 98403-3211 Fax: 253-272-6158. E-mail: bengilbert@wasa-shhh.org.

GILBERT, BENTLEY BRINKERHOFF, history educator, retired; b. Mansfield, Ohio, Apr. 5, 1924; s. John Hopkinson Gilbert and Mary Bentley Brinkerhoff; children: Bentley Brinkerhoff Jr., Margaret Mary, Louis Haviland, Francis Hopkinson; m. Elsie Louise Meyer, Jan. 1946 (div. 1967); m. Ellen Margaretta MacVeagh, 1968 (div. 1984). BA, Miami U. Ohio, 1949; MA, U. Cin., 1950; PhD, U. Wis., 1954. Instr. U. Cin., 1950-51; asst. prof. Colo. Coll., Colorado Springs, 1951-54, assoc. prof., 1954-67; prof. U. Ill., Chgo., 1967-97, dean Grad. Coll., 1971—72, chmn. dept. history, 1988-91, ret., 1997. Mem. adv. bd. First Nat. Bank Mansfield, Ohio, 1967-84. Author: The Evolution of National Insurance in Great Britain: The Origins of the Welfare State, 1966, reprinted 1974, 97, Britain Since 1918, 1967, revised, 1980, British Social Policy, 1970, David Lloyd George: A Political Life, Vol. I, The Architect of Change 1863-1912, 1987, David Lloyd George: A Political Life, Vol. II, The Organizer of Victory 1912-1916, 1992 (Soc. Midland Authors award for biography), Britain 1914-1945: The Aftermath of Power, 1996; editor: The Heart of the Empire, 1973; editor Jour. Brit. Studies, U. Chgo., 1978-83; contbr. articles to profl. jours. Mem. exec. com. Young Dems. Colo., Colorado Springs, 1961-67; vestryman St. Elisabeth Episcopal Ch., Glencoe, Ill., 1976-78. Tech. sgt. USAAF, 1942-45. Grantee Am. Philos. Soc., 1961-72, U. Ill. Chgo., 1973; fellow Nat. Libr. Medicine, NIH, 1963-71, Guggenheim Found., 1973-74, U. Ill. Inst. for the Humanities, 1982-83. Fellow Royal Hist. Soc. Gt. Britain; mem. Univ. Club Chgo., Westbrook Country Club (Mansfield, Ohio). Avocations: reading, traveling. Home: 681 Home Rd S Mansfield OH 44906-3363 Office: U Ill Chgo 601 S Morgan St # 922 Chicago IL 60607-7100

GILBERT, BLAINE LOUIS, lawyer; b. Phila., Aug. 26, 1940; s. Arthur I. and Marcia R. (Kaufman) G.; m. Sondra Gilbert; children: Beth M., Kimberly J. AA, Balt. Jr. Coll., 1961; postgrad., Am. U., 1962; JD, U. Balt., 1965. Bar: Md. 1966, U.S. Dist. Ct. Md. 1968, U.S. Supreme Ct. 1974. Exec. asst. ins. commr. State of Md., Balt., 1965-66; assoc. Polovoy & Polovoy, Balt., 1966-72; ptnr. Angeletti & Gilbert, Balt., 1972-79, Gilbert & Levin, Balt., 1979-92, Blaine L. Gilbert and Assocs. P.A., Balt., 1993—. Mem. ABA, Balt. Bar Assn., Am. Immigration Lawyers Assn., Am. Judicature Soc., Md. Trial Lawyers Assn. Avocations: music, screenwriting. Home: 2B Dorsett Hills Ct Owings Mills MD 21117-1131 Office: Blaine L Gilbert & Assocs PA Lower Level 200 E Lexington St Baltimore MD 21202-3530 Fax: 410-539-6440. E-mail: blglaw@aol.com.

GILBERT, BRADLEY, professional tennis coach, former professional tennis player, former Olympic athlete; b. Oakland, Calif., Aug. 9, 1961; m. Kim Gilbert; 2 children: Zachary, Julian Elizabeth. Student, Foothills Jr. Coll., Pepperdine. Ranked 9th in U.S. Tennis Assn., 1993; coach Andre Agassi, 1994—; played in over 35 USTA tour events. Recipient Bronze medal Olympics, Seoul, 1988. Achievements include winning 20 profl. singles titles. Office: USTA 70 W Red Oak Ln White Plains NY 10604-3602

GILBERT, CHARLES E., III, lawyer; b. Boston, Mass, Apr. 17, 1949; s. Charles and Margaret (Perkins) G.; m. Linda P. Gilbert, Dec. 22, 1974 (div. 1986); children: Stacey, Meredith; m. Peggy Bragdon, Oct. 12, 1986; children: Seth, Sean; stepchildren: Rachelle Dixon Maietta, Vanessa Dixon McDougall. BA, Harvard U., 1972; JD, Boston Coll., 1977. Bar: Maine 1977, Mass. 1977, US Dist. Ct. Maine 1978, US Ct. Appeals (1st cir.) 1987, US Supreme Ct. 1999. Law clk. Maine Supreme Jud. Ct., Rockland, Maine, 1977-78; assoc., then ptnr. Vafiades, Brountas & Kominsky, Bangor, Maine, 1978-88; ptnr. Gilbert & Heitmann, Bangor, Maine, 1988-90; prin. Gilbert Law Offices, P.A., Bangor, Maine, 1990—, Gilbert & Greif, P.A. (formerly Gilbert Law Offices, P.A.), Bangor, Maine. Trustee Hampden Congl. Ch., 1988-91, pres. 1991-95. Mem.: John Waldo Ballou Am. Inn Ct. (treas. 1999—2001), Penobscot County Bar Assn. (exec. com. 2000—), Nat. Bd. Trial Advocacy (cert. civil trial practice), Am. Jud. Soc., Maine Trial Lawyers Assn., Maine Bar Assn. (pub. affairs com. 1984—), Spee Club, Harvard Club (chmn. schs. and scholarships com. East Maine chpt.). Republican. Home (Summer): 16 Lower Rd Steadman's Landing Dover Foxcroft ME 04426 Office: Gilbert & Greif PA PO Box 2339 82 Columbia St Bangor ME 04402-2339 Fax: 207-941-9871. E-mail: ceg@yourlawpartner.com.

GILBERT, CHARLES RICHARD ALSOP, physician, medical educator; b. Phila., May 26, 1916; s. Chauncey McLean and Frances Marguerite (Young) G.; m. Helene Scher, Dec. 24, 1973; children: Anita Ivonne, Charles Richard Alsop Jr. MD, U. Va., 1944. Bar: Am. Bd. Abdominal Surgeons; diplomate: Am. Bd. Obstetrics and Gynecology. Rotating intern N.Y.C. Hosp., 1944-45, asst. resident in internal medicine, 1945-46; resident in surgery Nix Hosp., San Antonio, 1946; resident in gen. surgery, chief female abdominal surgery Ryder Meml. Hosp., Hunacao, P.R., 1952-55; house staff gynecology Johns Hopkins Hosp., Balt., 1948-49; asst. resident in obstetrics U. Md., 1949, chief resident in obstetrics, 1949-50, asst. resident in gynecology, 1950-51, chief resident in gynecology, 1951-52, assoc. in gynecology, instr. gynecol. pathology, 1952; asst. clin. prof. obstetrics and gynecology U. P.R., 1952-55, George Washington U., 1972-74, assoc. clin. prof. obstetrics and gynecology, 1974-93, clin. prof. ob/gyn., 1994—; chief gynecology Doctors Hosp., 1973—; sr. attending in obstetrics and gynecology Washington Hosp. Center. Instr. internal medicine Randolph Sch. Aviation, San Antonio, 1946; cons. U.S. Air Force in obstetrics, gynecology, female urology, 1952-54 Author: Childbirth-The Modern Guide to Expectant Mothers, 1960, Better Health for Women, 1964, Abdominal Pelvic Surgery, 1969; co-editor, editor: Symposiumon Abdominal Pelvic Surgery, 1966; contbr. articles to profl. jours.; Mem. editorial staff: Jour. Abdominal Surgery, 1964-74. Served with M.C. USAF, as chief internal medicine, 1946-48, Selfridge AFB, Mt. Clemens, Mich. Fellow ACS (founding fellow), Am. Coll. Obstetrics and Gynecology, Am. Soc. Abdominal Surgeons (teaching faculty 1964-74, mem. exec. com. 1964-74, v.p. 1969-70, pres. 1971-72), Internat. Coll. Surgeons (U.S. sect., regent, exec. com. 1981—, chmn. bd. regents 1983-84, sec. 1982-83, membership chmn. 1983, 2d pres.-elect 1985, pres.-elect 1986, pres. 1987-88, coordinator diplomatic relations 1985—, spl. advisor to pres. 1989-90, mem. internat. bd. govs. 1990, sec. N.Am. fedn. 1991-92, Regent of Yr. award 1981, emeritus 1992, bd. trustees 1993, 96-98, hon. fellow 1995); mem. Pan Am. Med. Assn., Med. Soc. D.C., AMA, Med. and Surgery Soc. Johns Hopkins Hosp., Douglass Obstet. and Gynecol. Soc., Nat. Rifle Assn., African Safari Club Washington (v.p. 1974-77, pres. 1977), Am. Outdoors Council (dir.), Hunting Hall of Fame Found. (dir. 1978), Jefferson Soc. Club: Boone and Crockett. Clubs: Boone and Crockett. Achievements include developing first audiovisual med. corr. teaching courses for continuing med. edn., 1973. Home and Office: 705 E Franklin Ave Silver Spring MD 20901-4707

GILBERT, CREIGHTON EDDY, art historian; b. Durham, N.C., June 6, 1924; s. Allan H. and Katharine (Everett) G. BA, NYU, 1942, PhD, 1955; DHL (hon.), Adelphi U., 1990, U. Louisville, 1997. Assoc. prof. Brandeis U., 1961-65, Sidney and Ellen Wien prof. history of art, 1965-69; prof. Queens Coll. City U. N.Y., 1969-77; Jacob Gould Schurman prof. art history Cornell U., 1977-81; prof. Yale U., 1981-2000, prof. emeritus, 2000—. Fulbright sr. lectr. U. Rome, 1951-52; fellow Netherlands Inst. for Advanced Study, 1972-73; vis. prof. U. Leiden, 1974-75; Zacks Found. vis. prof. Hebrew U. Jerusalem, 1985. Author: Change in Piero della Francesca, 1968, History of Renaissance Art, 1972, The Works of Girolamo Savoldo, 1986, Poets Seeing Artists' Work: Instances from the Italian Renaissance, 1991, Michelangelo On and Off the Sistine Ceiling, 1994, Piero della Francesca et Giorgione: Problèmes d'Interpretation, 1994, Caravaggio and His Two Cardinals, 1995, The Saints' Three Reasons for Paintings in Churches, 2001, How Fra Angelico and Signorelli Saw the End of the World, 2002; editor: Italian Art 1400-1500, Sources and Documents, 1979, enlarged Italian edit., 1988; editor-in-chief: The Art Bull, 1980-85; translator: Complete Poems and Selected Letters of Michelangelo, 1963, 3d edit., 1979. Recipient Mather award Coll. Art Assn., 1964 Fellow Am. Acad. Arts and Scis., Ateneo Veneto (fgn.). Office: Yale U Dept Art History Box 208272 New Haven CT 06520-8272

GILBERT, DAVID ERWIN, retired academic administrator, physicist; b. Fresno, Calif., June 23, 1939; s. Erwin Azel and Hester (Almond) G.; m. Carolyn Faye Parker, June 24, 1960; children: Ronald David, Joan Elaine. AB, U. Calif.-Berkeley, 1962; MA, U. Oreg., 1964, PhD, 1968. Prof. physics Eastern Oreg. U., La Grande, 1968-98, dean. acad. affairs, 1977-83, pres., 1983-98; pres. emeritus. Vis. rschr. Obs. Paris, 1975-82; commr. N.W. Assn. Schs. and Colls., 1982-88. Contbr. articles on physics to profl. jours. V.p. Ea. Oreg. Regional Arts Coun., 1979-80; vice chair, bd. dirs. Oreg. Ed-Net, 1989-97, Oreg. Pub. Broadcasting Found., 1991-93; mem. Oreg. Task Force Superconducting Super Collider, 1987, Oreg. Pub. Broadcasting Commn., 1991-01, Oreg. Bd. Forestry, 1991-2002, chair, 1996-2002; mem. Gov.'s Transition Team, 1990, Oreg. visibility adv. com. Dept. Environ. Quality, 1990-91; bd. dirs. Blue Mountains Natural Resources Inst., 1990-98, N.E. Oreg. Area Health Edn. Ctr., Gov.'s Telecomms. Forum Coun., 1996-97; bd. dirs. Keep Oreg. Green Assn., 1999-2001, Tillamook Forest Heritage Trust, 1999-

2002, North Ctrl. U., Ariz., 2002—. Grantee NATO; grantee Research Corp. U.S.A., U.S. Govt., pvt. founds. Mem. Am. Assn. Colls. and Univs. (bd. dirs. 1995-97, chmn. com. econ. and cmty. devel. 1990-92), Am. Assn. Physics Tchrs. (pres. Oreg. chpt. 1973-74), Pacific N.W. Assn. Coll. Physics (bd. dirs. 1970-74), Sigma Xi, Sigma Pi Sigma, Phi Kappa Phi. Democrat. Home: PO Box 36 Joseph OR 97846-0036 E-mail: deg@starband.net.

GILBERT, DAVID R. public relations executive; Press sec. to Gov. James Thompson, Ill.; pres. David R. Gilbert & Assocs.; gen. mgr. Golin/Harris Comms., Chgo., 1993-96; pres. Golin/Harris Internat., Chgo., 1996—2001. Office: Golin/Harris Internat 10th Fl 111 E Wacker Dr Fl 10 Chicago IL 60601-4305

GILBERT, DAVID WALLACE, retired aerospace engineer; b. Berkeley, Calif., June 20, 1923; s. Wallace William and Elizabeth Wilson (Findlay) G.; m. Jeanne Wilson Gillette, June 27, 1948; children: Laurence R., LeeAnn, Dean A., Barbara L., John L., Mary H. BSME, U. Calif., Berkeley, 1948. Flight test analyst Convair, San Diego, 1948-51, dynamics engr., 1951-55, design specialist, 1955-59, chief GN&C systems, 1959-62; mgr. GN&C JSC Apollo Project Office NASA, Houston, 1962-64, br. chief GN&C Systems div., 1964-89. With U.S. Army, 1942-45, ETO. Mem. AIAA (assoc. fellow). Achievements include technical development for numerous aspects of F-102, F 106, CV-880 and 990 aircraft and Apollo and space shuttle systems. Home: 10019 Cedarhurst Dr Houston TX 77096-5102 E-mail: SAM.Dave@worldnet.att.net.

GILBERT, DEBBIE ROSE, entrepreneur; b. Indpls., Jan. 18, 1961; d. James Taylor and Rosemary (Robinson) G. BA, Ind. U., 1984; diploma in computer literacy, St. Augustine Coll., Chgo., 1995. Student typing asst. Shortridge H.S./Indpls. Pub. Schs./Bd. Schs. Commrs., Indpls., 1978-79; substitute tchr. Indpls. Pub. Schs./Bd. Sch. Commrs., 1985-89, Washington Twp. Schs., Indpls., 1992; CHA housewatcher, clothes distbr. The Inner Voice, Inc., Chgo., 1994-95; vol. Lakefront Single Room Occupancy Employment Program, Chgo., 1997—. Dep. registrar O.N.E./Bd. Election Commrs., Chgo., 1996—; mem. People for the Am. Way, Chgo., 1995-96; mem. Access Living, Chgo., 1996—, mem. Southern Poverty Law Ctr., Tchg. Tolerance, Militia Task Force, Klanwatch Org., Montgomery, 1998—. Mem. ACLU, NOW, AAUW, NAACP, The Natl. Mus. of Women in the Arts Org., OWL (The Older Women's League), The Voice of Midlife & Older Women, Wash. D.C., Mental Health Consumer Edn. Consortium, Inc. Democrat. Baptist. Avocations: modeling, singing, race walking, Bingo, reading. Home: 5012 N Winthrop Ave Apt 224 Chicago IL 60640-3124 Office: 4753 N Broadway Ste 632/808 Chicago IL 60640-4986

GILBERT, DONALD ROY, lawyer; b. Phila., June 6, 1946; BA, Stanford U., 1968; JD, U. Calif., 1971. Bar: Calif. 1972, Ariz. 1972. Ptnr., dir. Fennemore Craig, Phoenix, 1972—. Mem. ABA, State Bar Ariz., State Bar Calif., Maricopa County Bar Assn. Office: Fennemore Craig 3003 N Central Ste 2600 Phoenix AZ 85012-2913

GILBERT, DOUGLAS BRAINERD, management executive; b. Miami, Fla., July 4, 1957; s. Thomas Marshall Gilbert Jr. and Jeanne Brainerd; m. Susan M. Pace, Apr. 28, 2001; 1 child, Joshua Daniel. BA in Philosphy/Theology, Boston Coll., 1979; MDiv, Maryknoll Sch. of Theology, 1983; MA in Counseling, Duquesne U., 1995. Microsoft cert. sys. engr., cert. project mgmt. profl. Cons. Worklife Solutions, Old Greenwich, Conn., 1997; assignment dir. Deloitte & Touche, LLP, N.Y.C., 1998-2000; sr. project mgr. Exodus Comms., Herndon, Va., 2000-01; svc. dir. Cable & Wireless, Sterling, Va., 2001—. Chmn. bd. SMA African Art Mus., 1997-98; exec. bd. Internat. Liaison of Lay Vols. in Mission, Washington, 1988-90. Recipient Eagle Scout Boy Scouts Am., 1974. Mem.: Am. Mgmt. Assn., Project Mgmt. Inst. Republican. Roman Catholic. Avocations: travel, fishing, ham radio. Office: Cable & Wireless 45901 Nokes Blvd Sterling VA 20166-6516 E-mail: dbg1999@hotmail.com.

GILBERT, ELAYNE RHODA, writer; b. Bklyn., Oct. 22, 1940; d. Henry Albert and Sara Gilbert. BA, U. Miami, Fla., 1964; MA, U. Miami, 1972; AA, Miami Dade C.C., 1996. With Dade County Cir. and County Cts., 1980—84; pollworker Dade County Election Day, 1998, 1990—2000, Broward County Election Day, 2001. Avocations: reading, plays and movies, music, book collecting.

GILBERT, ELMER GRANT, aerospace engineering educator, control theorist; b. Joliet, Ill., Mar. 29, 1930; s. Harry A. and Florence A. (Otterstrom) G.; m. Lois M. Verbrugge, Dec. 27, 1973. BSEE, U. Mich., 1952, MSEE, 1953, PhD in Instrumentation Engring., 1956. Instr. U. Mich., Ann Arbor, 1954-56, asst. prof., 1957-59, assoc. prof., 1959-63, prof. aerospace engring., 1963—. Founder, Applied Dynamics Inc., Ann Arbor. Patentee computer devices, 1968-74. Fellow IEEE (Control Engring. Field award 1994), AAAS; mem. Nat. Acad. Engring., Soc. Indsl. and Applied Math. Office: U Mich Dept Aerospace Engring Ann Arbor MI 48109-2140 E-mail: elmerg@umich.edu.

GILBERT, FREDERICK E. development planner, Africanist, consultant; b. Mpls., May 28, 1939; s. Eugene Lester and Anne Cecelia (Omlie) G.; m. Jane Arey, June 30, 1962; children: Erik O., Christopher A., Peter A. BA, U. Minn., 1961; MALD, Tufts U., 1963, PhD, 1976. Desk officer for Niger, Upper Volta, Cote d'Ivoire, Dahomey and Togo U.S. AID, Washington, 1974-76, asst. dir. Yaounde, Cameroon, 1976-80, chief Africa econ. policy and analysis Washington, 1980-81, dir. Sahel and West Africa, 1981-83, prin. officer Dar es Salaam, Tanzania, 1983-86, dep. mission dir. Khartoum, Sudan, 1986-88, mission dir., 1988-90, regional dir. Abidjan, Cote d'Ivoire, 1990-93; ind. cons., 1994-97; dir. Famine Early Warning Sys., 1998-2000; ind. cons. Falls Church, Va., 2000—. Mem. ACLU, Am. Fgn. Svc. Assn., Amnesty Internat., Sierra Club, World Resources Inst. (policy consultative group on natural resources mgmt. 1994-97). Episcopalian. Avocations: skiing, tennis, cycling.

GILBERT, GLENN GORDON, linguistics educator; b. Montgomery, Ala., Sept. 17, 1936; s. William H. and Margaret (Christensen) G.; m. Erika Wrede, Aug. 8, 1964 (div. Nov. 1993); children: Alexander Martin, Christa Selene; m. Sharon Wright Pape, July 23, 1994. AB in German Lang. and Lit., U. Chgo., 1957; postgrad., U. Frankfurt, Fed. Republic Germany, 1957-59; Diplôme de la Langue Française with honors, Sorbonne, U. Paris, 1960; PhD in Linguistics, Harvard U., 1963. Instr. Germanic langs. and lits. U. Tex., Austin, 1963-66, asst. prof. Germanic langs., 1967-70; vis. asst. prof. linguistics Can. Summer Sch. Linguistics, U. Alta., Edmonton, summer 1966; Fulbright lectr. linguistics U. Marburg, Fed. Republic Germany, 1966-67; assoc. prof. So. Ill. U., Carbondale, 1970-74, prof., 1975—, chmn. dept. linguistics, 1987—89, 1999—2002; Fulbright lectr. linguistics U. Mainz, Fed. Republic Germany, 1973-74; Z.W.O. research fellow in creole langs. U. Nijmegen, The Netherlands, 1984-85. Active numerous univ. linguistics coms. and councils; bd. dirs., mem. editorial bd., Ill. bus. rep. Papers in Linguistics, 1979-87; pres. Linguistic Research Inc., 1983-87. Founder, editor Journal of Pidgin and Creole Languages, 1985-2001; author: Linguistic Atlas of Texas German, 1972; editor: (books) Texas Studies in Bilingualism, 1970, The German Language in America, 1971, Pidgin and Creole Languages: Essays in Memory of John E. Reinecke, 1987, Pidgin and Creole Linguistics in the Twenty-First Century, 2002; co-editor (with Jacob Ornstein) Problems in Applied Educational Sociolinguistics, 1978; editor and translator: Pidgin and Creole Languages: Selected Essays by Hugo Schuchardt, 1980; editor: (book series) Studies in Ethnolinguistics, 1993—; contbr. numerous articles to profl. jours. and chpts. to books in field; also reviews. Translator, interpreter various cmty. orgns. NDEA fellow in Swedish, Harvard U., 1961-63; research grantee U. Tex.-Austin, 1963-70, Nat. Carl Schurz Meml. Fund, 1968, So. Ill. U.-Carbondale, 1970-84, NEH, 1981, Am. Philos. Soc., 1982; numerous invited lectures. Mem. Soc. Caribbean Linguistics, Soc. for Pidgin and Creole Linguistics. Home: 166 Union Grove Rd Carbondale IL 62901-7687 Office: So Ill U Dept Linguistics Carbondale IL 62901 E-mail: ggilbert@siu.edu., glenngilbert@msn.com.

GILBERT, GREG, former professional hockey coach; Profl. hockey player N.Y. Islanders, Chgo. Blackhawks, N.Y. Rangers, St. Louis Blues; bench boss St. Louis Blues Am. Hockey League affiliate, Worcester, Mass.; asst. coach Calgary Flames, 2000—01, head coach, 2001—02. Recipient AHL Coach of Yr., Louis A.R. Pieri Meml. award, Minor League Coach of Yr., The Sporting News.

GILBERT, HAMLIN MILLER, JR., publishing executive; b. Bridgport, Conn., Mar. 12, 1940; s. Hamlin Miller and Charlotte E. (Munn) G.; m. Emmy Lou Chatterton, July 20, 1963; children: Bradley, Kim. BA, Cornell U., 1962. Fin. analyst Chem. Bank, N.Y.C., 1963-64; sales rep. Continental Can Co., Teterboro, N.J., 1964-65, Time, Inc., N.Y.C., 1965-70; package goods mgr. Time Mag., 1970-75, travel advt. mgr., 1975-80, divsn. mgr., 1980-83, assoc. N.Y. dir., 1983-85, U.S. dir. spl. sect., 1985-92; N.Y. advt. sales dir. Smithsonian Mag., N.Y.C., 1992-95, dir. bus. devel., 1995-97, mktg. exec. web site, advt. svcs. dir., 1997-2000, ret., 2000. Editor spl. advt. sect., Time-Am. Cup, 1987, Time-Winter Olympic Preview, 1987. V.p. comm. New Canaan H.S. Sports Council, Conn., 1987-89; instr. U.S. Power Squadron, Darien, Conn., 1986—. Mem. Travel Rsch. Assn. (dir. 1979-81), Cornell U. Alumni Assn. (area dir. 1980-95), Woodway Country Club (bd. dirs. 1980-86), Austin Healey Club Am. Republican. Episcopalian. Avocations: sailing, skiing, golf, tennis, gardening, scuba diving (cert.). Home: 774 Norton St Longboat Key FL 34228-1448 E-mail: sandem133@aol.com.

GILBERT, HAROLD STANLEY, retired warehousing company executive; b. Ft. Worth, Jan. 22, 1924; s. Sydney Ralph and Reba Samuels (Lever) G.; m. Jeanne Schwarz, Apr. 6, 1950; children: Marsha Gilbert, Mark S. (dec. 1994), John L. BA, U. Tex., 1947, MEd., 1949; grad., Air Command and Staff Coll., 1961, Air War Coll., 1970, Indsl. Coll. Armed Forces, 1970. Sci. tchr., coach Houston Ind. Schs., 1949-51; asst. prin., head sci. dept., athletic dir., coach USAF Dependents Sch. System, Germany, 1953-55; v.p. Coastal Bag & Bagging Corp., Houston, 1968-71; exec. v.p., gen. mgr. Coastal Storehouse, Inc., Houston, 1968-88; chmn., CEO Gilbert & Sons Warehouse and Distbn., Houston, 1988-99; ret., 1999. Mem. def. strategy seminar Nat. War Coll., 1973. Parade marshal Bicentennial Armed Forces Week Parade, Houston, 1976; dir. gen. Armed Forces Week, 1977; bd. dirs. Houston Coun. USO, 1977-82, v.p., 1981; vol. St. Luke's Episcopal. Hosp. Aux., 1999—; docent Houston Zool. Gardens, 1999—; vol. M.D. Anderson Cancer Ctrs. Rotary House, 1999—; dir. The Chancellor's Coun., U. Tex. Sys., 2001. With AUS, 1943-45; USAF, 1951-53; col. USAF ret. Decorated Legion of Merit, Bronze Star, Meritorious Svc. medal, Purple Heart with oak leaf cluster, combat infantry badge; recipient USAFR Disting. Ednl. Achievement award, 1975, U.S. and Philippine Presdl. citations. Mem. Tex. Warehouse Assn. (charter, hon.), Houston Warehouse and Transfer Assn. (pres. 1980, 89-90), Air Force Assn. (life, v.p. chpt. 1977-78, pres. 1978-79, Tex. conv. chmn. 1976), Res. Officers Assn. (life, pres. Eric Ellington chpt. 1974-75, chmn. rules com. 1975, mem. Tex. mil. affairs com. 1975-78), Air War Coll. Alumni Assn. (life), Nat. Fedn. Temple Brotherhoods (dir.), Jewish Chautauqua Soc. (chmn. S.W. region 1964-70), Houston C. of C. (mil. affairs com. 1969—, vice-chmn. Air Force subcom. 1978-79), T Assn. U. Tex., Houston Tex. Ex-Students Assn., Mil. Order World Wars (life), Nat. Hist. Soc., Houston Livestock Show and Rodeo Assn. (life), Elks (life), Rotary (pres. activities Houston and Harris County clubs 1969-70, club sec. 1981-87, pres. University Area 1999-2000, Paul Harris fellow 1985), Phi Delta Kappa, Sigma Alpha Mu. Home: 476 N Post Oak Ln Houston TX 77024-5911 E-mail: colonelg@texas.net.

GILBERT, HARRY EPHRAIM, JR., retired hotel executive; b. Phila., Feb. 1, 1931; s. Harry Ephraim and Anna (Chilton) G.; children: Ronald C., Glen G.; m. Jacqueline J. Newton. BS in Hotel Adminstrn., Pa. State U., 1954. Resident mgr. Benjamin Franklin Hotel, Phila., 1954-71, gen. mgr., 1971-77, Cherry Hill Inns, N.J., 1977-78, Holiday Inn-City Line, Phila., 1978-80, Colony Inn, New Haven, 1980-81; sr. oper. analyst, gen. mgr. Aramark Corp., Phila., 1981-00; ret., 2000. Lectr. Hotel Sch., Pa. State U., 1956-58, Drexel U., Phila., 1962-63 Bd. dirs. Saratoga Council Boy Scouts Am., 1983-86; bd. dirs. Saratoga Conv. and Tourism Bur., 1985— ; mem. ch. council Luth. Ch., Saratoga Springs. Mem. N.Y. Hotel/Motel Assn., Phila. Hotel and Motor Inn Assn. (sec. 1971-72, v.p. 1973-74, pres. 1975-76), Pa. Hotel Restaurant Soc. (sec.-treas. 1973-74), Pa. Hotel Motor Inn Assn. (dir. 1975-76, treas. 1976-77), N.J. Hotel-Motel Assn. (dir. 1977-78), Hotel-Motel Greeter Internat., Pa. State Hotel Greeters (pres. 1952-54, 74-79), Phila. Press Assn., Pa. State Alumni Club Phila., Hotel Sales Mgrs. Assn., Chestnut St. Assn. (dir. 1971-76), Skal of N. Am. (treas. 1979-80, sec. 1980-86, v.p. 87-88) Clubs: Skal of North Am. (treas. 1979-80, sec. 1980-86, v.p. 1987-88). Home: 152 Fox Chase Dr Delran NJ 08075-2322 E-mail: hgilbert@webtv.net.

GILBERT, HEATHER CAMPBELL, manufacturing company executive; b. Mt. Vernon, N.Y., Nov. 20, 1944; d. Ronald Ogston and Mary Lodivia (Campbell) G. BS in Math. (Nat. Merit scholar), Stanford U., 1967; MS in Computer Sci. (NSF fellow), U. Wis., 1969. With Burroughs Corp., 1969-82, sr. mgmt. systems analyst, 1975-77, mgr. mgmt. systems activity Pasadena, Calif., 1977-82; mgr. software product mgmt. Logical Data Mgmt. Inc., Covina, Calif., 1982-83, dir. mktg., 1983, v.p. bus. devel., 1983-84, v.p. prof. svcs., 1984-85; mgr. software devel. Unisys Corp., Mission Viejo, Calif., 1985—. Founding bd. dirs., chmn. Breast Cancer Survivors Non-profit Orgn. Republican. Home: 21113 Calle De Paseo Lake Forest CA 92630-7037 Office: Unisys Corp 25725 Jeronimo Rd Mission Viejo CA 92691-2792 E-mail: MsHeatherG@mindspring.com., heather.gilbert@unisys.com.

GILBERT, HOWARD ALDEN, economics educator; b. Spokane, Wash., Feb. 1, 1935; s. Alden Phineas and Hester Anne (Warner) G.; m. Lucille Dorothy Weaver, June 28, 1957; children: Douglas Alden, Daniel William, Dawnna Faye Gilbert Berndt, Debra Anne Gilbert La Croix. BA, Cen. Bible Inst., Springfield, Mo., 1957; BS, Wash. State U., 1961, MA, 1962; PhD, Oreg. State U., 1967; postgrad., Vanderbilt U., 1971. Asst. prof. S.D. State U., Brookings, 1966-70, assoc. prof., 1970-76, prof., 1976—2001; ret., 2001. Expert witness retained by various attys. Mem. Mensa (pres. S.D. chpt. 1989-91, v.p. 1992-94, 96-97), Mortar Bd., Phi Kappa Phi (pres., v.p., sec., marshall), Pi Gamma Mu (sec., v.p., pres.), Gamma Sigma Delta (treas., pres.), Alpha Zeta, Omicron Delta Epsilon, Lambda Chi Alpha (head advisor 1967-97, ednl. advisor 1997—, order of merit, Alumni Hall of Fame). Democrat. Avocations: motorcycling, building restoration, running, piano, photography. Home: 708 8th St Apt 7 Brookings SD 57006-1559

GILBERT, HOWARD EARL, lawyer; b. Chgo., Apr. 3, 1947; BS, U. Ill., 1969; JD, DePaul U., 1972. Bar: Ill. 1972, U.S. Dist. Ct. (no. dist.) Ill. 1972, U.S. Tax Ct. 1973, U.S. Ct. Appeals (7th cir.) 1974, U.S. Supreme Ct. 1979, Fla. 1993. Atty. Altheimer & Gray, Chgo., 1972—74, Panter, Nelson & Bernfield, Chgo., 1974—75, Herman, Tannebaum, Levine & Gilbert, Chgo., 1975—82, Gilbert, Shapiro & Richman, Chgo., 1982—85, Howard E. Gilbert & Assocs., Wilmette, Ill., 1986—. Mem. ATLA, ABA, Ill. Trial Lawyers Assn., Ill. State Bar Assn., Chgo. Bar Assn., North Suburban Bar Assn., Aircraft Owners and Pilots Assn., Theta Chi Fraternity. Avocations: flying, boating. Home: 219 Beech St Highland Park IL 60035-4103 Office: 1000 Skokie Blvd Ste LL31 Wilmette IL 60091 E-mail: justiceb@aol.com.

GILBERT, HOWARD N(ORMAN), lawyer, director; b. Chgo., Aug. 19, 1928; s. Norman Aaron and Fannie (Cohn) G.; m. Jacqueline Glasser, Feb. 16, 1957; children: Norman Abraham, Harlan Wayne, Joel Kenneth, Sharon. PhB, U. Chgo., 1947; JD, Yale U., 1951. Bar: Ill 1951, U.S. Dist. Ct. (no. dist.) Ill. 1955, U.S. Ct. Appeals (7th cir.) 1956. Ptnr. Rusnak, Deutsch & Gilbert, Chgo., 1962-79, Aaron, Schimberg, Hess & Gilbert, Chgo., 1980-84; sr. ptnr. Holleb & Coff, Chgo., 1984-2000, Wildman, Harrold, Chgo., 2000—. Bd. dirs. Jewish Fedn. Met. Chgo., 1977-83; chmn. bd. dirs., pres. Mt. Sinai Hosp. Med. Ctr., Chgo., 1968-69; trustee Chgo. Hosp. Coun., 1979-84; mem. Bd. Jewish Edn., 1972-77; mem. vis. com. Coll. of U. Chgo., 1997-2003. Mem. ABA, Chgo. Bar Assn., Chgo. Coun. Lawyers, Ill. Soc. Health Lawyers, Standard Club, Bryn Mawr Country Club. Democrat. Jewish. Office: Wildman Harrold Allen & Dixon 225 W Wacker Dr Ste 3000 Chicago IL 60606-1224 E-mail: gilbert@wildmanharrold.com.

GILBERT, HOWARD WILLIAM, JR., lawyer; b. Washington, Dec. 10, 1931; s. Howard William and Mirian Keener (King) G.; m. Lillian Janine Poitte, Oct. 3, 1953 (div. Jan. 1983); children: Elizabeth, Linda, Wayne, Scott; m. Lois Histand, Apr. 23, 1983. AB, U. Md., 1953; JD, Georgetown U., 1961. Bar: Md. 1962, U.S. Dist. Ct. Md. 1965. Asst. mgr. underwriting GEICO, Washington, 1955-65; mem. Gilbert, Marks & DiGirolamo and predecessor firms, Hagerstown, Md., 1965—. Served to capt. USAF, 1953-55, 59-60. Mem. Washington County Bar Assn. (pres. 1981, 82), Md. State Bar Assn. Democrat. Presbyterian. Office: Gilbert Marks & DiGirolamo 35 E Washington St Hagerstown MD 21740-5605

GILBERT, J. PHIL, federal judge; b. 1949; BS, U. Ill., 1971; JD, Loyola U., Chgo., 1974. Ptnr. Gilbert & Gilbert, Carbondale, Ill., 1974-83, Gilbert, Kimmel, Huffman & Prosser, Carbondale, 1983-88; circuit judge First Jud. Circuit, Ill., 1988-92; fed. judge U.S. Dist. Ct. (so. dist.) Ill., Benton, 1992—, chief judge, 1993—. Spl. asst. atty. gen. Pub. Aid Enforcement Divsn., 1974-75; asst. city atty. City of Carbondale, 1975-78; active Nat. Coun. Govt. Ethics Laws, 1988—; mem. Ill. State Bd. Elections, 1982, vice chmn., chmn., 1983-85. Bd. dirs. Friends of Morris Libr., 1988—; active Edn. Coun. 100, 1989—, Boy Scouts Am. Mem. Ill. State Bar, Jackson County Bar Assn., Ill. Judges Assn. (mem. com. jud. retention), Phi Alpha Delta. Office: US Dist Ct 301 W Main St Benton IL 62812-1362

GILBERT, JAMES CAYCE, minister; b. Nashville, Feb. 26, 1925; s. Gettis and Delia Mae (Snyder) G.; m. Freda Mae Mitchell, Sept. 3, 1949; children—Elizabeth, Suzanne, Kathryn, Rosalie. BA, Bethel Coll., McKenzie, Tenn., 1945, D.D. (hon.), 1976; B.D., Cumberland Presbyn. Theol. Sem., McKenzie, 1947; MA, Scarritt Coll., Nashville, 1948. Ordained to ministry Cumberland Presbyn. Ch., 1944; asso. pastor West Nashville Cumberland Presbyn. Ch., 1947-48; pastor River Oaks Cumberland Presbyn. Ch., Houston, 1948-55, Trinity Cumberland Presbyn. Ch., Ft. Worth, 1956-64; exec. dir. Cumberland Presbyn. Children's Home, Denton, Tex., 1964-90, dir. devel., 1991-94; moderator gen. assembly Cumberland Presbyn. Ch., 1979-80. Stated clk., Red River Presbytery of the Cumberland Presbyn. Ch., 1993—. Mem. Nat. Assn. Homes Children, Southwestern Assn. Children's Home (past pres.), Tex. Assn. Execs. Homes Children (past pres.), Lions, Masons, K.T. Democrat. Home: 3720 W Biddison St Fort Worth TX 76109-2705

GILBERT, JAMES EASTHAM, academic administrator; b. Bridgeport, Conn., July 1, 1929; s. Carl Ludwig and Anna Maude (Eastham) G.; m. Betty Lee Blankenship, Aug. 26, 1953; 1 child, Gregory Eastham. BS in Psychology, U. N.Mex., 1952, MA in Psychology, 1959; PhD in Psychology, Am. U., 1969. Interviewer Va. State Employment Service, Alexandria, 1952-53; tng. officer Nat. Security Agy., Washington, 1953-55, rsch. psychologist Ft. Meade, Md., 1957-64, Hdqrs., Sec. to Air Staff, USAF, Washington, 1955-57; assoc. dean adminstrn. Northeastern U., Boston, 1964-71; assoc. vice-chancellor Ind. U.-Purdue U., Ft. Wayne, 1971-78; v.p. acad. affairs Pittsburg (Kans.) State U., 1978-86, interim pres., 1983; pres. East Stroudsburg (Pa.) U., 1986-96, pres. emeritus, 1996—; spl. asst. to provost Med. U. S.C., 1996—. NCES fellow, 1998. Mem. Sigma Xi, Psi Chi, Phi Kappa Phi, Omicron Delta Kappa. Democrat. Home: 1296 Waterfront Dr Mount Pleasant SC 29464-9493 E-mail: gilbertj@musc.edu.

GILBERT, JOAN STULMAN, retired public relations executive; b. NYC, May 10, 1934; m. Phil E. Gilbert Jr., Oct. 6, 1968; children: Linda Cooper, Dana McGrk, Patricia Novajosky. Student, Conn. Coll. Women, 1951-53. Br. coord. Vol. Svc. Bur., Westchester, NY, 1970-72; pub. rels. dir. Westchester Lighthouse, 1972-76; exec. dir. Westchester Heart Assn., 1976-77; mgr. cmty. rels. Texaco Inc., White Plains, NY, 1977-97. Vice chmn. ARC; chmn. The Street Theater, 1995—97; bd. dirs. Am. Heart Assn., Westchester Philharm., Jazz Forum Arts; former bd. dirs. Choate Rosemary Hall, United Way of Westchester; former bd. dirs., former trustee Westchester Coun. for the Arts; trustee, former bd. dirs. Teatown Lake Reservation. Recipient award, Youth Theater Interactions, Westchester Hispanic Coalition, Women in Comms., Am. Heart Assn., Am. Diabeters Assn., Westchester Putnam Affirmative Action Program, Arthritis Found., ARC, Urban League Westchester. Mem.: Sales and Mktg. Exec. Westchester (former dir.), Women in Comm. (award), Advt. Club (dir.), Pub. Rels. Soc. Am. (chpt. pres. 1977), Westchester County Assn. Home: The Croft 1595 Spring Valley Rd Ossining NY 10562-1634 E-mail: gilbertjs@aol.com.

GILBERT, JOHN B. retired electric and power company official; b. Wilmington, Del., Nov. 9, 1956; s. William Edgar and Helen (Ginn) G.; m. Meralyn Gilbert; children: Jamie, Amanda, Chris. BA, Rollins Coll., 1978; postgrad., U. Fla., 1980-82. Supr. corp. environ. affairs Savannah (Ga.) Electric and Power Co., 1982-96; ret., 1996. Recipient So. Superlative award So. Co., Atlanta, 1992. Mem. Navy League, Air Force Assn. Avocations: reading, computers, model building. Home: 118 W Gazebo Ln Savannah GA 31410-3949

GILBERT, JOHN HUMPHREY VICTOR, speech scientist, educator; b. Bath, Somerset, Eng., Mar. 19, 1941; s. Daniel and Nancy (Johns) G.; m. Carolyn; children: Eliot Daniel, Oliver Gaius, Kristen. Grad., U. London; PhD, Purdue U., 1966. Asst. prof. U. B.C., 1966-69, assoc. prof., 1969-74, prof., 1974—, Med. Research Council postdoctoral scholar, 1969-74, head div. audiology and speech sci., dir. Sch. Audiol. Speech Sci., 1980-88, acting dir. Sch. Rehab. Medicine, 1985-88; coord. health scis. Univ. B.C., Vancouver, Canada, 1995—2001; prin. Coll. Health Disicplins, 2001—. Mem. study sect. NIH, 1983; mem. senate U. B.C., 1984-87, 96—, chair senate libr. com. 93-99, vice-chair senate, 2000-2001; chmn. adv. com. B.C. Med. Svcs. Found., 1981-2000, chmn., pres. com. lectures, 1986-90; mem. health and welfare com. Vancouver Found.; bd. dirs. B.C. Rsch. Found., deputy chair, 1998-2002; mem. adv. com. Cmty. Care Found., 1994-2000. Mem. editl. bd. Cambridge U. Press, J. Child Lang. Recipient Dist. Svc. award BCIT, 2003; Fulbright scholar Purdue U., 1963-66; David Ross Rsch. fellow, 1965-66, sr. fellow Green Coll., U. B.C., 1996—; named Outstanding Alumnus, Purdue U., 1993. Mem. Can. Assn. Audiologists and Speech Lang. Pathologists (pres. 1984-85, chmn. com. on examinations 1986-88, medal for outstanding profl. achievement 1988), Internat. Assn. Child Lang. (exec. coun. 1983-89), Vancouver Club. Home: 3350 W 37th Ave Vancouver BC Canada V6N 2V6 Office: Univ BC Health Sci Office Rm 400 IRC 2194 Health Mall Vancouver BC Canada V6T 1Z3 E-mail: john.gilbert@ubc.ca.

GILBERT, JOHN JOUETT, aquatic ecologist, educator; b. Southampton, N.Y., July 18, 1937; s. Seymour Parker Gilbert and Louise Ross (Todd) Stanley; m. Caroline Spalding Colburn, June 16, 1959; children: John Spalding, Anne Gilbert Coleman. BA, Williams Coll., 1959; PhD, Yale U., 1963. Asst. prof. Princeton (N.J.) U., 1964-66; asst. prof. dept. biol. scis. Dartmouth Coll., Hanover, N.H., 1966-69, assoc. prof., 1969-74, prof., 1974—. Contbr. numerous articles to profl. jours. Recipient Career Devel. award, 1973-78; NSF, NIH, EPA grantee, 1965—. Fellow AAAS; mem. Ecol. Soc. Am., Am. Soc. Limnology and Oceanography (Lifetime Achievement award 2003), Internat. Soc. Theoretical and Applied Limnology (nat. rep. 1971-83). Avocation: fly fishing. Office: Dartmouth Coll Dept Biol Scis Hanover NH 03755

GILBERT, KENNETH G. art educator; b. Spencer, W.Va., Oct. 29, 1942; s. Delmer L. and N. Marie Gilbert. BA, Glenville (W.Va.) State Coll.; MA, Salem Internat. U.; postgrad., W.Va. U., U. Ky. Staff writer Encyclopedia of Appalachia East Tenn. State U.; owner, dir. Tile Design Studio, Parkersburg, W.Va. Author: Mountain Trace Book I, 1980, Book II, 1982, A Blennerhassett Sketchbook, 1995, Parkersburg High School History Book, 1985, Appalachian/Wildfood Cookbook, 1997; one man shows include Parkersburg Art Ctr., Smoot Theatre, Glenville State Coll., Tamarack Galleries. Apptd. human rights commr. Gov. of W.Va. Mem. Nat. Art Edn. Assn. Baptist. Home: 2323 Broad St Parkersburg WV 26101-2819

GILBERT, LEONARD HAROLD, lawyer; b. Hutchinson, Minn., Apr. 3, 1936; s. Sidney and Clara (Franzblau) G.; m. Jean Buchman, Apr. 21, 1963; children— Jonathan Stuart, Suzanne Elaine. BA, Emory U., 1958; LLB, Harvard U., 1961. Bar: Fla. 1961. With Carlton, Fields, Ward, Emmanuel, Smith & Cutler PA, Tampa, Fla., 1961-98, Holland & Knight, LLP, Tampa, Fla., 1998—. Bd. dirs. Gasparilla Sidewalk Art Festival, Tampa, 1970-74, United Way; trustee Tampa Bay Performing Arts Ctr., Lowry Park Zool. Soc., Univ. Cmty. Hosp.; chmn. Art Coun. Tampa, 1973-74; mem. Hillsborough County (Fla.) Bicentennial Commn., 1973-76, Tampa Charter Revision Com., 1975; chmn. bd. fellows U. Tampa, 1986-87, trustee, 1987-00; pres. Tampa Mus. Art, 1986-87. With USCGR, 1961-69. Fellow Am. Bar Found. (chair 1998, dir.), Fla. Bar Found. (dir.); mem. ABA (chmn. sect. gen. practice 1979-80, ho. of dels. 1980-90, chmn. creditors' rights com. corps. sect., mem. coun. sect. bus. law 2000—), Fla. Bar (chmn. sect. corp. banking and bus. law 1970-71, chmn. sect. gen. practice 1972-73, bd. govs. 1975-79, pres. 1980-81), Bar Assn. Hillsborough County (pres. 1974-75), Am. Judicature Soc. (dir.), Am. Law Inst., Am. Coll. Bankruptcy (dir. 1997—), Internat. Bar Assn., Internat. Insolvency Inst. (dir. and sec. 2000—), N.C. Banking Inst., Harvard Law Sch. Assn. Fla. (pres. 1986), Am. Coll. Comml. Fin. Lawyers (pres. 1999-2000), Tampa C. of C. (bd.

dirs.), Eleventh Cir. Hist. Soc. (trustee, v.p.). Clubs: The Tampa (pres. 1986-87). Lodges: Kiwanis (pres. 1972), Ye Mystic Krewe of Gasparilla. Office: Holland & Knight LLP PO Box 1288 Tampa FL 33601-1288 E-mail: lgilbert@hklaw.com.

GILBERT, MARGARET P. university educator, researcher; b. England; d. Peter and Miriam Gilbert. DPhil, Oxford U. Prof. philosophy U. Conn., Storrs, 1983—. Vis. prof. Princeton (N.J.) U., King's Coll., London; vis. fellow Wolfson Coll., Oxford; vis. mem., Herodotus fellow Inst. for Advanced Study, Princeton; rsch. fellow St. Hilda's Coll., Oxford, St. Anne's Coll., Oxford, England. Author: On Social Facts, 1989, Living Together: Rationality, Sociality, and Obligation, 1996, Sociality and Responsibility: New Essays in Plural Subject Theory, 2000, Marcher Ensemble: Essais sur les Fondements des Phenomenes Collectifs, 2003. Rsch. fellow, Am. Coun. Learned Socs., 1989—90, NEH fellow, 2003—. Office: U Conn U-2054 Storrs Mansfield CT 06269-2054

GILBERT, MARIE ROGERS, poet; b. Florence, S.C., Jan. 27, 1924; d. Frank Mandeville and Marie Barringer Rogers; m. Richard Austin Gilbert, Apr. 24, 1946; children: Richard Austin Jr., Laurie Gilbert Sanford. BA in Psychology and Theater Arts, Rollins Coll., 1945. Read poetry at Spoleto Festival, Charleston, S.C., 1999. Contbr. poetry to anthologies including Word and Witness: 100 Years of North Carolina Poetry, 1999; author: Brookgreen Oaks, 1999, Connexions, 1994, Myrtle Beach Back When, 1989, Forever New, 1987, The Song and the Seed, 1983, From Comfort, 1981. Driver ARC, Florence Army Air Base, summer 1943-44; trustee St. Andrews Presbyn. Coll., Laurinburg, N.C., 2002. Recipient Poet Laureate Sam Ragan Fine Arts award St. Andrews Presbyn. Coll., 1994. Mem. Poetry Soc. N.C. (v.p., 1988-89, pres. 1990-92), Poetry Soc. S.C. (1st pl. for lyric poetry 1987, 90), N.C. Writers Conf., N.C. Writers Network, Colonial Dames of Am. in state of N.C. (sec. 1990-91, v.p. 1992-93), Jr. League. Avocation: poetry readings and seminars. Home: 2 Saint Simons Sq Greensboro NC 27408-3833

GILBERT, MARILYN DEL BOSQUE, architectural engineer; d. Mario del Bosque Cardenas and Socorro del Bosque; m. Randy Dale Gilbert, Dec. 10, 2000. BS in Archtl. Engring., U. Tex., Austin, 1996; MBA (hon.), U. Tex., Edinburg, 1999. Grad. engr. Turner, Collie, and Braden, Pharr, Tex., 1997—98; energy mgr. Brownsville Ind. Sch. Dist., Tex., 1999—2000; key account mgr. Brownsville Pub. Utilites Bd., Tex., 2000—01, energy risk mgr., 2001—. Current mem. North Brownsville Rotary Club, Tex., 2001, Brownsville Jr. Svc. League, Tex., 2000; bd. mem. Brownsville Ind. Sch. Dist., Tex., 2001—, Tech Prep of Rio Grande Valley, Harlingen, Tex., 2000—. Recipient Minority Talent Roster award, Tex. Southmost Coll., 1992; Xerox grant, Xerox Corp., 1998. Mem.: ASCE, Nat. Soc. Archtl. Engrs. (assoc.; social chair 1994—96), Mes. Student Assn., U. Tex. Ex Alumni Assn. (life), Beta Gamma Sigma (assoc.). Catholic. Avocations: travel, tennis. Office: Brownsville Pub Utilities Bd 1425 Robinhood Dr Brownsville TX 78523 Office Fax: 956-983-6289. E-mail: mgilbert@brownsville-pub.com.

GILBERT, MELISSA, actress; b. Los Angeles, May 8, 1964; d. Paul and Barbara (Crane) G.; m. Bo Brinkman (div.); 1 son, Dakota; m. Bruce Boxleitner, Jan. 1, 1995; stepchildren: Lee, Sam. Student, U. So. Calif. Actress: (TV movies) Little House on the Prairie, 1974, Christmas Miracle in Caulfield, U.S.A., 1977, The Miracle Worker, 1979, The Diary of Anne Frank, 1980, Splendor in the Grass, 1981, Little House: Look Back to Yesterday, 1983, Choices of the Heart, 1983, Little House: Bless All the Dear Children, 1984, Family Secrets, 1984, Little House: The Last Farewell, 1984, Choices, 1986, Penalty Phase, 1986, Family Secrets, Killer Instincts, Without Her Consent, Forbidden Nights, 1990, Blood Vows: The Story of a Mafia Wife, Joshua's Heart, 1990, Donor, The Lookalike, 1990, Conspiracy of Silence: The Shari Karney Story, 1992, With Hostile Intent, 1993, Shattered Trust, 1993, House of Secrets, 1993, Dying to Remember, 1993, Cries From the Heart, 1994, Against Her Will: The Carrie Buck Story, 1994, The Babymaker: The Dr. Cecil Jacobson Story, 1994, Danielle Steel's 'Zoya', 1995, Christmas in My Hometown, 1996, Seduction in a Small Town, 1996, Childhood Sweetheart, 1997, Her Own Rules, 1998, Murder at 75 Birch, 1999, Switched at Birth, 1999, A Vision of Murder: The Story of Donielle, 2000, Sanctuary, 2001, Then Came Jones, 2003; (TV series) Little House on the Prairie, 1974-82, Little House: A New Beginning, 1983, Stand By Your Man, 1992, Sweet Justice, 1994-95 (TV spls.) Battle of the Network Stars, 1978, 79, 81, 82, Celebrity Challenge of the Sexes, 1980, Circus Lions, Tigers and Melissa, Too, 1977, Dean Martin Celebrity Roast, 1984, (stage prodns.) Night of 100 Stars, 1982, The Glass Menagerie, 1985, A Shayna Maidel, 1987 (Outer Critics Circle Award), (feature films) Nutcracker Fantasy, 1979, Sylvester, 1985, Ice House, 1989. Mem.: SAG (pres. 2001—).

GILBERT, MICHELLE DAWN, middle and secondary school educator; b. Mt. Vernon, Ohio, July 7, 1971; d. Franklin Gene and Carolea Jean Ruhl; m. Stan Lee Gilbert, Oct. 16, 1993; children: Dustin, Derek. AAS, North Ctrl. State Coll., Mansfield, Ohio, 1992; BS, Ashland U., 1996, BSBA, 1998; MPA, Ohio State U., 2000. Various positions Ashland (Ohio) U., 1992-98; grad. asst. Ohio State U., Columbus, 1998-99, 99-2000; tchr. at-risk students, ct. liaison Mid-Ohio Ednl. Svcs. Ctr., Mansfield, 2000—. Mem.: ASPA, Phi Alpha Theta. Office: 175 Mansfield Ave 4th Fl Shelby OH 44875 Office Fax: 419-342-4342.

GILBERT, NEIL ROBIN, social work educator, writer, consultant; b. N.Y.C., Sept. 18, 1940; s. Alan and Ida (Bedzin) G.; children: Evan Mallory, Jesse Arthur; m. Rebecca A. Van Voorhis, 2002; children: George Nathaniel, Nicole. BA, Bklyn. Coll., 1963; MSW, U. Pitts., 1965, PhD, 1968. Caseworker Interdepartmental Service Ctr., N.Y.C., 1963; dir. research Mayor's Com. on Human Resources, Pitts., 1967-69; prof. sch. social welfare U. Calif., Berkeley, 1969—, chmn. doctoral program, 1983—, acting dean sch. social welfare, 1986, 95-97, Milton and Gertrude Chernin prof. social welfare and social svcs., 1989—. Advisor Jour. Social Policy, 1982—. Author: Clients or Constituents, 1970, Capitalism and the Welfare State, 1983, (with others) Dimensions of Social Welfare Policy, 1974, 2d rev. edit., 1986, Dynamics of Community Planning, 1978, (with Barbara Gilbert) The Enabling State, 1989, Protecting Young Children from Sexual Abuse, 1989, Practical Program Evaluation, 1990, (with Jill Berrick) With the Best of Intentions, 1992, Welfare Justice, 1995, Transformation of the Welfare State, 2002; editor: (with Rebecca Van Voorhis) Activating the Unemployed; editor Social Welfare Series, 1977-83, Social Worker and Social Welfare Series, 1977—. Trustee Head Royce Sch., 1990-96; chair bd. dirs. Seneca Ctr. Fellow NIMH, 1966, U.N. Research Inst. for Social Devel., 1975; Fulbright scholar, U.S. Info. Agy, 1981; Fulbright Research fellow, London, 1981, Fulbright Western European scholar, 1987; recipient Medallion of Distinction U. Pitts., 1987. Mem. Nat. Assn. Social Workers, Assn. Pub. Policy Analysis and Mgmt. Avocations: skiing, moutaineering. Office: U Calif Sch Social Welfare Haviland Hl Berkeley CA 94720-0001

GILBERT, PAMELA, strategic services company executive; b. New Brunswick, NJ, Oct. 3, 1958; m. Charles R.E. Lewis, 1995; one child; one stepchild. BA, Tufts U., Medford, MA, 1980; JD, NYU, 1984. NY and DC bar assocs. Dir. consumer program U.S. Pub. Interest Rsch. Group, Washington; dir. Pub. Citizens Congress Watch, Washington; legis. counsel Malkin & Ross, Washington; exec. dir. Consumer Product Safety Commn., Bethesda, Md., 1996-2001; COO, M&R Strategic Svcs., Washington, 2001—. Office: M&R Strategic Svcs 2120 L St NW Ste 400 Washington DC 20037 E-mail: pgilbert@mrss.com.

GILBERT, PAUL H. engineering executive, consultant; b. Healdsburg, Calif., Apr. 23, 1936; s. Lindley D. and Beatrice G.; m. Elizabeth A. Gilbert, July 13, 1963; children: Christopher, Gregory, Kevin. BSCE, U. Calif., Berkeley, 1959, MSCE, 1960. Registered profl. engr. in 17 states. Project mgr. Calif. State Water Project, Sacramento, 1959-68; officer U.S. Army Corp Engrs., Heidleberg, Germany, 1960-61, capt., 1961-68; project mgr. Parsons Brinckerhoff, N.Y.C., 1969-73, regional mgr./ptnr. San Francisco, 1973-85, dir. N.Y.C., 1973-98, chmn. bd., 1990-98, sr. v.p., 1973—, project dir. supercollider design and constrn., 1990-95; vice chmn. Parsons Brinckerhoff Internat. Inc., 1993—99. Prin.-in-charge of award winning projects Glenwood Canyon I-70 tunnels, San Francisco Ocean Outfall, Seattle Bus. Tunnel, Hood Canal Floating Bridge and West Seattle High Level and Low Level Swing Bridges, others; Laser Interferometer Gravitational-Wave Obs. reviewer NSF, Washington, 1992—99; program mgmt. advisor Railtrack West Coast Modernization Project, London, GM Design Ctr. Modernization, Warren, Mich.; NRC spl. com. on rev. and oversigh U.S. Dept. Energy Project Mgmt. Program, 1999—2002; mem. U. Calif. Pres.'s Coun.; chmn. Project Mgmt. Panel for the UC Managed Three Nat. Labs., 2000—; mem. NRC Com. on Sci. and Tech. for Countering Terrorism; chair bd. on infrastructure and the constructed environment NRC; chmn. oversight com. for nat. radio astronomy obs. Atacama Large Millimeter Array Radio Obs. Trustee Assoc. Univs., Inc., 1998—. Recipient Lincoln Art Welding award, 1964; named disting. engring. alumnus U. Calif., Berkeley, 1998. Fellow: ASCE (Rickey medal 1969, Constrn. Mgmt. award 1994); mem.: Nat. Acad. Engring., Moles, Soc. Am. Mil. Engrs., Project Mgmt. Inst. Republican. Roman Catholic. Office: Parsons Brinkerhoff 999 3rd Ave Ste 2200 Seattle WA 98104-4020 E-mail: gilbert@pbworld.com.

GILBERT, PAUL THOMAS, chemical development engineer; b. Chgo., July 29, 1914; s. Paul T. and Ilse (Forster) G.; m. Phyllis A. Simons, Oct. 17, 1942 (div. July 1955); children: Susan R. Sorensen, John (dec.), Brian (dec.), Wendy E. Levy; m. Hazel L. Dalton, July 9, 1955 (dec. Jan. 1999); children: Michael L. Pinizzotto, Michele L. Urquhart; m. Erlinda M. Rodriguez, Apr. 10, 1999; children: Desiree A. Milling, Vincent L. Ruiz, Stephanie D. Ruiz, Donald P. Ruiz. BS in Chemistry, Northwestern U., 1936; postgrad., U. Wis., 1936-38; MA in Math., U. Minn., 1940; postgrad., Calif. Inst. Tech., 1941, U. Calif., Santa Barbara, 1971-74. Tchg. asst. math. U. Minn., Mpls., 1939-41; instr. math. Utah State Agrl. Coll., Logan, 1941, 43-44, U. Minn., Mpls., 1943; rsch. chemist Metalloy Corp., Mpls., 1944-46; rsch. scientist Beckman Instruments, South Pasadena, Calif., 1946-52, N.Am. Aviation, Downey, Calif., 1952-55, Beckman Instruments, Fullerton, Palo Alto, Calif., 1955-71; devel. engr. Chemistry Dept. U. Calif., Santa Barbara, 1971-93. Tchr. math. NW Mil. and Naval Prep. Sch., Mpls., 1939-41, 45; tech. translator, 1946—; cons. Atomics Internat., Canoga Park, Calif., 1956-59, lectr. Fullerton Youth Mus., 1963-65, bd. dirs. Co-author (translator) Chemical Analysis by Flame Photometry, 1963; translator: Fundamentals of Analytical Flame Spectroscopy, 1979; patentee in field; contbr. articles to profl. jours. Racecourse measurer Santa Barbara Athletic Assn., 1978—. Cadet USAF, 1941-43. Mem. AAAS, Am. Chem. Soc., Am. Math. Soc., Phi Beta Kappa, Sigma Xi, Phi Eta Sigma. Avocations: running, surfing, natural history, indexing, piano. Home: 715 Via Miguel Santa Barbara CA 93111-2743 Office: Univ Calif Dept Chemistry Santa Barbara CA 93106

GILBERT, REBECCA J. marketing executive; b. Pitts., June 30, 1972; d. Sheldon Ian and Shandel Sue Gilbert. BA in Psychology, U. Pa., 1993; MBA, Emory U., 1997. Mktg. analyst, planner Milliken & Co., Spartanburg, S.C., 1997-2001; owner Maps & Guides, Pitts., 2002—. Pres. RJG Translations, Pitts., 1998—. Mem. NAFE. Avocations: figure skating, foreign languages.

GILBERT, RICHARD ALLEN, lawyer; b. Pitts., Dec. 13, 1948; s. Donald T. Sr. and Sara Margaret (Fife) G.; m. Patricia Ann Ramsdale, Jan. 21, 1972; 1 child, Stephanie Ann. B.A., Miami U., Oxford, Ohio, 1970; J.D., U. Cin., 1973. Bar: Ohio 1973, Fla. 1974, U.S. Dist. Ct. (mid. dist.) Fla. 1975, U.S. Ct. Appeals (5th and 11th cirs.) 1975, U.S. Supreme Ct. 1985; cert. trial lawyer. Assoc. Fowler, White, Gillen, Boggs, Villareal & Banker, PA, Tampa, Fla., 1974-78; ptnr. de la Parte & Gilbert PA, Tampa, 1979—. Editorial bd. U. Cin. Law Rev., 1972. Co-chmn. United Way Tampa, 1984; mem. State Fla. Ethics Commn. Mem. Acad. Fla. Trial Lawyers, Assn. Trial Lawyers Am., Fla. Bar Assn., Ohio Bar Assn., ABA, Hillsborough County Bar Assn. Republican. Presbyterian. Home: 4141 Bayshore Blvd Tampa FL 33611-1800

GILBERT, RICHARD JOSEPH, economics educator; b. N.Y.C., Jan. 14, 1945; s. Michael N. and Esther (Dillon) G.; m. Sandra S. Waknitz, Sept. 7, 1974; children: Alison, David. BEE with honors, Cornell U., 1966, MEE, 1967; MA in Econs., PhD, Stanford U., 1976. Rsch. assoc. Stanford U., Calif., 1975-76; from assist. prof. to assoc. prof. econs. U. Calif., Berkeley, 1976-83; assoc. prof engring-econ. systems Stanford U., 1982-83; prof. econs. U. Calif., Berkeley, 1983—, dir. energy rsch. inst., 1983-93, prof. bus. adminstrn., 1990—; dep. asst. atty. gen. antitrust divsn. U.S. Dept. Justice, 1993-95. Prin. Law & Econ. Cons. Group, Berkeley, 1989—. Contbr. numerous articles to profl. jours.; editor scholarly jours. Adv. U.S. Dept. Energy, Washington, 1983—, World Bank, Washington, 1980—, NSF, Washington, 1985—, Calif. Inst. Energy Efficiency, Berkeley, 1990—. Fulbright scholar Washington, 1989; vis. scholar Cambridge U., 1979, Oxford U., 1979. Mem. Tau Beta Pi, Eta Kappa Nu, Sigma Xi. Office: U Calif Dept Economics Berkeley CA 94720-0001

GILBERT, RICHARD KEITH, education educator, researcher; b. St. Louis, Apr. 23, 1958; s. William Ray and Janice Sylvia (Rephlo) Gilbert. BA, U. Calif., Santa Barbara, 1981, MA, 1990, postgrad., 1993; PhD, U. So. Calif., 1997. Cert. secondary tchr. Calif. Rschr. Marine Sci. Inst., Santa Barbara, 1979-82; rschr., coord. Catalina Isl. Marine Inst., Calif., 1983-85; tchr. sci. LA Unified Sch. Dist., 1985-87; sci. and calculus educator Am. Internat. Sch., Johannesburg, 1987-89; rschr. psychotherapy U. Calif., Santa Barbara, 1990-92; cons. advanced tech. divsn. spl. projects Gen. Rsch. Corp., Santa Barbara, 1992-94; instr., rschr. U. So. Calif., LA, 1993—; head dept. sci. Valley HS, 2002—. Rschr., cons. Human Scis. Rsch. Coun., Pretoria, South Africa, 1995; cons. spl. project divsn. binary sys. and geog. area specialist Akela Corp., 1994; team leader, cons. Tertiary Edn. Linkages Project USAID, Pretoria, 1996; profl. expert rsch. and evaluation dept. alternative edn. L.A. County Office Edn.; adj. prof., rschr. U. So. Calif., 1993—; cons. tech. Capabilities, Assessment Geog. Info. Sys.; evaluator NSF, 1999—; adj. prof. rsch. U. Phoenix; evaluator MSP Projects NSF, 2002—; cons. UN Bangladesh Sci. Project, 2002; chair sci. dept. Hacienda La Punta Sch. Dist., 2002—. Active re-election campaign Hon. Robert Lagomarsino, Santa Barbara, 1992. Named Outstanding Tchr. Advanced Biol. Sci., NSF, Calif. State U. Northridge, 1986—87, Internat. Man of Yr. Sci. and Edn., 1996—97; fellow Calif. State U., U. So. Calif., 1993, Eisenhower fellow in marine rsch., NSF, 2002—, 2002; grantee Outstanding Mentor, NSF Rsch. Dir. Fellow Program, 2003, Evaluator TCP projects, NSF, 2003; Calif. Sci. Project fellow, 2002—, Robotics edn. grantee, NASA. Mem.: AAAS, Am. Ednl. Rsch. Assn., Comparative Internat. Edn. Soc., NY Acad. Sci., Order Internat. Ambs., Phoenix Soc. (Outstanding Achievement award 1987), US Naval Inst., Phi Beta Delta. Presbyterian. Avocations: scuba diving, photography, music, climbing, trekking. Home: 6285 Avenida Ganso Goleta CA 93117-2063 Office: 123 S Figueroa St Apt 702 Los Angeles CA 90012-5485 E-mail: richard.gilbert@mindspring.com.

GILBERT, RONALD RHEA, lawyer; b. Sandusky, Ohio, Dec. 29, 1942; s. Corvin and Mildred (Millikin) G.; children: Elizabeth, Lynne, Lisa; m. Wendy Wawrzyniak, Apr. 2, 2002; 1 stepchild, Joshua Sisco. BA, Wittenberg U., 1964; JD, U. Mich., 1967, postgrad., 1967-68, Wayne State U., 1973-74. Bar: Mich. 1968, U.S. Dist. Ct. (ea. and we. dists.) Mich. 1968, U.S. Ct. Appeals (6th cir.) 1968, U.S. Ct. Appeals (9th cir.) 1977, U.S. Ct. Appeals (7th cir.) 1984, U.S. Ct. Appeals (3d cir.) 1988, U.S. Ct. Appeals (4th cir.) 1989, U.S. Ct. Appeals (8th cir.) 1990, U.S. Ct. Appeals (10th cir.) 1991, U.S. Ct. Appeals (11th cir.) 1992, U.S. Ct. Appeals (2nd cir.), 1992. Assoc. prosecutor Wayne County, Mich., 1969; assoc. Rouse, Selby, Dickinson, Shaw & Pike, Detroit, 1969-72; ptnr. Charfoos, Christensen, Gilbert & Archer, P.C., Detroit, 1972-84; sole practice, 1984—. Instr. Madonna Coll., Detroit, 1977-81; mem. faculty Inst. Continuing Legal Edn., 1977—; speaker symposium on social security law Detroit Coll. Law, 1984; state bar grievance investigator; vol. chmn. Aquatic Injury Safety Found; mgr. web sites Found. for Spinal Cord Injury Prevention, Care and Cure (fscip.org), Found. for Aquatic Injury Prevention (aquaticisf.org). Co-author: Social Security Disability Claims, 1983; contbr. articles to legal jours. Founder, chmn. Aquatic Injury Safety Group, 1982-89, Found. for Aquatic Injury Prevention, 1988, Found. for Spinal Cord Injury Prevention, 1988; chmn. aquatic safety com. Nat. Safety Coun., 1987; data collection subcom. of Nat. Swimming Safety Com. for Consumer Products Safety Commn.; bd. dirs. Nat. Coordinating Coun. on Spinal Cord Injuries; patron Detroit Art Inst., Detroit Zool. Soc.; mem. Pres.' Club U. Mich.; mem. Detroit Council on World Affairs, 1968-73, Council for Nat. Coop. in Aquatics; mem. combined fed. campaign Nat. Health Agy. Mich.; founder Spinal Cord Injury Traumatic Brain Injury Adv. Com. Mich. Pub. Health Chronic Adv. Com.; co-founder Safe Kids Coalition Southeastern Mich.; mem. Nat. Safe Kids Coalition. Mem. ATLA, Mich. Trial Lawyers Assn., System Safety Soc., ABA, Mich Bar Assn., Detroit Bar Assn., Am. Arbitration Assn., Am. Judicature Soc., Nat. Spinal Cord Injury Assn. (sec. 1988, bd. dirs., exec. com., chmn. prevention com.), Nat. Head Injury Assn., Mich. Head Injury Assn., Am. Standards and Testing Materials (com. F-24 on water parks and playgrounds, mem. com. F-8), World Water Parks Assn., Nat. Environ. Health Assn., Nat. Pub. Health Assn., Nat. Eagle Scout Assn. (alumni), Blue Key, Pi Kappa Alpha, Pi Sigma Alpha, Pi Delta Epsilon, Fenton Rotary, Fenton Village Theatre, U. Mich. Club, Spring Meadows Country Club. Office Fax: 810-714-4782. E-mail: ron@fscip.org., ron@aquaticisf.org., rrgpc@aol.com.

GILBERT, SAMUEL LAWRENCE, publishing executive; b. Chgo., Mar. 3, 1950; s. Robert Augustus and Ruby Elizabeth (Gammon) Gilbert; m. Sharon Faye Warner, Nov. 3, 1972 (div. Oct. 1984); children: Shaundra, Shari, Sharita; m. Shermine R. Palmer, Dec. 3, 1999. AA in Health Care, Malcolm X Coll., Chgo., 1969; cert. in acctg., Bryant Stratton Coll., Chgo., 1989. Mail/shipping coord. Natural Gas Pipeline Co. Am., Chgo., 1970-82; mailroom asst. IBM Corp., Chgo., 1982-83; CEO Genesis Comics Group, Inc., Chgo., 1986-94; chmn., pub., CEO Genesis Pub., Ltd., Chgo., 1994—; pub. Gilben Comics, 2000—; sr. v.p. creative design Gilben Prodn. Ltd., 2000—, Gil Ben Comics. Editor: Gil Ben Prodns. Deacon Christ the King Temple Ch., Chgo., 1985—87; asst. pastor Greater Holy Rock MBC, Chgo., 1988—92, St. Titus MBC, Chgo., 1994—; assoc. min. Greater New Mt. Carmen, Chgo., 1992—94. Mem.: Rsch. Inst. Am., Am. Mgmt. Assn. Democrat. Baptist. Avocation: building model aircraft.

GILBERT, SCOTT FREDERICK, biologist, educator, author; b. N.Y.C., Apr. 13, 1949; s. Marvin Marshall and Elaine (Caplan) G.; m. Anne Marie Raunio, Dec. 30, 1971; children: Daniel, Sarah, David. BA, Wesleyan U., 1971; MA, PhD, Johns Hopkins U., 1976; PhD (hon.), U. Helsinki. Postdoctoral assoc. U. Wis., Madison, 1976-78, 1978-80; asst. prof. Swarthmore (Pa.) Coll., 1980-86, assoc. prof., 1986-92; prof., 1992—. Author: Developmental Biology, 1985, 88, 91, 94, 97, 2000, Embryology, 1997; zoology editor Jour. Irreproducible Results, 1979-93, Com. de Patronage, Annales Hist. Philosophie Sci.; mem. editl. bd. Am. Jour. Med. Genetics, Jour. Exptl. Zoology, Internat. Jour. Devel. Biol., Ency. of Life Scis.; contbr. articles to sci. jours. Grantee Dwight J. Ingle award Perspectives in Biology and Medicine, 1984, medal of François I, Coll. de France, 1996; Guggenheim fellow, 1999., Hon. Fel., St. Petersburg Soc. Nat., 2001. Fellow AAAS; mem. Soc. Devel. Biology (Viktor Hamburger prize 2002), Soc. Integrative Comparative Biology, Internat. Soc. for Differentiation (exec. bd.), Soc. Human Genetics, Hist. Sci. Soc., St. Petersburg Soc. Naturalists, Internat. Soc. Hist. Phil. Soc. Stud. Biology, Phi Beta Kappa, Sigma Xi. Democrat. Jewish. Home: 224 Cornell Ave Swarthmore PA 19081-1932 Office: Swarthmore Coll Dept Biology 500 College Ave Swarthmore PA 19081-1306 E-mail: sgilber1@swarthmore.edu.

GILBERT, STEPHEN ALAN, lawyer, organization executive; b. N.Y.C., Feb. 20, 1939; s. Ben Gilbert and Elsie (Alweiss) G. AB, Cornell U., 1960, JD, 1962. Bar: N.J. 1963, Fla. 1964, N.Y. 1984. From clk. to assoc. Carpenter, Bennett & Morrissey, Newark, 1961-63; assoc. Milton M. and Adrian M. Unger, Newark, 1963-67; pres. Preserver Goup, Inc. (formerly Motor Club Am.), Paramus, NJ, 1967—. Pres. MCA Ins. Co., 1988-92, Property-Casualty Co. MCA, 1988-93, Motor Club Am. Ins. Co., 1989—, Preserver Ins. Co., 1992—, Am. Colonial Ins. Co., 1999—2003, Mountain Valley Ind. Co., 2000—; chmn. bd. N.E. Ins. Co., 1999—. Asst. editor Plain Language Law Dictionary, 1979, assoc. editor, 1995. Active Boys and Girls Clubs, Newark, 1970—, pres., 1977-80, 96-97, chmn. bd., 1980-81, 97-2003; active Newark Mus. Coun., 1975-87, chmn., 1981; active Natural Sci. Solar Ctr., Milford, Pa., 1981-87, v.p., 1982-84; trustee Natural Sci. for Youth Found., 1984-87. Recipient Man and Boy award Boys Clubs, Newark, 1980. Mem. Nat. Assn. Ind. Insurers (bd. govs.). Jewish. Home: 8909 Francis Pl North Bergen NJ 07047-6001 Office: 95 Rte 17 S Paramus NJ 07653-0931 E-mail: sgilbert@preserver.com.

GILBERT, STEVEN JEFFREY, venture capitalist, screenwriter; b. N.Y.C., Apr. 6, 1947; s. Bernard and Ruth (Turner) G.; m. Anita Schneider, Apr. 25, 1987; children: Steven Turner, Anna Christina. BS in Econs., U. Pa., 1967; JD, Harvard U., 1970, MBA, 1972. Bar: Mass. 1970. Assoc. Morgan Stanley and Co., N.Y.C., 1972-76; v.p. Wertheim and Co., N.Y.C., 1976-78; mng. dir. E.F. Hutton, Internat., N.Y.C., 1978-80; pres., chief exec. officer Lion's Gate Films, Inc., Los Angeles, 1980-82; gen. ptnr. Cen. Devel. Ptnrs., N.Y.C., 1982-83; mng. gen. ptnr. Chem. Venture Ptnrs., N.Y.C., 1983-88; mng. dir. Commonwealth Capital Ptnrs., N.Y.C., 1988—; mng. gen. ptnr. Soros Capital, N.Y.C., 1992—; chmn. bd. Gilbert Global Equity Ptnrs., L.L.C., 1997—. Bd. dirs. A.C.X. Pacific, Inc., The Asian Infrastructure Fund, LCC Internat., Inc.; trustee NYU Med. Ctr. Screenwriter Chapter XI, 1982. Mem. Writers Guild Am., Young Pres. Orgn., Coun. on Fgn. Rels. Office: Gilbert Global Equity Ptnrs LLC 785 Smith Ridge Rd New Canaan CT 06840-3228

GILBERT, SUSAN LYNN, software engineer; b. Seattle, Aug. 18, 1956; d. Yowland Dewitt and Pauline Elanore Gilbert; m. Evan Cowart, June 25, 2000. BS, MS, MIT, 1978; MA, Johns Hopkins U., 1984; M of Software Engring., Tex. Christian U., 1995. Programmer Marcon Industries, Ft. Worth, 1984-85; sr. engr. Lockheed Martin Aeronautics Co., Ft. Worth, 1985-98; prin. software engr. L-3 Comms., Arlington, Tex., 1998—. Mem. AAAS, IEEE, Assn. for Computing Machinery, Am. Chem. Soc. Office: L-3 Comms MS 403 PO Box 5328 Arlington TX 76005-5328 E-mail: sgilbert@link.com.

GILBERT, WALTER, molecular biologist, educator; b. Boston, Mar. 21, 1932; s. Richard V. and Emma (Cohen) G.; m. Celia Stone, Dec. 29, 1953; children: John Richard, Kate. AB, Harvard U., 1953, AM, 1954; PhD, Cambridge U., 1957; DSc (hon.), U. Chgo., 1978, Columbia U., 1978, U. Rochester, 1979, Yeshiva U., 1981. NSF postdoctoral fellow Harvard U., Cambridge, Mass., 1957-58, lectr. physics, 1958-59, asst. prof. physics, 1959-64, assoc. prof. biophysics, 1964-68; prof. biochemistry, 1968-72, Am. Cancer Soc. prof. molecular biology, 1972-81, prof. biology, 1985-86, H.H. Timken prof. sci., 1986-87, Carl M. Loeb Univ. prof., 1987—, chair dept. cellular and devel. biology, 1987-93; chmn. sci. bd. Biogen, 1978-83, co-chmn., supervisory bd., 1979—81, chmn. supervisory bd., chief exec. officer, 1981—84; vice chmn., bd. dirs. Myriad Genetics, Inc., 1992—; chmn. bd. Paratek Pharms., Inc., 1996—; mng. ptnr. BioVentures Investors, 2001—; chmn. bd. dirs. Myriad Proteomics, Inc., 2001—; mng. ptnr. BioVentures Investors, 2001—. Mem. bd. sci. govs. The Scripps Rsch. Inst., 1994-; bd. dirs. ActivBiotics, Inc. (formerly Merlin Techs.); bd. dirs. Memory Pharms., Inc., mem. sci. adv. bd., 1998-; chmn. bd. dirs., sci. adv. bd. Pintex Pharms., Inc., 1999—; chmn. bd. dirs., mem. sci. adv. bd. Trankaryotic Therapies Inc., 2000-; chmn. bd. dirs. Myriad Protemics, Inc., 2001—; mem. bd. dirs. HospitalCareOnline.com., Inc., 2001—; V.D. Mattia lectr. Roche Inst. Molecular Biology, 1976. Recipient U.S. Steel Found. NAS, 1968, Ledlie prize Harvard U., 1969, Warren triennial prize Mass. Gen. Hosp., 1977, Louis and Bert Freedman Found. N.Y. Acad. Scis., 1977, Prix Charles-Leopold Mayer Academie des Scis., Inst. de France, 1977, Nobel prize in chemistry, 1980, New Eng. Entrepreneur of Yr. award, 1991; co-winner Louisa Gross Horwitz prize Columbia U., 1979, Gairdner prize, 1979, Albert Lasker Basic Sci. award, 1979; Guggenheim fellow, 1968-69; hon. fellow Trinity Coll., Cambridge, U.K., 1991. Mem. Am. Phys. Soc., Nat. Acad. Scis., Am. Soc. Biol. Chemists, Am. Acad. Arts and Scis., Scripps Rsch. Inst. (mem. bd. sci. govs. 1994-); fgn. mem. Royal Soc. Office: The Biol Labs 16 Divinity Ave Cambridge MA 02138-2020

GILBERT BARNESS, ENID, medical educator; b. Sydney, Australia; d. Christian Henry and Mabel (Milne) Fischer; m. James Bryson Gilbert (dec. Nov. 1986); m. Lewis A. Barness, July 5, 1987; children: Mary M., Elizabeth A., Jennifer E., Rebecca D. MBBS, U. Sydney, 1950, MD, 1983. Assoc. prof. U. W.Va., Morgantown, 1967-70, U. Wis., Madison, 1970-71, prof., 1971-93, emeritus prof., 1993—, Disting. prof., 1988—. Mem. editl. bds. Pediat. and Path. Med. jours., 1986—. Author: Introduction to Pathology, 1978, Genetic Aspects of Developmental Pathology, 1987, Pathology of Fetus and Infant, Metabolic Diseases, Atlas of Fetal and Infant Pathology; contbr. articles to profl. jours. NIH grantee, 1972—92. Mem.: Internat. Pediat. Pathology Assn. (pres. 1992—94), Soc. Pediat. Pathology (pres. 1986—87). Republican. Avocation: writing. Office: Tampa Gen Hosp Tampa FL 33601

GILBERT-BARNESS, ENID F. pathologist, pathology and pediatrics educator; b. Sydney, Australia, May 31, 1927; came to U.S., 1952, naturalized, 1975; d. Christian Henry and Mabel (Milne) Fischer; m. James Bryson Gilbert, Aug. 12, 1954; children: Mary M., Elizabeth A., James C. (dec.), Jennifer E., Rebecca D.; m. Lewis Barness, July 5, 1987. MBBS, U. Sydney, 1950, MD, 1983; DSc (hon.), U. Wis., 1999; MD (hon.), U. Sydney, 1999. Diplomate Am. Bd.

Pediats., Am. Bd. Clin. Pathology, Am. Bd. Anatomical Pathology, Am. Bd. Pediat. Pathology. Resident Children's Hosp., Boston, Phila., Washington, Brackenridge Hosp., Austin, Tex.; from asst. prof. to assoc. prof. U. W.Va., 1963-70; from assoc. prof. pathology and pediats. to prof. U. Wis., Madison, 1970-93, Disting. Med. Alumni prof., 1986-93, dir. pediat. pathology, 1970-93, prof. emeritus pathology and pediat., 1993—, Disting. Med. Alumni prof. emeritus, 1993—; prof. pathology, pediats. and ob-gyn. U. So. Fla., 1993—. Author: Introduction to Pathology, 1978, Genetic Aspects Developmental Pathology, 1987, Potters Pathology of the Fetus and Infant, 1997, Atlas Infant and Fetal Pathology, 1998, Metabolic Diseases, 2000, Atlas Embryo Fetal Pathology, 2002, Clinical Use of Pediatric Diagnostic Tests, 2003; also numerous chpts., articles. Recipient Disting. Pathologist award, Royal Coll. Pathologists (Australia), 2001; NIH grantee, 1972—. Mem. Am. Soc. Clin. Pathology, Soc. Pediat. Pathology (pres. 1986-87), Internat. Acad. Pathology, Internat. Pediat. Pathology Assn. (pres. 1990-92), Teratology Soc., Cardiovasc. Soc. S.Am. (hon.), Am. Pediat. Soc., Am. Acad. Pediat., U.S. Can. Acad. Pathology, Arthur Purdy Stout Soc. Surg. Pathology, N.Y. Acad. Sci., Alpha Omega Alpha. Home: 3301 Bayshore Blvd #403 Tampa FL 33629 Office: Tampa Gen Hosp Dept Pathology Tampa FL 33601 Fax: 813-844-1427. E-mail: egilbert@tgh.org.

GILBERTSON, BERNICE CHARLOTTE, artist; b. Boston, Nov. 11; d. Elmer Nordin and Otelia Sigurd (Peterson) G. Student, Boston U., 1941-44, Art Students League, 1948-49, Pratt Graphics, 1952-54, Atelier Fernand Leger, 1949-51. Asst. scenic designer William Pitkin, N.Y.C., 1950-57, Stewart Chaney, N.Y.C., 1953-62; asst. dir. Alexander Iolas Gallery, 1962-78; dir. Parks Gallery, 1984; news rm. asst., reviewer Cape Cod Times, Hyannis, Mass., 1987—. One woman shows include Bodley II, N.Y.C., 1971, 1977, As You Like It Gallery, Palm Beach, Fla., 1978, Galeria Bryna, Palm Beach, 1980, 81, 1st Nat. Bank, Palm Beach, 1987—; exhibited in group shows at Galerie Mai, Paris, 1949, Burr Galleries, N.Y.C., 1960, 61, 62, Inst. Contemporary Arts, Phila., 1965, Bklyn. Mus., 1968, Erik Nord Gallery, Mass., 1972-78, Flagler Mus., Fla., 1981, numerous others. With WAC, 1944-46. Mem. Art Student League (life), Visual Artists and Galleries Assn., Eng. Speaking Union, Nat. League Am. Pen Women (treas. Palm Beach br.). Republican. Avocations: writing, travel, lectures. Home (Winter): 151 Chilean Ave Palm Beach FL 33480-4436 E-mail: bcgweb@aol.com.

GILBERTSON, DAVID, state supreme court justice; Former judge S.D. Cir. Ct. (5th jud. cir.), Pierre; assoc. justice S.D. Supreme Ct., Pierre, 1995—2001, chief justice, 2001—. Office: 500 E Capitol Ave Pierre SD 57501-5070

GILBERTSON, ERIC RAYMOND, academic administrator, lawyer; b. Cleve., Mar. 5, 1945; s. Ewald R. and Esther V. (Johnson) G.; m. Cynthia F. Forrest, Jan. 25, 1974; children: Sara, Seth. BS, Bluffton Coll., 1966; MA in Econs., Ohio U., 1967; JD cum laude, Cleve. State U., 1970; DLitt (hon.), U. Mysore, Karnataka, India, 1993. Bar: Ohio 1970, Vt. 1984, U.S. Dist. Ct. (no. and so. dists.) Ohio 1971, U.S. Supreme Ct. 1981. Instr. econs. Kent State U., Ohio, 1969-70; law clk. Supreme Ct. of Ohio, Columbus, 1970-71; asst. atty. gen. State of Ohio, Columbus, 1971-73; exec. asst. to pres. Ohio State U., Columbus, 1973-79; assoc. Vorys, Sater, Seymore & Pease, Columbus, 1979-81; pres. Johnson State Coll., Vt., 1981-89, Saginaw Valley State U., University Center, Mich., 1989—. Bd. dirs. Citizens Bank. Contbr. articles to profl. jours. Exec. com. Mich. Campus Compact; pres. coun. State Univs. Mich.; cmty. affairs com. Diocese Saginaw; active Bay County Bus. and Edn. Adv. Coun., Mich. Cmty. Svc. Commn., Saginaw County Crime Prevention Coun., Vision Tri-County Steering Com.; bd. trustees Citizens Rsch. Coun. Mich. Mem. Am. Assn. State Colls. and Univs., Saginaw County C. of C., Torch Club, Saginaw Club, Bay City Country Club. Home: 7371 Glen Eagle Dr Bay City MI 48706-9316 Office: Saginaw Valley State U Office Of Pres University Center MI 48710-0001 E-mail: erg@svsu.edu.

GILBERTSON, OSWALD IRVING, marketing executive; b. Bklyn., Mar. 23, 1927; s. Olaf and Ingeborg Garbrielsen (Aase) Gilbertson; m. Magnhild Hompland, Sept. 11, 1954; children: Erik Olaf, Jan Ivar. Cert. electrotechnician, Sorlandets Teknise Skole, Norway, 1947; BSEE, Stockholms Teknisa Inst., Stockholm, Sweden, 1956. Registered profl. engr., Vt. Planning engr. test equipment design and devel. Western Electric Co., Inc., Kearny, N.J., 1957-61, planning engr. new prodn., 1963-67, engring. supr. test equipment, 63-67, engring. supr. submarine repeaters and equalizers, 1967-69; engring. mgr. comm. cables ITT Corp., Oslo, Norway, 1969-71; mktg. mgr. for ITT's Norwegian co. Std. Telefon og Kabelfabrik A/S (STK), 1971-87, STK factory rep., 1987-89, Alcatel Kabel Norge AS Factory rep., 1989-92, Alcatel Can. Wire Inc. Factory rep., 1992-95; divsn. mgr. Eswa Heating Sys., Inc., 1980-87, pres., 1987-89. Author: Electrical Cables for Power and Signal Transmission, 2000; patentee in field. With AUS, 1948-52. Named Hon. Norwegian Consul, 1981—; apptd. Knight 1st Class Norwegian Order Merit, 1989. Mem. IEEE, Norwegian Soc. Profl. Engrs., Soc. Norwegian Am. Engrs., Sons of Norway. Home and Office: 6240 Brynwood Ct San Diego CA 92120-3805

GILBERT-STRAWBRIDGE, ANNE WIELAND, journalist; b. Chgo. d. David and Joy (Arnold) Wiel; m. George Gale Gilbert III (dec.); children: Douglas, Christopher; m. James Murry Strawbridge. BS, Northwestern U. Columnist Chgo. Daily News, 1971-78, United Features Syndicate, 1978-81; reporter NBC-TV Sunday in, Chgo., 1973; guest expert NBC-TV, N.Y.C. Today, 1974—. Mem. Newspapers Features Council. Prodr.: WSNS-TV spl. Collectors World, 1971; performer TV programs, KETC-TV, St. Louis, Donahue, 1975, 77; owner syndicated radio spot The Antique Detective; author: Antique Hunters Guide: For Freaks and Fanciers, 1974, Collecting the New Antiques, 1975, How to Be an Antiques Detective, 1978, Investing in the Antiques Market, 1980, Collectors Guide to American Illustrator Art, 1991, Design and Memorabilia 40s-50s, 1995, Design and Memorabilia 70s-80s, 1996, Collecting of Quilts (syndicated news column) Antique Detective, 1983-2001. Mem. Soc. Illustrators (assoc.), Alpha Gamma Delta. Presbyterian. Address: 854 Pruitt Cove Rd Laurel Springs NC 28644-8349 E-mail: antique1@skybest.com.

GILBURNE, MILES R. communications executive; b. N.Y.C., Apr. 2, 1951; AB summa cum laude, Princeton U., 1972; JD cum laude, Harvard U., 1975. Bar: Calif. 1975. Ptnr. Weil, Gotshal & Manges, Menlo Park, Calif., sr. v.p. corp. devel. for AOL, 1998-2000; bd. dirs. Am. Online, Dulles, Va., 2000—01, AOL Time Warner, 2001—. Editor in chief Computer Lawyer, 1983-91; co-editor Computer Law Annual, 1985; contbr. articles to profl. jours. Mem. Am. Arbitration Assn. (panel arbitrators), State Bar Calif., Computer Law Assn. (bd. dirs. 1984-87). Office: AOL Time Warner Inc 75 Rockefeller Pl New York NY 10019*

GIL CASADO, PABLO, Romance languages educator; b. Santander, Cantabria, Spain, Aug. 17, 1931; came to U.S., 1954; s. Pablo Gil Benet and Agueda Casado Ortega; m. Stacey Lynn Dolgin, June 24, 1989. PhD, U. Wis., 1967. Asst. prof. dept. Romance langs. U. N.C., Chapel Hill, 1967-70, assoc. prof., 1970-80, prof., 1980—. Author: (novel) El Paralelepipedo, 1977, La Novela Social Espanola (1920-1971), 1967, 2d edit., 1973, La Novela Deshumanizada Espanola (1958-1988), 1990; editor, dir. Ojancano, jour. Spanish lit., 1988—. Mem. MLA, Asociacion de Licenciados y Doctores Españdes en los EEUU, Pen Club Español.

GILCHREST, BARBARA ANN, dermatologist; b. Port Chester, N.Y., 1945; MD, Harvard U., 1971. Diplomate Am. Bd. Dermatology, Am. Bd. Internal Medicine. Intern Boston City Hosp., 1971-72, resident internal medicine, 1972-73, resident dermatology, 1973-76; fellow photobiology Harvard U., Boston, 1974-75; chief dermatology U. Hosp., Boston, Boston City Hosp. (now Boston Med. Ctr.); prof., chmn. dermatology Boston U. Sch. Medicine, 1985—. Mem. AAAS, Am. Acad. Dermatology, Assn. Am. Physicians, Am. Soc. for Clin. Investigation, Inst. Medicine, Soc. for Investigative Dermatology. Office: Boston U Sch Medicine Dermatology 609 Albany St # J507 Boston MA 02118-2515

GILCHREST, THORNTON CHARLES, retired association executive; b. Chgo., Sept. 1, 1931; s. Charles Jewett Gilchrest and Patricia (Thornton) Thornton; m. Barbara Dibbern, June 8, 1952; children: Margaret Mary, James Thornton. BS in Journalism, U. Ill., 1953. Cert. tchr., Ill. Tchr. pub. high sch., West Chicago, Ill., 1957; exec. dir. Plumbing-Heating-Cooling Info. Bur., Chgo., 1958-64; asst. to pres. A.Y. McDonald Mfg. Co., Dubuque, Iowa, 1964-68; exec. dir. Am. Supply Assn., Chgo., 1968-77, exec. v.p., 1977-82, Nat. Safety Coun., Chgo., 1982-83, pres., 1983-95; chmn. Internat. Safety Coun., Chgo., 1992-95. Pres. Nat. Safety Coun. Found. for Safety and Health, 1986-95. Bd. dirs. Prevent Blindness Am., 1993. With USN, 1953-55. Mem. Am. Soc. Assn. Execs., Chgo. Soc. Assn. Execs. Methodist.

GILCHREST, WAYNE THOMAS, congressman, former high school educator; b. Rahway, N.J., Apr. 15, 1946; s. Arthur and Elizabeth Gilchrest; m. Barbara Rawley; children: Kevin, Joel, Katie. AA in Liberal Arts, Wesley Coll., 1971; BA in History, Del. State Coll., 1973; postgrad., Loyola Coll., Balt., 1984—. Tchr. social studies Warren Hills Jr. H.S., Washington, N.J., 1973-76; tchr. history St. Alban's City (Vt.) Elem. Sch., 1976-79, Kent County H.S., Worton, Md., 1979-90; mem. U.S. Congress from 1st Md. dist., 1991—; mem. resources com., transp. and infrastructure com., sci. com. Vol. Nat. Forest Svc., Bitterroot Nat. Forest, Idaho, 1986-87. Sgt. USMC, 1964-68, Vietnam. Decorated Purple Heart, Bronze Star. Mem. Kent Country Tchrs. Assn., VFW, Am. Legion, Mil. Order Purple Heart. Republican. Methodist. Office: US Ho of Reps 2245 Rayburn Hob Washington DC 20515-0001*

GILCHREST, YADIRA VELLON, computer scientist; d. Roberto Luis Vellon and Yadira Morales; m. Matthew Joseph Gilchrest. BS, U. Ctrl. Fla., 1998, MS, 2000. Computer scientist Naval Undersea Warfare Ctr, Newport, RI, 2000—. Spkr. in field. V.p., mem. RI Wind Ensemble, Providence, 2002—03. Mem.: Assn. Women Math., Am. Math. Soc., Soc. Indsl. Applied Math., Soc. Women Engrs. (Helen Martha Sternberg award 2002).

GILCHRIST, ANN ROUNDEY, hospice nurse; b. Utica, N.Y., Dec. 21, 1948; d. William Gilchrist and Adele (Cobb) Roundey; married; children: Kristie Ann Hughes, Megean Elizabeth Hughes Holden. Student, Cazenovia Coll., 1967-68; LPN, Utica Sch. Practical Nursing, 1972; postgrad., Mohawk Valley C.C., 1972-75; ADN, SUNY, Morrisville, 1976. RN, Nev.; CNOR. Obstetrics and med., surg. staff nurse St. Elizabeth Hosp., Utica, 1972-76; asst. charge nurse CCU and ICU Mohawk Valley Gen. Hosp., Ilion, N.Y., 1976-78; staff nurse operating room Tucson Med. Ctr., 1978-80, El Dorado Hosp., Tucson, 1978-80; staff nurse oper. room and post anesthesia care unit Tucson Gen. Hosp., 1980-85; charge nurse oper. room Desert Springs Hosp., Las Vegas, Nev., 1985-87, staff nurse GI Lab., 1988-90; charge nurse GI Lab, staff nurse operating room Lake Mead Hosp., Las Vegas, 1991-93; supr. operating room Red Rock Surg. Ctr., Las Vegas, 1993-95; staff nurse Endoscopy Lab., Sunrise Flamingo Surg. Ctr., Las Vegas, 1995-97; RN case mgr. Home Side, at Odyssey Hospice, Las Vegas, 1998—. Mem.: Assn. Hospice and Palliative Care Nurses, So. Nev. Land Cruisers. Avocations: professional doll artist, learther artist, ceramicist, equestrian. Home: 4552 Scott Ave Las Vegas NV 89102-8107 Office: 4011 Mcleod Dr Las Vegas NV 89121-4305 E-mail: annzart@msn.com.

GILCHRIST, DONNA ANN, librarian; b. Ames, Iowa, Jan. 28, 1955; d. Donald Merton and Angelyn Rosaland (Braland) G. AA, Des Moines Area Community Coll., 1975; student, U. Iowa, 1975-76; cert. library technician, Kirkwood Community Coll., 1979; BS in Secondary Edn., Library Sci., N.W. Mo. State U., 1983. Librarian NESCO Cmty. Schs., McCallsburg, Iowa, 1983—2002; oibrarian Colo-NESCO Sch. Dist., 1987—2002; librarian Sch. Dist. of University City, Mo., 2002—. Sec. NESCO Sch. Edn. Assn., 1984-85, pres., 1987-88. Mem. Alpha Beta Alpha (pres. 1981-82, sec.-treas. 1980-81). Lutheran. Home: 8646 Old Bonhomme Rd Apt A Saint Louis MO 63132 Office: Sch Dist of University City 8346 Delcrest Dr Saint Louis MO 63124

GILCHRIST, ELLEN LOUISE, writer; b. Vicksburg, Miss., Feb. 20, 1935; d. William Garth and Aurora (Alford) G.; children: Marshall Peteet Walker, Jr., Garth Gilchrist Walker, Pierre Gautier Walker BA in Philosophy, Millsaps Coll., 1967; postgrad., U. Ark., 1976; LittD (hon.), Millsaps Coll., 1987; LHD (hon.), U. So. Ill., 1988, U. Ark., 2000. Freelance writer, journalist. Commentator, morning edit. of news Nat. Pub. Radio, Washington, 1984, 85 Author: The Land Surveyor's Daughter, 1979, In The Land of Dreamy Dreams, 1981, The Annunciation (Book of Month Club alternate in U.S. and Sweden), 1983, Victory Over Japan (Am. Book award 1984), 1984, Drunk With Love, 1986, Falling Through Space, 1987, The Anna Papers, 1988, Light Can Be Both Wave and Particle, 1989, I Cannot Get You Close Enough, 1990 (Miss. Inst. Arts and Letters award 1990, fiction award Miss. Libr. Assn. 1990), Net of Jewels, 1992, Starcarbon, 1994, Anabasis, A Journey to the Interior, 1994, The Age of Miracles, 1995, Rhoda, A Life in Stories, 1995, The Courts of Love, 1996, Sarah Conley, 1997, Flights of Angels, 1998, The CABAL and Other Stories, 1999, Collected Stories, 2000, I, Rhoda Manning, Go Hunting with My Daddy, 2002; (poems) Riding Out the Tropical Depression; contbr. short stories poems to literary publs. Recipient Poetry award U. Ark., 1976, Craft in Poetry award N.Y. Quar., 1978, Fiction award The Prairie Schooner, 1981, Poetry award Miss. Arts Festival, 1968, Saxifrage award, 1983, Fiction award Miss. Acad. Arts and Sci., 1982, 85, Am. Book award Victory Over Japan, 1984, J. William Fulbright prize U. Ark., 1985, Lit. award Miss. Inst. Arts and Letters, 1985, 90, 91; 2 Pushcart prizes, O. Henry Short Story award, 1995; named Woman of Yr. Chi Omega, 2001; grantee NEA, 1979. Mem. Author's Guild

GILCHRIST, GERALD SEYMOUR, pediatric hematologist, oncologist, educator; b. Springs, Transvaal, South Africa, May 25, 1935; arrived in U.S.A., 1962; s. David and Anne (Lipschitz) G.; m. Antoinette E. Besset, May 7, 1967; children: Daniel J., Michael A., Lauren D. MB BCh, U. Witwatersrand Med. Sch., Johannesburg, South Africa, 1957; Diploma in Child Health, Royal Coll. Physicians and Surgeons, London, 1961. Diplomate Am. Bd. Pediatrics (chmn. Sub-Bd. Pediatric Hematology-Oncology 1990-92). Intern Johannesburg Gen. Hosp., 1958-59; resident Transvaal Meml. Hosp. for Children and Baragwanath Hosp., Johannesburg, 1959-60; resident in pediatrics Hosp. for Sick Children, London, 1961, Children's Hosp., Cin., 1962-63; fellow pediatrics, hematology/oncology Children's Hosp. of L.A., 1963-65, cons. hematology and blood banking, 1965-71; attending physician Childrens Hosp. L.A., 1968-71; asst. prof. pediatrics U. So. Calif., Los Angeles, 1966-71; assoc. prof. pediatrics Mayo Med. Sch., Rochester, Minn., 1972-78, chmn. dept. pediatrics, 1984-96; cons. pediatric hematology/oncology Mayo Clinic and Found., Rochester, 1971-2000; prof. pediatrics Mayo Med. Sch., Mayo Clinic and Found., Rochester, Minn., 1978-2000; Helen C. Levitt prof. Mayo Clinic and Found., Rochester, Minn., 1987-2000; prof. emeritus Mayo Found. and Med. Sch., 2000—. Mem. Commn. on Cancer ACS, 1982—85; bd. dirs. Hemophilia Ctr., Dept. Maternal and Child Health, Rockville, Md., 1978—2000; prin. investigator Children's Cancer Study Group Nat. Cancer Inst., Bethesda, 1981—99; mem. Accreditation Coun. Grad. Med. Edn. Residency Rev. Com. Pediat., 1997—2002. Co-author: You and Leukemia, 1976; contbr. chpts. to books, numerous articles to profl. jours. Med. advisor Northland Childrens Oncology Svcs., Rochester, Minn., 1978-80; bd. dirs. Minn. chpt. Nat. Hemophilia Found. Found., Mpls., 1981-84; chpt sec. Physicians for Social Respinsibility, Rochester, 1982-85; bd. dirs. Nat. Childhood Cancer Found., 1990-97; chair med. and scientific adv. bd. Nat. Children's Cancer Found., 1995-97. Fellow: Am. Acad. Pediat. (chmn. sect. on pediat. hematology-oncology 1988—90, chair coun. on sects. 1999—2002, com. on peidat. edn. 1999—, com. on pediat. workforce 2003—); mem.: Am. Soc. Pediat. Hematology/Oncology (trustee 1996—98), Soc. Pediat. Rsch. (mem. accrediation coun. grad. med. edn. residency rev. com. pediatrics 1997—2002), Am. Bd. Pediat. (chmn. sub-bd. pediat. hematology-oncology 1989—91, bd. dirs. 1990—91), Am. Pediat. Soc., Am. Soc. Hematology, Am. Soc. Clin. Oncology. Democrat. Jewish. Avocations: sailing, bicycling, kayaking, scuba diving.

GILCHRIST, JOHN MARK, otolaryngologist; b. Dallas, Dec. 10, 1959; s. Ronald Wallace Jr. and Patricia Gene G.; m. Melissa Paige LaBoon, Jan. 4, 1986; children: Sarah, Claire, Michael. BS, Wheaton (Ill.) Coll., 1982; MD, U. Okla., Oklahoma City, 1986. Diplomate Am. Bd. Otolaryngology. Intern U. Okla. Med. Ctr., 1986-87, resident otolaryngology, head and neck surgery, 1987-91; mem. staff Mercy Health Ctr., Oklahoma City, 1991—, Bapt. Med. Ctr., Oklahoma City, 1991—, Deaconess Hosp., Oklahoma City, 1991—; head, otolaryngology sect., dept. of surgery Mercy Health Ctr., Oklahoma City, 1995-2000; pvt. practice Okla. Otolaryngology Assocs., Inc., Oklahoma City, 1991—. Pres. Okla. Acad. of Otolaryngology, 1996-97. Mem. com. Young Life, Oklahoma City, 1987-97. Mem. AMA, Am. Acad. Otolaryngology-Head and Neck Surgery, Okla. Med. Assn., Okla. Acad. Otolaryngology (pres. 1996-97). Office: Okla Otolaryngology Assocs 4200 W Memorial Rd Ste 606 Oklahoma City OK 73120-8359

GILCHRIST, RICHARD IRWIN, real estate developer; b. L.A., Mar. 6, 1946; s. Dennis Samuel and Norma Elizabeth (Irwin) G.; m. Nina Newsom, June 21, 1969; children: Katherine Claire, Kimberly Ann, Brian Roy, Bradley Richard. Student, U. Copenhagen, Denmark, 1967; BA, Whittier (Calif.) Coll., 1968; JD, UCLA, 1971. Bar: Calif. 1972, U.S. Supreme Ct. 1972. Assoc. Flint & MacKay, L.A., 1972-74, ptnr., 1974-81, Thomas, Shafran, Wasser & Childs, L.A., 1981-83; founding ptnr. Gilchrist & Rutter, Santa Monica, Calif., 1983, of counsel, 1984—; gen. counsel Maguire Thomas Ptnrs., Santa Monica, Calif., 1983-85, ptnr., 1985-88, sr. ptnr., 1988-95; co-owner Sacramento Kings NBA Team, 1992—; prin. founding ptnr. Common Wealth Ptnrs., L.A., 1995-99, Alexandria, Va., 1999—; pres., CEO Commonwealth Atlantic Properties, Washington, 1997—. Instr. bus. law Calif. State U., L.A., 1973-74. Bd. dirs. Weingardt Ctr., 1993—, L.A. Met. YMCAs, 1993—; trustee Whittier Coll., 1996—. Mem. ABA, Calif. Bar Assn., Whittier Coll. Alumni Assn., UCLA Alumni Assn., Arltington (Va.) County C. of C. (bd. dirs. 1998—). Avocations: running, sports, travel. Home: PO Box 1338 Middleburg VA 20118 Office: Commnowealth Ptnrs 533 W 5th St Los Angeles CA 90013

GILCHRIST, VALERIE JEAN, medical educator; b. June 14, 1951; BS in Phys. Therapy with honors, McGill U., 1973; MD with honors, U. Toronto, 1977; postgrad., Kent State U., 1987. Bd. cert. Am. Bd. Family Physicians, 1980; recert. 1986, 1992, 1998; cert. Can. Coll. Family Physicians, 1979; recert. 1987, 1992. Staff phys. therapist Montreal Gen. Hosp., 1972; staff phys. therapist Royal Victoria Hosp., Montreal, 1972-73, Hosp. for Sick Children, Toronto, 1973-75; co-chairperson Alexandra Park Cmty. Health Ctr., Toronto, 1975-76; chief resident North York Gen. Hosp., Toronto, 1977-78; resident Toronto Western Hosp., 1978-79; chief resident Youngstown (Ohio) Hosp. Assn., 1979-80; staff physician (part-time) Mahoning County Planned Parenthood, 1979-80; assoc. dir. Family Practice Ctr. Western Res. Care Sys., Youngstown, 1980-86; assoc. program dir. Family Practice Residency Program Aultman Hosp., Canton, Ohio, 1986—; med. dir. Hartville (Ohio) Family Practice Ctr., 1988-92; interim program dir. Family Practice Residency Program Aultman Hosp., 1993; rsch. dir. Dept. Family Medicine Northeastern Ohio U. Coll. Medicine, Rootstown, 1993—, dir. Office of Women and Medicine, 1996-97, chair Dept. Family Medicine, 1997—. Asst. prof. Family Medicine Northeastern Ohio U. Coll. Medicine, 1981-84; assoc. prof., 1984-92; prof., 1993—. Author: Developing Collaborative Research in Primary Care, 1994; contbr. chpts. to other books, articles to profl. jours.; presenter in field. Bd. dirs. Family Counseling Svcs., Canton, 1987-89, Mahoning County Unit Am. Cancer Soc., 1980-85, Med. Adv. Bd. Hospice of Youngstown, 1980-84, Med. Adv. Bd. Easter Seal Soc. Mahoning and Columbiana Counties, 1980-84. Recipient Med. Alumni Assn. Graduate scholarship U. Toronto, 1977, Walter F. Watkins scholarship U. Toronto, 1976. Mem. Nat.Bd. Med. Examiners, Soc. Tchrs. Family Medicine (bd. dirs. 1995-97, 2001--, chair program com. 1995-97, long range planning com. 1989-91, program planning com. 1993—), Ohio Acad. Family Physicians, N.Am. Primary Care Rsch. Group (bd. dirs. 2000--). Office: Dept Family Medicine Coll Medicine Northeastern Ohio U PO Box 95 Rootstown OH 44272-0095 also: Family Practice Ctr Aultman Hosp 2600 7th St SW Canton OH 44710-1709 E-mail: vg@neoucom.edu.

GILCHRIST, WILLIAM AARON, architect; b. N.Y.C., Jan. 31, 1956; s. Johnie Aaron and Juanita Marcella (Hunt) G. BS, MIT, 1977, MArch, MS, MIT, 1982; postgrad., Harvard U., 1996. Registered arch., Ga., Ala., Nat. Coun. Archtl. Registration Bds. Project engr. H.J. Russell & Co., Atlanta, 1982-84, project mgr., 1987-88, project dir. Birmingham, Ala., 1988-90; br. mgr. H.J. Russell & Co., Birmingham, Ala., 1990-93; dir. planning and engring. City of Birmingham, 1993-97, dir. planning, engring. and permits, 1997—; architect intern Cherry Roberts Sullivan, Atlanta, 1984-87. Project dir. Birmingham Civil Rights Inst., 1988-91; mem. vis. com. dept. architecture MIT, Cambridge, 1997—; mem. adv. com. on cmty. devel. Auburn (Ala.) U., 1994—. Contbg. editor articles to Birmingham News, 1997—. Bd. dirs. Discovery 2000 Sci. Mus., Birmingham, 1991-93, Birmingham Festival of Arts, 1993—, Ala. Symphony Found., Birmingham, 1997-99. Recipient James C. Howland award Nat. League of Cities, 1995, Karl Taylor Compton prize, 1979, Chandler prize MIT, 1982; Aga Khan fellow MIT-Harvard U., 1981. Mem. AIA (Ala. state coun., mem. nat. task group regional urban design asst. team, mem. urban design com. 1999—), Am. Planning Assn. (del. 1996), Constrn. Specifications Inst., Urban Land Inst. (pub./pvt. partnership coun.), Kiwanis, Roman Catholic. Avocations: linguistics, photography, graphic arts, Aikido. Office: City of Birmingham 710 20th St N Birmingham AL 35203-2216

GILCREASE, JACK CHRISTOPHER, library science educator; b. Houma, La., Nov. 11, 1963; s. Jack Russell and Marlene Dusenberry G. BA, U. So. Miss., 1994, MLS, MA, 1998, MS, 1999. Commn. sales assoc. Sears Roebuck & Co., Houma, La., 1990-93; faculty libr. U. La., Lafayette, 1999—. Contbr. articles to profl. jours. Bd. dirs. La. Young Reps., 1989-90. Mem. Am. Hist. Assn., Soc. Historians Am. Fgn. Rels., Rotary, St. Andrew Soc., Phi Alpha Theta, Beta Phi Mu, Phi Beta Delta. Republican. Roman Catholic. Avocations: reading, golf, history, U.S. foreign policy, international relations. Home: 2314 Kaliste Salom Rd #1715 Lafayette LA 70508 Office: 302 E Saint Mary Blvd Lafayette LA 70503-2038

GILDAN, PHILLIP CLARKE, lawyer; b. West Palm Beach, Fla., July 17, 1959; s. Herbert Leonard and Kathleen (Yeager) G.; m. Laurie Beth Leinwand, Aug. 25,1985; children: Tyler Ross, Jacob Lee. AB magna cum laude, Dartmouth Coll., 1981; JD cum laude, Harvard U., 1984. Bar: Fla. 1984, U.S. Ct. Appeals (11th cir.) 1986, U.S. Supreme Ct. 1989. Assoc. Nason, Gildan, Yeager, Gerson & White, P.A., West Palm Beach, 1984-89, shareholder, 1989-96, Greenberg Traurig PA, West Palm Beach, 1997—. Lectr. Reinventing Govt. Symposium, Hollywood, Fla., 1994, Risk Mgmt. State Conf., Deerfield Beach, Fla., 1995. Contbr. articles to profl. jours. Dir. Com. for Good Govt., Palm Beach, Fla., 1990-94. Mem. Fla. Bar Assn., Palm Beach County Bar Assn., Am. Inns of Ct. LIV (exec. com. 1991-94), Phi Beta Kappa. Office: Greenberg Traurig PA 777 S Flagler Dr Ste 300 West Palm Beach FL 33401-6161

GILDART, CHARLES ROLLAND, JR., mechanical engineer; b. Shelbyville, Ky., July 28, 1928; s. Charles Rolland Gildart and Mary Charlotte Willis; m. Blanche Billingslea, June 17, 1961; children: Leslie Stanton, Charles Rolland Gildart III. BS in Mil. Sci., U.S. Mil. Acad., West Point, 1951; MSME in Guided Missile Sys., U. So. Calif., L.A., 1960. Commd. 2d lt. U.S. Army, 1951, advanced to lt. col., 1971, ret., 1990; ops. analyst Potomac Rsch., Inc., Baily's Crossroads, Va., 1971—72; prin. sys. engr. mil. compiler sys. Sperry Univac, St. Paul, 1972—76, staff engr., 1976—82; program mgr. B-1B electronic warfare sys. Eaton AIL Divsn., Deer Park, NY, 1982—89. E-mail: cgildar@juno.com.

GILDEA, BRIAN MICHAEL, lawyer; b. New Haven, Nov. 1, 1939; s. Thomas Michael and Lillian Frances (Reilly) G.; children: Larysa Albina, Stefan Bohdan. AS, New Haven U., 1964; BA, Providence Coll., 1967; JD, Suffolk U., 1970. Bar: Conn. 1970, U.S. Dist. Ct. Conn. 1971, U.S. Ct. Appeals (2d cir.) 1975, U.S. Ct. Appeals (3d cir.) 1979, U.S. Ct. Appeals (5th cir.) 1984, U.S. Supreme Ct. 1975. Legal adviser City of Boston, 1969-70; assoc. Celentano, Ivey & Gery, New Haven, 1970-73; ptnr. Celentano & Gildea, New Haven, 1973-74; pvt. practice New Haven, 1974—. Bd. dirs. St. Mary's High Sch., New Haven, 1975-77; mem. Bethany (Conn.) Town Charter Commn., 1976; del. U.S./Japan Bilateral Session, 1988, U.S./China Joint Session on Trade and Econ. Law, 1987. With USAF, 1958-62. Recipient Svc. award Providence Coll., New Haven, 1979, Friar award St. Mary's Alumni Assn., 1980. Mem. ABA, Def. Rsch. Inst., Conn. Bar Assn., New Haven County Bar Assn., Am. Lawyers Assn. Democrat. Roman Catholic. Avocations: bicycling, tennis, skiing, photography. Office: 512 Blake St New Haven CT 06515-1287

GIL DE GIBAJA, SUSANA, artist, small business owner; b. Havana, Cuba, May 15, 1959; arrived in U.S., 1961; AA, Miami Dade C.C., 1982; BFA, Fla. Internat. U., 1985. Cert. legal sec. One-woman shows include Infinite Possibilities Gallery, Hollywood, Fla., 1996, I've Been Framed Gallery, Miami, 1996, Mus. New Arts, Ft. Lauderdale, Fla., 1996, 97, Art and Culture Ctr.,

Hollywood, Fla., 1998; contbr. articles to profl. publs. Mem. Vivas Las Artes, Broward Art Guild, Hollywood Art Guild, Miami Watercolor Soc. Republican. Roman Catholic. Avocations: bicycling, book collecting, reading. Office: 7417 W 30th Ct Hialeah FL 33018-5207 E-mail: sgbarral@aol.com.

GILDEN, RICHARD HENRY, lawyer; b. Waterbury, Conn., May 28, 1946; s. Samuel and Adele (Lipshez) G.; m. Lorraine Ellen Bitner, Aug. 23, 1970; children: Sarah, Andrew. AB, Lafayette Coll., 1968; JD, Cornell U., 1971. Bar: N.Y. 1972, U.S. Dist. Ct. (no. dist.) N.Y. 1972. Assoc. Rosenman & Colin, N.Y.C., 1971-80, ptnr., 1980-86, Gelberg & Abrams, N.Y.C., 1986-87, Fulbright & Jaworski, N.Y.C., 1987-2000, Brobeck, Phleger & Harrison, N.Y.C., 2000—03, Kramer Levin Naftalis & Frankel, N.Y.C., 2003—. Bd. dirs. Cotswold Assn., 1983-89, Edgemont Community Coun. Inc., 1991-96. Mem. ABA, Assn. Bar City N.Y., N.Y. State Bar Assn. E-mail: rgilden@kramerlevin.com.

GILDEN, ROBIN ELISSA, elementary education educator; b. Albany, N.Y., Aug. 1, 1950; d. Avrom Irwin and Virginia (D'Arcangelo) G. BS, Pa. State U., 1972, cert. in teaching, 1977. Cert. elem. tchr., Pa. Tchr. West Allegheny Sch. Dist., Imperial, Pa., 1972—. Fundraiser Mary Rensel Meml. Fund, Pitts., 1992—, Fanconi Anemia, 1996—; participant Race for the Cure, 1998—. Recipient NASA Tchr. in Space Program, 1986. Mem. Pa. Edn. Assn. (bldg. rep. 1984-86, 91-93, 99—), Pa. Framework, PTA, Pa. State U. Alumni Assn., ASCD. Avocations: reading, travel, body building, theater. Home: 1256 Pennsbury Blvd Pittsburgh PA 15205-1638 Office: McKee Sch 1501 Oakdale Rd Oakdale PA 15071-3638 E-mail: rgilden@westallegheny.k12.pa.us.

GILDENBERG, PHILIP LEON, neurosurgeon; b. Hazleton, Pa., Mar. 15, 1935; s. Samuel and Ida (Kline) G.; m. Patricia O'Neill Franklin; children: Susan, Steven, Ronald, Laura, Alexandra. AB in Zoology with honors (Edward Pendleton scholar 1952-55), U. Pa., 1955; MD, MS in Exptl. Neurology (Pa. Senatorial scholar 1955-59), Temple U., 1959, PhD in Neurophysiology (Nat. Inst. Neurol. Diseases and Blindness 1966-67, spl. fellow 1967, NIH grantee 1966), 1970. Diplomate Am. Bd. Neurol. Surgery. Intern Grace Hosp., Detroit, 1959-60; resident in surgery Temple U. Hosp., 1962, resident in neurosurgery, 1963-67, lectr. neurosurgery Sch. Nursing, 1963-67, lectr. neurosurgery Philippine Nurse Exchange Program, Health Scis. Ctr., 1965-67; research fellow neurophysiology Max Planck Inst. Brain Research, Frankfurt, Fed. Republic of Germany, 1968; staff neurosurgeon Cleve. Clinic Found., 1968-72, head clinician neurosurg. research, 1969-72; prof., chief div. neurosurgery Med. Ctr., U. Ariz., Tucson, 1972-75, Med. Sch., U. Tex., Houston, 1976-82; clin. prof. neurosurgery Med. Sch. U. Tex., Houston, 1982-96, clin. prof. psychiatry and behavioral medicine, 1988-94; co-dir. pain clinic Med. Sch., U. Tex., Houston, 1975-83; chief neurosurg. service Hermann Hosp., Houston, 1975-82, 90-91; clin. prof. neurosurgery Tex. A & M. Med. Sch., College Station, 1992-94; clin. prof. neurosurgery, clin. prof. radiology Baylor Med. Coll., 1994—. Adj. asst. prof. Case Western Res. U., Cleve., 1970-72; vis. prof. Temple U. Med. Sch., 1978, 80, 94, Hahnemann Med. Sch., Phila., 1980, U. Fla. Med. Sch., 1981, U. Pa. Med. Sch., 1985, Wayne State Med. Sch., Detroit, 1988, U. Ariz. Med. Sch., 1995; dir. Houston Stereotactic Ctr., Houston; cons. Tucson VA Hosp., 1972-74; mem. numerous nat. med. coms. and study groups. Author numerous articles in field.; assoc. editor: Pain and Headache, Stereotactic and Functional Neurosurgery; mem. editorial bds. profl. jours. Bd. dirs. Houston Stereotactic Ctr., 1995—. Recipient Rsch. award U. Ariz. Med. Sch., 1973, Fan Kane Rsch. award, 1974, Speigel-Wyois medal, 1997; grantee NIH. Fellow: ACS; mem.: Am. Assn. Pain Medicine, Coun. Biology Editors (bd. dirs. 1989—93), Nat. Pain Found. (bd. dirs. 1987—92), Harris County Med. Soc., Am. Trauma Soc. (co-founder), Houston Neurol. Soc., Internat. Assn. Study Pain (co-founder), Soc. Neurosci., Rsch. Soc. Neurol. Surgeons, Soc. U. Neurosurgeons, Am. Physiol. Soc., Soc. Neurol. Surgeons, Congress Neurol. Surgeons, Am. Assn. Neurol. Surgeons (bd. dirs.), Am. Soc. Stereotactic and Functional Surgery (pres. 1999—2000), World Soc. Stereotactic and Functional Surgery (pres. 1993—96), Am. Acad. Neurology (assoc.). Republican. Jewish. Home and Office: 6620 W Holcombe Ste 309 Houston TX 77030 E-mail: hsc@stereotactic.net.

GILDENHORN, JOSEPH BERNARD, lawyer, businessman, former diplomat; b. Washington, Sept. 17, 1929; s. Oscar and Celia (Koval) G.; m. Alma Lee Gross, June 28, 1953; children: Carol Winer, Michael Saul. BS, U. Md., 1951; LLB, JD, Yale U., 1954. Bar: D.C. 1954, U.S. Ct. Appeals (D.C. cir.) 1954, U.S. Supreme Ct. 1954. Ptnr. Brown, Gildenhorn & Jacobs, 1955—; vice chmn. D.C. Nat. Sovran Bank, Washington, 1979-89; amb. to Switzerland Dept. State, Bern, 1989-93; ptnr. The JBG Cos. Adj. prof. George Washington U., D.C. Bar Assn.; pres. JBG Properties, Inc., 1956-88; vice chmn. adv. bd. D.C. metro region BB&T Bank, 1985-2003; bd. dirs. The Mills Corp.; D.C. chmn. George W. Bush for Pres., 2000, trustee U. Md. College Park Found., Inc.; chmn. bd. trustees Woodrow Wilson Internat. Ctr. for Scholars, 2002—. Mem. editl. bd. Yale Law Jour., 1954. D.C. campaign chmn. Bush-Quayle, 1988; past pres., bd. dirs. Hebrew Home Greater Washington, 1975-77; treas. Coun. Am. Ambassadors, 2000; bd. dirs. Washington Jewish Cmty. Found., Inst. for Study of Diplomacy, Georgetown U., Ctr. for Strategic and Internat. Studies, UN Watch, Geneva, Internat. Inst. Strategic Studies; treas. Am. Joint Distbn. Com., 1999-2003; pres. bd. dirs. Jewish Fedn. Greater Washington, 1988-89; vice chmn. D.C. Sports Commn., 1996-2003; participant Nat. Prayer Breakfast, 2000. With AUS, 1954-56. Recipient David Ben Gurion award State of Israel, 1977, Hyman Goldman Humanitarian award, 1984, B'nai B'rith Humanitarian award, 1985, Ourisman Cmty. Svc. award, 1987, Ottenstein Cmty. Svc. award, 1991, B'nai B'rith Disting. Alumnus award, 1983, Jewish Inst. for Nat. Security Affairs Leadership award, 1993, U. Md. Disting. Alumnus award, 1996, Leadership award Washington Inst., 1999, Corp. Citizenship award Woodrow Wilson Internat. Ctr. for Scholars, 2000; named Philanthropist of the Yr., Nat. Soc. of Fundraising Execs., 2000; named Washingtonian of Yr. Washingtonian mag., 1996. Mem. Order of Coif, Team 100, Presdl. Trust. Home: 2030 24th St NW Washington DC 20008-1608 Office: 4445 Willard Ave Chevy Chase MD 20815 Office Fax: 240-333-3610.

GILDERSLEEVE, THOMAS HENRY, retired civil engineer, consultant, photographer; b. Aug. 25, 1937; s. Charles Leland and Elizabeth Magdalena Gildersleeve; m. Elizabeth Ann Goldmann, July 3, 1965; children: Ann, Ellen, Kristin Gildersleeve Alford. BS, Stanford U., 1960. Registered profl. engr., Calif. Various civil engring. positions Calif. Dept. Transp., L.A., 1955—2000. Cons., 2000—. Photographer for books, mags., calendars, slides; author: Narrow Gauge...Then and Now, 1993. 1st lt. USAF, 1960-63; capt. USAFR. Mem.: Profl. Engrs. in Calif. Govt., L.A. R.R. Heritage Found., Friends Cumbres and Toltec Scenic R.R., Santa Clarita Valley Hist. Soc. (corr. sec. 1987—89), Rlwy. and Locomotive Hist. Soc. (bd. dirs. 1970—72), Quarter Century Club (dist. dir. 1996—2000). Avocations: photography, railroads. Office: Calif Dept Transp 120 S Spring St Los Angeles CA 90012 Fax: 661-799-3995. E-mail: tgilders@pacbell.net.

GIL DIAZ, FRANCISCO, minister of finance for Mexico; b. Mexico City, Sept. 2, 1943; m. Margarita White; 4 children. BA in economics, ITAM; M, U. Chgo.; PhD, U. of Chgo. Min. of fin. and pub. credit Govt. of Mexico, Col Centro, 2000—; former under-sec. for revenue Finance and Public Credit Secretariat; ceo Avantel, 1997—2000; vice gov. Mex. Ctrl. Bank. Bd. govs. Ctr. Bank; mem. governing bd. Iberoamericana U.; bd. visitors Anderson Sch. of Bus. at UCLA; exec. coun. Mex. Ctr. of the U. of Tex. at Austin. Office: Govt of Mexico/Palacio Nac primer patio Mariano 3 Col Centro 06066 Mexico

GILDRED, THEODORE E. former diplomat, real estate developer; b. Mexico City, 1935; m. Heidi Copin. Grad., Stanford U., 1959; postgrad., Sorbonne, U. Heidelberg; grad. Sch. Internat. Rels. and Pacific Area Studies, U. Calif. Pres. Gildred Found., 1967; founder Torrey Pines Bank (now Wells Fargo Bank), San Diego, 1979; U.S. amb. to Argentina, 1986-89; founder, chmn. bd. The Lomas Santa Fe Group, San Diego, 1989—. Bd. dirs. N.Am. Airlines, Grad. Sch. Internat. Rels. and Pacific Area Studies, U. Calif., San Diego, Security Pacific Nat. Bank; spkr. in field. Recipient hon. command pilot wings Ecuadorian Air Force, Orden de Mayo al Mèrito, en Grado de Gran Cruz, Pres. Carlos Menem, Argentina, 1992. Office: 265 Santa Helena Ste 200 Solana Beach CA 92075-1547 Fax: 858-755-6821. E-mail: Tegildred@lsfg.com.

GILDZEN, ALEX, writer; b. Monterey, Calif., Apr. 25, 1943; s. Al and Helen (Kovach) G. BA, Kent (Ohio) State U., 1965, MA, 1966. Intern Gen. Tire & Rubber, Akron, Ohio, 1965; lectr. English Kent State U. Libr., 1967-70, asst. curator, 1970-77, assoc. curator, 1977-84, curator spl. collections, 1984-93. Fellow Inst. for Bibliography and Editing, Kent State U., 1986-94; judge poetry contest Kaleidoscope: A Literary/Art Mag. by Persons with Disabilities, Akron, Ohio, 1983-84. Author: The Year Book, 1974, The Avalanche of Time, 1986, Mail and More, 2003; co-author: Joseph Chaikin, 1992; co-editor: A Gathering of Poets, 1992; playwright The New Girl, 1999, Lefthanded, 2000. Bd. dirs. Santa Fe Cares, 1997-99. Recipient Ohioana award Ohioana Libr. Assn., Columbus, 1993. Mem. ALA (mem. exhbn. catalog awards com. 1990-92). Avocation: movies. Home: 2328 Brother Abedon Way Santa Fe NM 87505-6926 E-mail: takis@cybermesa.com.

GILES, ALLEN, pianist, composer, music educator; b. Cambridge, Mass., Dec. 26, 1924; s. Allen Lester and Clara Lillian (Collins) G.; m. Marilla Jane Roberts, May 26, 1950 (div. 1970); children: Marilyn, Andrea, Cynthia; m. Anne Watson Diener, Sept. 26, 1970 (div. 1996); 1 child, Katherine Anne. MusB in Piano, Boston U., 1946, MA in Music, 1949; EdD in Music Edn., Columbia U., N.Y.C., 1981. performing pianist, soloist and chamber musician, U.S., Europe, Japan, 1945—; adjudicator for competitions nationwide, 1956—. Pvt. piano tchr., Mass., N.Y., Calif., 1944—; head piano dept., assoc. dir. music dept. SUNY, Buffalo, N.Y., 1952-64; chair, music dept., dir. Inst. of Music Villa Maria Coll., Buffalo, 1964-68; prof. music, chair performing arts Golden West Coll., Huntington Beach, Calif., 1972-93, prof. emeritus, 1993-2000; exec. dir. South Bay Conservatory, Torrance, Calif., 1997-98; owner, pres. GME Piano Video, 1984—; artistic dir. Learning Ctr. for Arts Excellence, Torrance, Calif., 1999-2000; DVD annotator Media Hyperium/Pioneer Classics, 2000—; piano and musicianship tchr. Rivers Music Sch., Weston, Mass., 2001—. Author: (books) Beginning Piano-An Adult Approach Vol. 1, 1978, Vol. 2, 1988, Beginning Piano Telecourse Student Study Guide, 1979; Learning To Play The Piano By Television, 1982; course designer, tchr. on camera (video series) Beginning Piano-An Adult Approach, 1978—; contbr. articles to profl. jours. Recipient Annual Piano Tchr. award SUNY, Fredonia, 1968; Radio and TV award for Noteworthy Achievement in Serious Music, Sigma Alpha Iota, 1980; named Master Tchr., Univ. Tex., Austin, 1986, Master Tchr. (piano), Music Tchrs. Nat. Assn., 1989. Mem. Music Tchrs. Nat. Assn., Nat. Piano Found., New Eng. Piano Tchrs. Assn. Home: 42 Windingwood Ln Lincoln MA 01773-4912 Office: GME Piano Video PO Box 0833 Lincoln MA 01773-0309 E-mail: gmegiles@aol.com.

GILES, BRIAN STEPHEN, baseball player; b. El Cajon, Calif., Jan. 20, 1971; m. Doddie Giles; children: Alexis, Avery. Grad., Granite Hills HS, 1989. Profl. baseball player Cleve. Indians, 1995—98, Pitts. Pirates, 1998—. Named 2 time Nat. League All-Star, 2000, 2001, 4 Time Nat. League Player of Week, 1999, 2000, 3 time Triple-A All-Star, 1994—96; recipient Robert Clemente award, BBWAA Pitts. chpt., 1999, 2000. Office: Pitts Pirates PNC Pk 115 Federal St Pittsburgh PA 15212 Business E-Mail: pirates.mlb.com.

GILES, CALVIN LAMONT, state legislator; b. Chgo., July 10, 1962; BA in Mgmt, Northeastern Ill. U. Mem. from dist. 8 Ill. Ho. Reps., 1993—, chmn. local govt. com. Office: 5255 W North Ave Chicago IL 60639-4429*

GILES, CONRAD LESLIE, ophthalmic surgeon; b. N.Y.C., July 14, 1934; s. Irving Samuel Giles and Victoria Ampole; m. Marilyn Toby Schwartz, June 20, 1955 (div. 1978); children: Keith Martin, Suzanne Speer, Kevin William, Brian Alan; m. Lynda Fern Schenk, Nov. 26, 1978; stepchildren: Jared Schenk, Jamie Schenk. MD, U. Mich., 1957, MS, 1961. Diplomate Am. Bd. Ophthalmology. Clin. assoc. NIH, Bethesda, Md., 1961-63; clin. asst. prof. Wayne State U. Sch. Medicine, Detroit, 1965-72, clin. assoc. prof. ophthalmology, 1973-89, clin. prof. ophthalmology, 1989—; chief ophthalmologist Children's Hosp. Mich., 1985-99, emeritus chief, 1999—, chief emeritus, 2000—. Contbr. articles to med. jours. Active Jewish Welfare Fedn., Detroit, 1981-86, pres., 1986-89; bd. govs. Jewish Agy. for Israel, 1995-2000; vice-chair United Jewish Communities, 2000—. Fellow: Am. Acad. Ophthalmology; mem.: AMA, Mich. State Ophthalmol. Soc., United Jewish Cmtys. (vice chair 2000—02), Mich. Jewish Conf. (pres. 1992—95), United Jewish Appeal Fedns. N.Am. (co-pres. 1997—99), Coun. Jewish Fedns. (v.p. 1992—95, treas. 1995—96, pres. 1996—99). Avocations: golf, tennis, skiing. Home: 6300 Westmoor Rd Bloomfield Hills MI 48301-1359 Office: 31500 Telegraph Rd Bingham Farms MI 48025 E-mail: clgiles@sbcglobal.net.

GILES, EUGENE, anthropology educator; b. Salt Lake City, June 30, 1933; s. George Eugene and Eleanor (Clark) G.; m. Inga Valborg Wikman, Sept. 9, 1964; children: Eric George, Edward Eugene. AB, Harvard U., 1955, AM, 1960, PhD, 1966; MA, U. Calif., Berkeley, 1956. Diplomate Am. Bd. Forensic Anthropology (bd. dirs. 1996-2002). Instr. in anthropology U. Ill., Urbana, 1964-66, assoc. prof., 1970-73, prof., 1973-99, head dept. anthropology, 1975-80; asst. prof. Harvard U., Cambridge, Mass., 1966-70; assoc. dean Grad. Coll. U. Ill., 1986-89, assoc. dean Liberal Arts and Scis. Coll., 1995-99, prof. emeritus, 1999—. Editor: (with J.S. Friedlaender, jr. editor) The Measures of Man: Methodologies in Biological Anthropology, 1976. Served with U.S. Army, 1956-58. NSF postdoctoral fellow, 1967-68; NSF grantee, 1970-72, NIH grantee, 1965-68 Fellow Am. Anthropol. Assn., AAAS, Am. Acad. Forensic Scis.; mem. Am. Assn. Phys. Anthropologists (exec. com. 1973-76, v.p. 1979-80, pres. 1981-83), Human Biology Assn. (exec. com. 1974-77), Phi Beta Kappa, Sigma Xi. Avocations: history of biological anthropology; rsch. in Papua New Guinea and Australia; forensic anthropology. Home: 1106 S Lynn St Champaign IL 61820-6331 Office: U Ill Dept Anthropology 607 S Mathews Ave Urbana IL 61801-3635 E-mail: e-giles1@uiuc.edu.

GILES, JACK MICHAEL, lawyer; b. Vancouver, B.C., Can., Feb. 6, 1936; s. Henry George and Alice Maude (Frewen) G.; m. Virginia Cumming Grant; children: J. Graham, David M., E. Peter. B of Commerce, U. B.C., 1956, LLB, 1959. Bar: B.C. 1960, created Queen's Counsel, 1982. Assoc. Farris, Vaughan, Wills & Murphy, Vancouver, 1959-67, ptnr., 1967-73, sr. ptnr., 1973—. Fellow Am. Coll. Trial Lawyers; mem. Can. Bar Assn. (past mem. provincial and nat. councils), Vancouver Bar (past bd. dirs.), Justice Inst. B.C. (past bd. dirs.), Lawyers Inn B.C. (pres. 1981-82). Home: 2665 Point Grey Rd Vancouver BC Canada V6K 1A4 Office: Farris Vaughan Wills & Murphy 2600-700 W Georgia St Vancouver BC Canada V7Y 1B3

GILES, JAMES FRANCIS, financial executive; b. Teaneck, N.J., Aug. 16, 1954; s. James Francis Giles Sr. and Regina Bianca (Renzo) Micera. BA, Fairleigh Dickinson U., 1977, MBA, 1980, cert. webmaster skills, 1999. Lic. real estate broker, N.J. Bus. mgr. Bradford Securities, Teaneck, 1977-78; self employed translator Emerson, N.J., 1978-82; real estate broker Micera Realty, Oradell, N.J., 1982-89, Nigito Realty, River Edge, N.J., 1989—; payroll adminstr. Butler Telecom, Montvale, N.J., 1996-97; pension adminstr. Nat. Assocs. Metro, Totowa, N.J., 1997-99. Adj. prof., lectr. Bergen C.C., Paramus, NJ, 1985—, chmn. real estate adv. com., 1993—95; adj. prof. William Patterson U., Wayne, NJ, 1993—; adj. prof. math. Felician Coll., Lodi, NJ, 2001—. Roman Catholic. E-mail: gilesmba@optonline.net.

GILES, JAMES LEE, artist, educator; s. Lee Conovie and Helen Isabelle (Cooper) Giles. BA in Black Studies and English, Ohio State U., Columbus, 1996, BA in Journ., BFA in Painting and Drawing, Ohio State U., Columbus, 1999. Exec. asst. Ednl. Alliance, N.Y.C., 1975—90; ednl. asst. Wexner Ctr. for the Arts, Columbus, Ohio, 1994—99; artist, tchr. Greater Columbus Arts Coun. and Children of the Future, Columbus, Ohio, 2001—. Author: The Hypocrites - Politics 2000, 2001, Attack on America: Declaration of War. Why?, 2002. Mem. Rep. Presdl. Task Force, 1989—. Mem.: Columbus Assn. Black Journalists, Nat. Assn. Black Journalists, Ronald Reagan Rep. Ctr., Ohio State U. Alumni Assn. Republican. Baptist. Avocations: reading, dancing. Home: 1761 Clifton Ave #10 Columbus OH 43203 Office: Greater Columbus Arts Coun Columbus OH 43215 E-mail: leegiles78@hotmail.com.

GILES, MAMYE RUTH, genealogy consultant, music voice educator; b. Laurel, Miss., Sept. 17, 1910; d. Henry Dodson and Cora Sampson (Farlow) G. MusB, Belhaven Coll., 1937; MA, Columbia U., 1949; postgrad., Juilliard Sch. of Music, 1943-45. Gen. music and vocal tchr. Laurel (Miss.) City Schs., 1929-33, 37-74; tchr. pvt. voice Laurel, 1937-74; nat. field rep. Columbia Artist Mgmt., Inc., N.Y.C., 1974-88; genealogy cons. Laurel, 1987—. Composer of song including Then April, 1937. Choir mem. St. John's Episcopal Ch., Laurel, 1937-88, soloist, 1945-74; organizer Laurel Community Concert Assn., 1943—, life bd. mem.; treas. Argus Club, Laurel, 1959-71, pres. 1987-89; v.p. Laurel-Jones County Hist. Soc., 1991; mem. St. Cecelia Choral Soc., N.Y., 1954-55; organizer Girl Scout Troop 1, 1937. Recipient Advanced Study award Ford Found., 1954-55; voice scholarship Miss. Fedn. of Music Clubs, 1933. Mem. Nat. Assn. Tchrs. Singing, Music Educators Nat. Conf. (life), Miss Geneal. Soc., First Families of Miss., DAR, Colonial Dames XVII, Daus. of Am. Colonists, Nat. Soc. Sons and Daus. of the Pilgrims, Mu Phi Epsilon, Delta Kappa Gamma. Republican. Episcopalian. Avocations: travel, needlepoint, bridge. Home: 723 6th Ave Laurel MS 39440

GILES, NORMAN HENRY, educator, geneticist; b. Atlanta, Aug. 6, 1915; s. Norman Henry and Alice (Guerard) G.; m. Dorothy Lunsford, Aug. 26, 1939 (dec. Jan. 1967); children: Annette Guerard, David Lunsford; m. Doris Vos Weaver, Aug. 1, 1969; stepchildren: Gayle Weaver (dec.), Alix Weaver. AB, Emory U., 1937, ScD (hon.), 1980; MA, Harvard U., 1938, PhD, 1940; MA (hon.), Yale U., 1951. Instr. botany Yale U., New Haven, 1941-45, asst. prof., 1945-46, assoc. prof., 1946-51, prof., 1951-61, Eugene Higgins prof. genetics, 1961-72; Fuller E. Callaway prof. genetics U. Ga., 1972-86, emeritus, 1986—. Prin. biologist Oak Ridge Nat. Lab., 1947-50; cons. AEC, 1954-64; mem. genetics study sect. NIH, 1960-64, genetics tng. com., 1966-70; ednl. adv. bd. John Simon Guggenheim Meml. Found., 1977-86. Mem. editorial bd. Radiation Research, 1953-58, Am. Naturalist, 1961-64, Devel. Genetics, 1979-86. Bd. dirs. U. Ga. Research Found., 1979-85. Parker fellow Harvard U., 1940-41, Fulbright and Guggenheim fellow Genetics Inst., U. Copenhagen, 1959-60, Guggenheim fellow Australian Nat. U., Canberra, 1966; recipient Bicentennial Silver medallion U. Ga., 1984, Lamar Dodd award for rsch. U. Ga., 1985, Thomas Hunt Morgan medal Genetics Soc. Am., 1988. Fellow Am. Acad. Arts and Scis., AAAS; mem. Nat. Acad. Scis. (chmn. genetics sect. 1976-79), Genetics Soc. Am. (treas. 1954-56, pres. 1970), Bot. Soc. Am., Am. Soc. Naturalists (pres. 1977), Am. Inst. Biol. Scis., Genetics Soc. Japan (hon.), Royal Danish Acad. Scis. and Letters (fgn.), Am. Ornithologists Union, Phi Beta Kappa, Sigma Xi. Home: 289 Hanover Dr Bogart GA 30622-1734 Office: U Ga Dept Genetics Athens GA 30602-7223 E-mail: norman413@charter.net.

GILES, PATRICIA CECELIA PARKER, retired art educator, graphic designer; b. Chgo., Mar. 8, 1925; d. Frederick Louis and Bernice Clara (Kennedy) Parker; m. Lewis Wentworth Giles, June 20, 1946 (div. 1960); children: Alan Julian, Kay Celeste. BS in Fine Arts, U. Ill., Urbana, 1946; postgrad., Howard U., Washington D.C., 1947, U. Mass., Amherst, 1974-75, Washington Sch. Psychology, 1962. Reg. sec. tchr. art Ill., 1972. Sec. tchr. art Randall Jr. High, Washington, D.C., 1947-48; art cons. Elem. Sch., Washington, 1952-53; tchr., chmn. art dept. Theodore Roosevelt H.S., Washington, 1959-60, Boys Sr. H.S., Washington, 1961-63, Carter G. Woodson Jr. H.S., Washington, 1963-72, Howard D. Woodson Sr. H.S., Washington, 1973-85; mgr. Foreverl Living Products, Washington, 1985—. V.p. D.C. Art Assn., 1964-65; cons. art-math. with humanities Upward Bounders U. Md., College Park, 1966-67; potential supr. of student tchg. in art therapy Planning Program Staff George Washington U., Washington, 1972; visual arts coord. D.C. Congress PTA Cultural Arts, Washington, 1972; artist-in-residence Washington Srs. Wellness Ctr., 1987-88, 97—, art therapist, 2002—; tennis instr. Tenn. Edn. Found.; calligraphy instr. D.C. Parks and Recreation, 34th Smithsonian Folklife Festival, 2000. Painter: (oil painting) Mud and Roots, 1971 (award), Mural: Infinite Joy, 1991 (Golden Dolphins Commendation award 1991), Kenkin, oils, 1992 (award); author: (poetry) Mud and Roots, 1976; illustrator: (children's book) Short Fuzzy Hair, 1999; exhibited at two Washington pub. librs., 2002. Taught art workshop in cmty. Fort DuPont Civic Assn., Washington, 1960, defining creative art WOOK-TV, Washington, 1963, comparing and interacting with cultures and govts. Am. Forum for Internat. Study, Senegal, Ghana, Ethiopia, Kenya, Tanzania, 1970; peer leader in tennis and yoga Washington Seniors Wellness Ctr., Washington, 1995-2000; charter mem. Nat. Mus. Art Women. Recipient Commendation award Ft. DuPont Civic Assn., Washington, 1960, 1st prize for watercolor Arch.'s Wives Assn., 1962, Gold medal D.C. Sr. Olympics in Tennis, 1993, 95-97, Silver medal, 1998-99, Gold medal in Swimming, 1993, 2 Gold medals Sr. Olympics in Tennis, 2000, 2d pl. Am. Tennis Assn. Nat. Competition 65 Doubles, 2002; named Orgn. Dir. of the Yr., US Tennis Assn./Washington Tenn. Assn., 2002. Mem. Nat. Conf. Artists, Am. Art League (D.C.), U.S. Tennis Assn., Swim Club Golden Dolphins (Outstanding Swimming Trophy 1993), Deltakas Social Club, Alpha Kappa Alpha. Democrat. Seventh Day Adventist. Avocations: tennis, swimming, yoga, gardening, painting. Home: 3942 Blaine St NE Washington DC 20019-3333

GILES, ROBERT EDWARD, JR., lawyer; b. Bremerton, Wash., Dec. 17, 1949; s. Robert Edward Sr. and Alice Louise (Morton) G.; m. Barbara Susan Miller, Aug. 21, 1971; children: Steven, William, Thomas, James. BA in Fin., U. Washington, 1971, JD, 1974. Bar: Wash. 1974, U.S. Tax Ct. 1974. From assoc. to fin. ptnr. Perkins Coie, Seattle, 1974-86, mng. ptnr., 1986—. Bd. dirs. Jr. Achievement, Seattle, 1984—; bd. dirs., sec. Wash. Coun. for Econ. Edn., 1981-91; v.p., chief Seattle coun. Boy Scouts Am., 1996-2002. Capt. U.S. Army, 1974. Mem. ABA, Wash. State Bar Assn., Greater Seattle C. of C. (trustee 1994-97, 2000—). Avocations: hiking, climbing. Home: 22018 NE 137th St Woodinville WA 98072-5802 Office: Perkins Coie 1201 3rd Ave 48th Fl Seattle WA 98101-3029

GILES, ROBERT HARTMANN, journalist, educator; b. Cleve., June 6, 1933; s. Robert Hamilton and Grace (Hartmann) G.; m. Nancy May Morgan, Feb. 6, 1960; children: David Morgan, Megan Elisabeth, Robert Hamilton II. BA, DePauw U., 1955; MS, Columbia U., 1956; D of Journalism (hon.), DePauw U., 1996. Reporter Newport News Daily Press, 1957-58; reporter Akron (Ohio) Beacon Jour., 1958-63, editorial writer, 1963-65, city editor, 1966-68, met. editor, 1968-69, mng. editor, 1969-73, exec. editor, 1973-76; spl. lectr. Sch. Journalism, U. Kans., 1976-77; exec. editor Gannett Rochester (N.Y.) Newspapers, 1977-81, editor, 1981-86; v.p., exec. editor Detroit News, 1986-89, editor, pub., 1989-97; sr. v.p. The Freedom Forum, 1997-2000; exec. dir. Media Studies Ctr., 1997-2000; curator Nieman Found. Harvard U., Cambridge, Mass., 2000—. Pres. Media Mgmt. Books Inc. Author: Newsroom Management: A Guide to Theory and Practice. Trustee William Allen White Found., U. Kans., 1978—. With AUS, 1956-58. Nieman fellow Harvard, 1965-66; co-recipient Pulitzer prize for local reporting, 1971, Scripps-Howard 1st Amendment award, 1978 Mem. AP Mng. Editors Assn. (pres. 1988), Am. Soc. Newspaper Editors (bd. dirs., treas. 1994, v.p. 1995, pres. 1996), Soc. Profl. Journalists, Found. Am. Comm. (chmn. 1993-97), Accrediting Coun. for Edn. in Journalism and Mass Comm. (pres. 1992-98), Alpha Tau Omega. Office: Harvard U One Francis Ave Cambridge MA 02138

GILES, SCOTT ANDREW, finance company executive; b. Ithaca, NY, Aug. 6, 1960; s. Peter Giles and Marilyn Kay Redman; m. Catherine Elizabeth Lalley, Oct. 10, 1987; children: Abagael Brennan, Eliza Roe, William Samuel. BA, St. Lawrence U., 1982; MA, U. Va., 1995, postgrad., 1995—. Spl. asst. to Hon. Frank Horton, Washington, 1982-84, legis. dir., 1984-86; assoc. Cassidy & Assocs., Washington, 1986-90, interim dir. rsch., 1991-92; pub. affairs cons. Charlottesville, Va., 1990-97; editl. asst. Biolaw, 1993—97; mem. profl. staff Senate Labor and Human Rels. Com., 1997-99, Senate Com. on Health, Edn., Labor and Pensions, 1999—2001; dep. staff dir. House Com. on Sci., 2001—03; v.p. policy, rsch. and planning Vt. Student Assistance Corp., 2003—. Presenter Am. Assn. Cmty. Colls., Nat. Leadership Acad.; keynote spkr. Calif. C.C., 1996. Adv. to bd. dirs. Tougaloo Coll., 1987-90; adv. to bd. Alexander Graham Bell Assn. for Deaf, 1986-92; mem. St. Marks Episcopal Ch. Mem. AAAS, Soc. for Health and Human Values, Soc. for Christian Ethics, Kennedy Inst., Hastings Ctr., Raven Soc. Home: 73 Yacht Haven Dr Shelburne VT 05482

GILES, WILLIAM ELMER, retired newspaper editor; b. Somerville, N.J., July 5, 1927; s. Elmer and Mary Jane (Reed) G.; m. Gloria Mastrangelo, June 4, 1949; children: William J., Michael E., Richard H. and Paul L. (twins), Joseph R. AB in Government, Columbia U., 1950, MS in Journalism, 1951. Reporter Plainfield Courier-News, N.J., 1946-47; copyreader, reporter Wall Street Jour., 1951- 58, mng. editor S.W. edit., 1958-61, news editor Washington bur., 1961; an organizer nat. weekly newspaper Nat. Observer, 1961, editor, 1962-71; asst. gen. mgr. Dow Jones & Co., Inc.; pub. Dow Jones & Co., Inc. (Wall Street Jour. and Nat. Observer), 1971-76; dir. mgmt. programs, mem. Dow Jones mgmt. com., 1972-76; disting. editor in residence Baylor U., 1976;

exec. editor Detroit News, 1976-77, editor, v.p., 1977-83; editor-in-residence, lectr. Mich. State U., East Lansing, 1983—; Sunday editor Singapore Monitor, 1984-85; v.p. Sandy Corp., Troy, Mich., 1985-87; prof. journalism La. State U., Baton Rouge, 1987-91, dir. Manship Sch. Journalism, 1988-91; prof. So. U., Baton Rouge, 1992-97; mng. editor The Washington Times, 1997—2002; ret., 2002. Mem. Assn. Educators in Journalism and Mass Comm., Soc. Profl. Journalists, Nat. Press Club. Home: 85 Dogwood Trl London KY 40741-7536 E-mail: billgiles75@hotmail.com.

GILES, WILLIAM JEFFERSON, III, lawyer; b. Manila, Apr. 10, 1936; came to U.S., 1938; s. William Jefferson and Gardner (Anderson) G.; m. Nancy Gifford Seff, May 9, 1957; children: William Jefferson IV, Gregory Gifford. BS, U. Calif., Berkeley, 1957; postgrad., Golden Gate Coll., 1958-59, Stanford U., 1960; JD, U. S.D., 1961. Bar: Iowa 1961, U.S. Dist. Ct. Iowa 1961, U.S. Ct. Appeals (8th cir.) 1971, U.S. Supreme Ct. 1971, Nebr. 1982, U.S. Ct. Appeals (9th cir.) 1988. Pvt. practice, Sioux City, Iowa, 1961—. Of counsel Whicher & Whicher, Sioux City, 1966 75, Whicher & Hart, Sioux City, 1975-77; lectr. in field. Contbr. articles to profl. jours. Bd. dirs. Sioux City Mus. and Hist. Soc., 1976-79, Sioux City Cmty. Theatre, 1974-76. Capt. USAR, 1957-68. Recipient Gold Seal award Phi Beta Kappa, 1953. Fellow Am. Acad. Matrimonial Lawyers (chmn. bankruptcy com. 1992-99), Internat. Acad. Matrimonial Lawyers; mem. ABA, ATLA, Iowa Bar Assn., Iowa Assn. Trial Lawyers, Comml. Law League Am., Sioux City Country Club, Phi Delta Phi, Phi Phi. Republican. Home: 3827 Country Club Blvd Sioux City IA 51104-1327 Office: 322 Frances Bldg 505 5th St Sioux City IA 51101 also: 3940 Hideaway Acres Crofton NE 68730-0088 also: 3 Sloane Gardens London SW1 W8EA England

GILFILLAN, DANIEL DAVID, language educator, consultant; b. Newport, Vt., Sept. 2, 1965; s. Gilbert E. and Marlene A. Gilfillan. BA, U. Vt., 1988, MA, 1990; PhD, U. Oreg., 2000. Rsch. assoc. Ctr. Study of Women in Soc., Univ. Oreg., Eugene, 2000—02; asst. prof. langs. and lit. Ariz. State U., Tempe, 2002—. Humanities computing cons. Ctr. Study of Women in Soc., U. Oreg., Eugene, 2002—. Fellow, Oreg. Humanities Ctr., 1994—95, Fulbright, 1990—91; DAAD Ann. grant, German Acad. Exch. Svc., 1993—94. Mem.: Modern Austrian Lit. and Culture Assoc., Rocky Mountain Modern Lang. Assoc., Soc. Cinema and Media Studies, German Studies Assn., MLA, Am. Assoc. Tchrs German (Transatlantisches interkulturelles Nachwuchsforderungs programm Deutsch als Fremdsprache award 1994—95), Delta Phi Alpha. Avocations: biking, reading, cooking, travel. Office: Ariz State Univ Lang & Lit PO Box 870202 Tempe AZ 85287-0202 E-mail: dgilfil@asu.edu.

GILFORD, DOROTHY MORROW, statistician, researcher; b. Ottumwa, Iowa, Feb. 19, 1919; d. Frank Bliss and Mabel Irene (Coate) Morrow; m. Leon Gilford, Mar. 31, 1950. BS in Math., U. Wash., 1940, MS in Math., 1942. Statistics lectr. Bryn Mawr (Pa.) Coll., 1944-45; asst. prof. statistics George Washington U., Washington, 1945-48; chief biometrics br. Civil Aeronautics Adminstrn., Washington, 1948-51; dep. dir. divsn. fin. statistics FTC, Washington, 1951-55; head math. stats. br. & logistics br., dir. math. sci. divsn Office Naval Rsch., Washington, 1955-68; asst. commr., dir. Nat. Ctr. Edn. Statistics, U.S. Office Edn., Washington, 1968-74, dir. bd. on human resource studies, 1975-77, sr. statistician, 1978-87; dir. bd. internat. edn. NRC, Washington, 1988-94; prin. ptnr. Gilford Assocs., Bethesda, Md., 1994—2001. Tech. adv. group Nat. Edn. Goals Panel, Washington, 1992 94; mem. adv. groups Coun. Chief State Sch. Officers, Washington, 1990-93, Nat. Ctr. for Edn. Statistics, Washington, 1987-2000. Editor: Rural America in Passage: Statistics for Policy, 1981, The Aging Population in the Twenty-First Century, 1988, Precollege Science and Mathematics Teachers, 1990, A Collaborative Agenda for Improving International Comparative Studies in Education, 1993; author: Women and Minority PhD's in the 1970's: A Data Book, 1977, Framework and Principles for International Studies in Education, 1990, Teacher Supply, Demand and Quality, 1992, Measures of Inservice Professional Development, 1996, Myths About U.S. Science and Mathematics Education, 1998, A Decade of Improvement in Statistics for an Aging Population, 2000, Status of Charter Schools, 2002. Econ. adv. coun. Montgomery County Govt., Rockville, Md., 1981-94; neighborhood coord. Montgomery County Hunger Relief Campaign, 1998. Recipient Fed. Women's award U.S. Civil Svc. Commn., 1965. Fellow Am. Statis. Assn. (v.p. 1974-76); mem. Internat. Statistics Inst., Am. Ednl. Rsch. Assn., Eistophos Sci. Club (corr. sec. 1997-99, program chair 2001-02), Conf. Bd. Math. Scis. (chmn. 1977-79, trustee 1972-75). Coun. Sci. Soc. Pres. (exec. bd. dirs. 1978-80, sec.-treas. 1979, com. on sci. edn. 1977-79), Women's Club of Chevy Chase, Phi Delta Kappa. Avocations: gardening, travel.

GILFORD, LEON, business executive and consultant; b. Warsaw, Feb. 14, 1917; came to U.S., 1922, naturalized, 1928; m. Dorothy Jeanne Morrow, Mar. 31, 1950. BA, Bklyn. Coll., 1939; MA, George Washington U., 1949. Mem. War Dept., 1941-42; chief ops. rsch. br. U.S. Census Bur., 1946-60; prin. scientist Ops. Rsch., Inc., Silver Spring, Md., 1960-71; chief statistician and dir. automatic data processing U.S. Tariff Commn., Washington, 1971-74; spl. asst. for reliability AEC, Germantown, Md., 1974-76; spl. asst. office of dir. U.S. Census Bur., Washington, 1977-81; v.p. rsch. and devel. Cobro Corp., Wheaton, Md., 1982-90. Mem. panel quality control nat. welfare program Nat. Acad. Scis., 1986-87; mem. adv. com. Dept. Energy, Washington, 1981-84, mem. adv. coun. Nat. Ctr. for Edn. Stats., 1979; expert witness testimony to U.S. Congress and Fed. Cir. Ct. Contbr. articles to profl. jours. Capt. U.S. Army, 1942-46. Recipient Silver medal Dept. Commerce, 1956. Fellow Am. Statis. Assn. (coun. 1968-70); mem. Washington Statis. Soc. (pres., v.p. 1963-65), Cosmos club (Washington).

GILFORD, STEVEN ROSS, lawyer; b. Chgo., Dec. 2, 1952; s. Ronald M. and Adele (Miller) G.; m. Anne Christine Johnson, Jan. 2, 1974; children: Sarah Julia, Zachary Michael, Eliza Rebecca. BA, Dartmouth Coll., 1974; JD, M of Pub. Policy Scis., Duke U., 1978. Bar: Ill. 1978, U.S. Dist. Ct. (no. dist.) Ill. 1978, U.S. Ct. Appeals (7th cir.) 1981, U.S. Ct. Appeals (D.C. cir.) 1984, U.S. Ct. Appeals (5th cir.) 1988, U.S. Dist. Ct. (ea. dist.) Mich. 1995. Assoc. Isham, Lincoln & Beale, Chgo., 1978—85, ptnr., 1985—87, Mayer, Brown, Rowe & Maw, Chgo., 1987—. Adminstrv. law editor Duke Law Jour., 1976-77. Participating atty. ACLU, 1983—2000; sec. Evanston (Ill.) YMCA, 1985, vice chmn., 1986—92; v.p. ACLU, Ill. chpt., 1995—96; elected mem. bd. edn. dist. 202 Evanston Twp. H.S., 1993—, v.p., 1995—96, 2003—, pres., 1996—98, mem. joint task force on safety, 1995—96; mem. Met. Family Svcs., Evanston Skokie Valley Cmty. Adv. Bd., 1997; mem., bd. dirs. Met. Family Svcs., 1998—; mem. Legal Aid Soc., 2001—; chmn. fin. com. Evanston Twp. H.S., 2001—; mem. exec. com. ED-RED, 2002—; Bd. dirs. Evanston (Ill.) YMCA, 1982—92; bd. dirs. Ill. ACLU, 1991—96; bd. dirs. Roger Bawldwin Found., 1993—96. Mem. ABA, Ill. Bar Assn., Chgo. Bar Assn. Home: 2278 Harrison St Evanston IL 60201-1216 Office: Mayer Brown Rowe & Maw 190 S La Salle St Ste 3100 Chicago IL 60603-3441

GILFOYLE, NATHALIE FLOYD PRESTON, lawyer; b. Lynchburg, Va., May 4, 1949; d. Robert Edmund and Dorothea Henry (Ward) Gilfoyle; m. Christopher Y.W. Ma, Sept. 9, 1978; children: Olivia Otey, Rohan James. BA, Hollins Coll., 1971; JD, U. Va., 1974. Bar: Mass. 1974, D.C. 1977. Staff counsel Rate Setting Commn., Boston, 1974-76; ptnr. Peabody, Lambert & Meyers, Washington, 1976-84, McDermott, Will and Emery, 1984-96; gen. counsel Am. Psychol. Assn., 1996—. Bd. dirs. ACLU Nat. Capital Area, Washington, 1980-83, St. Columbia's Nursery Sch., 1992-99, D.C. Bar Atty. Client Arbitration bd., chmn., 1994-95. Mem. APA, ABA, D.C. Bar Assn. (legal ethics com. 1998-2001), Mass. Bar Assn., Women's Bar Assn. Mem.: ABA, Mass. Bar Assn., Women's Bar Assn., DC Bar Assn. (legal ethics com. 1999—2001, gen. counsel 2002—). Episcopalian. Office: APA 750 1st St NE Washington DC 20002-4241 E-mail: ngilfoyle@apa.org.

GILFOYLE, TIMOTHY JOSEPH, historian; b. Harrisburg, Pa., Mar. 24, 1956; s. Joseph Daniel Gilfoyle and Mary Dorothy Norton; m. Mary Rose Alexander, Aug. 19, 1990; children: Maria Adele, Danielle Louise. BA, Columbia U., 1979, MA, 1980, PhD, 1987. Vis. prof. Sarah Lawrence Coll., Bronxville, N.Y., 1987-88, Barnard Coll., N.Y.C., 1988-89; asst. prof. Loyola U., Chgo., 1989-95, assoc. prof., 1995—2003, prof., 2003—. Author: (book) City of Eros: New York City, Prostitution, and the Commercialization of Sex, 1790-1920, 1992; assoc. editor: Encyclopedia of New York City, 1985-95, Jour. Urban History, 1995—; bd. editors: Encyclopedia of Chicago History, 1992—, N.Y. Jour. Am. History, 2002—; author: (Making History series) Chicago History, 1996—; editor Hist. Studies in Urban Am. series, U. Chgo. Press, 1999—. Bd. dirs., mem. Chgo. Met. History Fair, 1996—, Mus. of Sex., N.Y.C.; adv. bd. mem. Ency. Am. Urban History, 2002—. Recipient Allan Nevins prize Soc. Am. Historians, 1988; fellow John Simon Guggenheim Meml. Found., 1998-99, sr. fellow Nat. Mus. Am. History, Smithsonian Instn., 1997, NEH fellow Newberry Libr., 1993-94, fellow Minow Family Found., 2001-02. Mem. Am. Hist. Assn. (life), Am. Studies Assn. (life), Orgn. of Am. History (life), Urban History Assn. (life). Democrat. Roman Catholic. Avocation: basketball. Home: 718 W Aldine Ave Chicago IL 60657-3412 Office: Loyola U Dept History 6525 N Sheridan Rd Chicago IL 60626-5385 E-mail: tgilfoy@luc.edu.

GILFRICH, JOHN VALENTINE, retired chemist; b. Springfield, Mass., Sept. 14, 1927; s. John Valentine and Irene Frances (Connery) Gilfrich; m. Nancy Jane Tucker, Jan. 23, 1954; children: John T., N. Lynn, Beth Ann, Robert H., Georgia Ann. BA, Am. Internat. Coll., 1949; postgrad., George Washington U., 1954-56. Analytical chemist Nat. Bur. Stds., Washington, 1948-51, phys. chemist, 1951-52; analytical chemist Naval Ordnance Lab., Silver Spring, Md., 1952-60, phys. chemist, 1960-66; rsch. chemist x-ray optics br. Naval Rsch. Lab., Washington, 1966-71, head spectrochem. analysis sect., 1971-77, cons., 1977-81, assoc. head condensed matter physics br., 1981-82; ret., 1983; part-time cons. Condensed Matter Physics Br., 1983-87; cons. rsch. chemist Bethesda, Md., 1987—2000. Co-chmn. ann. Denver X-Ray Conf., 1986—98, mem. organizing com., 1999—. Contbr. articles to profl. jours. With USAAF, 1946—47. Recipient Meritorious Civilian Svc. award, USN, 1958, Birks award, X-ray Spectrometry 45th Ann. Conf., 1996, Jenkins award for Lifetime Achievement in use of X-rays for Material Analysis, 52d Ann. Denver X-ray Conf., 2003. Fellow: Am. Inst. Chemists; mem.: Soc. for Applied Spectroscopy, Microbeam Analysis Soc., Am. Chem. Soc. (life), Internat. Ctr. Diffraction Data, Am. Crystalographic Assn., Sigma Xi. Achievements include invention of method for analyzing materials. Address: 8710 Lowell St Bethesda MD 20817-3218 E-mail: jgilfrich@juno.com.

GILGEN, ALBERT RUDOLPH, psychologist, educator; b. Akron, Ohio, Sept. 19, 1930; s. Albert and Jeannette (Rufer) Gilgen; m. Carol E. Keyes, 1954; children: James D., Jeanne Elizabeth, Albert P. *Parents were Swiss immigrants. Wife, AB 1954 Bryn Mawr, MA 1964 Kent State, is a CPA who majored in Russian as an undergraduate and has co-authored or co-edited books on international and Russian psychology with Albert and Russian psychologists. Son Jim owns and manages a Cedar Falls store, Gilgen's Consignment Furnishings. Daughter Beth, married to Douglas Gerken, has a home day care center in Cedar Falls and is mother of 2 sons: Christopher and James. Son Bert is a music agent in Houston, Texas.* AB in Chemistry, Princeton U., 1952; MA in Psychology, Kent State U., 1963; PhD in Psychology, Mich. State U., 1965. Asst. then assoc. prof. Beloit (Wis.) Coll., 1965-73; prof., head of dept. U. No. Iowa, Cedar Falls, 1973-93, prof., 1993-2001, prof. emeritus, 2001—. Author: American Psychology Since World War II, 1982; co-author: Soviet and American Psychology During World War II, 1997; editor: Contemporary Scientific Psychology, 1970; co-editor: International Handbook of Psychology, 1987, Chaos Theory in Psychology, 1995, Post-Soviet Perspectives on Russian Psychology, 1996; contbr. With USN, 1952—55. Named Fulbright Exch. lectr., U. Coll. Galway, Ireland, 1971—72. Fellow: APA, Am. Psychol. Soc.; mem.: AAAS, Fulbright Alumni Assn. Avocations: reading, maintaining Victorian house. Home: 1107 Washington St Cedar Falls IA 50613-3069 E-mail: albert.gilgen@uni.edu.

GILGER, MARK ALAN, pediatrician, educator; b. Kansas City, Mo., May 19, 1954; s. Virgil Lee and Odillia Anne (Erker) G.; m. Donna Lee Short, Sept. 5, 1982; children: Michael Alan, Katherine Anne, Caroline Leigh. BA in Sociology, Creighton U., 1976, MD, 1980. Diplomate Am. Bd. Pediatrics, sub.-bd. Pediatric Gastroenterology and Nutrition. Resident in pediat. U. Rochester, 1981-83; clin. dir. USPHS Indian Health Svc., Yuma, Ariz., 1984-86; fellow in pediat. gastroenterology Baylor Coll. Medicine, Houston, 1986-89, asst. prof. pediat., 1989—96, assoc. prof. pediat., 1996—. Contbr. chpts. to books, articles to profl. jours. Served as comdr. USPHS, 1983-86. Recipient Health Emphasis Campaign Role Model award Indian Health Svc., 1985, Nat. Rsch. Svc. award NIH, 1987, 88, 95; Baylor Pediatric award for excellence in teaching. Fellow Am. Acad. Pediatrics; mem. N.Am. Soc. Pediatric Gastroenterology and Nutrition. Avocations: running, tennis, golf, woodworking, music. Office: Baylor Coll Medicine 1 Baylor Plz Houston TX 77030-3411

GILGER, PAUL DOUGLASS, architect; b. Mansfield, Ohio, Oct. 13, 1954; s. Richard Douglass and Marilyn Joan (Hawkins) G. BArch, U. Cin., 1978. Registered architect, Ohio. Architect Soulen & Assocs., Mansfield, Ohio, 1976-81, PGS Architecture/Planning, Los Gatos, Calif., 1981-82, Bottomline Systems, Inc., San Francisco, 1983-85; pvt. practice San Francisco Bay Area, 1985-90; set designer Nomad Prodns. Scenic Studios, San Francisco, 1985-87; architect James Gillam, Architect, San Francisco, 1987-90, Hedgpeth Architects, Santa Rosa, Calif., 1990—, Home Planners, Inc., Tucson, 1994—. Booking mgr. 1177 Club, San Francisco, 1985-86, City Cabaret, San Francisco, 1986-87; bd. dirs San Francisco Coun. Entertainment, 1987-90; project architect Lucasfilm Movie Studio Indsl. Light and Magic, San Rafael, Calif., 1991. Author: "Showtune", the Jerry Herman Musical Revue. Recipient Ohio Cmty. Theatre Assn. award, 1980, Theatrewest Acting award, 1983, 3 Bay Area Critics Cir. award, 1984, 85, 4 Cabaret Gold awards San Francisco Coun. Entertainment, 1985, 86, 3 Hollywood Dramalogue awards, 1985, 5 awards. 1996; San Francisco Focus award, 1985. Avocations: travel, piano, automobiles. Home: 530 Juilliard Park Dr Santa Rosa CA 95401-6312 Office: Hedgpeth Architects 2321 Bethards Dr Santa Rosa CA 95405-8536 Business E-Mail: paul@hedgpetharchitects.com. E-mail: gilger@sonic.net.

GILGUN, JANE FRANCES, social work educator; b. Wakefield, R.I., July 30, 1943; d. James Harold and Rosaria Elvera Costanza Gilgun. BA, Cath. U., 1965; licentiate, U. Louvain, Belgium, 1971; MA, U. R.I., 1979, U. Chgo., 1984; PhD, Syracuse U., 1983. Lic. clin. social worker, Minn. Tchr. Vets. Meml. H.S., Warwick, R.I., 1968-69; coord. family planning Providence Health Ctrs., 1969-70; health educator St. Joseph's Hosp., Providence, 1970-71; social worker R.I. Child Welfare Svcs., Providence, 1971-79; grad. asst. Syracuse (N.Y.) U., 1979-83, U. Chgo., 1983-84; prof. social work U. Minn., Mpls., 1984—. Cons. in field. Editor: Qualitative Methods in Family Research, 1992, The Methods and Methodologies of Qualitative Family Research, 1996; contbr. articles to profl. publs. Bd. dirs. Project Pathfinder, St. Paul, 1992-99, Stop It Now Minn., 2001—. Recipient Silberman award Silberman Found., 1993, 97; rsch. grantee St. Paul Found., 1986-88, Allina Found., 1996-98. Mem. NASW, Soc. for Rsch. in Social Work, Nat. Coun. Family Rels., Internat. Soc. for Prevention of Child Abuse, Am. Profl. Soc. on Abuse of Children, Soc. for Study of Symbolic Interactionism, Internat. Fed. of Social Workers. Avocations: equitation, swimming, creative writing, gardening, theater. Office: U Minn Sch Social Work 1404 Gortner Ave Saint Paul MN 55108-6160 E-mail: jgilgun@umn.edu.

GILHAM, HANNA KALTENBRUNNER, writer; b. Linz, Austria, July 1, 1943; arrived in U.S., 1977; d. Werner and Marianne Kaltenbrunner; m. Royce Edward Gilham, Sept. 13, 1971. BA, East Carolina U., 1994. Office worker Teekanne, Salzburg, Austria, 1959—64; ground hostess Lufthansa, Frankfurt, Germany, 1965—66; distbr. Oefag Car Dealership, Salzburg, 1966—67; receptionist Europea Hotel Mirabell, Salzburg, 1968—71; writer, 1971—. Author: (book) CET, Color Equals Time, 2000, Elite, 2000, VS-VE=EA, 2002. Roman Catholic. Avocation: painting. Home: 401 Summit St Greenville NC 27858

GILHOOLY, DAVID JAMES, III, artist; b. Auburn, Calif., Apr. 15, 1943; s. David James and Gladys Catherine (Schulte) G.; m. Camille Margot Chang, Aug. 23, 1983; children: David James, Andrea Elizabeth, Abigail Margaret, Peter Rodney, Hakan Yuatutsu, Kiril Shintora, Sorqan Subetei. BA, U. Calif., Davis, 1965, MA, 1967. Tchr. San Jose (Calif.) State Coll., 1967-69, U. Sask. (Can.), Regina, 1969-71, York U., Toronto, Ont., Can., 1971-75, 76-77, U. Calif.-Davis, summer 1971, 75-76, Calif. State U.-Sacramento, summers 1978-79; lectr. in field. One-man shows include San Francisco Museum Art, 1967, M. H. deYoung Meml. Mus., San Francisco, 1968, Matrix Gallery, Wadsworth Athenuem, Hartford, Conn., 1976, Mus. Contemporary Art, Chgo., 1976, Vancouver (B.C., Can.), Art Gallery, 1976, ARCO Ctr. for Visual Arts, Los Angeles, 1977, Mus. Contemporary Craft, N.Y.C., 1977, E.B. Crocker Art Mus., Sacramento, 1980, St. Louis Mus. Art, 1981, Smith-Anderson Gallery, Palo Alto, 1985, San Jose Mus. Art, 1992, De Saisset Mus., Santa Clara U., 1999, Hallie Ford Mus. Art, Salem, Oreg., 2000; group shows include U. Calif.-Berkeley Art Mus., 1967, Inst. Contemporary Art, Boston, 1967, Whitney Mus. Am. Art, N.Y.C., 1970, 74, 81, Musee d'art de la Ville Paris, 1973, Chgo. Art Inst., 1975, San Francisco Mus. Art and Nat. Collection Fine Art, Washington, 1976-77, Stedelijk Mus., Amsterdam, The Netherlands, 1979, Everson Mus. Art, Syracuse, N.Y., 1979, Whitney Mus. Am. Art, N.Y.C., 1981, Palm Springs Desert Art Mus., 1984, Oakland Mus., 1985, Stanford Mus. Art, 1987, Inst. Contemporary Art, Boston, 1994, DeSaisset Mus., Santa Clara, Calif., 1999, Hallie Ford Mus., Salem, Oreg., 2000; represented in permanent collections S. Bronfman Collection Can. Art, Montreal, Que., San Francisco Mus. Art, Phila. Mus. Art, Vancouver Art Gallery, Art Gallery Greater Victoria (B.C.), Albright-Knox Art Gallery, Buffalo, San Antonio Mus. Art, Oakland (Calif.) Mus. Art, Stedelijk Mus., Stanford U., Palo Alto, Calif., Australian Nat. Gallery, Canberra, Govt. Can., Calgary, Alta., Whitney Mus. Am. Art, Eugene (Oreg.) Ctr. Performing Arts. Can. Council grantee, 1975, 78. Mem. Royal Can. Acad. Republican. Mem. Ch. of Scientology. Office: 4385 Yaquina Bay Rd Newport OR 97365-9618 E-mail: dgllhooly@earthlink.net.

GILHOUSEN, BRENT JAMES, lawyer; b. Anacortes, Wash., Sept. 24, 1946; s. Darrell J. and Jean Sarah (Sabatine) G.; m. Sandra M. King, Aug. 13, 1983; 2 children: Lindsay Elizabeth, Shane Shroeder. BA, Wash. State U., 1968; JD, U. Oreg., 1973. Bar: Wash. 1973, U.S. Dist. Ct. (we. dist.) Wash. 1973, U.S. Ct. Appeals (9th cir.) 1973, U.S. Supreme Ct. 1980, Mo. 1981, U.S. Ct. Appeals (4th cir.) 1986. From atty.-advisor to sr. atty. U.S. EPA, Seattle, 1973-80; from environ. atty. to asst. gen. counsel-environ. Monsanto Co., St. Louis, 1980-97; asst. gen. counsel-environ. Solutia Inc., St. Louis, 1997—. Mem. Superfund Settlements Project, Washington, 1988-95, 2001—; legal com. Chem. Industry Inst. Toxicology, Rsch. Triangle Park, N.C., 1986-99; mem. environ. law adv. com. Nat. Chamber Litigation Ctr., Washington, 1992-97. Mem. editl. bd. Hazardous Waste Strategies Update, 1994-2001. With USAR, 1968-74. Mem. ABA (sect. environ., energy and resources, chair corp. counsel com. 1994-96, vice-chair hazardous waste com. 1991-99), Am. Chem. Coun. (mem. enforcement subgroup 1995—), Def. Rsch. Inst., Forest Hills Country Club, Indian Wells Country Club.. Republican. Avocations: skiing, golf, boating. Home: 1 Peakmont Ln Chesterfield MO 63005-6806 Office: Solutia Inc 575 Maryville Centre Dr Saint Louis MO 63141-5813 E-mail: bjgilh@solutia.com.

GILHULY, PETER MARTIN, lawyer; b. Stamford, Conn., Aug. 20, 1961; s. Robert T. and Anne (Kilby) G.; m. Namhee Han, Aug. 20, 1988; children: Emma, Thompson Young, John Daniel. BA with honors, Wesleyan U., Middletown, Conn., 1983; JD cum laude, Harvard U., 1990. Bar: Calif. 1990, U.S. Dist. Ct. (ctrl. dist.) Calif. 1990. Vol. U.S. Peace Corps, Argali, Nepal, 1983-86; assoc. Latham & Watkins, L.A., 1990-98, ptnr., 1998—, nat. chair pro bono com., 1998—2003. Mem. adv. bd. Pacific Gemini LLC, L.A., 1995-97. Contbr. articles to law jours. Bd. dirs. Pub. Counsel, L.A., 1995-96; bd. govs. Fin. Lawyers Conf., 1999-2002; chmn. bd. dirs. A Place Called Home, L.A., 2001—. Recipient President's award Los Angeles County Barristers, 1998. Avocations: skiing, running, tennis. Office: Latham & Watkins 633 W 5th St Ste 4000 Los Angeles CA 90071-2005

GILIBERTI, MICHAEL RICHARD, financial planner; b. Bklyn., July 5, 1949; s. Michael John and Rosemarie (Lucich) G.; m. Rosemary Kathryn Pettina, June 17, 1972, 1 child, Sean Michael. BS in Math., Duquesne U., 1971. Cert. fin. planner. Agt. Metropolitan Life, Pitts., 1972-74, sales mgr., 1974-78, acct. exec., 1978-92, fin. planner, 1992—. Mem. Nat. Assn. Life Underwriters, Pitts. Assn. Life Underwriters, Registry of CFP Licensed Practitioners. Home: 92 Phillips Ln Mc Kees Rocks PA 15136-1075 Office: MetLife Securities Inc 2 Gateway Ctr Pittsburgh PA 15222-1402

GILINSKY, STANLEY ELLIS, department store executive; b. Trenton, N.J., Aug. 7, 1918; s. Charles Edgar and Rose (Kohn) G.; m. Gerry Braslove, Nov. 25, 1945; children: Michael, Ellen. BS, Lehigh U., 1940; LL.B., JD, U. Pa., 1944. Bar: Pa. 1944. Law sec. Justice Horace Stern Supreme Ct. Pa., Phila., 1944-45; assoc. firm Wolf, Block, Schorr & Solis-Cohen, Phila., 1944-46; asst. budget dir. R.H. Macy Corp., Newark, 1946-50; research, planning dir. Gimbels, Phila., 1950-58; dir. corp. expansion, devel. Gimbel Bros., Inc., N.Y.C., 1958-64, dir., 1964-68, corp. v.p., sec., 1968-80, also v.p. charge expansion, planning, devel. for Gimbels and Saks Fifth Ave. subs., 1964-76; v.p. Saks & Co., 1968-76; sr. v.p. corp. devel. and real estate Saks Fifth Ave., 1975-83, Gimbels, 1977-80, sr. v.p. Batus retail div., 1980-83; vice chmn. The Harlan Co., 1985—91, also dir.; dir. Saks & Co., Saks Retailing Corp.; v.p., dir. Fifth Win Corp. of Saks Fifth Ave., 1997-99; pres., dir. Peruvian Ave. Corp., Palm Beach, Fla., 1986—. Rep. Saks 5th Ave., a prin. shareholder of the parking facilities. Mem. Teaneck (N.J.) Polit. Assembly, 1962, Teaneck Redevel. Authority, 1970-74. Mem. Am. Mktg. Assn., Phi Beta Kappa, Pi Lambda Phi. Home and Office: 10504 Red Maple Ln Richmond VA 23233-4177 E-mail: Stanley.gilinsky@verizon.net.

GILINSKY, VICTOR, physicist; b. Warsaw, May 28, 1934; came to U.S., 1941, naturalized, 1948; s. Shlome Faywysh and Luba (Kantorowicz) G.; m. Madeleine Gilinsky, 2000; children from previous marriage: David, Anessa. BS in Engring. Physics, Cornell U., 1956; PhD in Physics, Calif. Inst. Tech., 1961. Physicist Rand Corp., Santa Monica, Calif., 1961-71, head dept. phys. sci., 1973-75; asst. dir. policy and program rev. AEC, Washington, 1971-73; mem. U.S. Nuclear Regulatory Commn., Washington, 1975-84, cons., 1984—. Mem. IEEE, Am. Phys. Soc., Internat. Inst. Strategic Studies, Internat. Conf. on Large Elec. Sys.

GILJE, PAUL ARN, history educator; b. Bklyn., Aug. 3, 1951; s. Arne and Wladja (Trendowski) G.; m. Ann Elisabeth Liebermann, Aug. 10, 1973; children: Erik, Karin. BA, Bklyn. Coll., 1974; MA, Brown U., 1975, PhD, 1980. Asst. prof. history U. Okla., Norman, 1980-86, assoc. prof., 1986-94, prof., 1994—, Samuel Roberts Nobel Found. Presdl. prof. dept. history, 2000—. Author: The Road to Mobocracy, 1992, Rioting in America, 1996; editor: Wages of Independence, 1997, Revolution and New Nation, 1761-1812, vol 3, Ency. Am. History, 2003; co-editor: Keepers of the Revolution, 1992, American Artisans, 1995. Fellow Rockefeller Found., Johns Hopkins U., 1987-88, Ctr. for History of Freedom, Washington U., St. Louis, 1991. Mem. Am. Hist. Assn., Orgn. of Am. Historians, Soc. of Historians of the Early Republic, Inst. of Early Am. History and Culture. Lutheran. Home: 808 Tarkington Dr Norman OK 73026-0868 Office: Dept History Univ Okla Norman OK 73019-0001

GILKES, CHERYL LOUISE TOWNSEND, sociologist, educator, minister; b. Boston, Nov. 2, 1947; d. Murray Luke Jr. and Evelyn Annette (Reid) Townsend. BA, MA, PhD, Northeastern U.; postgrad., Boston U., 1988. Lectr. Univ. Coll. Northeastern U., Boston, 1973-78; instr. sociology Boston State Coll., 1974-78, U. Mass., 1976; asst. prof. sociology Boston U., 1978-87; MacArthur assoc. prof. African-Am. studies and sociology Colby Coll., Waterville, Maine, 1989-2000, MacArthur asst. prof., 1987-89, MacArthur prof. African Am. studies and sociology, 2000—. Vis. lectr. Tufts U., 1974; rsch. assoc., vis. lectr. sociology of religion Harvard U. Div. Sch., 1981-82, vis. lectr. African-Am. religious studies, 1992-93; vis. lectr. Afro-Am. studies Simmons Coll., Chgo. Theol. Sem., 1989, Iliff Sch. Theology, 1989, Temple U., 1989; faculty fellow Bunting Inst., Radcliff Coll., 1982-84; vis. scholar Episcopal Div. Sch., 1992-93; fellow W.E.B. DuBois Inst. for Afro-Am. Rsch., Harvard U., Inst. Advanced Study Religion, Yale U., 1999-2000; host gospel music radio sta. WMHB Waterville, 2002—. Author: If It Wasn't for the Women...: Black Women's Experience and Womanist Culture in Church and Community, 2000; gospel music radio show host Sta. WMHB, Waterville, 2002—; contbr. articles and revs. to profl. jours., chpts. to books. Sec. Cambridge Civic Unity Com., 1978-87; mem. adv. com. Schlessinger Libr., Radcliffe Coll., 1984-86; pres. Cambridge Black Cultural and Hist. Assn., 1978-87; parliamentarian, asst. dean congress Christian Edn. United Bapt. Conv., Mass., R.I. and N.H., 1986—; assoc. min. Union Bapt. Ch., Cambridge, Mass., 1982-97, asst. pastor, 1998—; mem. NAACP. Nat. Fellowships fund dissertation fellow, 1977-78, Socialization Tng. fellow Northeastern U., 1970-73. Fellow: Inst. Advanced Study Religion; mem.: NAACP, Urban League Ea. Mass., Assn. for Sociology of Religion, Soc. Study Black Religion, Soc. Sci. Study of Religion (exec. coun. 1995—97), Sociologists Women in Soc. (lectr. 2002—), Assn. Black Sociologists, Soc. Study of Sybolic Interaction, Am. Acad. Religion, Assn. Humanist Sociology, Soc. Study of Social Problems (v.p. 1990—91), Mass. Sociol. Assn., Ea. Sociol. Soc. (v.p. 1995—96), Am. Sociol. Assn. (Spivak dissertation fellow 1977—78, mem. coun. 1995—98), Delta Sigma Theta, Phi Kappa Phi. Office: Colby Coll Dept Sociology Waterville ME 04901

GILL, ALLEN (DALE GILL), environmental management service; b. London, Ky., Sept. 12, 1957; s. Roland And Edna (Hurley) G.; m. Beverley Joe Stull, Dec. 8, 1990; children: Brandon Michael, Heather Ann. Student, Laurel County Vocat. Tech., 1979-80, 84-86. With order dept. Griffin Pie Co., London, Ky., 1980-83; collection mgr. Sterchi Bros., Corbin, Ky., 1983-86; carpenter, mason London, 1986-89; environ. mgmt. dept. housekeeper VA, Lexington, Ky., 2001—. Author religious poems. With U.S. Army, 1975-79. Republican. Methodist. Avocations: swimming, family, woodworking, church activities. Home: 960 Hwy 1778 Kings Mountain KY 40442

GILL, ARDIAN C. actuary, photographer, writer; b. Griswold, Conn., Oct. 9, 1929; s. Lewis A. and Sarah (Geer) G.; m. Jill Freeman, May 29, 1954; children: Tracy, Claudia, John Freeman; m. 2d, Anna Hannon, Sept. 9, 1988. BA with honors in Math, U. Conn., 1951. With Travelers Ins. Co., 1951-54; with Mut. Life Ins. Co., N.Y., 1954-77, 2d v.p., actuary, 1965-66, v.p., actuary, 1966-70, sr. v.p., chief actuary, chief fin. officer, 1970-77; mgmt. cons. N.Y.C., 1977-78; v.p., prin., dir. Tillinghast, Nelson & Warren, N.Y.C., 1978-83; chmn. Gill & Roeser, Inc., 1983-92; pres. Gill & Roeser Life Intermediaries, Inc., N.Y.C., 1992—. Adj. prof. Coll. Ins., 1992—94; pres. Local Color, Author, Photographer. Trustee Village of Saltaire, 1970-72. Fellow Soc. Actuaries (bd. govs. 1974-76, 82-84, v.p. 1978-80), Can. Inst. Actuaries; mem. Acad. Actuaries (bd. dirs. 1987-90), N.Y. Actuaries Club (pres. 1971-72) Home: 316 W 79th St New York NY 10024-6125 Office: Studio 506 526 W 26th St New York NY 10001-5517 E-mail: agillr@aol.com.

GILL, BECKY LORETTE, retired psychiatrist; b. Phoenix, Mar. 16, 1947; d. David Franklin and Lorette (Cooper) Brinegar; m. Jim Shack Gill, Jr., Aug. 5, 1978. BA in Biology, Stanford U., 1968; MD, U. Ariz., 1973. Diplomate Am. Bd. Psychiatry and Neurology; cert. addiction counselor; substance abuse residential facility dir., addictions specialist, clin. supr. Clerk typist Ariz. Med. Ctr. Med. Libr., Tucson, 1970, asst. ref. libr., 1971; surg. extern Tucson Med. Ctr., summer 1970; med. extern Fed. Reformatory for Women, Alderson, W.Va., 1972-73; commd. lt. USN, 1974, advanced through grades to capt., 1992; intern in medicine USPHS Hosp., Balt., 1973-74; resident in psychiatry Nat. Naval Med. Ctr., Bethesda, Md., 1974-77; head alcohol rehab. svc./substance abuse dept., staff psychiatrist Naval Hosp., Camp Lejeune, N.C., 1977-85, head alcohol rehab. svc./substance abuse dept., head psych. Millington, Tenn., 1985-88, head alcohol rehab. dept. Long Beach, Calif., 1988-94; head Navy Addictions Rehab. and Edn. Dept., Camp Pendleton, Calif., 1994-2001; ret., 2001. Mem. tumor bd. Naval Hosp., Camp Lejeune, 1977-85, cons. Tri-Command Consolidated Drug and Alcohol Counseling Ctr. Agy., 1977-85, phys. fitness program com., 1980-85, med. liaison on substance abuse, 1982-85, drug/alcohol program advisor, 1983-85, Tri-Command Consolidated Drug and Alcohol Adv. Coun., 1983-85, controlled substance abuse review subcom. of pharmacy and therapeutics com., 1984-85; watch officer Acute Care Clinic, Naval Hosp., Millington, 1985-86, cons. Counseling and Assistance Ctr., 1985-88, mem. bioethics com., chmn. med. records, utilization review com., 1985-88, exec. com. med. staff, chmn., 1986-87, psychiatric cons. to NAS Brig, 1986-88, mem. quality assurance com., 1986, mem. credentials com., 1986-87, pharmacy and therapeutics com., 1986, pos. mgmt. com., 1986-87, dir. med. svcs., 1986-88, dir. surgical svcs., 1986, commd. duty watch officer, 1986-87, watch officer acute care clinic, 1987-88, mem. Navy Drug and Alcohol adv. coun., 1987-88, preceptor to social worker, 1987-88, pos. mgmt. com., 1988, mem. commd. retention coun., 1988; also, numerous coms. at Naval Hosp., Long Beach, Calif., Naval Hosp., Camp Pendleton, Calif. Capt. USN. Decorated Commendation medal USN, Meritorious Svc. medal, Legion of Merit, Army Commendation. Mem. Am. Acad. of Psychiatrists in Alcoholism and Addictions (founding mem.), Am. Soc. of Addiction Medicine, Addiction Profls. of N.C. (chmn. pub. info. com. 1979-80, ea. regional v.p. 1981-82, chmn. fall meeting planning com. 1983, sec. 1984-85), Nat. Assn. of Alcoholism and Drug Abuse Counselors, Am. Legion, VFW Aux. U.S. Lawn Tennis Assn. (hon. life), Stanford Cap and Gown, Stanford Alumni Assn., U. Ariz. Alumni Assn., Stanford Cardinal Club. Democrat. Avocations: tennis, swimming, jogging. Home: PMB 8187 PO Box 2428 Pensacola FL 32513-2428

GILL, CLAIR F. military career officer; b. Johnstown, Pa., July 7, 1943; m. Sherry Angello; children: Clair, Heidi, Christopher. Grad., U.S. Mil. Acad., 1965; MS in Civil Engring., U. Calif., Berkeley; postgrad., Harvard U.; grad., Command & Gen. Staff Coll., Army War Coll. Registered profl. engr., D.C. Commd. officer U.S. Army C.E., 1965, advanced through grades to maj. gen., various positions including platoon leader, 1965-71; asst. exec. officer to dean Mil. Acad., 1971-74; dir. facilities engring., dir. engring. and housing U.S. Mil. Cmty. Activity, Ansbach, Germany; exec. officer 16th Engr. Battalion, 1st Armored Divsn. U.S. Army, Germany, 1977-79, comdr. 14th Engr. Battalion; chief manpower and force programs analysis divsn. Office of the Chief of Staff, Washington; comdr. 7th Engr. Brigade VII Corps U.S. Army, Germany; comdr. Pacific Ocean divsn. U.S. Army C.E., Ft. Shafter, Hawaii; dep. chief staff, engr. U.S. Army Europe and Seventh Army, Heidelberg, Germany; dir. resource mgmt. U.S. Army Forces Command, Ft. McPherson, Ga.; commdg. gen./commandant U.S. Army Engr. Ctr., Ft. Leonard Wood; dep. asst. sec. Army for Budget Office of the Asst. Sec. of the Army. Decorated Legion of Merit with 3 oak leaf clusters, Bronze Star medal with 2 oak leaf clusters, Meritorious Svc. medal, Air medal. Office: Office of the Asst Sec of the Army 109 Army Pentagon Washington DC 20310-0109

GILL, DAVID BRIAN, electrical engineer, educator; b. Columbus, Ohio, Oct. 23, 1957; s. Emery Jr. and Norma Jean Gill; m. Karen Marie Schaar, June 25, 1988. BSEE with highest distinction, Purdue U., 1978, MSEE, 1979, MBA, 1981. Registered profl. engr., Tex. Systems design engr. Owens-Ill., Toledo, 1976-80; engr. Tex. Instruments Def. Group, Dallas, 1981-84, lead engr., 1984-86, mem. group tech. staff, 1986-88, br. mgr., 1988-95, sr. mem. tech. staff, 1995—2001; sr. fellow Raytheon, 2001—. Instr. Purdue U., West Lafayette, Ind., 1978-80, Richland Coll. Engring. Lab., Dallas, 1982-96. Editor lab. manual Control Systems Workbook, 1979. Krannert scholar, 1981. Mem. Purdue Alumni Assn. (life), IEEE, Assn. Old Crows, Phi Eta Sigma, Tau Beta Pi, Eta Kappa Nu, Beta Gamma Sigma, Phi Kappa Phi. Avocations: golf, skeet shooting, hunting. Office: Raytheon 2501 W University Dr Mc Kinney TX 75071-2813

GILL, DIANE LOUISE, psychology educator, university official; b. Watertown, N.Y., Nov. 7, 1948; d. George R. and Betty J. (Reynolds) G. BS in Edn., SUNY, Cortland, N.Y., 1970; MS, U. Ill., 1974, PhD, 1976. Tchr. Greece Athena High Sch., Rochester, N.Y., 1970-72; asst. prof. U. Waterloo, Ont., Can., 1976-78, U. Iowa, Iowa City, 1979-81, assoc. prof., 1981-86; assoc. prof. sport & exercise psychology U. N.C., Greensboro, 1987-89, prof. Greenboro, 1989—, assoc. dean Greensboro, 1992-97, head dept. exercise and sport sci., 1997-2000, dir. Ctr. for Women's Health and Wellness, 2002—. Author: Psychological Dynamics of Sport and Exercise, 1986, 2000; editor Jour. of Sport and Exercise Psychology, 1985-90; contbr. articles to profl. jours. Fellow AAHPERD (rsch. consortium pres. 1987-89), APA (pres. divsn. 47 exercise and sport 1999-2001), Am. Psychol. Soc., Assn. for Advancement of Applied Sport Psychology, Am. Acad. Kinesiology and Phys. Edn.; mem. N.Am. Soc. for Psychology of Sport and Phys. Activity (pres. 1988-91). Democrat. Office: U NC Dept Exercise and Sport Sci Greensboro NC 27402-6170 E-mail: diane_gill@uncg.edu.

GILL, DONALD GEORGE, education educator; b. O'Fallon, Ill., Dec. 3, 1927; s. Fred Kenneth and Anna (Mayer) G.; m. Betty Jo Brummal, Dec. 28, 1952; children— Donald Bruce, Ann Brummal, Gay Ellen. AB, Ill. Coll., 1951; MEd, U. Ill., 1954, EdD, 1969; LLD, Ill. Coll., 1981. Tchr. Waverly (Ill.) Public Schs., 1950-52; prin., elem. and jr. high schs. Taylorville, Ill., 1952-60; asst. dir., dir. Labs. Schs. Eastern Ill. U., Charleston, 1960-74; also prof. edn.; supt. schs. Volusia County, Deland Daytona Beach, Fla., 1974-80; supt. Ill. Dept. Edn., Springfield, 1980-85; DuPont prof. edn., chmn. div. edn. Stetson U., DeLand, Fla., 1985—. Chmn. Ill. Tchr. Cert. Bd., 1980-85; pres. trustees Ill. Tchr. Retirement System, 1980-85; Ill. commr. Edn. Commn. U.S., 1980-85 Contbr. articles to profl. jours. Mem. Charleston (Ill.) Twp. Bd., 1964-74. Served with USN, 1945-46. Mem. Am. Assn. Sch. Adminstrs., Council Chief State Sch. Officers, Fedn. Urban Suburban Sch. Dists. (exec. com.), Phi Delta Kappa, Omicron Delta Kappa. Office: Stetson Univ Chmn Div Edn Deland FL 32720 *From early in my youth onward I have had a deep commitment to the Democratic Ideal based upon the inherent dignity of man under the sovereignty of God.*

GILL, E. ANN, lawyer; b. Elyria, Ohio, Aug. 31, 1951; d. Richard Henry and Laura (Beeler) G.; m. Robert William Hempel, Aug. 4, 1973; children: Richard, Peter, Mary. AB, Barnard Coll., 1972; JD, Columbia U., 1976. Bar: N.Y. 1977, U.S. Supreme Ct. 1982. Assoc. Mudge, Rose, Guthrie & Alexander, N.Y.C., 1976-77, Dewey Ballantine L.L.P., N.Y.C., 1977-84, ptnr., 1985—. Mem. ABA, Nat. Assn. Bond Lawyers. Home: 255 W 90th St New York NY 10024-1109 Office: Dewey Ballantine 1301 Ave of the Americas New York NY 10019-6022 E-mail: agill@deweyballantine.com.

GILL, EVALYN PIERPOINT, editor, writer, publisher; b. Boulder, Colo. d. Walter Lawrence and Lou Octavia Pierpoint; m. John Glanville Gill; children: Susan Pierpoint, Mary Louise Glanville. Student, Lindenwood Coll.; BA, U. Colo.; postgrad., U. Nebr., U. Alaska; MA, Ctrl. Mich. U., 1968. Lectr. humanities Saginaw Valley State Coll., University Ctr., Mich., 1968-72; mem. English faculty U. N.C., Greensboro, 1973-74; editor Internat. Poetry Rev., Greensboro, 1975-92; pres. TransVerse Press, Greensboro, 1981—. Author: Poetry by French Women, 1930-1980, 1980, Dialogue, 1985, Southeast of Here: Northwest of Now, 1986, Entrances, 1996; editor: O. Henry Festival Stories, 1985, 87, Women of the Piedmont Triad: Poetry and Prose, 1989, Edge of Our World, 1990, A Turn in Time: Piedmont Writers at the Millennium, 1999. Bd. dirs. Eastern Music Festival, Greensboro, 1981-85, Greensboro Symphony, 1982-86, Greensboro Opera Co., 1982—, Weatherspoon Art Mus., 1980-; chmn. O Henry Festival, 1985, 95. Recipient numerous poetry prizes, Fortner award St. Andrews Coll., 1995, Altrusa Internat. Cmty. Arts award, Greensboro, 1998. Mem. MLA, Amn. Lit. Translators Assn., N.C. Poetry Soc., Phi Beta Kappa. Home: 2900 Turner Grove Dr N Greensboro NC 27455-1977

GILL, GENE, artist; b. Memphis, June 18, 1933; s. Edward Morris and Annie Zelma (Mondy) G. BFA, Chouinard Art Inst., L.A., 1962. One-man shows include Comara Gallery, L.A., 1970, 71, 74, Orlando Gallery, Sherman Oaks, Calif., 1995, Ronald Reagan Presdl. Libr., Simi Valley, Calif., 2000; exhibited in group shows Esplanade Gallery, Santa Monica, 1969, L.A. Art Assn. Galleries, 1970, R and W. Gallery, Memphis, 1971, Scripts Coll., 1971, San Diego Fine Arts Mus., 1971, Laguna Beach Mus. Art, 1971, 72, 77, Palm Springs Mus. Art, 1973, L.A. County Mus. Art, 1973, Van Straaten Gallery, Chgo., 1974, Mepl Art Gallery, L.A., 1976; represented in permanent collections L.A. County Mus. Art, Palm Springs Desert Mus. Art, Atlantic Richfield Corp, Northrop Corp., Container Corp. Am., Home Savings, Pattiz Found., Westside Jewish Cmty. Ctr., Ronald Reagan Libr., Tee Ridder Miniatures Mus., Roslyn Harbor, NY. With USN, 1954-58. Recipient numerous awards at juried art shows. Home: 3895 Valley Lights Dr Pasadena CA 91107-1345 E-mail: gene.gill@verizon.net.

GILL, GEORGE NORMAN, newspaper publishing company executive; b. Indpls., Aug. 11, 1934; s. George E. and Urith (Dailey) G.; m. Kay Baldwin, Dec. 28, 1957; children— Norman A., George B. AB, Ind. U., 1957. Reporter Richmond (Va.) News Leader, 1957-60; copy editor, reporter, acting Sunday editor, city editor, mng. editor Courier-Jour., Louisville, 1960-74; v.p., gen. mgr. Courier-Jour. and Louisville Times Co., 1974-79, sr. v.p. corp. affairs, 1979-80, pres., chief exec. officer, 1981-86. Chief exec. officer affiliates Standard Gravure Corp., WHAS, Inc., 1981-86; pres., pub. Courier-Jour. and Louisville Times Co., 1986-93. Served with USNR, 1954-56. Recipient Picture Editors award Nat. Press Photographers Assn., 1965 Mem. Am. Soc. Newspaper Editors, Asso. Press Mng. Editors, Alpha Tau Omega, Sigma Delta Chi. Home: PO Box 108 Pewee Valley KY 40056-0108 E-mail: gillg@BellSouth.net.

GILL, GEORGE WILHELM, anthropologist; b. Sterling, Kans., June 28, 1941; s. George Laurance and Florence Louise (Jones) Gill; m. Carol Anne Livesay, Aug. 11, 1962 (div. 1974); children: George Scott, John Ashton; m. Pamela Jo Mills, July 26, 1975 (div. 1988); children: Bryce Thomas, Jennifer Florence; m. Denise Ann Royer, Oct. 30, 2001. BA in Zoology with honors (NSF grantee), U. Kans., 1963, MPhil Anthropology (NDEA fellow, NSF grantee), 1970, PhD in Anthropology, 1971. Diplomate Am. Bd. Forensic Anthropology. Mem. faculty U. Wyo., Laramie, 1971—, prof. anthropology, 1985—, chmn. dept. anthropology, 1993—96. Forensic anthropologist law enforcement agys., 1972—; sci. leader Easter Island Anthrop. Expdn., 1981; bd. dirs. Am. Bd. Forensic Anthropology, 1985-91; chmn. Rapa Nui Rendezvous: Internat. Conf. Easter Island Rsch., U. Wyo., 1993. Author: articles, monographs; editor: (with S. Rhine) Skeletal Attribution of Race, 1990. Served to capt. U.S. Army, 1963-67. Recipient J.P. Ellbogen meritorious classroom tchg. award, 1983; rsch. grantee U. Wyo., 1972, 78, 82, Nat. Geog. Soc., 1980, Ctr. for Field Rsch. 1980, Kon-Tiki Mus., Oslo, 1987, 89, 94, 96, World Monuments Fund, 1989, Mus. Inventory and Curation grantee BLM, Bur. Reclamation, Wyo. DOT, Fish and Wildlife Svc., 1994-99. Fellow: Am. Acad. Forensic Scis. (sec. phys. anthropology sect. 1985—87, chmn. 1987—88); mem.: Wyo. Archaeol. Soc., Plains Anthrop. Soc., Am. Assn. Phys. Anthropologists. Republican. Presbyterian. Home: 649 Howe Rd Laramie WY 82070-6885 Office: U Wyo Dept Anthropology Laramie WY 82071 E-mail: ggill@uwyo.edu.

GILL, GERALD LAWSON, librarian; b. Montgomery, Ala., Nov. 13, 1947; s. George Ernest and Marjorie (Hackett) G.; m. Nancy Argroves, Mar. 5, 1977 (div. 1982). AB, U. Ga., 1971; MA, U. Wis., 1973. Cert. profl. libr., Va. Cataloger James Madison U., Harrisonburg, Va., 1974-76, reference libr., 1976-87, bus. reference libr., 1987-99, govt. documents libr., 1998—2003, head of reference and govt. documents, 2003—, instr., 1974-80, asst. prof., 1980-90, assoc. prof., 1990—2002, prof., 2002—. Lectr., spkr. nat. and regional groups; cons. in field; mem. faculty senate James Madison U., 1975-79, 96-98, sec. curriculum and instrn. com., 1976-78, chair, 1978-79, univ. coun., 1996-98. Mem. editl. bd. James Madison Jour., 1977-80; reviewer Am. Reference Books Ann.; contbr. articles to profl. jours. Mem. libr. adv. com. State Coun. for Higher Edn. in Va., 1986-87; virtual Va. Coord. Mgmt. Bus. com. Mem. ALA (chmn. bus. reference svcs. com. 1984-86, sec. law and polit. sci. sect. 1982-85, chmn. bus. reference svcs. discussion group 1986-87, chmn. bus. reference in acad. librs. com. 1988-91, Gale Rsch. award 1991), AAAS, Am. Soc. for Info. Sci., Va. Libr. Assn. (coun. 1986-87, parliamentarian 1979, 81), Spl. Librs. Assn. (treas. Va. chpt. 1983-85, pres. 1986-87), World Future Soc., Harrisonburg C. of C., Sierra Club. Democrat. Roman Catholic. Avocations: art collecting, travel. Home: 326 Westfield Rd Charlottesville VA 22901-1660 Office: James Madison U Library Harrisonburg VA 22807-0001 E-mail: gillgl@jmu.edu.

GILL, GORDON N. medical educator; b. Dec. 19, 1937; BA in Chemistry/Lit., Vanderbilt U., 1960, MD, 1963. Diplomate Am. Bd. Internal Medicine with subspecialty in endocrinology and metabolism. Intern in internal medicine Vanderbilt U. Hosp., Nashville, 1963-64; resident Yale-New Haven Hosp., 1964-66; fellow postdoctoral fellow metabolism/endocrinology NIH/Yale U., 1966-68; spl. postdoctoral rsch. fellow NIH/U. Calif., San Diego, 1968-69; asst. prof. medicine U. Calif., San Diego, 1969-73, assoc. prof., 1973-78, prof. medicine, 1978—, chief divsn. endocrinology dept. medicine, 1971-83, chief divsn. endocrinology/metabolism, 1983-95, assoc. chair sci. affairs, 1992-95, chmn. faculty basic biomed. scis., 1995—, dean sci. affairs, 2001—03, interim dir. Moores/UCSD Cancer Ctr., 2003—. Chmn. endocrinology study sect. NIH, 1979-80, chmn. task force on endocrinology, 1978, dir. tng. grant on exptl. endocrinology and metabolism, 1978—; prin. investigator interdisciplinary program to study macromolecules regulating growth and oncogenesis U. Calif., San Diego, 1988-95; chmn. Gordon Conf. on Hormone Action, 1979, Gordon Conf. on Peptide Growth Factors, 1990; mem. sci. adv. bd. BioCryst, 1990—; sci. and med. adv. bd. chair Whittier Inst., 1991-95; sci. adv. bd. Liver Ctr., U. Calif., San Francisco, 1991-95, Charles E. Culpepper Found., 1992—, Coun. for Tobacco Rsch. USA, 1991-97, ICN Pharms., 1992—; internat. adv. bd. dept. molecular and structural biology U. Grenoble, France, 1993—; S. Richardson Hill vis. prof. U. Ala., Birmingham, 1991; Berlin lectr. Northwestern U. Sch. Medicine, 1994, sci. adv. bd. Chau, Kirsch Found., 2001—. Mem. editl. bd. Jour. Cyclic Nucleotide and Protein Phosphorylation Rsch., 1974-84, Endocrinology, 1978-82, Am. Jour. Physiology, Cell Physiology, 1981-87, Jour. Biol. Chemistry, 1983-88, Jour. Cellular Biochemistry, 1984-89, Ann. Rev. Medicine, 1986-91, Analytical Biochemistry, 1980-92; editor Molecular and Cellular Endocrinology, 1974-92; cons. editor Jour. Clin. Investigation, 1992-97; sect. editor: Endocrinology, Best and Taylor Physiological Basis of Medical Practice, 11th-12th edits., Endocrinology and Metabolism, Cecil's Textbook of Medicine, 20th-22nd edit. Bd. dirs. Med. Rsch. and Edn. Found., The Agouron Inst., 1985—; mem. biochemistry and endocrinology sci. adv. com. Am. Cancer Soc., 1989-91; adv. com. Markey Charitable Trust, 1990-97; peer rev. com. Am. Heart Assn., 1991-96. Helen Hay Whitney Found. fellow, 1969-73; NIH Rsch. Career Devel. awardee, 1969-73, Merit award. Fellow ACP, Am. Acad. Arts and Scis.; mem. AAAS, Assn. Am. Physicians, Am. Fedn. Clin. Rsch., Am. Soc. Clin. Investigation, Am. Soc. Biol. Chemistry and Molecular Biology, Endocrine Soc., Western Assn. Physicians, Western Soc. for Clin. Investigation, Am. Soc. for Cell Biology, Phi Beta Kappa, Alpha Omega Alpha. Office: Univ Calif 9500 Gilman Dr La Jolla CA 92093-5003

GILL, HARDAYAL SINGH, electrical engineer; b. Amritsar, Punjab, India, Aug. 18, 1952; came to U.S., 1974; BSc with honors, Punjabi U., Patiala, 1971, MSc, 1973; PhD, U. Minn., Mpls., 1978. Sr. engr. Nat. Semiconductor, Santa Clara, Calif., 1978-81; mem. tech. staff Hewlett-Packard, Palo Alto, Calif., 1981-83, project leader, 1983-85, project mgr., 1985-90; sr. engr. IBM, San Jose, Calif., 1990-94, sr. tech. staff, 1994-97; IBM Disting. engr., 1997—. Contbr. over 100 articles to profl. jours. Fellow IEEE (chmn. Magnetics Soc. 1987-88, chmn. Santa Clara sect. 1992-93, adminstrv. com. Magnetics Soc. 1992-94); mem. Am. Phys. Soc. Achievements include over 100 U.S. patents on data storage devices. Avocations: tennis, bike riding. Office: IBM Corp MS N17/142 5600 Cottle Rd San Jose CA 95123-3696

GILL, HENRY HERR, photojournalist; b. Detroit, July 21, 1930; s. Henry Herr and Esther (King) G.; m. Mary Jane Brown, Aug. 26, 1957. Student, Vincennes U., 1948, Northwestern U., 1949, Ind. U., 1951, McNeese State U., La., 1952, U. Miami, 1962. Mem. publ. staff U. Miami, 1960; fgn. service photographer, then dir. photography Chgo. Daily News, 1976; dir. photography Chgo. Sun-Times, 1978-83; pres., exec. editor Globalfoto/Roma, 1983-87; pres., film dir. Fotostar Prodns., 1987—. Lectr. in field, exhibitor of photographs, 1964— Co-author: Mississippi Notebook, 1964; photographer: film A War of Many Faces, 1965, The Cocaine Express, 1982. Recipient photo reporting award on Vietnam Nat. Headliners Club, 1967, Overseas Press Club award, 1967, 81, Emmy award for documentary Nat. Acad. TV Arts and Scis., 1965, Best News Picture of Yr. award Inland Press Assn., 1968, 69, Faculty citation Vincennes U., 1979, Baker Meml. Journalism award, 1980; named to Journalism Hall of Fame, 1994. Mem. Internat. Press Club (Chgo.), Headliner Club (Chgo.), Sigma Delta Chi (Disting. Journalism award 1965). E-mail: gattolv@earthlink.net.

GILL, JO ANNE MARTHA, middle school educator; b. L.A., July 8, 1940; d. James Hurse Wilson and Martha Grace (Hanson) Wilson Horn; m. Richard Martin Gill, Apr. 18, 1959; 1 child, Richard James. BA in Interdisciplinary Studies, Nat. U., San Diego, 1989; MA in Edn. Adminstrn., Calif. State U., San Bernardino, 1992. Cert. tchr. pre-sch. through adult edn., social sci., adminstrn. Tchr. grades 6 and 7 Palm Springs (Calif.) Unified Sch. Dist., 1989-94, tchr. 8th grade U.S. history, gifted/regular, 1994-2001; prof. edn. Calif. State U., San Bernardino, 2001—; ednl. cons.; cons. tchr. PAR/BTSA, 2001—. Cons. Desert Schs. Consortium, Palm Springs, 1993-95, Inland Empire History/Social Studies, Riverside, Calif., 1991-95, Palm Springs Unified Sch. Dist.; adv. bd. Inland Empire Lit. Project, 1994-98; mem. leadership team Inland Area History/Social Sci. Summer Inst., U. Calif., Riverside, 1994-98; presenter in field. Contbr. articles to profl. jours. Mem. Calif. State History Standards and Course Models Commn.; coach mid. sch. demonstration program. Inland Area History/Social Sci. Adv. Acad. fellow, 1991, NEH fellow, 1993, Calif. History/Social Sci. Project/UCLA fellow, 1994; recipient 1st pl. award/tchr. multimedia group presentation Nat. History Day, 1996, 98. Mem. AAUW (home tour guide 1993), Calif. Coun. for the Social Studies (presenter conf. workshop 1993, 95, 96), Calif. Assn. for Gifted (presenter ann. conf. workshop 1994, 96, 98, Calif. Outstanding Middle Sch. Educator Area 9 1997), Inland Empire Coun. for the Social Studies (pres. 1994-96, Outstanding Middle Sch. Educator area 9 local award 1997), Delta Kappa Gamma (scholarship fundraising com. 1993-94, Theta Zeta Chi (pres. 1998-2000). Democrat. Roman Catholic. Avocations: hiking, fishing, reading, travel, writing. Office: Palm Springs Unified Schs 980 E Tahquitz Canyon Way Palm Springs CA 92262-6786

GILL, JOSEPH F. music educator; s. Joseph F. and Angela M. Gill; m. Evelyn R. Coen, Dec. 30, 1972. MusB, Millikin U., 1968—72. Cert. tchr. Ill. State Bd. Edn., 2001. Band dir. Decatur Sch. Dist. 61, Decatur, 1972—73, Paris Union Sch. Dist. 95, 1974—. Music instr., prep dept. Millikin U., 1972—74. Com. mem. Mabel Wells Fishback Scholarship Com., Paris, 1982—2003; publicity chmn. Edgar County Cmty. Concert Assn., Paris, 1985—87, com. mem., 1985—2000; dir. Paris Big Band, 1999—2000. Mem.: NEA, Music Educators Nat. Conf., Internat. Assn. Jazz Edn., Lionel Collectors Club of Am. Avocations: jazz, gardening, collecting toy trains. Office: Paris High Sch 309 S Main St Paris IL 61944 E-mail: gillj@paris95.k12.il.us.

GILL, KENNETH DUANE, minister, missiologist; b. Pomona, Calif., Apr. 23, 1946; s. Roy Heflin and Madelyn Ruth (Reed) G.; m. Judith Ann Haggerton, Apr. 25, 1970; children: Matthew Houston, Manola Roberta. BA, Pepperdine Coll., 1969; MA, Fuller Theol. Sem., Pasadena, Calif., 1977; MSLS, U. Ky., 1982; PhD, U. Birmingham, Eng., 1990. Ordained to ministry Ind. Pentecostal Ch., 1977. Assoc. pastor Parkview Christian Ch., Arcadia, Calif., 1976-77, missionary, 1977-84; assoc. pastor Jesus Chapel, El Paso, Tex., 1984-85; theol. libr. Billy Graham Ctr. Libr., Wheaton, Ill., 1985-96; acting dir. Billy Graham Ctr., Wheaton, 1996-98, assoc. dir., 1998—. Dir. EMIS, 1997—; coord. CINCOMEX, Mexico City, 1979-81. Book rev. editor The Christian Librarian, 1991-94. Mem. Am. Soc. Missiology (pub. 1989-2002), Assn. Christian Librs. (co-chair Commn. on Internat. Libr. Assistance 1989-97), Internat. Assn. Mission Studies, Soc. for Pentecostal Studies, Acad. for Evangelism in Theol. Edn. (book rev. editor 1999—), Evang. Missiological Soc. (v.p. for publs. 1999—). Office: Wheaton Coll Billy Graham Ctr Wheaton IL 60187 *It has always intrigued me that those who claim that we lack the capability to measure God's impact on the universe often posit a universe which precludes the possibility of his existence.*

GILL, MARY LOUISE GLANVILLE, educator of classics and philosophy; b. Alton, Ill., July 31, 1950; d. John Glanville and Evalyn Ruth (Pierpoint) G. BA, Barnard Coll., 1972; MA, Columbia U., 1974; BA, Cambridge (Eng.) U., 1976, MA, PhD, 1981. Instr. U. Pitts., 1979-81, asst. prof., 1981-88, assoc. prof., 1988-94, prof., 1994—2001, Brown U., Providence, 2001—. Vis. asst. prof. Dartmouth Coll., Hanover, N.H., 1984, Stanford (Calif.) U., 1985; dir. program in classics, philosophy, and ancient sci. U. Pitts., 1988-93; vis. prof. philosophy and classics Harvard U., Cambridge, Mass., 1998-99; vis. assoc. prof. UCLA, 1994; vis. prof. U. Calif., Davis, 1995; chair of classics U. Pitts., 1994-97; vis. scholar Princeton (N.J.) U., 1989; vis. fellow Clare Hall, Cambridge (Eng.) U., 1994; mem. Inst. for Advanced Study, Princeton, 1999-2000. Author: Aristotle on Substance, 1989; book review editor Ancient Philosophy Jour., 1983-88, co-editor, 1988—; co-translator, author introduction: Plato: Parmenides, 1996; co-editor: Self-Motion: From Aristotle to Newton, 1994, Unity, Identity and Explanation in Aristotle's Metaphysics, 1994; series editor: Ashgate Publs., 1999—; mem. editl. bd. History of Philosophy Quar., 1990-93, Philosophy and Phenomenological Research, 2002—. Faculty rsch. grant U. Pitts., 1981, Am. Coun. of Learned Socs. Travel grant, 1989; Ethel Wattis Kimball fellow Stanford Humanities Ctr., 1985-86; recipient Pres. Disting. Rsch. award U. Pitts., 1990. Mem. Am. Philol. Assn., Am. Philos. Assn., N.Y. Ancient Philosophy Colloquium. Home: 36 Bowen St Providence RI 02903 Office: Dept Philosophy Brown U Box 1918 Providence RI 02912

GILL, MILTON RANDALL, minister, artist; b. Cheverly, Md., Dec. 8, 1950; s. Milton Thomas and Patricia Georgiana (King) G.; m. Carroll Ann Bennett, Nov. 10, 1979; 1 child, Laura Grace. BS, U. Md., 1973; MDiv, Princeton Sem., 1977; DMin, South Fla. Ctr. Theol. Studies, Miami, 1995. Ordained to ministry Presbyn. Ch., 1979. Pastor First Presbyn. Ch., Theresa, N.Y., 1979-84, Weirsdale (Fla.) Presbyn. Ch., 1984-89, First Presbyn. Ch., Boynton Beach, Fla., 1989—. Adj. prof., Fla. Ctr. Theol. Studies, Miami, 2000-2001; sem. del. Gen. Assembly Presbyn. Ch. (U.S.A.), Balt., 1976; pres. Thousand Island Clergy Assn., Alexandria Bay, N.Y., 1982-83, Boynton Beach Ministerial Assn., 1994-96, 2000-02. Mem. Bd. Visitors Presbyn. Coll., Clinton, S.C., 1993-96; mem. adv. bd. Hospice of Palm Beach County, 1998-99; mem. Circle of Friends, Habitat for Humanity, Boynton Beach, Fla., 1998-99. Mem Rotary, Kiwanis (pres. Lake Weir, Fla. club 1986-87). Republican. Office: First Presbyn Ch 235 SW 6th Ave Boynton Beach FL 33435-5517 *God will make plain your path, if you acknowledge him every day.*

GILL, NIA H. state legislator; BA, Upsala Coll.; JD, Rutgers Law Sch. Law clk. McTeer, Walls & Bailey, Greenville, Miss., 1973; legis. aide Sen. Wynona Lipman, N.J., 1973-74; trial atty. N.J. Pub. Defenders Office, Essex & Passaic Counties, N.J., 1976-82; lawyer del. 3d Jud. Conf., 1987—; state legislator N.J. Ho. of Reps. Assembly N.J. State Dist. 27, 1994—, jud. law & pub. safety com. N.J. State Assembly, sr. citizen & social svc. coms., task force on juvenile crime, criminal justice subcom., Dem. task force on crime & corrections; ptnr. Gill & Cohen, P.C., Montclair. Trustee Montclair Pub. Libr., 1978-83, Cmty. Nursing Svc., Montclair, 1986-87; bd. adjustment Montclair Twp., 1985—; bd. dirs. Playwrights Theater N.J., 1993-94, Luna Theater, Montclair. Recipient legal profession award Nat. Coun. Negro Bus. Women, 1985, citizen award Montclair br. NAACP, 1988. Mem. ABA, Assn. Criminal Def. Lawyers N.J. (trustee 1986-89), N.J. State Bar Assn., Garden State Bar Assn., Essex County Bar Assn., Nat. Conf. Black Lawyers, Black Women Lawyers N.J., Assn. Trial Lawyers Am., Isis Literary Guild (pres.). Democrat. Office: NJ Senate Dist 34 425 Bloomfield Ave Ste 2 Montclair NJ 07042-3538*

GILL, PATRICK DAVID, lawyer; b. N.Y., Apr. 27, 1944; s. Patrick John and Ellen A. Gill; m. Ann Brooke, May 13, 1972; children: Elizabeth, Kimberly, Roger. BA, CUNY Queens, 1965; JD, NYU Sch. Law, 1968. Bar: N.Y. 1968, U.S. Ct. Internat. Trade 1968, U.S. Ct. Appeals (2nd cir.) 1969, U.S. Dist. Ct. (so. and ea. dists.) N.Y. 1977, D.C. 1980, U.S. Ct. Appeals (fed. cir.) 1982, U.S. Supreme Ct. 1990. Trial atty. U.S. Dept. Justice, N.Y., 1968-73; assoc. Sharretts, Paley, Carter & Blauvelt, N.Y.C., 1973—77; ptnr. Rode & Qualey, N.Y., 1977—. With USAR, 1968-74. Bd. dirs. Customs and Internat. Bar Assn. (chmn. adminstrn. practice com., 1981-90, sec. 1990-92, v.p. 1992-94, pres. 1994-96). Avocations: tennis, boating. Office: 55 W 39th St Ste 600 New York NY 10018-3803 E-mail: tradelaw@aol.com., gillpd@aol.com.

GILL, REBECCA LALOSH, aerospace engineer; b. Brownsboro, Tex., Sept. 17, 1944; d. Milton and Dona Mildred (Magee) LaLosh; m. Peter Mohammed Sharma, Sept. 1, 1965 (div.); m. James Frederick Gill, Mar. 9, 1985; children: Erin, Melissa, Ben. BS in Physics, U. Mich., 1965; MBA, Calif. State U., Northridge, 1980. Tchr., Derby, Kans., 1966; weight analyst Beech Aircraft, Wichita, Kans., 1966; weight engr. Ewing Tech. Design, assigned Boeing-Vertol, Phila., 1966-67, Bell Aerosystems, Buffalo, 1967; design specialist Lockheed-Calif. Co., Burbank, 1968-79; sr. staff engr. Hughes Aircraft Missile Sys., Canoga Park, Calif., 1979-82, project mgr. AMRAAM spl. test and tng. equipment, 1982-85, project mgr. GBU-15 guidance sect., Navy IR Maverick Missile Tucson, 1985-89, project mgr. Navy IR Maverick Missile, Slam Seeker Prodn., 1989-92, TOSH and TOW Internat. program mgr., 1992—. Sec. Nat. Cinema Corp. Com. chmn. Orgn. for Rehab. through Tng., 1971-75; spkr. ednl. and civic groups. Pres. Briarcliffe East Homeowners Assn.; coord. support group Am. Diabetes Assn., chmn. com. fundraising coun. mem. Tucson chpt., walk team capt., 1997, 98, 99; active NOW; block leader Neighborhood Watch. Recipient Lockheed award of achievement, 1977. Mem. NAFE, Soc. Allied Weight Engrs. (dir., sr. v.p., chmn. pub. rels. com.), Aerospace Elec. Soc. (dir.), Tucson Zool. Soc. (bd. dirs.), Hughes Mgmt. Club (bd. dirs., chmn. spl. events, chmn. programs, parliamentarian, 1st v.p., pres.), Women in Def. (sec., Ariz. chpt.), Las Alturas Homeowners Assn. (v.p., pres.), Raytheon Mgmt. Club (chmn. elections com.), Tucson Racquet Club. Republican. Office: Raytheon Missile Sys Bldg 801 MS G25A Tucson AZ 85734

GILL, RICHARD LAWRENCE, lawyer; b. Chgo., Jan. 8, 1946; s. Joseph Richard and Dolores Ann (Powers) G.; m. Mary Helen Walker, July 14, 1990; children: Kyla Marie, Matthew Joseph. BA, Coll. of St. Thomas, St. Paul, 1968; JD, U. Minn., 1971. Bar: Minn. 1971, U.S. Dist. Ct. Minn. 1971, U.S. Supreme Ct. 1979, U.S. Ct. Appeals (8th cir.) 1983, U.S. Ct. Appeals (4th cir.) 1990, Ill. 1992. Spl. asst. atty. gen. State of Minn., St. Paul, 1971-73; assoc. Maun, Hazel, Green, Hayes, Simon & Aretz, St. Paul, 1974-77; ptnr. Gill & Brinkman, St. Paul, 1978-84, Robins, Kaplan, Miller & Ciresi, Mpls., 1984—2002, of counsel, 2002—. Vol. Courage Ctr., Golden Valley, Minn., 1981—; youth football coach Maplewood (Minn.) Athletic Assn., 1978-80; youth basketball coach Orono (Minn.) Athletic Assn., 1999—; mem. athletics adv. bd. U. St. Thomas, 2002—. Mem. ABA, Minn. Bar Assn., Hennepin County Bar Assn., Ramsey County Bar Assn., Assn. Trial Lawyers Am., Minn. Trial Lawyers Assn., Town and Country Club. Avocations: skiing, tennis, golf. Office: Robins Kaplan Miller & Ciresi 800 Lasalle Ave Ste 2800 Minneapolis MN 55402-2015 E-mail: rlgill@rkmc.com.

GILL, ROBERT JEROME, education educator; b. Wilkes-Barre, Pa., Aug. 24, 1946; s. Francis Thomas and Patricia Jeramine (McGlynn) Gill; m. Maribel Rosales, Apr. 21, 1973; children: Yuri Esmeralda, Diana Marsela. AA in Liberal Arts, St. Charles Coll., 1966; BA in Philosophy, Passionist Monastic Sem. Coll., 1969; MA, Seton Hall U., 1971; EdD, Rutgers U., 1982. Cert. learning disabilities tchr. NJ. Tchr. St. Bernard's Sch., Plainfield, NJ, 1969—70; tchr., learning disabilities cons. Old Bridge (NJ) Twp. Pub. Schs., 1970—2000; part-time instr. Rutgers U., New Brunswick, NJ, 1986—2000, full-time instr., 2000—03; adj. instr. Nova Southeastern U. Cons. in field. Co-editor: Business and Professional Writing, 2001, Scientific and Technical Writing, 2001, Writing for Engineers, 2001; editor: (web courses) Technical Writing Essentials, 2002. Recipient NJ Gov.'s Tchr. Recognition award, State of NJ, 1995. Mem.: MLA, Nat. Coun. Tchrs. English. Roman Catholic. Avocations: recreational vehicle camping, travel, dancing. Home: 10626 W Sample Rd Pompano Beach FL 33065 E-mail: rjgill@rci.rutgers.edu.

GILL, STEPHEN PASCHALL, retired physicist, mathematician; b. Balt., Nov. 13, 1938; s. Robert Lee and Charlotte (Olmsted) G.; m. Margaret Ann Gaskins, Dec. 21, 1961; children: Elizabeth Olmsted, Richard Paschall. BS, MIT, 1960; MA, Harvard U., 1961, PhD, 1964. Cons. hypersonic aerodynamics Raytheon Corp., Bedford, Mass., 1963-64; research physicist Stanford Research Inst., Menlo Park, Calif., 1964-65, head high energy gasdynamics, 1965-68, Physics Internat. Co., San Leandro, Calif., 1968-70, mgr. shock dynamics dept., 1970-72; founder, pres. Artec Assocs., Inc., Hayward, Calif., 1972-77, chief scientist, 1977-91; founder, pres. Votan Corp., Hayward, Calif., 1979-91, chief scientist, chmn. bd., 1981-85; ret., 1999. Founder, chief scientist Magnetic Pulse Inc., 1985-99. Mem. San Francisco Symphony Assn.; mem. San Francisco Mus. Art. Mem. IEEE, Am. Phys. Soc., Am. Math. Soc., MIT Alumni Assn., Sigma Xi, Delta Kappa Epsilon. Clubs: MIT. Republican. Episcopalian. Home: 32 Flood Cir Atherton CA 94027-2151 E-mail: stephen_p_gill@hotmail.com.

GILL, SUKHDEEP, education educator, researcher; b. Shimla, Himachal Pradesh, India, July 9, 1957; d. Sohanjit S. and Surinder K. Atwal; m. Surinder P. Gill, Nov. 9, 1980; children: Karandeep S., Manan. PhD, Pa. State U., 1997. Assoc. prof. Punjab Agrl. U., Ludhiana, India, 1989—97; asst. prof. Pa. State U., York, 2001—. Contbr. rsch. pubs. Grantee Rsch. grant, Dorothy Rider Health Care Pool Trust, 1999—2003, The William Penn Found., 2000—02, The Marine Corps, 2001—. Mem.: Soc. for Rsch. in Child Devel., Am. Evaluation Assn., Soc. for Prevention Rsch., Pa. State Alumni Assn. (life). Office: The Pa State Univ 1031 Edgecomb Ave York PA 17403 Home Fax: 717-771-4062; Office Fax: 717-771-4062. Personal E-mail: sgill@psu.edu. E-mail: sgill@psu.edu.

GILL, SUZANNE, software book publisher; b. Quincy, Ill., June 30, 1941; d. Harry J. and Anne (McDonnell) Lutz; m. James H. Gill, June 25, 1966 (div.); children: Michael, Brian, Molly. BS, Fontbonne Coll., St. Louis, 1963; MS, U. Mich., 1967. Tchr., librarian Parkway Sch. Dist., St. Louis, 1963-66; coord. libr. tech. asst. program U. Toledo, Cuyahoga C.C., St. Louis C.C., 1967—84; pres. Info. Resources Cons., St. Louis, 1977—. Author: File Management and Information Retrieval Systems, 1981, 2d edit., 1988, 3d edit., 1993, Using Volunteers Effectively in a School Library Media Center, 2001; contbr. numerous mag. articles; developer numerous software programs and books, 1984—. Mem. Mo. Sch. Libr. Assn. (bd. dirs. 1997—), Mo. Libr. Assn., St. Louis Suburban Sch. Librs. (pres. 1997-2001), Chesterfield Hist. Soc., Am. Legion Aux. Republican. Roman Catholic. Home and Office: 1556 Walpole Dr Chesterfield MO 63017-4615 E-mail: s.l.gill@worldnet.att.net.

GILL, THOMAS GRANDON, information technology executive, educator; b. Boston, Apr. 26, 1955; s. Richard Thomas and Elizabeth B. Gill; m. Clare Ellen Barres, July 29, 1958; children: Thomas Richard, Jonathan Grandon. BA, Harvard Coll., 1975; MBA, Harvard U., 1982, D in Bus. Adminstrn., 1991. Pres. SnCorp, Inc., Dallas, 1982—83; sr. v.p. Agribus. Assocs., Wellesley Hills, Mass., 1983—86; assoc. prof. Fla. Atlantic U., Boca Raton, 1991—2001, U. South Fla., Tampa, 2001—. Author: (laminated study guides) CyberCue Cards, QuickStudy Guides, (case studies) HBS Pub., Prentice Hall; contbr. trade paperback. Lt. Submarine Force USN, 1975—80. Scholar Baker scholar, Harvard U., 1982. Conservative. Home: 9226 Highland Ridge Way Tampa FL 33647-2299 Office: University of South Florida IS&DS Dept 4202 E Fowler Ave CIS1040 Tampa FL 33620-7800 Home Fax: 509-472-6576; Office Fax: 813-974-6749. Personal E-mail: grandon@grandon.com. E-mail: ggill@coba.usf.edu.

GILL, THOMAS JAMES, III, physician, educator; b. Malden, Mass., July 2, 1932; s. Thomas James and Marguerite (Capobianco) G.; m. Faith Libbie Etoll, July 8, 1961; children: Elizabeth Ruth, Thomas James IV, Christopher Gregory. AB summa cum laude, Harvard U., 1953, AM in Chemistry, MD, Harvard U., 1957. Diplomate Am. Bd. Pathology. Asst. in pathology Peter Bent Brigham Hosp., Boston, 1957-58; intern N.Y. Hosp.-Cornell Med. Center, 1958-59; jr. fellow Soc. Fellows Harvard U., 1959-62, mem. faculty Harvard U. Med Sch., 1962-71, asso. prof. pathology, 1970-71; prof. pathology, chmn. dept. U. Pitts. Med. Sch., 1971-90; pathologist-in-chief Univ. Health Ctr. Pitts., 1971-90, Maud L. Menten prof. exptl. pathology, 1988—98, prof. human genetics, 1988-98, prof. emeritus human genetics and exptl. pathology, 1999—; prof. clin. immunology for postgrad. studies U. Rijeka, Croatia, 1996—; fellow U. Pitts. Ctr. for Philosophy Sci., 1996—98, assoc., 1999—2001; vis. scholar in biology Harvard U., 1998-2001. Affiliate of Eliot House, Harvard Coll., 1998—; cons. to govt. and industry; mem. sci. adv. bd. St. Jude Children's Rsch. Hosp., Memphis, 1969-77, chmn., 1974-76; mem. allergy and immunology rsch. com. Nat. Inst. Allergy and Infectious Diseases, 1973-76; mem. med. rsch. svc. merit rev. bd. in immunology VA, 1976-79, chmn., 1977-79; mem. sci. adv. com. Damon Runyon-Walter Winchell Cancer Fund, 1978-81; mem. com. on animal models and genetic stocks NRC, 1978-86, chmn. com., 1983-86, mem. com. on rabbit genetic resources, 1979-80, mem. coun. Inst. Lab. Animal Resources, 1986-92, mem. com. on preservation of lab. animal resources, 1985 90, com. on transgenic animals, 1991-92; mem. surgery, anesthesiology and trauma study sect. NIH, 1983-84; sci. adv. com. on immunology and immunotherapy Am. Cancer Soc., 1986-88; mem. Armed Forces Epidemiol. Bd., 1966-72; adj. prof. U. Milan, 1990-92; nutrition found. Italy lectr. U. Milan, 1986-97; trustee Am. Bd. Pathology, 1981-92, life trustee, 1992—, pres., 1992; mem. Maternal and Child Health com. Nat. Inst. Child Health and Human Devel., 1992-96; chmn., 1995-96; mem. immunology task force Nat. Inst. Allergy and Infectious Diseases, 1996-98; mem. adv. com. for the Rat Genome Project and Rat EST Project, Nat. Heart, Lung, and Blood Inst., 1998. Mem. editorial bd. several sci. and med. jours.; contbr. articles to profl. jours. Bd. dirs. Easter Seal Soc., Allegheny County, 1972-77, Univs. Asso. for Research and Edn. in Pathology, 1979-90 Recipient Lederle med. faculty award, 1962-65, rsch. career devel. award NIH, 1965-71, cert. of appreciation for patriotic civilian svc. Dept. Army, 1973, Spl. Qualification in Pathology: Immunopathology, 1983, Disting. Scientist award in genetics S.W. Found. for Biomed. Rsch., 1986, Charter with medal U. Rijeka, 1990, medal U. Pitts., 1990; named George H. Fetterman lectr. U. Pitts., 1981, George Hoyt Whipple lectr. U. Rochester, N.Y., 1984, Aron E. Szulman lectr. U. Pitts., 1993, Raymond O. Berry Meml. lectr. Tex. A&M U., 1995, Mühlblock lectr. Internat. Coun. for Lab. Scis., 1995, Spiridion Brusina award Croatian Soc. Natural Scis., 1997. Fellow Assn. Pathology Chairmen (pres. 1978); mem. AMA, Am. Assn. Immunologists, Am. Assn. Pathologists, Am. Soc. Molecular Biology and Biochemistry, Am. Soc. Human Genetics, Transplantation Soc. (v.p. 1982-84), Am. Soc. for Immunology of Reprodn. (v.p. 1988-89, Disting. Investigator award 1991, pres. 1995-96), Genetics Soc. Am., Internat. Acad. Pathology, Internat. Soc. Immunology of Reprodn. (pres. 1992-95, hon. pres. 1995—), Alps Adria Soc. for Immunology of Reprodn. (hon. pres. 1994—), Mass. Med. Soc., Harvard Club (Boston), Harvard Varsity Club. E-mail: gilliii@massmed.org.

GILL, THOMAS JAMES, IV, orthopedic surgeon; b. Boston, June 15, 1964; s. Thomas James Gill III and Faith Libbie (Etoll) Gill; m. Kathleen Margaret Buckley, Sept. 12, 1992; children: Thomas James Gill V, Olivia Margaret, Rebecca Buckley. AB, Harvard Coll., 1986; MD, Harvard Med. Sch., 1990. Bd. cert. Am. Bd. Orthopedic Surgery. Intern surgery Mass. Gen. Hosp., Boston, 1990—91; resident orthopedic surgery Hosp. for Spl. Surgery, N.Y.C., 1991—92; resident Harvard Combined Orthopedic Program, Boston, 1992—96; fellow Maurice E. Müller Fellow in Reconstructive Surgery, Bern, Switzerland, 1997, Steadman Hawkins Clinic, Vail, Colo., 1997—98; attending staff Mass. Gen. Hosp., Boston, 1998—. Team physician New Eng. Patriots, Boston Bruins, New Eng. Revolution, Boston Breakers. Contbr. articles to profl. jours. Recipient Rsch. award, Orthopedic Rsch. and Edn. Found., Chapel Hill, N.C., 2000; scholar Maurice E. Muller scholar, Muller Found., Bern, 1996. Fellow: Am. Assn. Orthopedic Surgeons; mem.: Major League Soccer Team Physicians Soc., Nat. Hockey League Team Physicians Soc., Nat. Football League Team Physicians Soc., Am. Orthopedic Soc. for Sports Medicine. Avocations: golf, tennis, jogging, skiing, rowing. Office: Mass Gen Hosp ACC-508 15 Parkman St Boston MA 02114

GILL, WILLIAM NELSON, chemical engineering educator; b. N.Y.C., Sept. 13, 1928; s. William Nelson and Frances (Murphy) G.; m. Chandlee Stevens, Aug. 13, 1982; children: Alison Louise, Christine Marie, Douglas Max, Max William. BSChemE, Syracuse U., 1951, MA, 1955, PhD, 1960. Field engr. Am. Blower Corp., 1951-55; mem. faculty Syracuse U., 1957-65, assoc. prof., 1963-65; prof. chem. engring., chmn. dept. Clarkson U., 1965-71; provost engring. and applied sci. SUNY, Buffalo, 1971-78, prof. chem. engring., 1982-87; Glenn Murphy Disting. prof. engring. Iowa State U., Ames, 1980-82; Russell Sage disting. prof. chem. engring. Rensselaer Poly. Inst., Troy, N.Y., 1987—. Cons. in field. Editor: Chem. Engring. Communications, 1979— ; mem. editorial adv. bd. Fuel, Processing Tech.; mem. bd. cons. editors Elsevier Texts in Engring.; editor Chem. Engring. series Elsevier Sci. Pub. Co.; author numerous articles in field. Named Alumnus of Yr., Bklyn. Tech. H.S., 1977; recipient William H. Wiley Disting. Faculty award in recognition of outstanding tchg. and scholarship Rensselaer Poly. Inst., 1994; Fulbright-Hays sr. rsch. scholar Univ. Coll., London, 1977-78, U. Queensland, Australia, 1986-87, Best Paper award Interconnect Scis. & Tech., Techcon 96 Semiconductor Rsch. Corp., 1996, Lecturship award Chem. Eng. Divsn. ASEE, 1992, Best Paper award Interconnect Modeling and Simulation, Techcon 98, Semiconductor Rsch. Corp., 1998. Fellow AIChE; mem. AAAS, AAUP, Am. Chem. Soc., Am. Soc. Engring. Edn. (lectureship award chem. engring. divsn. for fundamental contbns. to chem. engring. theory and practice 1992), N.Y. Acad. Scis., Sigma Xi. Office: Rensselaer Poly Inst Chem Engring Ricketts Troy NY 12180

GILL, WILLIAM ROBERT, soil scientist; b. McDonald, Pa., July 21, 1920; s. William Merle and Mary Della (Leiden) G.; m. Irene Victoria Majorkiewicz, July 10, 1947; children: William Robert, John Philip, David C., Michael J., Elaine N. BS, Pa. State U., 1942; MS, U. Hawaii, 1949; PhD, Cornell U., 1955. Asst. soil scientist Pineapple Rsch. Inst., Honolulu, 1949—50; rsch. soil scientist USDA-ARS, Auburn, Ala., 1955—80, dir., 1971—80. Adj. prof. agrl. engring. Auburn U., 1957-88; collaborator Nat. Soil Dynamics Lab. (formerly Nat. Tillage Machinery Lab.), Auburn, 1980—; exch. scientist in Soviet Union, 1970. Author: Soil Dynamics in Tillage and Traction, 1967, History of the National Tillage Machinery Laboratory, 1990, War Crimes Investigations in Japan 1945-48: A Personal Remembrance, 1995; contbr. articles to profl. jours. and tech. confs.; monographs on soil dynamics. Col. AUS ret., 1943-47, 51-52. Recipient recognition award Internat. Soil Dynamics Conf., 1985, 97; named to Officer Candidate Sch. Hall of Fame, 1993. Mem. Am. Soc. Agrl. Engrs. (Peer Recognition award 1985, Disting. Engr. award 1988, John Deere medal 1990), Soil Sci. Soc. Am. Achievements include translation of Russian soil dynamics articles into English, fgn. analysis and technology transfer for internat. audience.

GILLAM, LINDA DAWN, cardiologist, researcher; b. Corner Brook, Nfld., Can., Sept. 23, 1952; d. Donald Samuel and Vera (Pieroway) G.; m. Vincent Charles DiCola, Aug. 30, 1985 (div. 1995); children: John William DiCola, Laura Ann DiCola. BS, McGill U., Montreal, Que., Can., 1972; MD, Queen's U., Kingston, Ont., Can., 1976. Diplomate Am. Bd. Internal Medicine, Am. Bd. Cardiovascular Disease. Intern U. Toronto, 1976; resident in medicine St. Michaels Hosp., Toronto, 1977-79; fellow in cardiology U. Toronto, 1979-81, Mass. Gen. Hosp., Boston, 1981-83; instr. in medicine Harvard U. Med. Sch., Boston, 1983-86; clin. asst. prof. medicine U. Conn., Farmington, 1986-95, clin. assoc. prof., 1995—. Dir. echocardiography U. Conn. Health Ctr., Farmington, 1986-90, Hartford (Conn.) Hosp., 1990—; spkr. in field. Contbr. articles to profl. jours. Rsch. grantee Can. Heart Assn. Fellow: Am. Heart Assn. (chair com. on women in cardiology 2000—, task force on guidelines for echocardiography, exec. com. coun. on clin. cardiology, ARDMS chair adult echo exam task force), Am. Coll. Cardiology (gov. 1996—99, chpt. pres. 1996—99, govt. rels. com. 1997—, mem. steering com. bd. govs., chair task force on comm., mem. awards com., editl. bd. website, program com., Pac bd. medicare carrier adv. com.); mem.: AMA, Am. Soc. Echocardiography (legis. and regulatory affairs com. 1993—2001, bd. dirs. 1995—98, com. on sonographer tng. 1997—, treas. 2001—), Am. Bd. Echocardiography, Conn. State Med. Soc. Avocations: ballet, opera, classical music, aerobics, tennis. Office: Hartford Hosp 80 Seymour St Hartford CT 06102 8000

GILLAM, SIR PATRICK, oil company executive, banker; b. London, Apr. 15, 1933; s. Cyril Bryant and Mary Josephine (Davis) G.; m. Diana Echlin, Nov. 23, 1963; children: Jane, Luke. BA in History with honors, London Sch. Econs., 1954. With Fgn. Office, London, 1956-57, Brit. petroleum Co. p.l.c., London, 1957-91; v.p. BP (N.Am.) Inc. subs., N.Y., 1971-74, gen. mgr. supply, 1974-78; dir. BP Internat. Ltd., 1978-81, mng. dir., 1981-91; non-exec. dir. Comml. Union, 1991-96; bd. dirs. Standard Chartered p.l.c., 1988-91, dep. chmn., 1991-93, chmn., 1993—2003, Asia House, 2003. Chmn. ICC U.K., 1989-98, Booker Tate Ltd., 1991-93, Asda p.l.c., 1991-96, Royal & Sun Alliance, 1997-2003; mem. exec. bd. dirs. ICC World Wide, 1991-98. Chmn. Asia House, 2003—, Standard Chartered Bank, 1993—2003, Royal & Sun Alliance, 1997—2003; trustee Asia House, 2002—. Created knight, 1998; hon. fellow London Sch. Econs. and Polit. Sci. Avocation: gardening. Office: Asia House 105 Piccadilly London W1V 9FN England

GILLAN, GARTH JACKSON, writer, psychotherapist, deacon, emeritus educator; b. Washington, Feb. 14, 1939; s. James Joseph and Lolita Jackson G.; m. Mary Elizabeth Marlene (McCormick), Dec. 29, 1965; children: Johanna, Rebecca, Daniel, Susannah, Jonathan, Miriam. PhD, Duquesne U., 1966; MA in Pastoral Theol., St. Mary in the Woods Coll., 1992; MS in Edu. Psychology, So. Ill. U., 1991. Asst. prof. Seton Hill Coll., Greensberg, Pa., 1965-66, Canisius Coll., Buffalo, 1966-69, So. Ill. U., Carbondale, Ill., 1969-73, assoc. prof., 1973-82, prof., 1982-99, prof. emeritus, 1999—. Author: Horizons of the Flesh, 1973, From Sign to Symbol, 1982, Michel Foucault, 1982, Rising From the Ruins, 1997. Mem. Soc. Advancement Am. Philosophy, Soc. Phenomenology, Am. Assn. Pastoral Counselors, Am. Counseling Assn., Cath. Philos. Assn. Home: 120 Cooper St Spring Mills PA 16875-8102

GILLANI, NOOR VELSHI, atmospheric scientist, researcher, educator; b. Arusha, Tanzania, Mar. 8, 1944; came to the U.S., 1963, naturalized, 1976; s. Noormohamed Velshi and Sherbanu (Kassam) G.; children: Michael, Michelle, Nicole. Gen. Cert. of Edn., U. Cambridge, 1960; advanced level, U. London, 1963; AB cum laude, Harvard U., 1967; MSME, Washington U., St. Louis, 1969, DSc, 1974. Rsch. assoc. Washington U., 1975-76, rsch. scientist, 1976-77, asst. prof., 1977-80, assoc. prof., 1981-84, prof. mech. engring., 1984-91, faculty assoc. Ctr. Air Pollution Impact and Trend Analysis, 1979-91, dir. air quality spl. studies data ctr., 1981-88, dir., mech. engring. rsch. computing facility, 1988-90; pres. N.V. Gillani & Assocs., Inc., 1991—; prin. rsch. scientist NASA-UAH Nat. Space Sci. & Tech. Ctr., Ala., 1995—; adj. prof. atmospheric sci. U. Ala., Huntsville, 1995—. Vis. scientist Stockholm U., 1977, Brookhaven Nat. Lab., 1990—91, EPA/RTP, 1992—93, TVA Environ. Rsch. Ctr., 1994—95; organizer NATO CCMS 15th internat. tech. meeting on air pollution modeling and its applications, St. Louis, 1985; mem. Sci. Bd. NATO/Commn. for the Challenges of Modern Soc. Air Pollution Pilot Study, 1984—92; mem. tech. adv. bds. U.S. EPA, DOE and others, 1980—; hon. mem. Aga Khan Edn. Bd. for U.S.A. (AKEB/USA), 1987—90; vis. prof. NC State U., NC, 1993—94. Author: (with others) Critical Assessment Document on Acidic Depositions, 1984, EPA Criteria Document for Particulate Matter, 1994-95; editor: Air Pollution Modeling and Its Applications V, vol. 10, 1986; contbr. chpts. to book and articles to profl. jours. Dir., founder AKEB/USA Program (PIAR)for Parental Involvement in Children's Edn., 1987-97; pres. Pyar Found. for Humanitarian Assistance, 2000—. Scholar, Harvard Coll., 1963—67; Aga Khan travel grantee, 1961—63, grad. fellow, Washington U., 1967—74, rsch. grantee, EPA, DOE, Elec. Power Rsch. Inst., NASA, NOAA, NSF, TVA, Tex. Commn. Environ. Quality, 1978—. Mem. Am. Meteorol. Soc., Am. Chem. Soc., Am. Geophys. Union, Nat. Assn. for Edn. Young Children, N.Y. Acad. Scis. Achievements include research on superconductivity, bioengring., atmospheric scis., air pollution and Islamic humanism. Office: NASA-UAH Nat Space Sci and Tech Ctr 320 Sparkman Dr Huntsville AL 35805 E-mail: gillani@nsstc.uah.edu.

GILLELAND, JOHN ROGERS, technology company executive; b. Gadsden, Ala., Jan. 12, 1941; s. Earl Rogers and Margaret Eta Gilleland; m. Kim Denise Turos, Aug. 23, 1987. BS in Physics, Yale U., 1963; MS in Physics, U. Mich., 1964, PhD in Physics, 1969. Scientist Gulf Gen. Atomics, La Jolla, Calif., 1970-72, dir. Doublet III program, 1972-78, sr. v.p. fusion energy program, 1985-87; program dir. U.S.-Japan Fusion rsch. Collaboration, La Jolla, 1978-85; mng. dir. Internat. Thermonuclear Exptl. Reactor Project, Garching, Germany, 1987-91; v.p., chief scientist Bechtel Corp., San Francisco, 1991-98; pres., CEO Archimedes Tech. Group, San Diego, 1998—. Advisor space def. initiative Dept. Def., Washington, 1985-86; advisor Nat. Acad. Scis., Washington, 1984-87; dir. Fusion Power Assocs., Washington, 1994-00. Named Young Engr. of the Yr. Am. Nuc. Soc., 1980; recipient Achievement award Am. Nuc. Soc., 1992. Avocations: cello, squash, art installation, philosophy, carpentry. Home: PO Box 9154 Rancho Santa Fe CA 92067-4154 Office: Archimedes Tech Group 5405 Oberlin Dr San Diego CA 92121-1700

GILLEM, ELISE (MARIE) (ELISE MICHAELS), radio and television personality; d. Kenneth James and Mary Louise Fleckenstein; m. Mark Gillem; children: Charles, Gracie. Grad. high sch., Kalamazoo. Radio personality Sta. KTIL, Tillamook, Oreg., 1983-84; personality, news dir. Sta. KXIQ/KGRL, Bend, Oreg., 1984-88, Sta. KLRR/KBND, Bend, Oreg., 1988-94; promotion and pub. affairs dir. Sta. KTVZ-TV, Bend, Oreg., 1994-99; on-air personality Sta. KLRR/KBND/KTWS, Bend, 1999—. On-air personality, co-host Sta. KLRR, KBND, KTWS. Prodr. Living with Renal Failure, 1986 (hon. mention Oreg. AP); writer, host weekly TV show Your Next Home; creator, host, prodr. TV show The Earth Friendly Home; prodr., host Ctrl. Oreg. Today. Named Kidney Patient of Yr., Nat. Kidney Found. Oreg. and Wash., 1999. Office: KLRR 711 NE Butler Market Rd Bend OR 97701-8083

GILLEN, HOWARD WILLIAM, neurologist, medical historian; b. Chgo., Nov. 25, 1923; s. John Howard and Emily Elizabeth (Bayley) G.; m. Corinne V. Neese, July 24, 1948. BS, U. Ill., 1947; MD, U. Ill., Chgo., 1949. Hon. active neurologist New Hanover Regional Med. Ctr., Wilmington, N.C., 1973-93, emeritus neurologist, 1993—; cons. neurologist Cape Fear Meml. Hosp., Wilmington, 1973-93; clin. prof. neurology U. N.C., Chapel Hill, 1973-93, clin. prof. emeritus, 1993—. Adj. prof. biol. sci. U. N.C., Wilmington, 1986—; rsch. assoc. I.R.I.S.C., Wilmington, 1989-93, sr. investigator, 1993-99. Capt. USNR, ret. Home: 500 Sand Castle Ct Wilmington NC 28405-8386

GILLEN, JAMES ROBERT, lawyer, insurance company executive; b. N.Y.C., Nov. 14, 1937; s. James Matthew and Katharine Isabel (Fritz) G.; m. Rita Marie Wahleithner, June 15, 1963 (div. 1992); children: Jennifer Elaine, Nancy Louise, Paula Anne; m. Edda Lya Pacheco, Dec. 10, 1994. AB magna cum laude, Harvard U., 1959, LLB cum laude, 1965. Bar: N.Y. 1966, N.J. 1975. Assoc. firm White & Case, N.Y.C., 1965-72; v.p., assoc. gen. counsel Prudential Ins. Co. Am., Newark, 1972-77, sr. v.p., assoc. gen. counsel, 1977-80, sr. v.p. pub. affairs, 1980-84, sr. v.p., gen. counsel, 1984-98. Mem. bd. trustees Columbia Inst. Investor Project, 1981—97; legal adv. com. N.Y. Stock Exch., 1986—89; mem. adv. bd. Ascertain Solutions, Inc., 2001—02. Trustee United Way Essex and West Hudson Counties, 1981-90, pres., 1986-88; mem. Mendham Twp. (N.J.) Bd. Edn., 1981-82; trustee N.J. Shakespeare Festival, 1991-99, Mendham Twp. Libr., 1979-82; dir., chmn. Neurol. Inst. N.J., 1998—. Lt. (j.g.) USN, 1959-62. Mem. ABA, N.J. Bar Assn., Assn. Life Ins. Counsel, Harvard Club (N.Y.C.), Morris Country Golf Club. Home: 72 Washington Valley Rd Morristown NJ 07960-3332

GILLEN, PATRICK BERNARD, nurse; b. Toledo, June 6, 1950; s. Aloysius Martin and Edna Marie (Baugh) G.; m. Dolores Almeda Szabo, June 29, 1973; children: Abraham Joseph, Laura Marie, Kurtis Aloysius, Kathy Jean. BS, U. Toledo, 1973; Diploma in Nursing, Toledo Hosp. Sch., 1978; Enterostomal Therapy Nursing, Cleve. Clinic, 1980; MA in Internat. Rels., Webster U., 1997. Cert. enterostomal therapy nurse. Charge nurse med.-surg. Fulton County Health Ctr., Wauseon, Ohio, 1978-79; float nurse Flower Meml. Hosp., Sylvania, Ohio, 1979-80, enterostomal therapy nurse, 1980-88; pres. enterostomal therapy nurse practice Patient Care Assocs., Toledo, 1988-89; home health nurse Adrian (Mich.) Cmty. Health, 1988-89; commd. 1st lt. USAF Nurse Corps, 1989, advanced through grades to maj., 1998; med. surg., asst. charge nurse Keesler (AFB) Med. Ctr., Miss., 1989-91, nursing supr., 1992-93; flight nurse med. dir. 57th Aeromed. Evacuation, Scott AFB, Ill., 1993-94; instr., asst. charge tng. 375th Aeromed. Evacuation, Scott AFB, Ill., 1993—, flight examiner, 1995-97, asst. flight comdr. standards & evaluations, 1996-97; with USAF Med. Ctr., Wright-Patterson AFB, Ohio, 1997—; nurse mgr. surgery, clinic dep. nurse execs. surg. divsn. Enterostomal nurse cons. in field; CEO Gillen Acad. Cons. on Leadership, Bus., and Healthcare Issues. Contbr. articles to profl. jours. and chpt. to book. Con. United Ostomy Assn., 1980-89, Am. Cancer Soc., Fulton and Lucas Counties, Ohio, 1981-89, Toledo Cmty. Hosps. Oncology Program, 1984-86; leader Boy Scouts of Am., Ohio, 1981-87, counselor 1981-94). Named Nurse of Hope, Am. Cancer Soc. Mem. Aerospace Med. Assn., Am. Air Mus. in Britain, Secular Franciscan Order. Roman Catholic. Avocations: reading, running, writing, painting (oils), guitar, camping, modeling planes. Home: 4921 Honeywood Ct Dayton OH 45424-4804 Personal E-mail: gillcup@bww.com. E-mail: patrick.gillen@wpafb.af.mil.

GILLEN, SHAWN P. English language educator, writer; b. Denver, Jan. 4, 1962; s. Albert John and JoAnne Marie (Dyer) Gillen; m. Barbara Josephine Higgins, July 29, 1995; children: Claire, Niall. BA in English, St. John's U., Mpls., 1984; MA in English, U. Minn., 1992, PhD in English, 1994. Mng. editor, reporter Twin Cities Courier, Mpls., 1985-87; contbg. writer City Pages, Mpls., 1985-90; cmty. editor, writer Minn. Daily, Mpls., 1988-91; tchg. asst. U. Minn., Mpls., 1988-94; assoc. prof. English, Beloit (Wis.) Coll., 1994—, chmn. dept., 2001—. Vis. prof. Glasgow (Scotland) U., 2001; scholar-in-residence Newberry Libr., Chgo., 2002—. Editor: Retake the Falling Snow, 2001; contbr. articles to profl. publs., including Henry James Rev., Ency. Travel Writing, Colo. Rev. Named Midwest Faculty fellow, U. Chgo., 1996, Continuing Edn. and Extension fellow, U. Minn., 1993; recipient Mentor Writing award, The Loft, Mpls., 1992, Phee Boon Kang prize, 2003. Mem MLA, Henry James Soc. Avocations: bicycling, swimming, music. Office: Beloit Coll Dept English 700 College St Beloit WI 53511

GILLENWATER, JAY YOUNG, urologist, educator; b. Kingsport, Tenn., July 27, 1933; s. Jay King and Ann Marion (Young) G.; m. Shirley Joyce Brockman; children: Linda, Ann, Jay. BS, U. Tenn., 1954, MD, 1957. Diplomate Am. Bd. Urology (pres. 1988). Intern U. Pa. Grad. Hosp., 1958-59, resident, 1959-60, 62-65; asst. prof. U. Va. Med. Sch., Charlottesville, 1965-67, prof., chmn. urology dept., 1967-95; prof., 1995—. Mem. coun. Nat. Inst. Diabetes and Digestive and Kidney Diseases, NIH, 1987-93; pres. AUA, 1991-92. Editor: Adult and Pediatric Urology, 1987, 91, 95; editor Urology Yearbook, 1978-94; assoc. editor Jour.Urology, 1985-93, editor, 1994—. Capt. U.S. Army, 1960-62. Mem. Am. Urol. Assn. (exec. com. 1987—, pres. 1991-92, Hugh Young award, 1989, Mary Scott Hughes edn. award 1985, Ramon Gueteras award 1999), Health Svc. Found. (pres. 1980-91), Am. Bd. Urology (pres. 1988), Am. Found. Urol. Diseases (pres. 1992-99). Republican. Methodist. Avocation: gardening. Home: 648 Dry Bridge Rd Charlottesville VA 22903-7037 Office: U Va Hosps Dept Urology PO Box 800422 Charlottesville VA 22902-0422

GILLER, EDWARD BONFOY, retired government official, retired air force officer; b. Jacksonville, Ill., July 8, 1918; s. Edward Bonfoy and Ruth (Davis) G.; m. Mildred Florana Schmidt, July 2, 1943; children— Susan Ann, Carol Elaine, Bruce Carleton, Penny Marie, Paul Benjamin. BS in Chem. Engring, U. Ill., 1940, MS, 1948, PhD, 1950. Chem. engr. Sinclair Oil Refining Co., 1940-41; commd. 2d lt. USAAF, 1942; advanced through grades to maj. gen. USAF, 1968; pilot, 1941-46; chief radiation br. (Armed Forces Spl. Weapons Project), Washington, 1950-54; dir. research directorate Air Force Spl. Weapons Center, Albuquerque, 1954-59; spl. asst. to comdr. (Office Aerospace Rsch.), Washington, 1959-64; dir. sci. and tech. Hdqrs. USAF, 1964-67; asst. gen. mgr. for mil. application U.S. AEC, 1967-72; ret. from USAF, 1972; asst. gen. mgr. for nat. security AEC, 1972-75; dep. asst. adminstr. for nat. security U.S. ERDA, 1975-77; rep. of Joint Chiefs of Staff to Comprehensive Test Ban Negotiations, Geneva, Switzerland, 1977-84; sr. scientist Pacific-Sierra Rsch. Corp., Arlington, Va, 1984-92; v.p. Trans Mar Inc., Spokane, Wash., 1992-96; cons. Sandia Nat. Labs., Albuquerque, 1990—. Cons. in the field. Decorated Silver Star, D.S.M., Legion of Merit with oak leaf cluster, D.F.C., Air medal with 17 oak leaf clusters, Purple Heart; Croix de Guerre France). Fellow Am. Inst. Chemists; mem. Am. Inst. Chem. Engrs., Sigma Xi, Alpha Tau Omega. Episcopalian. Home: 14415 Soula Dr NE Albuquerque NM 87123-1941

GILLER, NORMAN MYER, banker, architect, author; b. Jacksonville, Fla., Feb. 14, 1918; s. Morris and Esther (Seltzer) Giller; m. Frances Schwartz, June 30, 1946 (dec. 1998); children: Ira D., Anita Giller Grossman, Brian; m. Vivian B. Giller, Jan. 9, 2000. Student, Ga. Inst. Tech., 1943-44; BArch, U. Fla., 1945; postgrad. in banking, Bankers Adminstrn. Inst., 1965-66. Chmn. bd. Norman M. Giller and Assocs., Architects, Miami Beach, Fla., 1945—; chmn. bd., pres. Interam. Nat. Bank, Miami Beach, 1964-68; vice chmn. Jefferson Bancorp, Miami Beach, 1968-97; pres., vice chmn. Jefferson Nat. Bank, Sunny Isles, Fla., 1968-97. Bd. dirs. Jefferson Nat. Bank, Miami Beach, Jefferson Nat. Bank of Palm Beach, Boca Raton, Fla., Jefferson Bank of Broward, Hollywood, Fla.; cons. U.S. Dept. State, Washington, 1961-70, Govts. Panama, Nicaragua, Brazil, Colombia, El Salvador, 1961-70. Author: An Adventure in Architecture, 1977, A Century in America, 1986; contbr. articles on architecture to profl. jours. Chmn. Miami Beach Housing Authority, 1970, Fla. State Bd. Architecture, Tallahassee, 1979, Design Rev. Bd. City of Miami Beach, 1985; pres. So. Fla. coun. Boy Scouts Am., 1961-63, Concerned Citizens of N.E. Dade County, Miami Beach, 1970; sec. Nat. Coun. Archtl. Registration Bd., S.E. Atlanta, 1981; mem. Sunny Isles Task Force, Fla., 1982; pres. Mosaic-Jewish Mus. Fla., 1992—, chmn. 1998. Lt. (j.g.) USNR, 1942-46. Named Man of Yr., Gold Coast C. of C., 1973; bridge named in his honor Fla. Legis., Miami Beach, 1983; recipient Man of the Decade award, 1989; named to Hall of Fame, Gold Coast C. of C., 1994. Fellow AIA (pres. South Fla. chpt. 1945—, Silver medal 1979); mem. Fla. Assn. Architecture (bd. dirs. 1945—, Cmty. Svc. award 1982), Am. Bankers Assn., Fla. Bankers Assn. (mem. com. 1965—), Fla. Bankers Holding Co. Assn., Miami Beach C. of C. (Citizen of the Yr. 1995, pres. 1970—). Lodges: Masons, Shriners. Democrat. Jewish. Avocations: photography, writing. Office: 975 Arthur Godfrey Rd Ste 401 Miami FL 33140-3343

GILLERAN, JAMES E. federal agency administrator; married; 2 children. Law degree, Northwestern Calif. U. CPA. Banking supt. State of Calif., 1989—94; chmn., CEO Bank of San Francisco, 1994—2000; dir. office thrift supervision U.S. Dept. Treasury, Washington, 2001—. Chmn. state liaison coun. Fed. Fin. Instns. Examination Coun., 1991—92; chmn. Conf. State Banking Suprs., 1993—94, mem. bankers adv. coun., 2000. Office: US Dept Treasury Office Thrift Supervision 1700 G St NW Washington DC 20552

GILLERS, STEPHEN, law educator, university official; b. 1943; BA, Bklyn Coll., 1964; JD, NYU, 1968. Bar: N.Y. 1968. Law clk. to Hon. Gus J. Solomon, Oreg., 1968-69; assoc. Paul, Weiss, Rifkind, Wharton & Garrison, N.Y., 1969-71; pvt. practice law N.Y.C., 1973-78; assoc. prof. NYU, N.Y.C., 1978-81, prof. law, 1981—, vice dean, 1999—. Mem. deptl. disciplinary com. N.Y. Supreme Ct., 1980-83. Editor: Looking at Law School, 4th edit., 1997, Regulation of Lawyers: Problems of Law and Ethics, 6th edit., 2002. Exec. dir. SALT, 1975-78, 78-80, bd. govs. Office: NYU Sch Law 40 Washington Sq S New York NY 10012-1099 E-mail: stephen.gillers@nyu.edu.

GILLES, BRUCE CARLSON, civil engineer; b. Meadville, Pa., Sept. 4, 1936; s. August John and Lillian Maude (Carlson) G.; m. Carolyn Ann Hilsdon, Sept. 1, 1967; children: James, Thomas. BA, Gannon U., 1962; MEd, U. Pitts., 1965, postgrad., 1980-82; BSCE, Int Corr. Sch., 1974; postgrad., U. Pitts., 1963-65, 80-82. Quality control engr. Alaska pipeline Mich. Baker Engrs., Beaver, Pa., 1974; civil engr. trainee Chgo. Bridge and Iron, Greenville, Pa., 1974-75; cons. Hendricks and Assocs., Erie, Pa., 1977-79; civil engr., asst. to v.p. Green Internat. Engrs., Sewickley, Pa., 1980-82; resident engr. Pitts. subway Parsons-Brinkerhoff, Pitts., 1983-86; asst. pub. works dir. USN, Adak (Alaska) Naval Sta., 1986; regional chief engr. Mazza Engrs., Aliquippa, Pa., 1986-91; chief quality assurance/quality control engr. Adak Alutian Constrn. Co., Anchorage, 1991-92; rsch. engr. Greiner Engrs., Denver, 1992—93; asst. rsch. engr. Monaloh Basin Engrs., Pitts., 1993—94; project mgr. Multi-Lynx Engrs., Inc., Pitts., 1994—99; rsch. engr. Warf Constrn., Anchorage, 1999—2001; cost engr. Laird Engrs., Erie, Pa., 2001—. Instr. weightlifting YMCA, Meadville, Pa., 1977—. Mem. ASCE (bd. dirs. N.W. Pa. br. 1990-91), NSPE. Republican. Methodist. Home: 373 Allegheny St Meadville PA 16335-1214

GILLESPIE, ADRIENNE AMALIA, artist, editor, researcher; b. N.Y.C., Feb. 26, 1937; d. Quirino and Anne (De Borrello) Galante; m. Gerald Ernest Paul Gillespie, Sept. 5, 1959. BA, Barnard Coll., 1958; MA, Ohio State U., 1960; student, U. Paris, 1960-61; MLS, U. Pitts., 1967. Tchg. asst. Ohio State U., Columbus, 1958-60; libr. State U. N.Y., Binghamton, 1968-73; reviewer Choice, N.Y., 1968-73; artist Palo Alto, Calif.; rschr. hist. preservation City of Palo Alto, 1997-99. Exhibited in numerous one-woman and group shows in midwest and on west coast, 1990—. Dir. Norton Gallery and cmty. svc. sites; founding mem. Filoli Art Com. Featured artist Encyclopedia Living Artists, 10th ed. Mem. Pacific Art League (1st v.p. 1993-98).

GILLESPIE, DANIEL CURTIS, SR., retired non-profit company executive, consultant; b. Shamokin, Pa., Sept. 22, 1922; s. John F. and Verna E. (Erdman) G.; m. Juliet Warren Yearns, Oct. 7, 1950; children: Julia W., Daniel Curtis, David R. BS, Pa. State U., 1943; MS in Chem. Engring., U. Mich., 1948. Devel. engr. Tidewater Associated Oil Co., Bayonne, N.J., 1943-44; jr. scientist Manhattan Project, Los Alamos Sci. Lab., 1946; with Dorr-Oliver Inc., Stamford, Conn., 1948-82, v.p. mktg., 1973-75, exec. v.p., 1975-76, pres. and chief exec. officer, 1976-82, also dir.; v.p. bus. devel. Sohio Chems. & Indsl. Products Co., 1982-84; pres., chief exec. officer Metropool, Inc., 1985-87; cons., 1987-92; ret., 1992. Served with U.S. Army, 1944-46. Fellow Am. Inst. Chem. Engrs.; hon. mem. Process Equipment Mfrs. Assn., Southwestern Area Commerce and Industry Assn. Home: 18 Pepper Bush Cir Savannah GA 31411-3009

GILLESPIE, ED, public affairs consultant, political organization executive; b. NJ; m. Cathy Hay; children: John Patrick, Carrie, Mollie Brigid. Grad., Cath. U. Am. Asst. to Andy Ireland, Fla., 1983—84; press spokesman Rep. Dick Armey, Tex., 1985—95; dir. comm. and congl. affairs Rep. Nat. Com., 1996; pres., CEO Policy Impact Comms., 1997—99; founder, prin. Quinn Gillespie and Assocs., Washington, 2000—; chmn. Rep. Nat. Com., 2003—. Editor: Contract with America, 1995 (NY Times bestseller list, 1995). Comm. dir. Pres. George W. Bush Inauguration, 2001; mgr. Phila. conv. Rep. Nat. Com., 2000; sr. comm. advisor George W. Bush Presdl. Campaign, Austin, 2000, spokesman for Fla. election recount, 2001; gen. strategist Elizabeth Dole Senate Campaign, NC, 2002. Office: Quinn Gillespie & Assocs LLC Fl 5 1133 Connecticut Ave NW Washington DC 20036 also: Rep Nat Com 310 First St SE Washington DC 20003*

GILLESPIE, EDWARD MALCOLM, hospital administrator; b. Mpls., Oct. 19, 1935; s. Harold Livingston and Alice May (Thompson) G.; children: Karin, Timothy, Kenneth. BS, U. Minn., 1957, MPA, 1959, MHA, 1962. Engaged in refugee adminstrn., Linz, Austria, 1958-60; asst. adminstr. Luth. Med. Ctr., Denver, 1962-66; asst. gen. sec. Meth. Bd. Health and Welfare Ministries, Evanston, Ill., 1966-69; adminstr. Meth. Hosp., Rochester, Minn., 1969-74, Univ. Hosp., Augusta, Ga., 1974-91, pres. Health Advance, 1991-92. Bd. dirs. Augusta Area Mental Health, Augusta Speech and Hearing Ctr., St. John's Towers, CSRA Blood Assurance; chmn. hosp. divsn. certification coun. Meth. Health and Welfare. Bd. dirs. local United Way, Boy Scouts Am., Blue Cross Ga., Bankers First; chmn. Augusta Resource Ctr. on Aging, Brandon Wilde. Fellow ACHA; mem. Am. Hosp. Assn., Ga. Hosp. Assn. (chmn.), Rotary Internat. (bd. dirs. Augusta chpt.). Methodist. Home and Office: Health Advance 12 Shadow Brook Cir Augusta GA 30909-3749

GILLESPIE, GARY DON, physician; b. Jackson, Mich., Apr. 23, 1943; s. Harold Don and Marion Estella (Diemer) G.; m. Nancy Bliven Hinkle, June 29, 1969 (div. July 1980; children: Brian James, Julie Elizabeth; m. Elaine Marie Beard, July 25, 1984. BS, U. Mich., 1966, D of Medicine, 1971. Diplomate Am. Bd. Family Practice. Intern Edward W. Sparrow Hosp., Lansing, Mich., 1971-72, resident in family practice, 1971-74; physician Dept. Family Practice, USN Med. Corps., Orlando, Fla., 1974-76; pvt. practice Okemos, Mich., 1976—2001; ret., 2001. Chmn. continuing edn., dept. family practice Edward W. Sparrow Hosp., 1976-91; asst. clin. prof. dept. family practice Mich. State U. Coll. Medicine, East Lansing, 1981-2001. Lt. comdr. USN, 1974-76. Mem. AMA, Am. Acad. Family Physicians, Am. Bd. Family Practice, Mich. Acad. Family Physicians (treas. Capitol chpt. 1982-92). Republican. Avocations: reading, music, photography, travel, golf.

GILLESPIE, GEORGE HUBERT, physicist; b. Dallas, Sept. 9, 1945; s. Hubert W. and Frieda S. Gillespie; children: James S., Colin H., Ian G. BA, MSEE, Rice U., 1968; MS, U. Calif., San Diego, 1969, PhD, 1974. Rsch. asst. U. Calif., San Diego, 1969-74; staff scientist Phys. Dynamics, Inc., San Diego, 1975-88; pres. G. H. Gillespie Assocs., Inc., San Diego, 1988—, AccelSoft Inc., San Diego, 1997—. Assoc. La Jolla Inst., San Diego, 1976-88; cons. Sci. Applications Internat., McLean, Va., 1985-87; mem. rev. com. for ANL, U. Chgo., 1991-93; mem. and/or chmn. program and organizing coms. for internat. sci. confs. Editor: Supernovae Spectra, 1980, High Current, High Brightness and High Duty Factor Ion Injectors, 1985; contbr. articles to profl. jours. Trustee Sky Mountain Life Sch., Vista, Calif., 1983-86. Capt. USAR, 1968-76. Mem. Am. Nuclear Soc. (treas. accelerator applications divsn. 1999-2000), Am. Phys. Soc. Office: G H Gillespie Assocs Inc 10855 Sorrento Valley Rd Ste 203 San Diego CA 92121-1616

GILLESPIE, GEORGE JOSEPH, III, lawyer; b. N.Y.C., May 18, 1930; s. George Joseph Jr. and Dorothy Elizabeth (McKenna) Gillespie; m. Eileen Tracy Dealy, July 27, 1955; children: Gail Gillespie Garcia, John D., Myles D., Eileen G. Fahey. AB magna cum laude, Georgetown U., 1952; LLB magna cum laude, Harvard U., 1955. Bar: N.Y. 1957. Assoc. Cravath, Swaine & Moore, LLP, N.Y.C., 1956-62, ptnr., 1963—. Bd. dirs. Washington Post Co., White Mountains Holdings, Inc. Trustee, pres. John M. Olin Found.; pres. Pinkerton Found., Arthur Rose Found., William S. Paley Found., Edward E. Ford Found., Edmond J. Safra Philanthropic Found.; bd. dirs., sec. Mus. TV and Radio; vice-chmn. exec. com. Madison Sq. Boys and Girls Club; chmn. emeritus, hon. life dir. Nat. Multiple Sclerosis Soc.; trustee Jackson Lab., Convent of the Sacred Heart, Greenwich, Conn. Frederick Sheldon Travel fellow, Harvard U., 1955—56. Mem.: Century Assn., Portland Country Club, Am. Yacht Club, Double Eagle Club, Falmouth Country Club, Prouts Neck Country Club, Winged Foot Golf Club. Republican. Roman Catholic. Office: Cravath Swaine & Moore Worldwide Pla 825 8th Ave Fl 43 New York NY 10019-7475

GILLESPIE, GERALD ERNEST PAUL, comparative literature educator, writer; b. Cleve., July 12, 1933; s. Francis and Nora Veronica (Quinn) G.; m. Adrienne Amalia Galante, Sept. 5, 1959. AB, Harvard U., 1956; postgrad., U. Tübingen, Germany, 1956-57; MA, Ohio State U., 1958, PhD, 1961; postgrad., U. Munich, 1960-61. Asst. prof. U. So. Calif., L.A., 1961-65; assoc. prof., then prof. SUNY, Binghamton, 1965-74; vis. prof. U. Pa., Phila., 1969, NYU, 1970; prof. Stanford (Calif.) U., 1974—. Vis. prof. U. Minn., Mpls., 1978, Peking U., Beijing, 1985, U. East Anglia, Norwich, Eng., 1988, U. Munich, 1993; hon. prof., Liaoning U., China. Author: German Baroque Poetry, 1971, Evolution of the European Novel, 1987, Garden and Labyrinth of Time, 1988, Proust, Mann, Joyce in the Modernist Context, 2003, By Way of Comparison, 2003; author, editor: Herkommen und Erneuerung, 1976, Studien zum Werk D.C. von Lohenstein, 1983, German Theater Before 1750, 1992, Romantic Drama, 1994, Narrative Ironies, 1997, Mallarmé in the Twentieth Century, 1998; translator, editor: Night Watches, 1972, Puss-in-Boots, 1974, Bohemian Lights, 1976; editor: Littérature Comparée, Littérature Mondiale, 1991, Visions in History, 1995, Powers of Narration, 1995; mem. editl. bd. Comparative Lit., 1977—, Internationales Archiv, 1975—. Utrecht Studies in Comparative Lit., 1987—, Recherche Littéraire, 1991—, Literary Imagination, 1998—; co-editor German Life and Letters, 1987—. Andrew Mellon Found. fellow, 1966-67; John S. Guggenheim Found. fellow, 1967-68; NEH sr. fellow, 1973-74; vis. fellow Clare Hall, Cambridge U., Eng., 1979 Mem.: MLA (mem. exec. com. comparative studies in romanticism and the 19th centur 1982—87, mem. nat. program com. 1985—88, mem. exec. com. classical studies and modern lit. 1986—91), Calif. Assn. Scholars (bd. dirs. 1992—), Assn. Literary Scholars and Critics (coun. 1998—2001), Renaissance Soc. Am., Brit. Comparative Lit. Assn., Am. Comparative Lit. Assn., Internat. Comparative Lit. Assn. (sec. 1979—85, mem. editl. bd. bull. 1979—85, v.p. 1985—88, pres. 1994—97), Berliner Wissenschaftliche Gesellschaft (corr.).

GILLESPIE, J. MARTIN, sales and distribution company executive; b. Detroit, Sept. 27, 1949; s. John Martin and Shirley Ann (Rees) G.; children: Heather, Tara. BBA, Xavier U., 1971; MBA, U. Mich., 1973. Account exec. Foote Cone & Belding, Chgo., 1973-76, account supr., 1976-77; mktg. mgr. Hansen Corp., Walled Lake, Mich., 1977-80, gen. mgr., 1980-82; chmn., CEO Hansen Mktg. Svcs., Inc., Walled Lake, 1982—. Recipient Merit award Nat. Alliance Businessmen, 1973. Mem. Assn. MBA Execs., Am. Mgmt. Assn., Nat. Acad. TV Arts and Scis., Nat. Assn. Credit Mgmt., Nat. Bldg. Materials Distbn. Assn. (chmn. govt. rels. com.), Alpha Kappa Psi. Office: Hansen Mktg Svcs Inc PO Box 638 1000 Decker Rd Walled Lake MI 48390-3218

GILLESPIE, JAMES DAVIS, lawyer; b. Elkin, N.C., Apr. 30, 1955; s. John Banner and Jerry Sue (Swaim) G.; m. Tommie Lee Johnson, Aug. 13, 1977 (div. Dec. 1995); 1 child, John Foster; m. Regina Lee Robinson, July 11, 1998. BA, U. N.C., 1977; JD, Samford U., 1980. Bar: N.C. 1980, U.S. Dist. Ct. (mid. dist.) 1982, U.S. Dist. Ct. (we. dist.) N.C. 1983, U.S. Ct. Appeals (4th cir.) 1984. Ptnr. Neaves & Gillespie, Elkin, 1980—. Mem. Surry-Yadkin Mental Health Authority, Mt. Airy, N.C., 1981-91, vice chmn., 1987-89, chmn. 1990-91. Bd. editors: Cumberland Law Rev., 1978-80. Commr. Town of Jonesville, N.C., 1983-85, mayor, 1985-93; mem. exec. com. N.W. Piedmont Coun. Govts., 1987, sec., 1988-89, chmn., 1990-91. Mem. ABA, Assn. Trial Lawyers Am., N.C. Bar Assn., N.C. Trial Lawyers Assn., Surry and Yadkin Counties Bar Assn., Elkin Jaycees (bd. dirs. 1981-83, v.p. 1983-84), N.C. Acad. Trial Lawyers, Greater Elkin-Jonesville C. of C. (charter, bd. dirs. 1987-90), Phi Alpha Delta, Soc. Curia Honoris. Democrat. Methodist. Avocations: tennis, basketball, reading, travel. Home: 516 Westbrook St Jonesville NC 28642-2658 Office: Neaves & Gillespie 124 W Main St Ste A Elkin NC 28621-3433 E-mail: neavesgillespie@aol.com.

GILLESPIE, JANE, lawyer; b. Cin., Aug. 18, 1935; d. William Pembroke and Elizabeth (Biermann) G. Student, Vassar Coll., 1953-55; cert. Polit. Sci. U. Strasbourg, France, 1956; BA, Northwestern U., 1958; LLB, Yale U., 1962. Bar; N.Y. 1964, U.S. Dist. Ct. (so. and ea. dists.) N.Y. 1972. with McLanahan, Merritt, Ingraham, N.Y.C., 1964-69, Olwine, Connelly, Chase, O'Donnell & Weyher, N.Y.C., 1969-78; atty. Interpublic Group of Cos., Inc., N.Y.C., 1978—, sec. various advt. agys. including McCann-Erickson, U.S.A., Inc., Muir, Cornelius & Moore, Inc., McCann Direct Inc., The Phillips-Ramsey Co., LUL Software Systems, Inc. Mem. Darien Rep. Town Meeting, Conn., 1980-84, Five Mile River Commn., 1981— . Mem. ABA (subcom. on fed. regulation securities 1969—), Assn. of Bar of City of N.Y., Yale Club (N.Y.C.). Office: Interpublic Group Cos Inc Ste 383 1271 Avenue Of The Americas Fl 44 New York NY 10020-1459

GILLESPIE, JOHN FAGAN, mining executive; b. Cleve., Aug. 16, 1936; s. James Patrick and Mary Isabelle (Fagan) G.; m. Rita Kirsch, 1956 (div.); children: John Joseph, Richard Anthony, Rita Therese, Margaret Mary, Veronica Gail; m. Dorothy May LaForest, July 6, 1962 (div. 1994); 1 child, Kelly Joseph. Student, John Carroll U., 1955-58, U. Tulsa, 1970-71. With Great Lakes Dredge and Dock Co., Cleve., 1955-63, project supt., 1962-63; owner, operator Tri-Angle Bldg. and Wrecking Co., Bay City, Mich., 1963-65; with Martin Marietta Corp., 1965-71, Aetna Portland Cement Co., Bay City, 1965-69, prodn. supt., 1968-69; maintenance supr. Dewey Rocky Mountain Cement Co., Tulsa, 1969-71; plant mgr. Kellstone Inc., Kelley's Island, Ohio, 1971-73, Lyon Sand and Gravel Co., Wixom, Mich., 1973-75; area mgr. J.P. Burroughs & Son, Inc., Aggregate div. subs. Blount Inc., Montgomery, Ala., 1975, asst. to pres., 1975-76, mgr. ops., 1976-78, gen. mgr., 1978-81; pres., CEO, chmn. bd. Tilcon N.Y. Inc., Haverstraw, N.Y., 1981—; pres., CEO JFG and Assocs., Inc., 1990—. Pres., CEO, Tilcon Quarries N.Y. Inc., 1981-91; ptnr. The Pasta-Bilities Cafe, Inc., sec., 1994—; pres., CEO The Pasta Co., 1994—; lobbyist, cons. to hospitality industry on indoor air quality; regional dir. Statewide Corp. Strategies Corp., 1995—; mem. Small Bus. Conf., State of Mich., 1977-81; cons. TT Materials, 1999—. Mem. bd. visitors Helen Hayes Hosp., 1985—; mem. corp. adv. coun. Columbia Presbyn. Hosp.; mem. adv. bd. to dean Columbia Presbyn. Dental Sch.; bd. dirs., chmn. Rockland C.C., 1985—; bd. dirs., chmn. bd. Rockland Econ. Devel. Corp., Nyack Hosp. Found., 1985—; bd. govs. Good Samaritan Hosp.; bd. dirs. Camp Ventura. Mem. Detroit Engring. Soc., Am. Mgmt. Assn., Pvt. Industry Coun. (bd. dirs. 1985—), Mich. Mineral Resources Assn. (past vice chmn.), Nat. Sand and Gravel Assn., Nat. Crushed Stone Assn. (chmn. flugas com.), Mich. Sand and Gravel Prodrs. Assn. (chief negotiator, sec.-treas.), Restaurant and Hospitality Assn. Rockland. Republican. Roman Catholic. Home: 11 Wildwood Rd Katonah NY 10536-1726 Office: 572 Route 303 Blauvelt NY 10913-1941 Home: 25 Juniper Ln Pawling NY 12564 E-mail: jfgassoc@peoplepc.com.

GILLESPIE, JOHN THOMAS, university administrator; b. Thunder Bay, Ont., Can., Sept. 25, 1928; came to U.S., 1954, naturalized, 1961; s. William and Jeannie (Barr) G. BA, U. B.C., 1948; MA, Columbia U., 1957; PhD, NYU, 1969. High sch. tchr., Powell River, B.C., Can., 1949-53; libr. Roslyn (N.Y.) Pub. Sch. Dist., 1955-63; mem. faculty Palmer Grad. Library Sch., C.W. Post Center, LIU, N.Y., 1963—, prof., 1975-80, dean, 1981-83; acad. v.p. C.W. Post Ctr., LIU, 1983-85. Vis. prof. Syracuse (N.Y.) U., SUNY, Albany; cons. in field. Author: Juniorplots, 1966, Introducing Books, 1970, Young Phenomenon, 1971, Creating the School Media Program, 1973, A Model School Media Program, 1973, Paperback Books for Young People, 3d edit., 1987, More Juniorplots, 1977, Best Books for Children, Administering the School Library Media Center, 1983, Elementary School Paperback Collection, 1985, Senior High School Paperback Collection, 1986, Juniorplots 3, 1987, Seniorplots, 1989, Best Books for Junior High Readers, 1991, Best Books for Senior High Readers, 1991, Juniorplots 4, 1993, Middleplots 4, 1994, Best Books for Children, 5th edit., 1994, Guides to Library Collection Development, 1994, The Newbery Companion, 1996, 2d edit. 2000, Characters in Young Adult Literature, 1997, Guides to Library Collection Development for Children and Young Adults, 1997, Best Books for Children, 7th edit., 2001, Best Books for Young Teen Readers, 1999, Teenplots, 2003. Mem. ALA, N.Y. Libr. Assn., Phi Delta Kappa, Kappa Delta Pi. Home: 360 E 72nd St New York NY 10021-4753 E-mail: bestgill@aol.com.

GILLESPIE, MARCIA LOU, accountant, tax preparer, musician; b. Grand Rapids, Mich., Nov. 26, 1942; d. Peter James and Bernice Lucille (DeReus) Muyskens; m. Norman Wayne Edwards, Aug. 15, 1964 (div. Apr. 1977); 1 child, Cary Ann Edwards; m. Eugene Scott Gillespie, Jan. 31, 1988. BA cum laude, U. Pitts., 1973. Enrolled agt. IRS. Acct. San Jose (Calif.) Symphony, 1977-78; agt. Prudential Ins., San Jose, 1978-81; acct. MicroFocus, Palo Alto, Calif., 1981-83; pianist, accompanist Opera Soc., Jr. Colls., San Jose and Napa, Calif., 1976—; contr. Gaston Snow, Palo Alto, 1983; acct. Accountemps, San Francisco, 1983-85, Bernheim Co., San Francisco, 1985-93; acct., tax preparer M.L. Gillespie Tax Svc., Emeryville, Napa, Calif., 1993—. Mem. Better Bus Bur., Oakland, Calif., 1996-97. Sgt., mem. Army Band, U.S. N.G., 1977-2000. Mem. Nat. Assn. Enrolled Agts. Democrat. Avocations: tennis, bowling, home decorating. Office: 1834 1st St # 5 Napa CA 94559-2353 E-mail: marciaea@msn.com.

GILLESPIE, MICHAEL ALLEN, social sciences educator, writer; b. Valley Forge, Penn., Jan. 24, 1951; s. Eileen L. Gillespie; m. Nancy S. Henley. AB, Harvard U., 1969—73; MA, U. Chgo, 1975, PhD, 1981. Instr. St. Olaf Coll., Northfield, Minn., 1978—80; Harper fellow U. Chgo., Ill., 1980—83; prof of polit. sci. and philosophy Duke U., Durham, NC, 1983—. Dir. Gerst Program in Polit., Econ. and Humanistic Studies Duke U., Durham, NC, 1998—. Author: Nihilism Before Nietzsche, 1996, Hegel, Heidegger, and the Ground of History, 1986; editor: Nietzsche's New Seas, 1991, Ratifying the Constitution, 1991. Grantee, Nat. Endowment for the Humanities, John Templeton Found., The Liberty Fund, German Academic Exch. Svc. (DAAD). Mem.: Am. Polit. Sci. Assn. (Leo Strauss award 1983). Office: Dept of Political Sci Duke Univ Box 90204 Durham NC 27708

GILLESPIE, PENNY HANNIG, business owner; b. Schenectady, N.Y., June 4, 1954; d. William Armand and Freda (Penney) H.; m. Kenneth Scofield Keyes, Jr., Sept. 2, 1984 (div. Aug. 1992). Student, U. Ariz., 1972-74. Cert. EMT, Ariz., N.Y.; completion in skills tng. for profls. in Hakomi psychotherapy, Oreg. Co-founder Ken Keyes Coll., Coos Bay, Ore., 1982-91; pvt. practice counseling Eugene, Ore., 1991-95; founder, pres. The Wellness Network, Eugene, Oreg., 1994—. Co-author: Gathering Power Through Insight and Love, 1986, Handbook to Higher Consciousness: The Workbook, 1989; editor: How to Enjoy Your Life in Spite of It All, 1980, The Hundredth Monkey, 1982, Your Heart's Desire, 1983, Your Life Is a Gift, 1987, Discovering the Secrets of Happiness, 1988, PlanetHood, 1988, The Power of Unconditional Love, 1990. Bd. dirs. Living Love Ch., 1980-91, sec., v.p.; founding bd. dirs., sec., sec.-treas., v.p. The Vision Foundation, Inc., 1982-91; founding bd. dirs., sec., sec.-treas. Cornucopia, The Living Love Ch. of Ky., 1982-91; vol. Victim Advocate Lane County Dist. Attys. Victim/Witness Svcs. Program, Oreg., 1993. Recipient peace award Coalition for Justice and Peace, Ariz. State U. and the Inst. Peace Edn., 1989; award as site mgr. for Anne Frank exhibit Jewish Fedn. Lane County, Ore., 1993. Avocations: piano, bicycling. Home: PO Box 41532 Eugene OR 97404 0369

GILLESPIE, RONALD JAMES, chemistry educator, researcher, writer; b. London, Aug. 21, 1924; arrived in Can., 1958; s. James Andrew and Miriam (Kirk) G.; m. Madge Garner, July 5, 1950; children: Ann, Lynn. BSc, London U., 1945, PhD, 1949, DSc, 1957; LLD (hon.), Concordia U., Montreal, Can., 1988, Dalhousie U., Halifax, Can., 1988; D Honoris causa, U. des Scis. et Techniques du Languedoc, 1991; DSc (hon.), McMaster U., 1993. Asst. lectr. dept. chemistry U. Coll., U. London, 1948-50, lectr., 1950-58; assoc. prof. dept. chemistry McMaster U., Hamilton, Ont., Can., 1958-60, prof., 1960-87, prof. emeritus, 1988—, chmn. dept., 1962-65. Vis. prof. U. Manchester (Eng.), 1965-66, U. des Scis. et Techniques du Languedoc, Montpellier, France, 1972-73, U. Geneva, 1976, U. Göttingen, Fed. Republic Germany, 1978, Australian Nat. U., Canberra, 1979, U. Melbourne, Australia, U. Auckland, New Zealand, 1980, Panjab U., Chandigarh, India, 1983; Nyholm lectr. Chem. Soc., London, 1978; Gillespie lectr. U. Coll., London, 1990; Muetterties vis. scholar U. Calif., Berkeley, 1990. Author: Molecular Geometry, 1972, (with others) Chemistry, 1986, 2d edit., 1989, (with I. Hargittai) The VSEPR Model of Molecular Geometry, 1991, (with others) Atoms, Molecules and Reactions: An Introduction to Chemistry, 1994, (with P. Popelier) Chemical Bonding and Molecular Geometry: From Lewis to Election Densities, 2001; contbr. over 370 articles to profl. jours. Recipient Can. Centennial medal, 1967, Coll. Chemistry Tchr. award Mfg. Chemists Assn., 1972, Silver Jubilee award, 1977, Excellence in Teaching award McMaster u. Students Union, 1983, Izaak Walter Killam Meml. Prize of Can. Coun. for Pure Sci., 1987; Commonwealth Fund fellow Brown U., 1953-54. Fellow Royal Soc. London, Royal Soc. Can. (Henry Marshall Tory medal 1983), Royal Soc. Chemistry (Harrison Meml. medal 1953), Royal Inst. Chemistry, Chem. Inst. Can. (Noranda award 1966, Union Carbide award 1976, medal 1977); mem. Am. Chem. Soc. (N.E. Region award 1971, Tour Speaker of Yr. award 1971, Disting. Svc. award 1973, fluorine chemistry award 1981). Avocations: sailing, skiing, travel. Office: McMaster U Dept Chemistry Hamilton ON Canada L8S 4M1 E-mail: gillespi@mcmaster.ca.

GILLESPIE, THOMAS STUART, business executive; b. Montreal, July 18, 1938; s. Alexander Robert and Lois Tully (O'Brien) G.; m. Caroline Pierce Doyle, June 28, 1963; children: Caroline Alexandra, Alexandra Olivia, Vanessa Margaret, Joshua William. BA, McGill U., 1959, BCL, 1963. Assoc., Ogilvy, Renault, Montreal, 1964-72, ptnr., 1972-89, sr. ptnr., 1989-2001; pres. Tyringham Investments Ltd., 2001—. Sec., bd. dirs. Bouverie Investments Ltd., Charlottetown Trust Co; chmn., bd. dirs. Shreve, Crump & Low, Ltd., Schwarzschild Jewelers, Inc. Bd. dirs. Carnegie Instn. Can., The Montreal Young Co., Ltd. Mem. Que. Bar Assn., Can. Bar Assn., Mt. Bruno Country Club, Orleans Fish and GameClub, Univ. Club, Tarratine Club, Toronto Golf Club. Roman Catholic. Home: 48 Aberdeen Ave Westmount QC Canada H3Y 3A4 Office: 1800 McGill College Ave Ste 2430 Montreal QC Canada H3A 3J6 E-mail: tgillespie@tyringham.ca.

GILLESPIE, THOMAS WILLIAM, theological seminary administrator, religion educator; b. L.A., July 18, 1928; s. William A. and Estella (Beers) G.; m. Barbara A. Lugenbill, July 31, 1953; children: Robyn C., William T., Dayle E. BA, George Pepperdine Coll., 1951; BD, Princeton Theol. Sem., 1954; PhD, Claremont Grad. Sch., 1971; DD (hon.), Grove City Coll., 1984; ThD (hon.), Theol. Acad. Debrecen, Hungary, 1988; DTh (hon.), Karoli Gaspar Reformed U., Budapest, Hungary, 1994; DPhil (hon.), Soong Sil U., Seoul, Korea, 1994; DD (hon.), U. St. Andrews, Scotland, 1996; LHD (hon.), King Coll., Bristol, Tenn., 1999. Ordained to ministry Presbyterian Ch., 1954. Pastor 1st Presbyn. Ch., Garden Grove, Calif., 1954-66, Burlingame, Calif., 1966-83; pres., prof. N.T. Princeton (N.J.) Theol. Sem., 1983—. Author: The First Theologians: A Study in Early Christian Prophecy, 1994. Chmn. bd. trustees Ctr. Theol. Inquiry, 1992—. With USMC, 1946-47. Recipient A.A. Hodge prize in systematic theology Princeton Theol. Sem., 1953; Disting. Alumnus award Claremont Grad. Sch., 1984; Disting. Alumnus award Pepperdine U., 1986. Mem. Soc. Bibl. Lit., Studiorum Novi Testamenti Societas, Rotary Internat. Republican. Home: Springdale 86 Mercer St Princeton NJ 08540-6819 Office: Princeton Theol Sem Office of Pres PO Box 552 Princeton NJ 08542-0552

GILLESPIE, WILLIAM HARRY, forestry executive, geology educator; b. Webster Springs, W.Va., Jan. 8, 1931; s. William Marston and Rosalie Casteel (Frazee) G.; m. Betty Jean Rasnick, Dec. 23, 1950; children: William A., Linda M., Clifton P., Laura L., James D. BS, W.Va. U., 1952, MS, 1954, postgrad., 1956-60. Forest biologist W.Va. Dept. Agr., Morgantown, 1956-66, asst. dir. plant pest control Charleston, 1966-67, dir. plant pest control, 1967-69, asst. commr., 1969-80, dep. commr., 1980-85; instr. dept. geology W.Va. U., Morgantown, 1958-74, from asst. prof. to prof., 1974—99, adj. prof., 2000—; dir. W.Va. Dept. Forestry, Charleston, 1985-93. Cons. forester-geologist, W.Va., 1993—; rsch. paleobotanist U.S. Geol. Survey, Reston, Va., 1974-95. Author: W.Va. Geology, Archaeology and Pedology, 1964, W.Va. Plant Fossils, 1978, Wild Foods of Appalachia, 1986; contbr. articles to profl. jours. Named to W.Va. Agr. and Forestry Hall of Fame, 1998; recipient Disting. Achievement in Earth Scis. award, Am. Fedn. Mineral. Socs., 1982, Outstanding Contbn. to Forestry award, W.Va. Forestry Assn., 1986, 2000, Outstanding Svc. award, Nat. Assn. State Foresters, 1993, Nat. Assn. State Depts. Agr., 1994, W.Va. U. Dept. Geology, 1995, W.Va. Coll. Agr. and Forestry, 1999, fossil plant genus Gillespieisporites named in his honor, J.A. Clendening, 1969, fossil plant genus Gillespia named in his honor, Erwin and Rothwell, 1989. Fellow: Soc. Am. Foresters; mem.: Assn. Cons. Foresters, Internat. Assn. Paleobotanists, Internat. Assn. Plant Taxonomists, Bot. Soc. Am., Am. Assn. Petroleum Geologists, Geol. Soc. Am., W.Va. Assn. Soil Conservation Suprs. (hon. life), Lions. Democrat. Avocations: woodworking, fishing, photography. Home and Office: 916 Churchill Cir Charleston WV 25314-1747

GILLET, HENRI ANTOINE DENIS CIARAN, mathematician, educator; b. Tangier, Morocco, July 8, 1953; m. Gail J. Holmberg, June 30, 1979; children: Victoria G., Maia M. BSc, U. of London, Kings Coll., 1975; PhD, Harvard U., 1978. Prof. of math. U. of Ill. at Chgo., 1988—, head dept. mscs, 1994—2001, assoc. prof. of math., 1986—88, asst. prof. of math., 1984—86; asst. prof. Princeton U., 1981—84, instr., 1978—81; prof. associe U. Paris Sud, 1985. Lectr. Columbia U.; mem. Isaac Netwon Inst., Cambridge, England, 1998, Inst. for Advanced Study, Princeton, NJ, 1987. Editor: Am. Jour. of Math, 1995—99, Internat. Math. Rsch. Notices, 1995—98, Ill. Jour. of Math.; contbr. articles to profl. jours. Rsch. fellowship, A. P. Sloan Found., 1986—89. Mem.: IHES, Am. Math. Soc. (elected mem. coun. 2002—), Lake Ripley Country Club. Achievements include research in in arithmetic geometry and algebraic K-theory, including development (with C. Soule) of higher dimensional Arakelov theory. Avocations: reading, travel, golf. Office: Dept MSCS m/c 249 UIC 851 S Morgan Chicago IL 60607-7045

GILLET, PAMELA KIPPING, special education educator; EdB in Elem. Edn., Chgo. Tchrs. Coll., 1963; MA in Mental Retardation, Northeastern Ill. U., 1966; PhD in Gen. Spl. Edn./Adminstrn., Walden U., 1976. Cert. elem. edn., early childhood edn., learning disabled, mental retardation, behavior disorders, supt., supr. and dir. spl. edn. 4th grade tchr. Dist. # 83 Mannheim, Frankling Park, Ill., 1963—64; h.s. spl. edn. tchr. Dist. # 207 Maine Twp., Park Ridge, Ill., 1964—67, prevocational coord., 1967—69, dept. chmn. spl. edn. dept., 1969—70; dir. EPDA tchr. tng. program Chgo. Consortium Colls. and Univs., Northewst Ednl. Coop., Palatine, Ill., 1970—71; prin. West Suburban Spl. Edn. Ctr., Cicero, Ill., 1971—73; supr. West Suburban Assn. Spl. Edn., Cicero, 1973—75; asst. dir. Northwest Suburban Spl. Edn. Orgn., Palatine, 1975—78, supt. Mt. Prospect, Ill., 1978—96; spl. edn. cons., 1996—. Adj. instr. Northeastern Ill. U., Chgo. State U., Corcordia Coll., Barat Coll. Nat. Coll. Edn., Roosevelt U.; mem. task forces ISBE, 1975—2007, cons. career edn. project, 1977—78, spl. edn. demandate study group, 1983—85; cons. Ednl. Testing Svc.; tchr. edn. coun. Northeastern Ill. U., 1981—97, dean's grant program, 1982—97; workshop leader, 1974—; lectr., cons. in field. Author: Auditory Processes, 1974, rev., 1992, Career Education for Children, 1978, Of Work and Worth: Career Education Programming for Exceptional Children and Youths, 1981; contbr. articles to profl. jours., chapters to books. Bd. dirs. Found. Exceptional Children, 1996—, pres., 1999—. Recipient Cmty. Svc. award, Am. Legion, 1976, 1980, Alumnus of Yr. award, Northeastern Ill. U., 1984, Learning Disabilities of Am. Contributors award, Coun. Understanding Learning Disabilities, 1992, Those Who Excel award of excellence, Ill. State Bd. of Edn., 1994, Outstanding Svc. award, Divsn. Mental Retardation and Devel. Disabilities, 1994, Sleznick award, Coun. of Admin. of Spl. Edn., 1996, Outstanding Contbr. award, Coun. Exceptional Children, 1996, Burton Blatt award, Divsn. on Metal Retardation and Devel. Disabilities, 1997, Spl. Edn. Leadership award, Ill. Adminstrs. of Spl. Edn., 1995, Outstanding Spl. Edn. Adminstr. of Yr. award, 1997. Mem.: ASCD, Found. for Exceptional Children (pres. 2000—), Ill. Adminstrs. Spl. Edn. (pres. 1994—95), Coun. Exceptional Children (pres. Ill. chpt. 1975—77, bd. govs. 1977—80, 1996—2000, pres. mental retardation divsn. 1983—85, bd. govs. 1986, exec. com. 1989—92, v.p. internat. 1992—93, pres.-elect 1993—94, pres. 1994—95, bd. dirs. 2000—, Meritorious Svc. award Ill. 1983), Assn. Children with Learning Disabilities, Am. Assn. Sch. Adminstrs. Home and Office: 413 Courtley Oaks Blvd Winter Garden FL 34787

GILLETT, ANNETTE DAMRON, retired speech and forensics educator; b. L.A., Dec. 17, 1905; d. George Wilshire Damron and Florence Frances Helm; m. Cecil Gillett, June 15, 1934 (dec. Mar. 1969); 1 child, Charles Lucky. BA, U. Calif., Berkeley, 1926. Tchr. English and Spanish local high schs., Ramona, Calif., 1927-30, Cen. Union H.S., El Centro, Calif., 1931-57; tchr. speech Cen. Cmty. Coll., El Centro, Calif., 1931-57. Active Nevada County Task Force on Housing, Nevada City, Calif., 1998-2001; mem. cen. com. Nevada County Dems., 1990-98. Recipient Vol. Svc. award Calif. Ret. Tchrs. Assn., 1997. Mem. LWV (life, vol. svc. award 1996), AAUW (life, pres. 1975-77), Pi Lambda Theta (life). Avocations: hiking, fishing. Home: 50 Rockwood Dr Grass Valley CA 95945

GILLETT, GARY LEE, music educator; b. Detroit, Mich., Apr. 15, 1953; s. Vincent B. and Maxine B. Gillett; m. Luanne Lucille Sausle; children: Kyle, Erin. MusB, U. Mich., 1975; MusM in Edn., U. Mont., 1987. Cert. K-12 music tchr. Mont. Music tchr. Owyhee Schools, Nev., 1975—79, Corvallis Pub. Sch., Mont., 1979—80; dir. bands Stevensville Pub. Sch., Mont., 1980—88, Sentinel H.S., Missoula, Mont., 1988—. Dir. Missoula City Band, 1992—. Mem.: Music Educators Nat. Conf. Home: 2203 42nd St Missoula MT 59803 Office: Sentinel High Sch 901 South Ave W Missoula MT 59801 Office Fax: 406-329-5959. Personal E-mail: ggillett@bigsky.net. E-mail: ggillett@mcps.k12.mt.us.

GILLETT, GROVER, author; b. Whitewright, Tex., June 22, 1927; s. Grover Cleveland and Gertrude (Holland) G.; m. Mary Margaret Landress, Aug. 16, 1963. BBA, Tex. Tech. U., 1949; MBA, U. Tex., 1951; postgrad., Columbia U., 1953. CPA, Tex. Auditor Lumberman's Mutual Casualty Co., Dallas, 1954-56; operational auditor Dept. of Def., Dallas, 1956-58; self-employed CPA Dallas, 1958-64; asst. prof. McMurry Coll., Abilene, Tex., 1964-66; sr. internal auditor Ling-Temco-Vought Aerospace Corp., Dallas, 1966-67; instr. El Centro Coll., Dallas, 1967-96. Author: Personnel Policies of Public Accounting Firms in Texas, 1951, (booklet) Marriage Quotables, 1999, 57 other books and booklets. Bd. dirs. Twenty-One Turtle Creek Homeowners Assn., Dallas, 1996-98; mem. Dallas Coun. on World Affairs. With USN, 1945-46, Korea, lt. (j.g.) USNR ret. Mem. AICPAs, Tex. Soc. CPAs, World Future Soc., Dallas UN Assn., S.W. Social Sci. Assn., Lions. Democrat. Unitarian Universalist. Avocations: reading, collecting antiques. Home and Office: Apt 1103 3883 Turtle Creek Blvd Dallas TX 75219-4426

GILLETT, JAMES WARREN, ecotoxicology educator; b. Sept. 18, 1933; s. Ira Elijah and Atha Arthela (Morlan) Gillett; m. Mary Francis Hebert, Aug. 7, 1970; children: Grant Jameson, Iain; m. Mary Alexia Stuart, June 26, 1958 (div. Apr. 1970); children: John Stuart, Peter Warren. BS, U. Kans., 1955; PhD, U. Calif., Berkeley, 1962. Postdoctoral rsch. chemist U. Calif., Berkeley, 1962-64; asst. prof. agrl. chemistry Oreg. State U., Corvallis, 1964-69, assoc. prof., 1969-74; rsch. ecologist EPA/Environ. Rsch. Lab., Corvallis, 1974-81, rsch. environ. scientist, 1981-83; prof. ecotoxicology dept. natural resources Cornell U, Ithaca, N.Y., 1983—, dir. superfund basic rsch. program, 1992—2001. Dir. Inst. for Comparative and Environ. Toxicology, 1986-92, Risk Analysis Studies minor field of grad study. Editor, pub.: Biological Impact of Pesticides in the Environment, 1971; editor: Terrestrial Microcosms, 1979; editor: (jour.) Hazard Assessment, Environ. Toxicology & Chemistry, 1988-93; contbr. articles to profl. jours. Chmn. bd. Oreg. Mus. Sci. and Industry, 1969-71, Cmty. Action Program, 1970-72; sec. Willamette Soccer League, 1970-74; coach Corvallis Womens Soccer Team, 1979-81; pres., founder Esophagal Cancer Awareness Assn., 2002-. Summerfield scholar, 1951-54. Mem. Soc. Environ. Toxicology and Chemistry (bd. dirs. 1984-88), Alpha Kappa Lambda, Toastmasters (pres. 1974). Office: Cornell U Ctr for Environment 216 Rice Hall Ithaca NY 14853 E-mail: jwg3@cornell.edu.

GILLETT, MARY CAPERTON, military historian; b. Richmond, Va., Apr. 28, 1929; d. Lewis Hopkins and Mary Caperton (Horsley) Renshaw; m. Richard Clark Gillett, June 7, 1949; children: Richard Clark Jr., Glenn Douglas, Mary Caperton, Priscilla Elizabeth, Blakeney Diana. Student, Wellesley Coll., 1946-49; BA, Am. U., 1966, MA, 1971, PhD, 1978. Historian U.S. Navy Dept., Washington, 1966-69, U.S. Dept. Army, Washington, 1972-96. Author: The Army Medical Department, 1775-1818, 1981, The Army Medical Department, 1818-1865, 1988, The Army Medical Department, 1865-1917, 1995; contbr. articles to profl. jours. Mem. Am. Assn. for History of Medicine, Nat. Wildlife Fedn., We. Hist. Assn., The Nature Conservancy, The Wilderness Soc., The Sierra Club, Nat. Audubon Soc., Audubon Naturalist Soc. Avocations: backpacking, gardening. E-mail: mcgillett@mindspring.com.

GILLETT, PATRICIA, family and acute care nurse practitioner, clinical nurse; b. Mass., Jan. 2, 1948; d. Clyde and Estelle (Carter) Gleason; m. Warren Gillett, July 1968; children: Michael, James. ADN, Berkshire Community Coll.; BSN, U. N.Mex.; MSN, U. Tex., El Paso; FNP, Tex. Tech. Univ. Nursing instr. U. Albuquerque, Albuquerque T-VI; critical care edn. coord. St. Joseph Med. Ctr., Albuquerque VA Med. Ctr.; faculty U. N. Mex., Coll. of Nursing. Mem. ANA, AACN (Outstanding Cricital Care Educator 1989), Am. Acad. Nurse Practitioners, N.Mex. Nurses Assn. (award for clin. excellence 1994), Sigma Theta Tau.

GILLETT, PAULA, humanities educator; b. N.Y.C., July 15, 1934; d. Ira and Sophie (Silvershein) Levy; m. Eric Gillett, June 23, 1956; children: Walter, Nadia, Noel. BA, Bklyn. Coll., 1955; MA, Yale U., 1956; PhD, U. Calif., Berkeley, 1979. Project dir. Grad. Sch. Edn., U. Calif., Berkeley, 1984-89; prof. San Jose (Calif.) State U., 1989—; lectr. U. Calif., Santa Cruz, 1979—80. Co-chair Com. on History in the Classroom, 1992-96; vis. scholar Inst. for Rsch. on Women and Gender, Stanford U., 1996-97. Author: Worlds of Art: Painters in Victorian Society, 1990, Musical Women in England, 1870-1914: Encroaching on All Man's Privileges, 2000. Project dir. New Faces of Liberty, San Francisco, 1985-89. Summer fellow Am. Coun. Learned Socs., 1994, Mellon fellow Harry Ransom Humanities Rsch. Ctr., U. Tex., Austin, 1996. Mem. Am. Hist. Assn., Phi Beta Kappa. Avocation: choral singing. Office: San Jose State U Humanities Dept San Jose CA 95192-0092 E-mail: pgillett@aya.yale.edu.

GILLETT, RICHARD CLARK, JR., physician, educator, health facility administrator; b. Richmond, Va., Mar. 27, 1950; s. Richard Clark and Mary Caperton (Renshaw) G.; m. Barbara Jean Bolecek, Aug. 12, 1972; children: Douglas Clark, Ann Caperton. BA, U. Va., 1971, MD, 1977. Diplomate Am. Bd. Family Practice. Tchr. Prince William County Schs., Manassas, Va., 1971-72; resident Roanoke (Va.) Meml. Hosp., 1977-80; family physician Family Practice Clinic, Inc., Radford, Va., 1981-82; emergency physician Montgomery Regional Hosp., Blacksburg, Va., 1982-83; pvt. practice Radford, Va., 1983-85; asst. prof. family medicine, asst. dean continuing med. edn. East Tenn. State U., Johnson City, 1986-91; dir. med. edn. Columbus (Ga.) Regional Healthcare Sys., 1991-2000. Bd. dirs. Stewert Cmty. Home, Columbus, 1996-99, Human Experience Theater, Columbus, 1997, Springer Theater, Columbus, 1993-94, 99-00. Mem. AMA (rep. sect. on med. schs. Chgo., 1996-2000), Am. Assn. Family Physicians, Med. Assn. Ga. (mem. com. med. schs.), Muscogee County (Ga.) Med. Soc. Avocations: gardening, flying. Fax: 706-571-1604. E-mail: gillettrc@knology.net., clark.gillett@crhs.net.

GILLETT, VICTOR WILLIAM, JR., title insurance company executive; b. El Paso, Tex., Feb. 4, 1932; s. Victor William and Alice Cecelia (Kemper) G.; m. Anita Johanne Dexter, Mar. 1, 1975; children: Victor William III, Blake Andrew. BBA, Tex. A&M U., 1953. V.p., dist. mgr. Stewart Title Guaranty Co., Corpus Christi, Tex., 1955-61; pres., CEO, Stewart Title & Trust Co., Phoenix, 1961-77, dir., 1965 77; sr. v.p. nat. mktg. dir. Stewart Title Guaranty Co., Houston, 1977-91, dir., 1981 91, sr. v.p. Irvine, Calif., 1988-91; pres. Old Republic Title Co. Bell County, Temple, Tex., 1992—2001; ret., 2001. Dir. Stewart Info. Svcs. Corp., 1983-91. Bd. dirs. Ariz. Heart Assn., 1970-73; bd. dirs., sec. Phoenix Civic Improvement Corp., 1974-76. With AUS, 1953-54. Mem. Am. Land Title Assn. (gov. 1969-71), Temple C. of C. (former bd. dirs.), Rotary, Assn. U.S. Army (pres., bd. dirs. 1968), Navy League, Former Students Assn. Tex. A&M U., 12th Man Found. (Tex. A&M U.). Home: 5007 Sterling Dr Temple TX 76502-7108

GILLETTE, DEBORAH JEAN, music educator; b. Kalamazoo, Mich., July 5, 1956; d. Robert Keith and Margaret M McLain; children: Sara Elizabeth, Peter Thomas, Charles James. Applied Piano Pedagogy, Mich. State U., East lansing, MI, 1974—80. Piano tchr. Trinity Internat. U., Deerfield, Ill., 1998—; dir. of music Antioch United Meth. Ch., Ill., 1998—. Bd. dirs., state com. North Shore Music Tchrs. Assn., Winnekta, Ill., 1998—; alto saxophone soloist Lakes Area Cmty. Band, Antioch, Ill., 1998—; handbell choir dir. Trinity Internat. U., Deerfield, Ill., 1998—. Vol. musician Lakes Area Cmty. Swing Band, Antioch, Ill., 1999—2003; organized Sept. 11th Svc. of Remembrance for city of Antioch in conjunction with the local village and area chs. Antioch United Meth. Ch., Antioch, Ill., 2002. Recipient Honored mem., Internat. Exec. Guild, 2002 to present. Mem.: Nat. Piano Guild (assoc.; adjudicator 1996—2003), North Shore Music Tchrs. Assn. (assoc.; aim chmn. and mem.state com. 2001—03). Avocations: gardening, reading. Home: 40272 Shady Ln Antioch IL 60002 Office: Trinity Internat Univ 2065 Half Day Rd Deerfield IL 60015 Personal E-mail: pianodeb@msn.com.

GILLETTE, DENNIS C. academic administrator, mayor; b. Mpls., Oct. 27, 1939; m. Terry J. Larson, Aug. 24, 1968. AA in Polit. Sci., Moorpark Coll., 1971; BA in Sociology, La Verne U., 1973; cert. tchr., U. Calif., Santa Barbara, 1974; MS in Adminstrn. of Justice, Calif. Luth. U., 1975. Asst. sheriff Ventura County (Calif.) Sheriff's Dept., 1963-88; v.p. adminstrv. svcs., treas. Calif. Luth. U., Thousand Oaks, 1988-2000. Mayor pro tem City of Thousand Oaks, 1998-99, mayor, 1999-2000; bd. dirs. Conejo Recreation and Park Dist., Thousand Oaks, 1987-98, chmn. bd., 1991, 96; vice chmn. Conejo Future Found., Thousand Oaks; gen. chmn. Conejo Valley Days, Thousand Oaks, 1989; chmn. bd. dirs. Los Robles Regional Med. Ctr., Thousand Oaks, 1993, Conejo Valley C. of C., Thousand Oaks, 1994-95; mem. Ascension Luth. Ch. With USMC, 1957-59. Recipient Conejo Family Family of Yr. award, 1983, Man of Yr. award Conejo Valley C. of C., 1987, Don Triunfo award Conejo Valley Hist. Soc., 1992. Mem. Am. Soc. Indsl. Security, Calif. Peace Officers Assn., Thousand Oaks Rotary, Elks, Masons. Office: 286 W Siolee St Thousand Oaks CA 91360

GILLETTE, EDWARD LEROY, radiation oncology educator; b. Coffeyville, Kans., May 21, 1932; s. Harold R. and Laura Belle (McLaughlin) G.; m. Carol J. Peterson, June 2, 1956 (div. Oct. 1981); children: William R., Jeffrey S., Timothy E., Jennifer L.; m. Sharon L. McChesney, Nov. 26, 1988. BS, DVM, Kans. State U., 1956; MS, Colo. State U., 1961, PhD, 1965. From instr. to prof. radiology and radiation biology Colo. State U., Ft. Collins, 1959-72, prof., 1972-2000, prof., chmn. emeritus, 2000—, dir. comparative oncology, 1974-98, chmn. dept. radiol. health scis., 1989-98, assoc. dean rsch. Coll. Vet. Medicine and Biomed. Sci., 1997-98; adj. clin. prof. dept. radiation oncology UCLA Med. Sch., 1998—. Adj. prof. dept. radiation oncology Duke U. Med. Coll., Durham, N.C.; bd. dirs. The Children's Hosp. Kempe Rsch. Ctr., Denver, 1984-90; vis. scientist M.D. Anderson Cancer Ctr. U. Tex., 1988. Assoc. editor Radiation Rsch., 1979-82, 86-90; assoc. editor, Internat. Jour. of Radiation Oncology Biology and Physics, 1990-95, mem. editl. bd., 1995—; contbr. articles to profl. jours. Bd. dirs. Colo. State Sci. Fair, 1984-90. 1st lt. U.S. Army, 1956-58. Recipient Outstanding Svc. to the Vet. Profession award Am. Animal Hosp. Assn., 1984, Ralston-Purina rsch. award, 1988, Kans. State U. Alumni Assn. Medallion award, 1999; U. Tex. fellow, 1968-69. Mem. AVMA, Am. Coll. Vet. Radiology (cert., pres. 1973-74), Am. Coll. Vet. Internal Medicine, Oncology (cert.), Am. Cancer Soc. (mem. exec. com. Colo. divsn. 1978-82, bd. dirs. Colo. divsn. 1984-90, pres. Larimer County chpt. 1977-81), Vet. Cancer Soc. (pres. 1982-84), Radiation Rsch. Soc. (councilor 1988-91), Am. Soc. Therapeutic Radiology and Oncology, Am. Assn. Cancer Rsch., Colo. State U. Alumni Assn. (Honor Alumnus award 1985). Republican. Avocation: reading. Office: Colo State Univ Animal Cancer Ctr Fort Collins CO 80523-0001

GILLETTE, HYDE, retired investment banker; b. Chgo., June 23, 1906; s. Edwin Fraser and Mabel (Hyde) G.; m. Marie Clarke Smith, Sept. 7, 1932 (dec. Sept. 28, 1994); 1 child, Marie Clarke Gerald. Grad., Exeter Acad., 1924; AB cum laude, Princeton U., 1928; MBA with distinction, Harvard U., 1930. With Glore, Forgan & Co., 1930-53, ptnr., 1950-53; dep. asst. and dep. under sec. USAF, 1953-57; asst. postmaster gen., bur. finance U.S. Post Office Dept., Washington, 1957-61; ptnr. Auchincloss Parker & Redpath, 1961-70; regional v.p. Thomson & McKinnon Auchincloss, Inc., Washington, 1970-73; v.p. Thomson McKinnon Securities, 1973-89, Prudential Securities, 1989-91. Exec. bd. Chgo. Area Project, 1936-53, chmn., 1948-53; bd. dirs., v.p. Nat. Capital area council Boy Scouts Am.; regent Nat. Eagle Scout Assn.; dir., vice chmn. budget com. Community Fund of Chgo., 1942; chmn. exec. com. Chgo. Opera Theatre, 1947; adv. bd. Dept. Public Welfare Ill., 1949-53; pres. Barrington Country Day Sch., 1941; v.p. Washington Heart Assn., 1961; bd. dirs. Am. Heart Assn., 1960-63. Served as lt. comdr. USNR, 1943-46. Recipient Exceptional Civilian Svc. award USAF, 1956; Disting. Svc. award U.S. Post Office Dept., 1960; disting. Eagle Scout Nat. award. Mem. Mayflower Descs., Soc. Colonial Wars, English Speaking Union (dir. 1977-86), Barrington Countryside Assn. (pres. 1949-50), Phi Beta Kappa. Clubs: Quadrangle (Princeton); Chevy Chase (Washington), Metropolitan (Washington); Beverly Yacht (Marion, Mass.), Kittanset (Marion, Mass.). Episcopalian. Home: Fox Hill Village 10 Longwood Dr Apt 404 Westwood MA 02090-1144

GILLETTE, LYNN G. dean; b. Aug. 15, 1953; BA in Econs., U. Richmond, 1975; PhD in Econs., Tex. A&M U., 1981. Asst. v.p. for acad. affairs James Madison U., Harrisonburg, Va., 1985-86; sr. lectr., coord. prins. of macroeconomics Tex. A&M U., College Station, 1986-90; assoc. v.p. for acad. affairs Truman State U., Kirksville, Mo., 1991-93, exec. asst. to pres., 1993-94; dean Sch. Bus., prof. econs. Hardin-Simmons U., Abilene, Tex., 1994-98, dean Coll. Bus. and Econs., prof. econs., 1998—. Vis. asst. prof. Ind. U., Indpls., 1990-91. Office: Houston Bapt U 7502 Fondren Rd Houston TX 77074

GILLETTE, P. ROGER, physicist, systems engineer; b. Mt. Vernon, Iowa, May 12, 1917; s. Clinton Edgar and Celia (Rogers) G.; m. Bettelaine Dunbar, Apr. 26, 1947 (dec. Mar. 1986); children: Kenneth Lee, Sandra Jo. BA in Physics, Cornell Coll., 1937; BS in Engring. Physics, U. Ill., 1938, MS in Physics, 1939, PhD in Physics, 1942. Staff mem. Radiation Lab, MIT, Cambridge, Mass., 1942-45; rsch. engr. Sperry Gyroscope Co., Great Neck, N.Y., 1945-48; physicist Hanford Works Gen. Electric Co., Richland, Wash., 1948-50; sr. rsch. physicist SRI Internat., Menlo Park, Calif., 1950-92, ret. Co-author: Pulse Generators, 1948. Bd. dirs. West Bay Opera Assn., Palo Alto, Calif., 1959—64, 1977—79, Inst. for Continued Learning, Willamette U., Salem, Oreg., 1996—98. Mem. AAAS, IEEE (sr. life), Am. Phys. Soc. (life), Am. Acd. Religion, Inst. on Religion in an Age of Sci., Sigma Xi, Phi Beta Kappa, Tau Beta Pi, Phi Kappa Phi. Achievements include development of

pulse transformer theory, of system design concepts for command, control, communications and intelligence systems, electronic combat systems, and air combat training systems. Home: 2385 Crestview Dr S, Salem OR 97302-5373

GILLETTE, PAUL CRAWFORD, pediatric cardiologist; b. Winston-Salem, N.C., Dec. 1, 1942; s. Crawford Paul and Eileen Marie (O'Rourke) G.; m. Vicki Lynn Zeigler, 1992; 2 children. BA in Chemistry, U.N.C., 1965; MD, Med. Coll. S.C., 1969. Intern, then resident in pediatrics Baylor U. Coll. Medicine, Houston, 1969-71, fellow in pediatric cardiology and cell biophysics, 1971-74, mem. faculty, 1974-84, assoc. prof. exptl. medicine, 1977-84, prof. pediatrics, 1980-84, Med. U. S.C., Charleston, 1984-96, chmn. promotions com., dept. pediatrics, 1989-96; dir. S.C. Children's Heart Ctr., Charleston, 1984-96; med. dir. Cook Children's Cardiology, 1996—, Cook Childrens Cardiac Ctr., Fort Worth, Tex., 1996—. Dir. electrophysiology and electrocardiography Tex. Children's Hosp.; co-dir. Palmetto Heart Inst., 1988-96; mem. tng. grant manpower rev. com. Nat. Heart, Lung and Blood Inst., 1989-93, chmn., 1992-93. Co-author: A Guide to Pediatric Cardiac Dysrhythmias, 1980, Pediatric Cardiac Dysrhythmias, 1981, A Practical Guide to Cardiac Pacing, 1986, Pediatric Electrophysiology, Arrythmia and Pacing, 1990, Pediatric Cardiac Pacing, 1995, Clinical Pediatric Arrythmias, 1999; edtl. bd. Circulation, Am. Heart Jour., Pediatric Cardiology, Jour. Am. Coll. Cardiology; contbr. articles to profl. jours. Mem. sports com., treas. St. Thomas More Sch., Houston; bd. dirs. Toler's Cove Homeowners Assn. Charleston, 1989-94, Ronald McDonald House of Ft. Worth, 2001—. Nat. Heart, Lung and Blood Inst. grantee; named Disting. Alumni, Medical Univ. S.C., 1991; recipient Rsch. award So. Med. Assn., 1994. Fellow Am. Acad. Pediatrics (exec. com. cardiology sect. 1979, ednl. grantee 1970, Young Investigator award 1975, trustee 1987—, chmn. rsch. rev. com. 1987-88 S.C. chpt.), Am. Coll. Cardiology (trustee 1984-90, learning ctr. com. 1984-88, strategic planning com. 1986-90, long range planning com. 1987-88, chmn. pacemaker com. 1990-95, mem. rsch. com. 1990—); mem. Soc. Pediatric Rsch., So. Soc. Pediatric Rsch., Southeastern Pediatric Cardiology Soc. (pres. 1987), N.Am. Soc. Pacing and Electrophysiology (pres. 1986-87, trustee 1987-90, program com. 1987, Pioneer in Cardiac Pacing and Electrophysiology award 1998), Am. Heart Assn. (chmn. rsch. peer rev. com. S.C. chpt. 1989, chmn. rsch. com. 1990, pres.-elect Ft. Worth chpt. 1998-98, pres. 1998-99), Tex. Pediatric Soc., Harris County Med. Soc., Houston Cardiology Soc., North Tex. Electrophynology Soc., Houston Pediatric Soc., S.C. Med. Soc., Charleston County Med. Soc., Tarrant County Med. Soc. (bd. dirs. 2001—), S.C. Heart Assn. (rschr. of the yr. 1991), Alpha Omega Alpha, Phi Chi. Republican. Roman Catholic. Office: Cook Childrens Cardiac Ctr 901 7th Ave Ste 301 Fort Worth TX 76104-2724

GILLETTE, RICHARD GARETH, neurophysiology educator, researcher; b. Seattle, Feb. 17, 1945; s. Elton George and Hazel I. (Hand) G.; m. Sally A. Reams, Feb. 17, 1978 (div. Nov. 1988); 1 child, Jesse Robert. BS, U. Oreg., 1968; MS, Oreg. Health Sci. U., 1976, PhD, 1993. Rsch. asst. dept. otolaryngology Oreg. Health Sci. U., Portland, 1969-72, grad. rsch. asst., 1973-80; instr. neurosci. Western State Chiropractic Coll., Portland, 1981-85, asst. prof. neurosci., 1985-93, assoc. prof. neurosci., 1993-99, prof. neurosci., 1999—. Lectr. neurosci. sch. optometry Pacific U., Forest Grove, Oreg., 1985-86; grad. rsch. asst. Neurol. Sci. Inst. OHSU, Portland, 1988-93, vis. scientist, 1993—. Contbr. articles to profl. jours. NIH Predoctoral Tng. fellow Oreg. Health Sci. U., 1973-76, Tarter fellow Med. Rsch. Found. Oreg., 1989; NIH grantee, 1990-99. Mem. AAAS, Soc. for Neurosci., Am. Pain Soc., Internat. Assn. for Study of Pain. Avocations: history studies, vocal music performance. Office: WSCC 2900 NE 132nd Ave Portland OR 97230-3014 E-mail: rgillette@wschiro.edu.

GILLETTE, W. MICHAEL, state supreme court justice; b. Seattle, Dec. 29, 1941; s. Elton George and Hazel Irene (Hand) G.; m. Susan Dandy Marmaduke, 1989; children: Kevin, Saima, Ali, Quinton. AB cum laude in German, Polit. Sci., Whitman Coll., 1963; LLB, Harvard U., 1966. Bar: Oreg. 1966, U.S. Dist. Ct. Oreg. 1966, U.S. Ct. Appeals (9th cir.) 1966, Samoa 1969, U.S. Supreme Ct. 1970, U.S. Dist. Ct. Vt. 1973. Assoc. Rives & Rogers, Portland, Oreg., 1966-67; dep. dist. atty. Multnomah County, Portland, 1967-69; asst. atty. gen. Govt. of Am. Samoa, 1969-71, State of Oreg., Salem, 1971-77; judge Oreg. Ct. Appeals, Salem, 1977-86; justice Oreg. Supreme Ct., Salem, 1986—. Avocation: officiating basketball.*

GILLETTE, WILLIAM, historian, educator; b. Bridgeport, Conn., Mar. 2, 1933; s. Samuel William and Lillian (Abeson) G.; m. Elisabeth L. Janes, May 23, 1971; children: Scott Douglas, Wendy Elisabeth. BS, Georgetown U., 1955; MA, Columbia U., 1956, postgrad., 1958-59; PhD, Princeton U., 1963. Instr. Ohio State U., 1962-64; acting asst. prof. U. Conn., Storrs, 1965-66; asst. prof. Bklyn. Coll. CUNY, 1966-67; asso. prof. Rutgers U., 1967-81, prof., 1981—. Fulbright prof. U. Salzburg (Austria), 1982-83, Japan Women's U. and Tsuda Coll., 1997-98. Author: The Right to Vote: Politics and the Passage of the Fifteenth Amendment, 1969, Retreat From Reconstruction, 1869-1879, 1979, Jersey Blue: Civil War Politics in New Jersey, 1995. Served with AUS, 1956-58. Social Sci. Research Council faculty fellow, 1970; recipient Landry award La. State U. Press, 1979, Chastain award So. Polit. Sci. Assn., 1980, award of merit Am. Assn. for State and Local History, 1996, McCormick award N.J. Hist. Commn., 1997; grantee Am. Philos. Soc., N.J. Hist. Commn. Mem. AAUP, N.J. Hist. Soc., Advs. for N.J. History. Democrat. Unitarian Universalist. Home: 43 South Dr East Brunswick NJ 08816-1134 Office: Rutgers U Dept History New Brunswick NJ 08901-1108

GILLEY, JAMES WADE, university president; b. Fries, Va., Aug. 15, 1938; m. Nanna Beverly, 1961; children: Cheryl Rice, Wade Jr. BS in Civil Engring., Va. Polytechnic Inst. and State U., 1961, MS in Civil Engring., 1964, PhD in Civil/Environ. Engring., 1966; postgrad., U. Fla., Harvard U. Design engr. Newport News (Va.) Shipbuilding and Drydock Co., 1961-62; asst. prof. engring./coord. off campus engring. programs Va. Polytechnic Inst., State U., Blacksburg, Va., 1962-66; dean Sch. Sci. and Tech. Bluefield (W.Va.) State Coll., 1966-67, pres., 1975-78, Wytheville and J. Sargeant Reynolds instns. Va. C.C. Sys., 1967-75; sec. edn. State of Va., 1978-82; sr. v.p., prof. syss. engring., prof. higher edn. George Mason U., Fairfax, Va., 1982-91; pres., prof. engring., prof. edn. Marshall Univ., Huntington, W. Va., 1991-99; pres. U. Tenn., Knoxville, 1999—2001. Author: Thinking About American Higher Education: the 1990s and Beyond, The Interactive University: A Source of American Revitalization, Searching for Academic Excellence, Administration of University Athletic Programs: Internal Control and Excellence, Leaning Forward: A Public President Confronts the New Realities; contbr. articles to profl. jours. Active Huntington Mus. Art, W. Va. Jobs Investment Trust, Huntington Area Devel. Coun., 5th Ave. Bapt. Ch., Edn. Commn. of the States, other orgns. Mem. W. Va. Roundtable, Huntington Rotary Club, Huntington C. of C., Guyan Country Club. Office: U Tenn Office of Pres 831 Andy Hope Tower Knoxville TN 37996-0001

GILLEY, MICKEY LEROY, musician; b. Natchez, Miss., Mar. 9, 1936; s. Arthur Philmore and Irene Frances (Lewis) G.; m. Vivian McDonald, Dec. 27, 1962; 1 son, Gregory Brent. Ptnr. Gilley's Club, Pasadena, Tex., 1971-89; owner Gilley's Theatre, Branson, Mo., 1990—; pres., owner Gilley's Tex. Cafe, 1992—, owner, 1995—2000, Gilley's Rest., Pasadena, Tex., 2002—. Appeared in night clubs in, Houston, New Orleans, Biloxi, Miss., Mobile, Ala., Lake Charles, La., 1957-59; appeared at, Nesadel Club, Houston, 1960-70. Named Most Promising Male Artist, Acad. Country Music 1974, Most Promising Male Artist, Record World 1974, Top New Country Singles Artist, Billboard 1974, Top New Male Vocalist in Album Category, Record World 1975, Most Promising Male Artist, Music City News 1976, Best Male Vocalist, Entertainer of the Year, Acad. Country Music 1976; recipient Star in Walk of Fame on Hollywood Blvd., 1984, over 17 #1 records, Grammy award for Orange Blossom Special Nat. Acad. Rec. Arts and Scis., 1981. Mem. Country Music Assn., Acad. Country Music, AFTRA, Musicians Local 65. Clubs: Moose. Office: 3737 Lily St Pasadena TX 77505-2927 E-mail: mickey@gilleys.com.

GILLHAM, JOHN KINSEY, chemical engineering educator; b. London, Aug. 7, 1930; came to U.S., 1959, naturalized, 1968; s. Gerald Albert and Doris (Kinsey) G.; m. Helen Alyce Currier, Sept. 18, 1961; children: Matthew, Jane, Martha. BA, Cambridge U., 1953, MA, 1957; PhD in Chemistry, McGill U., Montreal, 1959. Research chemist Am. Cynamid Co., Stamford, Conn., 1958-65; vis. research chemist Princeton U., 1964-65, mem. faculty, 1965—, prof. chem. engring., 1975-98, prof. emeritus, 1998—. Cons. to chem. and polymer industries; vis. fellow Japan Soc. Promotion Sci., 1983; vis. scholar Chinese Acad. Scis., 1984; sci. exchange visitor USSR Acad. Scis./Nat. Acad. Scis., 1986. Author papers in field. Recipient 1st prize for best tech. paper Roon Found. Awards Competition of Fedn. Socs. for Coatings Techs., 1983, 89, Outstanding Rev. Paper award Electronics Components Conf. of IEEE, 1985. Fellow Soc. Plastics Engrs. (Internat. Rsch. award 1988, Best Paper award 1991); mem. Am. Chem. Soc. (Borden award 1978, Doolittle award 1980, Roy W. Tess award 1996, fellow divsn. Polymeric Materials: Sci. and Engring. 2000), N.Am. Thermal Analysis Soc. (Mettler award 1978). Home: 11 Vernon Cir Princeton NJ 08540-5415 Office: Princeton U Dept Chem Engring Princeton NJ 08544-0001 E-mail: jkgillham@yahoo.com.

GILLHAM, NICHOLAS WRIGHT, geneticist, educator; b. NYC, May 14, 1932; s. Robert Marty and Elizabeth (Enright) G.; m. Carol Lenore Collins, June 2, 1956. AB, Harvard, 1954, A.M., 1955, PhD (USPHS fellow), 1962. From instr. to asst. prof. Harvard U., 1963-68; assoc. prof. zoology Duke U., 1968-72, prof., 1973-82, James B. Duke prof. biology, 1982—2002, chmn. dept. zoology, 1986—89, profl. emeritus, 2002—. Mem. biochemistry, molecular genetics and cell biology interdisciplinary cluster Pres.'s Biomed. Rsch. Panel, 1975; mem. study sect. in genetics NIH, 1976-80; mem. N.C. Gov.'s Bd. Sci. and Tech., N.C. Gov.'s Task Force on Sci. and Tech., chmn., bd. dirs. Am. Type Culture Collection, 1993-96. Author: (with R. Krueger and J. Coggin) Introduction to Microbiology, 1973, Organelle Heredity, 1978, Organelle Genes and Genomes, 1994, A Life Sir Francis Galton: From African Exploration to the Birth of Eugenics, 2001; mem. editl. bd. Genetics, 1975-78, Jour. Cell Biology, 1977-79, Intl. Review of Cytology, 1987-97; sr. editor Plasmid, 1977-86. Served to 1st lt. Med. Service Corps USAF, 1955-58. Postdoctoral fellow, 1962-63; Spl. fellow, 1967-68; Research Career Devel. Award grantee, 1972-77; all USPHS); Guggenheim fellow, 1984-85. Mem. Genetics Soc. Am., Sigma Xi. Home: 1183 Fearrington Post Pittsboro NC 27312 Office: DCMB Group PO Box 91000 Durham NC 27708-1000 E-mail: gillham@acpub.duke.edu.

GILLIAM, JAMES H., JR., lawyer, private investor, consultant; b. Balt., Apr. 21, 1945; BA in English, Morgan State U., 1967; JD, Columbia U., 1970. Bar: Del., N.Y. Assoc. Paul, Weiss, Rifkind, Wharton & Garrison, N.Y.C., 1970-73, Richards, Layton & Finger, Wilmington, Del., 1973-76; cabinet sec. Dept. Cmty. Affairs and Econ. Devel. State of Del., 1977-79; v.p. Legal Beneficial Corp., 1979-81; sr. v.p. legal Beneficial Corp., 1982-85, sr. v.p., 1986-89, gen. coun., 1986-89, sec., 1987-92, exec. v.p., 1989-98; pvt. practice Wilmington, Del., 1998—. Chmn., bd. dirs. Beneficial Nat. Bank, 1987-98; bd. dirs. Household Internat.; past trustee, past bd. dirs. Med. Ctr. Del.; trustee Howard Hughes Med. Inst., Nat. Geog. Soc. Former chmn., hon. life trustee Goldey Beacom Coll.; former chmn. bd. visitors Del. State U.; bd. visitors Columbia Sch. Law; former chmn. Wilmington 2000 Inc.; former chmn. Jud. Nominating Commn., Del. 1993-2000; past chmn., bd. dirs. Del. C. of C. Fellow Am. Bar Found.; mem. ABA, NBA, Del. Bar Assn., Brandywine Country Club, Knickerbocker Club (N.Y.C.), Wilmington Club, Wilmington Country Club, Rehoboth Beach Country Club, Monday Club, Natl. Guardsmen, Inc., Sigma Pi Phi, Kappa Alpha Psi. Avocations: tennis, golf, water sports. Office: Knickerbocker LLC PO Box 2205 Wilmington DE 19899-2205 Address: Brandywine Plz 105 Foulk Rd Ste 101 Wilmington DE 19803-3740

GILLIAM, JOHN A. lawyer; b. Goldthwaite, Tex., Nov. 3, 1935; s. Ed Burr and Emily Corine (Anderson) G.; m. Sara Ann Swindell, Dec. 26, 1963; children— Joanna, John, Jason. B.A., Baylor U., 1958; LL.B., U. Tex., 1961. Bar: Tex. 1961, U.S. Dist. Ct. (no. dist.) Tex. 1961, U.S. Dist. Ct. (ea. and we. dists.) Tex., U.S. Ct. Appeals (5th, 10th and 11th cirs.) Assoc. then ptnr. Thompson & Knight, Dallas, 1961-74; sr. ptnr. Jenkens & Gilchrist, Dallas, 1975— . Assoc. editor Tex. Law Rev., 1959. Fellow Tex. Bar Found., Am. Coll. Trial Lawyers; mem. Tex. Assn. Def. Counsel (dir.), Dallas Bar Assn. (dir. 1981-85), Order of Coif, Alpha Chi, Phi Delta Phi, Phi Gamma Delta. Baptist. Home: 4617 Meadowood Rd Dallas TX 75220-2014 Office: Jenkens & Gilchrist 1445 Ross Ave Ste 3200 Dallas TX 75202-2785

GILLIAM, JOHN CHARLES, economist, educator; b. Boulder, Colo., Sept. 19, 1927; s. Arthur Woodson and Marguerite (Hubbard) G.; m. Katherine Frances Mihevc, July 16, 1947; children: Bruce, Charles, Carol Ann. BA, Western State Coll., Colo., 1951; M.Bus.Ed., U. Colo., 1952; PhD, State U. Iowa, 1959. Instr. bus. Brush (Colo.) High Sch., 1952-55, State U. Iowa, 1955-57; asst. prof. commerce U. Wyo., 1957-62, asso. prof., 1962; asso. prof. bus. edn. Tex. Tech. U., 1962-66, prof., 1966-95; asso. dean Tex. Tech. U. (Coll. Bus. Adminstrn.), 1968-73, prof. econs., 1973-95, prof. emeritus, 1995; cons., 1995—. Program specialist Ford Found., Ammam, Jordan, 1966-68, cons. in edn. for bus.; cons. to Govt. Saudi Arabia, World Bank, 1993-94; vis. prof. several uivs., including U. Jordan, 1993; cons. bus. and econs.; vis. prof. Mid. East Tech. U., Ankara, Turkey; acad. cons., 1988-90, Jordan U. Sci. and Tech., Irbid, 1989-90; cons. Govt. Turkey, 1992-94. Contbr. articles to profl. jours. Served with USNR, 1945-47. Fulbright-Hays grantee study tour People's Rep. China, 1988; Fulbright-Hays grantee study tour Egypt, 1990. Mem. Beta Gamma Sigma, Omicron Delta Epsilon, Alpha Kappa Psi, Delta Pi Epsilon, Pi Omega Pi, Phi Beta Delta. Lodges: Elks. Episcopalian. Home: 9311 Utica Dr Lubbock TX 79424-4821

GILLIAM, MARSHA SAMPSON, state agency administrator; b. Plant City, Fla., Oct. 14, 1946; d. Moses William and Catherine (Bythwood) Sampson; m. Richard Douglas Gilliam, June 27, 1967; children: Maurice Shoats, Kathy Ann, Richard Douglas. AAS in Human Svcs., Hudson Valley C.C., Troy, New York, 1991. Cert. worker Christian and Missionary Alliance, 2003. Supr. NY State Taxation and Fin., Albany, NY, 1985—2001, clk. I, 1972—85; clk. II NY Taxation and Fin., Albany, NY, 2001—. Author: poems. Angel tree coord. Internat. Prison Fellowship, Albany, NY, 1996—2000; faciliator Wendy Christiano's Women's Rensselaer County Jail Bibles Study, Troy, NY. Home: 68 Rapp Rd Albany NY 12203 Office: New York State Taxation and Finance 110 State St Albany NY 12203

GILLIAM, MARY, travel executive; b. Pampa, Tex., Apr. 18, 1928; d. Roy and Hylda O. (Bertrand) Brown; divorced; 1 child, Terry K. AA, Amarillo (Tex.) Bus. Coll., 1949. Flight attendant Braniff Internat. Airways, Dallas, 1950-53; from reservation agt. to mgr. passenger sales Trans-World Airlines, various locations, 1953-81; exec. v.p. Lakewood (Colo.) Travel, 1981; mgmt. cons. Bank One Travel, Columbus, Ohio, 1981-82; pres. Icaria Travel, Inc., Tucson, Ariz., 1986—, Intensive Trainers Inst., Tucson, 1983-92. Mem. Ariz. Rep. Com., 1978—. Recipient Award of Excellence Trans-World Airlines, N.Y.C., 1972, Pres.' Hall of Fame award, 1973. Mem. Am. Soc. Travel Agts. (Industry Svc. award 1980), Inst. Cert. Travel Agts. Methodist. Avocations: reading, travel, music. Office: Icaria Travel Inc 616 W Rio San Pedro Green Valley AZ 85614-3927

GILLIAM, M(ELVIN) RANDOLPH, retired urologist, educator; b. Jan. 5, 1921; s. Adolphus and Grace (Thornsberry) Gilliam; m. Sara Dee Rainey, May 15, 1948; children: Elizabeth Neal, Virginia Dee, Bryan Randolph, Frank Stuart, Grace Carroll. Student, Centre Coll. of Ky., 1938-41; MD, U. Louisville, 1944. Diplomate Am. Bd. Urology. Intern Norfolk (Va.) Marine Hosp., 1944-45; resident in urology Nichols VA Hosp., Louisville, 1947-50; pvt. practice medicine specializing in urology Lexington, Ky., 1950-98; retired, 1998. Ptnr. Commonwealth Urology, P.S.C., Lexington, Ky., 1971—98; clin. prof. urology U. Ky. Med. Sch., 1964—98, prof. emeritus, 1998—; chief urology Good Samaritan Hosp.; staff mem. Ctrl. Bapt. Hosp., St. Joseph's Hosp. Capt. U.S. Army, 1945—47. Mem.: AMA, Fayette County Med. Soc. (past pres.), Ky. Med. Assn., Am. Urology Assn. Republican. Methodist. Home: 1244 Summitt Dr Lexington KY 40502-2273

GILLIAM, PAULA HUTTER, transportation company executive; b. N.Y.C. d. Irving and Edna Phyllis (Manes) Hutter; m. Stanley Spencer Rolnick (div.); children: Jeffry Hutter Gilliam, Pamela Sara Bielory; m. Peter Gilliam, 1981. AA, Centenary Coll., 1961. Pres. Paula Rolnick Sales, N.Y.C., 1970-74; mdse. mgr. Kirby Block Internat., N.Y.C., 1974-78; pres. P.M.G. Internat. Ltd, N.Y.C., 1981—. V.p. Rical Air Express, Inc., N.Y.C., Rical Ocean Forwarding, N.Y.C.; ptnr. The Golden Unicorn Restaurant; mem. adv. bd. for internat. bus. Fashion Inst. Tech., 1991—. Producer (Broadway show) Stardust, 1987; exec. producer (plays) Long Days Journey Into the Night, 1988, Ah Wilderness, 2003. V.p. Murray Hill Neighborhood Assn., N.Y.C., 1982—, chmn. block party, 1983-92, bd. dirs and sec. John Murray House Owners Corp., 1995—; bd. advisors 132 E 35th St., N.Y.C., 1984-86; vol. aide June Eisland Coun. Women, Riverdale, N.Y., 1979—; bd. dirs. Theater Off Park, 1983-88, Black Goat Entertainment and Enlightenment, 1994-2000, hon. trustee, 2003—. Mem. Women in Internat. Trade (bd. dirs. 1991-96), Women's Traffic Club, Met. Traffic Club. Democrat. Avocations: travel, horesback riding, gardening, theatre. Home and Office: 220 Madison Ave New York NY 10016-3422 E-mail: phgilliam@aol.com.

GILLIAM, STEVEN PHILIP, SR., lawyer; b. L.A., Feb. 5, 1949; s. Robert Walter Gilliam and Carlene (Fincher) Durkee; m. Susan Lynch, Nov. 7, 1971; children: Steven Philip Jr., Laney Evelyn. BBA in Econs., U. Ga., 1971, JD cum laude, 1974. Bar: Ga. 1974, U.S. Dist. Ct. Ga., U.S. Ct. Appeals (5th and 11th cirs.) 1974, U.S. Supreme Ct. 1980. Ptnr. Smith, Smith & Frost, Gainesville, Ga., 1974-83, Smith, Frost. Gilliam & Williams, 1983-86, Smith, Gilliam & Williams, 1986-99, Smith, Gilliam, Williams & Miles, 2000—. V. chmn. Gainesville Hall '96, 1993—; mem. magistrate selection com. U.S. Dist. Ct., 1998; bd. trustees Rabun Gap Nacoochee Sch., 1998—, vice chmn., 2002—. Trustee Leadership Ga., 1988—91; chmn. bd. trustees Elachee Nature Sci. Ctr., 2003—, pres., 2003—, bd. dirs., 1997—; bd. trustees Lanier Pk. Hosp., 1998—2001, chmn., 2001, Gainesville Coll. Found., 1987, hon. life trustee, 1997; chmn. Quality Growth Coun. Hall County, 2000—02; mem. U. Ga. Law Sch. Alumni Coun., 2000—. Named Hall County Young Man of Yr., 1983, Olympic Cmty. Hero Torchbearer, 1996, Man of Yr. Rotary, 1996. Fellow: Lawyers Found. Ga., Atlanta Lawyers Club; mem.: Gainesville-Hall C. of C. (v.p. 1987—89, chmn. 1998—99, Silver Shovel award 1986), Assn. Def. Trial Attys., Def. Rsch. Inst., Northeastern Bar Assn. (pres. 1982, Supreme Ct. commn. on pub. trust and confidence 2000—01), Ga. Bar Assn. (chairperson professionalism com. 1996—2000), ABA, Gridiron Secret Soc., Ga. Bulldog Club, Chattahoochee Country Club (pres. 1989). Presbyterian. Avocations: backpacking, hunting, kayaking, golf, flyfishing. Home: 1450 Heritage Rd Gainesville GA 30501 Office: Smith Gilliam Williams Miles PA 301 Green St NE Ste 200 Gainesville GA 30501 E-mail: sgilliam@sgwfirm.com.

GILLICE, SONDRA JUPIN (MRS. GARDNER RUSSELL BROWN), sales and marketing executive; b. Urbana, Ill. d. Earl Cranston and Laura Lorraine (Rose) Jupin; m. Gardner Russell Brown, Jan. 12, 1980; 1 child, Thomas Alan Gillice. BS, Lindenwood Coll., 1968; MBA, Loyola Coll., 1983. Pers. officer N.Y. Citibank, 1968-70, 1st Nat. Bank Chgo., 1970-72; mgr human resources Potomac Electric Power Co., Washington, 1973-81; dir. pers. U.S. Synthetic Fuels Corp., Washington, 1981-86; v.p. human resources Guest Svcs., Inc., 1987-90, v.p. sales and mktg., 1990-93; sr. v.p. govt. rels. Drake Beam Morin, Inc., 1994-98; pres. RusSon, Inc., 1998—. Bd. govs. Nat. Coal Coun., exec. com. Bd. dirs. KHG Dance Theatre, Nat. Womens Econ. Alliance, Life With Cancer; chmn. Career & Life Learning Sys., Inc. Mem. AAUW (pres. Falls Church br. 1976-78), Edison Electric Inst. (chair tng. and mgmt. devel. com.), Soc. for Human Resource Mgmt., Greater Met. Washington Bd. Trade, Soroptimists (pres. Washington chpt. 1979-80), DAR, Army Navy Country Club, Army Navy Club, Soc. Magna Charta Dames, Edgartown Yacht Club, Georgetown Club. Republican.

GILLICK, MURIEL RUTH, physician; b. N.Y.C., May 14, 1951; d. Peter H. and Ilse (Wulff) Garfunkel; m. Laurence S. Gillick, June 18, 1972; children: Daniel, Jeremy, Jonathan. BA, Swarthmore Coll., 1972; postgrad., Columbia U., 1973; MD, Harvard Med. Sch., 1978. Med. diplomate. Staff physician Bunker Hill Health Ctr./Mass. Gen. Hosp., Boston, 1982-87, Mt. Auburn Hosp., Cambridge, Mass., 1987-92, Hebrew Rehab. Ctr. for Aged, Boston, 1992—, physician-in-chief, 2000—03. Cons. in geriatrics Mass. Gen. Hosp., Boston, 1984-87; sr. fellow Harvard Med. Sch., 1989-91; asst. prof. medicine Harvard Med. Sch., 1993-99, assoc. prof., 1999—. Author: Choosing Medical Care in Old Age, 1994, Tangled Minds, 1998, Lifelines, 2000; contbr. articles to profl. jours. Geriatrics fellow Boston U. Med. Ctr., 1981-82, Mellon fellow MIT, Cambridge, 1982-83. Mem. ACP, Am. Med. Dirs. Assn., Am. Soc. Law, Medicine, and Ethics, Am. Geriatrics Soc., Phi Beta Kappa. Office: HRCA 1200 Centre St Boston MA 02131-1011 E-mail: mgillick@alum.swarthmore.edu.

GILLIE, R. BRUCE, internist; b. New Haven, Conn., Nov. 21, 1945; s. Robert Bowen and Marjorie (Kennedy) G.; m. Polly Jane Dubuque, June 12, 1982; children: R. Bowen, Anne Dubuque. BA, Brown U., 1967; PhD in Anatomy, U. Utah, 1973; MD, N.J. Coll. Medicine, Dentistry, 1974. Diplomate Am. Bd. Internal Medicine, Diabetes and Metabolism. From intern to sr. resident Tufts U. New Eng. Med. Ctr., Boston, 1974-77; pvt. practice Westerly, R.I.; mem. active staff The Westerly Hosp. Med. dir. Westerly Nursing Home, Watch Hill Manor, The Clipper Rehab. House; adv. curator of mammalogy The Kendall Whaling Mus. Contbr. articles to profl. jours. Paul Harris fellow Rotary Internat. Fellow ACP; mem. Am. Soc. Mammalogy, Am. Paleontol. Soc. Soc. Marine Mammalogy. Avocations: comparative anatomy/physiology, paleontology of mammalian evolution. Home: 20 Saratoga Ave Westerly RI 02891-1101 Office: 11 Wells St Westerly RI 02891-2998

GILLIES, DONALD RICHARD, marketing and advertising consultant, educator; b. Sioux Falls, SD, Jan. 14, 1939; s. Donald Franklin and Gladys O. (Gullickson) G.; m. Twyla Elaine Bloomquist, Apr. 7, 1962; children: Dawn, Trent, Tara. BA in Journalism/Advt., U. Minn., 1961. Writer, producer Sta. WCCO-TV, Mpls., 1954-60; mgmt. supr., sr. v.p., bd. dirs. Campbell-Mithun Advt., Mpls., 1960-86; pres., chief oper. officer Colle & McVoy Inc., Mpls., 1987-89; prin. Gillies group inc. (Gg), Minnetonka, Minn., 1989—. Adj. prof. U. St. Thomas, 1990-97, asst. prof., 2001—. Bd. dirs. Guthrie Theater, Mpls., 1979-84; ch. coun. Mt. Olivet Ch., Mpls., 1988-94; Midwest adv. rev. bd. BBB, 1996—. Mem. Am. Assn. Advt. Agencies (regional gov.), Minn. Advt. Fedn. (bd. dirs. 1973-76). Lutheran. Home and Office: Gillies group inc (Gg) 5942 Fairwood Ln Minnetonka MN 55345-6533 E-mail: dongillies@prodigy.net.

GILLIES, TRENT DONALD, television producer; b. Mpls., June 14, 1965; s. Donald Richard and Twyla Elaine (Bloomquist) G. BS in Journalism, Boston U., 1987. Prodn. asst. 60 Minutes, CBS News, N.Y.C., 1987-90, asst. prodr., 1990-91, assoc. prodr. 60 Minutes, 1991-95; prodr. investigative unit Am. Jour., King World, N.Y.C., 1995-97; prodr. Real Sports with Bryant Gumbel, HBO Sports, 1997-98; prodr. SportsCentury ESPN, 1998-99; prodr. Spl. Edit., MSNBC Investigates, MSNBC News, 1999—2002; prodr. CNN, 2002—. Lutheran. Avocations: music, skiing. Home: 321 E 43d St Apt 701 New York NY 10017

GILLIG, JOHN STEPHENSON, lawyer; b. Lexington, Ky., May 27, 1951; Bar: Ky. 1976, U.S. Dist. Ct. (ea. and we. dist.) Ky. 1984, U.S. Ct. Appeals (6th cir.) 1984, U.S. Supreme Ct. 1984. Law clk. Ky. Supreme Ct., Frankfort, 1976-77; policy analyst Congl. Sunbelt Coun., U.S. Ho. of Reps., Washington, 1981-83; asst. atty. gen. Ky. Atty. Gen., Frankfort, 1984-95, environ. spl. coun., 1992-95; counsel to spkr. Spkr.'s Office Ky. Ho. of Reps., Frankfort, 1995—, chief of staff Spkr.'s Office, 1999—. Mem. criminal rules adv. com. Ky. Supreme Ct., Frankfort, Ky., 1988-92, task force on ethics, 1989-91; mem. legis. task force on sentencing Legis. Rsch. Commn., Frankfort, 1990-91; commr. Ky. Emergency Response Commn., Frankfort, 1995, Nat. Conf. of Commissioners on Uniform Senate Laws, 1997—. Author: Kentucky Post-Conviction Manual, 1990; contbr. articles to profl. jours. Officer, bd. dirs. Ky. YMCA Youth Assn., Frankfort, 1987-94, 96—. Paul Harris fellow Rotary Internat., 1990; recipient Disting. Svc. award Ky. Commonwealth Attys. Assn., 1992. Methodist. Avocations: state and local history, naval history. Office: Office Spkr of the House State Capitol 700 Capitol Ave Ste 309 Frankfort KY 40601-3415

GILLIG, PAULETTE MARIE, psychiatry educator, researcher; b. Boston, Mar. 24, 1949; d. Franklin Joseph and Marie Robichaud (Collins) G.; m. Douglas K. Fairobent, June 13, 1981. BA cum laude hons. psychology, SUNY, Buffalo; MA, PhD, Ohio State U., 1973; MD, Med. Coll. Ohio, 1977. Diplomate Am. Bd. Psychiatry and Neurology, Am. Bd. Geriat. Psychiatry. Resident in neurology Med. Coll. Ohio, 1978-79, U. Mich., Ann Arbor, 1979-81; resident in psychiatry Ohio State U., Columbus, 1981-83; med. dir. North Ctrl. Mental Health Ctr., Columbus, 1985; clin. asst. prof. Ohio State U., Columbus, 1983-85; asst. prof. U. Cin., 1985-90; assoc. prof. Wright State U., Dayton, 1990-2000, prof. psychiatry, 2000—; chief clin. officer Mental Health Drug and Alcohol Svcs. Bd., Champaign and Logan Cos., 1995—. Prof. rural psychiatry Ohio Dept. Mental Health, 1997—; mem. strategic planning coun. Wright State U., Dayton, 1998—, faculty devel. com. Founding Bd. Domestic Abuse and Violence Inst. of Dayton, 2000; Patron Cin. Ballet Co., Xavier U.,

1988—, Humane Soc. U.S., Sorg Opera Co., Middletown, Ohio, 1989—, Lebanon Police Children's Fund, 1995—, Balletech Ohio, 2002—, Warren County Animal Shelter, 2002—; chair Domestic Violence Rsch. Group, 1999-2002. Recipient Clin. Neurosci. award, Med. Coll. Ohio; grantee Pruitt Found., 1992, Ohio Dept. Mental Health, 1995—. Fellow Am. Psychiat. Assn. (disting.; com. on homelessness, poverty and mental illness 1999—); mem. Am. Assn. Women Psychiatrists, Am. Assn. Cmty. Psychiatrists (Midwestern rep. 2002—, Moffic award 1999), Ohio Psychiat. Assn. (chmn. com. on minorities 1999-03, Pres.'s award 2001), World Health Orgn. (dir. internat. classification diseases), Univ. Club. Avocations: classical piano, opera, companion animals, dancing, horticulture. Office: Wright State U Dept Psychiatry PO Box 927 Dayton OH 45401-0927 E-mail: paulette.gillig@wright.edu.

GILLIGAN, SANDRA KAYE, private school director; b. Ft. Lewis, Wash., Mar. 22, 1946; d. Jack G. and O. Ruth (Mitchell) Wagoner; m. James J. Gilligan, June 3, 1972 (div. June 1998); 1 child, J. Shawn Gilligan. BS in Edn., Emporia State U., 1968, MS in Psychology, 1971; postgrad., Drake U., 1976, U. Mo., St. Louis, 1977-79. Tchr. Parklane Elem. Sch., Aurora, Colo., 1968-69, Bonner Springs (Kans.) Elem., 1970; stewardess Frontier Airlines, Denver, 1969; grad. teaching asst. Emporia (Kans.) State U., 1970-71; lead tchr. Western Valley Youth Ranch, Buckeye, Ariz., 1971-74; staff mem. program devel., lead tchr. The New Found., Phoenix, Ariz., 1974; ednl. therapist Orchard Pl., Des Moines, 1974-76; cdnl. cons. Spl. Sch. Dist. of St. Louis County, 1976-79; founding dir. The Churchill Sch., St. Louis, 1978—. Instr. Webster Coll., Webster Groves, Mo., 1978-80; adj. prof. Maryville Coll., St. Louis, summer 1985; keynote spkr. Miss. Learning Disabilities Assn. Conv., 1991; site visitor blue ribbon schs. program U.S. Dept. Edn., 1992; mem. Evaluation Review Com. Indep. Sch. of Ctrl. States; cert. trainer Human Potential Seminars; presenter in field. Mem. Learning Disabilities Assn., Internat. Dyslexia Assn., St. Louis Jr. League. Avocations: gardening, painting. Office: The Churchill Sch 1035 Price School Ln Saint Louis MO 63124-1596

GILLILAND, IRENE LYDIA, nursing educator; b. Phila., Nov. 30, 1950; d. Michael and Tatiana (Koziol) Chodan; m. Charles Donald Gilliland, Mar. 23, 1974 (div. Dec. 1990); children: Ami, Charles, Robert. BSN, Villanova U., 1972; MSN, U. Va., 1986. Lectr. nursing Radford (Va.) U., 1986-87; nursing instr. Va. Western C.C., Roanoke, Va., 1984-90, U. of Incarnate Word, San Antonio, 1991—. Hospice case mgr. Odyssey Health Care, San Antonio, 1998—; cost containment cons. ins. cos. in field, 1988—. Mem. ANA, AAUP, Women in Bus., Nat. Assn. Holistic Aromatherapy, Sigma Theta Tau. Avocations: herbal gardening, jazz. Home: 21527 Longwood San Antonio TX 78259-2101 Office: U of Incarnate Word Sch Nursing San Antonio TX 78209 E-mail: igilliland@satx.rr.com.

GILLILAND, JOHN CAMPBELL, II, lawyer; b. Bellefonte, Pa., June 4, 1945; s. John Campbell and Miriam Ruth (Forsythe) G.; m. Karen Gardner, Nov. 2, 1997; children: Jennifer, John, David. BA, Pa. State U., 1967; JD, Georgetown U., 1971. Bar: Pa. 1971, Ind. 1979, Ky. 1991, Ohio 1992. Ptnr. McQuaide, Blasko & Brown, Inc., State College, Pa., 1974-79, DeFur, Voran, Hanley, Radcliff & Reed, Muncie, Ind., 1979-90; prin. Gilliland & Assocs., Covington, Ky., 1991-2000; sr. counsel Locke Reynolds LLP, Indpls., 2000—01; prin. Gilliland Law Office, Indpls., 2001—02; ptnr. Gilliland & Caudill LLP, 2002—. Lectr. econs. dept. Ball State U., Muncie. Bd. dirs. United Way Delaware County, v.p., 1983-85; bd. dirs. Vis. Nurses Assn.; v.p. Muncie chpt. ARC, 1983-85; bd. govs. Friends of Bracken Libr. Served to capt. U.S. Army, 1971-72. Fellow Rotary Found., Queens Coll., Belfast, Ireland, 1968-69. Mem. ABA, Ind. Bar Assn., Ky. Bar Assn., Ohio Bar Assn., Am. Health Lawyers Assn., Ind. Soc. Hosp. Attys. (chmn. 1989), Pa. Soc. Hosp. Attys. (pres. 1978-79), East Central Ind. Pers. Assn. (bd. dirs.). Republican. Presbyterian. Home: 3446 Kenilworth Dr Indianapolis IN 46228- Office: 6650 Telecom Dr Ste 100 Indianapolis IN 46278 E-mail: jcg@gilliland.com.

GILLILAND, MARY MARGARETT, healthcare consultant; b. Leland, Miss., Dec. 23, 1942; d. Lindon Edward and Allie Earlene (Saulters) Palmore; m. Carl Ralph Gilliland, Jan. 12, 1963; children: Carl Ralph, Gini Lynn. Diploma in Nursing, Greenwood Leflore, 1963; B of Healthcare Adminstrn., East Tex. State U., 1976; M of Human Rels. and Mgmt., Abilene Christian U., 1978; BS, Tex. Woman's U., 1991, MS, 1993, PhD, 1999. RN, Tex. Staff nurse Sunflower County Health Dept., Indianola, Miss., 1965-66; asst. dir. nursing Presbyn. Hosp. Dallas, 1966-80, assoc. dir. nursing, 1980-87, assoc. exec. dir., 1987-91; healthcare cons. G&S Healthcare Cons., Allen, Tex., 1991—. Contbr. articles to profl. jours. Mem. ANA, Am. Orgn. Nurse Execs., Tex. Orgn. Nurse Execs., Tex. Nurses Assn. (continuing edn. com, Great 100 Nurses 1991), Nurses Alumni Assn. (sec.) Sigma Theta Tau, Phi Kappa Phi. Avocations: walking, reading, tae kwoon do. Home: 2101 Rigsbee Dr Plano TX 75074-4913 Office: G&S Healthcare Cons Raceway Profl Bldg I 200 Boyd Pl Allen TX 75013-2560 E-mail: mmpg@mindspring.com.

GILLILAND, RICK E. elementary education educator; b. Ottumwa, Iowa, July 9, 1948; s. Donald Franklin and Lorreta Vondean (Manos) White; m. Diane M. Gilliland, June 3, 1972; children: Michael, Gina. AA, Centerville Community Coll., 1968; BSEd, SE Mo. State U., 1970; MS, Western Ill. U., 1975. Cert. elem. edn. K-8th grades, secondary edn. 6th-12th grades, phys. edn. specialist K-14th grades. Phys. edn. tchr. K-6 Rock Island (Ill.) Sch. Dist., 1981—2002; dir. phys. edn. Clinton (Iowa) YMCA, 1970-71; elem. tchr. Rock Island Sch. Dist. 41, 1985—. Co-author: Rock Island School District Physical Education Curriculum Guide. Trustee Andalusia Village. Mem. Phi Delta Kappa, Phi Kappa Phi. Home: 853 2nd Ave W PO Box 272 Andalusia IL 61232-0272

GILLILAND, STANLEY EUGENE, dairy-food microbiology educator; b. Minco, Okla., June 24, 1940; s. Dale W. and Evelyn M. (Barnes) G.; m. Blanche D. King, June 2, 1960 (dec. July 1989); children: Stanley Jr., Stephen, Angela, Amy; m. Jerri Hall, May 26, 1990. BS, Okla. State U., 1962, MS, 1963; PhD, N.C. State U., 1966. Instr. N.C. State U., Raleigh, 1965-67, asst. prof., 1967-72, assoc. prof., 1972-76, Okla. State U., Stillwater, 1976-80, prof., 1980-86, regents prof., 1986-98, regents prof. and Sitlington endowed chair, 1998—. Editor: Bacterial Starter Cultures for Foods, 1985. Recipient Disting. Alumnus award, N.C. State U., 2002. Fellow Am. Acad. Microbiology; mem. Am. Dairy Sci. Assn. (bd. dirs., v.p., pres., Pfizer award 1979, Dairy Rsch. Found. award 1987, Milk Ind. Fedn. Tchr. award 1999, award of honor, 2003), Am. Soc. for Microbiology, Inst. Food Technologists, Coun. for Agrl. Sci. and Tech., Am. Fed. Soc. Food Animal Sci. (v.p., pres.). Baptist. Office: Okla State U Animal Sci Dept & Food and Agri Products Ctr Stillwater OK 74078-0001

GILLIN, CAROL ANN, middle school educator; b. Phila., July 19, 1942; d. Harry Joseph and Louise Dolores (Hewitt) G. AB in English Lit., Chestnut Hill Coll., 1972; MEd in Reading, Temple U., 1978, postgrad., 1990—. Cert. elem. educator, reading specialist, N.J., Pa. Tchr. Phila. and N.J. Parochial Schs., 1962-76; reading specialist Camden (N.J.) Bd. Edn., 1976-80, Corpus Christi Sch., Lansdale, Pa., 1980-82; asst. prof. edn., supr. student tchrs. Rosemont (Pa.) Coll., 1982-86, acting dir. edn., asst. acad. dean, 1985-88; mid. sch. tchr. Phila. Sch. System, 1988—. Tchr. cons. Phila. Writing Project; presenter, lectr. in field; mem. rsch. project Taking Stock, Making Change, U. Pa.; instr. Chestnut Hill Coll., 1998—; sr. career tchr. Phila. Sch. Sys., enhanced compensation project, 2003—; adv. bd. Schuylkill Ctr. Environ. Edn., Phila, 1999—; participant enhanced compensation sys. pilot, 2003 Bd. dirs. Archbishop Prendergast H.S. Alumnae, Drexel Hill, Pa., 1989-95. Mem. Internat. Reading Assn., Am. Assn. Univ. Adminstrs., Nat. Coun. Tchrs. English. Avocations: reading, needlepoint, walking club, cooking. E-mail: Carolanngillin@aol.com.

GILLIN, DONNA LYNN, lawyer; b. Plainview, N.Y., May 18, 1971; d. Carolyn Iacullo and Thomas McElhinney; m. Michael Edward Gillin, Dec. 12, 1999. BA, SUNY, 1993; JD, Touro Coll., 1996. Bar: N.J. 1996, N.Y. 1997. Paralegal Alice K. Berke, Esq., Albany, 1992—92; legislative asst. N.Y. State Assembly, Assemblywoman Donna Ferrara, 1993—93; rsch. asst. Prof. Jeffery Morris Touro Law Ctr., Huntington, 1995—95, legal intern Family Law Clinic, 1995—95; legal intern Nassau/Suffolk Law Services, Central Islip, 1995—95; paralegal Bijesse & Belford, St. James, 1996—96; dir. govt. affairs CMOR, Mt. Sinai, 1997—; leg. asst. coord. Port Jefferson, NY, 1994—95. Adv. bd. mem. Netscan iPublishing, Church Falls, Va., 2002—03. Office: Cmor 5507-10 Nesconset Hwy # 147 Mount Sinai NY 11766 Office Fax: 631-696-2372. E-mail: d_gillin@yahoo.com.

GILLIN, JAMES, pharmaceutical company executive; b. Floral Park, N.Y., Sept. 16, 1925; s. James and Frieda Rosa (Gilcher) G.; m. June Dolores Jacobi, June 11, 1949; children: Sheryl Claire, James Scott. BSChemE, Cornell U., 1947, PhD, 1951. Dir. chem. engring. Merck & Co. Inc., Rayway, N.J., 1962-69, exec. dir. adminstrn., 1969-71, v.p. devel. research, 1971-78, pres. div. MSD Agvet, 1979-87, pres. polit. action com. Patentee in field. Trustee, treas. Elizabeth (N.J.) Gen. Med. Ctr., 1982-91; chmn., trustee Animal Health Inst., Washington. Mem. NAE, AIChE, Am. Chem. Soc., N.Y. Acad. Scis., Echo Lake Country (trustee 1976-92), Lost Tree Club, (trustee 1991-95), Tau Beta Pi. Republican. Roman Catholic. Avocations: golf, swimming, tennis. E-mail: giltree@aol.com.

GILLIN, JOHN F. quality engineer; b. Agana, Guam, Sept. 8, 1956; s. George F. and Betsey (Berg) G.; m. Kimberly L. Hushin, Nov. 6, 1999; children: Katlin, Elizabeth. BS, SUNY, Stony Brook, 1978. Materials lab. asst. Lockheed Martin Fed. Sys., Great Neck, N.Y., 1979-81; materials engr. Lockheed Martin Undersea Sys., Mitchel Field, N.Y., 1981-90, quality/test engr., 1990—. Vol. Christ the King Youth Coun., Commack, N.Y., 1971-87. Recipient Joseph Furman Meml. award Christ the King Youth Coun., 1976, Cert. of Appreciation, 1982, 84, Letter of Commendation Dir. Strat. Sys. Program Office USN, 2001; Yon-Dan (4th degree) Black Belt Ju-Jutsu, 1998. Achievements include patent in Target Source for Ion Beam Sputter Deposition. Office: Lockheed Martin Undersea Sys Mail Sta A4-014 55 Charles Lindbergh Blvd Uniondale NY 11553-3682 E-mail: gillin.jf@worldnet.att.net.

GILLINGHAM, BRYAN REGINALD, music educator; b. Vancouver, B.C., Can., Apr. 12, 1944; s. Reginald Pearce and Ethel Gladys (Collier) G.; m. Helen Campbell, Aug. 11, 1970 (div. 1980); children: Gregory, Sara; m. Susanna Catharine Burton, Oct. 29, 1984; children: Gwendolyn, Miranda, Jeremy. BA, U. B.C., 1966, MusB, 1968; MusM, U. London, 1972; PhD, U. Wash., 1976. Lectr. Mt. Allison U., Sackville, N.B., Can., 1972-73, U. Alta., Edmonton, Can., 1975-76; prof., chmn. Carleton U., Ottawa, Ont., Can., 1976-83. Dir. Inst. Medieval Music, Ottawa, 1985—. Author: The Polyphonic Sequences in Codex Wolfenbüttel 677, 1982, Saint-Martial Mehrstimmigkeit, 1984, Medieval Polyphonic Sequences, 1985, Modal Rhythm, 1986, Secular Medieval Latin Song, 1993, A Critical Study of Secular Medieval Latin Song, 1995, The Social Background to Secular Medieval Latin Song, 1998, Chant & Its Peripheries, 1998; editor (with Donald Beecher) Dovehouse early music edits.; contbr. articles and book revs. to profl. jours. Avocations: wine making, squash, cross-country skiing. Office: Carleton U Dept Music Colonel By Dr Ottawa ON Canada K1S 5B6

GILLINGHAM, ROBERT FENTON, economist, consultant; b. Newark, Nov. 13, 1944; s. Evan Stevenson and Eleanor (Fenton) G.; m. Deborah Lynn Wickham, 1989; children: James Stevenson, Sarah Eleanor. BA, Haverford Coll., 1965; PhD, U. Pa., 1973. Economist Bur. Labor Stats., Washington, 1968-73, chief price rsch. div., 1973-82, dep. assoc. commr., 1982-85; dir. office econ. analysis Dept. Treasury, Washington, 1985-88, dep. asst. sec. for econ. policy, 1988 98; cons. Internat. Monetary Fund, Washington, 1998—. Assoc. editor Jour. Bus. and Econ. Stats., 1982-93; contbr. articles to profl. jours. Mem. Am. Econ. Assn., Am. Statis. Assn., Econometric Soc., Western Econ. Assn. (bd. dirs. 1995-98), Conf. on Income and Wealth, Nat. Acad. Social Ins. Home: 20448 Tappahannock Pl Sterling VA 20165-4786 Office: Internat Monetary Fund 700 19th St NW Washington DC 20431-0001

GILLINGHAM, STEPHEN THOMAS, financial planner; b. St. Paul, May 30, 1944; s. Thomas Elmwood and Barbara Alice (Sickles) G.; m. Carolyn Jean Alvey, June 5, 1976; children: Kenneth, Brett. BA, Juniata Coll., 1966; JD, The George Washington U., 1969. Bar: Va. 1971; CFP; ChFC. Tax specialist Price Waterhouse, Washington, 1969-71; tax law specialist IRS, Washington, 1971-77; sr. tax lawyer Internat. Paper Co., N.Y.C., 1977-83; dir. tax rsch. and planning The Singer Co., Stanford, Conn., 1983-88; tax counsel Am. Cyanamid Co., Wayne, N.J., 1988-95; fin. planner The Thompson Group, Inc., White Plains, N.Y., 1995—. Lectr. World Trade Inst., 1980-90. Contbg. editor Tax Lawyer, 1984-88. With U.S. Army, 1970—75. Named one of Outstanding Young Men in Am., Jaycees, 1979. Mem. Va. Bar Assn., N.J. Tax Group (chmn. 1991-95), Tax Execs. Inst., Fin.Planning Assn. Avocations: golf, swimming, hiking. Home: 4 Northway Hartsdale NY 10530-2109 Office: The Thompson Group Inc 244 Westchester Ave White Plains NY 10604-2907 E-mail: stgill@cyburban.com.

GILLINSON, ANDREW STUART, marketing communications executive; b. Stoke-on-Trent, Eng., Aug. 5, 1948; came to U.S., 1955; s. Roy Stuart and Joan Monica (Keatman) G. AB, Brandeis U., 1969. From copywriter to sr. creative group supr. W.B. Doner & Co., Balt., 1970-78; v.p., creative Vansant Dugdale & Co., Balt., 1978-81; sr. exec. writer SmithKline Beckman, Phila., 1981-84; v.p. and creative dir. Foote Cone & Belding, Phila., 1984-86; pres. Gillinson Mktg. Comms., Lancaster, Pa., 1986—. Active The English Speaking Union of the U.S., Phila., 1989, ARC, Phila., 1986. Mem. Am. Mktg. Assn. Avocations: public speaking, investment analysis, skiing. E-mail: gillinson@myrealbox.com.

GILLIOM, JUDITH CARR, government official; b. Indpls., May 19, 1943; d. Elbert Raymond and Marjorie Lucille (Carr) G. BA, Northwestern U., 1964; MA, U. Pa., 1966. Feature writer, asst. women's editor Indpls. News, summers 1961-63; rsch. asst. cultural anthropology Northwestern U., 1963-64, asst. instr. freshman English, 1964; editorial asst. to dir. div. cardiology Phila. Gen. Hosp., 1965-67; asst. to ophthalmologist-in-chief Wills Eye Hosp., Phila., 1967-69; editor, writer Nat. Assn. Hearing and Speech Agencies, Washington, 1969-70; free-lance speech writer White House Conf. Children and Youth, 1969-70; free-lance editor, writer, abstractor, 1971-78; free-lance speechwriter President's Com. Mental Retardation, 1971-78; from dir. publs. to dir. comm. Nat. Assn. Hearing and Speech Action, Silver Spring, Md., 1972-77; editor Hearing & Speech Action mag., 1969-70, 72-77; program mgr. Interagy. Com. on Handicapped Employees, 1978, dep. exec. sec., 1979-83; mgr. disability program Dept. Def., 1983—. Cons. U.S. Archtl. and Transp. Barriers Compliance Bd., 1976-77, Office Ind. Living for Disabled, HUD, 1977-78, Office for Handicapped Individuals, HEW, 1978, Women's com. Pres.'s Com. Employment Handicapped, 1985-86. Mem. Nat. Spinal Cord Injury Assn., 1970-90, editor, pub. conv. jour., 1974-82, bd. dirs. D.C. chpt., 1975-81, 89-90, nat. trustee, 1975-81, nat. bd. dirs., 1978-79; bd. dirs. Nat. Ctr. for a Barrier-Free Environment, 1979-84, v.p., 1980-81, pres., 1981-82; nat. bd. dirs., treas. League Disabled Voters, 1980-85; local bd. dirs. Easter Seal Soc. Disabled Children and Adults, 1985-90; active Montgomery County Commn. on People with Disabilities, 1989-95; mem. Taxicab Svcs. Adv. Com., 1995-99. Recipient Geico Pub. Svc. award, 1996, Civilian Career Svc. award Office of Sec. of Def., 1997; Woodrow Wilson fellow, 1965. Mem. Phi Beta Kappa, Delta Delta Delta. Home: 901 Arcola Ave Silver Spring MD 20902-3401 Office: Dept Def The Pentagon Rm 3a272 Washington DC 20301-0001

GILLIOM, MORRIS EUGENE, social studies and global educator; b. Bluffton, Ind., Feb. 10, 1932; s. William Orel and Zella Leota (Gallimore) G.; m. Bonnie Lee Cherp, Dec. 29, 1956; children: Gregor William, Julia Lee. BA, Heidelberg Coll., 1954; MA, Ohio State U., 1958, PhD, 1962. Cert. tchr., Ohio. Tchr. social studies Cleve. Pub. Schs., 1956-59; instr. Ohio State U., Columbus, 1959-62; asst. prof. San Francisco State Coll., 1962-65, U. Chgo., 1965-66; from assoc. prof. to prof. social studies, global edn. Ohio State U., Columbus, 1966-95, prof. emeritus, 1995—, dir. social studies edn. program abroad, 1969-95. Cons. TraveLearn, Lakeville, Pa., group leader programs worldwide; group leader Smithsonian Instn. Programs to China. Author, sr. editor: Practical Methods for the Social Studies, 1977; author, co-editor: Perspectives of Global Education, 1981; contbr. chpts. to books, articles to profl. publs. Mem. Heidelberg Coll. Fellows, Heidelberg Coll. Global Edn. Adv. Coun. With U.S. Army, 1954—56. Recipient Disting. Tchg. award Ohio State U., 1985; Malone fellow. Mem. Nat. Coun. Social Studies (coll. and univ. faculty assembly), Social Sci. Edn. Consortium (bd. dirs. 1986-90), Ohio Coun. Social Studies, Torch Club. Democrat. Avocations: photography, travel, skiing, reading. Home: 2495 Haverford Rd Columbus OH 43220-4203 Office: Ohio State U 1945 N High St Columbus OH 43210-1120 Fax: 614-451-1763. E-mail: genegilliom@mac.com.

GILLIS, CHRISTINE DIEST-LORGION, financial planner, stockbroker; b. San Francisco, Apr. 26, 1923; d. Evert Jan and Christine Helen (Radcliffe) Diest-Lorgion; children: Barbara Gillis Pieper and Suzanne Gillis Seymour (twins). BS, U. Calif., Berkeley, 1944; MS, U. So. Calif., 1968. Cert. fin. planner. Account exec. Winslow, Cohu & Stetson, N.Y.C., 1962-63, Paine Webber, N.Y.C., 1964-65; sr. investment exec. Shearson Hammill, Beverly Hills, Calif., 1966-72; fin. planner, asst. v.p. E.F. Hutton, L.A., 1972-87; 2d v.p. Shearson Lehman Hutton, Glendale, Calif., 1988; v.p. investments Dean Witter Reynolds, Glendale, Calif., 1988-90; fin. planner, asst. v.p. W.J. Gallagher & Co., Inc., Pasadena, Calif., 1991-2000; dir. San Pasqual Ptnrs., Pasadena, 2000—. Mem. AAUW (life; trustee ednl. found.), Town Hall. of Calif. (life; corp. sec. 1974-75, dir., gov. 1976-80), Women Stockbrokers Assn. (founding pres. N.Y.C. 1963), Women of Wall Street West (founder, pres. 1979-84), Navy League (life), U. Calif. Berkeley Alumni Assn. (life), U. So. Calif. Alumni Assn. (life), Town and Gown (life), Pasadena Bond Club. Episcopalian. Home: 1099 Pine Oak Ln Pasadena CA 91105 Office: Brookstreet Securities Inc 127 N Madison Ave Ste 200 Pasadena CA 91101 Fax: 626-397-2812. E-mail: cgillis3@earthlink.net.

GILLIS, JOAN, legal administrative assistant; b. Dallas, Mar. 10, 1944; d. John Malcolm and Nancy (Pollock) G.; m. Roger H. Sevigny, July 10, 1965 (div. Sept. 1982); children: R. Erik, Lisa M.; m. Allen R. Burrell, June 5, 1993. BA, Mt. St. Mary Coll., 1976; MBA, Rivier Coll., 1984. Admissions officer Mt. St. Mary Coll., N.H., 1976-77; adminstrv. asst. Weight Watchers of N.H., Nashua, 1977-79; sales assoc. Thelma Katz Real Estate, Manchester, N.H., 1979-80; program dir. N.H. Dental Soc., Concord, 1980-81; officer mgr. New Eng. Life, Bedford, N.H., 1981-87; adminstrn. mgr. Wiggin & Nourie, P.A., Manchester, N.H., 1987—. Mem. allocations com. United Way, Manchester, 1984-86, 98-99; bd. dirs. YWCA, Manchester, 1983-90, mem. membership com., 1996-97. Mem. Assn. Legal Adminstrs. (pres. 1999, sec. 1997-98). Avocations: bicycling, sewing. Office: Wiggin & Nourie PA 20 Market St Manchester NY 03101

GILLIS, JOHN LAMB, JR., lawyer; b. St. Louis, June 13, 1939; s. John L. and Carol (Randolph) G.; m. Nichola Mitchell, Aug. 1965; children: John Mitchell, Suzanne Lamb. Student, Brown U.; AB, Washington U., 1965; LLB, Stanford U., 1968. Bar: Mo. 1968. Ptnr., chmn. securities dept. Armstrong Teasdale LLP, St. Louis. Address: Armstrong Teasdale LLP 1 Metropolitan Sq Saint Louis MO 63102-2733 E-mail: jgillis@armstrongteasdale.com.

GILLIS, JOHN W. federal agency administrator; Grad., Calif. State U., L.A., U. So. Calif. Lt., asst. comdg. officer L.A. Police Dept., 1962—88; ret., 1988; dir. victims of crime U.S. Dept. Justice, Washington, 2001—. Commr. Calif. Bd. Prison Terms, acting chmn., 1991—93; mem. crime victims and corrections com. Calif. State Bar Assn.; mem. victim com. Am. Legis. Exch. Coun. Founder Justice for Homicide Victims, Coalition of Victims Equal Rights, Victims and Friends United; active Memory of Victims Everywhere, Parents of Murdered Children. Named, Am. Police Hall of Fame; recipient Nat. Crime Victim Svc. award, 1991, Spl. Commendation award, 1993. Office: US Dept Justice Victims of Crime 810 7th St NW Washington DC 20531

GILLIS, JUSTIN HOWARD, journalist; b. Lyons, Ga., Feb. 15, 1960; s. Clarence Jack Gillis and Reta Herndon. BA, U. Ga., 1982. Reporter, editor Miami (Fla.) Herald, 1983-95; met. reporter Washington Post, 1995-98, biotech. reporter, 1998—. E-mail: gillisj@washpost.com Avocations: wine, cooking, traveling. Office: Washington Post 1150 15th St NW Washington DC 20071

GILLIS, MALCOLM (STEPHEN GILLIS), academic administrator, economics educator; b. Dothan, Ala., Dec. 28, 1940; s. Stephen Malcolm and Eva May (Mac Kinnon) Gillis; m. Elizabeth Cifers, Aug. 18, 1962; children: Eva Leanora, Heather Elizabeth, Stephen Malcolm. BA, U. Fla., 1962, MA, 1963; PhD, U. Ill., 1968; LLD (hon.), Rocky Mountain Coll., 1992. Asst. prof. econs. Duke U., Durham, NC, 1967—69; lectr. in econs. Harvard U., Cambridge, Mass., 1969—73, inst. fellow, 1974—84; prof. econs., pub. policy Duke U., 1984—93, dean grad. sch., vice provost acad. affairs, 1986—91, Z. Smith Reynolds Disting. prof. pub. policy, 1990—93, dean faculty arts and scis., 1991—93; pres. Rice U., Houston, 1993—, Irvin Kenneth Zingler prof. econs., 1998—. Com. on energy taxation NRC/NAS, 1979—80; coun. econ. policy Office of Gov. State of Alaska, Juneau, 1982—83; mem. seminar on Southeast Asia in world affairs Columbia U., 1982—84; adv. com. energy divsn. Oak Ridge Nat. Lab., 1984—87, chmn. adv. com., 1985—86; internat. adv. bd. KPMG Peat Marwick Policy Econs. Group, 1988—; cons. World Bank, Washington; Disting. Fulbright prof. Cath. U., Chile, 1989; adv. bd. Internat. Ctr. for Econ. Growth, 1986—, Inst. for Policy Reform, 1990—; so. regional adv. bd. Inst. Internat. Edn., 1993—; bd. dirs. Houston Advanced Rsch. Ctr.; presenter in field; bd. dirs. Fed. Res. Bank, Dallas. Author (with others): Fiscal Reform For Colombia, 1971, Taxation and Mining, 1978, Tax and Investment Policies for Hard Minerals, 1980, Economics of Development, 1983; editor: Export Diversification and the New Protectionism, 1981, Public Policy and Misuse of Forest Resources, 1988, The Value-Added Tax in Developing Countries, 1991; mem. editl. bd.: Pakistan Devel. Rev., 1977—80, Quar. Jour. Econs., 1978—79, co-editor; mem. editl. bd.: Tex. Bus. Rev., 1979—83, Pakistan Jour. Applied Econs., 1980—83, Comparative Econ. Studies, 1986—88, referee: various jours.; contbr. articles to profl. jours. Adv. Navajo Indian Nation, Ship Rock, N.Mex., 1983—84; trustee Found. for Hosp. Art, 1989, Francisco Marroquin Found., 1989—, Friends of Edn. in Chile, 1989—, United Way of Tex. Gulf Coast; vice-chmn. higher edn. sector Houston area U.S. Savs. Bond Campaign, 1994; bd. adv. Houston Symphony, 1995; chmn. March of Dimes Gulf Coast Walk Am., 1995; chmn. bd. trustees Ctr. for World Environ. and Sustainable Devel., 1969, 1975, 1983—87, Harvard Inst. Internat. Devel., 1984—; bd. dirs. Am. Forestry Assn., 1989—92; chair U.S. Savs. Bonds, Gulf Coast Region, 2002—04; bd. dirs. South Main Ctr. Assn., 1993—, Greater Houston Partnership, 1993—, St. Luke's Episc. Hosp., 1994—2003, Amigos de las Ams., Consortium on Financing Higher Edn., 1994—, Ind. Colls. and Univs. Tex., 1995—; exec. com. Houston Advanced Res. Ctr. Bd., 1994—, Assn. Am. Univs., 1993—; mem. Houston Lifestock Show and Rodeo; bd. dirs. Indo-Am. C. of C., 2000—, Houston Tech. Ctr., 1999—, BioHouston, 2000—, Tex. Aviation Hall of Fame, 1998—. Grantee, U.S. AID, Washington, 1986—87. Mem.: Houston Philos. Soc., Assn. Pub. Policy Analysis and Mgmt., Nat. Tax Assn., Am. Econ. Assn. Republican. Episcopalian. Office: Rice U Office of Pres PO Box 1892 Houston TX 77251-1892

GILLIS, MARVIN BOB, retired chemical executive, consultant; b. Treutlen County, Ga., Apr. 5, 1920; s. Bob Lee and Pearl (Gillis) G.; m. Helen Reed, Dec. 23, 1946; children: Margaret Susan, Marvin Reed, Kenneth Robert. BSA., U. Ga., 1940; PhD, Cornell U., 1947. Rsch. assoc. Cornell U., 1947-51; sr. rsch. chemist Internat. Minerals and Chem. Corp., from 1947, asst. dir. rsch., 1956-57, dir. rsch., 1957-64, dir. animal health and nutrition, 1964-66, div. v.p., 1966-70, corp. v.p., 1970-72, sr. v.p., 1972-82; pres., dir. IMC Chem. Group, Inc., 1976-78; pres. Animal Products Group, 1978-82, cons. to exec. office, 1982-86; mng. gen. ptnr. Gillis Ltd. Partnership. Sec. Agrl. Rsch. Inst., NRC, 1958-59, v.p., 1960-62, 66-67, pres., 1962-63, 68-69, mem. Agrl. bd., 1962-67; bd. dirs Animal Health Inst., 1966-69 Author numerous papers in field; patentee in field Served to 1st lt. USAAF, 1942—45. Decorated DFC with oak leaf cluster, Air medal with 3 oak leaf clusters. Mem. North Shore Country Club (Glenview, Ill.), Sea Island (Ga.) Club, Blue Key, Sigma Xi, Gamma Alpha, Alpha Zeta, Phi Kappa Phi. Baptist. Home: 2500 Indigo Ln 409 Glenview IL 60025 also: 103 Cascades Saint Simons Island GA 31522

GILLISPIE, CHARLES COULSTON, history of science educator; b. Harrisburg, Pa., Aug. 6, 1918; s. Raymond Livingston and Virginia Lambert (Coulston) G.; m. Emily Ramsdell Clapp, Jan. 29, 1949. AB, Wesleyan U., Middletown, Conn., 1940, MA, 1942, DSc (hon.), 1971; student, MIT, 1940-41; PhD, Harvard U., 1949; DSc (hon.), Lafayette Coll., 2001. Teaching fellow, tutor history Harvard U., 1946-47; faculty Princeton U., 1947-87, prof. history sci., 1959-67, Shelby Cullom Davis prof. European history, 1967-73, Dayton-Stockton prof. history, 1973-87, prof. emeritus, 1987—, chmn. dept., 1971-73, dir. program in history and philosophy of sci., 1960-66, 76-80; A.J. Balfour prof. history sci. Weizmann Inst., Israel, 1972. Assoc. dir. studies Ecole des Hautes Etudes en Sciences Sociales, Paris, 1980-85. Author: Genesis and Geology, 1951, A Diderot Pictorial Encyclopedia of Trades and Industry, 2 vols, 1959, The Edge of Objectivity: An essay in the History of Scientific Ideas, 1960, Lazare Carnot, Savant, 1971, Science and Polity in France at the End of the Old

Regime, 1980, The Montgolfier Brothers and the Invention of Aviation, 1783-1784, 1983, Monuments of Egypt, 1987, Pierre-Simon LaPlace, A Life in Exact Science, 1997; editor-in-chief: Dictionary of Scientific Biography, 16 vols., 1970-80. Bd. mgrs. Bach Choir, Bethlehem, Pa., 1976-80. Served to capt. C.W.S. AUS, 1942- 46. Decorated officier Ordre des Palmes Académiques (France), 1989, Balzan prize History and Philosophy of Sci., 1997; fellow Am. Coun. Learned Socs., 1951-52, Guggenheim fellow, 1954-55, 70-71, NSF fellow, 1958-59, 62-63, fellow Ctr. for Advanced Study in Behavioral Scis., 1970-71; chaire d'histoire des Sciences, Fondation de France, 1980-85. Fellow AAAS, Brit. Acad. (corr.); mem. History Sci. Soc. (council 1952-55, 59-60, pres. 1964-66), Am. Acad. Arts and Scis., Académie Internationale d' Histoire des Sciences (v.p. 1965-68), N.Y. Acad. Scis. (hon. life mem.), Am. Philos. Soc., Princeton Club (N.Y.C.), Nassau Club, Phi Beta Kappa, Sigma Xi. Home: 2409 Windrow Dr Princeton NJ 08540

GILLISPIE, HAROLD LEON, minister; b. Levant, Kans., May 11, 1933; s. Harold Leon and Agnes Anne (Dryden) G. BA in Bus. Adminstrn., Kans. Wesleyan U., 1955. Youth dir. Cen. YMCA, Des Moines, 1957-61; exec. dir. West Des Moines br. YMCA, 1961-65; exec. dir. Aurora Br. YMCA, Denver, 1965-69, YMCA, McCook, Nebr., 1969-75, Junction City, Kans., 1975-79; owner H & R Block Franchise, Manhattan, Kans., 1979-91; lay pastor Presbyn. Ch., Oak Hill, Kans., 1996—; vice moderator Presbytery of No. Kans., 1999-00, moderator, 2000-01. Proofreader text H & R Block, Kansas City, Mo., 1986-92. Bd. dirs. Flint Hills Breadbasket, Manhattan, Kans., 1982-89, treas., 1987; bd. dirs. Big Bros. Big Sisters, Manhattan, 1981-85, pres., 1983-85; pres. Downtown Manhattan, Inc., 1986; bd. dirs. Manhattan Main Street, 1986-89; bd. dirs. Ecumenical Campus Ministry, Kans. State U., 1995-99, 2002—, chmn., 1996-98. Republican. Presbyterian. Avocations: theology, tennis, baking, working with youth. Home: 710 Bertrand St Manhattan KS 66502-5156 E-mail: pastogil@flinthills.com.

GILLISPIE, STEVEN BRIAN, systems analyst, researcher; b. Seattle, Oct. 19, 1955; s. Edwin B. and Claudia Mae (Cooper) G. BS in Physics with distinction, BS in Math., U. Wash., 1979, BS in Psychology, BA in Gen. Studies, U. Wash., 1983, MS in Math., 1998. Software specialist Fla. Computer Graphics, Seattle, 1983-84; data analyst coronary artery surgery study U. Wash., Seattle, 1985-87, sci. programmer dept. radiology, 1987-88, systems analyst dept. radiology, 1988—. Dir. devel. med. imaging software Viewbox, 1992; contbr. articles to profl. jours. Mem. Woodland Park Zool. Soc., Seattle, 1986—; contbg. mem. Nordic Heritage Mus., Seattle, 1991—; patron The High Desert Mus., Bend, Oreg., 1991—. Mem. Soc. for Indsl. and Applied Math., U. Wash. Alumni Assn. (life), So. Oreg. Hist. Soc. Office: U Wash Dept Radiology Box 356004 Seattle WA 98195-6004 E-mail: gillisp@u.washington.edu.

GILLISS, CATHERINE LYNCH, nursing educator; b. New Britain, Conn., Apr. 18, 1949; d. James A. and Lorraine Lynch; m. Thomas P. Gilliss, June 6, 1970. BS in Nursing, Duke U., 1971; MS in Nursing, Cath. U. Am., Washington, 1974; D of Nursing Sci., U. Calif., 1983; cert. adult nurse practitioner, U. Rochester, 1979. Staff and charge nurse Duke U. Med. Ctr., Durham, 1971, VA Hosp., Washington, 1971-72; asst. prof. U. Md., Balt., 1974-76, The Cath. U. Am., 1976-79; assoc. prof. U. Portland, Oreg., 1979-83; lectr. in nursing Sonoma State U., Rohnert Park, Calif., 1983-84; prof., chmn. dept. family health care U. Calif., San Francisco, 1984-98, prof. emeritus, 1999—; prof. Sch. Nursing Yale U., New Haven, Conn., 1998—, dean Sch. Nursing, 1998—. Chair NIH, Nat. Inst. Nursing Rsch. Study Sect., 1997-99. Co-author: Toward a Science of Family Nursing, 1989, The Nursing of Families, 1993; mem. editl. bd. Families, Systems and Health, 1994-98, jour. Family Nursing; contbr. articles to profl. jours. Bd. dirs. Conn. Inst. for Child Health and Devel., Am. Acad. Nursing, U. Calif. San Francisco Ctr. for the Health Professions. Recipient Disting. Alumna award Duke U., 1991; Pres.'s fellow U. Calif., 1983; Se. fellow Ctr. for Health Professions, 1996-99, Primary Care Policy fellow USPHS, 1993; Regent U. Portland, Oreg., 1994-2000. Fellow Am. Acad. Nursing (bd. dirs.); mem. ANA, Nat. Coun. on Family Rels., Nat. Orgn. Nurse Practitioner Faculty (pres. 1995), Primary Care Fellowship Soc. (pres. 1996-97). Office: Yale U Sch Nursing PO Box 9740 New Haven CT 06536-0740

GILLMAN, ARTHUR EMANUEL, psychiatrist; b. N.Y.C., June 6, 1927; s. Hyman David and Sadie Ruth (Ornstein) G.; m. Barbara E. O'Connell, June 29, 1961 (div. 1980); children: Theodore Jones, Sarah Ann; m. Harriet Oster, Aug. 27, 2000. BS, U. Vt., 1947; MD, N.Y. Med. Coll., 1950. Diplomate Am. Bd. Psychiatry and Neurology, Am. Bd. Child and Adolescent Psychiatry. Intern State U. Iowa Hosps., Iowa City, 1950-51; asst. resident in neurology Montefiore Hosp., Bronx, N.Y., 1951-52; asst. resident in psychiatry Bellevue Hosp., N.Y.C., 1952-53; resident in psychiatry Hillside Hosp., Glen Oaks, N.Y., 1953-54; fellow in child psychiatry Child Guidance Inst., Jewish Bd. Guardians, N.Y.C., 1954-56; clin. fellow in child psychiatry Bronx Mcpl. Hosp. Ctr./Albert Einstein Coll. Medicine, 1955-56; pvt. practice Mamaroneck, NY, 1956—80; cons., dir. evaluative studies, then rsch. dir. N.Y. Assn. for the Blind, 1986—95; pvt. practice Larchmont, NY, 1980—95; clin. dir. community svcs. Rockland Children's Psychiat. Ctr., Orangeburg, N.Y., 1985-95; chief physician child adolescent svcs. Bronx Lebanon Hosp., 1995-2001, attending physician, 2001—, dir. child adolescent forensic svcs., 2001—; asst. prof. psychiatry Albert Einstein Coll. Medicine, N.Y.C., 1995—. Asst. clin. prof. Columbia U., 1989-95; cons. psychiatrist, dir. evaluative studies, dir. rsch. devel., then dir. rsch. N.Y. Assn. for Blind, 1966-85; dir. curriculum in child psychiatry Montefiore Hosp., 1968-69; vis. lectr. Manhattanville Coll., Purchase, N.Y., 1974-76; dir. psychiat. clinic Jewish Guild for Blind, 1962-66; presenter at profl. confs. Contbr. articles to profl. publs. Fellow Am. Psychiat. Assn. (life), Am. Orthopsychiat. Assn. (life), Am. Acad. Child and Adolescent Psychiatry (life); mem. AMA. Mailing: 34 Pryer Manor Rd Larchmont NY 10538-3437 Office: Bronx Lebanon Hosptr Fulton Divsn 1276 Fulton Ave Bronx NY 10456 E-mail: Gillman3@optonline.net.

GILLMAN, DANIEL W. information scientist; b. Balt., Mar. 14, 1952; s. Robert D. and Katherine B. Gillman; m. Julie A. Black, Mar. 17, 1990; children: Ivan, Stephanie. BS in Math., U. Md., 1979, MA in Math., 1982. Mathematician U.S. Census Bur., Washington, 1982—88, info. scientist, 1988—2000, Bur. of Labor Stats., Washington, 2000—. Chair INCITS/L8 (Metadata) Standards Com., 1998—, UN/ECE Workgroup on Statis. Metadata, Geneva, 1999—, Terminology Workgroup, MetaNet Project, Edinburgh, Scotland, 2002—. Editor (author): (pub.) International Standard Specification and Standardization of Data Elements-Part 1, 1999; editor: technical reports; tech. contbr. Metamodel for Management of Sharable Data, Specification and Standardization of Data Elements All Parts, 2000, Metadata Registries-Part 3, 2003; contbr. numerous articles to profl. jours. Recipient Bronze medal, U.S. Dept. Commerce, 1999. Mem.: Data Documentation Initiative, Internat. Assn. for Social Sci. Info. Svc. Technologies, Am. Statis. Assn. Achievements include development of conceptual model for managing statistical metadata within U.S. and Canadian federal statistical offices. Office: Bureau of Labor Statistics 2 Massachusetts Ave NE Washington DC 20212 E-mail: Gillman.Daniel@BLS.gov.

GILLMAN, LEONARD, mathematician, educator; b. Cleve., Jan. 8, 1917; s. Joseph Moses and Etta Judith (Cohen) G.; m. Reba Parks Marcus, Dec. 24, 1938; children: Jonathan Webb, Michal Judith. Diploma (fellow in piano 1933-38), Juilliard Grad. Sch. Music, 1938; BS, Columbia U., 1941, MA (Carnegie fellow math. statistics 1942-43), 1945, PhD, 1953. Asst. in math. dept. Columbia U., 1941-42, lectr., 1942-43; ops. analyst Tufts Coll., MIT, 1943-51; from instr. to assoc. prof. math. Purdue U., 1952-60; prof. math., chmn. dept. U. Rochester, 1960-69; prof. math. U. Tex., Austin, 1969-87, prof. emeritus, 1987, chmn. dept., 1969-73. Mem. Inst. Advanced Study, Princeton, 1958-60; cons. editor W.W. Norton Co., Inc., 1967-80. Author: (with Meyer Jerison) Rings of Continuous Functions, 1960, 76, You'll Need Math, 1967, (with Robert H. McDowell) Calculus, 1973, 78, Writing Mathematics Well, 1987; mem. editorial bd. Topology and Its Applications, 1971-94. Guggenheim fellow, 1958-59; NSF sr. post-doctoral fellow, 1959-60. Mem. Am. Math. Soc. (assoc. sec. 1969-71, mem. com. to monitor problems in commn. 1972-77), Nat. Coun. Tchrs. Math., Math. Assn. Am. (bd. govs. 1973-95, treas. 1973-86, pres.-elect 1986-87, pres. 1987-89, past pres. 1989-90, Lester R. Ford award for expository writing 1994, 2003, Yueh-Gin Gung and Dr. Charles Y. Hu award for disting. svc. to math. 1999). Home and Office: 1606 The High Rd Austin TX 78746-2236 E-mail: len@math.utexas.edu., gillman@mail.utexas.edu.

GILLMER, THOMAS CHARLES, retired naval architect; b. July 17, 1911; s. Derr Oscar and Hazel May (Voit) G.; m. Anna May Derge, June 5, 1937; children: Christina Gesell Gillmer Erdmann, Charles Voit; m. Ruth N. Morgan, 1999. BS, U.S. Naval Acad., 1935; postgrad., Case Western Res. U., 1946, Johns Hopkins U., 1946. Commd. ensign USN, 1935, advanced through grades to lt. (j.g.), 1939, lt. comdr., 1944-46; mem. faculty U.S. Naval Acad., Annapolis, Md., 1946-68, prof., dir. Naval Arch., 1961-68, chmn. naval engring. dept., 1963-68; pvt. practice naval arch. Annapolis, 1968-2000; ret., 2000. Mem. panel experts FAO, UN, Rome, 1963-66; cons. to Navy Dept. Restoration USS Constitution, 1991—. Author: Construction and Stability of Naval Ships, 1959, Modern Ship Design, 1970, 2d edit., 1975, Working Water Craft, 1972, 2d edit., 1994, Chesapeake Sloops, 1981, Introduction to Naval Architecture, 1982, The Story of Baltimore Clippers, 1991, Old Ironsides, Rise, Decline, and Resurrection of USS Constitution, 1993; designer PRIDE of Balt., 1976-77, Lady Maryland, 1985, PRIDE of Balt. II, 1987-88, A History of Working Watercraft of the Western World, 1994; contbr. articles to profl. jours. and papers to profl. confs.; designer Kalmar nickel replica ship of Del., 1998; patentee in field. Mem. bd. govs. Chesapeake Bay Maritime Mus., 1981-91, emeritus, 1995, curatorial chmn., 1989-91. Recipient 1st Maritime Preservation award Chesapeake Bay Maritime Mus., 1992, Robert G. Albion/James Monroe award for maritime history Nat. Maritime Hist. Soc., N.Y.C., 1995. Mem. AAUP, Soc. Naval Archs. and Marine Engrs. (award for individual efforts to further body of knowledge 1988), Am. Soc. Naval Engrs., Soc. Nautical Rsch., PRIDE of Balt. (ops. com. 1979—), Hellenic Inst. Nautical Archaeology Athens (Bronze medal 1985), Annapolis Yacht Club, de Voile Club (France), New Providence Club.

GILLMING, KENNETH, church administrator; Pres. Bapt. Bible Fellowship Internat., Springfield, Mo. Baptist. Office: Bapt Bible Fellowship Internat PO Box 191 Springfield MO 65801-0191

GILLMOR, CHARLES STEWART, history and science educator, researcher; b. Kansas City, Mo., Nov. 6, 1938; s. Charles Stewart and Evelyn (Noland) G.; m. Rogene Marie Godding, Nov. 28, 1964; children: Charles Stewart III, Alison Bogue. BSEE, Stanford U., 1962; MA, Princeton U., 1966, PhD, 1968; postgrad., U. Colo., 1963. Ionospheric physicist Bur. Standards, Antarctica and Boulder, Colo., 1960-62; instr. history Wesleyan U., Middletown, Conn., 1967-68, asst. prof., 1968-72, assoc. prof., 1973 79, prof. history and sci., 1979—, chmn. dept. history, 1986-88, 91-94; cons. Office Sci. Edn., AAAS, 1973-75. Adv. com. Coun. Internat. Exch. Scholars, 1978—82; cons. NSF, 1983; Hennebach vis. prof. Colo. Sch. Mines, 1996—97; vis. prof. elec. engring. Stanford u., 1998—2001. Author: Coulomb and the Evolution of Physics and Engineering in 18th Century France, 1971; editor: The History of Geophysics, Vol. 1, 1984, Vol. 2, 1986, Vol. 4, 1990, Vol. 7, 1997; jour. editor: Transactions Am. Geophys. Union, 1983-86; mus. dir. Nutmeg Foxtrot-Jazz Orch., 1990-96; contbr. articles to profl. jours.; recording artist with Leo Records, 1998. Deacon Higganum Congl. Ch., Conn., 1978-96. Mt. Gillmor in Antarctica named in his honor, 1963; Social Sci. Research Council grantee, 1971; NSF research grantee, 1972-74, 75-77, 76-79; sr. Fulbright research scholar Cambridge U., Eng., 1976; NASA History scholar, 1980-81; U.S.-France NSF research fellow, Paris, 1984-85; Joseph J. Malone fellow to Tunisia Nat. Coun. U.S.-Arab Rels., 1989 Fellow Am. Phys. Soc. (sec.-treas. history of physics divsn. 1988-94, exec. com. 1996-98, chair 1997-98); mem. AAAS, IEEE, Am. Geophys. Union, History of Sci. Soc., Soc. History of Tech. (adv. coun. 1978-82), Sigma Xi. Home: 29 Spencer Rd Higganum CT 06441-4034 Office: Wesleyan Univ Dept History Middletown CT 06459-0002 E-mail: sgillmor@wesleyan.edu.

GILLMOR, HELEN, federal judge; BA, Queen's Coll. of CUNY, 1965; LLB magna cum laude, Boston U., 1968. With Ropes & Gray, Boston, 1968-69, Law Offices of Alexander R. Gillmor, Camden, Maine, 1970, Torkildson, Katz, Jossem, Fonseca, Jaffe, Moore & Hetherington, Honolulu, 1971-72; law clk. to Chief Justice William S. Richardson Hawaii State Supreme Ct., 1972; dep. pub. defender Office of Pub. Defender, Honolulu, 1972-74; dist. ct. judge per diem Family Ct. (1st cir.) Hawaii, 1977-83; per diem judge Dist. Ct., 1st circuit, 1983-85; pvt. practice Honolulu, 1985-94; district judge U.S. Dist. Ct. Hawaii, 9th circuit, 1994—. Counsel El Paso Real Estate Investment Trust, 1969; lectr. U.S. Agy. Internat. Devel., Seoul, South Korea, 1969-70, Univ. Hawaii, 1975. Office: Prince J K Kuhio Fed Bldg 300 Ala Moana Blvd Rm C-435 Honolulu HI 96850-0435

GILLMOR, JOHN EDWARD, lawyer; b. Phila., Oct. 26, 1937; s. John Edward and Louise Ann (Porter) G.; m. Allis Dale Brannon, Aug. 17, 1968; children: Sarah, Abigail, Susan, Eleanor, John, Matthew. BA, Swarthmore Coll., 1959; LL.B., U. Pa., 1962. Bar: D.C. 1962, N.Y. 1963, Tenn. 1972, Pa. 1980. Assoc. Dewey Ballantine Bushby Palmer & Wood, 1962-63, 66-71; v.p., corp. counsel Hosp. Affiliates Internat., Nashville, 1971-78, sr. v.p., gen. counsel, 1978-79; staff v.p., asst. gen. counsel INA Corp., Phila., 1980; sr. v.p., gen. counsel INA Health Care Group, 1981; partner Gillmor, Mills & Gillmor, 1981-83; dir., exec. v.p. Health Am. Corp., 1983-86; ptnr. Gillmor, Anderson & Gillmor, 1986-89, Dearborn & Ewing, 1989-92, Boult, Cummings, Conners & Berry, Nashville, 1992—. Trustee U. Sch. Nashville, 1990-2002; bd. dirs. Nashville Opera Assn., 1991-2002, pres.; bd. dirs. Hoosier CARE, Inc. With USMC, 1963-66. Mem. ABA, Assn. of Bar of City of N.Y., Nashville Bar Found., Tenn. Bar Assn., Nashville Bar Assn. Republican. Home: 1700 Graybar Ln Nashville TN 37215-2106 Office: Boult Cummings Conners & Berry 414 Union St Ste 1600 Nashville TN 37219-1744 E-mail: jgillmor@bccb.com.

GILLMOR, KAREN LAKO, state agency administrator; b. Cleve., Jan. 29, 1948; d. William M. and Charlotte (Sheldon) Lako; m. Paul E. Gillmor, Dec. 10, 1983; children: Linda D., Julie E., Paul Michael, Connor W., Adam S. BA cum laude, Mich. State U., 1969; MA, Ohio State U., 1970, PhD, 1981. Asst. to v.p. Ohio State U., Columbus, 1972-77, spl. asst. dean law, 1979-81, assoc. dir. Ctr. Healthcare Policy and Rsch., 1991-92; asst. to pres. Ind. Cen. U., Indpls., 1977-78; rsch. asst. Burke Mktg. Rsch., Indpls., 1978-79; v.p. pub. affairs Huntington Nat. Bank, Columbus, 1981-82; fin. cons. Ohio Rep. Fin. Com., Columbus, 1982-83; chief mgmt. planning and rsch. Indsl. Commn. Ohio, Columbus, 1983-86; mgr. physician rels. Ohio State U. Med. Ctr., Columbus, 1987-91; cons. U.S. Sec. Labor, Washington, 1990-91; mem. Regional Bd. Rev./Indls. Commn., Ohio, 1991-92; state senator Ohio Gen. Assembly, 1993-97; vice-chair State Employment Rels. Bd., 1997—. Legis. liaison Huntington Bancshares, Ohio, Ohio State U., Columbus; trustee Heidelberg Coll., 1999—, Rutherford B. Hayes Presd. Ctr., 2002—. Mem. adv. coun. The Childhood League Ctr., 2003—; bd. dirs. Congl. Childcare Ctr., 2003—. Grantee Andrew W. Mellon Found. 1978, Carnegie Corp. 1978; named Outstanding Freshman Ohio Legislator, 1994, Watchdog of the Treasury, 1994, 96; recipient Pres. award Ohio State Chiropractic Assn., 1994, Pub. Svc. award Am. Heart Assn., 1995, Outstanding Nat. Freshman Legislator of Yr., 1995; Ctr. Advancement and Study of Ethics award Capital U. and Trinity Luth. Seminary, 1996, U.S. Dept. of Army Cert. of Ach., 1997, Friend of Medicine award Ohio State Med. Assn., 1997, Legis. Ach. award Am. Acad. Pediatrics (Ohio chpt. 1997); inducted Hall of Fame, Rocky River H.S., 1998, Spirit of Women award, 1999. Mem. Women in Mainstream, Women's Roundtable, Ohio Fedn. Rep. Women, Am. Assn. Higher Edn., Coun. Advancement and Support Edn., DAR, Phi Delta Kappa. Methodist. Office: 65 E State St Ste 1200 Columbus OH 43215-4209

GILLMOR, PAUL E. congressman, lawyer; b. Tiffin, Ohio, Feb. 1, 1939; s. Paul Marshall and Lucy Jeannette (Fry) G.; m. Karen Lee Lako, Dec. 10, 1983; children: Linda Dianne, Julie Ellen, Paul Michael, Connor Sheldon, Adam William BA, Ohio Wesleyan U., Delaware, 1961; JD, U. Mich, 1964; LL.D. (hon.), Tiffin U., Ohio, 1985. Bar: Ohio, 1965. Mem. Ohio Senate, 1967-89, minority leader, 1978-81, 83-85, pres., 1981-83, 85-88; mem. U.S. Congress from 5th Ohio dist., Washington, 1989—; mem. energy and commerce com., fin. svcs. com., dep. majority whip. Assoc. firm Tomb and Hering, Tiffin, 1967-88; bd. dirs. Old Fort Banking Co., Ohio. Pres. Ohio Electoral Coll., Columbus, 1984. Served to capt. USAF, 1965-67. Recipient Gov.'s award, Ohio, 1980; Phillips medal of pub. service Ohio U. Coll. Osteopathy, 1981; Exec. Order, Ohio Commodores Assn., 1981; Disting. Citizen award Med. Coll. Ohio, 1982; named Legislator of Yr., Ohio VFW, 1994. Mem. ABA, Ohio State Bar Assn., Nat. Republican Legislators Assn. (named Outstanding Legislator of Yr. 1983). Republican. Methodist. Office: US Ho of Reps Office House Mems 1203 Longworth Bldg Washington DC 20515-3505*

GILLMOR, ROGENE GODDING, retired medical technologist; b. El Dorado, Kans., Jan. 25, 1939; d. Marc Antone and Verda May (Bogue) Godding; m. Charles Stewart Gillmor Jr, Nov. 28, 1964; children: Charles Stewart III, Alison Bogue. AA in Liberal Arts, Cottey Coll., 1958; BA in Biology, Stanford U., 1960; postgrad., Wesleyan U., U. Hartford, Foothills Coll. Rsch. asst. genetics Joshua Lederberg lab. Stanford U., 1960-62; assoc. scientist space biology/medicine Lockheed Missiles & Space Co., Palo Alto, Calif., 1962-64; rsch. asst. biology Princeton (N.J.) U., 1965-66, Wesleyan U., Middletown, Conn., 1967-69; lab. technician immunochemistry Hartford (Conn.) Hosp., 1978-84, instr. immunology clin. lab. edn. program, 1985-89, lab. supr. proteins/immunology dept. pathology/lab. medicine, 1986-99, ret., 1999. Researcher various labs France and Switzerland, 1984—85. Contbr. articles to profl jours. Leader Girl Scouts US, 1977—85; trustee, deacon Higganum Congregational Ch, Conn., 1980—. Recipient Achievement Award, Girl Scouts US, 1985. Mem.: Conn Hist Soc (secy 1970—72), Wesleyan Potters (pres 1982—84), Am Soc Clin lab Sci, Am Soc Clin Pathologists (cert immunology specialist), Am Asn Clin Chemistry, PEO Sisterhood, Haddam. Avocations: gardening, music, pottery. Home: 29 Spencer Rd Higganum CT 06441-4034 E-mail: rogenegillmor@hotmail.com.

GILLMORE, KATHLEEN CORY, lawyer; b. Louisville, July 10, 1947; d. Elmer Louis and Frances (Cory) Hoehn; m. David Newton Gillmore, Dec. 14, 1974. Student, U. Mich., 1965-66; B.A., Purdue U., 1969; J.D., Ind. U., 1972. Bar: Ind. 1972, D.C. 1973, Ky. 1979, Tex. 1986. Ptnr., firm E.L. Hoehn, Washington, 1972-78; staff atty. Ashland Oil, Inc., Ky., 1978-82, sr. atty., 1982-85; staff atty., Shell Oil Co., Houston, Tex., 1985-87, sr. environ. atty., 1987-96, sr. environ. counsel, 1996-98, 2002-; sr. environ. counsel Equiva Svcs. LLC, 1998-2002. Mem. ABA, D.C. Bar Assn., Ind. Bar Assn., Ky. Bar Assn., Tex. Bar Assn., Houston Bar Assn. (bd. dirs. environ. section 1994-98, 2002—), Am. Petroleum Inst. (vice chmn. subcomm. on environ. and health law 1995-95, chmn. 1996-98). Office: Shell Oil Co 910 Louisiana 1 Shell Plz Houston TX 77002-2463

GILLMORE, ROBERT, landscape designer, author, editor, publisher; b. Claremont, N.H., Jan. 21, 1946; s. Vern Winslow and Helen Marion (Tyre) G. BA in Polit. Sci. cum laude, Williams Coll., 1968; postgrad., London Sch. Econs., 1970; MA, U. Va., 1971, PhD, 1979. Editl. writer Daily Eagle, Claremont, 1965-66; reporter, editor The Transcript, North Adams, Mass., 1966; reporter Bennington Banner, Vt., 1967; editor, mem. editl. page staff Washington Post, 1970; instr. politics St. Anselm Coll., Manchester, N.H., 1972-73; editor, writer N.H. Times, Concord, 1973; editor N.H. Law Weekly, Manchester, 1974-79; lectr. constl. law New England Coll., Henniker, N.H., 1975; editor Supreme Ct. Bull., Goffstown, N.H., 1979-87; syndicated columnist Bull. Syndicate, Goffstown, 1983-90; pub., editorial dir. Great Walks guides, 1990—; prin. Robert Gillmore, Landscape Consulting, Contracting & Design, 1990—. Author: Liberalism and the Politics of Plunder: The Conscience of a Neo-Liberal, 1987, Great Walks of Acadia National Park and Mount Desert, 1990, Great Walks of Southern Arizona, 1990, Great Walks of Big Bend National Park, 1991, Great Walks of the Great Smokies, 1992, Great Walks of Yosemite National Park, 1993, Great Walks of Sequoia and Kings Canyon National Parks, 1994, Great Walks of Acadia National Park and Mount Desert Island, 1994, The Woodland Garden, 1996, Great Walks of the Olympic Peninsula, 1999, Beauty All Around You: How To Create Large Private Low-Maintenance Gardens, Even on Small Lots and Small Budgets, 2000. Mem. N.H. Ho. Reps., 1973-74; del. N.H. Constl. Conv., 1974, vice chmn. com. on form and style; mem. N.H. state adv. com. U.S. Commn. on Civil Rights, 1973-76. With U.S. Army, 1968-70, Vietnam. Office: Great Walks Inc PO Box 410 Goffstown NH 03045-0410

GILLMORE, VICKI LONGENECKER, health care administrator; b. Lancaster, Pa., Mar. 10, 1950; d. Harry Kreider and Doris Louise (Heisey) Longenecker; m. Jack L. Gillmore, Aug. 30, 1986. Diploma, Harrisburg Hosp. Sch. Nursing, 1971; BS, U. Md., 1976, MS, 1977, PhD, 1990. Lic. nursing home adminstr., Pa. Dept. Health. Adminstr. healthcare svcs. Masonic Homes, Elizabethtown, Pa., 1997—; coord. critical care Community Hosp. Lancaster, 1978-79; clin. specialist cardiovascular St. Joseph Hosp., Lancaster, 1979-85, asst. dir. nursing, 1985-91; nursing instr. Millersville (Pa.) U., 1981—; v.p. nursing Community Gen. Osteopathic Hosp., Harrisburg, 1991-94; dir. Keystone Health Plan Ctrl., Camp Hill, Pa., 1994-97. Mem. Pa. Orgn. Nurse Leaders, South Ctrl. Org. of Nurse Leaders, Sigma Theta Tau. Home: 1429 Drager Rd Columbia PA 17512-8701 E-mail: vgillmore@supernet.com., vickig@masonichomespa.org.

GILLOM, JENNIFER, professional basketball player; b. June 13, 1964; Basketball player Italian League, Milan, 1987—91, Ancona, 1991—94, Messina, 1995—96, Athens, Greece, 1996—97, Phoenix Mercury, WNBA, 1997—, Toronto, 2000. Named to All WNBA 1st Team, 1998; recipient Gold medal, Pan Am. Games, 1987, Olympic Games, 1988. Office: Phoenix Mercury 201 E Jefferson St Phoenix AZ 85004-2412

GILLON, STEPHEN JOHN, business educator, consultant; b. Ft. Sheridan, Ill., June 13, 1948; s. Eli and Joan Rodgers Gillon; children: Barron August, Sterling Joseph. AA, Reedley Coll., 1981; BS, U.S. Mil. Acad., 1972; MBA, Calif. State U., Fresno, 1984; MS in Accountancy, Calif. State U., Chico, 1989; D Edn., Boston U., 1997. Cert. airframe and powerplant mech., pvt. pilot, FAA. Sports info. officer Reedley (Calif.) Coll., 1978-81; instr. Calif. State U., Fresno, 1981, Chico, 1987-90, U. Alaska, Anchorage, 1991-94, Ivy Tech. C.C., Marion, Ind., 1996-97; instr., sys. mgr. MILA, Inc., Anchorage, 1991-94; asst. prof. Cleve. State C.C., 1997-2000, U. Alaska-Anchorage, Homer, 2000—. Mem. com. Vocat. Ednl. Task Force, Homer, Alaska, 2000—03; dir., treas. Homer Co. on Arts, 2001—03. Capt. USAF, 1973—77, Sam M. Walton fellow, 1997-2000. Mem. Exptl. Aircraft Assn. Home: 137 E Danview Homer AK 99603-0724 Office: U Alaska 533 E Pioneer Dr Homer AK 99603 Fax: (907) 235-2199. E-mail: gillon@uaa.alaska.edu.

GILLQUIST, PETER EDWARD, church organization executive; b. Mpls, Minn, July 13, 1938; s. William Parker and Louise E. (Blitsch) G.; m. Marilyn Joyce Grinder; children: Wendy, Gregory, Ginger, Terri Beth, Heidi, Peter Jon. BA, U. Minn., 1960; postgrad., Dallas Sem., 1960-61, Wheaton (Ill.) Grad. Sch., 1961-62. Regional dir. Campus Crusade, Chgo., 1960-68; dir. devel., exec. v.p. Found., U. Memphis, Tenn., 1969-72; sr. editor Thomas Nelson Publ., Nashville, 1975-86; dir. missions Antiochian Orthodox Ch., Santa Barbara, Calif., 1987—. Presiding bishop Evang. Orthodox Ch., Santa Barbara, 1979-87; pub. Conciliar Press, Ben Lomond, Calif., 1985—; v.p. Orthodox Christian Mission Ctr., St. Augustine, Fla., 1995-01. Author: Becoming Orthodox, 1989, Metropolitan Philip, 1991; editor: Coming Home, 1992, Orthodox Study Bible, 1993. Planning dir. Memphis Mayor's Drug Commn., 1970-72. Mem. Four Freshmen Soc., Order of St. Ignatius, Sigma Alpha Epsilon (nat. chaplain). Office: Antiochian Orthodox Ch Dept Missions-Evangelism 777 Camino Pescadero Santa Barbara CA 93117-4908

GILLULY, MARY SEANA, not-for-profit executive; d. Suzanne Hart and Richard Hart Gilluly; m. Kevin Noel Brensdal, Nov. 29, 1997; 1 child, Remi Trottier. BA, Carroll Coll., 1986; EdB, Mont. State U., Billings, 1992, MEd, 1994. Counselor supr. Yellowstone County Youth Svcs. Ctr., Billings, 1990—94; dir., field coordination and rsch. Senator Conrad Burns Campaign, Billings, 1994; coord. adult edn. Plentywood Pub. Schs., Plentywood, Mont., 1995—97; exec. dir. The Family Tree Ctr., Billings, 1997—. Dir. Mont. Coun. for Families, Missoula, Mont., 1998—; pres. elect Nat. Parent Aide Network, Toledo, 2003—, regional rep., Billings, Mont., 1999—; steering com. mem. Billings Promise, Billings, Mont., 2000—; dir. Treasure Trails Girl Scout Coun., Billings, Mont., 1998—2000. Contbr. articles. Dir. Treasure Trails Girls Scout Coun., Billings, 1998—2000; pres. elect Nat. Parent Aide Network, Toledo, 2003—; steering com. Billings Promise, 2000—; regional rep. Nat. Parent Aide Network, Toledo, 1999—; advocacy com. chair Mont. Coun. for Families, Missoula, 1998—. Mem.: Exchg. Club. Roman Catholic. Avocations: reading, outdoor activities. Home: 9640 McCranie Rd Shepherd MT 59079 Office: The Family Tree Ctr 1001 N 30th St Billings MT 59101 Office Fax: 406-256-3014. E-mail: familytree@mcn.net.

GILMAN, ALAN B. restaurant company executive; b. South Bend, Ind., Sept. 24, 1930; s. Sol M. and Lee R. (Rintzler) G.; m. Phyllis Schrager, Feb. 16, 1951; children: Bruce, Jeffrey, Lynn. AB with highest honors (Raymond Charles

Stoltz scholar), Ind. U., 1952, MBA (John H. Edwards fellow), 1954. With Lazarus Co. div. Federated Dept. Stores, Inc., Columbus, Ohio, 1954-64, div. mdse. mgr., 1961-64; with Sanger Harris div., 1965-74, chmn. bd., chief exec. officer, 1970-74, corp. v.p., 1974-80; with Abraham & Straus div., 1975-80, chmn. bd., chief exec. officer, 1978-80; pres. Murjani Internat. Ltd., N.Y.C., 1980-85; pvt. investor, 1985-87; chmn. At Ease of Newport Beach (Calif.) Inc., 1988-91; pres., chief exec. officer Consol. Products Inc., 1992—, Steak 'n Shake Inc. Vice chmn. bd. dirs. Ind. U. Found., nat. chmn. ann. giving, 1983, mem. presdl. search com., 1987-88; chmn. dean's adv. coun. Ind. U. Grad. Sch. Bus., 1976-86; mem. dean's adv. coun. Coll. Arts and Scis., Ind. U., 1989—, pres.'s cabinet, 1995; bd. dirs., pres., mem. exec. com. Greater N.Y. Fund-United Way, 1984-87; bd. dirs., mem. exec. com., chmn. strategic planning com. United Way of N.Y.C., 1982-88; dir. Corp. Comty. Coun., Indpls., Greater Indpls. Progress Com., Kelley Restaurants, Inc. Recipient Humanitarian of Yr. award Juvenile Diabetes Found., 1979, Disting. Alumni Svc. award Ind. U., 1996. Mem. Young Pres. Orgn. 49'er, Ind. U. Acad. Alumni Fellows, World Bus. Council, Phi Beta Kappa Assocs., Phi Alpha Theta, Beta Gamma Sigma (charter mem. dirs. table) Office: Consolidated Products Inc 500 Century Bldg 36 S Penn Ave Indianapolis IN 46204 *Value intellectual curiosity, an open mind, the greater import of tomorrow over yesterday, and recognize rapid change as the definition of opportunity while maintaining a sense of humor and honest humility.*

GILMAN, ALFRED GOODMAN, pharmacologist, educator; b. New Haven, July 1, 1941; s. Alfred and Mabel (Schmidt) Gilman; m. Kathryn Hedlund, Sept. 21, 1963; children: Amy, Anne, Edward. BS, Yale U., 1962; MD, PhD, Case Western Res. U., 1969; DSc (hon.), U. Chgo., 1991, Case Western Res. U., 1995; DMS (hon.), Yale U., 1997; DSc (hon.), U. Miami, 1999. Pharmacology rsch. assoc. NIH, Bethesda, Md., 1969—71; from asst. prof. to assoc. prof. pharmacology U. Va., Charlottesville, 1971—77, prof., 1977—81, dir. med. sci. tng. program, 1979—81; prof. pharmacology, chmn. dept. U. Tex. Southwestern Med. Ctr., Dallas, 1981—, Raymond and Ellen Willie disting. chmn. molecular neuropharmacology, 1987—, regental prof., 1994—; chmn. steering com. The Alliance for Cellular Signaling, 2000—. Mem. pharmacology study sect. NIH, 1977—81, mem. nat. adv. gen. med. scis. coun., 1992—95; bd. sci. counselors Nat. Heart, Lung and Blood Inst. NIH, 1982—86; sci. adv. com. Am. Cancer Soc., N.Y.C., 1982—86; adv. com. Lucille P. Markey Charitable Trust, Miami, 1984—96; sci. rev. bd. Howard Hughes Med. Inst., Bethesda, 1986—93; dir. Regeneron Pharmaceutics, 1989—, Eli Lilly and Co., Inc., 1995—; mem. vis. com. Sch. Medicine Case Western Reserve U., 1995—99; mem. sci. adv. bd. Huntsman Cancer Inst., U. Utah, 1995—2000, Ernest Gallo Clinic and Rsch. Ctr., U. Calif., San Francisco, 1996—2001. Editor The Pharmacological Basis of Therapeutics, 1975, 1980, 1985, 1990, consulting editor, 1996; consulting editor: The Pharmacological Basis of Therapeutics, 2001; contbr. over 240 articles to profl. jours. Recipient Poul Edvard Poulsson award, Norwegian Pharmacology Soc., 1982, Gairdner Found. Internat. Award, Can., 1984, Albert Lasker Basic Med. Rsch. award, 1989, Passano Sr. award, Passano Found., 1990, Waterford Biomed. Sci. award, Scripps Clinic and Rsch. Found., 1990, Basic Sci. Rsch. prize, Am. Heart Assn., 1990, City of Medicine award, Durham, N.C., 1991, Ciba-Geigy Drew award, 1991, Nobel prize in Physiology or Medicine, 1994, ACP award, 1995, Disting. Alumnus award, Case Western Reserve U., 1995, Am. Acad. Achievement award, 1995, Med. Honor award, Am. Cancer Soc., 1995. Mem.: NAS (Richard Lounsbery award 1987), Am. Acad. Arts and Scis., Inst. Medicine NAS. Am. Soc. Biol. Chemistry, Am. Soc. Pharmacology and Exptl. Therapeutics (John J. Abel award in pharmacology 1975, Louis S. Goodman and Alfred Gilman award 1990, Torald Sollman award 1997). Office: U Tex Southwestern Med Ctr Dept Pharmacology 5323 Harry Hines Blvd Dallas TX 75390-9041 E-mail: alfred.gilman@utsouthwestern.edu.

GILMAN, BENJAMIN ARTHUR, former congressman, lawyer; b. Poughkeepsie, N.Y., Dec. 6, 1922; s. Harry and Esther (Gold) G.; m. Jane Prizant, Oct. 19, 1952 (div. 1978); children: Jonathan, Harrison, Susan, David (dec.), Ellen (dec.); m. Rita Gail Keller Kelhoffer, Nov. 9, 1984 (div. 1996); m. Georgia Nickles Tingus, Jan. 12, 1997; children: Nicole, Peter. BS, U. Pa., 1946; LLB, N.Y. Law Sch., 1950; degree (hon.), St. Thomas Aquinas Coll., 1977, Mercy Coll., 1984, Yeshiva U., 1995, Dominican Coll., 2003. Bar: N.Y. 1952. Dep. asst. atty. gen. N.Y. Dept. Law, 1952-54, asst. atty. gen., 1954-55; ptnr. Gilman & Gilman, Middletown, N.Y., 1955-72; counsel N.Y. Assembly's Com. on Local Finance, 1956-64; mem. N.Y. State Assembly, 1967-72, 93d-97th Congresses from 26th N.Y. dist., 1972-82, Congress from 20th dist. N.Y., 1983—2002; sr. counsel Finkelstein & Ptnrs., New Windsor, NY, 2003—. Mem. Rep. Congl. Policy Com., 1997-2002; mem. Presdl. Commn. on World Hunger, 1978-80, co-chair Ad-Hoc Com. on Irish Affairs, Republican Task Force on Handicapped and Task Force on Econ. Policy; mem. U.S.-Mex. Consultative Mechanism Subcom. on Narcotics Trafficking; U.S. rep. to 36th session UN Gen. Assembly; mem. Spkrs.'s Task Force on Narcotics; chmn. House Task Force on Missing in Action, 1983-85; mem. World Hunger Yr. Bd.; mem. adv. com. N.Y. State Div. Youth's Start Ctr., 1962-67; mem. N.Y. State Southeastern Water Study Com., 1971-73, Lawyers' Com. for Civil Rights Under Law, 1963-75; mem. adv. com. Otisville Fed. Correctional Instn.; v.p., bd. dirs. Orange County Health Assn.; adv. coun. Lamont-Doherty Geol. Obs., Columbia U., 1979-82; chmn. House Internat. Com. on Fgn. Affairs, 1995-2001. Chmn. bd. dirs. Middletown Little League; bd. visitors U.S. Mil. Acad., 1973-83; lt. col. CAP. With USAAF, 1943-45, Japan. Decorated D.F.C., Air medal. Mem. ABA, D.C. Bar Assn., N.Y. State Bar Assn., Assn. of Bar of City of N.Y., Middletown Bar Assn., Orange County Bar Assn., Assn. Trial Lawyers Am., VFW (past county comdr.), Am. Legion, Masonic War Vets. (lt. comdr.), Jewish War Vets., Forty and Eight, Air Force Assn., Internat. Narcotics Enforcement Officers, N.Y. Law Sch. Alumni (bd. dirs.), N.Y. Soc. in Washington (pres.), Grange, La Société des 40 Hommes et 8 Chevaux, Masons (33 deg.), Shriners (Capitol Hill pres.), Elks. Republican. Jewish. Office: Finkelstein & Ptnrs 103 Executive Dr New Windsor NY 12553 also: The Gilman Group 1625 K St Ste 107 Washington DC 20006

GILMAN, J. PAUL, federal agency administrator; BA, MA, Johns Hopkins U.; PhD Ecology and Evolutionary Biology, John Hopkins U. Staff dir. subcom. energy rsch. and devel. U.S. Senate, Washington; exec. asst. to the Sec. of Energy; assoc. dir. Office Mgmt. and Budget Natural Resources, Energy and Sci.; exec. dir. life scis. and agrl. divsns. Nat. Rsch. Coun., Nat. Acads. Scis. and Engring.; dir. policy planning Celera Genomics, Rockville, Md.; asst. adminstr. rsch. and devel., sci. advisor to the adminstr. EPA, Washington, 2002—. Office: EPA Rsch and Devel 1200 Pennsylvania Ave NW MC 8101R Washington DC 20460

GILMAN, JOHN JOSEPH, research scientist; b. St. Paul, Dec. 22, 1925; s. Alexander Falk and Florence Grace (Colby) G.; m. Pauline Marie Harms, June 17, 1950 (div. Dec. 1968); children: Pamela Ann, Gregory George, Cheryl Elizabeth; m. Gretchen Marie Sutter, June 12, 1976; 1 son, Brian Alexander. BS, Ill. Inst. Tech., 1946, MS, 1948; PhD, Columbia, 1952. Research metallurgist Gen. Electric Co., Schenectady, 1952-60; prof. engring. Brown U., Providence, 1960-63; prof. physics and metallurgy U. Ill., Urbana, 1963-68; dir. Materials Research Center Allied Chem. Corp., Morristown, N.J., 1968-78; dir. Corp. Devel. Center, 1978-80; mgr. corp. research Amoco Co. (Ind.), Naperville, Ill., 1980-85; assoc. dir. Lawrence Berkeley Lab./U. Calif., Calif., 1985-87; sr. scientist Lawrence Berkeley Lab., Calif., 1987-93; adj. prof. UCLA, 1993—. Author: Micromechanics of Flow in Solids, 1969, Inventivity-The Art and Science of Research Management, 1992, Electronic Basis of the Strength of Materials, 2003; editor: The Art and Science of Growing Crystals, 1963, Fracture of Solids (with D.C. Drucker), 1963, Atomic and Electronic Structures of Metals, 1967, Metallic Glasses, 1973, Energetic Materials, 1993; editl. bd. Jour. Applied Physics, 1969-72; contbg. editor Materials Tech., 1994-99; contbr. over 325 papers, articles to tech. jours. Served as Ensign USNR, 1943-46. Recipient Mathewson gold medal Am. Inst. Metal Engrs., 1959, Disting. Service award Alumni Assn. Ill. Inst. Tech., 1962, Application to Practice award, 1985. Fellow AAAS, Am. Phys. Soc., The Materials Soc., Am. Soc. for Metals (Campbell lectr. 1966); mem. Nat. Acad. Engring., Phi Kappa Phi, Tau Beta Pi. Home: 2852 Forrester Dr Los Angeles CA 90064-4662 Office: UCLA 6532 Boelter Hl Los Angeles CA 90095-0001 E-mail: gilman@seas.ucla.edu.

GILMAN, JOHN RICHARD, JR., retired management consultant, sculptor; b. Malden, Mass., July 6, 1925; s. John Richard and Philomene (Gradie) F.; m. Julia Streeter, Feb. 6, 1960; children: Derek, Susan. AB, Harvard U., 1945; postgrad., Georgetown U., 1945-46; student, Art Students League, N.Y.C., 1953-55, Sculpture Ctr., 1972-76; MSW, NYU, 1983. Diplomate Am. Bd. Clin. Social Work; lic. clin. social worker, N.Y., R.I. Dir. publicity John H. Breck, Inc., Springfield, Mass., 1949-53, asst. advt. mgr., 1950-53, dir. new products, 1955-56, tech. dir., 1956-63; dir. new products Acco. Labs., Am. Cyanamid Co., Wayne, N.J., 1963; treas., exec. v.p. August Sauter of Am., Inc., N.Y.C., 1964, pres., CEO, 1965-79; pres. John R. Gilman Inc., N.Y.C., 1980-94, ret., 1994. Dir. Slee Internat., Inc., N.Y.C., Finex Mining Co., Reno; assoc. Fisher Cons. Internat. Inc. N.Y.C., 1980-86, C.M. Oppenheim & Co. Inc. N.Y.C., 1981-86; cons. Right Assocs., Inc., Providence, 1986-89. Filmmaker: Water, 1950, Dear Nancy, 1953; sculpture exhibitions include Convergence Internat., Providence, R.I., 1998, Von Liebig Art Ctr., Naples, Fla., 1999, Maine Art Gallery, Wiscasset, Maine, 1999, Winners Circle Art Coun., Fla., 2001. Trustee Sculpture Ctr., N.Y.C., 1977-90, mem. exhbn. com., 1980-82, v.p., 1983-86; trustee Augustus Saint-Gaudens Meml., N.Y.C., 1982—, 1st v.p., mem. exec. com., chmn. facilities com., 1988-91, pres., 1991-93, chmn. exhbn. com., 2000—, mem., 1994—, co-chmn. 2000—. mem. fin. com., 1988—, chmn. fin. com., 1998-2000, mem. meml. music com., 1997—; bd. dirs. Maine Art Gallery, Wiscasset, 1998—, chmn. exhbn. com., 1999. Served with USNR, 1943-46. Mem. Internat. Sculpture Soc., Art Students League (life), Art Club Washington D.C., Harvard Club (N.Y.C., Boston), Nat. Arts Club (N.Y.C.). Home and Office: 770 Bentwater Cir 101 Naples FL 34108-6776 also: 3 Waters Edge Ln Belfast ME 04915 6053 E-mail: jgill39@aol.com.

GILMAN, KAREN FRENZEL, legal assistant; b. Syracuse, N.Y., Jan. 11, 1947; d. Charles Henry and Cora Adell (Haith) Frenzel; m. Lawrence Sanford Gilman, June 5, 1970 (div. Feb. 9, 1977). AAS in Horticulture, SUNY, Morrisville, 1967; BS, Cornell U., 1969, MS in Floriculture and Ornamental Hort., 1971; attended, Syracuse Univ. Coll., 1983. Cert. legal asst. Floral designer Fortino of Fayetteville (N.Y.), 1965-69, 76-79, 81-84, Fallon's Florist, Raleigh, N.C., 1973-74; salesperson Finley Fine Jewelry, N.Y.C., 1979-80; legal asst. Agway, Inc., Dewitt, N.Y., 1984; legal asst. gen. legal Carrier Corp., Syracuse, N.Y., 1984-91, legal asst. intellectual property, 1992—. Mem. adv. bd. legal asst. program Syracuse U. Coll., 1986-90. Contbr. articles to profl. jours. Henry Strong Denison fellow, 1969. Mem. Pi Alpha Xi, Phi Theta Kappa. Avocations: gardening, biking. Office: Carrier Corp PO Box 4800 Carrier Pkwy Syracuse NY 13221

GILMAN, KENNETH B. retail executive; Formerly v.p., corp. contr. The Limited Inc., Columbus, Ohio, exec. v.p., chief fin. officer, 1987—93, vice chmn., chief adminstrv. officer, 1993—2001; vice chmn. Intimate Brands, Inc., Columbus, Ohio, 1998; CEO Lane Bryant, Reynoldsburg, Ohio, 2001; pres., CEO Asbury Automotive Group, Stamford, Conn., 2001—. Office: Three Landmark Square Ste 500 Stamford CT 06901*

GILMAN, PATRICIA ANN, artist, educator; b. Macon, Mo., July 2, 1929; d. Vernon Edward and Vangie (Crawford) Leist; m. B. Dale Gilman, Dec. 24, 1950; children: John David, Sharron Ann, Mark Crawford. BS in Edn., Mo. U., 1951, MA in Arts Edn., 1971. Art tchr. Mexico (Mo.) Pub. Schs., 1952-59, Kunsmiller Jr. H.S., Denver, 1959; art cons. grades K-6 City of St. Charles, Mo., 1968-95; mem. adj. faculty art edn. Lindenwood Coll., St. Charles, 1972-80, St. Charles County C.C., 1980-85, 87-96; instr. various media St. Peters (Mo.) Cultural Arts Ctr., 2000—04; moderator Presbyterian women St. Charles Presbyterian Ch. Illustrator: E is for Everybody (Nancy Politte), 1976; portraitist. Mem. St. Charles County Arts Coun.; moderator Presbyn. Women St. Charles Presbyn. Ch., 2002—. Recipient commendation, Mo. State Senate, Mo. Ho. of Reps. Mem. Nat. Art Educators Assn., Mo. Art Educators Assn. (Art Cons. of Yr. 1995), Mo. State Tchrs. Assn. (local pres., dist. pres. 1970-73, legis. com. 1973-75), P.E.O. Sisterhood (pres. 1982-84). Republican. Presbyterian. Avocations: family, church activities, seeking wisdom. Home: 4002 West Dr Saint Peters MO 63376

GILMAN, RICHARD CARLETON, retired college president; b. Cambridge, Mass., July 28, 1923; s. George Phillips Brooks and Karen Elise (Theller) G.; m. Lucille Young, Aug. 28, 1948 (dec. 1978); children: Marsha, Bradley Morris, Brian Potter, Blair Tucker; m. Sarah Gale, Dec. 28, 1984 (dec. 1986). BA, Dartmouth Coll., 1944; student, New Coll., U. London, Eng., 1947-48; PhD (Borden Parker Bowne fellow), Boston U., 1952, LHD, 1969; LLD, Pomona Coll., 1966, U. So. Calif., 1968, Coll. Idaho, 1968; LHD, Chapman Coll., 1984, Occidental Coll., 1988. Teaching fellow religion Dartmouth, 1948; mem. faculty Colby Coll., 1950-56, assoc. prof. philosophy, 1955-56; exec. dir. Nat. Council Religion Higher Edn., New Haven, 1956-60; dean coll., prof. philosophy Carleton Coll., 1960-65; pres. Occidental Coll., L.A., 1965-88, pres. emeritus, 1988—; pres., mng. trustee S.W. Mus., L.A., 1994-95. Past mem. bd. dirs. Am. Coun. on Edn., Assn. Am. Colls., Assn. Ind. Calif. Colls. and Univs., Coun. for Fin. Aid to Edn., Coun. on Postsecondary Accreditation, Nat. Coun. Ind. Colls. and Univs., Ind. Coll. Funds Am.; mem. Intergovtl. Adv. Coun. on Edn., 1980-84; mem. president's commn. NCAA, 1984-86; exec. asst., counselor to sec. of edn., 1979-80; mem. Calif. Student Aid Commn., 1988-92. Bbd. dirs. Wellness Cmty.-Foothills, pres., 1996-98; past mem. bd. dirs. Calif. Mus. Found., Cape of Good Hope Found., Exec. Svc. Corp. Calif., S.W. Mus., L.A. World Affairs Coun. Fellow Soc. for Values in Higher Edn.; mem. Calif. C. of C. (past bd. dirs.), Calif. Club L.A., Twilight Club (Pasadena), Phi Beta Kappa. Home: 131 Annandale Rd Pasadena CA 91105-1405 E-mail: rcgilman@earthlink.net.

GILMAN, RICHARD H. newspaper publishing executive; BA in Govt. and Journalism, U. Ariz., 1972; MBA, Harvard Bus. Sch., 1983. Circulation mgr. The New York Times, N.Y.C., 1983—87, responsible for pre-press operations, 1988—91, v.p., 1992, sr. v.p. ops., 1993; pub., chmn. The Boston Globe, Boston, 1999—. Office: Globe Newspapers Co PO Box 2378 135 Morrissey Blvd Boston MA 02107-2378*

GILMAN, RONALD LEE, judge; b. Memphis, Oct. 16, 1942; s. Seymour and Rosalind (Kuzin) Gilman; m. Betsy Dunn, June 11, 1966; children: Laura M., Sherry I. BS, MIT, 1964; JD cum laude, Harvard U., 1967. Bar: Tenn. 1967, U.S. Supreme Ct. 1971. Mem. Farris, Mathews, Gilman, Branan & Hellen, Memphis, 1967—97; judge U.S. Ct. Appeals (6th cir.), 1997—. Judge Tenn. Ct. Judiciary, 1979—87; lectr. trial advocacy U. Memphis Law Sch., 1980—97. Contbr. articles to profl. jours. Regional chmn. ednl. coun. MIT, 1968—88; active Chickasaw coun. Boy Scouts Am., 1993—2000; mem. Leadership Memphis; bd. dirs Memphis Jewish Home, 1984—87. Recipient Sam A. Myar Jr. Meml. award for outstanding svc. to legal profession and cmty., 1981. Mem.: ABA (ho. of dels. 1990—97), Am. Arbitration Assn. (mem. large, complex case panel 1993—97), Tenn. Bar Assn. (spkr. ho. of dels. 1985—87, pres. 1990—91), Memphis Bar Assn. (pres. 1987), Am. Coll. Trust and Estate Counsel, Am. Judicature Soc., Am. Law Inst., 6th Cir. Jud. Conf. (life). Democrat. Jewish. Office: Fed Bldg 167 N Main St Ste 1176 Memphis TN 38103-1824

GILMAN, SANDER LAWRENCE, German language educator; b. Buffalo, Feb. 21, 1944; s. William and Rebecca (Helf) G.; m. Marina von Eckardt, Dec. 28, 1969; children: Daniel, Samuel. BA, Tulane U., 1963, PhD, 1968, postgrad., U. Berlin and U. Munich, Ger.; LLD (hon.), U. Toronto, Ont., 1997 Lectr. German St. Mary's Dominican Coll., New Orleans, 1963-64; instr. Dillard U., New Orleans, 1967-68; asst. prof. Case Western Res. U., 1968-69; mem. faculty Cornell U., 1969-94, prof. German, 1976-94, prof. Near Eastern studies, 1984-91, prof. humane studies, 1984-87, Goldwin Smith prof., 1987-94, chmn. dept. German lit., 1974-81, 83-84; fellow dept. psychiatry Cornell U. Med. Coll., 1977-78; prof. history of psychiatry Cornell U., 1978-94; prof. German, history of sci. and psychiatry U. Chgo., 1994-2000, Henry R. Luce prof. Liberal Arts in Human Biology, 1995-2000, disting. svc. prof., 1999-2000; disting. prof. liberal arts & scis. and medicine U. Ill., Chgo., 2000—. O'Connor prof. Colgate U., 1982-83; Mellon prof. Tulane U., 1988, Old Dominion prof. English, Princeton U., 1988; Northrup Frye prof. of comparative lit. U. Toronto, Ont., Can., 1989; vis. prof. German lit. Free U. Berlin, 1989; vis. hist. scholar Nat. Libr. Medicine, 1991-92; vis. Rudolph prof. Jewish studies Syracuse (N.Y.) U., 1992; vis. prof. U. Witwatersrand, South Africa, 1994, U. Potsdam, 1996, U. Cape Town, 1996, Ctr. for Advanced Studies in the Behavioral Scis., 1996-97, Getty Inst. for Art and the Humanities, 1998, Am. Acad., Berlin, 2000-01. Author, editor.: Bertolt Brecht's Berlin, 1975, Nietzschean Parody, 1976, The Face of Madness, 1976, Klingers Werke, 1978, On Blackness Without Blacks, 1982, Begegnungen mit Nietzsche, 1981, Difference and Pathology, 1985, Jewish Self-Hatred, 1986, Oscar Wilde's London, 1987, Conversations with Nietzsche, 1987, Diseases and Representation, 1989, Sexuality: An Illustrated History, 1989, Nietzsche on Rhetoric and Language, 1989, The Jew's Body, 1991, Inscribing the Other, 1991, Rasse, Seuche, Sexualitat, 1992, Freud, Race, Gender, 1993, The Case of Sigmund Freud, 1993, Reading Freud Reading, 1993, Reemerging Jewish Culture in Germany, 1994, Jews in Today's German Culture, 1995, Health and Illness, 1995, Franz Kafka: The Jewish Patient, 1996, L'Autre et Le Moi, 1996, Smart Jews, 1996, Yale Companion to Jewish Writing and Thought in German Culture, 1997, Love and Marriage with Death, 1998, Creating Beauty to Cure the Soul, 1998, Making the Body Beautiful, 1999, Jurek Becker: Die Biographie, 2002; mem. editl. bd. Diacritics, 1971-72, Lessing Yearbook, 1974—, German Quar., 1977-86, Confinia Psychiatrica, 1978-80. Guggenheim fellow, 1972-73, IREX exch. fellow German Democratic Republic, 1976, Soc. for Humanities faculty fellow Cornell U., 1981-82, Nat. Libr. Medicine sr. historian, fellow, 1990-91, Ctr. for the Adv. Study of the Behaviorial Scis. fellow, Stanford, 1996-97, Am. Acad., Berlin, 2000—. Mem. MLA (pres. 1995), Lessing Soc., Am. Assn. Tchrs. German, Soc. Internat. d'Études Littéraires et Psychiatres, Internat. Assn. Germanists. Democrat. Jewish. Home: 5701 S Dorchester Ave Chicago IL 60637-1726 E-mail: sander34@aol.com.

GILMAN, SHELDON GLENN, lawyer; b. Cleve., July 20, 1943; BBA, Ohio U., 1965; JD, Case Western Res. U., 1967. Bar: Ohio 1967, Ky. 1971, Ind. 1982, Fla. 1984, D.C. 1985, Tenn. 1985, U.S. Supreme Ct. 1987. Assoc./ptnr. Louisville law firms, 1972—; ptnr. Lynch, Cox, Gilman & Mahan, P.S.C., Louisville, 1987—. Gen. counsel Louisville Assn. Life Underwriters, 1977, 78, 90; adj. prof. law U. of Louisville Sch. of Law. Author: Kentucky Estate Planning, 2d edit., 2003, (jour. article) Am. Coll. of Trust and Estate Counsel Jour., 2003, Kentucky Bench and Bar, 2003, (mag. article) Trusts and Estates, 2003. Bd. dirs., chmn. Louisville Minority Bus. Resource Ctr., 1975-80; pres. Congregation Adath Jeshurun, 1986-88; bd. dirs., v.p., sec. Louisville Orch., 1982-85; bd. dirs. City of Devondale, Ky., 1976, United Synagogue of Cons. Judaism, N.Y., 1989-98, also pres. Ohio Valley region. With JAGC, AUS, 1968-71. Fellow Am. Coll. Trust and Estate Counsel, Am. Bar Found.; mem. ACLU (bd. dirs. 1998—), Ky. Bar Assn. (ethics com. 1982—, ethics hotline com. 1990), Louisville Employee Benefit Council (pres. 1980). Office: Lynch Cox Gilman & Mahan 400 W Market St Ste 2200 Louisville KY 40202-3354 E-mail: SGilman@lcgandm.com.

GILMAN, SID, neurologist; b. L.A., Oct. 19, 1932; s. Morris and Sarah Rose (Cooper) G.; m. Carol G. Barbour. BA, UCLA, 1954; MD, 1957, FRCP, 2001. Intern UCLA Hosp., 1957-58; resident in neurology Boston City Hosp., 1960-63; from instr. to assoc. in neurology Harvard Med. Sch., 1965-68; from asst. prof. to prof. neurology Columbia U., N.Y.C., 1968-76; H. Houston Merritt prof. neurology, 1976-77; William J. Herdman prof., chair dept. neurology U. Mich., Ann Arbor, 1977—. Cons. VA Hosp., Ann Arbor, 1977—; mem. peripheral and ctrl. nervous sys. drugs adv. com. FDA, 1983-85, 86-87, 90-94, chmn., 1996-2000, cons., 2000—; adj. attending neurologist Henry Ford Hosp., Detroit; mem. chronic disease adv. com. Mich. Dept. Pub. Health, 1988-94; mem. neurol. sci. rsch. and tng. com. NIH, 1971-73, mem. neurol. disorders program project B com., 1976-80, mem. sci. programs adv. com. Nat. Inst. Neurol. Diseases, Communicative Disorders and Stroke, 1982-84, mem. nat. adv. neurol. disorders and stroke coun., 1994-97; mem. clin. trials subcom. Nat. Adv. Neurol. Disorders and Stroke Coun., 2001—; dir. Mich. Alzheimer's Disease Rsch. Ctr., 1991—; mem. rsch. adv. coun. United Cerebral Palsy Found.; mem. sci. adv. coun. Nat. Ataxia Found., Nat. Amyotrophic Lateral Sclerosis Found., Inc.; mem. profl. adv. bd. Epilepsy Found. Am.; mem. rsch. adv. com. Nat. Multiple Sclerosis Soc., 1986-90; mem. exec. bd. Nat. Coalition for Rsch., 1989-95, Nat. Found. for Brain Rsch., 1989-95; mem. rsch. adv. com. Dana Alliance; mem. sci. adv. bd. Merck, Inc., 2000-04, PPD Devel., 1999—, INC Rsch., 2000—; Henry Russel lectr. U. Mich., 2001. Author: (with J.R. Bloedel and R. Lechtenberg) Disorders of the Cerebellum, 1981, (with S.W. Newman) Manter and Gatz's Essentials of Clinical Neuroanatomy and Neurophysiology, 10th edit., 2003, (with J.C. Mazziotta) Clinical Brain Imaging: Principles and Applications, 1992, Clinical Examination of the Nervous System, 2000; sect. editor editl. bd. Exptl. Neurology, Current Opinion in Neurology and Neurosurgery, Neurology, Annals Neurology, Jour. Neuropathology and Exptl. Neurology, Neurobase Arbor Pub. Co.; editor-in-chief MedLink Neurology, 1992, Contemporary Neurology Series, 1995—, Neurology Network Commentary, 1996-2000, Lancet Neurology Network, 2000-02, Exptl. Neurology, 2003—; contbr. articles to profl. jours. Dir. Mich. Dem. Program, 1994-2000. With USPHS, 1958-60. Recipient Lucy G. Moses prize Columbia U., 1973, Weinstein Goldenson award United Cerebral Palsy Assn., 1981, UCLA Alumni Profl. Achievement award, 1992, UCLA Med. Alumni Profl. Achievement award, 1992. Fellow AAAS, Royal Soc. of Medicine, Royal Coll. Physicians, Am. Acad. Arts and Scis.; mem. Am. Neurol. Assn. (hon.; 1st v.p. 1985-86, pres.-elect 1987-88, pres. 1988-89), Mich. Neurol. Assn. (pres. 1987-88), Soc. Clin. Investigation, Am. Physiol. Soc., Am. Assn. Neuropathologists, Soc. Neurosci., Am. Acad. Neurology (vice chmn. geriatric neurology subcom. 1992-94, chmn. 1994-96, chmn. Decade of Brain com. 1990-95), Am. Epilepsy Soc., Assn. Rsch. in Nervous and Mental Disease, Inst. Medicine, Nat. Acad. Scis., The Nat. Acads. (nat. assoc.), Phi Beta Kappa, Alpha Omega Alpha. Home: 3411 Geddes Rd Ann Arbor MI 48105-2518 Office: U Mich Dept Neurology Ann Arbor MI 48109 E-mail: sgilman@umich.edu.

GILMAN, TODD SEACRIST, librarian, scholar, educator, musician; b. Cambridge, Mass., Feb. 15, 1965; s. Sidney and Linda Louise (Lamlein) G. BA, U. Mich., 1987; MA, U. Toronto, 1988, PhD, 1994; MS, Simmons Coll., 2001. Artistic dir. Arbor Oak Trio, Toronto, 1988-96; lectr., tutor, writing cons. U. Toronto, 1994-96; lectr. Boston U., 1996-97; vis. fellow Houghton Libr., Harvard U., Cambridge, Mass., 1996-97; lectr. dept. English, Suffolk U., Boston, 1997-99; lectr. lit. sect. MIT, Cambridge, 1998-99; libr. assoc. collection maintenance and pub. svcs. Mus. Libr., Mus. of Fine Arts, Boston, 2000-01; libr. for lit. in English, Sterling Meml. Libr., Yale U., New Haven, 2001—. Adj. asst. prof. dept. info. and libr. sci. and dept. English So. Conn. State U., 2002—. Book reviews editor: Yale Jour. Law and the Humanities, 2002—; contbr. articles to profl. jours. Bd. dirs. Toronto Early Music Ctr., 1993-95. Fletcher Jones fellow The Huntington Libr., San Marino, Calif., 1995, fellow Ezra Stiles Coll., Yale U., 2002-. Mem. ALA, MLA (field bibliographer English lang and lit. sect.), AAUP, Assn. Coll. and Rsch. Librs., Viola Gamba Soc. Am.-N.E., Am. Soc. 18th Century Studies (McMaster fellow 1994), Am. Handel Soc. (rsch. fellow 1998), Soc. Theatre Rsch. (travel grantee 1998), Early Music Am., Beta Phi Mu. Democrat. Office: Yale U PO Box 208240 New Haven CT 06520-8240 E-mail: toddgilman@aol.com.

GILMARTIN, CLARA T. volunteer; b. East Stroudsburg, Pa., Jan. 23, 1922; d. Harry and Clarissa (Snearley) Treible; m. John Gilmartin, Jan. 18, 1945 (dec. Feb. 1956); children: Ronald, Donald; m. William Gilmartin, Sept. 8, 2002. BA, Rutgers U., 1961, MA, 1966. Elem. sch. tchr. Union Beach (N.J.) Pub. Sch., 1956-61; lang. arts tchr. Holmdel Village (N.J.) Intermediate Sch., 1961-82; Fulbright exch. tchr. New Zealand, 1973-74; mem. adv. bd. Juvenile Conf. Com., 1986—. Chair bd. trustees Grace Meth. Ch., Union Beach, 1997—. Mem. Monmouth County Ret. Educators Assn., Am. Legion (Post 321 Color Guard, scholarship com., trustee, chaplain), Triad. Democrat. Home. PO Box 143 Keyport NJ 07735-0143

GILMARTIN, RAYMOND V. pharmaceutical company executive; b. Washington, Mar. 6, 1941; m. Gladys Higham; 3 children. BS in Elect. Engring., Union Coll., 1963; MBA, Harvard U., 1968. Sr. cons. Arthur D. Little Inc., 1968-76; v.p. corp. planning Becton Dickinson & Co., Paramus, N.J., 1976-79, pres. Becton Dickinson divsn., 1979-87, group pres., 1982-83, sr. v.p., 1983-86, exec. v.p., 1986-87, pres. Franklin Lakes, N.J., 1987-94, CEO, 1989-94, also bd. dirs.; chmn., pres., CEO Merck, Whitehouse Station, NJ, 1994—. Bd. dirs. Gen. Mills, Inc., Microsoft Corp.; chmn. Inter-faculty initiative in Health Policy. Trustee Valley Health Systems, Inc., Ridgewood, NJ, Healthcare Inst. NJ, Alliance for Healthcare Reform, Am. Enterprise Inst.; bd. dirs. Coll. Fund/United Negro Coll. Fund, Pharm. Rsch. and Mfrs. Am., Healthcare Leadership Coun.; active Bus. Coun., Bus. Roundtable, Pres. Export Coun.; exec. com. Coun. on Competitiveness. Mem.: Internat. Fed. Pharm. Mfrs. Assn. (chmn.). Office: Merck & Co 1 Merck Dr Whitehouse Station NJ 08889-0100

GILMER, ROBERT, mathematics educator; b. Pontotoc, Miss., July 3, 1938; s. Robert William and Lucy Marie (Jernigan) G.; m. Rachel Grace Colson, Aug. 24, 1963; children: David Patrick, Stephen Douglas. Student, Itawamba Jr.

Coll., 1955-56; BS, Miss. State U., 1958; MS, La. State U., 1960, PhD, 1961. Instr., Miss. State U., Starkville, 1958, vis. prof., 1962; research instr. La. State U., Baton Rouge, 1961-62; vis. lectr. U. Wis., Madison, 1962-63; mem. faculty Fla. State U., Tallahassee, 1963—, prof. math., 1968—, Robert O. Lawton Disting. prof., 1981—. Vis. prof. Latrobe U., Bundoora, Victoria, Australia, 1974, U. Tex., Austin, 1976-77; vis. rsch. prof. U. Conn., Storrs, 1982; visitor Inst. for Advanced Study, 1990; vis. scholar U. N.C., Chapel Hill, 1997. Author: Multiplicative Ideal Theory, 1967, 72, 92, Commutative Semigroup Rings, 1984; also articles; assoc. editor Am. Math. Mo., 1971-73; editorial bd. Jour. Communications in Algebra, 1974-85. Named Barrett Meml. Lectr., U. Tenn., Knoxville, 1994; Office Naval Rsch. fellow, 1962-63; Alfred P. Sloan Found. fellow, 1965-67; NSF grantee, 1965-89; Fulbright sr. scholar to Australia, 1974. Mem. Am. Math. Soc., Math. Assn. Am. (gov. Fla. sect. 1986-89, cert. meritorious svc. 1992). Baptist. Home: 2414 Perez Ave Tallahassee FL 32304-1329 E-mail: gilmer@math.fsu.edu.

GILMER, ROBERT WILLIAM, III, economist; b. Amarillo, Tex., July 4, 1946; s. Robert William and Gloria Zoe (Vinson) G.; m. Maryann Theodore Gilmer, Aug. 30, 1969; 1 child, Anna. BA, U. Tex., El Paso, 1968; MA, U. Tex., Austin, 1970, PhD, 1973. Economist Inst. Def. Analysis, Arlington, Va., 1973-76, Inst. Energy Analysis, Oak Ridge, Tenn., 1976-82; sr. economist TVA, Knoxville, Tenn., 1982-89; rsch. prof. Ball State U., Muncie, Ind., 1986-87; sr. economist, v.p. Fed. Res. Bank Dallas, Houston, 1989—2002, v.p. in charge El Paso, Tex., 2003—. Cons. U. Tenn., Knoxville, 1989—90. Contbr. articles to profl. jours. Mem. Internat. Assn. Energy Economists, Nat. Asns. Bus. Economists, Am. Econ. Assn., So. Econ. Assn. Home: 3811 Sweetgum Hill Ln Humble TX 77345-1085 Office: Fed Res Bank Dallas El Paso Br 301 E Main St El Paso TX 79901

GILMORE, ARTHUR WARHAM, aeronautical engineer, engineering educator; b. Louisville, Oct. 5, 1920; s. Frank Foster and Annie (Miller) G.; m. Beverly Mary Snow, Dec. 11, 1948; children— David, Beverly, Richard, Paul. BS in Aeroengring., Rensselaer Poly. Inst., 1942; MS, U. Colo., 1956. Registered profl. engr., NY Instr. aeroengring. Rensselaer Poly. Inst., Troy, NY, 1942-43; aerodynamicist Consol. Vultee, Fort Worth, 1943-45; asst. product engr. Sperry Gyroscope, Lake Success, NY, 1945-47; sect. head, dir. Grumman Aero Corp., Bethpage, NY, 1948-77; dir. grad. studies indsl. mgmt. SUNY-Stony Brook, 1978— ; cons. L.I. Lighting Co., Hicksville, NY, 1978-79, Am. Assn. Engring. Soc., NYC, 1977-84, Eaton Corp. AIL div., Deer Park, NY, 1984-85. Author numerous tech. papers and reports. Chmn. Engring. Manpower Commn., 1975-77; mem. Suffolk County Econ. Devel. Com., 1979-80; mem. Nat. Commn. Engring. Manpower, 1974. Mem. Sigma Xi (assoc.). Republican. Episcopalian. Avocations: boating, swimming, hiking. Home: 316 Oakwood Rd Port Jefferson NY 11777-1460

GILMORE, CLARENCE PERCY, writer, magazine editor; b. Baton Rouge, Feb. 8, 1926; s. Clarence Percy and Clara (Cobb) G.; m. V. Elaine Oliver, 1985; children: Robert Dillard, Patricia Anne. Student, La. State U., 1942-44, 46-48. Reporter various radio, TV stas., 1948-56; free-lance mag. writer, 1956—; sci. editor Metromedia TV, 1967-84; exec. editor Popular Sci. Mag., 1971-80, editor-in-chief, 1980-89; dep. editorial dir. Times Mirror Mags., N.Y.C., 1989-92, ret., 1992. Cons. in field. With USNR, 1944-46. Recipient Claude Bernard sci. journalism award Nat. Soc. Med. Rsch., 1969, Albert and Mary Lasker Found. award, 1969, Howard W. Blakeslee award Am. Heart Assn., 1969, Spl. Commendation for med. journalism AMA, 1969, 70, Sci. Writing award for physics and astronomy Am. Inst. Physics, 1970, Sci. Writing award AAAS, 1980. Home: 19725 Creek Round Ave Baton Rouge LA 70817-1915 E-mail: kgilmore@cox.net.

GILMORE, CONNIE SUE, educator; b. Nashville, Sept. 3, 1951; d. Earl C. and L. Louise (Coleman) G. AA, Stephens Coll., 1971; BA, Vanderbilt U., 1973; MA, Cumberland U., 1992, postgrad., 1992—. Cert. tchr., Tenn. Tchr. Bellevue Presbyn. Ch., Nashville, 1980-83, dir., 1983-86; presch. tchr. St. Henry's Ch., Nashville, 1985-89, dir., 1986-90; comparative fin. analyst Vanderbilt U., 1998—. Tutor BellSouth Grant Reading Program, Lebanon, Tenn., 1990. Editor, author: Leadership, 1992. Mem. Nat. Assn. for Edn. Young Children, So. Assn. for Children Under Six, Tenn. Assn. for Young Children, Nashville Area Assn. for Young Children, So. Literacy Soc. (charter)., Kappa Delta Pi

GILMORE, GORDON RAY, engineering executive; b. Mesa, Ariz., Sept. 7, 1935; s. Raymond Nelson and Maryette (MacDonald) G.; m. Carol Rae McMahan, 1957 (div. 1966); m. Donna K. Miller, July 28, 1979; stepchildren: Michael, Mitchell, Mathew, Monty. BS in Petroleum Engring., U. Corpus Christi, 1958; MS in Mgmt., Naval Postgrad. Sch., Monterey, Calif., 1968. Registered profl. engr., Wis. Commd. ensign USN, 1958, advanced through grades to capt., 1979; various assignments, Vietnam, Cambodia, Thailand, Japan, 1958-83; ret., 1983; mgr. engring. Lawrence-Allison & Assocs. West Inc., Houston, 1983-84, v.p., 1984-87, pres., 1987-90, also bd. dirs.; v.p. Trafalgar House Inc., Houston, 1987-95; pres. John Brown U.S. Svcs. Inc., Houston, 1993-95. Sustaining mem. Rep. Nat. Com., 1989—; v.p. Fruitvale Ednl. Found. Decorated Legion of Merit, Bronze Star with combat V, Navy-Marine Corps Medal for Heroism; recipient Disting. Svc. award Sec. of Energy, 2000. Mem.: NRA, Soc. Navy Civil Engr. Corps Officers, Ret. Officers Assn., Navy League, Am. Legion. Avocations: hunting, fishing, golf, tennis. Home: 1405 Corte Canalette Bakersfield CA 93309-7129 E-mail: ceccb27@aol.com.

GILMORE, HAYDN LEWIS, English educator; b. Wilkes-Barre, Pa., Dec. 13, 1929; s. Haydn and Hanna (Sylvanus) G.; m. Jean Meitrett (dec. Apr. 1995); children: James, Dwight; m. Marlene Lindberg, Nov. 3, 1996. AB, Temple U., 1950; ThM, Dallas Theol. Sem., 1954; MA, Syracuse U., 1970. Ordained pastor 1955. 1instr. Keystone Coll., LaPlume, Pa., 0968—1969; dir. pub. info. Messiah Coll., Grantham, Pa., 1970—71; dir. cmty. rels. Health & Hosp. Coun. Northeastern Pa., 1973—74; pastor Bapt. Ch., Nesque Honing, Pa., 1977—85; mgr. French Azilum, Wysox, Pa., 1985—86; prof. English Marywood U., Scranton, Pa., 1988—; instr. Luzerne C.C., Nanticoke, Pa., 1990—2001. Author: Jog for Your Life; contbr. articles to profl. jours. Mem. State Draft Bd., Pa., 1980-83. Capt., chaplain USAF, 1959-68. Scholar State Senatorial, 1946, Morris Found., 1946; recipient medal Freedoms Found., 1967. Mem. Assn. Literary Scholars and Critics (pres.), St. David's Soc., Wyoming County Chorale. Republican. Avocation: beekeeping. Home: 17 Hilltop Dr Tunkhannock PA 18657

GILMORE, JEFFERY MANDALE, artist, educator, musician, communications executive; b. Cin., July 19, 1959; s. Henry Taylor and Shirley Ann (Burrell) Gilmore; m. Michelle Renee Calhoun, Jan. 10, 1984; children: Kathryn, Krystle, Karen, Jeff Jr. Grad. H.S., Cin. Instr. art edn. Ional Sch., Mpls., 1996; profl. musician; head Royal Illustration, 2003—; student, tchr. Wonder Comix. Avocations: music, calligraphy, song writing, singing, basketball. Home: 915 Fairbanks Ave Cincinnati OH 45205-1807

GILMORE, JENNIFER A.W. computer specialist, educator; b. San Fernando, Trinidad, Jan. 12, 1954; came to U.S., 1972; d. Fitzroy Grant and Zelma (Williams) Oudkerk; m. Frederick R. Gilmore, June 17, 1983. BA, MA, Bklyn. Coll., 1984; BBA, MS, Baruch Coll., 1993; MBA, L.I. U., 1994; PhD, Walden U./Kennedy-Western U., 2001. COBOL programmer MetLife, N.Y.C., 1972-86; project mgr., human resources adminstrn. mgmt. info. sys. City of N.Y., 1990—. Adj. prof. N.Y.C. Coll. Tech., 1997, Kingsborough C.C., 1998, St. Francis Coll., Bklyn., 1998, Medgar Evers Coll., 1998, Borough of Manhattan C.C., 1998, Touro Coll., 1999—, Baruch Coll., 1999—2000, Monroe Coll., 1999—, U. Md., 2003—. Home: 47 Mckeever Pl Apt 16J Brooklyn NY 11225-2537 Office: NYC-HRA-MIS 111 8th Ave New York NY 10011-5201 E-mail: jgilmore102716560@yahoo.com.

GILMORE, JERRY CARL, lawyer; b. Memphis, Tex., Dec. 29, 1933; s. Hugh Bailey and Gladys Herd (Jones) G.; m. Martha Niendorff, Dec. 1, 1956; children: Daniel, Susan, Charles. BA, U. Tex., 1955, JD, 1957. Bar: Tex. 1957. Practice law, Dallas, 1957—. Pres. North Ctrl. Tex. Coun. Govts., 1974-75, gen. counsel, 1986—, also exec. bd.; chmn. steering com. transp. Nat. League of Cities, 1974; mem. Dallas City Coun., 1971-75. Mem. City of Dallas Transit Bd., 1979-80; former bd. dirs., pres. Suicide Prevention of Dallas; former chmn. bd. trustees Dallas County Mental Health-Mental Retardation Ctr.; trustee Dallas C.C. Dist., 1976-92, chmn. 1981-82, 85-86; trustee Meth. Med. Ctr., Dallas, 1986—, vice chmn., 1990-96, chmn., 1996—; bd. dirs. Meth. Hosp. Dallas, 1996—; ; bd. dirs. home mission bd. So. Bapt. Conv., 1979-85, chmn. 1983-85; active Dallas Area Rapid Transit Bd., 1993-95; bd. trustees Tex. Scottish Rite Hosp. for Children, 1994—. Named Outstanding Young Lawyer, Dallas Jr. Bar Assn., 1971; recipient Outstanding Community Service award Oak Cliff Civitan Club, 1972, Justinian award Dallas Lawyers Auxiliary, 2001. Mem. ABA, Dallas Bar Assn., Tex. Bar Assn., High Noon Club of Dallas (pres. 1967-68), Dallas Assembly, Oak Cliff C. of C., Masons, Lions, Delta Theta Phi. Methodist. Home: 19 Turtle Creek Bnd Dallas TX 75204-1635 Office: 1700 Pacific Ste 2800 Dallas TX 75201-7357

GILMORE, JOANNE R. librarian; b. Phila., Oct. 18, 1952; d. John Leo and Sarah Rita (McGinley) G.; m. Michael O'Donnell, Nov. 11, 1978 (div.); m. Paul A. Grygier, Oct. 21, 1989. BA, Marywood Coll., 1974; MLS, Rutgers U., 1976. Reference & info. svc. libr. Cecil County Pub. Libr., Elkton, Md., 1977-82; mgr. ACCESS info. svc. Cumberland County Pub. Libr., Fayetteville, N.C., 1982, dept. head info. svcs., 1982-86; mgr. gen. reference Columbus (Ohio) Met. Libr., 1987-89, dir. tech. svcs., 1989—. Mem. ALA, Pub. Libr. Assn. (chair cataloging needs com. 2000-02), Ohio Libr. Assn. (sec. tech. svc. 1992-94), Assn. Libr. Collections Tech. Svcs. Office: Columbus Met Libr 101 S Stygler Rd Columbus OH 43230

GILMORE, KATHI, state treasurer; b. Dec. 23, 1944; m. Richard Gilmore; children: Suzi, Barb, Jeff, Amy. Mem. N.D. Ho. of Reps. from Dist. 6, 1989-92; treas. State of N.D., 1993—. Mem. Bd. Tax Equalization, State Hist. Bd., State Investment Bd., Tchrs. Fund for Retirement Bd., State Canvassing Bd., Bd. of Univ. and Sch. Lands Mem.: Assn. Securities Profls. (hon. co-chair pension fund conf. 1994, Task Forces Orgnl. Planning and Coordinating Com. 1993), Retirement and Investment Office Internal Audit Com., Nat. Assn. State Treas. (pension com.). Democrat. Presbyterian. Office: State Treasurer 600 E Boulevard Ave Bismarck ND 58505-0660

GILMORE, LOUISA RUTH, retired nurse, retired firefighter; b. Pitts., Oct. 21, 1930; d. Albert Leonard and Bertha Christina (Birch) Huber; m. William Norman II Kemp (div. 1975); children: Jance Louise Kemp Lipson, Barbara Lea Kemp Bilharz, Robert William, Paul Lee, Charles Albert; m. Robert James Gilmore, Sept. 1, 1989; stepchildren: Robi Lynn Lee, Donna Elizabeth Singleton. Diploma in nursing, San Bernardino C.C., Needles, Calif., 1983. Office nurse Santa Fe Clinic, Needles, 1953-57; spl. duty nurse Needles Cmtys. Hosp., 1957-62; nurse supr. Santa Fe Clinic, 1962-79; staff nurse in surgery Needles Desert Cmtys. Hosp., 1979-90; Cell Tech ind. distbr. Reliv Products, Temple, Tex., 1991-95; with Fine Host Corp., 1996—2001; food or product demonstrator Sam's Club #6339, 2000-2001, demonstrator jewelry dept., door greeter, 2001—. Instr. CPR Needles Desert Cmtys. Hosp., 1987-90; med. officer San Bernardino County Fire Dept., Needles, 1980-83, pub. info. officer, 1983-85, vol. fire fighter, 1983-90; ind. distbr. Reliv Products, 1991-95, Cell Tech., 1996. Mem. Calif. State Fireman Assn., Needles Firefighters Assn. (treas. 1987, 88), Beta Sigma Phi-Zeta Gamma (treas. 1966, sec. 1967, v.p. 1968, pres. 1969, named Sweetheart Queen 1969), Order of Rose (life). Avocations: grandchildren, gardening, camping, travel, plastercraft and oil painting. E-mail: fireangel5318@yahoo.com., rgilmore@vvm.com., rolukg2@yahoo.com.

GILMORE, MARJORIE HAVENS, civic worker, lawyer; b. N.Y.C., Aug. 16, 1918; d. William Westerfield and Elsie (Medl) Havens; m. Hugh Redland Gilmore, May 8, 1942; children: Douglas Hugh, Anne Charlotte Gilmore Decker, Joan Louise. AB, Hunter Coll., 1938; JD, Columbia U., 1941. Bar: N.Y. 1941, Va. 1968. Rsch. asst. N.Y. Law Revision Commn., 1941-42; assoc. Spence, Windels, Walser, Hotchkiss & Angell, N.Y.C., 1942, Chadbourne, Wallace, Parke & Whiteside, N.Y.C., 1942-43; atty. U.S. Army, Washington, 1948-53. Sec., Thomas Jefferson Jr. High Sch. PTA, 1956-58; chmn. by-laws rev. com., Long Point Corp., Ferrisburg, Vt., 1981-93; parliamentarian Wakefield High Sch. PTA, 1959-60, chmn. citizenship com., 1960-61; publicity chmn. Patrick Henry Sch. PTA, sec., 1964-65; parliamentarian Nottingham PTA, 1966-69; mem. extra-curricular activities com. Arlington County Sch. Bd.; area chmn. fund drive Cancer Soc., 1955-56; active Girl Scouts U.S.A., 1963-70; mem. '41 com. Columbia Law Sch. Fund. Recipient Constl. Law award Hunter Coll., 1938. Mem. Arlington Fedn. Women's Clubs (rec. sec. 1979-80), No. Dist. Va. Fedn. Women's Clubs (rec. sec. 1979-80), No. Dist. Va. Fedn. Women's Clubs (chmn. legis. com. 1986-88, chmn. pub. affairs no. dist. 1988-90), Williamsburg Woman's Club of Arlington (corr. sec. 1970-72, 97-98, 1st v.p. 1972-74, pres. 1974-76, 98-99, chmn. comms. 1981-82, chmn. legis. com. 1982-86, 90-98, pres. 1998-2000, pub. affairs chmn. 2000—), Columbia Law Sch. Alumni Assn., Alpha Sigma Rho. Presbyterian. Home: 3020 N Nottingham St Arlington VA 22207-1268

GILMORE, MAURICE EUGENE, mathematics educator; b. NYC, Jan. 2, 1938; s. Maurice Eugene and Mary Wells (Barnes) G.; m. Julie Anne Rogers, June 20, 1964 (div. 1989); children: Peter Barnes, Christopher Alan, Jessica Lynn; m. Cathi Leslie Sonneborn, Sept. 1, 1991. BA, Georgetown U., 1959; MS, Syracuse U., 1961; PhD, U. Calif., Berkeley, 1967. Instr. Northeastern U., Boston, 1966-68, asst. prof., 1968-72, assoc. prof., 1972-78, prof., 1978—, chmn. math. dept., 1975-88. Vis. prof. U. Tecnica Del Estado, Santiago, Chile, 1968, U. of Sussex, Falmer, U.K., 1989. Grantee, NSF, 1979, 1992, 1999, CNSF, 1999, Nellie Mae, 2001. Mem.: Assn. Tchrs. Math. Mass., Nat. Coun. Tchrs. Math., Am. Math. Soc., Math. Assn. Am. Office: Northeastern U 360 Huntington Ave Boston MA 02115-5000 E-mail: gilmore@neu.edu.

GILMORE, ROBIN HARRIS, nursing administrator; b. Wilmington, N.C., Apr. 23, 1964; d. John Sidney and Emily (Newton) Harris; m. Christopher Alan Gilmore, Feb. 20, 1993. AAN, Southeastern C.C., 1987; BSN, U. N.C. (Pembroke), 2000. RN, ACLS, BTLS, PALS, MICN. From staff nurse to asst. nurse mgr. ER Columbus County Hosp., Whiteville, N.C., 1993-95, critical care nurse mgr., current CCU and emergency dept., 1995—. Mem. Emergency Nurses Assn., Columbus Co. Shrine Club. Republican. Methodist. Avocations: cooking, water skiing, snow skiing, four wheeling. Home: PO Box 1835 Whiteville NC 28472-1835 Office: Columbus County Hosp 500 Jefferson St Whiteville NC 28472-3696

GILMORE, ROGER, college consultant; b. Phila., Oct. 11, 1932; s. Wheeler and Edith Seal (Thompson) G.; m. Beatrice Reynolds, Sept. 17, 1952 (dec. Sept. 1994); children: Christopher, Jennifer E., Lesley Margaret; m. Elizabeth McOuat Lameyer, Oct. 1, 1995. AB, Dartmouth Coll., 1954; postgrad., U. Chgo. Div. Sch., 1958-63; DFA (hon.), Sch. Art Inst. Chgo., 1993; DHL (hon.), Maine Coll. Art, 2002. Social worker N.H. Dept. Pub. Welfare, Woodsville, 1954-55; adminstrv. asst. Furn Corp. Lisbon, N.H., 1955-56; office mgr., asst. to pres. Cole's Mill Inc., Littleton, N.H., 1956-58; acct., office supr. U. Chgo., 1958-61, asst. dir. fin. aid, 1961-63; asst. to dean Sch. Art Inst. Chgo., 1963-65, acting dean, 1965-68, dean, 1968-87, provost, v.p. for acad. affairs, 1987-89; pres. Maine Coll. Art (formerly Portland Sch. Art), 1989-2001, pres. emeritus, 2001—. Dir. Commn. Accreditation and Membership Nat. Assn. Schs. of Art and Design, 1975-78, v.p. 1984-87, pres., 1987-90; mem. Joint Commn. on Dance and Theatre Accreditation, 1978-82; bd. dirs. Internat. Coun. Fine Arts Deans, 1986-88; pres., bd. dirs. Ox-Bow Summer Sch. and Artists Colony, 1987-89; treas. Assn. Ind. Colls. Art and Design, 1991-95; mem. exec. com. Maine Higher Edn. Coun., 1991-95. Bd. dirs. Maine Alliance for Arts Edn., 1992-94, Greater Portland Landmarks, 1993-99, Stanley Mus., 1993-95, World Affairs Coun., 1993-95. Fellow Nat. Assn. Schs. Art and Design (life); mem. Maine Citizens for Hist. Preservation, Nat. Trust for Hist. Preservation, Maine Alliance for Arts Edn. Democrat. Episcopalian. Home: 24 Fairmount St Portland ME 04103-3051

GILMORE, THOMAS DAVID, biologist; b. Uniontown, Pa., Dec. 28, 1952; s. Thomas Hardie and Marian (Madeline) G. AB in English, Princeton U., 1974; PhD in Zoology, U. Calif., Berkeley, 1984. Grad. student U. Calif., Berkeley, 1978-84; postdoctoral fellow U. Wis., Madison, 1984-87; asst. prof. Boston U., 1987-93, assoc. prof., 1993—97, prof., 1997—. Grant reviewer NIH, Bethesda, Md., 1992, Am. Cancer Soc., Atlanta, 1991-93. Contbr. articles to profl. jours. Recipient postdoctoral fellowship Jane Coffin Childs, 1984-87, Faculty Rsch. award Am. Cancer Soc., 1988-91, 92-96, NIH grantee, 1988—, Tobacco Rsch. Coun. grant 1994-97. Mem. AAAS, Am. Soc. Microbiology. Democrat. Roman Catholic. Achievements include characterization of the rel oncogene. Office: Boston U Biology Dept 5 Cummington St Boston MA 02215-2406

GILMORE, TIMOTHY JONATHAN, paralegal; b. Orange, Calif., June 24, 1949; s. James and Margaret (Swanson) G.; m. Blanche Jean Panter, Sept. 3, 1984; children: Erin, Sean and Brian (twins). BA, St. Mary's Coll., Moraga, Calif., 1971; grad., Denver Paralegal Inst., 1996. Adminstrv. asst. Gov. Ronald Reagan, Sacramento, Calif., 1971-73; salesman Penn Mutual, Anaheim, Calif., 1973-76; asst. devel. dir. St. Mary's Coll., Moraga, 1976-81; devel. dir. St. Alphonsus Hosp., Boise, Idaho, 1981-83; adminstr. Blaine County Hosp., Hailey, Idaho, 1983-86; exec. dir. Poudre Hosp. Found., Ft. Collins, Colo., 1986-87; nat. recruiting dir. Power Securities Corp., Denver, 1987-89; cons. Horn, Fagan & Lund Exec. Search Cons., Ft. Collins, 1989; v.p. Jackson & Coker Locum Tenens, Inc., Denver, 1990-93; pres. Gilmore and Assocs., Ft. Collins, Colo., 1993-98; paralegal Brownstein, Hyatt & Farber PC, Denver, 1998—. Republican. Mem. Lds Ch. Avocation: fishing. Home and Office: 1527 River Oak Dr Fort Collins CO 80525-5537 E-mail: TG1527FC@aol.com.

GILMORE, VANESSA D. federal judge; b. St. Albans, N.Y., Oct. 26, 1956; BS, Hampton U., 1977; JD, U. Houston, 1981. Bar: Tex. 1982, U.S. Dist. Ct. (so. dist.) Tex. Fashion buyer Foley's Dept. Store, 1977-79; ptnr. Vickery, Kilbride, Gilmore & Vickery, Houston, 1981-85, 86-94; atty. Sue Schecter & Assocs., Houston, 1985-86; judge U.S. Dist. Ct. (So. dist.) Tex., Houston, 1994—. Spkr. ATLA, San Diego, 1990, ABA, Atlanta, 1991, N.Y.C., 1993, Leadership Tex., Austin, 1992, Hampton U. Alumni Assn., Dallas, 1992, Laredo Bus. and Profl. Women's Assn., 1993, XI Ann. Border Gov.'s Conf., Monterrey, Mex., 1993, Gov.'s Bus. Devel. Coun., Ausitn, 1993, Tex. A&M U., 1993, State Bar of Tex., Austin, 1993, Houston Bus. Coun., 1993, Minority Enterprise Devel. Week, Houston, 1993, Holman St. Bapt. Ch., 1994, Greater Houston Women's Found., 1994, The Kinkaid Sch., 1995, So. Meth. U., Dallas, 1996, South Tex. Coll. of Law, 1996, among others. Contbr. articles to profl. jours. Bd. dirs. Houston Ballet, Tex. So. Univ. Found., Neighborhood Recovery Community Redevel. Corp., 1992-95; chair African Am. Art Adv. Assn., Mus. Fine Arts; mem. scv. acad. nominations bd. Rep. Jack Fields, Tex., 1993, 94; active Texans for NAFTA; mem. Tex. Dept. Commerce, 1991-94, chairperson, 1992-94; mem. adv. bd. St. Joseph's Hosp.; mem. Leadership Tex. Named One of Houston's Black Achievers, Human Enrichment of Life Program, 1989; recipient Citizen of the Month award Houston Defender, 1990, YWCA award, 1991, Austin Met. Resource Bus. Ctr. award, 1991, Houston Bus. and Profl. Men's Club award, 1992, Disting. Svc. award Nat. Black MBA Assn., 1994, Cmty. Svc. award Holman St. Bapt. Ch., 1994. Mem. ABA, NAACP (chair chs. and orgns. com. Freedom Fund banquets 1989-93), ATLA, Am. Leadership Forum, Tex. Trial Lawyers Assn., Tex. Lyceum Assn., Houston Bar Assn., Houston Lawyers Assn., U. Houston Law Alumni (bd. dirs. 1993—), W.J. Durham Legal Soc., Links, Inc. (Mo. chpt., chair LEAD substance abuse and teen pregnancy prevention program 1990-91). Office: US Courthouse 515 Rusk Ave Rm 9513 Houston TX 77002-2605 E-mail: vanessa_gilmore@txs.us.courts.gov.

GILMORE, VOIT, travel executive; b. Winston-Salem, N.C., Oct. 13, 1918; s. John Merriman and Helen (Hensel) G.; m. Kathryn Kendrick, Jan. 21, 1945 (div. 1975); children: Kathryn, Geraldine, Susan, Peter, David.; m. Tatiana Dominick, July 4, 1982 (div. 1990); m. Josephine Baldwin, Nov. 23, 1990. BJ, U. N.C., 1939, M in Geography, 1985, PhD in Geography, 1987; grad., Nat. Inst. Pub. Affairs, Washington, 1940. Cert. travel counselor Inst. Cert. Travel Agts. Asst. to div. mgr. Pan Am. Airways, Miami, Fla., 1940-41; personnel mgr. Pan Am. Airways-Africa Ltd., Accra, Gold Coast, 1942-43; pub. relations dir. Pan Am. Airways, San Francisco, 1946-48; pres. Storey Corp. and affiliated cos., 1948-61, 64-83, Four Seasons Travel Service, Inc., 1971-95. Dir. U.S. Travel Svc., Washington, 1961-64, So. Nat. Bank of N.C., 1980-95; news corr. to Arctic, 1958, Antarctic, 1958, 60, 61, 63; mem. adv. coun. U.S. Travel and Tourism Adminstrn., 1990-96. Contbr. articles on polar exploration to newspapers, mags. Mem. town coun., mayor, Southern Pines, N.C., 1953-57; mem. N.C. Senate, 1965-69, N.C. Bd. Conservation and Devel., 1957-61; trustee U. N.C., Fayetteville, 1981-87; mem. Gov.'s Adv. Com. on Travel and Tourism, 1982, N.C. Forestry Adv. Com., 1986; candidate for U.S. Congress from 8th Dist. N.C., 1968; bd. dirs. U. N.C. Sch. Journalism Found., Chapel Hill; chmn. Clean N.C. 2000, 1999-01. Lt. (j.g.) USN, 1943-46, PTO. Recipient European Tourism Golden Helm award, West Berlin, 1986, Parker award Travel Coun. N.C., 1997, Order of Long Leaf Pine award Gov. N.C., 2003; elected to Travel Industry Assn. Hall of Leaders, 1988. Fellow Royal Geog. Soc. (life), Explorers Club (life); mem. Am. Soc. Travel Agts. (pres. 1988-90), Assn. of Am. Geographers, Am. Forestry Assn. (pres. 1973-75), Soc. Am. Travel Writers, Travel Coun. N.C. (pres. 1969-71), Bohemian Club, Cosmos Club, Country Club N.C., Heidelburg Prince Club. Home and Office: 1600 Morganton Rd D11 Pinehurst NC 28374-6842

GILMORE, WEBB REILLY, lawyer; b. Lake Forest, Ill., Dec. 9, 1944; s. Durward Wilson and Dorothy Angeline (DeField) G.; m. Denise Regina Dever, May 9, 1970; children— Kara Anne, Kimberly Erin, Katharine Reilly. B.S., U.S. Naval Acad., 1966; J.D., U. Mo.-Columbia, 1973. Bar: Mo. 1973. Assoc. firm Stinson Mag & Fizzell, Kansas City, Mo., 1973-77, ptnr., 1977-79; ptnr. firm Gaar & Bell, Kansas City, Mo., 1979-87, Gilmore & Bell (formerly Garr & Bell), Kansas City, Mo., 1987— ; dir. Glasgow Savs. Bank, Mo., 1970— ; dir. Oran State Bank, 1984—. Mem. Mo. Lottery Commn., 1985—. Served with USN, 1966-70. Mem. ABA, Mo. Bar Assn., Nat. Assn. Bond Lawyers. Democrat. Roman Catholic. Home: 833 Westover Rd Kansas City MO 64113-1121 Office: Gilmore & Bell 1200 Main St 40th Floor One Kansas City Pl Kansas City MO 64105

GILMOUR, D(AVID) JAMES, financial analyst, systems analyst; b. Phila., July 10, 1947; s. James William and Florence Elizabeth (Weisbrod) Gilmour; m. Deborah Anne Kaufold, July 2, 1977. BS, Muhlenberg Coll., 1969; MS in Adminstrn., George Washington U., 1974; MBA, Temple U., 1981; MS, U. Pa., 1995, MPhil, 1998. Analyst Nat. Security Agy., Ft. Meade, Md., 1970-74; programmer, analyst Rohm & Haas Co., Phila., 1974-77; staff economist Sun Oil Co., Radnor, Pa., 1977-85; project leader Arco Chem. Corp., Phila., 1985-87; asst. v.p. Corestates Fin. Corp., Phila., 1987-98, cons., 1998—. Ambassador Ctr. Orgnl. Dynamics U. Pa., Phila. Author: (book) An Economic Model of Core States Financial Corporations, 1994, How to Write Term Papers Real Good, 1996, The Corestates/University of Pennsylvania Strategic Planning Model, 1997, The Philadelphia Ethos, 1998, 1776 and All That: A Memorable History of Philadelphia, 2002. With USN, 1970—74. Mem.: NRA, Clan Morrison Soc., Mensa, Beta Gamma Sigma, Alpha Tau Omega (exchequer 1965—69, Thomas Arcle Clark award 1969). Republican. Anglican. Achievements include co-inventor semi-automatic pistol. Home and Office: 15 Keats Rd Yardley PA 19067-3219

GILMOUR, DOUG, hockey player; b. Kingston, Ont., Canada, July 25, 1963; With St. Louis Blues, 1983—88, Calgary Flames, 1988—92, Toronto Maple Leafs, 1992—97, N.J. Devils, 1997—98, Chgo. Blackhawks, 1988—99, Buffalo Sabres, 2000—01, Montreal Canadians, 2001—02, Toronto Maple Leafs, 2002—03. Recipient Red Tilson Trophy, 1982—83, Eddie Powers Meml. Trophy, 1982—83, Frank J. Selke Trophy, 1992—93, 1994. Achievements include Member of 1989 Stanley Cub championship team; Played in NHL All-Star game, 1993.

GILMOUR, EDWARD ELLIS, retired psychiatrist; b. Schenectady, N.Y., May 6, 1930; s. William Ellis and Adeline (Campbell) G. B.Engring., Yale U., 1952; MA in Philosophy, 1957; MD, Boston U., 1961. Diplomate Am. Bd. Psychiatry and Neurology with subspltys. in adult and child psychiatry. Intern St. Luke's Hosp., N.Y.C., 1961-62; resident in medicine, 1962-64; resident in psychiatry, 1964-66; child psychiatry, 1966-68; asst. attending, child psychiatry, 1968-80; assoc., 1980—; supr. residents, 1968—; pvt. practice specializing in adult, child, and adolescent psychiatry and pscyhoanalysis, 1968-82; pvt. practice specializing in adult, child, and adolescent Falmouth, Mass., 1982—; psychoanalytic tng. William Alanson White Inst., N.Y.C., 1969-74; attending psychiatrist Columbia U. Health Svc., N.Y.C., 1969-74; staff psychiatrist Ittleson Ctr. Child Rsch., Riverdale, N.Y., 1976-82; staff Falmouth Hosp., 1982—; mem. provisional staff St. Vincent Hosp., Santa Fe, N.Mex., 1995—; asst. clin. prof. NYU, 1979—. Cons. community psychiatry, 1973-75 Fellow

Am. Acad. Psychoanalysis, Am. Acad. Child Psychiatry; mem. Am. Psychiat. Assn., AMA, Mass. Med. Soc., William Alanson White Psychoanalytic Soc., Soc. Adolescent Psychiatry, Mass. Psychiat. Soc. Home: PO Box 10108 Santa Fe NM 87504-6108

GILMSON, SOPHIA, music educator; arrived in U.S.A., 1976; d. Rafail Solomonovitch and Tamara Semenovna Gilmson; 1 child, Vadim Rizov. MusB, Leningrad (Russia) Conservatory, MusM, 1973. Tchr. Ctrl. City Sch. Music, Leningrad, 1969—75; pvt. piano tchr. Houston, 1976—93; coord. keyboard studies Coll. of the Mainland, Tex. City, Tex., 1980—93, assoc. prof. Sch. Music U. Tex., Austin, Tex., 1993—. Music dir. Houston (Tex.) Young Artists Consort, 1987—; artistic dir. Austin (Tex.) Young Artists Concert, 1999—. Contbr. articles to profl. jours. Co-founder Music Clef, Houston, 1980—90. Recipient 1st prize, Young Artists in Recital, 1978, Grand prize, Internat. Recording Competition, 1979, mann & Everest award, Austin (Tex.) Critics Table, 2001. Mem.: Austin (Tex.) Music Tchrs. Assn. (named Tchr. of Yr. 1986, 1998), Tex. Music Tchrs. Assn. (Collegiate Tchr. of Yr. award 2001), Music Tchrs. Nat. Assn. Avocations: reading, fitness, travel, theater. Home: 4205 Zuni Drive Austin TX 78759-4248 Office: School of Music The University of Texas Austin TX 78759 E-mail: s.gilmson@mail.utexas.edu.

GILPATRICK, JANET, public affairs and public relations consultant; b. Seattle, Jan. 26, 1944; d. Donald Ernst Majer; m. Thomas S. Gilpatrick; children: Annie, Dawn. Dep. dir. Carter-Mondale Campaign, Wash. State, 1978-80; dist. dir. Spkr. of the House Thomas S. Foley, 1981-95; adminstr. asst. Office of Former U.S. Spkr. Thomas S. Foley, 1995-98; sr. cons. pub. affairs and pub. rels. Rockey-West Co., Spokane, 1998—. Bd. dirs. YWCA, Spokane, United Way, Women Helping Women, Mirabeau Point, Spokane Intercollegiate Rsch. Inst.; mem. Spokane Housing Commn.; mem. state bd. dirs. FEMA, Spokane. Office: Rockey-West Co 421 W Riverside Ave Ste 575 Spokane WA 99201-0402

GILPIN, PERI, actress; b. Waco, Tex., May 27, 1961; Former student, Dallas Theatre Ctr., U. Tex., Brit.-Am. Acad., London. Appeared in (TV series) Frasier, 1993-, Designing Women, Cheers, Wings, Hercules (voice), 1998, The Lionhearts, 1998, (TV movies) Fight for Justice: The Nancy Conn Story, 1995, The Secret She Carried, 1996, The Lionhearts, 1998, Laughter on the 23rd Floor, 2001, Finaly Fantasty: The Spirits Within (voice), 2001 (films) Spring Forward, 1999, How to Kill Your Neighbor's Dog, 2000; guest appearance Later with Greg Kinnear, 1994, Early Edition, 1996, The Outer Limits, 1995, Superman, 1996, Pride & Joy, 1995, Talk Soup, 1991, Matlock, 1986, 21 Jump Street, 1987. Recipient SAG award, 2000. Office: William Morris Agy One William Morris Place Beverly Hills CA 90212-2775

GILPIN, ROBERT GEORGE, JR., political science educator; b. Burlington, Vt., July 2, 1930; s. Robert George and Beatrice (Sandspra) G.; m. Jean Millis, Aug. 13, 1955; children— Linda, Elizabeth, Robert. BA, U. Vt., 1952; MS, Cornell U., 1954; PhD, U. Calif., Berkeley, 1960. Fellow Harvard U., 1960-61; lectr. Columbia U., 1961-62; faculty Princeton U., 1962—, prof. polit. sci., 1970-98, Eisenhower prof. internat. affairs, 1975-98, prof. emeritus, 1998—. Mem. Pres.'s Advisory Group Tech. and the Economy, 1975-76. Author: American Scientists and Nuclear Weapons Policy, 1962, France in the Age of the Scientific State, 1968, U.S. Power and the Multinational Corporation, 1975, War and Change in World Politics, 1981, The Political Economy of International Relations, 1987, The Challenge of Global Capitalism: The World Economy of the 21st Century, 2000, Global Political Economy: Understanding the International Economic Order, 2001; co-author (co-editor): Scientists and National Policy Making, 1964. Served with USNR, 1954-57. Congl. fellow, 1959-60, Guggenheim fellow, 1969, Rockefeller fellow, 1967-68, 76-77 Fellow AAAS; mem. Am. Polit. Sci. Assn. (v.p. 1984-85). Home: 134 Moore St Princeton NJ 08540-3359 E-mail: rggilpin@princeton.edu.

GILREATH, JERRY HOLLANDSWORTH, retired community planner; b. Smithville, Tenn., Jan. 19, 1934; s. Homer Freeman and Wallee (Hollandsworth) Gilreath; m. Ellen Johnston, June 15, 1974; 1 child, Kathryn Ann. BS, Mid. Tenn. State Coll., 1956; MS in Planning, U. Tenn., 1972. Editor UPI, Frankfurt, Fed. Republic of Germany, 1959-60; proofreader Jones Composition, Inc., Washington, 1961-62; publ. asst. Am. Geophysical Union, Washington, 1963-65; editorial asst. Library of Congress, Washington, 1965-67, adminstrv. asst., 1968-69; cmty. planner Nat. Capital Planning Commn., Washington, 1975—2002; ret., 2002. Lead planner in update Fed. Employment Facilities Element of Comprehensive Plan for Nat. Capital, 1999—2001; active D.C. Bd. Zoning Adjustment, 1999—2000, prin. planner, 2002. Mem.: Am. Planning Assn., Little Falls Swimming and Tennis Club (Bethesda, Md.). Avocations: tennis, swimming, bicycling, reading. Home: 5103 Baltimore Ave Bethesda MD 20816-1605 E-mail: jerel3178@aol.com.

GILROY, EILEEN M. speech pathology/audiology services professional, educator; m. Brian P Gilroy; children: Michael, Alison. BS, Marywood Coll., Scranton, Pa., 1982; MS, Pa. State U., 1984. Cert. in clin. competence Am. Speech Lang. and Hearing Assn., lic. speech/lang. pathologist N.Y. State, cert. tchr. speech speech and hearing handicapped N.Y. State. Speech pathologist Handicapped Children's Assn., Johnson City, NY, 1984—86; supr. of rehab. dept./speech lang. pathologist Lourdes Hosp., Binghamton, NY, 1986—. Facilitator-laryngectomee support group Am. Cancer Soc., Endicott, NY; adj. lectr. Ithaca Coll., NY, 1993—. Presenter (poster presentation asha) Role of Speech Pathologist in Hospice. Supporting mem. Am. Diabetes Assn.; mem. Sweet Kids-support group for children with diabetes, Binghamton, NY. Named Value Inspired Person (VIP), Lourdes Hosp. Mem.: Am. Speech Lang. Hearing Assn., So. Tier Speech and Hearing Assn., N.Y. State Speech Hearing Assn. Roman Catholic. Office: Lourdes Hospital Rehab Dept 169 Riverside Dr Binghamton NY 13905

GILROY, FRANK DANIEL, playwright; b. N.Y.C., Oct. 13, 1925; s. Frank B. and Bettina (Vasti) Gilroy; m. Ruth Dorothy Gaydos, Feb. 13, 1954; children: Anthony, John, Daniel. BA magna cum laude, Dartmouth Coll., 1950; postgrad., Yale Sch. Drama. Author became TV writer, (TV series) (originated) Burkes Law, (TV writer, scripts prod. on programs) Playhouse 90, U.S. Steel Hour, Omnibus, Kraft Theatre, Lux Video Theatre, Studio One; dir.(writer): 40 Gibbsville, 1975, The Doorbell Rang, 1977, Money Plays, 1997; author: (plays) Who'll Save the Plowboy? (presented off-Broadway, 1962), 1957, (completed) The Subject Was Roses, 1962, (presented on Broadway, 1964), 1962; presented (Broadway plays) That Summer-That Fall, 1967, The Only Game in Town, 1968, Last Licks, 1979, Any Given Day, 1993, (off Broadway plays) Contact With the Enemy, 1999, one-act (produced off-Broadway plays) The Next Contestant, 1978, Real to Reel, 1987, Match Point, 1990, A Way With Word, 1991, Give the Bishop My Faint Regards, 1992, Contact with the Enemy, 2000, Inspector Ohms, 2001; prodr.(writer, dir.): (films) Desperate Characters, 1970 (best screenplay award Berlin Film Festival), From Noon Till Three, 1977, The Gig, 1985, Once in Paris (original screenplay), 1978; writer, dir. (films) The Luckiest Man in the World, 1989; author: Present Tense, prod. off-Broadway, 1972, (novels) Private, 1970, (with Ruth Gilroy) Little Ego, 1970, From Noon till Three, 1973, (non-fiction) I Wake Up Screening-Everything You Need to Know About Making Independent Films Including A Thousand Reasons Not To, 1993, (screenplays) (with Russell Rouse) The Fastest Gun Alive, 1956, (with Beirne Lay Jr.) Gallant Hours, 1960, Desperate Characters, 1971, The Subject was Roses, The Only Game in Town, From Noon till Three, Once in Paris. Served with U.S. Army, 1943—46, ETO. Nominee Best Play N.Y. Drama Desk, 1999—2000; recipient Obie award for best Am. play, 1962, Outer Circle award, 1964, Drama Critics Circle award, 1964, N.Y. Theatre Club award, 1964—65, Antoinette Perry award, 1965, Pulitzer prize for drama, 1965. Mem.: Writers Guild Am., Dirs. Guild Am., Dramatists Guild (pres. 1969—71).

GILROY, JANE HAGAN, literature educator; b. Bklyn., N.Y., Aug. 14, 1936; d. Harry Joseph Hagan and Marcella Louise Druhan; m. Francis Henry Gilroy, Nov. 28, 1957; children: Arthur, Francis, Lawrence, Charles, Barbara. BA, Molloy Coll., Rockville Centre, NY, 1981; MA, Hofstra U., Hempstead, NY, 1985; PhD, Fordham U., Bronx, NY, 1999. Adj. instr. English Molloy Coll., Rockville Centre, NY, 1981—86, Hofstra U., Hempstead, NY, 1984—86; instr. English Molloy Coll., Rockville Centre, NY, 1986—91, asst. prof. English, 1991—2001, assoc. prof. English, 2001—. Contbr. books of poetry. Coord. Women Life, Rockville Centre, NY, 1969; pres. Com. Human Life, Merrick, NY, 1969; founding mem., pres. LI Chpt. U. Faculty for Life, Merrick, NY, 2000—03. Recipient Named to Pro-Life Hall of Fame, Elect Life PAC, 2001, Nominee Gov., NY State Right Life Party's Ind. Nominating Petition, 1970. Mem.: Soc. Cath. Social Scientists, Early English Text Soc., U. Faculty for Life. Right To Life Party. Roman Catholic. Avocations: poetry readings, public speaking, medieval mystics, gardening, photography. Office: Molloy College 1000 Hempstead Avenue PO Box 5002 Rockville Centre NY 11571-5002 Office Fax: 516-256-2243. E-mail: jgilroy@molloy.edu.

GILROY, JOSEPH M. civil engineer; b. Valley Stream, N.Y., Jan. 28, 1955; s. Anthony Francis and Elizabeth Patricia (Kenny) Gilroy; m. Rosemarie Iorio Gilroy, Aug. 9, 1986; children: Kathryn Marie, Steven Joseph. B in Engring., Cooper Union, 1977; MS in Transp. Planning and Engring., Poly. Inst. N.Y., 1978. Registered profl. engr., N.Y., Ill., Mo., cert. profl. traffic ops. engr. Transp. engr. TAMS Consultants, Inc., N.Y.C., Panama City, Panama, Lisbon, Portugal, 1978—87, head transp. planning dept. N.Y.C., 1989—91, assoc./design mgr. Belleville, Ill., 1991—97; port planner Port Authority of N.Y./N.J., N.Y.C., 1987—89; assoc./project mgr. Burns & McDonnell Engring. Co., O'Fallon, Ill., 1997—. Lectr. port planning Poly. Inst. N.Y., Bklyn., 1983—86. Mem.: KC, ASCE, Soc. Am. Mil. Engrs., Inst. Transp. Engrs. Roman Catholic. Office: Burns & McDonnell Eagle Ctr # 4 O Fallon IL 62269 Office Fax: 618-632-0307. Business E-Mail: jgilroy@burnsmcd.com.

GILROY, SUE ANNE, state official; b. Ind. m. Dick Gilroy; children: Emily (dec.), Grant. Grad. cum laude, DePauw U.; MA, Ind. U. Ordained elder Presbyn. Ch. Former profl. assoc. Office of Mayor Lugar; former dir. Parks and Recreation; asst. to pres. Ind. Ctrl. U. (now U. Indpls.); chair Mayor Steve Goldsmith's Transition Team, 1991-92; state dir. for Senator Richard Lugar, Ind., 1990-93; sec. of state State of Ind., 1994—. Cons. in fundraising and bus. adminstrn. Tabernacle Presbyn. Ch.; bd. dirs. St. Vincent Hosp Found., Cathedral H.S., U. Indpls.; mem. adv. bd. Salvation Army. Mem. Indpls. Rotary Club. Republican.

GILSINN, DAVID EDMUND, mathematician, researcher; b. Washington, Jan. 25, 1943; s. David Leo and Doris (Dyson) G.; m. Judith Helen Forward, Aug. 6, 1966; 1 child, James David. BS, Georgetown U., 1964, PhD, 1969; MS, Rutgers U., 1966. Mathematician Melpar, Inc., McLean, Va., 1969-70, Nat. Inst. Standards & Tech., Gaithersburg, Md., 1970—. Contbr. articles to profl. jours. Fundraiser, co-chair St. Rose Lima Cath. Ch., Gaithersburg, 1993-99. Recipient Bronze medal U.S. Dept. Commerce, Washington, 1994. Mem. ASME, Am. Soc. Precision Engring., Soc. Indsl. & Applied Math. Democrat. Office: Nat Inst Standards & Tech Rm 365 Bldg 820 100 Bureau Dr Stop 8910 Gaithersburg MD 20899-8910 E-mail: dgilsinn@nist.gov.

GILSON, ARNOLD LESLIE, retired engineering executive, consultant; b. Perrysburg, Ohio, Apr. 10, 1931; s. Leslie Clair and Velma Lillian (Hennen) G.; m. Phyllis Mary Seiling, Sept. 15, 1951 (dec. May 1982); children: David, Jeffrey, Luann, Suzanne. BSME, U. Toledo, 1962. Engr. Miller, Tillman & Zamis engrs., Toledo, 1962-67, regional mgr. Phoenix br., 1967-69; owner, mgr. ABS Tech. Svcs., Phoenix, 1969-98; ret. Patentee in several fields. With U.S. Army, 1952, Korea. Decorated Bronze Star; Comnd. extraordinary minister, 1975.. Mem. Nat. Mil. Intelligence Assn. (charter). Republican. Roman Catholic. Home: 8226 E Meadowbrook Ave Scottsdale AZ 85251-1739 E-mail: ADGILSON@JUNO.COM.

GILSTRAP, LARRY COWAN, obstetrician gynecologist; b. Jacksonville, Fla., Nov. 26, 1944; s. Larry Cowan Gilstrap and Clara Wilford; m. Jo Ellen Reed, Aug. 21, 1965; children: Lori Caroline Monk, Lisa Christine Campbell, Jennifer Erin Bagwell. BA, Fla. State U., 1965; MD, U. of Miami, 1970. Diplomate Am. Bd. of Ob-Gyn. Dir. of obstetrics Wilford Hall USAF Med. Ctr., San Antonio, 1980—86; prof. of ob-gyn. U. of Tex. Southwestern Med. Sch., Dallas, 1987—96; chmn. of dept. ob-gyn. U. of Tex. Houston Med. Sch., 1996—. Cons. to air force surgeon gen. USAF, San Antonio, 1982—86; assoc. editor Am. Jour. of Perinatology, N.Y.C., 1992—; obstetric mem. Neonatal Network Adv. Bd., NIH, Washington, 1997—; expert cons. Tex. State Bd. of Med. Examiners, Austin, 1991—; editl. bd. Infectious Diseases in Ob-Gyn., N.Y.C., 1993—; update editor Primary Care Update for Ob/GYN, Washington, 1995—; bd. of directors Soc. for Maternal Fetal Medicine, Washington, 1987—89; editl. bd. Obstetrics and Gynecology, 1984—87; bd. dirs. Am. Bd. Ob-Gyn., Dallas, 1997—, treas., 2002—, sci. program chmn., Washington, 1995—95, bd. examiner, Dallas, 1984—, bd. examiner divsn. maternal-fetal medicine, 1987—2001. Author: (medical textbook) Williams Obstetrics, 19th, 20th, and 21st edits., Study Guide for Williams Obstetrics, 19th, 20th, 21st edits.; editor: Operative Obstetrics, 1st and 2nd edits.; author: Operative Obstetrics 2nd edit. Study Guide, Case Files Obstetrics & Gynecology, Drugs and Pregnancy, 1st and 2nd edits., Infections in Pregnancy, 1st and 2d edits.; editor: (med. book) Guidelines for Perinatal Care, 5th edit.; guest editor (medical jour.) Operative Obstetrics. Bd. dirs. Meml. Hermann Healthnet Providers, Houston, 1999—2002. Col. USAF, 1966—86. Decorated Legion of Merit USAF; named one of Best Drs. for Women, Good Housekeeping Mag., 1997, Best Drs. in Am., Am. Health Mag., 1996; recipient Outstanding Svc. award, Soc. of Perinatal Obstetricians, 1998. Fellow: Am. Coll. of Obstetricians and Gynecologists (Outstanding Prof. award Armed dist. 1986); mem.: Houston Gynecol. and Obstet. Soc., Harris County Med. Soc., Am. Gynecologic and Obstetric Soc., Soc. of Gynecologic Investigation, Soc. of Maternal-Fetal-Medicine (bd. dirs. 1987—89, pres. 1993—93), Infectious Disease Soc. of Obstetrics and Gynecology (coun. mem. 1996—99), Tex. Assn. of Obstetricians and Gynecologists. Liberal. Methodist. Home: 3734 Bellefontaine Houston TX 77025 Office: U Tex Houston Med Sch Ste 3286 6431 Fannin Houston TX 77030 Personal E-mail: lgilst01@aol.com. E-mail: larry.c.gilstrap@uth.tmc.edu.

GILSTRAP, LEAH ANN, media specialist; b. Seneca, S.C., Sept. 12, 1950; d. Raymond Chester and Eunice Hazel (Long) G. AA, Anderson Coll., 1973; BA in History, Furman U., 1976, MEd, 1982; MLS, U. S.C., 1991. Cert. tchr., media specialist, S.C. Tchr. Greenville (S.C.) County Sch. Dist., 1978-92, media specialist, 1992—. Mem. NEA (del. 1991-95), ALA, S.C. Assn. Sch. Librs., S.C. Edn. Assn. (bd. dirs. 1994-96), Greenville County Edn. Assn. (bd. dirs. 1988-98, governance chair 1988-98, v.p. 1996-97, pres. 1997-98), Greenville County Coun. Media Specialists (bd. dirs. 1993-94). Democrat. Baptist. Avocations: travel, reading, ednl. studies. Home: 19 Anson Ct Simpsonville SC 29681-5560 Office: Bryson Mid Sch 3657 S Industrial Dr Simpsonville SC 29681-3295 E-mail: lgistra@greenville.k12.sc.us.

GILTON, DONNA LOUISE, library and information scientist, educator; b. Lynn, Mass., July 9, 1950; d. Rev. Charles Webster and Hattie Franklin Gilton. BA, Simmons Coll., 1972, MS, 1975; PhD, U. of Pitts., 1988. Pre-professional asst. Boston Pub. Libr., Boston, 1972—75, libr., 1975—79; head libr. Belize Teachers' Coll., Belize City, Belize, 1979—81; bus. reference libr. Western Ky. U., Bowling Green, Ky., 1984—88, Pa. State U., University Park, Pa., 1988—91; asst. prof. U. of RI, Kingston, RI, 1991—98, assoc. prof., 1998—. Mem.: ALA, R.I. Libr. Assn., Assn. of Libr. & Info. Sci. Educators. African Meth.Episcopal. Avocations: churchwork, reading, music. Office: University of Rhode Island 9 Rodman Hall Kingston RI 02881 Office Fax: 401-874-4964. Business E-Mail: dgilton@uri.edu.

GIMBEL, DAVID NELSON, archaeologist; BA, Wesleyan U.; MA, Inst. of Fine Arts, NYU; DPhil, U. of Oxford. Pres. Archaeos, Inc., NYC, 1999—2003. Mem.: Coll. Art Assn., Cognitive Sci. Soc., Brit. Sch. of Archaeology at Ankara, Brit. Inst. of Persian Studies, Brit. Sch. of Archaeology in Iraq, Am. Assn. of Museums, Am. Oriental Soc., Am. Inst. of Archaeology, Mind Assn., Internat. Cognitive Linguistics Assn., Am. Schools of Oriental Rsch.

GIMBEL, FRANKLYN M. lawyer; b. Milw., Mar. 18, 1936; s. Virginia Grace Pivar; m. Barbara Posner, Aug. 3, 1958 (div. May 1969); children: Tod, Joshua; m. Martha Anne Knewtson, July 24, 1982; children: Rachel, Noah. BBA, U. Wis., 1958; JD, Marquette U., 1960. Bar: Wis. 1960, U.S. Dist. Ct. (ea. dist.) Wis. 1960, U.S. Supreme Ct. 1966. Staff atty. U.S. Atty. Dept. Justice, Milw., 1963-68; ptnr. Gimbel, Reilly, Guerin and Brown, Milw., 1968—. Vice chair Milw. Fire and Police Commn., 1977-82; bd. dirs. Milw. Expn. and Conv. Ctr. and Arena, 1982-94, Greater Milw. Found., 2002—, Fed. Defender Program Ea. Dist. Wis., 2000—. Fellow Am. Bar Found., Wis. Bar Found., Am. Coll. Trial Lawyers; mem. Wis. State Bar Assn. (chair bd. govs. 1981-82, pres. 1986-87), Milw. Bar Assn. (pres. 1976-77, Lawyer of Yr. 1989, 98, Greater Milw. Com., Rotary (v.p. 1999-00, pres. 2000-01); chmn. bd. dirs. Wis. Ctr. Dist. 1994-. Jewish. Home: 3075 N Lake Dr Milwaukee WI 53211-3403 Office: Gimbel Reilly Guerlin and Brown 330 E Kilbourn Ave Milwaukee WI 53202-3170

GIMBEL, HERVEY WILLIS, public health physician, medical administrator; b. Calgary, Alta., Can., Nov. 25, 1926; s. Jacob Allen Gimbel and Ruth Helen Johnson; m. Ann Matterand Gimbel, Dec. 23, 1951; children: Shirley Tetz, Denise Job, Kenneth, Marlin, Beverly Kramer. BA, Walla Walla Coll., 1950; MD, Loma Linda U., 1955, MPH, 1978. Diplomate Nat. Bd. Medicine; cert. Am. Bd. Preventive Medicine. Med. dir. North Hill Med. Clinic, Calgary, 1957-82; assoc. prof. Loma Linda (Calif.) U., 1982-84; med. dir. Parkview Ctr. for Occupl. Medicine, Riverside, Calif., 1985-91, Rancho Canyon Occupl. Medicine, Temecula, Calif., 1991-2001, Steck Meml. Medica Ctr., Centralia, Wash., 2002. Cons. China Nat. Health Edn. Inst., Beijing, 1992—; dir. China-U.S.A. Health Project, Loma Linda, Calif., 1991—, Health Edn. Ctr., Calgary, 1969-82; guest prof. Huazhong U., Wuhan, China, 2002-2004. Contbr. articles to periodicals. Flight lt. Royal Can. Air Force Res., 1958—60. Recipient China Tobacco Control award Chinese Assn. Smoking and Health, 2000. Fellow Am. Coll. Preventive Medicine; mem. Am. Coll. Environ. and Occupl. Medicine, Med. Coll. Can. (licentiate), Delta Omega. Avocations: traveling, photography, history. Home: 911 Landing Way Centralia WA 98531 E-mail: gimbel@quik.com.

GIMBLE, JOHNNY, country musician; Musician (solo): Texas Fiddle Collection, Texas Honky-Tonk Hits, (single John Gimble & Texas album Swing Pioneers) Still Swingin. Recipient Grammy award Best Country Instrumental Performance, 1996. Office: c/o Nancy Fly Agy PO Box 90306 Austin TX 78709-0306

GIMBRONE, MICHAEL ANTHONY, JR., research scientist, pathologist, educator; b. Buffalo, Nov. 16, 1943; married, 1971; 3 children. AB, Cornell U., 1965; MD, Harvard U., 1970. Intern, resident fellow Mass. Gen. Hosp., Boston, 1970-72; staff assoc. Nat. Cancer Inst., Bethesda, Md., 1972-74; resch. assoc. Harvard Med. Sch., Boston, 1974-76, from asst. prof. to assoc. prof., 1979-85, Elsie T. Friedman prof. pathology, 1985—; chmn. dept. pathology Brigham and Women's Hosp., Boston, 2001—. Cons. Nat. Heart, Lung and Blood Inst., NIH, 1976—; established investigator Am. Heart Assn., 1977-82; head Vascular Pathophysiol. Rsch. Lab., 1977-85; dir. vascular rsch. div. Brigham and Women's Hosp., 1985—, dir. Ctr. for Excellence in Vascular Biology. Recipient Achievement award in cardiovascular scis. Bristol-Myers Squibb, 2001. Fellow AAAS, Nat. Acad. of Scis., Am. Acad. Arts and Scis.; mem. Inst. of Medicine, Am. Heart Assn. (Basic Rsch. prize 1993), Am. Soc. Cell Biologists, Tissue Culture Assn., Am. Soc. Hematology, Am. Assn. Pathologists (v.p. 1991-92), Am. Soc. Invest. Pathology (pres. 1992-93), Am. Assn. Physicians, Fedn. Am. Socs. for Exptl. Biology (Exptl. Pathologist award 1982, bd. dirs. 1990-94), N.Am. Vascular Biology Orgn. (founding pres. 1994—, J. Allyn Taylor Internat. prize in medicine). Achievements include research in cardiovascular pathophysiology, especially atherosclerosis, thrombosis and inflammation, vascular cell biology. Office: Brigham and Womens Hosp Dept Pathology 75 Francis St Boston MA 02115 E-mail: mgimbrone@rics.bwh.harvard.edu.

GIMELSTOB, JUSTIN, professional tennis player; b. Livingston, N.J., Jan. 26, 1977; Professional tennis player, 1996—. Office: c/o USTA 70 W Red Oak Ln White Plains NY 10604-3602

GIMENEZ, DANIEL, soil scientist, educator; b. San Miguel de Tucuman, Tucuman, Argentina, Dec. 21, 1957; s. Aurelio and Nelly Amanda Gimenez; m. Rita Josefina Pasini; children: Ignacio, Ana, Clara. BS, U. Nacional de Tucuman, Argentina, 1982; MS, Agrl. U. Wageningen, The Netherlands, 1989; PhD, U. Minn., 1995. Rsch. asst. U. Nacional de Tucuman, 1982—87, Agrl. U. Wageningen, Netherlands, 1989—90, U. Minn., St. Paul, 1990—95; soil scientist USDA-ARS, Beltsville, Md., 1995—97; asst. prof. Rutgers U., New Brunswick, NJ, 1998—. Soil conservationist, San Miguel de Tucuman, Tucuman, Argentina, 1983—87. Fellow Grad. fellow, Dutch Govt., 1987—89. Mem.: Am. Geophys. Union, Internat. Soc. Soil Sci., Soil Sci. Soc. Am. Personal E-mail: iglu@worldnet.att.net.

GIMENEZ, LUIS FERNANDO, physician, educator; b. Antofagasta, Chile, Mar. 3, 1952; came to U.S., 1979; s. Luis Sr. and Nelly (Basulto) G.; m. Diane Marie Salazar, Sept. 20, 1957; children: Luis Andres, Pilar Elizabeth, Nicholas Miguel, Catherine Anne. MD, U. Chile, Valparaiso, 1976. Diplomate Am. Bd. Internal Medicine, Am. Bd. Nephrology. Intern U. Chile Sch. Medicine, Valparaiso, 1975-76; resident U. Concepcion Sch. Medicine, Chile, 1976-77, U. Chile Sch. Medicine, Valparaiso, 1977-79; research fellow in nephrology Johns Hopkins U. Sch. Medicine, Balt., 1979-81; intern Johns Hopkins Hosp., Balt., 1981-82, resident, 1982-84, clin. fellow nephrology div., 1984-85; instr. Johns Hopkins U. Sch. Medicine, Balt., 1985-86, asst. prof. medicine, 1986—. Dir. dialysis unit The Good Samaritan Hosp., Balt., 1985—, chief renal div., 1990; mem. med. adv. bd. Am. Kidney Found., Balt., 1987—. Contbr. articles to profl. jours. Recipient Outstanding Civic Svc. award Chilean Med. Assn., Valparaiso, 1974. Mem. Am. Fedn. for Clin. Research., Am. Soc. Nephrology, Am. Coll. Physicians, Internat. Soc. Nephrology, Internat. Soc. Peritoneal Dialysis, Am. Coll. Clin. Pharmacology. Avocation: philatelist. Office: Johns Hopkins Hosp Renal Divsn 1830 Bldg Baltimore MD 21205-2109

GIMMESTAD, GARY GENE, physicist, researcher; b. Madison, Wis., Oct. 8, 1946; s. Victor Edward and Maude Lucille (Gray) G.; m. Beverly Jane Beyreuther Baartmans, Aug. 10, 1968 (div. Oct. 1989); children: Maryann Elizabeth, Katherine Dawn; m. Susan Claire Elm, Sept. 22, 1990. BA in Physics, St. Olaf Coll., 1968; MS in Physics, U. Colo., 1972, PhD in Physics, 1978. Rsch. scientist Mich. Tech. U., Houghton, 1978-86, assoc. prof. physics, 1979-86; prin. rsch. scientist Ga. Inst. of Tech., Atlanta, 1986—. Sr. faculty leader Ga. Inst. Tech., Atlanta, 1986—; Glen P. Robinson chair electro-optics, 2001—. Contbr. articles to profl. jours. Mem. IEEE (sr.) Optical Soc. of Am., Soc. of Photo-Optical Instrumentation Engrs., Sigma Pi Sigma. Achievements include contbns. to new techniques for atmospheric remote sensing; devel. of optical instrumentation. Office: GTRI-EOEML Ga Tech Atlanta GA 30332-0834 E-mail: gary.gimmestad@gtri.gatech.edu.

GIMPLE, W. THOMAS, sales executive; BSBA, U. So. Calif. Pres. Iwerks Touring Techs., Inc. (subs. Iwerks Entertainment), 1991-95; exec. v.p. Iwerks Entertainment, Inc., 1995-96; pres., CEO, dir. Tickets.com, CEO, co-chmn., dir., 1999—. Office: Tickets dot com Inc 555 Anton Blvd Fl 12 Costa Mesa CA 92626-7811

GINDIN, R. ARTHUR, retired neurosurgeon; b. Perth Amboy, N.J., Sept. 10, 1934; m. Sara Roberson, 1991. Undergrad., U. Richmond, 1955; MD, Va. Commonwealth U., Richmond, 1959. Diplomate Am. Bd. Neurol. Surgery. Intern U. Okla. Hosp., Oklahoma City, 1959-60; resident Montreal (Can.) Neurol. Inst., 1963-65, Med. Coll. Va., 1965-67; assoc. prof. neurological surgery Med. Coll. Ga., Augusta, 1967-78; practice medicine specializing in neurological surgery, 1978-97; ret., 1997. Mem. Am. Assn. Neurol. Surgery. Office: 821 Straley Ave Princeton WV 24740-2925 E-mail: harvey@gindinyori.org.

GINDIN, WILLIAM HOWARD, judge; b. Perth Amboy, N.J., Sept. 1, 1931; s. Jac Paul and Belle Ruth (Steinberg) G.; m. Jane Hersh, June 24, 1954; children: Thomas L., Suzanne Hinsdale; m. Emily Shimkin, Dec. 25, 1965; children: Geoffrey A. Drucker, Janine Drucker Gordon. AB, Brown U., 1953; JD, Yale U., 1956. Bar: N.J. 1956, U.S. Supreme Ct. 1965, U.S. Ct. Appeals (3d cir.) 1980. Assoc. Gindin & Gindin, Plainfield, N.J., 1956-62, ptnr. Plainfield & Bridgewater, N.J., 1962-82; adminstrv. law judge Newark, 1982-85; U.S. bankruptcy judge Trenton, 1985-90, 99—; chief, 1990-98. Adj. prof. Rutgers Camden Law Sch., 1988-93; lectr. Inst. Continuing Legal Edn., Profl. Edn. Systems, Inc.; bd. govs. Nat. Conf. Bankruptcy Judges (3d cir.), 1989-92. Mem. editl. bd. N.J. Bar Assn. Jour., 1962-72. Mem. Plainfield Human Relations Commn., 1965-72, chmn., 1968-72; pres. Temple Sholom, Plainfield, 1979-81; regional v.p. Union Am. Hebrew Congregations, 1983-86; trustee Princeton Jewish Ctr.1994-96, Jewish Cmty. Found. of Mercer-Bucks 1998-2000; mem. Opera Festival of N.J. Fellow: Assn. Fed. Bar (adv. bd.), Bankruptcy Inn of Ct. (pres. 1995—99), Am. Bar Found., Am. Coll. Bankruptcy; mem.: ABA, Am.

Judicature Soc., N.J. Bar Assn., Mercer County Bar Assn., Union County Bar Assn., Plainfield Bar Assn., Plainfield Rotary (Paul Harris fellow, pres. 1974—75). Home: 30 James Ct Princeton NJ 08540-2633 Office: US Bankruptcy Ct 402 E State St Trenton NJ 08608-1507

GINDROZ, RAYMOND L. architect; b. Aug. 4, 1940; s. Theodore Stevens and Harriet (McBride) G.; m. Marilyn Jane Miltenberger, May 27, 1967; 1 child, Monica Ruth Gindroz. BArch with honors, Carnegie Inst. Tech., 1963, MArch in Urban Design with honors, 1965. Registered architect, Pa., Mich., N.J., Va., N.Y., W.Va. With UDA Archs., Pitts., 1964, prin., 1967-87; mng. prin. UDA Architects, Pitts., 1987—. Vis. prof. urban design Grad. Ctr. CUNY, 1988-89; critic, lectr. in urban design Yale U., 1967-88; lectr. Exploring New Urbanism, Harvard Symposium, 1999, Congress for New Urbanism VI and VII, 1998, 99, AIA Conv., 1998, 99, HUD, 1995—, U. Paris, Porte Dauphine, 1994, NAHB Conf., 1995; The Netherlands Now as Design, Amsterdam, 1989, others; urban design cons. City of Norfolk, Va., 1990—. Exhbns. include U. Pitts., 1976, Frick Gallery, Contemporary Art Ctr., Cin., 1977, Yale U., 1980, Cooper Hewitt Mus., N.Y.C., 1983, Peninsula Fine Arts Ctr., Hampton, Va., 1995, Shelter by Design, Chgo. and Naat. Bldg. Mus., Washington, 1996, COD sketches for Alliance Francaise, Washington, 1999; author: Papal Porticoes and Methodist Porches, 1987, Building Communities Through Good Design, Hope VI Developments, 1998, A Better Neighborhood, 1998, Cross Sections in Time and Space, 1998; author (with others): Representation and Architecture, Urban Structure, The Growth of Cities, Restoring Community Through Traditional Neighborhood Design: A Case Study of Diggs Town Public Housing, 1998; selected urban design and planning projects include Celebration (Fla.) Pattern Book, 1994—, Park DuValle, Louisville, 1996—, Downtown Norfolk 2000, 1989—, Diggstown Pub. Housing Redesign, Norfolk, Va., 1992, Vision Plan for Bluegrass Tomorrow, Lexington, Ky., 1992, numerous others; architecture includes Crawford Sq., Pitts., 1994 Tidewater Cmty. Coll., 1992-94, others. Bd. mem. Congress for New Urbanism., 1999; co-chair Inner City Task Force, CNU. Fulbright fellow, 1965-66, Stewardson traveling fellow in architecture, 1963. Fellow AIA (chair com. on design 1998); mem. AAUP, Pa. Soc. Architects, Am. Planning Assn. Office: Gulf Tower 31st Fl 707 Grant St Pittsburgh PA 15219-1908

GINDY, BENJAMIN LEE, insurance company executive; b. July 23, 1929; s. Roy E. and Anne M. Gindy; m. Judith Youngerman, Dec. 20, 1955; children: Deborah, Daniel, David. BS, U. Fla., 1951. CLU. Field rep. Penn Mut. Ins. Co., 1957-59; brokerage mgr. Mass. Indemnity Co., Miami, Fla., 1959-68; gen. agt. Guardian Life Ins. Co. Am., Miami, 1968—. Pres. Internat. Risk Cons., Inc., Wealthcare, Inc.; mktg. dir. Party Magic, Inc., Archer Impact Mktg., Solarpath Energy Sys. & Theme Cameras; instr. Life Underwriter Tng. Council, C.L.U. diploma course U. Miami; past columnist Miami Rev.; guest speaker in field. Recipient Nat. Health Ins. award Guardian Life Ins. Co. Am., 1977, 83. Mem. Am. Soc. CLUs (past pres. Miami chpt., named Man of Yr. 1987), Am. Wind Energy Assn., Am. Solar Energy Soc., Internat. Solar Energy Soc., South Fla. Inter-Profl. Coun. (past pres.), Gen. Agts. and Mgrs. Assn. (past pres.), Miami Assn. Life Underwriters (past pres., Man of Yr. 1972), Sierra Club. Home: 1018 Aduana Ave Coral Gables FL 33146-3326 Office: Gindy Agy Guardian Life 7615 SW 62nd Ave Miami FL 33143-4906 E-mail: greenpower@solarpath.com.

GINGERICH, MARTIN ELLSWORTH, literature educator; b. Reedsville, Pa., May 24, 1933; s. Norman John and Kathryn Pauline (Graham) Gingerich; m. Jeanne Ellen Carroll, Nov. 20, 1985; m. Mary Elizabeth Morsillo, Aug. 3, 1958 (div. 1985); children: Darcy, Kevin, Jonathan, Marta. BS, Shippensburg (Pa.) U., 1967; MA, U. Maine, Orono, 1961; PhD, Ohio U., Athens, 1967. Asst. prof. East Stroudsburg (Pa.) U., 1961—64, Ohio U., Athens, 1967—68; prof. Western Mich. U., Kalamazoo, 1968—90, prof. emeritus, 1990—. Undergraduate dir. English dept. Western Mich. U., 1983—85. Author: (books) W.H. Auden: A Reference Guide, 1977, Contemporary Poetry in Am. and Eng., 1983; contbr. articles to literary jours. With USN, 1951—55. Mem.: Dylan Thomas Soc. (life). Independent. Avocations: reading, cooking, gardening, fishing, star gazing. Home: 388 Ponemah Tr Buckley MI 49620

GINGERICH, OWEN JAY, astronomer, educator; b. Washington, Iowa, Mar. 24, 1930; 3 children. BA, Goshen Coll., 1951; MA, Harvard U., 1953, PhD in Astronomy, 1962. Dir. obs. Am. U., Beirut, 1955-58, from instr. to asst. prof., 1955-58; lectr. astronomy Wellesley Coll., 1958-59; astrophysicist Smithsonian Astrophys. Obs., 1961-87, sr. astronomer, 1987-2000; from lectr. to assoc. prof. astronomy and history of sci. Harvard U., 1960-69, prof., 1969-2000, chmn. history of sci. dept., 1992-93, rsch. prof., 2000—; Sigma Xi nat. lectr., 1971; George Darwin lectr. Royal Astron. Soc., 1971. Astronomy cons. Harvard Project Physics, 1964-69; dir. ctrl. telegram bur. Internat. Astronomical Union, 1965-67, pres. commn. history astronomy, 1970-76, chmn. U.S. nat. com., 1982-84; adv. com. Ctr. Theol. Inquiry, Princeton, 1988-97; adv. bd. John Templeton Found., 1994-99, 2001-2003, trustee, 2003—. Assoc. editor: Jour. History Astronomy, 1975— ; mem. editorial bd. Am. Scholar, 1975-80; dir. Harvard mag., 1978-85, incorporator, 1986—. Overseer Boston Mus. Sci., 1979-96, 98—. Decorated Order of Merit comdr. class People's Republic of Poland, 1981 Fellow AAAS (chmn. sect. L 1974, sect D 1981); mem. Academie Internationale d'Histoire des Sciences, Am. Acad. Arts and Scis., Am. Philos. Soc. (v.p. 1982-85, John F. Lewis prize 1976, councilor 1994-2000), Am. Astron. Soc. (chmn. hist. astronomy div. 1983-85, Doggett prize 2000), Royal Astron. Soc. Can. (hon.), Phi Beta Kappa. Clubs: Examiner. Achievements include research and publications on model stellar atmospheres (to 1971) and in history of astronomy. Office: Harvard-Smithsonian Ctr for Astrophysics Cambridge MA 02138 Business E-Mail: ginger@cfa.harvard.edu. *Our most earnest ambitions are in effect unspoken prayers-they define our deepest views on the meaning of life far more precisely than any outward profession of religion or ethics.*

GINGLES, MARJORIE STANKE, music educator, educator; b. Bklyn., Jan. 30, 1938; d. E.C. and E.L. (Lewthwaite) Stromberg; m. Charles Frederick Stanke, Aug. 27, 1960 (div. Nov. 8, 1976); m. William Glen Gingles, Sept. 29, 1984. BS in Music Edn., W. Chester U., formerly W. Chester State Tchrs. Coll., 1959; MA in Edn., W. Chester U., formerly W. Chester State Tchrs. Coll., mem, 1969. Elem. music tchr. George Gray Elem. Sch., Wilmington, Del., 1959-60, Penn-Delco Pub. Schs., Aston, Pa., 1960-61; pvt. piano tchr. home studio Berwyn, Norwood, Devon, Malvern, Pa., 1963—; choral dir. Coterie Singers, Wayne, Pa., 1975-84; music dir. St. Francis-in-the-Fields Ch., Malvern, Pa., 1981-88; piano tchr. Acad. Cmty. Music, Fort Washington, Pa., 1997—. Mem. music com. Main Line Unitarian Ch, Devon, 1970—, chair music com., 1978-79; mem. music com. Dorothy Taubman Inst. Piano, Amherst Coll., 1988-97, adjudicator Pa. Govs. Sch. Arts, 1986; music dir. Pro-Arte Chorale, 1980-86, dir. world and area premieres of new works; instr. several vocal workshops in field; clinician PMTA Convention, 1999. Piano concert artist, Pa. and N.Y. State; duo pianist with William Gingles; performances (in Gingles Duo) Pa. Music Tchrs. Conv. Taubman Piano Study grantee Pa. Music Tchrs. Assn., 2000. Mem. Main Line Music Tchrs. Assn. (chair adult recitals, chair Prime Time Players). Unitarian-Universalist. Avocations: reading, swimming, decorating. Home and Office: 27 Cypress Ln Berwyn PA 19312-1004 E-mail: msgingles@worldnet.att.net.

GINGOLD, DENNIS MARC, lawyer; b. Plainfield, N.J., June 23, 1949; s. Michael Richard and Sally (Weiss) G.; m. Anne Carol Pearson, Sept. 4, 1970; children: Stacy Michele, Samantha Anne. BA, Rollins Coll., 1971; JD, Seton Hall U., 1974; postgrad., Princeton U., NYU, 1974-75; LLM in Internat. Legal Studies, NYU, 1975; postgrad., SUNY, Buffalo, 1975-76. Bar: N.J. 1974, U.S. Dist. Ct. N.J. 1974, Colo. 1981, U.S. Dist. Ct. Colo. 1981, U.S. Ct. Appeals (10th cir.) 1984, (9th cir.) 1991, (11th cir.) 1997, U.S. Supreme Ct. 1985, D.C. 1989, U.S. Dist. Ct. D.C. 1989. Atty.-advisor U.S. Compt. Currency, Washington, 1976-79, regional counsel 12th Nat. Bank Region Denver, 1979-80; ptnr. Gorsuch, Kirgis, Campbell, Walker & Grover, Denver, 1980-82, Kirkland & Ellis, Denver and Washington, 1982-85; lead banking ptnr. Squire, Sanders & Dempsey, Washington, 1985-88; ptnr. Foley, Hoag & Eliot, Washington, 1988-90, Dickstein, Shapiro & Morin, Washington, 1991-93. Adj. prof. law U. Denver, 1981-82. Sr. mem. Seton Hall U. Law Jour., 1972-73. Named one of the Top 20 Banking Lawyers in U.S. Nat. Law Jour., 1983; Reginald Heber Smith fellow, 1975-76. Mem. D.C. Bar Assn., Colo. Bar Assn., N.J. Bar Assn., Denver Bar Assn., Banking Law Inst. (adv. coun. 1983-86), Bethesda Country Club.

GINGOLD, GEORGE NORMAN, insurance company executive, lawyer; b. N.Y.C., Aug. 2, 1939; s. Josef and Gladys (Anderson) G.; m. Anne Brenda Davis, July 7, 1963; children— Rachel June, David Bruce AB magna cum laude, Harvard U., 1960, JD, 1963. Bar: Ariz. 1964, Conn. 1968, Mass. 1989. Pvt. practice law, Phoenix, 1964-65; atty. SEC, Washington, 1965-67; counsel AEtna Life & Casualty, Hartford, Conn., 1967-94; counsel, corp. sec. AEtna Life Ins. and Annuity Co., Hartford, 1981-94; pvt. practice ins. securities law, 1994—. Mem. com. on securities regulation Am. Council of Life Ins., Washington, 1978-94, chmn., 1986-88; instr. Hartford Coll. for Women, 1983-95. Author articles in field Vice pres., bd. dirs. United Cerebral Palsy Assn., Hartford, 1980-87; vice chmn. West Hartford Human Rights Commn., Conn., 1975-79; pres. West Hartford PTA, 1976-78 Mem. ABA (mem. fed. regulation of securities com. 1978—), Am. Soc. Corp. Secs., Fed. Bar Assn. (pres. Hartford County chpt. 1974-76) Lodges: B'nai B'rith Unity (pres. 1971-72). Avocations: classical music; theatre; chess. Office: PO Box 155 West Hyannisport MA 02672-0155

GINGOLD, NEIL MARSHALL, lawyer; b. Syracuse, N.Y., Jan. 3, 1946; s. Eli and Sarle (Greenhouse) G.; m. Susan Lite, Aug. 15, 1970; children— Scott, Jason, Samantha. AB in Polit. Sci., Syracuse U., 1967, JD, 1970. Bar: N.Y. 1971, U.S. Dist. Ct. (no. dist.) N.Y. 1971, U.S. Supreme Ct. 1977, U.S. Dist. Ct. (we. dist.) N.Y. 1988, U.S. Dist. Ct. (ea. dist.) Mich. 1989. Assoc. Michaels & Michaels, Syracuse, 1970-71; asst. atty. gen. N.Y. State Dept. Law, Syracuse, 1971-73; regional atty. N.Y. State Dept. Environ. Conservation, Syracuse, 1973-79; counsel N.Y. State Assembly, Albany, 1980; ptnr. Gingold & Gingold, Syracuse, 1980-82; asst. dist. counsel U.S. SBA, Syracuse, 1982-85; gen. counsel Envirosure Mgmt. Corp., Buffalo, 1985-88; assoc. Pinsky & Skandalis, Syracuse, 1988-92; sr. assoc. Hancock & Estabrook, LLP, Syracuse, 1992—. Co-chmn. fund raising CNY Charities Open, Inc., Syracuse, 1980-85; successively treas., v.p., pres. Jewish Family Service Bur., Inc., Syracuse, 1975-82; bd. dirs. Temple Adath Yeshurun, Syracuse, 1972-76, Syracuse Jewish Fedn., 1975-78, Upstate N.Y. chpt. Am. Diabetes Assn. Syracuse, 1981-85, U.S. Com. for Israel Environment, N.Y.C., 1981-85, Finger Lakes Land Trust, Ithaca, 1997—2000; mem. heart walk run com. Am. Heart Assn. Office: Hancock & Estabrook LLP 5178 WInterton Drive Fayetteville NY 13066 Office Fax: 315-445-7222.

GINGRAS, ANNE ELIZABETH, geriatrics, rehabilitation nurse; b. Attleboro, Mass., May 15, 1948; d. William Joseph and Anna Evelyn (McNaly) G. ADN, Ctrl. Fla. C.C., 1977; BS in Profl. Arts Edn., St. Joseph's Coll., 1988; grad. legal nurse cons., Kaplan Law Coll., 2000. BLS; CCRN. Staff nurse CCU/ICU Citrus Meml. Hosp., Inverness, Fla., 1978-80; staff nurse cardiac step down unit Monroe Regional Med. Ctr., Ocala, Fla., 1986-91; patient care asst., nursing instr. Marion County Community Edn., Ocala, Fla., 1988-89; nursing supr. Marion House Nursing-Rehab., Ocala, Fla., 1992; nurse Hospice Marion County, Ocala, 1992-93; nurse clinician Charter Behavioral Health Svcs., Ocala, 1993-95, with outpatient psychiatry unit Plant City, Fla., 1996-97; with nursing rehab. unit Health-South, Largo, Fla., 1998—; mem. adult rehab. nursing unit Health South, Largo, Fla., 2000-01; med.-surg. nurse Suncoast Hosp., Largo, 2000—. Instr. BLS, ARC, Ocala, 1988-89. Mem. Ocala Jaycees, Nurses for Christ. Avocations: free-lance writing, drawing, hiking, music.

GINGRAS, PAUL JOSEPH, real estate management company executive; b. Augusta, Maine, Mar. 10, 1948; s. Adolphe Joseph and Antoinette Marie (Lacombe) G.; m. Azucena Figuera Malaver, Nov. 13, 1976; children: Audrey Elena, Natali Elizabeth. BA Math., U. Maine, 1973; student, Boston Archtl. Ctr., 1974-76. Cert. shopping ctr. mgr. Property mgr. Coppola & Co., Boston, 1975-77; property acquisitions and mgmt. William Crocker Corp., White Plains, N.Y., 1979-82; v.p. Roebling Mgmt. Co. Inc., Paramus, N.J., 1983-86, pres., 1986-91, Parkway Asset Mgmt. Corp., Hackensack, N.J., 1992—. With U.S. Army, 1967-70. Mem. Internat. Coun. Shopping Ctrs. Avocations: guitar music, sports. Home: 497 Rutland Ave Teaneck NJ 07666-2925 Office: Parkway Asset Mgmt Corp 225 Moore St Hackensack NJ 07601-7417

GINGREY, PHIL, congressman; b. Augusta, Ga., July 10, 1942; m. Billie Gingrey; 4 children. BS, Ga. Inst. Tech.; MD, Med. Coll. Ga. Intern Grady Meml. Hosp., Atlanta; resident Med. Coll. Ga.; pvt. practice ob-gyn. Marietta, Ga.; mem. Ga. State Senate, 1999—2002; congressman 11th Dist. Ga. U.S. Ho. Reps., 2003—. Chmn. Marietta Sch. Bd. Republican. Office: 1118 Longworth House Office Bldg Washington DC 20515-1011*

GINGRICH, NEWT (NEWTON LEROY GINGRICH), former congressman; b. Harrisburg, Pa., June 17, 1943; s. Robert Bruce and Kathleen (Daugherty) G.; children: Linda Kathleen, Jacqueline Sue.; m. Marianne Ginther, Aug. 1981. BA, Emory U., 1965; MA, Tulane U., 1968, PhD in European History, 1971. Faculty W. Ga. Coll., Carrollton, 1970-78, asst. prof. history, until 1978; mem. 96th-105th Congresses from 6th Ga. dist. U.S. Ho. of Reps., Washington, 1979-99; speaker U.S. Ho. Reps., 104th-105th Congress, 1995-99; founder The Com. for New Am. Leadership, Washington. Speaker, chmn. emeritus GOPAC; co-founder Conservative Opportunity Soc., congl. mil. caucus, space caucus; mem. joint com. on printing, house adminstrn. com.; co-chmn. Leader's Task Force on Health; adj. prof. Reinhardt Coll., Waleska, Ga., 1994-95. Author: (with Marianne Gingrich) Window of Opportunity, 1984, Renewing American Civilization, 1995, (with William Forschen) 1945, 95, To Renew America, 1995. Named Man of Yr., 1995. Mem. AAAS, Ga. Conservancy. Lodges: Kiwanis, Moose. Republican. Baptist. Office: The Com for New Am Leadership 1800 K St NW Ste 714 Washington DC 20006-2211

GINIGER, KENNETH SEEMAN, publisher; b. N.Y.C., Feb. 18, 1919; s. Maurice Aaron and Pearl (Triester) G.; m. Carol Virginia Wilkins, Sept. 27, 1952 (dec. Aug. 1985); m. Bernice Dees Ellinger Cullinan, Apr. 13, 2002. Student, U. Va., 1935-39, N.Y. Law Sch., 1940-41. Ptnr. Signet Press, 1939-40; assoc. editor Arts and Decoration and The Spur, 1940-41; dir. pub. relations Prentice-Hall, Inc., 1946-49, editor-in-chief trade book div., 1949-52; v.p., gen. mgr. Hawthorn Books div., 1952-61; pres. Hawthorn Books, Inc., N.Y.C., 1961-65, K.S. Giniger Co., Inc., N.Y.C., 1965—, Consol. Book Pubs. div. Processing & Books, Inc., Chgo., 1969-74, Tradewinds Group div. IPC Ltd., Sydney, Australia, 1974-76. Lectr. New Sch. Social Rsch., 1948—49, NYU, 1979—81, adj. asst. prof., 1981—83, adj. assoc. prof., 1983—85; asst. to dir. CIA, 1951—52. Author: The Compact Treasury of Inspiration, 1955 (NCCJ Brotherhood Week citation), America, America, America, 1957, A Treasury of Golden Memories, 1958, (with Walter Russell Bowie) What Is Protestantism?, 1965, A Little Treasury of Hope, 1968, A Little Treasury of Comfort, 1968, A Little Treasury of Christmas, 1968, The Sayings of Jesus, 1968, (with Will Yolen) Heroes for Our Times, 1969, The Family Advent Book, 1979, Pope John Paul II: Pilgrim of Faith, 1987, (with Sir John Templeton) Spiritual Evolution, 1998; editor: Internat. Pub. News, 1983-91, European Bookseller Pub. World/Update Newsletter, 1991-92; mem. editorial bd.: RAM Reports, 1977-83, Communications and the Law, 1978-94. Sec. Com. Collective Security, 1952—65; nat. adv. bd. Found. Religious Action, 1956—94; dir. Layman's Nat. Bible Com., 1957—, pres., 1963—71, chmn., 1987—94, chmn. emeritus, 1994—; mem. adv. bd. Templeton Found., 1992—2000, Am. Theater Wing, 1999. Capt. AUS, 1941—45. Decorated chevalier French Legion of Honor. Mem. P.E.N., Garrick Club (London), Authors Club (London) Arts Club (London), Army and Navy Club (Washington), Players Club, Yale Club, Dutch Treat Club, Church Club (N.Y.C.), Phi Delta Phi. Republican. Episcopalian. Home: 1045 Park Ave New York NY 10028-1030 Office: 250 W 57th St New York NY 10107

GINN, JOHN ARTHUR, JR., insurance agent; b. Palatka, Fla., June 2, 1918; s. John Arthur and Violet Maude (Merwin) g.; m. Lou Eliska Cone, Feb. 4, 1945; children: Judith Ann, John Arthur III. BS, Fla. So. Coll., 1940. CLU; chartered fin. cons. Agt. N.Y. Life, Palatka, Fla., 1938—; v.p. Ginn Fin. Group, 1938—. Chmn. N.Y. Life Chmn. Coun., 1981; mem. N.Y. Life Adv. Bd. Dirs., 1981-95. Mem. Fla. Assn. Life Underwriters (pres. 1969), Nat. Assn. Life Underwriters. Republican. Methodist. Office: Ginn Fin Group Inc 421 Saint Johns Ave Ste 3 Palatka FL 32177-4700 E-mail: ginnfingrp@funport.net.

GINN, MARTIN E. writer, consultant; b. N.Y.C., Sept. 26, 1929; s. Joseph Edwin Ginn and Minnie Brenner; m. Diane Ecker, Nov. 29, 1948; children: Daryl Morrison, David S., Joanne S. Kurzmann. AB in Chemistry, NYU, 1952, MS in Chemistry, 1954; MBA, Ill. Inst. Tech., 1971; PhD in Indsl. Engring. and Mgmt. Sci., Northwestern U., 1983. Rsch. asst. Sanitary Engring. Lab. NYU, N.Y.C., 1952—54; rsch. chemist Monsanto and Co., Dayton, Ohio, 1954—62; lab. mgr., corp. advisor Armour and Co., Chgo., 1962—70; dir. R&D, v.p. Alberto-Culver Co. Masury-Columbia Dvisn., Chgo., 1970—78; tech. dir. Walton-March, Inc., Deerfield, Ill., 1978—80; rsch. assoc. Northwestern U., Evanston, Ill., 1980—83; assoc. prof., dir. exec. MBA Ill. Inst. Tech., Chgo., 1983—99; cons., author Skokie, Ill., 1999—. Lectr. in field. Author: The Creativity Challenge: Parts A&B, 1995; mem. editl. bd.: Jour. Mgmt. Sys., 1988—92; contbr. articles to profl. jours. Chief advisor Jr. Achievement, Dayton, 1957—60. Mem.: Soc. Childrens Books Assn., Am. Oil Chemists Soc. (assoc. editor 1970—85), Am. Chem. Soc. (emeritus). Avocation: writing. Home: 9327 N Kostner Ave Skokie IL 60076

GINN, ROBERT MARTIN, retired utility company executive; b. Detroit, Jan. 13, 1924; s. Lloyd T. and Edna S.; m. Barbara R. Force, 1948; children: Anne, Martha, Thomas. BS in Elec. Engring., MS in Elec. Engring., U. Mich., 1948. With Cleve. Electric Illuminating Co., 1948-89, contr., 1959-62, v.p. gen. svcs., 1963-70, exec. v.p., 1970—79, pres., 1979—83, chief exec. officer, 1979-88, chmn., 1983-89; chmn., CEO Centerior Energy Corp., Toledo Edison Co., 1986-88. Mem. Shaker Heights Bd. Edn., (Ohio), 1968-75, pres., 1973-74; pres. Welfare Fedn. Cleve., 1968-69; chmn. Cleve. Commn. on Higher Edn., 1983-86; trustee John Carroll U., 1983-89, exec.-in-residence, 1989—; trustee Martha Holden Jennings Found., 1975-2002; chmn. Cleve. Opera, 1986-91. With USAAF, 1943-46. Office: 1120 Chester Ave # 470 Cleveland OH 44114-3514

GINN, RONN, architect, urban planner, general contractor; b. Jacksonville, Fla., Apr. 17, 1933; s. Angus Theodore and Joan Adelaide (Bailey) G.; children: Sharon Lee, John Norman. AA, U. Fla., 1957, B.Arch., 1960, B.Landscape Architecture, 1961. Lic. bldg. ofcl., Fla. Urban design specialist Model Cities Adminstrn., HUD, Washington, 1967-68; pvt. practice landscape architecture, constrn., urban planning St. Petersburg, Fla., 1968—; pres. ARG Constrn. Corp., 1975-76, ARG Corp., 1977—, Ginn Corp., 1967-70, Atrium Corp., 1965-72. Urban design lectr. U. N.Mex., 1967; planning cons. State Dept., 1967-68; design cons. Am. Revolution Bicentennial Commn., 1967-69; vis. design critic Rice U., 1974; mem. Pinellas County (Fla.) Bd. Adjustments and Appeals, 1981-88; mem. Albuquerque Fine Arts Commn., 1965-67, St. Petersburg Design Goals Com., 1971-73; moderator radio program Design in Our Community WPKM, Tampa, Fla., 1971-72; founder, bd. dirs. Pinellas County Red Flag Charrette, 1972-76, Catalyst, St. Petersburg; bd. dirs. Fla. Council Clean Air, Fla. Red Flag Charrette; mem. Pinellas County Planning Council, 1972-73 Supervising architect, urban designer: Roswell (N.Mex.) Ctrl. bus. dist. redesign, 1964, Tucumcari (N.Mex.) ctrl. bus. dist. redesign, 1967, Treasure Island (Fla.) civic ctr. design, 1971; architect, urban designer, prin. Atrium One, Albuquerque, 1965-67; contbg. editor Urban Affairs Symposia, 1965-73; guest columnist St. Petersburg Evening Ind., 1974; important works include Albuquerque ctrl. bus. dist. redesign (nat. AIA award 1966), new town Fla. Ctr. (nat. Am. Soc. Landscape Architects award 1970), Brown residence (AIA merit award 1975), Penguin Restaurant, Treasure Island, Fla., 1973, Cross residence, 1974, Sheridan Gallery, 1974, Madeira Beach C. of C., 1975, Greenpepper Restaurant, 1975, Mixon Bldg., Ruskin, Fla., 1976, Congregation Beth Chai Synagogue, Seminole, Fla., 1979, Villa Dos Santos Master Plan, St. Petersburg Beach, Fla., 1979, Congregation Kol Ami Synagogue, Tampa, 1981, Markham residence, St. Petersburg, 1981, The Moorings, Tierra Verde, Fla., 1981, Ginn Residence, St. Petersburg, 1981, Congregation B'nai Israel Synagogue, Clearwater, Fla., 1981, Suncoast Seabird Sanctuary, St. Petersburg, 1982, Lilly Residence, Treasure Island, Fla., 1983, Anchor Bank Office Bldg., St. Petersburg, 1984, 1600 Pasadena Office Bldg., 1984 (nat. design patent), Lighthouse Harbor Marina, 1984, Tugaloo Environ. Edn. Ctr., 1989, Latorre Chiropractic Clinic, 1990, Johnnie Ruth Clarke Health Ctr., 1992, Jakabosi Studio, 1995, Jakabosi residence, 2001, Santeeteah (N.C.) Town Hall, 1998, Graham County (N.C.) EMS Bldg., 2002, Graham County Adminstrn. Bldg. DEsign Studies, 2002. Mayoral candidate City of Treasure Island, Fla., 1973; bldg. dir. City of Seminole, 1975-78; mem. Leadership St. Petersburg, 1978-79; mem. permitting task force City of St. Petersburg, 1999-2001. Recipient numerous archtl., landscape architecture, urban design awards, Addy awards, 1981, 82; named Spiffs Person of Courage, 1984 Mem. AIA (nat. com. on regional devel. 1969-76, vice chmn., commr. pub. affairs Fla. chpt.), Am. Inst. Planners, Constrn. Specifications Inst., Am. Inst. Landscape Architects, So. Bldg. Code Congress, Fla. Planning and Zoning Assn., Nat. Eagle Scout Assn. (chpt. chmn.). Republican. Presbyterian. Office: Jakabosi-Ginn Arch PO Box 1541 Robbinsville NC 28771-1541 E-mail: ronnginn@aol.com.

GINN, VERA WALKER, director; b. Jacksonville, Fla., Dec. 22, 1949; d. Grady and Pearl Walker; m. Perry L. Ginn, Mar. 16, 1969; children: Perry Jr., Spencer. BA in Edn., Fla. Atlantic U., 1972; MS, Nova U., 1985; specialist in edn., Barry U., 1991. Cert. ednl. leadership, reading, elem. edn. ESOL. Tchr. grades 3 and 4 Plantation (Fla.) Park Elem., 1973-82, Griffin Elem., Cooper City, Fla., 1982-85; tchr. grades 6-8 Seminole Mid., Plantation, 1985-90; lead tchr. Chpt. 1 Adminstrv. Office, Ft. Lauderdale, Fla., 1990-92, tchr. on spl. assignment, 1992-93, dir. title 1 migrant & spl. programs, 1997—. Advisor Fla. Future Educators Am., Plantation, 1990—91; adj. prof. Fla. Atlantic U., Ft. Lauderdale, 1995—97. Mem.: ASCD, Fla. Assn. Sch. Adminstrs., Fla. Reading Assn., Internat. Reading Assn., Fla. Assn. State and Fed. Ednl. Program Adminstrs., Phi Delta Kappa. Democrat. Baptist. Avocations: reading, travel, entertaining, bowling. Home: 6700 SW 20th St Plantation FL 33317-5107 Office: Title 1 Adminstrv Office 701 NW 31st Ave Fort Lauderdale FL 33311-6627

GINOS, JAMES ZISSIS, retired research chemist; b. Hillsboro, Ill., Feb. 1, 1923; s. Zissis and Nicoletta M. (Sakellaris) G.; m. Chrisilla Katsas, June 13, 1947; children: Geoffrey, Milton. BA, Columbia U., 1954; MS in Chem. Engring., Stevens Inst. Tech., 1962, PhD in Organic Chemistry, 1964. Chemist Colgate Palmolive Co., Jersey City, 1953-57; chief chemist Diamond Shamrock Corp., Newark, 1957-58; project coord. Nopco Chem. Co., Harrison, N.J., 1959-64; asst. scientist Brookhaven Nat. Labs., Upton, N.Y., 1964-68; rsch. asst. prof. Mt. Sinai Sch. Medicine, N.Y.C., 1968-70; assoc. scientist Brookhaven Nat. Labs., 1970-74, scientist, 1974-75; rsch. assoc. prof. Cornell U. Med. Coll., 1975-92, assoc. rsch. prof. neurosci., 1989-92; ret., 1992. Sr. rsch. assoc. neuro-oncology Lab. Meml. Sloan-Kettering Cancer Ctr., N.Y.C., 1980-84, assoc. lab. mem., 1984-89, assoc. lab. mem. nuc. medicine cyclotron core, 1989-93. Contbr. articles to profl. jours. Mem. AAAS, Am. Chem. Soc., Am. Soc. Pharmacology and Exptl. Therapeutics, N.Y. Acad. Sci., Soc. Nuc. Medicine, Harvey Soc. Achievements include research on synthesis of radiopharmaceuticals labelled with shortlived positron emitting radioisotopes used in positron emission tomography; patentee in field. Home: 200 Winston Dr Apt 3016 Cliffside Park NJ 07010-3234 E-mail: jamesginos@worldnet.att.net.

GINOZA, WILLIAM, former biophysics educator; b. L.A., Feb. 7, 1914; s. Shinkichi and Kame (Yamashiro) G.; m. Midori Sugita, Oct. 4, 1944 (dec. May 1987); children: Lillian, Donn. BA, U. Calif., Berkeley, 1937, MA, 1939; PhD, UCLA, 1952. Asst. rsch. biochemist dept. botany UCLA, 1952-55, rsch. scientist atomic energy commn., 1956-61; assoc. prof. dept. biophysics Pa. State U., University Park, 1961-67, prof., 1967-79, prof. emeritus, 1979—. Invited speaker ednl. instns. and sci. confs., including Internat. Congress Biochemistry, Vienna, 1958, Faraday Soc. meeting on nucleic acids, Birmingham, Eng., 1958; vis. fellow Yale U., New Haven, 1958-60; vis. prof. U. Kyoto, Japan, 1974. Co-author: Methods in Virology, Vol IV, 1968.; contbr. reviews to Ann. Reviews Nuclear Sci., Ann. Reviews Microbiology; contbr. articles to profl. jours. Fellow AAAS; mem. Biophys. Soc., Sigma Xi, Phi Lambda Upsilon. Achievements include illucidation of molecular structure of Tobacco Mosaic Virus and its RNA, mechanisms by which heat or high energy radiations destroy the biological functions of nucleic acids of viruses and bacteria. Home: 962 E McCormick Ave State College PA 16801-6529

GINSBERG, BARRY GAVRILLE, psychologist, consultant, trainer; b. Bklyn., July 25, 1936; s. Elias Ginsberg and Lea Schwartz Epstein; m. Mindi Silverberg, Feb. 22, 1962; children: Joshua, Neil Daniel, Jeremy Marc. BS in Pharmacy, columbia U., 1958; MS in Edn./Clin. Sch. Psychology, CCNY, 1969; PhD in Human Devel. and Family Studies, Pa. State U., 1971. Lic. pharmacist, N.Y., N.J., Calif., Fla.; cert. tchr., N.Y.C.; lic. psychologist, Pa., Mass.; diplomate in family psychology Am. Bd. Profl. Psychology; cert. play therapist/supr., cert. marriage and family therapist; nat. cert. sch. psychologist. Pharmacist, mgr. Ginsberg Pharmacy, Bronx, N.Y., 1958-63; tchr. jr. and sr. h.s.

N.Y.C. Bd. Edn., 1963-69; psychologist Bucks County Psychiat. Ctr., Chalfont, Pa., 1971-73; dir. child and family unit Lenape Valley Found., Chalfont, 1973-75, dir. cmty. svcs., 1975-78; psychologist dir. Ginsberg Assocs., Doylestown, Pa., 1978—; cons. and trainer, dir. Ctr. Relationship Enhancement, Doylestown, 1981—. Adj. assoc. prof. Temple U., 1975-85; cons. Bucks County Area Coun. Aging, 1988—, Bucks County Children and Youth, Doylestown, 1989—, Bucks County Head Start, Bucks County Assn. Retarded Citizens, Doylestown, 1982—; adj. prof. psychology Phila. Coll. Osteo Medicine, 1997; adj. prof. clin. psychology Chestnut Hill Coll., 2000; bd. dirs. Am. Bd. Family Psychology, 1997. Author: Relationship Enhancement Family Therapy, 1997, 50 Wonderful Ways to Be a Single Parent Family, 2002; columnist Parenting, 1988-89; co-host Cable TV program Parenting, 1994—. Bd. dirs. Big Bros./Big Sisters of Bucks County, 1972—, Bucks County Drug and Alcohol Commn., 1981-87, Network of Victims Asistance, 1990-95. Recipient Sterling Vol. award Ctrl. Bucks C. of C., 1996, Meritorious award Am. Bd. Profl. Psychology, 1992, Meritorious award Bucks County Drug and Alcohol Commn., 1987. Fellow APA (bd. dirs. divsn. family psychology, Meritorious awards divsn. family psychology 1986, 87, 88, 89), Pa. Psychol. Assn. (bd. dirs., pres. cmty. divsn.), Am. Assn. Marriage and Family Therapists (clin. mem., approved supr.), Ctrl. Bucks C. of C. (v.p., bd. dirs. 1975-89, chmn. parenting and family com. 1990—). Avocations: racquetball, folk dancing, nutcracker ballet. Office: Ctr Relationship Enhancement 17 W State St Doylestown PA 18901-4225

GINSBERG, BARRY HOWARD, physician, researcher; b. Bklyn., May 9, 1945; s. Emanuel and Ruth (Friedman) G.; m. Marjorie Ellen Kanef, Aug. 20, 1967; children: Susan, David. BA, SUNY, Binghamton, 1965; PhD, Yeshiva U., 1971, MD, 1972. Intern Beth Israel Hosp., Boston, 1972-73, resident in internal medicine, 1973-74; fellow in endocrinology NIH, 1974-77; asst. prof. U. Iowa, Iowa City, 1977-82, assoc. prof. medicine and biochemistry, 1982—87, prof., 1988-90, assoc. dir. Diabetes-Endocrinology Rsch. Ctr., 1982-84, dir., 1984-86, co-dir. diabetes control and complications trial, 1984—86, dir., 1986-90; med. dir. worldwide diabetes healthcare Becton Dickenson and Co., Franklin Lakes, NJ, 1990—98; v.p. med. affairs BD Consumer Healthcare, 1999—. Adj. prof. medicine Robert Wood Johnson Coll. Medicine. Contbr. chpts. to med. books. Comdr. USPHS, 1974-77. Mem. Am. Fedn. Clin. Rsch., Endocrine Soc., Ctrl. Soc. Clin. Rsch., Am. Diabetes Assn. (pres. Iowa chpt. 1982-84, bd. dirs. 1982-85, bd. dirs. N.E. chpt. 1989—). Avocation: computer programming. Office: Becton Dickinson and Co 1 Becton Dr Franklin Lakes NJ 07417-1880 E-mail: barry_ginsberg@bd.com.

GINSBERG, BENJAMIN, political science educator; b. Poking, Germany, Apr. 1, 1947; came to U.S., 1949, naturalized 1955. s. Herman and Anna (Wolfstein) G.; m. Sandra Joy Brewer, Dec. 15, 1968; children: Cynthia, Alexander. BA, U. Chgo., 1968, MA, 1970, PhD, 1973. Asst. prof. govt. Cornell U., Ithaca, N.Y., 1972-78, assoc. prof., 1978-83, prof., 1983-91, dir. Survey Rsch. Facility, 1985-86, dir. Inst. Pub. Affairs, 1987-91, dir. Washington program, 1988-91; David Bernstein prof. polit. sci., dir. Ctr. Govt. Studies, Johns Hopkins U., Balt., 1992—, dir. MA in Govt. program, 1993—. Cons. N.Y. Times, N.Y.C., 1984-85; Taft Meml. lectr. U. Cin., 1992; Exxon Found. lectr. U. Chgo., 1992. Author: Poliscide, 1976, The Consequences of Consent, 1982, Do Elections Matter?, 1985, The Captive Public, 1986, Freedom and Power in American Government, 1989, Politics by Other Means, 1990, 2d edit., 1998, American Government: Readings and Cases, 1992, The Fatal Embrace, 1993, Democrats Return to Power, 1994, Embattled Democracy, 1995, We the People, 1997, Downsizing Democracy, 2002, Making Government Manageable, 2003. Trustees' scholar U. Chgo., 1964-68; NIMH fellow U. Chgo., 1968-72; Jonathan Meigs grantee Cornell U., 1985, U.S. Dept. Justice grantee, 1984, Kellogg Found. grantee, 1987; recipient Oraculum award for excellence in teaching, 1993, George Owen award for outstanding tchg. and svc., 2000. Mem. Am. Polit. Sci. Assn. (pres. nat. capital area 2002). Jewish. Home: 10800 Tara Rd Potomac MD 20854-1340 Office: Johns Hopkins U Mergenthaler Hall Baltimore MD 21218 E-mail: bgin@jhu.edu.

GINSBERG, DAVID LAWRENCE, architect; b. N.Y.C., Sept. 21, 1932; s. Harry Seaman and Zena (Sagal)S.; m. Emily (Boor), Dec. 29, 1969; children: Stuart Samuel, Daniel Paul, Laura Ruth. BA rsch., Cornell U., 1955. Ptnr. charge N.Y. offices Perkins and Will, N.Y.C., 1957-78; exec. v.p. Perkins and Will, Chgo., 1978-79; exec. v.p. and chief planning officer Columbia-Presbyn. Health Svc., Inc., N.Y.C., 1979-92; v.p. Columbia-Presbyn. Health Sys., Inc., N.Y.C.; dep. to pres. Presbyn. Hosp., N.Y.C., 1993-95; ptnr. Larsen, Shein, Ginsberg, and Snyder LLP, N.Y.C., 1995—. A1A Health Care Facilities 2005, Nat. Guidlines Revision Com., NYS code advisory group, asst. clin. prof. pub. health, Columbia U., N.Y.C., 1979-97; sr. cons. U.S. Global Health Svc., 1992-94. Mem., Washington U. Parents Coun., St. Louis, 1988-91; mem., Scarsdale Planning Bd., 1980-90; sec. bd. trustees N.Y. Presbyn. Hosp. Infant and Child Care Ctr.; bd. dirs. Stephen Wise Free Synagogue. Recipient (medal) N.Y. Soc. Architects, 1955, recipient,(award), N.Y. Soc. for Health Planning, 1993. Fellow A1A (nat. guidlines revision com., co-chair, NYS Code adv. com. for Outpatient D&T Svc., Modern Healthcare Design award; mem. APHA, Acad. Architecture for Health, Forum for Healthcare Planning, Am. Hosp. Assn., Assn. Am. Med. Coll., Soc. Hosp. Planning, Regional Planning Assn., Gargoyle Soc. Office: Larsen Shein Ginsberg & Snyder LLP 170 Varick St New York NY 10013-1221 E-mail: dginsberg@Lsgsarchitects.com.

GINSBERG, DONALD MAURICE, physicist, educator; b. Chgo., Nov. 19, 1933; s. Maurice J. and Zelda Ginsberg; m. Joli D. Lasker, June 10, 1957; children: Mark D., Dana L. BA, U. Chgo., 1952, BS, 1955, MS (NSF fellow), 1956; PhD (NSF fellow), U. Calif. at Berkeley, 1960. Mem. faculty U. Ill., Urbana, 1959-97, prof. physics, 1966-97, prof. emeritus, 1997—. Vis. scientist in physics Am. Assn. Physics Tchrs.-Am. Inst. Physics, 1965-71; vis. scientist IBM, 1976; mem. evaluation com. for Nat. High-Field Magnet Lab., NSF, 1977-79, 85, 91; mem. rev. com. for solid state sci. div. Argonne Nat. Lab., 1977-83, chmn., 1980; mem. rev. panel for basic energy scis. div. Dept. Energy, 1981 Editor: Physical Properties of High Temperature Superconductors, Vols. 1, 2, 3, 4, and 5, 1989, 90, 92, 94, 96; contbr. to Ency. Britannica, 1971, 82, 88, 94, 96, Concise Ency. of Magnetic and Superconducting Materials, 1992. Alfred P. Sloan rsch. fellow, 1960-64, NSF fellow, 1966-67; U. Ill. scholar, 1994; recipient Daniel C. Drucker award U. Ill. Engring. Coll., 1992. Fellow Am. Phys. Soc. (winner Oliver E. Buckley Consensed Matter Physics prize 1998); mem. AAAS, Phi Beta Kappa, Sigma Xi. Achievements include research and publications on low temperature physics, superconductivity, cryogenic instrumentation. Home: 2208 Grange Cir Urbana IL 61801-6607 Office: Loomis Lab 1110 W Green St Urbana IL 61801-9013

GINSBERG, ERNEST, lawyer, banker; b. Syracuse, N.Y., Feb. 14, 1931; s. Morris Henry and Mildred Florence (Slive) G.; m. Harriet Gay Scharf, Dec. 20, 1959; children: Alan Justin, Robert Daniel. BA, Syracuse U., 1953, JD, 1955; LLM, Georgetown U., 1963. Bar: N.Y. 1955, U.S. Supreme Ct. 1964. Pvt. practice law, Syracuse, 1957-61; mem. staff, office chief counsel IRS, Washington, 1961-63; tax counsel Comptr. of Currency, Washington, 1964-65, assoc. chief counsel, 1965-68; v.p. legal affairs, sec. Republic Nat. Bank N.Y., N.Y.C., 1968-74; sr. v.p. legal affairs, sec. Republic Nat. Bank, N.Y.C., 1975-86, exec. v.p., gen. counsel, sec., 1984-86, vice chmn. bd., gen. counsel, 1986-94, vice chmn. bd., 1990-99. Sr. v.p., sec. legal affairs Republic N.Y. Corp., N.Y.C., 1974-84, exec. v.p., gen. counsel, sec., 1984-86, vice chmn. bd., gen. counsel, sec., 1986-94, vice chmn. bd., 1986-99, also bd. dirs.; bd. visitors Syracuse U. Coll. Law; bd. dirs. Safra Nat. Bank of N.Y., N.Y.C. Chmn. emeritus Roundabout Theatre Co., N.Y.C. With U.S. Army, 1955-57. Mem. Am. Bankers Assn. (bd. dirs. 1995-97), Am. Bankers Coun. (co-chmn. 1992-94), N.Y. State Bankers Assn. (pres. 1993-94), Bankers Roundtable (bd. dirs. 1995-97), Phi Sigma Delta, Phi Delta Phi.

GINSBERG, EUGENE STANLEY, lawyer, arbitrator, mediator; b. Bklyn., N.Y., 1929; BBA, CCNY, 1951; JD, NYU, 1954. Bar: N.Y. 1955, U.S. Dist. Ct. (ea. and so. dists.) N.Y. 1957, U.S. Ct. Appeals (2d cir.) 1966, U. S. Supreme Ct. 1966. Ptnr. Krainin & Ginsberg, N.Y.C., 1958-62; sole practice Bklyn. and Mineola, NY, 1962-70; ptnr. Jaspan, Ginsberg, Schlesinger, Silverman & Hoffman (and predecessor firms), Garden City, 1970-96; pvt. practice Garden City, NY, 1996—. Arbitrator Nassau County Dist. Ct., 1980— ; mem. nat. panel comml. arbitrators Am. Arbitration Assn., 1966—, nat. labor panel, 1991—; arbitrator BBB, 1982-86, among others; mediator EEOC, U.S. Dist. Ct., etc. With U.S. Army, 1953-55. Fellow Coll. Comml. Arbitrators, N.Y. Bar Found., Coll. of Labor and Employment Lawyers; mem. ABA (co-chmn. subcom. on profl. responsibility in labor arbitration 1977-83, subcom. on publ. of labor arbitration awards 1984-86, historian 1994—, ADR in labor and employment law com., formerly labor arbitration and law of collective bargaining agreements com., 1975—), N.Y. State Bar Assn. (ADR com. co-chmn. 2001-, exec. com. 1996-, labor and employment law sect.), Nassau County Bar Assn. (dir. 1997-2000, chmn. 1993-95, labor and employment law com. 1973—, ADR com. 1973—, chmn. 1985-87, grievance com. 1983-88). Home: 67 Hilton Ave Apt D26 Garden City NY 11530-2811 Office: 300 Garden City Plz Garden City NY 11530-3302 Business E-Mail: esginsberg@aol.com.

GINSBERG, HERSH MEIER, rabbi, religious organization executive; b. Vienna, July 8, 1928; s. Lazar Yonah Ginsberg and Perl Roth; m. Fradel Levy; children: Lazar Yonah, Meshulim, Chana. Dir. Union Orthodox Rabbis of U.S. and Can.; rabbinical ct. judge; dean Rabbi Jacob-Joseph Sch., N.Y.C., 1955-73. Founder Kolel Ohel Elemelech Rabbinical Coll., Jerusalem. Jewish. Office: Union Orthodox Rabbis US & Can 235 E Broadway New York NY 10002-5600

GINSBERG, LEON HERMAN, social work educator; b. San Antonio, Jan. 15, 1936; s. Sam and Lillian (Gindler) G.; m. Elaine Myrna Kaner, July 29, 1956 (div. 1983); children: Robert, Michael, Meryl Sue.; m. Connie Mooney, June 2, 1983; stepchildren: Claire, Kathleen Mooney. BA, Trinity U., 1957; MSW, Tulane U., 1959; PhD, U. Okla., 1966. Dist. dir. B'nai B'rith Youth Orgn., New Orleans, 1958-61; dir. cmty. activities Jewish Cmty. Coun., Tulsa, 1961-63; assoc. prof. Sch. Social Work U. Okla., Norman, 1963-68; prof., dir. Sch. Social Work W.Va. U., Morgantown, 1968-71, prof., dean, 1971-77; commr. human services State of W.Va., Charleston, 1977-84; chancellor W.Va. Bd. Regents for Higher Edn., 1984-86; Carolina disting. prof. Coll. Social Work U. S.C., Columbia, 1986—, interim dean, 2002—. Fulbright prof. U. Pontificia Bolivariana, Medellin, Colombia, fall 1974; cons. tng. programs Peace Corps, Head Start, Cmty. Action, Bur. Indian Affairs, pub. welfare depts. Okla., Pa., W.Va.; sec. S.C. Gov.'s Commn. on Women, 1999—. Author: Social Work Practice in Public Welfare, 1983, The Social Work Almanac, 1992, Understanding Social Problems, Policies and Programs, 1994; : 3d edit., 1999, Conservative Social Policy, 1998, Careers in Social Work, 1998, 2d edit., 2001, Social Work Evaluation, 2001, Thinking About a Social Work Career, 2002; co-author: Human Services for Older Adults, 1979, 2d edit., 1990, Human Biology for Social Workers, 2004; editor: Social Work in Rural Communities, 1976, 3d edit., 1998, Supplement Ency. Social Work, 1990, (book series) Social Issues and Social Problems, 1992—; co-editor: Life-Span Development Psychology, 1975, New Management for Social Workers, 1988, Understanding Social Problems, Policies, and Programs, 1994; : 3d edit., 1999, Information Technologies; editor: Adminstrn. in Social Work, Tchg. in Social Work. Mem., sec. Gov.'s Commn. on Women, 2001—. Capt. AUS, 1957-58. Recipient Disting. Service award W.Va. Welfare Conf., 1970; named W.Va. Social Worker of Yr., 1978, Outstanding Alumnus, Tulane U. Sch. Social Work, 1989. Mem. NASW (past nat. sec., comm. com. 1995-98, Rhoda G. Sarnat Internat. award 1998), Coun. Social Work Edn., Am. Pub. Welfare Assn. (past pres.), Nat. Ctr. for Social Policy and Practice (past chmn. bd.), Internat. Coun. on Social Welfare (past chmn. to U.S. com.), Child Welfare League Am., B'nai B'rith. Office: U SC Coll Social Work Columbia SC 29208-0001

GINSBERG, MARC C. former diplomat, investment company executive, b. N.Y.C., Oct. 18, 1950; m. Janet Louise Ginsberg; two children. BA, Am. U.; JD, Georgetown U. Legis. asst. to Sen. Edward Kennedy, 1973-76; spl. asst. to under sec. of mgmt. Dept. State, 1977-80; dep. sr. adviser to Pres. for Middle East affairs, 1980-81; atty. Surrey & Morse, D.C., 1981-87, Galland, Kharasch, Morse & Garfinkle, D.C., 1987-93; U.S. amb. to Morocco, 1993-98; pres. Georgetown Global Investments Corp., Washington, 1998-2000; CEO, mng. dir. Northstar Equity Group Inc, Washington, 2000—. Mem. ABA, D.C. Bar Assn. Office: Northstar Equity Group Inc 1615 L St NW Ste 900 Washington DC 20036-5623

GINSBERG, MARC DAVID, lawyer; b. Chgo., Aug. 14, 1951; s. Marshall Leonard and Gloria Barbara (Goldfus) G.; m. Janice Diane Gordon, Jan. 23, 1977; 1 child, Brian. B.A. with honors, U. Ill., 1972; M.A., Ind. U., 1975; J.D. with highest distinction, John Marshall Law Sch., 1977; LLM DePaul U., 1992. Bar: Ill. 1977, U.S. Dist. Ct. (no. dist.) Ill. 1977, U.S. Ct. Appeals (7th cir.) 1977, U.S. Supreme Ct. 1981. Law clk. to presiding justice Ill. Appellate Ct., Chgo., 1977-79; assoc. Tenney & Bentley, Chgo., 1979-83, Rooks, Pitts & Poust, Chgo., 1984— . Lead articles editor John Marshall Jour., 1976-77. Contbr. articles to profl. jours., chpts. to book. Recipient Hornbook award, West Pub. Co., 1977. Mem. Appellate Lawyers Assn. Ill., Am. Judicature Soc. E-mail: mginsberg@roohspitts.com.

GINSBERG, MYRON, computer scientist; b. Brockton, Mass., May 3, 1943; s. Frank and Evelyn Hazel (Spekin) G.; m. Judith Beverly Rosenbaum, Nov. 19, 1989; 1 child, Ellen Joy Hochberg. BA in Math., Boston U., 1965; MA in Math., Clark U., 1967; PhD in Computer Sci., U. Iowa, 1972. Instr. dept. computer sci. U. Iowa, Iowa City, 1969-72; from asst. prof. to assoc. prof. computer sci. So. Meth. U., Dallas, 1972-77, 77-79; NASA/ASEE rsch. fellow NASA Langley Rsch. Ctr, Hampton, Va., summer 1979, summer 2000; assoc. sr. rsch. scientist GM Rsch. Labs., Warren, Mich., 1979-81, sr. rsch. scientist, 1981-82, staff rsch. scientist, 1982-92; cons. sys. engr. EDS Advanced Computing Ctr., GM NAO R & D Ctr., Warren, 1992-96, EDS High Performance Computing Group, Troy, Mich., 1996-97; ind. cons. High Performance Computing Rsch. and Edn., Farmington Hills, Mich., 1997. Mathematician US Army Ballistics Rsch. Lab., Aberdeen Proving Ground, MD., summers, 1964-67; data sys. analyst NASA Electronics Rsch. Ctr., Cambridge, Mass., summers, 1968-69; adj. assoc. prof. U. Mich., Ann Arbor, 1990; mem. adv. bd. Cray Rsch. Fortran, 1991-92; grant rev. panelist NSF, 1992-93, 96-97; GM/EDS rep. to Supercomputing Automotive Applications Partnership, 1992-94; founder and first chmn. of AUTOBENCH Project of US Coun. for Automotive Rsch., 1995-96; coun. adv. Gerson Lehrman Group, Farmington Hills, Mich., 2002—. Editor: Supercomputers in the Auto Industry, 1985, Automotive Applications of Supercomputers, 1988, High-Speed and Large-Scale Computing: A Panoramic View, 1988, Automotive Applications of Vector/Parallel Computers: State-of-the-Art, 1992; contbr. articles to profl. jour.; mem. editl. bd. Computing Sys. in Engring., 1988-93. Grantee, Mobil Oil Found., 1975, US Army C.E., 1977-78, NSF, 1983-84, 77-79, Alfred P. Sloan Found., 1975-78. Fellow Assn. for Computing Machinery (lectr., bd. dir. SIGNUM 1976-80 editor-in-chief SIGNUM newsletter 1976-80); mem. IEEE (sr., program evaluator, 2003—), Computer Soc. of IEEE (lectr.), ASME (lectr.), Soc. for Indsl. and Applied Math. (lectr., spl. group on supercomputing), Soc. Automotive Engr. (founder, 1st chmn. com. on high performance computing stds. for automotive mfg. applications 1996-97, lectr., award for excellence in oral presentation 1985, 86, 87, Disting. Spkr. plaque 1988, Forest R. McFarland award 1994), Sigma Xi (lectr). Avocations: playing alto sax, tenor sax, soprano sax, clarinet and flute, listening to jazz and classical music. Office: HPC Rsch & Education 35764 Congress Rd Ste 100 Farmington MI 48335-1222 E-mail: m.ginsberg@ieee.org.

GINSBERG, MYRON DAVID, neurologist; b. Denver, Aug. 26, 1939; s. Morris Seymour and Evelyn (Fishman) G.; children: Deborah Mara, Emily Michelle. BA, Wesleyan U., 1961; MD, Harvard U., 1966. Intern, resident Harvard Med. Svc., Boston City Hosp., 1966-68; neurology resident, fellow Mass. Gen. Hosp., Boston, 1968-70, 72-73; staff assoc. Lab. Perinatal Physiology, NIH, Bethesda, Md., 1970-72; asst. prof., assoc. prof. dept. neurology U. Pa., Phila., 1973-79; assoc. prof. neurology U. Miami (Fla.) Sch. Medicine, 1979-81, prof. neurology, 1981—, dir. cerebral vascular disease rsch. ctr., 1981—, dir. neurotrauma clin. rsch. ctr., 1991-95, Peritz Scheinberg endowed chair of neurology, 1992—. Mem. study sect. NIH, Bethesda, 1982-86; nat. rsch. com. Am. Heart Assn., Dallas, 1986-91. Editor: Cerebrovascular Diseases, 16th Princeton Conf., 1989; editor Jour. Blood Flow and Metabolism, 1992-97; contbr. over 280 articles to profl. jours. Lt. comdr. USPHS, 1970-72. Recipient Fulbright scholarship U.S. Govt., 1961-62, Jacob Javits Neuroscience Investigator award NIH, 1985-92, Willis Lectr. award, Am. Stroke Assn., 2002. Fellow Am. Acad. Neurology; mem. Am. Neurol. Assn. (membership com. 1990-91), Am. Physiol. Soc., Internat. Soc. Cerebral Blood Flow & Metabolism (dir. 1985-89), Phi Beta Kappa, Alpha Omega Alpha. Office: U Miami Sch Medicine Dept Neurology D4-5 PO Box 016960 Miami FL 33101-6960

GINSBERG, PHILLIP H(ENRY), lawyer; b. N.Y.C., May 1, 1939; s. Benedict and Adele Harriett (Wall) G.; children: Elizabeth Clare Ginsberg-Lytle, Raphael Trapido Ginsberg-Lytle. AB, Princeton U., 1961; LLB, Harvard U., 1964. Bar: Ill. 1964, U.S. Dist. Ct. (no. dist.) Ill. 1964, Wash. 1970, U.S. Dist. Ct. (we. dist.) Wash. 1970, U.S. Dist. Ct. (ea. dist.) Wash. 1972, U.S. Ct. Appeals (7th cir.) 1967, U.S. Ct. Appeals (9th cir.) 1971. Assoc. Ross, Hardies & O'Keefe, Chgo., 1964-68; asst. prof. law U. Chgo., 1968-70; chief atty. Seattle King County Defender Assn., Seattle, 1970-74, dir., 1974-76; prin. Skellenger Ginsberg & Bender, Seattle, 1976-86; ptnr. Ginsberg & Stanich, Seattle, 1986—. Author books and articles in field. Mem. com. on appellate reorgn. Wash. Supreme Ct., 1976, com. on pattern jury instrns., 1974-78; mem. King County Adv. Com. for Indigent Def., 1984. Democrat. Jewish. Home: 6034 Lake Shore Dr S Seattle WA 98118-3038

GINSBERG, PHRAN See ROSENBAUM, FRANCES

GINSBERG, ROBERT E. philosophy educator, editor; b. Bklyn., May 18, 1937; s. Samuel and Rose (Dreifach) G.; m. Ellen Sutor, Apr. 5, 1962. BA, U. Chgo., 1955, MA, 1958; PhD, U. Pa., 1966. Lectr. English Gary Ctr. Ind. U., Gary, 1959-1960; prof. Am. civilization Internat. Lycée, St. Germain-en-Laye, France, 1962-63; lectr. philosophy U. Md., Istanbul and Karamürsel, Turkey, 1965; asst. prof. English Drexel Inst. Tech., Phila., 1966-67, asst. prof. philosophy Pa. State U., Delaware County, Pa., 1967-72, assoc. prof. philosophy, 1972-77, prof. philosophy, 1977—2002, prof. comparative lit., 2001—02, prof. emeritus, 2002—. Adj. asst. prof. philosophy Drexel U., Phila., 1969-71, adj. assoc. prof. philosophy, 1971-77; dir. Internat. Ctr. for Arts, Humanities and Value Inquiry, 2000—. Author: Welcome to Philosophy, 1977; editor: A Casebook on the Declaration of Independence, 1967, The Critique of War: Contemporary Philosophical Explorations, 1969, The Philosopher as Writer: The Eighteenth Century, 1987; editor-in-chief: Social Philosophy Research Institute Book Series, 1985-91; series editor: New Studies in Aesthetics, 1986—; exec. editor: The Journal of Value Inquiry, 1990-95, Value Inquiry Book Series, 1992-2001; gen. editor philosophy: Jones and Bartlett Pubs., 1991-96. Fulbright fellow U.S. Govt., Paris, 1960-61, 61-62, fellow NEH, Washington, 1972-73, fellow world order studies Inst. for World Order, 1982-83; recipient Laura S. Campbell award for excellence in tchg., Phila., 1974. Mem. Am. Soc. Value Inquiry (pres. 1986), Washington Philosophy Club (pres. 1980-81), Am. Philosoph. Assn., Internat. Soc. Value Inquiry (bd. dirs. 1988-98), Conf. Value Inquiry (co-exec. dir. 1991-95), Conf. Philosoph. Socs. (pres. 1986-88). Avocations: travel, gardening. Office: Pa State U Delaware County 25 Yearsley Mill Rd Media PA 19063-5596

GINSBERG, STANLEY ARTHUR, retired urologist, consultant; b. N.Y.C., Aug. 29, 1933; s. William and Ruth (Mutterperl) G.; m. Susan Judith Kabran, Aug. 20, 1967; children: Marnie, Jodi. BA, Amherst Coll., 1955; MD, Columbia U., 1959. Diplomate Am. Bd. Urology. Dir. urology Peninsula Hosp. Ctr., Far Rockaway, N.Y., 1964-2000; acting dir. urology St. John's Episc. Hosp., Far Rockaway, 1964-2000; ret., 2000. Cons. Long Beach (N.Y.) Hosp., 1964—. Home: 132 Saint Martin Dr Palm Beach Gardens FL 33418-4627

GINSBERG, STEPHEN D, neuroscientist; s. Donald and Harriette R Ginsberg; m. Jill P Ginsberg; children: Max J, Zoe L. PhD, Mt. Sinai Med. Ctr., 1993. Asst. prof. Nathan Kline Inst./NYU Sch. of Medicine, Orangeburg, NY, 2001—. Office: Nathan Kline Inst NYU Sch Med 140 Old Orangeburg Rd Orangeburg NY 10962 E-mail: ginsberg@nki.rfmh.org.

GINSBURG, CHARLES DAVID, lawyer; b. N.Y.C., Apr. 20, 1912; s. Nathan and Rae (Lewis) G.; m. Marianne Laïs; children by previous marriage: Jonathan, Susan, Mark. AB, W.Va. U., 1932; LLB, Harvard U., 1935. Bar: W. Va. 1935, U.S. Supreme Ct. 1940, D.C. 1946, U.S. Ct. Appeals (2d, 3rd, 4th, 7th, and Fed. cirs.) 1946, U.S. Claims Ct. 1960, U.S. Tax Ct. 1961. Atty. for public utilities div. and office of gen. counsel SEC, 1935-39; law sec. to Justice William O. Douglas, 1939; asst. to commr. SEC, 1939-40; legal adviser Price Stblzn. Div., Nat. Def. Adv. Com., 1940-41; gen. counsel Office Price Adminstrn. and Civilian Supply, 1941-42, OPA, 1942-43; pvt. practice law Ginsburg, Feldman and Bress, Washington, 1946-98; founding ptnr. Ginsburg, Feldman & Bress, 1946-98; sr. counsel, firm Powell, Goldstein, Frazer & Murphy, LLP, 1998; adminstrv. asst. to Senator M.M. Neely, W.Va., 1950; adj. prof. internat. law Georgetown U. (Grad. Sch. Law), 1959-67. Dep. commr. U.S. del. Austrian Treaty Commn., Vienna, 1947; adviser U.S. del. Council Fgn. Ministers, London, 1947; Mem. Presdl. Emergency Bd. 166 (Airlines), 1966; mem. Pres.'s Commn. on Postal Orgn., 1967; chmn. Presdl. Emergency Bd. 169 (Railroads), 1969; exec. dir. Nat. Adv. Commn. Civil Disorders, 1967 Author: The Future of German Reparations; Contbr. to legal jours. Bd. mem., chmn. exec. com. Nat. Symphony Orch. Assn., 1960-69; bd. govs. Weizmann Inst., 1965 (hon. fellow 1972); mem. vis. com. Harvard-Mass. Inst. Tech. Joint Ctr. on Urban Studies, 1969; trustee St. John's Coll., 1969-76, chmn. bd., 1974-76; overseers com. Kennedy Sch. Govt. Harvard, 1971—; mem. coun. Nat. Harvard Law Sch. Assn., 1972—, gen. counsel Dem. Nat. Com., 1968-70. Served from pvt. to capt. AUS, 1942-46; dep. dir. econs. div. Office Mil. Govt., 1945-46, Germany. Decorated Bronze Star, Legion of Merit; recipient Presdl. Cert. of Merit. Mem. ABA, Fed. Bar Assn, Am. Law Inst., Coun. on Fgn. Rels., Met. Club, Army and Navy Club, Phi Beta Kappa. Democrat. Home: 619 S Lee St Alexandria VA 22314-3819 Office: 1001 Pennsylvania Ave NW Washington DC 20004-2505 E-mail: DGinsbur@PGMF.com.

GINSBURG, DOUGLAS HOWARD, federal judge; b. Chgo., May 25, 1946; s. Maurice and Katherine (Goodmont) Ginsburg; m. Claudia De Secundy, May 31, 1968 (div. Sept. 1980); 1 child, Jessica DeSecundy; m. Hallee Perkins Morgan, May 9, 1981; children: Hallee Katherine Morgan, Hannah Maurice Morgan. Diploma, Latin Sch. Chgo., 1963; BS, Cornell U., 1970; JD, U. Chgo., 1973. Bar: Ill. 1973, Mass. 1982, U.S. Supreme Ct. 1984, U.S. Ct. Appeals (9th cir.) 1986. Assoc. Covington & Burling, Washington, 1972; law clk. to Hon. Carl McGowan U.S. Ct. Appeals, Washington, 1973—74; law clk. to Justice Thorogood Marshall U.S. Supreme Ct., Washington, 1974—75; prof. Harvard U., 1975—83; dep. asst. atty. gen. for antitrust divsn U.S. Dept. Justice, Washington, 1983—84; adminstr. for info. and regulatory affairs Exec. Office Pres., Office Mgmt. and Budget, Washington, 1984—85; asst. atty. gen. antitrust divsn. U.S. Dept. Justice, Washington, 1985—86; judge U.S. Ct. Appeals (D.C. cir.), 1986—2001, chief judge, 2001—. Vis. prof. law Columbia U., N.Y.C., 1987—88; lectr. law Harvard U., Cambridge, Mass., 1988—89; disting. prof. law George Mason U., Arlington, Va., 1988—93; Charles J. Merriam vis. scholar, sr. lectr. U. Chgo., 1990—. Author: Regulation of Broadcasting: Law and Policy Towards Radio, Television and Cable Communications, 1979, Antitrust, Uncertainty, and Technological Innovation, 1980; co-author: Regulation of the Electronic Mass Media, 1991; editor (with W. Abernathy): Government, Technology and the Future of the Automobile, 1980; contbr. articles to profl. jours. Recipient Casper Platt award, U. Chgo. Law Sch., 1972; scholar Mecham scholar, 1970—73. Mem.: ABA (jud. rep. sect. coun. 2000—), Mont Pelerin Soc., Am. Law and Econs. Assn., Am. Econ. Assn., Phi Kappa Phi, Order of Coif. Avocations: historic preservation, antiques, fox hunting. Office: US Ct Appeals 333 Constitution Ave NW Washington DC 20001-2866*

GINSBURG, GERALD J. lawyer, business executive; b. Poughkeepsie, N.Y., Aug. 29, 1930; s. Abraham and Anna (Murkoff) G.; children: Jason Andrew, Stephanie Carla. BS, Syracuse U., 1952; JD, Bklyn. Law Sch., 1958. Bar: N.Y. 1959. Pub. acct., 1954-59; v.p. fin. and ops., dir. Sheffield Watch Corp., N.Y.C., 1959-70, dir., 1967-70; exec. v.p., dir. Kurt Orban Co., Wayne, N.J., 1971-83; pres., dir. Pacific Marine Holdings Corp., 1983-87; pres. J&S Cons., Walnut Creek, CAlif. Dir. Ramapo Fin. Corp., Pilgrim State Bank Served with USNR, 1952-53. Mem. ABA, N.Y. Bar Assn. Office: PO Box 5314 Walnut Creek CA 94596-1314

GINSBURG, HELEN, economics educator; b. N.Y.C. d. William and Anna (Riegelhaupt) Lachs; m. Nathan Ginsburg. BA, Queens Coll., Flushing, N.Y.; MA, PhD, New Sch. Social Rsch., N.Y.C. Rsch. asst. Twentieth Century Fund, N.Y.C.; rsch. assoc. New Sch. Social Rsch., N.Y.C.; asst. prof. L.I. U., Bklyn.; rsch. assoc. prof. NYU, N.Y.C.; assoc. prof. Bklyn. Coll., CUNY, 1977-83, prof. econs., 1984—95, prof. emeritus, 1995—. Founder, mem. exec. com. New Initiatives for Full Employment, N.Y.C., 1986-94; co-founder, mem. exec. com. Nat. Jobs For All Coalition, 1994—. Author: Full Employment and Public Policy in the United States and Sweden, 1983, Unemployment, Subemployment and Public Policy, 1975; co-author (with Sheila D. Collins and Gertrude

Schaffner Goldberg) Jobs For All: A Plan For the Revitalization of America, 1994, chptrs. to books; editor: Poverty, Economics and Society, 1972; co-editor The Challenge of Full Employment in the Global Economy, 1997; mem. editorial bd. Jour. Econ. Issues, 1985-90. Recipient Rsch. awards Profl. Staff Congress CUNY, N.Y.C., 1983, 86, 94, Bicentennial award Swedish Inst., Stockholm, 1979, Faculty Rsch. award L.I. U., Bklyn., 1967, 68, 69, 70, Lawrence Klein award U.S. Dept. Labor/Bur. Labor Stats., Washington, 1986. Mem. Am. Econ. Assn., Internat. Indsl. Rels. Rsch. Assn., Indsl. Rels. Rsch. Assn., Assn. Evolutionary Econs., Com. on Status of Women in Econs. Jewish. Avocations: travel, reading. Office: Bklyn Coll Econs Dept Brooklyn NY 11210

GINSBURG, IONA HOROWITZ, psychiatrist; b. N.Y.C., Dec. 2, 1931; d. A. Eugene and Gertrude (Seidman) Horowitz; m. Selig M. Ginsburg, Aug. 15, 1954 (div. 1984); children: Elizabeth, Jessica. AB, Vassar Coll., 1953; MD, Columbia U., 1957. Diplomate Am. Bd. Psychiatry and Neurology. Pvt. practice, N.Y.C., 1961—; instr. psychiatry Columbia U., N.Y.C., 1961-81, asst. clin. prof. psychiatry, 1981-95, assoc. clin. prof. psychiatry, 1995—; psychiatrist student health svc. NYU, N.Y.C., 1978—2000. Cons.-liaison psychiatrist Columbia Presbyn. Med. Ctr., N.Y.C., 1982—. Contbr. articles to profl. jours. Med. adv. bd. Nat. Psoriasis Found. 1990-95. Recipient Josie Bradbury Travel award Psoriasis Assn. Gt. Britain. Mem. Am. Soc. Adolescent Psychiatry, N.Y. Soc. Adolescent Psychiatry (pres. 1986, cert. of appreciation 1986), Am. Psychiat. Assn., Am. Psychosomatic Soc., Met. Coll. Mental Health Assn. (pres. 1980), Assn. Psychocutaneous Medicine N.Am. (sec.-treas. 1994-95, v.p. 1995-98, pres. 1998-2000).

GINSBURG, MARK BARRY, comparative sociology of education educator; b. LA, Dec. 9, 1949; s. Norman Leslie and Blanche Dorothy (Burg) G.; m. Barbara Iris Chasin, Sept. 5, 1971; children: Jolie Richelle, Kevin Eran, Stefanie Alyse. AB in Sociology magna cum laude, Dartmouth Coll., 1972; MA in Sociology, UCLA, 1974, PhD in Edn., 1976. Lectr. U. Aston, England, 1976-78; asst. prof. U. Houston, Tex., 1979-82, assoc. prof. sociology of edn., 1982-87; dir. Inst. Internat. Studies in Edn. U Pitts., Pa., 1987-93, 96—, prof. edn. and sociology, 1989—, co-chair faculty social responsibility, 1990—95. Contbr. articles to profl. jours. Mem. steering com. Tex. Mobilization for Peace, Jobs and Justice, Houston, 1985—87; bd. dirs. Alliance for Progressive Action, 1990—; active Free South Africa Movement, Houston, 1985—87, Pitts. Peace Inst., 1989—98, co-chmn., 1990—92; bd. dirs. Pitts.-Matanzas (Cuba) Sister City Project, 1998—; treas. Metro Pitts. Labor Party chpt., 1997—99, steering com., 1997—. Rufus Choate scholar Dartmouth Coll., 1972. Mem.: United Faculty of the U. Pitts. (v.p. 1990-92, pres. 1992-), Coun. on Anthropology and Edn. (co-chmn. transnat. issues com. 1984-86), Brit. Sociol. Assn., Am. Ednl. Studies Assn. (exec. bd. 1988-91), Am. Ednl. Rsch. Assn. (exec. com. internat. studies spl. interest group, 1991-94, chmn. peace edn. spl. interest group 1992-96), Comparative and Internat. Edn. Soc. (v.p., pres.-elect, pres. 1989—93, co-editor 2003—), Phi Delta Kappa (rsch. rep. 1983-85). Avocations: bicycle touring, coin collecting. Home: 365 N Craig St 2 Pittsburgh PA 15213 Office: U Pitts Inst Internat Studies in Edn 5K01 Posvar Hall Pittsburgh PA 15260-7455 E-mail: mbg@pitt.edu.

GINSBURG, MARTIN DAVID, lawyer, educator; b. N.Y.C., June 10, 1932; s. Morris and Evelyn (Bayer) Ginsburg; m. Ruth Bader, June 23, 1954; children: Jane, James. AB, Cornell U., 1953; JD, Harvard U., 1958; LLD (hon.), Lewis and Clark Coll., 1992, Wheaton Coll., 1997. Bar: N.Y. 1959, D.C. 1980. Practiced in N.Y.C., 1959-79; mem. firm Weil, Gotshal & Manges, N.Y.C., 1963-79; of counsel firm Fried, Frank, Harris, Shriver and Jacobson, Washington, 1980—; Charles Keller Beekman prof. law Columbia U. Law Sch., N.Y.C., 1979-80; prof. law Georgetown U. Law Center, Washington, 1980—; lectr. U. Leiden, The Netherlands, 1982; lectr. Salzburg Seminar Austria, 1984; mem. tax divsn adv. group Dept. Justice, 1980-81; mem. adv. group to Commr. Internal Revenue, 1978-80; mem. adv. bd. U. Calif. Securities Regulation Inst., 1973-91. Adj. prof. law NYU, 1967—79; vis. prof. law Stanford U., Calif., 1978, Harvard U., Cambridge, Mass., 1986, U. Chgo., 1990, NYU, 1993; cons. joint com. on taxation U.S. Congress, 1979—80, acad. advisor, 2000—01; chmn. tax adv. bd. Commerce Clearing House, 1982—94; mem. bd. advisors NYU/IRS Continuing Profl. Edn. Program, 1983—88, co-chmn., 1986—88; sub coun. on capital allocation, co-chmn. taxation expert group Competitiveness Policy Coun., 1993—95; chmn. tax adv. bd. Little, Brown, 1994—96; bd. dirs. Millennium Chems., Inc., 1996—2003, Chgo. Classical Rec. Found.; lectr. various tax insts. Co-author: Mergers, Acquisitions, and Buyouts, 4 vols., 2003; contbr. articles to legal jours. Mem. vis. com. Harvard Law Sch., 1994—98. 1st lt. arty. U.S. Army, 1954—56. Recipient Chair named in his honor, Georgetown U. Law Ctr., 1986, Marshall-Wythe Medallion, Coll. of William and Mary Sch. Law, 1996, Outstanding Achievement award, Tax Soc. NYU, 1993, Viccenial medal, Georgetown U., 2000. Fellow: Am. Bar Found. (bd. dirs. 2000—03), Am. Coll. Tax Counsel; mem.: ABA (mem. com. corp. taxation, tax sect. 1973—, chmn. com. simplification 1979—81, mem. tax sect. coun. 1984—87, tax systems task force 1995—97), Assn. Bar City N.Y. (chmn. com. taxation 1977—79, mem. audit com. 1980—81), N.Y. State Bar Assn. (mem. tax sect. exec. com. 1969—, chmn. tax sect. 1975, ho. of dels. 1976—77), Am. Law Inst. (cons. Fed. Income Tax Project 1974—93). Office: 600 New Jersey Ave NW Washington DC 20001-2022 E-mail: ginsbma@ffhsj.com.

GINSBURG, NORTON SYDNEY, retired geographer; b. Chgo., Aug. 24, 1921; s. Morris and Sarah (Ginsberg) G.; m. Diana Roselle Peterson, Aug. 12, 1973; children: Jeremy, Alexander. BA, U. Chgo., 1941, MA, 1947, PhD, 1949. Geographer U.S. Army Map Service, 1941-42; prof. geography U. Chgo., 1947-86, assoc. dean Coll., 1963-66, assoc. dean social scis., 1967-69; dean academic program, sr. fellow Center for Study Democratic Instns., Santa Barbara, 1971-74; chmn. dept. U. Chgo., 1978-85; retired, 1986; dir. Environment and Policy Inst. East-West Ctr., Honolulu, 1986-91. Cons. Social Sci. Research Council, Ency. Brit., Ford Found. East-West Center, Nat. Acad. Sci., NRC, SCOPE, UN, UNESCO Author: Atlas of Economic Development, 1961, The Urban Transition: American and Asian Experiences, 1990; co-author, editor: Pattern of Asia, 1958, Malaya, 1958, Essays on Geography and Economic Development, 1960, China: Urbanization and National Development, 1980, China: The 80s Era, 1984, Geographic Perspectives on the Wealth of Nations, 1986; co-author, editor: The Extended Metropolis in Asia, 1991; co-editor: The Ocean Yearbooks, 1978-96. Served to lt. USNR, 1942-46. Guggenheim fellow, 1983 Mem. Assn. Am. Geographers (pres. 1970-71), Quadrangle Club, Cosmos Club, Phi Beta Kappa, Sigma Xi. Home: 1320 E Madison Park Chicago IL 60615-2917

GINSBURG, RUTH BADER, United States supreme court justice; b. Bklyn., Mar. 15, 1933; d. Nathan and Celia (Amster) Bader; m. Martin David Ginsburg, June 23, 1954; children: Jane Carol, James Steven. AB, Cornell U., 1954; postgrad., Harvard Law Sch., 1956—58; LLB Kent scholar, Columbia Law Sch., 1959; LLD (hon.), Lund (Sweden) U., 1969; LLD (hon.), Am. U., 1981, Vt. Law Sch., 1984; LLD (hon.), Georgetown U., 1985; LLD (hon.), DePaul U., 1985, Bklyn. Law Sch., 1987, Amherst Coll., 1991; LLD (hon.), Rutgers U., 1991; LLD (hon.), Lewis and Clark Coll., 1992, Radcliffe Coll., 1994, NYU, 1994; LLD (hon.), Columbia U., 1994; LLD (hon.), Smith Coll., 1994, L.I. U., 1994, U. Ill., 1995; LLD (hon.), Brandeis U., 1996, Wheaton Coll., 1997, Jewish Theol. Sem. of Am., 1997; LLD (hon.), George Washington U. Law Sch., 1997; DHL (hon.), Hebrew Union Coll., 1988. Bar: N.Y. 1959, D.C. 1975, U.S. Supreme Ct. 1967. Law sec. to judge U.S. Dist. Ct. (so. dist.) N.Y., 1959—61; rsch. assoc. Columbia Law Sch., N.Y.C., 1961—62, assoc. dir. project internat. procedure, 1962—63; asst. prof. Rutgers U. Sch. Law, Newark, 1963—66, assoc. prof., 1966—69, prof., 1969—72, Columbia U. Sch. Law, N.Y.C., 1972—80; U.S. Cir. judge U.S. Ct. Appeals, D.C. Cir., Washington, 1980—93; assoc. justice U.S. Supreme Ct., Washington, 1993—. Phi Beta Kappa vis. scholar, 1973—74; fellow Ctr. for Advanced Study in Behavioral Scis., Stanford, Calif., 1977—78; lectr. Aspen (Colo.) Inst., 1990, Salzburg (Austria) Seminar, 1984; gen. counsel ACLU, 1973—80, bd. dirs., 1974—80. Author (with Anders Bruzelius): Civil Procedure in Sweden, 1965; author: Swedish Code of Judicial Procedure, 1968; author: (with others) Sex-Based Discrimination, 1974, Sex-Based Discrimination, supplement, 1978; contbr. numerous articles to books and jours. Fellow: Am. Bar Found.; mem.: AAAS, Coun. Fgn. Rels., Am. Law Inst. (coun. mem. 1978—93). Office: US Supreme Ct One First St NE Washington DC 20543*

GINSBURG, SIGMUND G. management and executive search consultant; b. N.Y.C., Oct. 12, 1937; s. Saul and Rose (Rich) G.; m. Judith Ann Jacobson, July 4, 1965; children: Beth Alison, David Grant. BA magna cum laude, Dartmouth Coll., 1959; postgrad., London Sch. Econs., 1959-60; MPA, Harvard U., 1961. Mgmt. intern Office of Sec. of Def., Washington, 1961-62; asst. to pres. Hudson Inst., 1964; asst. mgr. pers. adminstrv. svcs., mgmt. analyst Port Authority of N.Y. and N.J., 1964-66; sr. mgmt. cons. and spl. asst. to dep. mayor Office of the Mayor, City of N.Y., City of N.Y., 1966-67, asst. city adminstr., 1967-72; v.p. for adminstrn. and planning, treas. Adelphi U., Garden City, N.Y., 1972-78; v.p. for fin., treas. U. Cin., 1978-84, adj. prof. higher edn. adminstrn., bus. adminstrn., 1980-84; v.p. fin. and adminstrn. Barnard Coll., N.Y.C., 1984-94; v.p. bus. devel. Am. Mus. Natural History, N.Y.C., 1994, sr. v.p. fin. and bus. devel., 1995—2002; exec. v.p. nonprofit practice DHR Internat., N.Y.C., 2003—; pres. Sigmund G. Ginsburg Cons., 2003—. Project exec. Rose Ctr. for Earth and Space, 1995-2000; adj. assoc. prof. Adelphi U., 1972-78; adj. asst. prof., lectr. CUNY, 1966-72; founder, dir. N.Y.C. Urban Fellows Program, 1969-72, adv. bd., 1994—; lectr. profl. mtgs..; cons. in field; mgmt. commentator Sta. WGUC, Cin., 1980; instr. Fordham U., 1985-95, New Sch. U., 1986, 91; mem. City Mgrs. Working Rev. Com. Cin. 2000 Plan, 1979-82; citizens adv. com. Wyo. Bd. Edn., 1980; adv. coun. Tchrs. Ins. and Annuity Assn.-Coll. Retirement Equities Fund, 1993-96, chmn., 1994-95. Co-author: Managing the Higher Education Enterprise, 1980; author: Management: An Executive Perspective, 1982, Ropes for Management Success: Climb Higher, Faster, 1984; editor: Paving the Way for the 21st Century: The Human Factor in Higher Education Financial Management, 1993, Managing With Passion: Making the Most of Your Job and Your Life, 1996; contbr. chpts. to books; contbr. over 100 articles to profl. jours. Lt. U.S. Army, 1962-64. Decorated Army Commendation medal; recipient Merit award City of N.Y., 1969, Neil O. Hines publ. award Nat. Assn. Coll. and Univ. Bus. Officers, 1992; Littauer fellow Harvard U., 1961, Disting. Svc. award N.Y.C. Urban Fellows Program, 1994. Mem. Phi Beta Kappa. Office: DHR Internat 280 Park Ave 43d Fl West New York NY 10017

GINSBURGH, BROOK, association executive; b. Phila., Oct. 4, 1942; d. Harrison Stanford and Florence Virginia (Campbell) G. Diploma in nursing, Chestnut Hill Hosp., 1963. RN, Pa. Pediatric nurse Chestnut Hill Hosp., Phila., 1963-66; pediatric charge nurse Ea. Pa. Psychiatric Inst., Phila., 1967-69, Nazareth Hosp., Phila., 1970-76; adminstrv. asst. Subcontractors Assn. Del. Valley, Ardmore, Pa., 1977-79; exec. dir. Am. Subcontractors Assn. Del. Valley, Ardmore, Pa., 1979—; editor monthly newsletter, pub. ann. directory, 1980—. Mem. NAFE, Am. Soc. Assn. Execs., Pa. C. of C. Avocations: volunteer in nursing home visitation programs, church guitar group. Office: Am Subcontractors Assn Del Vly PO Box 586 63 W Lancaster Ave Ardmore PA 19003-0586 E-mail: asadelval@aol.com.

GINSPARG, PAUL, physicist; AB in Physics, Harvard U., 1977; PhD in Physics, Cornell U., 1981. Asst. prof. physics Harvard U., 1984—86, assoc. prof. physics, 1986—90; mem. tech. staff Los Alamos Nat. Lab., 1990—2001; prof. physics, computer sic. Cornell U., 2001—. Vis. prof. CEN, Saclay, France, Princeton U.; vis. scientist Stanford Linear Accelerator Ctr.; vis. prof. U. Calif., Santa Barbara, vis. scientist, Berkeley; vis. prof. Hebrew U., Jerusalem. Contbr. articles to profl. jours. Named Outstanding Jr. Investigator, Dept. Def., 1986—91; recipient Physics, Astronomy and Math award, Spl. Libr. Assn., 1998; fellow A.P. Sloane fellow, 1986—90, MacArthur Found. fellow, 2002. Fellow: Am. Phys. Soc. Office: Cornell U 325 Clark Hall Ithaca NY 14853*

GINTER, CAROLYN AUGUSTA ROMTVEDT (CAROL AUGUSTA ROMTVEDT GINTER), retired bond underwriter; b. Toledo, Oreg., May 24, 1926; d. Fred and Mary Elizabeth (Whitney) Romtvedt; m. Paul Peter Ginter, June 2, 1951 (dec. Dec. 1995); children: Joan Paula, Teresa Ginter Ward, Philip M., Jeffrey G. Student, U. Oreg., 1945-46. Office and dispatch clk. Oregonian Newspaper, Portland, 1943-45; clk. typist USN Supt. of Ships, Portland, 1945; gen. ins. clk. Fidelity & Deposit Co., Portland, 1946-48; bond clk. Aetna Casualty & Surety Fireman's Fund, Transamerica, Portland, 1956-65; surety bond underwirter Cole, Clark & Cunningham/Rollins, Burdick Hunter, Portland, 1965-79; freelance publicity specialist Waldport, Oreg., 1986—. Pub., coord. family history: Fred Romtvedt, His Life and Loves, 1980. Lay min. Sacred Heart Cath. Ch., Newport, 1990—; vol. blood drive ARC, Newport, 2000-2001; mem. Oreg. Hist. Soc.; vol. Rep. Ctrl. com. Mem. Bayshore Women's Club (sec. 1984-94, 96, 98), Waldport C. of C. (vol. visitors ctr. 1995—), Lincoln County Hist. Soc., Alsi Hist. Soc., Bayshore Beach Club (bd. dirs. publicity), Yaquina Geneology Soc. (v.p. 2003), Daus. Union Vets. Civil War. Republican. Avocations: family reunion organization, water exercise, travel, gardening. Home: 1802 NW Canal St Waldport OR 97394-9424 E-mail: caginter@casco.net.

GINTER, VALERIAN ALEXIUS, urban historian, educator; b. Chgo., Nov. 4, 1939; s. Valerian Adalbert and Bernice (Podraza) G.; m. Linda Garner Tadlock, Feb. 24, 1968 (div. 1973). BS in Speech, Northwestern U., 1962; postgrad., L.I.U., 1979-81. Investigator Acme Secret Service Ltd., Chgo., 1960-62; producer, dir. Sta. WAAY-TV, Huntsville, Ala., 1965-68; comml. coordinator CBS TV, N.Y.C., 1968-70; buyer SSC&B Lintas Worldwide, Furman-Roth Inc., SFM Media Corp., N.Y.C., 1970-79; prin. Ginter-Gotham Urban History, N.Y.C., 1981—. Adj. lectr. Kingsborough C.C., N.Y., 1990—, LaGuardia C.C., N.Y., 1998—. Author: Manhattan Trivia: The Ultimate Challenge, 1985; contbr. articles to profl. jours., The Ency. N.Y.C., 1995. Cons., lectr. Mcpl. Art Soc., N.Y., 1975—, dir. video tng., St. Bartholomew's Cmty. House, N.Y.C., 1974-77. With U.S. Army, 1962-65. Mem. Theatre Hist. Soc., Victorian Soc. Am., Nat. Trust Historic Preservation, Soc. Archtl. Historians. Roman Catholic. Avocation: jazz accordionist. Home and Office: 50 W 72nd St Ste 312 New York NY 10023-4132 E-mail: gintgotham@aol.com.

GINTHNER, DELORES ANN, interior designer, educator; b. Mpls., Minn., Jan. 3, 1940; d. Malven Leonard and Ann O. (Noreen) Lunderberg. BS, U. Minn., 1958-62, MA, 1971-73. Assoc. prof. design U. Minn., St. Paul, 1973—. Prin., lighting designer Dee Ginthner Design, Mpls., 1973—. Mem. Interior Design Educators Coun., pres. Mem. Illuminating Engr. Soc., Am. Soc. Interior Designers, Internat. Assn. Lighting Designers. Home: 5574 Meister Rd Minneapolis MN 55432-6053 Office: U Minn/DHA 1985 Buford Ave Saint Paul MN 55108-6134 E-mail: dginthne@che.umn.edu.

GINTY, ROBERT, actor; b. N.Y.C., Nov. 14, 1948; s. Michael J. and Elsie (O'Hara) G.; m. Francine Tacker, May 23, 1980 (div. Oct. 1983; 1 child, James; m. Lorna Patterson, Nov. 23, 1983 (div. Mar. 1988); children: James, Marissa. Student, CCNY, 1966-68, Neighborhood Playhouse, N.Y.C., 1968-69, Yale U., 1970-72. Ind. actor, 1972—. Actor: (films) Bound for Glory, 1976, Coming Home, 1978, The Exterminator, 1980, Gold Raiders, 1981, The Alchemist, 1982, Scarab, 1983, The Act, 1983, Warrior of the Lost World, 1984, White Fire, 1984, Exterminator II, 1985, Three Kinds of Heat, 1986, Mania, 1987, Out on Bail, 1988, Loverboy, 1988, The Prophet's Game, 1999; actor, dir., writer (film) Bounty Hunter, 1988; actor (TV series) Baa Baa Blacksheep, Paper Chase, Hawaiian Heat, (Broadway prodns.) The Great God Brown, Don Juan, The Government Inspector, (off-Broadway prodns.) Indian Wants the Bronx, Silent Partner, Bring It All Back Home; screenwriter, actor: Mission Kill, 1985, Retaliator, 1986, Code Name Vengeance, 1987; exec. producer, scriptwriter, actor (TV pilot) Hardesty House, 1986; dir.: Early Edition, 1996—, Nash Bridges, 1996—, Charmed, 1998—. Democrat. Roman Catholic. Avocations: baseball, tennis, skiing. Office: care The Gersh Agy 16255 Ventura Blvd # 625 Encino CA 91436-2302

GINWAY, MARY ELIZABETH, language educator; b. NYC, Feb. 25, 1959; d. John Ralph and Ann Ginway; m. Cullen Ashley McAllen, May 25, 1991 (div. Aug. 19, 1996); 1 child, Matthew Ashley McAllen; m. David Arnold Pharies, July 25, 2003. BA in Comparative Lit., Smith Coll., 1981; MA in Spanish, Vanderbilt U., 1986, PhD in Spanish-Portuguese, 1989. Asst. prof. U. Ga., Athens, 1989—93; lectr. Emory U., Atlanta, 1994—95; vis. asst. prof. U. Fla., Gainesville, Fla., 1995—97, asst. prof., 1997—2003, assoc. prof., 2003—. Coord. program in Rio de Janeiro U. Fla., Gainesville, Fla., 1998—2000. Contbr. articles to profl. jours. Mem. Norton Elem. Sch. PTA, Gainesville, 2000—02. Lilly Tchg. fellow, U. Ga., Athens, 1990—91, Fulbright scholar, U.S. Govt., 1982—83. Mem.: MLA, Am. Assn. Tchrs. Spanish and Portuguese, Phi Beta Kappa (v.p. 2002—03, Zeta chpt.). Avocations: dancing, running, tennis. Office: Univ Fla Dept Romance Langs and Lit PO Box 117405 Gainesville FL 32611-7405

GINZBERG, ABIGAIL, video producer; b. NYC, June 6, 1950; d. Eli and Ruth (Szold) G.; 1 child, Sasha Sesser-Ginzberg. Student, London Sch. Econs., 1969-70; BA, Cornell U., 1971; JD, U. Calif., San Francisco, 1975. Bar: Calif. 1975, D.C. 1979, U.S. Supreme Ct. 1979. Instr. Boalt Hall Law Sch., Berkeley, Calif., 1975-76; atty. Zaks and Harris, San Francisco, 1976-79; litigation counselor U.S. Dept. Labor, Washington, 1979-80; staff counsel Cal/OSHA/Dept. Indsl. Rels., San Francisco, 1979-80; instr. New Coll. Sch. Law, San Francisco, 1980-84; video prodr. Ginzberg Video Prodns., Albany, Calif., 1983—. Pres. Nat. Lawyers Guild, San Francisco, 1988-91; cons. Dept. Labor, Washington, 1980-81, Dept. Health Svcs., Calif. and N.J., 1988-90, Bar Assn. of San Francisco, 1990-91. Prodr., dir.: (videos) Those Who Know Don't Tell, 1989 (Finalist award John Muir Med. Film Festival 1990, Silver Apple award Nat. Ednl. Film Festival 1990, Blue Ribbon award Am. Film and Video Festival 1990, Bronze award Houston Internat. Film Festival 1991, U.S. Environ. Film Festival award 1991), All Things Being Equal, 1989 (Golden Eagle award 1990, Finalist award Internat. Film and TV Festival N.Y. 1990), A Firm Commitment, 1990 (San Francisco AFTRA/SAG Am. Scene award 1991, silver plaque INTERCOM/Chgo. Film Festival 1991, Com. on Partnership award ABA 1992, Am. Scene award AFTRA/SAG 1992), All in A Day's Work, 1992 (E. Smythe Gambrell/ABA award 1993), Doing Justice: The Life and Trials of Arthur Kinoy, 1994 (Best of Festival award Vt. Internat. Film Festival 1994, CINE Golden Eagle award 1994, Silver Apple award Nat. Ednl. Film Festival, 1994), Inside/Out: A Portrait of Lesbian and Gay Lawyers, 1994, Breaking Down Barriers: Overcoming Discrimination Against Lawyers with Disabilities, 1994 (Silver plaque Intercom Film Festival 1995), Pulp Ethics, 1995 (Gold award World Fest Houston 1996, Gold plaque Intercom Film Festival 1996), The Unfinished Agenda: NIOSH's First 25 Years and Beyond, 1996 (Cert. of Merit, Intercom Film Festival 1996), Keeping the Door Open: Women and Affirmative Action, 1996 (Honorable mention Columbus Internat. Film Festival 1996), A Voice for Children, 1996, Movin' On Up, 1977, The Public's Health, 1997 (Gold award World Fest Houston 1998), Obstacle Courts, 1997 (Gold award Charleston World Fest 1997, others), Outlooks, 1998, Cracking the Habit: Drug Courts in Action, 2000 (CINE Golden Eagle 2001, Platinum award World Fest Houston 2001, Daughters of Justice 2001, Summary Judgments 2001, Silver award World Fest Houston 2002), others; co-prodr. Everyday Heroes, 2001, Recovering Lives, Uncovering Hope, 2002 (Gold award World Fest. Houston 2002), Growing Independence, 2002, If the Robe Fits, 2002, Changing Children's Lives, 2002; Bd. advisors KPFA, 1986-92; active Coalition for Civil Rights, San Francisco, 1988—, Ctr. Social Justice, U. Calif., Berkeley, 2002—; bd. dirs. Meiklejohn Civil Liberties Inst., 1991—; adv. bd. Impact Fund, 1993—. Recipient Cert. Recognition, Calif. Assembly, 1988, award Alice Toklas Dem. Club, 1988, Award of Merit from Bar Assn. San Francisco, 1994, Bronze Apple award Nat. Ednl. Media Network, 1997. Mem. ABA (standing com. Gavel awards 1997-2000), APHA, State Bar Assn. Calif., D.C. Bar Assn. Jewish. Avocations: swimming, photography. Home and Office: Ginzberg Video Prodns 1136 Evelyn Ave Albany CA 94706-2316

GINZBURG, VICTOR A. mathematics educator; b. Moscow, July 26, 1957; s. Alexander David Ginzburg and Marianna David Kaminskaya; m. Elizabeth Ginzburg; 1 child, Mikhail. PhD in Math., Moscow State U., 1984. Instr. math. U. Chgo. Lectr. Underground Jewish U., Moscow, 1980—81. Author: Representation theory and Complex geometry, 1997; contbr. Achievements include research in noncommutative geometry and string theory. Avocation: hiking. Office: U Chgo Math Dept 5734 S University Ave Chicago IL 60637 Personal E-mail: ginzburg@math.uchicago.edu. Business E-Mail: ginzburg@math.uchicago.edu.

GINZBURG, VITALY LAZAREVICH, physicist; b. Moscow, Oct. 4, 1916; s. Lazar and Augusta G.; m. Nina Ginzburg, 1946; 1 child. PhD, Moscow U., 1940. With P.N. Lebedev Phys. Inst. Russian Acad. Scis., 1940—, dir. I.E. Tamm dept. theoretical physics, 1971-88, adv., head theoretical group in P.N. Lebedev Physical Inst., 1988—; prof. Gorky U., 1945-68, Moscow Tech. Inst. Physics, 1968—. Author: Theoretical Physics and Astrophysics, 1979, Waynflete Lectures of Physics, 1983; author: (with S.I. Syrovatskii) Origin of Cosmic Rays, 1964; author: Propagation of Electromagnetic Waves in Plasma, 1970; author: (with V.M. Agranovich) Crystal Optics with Spatial Dispersion and Excitons, 1984; author: (with V.N. Tsytovich) Transition Radiation and Transition Scattering, 1990; author: (in Russian) On Physics and Astrophysics, 1995; author: About Science, Myself and Others, 1997, 2001, 2003, The Physics of a Lifetime, 2001; contbr. Decorated Order of Lenin; recipient Manelstam prize, 1947, Lomonosov prize, 1962, USSR State prize, 1953, Lenin prize, 1966, M. Smoluchovskii Medal Polish Physics Soc., 1987, Bardeen prize, 1991, Wolf Found. prize, 1994, 95, Vavilov Gold medal, 1995, Big Lomonosov Gold medal, 1995, UNESCO-Nils Bohr Gold medal, 1998, Nicholson Medal Am. Phys. Soc., 1998, Nobel prize in physics, 2003. Fellow Indian Acad. Sci. (hon.); mem. Acad. Sci. USSR (elected people's dep. mem. of Soviet Parliament 1989) Royal Soc. (London), Royal Astronomy Soc. London (assoc., Gold Medal 1991), Academia Europaea, Internat. Acad. Astronautics, Royal Danish Acad. Sci. (fgn.), NAS. Address: PN Lebedev Phys Inst RAN Leninsky Prospect 53 119991 Moscow Russia Fax: 095-135-85-33. E-mail: ginzburg@lpi.ru.

GINZEL, ANDREW H. artist; b. Chgo., July 14, 1954; s. Roland F. and Ellen (Laynon) G.; m. Kristin A. Jones, June 14, 1986. Student, SUNY, 1978-81, Bennington Coll., 1972-74. Sculpture faculty Sch. of Visual Arts, N.Y.C., 1986—. Artistic cons. Hudson River Park Conservancy, N.Y.C., 1997. Solo shows include: Metronome Union Square South Project, N.Y.C., 1999, TZ'Art, N.Y.C., 1996, Acqario Romano, Rome, 1995, Madison Art Ctr., Wis., 1992 93, Three Rivers Arts Festival, Pitts., 1991, Mpls. Coll. of Art and Design, 1991, Damon Brandt Gallery, N.Y.C., 1990, Kunsthalle, Basel, 1989, others; commns. include: Oculus, MTA, N.Y.C., 1999, Olympic Arts Festival, Atlanta, 1996, Battery Park City, N.Y.C., 1992, Pa. Conv. Ctr., 1994, Oreg. Conv. Ctr., Portland, 1990, Kunsthalle, Basel, Switzerland, 1989; group shows include Contemporary Artists and the Am. Acad. in Rome, 1995, 96, Equitable Gallery, N.Y.C., 1996, Paine Webber Gallery, N.Y.C., 1994, The Drawing Ctr., N.Y.C., 1993-94, numerous others; selected collections include: Bklyn. Mus., Beckton Dickinson and Co., Franklin Lakes, N.J., Bklyn. Mus., Centro per L'Arte Contemporanea Luigi Pecci, Prato, Italy, Hoffmann-La Roche, Inc., Pacific Enterprises, L.A., Progressive Corp., Cleve., The Prudential Life Ins. Co., others. Recipient Visual Arts fellowship Nat. Endowment for the Arts, 1986, 94, awards Pollack-Krasner Found., 1994, Louis Comfort Tiffany Found., 1991, fellowship for Indo-Am. Coun. for Internat. Exch. of Scholars, 1990, numerous others in field. Fellow Am. Acad. in Rome (Rome prize 1994-95). Home: 289 Bleecker St New York NY 10014-4106

GIOCONDA, THOMAS F. management consultant, retired military officer; BA in History, St. Joseph's U., 1970; grad., Squadron Officer Sch., 1974; MBA, U. Mont., 1975; grad., Air Command and Staff Coll., 1976; M in Ednl. Adminstrn., Seton Hall U., 1979; grad., Air War Coll., 1986. Commd. 2d lt. USAF, 1970, advanced through grades to brig. gen., 2001; stationed at Malmstrom AFB, Mont., 1970-75; asst. prof. aerospace studies AFROTC detachment 750 St. Joseph's U., Phila., 1975-76, prof., 1976-77, detachment comdr., detachment closure officer, 1976-77; adminstrn. officer, asst. prof. aerospace studies N.J. Inst. Tech., Newark, 1977-79; stationed at Vandenberg AFB, Calif., 1979-83; mission analyst strategic programs Hdqs. SAC, Offutt AFB, Nebr., 1983, congl. liaison br. chief, action officer, 1983-85; congl. affairs and resources planner, dep. chief of staff plans and ops. Hdqs. USAF, Washington, 1985-89; stationed at Whiteman AFB, Mo., 1989-91; dep. legis. asst. to chmn. joint chiefs of staff USAF, Washington, 1991-93, legis. asst. to chmn. joint chiefs of staff, 1993-97; prin. dep. asst. sec. mil. application Dept. Energy, Washington, 1997-99, acting asst. sec. energy for defense programs, 1999—2001; ret., 2001; program mgr. Bechtel Nat. Inc., 2001—. Mem.: Mil. Officers Assn. Am. (life), KC, Am. Legion (life), Soc. SAC (life), Kappa Delta Phi. Home: 4818 Hercules Ct Annandale VA 22003-4243

GIOFFRE, BRUNO JOSEPH, lawyer; b. June 27, 1934; s. Anthony B. and Louise (Giorno) G.; m. Kathleen M. Bartlik, Nov. 14, 1959; children: Kathleen, Lisa, Michael, Christopher, B. Scott, David, Kerry. BA, Cornell U., 1956, JD, 1958. Bar: N.Y. 1958, U.S. Dist. Ct. (so. dist.) N.Y. 1973. Sr. mem. Gioffre & Gioffre, P.C., Purchase, NY, 1958—99, prin. atty., 2000—. Justice Town of Rye, N.Y., 1965-99. Vice-chmn. bd. trustees United Hosp.; counsel Port Chester Pub. Libr.; chmn. bd. dirs. Sound Fed. Savs. Bank and Charitable Found. Mem.

ABA, N.Y. Bar Assn., N.Y. Magistrate's Assn., Westchester County Magistrate's Assn., Westchester Bar Assn., Port Chester-Rye Bar Assn., Elks, KC. Home and Office: 2900 Westchester Ave Purchase NY 10577-2552

GIOIA, (MICHAEL) DANA, poet, literary critic; b. L.A., Dec. 24, 1950; s. Michael and Dorothy (Ortiz) G.; m. Mary Hiecke, 1980; children: Michael (dec.), Theodore, Michael Frederick. BA, Stanford U., 1973, MBA, 1977; MA, Harvard U., 1975; PhD in Lit. (hon.), St. Andrews Coll., 2003. V.p. mktg. General Foods Corp., White Plains, N.Y., 1977-92; pres., bd. dirs. Story Line Press, 1992-2001; chmn. Nat. Endowment Arts, 2003—. Editor Sequoia mag., 1971-73, poetry editor, 1975-77; literary editor Inquiry mag., 1977-79, poetry editor, 1979-83; mem. bd. dirs. Wesleyan U. Writers Conf., 1985-99; commentator BBC Radio, 1992-2003; co-dir. West Chester Writers Conf., 1995-2002; music critic San Francisco mag., 1997-2003; librettist for opera Nosferatu, 2001; dir. Tchg. Poetry Conf., 2001-02. Author: (poetry) Daily Horoscope, 1986, The Gods of Winter, 1991, Interrogations of Noon, 2001, (criticism) Can Poetry Matter? Essays on Poetry an American Culture, 1992, 2d edit., 2002; editor: The Ceremony and Other Stories, 1984, Poems from Italy, 1985, New Italian Poets, 1990; co-editor: Literature: An Introduction to Fiction, Poetry and Drama, 2001, Longman Anthology of Short Fiction, 2000, Selected Short Stories of Weldon Kees, 2002; translator: Eugenio Montale's Mottetti: Poems of Love, 1990; contbr. to periodicals including New Yorker, Atlantic, Washington Post, Hudson Rev., Poetry. Recipient Frederick Bock prize Poetry, 1986, Am. Book award, 2002. Mem. Poetry Soc. Am. (v.p. 1992-2003), Nat. Fed. Coun. on Arts and Humanities. Office: Nat Endowment for Arts 1100 Pennsylvania Ave NW Washington DC 20004

GIOIA, DANIEL AUGUST, lawyer; b. Bellerose, N.Y., Dec. 23, 1950; s. Joseph Daniel and Concetta P. (Della Femina) Gioia; m. Helen Dumas, June 30, 1973; children: Martha Dumas Picarello, Thomas Joseph, David Albert, Carl Daniel. BA in Govt., Georgetown U., 1972; JD, Am. U., 1975. Bar: Ind. 1975, U.S. Dist. Ct. (no. and so. dist.) Ind. 1975. Ptnr. Spangler, Jennings & Dougherty, Merrillville, Ind., 1975—, mng. ptnr., 2002—. Adj. prof. med. malpractice Sch. of Law Valparaiso U., Ind., 1998—; mem. Commn. for C.L.E. Ind. Supreme Ct., 1992—98; mem. Conclave for Legal Edn., Ind. State Bar Assn., 1996, 2002. Mem.: Lake County Bar Assn. (bd. mgrs. 1987—91, pres. 1990), Valpo Soccer Club (pres. 1992—98), Am. Inn of Ct. (pres. Calumet chpt. 2003—). Roman Catholic. Avocations: soccer referee and coach, gourmet cooking, coin collecting. Home: 4221 Oak Grove Cir Valparaiso IN 46383-2084 Office: 8396 Mississippi St Merrillville IN 46410 E-mail: dhgioia@attbi.com., dgioia@sjdlaw.com.

GIOMBETTI CLUE, DIANE, writer; b. Framingham, Mass., Sept. 4, 1966; d. Robert Alfred and Anne Lauretta Giombetti; m. Kevin Andrew Clue, Oct. 7, 1995; 1 child, Domenic Martin Clue. BA cum laude, Mt. Holyoke Coll., 1988. Asst. acct. exec. ASR, Inc., Waltham, Mass., 1989—92; copywriting mgr. Thomson Fin., Boston, 1992—94; freelance writer Upton, Mass., 1994—. Mem.: Phi Beta Kappa. Roman Catholic. Avocations: foreign travel, antiques, reading, cooking.

GIONFRIDDO, MAURICE PAUL, aeronautical engineer, research and development manager; b. Medford, Mass., Feb. 19, 1931; s. Santo and Germaine Camille (Gaillard) G.; m. Joan Marie Powers, Apr. 21, 1956; children: Marianne E., Linda. BS in Aero. Engring., MIT, 1953, MS in Aero. Engring., 1969. Rsch. asst. Aeroelastic and Structures Rsch. Lab., MIT, Cambridge, Mass., 1953-54; aero. rsch. engr. Air Force Cambridge Rsch. Ctr., Bedford, Mass., 1956-57; aero. engr. Army Natick (Mass.) Rsch., Devel. and Engring. Ctr., 1957-94; cons. MPG Cons., Westborough, Mass., 1994—. Mem. Nat. Parachute Tech. Coun., 1991—. Class agt. MIT Class of 1953, 1968-78. 1st lt. USAF, 1954-56. Fellow AIAA (assoc., charter, aerodyn. decelerator tech. com. 1964-67, Aerodyn. Decelerator award 1990), Parachute Industry Assn. (Mem. of Yr. 2002). Roman Catholic. Home and Office: MPG Cons 20 Westminster Way Westborough MA 01581-3410 E-mail: mgion@pia.com.

GIONFRIDDO, PAUL, healthcare executive; b. Middletown, Conn., May 25, 1953; s. Valentine Louis and Catherine (Pugliese) G.; children: Timothy, Larissa, Elizabeth, Benjamin, Verena Hormuth; m. Pamela J. Hormuth, July 5, 2001. BA, Wesleyan U., 1975. Paralegal Conn. Legal Svcs., Meriden, 1977-78; mem. Conn. State Legislature, Hartford, 1979-89; mayor City of Middletown, 1989-91; instr. Nat. Ctr. for Health Stats. Applied Stats. Tng. Inst., 1994—97; exec. dir. Conn. Assn. for Human Svcs., Inc., 1995-2001, Indigent Care Collaboration, Austin, Tex., 2001—. Vis. lectr. in liberal studies Wesleyan U., 1993-2000; adj. lectr. pub. policy Trinity Coll., 1999-2001. Pres. People's Action for Clean Energy, Inc., Canton, Conn., 1976-2000; bd. dirs. Texans Care for Children, Inc., 2002—. Recipient Outstanding Pub. Svc. award Assn. for Retarded Citizens, Conn., 1984, Ira Hiscock award Conn. Pub. Health Assn., 1985, Legis. Leadership award Conn. Assn. for Human Svcs., 1988, Ofcl. citation Conn. Gen. Assembly, 1998, Bd. Svc. award Conn. Ctr. for Sch. Change, 2001. Mem. APHA, Rockfall Found. Democrat. Roman Catholic. Home: 1700 Windoak Dr Austin TX 78741 E-mail: pgionfriddo@juno.com.

GIOR, FINO (SERAFINO GIORDANO), electrology company executive; b. Hollywood, Calif., Sept. 8, 1936; s. Jack and Mary G.; m. Carole Chalupa, Sept. 23, 1961; children: John, Maryann, James, Matthew. Student, St. John's U., Queens, N.Y., 1955-57; cert., Kree Inst. Electrology, Manhattan, N.Y., 1958. Pres. N.Y. State Electrologists, Inc., N.Y.C., 1978-79; founder, pres. Internat. Guild Profl. Electrologists Inc., High Point, N.C., 1979-84; pres. Advanced Electrology Clinics Am., Great Neck, N.Y., 1958—. Advisor Internat. Guild Profl. Electrologists, Inc., 1980—; cons. and presenter various electrology-related orgns. Author: Modern Electrology, 1987, 3rd edit., 2000, First Official Standards For Electrology and Laser Research; contbr. articles to numerous nat. mags. and profl. publs. Sgt. U.S. Army N.G., 1954-59. Recipient E. Michael, MD award 1984. Mem. Internat. Guild of Electrologist Inc. (3d v.p.). Roman Catholic. Avocations: sports, art, reading, gardening, photography. Office: Advanced Electrology 15 Bond St Great Neck NY 11021-2002 E-mail: finogior@aol.com.

GIORDANO, ANDREW ANTHONY, retired naval officer; b. Passaic, N.J., May 17, 1932; s. Samuel and Sarah (Pollara) G.; m. Felice Rochman, Mar. 3, 1957; children: Andrew Anthony, II, Dean James, Catherine Lisa. BBA cum laude, CCNY, 1953; MBA with distinction, Harvard U., 1962; student, Naval War Coll., 1965; L.H.D. (hon.), Nat. U., San Diego, 1982. Commd. ensign U.S. Navy, 1953, advanced through grades to rear adm., 1978; supply officer U.S.S. Kitty Hawk, Vietnam, 1968-70; ops. officer Aviation Supply Office, Phila., 1970-72; dir. material div. Office of Chief of Naval Ops., Washington, 1977-81; comdr. Naval Supply Systems Command, Chief Supply Corps, 1981-84; sr. v.p. control and ops. Donaldson's of Mpls. unit Allied Stores, 1984-87; exec. v.p., CFO Lamonts Corp., 1987-93; assoc. prof. acctg. George Washington U., 1966-67, Nat. U., 1970-72; prin. The Giordano Group, Ltd., Arlington, Va., 1993—. Chmn. bd. dirs. Nomos, Inc., Jos. A. Bank, Inc. Treas., trustee Navy Marine Coast Guard Residence Found., 1993-98; pres., COO Graham Field, 1998; chmn., CEO Jos. A. Bank, Inc. Decorated Legion of Merit, D.S.M.; recipient Navy Civilian Svc. award. Mem. NAS (Naval studies bd. 1996), Army-Navy Country Club (chmn. bd. govs. 1993-96), Naval Supply Corps Assn. (hon. pres.). Roman Catholic. Address: PO Box 31059 Palm Beach Gardens FL 33420-1059

GIORDANO, ANTONIO, medical educator; b. Naples, Italy, Oct. 11, 1962; came to U.S., 1987; s. Giovan Giacomo and Maria Teresa (Sgambati) G.; m. Mina Massaro, July 4, 1992; children: Maria Teresa, Giovan Giacomo, Luca. MD summa cum laude, U. Naples, 1986; PhD in Pathology summa cum laude, U. Trieste, 1990. Intern U. Naples, 1983-86; postdoctoral fellow N.Y. Med. Coll., 1987-88, Cold Spring Harbor Lab., N.Y.C., 1988-92; fellow Irvington Inst. for Med. Rsch., 1990-92; asst. prof. pathology/biochemistry Temple U., Phila., 1992-94; pres., chmn. bd., founder Sbarro Inst. for Cancer Rsch. and Molecular Medicine, 1993—; asst. prof. pathology Thomas Jefferson U., Phila., 1994-96, assoc. prof., 1996—2001, prof., 2001—02, Temple U., Phila., 2002—. Adj. prof. Thomas Jefferson U., Phila., 2002—; prof. human pathology and oncology U. Siena, Italy, 2003. Editl. bd. Jour. Cellular Biochemistry, Jour. Cellular Physiology, Anticancer Rsch., La Clinica Terapeutica, Jour. Clin. Pathology and Molecular Pathology, Frontiers in Bioscience, Cancer Biology and Therapy, Women's Oncology Rev., Jour. Exptl. Clin. Cancer Rsch., Jour. Neurovirology; contbr. numerous articles to profl. jours. and books. Knighted by Pres. of Republic of Italy, 2001; recipient Nat. Achievement award in med. rsch., Nat. Italian-Am. Polit. Action Com., 2003. Mem. Societá Italiana Tumori, Am. Assn. for Cancer Rsch., N.Y. Acad. of Scis. Achievements include identification of a novel tumor suppressor gene and a development of a new test for lung cancer; patent for tumor suppressor protein pRB2, related gene products, and DNA encoding, patents include novel human cyclin-dependent kinase-like proteins and methods of using the same, human retinoblastoma-related, genomic DNA and methods of detecting mutations therein, lung, prostate, breast cancer screening on pRb2 gene expression; pRb2/p130 peptide inhibitors of cdk2 kinase activity; determination of cyclin dependent kinase inhibitor p27 as prognostic factor in cancer patient. Home: 1230 Gulph Creek Dr Radnor PA 19087-4686 Fax: 610-964-9834. E-mail: g_tonio@hotmail.com.

GIORDANO, BILL A. psychotherapist; b. Newark, June 15, 1957; s. John and Marie Giordano. BA in Polit. Sci. cum laude, Fairleigh Dickinson U., Rutherford, N.J., 1979; postgrad. cert. in clin. social wk., NYU, 1982, MSW, 1992, postgrad., 2003—. LCSW N.Y. Case worker Cath. Charities, N.Y.C., 1982; social worker Bklyn. Bur. C.C., 1986—89, primary therapist South Beach Psychiat. Ctr., S.I., 1989—93; sr. therapist day tx. coord. H.S.S. Cmty. Cons. Ctr., N.Y.C., 1993—. Cons., Think Tank mem. On Step Inst., N.Y.C., 1998—; presenter in field. Mem. Dem. Nat. Com., 1976—. Mem.: NASW. Achievements include research in on paternal instinct; symptoms of parental alienation and its implications for clinicians and patients; coordination of multicultural day treatment program; depression in men. Home: 98 Ann St Newark NJ 07105-3110 Office: On Step Inst 169 E 74th St New York NY 10021

GIORDANO, CATHERINE KOWKABANY, nurse; b. Bklyn., Feb. 18, 1956; d. Emil and Madeline (Asmar) Kowkabany; m. William Lawrence Giordano, Feb. 2, 1985; 1 child, Lawrence William. ADN, L.I. Coll., 1978; BS in Adminstrn. cum laude, St. Francis Coll., Bklyn., 1982. RN, N.Y.; cert. apheresis nurse. Educator Downstate Med. Ctr., Bklyn., 1979-84; counselor ARC, Bklyn., 1981-84; head nurse Blood Donor Ctr., Coney Island Hosp., Bklyn., 1982—; health svc. nurse Kingsborough Coll., 1999—. Office: Coney Island Hosp 2601 Ocean Pkwy Brooklyn NY 11235-7745

GIORDANO, DAVID ALFRED, retired internist, gastroenterologist; b. South Bend, Ind., Feb. 3, 1930; s. Alfred S. and Alice (Gracy) G.; m. Sally Kay Buchanan, Jan. 30, 1960; children: Steven David, Michael Bruce. BS, Northwestern U., 1951; MD, Ind. U., Indpls., 1955. Diplomate Am. Bd. Internal Medicine. Intern Univ. Hosp., Cleve., 1955-56; resident in internal medicine Ind. U. Med. Ctr., Indpls., 1958-60; instr. medicine Duke U. Med. Ctr., Durham, N.C., 1960-61, Ind. U. Med. Ctr., Indpls., 1961-63; cons. gastroenterology Vets. Hosp., Univ. Hosp., Indpls., 1961-63; pvt. practice Sarasota, Fla., 1963-99; ret., 1999. Active staff Sarasota Meml. Hosp., chief of staff, 1970-71, assoc. staff Drs. Hosp., Sarasota; mem. West Cen. Fla. Profl. Standards Review Orgn., 1976, Sarasota County Local Govt. Study Commn., 1967-69; sec. Sarasota County Comprehensive Health Planning Coun., 1969-70, exec. com., 1969-72; bd. dirs. Blue Shield, 1973-80, chmn. Governmental Affairs Com., 1978-80; rep. of state ins. commr. to Russia, Denmark, Sweden, Eng. and France, 1979. Contbr. articles to profl. jours. Med. advisor Planned Parenthood Assn., 1965-70; bd. dirs. Pines Sarasota, 2000—. Lt. comdr. USN, 1956 58. Fellow Am. Coll. Physicians (rep. Fla. coun. med. specialists 1973—, health and pub. policy com. 1987—, governing bd. 1987— Internist of Yr. Fla. chpt. 1997), Am. Coll. Gastroent.; mem. AMA, Fla. Soc. Internal Medicine (med. adv. coun. 1971-90), Fla. Gastroent. Soc. (pres. 1972), West Coast Acad. Internal Medicine (pres. 1977-78); Sarasota County Med. Soc. (co-chmn. peer review com. 1970-71), Fla. Med. Assn., Am. Soc. Internal Medicine, Fla. Med. Assn., Am. Soc. Gastrointestinal Endoscopy, Am. Gastroent. Assn. Avocations: sailing, tennis, nautical antiques. Home: 6 Lands End Ln Sarasota FL 34242-1148

GIORDANO, JOSEPH, JR., financial planner, investment consulting firm executive; b. Detroit, July 28, 1953; s. Joseph and Josephine Marie (Delicolli) G. BS in Fin., Bus. Econs., Wayne State U., 1977. Cert. fin. planner, 1986. Sr. cost analyst Nat. Bank Detroit, 1978-81; registered rep. Am. Express Fin. Svcs. Inc., Mpls., 1981-83; dist. mgr. IDS Fin. Svcs. Inc., Mpls., 1983-86; pres. Joseph James Fin. Svcs. Inc., Rochester Hills, Mich., 1986—, Investors Fin. Adv. Inc., Rochester Hills, 1986—. Instr. Macomb C.C., Warren, Mich., 1988; cons. various clients, 1988—. Mem. Nat. Assn. Security Dealers. Avocations: music, composing songs, biking, tennis, traveling. Office: Joseph James Fin Svcs Inc 705 Barclay Cir Ste 125 Rochester MI 48307-4575

GIORDANO, LAWRENCE FRANCIS, lawyer; b. Buffalo, Feb. 17, 1953; s. Anthony Jerome and Martha Ann (Taylor) G.; m. Elaine Kristie Thomas, May 29, 1976; children: Bradley Thomas, Evan Taylor. BS with highest honors in Psychology, Denison U., 1975; JD, Georgetown U., 1978. Bar: Tenn. 1978, U.S. Dist. Ct. (ea. dist.) Tenn. 1979, U.S. Ct. Appeals (6th cir.) 1980, U.S. Supreme Ct. 1983. Assoc. Stone & Hinds, P.C., Knoxville, Tenn., 1978-81, ptnr., 1981-88, Thomforde & Giordano, P.C., Knoxville, 1988-90, McCampbell & Young, P.C., Knoxville, 1990-91, London, Amburn & Giordano, Knoxville, 1991-92, Susano, Sheppeard & Giordano, Knoxville, 1993-94; spl. counsel Lewis, King, Krieg & Waldrop, P.C., Knoxville, 1994-97, shareholder, 1997—. Spl. judge Knox County Gen. Sessions Ct., 1988—; adminstrv. law judge State of Tenn. Dept. Edn., 1994-96; adj. prof. U. Tenn. Coll. Law, 1993—; instr. Knoxville Police Acad., 1989. Mem. exec. bd. Knoxville Metro Soccer League, 1980-85; mem. community network Knox County Youth Alcohol Hwy. Safety Project, Knoxville, 1987-90. Nat. Merit scholar, 1971-75, Kenneth I. Brown scholar, 1974. Mem. ABA, Tenn. Bar Assn. (Law Through Liberty award, 2000), Knoxville Bar Assn. (bd. govs. 1986-92, treas. 1986-90, sec. 1991-92), Def. Rsch. Inst., Am. Inns of Ct. (master of the bench 1991—, pres. 1994-95), Sertoma (v.p. chpt. 1987-89, pres. 1989-90), Phi Beta Kappa, Omicron Delta Kappa. Democrat. Roman Catholic. Avocations: soccer, gardening, reading, theater. Home: 1822 Nantasket Rd Knoxville TN 37922-5769 Office: Lewis King Krieg & Waldrop 620 Market St Fl 5 Knoxville TN 37902-2231

GIORDANO, NICHOLAS ANTHONY, stock exchange executive; b. Phila., Mar. 7, 1943; s. Nicola and Aida (Gioioso) G.; m. Joanne M. Pizzuto, Oct. 21, 1967; children: Jeannine, Colette and Nicholas (triplets). BS, LaSalle Coll., 1965. CPA, Pa. Mem. staff Price Waterhouse & Co., Phila., 1965-68; with various brokerage cos. Phila., 1968-71; controller stock exchange and stock clearing corp PBW (later Phila.) Stock Exch., Inc., 1971-72, v.p. ops., 1972-75, sr. v.p., 1975-76, exec. v.p., 1976-81, pres., CEO, 1981-97, bd. dirs.; interim pres. LaSalle U., 1998-99. Cons. to securities markets and fin. cos. Vice chmn. bd. trustees LaSalle U.; former chmn. bd. dirs. Mt. St. Joseph Acad.; trustee, bd. dirs. WT Mutual Fund, Kalmar Investments, Inc.; bd. dirs. Fotoball USA, Inc., Selas Corp., Greater Phila. Urban Affairs Coalition, Ind. Blue Cross, Union League Phila. Home: 1755 Governors Way Blue Bell PA 19422-2554 Office: PO Box 984 Blue Bell PA 19422-0984 Fax: 610-834-0898.

GIORDANO, SANDRA L. elementary school educator; b. Paterson, NJ, Oct. 22, 1969; s. Rocco and Marie Cammilleri; m. Salvatore Giordano, July 8, 1995; children: Christina Marie, Joseph Michael. BA in English, Felician Coll., 1991; postgrad., Montclair State U., 1993, William Paterson U. Cert. tchr. NJ. Tchr., curriculum developer Fair Lawn (NJ) Bd. Edn., 1995—99, Classical Acad. Charter Sch., Clifton, NJ, 2000—. Clin. faculty mem. NJ Network for Edn. Renewal, Montclair, 1996—98; judge Internat. Women's Day Writing Contest, NJ, 1999. Contbr. articles to publs. in field. Named Tchr. of Yr., NJ Charter Pub. Schs. Assn., 2001. Mem.: NJ Coun. Tchrs. English (state contest coord. 1998—2000, corr. sec. 1996—2000). Roman Catholic. Home: 21 Noll Terr Clifton NJ 07013

GIORDANO, SERAFINO **See GIOR, FINO**

GIORDANO, SONDRA BRITCHKY, nursing educator, medical and surgical nurse; m. Ralph Giordano; children: Lori, Daniel. BS, Adelphi U., 1965; MS, Russell Sage Coll., 1981. RN, N.Y. Albert Einstein Hsop. Clin. Rsch. Ctr., 1965; head nurse Maimonides Hosp. Ctr., Bklyn., 1965-66; clin. instr. Kings County Hosp. Sch. Nursing, Bklyn., 1966-68, Kingston (N.Y.) Hosp., 1970-72; SUNY Coll. Health Ctr., New Paltz, 1973-76; prof. Dutchess C.C., Poughkeepsie, NY, 1981—2002, prof. emeritus, 2002—. Mem. ANA, N.Y. State Nurses Assn., Sigma Theta Tau (mem. Alpha Omega and Mu Epsilon chpts.). Home: 8 North Rd Tillson NY 12486-1000 E-mail: giordano@sunydutchess.edu.

GIORDANO, THOMAS H. chemist, educator; b. Phila., Feb. 13, 1950; s. James A. and Margaret H. Giordano. BA in Chemistry, Millersville (Pa.) U., 1972; PhD in Geochemistry, Pa. State U., 1978. From post doctoral rschr. to prof. Dept. Geol. Scis. N.Mex. State U., Las Cruces, N.Mex., 1977—98, prof. Dept. Geol. Scis., 1998—. Vis. sci. Chemistry Divsn. Oak Ridge (Tenn.) Nat. Lab., 1987—93; vis. sci. Dept. Earth Scis. U. Manchester, Manchester, England, 1995. Editor: Ore Genesis and Exploration: The Roles of Organic Matter, 2000, Ore Geology Reviews, 1996. Mem.: N.Mex. Geol. Soc., The Am. Geophysical Union, The Geochemical Soc. Roman Catholic. Home: Las Cruces NM 88005 Office: Dept Geological Scis New Mex State Univ Box 3AB Las Cruces NM 88005

GIORLANDO, JEANNE A. labor and delivery nurse; b. Tooele, Utah, Dec. 13, 1957; d. Joseph Richard and Geraldine Ellen (Daniels) Giorlando; m. Francis J. Paglia, May 17, 1983 (dec. Oct. 7, 1985); 1 child, Karen Paglia-Hayes; m. John J. Hayes, Aug. 25, 1990 (div. Apr. 1999). BSN, Hunter Coll., 1978. RN, N.Y.; cert. nurse oper. rm.; cert. nurse inpatient obs., childbirth educator. Staff nurse med./surg. unit St. Vincents Med. Ctr. N.Y., N.Y.C., 1978-80; staff nurse labor and delivery, post-partum and nursery Bapt. Med. Ctr., Bklyn., 1980-81; staff nurse oper. rm., labor and delivery NYU Downtown Hosp., N.Y.C., 1981—. Mem. Assn. Women's Health, Obstetric and Neonatal Nurses, Comm. Workers Am. (union steward), Curtis H.S. Assn. Alumni and Friends (nominating chair bd. dirs.). Democrat. Roman Catholic. Avocations: yoga, meditation. Home: 7631 Amboy Rd Staten Island NY 10307-1418 Office: NYU Downtown Hosp 170 William St New York NY 10038-2649

GIORNO, JOHN, poet; b. N.Y.C., Dec. 4, 1936; BA, Columbia Coll., 1958. Author: Balling Buddha, Grasping at Emptiness, You Got to Burn to Shine; pres. Giorno Poetry Systems, a non-profit found. started in 1965, producing numerous record albums, CDs, cassettes and videopaks of poets working with music and performance including The Best of William Burroughs Box Set, 1998; invented Dial-A-Poem, 1968; originator Spoken Word, performance poetry. Founder AIDS Treatment Project, 1984. Tibetan Nyingma Buddhist. Home: 222 Bowery New York NY 10012-4216

GIOSEFFI, DANIELA (DOROTHY DANIELA GIOSEFFI), poet, novelist, educator, singer, literary critic; b. Orange, N.J., Feb. 12, 1941; d. Daniel Donato Gioseffi and Josephine Buzevska; m. Richard J. Kearney, Sept. 7, 1965 (div.); 1 child, Thea D. Kearney; m. Lionel B. Luttinger, June 6, 1986. BA, Montclair State Coll., 1963; MFA, Cath. U. of Am., 1966. Cons., poet Poets-in-the-Schs., Inc., N.Y.C., 1972-85. Freelance writer, lectr. at numerous univs. throughout U.S. and Europe; appeared on Nat. Pub. Radio, CBC, BBC; spkr. on world peace and disarmament, 1979—; keynote spkr. Am. Forum for Global Edn. Nat. Conf., Miami, Fla., 1994, State Coun. Tchrs. English conf., Orlando, Fla., 1995, So. Edn. Found. Internat. Conf. of Tchrs. of English, Atlanta, 1997, IV Feminist Internat. Book Fair, Barcelona, 1989, Miami Internat. Book Fair, 1990. Author: The Great American Belly, 1977, The Great American Belly, 4th edit., 1979; author: (collections of poems) Eggs in the Lake, 1979, Word Wounds and Water Flowers, 1995, Going On, 2000, Symbiosis, 2002; author: Earth Dancing: Mother Nature's Oldest Rite, 1981, Women on War: International Voices for the Nuclear Age, 1988 (Am. Book award, 1990), rev. edit., 2003, On Prejudice: A Global Perspective, 1993—, Dust Disappears: Translations of Carilda Oliver Labra of Latin America, 1995—, (short stories) In Bed With the Exotic Enemy, 1997—, (novella) The Psychic Touch, 1996—; author: (play) The Golden Daffodil Dwarf, 1988—, Care of the Body, 1988—, The Sea Hag in the Cave of Sleep, 1988—; author: (radio play) Fathers and Children, 1988—, 1998—; author: (short stories) Daffodil Dollars, — (PEN Short Fiction award, 1990, Lifetime Achievement award Assn. Italian Am. Educators, 2003); contbr. ;, performer (stage presentations throughout U.S. and Europe), composer (and lyricist), singer (many concert series) ; editor: PoetsUSA.com, —, NJ Poets.com, —; prodr.: The First Bklyn. Bridge Poetry Walk, 1978; verses carved in marble: Penn Sta., 2002. Pres. Bklyn. Citizens for Sane Nuclear Policy, 1987—89; mem. exec. bd., chmn. media watch com. Writers and Pubs. Alliance for Nuclear Disarmament, 1978—91. Named featured poet, The Peoples' Poetry Gathering: The Great Hall, 2003; recipient World Peace award, Ploughshares Fund, 1989, 1999, Lifetime Achievement award, Assn. of italian Am. Educators, 2003, End. Assn. N.Y., 2003; grantee poetry and fiction, Creative Artists' Pub. Svc. Program - N.Y. State Coun. on Arts, 1971—77, Thanks Be to Grandmother Winifred Found., 1996. Mem.: Poet's House, Nat. Book Critics Cir., Actors Equity Assn., Acad. Am. Poets, PEN Am. Ctr. Office: Box 8G 57 Montague St Brooklyn NY 11201-3356 E-mail: daniela@garden.net.

GIOVACCHINI, PETER LOUIS, psychoanalyst; b. N.Y.C., Apr. 12, 1922; s. Alex and Therese (Chicca) G.; m. Louise Post, Sept. 29, 1945; children: Philip, Sandra, Daniel. BS, U. Chgo., 1941, MD, 1944; postgrad., Columbia U., 1939; cert., Chgo. Inst. Psychoanalysis, 1954. Diplomate Am. Bd. Psychiatry and Neurology. Intern Fordham Hosp., N.Y.C., 1944-45; resident U. Chgo. Clinics, 1945-46, resident and research fellow, 1948-50; candidate Chgo. Inst. Psychoanalysis, 1949-54, clin. assoc., 1957—; clin. prof. U. Ill. Coll. Medicine, 1961-92, prof. emeritus, 1992—. Chief cons. psychodynamic unit Barclay Hosp., Chgo., 1979-81; cons. Wilmette (Ill.) Family Svc. Ctr. and United Charities, Boyer-Marin Lodge, Marin County, Calif., 1986—, Mario Martin Inst. for Psychotherapy, 1989—, Psychoanalytic Ctr. Calif., L.A., 1990—; vis. prof. Smith Coll., Mass.; tng. and supervising analyst Chgo. Ctr. for Psychoanalytic Studies, 1994—. Author: (with L.B. Boyer) Psychoanalytic Treatment of Schizophrenia and Characterological Disorders, 1967, Psychoanalytic Treatment, 1971, also several books on character structure, primitive mental states, psychopathology and psychoanalytic technique, psychoanalysis; also articles.; Co-editor: Annals of Adolescent Psychiatry, 1972-80. Capt. M.C. AUS, 1946-48. Fellow Am. Psychiat. Assn., Am. Orthopsychiat. Assn. (bd. dirs. 1979-83), Am. Coll. Psychoanalysts; mem. Am. Soc. Adolescent Psychiatry, Chgo. Soc. Adolescent Psychiatry (pres. 1972-73), Internat. Psychoanalytic Soc. (chmn. standing com. on rsch. in psychosis 1994—), Am. Psychoanalytic Assn., Chgo. Psychoanalytic Soc. Home: 270 Locust Rd Winnetka IL 60093-3609 Office: 505 N Lake Shore Dr Chicago IL 60611-3427

GIOVANELLI, JOHN, research chemist; b. Taree, NSW, Australia, Nov. 28, 1930; came to the U.S., 1965; s. Grantel Elwin and Doris Eileen (Dennison) G.; m. Edna Rosina Gankerseer, Sept. 13, 1959 (dec. July 1988); m. Martha Masa Tsukiyama, Apr. 15, 1989. BSc in Agr. with honors, U. Sydney, Australia, 1953; PhD, U. Calif., Berkley, 1957. Postdoctoral fellow Johns Hopkins U., Balt., 1957-59; from rsch. scientist to sr. rsch. scientist, lectr. Indsl. Rsch. Orgn. and U. Sydney, 1959-65; from vis. scientist to rsch. chemist NIMH, Bethesda, Md., 1965-2001, spl. vol., 2001—; ret., 2001. Author: Plant Biochemistry, 1964; editl. bd. mem. Plant Physiology, 1983-92, contbr. articles to profl. jours. Vol. NIMH. Pacific scholar English Speaking Union, San Francisco, 1954; recipient Peter Goldacre award Australian Soc. Plant Physiologists, Sydney, 1965. Avocations: ballroom dancing, hiking, gardening. Office: 36 Convent DrBldg 36 Rm 3D32 Bethesda MD 20892-4020 E-mail: giovanej@mail.nih.gov., giovanellijohn@hotmail.com.

GIOVANIELLI, DAMON VINCENT, physicist, consulting company executive; b. Teaneck, N.J., May 8, 1943; s. Dominick John and Marie Concetta (Conti) G.; m. Eleanor Ruth Rand, Aug. 18, 1968; children: Kira, Tina. AB, Princeton U., 1965; PhD in Physics, Dartmouth Coll., 1970. Instr. dept. engring. and applied sci. Yale U., New Haven, 1970-72; with Los Alamos (N.Mex.) Nat. Lab., 1972-93, leader physics divsn., 1987—93; ret., 1993; pres. Sumner Assocs., Sante Fe, 1993—; chmn. bd. dirs. La Mancha Co., 1997—. With J. Robert Oppenheimer Meml. Com. Contbr. articles to profl. jours. Mem. alumni schs. com. Princeton U.; trustee Coll. Santa Fe. Fellow AAAS, mem. AIAA, Am. Phys. Soc., Fusion Power Assocs., U.S. Space Found., Sigma Xi. Episcopalian. Home: 12 Loma Del Escolar Los Alamos NM 87544-2524 Office: Sumner Assocs 100 Cienega St Ste D Santa Fe NM 87501-2003

GIOVANONI, STEPHEN FRANCIS, music educator; b. Urbana, N.Y., June 10, 1964; s. Richard Louis and Mary Josephine Giovanoni; m. Lisa Kay Sheridan, May 20, 1988; children: Matthew, Tyler. MusB, W.Va. U., 1986; MusM, U. North Tex., 1990. Cert. tchr. Tex. Saxophonist 323d Army Band, San Antonio, 1993—99; band dir. Comfort (Tex.) Ind. Sch. Dist., 1999—2001, LaVernia (Tex.) Ind. Sch. Dist., 2001—02; music instr. San Antonio Coll., 2000—02; saxophone instr. Tex. Luth. U., Seguin, 2001—02; dir. bands Wharton (Tex.) County Jr. Coll., 2002—. Saxophonist Al Sturchio Orch., San

Antonio, 1993—2002; clinician various schs. in Tex.; saxophone performer various Tex. bands; arranger jazz band music. Served U.S. Army, 1993—99, Ft. Sam Houston. Mem.: Tex. Bandmasters Assn., Tex. Music Educators Assn. Avocations: music history, sports. Office: Wharton County Jr Coll 911 Boling Hwy Wharton TX 77488 E-mail: stepheng@wcjc.edu.

GIOVINAZZO, VIVIAN CURRY, writer; b. Gstaad, Switzerland, Dec. 7, 1945; arrived in U.S., 1949; d. Hugo Alexander and Beatrice Ferdinand (Wärtli) Curry; m. George Potts, Dec. 30, 1965 (dec.); m. Anthony Gioviazzo, Sept. 10, 1995 (dec. Apr. 18, 2002). HS, Lâchâtlaine, Switzerland, 1962—63; HS diploma, Edgewater High, Orlando, Fla.; student psychology. Author children's books; athletic (Tennis) Champion, Fla. and NY, 1950—59; author: (children's stories) Those Scary Dust Bunnies, 2001—02, Daddy, I Don't Want To Go To School, 2001—02, New Puppy on the Block, 2001—02, Bubbles for My Birthday, 2001—02. Named NY State Tennis Championship, FIA. Avocation: philately.

GIOVINCO, JOSEPH, nonprofit administrator, writer; b. San Francisco, Oct. 12, 1942; s. Joseph Bivona Giovinco and Jean Andrews; m. Sally Garey, Aug. 31, 1970 (div. Mar. 1982); 1 child, Gina Lorraine. BA, U. Oreg., 1964; MA in History, San Francisco State U., 1968; PhD in History, U. Calif., Berkeley, 1973. Asst. prof. history SUNY, Albany, 1974-76; instr. multicultural studies Sonoma State U., Cotati, Calif., 1976-79; exec. dir. Hist. Mus. Found., Sonoma County, Santa Rosa, Calif., 1977-80; exec. dir. no. Calif. affiliate Am. Diabetes Assn., San Francisco, 1980-81; exec. dir. San Francisco Sch. Vols., 1981-85, Calif. Hist. Soc., San Francisco, 1985-87; dir. Ctr. Advancement & Renewal of Educators, San Francisco, 1988—. Contbr. articles to profl. publs. Fellow, NEH and Harvard U., 1973; recipient scholarship U. Minn. Ctr. for Immigration History, Mpls., 1975; Rockefeller Found. grantee, 1977; recipient Covello prize Italian Am. Hist. Assn., 1976; named Alumnus of Yr., San Francisco State U., 1987. Roman Catholic. Avocations: rose gardening, classical music. Office: Ctr Advancement & Renewal Educators 25550 25th Ave San Francisco CA 94116

GIPPIN, ROBERT MALCOLM, lawyer; b. Cleve., Feb. 3, 1948; s. Morris and Helena (Weil) G.; children: Sarah, Joshua, Rebecca, Alanna; m. Susan Smith. AB, Dartmouth Coll., 1969; JD, Harvard U., 1973. Bar: Ohio 1973. Asst. to dir. Ohio Dept. Commerce, Columbus, 1973; exec. sec. Ohio Real Estate Commn., Columbus, 1974-75; pros. Mcpl. Ct., Cuyahoga Falls, Ohio, 1975; ptnr. Thompson, Hine, Cleve. Active exec. com. Summit County Dem. Party, Akron, 1975, Planned Parenthood; pres. Summit County Coun., 1982-84, Project Learn, 1997—. Mem. Akron Bar Assn., Ohio Bar Assn., Phi Beta Kappa. Jewish. Avocations: reading, tennis, cooking. Home: 929 Eaton Ave Akron OH 44303-1311 Office: Thompson Hine 3900 Key Ctr Cleveland OH 44114 E-mail: robert.gippin@thompsonhine.com.

GIPSON, JIM, wholesale distribution executive; Pres. Houchens Industries, chmn., CEO, 1994—. Office: Houchens Industries Inc 900 Church St Bowling Green KY 42101*

GIPSON, ROBERT EDGAR, lawyer; b. Boise, Idaho, Aug. 31, 1946; s. Tracy Greer and Marjorie (Lynch) G.; m. Penelope Helen Brandt, Aug. 20, 1966; children— Christopher, Jonathan, Elliot. A.B., Harvard U., 1967; J.D., Yale U., 1973. Bar: Calif. 1973. Assoc., Irell & Manella, Los Angeles, 1973-75, Armstrong Hendler & Hirsch, Los Angeles, 1975-82; ptnr. Gipson Hoffman & Pancione, Los Angeles, 1982— ; trustee Sundance Film Inst., Salt Lake City, 1981-84. Mng. editor Yale Law Jour., 1972-73. Served to 1st lt. U.S. Army, 1968-71, Thailand. Mem. ABA. Democrat. Methodist. Club: Century City. Lodge: Rotary. Home: 656 Westholme Ave Los Angeles CA 90024-3248 Office: Gipson Hoffman & Pancione Bldg 1100 1901 Avenue of the Stars Los Angeles CA 90067-6002

GIPSTEIN, MILTON FIVENSON, lawyer, psychiatrist; b. Schenectady, N.Y., Aug. 31, 1951; s. Milton and Evelyn G.; m. Carol Grace Gipstein, July 21, 1974; children: Steven Mark, Richard Seth. BA, Columbia U., 1972; MD, SUNY, Syracuse, 1976; JD, U. N.C., 1981. Bar: Mass., 1982; Diplomate Am. Bd. Psychiatry and Neurology. Resident psychiat. U. N.C., Chapel Hill, 1976-79; pvt. practice of psychiat. Dept. Corrections N.C., Raleigh, 1979-81; med. dir. Brockton (Mass.) Dist. Ct. Clinic, 1981-86, Bridgewater (Mass.) St. Hosp., 1986-87, Charter Hosp. of Aurora, Colo., 1988—91; med. dir. of forensic svcs. Columbine Psychiatric Hosp., Littleton, Colo., 1991—96; med. dir. forensic psychiatry divsn. Marvin Foote Youth Detention Facility, Englewood, Colo., 1997-2000. Cons. med.-legal N.C. Legal Aid Soc., Raleigh, 1976-81, forensic Mass. Treatment Ctr. Sexually Dangerous, Bridgewater, 1981-88, psychiat. La. Gov.'s Task Force Mental Health, Baton Rouge, 1982, Jefferson Ctr. Mental Health, 1996-98; med.-legal cons. Med. Evaluators, Inc., Denver, 1991-2000; legal counsel indigent clients mental health Com. Pub. Counsel Svcs., Boston, 1982-88; lectr. mental health legal advisors com. Law and Mental Health for Mass. Supreme Ct., Boston, 1982-88. Cons. Pub. Health Adv. Com. Town of Sharon, Mass., 1983-88, Mental Health Legal Advisors Com. Mass. Supreme Ct., Boston, 1985-88; v.p. cmty. affairs Heights Elem. Sch. PTA, Sharon, 1983-88; adv. com. gifted and talented Cherry Creek H.S., 1992-97, Campus Middle Sch., 1993-96. Mem. ABA, Mass. Bar Assn., Am. Profl. Practice Assn. Avocations: boating, antique documents, swimming.

GIRALDI, ROBERT NICHOLAS, film director; b. Paterson, N.J., Jan. 17, 1939; B.F.A., Pratt Inst., 1960. Assoc. creative dir. Young & Rubicam, N.Y.C., 1960-71; v.p., head creative dept. Della Femina, N.Y.C., 1971-73; ptnr. Ampersand Prodns., N.Y.C., 1973-74, dir.; pres. Giraldi Suarez Prodns., N.Y.C., 1974—. Head advt. and design, asst. dir. Sch. Visual Arts, N.Y.C., 1969-73, instr. 2002—; owner N.Y.C. restaurants, Vong Lipstick Cafe, Patria, Gigino, Jean-Georges, Prime, The Mercer Kitchen, Bread in Inkca. Dir.: (play) Laughing on the Outside, 1982, (music videos) Say Say Say, 1983, Love Is a Battlefield, 1984, Hello, 1984, Don't Drive Drunk, 1984, Beat It. (Michael Jackson), 1983, World Series (Baseball Hall Fame), (TV special) A Christmas to Remember with Dolly Parton and Kenny Rogers, 1985, (feature film) Hiding Out, 1987, (feature film) Dinner Rush with Danny Aiello, 2000, (short film) The Routine, 2001 (Best Drama award L.A. Internat. Short Film Festival), The Dream Begins for N.Y.C. 2012 Olympic Bid, 2002; art represented in permanent collection Mus. Modern Art, N.Y.C. Appears in numerous ads against AIDS. Recipient numerous gold awards Art Dirs. Club N.Y., N.Y.C., numerous Andy awards Advt. Club N.Y., N.Y.C., numerous Clio awards, numerous One Show awards Copy Club N.Y., N.Y.C., numerous N.Y. Festival awards, numerous Mobius awards, Gold award Cannes Film Festival, 1974, 76, 79, 81, 88, 96, AICP MOMA gold award, 1992, 94, London Internat. Film Festival gold award, 1992, Italian Key awards, 1990, numerous other awards for excellence in advt., 1993-96, MTV Best Male Video award Will Smith's Just The Two of Us; Herschel Levit Scholarship award Pratt Inst., 1994; named to N.Y. Dir.'s Hall of Fame, 1991. Mem. Dirs. Guild Am. Roman Catholic. Office: Giraldi Suarez Prodns 149 Wooster St 2d Fl New York NY 10012-3327 also: 329 N Wetherly Dr Beverly Hills CA 90211-1605 *If you do quality you will always do quantity, but it never works the other way around.*

GIRARD, ANDREA EATON, communications executive, consultant; b. N.Y.C., Oct. 16, 1946; d. Samuel Robert and Mimi (Eaton) G. Student, Syracuse U., 1964-66; BA cum laude, Finch Coll., 1968; MA, Columbia U., 1971. Talent coord./prodn. asst. Guber-Ford-Gross Prodns., N.Y., 1968-70; v.p. Charing Cross Press, N.Y.C., 1970-72; assoc. producer, talent dir.TV shows "To Tell the Truth" and "Snap Judgment" Goodson Todman Prodns., N.Y.C., 1972-80; programming exec. David Letterman-NBC, N.Y.C., 1980; dir. of talent, producer Daytime/Arts and Entertainment Networks (Hearst/ABC Video Enterprises), N.Y.C., 1981-84; dir. current programming acquisition, sr. producer Lifetime Network (Hearst/ABC/Viacom Entertainment Svcs.), N.Y.C., 1984-86; pres. Girard Communications, N.Y.C., 1986—, dir. med. communications advantage internat., 1990-91; v.p. PRNY, N.Y.C., 1990-92; CEO Panache Communications Inc., N.Y.C., 1992—. Judge Emmy awards Internat. Film and TV Festival; speaker pub. rels. coun. sch. of continuing edn. NYU; media cons. to med. industry, 1987—. Producer, writer (documentaries) Cave Dwellers of Crete, 1974, Sponge Divers of Kalymnos, 1979, Gypsies of the Camargue, 1983. Active fund raising bd. Jersey Wildlife Preservation Trust, N.Y.; active hospitality com. United Nations, N.Y., Big Apple Com. for the Benefit of the Image of N.Y. Mem. NATAS, NAFE, N.Y. Women in Film and TV, Nat. Assn. Women Bus. Owners, Internat. Assn. Cooking Profls., Delta Soc. Avocations: goldsmith, horseback riding, tennis. Office: Panache Comms 201 E 77th St Ste 7F New York NY 10021-2082 E-mail: panacheinc@aol.com.

GIRARD, FRANCOIS, film director; b. Lac St-Jean, Que., Can. Founder, prin. Zone Prodns., 1988-92, Velvet Camera, 1988-92. Writer, dir. feature films including Cargo, 1990, Thirty Two Short Films About Glenn Gould, 1993 (Best Film prix Genie award, 1993, Best Dir. prix Genie award, 1993, Best photography prix Genie award, 1993, Best Editing prix Genie award, 1993, mention Festival of Festival Toronto, 1993, mention Festival du Film de Vancouver, 1993, Prize Figueira Da Foz Festival de Lisbonne, 1994, Badeira Paulista award Mostra de Sao Paulo, 1994), Peter Gabriel's Secret World, 1994 (Prix du Pub. Festival Internat. du Nouveau Cinéma Mtl., 1994, silver rose for best concert film Montreux Film Festival, 1995, Internat. Grammy award for Music Video long version, 1996); dir. medium-length films including Le Dortoir, 1991 (Internat. Emmy award, Gold FIPA, Gemeau award), Le Jardin des Ombres, 1993, After Othello, 1994, Souvenirs d'Othello, 1994; dir. short films including Das Brunch, 1983, Human Scope, 1984, Le Train, 1985, Monsieur Léon, 1986, Tango Tango, 1986, Montréal Danse, 1988, Mourir, 1988, Supect No 1, 1989, CCA, 1989, Vie Et Mort De L'Architecte, 1989; co-dir. short films including Distance, 1984; co-writer: Thirty Two Short Films About Glenn Gould; dir. various commls.; dir.: The Red Violin, 1998 (8 Genie awards including best film and best dir., Oscar for best original soundtrack). Office: c/o Chantal Neveu 1435 St Alexandre Ste 500 Montreal QC Canada H3A 2G4 E-mail: chantal.neveu@sympatico.ca.

GIRARD, G. TANNER, state environmental officer; b. Jacksonville, Fla., May 15, 1952; s. Gerald Joseph and Paula Jean (Tanner) G.; m. Suellen Hill, Aug. 14, 1976; children: Anne Rachel, Justin Porter. BS, Principia Coll., 1974; MS, U. Cen. Fla., 1976; PhD, Fla. State U., 1979. Tchr., rsch. asst. U. Cen. Fla., Orlando, 1974-1975; tchr. asst. Fla. State U., Tallahassee, 1976-1977; prof. biology Principia Coll., Elsah, Ill., 1977-92; mem. Ill. Pollution Control Bd., Jacksonville, 1992—. Vis. prof. U. del Valle de Guatemala, 1988; dir. field study programs Mex., Guatemala, Costa Rica. Contbr. articles to profl. jours. Ornithologist Bartram Trail Canoe Expdn., Ga. and Fla. Bicentennial Commn., 1975; mem. Riverbend in 90's, Alton, Ill., 1989-92, Ill. Nature Preserves Commn., Springfield, Ill., 1987-94, chmn., 1989-92; organizer Mississippi River Conf., Alton, 1984-86; del. Gov.'s Environ. Forum, Springfield, 1986; dir. Ill. Audubon Soc., Wayne, Ill., 1983-92, pres., 1985-89; mem. Gov.'s Sci. Adv. Com., Ill., 1991-97; dir. Ill. Environ. Coun., 1984-92, v.p., 1985-87; trustee QEM Fire Protection Dist., 1998-99; bd. dirs. Great Rivers Land Trust, 1998-2002, Jubilee Habitat for Humanity, 2002—. Mem. Am. Ornithologists Union, Fla. Ornithol. Soc., Natural Lands Inst., Rotary Internat., Ill. Audubon Soc. Presbyterian. Avocations: canoeing, birding, travel, golf. Home: 857 W State St Apt 3 Jacksonville IL 62650-1983 Office: Pollution Control Bd 1021 N Grand Ave Springfield IL 62794

GIRARD, JONATHAN RICHARD, conductor; b. Fall River, Mass., Apr. 25, 1978; s. Richard Joseph and Janet Theresa Girard. MusB in Saxophone Performance Summa Cum Laude, Hartt Sch. Music, 2000. Music dir., organist St. Robert Bellarmine Ch., Windsor Locks, Conn., 1996—2000; asst. condr. Portland Opera Repertory Theatre, Portland, Maine, 1996—2000; assoc. condr. Brockton Symphony Orch., Mass., 1998—; orch. condr. Wellesley H.S., 2000—; music dir., organist Ch. of St. George, Framingham, 2000—02; music dir. Waltham Philharm., 2002—; music dir., organist St. Mary of the Assumption Ch., Boston, 2002—, Dedham, 2002—. Named one of Top 50 Orch. Condrs. U.S., Sch. Band and Orch. Mag., 2001; Conducting fellow, Pierre Monteux Sch., 2001—02. Mem.: Am. Guild Organists, Phi Kappa Lambda (hon.). Achievements include Premiered the work Tribute to Kerouac by composer David Alpher - Hartford, 2000. Avocations: flying, skiing, golf. Home: 114 Sarah Ave Somerset MA 02725 Personal E-mail: jg@jonathangirard.com.

GIRARD, LOUIS JOSEPH, ophthalmologist, educator; b. Spokane, Wash., Mar. 29, 1919; s. Harry and Agnes (Cain) G.; m. Bonita Crossnay, Mar. 31, 1945; children: Hilaire Michelle (Mrs. Cliff Richey), Bryan, Suzanne (Mrs. R. Thackston), Christina Ann, Michael Sanford (dec.), Hugh Ashley, Gabrielle Inez; m. Loraine McMurrey, June 30, 1967; 1 son, Louis McMurrey; m. Louise Bell, June 14, 1975. BA, Rice U., 1941; MD, U. Tex., 1944; postgrad., NYU, Med. Sch., 1947-48. Diplomate: Am. Bd. Ophthalmology. Intern Jersey City Med. Ctr., 1944-45; assoc. Dr. Conrad Berens, NYC, 1947—49; asst. attending St. Clare's Hosp., 1948—53; resident ophthalmology NY Eye and Ear Infirmary, 1949-51; asst. attending Willard Parker Hosp., 1949-53; dir. chronic infection project, 1949-52; asst. attending N. Country Community Hosp., 1951-53; assoc. Dr. Conrad Berens, 1951—53; asst. surgeon, 1951-53; assoc. dir. dept. rsch., 1953—57; asst. attending Nassau Hosp., 1951-53; cons. ophthalmologist Southside Hosp., 1951-53; attending ophthalmologist Jefferson Davis Hosp., 1953-59, VA Hosp., Houston, 1954—98, Tex. Children's Hosp., 1954—98, St. Luke's Episcopal Hosp., 1954—98, Meth. Hosp., 1955—98; cons. Montgomery County Hosp., 1955—, Tex. Children's Hosp., 1957—98; assoc. prof., assoc. chmn. dept. ophthalmology Baylor Coll. Medicine, Houston, 1957—70, prof., chmn. dept., 1957-70; cons. VA Hosp., Houston, 1958—98; sr. attending Ben Taub Gen. Hosp., 1959—98, Meth. Hosp., 1959—98; cons. St. Luke's Episcopal Hosp., 1961—98, St. Joseph's Hosp., 1965—98; chief ophthalmology, co-chief surgery Ctr. Pavilion Hosp., 1970-76; clin. prof. Baylor Coll. Medicine, Houston, 1971—. Coord. grad. course ophthalmology NYU Postgrad. Med. Sch., 1948-49, instr., 1951-53; clin. asst. prof. U. Tex. Postgrad. Sch. Medicine, 1953-57, lectr., 1946 ; assoc. mng. dir. Ophthal. Found., N.Y., 1951-55, cons., 1957; founder Tex. Med. Ctr.-Lions Eye Bank, 1953; exec. dir. Girard Ophthal. Found., 1971—; cons. Meth. Hosp., St. Luke's Hosp.; founder, exec. dir. Inst. Ophthalmology, Tex. Med. Ctr., 1958—70; founder ophthal. tissue culture lab. Baylor U., 1954; mem. Am. Orthoptic Coun., 1962-72; pres. Internat. Eye Film Library, 1967-71; med. adv. bd. Internat. Eye Bank, 1965-70; Pres. IX Pan Am. Congress Ophthalmology, 1972; presenter in field. Author: Advanced Techniques in Ophthalmic Microsurgery, Vol. I: Ultrasonic Fragmentation for Intraocular Surgery, 1979, Vol. II: Corneal Surgery, 1981; author, editor. over 7 books; prodr. 70 films.; editor: Corneal Contact Lenses, 1964, 2d edit., 1971, Corneal Scleral Contact Lenses, 1967, Proceedings of XI Pan Am Congress of Ophthalmology, 1974; mem. editl. bd. Ophthalmologica, 1965-72, Annals of Ophthalmology, 1968-74; contbr. articles to profl. jours.; cons. Highlights Ophthalmology, 1972; founded the Lions Ey Bank; founded the just Tissue laboratory devoted to ophthalmology in the world, 1959; established the first institute of ophthalmology in southwestern USA at Taylor College of Medicine, 1961. Recipient Alfred H. Bond award for rsch. in ophthalmology, 1950, Prof. Ignacio Barraquer Meml. award Inst. Barraquer, 1965, 2d prize Internat. Eye Film Festival, 1966, 1st prize, 1970, 1st prize, 1972, Golden Eagle award Internat. Film Festival Nantes, France, 1970, 71, Alumnus award Baylor U., 1984, First Disting. Alumnus award NY Eye and Ear Infirmary, 1984, Disting. Alumnus award Rice U., 1985, Disting. Alumnus award U. Tex. Med. Br. at Galveston, 1991; named to Hall of Fame, Alcon Labs., 1990. Fellow ACS (bd. gov. 1966-72); mem. Am. Acad. Ophthalmology (2d pl. award sci. exhibits 1960, Honor award, Sr. Honor award), Pan Am. Assn. Ophthalmology (1st pl. award sci. exhibits 1960, 62, vis. prof. 1967, v.p. 1972), Assn. Research Ophthalmology, N.Y. Acad. Medicine, NY Acad. Sci., Nassau, Houston ophthal. socs., French Soc. Ophthalmology, Houston Neurol. Soc., Jules Gonin Club, Tex. Ophthal. Assn., Alumni Assn. NY Eye and Ear Infirmary, AMA (certificate of merit sci. exhibit 1961), So. Med. Assn., Nat. Med. Found. Eye Care, Assn. Am. Physicians and Surgeons, Am. Assn. Ophthalomologists, Nat. Med. Found. Eye Care, Tex. Rehab. Assn., Harris County Med. Soc., Am. U. Prof. Ophthalmologists (founder, chmn. com. on ophthalmic asst.), Med. Rsch. Found. Tex., Contact Lens Soc. Ophthalmologists (Exceptional Merit award 1968), Inst. Horacio Ferrer (corr., lectr. 1959), Am. Eye Study Club (pres.) Achievements include inventing several instruments; originator numerous surg. techniques. Home: 20126 Indigo Lake Dr Magnolia TX 77355-3163

GIRARD, NETTABELL, lawyer; b. Pocatello, Idaho, Feb. 24, 1938; d. George and Arranetta (Bell) Girard Student, Idaho State U., 1957-58; BS, U. Wyo., 1959, JD, 1961. Bar: Wyo. 1961, D.C. 1969, U.S. Supreme Ct. 1969. Practiced in, Riverton, 1963-69; atty.-adviser on gen. counsel's staff HUD; assigned Office Interstate Land Sales Registration, Washington, 1969-70; sect. chief interstate land sales Office Gen. Counsel, 1970-73; ptnr. Larson & Larson, Riverton, 1973-85; pvt. practice Riverton, 1985—. Condr. course on women and law; lectr. in field. Editor Wyoming Clubwoman, 1966-68; bd. editors Wyo. Law Jour., 1959-61; writer Obiter Dictum column Women Lawyers Jour., Dear Legal Advisor column Solutions for Seniors, 1988-94; featured in Riverton Ranger, 1994; also articles in legal jours. Chmn. fund dr. Wind River chpt., ARC, 1965; chmn. Citizens Com. for Better Hosp. Improvement, 1965; chmn. subcom. on polit. legal rights and responsibilities Gov.'s Commn. on Status Women, 1965—69, mem. adv. com., 1973—93; local chmn. Law Day, 1966, 1967, county chmn., 1994—97; mem. state bd. Wyo Girl Scouts USA, sec., 1974—89, bd. dirs., 2001—; state vol. adv. Nat. Found. March of Dimes, 1967—69; legal counsel Wyo. Women's Conf., 1977; gov. apptd. State Wyo. Indsl. Siting Coun., 1995—2001; rep. Nat. Conf. Govs. Commn., Washington, 1966. Recipient Spl. Achievement award HUD, 1972, Disting. Leadership award Girl Scouts USA, 1973, Franklin D. Roosevelt award Wyo. chpt. March of Dimes, 1985, Thanks Badge award Girl Scout Coun., 1987, Women Helping Women award Riverton Club Soroptimist Internat., 1990, Spl. award 27 yrs. svc. Wyo. Commn. for Women, 1964-92, Appreciation award Wyo. Sr. Citizens and Solutions for Srs., 1994, Arts in Action Pierrot award for outstanding musician, 1998, Disting. Svc. award Wyo. Music Edn. Assn., 2003. Mem. AAUW (br. pres., condr. seminar on law for layman Riverton br. 1965), Wyo. Bar Assn., Fremont County Bar Assn. (Spl. Recognition cert. 1997), DC Bar Assn., Women's Bar Assn. DC, Internat. Fedn. Women Lawyers, Am. Judicature Soc., Assn. Trial Lawyers Am., Wyo. Trial Lawyers Assn., Nat. Assn. Women Lawyers (del. Wyo., nat. sec. 1969-70, v.p. 1970-71, pres. 1972-73), Wyo. Fedn. Women's Clubs (state editor, pres.-elect 1968-69, treas. 1974-76), Prog. Women's Club (pres.-elect. 1994-95), Riverton Chautaqua Club (pres. 1965-67, 2000-01), Riverton Civic League (pres. 1987-89), Kappa Delta, Delta Kappa Gamma (state chpt. hon.). Home: PO Box 687 Riverton WY 82501-0687 Office: 513 E Main St Riverton WY 82501-4440 *I believe first and foremost in the freedom of the individual: the right of the individual to be different, to be unique, and to pursue his or her particular heart's desire so long as that pursuit does not endanger the life or freedom of another. Perhaps because as a woman lawyer in predominately a man's profession, I have experienced the bitterness and dissolutionment of discrimination, I have actively worked through the equal rights movement toward the realization of individual freedom for all people. I support equality, not in the sense of "sameness," but in the realization of greater opportunities for individual development and differentiation.*

GIRARD, RENÉ NOEL, author, educator; b. Avignon, France, Dec. 25, 1923; came to U.S., 1947; s. Joseph and Thérèse (Fabre) G.; m. Martha McCullough, June 18, 1951; children: Martin, Daniel, Mary. Archiviste-paléographe, Ecole des chartes, Paris, 1947; PhD, Ind. U., 1950. Tchr. Romance langs. Ind. U., 1947-52, Duke U., 1952-53, Bryn Mawr Coll., 1953-57; faculty Johns Hopkins U., 1957-68, prof. French lit., 1961-68, chmn. dept. Romance langs., 1966-68, James M. Beall prof. French and humanities, 1977-80; disting. faculty prof. arts and letters SUNY, Buffalo, 1971-77; Andrew B. Hammond prof. French and Comparative Lit., Stanford U., 1981-95, courtesy prof. religious studies, 1986-95. Mem. Ctr. for Internat. Security and Arms Control, 1990-95, emeritus mem., 1995. Author: Mensonge romantique et vérité romanesque, 1961, 78, Marcel Proust: A Collection of Critical Essays, 1962, 77, Deceit, Desire and the Novel, 1967, 76, La Violence et le Sacré, 1972, English transl., 1977, Critique dans un souterrain, 1976, Des Choses cachées depuis la fondation du monde, 1978, To Double Business Bound, 1978, Le Bouc émissaire, 1982, La Route antique des hommes pervers, 1985, Things Hidden since the Foundation of the World, 1987, Job: the Victim of his People, 1987, Shakespeare: Les feux de l'envie, 1990, A Theater of Envy. William Shakespeare, 1991, Quand ces choses commenceront, 1994, The Girard Reader (ed. James Williams), 1996, Resurrection from the Underground: Feodor Dostoevsky (ed. James Williams), 1997, Je Vois Satan Tomber Comme L'Éclair, 1999, I see Satan fall like Lightning, 2001, Celui par qui le scandale arrive, 2001, La voix méconnue du réel, 2002; contbr. articles to profl. jours. Guggenheim fellow, 1960, 67; recipient Prix Médicis Essai, 1990, Premio Nonino, 1998. Mem. Acad. Arts and Scis., French Legion Honor, Acad. Francaise (Grand prix de philosophie 1996). Home: 705 Frenchmans Rd Stanford CA 94305-1004 also: 17 Av la Bourdonnais 75007 Paris France

GIRARD-DICARLO, DAVID FRANKLIN, lawyer; b. Bryn Mawr, Pa., Jan. 20, 1943; s. John J. Girard-DiCarlo and Elizabeth (Patton) Ward; m. Constance Jean Bricker, Apr. 5, 1973. BS, St. Joseph's U., 1970; JD, Villanova U., 1973. Bar: U.S. Dist. Ct. (ea. dist.) Pa. 1973, Pa. 1973, U.S. Ct. Appeals (3d cir.) 1973, U.S. Supreme Ct. 1978. Assoc., Wolf, Block, Schorr & Solis-Cohen, Phila., 1973-74; assoc. Dilworth, Paxson, Kalish, Levy & Kauffman, Phila., 1974-78, ptnr., 1979; ptnr. Fell, Spalding, Goff & Rubin, Phila., 1979-82; ptnr. Blank, Rome, Comisky & McCauley, Phila., 1982—, chmn. labor and employment law sect., 1982-86, adminstrv. ptnr., 1986-87, mng. ptnr., 1987—; mem. hearing com. Disciplinary Bd. of Supreme Ct. of Pa., Phila., 1981-84, chmn. hearing com., 1984-87; faculty mem. Workshop on Urban Mass Transp., Practicing Law Inst., San Francisco and Washington, 1978; bd. dirs. Midlantic Corp.; trustee Phila. Belt Line R.R. Co., 1992—; lectr. in field. Editor-in-chief Villanova Law Rev., 1972, Transit Law Rev., 1977-81; contbr. articles to legal jours. Mem. Phila. Cmty. Leadership Seminar Program, 1978-79; chmn. bd. Southeastern Pa. Transp. Authority, 1979-82; mem. transp. taxation task force Tax Commn. of Commonwealth of Pa., 1981-82; chmn. N.E. Corridor Commuter Rail Authorities Com., 1981-83; mem. Pa. Rep. State Fin. Com., 1982— ; bd. dirs. Greater Phila. Partnership, 1981-83, Urban Affairs Partnership, 1983-85, Hermitage Homeowners Assn., 1982-86; mem. World Affairs Coun., Phila., bd. dirs., 1993—; trustee Walnut St. Theatre, 1986-93, Harcum Jr. Coll., 1987-92, Drexel U., 1988-92, Phila. Acad. Music and Phila. Orch., 1988-95, mem. exec. com., 1988-95, vice chmn., 1991-94; mem. sch. of law bd. of consultors Villanova U., 1992—; chmn. transition team Pa. Gov. Elect Tom Ridge, 1994; bd. mgrs. The Phila. Found., 1994—; trustee St. Joseph's U., 1994—. Fellow Am. Bar Found.; mem. ABA, Pa. Bar Assn., Phila. Bar Assn., Am. Pub. Transit Assn. (bd. dirs. 1979-82, chmn. bd. dirs. 1982, chmn. legis. com. 1980-81, mem. exec. com. 1980-82, v.p. govt. affairs 1981-82, mem. various coms.), Greater Phila. C. of C. (bd. dirs., sec., mem. exec. com. 1990—). Episcopalian. Clubs: Union League of Phila., Vesper (Phila.), Waynesborough Country (Paoli, Pa.), Pyramid Club (Phila., bd. dirs. 1992—), Stonewall Golf Club, The Boulders (Carefree, Ariz.). Office: Blank Rome Comisky & McCauley 4 Penn Ctr Fl 10-13 Philadelphia PA 19103-2808

GIRARDEAU, MARVIN DENHAM, physics educator; b. Lakewood, Ohio, Oct. 3, 1930; s. Marvin Denham and Maude Irene (Miller) G.; m. Susan Jessica Brown, June 30, 1956; children— Ellen, Catherine, Laura. BS, Case Inst. Tech., 1952; MS, U. Ill., 1954; PhD, Syracuse U., 1958. NSF postdoctoral fellow Inst. Advanced Study, Princeton, 1958-59; research assoc. Brandeis U., 1959-60; staff mem. Boeing Sci. Research Labs., 1960-61; research assoc. Enrico Fermi Inst. Nuclear Studies, U. Chgo., 1961-63; assoc. prof. physics, research assoc. Inst. Theoretical Sci., U. Oreg., Eugene, 1963-67, prof. physics, research assoc., 1967—95, dir., 1967-69, chmn. dept. physics, 1974-76, prof. emeritus, 1995—; rsch. prof. optical scis. U. Ariz., 2000—. Contbr. articles to profl. jours. Recipient Humboldt Sr. U.S. Scientist award, 1984-85. NSF research grantee, 1965-79; ONR research grantee, 1981-87, 99—. Fellow Am. Phys. Soc.; mem. AAUP. Achievements include research on quantum-mech. many-body problems, statis. mechanics, atomic, molecular and chem. physics; Bose-Einstein condensation of atomic vapors, coherent control of quantum systems. Home: 288 N Bent Ridge Dr Green Valley AZ 85614-5949 Office: Optical Scis Ctr Univ Arizona Tucson AZ 85721-0001 E-mail: girardeau@optics.arizona.edu.

GIRARDI, FEDERICO PABLO, surgeon, educator; b. Rosario, Santa Fe, Argentina, Dec. 20, 1967; came to U.S., 1996; s. Hector Francisco Girardi and Martha Sylvia Malano; m. Maria Florencia Ferrero, May 4, 1996; children: Federico, Emilia. MD, 1991. Resident Hosp. de Clinicas Jose de San Martin, Buenos Aires U.; orthop. fellow Hosp. Spl. Surgery, N.Y.C., 1996-99, asst. attending orthop. surgeon, asst. scientist, 2000—; instr. Weill Coll. Medicine Cornell U., N.Y.C., 2000—. Dir. rsch. and edn. SpineCare Inst., Hosp. Spl. Surgery, N.Y.C., 2000—. Mem. AMA, N.Am. Spine Soc., Scoliosis Rsch. Soc., European Spine Soc., Med. Soc. State N.Y., N.Y. County Med. Soc. Office: Hosp Spl Surgery 535 E 70 St New York NY 10021 Fax: 212-472-1486. E-mail: GirardiF@hss.edu.

GIRARDI, JOSEPH ELLIOTT, baseball player; b. Peoria, Ill., Oct. 14, 1964; BS in Indsl. Engring., Northwestern U., 1986. Baseball player N.Y. Yankees, 1995-2000; catcher Chgo. Cubs, 2000—. Achievements include member of N.Y. Yankees World Series Champions, 1996. Office: Chgo Cubs Wrigley Field 1060 W Addison St Chicago IL 60613-4383

GIRARDS, JAMES EDWARD, lawyer; b. Manhasset, N.Y., Aug. 16, 1963; s. H.V. and Barbara (Davis) G.; m. Julie Ann Calame, June 27, 1987; children: Jessica Lauren, James Edward. BS, Baylor U., 1986; JD, St. Mary's Law Sch., 1989. Bar: Tex. 1989, U.S. Dist. Ct. (no., so. and ea. dists.) Tex. 1991, U.S. Ct. Appeals (5th cir.) 2000. Assoc. Law Offices Windle Turley, P.C., Dallas, 1989-94; prin. Tracy & Girards, Dallas, 1994-97, The Girards Law Firm, Dallas, 1997—. Contbr. articles to profl. jours. Recipient Am. Jurisprudence Contracts award AmJur Pub. Co., 1986. Mem. ATLA (pres.'s club 1999-), Tex. Trial Lawyers Assn. (dir. 1999—), Dallas Trial Lawyers Assn. (dir. 1998—), Dallas Bar Assn., Dallas Assn. Young Lawyers, State Bar Tex., Coll. of State Bar of Tex., Am. Mensa, Ltd., Million Dollar Advocates Forum. Office: 10000 N Central Expy Ste 750 Dallas TX 75231

GIRGENTI, JOHN ALEXANDER, state legislator; b. Paterson, N.J., Aug. 8, 1947; s. Joseph George and Angelina (Giovanelli) G.; m. Rose Nagle, 1982. BA cum laude, Seton Hall U., 1969; MA, St. John's U., 1972. Mem. N.J. Gen. Assembly, 1978-90, N.J. Senate, Dist. 35, Trenton, 1990—. Asst. minority leader N.J. State Assembly, 1986-90, dep. minority leader, 1990; dir. pub. rels. devel. Straight & Narrow, Inc., Paterson, N.J., 1974-77. Trustee, v.p. Hawthorne (N.J.) Sch. Bd., 1973-76; commr. Mental Health Bd., Passaic County, N.J., 1975-77; chmn. Hawthorne Dem. Town Com., 1976—; fin. aid coun. Passaic County C.C., 1973-74; dir. mental health Passaic County, 1977-78; pres. Dem. Club Passaic County, 1974-78; vol. Passaic Valley coun. Boy Scouts Am. Named man of yr. Judge Alfano Assn., 1978, Hawthorne Boy's Club, 1989; named outstanding young man N.J. Jaycees, 1981. Mem. Italian Cir. Paterson, Columbus Cir. Hawthorne, Lions. Office: 507 Lafayette Ave Hawthorne NJ 07506-2424*

GIRGIS-HANNA, MARY FAHIM, music educator; b. Assiut, Egypt, Mar. 6, 1935; arrived in U.S., 1989; d. Fahim Girgis and Emily Matta Boctor; m. Fadel M. Hanna, Nov. 25, 1954; children: Baher, Farid, Wagih. BA in Edn., Am. U., Cairo, 1958, MA in Sociology, 1978; ATCL in Piano Tchg., Trinity Coll. London, 1972; PhD in Spl. Edn., U. Toledo, 1997. Tchr. Manor House H.S., Cairo, 1967—69; pvt. piano tchr. Cairo, 1972—88; tchr. family sociology Prebyn. Sem., Cairo, 1984—88; cons. gerontology Egyptian Ministry of Health, Cairo, 1980—83; instr. sociology U. Toledo, 1989—2000; dir., founder Rhapsody Sch. Music, Toledo, 1994—. Founder, bd. dirs. Ctr. for Geriatric Svcs., Cairo, 1976—88. Author: The Gerontologist, 1983. Chmn., commr. internat. com. Christian Med. Commn., World Coun. of Chs., Geneva, 1980—83; bd. dirs. Lucas County Bd. Mental Retardation, Toledo, 1998—2000; Ohio rep. Trinity Coll. London, 1995—; organist Judson Bapt. Ch., Toledo, 1992—, deacon of missions, 1997—2002. Named Model Mother, Presbyn. Women's Assn., 1980. Mem.: Toledo Piano Tchr. Assn. (pres. 2001—03), Nat. Piano Tchr. Assn. Avocations: piano, organ, accordion, singing, reading. Home: 3006 E Lincolnshire Blvd Toledo OH 43606

GIRGUS, SAM B. English literature educator; b. Dec. 30, 1941; m. Judith Scot-Smith; children: Katya Roberts, Meighan St. John, Jennifer Scot-Smith. BA in American Studies, Syracuse U., 1962; MA in English, State U. Iowa, 1963; PhD in American Studies, U. N.Mex., 1972. Reporter, critic Providence (R.I.) Jour., 1967-69; asst. prof. in Am. studies and English U. Ala., 1972-75, dir., 1973-75; assoc. prof., chmn. dept. Am. studies U. N.Mex., 1975-84, prof. English and Am. studies, 1980-87; prof. English, dir. Am. studies U. Oreg., Eugene, 1987-90; prof. English Vanderbilt U., Nashville, 1990—, dir. Am. studies, 1990-92. Chmn. disciplinary adv. com. Fulbright Scholars Awards in Am. Culture, 1989-93; cons. USIA visit at Sofia U., Bulgaria, 1985, Los Andes U., Bogota, Columbia, 1992, Hankuk U., Seoul, Korea, 1993, Aarhus U., Odense U., Denmark, 1995; lectr. in field; Uppsala chair in Am. studies Uppsala U., Sweden, 1996. Author: The Law of the Heart: Individualism and the Modern Self in American Literature, 1979, The New Covenant: Jewish Writers and the American Idea, 1984, Desire and the Political Unconscious in American Literature, 1990, The Films of Woody Allen, 1993, 2d edit., 2002, Hollywood Renaissance: The Cinema of Democracy in the Era of Ford, Capra and Kazan, 1998, America on Film: Modernism, Documentary, and a Changing America, 2002; editor: The American Self: Myth, Ideology and Popular Culture, 1981, The New Eden: Consensus and Regeneration in America, 1988, The Outsider: Dissent and Alienation in America, 1988; guest editor: Am. Literary Realism 1870-1910, 1977; prodr., writer: (film) In Loco Amicis: The New Vanderbilt Story, 2001; contbr. articles to profl. jours. With USN, 1963-67. Rockefeller Humanities fellow, 1980-81; Sr. Fulbright lectr. U. Heidelberg, Germany, 1984. Mem. MLA, Cinema Studies Assn., Am. Studies Assn. Home: 402 Lynwood Blvd Nashville TN 37205-3435 Office: Vanderbilt U Dept English PO Box 1654 Sta B 318 Benson Hall Nashville TN 37235 E-mail: sam.b.girgus@vanderbilt.edu.

GIRGUS, SIGNE LINSCOTT, interior designer; b. Elizabeth, N.J., June 17, 1950; d. Andrew and Carol (Callahan) Girgus; m. Edward Jenkins Rhea, Oct. 7, 1989 (div. Jan. 1997); stepchildren: Alexander J., Jean Edwin M., Kenneth A.; m. Gordon Thornhill Jr., Dec. 22, 2002; 1 stepchild, Brittany S. Thornhill. BFA, Va. Commonwealth U., 1972; postgrad., Parsons Sch. Design, 1997—. Cert. interior designer Nat. Coun. Interior Design Qualification, Am. Soc. Interior Designers, 1975. Interior designer W & J Sloane Inc., Washington, 1972-76; exhibit design mus. aid Mus. Natural History, Smithsonian Instn., Washington, 1974; interior designer GSA Spl. Projects Divsn., Washington, 1976-78; sole staff interior designer Exec. Office of Pres., The White House, Washington, 1978—, assoc. dir. facilities mgmt., 1993-95, sr. preservation and facilities officer, 1995—2001, interior design & preservation mgr., 2001—. Design liaison Presdl. Boxes, Kennedy Ctr., Washington, 1978—; facilities mgr. Presdl. Inaugural Com., Washington, 1985; design cons. Ronald Reagan Retirement Office, L.A., 1989, George Bush Retirement Office, Houston, 1992. Named 100 Most Notable Alumni, Va. Commonwealth U., Richmond, 1994; recipient Lisa Taylor fellowship Cooper-Hewitt Nat. Design Mus. Paris Program, 1997. Mem. DAR, Am. Soc. Interior Designers, Coun. Fed. Interior Designers, Nat. Trust for Hist. Preservation, Washington Decorative Arts Forum, Jr. League Washington. Avocation: horsemanship.

GIRLING, PETER MICHAEL, analyzer systems engineer, consultant; b. London, Jan. 28, 1937; came to U.S., 1981; s. Frederick Atto and Doris Winifred (Martin) G.; m. Sonia Mavis Hickson, 1962 (div.); 1 child, Philippa; m. Patricia Anne Wade, Apr. 28, 1972; children: Anna, Simon, Katherine, Siobhan. Spl. degree in chemistry, Imperial Coll., London, 1957; assoc., Royal Coll. Sci., London, 1968; higher nat. cert., Borough Poly., London, 1965. European engr.; chartered engr., U.K. Asst. master London County Coun., 1959-61; devel. chemist Burt, bolton & Haywood, Belvedere, Kent, Eng., 1961-63; applications chemist Cray Valley Products, St. Mary Cray, Kent, 1963-64; asst. chief engr. GEC-Elliott, London, 1964-70; engring. assoc. Esso Engring. (Europe) Ltd., New Malden, Surrey, Eng., 1970-81; sr. engring. assoc. Air Products & Chems. Inc., Allentown, Pa., 1981-90; sr. assoc. engr. Mobil R & D Corp., Princeton, N.J., 1990—. Cons. PSkills, Allentown, 1975-91. Editor Process Control and Quality, 1990—; patentee in field. Sr. sci. officer CD Corps, London, 1959-67; chmn. cub pack 8 Boy Scouts Am., Allentown, 1982-84. Fellow Inst. Measurement and Control (U.K.); mem. Instrument Soc. Am. (sr.). Avocations: music, model construction.

GIRMAN, DEE-MARIE, iconographer, artist; b. Duquesne, Pa., Apr. 10, 1919; d. Michael Girman and Marie Schuster. Student, Pitts. Musical Inst., Fillion Ballet Sch.; studied dress design with Louise Salinger; student, Barry U. Singer, Pitts.; iconographer, artist Barry U., Miami Shores, Fla. Author: Sandtrap, The Mathematical Genius Dog, 2003. Entertainer specialist Spl. Svc., USAAC, 1942—45. Named to Hall of Fame, Barry U., 1995, Meml. Hist. Roll of Honor, Am. Meml. Found., 1997. Republican. Roman Catholic. Achievements include creation of over 26 icons of mother and child, 144 "Keyhole" mini-icons and other pieces of artwork. Avocation: golf. Home: 1779 San Silvestro Dr Venice FL 34292

GIRO, JORGE ANTONIO, languages educator, consultant; b. Havana, Cuba, Oct. 21, 1933; s. Jose A. and Catalina A. G.; m. Alicia T. Godoy, July 16, 1960; children— Alicia Marie, Christine Marie. B.A., Ind. State U., 1962, M.S., 1964; Ph.D., Jose Marti U., 1957. Tchr., Sch. City of Elkhart (Ind.), 1962-66; prof. dept. modern langs. Towson U. (Md.), Balt., 1966—. Home: 109 Ridgefield Rd Lutherville Timonium MD 21093-6320 E-mail: jgiro@towson.edu.

GIROD, ERWIN ERNEST, internist; b. L.A., Oct. 1, 1944; s. Dudley Leonard and Rena Merl (Hudson) G.; m. Jill Louise Johnson, Dec. 16, 1967; children: Jeffrey Johnson, Janette Renee. BA, Calif. State U., L.A., 1966; MD, U. Calif., Irvine, 1970. Diplomate Am. Bd. Internal Medicine. Med. intern L.A. County-U. So. Calif. Med. Ctr., 1970-71, resident in internal medicine, 1971-73; ward med. officer, dir. med. ICU, adminstrv. chief U.S. Naval Hosp., San Diego, 1973-75; dir. ICU Christian Med. Coll., Brown Meml. Hosp., Ludhiana, Punjab, India, 1976-77; asst. prof. medicine Punjab U., 1976-77; chief gen. medicine, asst. chief dept. medicine Loma Linda VA Hosp., 1978-80; pvt. practice Pasadena, Calif., 1981-86; internal medicine specialist Hanson Med. Group, Inc., San Gabriel, Calif., 1986—. Asst. prof. dept. medicine Loma Linda U., 1978-80; mem. staff Huntington Meml. Hosp., Pasadena, 1981—, St. Luke Med. Ctr., Pasadena, 1981—; assoc. staff mem. Meth. Hosp. So. Calif., Arcadia, Calif., 1986—; lectr. in field. Contbr. articles to profl. publs. Bd. dirs. Lifewater, Internat., Baldwin Park, Calif., 1984-89; med. advisor Overseas Missionary Fellowship, Orange, Calif., 1988-92. Lt. comdr. USN, 1973-75. Fellow ACP, Am. Biographical Inst., Internat. Biographical Ctr. (life); mem. Calif. Med. Assn., Christian Med.-Dental Soc., Ephebian Soc. L.A., Gideons Internat. (chaplain Pasadena camp 1992-95), World Inst. Achievement (Internat. Cultural Diploma of Honor 1989, World Decoration of Excellence Medallion 1989, Disting. Leadership award 1989), Phi Kappa Phi, Alpha Gamma Omega (Legion of Honor). Republican. Congregationalist. Avocations: swimming, music, roses. Home: 1195 Coronet Ave Pasadena CA 91107-1729

GIROIR, LEO JEAN JR. accountant; b. New Orleans, Nov. 5, 1941; s. Leo Jean and Evelyn Gerhardt G.; children from previous marriage: Lisa Marie, Wendy Ann Giroir-Colson; m. Louise Moore. BBA, Loyola U., 1963. CPA, Calif., La. Staff acct. Haskins & Sells CPAs, New Orleans, 1966-71; ptnr. Ross Landis & Pauw CPAs, Riverside, Calif., 1971-79, Easley & Giroir CPAs, Colton, Calif., 1979-81, McGladrey Hendrickson CPAs, Colton, 1981-84; shareholder Leo J. Giroir Jr. CPA, APC, Riverside, 1984—. Chair bd. dirs. Riverside Arts Found., 1991-97, Riverside County ARC, 1997—; treas. Riverside Ballet Theatre, 1991-92; bd. dirs. BBB, So. Calif., 1981—. Served in U.S. Army, 1964-66. Republican. Roman Catholic. Avocations: cooking, fishing. Home: PO Box 20259 Riverside CA 92516-0259

GIROIR, LOUIS ERIC, toxicologist; b. Shreveport, La., Apr. 9, 1961; s. Louis Elie Giroir and Jane Sims; m. Kelly Jane Robertson, Mar. 21, 1992 (div. Dec. 1998); 1 child, Mitchell Ryan. BS in Biochemistry, Tex. A&M U., 1983, PhD in Toxicology, 1990; MS in Biochemistry, La. State U., 1986. Metabolism chemist Analytical Biochem. Labs., Columbia, Mo., 1990-94; toxicologist Mo. Dept. Natural Resources, Jefferson City, 1994—. Recipient Program Dir. award Air Pollution Control Program, 1998. Mem. Am. Chem. Soc. Avocations: camping, hiking, fishing, running. Office: Air Pollution Control Program 205 Jefferson St Jefferson City MO 65101-2901

GIROIR, MICHAEL JAMES, software analyst; b. Taipei, Taiwan, Oct. 14, 1967; s. Russell Joseph and Mae Hui Giroir; m. Tammy Denise Ferrey; 1 child, James. BSEE, La. State U., 1989. Software engr. Intergraph, Huntsville, Ala., 1990—99; sr. software analyst APT Rsch., Huntsville, Ala., 1999—. Mem.: Eta Kappa Nu, Tau Beta Pi. Home: 102 Laurelmill Dr Harvest AL 35749 Office: APT Rsch Inc 4950 Research Dr Huntsville AL 35805 Office Fax: 256-837-7786. Personal E-mail: mjgiroir@hiwaay.net. Business E-Mail: mjgiroir@apt-research.com.

GIRON, ROBERT LEROY, English educator, writer; s. Robert and Carmen (V.) G. BA, U. Tex., El Paso, 1973; MA, So. Ill. U., 1975. Teaching asst. So. Ill. U., Carbondale, 1974-75; instr. El Paso C.C., 1975-81; adj. lectr. St. Mary's U., San Antonio, 1981-82; teaching asst. U. Tex., San Antonio, 1981; adj. instr. Austin (Tex.) C.C., 1982-83; prof. English, Montgomery Coll., Takoma Park, Md., 1986—, chmn. dept., 1992-95, acting dean, fall 1993, coord., advisor honors program; pub. Gival Press, LLC. Adj. lectr. George Washington U., Washington, summer 1986; assoc. T. J. Schmidt, Inc., Washington, 1985-86. Editor/writer Ednl. Challenges, Inc., Alexandria, Va., 1984-85; author 5 collections of poetry; contbr. poems to various publs. Advisor Circle K Internat., Montgomery Coll., 1986-89, Rotaract Club, Montgomery Coll., 1990. Mellon Found. fellow, 1979. Mem. Tchrs. ESOL (editor jour. Washington area 1989), Pub. Mktg. Assn., Coll. English Assn., Washington Ind. Writers, Tex. Writers League, Writer's Ctr., Poetry Soc. Am. Avocations: art, music, photography, travel, theater. Office: Montgomery Coll Fenton & Takoma Aves Takoma Park MD 20912

GIRONE, JOAN CHRISTINE CRUSE, realtor, former county official; b. Kingston, Ont., Can., Aug. 30, 1927; d. Arthur William and Helen Wilson Cruse; m. Joseph MIchael Girone, June 26, 1954; children: Susan, Richard, William. Buyer Franklin Simon, Inc., N.Y.C., 1946-54; supr. Midlothian dist. Chesterfield County (Va.) Bd. Suprs., 1976-88, vice chmn., 1976-82; Founding mem. Capitol Area Agy. on Aging, 1973-89, Med. Coll. Va. Women's Health Adv. Coun., 1990-97, Chesterfield County Citizens for Responsible Govt., 1991—; comml. real estate agent Long and Foster Realtors, Richmond. Bd. dirs. Cen. Va. Ednl. TV Corp., 1989-94; commr., chmn. Richmond (Va.) Regional Planning Dist. Commn., 1976-88; Va. Power Consumer adv. bd.; chmn. cmty. edn. adv. com. Va. Bd. of Edn., 1972-79; mem. Va. Gov.'s Adv. Bd. on Aging, 1980-82; chmn. Richmond Met. Transp. Planning Orgn., 1981-88; bd. visitors Va. State U., 1980-84. Vice chmn., exec. com. Gateway Bus. Assn.; mem. Ctrl. Va. River Basin Com., 1985; mem. evaluation task force United Way of Greater Richmond, 1985; adv. bd. Chesapeake Bay Local Assistance Bd. Adv. Com. Midlothian YMCA, 2000; chmn. steering com. Bon Air Village Preservation, 1995—; mem. Coun. Advocates Va. Supportive Housing, 2001—; chmn. Chesterfield County Com. to elect John Warner and Paul Trible to U.S. Senate, 1979, 1982, 1984; Chesterfield chmn. Marshall Coleman for Gov., 1981—; chmn. Women for Reagen-Bush, 1984; vice chair Rt. 288 Freeway Comm., 1996, exec. com.; mem. candidate recruitment com. Va. Fedn. Rep. Women, 1995; bd. dirs. Maymount Found., 1982—89, YMCA Greater Richmond Metro, ARC Va. Capital chpt.; bd. mgrs. Chesapeake Bay Local Assistance Bd. Adv. Com. Midlothian YMCA, 1999, bd. dirs., 1994—, Caucus Future Ctrl. Va., 1994—, Coalition for Greater Richmond. Recipient Good Govt. award Richmond First Club, 1985; Joan C. Girone Libr. named in her honor, Chesterfield County, 1995. Mem. Va. Assn. Counties (exec. bd. 1982-87), Richmond Metro C. of C. (bd. dirs. Chesterfield Bus. Coun. 1989—), Hugeunot Rep. Woman's Club (Rep. Woman of Yr. 1983). Home: 2609 Dovershire Rd Richmond VA 23235-2815 E-mail: joan.girone@longandfoster.com.

GIROTTI, ROBERT BERNARD, medical and surgical nurse; b. New London, Conn., Dec. 10, 1962; s. Alfred E. and Patricia (Turello) G.; m. Grace Edna Reidy, May 25, 2002. BS, U. Conn., 1985, MSN, 1995. RN, Conn.; cert. med.-surg. nurse; cert. CPR. Staff nurse respiratory unit Lawrence Meml. Hosp., New London, 1985-90, staff nurse float pool, 1990—2002; staff nurse Exeter (NH) Hosp., 2002—. Instr. clin. nursing U. Conn., 1997-2000. Contbr. articles to nursing newsletters. Mem.: Cath. Nurses Assn., Lawrence Meml. Alumnae Assn., Internat. Assn. Approved Basketball Ofcls., U. Conn. Alumni Assn. (S.E. chpt. bd. dir. 1994—99), U. Conn. Sch. Nursing Alumni Assn. (exec. bd. dir. 1985—2000), Phi Kappa Phi, Sigma Theta Tau. Home: 139 GH Carter Dr Danville NH 03819 E-mail: robrncms@aol.com.

GIROUARD, PEGGY JO FULCHER, ballet educator; b. Corpus Christi, Tex., Oct. 25, 1933; d. J.B. and Zora Alice (Jackson) Fulcher; m. Richard Ernest Girouard, Apr. 16, 1954 (div. Mar. 1963); children: Jo Linne, Richard Ernest; m. James C. Boles, May 4, 1996. BS in Elem. Edn., U. Houston, 1970. Ballet instr. Emmamae Horn Studio, Houston, 1951-81; owner, dir. Allegro Acad. Dance, Houston, 1981—. Artistic dir. Allegro Ballet Houston, 1976—; asst. mgr. Sugar Creek Homes Assn., Sugar Land, Tex., 1979-90; coord. 1st Regional Dance Am. Nat. Festival, Houston, 1997. Choreographer (with Glenda W. Brown) Masquerade Suite, 1983, Sebelius Suite, 1983, Shannan, 1984, Papa Shamus, 1986, Silhouettes, 1987, Aspirations, 1989, Here Come the Clowns, 1990. Mem. Cultural Arts Coun. Houston; founding officer Regional Dance Am., 1988, bd. dirs., 1988—, sec., 1996-2001. Mem. Dance Masters Am. (dir. 1977-80), S.W. Regional Ballet Assn. (chmn. craft of choreography 1983-85, coord. to nat. assn. 1983-2003, Stream award 1986). Democrat. Home: 9945 Warwana Rd Houston TX 77080-7609 E-mail: pgirouard77080@yahoo.com.

GIROUARD, SHIRLEY ANN, nurse, policy analyst; b. New London, Conn., Jan. 16, 1947; d. Maxime Albert Girouard and Irene Barbara (Arnold) Reid. BA in Sociology, Ea. Conn. State Coll., 1972; MA in Sociology, U. Conn., 1974; MSN, Yale U., 1977; PhD in Policy Analysis, Brandeis U., 1988. Nurse Woodstock (Conn.) Pub. Health Assn., 1968-70; staff nurse Clinton (Conn.) Convalescent Ctr., 1970-72; ins. edn. coord. Middlesex Meml. Hosp., Middletown, Conn., 1973-75; clin. nurse specialist Dartmouth Hitchcock Med. Ctr., Hanover, N.H., 1977-83, staff nurse, 1983-84; legis. cons., lobbyist N.H. Nurses Assn., Concord, 1985-87; program officer Robert Wood Johnson Found., Princeton, N.J., 1987-92; exec. dir. N.C. Ctr. Nursing, 1992-93, Am. Nurse's Assn., 1993-94; health policy and nursing cons. pvt. and pub. sector orgns., Washington, 1994-95; v.p. child health and financing Nat. Assn. Children's Hosps. and Related Instns., Alexandria, Va., 1995-99; cons., 1999—; assoc. prof. So. Conn. State U., 2001—. Pvt. practice cons., 1983-87; profl. devel. cons., Lebanon, N.H., 1983-87; health policy and nursing cons. Author: (chpt.) Health Policy and Nurse Services, 1989, 98, others; mem. editorial bd. Clin. Nurses Specialist Jour., 1986—, others; contbr. articles to profl. jours. State rep. N.H. Legislature, Concord, 1982-84; counselor City of Lebanon Coun., 1984-87. Fellow Am. Acad. Nursing; mem. ANA (project dir. 1986), Sigma Theta Tau. Democrat.

GIROUARD, TANDY DENISE, special education educator, psychology educator; b. Ft. Worth, Tex., Aug. 25, 1960; d. Nolan Ray and Barbara Gale (Miller) Rutledge; m. Jan. 22, 1980 (div. Dec. 1995); children: Michael, Christopher, Kaneissa. BS in Generic Spl. Edn., U. of Mary Hardin-Baylor. Tchr. asst. spl. edn. Hurst-Euless-Bedford Ind. Sch. Dist., Bedford, Tex., 1988; tchr. asst. in spl. edn. McLennan County Dept. Edn., Waco, Tex., 1988-90; tchr. spl. edn. Moody Ind. Sch. Dist., 1991—94; tchr. resource reading LaVega Ind. Sch. Dist., 1994—95; tchr. life skills Waco Ind. Sch. Dist., 1996—98; tchr. 2d grade/tchr. spl. edn. Emma L. Harrison Charter Sch., 1998—99; tchr. resource Belton Ind. Sch. Dist., 1999—2000; tchr. spl. edn. Connally Ind. Sch. Dist., 2000—02. Mem. Internat. Assn. of Pers. in Employment Security, Assn. Tex. Profl. Educators, PTA, Bedford-Euless Soccer Assn., Tex. State Edn. Assn., Pi Gamma Mu. Home: 500 Greenfield Dr Waco TX 76705-1705

GIROUARD, TINA, artist, curator; b. De Quincy, La., May 26, 1946; BFA, U. La. Established studio, N.Y.C., 1968—85, Cecilia, La., 1980—, Port-au Prince, Haiti, 1991—. One-woman shows include Univ. Gallery, Lafayette, La., 1968, 1973, 1974, 112 Greene St. Gallery, N.Y.C., 1971—73, 1975, Vehicule, Montreal, 1975, Alfred (N.Y.) U. Gallery, 1975, Memphis Acad., 1975, Holly Solomon Gallery, N.Y.C., 1976, 1978, 1980, Alexandra Monet Gallery, Brussels, 1979, Forum Stadtpark Mus., Graz, Austria, 1979, Elmhurst Park Gallery, Lafayette, 1981, De Vleeshal, Middelburg, Holland, 1982, Zeeuws Kuntenaarscentrum, 1982, Arthur Roger Gallery, New Orleans, 1983, Museo Tamayo, Mexico City, 1983, Fabric Workshop, N.Y.C., 1984, World's Fair, New Orleans, 1984, PS 1, L.I., 1985, Arthur Roger Gallery, New Orleans, 1985, Artist's Alliance, Lafayette, 1986, Contemporary Art Ctr., New Orleans, 1987, Quebec Delegation Gallery, Lafayette, 1987, C.A.C., New Orleans, 1989, Mus. Art, Alexandria, La., 1989, one-man shows include Atlantic Ctr. Arts, 1990, one-woman shows include Lafayette Regional Airport, 1990, Contemporary Arts Ctr., New Orleans, 1990, exhibited in group shows at 112 Green St. Gallery, N.Y.C., 1972, Leo Castelli Gallery, 1974, UCLA Gallery, 1976, Cin. Art Mus., 1978, Mus. Modern Art, Oxford, Eng., 1980, Holly Solomon Gallery, N.Y.C., 1982, Arthur Roger Gallery, New Orleans, 1984, Inst. Contemporary Art, 1987, Contemporary Art Ctr., La., 1990, numerous others, commns. include, Contemporary Art Ctr., New Orleans, 1989, Lafayette Regional Airport, 1990, videography includes, Maintenance I, 1971, Maintenance II, 1972, Maintenance III, 1973, Maintenance IV, 1975, Six of Hearts, 1976, Maintenance V, 1976, WAWA, 1979, 2 C 3 T S, 1981, others. CAPS grantee, Art Matters, Inc. grantee, Nat. Endowment Arts grantee, La. Divsn. Arts fellow, Nat. Endowment Arts fellow, Creative Artists Pub. Svc. fellow, 1973, Internat. Comm. Agy. fellow, 1979, Lila Wallace Arts Internat. fellow, 1993, Gottlieb Fatn fellow, 1997. Office: Tina Girouard Art Projects PO Box 64 Cecilia LA 70521-0064

GIROUX, EUGENE XAVIER, lawyer; b. Somerville, Mass., May 8, 1928; s. Eugene H. and Mary E. (Cotter) G.; married, May 9, 1953; children: Susan M., E. Mark, Jacqueline L. BA, Boston Coll., 1952, LLB, 1957. Bar: Mass. 1957. Safety engr. Merchants Mutual Ins., Boston, 1952-54; pvt. practice Boston, 1957-61, 64—; asst. U.S. atty. U.S. Dept. Justice, Boston, 1961-64. With U.S. Army, 1946-47, Korea. Mem. Mass. Bar Assn. Democrat. Roman Catholic. Avocations: grandchildren, boating, photography, travel, music. Home and Office: 8 Grant Ave Wellesley MA 02481-6002

GIROUX, ROBERT-JEAN-YVON, retired Canadian government official; b. Rockland, Ont., Can., Mar. 1, 1939; s. Leo-Romeo and Cecile-Marie (Brunet) G.; m. Therese A. Briand, Aug. 31, 1963; children— Benoit, Andre, Jean-Pierre BCom in Econs., U. Ottawa, 1961, M in Social Sci., 1970; LLD, McMaster U., 2001, Royal Mil. Acad. Can., 2003. Pay research officer Can. Civil Service Commn., 1961-65; asst. research dir. Pub. Service Can., 1965-70; dir. Dept. Regional Econ. Expansion, 1970-73; adminstr. Fitness and Amateur Sport, 1973-75; dir. gen. Pub. Service Commn., 1975-78; adminstr. Surface Transport Adminstrn., 1978-82; dep. minister Nat. Revenue Customs and Excise, Ottawa, Ont., Can., 1982-86; dep. minister pub. works Govt. of Can., Ottawa, 1986-90; pres. Pub. Svc. Comn., Ottawa, 1990-94; sec. Treasury Bd., 1994-95; comptr. gen. Canada, 1994-95; pres. Assn. Univs. and Colls. Can., Ottawa, 1995—. Lectr. U. Ottawa, 1964-65; bd. govs. Can. Comprehensive Auditing Found., 1994. Bd. dirs. U. Que., Hull, 1993-95, Ottawa Gen. Hosp., 1996-98, Ottawa Hosp., 1998-99, Pub. Policy Forum; mem. Can. Found. for Innovation, 1997; chmn. Inst. on Governance, 1996-2001; mem. Can. Millenium Scholarship Found., 1998; mem. Edn. Mktg. adv. bd., 1998; mem. Can. Ctr. Mgmt. Devel., 1999—; pres. Rivermead Gulf Club, 2002—. Named to Order of Can., 1997; recipient Trudeau medal U. Ottawa. Mem. Can. Pub. Pers. Mng. Assn., Nat. Film Bd., Inst. Pub. Adminstrn. Can. (bd. dirs. 1990-94, nat. pres. 1992-93). Avocations: golf, cycling. Home: 438 Cannes Gatineau QC Canada J8T 5M5 Office: Assn Univs and Colls Can 600-350 Albert Ottawa ON Canada K1R 1B1 E-mail: president@aucc.ca.

GIRTH, MARJORIE LOUISA, lawyer, educator; b. Trenton, N.J., Apr. 21, 1939; d. Harold Brookman and Marjorie Mathilda (Simonson) G. AB, Mt. Holyoke Coll., 1959; LLB, Harvard U., 1962. Bar: N.J. 1963, U.S. Supreme Ct. 1969, N.Y. 1976. Pvt. practice, Trenton, 1963-65; rsch. assoc. Brookings Instn., 1965-70; assoc. prof. law SUNY Law Sch., Buffalo, 1971-79, prof., 1979-91, assoc. dean, 1986-87; dean Ga. State U. Coll. Law, Atlanta, 1992-96, prof., 1992—. Vis. prof. U. Va. Law Sch., 1979-80; Southeastern Bankruptcy Law Inst. vis. prof. Emory Law Sch., spring 1991, vis. scholar, 1996; vis. legal educator W.Va. U. Coll. of Law Vis. Com., 1994-95; chancellor's search adv. com. Bd. of Regents, 1993-94. Author: Poor People's Lawyers, 1976, Bankruptcy Options for the Consumer Debtor, 1981, (co-author) Bankruptcy: Problem, Process, Reform, 1971. Bd. dirs. Buffalo and Erie County YWCA, 1972-76, Buffalo Unitarian-Universalist Ch., 1981-84, Feminist Women's Health Ctr., 1993-94, ACLU, Ga., 1995-2001, Unitarian-Universalist Congregation of Atlanta, 1999—; mem. commn. on peace, justice and human rights Internat. Assn. Religious Freedom, 1976-79; chmn. Erie County Task Force on Status of Women, 1985-87. Recipient award for pioneering achievements N.Y. State 8th Jud. Dist. Splty. Bar Assn. and Com. on Women in the Cts., 2000. Fellow Lawyers Found. Ga.; mem. ABA (mem. coun. bus. law sect. 1985-89, chmn. consumer bankruptcy com. 1983-86), Am. Arbitration Assn. (comml. arbitration panel 1997—), Assn. Am. Law Schs. (profl. devel. com. 2002—, nominations com. 1996), Am. Law Inst., N.Y. State Bar Assn. (mem. exec. com. bus. law sect. 1980-91, chmn. bankruptcy law com. 1980-82, chmn. banking corp. bus. law sect. 1986-87, mem. ho. of dels. 1990-91), Ga. Supreme Ct. (commn. on racial and ethnic bias in ct. sys. 1993-95, commn. on equality 1995—, sec. 1998-2000), Ga. Assn. Women Lawyers, Law Sch. Admissions Coun. (audit com. 1995-97, 1999—, fin. and legal affairs com., 1997-99), Mt. Holyoke Alumnae Assn. (centennial award 1972). Office: Ga State U Coll Law PO Box 4037 Atlanta GA 30302-4037 E-mail: mgirth@gsu.edu.

GIRTON, LANCE, economics educator; b. Brazil, Ind., July 20, 1942; s. John E. and Barbara (Woolad) G.; children: Derek, Lance Alan. BA in Econs., So. Ill. U., cre, 1964; MA in Econs., U. Chgo., 1967, PhD in Econs., 1976. Instr. econs. Elmhurst (Ill.) Coll., 1968-69; asst. prof. econs. Mich. Technol. U., Houghton, 1969-71; economist internat. fin. div. Bd. Govs. FRS, Washington, 1971-78;

prof. Pa. State U., College Park, 1983-84; vis. prof. U. Utah, Salt Lake City, 1977-78, prof., 1978—. Assoc. professorial lectr. George Washington U., Washington, 1975-76; v.p., head rsch. Citicorp Homeowners Inc., St. Louis, 1985-86; cons. Investment Cos. Inst., Washington, 1981-83, World Bank, Washington, 1982—, Congl. Budget Office, Washington, 1980; rsch. assoc. Ctr. for the Econ. Analysis of Law, 1996—; Murphy Endowment Fund vis. scholar U. Wis., La Crosse, 1979; presenter papers, participant profl. meetings, 1973—; seminar presenter Brown U., U. Chgo., U. Pa., Pa. State U., UCLA, U. Colo., also others; referee profl. jours. Contbr. articles to profl. jours. Univ. scholar So. Ill. U., 1961-64; fellow NIMH, 1966-68. Mem. Am. Econ. Assn. Office: U Utah Dept Econs Salt Lake City UT 84112

GIRVIGIAN, RAYMOND, architect; b. Detroit, Nov. 27, 1926; s. Manoug and Margaret G.; m. Beverly Rae Bennett, Sept. 23, 1967; 1 son, Michael Raymond. AA, UCLA, 1947; BA with honors, U. Calif., Berkeley, 1950; MA in Architecture, U. Calif.-Berkeley, 1951. With Hutchason Architects, LA, 1952-57; owner, prin. Raymond Girvigian, LA, 1957-68, South Pasadena, Calif., 1968—. Co-founder, advisor LA Cultural Heritage Bd., 1961—; vice chmn. Hist. Am. Bldgs. Survey, Nat. Park Svc., Washington, 1966-70; co-founder, mem. Calif. Hist. Resources Commn., 1970-78; co-founder, chmn. governing bd. Calif. Hist. Bldgs. Code, 1976-91, chmn. adminstrv. law, 1992—, chmn. emeritus, 1993—; chmn. Calif. State Capitol Commn., 1985-98, chmn. emeritus, 1998—. Co-editor, producer: film Architecture of Southern California for Los Angeles City Sch., 1965; hist. monographs of HABS Landmarks, Los Angeles, 1958-80; historical monographs of Calif. State Capitol, 1974, Pan Pacific Auditorium, 1980, LA Meml. Coliseum, 1984, Powell Meml. Libr., UCLA, 1989; designed: city halls for Pico Rivera, 1963, LaPuente, 1966, Rosemead, 1968, Lawndale, 1970 (all Calif.); hist. architect for restoration of Calif. State Capitol, 1975-82, Workman/Temple Hist. Complex, City of Industry, Calif., 1974-81, Robinson Gardens Landmarks, Beverly Hills, Calif., 1983-92, Pasadena (Calif.) Ctrl. Libr., 1982-92, 95—, Mt. Pleasant House Mus., Heritage Sq., LA, 1972-95. With US Army, 1944-46. Recipient Outstanding Achievement in Architecture award City of Pico Rivera, Calif., 1968, Neasham award Calif. Hist. Soc., 1982, Preservationist of Yr. award Calif. Preservation Found., 1987, LA Mayor's award for archtl. preservation, 1987, Gold Crown award for advancement of arts Pasadena Arts Coun., 1990, Golden Palm award Hollywood Heritage, 1990; named Hist. Architect Emeritus, Calif. Legislature, 1998, commendation for state and national career achievemtns hist. preservation, Calif. Legislature, 1998; co-recipient honor award for rehab. Los Altos Apts., Calif. Preservation Found., 1999, co-recipient Calif. Preservation Found., 2003 Design Award for Oaklawn Bridge Rehabilitation. Fellow AIA, 1972 (Calif. state preservation chmn. 1970-75, state preservation coord. 1970-89, co-recipient nat. honor award for restoration Calif. State Capitol 1983, co-recipient honor award for restoration Pasadena Cen. Libr., Pasadena chpt. 1988); mem. Soc. Archtl. Historians, Nat. Trust for Historic Preservation, Calif. Preservation Found., Calif. Hist. Soc., Xi Alpha Kappa. Episcopalian. Office: PO Box 220 South Pasadena CA 91031-0220 *I believe that we must all serve society in whatever way that we are best able; and if a worthy cause I have undertaken appears to have failed, I should ignore that possibility and press on with even greater determination and vigor to succeed. I would hope by that example to encourage others to join the cause and thereby futher the likelihood of a successful effort for the good of all.*

GIRVIN, EB CARL, biology educator; b. Georgetown, Tex., Dec. 27, 1917; s. Fitzhugh Bryson and Meta (Perlitz) G.; m. Virginia Lessor, Aug. 29, 1944; chilren: John Lessor, Eric Reed, Stacey Virginia. BA, U. Tex., 1940, MA, 1941, PhD, 1948. Prof. biology Millsaps Coll., 1948-53; prof. biology, head dept. Southwestern U., Georgetown, 1953-88. Mem. Tex. Bd. Examiners Basic Sci., 1960-79; Mem. div. coll. work Episcopal Diocese Tex., 1962-65 Contbr. articles to profl. jours. Mem. Georgetown City Coun., 1981-87. Lt. comdr. USNR, 1941-45. Mem. Tex. Acad. Sci. (bd. dirs.), AAAS, Sigma Xi. Home: 1703 E 16th St Georgetown TX 78626-7303

GIRVIN, SHIRLEY EPPINETTE, retired elementary education educator, journalist; b. New Orleans, Apr. 16, 1947; d. Woodie Trevillion and Thelma Elizabeth (Axline) E.; m. Russell Robertson Girvin, Nov. 30, 1996. AA, East L.A. Coll., 1967; BA, Calif. State U., L.A., 1969, postgrad., 1969-70, U. So. Calif., 1982, Chapman Coll., 1983, Loyola Marymount U., L.A., 1986-87. Elem. tchr. Covina-Valley Unified Sch. Dist., 1970-74, San Gabriel (Calif.) Sch. Dist., 1974-75, Alhambra (Calif.) City Sch. Dist., 1976-78; elem. and program mentor tchr., faculty rep. L.A. City Unified Sch. Dist., 1978—2003; ret., 2003. Rewrite editor, staff writer San Gabriel Valley Newspaper Publs., 1975-76. Contbr. articles to profl. pubs. Recipient TAP award Alhambra-San Gabriel dist. Soroptimist Club, 1975; Calif. State PTA scholar, 1981, Journalism Alumni Assn. scholar East L.A. Coll., 1967, Arthur J. Baum Journalism scholar Calif. State U., 1969. Mem. AAUW (mem. com. internat. rels. 1977-78, chmn. ednl. com. 1978-79), NEA, Calif. Tchrs. Assn., L.A. City Tchrs. Math. Assn., United Tchrs. L.A. (chpt. chairperson 1994-95), Women in Comm., Nat. Press Women, Humane Soc. U.S., Soc. for the Prevention of Cruelty to Animals, Handgun Control Inc., Sigma Delta Chi. Avocations: breeding, selling, and racing Thoroughbred race horses, gardening. Home: 8730 S East Ave Fresno CA 93725

GISH, ROBERT FRANKLIN, English language educator, writer; b. Albuquerque, Apr. 1, 1940; s. Jesse Franklin and Lillian J. Gish; m. Judith Kay Stephenson, June 20, 1961; children: Robin Elaine Butzier, Timothy Stephen, Annabeth. BA, U. N.Mex., Albuquerque, 1962, MA, 1967, PhD, 1972. Tchr. Albuquerque Pub. Schs., 1962-67; prof. U. No. Iowa, Cedar Falls, 1968-91; dir. ethnic studies, prof. English Calif. Poly. State U., San Luis Obispo, 1991-2000, prof., 1992-2000, prof. emeritus, 2000—. Vis. prof. U. N.Mex., 2001—. Author: Hamlin Garland: Far West, 1976, Paul Horgan, 1983, Frontier's End: Life of Harvey Fergusson, 1988, William Carlos Williams: The Short Fiction, 1989, Songs of My Hunter Heart: A Western Kinship, 1992, Frist Horses: Stories of the New West, 1993, North American Native American Myths, 1993, When Coyote Howls: A Lavaland Fable, 1994, Nueva Granada: Paul Horgan and the Southwest, 1995, Bad Boys and Black Sheep: Fateful Stories from the West, 1996, Beyond Bounds: Cross-Cultural Essays, 1996, Beautiful Swift Fox: Erna Fergusson and the Modern Southwest, 1996, Dreams of Quivira: Stories in Search of The Golden West, 1997. Avocation: guitarist. E-mail: rfg@robertfgish.com.

GISLASON, ERIC ARNI, chemistry educator; b. Oak Park, Ill., Sept. 9, 1940; s. Raymond Spencer and Jane Ann (Clifford) G.; m. Nancy Brown, Sept. 11, 1962 (dec. June 1994); children: Kristina Elizabeth, John Harrison; m. Sharon McKevitt Fetzer, Apr. 25, 1998. BA summa cum laude, Oberlin Coll., 1962; PhD, Harvard U., 1967. Postdoctoral fellow U. Calif-Berkeley, 1967-69; asst. prof. chemistry U. Ill., Chgo., 1969-73; assoc. prof. U. Ill.-Chgo., 1973-77, prof., 1977—; acting head chemistry dept. U. Ill., Chgo., 1993-94, head chemistry dept., 1994-99, interim dean Coll. Liberal Arts and Scis., 1997-98, interim vice chancellor rsch., 1999-2001, vice chancellor rsch., 2001—. Vis. scientist FOM Inst. Atomic and Molecular Physics, Amsterdam, 1977-78; prof. associé U. Paris South, 1985. Contbr. articles to profl. jours. Recipient Silver Circle Teaching award U. Ill., 1982, Excellence in Teaching award U. Ill., 1990. Mem. Am. Chem. Soc. (vis. assocs. program), Am. Phys. Soc., Phi Beta Kappa, Sigma Xi, Phi Kappa Phi. Congregationalist. Achievements include rsch. in theoretical studies of ion-molecule reactions, collision-induced dissociation, nonadiabatic transitions, molecular energy transfer and isotope effects. Home: 7227 Oak Ave River Forest IL 60305-1935 Office: U Ill-Chgo OCVR M/C 672 Rm 310 1737 W Polk St Chicago IL 60612-7727 E-mail: Gislason@uic.edu.

GISO, FRANK, III, lawyer; b. Haverhill, Mass., Feb. 14, 1949; s. Frank and Clementina Paula (Foresta) G; m. Deborah Jean Kracht, May 5, 1979; children: Christopher Anderson, Benjamin Hilding. BA Econs. magna cum laude, Brown U., 1971; JD magna cum laude, Cornell U., 1975. Bar: Mass. 1975, U.S. Dist. Ct. Mass. 1976, U.S. Ct. Appeals (1st cir.) 1976. Law clerk Mass. Superior Ct., Boston, 1975-76; assoc. Peabody & Brown, Boston, 1976-83, ptnr., 1983-88, Choate, Hall & Stewart, Boston, 1988—, chmn. real estate dept., 1988-98. Bd. dirs. Melrose (Mass.) Coop. Bank. Vice chmn. Melrose Housing Authority, 1986-98, chmn. 1998—. Mem. Mass. Bar Assn., Boston Bar Assn., Phi Beta Kappa, Order of Coif. Avocations: tennis, golf. Office: Exchange Pl 53 State St Boston MA 02109-2804

GISOLFI, DIANA (DIANA GISOLFI PECHUKAS), art history educator; b. N.Y.C., Sept. 12, 1940; d. Anthony M. and Eleanor (Hayes) Gisolfi; m. Philip Pechukas, June 15, 1963 (div. Sept. 1991); children: Rolf, Maria, Sarah, Fiona (dec.), Amy. Student, Manhattanville Coll., 1958-60; BA magna cum laude, Radcliffe Coll., 1962; postgrad., Yale U., 1962-63; MA, U. Chgo., 1964, PhD, 1976. Instr. CUNY, 1967-68, Marymount Manhattan Coll., N.Y.C., 1977-79; asst. prof. art history Pratt Inst., Bklyn., 1979-84, assoc. prof., 1984-90, prof., 1990—, chmn. dept., 1980-99. Vis. asst. prof. Pratt Inst., 1976-79; dir. Pratt in Venice, Italy, 1984—; spkr. Conv. on Veronese, Venice, 1988, Conv. on Tintoretto, Venice, 1994, Symposium on Italian Art in Am., Fordham U., 1993, Mass. Coll. Art, 1998, AM Berger lecture, Manhattanville Coll., 2001; invited participant Veronese Reconsidered, CASVA, Washington, 1988; spkr. in field. Illustrator (book) On Classic Ground, 1982; designer (book) Caudine Country, 1987; author: (with S. Sinding-Larsen) The Rule, the Bible, and the Council: The Library of the Benedictine Abbey at Praglia, 1998; contbr. articles on Veronese, Tintoretto and other sixteenth-century artists in North Italy and Venice to Art Bull., 1982, Artibus et Historiae 1987, 96, Arte Veneta 1989-90, Nuovi Studi su Paolo Veronese, 1990, Burlington Mag., 1995, Dictionary of Art, 1996, Tintoretto Convegno Acts, 1996, Renaissance Quar., 1997, 2000, 01, Encyclopedia of Italian Renaissance and Mannerist Art, 2000, and others. Coord. Park Slope Freeze, Bklyn., 1984-86, Peace and Justice Com., St. Francis Xavier, 1984-86. Am. Philos. Soc. grantee, 1989, Delmas Found. grantee, 1995-96. Mem. Italian Art Soc., Renaissance Soc., Coll. Art Assn., Caucus for Design History, Phi Beta Kappa. Democrat. Roman Catholic. Home: 843 President St Brooklyn NY 11215-1405 Office: Pratt Inst Dept Art History East 250 Brooklyn NY 11205 E-mail: dgisolfi@pratt.edu., Dianagisolfi@aol.com.

GISSEL, L. HENRY, JR., lawyer; b. Houston, Oct. 20, 1936; BA, Rice U., 1958; LLB, So. Meth. U., 1961; postgrad., Georgetown U. Bar: Tex. 1961. Of counsel Fulbright & Jaworski, Houston. Fellow Am. Coll. Trust and Estate Counsel (pres. 1995-96, regent 1981-87, 91-97, regent emeritus 1997—), Am. Bar Found. (bd. cert. estate planning and probate lab, Tex. bd. legal specialization); mem. ABA (sect. real property probate and trust law, chair 1988-89, Internat. Acad. Estate Trust Law (academician 1986-87), coun. 1981-90, 94-97), Am. Bar Assn. (sect. del. 1994-97), Houston Bar Assn. (chmn. probate trust sect. 1982-83). Office: Fulbright & Jaworski 1301 Mckinney St Ste 5100 Houston TX 77010-3031

GISSLER, SIGVARD GUNNAR, JR., journalist, educator, retired editor; b. Chgo., July 2, 1935; s. Sigvard Gunnar Sr. and Louisa (Anderson) Gissler; m. Catherine Engman, Oct. 23, 1954; children: Gary, Glenn, Gregory. BA in Am. Civilization, Lake Forest Coll., 1956, LLD (hon.). 1991; student, Northwestern U., 1958-61. News editor Ind. Register, Libertyville, Ill., 1958-59; exec. editor News-Sun, Waukegan, Ill., 1963-67; editl. writer Milw. Jour., 1967-77, editl. page editor, 1977-84, assoc. editor, 1984-85, editor, 1985-93; v.p. Jour. Comm., Milw., 1987-93, also bd. dirs.; sr. v.p. Jour./Sentinel Inc., Milw., 1987-93, also bd. dirs.; assoc. prof. grad. sch. journalism Columbia U., N.Y.C., 1994—, acting assoc. dean, 1997, founder, dir. workshops on journalism, race and ethnicity, 1998-2000, sr. advisor, 2000—, adminstr. Pulitzer Prizes, 2002—. Vis. prof. dept. comm. Stanford U., 1993; mem. jury Pulitzer Prize. Recipient Disting. Svc. citation, Lake Forest Coll., 1977, Pub. of the Yr. award, Wis. Newspaper Assn., 1987, 1991, 1992; Journalism fellow, Stanford U., 1976, Sr. fellow, Freedom Forum Media Studies Ctr. Columbia U., 1993—94. Mem.: Soc. Profl. Journalists (Tchr. of the Yr. award 1998), Internat. Press Inst., Am. Soc. Newspaper Editors, Phi Beta Kappa. Home: 101 W 79th St Apt 6D New York NY 10024-6475 E-mail: sg138@columbia.edu.

GIST, HOWARD BATTLE, JR., lawyer; b. Alexandria, La., Sept. 17, 1919; s. Howard Battle and Marcie (Luckett) G.; m. Rosemary Flynn, Sept. 30, 1950; children: Howard Battle III, Marcie, Stephanie, Robert C., Ellen K., William M. Student, Washington and Lee U., 1936—38; BA, Tulane U., 1941, JD, 1943. Bar: La. 1943. Mem. firm Gist, Methvin, Alexandria, 1946—. Bd. dirs. Security First Nat. Bank, Alexandria, chmn. bd., 1983-93, dir. emeritus, 1993. Named 2000 Disting. Atty., La. Bar Found., 2000. Fellow Am. Coll. Trial Lawyers; mem. La. State Bar Assn. (pres. 1977-78), Alexandria Bar Assn. (pres. 1967), La. City Attys. Assn. (past pres.), La. Def. Attys. (pres. 1972-73), La. State Law Inst. (mem. coun. 1964—, past v.p.). Office: Gist Methvin 4615 Parliament Dr Ste 101 Alexandria LA 71309-1871

GIST, JOHN MONTFORT, publishing executive, educator; b. Denver, Oct. 26, 1963; s. Christopher Gist and Phyllis Ann (Angevine) Jozwik. BA, U. Wyo., 1992; MFA, U. Alaska, 1996. Editor, pub. Exegesis Writing Svcs., Laramie, Wyo., 1992-96; tchr. English U. Alaska, Fairbanks, 1994-96; owner All-Terrain Writing Cons., 2000—; prof. creative non-fiction Western Carolina U., 2001—; editor-in-chief High Sierra Books, 2003—. Author: Crow Heart, 1999, Lizards Dreaming of Birds, 2003; editor: Plants for Profit, 1998, Perennial Plants for Profit, 1998; editor: The Greenhouse & Nursery Handbook, 1999, Illustrated Handbook of Landscape Plants, 2000, Make Money Growing Trees, 2000, Creation Through Evolution, 2000, The Voice of Creation, 2000, The Dawn of Satisfaction, 2001, The Liberty of Man & Eternity of Mind, 2002, Beyond Charles Darwin, 2003, Environmental Vitalism, 2003. Tchr. Acad. Decathlon, Fairbanks, 1994-96, Upward Bound, Laramie, 1998—. Mem. Poets and Writers, U. Alaska Alumni Assn., U. Wyo. Alumni Assn. Avocations: hunting, fishing, reading, quantum theory.

GIST, MARILYN ELAINE, organizational behavior and human resource management educator; b. Tuskegee, Ala., May 9, 1950; d. Lewis A. and Grace (Perry) G. BA in Edn., Howard U., 1972; MBA, U. Md., 1982, PhD in Bus. Aminstrn. Organizational Behavior, 1985. Tchr. Montgomery County Pub. Schs., Rockville, Md., 1972-76; mgmt. intern NASA Goddard Space Flight Ctr., Greenbelt, Md., 1976-79, procurement mgr., 1980-81, staff asst. to dir. mgmt. ops., 1983-85; dir. contracts OAO Corp., Greenbelt, 1981-83; prof. organizational behavior U. N.C., Chapel Hill, 1985-87; Boeing Endowed prof. bus. mgmt. U. Wash., Seattle, 1987—2002. Staff cons. U. Md., Coll. Park, 1979-84; adj. prof. human resources Cornell U., 1995-96; pres., exec. dir. Millennium Resources, Inc., 1999—. Contbr. articles to profl. jours. Recipient Outstanding Student award Alumni Assn. Internat. U. Md., 1985, Alan Nash Outstanding Doctoral Student award U. Md., 1985, Chancellor's Disting. lectr. award U. Calif., Irvine, 1993; U. Md. Acad. Rsch. grantee, 1982-85. Mem. APA, Acad Mgmt. (Outstanding Paper award 1987). Democrat. Roman Catholic. Avocations: stained glass, photography, guitar. Office: 1001 4th Ave Ste 3200 Seattle WA 98154

GIST, RICHARD MICHAEL, research scientist; b. Oakland, Calif., Dec. 19, 1949; s. Daniel Washington and Emma Lou Gist; m. Shannon Marie LaBelle, May 2, 1993; children: Grayson Daniel, Galen Charles. BA, U. Mo., Kansas City, 1974, MA, 1977, PhD, 1985. Test devel. spec City of Kans. City, Mo.; consultation and edn. dir Comp Mental Health Svcs., Independence, Mo., 1979—81; exec. dir. Kans. City (Mo.) Assn Mental Health, 1981—83; sr. ptnr. Cmty. Response Assocs., Kansas City, 1983—88; dir. of social sci. Johnson County C.C., Overland Park, Kans., 1988—98; prin. asst. to dir. Kans. City (Mo.) Fire Dept., 1998—. Cons., Kansas City, 1988—; adj. assoc prof psychology U. of Mo., Kansas City, 1997—. Editor: (text) Response to disaster, Psychosocial Aspects of Disaster; contbr. rev., rev. chpt., invited commentary; author: (invited article) Cognitive & Behavioral Practice; contbr. rev. chpt. Project team chair Safe Cities Initiative, Kansas City, 2001—02; invited participant Natl Cen. Disaster Psy. and Terrorism, Palo Alto, Calif.; expert rev. panel US CDC/OSHA Firefighter Fatality Surveillance Project, Washington, 1998—99; participant AAS Wingspread Task Force on Adolescent Suicide, Racine, Wis., 1987; svc. delivery com. ARC, Kansas City, 1998—2003. Recipient Victor Wilson scholarship, U. of Mo., Kansas City, 1974, Response to psychiat. treatment grant, NSF, 1974—75, Award of Merit, Corp. Coun. of Greater Kans. City, 1992, Mayoral commendation, City of Kans. City, Mo., 1993, Disting. Svc. award, Kans. City Fire Dept., 1995, Coun. resolution for svc. to cmty. award, City of Kans. City, Mo., 1998. Mem.: APA, Soc. for Cmty. Rsch. and Action, Soc. for Sci. of Clin. Psychology, Internat. Soc. for Traumatic Stress Studies. Roman Catholic. Home: 4014 NW Claymont Dr Kansas City MO 64116 Office: Kansas City Fire Dept 414 E 12th St Kansas City MO 64106 Office Fax: 816-513-1712. E-mail: richard.gist@kcmo.org.

GIST, WILLIAM CLAUDE, JR., retired dentist; b. Chattanooga, May 14, 1935; s. William Claude and Dorothy Virginia (Gibbs) Gist; m. Barbara Roppel Babcock, May 9, 2003. BSc, U. Tenn., Knoxville, 1958; DMD, U. Louisville, 1967. Diplomate Am. Bd. Forensic Dentistry, Am. Bd. Forensic Medicine, Am. Bd. Forensic Examiners. Pvt. practice, Louisville, 1967-2001. Chmn. celebrations Bicentennial of Pres. Zachary Taylor's Birth, Louisville, 1984; pres. Louisville Civil War Roundtable, 1990-91. Recipient Presdl. commendation Pres. Ronald Reagan, 1985, DAR medal of honor, 1996, DAR history award, 1985. Mem.: ADA (life), Gen. Soc. War 1812 (Ky. pres. 1986—88, v.p. gen. 1990—93, 2001—), Hereditary Order Descs. Loyalists-Patriots, Gen. Soc. Sons Revolution, Nat. Soc. Sons and Daus. of Pilgrims (Ky. gov. 1990—93), Colonial Order of Acorn, Gen. Soc. Colonial Wars, Jamestowne Soc., Order Ams. Armorial Ancestry, Magna Charta Barons (Somerset chpt.), Nat. Gavel Soc., Nat. Order of the Blue and Gray (comdg. gen. 1996—98), Continental Soc. Sons of Indian Wars (nat. gov. 1990—92), Nat. Soc. SAR (Ky. pres. 1985—86, nat. chmn. centennial observances com. 1985—90, nat. trustee 1986—87, v.p. gen. Ctrl. dist. 1989—90, nat. chmn. hdqrs. com. 1989—94, historian gen. 1991—93, registrar gen. 1993—94, sec. gen. 1994—95, pres. gen. 1995—96, nat. chmn. nominating com. 1996—97, dir. mus. 1998—, nat. chmn. ethics com. 1999—2003, Gold Good Citizenship award 1996, Minuteman award 1990, Disting. Svc. medal 1999), St. Matthews Hist. Soc. (life), Ky. Hist. Soc. (life), Louisville Dental Soc. (life), Ky. Dental Assn. (life), Aztec Club, Filson Club (life), Honorable Order of Ky. Cols., Order Stars-Bars (Ky. comdr. 1988—90), Kappa Sigma (asst. dist. grand master 1999—). Republican. Roman Catholic. Avocations: history, genealogy, historic preservation. Home: Springfield Zachary Taylor House 5608 Apache Rd Louisville KY 40207

GITELSON, ANATOLY AVRAAM, engineering educator; b. Nignjytagil, Sverdlovsk, Russia, July 19, 1942; arrived in Israel, 1990; s. Avraam Josef and Anna Solomon (Peselnick) G.; m. Galina Petr Keydan, Oct. 31, 1973; 1 child, Anna. MSc, Radiotech. Inst., Taganrog, Russia, 1963; PhD, Rostov-on-Don State U., 1972. Engr., head of lab. Design Office of Electronic Devices, Krasnodar, 1964-72; sr. scientist, head lab. solid state electronics Phys. Inst., Rostov-on-Don State U., 1973-77; sr. scientist Inst. Nuclear Rsch., Acad. of Scis. of USSR, Moscow, 1977-81; sr. scientist, head Remote Sensing Lab. Hydrochem. Inst. Environ. Protection Agy., Rostov-on-Don, 1981-89; prof. remote sensing lab. J. Blaustein Inst. for Desert Rsch., Ben-Gurion U. of Negev, Sede Boker, Israel, 1990-2000; prof. Ctr. for Advanced Land Mgmt. Info. Techs., U. Nebr. Sch. Natural Reouce Scis., Lincoln, 2000—. Cons. Inst. Environ. Protection Agy., Russia, 1964-90, Inst. of Environ. Agy. of Israel, 1992—. Contbr. numerous articles to profl. jours. Grantee, Nat. Acad. Scis. and Humanities, 1990—91, UNESCO/MEDPOL, 1991—92, Israeli Ministry of Sci. and tech., 1993—96, Israeli Ministry of Agr., Water Commn., 1993—95, 1997—98, U.S. Agy. for Internat. Devel., 1993—95, 1998—, Internat. Atomic Agy., 1994—95, 1996—98, U.S.-Israeli Bynat. Found., 1994—95, European Cmty., 1995—97, Israeli Ministry of energy and Infrastructure, 1995—98, Israeli Ministry of Scis., 1995—98, EPA, 2001—03, NASA, 2001—04. Mem. IEEE, Internat. Soc. for Optical Engrng. Avocations: jogging, classical music, reading. Office: U Nebr Ctr Advanced Mngmt 113 Nebraska Hall Lincoln NE 68588-0517 E-mail: gitelson@calmit.uni.edu.

GITELSON, SUSAN AURELIA, business executive, civic leader; b. N.Y.C. d. Moses Leo and Miriam Evelyn (Silverman) G. BA, Barnard Coll.; MIA, Columbia Sch. Internat. Affairs; PhD, Columbia U.; student, Univ. Calif., Berkeley. Trainee Rockefeller Found.; asst. prof. internat. rels. Hebrew U., Jerusalem; rsch. assoc. Columbia U., N.Y.C.; dir. internat. affairs and third world World Jewish Congress, N.Y.C.; pres. Internat. Cons., Inc., N.Y.C., Magic Touch Icewares Internat. Corp., N.Y.C. Author: Multilateral Aid for National Development and Self-Reliance; editor, author: Israel in the Third World; contbr. articles to profl. jours.; mem. editl. com. Jerusalem Papers on Peace Problems. Mem. nat. adv. coun., sponsor Gitelson Essay awards Ctr. for Study of Presidency, Washington; co-chair dean's coun. Columbia Sch. Internat. and Pub. Affairs; sponsor Dr. Susan Aurelia Gitelson Fund for Innovative Programs, Columbia Sch. of Internat. Pub. Affairs; pres. Dr. Susan Aurelia Gitelson Found. Inc.; mem. Columbia U. seminars; mem. bd. overseers Mus. Jewish Heritage--A Living Meml. to the Holocaust; sponsor Gitelson Lecture on Human Rights and U.S. Fgn. Policy, Columbia U., Gitelson award for human values in internat. affairs Columbia Sch. Internat. and Pub. Affairs, Gitelson-Meyerowitz Human Rights essay award Columbia Ctr. for Study of Human Rights, Gitelson Seminars on UN, City U. Grad. Ctr.; sponsor Gitelson Peace prize Truman Inst.; sponsor Gitelson Peace Papers and Publs., mem. bd. overseers Truman Inst. Hebrew U. Jerusalem; mem. internat. bd. govs. Hebrew U. Jerusalem; v.p. bd. dirs. Am. Friends of Hebrew U.; trustee Sutton Pl. Synagogue; mem. trustees Nat. Com. Am. Fgn. Policy; sponsor Gitelson-Meyerowitz Disting. Svc. award, Sutton Place Synagogue, Dr. Susan Aurelia Gitelson Fund Innovative Programs Columbia U. Faculty Arts and Scis. Recipient Outstanding Service award Columbia Sch. Internat. and Public Affairs; Alumni medal for conspicuous service Columbia U. Mem. Nat. Inst. Social Scis., Columbia Sch. Internat. and Pub. Affairs Alumni Assn. (pres. 1980-84), Columbia U. Alumni Fedn. (mem. exec. com.), Nat. Com. on Am. Fgn. Policy (mem. bd. trustees), Carnegie Coun. on Ethics and Fgn. Affairs, Fgn. Policy Assn., Am. Jewish Com. Home: 303 E 83d St New York NY 10028-4318 Office: 1201 Broadway New York NY 10001-7504 E-mail: susangitel@aol.com.

GITLER, BERNARD, cardiologist and critical care specialist; b. Munich, Aug. 14, 1950; arrived in U.S., 1953, naturalized, 1957; s. Abe and Lola (Greenberg) G.; m. Ellen Spielman, Aug. 4, 1974; children: Stefanie, Cynthia, Bryan. BS in Chemistry, BS in Life Scis., MIT, 1972; MD, Cornell U., 1976. Diplomate Nat. Bd. Med. Examiners, Am. Bd. Internal Medicine, Am. Bd. Internal Medicine-Cardiovascular Diseases, Am. Bd. Internal Medicine-Critical Care Medicine, Nat. Bd. Echocardiography; cert. Bd. Nuclear Cardiology. Resident in internal medicine Bronx Mcpl. Hosp. Ctr., Albert Einstein Coll. Medicine, Bronx, NY, 1976—79; cardiology fellow Montefiore Med. Ctr., Albert Einstein Coll. Medicine, Bronx, 1979—81, chief fellow, 1980—81; clin. instr. Albert Einstein Coll. Medicine, Bronx, 1981—84, asst. clin. prof. medicine, 1984—92, assoc. clin. prof. medicine, 1992—; attending cardiologist Sound Shore Med Ctr. Westchester, New Rochelle, NY, 1991—; chief divsn. cardiology Sound Shore Med. Ctr. Westchester, New Rochelle, NY, 2002—; assoc. attending cardiologist Montefiore Med. Ctr., Bronx, 1993—; pvt. practice cardiology Westchester Heart Specialists, New Rochelle, 1981—; asst. attending cardiologist Columbia-New York. Presbyn. Med. Ctr., N.Y.C., 1992—; asst. prof. clin. medicine Columbia U., N.Y.C., 1992—. Physician cons. Island Peer Rev. Orgn., N.Y., 1985-88; faculty senator Albert Einstein Coll. Medicine, 1987-89, co-dir. cardiology curriculum New Rochelle Hosp. Housestaff, 1985-92; attending cardiologist dept. electrocardiography Montefiore Med. Ctr., Bronx, 1983—; attending cardiologist dept. medicine Westchester County Med. Ctr., 2002—; pres. med. staff Sound Shore Med Ctr. Westchester, 1996-99, bd. govs., 1993-99; clin. cardiology rschr. SSMC of Westchester, 1985—. Referee Am. Heart Jour., 1983-95, Jour. Am. Coll. Cardiology, 1987-89, N.Y. State Jour. of Medicine, 1990-91, Chest, 1998—; contbr. articles to profl. jours. Recipient Attending of the Yr. award Montefiore Hosp. Med. House Staff, 1985, Tchr. of the Yr. award New Rochelle Hosp. and Med. Ctr., 1986, William C. Schraft Jr. Meml. Tchg. award New Rochelle Hosp., 1996, Preceptorship Award for Outstanding Tchg., ACP, 1996. Fellow ACP, Am. Soc. Echocardiography, Am. Coll. Cardiology, Am. Coll. Chest Physicians, Am. Heart Assn., N.Y. Cardioil. Soc.; mem. AMA, Soc. Critical Care Medicine, Am. Med. Athletic Assn., Am. Fedn. Med. Rsch., Am. Soc. Nuclear Cardiology, Phi Beta Kappa, Phi Lambda Upsilon, Mensa. Democrat. Jewish. Avocations: Blackbelt in Okinowan Gojuryu karate, marathon running. Office: 150 Lockwood Ave New Rochelle NY 10801-4916 E-mail: bgmd@aol.com.

GITLER, DANIEL, neurobiologist, researcher; b. Mexico City, Dec. 15, 1965; s. Carlos and Rebeca Gitler; m. Inbal Ben-Asher, Aug. 30, 1990; children: Daphna, Erran Nahum, Noam Ilan. BSc magna cum laude, Hebrew U. of Jerusalem, 1992, MSc, 1994, PhD, 1999. Tchg. asst. Hebrew U. of Jerusalem, 1992—99; rsch. assoc. Duke U. Med. Ctr., Durham, NC, 1999—. Capt. IDF. Recipient Wolf Prize for Masters Students, The Wolf Found., 1994, Grad. Student Excellence scholarship, The Clore Found., 1996—99, long-term postdoctoral fellowship, European Molecular Biology Orgn., 1999—2001, Pfizer postdoctoral fellowship, Life Scis. Rsch. Found., 2001—. Mem.: AAAS, Soc. For Neurosci. Achievements include research in Molecular mechanisms of neuronal transmission; Initial stages of neuronal regeneration. Office: Duke U Med Ctr Box 3209 Dept Neurobiology Durham NC 27710 Office Fax: 1-919-681-9866.

GITLIN, MELVIN CHARLES, anesthesiologist, educator; BA, NYU, 1969; MD, U. Pa., 1973. Bd. cert. anesthesiologist Am. Bd. Anesthesiology, 1986. Interim chmn. dept. anesthesiology Tulane U. Health Sci. Ctr., New Orleans, 2000—02, prof., chmn. dept. anesthesiology, 2002—. Office: Tulane Univ Health Scis Ctr 1430 Tulane Ave (SL-4) New Orleans LA 70112

GITLITZ, STUART HAL, lawyer; b. Bklyn., Sept. 22, 1951; s. Jerome I. and Ruth (Moskowitz) G.; m. Marilyn June Mittentag, Apr. 28, 1979; children: Gina Ilyse, Keith Vance. BA, SUNY-Binghamton, 1972; JD, U. Miami, 1975. Bar: Fla. 1976, D.C. 1975, U.S. Dist. Ct. (D.C.) 1976, N.Y. 1977, U.S. Supreme Ct. 1979, U.S. Dist. Ct. (so. dist.) Fla. 1979, U.S. Ct. Appeals (5th cir.) 1979, U.S. Ct. Appeals (D.C.) 1976, U.S. Ct. Appeals (11th cir.) 1983, U.S. Ct. Mil. Appeals 1984, U.S. Dist. Ct. (mid dist.) Fla. 1984. Asst. pub. defender Office Pub. Defender for 11th Jud. Cir., Miami, Fla., 1977-80; ptnr. Gitlitz & Keegan, Miami, 1980-81, Gitlitz, Keegan & Dittmar, P.A., Miami, 1981-87, Sheppard Faber, P.A., Coral Gables, Fla., 1987-89, Faber & Gitlitz, P.A., Coral Gables, 1989—. Prettyman fellow Georgetown U. Law Ctr., Washington, 1975-77. Mem. Mortgage Bankers Assn. Am., Mortgage Bankers Assn. Fla., Mortgage Bnkers Assn. Greater Miami, Atty.'s Title Ins. Fund Inc. Democrat. Jewish. Office: Faber & Gitlitz PA 1570 Madruga Ave Ste 300 Miami FL 33146-3013

GITLOW, ABRAHAM LEO, retired university dean; b. N.Y.C., Oct. 10, 1918; s. Samuel and Esther (Boolhack) G.; m. Beatrice Alpert, Dec. 12, 1940; children: Allan Michael, Howard Seth. BA, U. Pa., 1939; MA, Columbia U., 1940, PhD, 1947. Substitute instr. Bklyn. Coll., 1946-47; instr. NYU, N.Y.C., 1947-50, asst. prof., 1950-54, assoc. prof., 1954-59, prof. econs., 1959-89, prof. emeritus, 1989—; acting dean NYU Coll. Bus. and Pub. Adminstrn., 1965-66, dean, 1966-85, dean emeritus, 1989—. Hon. dir. Bank Leumi Trust Co. N.Y.; pres. bd. edn. Ramapo (N.Y.) Cen. Sch. Dist. 2, 1963-66; pres., sec. Samuel and Esther Gitlow Found., N.Y.C. Author: Economics of the Mt. Hagen Tribes, New Guinea, 1947, Economics, 1962, Labor and Manpower Economics, 1971, Being the Boss: The Importance of Leadership and Power, 1992, NYU's Stern School: A Centennial Retrospective, 1995, Reflections on Higher Education: A Dean's View, 1995; co-editor: General Economics: A Book of Readings, 1963; contbr. articles to profl. jours. Served to 1st lt. USAAF, 1943-46, PTO. Recipient Univ. medal Luigi Bocconi U., 1983 Mem. Am. Econ. Assn. Home and Office: 9 Island Ave Apt T3 Miami Beach FL 33139-1349 E-mail: abgit@earthlink.net.

GITNER, DEANNE, retired school system administrator; b. Lyons, NY, Jan. 8, 1944; d. Myron and Mary (Kurland) Gebell; m. Gerald L. Gitner, June 24, 1968; children: Daniel Mark, Seth Michael. AB, Cornell U., 1966. Cert. English tchr. Tchr. English Gates (N.Y.) Chili Cen. Sch., 1966-68, Wantagh (N.Y.) Jr. and Sr. High Sch., 1968-70, F. Weiner Sch., Houston, 1980-81; writer Bellaire Texan, Houston, 1980; rep. sales McDougal Littel & Co., Chgo., 1981-83; writer Millburn Short Hills Ind., New Providence, N.J., 1987-93; comm. coord. Millburn Twp. (N.J.) Pub. Schs., 1993—2002; ret., 2001. Contbr. articles to profl. publs. Bd. dirs. United Way of Millburn-Short Hills, NJ, 1998—2001, sec., 1999—2002. Mem.: NJ Sch. Pub. Rels. Assn., NJ Press Women (newsletter editor 1992, 2d prize comm. contest 1992, hon. mention 1990, 1st prize 1993, 1994, 3d prize nat. contest 1994, Hon. Mention Nat. Contest 1995), Nat. Fedn. Press Women, Soc. Profl. Journalists, Cornell Alumni Assn. Admissions Network (chmn. 1990—2001), Nat. Coun. Jewish Women (v.p. Houston sect. 1976—79, pres. 1980—81, pub. rels. com. 1981—90, v.p. Essex County NJ sect. 1983—88, chmn. nat. bull. subcom. 1990—93, Vol. award), Cornell Alumni Fedn. (bd. dirs. 1995—, v.p. 1999—), Cornell Club N.Y.C., Cornell Club No. NJ (v.p. 1992, 1993, pres. 1994, 1995, co-pres. 1997—98, bd. dirs. 1999—).

GITNER, FRED JAY, library administrator; b. N.Y.C., Nov. 28, 1951; s. Stanley and Sonia (Auerbach) G. AB, Hamilton Coll., 1973; MA, Middlebury Coll., 1976; MLS, Rutgers U., 1975. Asst. mgr. Christopher P. Stephens Bookseller, N.Y.C., 1975-76; libr. French Inst./Alliance Française, N.Y.C., 1976-84, libr. dir., 1984-94; spl. collections libr. N.Y. Acad. Medicine, N.Y.C., 1995; asst. head New Ams. Program Queens Borough Pub. Libr., Jamaica, N.Y., 1996—. Editor: Med. Trade Catalogs at the N.Y. Acad. of Medicine Libr., 1995; joint editor, contbr.: Bridging Cultures: Ethnic Services in the Libraries of New York State., 2001; contbr. articles to profl. jours. Decorated chevalier Ordre des Palmes Académiques (France). Mem. ALA, Pub. Libr. Assn., Internat. Rels. Round Table (chair com.), N.Y. Libr. Assn., Am. Assn. Tchrs. French. Democrat. Jewish. Avocations: breweriana collecting, theater going, reading, travel. Home: 382 Central Park W New York NY 10025-6054 Office: Queens Borough Pub Libr 89-11 Merrick Blvd Jamaica NY 11432 E-mail: fred.j.gitner@queenslibrary.org.

GITNER, GERALD L. air transportation executive, investment banker; b. Boston, Apr. 10, 1945; s. Samuel and Sylvia (Berkovitz) Gitner; m. Deanne Gebell, June 24, 1968; children: Daniel Mark, Seth Michael. BA cum laude, Boston U., 1966. Staff v.p. TransWorld Airlines, N.Y.C., 1972-74; sr. v.p. mktg. and planning Tex. Internat. Airlines, Houston, 1974-80; pres., founder People Express Airlines, Newark, 1980-82; chmn. Pan Am. World Svcs. Inc., N.Y.C., 1982-85, exec. v.p., chief fin. officer, 1983-85; vice chmn. Pan Am. World Airways, N.Y.C., 1982-85, Pan Am Corp., 1984-85; pres. Tex. Air Corp., Houston, 1985-86; CEO, pres. ATASCO USA, Inc., aircraft trading firm, N.Y.C., 1986-89; chmn. D. G. Assocs. Inc., 1986—, Avalon Group, Ltd., N.Y.C., 1990-98; co-chmn. Global Aircraft Leasing Ltd., 1991-98, 1990—; dir. TWA, Inc., 1993—. CEO, 1996-99, chmn., 1997—2002; chmn. bd. Kitty Hawk, Inc., 2002—. Bd. advisers econs. dept. Boston U.; mem. chancellors coun. U. Mo., St. Louis, 1997—2000. Trustee, mem. exec. com. Boston U., 1984—96; trustee Rochester (N.Y.) Inst. Tech., 1999—. Recipient Disting. Alumni award, Boston U., 1982, 1984. Mem.: Cornell Club N.Y., Sky Club, Phi Alpha Theta.

GITTELMAN, MARC JEFFREY, manufacturing and financial executive; b. N.Y.C., Nov. 26, 1947; s. Sidney and Trudy (Eidus) G.; m. Nanci V. Geiger, Apr. 9, 1988; 1 child, Brandon Michael. BBA, Hofstra U., 1969; MBA in Fin., Adelphi U., 1972; postgrad., U. Colo., Denver. Credit analyst Security Nat. Bank Long Island, Melville, N.Y., 1969-72; dir. adminstrn. Tiger Leasing Group Inc., Chgo., 1973-78; asst. treas. Storage Tech. Corp., Louisville, Colo., 1979-83; v.p., treas. Holnam Inc. (formerly Ideal Basic Industries), Dundee, Mich., 1984-91, Andrew Corp., Orland Park, Ill., 1992—. Bd. dirs. Food Bank of Rockies. Mem. Nat. Assn. Corp. Treas. Republican. Jewish. Office: Andrew Corp 10500 153rd St Orland Park IL 60462-3071

GITTELSON, BERNARD, public relations consultant, author, lecturer; b. N.Y.C., June 13, 1918; s. Sam and Gussie (Lefand) G.; m. Rosalind Weinstein, Mar. 1, 1945; children: Louise Barbara, Steven Henry. BA, St. John's U., 1939. Cons. on race relations N.Y. State War Council, 1939-41, N.Y. Com. on Industry and Labor Relations, 1941-42; dir. N.Y. State Legis. Com. on Discrimination, 1943-45; asso. coordinator Com. on Community Inter-relations, 1945-46; pres. Roy Bernard Co., Inc., 1946-65; chmn. Roy Bernard Co. Ltd., London, 1955-65; pres. Biorhythm Computers, Inc., Med. News. Service, Formulated Health Products, Fairfield Mktg. Corp., Advanced Health Research Products Inc.; chmn. bd. Time Pattern Research Inst., N.Y.C., U.S. Commemoratives Inc., Bernard Gittelson Cons. Inc. Cons. to govts., corps., instns. Author: Gittelson Biorhythm Code Book, Biorhythm, A Personal Science, How to Make Your Own Luck, Intangible Evidence, Special Stories for Children, Our America, Notre America, Nuestra America, Nossa America; syndicated writer column on biorhythm, 1987—; pub. Med. Hot Line. Mem. Am. Journalists and Authors, Authors Guild. Address: Mote Ranch 6808 Corral Cir Sarasota FL 34243-3858

GITTENS, ANGELA, airport executive; Dep. dir. San Francisco Internat. Airport, 1994; former gen. mgr. William B. Hartsfield Internat. Airport, Atlanta, regional dir. N.Am. for airport svcs., 1993—98; gen. mgr. Memphis Internat. Airport, 1998—. Office: PO Box 592075 Miami FL 33159*

GITTER, ALLAN REINHOLD, lawyer; b. Yonkers, N.Y., Aug. 26, 1936; s. George Reinhold and Katherine (Allan) G.; divorced; children: Alison, Ryne, Kent; m. Sandra Case Gitter, Apr. 2, 1988. BA, Washington & Lee U., 1958; LLB, U. Mich., 1961. Bar: N.C. 1963, U.S. Dist. Ct. (mid., ea. and we. dists.) N.C. 1964, U.S. Ct. Appeals (4th cir.) 1964, U.S. Dist. Ct. (mid. dist.) Pa. 1998. From assoc. to ptnr. Womble, Carlyle, Sandridge & Rice, Winston-Salem, N.C., 1969—. Fellow Am. Coll. Trial Lawyers; mem. Am. Bd. Trial Advs. Home: 1077 E Kent Rd Winston Salem NC 27104-1113 Office: Womble Carlyle Sandridge & Rice One W 4th St Winston Salem NC 27101 E-mail: agitter@wcsr.com.

GITTER, MAX, lawyer; b. Samarkand, Uzbekistan, Nov. 17, 1943; came to U.S., 1950; s. Wolf and Paula (Nissenbaum) G.; m. Elisabeth Karla Gesmer, June 22, 1969; children: Emily F., Michael A. AB, Harvard U., 1965; LLB, Yale U., 1968. Bar: N.Y., D.C., U.S. Dist. Ct. (so. and ea. dists.) N.Y., U.S. Ct. Appeals (2d, D.C., 4th and 9th cirs.), U.S. Supreme Ct. Instr. U. Chgo. Law Sch., 1968-69; assoc. Paul, Weiss, Rifkind, Wharton & Garrison, N.Y.C., 1969-76, ptnr., 1976-99, Cleary, Gottlieb, Steen & Hamilton, N.Y.C., 1999—. Vis. lectr. law Yale U., 1986-88; mem. Internat. Steering Com. on Free Trade with Israel; vice-chmn., Yivo Inst. for Jewish Rsch. Spl. counsel Mayor of N.Y.C. to Investigate Office of Chief Medical Examiner, 1985. Mem. Fed. Bar Coun., Assn. Bar City of N.Y. (vice chmn. com. on profl. and jud. ethics 1985-86), Am. Law Inst. (spkr., panelist 1985-89), Practicing Law Inst (spkr., panelist 1983-92), N.Y. State Bar Assn. (exec. com. sect. on comml. and fed. litigation 1994-99), Internat. Arbitration Inst. Office: Cleary Gottlieb Steen & Hamilton Rm 200 One Liberty Plz Ste 4300 New York NY 10006-1470 E-mail: mgitter@cgsh.com.

GITTERMAN, ALEX, social work educator; b. Kolomea, Poland; came to U.S., 1948; s. Paul and Fay (Hirsch) G.; m. Naomi Janet Pines, Sept. 1963; children: Daniel Paul, Sharon Lynn. BA, Rutgers U., 1960; MSW, Hunter Coll., 1962; EdD, Columbia U., 1972. Div. dir. Bronx River Settlement, 1962-65; dir. East Side House Millbrook Ctr., Bronx, 1965-66; mem. faculty Columbia U., N.Y.C., 1966—, prof., 1972—, assoc. dean, 1981-85; mem. faculty U. Conn. Sch. Social Work, 2000—. Cons. Manhattan VA, N.Y.C., 1974-80, Family Service of Westchester (White Plains), N.Y., 1978-80, Bur. Child Welfare, 1977-80, Drug Abuse Prevention Program, Archdiocese of N.Y., 1985—. Keio Acad.; vis. prof. U. Conn. Sch. Social Work, 2000-. Author: (with C.B. Germain) The Life Model of Social Work Practice, 1980, (with L. Shulman) Mutual Aid Groups and The Life Cycle, 1986, Handbook of Social Work Practice with Vulnerable Populations, 1991, Mutual Aid Groups, Vulnerable Populations and the Life Cycle, 1994, (with C.B. Germain) The Life Model of Social Work Practice: Advances in Theory and Practice, 1996, Handbook of Social Work Practice with Vulnerable and Resilient Populations, 2001; contbr. articles to profl. jours. Recipient Hexter award Hunter Coll., 1981 Mem. Con. on Social Work Edn., Nat. Assn. Social Workers Democrat. Jewish. Office: U Conn Sch Social Work 1798 Asylum Ave West Hartford CT 06117-2001 E-mail: Alex.Gitterman@uconn.edu.

GITTES, FREDERICK M. lawyer; b. Hampton, Va., June 4, 1947; s. Hymam R. and Pearl (Levin) G. Cert. achievement, U. Oslo, Norway, 1967; BA with honors, Rollins Coll., 1968; JD cum laude, Ohio State U., 1975. Bar: Ohio 1975, U.S. Supreme Ct., U.S. Ct. Appeals (6th cir.), U.S. Dist. Ct. (so. dist.) Ohio. Ptnr. Spater, Gittes, Schulte, Kolman, Columbus, Ohio, 1975—2001, Gittes & Schulte, Columbus, 2001—. Contbr. articles to profl. jours. Bd. dirs., founder Columbus Tenants Union, 1970-74; bd. dirs. Columbus Recycling Ctr., 1987-90, Columbus Legal Aid Soc., 1989-97. Walter J. Black Teaching fellow L.I. U., 1968-69. Fellow Columbus Bar Found., Coll. Labor and Employment Lawyers; mem. Nat. Employment Lawyers Assn. (bd. dirs. 1990, pres. 2001—), Ohio Employment Lawyers Assn. (state chair 1988-2001), Ohio State Bar Assn. (chair civil rights com. 1995-2000, chair labor/employment law sect. 2000-2002), Columbus Bar Assn., Ohio Acad. Trial Lawyer (bd. dirs. 1998—, pres.-elect 2003—). Office: Gittes & Schulte 723 Oak St Columbus OH 43205-1011

GITTES, RUBEN FOSTER, urological surgeon; b. Mallorca, Spain, Aug. 4, 1934; s. Archie and Cicely Mary (Foster) G.; m. K.S. Zipf, June 10, 1955 (div.); m. Rita R. Drum, Feb. 21, 1976 (div.); m. Vera Gomes, Feb. 9, 1996; children: Julia S., Frederick T., George K., Robert F. Grad., Phillips Acad., Andover, Mass., 1952; AB, Harvard U., 1956, MD, 1960. Intern, then resident in surgery and urology Mass. Gen. Hosp., Boston, 1960-67; asst. prof. UCLA Med. Sch., 1968-69; assoc. prof., then prof., chief urology U. Calif. at San Diego Med. Sch., 1969-75; prof. urol. surgery Harvard U. Med. Sch., chmn. Harvard program urology Longwood area, 1975-87; chmn. dept. surgery Scripps Clinic and Rsch. Found., La Jolla, Calif., 1987-98. Mem. study sects., task forces NIH, 1973— Author, editor publs. in field. Served with USPHS, 1963-65. NIH grantee, 1969— Mem. AAAS, Endocrine Soc., Soc. Univ. Surgeons, Soc. Univ. Urologists, Am. Assn. Genito-Urinary Surgeons, Clin. Soc. Genito-Urinary Surgeons (pres., 2003—), A.C.S., Am. Surg. Assn., Am. Urol. Assn., Am. Soc. Transplant Surgeons, Soc. Ancient Numismatics, 2003—), Kappa, Alpha Omega Alpha. Office: Scripps Clinic & Rsch Found 10666 N Torrey Pines Rd La Jolla CA 92037-1092

GITTINGER, D. WAYNE, lawyer; b. Kellogg, Idaho, Jan. 22, 1933; s. Daniel Reese and Evelyn Caroline (Knudson) G.; 1 child, Marni; m. Anne Elizabeth Nordstrom, Dec. 17, 1984; stepchildren: John Hopen, Susan Dunn. BA, U. Wash., 1955, JD, 1957. Bar: Wash. 1957, U.S. Ct. Appeals (9th cir.) 1957, Tax Ct. of U.S., U.S. Supreme Ct. Teaching assoc. Northwestern U. Law Sch., Chgo., 1957-58; ptnr. Lane Powell Spears Lubersky, Seattle, 1959—. Bd. dirs. Nordstrom, Inc. Active U. Wash. Alumni Assn., 1965—. Lt. USCGR, 1958-67. Mem. Vintage Club, Seattle Golf Club, Seattle Yacht Club, 101 Club, Overlake Golf and Country Club (past pres. 1978-79). Republican. Avocations: golf, yachting. Office: Lane Powell Spears Lubersky 1420 5th Ave Ste 4100 Seattle WA 98101-2338 E-mail: gittingerw@lanepowell.com.

GITTINS, ANTHONY J. theology studies educator; b. Feb. 16, 1943; MA, U. Edinburgh, Scotland, 1972, PhD, 1977. Lectr., head of dept. Missionary Inst., London, 1980-84; assoc. prof. theol. anthropology Chgo., 1984-90; Bishop F. X. Ford prof. missiology, 1998—. Author: Bread for the Journey, 1993, Gifts and Strangers, 1998, Reading The Clouds, 1999, Life and Death Matters, 2000, A Presence That Disturbs, 2002, Ministry at the Margins, 2002. Fellow Royal Anthrop. Inst.; mem. Am. Anthrop. Assn., Cath. Theol. Soc. Am., Am. Soc. Missiology, Assn. Social Anthropologists. Office: 4740 N Malden St Chicago IL 60640-4808 E-mail: tgittins@ctu.edu.

GITTIS, HOWARD, lawyer; b. Phila., Feb. 16, 1934; s. Herman and Sonia (Forman) Gittis; m. Sondra Hamberg, June 26, 1960; children: Caroline, Hope, Marjorie. BS Econ., U. Pa., 1955; LLB, 1958. Bar: Pa. 1958, US Supreme Ct. 1971, Fla. 1976. Ptnr. Wolf, block, Schorr and Solis-Cohen, Phila., 1965—; legal counsel mayor Phila. Lectr. in field. Mem.: Am. Law Inst., Am. Coll. Trial Lawyers, Am. Judicature Soc., Jud. Conf. of 3rd Cir., Phila. Trial Lawyers Assn., Fla. Bar Assn., Pa. Bar Assn., Phila. Bar Assn., ABA, Fedn. Jewish Agy. of Greater Phila., Thomas Jefferson U., Temple U., Mus. Am. Jewish History, Phila. Orch. Assn. Office: Wolf Block Schorr & Solis-Cohen 12 Floor Packard Bldg Philadelphia PA 19102

GITTLEMAN, ARTHUR PAUL, computer science and engineering educator; b. Bklyn., Oct. 7, 1941; s. Morris and Clara (Konefsky) G.; m. Charlotte Marie Singleton, June 1, 1986; 1 child, Amanda Eve. BA, UCLA, 1962, MA, 1965, PhD, 1969. Asst. prof. Calif. State U., Long Beach, 1966-70, assoc. prof., 1970-75, chair, math. and computer sci. dept., 1978-83, prof. computer sci. and engring., 1975—. Author: History of Mathematics, 1975, Computing with Java: Programs, Objects, Graphics, alt. 2d edit., 2002, Objects to Components with the Java Platform, 2000, Advanced Java Internet Applications, 2d edit., 2001, Computing with C# and the.NET Framework, 2003. Mem. Assn. for Computing Machinery, Math. Assn. of Am., Phi Beta Kappa. Avocations: running, piano. Office: Calif State U 1250 N Bellflower Blvd Long Beach CA 90840-8302

GITTLEMAN, SOL, university official, humanities educator; b. Hoboken, N.J., June 5, 1934; s. Frank and Edna (Schlanger) G.; m. Robyn Singer, Sept. 9, 1956; children: Julia, Peter Thomas. BA, Drew U., 1955; MA, Columbia U., 1956; PhD, U. Mich., 1961; LHD (hon.), Hebrew Coll., 1993, Stonehill Coll., 1996. Asst. prof., German Mt. Holyoke Coll., South Hadley, Mass., 1962-64; asst. prof. Tufts U., Medford, Mass., 1964-70, prof. German, 1971—, chmn. dept. German and Russian, 1966-81, McCollester prof. religious studies, 1978—, provost, 1981—2002, acad. v.p., from 1981, now sr. v.p., Alice and Nathan Gantcher prof. Judaic studies, 1992, disting. univ. prof., 2002—. Dir. summer seminars NEH Author: Frank Wedekind, 1969, Sholem Aleichem, 1974, From Shtetl to Suburbia, 1978. Recipient Harbison award Danforth Found., 1970; named Alice and Nathan Gantcher Prof. of Judaic Studies, 1992, Disting. Prof., 1992, Gantcher Univ. prof., 2002—. Mem. MLA, Am. Assn. Tchrs. Yiddish, Am. Assn. Tchrs. German Office: Tufts U Ballou Hall Medford MA 02155

GITTLER, JOSEPH BERTRAM, sociology educator; b. N.Y.C., Sept. 21, 1912; s. Morris and Toby (Rose) G.; m. Lami Shapiro, June 28, 1934 (dec. 1966); 1 child, Josephine; m. Susan Wolters, Sept. 15, 1968. BS, U. Ga., 1934, MA, 1936; PhD, U. Chgo., 1941. From instr. to assoc. prof. sociology U. Ga., 1936-43; research assoc. Va. Planning Bd., 1942-43, U. Chgo., 1944; prof. Iowa State U., 1945-54; prof. sociology, chmn. dept. Ctr. Study Group Relations, U. Rochester, 1954-61; dean faculty, prof. social scis. Queensborough Coll., CUNY, 1961-66; prof. sociology, dean Ferkauf Grad. Sch. Humanities and Social Scis., Yeshiva U., N.Y.C., 1966-78; disting. vis. prof. sociology George Mason U. of State U. Va., Fairfax, 1978-79, disting. vis. prof., 1980-90, dir. Ctr. for Study of Race and Ethnic Relations, 1987-90, emeritus prof. sociology, 1990—. Vis. prof. Cardoza Law Sch., 1978-79, Hiroshima (Japan) U., 1979-80; lectr. various univs., U.S., Japan, Spain, Germany, Eng., The Netherlands, France, Italy, Mex., Israel, Finland, Taiwan, Ireland, Austria; cons. in field, 1940—; mem. Rochester cmty. coun. N.Y. State Commn. Against Discrimination, 1955-60; chmn. regional selection com. Woodrow Wilson Fellowship Found., 1955-58; co-chmn. Brotherhood Week edn. com. NCCJ, 1950; coun. fellows Upland Inst., 1965-72; disting. vis. prof. dept. sociology Duke U., 1990-94, Disting. Scholar-in-residence, 1994-99; Fulbright scholar, vis. prof. Ben Gurion U., Israel, 1990-91. Author: Social Thought Among the Early Greeks, 1941, Virginia's People, 1944, Social Dynamics, 1952, Your Neighbor Near and Far: A Study of Racial and Ethnic Relations in Rural Iowa, 1955, Review of Sociology, 1957, Understanding Minority Groups, 1964, Ethnic Minorities in the U.S.: Perspectives from the Social Sciences, 1977, Jewish Life in the United States, 1977, Jewish Life in the United States, 1981; co-editor: Internat. Jour. Group Tensions, 1986-94; editor, contbg. author: Ann. Rev. Conflict Knowledge and Conflict Resolution, vol. 1, 1989, vol. 2, 1990, vol. 3, 1991, Research in Human Social Conflict Series, Racial and Ethnic Conflict: Perspectives from the Social Disciplines, 1995; editor in chief: Internat. Encyclopedia of Racial and Ethnic Relations, 2000, Ideas of Concord and Discord in Religion, 1999; contbr. numerous articles to profl. jours. Fulbright scholar, Hiroshima (Japan) U. scholar, 1979-80, Ben Gurion U. scholar, Israel, 1990-91; recipient Walter B. Hill prize philosophy U. Ga., 1934, poetry award, best tchr. award, Disting. Faculty award George Mason U., 1984. Fellow Am. Sociol. Assn., N.Y. Acad. Scis.; mem. PEN, Internat. Sociol. Soc., Inst. Internat. Sociology, So. Sociol. Soc., Assn. for Higher Edn., Am. Assn. Acad. Deans, Phi Beta Kappa, Phi Kappa Phi, Pi Mu Epsilon. Home: 5 Glenmore Dr Durham NC 27707-3923

GITTLER, STEVEN, lawyer, law educator; b. Breslau, Germany, May 21, 1926; m. Antonia Brne, Aug. 7, 1954; 1 child, Jean Elizabeth. Diploma, City Colls. Chgo., 1946—47; BA, Lake Forest Coll., 1948; MA, Wash. State U., 1949; attended, U. Ill., 1951, U. Mich., 1954—55; EdD, SUNY, Buffalo, 1961. Bar: NY 1981. Instr. Mich. State U., East Lansing, 1953—54; prof. edn. Buffalo State Coll., 1955—95; mgr. residence hall, rsch. instr. in edn. Kent State U.; arbitration panelist, U.S. Dist. Ct. (We. Dist. NY) Supreme Ct. State NY., Am. Arbitration Assn., Buffalo, 1999—. Lt. col. med. svc. corps, Us.army Res., Ret.; mediator & factfinder Nys Pub. Employment Rels. Bd., NY, 1973—; dir. Edn. Law Assn., formerly Nat. Assn. of Legal Problems in Edn. (NOLPE), 1967—69. Hearing officer City Ct. of Buffalo, NY State Supreme Ct., Erie, NY, 1993—2003. Pvt. first class U.S. Army, 1944—46. Mem.: Bar Assn. of Erie County (life), Mason (32nd Degree Mason 1965). Achievements include admitted to the U.S. Supreme Court, 1984.

GITTLER, WENDY, artist, art historian, writer; b. Manhattan, N.Y. d. Lewis Frederic and Esther (Becker) G. Studied with George Grosz, Art Students League, N.Y., 1958-59; studied with Camillio Egas, N.Y.C., 1960; BS in Art History, Columbia U., 1963; MA in Art History, Hunter Coll., 1967; postgrad., NYU, 1968; MFA, Bklyn. Coll., 1973; postgrad., U. Paris, 1977-78. Lectr. art NYU, N.Y.C., 1966-68, lectr. art history Fairleigh Dickinson U., Teaneck, N.J., 1966-68; lectr., art history Hunter Coll., N.Y.C., 1968-80; lectr. art history Sch. Visual Arts, N.Y.C., 1979-86; lectr. Met. Mus., N.Y.C., 1988-89; lectr. art history Parsons Sch. of Design, N.Y.C., 1989-96; lectr. N.Y. Studio Sch., N.Y.C., 1991—. Instr. studio U. Haifa, Israel, 1971; curator First Street Gallery, N.Y.C., 1992; lectr. Brown U., R.I., 1993, South Fla. Art Ctr., 1990, Lowe Art Mus., U. Miami, Fla., 1984; moderator artists panels, bd. dirs. v.p. Artists Equity, N.Y.C., 1995-2003. One-woman shows include 1st Street Gallery, N.Y.C., 1976, 82, 88, 95, 99, 2002, Artists Equity, 1999, 2001, 2002; exhibited in group shows at Blue Mountain Gallery, Atlantic Gallery, N.Y.C., 1995-2001, 2002, 2003, N.Y. Studio Sch., 1996-2003, Savannah Coll. Art and Design, 1997,, S.E. Mo. State U. Mus., 1997, Fordham U., 1996, Ashawag Hall, East Hampton, N.Y., 1995, LeHigh U., Bethlehem, Pa., 1984, Gallery of Fine Arts, N.Y.C., 1976, N.Y. City C.C., 1975, McKee Gallery, N.Y.C., 1998, 1999-2003, N.Y. Studio Sch., 1999-2003); represented in permanent collections S.E. Mo. State U. Mus., Savannah Coll.. Art and Design; contbg. author art jours., exhibit catalogues. Mem. Coll. Art Assn., Fedn. Modern Painters and Sculptors, Channel 13, Artist Equity (bd. dirs.), Internat. Assn. Art Critics. Avocations: archaeology, philosophy, travel. Home: 780 West End Ave New York NY 10025-5573

GITTMAN, ELIZABETH, retired educator; b. NYC, Mar. 15, 1945; d. Kallman and Rebecca (Santcroos) Gittman; children: Stephen Loeb, Leslie Gulkis, Sherry Loeb. BS, NYU, 1966; MS, CUNY Queens Coll., 1969; PhD, Hofstra U., 1979, Cert. Advanced Study, 1987. Cert. ednl. adminstr., N.Y. Tchr. NYC Bd. Edn., Kew Gardens, NY, 1966-68; instr. New Sch. for Social Rsch., NYC, 1980-81; ind. cons., 1981-84; coord. instl. rsch. and evaluation Bd. Coop. Ednl. Svc. of Nassau County, Westbury, NY, 1984-94; assoc. prof. NY Inst. Tech., Old Westbury, NY, 1994-97; cons., 1997-98; dir. instrnl. support svc. Commack Pub. Sch., NY, 1998-2000; ret., 2000; ind. cons., 2002—03. Adj. prof. L.I. U., Brookville, N.Y., 1987-93. Mem. high risk youth rev. com. Ctr. Substance Abuse Prevention, U.S. Dept. HHS, 1990-95; developer numerous ednl. programs. Recipient NYU Founders Day award, 1966; Hofstra U. Doctoral fellow, 1976. Mem.: ASCD, APA, Northeastern Ednl. Rsch. Assn. (membership com. 1989—90, program com. 1989—2003, nominating com. 1991—2003, program co-chair 1993, editor 1993—95, bd. dirs. 1993—98, treas. 1996—98), Nat. Coun. Measurement in Edn., Am. Evaluation Assn., Am. Ednl. Rsch. Assn., Phi Delta Kappa (rsch. rep. 1990—91, exec. bd. 1990—2003, sec. 1991—93, conf. co-chair 1992, v.p. 1993—94, pres. 1995—96, nominating com. 1996—2000, Svc. award 1998), Kappa Delta Pi. Republican. Jewish. Avocations: computer applications, reading, writing. E-mail: elarn@optonline.net.

GIUFFRÉ, JOHN JOSEPH, lawyer; b. Bklyn., Nov. 30, 1963; s. John B. and Marilyn N. G.; m. Lauren P. Dippel, Sept. 1, 1990; children: John Paul, Danielle Emily. BA, Columbia Coll., 1984; JD cum laude, U. Pa., 1987. Bar: N.J. 1987, N.Y. 1988, Conn. 1988, Pa. 1988, U.S. Dist. Ct. (so. and ea. dists.) N.Y. 1989. Assoc. labor and employment law sect. Morgan, Lewis & Bockius, N.Y.C., 1987-88; assoc. McLaughlin & McLaughlin, Bklyn., 1988-93; founding ptnr. Giuffré & Kaplan, PC, Hicksville, N.Y., 1994—. Editor: U. Pa. Jour. Comparative Bus. and Capital Market Law, 1985-86; sr. editor: U. Pa. Jour. Internat. Bus. Law, 1986-87. Vol. lawyer Bklyn. Bar Assn. Vol. Lawyer Project, 1992-93; trustee 1st Presbyn. Ch., Flushing, N.Y., 1991-92, pres. bd. trustees, 1993, elder, 1996—; bd. dirs. Flushing Christian Sch., 1994-2002. Mem. Nassau County Bar Assn., Phi Beta Kappa. Avocations: studying history, teaching sunday school, raising Johnny and Danielle. Office: Giuffré & Kaplan PC 28 E Old Country Rd Hicksville NY 11801-4207

GIULIANI, RUDOLPH W. former mayor, consultant, lawyer; b. N.Y.C., May 28, 1944; m. Donna Hanover (div. July 2002); children: Andrew, Caroline; m. Judith Nathan, May 24, 2003. AB, Manhattan Coll.; JD magna cum laude, NYU, 1968. Law clk. U.S. Dist. Ct. Judge, N.Y.C., 1968-70; asst. U.S. atty. So. Dist. N.Y., 1970-73; exec. asst. U.S. atty., chief narcotics sect., and chief spl. prosecutions sect. Dept. Justice, 1973-75, assoc. dep. atty. gen., 1975-77; assoc. atty. gen., 1981-83; U.S. atty. U.S. Dist. Ct. (so. dist.) N.Y., 1983-89; mem. firm Patterson, Belknap, Webb and Tyler, N.Y.C., 1977-81, White & Case, N.Y.C., 1989-90, Anderson Kill Olick & Oshinsky PC, N.Y.C., 1990-93; mayor N.Y.C.,

1994—2001; mgmt. and security cons. Giuliani Partners, New York, 2002—. Author: Leadership, 2002. Rep. candidate for mayor N.Y.C., 1989, 93. Named Person of the Year, Time Mag., 2001. Republican. Office: Giuliani Partners 5 Times Sq New York NY 10036*

GIULIANO, LOUIS J. industrial manufacturing company executive; BS in Chemistry, MBA in Mktg., Syracuse U. Various mgmt. positions Bendix, v.p., gen. mgr. Gen. Aviation Avionics divsn., v.p., group exec. Avionics Sys. Group; pres. Avionics Sys. Group Allied-Signal Aerospace Co.; v.p. def. ops. ITT Def., 1988; v.p. ITT Corp., 1988; sr. v.p. ITT Industries, Inc., pres., chief exec. def. and electronics, 1991-98, pres., COO, 1998—2001, chmn., pres., CEO, 2001—. Mem. Nat. Def. Indsl. Assn. (vice chmn., bd. dirs.), Aerospace Industries Assn. (bd. govs.). Office: ITT Industries Inc 4 W Red Oak Ln Fl 2 White Plains NY 10604-3617*

GIULIANO, MICHAEL PHILIP, arts journalist, educator; b. Somerville, N.J., Aug. 25, 1957; s. Michael N. and Marie M. Giuliano. BA, Johns Hopkins U., 1978, MA, 1979. Journalist Balt. News Am., 1979-86, WJHU-FM, 1986-88; freelance journalis Balt., 1988—. Contbr. Democrat. Roman Catholic. Home: 2317 N Calvert St Baltimore MD 21218-5202

GIULIANO, NEIL GERARD, mayor, academic administrator; b. Bloomfield, N.J., Oct. 26, 1956; s. Jacqueline Ann (Enright) G. BA, Ariz. State U., 1979, MEd, 1983. Pres. Circle K. Internat., Chgo., 1977-78, conv. cons., 1983-91; counselor disabled students Ariz. State U., Tempe, 1980-81, pres. associated students, 1982-83, coord. leadership devel., 1983-87, constituent dir., 1988-91, dir. fed. and community rels., 1991—; pres. Valley Achievement, Tempe, 1987—; mem. Tempe City Coun., 1990—94; vice mayor City of Tempe, 1992—94, mayor, 1994—. Speaker, trainer in field. Bd. dirs. Tempe Community Coun., 1990—2003, Valley Big Bros.-Big Sisters, Tempe, 1987—; pres. Tempe Leadership, Inc., 1990-91; mem. gov.'s task force on drug abuse, 1990—. Recipient Selected Participant award Ctr. for the Study of the Presidency Symposium, Washington, 1983. Mem. Tempe C. of C., Kiwanis (pres. 1986-87), Sigma Nu (conv. cons. 1988), Key Club Internat. (conv. cons. 1983-87). Republican. Roman Catholic. Avocations: reading, rock climbing, tennis. Home: 2007 E Balboa Dr Tempe AZ 85282-4004*

GIULIANO, ROBERT PAUL, pharmacist; b. N.Y.C., Mar. 7, 1943; s. Salvatore Anthony and Marie Rita (LoScalzo) G.; m. Maja Hreljanovic, July 2, 1966; children: Christopher Robert, Kenneth Paul. BS in Pharmacy, Fordham U., 1965; MS in Hosp. Pharmacy Adminstrn., L.I. U., 1970. Diplomate Am. Bd. Pharmacy, Nat. Registy Emergency Med. Technicians. Clin. pharmacist Columbia-Presbyn. Med. Ctr., N.Y.C., 1965-70; dir. pharmacy dept. St. Barnabas Hosp., N.Y.C., 1970-71; dir. dept. pharm. scis. Misericordia Hosp. Med. Ctr., N.Y.C., 1971-78, adminstrv. dir. material mgmt., 1978-79, asst. adminstrv. dir., 1979-81; pres. Apotheke Assos. Ltd., N.Y.C., 1980-81; pres., dir., CEO U.S. Home Health Care Corp. and Steri-Pharm subs., 1981-91; also chmn. bd.; mem. Tech. Adv. Svc. for Attys., 1988—. Pres. RPG Assoc., 1991—, pres. dir.; chmn. bd. Bryce Rx Labs Inc., 1995—; pres., dir. Red Rock Labs, Inc., 1997-99; v.p. Red Rock Rsch., Inc., 2001-; cons. Weleda Internat., 1991-92; affil. clin. instr. St. John's U., 1971-81; cons. Healix Health Care, 1992-96, Rye Beach Pharmacy, 1992-96, Champlain Valley Physicians Hosp., 1993-94, Columbia Presbyn. Med. Ctr., 1984-97, Transworld Home Health Corp., 1991-93, N.Y. Med. Coll., 1992-95, ROR Group, 1992-93, Geneva Gen. RegionalHosp., 1994-95; home health care cons. Alternative Care Svcs., Inc., 1988-90, Robert Wood Johnson Found., 1985; mem. clin. pharmacy adv. bd., 1971-81; mem. exec. com. Bronx Emergency Med. Svcs. Coun., 1975-80; sr. emergency med. technician instr./coord. N.Y. State Dept. Health, Bur. Emergency Med. Svcs., 1975-81; spkr.'s bur., CPR instr. AHA, 1975-81; CPR instr. Westchester Heart Assn., 1977-80; spkr.'s bur. Misericordia Hosp. Med. Ctr., Westchester County Soc. Hosp. Pharmacists. Author: (with others) RX Technician Manual, 1994; editor: Misericordia Hosp. Pharmacy Newsletter, 1971-78. Asst. master Cub Scouts, Eastchester, N.Y., 1976-78; coach youth baseball T.Y.A., Eastchester, 1975-83. Mem. Am. Pharm. Assn., Italian Pharm Assn., Am. Soc. Cons. Pharmacists, Am. Soc. Healthcare Pharmacists, N.Y. State Coun. Hosp. Pharmacists, Nat. Assn. Sr. Emergency Med. Technician Instrs., Nat. Assn. Emergency Technicians (founding), Am. Soc. Parenteral-Enteral Nutrition, League IV Therapists, Nat. IV Therapy Assn., Nat. Assn. Retail Druggists, Pharmacy Compounding Ctrs. Am., Internat. Acad. Compounding Pharmacists, Fordham U. Pharmacy Alumni Assn. (dir. 1982-98, 1st v.p. 1990-91, pres. 1992-95), N.Y. Athletic Club. Republican. Roman Catholic. Home: 157 Oakland Ave Eastchester NY 10709-5403 Office: PO Box 1 Eastchester NY 10709-1403 E-mail: rx@brycerx.com., bobgrx@optonline.net.

GIULIANTI, MARA SELENA, mayor, civic worker; b. N.Y.C., June 3, 1944; d. Leon and Bertha (Jablonky) Berman; m. Donald Giulianti, May 29, 1966; children: Stacey Alexander, Michael Alan. BA, Tulane U., 1966. Social worker L.A. County Social Svcs., 1966-68; adminstrv. asst. neurosurg. cons. D. Giulianti, MD, Hollywood, Fla., 1980-83; campaign mgr. City Commr. Suzanne Gunzburger, Hollywood, 1982; mayor City of Hollywood, 1986-90, 92—. Vice chmn. Broward Employment and Tng. Adminstrn., 1987-89, 92-94, 96-2000, 01-02, chmn., 1989-90, 94-96, 2000-01, Work Force One chmn., 2002—; mem. exec. bd. Fla. League Cities, Tallahassee, 1986-90, 92-94, bd. dirs., 1990-91, 94—; mem. econ. devel. pol. com. Nat. League Cities, Washington, 1987-90, human devel. policy com., 1992-94, fin., adminstrn. and intergovtl. rels. steering com., 1994-2002; mem. Broward County Met. Planning Orgn., 1986-90. Columnist The Digest, Hallandale, Fla., 2001-02, South Fla. Sun-Times, 2002—, Beach Digest, 2002-03; contbr. articles to local newspapers. Pres. Women in Distress, Broward County, 1982-83, bd. dirs., 1983-90, trustee, 1994-97; v.p. CHARLEE Family Care Homes, Broward County, 1986-88, bd. dirs., 1988-92; mem. Broward County Commn. on Status Women, 1984-86, Fla. Commn. on Drug and Alcohol Concerns, Tallahassee, 1984-85, Broward County Dem. Exec. Com., 1984-88; pres. Hills Dem. Club, 1991-94; bd. trustees Graves Mus. of Archeol. and Nat. History, Dania, Fla., 1993-97; bd. dirs. Hollywood Econ. Growth Corp., 1994-95, 98-99; chmn. Hollywood Cmty. Redevel. Agy., 1992—; v.p. South Broward unit Am. Cancer Soc., 1992-93, bd. dirs., 1993-99. Recipient Hannah G. Solomon award, 1983, Giraffe Stick Your Neck Out award Women's Advocacy - the Majority/Minority, 1986, Leadership award Leadership Hollywood Alumnni, 1987, City of Peace award Israel Bonds, Broward County, 1987, Broward County Woman of Yr., Am. Jewish Congress, 1988, Menorah award Histadrut, 1990; named Woman of Yr. Women in Comms., Inc., 1990, Crystal Vision award Hollywood Art and Culture Ctr., 2000, Honoree Boys & Girls Clubs of Broward, 2001, Govt. Leadership award, ArtServe, 2002, Gracias award Hispanic Unity, 2000, Cmty. Covenant award, Broward Outreach Ctr., 2001, Breaking the Glass Ceiling award, Ziff Jewish Mus. of Fla., 2002; inducted Broward County Women's Hall of Fame, 1996, Juliette Gordon Low award Girl Scouts Broward County, 1997, Govt. Leadership award Art Serve, Broward County, Fla., 2002, Woman of Valor award Broward County Jewish Cmty. Ctr., 2003. Mem. Nat. Coun. Jewish Women (nat. bd. dirs. 1985-89), Jewish Fedn. So. Broward (chair community rels. com. 1981-82, bd. dirs. 1982-90), Broward County Med. Aux. (br. pres. 1977-78), Nat. Jewish Community Rels. Adv. Coun. (exec. bd. 1985-87). Democrat. Avocations: writing, volunteer work, travel. Office: PO Box 229045 Hollywood FL 33022-9045 E-mail: mgiulianti@hollywoodfl.org.

GIULITTO, PAULA CHRISTINE, lawyer; b. Ravenna, Ohio, June 20, 1967; d. Joseph and F. Jean G.; m. Lawrence A. Sutter III, Nov. 22, 1997. BS, Miami (Ohio) U., 1989; JD, U. Akron, 1992. Bar. Ohio 1992. Assoc. Giulitto & Berger Attys. at Law, Ravenna, 1992—. Bd. dirs. ARC, Ravenna, 1994-2000, chair bd. 1997-2000; bd. dirs. Boys and Girls Club, Ravenna, 1996-2000. Mem. ABA, ATLA, Ohio State Bar Assn., Portage County Bar Assn. (pres. 2003—). Office: Giulitto & Berger 222 W Main St PO Box 350 Ravenna OH 44266-0350

GIUNTA, AGATINO JOHN, economics educator; b. Messina, Italy, Sept. 6, 1925; came to U.S., 1947, naturalized, 1963; s. Carmelo and Josephine (Savoca) G.; m. Santa Maria Molino, July 4, 1960; children— Carmen Joseph, Josephine-Ann, Lucia Catherine, Mary-Louise. B.S., SUNY-Binghamton, 1952; M.A., Syracuse U., 1954, Ph.D., 1956. Asst. prof. Western Md. Coll., Westminster, 1956-60; assoc. prof. U. Scranton, Pa., 1960-67, prof., 1967— . Author: Managerial Economics, 1966, An Introduction to Business Research, 1968. Mem. Scranton chpt. UNICO, 1966-72. Research grantee Schalkenback Found., 1982. Mem. Am. Econ. Assn. Democrat. Roman Catholic. Lodge: K.C. Avocations: home gardening, golf. Home: 1804 Monsey Ave Scranton PA 18509-1943

GIUNTA, JOSEPH, conductor, music director; b. Atlantic City, May 8, 1951; m. Cynthia Reid, June 5, 1982. MusB in Theory, Northwestern U., 1973, MusM in Conducting, 1974; DFA (hon.), Simpson Coll., 1986. Condr., music dir. Waterloo/Cedar Falls Symphony and Chamber Orch. of Iowa, 1974-89; music dir. Des Moines Symphony Orch., 1989—. Guest condr. numerous symphonies, orchs. including Chgo. Symphony, London Philharm., Philharmonia Orch. of London, Minn. Orch., Indpls. Orch., Phoenix Symphony, Fla. Symphony, Akron (Ohio) Symphony, Syracuse (N.Y.) Symphony, R.I. Philharm. Recipient Helen M. Thompson award; named Outstanding Young Condr. in U.S., 1984. Mem. Phi Mu Alpha, Pi Kappa Lambda. Office: Des Moines Symphony 221 Walnut St Des Moines IA 50309-2101

GIUSTI, JOSEPH PAUL, retired academic administrator, consultant; b. Harrisburg, Pa., Mar. 4, 1935; s. Joseph and Ellen C. (Carletti) G.; m. Marie D. Mazza, Jan. 30, 1960; children: Jeannine Carolyn, Lynn Christine, Susan Marie. BA in English Lit., Villanova U., 1957; MSBA, Pa. State U., 1959, PhD in Higher Edn. Adminstrn., 1962; LHD (hon.), St. Vincent Coll., 1976. Instr. dept. commerce and fin. Pa. State U., 1958-60, grad. asst., 1961-62, asst. to v.p., 1963-65, mem. grad. faculty, 1963-79, assoc. prof. higher edn., 1965-79; campus dir., chief exec. officer Beaver campus, 1965-79; chancellor univ., prof. higher edn. Ind. U.-Purdue U., Fort Wayne, 1979-85; prof. edn. Ind. U., 1985-87; dir. global human resource devel. edn. programs/scholarships AMP, Inc., 1987-98; ret., 1998; cons. AMP, Inc., 1998-99. Cons. hemolytic disease study group divsn. blood diseases and resources Nat. Heart, Lung and Blood Inst., NIH, 1975-79; mem. adv. com. Edn. Mgmt. Info. Sys., Commonwealth of Pa., 1971-79; mem. joint adv. coun. Ft. Wayne Med. Edn. Program, 1979-85; mem. exec. com. Ft. Wayne Future, Inc., 1979-85, Ft. Wayne Ednl. Found., 1979-85, Allen County (Ind.) United Way, 1979-80; sec. Beaver Campus Adv. Bd., 1966-79, dir. emeritus, 1979—; mem. Corp. Coun., Ft. Wayne, 1981-85, also bd. dirs. Contbr. articles on fin. mgmt. and ednl. adminstrn. to profl. publs.; contbr. chpts. to books on fin. mgmt. and edn. Bd. dirs. Med. Ctr. Beaver County, Pa., 1966-79, chmn. bd. dirs., 1972-75, dir. emeritus, 1979—; bd. dirs. Parkview Meml. Hosp., 1982-85. Recipient Beaver Campus Disting. Service award, 1974; Trustee award Community Coll. of Beaver County, 1972; Civic Improvement League award, 1972; Benjamin Rush award Med. Soc. of Beaver County, 1976; resolutions in his honor for contbrs. to edn. and health care delivery in state Pa. State Senate and Ho. Reps., 1979; Beaver Campus Community Cultural Ctr.'s 1000 seat amphitheater named in his honor, 1980; lit. collection named in his honor Beaver Campus Library, 1980 Mem. Greater Fort Wayne C. of C. (dir. 1981-85), Ind. U. Ft. Wayne Alumni Assn. (life dir. 1982—), Purdue U. Ft. Wayne Alumni Assn. (life dir. 1982—). Roman Catholic.

GIUSTI, KARIN F. artist, educator; MFA in Sculpture, Yale U. Head sculpture dept. Bklyn. Coll., CUNY, 1995—. Selected exhbns., installations and projects, U. Mass. Fine Arts Ctr., Hartford, 1993, Sculpture Ctr., N.Y.C., 1993, Roosevelt Island, 1993, Real Art Ways, Hartford, 1994, La Quinta (Calif.) Open Air Mus., 1994, Bklyn. Coll. CUNY, Bklyn., 1995, Thread Waxing Space, N.Y.C., 1995, Socrates Sculpture Park, Queens, N.Y., 1995, Bklyn. Bridge, 1995, Conn. Commn. Arts, 1995, The Lytman Allyn Art Mus., 1995, Statewide Mus. Collaborative, 1995, Conn. Resource Recovery Authority, Hartford, 1996, Woodson Art Mus., Wis., 1998, Anya von Gosslen Gallery, N.Y.C., 1998, Trans Hudson Gallery, 1998, St. Mary's Cathedral, Limerick, Ireland, 1998, others, commns., PECO Energy Co., Phila., Excell Techs., Enfield, Conn., Bank of Boston, Western, Mass., others, pvt. collections. Named artis in industry resident, John Michael Kohler Arts Ctr., 1992, internat. artist's resident Lila Wallace-Reader's Digest, Givernyy, France, 1995; recipient award for innovation pub. art project Divsn. Capitol Planning and Ops., 1% for Arts Program, Boston, 1988; Guggenheim fellow, 1997—98, grantee, Conn. Commn. on the Arts, 1991, NEA, 1991, New Eng. Found. Arts, 1991. Studio: 82 Wall St Ste 1105 New York NY 10005-3600 Office: Bklyn Coll Sculpture Dept Whitehead Hall Rm 103 2900 Bedford Ave Brooklyn NY 11210-2814

GIUSTI, WILLIAM ROGER, lawyer; b. N.Y.C., Oct. 27, 1947; s. John Eletto and Rita Marie (Lucarini) G.; m. Ingrid Gerke, Dec. 12, 1980. AB, Columbia Coll., 1969; postgrad., Oxford U., 1969-71; JD, Yale U., 1974. Bar: N.Y. 1975. Law clk. to judge U.S. Ct. Appeals (2d cir.), N.Y.C., 1974-75; assoc. Cravath, Swaine & Moore, N.Y.C., 1975-80, Shearman & Sterling, N.Y.C., 1980-82, ptnr., 1983—. Mem.: Yale (N.Y.C.). Roman Catholic. E-mail: wgiusti@shearman.com.

GIUSTO, THOMAS MICHAEL, broadcast journalist; b. Bklyn., May 29, 1953; s. Thomas Michael and Rose (Talarico) G. BS in Engring., Columbia U., 1974, MS in Journalism, 1975. Writer NBC News, N.Y.C., 1971-77; editor, prodr. Ind. TV News Assn., Washington, 1978-82; prodr. ABC News, Washington, 1982—. Mem. Writers Guild Am. East. Roman Catholic. Home: 508 Ft Williams Pkwy Alexandria VA 22304-1812 Office: ABC News 1717 Desales St NW Washington DC 20036-4407 E-mail: tmg20@columbia.edu.

GIVAN, RICHARD MARTIN, retired state supreme court justice; b. Indpls., June 7, 1921; s. Clinton Hodel and Glee (Bowen) G.; m. Pauline Marie Haggart, Feb. 28, 1945; children: Madalyn Givan Hesson, Sandra Givan Chenoweth, Patricia Givan Smith, Elizabeth Givan Whipple. LL.B., Ind. U., 1951. Bar: Ind. 1952. Ptnr. with Clinton H. Givan, 1952-59, Bowen, Myers, Northam & Givan, 1960-69; justice Ind. Supreme Ct., 1969-74, chief justice, 1974-87, assoc. justice, 1987-95; ret.; dep. pub. defender, 1952-53; dep. atty. gen., 1953—64; dep. pros. atty. Marion County, 1965-66; ret., 1995. Mem. Ind. Ho. Reps., 1967-68 Served to 2d lt. USAAF, 1942-45. Mem. Ind. Bar Assn., Indpls. Bar Assn., Ind. Soc. Chgo., Newcomen Soc. N.Am., Internat. Arabian Horse Assn. (past dir., chmn. ethical practices rev. bd.), Ind. Arabian Horse Club (pres. 1971-72), Indpls. 500 Oldtimers Club, Lions, Sigma Delta Kappa. Mem. Soc. Of Friends. Home: 6690 S County Road 1025 E Indianapolis IN 46231-2495

GIVANT, STEVEN ROGER, mathematician, computer scientist, educator; s. Paul and Irma Wilhemina Givant. BA, U. Calif., Berkeley, 1967, MA, 1969, PhD, 1975. Prof. math. and computer sci. Mills Coll., Oakland, Calif., 1975—. Contbr. articles to profl. jours. Founder, dir. Mills Summer Math. Inst., Oakland, 1991—95; dir. Project S.E.E.D., Oakland, Calif., 1966—73. Named Danforth Tchg. assoc., Danforth Found., 1978; fellow, German Academic Exch. Svc., 1967—68; grantee, IREX, 1991—92. Mem.: Assn. Symbolic Logic, Math. Assn. Am., Am. Math. Soc. Achievements include fundamental research in the theory of relations. Office: Mills College 5000 MacArthur Blvd Oakland CA 94613

GIVELBER, HARRY MICHAEL, pathologist; b. Cleve., Apr. 3, 1938; s. Myer and Hyla (Kanter) G.; m. Judith Gottlieb, June, 1960 (div. Jan. 1973); children: Rachel Joy, Joshua Mark, David Saul; m. Susan Margaret Hess, Feb. 3, 1973; children: Leah, Aron. AB, Harvard U., 1960, MD, 1964. Diplomate Am. Bd. Pathology. Clin. pathologist, hematologist NIH Clin. Ctr., Bethesda, Md., 1970-73; pathologist Geneva (N.Y.) Gen. Hosp., 1973—. Bd. dirs. Temple Beth El, Geneva, 1977-87, Geneva Free Libr., 1984-93. Fellow Coll. Am. Pathologists, Am. Soc. Clin. Pathology. Avocation: book collector. Office: Geneva Gen Hosp 196 North St Geneva NY 14456-1651

GIVEN, KENNA SIDNEY, surgeon, educator; b. Charleston, W.Va., Nov. 22, 1938; s. Virgil and Chessie Given; m. Charlene K. Given; children: Kari, Patrick, Amy. BA, W.Va. U., 1960; MD, Duke U., 1964. Diplomate Am. Bd. Surgery, Am. Bd. Plastic Surgery (chairperson-elect 1996-97, bd. dirs. 1992—). Intern Ind. U. Med. Ctr., Indpls., 1964-65; resident, then chief resident gen. surgery Grady Meml. Hosp./Emory U. Hosp., Atlanta, 1965-69; asst. resident, then chief resident plastic surgery Duke U. Med. Ctr., Durham, N.C., 1975-77; clin. instr. surgery Emory U., Atlanta, 1972-74; chief surgery Lanier Meml. Hosp., Langdale, Ala., 1974; prof., chief divsn. plastic surgery Med. Coll. Ga., Augusta, 1977—, med. dir. oper. rm., 1989-90. Assoc. dir. burn unit Med. Coll. Ga. Hosp.; cons. Augusta Correctional and Med. Instrn.; plastic surgery dir. Children's Med. Svc., 1981—; mem. Residency Rev. Commn. for Plastic Surgery, 1991—, chmn., 1994-96; chair Am. Bd. Plastic Surgery, Inc., 1997-99; chmn. residency rev. com. Accreditation Coun. for Grad. Med. Edn., 1994-96; lectr. in field. Contbr. articles to profl. jours. Pres. Med. Rsch. Found. Ga., 1985-88; trustee Plastic Surgery Edn. Found., 1994-97, pres.-elect, 1997; bd. dirs. Augusta Country Day Sch.; bd. dirs. Augusta Prep. Day Sch., 1988, trustee, 1989-90. Fellow ACS; mem. AMA, Am. Assn. Plastic Surgeons (trustee 1994-97), Assn. Acad. Chmn. in Plastic Surgery (pres. 1996-97, bd. dirs. 1985-88, 93—), Southeastern Plastic and Reconstructive Surgery (chmn. continuing med. edn. com. 1987, bd. dirs. 1992-95), Am. Soc. Plastic and Reconstructive Surgery (bd. dirs. 1988), Am. Assn. Hand Surgery, Am. Cleft Palate Assn., Am. Soc. Aesthetic Plastic Surgeons, Internat. Soc. Clin. Plastic Surgeons, Ga. Plastic Surgery Soc. (pres. 1985), Med. Assn. Ga., Richmond County Med. Soc., Southeastern Surg. Congress., So. Med. Assn., Southeastern Soc. Plastic and Reconstructive Surgeons (pres. 1997), So. Surg. Soc. Baptist. Home: 748 Tripps Ct Augusta GA 30909-1816 Office: Med Coll Ga Divsn Plastic Surgery HB-5049 Augusta GA 30912

GIVEN, MELISSA ANN, elementary school educator, educational consultant; b. Charleston, West Virginia, June 5, 1961; d. Robert Carl and Janet (Barnette) Rehe; m. Bruce Owen Given. BS, West Va. State Coll., 1983; MA, West Va. U., 1989. Cert. elem. edn., mental retardation K-12, preschool handicapped, severe,profound handicapped. Tchr. Kanawha County Sch., Charleston, 1984—91, Monongalia County Sch., Morgantown, W.Va., 1991—94, Gwinnett County Sch., Buford, Ga., 1995—98, Kanawha County Sch., Dunbar, W.Va., 1998—. Course grader W.Va. U., Morgantown, 1991—94; cons., cadre tchr. Office Spl. Edn. W.Va. Dept. Edn., Charleston, 1999—; qualified mental retardation profl. Braley & Thompson, St. Albans, W.Va., 2000—01; qualified mental retardation prof. cons., 1999—. Named Tchr. of the Yr., West Va. Fedn. Coun. Exceptional Children, 2001. Mem.: Coun. Exceptional Children, La Belle Garden Club (co-v.p. 2001—). Episcopalian. Avocations: boating, swimming, photography. Home: 848 Alta Rd Charleston WV 25314 Office: Kanawha County Sch Dunbar Middle Sch 325 27th St Dunbar WV 25064 Business E-Mail: Wvcatlover39@aol.com.

GIVENS, DAVID BRADLEY, anthropologist, educator; b. Whittier, Calif., July 15, 1944; s. Willis Bradley and Helen Tesora Givens; m. Doreen Kay McKenna, Aug. 21, 1974; children: Scott, Aaron Huffman. PhD, U. Wash., 1976. Dir. programs Am. Anthrop. Assn., Arlington, Va., 1985—97; exec. dir. Ctr. for Nonverbal Studies, Spokane, Wash., 1997—. Cons. U.S. Dept. of Def., Fort George G. Meade, Md., 2002. Author: The Nonverbal Dictionary of Gestures, Signs & Body Language Cues, 2002. Recipient award for excellence, The Ctr. for Anthropology and Journalism, 1994. Fellow: Am. Anthrop. Assn. Office: Ctr for Nonverbal Studies 204 W 23rd Ave Spokane WA 99203 E-mail: nonverbal2@aol.com.

GIVENS, FLORENCE ROSIE, author, editor, publishing executive, b. Spotsylvania, Va., Apr. 2, 1948; d. Edward and Carrie Mae Camp; m. Anderson Jackson Sr., Aug. 31, 1963 (dec. Oct. 1967); children: Anderson Jackson Jr., Freda A. Jackson, Mario D. Jackson; m. Josephus Givens Jr., Jan. 10, 2000; stepchildren: Alfreda, Roland, Dana, Deanna;1 child, Gregory T Wright Sr. Grad. high sch., Fredericksburg, Va. Acct., Stafford, Va., 1962—2003; legal clk. U.S. Fed. Govt., Washington, 1991—2001; author, editor, pub. Flo Bound Poems Pubs., Stafford, 1999—. Cons. Flobound Poems Pubs., 1999—. Author (editor): A Morning Without Coffee, 2000, Revisiting Friends: The Journey Home, 2001, The Ring of Friends: Forever, 2002, A Little More Cream Please, 2003. Recipient Highest Honor Spelling Bee, John J. Wright Consolidated Sch., Snell, Va., 1953, Pensmanship award, 1956. Democrat. Pentecostal Apostolic. Avocations: writing, reading, travel. Office: FloBound Poems Pubs PO Box 3101 Fredericksburg VA 22402-3101 E-mail: morningpormsflog@aol.com.

GIVENS, JOHN KENNETH, manufacturing executive; b. Highland Park, Mich., Aug. 21, 1940; s. John Hamilton and Marion Florence G.; children: Kevin John, Kirk David; m. Patricia Ann Bowlby, May 23, 1980. BA, Mich. State U., 1963. With Lincoln-Mercury divsn. Ford Motor Co., Cleve., 1963-71, sales promotion mgr. Lincoln-Mercury divsn. Dearborn, 1971-73; dir. sales and mktg. Ford South Africa, 1973-75; car advt. mgr. Ford Div., 1975-77; sr. v.p. Wells. Rich, Greene Advt., Los Angeles, 1977-79; v.p. mktg. Chrysler Corp., Highland Park, Mich., 1979-82; pres. Seal-Dry USA, Inc., Little Rock, 1982-92; chmn. Eastar, Inc. Holding Co., 1982-98, Spash Superpools, LLC, 1988—, SanduskyAthol Internat., 1992—, Deckrite, LLC, 1997—, Aqua Ventures, LLC, 2002—. Office: Splash LLC 3912 E Progress St North Little Rock AR 72114-5239 also: Sandusky Ltd 3130 W Monroe St Sandusky OH 44870-1811 E-mail: jg82140@aol.com.

GIVENS, MELISSA LOUISE, emergency physician; b. Oakes, N.D., Nov. 21, 1969; d. Marvin H. and Patricia A. Werner; m. Edward Wendell Givens, July 3, 1993; children: Aja Rae, Maya Mae. MD, Uniformed Svcs. U., 1997. Commd. 2d lt. U.S. Army, 1988, advanced through grades to capt., flight surgeon, brigade sureon, 1st cavalry divsn., 1998—2000; resident SAUSHEC, San Antonio, 2000—, chief resident, 2002—03. Contbr. articles. Named All Am. Powerlifter, 1991, 1992. Mem.: Am. Acad. Emergency Physicians, Am. Coll. Emergency Physicians (acad. affairs com. 2001—02). Office: Brooke Army Ctr Dept Emergency Medicine Fort Sam Houston TX 78234 Personal E-mail: egivens@satx.rr.com.

GIVENS, PAUL RONALD, former university chancellor; b. Wellsburg, W.Va., Nov. 16, 1923; s. George D. and Anna (Peters) G.; m. Leona Janssen, Dec. 20, 1945; children— Gregg, Stann, Rodney, Deborah. Student, Graceland Coll., 1941-43; BA, George Peabody Coll., 1948, MA, 1949; postgrad., U. Iowa, 1949-50; PhD, Vanderbilt U., 1953. Instr. Lawrence Coll., Appleton, Wis., 1949-51; counselor Vanderbilt U., Nashville, 1951-53; chmn. psychology dept. Birmingham (Ala.) So. Coll., 1953-60, U. So. Fla., Tampa, 1960-67; dean arts and scis. Ithaca (N.Y.) Coll., 1967-72; v.p. acad. affairs Millikin U., Decatur, Ill., 1972-79; chancellor U. N.C., Pembroke, 1979-89. Author: (with others) Human Behavior, 1966. Served with USN, 1943-46. Home: 704 Druid Hills Rd Tampa FL 33617-3810

GIVENS, RANDAL JACK, communications educator; b. Borger, Tex., Mar. 17, 1951; s. Fred Frank and Doris Mae (Bley) G.; m. Carol Marie Griffin, May 21, 1973; children: Mary Leanna, Anna Elizabeth. BA in Speech, Lubbock (Tex.) Christian Coll., 1973; MA in Speech Comm., Tex. Tech. U., 1974; MAR in Counseling Psychology, Harding U., Memphis, 1977, MAR in Missiology, MTh in Philosophy, 1978; diploma in French, IFCAD, Brussels, 1982. Diploma in French, I.F.C.A.D., Brussels, 1982. Missionary (in French) Eglise du Christ, Brussels, 1979-82; dir. Internat. Sch. Conversational English, Brussels, 1982-89; acad. dean Internat. Christian U., Vienna, Austria, 1989-94; chmn. dept. comm., dir. forensics York (Nebr.) Coll., 1994-97, dir. grants and program devel., 1997—. Counselor Memphis Mental Health Ctr., 1976-78; group therapy coord. Memphis Rehab. Svc., 1976-78; chief coord. of translating 2 internat. confs., Strasbourg, France, 1983, Metz, France, 1987; bd. dirs. Grant Profls. Cert. Inst., 2003—; lectr. in field; ind. grants cons., 1998—; bd. dirs. Grant Profls. Cert. Inst. Author: Induced Feedback, 1974; translator (book): Johnson's Notes, 1989; editor Vienna Views newsletter, 1989-94. Bd. dirs. Blue Valley Cmty. Action Agy., 2001—, Grant Profls. Cert. Inst., Blue Valley Cmty. Action Agy.; mem. tech. panel Grant and Program Devel. Inst., 1999—. Recipient Svc. award Lubbock Christian Schs., 1992; Tex. Tech. U. grantee, 1974, 91. Mem. Nat. Soc. Fundraising Execs., Speech Comm. Assn. Am., Nebr. Speech Comm. Assn. (liaison for univ. affairs 1994), Speech Comm. Assn., Martial Arts Black Belt Assn., L'Association de l'Ordinateur (mem. tech. panel grant and program devel. inst.), Am. Assn. Grant Profls. (founding pres. 1998, pres. 1999, 2000—). Republican. Ch. of Christ. Avocations: martial arts, drummer, woodworking, computers. Home: 1315 Blackburn Ave York NE 68467-2011 Office: York College 1125 E 8th St York NE 68467-2699

GIVENS, STANN WILLIAM, lawyer; b. Appleton, Wis., Feb. 20, 1950; s. Paul Ronald and Leona (Janssen) G.; m. Bonnie MacGregor, Aug. 28, 1971; children: Christian MacGregor, Emily Kate. BS, Bucknell U., 1971; JD, Fla. State U., 1973. Bar: Fla. 1974, U.S. Ct. Appeals (5th cir.) 1974, U.S. Dist. Ct. (mid. dist.) Fla. 1974. Asst. state atty. Hillsborough State Atty.'s Office, Tampa, Fla., 1973-75; asst. city atty. City of Tampa, 1975-77; atty. Stann W. Givens, P.A., Tampa, 1977-93, Knox and Givens, P.A., 1993—. Race dir. Gasparilla Distance Classic, Tampa, 1980-81, dir., 1977-85; elder Temple Terrace (Fla.) Presbyn. Ch., 1976—; moderator permanent jud. commn. Synod of South Atlantic of Presbyn. Ch., 1977-88. Recipient Outstanding Young Men Am.

award, 1980, 77, Outstanding Community Svc. award Boys Club Tampa, 1981, Professionalism award Family Law Inn of Tampa, 1999. Fellow: Am. Acad. Matrimonial Lawyers; mem.: Hillsborough County Bar Assn. (chair family law sect. 1988—89), Fla. Bar (cert. in marital and family law, past chair marital and family law bd. cert. com., chair 13th jud. cir. grievance com. 1999—2000). Presbyterian. Avocations: youth sports, golf. Office: Knox and Givens PA 607 W Horatio St Tampa FL 33606-2272 E-mail: givens@tampafamilylaw.com.

GIVENS, THEARTIS TINA MANSFIELD, primary school educator; b. Elizabeth, N.J., Oct. 17, 1950; d. Allen Nelson and Rebecca Moment Mansfield; m. Robert L. Givens Jr., Aug. 19, 1978 (div. Sept. 10, 1985); children: Quinn, DeKida. BA in Home Econs. K-12, Montclair (N.J.) State Coll., 1973; early childhood N.J. state cert., Kean Coll., 1983. Cert. home health aide. Elem. resource math., lang. arts tchr. Newark Pub. Schs., 1973—. Contbr. poetry (award, 2002). Avocations: writing, crocheting, piano, music. Home: 51-53 N Day St # 17 Orange NJ 07050 Office: Newark Pub Schs 87 Richelieu Ter Newark NJ 07106

GIVHAN, EDGAR GILMORE, physician, writer; b. Montevallo, Ala., Aug. 6, 1935; AB in German Lit., Washington and Lee U., 1956; MD, Washington U., St. Louis, 1960. Diplomate Am. Bd. Internal Medicine. Intern Vanderbilt U., 1960, resident in internal medicine, 1965, instr. in hematology, 1965-66, Auburn U. Sch. Lab. Tech., 1967-85; co-owner Commercial Garden Design, Montgomery, Ala., 1982—. Pres. med. staff Montgomery Bapt. Hosp., 1974-75; cons. physician Ala. Medicaid Program, 1982-86; bd. dirs., cons. Humana Hosp. East Montgomery; med. dir. Humana Ins. Co. Ala.; chmn. bd. Direct Care, 1995—; horticulture lectr. Author: (guide and video) How to Grow Great Southern Gardens, 1992, Flowers for South Alabama Gardens, 1980, Conversations with a Southern Gardener, 1999, (with others) Heritage Gardens, 1992, Alabama Gardens Great and Small, 2002; contbr. articles to profl. jours. Chmn. bd. South Montgomery YMCA, 1973; bd. dirs. ARC, Montgomery, 1970-73, med. dir. blood processing ctr., Montgomery, 1973-80; bd. dirs. Montgomery Symphony Orch., Blue Cross and Blue Shield Ala., 1979-85, Montgomery C. of C., 1980-84; bd. vis. for the humanities Auburn U. Capt. USAF, 1962-64. Vanderbilt U. fellow, 1965-66. Fellow ACP; mem. AMA, Ala. Soc. Internal Medicine, Montgomery Soc. Internal Medicine (pres. 1970), Montgomery County Med. Soc. (pres. 1976), Ala. Soc. Clin. Oncology (v.p. 1982), Am. Soc. Hematology, So. Garden History Soc. (pres., bd. dirs.), Phi Beta Kappa. Office: 300 Taylor Rd Ste 600 Montgomery AL 36117-3555

GIVHAN, ROBERT MARCUS, lawyer; b. Mineral Wells, Tex., May 10, 1959; s. Walter Houston Givhan and Marion Blackwell Callen Stothart; m. Janet Lee Dothard, May 6, 1989; children: Vivian Lee, Charlotte Ann, Virginia Mae. BA, U. Ala., Tuscaloosa, 1981; JD, Cumberland Sch. Law, Birmingham, Ala., 1986. Bar: Ala. 1987, D.C. 1989, U.S. Supreme Ct. 1989, U.S. Ct. Appeals (D.C. and 11th cirs.), U.S. Dist. Ct. (so., mid. and no. dists.) Ala. 1987. Assoc. Perry and Russell, Montgomery, Ala., 1987-88; dep. dist. atty. 15th Jud. Cir. of Ala., Montgomery, 1988-91; dep. atty. gen. Office of Atty. Gen. of Ala., Montgomery, 1991-95; ptnr. Johnston Barton Proctor & Powell LLP, Birmingham, 1995—. Contbr. articles. Fellow: Am. Coll. Pros. Attys.; mem.: Am. Health Lawyers Assn., Birmingham Bar Assn. (co-chmn. econs. law practice com. 1998, chmn. 1999, co-chmn. jud. and legal reform com. 2002, chmn. 2003), Ala. State Bar Assn., ABA (vice chmn. antitrust competition and trade regulation com. adminstrv. 1994—2000). Episcopalian. Avocations: whitewater rafting, hiking, music collecting, book collecting. Office: 2900 AmSouth/Harbert Plz 1901 6th Ave N Birmingham AL 35203-2618 Home. 1601 Shades Park Cove Birmingham AL 35209 E-mail: rmg@jbpp.com.

GIVHAN, THOMAS BARTRAM, lawyer; b. Lexington, Ky., Sept. 24, 1926; s. Thomas Holman and Eva Mae (Beck) G.; m. Sharon Rose Richard, June 10, 1949 (dec.); children: Elise Charles, Ellen Foster, Aaron Todd. JD, U. Ky., 1951. Bar: Ky. 1951, U.S. Dist. Ct. (ea. dist.) Ky. 1957, U.S. Dist. Ct. (we. dist.) Ky. 1957, U.S. Supreme Ct. 1972. City atty. City of Shepherdsville, Ky., 1953-57; county atty. Bullitt County, Shepherdsville, 1958-61, 66-73, 1982-89; mem. Ky. Ho. of Reps., Frankfort, 1974-78, chmn. judiciary com., 1976-78. Mem. Ky. Gov.'s Ad Hoc Com. on Jud. Reform, Frankfort, 1976. Chmn. Bullitt County Dem. Party, 1968-71; mem. Bullitt County Planning Commn., 1995—. With USMC, 1945-46, PTO. Mem. ABA, Ky. Bar Assn. (ho. of dels. 1964-68, character and fitness com. 1968-74, CLE award 1981), Bullitt County Bar Assn. (sec./treas. 1956-61). Office: Givhan & Spainhour PSC Profl Bldg 200 S Buckman St Ste 1 Shepherdsville KY 40165-0065 E-mail: tgivhan@aol.com.

GIVOGRE, JOHN LEE, pain medicine specialist, anesthesiologist; b. Iron Mountain, Mich., July 20, 1964; s. John Lee and Doreen Marie (McMahon) G.; children John Lee, Caroline. BS, U. Mich., 1986, MD, 1989. Diplomate Am. Bd. Anesthesiology, Am. Bd. Pain Medicine. Intern St. Joseph Mercy Hosp./CMHC, Ann Arbor, Mich., 1989-90; resident in anesthesiology Johns Hopkins U., Balt., 1990-93, fellow in pain mgmt., 1993-94, faculty, 1993-94; staff anesthesiologist Northeast Ga. Med. Ctr., Gainesville, 1994—, Lanier Park Hosp.. Ctr., Gainesville, 1996—. Contbr. articles to profl. jours. Mem. Am. Acad. Pain Medicine (cert.), Am. Assn. Orthopaedic Medicine, Am. Soc. Regional Anesthesia, Am. Soc. Anesthesiology, Am. Pain Soc., Christian Med. Dental Soc., Hall County Med. Soc. (pres. 2001—), Med. Assn. Ga. Office: Ga Pain and Preventive Medicine Specialists 530 Spring St SE Gainesville GA 30501-3740

GIVOT, WINNIE, artist, educator; b. Mount Holly, N.J., Dec. 29, 1944; d. Richard H. and Mary E.G. Rhoads; m. Irv Givot, Aug. 24, 1968; children: Rima M., John A. BA in Econs., Wheaton Coll., 1967; postgrad. in Econs., Brown U., 1968-70. With Givot Studio and Gallery, Sisters, Oreg., 1992—; workshop asst. Art in the Mountains, Bend, Oreg., 1996—2001. Interior design Two Rivers Farm, Aurora, Oreg., 1980-92, Metanoia Soc., Bend, Oreg., 1996-99; juror art shows Mirror Pond Gallery, Bend, Oreg., 1996-2001; watercolor and drawing instr., 1995—. Exhibited in numerous one-person and group shows; presented 24 paintings to U.S. Congressmen for hope and inspiration, 2002; represented in hundreds of pub. and pvt. collections. Recipient Chilean Congl. Medal of Hon., 2000. Mem.: Ga. Watercolor Soc., Arts Ctrl. (exhibit com. 1993—95), N.W. Watercolor Soc., Watercolor Soc. Oreg. Achievements include presented 24 paintings to U.S. congressmen, 2002. Home and Office: Givot Studio and Gallery 69953 Holmes Rd Sisters OR 97759-9706 E-mail: givots@outlawnet.com.

GIZA, DAVID ALAN, lawyer; b. Chgo., May 16, 1958; s. Bruno Frank and Marianne Theresa (Mozdren) G.; m. Karen Ann Van Maldegiam, Nov. 5, 1988. BS, DePaul U., 1981; JD, John Marshall U., 1984. Bar: Ill. 1985, U.S. Dist. Ct. (no. dist.) Ill. 1985. Atty. pvt. practice, Chgo., 1985-86; assoc. Larry Karchmar, Ltd., Chgo., 1986-87, Kovitz, Shifrin & Waitzman, Chgo., 1987; atty. W.W. Grainger, Inc., Skokie, Ill., 1987-91, Lincolnshire, Ill., 1991—, divsn. atty., 1993-96, sr. atty., 1996-98, asst. gen. counsel, 1998—2002; pvt. practice Corp. Law Assocs., Northfield, Ill., 2002—. Trustee Village of Libertyville, Ill., 1995—; chmn. Camp Lake (Wis.)/Ctr. Lake Rehab. Dist., 1990—. Mem. Am. Trial Lawyers Assn., Am. Corp. Counsel Assn., Ill State Bar Assn., Chgo. Bar Assn., Lake County Bar Assn. Republican. Roman Catholic. Avocations: politics, water sports, reading, travel, cooking. Office: Corp Law Assocs 400 Central Ave #150 Northfield IL 60093 Fax: 847-816-1799. E-mail: dave@corplawassociates.com.

GIZIS, EVANGELOS JOHN, biochemist; b. Tinos, Greece, Apr. 1, 1934; came to U.S. 1960; s. John Constantine and Anna (Sigalas) G.; m. Frances C. Murray, Oct. 21, 1967; children: John, Alexander, Paul-Robert. BS in Chemistry, Athens U., 1957; MS in Food Sci., Oreg. State U., 1962, PhD in Food Sci., Biochemistry, 1963. Postdoctoral fellow Mich. State U., E. Lansing, 1964-65; fellow Carnegie-Mellon U., Pitts., 1965-66; biochemist L.I. Jewish Hosp., N.Y.C., 1966-70; rsch. collaborator Brookhaven (N.Y.) Nat. Lab., 1967-69; acting pres., dean CUNY, Hostos CC, Bronx, 1970-77; chemist VA Hosp., Bklyn., 1970-73; adj. prof. Nutrition Dept. NYU, N.Y.C., 1978-99; v.p. Queens Coll., CUNY, Flushing, 1986-96; interim provost, v.p. Hunter Coll., N.Y.C., 1996—2000, interim pres., 2000—01; provost and sr. v.p. Queen's Coll., CUNY, 2001—. Acting pres., v.p. CUNY, Borough of Manhattan Community Coll., 1977-86; title III evaluator Community Coll. of Balt., 1980-97. Contbr. articles to profl. jours. Mem. Am. Inst. Nutrition, Inst. Food Technologists, Am. Chem. Soc., Soc. for Exptl. Biology and Medicine. Greek Orthodox. Home: 427 Ryder Rd Manhasset NY 11030-2761 Office: Queen's College Office of Provost Flushing NY 11367 Office Fax: 718-997-5879. E-mail: Evangelos_Gizis@qc.edu.

GJERTSEN, O. GERARD, lawyer; b. Bklyn., June 24, 1932; s. Ole Gerhard and Hilma (Jorgensen) G.; m. Carol Ann Jurkops, June 2, 1962; children: Gerard, Gary, Krista, Karen. BA, Columbia Coll., 1954; JD, NYU, 1958. Bar: N.Y. 1958, U.S. Dist. Ct. (so. dist.) N.Y. 1960. Ptnr., counsel Thacher Proffitt & Wood, N.Y.C., 1964—. Vice chmn. Tuckahoe (N.Y.) Urban Renewal Agy. With U.S. Army, 1954-55. Mem. ABA, N.Y. State Bar Assn., Assn. of Bar of City of N.Y., Westchester County Bar Assn., White Plains Bar Assn., Scarsdale Golf Club. Avocations: music, sports. Home: 262 Dante Ave Tuckahoe NY 10707-3015 Office: Thacher Proffitt & Wood 50 Main St White Plains NY 10606-1934

GJOVIG, BRUCE QUENTIN, entrepreneur coach, consultant, entrepreneur; b. Crosby, N.D., Mar. 24, 1951; s. Ronald Daniel and Agnes (Smedberg) G.; children: Mike Mohn, Todd Chaffee. BA, BS, U. N.D., 1974. Rsch. chemist Man-in-the-Sea Project, Grand Forks, N.D., 1975-76; campaign advisor Elkin for Gov. Com., Bismarck, N.D., 1976; exec. officer Grand Forks Bd. Realtors, 1977-81; devel. officer U. N.D. Found., 1981-84; founder, dir. Ctr. for Innovation, Grand Forks, 1984—. Bd. dirs. 1st Seed Capital Co., Grand Forks, SBIR Project West, Phoenix; founder, chmn. N.D. Entrepreneur Hall of Fame, 1985—; founder Rural Tech. Incubator, 1994—, N.D. Angel Capital Network, 1998—. Editor: The Business Plan: Step-by-Step, 1988, The Marketing Plan: Step-by-Step, 1990; author, editor: Boxcar of Peaches: Nash Finch Co., 1990, Pardon Me, Your Manners are Showing!, 1992; contbr. articles to profl. jours. Founder, sponsor 67th Patent & Trademark Depository Libr., 1991—; chair N.D. Mus. Art, U. N.D. Nordic Initiative. Named Friend of Small Bus., Fargo C. of C., 1988, U. N.D. Outstanding Greek Alumnus, 1990, ANSA Norseman of Yr., 2001, Rsch. Adv. of Yr. for N.D. and Six States in Regiona VIII, SBA, 2003; recipient Outstanding Svc. award U. N.D. Alumni Assn., 1984, Western U.S. SBIR Support Person award, 1997, Tibbetts award SBA, 1998, Kauffamn Leadership award 1998, SBA Nat. Vision 2000 award, 1999, Rsch. Advocate of Yr., 2003, others; named to N.D. Entrepreneur Hall of Fame, 2001. Mem. Assn. Univ. Tech. Mgrs., Assn. Univ. Related Rsch. Pks., Univ. Small Bus. Tech. Consortium (state dir. 1986-90), Alumni Inter-Fraternity Coun. (chmn. 1982-86, 90-95, Outstanding Alumnus 1990), Rotary, Delta Tau Delta. Republican. Episcopalian. Avocations: reading, politics, art collector, fund raising, entrepreneur history collector. Home: Condo # 31 2501 26th Ave S Grand Forks ND 58201-6454 Office: Ctr for Innovation PO Box 8372 Rural Tech Ctr Grand Forks ND 58202-8372 E-mail: bruce@innovators.net.

GJURICH, MICHAEL JOHN, music educator; b. Johnstown, Pa., Aug. 18, 1957; s. Samuel and Mary Gjurich; m. Christine Marie Esdinsky, Jan. 2, 1982; children: Michael Kristopher, Matthew Alexander. BS in Music Edn., U. of Pa., Edinboro, 1979. Cert. tchr. W.Va., 1980, Pa., 1994, Nev., 1996. Asst. band dir. elem. instrumental music Clay-Battelle Jr. Sr. HS and Feeder Schs., Blacksville, Va., 1980—83; instrumental music, head tchr. Cass Dist. Jr. HS, Osage, W.Va., 1983—89; dir. of bands and strings Clarion-Limestone Sch. Dist., Strattanville, Pa., 1989—96; dir. of instrumental music Virgin Valley Jr./Sr. HS, Mesquite, Nev., 1996—2001, The Meadows Sch., Las Vegas, 2001—. First chair french horn S.W. Symphony Orch., St. George, Utah, 1996—2001, first, sect., solo french horn, guest condr. Franklin Silver Cornet Band, Franklin, Pa., 1989—96; first sect. solo french horn, guest condr. Mercer (Pa.) Cmty. Band, 1989—2000; 1st and solo french horn, asst. condr. Clarion (Pa.) U. Cmty. Orch., 1990—92; 2nd french horn Butler (Pa.) Symphony Orch., 1990—92. Pres. Mesquite (Nev.) Arts Coun., 1997—2001, Copper Bluffs Home Owners Assn., Mesquite, Nev., 1997—99. Named Hon. Citizen, City of Osage, W.Va., 1988. Mem.: Am. Fedn. Musicians, Clarion County Music Educators Assn. (sec. 1990—96), Pa. Music Educators Assn., Nev. Music Educators Assn., Music Educators Nat. Conf., Internat. Horn Soc., Phi Mu Alpha (pres. 1977—79). Serbian Orthodox. Avocations: gardening, woodworking, model making, painting, reading. Home: 2201 North Buffalo Drive; #1080 Las Vegas NV 89128 Personal E-mail: mgju@sisna.com.

GLAAB, CHARLES NELSON, educator, historian; b. b Williston, N.D., Dec. 19, 1927; s. Reuben and Betty (Nelson) G.; m. Mary Ellen Anderson, Nov. 5, 1949; children— Martha Ann, John Reuben. BPh, U. N.D., 1951, MA, 1952; PhD, U. Mo., 1958. Rsch. assoc. history Kansas City project U. Chgo., 1956-58; from instr. to asst. prof. history Kans. State U., 1958-60; from assoc. prof. to prof. history U. Wis., Milw., 1960-68; dir. urban history sect. Wis. Hist. Soc., 1960-63; prof. history U. Toledo, 1968—. Dir. Fox Valley research project Wis. Hist. Soc., 1963-64; mem. Milw. Landmarks Commn., 1965-68, Toledo Landmark Com., 1968-70, Ohio Hist. Site Preservation Bd., 1979-81 Author: Kansas City and the Railroads, 1962, The American City: A Documentary History, 1963, (with A.T. Brown) A History of Urban America, 1967, (with L.H. Larsen) Factories in the Valley, 1969, (with Morgan A. Barclay) Toledo: Gateway to the Great Lakes, 1983; editor: Urban History Group Newsletter, 1962-68; co-editor, 1968-70, N.W. Ohio Quar., 1994-99; mem bd. editors Urban Affairs Quar., 1966-74, Sci. Press Wis, 1966-7 Jour. Urban History, 1973-88, Urban Affairs Ann. Rev, 1978-82, Frederick Law Olmsted Papers, 1985-90, Hayes Hist. Jour., 1987-91. Served with AUS, 1946-48. Mem. Orgn. Am. Historians, Am. Hist. Assn., Urban History Assn., VFW, Am. Legion, Phi Beta Kappa. Home: 3021 Hopewell Pl Toledo OH 43606-3105 E-mail: cgmg@glasscity.net.

GLACEL, BARBARA PATE, management consultant; b. Balt., Sept. 15, 1948; d. Jason Thomas Pate and Sarah Virginia (Forwood Pate) Wetter; m. Robert Allan Glacel, Dec. 21, 1969; children: Jennifer Warren, Sarah Allane, Ashley Virginia. AB, Coll. William and Mary, 1970; MA, U. Okla., 1973, PhD, 1978. Tchr. Harford County (Md.) Schs., 1970-71; tchr. Dept. Def. Schs., W.Ger., 1971-73; ednl. counselor U.S. Army, Germany, 1973-74; mgmt. cons. Barbara Glacel & Assocs., Anchorage, 1980-86, Washington, 1986-88; ptnr. Pracel Prints, Williamsburg, Va., 1981-85; sr. mgmt. tng. specialist Arco Alaska, Inc., 1984-85; gen. mgr. mgmt. programs Hay Systems, Inc., Washington, 1986-88; CEO VIMA Internat., Burke, Va., 1988-99, chmn. emeritus, 2000; 2d v.p., bd. dirs. Chesapeake Broadcasting Corp. Md.; prin. The Glacel Group, 2000—. Adj. prof. U. Md., 1973—74, Suffolk U., Boston, 1975—77, C.W. Post Ctr., L.I. U., John Jay Coll. Criminal Justice, N.Y.C., 1979—80, St. Thomas Aquinas Coll., N.Y.C., 1981, St. Mary's Coll., Leavenworth, Kans., 1981, Anchorage C.C., 1982; acad. adviser Ctrl. Mich. U., 1981—82; asst. prof. U. Alaska, Anchorage, 1983—85; mem. adj. faculty Ctr. for Creative Leadership, 1986—; guest lectr. U.S. Mil. Acad.; mem. U.S. Army Sci. Bd., 1986—90, U.S. Dept. Def. Sci. Bd. Quality of Life Panel, 1994—95, Def. Adv. Com. on Women in the Svcs., 2000—02, Consumer Rev. Bd. DOD Breast Cancer Rsch. Program, 2001—02; mem. adv. coun. Reves Ctr. for Internat. Studies Coll. William and Mary, 2001—; bd. dirs. The Fund for William and Mary, 2001—. Author: Regional Transit Authorities, 1983; (with others) 1000 Army Families, 1983, The Army Community and Their Families, 1989, Light Bulbs for Leaders, 1994, Hitting the Wall: Memoir of a Cancer Journey, 2001. Chmn. 172d Inf. Brigade Family Coun. Recipient Comdr.'s award for pub. svc. U.S. Dept. Army, 1984, U.S. Army Patriotic Civilian Svc. award 1991, U.S. Army Forscom Svc. award 1993, Dept. of Army Outstanding Civilian Svc. medal, 1999, Yellow Rose of Tex. award, 1999, Helping Hand Cmty. Svc. award, 1999, Coll. William & Mary Alumna medallion, 2001; AAUW grantee, 1977-78. Mem. ASTD (bd. dirs. Anchorage chpt.), APA, Soc. for Indsl. and Organizational Psychology, Instrnl. Systems Assn. (v.p. 1993-96), Soc. of Alumni Coll. of William and Mary (bd. dirs. 1992-98, v.p., 1997-98).

GLACEL, ROBERT ALLAN, retired military career officer; b. Frankfurt, Germany, Oct. 31, 1947; (parents Am. citizens); m. Barbara Pate; children: Jennifer, Sarah, Ashley. Grad., U.S. Mil. Acad., 1969; M in Civil and Mech. Engring., MIT, 1977; MBA, Boston U., 1977; grad., Command and Gen. Staff Coll., 1982, Indsl. Coll. Armed Forces, 1990. Commd. 2d lt. U.S. Army, 1969, advanced through grades to brig. gen., 1995, FO, fire dir. officer 3d bn., 319th field arty., 1970-71, comdr. B battery, 1st Bn., 10th Field Arty., 3rd Inf. Divsn., 1971-72, S-2 (Intelligence) Divsn. Arty., 1972-74, asst. prof. engring. U.S. Mil. Acad., 1977-81, ops. officer, exec. officer 1st Bn., 37th Field Arty. Ft. Richardson, Alaska, 1982-85, with office Dep. Chief of Staff Pers. Hdqrs., Pentagon Washington, 1985-87, comdr. 1st Bn., 4th Field Arty., 2d Inf. Divsn., 1987-89, polit. mil. planner J-5 (Plans), the Joint Staff, Pentagon, 1990-92, divsn. arty. comdr. 7th Inf. Divsn. (Light) Ft. Ord, Calif., 1992-93, exec. officer to the Under Sec. of the Army, Pentagon Washington, 1993-95; chief requirements and programs br. Office of Asst. Chief of Staff for Policy in SHAPE, Belgium, 1995-97; comdr. U.S. Army Test and Experimentation Command, Ft. Hood, Tex., 1997-99; ret. from active duty, 1999; v.p. America Online, Inc., Herndon, VA, 1999—. Decorated Legion of Merit, Bronz Star, Def. Meritorious Svc. medal, Meritorious Svc. medal, Disting. Svc. medal, Def. Superior Svc. medal. Office: America Online Inc 381 Elden St Herndon VA 20170-4842

GLACKIN, WILLIAM CHARLES, arts critic, editor; b. Sacramento, July 10, 1917; s. William Martin and Anita Ivy (Derr) G.; m. Helen Bateman, 1941 (div. 1960); children: Christine, Nancy; m. Sandra May Littlewood, Jan. 27, 1962; 1 child, Brendan. BS, St. Mary's Coll., Calif., 1939; postgrad., U. Calif., Berkeley, 1939-41. Tchr. Sacramento City Schs., 1941-43; reporter UPI, Sacramento, 1946-48; critic Sacramento Bee, 1948—, arts editor, 1948-76. Dir. criticism workshops Nat. Coll. Theater Festival, Sacramento, 1980's, various theater groups, Sacramento, 1948-62. Author: (musical) Anita, 1955. Sgt. U.S. Army, 1943-46. Nominated Pulitzer prize in criticism, 1980; named Conservator of Am. Arts Am. Conservatory Theater Found., 1984. Mem. Am. Newspaper Guild, Am. Theater Critics Assn., Music Critics Assn. Avocations: golf, tennis. Office: PO Box 95852 2100 Q St Sacramento CA 95816-6816

GLAD, DAIN STURGIS, aerospace engineer, consultant; b. Santa Monica, Calif., Sept. 17, 1932; s. Alma Emanuel and Maude LaVerne (Morby) Glad; m. Betty Alexandra Shainoff, Sept. 12, 1954 (dec. 1974); 1 child, Dana Elizabeth; m. Carolyn Elizabeth Giffen, June 8, 1979. BS in Engring., UCLA, 1954; MSEE, U. So. Calif., 1963. Registered profl. engr., Calif. Elec. engr. Clary Corp., San Gabriel, Calif., 1957-58; with Aerojet Electro Sys. Co., Azusa, Calif., 1958-72, 75-84; with missile sys. divsn. Rockwell Internat. Corp., Anaheim, Calif., 1973-75, with Electro-Optical Ctr., 1990-94; with support sys. divsn. Hughes Aircraft Co., 1984-90; cons., 1994—. Oper. mgr. V. C. D. Techs. LLC, 1997—2003. Contbr. articles to profl. jours. With USN, 1954—56, lt. (j.g.) USNR, 1956—57. Mem.: IEEE. Home: 1701 Marengo Ave South Pasadena CA 91030-4818 E-mail: dglad@socal.rr.com.

GLAD, JOAN BOURNE, retired clinical psychologist, educator; b. Salt Lake City, Apr. 24, 1918; d. E. LeRoy and Ethel G. (Rogers) Bourne; m. Donald D. Glad, Sept. 10, 1938 (dec. 1978); children: Dawn JoAnne Lundquist, Toni Ann Saunders, Sue Ellen Winmill, Roger Bruce. BA, UCLA, 1955; MA, U. Utah, 1960, PhD, 1965. Psychologist Utah State Dept. Health, Salt Lake City, 1960-65; founder, dir. adminstr. Child and Family Guidance Clinic, Primary Children's Hosp., Salt Lake City, 1965-68; dir. parent edn. Children's Hosp., Orange County, 1968-75; founder, adminstr. Family Learning Ctr., Santa-Ana Tustin Cmty. Hosp., Santa Ana, Calif., 1975-77; dir. Glad & Assocs., Tustin, Calif., 1977—2003, ret., 2003. Instr. Grad. Sch., Chapman Coll., Orange, Calif., 1970-73; cons. Calif. Assn. Neurologically Handicapped Children, Orange, 1970-77; lectr. self esteem Fullerton (Calif.) Coll., 1980-82; pres. Profl. Corp., Orange, Calif., 1999. Author: Reading Unlimited, 1965; editor newsletter Between You and Me, 1998—. Past Pres. Friends of Tustin (Calif.) Libr.; docent Tustin Hist. Soc. Mem. Assn. Holistic Health (a founder San Diego), Assn. Mormon Counselors and Psychotherapists, Redwood Psychol. Assn. Mem. Lds Ch. Home and Office: Glad & Assocs 309 Orangewood Dr Healdsburg CA 95448-4322 E-mail: joanglad@sonic.net.

GLAD, SUZANNE LOCKLEY, retired museum director; b. Rochester, N.Y., Oct. 2, 1929; d. Alfred Allen and Lucille A. (Watson) Lockley; m. Edward Newman Glad, Nov. 7, 1953; children: Amy, Lisanne Glad Lantz, William E. BA, Sweet Briar Coll., 1951; MA, Columbia U., 1952. Exec. dir. New York State Young Reps., N.Y.C., 1951-57; mem. pub. rels. staff Dolphin Group, L.A., 1974-83; scheduling sec. Gov.'s Office, Sacramento, 1983-87; dep. dir. Calif. Mus. Sci. and Industry, L.A., 1987-94; ret. Mem. Calif. Rep. League, Pasadena, 1969—; mem. Assistance League of Flintridge, 1970—, Flintridge Guild Children's Hosp., 1969-89. Mem. Sweet Briar Alumnae of So. Calif. (pres. 1972), Phi Beta Kappa, Tau Phi. Episcopalian. Avocations: reading, gardening.

GLADDEN, GARNETT LEE, educator, health consultant, psychologist; b. May 8, 1922; s. Martin L. and Beatrice G. (Palmer) Gladden; m. Vivianne C. Gladden, 1958; children: Mark L., Jeanne Sue. AB, U. Calif., 1943; MA, Claremont Coll., 1948; PhD, Honolulu U., 1989. Prof. emeritus Riverside (Calif.) City Coll., 1946-77; dir. Anza Human Rels. Ctr., Riverside, 1948—78; v.p. Golden State U., L.A., 1978-82; dean Grad. Studies, provost Honolulu U., 1982-98; scientific cons. Japan LifeLtd., L.A. & Tokyo, 1986-98. Adj. prof. San Bernardino Valley Coll., 2002. Author (with Vivianne Cervantes Gladden): How to Win the Aging Game, 1958. Home: 6148 Turnberry Dr Banning CA 92220

GLADDEN, JAMES WALTER, JR., lawyer; b. Pitts., Feb. 23, 1940; s. James Walter and Cynthia Unice (Hales) G.; m. Patricia T. Kuehn, Aug. 21, 1993; children: James, Thomas, Robert. AB, DePauw U., 1961; JD, Harvard U., 1964. Bar: Ill. 1964, U.S. Sup. Ct. 1978. Ptnr. Mayer, Brown, Rowe & Maw, Chgo., 1964—. Mem. ABA. Home: 1426 Chicago Ave Apt 5N Evanston IL 60201 Office: Mayer Brown Rowe & Maw 190 S La Salle St Ste 3900 Chicago IL 60603-3441 E-mail: jgladden@mayerbrownrowe.com.

GLADDEN, JOSEPH REAH, II, lawyer; b. Atlanta, Oct. 5, 1942; s. Joseph Rhea I and Frances (Baker) G.; m. Sarah Elizabeth (Bynum), Aug. 21, 1965; children: Joseph III, Elizabeth. BA, Emory U., 1964; LLB, U. Va., 1967. Bar: Ga., 1968; U.S. Dist. Ct. (no. dist.) Ga., 1968; U.S. Ct. Appeals (5th cir.), 1968; U.S. Ct. Appeals (11th cir.), 1985. Assoc. King and Spalding, Atlanta, 1967-73, ptnr., 1973-85; v.p., sr. staff counsel The Coca Cola Co., Atlanta, 1985-87, v.p., dep. gen. counsel, 1987-90, v.p., gen. counsel, 1990-91, sr. v.p., gen. counsel, 1991—99, exec. v.p., gen. counsel, 1999—2000; ret. Atlanta, 2001. Bd. dirs. Coca Cola Enterprises, Emory Healthcare; chmn. bd. dir. Wesley Woods Inc., Coca Cola Amatil. Chmn. bd. trustees Agnes Scott Coll.; bd. dir. Atlanta Ballet; trustee Lovett Sch.; Acad. Search Cons. Svc. Mem. ABA (com. corp. law, gen. counsel); Am. Corp. Counsel Assn.; Ga. Bar Assn.; State Bar Ga.; Assn. Gen. Counsel; Atlanta Bar Assn.; Commerce Club; Piedmont Driving Club. E-mail: sjgladden@mindspring.com.

GLADDEN, ROBERT WILEY, corporate executive; b. Barnesville, Ohio, Dec. 17, 1958; s. William R. Gladden and Clara M. (Sidebottom) Dimitro; m. Jorja Abernethy, Nov. 6, 1959; children: Teri Marie, Scott Robert, Corey William, Sara Sylvia, Bridget Kay. BS, West Liberty State Coll., 1981; MA, Bowling Green (Ohio) State U., 1983. Actuarial rsch. analyst Blue Cross of N.W. Ohio, Toledo, 1983-85; dir., actuarial svcs. Co-Med Inc., Dublin, Ohio, 1985-87; sr. v.p., rsch. and analysis McNerney Heintz, Inc., Barrington, Ill., 1987-93; exec. dir. managed care numerics Luth. Gen. Health System, Park Ridge, Ill., 1993-96; exec. Ernst & Young, LLP, Chgo., 1996-99; asst. v.p. Evanston Northwestern Healthcare, 1999—. Advancement chair, Cub Scout den leader, cubmaster, com. mem. Boy Scouts Am.; treas., dir., soccer coach Palatine Celtic Soccer; svc. unit cookie coord. Girl Scouts Am.; student fund acct. Palatine H.S. Music Dept.; team bus. mgr. N.W. Travelers Baseball; fin. chmn., treas., fin. com. chair Frst United Meth. Ch., Palatine, Ill. Avocations: shortwave radio, reading. Office: 1301 Central St Evanston IL 60201

GLADDEN, VIVIANNE CERVANTES, healthcare consultant, writer; b. Brookhaven, Miss., Oct. 8, 1927; d. Thomas James Guillory and Edna Beatrice Torry; m. Garnett Lee Gladden; children: Mark Lee, Jeanne Sue Wood. Grad., Edwin Lester Sch. Musical Theater, 1976; LittD (hon.), Union U., 1979; BA, Golden State U., 1980, PhD, DHL, Honolulu U., 1993. Ordained to ministry Cmty. Ch. of the Bay, 1985. Stage, film and TV actress, N.Y.C. and Hollywood, 1950—64; model Harry Conover, N.Y.C., 1951; mannequin Jacques Heim, Paris, 1951; featured singer La Vien Rose, N.Y.C., 1951—52, Copa City, Fla., 1951—52; nutritional cons. Ctr. Holistic Health Cedars-Sinai Hosp., L.A., 1975—77; health and lifestyle counselor Beverly Hills and Newport, Calif., 1977—; lectr., cons. health sci. and products All Natural Products, Honolulu, Japan Life Inc., Tokyo. Radio ministry KIEV, Glendale, Calif., 1985—86; mem. adv. bd. Nat. Acad. Sports Medicine, Chgo., 1993—2002. Author (with Lee Gladden): Heirs of the Gods, 1978 (Bronze Halo award So. Calif. Motion Picture Coun., 1982); author: (with Lee Gladden and Gary Couture) How to Win the Aging Game, 1979; author: Archeolinguistics, 1984. Chmn. Eco World, Hollywood, Calif., 1971; master of ceremonies Opening of Ahmanson Theatre,

L.A., 1976. Named to Hall of Fame, Oakwood Coll., Huntsville, Ala., 1956; recipient Gold award of merit, Martin Luther King Jr. Campaign Ctr., Port Arthur, Tex., 1988. Avocations: singing, piano, yoga, running.

GLADDING, NICHOLAS C. lawyer; b. Washington, 1945; BA, Yale U., 1967; JD, Vanderbilt U., 1970. Bar: Conn. 1970, U.S. Dist. Ct. Conn. 1974, U.S. Ct. Appeals (2d cir.) 1975, U.S. Supreme Ct. 1976, Mo. 1986, U.S. Dist. Ct. (ea. dist.) Mo. 1986, U.S. dist. Ct. (we. dist.) Mo. 1988. Assoc. Wiggin & Dana, New Haven, 1974-77; assoc. counsel Olin Corp., 1977-78, group counsel, 1978-82, group counsel, sr. counsel, 1982-86; ptnr. Husch & Eppenberger, St. Louis, 1986-88, Bryan Cave, St. Louis; pres. JCI Chems., Sarasota, Fla., 1999—2000. Lt. (j.g.) USN, 1970-74. Mem. ABA, Bar Assn. Met. St. Louis (chmn. environ. law com. 1990-92), Mo. Bar Assn., Conn. Bar Assn. Office: JCI Chems 808 Sarasota Quay 211 N Broadway Sarasota FL 34236

GLADE, WILLIAM PATTON, JR., economics educator; b. Wichita Falls, Tex., July 29, 1929; s. William Patton and Billie (Hatcher) G.; m. Marlene Louise Joseph, July 10, 1954; children: Anita, Genie, Patton, John. BBA, U. Tex., 1950, MA, 1951, PhD, 1955. Instr., asst. prof. econs. U. Md., 1957-60; asst., assoc. prof. U. Wis., Madison, 1960-65, prof. Sch. Bus. and dept. econs., 1996-71; prof. econs. U. Tex., Austin, 1970—, dir. Inst. L.Am. Studies, 1971-86, dir. Mex. Ctr., 1997-2001; sr. program assoc. Smithsonian Instn. Wilson Ctr., 1987-88, acting sec. L.Am. program, 1989, sr. scholar, 1990-2000; assoc. dir. USIA, 1989-92; mem. rsch. adv. coun. Ctr. for Arts and Culture, 1998—; Am. co-chair Mex.-U.S. Commn. for Ednl. and Cultural Exch./Fulbright Commn., 2002—. Author: Las empresas gubernamentales descentralizadas, 1959, The Political Economy of Mexico, 1963, The Latin American Economies, 1969, Marketing in a Developing Economy - The Case of Peru, 1970; co-editor (with Charles A. Reilly) Inquiry at the Grassroots, 1993; contbr., editor Privatization of Public Enterprises in Latin America, 1991; author, editor: Bigger Economies, Smaller Governments: The Role of Privatization in Latin America, 1996. Mem. Latin Am. Studies Assn. (v.p. 1978, pres. 1979), S.W. Coun. Latin Am. Studies Assn. (v.p. 1995, pres. 1996), Assn. for Cultural Econs., Assn. Evolutionary Econs. (bd. dirs. 1995-97), Cosmos Club. Office: U Tex Dept Econs Austin TX 78712

GLADECK, SUSAN ODELL, retired social worker; b. Honesdale, Pa., Apr. 28; d. Lester Albert and Esther Grace (Fleming) Odell; children: Amy Frances, Esther Lena. BA with honors, Cedar Crest Coll., 1960; M. Social Svc., Bryn Mawr Coll., 1962. Lic. clin. social worker, Va.; cert. piano tchr. Social worker Family Svc. of Phila. and Family Svc. of Del. County, Media, Pa., 1962-63, Lehigh U. Child Devel. Ctr., Bethlehem, Pa., 1966, South Terr. Area Neighborhood Ctr., Bethlehem, Pa., 1969-71, Lehigh County Children's Bur., Allentown, Pa., 1971-73; social worker II Fairfax (Va.) County Dept. Human Devel., 1987-90; sr. social worker adult svcs. Loudoun County Dept. Social Svcs., Leesburg, Va., 1990-94; pvt. practice McLean, 1994—2002; ret., 2002; pvt. piano, organ and voice tchr. Organist, choir dir. Chesterbrook Presbyn. Ch., Falls Church, Va., 1995—2001. Mem. NASW, Acad. Cert. Social Workers, Am. Coll. Musicians, Music Tchrs. Nat. Assn., Nat. Fedn. Music Tchrs., Va. Fedn. Music Tchrs., No. Va. Music Tchrs. Assn. Avocation: animal humane work. Home and Office: 6516 Fairlawn Dr Mc Lean VA 22101-5235

GLADFELTER, WILBERT EUGENE, physiology educator; b. York, Pa., Apr. 29, 1928; s. Paul John and Marea Bernadette (Miller) G.; m. Ruth Isabelle Ballantyne, Jan. 26, 1952; children: James W., Charles D., Mary A. AB magna cum laude, Gettysburg (Pa.) Coll., 1952; PhD, U. Pa., 1960. NSF fellow U. Pa., Phila., 1956-58, NIH fellow, 1958-59, asst. instr., 1954-56; instr. physiology W.Va. U., Morgantown, 1959-61, asst. prof., 1961-69, assoc. prof., 1969-96, prof. emeritus, 1996—. Contbr. articles to profl. jours. Treas., Monongalia County chpt. W. Va. Heart Assn., 1976-95. With USN, 1946-48. NSF fellow, 1956-58. Mem. Am. Physiol. Soc., Soc. Neurosci., Soc. for Integrative and Comparative Biology, Sigma Xi, Phi Beta Kappa, Beta Beta Beta. Lutheran. Home: 70 Pine Tree Ln Morgantown WV 26508-2929 Office: WVa U Health Sci Ctr Dept Physiology Morgantown WV 26506

GLADNER, MARC STEFAN, lawyer; b. Seattle, July 18, 1952; s. Jules A. and Mildred W. (Weller) G.; m. Susanne Tso (div. Feb. 1981); m. Michele Marie Hardin, Sept. 12, 1981; 1 child, Sara Megan. Student, U. Colo., 1970-73; JD, Southwestern U., 1976. Bar: Ariz. 1976, Navajo Tribal Ct. 1978. Law clk. jud. br. Navajo Nation, Window Rock, Ariz., 1976-77, gen. counsel jud. br., 1977-79; pvt. practice law Phoenix, 1979-83; ptnr. Seplow, Rivkind & Gladner, Phoenix, 1983-86, Crosby & Gladner, P.C., Phoenix, 1986—. Adj. instr. Coll. Ganado, Ariz., 1978-79. Democrat. Jewish. Avocation: stamp collecting. Office: Crosby & Gladner PC 1726 E Thomas Rd Phoenix AZ 85016-7604 E-mail: msgladner@candglaw.com.

GLADSTONE, ARTHUR M. artist, author; b. N.Y.C., Sept. 22, 1921; m. Margaret SeBastian, July 14, 1948 (dec. Mar. 1972); m. Helen Worth, Feb. 3, 1980 (dec. Aug. 2002). BA cum laude, NYU, 1942, MS in Chemistry, 1947. Cert. propulsion engr., U.S. Civil Svc. Rsch. chemist Am. Cyanamid, Bridgeville, Pa., 1947-48; rsch. supr. Pitts. Coke and Chem., 1978-53; product mgr. Nopco Chem., Harrison, N.J., 1953-59; v.p. Anchor Serum, St. Joseph, Mo., 1959-61; engr. advanced propulsion Hercules Powder, Rocket City, W.Va., 1961-68. Author (under pseudonym Margaret SeBastian): (novels) Miss Letty, My Lord, Rakehell, The Courtship of Colonel Crown, The Fortunate Belle, A Lesson in Love, Dilemma in Duet, A Keeper for Lord Linford; author: (as Maggie Gladstone) The Love Tangle, The Reluctant Debutante, The Impudent Widow, A Lesson in Love, others; author: (as Cilla Whitmore) His Lordship's Landlady. 1st lt. USAF, 1944—46, maj. USAF, ret. Decorated Meritorious Svc. medal USAF. Mem. Authors Guild, Va. Soc. Photographic Arts. Avocations: theatre organ, 19th century literature, cooking, cosmology. Home: 1701 Owensville Rd Charlottesville VA 22901 E-mail: gladstone@cville.net.

GLADSTONE, CAROL LYNN, education educator; b. N.Y.C., Aug. 14, 1944; d. Albert Ludwig and Jeanne Adler; m. Edward Gladstone, Nov. 20, 1973. BA, Hunter Coll., 1965; MA, CCNY, N.Y.C., 1967; PhD, Columbia Pacific U., 1988, postgrad., 1993-94. Cert. tchr. English, French, sch. dist. adminstr., Ariz., Conn., N.J., N.Y. English/reading tchr. Jr. High Sch. #120, N.Y.C., 1965-66; reading coord. Dewitt Clinton High Sch., Bronx, 1966-74; asst. chair John F. Kennedy High Sch., Bronx, 1974-85; asst. prin. James Monroe High Sch., Bronx, 1985-97, Morris High Sch., 1997-98, Flags H.S., 1998-99. Prin. PM/Saturday Sch. James Monroe H.S., 1993-94; trainer of adminstrv. staff Bronx. Supt.'s Office, 1992-2002, Manhattan Supt.'s Office, 1989-90; adj. prof. Coll. of New Rochelle, N.Y., 1988-89, Lehman Coll., Bronx, 1987-88, Manhattanville Coll., 1999-2002; grad. edn. advisor Mercy Coll., 2003—. Contbr. articles to profl. jours.; author: Competence in Cloze, 1989; author series of books: Gladstone Comprehensive Writing Program, 1986-88; study guides Broadway shows, 1999-2001, EverStar Classics and Related Readings, 2001—, Brooklyn Academy of Music's Screening Guides, 2001. Sec. Westchester (N.Y.) Alzheimer's Disease Assn., 1980-87; reporter Pub. Access Cable TV, Westchester, 1982-83. Named Supr. of Yr. Bronx Supt.'s Office, 1990-91, 94-95, Educator of Yr. Assn. Tchrs. N.Y., 1987-88, 90-91, Educator as Writer Mayor of City of N.Y., 1986; N.Y. Inst. for Humanities fellow, 1994. Mem. ASCD (assoc.), N.Y. State English Coun. (Educator of Excellence 1992-93, 95-96, regional dir. 1994-98, v.p. supervision 1998), N.Y. State Reading Assn., Bronx Assn. Prins. of English (chmn. 1990-98), N.Y.C. Assn. Asst. Prins. (exec. bd. 1995-98), Nat. Bd. for Profl. Teaching Standards, Nat. Coun. Tchrs. English (chancellor's com. new stds. 1997, ESL/ELA new stds., 1997, dist. literacy com., 1997). Avocations: travel, reading, gourmet cooking, computer technology.

GLADSTONE, GEORGE RANDALL, planetary scientist; b. North Vancouver, B.C., Can., May 20, 1956; s. George Wilfrid and Alma (Johnson) G.; m. Aileen LeProtti Corelli, Oct. 2, 1987; children: Eleanor Ann, Elizabeth Anne. BS, U. B.C., Vancouver, 1978; MS, Calif. Inst. Tech., 1980, PhD, 1983. Project scientist Ctr. for Rsch. in Earth and Space Sci., York U., North York, Can., 1982-84; rsch. assoc. Lab. for Atmospheric and Space Physics, U. Colo., Boulder, 1984-87; asst. rsch. physicist Space Scis. Lab., U. Calif., Berkeley, 1987-93; sr. rsch. scientist, then inst. scientist S.W. Rsch. Inst., San Antonio, 1993—. Contbr. rsch. articles to sci. jours. Mem. Am. Geophys. Union (assoc. editor Geophys. Rsch. Letters jour. 1994-97), Am. Astron. Soc. (divsn. planetary scis.). Home: 347 Brees Blvd San Antonio TX 78209-4825 Office: Southwest Rsch Inst Dept Space Sciences 6220 Culebra Rd San Antonio TX 78238-5100 E-mail: rgladstone@swri.edu.

GLADSTONE, HERBERT JACK, manufacturing company executive; b. N.Y.C., May 12, 1924; s. Joseph D. and Ella (Shabman) G.; m. Sylvia Rosenberg, Dec. 28, 1946; children: Alan, Linda, Karen. Student, Hamilton Coll., 1944, Harvard U., 1945; BBA, CCNY, 1947. Mem. staff Gershon & Strell, CPAs, N.Y.C., 1947-51; budget dir. F.M.C., N.Y.C., 1951-55; v.p., treas. Condec Corp., Old Greenwich, Conn., 1955-85; treas., chief fin. officer Cober, 1985-92; ret., 1992. Prof. acctg. Sacred Heart U.; lectr. MBA program U. Conn.; bd. dirs. Consol. Controls Corp., Hammond Valve Corp. Pres. PTA, 1956-57; asst. scoutmaster Toquam coun. Boy Scouts Am., 1960-63. Served with USAAF, 1943-46. Mem. AICPA, Fin. Execs. Inst. (dir.), N.Y. State Soc. CPAs. Clubs: Roxbury Country (dir.), Roxbury Tennis and Swim (trustee). Home: 284 W Hill Rd Stamford CT 06902-1713 E-mail: shglad284@aol.com.

GLADSTONE, ROBERT ALBERT, lawyer; b. Phila., June 2, 1942; s. Albert Frederick and Elizabeth (O'Neill) G.; m. Barbara M. Cranmer, June 21, 1964; children: Frederick Robert, Elizabeth Rose. BA, Ursinus Coll., Collegeville, Pa., 1964; JD, Rutgers U., Newark, 1968. Bar: N.J. 1968, U.S. Dist. Ct. N.J. 1968, U.S. Ct. Claims 1992. Assoc. Pellettieri & Rabstein, Trenton, N.J., 1968-71; ptnr. Brener & Gladstone, Trenton, 1971-74, Warren Goldberg & Berman, Princeton, N.J., 1975-82, Schaff, Motiuk, Gladstone & Reed, Flemington, N.J., 1982-90; city atty. City of Trenton, 1971-75; ptnr., shareholder Shanley & Fisher, P.C., Morristown, N.J., 1990-99, Drinker, Biddle & Shanley (merger Drinker, Biddle & Reath), Florham Park, N.J., 1999—. Twp. atty. Twp. of Lawrence, Lawrenceville, N.J., 1985-88; mem. com. on tax ct. N.J. Supreme Ct., 1982-86; chmn. D'Imperio Property Superfund Site Group, Hamilton Twp., N.J., 1994—; chmn. Lightman Yard Superfund Site Group, Winslow Twp., N.J., 2000—. Contbr. articles to law jours. Chmn. Mercer County Rep. Com., Trenton, 1977-80; chmn. bd. trustees Coll. of N.J., Ewing, 1977-2000; mem. devel. bd. Prevention Edn., Lawrenceville, 1992—, Greater Trenton Cmty. Mental Health Ctr., 1994—. Mem. ABA, N.J. Bar Assn. (chmn. local govt. law sect. 1981-84), Trial Attys. N.J. Avocations: golf, outdoor activities. Home: 297 Millstone River Rd Belle Mead NJ 08502-5607 Office: River House 297 River Rd Belle Mead NJ 08502 E-mail: gladlaw1@msn.com.

GLADSTONE, WILLIAM LOUIS, accountant; b. Bklyn., May 23, 1931; s. Archie C. and Bernice T. (Turk) G.; m. Mildred G. Rosenberg, June 21, 1953; children: Susan, Douglas. BS, Lehigh U., 1951; LLB, Bklyn. Law Sch., 1955; grad., Harvard U. Advanced Mgmt. Program, 1970; LLD (hon.), Lehigh U., 1992. CPA, N.Y. Staff acct. Arthur Young & Co., N.Y.C., from 1951, ptnr., 1963, mng. ptnr., 1981-88, chmn., 1985-89; co-chief exec. Ernst & Young, N.Y.C., 1989-91; pres. Tri-City ValleyCats, Inc. Baseball Club, 1992—. Lectr. acctg. Columbia U., N.Y.C., 1962-64; ptnr. N.Y.C. Partnership, 1989-91; bd. dirs. Nat. Baseball Hall of Fame and Mus., Inc. Contbr. articles to profl. jours. Mem. Corp. Congress N.Y. Pub. Libr., 1987-91, mem. conf. bd., 1987-93, trustee com. for econ. devel., 1988-94; bd. dirs. N.Y.-Pa. Baseball League, 1992—; trustee Nat. Asn. Profl. Baseball Leagues, 2000--. Lt. USAF, 1952-53. Mem. AICPA, N.Y. State Soc. CPAs, Lehigh Alumni Assn. (award 1976), Bklyn. Law Sch. Alumni Assn., Fin. Acctg. Found. (trustee 1988-91). Home: 30 Clubhouse Ln Scarsdale NY 10583-3146 Office: 5 Times Sq Ste 35014 New York NY 10036

GLADSTONE, WILLIAM SHELDON, JR., radiologist; b. Des Moines, Dec. 19, 1923; s. William Sheldon and Wanda (Rees) G.; m. Ruth Alice Jensen, June 19, 1944; children— Denise Ann, William Sheldon, Stephen Rees BA, State U. Iowa, 1954, MD, 1947. Diplomate Am. Bd. Radiology. Intern Hurley Hosp., Flint, Mich., 1947-48; gen. practice medicine Iowa Falls, Iowa, 1948-49; asst. dept. pathology State U. Iowa Coll. Medicine, Iowa City, 1949-50; resident in radiology Univ. Hosp., Iowa City, 1950-51, 53-54; practice medicine specializing in radiology Kalamazoo, 1954—84. Exec. v.p. Kalamazoo Radiology; clin. asst. prof. radiology Mich. State U. Coll. Human Medicine; chief radiology Bronson Meth. Hosp., Kalamazoo, 1973-75, 77-79 Bd. dirs. Kalamazoo County Tb Soc., 1955-59, Mich. Children's Aid, 1960-62, Am. Cancer Soc., Kalamazoo, 1964-66. Served with AUS, 1943-46; served to capt. USAF, 1951-53 Fellow Am. Coll. Radiology; mem. Kalamazoo Acad. Medicine, AMA, Mich. Radiologic Soc. (pres. W. Mich. sect. 1976), Mich. State Med. Soc., SW Mich. Surg. Soc., Am. Roentgen Ray Soc., Phi Beta Kappa (pres. SW Mich. chpt. 1963) Clubs: Kalamazoo Country. Lodges: Masons, Shriners. Republican. Episcopalian. Home: 1029 Essex Cir Kalamazoo MI 49008-2349 Office: 524 S Park St Kalamazoo MI 49007-5118

GLADWELL, GRAHAM MAURICE LESLIE, mathematician, civil engineering educator; b. Otford, Kent, Eng., Feb. 21, 1934; emigrated to Can., 1969; s. Basil Maurice Edwin and Doris Alexandra (New) G.; m. Joyce Eugenie Nation, Mar. 29, 1958; children: Graham Hugh, Geoffrey Norman, Malcolm Timothy. B.Sc., U. London, 1954, PhD, 1957, D.Sc., 1969. Lectr. U. London, 1956-60, U. West Indies, Jamaica, 1960-62; sr. lectr. U. Southampton, Eng., 1962-69; prof. dept. civil engring. U. Waterloo, Ontario, Canada, 1969-99, prof. dept. applied math., 1979-99, Disting. prof. emeritus, 2001—. Author: Matrix Analysis of Vibration, 1965, Contact Problems in the Classical Theory of Elasticity, 1980, Inverse Problems in Vibration, 1986, Inverse Problems in Scattering, 1993, Functional Analysis: Applications to Mechanics and Inverse Problems, 1996; editor: Computer Aided Engineering, 1971, Contact Mechanics and Wear of Rail/Wheel Systems, 1983; series editor Solid mechanics and its Applications, 1989—. Fellow Am. Acad. Mechanics (dir. 1979-82), Inst. Math. and Its Applications, Royal Soc. Arts, Royal Soc. Can. Presbyterian. Office: Dept Civil Engring Univ Waterloo Waterloo ON Canada N2L 3G1

GLAESSMANN, DORIS ANN, former county official, consultant; b. Northampton, Pa., Feb. 18, 1940; d. Frank G. and Theresa (Fischl) Zwikl; m. Edward Glaessmann, Sept. 1, 1962; children: Edward Jr., Robert F. Grad. high sch., Northampton, 1958. Sec., bookkkeeper John F. Moore Agy., Inc., Allentown, Pa., 1958-64; ct. clk. Criminal div. Clk. of Cts. Office, Allentown, 1968-69, asst. dep. clk., 1969-76, chief dep. clk., 1976-82; clk. of cts., criminal and civil divsns. Lehigh County, Allentown, 1982-95; cons., 1995-2000; ret., 2001. Den mother, sec. Cub Scout Pack 140, Allentown, Pa., 1973-78; mem., past bd. dirs.; mem. coun. St. Peter's Evang. Luth. Ch., Allentown, 1984-89. Mem. Pa. Prothonotaries and Clks. Assn. (past pres., treas. 1993—), Pa. Elected Women's Assn. (past. sec.-treas. and pres. Lehigh Valley chpt.), Quota Internat. of Allentown (pres. 1997-99). Democrat. Avocations: baking, reading, crocheting, walking. Home: 945 E Lynnwood St Allentown PA 18103-5250

GLAGOV, SEYMOUR, physician, educator, research scientist; b. N.Y.C., Aug. 8, 1925; s. Benjamin and Gussie (Sternberg) G.; m. Sylvia Held, May 18, 1946; 1 child, Hersh Monroe. BA in Physics, Bklyn. Coll., 1946; MD, U. Geneva, Switzerland, 1953. Diplomate: Am. Bd. Pathology. Intern Kings County Hosp., Bklyn., 1953-54; resident Beth-El Hosp., Bklyn., 1954-56; jr. pathologist Cook County Hosp., Chgo., 1956-57; resident Pathology U. Chgo. Clinics, 1957-58, mem. faculty, 1957—, prof. pathology, 1970—; mem. staff and faculty U. Chgo. Hosps. and Clinics Pritzker Sch. Medicine and the Coll., U. Chgo., also dir. autopsy service, coordinator undergrad. pathology teaching; practice medicine, specializing in pathology, 1956—95; ret., 1997; research fellow Am. Heart Assn., 1959-61, advanced research fellow, 1961-62, established investigator, 1962-67; vis. research assoc. Nuffield Inst. Med. Research, Oxford (Eng.) U., 1963-64; mem. cardiovascular study sect., research grant div. Nat. Heart and Lung Inst., 1970-74, 85-88; mem. research grant com. Am. Heart Assn., 1977-80. Assoc. editor translation supplement Fedn. Am. Socs. Exptl. Biology, 1962-66 Past assoc. editor: (Cardiovascular Disease) of Human Pathology, Am. Jour. Cardiovascular Pathology, Cardiovascular Research. Served with AUS, 1946-47. NIH grantee, 1960— Mem. AAAS, Am. Assn. Pathologists, Chgo. Pathol. Soc. (pres. 1976-77), Biophys. Soc., Am. Soc. CV Pathologists, Am. Assn. Study Liver Disease, Am. Heart Assn. (council on arteriosclerosis, chmn. com. on lesions and myocardial infarctions 1983-87), Sigma Xi, Alpha Omega Alpha. Home: 5233 S University Ave Chicago IL 60615-4405

GLAISTER, JUDY ALANE, nursing educator; b. mexico, Mo., Feb. 11, 1943; d. Herbert Lee Jeans, Dorothy Delphine Jeans-Halsey; m. Rufus Richard Orange, Feb. 7, 2000; children: Jesse Martin, Jamie Martin. AA, Stephens Coll., 1963; BSN, U. Mo., 1966; MSN, U.Mo., 1981; PhD, U.Tex., 2000. Cert. Clinical Specialist in Adult Psychiatric and Ment. ANA, 1986, Expert in Traumatic Stress, Diplomate, 2001. Staff nurse Ellis Fischel State Cancer Hosp., Columbia, Mo., 1966; instr. Mt. Sinai Hosp. Sch. Nursing, Cleve., 1966—69; clin. instr. Cuyahoga C.C., Cleve., 1975—76; staff nurse Staff Builders, Cleve., 1976; asst. instr. nursing U. Mo. Sch. Nursing, Columbia, 1979; mem. staff U. Mo. Health Sci. Ctr., Columbia, 1979—80; tchg. asst. U. Mo. Sch. Nursing, Coumbia, 1979—80, rsch. asst., 1980—81; graduate nurse III Mid-Missouri Mental Health Ctr., Coumbia, 1982; psychiatric nurse practitioner Fulton State Hosp., Fulton, Mo., 1982—83; substance abuse counselor & program nurse Fairbanks Substance Abuse Ctr., Fairbanks, 1983—84; counselot III Regional Ctr. for Alcohol and other Addictions, Fairbanks, 1984—85; pvt. practice Killeenn, Tex., 1985—98; assoc. prof. U. Tex. Med. Branch Sch. Nursing, Galveston, Tex., 1998—. Adv. bd. Women's Resource & Crisis Ctr. of Galveston County, Galveston, Tex., 2000—. Contbr. articles to profl. jours. Mem. bd. health Bell County, Killeen, Tex., 1989—92; bd. dir. Families in Crisis, Killeen, Tex., 1990—96. Recipient Counseling Vol. of Yr. award, Families in Crisis, 1988, Family Violence Counselor of Yr. award, 1990, Research award, Alpha Delta Chapter, Sigma Theta Tau International, 1999, Unsung Heroines of the Battered Women's Movement award, Tex. Coun. on Family Violence, 2001. Mem.: ANA (bd. dir. Tex. chpt. 1992—94), Tex. Coun.Family Violence, So.Nursing Rsch. Soc., Nursing Network on Violence Against Women Internat., The Am. Acad. Experts in Traumatic Stress, The National League of Nurses, Am. Psychiatric Nurses Assn., Crisis Support Team, Alpha Delta Chapter of Sigma Theta Tau International (pres.-elect 2001—). Office: The University of Texas Medical Branch 301 University Boulevard Galveston TX 77555 Home Fax: ; Office Fax: 409-747-0325. Personal E-mail: . Business E-mail: juglaist@utmb.edu.

GLANCY, ALFRED ROBINSON, III, retired public utility company executive; b. Detroit, Mar. 14, 1938; s. Alfred Robinson and Elizabeth A. (Tant) G.; m. Ruth Mary Roby, Sept. 15, 1962; children: Joan C., Alfred R. IV, Douglas Roby, Andrew Roby. BA, Princeton U., 1960; MA, Harvard U., 1962. V.p. corp. planning Am. Nat. Gas Svc., Detroit, 1976-79; econ. and fin. planning staff Mich. Consol. Gas Co., Detroit, 1962-64, supr. econ. studies and rates, 1965-67, mgr. econ. and fin. planning dept., 1967-68, treas., 1969-72, v.p., treas., 1972-73, v.p. customer and mktg. svcs., 1976-79, v.p. mktg./dist. ops., 1979-81, sr. v.p. mktg./customer svcs., 1981-83, sr. v.p. utility ops., 1983-84, chmn., CEO, 1984-92, MCN Energy Group Inc., Detroit, 1989-2001; ret., 2001. Bd. dirs., exec. com. UNICO Properties, Inc., Seattle. Past chmn. Detroit Symphony Orch., Detroit Renaissance Inc., exec. com.; past chmn. Detroit Med. Ctr., New Detroit, Inc. Mem. Princeton Club Mich., Country Club Detroit, Detroit Athletic Club. Republican. Office: Ste 405 400 Maple Park Blvd Saint Clair Shores MI 48081

GLANCY, HELEN DIANE, literature educator; b. Kansas City, Mo., Mar. 18, 1941; d. Lewis and Edith (Wood) Hall; m. Dwane Glancy, May 2, 1964 (div. Mar. 1983); children: David, Jennifer. MFA, U. Iowa. Prof. English Macalester Coll., St. Paul. Author: (novels) The Only Piece of Furniture in the House, 1996, Pushing the Bear, 1996, Flutie, 1998, Closets of Heaven, 1999, The Man Who Heard the Land, 2001, The Mask Maker, 2002, Designs of the Night Sky, 2002, Stone Heart: A Novel of Sacajawea, 2003; contbr. short stories and essays to publs.; author: numerous poems. Named Edlestein-Keller Minn. Writer of Distinction, U. Minn., 1998; recipient Native Am. Prose award, 1991, Am. Book award, 1993, Prose-Playwriting award, Wordcraft Cir. Native Writers, 1997, Loft award of distinction, McKnight Fellowship, 1999, Cherokee medal of honor, Cherokee Honor Soc., 2001, Disting. Alumna award, U. Mo., 2003, NEA, 2003, Juniper Prize, U. of Mass. Press, 2003; fellow Many Voices, Playwrights Ctr., Mpls., 2001, Native Am. Screenwriter's fellow, UCLA, Sundance Inst., 1998. Office: Macalester Coll 1600 Grand Saint Paul MN 55105 Office Fax: 651-696-6430. E-mail: glancy@macalester.edu.

GLANCY, WALTER JOHN, lawyer; b. L.A., Mar. 8, 1942; s. Walter Perry and Elva Thomasin (Douglass) Glancy; m. Jane Whetstone Schroeder, 1995; children from previous marriage: Jill Marie, Gregory Owens. AB, Princeton U., 1964; BA, Oxford U., Eng., 1966; LLB, Yale U., 1969. Bar: Tex. 1971. Law clk. to assoc. justice Byron R. White U.S. Supreme Ct., 1969-70; staff asst. Nat. Security Council, 1970-71; staff asst. to Peter M. Flanigan, The White House, 1971; assoc. then ptnr. Jackson, Walker, Winstead, Cantwell & Miller, Dallas, 1972-76; ptnr. Hughes & Luce and predecessor, Dallas, 1976-85, Baker & Botts, Dallas, 1985-88, Hughes & Luce, Dallas, 1988-90; pvt. practice Dallas, 1991-95, 97-99; cons. Meyer, Hendricks, Victor, Osborn & Maledon, Phoenix, 1991-95; ptnr. Weil, Gotshal & Manges LLP, Dallas, 1995-96. Sr. v.p., gen. counsel, dir. Holly Corp., 1999—; adj. lectr. corp. taxation So. Meth. U. Sch. Law, 1988. Note and comment editor Yale Law Jour., 1968-69. Bd. mgmt. Dallas YMCA Urban Svcs., 1975—84; bd. dirs. Dallas Family Guidance Ctr., 1982—96, pres. bd. dirs., 1985—86; bd. dirs. Child & Family Guidance Ctrs., Dallas, 1996—2003, pres. bd. dirs., 2001—02; bd. dirs. Dallas Opera, 1984—88, 1996—97; bd. trustees Hockaday Sch., Dallas, 1989—95; mem. adminstrv. bd. Lovers Ln. United Meth. Ch., Dallas, 1984—86, 1988—89; deacon Park Cities Bapt. Ch., Dallas, 1996—. Nat. Merit scholar, 1960-64, Marshall scholar, 1964-66. Mem.: ABA, State Bar Tex. (profl. ethics com. 1982—, chmn. tax sect. 1985—86, chmn. profl. ethics com. 1999—), Am. Law Inst., Dallas Bar Assn. (chmn. legal ethics com. 1980—81), Order of Coif, Park Cities Rotary Club (pres. 2003—), Phi Beta Kappa. Republican. Home: 9162 Clearlake Dr Dallas TX 75225-2001 Office: 100 Crescent Ct Ste 1600 Dallas TX 75201-6915

GLANCZ, RONALD ROBERT, lawyer; b. Bay City, Mich., Jan. 29, 1943; s. Alexander and Ella (Josehart) Glancz; m. Margie Joan Pensler, Dec. 28, 1969. BA in Pre-Legal Studies, U. Mich., 1964, JD cum laude, 1968. Bar: Mich. 1968, U.S. Ct. of Appeals (D.C. cir.) 1969, U.S. Supreme Ct. 1972, D.C. 1974. Atty. civil divsn. Appellate Sec. U.S. Dept. Justice, Washington, 1968-75, asst. dir. civil divsn., 1975-79; dir. litigation divsn. Office of the Comptr. of the Currency, Washington, 1979-84; asst. gen. counsel Fed. Deposit Ins. Corp., Washington, 1984-88; ptnr. Venable Baetjer Howard & Civiletti, LLP, Washington, 1991—. Contbr. Mem.: ABA (vice chair banking law com.), Jewish Found. for Group Homes (pres. 2001—02, past pres.), The Exchequer Club Washington, Order of Coif. Office: Venable Baetjer Howard & Civiletti LLP 1201 New York Ave NW Ste 1000 Washington DC 20005-6197

GLANSTEIN, JOEL CHARLES, lawyer; b. Jersey City, May 16, 1940; s. Harry I. and Katherine G.; m. Eleanor Elovich, July 2, 1966; children: David Michael, Stacey Alison. BA with honors, Lehigh U., 1962; LLB, NYU, 1965, LLM in Labor Law, 1969. Bar: N.Y. 1967, D.C. 1975, U.S. Ct. Appeals (2d cir.) 1970, U.S. Supreme Ct. 1971, U.S. Ct. Appeals (1st cir.) 1972, U.S. Ct. Appeals (3d cir.) 1978, U.S. Ct. Appeals (11th and 9th cirs.) 1981, U.S. Ct. Appeals (5th cir.) 1982, U.S. Ct. Appeals (6th cir.) 1984, U.S. Ct. Appeals (7th cir.) 1999. Assoc. Pressman & Scribner, N.Y.C., 1968-69; ptnr. Scribner, Glanstein & Klein, N.Y.C., 1970-72, Markowitz & Glanstein, N.Y.C., 1972-79, O'Donnell & Schwartz, N.Y.C., 1980-90, O'Donnell, Schwartz, Glanstein & Rosen, N.Y.C., 1991-99, O'Donnell, Schwartz, Glanstein, Rosen et al, LLP, N.Y.C., 1999-2001, O'Donnell, Schwartz & Glanstein, N.Y.C., 2001, O'Donnell, Schwartz, Glanstein & Lilly, LLP, N.Y.C., 2002—. Adj. assoc. prof. N.Y. Law Sch., N.Y.C., 1980-95. Fellow Coll. of Labor and Employment Lawyers, Inc.; mem. ABA (labor and employment law sect., com. on internat. labor law 1976, com. on law of alternative dispute resolution 1976), N.Y. State Bar Assn. (labor and employment law sect., chmn. 1987-88), N.Y. County Lawyers Assn., D.C. Bar Assn., Maritime Law Assn. U.S., Cornell Club (N.Y.C.). Office: O'Donnell Schwartz Glanstein & Lilly LLP 305 Madison Ave Rm 1022 New York NY 10165-0100

GLANVILLE, ROBERT EDWARD, lawyer; b. Binghamton, N.Y., Aug. 1, 1950; s. Robert S. and Betty J. (Garlick) G.; m. Susan Anne Kime, Sept. 3, 1970. BA magna cum laude, SUNY, Binghamton, 1972; JD magna cum laude, Cornell U., 1976. Bar: N.Y. 1977, U.S. Dist. Ct. (we. dist.) N.Y. 1978, U.S. Supreme Ct. 1981, U.S. Ct. Appeals (2d cir.) 1985, U.S. Ct. Appeals (D.C. cir.) 1991. Law clk. Appellate Divsn., 4th Dept., Rochester, 1976-78; from assoc. to ptnr. Phillips, Lytle, Hitchcock, et. al., Buffalo, N.Y., 1978-85, 88—; ptnr. Prahl & Glanville, Buffalo, 1986-88. Mem. ABA, N.Y. State Bar Assn., Erie County Bar Assn., Am. Gas Assn. Avocations: whitewater kayaking, sailing, mountaineering, flying. Home: 9385 S Hill Rd Boston NY 14025-9667 Office: Phillips Lytle Hitchcock 3400 HSBC Ctr Buffalo NY 14203-2887

GLANZER, MONA N. lawyer, arbitrator; b. N.Y.C., July 29, 1931; d. David and Henrietta (Schweitzer) Sorcher; m. Murray A. Glanzer, Sept. 20, 1953; children: Michael John, Marla Curtis, James S. LLB, Bklyn. Law Sch., 1953. Bar: N.Y. 1954, U.S. Dist. Ct. (so. and ea. dists.) N.Y. 1965, U.S. Supreme Ct. 1976, U.S. Ct. Appeals (2d cir.) 1981. Editor CCH Pension Plan Guide, Chgo., 1953—54; assoc. Harry H. Rains, Rains, Pogrebin & Scher, Mineola, NY, 1965—71; ptnr. Rains & Pogrebin, P.C., Mineola, 1971—2000. Arbitrator AAA Pension and Employee Benefits U.S. Dist. Ct., NY, 1985—, Nassau County Bar Employment Rels. Bd., mem. law panel; arbitrator CSEA Discipline Panel. Contbr. articles to profl. jours. Mem. adv. com. Recodification N.Y. State Workers' Compensation Law Project, 1985-87; bd. dirs. Suffolk County Coalition Against Domestic Violence, Project Literacy/Outreach Inc. Recipient Presdl. Pvt. Sector Initiative Commendation citation, Profl. Achievement award Nassau County Bar Assn. Fellow ABA Found.; mem. Am. Arbitration Assn. (panel 1987—, arbitrator), Coun. Lic. Physiotherapists N.Y. (hon.), N.Y. State Assn. Profl. Land Surveyors (hon.), N.Y. State Bar Assn. (chair labor and employment law sect. 1988-89, chair com. pension, welfare and related plans 1983-86, chair com. labor standards legis. 1986-87), Nassau-Suffolk Women's Bar Assn. (pres. 1986-87). E-mail: monanglanzer@aol.com.

GLASBERG, H(ERBERT) MARK, psychiatrist, educator; b. N.Y.C., Oct. 11, 1939; s. Joesph and Elsa (Haber) G.; m. Paula Drillman, June 19, 1960; children: Scot Bradley, Hilary Jennifer. BA, Yeshiva U., 1953; MS, Columbia U., 1954; MD, SUNY, 1958. Diplomate Am. Bd. Psychiatry and Neurology. Intern Maimonides Hosp., N.Y.C., 1958-59; resident in psychiatry Kings County Hosp., N.Y.C., 1959-60; resident in internal medicine Kingbridge VA Hosp. of Columbia U. Coll. Med. Program, N.Y.C., 1960-61; resident Payne Whitney Psychiat. Clin., N.Y. Hosp., 1963-65; psychiatrist pvt. practice, N.Y.C., 1968—; attending physician dept. psychiatry Columbia U. Coll. Physicians & Surgeons; instr. Cornell U. Med. Sch., 1966-68; assoc. prof. psychiatry Mt. Sinai Sch. Medicine, 1968-80; dir. psychiat. outpatient svcs. Beth Israel Hosp., N.Y.C., 1968-74, assoc. attending physician, 1968-74, chief psychiat. emergency & cons. svcs., 1974-75; attending psychiatrist & clin. prof. psychiatry Coll. Physicians & Surgeons, Columbia U., 1986—; neurosurgery Coll. Physicians & Surgeons, Columbua U., 1982, clin. prof. neurosurgery, 1995; clin. prof. neurosurgery, attending neurosurgeon Columbia Presbyn Hosp., 1995. Examiner Am. Bd. Psychiatry & Neurology, 1988—; cons. mem. panel of ind. psychiatrists N.Y.C. Mental Health Info. Svc., 1968—. Mem. Manhattan physicians com. United Jewish Appeal, 1970—; mem. com. admission sel. Cornell U. Med. Coll., Ctr. Alumni Assn. N.Y. Hosp. Col. M.C. AUS, 1961-63. Fellow N.Y. Hosp., 1965-66, spl. rsch. fellow Nat. Inst. Mental Health, 1966-68, Cornell U. Med. Sch. Fellow ACP, Am. Soc. Neurosurgeons, Am. Psychiat. Assn. (internat. platform com. 1980—); mem. APA, AAAS, Am. Psychosomatic Soc., N.Y. Acad. Scis., N.Y. Acad. Medicine, Soc. Adolescent Psychiatry, Internat. Platform Assn. Office: 14 E 73rd St New York NY 10021-4128

GLASBERG, LAURENCE BRIAN, private investor, business executive; b. N.Y.C., Apr. 28, 1943; s. William and Tillie (Liebowitz) G.; m. Lana Lucille Pollack, Aug. 10, 1963; children: Jeffrey Scott, Glenn David. BBA, CUNY, 1964, MBA, 1968. Mgr. bus. affairs Sta. WCBS-TV, N.Y.C., 1970-72, dir. planning and adminstrn., 1972-74; gen. auditor Ea. ops. CBS Inc., N.Y.C., 1975-76; v.p. fin. and adminstrn. CBS Publs., 1976-82, v.p., gen. auditor, 1982-88; sr. v.p. fin. and adminstrn. N.Am. ops. AEG Corp., 1988 89; pres. Nat. Mgmt. Resources Group Inc., 1990—. Mng. dir. Future Resource Sys., Inc., 1994-96, exec. v.p. Future Bus. Ctr., Inc., 1995-96; sr. v.p., CFO MacDonald Comms. Corp., 1996-98, bus. and fin. mgr. Mus. Mags., 1998-2000; co-chmn. Media Resources Group, LLC, 2001-02. Mem. fin. and tax com. Princeton Twp., N.J., 1991, elected committeeman, 1992, elected mayor, 1993; bd. dirs. AMAS Mus. Theatre, Inc., 1998-99. 1st lt. inf. U.S. Army, 1964-65. Mem. Fin. Execs. Inst. (nat. com. on govt. liaison, local bd. dirs. 1987-88, chpt. sec. 1989-92), Econ. Club (N.Y.C.). Avocations: physical fitness, outdoor and environmental activities, reading.

GLASBERG, SCOT BRADLEY, plastic surgeon; b. N.Y.C., June 30, 1964; s. H. Mark and Paula (Drillman) G.; m. Alisa Goldman, Oct. 17, 1999; 1 child, Alexander Zachary. BA cum laude, Columbia U., 1986; MD with honors, NYU, 1990. Diplomate Am. Bd. Plastic Surgery, Am. Bd. Surgery, Nat. Bd. Med. Examiners. Resident in surgery U. Conn./Hartford Hosp., 1990-95, chief resident, 1995-96; craniofacial rsch. fellow Inst. of reconstructive Plastic Surgery, NYU Med. Ctr., N.Y.C., 1992-93; fellow SUNY Health Sci. Ctr., Bklyn., 1996-98, assoc. program dir., dir. plastic surg. edn., 1998—2000. Contbr. articles to profl. jours. Mem. young plastic surgeons com. Plastic Surgery Ednl. Found., Am. Soc. Plastic Surgeons, 1996-97, 99—. N.Y. State Regents scholar, 1982-86. Fellow ACS; mem. AMA (del. to resident physician sect. 1990-93, 96—, plastic surgery caucus 1996-97, 99—, del. to young physicians sect. 1999—, YPS governing coun. 2002—), Am. Soc. Plastic Surgeons (vice chmn. govt. rels. com., plastypac bd. govs. 2001—, Maliniac cir.), Am. Soc. for Aesthetic Plastic Surgery (legis. com.), Northeastern Soc. Plastic Surgery (resident/fellows award 1997), Med. Soc. State of N.Y. (del. to AMA resident physician sect. 1996-98, to young physician sect. 1999—, Outstanding Svc. award 1990), N.Y. County Med. Soc., N.Y. Regional Soc. Plastic Surgeons (winner clin. paper competition 1997). Avocations: tennis, golf, swimming, card collecting. Office: 42A E 74th St New York NY 10021-2735 E-mail: Scotbg@Juno.com., info@DrGlasberg.com.

GLASCO, SUE ALICE, retired educator; b. Anna, Ill., Nov. 23, 1933; d. Robert Clyde and Katherine Ann (Rockenmeyer) Martin; m. Gerald Dean Glasco Sr., June 15, 1956; children: Katherine Glasco Cedar, Gerald Dean Jr., Jean Claire Glasco Eiler, Mary Ellen Glasco Taylor. BS in Edn., So. Ill. U., 1955, MS in Speech, 1972. Tchr., debate coach Evergreen Park (Ill.) H.S., 1955-56, Marion (Ill.) H.S., 1964-67; adj. instr. Shawnee Coll., 1972, John A. Logan Coll., 1982-83, 86-93; tchr. Johnston City (Ill.) H.S., 1983-85; county family edn. coord. Rend Lake Coll., Ina, Ill., 1992-98, ret., 1998. Adj. instr. Southeastern Ill. Coll., 1992, McKendree Coll., 1993; presenter in field. Author of short stories, poems and articles. Vol. church, Ill., 1953—; vol. for establishing Crab Orchard (Ill.) Pub. Libr., 1972-82; mem. Bedford County, Tenn. Hist. Assn., So. Ill. Geneal. Assn., Williamson County Hist. Assn., Johnson County Hist. Assn., Ill. State Hist. Assn., Nat. Multiple Sclerosis Soc. Mem. So. Ill. Writers Guild (program chair 1991-92, 2000-02, newsletter 1991-94), Ill. Speech and Theater Assn., So. Ill. Reading Coun., Ill. Reading Coun., Mulkeytown Hist. Assn. Baptist. Avocation: local history. Home: 17354 New Dennison Rd Marion IL 62959-6238

GLASER, ARTHUR HENRY, lawyer, mediator; b. Jersey City, May 1, 1947; s. Ned C. and Lorraine I. (Neil) G.; m. Waynelia Potter, Mar. 19, 1994; children: Kimberly N., Kevin M., Daniel J. BS, Hampden-Sydney Coll., 1968; JD, U. Va., 1973. Bar: Ga. 1973, U.S. Dist. Ct. (no. and mid. dists.) Ga., U.S. Ct. Appeals (11th cir.). Assoc. Swift, Currie, McGhee & Hiers, Atlanta, 1973-78, ptnr., 1978-83, Drew, Eckl & Farnham, Atlanta, 1983-98, Self, Glaser & Davis, LLP, Atlanta, 1999—; with Henning Mediation, 1999—. Mem. ABA, Ga. Bar Assn., Atlanta Bar Assn. Presbyterian. Home: 1540 Burnt Hickory Rd NW Marietta GA 30064-1308 Office: Self Glaser & Davis LLP Ste 1650 400 Interstate North Pkwy SE Atlanta GA 30339-5029 E-mail: ahg@sgdlaw.com.

GLASER, DANIEL, sociologist, educator; b. N.Y.C., Dec. 23, 1918; s. Samuel Jacob and Lena (Solway) G.; m. Pearl Bennett, Oct. 11, 1946 (dec. Apr. 1999); 1 child, Lenore Meryl. AB, U. Chgo., 1939, AM, 1947, PhD, 1954. Prisons officer U.S. Mil. Govt., Germany, 1946-49; sociologist-actuary Ill. Parole and Pardon Bd., Pontiac Prison, 1950-52, Joliet Prison, 1952-54; faculty U. Ill., 1954-68, prof. sociology, 1964-68, head dept., 1964-68; prof. Rutgers U., 1968-70, U. So. Calif., 1970-89, prof. emeritus, sr. rsch. assoc., 1989—. Vis. asso. prof. UCLA, summer 1961; vis. prof. Ariz. State U., 1963-64; cons. in field, 1956—; assoc. commr. charge research div. N.Y. State Narcotic Control Commn., 1968-1970 Author: The Effectiveness of a Prison and Parole System, 1964, rev., 1969, Crime in the City, 1969, Adult Crime and Social Policy, 1971, Social Deviance, 1971, Routinizing Evaluation, 1973, Strategic Criminal Justice Planning, 1975, Crime in Our Changing Society, 1978, Evaluation Research and Decision Guidance, 1988, Preparing Convicts for Law-Abiding Lives: The Pioneering Penology of Richard A McGee, 1995, Profitable Penalties, 1997; editor: Handbook of Criminology, 1974, Sociology and Social Rsch., 1973-76; assoc. editor: Am. Jour. Sociology, 1965-70, Social Problems, 1965-68, Jour. Rsch. on Crime and Delinquency, 1968-72, Fed. Probation, 1968-96, Law and Soc. Rev., 1975-79, Am. Sociol. Rev., 1978-81, Ency. of Crime and Justice, 1983; also numerous articles, pamphlets, chpts. in books; contbr. Ency. of Social Scis. Served with AUS, 1942-46. Recipient Disting. Emeritus award U. So. Calif., 1995. Fellow Western Soc. Criminology; mem. Ill. Acad. Criminology (pres. 1964-65), Am. Sociol. Assn. (chmn. criminology sect. 1965-66), Am. Soc. Criminology (E.H. Sutherland award 1976, August Vollmer award 1990, pres. 1979-80), Am. Justice Inst. (Richard A. McGee award 1987), Assn. Criminal Justice Rsch. (pres. 1980-81), Soc. Study Social Problems (chmn. crime and delinquency div. 1978-79), Pacific Sociol. Assn. (v.p. 1981-82, Disting. Sociol. Practice award 1995). Home: 865 Central Ave Needham MA 02492-1316 *To expand practical knowledge that can alleviate mankind's problems, seek not just precision, but the grounding of facts in abstract explanatory principles. This, I hope, is the main theme conveyed by my teaching, research and writing.*

GLASER, DAVID, painter, sculptor; b. Bklyn., Sept. 29, 1919; s. Samuel and Jennie (Offer) G.; m. Millie Sappol, Feb. 19, 1944; children: Susan, Sherry. Student, N.Y. Sch. Indsl. Art, 1937, N.Y. Sch. Contemporary Art, 1947-48, Bklyn. Mus. Art Sch., 1948-50. Illustrator, cartoonist comic books Popular Mechanics, Electronics Illustrated, Popular Sci., N.Y.C., 1939-42, 46-50; pres., designer, inventor Mosamics Co., Bklyn., 1948-50; art dir., advt. mgr. Univ. Loudspeakers, White Plains, N.Y., 1951-60; owner, mgr., graphic designer Studio Concepts, Wantagh, N.Y., 1957—. Artist Civilian Conservation Corps, Adirondacks, 1936; tchr. art Ctr. Island Jewish Sch., Freeport, N.Y., 1959; newspaper artist Bering Breeze, Aleutian Islands, 1945-46; co-founder North-west Pacific chpt. AVC Adak, 1945; worked with North Am. Philips (Amperex), Gen. Instruments, Gen. Signal (Cardion), Schweber Electronics, Singer-Telesignal; Veeco/Lambda Electronics, Plessey Inc.; Polytech. R&D, Univ. Loudspeakers, Harmon Kardon, Brit. Industries, Hohner Harmonicas; lectr. career guidance Mid. Sch. East students; presenter in field Author: (poetry) My Mother Died Dancing, 1960; designer, creator illuminated slide series L.I. Comty. chorus; contbr. poetry to anthologies; three-man show Heckscher Mus., Huntington, N.Y., 1964; exhibited in group shows Mcpl. Gallery, Jackson, Miss., 1943, Allied Artists of Am., 1957-85, Nat. Art Club, N.Y.C., 1959, Art Directions, 1959, ACA Galleries, 1960, Hofstra U., Adelphi U., Nassau C.C., 1980, L.I. Art Dirs. Exhbn. Firehouse Gallery, 1980, Nassau County Art Mus., 1980, Hempstead Harbor Art Assn., Glen Cove, L.I., 1982, Knickerbocker Artists, Islip Mus., 1983, Wantagh Libr., 1975, Levittown Libr., 1986, Freeport Libr., 1987, Plainview Libr., 2002; illustrator: Planets (Willie Ley); author, creator: American Indian, Crime and Punishment, Superstition and Parapsychology, 1947-50; prodr. bicentennial pictorial chronological map of Entire Am. Revolution, Spirit of '76, 1975; inventor process for mass prodn. ceramic and transparent mosaics, silk screen sys. for printing inside compound curves; creator innovative 2 color graphics method; new age art: developer combining chemically colored copper (sculpture) plastic, resins and reflective integral elements with electronics, 1973—; prodr. crossover filming of painting, sculpture and poetry recitation as ongoing creative product of Bridges of Mind, 1993—, Career Forum, 1999—. Designer war posters visual aids for U.S. Army, 1942-44; creator comic character Giggy F. Useless, used in basic tng. and theatre dramatizations and for Army newspaper, 1943-46. Sgt. AUS, 1942-46. Art Student's League scholar, 1936-37; recipient grand prize for redesign Levitt Home, 1967, Printing Industries, N.Y., 1973, numerous graphics awards, 1973-84, graphic excellence award Monadnock Mills, 1975, Desi grand award, 1980-82, poetry award Nassau County Fine Arts Mus., 1981, award of excellence IEEE, World Trade Ctr., N.Y.C., 1984, Vets. Soc. Am. Artists, 1984, award of excellence Long Beach Art League, 1989. Mem. Internat. Soc. Poets, Freeport Arts Coun., Allied Artists Am. (pres. 1985-86), Huntington Twp. Art League, DAV, Comic Artist Guild (treas.), Nature Conservancy, various environ. groups. Achievements include development of process for mass-producing mosaics, both traditional and current for architecture as well as home decor; transparent (per-stained glass) and opaque. Home and Office: 33 Downhill Ln Wantagh NY 11793-1817

GLASER, DONALD ARTHUR, physicist; b. Cleve., Ohio, Sept. 21, 1926; s. William Joseph Glaser. BS, Case Inst. Tech., 1946, ScD (hon.), 1959; PhD, Calif. Inst. Tech., 1949; ScD (hon.), U. Mich., 2002. Prof. physics U. Mich., 1949—59; prof. physics U. Calif., Berkeley, 1959—, prof. physics, molecular and cell biology, divsn. neurobiology, 1964—. Recipient Henry Russel award, U. Mich., 1955, Charles V. Boys prize, Phys. Soc., London, 1958, Nobel prize in Physics, 1960, Gold medal, Case Inst. Tech., 1967, Golden Plate award, Am. Acad. of Achievement, 1989; fellow NSF, 1961, Guggenheim, 1961—62, Smith-Kettlewell Inst. for Vision Rsch., 1983—84. Fellow: AAAS, Am. Physics Soc. (prize 1959), Neuroscis. Inst., Royal Swedish Acad. Sci., Royal Soc. Sci., Assn. Rsch. Vision and Ophthalmology, The Exploratorium (bd. dirs.), Fedn. Am. Scientists; mem.: NAS, Am. Philos. Soc., Internat. Acad. Sci., N.Y. Acad. Scis., Am. Assn. Artificial Intelligence, Sigma Xi, Theta Tau, Tau Kappa Alpha. Home: 41 Hill Rd Berkeley CA 94708-2131 Office: U Calif Dept Physics and Neurobiology 221 Donner Lab Berkeley CA 94720-0001

GLASER, EDWIN VICTOR, rare book dealer; b. N.Y.C., June 7, 1929; s. Simon and Dorothy (Goldwater) Glaser; m. Janice Briggs, May 1, 1959 (div. 1975); children: Peter, Daniel; m. Lorraine Vivian Glaser, June 17, 2001. BA, U. N.Mex., 1950; MS, Columbia U., 1951. Reporter Providence Jour.-Bulletin, 1951-55; sales mgr. R.E.C. Corp., New Rochelle, N.Y., 1955-69; owner Edwin V. Glaser Rare Books, Sausalito, Calif., 1969—. Faculty mem., antiquarian book seminar, U. Denver, 1979—. Contbr. numerous articles to profl. jours. Mem. Antiquarian Booksellers Assn. Am. (pres. 1986-87, gov.). Office: Glaser Rare Books PO Box 755 Napa CA 94559

GLASER, GARY A. bank executive; Grad., Baldwin-Wallace, Case Western Res. U. With Nat. City Corp., 1967-84; exec. v.p. of corp. banking group Nat. City Bank., 1984—88; pres., CEO Nat. City Bank, Columbus, Ohio, 1988—. Exec. v.p. Nat. City Corp., 1988—. Bd. mem. Am. Cancer Soc., Boy Scouts of Am., Ctr. of Sci. and Ind., Columbus Mus. of Art, Greater Columbus Area Growth Assn., United Way of Franklin County; hon. trustee Columbus Coun. on world Affairs. Mem.: Columbus Coun. for Ethics in Econ., Ohio Bankers Assn. Office: Nat City Bank 155 E Broad St Columbus OH 43215-3609

GLASER, GILBERT HERBERT, neuroscientist, physician, educator; b. N.Y.C., Nov. 10, 1920; s. Burnard Richard and Sidelle (Rogers) G.; m. Morfydd Mai Pugh, Mar. 17, 1946; children: Gareth Evan, Sara Elizabeth. AB, Columbia, 1940, MD, 1943, Med. Sc.D., 1951; MA (hon.), Yale, 1963. Diplomate: Am. Bd. Psychiatry and Neurology. Intern Mt. Sinai Hosp., N.Y.C., 1943-44; resident neurology N.Y. Neurol. Inst., 1944-46; research asst. to assoc. neurology Columbia Coll. Physicians and Surgeons, 1948-52; research scientist N.Y. Psychiat. Inst., 1948-50; head. sect. neurology Sch. Medicine Yale U., 1952-71, chmn. dept. neurology Sch. Medicine, 1971-86, asst. prof. neurology Sch. Medicine, 1952-55, assoc. prof. Sch. Medicine, 1955-63, prof. neurology Sch. Medicine, 1963-91, prof. neurology emeritus, 1991. Commonwealth Fund vis. prof. neurology U. London, Eng., 1965-66; cons. West Haven (Conn.) VA Hosp., 1955—, vis. prof. neurology Nat. Hosp., London, 1972, Park Hosp., Oxford, Eng., 1973-86, Hunan Med. Coll., Peoples Republic of China, 1986, U. Niigata, Kyoto, Japan, 1989; Fulbright Disting. prof. neurology Zagreb U., Yugoslavia, 1981; vis. scholar Green Coll. Oxford U., Eng., 1987-88; mem. neurology research adv. com. USPHS, 1956-60, 68-72, spl. cons., 1973, epilepsy adv. com., 1974-77, chmn. basic sci. subcom., 1977-80; mem. neurobiology rev. com. VA, 1975-78, chmn., 1977-78. Author: EEG and Behavior, 1963; Editor: Epilepsia, 1958-76; adv. editor, 1976-86; editor: Recent Advances in Clinical Neurology, 1978, 81, 84, Antiepileptic Drugs: Mechanisms of Action, 1980; mem. editorial bd.: Jour. Nervous and Mental Diseases; Contbr. articles to profl. jours. Capt. M.C. AUS, 1946-48. Recipient Janeway prize Columbia U., 1943, Bicentennial medal award, 1968, Book award Commonwealth Fund, 1975. Fellow Royal Soc. Medicine, ACP; mem. Am. Neurol. Assn. (1st v.p. 1977-78), Am. Acad. Neurology (pres. 1973-75 hon. mem. 1998), Am. Epilepsy Soc. (pres. 1963, Lennox lectr. 1985), Am. Electroencephalographic Soc. (council 1958-61, bd. qualifications), Eastern Assn. Electroencephalographers (pres. 1958), EEG Soc. (Gt. Britain), Assn. Brit. Neurologists, Soc. for Neurosci., Epilepsy Found. Am. (med. adv. bd.), Myasthenia Gravis Foundation (med. adv. bd. chmn. 1964-65), Multiple Sclerosis Soc. (chmn. research programs com. 1973-74, med. adv. bd.). Clubs: Athenaeum (London). Home: 205 Millbrook Rd North Haven CT 06473-4334 Office: Yale U Sch Medicine 333 Cedar St New Haven CT 06510-3289

GLASER, KATHERINE, pianist; b. Johnstown, Pa., July 16, 1919; d. Isaac Ziff and Helen Gross; m. Nathan M. Glaser (div. 1972); 1 child, Robert Saul. MusB in piano and sch. music, U. Mich., Ann Arbor; MusM, Julliard, NYC. Concert pianist. Cons. Composer: (children's piano music) Duets for You and Me; contbr. articles to profl. jours. Mem.: Ill. State Music Tchrs. Assn., Chgo. Music Tchrs. Assn., Music Tchrs. Nat. Assn. Jewish. Achievements include development of healthy hands trng. for pianists and computer operators. Avocations: swimming, dancing, writing, poetry, cooking. Home: #4405 505 N Lakeshore Dr Chicago IL 60611

GLASER, LUIS, biochemistry educator; b. Vienna, Mar. 30, 1932; came to U.S., 1953, naturalized, 1961; s. Hermann and Gisela (Kohn) G.; m. Ruth Walliser, May 18, 1961; children: Miriam, Nicole. BA, U. Toronto, Ont., Can., 1953; PhD, Washington U., St. Louis, 1956. Asst. prof. biol. chemistry Washington U., 1959-62, asso. prof., 1962-67, prof., 1967-75, chmn. dept. biol. chemistry, 1975-86; dir. Div. Biology and Biomed. Scis., 1980-86; exec. v.p., provost U. Miami, 1986—. Contbr. numerous articles on bacterial and mammalian metabolism to profl. jours.; editor Jour. Biol. Chemistry, 1969-74, 81-86, Jour. Supramolecular Structures, 1979-86, Jour. Cell Biology, 1981-92. Helen Hay Whitney fellow, 1956-59; NIH grantee; NSF grantee. Mem. Am. Soc. Biol. Chemists, Am. Chem. Soc., Am. Soc. Microbiology, Am. Soc. Neurochemists, AAAS. Democrat. Jewish. Office: PO Box 248033 Coral Gables FL 33124-8033 E-mail: lglaser@umiami.edu.

GLASER, PETER EDWARD, mechanical engineer, consultant; b. Zatec, Bohemia, Czechoslovakia, Sept. 5, 1923; came to U.S., 1948, naturalized July, 1954; s. Hugo and Helen (Weiss) G.; m. Eva F. Graf, Oct. 16, 1955; children: David, Steven, Susan. Diploma, Leeds Coll. Tech., Eng., 1943; 1st state exam, Czech Tech U., Prague, Czechoslovakia, 1948; MS, Columbia U., N.Y.C., 1951, PhD, 1955. Head design dept. Werner Mgmt. Co., N.Y.C., 1948-53; from mem. profl. staff to cons. Arthur D. Little, Inc., Cambridge, Mass., 1955—94, v.p., 1985, cons., 1994—99; pres. Power from Space Cons., Inc., Lexington, Mass., 1995—. Cons. NASA, Washington, 1963-67, mem. adv. coun., 1986; mem. case study task force Lunar Energy Enterprise, 1988-89; mgmt. adv. bd. Ctr. for Space Power, Tex. A&M U. System, 1990-94; sr. adv. bd. mem. Space Studies Inst., 1990—; mem. bd. assessment NIST program NRC, 1993-96; cons. NRC, Washington, 1960-62, panel mem., 1994-95, Heritage Found., Washington, 1982-83; adv. panelist Office Tech. Assessment, Washington, 1980-81; mem. Awards Adv. Coun. of Space Found., 1988-96. Editor: The Lunar Surface Layer, 1964, Thermal Imaging Techniques, 1964, Solar Power Satellites-The Emerging Energy Option, 1993, Solar Power Satellites-A Space Energy System for Earth, 2d edit., 1998, Solar Power Systems in Space; contbr. Standard Handbook of Powerplant Engineering, 1998; assoc. editor Space Power Jour., 1980-86; editor-in-chief Jour. Solar Energy, 1972-85, mem. editl. bd., 1985-93; mem. editl. bd. Space Policy, Space Power, Jour. Practical Applications in Space, Solar Energy; patentee solar power satellite, 1973; guest editor spl. issue of "Space Policy" on Space Solar Power, 1999-2000. Mem. bd. overseers Combined Jewish Philanthropies, Boston, 1984-88; voting mem. engring. coun. Columbia U., N.Y.C., 1984; advisor Space Solar Power Rsch. Soc., Japan, 1998—. Recipient Carl F. Kayan medal Columbia U., 1974, Farrington Daniels award Internat. Solar Energy Soc., Australia, 1983; named to U.S. Space Found. Space Tech. Hall of Fame, 1996. Fellow AAAS, AIAA; mem. ASME, Internat. Astron. Fedn. (chmn. space power com. 1984-89), Internat. Acad. Astronautics, Internat. Solar Energy Soc. (pres. 1967-72), Am. Astron. Soc. (bd. dirs. 1977-84), Sunsat Energy Coun. (pres. 1978-94, chmn. 1994—2000), Nat. Space Soc. (bd. advisors 1990-94, dir. 1994-97, bd. govs. 1997—), United Socs. in Space (regent 1997—), Am. Soc. for Macro-Engring., Cosmos Club (Washington). Jewish. Avocation: archeology of Southern Arabia. Home and Office: Power from Space Cons Inc 62 Turning Mill Rd Lexington MA 02420-1010

GLASER, ROBERT, communications company executive; CEO and chmn. Progressive Networks, Seattle; various pos. Microsoft Corp., 1983—93; founder, CEO RealNetworks, Seattle, 1995—. Office: Real Networks 2601 Elliott Ave Ste 1000 Seattle WA 98121-3307*

GLASER, ROBERT EDWARD, lawyer; b. Cin., Jan. 12, 1935; s. Delbert Henry and Rita Elizabeth (Arlinghaus) G.; m. Kathleen Eileen Grannen, June 17, 1961; children— Petra M., Timothy X., Mark G., Bridget M., Christopher D., Jenny M., Michael F. BS in Bus. Adminstrn. cum laude, Xavier U., Cin., 1955; LLB, U. Cin., 1960; LLM, U. Chgo., 1962; postgrad., U. Tuebingen, Fed. Republic of Germany, 1961. Bar: Ohio 1960, U.S. Dist. Ct. (no. dist.) Ohio 1963, U.S. Ct. Appeals (6th cir.) 1964, U.S. Tax Ct. 1970, U.S. Ct. Internat. Trade 1971, U.S. Ct. Fed. Claims 1992, U.S. Ct. Appeals (fed. cir.) 2000. Assoc. Arter & Hadden, Cleve., 1963-69, ptnr., 1970-2001, chmn., 1983-92; ret., 2001. Arbitrator Cuyahoga County Ct. Common Pleas, Ohio, 1972—, Med. Malpractice Panel, 1985—, Mediator Settlement Week, 1990; lectr. Cleve. Tax Inst., 1966—2000, mem. exec. com., 1980—84, chmn., 1982; lectr. Can.-U.S. Law Inst., 1980, Res. Officers Assn., 1970—, Ret. Officers Assn., 1995—; mem. qualified list of neutrals IRS Rev. Proc., 2003—. Contbr. articles to legal jours. Sec. Bay View Hosp., 1972-81; trustee Mental Health Rehab. and Rsch., Inc., 1975-86, mem. exec. com., 1977-81, pres., 1979-81; mem. men's com. Cleve. Play House, 1965-2003; mem. joint mental health and corrections com. Fedn. Cmty. Planning, 1978-81; mem. Cleve. Coun. on Fgn. Affairs, 1987-2002; mem. vis. com. Coll. Law Cleve. State U., 1987-97; mem. Soc. of Benchers, Case Western Res. Univ. Coll. Law, 1988—; trustee Univ. Circle, Inc., 1989-99, mem. exec. com., 1989-99. Col. U.S. Army, ret. Ford Found. grantee, 1960. Fellow Am. Bar Found. (life); mem. Ohio Bar Assn. (gen. tax com. 1998—, lawyer assistance com. 1999—), Nat. Bar Assn., Cleve. Bar Assn. (trustee 1983-87, chmn. bd. of com. grievance and discipline trial com. 1993, gen. tax com. 1983—, lawyer assistance com. 1999—), Legal Aid Soc. Cleve., Am. Judicature Soc., 8th Jud. Conf. (life), Am. Arbitration Assn. (nat. and internat. panel arbitrators 1969—), Citizens League Greater Cleve., Order of Coif, Union Club, Pentagon Officers Athletic Club, Serra Internat., Cleve. Club (exec. com. 1987-88, 90-91, 93-98, 2000—, pres. 1994-96, 2002—), KC. Roman Catholic. Home: 22895 Mastick Rd Cleveland OH 44126-3145 Office: Arter & Hadden 1100 Huntington Bldg 925 Euclid Ave Cleveland OH 44115-1475

GLASER, ROBERT HARVEY, SR., retired pastor; b. Phila., May 4, 1935; s. Harvey A. and Janet (McKechnie) G.; m. Joan Williams, Nov. 16, 1957 (div. July 1979); children: Linda Hartwell, Diane Lim Myra Ward, Linda Carrano, Robert Sr., Teresa Garcia, David Glaser; m. Virginia Sue Fischer, May 27, 1990. AB, Grove City (Pa.) Coll., 1957; MDiv, Princeton (N.J.) Theol. Sem., 1960. Pastor Smithfield Presbyn. Ch., Amenia, N.Y., 1960-64; organizing pastor Westminster Presbyn. Ch., Warner Robins, Ga., 1964-69, pastor 1st Presbyn. Ch., Forest Hills, N.Y., 1967-81; mem. ch. redevelopment Prospect Heights Presbyn. Ch., Bklyn., 1981-86; pastor Colcord (W.Va.) and Clear Creek Presbyn. Chs., 1987-89; interim pastor 1st Presbyn. Ch., Nitro, W.Va., 1989, pastor Hinton, W.Va., 1989-2000; ret., 2000. Moderator Presbytery of N.Y.C., 1976-77; cmn. Maj. Mission Fund, N.Y.C., 1979-81; bd. sec. Edwin Gould Svcs. for Children, N.Y.C., 1987-89. Mem. Second Chance panel D.A.'s Office, Queens, 1977-81. Named Eagle Scout Boy Scouts Am., 1950. Mem. Lions (treas. 1991—), Omicron Delta Kappa, Pi Gamma Mu. Home: 1519 Fayette St Hinton WV 25951-2018

GLASER, ROBERT JOY, retired physician, foundation administrator; b. St. Louis, Sept. 11, 1918; s. Joseph and Regina Glaser; m. Helen Louise Hofsommer, Apr. 1, 1949 (dec. Oct. 1999); children: Sally Louise, Joseph II, Robert Joy. SB, Harvard U., 1940, MD magna cum laude, 1943; DS (hon.), U. Health Scis.-Chgo. Med. Sch., 1972; DS (hon.), Temple U., 1973; DS (hon.), U. N.H., 1979, U. Colo., 1979; LHD, Rush Med. Coll., 1973; DS, Mt. Sinai Med. Sch., 1984; DS (hon.), Washington U., 1988, Thomas Jefferson U., 1991; DHL, Johns Hopkins U., 2000; DS (hon.), Watson Sch. of Biol. Scis., 2001. Diplomate Am. Bd. Internal Medicine. Med. intern Barnes Hosp., St. Louis, 1944, asst. resident physician, 1945—46, resident physician, 1946—47, asst. physician, 1949—57; asst. resident physician Peter Bent Brigham Hosp., Boston, 1944—45; NRC fellow med. scis. Wash. U. Med. Sch., 1947—49, instr. medicine, 1949—50, asst. prof., 1950—56, assoc. dean, 1947, asst. dean, 1953—55, assoc. prof., 1956—57, assoc. dean, 1955—57; dean, prof. medicine Med. Sch. U. Colo., 1957—63, v.p. for med. affairs, 1959—63; vis. physician Washington U. Med. Service, St. Louis City Hosp., 1950, chief service, 1950—53, cons., 1953—57; attending physician Colo. Gen. Hosp., Denver, 1957—63; prof. social medicine Harvard U., Boston, 1963—65; pres. Affiliated Hosps. Ctr., Inc., 1963—65; v.p. med. affairs, dean Sch. Medicine, prof.

medicine Stanford U., 1965—70, acting pres., 1968, cons. prof., 1972—97, prof. emeritus, 1997—; bd. dirs. Henry J. Kaiser Family Found., 1970—83, pres., chief exec. officer, 1972—83; attending physician Columbia-Presbyn. Med. Ctr., N.Y.C., 1971—72, clin. prof. medicine, 1971—72; dir. for med. sci. Lucille P. Markey Charitable Trust, 1984—97, trustee, 1989—97. Bd. dirs. Maxygen; cons. medicine VA Hosp., Denver, 1957—63, Fitzsimons Army Hosp., Aurora, Colo., 1957—63, Lowry AFB, Denver, 1957—63; mem. nat. adv. coun. NIMH, 1970—72, Harvard Fund Coun., 1953—56, Harvard Med. Alumni Coun., 1956—59, 1991—94, pres., 1993—94; assoc. mem. streptococcal commn. Armed Forces Epidemiologic Bd., 1958—61; chmn. com. study nat. needs biomed. and behavioral rsch. pers. NAS-NRC, 1974—77; mem. vis. com. Med. Sch. Harvard U., 1968—74, Sch. Pub. Health, 1971—77; bd. visitors Charles Drew Postgrad. Med. Sch., 1972—79; mem. com. on med. affairs Yale U., 1969—82, adv. bd. Sch. Orgn. and Mgmt., 1976—84; vis. com. Tufts Med. Sch., 1974—84. Editor: Pharos, 1962—97; editor emeritus:, 1997—; contbr. articles to sci. jours., chapters to books. Bd. regents Georgetown U., 1976—78; trustee Commonwealth Fund, 1969—88, v.p., 1970—72; trustee David and Lucile Packard Found., 1984—96, Pacific Sch. Religion, 1972—77, Washington U., St. Louis, 1979—87, 1988—, Albert and Mary Lasker Found., 1998—2003, Palo Alto Med. Found., 1974—, vice chmn., 1991—2000, trustee emeritus, 2000—; mem. Sloan Commn. on Govt. in Higher Edn., 1977—79; bd. dirs. Kaiser Found. Hosps., Kaiser Found. Health Plan, 1969—79, Coun. on Founds., 1974—79, Packard Humanities Inst., 1987—. Recipient William Greenleaf Eliot Soc. Search award, 1998, Hubert H. Humphrey Cancer Rsch. Ctr. award, Disting. Citizen award for outstanding leadership of med. edn. and rsch., Harvard Club of San Francisco. Master: ACP; fellow: AAAS, Royal Coll. Physicians London, Am. Philos. Soc., Am. Acad. Arts and Scis. (exec. bd., v.p. 1972—76); mem.: N.Y. Acad. Medicine (John Stearns award for lifetime achievement in medicine 2000), Inst. Medicine NAS (acting pres. 1970—71, chmn. membership com. 1970—72, mem. exec. com. 1971—73), Nat. Inst. Allergy and Infectious Disease (tng. grant com. 1957—60), Am. Soc. Exptl. Pathology, Western Assn. Physicians (councillor 1960—63), Assn. Am. Physicians, Assn. Am. Med. Colls. (asst. sec. 1956—60, chmn. com. edn. and rsch. 1958—63, mem. exec. coun. 1959—63, v.p. 1963—64, chmn.exec. coun. and assembly 1968—69, mem. exec. coun. 1976—79, Abraham Flexner award, Disting. Svc. award), Am. Soc. Clin. Investigation, Ctrl. Soc. Clin. Rsch. (councillor 1955—58), Am. Fedn. Clin. Rsch. (chmn. midwestern sect. 1954—55), Am. Clin. and Climatological Assn. (pres. 1982—83), Century Club, Harvard Club (N.Y.C.), Alpha Omega Alpha (bd. dirs. 1963—77), Sigma Xi.

GLASER, RONALD, microbiology educator, scientist; b. N.Y.C., Feb. 27, 1939; s. Irving and Pauline G.; m. Janice Kiecolt, Jan. 17, 1980; children: Andrew, Erik. BA, U. Bridgeport, 1962; MS, U. R.I., 1964; PhD, U. Conn., 1968; postgrad., Baylor Coll. Medicine, 1968-69. Asst. prof. microbiology Pa. State U., Hershey, 1970-73, assoc. prof., 1973-77, prof., 1977-78; prof. chmn. dept. med. microbiology and immunology Coll. Medicine Ohio State U., Columbus, 1978-92; reviewer NIH and NASA study sects.; assoc. dean for rsch. and grad. edn. Ohio State U. Med. Ctr., Columbus, 1992-94, assoc. v.p. health sci. rsch., 1994-2001, Gilbert and Kathryn Mitchell chair in medicine, 1995—, assoc. v.p. rsch., 2001—03. Editor: (with T. Gottleib-Stematsky) Human Herpes Virus Infections: Clinical Aspects, 1982; (with others) Epstein-Barr Virus and Human Disease, 1987; (with J. Jones) Human Herpes Virus Infections, 1994; (with J. Kiecolt-Glaser) Handbook of Human Stress, 1994. NIH postdoc. fellow, 1968-69; Franco-Am. Exch. Program; Fogarty Internat. Ctr.; NIH and INSRM fellow, 1975, 77; Leukemia Soc. Am. scholar, 1974-79. Fellow: Acad. Behavioral Medicine Rsch. (pres. psychoneuroimmunology rsch. soc. 2003); mem.: AAAS, Am. Soc. Microbiology. Office: Ohio State U 2175 Graves Hall 333 W 10th Ave Columbus OH 43210-1239 E-mail: glaser.1@osu.edu.

GLASER, VERA ROMANS, journalist; b. St. Louis, Apr. 21, 1916; d. Aaron L. and Mollie (Romans); m. Herbert R. Glaser, Apr. 16, 1939; 1 dau., Carol Jane Barriger. Student, Washington U., St. Louis, George Washington U., Am. U., 1937-40. Reporter-writer Nat. Aero. mag., 1943-44; reporter Washington Times Herald, 1944-46; pub. relations specialist Great Lakes-St. Lawrence Assn., 1950-51; promotion specialist, writer Congl. Quar. News Features, 1951-54; writer-commentator radio sta. WGMS, Washington, 1954-55; mem. Washington bur. N.Y. Herald Tribune, 1955-56; press officer U.S. Senator Charles E. Potter, 1956-59; dir. pub. relations, women's div. Rep. Nat. Com., 1959-62; press officer U.S. Senator Kenneth B. Keating, 1962-63; Washington corr. N.Am. Newspaper Alliance, 1963-69, bur. chief, 1965-69; columnist, nat. corr. Knight-Ridder Newspapers, Inc., 1969-81; assoc. editor Washingtonian Mag., 1981-88, contbg. editor, 1988—; columnist Maturity News Svc., 1988-94. Mem. Pres.'s Commn. on White House Fellows, 1969, Pres.'s Task Force on Women's Rights and Responsibilities, 1970; judge 1981 Robert Kennedy Journalism Awards. Free-lance writer nat. publs.; radio and TV appearances on Stas. WTOP-TV, ABC, PBS, C-SPAN. Mem. nat. bd. Med. Coll. Pa., 1977-88; bd. dirs. Washington Press Club Found., 1986-88; bd. dirs. Internat. Women's Media Found., 1990-98. Mem. White House Corrs. Assn., Nat. Press Club (bd. govs. 1988, 89), Washington Press Club (pres. 1971-72), Cosmos Club. Unitarian Universalist. Home and Office: 4201 Cathedral Ave NW Apt 304E Washington DC 20016-4953

GLASER, VICTORIA MERRYLEES, music educator, retired; b. Amherst, Mass., Sept. 11, 1918; d. Otto Charles G. and Dorothy (Gibbs) Merrylees BA cum laude, Radcliffe Coll., 1940, MA, 1943. Instr. Wellesley (Mass.) Coll., 1943-46; chair music theory, choral music Dana Hall, Wellesley, 1945-59; tchr. music theory New Eng. Conservatory Music Ext. Divsn., Boston, 1957-82; ret., 1982; tchr. theory and counterpoint Longy Sch. Music, Cambridge, Mass., 1972-93; ret., 1993. Guest illustrated lectr. inflection and body lang. in music, dept. psychiatry Beth Israel Hosp. Grand Rounds, Boston, 1983. Choral arranger, translator (book) Third Concord Anthem, 1956; instrumental arranger Airs for Trumpet and Organ, 1973, More Airs for Trumpet and Organ, 1981; composer Birthday Fugue, 1960, 65, 67, Pops; Fugue in Honor of Walter Piston, 1990, A Mozart Carol, 1999. Mem. adv. com. Comprehensive Plan for City of Cambridge, 1975-77. Anne Louise Barrett fellow, 1951, 52; Ella Lyman Cabot grantee, 1969. Mem.: Am. Soc. Composers, Authors and Pubs. (Std. award 1993, 1994, 1995, 1996, 1997, 1998, 1999, 2000, 2001, 2002). Democrat. Avocations: art, astronomy, chamber music. Address: Longy Sch Music 1 Follen St Cambridge MA 02138

GLASERGREEN, LAWSON SCOTT, designer; b. Owensboro, Ky., Aug. 16, 1959; s. Carlos Lee Green and Geraldine Beasley; m. Amy Elizabeth Glaser, June 19, 1993; children: Eve, Indra; m. Yvonne Adams, May 16, 1977 (div. Apr. 1983). AS, Ky. Wesleyan Coll., 1985, BA, 1991. Draftsperson Johnson, Depp & Quisenberry, Owensboro, Ky., 1977-78; draftsperson, quality control Modern Welding Inc., Owensboro, 1978-79; designer, on-site coord. David Hocker & Assocs., Owensboro, 1979-89; project mgr. Muller Assocs., Somerville, N.J., 1996-97; p.m. designer Wall Tech., Broomfield, Colo., 1997-98, Scott Coburn & Assocs., Boulder, Colo., 1998-99, Pear Interiors subsidiary U.S. Office Products, Denver, 1999, Gen. Svcs. Adminstrn., Lakewood, Colo., 1999—2000, Fluor Global Svcs. at IBM, Boulder, 2000—. Planner Fluor Global Svcs., IBM, Boulder, Colo.; art cons. Icshthus Studios, Owensboro, 1989-94; artist-in-residence Vista Vols. in Svc. to Am., 1991, Peace Corps, 1994. Prin. works include Ky. Wesleyan Coll., 1984, David Hocker & Assocs., 1985, J.B. Speed Mus., Ky., 1986, Dimensions 88 Nat., Kans., 1988, Brescia Coll., Ky., 1990, Owensboro Mus. Fine Art, 1993, The Capitol Arts Ctr., Ky., 1991, Trans Fin. Bank, 1991—93, Art Park, 1992—94, Louisville Artsfest, 1993—94, Centro de Promocion Cultural y Deportivo, Guatemala, 1995, El Atico, 1995—96, La Fuente, 1995—96, Taller Exptl. Pinturas y Escultura, 1996, Hunterdon Art Ctr. Stone Mill Shop, N.J., 1996—97, Scott Coburn and Assocs., Colo., 1998—99, Boulder County Aides Project, 1999, 2001, Rocky Mountain PBS, Colo., 2001, A Art House, 2001, The Mikaela Found., 2002. Tex. Gas scholar Tex. Gas Transmition Corp., Ky., 1989-91. Home: 104 Longs Peak Ave Longmont CO 80501 Office: Fluor Global Svcs at IBM PO Box 9275 6300 Diagonal Hwy Boulder CO 80301-9275

GLASGOW, AGNES JACKIE, social welfare administrator, therapist; b. El Paso, Tex., July 23, 1941; d. Carl Lecota Pace and Henrietta Ford (Cozart) Robertson; m. Morgan Walton, Sept. 20, 1958 (div. 1979); children: Scott Gene, Carley Earlene Walton DeVore; m. Phillip Sidney Glasgow, Aug. 9, 1986. Lic., Trinidad State Jr. Coll., Colo., 1968; AAS, Met. State Coll., Denver, 1979, BS, 1980; MPA, U. Colo., Denver, 1987. Cert. substance abuse counselor, Colo., Tenn. Pvt. practice Life Counseling Ctr., Denver, Memphis, 1980—; coord. masters program for substance abuse Met. State Coll., Denver, 1980—81; exec. dir. Concord Commons Counseling Ctr., Decatur, Ill., 1981—82; child care specialist Adams Cmty. Mental Health Ctr., Commerce City, Colo., 1982—84; adolescent family counselor Parkside Lodge Colo., Thornton, Colo., 1984—86; family therapist Charter Lakeside Hosp., Memphis, 1986—87; counselor, coord. Shelby State Cmty. Coll., Memphis, 1987—88; supr. adolescent and young adult program Meth. Outreach, Memphis, 1988—90; sr. mental health specialist dual diagnosis unit Meth. Hosp. Ctr., 1990—98, relapse prevention specialist, 1994—98; ret., 1998. Cons., part-time instr. Shelby State C.C., Memphis. Contbr. articles to profl. jours. Com. mem. Youth Suicide Task Force, Memphis, 1988—; pres. Memphis and Shelby County Children and Adolescent Assn., 1990-91. Recipient Vol. of Yr. award United Way, Decatur, Ill., 1982, Cmty. Svc. award scholarship Mental Health Soc., 1983, Outstanding Svc. award, 1989, Disting. Svc. award Sheriff Dept., Memphis, 1988; nominated Diamond award Memphis Mental Health Assn., 1994. Mem. Nat. Orgn. Human Svc. Workers, Nat. Orgn. Substance Abuse Counselors, Am. Assn. Counseling & Devel., Psi Chi (treas. 1979-80). Republican. Mem. Lds Ch. Avocations: reading, stained glass, hunting, fishing, sailing.

GLASGOW, JESSE EDWARD, newspaper editor; b. Monroe, N.C., Mar. 28, 1923; s. Jesse Edwin and Alma (Brown) G.; m. Beth BonDurant, June 25, 1949; children— Jeffrey David, Charles Christopher. BS, Wake Forest U., 1948. Reporter Kannapolis (N.C.) Ind., 1947, Durham (N.C.) Sun, 1948, Norfolk Virginian-Pilot, 1949-52; reporter Balt. Sun, 1953-59, financial editor, 1960—. Served with AUS, 1943-45. Democrat. Methodist. Home: 4904 Wilmslow Rd Baltimore MD 21210-2329 Office: Balt Sun Calvert And Centre St Baltimore MD 21278-0001 E-mail: jeglasgow@mindspring.com.

GLASGOW, KAREN, principal; b. N.Y.C., May 20, 1954; d. Douglas G. Glasgow. BS in Edn., U. Wis., 1976; MS in Spl. Edn., U. So. Calif., 1979; MA, Calif. State Univ., Los Angeles; PhD, Claremont Univ., 2001. Prin. Toluca Lake Elem. Sch., 2000—; adj. prof. Calif. State U. Northridge, Northridge, 2001—. Mem. Assoc. Adminstrs. L.A., Women in Ednl. Leadership, Assoc. of Calif. Sch. Adminstrn. of L.A.

GLASGOW, NORMAN MILTON, lawyer; b. Washington, Aug. 14, 1922; children: Norman M., Heather Glasgow Harris, Glenn. BS, U. Md., 1943; LLB, JD, BA, George Washington U., 1949. Bar: D.C. 1949, U.S. Supreme Ct. 1956, Md. 1960. Assoc. Wilkes, McGarraghy & Artis, Washington, 1949-55; ptnr. Wilkes & Artis, Washington, 1955-82; pres. Wilkes, Artis, Hedrick & Lane, Washington, 1982-86, sr. prin., 1988-2000; ptnr. Holland & Knight, LLP, Washington, 2001—. Bd. dirs., gen. counsel Greater Washington Bd. Trade, 1966, 87, 88; mem., chmn. Md. PAC, 1981-93; bd. govs. Washington Bldg. Congress; mem. Citizens Tech. Adv. Com. for Drafting Bldg. Code and Zoning Regulations, Washington, Commrs. Citizens Adv. Com. on Zoning, Washington, Balt. conv. Ctr. Authority Transp. Revenue Com., Gov.'s Salary Commn., Gov.'s Spl. Com. Vehicle Emissions Inspection Program, Gov.'s Adv. Redistricting Com.; chmn. Gov.'s Task Force Statewide Bldg. Performance Stds., Md. Stadium Authority, 1993-97, Md. Econ. Growth, Resource Protection and Planning Commn., co-chair subcom. for updating state planning and zoning laws, 1993-97; chmn. Md. Econ. Growth Task Force; mem. Gov.'s Western Md. Econ. Devel. Strategies Task Force, 1998—, co-chair Updating Md. Zoning and Planning Regulations (Article 66B). 1st lt. U.S. Army, 1942-46, ETO. Recipient Outstanding Alumni award George Washington U., 1985, Outstanding Svc. award D.C. Real Estate, Greater Washington Bd. Trade, 1978. Mem. Supreme Ct. Bar Assn., D.C. Bar Assn., Md. Bar Assn., Urban Land Inst., Am. Soc. Planning Ofcls., Washington Bldg. Congress, Nat. Assn. Bus. Economists, Nat. Conf. States in Bldg. Codes and Stds., Lambda Alpha. Avocation: gardening. Home: 9012 Brickyard Rd Potomac MD 20854-1634 Office: Holland & Knight 2099 Penn Ave NW Washington DC 20006-2803

GLASGOW, ROBERT EFROM, lawyer; b. Portland, Oreg., Nov. 13, 1944; s. Joseph and Lee (Friedman) G.; m. Lesley G. Veltman, June 16, 1968; children: Jordan Robert, Emily Samantha. BA, George Washington U., 1966, JD with honors, 1969. Bar: Oreg. 1969. Assoc. Dusenbery, Martin, Beatty, Bischoff & Templeton, Portland, 1969-72; ptnr. Martin, Bischoff, Templeton & Biggs, Portland, 1973-76, Glasgow & Kelly, Portland, 1977-79, Glasgow & Kelly, PC, 1980-85, pres., 1982-85, Glasgow & Wight, PC, 1985-92; of counsel Black Helterline LLP, Portland, 1992—. Trustee Multnomah County Legal Aid Svc., 1974-76, chmn., 1976; trustee Jewish Family and Child Svc., 1972-77, treas., 1976; trustee Jewish Cmty. Ctr., 1975-76, 86—, v.p., 1987—; trustee Mittleman Jewish Cmty. Ctr., 1975-76, 86-97, pres., 1991-93; trustee Oreg. Legal Svcs. Corp., 1980-82, Am. Jewish Com., Oreg., 1996—, treas., 1998-99, v.p., 1999-2000, pres., 2000-02; trustee, v.p. Oreg. Uniting, 2002—; activities coun. Oreg. Art Inst., 1984-87; Dem. precinctman, 1986-87. Mem. ABA, Oreg. Bar Assn., Multnomah Bar Assn., West Hills Racquet Club (Portland). Office: 1900 Fox Tower 805 SW Broadway Portland OR 97205 Business E-Mail: reg@bhlaw.com.

GLASHOW, SHELDON LEE, physicist, educator; b. NYC, Dec. 5, 1932; s. Lewis and Bella (Rubin) Glashow; m. Joan Glashow; children: Jason David, Brian Lewis, Rebecca Lee. AB, Cornell U., 1954; AM, Harvard U., 1955, PhD, 1959; DSc (hon.), Yeshiva U., 1978, U. Marseille, 1982, Adelphi U., 1989, Bar Ilan U., 1989, Gustave Adolphus Coll., 1989, Case Western Res. U., 2001. NSF fellow U. Copenhagen, Denmark, 1958—60; rsch. fellow Calif. Inst. Tech., 1960—61; asst. prof. Stanford U., 1961—62; asst. prof., assoc. prof. U. Calif., Berkeley, 1962—66; prof. physics Harvard U., 1967—84, Higgins prof. physics, 1979—2000; disting. sci. Boston U., 1984—2000; Mellon prof. scis. Harvard U., 1988—93, Higgins prof. of physics emeritus, 2000—; Arthur G.B. Metcalf prof. sci. Boston U., 2000—. Cons. Brookhaven Nat. Lab., 1964, 1966—73; vis. prof. U. Marseille, 1970, MIT, 1974; cons. Brookhaven Nat. Lab., 1975; mem. sci. policy com. CERN, 1979—84; vis. prof. MIT, 1980, Boston U., 1983; affiliated sr. scientist U. Houston, 1983—96; univ. scholar Tex. A&M U., 1983—86; hon. prof. U. Nanjing, 1998—. Author (with Ben Bova): Interactions, 1988; author: Charm of Physics, 1990, From Alchemy to Quarks, 1994; contbr. articles to profl. jours. and popular mags.; founding editor Quantum mag., 1989—2000. Pres. Andrei Sakharov Inst., 1980—85, Nat. Com. for Excellence in Edn., 1985—88. Recipient J.R. Oppenheimer Meml. prize, 1977, George Ledlie prize, 1978, Nobel prize in Physics, 1979, Castiglione di Sicilia prize, 1983, Erice Sci. for Peace prize, 1991; fellow NSF, 1955—60, Sloan, 1962—66, CERN vis., 1968. Fellow: AAAS, Am. Phys. Soc.; mem.: NAS, Am. Philosophical Soc., Costa Rica Acad. Sci. (fgn.), Korean Acad. Sci. (fgn.), Russian Acad. Sci. (fgn.), Am. Acad. Arts and Scis., Sigma Xi, Phi Beta Kappa. E-mail: slg@bu.edu.

GLASPEY, TERRY W. publishing executive, writer; b. Springfield, Oreg., Oct. 7, 1960; s. Larry W. Glaspey, Patricia A. Glaspey; m. Sally L. Barratt; children: Emma, Kathryn. MA, U. Oreg. Author: Children of a Greater God, 1995, Not a Tame Lion: The Spiritual Legacy of C.S. Lewis, 1996, Great Books of the Christian Tradition, 1996, Pathway to the Heart of God, 1998, Where the Grass is Always Greener, 2000, Booklovers Guide to Great Reading, 2001, The Ultimate Round, 2003. Office: Harvest House Publishers 990 Owen Loop North Eugene OR 97402

GLASRUD, CLARENCE ARTHUR, English educator; b. Cass County, N.D., Oct. 15, 1911; s. Claus Christian Glasrud and Anna Maren Skrove Haugan; m. Barbara Adams Crawford, June 19, 1948; 1 child, Charles Crawford. BS, Moorhead State Tchrs. Coll., 1933; MA, Harvard U., 1951, PhD, 1953. Tchr. Becker County (Minn.) Dist. 107, 1929-30, Jr. H.S., Pelican Rapids, Minn., 1935-36, H.S., Lake City, Minn., 1936-40, Mankato, Minn., 1940-42; prof. Moorhead (Minn.) State Tchrs. Coll., 1947-57, Moorhead State Coll., 1957-75, chmn. English dept., 1949-72; prof. Moorhead State U., 1975-77; ret. Editor: The Age of Anxiety, 1960, Hjalmar Hjorth Boyesen, 1963, A Heritage Deferred, 1981, Roy Johnson's Red River Valley, 1982, A Special Relationship, 1983, A Heritage Fulfilled, 1984, L'Heritage Tranquille, 1987, The Moorhead Normal School: A History, 1987, Moorhead State Teachers College: A History, 1989. Pres. Clay County Hist. Soc., Moorhead, 1960-78; rsch. dir. Red River Valley Hist. Soc., Moorhead, 1974-84; alderman City Coun., Moorhead, 1980-84. Tech. sgt. U.S. Army Air Corps, 1942-45, ETO. Named Disting. Alumnus, Moorhead State Coll., 1971, Century Alumnus, Moorhead State U., 1987. Mem. NEA (life), MLA (life), Norwegian Am. Hist. Assn. (life, bd. editors 1964-92), Studies in Am. Fiction (adv. editor 1974—), Rotary, Am. Legion. Avocations: tennis, gardening, travel. Home: 422 6th St S Moorhead MN 56560-2735

GLASS, ANDREW JAMES, newspaper editor; b. Warsaw, Nov. 30, 1935; came to U.S., 1941, naturalized, 1948; s. Martin Allan and Wanda (Mosewicka) G.; m. Eleanor Attianese Sorrentino, June 3, 1962; 1 child, Samuel Sorrentino. BA, Yale U., 1957. Fin. reporter N.Y. Herald Tribune, 1959-62, chief congl. corr., 1963-66; mem. nat. staff Washington Post, 1966-68; exec. asst. to Senator Charles Percy, U.S. Senate, Washington, 1968-70; sr. editor Nat. Jour., Washington, 1970-74; Washington corr. Cox Newspapers, 1974-77, chief Washington Bur., 1977-97, sr. corr., 1997—2001; mng. editor The Hill Newspaper, Washington, 2002—. Syndicated columnist N.Y. Times News Svc., 1980-2001. Chmn. Corr. Com. for Refugee Relief, 1975—78. With U.S. Army, 1958, mem. USAR, 1958—64. Fellow Shorenstein, J.F. Kennedy Sch. Govt., Harvard U., 2001. Mem.: Am. Soc. Newspaper Editors, Met. Club Washington. Office: The Hill 755 15th St NW Ste 1140 Washington DC 20005 E-mail: ajglass@cpcug.org., ajglass@thehill.com.

GLASS, CHRISTOPHER KEVIN, physician; b. Oakland, Calif., Aug. 13, 1955; s. William Charles and Arden Barbara (Rayson) Glass; m. Renee Fitzmorris; children: Erin Rose, Bryan James, Megan Christine, Sean William. BA Biophysics, U. Calif., Berkeley, 1977; MD, PhD Biology, U. Calif. San Diego, 1984. Intern dept. medicine Brigham & Women's Hosp., Boston, 1984—85, resident dept. medicine, 1985—86; fellow div. endocrinology U. Calif. San Diego, La Jolla, 1986—89, asst. prof. medicine, 1989—95, assoc. prof. medicine and cellular and molecular medicine, 1995—99, prof. medicine and cellular and molecular medicine, 1999—. Cons. Parke-Davis, Ann Arbor, Mich., 1994—95, Ligand Pharms., San Diego, 1994—95. Contbr. articles. Recipient Wilson S. Stone award, M.D. Anderson, Houston, 1989; scholar Lucille P. Markey scholar, Lucille P. Markey Trust, Miami, 1987. Fellow: Am. Heart Assn. (Established Investigator award 1995); mem.: Fedn. Am. Soc. Exptl. Biologists, Am. Soc. for Clin. Investigation, Endocrine Soc. (Ernst Oppenheimer award 2000). Achievements include discovery of retinoic acid receptors bind to DNA as hetrodimers; allosteric interactions between retinoic acid and retinoid x receptors, nuclear receptor co-activators and corepressors; antiinflammatory and antiatherogenic properties of the peroxisome proliferator-activated receptor gamma. Office: U Calif San Diego 9500 Gilman Dr 0651 La Jolla CA 92093-5003 E-mail: cglass@ecsd.edu.

GLASS, DAVID CARTER, psychology educator; b. N.Y.C., Sept. 17, 1930; s. Samuel and Dorothy (Braunstein) G.; m. Kathleen Kehoe, May 15, 1982. AB, NYU, 1952, MA, 1954, PhD, 1959, postdoctoral fellow, 1959-62. Mem. staff social psychologist Russell Sage Found., N.Y.C., 1963-71; assoc. prof. psychology Rockefeller U., N.Y.C., 1966-68; prof. psychology N.Y.U., N.Y.C., 1968-72; chmn., prof. dept. psychology U. Tex., Austin, 1972-75; vis. scholar Russell Sage Found., 1975-76; prof. psychology, dir. Lab. Biobehavior, CUNY Grad. Ctr., N.Y.C., 1976-82; prof. psychology and psychiatry SUNY, Stony Brook, 1982-94, vice provost for research and grad. studies, 1982-86, spl. advisor to provost, 1987-89, vice provost for rsch., 1990-93, prof. emeritus psychology, 1994—; vis. prof. psychology Inst. Health, Rutgers U., New Brunswick, N.J., 1994-96; interm dir. of rsch. Kessler Med. Rehab. Rsch. and Edn. Corp., West Orange, N.J., 1997-98; cons. in field. Author: Behavior Patterns, Stress and Coronary Disease, 1977; co-author: (with J.E. Singer) Urban Stress: Experiments in Noise and Social Stressors, 1972 (AAAS prize 1971); contbr. articles to profl. jours. Fellow Am. Psychol. Assn., AAAS; mem. Am. Psychosomatic Soc., Soc. Psychophysiol. Research, Soc. Exptl. Social Psychology, Acad. Behavioral Medicine Research (pres. 1981-82), Sigma Xi, Phi Kappa Phi. Home: 330 E 33rd St Apt 11J New York NY 10016-9437

GLASS, DAVID D. department store company executive, professional baseball team executive; b. Liberty, Mo., 1935; m. Ruth Glass; 3 children. Gen. mgr. Crank Drug Co., 1957-67; v.p. Consumers Markets Inc., 1967-76; exec. v.p. fin. Wal-Mart Stores Inc., Bentonville, Ark., to 1976, vice chmn., CFO, 1976-84, pres., 1984-2000, COO, 1984-88, CEO, 1988-2000, also bd. dirs., chmn. exec. commn., 2000—; CEO, chmn. bd. dirs. Kansas City Royals, 1993—. Office: Wal-Mart Stores Inc 702 SW 8th St Bentonville AR 72716-6299 also: Kansas City Royals PO Box 419969 Kansas City MO 64141-6969

GLASS, DOROTHEA DANIELS, physiatrist, educator; b. N.Y.C. d. Maurice B. and Anna S. (Kleegman) Daniels; m. Robert E. Glass, June 23, 1940; children: Anne Glass Roth, Deborah, Catherine Glass Barrett, Eugene. BA, Cornell U., 1940; MD, Woman's Med. Coll. Pa., 1954; postgrad., U. Pa., 1960-61; DMS (hon.), Med. Coll. Pa., 1987. Diplomate Am. Bd. Phys. Medicine and Rehab. (guest bd. examiner 1978, 89). Intern Albert Einstein Med. Center, Phila., 1954-55, clin. asst. dept. medicine, 1956-59, attending phys. medicine and rehab., 1968-70, chmn. dept. phys. medicine and rehab., sr. attending, 1971-85; chief rehab. medicine VA Med. Ctr., Miami, Fla., 1985-95; clin. prof. dept. orthopaedics and rehab. U. Miami Sch. Medicine, 1985—. Lois Mattox Miller fellow preventive medicine Woman's Med. Coll. Pa., 1955-56, instr. preventive medicine, 1956-59, instr. medicine, 1960-62; resident phys. medicine and rehab. VA Hosp., Phila., 1959-62, chief phys. medicine and rehab., 1966-68, cons., 1968-82; asst. clin. dir. Jefferson Med. Coll. Hosp., Phila., 1963-66, Camden County Stroke Program, Cooper Hosp., Camden, N.J., 1963-66; gen. practice medicine, Phila., 1956-59; asst. med. dir., chief rehab. medicine and rehab. Moss Rehab. Hosp., Phila., 1968-70, med. dir., 1971-82, sr. cons., 1982— ; mem. active staff Temple U., Phila., 1968—, assoc. prof. rehab. medicine, 1968-73, prof., 1973—, dir. residency tng. rehab. medicine, 1968-82; program dir. Rehab. Research and Tng. Center, 1977-80, chmn. dept. rehab. medicine, 1977-82; staff physician Hosp. Med. Coll. Pa., Phila., 1955-59, vis. asso. prof. neurology, 1973-79, clin. prof., 1977-82, vis. prof., 1982-96; mem. cons. staff Frankford Hosp., Phila., 1968-82, Phila. Geriatric Center, 1975-82; mem. active staff Willowcrest-Bamberger Hosp., Phila., 1980-82; asso. phys. medicine and rehab. U. Pa. Sch. Medicine, Phila., 1962-66; asst. prof. clin. phys. medicine and rehab., 1966-68; asst. clin. dir. dept. phys. medicine and rehab. Jefferson Med. Coll., Phila., 1963-66; cons. Vols. in Medicine Clinic, Stuart, Fla., 1996—. Contbr. articles to profl. jours. Mem. profl. adv. com. Easter Seal Soc. Crippled Children and Adults Pa., 1975-82; active Goodwill Industries Phila., 1973-82, Cmty. Home Health Svcs. Phila., 1974-82, Ea. Pa. chpt. Arthritis Found., 1968-82. Recipient humanitarian svc. cert. Gov.'s Com. on Employment Handicapped, 1974, Outstanding Alumnae award Commonwealth of Pa. Bd., Hosp. Med. Coll. Pa., 1975, humanitarian award Pa. Easter Seal Soc., 1981, John Eiselie Davis award Am. Kinesiotherapy Assn., 1988, Carl Haven Young svc. award, 1994, Disting. Career award Moss Rehab. Hosp., 1997, Outstanding Svc. and Accomplishments award Fla. Soc. Phys. Medicine and Rehab., 2001, Susan B. Anthony award LWV of Martin County, 2002. Mem. AMA, Am. Acad. Med. Dirs., Am. Acad. Phys. Medicine and Rehab. (disting. clinician award 1995, Krusen award 2000), Am. Assn. Electromyography and Electrodiagnosis (assoc.), Am. Assn. Sex Educators, Counselors and Therapists, Am. Burn Assn., Am. Coll. Angiology, Am. Coll. Utilization Rev., Am. Congress Rehab. Medicine (bd. govs. 1979-85, pres. 1986-87, gold Key award 1989), Am. Heart Assn. (coun. on cerebrovascular disease), Am. Lung Assn. Phila. and Montgomery County (bd. dirs. 1977-79), Am. Med. Women's Assn., Assn. Acad. Physiatrists, Assn. Med. Rehab. Dirs. and Coordinators, Coll. Physicians Phila., Emergency Care Rsch. Inst., Gerontol. Soc., Internat. Assn. Rehab. Facilities, Internat. Rehab. Medicine Assn., Pan Am. Med. Assn., Fla. Med. Assn., Fla. Soc. Phys. Medicine and Rehab. (pres. 1975-77, Award for Outstanding Svc. in Rehab. Medicine 2001), Pa. Med. Soc. (phys. medicine and rehab. adv. com. 1975-82), Pa. Thoracic Soc., Delaware Valley Hosp. Coun. Forum, Phila. Med. Soc., Phila. PSRO (bd. dirs. 1975-82), Phila. Soc. Phys. Medicine and Rehab. (pres. 1968-69), Laennec Soc. Phila., Royal Soc. Health, Alpha Omega Alpha. E-mail: glassrd@earthlink.net.

GLASS, DOUGLAS B. lawyer; b. Houston, Aug. 19, 1949; BA, U. Tex., 1971, JD, 1974. Bar: Tex. 1974. Mem. Vinson & Elkins L.L.P., London. Office: Vinson & Elkins Citypoint No 1 Ropemaker St London EC2Y 9UE England

GLASS, FRED STEPHEN, lawyer; b. Asheboro, N.C., Oct. 17, 1940; s. Emmett Frederick and Colene F. (Foust) G.; m. Gloria A. Grant, June 12, 1964; 1 child, Elizabeth Foust; m. Martha G. Daughtry, June 9, 1982. BA, Wake Forest U., 1963, JD, 1966. Bar: N.C. 1966, U.S. Dist. Ct. (ea. dist.) N.C. 1966, (mid. dist.) N.C., (we. dist.) N.C.; U.S. Ct. Appeals (4th cir.), U.S. Supreme Ct. Rsch. asst. presiding justice N.C. Supreme Ct., 1966-67; ptnr. Miller, Beck,

O'Briant and Glass, Asheboro, N.C., 1971-77; exec. dir. and legal counsel N.C. Democratic Party, 1977-78; dep. commr. N.C. Indsl. Commn., 1978; spl. Congl. asst. 4th Congl. Dist., N.C., 1979; ptnr. Harris, Cheshire, Leager and Southern, Raleigh, N.C., 1979-86, Poyner and Spruill, Raleigh, 1987-94, Brooks, Stevens & Pope, P.A., Cary, 1994-98; mng. ptnr. Glass & Vining, LLC, Cary, 1998-2000, Johnson, hearn, Vinegar & Gee PLLC, 2001—. Prof. law and govt. Asheboro Jr. Coll. Bus., 1973-76; bd. dirs. Capital Bank; mem. Gov.'s commn. mil. affairs, N.C., commn. Battleship N.C. Author: The Legal Handbook for North Carolina Businesses, 2003, Your Estate Planning Handbook, Business Considerations for North Carolina Healthcare Providers; contbg. editor: N.C. Will Drafting and Probate Practice Handbook, 1983; contbr. articles to profl. jours. Pub. chmn., United Appeal; bd. dirs., Randolph County Emergency Med. Technician Bd., Capital Bank; chmn.-elect Cary C. of C., bd. dirs., vice-chair govt. relations com.; mem. adv. bd. Naval War Coll. ops. law; active Dem. campaigns, Boy Scouts Am., council commr. for Roundtables, 1980-89, asst. dist. commr. 1979-84, asst. scoutmaster; mem. nat. com. Boy Scouts of Am., council ex. bd., council commr., chancellor, council commrs. coll., 1980-83, Boy Scouts Am. Nat. Com., 1987-90, coun. pres. 1994-96; force judge adv. COMRNCF, 1985-89; v.p. Healthcare Bus. Mgmt., LLC. Rear adm. JAGC, USNR. Disting. Svc. Medal award, 1996, Meritorious Svc. medal with gold star, Meritorious Unit Commendation, Nat. Meritorious Svc. award USNR, 1995, Navy Commendation medal with Gold Star, Nat. Defense Svc. medal with Bronze Star, Seabee Combat Warfare Specialist Cert.; recipient numerous Scouters Tng. award Boy Scouts Am., Disting. Eagle Scout award, 1991, Young Man of Yr. award City Asheboro. Mem.: ABA (standing com. on armed forces law), N.C. Bar Found., N.C. Coun. Entrepreneurial Devel., N.C. Def. Lawyers Assn. (computers in litigation support 1989), N.C. Bar Assn. (chmn. young lawyer sect. Randolph County, computers in law office 1995), 19th Jud. Dist. Bar Assn. (pres. 1974—75), Randolph County Bar Assn. (pres. 1971—74), Cary C. of C. (bd. dirs., chmn. elect), Club, Sovereign Mil. Order Temple Jerusalem, Naval Order U.S. Democrat. Methodist. Home: 243 Chimney Rise Drive Cary NC 27511-7216 Office: PO Box 1776 Raleigh NC 27602 Fax: 919-743-2201. E-mail: sglass@jhvglaw.com.

GLASS, GEOFFREY THEODORE, judge; b. Washington, June 17, 1954; s. C. Edwin and Irene Glass; m. Deborah Anne Bodeson, Nov. 11, 1989; children: Hannah Irene, Elliott Edwin. BA, Amherst Coll., 1976; JD, U. Va., 1980. Bar: Minn. 1980, U.S. Dist. Ct. Minn. 1981, Calif. 1982, U.S. Dist. Ct. (cen. dist.), Calif. 1983, (no. and ea. dist.) Calif. 1984, (so. dist.) Calif. 1985, U.S. Ct. Appeals (9th cir.) 1985. Assoc. Robins, Kaplan, Miller & Ciresi, Mnpls. & Newport Beach, Calif., 1980-86, ptnr. Newport Beach, Calif., 1986-97; judge Orange County Mcpl. Ct., 1997-98, Orange County Superior Ct., 1998—. Avocation: music. Office: Harbor Justice Ctr 4601 Jamboree Rd Newport Beach CA 92660-2527

GLASS, HENRY PETER, industrial designer, interior architect, educator; b. Vienna, Sept. 24, 1911; came to U.S., 1939; s. Ernst and Berta (Zaitschek) G.; m. Eleanor C. Knopp, Mar. 4, 1937; children: Ann Karin, Peter. Diploma architect, Wiener Tech. Hochschule, Vienna, 1933; M.Arch., Meisterschule Prof. Theiss, Vienna, 1935; Indsl. Design, Sch. Design, Chgo., 1953. Prin. architect Studio H. Glass, Vienna, 1935-38; designer Office Gilbert Rohde, N.Y.C., 1939-40, Morris Sanders, N.Y.C., 1940; head design dept. W.L. Stensgaard Assocs., Chgo., 1941-45; prin. Henry P. Glass, Assocs., Northfield, Ill., 1946—; prof. indsl. design Chgo. Art Inst., 1946-69. Designs include, Swingline, Children's Furniture; patentee in field; author: Design & Consumer, 1981, The Shape of Manmade Things, 1996, 100 Travel Sketches, 2000; one-man shows Hochschule Für Angewandte Kunst, Vienna, Austria, 1997, Chgo. Art Inst., 1999-2000; represented in private and permanent collections. Trustee Bd. of Northfield, 1966-67, pres. Am. Friends of Austria, 1990—. Recipient Ann. award Fine Hardwoods Assn., 1955, 56, Best Booth award Ski Show Expo Ctr., Chgo., 1972, Excellence in Design award Indsl. Design Mag., 1978, Golden Merit award City of Vienna, 1986, Cross of Honor for Arts and Scis., Republic of Austria, 1987, Good Design award Chgo. Atheneum, 1992. Fellow Indsl. Design Soc. Am. (chmn. Chgo. chpt. 1959-60, nat. vice chmn. 1960-62) Clubs: Am. Friends of Austria (v.p. 1976, then pres.); Austro Am. Council for the Mid-West (Chgo.) (pres. 1983-84). Roman Catholic. Home: 245 Dickens St Northfield IL 60093-3224 Office: Henry P Glass Assocs PO Box 52 Northfield IL 60093-0052 *A designer's Thoughts: Anything man can perceive with his senses that isn't made by God and which is not a one-time creation by an artist, had it's origin on a drawing board.*

GLASS, JANET LEVINE, primary and secondary education educator; b. N.Y.C., Nov. 13, 1947; d. Richard and Miriam Levine; children: Jessie, Lara. BA, SUNY, Binghamton, 1967; MS in Edn., Queens Coll., N.Y.C., 1973. Cert. tchr. Spanish, N.Y., N.J. Tchr. Spanish Jr. High Sch. 189, Queens, N.Y., 1969-76; bilingual guidance counselor Samuel Gompers H.S., Bronx, N.Y., 1976-79; co-dir. Grapevine Lang. Instrn., Cliffside Park, N.J., 1983-85; tchr. Spanish Dwight-Englewood Sch., Englewood, N.J.; 1985—. Coord. World Lang. Inst. Fairleigh Dickinson U., Teaneck, N.J., 1999—. Contbg. author Model Lessons, 1998. Group facilitator Ethical Culture Soc. and Gay and Lesbian Youth N.J., Teaneck, 1998—. NEH fellow, 1994; grantee NEH, 1995, 97, Columbia U., 1995, 97. Mem. Nat. Network for Early Lang. Learning (N.E. rep. 1997—), Am. Assn. Tchrs. Spanish and Portuguese (co-chair elem. lang. 2000—). Avocation: international folk dancing. Home: 8700 Boulevard E 2F North Bergen NJ 07047 Office: Dwight Englewood Sch 315 E Pasisade Ave Englewood NJ 07631 E-mail: IguanaJ@aol.com.

GLASS, JOHN DEREK See HOOPER, IAN

GLASS, KENNETH EDWARD, management consultant; b. Ft. Thomas, Ky., Sept. 28, 1940; s. Clarence E. and Lucille (Garrison) G.; m. Nancy Romanek, May 9, 1964; children: Ryan, Lara. ME, U. Cin., 1963, MS, 1965, grad. student, 1967. Registered profl. engr., Ohio. With Allis Chalmers Mfg. Co., Cin. and Eng., 1963-73; v.p. mfg. Fiat Allis Contrn. Machinery, Inc., Chgo., 1973-75; pres. Perkins Diesel Corp., Canton, Ohio, 1975-77; pres., chief exec. officer Massey-Ferguson, Inc., Des Moines, 1978, v.p., gen. mgr. N.Am. ops. Massey Ferguson Ltd., Des Moines, 1978; chmn., pres., chief exec. officer Union Metal Mfg. Co., Canton, Ohio, 1979-85; pres. Glass & Assocs. Inc., 1985—, chmn., 1996—; pres. Stony Point Group, Inc., 1996—, also bd. dirs.; chmn. Utica Corp., 2001—, UCA Holdings, 2001—, TECT Corp.; bd. dirs. Thames Water Holdings, Turnaround Mgmt. Assn., N.C. Outward Bound Sch.; trustee U. Cin. Found.; dir. N.C. Outward Bound Sch. Mem. Young Presidents Orgn., ASME, Soc. Automotive Engrs., Turnaround Mgmt. Assn., Assn. Cert. Turnaround Profls. (bd. dirs., v.p. 1993-94, pres. 1995-96), Am. Bankruptcy Inst., Pi Tau Sigma. Patentee in field.

GLASS, LAUREL ELLEN, gerontologist, developmental biologist, physician, retired educator; b. Selma, Calif., Oct. 1, 1923; d. Sydney L. and Marie (Damron) G. BA, U. Calif.-Berkeley, 1951; PhD, Duke U., 1958; MD, U. Calif., San Francisco, 1974. Teaching asst. zoology Duke U., 1953-56; rsch. assoc. Pathology Rsch. Lab. Med. Rsch. divsn. VA Hosp., Durham, N.C., 1957-58; instr. dept. anatomy U. Calif. Med. Sch., San Francisco, 1958-61, asst. prof., 1961-66, assoc. prof., 1968-72, prof., 1972-89, prof. emeritus, 1989—, prof. psychiatry, 1984-89, prof. emeritus, 1989—, dir. Ctr. on Deafness, 1984-89, adj. prof. family and community medicine, 1983-89; dir. project on adaptation to adult onset hearing loss Langley Porter Psychiat. Inst., U. Calif. Med. Sch., San Francisco, 1989-92. Mem. San Francisco adv. com. Child Health and Disability Prevention Program, 1974-79; mem. exec. com., bd. dirs. Mission Neighborhood Health Ctr., 1974-77; mem. med. adv. com. Coalition for Med. Rights of Women, 1974-87; mem. adv. bd. P.R. Orgn. Women Health Edn. Project, 1976-78; v.p. Developmental Disabilities Programs, Inc., 1976-87; Politzer vis. scholar Gallaudet U. Rsch. Inst., 1999; Powrie V. Doctor chair Deaf Studies Gallaudet U., 2000. Co-author: Beyond Refuge: Coping with Losses of Vision and Hearing in Later Life, 1989; co-editor: State of the Art: Research Priorities in Deaf-Blindness, 1985, Mental Health Assessment of Deaf Clients: A Manual, 1987, Mental Health Assessment of Deaf Clients: Special Conditions, 1989; contbr. articles to profl. jours. Mem. edn. commn. NAACP, Ocean View-Merced Heights Community Stblzn. and Improvement Project, exec. com. Ocean View-Ingleside Dist. Council, Bay Area Social Planning Council, 1969-73, adv. council Nat. Ctr. for Vision and Aging, 1986-94; bd. dirs. Service Com. on Pub. Edn., 1963-66, Constl. Rights Found., 1965-73, Deaf Counseling, Adv. and Referral Agency (DCARA), 1985-86, Hearing Soc. for the Bay Area, Inc., 1984-86, 93-96; trustee Self-Help for Hard of Hearing People, Inc., 1986-89, Glide Found., 1966-75, Gallaudet U., Washington, 1986-99; bd. govs. Pub. Advs. Inc., 1975-79; mem. San Francisco Bd. Edn., 1967-71, pres., 1969; regent Lone Mountain Coll., 1973-76; pres. United Meth. Congress of the Deaf, 1993-2001. Recipient Spl. Friend of Persons with Hearing Loss award, 1993. Mem. Am. Assn. Anatomists, Gerontol. Soc. Am., Am. Soc. on Aging, Self Help for Hard-of-Hearing People, Inc., Am. Deafness and Rehab. Assn., Phi Beta Kappa, Sigma Xi. Democrat. Methodist. Home: 1300 NE 16th Ave Apt 1408 Portland OR 97232-4405 E-mail: laurelglass@earthlink.net.

GLASS, NOAH F. music educator, web site designer; b. L.A., Oct. 25, 1970; s. Paula Zelda Glass. MusB in Performance and Secondary Edn., Queens Coll., Flushing, N.Y., 1994, MS in Edn., 1996; advanced profl. cert., New Sch. U., N.Y.C., 2001. Permanent lics. in orchestral music N.Y.C., cert. permanent pub. sch. tchr. N.Y., completion of probation. Concert band dir. Pub. Schs. 201 and 21, Queens, NY, 1994—95; concert and jazz band dir. Edward Bleeker Jr. HS 185, Flushing, 1995—2001; marching band dir. Tottenville HS, S.I., 1998—2001; concert and jazz band dir., arts dept. webmaster Oceanside (N.Y.) Mid. Sch., 2001—. Student tour dir. Musiker Student Tours, Roslyn, NY, 1996—; webmaster Oceanside Fine & Performing Arts Dept., Oceanside Fedn. Tchrs., Oceanside Profl. Devel. Ctr. Musician: N.Y.C. Bd. Edn., 1999, 2001. Mem.: Music Educators Nat. Conf., N.Y. State Sch. Music Assn., Tau Epsilon Phi (bursar, pledge master 1988—90). Avocations: web design, travel, sports, camping, moutain biking. Office: Oceanside Mid Sch 186 Alice Ave Oceanside NY 11572 Personal E-mail: glassmusic@hotmail.com.

GLASS, PHILIP, composer, musician; b. Balt., Jan. 31, 1937; s. Benjamin C. and Ida (Gouline) Glass; m. JoAnne Akalaitas (div.); children: Juliet, Zachary; m. Linda Burtyk, 1980 (div.); m. Candy Jernigan (dec. 1991); m. Holly Critchlow, 2001; 1 child, Cameron. AB, U. Chgo., Ill., 1956; MS in Composition, Julliard Sch. Music, 1964; composition student with, Nadia Boulanger, Paris, 1964—66. Composer in residence Pitts. Pub. Sch., 1962—64; founder, performer Philip Glass Ensemble, 1968—; owner Dunvagen Music Pubs. Former taxi cab driver. Composer: (incidental music) Play, 1965, (chamber and instrumental music) String Quartet, 1966, Strung Out, 1967, In Again Out Again, 1967, Pieces in the Shape of a Sq., 1967, How Now, 1968, Red Horse Animation, 1968, Two Pages, 1968; various European concert tours, 1968—; composer: Music in Similar Motion, 1969, Music in Contrary Motion, 1969, Music in Eight Parts, 1969, Music in Fifths, 1969, Gradus, 1969, Music with Changing Parts, 1970, Music in Twelve Parts, 1971—74; US tours, 1972—; composer: Music for Voices, 1972; founder (record co.) Chatham Sq. Prodns., NYC, 1972; composer: (opera) Einstein on the Beach, 1975, Another Look at Harmony, 1975, The Lost Ones, 1975, The St. and the Football Player, 1975, (vocal and choral music) Knee Play No. 3, 1976, Geometry of a Cir., 1979, Modern Love Waltz, 1977, (film music) North Star, 1977, Dressed Like an Egg, 1977, Fourth Series Part I, 1978, Music for a Performance/Reading by C. DeJong: Fourth Series Part II, 1978, Cascando, 1979, Mercier and Camier, 1979, Dance No. 4, 1979; composer: (with Robert Wilson) The Panther, 1980; composer: Dead End Kids, 1980, Satyagraha, 1980, Facades, 1981, Vessels, 1981, Habeve Song, 1982, The Photographer, 1982, Hymn to the Sun, 1982, Co., 1983, Akhnaten, 1983, The Civil Wars: A Tree is Best Measured When It Is Down, 1983, Pages from Cold Harbor, 1983, Floe, 1983, String Quartet No. 2: Co., 1983, Endgame, 1984, Glassworks, 1984, (pop albums) Songs from Liquid Days, 1986, (Rome sect.) Three Songs, 1986; composer: (with Robert Morau) Juniper Tree, 1986; author: Music by Philip Glass, 1987; composer: The Making of a Rep. for Planet 8, 1987, Itaipu, 1988, The Fall of the House of Usher, 1988, 1000 Airplanes on the Roof, 1988, String Quartet No. 4: Boczak, 1989, Orphée, 1993, Dance No. 2, 1979, Mad Rush: Fourth Series Part III, 1979; author (with C. DeJong): Satyagraha: M.K. Gandhi in South Africa 1893-1914, 1980; composer: Koyaanisqatsi, 1981; co-editor: (symphonies and orchestral music) Co., 1983; composer: Civil Wars, 1984, Low Symphony, 1993, Dance from Akhnaten, 1984, Music from the Civil Wars, 1984, String Quartet No. 3: Mishima, 1985, Mishima, 1985, Dialogue, 1986, Dead End Kids, 1986, The Light, 1987, Hamburger Hill, 1987, Powaqqatsi, 1987, Concerto for violin and orch., 1987, The Canyon, 1988, The Thin Blue Line, 1988, Hydrogen Jukebox, 1990, The Voyage, 1992, Candyman, 1992, A Brief History of Time, 1992, Candyman II: Farewell to the Flesh, 1994, La Belle et la Bete, 1994, Symphony No. 2, 1994, Tirol Concerto for Piano and Orch., 2000, In the Penal Colony, 2000, Passage, 2001, The Man in the Bath, 2001, Dancissimo, 2001, Notes, 2001, Diaspora, 2001, Nagoygatsi, 2001, Voices for Organ, Didgeridoo and Narrator, 2001, Concerto for Cello and Orch., 2001, The Elephant Man, 2002, Symphony No. 6 Plutonian Ode, 2002, (opera) Galileo Galilei, 2002, (film soundtrack) The Hours, 2002 (The Anthony Asquith Award for Achievement in Film Music, British Acad. Film Award (BAFTA), 2003), (spl. events) Ceremonial Music at 1984 Olympics; collaborators: Joanne Akalaitis, Robert Wilson, Paul Simon, Allen Ginsberg; composer: (concerto) Concerto for Harpsichord and Orchestra, 2002, (Pandemic) Facing AIDS (documentary), 2002. Named Musician of Yr., Musical Am. mag., 1985, composition grantee, Fulbright, 1966—67, Found. for Contemporary Performance Arts, 1970—71, Changes, Inc., 1971—72, Nat. Endowment for the Arts, 1974—75, Menil Found., 1974; recipient Broadcast Music Industry award, 1960, Lado prize, 1961—67, Benjamin award, 1961—62, Young Composer's award, Ford Found., 1964—66. Mem.: PRS, ASCAP. Office: Dunvagen Music Publs 632 Broadway Rm 902 New York NY 10012-2614 E-mail: info@dunvagen.com.

GLASS, RENÉE, educational health foundation executive; b. Elizabeth, N.J., Jan. 27, 1928; d. Samuel and Helen Peritz m. Milton L. Glass, Feb. 5, 1950; children: Jill S., Mikel L. Student, Tufts U., 1952, Northeastern U., 1954, U. Mass., 1984-85. Bd. dirs. Inst. of Contemporary Art, Boston, 1979-83; pres. Connoisier Network, Boston, 1981; founder, pres. Jaw Joints Found., Boston, 1982—. Dir. Goldberg Ctr., Northeastern U., Boston, 1993—, exec.-in-residence, 1994—, mem. wellness com., 1994—, dir. Ctr. Health in Soc., 1999; participant, lectr. health forums, NIH, 1982—; bd. dirs. Health Practice and Policy Inst. Author numerous booklets and pamphlets on temporomandibular joint disorders, 1982—; mem. editl. bd. Bus. Ethics Resource. Mem. examining com. Boston Pub. Libr., 1983-84; bd. dirs. Boch Ctr. for the Performing Arts, Cape Cod. Mem. Internat. Catacomb Soc. (bd. dirs. 1987-97). Office: Jaw Joints/Musculo-Skeletal Disorders Found Forsyth Inst 140 Fenway Boston MA 02115-3782

GLASS, RICHARD MCLEAN, psychiatry educator, medical editor; b. Phoenix, Sept. 25, 1943; s. Richard Kirkpatrick and Harriet Margaret (Bradshaw) G.; m. Rita Mae Catherine Denk, Mar. 4, 1967; children: Kathryn, Brendan Neil. BA, Northwestern U., 1965, MD, 1968. Diplomate Am. Bd. Psychiatry and Neurology. Asst. prof. psychiatry U. Chgo., 1975-82, assoc. prof., 1982-95, clin. prof., 1995—. Dir. adult psychiatry clinic U. Chgo., 1985-89. Mem. editl. bd. Archives of Gen. Psychiatry, 1984-2003; cons. editor JAMA, 1987-89, dep. editor, 1989—; contbr. articles to profl. jours. Served to major U.S. Army, 1970-72. Fellow Am. Psychiat. Assn. (disting.); mem. AAAS, AMA. Presbyterian. Avocations: tennis, music, trombone. Office: JAMA 515 N State St Chicago IL 60610-4325 E-mail: richard_glass@jama-archives.org.

GLASS, ROBERT EDWARD, retired music educator; b. Cin., Ohio, Jan. 13, 1943; s. Edward Boetler and Mildred M. Glass; m. Linda Morgan, June 6, 1981; 1 child, Bethany Lynn. BA, Morehead State U., Morehead, KY, 1966; MA, Miami U., Oxford, OH, 1980. Gen. music instr. Fairfield City Schools, Fairfield, Ohio, 1966—2001. Dir. select elem. singing groups Fairfield City Schools, Fairfield, Ohio, 1966—88, asst. band dir., 1966—70, elem. band dir., 1970—90; tuba player, Ohio, 2002—. Composer: Fairfield Alma Mater. V.p. and sec. Fairfield Residents Assn., Fairfield, Ohio, 1968—74; choir dir. Lindenwald Meth. Ch., Hamilton, Ohio, 1966—68, First United Meth. Ch., Hamilton, Ohio, 1976, St. Marks United Meth. Ch., Fairfield, Ohio, 1970—79. Achievements include design of the Fairfield City flag. Home: 6209 Morris Road Hamilton OH 45011

GLASS, ROBERT L. software engineering educator; b. Moscow, Idaho, Feb. 3, 1932; s. Leroy Conrad and Edith Helena (Huesing) G.; children— Holly, David, Steve, Carol. B.A., Culver-Stockton Coll., 1952; M.S., U. Wis.-Madison, 1954, Computing specialist N.Am. Aviation, Columbus, Ohio, 1954-57, Aerojet-Gen., Sacramento, 1957-65, The Boeing Co., Seattle, 1965-71, U. Wash., Seattle, 1971-72, The Boeing Co., Seattle, 1972-82; asst. prof. computer sci. Seattle U., 1982-87, Software Engring. Inst., 1987-88; pres. Computing Trends, Seattle, 1977—. Author: Computing Projects Which Failed, 1977, Software Reliability Guidebook, 1979, Software Maintenance Guidebook, 1981, Software Soliloquies, 1982, Real-Time Software, 1983, Computing Catastrophes, 1983, Computing Shakeout, 1987, Software Folklore, 1991, Building Quality Software, 1992, Facts and Fallacies of Software Engineering, 2003; editor emeritus Jour. Systems and Software; pub., editor The Software Practitioner. Fellow, mem. Assn. Computing Manchinery. Address: 1416 S Sare Rd Bloomington IN 47401-4431

GLASS, ROY LEONARD, lawyer; b. Littleton, N.H., Jan. 27, 1947; s. Jack Irving and Noreen (Leiuthwait) Kline; m. Suzanne Schmidt Goldstein, May 20, 1967 (div. Oct. 1978); 1 child, Shannon Renee; m. Patricia Lee Wimbish, Dec. 9, 1978 (div. 1988); 1 child, Ashley Leigh; m. Lauren Rachel Adams, Aug. 8, 1998. AA with honors, St. Petersburg Jr. Coll., Fla., 1971; BA, U. South Fla., 1972; JD, Fla. State U., 1975. Bar: Fla. 1976, U.S. Dist. Ct. (mid. dist.) Fla. 1977, U.S. Dist. Ct. (no. dist.) Fla. 1978, U.S. Supreme Ct. 1979, U.S. Ct. Appeals (11th cir.) 1983. Assoc. Meyers, Mooney & Adler, Orlando, Fla., 1976-78, Barrett, Boyd & Bajoczky, Tallahassee, 1978-79; sole practice Tallahassee, 1979-81; ptnr. Deserio & Glass, St. Petersburg, Fla., 1981-82; assoc. Battaglia, Ross, Hastings, Dicus & Andrews, St. Petersburg, 1982-85; sole practice St. Petersburg, 1985—. Lectr. Floridians Against Constl. Tampering, Fla., 1984. Capt. U.S. Army, 1966-70, Vietnam. Mem. ABA, ATLA, Am. Arbitration Assn., Fla. Acad. Trial Lawyers (mem. spkrs. bur.), Fla. Bar Assn. (health law com. 1984-85, chmn. health care profls. subcom. 1984-85, mem. exec. coun. health care sect. 1986-94, mem. spkrs. bur., chair client security fund com. 2003—), St. Petersburg Bar Assn. (legis. com. 1983-85, liaison med. soc., med. rels. com. 1985—, trial lawyers 1987—, mem. spkrs. bur.), Pinellas County Trial Lawyers Assn., St. Petersburg C. of C. (urban solutions task force 1983-84), Phi Delta Phi, Phi Kappa Phi, Beta Gamma Sigma. Clubs: Suncoast Tiger Bay (St. Petersburg, Fang & Claw award 1983), Breakfast Sertoma (Cert. of Appreciation 1984), Westgate High Twelve (Cert. of Appreciation 1987), Fla. Bar Health Law Sect. (Meritorious Svc. award 1994), Am. Coll. Barristers (sr. counsel), Roscoe Pound Inst. Office: 5501 Central Ave Saint Petersburg FL 33710-8050

GLASSCOCK, JOYCE H. state official; BJ magna cum laude, U. Mo., 1985; postgrad., George Washington U., 1993. Adminstrv. asst. Bailey, Deardourff, Sipple Polit. cons., McLean, Va., 1986; legis. corr. U.S. Senator John C. Danforth of Mo., Washington, 1987, press sec. Danforth for U.S. Senate, St. Louis, 1988; field rep. Dole for Pres., St. Louis, 1988; comms. cons. Eisenhower Centennial Found., Washington, 1989; dir .pub. affairs Econ. Devel. Adminstrn., U.S. Dept. Commerce, Washington, 1989-93; press sec. Congress Dave Hobson of Ohio, Washington, 1993-94; campaign dir. Bill Graves for Gov., Topeka, 1994; chief of staff Kans. Gov. Bill Graves, Topeka, 1994—2001; Sec. of Adminstrn. State of Kans., Topeka, 2001—. Democrat. Office: Sec of Aminstrn Curtis Bldg Topeka KS 66612

GLASSCOCK, KENTON, state legislator; m. Joyce Glasscock. BA, Kans. State U., 1976. State rep. Dist. 62 Kans. Ho. of Reps., 1991—, mem. taxation and energy and natural resources com., mem. joint com. on adminstrv. rules and regulations, chairperson calendar and printing com., vice-chairperson interstate cooperation com., majority leader, spkr., 2000—. Pres. Kans. Lumber Home-store. Home: PO Box 37 Manhattan KS 66505-0068 E-mail: glasscock@house.state.ks.us., kentglas@flinthills.com.

GLASSCOCK, LARRY CLABORN, insurance company executive; b. Cullman, Ala., Apr. 4, 1948; s. Oscar Claborn and Betty Lou (Norman) G.; m. Lee Ann Roden, Sept. 13, 1969; children— Michael, Carrie BA, Cleve. State U., 1970; postgrad., Am. Inst. Banking, Columbia U. Vice pres. personnel and orgn. AmeriTrust Co., Cleve., 1974-75, v.p. nat. div., 1976-78, v.p., mgr. credit card ctr., 1978-79, sr. v.p. consumer fin., 1980-81, sr. v.p. nat. div., 1981-83, exec. v.p. corp. banking adminstr., 1983-87; group exec. v.p. AmeriTrust Corp. and AmeriTrust Co., Cleve., 1987-92; senior v.p., COO Anthem Ins., Indpls., 1998—99, pres., CEO, 1999—; chmn. Council for Affordable Quality Healthcare, Washington, 2002—. Bd. dirs. AT Fin. Corp., AT Capital Corp., AmeriTrust Internat. Banking, AmeriTrust Devel. Bank, CT Leasing Corp., Community Mut. Ins. Co., The Gt. Lakes Constrn. Co. Trustee Cleve. State U. Devel. Found.; campaign chmn. Geauga County United Way, 1989; mem. adv. bd. Northeast Ohio Employee Ownership Ctr. Kent State U., 1987—. Served with USMC, 1970-76. Mem. Am. Inst. Banking, Am. Bankers Assn. (vice chmn. exec. com. comml. lending div.), Assn. Res. City Bankers, Greater Cleve. Growth Assn., Cleve.State U. Alumni Assn. (pres. 1987). Clubs: Union (Cleve.); Hillbrook (Chagrin Falls, Ohio); The Country (Pepper Pike, Ohio). Office: Anthem Ins 120 Monument Cir Indianapolis IN 46204-4906

GLASSE, JOHN HOWELL, retired philosophy and theology educator; b. Buffalo, June 1, 1922; s. John Alfred and Jessie Elizabeth (Howell) G.; m. Wanda Lou Howard, June 16, 1950; children: Jeffrey Howell, Paulding Howard. BA, Williamette U., 1945; B.D., Yale U., 1948, PhD, 1961. Ordained to ministry Presbyn. Ch., 1948. Dir. field work Christian Activities Council, Hartford, Conn., 1948-50, exec. dir., 1950-52; dir. Danish program Scandinavian Seminar, Inc., 1952-53; mem. faculty Vassar Coll., Poughkeepsie, N.Y., 1956—, prof. religion, 1969-90, prof. emeritus, 1990—, Frederick Weyerhaeuser chair, 1971-90, chmn. dept. religion, 1965-67, 77-83, 87-90. Vis. prof. Harvard Div. Sch., 1970, vis. scholar, 1962, 69; vis. scholar Columbia U., Union Theol. Sem., 1980-81. Contbr. articles to profl. jours. Trustee Scandinavian Seminar, 1950— . Hon. fellow Am. Scandinavian Found., 1952; grantee Am. Philos. Soc., 1964; grantee Am. Council Learned Socs., 1965, 67 Mem. Am. Acad. Religion, Am. Philos. Assn., Metaphys. Soc. Am., Soc. Values in Higher Edn., AAUP. Address: Box 347 Vassar Coll 124 Raymond Ave Poughkeepsie NY 12604-0347

GLASSELL, ALFRED CURRY, JR., investor; b. Cuba Plantation, La., Mar. 31, 1913; s. Alfred Curry and Frances (Lane) G.; m. Clare Attwell; children: Jean Curry, Alfred Curry III. BA, La. State U., 1934. Investor, 1936—; cons. Glassell Producing Co., 1938—. Past bd. dirs. Transco Cos., El Paso Nat. Gas, First City Bancorp. Trustee Houston Mus. Natural Sci., Internat. Oceanographic Found.; truste, chmn. emeritus Houston Mus. Fine Arts; former trustee Kinkaid Sch., Tex. Children's Hosp., Smithsonian Nat. Bd. Recipient Marine Sci. ann. award Internat. Oceanographic Found., 1971, Soc. Grand Founders medallion U. Miami, 1984, James Smithson award, 1991. Mem. Am. Geog. Soc., Am. Mus. Natural History, Tex. Angus Assn., Can. Chianini Assn., Houston Horse Show Assn., Tex. Cattle Breeders Assn., Am. Nat. Cattlemen's Assn., Tex. and Southwestern Cattle Raisers Assn., Mil. and Hospitaller Order St. Lazarus of Jerusalem. Clubs: Atlantic Tuna (Providence), Boston (New Orleans), Cabo Blanco Fishing (Peru), Tex. Game Fishing (Dallas), Tex. Corinthian Yacht (Kemah), Bay of Islands Swordfish and Mako Shark (New Zealand), Anglers of N.Y., Houston, Petroleum, Ramada, Bayou, Houston Country, River Oaks Country. Achievements include being a holder of the record of world's largest fish, former holder of numerous world record salt water game fish. Office: 1021 Main St Ste 2300 Houston TX 77002-6606

GLASSELL, CLAES, health products executive; MChemE, Chalmer U. Tech., Gothenberg, Sweden; cert. in adv. mgmt. program, Harvard U., 1997. Mng. dir. agrl. divsn. Berol Europe, Ltd., 1986—89; pres., CEO chemistry bus. Nordic, 1989—94; v.p. Cambrex Corp., East Rutherford, NJ, 1994—97, pres. internat., 1997—98, pres. pharm group, 1998—, COO, 2000—, pres., 2001—. Office: Cambrex Corp 1 Meadowlands Plz East Rutherford NJ 07073 Office Fax: 201-804-9853. E-mail: communications@cambrex.com.

GLASSENBERG, MYRON, neurologist; b. Chgo., Ill., Nov. 17, 1946; s. Harry and Muriel Glassenberg; m. Marsha Glassenberg, June 23, 1970; children: Daniel, Brian, Aaron. BA, Northwestern U., 1967; MD, U. Ill., 1971. Diplomate bd. diplomate Am. Bd. Neurology and Psychiatry, Am. Bd. Electrodiagnostic Medicine, Am. Bd. Electroencephelography. Cons. USPHS, Chgo., 1975—76; clin. asst. prof. neurology U. Ill. Med. Sch., Chgo., 1980—92; attending neurologist Swedish Covenant Hosp., Chgo., 1976—, Hinsdale (Ill.) Hosp., 1995—2000. Cons. neurologist North Suburban Clinic, Skokie, Ill., 1985—97, Neurospinal Ctr., Westmont, Ill., 2000—. Contbr. articles to profl. jours. Capt. USAR. Fellow: Am. Soc. for EMG and Electrodiagnosis; mem.: AMA, Nat. Headache Found., Am. Back Soc., Ill. State Med. Soc., Am. Acad. Neurology. Avocations: art, theology. Office: 2740 W Foster Chicago IL

GLASSER, ADRIAN, physiologist, researcher, scientist; b. Johannesburg, June 19, 1964; came to U.S., 1985; s. Leslie and Peta (Jaentsch) G. BS, SUNY, Albany, 1989, MS, 1990; PhD, Cornell U., 1994. Postdoctoral fellow U. Waterloo, Ont., Can., 1994-96; asst. scientist U. Wis., Madison, 1996-98; asst. prof. U. Houston, 1998—. Cons. numerous internat. pharm. cos.; expert in physiol. optics. Contbr. articles to profl. jours. and book chpts. Fellow Natural Scis. and Engring. Rsch. Coun. Can., 1994. Fellow: Am. Acad. Optometry; mem.: Assn. for Rsch. in Vision and Ophthalmology, Sigma Xi. Avocation: tennis. Office: U Houston Coll Optometry 505 J Davis Armistead Bldg Houston TX 77204-2020 E-mail: aglasser@uh.edu.

GLASSER, CHARLES EDWARD, university president; b. Chgo., Apr. 3, 1940; s. Julius J. and Hilda (Goldman) G.; m. Hannah Alex, Mar. 8, 1987; children: Gemma Maria, Julian David. BA in History, Denison U., 1961; MA in Polit. Sci., U. Ill., 1967; JD, John F. Kennedy U., 1970. Bar: Calif. 1970, U.S. Ct. Appeals (9th cir.) 1970. Pvt. practice Hineser, Spellberg & Glasser, Pleasant Hill, Calif., 1971-77; dean Sch. Law John F. Kennedy U., Orinda, Calif., 1977-83, pres., 1990—; v.p., gen. counsel Western Hosp. Corp., Emeryville, Calif., 1983-90. Author: The Quest for Peace, 1986. Mem. Calif. Bar Assn. Office: John F Kennedy U 12 Altarinda Rd Orinda CA 94563-2603

GLASSER, IRA SAUL, civil liberties organization executive; b. Bklyn., Apr. 18, 1938; s. Sidney and Anne (Goldstein) Glasser; m. Trude Maria Robinson, June 28, 1959; children: David, Andrew, Peter, Sally. BS in Math., Queens Coll., 1959; MA in Math., Ohio State U., 1960; LLD (hon.), N.Y. Law Sch., 2001. Instr. math. Queens Coll., N.Y.C., 1960—63; lectr. math. Sarah Lawrence Coll., Bronxville, NY, 1962—65; assoc. editor Current Mag., N.Y.C., 1962—64, editor, 1964—67; assoc. dir. N.Y. Civil Liberties Union, N.Y.C., 1967—70, exec. dir., 1970—78, ACLU, 1978—2001. Cons. U. Ill.-Champaign-Urbana, 1964—65; dir. Asian Am. Legal Def. and Edn. Fund, N.Y.C., 1974—; pres., bd. dirs. Drug Policy Alliance N.Y. (formerly Lindesmith Ctr./Drug Policy Found.), 1991—. Author: Visions of Liberty: The Bill of Rights for All Americans, 1991; co-author: Doing Good: The Limits of Benevolence, 1978; contbr. articles to profl. jours. Chmn. St. Vincents Hosp., N.Y.C., Cmty. Adv. Bd., N.Y.C., 1970—72. Recipient Martin Luther King, Jr. award, N.Y. Assn. Black Sch. Suprs., 1971, Gavel award, ABA, 1972, Allard K. Lowenstein award, Park River Ind. Dem., 1981, Malcolm, Martin, Mandela award, Greater Rapt. Trinity Ch., 1993, Justice in Action award, Asian Am. Legal Def. and Edn. Fund, 1999. Avocation: sports.

GLASSER, JAMES J. leasing company executive, retired; b. Chgo., June 5, 1934; s. Daniel D. and Sylvia G.; m. Louise D. Rosenthal, Apr. 19, 1964; children: Mary, Emily, Daniel. AB, Yale U., 1955; JD, Harvard U., 1958. Bar: Ill. 1958. Asst. states atty., Cook County, Ill., 1958-61; mem. exec. staff GATX Corp., Chgo., 1961-69, pres., 1974-96, chmn. bd., CEO, 1978-96, chmn. emeritus, 1996—, also dir. Gen. mgr. Infilco Products Co., 1969-70; v.p. GATX Leasing Corp., San Francisco, 1970-71, pres., 1971-74; bd. dirs. B.F. Goodrich Co., Harris Bankcorp, Inc., Harris Trust & Savs. Bank, Mut. Trust Life Ins. Co. Bd. dirs. Lake Forest Hosp., Northwestern Meml. Corp., Voices for Ill. Children; trustee Better Govt. Assn., Chgo. Zool. Soc., U. Chgo. Mem. Chgo. C. of C. (dir.), Chgo. Cen. Area Com. (dir.), Econ. Club of Chgo., Commercial Club, Casino Club, Chgo. Club, Racquet Club, Onwentsia Club (Lake Forest, Ill.), Shoreacres (Lake Bluff, Ill.), Tucson Country Club, Chi Psi. Home: 464 N Mayflower Rd Lake Forest IL 60045-2306 Office: 500 W Monroe St Chicago IL 60661-3630

GLASSER, JOSEPH, manufacturing and marketing executive; b. Phila., May 17, 1925; BS in Econs., U. Pa., 1947, MBA, 1948, postgrad., 1948-51. With NLRB, 1948-51; internal mgmt. cons., 1954-55; mem. faculty Sch. Bus. Adminstrn., U. Conn., 1955-81, prof. emeritus, 1981—; pres. Eljen Corp., 1971—. Arbitrator Fed. Mediation and Conciliation Service, VA, Nat. Mediation Bd., Soc. Security Adminstrn., Am. Arbitration Assn.; fact finder Mass. Bd. Mediation and Arbitration, Ct. Bd. Mediation and Arbitration, N.H. Pub. Employee Labor Relations Bd.; mediator Conn. Bd. Edn.; rev. officer FAA; mem. Nat. Def. Exec. Res.-Fed. Emergency Mgmt. Agy.; speaker seminars, also mgmt. groups in Eng., Austria and Hungary, Am. Mgmt. Assn. Author: Fundamentals of Applied Industrial Management; contbr. articles to profl. jours. Served to lt. col. USAF, ETO. Decorated Air medal with four oak leaf clusters, Air Force commendation medal. Mem. Soc. Profls. in Dispute Resolution, Indsl. Rels. Rsch. Assn., Nat. Assns. Mgmt. Educators (Innovative Mgmt. Edn. award 1976), Nat. Assn. Suggestion Systems (winner internat. papers competition 1975), Res. Officers Assn., Air Force Assn. Office: Eljen Corp 10 N Main St #216-217 Hartford CT 06107-1968

GLASSER, LYNN SCHREIBER, publisher; b. Chgo., Sept. 19, 1943; d. Alexander Paul and Beatrice (Bollard) Schreiber; m. Stephen A. Glasser, Dec. 30, 1965; children: Susan, Laura, Jeffrey, Jennifer. BA, Chatham Coll., 1965. Publs. editor Inst. CLE U. Mich. Law Sch., Ann Arbor, 1966-68; asst. to dir. Practising Law Inst., N.Y.C., 1968-71; v.p., COO Law Jour. Press and Law Jour. Seminars, N.Y.C., 1971-78; exec. v.p., pub. Law & Bus./Harcourt Jovanovich, Inc., N.Y.C., 1978-86; co-pres. Prentice Hall Law & Bus., Englewood Cliffs, N.J., 1986-94; cons. Simon and Schuster, N.Y.C., 1994-95; pres. Glasser Publ. Inc., Little Falls, N.J., 1995—. Organizer, originator over 1000 CLE seminars, 1986—; organizer Woman Advt. Conf., N.Y.C., Chgo. and San Francisco, 1993-94; chmn. Woman Bus. Lawyer Conf., N.Y.C. and San Francisco, 1994. Trustee N.J. Chamber Music Soc., Montclair, 1989—, Montclair Art Mus., 1998—; Cmty. Found. of N.J., Morristown, 1995—; co-donor Lynn & Stephen Glasser Scholarship Fund, Colgate U., 1988—, Bloomfield Coll., 1993—. Office: 150 Clove Rd Little Falls NJ 07424-2138

GLASSER, MICHAEL A. lawyer; b. Norfolk, Va., Nov. 17, 1953; BA with distinction, U. Va., 1975; JD, U. Richmond, 1978. Bar: (Va.) 1978, U.S. Dist. Ct. Va. (ea. dist.) 1978, U.S. Ct. Appeals (4th cir.) 1978, U.S. Supreme Ct. 1997. Ptnr. Glasser & Glasser, Norfolk. Mem.: Va. State Bar (pres. 2001—02). Office: Glasser & Glasser Crown Ctr Bldg 580 E Main St Ste 600 Norfolk VA 23510

GLASSER, PAMELA JEAN, musician, music educator; b. Livonia, Mich., June 26, 1953; d. Walter and Margaret Julia (Geersens) Glasser; m. Richard Barth Turner, Sept. 7, 1996. BEd in Music, Wayne State U., 1976; M of Music, Rice U., 1982. Prin. hornist Wyo. Symphony Orch., Casper, 1994—, Jackson Hole Symphony, 1999—2002; adj. prof. horn Casper Coll., 1998—2001; artistic dir. Casper Chamber Music Soc., 2001—; dir. music Fremont Sch. Dist. # 2, Dubois, Wyo., 2001—. Hornist music edn. programs Wyo. Arts Coun., 1993; hornist, solo performer Llangollen Eisteddfod North Wales, 1978. Mem.: SPLC, ACLU, NEA, Casper Chamber Music Soc. (ednl. liaison 1997—2001), Wyo. Edn. Assn., Am. Fedn. Musicians. Democrat. Episcopalian. Avocations: field and space science, organic gardening, cross country skiing, science fiction, crystal and mineral collecting, world music, religion. Home: PO Box 1357 Dubois WY 82513-1357 E-mail: pjglasser@yahoo.com.

GLASSER, PAUL HAROLD, sociologist, educator, social worker, university administrator; b. N.Y.C., Aug. 21, 1929; s. David and Rae (Startz) G.; m. Lois Hannah Naefach, Nov. 25, 1954 (div. June 1993); children: Heather Denys, Frederick Naefach. BS, CCNY, 1949; MS, Columbia U., 1951; PhD, U. N.C., 1961. Chief psychiat. social work sect. Mental Hygiene Clinic, Camp Chaffee Army Hosp., Ark., 1952-53; asst. dir. residence Child Guidance Home, Inc., 1953-55; instr. psychiat. group work, dept. psychiatry Med. Sch. U. Cin., 1953-55; asst. prof. U. Mich., Ann Arbor, 1958-63, assoc. prof., 1963-65, prof. Sch. Social Work, 1965-78; dean Grad. Sch. Social Work U. Tex., Arlington, 1978-88; dean Sch. Social Work Rutgers U., State U. of N.J., New Brunswick, 1988-92, prof. II, 1988—. Vis. prof. Paul Baerwald Sch. Social Work, Hebrew U., Jerusalem, spring 1987, City U. Hong Kong, fall 1993, Bar-Ilan Sch. Social Work, spring 1997, Tel Aviv U., 2002—. Author: Small Groups in Hospital Community, 1967, Families in Crisis, 1970, Social Work Education for Family and Population Planning, 1973, Individual Change Through Small Groups, 1974, 2d edit., 1985, Social Work Roles and Functions in Family and Population Planning, 1974, Child Abuse and Neglect: A Challenge to the Caring Community, 1977, Group Workers at Work: Theory and Practice in the 80's, 1986, The First Helping Interview: Engaging the Client and Building Trust, 1996, in Russian, 2003, Il Primo Colloquio: Coinvolgiemento e Relazione Nelle Professioni D'aruto, 1999; sr. editor: Ency. Social Work, 1971, LaRicerca Valutative, 1972; editor Jour. Health and Social Behavior, 1970-73, Jour. Social Work, 1965-69, Jour. Marriage and Family Counseling, 1974-82, Social Work with Groups, Hong Kong Jour. Social Work, 1998—, Jour. Social Work and Social Policy in Israel, 1988—. Bd. dirs. Washtenau County Family Service, 1964-66, 69-70. Served to 1st lt. AUS, 1952-53. Fulbright Hays lectr. Italy, 1971; Fulbright Hays lectr. U. Philippines, 1966-67; Fulbright Hays lectr. Australia, 1973-74 Mem. Nat. Assn. Social Workers (chpt. chmn. 1962-63), Am. Sociol. Soc., Masons. Office: State U of NJ Rutgers U Sch Social Work 536 George St New Brunswick NJ 08901-1167 E-mail: pglasser@rci.rutgers.edu. *The generation and the dispersal of knowledge are the two primary ways in which the academician contributes to the society. He is an agent of change as he studies what is, in order to suggest what might be, and communicates this to his students. My career has been devoted to these principles and to stimulating others to follow them.*

GLASSER, STEPHEN ANDREW, publishing executive, lawyer; b. Memphis, July 27, 1943; s. Melvin A. and Esther (Kron) G.; m. Lynn Schreiber, Dec. 30, 1965; children: Susan, Laura, Jeffrey, Jennifer. BA cum laude, Colgate U., 1965; JD, U. Mich., 1968. Bar: D.C., 1968. Asst. dir. Practising Law Inst., N.Y.C., 1968-71; exec. v.p., exec. editor N.Y. Law Pub. Co., N.Y.C., 1971-77; pres. Law & Bus. Inc. div. Harcourt Brace Jovanovich, N.Y.C., 1977-86, Prentice Hall Law & Bus. div. Simon & Schuster Profl Info Group, Englewood Cliffs, N.J., 1986-94; chmn. Glasser Publs. Inc., Little Falls, N.J., 1995—. Co-founder, editor, publisher Legal Times of Washington, 1978-86. Former trustee Mental Health Assn. of Essex County; trustee Bloomfield Coll., chmn. bd., 1999—2000, former chmn. fin. and property com., 2000—01, 1st vice chair, 2001—; trustee The Hospice Inc. Mem. ABA, D.C. Bar Assn., Assn. Bar City N.Y., Phi Beta Kappa, Montclair Golf Club. Home: 86 Highland Ave Montclair NJ 07042-1910 Office: Glasser Publs Inc 150 Clove Rd Ste 14 Little Falls NJ 07424-2149

GLASSER, WOLFGANG GERHARD, chemical engineering wood science researcher, educator; b. Oct. 9, 1941; came to U.S., 1969, naturalized, 2001; s. Joachim and Charlotte (Syjatz) G.; m. Heidemarie Reinecke, Mar. 18, 1969; children: Christine Glasser Sutherland, Stephan A. Degree in wood tech., U. Hamburg, Germany, 1966; PhD in Wood Chemistry, U. Hamburg, 1969. Rsch. assoc. U. Wash., Seattle, 1969-70, rsch. asst. prof., 1970-71; asst. prof. Va. Poly. Inst. and State U., Blacksburg, 1972-75, assoc. prof., 1975-80, prof. wood chemistry, 1980—2002, assoc. dean rsch. and grad. studies Coll. Forestry and Wildlife Resources, 1993-98, prof. emeritus wood sci. & forest products 2002—. Adj. prof. Inst. of Paper Sci. and Tech., Atlanta, 1999—; dir. Pulp and Paper Research Inst., Sao Paulo, Brazil, 1976, Biobased Materials Ctr., 1988-91; vis. prof. U. Grenoble (France), Centre de Recherche sur Macromolecules Vegetales, Grenoble, 1985, Nat. U. Singapore, 1993, Kyoto (Japan) U., 1998, U. Toulouse, France, 2000, Chalmers U. Tech., Gothenborg, Sweden, 2001-02; chmn. panel NAS, 1974-76. Mem. editl. adv. group Holzforschung, Braunschweig, Germany, 1985—, Cellulose Chem. Tech., 1987—, Cellulose, 1994-99, Jour. Wood Sci. (Japan), 1998—, Jour. Applied Polymer Sci., 1989—; patentee in field; contbr. articles to profl. jours.; book editor; editor-in-chief Cellulose, 2000—. Co-recipient George Olmsted award Am. Paper Inst., 1974; recipient Sci. Achievement award Internat. Union Forest Rsch. Orgns., 1986, Anselme Payen award Cellulose, Papr and Textile divsn. Am Chem. Soc., 2000. Fellow Internat. Acad. Wood Sci. Tech.; mem. Am. Chem. Soc. (fellow div. cellulose and renewable materials, alt. councilor 1983-85, pub. chmn. 1985-88, chmn.-elect 1989, chmn. 1990, councilor 1991-2000, program chmn. 1993-96), Soc. Wood Sci. Tech., Sigma Xi, Phi Beta Delta. Lutheran. Office: Va Tech 210 Julian Cheatham Hall Wood Sci Forest Products Blacksburg VA 24061 E-mail: wglasser@vt.edu.

GLASSGOLD, ISRAEL LEON, construction company executive, engineer, consultant; b. Phila., Oct. 14, 1923; s. Solomon Sidney and Anna (Blaukopf) G.; m. Iris Jacqueline Silverman, Dec. 21, 1952; children: Marc Steven, Lori Beth, Jill Ellen. BSCE, U. Pa., 1944, MSCE, 1948. Registered profl. engr., Pa. Instr. U. Pa., Phila., 1946-48; chief engr. Masonry Resurfacing and Constrn. Co., Balt., 1948—, pres., 1948-94. Contbr. articles to profl. jours. Vice pres. Chizuk Amuno Congregation, Balt., 1984-86, pres., 1986-88; trustee Balt. Hebrew U., 1991-97. Ensign USNR, 1944-45, PTO. Fellow: ASCE, Am. Concrete Inst. (pres. Md. chpt., bd. dirs. 1984—87, tech. activities com. 1980—86, Bloem award 1979, Turner award 1987, chpt. activities award 1988), Am. Concrete Inst. Internat. (hon.; pres. 1991—92); mem.: ASTM (C-9 1998, chair C09.46 shotcrete 1990—2002), Engrs. Club, Suburban Club, Tau Beta Pi. Democrat. Jewish. Office: Masonry Resurfacing & Constrn Co 33 Stahl Point Rd Baltimore MD 21226-1747 E-mail: 102126.1102@compuserve.com.

GLASSHEIM, ELIOT ALAN, editor, state legislator; b. N.Y.C., Feb. 10, 1938; s. Raymond S. and Edith (Ruthizer) G.; m. Patricia Sanborn, July 20, 1969 (div. Feb. 1979); children: Eagle, Don; m. Dyan Rey, Feb. 14, 1996. BA, Wesleyan U., 1960; MA, U. N.Mex., 1966, PhD, 1972. Copy boy, book reviewer Wash. Post, 1960-61; editl. proofreader Wall St. Jour., N.Y.C., 1962-64; mgmt. trainee Accessory Fashions, N.Y.C., 1964-66; asst. prof. English, Augusta (Ga.) Coll., 1968-70; fellow U. N.D., Grand Forks, 1971-73; mem. N.D. Ho. of Reps., Grand Forks, 1975-76, 93—, house appropriations com., 2001—, asst. Dem. leader, 2003—; grant writer, dir. oral history project of 97 flood N.D. Mus. Art, Grand Forks, 1993-99; owner used bookstore and Internet sales Dr. Eliot's Twice Sold Tales, Grand Forks, 1992—; policy analyst No. Great Plains, Inc., Grand Forks, 1999—. Dir. Population/Food Fund, Grand Forks, 1977-79; housing coord., grantswriter N.D. Migrant Coun., Grand Forks, 1979-81. Editor: Population and Food Issues, 1977, 1978, Voices from the Flood, 1999, Behind the Scenes, 2002, Toward New Horizons: Moving the Northern Great Plains Region to a Stronger Economic Future, 2002; author (poems): The Restless Giant, 1968. Exec. dir. Quad County Cmty. Action Agy., Grand Forks, 1981—87; field rep., office mgr. U.S. Senator Quentin Burdick, Grand Forks, 1987—92; mem. Grand Forks City Coun., 1982—, Grand Forks Planning and Zoning Com., 1984—96, mem. flood response com., 1997—2000, chmn. population task force, 2001; chmn. interim legis. Commerce Commn., 1999—2000; founder, dir. Red River Valley Habitat for Humanity, Grand Forks, 1988—99; chmn. Dist. 17/18 Dems., Grand Forks, 1980—81; bd. dirs. Prairie Pub. TV, 1997—2000. Home: 619 N 3rd St Grand Forks ND 58203-3203 E-mail: eglasshe@state.nd.us.

GLASSICK, CHARLES ETZWEILER, academic foundation administrator; b. Wrightsville, Pa., Apr. 6, 1931; s. Gordon J. and Melva G. (Etzweiler) G.; m. Mary Williams, Feb. 27, 1952; children: Bruce, Judith, Jeffrey, Robert, Jonathan. BS with honors, Franklin and Marshall Coll., 1953; MA, PhD, Princeton U., 1957; D.Sc. (hon.), U. Richmond, 1977; L.L.D. (hon.), Dickinson Sch. Law, 1986; LLD, Pepperdine U., 1996, Adrian Coll., 1997; LHD (hon.), Franklin & Marshall Coll., 1997. Research chemist Rohm & Haas Co., Phila., 1957-62; instr. gen. chemistry Temple U., Phila., 1957-62; prof. chemistry Adrian (Mich.) Coll., 1962-68; v.p. Great Lakes Colls. Assn., Ann Arbor, Mich., 1968-69; asso. dean for acad. affairs Albion (Mich.) Coll., 1969-71, v.p. for acad. affairs, 1971-72; pres. Va. Inst. Scientific Research, Richmond, 1972-77; provost, v.p. for acad. affairs U. Richmond, Va., 1972-77; pres. Gettysburg (Pa.) Coll., 1977-89, Woodruff Arts Ctr., Atlanta, 1990-96; sr. scholar Carnegie Found. for Advancement of Tchg., Menlo Park, Calif., 1989-90, acting pres., 1995, interim pres., 1996-97, sr. assoc., 1997-2001, sr. assoc. emeritus, 2001—; interim pres. N.C. Wesleyan Coll., 2000-01, Reinhardt Coll., 2001—02. Cons. NEH, 1971-72, NSF, 1963-67, Va. Coun. High Edn., 1972-76; mem. exec. com. Luth. Ednl. Conf. of N.Am., 1983-86; mem. Pres.'s Commn. Nat. Collegiate Athletic Assn., 1988-89; interim pres. Converse Coll., 1998-99; interim dir. Scholars Press, 1999-2000; vis. fellow Cambridge U., 2002. Mem. editorial bd. Liberal Education, 1978-82, Educational Record, 1985-97. Mem. Mental Health and Mental Retardation Task Force Manpower Devel., Richmond, 1975—77, ACE Commn. on Minorities; bd. dirs. Meth. Conf. Homes Aging, 1985—89, Hist. Gettysburg/Adams County, 1979—89, Midtown Alliance, 1991—97; mem. exec. com. Atlanta Cultural Olympiad, 1991—96; trustee, vice-chmn. Carnegie Found. Advancement in Tchg., 1991—97, Eisenhower Soc., 1985—95, Ga. Found. Ind. Colls., 1992—, Literacy Action, Inc., 1994—97, Found. Hosp. Art, 1994—; bd. curators Ga. Hist. Soc., 1997—99; bd. regents Am. Arch. Fedn., 1998—; Fulbright sr. scholar specialist, 2002—. Mem. AAAS, AAUP, Am. Chem. Soc., N.Y. Acad. Scis., Danforth Assocs., Am. Chem. Soc., Phi Beta Kappa (hon.), Beta Gamma Sigma, Omicron Delta Kappa, Alpha Chi Omega. Methodist. Home: 216 Mills Ave Spartanburg SC 29302 E-mail: CEGlassick@aol.com.

GLASSMAN, ALEXANDER HOWARD, psychiatrist, researcher; b. Chgo., Feb. 4, 1934; s. Morris and Mindelle (Sosna) G.; m. B. Judith Cohen, Mar. 28, 1958; children: Steven, Laura Glassman Hercher. BS, U. Ill., Chgo., 1956, MD, 1958. Diplomate Am. Bd. Neurology and Psychiatry. Resident in psychiatry Albert Einstein Med. Coll. Medicine, Yeshiva U., N.Y.C., 1954-62; USPH fellow, 1963-64; asst. prof. psychiatry Albert Einstein Coll. Medicine, Bronx, N.Y., 1964-65, cons. psychopharmacologist, 1972-78; dir. residency tng. Letterman Gen. Hosp., San Francisco, 1967-68, chief psychiatry svc., 1968-69; dir. affective diseases N.Y. State Psychiat. Inst., N.Y.C., 1973-78, chief clin. psychopharmacology, 1978—; prof. clin. psychiatry Coll. Physicians and Surgeons, Columbia U., N.Y.C., 1980—. Mem. merit rev. bd. VA, Washington, 1987-90. Editor: Treatment Strategies in Refractory Depression, 1990, also 5 other books; contbr. articles to jours. in field; patentee in field. Lt. col. U.S. Army, 1967-69. Recipient Established Investigator award Nat. Assn. for Rsch. Affective Diseases and Schizophrenia, 1990, N.Y. State Psychiat. Rsch. award, 1994; invited spkr. Nobel Com. Conf. of Depression, Stockholm, 1983; Plenery spkr. German Psychiat. Assn., Fed. Republic Germany, 1990, Plenery spkr. Japanese Neurosci. Soc., Nagoya, 1994. Fellow Am. Coll. Neuropsychopharmacology, Am. Psychiat. Assn. (Lifetime achievement prize 1989); mem. AAAS, Am. Psychopath. Assn. (trustee), N.Y. Acad. Sci. Achievements include patent for clonidine in smoking cessation; first to recognize unique treatment response of delusionally depressed patients, to demonstrate relationship between antidepressant drug treatment outcome and individual differences in drug metabolism, to describe the cardiac antiarrhythmic effects of antidepressant drugs, to describe relationship between depression and cigarette smoking. Office: Columbia U Dept Psychiatry 1051 Riverside Dr New York NY 10032-2695 E-mail: ahg1@columbia.edu.

GLASSMAN, ARMAND BARRY, physician, pathologist, scientist, educator, administrator; b. Paterson, N.J., Sept. 9, 1938; s. Paul and Rosa (Ackerman) G.; m. Alberta C. Macri, Aug. 30, 1958; children: Armand P., Steven B., Brian A. BA, Rutgers U., N.J., 1960; MD magna cum laude, Georgetown U., Washington, 1964. Diplomate Am. Bd. Pathology, Am. Bd. Nuclear Medicine. Intern Georgetown U. Hosp., Washington, 1964-65; resident Yale-New Haven Hosp., West Haven VA Hosp., 1965-69; asst. prof. pathology, Coll. Medicine U. Fla.; chief radioimmunoassary lab. Gainesville VA Hosp.; practice lab. and nuc. medicine, 1969-71; dir. clin. labs., assoc. prof., prof. pathology, cellular, molecular biology Med. Coll. Ga., Augusta, 1971-76; cons. physician in nuclear medicine Univ. Hosp., Augusta, 1973-76; med. dir. clin. labs. Med. U. S.C. Hosp., Charleston, 1976-87; attending physician in lab. and nuclear medicine Med. U. S.C., Charleston, 1976-87, assoc. med. dir. Med. U. Hosp. and Clinics, 1982-86; med. dir. clin. labs. Charleston Meml. Hosp., S.C., 1976-87; cons. VA Hosp., Charleston, 1976-87; prof., chmn. dept. lab. medicine Med. U. S.C., 1976-87, med. dir. MT and MLT programs, 1976-87, clin. prof. pathology, lab. medicine, and radiology, 1987—, acting chmn. dept. immunology and microbiology, 1985-87, assoc. dean Coll. Medicine, 1979-85, asst. and assoc. dean Coll. Allied Health Sci., 1984-87, chmn. hosp. exec. com., 1985-86, acting med. dir. Univ. Hosp. and Clinics, 1985-86; sr. v.p. med. affairs, prof. lab. medicine and nuclear medicine Montefiore Med. Ctr. and Albert Einstein Coll. Medicine, Bronx, N.Y., 1987-89; v.p., lab. dir. Nat. Reference Lab., Nashville, 1989-92; from clin. prof. to prof. dept. pathology Vanderbilt U., Nashville, 1990-94; dir. Vanderbilt Pathology Lab. Svcs., 1992-94; dir. clin. labs. Vanderbilt U. Med. Ctr., 1993-94, O. Stribling chair, prof., 1994—; head and chair divsn./dept. lab. medicine U. Tex., M.D. Anderson Cancer Ctr., Houston, 1994-96, also med. dir. Med. Tech. & Cytogenetic Tech. programs, 1994-96, 2001—, also dir. sect. cytogenetics, 1994—, also dir. sect. cytogenetic, 2002—, chair ops. and improvement mgmt. com. dept. hematopathology, 1998—2002, prof. Grad. Sch. Biol. Scis., 1994—. Adj. prof. Grad. Sch. Biol. Scis. and U. Tex. Health Scis. Med. Sch., 1994–; adv. coun. Trident Tech. Coll., 1976-87; bd. dirs. Fetter Family Health Ctr.; mem. steering com. pathology and lab medicine U. Tex. M.D. Anderson Cancer Ctr., 1998-2000, mem. radiation safety com., 1998-, pharmacy and therapeutics com., 2000-, credentials com., 2002—, radiation drug rsch. com., 2003—, chmn. task force on antiemetic drugs, 2003—; founding dir. Sealite, Inc., 1987-99, chmn. bd. dirs., 1995-99; med. adv. com. Nashville Red Cross Blood Ctr., 1991-94, acting med. dir., 1991-92; bd. sci. advisors Nat. Health Labs./Nat. Reference Lab., 1992-94; trustee, bd. dirs. Gulf Coast Cmty. Blood Ctr., 1994—; cons. in field. Editor, co-editor 4 books; bd. editors Annals of Clin. and Lab. Scis., 1981—; contbr. over 170 articles to profl. jours., 30 chpts. to books. Trustee Coll. Prep. Sch., 1979-84, chmn. bd. 1983-84; trustee, bd. dirs., v.p. Mason Prep. Sch., 1984-87; bd. dirs. United Way, 1983-87, Am. Cancer Soc., 1984-87; co-founder, bd. dirs. Glassman Family Fund, 1998—. With USMCR, 1956-64. Johnson and Avalon Found. scholar Georgetown U., 1961-64, State scholar Rutgers U., 1956-60. Fellow ACP, Coll. Am. Pathologists (numerous coms.), Assn. Clin. Scientists (Diploma of Honor 1987, pres. 1990-91, exec. com. 1990-95, Clin. Scientist of Yr. 1993, C.P. Brown lectr. 1995), Am. Soc. Clin. Pathology (coun. immunohematology and blood banking 1983-89, coun. grad. med. edn. and rsch. 1998—, Commr.'s award for Continuing Edn. 1989, nat. contbg. editor to Resident In-Svc. Exam. 2000-) Am. Bd. Pathology (transfusion medicine/blood bank test com. 1984-88), Am. Coll. Nuc. Medicine, N.Y. Acad. Medicine; mem. Internat. Acad. Pathology, Am. Assn. Pathologists, Soc. Nuc. Medicine (chmn. edn. com. 1973-77, acad. coun. 1979-92), AMA (Physician's Recognition award, instnl. rep. to sect. on med. schs., 1987-94, 2003—), So. Med. Assn., Am. Geriat. Soc. (founding fellow So. divsn.), Am. Soc. Microbiology, Am. Assn. Blood Banks (chmn. cryobiology com. 1974-83, edn. com. 1978-85, sci. program com. 1981-84, autologous transfusion com. 1979-83, bd. dirs. 1984-87, transfusion practices com. 1992-96), Assn. Schs. Allied Health Professions (bd. editors jour. 1979-83), Soc. Cryobiology (treas., bd. dirs. 1978-80), AAAS, N.Y. Acad. Scis., Acad. Clin. Lab. Physicians and Scientists (exec. coun. 1978-85, pres. 1982-83), S.E. Area Blood Bankers (pres. 1979-81, exec. coun. 1980-85), Tenn. Assn. Blood Banks (treas. 1993-94), Am. Coll. Physician Execs., Sigma Xi, Alpha Eta, Alpha Omega Alpha. Avocations: jogging, tennis, community service. Office: U Tex MD Anderson Cancer Ctr Hematopathology Unit 350 1515 Holcombe Blvd Houston TX 77030-4009 E-mail: aglassma@mail.mdanderson.org.

GLASSMAN, CAROLINE DUBY, state supreme court justice; b. Baker, Oreg., Sept. 13, 1922; d. Charles Ferdinand and Caroline Marie (Colton) Duby; m. Harry Paul Glassman, May 21, 1953; 1 son, Max Avon. LLB summa cum laude, Willamette U., 1944. Bar: Oreg. 1944, Calif. 1952, Maine 1969. Atty. Title Ins. & Trust Co., Salem, Oreg., 1944-46; assoc. Belli, Ashe, Pinney & Melvin Belli, San Francisco, 1952-58; ptnr. Glassman & Potter, Portland, Maine, 1973-78, Glassman, Beagle & Ridge, Portland, 1978-83; justice Maine Supreme Judicial Ct., Portland, 1983-97. Lectr. Sch. Law, U. Maine, 1967-68, 80 Author: Legal Status of Homemakers in State of Maine, 1977. Mem.: ATLA, Russian Am. Rule of Law Consortium, Maine Trial Law Assn., Maine Bar Assn., Calif. Bar Assn., Oreg. Bar Assn., Am. Law Inst. Roman Catholic. Home: 56 Thomas St Portland ME 04102-3639

GLASSMAN, CYNTHIA A. commissioner; BA in econo., Wellesley Coll.; MA, PhD in econo., U. Pa. With Economists Inc., 1987—89; mng. dir. Furash & Co., Financial Svcs., 1989—97; prin. Ernst & Young, 1997—2001; commr. US SEC, 2002—. Mem.: Commn on Savings and Investment in Am., Women in Housing and Finance, Fed. Res. Bd Credit Union, Nat Economists Club. Office: US SEC 450 Fifth St NW Washington DC 20549

GLASSMAN, EDWARD, public relations management creativity consultant; b. N.Y.C., Mar. 18, 1929; s. Jacob S. and Riesa (Bronfman) F.; children: Lyn Judith, Susan Fiona, Ellen Ruth, Marjorie Riesa. AB, NYU, 1949, MS, 1951; PhD, Johns Hopkins U., 1955. Mem. staff City of Hope Med. Ctr., Duarte, Calif., 1959-60; prof., faculty biochemistry dept. med. sch. U. N.C., Chapel Hill, 1960-90, head program for team effectiveness and creativity, 1981-90; prof. emeritus, 1990—; pres. Leadership Cons. Svcs., Inc., Creativity Coll., Chapel Hill, 1990—. Mem. grants and rev. study sect. NIMH, 1966-69, U. Calif., Irvine, 1978; vis. fellow Ctr. Creative Leadership, Greensboro, N.C., 1983; vis. scientist Stanford Rsch. Inst., Menlo Park, Calif., 1986; pres. Creativity Coll. divsn. Leadership Consulting Svcs., Inc., Chapel Hill. Author: Molecular Approaches to Neurobiology, 1967, For Presidents Only: Unlocking the Creative Potential of Your Management Team, 1990, Creativity Handbook, 1991, The Creativity Factor: Unlocking the Potential of Your Team, 1991; columnist Creativity at Work, Chapel Hill Newspaper, 1991-92, Triangle Bus. Jour., 1992-95, Chapel Hill Herald, 1992-94, Moore County Citizens News Record, 1994-96; mem. editl. adv. bd. Behavioral Biology, 1971-78, Pharmacology, Biochemistry and Behavior, 1973-88; mem. bd. advisors Neurochem.

Rsch., 1975-78; contbr. 95 articles to profl. jours. Pub. rels. specialist Lions Club, 1995—. Adam T. Bruce fellow, 1954-55; Am. Cancer Soc. fellow, 1955-57; NIH fellow, 1958-59; NIH Career Devel. award, 1961-71; Guggenheim fellow, 1968-69 Fellow AAAS, Royal Soc. Edinburgh; mem. Soc. Neurosci. (pres. N.C. chpt. 1974-75), Elisha Mitchell Sci. Soc. (v.p. 1965-66) Home and Office: 679 Cedar Pt Vass NC 28394-8686

GLASSMAN, GEORGE MORTON, dermatologist; b. N.Y.C., Sept. 7, 1935; s. Oscar and Jeanette (Bitterbaum) G.; m. Carol Beth Frankford, July 10, 1960; children: Keith F., Laurie C. BA cum laude, Brown U., 1957; MD, NYU, 1962. Diplomate Nat. Bd. Med. Examiners. Rotating intern Greenwich (Conn.) Hosp., 1962-63; resident in dermatology NYU Med. Ctr., N.Y.C., 1963-66; chief dermatology U.S. Navy, St. Albans, N.Y., 1966-68; pvt. practice White Plains, N.Y., 1968-96. Clinical asst. prof. Albert Einstein Coll. Medicine, Bronx, N.Y., 1970-75, N.Y. Med. Coll., Valhalla, N.Y., 1975-87; assoc. attending dermatologist Westchester County Med. Ctr., Valhalla, 1974-87, St. Agnes Hosp., White Plains, 1978-96; attending dermatologist White Plains Hosp., 1977-96. Contbr. articles to profl. jours. Lt. comdr. USN, 1966-68. Mem. Am. Acad. Dermatology (Continuing Med. Edn. award, 1980—), Westchester County Med. Soc., Westchester Acad. Medicine (pres. dermatology sect., 1990-91), N.Y. State Soc. Dermatology, AMA (Physician's Recognition award, 1980—), Soc. for Pediatric Dermatology. Home and Office: 268 Stuart Dr New Rochelle NY 10804-1423

GLASSMAN, GERALD SEYMOUR, metal finishing company executive; b. Hartford, Conn., July 6, 1932; s. Abram and Lena (Rulnick)) G.; m. Edwina Wellins, Dec. 1, 1963; children: Cynthia Anne Heilweil, Barbara Diane Dell, Richard Philip Glassman. BS, U. Vt., 1954. Exec. Bland Co., Hartford, Conn., 1954-63, Coleco Industries, Hartford, 1963-75; pres. Stanley Plating Co., Forestville, Conn., 1977-82; chmn. CBR Industries, Plainville, Conn., 1977-82; pres. Plainville Plating Co., 1975-97, chmn., 1998—; pres. Internat. Metal Finishing, Inc., 1986—; mem. regional adv. bd. Bank of Boston Ct., Plainville, 1979-89; mem. adv. bd. 1st Nat. Bank of New Eng., 1991—99. Pres. Tunxis C.C. Found., 1978-88; trustee Wheeler Clinic, 1979-89, Plainville YMCA, 1980—; mem. Assocs. U. Hartford. Mem. Nat. Assn. Metal Finishers, Conn. Assn. Metal Finishers (v.p.), Metal Finishers Assn. Conn. (pres.), NAM, Am. Electroplaters Soc., Plainville C. of C., Masons. Jewish. Home: 23 Hazen Dr Avon CT 06001 Office: 21 Forestville Ave Plainville CT 06062-2159 E-mail: gsglassman@aol.com.

GLASSMAN, IRVIN, mechanical and aeronautical engineering educator, consultant; b. Balt., Sept. 19, 1923; s. Abraham and Bessie (Snyder) G.; m. Beverly Wolfe, June 17, 1951; children: Shari Powell, Diane Geinger, Barbara Ann. B.E., Johns Hopkins U., 1943, D.Eng., 1950. Research asst. Manhattan Project, Columbia U., N.Y.C., 1943-46; mem. faculty Princeton U., N.J., 1950—, prof. mech. and aero. engring., 1964—, Robert H. Goddard prof. mech. and aero. engring., 1988—99, prof. emeritus, 1999—, dir. Ctr. for Energy and Environ. Studies, 1972-79. Cons. to industry; vis. prof. U. Naples, Italy, 1966-67, 78-79, Stanford U., 1975. Author: (with R.F. Sawyer) Performance of Chemical Propellants, 1971, Combustion, 1987, 3d edit., 1996; editor Combustion Sci. & Tech. Jour., also 3 books; contbr. articles to tech. jours. Served with U.S. Army, 1944-46. NSF fellow, 1966-67 Fellow AIAA (Propellants and Combustion award 1998); mem. AAUP, Nat. Acad. Engring., Combustion Inst. (Sir Alfred Egerton Gold medal 1982), Am. Soc. Engring. Edn. (Roe award 1984), Am. Chem. Soc., Tau Beta Pi. Achievements include 3 rocket propellant and burner patents. Home: 160 Longview Dr Princeton NJ 08540-5641 Office: Princeton U Dept Mech & Aero Engring Princeton NJ 08544-5261 E-mail: glassman@princeton.edu.

GLASSMAN, JAMES KENNETH, editor, writer, publishing executive; b. Washington, Jan. 1, 1947; s. Stanley G. and Elaine Ruth (Schiff) Garfield; children: Zoe Ann, Kate Julia. BA, Harvard, 1969. Editor, pub. Provincetown (Mass.) Advocate, 1971-72; editor-in-chief, exec. pub. Figaro, New Orleans, 1972-78; exec. editor Washingtonian Mag., 1979-81; pub. New Republic mag., Washington, 1981-84; pres. Atlantic mag., Washington, 1984-86; exec. v.p. U.S. News & World Report, Washington, 1984-86; editor-in-chief Roll Call, Washington, 1987-93; fin. and polit. columnist Washington Post, 1993—; resident fellow Am. Enterprise Inst., Washington, 1996—. Host Capital Gang Sunday, CNN-TV, 1995-98, Techno Politics, PBS-TV, 1995-99. Co-author: Dow 36,000, 1999; host www.TechCentralStation.com, 2000—; author: The Secret Code of the Superior Investor, 2002. Office: Am Enterprise Inst 1150 17th St NW Washington DC 20036-4603 Home: 15 Battle Hill Rd Falls Village CT 06031

GLASSMAN, JON DAVID, research and development company executive; b. N.Y.C., Jan. 8, 1944; s. J. and Dorothy (Witkin) G.; m. Francesca Regina Smoot, Dec. 31, 1986; 1 child, Amanda Louise; 1 stepchild, James Smoot Decherd. B in Fgn. Svc., U. So. Calif., 1965; MA, cert. Russian Inst., Columbia U., 1968, PhD, 1976. Joined Fgn. Svc. Dept. State, 1968; officer Am. Embassy, Madrid, 1968-70, Moscow, 1971-73, Havana, Cuba, 1977-79, Mexico City, 1979-81, Dept. State, Washington, 1974-77, 81-87; charge d'affaires Am. Embassy, Kabul, Afghanistan, 1987-89; dep. asst. for nat. security affairs to V.p. The White House, 1989-90, asst. to V.p. of U.S., 1990-91; amb. to Paraguay Asuncion, 1991-94; dept. state chair Indsl. Coll. of the Armed Forces, Washington, 1994-96; dep. for Balkan mil. stabilization Dept. State, Washington, 1996-97; v.p. internat. bus. devel. electronic sensors & sys. sector Northrop Grumman Corp., Balt., 1998—. Mem. bd. Bus. Coun. for Internat. Understanding, 1999—. Author: Arms for the Arabs, 1976. Bd. dirs. Bus. Coun. for Internat. Understanding. Recipient Presdl. Meritorious Svc. award, 1991. Mem. City Tavern Club. Home: 3240 Q St NW Washington DC 20007-3032 Office: Northrop Grumman Corp Elec Sensors & Sys Sector PO Box 1897 Baltimore MD 21203-1897

GLASSMAN, PAUL, library director, architecture educator; b. Providence, Dec. 19, 1952; s. Samuel H. and Stella Simons Glassman; life ptnr. Ernest H. Rubinstein. BA, Bowdoin Coll., 1974; MArch, U. Colo., 1979; MS in Libr. Sci., Simmons Coll., 1984. Asst. dir. Frank Lloyd Wright Preservation Trust, Oak Park, Ill., 1992—93; dir. Morris-Jumel Mansion, N.Y.C., 1993—95; art and arch. libr. and asst. prof. Pratt Inst., Bklyn., 1995—97; exec. dir. Old Ch. Cultural Ctr., Demarest, NJ, 1997—98; instr. arch. Yeshiva U., N.Y.C., 1994—; libr. dir. N.Y. Sch. Interior Design, N.Y.C., 1998—. Contbr. articles to profl. jours. Mem.: Am. Assn. Museums, Art Librs. Soc. N.Am. (editor 1999—, moderator art and design sch. libr. divsn. 2000—01). Home: 200 Cabrini Blvd New York NY 10033 Office: NY Sch Interior Design 170 East 70th St New York NY 10021

GLASSMAN, RICHARD, lawyer; b. Memphis, Nov. 11, 1946; s. Julius and Julia (Baker) G.; m. Susan Lawless, Nov. 23, 1980; children: Samantha, Lauran, Kathryn, Zoë. BS, Memphis State U., 1969, LLB, 1972. Bar: Tenn. 1972, U.S. Dist. Ct. (we. dist.) Tenn. 1972, U.S. Dist. Ct. (no. and mid. dists.) Miss., U.S. Ct. Appeals (6th cir.) 1973, U.S. Dist. Ct. (ea. dist.) Ark, 1980, U.S. Supreme Ct. 1982. Salesman Hertz Corp., Memphis, 1965-69; sr. ptnr. Glassman, Edwards, Wade & Wyatt PC, Memphis, 1974—. Mem. ABA (litigation sect. 1982), Am. Bd. Trial Advocates, Memphis Bar Assn., Shelby County Bar Assn. (fee dispute com. 1980-84). Home: 7787 Dogwood Rd Germantown TN 38138-4912 Office: Glassman Edwards Wade & Wyatt PC 26 N 2nd St Memphis TN 38103-2600 E-mail: rglassman@gewwlaw.com.

GLASSMAN, STEVEN J. lawyer; b. N.Y.C., 1944; BS, MIT, 1964; JD, Georgetown U., 1968. Bar: N.Y. 1970. Patent examiner U.S. Patent Office, 1964-65; asst. sect. chief, counsel tech. utilization Nat. Aeronautics and Space Adminstrn., 1966-71; asst. U.S. Atty. so. dist. N.Y. U.S. Atty's. Office, 1971-76, chief civil rights sect. so. dist. N.Y., 1974-75, chief civil appellate atty. so. dist. N.Y., 1975-76; ptnr. Kaye Scholer LLP, N.Y.C., 1979—. Editor Georgetown Law Jour., 1967-68. Mem. ABA, Assn. Bar City N.Y., Fed. Bar Coun., Phi Delta Phi. Office: Kaye Scholer LLP 425 Park Ave New York NY 10022-3506

GLASSMANN, MARVIN JEAN, marriage and family therapist; b. N.Y.C., June 13, 1935; s. Edward and Frances Blanche (Frankel) G.; m. Deanna Moskowitz, Dec. 27, 1959; children: Leonard, Steven, David. BA, Bklyn. Coll., 1957; MA, George Washington U., 1959; EdD, Columbia U., 1975. Diplomate Am. Bd. Family Psychology; lic. psychologist N.J., Ohio; cert. sch. psychologist N.Y.; Nat. Cert. Sch. Psychologist; Nat. Health Svc. Provider Psychology. Rehab. counselor Jewish Guild for the Blind, N.Y.C., 1959-62; sr. clin. psychologist Creedmoor State Hosp., Queens Village, N.Y., 1962-66; fellow L.I. Mental Health Ctr. (formerly L.I. Cons. Ctr.), Forest Hills, N.Y., 1963-65, psychotherapist and supr., 1965-85; sch. psychologist N.Y.C. Bd. Edn., Queens, N.Y., 1966-95; pvt. practice Huntington, Forest Hills, N.Y., 1966—; supr., dir. family therapy program L. Armstrong Mid. Sch., East Elmhurst, NY, 1999—; grad. student advisor, dept. marriage and family therapy Hofstra U., Hempstead, N.Y., 2000-01. Externship program Ackerman Inst. for Family Therapy, 1994-96. Co-author: Family Therapy, 1992; book reviewer Am. Jour. Family Therapy. Steward Town of Huntington, 1995—. Fellow: Acad. Family Psychology; mem.: APA, N.Y. Mental Health Counselors Assn., Nassau-Suffolk Horsemens Assn. (mem. exec. bd. 1994—, 1st v.p.), Ea. Group Psychotherapy Soc., L.I. Assn. Marriage and Family Therapy (membership chmn. 1980—98, pres.-elect 1997—98, pres. 1999—2000, past pres. 2001, mem.-at-large 2002, bd. dirs., referral chmn., Disting. Svc. award, Presdl. award), N.Y. Assn. Marriage and Family Therapy (mem. exec. bd. 1990—2000, nominating chmn.), Am. Assoc. Marriage and Family Therapy (clin. mem., approved supr., mem. N.Y. senate, mem. health adv. com. 2000—), Psi Chi. Democrat. Jewish. Avocations: horseback riding, scuba diving, photography, cross country skiing, running. Home and Office: 91 Chichester Rd Huntington NY 11743-6340 Office: 71-36 110th St Forest Hills NY 11375

GLASSMEYER, EDWARD, investment banker; b. Jersey City, Sept. 14, 1915; s. Edward and Claire (Stuckert) G.; m. Elizabeth Fellows, Jan. 5, 1939 (dec. Sept. 1982); children: Elizabeth Glassmeyer Treynor, Edward, Mary Glassmeyer Maloney, Edith Glassmeyer Heilman; m. Martha Moody, June 15, 1985. BA, Princeton U., 1936. Statistician Blyth & Co., Inc., N.Y.C., 1936-47, mgr. syndicate, 1947-50, v.p., 1950-62, sr. v.p., 1962-70; pres. Athens (Greece) Coll., 1970-73; chmn. bd. Inter-Am. Life Ins. Co. (subs. INA), Athens, 1973-76; ptnr. Grubb & Williams, Ltd., Atlanta. Adv. coun. dept. classics Princeton U. Trustee, v.p., past chmn. exec. com. Beekman Downtown Hosp., N.Y.C.; trustee emeritus Athens Coll., Near East Coll. Assn.; bd. dirs. Riverside Theater, Vero Beach, 1992-95; mem. Alumni Council, Princeton. Served with OSS, AUS, 1945-46, Germany. Named Hon. Alumnus, Cornell Coll., Mt. Vernon, Iowa, 1992, Hon. Trustee, 1998. Mem. Am. Numismatic Soc. (coun. 1983-88), Investment Bankers Assn. Am. (v.p., gov. 1958-60, chmn. N.Y. group 1959-60), Archeol. Inst. Am. (trustee 1966-85), Bond Club (pres. 1966-67), Princeton Club, Links Club (N.Y.C.), Reading Room Club (York Harbor, Maine), Riomar Yacht Club, Royal Yacht Club of Greece, Propellor of U.S. in Greece (pres. 1974-75). Republican. Presbyterian. Home: 4119 Indian River Dr Vero Beach FL 32963-1410

GLASSMOYER, THOMAS PARVIN, lawyer; b. Reading, Pa., Sept. 4, 1915; s. James Arthur and Margaretha (Parvin) G.; m. Frances Helen Thierolf, May 9, 1942; children— Deborah Jane Beck, Nancy Parvin Brittingham, Wendy Jean Parsons. AB, Ursinus Coll., 1936, LLB (hon.), 1972; LLB, U. Pa., 1939. Bar: Pa. 1940. Law clk. Common Pleas Ct. 6, Phila., 1939-40; assoc. Murdoch, Paxson, Kalish & Green, Phila., 1940-42; atty. Dept. Justice and Office Price Adminstrn., 1942-43; assoc. Schnader, Harrison, Segal & Lewis, Phila., 1946-50, ptnr., 1950-87, retired ptnr., 1988—, chmn. pension com., 1969-84, chmn. tax dept., 1972-84, chmn. investment com., 1984-86, chmn. bd. trustees of Retirement Trust, 1986-89. Sec. The Lawrewnce McFadden Co., Phila., 1992, dir., 1994—; lectr. NYU Inst. Fed. Taxation; adv. bd. U. Pa. Tax Conf., 1968-88. Author: (with Sherwin T. McDowell) Legal Problems in Tax Returns, 1949; editor-in-chief U. Pa. Law Rev., 1938-39 Past pres. Upper Dublin Twp. PTA Council; mem. Zoning Bd. Adjustment Upper Dublin Twp., Montgomery County, Pa., 1957-59, bd. commrs., 1959-71, pres., 1968-69; mem. Upper Dublin Environ. Control Bd., 1972-82; bd. dirs. Ursinus Coll., Collegeville, Pa., 1956—, 1st v.p., 1978-81, pres., 1981-90, chmn. exec. com., 1981-97; bd. dirs. Wissahickon Valley Watershed Assn., 1974-76; trustee Bernard G. Segal Found., Phila., 1969-98, Charlotte W. Newcombe Found., Princeton, N.J., 1982-2001. Served to 1st lt. JAG Dept., AUS, 1943-46. Recipient Eagle Scout award, Boy Scouts Am. Fellow Pa. Bar Found. (life, sec. 1993-2001); mem. ABA, FBA, Pa. Bar Assn. (ho. of dels. 1982-88, membership com., by-laws com.), Phila. Bar Assn., Judge Advs. Assn., Pa. Folklife Soc. (bd. dirs., sec.), Nat. Assn. Coll. and Univ. Attys., Lawyers Club Phila., Manorlu Club, Mfrs. Golf and Country Club, Union League of Phila., Order of Coif, Order of Arrow. Republican. Lutheran. Avocations: golf, philately. Home: 1648 N Hills Ave Willow Grove PA 19090-4231

GLASSNER, MICHAEL J. obstetrician, gynecologist; b. N.Y.C., Feb. 4, 1960; MD, Albany Med. Coll., 1984. Diplomate Am. Bd. Ob/gyn. Resident in ob/gyn. Med. Coll. Pa. Hosp., Phila., fellow; fellow in infertility and reproductive medicine Hosp. U. Pa., 1988-91; staff Lankenau Hosp., Wynnewood, Pa., Paoli Hosp., Pa., Bryn Mawr Hosp., Pa.; asst. clin. prof. Jefferson Med. Coll. Hosp., Phila. Mem. AMA, Am. Fertility Soc., Pa. Med. Soc., SART. Office: Paoli Pointe 11 Indsl Blvd Paoli PA 19096 also: Main Line Fertility Lankenau Med Bldg East 100 E Lancaster Ave Wynnewood PA 19096-3450

GLASSON, FRANK MICHAEL, musician (classical and jazz), music educator; b. La Jolla, Calif., Oct. 13, 1964; s. William J. Glasson and Maria Rosalas; m. Robyn Dreijer, Aug. 8, 1997; m. Janet Cox McBride, July 5, 1983 (div. Nov. 1, 1986). MusB in Jazz Studies, San Diego Sch. Performance, 1983—86; M in Orchestral Performing (hon.), U.S. Internat. U., 1989—90. Prin. trumpet Middle Deutsche Radio Orch., Leipzig, Germany, 1990—92, State Theater Orch., Pretoria, South Africa, 1992—95; asst. prin. trumpet Capetown Symphony, South Africa, 1995—97; trumpet Starlight Opera, San Diego, 1998—, Broadway San Diego, 2000—; 1st trumpet Lyric Opera, San Diego, 2001—, Old Globe Theater, San Diego, 2001—; jazz dir. Palomar Coll., San Marcos, Calif., 1998—. Condr. Pretoria Youth Symphony, 1993—95, Civic Youth Wind Symphony, San Marcos, 1999—. Soloist (concerto) Haydn Trumpet Concerto, 1992; performer: (orch.) Nelson Mandela's Inauguration, 1993. Mem.: Am. Fedn. Musicians (gov. bd., bd. mem. 2001—). Republican. Christian. Achievements include Trumpet tchg. method that has helped several students to obtain admissions & scholarships to top music conservatories in the U.S. Avocations: cycling, scuba diving, flying, exotic cars, body surfing. Office: Palomar Arts Dept Palomar Coll 1140 W Mission Rd San Marcos CA 92069-1487 E-mail: frglasson@aol.com.

GLASSON, LINDA, hospital security and safety official, healthcare; b. Nassawadox, Va., July 2, 1947; d. William Robert and Doris (Savage) G.; m. Charles William Lemon, Jr., Mar. 21, 1969 (div. 1973). Student, Eastern Shore Br. U. Va., 1965-67, J. Sargent Reynolds C.C., 1976-80, Old Dominion U., 1981, Va. Wesleyan Coll., 1985. Cert. ambulance emergency med. technician; cert. healthcare protection adminstr. Clk.-typist G.L. Webster Co., Inc., Cheriton, Va., 1962-70; tchrs. aide Cape Charles H.S., Va., 1970-72; dir. recreation and infirmary asst. United Meth. Children's Home, Richmond, Va., 1972-73; stockroom mgr. Flair Clothing Store, Richmond, Va., 1973-74; with med. record dept. Richmond Meml. Hosp., 1974-75, asst. utilization rev. coord., 1975-80, hosp. police sgt., 1977-80; dir. safety and security Maryview Hosp., Portsmouth, Va., 1980-97, chmn. hosp. safety com., 1980-97, mem. disaster com., 1980-97. Security mgmt. assoc. Safety & Security Solutions, Richmond, 1997-99; security mgr. Louise Obich Meml. Hosp., Suffolk, Va., 1999—. Contbg. author tng. manuals; contbr. articles to profl. publs. Instr. first aid and personal safety ARC, 1970-85, multimedia first aid instr., 1983-88, first aid chmn. bd.dirs. Henrico chpt., 1979-80, vol. emergency med. technician ambulance state fiar annually, 1974-99. Mem. Internat. Assn. Hosp. Security (sr., chmn. Region III 1985, v.p., sec. 1985-88, spl. appointee to bd. 1988-89), Am. Soc. Indsl. Security (mem. nat. standing com. healthcare security 1979-84, v.p. 1983-84), Internat. Assn. Healthcare Security & Safety (pres.-elect 1990, pres. 1991-92, past pres. 1993—), Internat. Healthcare Security and Safety Found. (pres. 1994-95). Baptist. Avocations: golf, softball, swimming, reading, classical music. Office: Louise Obici Meml Hosp 1900 N Main St PO Box 1100 Suffolk VA 23439-1100 E-mail: lglassen@obici.com.

GLASSON, LLOYD, sculptor, educator; b. Chgo. s. Albert and Fay G.; m. Cathleen Naso, 1968. BFA, Sch. Art Inst. Chgo., 1957; MFA, Tulane U., 1959. Mannequin sculptor, 1959-60; exhibits designer Newark Mus., 1961-62; prof. emeritus U. Hartford, (Conn.), 1964—. Co-founder Artists Tenants Assn., 1961— One-man shows Dorsky Gallery, N.Y.C., 1966, 74, Trinity Coll., Hartford, 1977, SaltBox Gallery, West Hartford, 1985, The Greene Art Gallery, Guilford, Conn., 1997, Sculpture Showcase, Ltd., New Hope, Pa., 1997; represented in permanent collections Wadsworth Atheneum, Hartford, Bushnell Auditorium, Hartford, Ch. of St. Helena, West Hartford, U. N.H., Karen Horney Inst., N.Y.C., Yale U., New Haven, Hartford Hosp., Forma Viva, Kostanjevica, Slovenia, ACMAT Corp., New Britain, Conn.; recreated the 2 bronze angels atop Soldiers and Sailors Meml. Arch, Hartford; designer, Albert Schweitzer Humanitarian award. Served with U.S. Army, 1952-54. Recipient Gold medal 52d ann. exhbn. Nat. Sculpture Soc., 1985, James E. and Frances W. Bent award for Creativity, 1989. Fellow Nat. Sculpture Soc.; mem. NAD (Thomas Proctor prize 1985, Gold medal 1986), Sculptors Guild.

GLASSROTH, JEFFREY, physican, medical educator; b. N.Y.C., Oct. 28, 1948; s. Murray and Marie (Cheynoweth) G.; m. Carol Holton, July 22, 1972; children: Marley, Drew. AB, Columbia U., 1969; MD, U. Cin., 1973. Diplomate Am. Bd. Internal Medicine. Intern U. Cin. Med. Ctr., 1973-74, intern, resident, 1973-75, 77-78, resident, 1974-75, 77-78; fellow in pulmonary and critical care medicine Boston U., 1978-81, instr. medicine, 1979-81; from asst. to assoc. prof. medicine Northwestern U., Evanston, Ill., 1981-90, prof. medicine, 1990—; prof. medicine, chair dept. Allegheny U. Health Scis., Phila., 1995 98; pres. Am. Thoracic Society, N.Y.C., 1999—2000; chmn., dept. of med. Univ. of Wisconsin, 1998—. Cons. Astra N.Am., Westboro, Mass., 1993—, Genentech/Novartis, San Francisco, 2000 ; mem. adv. coun. for elimination of Tb, CDC, Atlanta, 1993-97; mem. ad hoc study sect. NIH, Bethesda, Md., 1993, 97. Editor: Scientific Basis Respiratory Infection, 1993; assoc. editor Am. Jour. Respiratory Critical Care Medicine, 1999; mem. editl. bd. (jour.) Chest, 1988-93. Surgeon, USPHS, 1975-77, Atlanta. Rsch. grantee NIH, 1987-97, recipient Pulmonary Acad. awards, 1983-89. Fellow ACP, Am. Coll. Chest Physicians; mem. AAAS, Am. Thoracic Soc. (sec. 1996-97, v.p. 1997-98, pres.-elect 1998—), Ctrl. Soc. for Clin. Rsch. (pres. 2002-03), European Respiratory Soc., Internat. Union Against TB and Lung Disease. Avocations: skiing, distance running. Office: U Wis Dept Medicine 600 Highland Ave Madison WI 53792

GLATT, DANIEL J. physician; b. Rochester, N.Y., Sept. 24, 1964; s. William and Florence Bernice Glatt; m. April Spitzer, Mar. 16, 1996; 1 child, Evan Isaac. BA, U. Calif., 1987; MPH, Harvard U., 1992; MD, N.Y. Med. Coll., 1992. Diplomate Am. Bd. Internal Medicine, cert. in addiction medicine, med. rev. officer. Commd. USN, 1992; advanced through grades to LCDR; intern in internal medicine Nat. Naval Med. Ctr., Bethesda, Md., 1992-93; resident in internal medicine Naval Med. Ctr., San Diego, 1994-96; staff physician Naval Hosp. Great Lakes (Ill.), 1996-99; fellow addiction medicine VA Med. Ctr., San Francisco, 1999—2001; pvt. practice internal medicine and addiction medicine, 2001—. Gen. med. officer USMC, 1993-94. Decorated Navy and Marine Corps Achievement medal USN, 1999. Mem.: AMA (at-large resident sect. 1992—93), Am. Soc. Addiction Medicine (co-chair mems. in tng. com. 1988—92). Democrat. Jewish. Avocations: skiing, photography, scuba diving, travel. Office: 160 Country Club Dr South San Francisco CA 94080-4347

GLATT, MITCHELL STEVEN, business executive; b. N.Y.C., Sept. 2, 1957; s. Herbert and Gloria (Comita) G.; m. Randy Ginsburg, Oct., 1987. BA, NYU, 1978, MBA, 1980. Agt. trainee Internat. Creative Mgmt., N.Y.C., 1980-81; exec. asst. to chmn. bd. Bozell, Jacobs, Kenyon & Eckhardt, Inc., N.Y.C., 1981-87; chmn. of bd. Magla Products Inc., Chatham, 1987—. Pres. GiGi Products, Inc., pres. Am. Med. Acceptance Corp., 1998—. Cons. Statue of Liberty Ellis-Island Found., N.Y.C., 1983-87, Juvenile Diabetes Found., N.Y.C., 1987; adv. bd. NYU Sch. of the Arts; mem. Playwrights Theater N.J. Recipient Commendation Advt. Women of N.Y., N.Y.C., 1986. Mem. Am. Mgmt. Assn., Young Pres. Orgn. Office: Am Med Acceptance Corp 120 W 44th St New York NY 10036-4011

GLATZER, JENNA, writer; b. Bay Shore, N.Y., Nov. 27, 1975; d. Mark and Loretta Glatzer. BS in Comm., Boston U., 1997. Editor-in-chief Absolute Write.com, Rochester, NY, 1999—. Author: Taking Down Syndrome to School, 2002, Exploration of the Moon, 2002, Conquering Panic and Anxiety Disorders, 2002, greeting cards and slogans for gift products, Native American Festivals and Ceremonies, 2002; editor: Outwitting Writer's Block and Other Problems of the Pen, 2003, Words You Thought You Knew, 2003; contbr. Mem.: The Screenplayers (founding mem.), Nat. Writers Union. Episcopalian. Avocations: gardening, singing, reading, crocheting. Office: Absolute Write PO Box 93273 Rochester NY 14692

GLATZER, ROBERT ANTHONY, marketing and sales executive; b. N.Y.C., May 19, 1932; s. Harold and Glenna (Beaber) G.; m. Paula Rosenfeld, Dec. 20, 1964; m. Mary Ann Murphy, Dec. 31, 1977; children: Gabriela, Jessica, Nicholas. BA, Haverford Coll., 1954. Br. store dept. mgr. Bloomingdale's, N.Y.C., 1954-56; media buyer Ben Sackheim Advt., N.Y.C., 1956-59; producer TV commls. Ogilvy, Benson & Mather Advt., N.Y.C., 1959-62; dir. broadcast prodn. Carl Ally Advt., N.Y.C., 1962-63; owner Chronicle Prodns., N.Y.C., 1963-73; dir. Folklife Festival, Smithsonian Inst., Washington, 1973, Expo 74 Corp., Spokane, Wash., 1973-74; pres. Robert Glatzer Assocs., Spokane, 1974— ; ptnr. Delany/Glatzer Advt., Spokane, 1979-84; dir. sales/mktg. Pinnacle Prodns., Spokane; adj. faculty Ea. Wash. U., 1987—. Author: Beyond Popcorn: A Critic's Guide to Looking at Films, 2001; pub. radio film critic; host pub. radio program Movies 101. Bd. dirs. Riverfront Arts Festival, 1977-78; bd. dirs. Comprehensive Health Planning Council, 1975-78, Spokane Quality of Life Council, 1976-82, Allied Arts of Spokane, 1976-80, Art Alliance Wash. State, 1977-81, Spokane chpt. ACLU, 1979-83, Wash. State Folklife Council, 1983—, chair 1998—; commr. Spokane Arts, 1987—; mem. Spokane Community Devel. Bd., 1988—; mem. Shorelines Update Commn., 1988—; mem. Wash. State Small Bus. Improvement Coun., 1994—, chair 1998—. Recipient CINE Golden Eagle award (2). Mem. Dirs. Guild Am. Democrat. Jewish. Author: The New Advertising, 1970; co-scenarist Scorpio and other TV prodns.

GLATZER, WOLFGANG P. W. sociology educator; b. Hohenborau, Germany, Sept. 15, 1944; arrived in Fed. Republic Germany, 1945; s. Paul and Emmi (Dartsch) G.; m. Veronika S. Hess, Aug. 4, 1969; children: Katja Verena, Kolja Paul. Diploma in sociology, J.W. Goethe U., Frankfurt, Fed. Republic Germany, 1972; PhD, U. Mannheim, Fed. Republic Germany, 1978. Rsch. asst. social polit. indicator-decision system project J.W. Goethe U., Frankfurt, 1972-78; dir. spl. rsch. dept. 3 Microanalytical Founds. of Soc., Mannheim, 1979-84; prof. sociology J.W. Goethe U., 1984—, dean, 1991-92, 96-97. Confidant Friedrich-Ebert-Stiftung, Bonn, Germany, 1988—; pres. Internat. Soc. for Quality of Life Studies, 1993—94. Author: Sociological Almanac, 1975, Housing in the Welfare State, 1980, Quality of Life, 1984; author, editor: Household Production, 1986, Household Technization, 1991, Social Trends, 1992, Inequality and Social Policy, 1996; editor: Redistribution, 1978, Modernization, 1991, Social Structure, 1992, Living Conditions in Germany, 1992, Attitudes in Europe, 1993, Convergence or Divergence, 1994, Seperated Unified, 1995, Eastern Europe, 1996, Welfare for Everybody?, 1997, Quality of Life in Countries Undergoing Rapid Social Change, 1998, Revolution in Household Technology, 1998, Germany in Change, 1999, Views of Society, 1999, Social Change and Social Monitoring, 2002, Rich and Poor, 2002. Lt. Pioneer, 1964-66. Mem. Internat. Sociol. Assn. (pres. working group 6, 1998-2002), German Sociol. Assn. (bd. dirs., 1996-2000), Deutsche Gesellschaft Gerontologie, Internat. Soc. Quality of Life Studies, Club of Que. Home: Im Rothkopf 8 61440 Oberursel Hessen Germany Office: J W Goethe U Robert-Mayer-Str 5 60054 Frankfurt Germany E-mail: glatzer@soz.uni-frankfurt.de.

GLAUBERMAN, MELVIN L. lawyer; b. Bklyn., Nov. 3, 1927; s. Sam and Beatrice (Jacobs) G.; m. Maxine Dvorsetz, Dec. 25, 1955 (div.); children: David J., Nancy J., Jane C.; m. Naomi Alexander, Jan. 6, 1980. B.A., Bklyn. Coll., 1948; J.D., Harvard U., 1951. Bar: N.Y. 1951, U.S. Dist. Ct. (so. dist.) N.Y. 1953, U.S. Dist. Ct. (ea. dist.) N.Y. 1954, U.S. Supreme Ct. 1972. Sole practice, N.Y.C., 1951-56, 73-74, 88—; ptnr. Berman & Glauberman, N.Y.C., 1957-60, Berman, Glauberman & Raives, N.Y.C., 1960-72; sr. ptnr. Berman, Glauberman & Bernstein, N.Y.C., 1975-87; mediator under N.Y. State Alternative Dispute Resolution Procedures; N.Y. State no-fault ins. arbitrator. Contbr. to book Manual for Theatre Owners, 1955; contbr. NYU Tax Law Rev. Vice-pres. League in Aid of Crippled Children, Inc., N.Y.C., 1969; mem. Ins. Industry Ednl. Adv. Com. Mem. N.Y. State Trial Lawyers Assn. (lectr. 1984), Am. Arbitration Assn. (master arbitrator, 1978-88, lectr. 1982—, N.Y. state permanent profl. no-fault arbitrator 1988—). Home: 32 Sheffield Ct Ardsley NY 10502-1524 Office: 32 Sheffield Ct Ardsley NY 10502-1524

GLAUBINGER, LAWRENCE DAVID, retired manufacturing company executive; b. Newark, Nov. 26, 1925; s. Samuel I. and Pauline (Sandler) G.; m. Lucienne Lefebvre, Nov. 11, 1967. BS with honors, Ind. U., 1949; MBA, Columbia U., 1977; LLD (hon.), Ind. U., 1993. Adminstrv. asst. to pres. Ronson, Inc., Newark, 1949-51; mdse. mgr. United Mchts., N.Y.C., 1951-65; v.p. Marietta Silk Mills, Pa., 1965-66; pres., CEO Channel Textile Co. Inc., Bradford, Vt., 1966-75; chmn. bd., CEO Stern & Stern Industries, Inc., N.Y.C., 1977-2000, also bd. dirs.; ret., 2000. Pres. Lawrence Econ. Cons. Inc., Hallandale, Fla., 1977—; mgr. Beegee Trading Co. LLC, 2000—; bd. dirs. Leucadia Nat. Corp., Marisa Christina, Inc. Bd. overseers Columbia U. Sch. Bus., chmn. ann. funds campaigns, 1980-82; bd. dirs. Ind. U. Found.; mem. Ind. U. Bus. Sch. Acad. Alumni Fellows; bd. dirs. Ind. U. Varsity Club. Served with USCGR, 1943-46. Recipient Disting. Alumni Svc. award, Ind. U. Mem. Hoosier Hundred, Ind. U. Dean's Assocs., Columbia U. Bus. Assocs., Campaign for Columbia (co-chmn. bus. sch.), Am. Arbitration Assn., Princeton Club (N.Y.), Green Brook Country Club, Beta Gamma Sigma. Republican. Jewish. Home: 437 Golden Isles Dr Hallandale FL 33009-7582 Office: Lawrence Econ Cons PO Box 3567 Hallandale FL 33008-3567

GLAUTHIER, T. J. non-profit executive; b. Durham, N.C., Jan. 3, 1944; s. Theodore and Martha May (Myers) G.; m. Carrie L. Bostrom, June 11, 1966 (div. 1973); children: Jeff, Paul, Tad; m. M. Brigid O'Farrell, July 9, 1977; 1 child, Patrick O. AB, Claremont (Calif.) Men's Coll., 1965; MBA, Harvard Bus. Sch., 1967. Cons. Peat, Marwick, Livingston, L.A., 1967-68; with Applied Computer Tech., L.A., 1968-70; cons. Applied Decision Systems, Cambridge, Mass., 1970-74; v.p. Temple, Barker & Sloane, Inc., Lexington, Mass., 1974-90; head Pub. Policy Practice, 1980-90; head Washington office, 1986-90; dir. energy and climate change World Wildlife Fund, Washington, 1990-93; assoc. dir. nat. resources, energy and sci. U.S. Office Mgmt. and Budget, Washington, 1993-98; dep. sec., COO U.S. Dept. Energy, 1999-2001; pres., CEO Electricity Innovation Inst., Palo Alto, Calif., 2001—. Mng. public and private partnerships for electricity tech. R&D. Pres. Lake Barcroft Assn., 1989—94; assoc. Lake Barcroft Watershed Improvement Dist., 1989—2001; del. Va. State Dem. Conv., 1993, 1997. Democrat. Unitarian Universalist. Home: 1001 Ocean Blvd Moss Beach CA 94038 Office: Electricity Innovation Inst 3412 Hillview Ave Palo Alto CA 94304 E-mail: tj@eE2I.org., tjglauthier@aol.com.

GLAVIN, A. RITA CHANDELLIER (MRS. JAMES HENRY GLAVIN III), lawyer; b. Schenectady, N.Y., May 11, 1937; d. Pierre Charles and Helen C. (Fox) Chandellier; m. James H. Glavin, III, June 1, 1963; children: Helene, James, Rita, Henry. AB cum laude, Middlebury Coll., 1958; JD, Union U. Albany Law Sch., 1961. Bar: N.Y. 1961, U.S. Dist. Ct. (no. dist.) N.Y. 1961, U.S. Tax Ct. 1965, U.S. Supreme Ct. 1978. Assoc. Eugene Steiner, Albany, N.Y., 1961-64, Helen Fox Chandellier, Schenectady, 1965-76; mem. Glavin and Glavin, Waterford, Schenectady, 1965-86, 87—, Albany, 1965-86, 87—. Del. 4th Jud. Dist. Nominating Conv., 1966—67; confidential law clk. presiding justices N.Y. State Ct. Claims, 1968—71; surrogate judge Saratoga County, 1986; dir. assn. coun. mems. and coll. trustees SUNY, 1991—2002, sec., 1996—2002. Mem. editl. bd. Albany Law Rev., 1960-61. Sec. Bellevue Women's Med. Ctr., 2001—02; bd. dirs., chmn. fin. com. Schenectady YWCA, 1979—81; bd. dirs. Schenectady Jr. League, 1974, 1976; del. pub. affairs com. N.Y. State Jr. League, 1976; sec. Bellevue Maternity Hosp., Inc., 1966—2001, bd. dirs., 1966—83, bd. advisors, 1984—2001; bd. dirs. Bellevue Women's Med. Ctr., 2001—02; trustee Middlebury Coll., 1978—88, chmn. law com., 1982—88, vice chmn. bd. dirs., 1986—87; trustee Waterford Hist. Mus. and Cultural Ctr., Inc., 2000—, sec., 2002—; mem. univ. coun. SUNY, Albany, 1985—2002; tech. advisor HSA Northeastern N.Y. Maternity and Pediat. Com., 1976. Mem. N.Y. State Bar Assn. (mem. ho. of dels. 1987-88, nominating com. 1988-90), Saratoga County Bar Assn. (exec. com. 1981—, v.p. 1985, pres. 1986), Schenectady County Bar Assn., Phi Beta Kappa, Kappa Kappa Gamma. Office: Glavin & Glavin PO Box 40 69 2nd St Waterford NY 12188-2422

GLAVIN, JAMES EDWARD, landscape architect; b. Syracuse, N.Y., Aug. 18, 1923; s. James Edward and Florence Ellen (Nelson) G.; m. Helen Catherine Hartnett, Aug. 24, 1946; children— Kathleen Glavin Kopitsky, Timothy, David, Matthew, Martin, Maureen. BS in Landscape Architecture, SUNY Coll. Environ. Sci. and Forestry, Syracuse, 1948. City planner Syracuse Planning Commn., 1948-49; chief land planning dept. Sargent Webster Crenshaw & Folley, Syracuse, 1951-56; partner Hueber Hares Glavin (architects, landscape architects, and engr., and predecessor), Syracuse, 1956-88, James E. Glavin & Assos. (landscape architects), Syracuse, 1956-88, Syracuse Scale Models, 1968-88, Glavin & Van Iderstine Landscape Architects, 1980-88; pvt. cons., 1988—. Vis. juror, lectr. State U. Coll. Environ. Sci. and Forestry, 1959, 65, 69, State U. Coll. Agr., Cornell U., 1970—; mem. faculty adv. coun. Sch. Landscape Architecture, N.Y. State U. Coll. Environ. Sci. and Forestry, 1990—; cons. N.Y. State Council Arts, 1971; mem. N.Y. State Bd. Landscape Architects, 1987-91. Contbr. articles to profl. publs.; contbg.; editor: Empire State Architect, 1957-60. Mem. Citizens Found., Syracuse, 1957-77, St. Thomas More Found, 1965-88; bd. dirs. Hiawatha coun. Boy Scouts Am., 1980-88, mem. adv. bd., 1988-2003; bd. dirs. Adirondack Archtl. Heritage, 1993-2000, Clifton-Fine Hosp., 1998-2000; trustee Clifton Cmty. Libr., 1994-2000. Recipient Design award Am. Assn. Nurserymen, 1969, 71; named Outstanding Alumni, SUNY Coll. Environ. Sci. and Forestry Alumni Assn., 1994. Fellow Am. Soc. Landscape Architects (past co-chmn. pvt. practice com., Design award 1968, 71); mem. ASCE (past v.p. Syracuse chpt.), Sigma Lambda Alpha. Home and Office: PO Box 491 Cranberry Lake NY 12927-0491

GLAVIN, JAMES HENRY, III, lawyer; b. Albany, N.Y., Oct. 6, 1931; s. James Henry, Jr. and Elizabeth Mary (Gibbons) Glavin; m. A. Rita Chandelier, June 1, 1963; children: Helene Elizabeth, James C., Rita Marie, James Henry IV. AB, Villanova U., 1953; JD, Albany Law Sch., 1956. Bar: N.Y. 1956, U.S. Dist. Ct. (no. dist.) N.Y. 1957, U.S. Dist. Ct. (mid. dist.) Tenn. 1959, U.S. Ct. Mil. Appeals 1959, U.S. Supreme Ct. 1959, U.S. Ct. Appeals (DC cir.) 1976. Mem. Glavin and Glavin, Waterford, NY, 1960—. Chmn. regional bd. Key Bank, N.A., 1968—93. Author: (book) The Tour Broker and the Interstate Commerce Commission, 1977; editor: Administrative Law Practice in New York, 1988. Bd. dirs. Waterford Ctrl. Cath. Sch., 1969—; county chmn. Saratoga County Dems., NY, 1964—68; trustee St. Mary's Ch., Waterford, 1974—, Waterford Rural Cemetery; bd. dirs. Bellevue Maternity Hosp., 1968—2001. Served to capt. JAGC USAF, 1957—60. Mem.: ATLA, ABA, Mystery Writers Am., Internat. Soc. Gen. Semantics, Rensselaer County Bar Assn., Albany County Bar Assn., Saratoga County Bar Assn., Estate Planning Coun. Ea. N.Y., N.Y. State Bar Assn., Fed. Bar Assn., Nat. Health Lawyers Assn., Transp. Lawyers Assn., Am. Acad. Hosp. Attys., N.Y. Trial Lawyers Assn., Am. Psychology-Law Soc., Am. Acad. Polit. and Social Sci., Am. Soc. Law and Medicine, Assn. Former Intelligence Officers, Soc. Am. Baseball Rsch., Air Force Assn., Nat. Lawyers Club, KC, Lions. Roman Catholic. Home: 66 Saratoga Ave Waterford NY 12188-0040 Office: Glavin and Glavin PO Box 40 Waterford NY 12188-0040 E-mail: gglaw@mindspring.com.

GLAVIN, WILLIAM PATRICK, IV, lawyer; b. LaFayette, Ind., June 26, 1965; s. William Patrick III and Rosemary G.; m. Carrie Lynn Stack, Apr. 19, 1997. BA, North Ctrl. Coll., Naperville, Ill., 1985; JD, Pepperdine U., Malibu, Calif., 1988. Bar: Calif. 1988; cert. Family Law Specialist, 2000. Assoc. Fain, Kaufman & Young, Beverly Hills, Calif., 1988-94, Kolodny & Anteau, LLP, Beverly Hills, 1994-98; ptnr. Glavin & Kolter, LLP, L.A., 1998-99, Hermes & Glavin, LLP, L.A., 2000—. Pro bono atty. South Bay Free Clinic, Manhattan Beach, Calif., 1997—. Expert advice columnist So. Calif. Divorce Mag.; contbr. numerous articles to profl. jours. Legal adv. Grandparents as Parents. Mem. Beverly Hills Bar Assn., Los Angeles County Bar Assn., Palm Desert Bar Assn., Kiwanis Club. Republican. Avocations: whitewater rafting, scuba diving. Office: Law Offices Hermes & Glavin LLP 1880 Century Park E #914 Los Angeles CA 90067

GLAVINE, TOM (THOMAS MICHAEL GLAVINE), professional baseball player; b. Concord, Mass., May 25, 1966; m. Carri Dobbins, Nov. 7, 1992. Grad. high sch., Mass. Pitcher Atlanta Braves, 1987—2002, N.Y. Mets, 2002—. Recipient Cy Young award Baseball Writers' Assn. Am., 1991, 98, Silver Slugger award, 1991, 95; named Nat. League Pitcher Yr., Sporting News, 1991, named to Nat. League All-Star Team, 1991-93, 96-99. Tied as leader of Nat. League pitching victories, 1991-92. Office: NY Mets Shea Stadium 123 01 Roosevelt Ave Flushing NY 11368-1699*

GLAZE, LYNN FERGUSON, development consultant; b. Oakland, Calif., May 24, 1933; d. Kenneth Loveland and Constance May (Pedder) Ferguson; m. Harry Smith Glaze, Jr., July 3, 1957; children: Catherine, Charles Richard. BA, Stanford U., 1955, MA, 1966. Devel. dir. Greenwich Acad., Conn., 1982-84; devel. cons. Del. Learning Ctr., Brandywine Mus., Opera Del., others, 1984—. Author: Seasons of the Trail, 2000. Pres. Darien-Norwalk YWCA, Conn., 1973-76; sec. Darien Republican Town com., 1974-79; dist. chmn. Darien Rep. Meeting, 1974-76, mem. Rep. Nat. Conv. Platform Com., 1988; vestry St. Luke's Ch., Darien, 1979-82; justice of the peace, Darien, 1981-84; bd. dirs. Ingleside Homes, Inc., 1986-92, Henrietta Johnson Med. Ctr., 1994-97; pres. Del. ProChoice Med. Fund, 1997-99; mem. Gov.'s Small Bus. Coun., 1987, EEOC, New Castle County, 1991-94, Del. Common Cause, 1999-2003, Coro Found. fellow.

GLAZE, ROBERT HOWE, real estate executive; b. St. Joseph, Mo., Nov. 9, 1952; s. Andrew S. and Elizabeth H. Glaze. BA, Westminster Coll., 1975; MBA, So. Meth. U., 1976. Credit analyst credit dept. Boatmen's Nat. Bank, St. Louis, 1976-78; comml. banking rep. credit tng. program First Nat. Bank, Chgo., 1978-79; comml. banking officer retailing cos. divsn. U.S. Banking Dpet., 1979-82, asst. v.p. retailing cos. divsn., 1983-85; gen. mgr. acquisitions and sales The Prudential Realty Group, Chgo., 1985-93; pres. Weybridge Capital Investors, Inc., Chgo., 1993—. Mem. aux. bd. Art Inst., Chgo., 1992—; trustee Lawrence Hall Youth Svcs., 1996—; bd. assocs. Chgo. Child Care Soc., 1980-85; jr. bd. Lawrence Hall Sch. for Boys, 1980-88, 125th anniversary benefit com., 1990; mem. assoc. bd. Mental Health Assn., Greater Chgo., 1986-91, benefit chmn., 1989; mem. Met. Bd. Youth Guidance, Chgo., 1986-89, 91—; mem. com. fgn. affairs of the Chgo. Coun. on Fgn. Rels.; mem. Ravinia Festival Annual Fund, 1995—. Recipient Cmty. Svc. award Prudential Pacesetters, 1989. Mem. Internat. Coun. Shopping Ctrs., Urban Land Inst., Univ. Club. Home: 1109 W Webster Ave # 1 Chicago IL 60614-3510 Office: Weybridge Capital Investors Inc 2502 N Clark St Ste 230 Chicago IL 60614-1712 E-mail: rglaze@weybridgecapital.com.

GLAZE, THOMAS A. state supreme court justice; b. Jan. 14, 1938; s. Phyllis Laser; children: Steve, Mike, Julie, Amy, Ashley. BSBA, U. Ark., 1960, JD, 1964. Exec. dir. Election Research Council Inc., 1964-65; legal advisor Winthrop Rockefeller, 1965-66; staff atty. Pulaski County Legal Aid, 1966-67, asst. then dep. atty. gen., 1967-70, pvt. practice law, 1970-79, chancellor Ark. Chancery Ct., 6th Jud. Cir., 1979-80; judge Ark. Ct. Appeals, 1981-86; assoc. justice Ark. Supreme Ct., 1987—. Co-author Ark. Election Act, 1969, Ark. Consumer Act; lectr. U. Ark.; adj. faculty U. Ark., Little Rock. Past bd. dirs. Vis. Nurses Corp., Youth Home Inc. Office: Ark Supreme Ct Justice Bldg 625 Marshall St, 120 Justice Bldg Little Rock AR 72201-1054

GLAZEBROOK, JAMES GRINSTEAD, judge; b. 1955; AB, Middlebury Coll., 1977; JD, Case Western U., 1980. Bar: Fla. 1980, N.Y. 1984, DC 1984, U.S. Supreme Ct., U.S. Ct. Appeals (2d, 3d, 5th 10th and 11th). Law clk. to Hon. John A. Reed Jr. U.S. Dist. Ct. (mid. dist.) Fla., Orlando, 1980-82, asst. U.S. Atty., 1980-82, magistrate judge, 1996—. Chair Nat. Conf. Fed. Trail Judges, 2001. Mem.: FBA, ABA, Orange County Bar Assn., Am. Judicature Soc. Office: 80 N Hughey Ave Rm 218 Orlando FL 32801-2231

GLAZEBROOK, RITA SUSAN, nursing educator; b. St. Paul, Apr. 26, 1948; d. David L. and Beverly Ruth (Penhiter) Beccue; m. Harold L. Glazebrook, Dec. 20, 1986; children: Julie, Robert J., Scott, Robert M., Katherine. Diploma, RN, Abbott Hosp. Sch. Nursing, Mpls., 1970; BS in Nursing, Augsburg Coll., Mpls., 1979; MS in Nursing, U. Minn., 1981, PhD in Edn. Adminstrn., 1987. Mem. staff, asst. head nurse United Hosps., Inc., St. Paul, 1970-78; mem. staff Med. Pers. Pool, St. Paul, 1978-81; prof. nursing, chmn. dept. St. Olaf Coll., Northfield, Minn., 1981—. Contbr. articles to profl. jours. Faculty devel. grant Evan. Luth. Ch. Am. Mem. ANA, Minn. Nurses Assn., Assn. of Women's Health Obstetric and Neonatal Nurses, Sigma Theta Tau. Home: 8941 Jasmine Ln S Cottage Grove MN 55016-3422 E-mail: glazebro@stolaf.edu.

GLAZER, BARRY DAVID, lawyer; b. Cleve., Oct. 10, 1948; s. Jacob J. and Constance (Schwartz) Glazer; m. Deborah Werbner, Sept. 28, 1984. AB, Miami U., Oxford, Ohio, 1970; JD, Mich. Law Sch., 1973. Bar: Minn. 1973, U.S. Dist. Ct. Minn. 1973, France Conseil Juridique 1981. Assoc. Dorsey & Whitney, Mpls., 1973—78, ptnr., 1979—80, resident ptnr. Paris, 1980—86, London, 1986—91, mng. ptnr. Brussels, 1991—2000, London, 2001—. Mem.: Union Internat. des Avocats, Internat. Bar Assn., ABA. Office: Dorsey & Whitney LLP 21 Wilson St London EC2 England

GLAZER, BARRY MICHAEL, anesthesiologist; b. Indpls., Aug. 24, 1946; s. Dave A. and Sylvia M. G.; m. Jan E., Oct. 21, 1971; 1 child, Ann M. AB, Ind. U., 1967, MD, 1971. Intern, resident Ind. U. Hosps., 1971-74; anesthesiologist Vincennes, Ind., 1976-80, Indpls., 1980—. With U.S. Army, 1974-76. Mem. Am. Soc. Anesthesiologists (1st v.p. 1999-2000, pres.-elect 2000-01, pres. 2001-2002), Am. Inst. Parliamentarians (3d v.p. 1999-2001, 2d v.p. 2001-2003), Ind. Soc. Anesthesiologists (pres. 1994-96).

GLAZER, BENNETT J. wholesale distribution executive; CEO Glazer's Wholesale Drug, Dallas, 2003—. Office: Glazers Wholesale Drug 14860 Landmark Blvd Dallas TX 75254*

GLAZER, DONALD WAYNE, lawyer, business executive, educator; b. Cleve., July 26, 1944; s. Julius and Ethel (Goldstein) G.; children: Elizabeth M., Mollie S. AB summa cum laude, Dartmouth Coll., 1966; JD magna cum laude, Harvard U., 1969; LLM, U. Pa., 1970. Bar: Mass. 1970. Assoc. Ropes & Gray, Boston, 1970-78, ptnr., 1978-92, counsel, 1992-96; ptnr. Am. Bus. Ptnrs. LLC, Boston, 1996-98; pres. Mugar/Glazer Holdings, Inc., Boston, 1992-95; vice chmn. fin. New Eng. TV Corp. and WHDH-TV, Inc., Boston, 1992-93; adv. counsel Goodwin Procter LLC, Boston, 1997—; co-founder, corp. sec. Provant, Inc., Boston, 1998—, vice-chmn., 2002. Instr. corp. fin. Boston U. Law Sch., 1975; lectr. law Harvard U., Cambridge, Mass., 1978-91; trustee GMO Trust, Boston, 2000—. Co-author: Massachusetts Corporation Law and Practice, 1991, Glazer and FitzGibbon on Legal Opinions, 1992, 2d edit., 2001; co-editor First Ann. Inst. on Securities Regulation, 1970; contbr. articles to legal jours. Past chmn., trustee Cowen Slavin Found.; past trustee Santa Fe Neuroscis. Inst.; past dir. Newton Girls Soccer League, past co-chmn. intramural com.; past trustee, past treas. Hillel Founds. of Greater Boston Inc.; past trustee Program for Young Negotiators. Fellow Salzburg Seminar in Am. Studies, 1975 Mem. ABA (past chmn. legal opinions com., co-reporter Legal Opinion Prins., past chmn. subcom. on employee benefits and exec. compensation, fed. securities law com., past co-chmn. task force on sec. 16 devels.), Boston Bar Assn. (past chmn., corp. sec., past chmn. securities law com., past co-chmn. legal opinions com.), Am. Law Inst., Tri-Bar Legal Opinions Com. (co-reporter Third-party Closing Opinions). Jewish. Home: 225 Kenrick St Newton MA 02458-2731

GLAZER, GERALD SHERWIN, real estate broker; b. Milw., Sept. 26, 1942; s. David and Dorothy (Joseph) G.; m. Mildred Susan Cohen, July 4, 1965; children: Channa Glazer Skier, Laya Glazer Witty, Meir, Chaim. BS, U. Chgo., 1963; MS, Northwestern U., 1965. Instr. in math. U. Wis., Waukesha, 1967-74; regional claims mgr. MGIC Investment Corp., Milw., 1974-78; broker Lake Park Inv. Realty, Milw., 1978-80; acct. Astronautics Corp. of Am., Milw., 1980-82; instr. Milw. Area Tech. Coll., 1983-85; owner/broker Prime Properties, Milw., 1985-92; adminstrv. specialist Dept. of City Devel., City of Milw., 1992-94; real estate broker Jarvis Realty Inc., Milw., 1994—. Author: Foreclosed Homes, 1988. Ward committeeman Dem. Party, Milw. County, 1970-72; bd. dirs. Milw. Jewish Coun., 1985—2002, co-chmn. Task Force on Anti-Semitism and Constl. Law, 1998-2000; bd. dirs. Sherman Park Cmty. Assn., Milw., 1968-70. Alumni fellow U. Wis., 1966-67; recipient State Merit award State of Wis., 1969. Mem. Milw. Bd. Realtors (mem. issues com. 1997-2001), Jewish Sacred Soc. Milw. (v.p. 1980-82, pres. 1982-85), Am. Jewish Congress. Home: 2944 N 50th St Milwaukee WI 53210-1640 Office: Jarvis Realty Inc 5909 W North Ave Milwaukee WI 53208-1058

GLAZER, GUILFORD, real estate developer; b. Knoxville, Tenn., July 17, 1921; s. Aaron Usher and Ida (Bressoff) G.; children: Emerson, Erika; m. Diane Pregerson, Jan. 29, 1967. Mech. Engr., George Wash. U., 1939; Metallurgy, U. Louisville, 1943. Bd. dirs. The Torrance (Calif.) Co., 1990, Del Amo Fashion Ctr., Torrance, Calif., 1990; owner operator Allegheny Ctr., Pitts. Bd. dirs. Rand-UCLA Ctr. Study Soviet Internat. Behavior, L.A. Developer various shopping ctrs. and office bldgs. in U.S. Pres. Reagan Libr. Found., Nixon Libr. Foun.; trustee L.A. Holocaust Meml., Jerusalem Found., Stop Cancer, Bell Shelter for Homeless; founder Ford's Theatre, Washington, Am. Friends of the Israel Def. Force; mem. Wilshire Blvd. Temple, L.A.County Mus. Art, Unified Fund Music Ctr. With USN, 1942-45. Recipient Hon. Fellow U. Tel Aviv. Mem. World Affairs Coun., Tamarisk Club, Hillcrest Country Club, Monterey Country Club, Palm Desert Club. Jewish. Avocation: golf. Office: Krasne & Mellon LLP 9440 Santa Monica Blvd Ste 610 Beverly Hills CA 90210-4619

GLAZER, JACK HENRY, lawyer; b. Paterson, N.J., Jan. 14, 1928; s. Samiel and Martha (Merkin) G.; m. Zelda d'Angleterre, 1979. BA, Duke U., 1950; JD, Georgetown U., 1956; postgrad., U. Frankfurt, Germany, 1956-57; SJD, U. Calif., Berkeley, 1977. Bar: D.C. 1957, Calif. 1968. Atty. GAO and NASA, 1958-60; mem. maritime divsn. UN Internat. Labour Office, Geneva, Switzerland, 1960, spl. legal adv., 1960-62; atty. NASA, Washington, 1963-66; chief counsel NASA-Ames Rsch. Ctr., Moffett Field, Calif., 1966-88; gov. Calif. Maritime Acad., 1975-78; asst. prof. Hastings Coll. Law, 1985-87; prof., assoc. dean bus. sch. San Francisco State U., 1988-92; dir. San Francisco Palace Fine Arts, 1995. Contbr. articles to profl. jours. Comdr. Calif. Naval Militia, ret. Capt. JAGC, USNR, ret. Mem. Calif. Bar Assn., D.C. Bar Assn., White's Inn (reader). Office: White's Inn 37 White St San Francisco CA 94109-2609 E-mail: whitesinn@aol.com.

GLAZER, JOSEPH A. medical association administrator; b. Middletown, N.Y., Feb. 3, 1961; s. Richard B. and Patricia A. Glazer; 1 child, Jeremy. AA, Ulster County C.C., Stone Ridge, N.Y., 1981; BA, SUNY, Albany, 1983; JD, Albany Law Sch., 1989. Bar: N.Y. 1990. Legis. staff various legis. offices, Albany; counsel, legis. dir. N.Y. State Assn. Counties, Albany, 1989-92; outreach coord. Alliance for Consumer Rights, Albany, 1993-97; pres., CEO Mental Health Assn. N.Y. State, Inc., Albany, 1997—. Spokesperson in field. Legis. staff various state legislators, Albany, N.Y., 1980-89; campaign mgmt. and staff local, state and presdl. campaigns, N.Y., 1983-96; candidate N.Y. State Assembly 102nd Dist., Upper Hudson Valley, N.Y., 1992. Mem. Found. Advocacy for Mental Health, Inc. (founder, sec./treas. 1998-2001). Office: Mental Health Assn NYS Inc Ste 415 194 Washington Ave Albany NY 12210 Office Fax: 518-426-8676. E-mail: mhanys@mhanys.org.

GLAZER, MICHAEL, lawyer; b. L.A., Oct. 10, 1940; BS, Stanford U., 1962; MBA, Harvard U., 1964; JD, U. Calif., L.A., 1967. Bar: Calif. 1967. Law clk. to Hon. Roger J. Traynor Calif. Supreme Ct., 1967-68; commr. L.A. Dept. of Water & Power, 1973-76; chmn. Calif. Water Commn., 1976-78; asst. adminstr. nat. oceanic and atmospheric adminstrn. U.S. Dept. of Commerce, 1978-80; dir. Met. Water Dist. of So. Calif., 1984-91; ptnr. Paul, Hastings, Janofsky & Walker LLP, L.A. Articles editor U. Calif. at L.A. Law Rev., 1966-67. Mem. State Bar Calif. (com. on corps. 1986-87), L.A. County Bar Assn. (chair fed. securities regulation com. 1988-90, chair exec. com. bus. and corp. law sect. 1995-96), Order of the Coif, Phi Beta Kappa. Office: Paul Hastings Janofsky & Walker LLP 515 S Flower St Los Angeles CA 90071-2300

GLAZER, MICHAEL L. consumer products company executive; Pres. Bombay Co., 1991—95, Consol. Store Corp., 1995—2000; pres., CEO KB Toys, 1996—. Office: KB Toys 100 West St Pittsfield MA 01201*

GLAZER, RACHELLE HOFFMAN, lawyer; b. Dallas, Aug. 18, 1958; married; 4 children. BA, U. N.C., 1980; JD, So. Meth. U., 1983. Bar: Tex. 1983, US Dist. Ct. (no. dist.) Tex. 1983, US Dist. Ct. (so. dist.) Tex. 1987, US Ct. Appeals (5th cir.) 1988, US Dist. Ct. (we. dist.) Tex. 1994, US Dist. Ct. (ea. dist.) Tex. 1995. Assoc. Thompson & Knight, Dallas, 1983-89; shareholder, ptnr. Thompson & Knight, PC, Dallas, 1989—, Thompson & Knight, LLP, Dallas. Mng. editor Southwestern Law Rev., So. Meth. U., 1982-83. Mem. Phi Beta Kappa. Office: Thompson & Knight 1700 Pacific Ave Ste 3300 Dallas TX 75201-4693

GLAZER, REA HELENE See KIRK, REA HELENE

GLAZER, RONALD BARRY, lawyer; b. Phila., Jan. 13, 1943; m. Adele J. Kay, June 12, 1965; children: Jodi M. Glazer, Jennifer G. Shorr. AB cum laude, Dickinson Coll., 1964; LLB cum laude, U. Pa., 1967. Bar: Pa. 1967, Fla. 1975. Sr. ptnr. Wolf, Block, Schorr & Solis-Cohen LLP, Phila., 1987—. Lectr. Pa. Bar Inst. Author: Pennsylvania Condominium Law and Practice, 1975, 3d edit., 1995. Mem. ABA, Pa. Bar Assn., Phila. Bar Assn. (chmn. real property law sect. 1987), Internat. Coun. Shopping Ctrs., Am. Coll. Real Estate Lawyers, Cmty. Assns. Inst., Coll. of Lawyers. Office: Wolf Block Schorr 1650 Arch St Ste 2100 Philadelphia PA 19103-2029

GLAZIER, JAMES ALEXANDER, biophysicist, researcher; b. Cambridge, Mass., June 27, 1962; s. Ira Albert and Elaine Atlas (Smulekoff) G. B.A., Harvard Coll., Cambridge MA, 1980—83; M.A., U. of Chgo., Chicago, IL, 1984—87, Ph.D., 1987—89. Postdoctoral mem. of tech. staff AT&T Bell Laboratories, Murray HIll, NJ, 1989—91; vis. fellow Trinity Coll., Dublin, Ireland, 1991—91; cons. U. of Utah, Dept. of Genetic Epidemiology, Salt Lake City, Utah, 1989—94; vis. fellow U. of Western Australia, Perth, Australia, 1989—89; cons. Trade Link Corp., Chicago, Ill., 1987—88; nsf/jsps fellow Tohoku U., Sendai, Japan, 1991—93; asst. prof. U. of Notre Dame, Notre Dame, Ind., 1993—97, assoc. prof., 1997—2002; prof. Ind. U., Bloomington, Ind., 2002—; vis. prof. Tohoku U., Sendai, Japan, 1999—99; vis. scientist U. of Grenoble, Grenoble, France (incl. Monaco), 2000—00; dir. Interdisciplinary Ctr. for the Study of Biocomplexity, U. of Notre Dame, Notre Dame, Ind., 2001—02, Biocomplexity Inst., Indian U., Bloomington, Ind., 2002—. Cons. Trade Link Corp., Chgo., 1988-89, U. Utah, Salt Lake City, 1989-94; vis. fellow U. Western Australia, Perth, 1989. Grainger fellow Grainger Found., 1987-89, Nat. Young investigator NSF, 1993-97, Vis. fellow Royal Irish Acad., 1994. Mem. Am. Phys. Soc., Materials Rsch. Soc. Democrat. Achievements include study of fluid turbulence and chaos; study of soap froths; discovery of "Glazier's Law" for three dimensional grain growth; first to make quantitative predictions & exptl. measurement of cell sorting during embryological devel. Home: 1035 Maxwell Ln Bloomington IN 47401 Office: Indiana U Biocomplexity Instn Dept Physics 727 E 3rd St/ Wain W 159 Bloomington IN 47405-7105 Office Fax: 812-855-5533. E-mail: glazier@indiana.edu.

GLAZIER, JONATHAN HEMENWAY, lawyer; b. Hartford, Conn., May 14, 1949; s. Orman Hemenway and Susan (Micka) G.; children: Martin Hemenway, Gregory Stephen. Student, Australian Nat. U., Canberra, 1969; BA, Rice U., 1972; JD, George Washington U., 1980. Bar: Tex. 1980, U.S. Dist. Ct. (so. dist.) Tex. 1981, U.S. Ct. Appeals (5th cir.) 1981, U.S. Ct. Internat. Trade 1984, U.S. Ct. Appeals (D.C. and Fed. cirs.) 1984, D.C. 1986, U.S. Dist. Ct. D.C. 1989, U.S. Tax Ct. 1989, U.S. Supreme Ct. 1991. Assoc. Chamberlain, Hrdlicka, White, Johnson and Williams, Houston, 1980-84, Busby, Rehm and Leonard, Washington, 1984-88, Dorsey & Whitney, Washington, 1988-91; assn. counsel Nat. Rural Elec. Coop. Assn., Washington, 1992—. Thomas J. Watson fellow, 1972-73. Mem. ABA (chmn. sub. com. on internat. tax and trade, 1988-90), Fed. Cir. Bar Assn. Avocations: sailing, bicycling. Office: Nat Rural Elec Coop Assn 4301 Wilson Blvd Arlington VA 22203-1867 E-mail: jonathan.glazier@nreca.org.

GLAZIER, RAYMOND EARL, JR., social research executive, disability policy analyst; b. Coshocton, Ohio, Nov. 14, 1941; s. Raymond Earl Sr. and Dorothy Opal (Baker) G.; m. Martha Lane MacLeish, Sept. 15, 1963 (div. 1973); 1 child, Andrew Baker; m. Debra Lee Medeiros, May 1, 1983 (div. 2000); 1 child, Daniel Ray. BA in Social Rels. magna cum laude, Harvard U., 1964, postgrad., 1964-65; PhD, Heller Sch. of Brandeis U., 1999. Anthropology field asst. Aro Hosp., Abeokuta, Nigeria, 1961-62; co-dir., stats. dept. Age Ctr. of N.Eng., Boston, 1964; ednl. games designer Abt Assocs., Inc., Cambridge, Mass., 1965-66; curriculum designer Abt Assocs., Cambridge, Mass., 1966-69, dep. area mgr., human devel. area, 1972-75, founder and editor-in-chief, Games Cen., 1969-78, mktg. mgr., Abt Books Div., 1978-80, dir. corp. communications, 1980-84, mgr., corp. mktg. svcs. and sr. health policy analyst, 1985-91; dir. Abt Ctr. for Advancement of Rehab. and Disability Svcs., Cambridge, Mass., 1991—; tech. assistance coord. Abt Assocs., Inc., Cambridge, Mass., 1991-96, assoc., 1992—. AIDS rsch. presenter, Westboro (Mass.) State Hosp., 1987; ednl. game cons. dept. nutrition, U. Lavale, Quebec City, Can., 1976;

reader Simulation and Games, Beverly Hills, Calif., 1969-79, Simulation/Gaming, Moscow, Idaho, 1971-78; project dir. nat. tech. assistance coord. Am. Disabilities Act, 1991-96; co-prin. investigator Mass. Medicaid Infrastructure Improvement Grant, 2000—; dir. Abt Ctr. for Advancement of Rehab. & Disability Svc., 1992-. Author: How to Design Educational Games, 6 edits, 1969-76, Life of the Egba Yoruba, 1973, Life of the Kwakiutl Indians, 1972, Mobility-Impaired Americans' Needs for Adaptive Housing Features, 1988, Preference for Consumer Directed Personal Assistance Services, 1999; pub. numerous class room games; contbr. articles on AIDS and public policy to jours. and mags., disability and access issues to mags. and newspapers. Pres. Info. Ctr. for Individuals with Disabilities, Boston, 1984-90, v.p., 1991-96, trustee, 1977—; mem. housing com. Boston Ctr. for Ind. Living, Boston, 1985-87; chair Belmont (Mass.) Disability Access Commn. Woodrow Wilson Nat. fellow, 1964, NSF grad. fellow, 1964-65; Ind. Student Rsch. grantee NSF, 1962-64; named Employee of the Yr., Nat. Bus. & Disability Coun., 2003. Mem. Nat. Spinal Cord Injury Assn., Mass. Assn. of Paraplegics, Nat. Head Injury Found., Mass. Head Injury Assn. Home: 59 Underwood St Belmont MA 02478-4021 Office: Abt Assocs Inc 55 Wheeler St Cambridge MA 02138-1168 E-mail: ray_glazier@abtassoc.com.

GLAZIER, ROBERT CARL, publishing executive; b. Brandsville, Mo., Mar. 26, 1927; s. Vernie A. and Mildred F. (Beu) G.; m. Harriette Hubbard, June 5, 1949; children: Gregory Kent, Jeffrey Robert. Student, Drury Coll., 1944-46; BA, U. Wichita, 1949. Reporter Springfield (Mo.) Daily News, 1944-46; asst. city editor Wichita Eagle, 1946-49; journalism instr. U. Wichita, 1949-53; dir. pub. relations Springfield (Mo.) Pub. Schs., 1953-59; asso. dir. dept. radio and TV The Methodist Ch., Nashville, 1959-61; gen. mgr. WDCN-TV (Channel 2), Nashville, 1961-65, KETC (Channel 9), St. Louis, 1965-76; also exec. dir. St. Louis Ednl. TV Commn.; pres. So. Ednl. Communications Assn., 1976-80; chmn. bd. Springfield Communications, Inc., Mo., 1980—. Bd. dirs. Systematic Savs. & Loan Assn.; pres., bd. dirs. Cox Health Systems. Bd. dirs. Adult Edn. Council Greater St. Louis, 1965-76, United Meth. Communications, 1980-86, Springfield Area Council of Chs., 1980-86, Lester E. Cox Med. Ctrs., 1988—. Served with AUS, 1945-46. Mem. Nat. Sch. Public Relations Assn. (past regional dir.), Nat. Acad. TV Arts and Scis. (gov.), Mo. Instructional TV Council, Ill. Instructional TV Commn., Nat. Assn. Ednl. Broadcasters. Clubs: Rotary Internat. Methodist. Home: 2305 E Meadow Dr Springfield MO 65804-4536 Office: 520 S Union Ave Springfield MO 65802-2660

GLEACH, FREDERIC WRIGHT, anthropologist, educator; b. Richmond, Va., June 1, 1960; s. Richard Colton and Judith Ann (Wright) G.; m. Vilma Iris Santiago-Irizarry, Mar. 17, 1995. BS, Va. Commonwealth U., 1984; AM, U. Chgo., 1987, PhD, 1992. Archaeologist Va. Commonwealth U., Richmond, 1982-88; fellow U. Chgo., 1986—90; with Cornell U., Ithaca, NY, 1993—2003; asst. prof. Transylvania U., Lexington, Ky., 1994-95. Instr. DePaul U., Chgo., 1992. Author: Powhatan's World and Colonial Virginia: a Confict of Cultures, 1997, Silversmiths of Ithaca NY, 1805-1890, Including Jewelers and Watchmakers, 2003; editor: (with Regna Darnell) Celebrating a Century of the American Anthropological Association: Presidential Portraits, 2002, (with Lisa J. Lefler) Southern Indians and Anthropologists: Culture, Politics and Identity, 2002; mem. editl. bd. Algonquian Conf., Winnipeg, 1994—, Chgo. Anthropology Exchange, 1987-90, Critical Studies in the History of Anthropology, 1997-; contbr. articles to profl. jours. Century fellow, U. Chgo., 1986—90, Philips Fund Rsch. grantee, Am. Philos. Soc., Phila., 1991—92. Mem.: Puerto Rican Studies Assn., Latin Am. Studies Assn., Soc. for Study Indigenous Lang. of Ams., Orgn. Am. Historians, Soc. Humanistic Anthropology (treas. 1998—), Am. Soc. Ethnohistory (sec., treas. 1994—98), Am. Anthrop. Assn. (centennial exec. com. 1999—2002, Pres.'s award 2002), Phi Kappa Phi (elected as an undergraduate 1983).

GLEASON, ABBOTT, history educator; b. Cambridge, Mass., July 21, 1938; s. Sarell Everett and Mary Eleanor (Abbott) G.; m. Sarah Caperton Fischer, June 11, 1966; children— Nicholas Abbott, Margaret Holliday BA, Harvard U., 1961, PhD, 1969. Asst. prof. history Brown U., Providence, 1969-73, assoc. prof. history, 1973-78, prof. history, 1978—, Keeney prof. history, 1993—; sec. Kennan Inst. for Advanced Russian Studies, Woodrow Wilson Ctr., Washington, 1980-82, chmn. history, 1989-92; dir. Watson Inst., 1999-2000, dir. univ. rels., 2000—. Mem. overseers com. to visit Davis Ctr. for Russian Studies, Harvard U., Cambridge, 1981-85, 91-97; bd. dirs. Fabergé Arts Found. Author: European and Muscovite, 1972, Young Russia, 1980, Totalitarianism, 1995 (with William Taubman and Sergei Khrushchev), Nikita Khrushchev, 2000; co-editor: Bolshevik Culture, 1985, Shared Destiny, 1985, Nineteen Eighty-Four: George Orwell and our Future, 2003. Howard Found. fellow, 1973-74; Rockefeller fellow Aspen Inst., 1977; Mellon fellow Harvard U., 1985 Mem. Am. Hist. Assn., Am. Assn. Advancement Slavic Studies (del. to Am. Coun. Learned Socs. 1984-87, bd. dirs. 1991-97, exec. com. 1994-97, pres. 1995). Democrat. Home: 30 John St Providence RI 02906-1043 Office: Brown U Dept History 142 Angell St Providence RI 02912-9040 E-mail: abbott_gleason@brown.edu.

GLEASON, ALAN HAROLD, retired economics educator; b. Riverside, Calif., Feb. 4, 1917; s. Harold Allen and Marion Hammond (Norris) G.; m. Emily Eleanor Gilbert, June 19, 1950; children: Alan G., Ann N., James D. AB, Princeton U., 1939; MA, U. Rochester, 1941; PhD, MIT, 1950. From instr. to asst. prof. econs. U. Rochester, N.Y., 1946-56; from assoc. prof. to prof. econs. Internat. Christian U., Tokyo, Japan, 1956-69; chmn. social sci. divsn., 1963-69; vis. prof. U. Pitts., 1969-70; prof. econs. U. Toledo, Ohio, 1970-84, dept. chmn. econs., 1970-77, prof. emeritus, 1984—. Vis. prof. Internat. Christian U., Tokyo, 1985-86. Contbr. numerous articles and reviews to profl. jours., 1948—. Trustee, treas. Maumee Valley Habitat for Humanity, Toledo, 1990-99. Sgt. U.S. Army, 1943-46, ETO. Citation for meritorious svc. to edn., Ohio Ho. Reps., 1984, Emeritus citation, Univ. Toledo, 1984. Mem. AAUP, Phi Kappa Phi. Democrat. Mem. United Ch. of Christ. Avocations: choir, piano, composing. Home: 5931 San Reno Dr Sylvania OH 43560-1131

GLEASON, ANDREW MATTEI, retired mathematician, educator; b. Fresno, Calif., Nov. 4, 1921; s. Henry Allan and Eleanor Theodalinda (Mattei) G.; m. Jean Berko, Jan. 26, 1959; children— Katherine Anne, Pamela, Cynthia. BS, Yale, 1942; Jr. Fellow Soc. Fellows, Harvard U., 1946-50, MA (hon.), 1953. Asst. prof. math. Harvard U., Cambridge, Mass., 1950-53, assoc. prof., 1953-57, prof., 1957-92, Hollis prof. math. and natural philosophy, 1969-92, emeritus prof., 1992—. Chmn. organizing com., pres. The Internat. Congress of Mathematicians, 1986. Author: Fundamentals of Abstract Analysis, 1966. Served from ensign to lt. (s.g.) USNR, 1942-46; lt. comdr. 1950-52. Recipient Newcomb Cleveland prize AAAS, 1952. Fellow Soc. of Fellows (sr., chmn. 1989-96); mem. NAS, Am. Math. Soc. (pres. 1981-82), Math. Assn. Am. (Disting. Svc. award 1996), Am. Philos. Soc., Am. Acad. Arts and Scis., Cosmos Club (Washington). Home: 110 Larchwood Dr Cambridge MA 02138-4639 Office: Havard Univ 1 Oxford St Cambridge MA 02138-2901

GLEASON, CAROL ANN, mental health nurse, educator; b. Fairfield, Iowa, Mar. 6, 1945; d. Maurice Alvin and Geraldine (Cook) Crist; m. Michael Gleason Jr., Nov. 26, 1966 (div. Nov. 1980); children: Daniel Lee, Raymond Joe, Christopher John, Crystal Dawn. ADN, Indian Hills Coll., 1977; AS in Adminstrn., Des Moines Area Coll., 1982; BSPA in Health Care, St. Joseph's, 1985; cert. nurses aides edn., U. Iowa, 1989; BSN, Drake U., 1997; grad., Nat. Inst. Paralegal Arts Sci., 2002. Lic. nursing home adminstr., Iowa; cert. psychiat. and mental health, gerontology ANA. Staff night charge nurse Mahaska Manor Nursing Home, Oskaloosa, Iowa, 1977; dir. nursing Tower Park Nursing Home, Oskaloosa, 1977-78, Pleasant Park Nursing Home, Oskaloosa, 1978-85, adminstr., 1985-86; staff nurse ICU-CCU Ottumwa (Iowa) Regional Hosp., 1986; psychiat. nurse Knoxville (Iowa) Vets. Hosp., 1986—. Coord., instr. Iowa Ednl. inst., Oskaloosa, 1987—; cons. Tower Park Nursing Home, Oskaloosa, 1985-87, Siesta Park Nursing Home, 1985-87, Mahaska Manor, 1993-95. Mem.: NAFE, Am. Fedn. Govt. Employers. Democrat. Roman Catholic. Avocations: home bus./gifts, football games, walking, boating. Home: 220 Keomah Vlg Oskaloosa IA 52577-9671

GLEASON, HARRIET HALL, nurse; b. Otranto, Iowa, May 11, 1923; d. Roy Francis Sr. and Amy Ruth (Read) G. RN, Kahler Sch. Nursing, Rochester, Minn., 1947; BS, BA, Hartwick Coll., 1956. RN, N.Y. Office nurse Mayo Clinic, Rochester, 1947-53, various hosps., Oneonta, N.Y.C., 1953—56; instr. Fairview Hosp., Mpls., 1956-57; clin. instr. Swedish Hosp., Mpls., 1958-59; supr. sick children unit Mt. Sinai Hosp., 1959-60; ward nurse various temp. agys., N.Y.C., 1960-82; gen. and spl. duty nurse various vol. assignments, Morgantown, W.Va., 1982—. Author: (cookbooks) Therapeutic Diets, 1980, Be Brave, 1994, (essays) I Understand, 1994. Active ARC; membership com., vol. Rep. Party Caucus, Mpls., N.Y.C. and W.Va., 1960-82, 92, 93. Mem. AAUW, Tri Beta, Zeta Tau Alpha (Pan Hellenic rep.). Lutheran. Avocations: reading, spectator sports, volunteer work, music appreciation.

GLEASON, JAMES MULLANEY, lawyer, insurance executive; b. Sept. 27, 1948; s. Harry H. and Dorothy (Mullaney) Gleason; m. Margaret McGuire; children: Matthew, Katherine. BA, Briar Cliff Coll., 1973; JD, Creighton U., 1976. Bar: (Iowa) 1976, Nebr. 1976. From asst. counsel to asst. v.p. Woodmen of the World, Omaha, 1976—93, asst. v.p., 1993—. With U.S. Army, 1968—69. Fellow: Life Mgmt. Inst. (master), Life Office Mgmt. Assn.; mem.: Assn. Life and Health Claims, Nebr. Fraternal Congress (pres. 1993—94), Internat. Claim Assn. (pres. 2002—03, exec. com.), Assn. Fraternal Benefit Counsel. Democrat. Roman Catholic. Office: Woodmen of World Life Ins Soc 1700 Farnam St Ste 2200 Omaha NE 68102-2007 E-mail: jgleason2@cox.net.

GLEASON, JEAN BERKO, psychology educator; b. Cleve., Dec. 19, 1931; d. Arthur E. and Alice (Gelberger) Berko; m. Andrew Mattei Gleason, Jan. 26, 1959; children: Katherine, Pamela, Cynthia. AB, Radcliffe Coll., 1953, AM, 1955, PhD, 1958. USPHS fellow MIT, 1958—59; research assoc. VA Med. Ctr., Boston, 1961—2000; vis. asst. prof. psychology Boston U., 1972—73, assoc. prof., 1973—76, prof., 1976—, chairperson dept. psychology, 1985—89, acting chair dept. psychology, 1997, dir. grad program devel. psychology, 1975—78, 1982—85, dir. grad. program human devel., 1997—2002; research assoc. edn. Harvard U., Cambridge, Mass., 1968—70, prin. research assoc. psychiatry, 1970—72. Rsch. scholar in residence Inst. Linguistics, Hungarian Acad. Sci., 1981, 83; mem. mental retardation rsch. com. Nat. Inst. Child Health and Human Devel., 1981-85; trustee Ctr. for Applied Linguistics, Washington, 1989-94. Author: The Development of Language, 1983, 4th edit., 1997, 5th edit., 2001, You Can Take It with You, 1989, Psycholinguistics, 1993, 2nd edit., 1998; mem. editl. bd. Child Development, 1971—77, Discourse Processes, 1982—2002, assoc. editor Language, 1997—2000; contbr. articles. Recipient Editors award Jour. Speech and Hearing Research, 1970. Fellow: APA, AAAS (coun. del. 2002—); mem.: ACLU, Internat. Assn. for Study of Child Lang. (pres. 1990—93), Soc. for Rsch. Child Devel., Linguistic Soc. Am. (chmn. program com. 1980—81), Radcliffe Alumni Assn. (bd. dirs. 1969—72), Radcliffe Grad. Soc. (past pres.), Gypsy Lore Soc. (exec. bd. 1983—87, 1992—2002, pres. 1996—99, exec. bd. 2003—), Acad. Aphasia, Phi Beta Kappa (pres. Radcliffe chpt. 1965—68). Home: 110 Larchwood Dr Cambridge MA 02138-4639 Office: Boston U Dept Psychology 64 Cummington St Boston MA 02215-2407 E-mail: gleason@bu.edu.

GLEASON, JOHN PATRICK, JR., trade association executive; b. N.Y.C., Nov. 11, 1941; s. John Patrick Sr. and Ruth T. (Madigan) G.; m. Judith Peper (dec. 1980); children: John P. III, Megan K.; m. Susan Leigh Collier, Mar. 31, 1984; children: Kevin M., Colin P. BS in Fgn. Service, Georgetown U., 1963; PMD, Harvard Bus. Sch., 1972. Gen. mgr. Pappagallo, Inc., Washington, 1964-67; export project mgr. U.S. Dept. Commerce, Washington, 1967-68; investment banker Blyth, Eastman Dillon, Inc., Washington, 1968-70; with U.S. Dept. Commerce, Washington, 1970-77, chief staff domestic and internat. bus. adminstrn., 1970-77, dep. asst. sec. commerce, 1970-77; pres. Brick Inst. Am., Reston, Va., 1977-86, Portland Cement Assn., Skokie, Ill., 1986—. Bd. dirs., chmn. Coun. Masonry Rsch., Reston, 1985—, Masonry Industry Com., Washington, 1984—. Recipient Silver medal U.S. Dept. Commerce, Washington, 1978. Mem. Am. Soc. Assn. Execs., Chgo. Soc. Assn. Execs., River Bend Country Club (Great Falls, Va.), Carlton Club (Washington), Skokie Country Club (Glencoe, Ill.). Republican. Office: Portland Cement Assn 5420 Old Orchard Rd Skokie IL 60077-1053

GLEASON, KEN BELL, historian, educator, journalist; b. Manhattan, NY, Mar. 4, 1941; s. Arthur Kesten and Eleanor Mary (Bell) Gleason; m. Carole Ann Horchler Crowe, July 20, 1963 (div. Dec. 3, 1976); children: Tara Ann, Darren Kenneth;children: Colin, Alexis. BA in History Honors, Univ. Calif., Berkeley, 1989; MA in History, San Francisco State U., 1992. Reporter Newsday, Long Island, NY, 1965—66; wire news editor Suffolk LI Sun, 1966—69; asst. editor The Baltimore Sun, Md., 1969—77; copy editor San Jose Mercury News, Calif., 1983—84; instr. history Chabot Coll., Hayward, Calif., 1992—, Santa Rosa Jr. Coll., Calif., 1994—, Coll. of Alameda, Calif., 1995—. Exec. coun. mem. All Faculty Assoc., Santa Rosa, Calif., 1998—2001; del. Bay Faculty Assoc., Oakland, Calif., 1998—2001; exec. coun. mem. AFT (Am. Fedn. Tchr) Local 1603, 1999—2001. Mem. Peralta Cmty. Coll. Dist. Save Our Cmty. Coll. Comm., Oakland, Calif., 1998; polit. action comm. mem. Faculty Assoc. Calif. Cmty. Coll., Sacramento, 1999—2000. Grantee, Nat. Endowment for Humanities, 1993. Mem.: Orgn. Am. Historians. Democrat. Avocations: reading, jazz listening, baseball viewing. Home: Box 7302 Berkeley CA 94707-0302 Office: Chabot Coll 25555 Hesperian Blvd Hayward CA 94545 E-mail: kgleason@chabotcollege.edu.

GLEASON, MARY RENA, secondary education educator; b. Bridgeport, Conn., Feb. 19, 1948; d. John M. and Veronica (Small) G. BS, Russell Sage Coll., 1970; MA, cert. C.C. edn., NYU, 1972; Cert. of Advanced Study in Adminstrn., Fairfield U., 1988. Lectr. history Union Jr. Coll., Cranford, N.J., 1972; tchr. social studies Chalk Hill Mid. Sch., Monroe, Conn., 1972-78; tchr. Fawn Hollow Sch., Monroe, 1978-83; tchr. social studies Masuk High Sch., Monroe, 1983—. Past sec., v.p., pres. elect, and pres. Conn. Coun. Social Studies, 1972-89; organizing com. N.E. Regional Conf. for Social Studies, 1979-88. Mem. Fairfield (Conn.) Dem. Town Com., 1980-82, Fairfield Historic Dist. Com., 1980-85; mem. adv. panel Conn. Hist. Commn., 1982-83; mem. State of Conn. Statue of Liberty Ellis Island Commn., Hartford, Conn., 1984-86. Named Outstanding Young Woman of Am., 1978; EPDA fellow NYU, 1970-72, Fulbright fellow U.S. Govt., 1978. Mem. Fairfield U. Pres. Circle, Russell Sage Alumni. Democrat. Roman Catholic. Avocations: swimming, travel. Home: 34 Linley Dr Fairfield CT 06432-1664 Office: Masuk High Sch 1014 Monroe Tpke Ste 1 Monroe CT 06468-1915

GLEASON, STEPHEN CHARLES, physician; b. Leon, Iowa, June 30, 1946; s. Charles Gerald and Ferne Louise (Pollard) Gleason; m. Lisa Ann Corcoran, Aug. 22, 1981; adopted children: Julia, Alex children: Michael John, Timothy Charles, Christian Kelly, Sean Patrick, Keriann Louise. BS, Iowa State U., 1971; DO summa cum laude, Coll. Osteo. Medicine and Surgery, 1974; PhD, Washington U., St. Louis, 1999. Diplomate Am. Bd. Family Practice. Resident in family practice Meml. Med. Ctr., Corpus Christi, Tex., 1974, 75; family practice medicine Des Moines, 1975-93. Chmn. dept. family practice Mercy Hosp. Med. Center, Des Moines, 1979-82; pres., CEO chief med. officer Mercy Clinic System, 1984-97; mem. papal med. security team Pope John Paul's Am. Pilgrimage, 1979; asst. prof. Mayo Grad. Sch. Medicine, 1996—. Chmn. Iowa CARES Med. Found., 1987, Nat. Health Policy Coun., 1989-98; bd. dirs. Family Health Plan, HMO, 1985, Securecare, Inc., 1990-99; White House health advisor, 1992-94; v.p. med. ops. Cath. Health Initiatives, 1997-98; sr. health adv. Pres. Clinton Campaign, 1996; sr. med. advisor Health Care Financing Adminstrn., 1998-99; dir. Dept. Pub. Health, State of Iowa, 1999—; active med. mission in El Salvador during earthquake disaster, 2001. Recipient Outstanding Young Iowan, 1982, Iowa Physician of Yr., 1990. Mem. AOA, AMA, Am. Acad. Family Physicians, Sigma Alpha Epsilon, Sigma Sigma Phi. Democrat.

GLEASON III, CHARLES RICHARD, dental industry executive, business management consultant; b. Tifton, Ga., Oct. 1, 1957; s. Charles Richard Gleason, Jr. and Melinda Ater Gyorog; m. Laura Ann Brooks; children: Charles Richard Gleason IV, Brenna Jean Gleason, Austin Thomas Gleason. MBA, U. of Del., 1998, BS Entomology, 1980. Lab. technician E. I. du Pont de Nemours and Co., Wilmington, Del., 1981—84; strategic market analyst Nor-Am Chem. Co., Wilmington, 1984—87; product specialist W. L. Gore and Assoc., Inc., Newark, 1987—94; tech. product and sales rep. Closure Systems, Inc., Bensalem, Pa., 1994—96; tech. products/sales specialist SMC Pneumatics, Inc., Somerville, NJ, 1996—98; regional dir., bus. devel. Nat. Dentex Corp., Wayland, Mass., 1998—2000, group support mgr., 2000—01, group mgr., 2001—. Cons. in field, Newark, 1998—. Pres. Glen Brook Homeowner's Assn., Inc., Elkton, 2001, Country Hills Civic Assn., Newark, 2000—01; bd. dirs. Oaklands Pool, Newark, 2000—01. Avocation: sailing, gardening, automobiles, woodworking. Office: Nat Dentex Corp 526 Boston Post Rd Wayland MA 01778 Office Fax: 302.661.6016. Personal E-mail: chuckgleas@aol.com.

GLEASON-JORDAN, IRENE, pathologist; b. Maui, Hawaii; d. Yong Woon Ow and Charng Hee Loo; children: Barbara Irene, Edward Donald, Colin Sean. AA, San Mateo Jr. Coll., 1952; AB, Stanford U., 1947; MD, U. Calif., San Francisco, 1951. Intern pathology Harbor Gen. Hosp./L.A. County, L.A., 1951-52; resident pathology Bellevue Hosp., N.Y.C., 1951-54, VA Hosp., 1954-56, pathologist chief grade, 1956-67, acting chief lab. svcs., 1958-65, chief grade pathologist surg. pathology Long Beach, Calif., 1967-79, chief clin. pathology and quality control, Coll. Am. Pathologists inspector, 1967—; cons. FDA, 1970-79; lab. dir. Lancaster (Calif.) Cmty. Hosp., 1979-86, Temple Hosp., L.A., 1987-91; pathologist, dir. histopathology, chemistry & spl. chemistry King/Drew Med. Ctr., L.A., 1991-94, pathologist, dir. hematology, ctrl. receiving & phlebotomy, 1994-96, acting chair dept. pathology, 1996—. Rsch. asst. anatomy Sch. Biol. Scis., Stanford U., 1944-47; instr. dept. pathology NYU Sch. Medicine, 1952-54; dermatopathology cons., lectr. to med. students UCLA and U. Calif. Irvine Sch. Medicine, 1955-79; clin. instr. VA Hosp., L.A., Long Beach, 1956-67; clin. instr. dept. pathology UCLA Sch. Medicine, 1957-61, asst. clin. prof., assoc. clin. prof. dept. pathology, 1961-73, assoc. clin. prof. dept. pathology, 1979-91; assoc. clin. prof. dept. pathology, lectr. U. Calif. Irvine Sch. Medicine, 1967-79; lectr. dept. pathology UCLA Sch. Dentistry, 1967- 68; commr. Calif. Med. Bd., 1974-92; assoc. prof. dept. pathology Charles R. Drew U. Medicine and Sci., 1991-97, prof. step I career acad. series, 1997—, UCLA Sch. Medicine, 1997—; chmn. cancer com. King/Drew Med. Ctr., L.A., 1999—; cons. in field. Editor Radioassay News, 1961-79; contbr. articles to profl. jours. Judge, trustee, chmn. rsch. Am. Orchid Soc., 1962—; sponsor Planetary Soc., Pasadena, 1991. Carson scholar Stanford U., 1945-46, Sara Hoyt scholar UCLA Sch. Medicine, 1948; grantee USPHS, 1958-60. Mem. AMA, Coll. Am. Pathologists (accreditation com. 1967-79), N.Y. Acad. Scis., Phi Beta Kappa (UCLA selection com. Eta chpt. 1957-67).

GLEAVES, EDWIN SHEFFIELD, librarian; b. Nashville, Feb. 28, 1936; s. Edwin Sheffield and Hazel Boyd (Hunter) G.; m. Jane Ann Thompson, May 20, 1978; children: Susan Kay, David Hunter. BA, David Lipscomb Coll., 1958; MA, Emory U., 1960, PhD, 1964. Head libr., assoc. prof. english David Lipscomb Coll., Nashville, 1964-65; dir., chmn. dept. libr. and info. sci. Peabody Coll. Vanderbilt U., Nashville, 1967-87; state libr., archivist Tenn. State Libr. and Archives, Nashville, 1987—. Fulbright lectr., San Jose, Costa Rica, 1971; Univ. lectr., cons. Colombia, 1971, 84, 92, Mex., 1971, 74, 79-81, 85-86, 94, 96, Paraguay, 1977-79. Author (with others): Reference Services and Library Education: Essays in Honor of Frances Neel Cheney, 1982; contbr. over 150 articles to profl. jours. Mem. Bread for World, Washington, 1984—; chmn. Tenn. Hist. Records Adv. Bd., 1988—; bd. dirs. Tenn. Hist. Soc., 1994—, Tenn. Hist. Commn., 1987—. With USAFR, 1954-63. Mem. ALA (translator World Ency. 1986), Assn. Specialized and Coop. Libr. Agys. (chair state libr. agy. 1996-97), Tenn. Libr. Assn. (Frances Neel Cheney award 1986, Honor award 1990), Soc. Am. Archivists, Tenn. Hist. Soc. (bd. dirs.), Chief Officers State Libr. Agys. Democrat. Avocations: ornithology, tennis, classical music, computers. Home: 1004 Norfleet Dr Nashville TN 37220-1410 Office: Tenn State Libr & Archives 403 7th Ave N Nashville TN 37243-1409

GLEAVES, LEON ROGERS, marketing and sales executive; b. Louisville, May 4, 1939; s. Leon Rogers and Fain Mae (King) G.; m. Hallie Virginia Dumke, Apr. 9, 1966 (dec. Dec. 20, 1990); 1 child, Keith Browning; m Elizabeth Ann Smith, June 25, 2000 BS, U. Louisville, 1961, MBA, 1966. Sales mgmt. trainee GM, Louisville, 1965-67; advt. rep. The Christian Sci. Monitor, N.Y.C., 1967-72; mktg. and sales coord. White Lily Foods Co., Knoxville, Tenn., 1972-75; v.p. mktg. and sales Wilkins-Rogers, Inc., Ellicott City, Md., 1975—2002; pres., CEO, LRG, Ltd., 2002—. Spkr. in field. Bd. dirs. Bucknell U. Parents Assn., Lewisburg, Pa., 1992-95; adv. com. Md. Agrl. Edn. Found., Balt., 1993-96, Md. Food Bank, Inc., Balt.; home econ. adv. bd. Howard County Schs., Columbia, Md., 1993-2003, Balt. City Schs., 1994-97; mem. fin. com. So. Assn. State Depts. Agr., 1997, Md. Agrl. Commn., 2002-03; Md. Agrl. Commn., 2002-2003; spkr. Future Bus. Leaders Am., 1997-99. Mem. Balt./Washington Grocery Mfr. Rep., Md. Food Exporters Assn., Am. Mktg. Assn., Home Baking Assn (dir 1990-92), So. Assn. State Dept. Agr. (fin. com. 1997), Md. Agriculture Commn., 2002-2003. Avocations: tennis, classical and vintage jazz music, English mystery books and movies. Office: LRG Inc 27 Frederick Rd Ellicott City MD 21043-4759

GLEAZER, EDMUND JOHN, JR., retired education educator; b. Phila., Aug. 24, 1916; s. Edmund John and Jane Hunter (Laurie) G.; m. Charlene A. Allen, Apr. 14, 1940; children: Allen, Sandra Jo, John, Susan. AA, Graceland Coll., 1936; AB, U. Cal. at Los Angeles, 1938; Ed.M., Temple U., 1943; Ed.D., Harvard, 1953. Minister Reorganized Ch. of Jesus Christ of Latter Day Saints, Phila., 1938-43; pres. Reorganized Ch. of Jesus Christ of Latter Day Saints (So. Iowa dist.), 1943-46, Graceland Coll., Lamoni, Ia., 1946-57; exec. dir. Am. Assn. Jr. Colls., Washington, 1958-81; vis. prof. George Washington U., Washington, 1981-85. Mem. U.S. Tech. Edn. Del. to, USSR, 1961, 76; edn. survey team AID, Kenya, 1962; chmn. Def. Adv. Com. on Edn. in Armed Forces, 1962; mem. vis. com. Stanford U., Sch. Edn., 1962; mem. Pres.'s Commn. on Fgn. Lang. and Internat. Studies, 1979; v.p. for N. Am., Internat. Council for Adult Edn., 1979; vis. prof. c.c. leadership program U. Tex., 1981—. Author: This is the Community College, 1968, Project Focus: A Forecast Study of Community Colleges, 1974, The Community College: Values, Vision and Vitality, 1980; Editor: American Junior Colleges, 1960, 63, 67, 71. Mem. North Central Jr. Colls. (pres. council 1954), Am. Assn. Jr. Colls. (pres. 1957), Am. Council on Edn. (sec., award for outstanding lifetime contbns. to Am. higher edn. 1980), Phi Delta Kappa. Clubs: Rotary (Washington), Cosmos (Washington). Home: 8208 Woodhaven Blvd Bethesda MD 20817-3176 E-mail: egleazer@cs.com.

GLEBA, BETH ANN (BETH ANN COLEMAN), communications executive; b. June 27, 1970; Cert. of desktop pub., Moore Coll. Art, 1992; BA, Albright Coll., 1994; MA in Comm., LaSalle U. Mgr. internal comm. IKEA, Plymouth Meeting, Pa. E-mail: bethgleba@memo.ikea.com.

GLEESON, PAUL FRANCIS, retired lawyer; b. Bronx, June 20, 1941; s. William Francis and Julia Anne (Dargis) G.; children: Kevin F., Sean W., Brendan J., Colleen J. AB in History, Fordham U., 1963; JD, U. Chgo., 1966. Assoc. Vedder, Price, Kaufman & Kammholz, Chgo., 1966-73, ptnr., 1973-2000; ret., 2000. Adj. prof. DePaul U. Sch. of Law, 1991. Co-author (with Day, Green & Cleveland) The Equal Employment Opportunity Compliance Manual, 1978; columnist: (with B. Alper) Gleeson and Alper on Employment Law, Merrill's Illinois Legal Times, 1988-90. Capt. U.S. Army, 1966-68, Vietnam. Decorated Bronze Star; Floyd Russell Mechem scholar, 1963-66. Mem. Order of Coif, Phi Beta Kappa. Roman Catholic.

GLEESON, ROSLYN M. pediatric clinical nurse specialist/practitioner; b. New Haven, Mar. 2, 1952; BS, U. Conn., 1974; MSN, U. Pa., 1979. RN, Pa., Del.; cert. pediatric nurse practitioner, child and adolescent nurse. Staff nurse, charge nurse St. Christopher's Hosp. for Children, Phila., 1974-77; staff nurse, charge nurse pediatrics, neonatal ICU Med. Coll. Pa., Phila., 1978-79; pediatric clin. nurse specialist Alfred I. duPont Hosp. for Children, Wilmington, Del., 1979—, pediat. clin. nurse spec., spinal dysfunction program coord., 1979—. Instr. Neumann Coll. Sch. Nursing, Aston, Pa., 1991; mem. pediatric test devel. com. ANCC; clin. instr. Temple U., Phila., 1977, Delaware County C.C., 1982, U. Del. Sch. Nursing, 1989-95, Thomas Jefferson U. Sch. Nursing, Phila., 1991—; cons. in field; presenter at nat. and internat. profl. confs. Mem. editl. rev. bd. Pediatric Nursing, Jour. Pediatric Nursing, Am. Jour. Maternal-Child Nursing; contbr. articles to profl. pediatric nursing jours. Mem. March of Dimes Folic Acid Coalition, Wilmington. Mem. ANA, Nat. Assn. Clin. Nurse Specialists, Soc. Pediatric Nurses (mem. nat. program com.), Sigma Theta Tau. Avocations: travel, international foods, environmental issues, theatre, arthurian legend. Office: Alfred I duPont Hosp for Children 1600 Rockland Rd Wilmington DE 19803-3607 E-mail: rgleeson@nemours.org.

GLEESON, THOMAS ALEXANDER, retired meteorologist; b. N.Y.C., Aug. 11, 1920; s. John and Bertha Alexander Gleeson; m. Jeanette Lucas, Nov. 21, 1942; children: Vicki, Keith Thomas. BS, Harvard U., 1946; MS, NYU, 1947, PhD, 1950. Professional Member Am. Meteorol. Soc., Mass., 1945. Asst. prof.

Fla. State U., Tallahassee, 1949—54, assoc. prof., 1954—59, full prof., 1959—94. Cons. USN, Norfolk, Va., 1962—67, NASA, Huntsville, Ala., 1964—73; state climatologist U.S. Weather Svc., Tallahassee, 1984—94. Contbr. articles to profl. jours. First lt. U.S. Army, 1942—45, U.S. and Middle East. Fellow: Am. Meteorol. Soc. (hon.; com. chmn. 1974—75); mem.: Sigma Xi (corr.). Home: 2106 Old Bainbridge Rd Tallahassee FL 32303 Office: Univ Dept Meteorology Fla State Tallahassee FL 32306

GLEICH, GERALD JOSEPH, immunologist, medical scientist, educator; b. Escanaba, Mich., May 14, 1931; s. Gordon Joseph and Agnes (Ederer) G.; m. Elizabeth Louise Hearn, Aug. 16, 1955 (div. 1976); children: Elizabeth Genevieve, Martin Christopher (dec.), Julia Katherine; m. Kristin Marie Leiferman, Sept. 25, 1976; children: Stephen Joseph, David Francis, Caroline Louise, William Gerald. BA, U. Mich., 1953, MD, 1956. Diplomate Am. Bd. Internal Medicine, Am. Bd. Allergy and Immunology. Intern Phila. Gen. Hosp., 1956-57; resident Jackson Meml. Hosp., Miami, Fla., 1959-61; instr. in medicine and microbiology U. Rochester, NY, 1961—65; cons. in medicine, prof. immunology and medicine Mayo Clinic-Med. Sch., Rochester, Minn., 1965—2001; chmn. dept. immunology Mayo Clinic, Rochester, Minn., 1982-90, George M. Eisenberg prof., 1995—2001; disting. investigator Mayo Found., Rochester, 1988—2001; prof. medicine & dermatology U. Utah, Salt Lake City, 2001—. Mem. bd. sci. counselors Nat. Inst. Allergy and Infectious Disease, 1981-83; chmn. subcom. on standardization allergens WHO, Geneva, 1974-75; lectr. Am. Acad. Allergy, 1976, 82; mem., chmn. immunological scis. study sect. NIH, 1984-87; John M. Sheldon Meml. lectr., 1976, 82, 88; Steve Lang Meml. Lectureship, 1980, Stoll-Stunkard lectr. Am. Soc. Parasitologists, 1986, David Talmage Meml. lectureship, 1987, Disting. lectr. Med. Scis. Mayo Clinic, 1988; original mem. Highly Cited Rschrs. Database, 2002. Contbr. articles on eosinophilic leukocyte to profl. jours. Served to capt. USAF, 1957-59. Recipient Landmark in Allergy award, 1990; grantee Nat. Inst. Allergy and Infectious Disease, 1970—; AAAS fellow for studies of structure, biol. properties and role in pathogenesis of disease of basic proteins present in cytoplasmic granules of eosinophilic leukocytes, 1993. Fellow ACP, Am. Acad. Allergy and Immunology (hon. fellow award 1992), AAAS; mem. Am. Soc. Clin. Investigation, Am. Assn. Immunologists, Assn. Am. Physicians, Phi Beta Kappa, Phi Kappa Phi, Alpha Omega Alpha. Roman Catholic. Home: 4313 S Zarahemla Dr Salt Lake City UT 84124-4020 Office: Univ Utah 1D151 Sch Medicine 30 North 1900 East Salt Lake City UT 84132-2409

GLEICHMAN, JOHN ALAN, safety and loss control executive; b. Anthony, Kans., Feb. 11, 1944; s. Charles William and Caroline Elizabeth (Emch) G.; m. Martha Jean Cannon, July 1, 1966; 1 son, John Alan Jr. BS in Bus. Mgmt., Kans. State Tchrs. Coll., 1966. Cert. hazard control mgr.; cert. safety profl. with a speciality in constrn. safety; cert. safety exec. Office mgr. to asst. supt. Barton-Malow Co., Detroit, 1967-72, safety coord., 1972-76, corp. mgr. safety and security, 1976-89, dir. corp. safety and loss control, 1989—. Instr. U. Mich., Wayne State U., 1977-81, Lawrence Tech. U., 1994-96; mem. constrn. safety stds. commn. adv. com. for concrete constrn. and steel erection Bur. of Safety and Regulations, Mich. Dept. Labor, 1977—; rep. constrn. stds. com. Am. Nat. Stds. Inst., 1984—. Author: (with others) You, The National Safety Council, and Voluntary Standards, 1981, Construction Accident Analysis: The Inductive Learning Approach, 1991; mem. editl. adv. bd. Safety and Health: The Internat. Safety, Health and Environ. Mag., 1989—. Instr. multimedia first aid ARC, 1976-89; past trustee Apostolic Christian Ch., Livonia, Mich. Recipient Safety Achievement awards Mich. Mut. Ins. Co., 1979-83; Cameron award Constrn. sect. Indsl. divsn. Nat. Safety Coun., 1982, 87. Mem. Mich. Safety Conf. (pres. 1984-85), Am. Soc. Safety Engrs. (pres. Detroit chpt. 1982, nat. adminstr. constrn. divsn. 1988-89, bd. dirs. 1988-90, Safety Profl. of Yr. 1984), Nat. Safety Coun. (chmn. tech. rev. constrn. sect. indsl. divsn. 1980-84, chmn. stds. com. indsl. divsn. 1983-85, chmn. assn. com. indsl. divsn. 1986-87, dir. sects. group indsl. divsn. 1987-89, chmn. elect indsl. divsn. 1989-90, chmn. 1990-91, bd. dirs. 1987-92, Disting. Svcs. to Safety award 1993), Am. Arbitration Assn. (panel arbitrators 1985). Office: Barton Malow Co 26500 American Dr Southfield MI 48034 Office Fax: 248-436-5403.

GLEICHMANN, FRANCES EVANGELINE, retired elementary educator; b. Marion, N.C., Sept. 24, 1920; d. Alexander Rudolph and Margaret Katherine (McNeely) McCulloch; m. August O. Gleichmann, Dec. 1, 1945. Diploma, Pfeiffer Jr. Coll., 1940; BS in Edn., Asheville Coll., 1942; postgrad., Mount St. Agnes Coll., Johns Hopkins U., U. Md., U. R.I. Elem. tchr. Balt. City Pub. Schs., 1942-85. Cooperating tchr. for student tchrs. from Towson State U. Balt. City Pub. Schs., 1957-59. Co-author: Tales of the Smokies and Blue Ridge Mountains1, 1997; contbr. poetry to poetry.com, poetry to Internat. Libr. Poetry. Recipient Econ. Edn. Tchr, award Econ. Edn. Program Com., 1985, Disting. Alumni award Pfeiffer Coll., 1973, Tate award Balt. C. of C. and Tate Industries, 1975, Salute 13 award Sta. WJZ TV, 1980, Golden Poet award World of Poetry, 1985-88. Mem. NEA, Md. State Ret. Tchrs. Assn., Balt. City Ret. Tchrs. Assn., Alpha Delta Kappa (Md. state publicity chmn. 1988-90, Alpha Delta Kappa week chmn. 1986-88). Home: 10 Dungarrie Rd Baltimore MD 21228-3401

GLEISSER, MARCUS DAVID, writer, lawyer, journalist; b. Buenos Aires, Feb. 14, 1923; s. Ben and Riva (Kogan) G.; m. Helga Marianne Rothschild, Oct. 23, 1955; children: Brian Saul, Julia Lynne Wainblat, Hannah Tanya Sharnsky, Ellyn Ruth Klein. BA in Journalism, Case Western Res. U., 1945, MA in Econs., 1949; JD, Cleve. State U., 1958. Bar: Ohio 1958, U.S. Dist. Ct. (no. and ea. dists.) Ohio 1981, U.S. Supreme Ct. 1962. Police reporter Cleve. Press, 1942-44, copy editor, 1944-47; advt. copy writer McDonough-Lewy, Inc., 1947-50; copy editor Cleve. Plain Dealer, 1950-52, gen. assignment reporter, 1952-57, courthouse reporter, 1957-63, real estate editor, 1963-81, fin. writer and investment columnist, 1981—. Instr. journalism, fin., law Cuyahoga C.C., 2002—. Author: The World of Cyrus Eaton, 1965, Juries and Justice, 1968; also articles.; editor in chief: Cleve.-Marshall Law Rev., 1956, 57. Trustee Cleve. Coll. Alumni Assn., 1968, Euclid Mayor's Exec. Council, 1973-76, Euclid Charter Commn., 1975-76. Recipient Nat. Bronze medal Am. Newspaper Pubs. Assn., 1944, Nat. Silver Gavel award ABA, 1958, Bronze medal Nat. Legal Aid and Defender Assn., 1963, Loeb award for disting. bus. and fin. writing U. Conn., 1966; cert. of recognition NCCJ, 1967, Silver Medal award consistently outstanding spl. feature columns Nat. Headliners club, 1969, award Ohio Bar Assn., 1957, 58, 59, 60, 61, 62, award pub. svc. Cleve. Newspaper Guild, 1959, award for best column, 1976, award Nat. Assn. Real Estate Editors, 1965, 71, 72, 73, 80, 91, award Nat. Assn. Real Estate Bds., 1966, 67, 68, 69, 70, 71, 73, award Nat. Assn. Home Builders, 1970, 1st prize Nat. Assn. Realtors, 1980, Bus.-Fin. Writing award Press Club Cleve., 1969, Disting. Merit award Cleve. Assn. Real Estate Brokers, 1976, Excellence in Bus. Journalism award Press Club Cleve., 1983, 85, Fin. Writing award Pannell, Kerr & Forster, 1985, State and Dist. Winner Ohio Journalist Advocate of Yr., U.S. Small Bus. Adminstrn., 2002; runner-up Pulitzer Prize in Journalism for local reporting, 1973; named to N.E. Ohio Apt. Assn. Hall of Fame, 1996. Mem. Am. Newspaper Guild, Soc. Profl. Journalists (Disting. Svc. award Cleve. chpt. 1994), City Club. Clubs: City (Cleve.). Home: 647 Grand View Ln Aurora OH 44202 Office: 1801 Superior Ave E Cleveland OH 44114-2107 E-mail: gleisser@stratos.net. *Honest and honorable communication with my fellow man is of the utmost importance . . . to inform, debate, educate, understand, persuade, listen, be open to new thoughts-never to ignore.*

GLEKEL, JEFFREY IVES, lawyer; b. N.Y.C., Apr. 8, 1947; s. Newton and Gertrude (Burr) G.; m. Cynthia R. Leder, June 18, 1988; 1 child, David L. AB, Columbia U., 1969; JD, Yale U., 1972. Bar: N.Y. 1973, U.S. Supreme Ct. 1981, U.S. Ct. Appeals (2d cir.) 1974, U.S. Dist. Ct. (so. dist.) N.Y. 1974. Law clk. to judge U.S. Dist. Ct. (so. dist.) N.Y., 1972-73; asst. U.S. atty. So. Dist. N.Y., 1975-77; law clk. to justice Byron R. White U.S. Supreme Ct., Washington, 1977-78; ptnr. Skadden, Arps, Slate, Meagher and Flom, N.Y.C., 1980—. Editor, contbr.: Civil Litigation Practice, 1990; Business Crimes, 1982; note and comment editor Yale Law Jour., 1971-72; contbr. articles to law jours. Mem. Assn. Bar City of N.Y. (chmn. com. fed. legislation 1984-87), ABA. Office: Skadden Arps Slate Meagher & Flom 4 Times Sq New York NY 10036-6522

GLEN, NIKI, artist; b. Milw., Nov. 14, 1950; d. Alan and Janet (Marx) G.; children: Dana Alan Knops, Laramie Ann Glen. BS in Art Edn., U. Wis., 1973. Cert. in art edn. K-12. Pub. artist, muralist numerous orgns., various locations, 1973—; co-founder Madison (Wis.) Graphics, 1973-76; art educator various schs. various locations, 1973—; dir. S.W. Pub. Art Group, Phoenix, Ariz., 1996—. Exhibited in group shows Corcoran Gallery, Washington, 1986, Williams Ratliff Gallery, Sedona, Ariz., 1988, Veneble Neslage Galleries, Washington, 1989-92, Spirit of N.Mex. Art Exhbn., Washington, 1990, Marin-Price Galleries, Bethesda/Chevy Chase, Md., 1992, Am. Bank Gallery, Chevy Chase, 1994, Artisimo Gallery, Scottsdale, Ariz., 1995, Nat. Soc. Mural Painters Centennial Exhibit, N.Y.C., 1996, Exit Gallery, N.Y.C., 1996, 1st Internat. Pub. Art and Mural Congress, Mexico City, 1998, Exit Gallery, NYC, 2002, Sietz Gallery, Harrisburg, Pa., 2003 (art installation) Phoenix Coll., Ariz. Ctr. Blind and Visually Impaired, Phoenix Childrens Hosp.; featured in publs. including Community Murals, 1984, Street Murals: The Most Exciting Cities of America, Britain and Western Europe, 1982, The Art of Handmade Tile, also numerous covers and illustrations for textbooks and periodicals. Pres. Arts and Creativity in Early Chlidhood, 1993-96; bd. dirs. Gaynor Mus. and Found., 1993-95, Cmty. Built Assn., 2000-; mem. Ariz. Alliance for Art Edn., 1990-95. Recipient Orchid award City of Madison, 1975, Tempe Diablo award of excellence in edn., 1996, 97, Livable Cities award, 2001, Beautification award Art in Pvt. Devel.; Ariz. Artist Project grantee Ariz. Commn. on Arts, 1994, Phoenix Children's Hosp.; grantee numerous orgns. including Atlantic Richfield, City of Whitewater, The Mills Corp., Phoenix Arts Commn., Medtronics Inc., Phoenix (Ariz.) Coll., NEA, YMCA, City of Tempe. Mem. Nat. Soc. Mural Painters. Avocations: swimming, reading, sailing, dancing.

GLEN, PAUL MICHAEL, management consultant, educator; b. Chgo., Mar. 10, 1965; s. Marren Jay and Ann (Elcrat) G. BA, Cornell U., 1988; M in Mgmt., Northwestern U., 1991. Cons. SEI Info. Tech., Chgo., 1988-95, regional mgr. L.A., 1995-99; prin. C2 Consulting, Marina Del Rey, Calif., 1999—. Author: Healing Client Relationships: A Professional's Guide to Managing Client Conflict, 2001, Lending Geeks: How to Manage and Lead People Who Deliver Technology, 2002. Office: C2 Consulting 3253 Malcolm Ave Los Angeles CA 90036

GLEN, ROBERT ALLAN, history educator; b. Sioux Falls, S.D., Nov. 5, 1946; s. Clarence Rolland and Virginia Carol (Grieme) G. BA, U. Wash., 1968; MA, U. Calif., Berkeley, 1969; PhD, U. Calif., 1978. Teaching asst. U. Calif., Berkeley, Calif., 1972-74; instr. U. Wis., Parkside, Wis., 1975-77, U. Vermont, 1977-78; asst. prof. history U. New Haven, Conn., 1979-83, assoc. prof., chair dept. history, 1983-87, prof., 1987—, chair dept. history, 1994-96. Vis. faculty fellow Yale U., 1981-82. Author: Urban Workers in the Early Industrial Revolution, 1984; contbr. articles to profl. jours. Hist. cons. New Dimension Theatre Co., New Haven, 1979-81; tutor Lit. Vols., New Haven, 1985—. Fellow NEH, 1976, 85. Mem. Am. Hist. Assn., Am. Soc. 18th Century Studies, N.Am. Conf. on Brit. Studies, Hist. Assn., Econ. History Soc., Wesley Hist. Soc. Office: U New Haven 300 Orange Ave West Haven CT 06516-1996 E-mail: rglen@newhaven.edu.

GLENDENING, EVERETT AUSTIN, architect; b. White Plains, N.Y., May 20, 1929; s. Gilbert Leslie and Elsie Jane (Fanjoy) G.; m. Wilhelmina Louise Hanley, Nov. 26, 1949; children: Nancy, James, Thomas, Terry, Susan. B.Arch., U. Cin., 1953; M.Arch., M.I.T., 1954. With Duffy Constrn. Co., Cleve., 1951-55, SIS Architects, Cin., 1956-58, T.J. Moore (architect), Denver, 1959; prof. architecture U. Cin., 1960-67; pvt. practice architecture Cin., 1959—. Prin. works include Queen's Towers, Cin., 1964, Summit Chase, Columbus, Ohio, 1966, Norwood High Sch., Cin., 1972, W.Va. State Mus., 1978, Douglass Montessori Sch., Cin., 1979, Christie Lane Workshop, Norwalk, Ohio, 1980, Coll. Law U. Cin., 1981, Elks Lodge, Columbus, Ind., 1981, Geology/Physics Sci. Ctr. U. Cin., 1983, U. Rio Grande Dormitory, 1989, U. Rio Grande Student Ctr., 1994, U. Rio Grande Math-Sci.-Nursing Bldg., 1995, Planetarium, Shawnee State U., 1998, Sch. for Creative and Performing Arts Auditorium, Cin. Pub. Schs., 1997. Served as 1st lt. USAF, 1954-56. Fellow AIA (honor awards Ohio chpt. 1966-70, 74, 82, 90, 91, Cin. chpt. 1966-68, 70, 76, Bronze medal 1969, Apple award for arch. 1995, mem. U.S. delegation of architects to People's Republic China and Hong Kong 1990); mem. Architect's Soc. Ohio, Scarab. Methodist. Office: 8050 Montgomery Rd Cincinnati OH 45236-2950 Fax: (513) 791-2794. *A consistently positive point of view has perhaps been the single, most important factor in making possible what has been accomplished in my lifetime. I have always felt that anything was possible as long as I was willing to make the effort and, in fact, I can recall telling myself as a new college freshman that "while I may not be the most intelligent man in the class, there was no reason why I should not be the hardest working member of that class."*

GLENDENING, PARRIS NELSON, former governor, political science educator; b. Bronx, N.Y., June 11, 1942; m. Jennifer Elizabeth Crawford; 1 child, Raymond Hughes. AA, Broward County Jr. Coll., 1962; BA, Fla. State U., Tallahassee, 1964, MA, 1965, PhD, 1967. Asst. prof. U. Md., College Park, 1967-72, assoc. prof., 1972-94; coun. mem. Hyattsville City Coun., Md., 1973-74, Prince George's County Coun., Upper Marlboro, Md., 1974-82, coun. chmn., 1980, 81, county exec., 1982-95; gov. State of Md., 1995—2003. Vice chair state of Md.'s Chesapeake Bay Critical Area Commn., 1984-94; vice chair bd. dirs. World Trade Ctr., 1990-97; mem. bd. visitors U. Md. Sch. Pub. Affairs, 1990-97; trustee Ptnrs. for Livable Places, 1990-97. Author: (with Mavis Mann Reeves) Controversies of State and Local Political Systems, 1972, Pragmatic Federalism, 1977, 2nd edit., 1984; contbr. numerous articles to profl. jours. Del. to Dem. Nat. Conv., San Francisco, 1984, Atlanta, 1988, N.Y.C., 1992; bd. govs., steering com. Am.'s Clean Water Found. Recipient numerous awards, including City and State mag., Prince George's County, Prince George's High Sch. Prins. Assn., State Assn. Retarded Citizens, Nat. Bus. League So. Md., Spanish Speaking Communities Md., Inc., Rotary Internat., Md. Assn. Psychol. Svcs., Elizabeth and David Scull award for disting. leadership to Washington met. region Coun. Govts., 1995, Dr. Nathan Davis award The Am. Med. Assn., 1991; Disting. Alumni award Fla. State U. Coll. Social Svcs., 1993, Outstanding Alumni The Am. Assn. of Com. Coll., 1997. Mem. AAUP, AAAS (profl. ethics group 1988—), Nat. Assn. Counties (bd. dirs. 1992—, chair large urban county caucus 1992—), Am. Polit. Sci. Assn., ASPA (profl. ethics com. mem. 1989—, chmn. 1991-92, SIAM mem. 1991—), Nat. Coun. Elected County Execs. (1st v.p. 1989-90, pres. 1991-92), Md. Assn. Counties (pres. 1987-88), Nat. Assn. Counties (bd. dirs. 1992—, vice chmn. intergovtl. rels. policy steering com. 1987-90, chair 1990—, taxation and fin. steering com. 1984-87), Nat. Govs. Assn. (chair 2000-01). Democrat. Fax: (410) 974-3275. E-mail: governor@gov.state.md.us.*

GLENDENING, TERRY SKY, psychologist; b. Cin., Apr. 19, 1961; BA, Cornell U., 1983; MA, U. Cin., 1986, PhD, 1995. Lic. psychologist Ohio, Ky., cert. corrective thinking practitioner 1999. Dir. recreation Indian Hill Cmty. Edn., Cin., 1986—92; clin. psychologist, psychotherapist Cin., 1983—. Tchg. asst. Cornell U., Ithaca, NY, 1982—83; cons. IHHS Peer Counseling Program, Indian Hill, Ohio, 1987—96; lectr. in field. Author: (book) Thought Patterns in Depression and Somatization, 1986, Cognitive Specificity in Non-Clinical Depressive Manifestations of Distress, 1995, Timeless Parenting Techniques: Fair, Firm and Functional, 2002; author: (workshop series) Coping Skills for a New Millenium, 2000. Vol. recreation for disabled Camp Stepping Stones, Cin., 1997—98; vol. Spl. Olympics, Cin., 1997—98. Named Outstanding Young Woman of Am., 1986; recipient Sons and Daughters Am. Revolution award, 1974. Mem.: APA, Ohio Psychol. Assn., Psi Chi. Avocations: hiking, camping, art, sports, rock collecting.

GLENDENNING, DON MARK, lawyer; b. Dallas, Dec. 24, 1953; s. Don Thomas and Nancy (Malloy) G.; m. Carol Peterson, Dec. 30, 1979. BA, Rice U., 1976; JD, Stanford U., 1979. Bar: Tex. 1979. Assoc. Rain Harrell Emery Young & Doke, Dallas, 1979-85; ptnr. Rain, Harrell, Emery, Young & Doke, Dallas, 1985-87; shareholder Locke Liddell & Sapp (formerly Locke Purnell Rain Harrell, P.C.), Dallas, 1987-98; ptnr. Locke Liddell & Sapp LLP, Dallas, 1999—. Pres. Human Rights Initiative North Tex., Tex.; bd. dirs. Nat. Tree Trust, Dallas Trees and Park Found.; chmn. Thanks-Giving Found.; bd. dirs., pres. Scenic Dallas; bd. dirs. Scenic Tex., Dallas Zool. Soc. Republican. Presbyterian. Office: Locke Liddell & Sapp LLP 2200 Ross Ave Ste 2200 Dallas TX 75201-6776

GLENDON, MARY ANN, law educator; b. 1938; BA, U. Chgo., 1959, JD, 1961, M Comparative Law, 1963. Bar: Ill. 1964, Mass. 1980. Legal intern. EEC, Brussels, Belgium, 1963; assoc. Mayer, Brown & Platt, Chgo., 1963-68; prof. Boston Coll., 1968-86; vis. prof. Harvard U., 1974-75, prof., 1986—. Vis. prof. U. Chgo., 1983, 84, 86. Author: Rights Talk, 1991, A Nation Under Lawyers, 1994, A World Made New: Eleanor Roosevelt and the Universal Declaration of Human Rights, 2001. Foreign Law fellow U. Libre de Bruxelles, 1962-63, Ford Found. fellow, 1975-76. Mem. Am. Acad. Arts & Scis., Pres.'s Coun. Bioethics. Office: Harvard U Law Sch Cambridge MA 02138

GLENISTER, BRIAN FREDERICK, geologist, educator; b. Albany, Western Australia, Sept. 28, 1928; came to U.S., 1959, naturalized, 1967; s. Frederick and Mabel (Frusher) G.; m. Anne Marie Treloar, Feb. 16, 1956; children: Alan Edward, Linda Marie, Kathryn Grace. BSc, U. Western Australia, Perth, 1949; MSc, U. Melbourne, Australia, 1953; PhD, U. Iowa, 1956. Lectr., then sr. lectr. geology U. Western Australia, 1956-59; asst. prof. U. Iowa, Iowa City, 1959-62, assoc. prof., 1962-66, prof., 1966-74, chmn. geology dept., 1968-74, A.K. Miller prof. geology, 1974-97, A.K. Miller prof. geology emeritus, 1997—. Mem. AAAS, Paleontol. Soc. (pres. 1988-89), Geol. Soc. Am., Geol. Soc. Iowa (pres. 1991), Paleontol. Rsch. Inst. Home: 2015 Scales Bend Rd NE North Liberty IA 52317-9331 E-mail: brian-glenister@uiowa.edu.

GLENN, CONSTANCE WHITE, art museum director, educator, consultant; b. Topeka, Oct. 4, 1933; d. Henry A. and Madeline (Stewart) White; m. Jack W. Glenn, June 19, 1955; children: Laurie Glenn Buckle, Caroline Glenn Galey, John Christopher. BFA, U. Kans., 1955; grad., U. Mo., 1969; MA, Calif. State U., 1974. Dir. Univ. Art Mus. & Mus. Studies program, from lectr. to prof. Calif. State U., Long Beach, 1973—. Art cons. Archtl. Digest, L.A., 1980-89. Author: Jim Dine Drawings, 1984, Roy Lichtenstein: Landscape Sketches, 1986, Wayne Thiebaud: Private Drawings, 1988, Robert Motherwell: The Dedalus Sketches, 1988, James Rosenquist: Time Dust: The Complete Graphics 1962-92, 1993, The Great American Pop Art Store: Multiples of the Sixties, 1997; contbg. author: Encyclopedia Americana, 1995—, The Grove Dictionary of Art, 1989—, Double Vision: Photographs from the Strauss Collection, 2001, Carrie Mae Weems: The Hampton Project, 2000. Vice-chair Adv. Com. for Pub. Art, Long Beach, 1990-95; chair So. Calif. adv. bd. Archives Am. Art, L.A., 1980-90; mem. adv. bd. ART/LA, 1986-94, chair, 1992. Recipient Outstanding Contbn. to Profession award Calif. Mus. Photography, 1986, Disting. Scholarly and Creative Achievement award, Calif. State U. Long Beach, Women of Distinction award Soroptimist Internat., 1999. Mem. Am. Assn. Mus., Assn. Art Mus. Dirs. (trustee 2000-02), Coll. Art Assn., Art Table, Long Beach Pub. Corp. for the Arts (arts adminstr. of yr. 1989), Kappa Alpha Theta. Office: Univ Art Mus 1250 N Bellflower Blvd Long Beach CA 90840-0006

GLENN, FRANCES BONDE, retired dentist; b. Tampa, Fla., Nov. 29, 1933; Student, U. Fla., 1951-52; DDS, U. Pa., 1956. Resident Children's Hosp., Washington, 1956-57; pvt. practice dentistry Miami, 1957—. Vis. lectr. U. Miami, 1959—, Miami Dade Sch. of Dental Hygiene, 1979; cons. D.C. Tng. Ctr. for the Retarded and Handicapped, 1956-57; lectr. Lindsey Hopkins Vocat. Sch., 1981, U.S. and other countries; bd. overseers U. Pa. Sch. Dental Medicine; rschr. Pediat. Dent. Ortho. Author: How to Have Children with Perfect Teeth, 2000; contbr. articles to Lady's Home Jour., Parents Mag., Chicago Tribune Newspaper, Med. and Dent. Jour. Active Dade County Welfare and Planning Coun., 1959-61; vol. dentist Cerebral Palsy Clinic, 1959-63; advisor, cons. Crippled Children's Soc., 1976—; dental clinic staff mem. Coral Gables Jr. Women's Club, 1959-61. Recipient Alumni award merit U. Pa. Sch. Dental Medicine, 1984. Fellow Am. Acad. of Pedodontics; mem. Am. Orthodontic Soc. (diplomate of bd., Moore Disting. Svc. award 1994), Fla. Soc. Dentistry for Children, Am. Assn. Women Dentists. Achievements include discovering that children of expectant mothers who take sodium fluoride don't get cavities. Home: 1976 Ocean Ridge Cir Vero Beach FL 32963

GLENN, FURMAN EUGENE, industrial chemist; b. Gastonia, N.C., Nov. 3, 1944; s. John Frank and Stella Lucielle Glenn; m. Janet Brown, May 10, 1968; children: Furman Eugene, Kevin Lammont, Michael LeVar. PhD, Wayne State U., 1973. Rsch. chemist E.I. DuPont de Nemours & Co., Wilmington, Del., 1972—77, supr., tech. supt. Louisville, 1977—88, sr. chemist, 1988—92, rsch. fellow, 1992—96; sr. scientist, rsch. fellow Dupont Dow Elastomers, Louisville, 1997—. Chairperson Corp. Sci. Leadership Coun. Mem.: Am. Chem. Soc. (sr.), Sigma Xi. Democrat. Mem. United Methodist Ch. Achievements include patents for latex for adhesives. Avocations: reading, running, foreign languages, golf, tennis. Home: 4713 Nottinghamshire Dr Louisville KY 40299 Office: DuPont Dow Elastomers LLC 4242 Campground Rd Louisville KY 40216 Office Fax: 502-569-2184. E-mail: furmaneglenn@aol.com.

GLENN, GERALD MARVIN, marketing, engineering and construction executive; b. Greenville, S.C., Aug. 20, 1942; s. Oscar Marvin and Lorene (Ashmore) G.; m. Candice Wilson, Oct. 24, 1986; children: Regina Lynn, Gerald Marvin II, Charles Wilson. BSCE, Clemson U., 1964. With Daniel Constrn. Co., Greenville, S.C., 1964-77, Fluor Corp., Santa Ana, Calif., 1977-94, sr. v.p. mktg., 1982-85, pres. U.S. ops., 1985-86, exec. v.p., 1986, group pres., dir. Irvine, Calif., 1986-94; owner, prin. The Glenn Group LLC, Cimarron, Colo., 1994—, Eagle Glen Ranch LLC, Cimarron, Colo., 1994—; chmn., pres., CEO, Chgo. Bridge & Iron Co. N.V., The Woodlands, Tex., 1996—. Chmn. bd. dirs. Chgo. chpt. Am. Heart Assn., 1999—2001. Mem.: TAPPI, AIChE, Inst. Gas Tech. (dir.), Ill. Bus. Roundtable, Am. Petroleum Inst., Chgo. Soc., Chgo. Coun. Fgn. Rels. (mem. Chgo. com.), Econ. Club Chgo., Mid-Am. Club, Club at Carlton Woods, Woodlands Country Club, Ruth Lake Country Club, Univ. Club Houston, Execs. Club Chgo., Olympia Fields Country Club, Fairway Pines Golf Club. Republican. Methodist. Home: 23 Cypress Lake Pl The Woodlands TX 77382 Office: CB&I Ste 300 10200 Grogans Mill Rd The Woodlands TX 77380 Fax: 832-513-1778.

GLENN, GUY CHARLES, pathologist; b. Parma, Ohio, May 13, 1930; s. Joseph Frank and Helen (Rupple) G.; m. Lucia Ann Howarth, June 13, 1953; children: Kathryn Holly, Carolyn Helen, Cynthia Marie. BS, Denison U., 1953; MD, U. Cin., 1957. Diplomate Am. Bd. Pathology, Am. Bd. Radioisotopic Pathology. Intern Walter Reed Army Med. Ctr., Washington, 1957-58; resident in pathology Fitzsimons Army Med. Ctr., Denver, 1959-63; commd. 2d lt. U.S. Army, 1956; advanced through grades to col., 1972; demonstrator pathology Royal Army Med. Coll., London, 1970-72; chief dept. pathology Fitzsimons Army Med. Ctr., Denver, 1972-77. Past pres. med. staff St. Vincent Hosp., Billings, Mont.; past mem. governing bd. Mont. Health Sys. Agy. Contbr. articles to profl. jours. Fellow: Coll. Am. Pathologists (chmn. chemistry resources com., chmn. commn. sci. resources, mem. budget com., coun. on quality assurance, chmn. practice guidelines com., bd. govs., chmn. nominating com.); mem.: Midland Empire Health Assn. (past pres.), Soc. Med. Cons. to Armed Forces, Am. Registry Pathology (bd. dirs., exec. com., search com.), Am. Soc. Clin. Pathology, Rotary (bd. dirs. emeritus local chpt., chmn. Found. local chpt., Paul Harris fellow). Home: 3225 Jack Burke Ln Billings MT 59106-1113 E-mail: gcandlhglenn@earthlink.net.

GLENN, JAMES FRANCIS, urologist, educator; b. Lexington, Ky., May 10, 1928; s. Cambridge Francis and Martha (Morrow) G.; children: Cambridge Francis II, Sara Brooke, Nancy Carrick, James Morrison Woodworth; m. Gay Elste Darsie, Jan. 11, 2002. Student (Yale Regional scholar), Univ. Sch., Lexington, 1946; BA in Gen. Sci. (Bausch and Lomb Nat. Sci. scholar), U. Rochester, 1949; MD, Duke U., 1952; DSc, U. Ky., 1998. Diplomate Am. Bd. Urology (mem.), Nat. Bd. Med. Examiners. Intern Peter Bent Brigham Hosp., Boston, 1952-54; asst. resident urology Duke U. Med. Ctr., 1956-58, resident, 1958-59; instr. urology Duke U., 1958-59, prof., chief div. urology, 1963-80; asst. prof. Yale U., 1959-61; assoc. prof. Bowman Gray Sch. Medicine, Wake Forest Coll., 1961-63; practice medicine specializing in urology New Haven, 1959-61, Winston-Salem, N.C., 1961-63, Durham, N.C., 1963-80; prof. surgery, dean Med. Sch., Emory U., 1980-83; pres. Mt. Sinai Med. Ctr., 1983-87; prof. surgery U. Ky. Coll. Medicine, Lexington, 1987—; CEO Markey Cancer Ctr., 1989-93; chief staff Univ. Hosp., Lexington, 1993-95, chmn. dept. surgery, 1996-97. Sci. dir. Coun. for Tobacco Rsch. U.S.A., 1987-91, chmn. bd., 1991—. Contbg. author: Renal Neoplasia, 1967, Urodynamics, 1971, Textbook of Surgery, 1972, Plastic and Reconstructive Surgery of The Genital Area, 1973, Current Operative Urology, 1975, Campbell's Urology, 1977; author, editor: Diagnostic Urology, 1964, Ureteral Reflux in Children, 1966, Urologic Surgery, 1969, rev. edit., 1975, 84, 90; contbr. numerous articles to profl. jours. Capt. M.C., USAF, 1954-56. Mem. Am. Assn. Genitourinary Surgeons (pres. 1992-93, hon. 1998), Am. Surg. Assn., ACS, AMA (sec. sect. urology 1972-73, chmn. 1975-77), Assn. Am. Med. Colls., Internat. Urol Soc. (v.p. 1985-91, pres. 1991-94), Clin. Soc. Genito-Urinary Surgeons (pres. 1990-91), N.Y. Acad. Medicine, Soc. Pediatric Urology (pres. 1972-73), Soc. Pelvic Surgeons (pres. 1980-81), Soc. Univ. Surgeons, Soc. Univ. Urologists (pres. 1971-72), Royal

Coll. Surgeons (hon. fellow 1987), German Urol. Assn. (hon.), Australasian Urologic Soc. (hon.), Brit. Assn. Urologic Surgeons (hon.) Home: 101 Idle Hour Dr Lexington KY 40502-1166 Office: Univ Ky Med Ctr Hosp Adminstrn 800 Rose St Lexington KY 40536-0001 E-mail: drjglenn@aol.com.

GLENN, JERRY HOSMER, JR., retired language educator; b. Little Rock, Sept. 5, 1938; s. Jerry Hosmer and Anne (Matthews) G.; m. Renate Drexl, July 29, 1978. BA, Yale U., 1960; MA, U. Tex., 1962; postgrad., Free U. Berlin, 1962 63; PhD, U. Tex., 1964. Asst. prof. German U. Wis., Milw., 1964-67; asst. prof. German U. Cin., 1967-69, assoc. prof., 1969-72, prof., 1972—2003, dir. honors program, 1977-79, head dept., 1980-83, prof. emeritus, 2003—. Author: Deutsches Schrifttum der Gegenwart (ab 1945), 1971, Paul Celan, 1973, Paul Celan: Eine Bibliographie, 1989, Paul Celan: A Bibliography of English Lang. Secondary Lit. 1955-1996, 1996; (with Jeffrey Todd) Paul Celan: Die zweite Bibliographie, 1998; mng. editor: Lessing Yearbook, 1969-74; editor: (with Uwe Faulhaber and others) Exile and Enlightenment, 1987; (with Joachim Herrmann and Rebecca Rodgers) Alfred Gong, Early Poems, 1987, Max Kade Occasional Papers, 2001—; translator (with Jennifer Kelley) On the Wrong Track, 1993, International Zone, 1999, Too-Late, Too-Early, 2000, (with Clarise Samuels) Landing Attempts, 2000. Mem. Lessing Soc. (sec-treas. 1968-74), Mideast Honors Assn. (exec. sec. 1977-78, pres. 1979-80), Am. Assn. Tchr. German, Soc. German-Am. Studies (v.p. 1987-89). Republican. Home: 54 Fairway Dr Southgate KY 41071-3025 E-mail: jerry.glenn@uc.edu.

GLENN, JOHN HERSCHEL, JR., former senator, astronaut; b. Cambridge, Ohio, July 18, 1921; s. John Herschel and Clara (Sproat) G.; m. Anna Margaret Castor, Apr. 1943; children: Carolyn Ann, John David. Student, Muskingum Coll., 1939-42, B.Sc., 1962; naval aviation cadet, U. Iowa, 1942; grad. flight sch., Naval Air Tng. Center, Corpus Christi, Tex., 1943, Navy Test Pilot Tng. Sch., Patuxent River, Md., 1954. Commd. 2d lt. USMC, 1943, assigned 4th Marine Aircraft Wing, Marshall Islands campaign, 1944, assigned 9th Marine Aircraft Wing, 1945-46; with 1st Marine Aircraft Wing, North China Patrol, also Guam, 1947-48; flight instr. advanced flight tng. Corpus Christi, 1949-51; asst. G-2/G-3 Amphibious Warfare Sch., Quantico, Va., 1951; with Marine Fighter Squadron 311, exchange pilot 25th Fighter Interceptor Squadron USAF, Korea, 1953; project officer fighter design br. Navy Bur. Aero. Washington, 1956-58; astronaut Project Mercury, Manned Spacecraft Center NASA, 1959-65; pilot Mercury-Atlas 6, 1st orbital space flight launched from Cape Canaveral, Fla., Feb. 1962; ret. as col., 1965; v.p. corp. devel. and dir. Royal Crown Cola Co., 1966-74; pres. Royal Crown Internat.; U.S. senator from Ohio, 1975-99; mem.-at-large Ohio State Dem. Com., 1999—. Mem. Spl. Com. on Aging, Armed Svcs. Com., Senate Dem. Tech. and Comm. Com., Intelligence Com.; ranking minority mem. Govtl. Affairs Com.; vice-chmn. Senate Dem. Policy Com. Co-author: We Seven, 1962; author: P.S., I Listened to Your Heart Beat, Made first supersonic transcontinental flight, July 16, 1957; trustee Muskingum Coll. Decorated D.F.C. (six), Air medal (18); recipient Astronaut medal USMC, Navy unit commendation, Korean Presdl. unit citation, Disting. Merit award Muskingum Coll., Medal of Honor N.Y.C., Congl. Space Medal of Honor, 1978, Centennial awd., Nat. Geographic Soc., 1988, other decorations, awards and hon. degrees. Mem. Soc. Exptl. Test Pilots, Internat. Acad. of Astronautics (hon.) Democrat. Presbyterian. Office: Ohio State U John Glenn Inst 100 Bricker Hall 190 N Oval Mall Columbus OH 43210 1321

GLENN, LUCIA HOWARTH, retired mental health services professional; b. Bklyn., Apr. 21, 1930; d. Arthur Orrel and Kathryn (Wilcox) Howarth; m. Guy Charles Glenn, June 13, 1953; children: Kathryn Holly, Carolyn Helen, Cynthia Marie. BS, Denison U., 1952; MS, Eastern Mont. Coll., 1980. Lic. profl. counselor; nat. cert. counselor; CC mental health counselor. Staff therapist Pastoral Counseling Ctr., Billings, Mont., Christian Psychol. Svcs., Billings; pvt. practice psychotherapist Billings, 1984—96; ret., 1996. Cons. in field. Contbr. articles to profl. jours. Active mid.-Yellowstone affil. Habitat for Humanity, 1992—; 1st v.p. St. Andrew Presbyn. Ch., 1996—97, 2d v.p., 1992—98, elder, leader Christian Parenting Group, 1997—99; mem. coun. Yellowstone Presbytery, 1999—. Tng. and Rsch. grantee AACD, 1986-87. Mem. Mont. Mental Health Counselors Assn. (past pres.), Am. Mental Health Counselors Assn. (chair spl. interest network on gender issues 1991-96). Home: 3225 Jack Burke Ln Billings MT 59106-1113

GLENN, NORVAL DWIGHT, sociologist, educator; b. Roswell, N.Mex., Aug. 13, 1933; s. William N. and Mary F. (Cochrain) G. BA, N.Mex. State U., 1954; PhD, U. Tex., 1962. Instr. Miami U., Oxford, Ohio, 1960-61; instr. U. Ill., 1961-63, asst. prof., 1963-64, U. Tex., Austin, 1964-65, assoc. prof. sociology, 1965-70, prof. sociology, 1970-84, Ashbel Smith prof. sociology, 1984—, Raymond Dickson, Alton C. Allen and Dillon Anderson centennial prof., 1990-91, Stiles prof. Am. studies, 1991—. Author: (with Leonard Broom) Transformation of the Negro American, 1965, Cohort Analysis, 1977, (with Elizabeth Marguardt) Hooking Up, Hanging Out, and Looking for Mr. Right; editor: (with Charles Bonjean) Blacks in the United States, 1969, (with Marion Coleman) Family Relations, 1989; editor Contemporary Sociology, 1977-80, Jour. Family Issues, 1984-89; compiler: (with Jon Alston and David Weiner) Social Stratification: A Research Bibliography, 1969; contbr. articles to profl. jours. Mem. coun. Inter-Univ. Consortium for Polit. and Social Rsch., 1980-84, assoc. dir., 1984—2000. Served to 1st lt AUS, 1954-56. Mem. Am. Sociol. Assn., Am. Assn. Public Opinion Rsch., Nat. Coun. on Family Rels., Population Assn. Am. Home: 13309 Villa Park Dr Austin TX 78729-3733

GLENN, PAUL M. federal judge; b. 1945; BA, Fla. State U., 1967; JD, Duke U., 1970. Assoc., shareholder Mahoney, Hadlow & Adams, P.A., Jacksonville, Miami, Fla., 1970-81; pres., CEO Mobile Am. Corp. and subsidiaries, Jacksonville, 1981-85; shareholder Bledsoe, Schmidt & Glenn, P.A., Jacksonville, 1985-87; exec. v.p., chief adminstrv. officer The Dependable Ins. Group, Inc. Am. and subsidiaries, Jacksonville, 1987-88; shareholder Dale & Bald, Jacksonville, 1989-93; bankruptcy judge U.S. Bankruptcy Ct. (mid. dist.) Fla., Tampa, 1993—. Mem. ABA, Fla. Bar Assn. Office: 801 N Florida Ave Ste 840 Tampa FL 33602-3849 Fax: 813-301-5111.

GLENN, ROBERT EASTWOOD, lawyer; b. Catlettsburg, Ky., Dec. 24, 1929; s. Albert Sidney and Pauline Elizabeth (Eastwood) G.; m. Clydenne Reinhard, Mar. 16, 1956; children: Pauline Glenn O'Brien, Robert Eastwood Jr. BS cum laude, Washington and Lee U., 1951, JD cum laude, 1953. Bar: Va. 1952, U.S. Dist. Ct. (we. dist.) Va. 1958, U.S. Ct. Appeals (4th cir.) 1974, U.S. Supreme Ct. 1975, U.S. Tax Ct. 1994. Assoc. Eggleston & Holton, Roanoke, Va., 1957-60; ptnr. Glenn, Feldmann, Darby & Goodlatte, Roanoke, 1960—2003, of counsel, 2003—. Mem. Va. Bd. Bar Examiners, Richmond, 1982—, pres., 1993—. Mem. State Coun. for Higher Edn. for Va., 1980-84; rector Radford (Va.) U., 1975-79, bd. visitors, 1972-79; chmn. Roanoke City Rep. Com., 1968-70, Roanoke Valley ARC, 1974-76; mem. Va. Found. for Humanities, 1995-01. Fellow: Va. Bar Found., ABA Found.; mem.: ABA, Roanoke Bar Assn. (pres. 1980—81), Va. Bar Assn., Roanoke Regional C. of C. (pres. 1988), Shenandoah Club (pres. 2001—03), Roanoke Country Club, Order of Coif, Beta Gamma Sigma. Roman Catholic. Home: 3101 Allendale St SW Roanoke VA 24014-3118 Office: Glenn Feldmann Darby & Goodlatte 210 1st St SW Ste 200 Roanoke VA 24011-1607 E-mail: rglenn@gfdg.com.

GLENNEN, ROBERT EUGENE, JR., retired university president; b. Omaha, Mar. 31, 1933; s. Robert E. and La Verda (Elledge) G.; m. Mary C. O'Brien, Apr. 17, 1958; children: Maureen, Bobby, Colleen, Billy, Barry, Katie, Molly, Kerry AB, U. Portland, 1955, M.Ed., 1957; PhD, U. Notre Dame, 1962. Asst. prof. U. Portland, 1956-60; asst. prof., assoc. prof. Eastern Mont. Coll., Billings, 1962-65; assoc. dean U. Notre Dame, South Bend, Ind., 1965-72; dean, v.p. U. Nev.-Las Vegas, 1972-80; pres. Western N.Mex. U., Silver City, 1980-84, Emporia (Kans.) State U., 1984-97; acting vice-chancellor U. Ark., Montecello, 1999; interim provost U. So. Colo., 1999-2000, interim pres., 2001—02. Bd. dirs. Emporia Enterprises; cons. HEW, Washington, 1964-84 Author: Guidance: An Orientation, 1966. Contbr. articles to profl. jours. Pres. PTA, South Bend, Ind., 1970-71; bd. trustees Am. Coll. Testing Corp., Iowa City, 1977-80; chmn. Kans. Regents Coun. of Pres., 1986-87, 92-93, 95-96. Recipient award of excellence Nat. Acad. Advising Assn., Disting. Alumnus award U. Portland, 1993, Kans. Master Tchr. award, 1994; named Coach of Yr., Coach and Athletic mag., 1958, Pub. Adminstr. of Yr., 1994, Athletic Hall of Fame, Portland, 1995; Rotary Paul Harris fellow, 1995, Ford Found. fellow, 1961-62. Mem. Kans. C. of C. (bd. dirs.), Emporia C. of C. Regional Devel. Assn. (bd. dirs., Bank IV), Am. Personnel and Guidance Assn., Am. Assn. State Colls. and Univs. (chair pres's. commn. on tchr. edn.), Am. Assn. Higher Edn., Nev. Personnel and Guidance Assn., Assn. Counselor Educators and Suprs., Am. Assn. Counseling and Devel., Nat. Assn. Student Personnel Adminstrs. Republican. Roman Catholic. Avocations: racketball, walking, reading; hiking.

GLENNER, RICHARD ALLEN, dentist, dental historian; b. Chgo., Apr. 14, 1934; s. Robert Joseph and Vivian (Prosk) G.; m. Dorothy Chapman, July 13, 1957; children: Mark Steven, Alison, Scott Jay. BS, Roosevelt U., 1955; BS in Dentistry, U. Ill., 1958, DDS, 1959; student, Army Med. Svc. Sch., 1960. Pvt. practice, Chgo., 1962—. Cons. on dental history to Smithsonian Instn., ADA, various corps., librs., univs., museums, dental jours, Dr. Samuel D. Harris Nat. Mus. Dentistry; dental and anthropol. rschr. Nat. Park Svc., Nat. Mus. Health and Medicine, 1993—; lectr. to various orgns. Author: The Dental Office: A Pictorial History, 1984, How it Evolved: Dentistry's Pursuit for Excellence, 1997; co-author: The American Dentist, 1990, A Visit to the Dentist: Then & Now, 1996; appeared in PBS video Sci. Am. Frontiers: The Wild West, 1995; cons. editor A Bicentennial Salute to Am. Dentistry, 1976; contbr. articles to profl. and popular jours.; film maker The Dental Office, 1994; reviewer Jour. ADA, 1999 . Served to capt. AUS, 1960—68. Mem. ADA (life), Ill. Dental Assn., Chgo. Dental Soc., Acad. Gen. Dentistry, Assn. Mil. Surgeons U.S., Am. Acad. History of Dentistry (historian 1984, chmn. smithsonian Instn. adv. group 1987, Hayden-Harris award 1983, columnist Jour. History of Dentistry 1989—, mem. editl. bd. 1993—, hist. display com. 1993—, pub. com. 1993—, Hayden-Harris award com. 1995-99), Fedn. Dentaire Internat., Lindsay Soc. G.B., Ill. Dental Soc. (history com.), Pierre Fauchard Acad., Am. Med. Writers Assn., Sci. Instrument Soc., Jewish War Vets. U.S., Westerners, Titanic Hist. Soc., Titanic Internat. Soc. (rschr.), Alpha Omega. Home: 6715 N Lawndale Ave Lincolnwood IL 60712-3711 Office: 3414 W Peterson Ave Chicago IL 60659-3447

GLENNON, CHARLES EDWARD, retired judge, lawyer; b. Monticello, Ill., Apr. 5, 1942; s. William Edward and Beatrice Jane (Pierson) G.; m. Sylvia Ann McClintock, Aug. 24, 1965 (div. Aug. 1972); children: David, Caroline; m. Victoria Louise Pearre, Oct. 26, 1974 (div. May 2001); 1 child, Andrew. BA, U. Ill., 1964, JD, 1966. Bar: Ill. 1966, U.S. Supreme Ct. 1974. Assoc. Fellheimer & Fellheimer, Pontiac, Ill., 1968-73; ptnr. Gomien & Glennon Ltd., Dwight, Ill., 1973-75; cir. judge State of Ill., Pontiac, 1976-98; temporarily recalled to bench, 1999, 2003; chief judge 11th cir., 1991-95. Lectr., author criminal law Ill. Village atty., Dwight, 1973-75; chmn. Salvation Army Adv. Bd., Pontiac, 1976; chmn. criminal law com. Ill. Jud. Conf., 1989-99, del., mem. exec. com., 1993-98; former mem. Regional Youth Planning Commn., Livingston County Commn. on Children and Youth; mng. dir. Nat. Arts Found., 1998—. With U.S. Army, 1966-68. Fellow Ill. Bar Found.; mem. Livingston County Bar Assn. (pres. 1991-93), Ill. Bar Assn., Ill. Judges Assn., Am. Assn. Juvenile and Family Ct. Judges, Lions, Rotary, Elks. Republican. Episcopalian. Home: 402 Carol Ct Pontiac IL 61764 also: N1930 Beach Rd Lake Geneva WI 53147 E-mail: chasness@aol.com.

GLENZER, SIEGFRIED HEINZ, physicist, educator, researcher; b. Essen, Germany, June 27, 1966; came to U.S., 1994; s. Heinz and Hannelore (Reimers) G.; m. Anja Berkel, July 13, 1994; 1 child, Helena Ashley. Diploma, Ruhr-U. Bochum, Germany, 1990, D in Natural Scis., 1994. Tchg. asst. Ruhr-U. Bochum, 1987-90, sci. asst., 1990-94, sci. assoc., 1994; postdoctoral physicist Lawrence Livermore (Calif.) Nat. Lab., 1995-96, staff physicist, 1996—. Vis. scientist U. Provence, Marseille, France, 1994, vis. lectr. U. Calif., Berkeley, 1997-98, Ecole Polytechnique, Paris, 1998, U. Oxford, Eng., 1999, 2000, 01. Contbr. more than 70 articles to profl. jours. Fellow: Am. Phys. Soc.; mem.: Deutsche Physikalische Gesellschaft. Achievements include the demonstration of x-ray scattering and the introduction of Thomson scattering to measure temperatures in high-density inertial confinement fusion plasmas; contributions to plasma spectroscopy, short-wave length lasers, and fusion research. Office: Lawrence Livermore Nat Lab 7000 East Ave L-399 Livermore CA 94550-9516

GLESENER, ROBERT RICHARD, biologist, educator, biologist, researcher; b. Chgo., Oct. 7, 1947; s. Richard Frederick and June Koletsos Glesener; m. Judith Marie Glesener, May 31, 1969 (div. Dec. 1, 1994); children: Traci Nikole Higgins, Stefani Christine; m. Jennie Thompson, Jan. 27, 1995 (div. May 20, 2003); 1 child, Timothy Stephen. BS, U. Md., 1969; MS, U. Mich., 1971, PhD, 1978. Asst. prof. Brevard (N.C.) Coll., 1979—86, assoc. prof., 1986—. Dir. White Squirrel Rsch. Inst., NC, 1997; water quality adv. bd. Riverlink, Asheville, NC, 1999—. Contbr. articles to profl. jours.; webmaster http://tornado.brevard.edu/whitesquirrel. Apptd. mem. Human Rels. Coun., Transylvania County, NC, 1992—94. Mem.: N.C. Acad. Sci. Avocation: photography. Office: Ecology Program Brevard Coll Brevard NC 28712

GLESK, IVAN, physicist, educator, researcher; b. Martin, Czechoslovakia, Sept. 1, 1957; arrived in U.S., 1990; s. Pavol and Elena (Orszaghova) G.; m. Helena Gleskova, Aug. 18, 1984; 1 child, Ivan. BS, MS in Physics, Comenius U., Bratislava, Slovak Republic, 1981, PhD in Quantum Electronics and Optics, 1989; DSc, Slovak Acad. Scis., 1998. Asst. prof. Comenius U., Bratislava, 1986-95, assoc. prof., 1996—2002, prof., 2003—; vis. fellow Princeton (N.J.) U., 1990-91, vis. rsch. staff mem., 1991-94, rsch. staff mem., 1994-96, rsch. scientist in physics, 1996-2000, sr. rsch. scholar, 2000—. Chmn. Slovak Com. for Optics, 1998—; presenter at numerous confs. Contbr. over 160 articles to profl. jours., 2 US patents; contbr. chapters to books. IREX Bd. fellow, 1990. Mem.: SPIE, IEEE (sr.), Optical Soc. Am. Achievements include first 1st demonstration of ultrafast all-optically controlled routing switch capable of Tb/s operation; first demonstration of all-optical demultiplexing of TDM data at 250 Gb/s; first demonstration of 100 Gb/s optical shuffle network; work in ultra fast all-optical switching; first demonstration of 100 Gb/s optical comptuer interconnect; patents in field.

GLESMANN, SYLVIA-MARIA, artist; b. Spardorf/Erlangen, Germany, June 8, 1923; arrived in the US, 1925; d. Rolf-Joseph and Auguste (Schultheiss) Hoffmann; m. John Brainerd Glesmann, Apr. 30, 1948; children: Glenn M., Eric B., Jonathan M. Degree, Acad. Fine Arts, Nurnberg, Germany, 1940, Acad. Fine Arts, Munich, 1944. Instr. Somerville Adult Edn. Exhibited in group shows at Carrier Clinic, 1993, Bergen Mus., 1993, Morris Mus., 1993, Nabisco Brands, 1993, Cultural and Heritage Gallery, Somerville, NJ, 1993-95, Salmagundi Club, 1994, Garden State Water Color Assn., Princeton, NJ, 1994, Barrons Art Ctr., 1993, Art on the Ave. Group Show of Flowers, 1991, Nat. Assn. Women Artists, NYC, 1991, 1994, SoHo, 1994, Bridgewater NJ County Libr., 1996, 2001-02, Nat. Assn. Women Artists New World Art Ctr., Soho, NY, 1999, Children's Specialized Hosp., Westfield, NJ, July 2002, Barrons Art Ctr, Woodbridge, NJ, 2002; others; one-woman shows include Childrens Specialized Hosp., Mountainside, NJ, 2002, N.U.I. Corp., Bridgewater, 1987, Salmagundi Club, NYC, 1995, 2000, Am. Artists Profl. League, 1995-97, Somerset County Libr., Bridgewater, 1996, 2001-02, Barrons Art Ctr., Woodbridge, NJ, 1997, Barrons Art Ctr., Bridgewater Mcpl. Bldg, 1999-2001, Nat. Assn. Women Artists (NYC), Balt. Conv. Ctr., Balt., 2000 (Editors Choice 2002), Bridgewater Libr., 2001, Nat. Assn. Women Artists, UN Visitors Lobby, 2002, Georgio Zikos Gallery, New Hope, Pa., 2002-03; others; author numerous poems. Recipient over 50 awards in water color, Editor's Choice award, 1998, Poetry Editors Choice award, 2002, Poetry award for poem, 2003. Mem. Am. Artists Profl. League (pres. NJ chpt. 1988-91), 2001, Bridgewater NJ Artists shows, 2002-2003, Nat. Assn. Woman Artists, Raritan Valley Arts Assn. (pres. 1976-78), Somerset Art Assn. (chairwoman 10th outdoor art show), Nat. Assn. Women Artists, Salmagundi Club, Nat. Mus. for Women in Arts (charter mem.). Lutheran. Avocations: sports, music, reading, poetry. Home and Office: 36 Twin Oaks Rd Bridgewater NJ 08807-2343 *To be of cultural stamina in the arts - to help and influence the American public. To see the world through art-music poetry painting also Philosophy. To make people see and feel. And to look at nature as a miracle.*

GLESSNER, JOHN JACOB, III, lawyer; b. Boston, Oct. 28, 1931; s. John Jacob and Martha Greenfield (Sluder) Glessner; m. Susan LeBourgeois Crockett, June 17, 1972; children: John Jacob, Ian Macbeth, Elizabeth Charless. AB, Harvard U., 1953; LLB, Columbia U., 1962. Bar: Mass. 1962. Dept. supr. Dewey & Almy Chem. Co., Acton, Mass., 1956—59; assoc. Ropes & Gray, Boston, 1962—72; v.p., sec. Ea. Gas and Fuel Assocs., Boston, 1972—. Bd. dirs. Animal Rescue League Boston. Trustee White Mountain Sch. With U.S. Army, 1954—56. Mem.: ABA, Mass. Bar Assn., Union Club Boston, Cruising Am. Club. Office: 1 Beacon St Boston MA 02108-3107

GLETNE, JEFFREY SCOTT, forester; b. Mpls., Dec. 10, 1952; s. John Sanford Gletne and Lillian Helen (Berg) Oxford; m. Michelle R. Evans, Feb. 6, 1998; 1 child, John Steven; stepchildren: Sarah Evans, Emily Evans, Alyssa Evans. BS, U. Calif., Berkeley, 1976. Registered profl. forester, Calif. Logger, forester Wickes Forest Industries, Dinuba, Calif., 1975-82; owner Skyline Logging Inc., Dinuba, 1982-89; forester Sierra Forest Products, Terra Bella, Calif., 1989—. Mem, Bakersfield (Calif.) Coll. Agrl. Adv. Bd., 1993—; cons. Integrated Forest Mgmt., Springville, Calif., 1994-95; bd. dirs. Sierra Cascade Logging Conf. Pres. People for the West, Bakersfield, 1994, v.p. People for the West, Porterville, Calif., 1995-96. Mem. Soc. of Am. Foresters (vice-chair, sec.-treas. 1993-94, chmn. 1994-95), Calif. Lic. Foresters Assn., Eagles Lodge. Republican. Avocations: fishing, hunting, reading, sporting events, hiking. Home: 10480 Road 261 Terra Bella CA 93270-9727 Office: Sierra Forest Products PO Box 10060 Terra Bella CA 93270-0060 E-mail: jgletne@sierraforest.net.

GLETSOS, CONSTANTINE, chemist; b. Stylis, Phthiotis, Greece, Aug. 5, 1934; came to U.S., 1968, naturalized, 1974; m. Helen D. Kerr, Sept. 2, 1967; children: Evangelos R., Rizos W., Vasilios P., Elly E.H.E. Diploma in chemistry, U. Athens, 1958; MSc in Chemistry, U. B.C., Vancouver, Can., 1965, PhD, 1968. Lab. asst. CHROPEI-Pharm. Co., Moschato, Greece, summer 1957; lab. dir., instr. Army Labs., Malakasa, Greece, 1959-61; lab. dir., R&D staff Gen. Devel. Co., Aspropygros, Greece, 1961-63; analytical chemist Gen. Chem. Labs., Elefsis, Greece, 1963; tchg. asst. U. B.C., 1963-68; sr. R&D chemist Wyeth Labs., Inc., West Chester, Pa., 1968—89; sr. R&D scientist Wyeth-Ayerst, 1989—95; prin. rsch. scientist Wyeth-Ayerst Rsch., Pearl River, NY, 1995—2001; ret., 2001. Contbr. articles to profl. jours.; patentee in field. V.p. Am. Hellenic League, Phila., 1984-85; mem. KRIKOS, Inc., N.Y.C., 1978—; pres. Am. Hellenic Edn. Progressive Assn., Coatesville, Pa., 1985—. Scholar U. B.C., 1963-68; grantee Nat. Cancer Inst., 1963, NRC, 1965, Med. Rsch. Coun., 1968. Mem. Am. Chem. Soc., Can. Inst. Chemists, Greek Chem. Soc., Toastmasters Internat. (v.p. West Chester chpt.), Hellenic U. Club (pres. 1979-80) (Wilmington, Del.), Internat. Union of Pure and Applied Chemistry, Adirondack Mountain Club (pres. Ramapo chpt. 2003—), Catskills Mountain Club. Avocations: swimming, jogging, hiking, beekeeping, stamps. Address: 56 Halley Dr Pomona NY 10970-2003 E-mail: cgletsos@aol.com.

GLEUE, LORINE ANNA, elementary education educator; b. Lucas, Kans., Feb. 12, 1926; d. Otto Martin and Bertha Marie (Luker) Becker; m. Fred Christoph Gleue, June 12, 1947; children: David Jean, Steven Randolph, Paul Frederick. Assoc., Cloud County C.C., 1969; BS in Edn., Ft. Hays (Kans.) State Coll., 1971; MS in Elem. Edn., Ft. Hays State U., 1977; reading specialist degree, Kans. State U., 1984. Cert. tchr., Kans. Elem. tchr., Coffey County, Kans., 1944-47; libr. Belleville (Kans.) Pub. Libr., 1960-67, Carnegie Free Pub. Libr., Concordia, Kans., 1967-68; elem. tchr. Chester, Nebr., 1971-72, Washington (Kans.) Unified Sch. Dist. #222, 1972-75; Chpt. I program instr. Washington, Kans., 1975-87; tchr. Republic County Schs., Mankato, and USD #333, Concordia, 1987—. Producer, co-owner Gleue's-On-The-Go Shows, Flying Carpet Story Hours, Lorine's Letter Writing Svc. to Shut-ins and Small Fry, Mothers' Mender, Gleue-Gomoll Home-Loomed Rag Rugs; co-owner, developer Acres for Wildlife Resource Ctr., Belleville. Published poet; contbr. articles to profl. jours. Mem. book selection com. Kans. State Reading Cir., Topeka, 1979-81; mem. PTA, 1981-87; pres. Washington chpt. Tchrs. Assn., 1977-81. Recipient Golden Poet award, 3d Ann. Poetry Conv., Las Vegas, Nev., 1987, World of Poetry Golden Poet award, 1988, 1989, 1990, 1991, 1992, 3d pl. award, Poetry Rendezvous, 1991, Best of Fair award, 2000, 2001, Blue Ribbon award, 1990—2001, Celebrate Literacy award, Internat. Reading Assn., 1993, Kans. Gov.'s Leadership Commendation, 1979, 1981, Citation of Appreciation, Assn. Retarded Citizens, 1981, Kans. Nat. Edn. Assn., 1979, 1980. Mem. Kans. Authors Club, Kans. Reading Assn. (mem. thunderbird coun.), Internat. Soc. of Poets, Fort Hays Alumni Assn. (life), Washington Sign Lang. Club (charter). Avocations: reading, travel, originating scripts for 35mm slide presentation.

GLEZOS, MATTHEWS, consumer products and services company executive; b. Montreal, Aug. 27, 1927; s. George and Katerina (Bakalos) G.; m. Sophia Protonotarios, Sept. 23, 1953; children: George, Mary. B. in commerce, McGill U., 1952. Tax assessor taxation div. Govt. of Can., Montreal, 1953-55; tax mgr., treas. Imasco Ltd., Montreal, 1955-78, v.p., treas., 1978-84; pres. Imasco B.V., Amsterdam, 1984-89, ret., 1989. Mem. Royal Montreal Golf Club. Home: 366 Kindersley Mount Royal QC Canada H3R 1R9

GLIBERT, JOHN H. research scientist; life ptnr. Connie Gilbert, May 30, 1992; children: Kesley Leigh, Jonathan Cade. BS chemistry, Univ. N.C., Chapel Hill, N. C., 1985. Chemist Applied Analytical Industries, Wilminston, NC, 1985—89; group leader Carolina Med. Products, Farmville, NC, 1989—90; sales cons. Krakeler Sceienitific, Durham, NC, 1990—91; QC lab supr. Lederle Lab., Sanford, NC, 1991—93; scientist Magellan Lab., RTP, NC, 1993—95, mgr., 1995—97, sr. mgr., 1997—2002; assoc. dir. Cardinal Health, RTP, NC, 2002—. Bd. mem. Orange County TV Commn., Hillsborough, NC, 1997—. Mem.: Am. Assoc. of Pharm. Scientists. Office: Cardinal Health PO Box 13341 Durham NC 27709

GLICK, CYNTHIA SUSAN, lawyer; b. Sturgis, Mich., Aug. 6, 1950; d. Elmer Joseph and Ruth Edna (McCally) G. AB, Ind. U., 1972; JD, Ind. U.-Indpls., 1978. Bar: Ind. 1978, U.S. Dist. Ct. (so. dist.) Ind. 1978, U.S. Dist. Ct. (no. dist.) Ind. 1981, U.S. Supreme Ct. 2000. Adminstrv. asst. Gov. Otis R. Bowen of Ind., 1973-76; dep. pros. atty. 35th Jud. Cir., LaGrange County, Ind., 1980-82, pros. atty., 1983—90; pvt. practice LaGrange, Ind., 1979—. Campaign aide Ind. Rep. State Ctr. Com., Indpls., 1972-73; chmn. La Grange County Rep. Ctrl. com. Named Hon. Spkr., Ind. Ho. of Reps., 1972, Sagamore of the Wabash, Gov. of Ind., 1974. Fellow Ind. Bar Found.; mem. ABA, Ind. State Bar Assn., LaGrange County Bar Assn. (pres. 1983-86), DAR, Order Eastern Star, Phi Delta Phi, Delta Zeta. Methodist. Home and Office: 113 W Spring St Lagrange IN 46761-1843

GLICK, EARL A. retired lawyer; b. Chgo., Feb. 20, 1930; s. Simon and Eva (Cohen) G.; m. Janet Esther Klein, Aug. 22, 1953; children: Michael J., Daniel H., Linda J. Richardson, Steven B. BS, U. Ill., 1951; JD, Northwestern U., 1953. Bar: Ill. 1953, Calif. 1962. Asst. atty. gen. State of Ill., Chgo., 1953-57; ptnr. Gerwin & Glick, Chgo., 1957-61, Gendel, Raskoff, Shapiro & Quittner, L.A., 1962-90, Orrick, Herrington & Sutcliffe, L.A., 1990-2000; gen. counsel S & S Corp., Beverly Hills, Calif., 1961-62; ret., 2000; of counsel Murphy Noell Capital, LLC, Westlake Village, Calif., 2000—. Bd. govs. Fin. Lawyers Conf., L.A., 1965-2000. Fellow Am. Coll. Comml. Fin. Lawyers; mem. ABA (chair program com. fin. svcs. subcom., 1993-96). Republican. Jewish. Avocations: travel, walking, reading. Home: 5560 Ostin Ave Woodland Hills CA 91367-3976 E-mail: eglick@socal.rr.com.

GLICK, GARLAND WAYNE, retired theological seminary president; b. Bridgewater, Va., Jan. 27, 1921; s. John T. and Effie (Evers) G.; m. Barbara Roller Zigler, Jan. 1, 1943; children— Martha (Mrs. Carl Barlett), Ted, Mary. B.D., Bethany Bibl. Sem., Chgo., 1946; MA in N.T. U. Chgo., 1949, PhD in Ch. History, 1957; LL.D., Bridgewater Coll., 1969. Ordained to ministry Ch. of Brethren, 1942, United Ch. Christ, 1978. Pastor, Lombard, Ill., 1945-48; instr., then asst. prof. Bibl. studies Juniata Coll., Huntingdon, Pa., 1948-53; mem. faculty Franklin and Marshall Coll., 1955-65, assoc. prof. religion, 1958-65, prof., 1965, v.p., 1962-65, acting pres., 1962-63, dir. rsch. and long-range planning, 1960, asst. to dean, 1960-61, dean coll., 1961-65; pres. Keuka Coll., Keuka Park, N.Y., 1966-74; dir. Moton Center Ind. Studies, Gloucester, Va., 1975-78; pres. Bangor (Maine) Theol. Sem., 1978-86. Vis. prof. Lancaster (Pa.) Theol. Sem., 1958-60, 64; coord. cons. Knox Seminars Ednl. Mgmt., 1963-65; seminar dir. Nat. Cath. Assn. Long-Range Planning Seminars, 1968; bd. dirs. Empire State Found. Ind. Liberal Arts Colls., Fund for Theol. Edn. (pres. 1988-92), Lancaster Guidance Ctr. Author: Maker of Modern Theology: Adolf von Harnack, 1967, Songs for my God, 1998; contbr. to Ency. Brit. Mem. Nat. Assn. Bibl. Instrs., Am. Soc. Ch. History, Lancaster Cliosophic Soc. (pres. 1995-97), Am. Conf. Acad. Deans (treas. 1965-66), Societas Orphea, Pi Gamma Mu, Tau Kappa Alpha. Mem. United Ch. Of Christ. Home: 1834 Ridgeview Ave Lancaster PA 17603-4316 *Clearly, a revolution has taken place in the last generation. The meaning of that revolution is not yet clear. I believe the name of the revolution is "longing" and Augustine's "God and the soul I want to know, nothing more," demarks its direction.*

GLICK, J. LESLIE, bio and information technology entrepreneur; b. N.Y.C., Mar. 2, 1940; s. Arthur Harvey and Hilda Lillian (Lichtenfeld) G.; m. Judith Sumiye Mihara; children: Geoffrey Michael, Jessica Michele. AB, Columbia U., 1961, PhD, 1964. Nat. Cancer Inst. postdoctoral fellow Princeton U., 1964-65; sr., then asso. cancer research scientist Roswell Park Meml. Inst., Buffalo, 1965-69; assoc. research prof. physiology, physiology chmn. Roswell Park div. SUNY, Buffalo, 1968-70; from exec. v.p. to chmn. bd. Asso. Biomedic Systems, Inc., Buffalo, 1969-77; pres. Inst. Sci. and Social Accountability, Washington, 1975-79; pres., chief exec. officer Genex Corp., Gaithersburg, Md., 1977-87; chmn., CEO Bionix Corp., Potomac, Md., 1987-93. Chmn. HTI Corp., Buffalo, 1972-75; dir. Nat. Assn. Life Sci. Industries, 1975-77; rsch. prof. biology Niagara (N.Y.) U., Canisius Coll., Buffalo, 1968-70; mem. exec. com. SUNY Grad. Sch., Buffalo, 1968-70; vis. lectr. NATO Adv. Study Inst., Brussels, 1970; mem. biotech. tech. adv. com. U.S. Dept. Commerce, 1985-87; adj. prof. tech. mgmt. Grad. Sch., U. Md. Univ. Coll., 1988—, mem. adv. panel, 1988-2000, mem. grad. coun., 1992-94; professorial cons. NTU Satellite Network, Nat. Tech. U., 1989-90; vis. lectr. tech. mgmt. Johns Hopkins U., 1993-97, external examiner doctoral program Sch. of Mgmt. Asian Inst. Tech., 1998-99; mng. dir. Cooper Alport Prodns., 1998—; chmn. bd. Marco Polo Techs., Inc., 1998--; bd. dirs. Advanced Processing and Imaging, Inc., vice chmn. bd., 1999--; vice chmn. bd. Advanced Tracking Svcs., Inc., 2000-01, chmn. bd., 2001--; bd. dirs. Genesis Engring. Solutions, Inc. Author: Fundamentals of Human Lymphoid Cell Culture, 1980; also articles; patentee in field; mem. editorial advisors bd. Strategic Direction, 1984-87; mem. adv. coun. High Tech. Mktg. Rev., 1986-87; mem. indsl. adv. bd. Biotech. Process Engring. Ctr., MIT, 1986-87; mem. editorial bd. Accountability in Rsch.: Policies and Quality Assurance, 1989—; editor-in-chief Tech. Mgmt., 1992-2001. Bd. overseers Simon's Rock of Bard Coll., 1984-85; trustee Nat. Faculty Humanities, Arts and Scis., 1985-87. Mem. Internat. Assn. for Mgmt. Tech., Am. Physiol. Soc., Indsl. Biotech. Assn. (pres. 1981-83, bd. dirs.1981-84), N.Y. Acad. Scis., Sigma Xi. E-mail: jlglick@ix.netcom.com.

GLICK, JANE MILLS, biomedical researcher, educator; b. Memphis, Nov. 26, 1943; d. Albert Axtell Jr. and Mary Louise (Baynes) Mills; m. John Harrison Glick, May 25, 1968; children: Katherine Anne, Sarah Stewart. AB, Randolph-Macon Woman's Coll., 1965; PhD, Columbia U., 1971. Postdoctoral trainee NIH, Bethesda, Md., 1971-73; postdoctoral fellow Sch. of Medicine Stanford (Calif.) U., 1973-74; rsch. asst. prof. biochemistry Sch. Dental Medicine U. Pa., Phila., 1974-77; asst. prof. biochemistry Med. Coll. Pa., Phila., 1977-82, assoc. prof. biochemistry, 1982-90, prof. biochemistry, 1990-94; sr. rsch. investigator Inst. Human Gene Therapy, U. Pa. Sch. Medicine, 1994—2002; faculty adminstr. cell and molecular biology group Sch. Medicine U. Pa. Mem. metabolism study sect. NIH, 1993-97; adj. assoc. prof. U. Pa. Sch. Medicine, 1996—. Assoc. editor: Jour. Lipid Rsch., 1985-86, mem. editorial bd., 1987-99; contbr. articles to profl. jours. Trustee Episcopal Acad., Merion, Pa., 1989-95, Swarthmore Presbyn. Ch., 1995-97, pres. 1997. Recipient Rsch. Svc. award NIH, 1975-77, Young Investigator award, 1980-83, Teaching award Lindback Found., 1985. Mem. AAAS, AAUP (sec. 1990-92), Arteriosclerosis Coun. Am. Heart Assn. (program com. 1990-93), Am. Soc. for Biochemistry and Molecular Biology, Am. Soc. for Human Genetics, Phi Beta Kappa, Sigma Xi. Presbyterian. Office: U Pa Sch Medicine 652 BRB II/III 421 Curie Blvd Philadelphia PA 19104

GLICK, JOHN H. oncologist, medical educator; b. N.Y.C., May 9, 1943; s. Arthur W. and Sybil (Goldman) Glick; m. Jane Mills, May 25, 1968; children: Katherine, Sarah. AB magna cum laude, Princeton U., 1965; MD, Columbia U., 1969. Diplomate Am. Bd. Med. Oncology, (sec. subsplty. com. med. oncology 1976-83, mem. subsplty. bd. med. oncology 1983-87, chmn. 1987-89, cert. exam. com. 1986-88, mem. bd. govs. 1987-89) Am. Bd. Internal Medicine. Intern in medicine Presbyn. Hosp., N.Y.C., 1969-70, asst. resident in medicine, 1970-71; commd. surgeon, clin. assoc. medicine br. Nat. Cancer Inst., USPHS, Bethesda, Md., 1971-73; postdoctoral fellow in med. oncology Stanford (Calif.) U., 1973-74; asst. prof. medicine U. Pa., Phila., 1974-79, Ann B. Young asst. prof. cancer rsch., 1974, assoc. prof., 1979-83, prof., 1983—, Madlyn and Leonard Abramson prof. clin. oncology, 1988—; dir. clin. trials U. Pa. Cancer Ctr., Phila., 1977-79, assoc. dir. for clin. rsch., 1980-85, dir. Cancer Ctr., 1985—; mem. numerous acad. coms., dept. medicine coms., hosp. coms., 1974—; pres. Abramson Family Cancer Rsch. Inst., Phila., 1998—, also bd. dirs. Attending physician Hosp. U. Pa., 1974—, dir. Hematology-Oncology Clinic, 1974—76; cons. Phila. VA Hosp., 1974—; mem. clin. trials rev. com. NIH, 1980—83, mem. radiosensitizer /radioprotector working group, radiotheraphy devel. br., 1980—85, chmn. consensus devel. panel conf. adjuvant therapy for breast cancer, 1985; mem. com. accreditation med. oncology tng. programs Accreditation Coun. Grad. Med. Edn., 1983—, mem. appeals panel, 1984—94; prin. investigator Ea. Coop. Oncology Group, U. Pa.; pres., dir. Abramson Family Cancer Rsch. Inst., 1987—; dir. Pa. Cancer Ctr., 1985—. Mem. editl. bd.: Am. Jour. Clin. Oncology, 1983—89, Blood, 1983—86, Jour. Clin. Oncology, 1987—93, mem. bd. editors: Internat. Jour. Radiation Oncology, Biology and Physics; editor (assoc. editor): Cancer Rsch., 1984—88; contbr. articles to profl. jours. Recipient Faculty Rsch. award, Am. Cancer Soc., 1982—86; grantee Rsch., Nat. Cancer Inst., Ea. Coop. Oncology Group, Am. Cancer Soc., others. Fellow: ACP (mem. various splty. coms. 1983—84, master), Coll. Physicians and Surgeons; mem.: John Morgan Soc. U. Pa., Am. Fedn. Clin. Rsch., Am. Soc. Hematology, Am. Radium Soc. (mem. exec. com. 1986—87), Am. Assn. Cancer Rsch., Am. Assn. Cancer Edn., Am. Soc. Clin. Oncology (chmn. program com. 1983—84, nominating com. 1983—84, mem. pub. issue com. 1984—85, bd. dirs., pres. 1995—96), Alpha Omega Alpha, Phi Beta Kappa. Office: U Pa Cancer Ctr 3400 Spruce St Philadelphia PA 19104-4283

GLICK, KAREN LYNNE, college administrator; b. Bucyrus, Ohio, Sept. 2, 1945; d. Phillip Dole and Bernice Grace Glick; children: M. Todd, K. Christine. BSJ, Bowling Green State U., 1967, MA, 1979. Editor Bowling Green (Ohio) State U., 1972-74; account exec. Howard E. Mitchell, Jr., Advt., Findlay, Ohio, 1974-77; asst. to dir. Student Devel. Program Bowling Green State U., 1977-79; dir. pub. info. Bluffton (Ohio) Coll., 1980-83; asst. to v.p. for instl. advancement Findlay (Ohio) Coll., 1983-85; assoc. dir. devel. Bluffton Coll., 1985-90; assoc. dir. devnsl. support Miami U. Ohio, Oxford, 1990-93; sr. regional dir. devel. U. Ill. Found., Urbana, 1993—. Bd. dirs. Provena Behavioral Health. Mem. Fla. Sea Kayaking Assn., Bowling Green U. Press Club (charter 1983). Anglican. Office: U Ill Found Harker Hall MC-386 1305 W Green St Urbana IL 61801-2945 E-mail: glick@uif.uillinois.edu.

GLICK, LESLIE ALAN, lawyer; b. N.Y.C., May 22, 1946; s. Leo S. and Sylvia (Hall) G. BS, Cornell U., 1967, JD, 1970. Bar: N.Y. 1971, D.C. 1971, Md. 1974, U.S. Ct. Internat. Trade 1971, U.S. Supreme Ct. 1974. Ptnr. Porter Wright Morris & Arthur, Washington, 1987—. Author: Multilateral Trade Negotiations, 1984, Trading with Saudi Arabia, 1980, Guide to U.S. Customs and Trade Laws, 1991, 2d edit., 1996, Understanding the North American Free Trade Agreement, 1993, 2d edit., 1995; author, co-editor, contbr. Manual for the Practice of U.S. International Trade Law, 2001. Active Dem. State Cen. com., Md., 1982-84; chmn. adv. com. on Consumer Affairs, Montgomery County, Md., 1982-84. Mem. Fed. Bar Assn. (chmn. internat. law sect. 1986-88). Office: Porter Wright Morris & Arthur 1919 Pennsylvania Ave NW Washington DC 20006

GLICK, MARION SHEPHERD, psychology, educator; b. N.Y.C., Sept. 30, 1938; d. Hall Edward and Elizabeth (Whiteside) S.; 1 child, Jonathan. BA, Drew U., 1959; MA, Clark U., 1964, PhD, 1968. Lic. clin. psychologist Bd. Examiners Conn. Clin. psychologist Worcester (Mass.) Youth Guidance Ctr., 1963-64, Waterbury (Conn.) Child Guidance Clinic, 1966-68; prof. So. Conn. State U., New Haven, 1968-95; postdoctoral assoc. Yale U., New Haven, 1977-85, assoc. rsch. scientist, 1985-95, ret., 1995. Consulting clin. psychologist New Haven and Guilford, Conn., 1970-98. Author: (with E. Zigler) A Developmental Approach to Adult Psychopathology, 1986; contbr. chpts. to books and articles to profl. jours. Active Caucus of Conn. Dems., 1967-70, Dem. Town Com., Branford, 1968-70; mem., nat. rep. Women's Polit. Caucus, New Haven, Conn., 1970-72. Presdl. Rsch. fellow So. Conn. State U., New Haven, 1980; program project rsch. grantee NIH, Washington, 1985-95. Mem. APA, AAUP. Avocations: writing, travel, gardening. Home: 229 Stony Creek Rd Branford CT 06405-3201 E-mail: mhglick488@aol.com.

GLICK, MILTON DON, chemist, university administrator; b. Memphis, July 30, 1937; s. Lewis S. and Sylvia (Kleinman) G.; m. Peggy M., June 22, 1965; children: David, Sander. AB cum laude, Augustana Coll., 1959; PhD, U. Wis., 1965. Asst. prof. chemistry Wayne State U., Detroit, 1966-70, assoc. prof., 1970-74, prof., 1974-83, chmn. dept., 1978-83; dean arts & scis. U. Mo., Columbia, 1983-88; provost Iowa State U., Ames, 1988-91, interim pres., 1990-91; sr. v.p., provost Ariz. State U., Tempe, 1991—2002, exec. v.p., provost of the univ., 2002—. Contbr. articles to profl. jours. Fellow dept. chemistry Cornell U., Ithaca, N.Y., 1964-66. Office: Ariz State U Provost Adm A210 PO Box 872803 Tempe AZ 85287-2803 E-mail: glick@asu.edu.

GLICK, PAUL MITCHELL, lawyer, educator; b. N.Y.C., Dec. 7, 1948; s. Gene H. and Ethel (Scott) G.; m. Roberta Wallenstein, Aug. 8, 1970; children: Geoffrey, Peter. Student Columbia U., 1969; BA with distinction, U. Wis., 1970. JD cum laude, DePaul U., 1973. Bar: Ill. 1973, U.S. Dist. Ct. (no. dist.) Ill. 1973, U.S. Ct. Claims 1976, U.S. Tax Ct. 1976, U.S. Supreme Ct 1976. Ptnr. Friedman & Koven, Chgo., 1973-86, Neal, Gerber & Eisenberg, Chgo., 1986; ptnr., pres. Paul M. Glick, Chartered, Chgo., 1986—; adj. prof. DePaul U. Grad. Sch. Law, Chgo., 1977-83; Author: When Should Rabbi Trusts Be Used To Secure Non-Qualified Deferred Compensation Arrangements, Estate Planning, 1988; pub. mem. Ill. Pub. Employees Pension Laws Comm., 1983-84; mem. Ill. Task Force on Funding of State Retirement System, 1985. NSF grantee, 1969. Mem. ABA, Chgo. Bar Assn., Am. Judicature Soc., Ill. Bar Assn., Midwest Pension Conf., Profit Sharing Council Am. Home: 2505 Stonebridge Ln Northbrook IL 60062-8107 Office: 3500 Three First Nat Plz Chicago IL 60602

GLICK, RUTH BURTNICK, author, lecturer; b. Lexington, Ky., Apr. 27, 1942; d. Lester Leon and Beverly (Miller) Burtnick; m. Norman Stanley Glick, June 30, 1963; children: Elissa, Ethan. BA, The George Washington U., 1964; MA, U. Md., 1967. Lectr. S.W. Writers Conf., Houston, 1984, Nebr. Writers' Guild, Omaha, 1985, Bouchercon, Balt., 1986, Triangle Romance and Fiction Writers' Conf., Raleigh, 1988, Romantic Times Booklovers Conf., San Antonio, 1990, Orlando, 2001, Kansas City, 2003, Malice Domestic, Bethesda, 1993, Howard C.C., 1995—. Author: (with Nancy Baggett) Dollhouse Furniture You Can Make, 1977, Dollhouse Lamps and Chandeliers, 1979, Soup's On, 1985, Oat Bran Baking, 1989, Skinny Soups, 1992, 100 Percent Pleasure, 1994 (US Today list of 12 best cookbooks of 1994), Skinny Italian, 1996, One-Pot Meals for People with Diabetes, 2002, (with Eileen Buckholtz, Carolyn Males and Louise Titchener) Love Is Elected, 1982 (named one of best romances 1982), Southern Persuasion, 1983, (with Titchener) In the Arms of Love, 1983 (Romance best seller list), Brian's Captive, 1983 (Romance best seller list), Reluctant Merger, 1983 (Romance best seller list), Summer Wine, 1984, Beginner's Luck, 1984, Mistaken Image, 1985, Hopelessly Devoted, 1985, Summer Stars, 1985, Stolen Passion, 1986, Indiscreet, 1988, (with Baggett and Gloria Kaufer Greene) Don't Tell 'Em It's Good for 'Em, 1984, Eat Your Vegetables!, 1985, (with Buckholtz) End of Illusion, 1984, Space Attack, 1984, Mission of the Secret Spy Squad, 1984, Mindbenders, 1984, Doom Stalker, 1985, Captain Kid and the Pirates, 1985, The Cats of Castle Mountain, 1985, Logical Choice, 1986, Great Expectations, 1987, A Place in Your Heart, 1988, Saber Dance, 1988, Postmark, 1988, Roller Coaster, 1989 (Young Adult Best Seller List), Silver Creek Challenge, 1989, Needlepoint, 1989, Life Line, 1990, Shattered Vows, 1991, Whispers in the Night, 1991, Only Skin Deep, 1992, Trial By Fire, 1992, Hopscotch, 1993, Cradle and All, 1993, What Child is This, 1993, Midnight Kiss, 1994, Tangled Vows, 1994, Till Death Us Do Part, 1995, Prince of Time, 1995, Face to Face, 1996, For Your Eyes Only, 1997, Father and Child, 1997 (Peregrine Connection series) Talons of the Falcon, 1986, Flight of the Raven, 1986, In Search of the Dove, 1986 (Lifetime Achievement award for romantic suspense series 1987), (with Kathryn Jensen) The Big Score, 1989 (Young Adult Best Seller List), Night Stalker, 1989 (Young Adult Best Seller List), (sole author) Dollhouse Kitchen and Dining Room Accessories, 1979, Invasion of the Blue Lights, 1982, More Than Promises, 1985, The Closer We Get, 1989, Make Me a Miracle, 1992, Bayou Moon, 1992, Skinny One Pot Meals, 1994, The Diabetes Snack, Munch, Nibble, Nosh Book, 1998, Simply Italian, 1998, Nowhere Man, 1998, Shattered Lullaby, 1999, Midnight Caller, 1999, Never Too Late, 2000, Amanda's Child, 2000, Fabulous Lo-Carb Cuisine, 2001, The Man from Texas, 2001, Never Alone, 2001, Lassiter's Law, 2001, Body Contact, 2002 (Waldenbooks Series Best Seller List), From the Shadows, 2002, Phantom Lover, 2003, Killing Moon, 2003 (Berkley Sensation Launch Book), Intimate Strangers, 2003, Edge of the Moon, 2003, Witching Moon, 2003, others; contbr. articles to profl. jours. U. Md. Am. studies fellow, 1964-65; recipient Romantic Times Career Achievement award for Romantic Mystery, 1994, Golden Leaf award for Best Long Contemporary novel and Best Novella N.J. Romance Writers, 2001, Best Selling Author, NY Times, USA Today, 2003; nominee Best Series Romance Book of the Yr. 1993-94 Romantic Times, 1995, 99, 2001, nominee Series Storyteller of Yr., 1996, nominee Best Harlequin Intrigue of Yr., 1998, nominee Best Series Romantic Suspense Writer of Yr., 2000. Mem. Author's Guild, Romance Writers Am. (lectr. Detroit, 1984, Atlanta 1985, Dallas 1987, 96, Boston 1989, San Francisco 1990, New Orleans 1991, 2001, Denver 2002, N.Y.C. 2003), Washington Romance Writers (bd. dirs.), Sisters in Crime, Novelists Inc., Md. Romance Writers.

GLICKMAN, ALBERT SEYMOUR, psychologist, educator; b. Bklyn., Feb. 7, 1923; s. Irving and Molly Glickman; m. Blanche Buller, July 14, 1945; children: Ralph, Marc, Judith, Debra. BA summa cum laude, Ohio State U., 1943, MA, 1947, PhD, 1952. Asst. prof. psychology Ga. Inst. Tech., Atlanta, 1947-52; project dir. Am. Insts. Rsch., Newport, RI, Pitts., 1952-55; dir. psychol. rsch. dept. U.S. Naval Pers. Rsch. Activity, Washington, 1955-62; chief pers. rsch. staff U.S. Dept. Agr., Washington, 1962-67; dir. Inst. Rsch. Orgnl. Behavior, 1967—70; dep. dir. Washington office Am. Insts. Rsch., 1970—76; v.p. Advanced Rsch. Resources Orgn., Washington, 1976-78; eminent prof. psychology Old Dominion U., Norfolk, Va., 1979-90, eminent prof. emeritus, 1991—; pres. Orgn. Rsch. Group Tidewater, Inc., 1979-91; chmn. bd. Third Quarter: Inst. Retirement Rsch., 1985-91. Vis. prof. Tel Aviv U., 1986, Tulane U., 1994. Cons., editor: Jour. Applied Psychology, 1971—81; co-author: (book) Top Management Development and Succession, 1968, Police-Community Action: A Program for Change in Police-Community Behavior Patterns, 1973, Changing Schedules of Work: Patterns and Implications, 1974; editor: Changing Composition of Workforce: Implications for Future Research and Its Applications, 1982. Recipient Louis Brownlow Meml. Fund prize, Internat. Pub. Pers. Assn., 1965, Author award, Tng. and Devel. Jour., ASTD, 1967. Fellow: AAAS, Soc. Indsl. and Orgnl. Psychology, Internat. Assn. Applied Psychology, Am. Psychol. Assn., Am. Psychol. Soc.; mem.: Soc. Psychol. Study Social Issues, Phi Beta Kappa. Jewish. Home: 14400 Homecrest Rd Apt 30 Silver Spring MD 20906 *Old enough to appreciate tradition. Young enough to facilitate change.*

GLICKMAN, CARL DAVID, banker; b. Cleve., July 29, 1926; s. Jack I. and Dora R. (Rubinowitz) G.; m. Barbara H. Schulman, Oct. 16, 1960; children: Lindsay Dale, David Craig, Robert Todd. Student, U. Minn., 1944, Inst. Fin. Mgmt., Harvard U., 1970. Pres. Glickman Orgn., Cleve., 1953—; chmn. bd., chief exec. officer Computer Research, Inc., Pitts., 1964-67, Am. Steel & Pump Corp., N.Y.C., 1968-71, Shelter Resources Corp., Cleve., 1971-75; pres. Leader Bldg., Inc., Cleve., 1959—, Capital Bancorp., Cleve., 1971-75, Real Property Corp., Cleve., 1975—; spl. ltd. ptnr. Bear Stearns & Co., 1978-85, dir., 1985—. Chmn. exec. com. Franklin Corp., N.Y.C., 1986-98, Cook United Inc., Cleve., 1986-87, Capital Nat. Bank Cleve., 1970-75; chmn. bd. dirs. Univ. Nat. Bank, Chgo., 1968-70; ltd. ptnr. S.B. Lewis & Co., N.Y.C., 1980-89; gen. ptnr. Millbrook Assocs., Chester Union Assocs.; founding gen. ptnr. Park Ctrl. Assocs.; pres. LGT Industries, Durham, N.C., 1987-95; bd. dirs. Royal Petroleum Properties Corp., Jerusalem Econ. Corp., Israel, Custodial Trust Co., Alliance Tyre and Rubber Co., Tel Aviv,Tnuport Ltd., Tel Aviv, Indsl. Structures, Inc., Tel Aviv, Office Max, Inc., InfoTech, Englewood Cliff, NJ, Lexington Corp. Properties, NYC, presiding trustee, chmn. exec. com. Active Mayor's Com. Urban Renewal, 1965-67, Mayors Task Force on Higher Edn., 1967-69; trustee Cleve. Growth Assn., 1972-75; co-chmn. Herzog Loan Fund Cleve. State U., 1970-76; chmn. Med. Arts Hosp., Houston, 1976-86; bd. visitors Case Western Res. Sch. Law; trustee Montefiore Home Aged, Mt. Sinai Hosp.; grievance com. Cleve. Bar Assn., 1982-85; foreman Cuyahoga County Grand Jury, Cleve., 1984-85; trustee Cleve. State U., ARC, 2000—; disting. fellow Cleve. Clinic; nat. co-chmn. Glickman Urological Inst. Cleve. Clinic. With USAAF, 1944-46. Mem. Am. Bankers Assn., Am. Arbitration Assn. (arbitrator), Beechmont Country Club, Shaker Heights Country Club, Union Club (Cleve.), Standard Club (Chgo.), Harmonie Club, Town Club (NYC), Friars Club, Palm Beach Club (Fla.) Yacht Club, Masons, Phi Sigma Delta, Phi Eta Sigma. Office: 1140 Leader Bldg Cleveland OH 44114 also: 383 Madison Ave New York NY 10167-0002 also: 1 N Breakers Row Palm Beach FL 33480-4021

GLICKMAN, DANIEL ROBERT, former congressman; b. Wichita, Kans., Nov. 24, 1944; s. Milton and Gladys Anne (Kopelman) G.; m. Rhoda Joyce Yura, Aug. 21, 1966; children: Jonathan, Amy. BA, U. Mich., Ann Arbor, 1966; JD, George Washington U., Washington, 1969. Bar: Kans. 1969, Mich. 1970. Trial atty. SEC, 1969-70; assoc., then ptnr. Sargent, Klenda & Glickman, Wichita, 1971-76; mem. 95th-103rd Congresses from 4th Kans. Dist., 1977-95; mem. agrl. com. 95th-10rd Congresses from 4th Kans. Dist., mem. judiciary, sci., space and tech. coms.; chmn. permanent select com. on intelligence 103d Congress; sec. U.S. Dept. Agriculture, Washington, 1995-2001; sr. advisor pub. law and policy group Akin Gump Strauss Hauer & Feld LLP, Washington, 2001; dir. Inst. Politics, John F. Kennedy Sch. Govt. Harvard U., 2002—. Mem. Wichita Bd. Edn., 1973-76, pres., 1975-76. Mem. Order of Coif, Phi Delta Phi, Sigma Alpha Mu. Democrat. Jewish. Office: Harvard University John F Kennedy School of Government 79 John F Kennedy St Cambridge MA 02138*

GLICKMAN, FRANKLIN SHELDON, dermatologist, educator; b. Bklyn., Dec. 14, 1929; s. Arthur Zachary and Hilda (Kurtz) G.; m. Leatrice Sallie Alter, Mar. 29, 1953; children: Todd Scott, Jeff Bret. BA cum laude, Hofstra Coll., 1950; MD, SUNY-Bklyn., 1954; MS in Health Care Mgmt., NYU, 1990. Diplomate: Am. Bd. Dermatology. Intern Flushing (N.Y.) Hosp., 1954-55; resident in dermatology Kings County Hosp., Bklyn., 1957-58, Bronx VA Hosp., 1958-60; practice medicine specializing in dermatology Bklyn., 1960-94; mem. faculty dermatology dept. SUNY-Bklyn., 1960—82, clin. prof., 1982-93, adj. clin. prof., 1993—96; dir. med. edn. Wyckoff Heights Med. Ctr., Bklyn., 1990-96, chmn. dept. grad. med. edn., 1992-96. Author: General Dermatology, 1978, Fundamentals of Dermatology: A Study Guide, 1990; contbr. articles to profl. jours. Served to capt. M.C. USAF, 1955-57. Fellow N.Y. Acad. Medicine, ACP; mem. Am. Acad. Dermatology, Bklyn. Dermatol. Soc. (pres. 1970-72), N.Y. State Med. Soc., Kings County Med. Soc., AMA, N.Y. State Soc. Dermatology (pres. 1983-85), Phi Beta Kappa. Home: 6841 Treves Way Boynton Beach FL 33437-6485

GLICKMAN, FRED ELLIOTT, lawyer; b. N.Y.C., Sept. 1, 1946; s. Stanley and Anita (Lipow) G.; m. Margery Feinschreiber, Apr. 24, 1977; children—David, Michael, Laura. B.A., Dartmouth Coll., 1968; M.B.A., U. Chgo., 1971, J.D., Columbia U., 1974. Bar: Ill. 1974, Fla. 1982, U.S. Dist. Ct. (no. dist.) Ill. 1974, U.S. Dist. Ct. (so. dist.) Fla. 1983, U.S. Tax Ct. 1978. Assoc. Sonnenschein, Carlin, Nath & Rosenthal, Chgo., 1974-75; atty. Allied Van Lines, Broadview, Ill., 1975-76; assoc. Fishel and Kahn, Chgo., 1976-77, Laser Schostok, Kolman & Flank, Chgo., 1977-81; ptnr. Feinschreiber & Assocs., Key Biscayne and Miami, Fla., 1981-85; sole practice, Miami, 1985— . Contbr. articles to profl jours. Mem. S. Miami Kendall Bar Assn (bd. dirs. 1996—, pres. 2002—). Home: 13740 SW 78th Ct Miami FL 33158-1108 Office: Ste 508 9200 S Dadeland Blvd Miami FL 33156-2713

GLICKMAN, GLADYS, lawyer, writer; b. N.Y.C., Feb. 28, 1920; d. Reuben and Sadie (Levy) Glickman. BA, Bklyn. Coll., 1939; JD, DePaul U., 1959. Bar: Ill. 1959, N.Y. 1961. Editor Bur. Nat. Affairs, Inc., Washington, 1942-44, Research Inst. Am., N.Y.C., 1944-48; asst. dir., labor rels. rsch. Continental Can Co., N.Y.C., 1948-51; supr. Wage Stabilization Bd., N.Y.C., 1951-53; writer, editor Matthew Bender and Co. a subsidiary of Lexis-Nexis, Inc., N.Y.C., 1959—; corp. counsel Parents Magazine Enterprises, Inc., N.Y.C., 1961-78; v.p. legal Gruner and Jahr, USA Pub., N.Y.C., 1978-93. Author: Franchising, 1969, (with others) and quadrennial supplements Warrens Forms of Agreement, 1964. Mem. ABA, N.Y. County Lawyers Assn. (com. mem.), Ill. State Bar Assn. Jewish. E-mail: Glickfran@aol.com.

GLICKMAN, MARLENE, non-profit organization administrator; b. Evansville, Ind., May 13, 1936; d. Morris Jack and Sarah (Krawll) Foreman; m. Marshall Levi Glickman, Jan. 9, 1956 (dec. 2002); children: Cynthia Anne, Joseph Leonard. Student, Ohio State U., 1954-56. Area dir. Am. Jewish Com., Buffalo, 1981-2000; v.p. adminstrn. and fin. Network of Religious Cmtys., 2000—. Pres. Meals on Wheels of Buffalo and Erie County, 1981—83, Coun. Congl. Pres. Erie County, 1979—81; vice chair gen. campaign United Jewish Appeal, 1980, chair woman's divsn., 1979; pres. N.E. Lakes coun. Union Am. Hebrew Congregations, 1982—86; pres. Temple Beth Am, 1978—80, Sisterhood Temple Beth Am, 1969—71, 1976—77, Temple Beth Am, 2002—; agy. allocations com. United Way, chair Towns and Villages divsn., 1981; pres. Human Rights Adv. Coun. Western N.Y., 1988—96; bd. dirs. YWCA, Buffalo and Erie County, 1990—96, Buffalo Fedn. Neighborhood Ctrs., Inc., 1994—98; exec. com., sec. Sheehan Meml. Hosp., Inc., 1994—98; pres., bd. dirs. Western N.Y. Martin Luther King Jr. Commn., 1991—97; mem. Western N.Y. Vision for Tomorrow 2000 C. of C./Buffalo Partnership. Recipient Abraham Pugash Cmty. Rels. award for establishing Kosher Meals on Wheels, Jewish Family Svc., Buffalo and Erie County, N.Y., 1975, NAACP Human Rels. award, 1997, Cmty. Rels. award Am. Jewish Com. Western N.Y., 2001; Am.-Pol Eagle Citizen of Yr., 1995. Mem. NAACP (life), Union Am. Hebrew Congregations (exec., bd. dirs. 1982-99, exec. com.), Commn. on Synagogue Music, Joint Cantorial Placement Commn., FRJ Admin. (budget and finance), New Congregations, Maintenance of Union Membership, Hadassah (life), Assn. Reform Zionists Am. (del. to Israel 1987), Brandeis Women's Com., Nat. Coun. Jewish Women (life, Hannah G. Solomon award 1985), Assn. Jewish Comty. Rels. Workers, Jewish Communal Svc. Assn., Arza/World Union (bd. dirs. 1992-2000). Avocation: singing. Home: 94 Broadmoor Dr Tonawanda NY 14150-5532 Office: M&M Connections 94 Broadmoor Dr Tonawanda NY 14150-5532 also: PMB 361 425 Carr 693 Dorado PR 00646 E-mail: mglickman5@cs.com.

GLICKMAN, MICHAEL RICHARD, social studies educator; b. N.Y.C., Nov. 15, 1946; s. George Osiris Glickman and Hilda Ann Milmed; m. Irma S. Glickman, June 10, 1990; stepchildren: Scott D., Shari E. BA, Franklin (Ind.) Coll., 1969; MS, Coll. of S.I., 1997. Cert. tchr. social studies, N.Y. Paraprofl. N.Y.C. Bd. of Edn., Bklyn., 1974-92, tchr. social studies, 1992—. Adj. prof. sociology Kings Borough Coll., Bklyn., 1998—; tutor Williamsburg Settlement House, Bklyn., 1966-67; computer svcs. for children John Jay H.S., 1990-91. Head Young Dems., Dem. Party, Franklin Coll., Ind., 1968; vol. VISTA, 1969-70; tchr. Literacy Program John Jay H.S. Mem. United Fedn. of Tchrs., Am. Fedn. of Tchrs. Republican. Jewish. Avocations: reading, astronomy, computers, painting, music. Home: 1111 Schmidt Ln North Brunswick NJ 08902 Office: Murray Bergtraum High School 411 Pearl St New York NY 10002 E-mail: glickmoid13@cs.com.

GLICKMAN, NORMAN JAY, economist, urban policy analyst; b. Bklyn., July 27, 1942; s. Harry and Beatrice (Frankel) G.; m. Elyse M. Pivnick, May 8, 1983; children: Katy Rose, Madeline Claire. BA, U. Pa., 1963, MA, 1967, PhD, 1969. Prof. urban and regional planning U. Pa., Phila., 1980-82; Hogg prof. urban policy U. Tex., Austin, 1983-89; State of N.J. prof. urban planning Rutgers U., New Brunswick, 1989, dir. Ctr. for Urban Policy Rsch. State of N.J., 1989—, Disting. Univ. prof., 2000—. Vis. scholar U.S. HUD, Washington, 1978-79; fellow Netherland Inst. Advanced Studies, Wassenaar, 1981-82; sr. rsch. scholar Internat. Inst. Applied Systems Analysis, Laxenburg, Austria, 1977; appointee N.J. Coun. on Job Opportunities, N.J., 1992—. Co-author: The New Competitors, 1989 (Top 10 Bus. Week 1989). Chmn. Econ. Devel. Commn., Austin, 1985-89. Recipient Lindback award U. Pa., 1976, named Disting. Fulbright Prof., Monterrey (Mex.) Inst. of Tech., 1985; fellow Japan Found., 1976. Mem. EEFMS (charter), Regional Sci. Assn. (v.p. 1988-89), Am. Econ. Assn. Office: Rutgers U Ctr Urban Pol Rsch 33 Livingston Ave Ste 400 New Brunswick NJ 08901-1982

GLICKMAN, ROBERT MORRIS, physician, educator; b. Bklyn., June 23, 1939; s. David B. and Sally G.; m. Mary Holahan, June 20, 1961; children: Jonathan, Michael. BA magna cum laude, Amherst Coll., 1960; MD cum laude, Harvard U., 1964. Diplomate Am. Bd. Internal Medicine. Intern Harvard U. Med. Services, Boston City Hosp., 1964-65, resident in medicine, 1965-66; research fellow in medicine Med. Sch., Harvard U., Boston, 1966-68; from instr. medicine to assoc. prof. Harvard U. Med. Sch., Boston, 1970-77; clin. and rsch. fellow in medicine Mass. Gen. Hosp., Boston, 1966-68, asst. in medicine, 1970-74, asst. physician, 1974-75; chief divsn. gastroenterology, assoc. physician Beth Israel Hosp., Boston, 1975-77; chief divsn. gastroenterology Coll. Physi-

cians and Surgeons, Columbia U., N.Y.C., 1977-84, chmn. gastrointestinal sect. abnormal biology, 1978-84, from assoc. prof. to prof., 1977-82, prof., 1981-82, Samuel Bard prof. medicine, chmn. dept. medicine, 1982-90; dean NYU Sch. of Med., N.Y.C., 1998—; ceo NYU Hospitals Cntr. at NYU Med. Cntr., N.Y.C. Dir. med. svc. Presbyn. Hosp., N.Y.C., 1982-90, attending physician, 1981-90; Herrman L. Blumgart Prof. Med. Harvard Med. Sch., Boston, 1990—, chmn. exec. com. dept. medicine, 1996—; physician-in-chief Beth Israel Hosp., 1990-96, Beth Israel Deaconess Med. Ctr., 1996—, sr. v.p. acad. and clin. strategies, 1996; mem. Nat. Digestive Diseases Adv. Bd., 1985—. Mem. editorial bd. Jour. Lipid Research, 1978-79, Jour. Clin. Investigation, 1979-84, Am. Jour. Medicine, 1981—; contbr. articles to med. jours. Maj. M.C. U.S. Army, 1968-70. Fellow ACP; mem. Am. Fedn. Clin. Rsch. (councillor Eastern sect. 1975-79, sec.-treas. 1976-79), Am. Gastroent. Assn. (v.p. 1985-87, pres. elect 1987, pres. 1988), N.Y. Acad. Medicine (inst. of medicine 1995—), Harvey Soc., Interurban Clin. Club, Assn. Am. Physicians (councillor 1992, v.p. 1997), Nat. Found. Ileitis and Colitis (mem. sci. adv. bd. 1978), Am. Soc. Clin. Investigation (councillor 1981-84, pres. elect 1983, pres. 1984-85), Assn. Profs. Medicine (councillor 1989-94, pres. 1992-93), Am. Bd. Internal Medicine (sub-splty. bd. on gastroenterology 1988-93), Harvard Soc., Phi Beta Kappa, Sigma Xi, Alpha Omega Alpha. Office: NYU Sch of Med 550 First Avenue New York NY 10016

GLICKMAN, STEPHEN, state supreme court justice; Ptnr. Zuckerman, Spaeder, Goldstein, Taylor & Kolker, 1980-99; judge D.C. Ct. Appeals, 1999—. Office: DC Ct Appeals 6th Pl 500 Indiana Ave NW Ste 2 Washington DC 20001-2131*

GLICKSMAN, ARVIN S(IGMUND), radiation oncologist; b. Bklyn., Mar. 14, 1924; s. Charles and Myrtle (Fetner) G.; m. Bernice R. Grobstein, Jan. 30, 1956; children: Jonathan, Jane Ellen, Merrylee, Caroline, Jeanette. MB, MD, Chgo. Med. Sch., 1949. Intern Kings County Hosp., Bklyn., 1948-50; AEC postdoctoral research fellow Duke U., 1950-51; postgrad. rsch. fellow Brookhaven Nat. Labs., Upton, N.Y., 1951-52; resident in medicine Meml. Hosp., N.Y.C., 1952-54, clin. asst. physician in medicine, 1955-64, asst. attending radiation therapist, 1964-65; rsch. fellow Sloan-Kettering Inst., N.Y.C., 1954-60, assoc., 1960-65; mem. med. rsch. inst. Michael Reese Hosp., Chgo., 1964-65, assoc. chmn. dept. radiation therapy, 1965-67; dep. dir. radiotherapy Mount Sinai Hosp., N.Y.C., 1967-73; prof. radiotherapy Mount Sinai Sch. Medicine, 1971-73; dir. radiation oncology R.I. Hosp., Providence, 1973-84, chmn. dept. radiol. medicine and biol. rsch., 1984-89; prof. med. scis. Brown U., 1973-95, prof. emeritus, 1995—; chmn. dept. radiation oncology Roger Williams Med. Ctr., 1989-95; practice medicine specializing in radiation oncology. Hon. med. cons. NIH, Royal Marsden Hosp.; mem. cancer clinic, investigation rev. com. Nat. Cancer Inst., 1975-79, mem. radiation oncology com., 1976-86, mem. cancer intervention study sect., 1991-94. Editor: (with others) Computers in Radiotherapy, 1970, 73; contbr.: numerous articles to profl. jours. Mem. exec. com. Am. Cancer Soc., R.I., 1987-96—, pres., 1987-89, nat. bd. dirs., 190-93; chmn. radiotherapy com. Cancer and Leukemia Group B.; dir. Quality Assurance Rev. Ctr., R.I. Cancer Control Bd., 1980-98, chmn. task force info. sys., mem. exec. com.; co-chmn. exec. com. ASSIST Program Nat. Cancer Inst./Am. Cancer Soc., 1991-98; exec. dir. R.I. Cancer Coun., 1999—. Dillon fellow Royal Marsden Hosp., Surrey, Eng., 1961-62, Rsch. Career Devel. awardee NIH, 1962-64; Fulbright sr. scholar, 1986-87; recipient St. George medal Am. Cancer Soc., 1991. Fellow Am. Coll. Radiology; mem. New England Soc. Radiation Oncologists (pres. 1975-76), N.Y. Roentgen Ray Soc. (chmn. sect. therapeutic radiology 1972-73), Am. Soc. Clin. Oncology, Am. Assn. Cancer Edn., Am. Assn. Cancer Rsch., Am. Radium Soc., Am. Soc. Therapeutic Radiologists, Brit. Inst. Radiology. Home: Old Blackstone Rd AKA Brown Terrace Uxbridge MA 01569 Office: RI Cancer Coun Inc 249 Roosevelt Ave Ste 201 Pawtucket RI 02860-2134 Fax: 401-728-4816.

GLICKSMAN, ELLIOT BORIS, educator, lawyer; b. Detroit, Jan. 25, 1942; s. B.H. and Sylvia (Bier) G.; m. Thea Schwartz, Dec. 27, 1970. B.A., Eastern Mich. U., 1964; M.A., Wayne State U., 1966; J.D., U. Detroit, 1969. Bar: Mich. 1969. Practice, Detroit, 1969-70; asst. pros. atty. Wayne County (Mich.), 1970-72; staff atty. Burroughs Corp. UNYSIS, Detroit, 1972-75; assoc. prof. law Thomas H. Cooley Law Sch., Lansing, Mich., 1975-80, prof. law, 1980—; lectr. Nat. Jud. Coll., U. Nev. Reno, Mich. Jud. Inst., Lansing;ad hoc hearing referee Mich. Dept. Civil Rights, 1975— ; vis. reseach fellow, faculty of law U. Birmingham (Eng.), 1984-85. Recipient Faculty award Mich. Jud. Inst., 1981-88, Disting. Men of Achievement award Cambridge U., 1986. Mem. Mich. Bar Assn., Ingham County Bar Assn. (10 yr. award, Disting. alumnus award 1997), ABA (select com. on rules on criminal procedure and evidence, Assn. Trial Lawyers Am., Scribes, Thomas M. Cooley Law Sch. Faculty Writers Assn. (charter). Contbr. chpts. to books, articles to profl. jours. Office: Thomas M Cooley Law Sch 300 S Capitol Ave PO Box 13038 Lansing MI 48901-3038

GLICKSMAN, MARTIN EDEN, materials engineering educator; b. N.Y.C., Apr. 4, 1937; s. Nathan Henry and Ruth Elaine (Rosensaft) G.; m. Lucinda Jeanette Mulder, May 7, 1967 B in Metall. Engring., Rensselaer Poly. Inst., 1957, PhD, 1961. Metall. engr. Procter & Gamble Co., Cin., 1957-58; research metallurgist Naval Research Lab., Washington, 1961-75, assoc. supt. materials sci. divsn., 1974-75; chmn. materials engr. dept. Rensselaer Poly. Inst., Troy, N.Y., 1975-86, prof., 1986—; prof. materials engring., chmn. dept. materials engring. Rensselaer Poly. Inst., Troy, N.Y., 1975-86, John Tod Horton prof. materials engring., 1986—. Van Horn lectr. Case Western Res. U., 1984; cons. in field. Author: Diffusion in Solids, 2000; contbr. articles to profl. jours. Recipient Pure Sci. Rsch. award Rsch. Soc. of Am., 1968, Arthur Flemming award Washington Jr. C. of C., Space Processing medal AIAA, 1998; Minerals Metals and Materials Soc. fellow AIME, 1994. Fellow AAAS, ASM (M.E. Grossman award 1971); mem. AIME (Bruce Chalmers award 1992), Am. Soc. Metals Internat. (Gold medal 2003), Univ. Space Rsch. Assn. (chmn. bd. trustees 1986, dir. microgravity divsn. 1986—), Nat. Acad. Engring. (Alexander von Humboldt Rsch. prize, 2001). Home: 22 Schuyler Hills Rd Albany NY 12211-1445 Office: Rensselaer Poly Inst CII-9111 Troy NY 12180-3590

GLICKSMAN, MAURICE, engineering educator, former dean and provost; b. Toronto, Ont., Can., Oct. 16, 1928; came to U.S., 1949, naturalized, 1961; s. Robert Maxwell and Fanny Bella (Lachowitz) G.; m. Yetta Leich, Dec. 18, 1949; children: Howard David, Roslynn Sue, Marcie Ann. Student, Queen's U., 1946-49; M.Sc., U. Chgo., 1952, PhD, 1954; ScD (hon.), Brown U., 1997. Research asso. Inst. Nuclear Studies, U. Chgo., 1954; mem. tech. staff RCA Labs., Princeton, N.J., 1954-61, head Plasma Physics Group, 1961-63; dir. research RCA Research Labs., Tokyo, 1963-67; head Gen. Research Group, Princeton, 1967-69; Univ. prof., prof. engring. Brown U., 1969-94, dean Grad. Sch., 1974-76, dean faculty and acad. affairs, 1976-78, provost, dean faculty, 1978-86, provost, 1986-90, prof. physics, 1990-94, prof. engring. rsch., 1994—2002, provost emeritus, 1990—, univ. prof. emeritus, 1994—, prof. engring. and physics emeritus, 1994—. Cons. RCA Corp., 1969-77; vis. scientist MIT, 1983-84; chmn. com. materials for radiation detection devices NAS, 1971-74; chmn. vis. com. U. Pa., 1977-83, Vanderbilt U., 1977-81; mem. vis. com. Emory U., 1981—, U. Miami, 1990—, Northwestern U., 1991, U. N.C., Greensboro, 1992; bd. dirs. Ctr. Rsch. Librs., 1981-87, chmn., 1983-84; mem. bd. overseers Fermilab, 1983-99, chmn., 1989-94; trustee OCLC, Dublin, Ohio, 1993—, vice chmn., 2002--; dir. Manisses Comm. Group, Providence, 1993—; dir. Lifespan Corp., Providence, 1994-2000. Contbr. research articles to profl. jours.; patentee frequency multipliers, hall-effect devices, semiconductor devices and circuits. Pres. Jewish Ctr., Princeton, 1962-63; v.p. cultural and ednl. affairs Jewish Cmty. Ctr., Tokyo, 1965-67; mem. Bur. Jewish Edn., R.I., 1974—, v.p., 1975-80; v.p. Jewish Fedn. R.I., 1980-83; trustee Miriam Hosp., 1979-85, 87—, chmn., 1993-97; v.p. Jewish Srs. Agy. R.I., 1998-2000, pres., 2000—03; chmn. World Affairs Coun. R.I., 1999—; pres. Tamarisk, Inc., 2003—. Recipient Outstanding Achievement award RCA, 1956, 62 Fellow IEEE, Am. Phys. Soc.; mem. AAAS, Am. Soc. Engring. Edn., N.Y. Acad. Scis., Phi Beta Kappa (pres. R.I. Alpha chpt. 1993-96.), Sigma Xi. Home: 10 Westwood Ln Barrington RI 02806-2614 Office: Brown U Box D 79 Waterman St Providence RI 02912-9079 E-mail: maurice_glicksman@brown.edu.

GLICKSTEIN, HOWARD ALAN, law educator; b. N.Y.C., Sept. 14, 1929; s. Samuel and Fannie (Greenblat) G. BA magna cum laude, Dartmouth Coll., 1951; LLB, Yale U., 1954; LLM, Georgetown U., 1962. Bar: N.Y. 1954, U.S. Supreme Ct. 1962, D.C. 1980. Assoc. Proskauer, Rose, Goetz & Mendelsohn, N.Y.C., 1956-60; staff atty. Civil Rights divsn. Dept. of Justice, 1960-65; gen. counsel U.S. Commn. on Civil Rights, Washington, 1965-68, staff dir., 1968-71. Cons. in law, 1971-73; adj. prof., dir. Ctr. for Civil Rights U. Notre Dame, 1973-75; prof., dir. equal employment litigation clinic Howard U. Sch. Law, Washington, 1976-80; dir. Task Force on Civil Rights Reorgn., Exec. Office of Pres., Washington, 1977-78; dean, prof. U. Bridgeport Sch. Law, Conn., 1980-85, Touro Coll. Law, 1986—. Contbr. articles to profl. jours. Bd. dirs. Fund for Modern Cts.; commr. Suffolk County Human Rights Commn.; chair Town Huntington Bd. Ethics and Fin. Disclosure, 1999—. With U.S. Army, 1954-56. Mem. ABA (former chmn. affirmative action com., sect. legal edn. and admissions to bar), Soc. Am. Law Tchrs. (bd. dirs., former pres.), N.Y. State Commn. on Fiduciary Appointments, N.Y. State Bar Assn. (mem. spl. com. pub. trust and confidence in the legal sys.). Office: Touro Coll Sch Law Jacob D Fuchsberg Law Ctr 300 Nassau Rd Huntington NY 11743-4346

GLICKSTEIN, STEVEN, lawyer; b. Bklyn., Jan. 3, 1952; s. Alexander and Esther (Camhi) G. BA, Lehigh U., 1973; JD, Columbia U., 1976. Assoc. Kaye Scholer, LLP, N.Y.C., 1976-84, ptnr., 1985—. Mem. ABA, D.C. Bar Assn., Fla. Bar Assn., N.Y. State Bar Assn. Home: 1619 3rd Ave Apt 9ae New York NY 10128-3459 Office: Kaye Scholer LLP 425 Park Ave New York NY 10022-3506

GLIDDEN, JOHN REDMOND, lawyer; b. Sanford, Maine, July 24, 1936; s. Kenneth Eugene and Kathryn (Gilpatrick) G.; m. Jacqueline R. Scales, Aug. 6, 1964; children— Ian, Claire, Jason Student, U. Wis., 1954-55; BS, Coe Coll., 1958; LL.B., U. Iowa, 1961. Bar: Iowa 1961, Ill. 1965. Assoc. firm Williams & Hartzell, Carthage, Ill., 1965-67; ptnr. Hartzell, Glidden, Tucker & Hartzell and predecessor firms, Carthage, 1969—. City atty. City of Carthage, 1969— Capt., judge advocate USAF, 1961-65. Mem. ABA, Fed. Bar Assn., Ill. Bar Assn., Iowa Bar Assn., Hancock County Bar Assn., Am. Trial Lawyers Assn., Ill. Trial Lawyers Assn. (governing bd. 1973-80), Am. Legion, Carthage Golf Club (bd. dirs. 1967—), Phi Delta Phi, Sigma Nu. Home: PO Box 70 1625 N Highway 94 Carthage IL 62321-3435 Office: PO Box 70 Carthage IL 62321-0070

GLIDDEN, ROBERT BURR, academic administrator, musician, educator; b. Rippey, Iowa, Nov. 29, 1936; s. Burr Harold and Lora Elsie (Groves) Glidden; m. Rene Colete Siefken, Apr. 26, 1964; children: Melissa, Michele, Briana. BA, U. Iowa, 1958, MA, 1960, PhD, 1966. Tchr. instrumental music Morrison Community High Sch., Ill., 1958-63, Univ. Schs., Iowa City, 1963-66; asst. prof. music Wright State U., Dayton, Ohio, 1966-67, Ind. U., Bloomington, 1967-69; also asst. dir. bands, 1969-72; assoc. prof. music U. Okla., Norman; dir. grad. studies in music, exec. dir. Nat. Assn. Schs. Music, Washington, 1972-75, treas., 1977-82, v.p., 1982-85, pres., 1985-88; dean Coll. Musical Arts, Bowling Green State U., Ohio, 1975-79; dean Sch. Music Fla. State U., Tallahassee, 1979-91, provost, v.p. for acad. affairs, 1991-94; pres. Ohio U., Athens, 1994—. Cons., higher edn., condr.; chmn. Coun. Specialized Accrediting Agys., 1976—77; chair Am. Coun. Edn. Commn. Leadership and Instnl. Effectiveness, 1998—2000; chair coun. pres. Mid-Am. Conf., 1997—99. Bd. dirs. Coun. on Postsecondary Accreditation, 1977—84, exec. com., 1979—84, chmn., 1981—83; bd. dirs. Arts, Edn. and Ams., Inc., 1978—81; chmn. advanced placement music com. Coll. Bd., 1977—79; mem. Coun. on Arts Task Force on Edn. Tng. and Devel. Profl. Artists and Art Educators, 1977—78; mem. adv. coun. on accreditation Nat. League for Nursing, 1977—81; mem. edn. adv. com. Nat. Endowment for Arts, 1987, adv. com. for arts in edn., 1989—90. Mem.: Ohio Inter-Univ. Coun. (chair 2001—02), Ohio Campus Compact (exec. com. 2000—), Ohio Aerospace Inst. (exec. com. 1995—, chair 1998—2000), Ohio Supercomputer Ctr. (governing bd. 1996—), Ohio Higher Edn. Funding Commn., Ohio Sci. and Tech. Coun. (biotech. com.), So. Assn. Colls. and Schs. (commn. on coll. 1993—94), Coun. for Higher Edn. Accreditation (chair bd. dirs. 1996—98), Assn. Specialized and Profl. Accreditors (bd. dirs. 1994—96), Coll. Music Soc. (chmn. govt. rels. com. 1976—78, task force on edn. coll. music tchrs. 1987), Mortar Bd., Pi Kappa Lamdba (nat. v.p. 1979—81, pres. 1981—85), Omicron Delta Kappa, Phi Kappa Phi, Phi Beta Kappa. Episcopalian. Home: 29 Park Pl Athens OH 45701-2910 Office: Ohio Univ Cutler Hall Athens OH 45701-2979 E-mail: gliddenr@ohio.edu.

GLIEBERMAN, HERBERT ALLEN, lawyer; b. Chgo., Dec. 6, 1930; s. Elmer and Jean (Gerber) G.; m. Evelyn Eraci; children— Ronald, Gale, Joel Student, U. Ill., 1947, Roosevelt U., 1948-50; JD, Chgo. Kent Coll. Law, 1953. Bar: Ill. 1954, D.C. 1987. Pvt. practice, Chgo., 1954—; lectr. Chgo. Kent. Coll. Law, Ill. Inst. Continuing Legal Edn. Lectr. in field numerous instns. including ABA, ATLA, Am. Acad Matrimonial Lawyers, Inst. Law Inst., others. Author: Some Syndromes of Love, 1965, Know Your Legal Rights, 1974, Confessions of A Divorce Lawyer, 1975, Closed Marriage, 1978, Four Weekends to an Ideal Marriage, 1981; former host 2 radio shows for NBC Sta. WMAQ: Ask the Lawyer, Law and Controversy; contbr. articles to profl. jours. Former trustee Chgo. Kent. Coll. Law; former bd. dirs. Chgo. Coun. on Alcoholism. Mem. Am. Acad. Matrimonial Lawyers (cert. of appreciation 1967), Decologue Soc. Lawyers (cert. of appreciation 1965, 66, 68), Assn. Trial Lawyers Am. (cert. of appreciation 1973), Ill. Trial Lawyers Assn. (cert. of appreciation 1974), ABA, Ill. State Bar Assn., Chgo. Bar Assn., N.C. Bar Assn., Idaho Bar Assn., Internat. Law Inst., Wash., D.C. Jewish (bd. dirs., pres. Temple) Office: 19 S La Salle St Chicago IL 60603-1401 Fax: (312) 236-3417. E-mail: hglieber@aol.com.

GLIEGE, JOHN GERHARDT, lawyer; b. Chgo., Aug. 3, 1948; s. Gerhardt John and Jane (Heidke) Gliege; children: Gerhardt, Stephanie, Kristine. BA, Ariz. State U., 1969, MPA, 1970, JD, 1974. Bar: Ariz. 1974. Pvt. practice, Scottsdale, Ariz., 1974-81, Flagstaff, Ariz., 1981-94, 98—, 1998—, Sedona, Ariz., 1994-97, Williams, Ariz., 1997-98. Prof. paralegal studies No. Ariz. U., Flagstaff, 1981—83, prof. urban planning and cmty. devel., 1984—99; prof. paralegal studies Yavapai C.C., Prescott, Ariz., 1995—97, Coconino C.C., 2001—. Address: PO Box 1388 Flagstaff AZ 86002-1388 E-mail: jgliege@earthlink.net.

GLIJANSKY, ALEX, psychiatrist, psychoanalyst; b. Caracas, Venezuela, Oct. 6, 1948; came to U.S., 1975; s. Natalio and Ghenea (Rechtman) G.; m. Belinda Matyas, Aug. 12, 1973; children: Ghena, Avi. MD, Universidad Cen. de Venezuela, 1971, MS, 1974. Resident in psychiatry Hahnemann U., Phila., 1978; med. dir. Fishtown/Lower Kensington Mental Health Ctr., Phila., 1978—82; assoc. psychiatrist dept. psychiatry Abington (Pa.) Meml. Hosp., 1982—. Clin. asst. prof. psychiatry Drexel U. Sch. Medicine, Phila., 1978. Fellow Am. Psychiat. Assn.; mem. Pa. Psychiat. Soc., Phila. Psychiat. Soc., Phila. Assn. for Psychoanalysis, Am. Psychoanalytic Assn. Avocation: golf. Office: 8302 York Rd Ste B5 Elkins Park PA 19027-1529 E-mail: aglijansky@compuserve.com.

GLIKIN, ANTON ARKADIEVICH, architectural designer, artist; b. St. Petersburg, Russia, Mar. 26, 1971; arrived in U.S.A., 1999; s. Arkady Glikin and Elena Kotelnikova; m. Irina Shumitskaya, Mar. 2, 2002. MA in Arch. and Bldg. Arts, The Prince of Wales Inst. of Arch., 1996, MA in Arch. and Fine Arts, St. Petersburg Acad. Fine Arts, 1997. Arch. and interior designer Patricia Howard Assocs., London, 1996—99; arch. Peter Pennoyer Archs. P.C., N.Y.C., 1999—. Contbr. ; prin. works include The Prince of Wales Olympic Monument, Atlanta, Ga., 1997— (First prize, 95), The Millenium Monument, Washington, D.C., 2000— (Competition prize, 00). Recipient The Measured Drawing prize, The Worshipful Co. Chartered Archs., 1999, Arthur Ross award for excellence in classical tradition, Inst. Classical Architecture and Classical Am., N.Y.C., 2003; grantee Study grant, The Prince of Wales' Inst. Arch., 1995, Calder Loth grantee, 1996. Avocations: history, philosophy, music, travel.

GLIMCHER, ARNOLD B. art gallery executive; b. Duluth, Minn., Mar. 12, 1938; s. Paul and Eva (Fishman) G.; m. Mildred Louise Cooper, Dec. 20, 1959; children: Paul William, Marc Cooper. BA, Mass. Coll. Art., 1969; postgrad., NYU Sch. Psychology, Boston U. Founder, owner Pace Gallery, Boston, 1961-63; founder, chmn. Pace Wildenstein, N.Y.C., 1963—; founder Pace Editions, 1968—. Author: Louise Nevelson, 1972, paperback edit., 1976; (with Paul Vitz) Modern Art and Modern Science: The Parallel Analysis of Vision; contbr. articles to art jours.; prodr.: (films) Gorillas in the Mist, The Good Mother; prodr., dir.: (film) The Mambo Kings, Just Cause; editor, cataloger, text writer for various art vols. selector, installer various mus. exhibits and retrospectives. Fellow Israel Mus. (chmn. devel. com. 1976-77); mem. Am. Acad. Arts and Letters, Officier des Arts and Lettres. Art Dealers Assn. Am. (bd. dirs.). Office: Pace Wildenstein 32 E 57th St New York NY 10022-2513

GLIMCHER, MELVIN JACOB, orthopedic surgeon; b. Brookline, Mass., June 2, 1925; s. Aaron and Clara (Fink) Glimcher; m. Karin Wetmore, Mar. 8, 2000; children from previous marriage: Susan Deborah, Laurie Hollis, Nancy Blair. Student, Duke U., 1943-44; BS in Mech. Engring. with highest distinction; BS in Physics with highest distinction, Purdue U., 1946; MD magna cum laude, Harvard, 1950; postgrad., Mass. Inst. Tech., 1956-59. Intern surgery Strong Meml. Hosp., Rochester, N.Y., 1950-51; 3d asst. resident surgery Mass. Gen. Hosp., Boston, 1951-52, 2d asst. resident, 1952-53, asst. resident orthopedic surgery, 1954-55, chief resident, 1956, chief orthopedic service, 1965-71, chmn. dept. orthopedic surgery, 1968-71; asst. resident orthopedic surgery Children's Med. Center, Boston, 1953-54, jr. resident, 1955-56; mem. faculty Harvard Med. Sch., 1956—, Edith M. Ashley prof. orphopedic surgery, 1965-71, Harriet M. Peabody prof., 1971—; also chmn. dept.; orthopedic surgeon-in-chief Children's Hosp. Med. Center, Boston, 1971-81, dir. Lab. for Study of Skeletal Disorders and Rehab., 1980—. Trustee Forsyth Dental Infirmary, New England Sinai Hosp. With USMCR, World War II. Recipient Soma Weiss award Harvard Med. Sch., 1950, Borden Research award, 1950; Kappa Delta award, 1959; Internat. Assn. Dental Research award, 1964; Ralph Pemberton award Am. Rheumatism Soc., 1969; Bristol-Meyers/Zimmer instl. grant for excellence; Disting. Achievement in Orthopaedic Research award Orthopaedic Research Edn. Found.; William Neuman award Am. Soc. Bone and Mineral Rsch., 1996; Physician Achievement award Arthritis Found., 1996. Fellow Am. Acad. Arts and Scis., Am. Acad. Orthopaedic Surgeons (Silver anniversary Kappa Delta prize 1974, Alfred Shands award jointly awarded with Orthop. Rsch. Soc 1997), Am. Orthopedic Assn.; mem. Orthopedic Research Soc. (past pres.), Assn. Bone and Joint Surgeons (Nicholas Andry award 1978), Internat. Soc. for Study Lumbar Spine (Volvo award 1983), Societe Internationale de Chirurgie Orthopedique et de Traumatologie. Office: 300 Longwood Ave Boston MA 02115-5724

GLIMM, JAMES GILBERT, mathematician, educator; b. Peoria, Ill., Mar. 24, 1934; s. William Frederick and Barbara Gilbert (Hooper) G.; m. Adele Strauss, June 30, 1957; 1 dau., Alison. AB, Columbia U., 1956, A.M., 1957, PhD, 1959. From asst. prof. to prof. math. MIT, 1960-69; prof. Courant Inst., NYU, 1969-74; prof. math. Rockefeller U., N.Y.C., 1974-82; prof. Courant Inst., NYU, N.Y.C., 1982-89, disting. prof., chair dept. applied math. and statis. SUNY, Stony Brook, 1989—, dir. Inst. for Math. Modeling, 1989—; dir. Ctr. for Data Intensive Computing Brookhaven Nat. Labs., 1999—. Co-author: Quantum Physics, 1981; Collected Papers, Vols. I and II, 1985; mem. editorial bds. profl. jours.; contbr. articles to sci. publs. Recipient Dannie Heineman prize in math. physics, 1980; Guggenheim fellow, 1963, 65. Mem. NAS, Internat. Assn. Math. Physicists, Am. Phys. Soc., Am. Math. Soc. (Leroy P. Steele prize 1992), Soc. Indsl. and Applied Math., Math. Assn. Am., Am. Acad. Arts and Scis., Soc. Petroleum Engrs., N.Y. Acad. Scis. (award in phys. and math. scis. 1979) Office: Stony Brook U Dept Applied Math and Stats Math Bldg Rm P-138A Stony Brook NY 11794-3600 Business E-Mail: glimm@ams.sunysb.edu.

GLINDEMAN, HENRY PETER, JR., real estate developer; b. Coeur d'Alene, Idaho, Sept. 26, 1924; s. Henry Peter and Laura Mae (Buchanan) G.; children: Pamela, Henry Peter III, John. BS, U.S. Naval Acad., 1945; postgrad., U.S. Naval War Coll., 1959-60. Commd. ensign U.S. Navy, 1945, advanced through grades to rear adm., 1973; exec. officer, comdg. officer Fighter Squadron 154, 1962-63; comdr. Attack Carrier Air Wing 15 Attack Carrier Air Wing 15, 1964-65; tng. officer attack carrier air wing, staff, comdr. U.S. Naval Air Forces, U.S. Pacific Fleet, 1965-66; readiness officer, staff comdr. U.S. First Fleet, 1966-68; comdg. officer U.S.S. Passumpsic, 1968-69; head Attack Carrier Weapons Requirements br. Office Chief Naval Ops., 1970-71; comdg. officer U.S.S. Ranger, 1971-73; chief Fleet Coordinating Group, 1973-74; dir. Office Program Appraisal, Office Sec. Navy, 1974-75; comdr. Carrier Group 7, 1975-76; comdr. Carrier Group 3, 1976; comdr. Carrier Group 5, Carrier Strike Force, 7th Fleet, 1976-77; comdr. Naval Safety Center, 1977-78; pres. Mr. Quick Lube Inc., Clearwater, Fla., 1978 81; v.p. Fla. Light and Save Inc., 1981-83; real estate developer, 1983-85; pres. GBS Devel. Inc., Redwood City, Calif., 1985-87; chmn., CEO Stormy Weather Guard, Inc., Clearwater, Fla., 1988-94. Bd. dirs., sec.-treas. Guardian Marine Corp., 1990-91; pres. Fiber Am. Inc., Clearwater, Fla., 1991-96. V.p., Edgar Allan Poe Jr. High Sch. PTA, Annandale, Va., 1960-61, Annandale Am. Little League, 1961-62; sec. exec. com. Troop 674, Boy Scouts Am., Annandale, 1961-62; chmn. bd. dirs. USS Ranger Mus. Found., 2001—. Decorated Legion of Merit with 4 gold stars, D.F.C., Air medal with gold star, Navy Commendation medal with Combat V. Mem. U.S. Naval Acad. Alumni Assn., Navy League, Mil. Order World Wars, Assn. Naval Aviation, Mil. Officer Assn. Am., Tailhook Assn., Golden Gate Club, Breakfast Club (San Francisco). Episcopalian. Home: 3976 Long Leaf Dr Melbourne FL 32940-1464 E-mail: radmu@earthlink.net.

GLINER, ERAST BORIS, theoretical physicist; b. Kiev, USSR, Feb. 3, 1923; came to U.S., 1980; s. Boris Moses Gliner and Bella Boris (Pauckman) Rubinstein; m. Galina Ilchenko, Dec. 12, 1944; children: Bella, Arkady. MS in Physics, Leningrad U., USSR, 1963; PhD in Physics, Tartu U., Estonia, 1972. Head theoretical dept. Spl. Design Office, Leningrad, 1954-63; sr. scientist A Ioffe Inst. for Physics and Tech. of Soviet Acad. Scis., Leningrad, 1963-80; vis. fellow Joint Inst. Lab. Astrophyiscs U. Colo., Boulder, 1982-83; rsch. assoc. McDonnel Ctr. Space Sci. Washington U., St. Louis, 1983-86. Guest nuc. physics divsn. Lawrence Berkeley Lab., 1987; vis. scientist Stanford Linear Acceleration Ctr., Palo Alto, Calif., 1987-2003, user, 2003—. Co-author: Differential Equation of Mathematical Physics (English, Russian, Japanese edits.), 1962-65; contbr. articles to profl. jours. Polit. prisoner USSR, 1945-54. Sgt. field arty. Soviet Army, 1942-44. Decorated Russian Orders Red Star and Patriotic War; recipient rsch. award USSR Govt., 1958-60, USSR Acad. Scis., 1977, 78. Mem. Am. Phys. Soc. Jewish. Achievements include patents in field (USSR); research in solar physics (combined effect of global and upper magnetic fields on solar atmosphere, coronal asymmetry as evidence of solar quadrupole magnetic field), and in Einstein gravitational theory (introduction of vacuumlike state of matter and non-singular Friedmann cosmology, covaiant energy description in general relativity, foundation of general relativity on the basis of Sakharov's concept of gravity; investigation of non-singular black hole geometry; non-singular Friedmann cosmology; general relativistic background of quantum non-locality). Office: Stanford U SLAC PO Box 4349 Palo Alto CA 94309-0450 E-mail: erast@hotmail.com.

GLINES, CARROLL VANE, JR., magazine editor; b. Balt., Dec. 2, 1920; s. Carroll Vane and Elizabeth Marion (Cross) G.; m. Mary Ellen Edwards, Oct. 1, 1943; children: Karen Ann, David Edwards, Valerie Jean. Student, Drexel Inst. Tech., 1938-40, Canal Zone Jr. Coll., 1946-48, U. Munich, 1948; BBA, U. Okla., 1952, MBA, 1954; MA, Am. U., 1969. Commd. 2d lt. USAF, 1942, advanced through grades to col., 1965, military service, 1941-68; mgr. publs. Nat. Bus. Aircraft Assn., Washington, 1968; assoc. editor Armed Forces Mgmt. mag., Washington, 1969-70; editor Air Cargo mag., Washington, 1970-71, Air Line Pilot mag., Washington, 1971-85, cons. editor, 1985-86, contbg. editor, 1989—; sr. editor Aviation Space mag., 1982-85; editor Profl. Pilot Mag., Alexandria, Va., 1986-88, sr. contbg. editor, 1988—, Aviation History mag. (formerly Aviation Heritage mag.), Leesburg, Va., 1990—. Mgr. publs. Air Line Pilots Assn., 1971-85, dir. comms., 1983-85; lectr. U. Dayton, U. Alaska, Am. U. Author 35 books; contbr. articles to mags.; gen. editor MacMillan, Air Force Acad. series, 1970-74; cdtl. cons. Van Nostrand Reinhold, 1980-85; contbg. editor Nation's Bus., 1981-86; mem. adv. bd. Hist. of Aviation Collection, U. Tex., Dallas, 1981-90, 95—, Alaska Aviation Heritage Mus., Anchorage, 1993-99; curator Doolittle Libr., U. Tex., Dallas, 1995—. Asst. to v.p. for spl. projects Evergreen Internat. Aviation, 1988-93; active Frontiers of Flight Mus., Dallas. Recipient numerous awards from press assns. Freedoms Found.; inducted into Interboro Hall of Fame, 2003. Mem. Aviation-Space Writers Assn. (Lauren D. Lyman award), Air Force Assn., Air Force Hist. Found., Soc. Aerospace Communicators, Quiet Birdmen, Soc. Profl. Journalists, Order of Daedalians. Home: 1531 San Rafael Dr Dallas TX 75218-4444 E-mail: ceevee1531@aol.com.

GLINN, FRANKLYN BARRY, lawyer; b. Newark, Oct. 22, 1943; s. Dave and Gertrude (Weinstein) G.; m. Sandra Lee Scales, Nov. 3, 1943; children: MacAdam Jordan, Dara Elisabeth, Daniel Garrett. BAE, U. Fla., 1965, JD, 1968. Bar: Fla. 1969, U.S. Ct. Appeals (5th cir.) 1969, U.S. Dist. Ct. (so. dist.) Fla. 1970. Assoc. Ser, Greenspahn & Keyfetz, Miami, Fla., 1969-70, Ser & Keyfetz, 1970-72, Rabin, Sassoon & Ratiner, Miami, Fla., 1972-74; ptnr.

Ratiner & Glinn, Miami, Fla., 1974—2000, Glinn & Somera, P.A., Miami, Fla., 2000—. Mem. ABA, Am. Judicature Soc., Am. Trial Lawyers Assn., Acad. Fla. Trial Lawyers, Am. Arbitration Assn. Democrat. Jewish. Office: Ste 401 2100 Coral Way Miami FL 33145-2657

GLINSEK, GERALD JOHN, lawyer; b. Akron, Ohio, Jan. 16, 1939; s. Rudolph Paul and Angela Louise (Stanger) G.; m. Karen Rosemary Mehen, Oct. 17, 1968 (div. Aug. 1990); children: Kelli, Daniel; m. Maureen Louise Nuosce, May 7, 1994 (dec. Aug. 1998); 1 child from previous marriage, Rebecca Ann; m. Debra K. Gable, Oct. 22, 2002. BA, U. Akron, 1963, JD, 1967. Bar: Ohio 1967, U.S. Dist. Ct. (no. dist.) Ohio 1969, U.S. Ct. Appeals (6th cir. 1986), U.S. Supreme Ct. 1986. Asst. pros. atty. Summit County Prosecutors Office, Akron, 1967-71; pvt. practice Akron, 1971—. With U.S. Army, 1957. Mem. ABA, Ohio Bar Assn., Akron Bar Assn. (treas. 1981), Summit County Legal Aid Soc. (pres. 1978-82), Phi Kappa Tau (advisor 1982—). Democrat. Roman Catholic. Avocations: travel, skiing. Home: 1861 Wiltshire Rd Akron OH 44313-6101 Office: 88 S Portage Path Akron OH 44303-1023

GLINSKI, HELEN ELIZABETH, operating room nurse; b. Gouverneur, N.Y., Apr. 9, 1944; d. Arthur Andrew and Lillian May (MacKenzie) Turnbull; m. David Lee Joseph Glinski, May 13, 1967; children: David Lee Joseph II, Christopher John. Diploma of Nursing, House of Good Samaritan, Watertown, N.Y., 1965; registered nurse 1st asst., Del. County C.C., 1992; student, St. Joseph's Coll., Maine, 1999—. RN, N.Y., Cert. Nurse Operating Room. Staff nurse operating rm. House of Good Samaritan, Watertown, N.Y., 1965-66, Cmty. Gen. Hosp., Syracuse, N.Y., 1966-68, acting headnurse operating rm., 1968-69, 70, acting asst. head nurse, inservice instr., 1969-70, 70-71; staff nurse operating rm. E.J. Noble Hosp., Gouverneur, N.Y., 1971-72; head nurse, supr. operating rm. Edward John Noble Hosp., Gouverneur, N.Y., 1972-77; sr. staff nurse operating rm. Mercy Hosp., Watertown, N.Y., 1978-79; staff nurse operating rm. Roswell Pk. Meml. Inst., Buffalo, 1979-85, Buffalo VA Med. Ctr., 1985-95; nurse 1st asst. oper. rm. VA Med. Ctr., West Palm Beach, Fla., 1995-97, established/coordinate preoperative clinic, coordinate surg. risk clinic, nursing facilitator Pre Operative Clinic, 1997-2000; reg. nurse first asst. Urology Svc., 1999—. Mem. RN First Asst. Spl. Assembly, 1992—; adv. com. N. Tech. Edn. Ctr., Riviera Beach, Fla., 2000. Collector Am. Cancer Assn., Buffalo, 1991-93. Recipient Performance award Dept. Vet. Affairs, Buffalo, 1988, 91, 93. Mem.: Soc. Urologic Nurses and Assocs., Fla. Assn. RN First Assn. (treas. 1998—), Fla. Coun. Oper. Rm. Nurses, Assn. Oper. Rm. Nurses (corr. sec. 1986—91, bd. dirs. 1992—93, pres.-elect 1993—94, pres. 1994—95, bd. dirs. 1996—98, officer western N.Y. chpt., nominating com. 2000—02, pres.-elect 2002—). Episcopalian. Avocations: knitting, motorcycling, computers, sewing, gardening. Home: 6940 43rd Terrance West Palm Beach FL 33404 Office: 7305 N Military Trl West Palm Beach FL 33410-6415 E-mail: glinskihel@aol.com.

GLINSKY, ALBERT VINCENT, composer, educator; b. N.Y.C., Dec. 9, 1952; s. Vincent Glinsky and Cleo Hartwig; m. Linda Kobler, June 10, 1979; children: Luka Emmanuel, Allegra Cleo. BM, The Juilliard Sch., 1976, MM, 1978; PhD, NYU, 1992. Instr. Montclair State U., NJ, 1983-87; prof. music Mercyhurst Coll., Erie, Pa., 1987—. Resident artist Ucross (Wyo.) Found., 1987; resident composer Pa. Composers Conf., Pitts., 1988; mem. instrumental and jazz adv. panel Pa. Coun. on Arts, Harrisburg, 1991-93; BMI composer-in-residence Vanderbilt U., 1996. Author: Theremin: Ether Music and Espionage, 2000 (Deems Taylor award ASCAP, 2001); composer numerous pieces including High Flight, 1990, Six Miniatures for Solo Violin, Day Walker, Night Wanderer, 1995; performances include Aspen Music Festival, Pitts. New Music Ensemble, Concerto Soloists of Phila., Zurich Chamber Orchestra, Joffrey II Ballet, others. Nat. Endowment for Arts fellow, 1980, Pa. Coun. on Arts fellow, 1988, 96, 98, 2000; recipient Hinrichsen award Am. Acad. Arts and Letters, 1998; grantee Jerome Found., 1982, N.Y. State Coun. on Arts, 1983, Astral Found., 1991, Haydn Found., 2001. Mem. Am. Composers Alliance, Broadcast Music Inc. Avocations: drawing, poetry. Office: Mercyhurst Coll 501 E 38th St Erie PA 16546

GLISE, ANTHONY LEROY, musician, composer, writer; b. St. Joseph, Mo., Jan. 17, 1956; s. Wyllis LeRoy Glise and Alma Jeannine Borngesser. M. Music (Performance), New England Conservatory, Boston, 1982; Diplom, Academie "L'Ottocento", Vigevano, Italy, 1991, Assn. Romana Cultori dela Musica, Rome, 1992, U. Vienna, 1983; Diploma, U. Cath., Lille, France, 1997. Rec. artist Young Rec. Artists, Eclipse, HEM, 1985—; pres. Eclipse Recordings, Lille, France, 1998—; author, composer, editor Mel Bay Publs., Pacific, Mo., 1995—; host, "Glise on Guitar" NPR Internat. Satellite Radio Program, 1989—; pres. Aveia Group, Ltd., St. Joseph, Mo., 1990—. Author: (textbooks) Classical Guitar Pedagogy - A Handbook for Teachers, 1998, Handbook for American Musicians Overseas, 2003, Help! My Kid is Taking Music Lessons, 2003; composer: (complete compositions (roughly 60 works) Anthony Glise Original Compositions & Studies, 1998, (Anthony Glise Urtext Editions) critical editions of musical compositions from Willis Music Co. (Cincinnatti, USA), 1987, critical editions of musical compositions from Mel Bay Publications (Pacific, USA), 1998, (original compositions) Original compositions include works for classical guitar, chamber music, orchestra and ballet (including "Noah," the largest ballet of the late 20th Century for full orchestra and 130 dancers); founder, performer : Nova Project ensemble; performer, composer, dir. (concerts) Carnegie Hall; performer : Lincoln Ctr.; Vienna Internat. Ctr.; Nouveau Siecle. Vol. active in work with children diagnosed with cancer and other terminal illnesses; arts advocate active in programs for pub. awareness for the arts. Recipient First prize, Internat. Toscanini Competition (Italy), 1991, diploma, Nemzetközi Gitárfestivál (Hungary) (for Composition), 1989, Festival Ville Sable sur Sarthe (France) (for Composition), 1985, Spl. prize for Performance, Internat. Toscanini Competition (Italy), 1989, Individual Mayor's award for the Arts, St. Joseph Arts Alliance, 2000. Mem.: Guitar Found. Am. (voting mem.), Phi Mu Alpha Sinfonia. Avocations: sailing, fencing, fishing, hunting, languages. Office: Aevia Group Ltd PO Box 7242 Saint Joseph MO 64507

GLISMANN, CLEMENTINE, elementary school educator, researcher; b. Oakland, Nebr., Aug. 4, 1917; d. Louis Martin Larson, Edvinna Josephine Young; m. Leonard William Glismann, Feb. 24, 1940 (dec. Feb. 1997). BA, Midland Luth. Coll., Fremont, Nebr., 1939; postgrad., U. Nebr., 1942—43, Weber Coll., Ogden, Utah, 1945—47, U. Utah, 1963—78. Tchr. 1st grade Bd. Edn., Norfolk, Nebr., 1939—40, secondary tchr. Madrid, Nebr., 1941—42, 3d grade tchr. Ogden, Utah, 1945—56, 4th grade tchr., 1957—63, Salt Lake City, 1964—79; ret., 1979. Traveling dealer Lenswood, 1977—91. Author: (TV series) Wheels; prodr.: (TV series) Wheels; author: (TV series) Paper; prodr.: (TV series) Paper; author: (TV series) Rubber; prodr.: (TV series) Rubber; author: (TV series) Clothes; prodr.: (TV series) Clothes; author: (TV series) Historical Masquerade (Great Americans); prodr.: (TV series) Historical Masquerade (Great Americans); author: (TV series) Mother Earth's Rock Family, 1952—63; prodr.: (TV series) Mother Earth's Rock Family, 1952—63. State chmn. Luth. Ch. Women, Utah, 1963. Mem.: Golden Spike Gem and Mineral Soc., Delta Kappa Gamma. Republican. Lutheran. Avocations: faceting gemstones, writing poetry.

GLITMAN, MAYNARD WAYNE, foreign service officer; b. Chgo., Dec. 8, 1933; s. Ben and Reada (Kutok Klass) G.; m. G. Christine Amundsen, Dec. 22, 1956; children: Russell M., Erik W., Karen C., Matthew M., Rebecca S. BA with highest honors, U. Ill., 1955; MA, Fletcher Sch. Law and Diplomacy, 1956; postgrad., U. Calif., Berkeley, 1965-66. Joined fgn. service Dept. State, 1956, economist, 1956-59; vice consul Nassau, Bahamas, 1959-61; econ. officer Am. Embassy, Ottawa, Ont., Can., 1961-65, Dept. State, 1966-67; mem. U.S. Del. to UN Gen. Assembly, 1967, Nat. Security Council staff, 1968; polit. officer, 1st sec. Am. Embassy, Paris, 1968-73; dir. Office of Internat. Trade, Dept. State, Washington, 1973-74, dep. asst. sec. of state for internat. trade policy, 1974-76, dep. asst. sec. def. for Europe and NATO affairs, 1976-77; dep. U.S. permanent rep. to NATO, Brussels, Belgium, 1977-81; ambassador, dep. chief U.S. del. Intermediate Nuclear Forces Negotiations, ACDA, Geneva, Switzerland, 1981-84; ambassador, U.S. rep. Mut. Balanced Force Reductions Negotiations, Vienna, Austria, 1985; ambassador, chief negotiator Intermediate Nuclear Force Negotiations, Geneva, Switzerland, 1985-88; U.S. ambassador to Belgium, 1988-91; diplomat in residence U. Vt., Burlington, 1991-94. Adj. prof. U. Vt., Burlington, 1994—. Served with U.S. Army, 1957. Recipient Outstanding and Disting. Pub. Svc. medals U.S. Dept. Def., 1977, 81, Presdl. Svc. award, 1984, 87, Howard Weil award SUNY, 1988, Joseph C. Wilson award, Rochester, N.Y., 1989, Presdl. Disting. Svc. award, 1989. Mem. Phi Beta Kappa. Home: PO Box 438 Jeffersonville VT 05464-0438 Office: U Vermont Dept Polit Sci PO Box 54110 Burlington VT 05405-0001

GLOBOKE, JOSEPH RAYMOND, accountant; b. Kansas City, Kans., Mar. 9, 1955; s. Anthony Joseph and Loretta Margaret (Bartkoski) G.; m. Debra Ruth Neumann, Nov. 13, 1982 (div. May, 2002); children: Theresa Renee, Michael Richard, William Robert. BSBA, Rockhurst Coll., 1977. CPA, Mo., Kans. Intern Ernst & Whinney, Kansas City, Mo., 1976-77; staff acct. Troupe Kehoe Whiteaker & Kent, Kansas City, 1977-84, mgr., 1984-88; sr. acct. Kennedy & Coe, Salina, Kans., 1988-91; audit supr. Robert Garrison & Assocs., Grandview, Mo., 1991-93; sr. staff actt. Logan & Schmidt, Kansas City, Kans., 1993-96; mgr., 1996—. Bd. dirs., treas. Children's Mus. of Kansas City; mem. Boy Scouts. Mem. AICPA, Kans. Soc. of CPA (v.p. metro chpt.), K.C. Roman Catholic. Avocations: reading, gardening. Home: 1719 N 85th St Kansas City KS 66112 Office: Logan Schmidt & Lerner 1300 N 78th St Ste 100 Kansas City KS 66112-2493

GLOCK, CHARLES YOUNG, sociologist, writer; b. N.Y.C., Oct. 17, 1919; s. Charles and Philippine (Young) G.; m. Margaret Schleef, Sept. 12, 1950; children: Susan Young, James William. BS, N.Y. U., 1940; MBA, Boston U., 1941; PhD, Columbia U., 1952. Research asst. Bur. Applied Social Research, Columbia U., 1946-51, dir., 1951-58, lectr., then prof. sociology, 1956-58; prof. sociology U. Calif. at Berkeley, 1958-79, prof. emeritus, 1979—, chmn., 1967-68, 69-71; dir. Survey Research Center, 1958-67; adj. prof. Grad. Theol. Union, 1971-79; Luther Weigle vis. lectr. Yale U., 1968. Co-author: American Piety, 1968, Wayne Shepherds, 1971, Anti-Semitism in America, 1979, The Anatomy of Racial Attitudes, 1983; author (sr.): Religion and Society in Tension, 1965, Christian Beliefs and Anti-Semitism, 1966, To Comfort and To Challenge, 1967, Adolescent Prejudice, 1968, The Apathetic Majority, 1975; contbg. editor: Rev. Religious Rsch. Sociol. Analysis; editor: Survey Research in the Social Sciences, 1967, Prejudice U.S.A., 1969, Beyond the Classics, 1973, Religion in Sociological Perspective, 1973, The New Religious Consciousness, 1975, Unison-Newsletter of One Voice, 1990—90, contbr. numerous articles on social scis. Active parish edn. Luth. Ch. Am., 1970-72; mem. mgmt. com. Office Rsch. and Planning, 1973-80; bd. dirs. Pacific Luth. Theol. Sem., 1962-74, 80-86, Inst. Rsch. in Social Behavior, 1962-90, Interplayers, 1990-92, Sandpoint Christian Connection, 1995-97; pres. Cornerhouse Fund, 1982-92, One Voice, 1994-95, bd. dirs., 1995-97; mem. adv. com. Office Rsch. and Evaluation Evang. Luth. Ch. Am., 1988-94; mem. history com. Soc. Study of Religion, 1993-94; v.p. Sandpoint chpt. Idaho Writers' League, 2003—. Capt. USAAF, 1942-46. Decorated Bronze Star, Legion of Merit; recipient Roots of Freedom award Pacific bd. Anti-Defamation League, 1977, Garman-Hidy award for Disting. Contbn. to Life of Luth. Ch. in the West, 1999; Berkeley citation U. Calif., Berkeley, 1979; Rockefeller fellow, 1941-42; fellow Center Advanced Study Behavioral Scis., 1957-58; fellow Soc. for Religion in Higher Edn., 1968-69 Fellow Soc. Sci. Study Religion (Western rep., pres. 1968-69); mem. Am. Assn. Pub. Opinion Research (v.p., pres. 1962-64, pres. Pacific chpt. 1959-60), Am. Sociol. Assn. (v.p. 1978-79), Religious Research Assn., Sociol. Research Assn. Home: 319 S 4th Ave Sandpoint ID 83864-1219

GLOCKER, THEODORE WILLIAM, lawyer, accountant; b. Washington, Sept. 20, 1953; s. Theodore Wesley and Julia (Ely) G.; m. Martha Harlow Carr, June 28, 1975; children: Theodore Wesley, Sean Ellis, Samuel Ross. BBA, Emory U., 1975, JD, 1983. Bar: Fla. 1984, U.S. Dist. Ct. (mid. dist.) Fla. 1984, U.S. Tax Ct. 1984; CPA, Ga. Acct. The Coca-Cola Co., Atlanta, 1975-80; assoc. Theodore W. Glocker, Jr., PA, Jacksonville, Fla., 1983-84; ptnr. Glocker & Glocker, Jacksonville, 1984-94; shareholder Martin Ade Birchfield & Mickler PA, Jacksonville, Fla., 1994—2001, Stoneburner, Berry & Simmons PA, Jacksonville, Fla., 2001—. Bd. dirs. Cath. Charities Housing Bur., Inc., Jacksonville, 1987—; San Jose Cath. Housing Assn., Inc., Jacksonville, 1997-, Cath. Found. Diocese of St. Augustine, Inc., Jacksonville, 2001-. Recipient Estate Planning award Ga. Bankers Assn., 1983. Mem. Fla. Bar Assn. (tax sect., real property, probate and trust law sect.). Republican. Roman Catholic. Avocations: surfing, hiking, reading. Office: Stoneburner Berry & Simmons PA 1 Independent Dr Ste 2000 Jacksonville FL 32202-5024

GLOCKMANN, WALTER FRIEDRICH, physicist, consultant; b. Gera, Germany, June 3, 1932; came to U.S., 1987; s. Walther Richard and Dorothee Luise (Woehler) G.; m. Waltraut Frieda Meier, Nov. 10, 1951; children: Harald, Eveline, Dagmar. Degree in physics and math., U. Frankfurt, Germany, 1958; degree in physics, U. Mainz, Germany, 1969. R & D mgr. Heimann GmbH, Wiesbaden, Germany, 1969-78; v.p., gen. mgr. Heimann Sys. Co. and Siemens Components, Inc., Iselin, N.J., 1978-91; pres. Argus Security, Inc., Stirling, N.J., 1992—. Cons. Capintec, Inc., Ramsey, N.J., 1992-94, Heitronics GmbH, Wiesbaden, 1995—, Vivid Techs., Inc., Woburn, Mass., 1995-99, Alpha-ES GmbH Geretsried, Germany, 1998-2002, Omega Electronics Sys. Ltd., London, 1999-2001. Co-author: Handbuch Technische Temperaturmessung, 1976, Temperaturmessung in der Technik, 1976; contbr. article to tech. jour. Sensors, 1994. Mem. ASTM, SPIE. Achievements include U.S. and European patents on x-ray scanner for detecting plastic articles, European and German patents on optical smoke detectors, and design and development of infrared sensing systems, temperature sensing, intrusion alarms. Home: 162 Pleasant Plains Rd Stirling NJ 07980-1017 Office: Argus Security Inc 50 Division Ave Millington NJ 07946-1358 E-mail: glock@wintron.com.

GLOCKNER, PETER G. civil and mechanical engineering educator; b. Moragy, Hungary, Jan. 26, 1929; emigrated to Can., 1949; BSc in Civil Engring., McGill U., Montreal, Que., Can., 1955; MSc in Civil Engring., MIT, 1956; PhD in Civil Engring., U. Mich., 1964. Asst. prof. applied mechanics U. Alta., Can., 1958-60; from asst. prof. to prof. emeritus U. Calgary, Alta., 1960-94, prof. emeritus, 1994—, chmn. dept. mech. engring., 1976-87. Author: A Place of Ingenuity, more than 300 articles on shell theory, stability and non-linear behavior of thin-walled structures, dielectrics and non-linear constitutive theory. Whitney fellow, 1955-56, Ford Found. fellow, 1962-64; recipient CANCAM medal, 1993. Fellow ASCE (Moisseiff award and medal 1983), Can. Soc. Mech. Engring., Engring. Inst. Can. (Gzowski Gold medal 1971), Am. Acad. Mechanics (pres. 1995-96); mem. Can. Soc. Civil Engring., Assn. Profl. Engrs., Geologists and Geophysicists Alta, Order of Univ. Calgary. Home: 2536 Charlebois Dr Calgary AB Canada T2L OT6 E-mail: glockner@ucalgary.ca.

GLOD, CAROL ANN, nursing educator; b. Niagara Falls, N.Y., July 10, 1958; d. William Vincent and Genevieve (Styczen) G. BSN cum laude, U. Rochester, 1980; MS, Boston Coll., 1983, PhD, 1994. Co-investigator, assoc. dir. McLean Hosp., Belmont, Mass., 1989-97, dir. nursing rsch., 1999—; asst. prof. Northeastern U., Boston, 1994-99, assoc. prof., 1999—; lectr. dept. psychiatry Harvard Med. Sch., Boston, 1993—. Co-investigator, prin. investigator McLean Hosp., 1989—; ind. investigator Nat. Alliance Rsch. on Schizophrenia and Depression, 2000. Author: Contemporary Psychiatric Nursing, 1998; contbr. articles to profl. jours. Cons. Big Sister Assn., Boston, 1998-2000, ABC News, Boston, 2000—, VA, Bedford, Mass., 1998—. Recipient Dissertation award Sigma Theta Tau, 1994. Mem. ANA, Am. Psychiat. Nurses Assn. (bd. dirs. 1992-2001, rsch. award 1994), Sigma Theta Tau (dissertation award 1994). Avocations: biking, cooking. Office: Northeastern Univ 106 D Robinson Hall Boston MA 02115 E-mail: c.glod@neu.edu.

GLODAVA, MILA GARCIA, entrepreneur, educator, consultant; b. Bauan, Batangas, Philippines, May 27, 1945, came to U.S., 1972; d. Francisco Ramos and Rosalia Manalo (Coronel) Garcia; m. Mark Jeffrey Glodava, Jan. 29, 1972; children: Kirsten Angela, Kevin Marc. B.S. in Edn., St. Paul Coll., Manila, 1969. Tchr. Mt. Carmel High Sch., Polillo, Quezon, P.I., 1969-72; bookkeeper First Nat. State Bank of N.J., Newark, 1972-74; owner Glodava Bus. Svcs., Arvada, Colo., 1980-99, Mila Glodava, Inc., 2000—; founding pres Metro Infanta Found., Inc., 1996—. Rep. to first White House briefing on Asian/Pacific women, 1985; bd. dirs. Asian Pacific Ctr. for Human Devel.; communications dir. St. Joan of Arc Ch., 1987-89, St. Thomas More Cath. Ch., 1989—; co-chair Festival Asian Arts and Culture, 1990. Recipient Minoru Yasui Community Vol. award, 1989. Fellow Asian Pacific Am. Women's Leadership Inst. Mem. Nat. Network of Asian and Pacific Women, Colo. Network of Asian and Pacific Women (pres.-elect). Co-author: Mail-Order Brides: Women for Sale, 1994, Labong ng Kawayan: Walking Through the Pathways and Streets of Infanta, 2002. Home and Office: 7350 Braun Way Arvada CO 80005-2843

GLOE, DONNA, systems change manager; b. Moberly, Mo., Apr. 24, 1951; d. James F. and E. Emogene (Semones) Osborn; m. Lloyd R. Gloe, Feb. 14, 1975; children: Darin Robert, Leslie Renee. BA, U. Mo., 1973; MEd, Lincoln U., Jefferson City, Mo., 1977; diploma, St. John's Sch. Nursing, Springfield, Mo., 1983; BSN, Southwest Mo. State U., 1999; EdD, Nova Southeastern U., 1996; MSN. Cert. nursing informatics; cert. nursing staff devel. and continuing edn. Family therapist Burrell Mental Health Ctr., Springfield; edn. coord., staff nurse surg. ICU St. John's Regional Health Ctr., Springfield, knowledge info. module mgr.; clin. analyst applicat. delivery clin. team-comp. med. rec. St. John's Health Sys., Springfield, 1999—. Adj. faculty S.W. Bapt. U., 1992. Contbr. articles to profl. jours.; author video. Mem. AACN, Nat. Nursing Staff Devel. Orgn., Mo. Assn. Hosp. Educators, Am. Nursing Credentialing Ctr. (mem. nursing staff devel. and continuing edn.). Home: 335 Big Timber Rd Marshfield MO 65706-2509

GLOGOWER, MICHAEL HOWARD, public housing senior functional specialist; b. Louisville, Jan. 6, 1944; s. Louis R. and Elaine R. (Switow) G. Student, Louisville Country Day Sch., 1958-61; BA in Polit. Sci., Kenyon Coll., 1965. Lic. real estate broker, Ky., Fla. Asst. gen. mgr. Mail Photo Svc. Inc., Louisville, 1966-69; pres. Mi-Glo Corp., Louisville, 1969-70; v.p. ops. Cherokee Coal Co. Inc., Louisville, 1970-71; area mgr. Owens/Corning Fiberglas Corp., Toledo, 1971-73; gen. mgr. Redd's Auto Parts Inc., Louisville, 1973-74; dist. mgr. Hackney Corp., Birmingham, Ala., 1974-75; area sales rep. J&W Fence Supply Co. Inc., Indpls., 1975-76; broker, salesman comml./investment divsn. Bass & Weisberg Realtors, Louisville, 1976-79; owner Michael H. Glogower Investment Realtor & Bus. Consulting, 1979—; housing programs specialist office pub. and Indian housing HUD, Washington, 1991-96, sr. functional specialist Honolulu, 1996-98, Miami, Fla., 1998—. Former mem. edn. com. Bd. Realtors, Louisville; former subs. instr. Jefferson C.C., Louisville; former moderator, ace designee, counselor Acad. Network II-Nat. Real Estate Exch. Former pres. bd. dirs. Waterford House Condo Assn., Arlington, Va., 1993—96; bd. dirs. Palace Condominium Assn., Miami, 1999—2002; pres. Am. Fedn. Govt. Employees HUD Union Local 1516, 1999—2001; pres. bd. dirs. Costa Brava Condo. Assn., Miami Beach, Fla., 2003—. Avocations: photography, real estate investment, antique and art collection, design work. Home: Apt 1012 11 Island Ave Miami Beach FL 33139-1323 Office: US Dept HUD 909 SE 1st Ave Ste 500 Miami FL 33131-3042 E-mail: michael_h._glogower@hud.gov. *Living different places, doing different things, I have never ceased to be impressed by the resiliance and humanity of my fellow human beings. We should never sell our fellow man short.*

GLOMAN, DAVID J. artist; b. Bryn Mawr, Pa., 1958; Student, Yale U., 1982, MFA, 1986; BFA, Ind. U., 1983. Tchg. asst. Yale U. Sch. Art, 1985-86, Ind. U., Herron Sch. Art, Indpls., 1988-89, Smith Coll., Northampton, Mass., 1990, lectr., 1995-98; tchg. asst. Amherst (Mass.) Coll., 1992-94, 97-98, instr. ASA Studio Art Program, 1993-97. Vis. asst. prof. Hampshire Coll., Amherst, 1994—95. One-man shows include Belleview Gallery, Bloomington, Ind., 1989, Fontbonne Coll., St. Louis, 1991, Northampton Ctr. Arts, 1993, Eli Marsh Gallery Amherst Coll., 1994, Rolly-Michaux Gallery, Boston, 1996, exhibited in group shows at Hudson Walker Gallery, Provincetown, Mass., 1986, East End Gallery, 1987, Provincetown Group Gallery, 1988, Julie Heller Gallery, Provincetown, 1989, 1990, Babcock Galleries, N.Y.C., 1991, Hart Gallery, Northampton, Mass., 1992, Northampton Ctr. Arts, 1992, 1993, Vt. Studio Ctr., Johnson, 1994, The Gallery in Monterey, Mass., 1994, Mead Art Mus., Amherst (Mass.) Coll., 1995, Bowery Gallery, N.Y.C., 1995, Rolly-Michaux Gallery, Boston, 1995, 1996, WM Baczak Fine Arts, Northampton, 1997, Hackett-Freedman Gallery, San Francisco, 1997, Pepper Gallery, Boston, 1997.

GLOMSKI, EDWARD EARL, electronic company executive; b. Royal Oak, Mich., July 21, 1955; s. Edward James and Lorraine Anne Glomski; 1 child from previous marriage, Hannah Michelle; m. Shellee Anita Habig. Grad. with honors, Nat. Inst. of Tech., 1983. Owner The Book Nook, Akron, Ohio, 1999; purchasing mgr. Stellar Pvt. Cable, Akron, 1997—. With USN, 1974-76. Mem. East Ctrl. Ohio Mensa (exec. bd. 1997-99), Intertel (jour. editor 1998—, area. coord. Ohio 1997—). Home: 300 Malacca St Akron OH 44305-3652

GLORIOD, PAUL, architectural firm executive; BA architecture, Univ. of Houston, Houston, Tex., 1976. Sr. project mgr. FKP Architects, Houston, 1985—. Mem.: Nat. Coun. of Architectural Reg. Bd., Am. Coll. of Healthcare Architects (founding mem.), Nat. Fire Protection Assoc. Avocation: 1932 Little Deuce Coupe street rod and a 1976 VW Bug Convert.. Office: FKP 8 Greenway Plaza Houston TX 77046-0899 also: FKP 8144 Walnut Hill Lane, ste 100 Dallas TX 75231-9900*

GLOSBAND, DANIEL MARTIN, lawyer; b. Salem, Mass., July 3, 1944; s. Leon Glosband and Ruth Pauline (Wentworth) Glosband School; m. Merrily Cotton, Dec. 23, 1967; children: Alexander, Gabriel, Oliver. BA, U. Mass., 1966; JD, Cornell, U., 1969. Bar: Mass. 1969, U.S. Dist. Ct. Mass. 1970, U.S. Ct. Appeals (1st cir.) 1971, U.S. Dist. Ct. Conn. 1971, U.S. Dist. Ct. Vt. 1974, U.S. Supreme Ct. 1982. Assoc., then ptnr. firm Widett & Widett, Boston, 1969-75; ptnr. Goldstein & Manello, Boston, 1976-87, Goodwin, Procter LLP, Boston, 1988—. Advisor Am. Law Inst. Transnat. Insolvency Project, 1994—2000. Contbr. numerous articles on bankruptcy to profl. jours. Fellow: Mass. Bar Found., Am. Bar Found., Am. Coll. Bankruptcy (sec. 2001—); mem.: ABA (sect. on corps., chmn. internat. bankruptcy com. 1990—95), Boston Bar Assn. (chmn. bankruptcy com. 1977—80), Mass. Bar Assn. (chmn. bankruptcy com. 1980—83), Internat. Bar Assn. (sect. bus. law, vice chmn. insolvency and creditors rights com. 1997—2000, del. UN Commn. Internat. Trade Law). Democrat. Jewish. Home: 34 Atlantic Ave Swampscott MA 01907-2404 Office: Goodwin Procter LLP Exchange Pl Boston MA 02109-2803 E-mail: dglosband@goodwinprocter.com.

GLOSS, LAWRENCE ROBERT, fundraising executive; b. Colorado Springs, Colo., Oct. 31, 1948; s. Kenneth Edwin and Clara U. Gloss; children: Alexander Edwin, Carolyn Claire. BA, U. Denver, 1970. Vol. Peace Corps, Colombia and Peru, 1970-75; dir. natl. congress on volunteerism and citizenship NCVA, Washington, 1975-76; dir. devel. Vis. Nurses Assn., Washington, 1976-77; devel. cons. Am. Lung Assn., Washington and N.Y.C., 1977-78; exec. dir. Colo. Conservation Fund, Denver, Colo., 1978-79; dir. devel. Rose Med. Ctr., Denver, 1985-86; exec. dir. Rose Found., Denver, 1979-86; sr. campaign dir. J. Panas, Young and Ptnrs., San Francisco, 1986-88; pres. Gloss and Co., Denver, 1988—. Adv. coun. non-profit mgmt. Metro State Coll., Denver, 1994; cons. Native Am. Rights Fund, Boulder, Colo., Arts at the Sta., Denver, 1994, Up With People, 1995-96, Emily Griffith Ctr. Found., 1995-96, Colo. CASA, 1998-99, Women of the West Mus., 1998, 2000, Sister Cities-Denver and Kumming, China, 1999, sec. bd. Ctr. for Tax Policy. Guest spkr. Tech. Assistance Ctr., Denver, 1992—94; bd. dirs. Alzheimer's and Related Disorders Assn., Denver, 1985—86, Woman's Sch. Network, Denver, 1984—85, Colo. PTA, Englewood, 1991—92; active Emily Griffith Ctr. Found., 1997, U. Denver, Episcopal Ministries U. Colo., Boulder, 1996—2001, Colo. Pub. Expenditure Coun., 1998—, Columbine H.S. Permanent Meml., Srs. Resource Ctr., 1998—99, Am. Humane Assn., 1998—99, Colo. Mil. History Mus., 2001—, Noah's Ark Pk., 2001—, Humane Soc. Pagosa Springs, 2001—; mem. BMH-BJ Congregation, 1999—2003, sec., 2001. Mem.: Acad. Charter Schs., Assn. Profl. Rschrs. Advancement, Assn. Healthcare Philanthropy (region XII 1993—94), Am. Prospect Rsch. Assn., Nat. Com. on Planned Giving, Assn. Fund-Raising Profls., Assn. Profl. Fundraisers (Colo. chpt. 1992—94, bd. dirs.), Am. Lung Assn. of Colo., Colo. Planned Giving Roundtable, Women of the West Mus., Englewood Hist. Soc., Arapahoe Ho., Nat. Assn. Mus. Exhibitors, Soccer Ofcls. Assn. Colo., Colo. State Youth Soccer Assn., U.S. Soccer Assn., Rotary Club of Denver. Lutheran. Avocations: dressage, art, soccer. Office: Gloss and Co 2755 S Locust St Ste 113 Denver CO 80222-7131 E-mail: larrygloss@msn.com.

GLOSSER, JEFFREY MARK, lawyer; b. 1936; married; 1 child. BS in Econs. with distinction, U. Pa., 1958; LLB, Harvard U., 1961. Bar: D.C. 1962. Law clk. U.S. Ct. Claims, 1963-64; assoc. Emery & Wood, Washington, 1965-69; ptnr. Jeffrey M. Glosser, P.C., Washington, 1969-86, Whiteford, Taylor & Preston, Washington, 1987-95. Instr. CLE courses sponsored by D.C. Bar, 1976-95. Mem. ABA (adminstrv. law sect., various coms.), D.C. Bar Assn. (numerous coms.), Fed. Bar Assn. (U.S. Claims Ct. com.), Fed. Cir. Bar Assn. (rules com. 1985-95). E-mail: glosser@mac.com.

GLOSSER, WILLIAM LOUIS, lawyer; b. Johnstown, Pa., Aug. 30, 1929; s. Saul I. and Eva (Hurwitz) G.; m. Patricia Freeman, Feb. 5, 1932; children: Alix Paul, Jill P., Jonathan. BS, Temple U., 1951; LLB, U. Pa., 1954. Bar: Pa. 1954, Fla. 1956, U.S. Dist. Ct. (we. dist.) Pa. 1956, U.S. Dist. Ct. (so. dist.) Fla. 1957. Assoc. Broad and Cassel, Miami Beach, Fla., 1956-57; sole practice Coral Gables, Fla., 1957-61, Johnstown, 1962—. Magistrate judge U.S. Dist. Ct. (we. dist.) Pa., 1972-93; corp. sec., dir. Glosser Bros., Inc., Johnstown, 1969-85; of counsel Smorto, Persio, Webb & McGill, Johnstown, 1988—. Bd. dirs. Lee Hosp., Johnstown, Greater Johnstown (Pa.) Cmty. Found., ret.; mem. Johnstown adv. coun. Pa. Human Rels. Commn.; pres. United Jewish Fedn. Johnstown, 1970-75, 2000—; chmn. fund drive United Way, 1985, pres., 1987-88; bd. dirs. Mt. Aloysius Coll., 1980-84, Cmty. Found. Greater Johnstown, Pa., 1990—. With U.S. Army, 1954-56. Mem. Pa. Bar Assn., Fla. Bar Assn., Cambria County Bar Assn., Greater Johnstown C. of C. (pres. 1985), Rotary (pres. 1990), B'nai B'rith (pres. lodge 1965-67, 83-84). Jewish. Home: 521 Luzerne St Johnstown PA 15905-2324 Office: Smorto Persio Webb & McGill 430 Main St Johnstown PA 15901-1823

GLOSSINGER, DONALD LEO, library director; s. Marshall Hamilton and Betty Jean Vanderpool; m. Caryn V. Tolchinsky, Nov. 28, 1981; 1 child, Micah Lee. B in Gen. Studies with distinction, Ind. U., Gary, 1990; MLS, Ind. U., Bloomington, 1993. Cert. profl. mgr., adminstrv. mgr., Libr. I Ind. State Libr., Indpls. Congl. aide U.S. Rep. Katie Hall, Gary, Ind., 1983—85; employer rep. Kankakee Valley Job Tng. Program, LaPorte, Ind., 1985—90; supr. Michigan City Pub. Libr., 1990—93, dept. head, 1993—96, asst. dir., 1996—2000, dir., 2001—. Mem.: Mensa, DFC Soc. (assoc.). Home: 7255 W Peppel Pky Michigan City IN 46360-9171 Office: Michigan City Pub Libr 100 E 4th St Michigan City IN 46360-9171 Office Fax: 219-873-3475. E-mail: dgloss@mclib.org.

GLOTFELTY, JOHN WILLIAM, ophthalmologist; b. Jefferson County, Iowa, Sept. 28, 1928; s. Floyd and Susan (Boley) G.; m. Bonnie Jeanne Dunnuck, May 27, 1949; children: John David, Robert, Jeanne, Michael, William Randolph, Edward Neil. BS, Parsons Coll., Fairfield, Iowa, 1945-48; postgrad., U. Iowa, 1948-49; MD, U. Louisville, 1953. Mem. Fla. Bd. Medicine, 1991—, 1st vice chmn., 1997. Intern USPHS, Norfolk, Va., 1953-54, acting chief ears, eyes, nose and throat, 1954-55, chief ears, eyes, nose and throat, 1960-61, resident in ears, eyes, nose and throat Staten Island, N.Y., 1955-60; pvt. practice Lakeland, Fla., 1961—, Lakeland Eye Clinic. Attending physician Lakeland Regional Med. Ctr.; mem. staff Lakeland Gen. Hosp., 1961—, mem. exec. com. 1975-77, pres. staff, 1976-77; instr. Polk Gen. Hosp., U. Fla., U. Guadalajara. Active Rsch. to Prevent Blindness; mem. med. adv. com. Fla. Divsn. Vocat. Rehab., chmn. membership com.; mem. adv. com. Sunshine State Workers for Blind; dist. chmn. Fla. Polit. Action Com., v.p., 1975-76, pres., 1977, bd. dirs., 1977-88, nat. key contact physician, state key contact physician; mem. med. adv. com. Fla. Soc. to Prevent Blindness; advisor eye screening program Polk County Sch. Bd., 1975-78; v.p. 10th jud.-med. legal com. Recipient Med. Achievement award Sunshine State Assn. for the Blind, 1975, Fla. Svc. Ribbon, N.G., 1987, Army Achievement medal, 1987, Guardsman award, 1988. Mem. AMA, Fla. State Med. Assn. (ho. dels. 1964—, reference com., chmn. credentials com., consulting editor jour., adv. com. Fla. State Sch. Health Coun., state key contact physician, nat. key contact physician), Fla. Soc. Ophthal. (program chmn., legis. chmn., pres.-elect 1974-75, pres. 1975-76, exec. com. 1970-76, com. on ethics, state key contact physician), Fla. Bd. Medicine, Tampa Bay Ophthal. Soc. (charter, pres. 1982-84), Polk County Med. Assn. (editor bull. 1964-93, exec. com. 1964-87, pres.-elect, pres., trustee 1972-77, 87-92, com. profl. malpractice rev., legis. com., state and nat. key contact physician), Kiwanis (bd. dirs., chmn. pub. and bus. affairs com.), Alpha Omega Alpha, Phi Beta Phi. Home: 2233 Nottingham Rd Lakeland FL 33803-3523 Office: 1247 Lakeland Hills Blvd Lakeland FL 33805

GLOTTA, RONALD DELON, lawyer; b. Lajunta, Colo., Mar. 18, 1941; s. John Wallace and Marian (Kisner) G.; m. Sharon S. Glotta, Aug. 27, 1961 (div. Mar. 1986); children: Holly Ann, Jeffrey Delon; m. Marietta Lynn Baba, June 23, 1990 (div. Oct. 1998). BA with honors, U. Kans., 1963; JD, U. Mich., 1966. Bar: Mich. 1966. Atty. Marcus, McCroskey, Libner, Reamon, Williams & Dilley, Muskegon, Mich., 1966-68; ptnr. Philo, Maki, Moore, Pitts, Ravitz, Glotta, Cockrel & Robb, Detroit, 1968-70; prin. Glotta & Adelman, Detroit, 1970-85, Glotta, Rawlings & Skutt, Detroit, 1985-96, Glotta, Skutt & Assts, Detroit, 1996—. Mem. Phi Beta Kappa. Home: 2065 Hyde Park Rd Detroit MI 48207-3885 E-mail: rglotta@winstarmail.com.

GLOTZBACH, GEORGE LINUS, retired insurance executive; b. New Ulm, Minn., Aug. 4, 1931; s. Linus Charles and Lucille Holly (Kuske) G.; m. Annette Terese Meyer, Aug. 22, 1959; children: Karl, Paul, Mary, Anne. BBA, U. Minn., 1953. Cert. Life Underwriters Tng. Coun. Group sales promotion mgr. Minn. Mut. Life, St. Paul, 1958-64; exec. v.p., pres. Paul Burke and Assocs. Inc., Mpls., 1965-76; exec. v.p. Trust Life Ins. Co. Am., Mpls., 1978-79; vice chmn., CEO Benefacts, Inc., Balt., 1979-83; v.p. Alexander & Alexander Inc., Balt., 1984-89; ret., 1989. Pres. Pilots Internat. Assn., Mpls., 1965-76; cons., Santa Fe, N.Mex., 1994—. Prodr. video: The Glotzbach Family from Saxony to Minnesota, A Genealogy and History 1746-1997, 1998 (Telly award 1999). Alternate del. Dem. Nat. Conv., Atlantic City, N.J., 1964; bd. dirs. Wildlife Forever, 1989-95; pres. Newcomers of Santa Fe, 1997; participant Nat. Sr. Games Assn., Orlando, Fla., 1999; observer Nat. Weather Svc. Capt. USAF, 1954-57. Recipient Newest DXer award Adventist World Radio, 1999. Mem. Nat. Geneal. Soc., N.Am. Shortwave Assn., Cath. League for Religious and Civil Rights, Jr. Pioneers of New Ulm, Eldorado Cmty. Improvement Assn., Phi Sigma Kappa (founders award 1991, bd. dirs. found. 1989-95). Roman Catholic. Avocations: cycling, shortwave radio, germanic studies, genealogy, art history research. Home: 5 Herrada Ct Santa Fe NM 87508

GLOTZBACH, PHILIP A. academic administrator; m. Marie B Glotzbach; children: Jason, Elizabeth. BA summa cum laude, U. Notre Dame, 1972; PhD, Yale U., 1979. Assoc. prof. to chair of Philosophy dept. to chair of the faculty sen. Denison U., Granville, Ohio, 1977—92; dean of coll. of arts then v.p. for academic affairs U. of Redlands, 1992—2003; pres. Skidmore Coll., 2003—. Mem.: Phi Beta Kappa. Office: Skidmore Coll 815 N Broadway Saratoga Springs NY 12866

GLOVER, ALBERT DOWNING, retired veterinarian; b. Newark, Mo., Dec. 4, 1907; s. Albert D. and Mattie O. (Downing) G.; m. Mildred Elva Haselwood; children: Allen, Gary, Janet. BS in Agr., U. Mo., 1932; DVM, Colo. State Coll., 1936. Former chmn. City Coun., Canton, Mo., other civic activities. Mem. Mo. VMA (pres. 1951, legis. commn.), AVMA (v.p. 1952), Mo. Vet. Examining Bd., Am. Legion (past comdr.), Shriners, others. Home: 806 Lewis St Canton MO 63435-1449

GLOVER, CLIFFORD CLARKE, retired construction company executive; b. Newnan, Ga., May 15, 1913; s. Howard Clarke and Fannie Virginia (Jones) G.; m. Louise Liles, Jan. 16, 1937; children: Edmund Cook, Nancy Liles Glover Kennedy, Virginia Johnston Glover Lee, Laura Clarke Glover Thatcher. BCE, U. N.C., 1934. With Batson-Cook Co., West Point, Ga., 1934-94; ret., 1994. Mem. West Point Sch. Bd., 1951-69, chmn., 1964-68; chmn. West Point Planning Bd., 1964-2000; trustee LaGrange Coll.; pres. George H. Lanier council Boy Scouts Am., 1977-78, dir. Southeast regional bd., 1987, recipient Silver Antelope award, 1992; bd. dirs. Joint Tech. Ga. Devel. Fund, 1987. Served with USNR, 1945-46. Recipient Silver Beaver award Boy Scouts Am., Silver Antelope award Boy Scouts Am.; Presdl. award George H. Lanier Coun. Boy Scouts Am., Disting. Citizen's award, 1988; Award of Merit Greater Valley C. of C., 1984; Golden Hammer award Profl. Constrn. Estimators Assn. Am., 1988; fellow La Grange Coll. Mem. Assoc. Gen. Contractors (past pres. Ga. br., Skill, Integrity and Responsibility award 1991) Methodist (ofcl. bd.). Clubs: Rotary (Paul Harris fellow); Capital City (Atlanta); Riverside (West Point). Office: Batson-Cook Co PO Box 151 West Point GA 31833-0151 E-mail: glover@batson-cook-wp.com.

LOVER, DOUGLAS DENNIS, obstetrics, gynecology and pharmacology ucator; b. Rowlesburg, W.Va., Feb. 7, 1929; s. Douglas and Iva (Hughes) G.; Barbara Anne Brady, Sept. 6, 1958; children: Joseph, William, Donald, offrey, Robert. BS in Pharmacy, W.Va. U., 1951, BS in Medicine, 1959; MD, ory U., 1961. Diplomate Am. Bd. Ob-gyn. Intern Grady Meml. Hosp., nta, 1961-62, resident, 1962-65; pvt. practice, Marietta, Ga., 1965-82; prof. ob/gyn. Marshall U. Sch. Medicine, Huntington, W.Va, 1982-87, W.Va. U., Morgantown, 1987—, prof. Sch. Pharmacy, 1987—. Vis. prof. Zhejiang Med. U., Hangzhou, People's Republic of China, 1993; operator 4 rural obstet. outreach clinics for disadvantaged pregnant women; mem. Consortium on Devel. and Reproductive Health Editor: Current Therapy in Obstetrics, 1988; mem. editl. bd. Gynecologic and Obstet. Investigation, Obstetrics and Gynecology; contbr. articles to profl. jours.; rschr. in placental metabolism and pharmacokinetics of drugs during pregnancy; patentee in field. Mem. U.S. Pharmacopeial Convention, Inc., 1990-; mem. gen. revision com., 1990-2000, chmn. ob-gyn adv. panel, 1990-2000, mem. expert com. on nomenclature and labeling, 1990-. Served to 1st lt. AUS, 1952-53, Korea. Decorated Bronze Star, Purple Heart; recipient Outstanding Svc. award W.Va. U., 1972, 87, Outstanding Alumnus award W.Va. U. Sch. Pharmacy, 1982, James H. Beal award W.Va. Pharmacists Assn., 1989. Fellow Am. Coll. Ob-Gyn., Am. Soc. Reproductive Medicine (co-chair sessions mgmt. com. 1990—, chair registrations com. 1992-98), Internat. Infectious Diseases Soc. for Ob-Gyn. (mem. nat. steering com.), Masons (32d deg.), Sigma Xi, Phi Delta Theta (chpt. advisor 1988-2000), Phi Chi, Phi Lambda Sigma. Republican. Presbyterian. Avocation: military history. Home: 5 Maple Ave Morgantown WV 26501-6542 Office: Dept Ob/Gyn WVa U Morgantown WV 26506 E-mail: dglover2@wvu.edu.

GLOVER, DOUGLAS HERSCHEL, writer, educator, editor; b. Simcoe, Ont., Can., Nov. 14, 1948; s. Murray Glover and Jean Ross; children: Jacob, Jonah. BA, York U., Toronto, 1969; MLitt, U. Edinburgh, 1971; MFA, U. Iowa, 1982. Lectr. philosophy U. New Brunswick, Saint John, Can., 1971-72, writer in residence Fredericton, 1987-88, U. Lethbridge, Alberta, Canada, 1988, N.Y. State Writers Inst., U. Albany SUNY, 1992-94; vis. prof. English Colgate U., Hamilton, N.Y., 1995; lectr. English U. Albany, SUNY, 1996-2000; vis. writer in residence Skidmore Coll., Saratoga Springs, N.Y., 1998-2000; faculty mem. Vermont Coll., Montpelier, 1994—. Vis. prof. English U. Albany, SUNY, 2000-01; host, prodr. The Book Show Sta. WAMC-FM, Albany, 1994-96. Author: The Mad River, 1981, Precious, 1984, Dog Attemps to Drown Man in Saskatoon, 1985, The South Will Rise at Noon, 1989, A Guide to Animal Behaviour, 1991, The Life and Times of Captain N, 1993, Notes Home from a Prodigal Son, 1999, 16 Categories of Desire, 2000, Bad News of the Heart, 2003, Elle, 2003; editor: Best Canadian Stories, 1996—, Coming Attractions, 1990-95. Recipient Gold medal Can. Nat. mag. awards 1990, 20 Kilometre Road Race Championship, Can. Amateur Athletic Union, 1979; fellowship N.Y. Found. for the Arts, 1994; Arts grantee Can. Coun., others. Mem. The Writers Union of Can., The Author's Guild. E-mail: DHGlover@aol.com.

GLOVER, DURANT MURRELL, lawyer; b. Wilmington, N.C., Mar. 6, 1951; s. Murrell Kelso and Erma Elizabeth (Williams) G.; m. Carol Ann Marquett, Dec. 16, 1978. AB, Duke U., 1973; JD with honors, U. N.C., 1976. Bar: N.C. 1976, U.S. Dist. Ct. (mid. dist.) N.C. 1976, U.S. Ct. Appeals (4th cir.) 1977, U.S. Supreme Ct. 1980. Assoc. Frassineti & Shaw, Greensboro, N.C., 1976-77; ptnr. Frassineti & Glover, Greensboro, 1977—. Mem., counsel Tarheel Triad Girl Scout Council Inc., Colfax, N.C., 1980-98. Mem. N.C. Bar Assn., Greensboro Bar Assn. (editor Greensboro Bar News 1983-87, bd. dirs. 1987-89), Order of Coif. Republican. Presbyterian. Home: 405 Staunton Dr Greensboro NC 27410-6070 Office: Frassineti & Glover PO Box 1799 Greensboro NC 27402-1799 E-mail: dmglover@bellsouth.net.

GLOVER, ERYN M. music educator; b. Olney, Ill., Apr. 27, 1975; d. David Kent and Paula Jean Glover. MusB, Ill. State U., 1998; postgrad., So. Ill. U., 2002—. Cert. cert. music therapist. Music therapist Tenet Hosps., St. Louis, 1998—99, Cedar Ridge Healthcare Ctr., Lebanon, Ill., 1999—2001; Ill. Outreach coord. Alzheimer's Assn., St. Louis, 2001—02; prof. McKendree Coll., Lebanon, Ill.; grad. asst., keyboard devel. instr. So. Ill. U., Edwardsville, 2002—. Pvt. piano instr., Edwardsville, 1998—. Com. chair Memory Walk Alzheimer's Assn., Collinsville, Ill., 2000—02. Mem.: Music Tchrs. Nat. Assn.; Gateway Arch (East chpt.). Republican. Roman Catholic. Avocations: playing board games, music, gardening, softball, sports.

GLOVER, FRED WILLIAM, artificial intelligence and optimization research director, educator; b. Kansas City, Mo., Mar. 8, 1937; s. William Cain and Mary Ruth (Baxter) G.; m. Diane Tatham, June 4, 1988; 1 child, Lauren Glover; children from previous marriage: Dana Reynolds, Paul Glover. BBA, U. Mo., 1960; PhD, Carnegie-Mellon U., 1965. Asst. prof. U. Calif., Berkeley, 1965-66; assoc. prof. U. Tex., Austin, 1966-69; prof. U. Minn., Mpls., 1969-70; John King prof. U. Colo., Boulder, 1970-87, US West chair in sys. sci., 1987-98, Media One chair in sys. sci., 1998—; rsch. dir. Artificial Intelligence Ctr., Boulder, 1984-90; disting. rschr. Hearin Ctr. for Enterprise Sci., U. Miss., 2000—. Invited disting. lectr. Swiss Fed. Inst. Tech., Lausaunne, 1990-91, 2002-03, IMAG Labs., U. Grenoble, France, 1991, U. Canterbury, New Zealand, 1997, U. Paris, 1998; vis. Regents Chair in Engring., U. Tex., Austin, 1989; cons. U.S. Congress, 1984, Nat. Bur. Stds., 1986, also over 70 U.S. corps. and govt. agys., 1965—; lectr. NATO, France, Italy, Germany, Denmark, 1970, 78, 80, 82, 89, Inst. Decision Scis., 1984; bd. dirs. Heuristec, Boulder, OptTek, Boulder, Decision Analysis, Rsch. & Computation, Austin, 1971-83; head, rsch. assoc. Global Optimization Space Contrn. Ctr., Boulder, 1988—; rsch. prin. U. Colo.-U.S. West Joint Rsch. Initiative, 1990—; prin. investigator Air Force Office Sci. Rsch., Office Naval Rsch., 1990—; invited rsch. scholar U. B.C., 1994. Author: Netform Decision Models, 1983 (DIS award 1984), Tabu Search I, 1989, Tabu Search II, 1990, Tabu Search (book and special vols.) 1993, 97, 98, 2003, Ghost Image Processes for Neural Networks, 1993, Linkages with Artificial Intelligence, 1990, Network Models in Optimization and Their Application in Practice, 1992, Handbook of Metaheuristics, 2003, others; contbr. over 300 articles on math. optimization and artificial intelligence to profl. jours. Participant Host Vis. Exchange, Nat. Acad. Scis., 1981; mem. grants com. Queen Elizabeth II fellowships, Australia and U.S., 1984; mem. U.S. nat. adv. bd. Univ. Rsch. Initiative on Combinatorial Optimization. Recipient Internat. Achievement award Inst. Mgmt. Scis., 1982, Energy Rsch. award Energy Rsch. Inst., 1983, Univ. Disting. Rsch. Lectr. award U. Colo., 1988, Rsch. Excellence prize Ops. Rsch. Soc., 1989, Nat. Best Theoretical/Empirical Rsch. Paper award Decision Scis. Inst., 1993, Computer Sci. Rsch. Excellence award Ops. Rsch. Soc. Am., 1994, Nat. Rsch. Excellence award Comp. Sci. Ops. Rsch. Soc., 1994, John Von Neumann Theory award INFORMS, 1998; named first U.S. West Disting. fellow, 1987. Fellow: AAAS, ICC Inst., Am. Assn. Collegiate Schs. Bus., Am. Inst. Decision Scis. (lectr. 1984, Outstanding Achievement award 1984); mem.: NAE, Alpha Iota Delta. Achievements include design of software systems used throughout the U.S. and abroad. Office: U Colo Coll Bus Box 419 Boulder CO 80309-0419

GLOVER, GENE ALAN, banking risk analyst; b. Jacksonville, Fla., Sept. 10, 1959; s. John Eugene Glover and Juanita Courtoy; m. Sandra Gail Pelchat, Sept. 11, 1956; 1 child, Matthias Gene. B of Econs., U. of North Fla., Jacksonville, 1993; BD, Blue Ridge Bible Inst., Valdese, N.C., 2002. Bass guitarist Johnny Van Zant Band, Jacksonville, Fla., 1975—78; loan officer U.S. Life Credit, Jacksonville, 1980—81, ITT Aetna Fin. Corp., Jacksonville, 1981—83; teen emergency shelter dir., social worker Bapt. Home for Children, Jacksonville, 1984—89; v.p. risk analyst Bank of Am., Jacksonville, 1989—. Team capt. Bank of Am. Vol. Math Tutors, Jacksonville, 2002—. Author: (poetry, music, lyrics) The Collective Works of Gene Glover. Bd. dirs. Citizens Against Pornagraphy, Jacksonville, 1991—93. Cpl. USMCR, 1979—82. Recipient Citizenship award, DAR, 1971, IMPACT award, NationsBank Corp. Risk Mgmt., 1998, Top 10 % - U.S. 15K Distance Championship, USA Running Circuit (USARC), 1998—99, Ortega 5 Mile River Run Race - 2nd Pl. Age Group award, Jacksonville Track Club, 1999. Mem.: Omicron Delta Epsilon. Conservative. Baptist. Avocations: piano, guitar, running, reading. Home: 8825 Chambore Dr Jacksonville FL 32256 Office: Bank of Am 9000 Southside Blvd Jacksonville FL 32256 Personal E-mail: genechord@juno.com.

GLOVER, JANET BRIGGS, artist; b. Allahabad, India, June 22, 1919; came to U.S., 1924; d. George Weston and Mary Ames (Hart) Briggs; m. Alan Marsh Glover, Feb. 5, 1949; children: Keith Terrot, John Carroll, Beth Marsh Glover Wittig. BA, Bennington Coll., 1943; postgrad., New Sch. Social Rsch., 1969-70. Artist, draftsman Chartmakers, Inc., N.Y.C., 1943-45; apprentice to Oscar Ogg Book of Month Club, N.Y.C., 1946; 2d grade tchr. Hartridge Sch., Plainfield, N.J., 1947-48, Country Day Sch., Lancaster, Pa., 1948-49; chmn. art dept. Women's Club Chatham, N.J., 1964-65, lectr. art, 1981-86; publicity chmn. N.J. Ctr. Visual Arts, Summit, 1980-81. One-man shows include Present Day Club, Princeton, N.J., 1967, Gallery 9 Upstairs, Chatham, 1978; group shows include Key Gallery, N.Y.C., 1980; contbg. editor N.J. Music and Arts Mag., 1970-71; art critic Madison Eagle, 1975-78. Recipient 1st prize Morris County Art Assn., 1966, Princeton Art Assn., 1969, Cmty. Art Assn., 1980. Mem. Chatham Twp. Art League (co-founder, 1st pres. 1988-90, editor Artist's Album 1993—, editor newsletter, 1996—), Drew U. Art Assn. (membership chmn. 1990-94, mem. directory illustrated 2000—). Democrat. Unitarian Universalist. Avocations: poetry, music. Home: 30 Oak Hill Rd Chatham NJ 07928-1552

GLOVER, JERE WALTON, lawyer; b. Brownsville, Tenn., June 20, 1944; s. William Lloyd and Betty Ruth (Shropshire) G.; m. Doris Ann Henderson, Mar. 30, 1968. BS, Memphis State U., 1966, JD, 1969; LLM, George Washington U., 1972. Bar: Tenn. 1969, Md. 1981, D.C. 1970. Trial atty. FTC, Washington, 1968-75; dir. legal div. Consumer Product Safety Commn., Washington, 1975-77; counsel small bus. com. Ho. of Reps., Washington, 1978; dep. chief counsel SBA, Washington, 1981, chief counsel advocacy, 1994-2001; pvt. practice Washington, 1981-94; counsel Senate Small Bus. Com., Washington, 2002—. Pres. Met. Lithotripsy Ctr., Inc., Washington, 1987-94; v.p. Scan Am., Inc., Washington, 1986-94. Mem. Md. Bar Assn., D.C. Bar Assn., Tenn. Bar Assn., Alliance for Affordable Health Care (pres. 1991-94), Small Bus. Legis. Coun. (bd. dirs. 1981-87). Democrat. Avocation: sailing. Home: 1005 York Ln Annapolis MD 21403-4222 Office: 923 Fifteenth St NW Washington DC 20005 E-mail: jereglover@brand-frulla.com.

GLOVER, JOHN, actor; b. Salisbury, Md., Aug. 7, 1944; s. John S. and Cade (Mullins) G. Student, Towson State Coll. Appeared in plays Look Homeward Angel, 1963, A Scent of Flowers, 1969, Subject to Fit, 1971, House of Blue Leaves, 1971, The Great God Brown, 1972, Don Juan, 1972, The Selling of the President, 1972, The Visit, 1973, Chemin de Fer, 1973, Holiday, 1973, Rebel Women, 1976, The Importance of Being Earnest, 1977, Treats, 1977, A Man for All Seasons, 1979, Frankenstein, 1981, Hedda Gabler, 1981, Booth, 1982, The Doctor's Delemma, 1982, A Doll's House, 1982, Whodonnit, 1982-83, Criminal Minds, 1984, Design for Living, 1984, Linda Her and the Fairy Garden, 1984, Digby, 1985, Henceforward, 1991, Love! Valour! Compassion!, 1994 (Tony award Featured Actor in a Play, 1995); films include Shamus, 1972, Annie Hall, 1977, Julia, 1977, Somebody Killed Her Husband, 1978, The Last Embrace, 1979, American Success Company, 1979, Mountain Men, 1980, Melvin and Howard, 1980, Brubaker, 1980, The Incredible Shrinking Woman, 1981, A Little Sex, 1982, The Evil That Men Do, 1984, A Flash of Green, 1985, White Nights, 1985, Willy/Milly, 1985, My Sister's Keeper, 1986, 52 Pick-up, 1986, Masquerade, 1988, A Killing Affair, 1988, Rocket Gibraltar, 1988, The Chocolate War, 1988, Scrooged, 1988, Meet the Hollowheads, 1989, Gremlins 2: The New Batch, 1990, Robocop 2, 1990, Dora Was Dysfunctional, 1993, Ed and His Dead Mother, 1993; TV movies include The Face of Rage, 1983, Ernie Kovacs: Between the Laughter, 1984, An Early Frost, 1985, Moving Target, 1988, Hot Paint, 1988, David, 1988, The Traveling Man, 1989, Twist of Fate, 1989, Breaking Point, 1989, El Diablo, 1990, What Ever Happened to Baby Jane?, 1991, Dead on the Money, 1991, Drug Wars: The Cocaine Cartel, 1992, Majority Rule, 1992, Assault at West Point, 1994, Night of The Running Man, 1995, In the Mouth of Madness, 1995, Schemes, 1995, Batman & Robin, 1997, Love! Valour! Compassion!, 1997, The Broken Giant, 1998, Dead Broke, 1999, Payback, 1999; mini-series include Kennedy, 1983, Rage of Angels, 1983, George Washington, 1984, Nutcracker: Money, Madness and Murder, 1987, Grass Roots, 1992; TV series appearances include (voice) The Adventures of Batman and Robin, 1992, South Beach, 1993, (voice) Batman: Gotham Knights, 1997, Dead Man's Gun, 1997, The Tempest, 1998, Brimstone, 1998, Macbeth in Manhattan, 1999, Dead Broke, 1999, On Edge, 2001, Sex & Violence, 2002, Mid-Century, 2002, Sweet Union, 2003, Tricks, 2003; (TV series) Smallville, 2001. Office: The Gersh Agy care Ken Kaplan 232 N Canon Dr Beverly Hills CA 90210-5302*

GLOVER, JOHN TRAPNELL, real estate executive; b. Newnan, Ga., May 30, 1946; s. Howard Clarke Jr. and Margaret Farmer (Trapnell) G.; m. Sandra Barron, May 27, 1967; children: John Trapnell Jr., Jeffrey Barron. BA with highest honors, Emory U., 1968; JD summa cum laude, U. Ga., 1972; B Civil Law with first class honors, Oxford (Eng.) U., 1973. Assoc. King & Spalding, Atlanta, 1973-78, ptnr., 1979-84; pres. Post Properties, Inc., Atlanta, 1984-2000, vice chmn., 2000—. Bd. dirs. SunTrust Bank. Editor-in-chief Ga. Law Rev., 1971-72. Chmn. Atlanta Symphony Orch., 1994—96; trustee Emory U., Atlanta, 1994—, Robert W. Woodruff Arts Ctr., Inc., Atlanta, 1992—2002, Lovett Sch., Atlanta, 1990—, chair, 1997—2002; bd. councilors Carter Ctr., Atlanta, 1991—. Stipe scholar, 1966-68. Mem. Nat. Realty Com. (vice chmn. 1993-96), Nat. Multi Housing Coun. (bd. dirs. 1990-99), Urban Land Inst., Atlanta C. of C. (bd. dirs. 1990-92), Wilderness Soc. (governing coun. 1993-96), Phi Beta Kappa. Avocations: golf, fly fishing, bird hunting. Office: Post Properties Inc 4401 Northside Pkwy NW Ste 800 Atlanta GA 30327-3093

GLOVER, KAREN E. lawyer; b. Nampa, Idaho, Apr. 14, 1950; d. Gordon Ellsworth and Cora (Frazier) G.; m. Thaddas L. Alston, Aug. 17, 1979; children: Samantha Glover Alston, Evan Glover Alston. AB magna cum laude, Whitman Coll., 1972; JD cum laude, Harvard U., 1975. Bar: Wash. 1975, U.S. Dist. Ct. (we. dist.) Wash. 1975. Assoc. Preston, Thorgrimson Ellis & Holman, Seattle, 1975-80; ptnr. Preston Gates & Ellis LLP, Seattle, 1981—. Bd. dirs. Adaptis, Inc., 2001—. Chmn. bd. dirs. United Way King County, Seattle, 1993-94; trustee Whitman Coll., Walla Walla, Wash., 1998—, King County Libr. Sys., Seattle, 1992-2001. Mem. Wash. State Bar Assn. (corp. and tax sects.), Seattle Pension Roundtable, Columbia Tower Club, Rainier Club. Episcopalian. Office: Preston Gates & Ellis LLP 701 5th Ave Fl 50 Seattle WA 98104-7097

GLOVER, LISA MARIE, transportation consultant; b. Detroit, Oct. 14, 1963; d. Ronald and Denise (Wellons) Glover. BS, Tuskegee U., 1986; MS, Morgan State U., 1988. Cert. Microsoft profl. Summer intern IBM, Charlotte, NC, 1982, GM, Pontiac, Mich., 1983-85, Turner Constrn., Detroit, 1986; grad. intern State of Md., Dept. Transp., Balt., 1987-88; planner Dept. Transp., Detroit, 1988-90, asst. to dir., 1990-91, mgr. Office of Contract Compliance, 1991-93; transp. engr., cons. M2 Internat., Detroit, 1993-94; transportation cons. Trans. Svcs., Inc., 1994-95; asst. venue transp. mgr. Atlanta Com. Olympic Games, 1996; ind. contractor, 1997-2000; staff asst., sta. svcs. Met. Atlanta Rapid Transit Authority, 1998, bus. analyst, info. tech., 1998, rsch. asst., strategic planning, 1999, rsch. analyst, project mgr. transit rsch., 1999-2000; ind. contractor tech. support McDermott Sys., tech. support, 1999; sr. transp. planner Dekalb County Planning Dept., Decatur, Ga., 2000—. Ind. contractor, 1997; spl. events planner Von Creatins, Inc., 1998; rep. trans. coord. com. Dekalb County Atlanta (Ga.) Regional Commn., 2000—; mem. steering com. No. Sub-Area Study Ga. Regional Trans. Authority, 2001—; mem. host com. RAIL-VOLUTION, Atlanta, 2001—03. Corr. sec. Metro Atlanta chpt. Nat. Congress Black Women, 2001—; math. tutor Ednl. Guidance and Tutoring Ctrs., Inc., 1995; nat. nominating bd. Outstanding Young Ams., 1995—96; mem. 14th Congl. Dist. Young Dems., spl. projects com., 1992; mem. Total Praise choir New Birth Missionary Bapt. Ch., Lithonia, Ga., 1997—, co-chair engring. ministry, 1999—2000, vol. registrar Lay Inst. Equipping, 1999—2000. Recipient cert. of Merit, Mayor Coleman A. Young City of Detroit, 1980. Mem.: NAACP (young adults com. 1989—91), NAFE, Women Transp. Seminar (scholarship coord. 1888—2001, bd. dirs. 2003—), Conf. Minority Transp. Ofcls., Assn. Gen. Contractors Am. (pres. 1985—86), Morgan State U. Alumni Assn., Tuskegee Nat. Alumni Assn., Internat. Olympic Family, Morgan State Student Transp. Assn. (sec. 1986—87), Atlanta Regional Leadership Inst., Sigma Lambda Chi (charter), Delta Nu Alpha, Alpha Kappa Alpha (sponsor teen group 1989—95). Democrat. Baptist. Avocations: art, classical/jazz/gospel music, travel, remodeling projects. E-mail: gloveret@msn.com.

GLOVER, NATHANIEL, JR., sheriff; b. Jacksonville, Fla., Mar. 29, 1943; BS, Edward Waters Coll., Jacksonville, 1966; MS, U. North Fla., 1987; grad., FBI Nat. Acad., Quantico, Va.; LLD (hon.), Edward Waters Coll., 1995. With Jacksonville Sheriff's Office, 1966-69, investigator, 1969-74, sgt., 1974-86, leader hostage negotiation team, 1975-86, chief of svcs., 1986-88, dep. dir. police svcs., 1988-91, dir. police svcs., 1991-95, sheriff, 1995—. Participant White House Leadership Conf. on Youth, Drug Use and Violence. Recipient Martin Luther King Humanitarian award Jacksonville Jewish Commn., 1996. Office: Jacksonville Sheriff's Office 501 E Bay St Jacksonville FL 32202-2927

GLOVER, SHEENA, academic administrator; BS, U. So. Miss., 1995, MEd, 1996, specialist in edn., 1998. Instr., chmn. dept. Antonelli Coll., Hattiesburg, Miss., 1996—97; coord. univ. programming and Greek affairs Edinboro (Pa.) U. Pa., 1998—2000; asst. dir. minority student svcs. Ctrl. Mich. U., Mt. Pleasant, 2000—01; dir. student activities ctr. Ga. So. U., Statesboro, 2001—. Grantee, Mich. Career Devel. Ctr., 2000. Mem.: Nat. Assn. Student Pers. Adminstrs., Delta Sigma Theta (mem. cons./advisement adv. bd., pres. 2002—03). Avocations: shopping, travel, reading, music. Office: Ga So U PO Box 8094 Statesboro GA 30460-8094 Fax: 912-486-7359. E-mail: sheenalglover@hotmail.com.

GLOVICZKI, PETER, surgeon; b. Nyiregyhaza, Hungary, May 5, 1948; m. Marta Matray; children: Peter Jr., Julia. Diploma, Benedictine Abbey, Pannonhalma, Hungary, 1966; MD, Semmelweis Med. U., Budapest, Hungary, 1972; postgrad., Mayo Grad. Sch. Medicine, 1981—83. Cert. vascular surgery Am. Bd. Surgery, gen. surgery Am. Bd. Surgery. Intern dept. pathology Semmelweis Med. U., Budapest, 1970—72, resident surg. clinic, 1972—75, resident Inst. Vascular Surgery, 1976—77, fellow vascular surgery Inst. Vascular Surgery, 1977—79, staff mem., 1979—81; resident cardiovasc. surgery Hosp. St. Michel and Hosp. St. Joseph, Paris, 1975—76; sr. assoc. cons. in vascular surgery Mayo Clinic, Rochester, Minn., 1987—89, vice chair divsn. vascular surgery, 1995—2000, chair divsn. vascular surgery, 2000—, dir. Gonda Vascular Ctr., 2002—. Rsch. dir. Mayo Clinic Vascular Surgery, Rochester, 1987—2002; mem., Cheselden vis. prof. St. Thomas's Hosp., London, 1999. Editor: Handbook of Venous Disorders, 1996, Atlas of Endoscopic Perforator Vein Surgery, 1997, Handbook of Venous Disorders, 2001; course dir., editor: CD-ROM Advances and Controversies in the Multidisciplinary Management of Vascular Disease, 1997, editor-in-chief: Perspectives in Vascular Surgery and Endovascular Therapy, 2000—, Outlook in Vascular Surgery and Endovascular Therapy, 2000—, assoc. editor: Internat. Angiology, 1998—, Vascular Surgery, 1998—, mem. editl. bd.: Jour. Vascular Surgery, Annals Vascular Surgery, Jour. Phlebology, Angiology News, Jour. Cardiovasc. Surgery, Giornale Italiano di Chirurgia Vascolare, Clinica Chirurgica e Microchirurgia, Linfologia, Brazilian Vascular Jour., guest editor: Seminars in Vascular Surgery. Fellow: ACS; mem.: Midwest Vascular Surgery Soc. (treas., mem. exec. coun. 2000—), Soc. for Clin. Vascular Surgery (mem. program com. 1995, chair constn. and by-laws com. 1996—, pres.-elect 1998—99, pres. 1999—2000, Allastair Karmody Essay award 1994), Internat. Union Angiology (sec. N.Am. chpt. 1989—94, v.p. N.Am. chpt. 1994—97, 2000—, pres. 2002—, pres.-elect 2000—02), Am. Venous Forum (chmn. membership com. 1994, chmn. com. on issues 1995, councillor at large 1996—, mem. internat. rels. com. 1997, mem. Sigvaris traveling fellowship com. 1997, councillor exec. com. 1997—, chmn. internat. rels. com. 1998, pres. 2002—, mem. ad hoc com., pres. elect 2001—02), Soc. for Vascular Surgery (treas., Edwin Jack Wylie Traveling Fellowship award 1987). Avocation: magic. Office: Mayo Clinic 200 First St SW Rochester MN 55905

GLOVSKY, SUSAN G. L. lawyer; b. Boston, Apr. 16, 1955; d. Leonard B. and Marilyn S. (Shapiro) Loitherstein; m. Steven M. Glovsky, May 25, 1980; 1 child, Lowell Eliott. BS in Chemistry, U. Vt., 1977; JD, Boston U., 1980. Bar: Mass. 1980, Mich. 1980, U.S. Dist. Ct. (ea. dist.) Mich. 1980, U.S. Patent Office 1981, N.Y. 1982, U.S. Dist. Ct. Mass. 1982, U.S. Ct. Appeals (1st cir.) 1982, U.S. Ct. Appeals (fed. cir.) 1991, U.S. Supreme Ct. 1995. Assoc. Levin, Levin, Garvett & Dill, Southfield, Mich., 1980-81, Ladas & Parry, N.Y.C., 1981-82, Dahlen & Gatewood, Boston, 1982-83; ptnr. Dahlen & Glovsky, Boston, 1983-85; pvt. practice Boston and Salem, Mass., 1985-93; of counsel Hamilton, Brook, Smith & Reynolds, Mass., 1993-97, prin., 1998—. Adj. prof. Suffolk U. Law Sch. Mem. ABA, Mass. Bar Assn., Boston Bar Assn., Boston Patent Law Assn. (past pres., chmn. litigation com. 1989-2001), Am. Arbitration Assn. (panel arbitrators 1985—, co-chmn. intellectual property adv. com. 1999—). Jewish. Avocations: swimming, skiing. Home: 36 Shaw Dr Wayland MA 01778-3214 Office: Hamilton Brook Smith & Reynolds 530 Virginia Rd PO Box 9133 Concord MA 01742 E-mail: susan.glovsky@hbsr.com.

GLOWINSKI, ROLAND, mathematics educator; b. Paris, Mar. 9, 1937; s. Nathan and Anna (Cukiernik) G.; m. Angela Rimok, Nov. 3, 1963; children: Anne, Tania. B, Ecole Polytechnique, Paris, 1960; M, Ecole Nationale Supérieure des Télécommunications, Paris, 1963; PhD, U. Paris, 1971. Registered profl. engineer; cert. prof. math. Rsch. engr. Office de Radio et Télévision Françaises, Paris, 1963-68, Institut National de Recherches en Informatique et Automatique, Paris, 1968-70; prof. U. Paris VI, 1970—98, chmn. math dept., 1981-85; Disting. prof. U. Houston, 1985—. Adj. prof. Rice U., Houston, 1986—; Sherman Fairchild Disting. visitor Calif. Inst. Tech., 1988-89; cons. CNET, Paris, 1968-85, Sci. Rsch. Coun., London, 1978-81; bd. dirs. Electricite de France, Paris, 1990-96, U. Leonardo da Vinci, Paris; dir. Centre Européen de Recherches et de Formation Avancée en Calcul Scientifique, Toulouse, France, 1992-94; docent prof. U. Jyvaskyla, Finland, 2001—. Lt. France Signal Corps, 1958-61. Decorated officer Nat. Merit, knight Order of Acad. Palms, knight Order Legion of Honor, France; recipient Cray prize Selected Jury, Paris, 1988, Marcel Dassault prize French Nat. Acad. Scis., 1996, Zienkiewicz Disting. lectureship, 1999, IMA, 1999, others. Mem. Soc. for Indsl. and Applied Math., Am. Math. Soc., French Acad. Scis. (correspondent 1987), Academia Europea (London), French Nat. Acad. Tech. Office: U Houston Dept Math 651 Philip G Hoffman Hall Houston TX 77204-3008 E-mail: roland@math.uh.edu.

GLOYD, LAWRENCE EUGENE, retired diversified manufacturing company executive; b. Milan, Ind., Nov. 5, 1932; s. Oran C. and Ruth (Baylor) G.; m. Delma Lear, Sept. 10, 1955; children: Sheryl, Julia, Susan. BA, Hanover Coll., 1954, Hon D in Bus. Adminstrn., 1994; postgrad., Rockford Coll., 1999. Salesman Shapleigh Hardware, St. Louis, 1956-60, W. Bingham Co., Cleve., 1960-61, Amerock Corp., Rockford, Ill., 1961-68, regional sales mgr., 1968-69, dir. consumer products mktg., 1969-71, dir. merchandising, 1971-72, dir. mktg. and sales, 1972-73, v.p. mktg. and sales, 1973-81, exec. v.p., 1982—86, pres., gen. mgr., 1982-86; v.p. Hardware Products Group, Anchor Hocking Corp., Lancaster, Ohio, 1986—88; pres., COO, CEO CLARCOR, Rockford, Ill., 1988—2000, chmn. bd., CEO, 1988-2000, also bd. dirs., chmn. emeritus, 2000—. Bd. dirs. Amcore Fin. Inc., Rockford, Thomas Industries Inc., Louisville, Woodward Gov. Co., Rockford, Ill., Genyte Thomas Group, Louisville, Group Dekko, Kendalville, Ind.; past. chmn. bd. trustees Rockford Coll.; bd. dirs., past chmn. SwedishAm. Corp. Past chmn. bd. dirs. Coun. of 100; past mem. bd. dirs. Ill. Coun. on Econ. Edn.; nat. bd. dirs. Big Bros./Big Sisters; bd. trustees Hanover (Ind.) Coll. Recipient Master Entrpreneur of Yr. Ill./N.W. Ind. award Ernst & Young, 1999, Lambda Chi Alpha Nat. Order Achievement award, 1999, Alumni Achievement award Hanover Coll., 1994. Mem. Am. Hardware Mfrs. Assn., Ill. Mfrs. Assn., Nat. Assn. Mfrs., Hardware Group Assn., Pres. Assn., Masons. Republican. Office: Clarcor Inc 6367 Sebring Way Loves Park IL 61111

GLOYNA, EARNEST FREDERICK, environmental engineer, educator; b. Vernon, Tex., June 30, 1921; s. Herman Ernst and Johanna Bertha (Reithmayer) G.; m. Agnes Mary Lehman, Feb. 17, 1946; children: David Frederick, Lisa Anna. BS in Civil Engring., Tex. Technol. U., 1946; MS in Civil Engring., U. Tex., 1949; Dr. Engring., Johns Hopkins U., 1953. Registered profl. engr.; diplomate environ. engring. Jr. engr. Tex. Hwy. Dept., 1945-46; office engr. Magnolia Petroleum Co., 1946-47; instr. civil engring. U. Tex., Austin, 1947-49, asst. prof., 1949-53, assoc. prof., 1953-59, prof., 1959-70, Joe J. King prof. engring., 1976—87, dir. Environ. Health Engring. Labs., 1954-70, dir. Ctr. for Rsch. in Water Resources, 1963-73, dean Coll. Engring., 1970-87, dir. Bur. Engring. Rsch., 1970-87, Bettie Margaret Smith chair in environ. engring., 1987-2001, Bettie Margaret Smith chair emeritus in environ. engring., 2001—. Cons. on water and wastewater treatment and water resources, 1947—; dir. Parker Drilling Co., 1978—2001; cons. numerous industries, WHO, World Bank, U.S. Air Force, U.S. Army, U.S. Senate, fgn. cities and govts.; mem., past chmn. sci. adv. bd. EPA; chmn. various coms. NAS, NAE, 1970—85; chmn. Tex. State Bd. Registration Profl. Engrs., 1992—93. Author: Waste Stabilization Ponds, 1971 (also French and Spanish edits), (with Joe O. Ledbetter) Principles of Radiological Health, 1969; Editor: (with W. Wesley Eckenfelder, Jr.) Advances in Water Quality Improvement, 1968, Water Quality Improvement by Physical and Chemical Processes, 1970, (with William S. Butcher) Conflicts in Water Resources Planning, 1972, (with Woodson and Drew) Water Management by Electric Power Industry, 1975, (with Malina and Davis) Ponds as a Wastewater Treatment Alternative, 1976, (with Richard B. McCaslin) Commitment to Excellence, 1990; contbr. 250 articles to profl. jours., seven patents in field. Served with Corps Engrs. AUS, 1942-46, ETO, lt. col. Ret. Named Disting. Engr. Grad. Tex. Tech. U., 1971, Disting. Alumnus, 1973, Disting. Engring. Grad. U. Tex., Austin, 1982, Disting. Alumnus, 1992, Disting. Alumnus Johns Hopkins U., 1993; recipient Joe J. King award U. Tex., Austin, 1982; EPA regional environ. educator award, 1977, Nat. Environ. Devel. award, 1983, Sci. award Nat. Wildlife Fedn., 1986, Order of Henri Pittier, Nat. Conservation medal Venezuela, 1983, Gabriel Narutowicz medal, Republic of Poland, 1993. Fellow: ASCE (Meritorious Paper award Tex. sect. 1968, Award of Honor Tex. sect. 1985, Simon W. Freese Environ. Engr. award 1986, Lifetime Achievement award 2002, OPEL award 2003, Hon. Mem. award); mem.: AIChE, NSPE (past. dir., Steinman medal 1970, NSPE award 1994, NSPE fellow 2000), NAE (past councilman), Am. Acad. Environ. Engrs. (diplomate, past pres., Gordon Maskew Fair award 1982, Hon. Diplomate award 2003), Soc. Mexicana de Aguas (Jack Huppert award), Nat. Acad. Scis. Venezuela (fgn. corr. mem.), Nat. Acad. Engring. Mex. (fgn. corr. mem.), Southwestern Soc. Nuc. Medicine, Tex. Soc. Profl. Engrs. (pres. 1986, Engr. of Yr. award Travis chpt. 1972, Award of Honor 1985, Engr. of Yr. 1994, Dream Team award 2001), Water Environ. Fedn. (past pres., hon. mem., Harrison Prescott Eddy medal 1959, Gordon Maskew Fair awardr 1982, Arthur Bedell award 1991), Am. Soc. for Engring. Edn. (Centennial Medallion award 1993), Assn. Environ. Engring. Profls. (past pres.), Am. Water Works Assn. (life), Headliners, Cosmos Club, Rotary, Tau Beta Pi, Sigma Xi, Omicron Delta Kappa, Pi Epsilon Tau, Phi Kappa Phi, Chi Epsilon. Office: U Tex Coll Engring Dept Austin TX 78712 E-mail: e.gloyna@mail.utexas.edu.

GLUBE, CONSTANCE RACHELLE, Canadian chief justice; b. Ottawa, Ont., Can., Nov. 23, 1931; d. Samuel and Pearl (Slonemsky) Lepofsky; m. Richard Hillard Glube, July 6, 1952 (dec.); children: John B., Erica D. Glube Kolatch, Harry S., B. Joseph. BA, McGill U., Montreal, Can., 1952; LLB, Dalhousie U., Halifax, Can., 1955, LLD (hon.), 1983, Mount St. Vincent U., 1998, St. Mary's U., 2000. Bar: N.S. 1956, created queen's counsel, 1974. Assoc. Kitz, Matheson, Halifax, 1964-66; ptnr. Fitzgerald & Glube, Halifax, 1966-68; sr. solicitor City of Halifax, 1969-74, city mgr., 1974-77; puisne judge Supreme Ct. of N.S., Halifax, 1977-82; chief justice Supreme Ct., Halifax, 1982-98, Nova Scotia, 1998—, Ct. Appeals, 1998—. Vice chair Can. Judges Conf.; interim bd. dirs. Nat. Jud. Ctr., 1987; bd. dirs. Nat. Jud. Inst., 1998—, Can. Inst. Adminstrs. Justice. Contbr. articles and papers to profl. publs. Co-chair Can. Coun. Christians and Jews; bd. dirs. Halifax Heritage Found., 1984—95; chmn. bd. N.S. Archives, 1998—; chair (hon.) N.S. divsn. Can. Mental Health Assn., 1984—98; mem. adv. coun. Order N.S., 2001—. Recipient award of merit City of Halifax, 1977, Frances Fish award, 1997, N.S. Women Lawyers Achievement award. Mem.: Nat. Judicial Inst., Can. Jud. Coun. (adminstrn. of justice com. 1992—94, chmn. edn. com. 1986—88, equality com. 1994—99, jud. benefits com. 1994—99, fin. com. 1999—2002, chmn. edn. com. 2000—, exec. com. 2001—, vice chair jud. conduct com. 2001—), Can. Bar Assn. Jewish. Avocations: swimming, gardening. Home: 5920 Inglewood Dr Halifax NS Canada B3H 1B1

GLUCK, ANDREW LEE, vocational economic analyst, counselor, philosopher; b. N.Y.C., Mar. 21, 1944; s. Irving and Rhoda (Ross) G.; m. Denise Bernard, Mar. 18, 1968; children: Aaron, Max, Sarah. BA in Econs. and Philosophy, U. Fla., 1965; MA in Religion and Edn., Columbia U., 1972, MEd in Counseling Psychology, 1977, EdD in Philosophy and Edn., 1997; MS in Mgmt., NYU, 1990. Cert. rehab. counselor. Counselor Tchrs. Coll., Columbia U., N.Y.C., 1971-72; caseworker N.Y.C. Housing and Devel. Adminstrn., 1972-76; psychologist N.Y. State Dept. Mental Health, Wingdale, 1977-78; vocat. rehab. counselor N.Y. State Edn. Dept., Hempstead, 1978-89; coord. vocat. and ednl. programs N.Y. Assn. for New Ams., N.Y.C., 1989-92; vocat. econ. analyst Vocat. Econ. Inc., Louisville, 1993-97, sr. analyst, 1997—. Empire State Coll., SUNY, NYC, 1998—, lectr. Bromson ORT, 1994-1997, adj. faculty Berkely Coll., 1997-1998, adj. prof. Hofstra U. 1998-2001, ad. prof. St. John's Univ., NYC, 2003-; presenter in field Editl. bd. reviewer The Jour.: Counseling and Values; contbr. articles to profl. jours. Mem. Am. Philos. Assn., Am. Law and Econs. Assn., Nat. Assn. Forensic Econs. Republican. Jewish. Avocations: dogs, horses, travel, bicycling, art, antiques. Home: 284 Route 27B Hudson NY 12534-3919 Office: Vocat Econs Inc 62 William St New York NY 10038-3901 E-mail: andy_gluck@msn.com., andrewg@vocecon.com.

GLUCK, CAROL, history educator; b. Newark, Nov. 12, 1941; d. David E. and Doris S. Newman; m. Peter L. Gluck, May 1, 1966; children: Thomas Edward, William Francis. Student, U. Munich, 1960-61, U. Tokyo, 1972-74; BA, Wellesley Coll., 1962; MA, Columbia U., 1970, PhD, 1977. Asst. prof. Columbia U., N.Y.C., 1975-83, assoc. prof., 1983-86, prof., 1986-88, George Sansom prof. history, 1988—. Vis. rsch. assoc. faculty law Tokyo U., 1978-79, 85-86, 92; vis. prof. Harvard U., Cambridge, Mass., 1991, Inst. Social Sci. Tokyo U., 1993, Ecole des Hautes Etudes en Scis. Sociales, Paris, 1995, 98; fellow Inst. for Advanced Studies in the Behavioral Scis., 1999-2000; publs. bd. Columbia U. Press, N.Y.C., 1991-96; co-dir. project on Asia in the core Curricuulm NEH, N.Y.C., 1987—; Am. adv. com. Japan Found., 1986-96, chair, 1991-96; disting. lectr. N.E. Area Coun., 1988, Japan Soc. for Promotion of Sci., 1989. Author: Japan's Modern Myths, 1985 (Fairbank prize 1986, Trilling award 1987); co-editor: Showa: The Japan of Hirohito, 1992, Asia in Western and World History, 1997; contbr. numerous articles to profl. publs. Mem. Coun. on Fgn. Rels., U.S.-Japan Friendship Commn., 1994—2001; mem. com. on rsch. librs. N.Y. Pub. Libr., 1987—, mem. humanities adv. coun., 1996—. Recipient Fulbright 50th Anniversary Disting. Fellow award, 2002; fellow, Woodrow Wilson Found., Fgn. Area fellow; grantee Fulbright grantee, 1985—86, Japan Found. grantee. Fellow: Am. Acad. Arts and Scis.; mem.: Am. Philos. Soc., Asia Soc. (trustee 1992—98, 2002—), Japan Soc. (bd. dirs. 1990—), Assn. Asian Studies (coun. 1981—84, nominating com. 1985—86, pres. 1996—97, bd. dirs. 1995—99), Am. Hist. Assn. (coun. 1987—90), Phi Beta Kappa. Home: 440 Riverside Dr New York NY 10027-6828 Office: Columbia U East Asian Inst 420 W 118th St New York NY 10027-7213

GLUCK, JEFFREY WILLIAM, electrical engineer; b. Norfolk, Va., July 26, 1960; s. Howard Lawrence and Marlies (Muhlfelder) G.; m. Carrie Ellen Freedman, Feb. 25, 1990; 1 child, Rena Lorraine. BS in Engring., Princeton U., 1982; MS in Elec. and Computer Engring., U. Mass., 1984; PhD, U. Md., 1988; JD, Georgetown U., 2003. Engr. M/A-COM LINKABIT, Inc., Vienna, Va., 1984-85; fellow U.S. Naval Rsch. Lab., Washington, 1985-88; asst. prof. dept. elec. engring. and computer sci. U. Ill., Chgo., 1988-93; dir. comm. sys. rsch. Info. Sys. Labs., Inc., Vienna, Va., 1993-94; patent examiner elec. engring. U.S. Patent and Trademark Office, Arlington, Va., 1994-99; patent agt. Venable LLP, Washington, 1999—2003, atty., 2003—. Reviewer Houghton-Mifflin Co., Inc., N.Y.C., 1989-93; session chair Conf. on Info. Scis. and Sys., Princeton, 1990. Contbr. articles to profl. jours. Travel grantee NATO/NSF, 1986, NSF, 1991, Univ. Rsch. grantee U. Ill., 1990. Mem. IEEE (reviewer jour. and conf. papers 1986-98), ABA, Am. Intellectual Property Assn. Avocations: music, sports. Home: 10813 Meadowhill Rd Silver Spring MD 20901-1531 Office: Venable Baetjer Howard and Civiletti LLP 1200 New York Ave NW Ste 1000 Washington DC 20005-3928 E-mail: jwgluck@venable.com.

GLÜCK, LOUISE ELISABETH, poet, educator; b. N.Y.C., Apr. 22, 1943; d. Daniel and Beatrice (Grosby) G.; m. Charles Hertz (div.); 1 child, Noah Benjamin; m. John Dranow, 1977 (div.). Student, Sarah Lawrence Coll., 1962, Columbia U., 1963-65; LLD, Williams Coll., 1993, Skidmore Coll., 1995, Middlebury, 1996. Vis. poet Goddard Coll., U. N.C., U. Va., U. Iowa; Elliston prof. U. Cin., 1978; vis. faculty Columbia U., 1979; faculty M.F.A. program Goddard Coll., also Warren Wilson Coll., Swannanoa, N.C.; Holloway lectr. U. Calif., Berkeley, 1982; vis. prof. U. Calif.-Davis, 1983; Scott prof. poetry Williams Coll., 1983, faculty, 1984—, Preston Parrish 3d century prof., 1997—; Regents prof. poetry UCLA, 1985-88. Vis. prof. Harvard U., 1995; Hurst prof. poetry Brandeis U., 1996; delivered Phi Beta Kappa poem Harvard U. commencement, 1990; baccalaureate spkr. Williams Coll.; Hopwood lectr. U. Mich.; spl. cons. Libr. of Congress, 2000; judge poets competition Yale U. Press, 2003—. Author: Firstborn, 1968, The House on Marshland, 1975, Descending Figure, 1980, The Triumph of Achilles, 1985, Ararat, 1990, The Wild Iris, 1992 (Pulitzer Prize for poetry 1993), Proofs and Theories (collected essays), 1994, Meadowlands, 1996, Vita Nova, 1999, The Seven Ages, 2001. Grantee Rockefeller Found., Nat. Endowment for Arts, 1969-70, 79-80, 88-89, Guggenheim Found., 1975-76, 87-88, NEA, 1988-89; recipient lit. award Am. Acad. and Inst. Arts and Letters, 1981, award in poetry Nat. Book Critics Cir., 1985, Melville Cane award Poetry Soc. Am., 1986, Sara Teasdale Meml. prize Wellesley Coll., 1986, Bobbitt Natil prize Libr. Congress, 1992, Pulitzer prize, 1993, William Carlos Williams award, 1993, PEN/Martha Albrand award Non-Fiction, 1995, Lannan Found. award in poetry, 1999, New Yorker mag. award, 1999, Ambs. award English Spkg. Union, 1999, 50th Anniversary medal MIT, 2000, Bollingen prize, 2001; named Poet Laureate of Vt., 1994. Fellow Am. Acad. Arts and Scis.; mem. Am. Acad. Arts & Letters, Am. Acad. Poets (chancellor 1999—), Phi Beta Kappa (hon.). Office: Williams Coll Dept Engring Williamstown MA 01267

GLUCKMAN, JACK LOUIS, otolaryngologist, educator, dean; b. Johannesburg, Aug. 15, 1945; s. Samuel V.P. and Martha G.; children: Nick, Kate, Simon, Jonathan. MD, U. Cape Town, 1967. Asst. prof. dept. otology U. Cin., Ohio, 1977, assoc. prof. dept. otology, 1981, prof. dept. otology, 1985; assoc. dean clin. affairs, chief staff U. Cin., Univ. Hosps., Ohio, 1987, chmn. dept. otology, 1991. Mem. Am. Acad. Otolaryngology (pres. 2000-01). Home: 3 Grandin Ln Cincinnati OH 45208-3358 Office: U Cin Med Sci Bldg Cincinnati OH 45267-0001 E-mail: jack.gluckman@uc.edu.

GLUCKSBERG, SAM, psychology educator; b. Montreal, Que., Can., Feb. 6, 1933; came to U.S., 1945; s. Murray and Sonia (Afrin) G.; children: Matthew, Kenneth, Nadia Glucksberg. BS, CCNY, 1956; PhD, NYU, 1960. Instr. NYU, N.Y.C., 1958-60; chair psychology dept. Princeton (N.J.) U., 1974-80, from instr. to prof., 1963—. Cons., Princeton, 1980—. Author: Psychology, 5th edit., 1991; editor Jour. Exptl. Psychology: Gen., 1984-89, Psychological Science, 2000; author 100 sci. articles, book chpts., 3 books. Capt. U.S. Army, 1958-63. Fellow APA (pres. div. exptl. psychology 1988-89), AAAS, Soc. Exptl. Psychologists (sec.-treas. 1987-90), Am. Psychol. Soc. Avocations: music, theater, cooking. Home: 29 Bainbridge St Princeton NJ 08540-3901 Office: Princeton U Dept Psychology Princeton NJ 08544-0001

GLUCKSTEIN, FRITZ PAUL, veterinarian, biomedical information specialist; b. Berlin, Jan. 24, 1927; came to U.S., 1948; s. Georg Jakob and Hedwig Emilie (Heinrich) G.; m. Ethel Gold, July 31, 1955 (dec. Nov. 1993); 1 child, Ruth; m. Maran Ostchega, Nov. 29, 1996. BS, U. Minn., 1953, DVM, 1955; MLS, U. Md., 1984. Diplomate Am. Coll. Vet. Preventive Medicine. Vet. meat insp. U.S. Dept. Agr., South St. Paul, Minn., 1955-56, asst. vet. pathologist Ames, Iowa, 1958-59, vet. analyst Washington, 1959-63; chief microbiology br. Sci. Info. Exchange Smithsonian Instn., Washington, 1963-66; coordinator for vet. affairs Nat. Library of Medicine, Bethesda, Md., 1966-93; biomed. info. cons., 1993—. Mem. coordinating com. for research animal resources NIH, 1982-93; adv. sci. bd. Gorgas Meml. Inst. Tropical Preventive Medicine, Washington, 1967-70; chmn. continuing edn. com. 1989-90. Author: (annotated bibliography) Laboratory Animal Welfare, 1984-93; contbr. chpts. to books. Served to 1st lt. U.S. Army, 1956-58; commd. officer USPHS, 1966-93. Recipient cert. merit U.S. Dept. Agr., 1962 Fellow Royal Soc. Health (London); mem. AVMA, APHA, Assn. Mil. Surgeons of U.S., Am. Assn. Lab. Animal Sci., Am. Soc. Lab. Animal Practitioners, Med. Libr. Assn., Beta Phi Mu. Avocation: music. Home: 11801 Rockville Pike Apt 812 Rockville MD 20852-2723 E-mail: opera.buff@verizon.net.

GLUCKSTERN, ROBERT LEONARD, physics educator; b. Atlantic City, N.J., July 31, 1924; BEE, CCNY, 1944; PhD, MIT, 1948. Asst. prof. physics Yale U., New Haven, Conn., 1950-57, assoc. prof., 1957-64; prof. physics U. Mass., Amherst, 1964-75, head dept., 1964-69, asso. provost, 1969-70, provost, vice chancellor for acad. affairs, 1970-75; prof. physics U. Md., College Park, 1975-97, chancellor, 1975-82, sr. rsch. scientist, 1997—. Vis. prof. U. Tokyo, Japan, 1969; cons. on theory of high energy particle accelerators Brookhaven Nat. Lab., Fermi Nat. Accelerator Lab., Lawrence Berkeley Nat. Lab., Los Alamos Nat. Lab., Stanford Linear Accelerator Ctr. With USNR, 1944-46. AEC fellow U. Calif., Berkeley, 1948-49, Cornell U., Ithaca, N.Y., 1949-50, Yale fellow, 1961-62. Fellow AAAS, Am. Phys. Soc.; mem. SSC (bd. overseers 1990-93), SURA (trustee 1982-98, chmn. bd. trustees 1994-96, high energy physics adv. panel 1990-93), Fedn. Am. Scientists, Am. Assn. Physics Tchrs. Office: U Md Physics Dept College Park MD 20742-0001 E-mail: RLG@physics.umd.edu.

GLUECK, MARY AUDREY, retired psychiatric and mental health nurse; b. Bridgetown, Barbados; arrived in U.S., 1952; d. Hubert and Christina Cumming; m. Stephen G. Glueck (dec.). Grad. sch. nursing, St. Joseph's Mercy Hosp., Georgetown, Guyana; paralegal diploma, Profl. Career Devel. Inst., 2000. RN, Calif. Asst. nursing educator in new employee orientation San Mateo County Gen. Hosp., San Mateo, Calif., also facilitator video insvcs. for nursing staff, tchr. safety and emergency response procedures to staff, ret., 1998. Mem. Mid. Mgrs. Assn., Am. Psychiat. Nurses Assn. Home: 4505 Sandra Ct Union City CA 94587-4853 E-mail: glueck69@msn.com.

GLUECK, MICHAEL WELLS, retired investment analyst, freelance/self-employed editor; b. Cin., Jan. 25, 1938; s. Harry and Lillian Wells G. AB magna cum laude, Kenyon Coll., Gambier, Ohio, 1959; MA with high honors, Columbia U., 1961, postgrad., 1961-65. Asst. portfolio mgr. Met. Life, N.Y.C., 1976-78; dir. investor rels. Echlin Mfg. Co., Branford, Conn., 1979; asst. v.p. Axe Houghton Funds, Tarryton, N.Y., 1980; v.p. Crocker Bank, San Francisco, 1980-85, Bank of Am., San Francisco, 1986-87; asst. v.p., investment analyst Credit Suisse, Zürich, Switzerland, 1989-92, Guyerzeller Bank, Zürich, 1992-94. Author: Living Among the Swiss, 1998. Nat. fellow Woodrow Wilson Found., 1959, N.Y. State Regent's fellow, 1962-63, N.Y. State Coll. Tchg. fellow, 1964. Fellow Assn. Investment Mgmt. and Rsch.; mem. N.Y. Soc. Security Analysts, Security Analysts San Francisco, Boston Security Analysts Soc. Avocations: playing piano, classical music, photography, skiing, hiking.

GLUECK, SYLVIA BLUMENFELD, writer; b. Tulsa, Dec. 23, 1925; d. Maurice and Sina (Turk) Blumenfeld; m. Norton Shushan Glueck, June 15, 1947; children: Nancy Eisen, Milton. BJ, U. Mo., Columbia, 1949. Publicity dir. Sta. WDSU, New Orleans, 1946-47; advt. copywriter Swiftway Direct Mail, New Orleans, 1961; freelance writer New Orleans, San Antonio, 1965—. Author book; contbr. articles to mags. and newspaper features, (Golden Pro award, 1986). Mem.: AAUW, Mensa. Home and Office: PO Box 12051 San Antonio TX 78212-0051

GLUHOVSKY, ILYA, statistician, researcher; b. Moscow, July 26, 1975; arrived in U.S., 1991; s. Alexander Gluhovsky. BS in Math. honors with highest distinction, Purdue U., 1995; PhD in Stats., Stanford U., 1999. Postdoctoral fellow IBM T.J. Watson Rsch. Ctr., Yorktown Heights, NY, 1999—2000; staff rschr. Sun Microsystems Labs., Mountain View, Calif., 2000—. Contbr. rsch. papers to profl. jours. Recipient Arthur Rosenthal scholarship, Purdue U., 1994, 1995; fellow, NSF, 1995—98. Mem.: Phi Beta Kappa, Phi Kappa Phi. Achievements include patents pending for. Home: #332 333 Escuela Ave Mountain View CA 94040 Office: Sun Microsystems Labs MTV29-120 2600 Casey Ave Mountain View CA 94043 E-mail: gluk@eng.sun.com.

GLUSCHENKOV, OLEG, electrical engineer; b. Samara, Russia, July 12, 1970; came to the U.S., 1992; s. Vladimir and Kaleria G. Diploma, Moscow Inst. Physics & Tech., 1992; MSEE, U. Ill., 1997, PhDEE, 2000. Rsch. fellow, asst. Dartmouth Coll., Hanover, N.H., 1992-94; rsch. asst. U. Ill., Champaign-Urbana, 1994-99; mem. devel. staff semiconductor rsch. and devel. ctr. IBM Microelectronics, Hopewell Junction, N.Y., 1999—. Contbr. articles to profl. jours.; patentee in field. Mem. IEEE, Am. Vacuum Soc., Electrochem. Soc. Office: IBM 2070 Rte 52 Z/33A Hopewell Junction NY 12533

GLUSHIEN, MORRIS P. lawyer, arbitrator; b. Bklyn., Oct. 15, 1909; s. Isaac and Minnie (Hoffman) G.; m. Anne Williams, Nov. 18, 1945; children: Minna Taylor, Ruth Wedgwood. AB with honors, Cornell U., 1929, JD with honors, 1931. Bar: N.Y. 1932, U.S. Supreme Ct. 1940. Pvt. practice, Bklyn., 1932-38; mem. faculty Cornell Law Sch., 1938-39, New Sch. for Social Rsch., 1977-78; chief U.S. Supreme Ct. sect., assoc. gen. counsel NLRB, 1939-47; gen. counsel Internat. Ladies Garment Workers Union, AFL-CIO, 1947-72; arbitrator 1972—; spl. master fed. ct., 1976-78. Mem. Nat. Acad. Arbitrators; mem arbitration panels Am. Arbitration Assn., Fed. Mediation and Conciliatio Service, various state and city agys. Editorial bd.: Cornell Law Quar, 1930-3 Contbr. legal periodicals. Bd. dirs. Nat. Legal Aid and Defender Assn., 1954-7 Served with AUS, as cryptanalyst, 1942-45. Mem. ABA (past chmn. labor l sect.), N.Y. State Bar Assn. (labor rels. com.), Assn. of Bar of City of N.Y. (p

chmn. com. labor and social security legis.), Indsl. Rels. Rsch. Assn., Practicing Law Inst., Am. Jewish Congress (com. law and social action), Am. Judicature Soc., AFL-CIO (past mem. nat. legis. coun.), Civil Svc. Reform Assn. (exec. com.), N.Y. Com. for Modern Cts. (past v.p., bd. dirs.), Nat. and N.Y. State Against Discrimination in Housing Coms., ACLU (com. free speech and assn.), Ams. for Dem. Action, NYU Conf. on Labor, Curia, Phi Beta Kappa, Phi Kappa Phi. Home: 2228 Westwood Blvd Los Angeles CA 90064-2018

GLUSHKO, GAIL MARIE, physician, military officer; b. Griffiss AFB, N.Y., Apr. 22, 1960; d. Wasil and Mary Patricia (Hanchowsky) Glushko. BA, Miami U., Oxford, Ohio, 1982; MD, Wright State U., 1993. From cashier to asst. mgr. Scarff's Garden Ctr., New Carlisle, Ohio, 1983-85; intelligence rsch. specialist Fgn. Tech. Divsn., Wright Patterson AFB, Ohio, 1985-89; commd. 2d lt. U.S. Army, 1989, advanced through grades to maj., 1999; resident in internal medicine William Beaumont Army Med. Ctr., El Paso, Tex., 1993-96; staff internist U.S. Army Aeromed. Ctr., Ft. Rucker, Ala., 1996-99; flight surgeon US Army Aeromed. Ctr., Ft. Rucker, Ala., 1998—; fellow in allergy and immunology Walter Reed Army Med. Ctr., Washington, 1999-2001; chief Allergy & Immunology Clinic Martin Army Cmty. Hosp., Ft. Benning, Ga., 2001—, chief dept. medicine, 2002—. Contbr. articles to profl. jours. Mem.: ACP-ASIM, Am. Coll. Allergy, Asthma and Immunology, Assn. Mil. Surgeons U.S., Phi Rho Sigma. Russian Orthodox. Avocations: gardening, most sports. Office: Dept Medicine 7950 Martin Loop Martin Army Cmty Hosp Fort Benning GA 31905

GLUSKER, JENNY PICKWORTH, chemist; b. Birmingham, Eng., June 28, 1931; came to U.S., 1955, naturalized, 1977; d. Frederick Alfred and Jane Wylie (Stocks) P.; m. Donald Leonard Glusker, Dec. 18, 1955; children: Ann, Mark John, Katharine. BA in Chemistry, Oxford (Eng.) U., 1953, MA, DPhil, Oxford (Eng.) U., 1957; DSc (hon.), Coll. of Wooster, Ohio, 1985. Postdoctoral rsch. fellow Calif. Inst. Tech., Pasadena, 1955-56; rsch. fellow Inst. Cancer Rsch., Phila., 1956, rsch. assoc., 1957-67, asst. mem., 1967, assoc. mem., 1967-79, sr. mem., 1979—. Adj. prof. U. Pa.; mem. U.S. Nat. Com. for Crystallography, 1974—90, sec.-treas., 1977—79, chmn., 1982—84; vis. fellow Oriel Coll., Oxford, England, 1994—95; vis. prof. Internat. Union Crystallography, Egypt, 1997, Nat. Inst. Health, Biophysics/Biochemistry A Study Sect., 1972—76; mem. Biotech. Rsch. Rev. Com., 1977—80, chmn., 1979—80; mem. Metallo Biochem. Study Sect., 1983—87, Divsn. Rsch. Grands Adv. Com., 1989—92, Rsch. Coun., 1995—99; mem. gov. bd. Cambridge Structural Database, England, 1988—2001, vice chmn., England, 1998 -2001; mem. computer graphics lab. adv. com. U. Calif., San Francisco, 1985—, chmn., 1988—; cons., lectr. in field. Co-author (with K.N. Trueblood): (book) Crystal Structure Analysis: A Primer, 1972, Crystal Structure Analysis: A Primer, 2d edit., 1985; co-author: (with Dodson, Ramaseshan and Venkatesan) The Collected Works of Dorothy Crowfoot Hodgkin; editor: Structural Crystallography in Chemistry and Biology, Structures of Molecules of Biological Interest, 1981; co-editor (with McLachlan): Crystallography in North America, 1982; co-editor: (with S. Parthasarathy) Aspects of Crystallography in Molecular Biology, 1997; editor: Acta Crystallographcia sect. Biological Crystallography; co-editor (with M. Lewis, M. Rossi): Crystal Structure Analysis for Chemists and Biologists, 1994; co-editor: (with Patterson and Rossi) Patterson and Pattersons, 1987; mem. adv. bd. Molecular Structures in Biology, 1991, mem. editl. bd. Biophys. Jour., 1981—86; contbr. Hon. fellow Somerville Coll., Oxford (Eng.) U., 2001. Fellow AAAS; mem. Am. Assn. Cancer Rsch., The Chem. Soc., Am. Soc. Biol. Chemists, Biophys. Soc., Am. Crystallog. Assn. (pres. 1979, Pub. Svc. award 1991, Fankuchen Meml. award 1995), Am. Chem. Soc. (Phila. sect. award 1978, Garvan medal 1979), Am. Phys. Soc., Sigma Xi. Home: 1011 Anna Rd Huntingdon Valley PA 19006 8610 Office: Inst Cancer Rsch Fox Chase Cancer Ctr Philadelphia PA 19111 E-mail: jpglusker?@comcast.net., jp_glusker@fccc.edu.

GLUSKIN, LISA L. poet, editor, writer; b. Stockton, Calif., Jan. 31, 1968; d. Neil Edward and Melanie Ann (Levin) Gluskin. BA in Am. studies, Yale U., New Haven, 1990; at, Warren Wilson Coll., Swannansa, N.C., 2003—. Prodn./copy editor Miller Freeman, Inc., San Francisco, 1992—93; editor and pub.1995 And Mag.: San Francisco Arts and Culture, San Francisco, 1992—95; editor in chief Fashion Internet, NYC, 1995—96; contr. editor Critique: The Mag. of Graphic Design Thinking, Palo Alto, Calif., 1997—2001; freelance writer/editor DBA Ampersand Editl. Svcs., San Francisco, 1996—. Contbr. poetry to jours. Poet-tchr. Calif. Poets in the Sch. Recipient James Duval Phelan award, 2001, Emily Dickinson award, 2003. Mem.: Women in Bus., Media Alliance, Poets and Writers (listed poet), Bay Area Editors Forum. E-mail: lisa@ampedit.com.

GLUSMAN, DAVID H. litigation support consultant; s. Jack A. and Miriam P. (Pinkser) G.; m. Janis F. finkel, June 27, 1971; children: Sharon, Brian. BS, Pa. State U., 1971. CPA, Pa. Staff acct. Laventhal & Horwath, Phila., 1971-75; contr. Panchraina, Inc., Ardmore, Pa., 1975-76; mgr. Harry K. Cohen & Co., Phila., 1976-77, Silver & Co., Bala Cynwyd, Pa., 1977-80; ptnr. Shotz, Miller & Glusman, Phila., 1980-97, BDO Siedman, LLP, Phila., 1997—2001; prin. Margolis & Co., PC, Bala Cynwyd, Pa., 2001—. Editl. advisor CPA Health Niche Advisor, San Diego, 1997—, CPA Litigation Advisor, San Diego, 1985-92. Internat. treas. Juvenline Diabetes Found., N.Y.C., 1983-86, internat. v.p., 1986-98, chmn., Phila., 1991-94; trustee Main Line Reform Temple Beth Elohim, Wynnewood, Pa., 1997—. Named Vol. of Yr., Juvenile Diabetes Found., Phila., 1997. Avocations: scuba diving, bike riding, photography. Home: 540 Putnam Rd Merion Station PA 19066-1021 Office: Margolis & Co PC 401 E City Ave # 600 Bala Cynwyd PA 19004 Fax: 610-668-8220. E-mail: dglusman@marg.com.

GLUTH, ROBERT C. management company executive; b. 1924; married. BBA, U. Wis., 1949. With The Marmon Group Inc., Chgo., 1963—, exec. v.p., 2002—, also bd. dirs. Office: Marmon Group Inc 225 W Washington St Chicago IL 60606-3418

GLUYS, CHARLES BYRON, retired marketing management consultant; b. Richmond, Ind., Apr. 16, 1928; s. J. Howard and Reba Anna (Macy) G.; children: Gary William, Robert Lee, Marcia Kay, James Duke. BS in Indsl. Econs., Purdue U., 1955. Sales mgr. Carlyle Constrn., Columbus, Ohio, 1958; asst. product mgr. Palmer-Donavin Mfg., Columbus, 1958-61; new product mgr. KCL Corp., Shelbyville, Ind., 1963-64; prin. Gluys & Assocs., Greenfield, Ind., 1964—. Asst. scoutmaster Boy Scouts Am., Greenfield, 1953-54, Columbus, 1958-60, chmn. orgn. and extension com., Columbus, 1960-61; vol. counselor Small Bus. Adminstrn., 1976-. Mem. Am. Mktg. Assn. (bd. dirs. 1970-73), Inventors Assn. Ind. (1st v.p. 1986), Assn. Indsl. Advertisers (treas. 1971-72), Masons.

GLYMPH, DIANNE TYLER, librarian; b. Burlington, N.C., Sept. 10, 1958; d. Earle Goodson and Mayme Alcora (Ellis) Tyler; m. Michael Joe Glymph, Sept. 26, 1981. BA cum laude, Presbyn. Coll., 1980; MLS, Univ. S.C., 1981. Head libr. Christ Ch. Episc. Sch., Greenville, S.C., 1981-83; reference libr. Greenville County Libr., 1983-90, br. mgr., 1990; reference libr. Midlands Tech. Coll., Columbia, S.C., 1991-94. Reference libr./webmaster Trident Tech. Coll., Charleston, SC, 1996—99; libr. Drug Free Am. Found., St. Petersburg, Fla., 2001—. Contbr. to profl. jours. Singer Greenville Chorale, 1982-90; bd. dirs. Walter Johnson Club of Presbyn. Coll., 1987-89, Pebble Ridge Homeowners Assn., 1989-90. Mem. S.C. Libr. Assn. (sec. archives and spl. collections 1987-88), Piedmont Libr. Assn., Staff Assn. Greenville County Libr. (pres. 1987-88), Alumni Assn. Presbyn. Coll. (bd. dirs. 1999—). Avocations: music, calligraphy. Home: 2212 Riverside Dr N Clearwater FL 33764-6722

GLYNN, CARLIN (CARLIN MASTERSON), actress; b. Cleve., Feb. 19, 1940; d. Guilford Cresse and Lois Carlin (Wilks) G.; m. Peter Masterson, Dec. 29, 1960; children: Carlin Alexandra, Mary Stuart, Peter C.B. Student, Sophie Newcomb Coll., 1957-58. Prof. Columbia U. Grad. Film Sch., N.Y.C.; prof. MFA program Actors Studio at New Sch. for Social Rsch. Creative advisor Sundance Inst. Film Lab. Appeared in N.Y. as Miss Mona in: The Best Little Whorehouse in Tex., 1978-80; in London, 1981; starred in Pal Joey, Goodman Theatre, Chgo., 1988 (Joseph Jefferson award 1988), Cover of Life, Am. Place Theatre, N.Y., 1994, The Young Man from Atlanta, Signature Theatre Co., 1995 (Pulitzer prize for drama 1995), Amazing Grace, 1998, The Chemistry of Change, 1999, Frame 312, 2002, Safe, 2003; films include Three Days of the Condor, 1974, Resurrection, 1978, Continental Divide, 1981, Sixteen Candles, 1984, The Trip to Bountiful, 1985, Blood Red, Night Game, Convicts, 1989, Blessing, 1992, Judy Berlin, 1997, West of Here, 2001, Lost Junction, 2001; TV series Mr. President, 1987; dir. short film Love Divided By, 1993. Recipient Theatre World award, 1978, Antoinette Perry award, 1979, best actress award in musical Soc. West End Theatres, Lawrence Olivier award, London, 1981 Mem. SAG, AFTRA, Actor's Studio (bd. dirs.), Actors' Equity Assn. Episcopalian.

GLYNN, EDWARD, college administrator; b. Clarks Summit, Pa., Oct. 6, 1935; s. John J. G. AB, Fordham U., 1960, PhL, 1961, MAT, 1962; STB, Woodstock Coll., 1967; STM, Yale Divinity Sch., 1968; ThD, Grad. Theol. Union, 1971; LLD (hon.), Monmouth Coll., 1984, U. Scranton, 1990; LHD (hon.), Seton Hall U., 1989, St. Peter's Coll., 1990, Loyola Coll., 1993. Entered Soc. Jesus 1955; ordained 1967. Instr. Gonzaga H.S., 1961—64; asst. prof. Georgetown U., 1971-77; acad. v.p. Gonzaga U., Spokane, 1977-78, pres., 1996—97, St. Peter's Coll., Jersey City, N.J., 1978-90; provincial Md. Province Soc. of Jesus, Balt., 1990-96; interim provost U. Mass., Boston, 1997—98; pres. John Carroll U., Cleve., 1998—. Acting dir., mem., bd. dir. Churches' Ctr. for Theology and Pub. Policy, 1976-77; exec. dir. Woodstock Theol. Ctr., Washington, 1974-76, bd. dirs., 1974-76. Contbr. articles to profl. jours. Bd. dirs. U. Scranton, 1973-78, Fordham U., 1981-87, Canisius Coll., 1982-88, 2001 —, LeMoyne Coll., 1983-89, 2000—, St. Louis U., 1986-91, John Carroll U., 1987-90, 98—, Seton Hall U., 1990-96, St. Mary's Sem. and U., 1991-96, Weston Sch. Theology, 1990-96, NCAA's Pres. Commn., 1984-88, Commn. on Higher Edn., Mid. States Assn., 1988-90, Fairfield U., 1997-, Marquette U., 1998-, U. Detroit Mercy, 1999-, Am. Coun. of Edn., 2001—, U.S. Dept. of Edn. (nat. adv. bd. 1999-2001), Fund for Improvement of Post Secondary Edn. Mem.: FIPSE. Office: John Carroll U Office of Pres University Heights OH 44118-0087

GLYNN, ERNEST B. civil engineer, environmental engineer; b. Cambridge, Mass., Dec. 19, 1911; s. Frederick Stanley G. and Maude Lillian Landers; m. Beatrice Beverly Bakerink, Jan 27, 1951; children: Nancy Belva, Priscilla Beverly. Diploma Structural Design, MIT, 1939; BS, U. Md., 1956. Registered profl. engr., Washington. Archtl. engr. Office Chief of Engrs. U.S. Army, Washington, 1942, 45-47, archtl. engr. Hq. 2nd Army Balt., 1947-48, ports engr. bd. engr. river and harbors Washington, 1948-51, engr., intelligence specialist, asst. chief of staff G-2, 1951-63; sr. engr. rsch. specialist Def. Intelligence Agy., Washington, 1963-73; pvt. practice Washington, 1973-85, Alexandria, Va., 1985—; prof. engring. George Washington U., Washington, 1982-85. Presenter, lectr. in field. Contbr. over 30 articles to profl. jours. Mem. Mt. Vernon dist. Fairfax (Va.) Falls Ch., 1959-65; mem. citizen adv. com. Met Wash COG, Washington, 1965-96. Served in U.S. Army, 1942-45. Decorated Croix de Guerre with palm, France; recipient two presdl. citations. Fellow Am. Soc. Civil Engrs. (chair solid waste com. 1950, 51); mem. Am. Acad. Environ. Engr. (diplomate), Va. Soc. Profl. Engrs., Nat. Soc. Profl. Engr. (pres. George Washington chpt. 1976, outstanding engr. 1976, engr. of yr. award 1984), Solid Waste and Environ. Protection, Masons (master lodge 4 Washington). Home and Office: 4306 Ferry Landing Rd Alexandria VA 22309-3025

GLYNN, JAMES A. sociology educator, author; b. Bklyn., Sept. 10, 1941; s. James A. and Muriel M. (Lewis) G.; m. Marie J. Gates, Dec. 17, 1966 (div. Apr. 1995); 1 child, David S. AA, Foothill Coll., 1961; BA in Sociology, San Jose (Calif.) State U., 1964, MA in Sociology, 1966; PhD, U. Calif. at Riverside, 1972. Instr. in sociology Bakersfield (Calif.) Coll., 1966-98, prof. sociology, 1972—; prof. sociology State Ctr. Cmty. Coll. Dist. Clovis Ctr. and Madera Ctr., 1998—2002, prof. emeritus State Ctr. Cmty. Coll. Dist., 2003. Adj. prof. Fresno (Calif.) State U., 1971-72, Chapman Coll., Orange, Calif., 1972, Calif. State U., Bakersfield, 1989-98, Chapman U., Visalia, Calif., 1997-98; del. acad. senate Calif. C.C., Sacramento, 1980-89; mem. coun. Faculty Assn. Calif. C.Cs., 1981—; columnist Madera Tribune, 1999-2001, www.maderainfo.com. Author: Studying Sociology, 1979, Writing Across the Curriculum Using Sociological Concepts, 1983, Hands On: User's Manual for Data Processing, 1986; (with Elbert W. Stewart) Introduction to Sociology, 1972, 4th edit., 1985; (with Crystal Dea Moore) Guide to Social Psychology, 1992, Understanding Racial and Ethnic Groups, 1992, 98, 2001, Guide to Human Services, 1994, Focus on Sociology, 1994, 98; (with Charles F. Hohm and Elbert W. Stewart) Global Social Problems, 1996; contbg. editor Introduction to Sociology, 1996; contbg. author: California's Social Problems, 1997; editor, contbg. author (with Charles F. Hohm) California's Social Problems, 2d edit., 2001 Mem. Madera County Arts Coun., 2000—, co-chair fin. com., 2001—02, pub. rels. chmn., exec. bd., 2001—, v.p., 2002—03, pres., 2003—04. Recipient Innovator Yr. award League Innovations C.C., 1989, Innovator Yr. award Kern C.C. Dist., 1992. Mem. Am. Sociol. Assn., Calif. Sociol. Assn. (founder, treas. 1990-92, editor newsletter 1991-92, pres. 1992 93, exec. dir. 1993-2001), Commn. on Tchg., Pacific Sociol. Assn. (mem. editl. bd. Sociol. Perspectives 1996-99, awards com. 2000-03, Disting. Prof. award for Contbn. to Edn. 1997,), Population Reference Bur., World Watch Inst., World Future Soc., Kiwanis (editor newsletter 2001—, pres. 2001-02). Democrat. Home: 135 N Park Dr Madera CA 93637-3041 Home Fax: 559-674-4490.

GLYNN, PETER ALEXANDER RICHARD, healthcare consultant; b. Toronto, Ont., Can., Oct. 14, 1944; s. John Richard Lewis and Jessie Mackenzie Glynn; m. Arlene Dawne Whalen, Aug. 13, 1966; children: Jennifer Dawne, Jeffrey Alexander. B Engring., Royal Mil. Coll., Kingston, Ont., 1965; MASc, U. Waterloo, Ont., 1967, PhD, 1972. Dir. dept. continuing edn. Province of Sask., Regina, Can., 1975-80, exec. dir. prescription drug plan, 1980-81; assoc. dep. min. Sask. Ministry Health, Regina, 1981-84; asst. dep. min. Can. Health and Welfare, Ottawa, Ont., 1984-91; pres., CEO, Kingston (Ont.) Gen. Hosp., 1991-2000. Bd. dirs. Inst. for Clin. Evaluative Scis., Toronto. Capt. Can. Army, 1961-69. Recipient Special Recognition award Can. Cancer Soc., 1991, Alumni Achievement medal U. Waterloo, 1998, Dedicated Svc. award Heart and Stroke Found. Can., 2002. Avocations: bicycling, hiking, kayaking.

GLYNN, ROBERT D., JR., electric power and gas industry executive; b. Orange, N.J., 1942; BSME, Manhattan Coll.; MS in Nuclear Engring., L.I. U.; postgrad., U. Mich., Harvard U. With L.I. Lighting Co., 1964-72; exec. v.p., prin., dir. Woodward Clyde Cons., 1972-84; with PG&E Corp., San Francisco, 1984—, CEO, pres., 1997—, chmn. bd., 1998—. Chmn. bd. dirs. Pacific Gas and Electric Co. subs. PG&E Corp. Bd. govs. San Francisco Symphony. Office: PG&E Corp One Market St Spear Tower Ste 2400 San Francisco CA 94105

GMEINER, WILLIAM HENRY, science educator; b. East Cleveland, Ohio, May 12, 1961; s. Francis James and Thelma Ruth G.; m. Susan Cathryn Stucki, Sept. 10, 1988; children: Robert James, Michael William, Karl Henry. BA, U. Chgo., 1982; PhD, U. Utah, 1989. Rsch. assoc. U. Alta., Edmonton, Canada, 1989-91; asst. prof. U. Nebr. Med. Ctr., Omaha, 1991-97, assoc. prof., 1997-2000; prof. Wake Forest U., Winston-Salem, NC, 2000—, chair, 2000 -03. Vis. prof. U. Calif., San Francisco, 1998; mem. edn. com. Am. Med. Grad. Dept. Biochemistry, 2001-03; vis. scholar Duke U., 2002-03; pres. Wake Forest U., Sigma Xi, 2002; cons. in field. Inventor/patentee in field. Pres. Habitat for Humanity, Omaha, 1999—2000, Neighbor's South Coalition; chair property com. St. Matthew's Evang. Luth. Ch., Omaha, 1996—2000; active Luth. Ch. of the Epiphany, Winston-Salem, 2000—. Recipient Chmn.'s Challenge award, 2002; Alta. Heritage Med. Rsch. fellow, Edmonton, 1990-91. Mem. Am. Chem. Soc., Am. Assn. Cancer Rsch., Fedn. Am. Socs. Exptl. Biology, Internat. Soc. Antiviral Rsch. Democrat. Lutheran. Avocations: camping, reading, sports, music. Office: Wake Forest U Dept Biochemistry Med Ctr Blvd Winston Salem NC 27157-1016 E-mail: bgmeiner@wfubmc.edu.

GNANADESIKAN, RAMANATHAN, retired statistics educator, researcher; b. Madras, India, Nov. 2, 1932; came to U.S., 1953; s. Ambalavanan and Jegathambal Ramanathan; m. Mrudulla G., Feb. 18, 1965; children: Anand, Mukund. BSc with honors, U. Madras, 1952, MA, 1953; PhD, U. N.C., 1957. Sr. rsch. statistician Procter & Gamble Co., Cin., 1957-59; tech. staff Bell Telephone Labs., Murray Hill, N.J., 1959-68, dept. head, 1968-83; divsn. mgr. Bellcore, Morristown, N.J., 1983-86, asst. v.p., 1986-91; prof. stats. Rutgers U., Piscataway, N.J., 1991-98; prof. emeritus, 1998—. Adv. com. U.S. Bur. Census, Washington; math. scis. edn. bd. NAS, Washington; adv. com. NSF, Washington; panel chmn., NRC; various other coms. Author: Methods for Statistical Data Analysis of Multivariate Observations, 1977, 2d edit., 1997. Vol. Mended Hearts, N.J., 1995-99, Tucson, Ariz., 2000-, Northwest Interfaith Ctr., Tucson, 1999—, Elder Svcs., Edgartown, 2000—; v.p. Down Harbor Assn., Martha's Vineyard, Mass., 1979-81, pres., 1999-2002; bd. dirs. Katama Assn., Martha's Vineyard, 1997-2001. Recipient Ann. Recognition award Asian Indian Assn., 1989, Founders award, Am. Statis. Assn., 1997; cited for contbns. to State of N.J., N.J. State Legis., Trenton, 1989. Mem. Internat. Statis. Inst. (v.p. 1997-2001). Avocations: world travel, gourmet foods, boating, fishing, photography. E-mail: RG@stat.rutgers.edu.

GNAT, RAYMOND EARL, librarian; b. Milw., Jan. 15, 1932; s. John and Emily (Syperek) Gnat; m. Jean Helen Monday, June 19, 1954; children: Barbara, Richard, Cynthia. BBA, U. Wis., 1954, postgrad., 1959; MS, U. Ill., 1958; MPA, Ind. U., Indpls., 1981. Page Milw. Pub. Libr., 1950-53, jr. libr., 1954, librarian, 1958-63; circulation asst. U. Ill., 1956-57, serials cataloger, 1957-58; asst. dir. Indpls.-Marion County Pub. Libr., 1963-71, dir., 1972-94. Exec. dir. Ind. Nat. Libr. Week, 1965. With AUS, 1954—56. Mem.: ALA, Bibliog. Soc. Am., Ind. Libr. Assn. (pres. 1980), Portfolio Club, Lit. Club. Home: 8246 Shadow Cir Indianapolis IN 46260-2761

GNEHM, EDWARD W., JR., ambassador; b. Nov. 10, 1944; s. Edward Sr. and Beverly (Thomasson) G.; m. Margaret Scott, June 13, 1970; children: Cheryl Lynn, Edward William III. BA, George Washington U., 1966, MA, 1968; postgrad., Am. U., Cairo, 1966-67; LLD, Thiel Coll., 2000. Head U.S. liaison office Dept. of State, Riyadh, Saudia Arabia, 1976-78, dep. chief of mission Am. Embassy Sanaa, Yemen, 1978-81, dir. jr. officer div. pers. Washington, 1982-83, dir. secretariat staff, 1983-84, dep. chief mission Am. Embassy Amman, Jordan, 1984-87; dep. asst. sec. def. for Near East and South Asia Dept. of Def., 1987-89, dep. asst. sec. state Bur. Near East and South Asian Affairs, 1989-90, U.S. amb. to Kuwait, 1990-94, dep. U.S. Permanent Rep. to UN, 1994-97; dir.-gen. of fgn. service, dir. personnel U.S. Dept. of State, Washington, 1997-2000; U.S. amb. to Australia, 2000-2001; U.S. amb. to Jordan, 2001—. Trustee George Washington U.; mem. 4th Presbyn. Ch., Bethesda, Md. Recipient Presdl. Disting. Honor award, 2000. Mem. Am. Philatelic Soc., Omicron Delta Kappa, Sigma Chi. Avocations: history, cycling, stamps, hiking. Office: Embassy of USA Jordan Apo AE 09892 E-mail: gnehmew@state.gov.

GNEPP, DOUGLAS ROBBIN, anatomic pathologist; b. Phila., Oct. 23, 1946; BSME, Drexel U., Phila., 1969; MS, MD, Duke U., 1974; MA (hon.), Brown U., 1993. Diplomate Am. Bd. Pathology. Intern and residency Barnes Hosp.-Washington U., St. Louis, 1974-77; from instr. to asst. prof. pathology W.Va. U. Sch. Medicine, Morgantown, 1977-81; asst. prof. to prof. St. Louis U. Sch. Medicine, 1981-91; prof. pathology R.I. Hosp./Brown U. Sch. Medicine, Providence, 1991—, diagnostic surg. pathology of head and neck, 2001. Editor: Pathology of the Head and Neck, 1988, Surgical Pathology of the Salivary Glands, 1991. Office: Rhode Island Hosp 593 Eddy St Providence RI 02903-4923

GNICHTEL, WILLIAM VAN ORDEN, lawyer; b. Summit, N.J., Jan. 11, 1934; s. William Stone and Edith Parrot (Van Orden) G.; m. Emily Hopkins Martenet, July 11, 1959 (dec.); children: William Van Orden Jr., Edwin Martenet; m. Mary B. Gayley, June 7, 1996. BA, Trinity Coll., 1956, LLB, Columbia U., 1959. Bar: N.Y. 1961, Mass. 1997. Ptnr. Whitman & Ransom, N.Y.C., 1968-88, resident ptnr., 1980-85; ptnr. Chadbourne & Parke, N.Y.C., 1988-92; spl. counsel Law Firm of Salah Al-Hejailan, Riyadh, Saudi Arabia, 1986-95. Co-chmn. pub. policy com. bus. law sect. Boston Bar Assn.; lectr. in field. Contbr. articles to profl. jours. Mem. Assn. of Bar of City of N.Y. (co-chmn. subcom. Com. Internat. Security Affairs), Union Club, Knickerbocker Club (N.Y.C.), Onteora Club (Tannersville, N.Y.; exec. vp. 1974-75, pres. 1976-77, bd. dirs. 1970-77), Masons, Phi Delta Phi. Episcopalian. Address: PO Box 431 Lincoln MA 01773-0431 E-mail: WVOGLAW@mindspring.com.

GNIEWEK, RAYMOND LOUIS, newspaper editor; b. Freeport, N.Y., Sept. 3, 1947; s. Edward and Jane (Park) G.; m. Noreen Ann Kopenhaver; 1 child, Edmond Louis; children by previous marriage: Brett Elizabeth, Jared Michael. BA, NYU, 1969; BS, SUNY, Brockport, 1980. Page one editor USA Today, 1982—89, sr. editor, 1989—. Theatre, dance photographer, 2001. Author computer pagination programs, 1985—. With U.S. Army, 1970-73, Vietnam. Decorated Bronze Star. Office: USA Today 7950 Jones Branch Dr Mc Lean VA 22102 E-mail: rgniewek@comcast.net.

GO, BENEDICT ANTHONY, internist; b. Sept. 28, 1964; s. Fernando and Elsa (Lim) Go. MD, U. of the Philippines Coll of Medicine, Manila, 1990; JD, U. of Detroit Mercy Sch. of Law, 2001. Bar: Mich. 2001; diplomate Am. Bd. Internal Medicine, lic. Mich., 1991. Med. dir. Oakwood Healthcare-Brownstown, Brownstown, Mich., 1997—98; asst. med. dir. Oakwood Healthcare-Southgate, Southgate, Mich., 1998—2002. Contbr. articles. Mem. Assn. of Chinese Ams., Detroit, 2001—. Recipient Excellent Achievement in the Study of Health Law, CALI Excellence for the Future Award Program, 2001. Mem.: Am. Soc. Internal Medicine, Detroit Met.Bar Assn., ABA, ACP, Phi Kappa Phi. Home: 9970 Hawthorn Glen Grosse Ile MI 48138 Office: 1700 King Rd Trenton MI 48183 Business E-Mail: drbenesq@hotmail.com.

GO, HOWARD TIANG, management consulting firm executive, educator; b. Solo, Indonesia, Nov. 15, 1933; came to U.S., 1960; s. Joe G. and Erkien (Oei) G.; m. Mary Thouw; children: Joan Maychu-Fitzharris, Brian Mingtao. D in Engring., U. Tech., Delft, Netherlands, 1958; PhD in Bus. Adminstrn., Calif. Western U., 1979. Cert. profl. engr., Md. Devel. engr. Philips Lamp, Eindhoven, Holland, 1957-60; mgr. quality and reliability assurance Transitron Electric, Wakefield, Mass., 1960-63; product assurance cons., fellow engr. Westinghouse Electric, Balt., 1963-66; dir. prodn. assurance Fairchild Industries, Germantown, Md., 1966-68; pres. Intersci. Mgmt., Columbia, Md., 1968-71, Mgmt. Adv. Svc. Inc., Columbia, 1971—; assoc. prof. U. Md., Balt., 1974-84; faculty Johns Hopkins U., Balt., 1972-89; advisor Community Pediatric Ctr., Balt., 1978-84; bd. dirs. Milisecond Pub. Co. Inc.; chief exec. officer Masinc Internat., 1972—. Co-author (reference books): Integrated Electronic Systems, 1970, Management Handbook, 1970; developer PEST forecasting method, 1976, POS Process Method, 1989. Bd. dirs. Bethany Community Orgn., Ellicott City, Md., 1972—. Deventer-Maas scholar, The Netherlands, 1956-58; recipient Eastman Kodak R & D award, Kodak Ltd., U.K., 1988. Mem. Am. Assn. Coll. Profs., Am. Mgmt. Assn. (Mgmt. award 1972), Am. Soc. Quality Control (sr.). Republican. Methodist. Achievements include development and implementation of Strat Capex system for longest gas pipeline in South America; development of CHAPS system for self adaptable processes with self learning ability. Office: Mgmt Adv Svcs Inc 5501 Twin Knolls Rd Ste 104 Columbia MD 21045-3260

GO, JOSIAH LIM, business executive, educator; b. Manila, Philippines, Apr. 22, 1962; s. Charles S. and Nelly (Lim) Go; m. Carolina Mojica Escareal, Apr. 30, 1984; children: Chase Gosingtian, Josiah Gosingtian Jr., Ma Patricia Gosingtian, Charles Matthew Gosingtian. BSc in Bus. Mgmt., De La Salle U., Manila., 1982, postgrad., 1982-85. Pres. Waters, Philippines, 1994—, Achievers Lending Corp., 1995—. Pres., mng. cons. Mansmith and Fielders, Inc., Quezon City, Philippines, 1989—; lectr. De La Salle U., Philippines; chmn. Josiah Go Found., Inc. Author: Contemporary Marketing Strategy in the Philippine Setting, 1992, Marketing Mix Strategy in the Philippine Setting, 1993, The Marketing Mentors, 1993, Marketing 101: An A To Z Quick Guide, 1994, Marketing Plan, 1997, Marketing Excellence in Good Times and Bad, 1998, Build, Grow and Sustain Your Network Marketing Distributor Business, 2000, Marketing Shift: From Basics to Breakthrough, 2001, Fundamentals of Marketing, 2001, The Direct Selling Entrepreneurial Mindset, 2002. Named one of Ten Outstanding Young Men, Philippine Jaycees, 2001, Ten Outstanding Young Persons of the World, Jaycees Internat., 2002. Mem. Philippine Mktg. Assn. Inc. (nat. pres.), Assn. Mktg. Educators (advisor, recipient Tanglaw ng Karwnungan award), Direct Selling Assn. of Philippines (chmn.). Home: Gracecourt Mariposa St Cubao Quezon City Philippines E-mail: josiah@i-manila.com.ph.

GOAD, DANNY HARLAN, mechanical engineer; b. July 15, 1961; BS in Mech. Engring., Va. Tech. U., 1989; MBA, Coll. William and Mary, 1993. Engr. Newport News (Va.) Shipbuilding, 1989-96, Hoechst Celanese, Narrows, Va., 1996-98; prodn. supt. Indsl. Mfg., Albany, Ga., 1998-2000; engr. Aerofin Corp., Lynchburg, Va., 2000—01; realtor Owens and Co., 2001 -. Address: 5075 Cove Rd NW Roanoke VA 24019-3503 E-mail: dhgoadpe@msn.com.

GOATES, PAT LANETTA, social worker, consultant; b. Waxahachie, Tex., Aug. 3, 1943; d. Elmer B. Owens, Bennie Inez Owens; m. Donald Ray Goates, June 7, 1963; children: Gretchen Brickhouse, Sunnae Hiler;1 child, Donald Goates II. BMEd, Hardin-Simmons U., 1986, MEd, 1987; MSSW, U. Tex., Arlington, 1999. LMSW. Program adminstr. Tex. Dept. Protective and Regulatory Svc., Fort Worth, 1987—99; adj. prof. sociology Tarrant County Coll. and Weatherford Coll., Fort Worth, Tex., 1999—2001; v.p. BEACON Endeavors, Inc., Weatherford, Tex., 2000—. Trainer Ct. Apptd. Spl. Advocates, Fort Worth, 1996—99; cons. sexually abused children, Fort Worth, 1988—99; founder, CEO Counseling and Resource Endorsement, Inc., Fort Worth, 2000—; founder, pres. Social Svcs. Mgmt. Cons., Inc., Fort Worth, 2001—; music tchr. Tarver-Rendon Elem. Sch., Rendon, Tex. Contbr. Presenter Tex. Legis. Sunset Commn., Austin, 1997—98; neighborhood chmn. Mother's March for March of Dimes, Fort Worth, 1988—91; selection com. bd. dirs. United Way of Tarrant County, Fort Worth, 1995—99. Mem.: NASW, Am. Bus. Women's Assn. (celebrity chpt.), Order of the Eastern Star. Baptist. Avocations: hunting, fishing, crocheting, music, cooking. Home: 7245 CR 1204 Cleburne TX 76031 Office: Counseling and Resource Endorsement, Inc 2944 Hemphill Fort Worth TX 76110 Home Fax: 817-373-2095. Personal E-mail: pogog@digitex.net. Business E-Mail: CareInc@digitex.net.

GOBAR, ALFRED JULIAN, retired economic consultant, educator; b. Lucerne Valley, Calif., July 12, 1932; s. Julian Smith and Hilda (Millbank) G.; m. Sally Ann Randall, June 17, 1957; children: Wendy Lee, Curtis Julian, Joseph Julian. BA in Econs., Whittier Coll., 1953, MA in History, 1955; postgrad., Claremont Grad. Sch., 1953-54; PhD in Econs., U. So. Calif., 1963. Asst. pres. Microdot Inc., Pasadena, Calif., 1953-57; regional sales mgr. Sutorbilt Corp., L.A., 1957-59; mkt. rsch. assoc. Beckman Instrument Inc., Fullerton, Calif., 1959-64; sr. marketing cons. Western Mgmt. Consultants Inc., San Diego, 1964-66; ptnr., prin., chmn. bd. Darley/Gobar Assocs., Inc., San Diego, 1966-73; pres., chmn. bd. Alfred Gobar Assocs., Inc., Placentia, Calif., 1973—. Asst. prof. finance U. So. Calif., L.A., 1963-64; assoc. prof. bus. Calif. State U., L.A., 1963-68, 70-79, assoc. prof. Calif. State U.-Fullerton, 1968-69; mktg., fin. adviser 1957—; bd. dirs. Quaker City Bancorp, Inc.; pub. spkr. seminars and convs. Contbr. articles to profl. publs. Trustee Whittier Coll., 1992—. Home: 1100 W Valencia Mesa Dr Fullerton CA 92833-2219 Office: 721 W Kimberly Ave Placentia CA 92870-6343 E-mail: agobar@gobar.com. *I try not to be too quick to cast aside the social protocol that has taken centuries to evolve and test in order to define effective behavior.*

GOBBEL, LUTHER RUSSELL, lawyer, business executive; b. Durham, N.C., May 17, 1930; s. Luther and Marcia R. (Russell) G.; m. Jean M. Mollison, Apr. 4, 1959; children— Robert R., Katharine S. A.B., Duke U., 1952; J.D., Harvard U., 1955. Bar: Tenn. 1955, Md. 1972. Asst. counsel Bur. Ordnance, Navy Dept., Washington, 1955-59, asst. counsel Bur. Naval Weapons, San Diego, 1959-65; sr. atty. elec. div. Gen. Dynamics Corp., Rochester, N.Y., 1965-70; counsel Amecom div. Litton Systems, Inc., College Park, Md., 1970— ; adv. bd. Bur. Nat. Affairs Fed. Procurements Report, Washington, 1968-79. Mem. Harper's Choice Village Bd., Columbia, Md., 1972-75; chmn. Columbia Combined Bds., 1973; Mem. Howard County Criminal Justice Task Force, Md., 1975-76; mem. Howard County Police Tng. Adv. Bd., 1976; mem. Howard County Charter Rev. Com., 1979, Md. Gen. Assembly Compensation Commn., 1984—, Prince Georges County Econ. Devel. Adv. Commn. Mem. ABA, Md. Bar Assn., Fed. Bar Assn. (nat. council 1962-71, nat. v.p. for 9th dist. 1963-64, pres. San Diego chpt. 1962-63), Am. Arbitration Assn. (panel of arbitrators 1969—). Democrat. Methodist. Home: 10701 Symphony Way Columbia MD 21044-4922 Office: Litton Systems Inc 5115 Calvert Rd College Park MD 20740-3808

GOBEL, JOHN HENRY, lawyer; b. Oak Park, Ill., Oct. 21, 1926; s. Henry Andrew and Mary Ann (Coughlan) G.; m. Carol Zvara, Mar. 8, 1969; children: Kristina, Gregory. BA cum laude, DePaul U., 1950, JD cum laude, 1952. Bar: Ill. 1951, Md. 1975, Ohio 1976. Various positions law dept. Chgo. and North Western R.R. Co., Chgo., 1952-60, Balt. and Ohio R.R. Co., Balt., 1960-75; asst. gen. counsel Chesapeake and Ohio Ry. Co., Cleve., 1975-77, gen. solicitor, 1977-80, gen. counsel, 1980-82; v.p. govt. relations CSX Corp., Cleve., 1982-86; v.p., regional trial counsel CSX Transp., 1987. Served with U.S. Army, 1945-46. Fellow Internat. Soc. Barristers; mem. ABA (spl. com. on rules 1967-71), Ill. Bar Assn. (chmn. profl. ethics com., mem. assembly 1973-74), Nat. Assn. R.R. Trial Counsel (nat. sec. 1971-75), Soc. Trial Lawyers Ill. (dir. 1968-70), Ohio C. of C. (bd. dirs.), Ohio Pub. Expenditures Council (v.p. 1979-88), Ohio R.R. Assn. (chmn. 1979-87), W.Va. R.R. Assn. (chmn. 1975-87). Clubs: Union League (Chgo.), Law (Chgo.). E-mail: gobel-john@webtv.net.

GOBER, JAMES RICHARD, writer, cartographer; b. Denver, Colo., June 10, 1927; s. John David and Jimmye Irene Bowersock, Richard Fly and Fanny Gober; m. Tuyet Vo, Dec. 26, 1972; m. Betty Lou Williams, June 3, 1949 (div. Sept. 0, 1972); children: Lynn Scott, Margaret Carlisle Reheard, Julie Kim Gober-Young, Cindi Irene Robinson, Catherine Ann Davis, James Richard Gober, Jr. BS, U.S. Naval Acad., 1945—49; MS in Mech. Engring., N.Mex State U., 1958—60; MA in Mgmt., Webster U. Profl. engr., N.J. State Bd. Profl. Engineers, 1970. Col. U.S. Army, 1949—79; project mgr.-wind energy systems Raytheon Svc. Co., Burlington, Mass., 1979—81; mgr. indsl. engring. GTE Comm. Systems, Albuquerque, N.Mex., 1981—85, mgr. inds. engring. El Paso, 1981—85, mgr. advanced mfg. engring. Albuquerque, N.Mex., 1986—88; mgr., engring. change & documentation control Siemens Transmission Systems, Albuquerque, 1989—93. Author/editor: nonfiction Cowboy Justice-Tale of a Tex. Lawman (First Pl., Nonfiction Book-Southwest Writers, 1994), (Best Book of 1997-Westerners Internat., 1997). Decorated Viet Nam Army Disting. Svc. Medal-2d Class Republic of Viet Nam Joint Gen. Staff, Legion of Merit-1st Oak Leaf Cluster U.S. Army-Viet Nam. Roman Catholic. Avocations: walking, rsch., humanitarian aid work overseas. Home: 1408 Wells Dr NE Albuquerque NM 87112-6382 Office: Asian Humanitarian Aid 1408 Wells Dr NE Albuquerque NM 87112-6382 Personal E-mail: jrg_cowboyjustice@hotmail.com.

GOBERN, CAMITA ANTOINETTE, internist; b. Trelawney, Jamaica, Aug. 29, 1968; d. Fitzroy Anthony and Carmeta Vinette Gobern. BS, U. W.I., Kingston, Jamaica, 1989; MD, Temple U., 1995. Diplomate Am. Bd. Internal Medicine. Resident Temple U. Hosp., Phila., 1995-98; attending physician Albert Einstein Med. Ctr., Phila., 1998-99, Washington Hosp. Ctr., 1999—. Mem. AMA, ACP, Alpha Omega Alpha. Office: Washington Hosp Ctr 110 Irving St NW # Rmgb10 Washington DC 20010-2975

GOBES, LANDY, psychotherapist; b. Indpls., Oct. 12, 1933; d. Nathan Morr Beery and Mary Rebecca Decker; m. James Atherton Gobes, May 26, 1956 (div. May 1979); children: Catherine Elizabeth, James Atherton Gobes, Jr., Michael Edward, Anne Rebecca Gobes Arcata, Peter John, Mary Virginia. BA, Ind. U., 1955; MSW, U. Conn., 1979. Diploma clin. social work, LCSW Conn., lic. marriage and family therapist. Clin. social worker Family Svc., Inc., New Britain, Conn., 1979—83; pvt. practice psychotherapy West Hartford, Conn., 1979—; pvt. practice psychotherapy supr. and trainer, 1980—. Contbr. articles to profl. jours. Co-chair United Way Collection Campaign, West Hartford, 1966; organizer FISH of West Hartford, West Hartford, 1970—76; organist, choir dir. Bloomfield (Conn.) United Meth. Ch., 1963—2003. Fellow: Inst. Integrative Psychotherapy; mem.: NASW (mem. com. inquiry 1998—2003), Am. Group Psychotherapy Assn., Internat. Transactional Analysis Assn. (trustee 1987—89, chair transactional analysis cert. coun. 1989—93, tchg. and supervising transactional analyst). Democrat. Methodist. Avocations: piano, reading, travel, genealogy, hiking. Home: 1168 New Britain Ave West Hartford CT 06110

GOBLE, PAUL, author, illustrator, artist; b. Haslemere, Eng., Sept. 27, 1933; s. Robert John and Elizabeth Marian (Brown) G.; m. Janet A. Tiller, June 2, 1978; 1 son, Robert George; children by previous marriage: Richard, Julia. Nat. Diploma in Design with distinction, Central Sch. Art and Design, London, 1959; LHD (hon.), S.D. State U. Vis. lectr. indsl. design Central Sch. Art and Design, London, 1960-68; sr. lectr. indsl. design Ravensbourne Coll. Art and Design, London, 1968-77. Author, illustrator numerous children's books including: Custer's Last Battle, 1969, The Fetterman Fight, 1972, Lone Bull's Horse Raid, 1973, The Friendly Wolf, 1974, The Girl Who Loved Wild Horses, 1978 (Caldecott medal), The Gift of the Sacred Dog, 1980, Star Boy, 1983, Buffalo Woman, 1984, The Great Race, 1985, Death of the Iron Horse, 1987, Her Seven Brothers, 1988, Iktomi and the Boulder, 1988, Beyond the Ridge, 1989, Iktomi and the Berries, 1989, Dream Wolf, 1990, Iktomi and the Ducks, 1990, Iktomi and the Buffalo Skull, 1991, I Sing for the Animals, 1991, Crow Chief, 1992, Love Flute, 1992, The Lost Children, 1993, Iktomi and the Buzzard, 1994, Adopted by the Eagles, 1994, Hau Kola—Hello Friend, 1994, The Return of the Buffaloes, 1996, Remaking the Earth, 1996, The Legend of the White Buffalo Woman, 1998, Iktomi and the Coyote, 1998, Iktomi Loses His Eyes, Paul Goble Gallery: Three Native American Stories, 1999, Storm Makers Tipi, 2001, Mystic Horse, 2003. Fellow Royal Soc. Arts, Soc. Indsl. Artists and Designers, Grey Owl Soc. (hon.), Eagle Cir. Soc. (hon.). *I have felt the pull of the Native American tradition as long as I can remember, probably since the time my mother read to me stories of Grey Owl and Ernest Thompson Seton. As I grew up in England, I read everything I could lay my hands on about Indians. It was the books concerning the wisdom of Black Elk which finally determined my life's orientation.*

GOBLE, PHILLIP E. writer, biblical scholar, translator; b. Princeton, Ind., May 2, 1943; s. Earl and Iva G. BA in Drama, Ind. U., 1965, M in Theatre Arts, 1966; D of Ministry, Fuller Theological Seminary, Pasadena, Calif., 1975. Author: Everything You Need to Grow a Messianic Synagogue, 1974, Everything You Need to Grow a Messianic Yeshiva, 1980, The Rabbi From Tarsus, 1981, New Creation Book for Muslims, 1986, The Orthodox Jewish Brit Chadasha, 1996, The Orthodox Jewish Bible - Tanakh and Brit Chadasha, 2002; actor, 1966-78, 79-95. Office: Artists for Israel PO Box 2056 New York NY 10163-2056 E-mail: pegoble@aol.com.

GOCEK, MATILDA ARKENBOUT (MRS. JOHN A. GOCEK), librarian; b. Hoboken, NJ, Feb. 18, 1923; m. Harry Francis Decker, May 15, 1939 (div. Nov. 1955); children: Ruth Ann Decker Robinson, Dianne Karen Decker McKinstrie; m. John A. Gocek, Nov. 18, 1956; 1 child, John Jacob. AA, Orange County CC, 1961; BA, SUNY, New Paltz, 1964; MLS, SUNY, Albany, 1967; PhD, Colo. State Christian Coll., 1973. Libr. dir. Monroe Free Libr., NY, 1958—61; dir. Tuxedo Pk. Libr., NY, 1963—76; historian Town of Tuxedo, 1973—76; dir. Suffern Free Libr., 1977—90; pres., CEO Libr. Rsch. Assoc., Inc., Monroe, NY, 1990—. Libr. cons. Tuxedo Union Free Sch., 1967—69. Editor: Libr. Rsch. Assoc., 1968; author: (weekly columnist) Times Herald Rec., 1977—80. Vice chmn. Montgomery Expdn. Meml. Observance, 1973; mem., publicist Monroe Hist. Soc., NY, 2002—, bd. dirs. Tuxedo Park Sch.; trustee, pres. Mus. Village of Orange County, NY, 1980—83. Mem.: Ramapo Catskill Libr. Sys. Assn. (exec. bd. 1986—88), Libr. Assn. Rockland County (goals com. 1977, exec. bd. 1980—83), Southeastern NY Libr. Ref. Resource Coun., NY Libr. Assn., Orange-Sullivan Pub. Libr. Assn. (pres. 1967—70). Home and Office: 474 Nininger Rd County Rte 64 Monroe NY 10950

GOCHBERG, THOMAS, real estate investor, financial executive; b. Boston, Jan. 18, 1939; s. Hyman and Lee (Goredetsky) G.; m. Leatrice Eckber, Mar. 28, 1965; children: John, Sarah. AB, Columbia U., 1961. Pres., CEO Smith Barney Real Estate Corp., N.Y.C., 1969-84; dir. Smith Barney, Inc., N.Y.C., 1980-84; pres., CEO Security Capital Corp., N.Y.C., 1978—90, dir., 1978—2000. Chmn. Benjamin Franklin Savs. Assn. 1985-89, dir. 1981-89; chmn. Foster Mortgage Co., 1985-89, dir. 1981-89; pres., sole shareholder TJG Holdings Inc., 1991—; ptnr. TGM Assocs. L.P., 1991—; pres., dir. TGM Realty Corp. I, II, III, IV, V, VI, VII, X, XX, XXX, XL, 1993—. V.p. Rep. County Com. of N.Y., 1985—95, 2001—; trustee, treas. Nat. Maritime Hist. Soc., 1990—92; bd. dirs. Am. Sail Tng. Assn., 1994—2003, exec. com., chmn. devel. com., 1996—98, vice chair, 1999—2003; trustee Birch Wathan Sch., N.Y.C., 1980—88, South Street Seaport Mus., N.Y.C., 1992—, co-chair waterfront com., 1995—98, co-chair devel. com., exec. com.; bd. assocs. The Whitehead Inst. Biomed. Rsch., 1995—. With U.S. Army, 1960—63. Mem.: Pension Real Estate Assn. (pres. 1982—84, chmn. 1984—85), Ocean Cruising Club, Cruising Club of Am. (treas. NY sta. 1996—2000, rear commodore NY sta. 2000—02), Royal Western Yacht Club Eng., Univ. Club (N.Y.C.), NY Yacht Club (seamanship com. 1995—, membership com. 1998—2001). Jewish. Home: 791 Park Ave New York NY 10021-3551 Office: TGM Assocs 650 5th Ave Fl 28 New York NY 10019-6108

GOCHNAUER, RICHARD WALLIS, consumer products company executive; b. Kansas City, Mo., Dec. 3, 1949; s. Harry Wallis and Janet Elizabeth (Huff) G.; m. Beth Andrea Splinter, Dec. 18, 1971; children: Grant D., Mary E. BS in Indsl. Engring., Northwestern U., 1972; MBA, Harvard U., 1974. From shift supr. to pres. Schreiber Internat., Schreiber Foods, Green Bay, Wis., 1974-82; exec. v.p., gen. mgr. Dial Corp., Phoenix, 1989—93; pres. cheese div. Universal Foods, Milw., 1982-89; pres. Golden State Foods, 1993—2002; COO United Stationers Inc., Des Plaines, Ill., 2002, pres., CEO, 2002—. V.p. Nat. Cheese Inst., Washington, 1988-89. Chmn. bd. dirs. YMCA, Green Bay, 1981, Milw., 1988; mem. met. bd. dirs. YMCA, Phoenix, 1990. Mem. Soap and Detergent Assn. Office: United Stationers Inc 2200 E Golf Rd Des Plaines IL 60016*

GOCKE, DAVID JOSEPH, immunology educator, physician, medical scientist; b. Fairmont, W.Va., June 10, 1933; s. Charles and Josephine G.; m. Barbara Donohoe, Apr. 12, 1958; children: Christopher, Susan, John, Gregory, Patricia, Robert, Mary Anne, Meghan. Ed., St. Vincent's Coll., Latrobe, Pa., 1954; MD, U. Pa., 1958. Diplomate Am. Bd. Internal Medicine, Am. Bd. Allergy and Immunology. Intern Columbia-Presbyn. Hosp., N.Y.C., 1958-59, asst. resident, 1959-60, program dir. clin. research center, 1971-73; fellow in microbiology Johns Hopkins Sch. Medicine, Balt., 1960-63; from asst. prof. to assoc. prof. medicine Columbia U. Coll. Physicians and Surgeons, N.Y.C., 1963-73; prof. medicine and microbiology, chief div. immunology and infectious disease Robert Wood Johnson Med. Sch., Rutgers U., New Brunswick, N.J., 1973-77, 78—, dean med. sch., 1977-78. Spl. cons. Nat. Research Council on Hepatitis. Co-author: Viral Hepatitis, 1978; contbr. articles on infectious diseases and immunology to profl. jours. Mem. Am. Soc. Clin. Investigation, Infectious Diseases Soc. Am., Am. Assn. Immunologists, Am. Assn. Study of Liver Disease, Am. Fedn. Clin. Research, AAAS, Alpha Omega Alpha. Roman Catholic. Office: Robert Wood Johnson Med Sch CN 19 New Brunswick NJ 08903

GOCKEL, JOHN RAYMOND, construction executive; b. Ft. Madison, Iowa, June 12, 1947; s. Carl R. and Virginia Jeanne (Schultz) G.; m. Joleen E. Gunst, Sept. 9, 1989; children: Rose M. Van Zandt, Chrstina Ann Rathman. BSCE, Iowa State U., 1970. Registered profl. engr., Mich., Minn., Wis. Cost estimator Barton Malow Co., Detroit, 1975-76, project mgr., 1976-82, project administr., 1982-83; project exec. Gilbane Bldg. Co., Maplewood, Minn., 1983-84; constrn. mgr., dir. phys. plant Minn. Racetrack, Inc., Shakopee, 1984-85; v.p. Scottland, Inc., Shakopee, 1985-86, Knutson Constr. Co., Mpls., 1987-88, Encompass Inc., Bloomington, Minn., 1988-89; ind. constrn. cons. Bloomington, 1989—; pres. John R. Gockel & Assocs., Inc., 1990—. Project mgr. Mpls. Metrodome; constrn. mgr. Canterbury Downs, Mpls.; constrn. cons. to owners and attys.; lectr. various civic profl., acad. groups, Minn. Arbitrator Am. Arbitration Assn., throughout Midwest, 1982. Recipient Honor award Cons. Engrs. Coun., Minn., 1985. Mem. Am. Acad. Forensic Examiners, Internat. Congress Bldg. Ofcls., Profl. Engrs. in Constrn. (v.p. 1983, pres. 1984, bd. dirs. 1984-93), Minn. Soc. Profl. Engrs. (bd. dirs. 1985-86, Seven Wonders of Engring. award 1982, 85), Iowa State U. Alumni Assn., Tau Beta Pi. Republican. Roman Catholic. Avocations: history, woodworking, boating, fishing. Home and Office: 11120 Stanley Cir S Minneapolis MN 55437-3315 Fax: 612-888-9814. E-mail: jrgockel@aol.com.

GOCKLEY, DANIEL L. academic administrator; s. Paul L. and Susan M. Gockley; m. Emily K. Moore, May 25, 1974; 1 child, Mary Kate. BA, U. of Ky., 1995, MA, 1998. Coord. of environment U. Md. BaltimoreCounty, Balt., 1998—2001; asst. dir. of residential life Ithaca (N.Y.) Coll., Ithaca, 2001—. Home: 15 Front St Van Etten NY 14889 Office: Ithaca Coll 953 Danby Rd Ithaca NY 14850 Office Fax: 607-274-1589. E-mail: dgockley@ithaca.edu.

GOCKLEY, DAVID (RICHARD DAVID GOCKLEY), opera director; b. Phila., July 13, 1943; s. Warren and Elizabeth S. Gockley; m. Adair Lewis; children: Meredith, Lauren, Adam. BA, Brown U., 1965; MBA, Columbia U., 1970; DHL (hon.), U. Houston, 1992; DFA (hon.), Brown U., 1993. Dir. music Newark Acad., 1965-67; dir. drama Buckley Sch., N.Y.C., 1967-69; mgr. box office Santa Fe Opera, 1969-70; bus. mgr. Houston Grand Opera, 1970-71, assoc. dir., 1971-72, gen. dir., 1972—. Co-founder Houston Opera Studio, 1977. Prodr. (operas): Nixon in China (Emmy award 1988), Harvey Milk, Florencia en el Amazonas, Porgy and Bess (Tony award, Grammy award 1977), Treemonisha, A Quiet Place, Willie Stark, Resurrection, Carmen. Bd. dirs. Tex. Inst. Arts in Edn.; past pres. OPERA Am.; past chmn. Houston Theater Dist. Recipient Tony award League of N.Y Theaters and Producers, 1977, Dean's award Columbia Bus. Sch., 1982, Music Theater award Nat. Inst. Music Theater, 1985, William Rogers award, Brown U., 1995; named one of Outstanding Men Am., Nat. Jr. C. of C., 1976. Mem. Opera Am. (pres. 1985—). Avocation: tennis. Office: Houston Grand Opera 510 Preston St Ste 500 Houston TX 77002-1504 E-mail: gockley@houstongrandopera.org.*

GODAGER, JANE ANN, retired social worker; b. Blue River, Wis., Nov. 29, 1943; d. Roy and Elmyra Marie (Hood) G. BA, U. Wis., 1965; MSW, Fla. State U., 1969. LCSW. Social worker III State of Wis. Dept Corrections, Wales, 1965—71; supervising psychiat. social worker I State of Calif., San Bernardino, 1972—75, La Mesa, 1975—77, psychiat. social worker San Bernardino, 1978—85; supr. mental health services Riverside (Calif.) County Dept. Mental Health, 1985—86; mental health counselor Superior Ct. San Bernardino County, 1986—2001; staff asst. to dist. dir. Calif. State Assembly, Calif., 2002, ret., 2002. Former mem. adv. bd. Grad. Sch. Social Work Calif. State U., San Bernardino, Mental Health Assn.; mem. County Hosp. Re-Use Com. Mem. commn. on sr. affairs City of San Bernardino, Calif. Mem. Nat. Assn. Social Workers, Acad. Cert. Social Workers (diplomate), Kappa Kappa Gamma Alumnae Assn. Avocations: travel, reading, music.

GODARD, JERRY HOLTON CARIS, psychology educator, college dean; b. Durham, N.C., May 13, 1936; s. James McFate and Aura Holton Godard; m. Jane Godard Caris, Apr. 1977; children: Ginger Elise, Renée Denise, Michelle Leigh. BS, Auburn U., 1958; EdD, Columbia U., 1966. Asst. dean, instr. Auburn U., Ala., 1958-62; adminstrv. asst., instr. Columbia U., N.Y.C., 1962-64; dean students, asst. prof. Earlham Coll., Richmond, Ind., 1964-66; exec. dean, assoc. prof. Guilford Coll., Greensboro, N.C., 1966-73, Dana prof. psychology and lit., 1975—2002, exec. v.p., dean, 2000—; dean coll., prof. Warren Wilson Coll., Asheville, NC, 1973-75. Author: Color Them Motley, 1967, Mental forms Creating: William Blake Anticipates Freud, Jung and Rank, 1984, Eros Plays: Parts and Pieces from a Left-Handed Psychology, 1990; contbr. articles to profl. jours. Fellow NEH, Yale U., 1986. Avocations: canoeing, kayaking, running, hiking. Home: 4331 Four Farms Rd Greensboro NC 27410 Office: Guilford Coll Office of Exec VP Greensboro NC 27410 E-mail: jgodard@guilford.edu.

GODBEE, GARY RUSSELL, artist; b. Miami, Fla., Jan. 20, 1952; s. Jack O. and Phyllis Godbee; m. Irene C. Burtyk, Sept. 17, 1988; children: Nina, Julia. BFA, Boston U., 1974. Gallery artist First St. Gallery, N.Y.C., 1981-89; rep. artist Cudahy's Gallery, N.Y.C., 1990-92; artist Gary Godbee Fine Arts, Westfield, N.J., 1993—; painting/drawing instr. Acad. Realist Art, Workshop Program, Santa Fe, 1994, 95; painting instr. Montclair (N.J.) Art Mus. Sch., 1993—; artist Gary Godbee Portraits, Westfield, 1990—; illustrator Gary Godbee Illustration, Westfield, 1997—; commd. artist State of N.J., Dept. of Labor, Trenton, 1999-00. Guest instr. Art Student's League, N.Y.C., 1992-93; guest lectr. DuCret Sch. Arts, Plainfield, N.J., 1993; instr. painting Somerset Art Assn., 2001—. Recipient Painting fellowship N.J. State Coun. on Arts, 1993, Merit award The Portrait Inst., 1996, Cert. of Merit, Soc. of Illustrators, 1998. Fax: 908-301-1734.

GODBEY, LUTHER DAVID, architectural and engineering executive; b. Friend, Nebr., May 28, 1938; s. Luther Dobbs and Ruth (Thomas) G.; m. Priscilla White, Oct. 6, 1963 (div. May 1985); children: Emily, Patrick David. BArch, U. Nebr., 1961. Registered architect, Tex. Archtl. designer Selmer A. Solheim & Assoc., Lincoln, Nebr., 1961-63; architect, prin. Golemon & Rolfe Assoc. Inc., Houston, 1963-88; v.p. CRSS, Houston, 1988-90; dir. Corp. program Henningson Durham & Richardson, Dallas, 1990-92; asst. dir. phys. plant Tex. A&M, College Station, 1992—. Author: 52 Ways to Overcome Tennis Elbow, 1980; prin. works include 5000 Montrose Condos., Houston, 1979, Richmond Commerce Bank Office Bldg., Houston, 1980, One Capitol Sq. Office Bldg., Austin, 1985, Marriott Riverwalk Hotel, San Antonio, 1980, Westin O'Hare Hotel, Chgo., 1985, Wyndham Hotel, San Antonio, 1986, L'Hotel Sofitel, Miami, Fla., 1987, Bell Northern Rsch. Ctr., Ottawa, Can., 1988, Yukon Ltd. R & D Complex, Taejon, Korea, 1990, Godbey Residence, Bryan, Tex., 1995; watercolor exhibits include Jefferson Nat. Exhibition, New Orleans, 1963, Houston Art League Show, 1968, Southwestern Watercolor Soc. Regional Exhibition, Dallas, 1969, Houston Arts Festival, 1969, 72, Watercolor U.S.A., Springfield, Mo., 1970, circuit exhibition, 1970-71, 48th Ann. Regional Jury Exhibition Shreveport (La.) Art Guild, 1970, Southwestern Watercolor Soc. 2d Ann. Jury Exhibition, Houston, 1972. Mem. Bryan Zoning Bd. Adjustment, 1997-99. Mem. AIA (Brazos chpt. 1992—, pres. 1999, design citation 2001), Tex. Soc. Archs. (honor award 1972), Tex. Assn. Phys. Plant Adminstrs. Avocations: vocal soloist, running, watercolor, guitar, fiddle, squash. Office: Tex A&M Phys Plant Ms 1371 College Station TX 77843-0001

GODBEY, ROBERT CARSON, lawyer; b. Houston, June 7, 1953; s. Charles Perry and Bobbye Lee Godbey; m. Ellen Carson, June 2, 1979. BS, BSEE magna cum laude, So. Meth. U., 1975; JD cum laude, Harvard U., 1980. Bar: U.S. Patent Office, 1981, Hawaii 1988. Telecommunications engr. Southwestern Bell, Dallas, 1975-76, Tex. Instruments, Dallas, 1976-77; assoc. Peabody, Lambert & Meyers, Washington, 1980-84; asst. U.S. atty. U.S. Dept. of Justice, Washington, 1984-87, Honolulu, 1987-91; prtnr. Godbey Griffiths Reiss, 1991—. Mem. ABA, IEEE, Hawaii State Bar Assn. (past chmn. intellectual property sect. 1994-96, past chmn. tech. com., 1995-97), Phi Beta Kappa, Tau Beta Pi. Office: 2300 Pauahi Tower 1001 Bishop St Honolulu HI 96813-3429

GODBEY, RONALD LEE, lawyer, meteorologist; b. Milford, Tex., July 11, 1934; s. Paschal Lee and Catherine Esta (Williams) G.; m. Martha Jane Worsham, May 14, 1954; children— Gary Lee, Julie Ann. B.S., North Tex. State U., 1960; postgrad. Tex. A&M U., 1960-61; J.D., So. Meth. U., 1971. Bar: Tex. 1971, U.S Dist. Ct. (no. dist.) Tex. 1971, Ill. 1982. Quality control mgr. Gen. Dynamics Corp., Ft. Worth, 1955-57; meteorologist WBAP TV and Radio, Ft. Worth, 1964-78; mem. firm Godbey, Simpson, Lynch & Wiley, Ft. Worth, 1971-81; lawyer Dept. Def., Belleville, Ill., 1982— ; cons. meteorologist, Ft. Worth, 1972-81; mcpl. ct. judge City of Keller, Tex., 1974-78. Co-author: Texas Weather, 1976. Bd. dirs. Grapevine Meml. Hosp., Tex. 1973-77. Served with USAF, 1960-64, Korea. Mem. Tex. Trial Lawyers Assn., Ill. Bar Assn. (environ. council 1983—), Ill. Trial Lawyers Assn., Am. Meteorol. Soc. (cert. cons. meteorologist, TV seal of approval), Nat. Guard Assn. U.S., DAV, VFW, Chi Epsilon Pi Democrat. Methodist. Club: Ft. Worth Lions.

GODBEY, TERRY, poet, newspaper copy editor; b. Bangor, Maine, Aug. 15, 1955; d. J.R. Godbey and Gladys Clark; m. Barry Glenn; 1 child, Tyler Glenn. BSJ, U. Fla., 1983. Copy editor Orlando (Fla.) Sentinel, 1994—, 1983—89, chief wire editor, 1989—94. Bd. dirs. Lake Sybelia Elem. Sch. PTA, Maitland, Fla., 2000—03. Avocation: reading, bicycling, hiking, scrapbooking.

GODBOLD, FRANCIS STANLEY, investment banker, securities firm executive; b. Charleston, S.C., Mar. 4, 1943; s. Francis Stanley and Ula Leigh (Waddey) G.; m. Lelia Elizabeth Harman, Sept. 24, 1966; children: John A., Laura H. Blair. BS in Indsl. Engring. with honors, Ga. Inst. Tech., 1965; MBA, Harvard U., 1969. V.p. Raymond, James & Assocs., Inc., St. Petersburg, Fla., 1969-74, sr. v.p., 1974-78, exec. v.p., 1978—; pres. Raymond James Fin., Inc., 1987—2002, vice chmn., 2002—. Mem. regional firms adv. com. N.Y. Stock Exch., 1990-93; bd. dirs. Raymond James Bank. Pres. Baypoint Mid. Sch. Parent Action Com., 1982-83, Bay Vista Parent Action Com., 1979-80; mem. Leadership St. Petersburg, 1974—; mem. Lakewood H.S. Parent Action Com., 1984-90, pres., 1987-88, trustee Ga. Tech. Found., Inc., 2003—; dir. Ga. Tech. Indsl. and Sys. Engring. Alumni award, 1997, mem. Tampa Bay area regional devel. coun., 1995; bd. dirs. Acad. Prep., 1999—. Capt. AUS U.S. Army, 1965—67. Mem. Securities Industry Assn. (vice chmn. so. dist. 1980, chmn. 1987, treas. 1986, exec. com. 1988-96, nat. dir. 1995-97, regional firms com. 1995-99, chmn. regional firms com. 1998, tax policy com. 1995-97, nominating com. 1997), Ga. Tech. Alumni Assn. (trustee 2002—), Harvard Club of West Coast Fla. (sec.-treas 1971-72, v.p. 1972-73, pres. 1973-74), Harvard Bus. Sch. Club (treas. 1984), St. Petersburg Country Club, Elk River Club, Tau Beta Pi, Phi Kappa Phi, Alpha Pi Mu, Phi Delta Theta. Republican. Office: Raymond James Fin Inc 880 Carillon Pkwy Saint Petersburg FL 33716-1100

GODBOLD, GENE HAMILTON, lawyer; b. Mullins, S.C., June 14, 1936; s. John Dalton and Mildred (Stalvey) G.; m. Janice Louise McKay, June 24, 1960; children: Lori McKay, Scott Hamilton, Stephanie Louise. BA, Furman U., Greenville, S.C., 1958; LLB, Tulane U., 1963. Bar: Fla. 1963, U.S. Dist. Ct. (mid. dist.) Fla. 1964, U.S. Ct. Appeals (5th cir.) 1964. Assoc. Maguire, Voorhis & Wells, Winter Park, Fla., 1963-68, ptnr., 1968-84, pres., 1978-84, Godbold, Allen, Brown and Builder, P.A., Winter Park, 1984-88, Goldbold & Downing, P.A., 1988-94, Godbold, Downing, Sheahan & Bill, P.A., 1994—. Served to 1st lt. U.S. Army, 1958-60. Mem. Fla. Bar, Orange County Bar Assn (mem. exec. com. 1968-72, pres. 1971-72), Interlachen Country Club. Address: 222 W Comstock Ave Ste 101 Winter Park FL 32789-4272 E-mail: ggodbold@gdsblaw.com.

GODBOLD, JOHN COOPER, judge; b. Coy, Ala., Mar. 24, 1920; s. Edwin Condie and Elsie (Williamson) Godbold; m. Elizabeth Showalter, July 18, 1942; children: Susan, Richard, John C., Cornelia. BS, Auburn U., 1940; JD, Harvard U., 1948; LLD (hon.), Samford U., 1981, Auburn U., 1988, Stetson U., 1994. Bar: Ala. 1948. With firm Richard T. Rives, Montgomery, 1948-49; ptnr. Rives & Godbold, 1949-51, Godbold & Hobbs and successor firms, 1951-66; cir. judge U.S. Ct. Appeals (5th cir.), 1966-81, chief judge, 1981, U.S. Ct. Appeals (11th cir.), 1981-86, sr. judge, 1987—; dir. Fed. Jud. Ctr., Washington, 1987-90. Mem. Fed. Jud. Ctr. Bd., 1976—81. With field arty. U.S. Army, 1941—46. Mem.: FBA, ABA, Montgomery County Bar Assn., Ala. Bar Assn., Phi Kappa Phi, Omicron Delta Kappa, Alpha Tau Omega. Episcopalian. Office: US Ct Appeals 11th Circuit One Church Street Montgomery AL 36104

GODBOUT, ARTHUR RICHARD, JR., lawyer; b. Hartford, Conn., Oct. 7, 1957; s. Arthur Richard and Elizabeth Anne (Desmond); m. Elizabeth G. Godbout. BSBA, Georgetown U., 1979, JD, 1986. Bar: Conn. 1987. Pres. A.R. Godbout & Co., Avon, Conn., 1987—. Home: 8 Cheltenham Way Avon CT 06001-2444 Office: PO Box 1175 Avon CT 06001-1175

GODDARD, BRYAN LANCE, physician, director; b. July 13, 1954; s. Charles William and Alice Lance Goddard; m. Nancy Baumback, June 24, 1978; children: David, Jonathan. MD, NY Med. Coll., 1980. Diplomate Am. Bd. of Family Practice, 1983. Pvt. practice Self-employed, Gloversville, NY, 1983—87; residency faculty Wilson Family Practice Residency, Johnson City, NY, 1987—; med. dir. Johnson City Family Care Ctr., NY, 1983—91; med. dir. info. technologies United Health Services, Johnson City, NY, 1998—. Domestic cons. Lockheed-Martin Healthcare Systems, Owego, NY, 1999—2000; chmn., aids policy group NY Penn Health Systems Agy., Binghamton, 1988—89; med. cons. Broome County Child Protective Services, Binghamton, 1989—98; bd. mem. Rural Health Network of South Ctrl. NY, Whitney Point, NY, 2001—. Contbr. articles to profl. jours. Recipient Recognition for Outstanding Svc., Broome County Child Abuse Coun., 1989—97. Fellow: Am. Acad. of Family Physicians; mem.: Am. Med. Informatics Assn., Soc. of Teachers of Family Medicine. Christian, United Methodist. Office: United Health Services 40 Arch St Johnson City NY 13790 Office Fax: 607-763-5415.

GODDARD, CLAUDE PHILIP, JR., lawyer; b. Long Beach, Calif., Oct. 31, 1952; s. Claude Philip and Doris Marian (Dow) G.; m. Ellen Kohn, May 23, 1981; children: Marian Laura, Nora Margaret. BS with distinction, U.S. Naval Acad., 1974; JD cum laude, U. Pa., 1979. Bar: N.H. 1979, D.C. 1985, Va. 1999, U.S. Dist. Ct. D.C. 1989, U.S. Ct. Appeals (9th cir.) 1985, U.S. Ct. Appeals (fed. cir.) 1991. Ensign U.S. Navy, 1974, advanced through grades to lt. comdr., 1987, atty., 1979-87, resigned, 1987; assoc. Keck, Mahin & Cate, Washington, 1987-89, ptnr., 1990, Jenner & Block, Washington, 1990-95; shareholder Kilcullen, Wilson and Kilcullen, Chartered, Washington, 1995-99, Wickwire Gavin, P.C., Vienna, Va., 1999—. E-mail: cgoddard@wickwire.com.

GODDARD, EDWARD DEAN, stockbroker, accountant; b. Danville, Ill., Oct. 13, 1929; s. Oscar E. and Dorothea Goddard; m. Mary Lenny, Jan. 29, 1955; children: James, Daniel, Steven, Mark. BS in Acctg., U. Ill., 1955. CPA, Ill. Auditor Ernst & Ernst, Chgo., 1955-58; comptr., treas. various small/large corps., Chgo./Grand Rapids, Mich., 1958-69; stockbroker Kenower McArthur/The Ohio Co., Grand Rapids, 1969-80, Morgan Stanley Dean Witter, Orlando, Fla., 1980—. Writer, prodr. host TV shows: Relax It's Income Tax 13 Weeks, 1981, 89, Corporate Profile Weekly, 1982-87, Ballroom Dance Class, 13 weeks series, 1989. Candidate U.S. Congress, Dist. 7, 1994. With U.S. Army, 1946-48, Korea. Mem. Maitland Toastmasters Club (pres. 1997-98, gov. area 49 1998-99, Disting. Toastmaster 1999). Democrat. Episcopalian. Avocations: ballroom dance instructing, stamp collecting. Home: 1316 Classic Dr Longwood FL 32779-5817 E-mail: edgoddard1@juno.com.

GODDARD, FRANCES BYRD, clinical social worker; b. Greensboro, N.C., Aug. 11, 1939; d. Henry Davis and Blanche Leavell Blake; m. Anthony Edward Goddard, Oct. 10, 1964; 1 child, Caroline Stuart. BA in Sociology with honors, Converse Coll., 1961; MSW, U. N.C., 1963. Lic. social worker; diplomate Nat. Assn. Social Workers. Social worker Children's Home Soc., Richmond, Va., 1964-71; supr. of svcs. Coun. of Culpeper, Va., 1971-74; dir. Culpeper Mental Health, 1974-76, Culpeper Family Counseling, 1976—; exec. dir. Am. Assn. State Social Work Bds., Culpeper, 1989-94. Bd. dirs. Va. Mental Health Assn. Author: 5 books in field, studies in field. NIMH traineeship NIMH. Mem. Holloway-Amiss-Leave II Soc. (sec./treas. 1990—), Nat. Clearinghouse on Licensure, Enforcements and Regulations, Nat. Orgn. of Competency Assurance, am. Soc. Assn. Exec., Va. Commonwealth U. Social Work Adv. Bd. (past chmn.), numerous others. Episcopalian. Avocations: reading, travel, art, needlework. Office: Culpeper Family Counseling Ste A 400 South Ridge Pkwy Culpeper VA 22713

GODDARD, HAZEL BRYAN, religious organization administrator; b. Mineral, Ill., Aug. 17, 1912; d. Thomas Benton and Maude Carrie (Riley) B.; m. John Howard Goddard; children: David Bryan, Joan Kathryn. BA, Judson Coll., 1966; MS, No. Ill. U., 1973; LittD (hon.), Calif. Grad. Sch. Theology, 1981. Lic. Marriage and family therapist, Fla., Colo. Clin. counselor Warrenville (Ill.) Med. Clinic, 1958-78; pres. Christian Counseling Ministries, Buena Vista, Colo., 1978-99, lectr., cons., 1978—, pres. emeritus, 1999. Auhtor: Can I Hope Again, 1971, Mama, Are You There?, 1996, Somebody Else's Girl, Connie, Bob Bronson; contbr. articles to jours. Mem. Am. Pychotherapy Assn. (diplomat), Am. Assn. Marriage and Family Therapists (clin.), Nat. Assn. Social Workers, Am. Assn. Counseling and Devel. Republican. Baptist. Avocations: writing, music, hiking, fishing, travel. Home: PO Box 1366 Buena Vista CO 81211-1366 E-mail: hazelg@chaffee.net.

GODDARD, JOHN WESLEY, cable television company executive; b. Aberdeen, Wash., May 4, 1941; s. Fred G. and Winifred (Vaughan) G.; m. Susan Ehrhart, Dec. 29, 1962 (div. Oct. 1978); 1 child, John Wesley Jr.; m. Joan Marie McGiff, Sept. 13, 1980. Grad., Stanford U.; MBA in Fin., U. Calif., Berkeley. Asst. mgr. Tele-Vue Systems Inc., Dublin, Calif., 1966, mgr., 1967-69, contr., 1969-74, pres., 1974-78; exec. v.p. Viacom Cable, Pleasanton, Calif., 1978-80, pres., 1980—. Dir. Viacom Internat. Inc., N.Y.C., 1983-87; treas. Nat. Cable TV Assn., Washington, 1984, sec., 1985-86, vice chmn., 1987, chmn., 1988, bd. dirs., 1981—. Republican. Episcopalian. Office: Viacom Cable 2166 Rheem Dr Pleasanton CA 94588-2613

GODDARD, LISA, meteorologist; b. Sacramento, Calif., Sept. 23, 1966; d. Glenn Kenneth Goddard and Marie Eleanor Betts; m. David Jeffrey Cooperberg, May 2, 1998; 1 child, Samuel Jonathan Cooperberg. PhD, Princeton U., 1995. Project scientist, Internat. Rsch. Inst. Climate Prediction, Forecasting Group, climate rsch. divsn. Scripps Inst. Oceanography, La Jolla, Calif., 1995—99; rsch. scientist, Internat. Rsch. Inst. Climate Prediction, The Earth Inst. Columbia U., Palisades, NY, 2000—. Contbr. articles and revs. to profl. jours. Global Change fellow, NASA, 1993—95. Mem.: AAAS, Americian Geophys. Union, Am. Meteorol. Soc. Office: IRI Earth Inst of Columbia U 61 Route 9W Palisades NY 10964 E-mail: goddard@iri.columbia.edu.

GODDARD, SANDRA KAY, elementary education educator; b. Steubenville, Ohio, Oct. 31, 1947; d. Albert Leonard and Mildred Irene (Hill) G. BS in Edn., Miami U., Oxford, Ohio, 1969; MEd, Miami U., 1973. Tchr. Gregg Elem. Sch., Bergholz, Ohio, 1969; tchr. elem. grades Springfield Mid. Sch., Bergholz, 1999—, media club advisor, 2002—; Praxis III assessor Ohio Dept. Edn., 2002—. Curriculum and textbook com. Jefferson County Schs., Steubenville, 1994-95, textbook com., 2002; cooperating tchr. Franciscan U., 1972-77, 2002; presenter Ohio Regional Tchrs. Workshop, 1998, County Tchrs. Workshops for ARC/Jefferson County Tchrs., 1992-97, Jefferson County coord. Presch./Kindergarten Workshop for ARC first aid course, 2000, 2002. Publicity chmn., rec. sec., box office chmn., lead actress, asst. dir. Steubenville Players, 1981-83; mem. Edison Local Adv. Coun. on Drug Edn., 1987-99; mem. Edison Local Curriculum Instrn. Com., 1993-99; state judge Ashland Oil Tchr. Achievement awards, 1988-90; regional and state judge Odyssey of the Mind, 1992-97, bd. dirs. Region XI, 1993-97, regional dir., chair governing bd., bd. dirs. Ohio chpt., 1994-97; exec. com. Gregg Elem. PTO, 1990-92; instr. 1st aid and CPR, ARC, 1990—, county disaster team, profl. rescuer status, 1997—, instr. trainer educator, 2002; instr. CPR for Profl. Rescuer, 2002—. Martha Holden Jennings scholar, 1972-73; mini-grantee Jefferson County Schs., 1991, 94. Mem. NEA (del. to rep. assembly 1979, 85-88), Ohio Edn. Assn. (exec. com. 1983-89, pres.'s cabinet 1985-87, appeals bd. 1994-2002), Ea. Ohio Edn. Assn. (pres. 1978-79, exec. com. 1983-89), Edison Local Edn. Assn. (pres. 1974-75, v.p. 1986 91, exec. com. 1991-94, negotiation's team 1987, 90, 93), Ohio Valley UNISERV Coun. (treas. 1986-92), Delta Kappa Gamma (legis. chair 1990-92). Democrat. Methodist. Avocations: singing, reading, theater, collecting hummels and bells, photography. Home: 200 Fernwood Rd Apt 11 Wintersville OH 43953-9200 Office: Springfield Mid Sch 4569 County Hwy 75 Bergholz OH 43908-9801

GODDARD, TERRY, state attorney general; BA, Harvard U., 1969; JD, Ariz. State U., 1976. Mayor City of Phoenix, 1983-90; of counsel Bryan Cave, Phoenix, 1990-94; atty. gen. State of Ariz., 2003—. Bd. dirs. Ariz. Theater Co., Neighborhood Coalition of Phoenix; former pres. Nat. League of Cities, 1989; former chmn. Ariz. Mcpl. Water Users Assn., Maricopa Assn. Govts., govt. and non-profit group Valley of the Sun United Way, Regional Pub. Transp. Authority, Rebuild Am. Coalition; adv. bd. State and Local Legal Ctr. Comdr. USNR, 1970—98, ret. Mem. ABA, State Bar Ariz., Maricopa County Bar Assn. Democrat. Office: Atty Gen 1275 W Washington St Phoenix AZ 85007

GODDARD, THELMA TAYLOR, critical care nurse, nursing educator; d. James Oscar and Goldie Pearl (Hawkins) Taylor; m. Kenneth L. Goddard; children: Catherine, Sharon, K. John. ADN, W.Va. No. C.C., Weirton, 1980; BSN, West Liberty State Coll., 1986; MSN, W.Va. U., 1991, postgrad. Staff critical care nurse Weirton (W.Va.) Med. Ctr., Pitts., West Pa. Hosp., Pitts.; instr. nursing W.Va. No. C.C.; staff critical care nurse Cen. Med. Ctr., Pitts.; nursing instr. Waynesburg (Pa.) Coll., 1991-92, Carlow Coll., Pitts., 1992-94; instr. nursing Allegheny County C.C., Pitts., 1993-94; asst. prof. Wheeling (W.Va.) Jesuit Coll., 1994-97; instr. nursing U. Pitts., 1997-98, Allegheny Gen. Hosp., Pitts., 1987-88. Critical care nurse St. Francis Ctrl. Hosp., 1990-94; vis. faculty C.C. Allegheny County, Pitts., 1999, prof. biology, 1999—. Mem. ANA, AACCN, Sigma Theta Tau, Phi Theta Kappa.

GODDEN, JEAN W. columnist; b. Stamford, Conn., Oct. 1, 1933; d. Maurice Albert and Bernice Elizabeth (Warvel) Hecht; m. Robert W. Godden, Nov. 7, 1952 (dec. Dec. 1985); children: Glenn Scott, Jeffrey Wayne. BA, U. Wash., 1974. News editor Univ. Dist. Herald, Seattle, 1951-53; bookkeeper Omniarts Inc., Seattle, 1963-71; writer editorial page Seattle Post-Intelligencer, Seattle, 1974-80, editorial page editor, 1980-81, bus. editor, 1981-83, city columnist, 1983-91, Seattle Times, 1991—. Author: The Will to Win, 1980, Hasty Put Ins, 1981. Communicator of the Yr. U. Wash. Sch. of Comm., 1995. Mem. LWV (dir. 1969-71), Wash. Press Assn. (Superior Performance award 1979), Soc. Profl. Journalists, Mortarboard, City Club, Phi Beta Kappa. Office: The Seattle Times PO Box 70 Seattle WA 98111-0070

GODDESS, LYNN BARBARA, commercial real estate broker; b. N.Y.C., Mar. 3, 1942; d. Eugene Daniel and Hazel Cecile (Kinzler) G.; divorced. BS, Columbia U., 1963, postgrad., 1964-66. Coord. John M. Burns Assembly Campaign, N.Y.C., 1963; dir. spl. events, projects Kenneth B. Keating Senatorial Campaign, N.Y.C., 1964; dist. dir. fund raising Muscular Dystrophy Assn. Am. Inc., N.Y.C., 1965-66; exec. acct. fund raising, pub. relations Victor Weingarten Co., N.Y.C., 1966-67, Oram Group (formerly Harold L. Oram Inc.), N.Y.C., 1967-70; dir. devel. City Ctr. Music Drama Inc., N.Y.C., 1970; sales person Whitbread-Nolan, N.Y.C., 1971-73; from asst. v.p. to sr. v.p. Cross and Brown Co., N.Y.C., 1973-1985; sr. dir., commercial real estate Cushman & Wakefield, Inc., N.Y.C., 1985—. Trustee Young Adult Inst.; founder, chmn. The Hazel K. Goddess Fund for Stroke Rsch. in Women., 2000—. Mem. Nat. Soc. Fund Raisers, Assn. Fund Dirs., Real Estate Bd. N.Y. (named Most Ingenious Broker Yr. 1975), Women's Forum (bd. dirs.). Office: Cushman & Wakefield Inc 51 W 52nd St Fl 11 New York NY 10019-6119 E-mail: lgoddess@cushwake.com.

GODECKI, MARK ALEXANDER, obstetrician-gynecologist; b. Chmielnik, Poland, Apr. 25, 1947; MD, Acad. Medicine, Cracow, Poland, 1970. Diplomate Am. Bd. Ob-gyn. Intern, then resident Maimonides Med. Ctr., N.Y.C., 1974-79; pvt. practice Med. Arts Ob-gyn. P.C., Utica, N.Y.; clin. instr. SUNY, Syracuse; mem. staff St. Luke's Meml. Hosp., Utica. Office: Med Arts Ob-Gyn PC 1522 Old Burrstone Rd Utica NY 13502-4854

GODEKE, RAYMOND DWIGHT COOK, insurance company executive, accountant; b. San Diego, Nov. 26, 1947; s. Robert Carroll and Julia Mae (Caeser) G.; m. Norma Dean Rhodes, Oct. 31, 1966(div. 1970); 1 child, Melyssa Dawn; m. Vicki Lorraine Coleman, Feb. 19, 1972; 1 child, Kristin Francine. AA, Fullerton Coll., 1976; BA, Calif. State U.-Fullerton, 1978; MBA, Pepperdine U., 1980. Acct. Robert Johnston & Assocs., Lynwood, Calif., 1974-75; mem. acctg. staff Denny's, Inc., La Mirada, Calif., 1975-82, div. contr., 1982-87, Foster Farms, Livingston, Calif., 1987-90; indsl. healthcare exec. TriCare, Irvine, Calif., 1990-92; produce distbn. exec. J.C. Produce, L.A., 1992-94; contr. Zacky Farms, South El Monte, Calif., 1994-98, Word & Brown Ins. Adminstrs. Inc., Orange, Calif., 1998—. Chmn. Arrowhead dist. Boy Scouts Am., 1986. With USMC, 1970-74. Mem. NRA, Nat. Assn. Accts. (bd. dirs. 1982-83), Inst. Internal Auditors (cert.), Inst. Mgmt. Accts. (cert.), Cert. Mgmt. Acct. Soc. So. Calif. (pres. 1999-2000), Masons (past master), Shriners. Republican. Presbyterian. Avocations: golf, reading. Office: Word & Brown 721 S Parker St Ste 300 Orange CA 92868-4732 E-mail: rgodeke@wordandbrown.com.

GODENNE, GHISLAINE DUDLEY, physician, psychoanalyst, educator; b. Brussels; came to U.S., 1951; d. Pierre and Olive Dudley (Short) G. BS, Universite Catholique de Louvain, Belgium, 1948, MD, 1952. Intern Providence Hosp., Washington, 1951-52; resident in pediatrics, 1952-54; fellow in pediatrics Mayo Clinic, Rochester, Minn., 1954-57; fellow in pediatric research Johns Hopkins U., 1957-58, assoc. prof. mental hygiene, 1966-82, assoc. prof. psychiatry and pediatrics, 1966-82, psychoanalyst, 1972—, prof. psychology, 1973-90, prof. psychiatry, pediatrics, and mental hygiene, 1982—; resident in psychiatry Johns Hopkins Hosp., Balt., 1958-62, chief adolescent psychiat. service, 1964-73, dir. counseling and psychiat. services, 1973-90, dir. health svcs., 1978-88, dir. emeritus, 1990—; mem. staff various hosps. Balt., 1978-88; clin. prof. psychiatry U. Md., Balt., 1986—. Cons. psychiatrist Cylburn Children's Home, Balt., 1960-81, Catonsville (Md.) C.C., 1968-75, Good Shepherd Ctr., Balt., 1970-74, Assoc. Cath. Charity, Balt., 1970-77, Jewish Family of Children's Svcs., Balt., 1972-77, Mt. Washington Pediat. Hosp., Balt., 1974-81, Sheppard and Enoch Pratt Hosp., Balt., 1973-80, Loyola Coll., Balt., 1990-92. Mem. editorial bd.: Adolescent Psychiatry, 1978-83, Clinical Update Adolescent Psychiatry, 1982-85; contbr. articles to profl. jours. Bd. dirs. Balt. Girl Scouts Assn., 1958-60, 81-82, Met. Balt. Assn. Mental Health, 1965-69, Florence Crittendon Home, 1966-68; trustee McDonough Sch., 1975-83; pres. bd. Trustees Richmond Fellowship Md., 1975-77. Decorated Knight and Officer Order of Leopold (Belgium 1972-84), recipient Christophe Plantin prize (Belgium), 1989; awarded Nobility Concession with the title of Baroness (Belgium) 1991; recipient Career Teaching award NIMH, 1963-65, Schonfeld award Am. Soc. Adolescent Psychiatry, 1995; grantee Fulbright Found., 1951-52, Parke Davis Co., 1957-58, NIMH, 1961-63. Fellow ACP, Am. Psychiat. Assn. (life), APHA (life), Am. Orthopsychiat. Assn. (life), Am. Soc. Adolescent Psychiatry (life, pres. 1981-82), Am. Coll. Health Assn.; mem. AAUP, Am. Psychoanalytic Soc., Md. Soc. Adolescent Psychiatry (pres. 1968-69), Md. Psychiat. Soc. (past chmn. program com., co-chmn. women's com. 1991-96), Md. State Conf. Social Welfare (past mem. child welfare com.), Am. Soc. Adolescent Medicine (charter), Am. U. and Coll. Counseling Ctr. Dirs., Internat. Soc. Adolescent Psychiatry (v.p. 1989-92, sec.-gen. 1992-95, v.p. 1995-99, co-editor monograph 2000—), Women's Club of Johns Hopkins U. (pres. 1999-2000). Home: 15 Edgevale Rd Baltimore MD 21210-2215 E-mail: gigodenn@jhmi.edu.

GODET-CALOGERAS, JEANFRANÇOIS, historian, educator; b. Etterbeek, Brabant, Belgium, July 10, 1946; s. René Godet and Suzanne Geerts; m. Athena Calogeras, Feb. 14, 1992. PhD, Cath. U. of Louvain, Belgium, 1963—74. Tchr. St. J.B. de La Salle H.S., Brussels, 1967—71; asst. prof. Cath. U. of Louvain, Louvain, Belgium, 1974—79; assoc. editor Franciscan Inst. Publications, St. Bonaventure, NY, 1999—2003; scholar Sch. of Franciscan Studies, St. Bonaventure, NY, 2003—. Office: School Franciscan Studies St Bonaventure U Saint Bonaventure NY 14778 Office Fax: 716-375-2156. E-mail: jefgocal@sbu.edu.

GODFREY, ALDEN NEWELL, communications educator; b. Quincy, Mass., Jan. 8, 1924; s. Edgar and Lela Winifred (Smith) G.; m. Ruth Mildred Mix, July 20, 1949 (div. Sept. 1968); children: Craig Alden, Brian Kent (dec.); m. Elvena Marie Ulrich, July 20, 1972. BA, Boston U., 1950; MA, U. Minn., 1951; D Divinity, Missionary of New Truth, Chgo., 1971. Info. officer U.S. Dept. of State, Manila, 1951-55; exec. various newspapers, Boston, Wilmington, N.C. and San Diego, 1955-68; exec. dir. United Way of Desert, Palm Springs, Calif., 1968-73, Combined Arts and Edn. Coun., San Diego, 1973-75, Inland Empire Cultural Found., Colton, Calif., 1975-79; v.p. Campaign Mgmt., Ltd., Palm Springs, Calif., 1979-83, pres., 1983-85; adj. prof. Coll. of Desert, Palm Desert, Calif., 1991—. Pres. Alliance of Calif. Arts Couns., San Francisco, 1975-77, San Diego chpt. Pub. Rels. Soc. Am., 1965-66, San Diego Press Club, 1966-67; v.p. Calif. Confedn. of Arts, L.A., 1978-79; campaign mgr. Maryanov for Mayor, Palm Springs, 1993; chmn. Wilson for Supr., Palm Springs, 1995, 98, Mayor's H.O.S.T. Com., San Diego, 1968; mem. Atty. Gen. Adv. Coun., Sacramento, 1964-68, Palm Springs Pub. Arts Commn., 2000. 1st lt. U.S. Army, 1942-46. Mem. Soc. Profl. Journalists, United Way Exec. Assn., Coll. of Desert Adj. Assn., Kiwanis, Press Club of Desert (treas.). Avocations: golf, travel. Home: 467 N Calle Rolph Palm Springs CA 92262-0708 Office: Coll of the Desert 43-500 Monterey Ave Palm Desert CA 92260 E-mail: pandapsp@aol.com.

GODFREY, CULLEN MICHAEL, lawyer, academic administrator; b. Ft. Worth, Apr. 8, 1945; s. Cullen Aubrey and Agnes (Eiland) Godfrey; m. Melinda McDonald, Aug. 29, 1970. BA, U. Tex., 1968, JD, 1970. Bar: Tex. 1969, U.S. Dist. Ct. (we. dist.) Tex. 1971, U.S. Ct. Appeals (5th cir.) 1979, U.S. Ct. Appeals (11th cir.) 1981. Ptnr. Sloan, Muller & Godfrey, Austin, Tex., 1969-72; staff atty. Hunt Oil Co., Dallas, 1972-74, Tesoro Petroleum Corp., San Antonio, 1974-75, sr. atty., 1975-78, asst. gen. counsel, 1978-82, FINA, Inc., Dallas, 1982-88, gen. counsel, 1988-90; v.p., sec., gen. counsel Am. Petrofina, Inc. (now FINA, Inc.), Dallas, 1990-95, sr. v.p., sec., gen. counsel, 1995-2000; vice chancellor, gen. counsel U. Tex. Sys., Austin, 2000—. Author: (book) Legal Aspects of the Purchase and Sale of Oil and Gas Properties, 1992; contbr. articles to profl. jours. Trustee Dallas Mus. Art, 1993—95, 1998—2000; bd. dirs. United Way Met. Dallas, Inc., 1999—2000, gen. campaign chmn., 1999; bd. dirs. Dallas County Heritage Soc., 1998—2000; mem. exec. bd. dirs. Cir. 10 Boy Scouts Am., 1999—2000. Recipient Excellence in Corp. Practice award, Am. Corp. Counsel Assn., 1998, Jurisprudence award, Anti-Defamation League, 1999. Fellow: Dallas Bar Found. (sustaining life fellow), Tex. Bar Found. (life); mem.: ABA (chmn.subcom. on fgn. investment reporting, internat. law sect. 1984—87), Am. Law Inst., Ctr. Am. and Internat. Law (rsch. fellow), Greater Dallas Crime Commn. (bd. dirs. 1991—2000, chmn. bd. dirs. 1997—99), Tex. Bus. Law Found. (bd. dirs. 1990—, chmn. bd. dirs. 1995—98), Tex. Bd. Legal Specialization (bd. cert. oil, gas and mineral law), State Bar Tex. (coll. mem. 1989—, coun. oil, gas and mineral law sect. 1992—95, coun. bus. law sect. 1998—, chmn. bus. law sect. 2002—03, Cert. Merit 1999, 2003). Office: U Tex Sys Office Gen Counsel 201 W 7th St Austin TX 78701 E-mail: mgodfrey@utsystem.edu.

GODFREY, DONAL CHARLES, priest; b. Liverpool, Eng., Jan. 8, 1959; s. Robin Patrick Godfrey and Mary Frances McCambridge. BCL, Univ. Coll., Cork, Ireland, 1980; BL, The Hon. Soc. of King's Inns, Dublin, 1982; BPhil, Milltown Inst. of Theology and Philosophy, Dublin, 1986; MDiv/STB, U. Toronto, 1991; STL, Jesuit Sch. of Theology, Berkeley, Calif., 1993; D in Ministry, Ch. Divinity Sch. of Pacific, Berkeley, Calif., 2003. Bar: Dublin (Mem. Irish Bar) 1982; cert. Mem. Soc. of Jesus (Jesuits) Dublin, 1984. Tchr. Clongowes Wood Coll., Ireland, 1986—88; assoc. dir. campus ministry U. San Francisco, 1993—95; reconciliation worker Jesuits, Belfast, Ireland, 1994—98, sabbatical Sydney, Australia, 1998—99; resident min. U. San Francisco, 1999—2003; coord. Magis program Loyola U., Chgo., 2003—. Deacon Most Holy Redeemer Ch., San Francisco, 1991—92; adj. prof. theology dept. U. San Francisco, 1993—94. Contbr. articles. Sec. interchurch fellowship Clergy Network, Belfast, 1997—99. Recipient Gold medal, Philos. Soc., Cork, Ireland, 1979, Law Soc., Cork, 1980; grantee grant to run ecumenical retreats, No. Ireland Govt., 1997—99. Mem.: Amnesty Internat. Avocation: hiking, novels, films, Bonsai. Home: Loyola U 6525 N Sheridan Rd San Francisco CA 60626 E-mail: donalgodfrey@yahoo.com.

GODFREY, JOHN CARL, medicinal chemist; b. Cornelius, Oreg., Mar. 11, 1929; s. Carl H. and Ruth Emma (James) G.; m. Nancy Jane Williams, June 12, 1954; children: Laura Alexis, Helen Rebecca, Sabrina Lee. BA in Chemistry, Pomona Coll., Claremont, Calif., 1951; PhD in Organic Chemistry, U. Rochester, 1954. Rsch. chemist Shell Devel. Co., Emeryville, Calif., 1954-55; instr. chemistry Rutgers U., New Brunswick, N.J., 1955-59; asst. dir. clin. rsch. Bristol Labs., Syracuse, N.Y., 1959-79, Revlon Health Care, Tuckahoe, N.Y., 1979-86; assoc. dir. clin. rsch. Rorer Pharm. Corp., Horsham, Pa., 1986-90; pres. Godfrey Sci. & Design, Inc., Huntingdon Valley, Pa., 1979—, cons., 1990—. Mem. sci. adv. bd. Quigley Corp., Doylestown, Pa., 1992—. Contbr. more than 60 articles to profl. jours. NSF fellow, 1951; DuPont fellow, 1952-53. Fellow Am. Inst. Chemists; mem. AAAS, Am. Soc. Microbiology, Am. Chem. Soc. Achievements include patents for formulation to deliver active zinc in treatment of common cold (U.S., U.K., Can., Europe), 51 total in U.S.; elucidation of mechanism of action of zinc against common cold in humans; development of major common cold intervention lozenges; invention of Godfrey Stereomodels which uniquely demonstrate mechanisms of formation, properties and reactions. Office: Godfrey Sci & Design 1649 Old Welsh Rd Huntingdon Valley PA 19006-5835 Office Fax: 215-914-0150. E-mail: jcandnj@aol.com.

GODFREY, JOHN MUNRO, economic consultant; b. San Antonio, Mar. 20, 1941; s. George Phillips and Frieda (Allen) G.; m. Nancy Porter, June 4, 1966 (div. 1976); 1 son, John Munro, Jr.; m. Flavel Mcmichael, July 30, 1994. AA, Armstrong State Coll., 1964; BBA, U. Ga., 1964, PhD, 1976. Rsch. officer, sr. fin. economist Fed. Res. Bank, Atlanta, 1969-81; sr. v.p., chief economist Barnett Banks Inc., Jacksonville, 1981-93; prin. Fla. Econ. Assocs., Jacksonville. Adj. prof. econs. and fin. Davis Coll. Bus., Jacksonville (Fla.) U., 1993-97; mem. Gov.'s Econ. Adv. Com.; mem. econ. adv. com. Am. Bankers Assn. Author: Monetary Expansion in the Confederacy, 1977. Mem. econ. adv. com. U.S. C. of C.; bd. dirs. Fla. Ballet at Jacksonville, Jacksonville Symphony Orch., Cummer Mus. of Art and Gardens, St. Vincent's (Hosp.) Found.; trustee St. Johns Country Day Sch.; vestryman St. Marks Episcopal Ch., Jacksonville; trustee, treas. St. Marks Episcopal Ch. Found. Recipient Disting. Alumnus award Terry Coll. of Bus., U. Ga., 1994. Mem. Econ. Roundtable of Jacksonville (pres. 1982-89), Nat. Assn. Bus. Economists (dir.), Am. Econ. Assn., So. Econ. Assn., U. Ga. Coll. Bus. Alumni Assn. (bd. dirs., pres.), Ponte Vedra Club, Fla. Yacht Club (bd. dirs.), Meninak Club (bd. dirs. Jacksonville chpt.), River Club, Timuquana Country Club. Episcopalian. Home: 4652 Ortega Forest Dr Jacksonville FL 32210-5823 Office: Fla Econ Assocs 2905 Corinthian Ave Ste 1 Jacksonville FL 32210-4464 E-mail: godfreyjon@aol.com.

GODFREY, JOHN WILLIAM, retired music educator; b. Utica, N.Y., July 24, 1946; s. Raymond Otis and Rose Ethel Godfrey; m. Maxine Ellen Lippincott, Dec. 10, 1933. BS in Music Edn., CUNY, 1968; M in Music Edn., Ithaca Coll., 1972. Cert. Music Tchr. State of N.Y., 1968. Tchr. elem. band Corfu-East Pembroke Ctrl. Sch., Corfu, NY, 1968—71; grad. asst. - student tchrs. Ithaca Coll., Ithaca, NY, 1971—72; tchr. jr. sr. high band Dryden Ctrl. Sch., Dryden, NY, 1972—90; tchr. elem. orch. Kyrene Elem. Sch. Dist., Tempe, Ariz., 1990—92; tchr. elem. gen. music and band Mesa Pub. Schools, Mesa,

Ariz., 1992—94, tchr. jr. high band, 1994—2002; ret., 2002. Dir. band Ahwatukee Cmty. Band, Phoenix, 1993—95; dir. music Dryden Ctrl. Sch., Dryden, NY, 1972—88. Mem.: Ariz. Music Educator's Assn., Nat. Music Educators Assn., Tompkins County Music Educator's Assn. (pres.), Nat. Assn. for Music Educators. Home: 12021 S 45th St Phoenix AZ 85044

GODFREY, RAYMOND MICHAEL, information systems educator; b. Washington, Sept. 10, 1946; s. Raymond Vincent Godfrey and Agnes Watt Mulvey; m. Nancy Hibbard Roberts; 1 child, Brenton. BA in Physics, Amherst Coll., 1968; MPA in Gen. Mgmt., U. So. Calif., L.A., 1975, PhD in Pub. Adminstrn., 1984. Cert. CDP Inst. for Certification of Computer Profls., N.Y. Physicist Assoc. Aero Sci. Labs., Ridgecrest, Calif., 1968—69; gen. mgr. Entropy Minus Mining & Milling, Johannesburg, Calif., 1969—72; software engr., test analyst Control Data Corp., China Lake, 1969—72; software engrng. project mgr. Computer Scis. Corp., China Lake, 1973—75; pres. EM Sys. Assocs., Irvine, Calif., 1975—2002; prof. info. sys. Antioch U., Santa Monica, Calif., 1983—85, Calif. State U., Long Beach, 1995—2001. Sr. cons. RMG Assocs., L.A., 1975—90; editl. reviewer info. sys. textbooks and jours. Mem. supr.'s forum Long Beach Unified Sch. Dist., Long Beach, 1993—95; acad. program reviewer Irvine Unified Sch. Dist., Irvine, 1996—2003; co-developer U./K-12 Cmty. Svc. Learning Partnerships, Long Beach, 1999—2002; Bd. dirs. Vision for Long Beach, Long Beach, 1991—93. Named univ. del. Nat. Forum on Tchg. Excellence, AAHE, 1994; fellow, UN (UNIDO), 1992, vis. scholar fellow, Claremont (Calif.) Grad. Sch. & Sch. of Theology, 1990—91. Mem.: IEEE, Ctr. for Process Studies (Claremont), Acad. Mgmt., Assn. for Computing Machinery, S.Am. Explorers Club. Office: EM Sys Assocs 4092 Manzanita St Irvine CA 92604

GODFREY, RICHARD CARTIER, lawyer; b. Harvey, Ill., Sept. 25, 1954; s. Richard L. and Rosemary (Cartier) G.; m. Alice Bacon Woolsey, Aug. 27, 1983; children: John Cartier, Polly Woolsey. BA magna cum laude, Augustana Coll., 1976; JD magna cum laude, Boston U., 1979. Bar: Ill. 1979, U.S. Dist.Ct. (no. dist.) Ill. 1979, U.S. Dist.Ct. (cen. dist.) Ill. 1988, U.S. Dist.Ct. (we. dist.) Mich. 1990, U.S. Dist.Ct. (no. dist.) Ind. 1999, U.S. Dist. Ct. Colo. 2002, U.S. Ct. Appeals (7th cir.) 1983, U.S. Ct. Appeals (6th cir.) 1988, U.S. Ct. Appeals (8th cir.) 1994, U.S. Ct. Appeals (10th cir.) 1996, U.S. Ct. Appeals (11th cir.) 1997, U.S. Ct. Appeals (5th & 9th cirs.) 1999, U.S. Ct. Appeals (2d. cir.) 2002, U.S. Ct. Appeals (1st cir.) 2003, U.S. Ct. Appeals (3d cir.) 2003, U.S. Claims Ct. 1990, U.S. Supreme Ct. 2000. Assoc. Kirkland & Ellis, Chgo., 1979-85, ptnr., 1985—. Mem. ABA, Ill. Bar Assn., Chgo. Bar Assn. Home: 623 N Euclid Ave Oak Park IL 60302-1619 Office: Kirkland & Ellis Ste 6048 200 E Randolph Dr Chicago IL 60601

GODFREY, RICHARD GEORGE, real estate appraiser, consultant; b. Sharon, Pa., Dec. 18, 1927; s. Fay Morris and Elisabeth Marguerite (Stefanak) G.; m. Golda Fay Goss, Oct. 28, 1951; children: Deborah Jayne, Gayle Rogers, Bryan Edward. BA, Ripon Coll., 1949. V.p. 1st Thrift & Loan Assn., Albuquerque, 1959-61; pres. Richard G. Godfrey & Assocs., Inc., Albuquerque, 1961-93, owner, 1993—. Mem. Appraisal Inst. (v.p. 1981-82), Counselors of Real Estate. Baptist. Home: 1700 Columbia Dr SE Albuquerque NM 87106-3311 Office: 523 Louisiana Blvd SE Albuquerque NM 87108-3842 E-mail: godfreyappraisal@cs.com.

GODFREY, ROBERT DOUGLAS, lawyer; b. Danbury, Conn., Sept. 11, 1948; s. Douglas and Rita (Cardinale) G. BA, Fordham U., 1970; JD, U. Conn., 1985. Bar: Conn. 1985. Com. clk. Conn. Gen. Assembly, Hartford, 1977-78; v.p. pub. affairs Greater Danbury C. of C., 1978-82; law clk. to presiding judge Probate Ct., City of Danbury, 1983; atty. Conn. Bank & Trust Co., Hartford, 1986-90; justice of the peace State of Conn., 1977—. Mem. U.S. Internet Coun., 1998. Councilman Common Coun. of Danbury, 1985-89; mem. Charter Rev. Commn., Danbury, 1988; with Conn. Ho. of Reps., 1989—, dep. maj. leader, 1995—; mem. exec. com. Coun. State Govts., 1997-99; mem. exec. com. Ea. Regional Coun., Coun. State Govts., 2000—; bd. dirs. AIDS Project Greater Dangury, 2003—. With USNR, 1970-77. Recipient reproductive rights award Conn. Coalition for Choice, 1990, environ. e nergy award Peoples Action for Clean Energy, 1992; named Champion for Children, Conn. Coalition for Children, 1990, Legislator of Yr., Conn. Police Chiefs Assn., 1993; recognized Conn. Coalition Against Gun Violence, 1993, spl. recognition award Danbury Dept. Elderly Svcs., 1995, legis. leadership award Housing Authority Danbury, 1995, legis. svc. award Conn. Med. Assn., 1996, cmty. svc. award Midwestern Conn. Coun. on Alcoholism, 1998, Outstanding State Legislator award AFL-CIO, 2000, Apple Pie award Million Mom March, 2001; recognized sponsor youth andgovt. Conn. YMCA. Cath. War Vets. (judge advocate 1978—) Home: 13 Stillman Ave Danbury CT 06810-8007 Office: Conn Ho of Reps Legis Office Bldg Rm 4107 Hartford CT 06106 E-mail: bob.godfrey@po.state.ct.us., robert.godfrey@snet.net.

GODFREY, ROBERT GORDON, physician; b. Wichita, Kans., June 11, 1927; s. Henry Robert and Pearl Madeline (Gaston) G.; m. Margaret Scott Ingling, June 24, 1951; children: Timothy, Katherine, Gwendolyn, Melissa. BA, U. Wichita, 1952; MD, U. Kans., 1958. Intern Boston City Hosp., 1958-59; resident in internal medicine Peter Bent Brigham Hosp., Boston, 1959-60, Colo. Gen. Hosp., Denver, 1961-63; asst. in medicine Peter Bent and Robert Brigham Hosp.-Harvard Med. Sch., 1959-61; fellow in rheumatology Robert B. Brigham Hosp., 1960-61, U. Colo., Denver, 1963-64; instr. medicine U. Kans. Med. Ctr., Kansas City, 1964-65, asst. prof. med., 1965-95, staff physician, chief arthritis sect., 1965-75; ret., 1995; assoc. chief of staff for ambulatory care VA Med Ctr., Kansas City, Mo., 1978-80; staff physician, sr. rheumatologist VA Med. Ctr., Kansas City, Mo., 1980-84; chief rheumatology sect., assoc. chief med. service ambulatory care Leavenworth VA Med. Ctr., Kans., 1984-88; cons. rheumatology Physicians Associated, Overland Park, Kans., 1988-93; pvt. cons. rheumatology, 1995—. Served with M.C., U.S. Army, 1945-47. Recipient Disting. Service award Kans. Arthritis Found., 1975 Fellow ACP, Am. Coll. Rheumatology (founding fellow original Am. Rheumatism Assn.); mem. Am. Soc. Clin. Rheumatology, Sigma Xi, Alpha Omega Alpha. Republican. Office: U Kans Med Ctr Divsn Allergy Clin Immunol Rheumatol 3901 Rainbow Blvd Kansas City KS 66160-0001 E-mail: rgodfrey@sound.net.

GODFREY, ROBERT R. financial services executive; b. Sweetwater, Tex., May 22, 1947; s. Ross R. and Lillian L. (Bradford) G.; m. Diane M. Kalinowski, June 30, 1972. BBA, Tex. Tech. U., 1969, postgrad. in Bus. Adminstrn., 1969-71; postgrad. in Acctg., Sacred Heart U., 2000. Underwriter Aetna Life and Casualty Co., Hartford, Conn., 1969-72; tchg. fellow Tex. Tech. U., Lubbock, Tex., 1969-71, Ctrl. Conn. State Coll., New Britain, 1972; asst. mgr. Gulf Ins. Group, Dallas, 1972-76; asst. v.p. Scor Reins. Co., Dallas, 1976-79; pres. Rollins Burdick Hunter Mgmt. Co., N.Y.C., 1979-81; founder, pres., dir. St. Regis Ins. Group/Drum Fin. Corp., N.Y.C., 1981-85; exec. v.p. MBIA, Inc., Armonk, N.Y., 1985-95; chmn., founder N/W Capital, Inc., Stamford, Conn., 1995—. Dir. Lebenthal Mut. Funds Group, 1995—, dir. MBIA Ins. Corp., 1987-95; corp. adv. coun. NYU Salomon Ctr., 1990-95. Author: Risk Based Capital Charges for Municipal Bonds, 1990, Higher Bond Yields: The Insured Triple A Advantage, 1993, The Municipal Bond Handbook, 1994. Trustee Citizens Budget Commn. of N.Y., 1990-96; interim chmn. Town Dem. Com. New Canaan, 2000. With U.S. Army, 1970. Mem. Union League (mem. pension and endowment coms.). Office: 1177 High Ridge Rd Stamford CT 06905-1203

GODFREY, WILLIAM ASHLEY, ophthalmologist; b. Arkansas City, Kans., May 19, 1938; BA, U. Kans., Lawrence, 1960; MD, U. Kans., Kansas City, 1965. Diplomate Am. Bd. Ophthalmology. Intern Tulane U., New Orleans, 1965-66; resident U. Kans. Sch. Medicine, 1968-71; rsch. fellow U. Calif., San Francisco, 1971-73; asst. prof., then assoc. prof. U. Kans. Sch. Medicine, 1973-84, prof. ophthalmology, 1984—. Mem. staff St. Luke's Hosp., Kansas City, Mo., 1973—, Kansas U. Med. Ctr., Kansas City, 1973— ; cons. Kansas City Vets Hosp., Mo., 1973-89. Contbr. articles to profl. pubs. With USAF, 1966-68. NIH fellow, 1971-73. Fellow ACP, Am. Acad. Ophthalmology (honor ward 1983), Am. Uveitis Soc.; mem. Am. COll. Physicians, AMA, Am. Fedn. Clin. Rsch., Am. Rheumatism Assn., Assn. Rsch. in Vision and Ophthalmology, Am. Math. Soc., Ocular Immunology and Microbiology Soc., Kansas City Soc. Ophthalmology, Kans. Med. Soc., Mo. Ophthalmology Soc., Jackson County Med. Soc., Am. Ophthal. Soc., Wyandotte County Med. Soc., Johnson County Med. Soc., Soc. Heed Fellows, Assn. Proctor Fellows, Kans. Ophthal. Soc., Alpha Omega Alpha. Office: Hunkeler Vision Ctr 4321 Washington St Ste 6000 Kansas City MO 64111-5933

GODILO-GODLEVSKY, EUGENE ALEXANDERSON, poet; b. Bklyn., July 13, 1956; s. Alexander Evgenievich and Paula (Nipp) G.-G. BA in English, Fordham U., 1979, MA in English, 1991. Author: Poems of Faith and Love, 1992, Five-Beat Poems, 1993, Four-Beat Poems, 1994, Migration of the Soul, 1995, The Judgment of Pilate, 1996, Stefan and the Bird of Paradise, 1998, Various Verses, 1998, Narrative Poems, 2000, Hymns, 2000, Imaginings, 2000, Theologies, 2001, Songs Without Scores, Tunes Without Tones, 2002. Deacon Mt. Kisco (N.Y.) Presbyn. Ch., 1992-98, ch. choir. Recipient Golden Poet award World of Poetry, 1989, Editor's Choice award Nat. Libr. Poetry, 1994. Avocations: walking, yoga. Home: 520 Tuckahoe Rd Apt 2A Yonkers NY 10710-5718

GODINE, DAVID RICHARD, publishing company executive; b. Cambridge, Mass., Sept. 4, 1944; s. Morton Robert and Bernice (Beckwith) G.; m. Sara Eisenman, 1987; children: Addison Reuben, Madeline Sangree. BA (Sr. fellow), Dartmouth Coll., 1966; Ed.M., Harvard U., 1968. Founder David R. Godine, Pub., Inc., Boston, 1969, pres., 1969—, pub., editor, 1969—. Author: Renaissance Books of Science, 1970. Trustee Mass. Hort. Soc. Served with AUS, 1967. Fellow Pierpont Morgan Libr.; mem. Mass. Hist. Soc., Am. Antiquarian Soc., Soc. Printers, St. Botolph Club (Boston), Grolier Club (N.Y.C.). Office: David R Godine Pub Inc 9 Hamilton Pl Boston MA 02108-4715

GODINER, DONALD LEONARD, lawyer; b. Bronx, N.Y., Feb. 21, 1933; s. Israel and Edith (Rubenstein) G.; m. Caryl Mignon Nussbaum, Sept. 7, 1958; children: Clifford, Kenneth. AB, NYU, 1953; JD, Columbia U., 1956. Bar: N.Y. 1956, Mo. 1972. Gen. counsel Stromberg-Carlson, Rochester, N.Y., 1965-71; assoc. gen. counsel Gen. Dynamics Corp., St. Louis, 1971-73; v.p., gen. counsel Permaneer Corp., St. Louis, 1973-75; ptnr. Gallop, Johnson, Godiner, Morganstern & Crebs, St. Louis, 1975-80; sr. v.p., gen. counsel, sec. Laclede Gas Co., St. Louis, 1980-98; of counsel Stone, Leyton and Gershman, P.C., St. Louis, 1999—. Editor Columbia U. Law Rev., 1955-56. Served with U.S. Army, 1956-58. Mem.: ABA, Bar Assn. of Metropolitan St. Louis. Home: 157 Trails West Dr Chesterfield MO 63017-2553 Office: Stone Leyton & Gershman PC 7133 Forsyth Blvd Ste 500 Saint Louis MO 63105-2122

GODINEZ, MAGDALENA, cardiology nurse; b. Brownsville, Tex., Dec. 30, 1956; d. Ramon Jr. and Virginia (Flores) Godinez; 1 child, Juan Ramon. Diploma, Tex. Southmost Coll., 1979, student. LVN. Surg. scrub nurse Brownsville (Tex.) Med. Ctr., 1979-80; pediatric/cardiology nurse physician's office, Brownsville, 1980-84, ophthalmology nurse, 1985-89; cardiology nurse Heart Clinic, Inc., Brownsville, 1989—2001; cardiology nurse, office mgr. Valley Cardiac Care Ctr., 2001—02; cardiology nurse, nuclear dept. Heart Clinic PA, McAllen, Tex., 2002—03; nurse Mi Jardin Adult Day Care, Brownsville, 2003—.

GODINEZ FLORES, RAMON, bishop; b. Jamay, Jalisco, Mexico, Apr. 18, 1936; s. Ortega J. Cleofas G. and Maria del Refugio (Flores). Lic. in Philosophy, Sem. Guadalajara, (Jalisco, Mexico); theology degree, postgrad. in canon law, U. Gregoriana, Rome. Ordained priest Roman Catholic Ch., 1959. Prof., superior Diocesan Sem., Guadalajara; chaplain religious communities, Templo de San Jorge, Vallarta-San Jorge, Guadalajara; pastor Parroco de Nuestra Senora de la Luz, Guadalajara; sec. Archdiocese of Guadalajara, 1972—80, aux. bishop, 1980—. Sec. gen. Conferencia del Episcopado Mexicano, 1991—98; bishop of Aguascalientes, Mex., 1998. Contbr. articles to religious jours. Home and Office: Galeana 105 Norte Apartado Postal 167 CP 20000 Aguascalientes Mexico

GODINO, MARC LAWRENCE, lawyer, musician; b. N.Y.C., Sept. 10, 1961; s. Rino L. and Dolores E. Godino. BS, Susquehanna U., 1983; JD, Whittier Coll., 1995. Bar: Calif. 1996, U.S. Dist. Ct. (cen. dist.) Calif. 1998, (ea., so., and no. dists) 1999, Colo. 2000. Assoc. Stull Stull & Brody, L.A., 1996—. Mem. ABA, L.A. County Bar Assn., Soc. Am. Magicians. Avocations: golf, tennis, music, fitness. Office: Stull Stull & Brody 10940 Wilshire Blvd Ste 2300 Los Angeles CA 90024-3916 E-mail: sonofrino@aol.com., mgodino@secfraud.com.

GODLESKI, JOHN JOSEPH, pathologist; b. Nanticoke, Pa., July 24, 1943; s. John and Sophie (Pretko) Godleski; m. Mary Lou Moss, June 14, 1969; children: Teresa Louise, Daniel Peter. BS, King's Coll., Wilkes-Barre, Pa., 1965; MD, U. Pitts., 1969. Intern, resident Mass. Gen. Hosp., Boston, 1969-71; rsch. fellow Harvard Sch. Pub. Health, Boston, 1971; USPHS officer EPA, Research Triangle Park, N.C., 1971-73; asst. prof. Med. Coll. of Pa., Phila., 1973-78, Brigham & Women's Hosp., Boston, 1978-85, assoc. prof., 1985—. Contbr. Rsch grant, NIH, 1979—. Roman Catholic. Home: 421 Conant Rd Weston MA 02493-1830 Office: Brigham & Womens Hosp 75 Francis St Boston MA 02115-6106

GODMAN, GABRIEL CHARLES, pathology educator; b. Albany, N.Y., Jan. 24, 1921; s. Hyman S. and Bertha R. Godman. AB, NYU, 1941, MD, 1944. House officer medicine Bellevue Hosp., N.Y.C., 1944-45; resident in pathology New Haven Hosp.; asst. in pathology Yale U. Med. Sch., New Haven, 1948-50; fellow in pathology Mt. Sinai Hosp., N.Y.C., 1950-51; mem. faculty Columbia U. Coll. Physicians and Surgeons, N.Y.C., 1952—; prof. pathology Columbia U. Coll. Physicians and Surgeons., N.Y.C., 1969—. Assoc. Rockefeller U., 1957-60. Contbr. articles and chpts. to jours. and texts in field. Served to capt. M.C., U.S. Army, 1945-47. Mem. Am. Assn. Pathologists, Am. Soc. Cell Biology, Harvey Soc., Internat. Acad. Pathology, Assn. U. Pathologists. Home: 900 W 190th St New York NY 10040-3633 Office: 630 W 168th St New York NY 10032-3702 E-mail: gcg2@columbia.edu.

GODOFF, ANN, book editor; b. N.Y.C., July 22, 1949; d. Boris and Marilyn (Rosenstock) G. BFA, NYU, 1972. Sr. editor Simon & Schuster, N.Y.C., 1980-86; editor in chief Atlantic Monthly Press, N.Y.C., 1986-91; exec. editor Random House Inc., N.Y.C., 1991-96, pres., editor-in-chief, 1997—2003.

GODOFSKY, LAWRENCE, lawyer; b. Yonkers, N.Y., Mar. 30, 1938; s. Eli and Lily (Deutsch) G.; m. Thea Grace Schimel, June 11, 1961; children: Randee Felicia, Howard Charles. BA, Columbia U., N.Y.C., 1960, LLB, 1965. Bar: N.Y. 1965, Fla. 1974. Asst. counsel Mut. Life Ins. Co. of N.Y., N.Y.C., 1964-73; mem. Swann and Glass and predecessor firm, Miami, Fla., 1973-74; v.p., gen. counsel Diversified Mortgage Investors (formerly Diversified Advisors, Inc.), Miami, 1974-76; mem. Greenberg, Traurig P.A., Miami, 1976—. Mem. bd. dirs. Infants in Need, Inc., Miami, 1991—. Mem. ABA, Fla. Bar Assn., Am. Coll. Real Estate Lawyers, Am. Land Title Assn. (assoc.). Office: Greenberg Traurig PA 1221 Brickell Ave Miami FL 33131-3224

GODOFSKY, STANLEY, lawyer; b. N.Y.C., May 24, 1928; s. Eli and Lily (Deutsch) G.; m. Elaine Gloria Weiss, Dec. 15, 1951 (dec. Feb. 1994); m. Phyllis A. Schaevitz, Jan. 16, 2000. AB, Columbia U., 1949, JD, 1951. Bar: N.Y. 1951, U.S. Supreme Ct. 1961. Assoc. Rogers & Wells, and predecessors, N.Y.C., 1951-64, ptnr., 1965-89. Co-adj. lectr. Rutgers Law Sch., 1990-91, adj. prof., 1992-93; adj. prof. Nova U. Law Sch., 1991-93; spl. asst. counsel N.Y. State Crime Commn., 1952. Bd. editors Columbia Law Rev., 1950, bd. revising editors, 1951. Trustee Jewish Community Ctr. White Plains, N.Y., 1983-89; mem. commn. on law and social action Am. Jewish Congress, 1986-98. Mem. ABA, Am. Law Inst., N.Y. State Bar Assn., Assn. of Bar of City of N.Y., Internat. Assn. Jewish Lawyers and Jurists (bd. govs. Am. sect. 1990-98, exec. com. and coun. 1999—). Home: 17858 Deauville Ln Boca Raton FL 33496-2457 E-mail: jenice45@bellsouth.net.

GODONE-MARESCA, LILLIAN, lawyer; b. Buenos Aires, June 9, 1958; d. Armand C.E. Godone-Signanini and E. Nydia Soracco-Godone; m. Paul Alexander Maresca-Lowell (dec.); children: Catherine Victoria, Gerard Frank, Warren Paul. BA, Cath. U. Buenos Aires, 1975, MA, 1977, JD summa cum laude, 1979, advanced tchg. degree in jud. sci., 1981. Bar: Dist. Ct. Buenos Aires 1980, Calif. 1995, U.S. Dist. Ct. (ea. dist.) Calif. 1995, U.S. Dist. Ct. (so. dist.) Calif. 1998; lic. real estate broker, Calif. Advisor Sub-Sec. of State for Fgn. Trade, Buenos Aires, 1982; pvt. practice law Buenos Aires, 1982-86; therapist Ocean Pkwy. Developmental Ctr., N.Y., 1992; pvt. practice law Sacramento, 1995-96, San Diego, 1997—. Asst. instr. Cath. U., Buenos Aires, 1983-86; adj. instr. U.S. Internat. U., San Diego, spring 1998. Contbr. articles to profl. jours.; author of poetry. Vol. San Diego Vol. Lawyer Program, 1993-94, Legal Svcs. No. Calif., Sacramento, 1995-96; catechist St. Ignatius, Sacramento, 1995-96, St. Michael's, Poway, Calif., 1997-98. Mem. Internat. Soc. Poets (disting.), State Bar Calif., Mothers Twins Club. Republican. Roman Catholic. Avocations: spending time with her children, the right to life, writing. Home: 202 Calle Florecita Escondido CA 92029

GODOSKY, ROBERT E. lawyer; b. N.Y.C., Jan. 1, 1963; s. Richard and Marcia Godosky; m. Laurie L. Pridgeon, Oct. 12, 1996; children: Jacob, Joshua. BA, Hamilton Coll., 1985; JD, Fordham U., 1988. Bar: Conn. 1988, N.Y. 1989; U.S. Dist. Ct. (ea. and so. dists.) N.Y. 1989. Atty. Gair, Gair & Conason, N.Y.C., 1988-96, Godosky & Gentile, P.C., N.Y.C., 1996—. Mem. ABA, ATLA, N.Y. State Trial Lawyers (instr. 1997—), N.Y. County Lawyers Assn., N.Y. State Bar Assn. Democrat. Jewish. Avocations: golf, reading. Office: Godosky & Gentile PC 61 Broadway New York NY 10006-2701 E-mail: robertg@godoskyandgentile.com.

GODSCHALK, DAVID ROBINSON, architect, urban development planner, educator; b. Enid, Okla., May 14, 1931; s. Harold J. and Helen Faye (Robinson) G.; m. Lallie Moore Kain, June 27, 1959; 1 child, David Kennedy. BA, Dartmouth Coll., 1953; B.Arch., U. Fla., 1959; M.Regional Planning, U. N.C., 1964, PhD, 1971. Vice pres. Milo Smith Assos., Tampa, Fla., 1959-61; planning dir. City of Gainesville, Fla., 1964-65; asst. prof. Fla. State U., Tallahassee, 1965-67; editor AIP Jour., Chapel Hill, N.C., 1968-71; assoc. prof. U. N.C., Chapel Hill, 1972-77, prof., 1977-94, Stephen Baxter prof. planning, 1994—, chmn. dept. city and regional planning, 1978-83. Cons. and expert witness in field. Author: (with others) Constitutional Issues of Growth Management, 1979, Land Supply Monitoring, 1986, Planning in America: Learning from Turbulence, 1974, Catastrophic Coastal Storms: Hazard Mitigation and Development Management, 1989, Urban Land Use Planning, 1995, Pulling Together: A Planning and Development Consensus Building Manual, 1994, Cooperating with Nature: Confronting Natural Hazards with Land Use for Planning Sustainable Communities, 1998. Natural Hazard Mitigation: Recasting Disaster Policy and Planning, 1999, Monitoring Land Supply with Georgaphic Information Systems, 2000; editor: (with others) Understanding Growth Management, 1989, The Planner as Dispute Resolver, 1989; editor Am. Inst. Planners Jour., 1968-71; mem. editl. bd. Jour. Planning Edn. and Rsch., 1983-89, 93-97, Jour. Am. Planning Assn., 1983-96, Jour. Archtl. Planning Rsch., 1991—, Australian Planner, 1997. Active Town Coun., Chapel Hill, 1985-89, NC Legis. Rsch. Commn. on Statewide Comprehensive Planning, 1991-93, NC Legis. Commn. on Smart Growth, 1999-2001. With USNR, 1953-56, 61-62; comdr. Res.; ret., 1980. Recipient Disting. Alumnus award Dept. City and Regional Planning, U. N.C., 1996; Disting. Grad. Tchg. awd., U.N.C., 1999. Fellow AICP; mem. Am. Planning Assn. (bd. govs. 1978-79, Profl. Achievement award 1983, Elected Ofcl. award N.C. chpt. 1990), Am. Soc. Planning Ofcls. (bd. dir. 1974-77), Am. Inst. Cert. Planners (Svc. medal 1971), Assn. Collegiate Schs. Planning (Disting. Educator award 2002). Office: Univ NC Dept City & Regional Planning Chapel Hill NC 27599-3140 E-mail: dgod@email.unc.edu.

GODSEY, JEFFREY LYNN, actor, educator; b. Cookeville, Tenn., July 11, 1968; s. Phillip Wayne (Stepfather) and Anne (Sewell) Godsey, Rex Herron. BFA Theatre Performance magna cum laude, Memphis State U., 1990; postgrad., U. Memphis, 2001—. Acting intern New Stage Theatre, Jackson, Miss., 1990-91; exec. asst. So. Coalition, Jackson, 1991-92; vol. coord. Miss. Mus. Art, Jackson, 1994; theatre prof. St. Joseph Cath. Sch., Jackson, 1994-95, 96; adminstrv. cons. Americorps, Jackson, 1995-96; exec. asst., devel. assoc. Memphis Coll. Art, 1998—2002; adminstv. dir. Delta Axis Power House, 2002—03. Voice-over actor Delta Casting, Memphis, 2000-2001; actor Circuit Playhouse, Memphis, 1999-2001, Theatre Memphis, 1998-2001, Take Note Prodns., Memphis, 1999, Playhouse on the Square, Memphis, 2001-02. Mem. steering com. Indie Memphis, 1999-2000; art acquisitions com. Hearts Against AIDS, Jackson, 1995; grants adjucator Hinds County Arts Alliance, Jackson, 1994. Democrat. Avocations: reading, writing, running, american popular music history.

GODSEY, JOHN DREW, minister, theology educator emeritus; b. Bristol, Tenn., Oct. 10, 1922; s. William Clinton and Mary Lynn (Corns) G.; m. Emalee Caldwell, June 26, 1943 (dec. Oct. 1993); children: Emalee Lynn Godsey Murphy, John Drew Jr., Suzanne Godsey Douglas, Gretchen Godsey Brownley; m. Cozette Hapney Barker, Sept. 23, 1995. BS, Va. Poly. Inst. and State U., 1947; BD, Drew U., 1953; D.Theol., U. Basel, Switzerland, 1960. Ordained to ministry United Methodist Ch., 1952. Instr. systematic theology, asst. dean Drew U., Madison, N.J., 1956-59, asst. prof., 1959-64, assoc. prof., 1964-66, prof., 1966-68; prof., assoc. dean Wesley Theol. Sem., Washington, 1968-71, prof. systematic theology, 1971-88, emeritus prof., 1988—. Fulbright scholar U. Goettingen, W. Germany, 1964-65 Author: The Theology of Dietrich Bonhoeffer, 1960, Karl Barth's Table Talk, 1963, Preface to Bonhoeffer, 1965, Introduction and Epilogue to Karl Barth's How I Changed My Mind, 1966, The Promise of H. Richard Niebuhr, 1970; co-editor: Ethical Responsibility: Bonhoeffer's Legacy to the Churches, 1981, Dietrich Bonhoeffer, Discipleship, 2000. Mem. Montgomery County Fair Housing Assn., Md. Served with AUS, 1943-46. Recipient Disting. Svc. Alumni award, Drew U. Theol. Alumni Assn., 1995; Faculty fellow, Am. Assn. Theol. Schs., 1964—65. Mem. Am. Acad. Religion, Am. Theol. Soc. (pres. 1985-86), Bibl. Theologians, Internat. Bonhoeffer Soc. (editor newsletter 1989-92), Karl Barth Soc. N.Am., New Haven Theol. Discussion Group, Am.'s Registry of Outstanding Profls., Common Cause, Omicron Delta Kappa, Phi Kappa Phi, Alpha Zeta Democrat. Home: 8306 Bryant Dr Bethesda MD 20817-3137 Office: Wesley Theol Sem 4500 Massachusetts Ave NW Washington DC 20016-5690 *My goal has been to serve others with integrity, to do every job to the best of my ability, and to respect and further the rights and welfare of my fellow creatures on planet earth. Thus should my life be a testimony to my faith.*

GODSEY, MARTHA SUE, speech-language pathologist; b. Abilene, Tex., Jan. 24, 1956; d. John Holbrook and Stella Mae (Blankenship) Chalmers; children: Bo Kilpatrick, Ryan Smith; married, Dec. 18, 1993; 1 child, J. Jordan Godsey. BSN, Tex. Chritian U., 1979; MA, Abilene Christian U., 1988. RN, Tex. RN Hendrick Med. Ctr., Abilene, 1979-80; speech pathologist Abilene Ind. Sch. Dist., 1989-92, Tri-County Edn. Co-op, 1992-94; pvt. practice, 1994-96; speech therapist Therapy Assocs., Inc., 1996-97, Sundance Rehab. Corp., 1997, West Tex. Rehab. Ctr., 1997-99, Abilene Ind. Sch. Dist., Tex., 1999—. Mem. Am. Speech/Lang. and Hearing Assn., Tex. Speech/Lang. and Hearing Assn. Avocation: reading. Home: 421 Pollard Abilene TX 79602

GODSEY, R(ALEIGH) KIRBY, university president; b. Birmingham, Ala., Apr. 2, 1936; m. Joan Stockstill; children— Raleigh, Hunter, Erica, Stephanie BA, Samford U., 1957; BD, New Orleans Baptist Theol. Sem., 1960, ThD, 1962; LHD, 1996; MA, U. Ala., 1967; PhD, Tulane U., 1969; LHD, U. S.C., 1984; LLD, Averett Coll., 1996. Asst. prof. philosophy and religion Judson Coll., Marion, Ala., 1962-67; Danforth assoc. Danforth Found., 1964-67; v.p., dean Averett Coll., Danville, Va., 1969-77; dean Coll. Liberal Arts Mercer U., Macon, Ga., 1977-78, exec. v.p., 1978-79, pres., 1979—. Trustee So. Assn. Colls. and Schs.; pres. Ga. Fund Ind. Colls.; chief cons. Comprehensive Instl. Devel. Project; cons. Mgmt. Higher Edn. and Organizational Devel. Problems, Planning and Data Systems for Pvt. Colls., Carnegie Found., Task Force on Acad. Affairs for Council of Ind. Colls.; mem. exec. com. Nat. Workshop on Faculty Devel., Lilly and Kellogg Founds.; lectr. Confs. on Personnel Relations, New Orleans, Chgo., Detroit, Seminars on Philos. Ethics for Med. Students, Tulane U., regional confs. and workshops, Chgo., St. Louis, Atlanta, Kansas City Author: When We Talk About God...Let's Be Honest; contbr. articles to profl. jours. Speaker at civic clubs and organs. and bus. and profl. groups including Rotary, Kiwanis, Exchange, Civitan, Sertoma Recipient Citizenship award, Danville, Va., 1971 Mem. Am. Assn. Higher Edn. (chmn. conf. on institutional planning), Am. Philosophical Assn., So. Soc. for Philosophy and Psychology, Macon C. of C. (bd. dirs.), Phi Alpha Theta, Phi Kappa Phi Lodges: Rotary. Baptist. Office: Mercer Univ Cen Office 1400 Coleman Ave Macon GA 31207-0001*

GODSEY, WILLIAM COLE, physician; b. Memphis, Dec. 11, 1933; s. Monroe Dowe and Margaret Pauline (Cole) G.; m. Norma Jean Wilkinson, June 18, 1958; children: William Cole, John Edward, Robert Dowe. BS, Rhodes Coll., 1955; MD, U. Tenn., 1958. Diplomate Am. Bd. Psychiatry and Neurology, Am. Bd. Forensic Medicine. Intern John Gaston Hosp., Memphis, 1958-59;

resident in psychiatry Gailor Meml. Hosp., Memphis, 1960-63; pvt. practice specializing in psychiatry and neurology Memphis, 1963—; asst. supt. Memphis Mental Health Inst., 1965-74; supt. Ctrl. State Hosp., Nashville, 1974-75; med. dir. Whitehaven Mental Health Ctr., Memphis, 1975-84, St. Joseph Hosp. Life Ctr., 1984-88; pres. Civilian Material Assistance, Memphis, 1988. Mem. staff Delta Med. Ctr.; asst. prof. U. Tenn. Coll. Medicine, 1965-74, Coll. Pharmacy, 1972-75; chief of staff Lakeside Hosp., Memphis, 1976-77; songwriter, pub.; pres. Memphis Country Music, Inc. Fellow Am. Psychiat. Assn. (life; past pres. West Tenn. chpt.); mem. NRA, Tenn. Psychiat. Assn. (exec. coun., past pres.), Am. Coll. Forensic Examiners, Moose. Methodist. Office: 3960 Knight Arnold Rd Ste 303 Memphis TN 38118

GODSOE, PETER COWPERTHWAITE, banker; b. Toronto, May 2, 1938; s. J. Gerald and Margaret (Cowperthwaite) G.; m. Shelagh Cathleen Reburn, Nov. 30, 1963; children: Craig, Cynthia, Eden. BSc in Math. and Physics, U. Toronto, 1961; MBA, Harvard U., 1966. Chartered acct., Can. Joined The Bank of N.S., various locations, 1966-71, various positions with internat., corp. banking divsn., 1971-82, vice chmn. bd., bd. dirs., 1982-92, pres., COO, vice chmn. bd., 1992, dep. chmn. bd., pres., CEO, 1993, chmn. bd., CEO, 1995—, Bd. dirs. Empire Co. Ltd., Bank N.S. Jamaica Ltd., Bank N.S. Trust Co. (Bahamas) Ltd., Bank N.S. Trust Co. (Cayman) Ltd.; dir. Lonmin Plc, Ingersoll Rand Co. Bd. dirs. Can. Coun. of Christians and Jews, Toronto, 1972—, Mt. Sinai Hosp., 1986; past pres. Bd. of Trade, Toronto, 1984-85; mem. adv. com. Western Bus. Sch., Richard Ivey Sch. Bus.; assoc. mem. bd. govs. Dalhousie U.; mem. chancellor's coun. Victoria U.; mem. adv. bd. Ctr. Rsch. Neurodegenerative Diseases; dir. (hon.) Sheena's Pl. Fellow Inst. Chartered Accts.; mem. Can. Bankers Assn. (past chmn.), Jr. Achievement of Met. Toronto and York Region (bd. govs.), Can. Club (past pres. 1982-83). Office: Bank of Nova Scotia Scotia Plz/44 King St W Toronto ON Canada M5H 1H1 E-mail: email@scotiabank.com.

GODSON, ROY SIMON, political scientist, think tank executive; b. Bklyn., Oct. 17, 1942; s. Joseph and Rose (Milner) G.; m. Christine Watson, Aug. 27, 1971. BA with honors, Middlebury Coll., 1964; MA, Columbia U., 1967, PhD, 1972. Instr. Carnegie-Mellon U., Pitts., 1967-69; dir. edn. World Affairs Coun. Pitts., 1967-69; prof. govt. Georgetown U., Washington, 1969—, dir. internat. labor program, 1971-86; with Nat. Strategy Info. Ctr., Washington, 1969—, pres., 1993—, coord. Consortium for Study of Intelligence, 1979—. Cons. U.S. agys., 1982—. Pres.'s Fgn. Intelligence Adv. Bd., 1982—89, Nat. Security Coun., 1982—86, UN, 1999—. Author: American Labor and European Politics: The AFL as a Transnational Force, 1976, Labor in Soviet Global Strategy, 1984; actor: Dirty Tricks or Trump Cards: U.S. Covert Action and Counterintelligence, 1995; co-author: Eurocommunism: Implications for East and West, 1978, Dezinformatsia: Active Measures in Soviet Strategy, 1984, The CIA and the American Ethic: An Unfinished Debate, 1985; editor: Intelligence Requirements for the 1990s: Collection, Analysis, Counterintelligence, and Covert Action, 1988, Comparing Foreign Intelligence: The US, USSR, UK and the Third World, 1988, Security Studies for the 21st Century, 1998—, Organized Crime & Democratic Governability: Mexico and the U.S.-Mexican Borderlands, 2001, Intelligence Requirements for the 1980s, 5 vol. series, Trends in Organized Crime, 1995—. Avocation: riding toward the light. Office: Georgetown Univ Dept Govt Washington DC 20057-0001

GODWIN, GAIL KATHLEEN, writer; b. Birmingham, Ala., June 18, 1937; d. Mose Winston and Kathleen (Krahenbuhl) G.; m. Douglas Kennedy, 1960 (div. 1961), m. Ian Marshall, 1965 (div. 1966). Student, Peace Jr. Coll., Raleigh, N.C., 1955-57; BA in Journalism, U. N.C., 1959; MA in English, U. Iowa, 1968, PhD, 1971, U. N.C., 1987, U. So.-Sewanee, 1994, SUNY, 1996. News reporter Miami Herald, 1959-60; rep., cons. U.S. Travel Service, London, 1961-65; editorial asst. Saturday Evening Post, 1966; instr. Univ. Iowa, Iowa City, 1967-71; lectr. Iowa Writer's Workshop, 1972-73, Vassar Coll., 1977, Columbia U. Writing Program, 1978, 81. Author: (novels) The Perfectionists, 1970, Glass People, 1972, The Odd Woman, 1974 (Nat. Book award nomination 1974), Violet Clay, 1978 (Am. Book award nomination 1980), A Mother and Two Daughters, 1982 (Am. Book award nomination 1982), The Finishing School, 1985, A Southern Family, 1987, Father Melancholy's Daughter, 1991, The Good Husband, 1994, Evensong, 1999, Evenings at Five, 2003; (short stories) Dream Children, 1976, Mr. Bedford and The Muses, 1983; editor: (with Shannon Ravenel) The Best American Short Stories 1985, 1985, Heart: A Personal Journey Through Its Myths & Meanings, 2001; librettist: (with Robert Starer) The Last Lover, 1975, Journals of a Songmaker, 1976, Apollonia, 1979, Anna Margarita's Will, 1981, Remembering Felix, 1987, Gregory The Great, 1996, The Other Voice: A Portrait of Hilda of Whitby in Words and Music, 1998, Magdalene At The Tomb, 1999, Abraham Remembers, 2000. Recipient Thomas Wolfe Meml. award Lipinsky Endowment of Western N.C. Hist. Assn., 1988, Janet Heidinger Kafka award U. Rochester, 1988; fellow Center for Advanced Study, U. Ill., Urbana, 1971-72; Am. specialist USIS, 1976; Nat. Endowment Arts grantee, 1974-75; Guggenheim fellow, 1975-76; recipient award in lit. Am. Acad. and Inst. of Arts and Letters, 1981 Mem. ASCAP, Authors Guild, Authors League. Home: PO Box 946 Woodstock NY 12498-0946

GODWIN, HAROLD NORMAN, pharmacist, educator; b. Ransom, Kans., Oct. 9, 1941; s. Harold Joseph and Nora Elva (Welsh) G.; m. Judy Rae Ricketts, June 9, 1963; children: Paula Lynn, Jennifer Joy. BS in Pharmacy, U. Kans., 1964; MS in Hosp. Pharmacy, Ohio State U., 1966. Lic. pharmacist, Kans., Ohio. Instr. Ohio State U. Coll. Pharmacy, Columbus, 1966-69; asst. dir. pharmacy Ohio State U., Columbus, 1966-69; dir. pharmacy U. Kans. Med. Ctr., Kansas City, 1969—; asst. prof. U. Kans. Sch. Pharmacy, Kansas City, 1969-74, assoc. prof., 1974-80, prof. pharmacy, 1980—, asst. dean pharmacy, 1975-89, assoc. dean pharmacy, 1989—, chmn. pharmacy practice, 1984—. John W. Webb lectr., vis. prof. Northeastern U., 1999; chmn. pharmacy exec. com. U. HealthSys. Consortium, 2001—. Author: Implementation Guide to IV Admixtures, 1977; (with others) Remington's Pharmaceutical Sciences, 1980, 85, 90, 95, 2000; contbr. over 100 articles to profl. jours. Recipient Clifton J. Latiolais award Ohio State U. Residents Alumni, 1986, Disting. Alumni award Ohio State U. Coll. Pharmacy, 1995; named Tchr. of the Yr., U. Kans. Sch. of Pharmacy, 2001. Fellow: Am. Soc. Health System Pharmacists (bd. dirs. 1978—81, pres. 1982—83, bd. dirs. rsch. and edn. found. 2002—, Harvey A.K. Whitney award 1991); mem.: Am. Coun. Pharm. Edn. (bd. dirs. 1988—2000, pres. 1992—96), Greater Kansas City Soc. Hosp. Pharmacists (pres. 1972), Kans. Soc. Hosp. Pharmacists (Kans. Hosp. Pharmacist of Yr. 1982, Harold N. Godwin award 1984), Kans. Pharmacists Assn. (pres 1977, Kans. Pharmacist of Yr. 1982), Am. Pharm. Assn. (Disting. Achievement award 2000). Republican. Methodist. Avocations: tennis, biking, cooking, wine tasting. Home: 10112 W 98th St Shawnee Mission KS 66212-5238 Office: U Kans Med Ctr Rainbow Blvd At 39th St Kansas City KS 66106-7231

GODWIN, JAMES BECKHAM, retired landscape architect; b. Richmond, Va, Nov. 17, 1918; s. James Bunyan and Carrie (Beckham) G.; m. Rebecca Maude Cade, Feb. 5, 1949 BS, N.C. State U., 1950. Assoc. R.D. Tillson & Assocs., High Point, N.C., 1950-55; ptnr. Godwin & Bell, Raleigh, N.C., 1955-61; pres. James B. Godwin & Assocs., Inc., Raleigh, N.C., 1961—. Pres., Gov.'s Beautification Com., Raleigh, 1967-69; bd. dirs. Keep N.C. Beautiful, Raleigh, 1971— ; bd. visitors Louisburg (n.C.) Coll., 1971-80; chmn. travel com. N.C. Art Soc., Raleigh, 1983-84. Served to capt. U.S. Army, 1941-46, PTO Fellow Am. Soc. Landscape Architects (trustee 1966-72). Democrat. Methodist. Avocations: reading; history; gardening; travel. Home and Office: 707 Smedes Pl Raleigh NC 27605-1140

GODWIN, JOHN THOMAS, pathologist, nuclear medicine specialist; b. Social Circle, Ga., Dec. 2, 1917; s. Hubert O. and Georgia (Adams) G.; m. Sara Moak, Mar. 5, 1948; children: Elizabeth, Thomas A., Patricia A. AB, Emory U., 1938, MD, 1941. Diplomate Am. Bd. Pathology, Clin. Pathology, Nuclear Medicine. Resident Touro Infirmary, New Orleans, 1941-42, 47-48; intern U.S. Naval Hosp., Pensacola, Fla., 1942-43; fellow Meml. Hosp., Sloan Kettering Inst., N.Y.C., 1948-51; pathologist Ochsner Found. Hosp., New Orleans, 1950-51; sr. scientist Brookhaven Nat. Lab., Upton Long Island, N.Y., 1951-55; attending pathologist Meml. Hosp., Sloan Kettering Inst., N.Y.C., 1951-55; dir. labs. St. Joseph's Hosp., Atlanta, 1955-78; chmn. dept. pathology King Faisal Specialist Hosp. and Rsch. Ctr., Riyadh, Saudi Arabia; dir. labs. Met-Path, Atlanta, 1978-91; pathologist West Paces Med. Ctr., Atlanta, 1991—. Rsch. scientist Ga. Inst. Tech., Atlanta; prof. pathology Sch. Dentistry, Emory U., Atlanta, 1959—; clin. prof. pathology Moorehouse Med. Sch., Atlanta; cons. to asst. sec. HEW, Washington, 1966. Contbr. articles to profl. jours. Mem. Republican Senatorial Inner Circle, Washington. Recipient 1st prize Radiol. Soc. N.Am., 1st prize So. Med. Assn. Fellow Am. Soc. Clin. Pathology (councilor 1961-63, silver medal, gold medal), James Ewing Soc. (treas. 1974-78, exec. com. 1972-73), Meml. Hosp. Pathology Alumni Soc. (pres. 1982). Republican. Methodist. Achievements include first to give description of at least two new neoplasms, training programs in medical technology; research in Thermal Neutron Capture Therapy for brain tumors. Home: 4691 Sentinel Post Rd NW Atlanta GA 30327-3915 Office: West Paces Med Ctr 3200 Howell Mill Rd NW Atlanta GA 30327-4101

GODWIN, JOSCELYN, humanities educator, writer; b. Kelmscott, Oxfordshire, U.K., Jan. 16, 1945; arrived in U.S., 1966; s. Edward Fell Godwin and Stephanie Mary Allfree; m. Janet Mattews, Nov. 21, 1979; 1 child, Ariel; m. Sharyn Cook, July 31, 1971 (div. May 18, 1979). BA, Magdalene Coll., Cambridge, U.K., 1965, MusB, 1966; PhD, Cornell Univ., Ithaca, N.Y., 1969. Instr. Cleve. State Univ., Cleve., 1969—71; prof. Colgate Univ., Hamilton, NY, 1971—. Author: Robert Fludd, 1979, Athanasius Kircher, 1979, Mystery Religions in the Ancient World, 1981, Harmonies of Heaven & Earth, 1987, The Mystery of the Seven Vowels, 1991, Arktos, 1993, The Theosophical Enlightenment, 1994, Music and the Occult, 1995, J.F.H. von Dalberg, 1998, The Pagan Dream of the Renaissance, 2002. Office: Colgate Univ Music Dept 13 Oak Dr Hamilton NY 13346

GODWIN, KIMBERLY ANN, federal agency administrator, lawyer; b. Fargo, N.D., July 18, 1960; d. Robert Chandler and Kathryn Marie (Haney) G. BA in Polit. Sci., U. N.H., 1980; MS in Mass Comm., JD, Boston U., 1984. Bar: D.C. 1984, U.S. Supreme Ct. 1990. Legal intern Army Corps of Engrs., Waltham, Mass., 1983-84; assoc. Booz, Allen & Hamilton, Inc., Bethesda, Md., 1986-88; cons. Dept. State, Washington, 1984-86, asst. dir. comm. interagy. affairs, 1988-92, chief of policy diplomatic telecom. svc., 1992-96, dir. external affairs, 1997—. Cons. Elton Assocs., Inc., Arlington, Va., 1984—. Mem. ABA (vice chmn. internat. comm. com. 1989—), Phi Beta Kappa, Pi Sigma Alpha. Avocations: flying, tennis, skiing. . Home: 6215 Walhonding Rd Bethesda MD 20816-2138 Office: Dept State IRM/EA Rm 4428 2201 C St NW Washington DC 20520-0001

GODWIN, KIPLING ELIGA, academic administrator; b. Whiteville, NC, Jan. 5, 1965; s. David Eliga and Walneta Caulder G.; m. Myra Lynn Tyner, Sept. 18, 1999. BS, N.C. State U., 1988, MEd, 1992. Owner Carolina Designs, 1988—; student svcs. specialist Nat. FFA Orgn., Alexandria, Va., 1989—92; exec. dir. N.C. FFA Found., Inc., Whiteville, 1992—2001; prin., owner Kipling Godwin & Assocs., Whiteville, NC, 2001—03; dir. Sylvan Learning Ctr., 2003—. Chmn. Columbus County ARC, Whiteville, 1996-99, Columbus County Partnership Children, Inc., Whiteville, 1997-2000, Columbus County Cmty. Disaster Response, Inc., Whiteville, 2000-01, Columbus County Job Ready Partnership, Whiteville, 2001-02; commr. Columbus County, 2002—; active Columbus County Com. of 100, Inc., Southeastern Regional Econ. Devel. Commn., Cape Fear Resource Conservation & Devel. Recipient Outstanding Young Alumnus award, N.C. State U., 1997. Mem. Nat. Assn. Counties, Assn. Execs. NC, NC Assn. County Commissioners, Nat. FFA Alumni Assn. (life). Democrat. Baptist. Avocations: photography, travel. Office: Columbus County Commr Carolina Designs PO Box 1844 Whiteville NC 28472 E-mail: kipgodwin@intrstar.net.

GODWIN, MARY JO, editor, librarian consultant; b. Tarboro, N.C., Jan. 31, 1949; d. Herman Esthol and Mamie Winifred (Felton) Pittman; m. Charles Benjamin Godwin, May 2, 1970. BA, N.C. Wesleyan Coll., 1971; MLS, East Carolina U., 1973. Cert. libr., N.C. From libr. asst. to asst. dir. Edgecombe County Meml. Library, Tarboro, 1970-76, dir., 1977-85; asst. editor Wilson Library Bull., Bronx, N.Y., 1985-89, editor, 1989-92; dir. govt. sales The Oryx Press, Phoenix, 1993-95, dir. mktg. svc., 1995-96, dir. mktg., sales and promotional svcs., 1996-2000; sr. mktg. mgr. Oryx, Greenwood Pub. Group, Westport, 2000—02; dir. mktg. Scarecrow Press and Scarecrow Edn., Rowman & Littlefield Pub. Group, Lanham, Md., 2002—. Mem. White House Conf. on Librs. and Info. Svcs. Task Force; bd. dirs. Libr. Pub. Rels. Coun., 1992-95. Bd. dirs. Friends of Calvert County Pub. Libr., 1994, Osborn Edn. Found., sec., 1997-98; mem. Ariz. Ctr. for the Book. Recipient Robert Downs award for intellectual freedom U. Ill. Grad. Sch. of Libr. Sci., 1992. Mem. ALA (3M/Jr. Mem. Roundtable Profl. Devel. award 1981), N.C. Libr. Assn. (sec. 1981-83), Info. Futures Inst., Ind. Librs. Exchange Roundtable (v.p., pres. elect 1994, pres. 1995-96). Democrat. Episcopalian. Office: Scarecrow Press 4501 Forbes Blvd Ste 200 Lanham MD 20706 E-mail: mjgodwin@comcast.net.

GODWIN, PAMELA JUNE, financial services executive; b. Council Bluffs, Iowa, Mar. 29, 1949; d. Fred Norman and Carol Ethel (Hatfield) Humphrey; m. Wallace Gill Godwin, Dec. 20, 1970; 1 child, Christopher Humphrey. BA in French, Pa. State U., 1970; postgrad., West Chester (Pa.) State U., 1971-74. Tchr. various schs., Phila., 1971-74; various underwriting/tng. positions Colonial Penn Ins. Co., Phila., 1974-77, mgr., 1977-81, dir., 1981-84, v.p., 1984-86, Colonial Penn Group, Inc., Phila., 1986-87, sr. v.p., 1987-88; sr. v.p. customer mgmt. Nat. Liberty Corp., Valley Forge, Pa., 1988-93; pres., COO, Acad. Ins. Group, Frazer, Pa., 1993-95, Nat. Home Life Assurance Co., Frazer, Pa., 1993-95; pres. Change Ptnrs., Inc., Havertown, Pa., 1995—96, 2002—; acting pres. Womens Way, Phila., 1998-99; pres., COO agy. divsn. GMAC Ins. Personal Lines (formerly Integon Corp.), Winston-Salem, NC, 1999—2001; pres. Change Ptnrs., Inc., Havertown, 2001—. Bd. dirs. Wheels, Inc., J.F. Kennedy Vocat. Tech. Sch., Phila., 1987-88; bd. dirs. Gt. Valley Cmty. Edn. Found., 1991-95, past pres.; mem. Westgate Hills Civic Assn., Havertown, 1974—; mem. Wharton Exec. Edn. adv. bd.; mem. Pa. State Great Valley adv. bd., 1996-2000; bd. dirs. Winston-Salem C. of C., 1996-2001; mem. Com. of 200, 2000—. Named to Pa. Honor Roll of Women, 1996. Mem. Phila. Forum of Exec. Women (pres. 1998-99), Soc. Property and Casualty Underwriters (past pres. Phila. chpt. 1987-88), Phi Beta Kappa, Phi Sigma Iota. Democrat. Lutheran. Avocations: skiing, walking, reading. E-mail: ChangePrtners@aol.com.

GODWIN, RALPH EDWARD, retired computer operator; b. Wilmington, Del., Sept. 6, 1952; s. Ralph Winfield and Margaret Suzanne (Phillips) G. Diploma, U.S. Army S.E. Signal Sch., Fort Gordon, Ga., 1971, Armed Forces Air Intelligence, Lowry AFB, Colo., 1977, Control Data Inst., 1979; AAS, Del. Tech. & C.C., 1987. File clk. FBI, Washington, 1973-76, coding clk., 1978-79; data technician Carter/Mondale Presdl. Com., Inc., Washington, 1979-80; computer operator I Beneficial Nat. Bank (USA), Wilmington, Del., 1984-87; page Del. State Senate, Dover, Del., 1991; computer operator I New Castle County, Wilmington, 1988—2001. Dem. dist. committee person 22nd Del. State Rep. Dist. Dem. Com., Newark, Del., 1983-90; political strategist Dem. Nominee Richard A. DiLiberto, Jr., Del. State Ho. of Reps., 14th State Rep. Dist., Newark, 1992; co-campaign mgr. Dem. Nominee Barbara L. Erskine, Del. State Ho. of Reps., 27th State Rep. Dist., 1994; mem. nat. steering com. Clinton/Gore '96, 1995-96. Airman 1st class USAF, 1976-78. Named Un-sung Hero-1994 Polit. Campaign, Del. Dem. Women's Club, 1995. Mem.; William J. Clinton Presdl. Found. (founding), Am. Legion (sgt.-at-arms Newark chpt. 1994—97), Colonial Williamsburg Found. (hon. citizen 1993—), Carter Ctr., Concord Coalition, Woodrow Wilson Internat. Ctr. for Scholars, Nat. Trust for Hist. Preservation, John F. Kennedy Libr. Found. (founding mem. hon. fellows), Smithsonian Assocs. Democrat. Episcopalian. Avocations: politics, photography, travel, reading. Home: 7 Wedgewood Rd Newark DE 19711-2055

GODWIN, RALPH LEE, JR., real estate executive; b. Raleigh, N.C., July 20, 1954; s. Ralph Lee Sr. and Hilda Faye (Sellars) G. BS in Commerce, U. Va., 1976; MBA, Dartmouth Coll., 1982. Fgn. exchange trader N.C. Nat. Bank, Charlotte, 1976-78; mgr. N.Y. office 1st Nat. Bank Atlanta, N.Y.C., 1979-80; assoc. corp. fin. Goldman Sachs & Co., N.Y.C., 1982-84; assoc. Eastdil Realty, Inc., N.Y.C., 1984-88; dir. Jones Lang Wootton, U.S.A., N.Y.C., 1988-92; mng. dir., head real estate group Gruntal & Co., Inc., N.Y.C., 1993-98; sr. mng. dir., head equity capital markets Landauer Assocs., Inc., N.Y.C., 1998-99; gen. ptnr. Centurion Realty Ptnrs., L.P., Cochecton, N.Y., 1999—. Recipient Devel. cert. DARE Inc., Wilmington, 1984, 88. Mem. NAREIT, Real Estate Bd., N.Y., Urban Land Inst., N.C. Soc. N.Y., U. Va. Alumni Assn., Dartmouth Coll. Alumni Assn., N.Y. Athletic Club, Omicron Delta Kappa. Republican. Roman Catholic. Avocations: fishing, bridge, golf, tennis.

GODWIN, ROBERT ANTHONY, lawyer; b. Phila., Apr. 24, 1938; s. Robert Anthony and Mary (MacElderry) G.; m. Isabel A. Tumelty; children: Cara G., Marisa A., Elise D. BS, Villanova U., 1960, JD, 1963. Bar: Pa. 1964, U.S. Dist. Ct. (ea. dist.) Pa. 1964, U.S. Ct. Appeals (3d cir.) 1964, U.S. Supreme Ct. 1980. Vol. defender, Phila., 1964; assoc. Eastburn & Gray, Doylestown, Pa., 1968-70; asst. pub. defender Bucks County, Pa., 1969-71; sole practice Newtown, Pa., 1971—73; ptnr. Timby and Godwin, 1973—75; atty. Robert A. Godwin & Assocs., 1975— . Served with JAG, USMC, 1964-68, JAG, USMCR, 1968-92, col. USMCR, ret. Mem. Pa. Bar Assn., Pa. Trial Lawyers Assn., Bucks County Bar Assn., Rotary. Office: Box 450 110 S State St Newtown PA 18940-3508

GODWIN, ROBERT DUANE, language educator; b. Marquette, Kans., May 22, 1930; s. Cleo Edward Godwin and Roberta Louise Mann-Godwin; m. Leonor Elena Dania, Dec. 22, 1961; children: Edward Isaac, Marcia Elizabeth, Holly Suzanne Miller. BA, Tex. Western U., 1960; MA, U. Tex., El Paso, 1963. Instr. Tarleton State Coll., Stephenville, Tex., 1961—69; from asst. prof. to prof. Spanish and English Tarleton State U., Stephenville, Tex., 1972—; Fulbright prof. U. Santiago, Santiago de Compostela, Spain, 1970—72. Staff sgt. USAF, 1951—54. Master: Hiawatha Lodge; mem.: Masons (32nd degree Mason). Avocation: private aviation. Office Fax: 254-968-1931.

GODWIN, SARA, writer; b. St. Louis, Feb. 18, 1944; d. Robert Franklin, Jr. and Annabelle Godwin; m. Charles D. James, May 1, 1990; children: Jane, Josh. BA, Calif. State U., 1967; postgrad., UCLA, 1968-70, U. Calif., Berkeley, 1970-71, W.I. Inst. Fairleigh Dickinson U., St. Croix, V.I., 1971-72; MA, Dominican Coll., 1974. Writer, editor Ortho Books, Std. Oil Calif., San Francisco, 1975-77; writer, editor Gannett Corp., San Rafael, Calif., 1977-79; sr. writer Shaklee Corp., San Francisco, 1979-88; freelance writer Marin County, Calif., 1988—. Featured spkr. Ask the Gardener Sta. KSFO, San Francisco, 1980—81; contbr., prodr. Raw Radio Travel, 1998—. Author: (book) Seals, 1990, Gorillas, 1990, The Angler's Companion, 1992, Hummingbirds, 1991, The Gardener's Companion, 1992 (N.Y. Times Rev., Garden Book Club selection), Landscaping Decks and Patios, 1994, Scott's See and Do: Lawns and Groundcovers, 1995; contbr. book (Lit. Guild selection); author (with others): (book) Smith and Hawken Book of Outdoor Gardening, 1996; author: (screenplays) Discover Canada, Discovering The USA; manuscript editor: All About Perennials, 1992, prin. lexicographer: Nat. Gardening Assn. Dictionary of Horticulture, 1994; scriptwriter, prodr. : China: The Middle Kingdom; contbr. CD ROM, articles to numerous U.S. and fgn. mags. Recipient 1st prize for personal column, Calif. Press Women, 1984. Mem.: PEN, Garden Writers Assn. Am., Am. Soc. Journalists and Authors, Authors Guild. Avocations: reading, travel, gardening, fly fishing. Home: PO Box 1503 Ross CA 94957-1503

GOEBEL, EDWIN M. microbiology educator, school administrator; b. Youngstown, Ohio, Aug. 10, 1951; s. Mark E. and Jeanne W. Goebel; m. Linda J. Blombach, June 15, 1945; children: Scott Rhoad, Bradley Rhoad. BS in Microbiology, Pa. State U., 1973; MS in Microbiology, U. Ill., 1975; PhD in Microbiology, Va. Poly. Inst. and State U., 1980. Asst. prof. biol. scis. Ind. U.-Purdue U., Ft. Wayne, 1981-87; microbiologist, sci. team leader Ill. Math. and Sci. Acad., Aurora, Ill., 1987-93, microbiologist, asst. prin. for ops., 1993—. Mem. Am. Soc. for Microbiology (pre-coll. edn. com. 1989-91). Office: Ill Math and Sci Acad 1500 W Sullivan Rd Aurora IL 60506

GOEBEL, JOEL ALAN, otolaryngologist; b. South Bend, Ind., 1954; BA summa cum laude, Notre Dame, 1976; MD, Washington U., St. Louis, 1980. Diplomate Am. Bd. Otolaryngology. Intern Jewish Hosp., St. Louis, 1980-81; resident in otolaryngology Barnes Hosp./Washington U., St. Louis, 1981-85; active staff Barnes Hosp., St. Louis; asst. prof. Washington U., St. Louis, 1986-94, assoc. prof. otolaryngology, 1994—2000, prof., 2000—02, prof., vice chmn. dept., 2002—. Fellow ACS; mem. Am. Acad. Otolaryngology, Head and Neck Surgery, Am. Otological Soc., Triological Soc., Barany Soc., Am. Neurotology Soc. Office: Washington U Sch Medicine Dept Otolaryngology 660 S Euclid Ave CBox 8115 Saint Louis MO 63110-1010

GOEBEL, JOHN J. lawyer, director; b. St. Charles, Mo., Feb. 3, 1930; s. Francis Joseph and Elizabeth (Lawler) G.; m. Margaret Mary Rooney, May 10, 1958; children— Laura, Margaret, John, Matthew BS, LL.B., St. Louis U., 1953. Bar: Mo. 1953, U.S. Dist. Ct. (ea. dist.) Mo. 1957. Jr. exec., Constrn. Escrow Service Inc., St. Louis, 1955-56; jr. ptnr. Bryan Cave LLP, St. Louis, 1956-66, ptnr., 1966-98, sr. counsel, 1998—. Served to 1st lt. USAF, 1953-55 Mem.: ABA, Mo. Bar Assn., St. Louis Bar Assn., Port Royal Club, Noonday Club, St. Louis Club, Bellerive Country Club. Roman Catholic. Home: 245 Little Harbour Ln Naples FL 34102-7606 Office: Bryan Cave 1 Metropolitan Sq Ste 3600 Saint Louis MO 63102-2750 E-mail: jjgoebel@bryancavellp.com.

GOEBEL, KATHRYN MARY, nurse; b. Denver, Dec. 8, 1958; d. Jack F. and Beverly Jean (Hummel) Vogt; children: Allison Mae, Hannah Jean. Diploma, Presbyn. Sch. Nursing, 1980; BSN, U. Phoenix; postgrad., Arapahoe Community Coll. Charge nurse neurosurgery Swedish Med. Ctr., Englewood, 1980-87, relief nurse float pool, 1987-91, clin. coord. Epilepsy Ctr., 1989-92; clin. nurse Kaiser Permanente, Littleton, Colo., 1992—99, triage nurse, 2000—01, clin. coord. diabetic foot clinic, 2001—; staff nurse Forensic Med. Unit-Correctional Care Denver Health Med., 1999—2000. Mem. Epilepsy Found. of Colo. (profl. adv. bd., client svcs. com., tng. and placement svcs. profl. adv. bd.). Home: PO Box 2364 Littleton CO 80161-2364

GOEBEL, WILLIAM HORN, lawyer; b. N.Y.C., Dec. 7, 1941; s. Harry H. and Maxine (Hamburger) G.; m. Barbara Golden, July 30, 1966; children: Jason, Pamela. AB, Columbia U., 1963; JD, NYU, 1966. Bar: N.Y. 1966. Assoc. Bernard Trencher, N.Y.C., 1966-69; real estate atty. J.C. Penney Co., Inc., N.Y.C., 1969-71; assoc. gen. counsel N.K. Winston Corp., N.Y.C., 1971-72, Teachers Ins. and Annuity Assn. Am./Coll. Retirement Equities Fund, N.Y.C., 1972-2000; bus. devel. and legal cons. Stewart Title Ins. Co., 2000—. Lectr. NYU Sch. Continuing Edn., 1985—; mem. adv. bd. Commonwealth Land Title/Transamerica Title Ins. Co., 1992-2000; v.p. M.O.A. Enterprises, Inc./M.O.A Holdings, Inc., 1992-2000. Pres. Oyster Bay Jewish Ctr., 1976—78. Mem. Assn. of Bar of City of N.Y., N.Y. State Bar Assn. (fin. subcom. of real estate sect. 1998—, subcom. on zoning and land use planning), Barnard-Columbia Hillel Soc. (pres.'s coun. 2002—). Office: Stewart Title Ins Co 4th Fl 300 E 42nd St New York NY 10017 E-mail: bgoebel@optonline.net., bgoebel@stewart.com.

GOEBLE, DEBORAH SQUIRES, clinical social worker; b. Cleve., Jan. 5, 1950; d. Eugene Bernard and Phyllis Ann (Jay) Squires; children: Jason David, Jaimie Rebecca. MSSA, Case Western Res. U., 1979. Lic. clin. social worker, Ohio. Mem. staff Crisis Intervention Team Mental Health Svcs., Cleve., 1976-89; pvt. practice Lyndhurst, Ohio, 1980—.

GOEDDE, ALAN GEORGE, financial company executive; b. Irvington, N.J., Feb. 27, 1948; s. Albert and Herta (Konrad) G.; m. Julie S. Withers, June 30, 1981. BS in Engring., Duke U., 1970, PhD in Econs., 1978. Economist U.S. Treasury, Washington, 1976-79, Export-Import Bank, Washington, 1979-81; mgr. Arthur Andersen & Co., Chgo., 1981-84; v.p. bus. planning 1st Nat. Bank Chgo., 1984-86; dir. strategic planning The NutraSweet Co., Chgo., 1986-87; pres., CEO Mentor Internat., Northbrook, Ill., 1987-88; cons. Coopers & Lybrand, Chgo., 1988-90, Freeman & Mills, L.A., 1990-94, Putnam, Hayes and Bartlett, L.A., 1994-2000, Freeman & Mills, L.A., 2000—. Office: Freeman & Mills Inc 350 S Figueroa St Ste 900 Los Angeles CA 90071

GOEHRING, KENNETH, artist; b. Evansville, Wis., Jan. 8, 1919; s. Walter A. and Ruth I. (Rossman) G.; m. Margretta M. MacNicol, Dec. 1, 1945. Student, Cass Tech. Inst., 1933-35, Meinzinger Sch. Applied Art, 1945-46, Colorado Springs Fine Arts Ctr., 1947-50. Works have appeared in over 100 exhibitions in 17 states and 20 museums; 17 one-man shows; exhibitor, Terry Inst., Miami, Symphony Hall, Boston, de Cordova Mus., Fitchburg Mus., Mass., Farnsworth Mus., Maine, Corcoran, Washington, Joslyn Meml. Mus., Nebr., Detroit Inst. Arts, Nebr. Galleries, Stanford U. Galleries, Calif, De Young Mus., San Francisco, Denver Art Mus., Okla. Art Ctr., La Jolla Art Ctr., Calif., Colorado Springs Fine Arts Ctr., 1998, 99, Boulder Mus. Avant Garde Art, 1999, others; represented in permanent collections, Sheldon Art Ctr., Lincoln, Nebr., Colorado Springs Fine Arts Ctr., Foothills Gallery, Golden Colo., Canon City Fine Arts Ctr., Colo., Washburn U. Gallery, Wichita, Kans., Swedish Consulate,

Washington, El Pomar Found., Colo. Springs, in many pvt. collections throughout U.S. Purchase awards include Colorado Springs Fine Arts Ctr., 1958; Washburn U., 1957; Am. Acad. Design, 1977 Address: 2017 W Platte Ave Colorado Springs CO 80904-3429

GOEHRING, MAUDE COPE, retired business educator; b. Persia, Tenn., Jan. 5, 1915; d. James Lawrence and Bobbie C. (Ross) Cope; m. Harvey John Goehring Jr., Aug. 12, 1950 (dec. Mar. 1992). Student, Lebanon Valley Coll., 1944-45; grad., Am. Inst. Banking, 1945; BS in Edn., Indiana U. of Pa., 1948; MEd, U. Pitts., 1950. Tchr. Penn Hills Sr. High Sch., Pitts., 1948-68, U. Pitts., 1959-60, ret., 1968; vol. chmn. ICU, operating rm. info. desk Margaret R. Pardee Meml. Hosp., Hendersonville, N.C., 1989-95; vol. Carolina Village Health Ctr., 1994-99. Coord. Henderson County Ct. House Vols., Hendersonville, 1983-89; cons., counselor tax aid program Am. Assn. Ret. Persons, Hendersonville, 1981-96. Neighborhood chmn. Girl Scouts U.S., Butler County Pa., 1976-79; bd. dirs. ARC, Hendersonville, 1986-91; sec.-treas., bd. dirs. Crime Stoppers of Henderson County, 1991-96; nat. bd. dirs. Second Wind Hall of Fame, 1991-95. Mem. AAUW (officer 1975-76), Gideon Internat. Aux. (pres., sec. 1969-70), Delta Pi Epsilon (life, Gamma chpt., pres., sec. 1956-59, nat. del. 1957). Republican. Lutheran. Avocations: gardening, crafts, sewing, reading.

GOEI, BERNARD THWAN-POO (BERT GOEI), architectural and engineering firm executive; b. Semarang, Indonesia, Jan. 27, 1938; came to U.S., 1969; naturalized, 1976; s. Ignatius Ing-Khien Goei and Nicolette Giok-Nio Tjioe; m. Sioe-Tien Liem, May 26, 1966; children: Kimberley Hendrika, Gregory Fitzgerald. BA in Fine Arts, Bandung Inst. Tech. State U. Indonesia, 1961, MA in Archtl. Space Planning, 1964; postgrad., U. Heidelberg, Germany, 1967-68. Co-owner, chief designer Pondok Mungil Interiors Inc., Bandung, 1962-64; dept. mgr., fin. advisor Gumarna Architects, Engrs. and Planners, Inc., Bandung, Jakarta, Indonesia, 1964-67; shop supr., model maker Davan Scale Models, Toronto, Ont., Can., 1968-69; chief archtl. designer George T. Nowak Architects and Assocs., Westchester, Calif., 1969-72; sr. archtl. designer Krisel & Shapiro Architects and Assocs., L.A., 1972-74; sr. supervising archtl. designer The Ralph M. Parsons A/E Co. (now Parsons Infrastructure and Tech. Group Inc.), Pasadena, Calif., 1974—. V.p. United Gruno U.S.A. Corp. Import/Export, Monterey Park, Calif., 1980-89. Mem. Rep. Presdl. Task Force, Washington, 1982—, Nat. Rep. Senatorial Com., Washington, 1983—, Nat. Rep. Congrl. Com., Washington, 1981—, Rep. Nat. Com., Washington, 1982—; active Am. Indonesian Cath. Soc. Recipient Excellent Design Achievement commendation Magneto-Hydro-Dynamics Program, 1976, Strategic Def. Initiative "Star Wars" Program, 1988, USAF Space Shuttle Program, West Coast Space-Port, 1984; scholar U. Heidelberg, 1967-68. Mem. NRA, Am. Air Gunner Assn., Tech. Comm. Soc., Indonesian Am. Soc., Dutch Am. Soc., Second Amendment Found., The Right to Keep and Bear Arms Com. Republican. Roman Catholic. Avocations: fire arms and daggers, photography, hi-tech electronics, stamps and coins, world travel. Home: 154 Ladera St Monterey Park CA 91754-2125 Office: Parsons Infrastructure & Tech Group Inc 100 W Walnut St Pasadena CA 91124-0001

GOEL, AJAY, molecular biologist, researcher; b. Ferozepur, Punjab, India, Aug. 23, 1968; came to U.S., 1996; s. Rajinder Kumar and Urmila (Gupta) G.; m. Shivali Garg, Nov. 25, 1997. BSc in Biophysics with honours, Panjab U., Chandigarh, India, 1988, MSc in Biophysics with honours, 1990, PhD in Biophysics, 1996. Jr. rsch. fellow biophysics dept. Panjab U., 1988-90, scientist Regional Sophisticated Instrummentation Ctr., 1991—, sr. rsch. fellow biophysics dept., 1992-96; rsch. assoc. Dept. molecular physics and biophysics U. Va., Charlottesville, 1996—. Author: Advances in Biological Sciences, 1995; contbr. articles to sci. jours. Recipient Best Rsch. in Cancer Young Investigation award AACR-Pharmacia Upjohn, 1999, Presdl. award for best paper Intenrat. Gastroenterol. Meeting, 1999; nat. merit scholar Indian Ministry Edn., 1988-90, scholar Internat. Fedn. Socs. for Electron Microscopy, 1994. Mem. Microscopy Soc. Am., Soc. Biophysicists India, Electron Microscope Soc. India, Assn. Med. Physicists India, Nutrition Soc. India, Soc. Biol. Chemists India, Am. Assn. Cancer Rsch., Am. Gastroenterology Assn. Avocations: surfing the internet, watching cricket and football, hiking, reading science fiction. Home: 9211 Garland Rd # 4418 Dallas TX 75218 Office: Baylor U Med Ctr Gastroenterology Cancer Rsch Lab Dallas TX 75246

GOEL, MAHESH CHAND, urologist, renal transplant surgeon; b. Delhi, India, Feb. 20, 1962; s. Krishan Chand and Bhagwanti (Devi) G.; m. Meenu Rani, June 24, 1991; children: Shokhi, Mrieshka. M.B.BS, Delhi U., 1987; MS in Surgery, Punjabi U., Patiala, India, 1991; MCh in Urology, Sanjay Gandhi PGI, Lucknow, India, 1995; Edn. Commn. Fgn. Med. Grads. cert., 2001. Lic. U.S., 2001. Clerkship/house surgeon Safdarjang Hosp., Delhi, 1986-88; postgrad. in surgery Rajendra Hosp. and Govt. Med. Coll., Patiala, 1989-91; sr. registrar Swami Dayanand Hosp. and GTB Hosp., Delhi, 1991-93, Sanjay Gandhi Postgrad. Inst. Med. Scis., Lucknow, 1993-96; cons. Dhanwantari Tomer Hosp., Bareilly, India, 1996; fellow Royal Liverpool U. Hosp., 1996-97; registrar in urology Univ. Hosp. of Wales, Cardiff, 1997-98; sr. registrar in urology South Wales Healthcare, Wales, 1998—2000. Fellow in urology Cleve. Clinic Found., 2001; mem. reviewing panel Jour. of Postgrad. Medicine, Bombay, 2000—; lectr. in field. Contbr. articles to profl. jours. Recipient Best Young Scientist award for Sci. Model, Nat. Sci. Exhbn., 1975, Vivekanand Gold Medal, Vivekanand Soc., 1977; Urol. Soc. North Zone Travelling fellow, 1995; recipient essay awards Dallas Endocrinology Soc., 2002. Fellow: Royal Coll. Physicians and Surgeons (Glasgow); mem.: Am. Med. Assn., Am. Soc. Transplant Surgeon (travelling fellow 2002, 2003), Am. Soc. Transplantation (fellowship 2002), The Transplantation Soc., Internat. Transplant Soc., Am. Urol. Assn., Brit. Med. Assn., Indian Soc. Organ Transplantation, Urol. Soc. India, Brit. Transplant Assn., European Assn. Urology (jr.). Avocations: computer sciences, cricket, tennis, cooking, reading. E-mail: mahesh_goel@yahoo.co.uk., mahesh_goel@hotmail.com.

GOEL, RAKESH K. engineering educator; b. Delhi, India, July 26, 1959; BTech, Indian Inst. Tech., New Delhi, 1982; MS, U. Calif., Berkeley, 1985, PhD, 1990. Registered profl. engr., Calif. Jr. engr., mgmt. trainee EIL, New Delhi, 1982-84; sr. engr. PMB Sys. Engring., Inc., San Francisco, 1985-86; asst. prof. Syracuse (N.Y.) U., 1995-97; from asst. prof. to prof. Calif. Poly. State U., San Luis Obispo, 1997—. Contbr. rsch. articles to profl. jours. Mem. ASCE (Amman rsch. fellow 1989, Huber Rsch. prize 2000, Norman medal 2001), Earthquake Engring. Rsch. Inst. Office: Calif Poly State U Dept Civil/Environ Engring San Luis Obispo CA 93407 Fax: (805) 756-6330. E-mail: rgoel@calpoly.edu.

GOELA, JITENDRA SINGH, researcher, consultant; b. Delhi, India, Apr. 20, 1951; s. Late Umrao Singh and Sushila Devi (Singal) G.; m. Geeta Gupta, Mar. 4, 1979; children: Naveen, Vikas. B in Tech., Indian Inst. of Tech., Delhi, India, 1972; MS, Brown U., Providence, R.I., 1974, PhD, 1976; MBA, Northeastern U., Boston, 1991. Prin. sci. Phys. Sci., Inc., Andover, Mass., 1976-78; asst. prof., lectr. Indian Inst. of Tech., Kanpur, India, 1978-84; prin. sci. Morton Internat. CVD Inc., Woburn, Mass., 1984—. Cons. Phys. Sci. Inc., Andover, 1979-80, CVD Inc., Woburn, 1983, Sanders Assoc., Nashua, N.H., 1985-86, Efficient Systems, Inc., Andover, 1987-89. Editor: Lasers and Applications, 1983; contbr. articles to profl. jours. Recipient Arthur L. Williston medal, Am. Soc. of Mech. Engr., 1978, Young Sci. medal, Indian Nat. Sci. Acad., 1982, Polycrystalline Si Property Data, Air Force, Wright-Patterson, Ohio, 1985, Lightweight Si/SiC LIDAR Mirrors, Nasa Langley Rsh. Ctr., Norfolk, Va., 1987, High Temp SiC Fibers, Nasa Lewis Rsch. Ctr., Cleve., 1987. Mem. Am. Soc. of Mech. Engrs., Am. Phys. Soc., Optical Soc. of Am. (Engring. Excellence award 1991), Soc. of Photo-optical and Instrumentation Engrs., Am. Ceramic Soc. Achievements include patents for fabrication of lightweight ceramic mirrors by means of a chemical vapor deposition process, method of fabricating lightweight honeycomb type structure, selective area chemical vapor deposition, a triangular deposition chamber, highly polishable, highly thermally conductive SiC, hard disc drives and read/write heads, chemical vapor deposition furnace and furnace apparatus, chemical vapor deposition produced SiC having improved properties, precision replication by chemical vapor deposition, bonding of SiC components. Home: 12 Messinia Dr Andover MA 01810-6027 Office: Rohm and Haas 185 New Boston St Woburn MA 01801-6278

GOELE, DHRUV (OSTARO), publisher, financial consultant; b. Delhi, India, May 25, 1937; came to U.S., 1973; s. Shri Shiam Lal and Smt. Luxmi Goel; m. Zoa D. Rued, Oct. 1965. Student, U. Delhi, 1959-61. Registered SEC. With The Times of India, 1957—63; vol. Svc. Civil Internat., 1963—68; editor, pub. Astronews, pres. Cardinal Star Corp., N.Y.C., 1976-80, pub. Ostaro's Market Newsletter, 1980—; Host Ostaro Show Manhattan Cable TV, N.Y.C., 1974—. Pres., lectr. Internat. Devel. Improvement & Assistance Inc., N.Y.C, 1979—; guest many radio stations including WMCA, WOR, WABC, WTOP, others Author: The Art and Craft of Success: 10 Steps, 2001; contbr. articles to profl. jours.; movies include: Stardust Memories, The Laser Man. Founder Inter-Nat. Devel., Improvement and Assistance, Inc., 1979. Mem. AFTRA, Nat. Acad. TV Arts Scis., Screen Actors Guild, Soc. for Investigation of Recurring Events. Lodges: Rosicrucians. Avocations: classical music, reading, metaphysical research, poetry, bicycling. Home: 402 E 74th St New York NY 10021-3917

GOELET, ROBERT G. investment executive; b. Sandricourt, France, Sept. 28, 1923; s. Robert Walton and Anne Marie (Guestier) G.; m. Alexandra Gardiner Creel, Sept. 9, 1976. AB, Harvard U., 1945. Trustee Am. Mus. Natural History, 1958—, pres., 1975-88, chmn., 1988-89; trustee Boscobel Restoration Inc., 1976—, French Inst.-Alliance Francaise N.Y., 1951—, pres., 1967-93; trustee N.Y. Zool. Soc., 1951—, pres., 1971-75; trustee Carnegie Instn. of Washington, 1980—, Mus. Comparative Zoology, 1980—, N.Y. Geneal. & Biographical Soc., 1998—. Office: 540 Madison Ave Ste 21A New York NY 10019-3398

GOELL, ABBY JANE, painter, collage artist, artist; b. N.Y.C. d. Stanley Mendel and Anne (Bellin) Wershof; 1 child, Mark Jordan. BA, Syracuse U.; cert., N.Y. Sch. Interior Design; MFA, Columbia U., 1965; postgrad., Attingham Park, Shropshire, Eng., summer 1963, Pratt Graphic Art Ctr., 1966. Pub. Arcadia Press, N.Y.C., 1980—; tchr. Hunter Coll., 1967, Lab. Inst. Merchandising, 1967—70; artist-in-residence Banff Ctr. for the Arts, 2001. Editor: English Silver 1675-1825, rev. edit., 1980; one-woman show Automation House, N.Y.C., 1973; group shows include Lumley-Cazalet, London, 1976, AAAL, 1977, Childe Hassam Purchase Exhbn., N.Y.C., 1977, Dept. State, Havana, Cuba, 1979, Sculpture Ctr., N.Y.C., 1981, Silvermine Ann., 1981, 82, TAGA Pratt Graphic Exhbn., Caracas, 1982, John Szoke Gallery, N.Y.C., 1988, Fotouhi-Kramer Gallery, N.Y.C., 1996, Kavehaz Gallery, N.Y., 1996, Cooperstown (N.Y.) Art Assn. Ann., 1999; represented in permanent collections Mus. Modern Art, N.Y.C., Chase Manhattan Bank, Princeton U. Mus., Atlantic Richfield Oil Co., Yale U., Sloane-Kettering Meml. Ctr., N.Y.C., Grafisches Kabinet, Munich, Germany, Neuberger Mus., Purchase, N.Y., Print Room, N.Y. Pub. Libr., Smith Coll. Art Mus., Northampton, Mass., Zimmerli Mus., Rutgers U., NJ, Libr. of Congress, Newark Pub. Libr. and others. Yaddo fellow, 1968; Va. Ctr. for Creative Arts fellow, 1981; artist-in-residence Found. Samuel Buffat, Geneva, 1997, Banff Ctr. for Arts, Alta., Can., 2001. Mem.: Appraisers Assn. Am. (sr.), Yeats Soc. N.Y. (founding bd. dirs.), Nat. Trust Hist. Preservation, Art Students League N.Y. (life). Democrat. Home and Office: 37 Washington Sq W New York NY 10011-9181 E-mail: abbygoell@earthlink.net.

GOELL, JAMES EMANUEL, electronics company executive; b. N.Y.C., Oct. 13, 1939; s. Milton Jacob and Amy (Jacob) G.; m. Tamara Greenberg, Sept. 11, 1960; children: Lisa Sue, Fredric Scott. BEE, Cornell U., 1962, MS, 1963, PhD, 1965. Tech. staff Bell Labs., Holmdel, N.J., 1965-74; v.p., dir. engring., dir. fiber optics lab. Electro-Optical Products div. ITT, Roanoke, Va., 1974-81; pres. Lightwave Technologies, Inc., Van Nuys, Calif., 1981-85; v.p. mktg. PCO, Chatsworth, Calif., 1985-91; program mgr. HBT Ericsson Components, L.A., 1991-92; dir. engring. end-user bus. AMP, Harrisburg, Pa., 1992-97; dir. Netconnect Engring. Amp, Harrisburg, Pa., 1997-2000; mng. dir. program mgmt. TyCom, Eatontown, NJ, 2000—02; v.p. engring. Omni Guide, Cambridge, Mass., 2002—. V.p. Middletown Twp. (N.J.) Bd. Edn. Fellow IEEE; mem. Optical Soc. Am., Am. Phys. Soc., Sigma Xi, Eta Kappa Nu, Tau Beta Pi, Phi Kappa Phi. Home: 6 Boxwood Ln Lexington MA 02420 Office: Omni Guide Bldg 100 Flr 3 One Kendall Sq Cambridge MA 02139

GOELLNER, JACK GORDON, publishing executive; b. Cleve., Aug. 16, 1930; s. Fred William and Ella (Rohde) G.; m. Sarah Frances Williams, Aug. 16, 1952 (div. Sept. 28, 1982); children: Katherine, Ellen, Michael, Kirsten.; m. Barbara B. Lamb, Apr. 14, 1984. BA, Allegheny Coll., 1952, Litt.D., 1979; MA, U. Wis., 1953. Reporter Springfield (Ohio) Sun, 1955-57; sr. writer, pub. information Cleve. Electric Illuminating Co., 1957-61; mgr. sales and advt. Johns Hopkins U. Press, Balt., 1961-65, editorial dir., 1965-73, asso. dir., 1973-74, dir., 1974-95; dir. emeritus, 1996; dir. Am. Univ. Press Services, 1963-66, treas., 1972-74, chmn. bd., 1979-80. Dir. York Press; bd. dirs. Johns Hopkins Press Ltd., 1974-88; bd. dirs. Internat. Book Bank; mem. nat. adv. bd. and exec. com. Ctr. for the Book, Libr. of Congress, 1979-85; mem. U.S. Govt. Adv. Com. on Internat. Book and Libr. Programs, 1975-78; head pubs. mission to Ea. Europe, Dept. State, 1977; cons. NEH, 1977-84; mem. acad. affairs com. Winterthur Mus.; mem. bd. advisers The Papers of Dwight D. Eisenhower. Mem. editorial bd. Scholarly Pub., 1980—, Book Rsch. Quar., 1983-88; mem. adv. bd. Lit. Classics of U.S, 1980-86; contbr. articles to profl. and popular jours. Bd. govs. U. Press of New Eng.; mem. mgmt. bd. MIT Press; mem. adv. bd. Brookings Instn. Press; bd. dirs. Sidran Found., Johns Hopkins Fed. Credit Union, 1994—. Recipient Frank Bradway Rogers Info. Advancement award Med. Libr. Assn., 1991; Am. Coun. Learned Socs. fellow, 1952-53; Danforth fellow, 1952-53 Mem. Assn. Am. Univ. Presses (dir. 1972-74, 78-81, treas. 1972-74, pres. 1979-80), Soc. Scholarly Pub. (dir. 1978—), Assn. Am. Pubs. (mem. exec. council profl. and scholarly pub. div. 1981-85, bd. dirs. 1986-90), Md. Fly Anglers (sec. 1970-72), Trout Unltd., Md. Hist. Soc., Phi Beta Kappa. Clubs: Tudor and Stuart, Hamilton St. Democrat. Episcopalian.

GOELTZ, RICHARD KARL, distilled spirits and wine company executive; b. Chgo., Sept. 11, 1942; s. Karl George and Adeline Caroline (Hoffeins) G. AB, Brown U., 1964; MBA, Columbia U., 1966; student, London Sch. Econs., 1962-63. Fin. analyst Office Treas. Exxon Corp., N.Y.C., 1966-70; asst. treas. Joseph E. Seagram & Sons, Inc., N.Y.C., 1970-73, exec. v.p. fin., 1976-92; bd. dirs., CFO Nat. Westminster Bank, London, 1992—. Trustee 59 Wall Street Fund, N.Y., 1984—. Bd. dirs., past pres. Opera Orch. of N.Y., 1980—, New Germany Fund. With USAR, 1966-72. Mem. Beta Gamma Sigma, Sleepy Hollow Country Club, Met. Opera Club, Racquet and Tennis Club, Brook Club. Republican. Episcopalian. Home: 21 Chester Sq London SWIW 9HS England Office: Natwest Group 41 Lothbury London EC28 2BP England

GOELTZ, THOMAS A. lawyer; BA in Econs. summa cum laude, DePauw U., 1969; JD magna cum laude, Mich. U., 1973. Assoc. Riddell, Williams, Ivie, Bullitt & Walkinshaw, Seattle, 1973-75; dep. prosecuting atty. civil divsn. King County Prosecuting Atty.'s Office, Seattle, 1976-79; prin. Cohen, Keegan & Goeltz, Seattle, 1979-86; ptnr. Davis Wright Tremaine, Seattle, 1986—. Cons. state and local govt. agencies on environ. land use issues; adv. shoreline mgmt. City of Seattle; part-time lectr. Law Sch. U. Wash., Seattle, 1976-79. Editor Mich. Law Rev. Active Gov. Task Force on Regulatory Reform, 1993-95. Mem. ABA (urban, state & local govt. law sect.), Wash. State Bar Assn. (real property sect., past chair land use and environ. law sect.), Seattle-King County Bar Assn., Am. Coll. Real Estate Lawyers, Nat. Assn. Indsl. and Office Park, ICSC, Order of Coif. Office: Davis Wright Tremaine 2600 Century Sq 1501 4th Ave Seattle WA 98101-1688

GOELZ, PAUL CORNELIUS, university dean; b. Bartelso, Ill., Oct. 7, 1914; s. Peter Paul and Clara (Bross) G. Cert., St. Louis U., 1939; BBA, U. Dayton, 1943, MA, 1946; MBA, Northwestern U., 1951, PhD, 1954. Credit mgr. Adjustable Shoe Co., St. Louis, 1937-39; asst. comptr. Key Refinery Equipment Co., St. Louis, 1939-40; auditor GMAC, St. Louis, 1940-41; instr. Southside High Sch., St. Louis, 1943-46; chmn. dept. mktg. St. Mary's U., San Antonio, 1946-62; dean Sch. Bus. Adminstrn., 1962-77; Myra Stafford Pryor prof. free enterprise, 1978-85; dir. Algur H. Meadows Ctr. Entrepreneurial Studies, 1985—. Vis. lectr. staff Army Mgmt. Engring. Tng. Agy., U.S. Dept. Def., Rock Island Arsenal; lectr. Exec. Devel. Insts. in, U.S. and Mexico; cons. to bus. and govt. Chmn. spl. series of sessions at Internat. Conf. Am. Inst. Indsl. Engrs., 1963; lectr. univs. in Moscow and Kiev, 1992. Editor: Philosophy of the Market System of Economics, 5 vols., 1979, 81, 83, 87, 90; contbr. articles to profl. pubs. Bd. trustees World Affairs Coun. of San Antonio. Recipient awards Freedoms Found. at Valley Forge, 1978, 79, 84, 85, 90, Liberty Bell award Young Lawyers Assn., 1982, Entrepreneur of the Yr. award, 1988; inducted into The Inst. Am. Entrepreneurs. Mem. Acad. Mgmt., Am. Mktg. Assn., Sales and Mktg. Execs. Internat., Am. Inst. Indsl. Engrs., San Antonio C. of C., Nat. Assn. Bus. Economists, Southwestern Assn. Bus. Sch. Deans (pres. 1968-69), Fin. Execs. Inst., Assn. Pvt. Enterprise Edn. (pres. 1982-83), Am. Assembly Collegiate Schs. Bus. (bd. dirs.), Delta Epsilon Sigma, Alpha Sigma Tau, Pi Sigma Epsilon. Home: 1 Camino Santa Maria San Antonio TX 78228-5433 E-mail: pgoelz@stmarytex.edu.

GOELZ, ROBERT DEAN, lawyer; b. Passaic, N.J., July 3, 1951; s. Robert M. and Catherine (Witte) G.; m. Pamela A. Wahrer, Oct. 18, 1975. BA in Econs., U. Dayton, 1973, JD, 1978. Bar: Ohio 1978, U.S. Dist. Ct. (so. dist.) Ohio 1978, U.S. Ct. Appeals (6th cir.) 1980, U.S. Supreme Ct. 1982. Asst. pros. atty. Montgomery County, Dayton, Ohio, 1979-84; assoc. Flanagan, Lieberman, Hoffman & Swaim, Dayton, 1984-89, ptnr., 1990—. Mem. ABA, Ohio State Bar Assn., Dayton Bar Assn. Republican. Roman Catholic. Avocations: gourmet cook, oenophile. Office: Flanagan Lieberman Hoffman & Swaim 318 W 4th St Dayton OH 45402-1437 E-mail: Rgoelz@flhslaw.com.

GOELZER, DANIEL LEE, lawyer; b. Milw., Feb. 14, 1947; s. Gerald Howard and Roberta (Hart) G.; m. Angela C. Carcone, Jan. 9, 1988; children: Christina H., Mary E.; 1 child by previous marriage, Michael W. BBA, U. Wis., 1969, JD, 1973; LLM, George Washington U., 1979. Bar: Wis. 1973, D.C. 1979, U.S. Dist. Ct. (we. dist.) Wis. 1973, U.S. Ct. Appeals (7th cir.) 1974, U.S. Ct. Appeals (2d, 9th and D.C. cirs.) 1975, U.S. Supreme Ct. 1976. Auditor Touche, Ross & Co., Milw., 1969-70; law clk. U.S. Ct. Appeals, Chgo., 1973-74; atty. SEC, Washington, 1974-78, exec. asst. to chmn., 1978-83, gen. counsel, 1983-90; ptnr. Baker and McKenzie, Washington, 1990—2002; bd. mem. Pub. Co. Acctg. Oversight Bd., Washington, 2003—. Adj. prof. Georgetown U. Law Ctr., Washington, 1986-92. Contbr. articles to profl. jours. With USAR, 1969-75. Mem. ABA, AICPA, Fed. Bar Assn. Republican. Congregationalist. Avocation: amateur radio. Home: 5941 Searl Ter Bethesda MD 20816-2022 Office: Pub Co Acctg Oversight Bd 1666 K St NW Washington DC 20006 E-mail: dgoelzer@aol.com.

GOEN, BOB, television show host; b. Dec. 1, 1954; Grad., San Diego State U. DJ Stint Sta. KPRO-FM, Riverside, Calif., 1977-81; achor, reporter, prodr., writer, editor Sta. KESQ-TV, Palm Springs, Calif., 1981-86; game show host Perfect Match, 1986, The Home Shopping Game, Blackout; daytime host Wheel of Fortune, 1989-92; game show host The Hollywood Game, 1992; co-host Entertainment Tonight, 1996—. Host Miss Universe, Miss USA, Miss Teen USA, 1993—.

GOEPP, ROBERT AUGUST, dental educator, oral pathologist; b. Chgo., Nov. 3, 1930; s. Charles August and Ernestine Josephine (Mertz) G.; m. Iraida Pineiro, July 9, 1960; children— Robert C., Heidi M., Myra J. BS in Biology, Loyola U.-Chgo., 1954, D.D.S., 1957; MS in Pathology, U. Chgo., 1961, PhD in Pathology, 1967. Instr. to assoc. prof. Sch. Medicine, U. Chgo., 1961-75, prof. dentistry and pathology, 1975-96, prof. emeritus, 1996—. Med. Med. Radiation Adv. Coun. FDA, 1979-82; mem. Nat. Coun. Radiation Protection, Washington, 1976-94. Contbr. articles to profl. jours. Recipient Career Devel. award USPHS, 1970 Fellow Am. Coll. Dentists, Internat. Coll. Dentists, Am. Acad. Oral Pathology, Am. Acad. Dental Radiology (pres. 1974), Ill. Soc. Oral Pathologists (pres. 1977-78), Inst. Medicine Chgo., Odontographic Soc. Chgo. (bd. dirs., treas. 1993-99, chmn. 2001—); mem. ADA (chmn. coun. dental rsch. 1981-82). Roman Catholic. Avocations: music; piano.

GOERDT, ANN RENEE, physical therapist, consultant; b. Dubuque, Iowa; d. Cletus Goerdt and Loyola Bohlke. BS in Phys. Therapy, St. Louis U., 1966; MA in Edn. & Anthropology, NYU, 1972, PhD in Internat. Cmty. Health Edn., 1984. Lic. phys. therapist, N.Y. Staff phys. therapist Rusk Inst. NYU, 1966-68, supr. clin. edn. Goldwater Meml. Hosp., 1969-72, instr. phys. therapy, 1973-80; rschr. NIMH, Barabados, 1980-81; cons. rehab. various, 1982-88; scientist rehab. unit WHO, Geneva, Switzerland, 1988-95; coord. DPhys. Therapy program for practing phys. therapists NYU. Co-author: Training in the Community for People with Disabilities, 1989; Global Burden of Disease: A Comprehensive Assessment of Mortality and Disability from Disease, Injuries, Risk Factors in 1990 and Projected to 2020, 1996; contbr. articles to profl. jours. Fellow Orgn. Am. States, 1980; Fulbright grantee, 1980. Mem. APHA, Am. Phys. Therapy Assn. Democrat. Avocations: golf, photography, art history. E-mial. Home: 300 E 71st St New York NY 10021-5234 E-mail: agoerdt@aol.com.

GOEREE, JACOB KLAAS, economist, educator; b. Emmen, Netherlands, Aug. 7, 1966; arrived in U.S., 1996; s. Janny (Pol) and Gerke Goeree; m. Michelle Sovinsky. BA in Econs., U.of Amsterdam, Netherlands, 1993—94; PhD in Econs., U.of Amsterdam, 1997; BS in Physics, U.of Utrecht, Netherlands, 1989; PhD in Physics, U.of Utrecht, 1993—93. Asst. prof. econs. U. of Va., Charlottesville, Va., 1996—99, assoc. prof. of econs., 2000—. Contbr. articles to profl. jours including; ; author: (article) journal: American Economic Review, 2001 (cited in: BusinessWeek, NY Times, 2002). Grantee, NSF, 1996-1999, 1999-2001, 2001-2005; Alfred P. Sloan Found. fellow, 2003—. Mem.: Am. Econ. Assn. Home: 1292 Clifden Greene Charlottesville VA 22901 Office: Univ Virginia 114 Rouss Hall Charlottesville VA 22904 Office Fax: 434-924-7659. Personal E-mail: jg2n@virginia.edu. Business E-Mail: jg2n@virginia.edu.

GOERKE, GLENN ALLEN, university administrator; b. Lincoln Park, Mich., May 15, 1931; s. Albert W. and Cecile P. (Crowl) Goerke; m. Joyce Leslie Walker, Mar. 3, 1973; children: Lynn, Jill, Kurt. AB, Eastern Mich. U., 1952, MA, 1955; PhD, Mich. State U., 1964; LhD (hon.), U. Tech. Santiago, Domincan Republic, 1995, U. Houston, 1997. Dean univ. svcs. Fla. Internat. U., Miami, 1970—71, assoc. dean faculty, 1971—72, assoc. v.p. acad. affairs, provost North campus, 1972—73; v.p. community affairs Fla. Internat U., Miami, 1973—78; dean coll. continuing edn. U. R.I., 1978—81; chancellor Ind. U. East, Richmond, 1981—86; pres. U. Houston, Victoria, 1986—89; interim chancellor U. Houston Sys., 1989; pres. U. Houston, Clear Lake, 1991—95, 1995—97, pres. emeritus, 1997; dir. Inst. for Future of Higher Edn., U. Houston, 1997—98. Recipient Disting. Alumni award, Eastern Mich. U., 1982. Mem.: Internat. Assn. Univ. Pres. (bd. dirs., v.p. 1991—98), Am. Assn. Univ. Adminstrs. (bd. dirs. 1991—96), Nat. Univ. Continuing Edn. Assn. (pres. 1973—74), Golden Key, Phi Delta Kappa, Phi Kappa Phi, Omicron Delta Kappa.

GOERLICH, SHIRLEY ALICE BOYCE, publishing executive, educator, media consultant; b. Oneonta, N.Y., May 17, 1937; d. John Orlo and Nella Virginia (Bartow) Boyce; m. Robert Frank Goerlich, Aug. 19, 1967; children: Robert John, Daniel Lee. AAS, SUNY, Cobleskill, 1957; BA, Parsons Coll., 1962. Cert. tchr. N.Y., bus. owner N.Y. Tchr. Milw. Pub. Schs., 1962-64, Huntington (N.Y.) Pub. Schs., 1964-67, Fairfax (Va.) County Adult Edn., 1970-76; pvt. practice Greene, NY, 1979-83; prin., owner RSG Pub., Sidney, NY, 1984—. Cons. Cemetery Bds. Trustees, Chenango, Delaware and Otsego counties. Author: (book) Genealogy: A Practical Research Guide, 1984 (CSG award, 1987), 2d edit., 1995, At Rest in Unadilla, Otsego Co., N.Y. 1987 (CSG award, 1988, Otsego County Local History award, 1993), Etched in Stone in Sidney, Delaware County N.Y., 1997, East Guilford Cemetery, 1997, History of Unadilla, 4 vols., 1998, History of West Unadilla, 1999, Town of Guliford, Chenango County, N.Y., Book 2 (Guilford, Chenango County, N.Y.) Cemeteries and Burial Grounds, 2000; pub.: Author Unknown, 2001, transcribed and pub.: N.Y. State Censuses for Guilford, Chenango County, N.Y., 1855, 1865, 1875, 1905, Sidney (Delaware County, N.Y.) 1850, Masonville (Delaware County, N.Y.) 1845 along with the Civil War Roster for this town, transcriber, pub.: N.Y. State censuses for Unadilla, N.Y., 1855, 1865, 1875, 1892, Civil War roster town of Franklin, Delaware County, N.Y. Historian Town of Unadilla, NY, 1989—98; trustee Evergreen Hill Cemetary Assoc., Unadilla, 1996—2000, advisor, 2001—; v.p. Prospect Hill Cemetary Assn., Sidney, NY, 2000, bd. dirs., 2001—, v.p. bd. dirs., 2001, pres., 2002—03, sexton, 2003—. Recipient Nat. award, Nat. Soc. New Eng. Women, 1989, award for Excellence, Otsego County Local History Adv. Com., 1995, Civil War Re-enactors award, Bainbridge Hist. Soc., 2002. Mem.: Nat. Soc. New Eng. Women, N.Y. State Hist. Assn., Conn. Soc. Genealogists (Spl. Outstanding award 1989), Nat. Soc. Daus. Union Vets., Nat. Soc. DAR (chmn. 1989—91, organizing regent Gen. John Paterson chpt. 1978, Nat. Lineage Rsch. award 1987, 1988, 1989), Sidney Hist.

Assn. (life). Republican. Presbyterian. Avocations: cooking, painting. Home: 217 County Highway 1 Bainbridge NY 13733-9307 Office: RSG Publishing 217 County Highway 1 Bainbridge NY 13733-3399 Home (Winter): PO Box 441 Sidney NY 13838-0441

GOERTZ, AUGUSTUS FREDERICK, III, artist; b. N.Y.C., Aug. 15, 1948; s. Augustus Frederick and Esther (Meyer) G.; m. Christine Matthai, Sept. 2, 1978. BFA with honors, San Francisco Art Inst. Dir. Art. Time Found., N.Y.C.; cons. Downtown Ventures, N.Y.C. One-man shows include N.Y. Law Sch., 1977, Sarah Rentschler Gallery, 1978-2000, U. Brussels, 1981, Patricia Correia Gallery, L.A., 1994-99, Somers Gallery, N.Y., The Gallery, N.Y.; exhibited in group shows at San Francisco Art Inst., 1971, Adlrich Mus. Contemporary Art, 1973-78, New Britain (Conn.) Mus., 1974, Soho Ctr. for Visual Artists, N.Y.C., 1975, Art Fiera, Bologna, Italy, 1978, Todd Capp Gallery, N.Y.C., 1986-88, Art in Gen., N.Y.C., 1987, Neo Persona Gallery, N.Y.C., 1991, Robin Rice Gallery, N.Y.C., 1992, Patricia Correia, L.A., 1992-2000, Kim Foster Gallery, N.Y.C., 1996-2001; represented in permanent collections Lever House, N.Y.C., Am. Gen. Aetna Bldg., Harrison, N.Y., Huntington Bank of Ohio Collection, Aldrich Mus. Contemporary Art, Chgo. Art Inst., San Francisco Art Inst., N.Y. Law Sch., Harmonious Arts Found. N.Y., Shearson-Lehman, Chubb, Avatar Brokerage, Seimens Electric, The Port Authority of N.Y. and N.J., Duke Power, Durham, N.C., Sungard Tech, N.Y.C., Progress Energy, Raleigh, N.C., others. Mem. Orgn. Ind. Artists, San Francisco Art Inst. Alumni Assn., Works Project Assn., Inc., Amnesty Internat. Democrat. Address: 319 Greenwich St # 2 New York NY 10013-3339 also: care Kim Foster Gallery 429 W 20th St Chelsea New York NY 10012-4410 Fax: 212-431-4806. *Every person has a responsibility to evolve away from materialistic environmental destruction, and towards linking intellect, spirit, body, and expanding universe.*

GOERTZ, ROGER LAMAR, retired education counselor; b. Freer, Tex., Apr. 24, 1938; s. Albert F. and Dorothy N. Goertz; m. Jean L. Humphrey, Mar. 29, 1980. BA, S.W. Tex. State U., 1964; MEd, Sul Ross State U., 1974. Cert. vocat. and spl. edn. counselor. Tchr., coach Knippa (Tex.) Schs., 1964-65, Sanderson (Tex.) Schs., 1965-69, Big Spring (Tex.) Schs., 1969-76, vocat. counselor, 1981-94, career svcs. coord., 1994-98; plan a counselor Plainview (Tex.) Schs., 1976-78; vocat. counselor Svc. Ctr. XV, San Angelo, Tex., 1978-81; ret., 1998. Mem. goals com. Future Goals City of Big Spring, 1995. Mem.: Big Spring Optimist Club (pres. 2000—02). Lutheran. Avocations: plays, jazz concerts, athletic events.

GOERTZEL, TED GEORGE, sociologist, educator; b. Visalia, Calif., Nov. 20, 1942; s. Victor and Mildred Goertzel; life ptnr. Linda Lawton; children: Benjamin, Rebecca. PhD, Washington U., St. Louis, 1970. Prof. sociology Rutgers U., Camden, NJ. Author: (books) Fernando Henrique Cardoso: Reinventing Democracy in Brazil, Linus Pauling: A Life in Science and Politics, Turncoats and True Believers. Home: 155 Algonquin Trail Medford NJ 08055 Office: Rutgers University 311 N Fifth St Camden NJ 08055 E-mail: goertzel@camden.rutgers.edu.

GOERTZEN, IRMA, hospital executive; BSN, U. Wash., 1967, MS, 1968, DS in Pub. Svc., 1998, D Humanities, 2000. Pres., CEO Magee-Women Hosp. & Rsch. Inst., 1989—. Office: 300 Halket St Pittsburgh PA 15213-3108

GOERZ, MARY ELIZABETH LARSEN, civic worker; b. Mpls., Apr. 1, 1935; d. David Paul and Myrtle Mary (Grunnet) Larsen; m. David J. Goerz, Jr., Jan. 26, 1962; children: David J. III, Karen Goerz Preston, Julie Goerz Mulvaney. BA, Stanford U., 1957. Mem. pers. staff Hewlett-Packard Corp., Palo Alto, Calif., 1960—62. Bd. dirs. Packard Children's Hosp., Stanford, Calif., 1985-96, Ch. of the Pioneers Found., Menlo Park, 1991—, Lucile Packard Found. for Children's Health, Stanford, 1996-2001; founder Roth Aux. of Packard Children's Hosp., 1989, pres. Assn. of Auxs., 1986-89; pres. of corp. Menlo Park Presbyn. Ch., 1989-91, moderator women's ministries, 1989-91; pres. PTA, La Entrada Sch., Menlo Park, 1976-77; sec. Mid-Peninsula Access Corp., 1986-87. Mem. Stanford Alumni Assn., Stanford Club of Palo Alto (dir. 1971-73). Home: 11 Shasta Ln Menlo Park CA 94025-7049

GOES, KATHLEEN ANN, secondary education educator, choral director; b. New Bedford, Mass., Jan. 13, 1951; d. Filento Andrade and Lillian (Cabral) G. BA in Psychology, U. Mass., North Dartmouth, 1976; postgrad., Ctrl. Conn. State U., 1987—98. Cert. K-8 elem. tchr., K-12 music tchr., Mass. Social worker Dept. Social Svcs., Cambridge, Mass., 1980-85; pvt. tchr. voice and piano, New Bedford, 1985-88; tchr. vocal music New Bedford Pub. Sch., 1985-90; tchr. music, choral dir. Fairhaven (Mass.) H.S., 1991—. Singer, actress, southeastern New Eng., 1974—; dir. music ministry St. Mary's Ch., South Dartmouth, Mass., 1988—; bd. dirs., sec. New Bedford Festival Theatre, 1990-97, v.p., 1997-99, mem. adv. bd., 1999—. Dir. musicals The Sound of Music, Cinderella, My Fair Lady, Bye, Bye Birdie, You're a Good Man Charlie Brown, How to Succeed in Business Without Really Trying, Little Shop of Horrors, The Boyfriend, Godspell, Jesus Christ Superstar; performed the mother in Amahl and the Night Visitors; actress, singer in musicals Fiddler on the Roof, Godspell, Phantom, The Sound of Music. Bd. dirs. New Bedford Symphony Orch., 1994-96. Named Promising Young Artist, Crescendo Club, Boston, 1981; recipient outstanding leadership award Fairhaven Assn. for Music Edn., 1995. Mem. NEA, Am. Choral Dirs. Assn., Nat. Pastoral Musicians Assn., New Eng. Theatre Conf., Drama League, Music Educators Nat. Conf., Mass. Tchrs. Assn., Mass. Music Educators Assn., Whale Hist. League. Roman Catholic. Avocations: cooking, crafts, computers, boating, scenic design. Home: 363 Maple St New Bedford MA 02740-1075 Office: Fairhaven HS 12 Huttleston Ave Fairhaven MA 02719-3122

GOESTENKORS, GAIL, head basketball coach; b. Waterford, Mich., Feb. 26, 1963; m. Mark Simons. BA, Saginaw Valley State U., 1985. Grad. asst. Iowa State U., 1985-86; asst. coach basketball Purdue U., West Lafayette, Ind., 1986-92; head basketball coach Duke U., Durham, N.C., 1992—. Coach U.S. Jones Cup Team, taiwan; head coach Festival Trials, 1991, 95; coach 1994 ACC All-Star Team, Latvia, Lithuania. Named ACC Coach of the Yr., 1995-96, 97-98, 98-99, Nat. Coach of Yr. 1999. Office: Duke University Cameron Indoor Stadium PO Box 90555 Durham NC 27708-0555

GOETHE, ELIZABETH HOGUE, music educator; b. Balt., May 4, 1943; d. Paul Robert and Charlotte H. (Rigney) H.; m. Frederick Martin Goethe, June 30, 1973; children: Elizabeth Anne, Jonathan David. BS, Towson U., 1965; MEd in Music, U. Md., 1972. Cert. tchr. piano. Accompanist Vera Hax Dance Studio, Balt., 1962-66; music tchr. Balt. County Pub. Schs., 1965-74; ch. choir dir. Glyndon, Ellicott City, Md., 1976-79; class piano tchr. Balt. County Pub. Schs., 1980—83; piano tchr. Reisterstown, Md., 1978—; pvt. piano tchr., 1978—; music tchr. St. John's Episcopal Pre-Sch., Glyndon, 1978—2000. Mem Choristers Guild, 1976-79. Mem. Music Tchrs. Nat. Assn. (ea. divsn. sec. 1996-98), Md. State Music Tchrs. Assn. (convention chair 1991-93, v.p. student activities 1993-97, cert. com. 1991-97), Greater Columbia Music Tchrs. Assn. (sec. 1996-98), Greater Balt. Music Tchrs. Assn. (treas. 1997—), Nat. Guild of Piano Tchrs. (adjudicator), Am. Coll. Musicians. Republican. Episcopalian. Avocations: family, teaching, profl. activities. Home and Office: 120 Nicodemus Rd Reisterstown MD 21136-3245

GOETHEL, STEPHEN B. lawyer; b. Grand Rapids, Mich., Apr. 10, 1953; S. Warren B. Goethel and Beverly (Hendrick) Barrett; children: Dana, Erica, Matthew. BA, Mich. State U., 1975; JD, Detroit Coll. Law, 1979. Bar: Mich. 1979, U.S. Dist. Ct. (ea. dist.) Mich. 1979. Asst. prosecutor, Oakland County, Mich., 1979-80; assoc. Carlin, Ranno & Goethel, Southfield, Mich., 1980-83; pvt. practice Pontiac, Mich., 1983—85; ptnr. Stein, Moran & Westerman, Ann Arbor, Mich., 1985—91, Stein, Moran, Raimi & Goethel, Ann Arbor, 1991—2001, Moran, Raimi & Goethel, Ann Arbor, 2002—. Bd. dirs. Old West Side Assn., Ann Arbor, 1984-86. Mem. ATLA, Mich. Trial Lawyers Assn., State Bar of Mich., Washtenaw County Bar Assn. Office: 320 N Main St Ann Arbor MI 48104-1127 E-mail: sgoethel@aol.com.

GOETSCH, CHARLES CARNAHAN, lawyer, legal historian; b. New Haven, Nov. 9, 1950; s. John Black and Miriam Goetsch; m. Cecilia Cartwright Moffitt, Mar. 31, 1980; children: Benjamin John, Megan Elizabeth. AB magna cum laude, Brown U., 1973; JD, U. Conn., 1976; LLM, Harvard U., 1977; postgrad., Yale Law Sch., 1978-79. Bar: Conn. 1978, N.Y. 1984, U.S. Dist. Ct. Conn. 1978, U.S. Dist. Ct. (so. dist.) N.Y. 1982, U.S. Ct. Appeals (2d cir.) 1982, U.S. Supreme Ct. 1984. Law clk. to judge U.S. Dist. Ct. Conn., 1978-79, U.S. Ct. Appeals 2d cir., 1979-80; assoc. Tyler, Cooper & Alcorn, New Haven, 1980-81; ptnr. Cahill & Goetsch, P.C., New Haven, 1982—. Chmn. civil justice adv. group U.S. Dist. Ct. Conn., 1990-95. Author: Essays on Simeon E. Baldwin, 1981, The Autobiography of Thomas L. Chadbourne, 1985; contbr. articles to legal jours.; editor Conn. Law Rev., 1974-76, Conn. Bar Jour., 1983-95. Am. Bar Found. fellow, 1978, NEH fellow, 1979. Fellow Am. Bar Found.; mem. ABA, Am. Trial Lawyers Assn., Conn. Bar Assn. (fed. practice com., chmn. legal history com.), Am. Soc. Legal History, Harvard Club, Brown Club (N.Y.C.), Phi Beta Kappa. Home: 39 Round Hill Rd Woodbridge CT 06525-1228 Office: 43 Trumbull St New Haven CT 06510-1003 E-mail: charlie@trainlaw.com.

GOETSCH, JOHN HUBERT, consultant and retired utility company executive; b. Merrill, Wis., Apr. 28, 1933; s. John Albert and Ada (Natzke) G.; m. Joyce A. Wilke, June 16, 1956; children: Jody A. Goetsch Beauvais, Jacklyn L., John C., James W. BS in Commerce magna cum laude, U. Notre Dame, 1955; MBA, Ind. U., 1956. Jr. analyst Wis. Electric Power Co., Milw., 1958-62, sr. specialist, 1962-63, adminstrv. asst., 1963-67, asst. sec., 1967-79, sec., 1979-88, v.p., sec., 1988-93; asst. sec. Wis. Natural Gas Co., Milw., 1969-79, sec., 1979-93; asst. sec. Badger Svc. Co., Milw., 1975-79, sec., 1979-95; asst. sec. Wis. Mich. Investment Corp., Milw., 1978-79, sec., 1979-95, Wis. Energy Corp., Milw., 1981—93, v.p., sec., 1994—95; sec. Wispark, Wisvest, Witech Corps., Milw., 1984-95; v.p., sec. Wis. Energy Corp., Milw., 1994-95. 1st Lt. USAF, 1956-58. Mem. Am. Soc. Corp. Secs. (pres., v.p., sec., treas. Milw. chpt. 1981-85, nat. dir. 1989-95, nat. chmn. 1993-94). Avocations: spectator sports, fishing, swimming. Home: 2301 W Brantwood Ave Milwaukee WI 53209-3331 E-mail: goejac@webtv.net.

GOETSCHEL, ROY HARTZELL, JR., mathematician, researcher; b. Oak Park, Ill., Apr. 19, 1930; s. Roy Hartzell and Elizabeth Wilhelmina Johanna (Gaude) G.; m. Jane Peterson, June 6, 1971. BS, Northwestern U., 1954; MS, DePaul U., 1958; PhD, U. Wis., 1966. Asst. prof. math. Sonoma State U. of Calif., Rohnert Park, Calif., 1966-69; prof. math. U. Idaho, Moscow, Idaho, 1969-97, prof. emeritus math., 1997—. Author: Advanced Calculus, 1981; contbr. articles to Fuzzy Sets and Systems. Mem. N.Y. Acad. Scis. Achievements include introduction and development of concept of fuzzy darts and fuzzy dart representations of fuzzy numbers; introduction of the topic of fuzzy hypergraphs including methodology and applications (especially Hebbian structures) to the literature through papers published in Fuzzy Sets and Systems; conceptualization and development of the basis of a fuzzy matroid theory. Home: 1721 Atsirk St Moscow ID 83843-9302

GOETSCHEL, WILLI, literary and intellectual historian, philosopher, educator; b. Zürich, Switzerland, Mar. 13, 1958; came to U.S., 1983; s. Robert and Charlotte (Hayum) G.; m. Samira Afrasiabi; 1 child, Daniel. MPhil, U. Zürich, 1982; PhD, Harvard U., 1989. Instr. Harvard U., Cambridge, Mass., 1988-89; vis. asst. prof. Bard Coll., N.Y., 1989-91; asst. prof. Columbia U., N.Y.C., 1991-97, assoc. prof., 1997-2000, U. Toronto, Ont., Can., 2000—. Book rev. editor Germanic Rev., 1996, exec. editor, 2000—. Author: Constituting Critique: Kant's Writing as Critical Praxis, 1994, Spinoza's Modernity: Mendelssohn, Lessine and Heine, 2003; editor: Wege des Widerspruchs, 1984, Perspektiven der Dialogik, 1994, Werkausgabe Hermann Levin Goldschmidt, 9 vols., 1999; contbr. articles to profl. jours. Pres. Dialogik Found., Zürich, 1998—. Humboldt Found. fellow, 1996-97. Office: U Toronto German Dept 50 St Joseph St Toronto ON Canada M5S 1J4 E-mail: w.goetschel@utoronto.ca.

GOETTEL, GERARD LOUIS, federal judge; b. N.Y.C., Aug. 5, 1928; s. Louis and Agnes Beatrice (White) G.; m. Elinor Praeger, June 4, 1951; children: Sheryl, Glenn, James. Student, The Citadel, 1946-48; BA, Duke U., 1950; JD (Harlan Fiske Stone scholar), Columbia U., 1955. Bar: N.Y. 1955. Asst. U.S. atty. So. Dist. N.Y., N.Y.C., 1955-58; dep. chief atty. gen.'s spl. group on organized crime Dept. Justice, N.Y.C., 1958 59; assoc. firm Lowenstein, Pitcher, Hotchkiss, Amann & Parr, N.Y.C., 1959-62; counsel N.Y. Life Ins. Co., N.Y.C., 1962-68; with Natanson & Reich, N.Y.C., 1968-69; asso. gen. counsel Overmyer Co., N.Y.C., 1969-71; asst. counsel N.Y. Ct. on the Judiciary, 1971; U.S. magistrate U.S. Dist. Ct., So. Dist. N.Y., 1971-76; U.S. dist. judge U.S. Dist. Ct., Conn. Dist. Ct., Waterbury, 1976—, now sr. judge. Adj. prof. law Fordham U. Law Sch., 1978-87, Pace U. Law Sch., 1988-91; mem. com. on criminal justice act Jud. Conf. U.S., 1981-87, mem. cir. com. on pretrial phase of civil litigation, chmn. dist. coms. on discovery and criminal justice act 1982-85. Mem. council Fresh Air Fund, N.Y.C., 1961-64; bd. dirs. Community Action Program, Yonkers, N.Y., 1964-66. Served to lt. (j.g.) USCG, 1951-53. Mem.: Greenwoods Country (Winsted, Conn.), Boyne South Golf Club (Naples, Fla.), Greenwood Country Club (Winsted, Conn.). Office: 14 Cottage Pl Waterbury CT 06702-1904

GOETZ, ANGELLA MARIE, infection control nurse, researcher; b. Stamford, Conn., Dec. 2, 1935; d. James Vincent and Mary (Marciano) Preteroti; m. Albert Frank Goetz, Oct. 12, 1963; 1 child, Lisa Marie. Diploma, Allegheny Gen. Hosp. Sch. Nursing, Pitts., 1956; BSN, U. Pitts., 1975, M Nursing Edn., 1977. RN, Pa; cert. in infection control. Staff nurse Allegheny Gen. Hosp., 1956-58, 59, head nurse, 1959-64, team leader, 1967-72; staff nurse Multnomah County Hosp., Portland, Oreg., 1958-59, Hotel Dieu Hosp., El Paso, 1964-66; instr. Western Pa. Hosp. Sch. Nursing, Pitts., 1977-78, infection control nurse, 1978-81, VA Med. Ctr., Pitts., 1981-97, dir. IV team, 1991-97. Adj. instr. U. Pitts., 1991-99; rschr. in field; bd. dirs. Cert. Bd. Infection Ctrl., 1997-02. Mem. editl. bd. Am. Jour. Infection Control, 1987-97, 2003—, Infection Control and Hosp. Epidemiology, 1987-90; contbr. articles to profl. jours. Named Disting. Alumna of Yr., Allegheny U. Health Scis., 1998. Mem. ANA, Assn. for Profls. in Infection Control and Epidemiology (cert. treas. adv. com. 1985—, Carole DeMille Achievement award 1994, Lifetime award 2002), Soc. for Healthcare Epidemiologists Am. Avocations: reading, music, traveling. E-mail: afgamg@aol.com.

GOETZ, CLARENCE EDWARD, retired judge, retired chief magistrate judge; b. Balt., Feb. 4, 1932; AA, U. Balt., 1961, LLB, 1964. Bar: Md. 1964. Assoc. Hackney & Yourtee, Anne Arundel County, Md., 1965-66; asst. U.S. atty. for Md., 1966-70; U.S. magistrate judge for Md., 1970-97. Asst. prof. U. Balt., 1975, Towson State Coll., 1976; cons., arbitrator, mediator. Mem. Fed. Magistrate Judges Assn. E-mail: CKGoetz@comcast.net.

GOETZ, GARY D., SR., writer, retired chef, restaurateur; b. Cleve., Feb. 3, 1952; s. Wilmer F. and Dorothy (Moody) G.; m. Oliva G., May 25, 1987; children: Michael Anthony, Jason William, Laura Gresham, Raymond Daryan, Luis G., Gary Jr. AA, La. Tech. U., 1975; grad., Culinary Arts Inst., Norfolk, Va., 1977. Restaurant mgr. Bonanza Internat., Shreveport, La., 1977-79; plant mgr., cons. chef Chef Shorty Lenard's Gumbo, Shreveport, La., 1979-80; dept. head, El Bandido's Restaurant Dillard's, Shreveport, La., 1980-81; owner Night Moves Restaurant, Panama Reds Restaurant, Shreveport, La., 1981-82; v.p. sales Jim Wilson Constrn., San Antonio, 1982-83; disabled postal worker U.S. Postal Svc., San Antonio, 1983-91; shop steward, rep. EEOC. Author: Biologically Incorrect, 1996; contbr. poems and essays to publs.; TV and radio guest personalist, Southern Tex., 1996—, pub. 7 books of poetry, —, 2 cassettes of top 10 American Poets featuring one poem in each, —, lyricist, musician, actor (films) Selena. Treas. Brush Country Homeschoolers, Pleasanton, Tex., 1993—97; asst. comdr., organizer Atascosa Militia, Atascosa County, Tex., 1996—97; coach children's baseball and basketball San Antonio, 1992—; apptd. state rep. Tex. Rep. Party, 1996; county precinct chmn. Atascosa County, 1994—98; treas. South Tex. Assn. Reps., 1996—98; apptd. temp. county judge for election Atascosa County; deacon 1st Presbyn. Ch., Pleasanton, 2000, children's guitarist. With USAF, 1971—75, Vietnam. Named Poet of Merit, Internat. Soc. Poets, 1998, Poet of Yr., 2000—02; recipient Outstanding Bus. award, Muscular Dystrophy Assn., Shreveport, 1977, Editor's Choice award, Nat. Libr. Poetry, 1999, 2000, (4) various other Editor's Choice awards. Mem. DAV, NRA, Christian Coalition, Lions Club. Libertarian. Lutheran/Presbyterian. Avocations: herbal and natural cures, guitar, sports, movies, gardening. Home: Apt K4 2408 NW 52nd St Lawton OK 73505-1484 E-mail: gdgoetzpoetofmerit@yahoo.com.

GOETZ, JACK RALPH, dean; b. L.A., Mar. 4, 1955; s. Theodore Arthur G. and Jane Small; m. Reva Garfunkel, Aug. 1, 1982; children: Rachelle Elisabeth, Jason Randall. BA, San Diego State U., 1976; JD, Boston U., 1979; MBA, Pepperdine U., 1990. 2d v.p. Harcourt, Brace & Jovanovich Legal & Profl. Pubs., Inc., Chgo., 1979-89; CEO Am. Profl. Testing Svcs., Inc., Santa Monica, Calif., 1989-95; v.p. West Profl. Tng. Programs, Inc., Mpls., 1995-97, Kaplan Ednl. Svcs., Inc., N.Y.C., 1997—; pres., dean Concord U. Sch. Law, L.A., 1998—. Trustee Distance Edn. and Tng. Coun., 2000-2002; mem. Law Sch. Coun., 2001—. Mem. State Bar Calif., Cheviot Hills Pony Baseball Assn. (bd. dirs. 1996-2001). Avocations: historian, sports.

GOETZ, KENNETH LEE, cardiovascular physiologist, research consultant, writer; b. Java, S.D., Jan. 7, 1932; m. Shirley Anne Caldwell, July 14, 1962; children. Gregory Earl, Anne Katherine. PhD, U. Wis., 1963; MD, U. Kans., 1967. Instr., asst. prof. dept. physiology U. Kans. Med. Ctr., Kansas City, 1963-69, med. intern St. Luke's Hosp., Kansas City, 1969, head, div. of exptl. medicine, 1970-91, dir. rsch., 1980-91. Adj. prof. dept. physiology U. Kans. Med. Ctr., 1976-92; vis. prof. U. Kuopio, Finland, 1985, 91, U. Munich, 1992; vis. scientist German Inst. Aerospace Medicine, Cologne, 1993-94. Author (memoir): Bending the Twig, 2002. Recipient Alexander von Humboldt award, 1992. Fellow Am. Phys. Soc. (circulation sect.); mem. Am. Physiol. Soc., Alexander von Humboldt Assn. of Am. Achievements include research in Neurohumoral control of body fluid balance; influence of vasoctive peptides on hemodynamics; Vasopressin, atriopeptin, renal natriuretic peptide, endothelin; reflex control of the circulation. Home: 4856 Black Swan Dr Shawnee Mission KS 66216-1237

GOETZ, LEWIS J. architect; Prin. and founder Greenwell Goetz Archs., 1978—2000; CEO and founding prin. Group Goetz Archs., PC, 2001—. Mem.: AIA, Internat. Interior Design Assn. (pres.-elect 2002—, v.p. comm.). Office: Group Goetz Archs 2000 L St NW Ste 410 Washington DC 20036*

GOETZ, MAURICE HAROLD, lawyer; b. N.Y.C., Mar. 29, 1924; s. Morton M. and Elsie (Klein) G.; m. Pearl Goldberg, Sept. 12, 1948; children: Susan Goetz Zwirn, Janet L., Jill K. B Social Scis. in Econs. and History, CCNY, 1947; JD, Harvard U., 1950. Bar: N.Y. 1951. Assoc. Bandler Haas & Kass, N.Y.C., 1951-57; ptnr. Bandler Kass & Goetz, N.Y.C., 1957-66, Friedlander, Gaines, Ruttenberg & Goetz, N.Y.C., 1966-74, Rosenman & Colin, N.Y.C., 1974-92; of counsel KMZ Rosenman, N.Y.C., 1993—. Lectr. on labor law Contbr. articles to Nat. Law Jour., Fed. Publs., Inc., others. Office: KMZ Rosenman 575 Madison Ave New York NY 10022-2585

GOETZ, ROGER MELVIN, minister; b. Chgo., May 17, 1940; s. Charles Albert and Sidonia Helene (Heck) G.; m. Betty Jean Bokelheide, Nov. 22, 1969; 1 child, Anne Katharine. BS in Chemistry, Iowa State U., Ames, 1962, BS in Math., 1967; MDiv, Concordia Theol. Sem., 1967; STM, Luth. Theol. Sem., 1972. Ordained minister Luth. Ch., 1968. Asst. pastor, dir. music Gethsemane Luth. Ch., St. Paul, 1968 80; assoc. pastor, kantor St. John's Luth. Ch., Topeka, 1980—; instr. Walther Luth. Jr. H.S., St. Paul, 1968-80; archivist Kans. Dist. Luth. Ch.-Mo. Synod, Topeka, 1985-89, chmn. worship com., 1985-94, chair floor com. edn., 2000; instr. organ Luth. Ch. - Mo. Synod, 2000—02. Organ recitalist various Luth. chs., 1970—. Author: The Descendants of Johann Georg Götz, 1976, Double Cousins by the Dozens, 1982; editor: A Century of Grace: Centennial History of the Kansas District, 1888-1988, 1988; contbr. articles to profl. jours. including Luth. Witness and Concordia Hist. Inst. Quarterly; composer work for double mixed chorus. Bd. edn. Topeka Luth. Sch., 1996—; Rep. precinct committeeman Ward 11/Precinct 3, Topeka, 1996-98, 2002—. Mem.: Alpha Chi Sigma, Am. Guild Organists (chpt. pres. 1983—84, chpt. chaplain 1994—2001, v.p. 2001—02), Cosmopolitan Internat., Phi Mu Alpha. Office: St Johns Luth Ch 901 SW Fillmore St Topeka KS 66606-1445 *In my life I have found that the less I try to control things and people and rather leave things in the hands of my loving God, the more God brings gifts and joy into my life.*

GOETZ, THOMAS HENRY PAUL, French literature educator; b. Phila., Feb. 9, 1936; s. John Thomas and Anna Marie (O'Neill) G.; m. Joanne E. Smith, June 27, 1970; 1 son, Justin Paul. BA, LaSalle U., Phila., 1961; MA, Syracuse U., 1963, PhD, 1967. Asst. prof. Ill. Wesleyan U., Bloomington, 1966-67; faculty mem. SUNY, Fredonia, 1967—, prof. French lit., 1978—, chmn. fgn. lang. dept., 1979—89, 2000—02, disting. svc. prof., 1991. Cons. La. Bd. Regents, Baton Rouge, 1982. Author: Taine and the Fine Arts, 1973; editor: Nineteenth Century French Studies jour., 1972-99; contbr. articles to profl. jours. With AUS, 1954-57. Syracuse U. Coll. tchg. fellow in humanities, 1964-66, SUNY Rsch. Found. fellow, 1969, 75, 80, Nat. Endowment for Humanities Coll. fellow, 1977, 79, 84, 87, 88; recipient N.Y. State UUP Excellence award 1990. Mem. Assn. des Membres de l'Ordre des Palmes Academiques (officer), MLA (del. 1979-81, 19th Century French studies colloquia com., 1978-99, exec. com. divsn. on 19th Century French lit. 1984-88). Democrat. Roman Catholic. Home: 6 Pine Dr Fredonia NY 14063-2218 Office: SUNY Dept Fgn Langs and Lits Fenton Hall Fredonia NY 14063 E-mail: goetz@fredonia.edu.

GOETZE, RICHARD B., JR., association administrator; Grad., USAF Acad.; MA in Latin Am. Studies, Am. U., Washington, 1967, PhD in Internat. Studies, 1973. Cert. flight instr. FAA. Commd. 2d lt. USAF, 1959, advanced through grades to maj. gen., 1989; pres., CEO Coll. Aeronautics, Queens, NY, 1992—97; cons. TRIAD Enterprises, 1997—; pres. Aerospace Edn. Found., 2000—. Adj. faculty Am. Mil. U., Ctr. for Civil-Mil. Rels. of Naval Postgrad. Sch., Monterey, Naval War Coll.; trustee Aerospace Edn. Found., 1995—, chmn. scholarship, nominating and partnership com.; trustee Univ. Aviation Assn.; bd. dirs. Am. Mil. U. Decorated D.S.M.; recipient Postgrad. scholarship, George Olmsted Found. Office: c/o Aerospace Edn Found 1501 Lee Hwy Arlington VA 22209-1198

GOETZINGER, LAUREL ELDREDGE, music educator; b. Chgo., May 13, 1947; d. Don Herbert and Frances Cain Eldredge; m. Mark A Goetzinger; children: Benjamin Ross, Katherine Elizabeth. BS in Edn., Ill. State U., 1969; MusM, U. of Ill., 1974. Asst. prof. Butler U., Indpls., 1989—97; adj. asst. prof. DePauw U., Greencastle, Ind., 1996—99, Miami U., Oxford, Ohio, 1997—99; assoc. prof. Anderson (Ind.) U., 1999—, dir. opera and mus. theater, 1999—. Singer, actor, dir. (opera and musical theatre) various operas, musicals, plays. Mem.: Actors Equity Assn., Opera Am., Nat. Opera Assn., Coll. Music Soc., Nat. Assn. of Teachers of Singing (state auditions co-chair 2003), Phi Kappa Lambda. Methodist. Avocation: needlework.

GOETZMAN, BRUCE EDGAR, architecture educator; b. Rochester, June 6, 1931; s. Benjamin Byron and Ila Flowers G.; m. Jane Grady McRae,June 25, 1955; children: Adam Brit, Ben Evan. BArch, Carnegie Mellon U., 1954; MS in Architecture, Columbia U., 1956; M in Cmty. Planning, U. Cin., 1965; postgrad., U. London, 1968. Asst. prof. Univ. Cin., 1956-66; prin. Bruce Goetzman & Assocs., Cin., 1965-77; acting chmn. grad. div. Univ. Cin., 1966-67, assoc. prof., 1967-99; prof. emeritus, 1999; ptnr. Goetzman & Follmer Architects, Cin., 1977-85; prin. Bruce Goetzman, Restoration Architect, 1985--. Trustee Miami Purchase Assn. Hist. Preservation, Cin., 1972-91, Ohio Hist. Sites Preservation Adv. Bd., 1980-92; trustee Ohio Hist. Soc., 1986-96, pres., 1995-96; pres. Ohio Preservation Alliance, 1986-88; trustee Cin. Preservation Assn., 1993-2000. Mem.: AIA, Assn. Preservation Tech., Architects Soc. Ohio, Cincinnatus Assn. Democrat. Home: 187 Greendale Ave Cincinnati OH 45220-1223

GOFF, BETSY KAGEN, lawyer, international management group executive; b. York, Pa., July 3, 1948; d. Kenneth Stanford Kagen and Charlotte (Senn) Isen; m. William Miller Goff, Mar. 8, 1973; 1 child, Kenneth Steven. B.S. in Econs., U. Pa., 1970; J.D., Temple U., 1974. Bar: N.Y. 1975. Asst. exec. dir. Writers Guild of Am., N.Y.C., 1974-75; contract atty. ABC Sports, N.Y.C., 1975-78, asst. gen. atty. ABC News, N.Y.C., 1978-81; N.Y. v.p. Internat. Mgmt. Group Trans World Internat., N.Y.C., 1981— ; atty.-on-call Vol. Lawyers for the Arts, N.Y.C., 1974—, NOW, N.Y.C., 1975-79; dir. Living Arts, Inc., N.Y.C. Mem. Voters for Choice, Women in Sports. Office: Internat Mgmt Group 22 E 71st St New York NY 10021-4975

GOFF, CHRISTOPHER WALLICK, pediatrician; b. Phila., Jan. 24, 1948; s. Donald Heiserman and Jean Christman Wallick G.; m. Holly Lynn Housner, Aug. 1970; children: Heather Elizabeth, Rebecca Ann, Abigail Christine. BA in Psychology, Yale U., 1970; MD, U. Pa., 1974. Diplomate Am. Bd. Pediatrics, Pediatric Endocrinology, Nat. Bd. Med. Examiners. Intern, then resident in pediatrics Yale-New Haven (Conn.) Hosp., 1974-76, chief resident in pediatrics, 1977; pvt. practice specializing in pediatrics Wildwood Pediatrics, Essex, Conn., 1977—; alternate dir. Health Town of Essex, 1980-81, dir. Health, 1981—; co-dir. Child Diagnostic Assocs., Essex, 1983—; assoc. staff Yale-New Haven Hosp., 1977-80, attending staff, 1980—. Clin. instr. Pediatrics Yale U. Sch. Med., 1977-79, clin. asst. prof., 1979-97, clin. assoc. prof., 1997—; bd. dirs. Wildwood Med. Ctr. Assn., 1986-89, treas. 1988—; co-med. adviser Mt. St. John Sch., Deep River, Conn., 1977—, Oxford Acad., Westbrook, Conn., 1990-95; acting med. adviser Essex Elem. Sch., 1981—; med. adviser Old Saybrook Sch. sys., 1992-97. Reviewer Clinical Pediatrics; clin. reactor Contemporary Pediatrics; contbr. articles to prof. jours. Chmn. prof. adv. com. Visiting Nurses Lower Valley, 1980—, med. dir., 1996—; devel. bd. Tri-Town Youth Svc. Bur., 1987-88; mem. Sexual Abuse Prevention Task Force, 1987-95, Tri-Town Substance Abuse Task Force, 1988-95, Westbrook Sexual Abuse Prevention Task Force, 1988-93, Shoreline Child Protection Team, 1988-93, Tri-Town Sexual Abuse Response Team, 1990-91; vestryman St. John's Episcopal Ch., Essex., 1978-79, sr. warden, 1979-83, coord. Youth Ministry program, 1986-90, treas. 1994-96; lector 1989-96; pres. Marlins Parents Club, 1989-91; bd. dirs. Lower Valley Cmty. Health Svcs., 1979-80, Essex Ambulance Assn., 1985-89, Cougar Aquatic Team, 1992-96, v.p. 1992-93, treas. 1993-94. Recipient Joel Gordon Miller award, 1974. Fellow Am. Acad. Pediatrics; mem. AMA, N. Am. Soc. Pediatric and Adolescent Gynecology, New England Soc. Clin. Hypnosis, Conn. State Med. Soc. (malpractice claims rev. bd., 1981-84), New Haven County Med. Soc., Lawson Wilkins Pediatric Endocrine Soc. Republican. Avocations: sailing, skiing, ballroom dancing, stamp collecting, golf. Office: Wildwood Pediatrics and Adol Med 1 Wildwood Medical Ctr Essex CT 06426-1190

GOFF, HARRY RUSSELL, retired manufacturing company executive; b. San Francisco, May 24, 1915; s. Harry Roy and Ethel S. (Ludwigsen) Goff; m. Kathleen K. Kloster, Feb. 10, 1940; children: Kathi, Karen, Betsi. BA, Stanford U., 1937; MBA, Harvard U., 1939. With Nat. Lead Co., San Francisco, 1939—41; ptnr. James D. Dole & Assocs., San Francisco, 1946—60; pres. James Dole Corp., San Francisco, 1955—79; chmn. bd., dir. emeritus Pacific Sci. Co., Newport Beach, Calif., 1979—91. Mem. adv. coun. Stanford U. Libr. Assn., 1979—; mem. Nat. Pub. Adv. Com. on Regional Econs. Devel., 1974—76; trustee Am. Sch. Oriental Rsch., 1978—82, Calif. Hist. Soc., 1993—. Lt. comdr. USNR, 1941—46. Mem.: Inst. Food Technologists, Book Club Calif. (past pres.), Roxbourghe Club Calif., Los Altos Golf and Country Club, Univ. Club San Francisco, Bohemian Club. Republican. Home: 868 Southampton Dr Palo Alto CA 94303-3439

GOFF, JAMES FRANKLIN, physicist, consultant; b. Louisville, Aug. 1, 1928; s. James Robert and Mary Louise (Kubaugh) Goff; m. Barbara Louise Kral, June 20, 1959; children: Sidra Denise, Alexandra Kral. BS in Physics, MIT, 1950; PhD in Physics, Purdue U., 1962. Rsch. physicist Naval Ordnance Lab., Silver Spring, Md., 1961-80; dir. materials applications office Naval Surface Weapons Ctr., Silver Spring, Md., 1980-90. Editor: Gaelic Jour. of An Comunn Gaidhealach Am., 1993—2000; contbr. articles to profl. jours. With U.S. Army, 1953—55. Fellow: Washington Acad. Scis. (pres. 1982); mem.: Philos. Soc. Washington (pres. 1980), Cosmos Club (program chmn. 1986—90). Achievements include research in reformulation of thermoelectric figure-of-merit so that it could be computed from realistic band structure and scattering; electron-phonon interactions in Ge at low temperatures, contributions of real density states to anomalous electronic transport properties of transition metals and alloys. Home: 3405 34th Pl NW Washington DC 20016-3135

GOFF, JANE E. secondary school educator; b. Denver, Nov. 12, 1949; d. Donald F. and Susanna L. (Commerford) Gallion; m. Harry M. Goff, June 12, 1982. BA, Colo. State U., 1971; student, U. Colo. Cert. modern lang. tchr., Colo. Tchr. French Jefferson County Pub. Sch., Golden, Colo. Adminstr. Alternative Compensation/Student Outcomes Task Forces; project dir. Tchr. Performance Pay Pilot, 1995-98, Columbine anniversary com., Coordinator of World Lang. and Internat. Student Exchange Program, 2003-; mem. Nat. Bd. for Profl. Tchg. Std. Workgroup. Hon. chmn. West Chamber Good News Breakfast; design group West Chamber Links for Learning; mem. Jefferson County Sch. Anchor Group, 1998-2000, Jefferson County Sch. Fin. Task Force, Leadership Jefferson County Steering Com., Jefferson County Schs. 50th Anniversary Com.; bd. dir., v.p. for edn. programs Jefferson Symphony. Mem. NEA, Am. Assn. Tchr. French, Colorado Congress of Fgn. Lang. Tchrs. Jefferson County Edn. Assn. (bd. dir., by-laws chair, bldg. rep., sec. 1990-94, v.p. 1994-98, pres. 1998-2000, budget com./negotiations team, JCEA Award 2003), Colo. Edn. Assn. (v.p. 2000—, quality tchg. task force, pub. edn. advocacy team)Western States Quality Schs. Cadre, Jefferson County Coun. PTA (bd. dirs. 1990-2000), Phi Delta Kappa Internat. E-mail: jgoff@nea.org.

GOFF, KENNETH WADE, electrical engineer; b. Salem, W.Va., June 14, 1928; s. Wetzel and Alma (Beeghley) G.; m. Hazel Lucille Sullivan, July 1, 1950; children— Jerry Kenneth, Deborah Lucille, Brian Lee. BS, W.Va. U., 1950; MS, M.I.T., 1952, Sc.D., 1954. Cons. engr. Bolt Beranek & Newman, Inc., Cambridge, Mass., 1954-56; project mgr. Gruen Precision Labs., Cin., 1956-57; mgr. systems analysis Leeds & Northrup Co., North Wales, Pa., 1957-69, mgr. systems devel., 1969-84, corp. scientist, 1984-85; v.p. advanced tech. Performance Controls, Inc., Horsham, Pa., 1986-98, also dir.; v.p. advanced tech. MTS Automation-Performance Controls, Horsham, Pa., 1998—2001; cons. adv. tech. MTS Automation, Montgomery, Pa., 2001—03. Trustee Eastern U.; vis. lectr. Franklin Inst., 1962, 63. Contbr. articles to profl. jours.; patentee in field. M.I.T. acoustical materials fellow, 1954 Fellow Instrument Soc. Am., IEEE; mem. Acad. Disting. Alumni of W.Va. U. Elec. and Computer Engrng. Dept., Sigma Xi, Tau Beta Pi, Eta Kappa Nu. Baptist. Home: 1815 Cathedral Rd Huntingdon Valley PA 19006-5003

GOFF, KIMBERLY (KIMBERLY KNOLLENBERG), art dealer, painter, writer; b. Phila., Apr. 6, 1955; d. Warren Goff and Elaine Benson; m. Kenneth Knollenberg, Apr. 6, 1985 (dec. July 1997). Owner Kimberly's E., Bridgehampton, N.Y., 1974-86; artist Baja Califonia, Mex., 1986-92; apprentice Elaine Benson Gallery, Bridgehampton, 1993-95, co-dir., 1996-98, owner, dir., 1999—. Mem. adv. bd. Nurture Art, N.Y.C., 1997—, Internat. Toy Bank, L.A., 2000—. Columnist and photographer Dan's Papers, 1999—. Bd. dirs. Bridgehampton Child Care and Recreation Ctr., 1997—; co-chair John Steinbeck Com., Southampton, N.Y., 1999—, Southampton Cultural Ctr., 1999—, Robert Wilsons' Watermill Cmty. Ctr., 1999—, Fish Unltd., Shelter Island, N.Y., 2000—, South Fork Natural History Mus., 2003—. Avocations: painting, ceramics, kayaking, fishing, whale watching. Office: Elaine Benson Gallery PO Box 3034 2317 Montauk Hwy Bridgehampton NY 11932-3034 Home (Winter): Pto A Lopez Mateos Baja California, Sur Mexico E-mail: goffkimber@msn.com.

GOFF, MICHAEL HARPER, retired lawyer; b. Hartford, Conn., Aug. 4, 1927; s. Charles Weer and Fern (Harper) G.; m. Katharine Lyman Bliss, Feb. 11, 1949 (div.); children— Carlin Weer, Peter Lyman; m. Patricia Darilyn King, Apr. 20, 1984 Student, Loomis Sch., Conn., 1942-45, Bethany Coll., 1945, Trinity Coll., Conn., 1949; BA, Swarthmore Coll., 1950; LL.B., Columbia U., 1953. Bar: N.Y. 1953. Assoc. Debevoise & Plimpton, 1953-60, ptnr., 1961-91; asst. to dir. Legis. Drafting Rsch. fund, 1951-53. Lectr. Banking Law Inst., 1966; cons. Atty. Gen. State of N.Y., 1977; spl. cons. Temp. Commn. to Study Orgnl. Structure City N.Y., 1953-54 Served with USNR, 1945-46; to 2d lt. F.A., AUS, 1946-48 Harlan Fiske Stone Scholar, Columbia U., 1951-52; Robert Noxon Toppan prize, Columbia U., 1952; E. B. Convers Prize, Columbia U., 1953 Mem. ABA, N.Y. State Bar Assn., Assn. Bar City N.Y., Moorings Club (Fla.), Phi Delta Phi, Kappa Sigma. Democrat. Episcopalian. Home: 151 Anchor Dr Vero Beach FL 32963-2957

GOFF, R. GAREY, architect; b. Nashville, Feb. 2, 1943; s. R. C. and Martha Ann (Garey) G.; m. Diana R. Richardson; children: Gina Leigh, Susan Kimberly. Student, Vanderbilt U., 1961-65; BArch, U. Fla., 1968. Intern architect Earl Swensson Assocs., Nashville, 1968-70; project architect Sverdrup & Parcel, Nashville, 1970-73, Gresham, Smith and Ptnrs., Nashville, 1973-76, dir. of architecture, 1976-81, prin., assoc., 1981-83, Charleston, S.C., 1983-84; prin. Goff Assocs., Charleston, 1984-89, NBBJ/Goff-D'Antonio, Charleston, 1989-91, Goff-D'Antonio Assocs., Charleston, 1991—. Mem. Trident 100, Charleston. Recipient Bell System awards Southeastern Bell, 1970, Spl. Recognition awards Prestressed Concrete Inst., Chgo., 1987, 88, Design award Gen. Svcs. Adminstrn., Dept. of Transp., Washington, 1990, AIA award, 1998, Coastal Living award, 2000. Mem. Rotary Internat. Republican. Episcopalian. Avocations: golfing, travel, boating. Office: Goff-D'Antonio Assocs 34 Radcliffe St Charleston SC 29403-3154

GOFF, ROBERT BURNSIDE, retired food company executive; b. Arcadia, La., Aug. 8, 1924; s. Carl and Ruth (Capers) G.; m. Mary Jane Ellis, June 14, 1947; children— Gayle M., Robert B. BS, Rice U., 1947. Engr. Tex. Pipe Line Co., Tulsa, 1947-48; v.p., dir. Comet Rice Mills, Inc., Houston, 1948-58; sr. v.p., dir. Riviana Foods, Inc., Houston, 1958-75; pres., dir. Food Corp. Internat., Houston, 1975-86. Trustee Found. for Retarded, 1982-90. Served to lt. (j.g.) USNR, 1942-46. Mem. Rice U. Alumni Assn. (exec. bd. 1985-88), River Oaks Country Club. Presbyterian. Home: 2710 Essex Ter Houston TX 77027-5212

GOFF, ROBERT EDWARD, health care executive; b. Worcester, Mass., Nov. 19, 1952; s. Julius Lewis and Doris (Katz) G.; m. Jinny Sue Yaver, June 30, 1985; 1 child, Blake Adam. BSBA with honors, Northeastern U., Boston, 1976; MBA with honors, Babson Coll., 1978; cert., Cornell U., 1981. Adminstrv. dir. Adirondack PSRO Inc., Glens Falls, N.Y., 1977-80; v.p. No. Met. Hosp. Assn., Newburgh, N.Y., 1980-83, Good Samaritian Hosp., Suffern, N.Y., 1983-85; exec. dir., chief exec. dir. WellCare N.Y., Inc., Newburgh, 1985-97; pres. Wellcare Leasing Corp., Newburgh, N.Y., 1990-96, Well Care Med. Mgmt. Inc., 1992-96; exec. v.p. Well Care Mgmt. Group, Inc., 1992-97; prin. The ABER Group, 1997-98; exec. dir., CEO Univ. Physicians Network, 1998—. Pres., CEO, UPT Trust, mng. dir.; bd. dirs. Wellcare Mgmt. Group Inc.; pres. Wellcare Med. Mgmt.; mem. adj. prof. New Sch. Univ., N.Y.; cons. in field. Bd. dirs. Hospice Care, Inc., Hospice of Orange Inc. Recipient Vigil Honor award Order Arrow, 1969, Eagle Scout award Boy Scouts Am., 1970. Mem. Hudson Valley Hosp. Exec. Assn. (pres., bd. dirs. 1982-85), Healthcare Fin. Mgmt. Assn., Am. Coll. Hosp. Adminstrs., Beta Gamma Soc. Home: 93 Old Castle Point Rd Wappingers Falls NY 12590-7061 Office: 1 Park Ave Fl 9 New York NY 10016-5802 E-mail: robert.goff@med.nyu.edu.

GOFF, ROBERT WILLIAM, JR., lawyer; b. Houston, Apr. 22, 1946; s. Robert William and Emma Kate (Richey) G.; m. Donna M. Davidson, Dec. 22, 1968 (div. 1971); m. Sandra Kaye Chenault, June 22, 1974; 1 child, Melinda Kaye. BBA, Tex. Tech U., 1968; JD, U. Tex., Austin, 1971. Bar: Tex. 1971, U.S. Dist. Ct. (no. dist.) Tex.; cert. in estate planning and probate law. Atty. Sherrill, Crosnoe & Goff, Wichita Falls, Tex., 1971—. Bd. dirs. North Tex. Rehab. Ctr. Found. Bd. dirs. Bethania Regional Health Care Found., Wichita Falls, 1988-98, North Tex. Rehab. Ctr., Inc., 1994-98, United Regional Health Care Sys., 1998-2001, United Regional Health Care Found., 1998-99; trustee Bethania Regional Health Care Ctr., Wichita Falls, 1994-97. Mem. ABA, Wichita County Bar Assn. (pres. 1980-81), Wichita Club (pres., bd. dirs. 1981-85), Wichita Falls Country Club (bd. dirs. 1987-90). Avocations: golf, hunting, fly fishing. Home: 2503 Elmwood Cir N Wichita Falls TX 76308-3915 Office: Sherrill Crosnoe & Goff 2301 Kell Blvd Ste 200 Wichita Falls TX 76308-1042

GOFF, WILMER SCOTT, retired photographer; b. Steubenville, Ohio, July 11, 1923; s. Floyd Orville and Ellen Armenia (Funk) G.; m. Mary Elizabeth Fischer, Dec. 7, 1950; children: Carolyn, Christopher. BFA with honors, Ohio U., 1949. Photographer Columbus (Ohio) Dispatch, 1949-52, Warner P. Simpson, Columbus, 1952-53; owner Willy Goff Photo Studio, Grove City, Ohio, 1954-59; photographer N.Am. Rockwell, Columbus, 1953-70; supr. Transp. Rsch. Ctr. Ohio, East Liberty, 1970-89; adult edn. instr. photography Upper Arlington and Worthington Schs., 1989-99. Photography instr. Columbus Coll. Art and Design, 1949-71; photography judge Ohio State Fair, 1966-68; judge Greater Columbus Film Festival, 1970-72; photographer John Glenn campaign, 1974. One man shows include 100 print exhibit Southern Hotel, Columbus, 1953. Recipient Public's Choice award Columbus Art Gallery, 1958, Photo-Pictoral 1st Pl. award Dix Newspapers, 1960, Best of Show award Balloon Show Competition, 1985. Mem. Aircraft Camera Club (pres. 1954-55), Grove City Camera CLub (pres. 1959-60). Republican. Roman Catholic. Avocations: stamp collecting, recording, cycling. Home: 6110 Darby Ln Columbus OH 43229-2628 *Personal philosophy: My philosophy of a successful life is to pursue a career of choice regardless of monetary gain. My photography career has been exciting and fullfilling. I feel I have accomplished my goals and one for which I had not planned, being included in Who's Who in the America.*

GOFFART, WALTER ANDRÉ, history educator; b. Berlin, Feb. 22, 1934; emigrated to U.S., 1943, naturalized, 1959; s. Francis Leo and Andrée Juliette (Steinberg) G.; m. Ellen Horvath, May 19, 1961; children: Vivian, Andrea Judith; m. Roberta Frank, Dec. 31, 1977. AB, Harvard U., 1955, AM, 1956, PhD, 1961; postgrad., École pratique des Hautes-Études, Paris, France, 1957-58. Lectr. history U. Toronto, Ont., Can., 1961-63, asst. prof., 1963-66, assoc. prof., 1966-71, prof., 1971-99, acting dir. Ctr. for Medieval Studies, 1971-72, prof. emeritus, 1999; sr. rsch. scholar and lectr. history Yale U., 2000—. Vis. asst. prof. U. Calif. at Berkeley, 1965—66; vis. fellow Inst. Advanced Study, Princeton, NJ, 1967—68, Dumbarton Oaks Ctr. Byzantine Studies, Washington, 1973—74; residency Rockefeller Found. Study and Conf. Ctr., Bellagio, Italy, 2001. Author: The Le Mans Forgeries, 1966, Caput and Colonate, 1974, Barbarians and Romans, A.D. 418-584, 1981; The Narrators of Barbarian History: Jordanes, Gregory of Tours, Bede, and Paul the Deacon, 1988, Rome's Fall and After, 1989, Historical Atlases: The First Three Hundred Years, 1570-1870, 2003; translator: The Origin of the Idea of Crusade (C. Erdmann), 1978. Fellow Berkeley Coll. (Yale). Recipient Haskins medal Medieval Acad. Am., 1991; Can. Coun. fellow, 1967-68; Am. Coun. Learned Socs. fellow, 1973-74; Guggenheim fellow, 1979-80; Connaught sr. fellow in humanities U. Toronto, 1983-84; Newberry Libr. fellow, 1989. Fellow Medieval Acad. Am. (councillor 1977-80), Royal Hist. Soc., Royal Soc. Can.; mem. Internat. Soc. Anglo-Saxonists, Hagiography Soc., Phi Beta Kappa. Office: Yale U Dept History PO Box 208324 New Haven CT 06520-8324

GOFFEN, RONA, art educator, educator; b. N.Y.C., June 7, 1944; d. William and Stella (Friedman) G. AB cum laude, Mt. Holyoke Coll., 1966; MA, Columbia U., 1968, PhD with distinction, 1974. Lectr. dept. fine arts Ind. U., Bloomington, 1971-73; lectr. dept. art and archaeology Princeton (N.J.) U., 1973-74, asst. prof. art, 1974-78; asst. prof. dept. art and art history Duke U., Durham, N.C., 1978-80, assoc. prof. art, 1980-86, chmn. dept. art and art history, 1983—, prof. art, 1986-88; Disting. prof. Rutgers U., New Brunswick, N.J., 1988-98, chmn. dept. art history, 1990-96, bd. govs. prof., 1998—. Vis. assoc. prof. Barnard Coll. Columbia U., N.Y.C., 1980; vis. scholar Am. Acad. Rome, 1976, Inst. Advanced Study, 1999—2000; Robert Sterling Clark vis. prof. Williams Coll., 1997; vis. prof. UCLA, 2001, Ecole des Hautes Etudes, Paris, 2002. Author: Piety and Patronage in Renaissance Venice, 1986, Spirituality in Conflict, 1988, Giovanni Bellini, 1989, Titian's Venus of Urbino, 1997, Titian's Women, 1997, Masaccio's Trinity, 1998, Renaissance Rivals, 2002; co-editor: Life and Death in Fifteenth-Century Florence, 1989; co-editor/co-author: Il colore Ritrovato: Bellini a Venezia, 2000, bd. editors: Art History, Venezia Cinquecento; contbr. articles to profl. publs. Am. Philos. Soc. grantee, 1979, NEH grantee, summer 1986; Harvard U. Ctr. Italian Renaissance Studies fellow, Florence, Italy, 1976-77, Am. Council for Learned Socs. fellow, 1976-77, Nat. Humanities Ctr. fellow, Research Triangle Park, N.C., 1986-87, Guggenheim fellow, 1986-87. Mem. Coll. Art Assn., Renaissance Soc. Office: Rutgers U Dept Art History Voorhees Hall New Brunswick NJ 08901

GOFFMAN, THOMAS EDWARD, radiation oncologist, researcher; b. Chgo., Apr. 16, 1953; s. E. and A. (Choate) G.; divorced; 1 child, James Edward. BA, Yale U., 1975; MD, Hahnemann U., 1979. Diplomate Am. Bd. Radiology, Am. Bd. Internal Medicine, Am. Coll. Radiation Oncology. Intern, resident Georgetown U. Hosp., Washington, 1979-82; med. staff fellow, epidemiology tng. program Nat. Cancer Inst., NIH, Bethesda, Md., 1982-83; resident in radiotherapy, Joint Ctr. for Radiation Therapy Harvard U. Med. Sch., Boston, 1983-86; instr. in radiation oncology Columbia U., N.Y.C., 1986-87, asst. prof. of radiation oncology, 1987; attending in radiation oncology Washington Hosp. Ctr., 1987-89, vice chmn. dept. radiation oncology, 1988-89; asst. dir. radiation oncology Sibley Meml. Hosp., 1989; asst. clin. prof. radiation medicine Georgetown U., 1989—; assoc. prof. dept. radiation oncology/biophysics, med. dir. Sentora Norfolk (Va.) Gen. Hosp., 1997—, chief radiation oncology, 1997—99. Head clin. therapy sect., radiation oncology br., Nat. Cancer Inst., Bethesda, 1989—; asst. prof. radiology USUHS, Bethesda, 1989-91; dir. radiation oncology tng. USUHS, Bethesda, 1989-92; dir. radiation oncology tng. Nat. Cancer Inst., USUHS, Bethesda, 1990-92; assoc. prof. radiology USUHS, 1991-92; dir. radiation oncology St. Agnes Hosp., Balt., 1992-93; rschr. internat. epidemiology nat. radiation NIH, 1983-84; med. dir. radiol. oncology Sentara Norfolk Gen. Hosp., 1999-2000. Contbr. articles to profl. jours. Bd. dirs. Lee's Friends, 2000—. Recipient Mosby scholarship for acad. achievement, 1979, Excellence in Medicine award, 1979, Blue Ribbon award, 1979, Nat. Rsch. Svc. award, 1983, Epidemiology Tng. fellowship Nat. Cancer Inst.-NIH, 1983. Fellow ACP; mem.AAAS, ACP, ACS (oncology com. 2001—), ACS Oncology Group, Am. Soc. Clin. Oncology, Am. Soc. Therapeutic Radiology and Oncology, N.Y. Acad. Scis., Com. on Physicians Assn., D.C. Med. Soc. (legis. com.), Nat. Cancer Inst. (internal rev. bd. 1989-90, biol. operating com. 1991-, Va. Med. Soc.

GOFFMAN, WILLIAM, mathematician, educator; b. Cleve., Jan. 28, 1924; s. Sam and Mollie (Stein) G.; m. Patricia McLoughlin, Feb. 7, 1964. BS, U. Mich., 1950, PhD, 1954. Math. cons., 1954-59; research asso. prof. Case Western Res. U., Cleve., 1959-71; dean Case Western Res. U. (Sch. Library Sci.), 1971-77; dir. Case Western Res. U. (Complex Systems Inst.), 1972-75. Contbr. numerous publs. to sci. jours. Served with USAAF, 1943-46. Recipient research grants NSF, research grants NIH, research grants USAF, research grants others. Fellow AAAS Home: 2 Bratenahl Pl Bratenahl OH 44108-1183 Office: Case Western Res Univ Cleveland OH 44106

GOFORTH, AUGUSTUS JOHNSON, III, physician; b. Greenville, S.C., Nov. 24, 1953; s. Augustus Johnson Jr. and Eula Campbell (Sullivan) G.; m. Rhonda Lee Calcutt, June 21, 1980; children: Austin Johnson, Lee Anne. BS, Furman U., Greenville, 1975; MD, Med. U. S.C., Charleston, 1980. Diplomate Am. Bd. Otolaryngology. Intern Med. U. S.C., Charleston, 1980-81, resident, 1981-85; with Carolina ENT, Greenville. Deacon 1st Presbyn. Ch., Greenville, 1992-95. Mem. AMA, S.C. Med. Soc., Greenville County Med. Soc., Am. Acad. Otolaryngology, Head and Neck Surgery. Avocations: golf, skiing, running, boating. Home: 403 Spaulding Lake Dr Greenville SC 29615-6035 Office: Carolina ENT 131 Commonwealth Dr Ste 230 Greenville SC 29615-4887

GOFORTH, MARY ELAINE DAVEY, secondary education educator; b. Barnesville, Ohio, Sept. 9, 1922; d. Frederick Richard and Lola (Knox) Davey; m. Richard Eugene Goforth, Sept. 9, 1944; 1 child, Diane Lynell Goforth-Ohning. B.M.Ed., Oberlin Coll., 1944; MA in Edn., Coll. of Mt. St. Joseph, 1987. Cert. edn. Music tchr., Leipsig, Ohio, 1944-45, Perry Local, 1945-47; English tchr. Ohio No. Univ., 1946; English and music tchr. Perry Sch., Lima, Ohio, 1945-47; English tchr. Stone Creek (Ohio) Sch., 1947—51, Conotton Valley Sch., Bowerston, Ohio, 1961—68, New Philadelphia (Ohio) Sch., 1973—88, Indian Valley Sch., Midvale, Ohio, 1988—93. Author poems. Pres. New Philadelphia (Ohio) Tchrs.' Assn., 1967. Named Indian Valley Tchr. of Yr., 1985, Candidate for Ohio Tchr. of the Yr., 1985; Martha Holden Jennings scholar, 1985. Home: 2123 E High Ave New Philadelphia OH 44663-3323

GOFORTH, NATHAN DAN, protective services official; b. Phoenix, Sept. 12, 1951; s. Nathan and Mabel Lettie (Deal) G.; m. Lori Ann Petersen (div. 1984). AA in Bus. Adminstrn., Glendale Community Coll., Ariz., 1974, AA in Adminstrn. Justice, 1976; BS in Pub. Programs, Ariz. State U., 1985. Second asst. mgr. Smittys Big Town, Phoenix, 1967-73, sales rep., 1975-76; sr. inventory auditor Motorola Semiconductor, Phoenix, 1973-74; police officer City Glendale, Ariz., 1976—. Interpreter for deaf Glendale Police Dept., 1976—, peer counselor, 1989—, field tng. officer, 1980—; vol. tchr. Glendale Community Coll. Police Res. Acad., 1989-94; pub. safety vol. program, coord. Glendale Police Dept., 2001-. Res. hwy. patrolman Ariz. Dept. Pub. Safety, Phoenix, 1975-76; advisor Glendale Explorer Post 469, 1978—, instl. head, 1992; bd. dirs. Theater Works, 1994-97, v.p., 1995-97. Recipient Dedication to DAV award, 1990-91, Cert. of Appreciation award Independence High Sch., 1990, Outstanding Vol. Svc. award MADD, 1991. Mem. Ariz. State U. Alumni Assn., Internat. Police Assn., Frat. order of Police (treas. 1990-94, v.p. 1994-95, 96-00, trustee 1995—), Critical Incident Stress Debriefing (S.W. region), Sons of Am. Legion. Avocations: volleyball, racquetball, camping, traveling europe. Office: Glendale Police Dept 6835 N 57th Dr Glendale AZ 85301-3218

GOFORTH, WILLIAM H. lawyer; b. Norfolk, Va., Nov. 28, 1947; s. Solomon Frank and Thelma Goforth; m. Glenna K. Ford, Nov. 24, 1972; 1 child, Jeff. BS, Troy State U., Fort Benning, GA, 1977; JD, La. State U., Baton Rouge, LA, 1982. Cert.: Nat. Bd. Trial Advocacy (Civil Trial Advocate). Pvt. practice, Lafayette, La., 1984—2000; shareholder Goforth & Lilley PLC, Lafayette, La., 2000—02. Bd. directors La. Trial Lawyers, Baton Rouge, 1993—93, Lafayette Vol. Lawyers, Lafayette, La., 2002—. Del. La. Rep. Conv., Baton Rouge, La., 2002—02. Sp5 US Army Security Agy., 1965—69, Southeast Asia. Mem.: Lafayette Parish Bar Assn. (bd. directors 2002—02), LTLA, ATLA, Million Dollar Advocates Forum, Lafayette Barrister's Club, Vietnam Veterans Am. Avocations: fishing, boating. Home: 160 Acacia Lafayette LA 70508 Office: Goforth & Lilley PLC 109 Stewart Street Lafayette LA 70501

GOGATE, LAKSHMI J. psychologist, researcher; b. Bombay, Jan. 7, 1962; d. Balakrishna M.S. and Leela Rao; m. Jagadish P. Gogate, July 12, 1985; 1 child, Vishal. PhD, Rutgers U., 1995. Post doctoral rsch. fellow in psychology Fla. Internat. U., Miami, 1994—97, asst. rsch. scientist, 1998—99; asst. prof. U. Del., Newark, 1997—98; asst. prof. Health Sci. Ctr. SUNY, Bklyn., 1999—. Reviewer Child Devel. Soc. Rsch. in Child Devel., Ann Arbor, Mich., 2000; Reviewer MIT press, Cambridge, MA. Contbr. articles to profl. jours. Mem.: APA (reviewer Psychol. Sci. 2001, Dissertation Rsch. award Sci. Directorate 1994), Internat. Soc. Infant Studies. Avocations: hiking, travel, gardening. Office: SUNY Health Sci Ctr @ Bklyn 450 Clarkson Ave Brooklyn NY 11203

GOGGIN, JOHN R. software quality engineer; b. Lynwood, Calif., June 26, 1951; s. John R. and Pauline Ruth (Robinson). BA in Math. and Computer Sci., U. Tex., 1974. Programmer, analyst Potomac Electric Power Co., Washington, 1974-75; assoc. Analytics, Inc., McLean, Va., 1975-79; sr. analyst Pattern Analysis & Recognition, Colorado Springs, 1979-80; research assoc. Colo. State U., Ft. Collins, 1980-81; software engr. Ford Aerospace, Colorado Springs, 1982-84; software design engr. Hewlett Packard Co., Colorado Springs, 1985-88; sr. software engr. Kentek Info. Systems, Boulder, Colo., 1988—89, Array Tech. Corp., Boulder, Colo., 1990-93; adv. software quality engr. StorageTek Corp. Mem.: Am. Soc. for Quality, Mensa. Avocations: skiing, high altitude mountaineering, bicycling, rock and ice climbing, fishing.

GOGGIN, MARGARET ENID (KNOX), librarian, educator; b. Nyack, N.Y., Feb. 24, 1919; d. Henry Julian and Eleanor (Green) Knox; m. John Mann Goggin, Nov. 22, 1962. AB, Maryville Coll., 1940; BS, Peabody Coll., 1942; MS, U. Ill., 1948, PhD, 1957. Tchr., librarian Flintville (Tenn.) High Sch., 1940-42; reference asst. Joint U. Library, Nashville, 1942-43, acting reference librarian, 1943-45; vis. instr. Peabody Library Sch., Nashville, 1943-45; readers adviser Youngstown (Ohio) Pub. Library, 1945-46; bibliographer, reference librarian Office Tech. Services Dept. Commerce, Washington, 1946-47; reference asst. U. Ill., 1948-49; asst. to dir. U. Fla. Libraries, asst. prof. library sci., 1949-50, head dept. reference and bibliography, asso. prof. library sci., 1950-62; asst. dir. U. Fla. Libraries (Readers Services), asso. prof. library sci., 1965-66, asst. dir. libraries, prof. library sci., 1966, acting dir. libraries, 1967-68; dean Grad. Sch. Librarianship, U. Denver, 1968-79, prof., 1979-84, prof. emeritus, 1984—. Vis. lectr. U. Okla. Libr. Sch., summer 1959, Emory U. Sch. Librarianship, 1965; dir. Satellite Libr. Info. Network, 1974-76; prin. investigator Telefax Libr. Info. Network, 1978-79; cons. U.S. Office Edn. divsn. Libr. Programs, 1968-69, 87, Aims C.C., Greeley, Colo., 1973, Wash. State Libr., 1978-79, Loretto Heights Coll., Denver, 1981; co-owner Book Seminars, Inc., 1986-95; interim dir. Collection Mgmt., Emory U., 1986-88; owner Margaret K. Goggin Books, 1994—. Recipient Colo. Libr. of Yr. award, 1979, Outstanding Svc. award U. Denver, 1985, Alumni citation Maryville Coll., 1987, Disting. Alumnus award Peabody Coll., 1987; Rockefeller Found. grantee, Haiti and Paris, 1958, 61-62, Fulbright grantee, 1972, OAS grantee for multi-nat. libr. edn. program, 1974-75 Mem. ALA (past div. pres.), Colo. Libr.

Assn. (dir. 1978-79), Mountain Plains Libr. Assn. (dir. 1978-79), Assn. For Library and Info. Sci. Edn. (pres. 1977), Nat. League Am. Pen Women, Fla. Ctr. for the Book (mem. exec. bd. 1988—), Delta Kappa Gamma, Beta Phi Mu (past dir.), PEO. Clubs: Altrusa (bd. dirs. Denver 1974-76, 80-82, pres. 1983-84). Home: 4024 NW 15th St Gainesville FL 32605-1912 E-mail: gog@gnv.fdt.net.

GOGGINS, JEAN, biomedical engineer, foundation administrator; BS in Biology, Molloy Coll., 1969; MS in Biology, Fordham Univ,, 1973; PhD in Biomedical engring., Case Western Res. U., 1985. Tchr. N.Y. schools., 1969—71, 1975—79; rsch. technician GTE Labs., Inc., Bayside, NY, 1971; supr. ultra structure lab. Fordham U., Bronx, NY, 1971-72; electron micro scopist Yale U. Sch. Medicine, New Haven, 1972-74; rsch. asst. Mt. Sinai Sch. Medicine, N.Y.C., 1979-80; grad. fellow dept. biomedical engring. Case Western Res. U., Cleve., 1980-85; sr. rsch. scientist Meadox Medicines., Inc., Oakland, NJ, 1985-86, mgr. R&D, 1986-90, mgr. med./tech. rels., 1990-93, dir. med./tech. rels., 1993-95; med. dir. Meadox Boston Sci. Corp., Oakland, NJ, 1995-97; dir. stent devel. and clin. affairs Medtronic Interventional Vascular, San Diego, 1997-98, dir. coronary stent devel., 1998-99; dir. William J. von Liebig Found., 1999—2002. Ind. cons. in med. devices, cardiovascular implants, vascular implants, endovascular devices, stents, implant materials, mechanical, chem. and physiol. interactions of implants; presenter, panelist in field; convenor internat. std. working group, mem. editl. bd. Jour. Biomed. Materials Rsch., 1996—. Contbg. articles to profl. journals. N.Y. State Regents scholar, 1965; NSF grantee, 1978; Timken Honors fellow, 1980-84, Cross-Jones Med. Rsch. Found. fellow, 1984-85. Fellow Am. Inst. Med. and Biol. Engring.; mem. Am. Heart Assn.; Internat. Soc. Applied Cardiovascular Biology; Internat. Soc. Endovascular Surgery; N.Y. Acad. Sci., Soc. Biomaterials; Sigma Xi. Personal E-mail: jagbme728@yahoo.com.

GOGLIA, CHARLES A., JR., lawyer; b. Phila., Aug. 26, 1931; s. Charles and Marie A. (Beckman) G.; m. Patricia A. Morrissey, July 26, 1958; children: Philip L., Catherine A. BS, St. Joseph's U., Phila., 1953; LLB, Boston Coll., 1958. Bar: Mass. 1958, U.S. Dist. Ct. Mass. 1959, U.S. Ct. Appeals (1st cir.) 1964, U.S. Tax Ct. 1977, U.S. Supreme Ct. 1993. Atty. Sheff & Gens, Boston, 1958-61, Foley, Hoag & Eliot, Boston, 1961-68, ptnr., 1968-74; pvt. practice Wellesley, Mass., 1974—. Corporator, trustee, mem. bd. investment, exec. com. Bank Five for Savs., Burlington, Mass., 1974-92; mem. hearing com. Bd. Bar Overseers, Boston, 1984-86; arbitrator Nat. Assn. Dispute Resolution, Inc., 2002—. Counsel Town of Nantucket, Mass., 1970-82, spl. counsel, 1982-85, Town of Weston, Mass., 1974-85, town counsel, 1986-92, spl. counsel, 1992—, mem. zoning bd. appeals, 1964-66, 74-85, mem. planning bd., 1973-74; spl. counsel Mass. Cable TV Commn., Boston, 1973-74. With USNAR, 1951-59. Mem. Wellesley Country Club (past pres.). Avocations: golf, travel. Home: 1 Hopewell Farm Rd Natick MA 01760-5570 Office: Wellesley Office Pk 65 William St Wellesley MA 02481-3802

GOGLIA, RICHARD A. corporate financial executive; BS, Bucknell U., Lewisburg, Pa., 1973; MBA, Wharton Sch., 1977. Head mergers and acquisitions Gen. Signal, 1980—81; fin. and corp. devel. GE Co., 1981—97; dir. internat. fin. Raytheon Co., Lexington, Mass., 1997—99, v.p., treas., 1999—. Office: Raytheon Co 141 Spring St Lexington MA 02421*

GOGLIETTINO, JOHN CARMINE, insurance broker; b. Danbury, Conn., Sept. 5, 1952; s. Nicholas and Josephine (Staffieri) G.; m. Deborah Ann Russo, Sept. 25, 1976. BA in History, Western Conn. State Coll., 1975. Sales rep. Mct. Life Ins. Co., Danbury, 1978-81; account exec. Thomas A. Settle, Inc., Danbury, 1981-88, Hodge Ins. Agy., Danbury, 1988-93; owner, mgr. John C. Goglietttino, ins. broker, Danbury, 1993—. Chmn. Life Underwriters Polit. Improvement Com., to 1996. Editor: (newspaper) Yankee Doodler, 1983-84; prodr. (TV show) Cmty. Forum, 1995—. Rec. sec. Conn. Bd. Vet. Medicine, Hartford, 1984-94; candidate Danbury Dem. Town Com., 1986, mem., 1988-2000, fin. chmn., 1990-92, treas., 1992-94, sec., 1996-98; active Italian Heritage Soc.; trustee, v.p. Scott-Fanton Mus., 1985-91; bd. dirs. Friends Danbury Libr., 1991-96, pres., 1994-96; candidate for state rep. 138th Assembly Dist., 1992; mem. Environ. Impact Commn., 1991-99, chmn., 1998-99; pres. coun. St. Peter's Ch., 1995-98; mem.-at-large City Coun., Danbury, 1999—; active fundraising and allocations United Way of No. Fairfield County, 1995—. Recipient Statesman award Conn. Jaycees 1983, Disting. Svc. award 1990, City of Danbury 1990; named one of Outstanding Young Men of Am. Jaycees, 1982, 90, Conn. Outstanding Young Citizens award Channel 30 and Conn. Jaycees. Mem. Danbury Life Underwriters Assn. (cert., bd. dirs., pres. 1996-98), Health Underwriters Assn., Danbury Ins. Men's Orgn., Western Conn. State U. Alumni Assn. (activator memberships 1985-87), No. Fairfield County Bus. Assn. (pres. 1995, 99), Danbury Jaycees, Kiwanis (v.p. Danbury chpt. 1984-86, pres. 1989-92), Elks, Order Sons of Italy Conn. (grand trustee 1991-94). Roman Catholic. Avocations: hiking, bicycling, reading, coin collecting, stamp collecting. Home: PO Box 2598 Danbury CT 06813-2598 E-mail: jcgogliettino@aol.com.

GOGOLIN, MARILYN TOMPKINS, language pathologist, retired educational administrator; b. Pomona, Calif., Feb. 25, 1946; d. Roy Merle and Dorothy (Davidson) Tompkins; m. Robert Elton Gogolin, Mar. 29, 1969. BA, U. LaVerne, Calif., 1967; MA, U. Redlands, Calif., 1968; postgrad., U. Wash., 1968-69; MS, Calif. State U., Fullerton, 1976. Cert. clin. speech pathologist; cert. teaching and sch. adminstrn. Speech and lang. pathologist Rehab. Hosp., Pomona, 1969-71; diagnostic tchr. L.A. County Office of Edn., Downey, Calif., 1971-72, program specialist, 1972-74, cons. lang., 1975-76, cons. orgns. and mgmt., 1976-79, dir. administrv. affairs, asst. to supt., 1979-95; dep. supt., 1995—2001; acting supt. L.A. County Office of Edn., Downey, Calif., 2001—02; COO Pulliam Group, 2003—. Cons. lang. sch. dists., Calif., 1975—79; cons. orgn. and mgmt. and profl. assns., Calif., 1976—; exec. dir. L.A. County Sch. Trustees Assn., 1979—2003; treas. L.A. County Edn. Found., 1996—2003; mem. NAEP task force, 1998; mem. adv. bd. Lightspan Partnerships, 2001. Founding patron Desert chpt. Kidney Found., Palm Desert, Calif., 1985. Doctoral fellow U. Washington, 1968; named One of Outstanding Young Women Am., 1977. Mem. Am. Mgmt. Assn., Am. Speech/Hearing Assn., Calif. Speech/Hearing Assn., Am. Edn. Research Assn. Baptist. Avocation: travel. Office: The Pulliam Group 1980 Orange Tree Ln Redlands CA 92374-

GOGOTSI, YURY, materials science educator; b. Kiev, Ukraine, Dec. 16, 1961; s. George A. and Svetlana (Potarykina) G.; m. Larissa Ganzha, Mar. 18, 1989; children: Pavel, Natalie. MS, Kiev Poly., 1984, PhD, 1986; DSc, Ukrainian Acad. Sci., Kiev, 1996. Rsch. assoc. Ukrainian Acad. Sci., 1986-90; Alexander von Humboldt fellow U. Karlsruhe, Germany, 1990-92; Japan Soc. Promotion of Sci. fellow Tokyo Inst. Tech., 1992-93; NATO rsch. fellow U. Oslo, 1993-95; rsch. assoc. U. Tübingen, Germany, 1995-96; asst. prof. U. Ill., Chgo., 1996-99, assoc. prof., asst. dir. Rsch. Resources Ctr., 1999-2000; assoc. dean, dir. A.J. Drexel Nanotech. Inst., 2003—; assoc. dean Coll. Engring., prof. materials engring., mech. engring. and chemistry Drexel U., Phila., 2000—. Author: Corrosion of Structural Ceramics, 1989, Corrosion of High-Performance Ceramics, 1992 (I.N. Frantsevich prize 1993); editor: Materials Science of Carbides, Nitrides and Borides, 1999, Nanostructured Materials and Coatings for Biomedical and Sensor Applications, 2003, High Pressure Surface Science and Engineering, 2003; issue editor Jour. Materials Mfg. and Processing Sci., 1998. Grantee NSF, 1999. Mem. AAAS, Am. Ceramic Soc., Materials Rsch. Soc., Electrochem. Soc. Christian Orthodox. Avocations: travel, reading. Office: Drexel U Dept Materials Engring 3141 Chestnut St Philadelphia PA 19104 Fax: 215 895-6760. E-mail: gogotsi@drexel.edu.

GOGUEN, HEALFDENE HROTHGAR, computer scientist, consultant; b. Berkeley, Calif., Dec. 25, 1967; s. Joseph Amadee and Nancy Hammer G.; m. Adriana Compagnoni; 1 child, Nicholas Daniel Goguen-Compagnoni. PhD, U. Edinburgh, U.K., 1994. Rsch. asst. U. Edinburgh, 1995-98; prin. tech. me. of staff AT&T Labs., Florham Park, NJ, 1998—. Tenor St. Peter and Paul Ch. choir, 2000-2002. Avocations: bicycling, singing, languages, acting, traveling. Office: AT&T Labs 180 Park Ave Florham Park NJ 07932

GOH, ANTHONY LI-SHING, marketing professional; b. Cleve., Apr. 14, 1954; m. Renee Kropat, Oct. 3, 1981; children: Anthony, Andrew. BSEE, U. Mich., 1975; MBA, U. Dayton, 1982. Sales engr. Toledo Scale, Mpls., 1975-76, application engr. Columbus, Ohio, 1976-77, product specialist, 1977-78, product mgr., 1978-80, internat. mktg. mgr., 1980-82, modifications mgr., 1983, mktg. mgr. heavy capacity, 1984-86; v.p., gen. mgr. Ricton Corp., Columbus, 1987-92; owner Li-Shing Enterprises, Westerville, Ohio, 1992-95; product mgr. Mettler-Toledo, Inc., Worthington, Ohio, 1995-97, mktg. mgr., 1997—2002, strategic product group leader, 2002—. Industry rep. Nat. Bur. Standards, Washigton, 1984-85; distributors coun. Mitel Trillium Phone Systems, Boca Raton, Fla., 1990-91. Mem. Nat. Assn. Telecommunications Dealers (mem. ethics com. 1990). Avocations: squash, swimming, family activities. Home: 89 W College Ave Westerville OH 43081-2031 also: 1150 Dearborn Dr Worthington OH 43085-4766

GOH, CHAN HON, ballerina; b. Beijing, Feb. 1, 1969; arrived in Can, 1977; d. Choo Chiat and Lin Yee Goh. Dancer Goh Ballet Tng. Co., Vancouver, B.C., Can., 1986-87; corp de ballet dancer Nat. Ballet of Can., Toronto, 1988-90, second soloist, 1990-92, first soloist, 1992-93, prin. dancer, 1994—. Advisor in dance Met Toronto Arts Coun, 1992—94; guest artist Royal Danish Ballet, Hong Kong Ballet, Singapore Dance Theatre, Washington Ballet, Nat Ballet China, Suzanne Farrell Ballet, N.B.A. Ballet, Japan, Vail Internat Dance Festival. Dancer Prin role The Sleeping Beauty, La Fille Mal Gardée, Don Quixote, Romeo & Juliet, The Merry Widow, The Nutcracker, Taming of the Shrew, Onegin, Swan Lake, Giselle, Cinderella, La Boutique Fantasque, Tales of Arabian Night, La Sylphide, Jewel, prin. role Tristan and Isolde, other maj roles Sylvia Pas de deux, Paquita, Dream Dances, Divertimento No. 15, Les Sylphides, Theme and Variations, Désir, The Four Temperaments, La Ronde, Dahnis and Chloe, Mozartiana, Song of the Earth, LaBayadere Act II, Etudes, Apollo, other maj. role Chaconne, Serenade, Napolie Act 3, Firebird, Scotch Symphony, La Sonnombula, The Man I Love (pas des deux from Who Cares?), Afternoon of a Faun, Chaccoon, Can premieres include Madame Butterfly (Stanton Welch), Jewels (George Balanchine), Concerto for Flute and Harp (John Cranko), 1990, The Leaves are Fading (Anthony Tudor), 1990, Pastorale (James Kudelka), 1990, Musings (Kudelka), 1991, (ballets) The Actress (Kudlka), 1993, Now and Then (John Neumeier), 1993, The Four Seasons (Kudelka), 1997, Terra Firma (Kudelka), Forgotten Land (Kylian), lead and organized stars of N.Am. Ballet, 2002; author: (autobiography) Beyond the Dance: A Ballerina's Life, 2002. Nominee Norma Fleck award, for "Beyond the Dance, A Ballerina's Life", Tundra Books, 2002; recipient Prix de Lausanne, 1986, Solo Award, Royal Acad Dancing, 1987, Silver Medal, Adelene Genee Comp, London, 1988; grantee, Can Coun, 1987. Office: Nat Ballet of Canada 470 Queens Quay W Toronto ON Canada M5E 3K4

GOH, DAVID SHUH-JEN, psychology educator; b. Nanjing, Kiangsu, China, July 9, 1941; came to U.S., 1967; s. Yinghwa and Pei-sue (Cho) G.; m. Jane C.; children: Alice, Nancy, Tiffany. BA, Nat. Taiwan C.K. U., 1963; MS, Ill. State U., 1969; PhD, U. Wis., 1973. Psychologist Lincoln (Ill.) Devel. Ctr., 1969-70; asst. prof. U. Wis., La Crosse, 1973-75; assoc. prof. Cen. Mich. U., Mt. Pleasant, 1975-80; prof., dir. So. Ill. U., Carbondale, 1980-88; prof. and dept. chmn. CUNY, Queens Coll., Flushing, 1988—. Author: Psychological Testing and Assessment, 2001; contbr. articles to profl. jours. Fellow APA, Am. Psychol. Soc., Am. Assn. of Applied and Preventive Psychology; mem. Asian Am. Psychol. Assn. (pres. 1991-92), numerous others. Home: 34 Angler Ln Port Washington NY 11050-1702 E-mail: dgohcuny@aol.com.

GOHEEN, JANET MOORE, counselor, sales professional; b. Everett, Mass., Sept. 29, 1945; d. Franklin Pierce and Virginia Louise (Murphy) Moore; m. Peter Arthur Goheen, Apr. 2, 1967; children: Kevin Murphy Moore Goheen, Andrew Hudson Moore Goheen. BA, Ohio Wesleyan U., 1967; MS, U. Bridgeport, 1979. Cert. profl. guidance counselor, Ohio. Tchr. English Nordinia Hills High Sch., Macedonia, Ohio, 1967-69, White Plains (N.Y.) High Sch., 1969-71, Hudson (Ohio) High Sch., 1982-83; tchr. emotionally disturbed Palisades Learning Ctr., Paramus, N.J., 1986-87; sales cons. The Longaberger Co., Dresden, Ohio, 1983-84, br. advisor, 1984-90, regional advisor, 1990—; middle sch. counselor Hudson Middle Sch., 1988—. Tchr. ESL Hitchcock Presbyn. Ch., Scarsdale, N.Y., 1976-79, Aurora (Ohio) City Schs., 1979-81, Hudson Local Schs., 1980-82. Mem. Jr. League of Scarsdale, 1976-79, Jr. League of Akron, 1979-82, Jr. League No. N.J., Ridgewood, 1983-85; mem. alumni bd. dirs. Ohio Wesleyan U., Delaware, Ohio, 1990-93; trustee Am. Found. for Suicide Prevention N.E. Ohio, 1997—; founder Hudson Presbyn. Ch., 1980; founder Anna Lee chpt. Questers, Hudson, 1981. Mem. Am. Sch. Counselors Assn., Ohio Sch. Counselors Assn., Kappa Kappa Gamma, Kappa Delta Pi. Home: 97 Manor Dr Hudson OH 44236-3406 Office: Hudson Middle Sch 77 N Ovlatt St Hudson OH 44236-3043

GOHEEN, ROBERT FRANCIS, classicist, educator, former ambassador; b. Vengurla, India, Aug. 15, 1919; s. Robert H.H. and Anne (Ewing) G.; m. Margaret M. Skelly, June 21, 1941; children: Anne Goheen Crane, Gertrude Goheen Swain, Stephen, Margaret Goheen Lower, Elizabeth, Charles. BA, Princeton U., 1940, MA (Woodrow Wilson fellow), 1947, PhD (Procter fellow), 1948; hon. degrees from 26 univs. and colls. Instr. classics Princeton U., 1948-50, asst. prof., 1950-57, prof., 1957, pres., 1957-72, emeritus, 1972—; chmn. Coun. on Founds., 1972-77; pres. Edna McConnell Clark Found., 1977; amb. to India, 1977-80; sr. fellow Woodrow Wilson Sch., 1981—. Dir. Mellon Fellowships in the Humanities, 1981-92; mem. adv. com. Nat. Fgn. Lang. Ctr., Ctr. for Advanced Study of India. Author: The Imagery of Sophocles' Antigone, 1951, The Human Nature of a University, 1969. Trustee Bharatiya Vidya Bhavan (USA), Nat. Humanities Ctr., Village Charter Sch., Trenton, N.J., Woodrow Wilson Nat. Fellowship Found. Decorated Legion of Merit, Bronze Star. Mem. Am. Philos. Soc., Coun. Fgn. Rels., Am. Acad. Arts and Scis., Am. Acad. Diplomacy, Phi Beta Kappa, Princeton Club (N.Y.C.), Century Assn. (N.Y.C.), Cosmos Club (Washington), Nassau Club (Princeton), Springdale Club (Princeton), Eastward Ho Club (Mass.), Gymkhana and Delhi Golf Club (India). Address: 1 Orchard Cir Princeton NJ 08540-3025 E-mail: rfgoheen@princeton.edu.

GOIN, PETER JACKSON, art educator; b. Madison, Wis., Nov. 26, 1951; children: Kari, Dana. BA, Hamline U., 1973; MA, U. Iowa, 1975, MFA, 1976. Prof. art U. Nev., Reno, 1984—. Author: Tracing the Line: A Photographic Survey of the Mexican-American Border, 1987, Nuclear Landscapes, 1991, Arid Waters: Photographs from the Water in the West Project, 1992, Stopping Time: A Rephotographic Survey of Lake Tahoe, 1992, Humanature, 1996, Atlas of the New West, 1997, A Doubtful River, 2000, Changing Mines in America, 2003; one-man shows include Duke U. Mus. Art, Durham, N.C., 1992, Phoenix Mus. Art, 1992, Indpls. Mus. Art, 1992, Savannah (Ga.) Coll. Art and Design, 1992, Nev. Humanities Com. Traveling Exhibit, 1992, NICA, Las Vegas, Nev., 1997, Mus. for Photographie, Braunschweig, Germany, 1997, U. Oreg. Mus. of Art, Eugene, 1997, Nev. Mus. Art, Reno, 1996, 99, Princeton (N.J.) U. Art Mus., 1996, Whitney Mus. Am. Art, N.Y.C., 1996, Museet for Fotographie, Denmark, 1999, Recipient Millennium award for Excellence in Arts, 1999; grantee NEA, 1982, 90. Office: Univ Nev Dept Art Reno NV 89557-0007 E-mail: pgoin@unr.edu.

GOINES, LEONARD, music educator, consultant; b. Jacksonville, Fla., Apr. 22, 1934; s. Buford and Willie Mae (Lamar) G.; m. Margaretta Bobo (div.); 1 child, Lisan Lynette. *Daughter Lisan Lynette Goines, BA 1995 Harvard University, JD 1999 Columbia University Law School, is currently an associate at the law firm of Sullivan & Cromwell in New York City.* BMus, Manhattan Sch. Music, 1955, MMus, 1956; Cert., Fontainebleau Sch. Music, France, 1959; MA, Columbia U., 1960, profl. diploma, 1961, EdD, 1963; BA, New Sch. Social Rsch., 1980; MA, NYU, 1980; cert. in clin. counseling, Postgrad. Ctr. for Mental Health, N.Y.C., 1983; CAS, Harvard U., 1984. Lectr. music Queens Coll. CUNY, 1969, York Coll. CUNY, 1969, NYU, 1970—; trumpeter Symphony New World, N.Y.C., 1965-76; assoc. prof. music Morgan State Coll., Balt., 1966-68, Howard U., Washington, 1970-72; prof. Manhattan C. C. CUNY, N.Y.C., 1970—; freelance musician Broadway shows, theater, orchestras, recording ensembles, jazz groups, 1959—. Vis. prof. Williams Coll., Williamstown, Mass., 1984, Vassar Coll., Poughkeepsie, N.Y., 1985; co-exec. prodr., Bklyn. Acad. Music Majestic Theatre, 1988-96; dist. vis. prof. Lafayette Coll., Easton, Pa., 1986; postdoctoral fellow Harvard U., Cambridge, Mass., 1982-85; ptnr. Shepard & Goines Organizational and Ednl Art. cons., Jazz rsch. cons. Nat. Endowment Arts, 1983; appointee U.S. Dept. Interior, Smithsonian Inst.; mem. Preservation Jazz Adv. Commn., 1992-93; cons. in field. Contbr. articles to profl. jours. Folklore cons., field rschr., African Diaspora, Smithsonian Instn., 1972-76; trustee Nat. Assn. Community Schs. of Arts, N.Y.C., 1982-85; chmn. spl. arts section panel N.Y. State Council on Arts, N.Y.C., 1982-85; music panelist Arts Connection, N.Y.C., 1985. Recipient Pub. Svc. award U.S. Dept. Labor, 1980, Scholar Incentive award CUNY, 1983-84; named Hon. Citizen City of Winnipeg, Can., 1958; Coll. Tchrs. fell NEH, 1982-83; Faculty Rsch. grantee Howard U., CUNY, NYU, 1971-73. Mem. Local 802 of Am. Fedn. Musicians, AAUP, Nat. Acad. Rec. Arts and Scis., Phi Delta Kappa, Phi Mu Alpha. Democrat. Episcopalian. Avocations: running, photography, travel. Home: 221 W 131st St New York NY 10027-2030 Office: CUNY Manhattan Community Coll 199 Chambers St New York NY 10007-1044

GOINES, VICTOR LOUIS, music educator; b. New Orleans, Aug. 6, 1961; s. Joseph and Rosemary Goines; m. Renee Denise Goines, Jan. 4, 1964. MusB in Edn., Loyola U., New Orleans, 1984; MusM, Va. Commonwealth U., 1990. Math. instr. St. Augustine H.S., New Orleans, 1984—87; prof. music Loyola U., 1989—90; assoc. prof. music U. New Orleans, 1990—93; prof. music Fla. A & M U., Tallahassee, 1997—98; artistic dir. jazz studies The Juilliard Sch., N.Y.C., 2000—. Musician The Lincoln Ctr. Jazz Orch., N.Y.C., 1993—. Musician: (compact disc musical recording) Sunrise to Midnight, To Those We Love So Dearly, 1998-1999, Joe's Blues, 1996-1998, Genesis, 1990-1992; composer: (commisioned musical work) Base Line. Office: The Juilliard Sch 60 Lincoln Ctr Plz New NY 10023-6588 Home Fax: 718-432-2560; Office Fax: 212-769-7416. Personal E-mail: romjos@aol.com. E-mail: vgoines@juilliard.edu.

GOINGS, AUSTIN NELSON, sales executive; b. Brookhaven, Miss., Jan. 28, 1954; s. Nelson Porter and Mary Elizabeth Goings. Student, La. State U., 1972-77. Pvt. practice oil and gas landman, New Orleans, 1978-83; sales mgr. Telescan, Houston, 1983-88, Paradigm Techs., Houston, 1988-94, Landmark Graphics, Houston, 1995—98; regional mgr. Vignette Corp., Houston, 2001—; dir. sales Centical region Softface, Inc., 2001—. Founder, bd. dirs. Texchange, Houston, 2000—; spkr. in field. Bd. dirs. Houston Sigma Chi Alumni Assn., Houston, 1986-88; mem. leadership com. Cystic Fibrosis, 2002-; pres. Montgomery Mcpl. Utility Dist., 2001-. Mem. Coastal Conservation Assn. (bd. dirs. 1993-2001, pres. Houston chpt. 1994-96, state bd. dirs. 1996—, state exec. com. mem. 1996—, nat. bd. dirs. 2002-. Man of Yr. 1997), U. Club Houston, La. State U. Alumni Assn., Sigma Chi Alumni Assn. Office: Vignette Corp Ste 500 2603 Augusta Houston TX 77057 Office Fax: 713-974-9371. E-mail: agoings@sunbelt.net.

GOINGS, RALPH, artist; b. Corning, Calif., May 9, 1928; Student, Calif. Coll. Arts and Crafts, 1953; MA, Calif. State U., Sacramento, 1966. Solo. exhbns. Artists Coop. Gallery, Sacramento, 1960, 62, Artists Contemporary Gallery, Sacramento, 1968, O.K. Harris Works of Art, N.Y.C., 1970, 73, 77, 80, 83, 96, Solomon Dubnik Gallery, Sacramento, 1997, Bernarducci Meisel Gallery, N.Y.C., 2003; group shows include U. Oshkosh, Wis., 1983, Contemporary Art Ctr., New Orleans, 1982, Pa. Acad. Fine Arts European tour, 1982-83, Brainerd Art Gallery, SUNY-Potsdam, 1982, Stockholm Internat. Art Expo., Sweden, 1982, O.K. Harris West, Scottsdale, Ariz., 1982, Butler Inst. Am. Art, Youngstown, Ohio, 1982, Mus. Contemporary Art, L.A., 1984-85, Boise (Idaho) Gallery Art, 1985, Mus. of Art-R.I. Sch. Design, Providence, 1985, Isetan Mus., Tokyo, 1985, San Francisco Mus. Modern Art, 1985-87, Norton Ctr. for Arts, Danville, Ky., 1985, Wichita (Kans.) Art Mus., 1985-86, Mus. of Fine Arts, Boston, 1986-87, Tucson Mus. Art, 1986-87, Tucso Mus. AKt, 2002, Chiostro del Bramante, Rome, 2003, others; represented in permanent collections, Mus. Modern Art, Guggenheim Mus., N.Y.C., Whitney Mus. Am. Art, N.Y.C., Mus. Contemporary Art, Chgo.; contbg. author chpts. in books; contbr. numerous articles in field. Office: OK Harris Works of Art 383 W Broadway New York NY 10012-4398

GOIN-HARDING, CECILIA MARGARET, poet; b. Mansfield, Ohio, June 30, 1957; d. Cecil Eugene and Sara Jane Goin. Student, St. John's Coll., Annapolis, Md., 1977—78; BA in English, Case Western Res. U., 1984; grad., Cleve. Sch. Ballet, 1984; postgrad., U. Geneva, 1984, postgrad., 1999—2000, Cornell U., 1985; diploma, Supérieure d'Etudes Françaises Modernes; student, Coconut Grove Ballet Sch., Miami, Fla., 2001—, Martha Mahr Sch. Ballet, 2003—, Miami-Dade Equestrian Ctr., Homestead, Fla., 2003—. Governess pvt. family, Woody Creek, Colo., 1975; legis. aid Annapolis (Md.) Legislature, 1977; swimming instr. YMCA/YWCA, Mansfield, Ohio, 1979; proof reader Sun Press, Cleve., 1979; tchr. Am.-Nicaraguan Sch., Managua, Nicaragua, 1986, Cuyahoga C.C., Cleve., 1992, Cleve. State U., 1992. Model Parson's Sch. Design, N.Y.C., NY, 1975, Image Model, Miami, 1975, Cleve. Inst. Art, 1988—92, Image Models and Talent Agy., 2003—; translator Adriana Schaked LLC, Miami, Fla., 2000—, ALS. Exhibitions include The Art Ctr., Mansfield, Ohio, 1977; author (poetry): Figures Of A Voyage: Collected Poems (1984-2000), 2002, numerous poems. Vol. Kingwood Ctr., Mansfield, 1981, NAMI, Miami, 1995. Recipient divisional medalist, U.S. Ski Assn., 1970. Mem.: Broadcast Music Inc., Fairchild Tropical Garden, Nat. Tropical Bot. Garden. Avocations: ice skating, soccer, learning to play new instruments, mathematics, prose writing. Home: 4060 Battersea Rd Miami FL 33133

GOINS, FRANCES FLORIANO, lawyer; b. Buffalo, Jan. 30, 1950; d. William and Anita (Graziano) Floriano; m. Gary Mitchell Goins; children: Matthew W., Mark W. MusB, Cleve. Inst. Music, 1971; MusM, Case Western Res. U., 1973, JD, 1977. Bar: Ohio 1977, U.S. Dist. Ct. Ohio 1978, U.S. Ct. Appeals (6th cir.) 1979, N.Y. 1984, U.S. Dist. Ct. NY 1984, U.S. Supreme Ct. 2002. Law clk to Hon. Frank J. Battisti U.S. Dist. Ct. (no. dist.) Ohio, Cleve., 1977-78; ptnr. Squire, Sanders & Dempsey, Cleve., 1986—. Mem. vis. com. bd. overseers Case Western Res. U., Cleve., 1984-2000; faculty Nat. Inst. Trial Advocacy, Cleve.; faculty, lectr. trial advocacy seminar Cleve. State U. Sch. Law, 1989-90. Editor-in-chief law rev. Case Western Res. Sch. Law, 1976-77. Trustee, chairperson devel. com. Lyric Opera Cleve., 1985-92, 2003—; founding trustee Shoreby Club Cleve.; v.p. bd. trustees Bay Village Montessori Sch., 1994-96; chmn. bd. trustees No. Ohio Breast Cancer Coalition, 2003—. Mem. ABA (bus. law sect., bus. lit. com., governance com. 1995—, fed. regulation of securities com., subcom. on civil litigation and SEC enforcement 1992—), Ohio Women's Bar Assn. (founding mem.), Ohio State Bar Assn. (ad hoc com. on bus. cts. 1994-99), Cleve. Bar Assn. (com. on women and the law 1987-2000, ethics com. 1988-90, securities law inst., jud. selection com. 1996-2001). Democrat. Roman Catholic. Office: Squire Sanders & Dempsey 4900 Key Tower 127 Public Sq Ste 4900 Cleveland OH 44114-1304

GOINS, RICHARD ANTHONY, lawyer, educator; b. New Orleans, Mar. 1, 1950; s. James Milton and Vivian (Wiltz) G.; m. Jane Parker, Aug. 18, 1973 (div. Sept. 1987); m. Nannette Smith, Mar. 3, 1990. BA in History cum laude, Yale U., 1972; JD, Stanford U., 1975. Bar: La. 1975, Calif. 1977. Dep. dir. New Orleans Legal Asst. Corp., 1977-78, exec. dir., 1978-81; law clk. to Hon. A. Duplantier U.S. Fed. Dist. Ct., New Orleans, 1982; asst. prof. Loyola U. Law Sch., New Orleans, 1981-84; ptnr. Adams and Reese, New Orleans, 1987-96, The Goins Law Firm, New Orleans, 1997-99; shareholder Goins Aaron, PLC, 2000—. Asst. bar examiner torts La. Bar Exam., 1991-96, bar examiner civil procedure, 1996—; mem. merit selection panel for selection and appt. of U.S. Magistrate for Ea. Dist. La., 1992-95, 2000; mem. host com. jud. conf. Fed. 5th Cir. Ct. Appeals, 1995; adj. prof. Loyola U. Law Sch., New Orleans, 1984-92, 2003—. Mem. Mayor of New Orleans Overall Econ. Devel. Plan Com., 1991, Orleans Intercmty. Coun., 1992; mem. spl. gifts. com. Yale Alumni Fund, 1991-92; bd. dirs. New Orleans Home Mortgage Authority, 1991-94, City Trust, New Orleans, 1983-94, State Mental Health Advocacy Sys., New Orleans, 1983-84, New Orleans Legal Assistance Corp., 1982-83, Milne Asylum for Destitute Orphan Boys, Inc., 1994-97. Reginald Heber Smith fellow, 1975; Nat. Achievement scholar Yale U., 1968-72, Leadership La. scholar, 1992. Master Thomas Moore Inn of Ct.; mem. ABA (Conf. of Minority Ptnrs. 1990-96), La. State Bar Assn. (legal aid com. 1978-81, uniform fed. rules com. 1991-92, fed. ct. bench-bar liaison com. 1993-99), Nat. Bar Assn. (comml. law sect. 1989—), Fed. Bar Assn. (bd. dirs. New Orleans chpt. 1992-99), 5th Cir. Bar Assn., Calif. State Bar Assn. Democrat. Roman Catholic. Home: 4412 Mandeville St New Orleans LA 70122-4928

GOINS, SHEILA LEWIS, elementary school educator, researcher; b. St. Louis, Mo., Feb. 26, 1959; d. William Merlin and Ivadell Crawley Lewis; m. Thomas Greg Goins Sr., June 22, 1979; children: Crystal Goins Matthews, Thomas Greg Jr., Kayla Rachel. BSc, La. State U., Baton Rouge, 1991, MA, 2000. Cert. EdS La. State U., 2001. Tchr. math and sci. West Baton Rouge Pub. Sch., Port Allen, La., 1991—99; sci facilitator West Baton Rouge - Iberville Hands-on Sci. Ctr., Port Allen, La., 1999—. Author (grantwriter). Interactive Tech., Dow, 1999, Integrating Tech. in the Classroom, Exxon, 1998, Life

Experiences, Dow, 1996, Quality Sci. and Math grant, 1995, 1996. Mem.: La. Sci. Tchrs. Assn., Nat. Sci. Tchrs. Assn., Assn. of Sci. Materials Ctr. Avocations: reading, gardening, sewing, fishing. Home: 2140 Fairview Port Allen LA 70767

GOITEIN, BERNARD JOEL, management educator, researcher; b. N.Y.C., July 7, 1950; s. Percy Lionel Goitein and Denise Rachel Galperin; m. Patricia Louise Ostler, Oct. 9, 1979; children: Zachary, Daniel, Annie. BA, Hebrew U., 1972, MA, 1975; PhD, U. Mich., 1982. Rsch. and tchg. asst. Hebrew U., Jerusalem, 1970—75; asst. study dir. U. Mich., Ann Arbor, 1977—80, rsch. assoc., 1976, course coord., 1979—81, course instr., 1981; prof. mgmt. dept. Bradley U., Peoria, Ill., 1981—, dir. survey rsch., 1985—. Self-employed cons., Peoria, 1985—. Contbr. articles and book revs. to profl. jours., chapters to books. Mem. Peoria area Census 2000 Commn., 1999—2001; chair Spl. Population Census 2000, Peoria, 1999—2000; treas. bd. dirs. Northside Housing Svc., Peoria, 1997—. Named Caterpillar fellow, Bradley U., 1984; recipient Faculty Rsch. award, FCBA Nat. Adv. Coun., Peoria, 1987; grantee, Bradley U., 2001. Mem.: Soc. Judgement and Decision Making, Internat. Inst. Forecasters, Acad. Mgmt. Home: 1625 W Columbia Terr Peoria IL 61606 Office: Bradley Univ 1501 W Bradley Ave Peoria IL 61625 Office Fax: 309-677-3257 . Business E-Mail: bjg@bradley.edu.

GOKCEKUS, OMER, education educator; b. Gonyeli, Cyprus, July 21, 1964; s. Rifat and Yucel G.; m. Rumeysa Sare Bezci, July 1, 1990; childre: Samin, Eugell. BS in Econs., Mid. East Tech. U., Turkey, 1986, MS in Econs., 1988; PhD in Econs., Duke U., 1994. Asst. prof. econs. NC Ctrl. U., Durham, 1995—2003; assoc. prof. econs. Seton Hall U., South Orange, NJ, 2003—. Cons. The World Bank, Washington, 1999—. Contbr. articles to profl. jours. Recipient Alcoa Rsch. award, N.C. Ctrl. U. Office: Seton Hall Univ Sch Diplomacy South Orange NJ 07079 Fax: 919-489-0794. Business E-Mail: gokcekom@shu.edu.

GOKEL, GEORGE WILLIAM, organic chemist, educator; b. June 27, 1946; s. George William and Ruth Mildred G.; m. Kathryn Smiegocki, June 2, 1978; children: Michael Robert, Matthew George, Mark Arlington. BS in Chemistry, Tulane U., 1968; PhD in Organic Chemistry, U. So. Calif., 1971. Postdoctoral fellow UCLA, 1972-74; chemist cen. rsch. dept. E.I. Du Pont de Nemours & Co., Wilmington, Del., summer 1974; asst. prof. chemistry Pa. State U., University, 1974-78; assoc. prof. chemistry U. Md., College Park, 1978-82, prof. chemistry, 1982-85, U. Miami, Coral Gables, Fla., 1985-93, prof. dept. molecular biology and pharmacology Sch. Medicine, 1993—; dir. bioorganic chemistry program Washington U., 1993—. Cons. W.R. Grace Co., 1977-86, Lion Detergent Co., Tokyo, 1985—, Seal Sands Chem. Co., Stockton-on-Tees, Eng., 1983-88, Monsanto Co., St. Louis, 1989-91, A.H. Marks, Eng., 1990-99; dean's adv. com. Tulane U., 1997—; lectr. in field. Editor Supramolecular Chemistry jour., 1992-2000, Advances in Supramolecular Chemistry, 1990—, Jour. Supramolecular Chemistry, 2001—; mem. editl. adv. bd. Chemical Communications, 1998—; mem. editl. bd. New Jour. Chemistry, 2001—; author: Phase Transfer. Recipient Allan C. Davis medal Md. Acad. Sci., 1979; Leo Schubert award Washington Acad. Scis., 1980, Macrocycle Chemistry award Izatt-Christensen, 1996, Tomen Agro award excellence, 2000; Petroleum Rsch. Fund grantee, 1976-78; grantee NIH, 1979—, NSF, 1998—. Fellow AAAS; mem. Biophys. Soc., Protein Soc., Am. Chem. Soc., Chem. Soc. (London), Sigma Xi, Alpha Chi Sigma. Republican. Methodist. Home: 1817 Stenton Path Chesterfield MO 63005-4733 Office: Washington U Sch Medicine Dept Molecular Biology & Pharmacology Saint Louis MO 63110

GOKULANATHAN, KARAKAT SANKARAN, pediatrician, educator; b. Ernakulam, Kerala State, India, Oct. 27, 1933; parent Vallath Kozhipillil Sankara Menon, Karakat Thankamma; m. Indira Vadassery Indira; 1 child, Prasan. Diploma, Maharaja's Coll., Ernakulam, India, 1951; MD, Trivandrum Med. Coll., Tiruvanandapuram, India, 1956. Diplomate Am. Bd. Pediatrics. Lectr. physiology Kerala Med. Coll., Kozhikode, India, 1956—58; asst. surgeon Kerala State Med. Svc., Ernakulam, India, 1958—59; intern St. Paul's Hosp., Dallas, 1959—60; sr. intern pediat. Regina Gen. Hosp., Canada, 1960—61; jr. to chief resident pediat. D.C. Gen. Hosp., 1961—63; resident in medicine Bronx Mcpl. Hosp. Ctr., NY, 1963—64; resident in pediat. St. Joseph's Hosp., Toronto, Canada, 1964—65; founding dir. Ernakulam Polyclinic, Ernakulam, India, 1965—67; asst. prof. pediat. Howard U. Coll. Medicne, Washington, 1967—71; clin. asst. prof. pediat. Georgetown U. Coll. Medicine, Washington, 1970—. Dir. program in children's hosp. Howard U., Washington, 1967—69; courtsey staff Children's Hosp. D.C., 1967—69; attending physician Prince George's Hosp. Ctr., Cheverly, 1969—95; staff Freedmen's Hosp, Washington, 1967—75; courtsey staff Providence Hosp., Washington, 1970—80; sr. meritorius Prince George's Hosp. Ctr., Cheverly, 1995—. Author: Child Care in a Developing Community, 1969; contbg. author (book chpts.) Adolescence in Matriarchal Society: Changing Cultural and Social Patterns After Industrialization, 1974, contbg. author Child Care of Asian Indians in the United States, 1974, contbr. author Encyclopedia of Hinduism and Indic Religions, 2002; contbr. articles. Recipient Vicennial medal, Georgetown U. Coll. Medicine, 1970—90, Ambady Krishna Menon Gold medal, 1956. Fellow: Royal Soc. Health London, Am. Anthropol. Assn., Royal Coll. Physicians and Surgeons Can., Am. Acad. Pediat. (sr.); mem.: Gen. Med. Coun. U.K., Indian Med. Coun., Md. State Med. Bd., D.C. Med. Bd., Am. Pub. Health Assn., N.Y. Acad. Sci., Am. Coll. Allergists, Soc. Med. Anthropolgy, Ednl. Coun. Foreign Med. Grad., Physician's Com. Responsible Medicine, Assn. Kerala Med. Grad. (pres. 1980—82, Founder award 2001), Nat. Geog. Soc., Med. and Chirurgical Faculty State of Md., Prince George's County Med. Soc. Hindu. Avocations: traveling, reading, writing, horticulture, interior decorating. Office: KS & IV Gokulanathan MD 9470 Annapolis Rd # 311 Lanham Seabrook MD 20706-3022

GOLAN, DAVID ERIC, biophysicist, pharmacologist, hematologist, medical educator; b. Boston, Mar. 10, 1953; s. Harold Philip and Irene Judith (Soble) G.; m. Laura Carolyn Green, Nov. 29, 1981; children: Liza Green-Golan, Sarah Green-Golan. AB, Harvard Coll., 1975; MD, Yale U., 1979, PhD, 1982. Diplomate Am. Bd. Internal Medicine, Am. Bd. Hematology. Clin. and rsch. fellow Harvard Med. Sch., Brigham and Women's Hosp., Boston, 1979-83; intern Brigham & Woman's Hosp., Boston, 1979-80, resident in internal medicine, 1980-83, fellow in hematology/oncology, 1983-85; instr. Harvard Med. Sch., Brigham and Women's Hosp., Boston, 1983-87, asst. prof., 1987-94, assoc. prof., 1994-2001, prof., 2001—; assoc. physician Brigham and Women's Hosp., Boston, 1985-92, physician, 1992—; co-dir. MD-PhD program Harvard-MIT, 2000—. Reviewer NIH study section, 1997—; mem. med./sci. adv. bd. Alza Corp., 1994-2000; Applied Pharm. Task Force and Test Material Devel. com. Nat. Bd. Med. Examiners, 1996-98, Pharm. Test Com. and Test Material Devel. Com. 1998-2001, Interdisciplinary Test Com., 1999-2000; founding mem. Harvard Med. Sch. Acad. Contbr. over 75 articles to profl. jours.; author: (software) Pharm Aid, 1991. Recipient Faculty prize for excellence in tchg, 1996, Merit award, NIH, 1997—, Student award for excellence in tchg., Harvard Med. Sch., 1998—2003; fellow Rsch., Med. Found., 1985—87. Fellow Molecular Med. Soc.; mem. ACP, Acad. at Harvard Med. Sch. (founder), Biophys. Soc., Am. Soc. for Cell Biology, Am. Chem. Soc., Am. Soc. Hematology, Am. Soc. for Clin. Investigation. Achievements include demonstration of control of transmembrane protein diffusion by membrane skeletal proteins in human red blood cells, development of novel system for visualization of contact area between cell membrane and target membrane, and elucidation of molecular mechanisms by which cells respond to ac electric fields. Office: Harvard Med Sch 250 Longwood Ave Boston MA 02115-5731 E-mail: dgolan@hms.harvard.edu.

GOLAN, LAWRENCE PETER, mechanical engineering educator, energy researcher; b. Newark, June 20, 1938; s. Joseph and Francis (Duda) G.; m. Helen Imelda Hemko, June 30, 1962; children: Lisa Marie, Wanda Marie, Lawrence P. II. BSME, W.Va. U., 1961, MSME, 1964; PhD, Lehigh U., 1968. Mech. engr. Picatinny Arsenal, Dover, NJ, 1961—62; instr. W.Va. U., Morgantown, 1962—64, Lehigh U., Bethlehem, Pa., 1964—68; engring. assoc. Exxon Rsch. and Engring., Florham Park, NJ, 1968—86; dir. SC Inst. Energy Rsch., Clemson, 1986—2003, spl. asst. to v.p. rsch., 2003—; prof. mech. engring. Clemson U., 1986—, mgr. DOE sponsored univ. advanced turbune sys. rsch. program, 1992—2001, mgr. advanced waste tech. program, 1992—97, mgr. Energy Sys. Lab., 2000—, mgr. doe high efficiency engines and turbinos (HEET) program, 2002—. Chmn. 2d World Congress Chem. Engring. on Coal Utilization; cons. State of Ill. Ctr. for Coal Rsch., 1987-90; mem. S.C. Energy Products Evaluation Com.; chair Nat. HEat Transfer Conf., 1996. Contbr. articles to profl. jours. Mem. adv. com. W.Va. U., 1985—; mem. adv. com. Strom Thurmond Inst., 1996—. Mem. AIChE (exec. officer heat transfer divsn. 1973-76, 89-92, 96-99, divsn. chair 1995, 99, East Coast membership chmn., vice chair nat. meeting 1991, chair 1991, co-chair 1992, nat. heat transfer conf. best paper 2000, 01, chair AIChE Kern award 1994, 2002, chair ASME-AIChE Jakob award 1994, 2000, 02, vice-chmn. task force, 2002), Am. Petroleum Inst. (chmn. sampling project 1985-89, chair Internat. Gas Turbine Inst. distributed generation panel), S.C. Energy Mgrs. Roman Catholic. Avocations: jogging, woodworking. Home: 333 Lowkirk Aly Seneca SC 29672-2273 Office: SC Inst for Energy Studies 386 College Ave Ste 2 Clemson SC 29631-1475 E-mail: glawren@clemson.edu.

GOLAN, STEPHEN LEONARD, lawyer; b. Chgo., Oct. 22, 1951; s. Leonard Walter and Carol (Pepper) G.; m. Sharon D. Robson, Aug. 16, 1980; children: Brianna, Jenna, Melissa. BA, Claremont (Calif.) Men's Coll., 1974; MBA, JD, Northwestern U., 1978. Bar: Ill. 1978, U.S. Dist. Ct. (no. dist.) Ill. 1978, U.S. Ct. Appeals (7th cir.) 1993. Ptnr. Seyfarth, Shaw, Fairweather & Geraldson, Chgo., 1978-93; founding ptnr. Field & Golan, Chgo., 1993—. Mem. ABA, AICPA, Nat. Assn. JD-MBA Profls. (bd. dirs. 1984-86), Ill. Bar Assn., Chgo. Bar Assn., Tavern Club (mem. jr. com. 1984-86), Exmoor Country Club (Highland Park, Ill.), Lake Forest Caucus. Republican. Episcopalian. Office: Field & Golan LLP 70 W Madison St 15th Fl Chicago IL 60602 E-mail: slgolan@fieldgolan.com.

GOLB, NORMAN, historian, writer; b. Chgo., Jan. 15, 1928; s. Joseph and Rose Golb; m. Ruth Magid, Sept. 17, 1949; children: Joel, Judith, Raphael. BA, Rossevelt U., Chgo., 1948; PhD, Johns Hopkins U., Balt., 1954; docteur hist. (hon.), Univ. de Rouen, France, 1986. Postdoctoral rschr. The Hebrew U., Jerusalem, 1955—57; lectr. U. Wis., Madison, 1957—58; asst. prof. Hebrew Union Coll., Cin., 1958—63, U. Chgo., 1963—66, assoc. prof., 1966—76, prof. Hebrew and Judaeo-Arabic studies, 1973—89, Rosenberger prof. Jewish history and civilization, 1989—. Author: Khazarian Hebrew Documents of the Xth Century, 1982, Who Wrote the Dead Sea Scrolls, 1995, Les Juifs de Rouen au Moyen Age, 1985, The Jews of Medieval Normandy, 1998, several more books and 65 monographs and articles. Guggenheim fellow, N.Y.C., 1964, 1966. Mem.: Clare Hall, Univ. Cambridge (life), Ordre des Canadiens (founder Chgo. br. 1992), Internat. Soc. of Judaeo-Arabic Studies (founder 1983), Union League Club of Chgo. (chmn. and orgn. of Embassy to France program 1997—98, pub. affairs com. 1999—). Jewish. Achievements include discovery of numerous documentary manuscripts of the Cairo Genizah revealing new aspects of medieval history. Profiles in the N.Y. Times, Le Monde, Jerusalem Post; development of the hypothesis of Jerusalem origin of the Dead Sea Scrolls in various articles and 1995 book, which was a major dual selection of the Hist. Book Club. Avocations: bicycling, tennis, music, poetry. Office: Oriental Inst Univ Chgo 1155 E 58th St Chicago IL 60637

GOLBUS, JOSEPH, rheumatologist; b. Chgo., Mar. 16, 1955; BS summa cum laude, U. Ill., 1977; MD, U. Ill., Chgo., 1981. Diplomate Am. Bd. Internal Medicine, Am. Bd. Rheumatology, Nat. Bd. Med. Examiners. Intern in internal medicine Northwestern U. Med. Sch./Evanston (Ill.) Hosp., 1981-82, resident in internal medicine, 1982-84; fellow Rackham Arthritis Rsch. Unit divsn. rheumatology U. Mich. Hosp., Ann Arbor, 1984-87; asst. attending physician, tchg. chief divsn. rheumatology Evanston Hosp., 1987-89, head divsn. rheumatology, 1988—, sr. attending physician, 1994—; assoc. prof. sect. arthritis and connective tissue diseases Northwestern U. Med. Sch., Evanston, 1993—; pres. ENH med. group Evanston Northwestern Healthcare, 1998—. Chmn. bd. dirs. Arthritis Found. Greater Chgo., 1995-97; spkr. in field Contbr. numerous articles to profl. jours., chpts. to books. James scholar, 1975-77, Schwartz scholar, 1979; Rice Found. fellow, 1990; AMA Edn. and Rsch. Found. grantee, 1985. Fellow: ACS, Am. Rheumatism Assn. (Ctrl. Region Fellows award 1985, nat. sr. fellows scholar award 1996), Am. Coll. Rheumatology (sec./treas. ctrl. region 1995—97, ctrl. region meeting program com. 1997, nat. meeting planning com. 1997—2000, vice chmn. Rsch. and Edn. Found. 1999—2001, chmn. Rsch. and Edn. Found. 2001—03, bd. dirs. 2003—); mem.: AAAS, Am. Coll. Physician Execs., Am. Coll. Healthcare Execs., W.D. Robinson U. Mich. Rheumatology Soc., Lupus Found. No. Ill., Lupus Found. Am., Chgo. Rheumatism Soc., Arthritis Found. (bd. dirs. 1991—, exec. com. 1992—, strategy 2000 strategic planning task force 1995—96, chmn. bd. dirs. Ill. chpt. 1995—97, resource devel. com. 1996—99, Blue Ribbon com. on quality of life 1997—99, trustee 1997—99, human subjects rev. bd. 1997—2000, Gold Achiever award Ill. chpt. 1995—99, Freedom of Movement award 2003), Am. Fedn. Clin. Rsch., Am. Soc. Internal Medicine, Phi Eta Sigma, Phi Kappa Phi, Phi Beta Kappa. Office: Evanston Northwestern Healthcare 1301 Central St Evanston IL 60201-1613

GOLBY, JAMES L. school system administrator; b. Kewanee, Ill., Mar. 2, 1927; s. John Thomas and Margaret Elizabeth (Larkin) G.; m. Alice Ann Simons, July 25, 1964; children: Katherine Golby Stewart, Margaret Golby Gustafson, Angela, James. BA, U. Ill., 1950, MA, 1952; postgrad., Bradley U., U. Chgo. Cert. tchr., Ill. Agrl. instr. Geneseo (Ill.) H.S., 1950-51; agrl. and sociology instr. Kewanee (Ill.) H.S., 1951-62, prin., 1962-67; supt. Kewanee Cmty. Unit Schs., 1967-98, supt. emeritus, 1998—. Bd. dirs. Kewanee Devel. Corp., 1970s. Sgt. U.S. Army, 1945-46. Named one of Outstanding Young Men in Am., Kewanee Jaycees, 1965, Citizen of Yr., City of Kewanee, 1984, Outstanding Adminstr., State of Ill. Supts. Office, 1977, Hon. State Farmer, Future Farmers Am., 1958; named to Hall of Fame, Blackhawk Coll., 1992. Mem. Am. Assn. Sch. Adminstrs., Ill. Assn. Sch. Adminstrs., Kewanee C. of C. (bd. dirs. 1970s), Kiwanis (pres. 1966, George Hixson award 1997). Democrat. Roman Catholic. Home: 611 McKinley Ave Kewanee IL 61443-3015 Office: Kewanee Cmty Unit Sch Dist 1101 E Third St Kewanee IL 61443-2951

GOLD, ALAN B. former Canadian chief justice; b. Montreal, July 21, 1917; m. Lynn Lubin; children: Marc, Nora, Daniel. BA, Queen's U., Kingston, Ont., Can., 1938; LLD (hon.), Queen's U., 1982; LLL cum laude, U. Montreal, 1941, LLD (hon.), 1978, McGill U., 1984, Yeshiva U., 1987. Bar: Que. 1941; Queen's counsel. Lectr. Faculty of Law McGill U., Montreal, 1957-71; dist. judge, vice chmn. Labour Rels. Bd., Que., 1961-65; assoc. chief judge Provincial Ct., P.Q., 1965-70, chief judge, 1970-83, pres. Jud. Coun., 1978-83, chmn. Conseil du Referendum, 1980; chief justice Superior Ct., P.Q., 1983-92; chancellor Concordia U., 1987-92; sr. counsel, chmn. dept. alternative dispute resolution Davies Ward Phillips & Vineberg LLP, Montreal, 1992—, chair alternative dispute resolution dept.; chancellor emeritus Corcordia U., 1992—. Chief arbitrator under collective labour agreements between Govt. P.Q. and Employees, 1966-83, between Shipping Fedn. Can. Inc. and Maritime Employers Assn. and Internat. Longshoremen's Assn., 1967-75; mem. multi-nat. panel Arbitration and Mediation Ctr. Ams.; spl. mediator and arbitrator in disputes concerning Fgn. Svc., Rys., Airlines, Royal Mint, Can. P.O., constrn. industry, other areas of pub., para-pub., pvt. sectors; scholar in residence McGill U. Faculty of Law, 1982; pres. Jr. Bar Assn., Montreal, 1951-52; mem. coun. Bar of Montreal, 1952-53, various other coms.; mem. bd. examiners Bar of P.Q., 1952-61, various other coms.; founder, dir., officer Legal Aid Bur., Montreal, 1956-60; mem. multinat. panel arbitrators and mediators concerning N.Am. Free Trade Agreement, Comml. Arbitration Mediation Ctr. Ams. Bd. dirs., exec. coun. Regie de la Place des Arts, 1973-82; mem., vice-chmn. Societe de la Place des Arts de Montreal, 1982—; pres. Jewish Pub. Establishments Commn., Fedn. CJA, 1993-97, bd. dirs. Fedn. CJA 1993-97; pres. bd. dirs. Jerusalem Found. Can. Inc., 1980-83; bd. govs. McGill U., 1974-83, chmn. 1978-82, gov. emeritus, 1984—; gov. Soc. Pro Musica, 1970—, I Musici de Montreal, 1988—; bd. dirs., chmn. Conseil d'adminstrn. de l'orchestre, 1997—. Decorated officer Order of Can., Ordre Nat. du Qué.; recipient Human Rels. award Can. Coun. Christians and Jews, 1985, Disting. Bora Laskin award Yeshiva U., 1987, Médaille du Premier Ministre du Qué., 1987, Montreal medal Queen's U., 1985, Bar of Québec medal, 1990-91, Nat. Assembly of Québec medal, 1992, Université de Montréal medal, 1992, Samuel Bronfman Can. Jewish Contress, 1992, Commemorative medal for 125th anniversary of Can., Case District I, Disting. Friend of Edn. award, 1993, Pres.'s award Tel Aviv U., 1998. Mem. Bar Province Quebec, Montreal Bar (various offices) Nat. Acad. Arbitrators (hon., life, U.S.), Soc. Profls. in Dispute Resolution (charter, U.S., Spl. award for excellence 1981), Corp. Professionnelle des Conseillers en Rels. Industrielles de law Province de Quebec, Conseil de l'Order (pres. 1989-91), Acad. Grands Montréalais, Clin. Rsch. Inst. Montreal (chmn. ethics com. 1990-94), Phi Delta Phi. Office: Davies Ward Phillips & Vineberg LLP 1501 McGill College Ave Fl 26 Montreal QC Canada H3A 3N9 E-mail: agold@dwpv.com.

GOLD, ALBERT, artist; b. Phila., Oct. 31, 1916; s. Rubin and Dora (Sklar) G.; m. Aurora Mary Vannelli, May 3, 1953; children: Madelaine, Robert. Grad., Pa. Mus. Sch. Indsl. Art, 1938. Tchr. pictoral expression Pa. Mus. Sch., Phila., 1945-48; dir. dept. illustration Phila. Mus. Coll. Arts; prof. emeritus Phila. Coll. Art; tchr. art ctrs., pvt. classes. Exhibited at maj. ann. shows including Pa. Acad. Fine Arts, Corcoran Gallery, Met. Mus., Art Inst. Chgo., Carnegie Inst., World's Fair, N.Y.C., 1939, Nat. Gallery, London, 1943, Musee Galliera, Paris, 1944, La Tausca exhbn., Burlington Acad. Galleries, 1962, Phila. Coll. Art (Alumni grant), 1968; one man shows include Pa. Acad. Fine Arts, Phila. Art Alliance, Hahn Gallery, Chestnut Hill, Pa., Wigmore Fine Arts, N.Y.C., 1991; represented in collections Libr. of Congress, Soc. Illustrators, N.Y.C., N.Y. Pub. Libr., Phila. Mus. Art, War Dept., Pentagon Bldg., U. Pa., Phila., U. Del., Newark, U. Minn., Smithsonian Instn., Atwater-Kent Mus., Phila., New Britain (Conn.) Mus. Am. Art, Forbes Collection, Ford Collection, Pa. Acad. Fine Arts, Soc. Illustrators, N.Y.C., Fogg Mus., U. Pa., Harvard U., Gimbel Pa. Collection, Free Libr. Phila., Balch Inst. for Ethnic Studies, Brown U. Libr. Mil. Collection, Phila. Mus. Art; numerous pvt. collections; commd. to paint various documentary series; illustrator various mags.; (book) The Commodore (Robert L. Abrahams), 1954; illustrator: (book) This Was Our War (Frank Brookhouser), 1961, The Court Factor, 1964, The Captive Rabbi (Lillian S. Freehof), 1965; contbr. articles to Step-By-Step Graphics, Retrospective Exhibition 1996, Philadelphia Art Alliance. Decorated Order Brit. Empire, Brit. Empire medal; recipient John Gribbel Meml. prize Phila. Print Club, 1939, Prix de Rome, Am. Acad. in Rome, 1942, Geizel award Phila. Sketch Club, 1982, 83, Tiffany Found. grant, 1947-48, Jennie Sesnan Gold medal, 1950, Dorothy Kohl prize Phila. Art Alliance, 1953, Am. Artist citation Am. Water Color Soc., 1954, Am. Artists Guild award Am. Water Color Soc., 1955, Regional Water Color prize Phila. Art Alliance, 1955, Wm. W. Esty prize Am. Water Color Soc. Ann., 1961, award for series of illustrations Brandywine Ohio State U. Sch. Journalism, prize Phila. Watercolor Club, 1977, Silver Star award Phila. Coll. Art, 1979, Sawin award Phila. Watercolor Club, 1989; Woodmere Endowment Fund grantee, 1968; Tiffany Found. grantee, 1946 and 47. Mem. Artists Equity (dir.), AAUP. Achievements include being selected by War Dept. as one of 12 men in U.S. Army to make pictorial record of war, 1943, spent 3 yrs. in Eng., France and Germany on project contributing hundreds of war paintings and drawing at the Pentagon 1945. Home: 6814 Mccallum St Philadelphia PA 19119-3001 Office: Gallery D Wigmore Fine Arts Inc 22 E 76th St New York NY 10021-2611 *I have endeavored to "be myself" in my behavior and in my work as an artist. I've always felt that the surest way to oblivion was to "follow the herd". "Style" in art should be as personal as one's handwriting.*

GOLD, ALLAN HAROLD, architect, structural engineer, educator; b. Chgo., Jan. 12, 1942; s. Melvin King and Estelle M. (Zucker) G.; m. Barbara Gail Edelstein, June 20, 1967 (div. Feb. 1989); children: Grant, Ross, Susan; m. Susan Carlucci, Dec. 30, 1989. BArch, U. Ill., Urbana, 1966, MS, 1967. Registered architect, Conn., Colo., Ill., Ind., La., Okla., Wis.; registered structural engr., Ill; registered profl. engr., Ind., La., Okla., Wis., Tex., Mich.; cert. Nat. Coun. Archtl. Registration Bds. (juror registration exam. 1985), Nat. Coun. Examiners Engrin. and Surveying Certification. Architect, project engr. various archtl., engring. cos., Chgo. area, 1963—68; project structural engr. Perkins & Will Archs., Chgo., 1968—70; structural engr. Chgo. Dept. Bldgs., 1970—73; owner, operator Allan H. Gold & Assocs., Architects/Cons. Structural Engrs., Hazel Crest, Ill., 1973—81; project mgr., sr. structural engr. HKS/Structures, Dallas, 1981—84; dir. architecture and structural engring. dept. URS Engrs., Dallas, 1984; owner, operator Allan H. Gold, Architect/Structural Engr., Dallas, 1985—88; project mgr. Hoffmann Architects, North Haven, Conn., 1988—90; prin. Allan H. Gold, Archt. & Structural Engr., Chgo., 1990—93; v.p. Salse Engrs., Northbrook, Ill., 1993—96; assoc. Thornton-Tomasetti Engrs./LZA Tech., Chgo., 1996—2001; prin. Allan H. Gold Structural Engr., Chgo., 2001—; asst. prof. archtl. tech. dept. constrn. tech. Purdue U., Hammond, Ind., 1976—80; assoc. prof. architecture U. Okla., Norman, 1980—81. Adj. assoc. prof. architecture U. Tex., Arlington, 1983-85; guest lectr. U. Wis. Ext., 1981. Structural engr. Century Shopping Ctr., Chgo., 1973, Phoenix Tower, Houston, 1983, Xerox II, Irving, Tex., 1984. Mem. Village of Hazel Crest Plan Commn., 1979-81. Fellow: ASCE (tall bldgs. com. 1983—86, std. com. design loads on structure during constrn. 1989—, std. com. design engineered wood constrn. 1989—, editl. bd. Jour. Archtl. Enging. 1995—); mem.: AIA, Am. Arbitration Assn., Structural Engrs. Assn. Ill., Am. Concrete Inst., Shriners, Scottish Rite, Masons. Jewish. Home: 360 E Randolph St # 4204 Chicago IL 60601-7341 Office: Allan H Gold Structural Engr 120 W Madison St Ste 702 Chicago IL 60602 E-mail: ahgold@ameritech.net.

GOLD, ARNOLD HENRY, judge; b. Santa Monica, Calif., Apr. 12, 1932; s. Louis and Rose (Shalat) G.; m. Gloria Victor; children: Jeffrey Alan, Kenneth Clarke, Susan Elizabeth. AB with distinction, Stanford U., 1953, JD, 1955. Bar: Calif. 1955, U.S. Dist. Ct. (so., ctrl. and no. dists.) Calif. 1955, U.S. Ct. Appeals (9th cir.) 1955, U.S. Supreme Ct. 1955. Law clk. to Hon, John W. Shenk Supreme Ct. of Calif., San Francisco, 1955-56; assoc. atty. Loeb & Loeb, L.A., 1956-61; pvt. practice Beverly Hills, Calif., 1961-70; prin. Pachter, Gold & Schaffer, and predecessors, L.A., 1970-88; judge Calif. Superior Ct. for County of L.A., 1988-2001, supervising judge probate dept., 1993-94. Chmn. probate and mental health com. Calif. Judges Assn., 1995—96; lectr. Calif. Jud. Edn. and Rsch. Probate and Mental Health Insts., 1994—2002, Civil Practice Inst., 1993, Family Law Inst., 1992, Calif. Continuing Edn. of Bar, 1969, 1976—77, 1979—82, 1984—88, 1992, 2001—03; mem. Calif. Atty. Gen.'s Com. on Charitable Reporting Stds., 1970—71, Calif. Atty. Gen.'s Task Force on Charitable Solicitation Legis., 1975—78, Calif. Jud. Coun. Probate and Mental Health Adv. Com., 1997—; mem. exec. com. Stanford Law Soc. So. Calif., 1973—77. Co-author: Probate Module, California Civil Practice, 1993; contbg. author: California Family Law Handbook, California Nonprofit Corporations Handbooks; mng. editor, bd. editors Stanford Law Rev., 1954-55. Mem. ABA, State Bar Calif. (vice chmn. conf. dels. 1986-87), L.A. County Bar Assn. (trustee 1981-83), Los Angeles County Bar Found. (bd. dirs. 1985-91), Mulholland Tennis Club, Phi Beta Kappa, Alpha Epsilon Pi, Phi Alpha Delta, Delta Sigma Rho. Office: 10842 Alta View Dr Studio City CA 91604-3901 Home: 10842 Alta View Dr Studio City CA 91604-3901 E-mail: judgeagold@aol.com.

GOLD, ARNOLD P. pediatric neurologist; b. N.Y.C., Aug. 8, 1925; s. Michael and Rebecca (Perlman) Gold; m. Sandra Orenberg, Nov. 17, 1969; children: Jeffrey, Stephen, Jennifer, Amelia, Margaret. BA, U. Tex., 1947; MS, U. Fla., 1949; MD, U. Lausanne, 1954; D (hon.), U. Medicine & Dentistry N.J., 2001. Diplomate Am. Bd. Pediatrics; diplomate in neurology and in pediatric neurology Am. Bd. Psychiatry and Neurology. Intern Charity Hosp of La., New Orleans, 1954-55; resident, chief resident in pediatrics Children's Hosp, Cin., 1955-58; NIH fellow in pediatric neurology Columbia Presbyn. Med. Ctr., N.Y.C., 1958-61; prof. clin. neurology Columbia U., N.Y.C., 1976—, prof. clin. pediatrics, 1976—; attending neurologist Columbia Presbyn. Med. Ctr., 1976—, attending pediatrician, 1976—. Pres. Arnold P. Gold Found., Englewood Cliffs, NJ, 1989—; trustee, sec. AMA Found., 1999—; mem. interdisciplinary coun. Devel. and Learning Disabilities, Bethesda, Md., 1997—; pres. Myoclonus Rsch. Found., NJ, 1992—. Editor, 80, Author: Neurology of Infancy and Childhood, 1974, Pediatric Therapy, 1963, 80, Pediatrics, 1968, 96; author: Merritt's Textbook of Neurology, 1984-2003. Bd. dirs. Homes for the Developmentally Disabled, N.J., 1984-2001; cons. Cmty. Sch., Teaneck, N.J., 1975—; mem. adv. coun. Naomi Berrie Diabetes Ctr., N.Y.C., 1997—; mem. admissions com. Ben Guron U., Beer-Sheva, Israel, 1997-98; trustee, bd. advisors N.J. Med. Sch., 2001-03. Recipient Disting. Svc. award, Columbia U., 1999, Miracle Maker of N.Y., Children's Miracle Network, 1994, Brennerman award in pediatrics, 1968, Disting. Svc. award, Speech-Lang.-Hearing Assn., 1993, Lifetime Cmty. Svc. award, Autism Soc. Am., 2000, Man of Yr. award, Assn. Brain Injured Children, 1968, Practitioner of Yr. award, Columbia Presbny. Med. Ctr., 1992, Best Dr. in Am., Am. Health March issue, 1996, Best Dr. in N.Y., 1997, 1998, 1999, 2000, 2001, Humanitarian award, Sinai Inst., 2002. Fellow Am. Acad. Pediatrics, Am. Pediatric Soc., Am. Acad. Neurology, Child Neurology Soc., Internat. Child Neurology Soc. Avocations: gardening, stamp and coin collecting. Office: Neurol Inst NY 710 W 168th St New York NY 10032-2603 E-mail: apg1@columbia.edu.

GOLD, BELA, economist, educator; b. Kolozsvar, Hungary, Jan. 30, 1915; came to U.S., 1920, naturalized, 1927; s. Leo and Esther (Ludwig) G.; m. Sonia Steinman, July 5, 1938; 1 son, Robert. BS in Mech. Engring, NYU, 1934; PhD (Univ. fellow 1936-37), Columbia U., 1948. Research cons. Life Ins. Sales Research Bur., Hartford, Conn., 1938-39; asst. head div. program surveys Bur. Agr. Econs., 1939-42; econ. cons. subcom. war mblzn. U.S. Senate, 1943-44; econ. adviser FEA and Dept. Commerce, 1944-46; prof. indsl. econs. U. Pitts. Grad. Sch. Bus., 1947-66; Timken prof. and William E. Umstattd prof. indsl. econs., dir. research program indsl. econs. Case Western Res. U., 1966-83, chmn. dept. econs., 1967-73; Fletcher Jones prof. tech. and mgmt. Claremont Grad. Sch. (Calif.), 1983-2000; pres. Indsl. Econs. and Mgmt. Assocs., 1980-2000. Vis. professorial fellow Nuffield Coll., Oxford (Eng.) U., 1964; vis. prof. Imperial Coll. Scis. and Tech., London, 1967, 73; Disting. Internat. Sr. Rsch. fellow Centre Internat. Rsch. on Computer and Info. Tech., Melbourne, Australia, 1989, Adminstrv. Staff. Coll. India, Hyderabad, 1992, Rand Afrikaans U., South Africa, 1995; cons. to industry and ednl. instns., 1950—; mem. com. on steel industry Nat. Acad. Scis.-Nat. Materials Adv. Bd., 1977-78; mem. assembly of engring. com. on computer-aided mfg. NRC, 1978-82, mem. mfg. studies bd., 1982-86, mem. com. on machine tool industry, 1982-84; mem. Interdepartmental Adv. Com on Fed. Policy on Indsl. Innovation, 1978-79, mem. ferrous metals panel Nat. Acad. Engring., 1980-84, panel on improving the competitiveness of U.S. Industries, 1985. Author: Wartime Economic Planning in Agriculture, 2d edit., 1969, How is Higher Education Financed, 1959, Foundations of Productivity Analysis, 1955, Explorations in Managerial Economics, 1971, Japanese edit., 1977, Technological Change: Economics Management and Environment, 1975, 80, Applied Productivity Analysis for Industry, U.K. edit., 1976, Russian edit., 1981, Chinese edit., 1982, Research, Technological Change and Economic Analysis, 1977, Productivity, Technology and Capital, 1979, 2d edit., 1982, Evaluating the Effects of Technological Innovations, 1980, Appraising and Stimulating Technological Advances in Industry, 1980, Improving Managerial Evaluations of Computer-Aided Manufacturing, 1981, Technological Progress and Industrial Leadership, 1984, 85, On the Increasing Role of Technology in Corporate Policy, 1991, Strengthening Corporate and National Competitiveness Through Technology, 1992, New Technological Foundations of Strategic Management: Some International Perspectives, 1993, Needed Technological Responses to International Competition, 1994, Emerging Technological Frontiers in International Competition, 1995, Changing the Technological Determinants of International Competitiveness, 1996, Advancing the International Competitiveness of U.S. Manufacturing, 1999; mem. editl. bd. Acad. Mgmt. Jour., 1962-73, Omega: Internat. Jour. Mgmt. Scis., 1972-99, Jour. Product Innovation Mgmt., 1983-99, Internat. Jour. Tech. Mgmt., 1989-99; corr. mem. editl. bd. Revue d'Économie Industrielle, 1978-90; mem. adv. editl. bd. Jour. Computer Integrated Mfg., 1985—,Transactions in Engring. Mgmt., 1986—, Jour. Engring. and Tech. Mgmt., 1988—, Mfg. Rev., 1989—, Prodn. and Ops. Mgmt., 1991—, Mng. Tech. Today, 1992—; contbr. numerous articles to profl. jours., chpts. in books. Social Sci. Research Council fellow, 1937-38, 77, 83; Ford Found. fellow, 1961-62, 66-67, 72 Mem. Am. Econ. Assn., Inst. Mgmt. Scis. (chmn. Coll. on Mgmt. of Technol. Change 1970-85), Nat. Assn. Accts. (subcom. on productivity measurement 1977-79), AAUP. Home: The Classic 6380 Common Cir West Palm Beach FL 33417-4266

GOLD, BETTY VIRGINIA, artist; b. Austin, Tex., Feb. 15, 1935; d. Julius Ulisses and Jeffie Mae (Meek) Lee; 1 child, Laura Lee Gold Bousquet. Student(hon.), U. Tex. Lectr. Gazi U., Ankara, Turkey, 1988, NAshida Gallery, Nara, Japan, 1989, Met. State Coll. Denver, 1992, Downey Mus., Calif., 1993, Foothills Art Ctr., Golden, Colo., 1994, Triskel Art Ctr., Cork, Ireland, 1994, ARmand Hammer Mus., L.A., 1994, Austin Art Mus., 1996. One-woman shows include Sol Del Rio Gallery, San Antonio, 1971, Parkcrest Gallery, Austin, 1972, Rubicon Gallery, L.A., 1973, Downtown Gallery, Honolulu, 1974, Esther Robles Gallery, L.A., 1975, Laguna Gloria Art Mus., Austin, 1976, Charles W. Bowers Meml. Mus., Santa Ana, Calif., 1977, Phoenix Art Mus., 1979, Baum-Silverman Gallery, L.A., 1988, Del. Art Mus., Wilmington, 1981, Univ. Art Mus., Austin, 1981, Decias Art, LaJolla, Calif., 1982, Patrick Gallery, Austin, 1983, Jan Baum Gallery, L.A., 1984, Boise State U., 1985, Purdue U., West Lafayette, Ind., 1986, Walker Hill Art Ctr., Seoul, Korea, 1987, Nishida Gallery, Nara, Japan, 1989, Armeson Fine Arts, Ltd., Vail, Colo., 1991, Downey Mus., Calif., 1993, ARt Mus. South Tex., Corpus Christi, 1995, Austin Art Mus., Austin, 1996, The Czech Mus. Fine Arts, Prague, 1998, Elite Gallery, Venice, 1998, others; group shows include Enhol Gallery, Dallas, 1971, Bestart Fallery, Houston, 1972, Gargoyle, Inc., Aspen, Colo., 1975, Aronson Gallery, Atlanta, 1976, Shidoni Gallery, Sante Fe, N.Mex., 1977, Elaine Horwich Gallery, Scottsdale, Ariz., 1981, Fordham U., Bronx, 1983, Nat. Mus. Contemporary Art, Seoul, 1987, John Thomas Gallery, Santa Monica, Calif., 1989, La Quinta Sculpture Park, Calif., 1994, Bova Gallery, L.A., 1995, Museo Nacional Centro de Arte Reina Sofia, Madrid, Spain, 1997, Threshold Gallery, Santa Monica, 1998, others; represented in permanent installations at RCA Bldg., Chgo., Cedars Sinai Hosp., L.A., Sinai Temple, L.A., Hawaii State Fond. Arts, Apollo Plastic Corp., Chgo., Houston First Savs., Pepperdine U., Malibu, Calif., No. Ill. U., Dekalb, Mus. Nacional-Centro de Arte Reina Sofia, Madrid, Texas U., Austin, City of Palma de Mallorca (1999), Spain, Duke U. Med. Ctr. (1999), Mary Baldwin Coll., Staunton, Va., 2001, Baylor U., Waco, Tex., 2002, Pres. Garden, Slovakia Republic (gift from U.S. Embassy), Pepperdine U., Malibu, Calif, 2003, others. Fax: 310-399-3745. E-mail: bgold1324@earthlink.net.

GOLD, CALLA GISELLE, jewelry designer; b. L.A., Dec. 1, 1958; d. Robert Frederick Skeetz and Ruth Mary Connelly; m. Jeremy Peter Gold, July 15, 1979; 1 child, Daniel Jason. Grad. high sch., Berkeley, Calif. Sales rep. Fuller Brush, 1977-83; owner Cinderella Svcs., Santa Barbara, Calif., 1979-82, Ceiling Cleaning Co., Santa Barbara, Calif., 1982-83, Calla Gold Jewelry, Santa Barbara, Calif., 1983—. Spkr. Profl. Jeweler Show and Conf., Las Vegas, 2000. Contbg. author Profl. Jeweler mag., 1997, 98, 99. Orchard to Ocean run food dir. Carpinteria (Calif.) Edn. Found., 1999; fundraiser Kinderkirk Presch., Carpinteria, 1996; specific event fundraiser Villa Majella, Santa Barbara, 1997-2002, Holderman Endowment for La Patera, Lompoc Aquarium, 2000-02, Santa Barbara Women's Health Coalition, Santa Barbara County Med. Soc. Alliance; bd. dirs. Leads Club, 1995. Recipient Leadership award, Leads Club, 1996. Mem. Am. Jewelers Assn., Calif. Jewelers Assn., Santa Barbara Event Profls., Santa Barbara Jewelers Guild, South Coast Bus. Network, Toastmasters (competent Toastmaster 1991). Avocations: hiking, horseback riding, reading, scrapbooking. Office: Calla Gold Jewelry PO Box 40102 Santa Barbara CA 93140-0102 E-mail: gold2@cox.net.

GOLD, CAROL SAPIN, international management consultant, speaker; b. N.Y.C. d. Cerf Saul and Muriel Louise (Fudin) Rosenberg; children: Kevin Bart Sapin, Craig Paul Sapin, Courtney Byrens Sapin. BA, U. Calif., Berkeley, 1955. Asst. credit mgr. Union Oil Co., 1956; with U.S. Dept. State, 1964-66; mem. dept. pub. rels. Braun & Co., L.A., 1964-66; corp. dir. pers. tng. Gt. Western Fin. Corp., L.A., 1967-71; pres. Carol Sapin Gold & Assocs., L.A., 1971—. Bd. dirs. Marathon Nat. Bank, L.A.; cons., profl. spkr., Bath, Eng., 1987-90; cons., Can., Mex., India, Australia, New Zealand; host radio program The Competitive Edge; mem. expdn. to Syria and Jordan, 1994, to Morocco, 1995; mem. WORID Bus. Acad.; instr. Learning Annex; presenter Expertise Forum Presentations, Malaysia, Bangkok, 1997; instr. Asian program U. So. Calif., 1998. Author: Solid Gold Customer Relations, Travel for Scholars, Paris, 1999; featured in tng. films Power of Words; Author: Cassette Libraries, Sound Selling. Bd. dirs. Ctr. Theatre Group, Town Hall, Music Ctr., Odyssey Theater; asst. dir. Burnhill Prodns., 1992—, Cabaret, Palisades Theatre; dir. Improv Corp.; vol. Exec. Svc. Corp., 1996—. Mem. ASTD, Am. Film Inst. Assn., Sales and Mktg. Execs., Nat. Spkrs. Assn., Nat. Platform Assn., Women in Bus., KCET Women's Coun., Exec. Svc. Corps, World Affairs Coun., Blue Ribbon, Women in Arts, Women in Film, Manuscript Soc. Forum Scotland, Plato Soc., Brandeis Univ. Women, Sierra Club (Toure de Mt. Blanc), Supreme Ct. Hist. Soc., Dispute Resolution Svcs., Women of L.A., Marina Del Rey C. of C. Avocations: collecting famous manuscripts, training public speakers. Office: PO Box 11447 Marina Del Rey CA 90295 E-mail: cconsult@aol.com.

GOLD, DANIEL HOWARD, ophthalmologist, educator; b. N.Y.C., Sept. 21, 1942; s. Isadore and Leona (Cotton) G.; m. Joann Aaron, Oct. 22, 1966 (div. Sept. 1985); m. Barbara Wood, June 19, 1988; children: David, Abigail, Michael. Student, U. Mich., 1959-66. Diplomate Am. Bd. Ophthalmology. Asst. chief dept. ophthalmology Walter Reed Army Med. Ctr., Washington, 1972-74; asst. prof. dept. ophthalmology Montefiore Hosp. Med. Ctr., Bronx, N.Y., 1974-76; asst. clin. prof. med. br. U. Tex., Galveston, 1977-85, assoc. clin. prof. med. br., 1986-91; physician, ophthalmologist Eye Clinic of Tex., Galveston, 1977—; clin. prof. ophthalmology med. br. U. Tex., Galveston, 1991—. Mem. med. staff exec. com. St. Mary's Hosp., Galveston, 1989-90, 95-96, chmn. dept. surgery, 1995-96. Editor: (textbook) The Eye in Systemic Disease, 1990, Color Atlas of the Eye in Systemic Disease, 2001, Clinical Eye Atlas, 2002; contbr. articles to profl. jours. Pres. United Orthodox Synagogues, Houston, 1997-2000. Maj. U.S. Army, 1972-74. Fellow: N.Y. Acad. Medicine, Royal Coll. Ophthalmologist Gr. Britain, Am. Acad. Ophthalmology (self-assessment com. 1989—92, editl. adv. bd. EyeNet 1996—2002, Honor award 1985, Sr. Honor award 2001); mem.: Tex. Med. Assn. (coun. on pub. health 1995—97), Galveston Physicians Svc. Assn. (bd. dirs. 1985—2000, pres. 1993—2000), Pan Am. Assn. Ophthalmology, Assn. Rsch. Vision and Ophthalmology, Macula Soc. Jewish. Office: Eye Clinic Tex 2302 Avenue P Galveston TX 77550-7992

GOLD, EDWARD DAVID, lawyer; b. Detroit, Jan. 17, 1941; s. Morris and Hilda (Robinson) Gold; m. Francine Sheila Kamin, Jan. 8, 1967; children: Lorne Brian, Karen Beth. Student, Wayne State U., 1958-61; JD, Detroit Coll. Law, 1964 Bar: Mich. 1965, U.S. Dist. Ct. (ea. dist.) Mich. 1965, U.S. Ct. Appeals (6th cir.) 1965, D.C. 1966. Atty. gen. counsel FCC, Washington, 1965-66; ptnr. Conn, Conn & Gold, Detroit, 1966-67, May, Conn, Conn & Gold, Livonia, Mich., 1967-69, Hyman, Gurwin, Nachman, Gold & Alterman, Southfield, Mich., 1971-88, Butzel Long, Bloomfield Hills, Mich., 1988—. Mem. Oakland County Criminal Justice Coordinating Coun., 1976—77; chmn. Friend of the Ct. Adv. Com., Lansing, Mich., 1982—88; contbr. lectr. Inst. Continuing Legal Edn., Ann Arbor, Mich., 1981—, Mich. Trial Lawyers Assn.; adj. prof. U. Detroit Mercy Sch. Law, 2001—. Author: (book) Michigan Family Law, 1988; contbr. articles to legal jours. Mem. Southfield Transp. Commn., 1975—77; chairperson atty. disp. bd. Tri-County Hearin Panel 71, 1994—2002; chmn. attys.' divsn. Jewish Welfare Fedn., Detroit; mem. nat. young leadership cabinet United Jewish Appeal, N.Y.C., 1978—80; pres. Jewish Family Svc., Detroit, 1988—90; bd. dirs. Oakland County Legal Aid Soc., 1979—84. Scholar Tau Epsilon Rho, 1963. Fellow: Am. Acad. Matrimonial Lawyers (bd. dirs. 1988—93, pres. Mich. chpt. 1992—93, nat. bd. govs. 1988—2001, nat. v.p. 2001—), Am. Coll. Family Trial Lawyers; mem.: Am. Arbitration Assn., Bar Assn. D.C., Southfield Bar Assn. (pres. 1975—76), Oakland County Bar Assn. (bd. dirs. 1984—93, pres. 1992—93), Mich. Bar Assn. (coun. real property law sect. 1973—81, coun. family law sect. 1974—75, 1977—82, chmn. family law sect. 1981—82, rep. assembly 1978—82, Lifetime Achievement award), Alpha Epsilon Pi (nat. pres. 1976—77, Order of Lion award 1986). Avocation: golf. Office: Butzel Long Ste 200 100 Bloomfield Hills Pkwy Bloomfield Hills MI 48304 E-mail: Gold@Butzel.com.

GOLD, EVAN BRUCE, ophthalmologist; b. New Brunswick, N.J., Nov. 6, 1958; s. Robert D. and Marion (Beitel) G.; m. Sharon Cohen, Sept. 5, 1993. BS in Biology, SUNY, 1980; MD, U. Miami, Fla., 1984. With anat. pathology Jackson Meml. Hosp., Miami, 1984-85; with internal medicine Miami Sinai Med. Ctr., Miami Beach, 1985-86; with opthalmology Boston U. Assoc. Hosps., 1986-89; ophthalmologist Eye Sight & Surgery Assocs., Springfield, Mass., 1989-91, Harvard Vanguard Med. Assn., Chelmsford, Mass., 1991—; pvt. practice Needham, Mass., 1991—. Fellow Am. Acad. Ophthalmology, mem. New Eng. Ophthalmologic Soc. Avocations: cooking, travel.

GOLD, GEORGE MYRON, lawyer, editor, writer, consultant; b. Bklyn., June 28, 1935; s. Harry and Rose Miriam (Meyerson) G.; m. Bunny Winters, Dec. 24, 1960; 1 child, Seth Harris AB, U. Rochester, 1956; JD, NYU, 1959. Bar: N.Y. 1960. Practice, N.Y.C., 1960-64, 67-78; legal editor Prentice-Hall, Inc., Englewood Cliffs, N.J., 1960-62; assoc. Speiser, Shumate, Geoghan & Law, N.Y.C., 1962-64; assoc. editor Rsch. and Rev. Svc. Am., Inc., Indpls., 1964-67; dir. publs., mng. editor Estate Planners Quar., Farnsworth Pub. Co., Inc., Rockville Centre, N.Y., 1967-69; editor-in-chief Trusts & Estates, N.Y.C., 1969-76; mng. editor Trust News, N.Y.C., 1976-78; dir. news publs. and info. ABA, Chgo., 1978-83; sr. assoc. editor and dir. book divsn. ABA Jour., Chgo., 1984-87; dir. publs. and editor Trial Mag. Assn. Trial Lawyers Am., 1988-89; cons. North Potomac, Md., 1989-90; exec. sr. law editor Mead Data Cen., Dayton, 1990-93; exec. editor Stevens Pub., Washington, 1993-94, corp. editl. dir., 1994-95, v.p. editl., 1995—2001; dir. new product devel. Pike & Fischer, Silver Spring, Md., 2001—. Cons., Ashburn, Va., 1995—. Author: The Propriety, Procedure and Evidentiary Effect of a Jury View, 1959, Investments by Trustees, Executors and Administrators, 1961, What You Should Know About Intestacy, 1962, What You Should Know About the Common Disaster, 1962, The Powers of Your Trustee, 1962, What You Should Know About the Antenuptial Agreement, 1963, Who May Be the Beneficiary of Your Will, 1963, What You Should Know About The Spendthrift Trust, 1963, Comprehensive Estate Analysis, 1966, You're Worth More Than You Think, 1966, Medicare Handbook, 1966, The ABCs of Administering Your Estate, 1966, The Will: An Instrument for Service and Sales, 1966, A Tax-Sheltered Pension Plan for the Close-Corporation Stockholder, 1968, Social Security Law in Nutshell, 1968, What You Should Know About Custodial Gifts to Minors, 1968, The Short-Term Trust and Estate Planning, 1976, The Importance of a Will, 1976, The Need for an Experienced Executor, 1976, Tax Tips-99 Ways to Reduce the Bite, 1976, Investment Management: No Job for the Amateur, 1971, Who Manages Your Securities, 1972, A Woman's Need for Financial Planning, 1972, The Lawyer's Role in the Search for Peace, 1982, True Counselors: Helping Clients Deal with Loss, 1983, Evaluating and Settling Personal Injury Claims, 1991, Cite Checking: A Guide to Validating Legal Research, 1992, The Compliance Pak for HR Managers-Book I (Hiring, Evaluation & Separation), Book II (Severance), 1993, Selling Life Insurance: Overcoming Objections, 1996; editor: Fundamentals of Federal Income Estate and Gift Taxes, 1965-67, The R & R Tax Handbook, 1965-67, Tax-Free Reorganizations, 1968, Guide to Pension and Profit Sharing Plans, 1968, A Life Underwriter's Guide to Equity Investments, 1968, The Tired Tirade, 1968, A Handbook of Personal Insurance Terminology, 1968, The 15th Anniversary Edition of Estate Planners Quar., 1968, You, Your Heirs and Your Estate, 1968, The Farnsworth Letter for Estate Planners, 1968-69, How to Use Life Insurance in Business and Estate Planning, 1969, Human Drama in Death and Taxes, 1970, Don't Bank on It, 1970, The Feldman Method, 1970, Directory of Trust Instns. (ann.), LawTalk, 1986-87, The Supreme Court and Its Justices, 1987, Aaron J. Broder on Trial: Reflections of a Famous Litigator, 1994, Examining the Science Behind Nutraceuticals, 2001. Mem. Soc. Law Writers (dir. 1972-75), ABA, Am. Law Inst., N.Y. State Bar Assn., Assn. Bar City N.Y., Estate Planning Council N.Y.C., Nat. Press Club, Soc. Bus. Press Editors, Soc. Scholarly Publ., Soc. Human Resources Mgmt., Am. Soc. Assn. Execs., Newsletter and Electronic Publishers Assn., Washington Independent Writers, Loudoun County Cable TV Adv. Commn., Kappa Nu, Pi Alpha Lambda. Clubs: KP. Office: 1010 Wayne Ave Silver Spring MD 20910 E-mail: gmgold@erols.com.

GOLD, GERALD SEYMOUR, lawyer; b. Cleve., Feb. 2, 1931; s. David N. and Geraldine (Bloch) G.; 1 child, Anne; m. Rosemary Grdina, 1994. AB, Case-Western Res. U., 1951, LLB, 1954. Bar: Ohio 1954, U.S. Supreme Ct. 1961. Practiced in, Cleve., 1954-60; chief asst. legal aid defender Cuyahoga County, Cleve., 1960-61, chief legal aid defender, 1961-65; assoc. Ulmer, Byrne, Laronge, Glickman & Curtis, Cleve., 1965-66; ptnr. Gold, Rotatori, Schwartz & Gibbons, Cleve., 1966—. Instr. in law Case Western Res. U., 1965-66, Cleve. State Law Sch., 1968-69, Case-Western Res. Law-Medicine Center, 1961-77; lectr. to bar assns. commr. Cuyahoga County Pub. Defender, 1977-81. Contbg. author: American Jurisprudence Trials, 1966; Contbr. articles to law revs. Fellow Am. Coll. Trial Lawyers, Am. Bd. Criminal Lawyers, Ohio State Bar Found., Internat. Soc. Barristers; mem. ABA (criminal justice coun.), Cuyahoga County Criminal Ct. Bar Assn. (chmn., Lifetime Achievement award 1995), Ohio Bar Assn. (chmn. criminal law sect. 1974-78, ho. of dels. 1986—), Greater Cleve. Bar Assn. (Merit award 1974, trustee 1978—, pres. 1982-83), Nat. Assn. Criminal Def. Lawyers (pres. 1977, Merit award 1975), Ohio Acad. Trial Lawyers (chmn. criminal law sect. 1970-75), Ohio Assn. Criminal Def. Lawyers (bd. dirs. 1990), Case-Western Res. U. Law Alumni Assn. (pres. 1974-75, Outstanding Alumnus award 1991), Soc. Benchers, Court of Nisi Prius Club, Cleve. Skating Club. Home: 33000 Pinetree Rd Pepper Pike OH 44124-5514 Office: 526 Superior Ave E Ste 1140 Cleveland OH 44114-1497

GOLD, HAROLD ARTHUR, lawyer; b. Pitts., Jan. 13, 1929; m. Anita Hubert, Aug. 18, 1937; children: Howard, Bradley. BBA, U. Pitts., 1952; JD, Georgetown U., 1956. Bar: Pa. 1956, D.C. 1956. Sole practice law, Pitts., 1956-64; atty. City of Pitts., 1960-69; ptnr. Baskin and Sears, Pitts., 1965-84, Reed, Smith, Shaw & McClay, Pitts., 1985-93; pres., chief exec. officer Coventry Care, Inc., Monongahela, Pa., 1970-86, chmn. bd., chief exec. officer, 1986-87. Adj. prof. law Duquesne U. Pres. Young Dem. Club of Pitts., 1960-66; presdl. elector Pa., 1960; chmn. bd. Mayview State Hosp., Pitts., 1971-75. Served to lt. U.S. Army, 1948-49, 52-53. Mem. ABA, Pa. Bar Assn., Allegheny County Bar Assn. (real property council 1983-86). Office: The Pitt Bldg 213 Smithfield St Pittsburgh PA 15222-2224

GOLD, HERBERT, author; b. Cleve., Mar. 9, 1924; s. Samuel and Frieda (Frankel) G.; m. Edith Zubrin, Apr. 1, 1948 (div. 1956); children: Ann, Judy; m. Melissa Dilworth, Jan. 26, 1968 (div. 1975); children— Nina, Ari, Ethan BA, Columbia, 1948, MA, 1949; postgrad., U. Paris, France, 1949-51; LHD (hon.), Baruch Coll. of CUNY, 1988. Vis. prof. Cornell U., 1958, U. Calif. at Berkeley, 1963, Harvard, summer 1964, Stanford, 1967, U. Calif. at Davis, 1973-79, 85 Author: novels Birth of a Hero, 1951, The Prospect Before Us, 1954, The Man Who Was Not With It, 1956, The Optimist, 1958, Therefore Be Bold, 1961, Salt, 1963, Fathers, 1967, The Great American Jackpot, 1970, Swiftie the Magician, 1974, Waiting for Cordelia, 1977, Slave Trade, 1978, He/She, 1980, Family, 1981, True Love, 1982, Mister White Eyes, 1984, A Girl of Forty, 1986, Dreaming, 1988, She Took My Arm As If She Loved Me, 1997, Daughter Mine, 2000; short stories Love and Like, 1960, The Magic Will, 1971, Lovers & Cohorts: Collected Stories, 1986; essays The Age of Happy Problems, 1962, Biafra Goodbye, 1970, My Last Two Thousand Years, 1973, A Walk on the West Side: California on the Brink, 1981, Travels in San Francisco, 1990, Best Nightmare on Earth: A Life in Haiti, 1991; Bohemia: Where Art, Angst, Love, and Strong Coffee Meet, 1993. Recipient award for best novel Commonwealth Club, 1982; Fulbright fellow, 1950-51; Hudson Rev. fellow, 1956; Guggenheim fellow, 1957; Ford Found. grantee, 1960; recipient award Am. Inst. Arts and Letters, 1957, Longview award, 1959, Sherwood Anderson prize for fiction, 1989. Address: 1051 Broadway St # A San Francisco CA 94133-4205 *As a writer, I try to express a contradictory truth— that life is both tragic and a festival. To combine these two ideas is the highest intention of story.*

GOLD, HYMAN, cellist; b. Cleve., Aug. 26, 1914; s. Isaac and Fanny (Liebenson) g.; m. Ruth Olgin, Feb. 4, 1936; 1 child, Ronald Kenneth; m. Sue DiCicco, Oct. 2, 1982. Student, Cleve. Inst. Music, 1932-38; studies with Victor DeGomez, Cleve., 1938-40; studies with Leonard Rose, 1941-43. Cellist Gold Trio, Cleve., 1935-46, Paul Whiteman and Cleve. Orch., 1940; musician, actor 200 films numerous studios, Los Angeles and Las Vegas, Nev., 1947—; musician, actor Jack Benny TV Show, L.A., 1953-70; musician, actor Phil Harris/Alice Faye Radio Show, 1950—56; cellist numerous symphonies and ballet cos., L.A., 1955-65; condr. Beverly Hills (Calif.) Ensemble, Las Vegas, 1965—; cellist TV commls., L.A., 1960-73; condr. Las Vegas Pops Orch., 1977—; prin. cellist/soloist Nat. Sr. Symphony, New London, Conn., 1990-95; prin. cellist, soloist Las Vegas Civic Symphony, 1994—. Pres. Gold 'N' Cello Rec. Co., 1964—. Performer numerous recs. and club shows, Los Angeles and Las Vegas, 1947—. Grantee Cleve. Inst. Music, 1935, 36, Nev. State Council for Arts, 1977-80. Mem. SAG, Am. Fedn. Musicians, B'nai B'rith. Clubs: Scrabble (Las Vegas). Democrat. Jewish. Avocations: gardening, tennis, bowling, travel. Home and Office: 2416 Laurie Dr Las Vegas NV 89102-2104

GOLD, I. RANDALL, lawyer; b. Chgo., Nov. 2, 1951; Albert Samuel and Lois (Rodrick) G.; m. Marcey Dale Miller, Nov. 18, 1978; children: Eric Matthew, Brian David. BS with high honors, U. Ill., 1973, JD, 1976. Bar: Ill. 1976, U.S. Dist. Ct. (no. dist.) Ill. 1976, Fla. 1979, U.S. Dist. Ct. (so. dist.) Fla. 1979, U.S. Ct. Appeals (5th and 7th cirs.) 1979, U.S. Tax Ct. 1979, U.S. Ct. Appeals (11th cir.) 1981, U.S. Supreme Ct. 1982, U.S. Dist. Ct. (mid. dist.) Fla. 1987; CPA, Ill., Fla. Tax staff Ernst & Ernst, Chgo., 1976-77; asst. state atty. Cook County, Ill., 1977-78, Dade County, Miami, Fla., 1978-82; spl. atty. Miami Strike Force U.S. Dept. Justice, Fla., 1982-87; pvt. practice Miami, 1987-92; asst. U.S. atty. U.S. Dist. Ct. (mid. dist.) Fla., 1992—, dep. chief Orlando div., 2002—. Lectr. Roosevelt U., Chgo., 1976-77; vice chmn. fed. practice com. on criminal sect. Fla. Bar, 1986-88, profl. ethics com., 1992-2001, instr. Rollins Coll. paralegal program, 1992-97; adj. prof. criminal justice program U. Ctrl. Fla., 1994—; adj. prof. law U. Orlando, 1998-99; online faculty U. Phoenix, 2003—. Co-author: Supplement to Vol. 2 of Tax Fraud and Evasion, 6th edit. Co-chmn. Greater Oviedo Cmty. Devel. Program, 1992-93; adviser Jr. Achievement, Chgo., 1976-78, Miami, 1982-84; coach, judge Nat. Trial Competition, U. Miami Law Sch., 1983-86, 88, 90; mentor Seminole County Sch., 1994—; coach mock trial program legal project Dade County Pub. Schs., 1985-89, 91-92, ptnr. program, 1989-92. Mem.: FBA, ATLA, ABA (govt. litigation counsel, complex crimes com.litigation sect.), AICPA, Am. Inns of Ct. (master), Am. Assn. Atty. CPAs, Seminole County Bar Assn., Orange County Bar Assn. (bankruptcy com.), Ctrl. Fla. Bankruptcy Lawyers Assn., Fla. Inst. CPAs (com. on rels. with Fla. Bar 1985—86, bd. dirs. South Dade chpt. 1987—92), Ill. Soc. CPAs, Ill. Bar Assn., Fla. Bar, U. Ill. Alumni Club (v.p.), Delta Sigma Pi. Jewish. Office: 80 N Hughey Ave Ste 201 Orlando FL 32801-2224

GOLD, JAMES PAUL, museum director; b. Seattle, Sept. 26, 1944; s. William J. and Madlyn (Hunsberger) G.; m. Cheryl Magruder, Apr. 6, 1968. BA, Hiram Coll., 1966; MA, Cooperstown Sch. SUNY, 1967. Tchr., curator Elwood Mus., Amsterdam, N.Y., 1968-71; dir. New Eng. Fire and History Mus., Brewster, Mass., 1972-74; site mgr. Senate House, N.Y. State Parks Recreation and Hist. Preservation, Kingston, 1974-77; regional historic sites supr. Bear Mountain, 1977-79; dir. N.Y. State Bur. Historic Sites and Resource Ctr., Waterford, 1979—. Chair Design Rev. commn. Saratoga springs, 1992-2002; mem. N.Y. State Document Conservation Adv. Coun., 1984-87. Mem. Cooperstown Grad. Assn. (bd. dirs. 1983-93), N.Y. State Assn. Museums (bd. dirs. 1985-92), Am. Assn. Museums (bd. dirs. 1988-93), Am. Assn. State and Local History, Assn. Preservation Tech., Mid-Atlantic Assn. Mus. (bd. dirs. 1988-93, 94-98, pres. 1994-97). Democrat. Unitarian Universalist. Avocations: photography, architecture, gardening. Home: 197 Woodlawn Ave Saratoga Springs NY 12866-1507 Office: NY State Parks Recreation and Historic Preservation Peebles Island Waterford NY 12188

GOLD, JEFFREY MARK, investment banker, financial adviser; b. Bronx, N.Y., Jan. 7, 1945; s. Samuel L. and Sylvia E. Gold; m. Lenore N., May 29, 1966; children: Brian, Steven, Samuel. BBA in Acctg, Pace U., 1967. Sr. acct. KPMG Peat, Marwick, N.Y.C., 1967-71; v.p., corp. controller Nat. Patent Devel. Corp., N.Y.C., 1971-78; exec. v.p. fin. and adminstrn., chief fin. officer Esquire, Inc., N.Y.C., 1978-84; exec. v.p. strategic planning and corp. devel. Simon & Schuster div. of Paramount Communications, N.Y.C., 1984; pres. Goldmark Advisers, Inc., N.Y.C., 1985—; chmn. Quarto Holdings, Inc., 1994—; dir. Vision Fund Am., 2002—. Home: 515 E 72nd St New York NY 10021-4032 Office: Goldmark Advisers Inc 276 5th Ave Rm 205 New York NY 10001-4509 E-mail: gold1745@aol.com.

GOLD, JOSEPH, medical researcher; b. Binghamton, N.Y., Jan. 17, 1930; s. Leon and Gertrude J. G.; m. Judith Barbara Taylor, June 12, 1955; children: Shannon Gabriel, Skye Raphael. AB, Cornell U., 1952; MD, Upstate Med. Univ., Syracuse, 1956. Diplomate Nat. Bd. Med. Examiners. Fellow dept. pharmacology Upstate Med. Univ., Syracuse, 1961—62, rsch. asst. prof., 1962—64, asst. prof. pathology, 1964—65; dir. Syracuse Cancer Rsch. Inst., 1965—, trustee, 1965—. Editor: Monsters and Madonnas, The Roots of Christian Antisemitism, 1999; contbr. numerous articles on cancer research and therapy; contbr. chpts. to books. Served with USAF, 1958-61. Recipient Presdl. citation for work in Mercury Astronaut Selection Program, 1960; USPHS postdoctoral rsch. fellow U. Calif. Sch. Medicine, 1956-58; named Disting. Grad. Binghamton Sch. Dist., 1994. Mem. Am. Assn. Cancer Rsch., Am. Assn. for Lab. Animal Sci., N.Y. Acad. Scis., Onondaga County Med. Soc., Med. Soc. State N.Y. Achievements include pioneering work in proposing gluconeogenesis as a biochemical mechanism of cancer cachexia, 1968; development of hydrazine sulfate, 1st specific anti-cachexia drug to be used in human cancer; invention of process for the synthesis and prodn. of DL-Glyceraldehyde-3-phosphate in a pure and stable form; patentee in field. Home: 127 Edgemont Dr Syracuse NY 13214-2010 Office: 600 E Genesee St Syracuse NY 13202-3111

GOLD, JUDITH HAMMERLING, psychiatrist; b. N.Y.C., June 24, 1941; d. James S. and Anne (Linder) Hammerling; m. Edgar Gold, June 27, 1965. MD, Dalhousie U., 1965; DHumL (hon.), Mt. St. Vincent U., 2002. Intern Victoria Gen. Hosp., Halifax, N.S., Can., 1964-65; resident Dalhousie U., Halifax, 1967-71; practice medicine specializing in psychiatry Halifax, 1971—2002; staff psychiatrist Dalhousie U. Student Health Clinic, 1971-73; vis. colleague U. Wales Med. Sch., 1973-75; asst. prof. dept. psychiatry Dalhousie U., Halifax,

1975-78, assoc. prof., 1978-80, part-time, 1980-87; pvt. practice Brisbane, 1998—. Vis. prof., reader in psychotherapy studies U. Queensland Dept. of Psychiatry, Brisbane, 1998-99. Editor: Clinical Practice Series, 1987-2001, 5 books; contbr. articles to profl. jours. Bd. govs. Mt. St. Vincent U., 1981-87, chmn., 1986-87. Med. Research Council Can. fellow, 1973-75; Health and Welfare Bd. Can. grantee, 1976-78 Fellow Am. Psychiat. Assn., Am. Coll. Psychiatrists (1st v.p. 1990-91, pres.-elect 1991-92, pres. 1992-93); mem. Can. Psychiat. Assn. (pres. 1981-82), Royal Coll. Phys. Surgeons Can. (exec. mem. 1992-94, coun. 1991-98), Order Can., Alpha Omega Alpha. Home: 141/501 Queen St Brisbane QLD 4000 Australia E-mail: judithgold@compuserve.com.

GOLD, KAREN F. operations research specialist, educator; b. Boston, Mass., Aug. 19, 1961; d. David and Anna Lee Gold; m. Avner Cohen, June 27, 1999. PhD, UCLA, Los Angeles, CA, 1983—91. Dir. biostatistics and outcomes rsch. ABT Assocs., Bethesda, Md., 1999—; prof. Georgetown U., Wash., DC, 1994—. Recipient Presdl. Award for Undergraduate Rsch. in Math., SUNY, Albany, 1983; fellow U Fellow, U.C.L.A., 1988—90, Psychometrics Fellowship, ETS, Princeton, 1990—92; grantee Investigator on Grants, NIH, NCI, AHRQ, ACAAI and DOD, 1994—; scholar Invited Vis. Scholar, U. of Gothenberg, Sweden, 1993. Fellow: Inst. for Health Care Rsch. and Policy, Georgetown Univ.; mem.: ISPOR (assoc.). Achievements include research in Extensive Pub. in Patient Reported Outcomes Rsch. Avocations: numismatics, glass, Go. Home: 306 Mississippi Ave Silver Spring MD 20910 Personal E-mail: goldk@georgetown.edu. E-mail: karen_gold@abtassoc.com.

GOLD, KEITH DEAN, advertising and design executive; b. Pique, Ohio, Mar. 7, 1956; s. Russell D. and Sondra E. (Reid) Gold; m. Karen L. Bell, May 28, 1977; 2 children. Student, Ringling Sch. Art, 1974—74, U. Fla., 1975—76; BA, U. No. Fla., 1977. Art dir. Market Assocs., Jacksonville, Fla., 1975-76, Ambrose Design, Jacksonville, 1976-77; prin. Gold Advt. and Design, Atlanta, 1977—78; exec. art dir., assoc. creative dir. Bates Worldwide Lewis, Clark and Graham, Atlanta, 1978-81; assoc. creative dir. Price/McNabb, Asheville, NC, 1981—83; sr. v.p., dir. creative svcs., ptnr. Earle, Palmer, Brown, Tampa, Fla., 1983—87; exec. v.p., ptnr., dir. creative svcs. Omnicom, Ann Arbor, Mich., 1987-88; pres., CEO, creative dir. GOLD & Assocs, Ponte Vedra Beach, Fla., 1988—; exec. creative dir, mng. dir. DMB&B/Gold & Assocs., Atlanta, 1993-94. Prof. Kennesaw Coll., Atlanta, 1977-80; bd. dirs., ptnr. Package Material Sales, Inc., Tampa, Fla.; owner GOLD Investments, Inc., Ponte Vedra Beach, Fla.; lectr. in field. Author: Setting the Course of Excellence, 1986, Controlling The Weather, 1999; featured in Kodansha Pubs. World Graphic Design; designer U.S. postage stamp, Olympic posters, numerous books and CD covers; exhibited in shows at Mus. Modern Art, N.Y.C.; work represented in Libr. of Congress, Ringling Mus. Art, Sarasota, Fla. Recipient over 850 awards including 1st pl. awards from Advt. Club N.Y., AIGA, Am. Graphic Design, Clio awards, Vision awards, Communications Arts, Graphis, Zurich Internat. Advt. Festival of N.Y., Internat. Poster Festival, N.Y. Soc. Illustrators, Pub. Broadcasting Sys., Print Mag., Telly awards, Internat. Film and TV Festival N.Y., London Internat. Advt., Global Creative awards, N.Y. Art Dirs. Club, The One Show, Global Mktg. awards, Internat. Festivals, N.Y. Advt. Festival, N.Y. Film Festival, Graphic Design: U.S.A., Creativity, Print Mags. Design Annual, Photo Design; named one of Fla.'s Top All Time Coll. Grads. Fla. Bd. Regents, 1989, U. North Fla. Outstanding Alumnus of Yr., 1999; named one of Top 10 Ad Execs. of the 1980's Wall St. Jour., 50 Comm. Execs. to Watch in the New Millenium Graphic Design: USA. Mem.: Am. Inst. Graphic Arts. Republican. Presbyterian. Avocations: painting, writing, golf, duck hunting. Office: Gold & Assocs Gold Bldg 6000C Sawgrass Village Cir Ponte Vedra Beach FL 32082-5026 Home: 204 Clearwater Dr Ponte Vedra Beach FL 32082

GOLD, KENNETH R. computer software consulting executive; b. Providence, Ky., Aug. 9, 1934; s. R. Vernon Gold and Irene Frances Mitchell; m. Olga Ann Szakacs, Aug. 23, 1958; children: Victoria, Rebecca, Jennifer. AB, Wayne State U., 1960; MBA, Fla. State Christian Coll., 1971. Mktg. mgr. IBM Corp., 1960-70; dir. product devel. GTE Data Svcs., Tampa, Fla., 1970—73; internat. dir. Cincom Systems, Cin., 1973—79; internat. v.p. Mathematica, Princeton, NJ, 1980—88; founder, CEO 4 GL Inc., Miami, Fla., 1989—96, Seaplane Tech., Ft. Myers, Fla., 1996—. Instr. info. tech. U. Toledo, 1968-70. Contbr. articles to profl. jours. With USN 1952-56. Republican. Presbyterian. Avocations: flying, travel. Home: 8005 Wren Ave Hobe Sound FL 33455

GOLD, LEONARD SINGER, librarian, translator; b. Bklyn., July 3, 1934; s. Hyman B. and Gertrude (Singer) G.; m. Stella Schmidt, June 5, 1960; children: Yael, Dalia. BA, McGill U., 1956; MS in Libr. Service, Columbia U., 1966; MA, NYU, 1967, PhD, 1975; student, C. Redmond Art Students League, 1998—2001. Cert. profl. librarian, N.Y. Tchr. high sch., Kiryat Hayim, Israel, 1960-61; tchr. Hugim High Sch., Haifa, Israel, 1961-63; tech. asst. N.Y. Pub. Libr., N.Y.C., 1963-66, chief Jewish div., 1971-98, Dorot chief libr. Jewish div., bibliographer Jewish studies, 1987-98, asst. dir. Jewish, Oriental and Slavonic studies, 1980-88. Chmn. Jewish and Middle East studies program com. Rsch. Librs. Group, Inc., 1989-91; curator hist. exhbns. A Sign and A Witness: 2000 Years of Hebrew Books and Illuminated Manuscripts, N.Y. Pub. Libr., 1988-89, The Dead Sea Scrolls: Ancient Civilization, Modern Scholarship, N.Y. Pub. Libr., 1993-94. Translator (Nathan Shaham): The Other Side of the Wall, 3 novellas, 1983; editor: A Sign and A Witness: 2000 Years of Hebrew Books and Illuminated Manuscripts, 1998; exhibitions include Bob Laurie Gallery, N.Y.C., 2000, Broome St. Gallery, 2001, 2002; assoc. editor: Jewish Book Annual, 1979—94; contbr. Astor fellow, 1986-87. Mem. Assn. Jewish Librs. (pres. 1974-76, lifetime mem. award 1998), Coun. Archives and Rsch. Librs. in Jewish Studies (pres. 1978-80, disting. svc. award 1998), Jewish Book Coun. (v.p. 1980-90, pres. 1990-94), Assn. Jewish Studies, Rsch. Librs. Group (chmn. Jewish and Mid. East studies program com. 1989-91, mem. programs adv. group 1991-92), Jewish Publ. Soc. (editl. com. 1986-2002, nat. coun. 2002—). E-mail: LGold10545@aol.com.

GOLD, LOIS MEYER, artist; b. N.Y.C., June 2, 1945; d. Seymour Roy and Carol (Rubin) Meyer; m. Leonard Marshall Gold, Oct. 14, 1971 (dec. 1998); 1 child, Eric Marshall. BA, Boston U., 1967; MA, Columbia U., 1970. Tchr. Lenox Sch., N.Y.C., 1972-84, Columbia Grammar Sch., N.Y.C., 1975-76; artist, freelance N.Y.C., 1976—; represented by Lizan-Tops Gallery, Easthampton, NY, Canyon Ranch, Lenox, Mass., Martha Keats Gallery, Santa Fe, Karin Zatt, L.A., Ruzetti and Gow, N.Y.C. Prin. works include Canyon Ranch, Bristol Myers Squibb, Imperial Oil, Bed, Bath and Beyond, Boston U., others, exhibitions include juried selection Florence Bienniale, 2003, Represented in permanent collections Herbert F. Johnson Mus. Art, Ithaca, N.Y., Boston U. Libr., corp. collections including Bklyn. Union Gas Co.; featured artist The Artists Mag., 1993, 2000 (Landscape award, 1993), Dan's Papers, 1999—2003, Pastel Artist Internat., 1999, Decor, 1999, Southwest Art, 2001, others, poster art represented in (films) My Fat Greek Wedding, Art International, 2003; various original posters, Romm Art; contbr. works to profl. jours., work to books. Recipient Artists Mag. Landscape award, 1991, 1993, juried invitation, Florence Biennial, 2003; scholar Pastel Soc. Am. Juried, 1994—95. Mem.: Studio Ctr. Artist's Assn., Cassatt Pastel Soc., Nat. Assn. Women Artists (Pauline Law award 1988, Works on Paper award 1988), Pastel Soc. Am., Internat. Assn. Pastel Socs. Avocations: bicycling, ballroom dancing, tennis, skiing, bicycling. Home: 45 E End Ave New York NY 10028-7953

GOLD, LORNE W. Canadian government official; b. Saskatoon, Sask., Can., June 7, 1928; s. Alexander Stewart and Grace Dora (Davis) G.; m. Elizabeth Joan L'Ami, Sept. 8, 1951; children: Catherine Anne, Patricia Ellen, Judith Sharon, Kenneth Robert. BSc, U. Sask., 1950; MSc in Physics, McGill U., 1952, PhD, 1970. Research officer div. bldg. research Nat. Research Coucil Can., Ottawa, Ont., 1950-52, head snow and ice sect., 1953-69, head geotech. sect., 1969-74, asst. dir. div., 1974-79, assoc. dir. div., 1979-86, chmn., assoc. com. geotech. research, 1976-83, guest worker inst. research on constrn., 1987; rschr. emeritus Nat. Rsch. Coun. of Can., Ottawa, Ont., 1988—. Canadian del. to Intern. Union of Testing and Research Labs. for Materials and Structures, 1982-87, bd. dirs. Coun. Internat. du Batiment, 1983-86; sr. visiting scientist Ctr. for Cold Oceans Resources Engring., Meml. U. of Newfoundland, 1987-88; vis. rschr. Inst. for Marine dynamics, NRC of Can., 1990-91. Author: The Canadian Habbakuk Project, 1993. Chair coun. Radiau Park United Ch., Ottawa, 2003—. Fellow Royal Soc. Can. (sec. Acad. Sci. 1997-2001), Can. Acad. Engring., Engring. Inst. Can., Can. Soc. Civil Engrs. (Horst Leipholz medal 1991); mem. Internat. Glaciol. Soc. (pres. 1978-81), Assn. Profl. Engrs. Ont., Engring. Inst. Can. (hon. treas. 1991-96), Can. Geotech. Soc. Mem. United Ch. of Canada. Home: 1903 Illinois Ave Ottawa ON Canada K1H 6W5 Office: Nat Rsch Coun of Can Inst for Rsch in Constrn Ottawa ON Canada K1A 0R6

GOLD, MARK STEPHEN, psychopharmacologist, physician; b. N.Y.C., May 6, 1949; s. Meyer M. and Helene (Levy) G.; m. Janice Finn, June 19, 1971; 4 children. BA, Washington U., 1971; MD, U. Fla., 1975. Neurobehavior fellow Yale U. Sch. Medicine, 1975-78; dir. rsch. Fair Oaks Hosp., Summit, N.J., 1978-91; vis. prof. psychiatry and neurosci. Coll. Medicine U. Fla., 1991—, prof. dept. neurosci., psychiatry, cmty. health, family med., 1992—, disting. prof., 1999—. Cons. substance abuse unit Yale U. Sch. Medicine, 1979—89; founder Nat.Cocaine Hotline 800-COCAINE, 1983; cons. Office Drug Abuse Policy White House, 1988, William Bennett Kitchen Cabinet, 1988—90; spl. cons. Office Nat. Drug Policy, 1995—, DEA Mus., P.R.I.D.E., Physicians for Prevention, DARE, Child Welfare League, Nat. Families in Action, Gateway Rehab. Svcs.; spl. cons. alumni bd. U. Fla. Coll. Medicine; spl. cons. student life Washington U. Author: 800-Cocaine, 1984, Stop Drugs at Work, 1986, Wonder Drugs, 1987, The Good News About Depression, 1987, rev. edit., 1995, The Facts About Drugs and Alcohol, 1987, Marijuana, 1989, The Good News About Panic, Anxiety and Phobias, 1989, Alcohol, 1991, Dual Diganosis in Substance Abuse, 1991, The Good News About Drugs and Alcohol, 1991, Cocaine, 1993, Pharmacological Therapies for Drug and Alcohol Addiction, 1995, Tobacco, 1995, Smoking and Illicit Drug Use, 1999, Facts About Tobacco, Alcohol and Other Drugs; co-editor: Internat. Jour. Psychiatry in Medicine, Advances in Substance and Alcohol Abuse, Jour. Substance Abuse Treatment, ASAM Prins. Addiction Medicine, Am. Jour. Drug and Alcohol; editor: drugs and alcohol lifescape.com; contbr. ; patentee in field. Named Disting. Alumni, Washington U.; named one of Today's Most Valuable Persons, USA Today, 1986, People of Yr., 1987, Best Psychiatrists in Am., Good Housekeeping, 1995, Best Doctors in Am., 1993—; named to Disting. Alumni Wall of Fame, U. Fla. Coll. Medicine; recipient Seymour F. Lustman award for rsch., Yale U. Sch. Medicine, 1978, Founds Fund prize for rsch. in psychiatry, Am. Psychiat. Assn. Found, 1981, Presdl. award for disting. leadership in pychiat. rsch., Nat. Assn. Pvt. Psychiat. Hosps., 1982, Silver Anvil award, Am. Coun. Drug Edn., 1984, Nat. Fedn. Parents Award, 1986; grantee, NIMH. Fellow Am. Coll. Clin. Pharmacology, Am. Psychiat. Assn., Am. Coll. Forensic Medicine; mem. AAAS, Am. Acad. Psychiatrists in Alcoholism and Addiction, Am. Soc. Addiction Medicine, Soc. Neurosci., Biol. Psychiatry, Internat. Soc. Psychoneuroendocrinology, Coll. on Problems of Drug Dependence. Office: McKnight Brain Inst Depts Neurosci and Psychiatry PO Box 100183 Gainesville FL 32610-0183 Fax: 352-294-0197. E-mail: msgold@psych.med.ufl.edu.

GOLD, MARTIN ELLIOTT, lawyer, educator; b. N.Y.C., Jan. 6, 1946; s. Herman and Rose (Zippin) G.; 1 stepchild, Ariane. BA, Cornell U., 1967; JD, Harvard U, 1970, MPA, 1971. Bar: N.Y. 1972, U.S. Dist. Ct. (so. and ea. dists.) N.Y. 1974, U.S. Ct. Appeals (2d cir.) 1974. With Operation Crossroads Africa, The Gambia, 1965; cons. U.S. Dept. Justice, 1968; assoc. Freshfields, London, 1969; rsch. fellow Ctr. Law and Devel. Sri Lanka, Cambridge, Mass., 1971-73; assoc. Debevoise & Plimpton, N.Y.C., 1973-78; chief econ. devel. divsn. N.Y.C. Law Dept., 1978-85, N.Y.C. dir. corp. law, 1980-85; ptnr. Sidley Austin Brown & Wood, N.Y.C., 1985—. Adj. prof. Columbia U., 1987—; guest lectr. Fordham U., Yale U., Cornell U., U.S. Conf. of Mayors, U.S. Justice Dept., others. Author: Law and Social Change: A Study of Land Reform in Sri Lanka, 1977; contbr. articles to profl. jours. Mem. Legal Aid Soc., 1975-81, Cornell Real Estate Coun., 1988—; bd. dirs. Environ. Action Coalition, 1988-2002, INFORM, 1989—, J.F. Kennedy Sch., Tri State Coun., 1991-97; chmn. Ridgefield Coun. Lake Assns. Recipient awards Rockefeller Bros. Fund, 1979, 80, Fund for City N.Y., 1981, Leadership award J.F. Kennedy Sch. Mem. ABA, Internat. Assn. Attys. and Execs. in Corp. Real Estate, Nat. Coun. for Pub. and Pvt. Partnerships, Natural Resources Def. Coun., Assn. Bar City N.Y. (environ, mcpl., energy and real poperty and housing law coms.), Common Cause, Cornell Club.

GOLD, MICHAEL EVAN, law educator; b. Oakland, Calif., Apr. 14, 1943; s. Ellis and Ruth Lorraine Gold; m. Sarah Dogbe, Apr. 20, 1971; children: Elijah Laoba, Kebbeh Calypso. BA, U. Calif., Berkeley, 1965; LLB, Stanford U., 1967. Bar: Calif. 72, NY 78, U.S. Supreme Ct. 78. Vol. Peace Corps, Liberia, 1968—70; atty. Schwartz, Steinsapir & Dohrmann, LA, 1972—75; assoc. prof. San Fernando Valley Coll. Law, LA, 1975—77, Cornell U., Ithaca, NY, 1977—. Author: A Dialogue on Comparable Worth, 1983; contbr. articles to profl. jours. Home: 102 Oxford Pl Ithaca NY 14850-4720 Office: Cornell U Ives Hall Ithaca NY 14853-3901 Office Fax: 607-255-6840 . Business E-Mail: meg3@cornell.edu.

GOLD, PAUL ERNEST, psychology educator, behavioral neuroscience educator; b. Detroit, Jan. 7, 1945; s. Hyman and Sylvia Gold; children: Scott David Gold, Zachary Alexander Korol-Gold. BA, U. Mich., 1966; MS, U. N.C., 1968; PhD, 1971. NIH postdoctoral fellow, lectr. psychobiology U. Calif., Irvine, 1972-76; asst. prof. U. Va., Charlottesville, 1976-78, assoc. prof., 1978-81, prof., 1981-97, Commonwealth prof., 1997—99, dir. neurosci. grad. program, 1991-95; prof. Binghamton (N.Y.) U., 1999-2000, U. Ill., Urbana-Champaign, 2000—. Dir. Med. Scholars Program U. Ill. Coll. Medicine, Urbana-Champaign, 2000—02, mem. exec. com. Inst. Aging, 2001—. Editor Psychobiology, 1990-97, Neurobiology of Learning and Memory, 1998—; contbr. numerous articles to sci. publs. Mem. Commonwealth of Va. Alzheimer's and Related Disorders Commn., 1998-99. Recipient James McKeen Cattell award, 1983, Sesquicentennial Assn. award, U. Va., 1983, 90-93, Disting. Alumni award U. N.C., Chapel Hill, 2000; named APA Master Lectr., 2000; NIH fellow, 1967. Fellow APA (com. animal rsch. & ethics), AAAS, Am. Psychol. Soc. (mem. com. 1990-91, program com. 1991); mem. Soc. for Neurosci. (com. on animals in rsch. 1993-98), NSF Adv. Panel for Behavioral and Computational Neurosci., 1993-96. Office: U Ill at Urbana-Champaign Dept Psychology Champaign IL 61820 E-mail: pgold@uiuc.edu.

GOLD, PETER FREDERICK, lawyer; b. N.Y.C., Nov. 10, 1945; s. John and Dolores (Soyer) G.; m. Dee Crafferty, June 6, 1982; children: Joshua, Katharine. BA, Cornell U., 1967; MSc, London Sch. Econs., 1968; JD, NYU, 1971. Bar: D.C. 1988, N.Y. 1972, U.S. Dist. Ct. (so. dist.) N.Y. 1972, U.S. Dist. Ct. (ea. dist.) N.Y. 1972. Assoc. atty. Paul, Weiss, Rifkind, Wharton & Garrison, N.Y.C., 1971-75; legis. dir. Senator Gary Hart, Washington, 1975-81; ptnr. Wellford, Wegman, Krulwich, Gold & Hoff, Washington, 1981-84, Winthrop, Stimson, Putnam & Roberts, Washington, 1984-94; pres. The Gold Group, Chartered, Washington, 1994—, C.G. Sloan & Co., Inc., 1995-97. Editor in chief Review of Law and Social Change, 1970. Nat. policy dir. Hart for Pres. Campaign, Washington, 1984; chmn., founder First Book, Washington, 1992—; dir. Share Our Strength, Washington, 1990—; mem. Clinton-Gore Transition Team, Washington, 1992. Recipient Disting. Visitor Program European Econ. Community, Brussels, Belgium, 1982. Mem. D.C. Bar Assn., Fed. Bar Assn., N.Y.C. Bar Assn., Kenwood Golf & Country Club, Four Streams Golf Club. Democrat. Jewish. Avocations: tennis, golf. Home: 13640 Glenhurst Rd North Potomac MD 20878-3921 Office: The Gold Group Chartered 1319 F St NW Ste 1000 Washington DC 20004-1106

GOLD, PHIL, immunologist, educator, researcher; b. Montreal, Sept. 17, 1936; m. Evelyn Katz; 3 children. BSc in Physiology with honors, McGill U., Montreal, 1957, MSc, MD, 1961, PhD in Physiology, 1965; DSc (hon.), McMaster U., 1986. Licentiate Med. Coun. Can. Jr. rotating intern Montreal Gen. Hosp., 1961—62, jr. asst. resident in medicine, 1962—63, sr. resident in medicine, 1965—66, jr. asst. physician, asst. and assoc. physician, 1967—73, sr. physician, 1973—2003, physician-in-chief, 1980-95, dir. divsn. clin. immunology and allergy, 1977—80, dir. McGill U. Med. Clinic, 1980—95, also sr. investigator Research Inst.; faculty dept. physiology McGill U., 1964—, mem. faculty of medicine, 1965—, prof. medicine and clin. medicine, 1973—, chmn. dept. medicine and clin. medicine, 1985—90, prof. physiology, 1974—, prof. oncology, 1989—, mem. faculty of medicine exec. com. representing clin. depts., 1985—, D. G. Cameron prof. medicine (inauguaral), 1987—; exec. dir. Clin. Rsch. Ctr. Mont. Gen. Hosp. and McGill U. Hosp. Ctr., 1995—. Vis. scientist Pub. Health Research Inst. N.Y.C., 1967-68; Chester M. Jones Meml. lectr. Mass. Gen. Hosp., 1974; vis. prof. U. Caracas, Venezuela, 1974; Squires Club vis. prof. Wellesley Hosp., Toronto, 1983; Cecil H. and Ida Green vis. prof., 1984 autumn lectures U. Brit. Columbia; cons. in allergy and immunology Mt. Sinai Hosp., St. Agathe des Monts, Quebec, 1975—; hon. cons. dept. medicine Royal Victoria Hosp., Montreal; cons. dept. internal medicine Douglas Hosp. Ctr., Montreal; vice chmn. med. adv. com. Council of Physicians, Dentists and Pharmacists, 1985-90; mem. Conseil d'Adminstrn., Found. Quebecoise du Cancer, 1986-88, adv. com. Burroughs Wellcome fellowship fund, 1998—; health com. mem. Centre d'Entreprises et d'Innovation de Montreal, 1996—; Sir Arthur Sims travelling prof., 1998. Mem. editorial bd. Clin. Immunology and Immunopathology, 1972—, Immunopharmacology, 1978—, Diagnostic Gynecology and Obstetrics, 1978-83, Oncodevelopmental Biology and Medicine, 1979—, Modern Medicine of Can., 1984-90, Jour. Internal Medicine, 1988—, Canadians for Health Rsch., 1989—, Current Therapeutic Rsch., 1992—, Nutrition Quar., 1992—; editorial cons. Jour. Chronic Diseases, 1981-84; mem. editorial adv. bd. Cancer Research, 1971-73, assoc. editor 1973-80; contbg. editor Practical Allergy and Immunology, 1991—; editl. bd. Can. Jour. Allergy & Clin. Immunology, 1996—; contbr. over 140 articles to med. jours. External referee Can. Red Cross Soc. Recipient Hiram Mills Gold medal, Mosby Scholarship Book award, Wood Gold medal, E.W.R. Steacie prize Nat. Rsch. Coun. Can., 1973, Can. Silver Jubilee medal, 1977, Johann-Georg-Zemmerman prize for cancer rsch. Medizinische Hochschule, Hannover, Germany, 1978, Gold medal award of merit Grad. Soc. McGill U., 1979, Internat. award Gardner Found., Ernest C. Manning prize, F.N.G. Starr award Izzak Walton Killam prize Can. Coun., 1985, Tower of Hope award Israel Cancer Rsch. Fund, 1985, Sci. Achievement medal Govt. of Italy, 1990, Agora trophy Ambassador's Club, 1991, Internat. Soc. Oncodevel. Biol. Medicine Internat. Abbott award, 1992, Commemorative medal 125th Anniversary of Can. Confedn., Govt. of Can., 1992, Carl Goresky Meml. award, 1999, Christie award Can. Assn. of Profs. of Medicine, 1999, 20th Anniversary of L'Actualité Medicale award for outstanding contbns. to medicine, 2000, Queen Elizabeth II Golden Jubilee medal, 2002; named Most Outstanding Can. Med. Personality of the past 25 years, MacLean's Mag., 1986; decorated companion Order of Can., officer L'ordre nat. du Quebec, Great Montrealer, 1986; Knight Comdr., Sovereign Order St. John Jerusalem, Knights of Malta, 1986; MacDonald scholar, J. Francis Williams scholar, Univ. scholar. Fellow AAAS; mem. Internat. Assn. Health Profls. (chmn. 1998). Achievements include discovery of Carcinoembryonic Antigen (CEA). Office: Clin Rsch Ctr Montreal Gen Hosp 1650 Cedar Ave Montreal QC Canada H3G 1A4 E-mail: phil.gold@mcgill.ca.

GOLD, PHRADIE KLING **See KLING, PHRADIE**

GOLD, RICHARD N. management consultant; b. Chgo., May 27, 1945; s. Irving Louis and Victoria (Saltzman) G.; m. Renee Bonnie Rein, Nov. 3, 1968; children: Jedd Steven, Amanda Caryn. BSI, U. Wis., 1967; MBA with honors, Columbia U., 1971; MA with honors, NYU, 1971. Tchr., supr. Ocean-Hill Brownsville, N.Y.C. pub. schs., 1968-71; brand mgr. packaged soap and detergent divsn. Procter & Gamble Co., Cin., 1971-76; exec. v.p. Glendinning Assocs., Westport, Conn., 1976-81; pres. R.N. Gold & Co., 1981—; producer, ptnr. Enterplan, N.Y.C., 1983-85; dir. mktg. Downtown Coun., Cin., 1975-77. Bd. dirs. Hampton Products Internat. Corp., SoftLock.com Inc., MF&A Inc., Autolink.com Data Nat. Corp.; bd. advs. L.A. Brewing Co., Designer Fragrances Internat., Evolve Products Inc., CursorMate.com. Mem.: Am. Mgmt. Assn., Pres. Assn. Avocations: sports, theatre, collecting antique electronic musical devices. Office: RN Gold & Co 19 Rowayton Ave Rowayton CT 06853-1627 E-mail: rngoldco@aol.com.

GOLD, RICK L. federal agency administrator; b. Rexburg, Idaho, June 25, 1946; s. Raymond Russell and Thelma (Lee) G.; m. Anamarie Sanone, May 14, 1988; children: Nanette Phillips, Russell. BSCE, Utah State U., 1968, MSCE, 1970. Registered profl. engr., Colo., Mont., Utah. Hydraulic engr. U.S. Bur. Reclamation, Provo, Utah, 1969-73, project hydrologist Durango, Colo., 1973-75, regional hydrologist Billings, Mont., 1975-81, spl. asst. to regional dir. Washington, 1981-82, asst. planning officer Billings, 1982-83, projects mgr. Durango, Colo., 1983-88, regional planning officer Salt Lake City, 1988-90, asst. regional dir., 1990-94, dep. regional dir., 1994—2000, regional dir., 2001—. Mem. water quality com. Internat. Joint Commn. Study on Garrison Divsn. Unit, Billings, 1975-77; fed. negotiator Cost Sharing and Indian Water Rights Settlement, Durango, 1986-88; chmn. Cooperating Agy. on Glen Canyon Dam EIS, Salt Lake City, 1990-94. Contbr. articles to profl. jours.; author papers. Mem. Rotary Internat., Durango, 1985-87; bd. dirs. United Way of La Plata County, Durango, 1983-88; chmn. Combined Fed. Campaign, La Plata County, 1985; bd. dirs. U.S. Com. on Irrigation and Drainage, 1994-2000. Mem. ASCE. Office: US Bur Reclamation 125 S State St Salt Lake City UT 84138-1102

GOLD, ROSLYN, social worker, educator; b. Bklyn., July 17, 1924; d. Abraham and Esther (Steinberg) Smith; m. Simon Gold; children: Jay Alexander, Alice Louise. BS, Queens Coll., 1972; MSW, Yeshiva U., N.Y.C., 1977; M in Gerontalogy, Yeshiva U., 1980; DSW, Yeshiva U., N.Y.C., 1990. Cert. psychoanalytical psychotherapy, group psychotherapy. Tchr. home econs., food and nutrition, family and child enrichment N.Y. Bd. Edn., Queens, 1972-75; dir. sr. ctr. Jewish Assn. for Svcs. to the Aged, Queens, 1977-81; case mgr. JASA, Queens, 1981-85; pvt. practice Queens, 1985—; dir. svcs. to the aged L.I. Consultation Ctr., 1988-90; pvt. practice Forest Hills, N.Y., 1987—; founder/dir. Hillcrest Leisure Group, 1992—. Mem. (pres. Queens chap. 1990-92) N.Y. Soc. Clin. Social Workers. Home: Bldg 1-26D 27126 Grand Central Pkwy Floral Park NY 11005-1209 Office: 10923 71st Rd Apt 2J Forest Hills NY 11375-4856 E-mail: gzahav@aol.com.

GOLD, RUTH FORMAN, education educator; b. Bklyn., Oct. 10, 1932; d. Louis and Bertha (Wolkowitz) Forman; m. Bernard Gold, Nov. 23, 1952 (dec. May 1994); children: Alan Mark, Anyta Joan Costales. BA, Bklyn. coll., 1953, MA, 1955; EdD, Columbia U., 1973. Tchr. N.Y.C. Pub. Schs., Bklyn., 1953-58, East Meadow (N.Y.) Schs., 1958-60; lectr. Hofstra U., Hempstead, N.Y., 1961-72; from asst. prof. to prof. Adelphi U., Garden City, N.Y., 1972-86; prof. spl. edn. Hofstra U., 1986—2000, chair dept. counseling, rsch., spl. edn. and rehab., 1993-96, coord. gerontology, 1996—2003, dir. Ctr. for Gerontology, 1997—. Mem. adv. bd. C.W. Post Tchr. Tng. Grant, Greenvale, N.Y., 1992-95, C.W. Post Tapp Project, 2001-2002; cons. Ctr. for Devel. Disabilities, Woodbury, N.Y., 1991-94. Co-author: Education the Learning Disabled, 1982; contbr. chpts. to books. Named Person of the Yr. Long Is. Assn. Spl. Edn. Adminstrs. Mem. Assn. for Children with Learning Disabilities (mem. adv. bd. 1972-84, bd. dirs. 1984-90, bd. trustees 1990—), Coun. for Exceptional Children (v.p. N.Y. State chpt. 1987-88, pres. N.Y. state divsn. for early childhood 1984-85). Office: Hofstra U Hempstead Tpke Hempstead NY 11549-0001

GOLD, SHARON CECILE, artist, educator; b. N.Y.C., Feb. 28, 1949; d. Henry Joseph and Betty (Kopan) G.; m. William McKay Watson III, July 12, 1992; 1 child, Miranda Cecile. Student, CUNY, 1967-68, Columbia U., 1968-70; BFA, Pratt Inst., 1976. Adj. prof. Art NYU, 1983; vis. artist SUNY, Purchase, 1985; assoc. prof. painting and critical theory Syracuse (N.Y.) U., 1986—; vis. artist The Art Inst. Chgo., Chgo., 1990. Lectr. in field; guest critic Sch. Visual Arts, N.Y.C., 1987, N.Y. Studio Sch., 1988. Solo exhibits include Stephen Rosenberg Gallery, N.Y.C., 1987, 89, 91, 55 Mercer St., N.Y.C., 1986, John Davis Gallery, Akron, Ohio, 1986, Pam Adler Gallery, N.Y.C., 1986; group exhibits include IRIS House, N.Y.C., 1992, Everson Mus. of Art, Syracuse, 1991, ARTSTAR, L.A., 1991, Stephen Rosenberg Gallery, N.Y., 1991, Rose Art Mus. Brandeis U., 1990, Robert Pardo Gallery, N.Y.C., 2001; performance/video works include A Video Tape 1990-1991 Stephen Rosenberg Gallery, 1991, North South Consonance St. Stephen's Ch., N.Y.C., 1984. Pratt Inst. Acad. fellow, 1974-76, NEA grantee, 1981, Penny McCall Found. grantee, 1988. Home: 10 Leonard St New York NY 10013-2929 E-mail: scgold@ix.netcom.com.

GOLD, SIMEON, lawyer; b. Hartford, Conn., Jan. 3, 1949; s. Charles and Claire (Goldschein) G.; m. Heide Aline Turkel, Aug. 30, 1970; children: Jana, Craig. BS, Cornell U., 1970; JD, Harvard U., 1973. Bar: N.Y., U.S. Dist. Ct. (so. dist.) N.Y., U.S. Ct. Appeals (2d cir.). Assoc. Weil, Gotshal & Manges LLP, N.Y.C., 1973-81, ptnr., 1981—. Bd. dirs. Lawyers Alliance for N.Y. Contbr. articles to profl. jours. Mem. Coun. of Bus. Exec. Assn. for Help of Retarded Children, N.Y.C., Legal Aid Soc., N.Y.C.; bd. trustees Dalton Sch., 1997-2000. Mem. ABA, N.Y. State Bar Assn. (chair bus. law sect. 2000-01, chair corp. law com. 1993-97), Assn. of Bar of City of N.Y., N.Y. County Lawyers Assn., Harmonie Club, Old Oaks Country Club. Avocations: skiing, tennis, golf, travel. Office: Weil Gotshal & Manges LLP 767 5th Ave Fl Conc1 New York NY 10153-0119 E-mail: simeon.gold@weil.com.

GOLD, STANLEY PHILLIP, diversified investments executive; b. 1942; AB, U. Calif., 1964; JD, U. So. Calif., 1967. Ptnr. Gang Tyre and Brown, 1967-85, Shamrock Holdings Inc., Burbank, Calif., 1985—; pres., CEO, Shamrock Holdings, Burbank. Office: Shamrock Holdings Inc 4444 W Lakeside Dr Burbank CA 91505-4054 E-mail: sgold@shamrock.com.

GOLD, STEPHEN ALLEN, lawyer; b. Bklyn., May 24, 1942; s. George and Rose (Kaplan) G.; m. Winifred Atlas, June 5, 1966; children— Aliza, Shoshana. A.B., Columbia U., 1964; J.D., St. Johns U., 1967. Bar: N.Y. 1968, D.C. 70, U.S. Ct. Appeals (D.C. cir.) 1971, U.S. Supreme Ct. 1972. Atty., adviser FCC, Washington, 1967-68; assoc. law offices Samuel Miller, Washington, 1968-72; asst. gen. counsel Nat. Cable TV Assn., Washington, 1972-74; trial atty. U.S. Postal Rate Commn., Washington, 1974-75, dep. gen. counsel, 1975-82, consumer advocate, 1982— . Contbr. articles to legal jours. Pres. Lawyers North Civic Assn., Vienna, Va., 1981-83. Mem. Fed. Bar Assn. (chmn. postal law com. 1980-82), Am. Contract Bridge League (No. Va.). Jewish. Home: 2202 Loch Lomond Dr Vienna VA 22181-3231 Office: US Postal Rate Commn 1333 H St NW Washington DC 20005-4707

GOLD, STEVEN BRUCE, lawyer; b. Long Beach, Calif. s. Larry and Ruth (Geller) G.; m. Michelle Gonzalez-Gold; children: Ellena, Shannon, Erica, Samantha. BA in Environ. Studies with high honors, U. Calif., Santa Barbara, 1985; JD, U. Calif., Davis, 1988; cert. in hazardous materials mgmt, U. Calif., San Diego, 1992, OSHA HAZWOPER cert., 1999. Bar: Calif. 1988, U.S. Dist. Ct. (so. dist.) 1988. Dep. city atty. San Diego City Atty's. Office, 1989—, spl. dep. dist. atty., 1990-95, 97—. Instr. Office Spl. Investigations USAF, 1992-96, Univ. San Diego, 1992-95, Calif. Dist. Atty's. Assn., 1990—, Fed. Law Enforcement Tng. Ctr. Co-author: The Complete Guide to Hazardous Material Enforcement and Liability, 1987; contbr. articles to mags. Bd. dirs. Kids on the Block, San Diego, 1996—, pres. 1998—; reviewer Boy Scouts Am., 1994—. Recipient Gov.'s Restitution award, 1998, 40 Under 40 award San Diego Met. Mag., 2000; named Prosecutor of Yr., 2000. Mem. State Bar Calif. (environ. law sect.), Air and Waste Mgmt. Assn. (chair pub. rels. 1997-98, 2002-03), Eagle Scout Alumni Assn. Office: San Diego City Atty Office Consumer Environ Prot Unit 1200 3rd Ave Ste 700 San Diego CA 92101-4103 E-mail: sgold@sandiego.gov.

GOLD, STEVEN MICHAEL, lawyer; b. Bklyn., Sept. 19, 1953; s. Joseph and Gladys (Guss) G.; m. Susan Schwartz, Jan. 9, 1977; children: Rachel, David, Hannah. BA, Hobart Coll., 1975; JD, Cornell U., 1978. Bar: Conn. 1979, N.Y. 1979, U.S. Dist. Ct. Conn. 1979, U.S. Dist. Ct. (no. dist.) N.Y. 1979. Confidential law asst. 3d dept. appellate div. N.Y. Supreme Ct., Albany, 1978-79; assoc. Schatz & Schatz, Ribicoff & Kotkin, Hartford & Stamford, Conn., 1979-86, ptnr. Stamford, 1987-96, Shipman & Goodwin, LLP, Stamford, 1996—. Treas. Cmty. Coun. Westport/Weston, Conn., 1985, 1st v.p., 1987, bd. dirs., 1985-87; bd. dirs., counsel Urban League Greater Bridgeport, 1987-92; bd. dirs., v.p. Stamford Symphony Soc., 1990-95, counsel, 1994-95; bd. dirs. Nursing and Home Care, 1996-97, Women's Bus. Devel. Ctr., 2001-. Mem. ABA, N.Y. State Bar Assn., Conn. Bar Assn., Stamford/Norwalk Regional Bar Assn. (dir. 2002—), Assn. Comml. Fin. Attys., Assn. Corporate Growth, Nat. Assn. Transp. Practitioners (treas. Conn. chpt. 1983-85), Entrepreneurship Inst. (adv. bd. 1989-91), Phi Delta Phi, Pi Gamma Mu. Democrat. Jewish. Avocation: squash. Office: Shipman & Goodwin LLP One Landmark Sq Stamford CT 06901 E-mail: sgold@goodwin.com.

GOLD, STUART WALTER, lawyer; b. N.Y.C., Mar. 3, 1949; s. Morris I. and Barbara (Walters) G.; m. Michele M. Cardella, June 26, 1983. BA in Polit. Sci., Bklyn. Coll., 1969; JD, NYU, 1972. Bar: N.Y. 1973, U.S. Supreme Ct. 1983, U.S. Ct. Appeals (2d, 3d, 7th, 8th, 9th and D.C. cirs.). Law clk. to judge U.S. Dist. Ct. (so. dist.) N.Y., 1972-73; assoc. Cravath, Swaine & Moore LLP, N.Y.C., 1973-80, ptnr., 1980—. Bd. dirs. N.Y. Lawyers for Pub. Interest, N.Y.C., 1982—. Mem. ABA, N.Y. State Bar Assn., Assn. of Bar City of N.Y. Democrat. Avocations: tennis, travel. Office: Cravath Swaine & Moore 825 8th Ave Fl 39 New York NY 10019-7475

GOLD, THOMAS, astronomer, educator; b. Vienna, May 22, 1920; s. Max and Josefine (Martin) G.; m. Merle Eleanor Tuberg, June 21, 1947; children— Linda, Lucy, Tanya; m. Carvel Lee Beyer, Dec. 27, 1972; 1 dau., Lauren. BA, Cambridge (Eng.) U., 1942, MA, 1945, Sc.D., 1969; fellow, Trinity Coll., Cambridge, 1947; MA (hon.), Harvard, 1957. Lectr. physics Cambridge (Eng.) U., 1948-52; chief asst. to Astronomer Royal, Gt. Britain, 1952-56; prof. astronomy Harvard, 1958, Robert Wheeler Willson prof., 1958-59; prof. astronomy, dir. Center Radiophysics and Space Research Cornell U., 1959-81, chmn. dept., 1959-68, asst. v.p. for research, 1970-71, John L. Wetherill prof., 1971-86. Contbr. articles to profl. jours. Hon. fellow Trinity Coll., Cambridge, 1986—. Fellow Royal Soc. London, Am. Geophys. Union; mem. U.S. Nat. Acad. Sci., Am. Philos. Soc., Am. Acad. Arts and Scis., Royal Astron. Soc. (Gold medal 1985; past councillor), Am. Astron. Soc. Home and Office: 7 Pleasant Grove Ln Ithaca NY 14850-2548 E-mail: tg21@cornell.edu.

GOLD, WILLIAM ELLIOTT, health care management consultant, educator; b. Bklyn., Oct. 21, 1948; s. Theodore David and Debra (Fridovich) G.; m. Nili Rachel Scharf, June 1, 1972; children: Avitai, Doria Michelle. BA, SUNY, Stony Brook, 1970; MSS, Hebrew U. of Jerusalem, Israel, 1972; PhD, U. Minn., 1982. Rsch. asst. Hebrew U. of Jerusalem, 1971-72; cons. Dept. Health, Mpls., 1973-74; researcher Mt. Sinai Hosp., Mpls., 1973-74; hosp. adminstrn. instr. U. Minn., Mpls., 1974-75; coord., dir. Blue Cross/Blue Shield Greater N.Y. HMO, N.Y.C., 1975-85; pres. ANCHOR, Chgo.; v.p. Rush-Presbyn. St. Luke's Med. Ctr., Chgo., 1985-88; pres. Gold Health Strategies Inc., N.Y.C., 1988—. Bd. dirs. N.Y. Bus. Group on Health, chmn. managed care task force, 1989—; vice chmn. The HMO Group, 1987-88; steering com. U. Mo.-KC Nat. Ctr. for Managed Care Adminstrn., Kansas City, 1986-98; asst. adj. prof. Columbia U., N.Y.C., 1989-99, clin. prof., Columbia U. Sch. Pub. Health, 1999—. Founding editor Managing Employee Health Benefits. Fellowship Caldwell B. Esselstyn Found., 1991-92; mem. task force pub. health and managed care PEW Charitable Trust, 1995-96; mem. task force improving cardiovascular health Am. Heart Assn., N.Y.C., 1995-96. Avocations: clarinet, music, sports, photography. Home: 322 W 72nd St # 14B New York NY 10023-2676 Office: Gold Health Strategies Inc 250 Park Ave Ste 1300 New York NY 10177-0001 E-mail: billgold@worldnet.att.net, bgold@goldhealthstrategies.com.

GOLDANSKII, VITALII IOSIFOVICH, chemist, physicist; b. Vitebsk, USSR, June 18, 1923; s. Iosif Efimovich and Yudif' Iosifovna (Melamed) G.; m. Lyudmila Nikolaevna Semenova; children: Dmitrii, Andrei. Grad. in Chemistry, Moscow U., 1944, M of Chemistry, 1947, DSc in Physics, 1954. Scientist Inst. Chem. Physics-USSR Acad. Scis., Moscow, 1942-52, 1961—, from div. head to dir., 1988—; sr. scientist P.N. Lebedev Phys. Inst.-USSR Acad. Scis., Moscow, 1952-61; asst. prof. Phys.-Tech. Inst., Moscow, 1947-51; asst. prof., then prof. Inst. Phys. Engring., Moscow, 1951—. Author: Kinematics of Nuclear Reactions, 1959, Mossbauer Effect and its Applications in Chemistry, 1963, Physical Chemistry of Positron and Positronium, 1968, Tunneling Phenomena in Chemical Physics, 1986, many others; contbr. numerous articles and revs. to profl. jours.; patentee (numerous) in field. Chmn. Russian Pugwash Com., Moscow, 1987—; people's dep. of USSR; mem. com. fgn. affairs Supreme Soviet of USSR, 1989-92. Decorated Lenin Order, Order of October Revolution, numerous other orders and medals; recipient Lenin prize, 1980; Golden Mendeleev medal USSR Acad. Scis., 1975, Karpinsky prize Friedrich von Schiller Found., Hamburg, Germany, 1983, Boris Pregel award N.Y. Acad. Scis., 1990, Alexander von Humboldt award, Germany, 1991, Golden Semenov medal Russian Acad. Scis., 1996. Fellow Am. Chem. Soc. (hon.), Am. Phys. Soc., Am. Acad. Arts and Scis., Am. Philos Soc., Acad. Scis. German Dem. Republic, Royal Swedish Acad. Scis., Royal Danish Acad. Scis. and Lettrs, Deutsche Akademie der Naturforscher Leopoldina, World Acad. Arts and Sci., Hungarian Eotvos Lorand Phys. Soc.; mem. NAS USA (fgn., assoc.), N.Y. Acad. Scis. (life.), Russian Acad. Scis., Finnish Acad. Scis. (fgn.), Acad. Europaea, Acad. Georgia. Avocations: writing humor and aphorisms, record collecting, movies, cds, videos. Home: Bldg 8 Apt 66 Ulitsa Zelinskogo 38 Moscow 117334 Russia Office: Russian Acad of Scis Inst Chem Phys Ulitsa Kosygina 4 Moscow 117334 Russia

GOLDBECK, ROBERT ARTHUR, JR., physical chemist; b. Evanston, Ill., July 25, 1950; s. Robert Arthur Sr. and Ruth Marilyn (Nordwall) G.; m. Jennifer Jane Tollkuhn, Aug. 19, 1989; stepchildren: Jessica Kathleen Tollkuhn, Brenna Maurin Tollkuhn. BS, U. Calif., Berkeley, 1974; PhD, U. Calif., Santa Cruz, 1982. Postdoctoral fellow Stanford (Calif.) U., 1983-84, rsch. assoc., 1984-87; rsch. chemist U. Calif., Santa Cruz, 1987—. Lectr. in chemistry U. Calif., 1980, 84, 86. Contbr. articles to Biophys. Jour.; contbr. articles to profl. jours. Mem. AAAS, Am. Chem. Soc., Biophys. Soc., Sigma Xi. Achievements include development of nanosecond time-resolved magnetic circular dichroism spectroscopy; research in the time-resolved MCD and natural CD of photolyzed hemeprotein-ligand complexes. Office: U Calif Dept Chemistry Biochem Santa Cruz CA 95064

GOLDBERG, ALAN MARVIN, toxicologist, educator; b. Bklyn., Nov. 20, 1939; s. William and Celia Ida (Rudman) G.; m. Helene Schoenbach, Aug. 14, 1960; children: Michael David, Naomi Jill BS, Bklyn. Coll. Pharmacy, 1961; PhD in Pharmacology, U. Minn., 1966; DSc (hon.), L.I. U, 1995. Rsch. asst. U. Wis., 1961-62, U. Minn., 1962-66; rsch. assoc. Inst. Psychiat. Rsch. Ind. U., 1966-67, asst. prof. dept. pharmacology, 1967-69; asst. prof. environ. medicine Johns Hopkins U., Balt., 1969-71, assoc. prof., 1971-78, prof. dept. environ. health scis., 1978—, assoc. chmn. dept., 1978-80, acting dir. div. toxicology, 1979-80, dir. div. toxicology, 1980-82, dir. Ctr. Alternatives to Animal Testing, 1981—, assoc. dean rsch., 1984-94; assoc. dean corp. affairs Sch. Pub. Health, Balt., 1994-99; adminstrv. head health edn. program Johns Hopkins U./Nat. Basketball Player Assn., 1990-95; cons. OECD, Paris, 1998—. Prin. rsch. scientist Chesapeake Bay Inst., 1979-84; mem. health hazard evaluation team of chem. waste dumps State of Tenn., 1980; mem. rev. panel EPA, 1980-82; mem. working group on harmonization of in vitro methods Orgn. Econ. and Cmty. Devel., 1995—; organizer 1st World Congress on Alternative and Animal Use in Life Scis., 1993; sci. adv. bd. subcom. on toxicology U.S. FDA, 1996-2001; mem. interagy. coord. com. for validation of alternative method HHS, 1998-2002; bd. sci. advisors Xenogen, Inc.; mem. sci. adv. com. Alternative Tchg. Methods, NIEHS, 2002— vis. prof. U. Utrecht Ctr. Animals and Society, 2002. Mem. editorial bd. Jour. Am. Coll. Toxicology, assoc. editor In Vitro Toxicology; contbr. articles to profl. jours. Trustee Hildergard Doerenkamp-Gerhard Zbinden Found., 1985-2001, hon. mem., 2002-. Recipient award Ind. Neurol. Soc., 1967, Russell and Burch award Human Soc. of U.S., 1991; named Disting. Alumnus, L.I. Univ., 1992. Mem. AAAS, Am. Soc. Pharmacology and Exptl. Therapeutics, Soc. Neurosci. (pres. Balt. chpt. 1971-73), Am. Soc. Neurochemistry, Am. Epilepsy Soc., Assn. Univ. Tech. Mgrs., Internat. Soc. Neurochemistry, Soc. Toxicology (Ambassador Mid-Atlantic sect. 1998), Soc. Toxicology (Enhancement of Animal Welfare award 2001, Hildergard Doerenkamp-Kerhard Zbinden award 2001), Internat. Study Group on Memory Disorders, Internat. Union Pharmacology, Office of Tech. Assessment Panel on Alternatives to Animal Use in Rsch. Testing and Edn. and Frontiers in Neuroscience, Nat. Acad. Sci., Inst. for Lab. Animal Resources. Office: 111 Market Pl Ste 840 Baltimore MD 21202-7113 E-mail: goldberg@jhsph.edu.

GOLDBERG, ALAN MICHAEL, music educator; b. San Angelo, Tex., June 1, 1954; s. Walter and Bertha Willick Goldberg; m. Marilyn Sable, Sept. 12, 1982; children: Stefanie, Jonathan. MusB in Performance-Violin, MusM in Performance-Violin, Manhattan Sch. Music; MEd in Music, Columbia U. Cert. tchr. N.Y., N.Y.C., Conn. Dir. instrumental music Rippowam H.S., Stamford, Conn., 1985—89; orch. dir. Mamaroneck H.S./Hommocks Mid. Sch., Mamaroneck, NY, 1989—92, John Dewey and Adlai E. Stevenson H.S., N.Y.C., 1992—96; instrumental music tchr. F. H. LaGuardia H.S. of Music and Art and Performing Arts, N.Y.C., 1996—2001; instrumental music tchr. in strings Irvington Pub. Schs., Irvington, NY, 2001—. Condr. N.Y.C. All-City H.S. Orch., 1993—2002. Musician (music dir.): (competition/performance for jazz bands) Essentially Ellington Competition, Wynton Marsalis, Artistic Director, 1996 (3rd Pl. Winner, 1996); condr.: performance Words and Music Series @ Bryant Part, 1998; musician: (orch.) Music Educators Nat. Conf., 1998. Recipient Disting. Svc. award, The Commn. Project, 2002. Mem.: Westchester County Sch. Music Assn., Music Educators Assn. N.Y.C., Am. String Tchrs. Assn., Music Educators Nat. Conf., Condrs. Guild, Kappa Delta Pi. Avocations: swimming, building, piano tuning.

GOLDBERG, ANNE CAROL, physician, educator; b. Balt., June 12, 1951; d. Stanley Barry and Selma Ray (Freiman) G.; m. Ronald M. Levin, July 29, 1989. AB, Harvard U., 1973; MD, U. Md., 1977. Diplomate Am. Bd. Internal Medicine, Am. Bd. Endocrinlolgy and Metabolism. Intern in medicine Michael Reese Hosp., Chgo., 1977-78, resident in medicine, 1978-80; fellow in endocrinology Washington U., St. Louis, 1980-83, instr. medicine, 1983-85, asst. prof. medicine, 1985-94, assoc. prof. medicine, 1994—. Fellow ACP, Am. Heart Assn.; mem. AMA, Am. Diabetes Assn., Am. Med. Women's Assn., Endocrine Soc., Alpha Omega Alpha. fellow, Am. Heart Assn. Democrat. Jewish. Avocation: needlepoint. Office: Washington U Med Sch Box 8127 660 S Euclid Ave Saint Louis MO 63110-1010 E-mail: agoldber@im.wustl.edu.

GOLDBERG, ARNOLD IRVING, psychoanalyst, educator; b. Chgo., May 21, 1929; s. Morris Henry and Rose (Auerbach) G.; m. Constance Obenhaus; children: Andrew, Sarah. BS, U. Ill., 1949; MD, U. Ill., Chgo., 1953. Diplomate Am. Bd. Psychiatry and Neurology; cert. psychoanalyst. Intern Cin. Gen. Hosp., 1954-55; psychiat. resident Michael Reese Hosp., Chgo., 1957-59; tng. and supervising analyst Chgo. Inst. for Psychoanalysis, 1970—, dir., 1990-92; assoc. psychiatrist Rush Presbyterian St. Lukes Hosp., Chgo., 1982—; prof. psychiatry Rush Med. Coll., Chgo., 1982-97, Cynthia Oudejans Harris MD prof. psychiatry, 1997—. Author: Models of the Mind, 1973, A Fresh Look at Psychoanalysis, 1988, The Prisonhouse of Psychoanalysis, 1990, The Problem of Perversion, 1995, Being of Two Minds, 1999; editor: Future of Psychoanalysis: Progress in Self Psychology, Vols. 1-16, 1976-99, Errant Selves, 2000; contbr. numerous articls to profl. jours. Capt. U.S. Army, 1955-57. Fellow Am. Psychiat. Assn. (life); mem. Am. Psychoanalytic Assn. Home: 844 W Chalmers Pl Chicago IL 60614-3223 Office: Inst for Psychoanalysis Chgo 122 S Michigan Ave Ste 1305 Chicago IL 60603-6107 E-mail: Docaiq@aol.com.

GOLDBERG, ARTHUR ABBA, merchant banker, financial advisor; b. Jersey City, Nov. 25, 1940; s. Jack Geddy and Ida (Steinberg) G.; m. Jane Elizabeth Gottlieb, Aug. 10, 1968; children: Ari Matthew, Shoshana Eve, Benjamin Saul, Talia Akiva. AB with honors, Am. U., 1962; JD, Cornell U., 1965; PhD (hon.), HHD (hon.), Natchez Coll., 1992. Intern, staff mem. to senator, 1962; law clk. DeSevo & Cerutti, Jersey City, 1964; pvt. practice Jersey City, 1965-89; asst. prof. law U. Conn. Sch. Law., 1965-67; cooperating atty. NAACP Legal Def. Fund, 1965-72; adminstrv. asst. to congressman Ohio, 1966-67; dep. atty. gen. N.J., counsel Dept. Community Affairs and Housing Finance Agy., 1967-70; exec. v.p., dir., mgr. mcpl. fin. dept. Matthews & Wright, Inc., N.Y.C., 1970-88; exec. v.p., dir. Landamatic Systems Corp., N.Y.C., 1982-85; vice chmn. Matthews & Wright Realty, N.Y.C., 1986-88, Matthews & Wright Pacific, N.Y.C., 1986-88; pres. New Am. Fed. Credit Union, 1981-87; dir., treas. Fedn. Community Devel. Credit Unions, 1985-88; v.p. Alfus Corp., 1958-85, Basow Corp., 1965-86; ptnr. Shayna Enterprises, York Builders, Hudson Mgmt. Svcs., 1978-87; dir. investment strategies Capital Corp., 1998-99. Mng. ptnr. Bank Bldg. Assocs., 1974—86, Inst. Profl. and Exec. Devel.; vis. lectr. Rutgers U., 1971—80, Practising Law Inst., 1969—76; mem. exec. com. N.J. Commn. Discrimination in Housing, 1975—80; mem. urban adv. coun. Anti-Defamation League, 1965—72; spl. cons. Exclusionary Zoning Nat. Com. Discrimination in Housing, 1965—70; cons. scholarship edn. Def. Fund for Racial Equality, 1965—72; gen. counsel N.J. chpt. Mcpl. Fin. Officers Assn., N.J. chpt. Nat. Assn. Housing and Redevel. Ofcls., 1966—74; chmn. Com. for Absorption of Soviet Emigrees (CASE), 1973—; pres. CASE-UNA Cmty. Devel. Corp., 1976; co-dir. Jews Offering New Alternatives to Homosexuality (JONAH), 1999—; v.p. Ophthalmic Mission Trust, India, 1988—91; fin. advisor Nat. Found. Manufactured Home Owners, 1994—, Ednl. Video Conference, Inc. (EVCI) Career Colls., 1997—; adv. bd. Parents and Friends of Ex-gays and Gays, 2001—, Internat. Healing Found., 2000—; chair monitoring of rsch. com. Nat. Assn. Rsch. Therapy Homosexuality, 2001—02; pres. Positive Alternative to Homosexuality, 2003. Author: Financing Housing and Urban Development, 1975, Zoning and Land Use, 1972; adv. bd. Housing and Devel. Reporter, 1975-89; contbr. articles to law revs. Co-pres. New Synagogue, Jersey City, 1974-80; bd. dirs. Jersey City Hebrew Free Loan Assn., 1976-77; pres. Met. N.Y. Coord. Com. for Resettlement of Soviet Jewry, 1978-80; treas. Hebrew Free Loan N.J., 1977-90, pres., 1995—; bd. dirs. Hillel Acad., 1985-87; dir. Bayonne Jewish Cmty. Ctr., 1987-88, Jersey City United Jewish Appeal, 1984—, chmn. allocation com., 1994, chmn. nominating com., 1996; bd. dirs. South Bronx Cmty. Housing, Inc., 1977-81; chmn. Novy Americanitz, 1980-84; bd. dirs. Citizens Housing and Planning Coun., 1980-84, Boys Club of Jersey City, 1975-92; pres. CASE Mus. Contemporary Russian Art, 1980—; pres. Freedom Synagogue, 1982—; mem. Settlement House Fund; treas. Coun. Jewish Orgns., Jersey City, 1977; mem. bd. edn. Yeshiva of Hudson County, 1977-85; pres. Hudson Yeshiva Parents Orgn., 1980-88. Mem. Conn. Assn. Mcpl. Attys. (exec. com., editor newsletter 1965-68), Nat. Housing Conf., Am. Polit. Sci. Assn., Nat. Acad. Polit. and Social Sci., Nat. Leased Housing Assn. (nat. pres. 1972-74, chmn. emeritus 1975—), Public Securities Assn. (legis. com. 1978), Nat. Housing Rehab. Assn. (dir. 1982-89, v.p. 1985), Omicron Delta Kappa, Pi Gamma Mu, Pi Sigma Alpha, Pi Delta Epsilon, Phi Alpha Delta. Home: 83 Montgomery St Jersey City NJ 07302-3723 Office: 80 Grand St Jersey City NJ 07302-4522 E-mail: agoldberg@evcinc.com.

GOLDBERG, ARTHUR H. brokerage services company executive; b. N.Y.C., May 13, 1942; s. Irving and Pearl (Ruben) G.; m. Hedy S. Krauss; children: Jill Marla, Mia Joy. BS, NYU, 1963, JD, 1966. Atty. Javits & Javits, N.Y.C., 1966-69; exec. Integrated Resources, Inc., N.Y.C., 1969-73, pres., 1973-89, pres., CEO, 1989—; chmn., CEO Vantage Securities, Inc., N.Y.C., 1989-92; chmn. Reich & Co., Inc., N.Y.C., 1992-94, Vantage Internat. Corp., 1992—; bd. dirs. Martin Simpson & Co., Inc. Chmn. bd. Resources Life Ins. Co., Vantage Internat. Group; chmn., CEO, Vantage Fin. Svcs., Inc., Edison, N.J., 1990—; trustee RPS Realty Trust, Ramco Gershelson Property Trust; bd. dirs. Providence Life Ins. Co., Guardsman Life Ins. Co., Integrated Resources Life Ins. Co., Capitol Life Ins. Co., Odin and Newkirk, Martin Simpson, Inc.; pres. Manhattan Assoc. LLC, 1994-2001; chmn. Fienslending Corp., 1994—; mng. dir. Corp. Solutions Group, an Am. Express Mktg. Ptnr.; mng. dir. Corp. Solutions Group, 2001. Bd. advisors Middle East Quar. Trustee Am. Friends Haifa U., Jerusalem Inst. Mgmt., Boston, Children's Med. Fund of N.Y., N.Y.C.; assoc. trustee North Shore U. Hosp.; bd. of trustees Anti Defamation League of Long Island; bd. dirs. Chamah Internat. Orgn. to Aid Soviet Jewry; bd. overseers NYU; charter mem. Dems. Exec. Com., NYU. Named Man of Yr. Boys Town Jerusalem, 1982; recipient John Madden award NYU Alumni, 1986 Mem. N.Y. State Bar Assn., Young Presidents Orgn., Am. Bus. Conf. (trustee), Investment Partnership Assn. (chmn. bd. trustees), Order of Coif.

GOLDBERG, AUBREY, lawyer; b. Suffolk, Va., Dec. 2, 1940; s. Meyer R. and Miriam (Pear) G.; m. Joanne Holland, Aug. 25, 1963; children: Devon Jon, Jennifer Jonine. BA, Coll. William & Mary, 1963, JD, 1966. Bar: Va. 1966, Nev. 1968, U.S. Dist. Ct. Nev. 1968, U.S. Ct. Appeals (9th cir.) 1985. Ptnr. Greenman, Goldberg, Raby & Martinez, Las Vegas, 1970—; settlement judge Nev. Supreme Ct., 1997—. Served to capt. USAF, 1966-70 Vietnam; lt. col. USAFR. Mem. ABA, Nev. Bar Assn. (bd. govs. 1986-93, pres. 1992-93), Clark County Bar Assn. (pres. 1978, 1st annual pres. award 1985), Las Vegas C. of C., Assn. Trial Lawyers Am., Nev. Trial Lawyers Assn. Democrat. Jewish. Avocations: tennis, weight lifting, jogging. Office: Greenman Goldberg Raby & Martinez 601 S 9th St Las Vegas NV 89101-7012

GOLDBERG, BERTRAM J. social agency administrator; b. Bklyn., Oct. 23, 1942; s. Ralph Goldberg and Geraldine Janith (Herzog) Gerber; m. Lorri Ann Schwartz, Oct. 19, 1980; children: Ilissa, Andrea, Joshua, Randi. BA, Fairleigh Dickinson U., 1964; MSW, U. Pa., 1966. Diplomate Acad. of Cert. Social Workers. Tween worker Bernard Horwich Jewish Community Ctr., Chgo., 1966-68; dir. group svcs. Seattle Jewish Community Ctr., 1968-70; chief centralized intake Eastside Mental Health Ctr., Bellevue, Wash., 1970-73; coord. coll. age youth svcs. Jewish Fedn., Chgo., 1973-74; exec. dir. Jewish Family Svc., Allentown, Pa., 1974-77, Orange County, Calif., 1977-86; pres., CEO, Assn. Jewish Family and Children's Agys., East Brunswick, N.J., 1986—. Mem. NASW, Jewish Social Svc. Profls. Assn. (bd. dirs. 1977-97), Jewish Communal Svc. Assn. N.Am. (bd. dirs. 1979, pres. 1994-96), World Coun. Jewish Communal Svc. (bd. dirs. 1989—, treas. 1998—). Democrat. Jewish. Avocations: computers, reading. Office: Assn Jewish Family/Children's Agys 557 Cranbury Rd East Brunswick NJ 08816-5419 E-mail: BGoldberg@AJFCA.org.

GOLDBERG, BEVERLY, foundation administrator, consultant; b. N.Y.C., Sept. 29, 1940; d. Solomon and Bess Goldberg; m. Laurence Mark Janifer (div.); children: Meg Janifer, Seth Janifer. BA, Hunter Coll., N.Y.C., 1961; MA, CUNY, 1963. Cons. editor Washington Sq. Press, N.Y.C., 1964—66; sr. editor Funk & Wagnall's New Standard Reference Ency., N.Y.C., 1967—69; chief editl. svcs. Noble & Noble, a Divsn. of Dell Books, N.Y.C., 1969—72; v.p., dir. pubs. The Century Found., N.Y.C., 1972—; founding ptnr., exec. editor Brown Herron Pub., 2002—. Cons. Siberg Assocs., N.Y.C., 1989—99. Co-author: Dynamic Planning: The Art of Managing Beyond Tomorrow, 1994, Corporation on a Tightrope: Balancing Leadership, Governance, and Technology in an Age of Complexity, 1996; author: Overcoming High-Tech Anxiety: Thriving in a Wired World, 1999, Age Works: What Corporate America Must Do to Survive the Graying of the Workforce, 2000; contbr. articles. Office: The Century Foundation 41 E 70th St New York NY 10021 Business E-Mail: goldberg@tcf.org.

GOLDBERG, BRUCE EDWARD, hypnotherapist; b. N.Y.C., Nov. 18, 1948; s. Samuel and Florence (Nussbaum) G. BA in Biology/Chemistry magna cum laude, So. Conn. State Coll., 1970; DDS, U. Md., 1974; MS in Counseling and Psychology, Loyola Coll., Balt., 1984. Dentist, Balt., 1976-89; hypnotherapist, 1976-89, L.A., 1989—. Pres. L.A. Acad. Clin. Hypnosis, 1990—; cons. Westinghouse TV, CBS, NBC, ABC, 1985—. Author: Past Lives-Future Lives, 1988, The Search for Grace, 1994; cons., tech. advisor film The Search for Grace, 1994, Soul Healing, 1997, Secrets of Self-Hypnosis, 1997, Peaceful Transition, 1997, Unleash Your Psychic Powers, 1997, Look Younger, Live Longer, 1997, New Age Hypnosis, 1998, Protected by the Light, 1998, Astral Voyages, 1999, Time Travelers from our Future, 1999; contbr. articles to profl. jours. Acad. Gen. Dentistry fellow, 1982; recipient Sealah award Assn. for Parapsychology Healing and Rsch., 1987. Mem. ASCD, Am. Psychol. Soc., Acad. Psychosomatic Medicine, Assn. for Past Life Rsch. and Therapy (life). Avocations: parasailing, tennis, parapsychology. Home and Office: 4300 Natoma Ave Woodland Hills CA 91364-5625 Fax: 818-704-9189. E-mail: karma4u@webtv.net.

GOLDBERG, BURTON DAVID, pathologist, researcher, educator; b. Milw., Jan. 6, 1927; s. Israel and Martha Goldberg; m. Geraldine Anne Yencha, Dec. 15, 1984. BS, Northwestern U., 1948, MD, 1950. Internship Cin. Gen. Hosp., 1951-52; residency in pathology Mallory Inst. Boston City Hosp., 1952-55; rsch. fellow in biochemistry MIT, Cambridge, 1955-57; asst. prof. pathology NYU Med. Sch., 1957-59, assoc. prof. pathology, 1959-71, prof. pathology, 1971-84; prof., chmn. dept. pathology U. Wis. Med. Sch., Madison, 1985-93, prof. emeritus, 1993—. Vis. scientist Inst. Pasteur, Paris, 1993-94. Contbr. articles to profl. jours.; contbr. chpt. to Connective Tissue in Histology, 1988. With USN, 1944-45. NIH grantee, 1959—; recipient Career Devel. award USPHS, 1960-70. Mem. Am. Soc. Experimental Pathology, Am. Soc. Biol. Chemistry and Molecular Biology, Am. Soc. Cell Biology.

GOLDBERG, CHARLES NED, lawyer; b. San Antonio, Dec. 6, 1941; s. Harry and Mamie G.; children— Donald Harris, Allison Beth, William Korash. B.B.A., U. Tex., 1963, J.D., 1966. Bar: Tex. 1966, U.S. Dist. Ct. (so. dist.) Tex. 1969, U.S. Ct. Appeals (5th cir.) 1972. Mng. ptnr. Goldberg Brown, Houston, 1980— ; sec., dir. Affiliated Capital Corp., Houston, 1968-80. Mem. Southwest regional bd. Anti Defamation League, Houston, 1978—, mem. nat. commn., N.Y.C., 1982 ; bd. govs. Houston Grand Opera, 1983-85. Served to capt. U.S. Army, 1966-68. Home: 1310 Chardonnay Dr Houston TX 77077-3102 Office: Goldberg Brown 5918 San Felipe St Apt 12 Houston TX 77057-1950

GOLDBERG, DANIEL BERNEY, eye surgeon; b. Newark, Oct. 18, 1948; s. Bernard R. and Ruth V. (Berney) G.; m. Catherine A. Connelly, Sept. 12, 1976; children: Adam, Jeffrey. BA, U. Calif., Berkeley, 1970; MD, SUNY, Bklyn., 1974. Intern George Washington U. Hosp., Washington, 1974-75; resident SUNY Downstate Med. Ctr., Bklyn., 1975-78; surgeon Atlantic Eye Physicians, Long Branch, N.J., 1979—. Chmn. N.J. Eye Care, 1996—; pres., bd. chmn. N.J. Acad. Ophthalmology, 1988; dir. ophthalmology Monmouth Med. Ctr., Long Branch, 1984-93. Contbr. articles to profl. jours. Fellow Am. Acad. Ophthalmology (councillor 1990-95), Am. Coll. Eye Surgeons; mem. Am. Soc. Cataract

and Refractive Surgery, Soc. Surgeons N.J., Internat. Soc. Refractive Surgery, Castroviejo Cornea Soc. Jewish. Avocations: skiing, golf, photography. Office: Atlantic Eye Physicians 279 3rd Ave Long Branch NJ 07740-6205 E-mail: dangold@att.net.

GOLDBERG, DAVID, lawyer, law educator; b. N.Y.C., Dec. 31, 1934; s. Philip and Esther (Dobbs) G.; m. Emily Ruth Messing, Aug. 17, 1958; children: Sara, Ari. BA, CUNY, 1956; LLB, Yale U., 1959. Bar: N.Y. 1960. Law clerk to judge U.S. Dist. Ct., N.Y.C., 1960-62; assoc. Kaye, Scholer, Fierman, Hays and Handler, N.Y.C., 1962-68, ptnr., 1969-83, Cowan, Liebowitz and Latman, N.Y.C., 1983—. Adj. prof. law NYU, 1976-96. Contbr. articles on copyright and trademark law to N.Y. Law Jour., other profl. jours. Pres. Hillcrest Jewish Ctr., Jamaica Estates, N.Y., 1987-89. Served as sgt. U.S. Army, 1959-60. Mem. ABA (fin. officer sect. intellectual property law 1986-89, spkr. on copyright devels. 1984, 85, 87, 90, 2000), Copyright Soc. USA (pres. 1978-80, hon. trustee 1980—, spkr. on copyright devels. annually 1984—), U.S. Trademark Assn. (spkr. on trademarks and copyright overlap 1987). Democrat. Avocation: fishing. Office: Cowan Liebowitz and Latman 1133 Avenue of the Americas New York NY 10036-6710 E-mail: dxg@cll.com.

GOLDBERG, DAVID ALAN, investment banker, lawyer; b. N.Y.C., Oct. 31, 1933; s. Joseph R. and Rose (Trutt) G.; m. Victoria Liebson, July 7, 1957 (div. Mar. 1976); children: Eric S., Jeremy P. AB magna cum laude, Harvard U., 1954, JD, 1957, postgrad. in bus. adminstrn, 1956-57. Bar: N.Y. 1958. Counsel firm R.W. Pressprich & Co., Inc., N.Y.C., 1958-64, gen. partner, 1965-68, exec. v.p., 1968-78, also chmn. exec. com. Bd. dirs. Charterhouse Assocs., Ltd., Gen. Atomics, Gen. Atomics Techs. Corp., Newbridge, Inc. Trustee Beth Israel Med. Center, N.Y.C., Continuum Health Ptnrs. Inc., St. Luke's-Roosevelt Hosp. Ctr.; trustee, bd. regents The L.I. Coll. Hosp. Served with AUS, 1957-58. Mem. Harvard Club (N.Y.C.), Phi Beta Kappa.

GOLDBERG, EDWARD DAVIDOW, geochemist, educator; b. Sacramento, Aug. 2, 1921; s. Edward Davidow and Lillian (Rothholz) G.; m. Kathe Bertine, Dec. 26, 1973; children— David Wilkes, Wendy Jean, Kathi Kiri, Beck Bertine. BS, U. Calif.-Berkeley, 1942; PhD, U. Chgo., 1949. Mem. faculty Scripps Instn. Oceanography, La Jolla, Calif., 1949—, prof. chemistry, 1960—; provost Revelle Coll., U. Calif. at San Diego, 1965-66. Condr. research and author publs. on subjects including marine pollution, chem. composition of sea water, sediments, marine organisms, environmental management; vis. prof. chemistry U. Otago Dunedin, New Zealand, 1988; H. Barr Steinbach vis. scholar Woods Hole Oceanog. Instn., 2001. Author: (with J. Geiss) Earth Sciences and Meteorites, 1964, Guide to Marine Pollution, 1972, North Sea Science, 1973, The Sea: Marine Chemistry, vol. V, 1974, The Health of the Oceans, 1976, Black Carbon in the Environment, 1985, Coastal Zone Space: Prelude to Conflict, 1994; contbr. articles to profl. jours. Recipient B.H. Ketchum award Woods Hole Oceanographic Instn., 1984, Ruth Patrick award for environ. problem solving Am. Soc. Limnology and Oceanography, 1999; co-recipient Tyler prize U. So. Calif., 1989; Guggenheim fellow, 1961, NATO fellow, 1970; NAS exch. scholar, 1987. Fellow Am. Geophys. Union, AAAS; mem. Geochem. Soc., U.S. Acad. Scis., Sigma Xi. Home: 750 Val Sereno Dr Encinitas CA 92024-6919

GOLDBERG, EDWARD JAY, general contractor; b. Atlanta, Apr. 30, 1950; s. J. Elliott and Sarah (Spiegelman) G.; m. Susan Ellen Jacobson, Dec. 19, 1976; children: Marc Samuel, Robin Beth, Allison Gayle. BS in Fin., U. Ga., 1972. Acctg. coordinator Panasonic, Atlanta, 1972-76; account supr. Oscar Mayer Co., Birmingham, Ala., 1976-81; pres. Alscan, Inc., Birmingham, 1981—. Mem. Birmingham Mus. Art, 1987, Birmingham Symphony Orch., 1987; bd. dirs. Temple Beth-El, Young Leadership Cabinet; v.p. Birmingham Jewish Fedn., 1992-93, gen. campaign chmn., 1993-95, pres., 1998—; bd. dirs., treas. Birmingham Jewish Day Sch.; chmn. ways and means Birmingham Jewish Cmty. Ctr. Mem. Am. Soc. Indsl. Security, Associated Gen. Contractors, Ala. Alarm Assn., Birmingham C. of C., Pine Tree Country Club, B'nai B'rith (v.p. 1981-83). Jewish. Avocations: golf, organizational work. Home: 3504 Branch Mill Rd Birmingham AL 35223-1608 Office: Alscan Inc 237 Oxmoor Cir Ste 101 Birmingham AL 35209-6480

GOLDBERG, FRANKLIN H. psychotherapist; s. Samuel and Julia (Schwartz) G.; m. Leonore H., June 4, 1955; children: Diana, Terry Ann. BA, NYU, 1952, PhD, 1962. Intern Bellevue Psychiat. Hosp., N.Y.C., 1954-55; tng. intern VA Hosp., East Orange, N.J., 1955-56, Montrose, N.Y., 1956-57, VA Regional Office, N.Y.C., 1957-58; researcher Rsch. Ctr. for Mental Health/NYU, 1958-59; adminstr. psychol. svcs./programs NYU Reading Inst., 1958-68; dir. psychol. svcs. Jewish Child Care Assn., NYC, 1968—2002; psychologist Jewish Agy., N.Y.C., 1972-92; supr. postdoctoral program NYU, 1991—; pvt. practice N.Y.C., New Rochelle, 1962—. With Peace Corps, Washington, 1967, Jewish Bd. Guardians, N.Y.C., 1960-63; tchr. Bklyn. Coll., 1962-63, 65-67; with City Hosp. at Elmhurst, Queens, N.Y., 1963, Coney Island Mental Health Ctr., Bklyn., 1965; others; faculty and supr. Manhattan Inst. for Psychoanalysis, 1980—. Contbr. articles to profl. jours. Mem. APA (divsn. psychoanalysis, various offices including pres. sect. 5 1992-93), Am. Orthopsychiat. Assn., N.Y. State Psychol. Assn. (various offices including pres. 1996-98). Home: 5 Indian Hill Rd New Rochelle NY 10804 Office: 30 5th Ave New York NY 10011-8859 E-mail: fhgphd@optonline.net.

GOLDBERG, GERALD JAY, writer, educator; b. N.Y.C., Dec. 30, 1929; m. Nancy Marmer, Jan. 23, 1954; 1 child, Robert. BS, Purdue U., 1952; MA, NYU, 1954; PhD, U. Minn., 1958. Tchg. asst., instr. U. Minn., Mpls., 1954-57; instr., asst. prof. Dartmouth Coll., 1958-64; asst. prof. UCLA, 1964-67, assoc. prof., 1968-73, prof. English and Am. lit., 1974-91, prof. emeritus, 1991—. Adv. panelist NEH TV series The Am. Short Story, 1975-81; lectr. Harvard U., 1979, U. Rennes, 1963, U. Valencia; vis. prof. Queens Coll., 1985-87, Williams Coll., 1981. Author: (fiction) Notes from the Diaspora, 1962, The National Standard, 1968, The Lynching of Orin Newfield, 1970 (N.Y. Times Book of Yr., Pulitzer prize nomination), 126 Days of Continuous Sunshine, 1972, Heart Payments, 1982; (non-fiction) (with Nancy Marmer Goldberg) The Modern Critical Spectrum, 1962, The Fate of Innocence, 1965, (with Lionel Trilling, Ihab Hassan, Karl Keller and Clifton Fadiman) American Literature Since 1945, 1971, (with Robert Goldberg) Anchors: Brokaw, Jennings, Rather and the Evening News, 1990, (with Robert Goldberg) Citizen Turner: The Wild Rise of an American Tycoon, 1995; contbr. short stories, revs. to profl. pubs. Fulbright prof., 1962-63; fellow U. Calif. Inst. Arts, 1966-67, U. Calif., 1976-77 Mem. PEN, Authors Guild.

GOLDBERG, GREGORY EBAN, lawyer; b. Denver, Oct. 9, 1967; BA, Dartmouth Coll., 1990; JD, Columbia Law Sch., 1995. Bar: Colo. 1995, U.S. Dist. Ct. Colo. 1995, U.S. Ct. Appeals (10th cir.) 1995. Law clk. to Judge Paul J. Kelly Jr. U.S. Ct. Appeals (10th cir.), Santa Fe, 1995-96; assoc. Arnold & Porter, Denver, 1996-99; asst. U.S. atty. Maj. Crimes & Appellate divsn., Denver, 1999—2003; of counsel Holland & Hart, Denver, 2003—. Bd. dirs. Anti-Defamation League, Denver, 1998—. Recipient U.S. Dept. of Justice Dirs. award, 2002. Mem. Colo. Bar Assn., Dartmouth Alumni Assn. (bd. dirs.), Graland Alumni Assn. (bd. dirs. 1995-2000). Avocations: snowshoeing, mountain biking, backpacking, home renovations. Office: Holland & Hart 555 17th St Ste 3200 Denver CO 80202 E-mail: ggoldberg@hollandhart.com.

GOLDBERG, HAROLD SEYMOUR, electrical engineer, educator; b. Bklyn., Jan. 22, 1925; s. David and Rose (Maslow) G.; m. Florence Meyerson, May 29, 1949 (dec.); children: Lawrence, Irene. BEE (Schweinberg scholar), Cooper Union, 1944; MEE, Poly. Inst. Bklyn., 1949; student, Columbia U. Engring. draftsman Cole Electric Products Co., 1944-45; radio engr. Press Wireless, Inc., 1945-47; asst. project engr. Radio Receptor Co., 1947-48; project engr. No. Radio Co., 1948-50; mgr. prodn. test, test equipment design sects. Allen B. DuMont Labs., Inc., 1950-56; mgr. engring. fabrication dept. Emerson Radio & Phonograph Corp., 1956-57; chief devel. engr. Consol. Avionics Corp., Westbury, N.Y., 1957-59; engring. mgr. data systems EPSCO, Inc., Cambridge, Mass., 1959-62; v.p. research Lexington Instruments Corp., Waltham, Mass., 1962- 66; prin. research engr. AVCO-Research div., Everett, Mass., 1966-68; ops. mgr. Orion Research Inc., 1968-70; v.p. applications Analogic Corp., Wakefield, Mass., 1970-71; pres. Data Precision Corp., Danvers, Mass., 1971-82; v.p. Analogic Corp., 1979-85; pres. Acrosystems Corp., Beverly, Mass., 1984-88; assoc. dean Gordon Inst., Wakefield, Mass., 1988-92; assoc. dean Gordon Inst. Tufts U., Medford, Mass., 1992-93. Lectr. Tufts U., 1993—; cons. Analogic Corp., 1988-2003, acting mgr. test and measurement divsn., 2002-03. Served with AUS, 1945-47. Recipient award of distinction Poly. Inst. N.Y., 1980, John Fluke Sr. Pioneer award, 1989, Haraden Pratt award, IEEE, 1993, Allen Ploss award Electro, 1992; N.Y. State Vets scholar, 1957. Fellow IEEE (life, chmn. Boston group on medicine and biology 1965-66, exec. com. Boston sect. 1967—, vice chmn. Boston 1969-70, chmn. Boston 1970-71, internat. bd. dirs. 1971-75, 89-90, v.p. 1975, dir. Electro 1975-89, editor Reflector 1976—, treas. tech. activities bd. 1991, chmn. tech. bd. pub. rels. com. 1992-96, citation of honor U.S. activities bd. 1978, Region 1 award 1994, William Terry Disting. Lifetime Svc. award 1999, Third Millennium medal 2000); mem. Instrumentation and Measurement Soc. IEEE (sec.-treas. 1983, pres. 1985-87, columnist mag. 1994—, gen. chmn. tech. conf. 1995, 2001, Disting. Svc. award 1988), Tau Beta Pi. Office: 8 Centennial Dr Peabody MA 01960-7902 E-mail: Halgold1@aol.com. *The highest achievement to which a person can aspire is that the world be a better place after he leaves it than before and that this be partly the result of his contributions to it.*

GOLDBERG, HARVEY, financial executive; b. Bklyn., Jan. 30, 1940; s. Joseph and Regina (Goldkrantz) G.; m. Joyce Baron, Nov. 22, 1962; children: Keith, Jodi. BS in Acctg., Bklyn. Coll., 1962; postgrad., CCNY, 1963. CPA, N.Y. Sr. acct. Schwartz, Zelin & Weiss CPA's, N.Y.C., 1962-66; mgr. fin. analysis Columbia Records div. CBS, Inc., N.Y.C., 1966-70; asst. controller Revlon, Inc., N.Y.C., 1970-71; treas. Ctrl. Textile, Inc., Jersey City, 1971-74; controller Marcade Group, Inc., Jersey City, 1974-81, v.p., controller, 1981-86; v.p., CFO Paul Marshall Products, Inc., subs. Marcade Group, Long Beach, Calif., 1982-86, Player's Internat., Inc., Calabasas, Calif., 1988-93, sr. v.p., CFO, 1988-93; exec. v.p., CFO Adesso, Inc., Culver City, Calif., 1994-98; CFO, dir. Hollywood Beauty Corp., Encino, Calif., 1997-99; CFO YellowOnline.Com, Inc., L.A., 1999; fin. cons., 1999—; bd. dirs. Tarzana Improvement Assn., 2000—. County committeeman Monmouth County Dem. Com., N.J., 1979-80; chmn. adv. bd. High Point Ctr., Marlboro, NJ, 1978-82; active Marlboro Twp. Bd. Edn., 1980-82, v.p., 1981-82; bd. dirs. Family Consultation Ctr., Freehold, NJ, 1982-83; treas., bd. govs. Tarzana Neighborhood Coun., 2003—. Mem. AICPA, N.Y. State Soc. CPA's. Home and Office: 19798 Greenbriar Dr Tarzana CA 91356-5442 E-mail: harveygoldberg98@yahoo.com.

GOLDBERG, HARVEY LEE, internal medicine; b. N.Y., Oct. 29, 1950; MD, Cornell Univ., 1976. Intern N.Y. Hosp., 1976, resident internal medicine, 1977-79, fellow cardiology, 1979-81; assoc. prof. Cornell Univ., with N.Y. Hosp. Fellow Am. Coll. Cardiology, Am. Heart Assn. Office: NY Cardiology Assocs 425 E 61st St New York NY 10021-8722 Fax: 212-752-5822.

GOLDBERG, HERB, psychologist, educator; b. Berlin, July 14, 1937; came to U.S., 1941; s. Jacob and Ella (Nagler) G.; 1 child, Amy Elisabeth. BA cum laude, CUNY, 1958; PhD, Adelphi U., 1963. Lic. psychologist, Calif. Pvt. practice, L.A., 1965—; prof. Calif. State U., L.A. Author: Creative Aggression, 1972, The Hazards of Being Male, 1976, Money Madness, 1978, The New Male, 1979, The Inner Male, 1986, The New Male/Female Relationship, 1982, What Men Really Want, 1991. Mem. APA, Phi Beta Kappa. Office: 3739 Mayfair Dr Los Angeles CA 90065-3208

GOLDBERG, HOMER BERYL, English language educator; b. Chgo., Feb. 4, 1924; married, 1956; 2 children. AB, U. Chgo., 1947, AM, 1948, PhD in English, 1961. Instr. English U. Chgo., 1950-54, asst. prof., 1954-60, Haverford (Pa.) Coll., 1960-61; assoc. prof. SUNY, Stony Brook, 1961-70, prof. English, 1970-88, Disting. teaching prof., 1988—, emeritus, 1991—. Fulbright lectr., Italy, 1956-57; dir. NDEA English Inst., 1965-66; editl. cons. L.I. Rsch. Inst., 1992-97. Author: The Art of Joseph Andrews, 1969; editor: Norton Critical Edition of Joseph Andrews and Shamela, 1987; contbr. articles to profl. jours. Mem. Suffolk County Campaign Fin. Bd., 1999—. Recipient Chancellor's award for Excellence in Teaching SUNY, 1973, Pres.'s award for Excellence in Teaching SUNY, 1987, others; faculty rsch. fellow SUNY, 1962, 67, 69. Mem. MLA. Office: SUNY Dept English Stony Brook NY 11794-5350

GOLDBERG, IRVING HYMAN, molecular pharmacology and biochemistry educator; b. Hartford, Conn., Sept. 2, 1926; s. Morris Wolfe and Rose (Krechevsky) Goldberg; m. Margaret Field Ziskin, Apr. 15, 1956; children: Daniel Eliot, Nancy Elizabeth. BS, Trinity Coll., 1949; MD, Yale U., 1953; PhD, Rockefeller U., 1960; AM (hon.), Harvard U., 1964. Intern Columbia-Presbyn. Med. Ctr., N.Y.C., 1953—54; asst. resident, chief resident, instr. medicine Columbia-Presbyn. Med. Ctr. (Coll. Phys. and Surgs.), 1954—57; asst. prof. medicine, biochemistry U. Chgo., 1960—64, assoc. prof., 1964; assoc. prof. medicine Med. Sch. Harvard, 1964—68; prof. medicine Med. Sch. Harvard U., 1968—, chmn. divsn. med. scis. Faculty Arts and Scis., 1968—70, Gustavus Adolphus Pfeiffer prof. pharmacology, 1972—83, chmn. dept. pharm., 1972—86, Otto Krayer prof. pharmacology, 1983—86, Otto Krayer prof. biol. chemistry and molecular pharmacology, 1986—; chief endocrinology-metabolism unit Beth Israel Hosp., 1964—68, physician, 1964—72, mem. bd. consultation in medicine, 1972—; cons. in pharmacology Dana-Farber Cancer Inst., Boston, 1980—87. Mem. rev. panel internat. program Howard Hughes Med. Inst., 1994; cons. in clin. pharmacology Children's Hosp. Med. Ctr., Boston, 1972—91; mem. rsch. com. Med. Found., Boston, 1968—77; mem. exptl. therapeutics study sect. NIH, 1974—77; mem. com. proposed legis. to restructure FDA Assembly Life Scis. NAS-NRC, Inst. Medicine, 1976; mem. sci. adv. com. Damon Runyon-Walter Winchell Cancer Fund, 1982—86; mem. life scis. panel NRC, 1992—93. Editl. bd. Endocrinology, 1964—68, Antimicrobial Agents and Chemotherapy, 1974—88, hon. editl. adv. bd. Jour. Biochem. Pharmacology, 1973—84, mem. editl. adv. bd. Biochemistry, 1986—97. Rev. panel Internat. Program Howard Hughes Med. Inst., 1994. Served with USNR, 1945—46. Recipient Faculty Rsch. award, Am. Cancer Soc., 1960—71; fellow Guggenheim, dept. genetics, Oxford (Eng.) U., 1970—71, sr., Trinity Coll., 1974—76. Mem.: Brit. Pharm. Soc., Am. Soc. Microbiology, Am. Soc. Pharmacology and Therapeutics (Otto Krayer award 1994), Am. Chem. Soc., Assn. Am. Physicians, Am. Acad. Arts and Scis., Am. Soc. Clin. Investigation, Am. Soc. Biochemistry and Molecular Biology, Inst. Medicine NAS, Alpha Omega Alpha, Sigma Xi, Phi Beta Kappa. Home: 987 Memorial Dr Apt 472 Cambridge MA 02138-5737 Office: Harvard U Med Sch 45 Shattuck St Boston MA 02115-6091 E-mail: irving_goldberg@hms.harvard.edu.

GOLDBERG, IVAN BAER, real estate executive; b. Newport News, Va., Apr. 20, 1939; s. David and Sara (Levy) G.; m. Mary Linda Caffee, Oct. 27, 1968 (div. 1978); children: Stephen Morris, Michael Scott; m. Rachel Bradley Tyler, Dec. 24, 2002. Student, U. Va., 1957-58, Coll. of William and Mary, 1958-60. Exec. v.p. Bedding Supply Co., Inc., Newport News, 1961-72; sec.-treas. Mut. Realty Corp., Newport News, 1972—; pres. Goldkress Corp., Newport News, 1972—; gen. ptnr. Goldkress Investment Co., Newport News, 1972—. Bd. dirs. Goldkress Corp., Mut. Realty Corp. With USCGR, 1962. Mem. Newport News-Hampton Bd. Realtors, Nat. Assn. Realtors. Jewish. Home: 15 Ferguson Cv Newport News VA 23606-2016 Office: Mut Realty Corp 11116 Jefferson Ave Newport News VA 23601-2551

GOLDBERG, JACK, hematologist; b. Ulm, Germany, Feb. 7, 1948; came to U.S., 1952; s. Isaac and Mary (Selitska) G.; m. Doreen, July 28, 1970; children: Joshua, Alexis. BA, Boston U., 1969; MD, SUNY, 1973. From asst. prof. medicine to prof. medicine SUNY Health Sci. Ctr., Syracuse, 1977-89; prof. medicine Robert Wood Johnson Med. Sch., Camden, NJ, 1989—, Am. Cancer Soc. prof. clin. oncology, 1992—; head divsn. hematology-oncology U. Pa. Presbyn. Med. Ctr., 2003—; vice chmn. Abramson Cancer Ctr. U. Pa. Network. Prof. medicine Coriell Inst. for Med. Rsch., Camden, 1990-2002; med. dir. blood bank Cooper Hosp., Camden, 1990-2002, head divsn. hematology/oncology, 1989-2002; med. dir. CorCell, Camden, 1996—; head Cooper Cancer Inst., 1998-2002. V.p. N.J. divsn. Am. Cancer Soc., 1989-99; vol. Leukemia Soc., Camden, 1990—. Fellow Am. Coll. Medicine. Jewish. Avocations: exercise, travel. Office: Penn Medicine at Cherry Hill 409 Rte 70 East Cherry Hill NJ 08034 E-mail: Jack.Goldbert@uphs.upenn.edu.

GOLDBERG, JAMES R. lawyer; b. East Cleveland, Ohio, Aug. 12, 1938; s. William and Celia (Schwartz) G.; m. Marilyn A. Goldberg; children: Bonnie Kraus, Laura Hudak. BS, Ohio State U., 1960; JD, Case Western Res. U., 1964. Bar: Ohio 1964, U.S. Dist. Ct. (no. dist.) Ohio, U.S. Claims Ct. V.p. Weisman, Kennedy & Berris Co. LPA, Cleve., 1964—. With U.S. Army, 1961. Office: Weisman Kennedy Berris Co LPA 1600 Midland Bldg Cleveland OH 44115

GOLDBERG, JAY, lawyer; b. N.Y.C., Jan. 2, 1933; s. Joseph and Lillian (Adler) G.; m. Rema, Dec. 27, 1959; children: Justin, Julie. BA, Bklyn. Coll., 1954; JD, Harvard U., 1957. Bar: N.Y. 1957, U.S. Ct. Appeals (2d, 4th and 9th cirs.) 1971, U.S. Supreme Ct. 1961. Asst. dist. atty. N.Y. County Dist. Atty. Office, N.Y.C., 1957-61; spl. asst. to atty. gen. Washington, 1961-63; spl. asst. to U.S. Atty. NJ Hammond, Ind., 1961-67; lawyer, sole practice N.Y.C., 1963—. Lectr. trial practice Harvard Law Sch., 1976-88; com. on grievances U.S. Dist. Ct. (so. dist.) N.Y., 1989—. Editorial mgr. White Collar Crime Law Reporter, 1989—; contbr. articles to profl. jours. Recipient Merit award for Advocacy of Individual Rights for Persons Advised, N.Y. Criminal Bar Assn., 1989. Mem. Friars Club (gov. 1988-92). Home: 200 E 65th St New York NY 10021-4451 Office: 250 Park Ave New York NY 10177-0001

GOLDBERG, JEROLD S. dean; BS, Case Western Res. U., 1966, DDS, 1970; dental internship, Newark Beth Israel Hosp.; resident oral surgery, U. Hosps. Cleve. Dean, Sch. Dentistry Case Western Res. U., 1997—, interim dean, Sch. Medicine, 2002—. Rschr. in field. Bd. mem. Ohio Dental Assn. Found. Mem.: Ohio Dental Assn. (mem. Ohio Dental Assn. Coun. on Dental Edn. and Licensure, del. and alt., House of Dels.). Office: Case Western Res U 10900 Euclid Ave Cleveland OH 44106-4920

GOLDBERG, JOEL HENRY, lawyer; b. Lewiston, Maine, Feb. 7, 1945; s. George and Evelyn Anne (Mackin) G.; m. Allyne Ross; 1 child, Ross Lewis. BA, Brandeis U., 1967; JD, Columbia U., 1970. Bar: N.Y. 1971, D.C. 1980. Dir. div. investment mgmt. SEC, 1981-83; ptnr. Shearman & Sterling, N.Y.C. Mem.: Assn. of the Bar of the City of N.Y. (sec., com. on investment co.), ABA. Jewish.

GOLDBERG, JOSEPH, lawyer; b. Washington, Aug. 21, 1950; s. Morris and Rose (Levin) G.; m. Christine Marie Riggott, Mar. 29, 1980; children: Benjamin R., Louis E. BS, Ohio U., 1972; JD, U. Pa., 1975. Bar: Pa. 1975, N.J. 1981, D.C. 1980, U.S. Ct. Appeals (3d cir.) 1980, U.S. Dist.Ct. (mid. dist.) Pa. 1987, U.S. Supreme Ct. 1989. Assoc. Margolis, Edelstein & Scherlis, Phila., 1975-81; ptnr. Margolis Edelstein, Phila., 1982—. Author: State and Local Government Immunity to Tort Claims, 1992, 2d edit., 1997. Mem. ABA, Pa. Def. Rsch. Inst., Pa. Jud. Rules Com., Phila. Assn. Def. Counsel, Phila. Bar Assn. Avocation: scuba diving. Office: Margolis Edelstein The Curtis Ctr 4th Fl Independence Sq West Philadelphia PA 19106

GOLDBERG, KIRSTEN BOYD, science journalist; b. San Bernardino, Calif., Oct. 29, 1963; d. Jerry Dock and Jewel Marie (Purkiss) Boyd; m. Paul Boris Goldberg, Aug. 25, 1985; children: Katherine, Sarah. BA, U. Calif., Berkeley, 1984. News editor Reston (Va.) Connection, 1985-86; reporter Edn. Week, Washington, 1986-88; assoc. editor Cancer Letter Inc., Washington, 1989-90, editor, pub., 1990—. Editor newsletter The Clin. Cancer Letter. Mem. Nat. Assn. Sci. Writers, Newsletter Pubs. Assn., Soc. Profl. Journalists (Washington Dateline award 1998), D.C. Sci. Writers Assn. Jewish. Office: Cancer Letter Inc PO Box 9905 Washington DC 20016-8905

GOLDBERG, LAWRENCE SPENCER, science foundation engineering administrator, physicist; b. St. Louis, June 11, 1940; s. Albert I. and Zelda (Becker) Goldberg; m. Jolande E. Goldberg, Sept. 7, 1969; children: Daniel, Elisa, Clarissa. BS, Wash. U., 1961; PhD, Cornell U., 1966. Laser scientist Naval Rsch. Lab., Washington, 1967-85; program dir. NSF, Arlington, Va., 1985-93, divsn. dir., 1993-98, sr. engr. advisor, 1998—. Sci. officer Office Naval Rsch., Arlington, 1972; postdoctoral rsch. U. Frankfurt, Germany, 1966—67; sabbatical Imperial Coll., London, 1976—77; acting head NSF, Tokyo, 1989. Contbr. articles to profl. jours. Pres. Hollin Hills Civic Assn., 1986. Fellow: IEEE, Optical Soc. Am. Achievements include patents in field. Office: NSF 4201 Wilson Blvd Arlington VA 22230 E-mail: Lgoldber@nsf.gov.

GOLDBERG, LEE DRESDEN, endocrinologist, medical educator; b. Point Pleasant, N.J., July 29, 1937; s. Milton J. and Maude (Dresden) G.; m. Lana Ditchek, July 23, 1967 (dec. 1991); children: Marissa Julie, Sara Amy, Rachel Sherry; m. Rhoda Kuperman, Mar. 10, 1994. BS summa cum laude, Yale U., 1959, MD, 1963. Diplomate Am. Bd. Internal Medicine, Am. Bd. Endocrinology, Nat. Bd. Med. Examiners. Rotating intern Mt. Sinai Hosp., N.Y.C., 1963-64; resident in internal medicine Montefiore Hosp., Bronx, N.Y., 1964, 66-68; clin. rsch. fellow in endocrinology Albert Einstein Coll. Medicine, Bronx, 1968-69; fellow in endocrinology Bellevue Hosp.-NYU Med. Ctr., N.Y.C., 1969-70; pvt. practice, Miami, Fla., 1970—. Co-chief endocrinology Mt. Sinai Hosp., Miami Beach, Fla., 1974-91, chief endocrinology, 1991—; tchg. asst. NYU Sch. Medicine, 1969-70; clin. instr. medicine U. Miami Sch. Medicine, 1970-71, clin. asst. prof., 1971-80, clin. assoc. prof., 1980-99, vol. prof. medicine, 1999—; chief internal medicine South Shore Hosp., Miami Beach, 1975-79; assoc. chmn. med. svcs. St. Francis Hosp., Miami Beach, 1977-78. Author: (with Goldberg) The Jewish Student's Guide to American Colleges, 1989; contbr. articles on endocrinology to med. jours. Bd. dirs. Hebrew Acad. Greater Miami, 1975-79. Lt. M.C., USNR, 1964-66. Fellow ACP, Am. Coll. Endocrinology; mem. Endocrine Soc., Am. Diabetes Assn. (past dir. Miami chpt.), Am. Assn. Clin. Endocrinologists, Yale Club, B'nai B'rith, Phi Beta Kappa, Sigma Xi. Office: 4302 Alton Rd Ste 550 Miami FL 33140-2876

GOLDBERG, LEE WINICKI, furniture company executive; b. Laredo, Tex., Nov. 20, 1932; d. Frank and Goldie (Ostrowiak) Winicki; m. Frank M. Goldberg, Aug. 17, 1952; children: Susan, Arlene, Edward Lewis, Anne Carri. Student, San Diego State U., 1951-52. With United Furniture Co., Inc., San Diego, 1953-83, corp. sec., dir., 1963-83, dir. environ. interiors, 1970-83; founder Drexel-Heritage store Edwards Interiors subs. United Furniture, 1975; founding ptnr., v.p. FLJB Corp., 1976-86; founding ptnr., sec., treas. Sea Fin., Inc., 1980; founding ptnr. First Nat. Bank San Diego, 1982. Den mother Boy Scouts Am., San Diego, 1965; vol. Am. Cancer Soc., San Diego, 1964-69; chmn. jr. matrons United Jewish Fedn., San Diego, 1958; del. So. Pacific Coast region Hadassah Conv., 1960, pres. Galilee group San Diego chpt., 1960-61; supporter Marc Chagall Nat. Mus., Nice France, U. Calif. at San Diego Cancer Ctr. Foun., Smithsonian Instn., Los Angeles County Mus., San Diego Mus. Contemporary Art, San Diego Mus. Art; pres. San Diego Opera, 1992-94. Recipient Hadassah Service award San Diego chpt., 1958-59; named Woman of Dedication by Salvation Army Women's Aux., 1992, Patron of Arts by Rancho Santa Fe Country Friends, 1993. Democrat. Jewish.

GOLDBERG, LESLIE PHILIP, ophthalmologist; b. Tampa, Fla., Mar. 22, 1945; s. Oscar and Irma Ruth (Rosner) G.; m. Zehava Kupperman, Jan. 24, 1970; children: Shelley, Michael. BA, Cornell U., 1966; MD, The Chgo. Med. Sch., 1970. Diplomate Am. Bd. Ophthalmology. Intern Columbia-Presbyterian Med. Ctr., N.Y.C., 1970-71; resident, chief resident in ophthalmology NYU Med. Ctr., N.Y.C., 1973-76; pvt. practice L.I. Eye Surgeons, P.C., Manhasset, N.Y., 1976—. Chief of ophthalmology, St. Francis Hosp., Roslyn, N.Y., 1993—; mem. staff North Shore U. Hosp., Manhasset, L.I. Jewish Med. Ctr., New Hyde Park, N.Y.; clin. asst. prof. ophthalmology NYU Med. Ctr., N.Y.C. Capt. U.S. Army, 1971-73. Recipient Achievement award Upjohn Pharm. Co., 1970. Fellow Am. Acad. Ophthalmology, Am. Coll. Surgeons; mem. Am. Soc. Cataract and Refractive Surgery, Med. Soc. State of N.Y., Nassau County Med. Soc., N.Y. State Ophthalmol. Soc., L.I. Opthalmol. Soc., Alpha Omega Alpha. Avocations: bicycling, skiing, automobiles. Office: LI Eye Surgeons PC 2110 Northern Blvd Manhasset NY 11030-3500 E-mail: lpgmd@aol.com.

GOLDBERG, LOIS D. health facility administrator, disability analyst; b. Mar. 30, 1940; m. Gerald Allen Goldberg, Dec. 18, 1960; children: Sheri, Nancy, Karen. BS, U. Wis., Milw., 1961, MS, 1977. Cert. Am. Inst. Hypnotherapy and Psychotherapy, disability analyst. Health svcs. adminstr. Eastside Clinic, Milw., 1985—; acupuncture detox specialist, 1992-98. Pres. Fox Point PTA, Milw., 1980; bd. dirs. Close Encounters Chamber Music. Recipient Fighting Back Initiative cert. of recognition, Milw. County for Reduction of Substance Abuse and Improvement of Life of Milw. County Residents, 1995. Mem.: Pi Lambda Theta (assoc. v.p. 1982). Avocations: music, swimming, tennis. Address: 806 Cypress Blvd Apt 507 Pompano Beach FL 33069-4034 E-mail: LG507@aol.com.

GOLDBERG, LUELLA GROSS, corporation executive; b. Mpls., Feb. 26, 1937; d. Louis and Beatrice (Rosenthal) Gross; m. Stanley M. Goldberg, June 23, 1958; children: Ellen Goldberg Luger, Fredric, Martha Goldberg Aronson. BA, Wellesley Coll., 1958; postgrad. in philosophy, U. Minn., 1958-59. Dir. Reliastar Fin. Corp., 1978-2000, NRG Energy, Inc., Mpls., 2001—. Bd. dirs. Northwestern Nat. Life Ins. Co., Mpls. TCF Fin. Corp., Mpls., Hormel Foods Corp., Austin, Minn., Personnel Decisions Internatl., dir. Communications System, Inc., ING Group, Amsterdam, 2001—. Pres. Minn. Orch. Women's Assn., Mpls., 1972-74; bd. dirs. Minn. Orch. Assn., 1972—, chmn., 1980-83, Mpls. chpt. United Way, 1978-88, Ind. Sector, Washington, 1984-90; regent St. John's U., Collegeville, Minn., 1974-83; trustee U. Minn. Found., Mpls., 1978—, chmn. bd. trustees, 1996-98; mem. bd. overseers Sch. Mgmt., U. Minn., Mpls., 1980—; chmn. bd. trustees Wellesley (Mass.) Coll., 1985-93, acting pres., 1993; trustee Wellesley Coll., 1978-96, emerita, 1996—, Northwest Area Found., 1994—. Recipient Disting. Svc. award, Minn. Orch. Assn., 1983, Community Svc. Leadership award, Mpls. YWCA, 1986, Disting. Svc. to Higher Edn. award, Minn. Pvt. Coll. Coun., 1992, Humanitarian award, NCCJ, 1992, Regents award, U. Minn., 2000, Alumnae Achievement award, Wellesley Coll., 2002, Disting. Women's award, Northwoods U., 2001, Lifetime Achievement award as Outstanding Dir., Twin Cities Bus. Monthly, 2001. Mem. Minn. Women's Econ. Round Table, Cosmopolitan Club (N.Y.C.), Mpls. Club, Phi Beta Kappa. Avocations: water skiing, wind surfing, traveling. Home: 7019 Tupa Dr Minneapolis MN 55439-1643

GOLDBERG, MARC EVAN, biotechnology venture capitalist; b. Boston, Mar. 14, 1957; s. Ray Allan and Thelma (Englander) G.; m. Pamela Girouard, Nov. 28, 1998; children: Frederick Warren, Alyssa Rachel, Meredith Hayley. AB, Harvard U., 1979, MBA, JD, 1983. Bar: Mass. 1985. Mgr. bus. devel. Genetics Inst., Inc., Cambridge, Mass., 1983-87; v.p. fin. and corp. devel., chief fin. officer, treas. Safer, Inc., Newton, Mass., 1987-91; pres., chief exec. officer Mass. Biotech. Rsch. Inst., Worcester, Mass., 1991-97; mng. dir. BioVentures Investors, Cambridge, 1997—. Bd. dirs. Pintex Pharms., Inc., Enanta Pharms., Inc., AngioLink Corp.; founder Mass. Biotech. Coun., bd. dirs., 1985-97, pres., 1985-87, 90-92. Mem., prin. author Gov.'s Task Force on Biotech., 1991—98; trustee Worcester State Coll., 1991—2002, vice chmn., 1993—95, chmn., 1995—97; trustee Harvard Yearbook Pubs., 1981—; mem. exec. adv. bd. Harvard Varsity Club, 1982—, bd. dirs., 2001—; mem. adv. com. town of Wellesley, 1992—94, mem. town meeting, 1993—95; trustee Mass. Taxpayers Found., 1993—99; mem. rsch. and tech. devel. com. Beth Israel Deaconess Med. Ctr., 1990—. Mem. Mass Bar Assn., New Eng./Israel C. of C. (trustee 1993-2000), Harvard Bus. Sch. Assn. Boston (bd. govs. 1993-96). Office: BioVentures Investors 245 1st St 14th Fl Cambridge MA 02142

GOLDBERG, MARCIA B. medical educator; b. Boston, July 29, 1957; AB in Biology summa cum laude, Harvard U., 1979, MD, 1984. Diplomate Am. Bd. Internal Medicine, Am. Bd. Infectious Diseases. Intern in primary care internal medicine Mass. Gen. Hosp., Boston, 1984—85, jr. and sr. resident in primary care internal medicine, 1985—87, clin. and rsch. fellow in medicine, 1987—90; rsch. fellow in medicine Harvard Med. Sch., Boston, 1987—90; rsch. fellow Unite de Pathogenie Microbienne Moleculaire, Inst. Pasteur, Paris, 1991—93; asst. prof. Dept. Microbiology and Immunology, Dept. Medicine divsn. Infectious Diseases Albert Einstein Coll. of Medicine, Bronx, NY, 1993—98, assoc. prof. dept. microbiology and immunology, 1998—99, assoc. dir. med. scientist tng. program, 1995—99; assoc. prof. medicine divsn. infectious disease Mass Gen. Hosp., Boston, 1999—. Contbr. articles and revs. to profl. jours. Recipient Rsch. award, Fundaciion para la Edn. Superior, 1981, Proctor-Wellington Fund award, 1987, Stuart Pharms. Travel award, Nat. Found. Infectious Diseases, 1990, Young Investigator award, Maxwell Finland, 1991, Intersci. Conf. on Antimicrobial Agents and Chemotherapy, 1991, Established Investigator award, Am. Heart Assn., 1996; fellow, Inst. Nat. de la Sante et de la Recherche Med., 1991, Moseley Traveling, Harvard Med. Sch., 1991—92; scholar Hon. Nat., Radcliffe Coll., 1975, Fulbright, 1991—92, Pew, 1994—98. Mem.: Infectious Diseases Soc. Am., Am. Soc. Microbiology, Phi Beta Kappa. Office: Mass Gen Hosp Divsn Infectious Disease 55 Fruit St Boston MA 02114-2696

GOLDBERG, MARK ARTHUR, neurologist; b. N.Y.C., Sept. 4, 1934; s. Jacob and Bertha (Grushlawska) G.; 1 child, Jonathan. BS, Columbia U., 1955; PhD, U. Chgo., 1959, MD, 1962. Resident neurology N.Y. Neurol. Inst., N.Y.C., 1963-66; asst. prof. neurology Columbia U. Coll. Phys. and Surgs., N.Y.C., 1968-71; assoc. prof. neurology and pharmacology UCLA, 1971-77, prof. neurology and pharmacology, 1977—; chair dept. neurology Harbor UCLA Med. Ctr., Torrance, 1977—. Contbr. articles to profl. jours., chpts. to books. Capt. U.S. Army, 1966-68. Fellow Am. Neurol. Assn., Am. Acad. Neurology; Am. Soc. Neurochemistry, Assn. Univ. Profs. Neurology. Avocation: oriental cusine.

GOLDBERG, MARK JOEL, lawyer; b. Pitts., June 2, 1941; s. Charles J. and Eleanore (Letwin) G.; m. Wendy Witt, Dec. 23, 1988; children: Michael, Wendy, Josh, Jamie. BA, Washington and Jefferson Coll., 1963; JD, Case Western Res. U., 1966. Bar: Pa. 1966, Ohio 1966, U.S. Tax Ct. 1969, U.S. Supreme Ct. 1972. Assoc. Jerome Silver, Cleve., 1966-67; pvt. practice, Pitts., 1967-69; ptnr. Goldberg & Wedner, Pitts., 1969-80; ptnr., shareholder Gillotti Goldberg & Capristo, Pitts., 1981-91, Goldberg Gentile & Voelker, Pitts., 1991-92, Goldberg, Gruener, Gentile, Horoho & Avalli, P.C., Pitts., 1992—. Mem. drafting com. Pa. Divorce Code, 1978-80, 88; frequent lectr. Pa. Bar Inst., Pa. Trial Lawyers Assn., Am. Acad. Matrimonial Lawyers. Contbr. articles to profl. jours. Committeeman Dem. Party, Pitts., 1970's; pres. bd. dirs. Parent and Child Guidance Ctr., Pitts., 1984-86. Fellow Am. Acad. Matrimonial Lawyers (pres. Pa. chpt. 1988-90, nat. bd. govs. 1991-95); mem. Am. Coll. Family Trial Lawyers (diplomate, officer), Allegheny County Bar Assn. (coun. mem. family law sect. 1972—, chmn. 1982-84), Pa. Bar Assn. (family law sect. chmn. 1986-88), Westmoreland Country Club, Rivers Club. Jewish. Avocations: golf, travel. Home: 14 Carmel Ct Pittsburgh PA 15221-3618 Office: Goldberg Gruener Et Al 230 Grant Bldg Pittsburgh PA 15219-2200 E-mail: mgoldberg@gggha.com.

GOLDBERG, MARTIN, physician, educator; b. Phila., Sept. 15, 1930; s. Samuel and Esther (Shreibman) Goldberg; m. Lynn Taksey, June 17, 1951 (dec. Aug. 31, 1976); children: Meryl I, Karen L, Dara S; m. Marion Lindblad, May 26, 1978. BA, Temple U., 1951, MD, 1955; MA (hon.), U. Pa., 1971. Diplomate Am Bd Internal Med (chmn nephrology comt 1976-79, bd govs 1976-79), Nat Bd Med Examiners. Intern Phila. Gen. Hosp., 1955-56, resident, 1957-59, sr. attending physician, 1970-76; resident Cleve. Clinic, 1956-57; fellow nephrology Hosp. U. Pa., Phila., 1959-61, sr. attending physician, 1962-79; mem. faculty U. Pa. Sch. Medicine, 1960-79, prof. medicine, 1970-79, chief renal electrolyte sect., 1966-79, acting chmn. dept. medicine, 1975-76; sr. attending physician Phila. VA Hosp., 1968-79; Gordon and Helen Hughes Taylor prof. medicine U. Cin., 1979-86; chmn. internal medicine U. Cin. Coll. Med. and Hosp., 1979-86; prof. medicine Temple U. Sch. Medicine, Phila., 1986-96, dean, vice pres., 1986-89, prof. emeritus, 1997—, asst. to dean for computer assisted instrn., 1997-2000; chmn. sci. adv. com. Gen. Clin. Rsch. Ctr. Temple U. Hosp., 1993—. Study consult NIH, 1968—72, 1982—85; mem sci adv bd Nat Kidney Found, 1970—76; chmn kidney coun Am Heart Asn, 1973—74; bd mgrs St Christopher's Hosp Children, 1986—89. Mem. editl. bd.: Jour Clin Investigation, 1969—70, Kidney Int, 1972—74, Jour Mineral and Electrolyte Metabolism, 1977—91, Am Jour Hypertension, 1990—97; editor (physician-ed): Nephrology MKSAP Am Col Physicians, 1991—94; editor: (assoc ed) MKSAP 11, MKSAP 12, ACP, 1996—2000; mem. editl. adv. bd.: PDxMD, 2000. Recipient Alumni Prize, Temple Univ Sch Med, 1955, Research Career Develop Award, NIH, 1963—70, Lindback Award for Distinguished Teaching, Univ Pa, 1972, Distinguished Med Scientist of the Yr Award, Med Alumni Temple Univ Sch Med, 1985, Honoree of the Yr Award, Greater Del Valley Kidney Found, 1997, A N Richards Award for Distinguished Contbns to Nephrology, Univ Pa, 1998, Centennial Award, Asn Chmn Depts Physiology, 1989; grantee Research, NIH, 1962—89, John Hartford Found, 1970—73. Fellow: ACP (nat sci program comt 1976—81), Royal Soc Med, Am Col Clin Pharmacology; mem.: Physicians for Social Responsibility (adv bd Philadelphia chpt 1988—98), Col Physicians Philadelphia, Am Med Informatics Asn, Int Soc Nephrology (coun 1975—84), Am Soc Nephrology (secy-treas 1975—78), Am Fedn Clin Research (chmn eastern sect 1967), Am Physiological Soc, Am Soc Clin Investigation, Asn Am Physicians, Asn Am Med Cols (coun deans 1986—89), Interurban Clin Club, Alpha Omega Alpha. Achievements include research in renal physiology and disease; electrolyte and acid-base metabolism, computer assisted instruction and diagnosis. Office: Temple Univ Hosp Nephrology Parkinson Pavilion Philadelphia PA 19140

GOLDBERG, MARTIN STANFORD, retired lawyer; b. Youngstown, Ohio, July 11, 1924; s. George and Bee (Walker) G.; m. Donna Mae Lowry, Nov. 18, 1962; children: Jeffrey A., Jeralyn Goldberg Mercer. BA, JD, Ohio State U., 1952. Bar: Ohio 1952, Calif. 1981. Sole practice law, Youngstown, Ohio, 1952—2001. Served with USAF, 1942-45, PTO. Decorated D.F.C. Mem. ABA, Calif. Bar Assn., Ohio Bar Assn., Mahoning County Bar Assn., Am. Trial Lawyers Assn. Clubs: Lodges: Masons, Friars Club. Republican. Jewish. Avocations: reading, writing, music. Home: 74513 Old Prospector Trl Palm Desert CA 92260-5624

GOLDBERG, MARVIN ALLEN, lawyer, business consultant; b. Phila., Jan. 9, 1943; s. Daniel and Elizabeth (Katz) G.; m. Kathryn Elizabeth Balotsky, Apr. 27, 1974; children: Robert Andrew, MaryBeth Anne. BS, Temple U., 1964, JD, 1967. Bar: Pa. 1968, U.S. Dist. Ct. (ea. dist.) Pa. 1980, U.S. Supreme Ct. 1976. Estate tax atty. IRS, Phila., 1967—68; staff atty. Legal Aid Soc. Northampton County, Easton, Pa., 1969-70, Northampton County Pub. Defender, Easton, Pa., 1969-70; pvt. practice law Phila., 1970-76, tchr. Inst. for Paralegal Tng., Phila., 1973; staff atty. Legal Aid Soc. Phila., 1974-76; CEO Goldberg & Assocs., P.C., Phila., 1976—. Cons. Butcher Trade Exchange, Ft. Washington, Pa., 1982-92. Mem. Chestnut St. Assn., Phila; dir. Sr. Citizen Judicare Project, Phila., 1977. With USAF, 1967-73. Fellow Roscoe Pound Inst.; mem. ABA, Phila. Bar Assn., Phila. Trial Lawyers Assn., Assn. Trial Lawyers Am., Pa. Trial Lawyers Assn., Attys. Across Am. (founding mem.), Jewish War Vets, Beta Gamma Sigma, Phi Alpha Delta. Avocations: running, flying, sailing, chess, algebra, 19th century physics. Office: Goldberg & Assocs PC 1334 Walnut St Fl 5 Philadelphia PA 19107-5311

GOLDBERG, MAUREEN MCKENNA, state supreme court justice; b. Pawtucket, R.I., Feb. 11, 1951; m. Robert D. Goldberg. Grad., St. Mary's Acad., 1969; AB cum laude, Providence Coll., 1973; JD cum laude, Suffolk U., 1978. Bar: R.I. 1978, Mass. 1978, U.S. Ct. of Appeals (1st cir.) 1979. Asst. atty. gen. Adminstr. of the Criminal Divsn., 1978-84; town solicitor South Kingstown, 1985-87, Town of Westerly, 1987-90, acting town mgr., 1990; spl. legal counsel R.I. State Police; apptd. assoc. justice Superior Ct., 1990-96; assoc. justice R.I. Supreme Ct., 1997—. Mem. ABA, R.I. Bar Assn., R.I. Trial Judges Assn., Pawtucket Bar Assn. Office: Rhode Island Supreme Ct 250 Benefit St 7th Fl Providence RI 02903-2719*

GOLDBERG, MELVIN ARTHUR, communications executive; b. N.Y.C., Feb. 5, 1923; s. Louis and Anna (Bergman) G.; m. Norma N. Nertz, Oct. 18, 1956; children: Ronald, Richard, Joan Sandra. BS, CCNY, 1942; AM, Columbia U., 1950. Mem. staff Bur. Applied Social Rsch., Columbia, 1946-47; news editor, rsch. dir. TV mag., 1947-49; dir. sales planning and rsch. DuMont TV Network, 1949-52; dep. dir. Office Rsch. and Evaluation, U.S. Info. Agy., 1952-53; exec. sec. Ultra-High Frequency TV Assn., 1953-54; cons., chief of rsch. M-G Rsch., 1954-56; dir. rsch. Westinghouse Broadcasting Co., 1956-62; v.p., dir. rsch. Nat. Assn. Broadcasters, 1962-64; v.p. planning and rsch. John Blair & Co., 1964-69, pres. Melvin A. Goldberg Inc., N.Y.C., 1969-77; v.p. primary and social rsch. ABC-TV, 1977-80, v.p. news, social and tech. rsch., 1980-85; v.p. market planning, tech. and social rsch. ABC Inc.; exec. dir. Electronic Media Rating Coun., 1985-93; pres. Melvin A. Goldberg Inc., N.Y.C., 1993—. Former mem. ABA Commn. on Pub. Understanding About the Law. Mem. editorial bd. TV Quar.; Contbr. articles to profl. publs. Mem. Great Neck/North Shore Cable Commn., chmn. long range planning com. Decorated D.F.C., Air medal with clusters. Mem. Am. Assn. Pub. Opinion Rsch., Radio-TV Rsch. Coun., Nat. Acad. TV Arts and Scis. Home: 17 North Dr Great Neck NY 11021-1337 Office: Melvin A Goldberg Inc Comm 17 North Dr Great Neck NY 11021-1337

GOLDBERG, MICHAEL ELLIS, neurologist, neuroscientist; b. New York, N.Y., Aug. 10, 1941; s. Samuel Goldberg; m. Deborah Baron Goldberg, July 31, 1966; children: Joshua, Jonathan. AB, Harvard Coll., 1963; MD, Harvard Med. Sch., 1968. Asst. prof. to prof. neurology NIH Georgetown U. Sch Medicine, Washington, 1978—2001; med. rsch. officer Lab. Sensorimotor Rsch. Nat. Eye Inst., Bethesda, Md., 1978—2001; David Mahoney prof. brain and behavior, dept. neurology, psychiatry, and the Center for Neurobiology and Behavior Columbia U. Coll. Physicians and Surgeons, N.Y.C., 2001—. Guest investigator Lab. Sensorimotor Rsch. Nat. Eye Inst., 2001—02; James M. Sprague lectr. U. Pa., 2000. Author: (Journal Articles) Science, Nature, Journal of Neurophysiology, Journal of Neuroscience, Experimental Brain Research, Vision Research, 2001; contbr. articles to profl. jours. Grantee rsch. grantee, Whitehall Found., 2001—. Mem.: Internat. Neuropsychol. Symposium (pres. 1990—94), Soc. Neurosci. (Spl. Achievement award 2000), Am. Neurol. Assn. Personal E-mail: meg2008@columbia.edu. Business E-Mail: meg2008@columbia.edu.

GOLDBERG, MORRIS, internist; b. Jan. 23, 1928; s. Saul and Lena (Schanberg) G.; m. Elaine Shaw, June 24, 1956; children: Alan Neil, Seth David, Nancy Beth. BS in Chemistry cum laude, Poly. Inst. Bklyn., 1951; MD, SUNY, Bklyn., 1956. Diplomate Am. Bd. Internal Medicine. Intern Jewish Hosp., Bklyn., 1956-57, resident, 1957-58, 61-62, renal fellow, 1958-59; practice medicine specializing in internal medicine N.Y.C., 1962-71, Phoenix, 1971—. Instr. to asst. clin. prof. internal medicine State U. N.Y. Coll. Medicine, Bklyn., 1962-71; clin. investigator, metabolic research unit Jewish Hosp. Bklyn., 1962-71; cons. in field; mem. staff Phoenix Bapt., Good Samaritan, St. Joseph's Hosp., Vets. Affairs Med. Ctr., Phoenix. Contbr. articles to med. jours. Capt. M.C., U.S. Army, 1959-61. Fellow ACP; mem. AMA, Am. Soc. Internal Medicine, Am. Coll. Nuclear Physicians (charter mem.), Am. Soc. Nephrology, Am. Soc. Hypertension (charter mem.), Ariz. Med. Assn., 38th Parallel Med. Soc., S. Korea, Ariz., Maricopa County Med. Assn., Sigma Xi, Phi Lambda Upsilon, Alpha Omega Alpha. Office: Vets Affairs Med Ctr 650 E Indian School Rd Phoenix AZ 85012-1839

GOLDBERG, MORTON EDWARD, pharmacologist; b. Phila., July 11, 1932; s. Herman and Ethel (Shill) G.; m. Janet Louise Werlin, Aug. 15, 1954; children— Shellie, Ellen, David. BS, Phila. Coll. Pharmacy and Sci., 1954, MS in Pharmacology, 1955, DSc in Pharmacology, 1958. Sr. pharmacologist Abbott Labs., North Chicago, Ill., 1958-60; asst. dir. pharmacology Union Carbide Corp., Tuxedo, N.Y., 1960-69; dir. pharmacodynamics Warner Lambert Research Inst., Morris Plains, N.J., 1969-73; dir. pharmacology Squibb Inst. Med. Research, Princeton, N.J., 1973-77; v.p. biomed. research Stuart Pharms. div. ICI Americas, Wilmington, Del., 1977-84; v.p. rsch., devel., and regulatory affairs ICI Pharm. Group divsn. ICI Ams. (now Astra Zeneca Pharm.), Wilmington, Del., 1984-92; clin. prof. pharmacology and exptl. therapeutics Dept. Pharmacology U. Pa. Sch. Medicine, Phila., 1992-96. Vis. prof. toxicology Phila. Coll. Pharmacy and Sci.; vis. prof. pharmacology, Allegheny U. Med. Sch., Phila., 1978-2001, U. Pa. Sch. Med., Phila., 1996-2001; cons. to pharm. industry in drug discovery and devel., 1992—; mem. extramural sci. adv. bd. NIDA, 1993-95, mem. nat. adv. bd. 1996-2000. Editor-in-chief: series Pharmacological and Biochemical Properties of Drug Substances; contbr. articles to profl. jours. Asst. scoutmaster Boy Scouts Am., Glen Rock, N.J., 1968-72. NIH grantee, 1961-64 Fellow Acad. Pharm. Sci., AAAS, N.Y. Acad. Sci.; mem. Am. Soc. Pharmacology and Exptl. Therapeutics, Behavioral Pharmacology Soc., Internat. Soc. Biochem. Pharmacology, Soc. Toxicology (charter), Sigma Xi, Rho Chi. Home: 715 Severn Rd Wilmington DE 19803-1725 E-mail: mjgold854@aol.com.

GOLDBERG, NANCY G. business owner, community volunteer; b. Pitts., 1942; d. Henry and Rose Gross; m. Gerald Sanford Goldberg, 1966; children: Brian Michael (dec.), Sheri Goldberg Glickman. Student, U. Laval, Que., Can., 1962; BA, U. Pitts., 1963; MAT, Johns Hopkins U., 1965. French tchr. secondary schs., Balt., 1965, Arlington, Va., 1965-68; travel agt. with various agys., Plantation, Fla., 1984-94; interior decorator Nancy G. Goldberg, Interiors, Plantation, 1983-92; pres., owner Creative Inspirations, Inc., Plantation, 1992—. Owner, dir. Creative Inspirations Gallery, Fort Lauderdale, Fla., 1994—96; bd. dirs. Child Advocacy, 1978—81, Jewish Family Svcs., 1982; owner, dir. Creative Inspirations Gallery, Plantation, Fla., 1996—98, Delray Beach, Fla., 2001—02; owner ArtisticJewelry.com, DecoratorPaintings.com, Ci-Gallery.com. Chair for internat. health Broward County Med. Assn. Aux., 1982—83, mem., 1974—85; bd. dirs., chair for Broward County Mosaic, Jewish Life in Fla., Ft. Lauderdale, 1977—81; mem. Brandeis Univ. Women's Com., 1975—; numerous other civic activities; bd. dirs. Greater Ft. Lauderdale Sister Cities Internat., 1999—. Recipient awards for cmty. svc. Mem.: NOW, Nat. Coun. Jewish Women (offices), Am. Craft Coun., Women's Am. ORT, Phi Beta Kappa, Sigma Kappa Phi. Democrat. Jewish. Avocations: art, gourmet cooking, gardening, world travel.

GOLDBERG, NEIL A. lawyer; b. N.Y.C., Dec. 24, 1947; s. Bernard G. Goldberg; children: Jane Hana, Robert Saul. BA cum laude, SUNY, Stony Brook, 1969; JD cum laude, SUNY, Buffalo, 1973. Bar: N.Y. 1974, U.S. Dist. Ct. (we. dist.) N.Y. 1974. Sr. ptnr. Saperston & Day P.C., Buffalo, 1974—2001, Goldberg Segalda, Buffalo, 2001—; pres. DRI, 2000—01. Editor Products Liaility in New York, 1997; co-editor in chief Preparing for and Trying the Civil Lawsuit. Mem.: ABA, Lawyers for Civil Justice (pres.-elect 2003), Erie County Bar Assn., N.Y. State Bar Assn. (ins. and compensation law sect. 1986—, past chmn. product liability com. torts), Am. Arbitration Assn. (bd. dirs. 1985—, product liability adv. coun.), Def. Rsch. Inst. (past pres.), Internat. Assn. Def. Counsel. Office: Goldberg Segalla 120 Delaware Ave Ste 500 Buffalo NY 14202 Office Fax: 716-566-5401. Business E-Mail: ngoldberg@goldbergsegalla.com.

GOLDBERG, NORMA LORRAINE, retired public welfare administrator; b. South Bend, Ind., May 6, 1929; d. James Albert and Minnie Sylvia (Kaplan_ Seamon; m. Albert Goldberg, Apr. 19, 1959 (dec. Dec. 1976); children: Lisa Ann, Paul Ephraim. BS, Ind. U., Bloomington, 1950; postgrad., Ind. U., 1950-52. Social worker Indpls. Pub. Schs., 1951-53; with Marion County Dept. Pub. Welfare, Indpls., 1953-66, 71-73, asst. dir., 1961-64, dir., 1964-66, intake supr., 1971-73; asst. dir. Ind. Dept. Pub. Welfare, Indpls., 1973-79, dir., 1979 87, regional adminstr., 1987-91; spl. project officer Adminstrn. Children and Families, 1991-94, asst. regional adminstr., 1994-95. Steering com. Whitehouse Conf. on Children and Youth, Indpls., 1982-83; program com. Gov.'s Conf. on Children and Youth, Indpls., 1982-83. Founder Welfare Service League, Indpls., 1968, pres., 1968-71, mem., 1968—. Mem. steering com. Indpls. sect. Nat. Coun. Jewish Women, 1982-87; steering com. Guardian ad Litem Project; mem. Rep. Round Table, Indpls., 1983-87; city chmn. adult bd. B'nai B'rith Youth Orgn., 1985-86; mem. People of Vision, Indpls. Mus. Art, Social Action Com., Indpls. Hebrew Congregation, Indpls. Newcomers Club. Recipient Gov.'s Vol. Action Program Cmty. Svc. award Gov. Ind., 1980. Mem. Assn. Women Execs., Dallas Coun. World Affairs, Dallas Women's Found., Ind. Conf. on. Social Concerns (state coord. 1963-64), Network Women in Bus., Indpls. Coun. Women (program chmn. 1968-71), The 500 Club, Inc., Meridian Hills Kiwanis, Northside Investment Club. E-mail: gold@in.net.

GOLDBERG, NORMAN ALBERT, music publisher, writer; b. Belleville, Ill., Mar. 11, 1918; s. Charles S. and Bessie (Tenenbaum) G.; m. Ruth E. Rodenberg, Dec. 29, 1940; children: Marcia Lee, Marc Edwin. BS, U. Ill., 1939, M in Music, 1942. Instr. U. Ill., Urbana, 1939-41; mem. faculty U. Iowa, Iowa City, 1941-42, Mo. High Sch., Univ. City, 1944-48; owner Baton Music Co., St. Louis, 1948-73; pres. Magnamusic-Baton Inc. (name now MMB Music), St. Louis, 1964—, G. Henle, USA, 1981-86, Norruth Music, Inc., 1985—; pub. Internat. Jour. Arts Medicine; pres. Contemporary Arts Corp., St. Louis, 1993—. Edn. com. St. Louis Symphony. Composer various works for alto and bass clarinets; arranger various symphony orchs. and bands. Bd. dirs. Internat. Assn. Music for Handicapped, Provo, Utah, St. Louis Conservatory and Sch. for the Arts (now Webster U. Cmty. Music Sch.), 1991—94, Rhythm for Life, 1992—96, Music Brain Info. Ctr., 1992—; mem. adv. coun. Webster U. Coll. Fine Arts, 2002—. With U.S. Army, 1943. Recipient Presdl. award Nat. Assn. Music Therapy, 1993, Constituent Leadership award U. Ill. Alumni Assn., 1997, Lifetime Achievement in the Arts award St. Louis Arts and Edn. Coun., 1999. Mem. Music Industry Conf. (bd. dirs. 1972-84, past pres. 1982-84, Outstanding Svc. award 1986), Univ. City C. of C. (past pres. 1971), Am. Assn. Music Therapy (bd. dirs. 1988-98, Joint Presdl. award with Nat. Assn. Music Therapy 1995, Lifetime Achievement award 1996), Jewish War Vets. (past dep. comdr. 1953), Univ. Ill. Alumni Assn. (bd. dirs. 1990-96, chair constituents com. 1994-96, Constituent Leadership award 1997), Am. Orff-Schulwerk Assn. (life, bd. dirs. 1970-75, First Industry Svc. award 1998), St. Louis chpt. AOSA (life), Music Educators Nat. Conf. (exec. bd. 1982-84), Internat. Soc. for Music in Medicine, Internat. Arts Medicine Assn. (bd. dirs. 1990-99, v.p. 1997-2000, Bridge Builder award 1997), Am. Music Therapy Assn. Norman Goldberg Libr., B'nai El Cong. (life, past pres., First Eternal Light award with Ruth Goldberg 1999), Internat. Arts Med. Assn. (v.p. 1997-99), Soc. for the Arts in Healthcare (bd. dirs. 2000-01), Phi Mu Alpha, Rotary (past pres. 1967-78, Univ. City chpt.), Shriners, Mason. Democrat. Jewish. Avocations: woodworking, metalsmithing, reading. Home: 790 Dielman Rd Saint Louis MO 63132-3520 Office: MMB Music Inc Contemporary Arts Bldg 3526 Washington Ave Saint Louis MO 63103-1019

GOLDBERG, PAMELA WINER, finance educator, director; b. Boston, Oct. 14, 1955; d. Arthur Leonard and Marilyn (Miller) Winer; children from previous marriage: Frederick Warren, Alyssa Rachel, Meredith Hayley. BA, Tufts U., 1977; MBA, Stanford U., 1981. Day care dir. Cmty. Action Inc., Haverhill, Mass., 1977-79; lending assoc. Bankers Trust Co., N.Y.C., 1980-81; mgr., bank officer, corp. fin. dept. Citicorp, N.Y.C., 1981-82; assoc. dir., mergers and acquisitions group State St. Bank, Boston, 1983-85; ind. strategic cons. Wellesley, Mass., 1986-97; dir. bus. rels. Babson Coll., Wellesley, 1998—2002; prof., dir. Ctr. for Entrepreneurial Leadership Tufts U., 2002—. Bd. friends Beth Israel Hosp., Boston, 1987—96; trustee Recuperative Ctr., Boston, 1988—95; mem. Hunnewell Sch. PTO Bd., 1991—96; mem. exec. bd. trustees Temple Beth Elohim, Wellesley, 1992—2000, treas., 1997—2000, Synagogue 2000 com., 2000—; bd. dirs. Wellesley LWV, 1995—98. Avocations: swimming, tennis, singing. Home: 34 Ivy Rd Wellesley MA 02482-4554 Office: Tufts University 4 Colby St Medford MA 02155 Business E-Mail: pamela.goldberg@tufts.edu. E-mail: pwg14@aol.com.

GOLDBERG, PAUL BERNARD, gastroenterologist, clinical researcher; b. Bklyn., Apr. 11, 1950; s. Samuel and Eva (Turkenitz) G.; m. Harriet Ruth Ferrer, July 8, 1973 (div. 1987); children: Deborah Lynn, Susan Michelle; m. Mary Alice Denaro, June 23, 1990; 1 child, Laura Alicia. BA in Chemistry summa cum laude, Cornell U., 1967-71, MD, 1971-75. Diplomate Am. Bd. Internal Medicine, Am. Bd. Gastroenterology. Intern in medicine Hosp. of U. of Pa., Phila., 1975-76, resident in medicine, 1976-78, fellow in gastroenterology, 1978-80, fellow in nutritional support svc., 1979-80; med. coord. and founder nutritional support svc. Lakeland (Fla.) Gen. Hosp., 1980-81; attending physician Halifax Med. Ctr., 1980—, Ormond Meml. Hosp., 1980—, Atlantic Med. Ctr., 1980-2000, Fish Meml. Hosp., New Smyrna Beach, Fla., 1989-99, Peninsula Med. Ctr., 1989-94. Pres. Sunshine Health Care Plan, Inc., 1983-86, v.p., 1986-87; chief staff Humana Hosp., Daytona Beach, 1986-88, trustee, 1986-89, mem. exec. com., 1984-91; mem. rev. bd. Coastal Instnl. Rev., 1990-93, chmn. rev. bd., 1993-96; expert reviewer Fla. Dept. Profl. Regulation, 1990—; pres. med. staff Halifax Hosp., 1996-97; clin. asst. prof. medicine dept. family medicine U. South Fla. Rschr. and author in field. Physician adv. Daytona chpt. Crohn's and Colitis Found., 1991-95. Recipient Nat. award Ford Future Scientists of Am., 1967, Westinghouse Sci. Talent Search finalist, 1967. Fellow ACP, Am. Coll. Gastroenterology; mem. Am. Gastroent. Soc., Am. Soc. Gastrointestinal Endoscopy, Am. Soc. for Parenteral and Enteral Nutrition (pres. Fla. chpt. 1991-92), Volusia County Med. Soc. (exec. com. 1991-94, co-chmn. mini internship program 1992-94, 2000-01), Fla. Gastrointestinal Soc., Fla. Med. Assn. (alt. del. to ho. of dels. 1990-95), Fla. Assn. Nutritional Support (1st pres.), Rotary, Phi Beta Kappa, Alpha Omega Alpha. Office: 1070 N Stone St Ste D Deland FL 32720 E-mail: pbgoldberg@aol.com.

GOLDBERG, RAY ALLAN, agriculturist, educator; b. Fargo, ND, Oct. 19, 1926; s. Max and Anne G.; m. Thelma R. Englander, May 20, 1956; children: Marc E., Jennifer E., Jeffrey L. AB, Harvard U., 1948, MBA, 1950; PhD, U. Minn., 1952; D of Pol. Sci. (hon.), U. Buenos Aires, Argentina, 2000. Officer, dir. Moorhead (Minn.) Seed & Grain Co., 1952-62; dir. Experience, Inc., Mpls., 1963-78, Arbor Acres Farm, Inc., N.Y.C., H.K. Webster Co.; mem. faculty Harvard U. Grad. Bus. Sch., 1955—, Moffett prof. agr. and bus., 1970-97; Moffett prof. agr. and bus. emeritus, 1997—; also dir. continuing edn. programs, participant seminars Harvard U. Grad. Bus. Sch. Bd. dirs. All-Flow, Inc., Daymon Assocs., Food One, Internet Commerce Sys., Inc., Veritec, Smithfield Foods; hon. prof. Royal Agrl. Coll., Cirencester, England, 1996; vis. prof. U. Minn. Grad. Sch., 1960; adv. coun. Foods Multinat., Inc., 1972-77; agrl.

investment com. John Hancock Ins. Co., 1971-95; cons. in field; adviser Instituto Centroamericano de Administracion de Empresa, Managua, Nicaragua, 1973—, Inst. Panamericano de Alta Direccion de Empressa, Mexico City, 1973—, U.S. Comptroller of Currency, 1975—, Food and Agr. Policy Project, Ctr. Nat. Policy, 1984—; study team, subgroup chmn. world food and nutrition study NRC, 1975—; com. tech. factor contbg. to nation's fgn. trade positions Nat. Acad. Engring., 1976—; chmn. agribus. adv. com. on Caribbean Basin USDA, 1982—; com. on indsl. policy for developing countries Commn. on Engring. and Tech. Systems, NRC, 1982—; task force on agr. Fowler-McCracken Commn., 1984—; adv. bd. The First Mercantile Currency Fund Inc., 1985—; internat. adv. bd. Atlantic Exchange Program, 1987—; mem. V.I. Lenin All-Union Acad. of Agrl. Scis., 1988—; mem. U.S. Presdl. Econ. Del. to Poland, Nov., 1989; scientific adv. bd. Sepragen Corp., 1993—, Inst. Food Technologists, 1999—; chmn. joint bus. scientific pub. policy consumer policy tech. com. U.S. Food System and Seminar, 1994—; internat. bd. vis. Zamorano, 1995—; adv. com. Foodfit.com., 1999—, sci. adv. bd., IFT/FDA Rsch. Contract, 1999, chmn. adv. panel for World Bank Guide to Developing Agrl. Markets and Agro-Enterprises, 1999, chmn. of suncommittee on Econ. and Social Devel. in a Global Context, Nat. Rsch. Coun., 2002; chmn. Task Force to utilize Tobacco Funds for Econ. Devel., Ky., Long Term Plan for Agricultural and Rural Development for the state of Kentucky, 2001, chmn. sub. com. on Econ. and Social Devel. in a Global Context for com. on opportunities in Agr.- NRC Bd. on Agr.; and Natural Resources, 2001. Author: Agribusiness Management for Developing Countries-Latin America, 1974, (with Lee F. Schrader) Farmers' Cooperative and Federal Income Taxes, 1974, (with John T. Dunlop et al) The Lessons of Wage and Price Controls-The Food Sector, 1977, (with Richard C. McGinity et al), Agribusiness Management for Devloping Countries-Southeast Asia Corn Study, 1979; editor: Research in Domestic and International Agribusiness Management, Vol. 1, 1980, Vol. 2, 1981, Vol. 3, 1982, Vol. 4, 1983, Vol. 5, 1984, Vol. 6, 1986, Vol. 7, 1987, Vol. 8, 1988, Vol. 9, 1989, Vol. 10, 1981, Vol. 11, 1995, Vol. 12, 1996; co-editor; (with Gerald E. Gaul) New Technologies and the Future of Food and Nutrition, 1991, The Emerging Global Food System: Public and Private Sector Issues, 1993; contbr. numerous articles to profl. jours.; chmn. editl. adv. bd. Agribus.: An Internat. Jour., 1983—. Bd. govs. Internat. Devel. Rsch. Ctr., Govt. of Can., 1978—; trustee Roxbury Latin Sch., Boston, 1973-76, Beth Israel Hosp., Boston, 1978—, mem. com. on patents and tech. transfer, 1982—, chmn. gerontology com., 1991—; mem. adv. com. to prep. sch. New Eng. Conservatory Music, 1974—, assoc. trustee, 1978—; vice chmn. bd. Spoleto Festival U.S.A., 1993; adv. mem. Polish Investment Fund, 1994—; chmn. adv. com. Sonoma Internat. Capital Assocs., 1994—; trustee Global Conservation Trust, Rome, 2002. Recipient Outstanding Alumni award, Dept. Agrl. Econs. U. Minn., 1992, 2d pl. McKinsey award, Harvard Bus. Rev., 2000, Disting. Svc. award, Harvard Grad. Sch. Bus. Adminstrn., 2001. Mem. Royal Agrl. Coll. Eng. (hon. prof. 1996—), V.I. Lenin All-Union Acad. Agrl. Scis. (fgn.), Am. Agrl. Econs. Assn. (editl. coun. 1974-78, nat. agribus. edn. commn. 1988—), Internat. Agribus. Mgmt. Assn. (pres. 1990-92, bd. dirs. 1990—, chmn. Russian food mgmt. program sponsored rsch. project 1994—, coord. non-partisan ednl., govt., pvt., sci., med. and consumer group for food, safety, nutrition and environ. 1994—, chmn. subcom. econ. and social devel.), Agribus. Inst. Cambridge (chmn. bd., treas. 1991-93), Am. Mktg. Assn., Am. Dairy Sci. Assn., Food Distbn. Rsch. Soc., Harvard Club (Boston and N.Y.C.), Bus. Coun. for Sustainable Devel. (adv. group for sustainable paper cycle project 1994—). Address: 975 Memorial Dr Apt 701 Cambridge MA 02138-5803 E-mail: rgoldberg@hbs.edu.

GOLDBERG, RICHARD ROBERT, lawyer; b. New York, Apr. 27, 1941; s. Joseph and Anne (Blumfield) G.; m. Rita Ann Zieve, June 30, 1963; 1 child, Andrew Louis. BA, Pa. State U., 1961; LLB, U. Md., 1964. Bar: Md. 1964, U.S. Ct. Appeals (4th cir.) 1970, U.S. Supreme Ct. 1974, U.S. Ct. Appeals (5th cir.) 1978, U.S. Ct. Appeals (D.C. cir.) 1992, Pa. 1994, N.J. 1994. Asst. city solicitor to Mayor and City Coun. City of Balt., 1965-70; atty. The Rouse Co., Columbia, Md., 1970-78, v.p., assoc. gen. counsel, 1978-94; ptnr. Ballard, Spahr, Andrews & Ingersoll, Phila., 1994—. Author: Real Estate Development of Downtown Projects, 1981; author and editor: (handbooks) Commercial Real Estate Leasing, Commercial Real Estate Financing; contbr. numerous articles to profl. publs. Chmn. Jewish Coun. of Howard County, Md., 1975-77, chmn. ann. campaign, 1978, 80, 87; pres. Temple Isaiah, Columbia, 1978-79; bd. trustees Jewish Fedn. Howard County, 1993-94. Mem. ABA (sec. real property, probate and trust law, chmn. prohibited transactions com. 1983-85, chmn. mgmt. property com. 1985-87, chmn. nat. insts. and satellite programs 1987-89, advisor UCC drafting com. article 1, article 3, article 9), Md. State Bar Assn., Pa. Bar Assn., Phila. Bar Assn., Am. Law Inst. (advisor restatement of the law of mortgages), Anglo-Am. Real Property Inst. (sec. 1990-92, chair-elect 1994, chair 1995), Am. Coll. Real Estate Lawyers (v.p. 1989-90, pres.-elect 1990-91, pres. 1991-92), Urban Land Inst., Am. Coll. of Mortgage Attys., Internat. Coun. Shopping Ctrs. (past chmn. law conf. com., mem. govtl. affairs com., econ. affairs subcom.). Home: 325 S 2nd St Philadelphia PA 19106-4317 Office: Ballard Spahr Andrews & Ingersoll 1735 Market St Ste 5100 Philadelphia PA 19103-7599 E-mail: goldbergr@ballardspahr.com.

GOLDBERG, RITA MARIA, foreign language educator; b. N.Y.C., Oct. 1, 1933; d. Abraham Morris and Hilda (Weinman) G. BA, Queens Coll., 1954; MA, Middlebury Coll., 1955; PhD, Brown U., 1968. Mem. faculty Queens Coll., N.Y.C., 1956, Oberlin (Ohio) Coll., 1957; mem. faculty St. Lawrence U., Canton, NY, 1957—2001, Dana prof. modern langs., 1975—2000, emerita, 2001—, chmn. dept., 1972-75, 83-91, chief reader Advanced Placement Program Spanish, 2001—. Chmn. Regional Conf. Am. Programs in Spain, 1979-81; mem. Nat. Fulbright Selection Com., 1990-92; mem. advanced placement devel. com. for Spanish, Ednl. Testing Svc., 1993-2000, chair, 1996-99. Spanish Ministry of Fgn. Affairs scholar, 1954-56; Danforth grantee, 1960-62, 63-64; N.Y. State Regents scholar, 1954, Brown U. scholar, 1960-62. Mem. Am. Assn. Tchrs. Spanish and Portuguese, AAUP, MLA, Am. Council Teaching of Fgn. Langs., N.E. Modern Lang. Assn., N.Y. State Assn. Fgn. Lang. Tchrs., Phi Beta Kappa, Sigma Delta Pi. Roman Catholic. Office: St Lawrence U Dept Modern Langs Lits Canton NY 13617 Address: Maria Guilhou 2 28016 Madrid Spain E-mail: ritagoldberg@stlawu.edu.

GOLDBERG, ROBERT THEODORE, ophthalmologist, educator; b. N.Y.C., Nov. 5, 1931; s. Benjamin and Lillian (Mermelstein) G.; m. Phyllis Evelyn White, June 20, 1956; children: Paul Kenneth, Lauren Ruth. BS summa cum laude, Queens Coll., 1952; MD, NYU, 1956. Diplomate Am. Bd. Ophthalmology. Intern SUNY, Downstate Med. Ctr., 1956-57, resident, 1960-63; fellow ophthalmology NYU Med. Ctr., 1963-65; dir. ophthalmology N.Y. Hosp. Med. Ctr. of Queens, 1972—. Assoc. clin. prof. ophthalmology NYU; clin. asst. prof. ophthalmology Weill Med. Coll., Cornell U. Collaborating staff Am. Jour. Ophthalmology, 1966-71, sci. referee, 1992-97. Capt. U.S. Army, 1957-59 Fellow: ACS; mem.: Am. Acad. Ophthalmology, Phi Beta Kappa. Office: 142-10 B Roosevelt Ave Flushing NY 11354-6046

GOLDBERG, RON, plastics broker executive; b. N.Y., Dec. 1, 1954; BA, Queens (N.Y.) Coll., 1976. V.p. Standard Polymers Corp., Tenafly, N.J., 1975-91; pres. RSG Polymer Corp., Stony Brook, N.Y, 1991—. Office: RSG Polymers Corp PO Box 2241 Valrico FL 33595

GOLDBERG, SABINE RUTH, soil scientist; b. Erlangen, Bavaria, Fed. Republic Germany, Mar. 25, 1958; came to U.S., 1967; d. Reinhold and Anneliese Elisabeth (Schmidt) Grimm; m. Gary Gene Goldberg, Aug. 9, 1980. BS in Agr., U. Fla., 1977; PhD, U. Calif., Riverside, 1983. Soil scientist USDA-Agrl. Rsch. Svc., Riverside, 1983—. Contbr. articles to Soil Soc. Am. Jour., Communications in Soil Sci. & Plant Analysis, Clays and Clay Minerals, Soil Sci., Jour. Colloid and Interface Sci. Grad. Regents fellow U. Calif., Riverside, 1980, 81. Fellow Soil Sci. Soc. Am.; mem. Am. Chem. Soc., Clay Minerals Soc., Toastmasters Internat. Club (pres. 1985, Able Toastmaster award 1988), Phi Kappa Phi, Sigma Xi, Gamma Sigma Delta. Office: USDA ARS George E Brown Salinity Lab 450 W Big Springs Rd Riverside CA 92507-4617 E-mail: sgoldberg@ussl.ars.usda.gov.

GOLDBERG, SAMUEL, retired mathematician, foundation officer; b. N.Y.C., Mar. 14, 1925; s. Gedalia and Fannie (Lieberman) G.; m. Marcia Chinitz, June 21, 1953; 1 son, David. BS, CCNY, 1944; PhD, Cornell U., 1950. Instr., then asst. prof. math. Lehigh U., Bethlehem, Pa., 1950-53; mem. faculty Oberlin (Ohio) Coll., 1953—, prof. math., 1961-85, emeritus prof., 1985—; program officer Alfred P. Sloan Found., N.Y.C., 1985-90, cons., 1990—. Vis. assoc. prof. Harvard U. Grad. Sch. Bus. Adminstrn., 1959-60; vis. prof. U. W.Australia, 1976; mem. com. math. in social scis. Social Sci. Research Council, 1979; participant African Math. Project, Mombasa, Kenya, 1965, 68 Author: Probability: An Introduction, 1960 (translated into Greek, German and Spanish, paperback edit.), Introduction to Difference Equations, 1958 (translated into Spanish, German and Japanese, also paperback edit.), Some Illustrative Examples of the Use of Undergraduate Mathematics in the Social Sciences, 1977, Probability in Social Science, 1983. Bd. dirs. Allen Meml. Hosp., Oberlin, 1980-85, 92-2000. Served with AUS, 1944-46. NSF sci. faculty fellow, 1960-61, 67-68 Mem. Math. Assn. Am., Am. Math. Soc., Phi Beta Kappa, Sigma Xi.

GOLDBERG, SETH A. lawyer; b. N.Y.C., Aug. 20, 1953; s. Seymour I. and Florence (Rovensky) Goldberg; m. Joan E. Shapiro, July 29, 1978; children: David, Emily. BA in History, SUNY, Binghamton, 1975; JD, Stanford U., 1978. Bar: D.C. 1978, Calif. 1991. Assoc. Steptoe & Johnson, Washington, 1978-86, ptnr., 1986—. Mem.: ABA, Environ. Law Inst., Prettyman-Levanthal Am. Inn Ct. Home: 8303 Whittier Blvd Bethesda MD 20817-3124 Office: 1330 Connecticut Ave NW Washington DC 20036-1704

GOLDBERG, SIDNEY, editor; b. N.Y.C., Mar. 1, 1931; s. Emanuel and Florence (Fischbein) G.; m. Lucianne Steinberger, April 10, 1966; children: Joshua John, Jonah Jacob. BA, U. Mich., 1950, MA, 1952; postgrad., NYU, 1952-53. Editor North Am. Newspaper Alliance, N.Y.C., 1957-71, Bell-McClure Syndicate, N.Y.C., 1957-71, pres. N. Am. Newspaper Alliance, 1971-72; reporter clk. Washington Post, 1955; fgn. editor World Week Mag., N.Y.C., 1956-57; v.p., dir. internat. newspaper ops. United Media, N.Y.C., 1972-94, sr. v.p., gen. mgr., 1994—2002, cons., 2002—; dir. Lucianne.com Media, Inc., 2003—. Pres. Newspaper Features Coun., 1999—2001. With AUS, 1953—55. Mem. Nat. Cartoonists Soc., Internat. Press Inst., Interam. Press Assn. Soc. of Silurians, Dutch Treat Club, Sigma Delta Chi. Jewish. Home: 255 W 84th St New York NY 10024-4321 Office: Lucianne Goldberg Agy 255 W 84th St New York NY 10024 E-mail: SidneyGoldberg1@aol.com.

GOLDBERG, STANLEY IRWIN, real estate company executive; b. Newport News, Va., May 13, 1934; s. David and Sara (Levy) G.; m. Marilyn Levin, Nov. 22, 1963 (dec. Oct. 1970); 1 child, Andrew Garfield. Student, Coll. William and Mary, 1952-54, U. Va., 1954-55. Lic. real estate broker, Va. V.p. Bedding Supply Co., Inc., Newport News, 1956-59, exec. v.p., 1960-61, pres., 1962-70; mng. ptnr. Goldkress Investment Co., Newport News, 1970—, also bd. dirs.; pres. Mutual Realty Corp., Newport News, 1973—. Trustee Temple Sinai, Newport News. Served with USAF, 1957-58. Mem. Nat. Assn. Realtors, Va. Assn. Realtors, Va. Peninsula Assn. of Realtors. Lodges: Elks. Home: 19 Hopemont Dr Newport News VA 23606-2146 Office: 11116 Jefferson Ave Newport News VA 23601-2551

GOLDBERG, TERI ANNE, writer, editor; Student, Oberlin (Ohio) Coll.; BA in Geology, U. Calif., Berkeley; MS in Journalism, Columbia U. Cons. EPA, N.Y.C. and Lakewood, Colo., 1984-89; writer, editor, 1990-98; columnist MSNBC.com, 1998—. Recipient Front Page award, The Newswomen's Club of N.Y., 2001. Home and Office: 454 7th Ave Brooklyn NY 11215-5514 E-mail: tgoldberg@nyc.rr.com.

GOLDBERG, VICTOR JOEL, retired data processing company executive; b. Chgo., Oct. 19, 1933; s. Albert J. and Ruth R. (Rosenberg) Goldbert; m. Harriet A. David, June 1, 1958 (dec. Apr. 1998); children: Susan A., Alan J.; m. Patricia A. Waldeck, Aug. 11, 2001. BS, Northwestern U., 1955, MBA, 1956. With IBM Corp., Armonk, N.Y., 1959-93, corp. dir. bus. plans, 1977-78, v.p. communications, 1979-81, corp. v.p., pres. communication products div., 1981-83, pres. nat. distbn. div., 1983-86, v.p. asst. group exec. marketing, 1986-88, v.p. mgmt. systems, 1988-93; dir. Edn. Through Music, 1998—. Mem. Forum for World Affairs, 1988-97; mem. planning bd. Village of Scarsdale, 1999—, chmn., 2002—; bd. govs. Am. Jewish Com., 1998—; trustee Inst. Internat. Edn., 1978—, mem. exec. com., 1984—, vice chmn., 1988—; trustee Mental Health Assn., Westchester, 1984-99, exec. v.p., 1997-99; trustee Westchester Reform Temple, 1995-98, Scarsdale Found., 1998—, treas. 1999—; dir. Actors Shakespeare Co., 1995-98; chmn. adv. com. Long Term Care Ombudsmen Program, Westchester County, 1995-98; trustee New Alternatives for Children, 1997-2001, treas., 1998-2001; v.p. Thanks to Scandavia, Inc., 2001—; trustee Ford Found. Internat. Fellowships program, 2001—. With U.S. Army, 1956-59. With U.S. Army, 1956—59. Mem. Beta Gamma Sigma.

GOLDBERG, WHOOPI (CARYN JOHNSON), actress; b. N.Y.C., Nov. 13, 1955; d. Robert and Emma (Harris) Johnson; m. David Claessen (div.); m. Lyle Trachtenberg, Oct. 1, 1994 (div. Oct. 1995); 1 child from previous marriage, Alexandrea Martin. Mem. San Diego Repertory Theatre, 1975—80, Blake St. Hawkeyes, Berkeley, Calif., 1980—84. Author: (novels) Alice; actor: (Broadway plays, one-person show) Whoopi Goldberg on Broadway, 1984—85; (plays) Living on the Edge of Chaos, 1988 (Calif. theatre award outstanding achievement, 1988); (films) The Color Purple, 1985, Jumpin' Jack Flash, 1986, Burglar, 1986, Telephone, 1987, Fatal Beauty, 1987, Clara's Heart, 1988; (films, cameo) Beverly Hills Brats, 1989; (films) Homer and Eddie, 1989, The Long Walk Home, 1990, Ghost, 1990 (Acad. award best supporting actress, 1991), Soapdish, 1991; (films, cameo) House Party 2, 1992; (films) The Player, 1992, Sister Act, 1992, Wisecracks, 1992, Sarafina!, 1992, Made in America, 1993, National Lampoon's Loaded Weapon 1, 1993, Sister Act 1: Back in the Habit, 1993; (films, voice) The Lion King, 1994; (films) The Little Rascals, 1994; (films, cameo) Naked in New York, 1994; (films) Corrina, Corrina, 1994, Star Trek: Generations, 1994; (films, voice) The Pagemaster, 1994; (films) Boys on the Side, 1995, Bogus, 1996, The Ghost of Mississippi, 1996, Eddie, 1996, Tales from the Crypt Presents: Bordello of Blood, 1996, The Associate, 1996, An Allen Smithee Film: Burn Hollywood Burn, 1998, How Stella Got Her Groove Back, 1998, A Knight in Camelot, 1998, The Rugrats Movie, 1998, Deep End of the Ocean, 1999, Jackie's Back!, 1999, Girl, Interrupted, others, 1999; (TV films) Kiss Shot, 1989, My Past Is My Own, Cinderella, 1997, Alice in Wonderland, 1999; (TV series) Star Trek: The Next Generation, 1988—94, Bagdad Cafe, CBS, 1990, In the Gloaming, 1997; (TV series, specials include) Tales from the Whoop: Hot Rod Brown, Class Clown, 1990; (TV series, voice) Happily Ever After: Fairy Tales for Every Child, 1997; host : (TV series, talk show) The Whoopie Goldberg Show, 1992—93; actor: (TV series) Whoopi, 2003—; prodr.: Hollywood Squares, 1998—2002; actor: (TV films) Jackie's Back!, 1999, The Magical Land of the Leprechauns, 1999, What Makes a Family, 2001; (TV films) Call Me Claus, 2001, It's a Very Muppet Christmas Movie, 2002, Good Fences, 2003; voice (TV films) Madeline: My Fair Madeline, 2002. Nominee Emmy, 1996; named Entertainer of the Yr., NAACP, 1990; recipient Humanitarian of Yr. award, Starlight Found., 1989, Hans Christian Andersen award for outstanding achievement by a dyslexic, 1987, Grammy award for album of Broadway show, 1985.

GOLDBERG, WILLIAM JEFFREY, accountant, financial planner; b. Chgo., Jan. 18, 1950; s. Harry and Bernice Dorothy (Benson) G.; m. Brenda Liebling; children: Leslie Claire, Melissa Liebling. BA, Knox Coll., 1971; JD, Cornell U., 1974; postgrad., U. Chgo., 1976-78. Bar: Ill. 1974, U.S. Dist. Ct. (no. dist.) Ill. 1974; CPA. Fin. counseling officer Continental Ill. Nat. Bank, Chgo., 1974-79; supr. KPMG Peat Marwick, Houston, 1979-80, mgr., 1980-82, ptnr., 1982—. Nat. dir. Personal Fin. Planning Svcs., 1984-93, southwest ptnr.-in-charge personal fin. planning, 1993—; instr. law Ill. Inst. Tech. Chgo. Kent Coll. Law, 1977-78; del. nat. summit on retirement savings, 1998. Dir. Acad. Fin. Svcs., 1988-89; trustee Jewish Fedn. Greater Houston, 1985-99, 2002—, Houston Jewish Cmty. Found., 1997—, chmn., 2002—, Contemporary Arts Mus., 2000—. Recipient Best Fin. Adviser, Worth Mag., 1996—. Mem. AICPA (personal fin. planning divsn., exec. com. 1986-89, 94—, chmn. exec. com. 1996-98, chmn. legis and regulation subcom. 1989-91), Tex. Soc. CPAs, Houston Estate & Fin. Forum, Houston Bus. and Estate Planning Coun., Knox Coll. Club Houston (pres. 1981-82), Shadow Hawk Golf Club. Office: KPMG LLP 700 Louisiana St Ste 3000 Houston TX 77002-2776

GOLDBERGER, ALLEN SANFORD, lawyer; b. N.Y.C., Apr. 18, 1933; s. William S. and Elsa (Goldman) G.; m. Gail Davidman, Jan. 15, 1966; children— Michael, Lynn. B.A., NYU, 1954; J.D., Boston U. 1959. Bar: N.J. 1960, N.Y. 1982, U.S. Dist. Ct. N.J., U.S. Supreme Ct. Ptnr. Goldberger Seligsohn & Shinrod and predecessor firms, West Orange, N.J., 1981—. Served with U.S. Army, 1954-56. Mem. N.J. State Bar Assn. (chmn. workers compensation sect. 1983-85, exec. com.), Assn. Trial Lawyers Am., Essex County Bar Assn. (chmn. workers compensation sect.), N.J. State Bar Assn., N.Y. Workers Compensation Bar Assn. Jewish.

GOLDBERGER, ARTHUR EARL, JR., industrial engineer, executive; BS in Systems Engring., U. Ariz., 1974, BS in Indsl. Engring., 1975; MS in Indsl. Engring., Tex. A&M U., 1977, postgrad., 1991—. Cert. Novell engr.; cert. Microsoft sys. engr.; registered profl. engr., Ky., Tex., Mo., Ariz., Fla. Gen. engr. DARCOM/RRAD, Texarkana, Tex., 1975-77; mgr. DARCOM/AVSCOM, St. Louis, 1977-81; div. dir. prodn. improvement McDonnell Douglas, St. Louis, 1981-90; pres. Spectrum Techs., Inc., St. Louis, 1990—. Founder Salientinfo, 2001; chmn. CAD/Expert System Tool Design, Seattle, 1991; internat. cons. in field. Author: Real Leadership, 1993, Radical Leadership, 1997; contbr. articles to profl. jours. Bd. dirs. Engrs. Club St. Louis, 1978, Nat. Com. on U.S. Competitiveness, Washington, 1989—; judge, coach Scientific Olympiad, Mo., 1989. Recipient Quality Leadership award McDonnell Douglas Corp., 1988; recognized as expert in inventory and prodn. mgmt. Am. Prodn. and Inventory Control Soc. Mem. IEEE (chmn. 1987-88, vice chmn. vehicle tech. soc. conf. 1991, bd. dirs. nat. com. on U.S. competitiveness, Leadership award 1988), Inst. Indsl. Engrs., Soc. Mfrg. Engrs., Data Mgmt. Assn. (bd. dirs. 1999—), Alpha Pi Mu. Achievements include research, consulting and executive leader in information systems, manufacturing technology, process engineering healthcare operations and management, RF and Network Communications, operations analysis, integration, and six sigma quality/process improvement.

GOLDBERGER, ARTHUR STANLEY, economics educator; b. N.Y.C., Nov. 20, 1930; s. David M. and Martha (Greenwald) G.; m. Iefke Engelsman, Aug. 19, 1957; children: Nina Judith, Nicholas Bernard. BS, N.Y.U., 1951; MA, U. Mich., 1952, PhD, 1958. Acting asst. prof. econs. Stanford U., 1956-59; assoc. prof. econs. U. Wis., 1960- 63, prof., 1963-70, H.M. Groves prof., 1970-79, Vilas research prof., 1979-98, prof. emeritus, 1998—. Vis. prof. Center Planning and Econ. Rsch., Athens, Greece, 1964-65, U. Hawaii, 1969, 71, Stanford U., 1990, 96, 2000; Keynes vis. prof. U. Essex, 1968-69. Author: (with L.R. Klein) An Econometric Model of the United States, 1929-52, 1955, Impact Multipliers and Dynamic Properties, 1959, Econometric Theory, 1964, Topics in Regression Analysis, 1968, Functional Form and Utility, 1987, A Course in Econometrics, 1991, Introductory Econometrics, 1998; editor: (with O.D. Duncan) Structural Equation Models in the Social Sciences, 1973, (with D.J. Aigner) Latent Variables in Socioeconomic Models, 1976; Assoc. editor: Jour. Econometrics, 1973-77; bd. editors: Am. Econ. Rev, 1964-66, Jour. Econ. Lit, 1975-77. Fulbright fellow Netherlands Sch. Econs., 1955-56, 59-60; fellow Ctr. for Advanced Study in Behavioral Scis., Stanford, 1976-77, 80-81; Guggenheim fellow Stanford U., 1972-73, 85. Fellow Am. Statis. Assn., Econometric Soc. (council 1975-80, 82-87), Am. Acad. Arts and Scis., AAAS; mem. Am. Econ. Assn. (Disting. fellow 1988), Nat. Acad. Scis., Royal Netherlands Acad. Scis. Home: 2828 Sylvan Ave Madison WI 53705-5228 Office: U Wis Dept Econs 1180 Observatory Dr Madison WI 53706-1320 E-mail: asgoldbe@facstaff.wisc.edu.

GOLDBERGER, BLANCHE RUBIN, sculptor, jeweler; b. N.Y.C., Feb. 2, 1914; d. David and Sarah (Israel) Rubin; m. Emanuel Goldberger, June 28, 1942 (dec. 1994); children— Richard N., Ary Louis. B.A., Hunter Coll., N.Y.C., 1934; M.A., Columbia U., 1936; Certificat d'Etudes, Sorbonne, Paris, 1936; postgrad. Westchester Arts Workshop Sculpture and Jewelry, White Plains, 1961-70, Silvermine Coll. Arts, 1962, Nat. Acad. Arts, N.Y.C., 1968. Tchr. French and Hebrew, N.Y.C. High Sch. System, Scarsdale Jr. and Sr. High Schs. One-woman shows include: Bloomingdale's, Eastchester, N.Y., 1975, Scarsdale Pub. Library, N.Y., 1976, Temple Israel, White Plains, N.Y., 1975, Greenwich Art Barn, Conn., 1972 Westlake Gallery, White Plains, N.Y., 1981; exhibited in group shows at Hudson River Mus., Yonkers, N.Y., 1978, Silvermine-New Eng. Ann., Silvermine, Conn., 1979; represented in permanent collection at Scarsdale High Sch. Library, N.Y.; sculpture commn. Jewish Community Ctr. White Plains, N.Y., 1988; commn. Manchester, Vt.; also pvt. collections. Recipient award Beaux Arts of Westchester, White Plains, N.Y., 1967, First Prize, White Plains Art Show, Holocaust Meml. Bronze Plaque for Synagogue Congregation Israel, Manchester, Vt.; various commns. for calli collis calligraphic collages. Mem. Nat. Assn. Women Artists, Nat. Assn. Tchrs. French, Scarsdale Art Assn. (bd. dirs.; first prizes for sculpture). Jewish. Avocations: lecturing on sculpture, reading contemporary lit. in Hebrew, the violin, classical music concerts, callicollies.

GOLDBERGER, GEORGE STEFAN, finance company executive; b. Oradea, Romania, July 3, 1947; arrived in U.S., 1962; s. Ladislau and Margareta (Schwartz) Goldberger; 1 child, David Michael. BS in Systems Engring., Bklyn. Poly. U., 1969; MBA in Fin., U. Pa., 1975. Sys. analyst Grumman Corp., Bethpage, NY, 1969-73; ops. analyst Internat. Paper Co., NYC, 1973-74; mgmt. cons. Booz, Allen & Hamilton, NYC, 1975-77; asst. to chmn. W.R. Grace & Co., NYC, 1977-85; pres. Citizens Against Govt. Waste, Washington, 1986-89; COO Pres.'s Pvt. Sector Survey on Cost Control (Grace Commn.), Washington, 1986-89; dir. mergers and acquisitions Figgie Internat., Inc., Willoughby, Ohio, 1989-90; pres. Goldberger & Assoc., Inc., NYC, 1991-98; chief bus. officer Progenitor Cell Therapy, LLC, Saddle Brook, NJ, 1999—. Contbr. articles to publs. Avocation: skiing. E-mail: georgegoldberger@aol.com.

GOLDBERGER, LEO, psychologist, educator; b. Vukovar, Yugoslavia, June 28, 1930; came to U.S., 1952; naturalized, 1959; s. Eugene and Helen (Berkovits) G.; m. Nancy R. Rule, Aug. 19, 1970; 1 child, Jessica. BA, McGill U., 1951; PhD, NYU, 1958; diploma, N.Y. Psychoanalytical Inst., 1967. Rsch. psychologist Cornell U. Med. Coll., N.Y.C., 1955-56; prof., dir. Rsch. Ctr. Mental Health, NYU, N.Y.C., 1969—. Cons. in field. Editor in chief Psychoanalysis and Contemporary Thought, 1970—; editor: (with S. Breznitz) Handbook of Stress, 1982, 2d edit., 1993, (with others) LSD: Personality and Experience, 1972; editor: The Rescue of the Danish Jews, 1987; contbr. articles to profl. jours. NIMH rsch. career devel. awardee, 1956-58; USAF grantee, 1958-61; NIMH grantee, 1963-77; recipient Knight's Cross by Queen Margrethe II of Denmark, 1993. Fellow Am. Psychol. Assn.; mem. Am. Psychoanalytic Assn., Internat. Psychoanalytic Assn. Office: NYU Dept Psychology 6 Washington Pl Dept New York NY 10003-6634 E-mail: leo.goldberger@nyu.edu.

GOLDBERGER, MARVIN LEONARD, physicist, educator; b. Chgo., Oct. 22, 1922; s. Joseph and Mildred (Sedwitz) G.; m. Mildred Ginsburg, Nov. 25, 1945; children: Samuel M., Joel S. BS, Carnegie Inst. Tech., 1943; PhD, U. Chgo., 1948. Research assoc. Radiation Lab., U. Calif., 1948-49; research assoc. Mass. Inst. Tech., 1949-50; asst.-assoc. prof. U. Chgo., 1950-55, prof., 1955-57; Higgins prof. physics Princeton U., 1957-77, chmn. dept., 1970-76, Joseph Henry prof. physics, 1977-78; pres. Calif. Inst. Tech., Pasadena, 1978-87; dir. Inst. Advanced Study, Princeton, N.J., 1987-91; prof. physics UCLA, 1991-93, U. Calif., San Diego, 1993-2000, dean divsn. natural scis., 1994-99, prof. emeritus, 2000—. Mem. President's Sci. Adv. Com., 1965-69; chmn. Fedn. Am. Scientists, 1971-73. Fellow Am. Phys. Soc., Am. Acad. Arts and Scis.; mem. Nat. Acad. Scis., Am. Philos. Soc., Council on Fgn. Relations. E-mail: mgoldberger@ucsd.edu.

GOLDBERGER, MELVIN TOBIAS, executive investment banker; b. Knoxville, June 6, 1919; s. Harry and Grace (Reich) G.; m. Betty Knox, June 4, 1944; children: Diane, Susan, Margy. BSBA, Ohio State U., 1940; postgrad., U. Tenn., 1940-41. Pres. Sq. Supply Co., Knoxville, 1946-64; chmn. Vector Co., Knoxville, 1965-72; pres. Seventh Investment Bancing Corp., Boca Raton, Fla., 1973—, Regency Highland Corp., Boca Raton, 1973—81. Treas. Fla. Philharm. Orch., Ft. Lauderdale, Fla., 1985-94, life bd. dirs., hon. life treas. emeritus, 1992-. Shrine mem. Kerbela Temple, 1947—; vice chmn. bd. dirs. Mae Volen Sr. Ctr., Boca Raton, 1989-2000, chmn. bd. dirs., 2001-02. Capt. Med. Adminstrn. Corps, U.S. Army, 1943-46. Mem. Elks Club. Avocations: golf, tennis, sports. Home: 7050 Islegrove Pl Boca Raton FL 33433-7461 Office: Seventh Investment Bancing Corps 1599 NW 9th Ave Boca Raton FL 33486

GOLDBERGER, ROBERT D. food products company executive; b. 1935; V.p. King Foods, Inc., Newport, Minn., 1956-73; with GFI America, Mpls., 1973—, pres., CEO. Office: GFI America 2815 Blaisdell Ave Minneapolis MN 55408-2385

GOLDBERGER, ROBERT R. lawyer; b. N.Y.C., May 16, 1908; s. Charles Kalman and Ann (Green) G. BA, Yale U., 1930, LLB, 1933. Bar: Conn. 1933, U.S. Dist. Ct. Conn. 1935. Factfinder, arbitrator Superior Ct. Fairfield County, Bridgeport, Conn., 1983, atty., trial referee, 1984—. Arbitrator Am. Arbitration Assn., Conn., 1976-82. Served with AUS, 1942-45. Mem. Greater Bridgeport Bar Assn. (pres. 1975-77), Conn. Bar Assn. (50 Yr. Pin 1983, ho. of dels. 1977-78, bd. govs. 1978-80), Am. Legion, Grasso-Seavey Club (comdr. 1947-49), Yale Club of Ea. Fairfield County (bd. dirs. 1972-75), 25 Sportsmen Club Bridgeport (pres. 1959—). Republican. Jewish. Home: 195 Jackman Ave Fairfield CT 06432-1727 Office: 955 Main St Bridgeport CT 06604-4300

GOLDBERGER, STEPHEN HENRY, otolaryngologist; b. Bronx, N.Y., May 7, 1947; s. Martin and Laura G.; m. Diane Jean Lenke, Dec. 10, 1977; children: Jennifer, Joshua, Shana. MD, Boston U., 1973. Diplomate Am. Bd. Otolaryngology. Intern Montefiore Hosp., Bronx, N.Y., 1973-74, resident in gen. surgery, 1974-75; resident in otolaryngology U. Calif. Irvine Med. Ctr., 1975-78; staff Huntington Beach Hosp., Pacifica Hosp., Calif., 1978-92, Fountain Valley Regional Hosp., Calif., 1980-92, Hoag Meml. Hosp., Newport Beach, Calif., 1980-92, UCI Med. Ctr. Hosp., Orange, Calif., 1980-92, United Hosp., Grand Forks, N.D., 1992-95, Rehab. Hosp. U. N.D., Grand Forks, 1992-95; clin. asst. prof. U. Calif., Irvine, 1980-87, U. N.D. Sch. Medicine, 1993-95; staff Brookwood Med. Ctr., Birmingham, Ala., 1995-98, Shelby Med. Ctr., Alabaster, Ala., 1995-98, St. Vincent's Hosp., Birmingham, 1995-98, Bluefield Reg. Hosp., W.V., 1998-99, Columbia St. Luke's, 1998-99, Three Rivers Health Care, Poplar Bluff, Mo., 1999—2001, Nevada Regional Med. Ctr., 2002—, Cedar County Meml. Hosp., 2002—, Barton County Meml. Hosp., 2002—. Fellow ACS, Am. Acad. Otolaryngology/Head and Neck Surgery, Am. Acad. Otolaryngic Allergy; mem. AMA, Mo. State Med. Assn., West Central Mo. Med. Soc., Nevada Country Club, Nevada C. of C., Rotary., Summit Club. Home: RR 6 Box 24 Nevada MO 64772 Office: 124 W Walnut Nevada MO 64772 E-mail: AuenHands@aol.com.

GOLDBERG-SCHAIBLE, JOCELYN HOPE SCHNIER, market research professional; b. NYC, Mar. 29, 1953; d. Alex and Eileen Rosalie (Firstenberg) Schnier. AB, Princeton U., 1974; MBA, Harvard U., 1977. Statis. technician John Hancock Inc., Boston, 1974-75; product mgr. Gen. Foods Corp., White Plains, N.Y., 1977-78; strategic and tactical bus. planning analyst Bausch & Lomb Corp., Rochester, N.Y., 1979-81; mgmt. assoc. Gordon S. Black Corp., Rochester, 1981-84; pres. Rochester Rsch. Group, 1985—. Dirs. adv. coun. M&T Bank. Bd. dirs. U. Rochester Med. Ctr., 1991-98, JCC Greater Rochester, 1998—; trustee Geva Theater, 1992 99; v.p. class of '74, Princeton U., 1999—. Recipient achievement award Wall Street Jour., 1977; nominee Athena award, 2001. Mem. Profl. Ski Instrs. Am. (cert.), Harvard U. Bus. Sch. Club (bd. dirs.). Home: 1666 Strong Rd Victor NY 14564-9133 Office: PO Box 22954 Rochester NY 14692-2954

GOLD-BIKIN, LYNNE Z. lawyer; b. N.Y.C., Apr. 23, 1938; d. Herbert Benjamin Zapoleon and Muriel Claire (Wimpfheimer) Sarnoff; m. Roy E. Gold, Aug. 20, 1956 (div. July 1976); children: Russell, Sheryl, Lisa, Michael; m. Martin H. Feldman, June 28, 1987. BA summa cum laude, Albright Coll., 1973; JD, Villanova Law Sch., 1976; hon., 1996. Bar: Pa. 1976, U.S. Dist. Ct. (ea. dist.) Pa. 1976, U.S. Supreme Ct. 1979. Assoc. Pechner, Dorfman, Wolffe, Rounick & Cabot, Norristown, Pa., 1976-81; ptnr. Olin, Neil, Frock & Gold-Bikin, Norristown, 1981-82, pres. Gold-Bikin, Welsh & Assocs., Norristown, 1982-96, Wolf, Block, Schorr & Solis-Cohen, Norristown, 1996—. Course planner for 12 manuals on continuing legal edn., 1978—; pres. coun. Albright Coll., Reading, Pa., 1982-87. Author: Pennsylvania Marital Agreements, 1984, Divorce Practice Handbook, 1994, The Divorce Trial Manual, 2003; contbg. editor, Fairshare Mag., 1987—. Named to Pa. Honor Roll of Women, 1996. Fellow Am. Acad. Matrimonial Lawyers, Internat. Acad. Matrimonial Lawyers, Am. Coll. Matrimonial Trial Lawyers, Am. Bar Found., Am. Law Inst., Pa. Bar Found.; mem. ABA (family law sect. chair 1994-95, ho. of dels. 1995, bd. govs. 1998-2001), Pa. Bar Assn. (family law sect. coun. mem. 1980-89), Montgomery County Bar Assn. (chmn. family law com. 1984-86), Pa. Trial Lawyers Assn. (chmn. family law sect. 1988-90). Office: Wolf Block Schorr & Solis-Cohen PO Box 869 Norristown PA 19404-0869

GOLDBLATT, BARRY LANCE, manufacturing executive; b. Palo Alto, Calif., July 29, 1945; s. Samuel and Joan Charlotte (Morton) G. BS, U. So. Calif., 1967, MBA, 1968. Supr. market rsch. for brands Procter & Gamble Co., Cin., 1968-71; mgr. market rsch. Personal Products Co. subs. Johnson & Johnson, 1971-74; assoc. dir. consumer rsch. Johnson & Johnson Baby Products Co., Skillman, N.J., 1974-87; dir. market rsch. Johnson & Johnson Dental Care Co., New Brunswick, N.J., 1987-89, Johnson & Johnson Consumer Products Inc., Skillman, 1989-93; exec. dir. mktg. rsch. Johnson & Johnson Consumer Products Worldwide, 1994—2002; dir. market rsch. Church & Dwight Co., Inc., Princeton, NJ, 2002—. Bd. dirs. New Brunswick Hot Line, 1973; vol. Urban Cons. Group, 1977—. Recipient Cert. of Recognition Nat. Symposium Hispanic Bus. and Economy, Chgo., 1981, Cert. of Appreciation U. So. Calif., 1981. Mem. Am. Assn. Pub. Opinion Rschrs., U. So. Calif. MBAs, U. So. Calif. Commerce Assocs., Advt. Rsch. Found., Am. Mktg. Assn., Assn. MBA Execs., Mktg. Rsch. Coun.-The Conf. Bd., Am. Philat. Soc., U. So. Calif. Assocs., U. So. Calif. Alumni Club, Skull and Dagger, U. So. Calif. Alumni of N.J. (pres.), Zeta Beta Tau (asst. chpt. advisor Princeton U.). Republican. Home: 20 Andrews Ln Princeton NJ 08540-7633 Office: Church & Dwight Co Inc 469 N Harrison St Princeton NJ 08543

GOLDBLATT, EILEEN WITZMAN, art director, director, management consultant; b. N.Y.C. d. Ben and Sylvia Witzman; m. Myron Everett Goldblatt Jr.; children: Tracy Ellen, David Laurence. BS, Russell Sage Coll., 1967; MS, Bank Street Coll, 1980. Tchr., tchr. trainer N.Y.C. Bd. Edn., 1967-73, dir. mus. and cultural programs, 1984-89; ednl. cons. Cooper-Hewitt Mus., N.Y.C., 1979-80; dir. mus., collaborative sch./cultural voucher programs Mus. Collaborative, Inc., N.Y.C., 1981-84; exec. dir. Young Audiences/N.Y., 1990-97; pres., CEO Nat. "I Have a Dream" Found., N.Y.C., 1997 2000, LBD Systems, Inc., 2001—; supr. regional arts N.Y.C. Dept. Edn., 2003—; internet cons. Creator N.Y.C. Arts and Cultural Edn. Network and Arts and Cultural Edn. Network Menu, 1986-90, Cultural Instn. Network Menu, 1984-85; creator N.Y.C. Cultural Instn. Network. Author: (workbook) Electroworks, 1980, (exhbn. guide) Smithsonian: A Treasure Hunt, 1979, (curriculum) The Ancient Egyptians, 1980. Trustee N.Y.C. Sch. Art League; mem. cultural del. People to People Internat., People's Republic China, 1988, 96, India Initiative, 1997; mem. Class of 1990 Leadership Am. Mem. Am. Assn. Mus., Nat. Arts Club, Women's City Club N.Y.

GOLDBLATT, HAL MICHAEL, photographer, accountant; b. Long Beach, Calif., Feb. 6, 1952; s. Arnold Phillip and Molly (Stearns) G.; m. Shawn Naomi Doherty, Aug. 27, 1974; children: Eliyahu Yonah, Tova Devorah, Raizel, Shoshana, Reuven Lev, Eliezer Noach, Esther Bayla, Rochel Leah, Zalman Ber, Perle Sara. BA in Math., Calif. State U., Long Beach, 1975. Owner Star Publs., Las Vegas, 1975—; treas. Goldblatt, Inc., Las Vegas, 1980—; pres. SDG Computer Svc., Las Vegas, 1985—; chief fin. officer Martin & Mills Ltd., Las Vegas, 1992-93; controller Amland Devel., Las Vegas, 1993-95; CFO Stewart Constrn., Las Vegas, 1995-96; CEO Goldblatt, Inc., Las Vegas, 1996-97; cost acct. Ameristar Casinos, Inc., Las Vegas, 1997-99; dir. spl. projects Chabad So. Nev., Las Vegas, 1999-2000; dir. photography Lightons Creations, Las Vegas, 2000 ; contr. Nev. Hand, Las Vegas, 2001—, exec. MBA Trinity So. Univ., 2003. Photographer: (photo essays) Mikveh Yisroel, 1978, Chassidic Fabrengen, 1979, A Day at Disneyland, 1985, Shavous Trek, 1997, Garth Brooks World Tour, 1998, Care for Kids Telethon, 1998, 99, Chanukah - Festival of Lights, 1998-00; prodr., engr.: (audio cassettes) From the Heart of My Dreams, 1980, Middle Class Dreams, 1981, Uforatzta Trio, 1982. Founder, pres. Jews for Judaism, Long Beach, 1975-82, v.p., 1983—; fundraising chmn. Friends of Lubavitch, Long Beach, 1977; bd. dirs. Congregation Lubavitch, Long Beach, 1987, 91-92; treas. Actor's Repertory Theatre, 1995-98, mem. adv. bd., 1998-2003. Recipient Gold Press Card award Forty Niner Newspaper, 1973, 74, Floyd Durham Meml. award for Outstanding Community Svc., 1973, Georgie award Actor's Repertory Theatre, 1995, ART Disting. Svc. award, 1996. Office: Nevada Hand 295 E Warm Springs Rd Ste 101 Las Vegas NV 89119 Fax: 702-739-3305. E-mail: hgoldblatt@nevadahand.org.

GOLDBLATT, LAWRENCE, dean, educator, researcher; Undergrad., Georgetown U., DDS cum laude, 1968; grad. oral pathology residency program, Ind. U., 1971, MSD, 1973. Diplomate Am. Bd. Oral and Maxillofacial Pathology . Rotating dental intern U.S. Naval Hosp., St. Albans, NY; lt. to comdr. U.S. Naval Res. U.S. Navy Dental Corps., 1971—89, ret., 1989; asst. prof. oral pathology; assoc. prof. Ind. U., 1977, prof., 1982, assoc. dean, grad. and postgrad. edn., 1988, assoc. dean acad. affairs, 1990, acting assoc. dean acad. affairs, dean, 1997—, Case Western Res. U. Sch. Dentistry, 1994—96. Tchr., rschr. in field; commr. ADA Commn. Dental Accreditation. Contbr. scientific papers, articles to peer-reviewed jours. Fellow: Internat. Coll. Dentists, Am. Coll. Dentists; mem.: Ind. U. Sch. Dentistry Alumni Assn. (ad hoc mem. assn.'s bd. dirs.), ADA Joint Commn. on Nat. Dental Exams. (past commr., chmn.), Am. Dental Edn. Assn. (adminstrv. bd. coun. deans), Am. and Internat. Assns. Dental Rsch., Am. Acad. Oral and Maxillofacial Pathology, Omicron Kappa Upsilon (past pres. Supreme chpt.). Office: 1121 West Michigan St Indianapolis IN 46202

GOLDBLATT, STANFORD JAY, lawyer; b. Chgo., Feb. 25, 1939; s. Maurice and Bernice (Mendelson) G.; m. Ann Dudley Cronkhite, June 17, 1968; children: Alexandra, Nathaniel, Jeremy. BA magna cum laude, Harvard U., 1960, LLB magna cum laude, 1963. Bar: Ill. 1963. Law clk. U.S. Ct. Appeals, 5th Jud. Circuit, New Orleans, 1963-64; mem. firm Winston & Strawn, Chgo., 1964-67; v.p. Goldblatt Bros., Inc., Chgo., 1967-76, pres., chief exec. officer, 1976-77, chmn. exec. com., 1977-78; ptnr. Hopkins & Sutter, 1978-97, Winston & Strawn, Chgo., 1997—. Bd. dirs. MacLean-Fogg Co., Divergence, Inc. Trustee U. Chgo., Cancer Rsch. Found., U. Chgo. Hosps. Mem. Econ. Club, Racquet Club, Comml. Club. Office: Winston & Strawn 35 W Wacker Dr Ste 4200 Chicago IL 60601-9703

GOLDBLATT, STEVEN HARRIS, law educator; b. Bklyn., Apr. 30, 1947; s. J. Irving and Ethel (Epstein) G.; m. Irene P. Burns, June 12, 1981; children: Sarah P., Elizabeth G.B. BA, Franklin & Marshall Coll., 1967; JD, Georgetown U., 1970. Bar: Pa. 1970, D.C. 1981. With Phila. Dist. Atty.'s Office, 1970-81; dir. Appellate Litigation Program Georgetown U. Law Ctr., Washington, 1981-83, prof. law, dir. Appellate Litigation Progam, 1983—. Chair rules adv. com. U.S. Ct. Appeals for Armed Forces, 1998—. Co-author: Analysis and Commentary to the Pennsylvania Crime Code, 1973, Three Prosecutors Look at the Crimes Code, 1974, Ineffective Assistance of Counsel: Attempts to Establish Minimum Standards for Criminal Cases, 1983; reporter Criminal Justice in Crisis, 1988, Achieving Justice in a Diverse America, 1992, An Agenda for Justice: ABA Perspectives on Criminal and Civil Justice Issues, 1996. Mem. ABA (criminal justice sect. chmn. amicus curiae briefs com. 1981-99, crisis in criminal justice com. 1990-91, criminal justice standards com.). Office: Georgetown U Law Ctr 600 New Jersey Ave NW Washington DC 20001-2075 E-mail: goldblat@law.georgetown.edu.

GOLDBLOOM, VICTOR CHARLES, b. Montreal, Que., Can., July 31, 1923; s. Alton and Annie (Ballon) G.; m. Sheila Barshay, June 15, 1948; children: Susan, Michael, Jonathan. MD, McGill U., Montreal, 1945, LLD (hon.), U. Toronto, Ont., Can., 1980, Concordia U., Montreal, 1993, St. Anne's U., N.S., Can., 1996; LittD, McGill U., Montreal, 1992; Dr. of Univ., U. Ottawa, Ont., 1994. Intern Montreal Children's Hosp., 1945-47, 1949-50; resident Babies Hosp., N.Y.C., 1947-48; pvt. practice, 1950-80; min. environment and mcpl. affairs Govt. of Province Que., Quebec, 1970-76; pres., CEO Can. Coun. Christians and Jews, Toronto, 1979-87; pres. Internat. Coun. Christians and Jews, 1982-90, Que. Environ. Pub. Hearings Bd., Quebec, 1987-90; exec. dir. Fonds de la recherche en santé du Qué., Montreal, 1990-91; commr. Official Langs., Ottawa, 1991—99. Can. del. UN Environment Conf., Stockholm, 1972, UN Habitat, Vancouver, B.C., 1976; tchr. McGill U., 1950—66; chair Montreal Regional Health and Social Svc. Bd., 2002—. Pres. (hon.) Jules and Paul-Emile Léger Found., Montreal. Decorated Companion Order of Can., officier Ordre Nat. du Que.; recipient Govt. of Can. award, 1990, James H. Graham award, Royal Coll. Pysicians and Surgeons of Can., 1996, Centennial medal, Assn. médecins langue française du Can. Mem.: Allied Jewish Cmty. Svcs. Motreal (Samuel Bronfman medal 1989, Samuel Bronfman medal 1989), Alliance Israelite Universelle (Rene Cassin medal 1987, Rene Cassin medal 1987). Avocations: opera, lieder singing. Home: 5 Grove Pk Montreal QC Canada H3Y 3E6

GOLDBLUM, A. PAUL, lawyer; b. N.Y.C., July 26, 1925; s. Meyer and Rebecca (Glassman) G.; m. Chantal Mona Laurent, Sept. 2, 1951. B.S. cum laude, Harvard U., 1947, LL.B., 1950. Bar: N.Y. 1951, U.S. Dist. Ct. (ea. and so. dists.) 1952, U.S. Ct. Appeals (2d cir.) 1973. Trial atty. Liberty Mutual Ins. Co., N.Y.C., 1950-55, sr. trial atty., 1962-76, N.Y. div. gen. atty., appellate counsel, 1977— ; ptnr. Dent, Goldblum & Witschieben, N.Y.C., 1956-62; asst. counsel Ambulance Chasing Investigation, Bklyn., 1958-59. Contbr. articles to law jours. Chmn. law com. N.Y. Com. for Dem. Voters, 1956-60, 2d and 11th Jud. Dists. grievance com., 1974-82; bd. dirs. Greater Jamaica Devel. Corp., 1981— ; vice chmn. adv. bd. Paralegal Inst. Queens Coll., 1980—; mem. exec. com. Flushing Meadows-Corona Park Corp., 1987—. Served to lt. (j.g.) USN, 1943-46, PTO. Fellow N.Y. Bar Found.; mem. Queens County Bar Assn. (pres. 1979-80, chmn. com. profl. ethics 1984-88), N.Y. State Bar Assn. (del. 1981-87, v.p. 11th Jud. Dist. 1987—, chmn. Com. on Profl. Discipline 1978-81, vice chmn. Com. to Improve Ct. Facilities 1983—), Assn. of Bar of City of N.Y. Club: Harvard (N.Y.C.); Huguenot Yacht (New Rochelle, N.Y.). Home: 34-21 80th St Jackson Heights NY 11372

GOLDE, DAVID WILLIAM, physician, educator; b. N.Y.C., Oct. 23, 1940; BS in Chemistry, Fairleigh Dickinson U., 1962; MD, McGill U., 1966. Diplomate: Am Bd. Internal Medicine, Am. Bd. Med. Oncology, Nat. Bd. Med. Examiners. Asst. research chemist Gen. Foods Corp., 1962; intern. U. Calif. Hosps., San Francisco, 1966-67, resident in medicine, 1970-72, fellow Cancer Research Inst., 1971-72; staff cons. continuing edn. and tng. br. div. regional med. program (NIH), 1967-68, resident in clin. pathology, 1968-70; hematology fellow NIH, 1969-70; instr. medicine U. Calif., San Francisco, 1972-73, asst. prof., 1973-74; asst. prof. medicine UCLA, 1974-75, assoc. prof., 1975-79, prof., 1979-91, chief divsn. hematology-oncology, 1981-91, prof. emeritus, 1991—, co-dir. Clin. Rsch. Ctr., 1974-87, dir., 1987-91, dir. AIDS Ctr., 1986-90; Enid A. Haupt prof. hematologic oncology Meml. Sloan-Kettering Cancer Ctr., N.Y.C., 1991—, attending physician Meml. Hosp. for Cancer and Allied Diseas, 1991—; head divsn. hematologic oncology, 1991-96; mem. Sloan-Kettering Inst. for Cancer Rsch., 1991—; prof. medicine Cornell U. Med. Coll., N.Y.C., 1991—; prof. molecular pharmacology and therapeutics Cornell U. Grad. Sch. Med. Scis., N.Y.C., 1992—; physician-in-chief Meml. Hosp. Cancer and Allied Diseases, 1996—2002. Mem. editl. bd. Blood, 1978-81, Peptides, 1979-83, Leukemia, 1986—; Scandinavian Jour. Haematology (now European Jour. Haematology), 1986-99; editor: Blood Revs., 1986-93, Cytokines, Cellular & Molecular Therapy, 1997—; assoc. editor: Cancer Rsch., 1989—; contbr. numerous articles to profl. jours. With USPHS, 1967-70. Fellow ACP; mem. AAAS, Am. Assn. Cancer Rsch., Am. Fedn. Clin. Rsch., Am. Soc. Clin. Investigation, Am. Soc. Clin. Oncology, Am. Soc. Hematology, Assn. Am. Physicians, Endocrine Soc., Internat. Soc. Exptl. Hematology (councillor 1995-97), Soc. Biol. Therapy, Internat. Assn. for Comparative Rsch. on Leukemia, Soc. Exptl. Biology and Medicine, Western Soc. Clin. Investigation (pres. 1989-90), Western Soc. Clin. Rsch., Alpha Omega Alpha. Office: Meml Sloan-Kettering Cancer Ctr 1275 York Ave New York NY 10021-6094 E-mail: d-golde@ski.mskcc.org.

GOLDEN, ARCHIE SIDNEY, pediatrician; b. Danbury, Conn., Feb. 9, 1931; s. Isadore Leon and Evelyn Sacartoff Golden; m. Sylvia Colon (dec.); children: Jenifer, Judith, Justine. BA, U. Conn., 1953; MD, U. Vt., 1957; MPH, Johns Hopkins U., 1966; MD (hon.), U. Cartagena, Colombia, 1969. Diplomate Am. Bd. Pediatrics. Rotating intern Lenox Hill Hosp., N.Y.C., 1957—58; resident in pediat. Bellevue Hosp., N.Y.C., 1959—60, 1961—62; pediatrician, educator Project Hope, Peru and Colombia, 1962—69; vis. prof. pediats. U. Trujillo Sch. Medicine, Peru, 1962—65, U. Cartagena Sch. Medicine, Cartagena, Colombia, 1966—69; assoc. prof. internat. health Sch. Pub. Health Johns Hopkins U., Balt., 1978—98, from asst. to assoc. prof. pediats., 1970—; chmn. dept. pediats. Johns Hopkins Bayview Med. Ctr., Balt., 1984—98, pediatrician. Author, editor: The Art of Teaching Primary Care, 1981; author: An Inventory for Primary Health Care Practice, 1976. Capt. Med. Corps U.S. Army, 1959—61, Korea. Named to Hall off Fame, Anne Arundel County Sr. Softball League, 1999; recipient Disting. Alumnus for Svc. to Medicine and Cmty., U. Vt. Coll. Medicine, 1995. Fellow: Am. Acad. Pediats. (chmn. com. on internat. child health 1970—79, chmn. sect. on cmty. health 1982—89, Pediatrician of Yr., Md. chpt. 1999). Avocations: softball, gardening, baseball history. Office: Johns Hopkins Bayview Med Ctr 4940 Eastern Ave Baltimore MD 21224 Fax: 410-550-1276.

GOLDEN, ARTHUR F. lawyer; b. Bklyn., Apr. 14, 1946; s. Isadore and Dorothy (Schisel) G.; m. Elisabeth Lee Smith, Aug. 28, 1971; children—Frederick Tucker, James Alexander, Eliza Emerson BS, Rensselaer Poly. Inst., 1966; JD, NYU, 1969. Bar: N.Y. 1970, U.S. Ct. Appeals (2d cir.) 1970, U.S. Dist. Ct. (so. dist.) N.Y. 1972, U.S. Supreme 1975, U.S. Ct. Appeals (D.C. cir.) 1979, D.C. 1980, U.S. Dist. Ct. D.C. 1980, U.S. Dist. Ct. (ea. dist.) N.Y. 1972, U.S. Dist. Ct. (no. dist.) Ohio 1985, U.S. Ct. Appeals (6th cir.) 1985, U.S. Ct. Appeals (7th cir.) 1996. With Davis Polk & Wardwell, N.Y.C., 1969—, ptnr., 1978—; mgmt. com., 1996—; co-founder Washington office Davis Polk, 1980-82, bd. dirs. Bd. dirs. Emerson Electric Co., 2000-, mem. pension and nominating com., ESCO Electronics Corp., mem. exec. com., chmn. compensation com., 1990-96, Burns Internat. Svs. Corp., mem. exec. and audit and fin. coms., 1996-2000, Allegiance Corp., mem. audit and pub. policy com., 1996 99. With USAR, 1968—74. Mem. ABA, Assn. of Bar of City of N.Y., N.Y. State Bar Assn., N.Y. State Communities Aid Assn. (bd. mgrs. 1986-89), New Canaan Winter Club (pres. 1988-91, bd. govs. 1987-93), Country Club New Canaan, River Club N.Y.C. Home: 72 Saint George Ln New Canaan CT 06840-2032 Office: Davis Polk & Wardwell 450 Lexington Ave Fl 29 New York NY 10017-3911

GOLDEN, BRUCE PAUL, lawyer; b. Chgo., Dec. 4, 1943; s. Irving R. and Anne K. (Eisenberg) G. SB in Elec. Sci. and Engring., MIT, 1965, SM in Elec. Engring., 1966; JD, Harvard U., 1969. Bar: Ill. 1969, U.S. Dist. Ct. (no. dist.) Ill. 1970, U.S. Ct. Appeals (7th cir.) 1994, U.S. Supreme Ct. 1995, cert.: (arbitrator); lic. real estate broker. Assoc. McDermott, Will & Emery, Chgo., 1970-75, ptnr., 1976-91; of counsel Fishman & Merrick, P.C., Chgo., 1991-92, Coffield, Ungaretti & Harris, Chgo., 1992-96; Bruce P. Golden and Assocs., Chgo., 1996—; gen. counsel Piranha, Inc., 2000—02. Officer, dir. various corps.; speaker bank law, securities law, venture capital seminars Contbr. articles to Banking Law Jour., contbg. editor, 1979— Chmn. MIT Enterprise Forum Chgo.; bd. dirs. Entrepreneurship Inst. Chgo., Chgo. chpt. U.S. Entrepreneurs Network, Ill. Small Bus. Devel. Ctr., Kellogg Sch. Bus. community services com. Mem. MIT Alumni of Chgo. (dir. 1993—), Union League. Home and Office: 4137 N Hermitage Ave Chicago IL 60613-1820

GOLDEN, DANIEL LEWIS, lawyer; b. N.Y.C., May 7, 1913; s. Louis and Rose (Rosen) G.; m. Evelyn Shayevitz, July 9, 1941 (dec.); children: Roger M., Leslie Rosemary; m. Eugenia Alice Norman, Feb. 14, 1997. BS, Lafayette Coll., 1934; LLD.(hon.), 1993; JD, Rutgers U., 1938. Bar: N.J. 1939, D.C. 1976, U.S. Supreme Ct. 1957. Practice, South River, 1940—; now of counsel Greenbaum, Rowe, Smith, Ravin, Davis & Himmell LLP, Woodbridge, N.J. Active survey legal systems USSR, East Europe for State Dept. Exchanges Programs, also for ABA, N.J. Bar Assn., 1961-75. Chmn. ethics Com., 1967; mem. N.J. Gov.'s Commn. on Individual Liberty and Personal Privacy, 1977-84; bd. trustees Lafayette Coll., 1975-80. Lt. USAAF, 1942-45. Recipient Kidd hon. citation for law Lafayette Coll., 1970, Bell Disting. Svc. Alumni award, 1985; Rutgers Law award, 1971, Lawyer of Yr. N.J. Commn. on Professionalism, 1998. Fellow Am. Bar Found. (state chmn. 1985-90, nat. chmn. 1992-93), Am. Acad. Martimonial Lawyers; mem. ABA (ho. of dels. 1972-90, chmn. adv. commn. on election law), N.J. Bar Assn. (pres. 1970-71, editorial bd. N.J. Lawyer mag. 1969—), Middlesex County Bar Assn. (pres. 1960-61), Assn. Trial Lawyers Am., Trial Attys. N.J. (bd. trustees 1969—, Lifetime Achievement award 1986), N.J. Bar Found. (Medal of Honor award 1991), Pi Lambda Phi (honoree 1997). Office: Greenbaum Rowe Smith Ravin Davis & Himmel LLP PO Box 5600 Metro Corp Campus One Woodbridge NJ 07095

GOLDEN, DAVID EDWARD, physicist; b. N.Y.C., May 27, 1932; s. Barnet Dade and Rose (Rosenbaum) G.; m. Paula Englander, July 18, 1962; children: Jeffrey Bertram, Leila Justine. AB, NYU, 1954, PhD in Physics, 1960. Asst. prof. NYU, 1960-61, Adelphi U., Garden City, N.Y., 1961-62; engring. specialist GTE Lab., Palo Alto, Calif., 1962-63; staff scientist Lockheed Lab., Palo Alto, 1963-68; vis. prof. U. Bari, Italy, 1968-69; sr. scientist Sylvania Electric Products, Danvers, Mass., 1969-70; prof. U. Nebr., Lincoln, 1970-75; George Lynn Gross rsch. prof., chmn. U. Okla., Norman, 1975-85; provost, v.p. acad. affairs, prof. physics U. North Tex., Denton, 1985-89, prof., dir. ctr. for materials characterization, 1989-94, regents prof., 1993—. Cons. autometric divsn. Paramount Pictures, N.Y.C., 1961-62, Tracor, Austin, Tex., 1969-74, Lawrence Radiation Lab., Livermore, Calif., 1975-78, Minn. Mining and Mftg., Mpls., 1984-86, Motorola, 1997-2000, Charles Evans & Assocs., 1998—; hon. lectr. Mid-Am. State U. Assn., 1982-83; chmn. Tex. Higher Edn. Coordinating Bd. Com. on Satellite Ednl. Delivery Systems, 1986; lectr. in field. Contbr. articles to profl. jours., chpts. to books. Sr. cons. Say It Straight Found. Grantee various orgns.; fellow Centennial Edn. Program U. Nebr., 1974-75. Fellow Am. Phys. Soc. (com. mem.); mem. AAAS, Materials Rsch. Soc., Sigma Xi. Lodges: Kiwanis. Avocations: jogging, tennis. E-mail: golden@unt.edu.

GOLDEN, DONALD ALAN, lawyer; b. Olean, N.Y., Aug. 31, 1953; s. Clayton Alexander and Dorothea Ann (Pfeil) G.; m. Carol Anne Metz, Jan. 1, 1982; children: Allyson Michelle, Christina Ann. BS, SUNY, Brockport, 1975; JD, U. Miami, 1978. Bar: Fla. 1979. Asst. counsel Am. Title Ins. Co., Miami, Fla., 1980; assoc. corp. counsel Burger King Corp., Miami, 1980-82; ho. counsel Senior Corp., Miami Beach, Fla., 1982-86; assoc. Blackwell, Walker, Fascell & Hoehl, Miami, 1986-87, ptnr., 1988; prin. Moretz Walker & Golden P.A., Miami, 1988-91, Donald A. Golden, P.A., Miami, 1991-93, 97—, Wampler, Buchanan & Breen, P.A., Miami, 1993-97. Mem. Fla. Bar Assn. Avocation: golf. Home: 11755 SW 62nd Ave Miami FL 33156-4909 Office: Donald A Golden PA 11755 SW 62nd Ave Miami FL 33156-4909 Fax: (305) 740-0513. E-mail: goldmiami@mindspring.com.

GOLDEN, E(DWARD) SCOTT, lawyer; b. Miami, Fla., Sept. 25, 1955; s. Alvan Leonard and Fay Betty (Gray) G.; m. Jane Eileen DeKlavon, June 9, 1979; children: Daniel Bryan, Kimberly Michelle. Student, So. Fla. Christian Coll., 1975-76; BS, MIT, 1978; JD, Harvard U., 1981. Bar: Fla. 1981, U.S. Dist. Ct. (so. dist.) Fla. 1982, U.S. Tax Ct. 1982, U.S. Supreme Ct. 1991, U.S. Dist. Ct. (mid. dist.) Fla. 1993, Eleventh Circut Ct. of Appeals, 2003. Assoc. Roberts and Holland, Miami, 1981-82, Valdes-Fauli, Richardson, Cobb & Petrey, P.A., Miami, 1982-83; v.p. Buck and Golden, P.A., Ft. Lauderdale, Fla., 1983-88; sole practice Ft. Lauderdale, Fla., 1988—. Judge negotiations competition Nova Southeastern U. Editor-in-chief Harvard Jour. of Law and Pub. Policy, 1980-81; contbr. articles to profl. jours. Mem. West Lauderdale Bapt. Ch., Broward County, Fla., 1982-98, chmn. deacons, 1984-86, 87-88, elder, 1994-98; mem. MIT Ednl. Coun., 1995—; del. Fla. Rep. Conv., 1987, 90; mem. Rep. Exec. Com., Broward County, 1984-94. Named one of Outstanding Young Men of Am., 1986; nominee Order of Silver Knight; Western Electric grantee, 1972-74. Mem. Christian Legal Soc., Broward County Christian Legal Soc. (pres. 1985-86, 94-95, 2000), Zeta Beta Tau. Lodges: Optimists (treas. Dade County Carol City High Sch., 1971-72). Avocations: sports, politics, bible study. Home: 5410 Buchanan St Hollywood FL 33021-5708 Office: 644 SE 4th Ave Fort Lauderdale FL 33301-3102 E-mail: esglaw@bellsouth.net.

GOLDEN, EDWIN HAROLD, insurance company executive; b. Corsicana, Tex., Dec. 14, 1931; s. Mace Benjamin and Sarah (Alterman) G.; m. Dolly Moskowitz, Aug. 3, 1952; children: Jeffrey L., Beth Golden Marsh. BBA, U. Tex., 1953. Agt. N.Y. Life Ins. Co., Austin, Tex., 1955-80; ptnr. Hodges, Golden & Duckworth, Austin, 1967-77; owner Ed Golden & Assocs., Austin, Tex., 1977—. Pres. Golden World Travel, Austin, 1993. Chmn. bd. trustees City of Austin Retirement Sys., 1975—; bd. dirs. James Dick Found. for Performing Arts, Round Top, Tex., 1979—. With U.S. Army, 1953-54. Mem. CLU (Austin chpt., certs. in pension planning and estate planning), Nat. Assn. Life Underwriters, Million Dollar Round Table (life), Top of the Table (charter), Am. Soc. Pension Actuaries, Internat. Found. Employee Benefit Plans, Shriners, Masons, Travelers' Century Club. Jewish. Avocation: travel. Office: Ed Golden and Assocs 5407 Parkcrest Dr Austin TX 78731-4911 E-mail: ed_g31@yahoo.com.

GOLDEN, ELLIOTT, judge; b. Bklyn., June 28, 1926; s. Barnet David and Rose (Fistel) G.; m. Ana Valbuena, July 8, 1990; children: Jeffrey Stephen, Marjorie Ruth, Peter Michael (dec.); stepchildren: Robert, Elizabeth, William,

John. Student, Maritime Acad., 1944-46, NYU, 1947-48; LLB, Bklyn. Law Sch., 1951. Bar: N.Y. 1952, U.S. Dist. Ct. (ea. dist.) N.Y. 1953, U.S. Tax Ct., U.S. Dist. Ct. (so. dist.) N.Y. 1953, U.S. Supreme Ct. 1961. Assoc. Golden & Golden, 1952-64; asst. dist. atty. Kings County, N.Y., 1956-64, chief asst. dist. atty., 1964-76, acting dist. atty., 1968; judge Civil Ct. of City of N.Y., 1977-78; justice Supreme Ct. State of N.Y., 1979-98, jud. hearing officer, 1998-2000. Adj. assoc. prof. N.Y.C. Tech. Coll., 1987-93; arbitrator, mediator Nat. Arbitration & Mediation, 1998—; cons. in field. Contbr. articles to profl. jours. Bd. trustees Greater N.Y. coun. Boy Scouts Am.; hon. vice chmn. March of Dimes; bd. dirs. Bklyn. Philharmonia; mem. adv. bd. Bklyn. PAL; chmn. Bklyn. Lawyers div. Fedn. Jewish Philanthropies; co-chmn. Bklyn. Lawyers div. State of Israel Bonds; assoc. trustee Temple Beth Emeth of Flatbush; mem. exec. com. Lawyers div. United Jewish Appeal; past pres. counsel Hosp. Relief Assn.; bd. dirs. Kings Bay YM-YMHA of Bklyn.; bd. dirs. Bklyn. ARC, Archway Sch. for Spl. Children, Bklyn. Sch. for Spl. Children. Recipient Cert. of Merit, Hosp. Relief Assn., numerous plaques, awards and certs. of appreciation various civic orgns. Mem. Nat. Dist. Attys. Assn. (dir. 1976-77, Disting. Svc. award), Combined Coun. Law Enforcement Ofcls. State N.Y., N.Y. State Dist. Attys. Assn. (sec. 1965-77), K.P. (supreme coun.). Avocations: golf, fishing, computers. Home and Office: 49 E Glenwild Dr PO Box 762 Smallwood NY 12778-0762 E-mail: egolden@hvc.rr.com.

GOLDEN, ELOISE ELIZABETH, community health nurse; b. Hope, Ind., Nov. 20, 1938; d. John M. and Hazel E. (Gosch) Holder; m. Don Golden, Aug. 2, 1959; children: David, Susanne. Diploma, Ball State U., 1959. RN. Office nurse, Columbus, Ind.; staff nurse Pub. Health Dept. Bartholomew County, Columbus; parish nurse, clinicare staff nurse, housecall coord. Bartholomew County Hosp., Columbus, intake coord. Hospice, 1991-2001; ret., 2001. Lutheran. Home: 11635 E 600 N Hope IN 47246

GOLDEN, GERALD SAMUEL, retired national medical board executive; b. Newark, N.J., June 8, 1935; s. Clement Harold and Jeanette (Bellat) G.; m. Deborah Ann Berlatsky, March 22, 1959 (dec. 1984); children: Leah Rachel, Ruth Naomi; m. Constance Reisa Abramson, Jan. 26, 1985. AB, Princeton U., 1957; MD, Columbia U., 1961. Diplomate Am. Bd. Pediatrics, Am. Bd. Psychiatry and Neurology. Asst. prof. of neurology and pediatrics Albert Einstein Coll. of Medicine, Bronx, N.Y., 1967-73, assoc. prof., 1973-77; prof. pediatrics and neurology U. Tex., Galveston, 1977-84; prof. pediatrics and neurology, dir. ctr. for devel. disabl. U. Tenn., Memphis, 1984-92; v.p. Nat. Bd. Med. Examiners, Phila., 1993—2002. Adj. prof. neurology U. Pa., 1993—98. Author: Textbook of Pediatric Neurology; assoc. editor: Pediatric Neurology Jour., 1987-92, Jour. of Devel. and Behavioral Pediatrics, 1987-2000, Jour. Epilepsy, 1987-92; contbr. numerous articles to profl. jours. Bd. dirs. Harwood Day Tng. Ctr., Memphis, 1987-92 Memphis-Shelby County Assn. for Retarded Citizens, 1987-92, Memphis Oral Sch. for the Deaf, 1987-92, Temple Israel Memphis, 1989-92. Recipient fed. grant Adminstrn. on Devel. Disabilities, 1990, Dept. of Human Svcs., 1990. Fellow Am. Acad. Pediatrics (neurology sect. head 1981-83), Am. Assn. Mental Deficiency (v.p. for medicine, 1984-86); mem. Am. Assn. U. Affiliated Programs (bd. dirs. 1987-92, pres. elect 1988-89, pres. 1989-90). Democrat. Jewish. Avocations: amateur radio, travel, bird watching.

GOLDEN, HARRY W. writer; AB, Coll. of the Holy Cross, Worcester, Mass., 1968; MS, U. Conn., 1979; MBA, U. New Haven, 1994.

GOLDEN, HERBERT HERSHEL, retired Romance languages educator; b. Boston, Nov. 1, 1919; s. Max and Minnie (Turetzky) G.; m. Hilda Rachel Lazerow, June 13, 1943 (dec. May 1964); children: Robert Sherman, Barry Allen (dec. Aug. 2003), Steven Eliot; m. Evelyn Pauline Sowa, Oct. 7, 1965. BA, Boston U., 1941, MA, 1942, Harvard U., 1947, PhD, 1951. Lectr. Spanish and French, Boston U., 1945-49, instr. Romance langs., 1949-53, asst. prof., 1953-57, assoc. prof., 1957-63, prof., 1963-85, prof. emeritus, 1985—. Cons. for NDEA lang. insts. U.S. Office Edn., HEW, Washington, 1955-56; asst. to mng. editor Modern Lang. Jour., Nat. Fedn. Modern Lang. Tchrs. Assns., Boston, 1955-58; instr. French and Italian, Harvard U. Ext., Cambridge, Mass, 1960-79; mem., editor, mem. adv. com. on fgn. langs. Mass. Dept. Edn., Boston, 1960-69; Fulbright lectr. U. Rome, 1962-63. Co-author: Modern French Literature and Language: A Bibliography of Homage Studies, 1953, reprinted 1971, Modern Iberian Language and Literature: A Bibliography of Homage Studies, 1958, reprinted 1971, Modern Italian Language and Literature: A Bibliography of Homage Studies, 1959, reprinted 1971, Histoire de France à Travers les Journaux du Temps Passé (1715-1789). Lumières et Lueurs du XVIII Siècle, 1986; editor: Studies in Honor of Samuel Montefiore Waxman, 1969, Giulio Bertoni and the Aesthetic Factor in Linguistics, 1969; contbr. articles and revs. to profl. jours. With U.S. Army, 1942-45, ETO. Decorated Purple Heart, Bronze Star, Gold medal of cultural merit (Italy); recipient diploma of merit Internat. Assn. for Study Italian Lang. and Lit., 1973, diploma of appreciation, France, 2001; Rsch. fellow Marion and Jasper Whiting Found., 1979-80. Mem. MLA (steering com. fgn. lang. program 1956-59), Am. Soc. for 18th Century Studies (editor Festschriften: 18th Century Bibliography), Am. Assn. Tchrs. Italian (sec.-treas. 1959-64, pres. 1964-66), French Soc. 18th Century Studies, Masons, Phi Beta Kappa (pres. Mass. Epsilon chpt. 1970-72, cert. disting. merit 1985). Avocations: classical music, collecting French films on video, reading. Home: 29 Thorndike St Brookline MA 02446-2405

GOLDEN, JOHN F. packaging company executive; b. N.Y.C., Feb. 5, 1949; s. David and Sylvia G.; m. Marguerite Ann Sellars, May 30, 1981; 1 child, Rachel Jeanne. Student, Bowling Green State U., 1967-69; BA, U. Colo., 1971. Exec. v.p. Stephen Gould Paper Co., Inc., Whippany, N.J., 1973—. Office: Stephen Gould Paper Co Inc 35 S Jefferson Rd Whippany NJ 07981-1043

GOLDEN, JOHN JOSEPH, JR., information systems executive; b. New Milford, Conn., Jan. 13, 1943; s. John Joseph and Anne Munroe (Hope) G.; m. Carolyn Joan Pachesa, May 29, 1965 (div. July 1984); children: Elizabeth Susan, Jennifer Leigh, John Joseph III, Matthew Benjamin; m. Ethel M. (Piercy) O'Neill, June 8, 1991; 1 stepchild, Michael Joseph. BS, MIT, 1966. V.p. systems devel. Quantum Computing Corp., Newton, Mass., 1968-70; mgr. computer ops. Polaroid Corp., Cambridge, Mass., 1970-75; dir. info. processing Schering-Plough Corp., Kenilworth, N.J., 1975-78; dir. info. systems Compugraphic Corp., Wilmington, Mass., 1978-80; dir. info. systems electro-optics div. Honeywell, Lexington, Mass., 1981-83, dir. adminstrn. electro-optics div. Wilmington, Mass., 1983-87, dir. materials elecro-optics div. Marlboro, Mass., 1987-90; dir. ops. Micracor, Acton, Mass., 1990-96; dir. info. sys. Fresenius Med. Care, Lexington, Mass., 1996-97; mgr. computing and telecom. U.S. Postal Svc., Washington, 1997-2000; sr. v.p. ops. Ethentica., Lake Forest, Calif., 2000—01; dir. bus. devel. Legato, Inc., Mountain View, Calif., 2001—. With USAR, 1964-70. Mem. IEEE, Assn. for Computing Machinery, MIT alumni Orgn., Mass. Iota Tau Assn. (treas. 1970—), Sigma Alpha Epsilon. Roman Catholic. Home: 5013 Ox Rd Fairfax VA 22030-4561 Office: Legato Fairfax VA 22030

GOLDEN, JUDITH GREENE, artist, educator; b. Chgo., Nov. 29, 1934; d. Walter Cornell and Dorothie (Cissell) Greene; m. David T. Golden, Oct. 10, 1955 (div.); children: David T. Golden III, Lucinda Golden Rizzo. BFA, Art Inst. Chgo., 1973; MFA, U. Calif., Davis, 1975; PhD Art (hon.), Moore Coll. Art, 1990. Assoc. prof. art U. Ariz., Tucson, 1981-88, prof. art, 1989-96, prof. emerita, 1996—. NEA forum pub. grants panelist, 1987; project dir. U. Calif. L.A. NEA Lecture series, 1979, 84. One woman shows include Women's Bldg., L.A., 1977, G. Ray Hawkins Gallery, L.A., 1977, Quay Gallery, San Francisco, 1979, 81, A. Nagel Galerie, Berlin, 1981, Ctr. Creative Photography, U. Ariz., 1983, Colburg Gallery, Vancouver, Can., 1985, Etherton Gallery, Tucson, 1985, 89, 91, 95, Mus. Photog. Arts, San Diego, 1986, Friends of Photography, Carmel, Calif., 1987, Tucson Mus. Art, 1987, Mus. Contemporary Photography, Chgo., 1988, Visual Arts Ctr., Anchorage, Alaska, 1990, Temple Music and Art, Tucson, 1992, 97, Scottsdale (Ariz.) Ctr. Arts, 1993, Arte de Oaxaca, Mex., 1995, Etherton Gallery, Tucson, 1995, Columbia Art Ctr., Dallas, 1997, U. Arts, Phila., 2002; exhibited in group shows at Centre Georges Pompidou, Paris, 1981, Security Pacific Bank, L.A., 1985, Phoenix Mus. Art, 1985, L.A. County Mus. Art, 1987, Tokyo Met. Mus. Photography, 1991, Laguna Art Mus., 1992, U. N.M. Mus. Art, Albuquerque, 1993, L.A. County Mus., 1994, Hara contemporary Mus., Tokyo, 1995, Mus. Women in Arts, Washington, 1997, Santa Barbara Mus. Art, Calif., 1997, Mus. Cont. Photography, 1998, Tucson Mus. Art, 1999, Calif. Mus. Photography, 1999, Ctr. for Creative Photography, 1999, Santa Barbara Mus. Art, 1999, Mus. Fine Arts, Santa Fe, N.Mex., 2002, U. Ariz. Mus. Art, 2003, Akron (Ohio) Mus. Art, numerous others; represented in permanent collections at Art Inst. Chgo., Calif. Mus. Photography, Ctr. Creative Photography U. Ariz., Denver Art Mus., Fed. Reserve Bank San Francisco, Fogg Mus. Art, Grunwald Ctr. Graphic Arts, Internat. Mus. Photography George Eastman House, L.A. County Mus. Art, Mpls. Inst. Arts, Mus. Photographic Arts, San Diego, Calif., Mus. Fine Arts, Santa Fe, N.Mex., Newport Harbor Mus. Art, Oakland Mus. Art, Photography Mus. Osaka, Polaroid Corp., San Francisco Mus. Modern Art, Security Pacific Bank, Tokyo Met. Mus. Photography, Tucson Mus. Art, Weisman Found., L.A., Mus. Cont. Photography, Chgo., Seattle Art Mus., Wash., Akron (Ohio) Art Mus., Avon Collection, N.Y.C. Individual artist grantee Tucson Pima Arts Coun., 1987; faculty rsch. grantee U. Ariz., 1986-87, 93-94; Ariz. Found. grantee U. Ariz., 1984; fellow Ariz. Commn. Arts, 1984; individual photography fellow NEA, 1979; Regent's faculty fellow Creative Rsch. U.Calif. L.A., 1977. Achievements include appearance of works in archive of artists' works and other material established at Center for Creative Photography.

GOLDEN, KELLY PAUL, electronic engineer, computer scientist; b. Detroit, Oct. 12, 1943; s. Harold Randolph and Shirley (Kelly) G.; m. Patricia Elaine Wright, June 20, 1964; children: Edward Stanley, Susan Marie. BSEE, Mich. State U., 1965, MSEE, 1967, PhDEE, 1971. Rsch. scientist Owens Ill. Corp., Okemos, Mich., 1968-73; sr. rsch. assoc. DuPont Co., Wilmington, Del., 1973-96; chief engr. Golden Systems, Inc., Bear, Del., 1996—. Tech. cons.; presenter seminar in thermal imaging 7th Internat. Congress on Advances in Nompact Printing, 1991. Author: (with others) Electronic Designers Handbook, 1974; patentee in field. Mem. IEEE (sr.), Sigma Xi. Avocation: computer system integration. Office: Golden Systems Inc PO Box 1340 Bear DE 19701-7340

GOLDEN, KIMBERLY KAY, critical care, flight nurse; b. Munich, July 31, 1961; arrived in US, 1961; d. Henry Davis and Mary Walker G. AA, Hinds Jr. Coll., Raymond, Miss., 1980, ASN, 1984; BSN, U. Miss., Jackson, 1987, AS in EMT-Paramedic, 1990; postgrad., U. Health Scis., Antigua, W.I., 1997—. Cert. ACLS, PALS provider and instr.; emergency nurse, crit. care RN; cert. paramedic, Miss., Tenn. Staff nurse neuro ICU U. Miss. Med. Ctr., 1984-85, staff nurse surg. ICU, 1985-87; staff nurse emergency rm. Rankin Gen. Hosp., Brandon, Miss., 1987-88, flight nurse Lifestar Helicopter Flight Svc., 1988-91; staff nurse emergency rm., ICU Nightingale Nursing, Jackson, 1988-91, Riveroaks Hosp., Jackson, 1990-91; staff RN emergency rm., Aerovesta flight Midland Meml. Hosp., Tex., 1991-93; flight nurse Hosp. Wing BTLS, Memphis, 1993-99, U. Health Sci. Med. Sch., Antigua, West Indies, 1997—; nurse Univ. Health Scis./Antigua Sch. Medicine, 1997—; emergency rm. staff nurse U. Nebr. Health Systems, 2001—. Examiner Nat. Registry EMT-P; advanced trauma life support station instr.; affiliate faculty paramedic program U. Miss. Faculty scholar Hinds Jr. Coll., 1983. Mem. AACN, Nat. Flight Assn., Emergency Nurses Assn. Baptist. Avocations: Karate, skiing, horse back riding, camping. Office: PO Box 140466 Austin TX 78714-0466

GOLDEN, LEON, classicist, educator; b. Jersey City, Dec. 25, 1930; s. Nathan and Regina (Okun) G. BA, U. Chgo., 1950, MA, 1953, PhD, 1958. Instr. ancient langs. Coll. William and Mary, 1958-60, asst. prof. ancient langs., 1960-65; assoc. prof. classical langs. Fla. State U., Tallahassee, 1965-68, prof., 1968—, dir. program in humanities, 1976—, chmn. dept. classics, 1986-95. Bd. dirs. Fla. Endowment for Humanities, 1983-87. Author: In Praise of Prometheus: Humanism and Rationalism in Aeschylean Thought, 1966, (with O.B. Hardison Jr.) Aristotle's Poetics, 1968, Aristotle: On Tragic and Comic Mimesis, 1992, Horace for Students of Literature, 1995. With AUS, 1953-55. Fellow coop. program humanities U.N.C. and Duke, 1964-65; fellow coop. program humanities Soc. for Religion in Higher Edn., 1971-72 Mem. Am. Philol. Assn., Archeol. Inst. Am., Classical Assn. Mid. West and South (pres. So. sect. 1972-74), Phi Beta Kappa. Office: Fla State U Dept Classics Tallahassee FL 32306

GOLDEN, MARC ALAN, investment banker; b. Phila., Dec. 26, 1953; s. Mano Robert and Sue E. (Aronsohn) G. B.A., Yale Coll., 1975; M.B.A., J.D., Harvard U., 1980. Bar: N.Y. 1981, U.S. Dist. Ct. (so. and ea. dists.) N.Y. 1984, U.S. Supreme Ct. 1985. Legis. asst. U.S. Senator Richard Stone (Fla.), Washington, 1975; legis. aide, issues analyst U.S. Rep. William Green (Pa.), Washington, 1975-76; legis. counsel U.S. Senate Com. on Vets. Affairs, Washington, 1976; asst. to dep. dir. Fed. Jud. Ctr., Washington, 1978; assoc. Cravath, Swaine & Moore, N.Y.C., 1981-86; v.p. Goldman, Sachs & Co., N.Y.C., 1986-88, mng. dir., head takeover def. and recapitalization group Prudential-Bache Capital Fundings, N.Y.C., 1988—. Active N.Y. chpt. Lawyers' Alliance for Nuclear Arms Control, 1983— . Mem. ABA, N.Y. State Bar Assn., Assn. Bar City N.Y. Office: Prudential Bache Capital Funding 199 Water St Fl 24 New York NY 10038-3592

GOLDEN, MARITA, English language educator, foundation executive; b. Washington, Apr. 28, 1950; d. Francis Sherman and Beatrice Lee Golden; m. Joseph Butlar Murray, Aug. 23, 1991; 1 child, Akintunde Michael Kayode. BA, Am. U., 1972; MSc, Columbia U., 1973; LittD (hon.), U. Richmond, 1998. Lectr. U. Lagos, Nigeria, 1975-79; asst. prof. Roxbury C.C., Boston, 1979-81, Emerson Coll., Boston, 1981-83; assoc. prof. George Mason U., Fairfax, Va., 1989-94; prof. English, Va. Commonwealth U., Richmond, 1994—2001. Author: Migrations of the Heart, 1983, A Woman's Place, 1986, Long Distance Life, 1989, And Do Remember Me, 1992, Wild Women Don't Wear No Blues, 1993, Saving Our Sons, 1995, Skin Deep, 1997, The Edge of Heaven, 1998, A Miracle Everyday, 1999, Gumbo, An Anthology of African American Writing, 2003. Pres. Hurston Wright Found., Hyattsville, Md., 1990—. Recipient Disting. Alumni award Am. U., 1994, Woman of Yr. award Zeta Phi Beta, 1997, Writers for Writers award Poets and Writers mag., 2001, Authors Guild Disting. Svc. award, 2002; named to Literary Hall of Fame, Chgo. State U., 2000. Mem. African Am. Writers Guild (pres. Washington 1986-90). Office: Hurston Wright Found Ste 531 6525 Belcrest Rd Hyattsville MD 20782

GOLDEN, OLIVIA A. human service agency administrator; b. N.Y.C., May 23, 1955; BA in Philosophy and Govt., MPP, PhD, Harvard U. Budget dir. office human svcs. State of Mass., 1983-85; lectr. in pub. policy J.F. Kennedy Sch. Govt. Harvard U., Cambridge, Mass., 1987-91; dir. programs and policy Children's Def. Fund, Washington, 1991-93; commr. on children, youth and families HHS, Washington, 1993-97, prin. dep. asst. sec. for children and families, 1997, asst. sec. for children and families, 1997—2001; dir. D.C. Child and Family Svcs. Agy., 2001—. Mem. adv. com. children and youth City of Cambridge. Author: Poor Children and Welfare Reform, 1992. Candidate for senator, Mass. Office: Chid and Family Svcs Agy 400 6th St SW 5th Fl Washington DC 20024

GOLDEN, RAYMOND LEE, retired theology studies educator, retired minister; b. Canton, TX, Dec. 11, 1920; s. Eddie Lloyd and Annie Mae (Phillips) Golden. Diploma jr. coll., E Ctrl. Clark Memorial, Newton, Miss., 1946—48; BA sr. coll., Miss. Coll., Clinton, Miss., 1950; Theology, New Orleans Theology, New Orleans, La., 1950—53. Cert. locksmith home bus./ Pixley, CA, 2002. Salesman Book and Bible sales, student aid, Charleston, NC, 1950; tchr. Scott County Sch. Dist., Sabastopool, Miss., 1952—53; air craft repairman Hayes Aircraft Corp., Birmingham, Ala., 1953—55; mission pastor so. Bapt., Plainview, Calif., 1955—57; sr. case worker county welfare, Visalia, Calif., 1957—59; tchr. Tulare County Sch., Tulare, Calif., 1959—69; kennel care Kennel Farm, Pixley, Calif., 2002. Family hist.: family tree Genealogy, 1982—86; author (correspondance): (letters) letters; author: (novels) (autobiography) This Happened to Me. Comdt. of cadets Civil Air Patrol, Visalia, Calif., 1957—59. Corp. USAAF, 1942—45, Pacific. Republican. Southern Baptist. Avocations: pilot, photography, bicycling, hiking, travel, reading. Home: 11260 Rd 144 general delivery Pixely CA 93256-9999

GOLDEN, REYNOLD STEPHEN, geriatrician, educator; b. Herkimer, N.Y., Jan. 11, 1937; s. Harold Theodore and Ethel Anne (Myers) G.; m. Gale Holtz, Nov. 26, 1959 (div. May 1978); children: Nathan Myers, Jennifer Lynn (dec.), Laura Beth (Lieba); m. Ellen Jeanne Moore, Sept. 9, 1978; children: Melissa Nan, Benjamin Harold. AB cum laude, Harvard Coll., 1958; MD, SUNY, Syracuse, 1962. Diplomate Am. Bd. Family Practice, Am. Bd. Internal Medicine; cert. added qualifications in geriatrics. Intern Lankenau Hosp., Phila., 1962-63; resident in internal medicine SUNY, Syracuse, 1963-66; pvt. practice Utica, N.Y., 1966-78; dir. family practice residency St. Elizabeth Hosp., Utica, 1978-92, St. Francis Hosp., Poughkeepsie, N.Y., 1992-95; clin. assoc. prof. dept. family medicine SUNY, Syracuse, 1991-96; chief of geriatrics Unity Med. Group (formerly Rochester Park Med. Group), 1995—; med. dir. continuing care svcs. Park Ridge Health Sys. (now Unity Health Sys.), Rochester, 1995—; clin. asst. prof. dept. internal medicine U. Rochester, 1999—. Cons. residency assistance program, Kansas City, Mo., 1988-96; pres. med. staff St. Elizabeth Hosp., Utica, N.Y., 1978-80; charter mem. N.Y. State Coun. on Grad. Med. Edn., N.Y.C., 1987-89. Editor N.Y. Family Physician, 1987-92. Recipient Vincentian Award, Unity Health Sys., 2000. Jewish. Avocations: travel, computers, music, theater, wine. Office: Ste 216 1561 Long Pond Rd Rochester NY 14626 E-mail: GoldenREN@aol.com.

GOLDEN, ROBERT CHARLES, financial services executive; b. Bklyn., July 12, 1946; s. Charles Joseph and Audrey (Griffin) G. BS in Acctg., Fordham U., 1968, MBA in Fin., 1978. V.p. internal audit Walston & Co., Inc., N.Y.C., 1969-73; v.p.-fin. Acan X-Ray Co., Inc., Detroit, 1973-76; exec. v.p. Prudential Securities Inc., N.Y.C., 1976-97, Prudential Ins. Co. Am., Inc., Roseland, N.J., 1997—. Bd. dirs. HeartShare Human Svcs. of N.Y., 1985—; trustee Xaverian H.S., Bklyn., 1987-93. Named Educator of Yr., Assn. of Tchrs. of N.Y., 1986, Cath. Guardian Soc. Humanitarian of Yr., 1985, Chief Brehon of the Great Irish Fair, 1992, Knight of the Sovereign Mil. Order of Malta, 1995, Man of Yr., Cath. Big Bros. and Big Sisters, 2002; named one of Top 50 Irish Ams. on Wall St., Irish Am. Mag., 1999, 2000, 2001, 2002, 2003; named to Diocesan Ct. of Honor, Diocese of Bklyn., Assembly of Stewarts, Diocese of N.Y., 1995, Knights of the Equestrian Order of the Holy Sepulchre, 1998; recipient citation, Coun. of the City of N.Y., Franciscan Heritage award, Franciscan Sisters of the Poor at Pla. Hotel, 1987, Apple award, Prudential Pacesetters, 1989, St. Francis Xavier Soc. award, Xaverian Bros., 1990, Thomas J. Cuite award, Irish Am. Heritage Wk. Com. of N.Y.C. Hall, 1991, Crystal Shield award, Salvation Army, 1992, Disting. Alumni award, Xaverian High Sch., 1993, Constance O. Garreson award, Minority Interchange, Inc., 1999, Ellis Island medal of honor, 2000, Bishop's Humanitarian award, Cath. Charities Diocese, Bklyn., 2001, Bus. 100 award, Irish Am. Mag., 2001, 2002, Disting. Leadership award, N.Y. Aquarium, 2001, Caritas award, Catholic Tchr. Assn, Diocese of Brooklyn, 2003. Mem. Securities Industry Assn., Mcpl. Club Bklyn., St. Patrick Soc. Bklyn., Emerald Assn. L.I. (past pres.), Ft. Hamilton Hist. Soc., Acad. Magical Arts, The Friendly Sons St. Patrick City N.Y., Cathedral Club of Bklyn. (past pres., Man of Yr. 1994), Bay Ridge Men's Club, Fordham U. Pres. Club, Bishop's Coat of Arms Club, Ancient Order of Hibernians (divsn. 22), KC, Bayfort Benevolent Assocs. (past pres.). Roman Catholic. Home: 33 Columbia Ave Staten Island NY 10305-3739 Office: Prudential Fin Inc 80 Livingston Ave Roseland NJ 07068-1798

GOLDEN, T. MICHAEL, state supreme court justice; b. 1942; BA in History, U. Wyo., 1964, JD, 1967; LLM, U. Va., 1992. Bar: Wyo. 1967, U.S. Dist. Ct. 1967, U.S. Ct. Appeals (10th cir.) 1967, U.S. Supreme Ct. 1970. Mem. firm Brimmer, MacPherson & Golden, Rawlins, Wyo., 1971-83, Williams, Porter, Day & Neville, Casper, Wyo., 1983-88; chief justice Wyo. Supreme Ct., Cheyenne, 1994—96, justice, 1988—. Mem. Wyo. State Bd. Law Examiners, 1977-82, 86-88. Capt. U.S. Army 1967-71. Office: Wyo Supreme Ct Bldg 2301 Capitol Ave Cheyenne WY 82002*

GOLDEN, WILLIAM THEODORE, trustee, corporate director; b. N.Y.C., Oct. 25, 1909; s. S. Herbert and Rebecca (Harris) G.; m. Sibyl Levy, May 2, 1938 (dec. 1983); children: Sibyl Rebecca, Pamela Prudence; m. Jean E. Taylor, July 8, 2001. AB, U. Pa., 1930, LLD (hon.), 1979; postgrad. bus. adminstrn., Harvard U., 1930-31; DSc (hon.), Poly. Inst. N.Y., 1975, Bard Coll., 1988; MA, Columbia U., 1979, LLD (hon.), 1986, Hamilton Coll., 1987; DHL (hon.), CUNY, 1997, Mt. Sinai Sch. Medicine, NYU, 2000. Lic. amateur radio operator, 1922—, station 2AEN. Asst. to pres. Cornell, Linder & Co., N.Y.C., 1931-34; with Carl M. Loeb & Co., Carl M. Loeb, Rhoades & Co., 1934-41; dir. Woodward Iron Co., 1940-68; asst. to commr. AEC, Washington, 1946-50, cons., 1950-58; chmn. bd. Nat. U.S. Radiator Co. (and successor cos.), 1952-74; dir. Pitts. Railways Co., 1952-63, United Carbon Co., 1957-63, Crowell-Collier and Macmillan, Inc., 1964-71, Paribas Corp., 1965-69; trustee Mitre Corp., 1958-72, 76-85, System Devel. Corp., 1957-66, chmn. bd. trustees, 1961-66. Spl. cons. on rev. govt. sci. activities Pres. Truman, Washington, 1950-51; advisor on NSF to dir. Bur. Budget, 1950-51; mem. mil. procurement task force Commn. on Orgn. Exec. Br. Govt., Hoover Commn., 1954-55; mem. adv. com. on pvt. enterprise in fgn. aid, U.S. State Dept., 1964-65; pub. mem. Hudson Inst., 1964-94; mem. commn. on delivery personal health services Mayor's Piel Commn., 1966-68; mem. adv. council Sch. Gen. Studies, Columbia U., N.Y.C., 1966—; mem. vis. com. on astronomy Princeton (N.J.) U., 1969—, chmn., 1976-89; mem. vis. com. on engring. and applied physics and on medicine and dental medicine Harvard U., Cambridge, Mass., 1969-77, mem. vis. com. on astronomy, 1976-90; mem. vis. com. Assn. Univs. for Research in Astronomy, 1973-76, dir. at large, 1988-91, Disting. advisor, 1991—; mem. vis. com. Space Telescope Sci. Inst., 1982-87; mem. adv. panel on space transp. ops. NASA, 1976-77; mem. adv. panel U.S. Postal Service, 1981-83; vice chmn. Mayor's Commn. on Sci. and Tech., 1983-91, hon. chair, 1992—, Commn. Coll. Retirement, 1984-88, Scientists Inst. Pub. Info., 1985-94; co-chmn. Carnegie Commn. on Sci., Tech. and Govt., 1988-96; bd. dirs. Verde Exploration, Ltd., Inc., Block Drug Co., Inc.; bd. dirs. emeritus Gen. Am. Investors Co.; founder Carnegie Group of Ministers of Sci. and Sci. Advisors to Heads of G8 countries, Russia and European Union, 1991—. Editor, co-author: Science Advice to the President, 1980, 2d rev. edit., 1993, Science and Technology Advice to the President, Congress and Judiciary, 1988, 2d rev. edit., 1993, Worldwide Science and Technology Advice to the Highest Levels of Governments, 1991; contbr. articles on govt. and sci. to various publs. Trustee Hebrew Free Loan Soc., 1935—, treas., 1985—, United Neighborhood Houses, 1952-61, Associated Hosp. Service N.Y., 1959-74, Univ. Corp. for Atmospheric Research, 1965-74, Riverside Research Inst., 1967-76, N.Y.C.-Rand Inst., 1969-75, Ctr. for Advanced Study Behavioral Scis., 1970-76, Bennington Coll., 1971-76, Haskins Labs., 1971-92, SIAM Inst. Math. and Soc., 1973-91, Columbia U. Press, 1974-77, John Simon Guggenheim Meml. Found., 1976-81, Nat. Humanities Ctr., 1978-90, emeritus, 1990—; trustee The Population Council, 1979-89, Catskill Ctr. for Conservation and Devel., 1981—, U. Pa. Press, 1985—; mem. Marine Biology Lab., Woods Hole, Mass., 1968—, trustee, 1968-87, trustee emeritus, 1987; trustee Mt. Sinai Hosp., N.Y.C., 1955—, vice chmn., 1977—; mem. governing council Courant Inst. Math. Scis., NYU, 1962-91, vice chmn., 1962-86, chmn., 1986-91; trustee Mt. Sinai Med. Sch., 1963—, vice chmn., 1977—; trustee N.Y. Found., 1963-84, treas., 1974-78; chmn. bd. trustees City Univ. Constrn. Fund, 1967-71; mem. exec. com. Health Research Council, City of N.Y., 1968-75; trustee Am. Mus. Natural History, 1968—, v.p., 1971-88, vice chmn., 1988-89, chmn., 1989-94, chmn. emeritus, 1994—; trustee Carnegie Instn. Washington, 1969—, sec., 1971-99, sr. trustee, 2000—; trustee Barnard Coll., 1973—, vice chmn., 1975-79, 86-92, treas. 1980-83, hon. vice chmn., 1992-98, emeritus, 1998—; trustee N.Y. Council for Humanities, 1975-78, chmn., 1976-78; bd. overseers Sch. Arts and Scis., U. Pa., Phila., 1976-97, emeritus, 1997—; mem. council Rockefeller U., 1978—; mem. bd. visitors Grad. Sch. and Univ. Ctr., CUNY, 1979-96, mem. bd. Grad. Ctr. Found., 1996—; trustee Am. Trust for Brit. Library, 1980-92, 98—, vice chmn., 1985-92, co-chmn., treas., 1998—; trustee Neurosci. Research Found., 1981-99, chmn., 1981-87; bd. dirs. Grad. Sch. of Arts and Sci. Alumni Assn., Columbia U., 1984-93, vice chmn. 1984-91; chmn. Black Rock Forest Consortium, 1988—; mem. adv. bd. Johns Hopkins Sch. Hygiene and Pub. Health, 1995-98; bd. dirs. Internat. Univ. Exch., Inc., 1996—; trustee, The After School Corp., 1999—. Served to lt. comdr. USNR, 1941—. Recipient Letters of Commendation with ribbon Sec. of Navy and chief Bur. Ordnance for invention of naval gunfire device used in WWII, Pub. Svc. award Mus. City of N.Y., 1981, Disting. Pub. Svc. award NSF, 1982, Tribute of Appreciation, Nat. Sci. Bd., 1991, Pub. Welfare medal NAS, 1996, medal of distinction Barnard Coll., Columbia U., 1999, Dean's award for disting. achievement Grad. Sch. A&S, Conversatoin Citizen award, Ctr. Environ. Rsch. and Conservation, 2003. Fellow AAAS (treas., bd. dirs. 1969-2000, treas. emeritus 2000, Lifetime Achievement award 2001), N.Y. Acad. Scis. (mem. bd. govs. 1977—, pres. 1988, chmn. 1989, life gov. 1991), Am. Acad. Arts and Scis. (Scholar-Patriot award 2001), Assn. Women in Sci., New York Acad. of Medicine; mem. Nat. Acad. Pub. Adminstrn., Am. Philos. Soc. (mem. coun. 1985-91, v.p. 1992—, Benjamin Franklin award for disting. pub. svc. 1995), History of Sci. Soc., Coun. Fgn. Rels., Army and Navy Club, Cosmos Club (Washington), Century Assn. Home: 730 Park Ave New York NY 10021-4945 Office: 500 Fifth Ave 50th Fl New York NY 10110-5099

GOLDEN, WILLIE MALCOME, JR., band director, music educator; b. Galveston, Tex., Oct. 24, 1966; s. Willie Malcome and Helen Jean G.; m. Nancy Elizabeth Richard, July 20, 1991; children: Willie Malcome III, Hunter Dean. B in Music Edn., McNeese State U., Lake Charles, La., 1991; MEd, McNeese State U., Lake Charles, LA, 2002. Cert. instrumental edn. K-12, adminstrn., supervision-principalship. Dir. of bands Lake Arthur H.S., Lake Arthur, La., 1991—94, Iowa H.S., Iowa, La., 1994—96, Northside Jr. H.S., Jennings, La., 1996—; dir. bands Bonlcie H.S., Bonlcie, La., 1990—91. Adminstrv. asst. Northside Jr. H.S., Jennings, La., 2001—. Music min. Holy Trinity Episcopal Ch., Sulphur, La., 1999—2002. Mem.: AFT/LFT, LMEA, MENC. Episcopalian. Avocation: camping. Home: 2013 Marge Ln Sulphur LA 70663 Office: Northside Jr High Sch 308 Shankland Ave Jennings LA 70546 Personal E-mail: mgolden104@netzero.net. E-mail: njhsband@hotmail.com.

GOLDEN, WILSON, lawyer; b. Holly Springs, Miss., Feb. 15, 1948; s. Woodrow Wilson and Constance Annette (Harris) G.; m. Krista Nix, July 10, 1999; children from previous marriage: Wilson Harris, Lewis Hamilton, Pamela Camille. BPA, U. Miss., 1970, JD, 1977. Bar: Miss. 1977, U.S. Dist. Ct. (no. and so. dists.) Miss. 1977, U.S. Ct. Appeals (5th cir.) 1977. Pub. affairs journalist PBS/Miss. Authority for Ednl. TV, Jackson, 1970-72; asst. sec. Miss. State Senate, Jackson, 1972-76; ptnr. Lane & Henderson, Greenville, Miss., 1977-80, Watkins Ludlam & Stennis, Jackson, 1980-89; pvt. practice Jackson, Washington, 1990-96; v.p. govt. rels. ICF Kaiser Internat., Inc., Fairfax, Va., 1996—99; sr. congl. liaison U.S. Dept. Transp., Washington, 1999-2001; v.p. Jefferson Govt. Rels., Washington, 2001—. Mem. Dem. State Exec. Com., 1976-84, 88-96; mem. Miss. Gov.'s Constl. Study Commn., 1986; mem. Dem. Nat. Com., 1990-92; charter mem. Dem. Leadership Coun. NETWORK, 1988; USDOT rep. Miss. Spl. Task Force for Econ. Devel. Planning, 2000—. Major USAR, 1970-90. Recipient Disting. Reporting award Am. Polit. Sci. Assn. 1971, U.S. Law Week award Bur. Nat. Affairs, Inc., Washington, 1978. Mem.: Miss. Bar Assn. Democrat. Presbyterian. Home: 7037 E Haycock Rd Falls Church VA 22043-2319 E-mail: Wilsongolden@aol.com.

GOLDENBERG, CHARLES LAWRENCE, real estate company executive; b. N.Y.C., Sept. 4, 1933; BS, NYU, 1955, JD, 1958. Associated with Brown, Harris, Stevens, Inc., 1955-75, officer, 1960-75, sr. v.p., dir. fin. dist. office; pres., CEO Sylan Lawrence Co., Inc., N.Y.C., 1975—. Former adj. prof. real estate NYU; cons., lectr. in field. Contbr. articles to N.Y. Times, Real Estate Weekly, and other profl. jours. Mem. Nat. Assn. Real Estate Bds., Internat. Real Estate Fedn., Real Estate Bd. N.Y. Inc. (gov.). Office: Sylvan Lawrence Co Inc 1350 Ave of the Americas New York NY 10019-4702 Fax: 212-344-8271. E-mail: clg_ny@yahoo.com.

GOLDENBERG, ELIZABETH LEIGH, editor; b. Dayton, Ohio, Oct. 29, 1963; d. Neal and Myrna (Gallant) G. AB in Philosophy and Politics, Mount Holyoke Coll., 1985. Intern, spokeswoman The White House, Washington, 1984; trainee Nat. Westminister Bank USA, N.Y.C., 1985-86, asst. to v.p. fin. and strategic planning ops. div., 1986-87; asst. dealer Toronto-Dominion Bank, N.Y.C., 1987-88, dealer money markets, 1988-90, sr. dealer money markets, 1990-91, sr. dealer, mgr. short term asset trading, 1991-93; sr. dealer, sr. mgr. short term loan participation TD Securities, Inc., N.Y.C., 1993-97, v.p., dir. short term money-market trading and origination, 1997-99; freelance journalist, author, 2000; reporter Bloomberg News, 2000—01, editor team leader, 2001—02, mng. editor bonds, currencies and derivatives, 2002—. Econ. commentator, 1993-2000. Contbr. articles and photographs to mags. Bd. dirs. USA Rugby Met. N.Y., 1987-89, N.Y. Rugby Club, 1995-98; publicist, spokesperson, com. on image and mktg. USA Rugby, 1993; U.S.A. Eagles publicist USA Rugby, Colorado Springs, Colo., 1989-94; chair Youth Rugby for Harlem Devel. Com., 1994-95. Mem. Pub. Securities Assn. (chmn. money market com. 1990-92, bd. dirs. 1990-92, mem. polit. action com. 1990-92, program com. 1990-92, awards com. 1991-93, chmn. money market com. 1997-99, bd. dirs. 1997-99). Avocations: photography, rugby, cooking, baking, ballet. Home: 355 S End Ave Apt 20J New York NY 10280-1007 E-mail: egoldenberg2@bloomberg.net.

GOLDENBERG, EVA J. lawyer; b. Nürnberg, Germany, Nov. 24, 1961; came to U.S., 1968; d. David M. Goldenberg and Hildegard (Grünbaum) Katz; m. Benjamin P. Michel. BA, U. Chgo., 1984; JD, Benjamin N. Cardozo Law Sch., N.Y.C., 1987. Bar: N.Y., N.J. Assoc. Riker, Danzig, Scherer, Hyland & Perretti, Morristown, N.J., 1987-90, Kelley, Drye & Warren, N.Y.C., 1990-94; asst. gen. counsel Russ Berrie & Co., Inc., Oakland, N.J., 1994-98, assoc. gen. counsel, 1999, dir. human resources, 1999-2000, v.p. human resources, 2000—. Office: 111 Bauer Dr Oakland NJ 07436-3123 E-mail: egoldenberg@russberrie.com.

GOLDENBERG, GEORGE, retired pharmaceutical company executive; b. N.Y.C., Mar. 12, 1929; s. Gersh and Rose (Kolpacci) G.; m. Arlene Sandra Yudell, May 22, 1955; children: Steven Alan, Heidi Michele Goldenberg Handelsman, Jeffrey Evan. Student, Bklyn. Coll., 1946-47; BS, Bklyn. Coll. Pharmacy L.I. U., 1951. Pharmacist Dolcorts Pharmacy, N.Y.C., 1951-56; export mgr. Chem. Specialties Co., Inc., N.Y.C., 1956-58; sales mgr. Syntex Chem. Co., Inc., N.Y.C., 1958-60; asst. to pres. Syntex Labs., Inc., N.Y.C., 1960-61; gen. sales mgr. Panray-Parlam Corp., Englewood, N.J., 1961-63; v.p. Ormont Drug & Chem. Co., Inc., Englewood, 1963-64, exec. v.p., dir., 1964-66, pres., dir., 1966-81; sec., dir. Goldleaf Pharmacal Co., Inc., Englewood, 1966-81; pres., dir. Moleculon, Inc., 1982-88; pres., CEO, dir. Argus Pharms. Inc., The Woodlands, Tex., 1988-92. Bd. dirs. Fed. Pharmacal Co., Ft. Lauderdale, Fla., Bedford Acme Surg. Co., Inc., Bklyn., Lawton Labs., Inc., Englewood, Ormont Diagnostics Ltd., London. Trustee L.I. U., Bklyn. Coll. Pharmacy. Mem. Bklyn. Coll. Pharmacy Alumni Assn. (pres.), Fedn. Alumni Assns. L.I. U. (pres.), Am. Pharm. Assn., Englewood Jr. C. of C., Young Pres. Orgn., Am. Mgmt. Assn., Drug and Allied Trades Assn., Delta Sigma Theta. Clubs: B'nai B'rith, The Polo Club of Boca Raton (past pres. bd. govs.). Home: 16730 Colchester Ct Delray Beach FL 33484-6946 E-mail: aggpolo@aol.com.

GOLDENBERG, KIM, academic administrator, internist; BS, SUNY, Stonybrook, 1968; MS, Polytech. Inst. N.Y., 1972; MD, Albany (N.Y.) Med. Coll., 1979. Test engr. lunar lander and naval jets, Grumman, NY, 1968—75; resident internal medicine We. Res. Care Sys., Youngstown, Ohio, 1979—82; dir. gen. internal medicine Wright State U. Sch. Medicine, Dayton, Ohio, 1983—89, vice chair medicine, 1988—89, assoc. dean for students and curriculum, 1989—90, dean, 1990—98, pres., 1998—. Office: Wright State U Office of Pres Dayton OH 45435

GOLDENBERG, MARVIN MANUS, pharmacologist, pharmaceutical developer; b. N.Y.C., July 7, 1935; s. Jacob and Sarah Goldenberg; m. Esther K. Gelman, Sept. 8, 1957; children: Sol Jeffrey, Lisa Shari. BS, Bklyn. Coll. Pharmacy, 1957; MS, Temple U., 1959; PhD, Med. Coll. Pa., 1965. Lic. pharmacist, N.Y., Pa. Group leader Procter & Gamble Pharms., Norwich, N.Y., 1965-80; dir. immunopharmacology rsch. Merck Sharp & Dohme, Rahway, N.J., 1980-85, asst. dir. clin. rsch., 1985-88; dir. ophthalmic R&D Am. Cyanamid, Pearl River, N.Y., 1988-89, dir. ophthalmic rsch., 1989-91; v.p. pharm. product devel. and mfg. Reed and Carnrick div. Block Drug Co., Jersey City, N.J., 1991-92; v.p. pharmacology & clin. design, 1992-93; v.p. pharmacology clin. design, pres. Mt. Sinai Med. Ctr., N.Y.C., 1994-99; investigational drug mgr. drugs internal rev. bd.; sr. dir. clin. product devel. Managed Health Care Assocs., Inc., Florham Park, N.J., 1999-2000; freelance med. writer, cons. medicine and healthcare, publs. in pharm. and med. jours.; sr. tech. dir., cons. MMG Assocs., 2000—. Grant reviewer NIH and DRG, Bethesda, Md., 1978-95, fellowship reviewer, 1984-89; cons. in field; med. writer for clin. asst. programs; adminstr. for ACPE-approved continuing edn. programs for pharmacists. Author: The Role of Arachidonic Acid Oxygenation Products, 1984, Gastric Cytoprotection with Prostaglandins, 1985, Critical Review of Losartan, 1995, Analysis of the Asthma Drug Ziluton, 1996, Critical Drug Appraisal: Mesalamine in IBD Fundamentals of the Clinical Trial, 1997, Critical Drug Appraisal: Misoprostol in NSAID-Induced Gastrointestinal Injury, 1998;, Oncology Reviews of New Drugs, 2001; sect. editor New Drugs: Jour. Clin. Therapeutics; column editor New Drugs: Jour. Pharmacy and Therapeutics; mem. editl. bd. Clin. Therapeutics; med. writer New Drugs: Clin. Trials; contbr. numerous articles to profl. jours.; inventor on numerous patents. Pres. Temple, Norwich, N.Y., 1972. Fellow Am. Soc. for Pharmacology, Am. Gastroent. Assn., Inflammation Rsch. Assn., Soc. of Clin. Pharmacology; mem. Am. Assn. Pharm. Scientists, N.Y. Soc. Health Care Specialists, Masons (pres. Norwich, N.Y. 1975). Achievements include patents relating to use of chemical entities in inflammation, pain and gastrointestinal disorders. E-mail: mmgpotter@comcast.net.

GOLDENBERG, MIKHAIL, mathematics; b. Ukraine, Sept. 24, 1939; arrived in USA, 1997, permanent resident, 2003; s. Mikhail Ya Godenberg and Anna Moses (Koytickh) Goldenberg; m. Nadezhda Ghernyak, Aug. 19, 1965; 1 child, Esther. Masters math., Odessa U, Odessa, Ukraine, 1961; PhD math., Ekaterinburg U, Ekaterinburg, Russia, 1970. Tchr. Kirov School, Donetsk, Ukraine, 1961—63; asst. prof. South-Ural U, Chelyabinsk, Russia, 1963—70, assoc. prof., 1970—97; tchr.-math, part time Tchr. Tng. Sch., Chelyabinsk, Russia, 1980—97; tchr. and coord.-math The Ingenuity Project, Baltimore, Md., 1997—2000, math dept. head, 2000—. Tests preparation group head Tchr. Tng. Sch., South-Ural U, Chelyabinsk, Russia, 1975—95; math con. of engr. South Ural U, Chelyabinsk, Russia, 1980—95. Contbr. articles to profl. publs. Avocations: poetry, classical, fencing. Home: 111Glyndon Drive, A-2 Reisterstown MD 21136 Office: Baltimore Polytechnic Inst 1400 W Cold Spring Ln Baltimore MD 21209-4904

GOLDENBERG, NANCY ANN, city planner; b. Cin., Aug. 28, 1956; d. Isadore and Carolyn (Cohen) G. BA, George Washington U., 1978; M in City Planning, U. Pa., 1980. Project mgr. Reading (Pa.) Ctr. City Devel. Fund, 1980-82; city planner Venturi, Rauch and Scott Brown, Phila., 1982-84; legis. asst. City Coun., Phila., 1984-89; mng. ptnr. Resources for Growth, Inc., Phila., 1989-90; asst. twp. mgr. Lower Merion Twp., Ardmore, Pa., 1990-93; dir. of pub. info. Ctr. City Dist., Phila., 1993-97; program adminstr. Fairmount Park Natural Lands Restoration and Environ. Edn., Phila., 1997-2000; dep. exec. dir. Center City Dist., Phila., 2000—. Bd. dirs. Preservation Coalition of Greater Phila., 1988-94, adv. bd. 1994. Mem. adv. bd. Fairmont Park, 1995-2000; founder Mt. Airy Arts Alliance, 1989—, Phila. Outward Bound, 1992—; trustee Hurricane Island Outward Bound Sch., 1994-99, 2001--; bd. dirs. Cliveden of the Nat. Trust, 1994-96, West Mt. Airy Neighbors Assn., 1984-86, Friends of Phila. Parks, 1996-2002, Reading Terminal Market Preservation Fund, 1997—. Mem. Phi Beta Kappa, Phi Eta Sigma. Avocations: swimming, hiking, travel, photography. Office: Center City Dist 917 Filbert St Philadelphia PA 19107 E-mail: ngoldenberg@centercityphila.org.

GOLDENBERG, PHILIP THEODORE, physician; b. Hartford, Conn., Aug. 17, 1920; s. Joseph and Esther (Taylor) G.; m. Gloria Rose Lavitt, Jan. 20, 1952; children: Jeffrey, Andrew, Lori. BA, Cornell U., 1943; MD, Boston U. Sch. Med., 1946. Diplomate Am. Bd. Internal Medicine. Physician, Hartford, 1952—. Pres. Hartford Med. Soc., 1977. Capt. U.S. Army, 1947-49, Germany. Fellow ACP. Home: 18 Shibah Way Bloomfield CT 06002-1541

GOLDENBERG, STEPHEN BERNARD, lawyer; b. Cambridge, Mass., Feb. 10, 1943; s. Alexander M. and Gertrude (Perlmutter) G. AB, Kenyon Coll., 1964; postgrad., Georgetown U. Law Sch., 1964-65; JD, Boston Coll., 1967. Bar: Mass. 1967, Fla. 1990, U.S. Supreme Ct. 1994. Assoc. Myer Israel, Boston, 1968—74; ptnr. Israel & Goldenberg, 1974—91, Goldenberg, Walters & Lipson, Brookline, 1991—98, Goldenberg, Walters & Popkewitz, 1998—. Chmn. rent control bd., Brookline, 1972-75; mem. Brookline Bd. Selectmen, 1976-85, chmn., 1983-84. Mem. ABA, Mass. Bar Assn., Mass. Conveyancers Assn., Brookline C. of C. (pres.). Democrat. Office: Goldenberg Walters et al 7 Harvard St Brookline MA 02445-7970 E-mail: sbgat23@aol.com.

GOLDENBERG, STEVEN SAUL, lawyer; b. Monticello, N.Y., Apr. 11, 1952; s. Joseph and Lillian (Stone) G.; m. Barbra Ellen Tucker, June 27, 1976; children: Matthew, Jenna, Alycia. BA cum laude, SUNY, Oneonta, 1974; MPA cum laude, NYU, 1976; JD, Benjamin N. Cardozo Sch. Law, 1980. Bar: N.J. 1981, N.Y., U.S. Dist. Ct. N.J., U.S. Dist. Ct. (so. dist.) N.Y. Law sec. Hon. David B. Follender, Hackensack, N.J., 1980-81; atty. Saiber Schlesinger Satz & Goldstein, Newark, 1981-94; atty., legis. agt. Buchanan Ingersoll, Princeton, N.J., 1994-95, Greenbaum Rowe Smith Ravin Davis & Himmel, Woodbridge, N.J., 1995—. Spl. counsel N.J. Bd. Pub. Utilities, Dept. Environ. Protection, Newark, 1984-91; N.J. Legislature Agt., Trenton, 1996—; counsel to competitors of N.J.'s investor-owned elec. and natural gas utilities in restructuring hearings N.J. Bd. Pub. Utilities. Named one of Top 10 N.J. Lawyer/Lobbyists N.J. Law Jour., Newark; named among Top Lawyers, N.J. Monthly mag. Mem. N.J. Bar Assn., N.Y. Bar Assn., N.J. Bus. and Industry Assn. (legal affairs com. 1995—). Avocations: Karate, physical fitness, computers, music. Office: Greenbaum Rowe Smith Ravin Davis & Himmel PO Box 5600 Woodbridge NJ 07095-0988 E-mail: sgoldenberg@greenbaumlaw.com.

GOLDENBERG, WILLIAM BRUCE, music educator, musician; b. Cleve., Nov. 1, 1950; s. DAvid and Helen Goldenberg. BA, Oberlin Coll., 1972; MusM, SUNY, Stony Brook, 1972, Juilliard Sch., 1974; MusD, Ind. U., 1991. Head tchg. asst. SUNY, Stony Brook, 1972—74; piano tchg. fellow and accompanist Juilliard Sch., N.Y.C., 1974—76; personal asst. to Menahem Pressler Ind. U. Sch. of Music, Bloomington, 1976—80; disting. prof. piano and chamber music No. Ill. U., DeKalb, 1980—; chair dept. piano and collaborative piano No. Ill. U. Sch. Music, DeKalb, 1996—. Concert pianist Idyllwild (Calif.) Arts Music Festival, 1995—, Grand Teton Music Festival, Jackson Hole, Wyo., 1983—84; guest prof. Ind. U., 1995; adjudicator Joanna Hodges Piano Competition, Palm Springs, Calif., 1983, Grace Welsh Internat. Piano Competition, Chgo., 2002, Music Tchrs. Nat. Assn., Decatur, Ill., 2003, St. Charles (Ill.) Internat. Art and Music Festival Piano Competition, 1987—88; masterclass tchr. Shanghai Conservatory of Music, 2001; tchr. Lisa Acad., Budapest, 2003—. Musician: (CDs) Violin Sonatas with Vermeer Quartet Violinist Pierre Menard, Contemporary Chamber Music, Door County Suite, Petite Suite for my Grandchildren, also numerous live concert performances, collaborations. Named winner Concerto Competition, Oberlin Coll., 1971, Ind. U., 1978; Piano fellow, Tanglewood Music Festival, 1975. Mem.: East Meets West Music Arts- Chgo. (adv. bd. 1993—2003), Pi Kappa Lambda, Phi Beta Kappa. Achievements include research in non-traditional repertoire from diverse cultures (Asian, Hispanic, Black) and contemporary music. Home: PO Box 165 DeKalb IL 60115 Office: No Ill U DeKalb IL 60115

GOLDENFARB, PAUL BENNETT, internist, oncologist; b. Medford, Mass., Jan. 11, 1941; MD, Boston U., 1966. Diplomate Am. Bd. Internal Medicine, Am. Bd. Oncology. Intern Boston City Hosp., 1966-67, resident medicine, 1967-68, Duke U. Med. Ctr., 1970-71; fellow hematology/oncology Yale U., 1971-73; mem. staff Morton F. Plant Hosp., Clearwater, Fla., 1973—; pvt. practice Clearwater, 1973—. Mem. ACP, AMA, Am. Soc. Hematology, Am. Soc. Clin. Oncology, Fla. Med. Assn. Office: 1200 Druid Rd S Ste 8 Clearwater FL 33756-1926

GOLDENHERSH, ROBERT STANLEY, lawyer; b. St. Louis, July 23, 1922; s. Boris and Sarah (Lapushin) G.; m. Jeanne Waldman, June 18, 1950; children: Lawrence E., Margaret J., Louise E. JD, Washington U., 1947; LLM in Taxation, NYU, 1948. Bar: Mo. 1947, U.S. Dist. Ct. (ea. dist.) Mo., U.S. Ct. Appeals (8th cir.), U.S. Supreme Ct. 1956. Sr. ptnr. Rosenblum, Goldenhersh, Silverstein & Zafft P.C., St. Louis, 1953—. Pres. Congregation Temple Israel, St. Louis, 1975-76; chmn. law sch. div. Elliot Soc. of Washington U., St. Louis, 1984; charter mem. Creve Couer Squires (Mo.), 1980—. Mem. ABA, Mo. Bar Assn., St. Louis Co. Bar Assn., Bar Assn. City of St. Louis, Order of the Coif. Clubs: Westwood Country. Democrat. Jewish. Avocations: tennis, golf, fishing. Home: 211 Rondelay Ct Saint Louis MO 63141-7702 Office: Rosenblum Goldenhersh et al 4th Fl Pierre Laclede Ctr 7733 Forsyth Blvd Ste 400 Saint Louis MO 63105-1812

GOLDENSHTEYN, VLADIMIR LEV, civil engineer; b. Kiev, Jan. 30, 1937; came to U.S., 1979; s. Lev Abram and Tanya Lev (Tsymberg) G.; m. Klara Shlema Sigal, Sept. 30, 1961; 1 child, Lena. Technician, Bldg. Technicum, Kiev, USSR, 1959; Civil Engr., Civil Engring. Inst., Voronezh, USSR, 1967. Technician, engr., dept. chief, chief specialist State Inst. of Design of Installations for Transport & Purification of Water for Indsl. Enterprises; technician, engr., project coord., engr.-in-charge City of N.Y., Dept. Environ. Protection, Divsn. Sewers, 1980—. Author computer programs hydraulic etc. calculations for water/sewer sys. Life mem. Rep. Presdl. Task Force. Mem. Profl. Engrs. Soc. Avocation: fishing. Office: City NY Dept Environ Prot Permit Control Office 120-55 Queens Blvd Jamaica NY 11424

GOLDENSOHN, BARRY NATHAN, poet, retired language educator; b. NYC, Apr. 26, 1937; s. Joseph Benjamin and Shirley (Friedburg) G.; m. Lorrie Myer, Aug. 5, 1956; children: Matthew, Rachel. BA, Oberlin (Ohio) Coll., 1957; MA, U. Wis., 1959. Instr. IIT, Chgo., 1959-61, Kent (Ohio) State U., 1961-62; co-founder, tchr., dir. Pacific High Sch., Portola Valley, Calif., 1962-65; tchr. Goddard Coll., Plainfield, Vt., 1965-70; vis. prof. Writers Workshop, U. Iowa, Iowa City, 1970-72; tchr. Goddard Coll., 1972-77; dean humanities and arts Hampshire Coll., Amherst, Mass., 1977-82; prof. English Skidmore Coll., Saratoga Springs, NY, 1982—93; ret., 1993. Author: (poetry) St. Venus Eve, 1972, Uncarving the Block, 1978, The Marrano, 1988, Dance Music, 1992, East Long Pond (with Lorrie Goldensohn), 1997; editor: Swift's Gullivers Travels, 1961; contbr. articles to profl. jours.; author numerous poems. Grantee NEH, 1977-78, Vt. Coun. of Arts, N.Y. Found. for the Arts. Home: 608 N Camp Rd Cabot VT 05647-9801 Office: Skidmore Coll English Dept Saratoga Springs NY 12866

GOLDENTHAL, ELLIOT, composer; Film scores include Pet Semetary, 1989, Drugstore Cowboy, 1989, Grand Isle, 1991, Alien 3, 1992, Fool's Fire, 1992, Demolition Man, 1993, Interview with the Vampire, 1994 (Academy award nomination best original score 1994), Cobb, 1994, Batman Forever, 1995, Sphere, 1998, In Dreams, 1999, Titus, 1999, Final Fantasy: The Spirits Within, 2001, Frida, 2002 (Best Musical Score Academy award, 2003). Office: Gorfaine-Schwartz Agy Inc 13245 Riverside Dr Ste 450 Sherman Oaks CA 91423-2172*

GOLDER, HERBERT ALAN, classics educator; b. Oct. 29, 1952; BA, Boston U., 1975; MA, Yale U., 1977, MPhil, 1979, PhD, 1984; postgrad., Oxford U., 1982. Tchg. fellow, instr. in classics Yale U., New Haven, Conn., 1977-80; asst. prof. of classics Syracuse (N.Y.) U., 1982-85, Emory U., Atlanta, 1985-87, Boston U., 1988-93, assoc. prof. of classics, 1993—. Vis. asst. prof. classics Emory U., Atlanta, 1984-85. Asst. dir. (to Werner Herzog): (documentary film) Little Dieter Needs to Fly, 1997 (Emmy nomination 1999, Disting. Achievement award Internat. Documentary Assn. 1998, Spl. Jury prize Amsterdam Internat. Documentary Film Festival 1997), Wings of Hope, 1999, My Best Fiend, 1999, The Lord and the Laden, 2000; asst. dir. (to Werner Herzog), co-writer, actor (feature film) Invincible, 2002; gen. editor: (with William Arrawsmith) The Greek Tragedy in New Translations, 1985-96, editor-in-chief: Arion, A Jour. of Humanities and the Classics, 1990— (winner CELJ Phoenix award for Significant Editl. Achievement 1992); writer: (books) Sophocles' Aias, 1999 (nominated for PEN/Book of Month Club Translation prize 1999), Euripides' Bacchae, 2001. Office: 621 Commonwealth Ave Boston MA 02215 E-mail: redlog@bu.edu.

GOLDES, JORDAN, legislative staff member, press secretary; b. Manhattan, N.Y. Student, N.Y. Inst. Tech., 1985-86; BA in Comm., SUNY, Oswego, 1989. Freelance tv prodr. Nat. Video Ctr., N.Y.C., 1988-89; prodr., asst. prodr. 1010 WINS Radio, N.Y.C., 1989-93, on air reporter, 1992-94; press sec., media advisor U.S. Congressman Gary Ackerman, Queens, N.Y., 1994—. Freelance on air reporter Radio Pacific, 1993—, Can. Broadcasting Corp., 1993—. Avocations: bike riding, roller blading, internet surfing, amateur video/photography, music. Home: 28 Vista Hill Rd Great Neck NY 11021-1528 Office: 21814 Northern Blvd Bayside NY 11361-3580

GOLDEY, JAMES MEARNS, retired physicist; b. Wilmington, Del., July 3, 1926; s. Robert Perkins and Ellen (Mearns) G.; m. Jeanne Calvert Potts, June 29, 1951; children: James P., Kristina. BS with honors, U. Del., 1950; PhD in Physics, M.I.T., 1955. Mem. tech. staff Bell Labs. (now Lucent Techs.), Murray Hill, N.J., 1954-56, supr., 1956-59, head integrated cir. and silicon transistor dept., 1959-60; dir. integrated cir. customer svc. lab. Bell Labs., Allentown, Pa., 1981-84, dir. linear and high voltage integrated cir. lab Reading, Pa., 1984-89; devel. v.p. high performance integrated cir. devel. AT&T Microelectronics, Reading, 1988-89, ret., 1989. Contbr. articles in field to profl. jours.; patentee in field. Served with U.S. Army, 1944-46. Fellow IEEE. Republican. Presbyterian. Home: 3930 Azalea Rd Allentown PA 18103-9743 E-mail: mosgolfi@aol.com.

GOLDFARB, ALISAN BETH, surgeon, educator; b. N.Y.C., Apr. 3, 1949; MD, Mt. Sinai U., 1975. Cert. in surgery, recert. Intern Mt. Sinai Hosp., N.Y.C., 1975-76, resident in surgery, 1976-80, asst. attending, 1980—; asst. clin. prof. Mt. Sinai Sch. Medicine, 1980—. Fellow ACS. Office: 1185 Park Ave New York NY 10128-1308

GOLDFARB, ARTHUR A. allergist and immunologist, educator; b. N.Y.C., May 29, 1917; s. Charles Goldfarb and Tillie Konig; m. June Florence Wax, June 3, 1945; children: Barbara Joan Offringa, Susan Lynn Grossman. BS in Biology, NYU, 1938, MD, 1942. Diplomate Am. Bd. Allergy and Immunology, Am. Bd. Pediats., subcert. pediat. allergy. Pvt. practice, Bronx, NY, 1946—51, 1953—57; asst. clin. in allergy Mt. Sinai Hosp., N.Y.C., 1946-57; asst. clin. prof. Albert Einstein Coll. Medicine, Bronx, 1957-78; pvt. practice Teaneck, NJ, 1957—88; attending chief of svc. dept. allergy and immunology Holy Name Hosp., Teaneck, 1959-88; clin. asst. prof. Albert Einstein Coll. Medicine, Bronx, 1988-99. Attending, chief of svc. allergy and immunology Engelwood (N.J.) Hosp., 1966-74. Contbr. med. articles to profl. jours. Lt. comdr. USPHS, 1951-52. Fellow Am. Acad. Allergy and Immunology, Coll. Allergy and Immunology; mem. Bergen County Med. Soc. (pres. 1969-70, trustee 1968-79), N.J. Allergy Soc. (pres. 1977-79, bd. dirs.), Phi Beta Kappa. Avocations: tennis, running. Home: 6323 Tall Cypress Cir Greenacres FL 33463

GOLDFARB, BERNARD SANFORD, lawyer; b. Cleve., Apr. 15, 1917; s. Harry and Esther (Lenson) Goldfarb; m. Barbara Brofman Goldfarb, Jan. 4, 1966; children: Merdeith Stacy, Lauren Beth. AB, Case Western Res. U., 1938, JD, 1940. Bar: Ohio 1940. Since practiced in, Cleve.; sr. ptnr. firm Goldfarb & Reznick, 1967-95; pvt. practice Cleve., 1997—. Spl. counsel to atty. gen. Ohio, 1950, 1971—74; mem. Ohio Commn. Uniform Traffic Rules, 1973—80. Contbr. legal jours. Served with USAAF, 1942-45. Mem.: ABA, Cuyahoga County Bar Assn., Greater Cleve. Bar Assn., Ohio Bar Assn. Home: 39 Pepper Creek Dr Pepper Pike OH 44124-5279 Office: 55 Public Sq Ste 1500 Cleveland OH 44113-1998

GOLDFARB, DAVID, investment banking executive; Ptnr. Ernst & Young; contr., CFO Lehman Bros. Inc.; CFO Lehman Bros. Holdings Inc., 2000—. Mem. Lehman Bros. Operating com. Office: Lehman Bros Holdings Inc 745 7th Ave 31st Fl New York NY 10019-6801

GOLDFARB, DONALD, industrial engineering educator; b. N.Y.C., Aug. 14, 1941; s. Leon and Hannah (Marcus) G.; m. Ranny Lichtman, June 29, 1968; children: Benjamin, Cora. B.Chem. Engring., Cornell U., 1963; MA, Princeton U., 1965, PhD, 1966. Asst. research scientist Courant Inst. Math. Sci., N.Y.C., 1966-68; mem. faculty CCNY, 1968-83, prof. computer sci., 1977-83; prof. indsl. engring. and ops. research Columbia U., N.Y.C., 1982—, chmn. dept. indsl. engring. and ops. research, 1984, 1995—2002, acting dean Sch. Engring. and Applied Sci., 1994-95, Alexander and Hermine Avanessians prof. indsl. engring. and ops. rsch., 2002—. Mem. com. recommendations U.S. Army Basic Sci. Rsch. of NRC; rsch. faculty mem. T.J. Watson Rsch. Lab., IBM, Yorktown Heights, N.Y., summers 1972, 76, 91; rsch. assoc. Atomic Energy Rsch. Establishment, Harwell, Eng., 1974-75; vis. prof. Cornell U., Ithaca, N.Y., 1979-80; mem. adv. coun. dept. civil engring. and ops. rsch. Princeton (N.J.) U.; cons. in field. Editor SIAM Jour. Numerical Analysis, 1982-84, SIAM Jour. on Optimization, 1989-95; editor-in-chief Math. Programming, Series A, 1994-99; assoc. editor Math. of Computation, 1969-90, mem. editl. com., 1982-85; assoc. editor Ops. Rsch., 1983-95, Math. Programming, 1983-95, 99—. NSF fellow, 1963-66; grantee NSF, 1973-75, 80—, ARO, 1977-80, 82-85, ONR, 1987-90, DOE, 1992—. Mem. Inst. for Ops. Rsch. and Mgmt. Scis. (prize for rsch. excellence in the interface between ops. rsch. and computer sci. 1995), Am. Math. Soc. (mem. coun. 1985-87), Soc. Indsl. and Applied Math., Math. Programming Soc. (mem. coun. 1982-85, Hon. Mention prize SIAG/OPT 1996). Home: 6 Peter Cooper Rd Apt 8C New York NY 10010-6709 Office: Columbia U Dept Indsl Engring Ops Rsch 316 SW Mudd Bldg New York NY 10027 E-mail: goldfarb@columbia.edu.

GOLDFARB, ERIC DANIEL, information technology executive, computer industry analyst; b. Kalamazoo, Mich., Apr. 29, 1964; s. Russell Marshall and Clare Sara (Rosett) Goldfarb; m. Gwen Julia Oberman, Aug. 20, 1989; children:

Adam, David. Bachelors, U. Mich., 1986. Project leader Domino's Pizza, Inc., Ann Arbor, Mich., 1986—90; mgr. info. systems Interpublic Group (Lintas), Warren, Mich., 1990-91; mgr. bus. sys. The Ltd. Inc. (Express), Columbus, Ohio, 1991-94; v.p., CIO Elder-Beerman Stores Corp., Dayton, Ohio, 1994—96; v.p., CIO/CTO Pearson plc (Viacom-Macmillan), Indpls., 1996—2001; CIO (worldwide) Global Knowledge Inc., Cary, NC, 2001—02; exec. v.p., CEO PRG-Schultz Internat., Inc., Atlanta, 2002—. Contbr. articles to profl. jours. Named Premier 100 IT Leader, IDG ComputerWorld, 2003; recipient nat. Arthur D. Little "Best of the Best" award. Republican. Avocations: sailing, golfing. Office: 600 Galleria Pkwy Atlanta GA 30339

GOLDFARB, HELENE DIANE, school counselor, retired; b. N.Y.C., Sept. 24, 1929; d. Joseph and Fay E. (Hirschhorn) G. BA, Hunter Coll., 1951; MA, NYU, 1953. Sci. and social studies tchr. Hunter Coll. H.S., N.Y.C., 1951-53; sci. tchr. Isaac E. Young Jr. H.S., New Rochelle, N.Y., 1953-56; asst. prodr. Tic Tac Dough-NBC, N.Y.C., 1956-59; sci. tchr. Albert Leonard Jr. H.S., New Rochelle, 1960-68; guidance counselor, key counselor Albert Leonard Jr. H.S. and Mid. Sch., New Rochelle, 1968-95; ret., 1995. Adminstr. O'Neill Critics Inst., Eugene O'Neill Theater Ctr., Waterford, Conn., summers 1981-86, 94-; sec. bd. dirs. Westchester Arts and Sci. Program, Scarsdale, N.Y., 1970-97; bd. dirs. New Rochelle H.S. Scholarship Fund, 1975-95. Pres. Alumni Assn. Hunter Coll., N.Y.C., 1979—81, 1996—99, treas., pres. Queens chpt., 1953—, 1st v.p. Scholarship and Welfare Fund, 1999—; bd. dirs. Hunter Coll. Found., 1996—99, chair subcom. on planned giving; mem. fin. com., bd. dirs. Lenox Hill Neighborhood Ho., N.Y.C., 1979—; treas. The Caring Neighbor, 2003—; chair bd. The Feminist Press at CUNY, 1987—2002, nat. chair, 1999—, Thomas Hunter Soc.; bd. dirs. Hunter Coll. Hillel Found., 2001—; chmn. subcom. planned giving HC Found. Recipient Alumni Recognition award Alumni Assn. Hunter Coll., 1984, Pres. medal Hunter Coll., 1999, Femmy award Feminist Press at CUNY, 1995; named to Hall of Fame, Hunter Coll. Alumni Assn., 1978. E-mail: hdgoldfarb@aol.com.

GOLDFARB, IRENE DALE, retired financial planner; b. Newark, N.J., Jan. 13, 1929; d. Philip and Lucie (Mintz) Dale; m. Samuel Goldfarb, Jan. 28, 1951; children: Ruth Goldfarb Koizim, David Alan, Sally Fay, Judith Valerie. BS in Chemistry, Rutgers U., 1950; MBA, U. Pa., 1979. CFP. Asst. to assoc. provost Princeton (N.J.) U., 1968-70, asst. to provost, 1970-72, tech. staff, 1972-74, mgr. pers. svcs., 1974-75, asst. dir. pers. svcs., 1975-84; fin. planner, mgr. A.L. Herst Assocs., Inc., Princeton, 1984-86; pvt. practice Princeton, 1986-90; v.p. A.L. Herst Assocs., Inc., Princeton, 1990-92; fin. planner Glenmede Trust Co. N.J., Princeton, 1992—2001; ret., 2002. Cons. in field. Mem. Fin. Planning Assn. (founding officer Princeton-Western N.J. chpt. 1986-98, pres. 1988-89, chmn. 1989-90), Assoc. Alumnae Douglass Coll. (chmn. ann. fund 1982-84, v.p. adminstrn. 1988-94), Phi Beta Kappa. Avocations: music, gardening, travel. Home and Office: 69 Balsam Ln Princeton NJ 08540-5326

GOLDFARB, KATHLEEN BLISS, interior designer; b. Bay Village, Ohio, Nov. 25, 1951; d. Burt Charles and Marilyn Jean (Barnhart) Bliss; divorced; children: Julie Diane, Wendy Claire, Zachary David. BS in Interior Design, Miami U., Oxford, Ohio, 1974. Interior designer Higbee Co., Cleve., 1974-77; sales account exec. Skyline, Inc./Chelsea House Fabrics, Columbus, Ohio, 1977-78; interior designer Cuyahoga Cos., Lakewood, Ohio, 1978-79, Wright Designs, Inc., Cleve., 1979-80; mgr. interior design H.W.H. Affiliates, Inc., Cleve., 1980-86; owner, prin. Interspective, Chagrin Falls, Ohio, 1986—. Cons. Smart Home Automation and Kitchen and Bath, 2001—. Head com. Am.'s City Halls Exhibit, Cleve., 1983; bd. dirs. Cleve. Restoration Soc., 1981-86. Mem. Am. Soc. Interior Designers (profl.; sec. 1983-84, bd. dirs. 1985-87, membership chmn. 1987—), Chagrin Valley Jr. Women's Club (Chagrin Falls). Avocations: fitness, running, bicycling, skiing. Office: Interspective Design Unltd 17552 Fairlawn Dr Chagrin Falls OH 44023-6420

GOLDFARB, MARSHA GEIER, economics educator, health services researcher; b. Lancaster, Pa., June 13, 1942; d. Sygmund Louis Geier and Pearl (Brand) Weisman; m. Robert Stanley Goldfarb, Nov. 27, l969; l child, Steven. BA, Brown U., l964; PhD, Northwestern U., l968. Asst. prof. econs. Yale U., New Haven, l968-73; prof. econs. U. Md. Balt. County, 1973—. Economist Agy. for Health Care Policy and Rsch., Rockville, Md., 1974-95; vis. assoc. prof. Harvard U. Sch. Pub. Health, Boston, 1986. Contbr. articles to profl. jours. Mem. Am. Econ. Assn., Am. Pub. Health Assn. Jewish. Home: 13309 Old Forge Rd Silver Spring MD 20904-6328 Office: U Md Baltimore County 5401 Wilkens Ave Baltimore MD 21250-1000

GOLDFARB, MARTIN, sociologist, researcher; b. Toronto, Ont., Can., May 6, 1938; s. David and Sonia (Silverstein) G.; m. Joan Freedman, June 7, 1961; children— Alonna, Baila, Rebecca, Daniel, Avi BA, U. Toronto, 1961, MA, 1965. Tchr. North York Bd. Edn., Toronto, 1965-67; chmn., pres. CEO The Goldfarb Corp., Toronto, 1987—; chmn., CEO Goldfarb Cons., 1967—. Past bd. govs. York U., Toronto; bd. dirs. CLC Downsview Inc., Fleming Packaging Corp., chmn. SMK Speedy Internat., Inc., Altamira Workbrain. Author: The Goldfarb Report, 1981-99, Marching to a Different Drummer, 1988; contbr. articles to profl. jours. Past bd. dirs. Toronto Symphony Orch., Shaw Festival, Niagara-on-the-Lake, Can. Coun. Christians and Jews, Can. Opera Co., Toronto, Coun. for Can. Unity; trustee The Martin Goodman Trust for Canadian Nieman Fellows. Avocations: skiing, tennis. Office: The Goldfarb Corp 4950 Yonge St Toronto ON Canada M2N 6K1 E-mail: m.goldfarb@goldfarbconsultants.com.

GOLDFARB, MARVIN AL, retired civil engineer; b. Memphis, Tenn., Dec. 12, 1928; s. Al Bohne and Melba (Pollock) G.; m. Lorene Shelton, June 13, 1965 (div. 1974); children: David Al, Julie Lin. BSCE, U. Tenn., 1950; MS in Engring. Mgmt., U. Mo., 1971. Registered profl. engr., Ala., Mo. Field engr. Inter-Am. Geodetic Survey, Panama, 1950-53; engr., supr. Rust Engring. Co., Birmingham, Ala., 1956-64; engr., prin. Monsanto Co., St. Louis, 1964-90, ret., 1990. Author: An Owner's Approach to Project Scheduling, 1975. Chmn. troop com. Boy Scouts Am., 1980—; councilman City of Maryland Heights, Mo., 1985-86, mem. Planning and Zoning Commn., chmn., 1986-98. Mem. VFW, Mo. Soc. Profl. Engrs. (pres. 1985-86), Profl. Engrs. Industry (regional vice chmn. 1980-82), Am. Legion (comdr. post 213 1991-93). Jewish. Home: 1474 Glenmeade Dr Maryland Heights MO 63043 E-mail: marvfarb1@aol.com.

GOLDFARB, MURIEL BERNICE, marketing and advertising consultant; b. Bklyn., Mar. 29, 1920; d. Barnett Goldfarb and May (Steinberg) Goldfarb Oshman; BA, U. Miami, Coral Gables, Fla., 1942; postgrad. CCNY, 1950. Pub. info. asst. UNESCO, Paris, 1946-47; advt. mgr. Majestic Specialties Co., N.Y.C., 1947-50; retail promotion mgr. Glamour Mag., 1955-61; advt. dir. Country Tweeds Co., N.Y.C., 1961-65; advt. dir. S. Augstein & Co., N.Y.C., 1966-72, Feature Ring Co., Inc., Gotham Ring Co., Inc., Fidco Inc., N.Y.C., 1972-77; dir. advt. and promotion Wasko Gold Products Corp., N.Y.C., 1977-81; advt. and mktg. cons. specializing in promotions and sale of vintage jewelry and Bric á Brac. Lt. WAVES, 1943-46. Mem.Women's Jewelry Assn. (corr. sec. 1983-85). Jewish.

GOLDFARB, ROBERT PAUL, neurological surgeon; b. St. Paul, July 17, 1936; s. Jack and Frances S. (Singer) G.; m. Lesley G. Zatz, Aug. 11, 1963; children: Jill, Pam. BA with distinction, U. Ariz., 1958; MD, Tulane U., 1962. Diplomate Am. Bd. Neurol. Surgery. Intern Michael Reese Hosp., Chgo., 1962-63; resident gen. surgery Presbyn. St. Luke's Hosp., Chgo., 1963-64; resident neurol. surgery U. Ill. Rsch. Hosp., Chgo., 1963-67; pres. med. staff Crippled Children's Svc. So. Ariz., Tucson, 1973-75; chief staff Tucson Med. Ctr., 1978-80; neurol. surgeon Western Neurosurgery, Ltd., Tucson, 1980—. Bd. dir. S.W. Physician Network; neurosurg. cons. U. Ariz. athletic teams, Tucson, 1980—; trustee El Dorado Hosp., 1999—; mem. Ariz. Bd. Med. Examiners, 2002, 2003. Maj. USAFR, 1962-70. Baird scholar U. Ariz., 1958. Fellow ACS; mem. Am. Assn. Neurol. Surgeons, Congress Neurol. Surgeons, Am. Coll. Physician Exec., Rocky Mountain Neurosurg. Soc. (v.p. 1979). Office: Western Neurosurgery Ltd 4753 E Camp Lowell Dr Tucson AZ 85712

GOLDFARB, RONALD LAWRENCE, lawyer, writer; b. Jersey City, N.J., Oct. 16, 1933; s. Robert S. and Aida J. (Weintraub) G.; m. Joanne Jacob, June 9, 1957; children: Jody, Nicholas, Maximilian Goldfarb. AB, Syracuse U., 1954, LLB, 1956; LLM, Yale, 1960, JSD, 1962. Bar: N.Y. 1956, Calif. 1959, D.C. 1962, U.S. Supreme Ct. 1965. Spl. asst. to U.S. atty. gen. (organized crime sect.), 1961-64; ptnr. Goldfarb and Assocs. and predecessor law firms, 1966—. Dir. Brookings Instn. program on cts. and adminstrn. Justice, 1966-67; mem. staff counsel com. on law and social action Am. Jewish Congress, 1960-61; cons. Pres.'s Poverty Program, 1964, Riots Commn., 1967-68 Author: The Contempt Power, 1963, Ransom: A Critique of the American Bail System, 1965, (with Alfred Friendly) Crime and Publicity, 1967, (with Linda Singer) After Conviction--A Review of the American Correction System, 1973, Jails: The Ultimate Ghetto, 1975, Migrant Farm Workers: A Caste of Despair, 1981, (with James Raymond) Clear Understandings: A Guide to Legal Writing, 1983, (with Gail Ross) The Writer's Lawyer: Essential Legal Advice for Writers and Editors in All Media, 1989, Perfect Villains, Imperfect Heroes: Robert F. Kennedy's War Against Organized Crime, 1995, TV or Not TV: Television, Justice and Courts, 1998. Served to capt. JAG Corps USAF, 1957-60. Capt. JAG Corp. USAF, 1957—60. Arthur Garfield Hays fellow N.Y.U., 1960-61; Woodrow Wilson fellow. Mem. ACLU, D.C. Bar Assn., N.Y. Bar Assn., Calif. Bar Assn., Cosmos Club, Sigma Alpha Mu., Phi Delta Phi. Office: 1501 M St NW Washington DC 20005-1700

GOLDFARB, RUTH, poet, educator; b. Bklyn., Aug. 13, 1936; d. Nathan Alter and Florence Goldfarb. BA in Psychology, L.I. Univ., 1980; MA in Edn., NYU, 1984. Tchr. kindergarten N.Y.C. Bd. Edn., 1963-64, early childhood tchr., 1993-94, N.Y.C., Bklyn., 1970-84; tchr. common br. Bklyn. Bd. Edn., 1986-93; clk. Primary Health Care Ctr. North Broward Med. Ctr., Pompano Beach, Fla., 1998—. Author (poetry) Whispers and Chants, 1997; CD recs. include Christmas Memories, 1999, The Miracle of Christmas, 2000, Songs of Praise, 2000. Mem.: AARP, Gold Coast Poetry Group, Acad. Am. Poets, Internat. Soc. Poets. Avocations: poetry, music, sculpture, writing stories.

GOLDFARB, WARREN (DAVID GOLDFARB), philosophy educator; b. N.Y.C., Aug. 25, 1949; s. Norman J. and Ella (Kaback) G. AB, Harvard U., 1969, A.M., 1971, PhD, 1975. Asst. prof. philosophy Harvard U., Cambridge, Mass., 1975-80, assoc. prof., 1980-82, prof., 1982—, Pearson prof. math. logic, 1995—, chmn. dept. philosphy, 1984—91, 1993—94, 1999—2000. Vis. prof. U. Calif.-Berkeley, 1984 Author: Deductive Logic, 2003, (with Burton Dreben) The Decision Problem, 1979; editor: Jacques Herbrand, Logical Writings, 1971; co-editor: K. Godel, Collected Works, vol. III, 1995, vols. IV-V, 2003. Mem. Am. Philos. Assn., Assn. Symbolic Logic (exec. com. 1982-84) Office: Harvard U Dept Philosophy Cambridge MA 02138 E-mail: goldfarb@fas.harvard.edu.

GOLDFIELD, EDWIN DAVID, statistician; b. N.Y.C., Oct. 26, 1918; s. Maurice and Sarah (Spears) G. BS, CUNY, 1939; MA, Columbia U., 1940; postgrad., Am. U., 1940-46. Rsch. assoc. dept. investigation, N.Y.C., 1938-39; statis. adviser Ct. Spl. Sessions, N.Y.C., 1939; with Bur. Census, Washington, 1940-75, asst. dir., 1967-71, chief internat. programs, 1971-75; with NAS, Washington, 1975—, study dir., 1975-78, exec. dir. com. on nat. statis., 1978-87, sr. assoc., 1987—. Cons. in field, 1951— ; staff dir. subcom. census and statistics Ho. of Reps., 1959-60, 67. Contbr. articles. Editor: Papers on Labor Force Statistics in the United States, 1952. Recipient Meritorious Svc. award Dept. Commerce, 1954. Fellow Am. Statis. Assn.; mem. Washington Statis. Soc. (past pres.), Am. Econ. Assn., Population Assn. Am., Inter-Am. Statis. Inst., Internat. Assn. Survey Statisticians, Internat. Statis. Inst., Phi Beta Kappa. Home: 4311 23rd Pkwy Apt 1102 Temple Hills MD 20748-4462 Office: NAS 2101 Constitution Ave NW Washington DC 20418-0007

GOLDFIELD, EMILY DAWSON, finance company executive, artist; b. Bklyn., May 31, 1947; d. Martin and Renee (Solow) Dawson; m. Stephen Gary Goldfield, June 17, 1973; children: Stacy Rose, Daniel James. BS, U. Mich., 1969; MEd, Pa. State U., 1971; PhD, U. So. Calif., 1977. Chmn. bd. Union Home Loan, Inc. Author: The Value of Creative Dance, 1971; Development of Creative Dance, 1977. U. Mich. scholar, 1969; Pa. State U. fellow, 1970, U. So. Calif. fellow, 1972. Mem.: Pastel Soc. San Diego, Allied Artists of the Santa Monica Mountains, Pastel Soc. of the West Coast, Calif. Art Club, Calif. Mortgage Assn. Office: 23586 Calabasas Rd Ste 201 Calabasas CA 91302-1322

GOLDFINE, ALAN, obstetrician, gynecologist; b. Phila., Feb. 10, 1933; MD, Temple U., 1959. Diplomate Am. Bd. Ob-Gyn. Intern Albert Einstein Med. Ctr., Phila., 1959-60; resident Sinai Hosp., Balt., 1960-63; mem. staff Brandywine Hosp., Coatesville, Pa., 1967—, South Chester County Med. Ctr., West Grove, Pa., 1967—; pvt. practice Coatesville, Pa.; ret., 2000. Fellow ACOG; mem. AMA, Chester County Med. Soc., Obstet. Soc. Pa., Pa. Med. Soc. E-mail: agoldfine@msn.com.

GOLDFISCHER, JEROME D. cardiologist; b. N.Y.C., Mar. 14, 1930; s. Sidney and Bella (Bernstein) G.; m. Joan Lila Goldfarb, June 28, 1953 (dec. Oct. 1996); children: Mindy Ann, Robin Lisa, Cathi Sue, Marilyn Lori. BS in Biology, Rutgers U., 1951; MD, NYU, 1955. Diplomate Am. Bd. Internal Medicine, Am. Bd. Cardiology. Researcher Polio Found. Irvington (N.J.) House, 1953; intern Montefiore Hosp., N.Y.C., 1955-56, jr. asst. resident in medicine, 1956-57, asst. resident in medicine, 1959-60, resident in cardiology, 1960-61, USPHS postdoctoral rsch. fellow in cardiology, 1961-63, rsch. asst. cardiology, attending medicine physician, 1963—; pvt. practice cardiology Ft. Lee, N.J. Mem. attending staff Englewood (N.J.) Hosp., 1963—; mem. electrocardiography dept. Montefiore Hosp., 1961—; chmn. cardiac care com. Englewood Hosp., 1976-91, dir. coronary care unit, 1963-81, acting chief cardiology, 1966-71, chief cardiology, 1971-81, chief medicine, 1981-92, dir. electrocardiography dept., 1966-2003; instr. medicine Albert Einstein Coll. Medicine, 1967-77, asst. clin. prof., 1978—. Contbr. articles to profl. jours. Mem. Bergen County Cmty. Coun., 1973-81. Capt. USAF, 1957-59. Fellow ACP, Am. Coll. Cardiology, Am. Heart Assn. (coun. clin. cardiology 1976, bd. dirs. Bergen County chpt. 1966-81, exec. com. 1969-81, chmn. cardiopulmonary resuscitation com. 1966-79, chmn. com. emergency coronary care 1973-80, other offices); mem. Assn. Advancement of Med. Instrumentation, Bergen County Med. Soc., Bergen County Heart Assn. Office: 1555 Center Ave Fort Lee NJ 07024-4612

GOLDFRANK, LEWIS ROBERT, physician; b. N.Y.C., Sept. 8, 1941; s. Herbert John and Helen (Colodny) G.; m. Susan M. Harrington, Aug. 29, 1964; children: Michelle, Andrew, Jennifer, Rebecca. BA, Clark U., 1963; MD, U. Brussels, Belgium, 1970. Diplomate Am. Bd. Med. Toxicology (dir., chmn. 1985-90). Resident Montefiore Hosp., Bronx, N.Y., 1971-73; dir. emergency medicine Morrisania Hosp., Bronx, 1973-76, North Cen. Bronx Hosp., 1976-79, Montefiore Hosp., 1976-79, Bellevue Hosp., N.Y.C., 1979—, NYU Med. Ctr., N.Y.C., 1979—; dir. N.Y.C. Poison Ctr., 1979—. Author, editor: Goldfrank's Toxicologic Emergencies, 1978, 7th edit., 2002, Emergency Doctor, 1987, Diagnostic Testing in the Emergency Department, 1984, 2d edit., 1995; editor: Preparing for Terrorism, 2002. Recipient hon. mention Am. Med. Writers Assn., 1988, Disting. Tchr. award NYU, 2003; faculty scholar NYU, 1999. Fellow: ACP, Am. Acad. Clin. Toxicology, Am. Coll. Emergency Physician; mem.: NAS (Inst. Medicine), Soc. for Acad. Emergency Medicine (Hal Jayne Acad. Excellence award 1990, Leadership award 1999). Avocation: gardening. Home: 55 Grace Ln Ossining NY 10562-2129 Office: Bellevue Hosp Ctr 1st Ave and 27th St New York NY 10016 Fax: 212-562-3001. E-mail: goldfl03@popmail.med.nyu.edu.

GOLDGAR, BERTRAND ALVIN, literary historian, educator; b. Macon, Ga., Nov. 17, 1927; s. Benjamin Meyer and Annie (Shapiro) G.; m. Corinne Cohn Hartman, Apr. 6, 1950; children: Arnold Benjamin, Anne Hartman. BA, Vanderbilt U., 1948, MA, 1949, Princeton U., 1957, PhD, 1958. Instr. in English Clemson (S.C.) U., 1948-50, asst. prof., 1951-52; instr. English Lawrence U., Appleton, Wis., 1957-61, asst. prof., 1961-65, assoc. prof., 1965-71, prof. English, 1971—, John N. Bergstrom prof. humanities, 1980—. Mem. fellowship panel NEH, 1979 Author: The Curse of Party: Swift's Relations with Addison and Steele, 1961, Walpole and the Wits: The Relation of Politics to Literature, 1722-1742, 1976; editor: The Literary Criticism of Alexander Pope, 1965, Henry Fielding's The Covent-Garden Jour., 1988, Henry Fielding's Miscellanies, Vol. 2, 1993, Jonathan Wild, 1997, The Grub Street Jour. 1730-1733, 2002; adv. editor: 18th Century Studies, 1977-87. With AUS, 1952-54. Fellow, Am. Coun. Learned Socs, 1973-74, NEH, 1980-81. Mem. Am. Soc. 18th Century Studies, Johnson Soc. Cen. Region. Home: 914 E Eldorado St Appleton WI 54911-5536 Office: Lawrence U Dept English Appleton WI 54912 E-mail: bertrand.a.goldgar@lawrence.edu.

GOLDHABER, GERALD MARTIN, communication educator, author, consultant; b. Brookline, Mass., Jan. 23, 1944; s. Robert and Ruth Irene Goldhaber; m. Marylynn Blaustein, Aug. 17, 1969; children: Michelle, Marc. BA, U. Mass., 1965; MA, U. Md., 1967; PhD, Purdue U., 1970. Asst. prof. communication U. N.Mex., 1970-74; assoc. prof., assoc. chmn. dept. communication SUNY, Buffalo, 1974-78, chmn. dept., 1979-88; owner Goldhaber Research Assocs., Buffalo, 1975—; polit. analyst N.Y. Post, CKO-Radio Can., WEBR Radio, Buffalo, WGRZ-TV, Buffalo, WBEN Radio, Buffalo, WIVB-TB, Buffalo. Consult polit cands, pollster. Author: (book) Organizational Communication, 1974, 2002; author: (with B Peterson and R W Pace) (book) Communication Probes, 1974, 1982; author: (with L Rosenfeld and V Smith) Experiments in Human Communication, 1975; author: (with M B Goldhaber) Transactional Analysis, 1976; author: (with E Zannes) Stand Up and Speak Out, 1978, 1982; author: (with H Dennis G Richetto and O Wilo) Information Strategies: New Pathways to Corporate Power, 1979, 1983; author: (with D Rogers) Auditing Organizational Communication Systems: The ICA Communication Audit, 1979; author: (with G Barnett) The Handbook of Organizational Communication, 1988; contbr. chapters to books; editor (rev ed): (book) Organizational Communication Abstracts; contbr. articles to profl jours. Bd dirs Rep polit pollster, Erie County, NY, Temple Beth El, Buffalo, 1980—, pres, 1992—94; chmn bd dirs Shea's Performing Arts Ctr, 1997—2000. Recipient Distinguishing Alumnus Award, Univ Mass, 1983, numerous teaching awards and grants. Fellow: Inst Int Sociological Research (life); mem.: Am Asn Pub Opinion Research, Human Factors Soc, Nat Communications Asn, Mkt Research Asn, Human Factors and Ergonomics Soc, Int Communication Asn (vpres, dir 1974—76). Home: 48 Jamstead Ct Buffalo NY 14221-4642 Office: SUNY-Buffalo Dept Communication Buffalo NY 14260-0001 E-mail: comgerry@ascu.buffalo.edu. *I have always believed that the search for excellence should govern the lives of all people. There is virtually nothing that a human being cannot achieve if he or she lives in accordance with this standard and possesses a strong sense of morality and a good sense of humor. I have lived my entire life according to these precepts and owe much to those who have stood with me for excellence.*

GOLDHABER, GERSON, physicist, educator; b. Chemnitz, Germany, Feb. 20, 1924; came to U.S., 1948, naturalized, 1953; s. Charles and Ethel (Frisch) G.; m. Judith Margoshes, May 30, 1969; children: Amos Nathaniel, Michaela Shally, Shaya Alexandra M.Sc., Hebrew U., Jerusalem, 1947; PhD, U. Wis., 1950; PhD honoris causus, U. Stockholm, 1986. Instr. Columbia U., N.Y.C., 1950-53; acting asst. prof. physics U. Calif., Berkeley, 1953-54, asst. prof., 1954-58, assoc. prof., 1958-63, prof. physics, 1963-92, prof. physics emeritus, 1992—; Miller research prof. Miller Inst. Basic Sci. U. Calif.-Berkeley, 1958-59, 75-76, 84-85, prof. Grad. Sch., 1994—; Morris Loeb lectr. in physics Harvard U., 1976-77. Named Calif. Scientist of Yr., 1977, Sci. Assoc., CERN, 1986; Ford Found. fellow CERN, 1960-61; Guggenheim fellow CERN, 1972-73 Fellow Am. Phys. Soc. (Panofsky prize 1991), Sigma Xi; mem. Am. Astron. Soc., Royal Swedish Acad. Sci. (fgn.), Nat. Acad. Sci. Office: Lawrence Berkeley Nat Lab Physics Ms 50 R5008 Berkeley CA 94720-0001 Fax: 510 486-6738. E-mail: gerson@lbl.gov.

GOLDHABER, JACOB KOPEL, retired mathematician, educator; b. Bklyn., Apr. 12, 1924; s. Joseph and Shirley (Heller) G.; m. Ruth Last, Dec. 25, 1951; children: Doreet, David, Aviva. BA, Bklyn. Coll., 1944; MA, Harvard, 1945; PhD, U. Wis., 1950. Instr. math. U. Conn., Storrs, 1950-53; instr. Cornell U., Ithaca, N.Y., 1953-54; asst. prof. Washington U., St. Louis, 1954-59, assoc. prof., 1959-61, U. Md., College Park, 1961-62, prof., 1962-93, chmn. math. dept., 1968-77, acting dean grad. studies and rsch., 1984-86, 87-92, acting v.p. acad. affairs, provost, 1992-93, prof. emeritus, 1993—. Exec. sec. Office Math. Scis., NRC, 1976-82; vis. rsch. assoc., NSF sci. faculty fellow U. London, 1966-67. Author: (with Gertrude Ehrlich) Algebra, 1970; contbr. papers to profl. jours. Mem. AAAS, Am. Math. Soc., Math. Assn. Am., Sigma Xi. Home: 2801 New Mexico Ave NW Washington DC 20007-3921 E-mail: jkg@jgoldhaber.com.

GOLDHABER, MAURICE, physicist, researcher; b. Lemberg, Austria, Apr. 18, 1911; arrived in U.S., 1938, naturalized, 1944; s. Charles and Ethel (Frisch) Goldhaber; m. Gertrude Scharff, May 24, 1939; children: Alfred S., Michael H. PhD, Cambridge U., Eng., 1936, Tel Aviv U., 1974; D (hon.), U. Louvain-La-Neuve, Belgium, 1982; DSc (hon.), SUNY, Stony Brook, 1983, U. Notre Dame, 1992. Bye fellow Magdalene Coll., Cambridge, 1936—38; asst. prof. physics U. Ill., 1938—43, assoc. prof., 1943—45, prof., 1945—50; sr. sci. Brookhaven Nat. Lab., 1950—60, chmn. dept. physics, 1960—61, dir., 1961—73, distinguished scientist emeritus, 1973—. Cons. labs. AFC; Morris Loeb lectr. Harvard U., 1955, 93, Rabi Scholar lectr., 55; adj. prof. physics SUNY, Stony Brook, 1965—; Royal Soc. Rutherford Meml. lectr., Canada, 1987; nuc. sci. com. NRC. Assoc. editor Phys. Rev., 1951—53; contbr. articles on nuc. physics to sci. jours. Bd. govs. Weizmann Inst. Sci., Rehovoth, Israel, Tel Aviv U.; trustee Univs. Rsch. Assn. Co-recipient Rossi prize, Am. Astron. Soc., hign energy physics divsn., 1989; recipient citation for meritorious contbns., U.S. AEC, 1973, J. Robert Oppenheimer Meml. prize, 1982, Nat. medal of Sci., 1983, Am. Acad. Achievement award, 1985, Wolf Found. prize in physics, Jerusalem, 1991, Enrico Fermi award in physics, 1998. Fellow: AAAS, Am. Acad. Arts and Scis., Am. Phys. Soc. (pres. 1982); mem.: NAS, Am. Philos. Soc. (Tom W. Bonner prize in nuc. physics 1971). Office: Brookhaven Nat Lab Bldg 510 Upton NY 11973*

GOLDHABER, PAUL, dental educator; b. N.Y.C., Mar. 16, 1924; m. Ethel Gurland, 1949; children: Samuel Zachary, Joshua Irving. DDS, NYU, 1948; BS, CCNY, 1954; MA (hon.), Harvard U., 1962. Diplomate Am. Bd. Periodontics. Asst. ophthalmology rsch. Harvard Med. Sch., Boston, 1948—50; asst. dentist Sch. Dental and Oral Surgery Columbia U., N.Y.C., 1950; rsch. fellow dental medicine Harvard Sch. Dental Medicine, Boston, 1954—55, rsch. assoc. oral pathology, 1955—56, assoc., 1956—59, from asst. prof. to assoc. prof., 1959—62, from assoc. prof. to prof., 1962—66, dir. postdoctoral studies, 1962—68, dean, 1968—90, prof. periodontics, 1966—, emeritus dean, 1990—. Vis. rsch. fellow Sloan-Kettering Inst. Cancer Rsch., 1954—55, rsch. fellow, 1955—56; sr. rsch. fellow USPHS, 1956—61; chmn. dental study sect. NIH, 1968—71. Mem.: Internat. Assn. for Dental Rsch. (pres. 1985—86), Inst. Medicine of NAS, Am. Assn. Dental Rsch. (pres. 1973—74). Office: Harvard U Sch Dental Medicine 188 Longwood Ave Boston MA 02115-5819 E-mail: pgoldhaber@hms.harvard.edu.

GOLDIN, CLAUDIA DALE, economics educator; b. N.Y.C., May 14, 1946; d. Leon and Lucille (Rosansky) G. BA magna cum laude with distinction, Cornell U., 1967; MA, U. Chgo., 1969, PhD, 1972; MA (hon.), U. Pa., 1985, Harvard U., 1990; DHL (hon.), U. Nebr., Lincoln, 1994. Asst. prof. econs. U. Wis., Madison, 1971-73; asst. prof. Princeton (N.J.) U., 1973-79, vis. fellow indsl. relations sec., 1987-88; vis. lectr. Harvard U., Cambridge, Mass., 1975-76, prof., 1990—; assoc. prof. U. Pa., Phila., 1979-85, prof., 1985-90; vis. fellow The Brookings Instn., 1993-94. Mem. Inst. Advanced Study, Princeton, 1982-83; rsch. assoc., project dir. Nat. Bur. Econ. Rsch., Cambridge, 1979—; vis. fellow Russell Sage Found., 1997-98. Author: Urban Slavery in the American South, 1976, Understanding the Gender Gap, 1990; editor: Strategic Factors in 19th Century American Economic History, 1992, The Regulated Economy, 1994, The Defining Moment: The Great Depression and the American Economy in the 20th Century, 1998, Jour. Econ. History, NBER Series on Long-Term Factors in Econ. Devel.; mem. editl. bd. Am. Econ. Rev., 1985-91, Quar. Jour. Econs., 1992—, Rev. Econs. and Stats., Jour. Interdisciplinary History; contbr. articles to profl. publs. Recipient NSF award, 1975-77, 79-81, 81-82, 84-86, 87-89, 92-93, 96-99, Spencer Found. rsch. award, 1996, 2001—; Guggenheim fellow, 1987-88. Fellow Econometric Soc.; mem. Am. Acad. Arts and Scis., Am. Econ. Assn. (v.p. 1990-91), Econ. History Assn. (pres. 1999-00, trustee 1984—, v.p. 1988-89). Avocations: aerobics, hiking, bird watching. Office: Harvard U Dept Econs Cambridge MA 02138 E-mail: cgoldin@harvard.edu.

GOLDIN, DANIEL S. former federal agency administrator; b. N.Y.C., July 23, 1940; m. Judith Linda Kramer; children: Ariel, Laura. BS in Mech. Engring., CCNY, 1962; PhD (hon.), Case Western Res. U., Cen. State U., CCNY, Fla. Inst. of Tech., Framingham State U., Poly. U. of N.Y., U. Ariz., U. Md., U. Mich. Rsch. scientist Lewis Rsch. Ctr., NASA, Cleve., 1962-67; with TRW, from 1967, mem. tech. staff, 1967; v.p., gen. mgr. Space & Tech. Group, TRW, Redondo, Calif., 1987-92; adminstr. NASA, Washington, 1992—2001; speaker

Leading Authorities, Inc., Washington, 2002; sr. fellow Council on Competitiveness, 2002—. Recipient 1996 Chmn. award Am. Assn. Engring. Societies, 1997, Civilian Kitty Hawk Sands of Time award, Goddard Quality award, Heald award Ill. Inst. of Tech., Nelson P. Jackson Aerospace award Nat. Space Club, Internat. Von Karman Wings award Aerospace Hist. Soc., Meritorious award (2) Nat. Assn. of Small and Disadvantaged Businesses, President's medal N.Y. Inst. of Tech., Nat. award for Space Achievement, Rotary, Space Pioneer award Nat. Space Soc.; named one of 100 Most Influential in Govt. Nat. Jour., One of 40 Most Influential Def. Industry Leaders, Def. Bus. mag. Fellow AIAA (Piper Gen. Aviation award), Am. Astronom. Soc. (John F. Kennedy Astronautics award), Inst. for Advancement of Engring. Achievements during his tenure at TRW include the building of 13 spacecraft, the launch and operation of NASA tracking and Data Relay Satellite-5 and the Compton Gamma Ray Observatory. The group also has worked on other NASA programs including the successfull grinding and testing of the worlds two largest X-ray mirrors fot the Advanced X-ray Astrophysics Facility. Office: Council on Competitiveness 1500 K St. NW Ste. 850 Washington DC 20005

GOLDIN, IAN ANDREW, executive; b. Pretoria, South Africa, Mar. 3, 1955; s. Harry and Alice (Widrich) G.; m. Theresa Ruth Webber, Aug. 23, 1992; children: Olivia, Alexander. BS in Math., U. Cape Town, South Africa, 1976, BA in Econs. (hon.), 1977; MS in Econs., London Sch. Econs., 1979; D, Oxford U., England, 1983. Lectr. econs. Oxford U., England, 1981-83; dir. Landell Mills Com., London, 1984-88; dir. programs OECD, Paris, 1988-92; prin. economist World Bank, Washington, 1992-95; sr. economist EBRD, London, 1995-96; chief exec., mng. dir. DBSA, Johannesburg, 1996-2001; v.p. World Bank, 2001—. Dir. Nat. Housing Fin. Corp., 1996—, Lesotho Highlands/South Africa Water Corp., 1997—, Khula Small and Medium Enterprise Fin. Co., 1996—, Commonwealth Africa Investment Fund, 1996—, Africa Infrastructure Fund. Author: Trade Liberalization: Global Economic Implications, 1996, others; author, editor: Open Economics, 1992, The Economics of Sustainable Development, 1995; co-author: Economic Reform, Trade and Agriculture Development, 1994; contbr. articles to profl. jours. Dir. Cape Town 2004 Olympic Bid Co., 1996—. Recipient French Chevalier award. Fellow Ctr. Econ. Policy Rsch. WEF Global Leader. Avocations: music, saxophone, skiing, scuba, cinema, hiking.

GOLDIN, LEON, artist, educator; b. Chgo., Jan. 16, 1923; s. Joseph P. and Bertha (Metz) G.; m. Meta Solotaroff, July 30, 1949; children: Joshua, Daniel. BFA, Art Inst. Chgo., 1948; MFA, U. Iowa, 1950. From instr. to assoc. prof. Columbia U., N.Y.C., 1964-82, prof., 1982-92, prof. emeritus, 1992—, 1992—. Former tchr. Calif. Coll. Arts and Crafts, Phila. Coll. Art, Queen's Coll., Cooper Union; vis. prof. painting Stanford, summer 1973 One-man shows Oakland Art Mus., 1955, Felix Landau Gallery, L.A., 1956, 57, 59, Galleria L'Attico, Rome, 1958, Kraushaar Galleries, N.Y.C., 1960, 64, 68, 72, 84, 88, 90, 93, 96, 98, 2001, U. Houston, 1981, Binghamton U. Art Mus., 2000, Ctr. for Maine Contemporary Art, 2000; represented in permanent collections Bklyn. Mus., City Mus. St. Louis, Worcester Mus., Addison Gallery Am. Art, Pa. Acad. Fine Arts, L.A. County Mus., Santa Barbara Mus., Oakland Art Mus., Munson Proctor Inst., Va. Mus. Fine Arts, Portland (Maine) Mus., Everson Mus., U. Ark., Okla. Art Ctr., Cleve. Mus. Fine Art. Served with AUS, 1943-46, ETO. Recipient Prix de Rome, Am. Acad. Rome, 1955 58, Jennie Sesnan Gold medal Pa. Acad. Fine Arts, 1966, Benjamin Altman Landscape prize Nat. Acad. Design, 1993, Adolph and Clara Obrig prize NAD; Tiffany grantee, 1951; Fulbright scholar to France, 1952; Guggenheim fellow, 1959, Nat. Endowment for Arts grantee, 1967, 80; Nat. Inst. Arts and Letters grantee, 1968; N.Y. Caps grantee, 1981, Benjamin Altman prize, NAD, 2003. Mem. NAD. Home: 438 W 116th St New York NY 10027-7203

GOLDIN, MARION FREEDMAN, television news producer, reporter; b. N.Y.C., Sept. 5, 1940; d. Milton I. and Alice S. Freedman; m. Norman W. Goldin, Mar. 19, 1967 (dec. Sept. 1992). BA, Barnard Coll.; MA, Harvard U. Sec./researcher Eric Sevareid, 1963-69; researcher/assoc. producer CBS Morning News, 1969-72; producer "60 Minutes" CBS News, 1972-82, 84-88; sr. producer, asst. to exec. producer "20/20" ABC News, 1982-84; sr. producer "Expose" NBC News, 1990-91; pres. Marigold Unltd., 1988-90, 92—. Avocations: tennis, art, music, travel. E-mail: mariongoldin@worldnet.att.net.

GOLDIN, MARTIN BRUCE, financial executive, consultant; b. Teaneck, N.J., May 18, 1938; s. Arthur Daniel and Shirley Edith (Holland) G.; m. Joyce Anne Rossin, Aug. 22, 1960; children: Melissa Beth, Julie Amber, Kevin James, Sabrina Nicole. BBA, U. Miami, 1960; postgrad., Detroit Coll. Law, 1967. Fin. analyst Chrysler Corp. Detroit, London, Eng., 1967-70; CFO Chrysler de Mex., Mexico City, 1971—77, Chrysler Australia Ltd., Adelaide, 1978—80, Internat. Harvester De Mex., Mexico City, 1980—85; comptroller Citicorp Diners Club, Denver, 1985—87, CFO, exec. v.p. Chgo., 1988—96; v.p. fin. Deluxe Corp., Shoreview, Minn., 1997-98. Fin. cons. Rossin-Goldin, Detroit, 1960—, La Torre de Acapulco (Mex.), 1980-88. Office: Rossin-Goldin Co 2634 Red Arrow Dr Las Vegas NV 89135 E-mail: mbgcfo@cox.net.

GOLDING, BRAGE, university president; b. Chgo., Apr. 28, 1920; s. Leon M. and Viola B. (Brage) G.; m. Hinda F. Wolf, Dec. 21, 1941; children: Brage, Susan, Julie. BS, Purdue U., 1941, PhD, 1948; LLD, Wright State U., 1975. Assoc. dir. research Lilly Varnish Co., Indpls.; also research assoc. Purdue U., 1948-57; vis. prof. engring. Purdue U., dir. research Lilly Varnish Co., 1957-59; head Sch. Chem. Engring. Purdue U., 1959-66; v.p. Ohio State U. and; Miami U., 1966-67; pres. Wright State U., Dayton, Ohio, 1967-72, San Diego State U., 1972-77, Kent State U., 1977-82, Met. State Coll., Denver, 1984-85; acting pres. Western State Coll., Gunnison, Colo., 1985, ret. Cons. Dept. Higher Edn., Pa. and N.J. Author: Polymers and Resins, 1959; Contbr. articles to profl. jours. Fellow AAAS; mem. Am. Chem. Soc., Phi Beta Kappa (hon.) Address: 12179 Branicole Ln San Diego CA 92129-5037 E-mail: bgolding@mail.sdsu.edu.

GOLDING, CAROLYN MAY, former government senior executive, consultant; b. Essex County, N.J., July 1, 1941; d. Wesley Irwin and Florence Grace (Smith) G.; m. Gary Anthony Derosa, Oct. 18, 1975 (div. Sept. 1982). BA, Duke U., 1963, postgrad., 1965 66. English tchr. Parkersburg (W.Va.) H.S., 1963; asst. to registrar Duke U., Durham, N.C., 1963-65; mgmt. intern Dept. Labor, Washington, 1966-67, various other positions, 1967-72; dep. assoc. regional adminstr. Employment and Tng. Adminstrn., San Francisco, 1972-77, comptroller Washington, 1977-78, regional adminstr. San Francisco, 1979-82, dir. Unemployment Ins. Svc. Washington, 1982-87, adminstr. employment security, 1987-88, dep. asst. sec. employment and tng., 1988-96. Cons. on mgmt., labor force, long-range planning, workforce edn. issues and exec. coaching, 1996—. Recipient Disting. Career Svc. award Dept. Labor, 1979, Fed. Women's Career award Sec. Labor, 1983, Presdl. Meritorious rank, 1987, 95, Philip Arnow award Dept. Labor, 1988. Mem. Internat. Women's Forum of Washington, Coun. for Excellence in Govt. (prin.). Episcopalian.

GOLDING, MARTIN PHILIP, law and philosophy educator; b. N.Y.C., Mar. 30, 1930; s. Sidney Israel and Mildred (Lewis) G.; m. Naomi Holtzman, Apr. 8, 1951; children— Shulamith, Belinda, Joshua. BA, UCLA, 1949, MA, 1952; PhD, Columbia U., 1959. From asst. to assoc. prof. philosophy Columbia U., 1957-70, adj. prof., 1971-80; prof. philosophy John Jay Coll. Criminal Justice, City U. N.Y., 1970-76; prof. philosophy and law Duke U., Durham, N.C., 1976—. Vis. prof. jurisprudence Faculty Law, Bar-Ilan U., Israel, 1971-72 Author: The Nature of Law, 1966, Philosophy of Law, 1975, Legal Reasoning, 1984, Jewish Law and Legal Theory, 1994, Free Speech on Campus, 2000, also articles. Mem. Am. Soc. Polit. and Legal Philosophy, Internat. Soc. Legal and Social Philosophy, Am. Philos. Assn. Jewish. Office: Duke U Philosophy Dept Durham NC 27708

GOLDING, SUSAN, former mayor; b. Muskogee, Okla., Aug. 18, 1945; d. Brage and Hinda Fay (Wolf) G.; children: Samuel, Vanessa. Cert. Pratique de Langue Francaise, U. Paris, 1965; BA in Govt. and Internat. Rels., Carleton Coll., 1966; MA in Romance Philology, Columbia U., 1974. Assoc. editor Columbia U. Jour. of Internat. Affairs, N.Y.C., 1968-69; teaching fellow Emory U., Atlanta, 1973-74; instr. San Diego Community Coll. Dist., 1978; assoc. pub., gen. mgr. The News Press Group, San Diego, 1978-80; city council mem. City of San Diego, 1981-83; dep. sec. bus., transp., housing State of Calif., Sacramento, 1983-84; county supr. dist. 3 County of San Diego, 1984-92; mayor City of San Diego, 1992—2000; pres. & CEO The Golding Group, Inc., San Diego, 2000—; head Homeland Security Office, Titan Corp., San Diego, 2000—. Chmn. San Diego Drug Strike Force, 1987-88, Calif. Housing Fin. Agy., Calif. Coastal Commn.; bd. dirs. San Diego County Water Authority; trustee So. Calif. Water Com., Inc.; founder Mid City Comml. Revitalization Task Force, Strategic Trade Alliance, 1993, Calif. Big 10 City Mayors, 1993; mem. Gov. Calif. Mil. Base Reuse Task Force, 1994; established San Diego World Trade Ctr., 1993, San Diego City/State/County Regional Permit Assistance Ctr., 1994; mem. adv. bd. U.S. Conf. of Mayors, 1994; chair Gov. Wilson's Commn. on Local Governance for 21st Century. Bd. dirs. Child Abuse Prevention Found., San Diego Conv. and Vis. Bur., Crime Victims Fund, United Cerebral Palsy, San Diego Air Quality Bd., San Diego March of Dimes, Rep. Assocs.; adv. bd. Girl Scouts U.S.; trustee So. Calif. Water Comm.; mem. Rep. State Cen. Com.; co-chair com. Presidency George Bush Media Fund, Calif.; chair San Diego County Regional Criminal Justice Coun., race rels. com. Citizens Adv. Com. on Racial Intergration, San Diego Unified Sch. Dist.; hon. chair Am. Cancer Soc's. Residential Crusade, 1988. Recipient Alice Paul award Nat. Women's Polit. Caucus, 1987, Calif. Women in Govt. Achievement award, 1988, Willie Velasquez Polit. award Mex. Am. Bus. and Profl. Assn., 1988, Catalyst of Chance award Greater San Diego C. of C., 1994, Woman Who Means Bus. award San Diego Bus. Jour., 1994, Internat. Citizen award World Affairs Coun., 1994; named One of San Diego's Ten Outstanding Young Citizens, 1981, One of Ten Outstanding Rep. County Ofcls. in U.S.A., Rep. Nat. Com., 1987, San Diego Woman of Achievement Soroptimists Internat., 1988. Mem. Nat. Assn. of Counties (chair Op. Fair Share, mem. taxation and fin. com.), Nat. Women's Forum. Republican. Jewish. Office: The Golding Group Inc 9276 Scranton Rd Ste 600 San Diego CA 92121 : Titan Corp 3033 Science Park Rd San Diego CA 92121 E mail: commerce@golding.org.

GOLDING, TERRY DAVID, engineering educator, researcher; b. Watford, Eng., Aug. 28, 1963; s. Ian David and Gillian Golding; m. Kathryn Smith, Dec. 12, 2001; m. Lisa Taratooty, Aug. 11, 1989 (div. Feb. 3, 1994); children: Alexander David, Myles David, Tarah-Rose. BS in Physics (hons.), U. of Leicester, Eng., 1985; PhD in Semiconductor Physics, Cambridge U., Eng., 1989. Rsch. scientist U.S. Army Night Vision Labs., Alexandria, Va., 1986—88; asst. prof. physics U. of Houston, 1989—93, assoc. prof. physics, 1993—2000; prof. physics and materials sci. and engring. U. of North Tex., Denton, 2000—. Pres. GEM Rsch. Inc, Houston, 1996—, Sigma Xi North Tex. Chpt., Dallas, 2002. Recipient Sci. and Engring. award, UK Rsch. Coun., 1985, 1986, 1987, Collaborative Award in Sci. and Engring., GE, 1985, 1986, 1987, 1988. Mem.: Sigma Xi (pres. 2002), Materials Rsch. Soc. (assoc.). Achievements include research in Properties of semiconductors, nanostructures, and novel electro-optical materials. Office: Dept of Physics 211 Ave A Denton TX 76203 Office Fax: 940-565-2515. Personal E-mail: golding@unt.edu.

GOLDMAN, ALAN IRA, investment banking executive; b. N.Y.C., July 29, 1937; s. Julius and Florence (Blum) G.; m. Joanne T. Marren, AB, Cornell U., 1958; MBA, NYU, 1962, grad., Stonier Grad. Sch. Banking, 1967. Methods analyst, personnel-researcher Fed. Res. Bank of N.Y., N.Y.C., 1958-62; platform asst. Bankers Trust Co., N.Y.C., 1962-63, asst. mgr., 1963-64, mgr., 1964-65, asst. treas., 1965-66, asst. v.p., 1967-69; assoc. investment banking dept. Lehman Bros., N.Y.C., 1969-70; v.p. fin., chief fin. officer, treas. Interway Corp., N.Y.C., 1970-74; mgmt. cons. Montclair, N.J., 1974-75; v.p. fin. Mgmt. Assistance Inc., N.Y.C., 1975-80, sr. v.p. fin., 1980-85; ind. investment banker, bus. cons., 1985—; pres. Goldmark Capital, 1987-88. Lectr., adv., examiner Stonier Grad. Sch. Banking, 1968-71; lectr. Am. Inst. Banking, 1968-69; chair SGA Interactive Corp.; chair SGA Interactive, Inc. Co-chmn. Montclair chpt. campaign ARC, 1970-73; chmn. Cornell Funds' N.Y. Area Phonathons, 1972-74, UN Week, Montclair, 1973; trustee, treas., co-chair Cocteau Repertory Theatre, 1985-2000; bd. dirs. Planned Parenthood Fedn. Am., 1986-88; bd. dirs., treas. Planned Parenthood Met. N.J.; bd. dirs., chair, treas. Montclair ARC; adv. coun., vice chair Columbia U. Mailman Sch. Pub. Health; advisor Productivity Technologies Corp. Mem. West Point Soc. N.Y., Orange Lawn Tennis Club, Univ. Club (N.Y.C.), Aspatuck Tennis Club, Surf Club of Quogue, Phi Beta Kappa, Phi Kappa Phi, Zeta Beta Tau. E-mail: alangoldman@comcast.net.

GOLDMAN, ALAN STUART, chemistry educator; b. N.Y.C., Aug. 3, 1958; s. Leonard Montague Goldman and Rhoda (Dobowitz) Blau; m. Danuta Szwajkajzer. BA, Columbia U., 1980, PhD, 1985. IBM postdoctoral fellow U. Chgo., 1985-87; asst. prof. chemistry Rutgers U., Piscataway, N.J., 1987—. Recipient Disting. New Faculty Mem. award Camille and Henry Dreyfus Found., 1987; Alfred P. Sloan Found. fellow, 1992. Office: Rutgers U Dept Chemistry Piscataway NJ 08855

GOLDMAN, ALFRED EMMANUEL, marketing research consultant; b. Bklyn., Dec. 19, 1925; s. Samuel and Julia (Schwartz) G.; m. Adele Lieb, Mar. 30, 1952; children: Julia Madelaine, Marshall Scott. BS, CCNY, 1949, MA, cert. in clin. sch. psychology, 1950; PhD in Clin. Psychology, Clark U., 1955. Research clin. psychologist Boston State Hosp., 1953-54; asst. prof. Northeastern U., Boston, 1954-55; research assoc. Sch. Public Health, Harvard U., 1955-56; asst. dir. psychol. services Norristown (Pa.) State Hosp., 1956-60; dir. rsch. devel. Nat. Analysts Inc., 1960-64, exec. v.p., dir. rsch., 1964-70; pres. Nat. Analysts div. Booz Allen and Hamilton Inc., 1970-82, sr. v.p., 1982-91; pvt. practice mktg. rsch. cons. Bryn Mawr, Pa., 1991—. Founding chmn. Coun. Am. Survey Rsch. Organs, 1975-77. Author: The Group Depth Interview: Principles and Practice, 1986; contbr. articles in field to various publs. Served with USAAF, 1944-46. Fellow Am. Psychol. Assn.; mem. Phi Beta Kappa.

GOLDMAN, ALLAN BAILEY, lawyer; b. Auburn, N.Y., Jan. 1, 1937; s. Charles and Rose Hortense (Abrahams) G.; m. Eleanor Ruth Levy, May 26, 1963; children; Jennifer Brooke Horwitz, Andrea Allison Gellert. AB magna cum laude, Harvard U., 1958, JD, 1963; LHD (hon.), Hebrew Union Coll.-Jewish Inst. Religion, 1992. Bar: Calif. 1964, D.C. 1977, U.S. Supreme Ct. 1977. Assoc. Wyman, Bautzer, Kuchel & Silbert, Beverly Hills, Calif., 1963-67, ptnr. L.A., 1967-91, Katten, Muchin, Zavis & Rosenman, L.A., 1991—. Judge pro-tem Calif. Mcpl. and Small Claims Cts.; arbitrator Calif. Superior Ct. Contbr. articles to profl. jours. Chmn. Attys. for Brown for Gov., officer Brown for Pres., 1976; founder L.A. Com. for Civil Rights Under Law, Mus. Contemporary Art., L.A., Fraternity of Friends of L.A. Music Ctr.; trustee Calif. Mus. Sci. and Industry, 1981-89, St. John's Hosp. and Health Ctr. Found., 1978—, exec. com., 1979-89, bd. dirs., 1989-95, treas., 1990-94, chmn., 1994-95; chmn. nat. bd. trustees Union of Am. Hebrew Congregations, 1987-91; bd. govs. Hebrew Union Coll. Jewish Inst. Religion, 1988—, bd. overseers L.A. campus, 1981-85, 88—; trustee SKirball Cultural Ctr., 1997—; pres. Leo Baeck Temple, L.A., 1975-77; mem. Conf. Pres.'s Major Jewish Orgns., 1987-91; mem. synagogue funding com. Jewish Fedn. Coun. of Greater L.A., 1979, chmn., 1985-88; Calif. Commn. Jud. Nominees Evaluation, 1999-2002. Lt. USNR, 1958-60. Mem. Calif. Bar Assn., D.C. Bar Assn., Regency Club. Democrat. Jewish. Avocations: trekking, running, tennis. Home: 347 Conway Ave Los Angeles CA 90024-2603 Office: Katten Muchin Zavis Rosenman 2029Century Park E Ste 2600 Los Angeles CA 90067 E-mail: allan.goldman@kmzr.com.

GOLDMAN, ALLEN MARSHALL, physics educator; b. N.Y.C., Oct. 18, 1937; s. Louis and Mildred (Kohn) G.; m. Katherine Virginia Darnell, July 31, 1960; children: Matthew, Rachel, Benjamin AB, Harvard U., 1958; PhD, Stanford U., 1965. Rsch. asst. Stanford U., Calif., 1960-65, rsch. assoc., 1965; asst. prof. physics U. Minn., Mpls., 1965-67, assoc. prof., 1967-73, prof., 1974—, inst. tech. prof., 1992—, dir. Ctr. for Sci. and Application of Superconductivity, 1989—, head Sch. of Physics and Astronomy, 1996—. Co-chmn. Gordon Conf. on Quantum Liquids and Solids, 1981; dir. NATO Advanced Study Inst., 1983; mem. materials rsch. adv. com. NSF, 1985-88; mem. vis. com. Francis Butter Nat. Magnet Lab., 1986-89, chmn., 1987-89; mem. vis. com. Nat. Nanofabrication Facility at Cornell, 1988-90, mem. user com., 1997-99; mem. vis. com. U. Chgo. Materials Program of Argonne Nat. Lab., 1992-98, chmn. 1995; mem. Buckley prize com., 1994-95, London prize com., 1994-98; mem. Helium Res. com. NAS/NRC, 1998-99. Mem. publs. oversight com. Am. Phys. Soc., 1996-99, chair 1997; mem. pub. policy com. Am. Inst. Physics, 1999—, assoc. editor Revs. of Modern Physics, 1999—; contbr. articles to profl. jours. Com. of vis. divsn. materials rsch. NSF, 1999. Alfred P. Sloan Found. fellow, 1966-70. Fellow AAAS, Am. Phys. Soc. (divisional councilor divsn. condensed matter physics 1994-96, 99—, mem. exec. com. 2001—, Fritz London Meml. prize 2002). Jewish. Home: 1015 James Ct Mendota Heights MN 55118-3640 Office: U Minn Sch Physics and Astronomy 116 Church St SE Minneapolis MN 55455-0149 E mail: goldman@physics.umn.edu., amgoldman@attbi.com.

GOLDMAN, ALVIN LEE, lawyer, educator, arbitrator; b. N.Y.C., Feb. 27, 1938; s. Joseph I. and Emma (Berger) G.; m. Elisabeth C. Paris, Nov. 23, 1956; children— Paula, Douglas AB, Columbia U., 1959; LL.B., NYU, 1962. Bar: Ky. 1969. Assoc. Parker, Chapin & Flattau, N.Y.C., 1962-65; mem. faculty U. Ky., Lexington, 1965—, prof. law, 1972—. Prof. in residence NLRB Zagoria staff, 1967-68; vis. scholar Inst. for Labor Law, U. Lueven, 1973; vis. prof. U. Calif., Davis, 1976-77. Author: Processes for Conflict Resolution, 1972, The Supreme Court and Labor-Management Relations Law, 1975, Labor Law and Industrial Relations in the USA, 2d edit., 1983, (with R. Covington) Legislation Protecting the Individual Employee, 1982, (with M. Finkin, C. Summers and K. Dau-Schmidt) Legal Protection for the Individual Employee, 1989, 2d edit., 1995, 3d edit., 2002, Settling for More: Mastering Negotiating Strategies and Techniques, 1991, Labor and Employment Law in the United States, 1996, (with J. Rojot) Negotiation: Theory and Practice, 2003. Bd. dirs. Central Ky. Jewish Assn., 1978-80, 81-84 Mem. ABA, Ky. Bar Assn., Nat. Acad. Arbitrators (bd. govs. 1994-97), Labor Law Group Trust (chmn. 1988-94), Internat. Soc. Labor Law (internat. v.p. 2000-03, exec. bd. U.S. br. 1982-85, 88—, vice-chair 1995-2001, chair 2001—), Internat. Indsl. Rels. Assn. Democrat. Home: 2063 Bridgeport Dr Lexington KY 40502-2615 Office: U Ky Coll of Law Lexington KY 40506-0048 E-mail: agoldman@pop.uky.edu.

GOLDMAN, ARTHUR JOSEPH, retired research and development company executive; b. New York City, Ny, Aug. 14, 1934; s. Henry Julius and Lottie (Schumer) G.; m. Joan Marilyn Broder, Jan. 27, 1957; children: Jeffrey Howard, Rona Beth. Ph D, NY U., New York City, NY, 1961—66, MChemE, 1958—61; BChemE cum laude, CCNY, New York City, NY, 1952—57; MBA, U of Chgo., Chicago, IL, 1978—80. Sr. engr. NDA/United Nuc. Corp, White Plains, NY, 1957—66; project mgr. Esso Math and Systems, INC, Florham Park, NJ, 1966. Adj. assoc. prof NY U., New York city, NY, 1966—71; vp and tech. dir. Nuc. Tech. Corp, White Plains, NY, 1967—70; dir. of fuel mgmt. SM Stoller Corp, New York City, NY, 1971; vp of applied sciences Transfer Systems Inc, North Haven, Conn., 1972; assoc. divsn. dir. Argonne Nat. Lab, Argonne, Ill., 1973—92, dir. quality mgmt., 1992—95, dep. chief ops. officer, 1995—98. Contbr. articles to profl. jours. Mem., bd. of edn. Oak Pk. Pub. Schools, Oak Park, Ill., 1975—78; mem. of adv. coun. Inst. Learning in Retirement; mem. of governing coun. Inst. for Learning in Retirement, Chicago, Ill.; pres. of vol. coun. Mus. of Sci. and Industry, Chicago, Ill., 2002—. 1st lt. U.S. Army Corps Engineers, 1957, Ft Belvoir, Va. Recipient AIC Medal, Am. Inst. of Chemists, 1956, Henry Masson Award, NY U., 1966; fellow AEC Fellow, AEC, 1964 - 1966; scholar Tremain Scholar, CCNY, 1953 - 1957. Achievements include patents for Three patents in nuclear technology. Home: 100 E Bellevue Place Apt 18D Chicago IL 60611 Office: Argonne National Laboratory 9700 S Cass Avenue Argonne IL 60439 E-mail: agoldman@anl.gov.

GOLDMAN, BENJAMIN ALLEN, statistician, writer; b. Phila., Oct. 21, 1960; s. Allen Seymour and Mary (Lemann) G.; m. Lois Marjorie; children: Emma Jennette, Brebna Gavriel. Student, Univ. Coll., London, 1980-81; BA, Vassar Coll., 1982; MPhil, PhD, NYU, 1993; student, Sch. Mus. Fine Arts, 1996. Project dir. Coun. on Econ. Priorities, N.Y.C., 1982-86; assoc. dir. Radiation and Pub. Health Project, N.Y.C., 1989-92; pres. Pub. Data Access, Inc., N.Y.C., 1986-92; exec. dir. Citizens Network for Sustainable Devel., N.Y.C., 1992-93; assoc. dir. Jobs and Environ. Campaign, Boston, 1993—95; mem. President's Coun. on Sustainable Devel. (task force comtys.), Washington, 1994—95; advisor, Nat. Environ. Justice Adv. Coun. U.S. Environ. Protection Agy., Washington, 1994—. Cons. Commn. for Racial Justice, N.Y.C., 1986, Greenpeace, U.S.A., Washington, 1988, Nat. Toxics Campaign, Boston, 1990, Nat. Wildlife Fedn., Washington, 1993, Natural Resources Def. Coun., N.Y.C., 1993, speaker in field, lectr. Tufts U., 1994-95. Author: (with J. Hulme and C. Johnson) Hazardous Waste Management, 1986, (with J. Gould) Deadly Deceit, 1990; The Truth About Where You Live, 1991, Discounting Human Lives, 1994, also monographs; contbr. articles to profl. jours. Founder Weehawken C. of C., 2002—. Scholar NYU, 1985-93; artist in residence grantee Newark Mus., 2002, grantee Vt. Studio Ctr., Johnson, 2003.

GOLDMAN, BERT ARTHUR, psychologist, educator; b. N.Y.C., Apr. 4, 1929; children: Lisa, Linda. BA, U. Md., 1951; M.Ed., U. N.C., 1956; Ed.D., U. Va., 1960. Mem. faculty U. N.C., Greensboro, 1965—, prof. ednl. psychology, 1971-85, dean acad. advising, 1970-85, prof. higher ednl. adminstrn., 1985—86, acting chair dept. ednl. adminstrn., higher edn. and ednl. rsch., 1987-88, dept. coord. of higher edn., 1991—. Served with U.S. Army, 1951-53. Mem. APA, Am. Coun. Measurement Edn., N.C. Assn. for Rsch. in Edn., Am. Ednl. Rsch. Assn. Office: U NC at Greensboro Dept Curriculum and Instrn PO Box 26170 Greensboro NC 27402-6170

GOLDMAN, BRIAN ARTHUR, lawyer, accountant; b. Balt., June 30, 1946; s. Marvin L. and Edythe R. Goldman; m. Eileen G. Safro, Aug. 22, 1970; children: Jonathan S., Evan M. BS in Real Estate Planning, Am.U., 1968; JD, U. Md., 1971. Bar: Md. 1972, U.S. Dist. Ct. Md. 1972, U.S. Tax Ct. 1977, U.S. Supreme Ct. 1977. Acct., Balt., 1974—; mem. Burke, Gerber & Wilen, 1972-77, Sapero & Sapero, 1977-78; pvt. practice, 1978-83; ptnr. Goldman and Fedder, P.A., Balt., 1983-85, Fedder & Garten, P.A., 1986-88, Goldman & Vetter, P.A., 1989—. Asst. prof. income taxation U. Balt., 1974-75. Mem. ABA, Md. Bar Assn., Balt. City Bar Assn., Md. Assn. CPAs, Ctr. Club, Woodholme. Office: Goldman & Vetter PA 36 S Charles St Ste 2401 Baltimore MD 21201-3108 E-mail: bgoldman@goldmanvetter.com.

GOLDMAN, CHARLES NORTON, retired corporate lawyer; b. N.Y.C., Feb. 15, 1932; s. Morris and Mary Celia (Tames) G.; m. Jane Barbara Webbink, July 21, 1968; children: Alexander Daniel, Jeffrey David. AB with honors, Columbia U., 1953, LLB, 1955. Bar: N.Y. 1956 Practiced in, N.Y.C., 1955-60; atty.-advisor AID, Washington, 1960-62; regional legal advisor for India, Nepal and Ceylon AID mission to India, New Delhi, 1962-64; asst. gen. counsel for Latin Am. AID, 1965-68, dep. gen. counsel, 1968-69; staff counsel for Latin Am. ITT, N.Y.C., 1969-72, sr. counsel, asst. to gen. counsel, 1972-74, sr. counsel for Latin Am., 1974-75; v.p., gen. counsel ITT Europe Inc., Brussels, 1975-81; v.p. ITT, 1976-95, assoc. gen. counsel, 1981-95. Mem. Overseas Devel. Coun., 1988-95, Bretton Woods Com., 1992-95. Dir. Jewish Repertory Theater Inc., 1999—2001; bd. dirs. The Internat. Shakespeare Globe Ctr. Ltd., 2003—, Alliance of Resident Theatres, N.Y.C., 1996—98, The Shakespeare Globe Ctr. (USA) Inc., 1996—, pres., 2001—. Mem. Coun. on Fgn. Rels., Mid-Atlantic Club N.Y. Inc. (pres. 1996-2001), Univ. Club, Phi Beta Kappa. Home: 139 E 94th St New York NY 10128-1761 E-mail: chgoldman@aol.com.

GOLDMAN, DARA ELLEN, education educator; b. N.Y.C., Feb. 21, 1971; d. Clifford Howard and Karen P. Goldman. BA, Columbia U., N.Y.C., 1992, MA, 1994; PhD, Emory U., Atlanta, 2000. Asst. prof. U. of Ill., Urbana, 1999—. Grantee Rsch. Funding, Campus Rsch. Bd., U. of Ill., 2000, 2002—03; scholar Dean's Tchg. Fellowship, Emory U., 1999. Mem.: Puerto Rican Studies Assn., Latin Am. Studies Assn., Instituto de Literatura Iberoamericnana, Am. Studies Assn., Am. Comparative Lit. Assn., MLA. Liberal. Jewish. Office: U of Ill 4080 FLB MC-176 707 S Mathews Ave Urbana IL 61801 Office Fax: 217-244-8430.

GOLDMAN, DORIS TORAN, not-for-profit developer; b. Phila., Feb. 5, 1932; d. Samuel Joshua and Bella Adler Nimoityn; m. Jule Goldman, Oct. 16, 1978 (dec. Mar. 1, 1980); m. Alan L. Toran, Mar. 15, 1953 (div. Nov. 1972); children: Nancy Duitch, Jack Steven Toran(dec.), Sharon Turner Turner(dec.). Student, Temple Univ., Phila., 1950—53. Admin. asst. Del. County Commr., Media, Pa., 1972—80; office ops. supr. 1980 U.S. Census, Media, Pa., 1980; area dir. Am. Jewish Com., Phila., 1986—90; nat. dir. Cardiac Arrhyhimias Rsch. and Edn. Found., Irvine, Calif., 1996—. Co-founder C.A.R.E. Found. Inc., Irvine, Calif., 1995—; bd. Orange County Interfaith Coun., Newport Beach, Calif., 1990—95, Am. Jewish Com., Irvine, Calif., 1996—99. Campaign coord. Del. County Dem. Commn., Media, Pa., 1972; chair Young Citizens for Johnson, Phila., 1965; coord. Citizens for Hart, Montgomery County, Pa., 1984. Recipient Nat. Human Rels. award, Am. Jewish Assn., 1996, Heart of A Child award, C.A.R.E. Found., 1997. Mem.: Operation Heartbeat (steering com. 2000—), Pub. Interest Orgn. NHLBI. Democrat. Jewish. Avocations: reading, bridge, walking, public speaking. Office: Cardaic Arrythmias Rsch & Edn Found 2082 Michelson Dr #301 Irvine CA 92612-1212

GOLDMAN, ELISABETH PARIS, lawyer; b. Pitts., Jan. 11, 1939; d. Harold H. and Silvia F. (Koenigsberg) Paris; m. Alvin Lee Goldman, Nov. 23, 1956; children: Polly, Douglas. BA, Queens Coll., 1964; JD, U. Ky., 1975. Bar: Ky. 1975, Calif. 1977. Chief law clk. Supreme Ct. Ky., Frankfort, 1975-76; pvt. practice Elisabeth Goldman PSC, Lexington, Ky., 1977—. Bd. dirs. ACLU Louisville, Ky., 1987-90, Hadassah, Chamber Music Soc., Fayette County Health Care Bd.; pres. Ctrl. Ky. Jewish Fedn., 1993-95, Ctrl. Ky. Civil Liberties Union, 1988-90, James Lane Allen PTA, Lexington, Ky., 1971-72. Recipient Pro-Bono Svc. award Ky. Bar Assn., Frankfort, 1994-2001. Mem. Am. Acad. Adoption Attys., Order of Coif, Phi Beta Kappa. Democrat. Avocations: skiing, hiking, dog training. Office: Elisabeth Goldman PSC 118 Old Lafayette Ave Lexington KY 40502-1704 E-mail: egoldman@adoptionattorneys.org.

GOLDMAN, ELLIOTT STANLEY, writer; b. N.Y.C., Apr. 25, 1913; s. Maurice and Ethel (Rosenstein) G.; m. Virginia Harris, Sept. 18, 1938; children: Richard H., Susan E. Cert. edn., U. Wis., 1932; BA, U. Pitts., 1934. Pres. J. Grant Co., Pitts., 1939-42, The Technics Co., Plainfield, N.J., 1946-62, Trees Place Inc., Orleans, Mass., 1962-80. Author: Big Chocolate Cookies, 1987, (story collection) Earthly Justice, 1990, The Palmer Method, 1995, (memoir; pen name Aaron Alterra) The Caregiver, 1999. Lt. USNR, 1942-45. Recipient Best Fiction Book award Wm. Goyen prize Triquar. Pub., Northwestern U., 1990. Mem. PEN. Democrat. Unitarian Universalist. Avocation: gardening. Home: PO Box 561 18-B Pershing Ln South Orleans MA 02662

GOLDMAN, ERIC A. film company executive; b. Phila., May 3, 1950; s. Ephraim L. and Belle J. (Finkelstein) G.; m. Susan L. Garmaise, May 28, 1978; children: Reisha, Arielle, Dori. B of Hebrew Lit., Gratz Coll., 1970; BA, Temple U., 1972; MFA, Brandeis U., 1974, MA, 1975; PhD, NYU, 1979. Dir. New Jewish Media Project, N.Y.C., 1974-76; curator of film YIVO Inst. for Jewish Rsch., N.Y.C., 1976—78; dir. Jewish Media Svc./JWB, N.Y.C., 1978-87; pres., founder Ergo Media Inc., Teaneck, NJ, 1987—. Adj. Ramapo Coll., 1989-97; juror Internat. Jewish and Israel Film Festival, Tiberias, 1989, Jerusalem Internat. Film Festival, 2000; cons. on film Mus. Jewish Diaspora, Tel Aviv, 1983-88; ednl. adv. com. U.S. Holocaust Meml. Mus., Washington, 1979-81; moderator 92d St. Y, N.Y.C., 1984-93, 98; adj. fellow Ctr. for Advanced Judaic Studies, U. Pa., 2000-2001; adj. Fairleigh Dickinson U., 2002—; adj. asst. prof. Queens Coll., 2003—; artistic dir. Jack Wolgin Film Festival, Phila., 1999—; prof. in residence Skidmore Coll., 2001; film program curator/moderator YIVO Inst. for Jewish Rsch./Ctr. for Jewish History, 2000—. Author: Visions, Images and Dreams: Yiddish Film Past and Present, 1983; dir., prodr.: (video) How to Trace Your Jewish Roots: A Journey With Arthur Kurzweil, 1995 (Parents Choice honors 1995, Spl. Jury award Internat. Jewish Video Competition 1996); editor Medium: a Jewish Media Rev., 1978-87; creator, prodr.: (radio) Song of the Sabras, 1970-72; film critic The Jewish Standard, 1993—. Bd. dirs. Holocaust and Genocide Ctr., Mahwah, N.J., 1989-97; edn. com. Solomon Schechter Day Sch., New Milford, N.J., 1980-94; mem. Congregation Beth Sholom. Weinreich Ctr. for Advanced Jewish Studies fellow, 1976-79, Meml. Found. for Jewish Culture fellow, 1977-78. Mem. Chavurat Reyim, Spl. Interest Video Assn., Assn. Jewish Book Pubs. Avocations: tennis, hiking, skiing, camping, singing. Office: Ergo Media Inc 668 American Legion Dr PO Box 2037 Teaneck NJ 07666-1437

GOLDMAN, ERIC SCOT, lawyer; b. Quincy, Mass., Mar. 5, 1957; s. Terry and Harriet (Goldstein) G.; m. Lora Anderson, June 18, 1983; children: William, Daniel, Leigh. BA, Boston Coll., 1979; MS in Criminal Justice, Northeastern U., 1980; JD, Suffolk U., 1987. Bar: Mass. 1987, U.S. Dist. Ct. Mass. 1987, U.S. Mil. Ct. Appeals. Adminstr. McLean Hosp., Belmont, Mass.; caseworker Norfolk County Dist. Atty.'s Office, Dedham, Mass.; atty. McDermott & Padis, Milton, Mass., 1983-93; assoc. Lynch & Lynch, South Easton, Mass., 1993-98, Lang & Morgera, Boston, 1998-99; ptnr. Finneran, Byrne & Drechsler, LLP, Boston, 1999—. Mediator Norfolk-Plymouth County; bd. dirs. Criminal Justice Scis. Inst., Washington. Recipient Cert. of Recognition, Norfolk County Dist. Atty., Commonwealth of Mass. Dist. Ct. Mem. Mass Acad. Trial Attys., Norfolk, Plymouth and Bristol County Bar Assn., Braintree Rifle and Pistol Club (pres. 1988—). Avocations: scuba diving, Karate, music, firearms training. Home: 36 Forge Way Duxbury MA 02332-4743 Office: Finneran Byrne & Drechsler Eastern Harbor Office Pk 50 Redfield St Boston MA 02122-3630

GOLDMAN, ETHAN HARRIS, finance executive; b. Boston, Jan. 2, 1956; s. Marshall Irwin and Merle Dorothy (Rosenblatt) G.; m. Julie Ellen Hurwitz, Sept. 11, 1982; children: Jessica, Todd, David, Lauren. BA, BS in Econs., U. Pa., 1978; MBA, Harvard Coll., 1982. CPA, Md. Pub. acct. Touche Ross, Balt., 1979-80, Coopers and Lybrand, Boston, 1982-84; mgr. fin. planning Hit or Miss Stores subs. Zayre Corp., Stoughton, Mass., 1984-86; asst. v.p. ops. planning/new bus. ventures Zayre Stores subs. Zayre Corp., Framingham, Mass., 1986-88, asst. v.p. mdse. logistics, 1988-89; housewares buyer Ames Stores, Rocky Hill, Conn., 1989-90, dir. mdse. planning and adminstrn., 1990-91, dir. pull replenishment, 1991-93, divisional mdse. mgr., 1993-95; dir. fin. analysis ADVO, Inc., Windsor, Conn., 1995-98, v.p. strategic bus. devel., 1999—2001, v.p. network planning (strategic planning), 2001—02; CFO Flexcon, Inc., Spencer, Mass., 2002—. Coach West Hartford Youth Soccer. 2d lt. U.S. Army, 1978-79, maj. Res., 1979—. Mem. No. Conn. Harvard Bus. Sch. Club (bd. dirs.-at-large 1992—). Jewish. Avocations: distance running, soccer, stamp collecting, tennis, history. Home: 9 Vardon Rd West Hartford CT 06117-2848 Office: One Flexcon Industrial Park Spencer MA 01562-2642

GOLDMAN, FATIMA, social services administrator; BA, CUNY; MA, Bank St. Coll. Edn. With Human Resources Adminstrn., University Heights Day Care Ctr., Hartley Ho. Family Day Care, Graham-Windham Svcs. Families and Children; exec. dir. Brookwood Child Care, 1994—2002; v.p. Coun. Family and Childcare Agys., 2000—; exec. dir., CEO Fedn. Protestant Welfare Agys., N.Y.C., 2003—. Mem. adv. bd. Am. Cancer Soc., Resources Children with Spl. Needs. Office: 281 Park Ave S New York NY 10010*

GOLDMAN, GARY CRAIG, lawyer; b. Dec. 28, 1951; s. Ronald Walter and Connie Sylvia (Stein) G.; m. Diane Rose Lane, Oct. 1, 1977; children: Justin Edward, Gregory David. BA magna cum laude, Temple U., 1973; JD, Villanova U., 1976. Bar: Pa. 1976, U.S. Dist. Ct. (ea. dist.) Pa. 1981. Jud. law clk. Common Pleas Ct., Northampton County, Pa., 1976-77; asst. atty. gen. office of legal counsel Pa. Dept. Pub. Welfare, Phila., 1977-81, asst. counsel, 1981-84; staff counsel CDI Corp., Phila., 1984-86, v.p., assoc. gen. counsel, 1986—. Mem. faculty, planning chmn. Nationwide Comml. Real Estate Leasing Programs. Author: Drafting a Fair Office Lease, 1989, 2d edit., 2000; contbg. author: The Commercial Real Estate Tenant's Handbook, 1987, The Practical Real Estate Lawyer's Manual, 1987, Commercial Tenants' Leasing Transactions Guide, 1991, Office Planning and Design Desk Reference, 1992, Negotiating and Drafting Office Leases, 1995; assoc. editor: Villanova Law Rev., 1974-76; contbr. articles to legal jours. Mem. ABA, Am. Corp. Counsel Assn., Phila. Bar Assn. Republican. Jewish. Avocation: golf. Home: 210 Fox Hollow Dr Langhorne PA 19053-2477 Office: CDI Corp 1717 Arch St Fl 35 Philadelphia PA 19103-2713

GOLDMAN, GERALD HILLIS, beverage distribution company executive; b. Omaha, July 26, 1947; s. Lester Jack and Lilyan Haykin (Weiskopf) G.; m. Cathy Evelyn Brightman, Dec. 15, 1973; children: Lori, Jeffrey. BSBA, U. Nebr., 1969; MBA, U. So. Calif., 1975. C.P.A., Calif., Nebr. Sr. acct. Arthur Andersen & Co., Los Angeles, 1969-72; exec. v.p., CFO CORE-MARK Internat., Inc., Richmond, B.C., Can., 1972-86, exec. v.p., 1986-87; pres. Gen. Acceptance Corp., Los Angeles, 1986-87; CFO, sr. v.p. fin. and ops. Alaska Distbrs., Inc., Seattle, 1987—. Mem. AICPA, Calif. Soc. CPAs, Fin. Execs. Inst.

GOLDMAN, GLENN, architecture educator, architect; b. N.Y.C., Apr. 7, 1952; s. Herbert and Tamara G.; m. Elizabeth Anne Strub, May 31, 1982; children: Aaron, Nathan, Jacob. BA, Columbia U., 1974; M in Architecture, Harvard U., 1978. Registered arch. and planner. Instr. career discovery program Harvard U., Cambridge, Mass., 1978; asst. prof. architecture Iowa State U., Ames, 1978-80; design critic Boston Architectural Ctr., 1981; prof., dir. imaging lab. N.J. Inst. of Tech., Newark, 1982—. Graphic designer Skidmore, Owings and Merrill, Boston, 1975; designer Moshe Safdie Archs., Ltd., Jerusalem, 1976; arch. Jung/Brannen Assocs., Boston, 1980-82, J.F. Caulfield Assocs., Hoboken, N.J., 1983-86, Glenn Goldman, Arch., Tenafly, N.J., 1984—. Author: Architectural Graphics: Traditional and Digital Communication, 1997; co-author, photographer: (video) Iowa: Downtowns in Transition, 1980; co-editor: Reality and Virtual Reality, 1991; contbr. articles to profl. jours. Recipient Applied Rsch. citation, Progressive Architecture Awards Program, 1991; grantee Tech. Engring. Pre-Visualization Archl. Design grantee, N.J. Dept. Higher Edn., 1985, 1989, Imaging Lab grantee, numerous corp. sponsors, 1990—2003. Mem.: AIA (honorable mention edn.honors program 1989), Assn. Computer Aided Design in Architecture (pres. 1996—97), N.J. Soc. Archs. (edit. bd. Architecture N.J. 1983—93), Assn. Computing Machinery Spl. Interest Group in Graphics, Tenafly United Soccer Club (youth soccer coach 1999—, v.p.), Tenafly Swim Club (trustee 1999—, pres. 2001—). Home: 11 Ravine Rd Tenafly NJ 07670-2124 Office: NJ Inst Tech Sch of Architecture Newark NJ 07102 E-mail: glenn_goldman@hotmail.com.

GOLDMAN, IRA STEVEN, gastroenterologist; b. Bronx, NY, May 19, 1951; s. George David and Belle (Hans) G.; m. Niki Ellen Kantrowitz, Jan. 20, 1980; children: Zachary, Joshua. BA, U. Rochester, 1973; student, Oxford U., 1972; MD, Columbia U., 1977. Diplomate Am. Bd. Internal Medicine, Am. Bd. Gastroenterology. Intern Columbia Presbyn. Med. Ctr., N.Y.C., 1977-78, resident in internal medicine, 1978-80; fellow in gastroenterology and liver diseases U. Calif. Sch. Medicine, San Francisco, 1980-83; instr. in anatomy Columbia U., N.Y.C., 1978; asst. prof. medicine U. Calif., San Francisco, 1983-85, Cornell U. Med. Coll., N.Y.C., 1985-91, assoc. prof. clin. medicine, 1991-96; attending physician North Shore Univ. Hosp., Manhasset, N.Y., 1985—; assoc. prof. clin. medicine NYU Sch. Medicine, 1996—. Attending physician St. Francis Hosp., Roslyn, N.Y.; physicians adv. bd. Am. Liver Found., Greater N.Y. chpt., 1985—; sci. adv. commn. L.I. chpt. Nat. Found. for Ileitis and Colitis, 1985-91; vice chair clin. practice sec. Am. Gastroent. Assn., 1995-97, chmn., 1997-2000. Reviewer jours. Gastroenterology; contbr. articles, book chapts. to profl. jours. Rsch. fellow Am. Liver Found., 1982, Clin. Investigator award NIH, 1983. Fellow ACP, Am. Coll. Gastroenterology; mem. Am. Assn. for Study of Liver Diseases, Med. Soc. State of N.Y., Nassau County Med. Soc., Nassau County. Acad. Medicine, N.Y. Soc. for Gastrointestinal Endoscopy (pres. 1996-97), Alpha Omega Alpha. Avocations: sailing, tennis. Office: 310 E Shore Rd Great Neck NY 11023-2432

GOLDMAN, ISRAEL DAVID, hematologist, oncologist; b. Jersey City, N.J., Nov. 17, 1936; married; 3 children. BA, NYU, 1958; MD, U. Chgo., 1962. Diplomate Am. Bd. Internal Medicine; lic. physician, N.C., Va., N.Y. Intern internal medicine U. Chgo. Hosps., 1962-63, jr. and sr. asst. resident internal medicine, 1963-65; fellow biophysics biophys. lab. Harvard Med. Sch., Boston, 1965—66; from rsch. assoc. to sr. investigator Nat. Cancer Inst., Bethesda, Md., 1966—69; asst. prof. medicine U. N.C., Chapel Hill, 1969-72, assoc. prof. medicine and pharmacology, 1972-74; assoc. prof. medicine, vice-chmn. dept. medicine Med. Coll. Va., Richmond, 1974-83, prof. medicine and pharmacology, 1979—95, prof. medicine and pharmacology, chmn. divsn. hematology/oncology, 1982—95, dir. Massey Cancer Ctr., 1988—95; prof. medicine and molecular pharmacology, dir. cancer rsch. ctr. Albert Einstein Coll. Medicine, 1995—. Mem. exptl. therapeutics study sect. Nat. Cancer Inst., 1976-80, bd. sci. counselors divsn. cancer treatment, 1982-86; sci. adv. com. Damon Runyon-Walter Winchell Cancer Fund, 1986-90; mem. tobacco related disease study sect. U. Calif., 1992-94. Mem. editl. bd. Biochem. Pharmacology, 1984—, Jour. Biol. Chemistry, 1996—2001, Clin. Cancer Rsch., 1999—, Molecular Cancer Therapy, 1992—. With USPHS, Nat. Cancer Inst., NIH, Bethesda, Md., 1966-69. Recipient Rsch. Career Devel. award Nat. Cancer Inst., 1973-78, Outstanding Investigator award Nat. Cancer Inst., 1985-92, 92-99. Fellow ACP; mem. Am. Soc. Clin. Investigation, Assn. Am. Physicians. Home: 231 Loring Ave Pelham NY 10803-2254 Office: Albert Einstein Coll Med Cancer Ctr 1300 Morris Park Ave Bronx NY 10461-1926

GOLDMAN, JANIS MERESMAN, lawyer, law firm executive; b. N.Y.C., Oct. 13, 1944; d. Harry and Helen (Chafets) Meresman; m. Michael David Goldman, Dec. 26, 1965; children— Melissa Lee, Lori Michelle. B.A. with honors in Psychology, U. Pa., 1965; J.D., Georgetown U. Law Center, Washington, 1969. Bar: D.C., Md. Sole practice, Washington, 1971-77; assoc. David Epstein, Esq., Washington, 1977-80; cons. Margolius, Davis & Finkelstein, Washington, 1980-82; pres. Lawyer's Lawyer, Inc., Washington, Chevy Chase, Md., 1983—, also chmn. bd. Co-author article in field. Chmn. U. Pa. Secondary Schs. Admissions Committee, Md., 1980— ; trustee D.C. Bd. Library Trustees, 1972-74; bd. dirs. Washington Urban League, 1972-74. New York State Regents scholar, 1961. Mem. D.C. Bar Assn., Montgomery County Bar Assn., Supreme Court Bar. Home: 118 Quincy St Chevy Chase MD 20815-3321

GOLDMAN, JAY, industrial engineer, educator, former dean; b. Norfolk, Va., Apr. 15, 1930; s. Louis H. and Rose O. Goldman; m. Renitta Librach, Dec. 20, 1959 BSME, Duke U., 1950; MSME, Mich. State U., 1951; DSc in Indsl. Engring., Washington U., St. Louis, 1955. Registered profl. engr., Mo. Lectr. indsl. engring. Washington U., 1952-56, asst. prof., 1956-64, acting chmn. human and orgn. factors, 1963-64; dir. dept. indsl. engring. Jewish Hosp., St. Louis, 1960-64; research assoc. dept. hosp. adminstr. U. N.C., Chapel Hill, 1964-68; prof., grad. adminstr. dept. indsl. engring. N.C. State U., Raleigh, 1964-68; prof., chmn. dept. indsl. engring. U. Mo., Columbia, 1968-84, prof. bioengring., 1969-75, prof. bioengring. and advanced automation, 1975-84; Disting. Svc. prof. and dean emeritus U. Ala., Birmingham, 1984—, dean, 1984-96. Cons. to fed., state agys., pvt. industry Contbr. to textbooks, profl. jours.; producer 6 tech. motion pictures; patentee in field V.p. Boone County Cmty. Svcs. Coun., 1973-76; v.p., exec. com., treas. Cmty. Rels. Coun.; bd. dirs. Birmingham Jewish Fedn.; vice-chmn., bd. dirs. Sloss Furnaces Nat. Hist. Landmark, bd. dirs., treas. Jewish Family Svcs. Named Ala. Engr. of Yr., ASPE; recipient Editl. award, Hosp. Mgmt. mag., 1969, U. Mo. Faculty Alumni award, 1981, Outstanding Engr. Educator in State award, ASPE. Fellow Inst. Indsl. Engrs. (trustee, exec. v.p., regional v.p., chpt. pres., v.p. edn. and profl. devel., editl. bd. Trans., Health Svcs. Devel. award 1981, Fred C. Crane award 1999), Accreditation Bd. Engring. and Tech. (dir., treas., fellow); mem. NSPE, Soc. Health Sys. (bd. dirs., pres.), Nat. Coun. Indsl. Engrs. Acad. Dept. Heads (chmn.), Ala. Soc. Profl. Engrs., Am. Soc. Engring. Edn., Sigma Xi, Alpha Pi Mu, Tau Beta Pi, Phi Kappa Phi, Omicron Delta Kappa. Home: 4631 Pine Mountain Rd Birmingham AL 35213-1834 Office: U Ala-Birmingham Sch Engring 1075 13th St S Ste 310 Birmingham AL 35205-3430

GOLDMAN, JERRY STEPHEN, lawyer; b. Bklyn., Sept. 7, 1951; s. Bernard I. and Charlotte (Emerling) G.; children by previous marriage: Rachel Dawn, Samantha. BA with honors, NYU, 1973; JD, Boston U., 1976; LLM in Taxation, Temple U., 1983. Bar: Mass. 1977, N.Y. 1977, U.S. Dist. Ct. (ea. and so. dists.) N.Y. 1980, U.S. Supreme Ct. 1981, Pa. 1982, U.S. Tax Ct. 1983, U.S. Dist. Ct. (ea. dist.) Pa. 1983, U.S. Ct. Appeals (3d cir.) 1983, U.S. Dist. Ct. Mass. 1997, U.S. Ct. Appeals (1st cir.) 1997. Sr. asst. dist. atty. Kings County Dist. Atty.'s Office, Bklyn., 1976-82; pvt. practice N.Y.C., Phila., 1982—; mng. ptnr. Law Offices of Jerry S. Goldman. Dir., pres. Huntingdon Brook Cmty. Assn., Bucks Co, Pa., 1985-89. Chmn. Upper Southampton Planning Commn., 1984—90; bd. dirs., counsel Citizens Crime Commn., Phila., 1983—95; bd. dirs. NYU Alumni Assn.; v.p. Coll. Arts and Scis.; mem. Phila. Estate Planning Coun., N.Y. Estate Planning Coun., Delaware Valley Venture Group; atty. Phila. Vol. Lawyers for the Arts, 1983—. Mem. ABA, N.Y. State Bar Assn., Pa. Bar Assn., Phila. Bar Assn., Fed. Bar Assn., N.Y. New Media Assn. Avocations: cross-country skiing, music. Office: 1601 Market St Philadelphia PA 19103 also: 13th Fl 111 Broadway New York NY 10006 E-mail: jgoldman@goldmanlawyers.com.

GOLDMAN, JOEL J. retired lawyer; b. N.Y.C., Sept. 7, 1940; s. Myron and Pearl (Jacobs) G.; m. Jane I. Stalker, July 23, 1973; children: Elizabeth Ann, Rebecca Lynn. BS, U. Va., 1962; JD, Syracuse U., 1965. Bar: N.Y. 1966, U.S. Dist. Ct. (we. dist.) N.Y. 1966. Law clk. Myron Goldman, N.Y.C., 1965; staff atty., chief trial counsel Legal Aid Soc., Rochester, N.Y., 1966-73; ptnr. Kaman, Berlove, Marafioti, Jacobstein & Goldman, Rochester, 1973-97; ret., 1997. Lectr. family law; spl. investigator N.Y. State Spl. Commn. on Attica, 1972; mem. panel arbitrators Am. Arbitration Assn..; mem. faculty Nat. Bus. Inst., 1985-97. Author continuing edn. materials; contbg. editor Bender's Forms for Civil Practice, 1986, Medina's Bostwick, 1986. Referee Ea. Assn. Inter-Collegiate Football Ofcsls., 1974-95, v.p. Empire chpt., 1988, pres., 1989, Observer, Ea. Coll. Athletic Conf., 1996—. Inductee Jewish Athletes Sports Hall of Fame, 1996. Fellow Am. Acad. Matrimonial Lawyers (ret.); mem. ABA, N.Y. State Bar Assn. (exec. com. family law sect. 1982, mem. exec. com. 1981-97), Monroe County Bar Assn. (chmn. family law sect. 1982, exec. com. 1981-86), Assn. Trial Lawyers Am. Jewish. Home: 67 Mountain Rd Rochester NY 14625-1816 also: 21 Bluebill Ave Apt 1005B Naples FL 34108-1765 E-mail: jjgesq@att.net.

GOLDMAN, JOSEPH ELIAS, retired advertising executive; b. N.Y.C., Nov. 26, 1923; s. A. Milton and Caroline (Elias) G.; m. Barbara Van Gelderen, Mar. 22, 1947; children: Carlee Georgette Goldman Paddock, Richard Jonathan. Student, Pratt Inst. Sch. Fine Art, 1941-42, 47-48. Gen. artist, designer Maxon, Inc., N.Y.C., 1948-50; officer, creative dir. Gamut, Inc., Garden City, N.Y., 1952-64; pres., chmn. bd. Adways, Inc., Jericho, N.Y., 1965-74; pres. Goldman Van Gelderen, Inc., Greenville, S.C., 1974-80; also bd. dirs.; pres. Gamut Agy., Inc., Hempstead, N.Y., 1975-77; v.p. Graphics Plus, Inc., Greenville, 1983-86; ret., 1986. Bd. dirs. Urban League L.I., 1976-77. With USMCR, 1942-46. Mem. League Advt. Agys. (pres. 1964-65), Art Dirs. Club L.I. (co-founder, pres. 1971-72, 72-73), Greenville Artists Guild (pres. 1986, bd. dirs. 1987), Upstate Visual Artists, Plein Air Artists Soc., Nat. Caricaturists Network, Alpha Delta Sigma. E-mail: jgvanart@aol.com.

GOLDMAN, L. BARTON, physician; b. Uniontown, Pa., Dec. 5, 1954; s. Mark Howard Goldman and Ann Louise Roman; m. Karen Jane Houser, Nov. 1, 1982; children: Elysa Brett, Eric Mitchell. BA with high distinction, Pa. State U., 1977; MD, Hahnemann U., 1984. Diplomate Am. Bd. Phys. Medicine and Rehab., Nat. Bd. Med. Examiners, Am. Bd. Ind. Med. Examiners. Intern, resident in phys. medicine and rehab. Temple U. Hosp., 1984-87; med. dir. Ctr. for Spine and Orthopedic Rehab., Englewood, Colo., 1987-96, CRPS Svc., Colo. Neurol. Inst., Englewood, 1991-96, R-Vision Corp., Denver, 1993-99; pres. Rehab. Assocs. Colo., P.C., Englewood, 1993-96; med. dir. HealthOne Occupl. Medicine, Denver, 1996—99, HealthOne Clinic Svcs., 2000—. Bd. mem. Colo. Health Care Rsch. Corp., Denver; chmn. Colo. Divsn. Workers Compensation Low Back Pain Guidelines Task Force, 1990-2000, Colo. Divsn. Workers Compensation Med. Care Adv. Com., Denver, 1991—. Sr. editor (newsletter) Neuropractice, 1994-2000; contbr. articles to profl. jours. Fund-raiser Nat. MS Soc., 1989-92, Rocky Mountain Stroke Assn., Littleton, Colo., 1999; bd. mem. Colo. Neurol. Inst., Englewood, 1990-97, Spalding Rehab Hosp., Denver, 1991-96. Fellow Am. Acad. Phys. Medicine and Rehab., Physiatric Assn. for Sports, Spine and Occupl. Rehab.; mem. Am. Acad. Med. Acupuncture, Am. Coll. Occupl. and Environ. Medicine, Am. Coll. Physician Execs., Rocky Mountain Rehab. Soc. (pres. 1995-99). Avocations: cycling, skiing, hiking, yoga. Office: HealthOne Clinic Svcs 3900 E Mexico Ave Ste 200 Denver CO 80210-3942 E-mail: lawrencebarton@msn.com.

GOLDMAN, LAWRENCE, music educator; b. Santa Rosa, Calif., Feb. 26, 1950; s. Stanley and Bernice Goldman. BA, U. Calif., Santa Barbara, 1972; MM, U. Mich., 1974; D Musical Arts, U. So. Calif., 1977. Asst. prof. music U. Southwestern La., Lafayette, 1977—79, Ala. State U., Montgomery, 1979—80; prof. music Miss. Valley State U., Itta Bena, Miss., 1980—. Mem.: Coll. Music Soc., Music Tchrs. Nat. Assn. Home: 1207 Wright St Greenwood MS 38930-2238 Office: Miss Valley State U Dept Fine Arts 14-000 Hwy 82 W #7255 Itta Bena MS 38941 Fax: 708-575-7438. E-mail: goldman@mvsu.edu.

GOLDMAN, LAWRENCE SAUL, lawyer; b. Phila., Mar. 25, 1942; s. Ephraim Lederer and Belle Joan (Finkelstein) G.; m. Kathi Sue Schleifer, June 20, 1965; children: Carolyn, Jonathan. BA, Brandeis U., 1963; JD, Harvard U., 1966. Bar: N.Y. 1966. Asst. dist. atty. New York County, N.Y.C., 1966-71; asst. gen. counsel N.Y. State Commn. To Investigate N.Y.C., 1971-72; pvt. practice N.Y.C., 1972-2001; principal Law Offices of Lawrence S. Goldman, 2001—. Cons. N.Y.C. Commn. on Police Corruption, 1972. Contbg. author: Criminal Trial Advocacy, 1980-99. Trustee Congregation Rodeph Sholom, N.Y.C., 1983-92; bd. dirs. William F. Ryan Cmty. Health Ctr., N.Y.C., 1986-88, Bronx Defenders, 1997—; mem. N.Y. State Commn. on Jud. Conduct, 1990—, mem. adv. com. on the criminal law, 1992—. Recipient Man of Yr. award Hogan Assocs., 1984. Mem. NACDL (chmn. ethics adv. com. 1988-92, white collar com. 1992-97, Robert C. Heeney award 1998, pres. 2001-2002), N.Y. State Assn. Criminal Def. Lawyers (pres. 1987-89, Thurgood Marshall award 1999), N.Y. Criminal Bar Assn. (pres. 1982-85, Outstanding Practitioner award 1994), N.Y. State Bar Assn. (Outstanding Practitioner award criminal justice sect. 1996), Harvard Club. Democrat. Office: 500 Fifth Ave New York NY 10110-0002 E-mail: lsgoldman2@hotmail.com., lsg@lsgoldmanlaw.com.

GOLDMAN, LOIS M. transportation planner; d. Conrad D. and Mimi P. Geller; m. Ben A. Goldman, Oct. 13, 1991; children: Emma Jeannette, Breena Gavriele. BA, SUNY, Stony Brook, 1985; M in City Planning, Boston U., 1996. Assoc. City of N.Y. - Cmty. Bd. 2, 1990—93; prin. planner North Jersey Transp. Planning Authority, Newark, 1997—. Founding mem. Friends of the Weehawken (N.J.) Waterfront, 1999—2003; pres. Dias y Flores Cmty. Garden, N.Y.C., 1990—93; founding mem. Lower East Side Coalition for a Healthy Environment, N.Y.C., 1990—93; trustee Weehawken Environment Com., 1998—2000; bd. dirs. Good Old Lower East Side, N.Y.C., 1992—93; founding mem. Weehawken Initiative Now, 2001; mem. Manhattan Solid Waste Adv. Bd., 1991—93. Mem.: Am. Inst. Certified Planners, Am. Planning Assn. Office: N Jersey Transp Planning Auth 1 Newark Ctr 17th Fl Newark NJ 07102

GOLDMAN, LOUIS BUDWIG, lawyer; b. Chgo., Apr. 11, 1948; s. Jack Sydney and Lorraine (Budwig) G.; m. Barbara Marcia Berg, Oct. 2, 1983; children: Jacqueline Ilyse, Annie Dara, Michael Louis. BA magna cum laude, U. Calif., Berkeley, 1970; JD cum laude, U. Chgo., 1974. Bar: Calif. 1975, U.S. Dist. Ct. (no. dist.) Calif. 1975, U.S. Ct. Appeals (9th cir.) 1975, N.Y. 1976, U.S. Dist. Ct. (so. and ea. dists.) N.Y. 1976, U.S. Ct. Appeals (2nd cir.) 1976, Ill. 1991, Czech Republic, 1997; registered fgn. lawyer, Eng. 1999, Wales 1999. Law clk. U.S. Dist. Ct., San Francisco, 1974-75; assoc. Cleary, Gottlieb, Steen & Hamilton, N.Y.C. and Paris, 1975-81, Edwards & Angell, N.Y.C., 1981-83, ptnr., 1986-88, Wald, Harkrader & Ross, N.Y.C., 1983-86, Altheimer & Gray, Chgo., 1989—, co-chmn., 1999—. Mng. dir. Abacus & Assocs. Inc., N.Y.C.; supervisory bd. Pudliszki S.A. Mem. U. Chgo. Law Rev.; contbr. articles to profl. jours. Mem. Chgo.-Prague Sister Cities Com., Chgo.-China Sister Cities Com.; bd. dirs. Lyric Opera Ctr. for Am. Artists, New Trier Swim Club; sec. class of 1970, U. Calif., Berkeley; bd. trustees The Ravinia Festival. Mem. ABA (com. on privatization), Calif. Bar Assn., N.Y. State Bar Assn. (com. on internat. banking, securities and fin. transactions), Assn. of the Bar of City of N.Y., N.Y. County Lawyers Assn., Chgo. Bar Assn., Ill. State Bar Assn., Internat. Bar Assn., Order of Coif, Northwestern Assocs., Chgo. China Sister Cities Comm., Old Willow Club, The Law Club, Phi Beta Kappa. Home: 465 Grove St Glencoe IL 60022-1844 Office: Altheimer & Gray 10 S Wacker Dr Ste 4000 Chicago IL 60606-7407 E-mail: goldmanlb@yahoo.com.

GOLDMAN, LYNN ROSE, medical educator; b. Galveston, Tex., Apr. 24, 1951; d. Armond Samuel and Barbara Jean (Bangert) G.; m. Douglas George Hayward. BS, U. Calif., 1976; MPH, Johns Hopkins U., 1981; MS, U. Calif., Berkeley, 1979; MD, U. Calif., San Francisco, 1981. Diplomate Am. Bd. Pediatrics; lic. physician, Calif. Resident in pediatrics Children's Hosp. Med. Ctr., Oakland, Calif., 1985; resident in preventive medicine U. Calif., Berkeley, 1985; pub. health med. officer Calif. Dept. Health Svcs., Berkeley, 1985-91, pub. health med. adminstr., 1991-93; asst. adminstr. Office of Prevention, Pesticides and Toxic Substances, EPA, Washington, 1993-98; prof. Sch. Hygiene and Pub. Health, Johns Hopkins U., Balt., 1999—. Democrat. Office: Johns Hopkins U Bloomberg Sch Pub Health 615 N Wolfe St Rm W511 Baltimore MD 21205-1900 E-mail: lgoldman@jhsph.edu.

GOLDMAN, MARION SHERMAN, sociology and religious studies educator, consultant on cults; b. Chgo., July 31, 1945; d. Mandel and Marjorie Lipman Sherman; m. Paul Goldman; children: Michael, Henry. BA, U. Calif., Berkeley, 1967; PhD, U. Chgo., 1977. Prof. sociology and religious studies U. Oreg., Eugene, 1996—. Author: A Portrait of the Black Attorney in Chicago, 1971, Gold Diggers and Silver Miners: Prostitution and Social Life on the Comstock Lode, 1981 (Alice and Edith Hamilton prize U. Mich. Press 1980), Passionate Journeys: Why Successful Women Joined a Cult, 1999; co-editor: Advances in Psychoanalytic Sociology, 1987, Sex, Lies and Sanctity, 1995; mem. editl. bd. Sociology of Religion, 2003. Bd. dirs. Friends of the Knight Libr., Eugene, 2000—. Mem. Soc. for Sci. Study of Religion, Assn. for Sociology of Religion. Office: Dept Sociology U Oreg Eugene OR 97403 Fax: (541) 346-5026. E-mail: mgoldman@oregon.uoregon.edu.

GOLDMAN, MARSHALL IRWIN, economist, educator; b. Elgin, Ill., July 26, 1930; s. Sam and Bella Goldman; m. Merle Rosenblatt, June 14, 1953; children— Ethan Harris, Avra Lea, Karla Ann, Seth Abraham. BS, Wharton Sch. of U. Pa., 1952; MA, Harvard, 1956, PhD, 1961; LLD (hon.), U. Mass., 1985. Mem. faculty Wellesley Coll., 1958—2002, prof. econs., 1967-75, Class of 1919 prof. econs., 1975-89, chmn. dept., 1971-77, Kathryn W. Davis prof. Russian econs., 1989—98; assoc. dir. Davis Ctr. for Russian Studies, Harvard U., 1975—. Vis. asst. prof. Brandeis U., 1961-62; Fulbright vis. lectr. Moscow State U., 1977; cons. in field; bd. dirs. Century Bank and Trust Co., Somerville, Mass.; mem. Mass. Fiduciary Advisors Coun., 1985-88. Author: Soviet Marketing: Distribution in a Controlled Economy, 1963, Comparative Economic Systems: A Reader, rev. edit, 1971, Soviet Foreign Aid, 1967, Controlling Pollution: The Economics of a Cleaner America, 1967, The Soviet Economy: Myth and Reality, 1968, The Spoils of Progress: Environmental Pollution in The USSR, 1972, Ecology and Economics: Controlling Pollution in the 70's, 1972, Detente and Dollars: Doing Business with the Soviets, 1975, The Enigma of Soviet Petroleum: Half Empty or Half Full, 1980, U.S.S.R. in Crisis: The Failure of an Economic System, 1983, Gorbachev's Challenge: Economic Reform in the Age of High Technology, 1987, What Went Wrong with Perestroika, 1991, Lost Opportunity: What Has Made Economic Reform in Russia So Difficult, 1996, The Piratization of Russia, 2003. Mem. Wellesley Clean Air Com., 1969-71, Wellesley Town Meeting, 1969-77; mem. Wellesley Town Dem. Com., 1964-77, sec., 1969; trustee Noble and Greenough Sch., 1983-89, Commonwealth Sch., 1996-98; pres. Banchetto Musicale, 1991-92; bd. dirs. Boston Baroque; bd. dirs. Jamestown Found., 2000—. With AUS, 1953-55. Huber Found. study grantee, 1959; Brookings Instn. research prof., 1964 Mem. Am. Acad. Arts and Scis., Am. Econ. Assn., Assn. Comparative Econs. (exec. com. 1968-70), Coun. Fgn. Rels., Boston Com. of Fgn. Affairs (exec. com. 2002—), Boston Econ. Club, Boston World Affairs Coun. (exec. com. 1985-2001), The Wellesley Club (exec. com. 2000-02). Clubs: Harvard (N.Y.C.); Cosmos (Washington). Home: 17 Midland Rd Wellesley MA 02482-6927 Office: Davis Ctr for Russian Studies 625 Mass Ave Cambridge MA 02139

GOLDMAN, MARVIN GERALD, lawyer; b. L.A., June 1, 1939; s. Harry Eli Goldman and Esther Cynthia Brodsky; m. Marilynn Sue Cohen, Oct. 11, 1964; children: Daniel, Sharon, Haviva. AB, UCLA, 1960, JD, 1963; LLM in Comparative Law, NYU, 1964. Bar: Calif. 1964, N.Y. 1966, D.C. 1981. Assoc. Reid & Priest, N.Y.C., 1965—73; ptnr. Thelen Reid & Priest, N.Y.C., 1974—. Author: El Al: Star in the Sky, 1990; editor Thelen Reid & Priest Internat. Bus. Transactions Newsletter, 1983-99. Ford Found. grantee NYU Sch. Law, 1963-64; Fulbright grantee U.S. Govt. Mexico, 1964-65; UCLA Law Rev. award 1963. Mem. ABA (sect. internat. law and practice, chmn. internat. coml. arbitration com. 1979-83), Internat. Bar Assn. (internat. constrn. projects com.), Am. Arbitration Assn. (internat. arbitration com.), U.S. Coun. for Internat. Bus. (arbitration com.), World Airline Hist. Soc. Avocations: civil aviation history, antique airline postcards, javanese gamelan, philately, fluorescent minerals. Office: Thelen Reid & Priest LLP 875 3d Ave New York NY 10022-6225 E-mail: mgoldman@thelenreid.com.

GOLDMAN, MIA, film editor; b. N.Y.C., Sept. 26, 1954; d. Bo Goldman and Mab Ashforth. BA, Vassar Coll., 1977. Film editor Choose Me, 1984, 2010, 1984, Silverado, 1985, The Big Easy, 1986, Cross My Heart, 1987, Dead Man Out, 1989, Crazy People, 1990, Prisoner of Honor, 1991, Untamed Heart, 1992, Flesh and Bone, 1994, Something to Talk About, 1995, Dick, 1999, My Big Fat Greek Wedding, 2002, The In-Laws, 2003; editl. cons. In The Bedroom, 2001. Mem. Am. Cinema Editors, Acad. Motion Picture Arts and Scis.

GOLDMAN, MICHAEL DAVID, lawyer; b. Jersey City, Oct. 16, 1942; s. Nathaniel J. and Ruth Goldman; m. Faith I. Frankel, June 5, 1966; children: Leigh S., Amy P. AB, Pa. State U., 1964; JD, Villanova (Pa.) U., 1967. Bar: Del. 1968. Law clk. to presiding judge Ct. Chancery, Wilmington, Del.; ptnr. Potter Anderson & Corroon, Wilmington, 1974—, chmn., 1999—. Chmn. bd. Bar Examiners State of Del., 1988-90, vice chmn., 1986-87; spkr., planning com. Tulane Corp. Law Inst., 1988—. Contbr. articles in field to profl. jours. Mem. state exec. bd. Muscular Dystrophy Assn., 1974-76; chmn. atty. div. United Way, Del., 1977, chmn. profl. div., 1978, 80-81; chmn. Am. Jewish Com., Del., 1981-82; chmn. Jewish Community Rels. Com., 1982; bd. dirs. Jewish Fedn. Del., 1982-85. Mem. ABA (bus. sect., corp. laws com. 1995—), Del. Bar Assn. (chmn. sect. on Del. corp. law 1990-92, chmn. subcom. bus. combination statute). Office: Potter Anderson & Corroon Hercules Plz PO Box 951 Wilmington DE 19899-0951 E-mail: mgoldman@potteranderson.com.

GOLDMAN, NATHAN CARLINER, lawyer, educator; b. Charleston, S.C., Mar. 19, 1950; s. Reuben and Hilda Alta (Carliner) G.; m. Judith Tova Feigon, Oct. 28, 1984; children: Michael Reuben, Miriam Esther. BA, U. S.C., 1972; JD, Duke U., 1975; MA, Johns Hopkins U., 1978, PhD, 1980. Bar: N.C. 1975, Tex. 1985, U.S. Dist. Ct. (mid. dist.) N.C. 1975. Paralegal City Atty.'s Office, Durham, N.C., 1975-76; asst. prof. govt. dept. U. Tex., Austin, Tex., 1980-85; pvt. practice Houston, 1985-86; assoc. Liddell, Sapp, Zivley, Hill & LaBoon, Houston, 1986-88; pvt. practice Houston, 1988-2000; atty. Amour Law Office, 2000—. Adj. prof. space law U. Houston, 1985-88; rsch. assoc. Rice U. Inst. Policy Analysis, 1986—; lectr. bus. law, 1988-95; mem. coordinating bd. Space Architecture, U. Houston, 1985—; v.p. Internat. Design in Extreme Environments Assn., U. Houston, 1991—; vis. asst. prof. U. Houston-Clear Lake, 1989-91, 99—; adj. prof. South Tex. Coll. Law, 1994-95; gen. counsel Internat. Space Enterprises, 1993—, Globus Ltd. Co., 1994—; info. officer Israel Consulate, 1996-97, atty. Judith G. Cooper, P.C. Author: Space Commerce, 1985, American Space Law, 1988, 2d edit., 1996, Space Policy: A Primer, 1992; editor: Space and Society, 1984; assoc. editor Jour. Space Commerce, 1990-91; exec. editor Space Governance, 1996-99; also articles. Mem. com. on governance of space U.S. Bicentennial Commn., 1986-88, Clear Lake (Tex.) Area Econ. Devel. Found., 1987, Space Collegium, Houston Area Rsch. Ctr., 1987; pres. Windermere Civic Assn., 1990-92; bd. dirs. Hebrew Acad., 1994-96, Men's Club United Orthodox Synagogues, 1994—, pres., 1999-2002. U.S. Dept. Justice grantee, 1979-80, U. Tex. Inst. for Constructive Capitalism U. grantee, 1983; E.D. Walker Centennial fellow, 1984; NASA Summer fellow U. Calif., 1984. Fellow Internat. Inst. Space Law; mem. ABA, Tex. Bar Assn., Nat. Space Soc. (v.p. 1989-91), Inst. for Social Sci. Study Space (mem. adv. bd. 1990, editor Space Humanization Jour. 1993-2000), Am. Astronautical Soc., Inst. for Design in Extreme Environment Assn. (v.p. 1991-96), Space Bus. Roundtable. Avocations: reading, hiking, baseball, softball. Home: 9406 Cliffwood Dr Houston TX 77096

GOLDMAN, NEIL, association administrator; b. St. Louis; married; 3 children. Student, Washington U. Nat. ins. chmn. Nat. Mus. Am. Jewish Mil. History, Washington, nat. outreach chmn., vice chmn. nat. centennial com., pres., 1999—; buyer, merchandiser Mays, St. Louis, sr. buyer, merchandiser Dallas; owner bus. Mem. Dallas Holocaust Ctr., Yad V'Shem Holocaust Mus., Jerusalem. Mem.: Disabled Am. Vets. Office: Nat Mus Am Jewish Mil History 1811 R St NW Washington DC 20009-1603

GOLDMAN, NORMAN LEWIS, chemistry educator; b. Bklyn., Aug. 11, 1933; s. Sam and Rose (Schrager) G. BS, CCNY, 1954; AM, Harvard U., 1956; PhD, Columbia U., 1959, Postdoctoral NSF fellow, 1959-60; NIH postdoctoral fellow, Columbia U., N.Y.C., 1960-61. Mem. faculty Queens Coll., CUNY, 1961—, prof. chemistry and biochemistry, 1976-98; prof. chemistry emeritus Queens Coll., 1998—; chmn. dept. Queens Coll., CUNY, 1972-77, acting assoc. dean faculty, 1977-78, acting dean faculty, div. math. and natural scis., 1978-79, dean faculty, div. math. and natural scis., 1979-98. Contbr. articles to profl. jours. Mem. Am. Chem. Soc., Y. Acad. Sci. (vice chair chem. sci. sect. 1998-99, chair 1999-2000), Sigma Xi, Phi Beta Kappa. Home: 75-10 Grand Central Pky Forest Hills NY 11375-5562 Office: CUNY Queens Coll 120 Remsen Hall Flushing NY 11367-1597 E-mail: norman_goldman@qc.edu.

GOLDMAN, PETER LOUIS, writer; b. Phila., Feb. 8, 1933; s. Walter and Dorothy (Semple) G.; m. Helen Dudar, July 16, 1961. BA, Williams Coll., 1954; MS, Columbia U., 1955. Staff writer St. Louis Globe Democrat, 1955-62; assoc. editor Newsweek, N.Y.C., 1962-64, gen. editor, 1965-68, sr. editor, 1968-88, contbg. editor, 1988—. Author: Civil Rights: The Challenge of the Fourteenth Amendment, 1965, Report from Black America, 1970, The Death and Life of Malcolm X, 1973, rev. 2d edit., 1979; co-author: Charlie Company: What Vietnam Did to Us, 1983, The Quest for the Presidency 1984, 1985, The Quest for the Presidency 1988, 1989, Quest for the Presidency 1992, 1994, The End of the World That Was, 1986, Brothers, 1988; editor: The Attentive Eye: Selected Journalism by Helen Dudar, 2002. Nieman fellow, Harvard U., 1961; recipient Sigma Delta Chi award 1962, Robert F. Kennedy Journalism award 1972, ABA Silver Gavel award 1972, Page One awards N.Y. Newspaper Guild, 1967, 72, 86, 88, 89, Nat. Mag. award, 1982, 92, Freedom Found. award, 1982, Am. Legion Fourth Estate award 1982, N.Y. Bar Media award, 1984. Home: 36 Gramercy Park E New York NY 10003-1741 Office: Newsweek 251 W 57th St New York NY 10019 E-mail: petergoldman@msn.com.

GOLDMAN, RACHEL BOK, civic volunteer; b. Phila., Mar. 28, 1937; d. W. Curtis and Nellie Lee (Holt) Bok; m. James Nelson Kise, Dec. 20, 1958 (div. May 1974); children: Jefferson B, C. Curtis; m. Allen S. Goldman, Nov. 28, 1981; stepchildren: Jonathan, Benjamin Allen, Adam Louis. Student, Sweet Briar (Va.) Coll., 1955-57; BA in Art History, U. Pa., 1977. Bd. dirs. Arts Exchange mag., 1977-79, chmn. bd. dirs., 1977-79. Mem. com. Soc. for Contemporary Art, Art Inst. Chgo., 1986—92, exhibitrix-selection subcom., 1987—88; mem. collectors' group Mus. Contemporary Art, Chgo., 1986—92; bd. dirs. Art Resources in Tchg., 1987—93, Craniofacial Ctr., 1989—95, AboutFace, 1993—95, Bay Chamber Concerts Inc., 1993—95, Coastal AIDS Network, 2001—, sec of the bd., 2002—; bd. dirs. The Am. Found., 1955—83, sec.-treas., 1980—83; mem. collectors cir. Pa. Acad. Fine Arts, 1983—85; mem. exhbn. selection Morris Gallery, 1979—82; mem. Rittenhouse Sq. women's com. Pa. Orch., 1979—85; mem. Indian com. Pa. Yearly Meeting, 1971—75; mem. ladies' com. Powel House, 1965—69; founder, pres. Friends of Curtis Inst. Music, 1982—, chmn., 1982—85; bd. dirs. Mary Louis Curtis Bok Found., 1982—2001, The Curtis Inst. Music, 1982—2002, The Buten Mus., 1982—84, Brady Cancer Rsch. Inst., 1983—, Settlement Music Sch., 1984—87, The Phila. Award, 1970—, Elfreth's Alley Assn., 1962—65, sec., 1963—65; bd. dirs. The Comm. Sch. of Phila., 1971—74, chmn. bd. dirs., co-founder, adminstr.; bd. dirs. Women in Transition, 1973—78, div. counselor, 1974—76; bd. dirs. Friends of Phila. Mus. Art, 1977—83, sec., 1979—81, program chmn., 1981—82; bd. dirs. Samuel Yellin Found., 1977—86, co-founder, sec., 1977—84. Mem. Camden (Maine) Yacht Club, Cosmopolitan Club of Phila. (house com. 1981-84). Democrat. Avocations: boating, art, needlepoint, travel, gardening.

GOLDMAN, RALPH FREDERICK, research physiologist, educator; b. Boston, Mar. 3, 1928; s. Harry and May (Field) G.; m. Joan R. Krinsky, May 27, 1957; children: Harry, Ellen. BS in Chemistry, U. Denver, 1949; MA in Physiology, Boston U., 1951, PhD in Physiology, 1954; MS in Engring., Northeastern U., Boston, 1962. Rsch. physiologist Natick (Mass.) Labs., U.S. Army, 1955-61; dir. div. environ. medicine U.S. Army Rsch. Inst., Natick, 1961-82; prin. cons. Dept. of Army for Environ. Physiology, Natick, 1971-82; chief scientist Multi-Tech Corp., Natick, 1982-88; chief scientist, R&D, clothing and human comfort Comfort Tech., Inc., Framingham, 1989—; sr. cons. tech. and product devel. Arthur D. Little, Inc., Cambridge, Mass., 1993-97. Adj. prof. Boston U., 1970—, N.C. State U., 1989—; lectr. MIT, Cambridge, 1974-94; vis. scientist Peoples Rep. of China, 1981—; vis. scholar lectr. Springfield (Mass.) Coll., 1977, Ohio State U., 1977, 88; chmn. rsch. group biomed. effects of clothing, NATO, 1981-86. Author: 2 books; contbr. over 500 articles, abstracts and tech. reports to profl. jours., 20 chpts. to books. Scoutmaster Boy Scouts Am., Framingham, Mass., 1956-90, exec. bd., 1991-2002; mem. town meeting Town of Framingham, 1983-88. Recipient Meritorious Civilian Svc. award U.S. Army R&D Command, 1963, Exceptional Civilian Svc. award Sec. of Army, 1976, Sr. Exec. Svc. award U.S. Civil Svc., 1979, Silver Beaver award Boy Scouts Am., 1981. Fellow: ASHRAE (life; bd. dirs. 1982—85, assoc. editor HVAC&R Rsch. 1995—2001, Disting. Fellow award 1992), Am. Coll. Sports Medicine (editl. bd. 1979—85), Ergonomics Soc. (hon.); mem.: ASTM, IEEE (life; AEMB Coun. 1978—84), Assn. Mil. Surgeons U.S., Am. Physiol. Soc. (editl. bd. 1972—78), Framingham Amateur Radio Assn. (treas. 1970—84), Tarpon Cove Yacht and Racquet Club, Naples, Fla., Cape Cod Yacht Club, Falmouth, Mass. Jewish. Avocations: piano, gardening, duplicate bridge, tennis. Office: Comfort Tech 45 Foxhill Rd Framingham MA 01701-3761 E-mail: ralphgoldman@cs.com.

GOLDMAN, RALPH MORRIS, political science educator; b. Bklyn., May 14, 1920; s. Benjamin and Rose (Smotritski) G.; m. Joan Alicia Walsh, Oct. 20, 1953 (div. Feb. 1990); children: Peter Timothy, Marjorie Edythe; m. Barbara Elizabeth Alban, Mar. 24, 1990. BA, NYU, 1947; MA, U. Chgo., 1948, PhD, 1951. Rsch. assoc. Brookings Instn., Washington, 1953-56; asst. prof., then assoc. prof. Mich. State U., East Lansing, 1956-62; prof. San Francisco State U., 1962-86, prof. emeritus, 1987—, dir. Inst. for Rsch. on Internat. Behavior, 1964-67, dean faculty rsch., 1965-67, chmn. dept. polit. sci., 1971-74. Pres. Ctr. for Party Devel., Washington and Seattle, 1992-2003; dir. Congrl. Studies Program Cath. U., Washington, 1992-96; vis. prof. Am. U., Washington, 1955, 85, 90, U. Chgo., 1961-62, U. Calif., Berkeley, 1963, Stanford (Calif.) U., 1966, U. Calif., San Diego, 1979; cons. rsch. divsn. Dem. Nat. Com., Washington, 1952, 86; cons. Ednl. Testing Svc., Princeton, N.J., 1976-77, CEELI ABA, 1993-96; commentator on pub. affairs Voice of Am., Washington, 1985-86; sr. cons. Nat. Dem. Inst. for Internat. Affairs, Washington, 1986-89. Author: Contemporary Perspectives on Politics, 1972, Behavioral Perspectives on American Politics, 1973, Search for Consensus: The Story of the Democratic Party, 1979, Arms Control and Peacekeeping: Feeling Safe in This World, 1982, Dilemma and Destiny: The Democratic Party in America, 1986, The National Party Chairmen and Committees: Factionalism at the Top, 1990, From Warfare to Party Politics: The Critical Transition to Civilian Control, 1990, How to Build and Maintain a Democratic Party System, 1993, The United Nation in the Beginning: Conflict Processes, Colligation, Cases, 2001, The Future Catches Up: Selected Writings of Ralph M. Goldman, 4 vols., 2002, The Mentor and the Protege: The Story of Presidents Calles and Cardenas, 2003; co-author: The Politics of National Party Conventions, 1960, Political Science Concept Inventory, 1979, Building Trust: An Introduction to Peace Keeping and Arms Control, 1997; also contbr. chpts. to books and encys.; editor: Transnational Parties; Organizing the World's Precincts, 1983; co-editor: Presidential Nominating Politics in 1952, 1954, Promoting Democracy: Opportunities and Issues, 1988; contbg. editor: Encyclopedia of American Political Parties and Elections, 1991; mem. editorial com. Background jour., 1963-66; mem. editorial bd. Ctr. for Study of Armament and Disarmament, 1984—; founding editor Party Devels., 1993-99. Bd. dirs. Frederic Burk Found. for Edn., San Francisco, 1967-78, chmn. bd., 1968-71; coord. Peace Force Proposition Campaign, San Francisco, 1972-73. Capt. U.S. Army, 1946. Edward Hillman fellow U. Chgo., 1948-49, Social Sci. Rsch. Coun. fellow, 1949-50, Air Force Office of Sci. Rsch., 1958; grantee U.S. Office of Naval Rsch., 1968, NSF, 1968-69. Mem. Am. Polit. Sci. Assn. (life), Internat. Polit. Sci. Assn., Internat. Studies Assn., Assn. to Unite the Democracies (bd. dirs. 1989-95). Democrat. Avocation: ballroom dancing. Home: 6825 117th Ave NE Kirkland WA 98033-8451 E-mail: rmgoldman@aol.com.

GOLDMAN, RENITTA LIBRACH, special education educator, consultant; b. St. Louis, Aug. 15, 1938; d. Frank and Sally (Krantz) Librach; m. Jay Goldman, Dec. 20, 1959. BA, Washington U., St. Louis, 1960; MS, N.C. State U., 1967; PhD, U. Mo., 1978. Cert. tchr., Mo.; cert. sch. psychometrist, Mo., Ala. Tchr. English and social sci. University City (Mo.) Pub. Schs., 1960-61; substitute tchr. St. Louis County Schs., St.Louis, 1961-64; rsch. asst. N.C. State U., Raleigh, 1967-68; counselor Columbia (Mo.) Pub. Schs., 1968-85; adj. asst. prof. U. Mo., Columbia, 1978-85; prof. spl. edn. U. Ala., Birmingham, 1985—; cons. Birmingham, 1985—. Sr. scientist Injury Prevention Rsch. Ctr., U. Ala., Birmingham, 1990—; invited speaker local, state, nat. and internat. profl. meetings. Author: Silent Shame: The Sexual Abuse of Children, 1986; co-author: Issues and Trends in Education, 2002; sr. editor: Children at Risk, 1990; contbr. articles to profl. jours. Bd. dirs. Healthcare for Homeless, Birmingham, 1990—, Jefferson County Prevention of Child Abuse, 1986—; bd. dirs., officer Jewish Family Svc., Birmingham, 1988—. Grantee UAB Injury Prevention Ctr., 1987, UAB, 1990, U.S. Office of Edn., 1999, 2002. Mem. Ala. Council for Children with Behavior Disorders (pres. 1988-89), Coun. for Exceptional Children, Assn. Children with Learning Disabilities, Am. Assn. for Counseling Devel., U. Ala. Birmingham Faculty Women's Club, Phi Beta Kappa, Phi Kappa Phi, Phi Delta Kappa. Avocation: reading. Home: 4631 Pine Mountain Rd Birmingham AL 35213-1834 Office: U Ala 210A Edn Bldg Univ Sta Birmingham AL 35294

GOLDMAN, RICHARD PAUL, educational administrator; b. N.Y.C., Mar. 31, 1935; s. Edward and Dorothy (Myer) Goldman; m. Claire Elaine Taylor, Aug. 16, 1975; stepchildren: Lisa Backe, Nina Backe. BA magna cum laude, Yale U., 1956; MA, Middlebury Coll., 1965. Tchr., adminstr. Wilbraham (Mass.) Acad., 1959-72; asst. headmaster Germantown Friends Sch., Phila., 1972-92, interim head, 1992-93, assoc. head, 1993—2002. Cons. The Franklin Group, 1985-92. Editor: (book) Sportswriters' Choice, 1959, (mag.) Studies in Education, 1972—; author: Profession at Risk, 1988; contbr. articles to profl. jours. Trustee Wilbraham and Monson Acad. Mem. Council for Advancement and Support of Edn., Phi Beta Kappa. Clubs: Yale. Democrat. Jewish. Avocations: reading, travel, walking, theater. Home: 107 W Allens Ln Philadelphia PA 19119-4101

GOLDMAN, STANFORD MILTON, medical educator; b. Salt Lake City, Nov. 28, 1940; s. Osher and Miriam (Solomon) G.; m. Harriet Kaplow, Apr. 2, 1965; children: Etan, Nava. BA, BRE, Yeshiva U., 1961; MD, Einstein Coll. Medicine, 1965. Intern Jefferson U. Sch. Medicine, Phila., 1965-66; resident Einstein Coll. Medicine, Bronx, 1966-69; chmn. dept. radiology USPHS Phoenix Indian Med. Ctr., 1969-71; asst. prof. radiology Einstein Coll. Medicine, Bronx, 1971-72; from instr. to asst. prof. radiology Johns Hopkins U. Sch. Medicine, Balt., 1972-79; from asst. prof. to assoc. prof. U. Md., Balt., 1975-81; assoc. prof. Johns Hopkins U., 1979-86; clin. prof. Uniformed Svcs. U., Bethesda, Md., 1981-94; prof. radiology Johns Hopkins U., 1986-94, prof. urology, 1988-93; prof., chmn. radiology U. Tex. Med. Sch., Houston, 1993—2000, prof. urology, 1995—, prof. radiology, 1993—. Adj. prof. radiology and urology Baylor Coll. Medicine, Houston, 1994—; med. dir. radiol. sch. tech. Houston C.C., 1994, ultrasound sch. tech., 1999—; prof. radiology M.D. Anderson Cancer Ctr., Houston, 1995—. Editor: Computed Tomography of Kidneys & Adrenals, 1983, CT & MRI of the Genitourinary Tract, 1990, Tc E Rm Del Trattos Genito-Urinario, 1994; assoc. editor: Urologic Radiology, 1982-85, Radiology, 1986-94; cons. editor Urology, 1998—. Mem. Radiation Control Adv. Bd., Md., 1989—93. Lt. comdr. USPHS, 1969—71. Recipient Albert Einstein Disting. Alumni award, 1996. Mem.: AMA (CPT adv. bd. 1995—2000), Johns Hopkins Med. and Surg. Assn., Assn. Univ. Radiologists (rep. AMA CPT adv. bd. 1995—2000, ethics com. 1997, nominating com. 1997—98), European Soc. Urogenital Radiology, Houston Radiol. Soc. (treas. 2000—, pres.-elect 2001, pres. 2002, past pres. 2003, chmn. nominating com. 2003—), Houston Med. Soc., Tex. Radiol. Soc. (program com. 1994—96, chmn. long range planning com. 1996—97, bd. dirs. 1996—, fellowship nominating com. 1998—2000, 2d v.p. 2001, 1st v.p. 2002, chmn. program com. 2002—03, exec. com., pres.-elect 2003, chmn. legis. com.), Tex. Med. Soc., Soc. Uroradiology (bd. dirs. 1992—98, med. equipment com. 2000—01, ethics com.), Radiol. Soc. N.Am. (chmn. sci. exhibits awards com. 1988—90, chmn. program coms. subcom. on gu radiology 1996—99), Am. Urol. Assn. (hematuria guidelines panel 1998—99), Am. Soc. Emergency Medicine (bd. dirs. 1994—, indsl. com. 1994—, abstract com. 1995—97, chmn. audit com. 1995—99, chmn. sci. program com. 1996—97, fin. com. 1996—98, site com. 1996—98, vice chair program com. 1996—, ad hoc audit com. 1996—, sec. treas. 1998—2000, 2001, pres.-elect 2001—02, nominating com. 2002—, chair site selection com. 2002—, pres. 2002—, site selection com.), Am. Roentgen Ray Soc., Am. Coll. Radiology (alt.-counselor from Tex. 1995—96, counselor from Tex. 1996—2002, mem. com. on coding and nomenclature of commn. on econs. 1996—, nominating com. 1999, co-chmn. nominating comm. 2000—01, alt. counselor 2002—03), U.S.-Israel Bi-Nat. Sci. Found., Albert Einstein Alumni Assn. (bd. dirs. 1991—, Disting. Alumni award 1996), U. Md. Alumni Assn. (assoc.). Jewish. Avocations: swimming, music. Office: U Tex Med Sch Dept Radiology 6431 Fannin St Ste 2100 Houston TX 77030-1501

GOLDMAN, STANLEY IRWIN, lawyer; b. Richmond, Va., Sept. 19, 1939; s. Robert and Alice Dorothy (Feldman) G.; m. Patricia Mae Samuel, Apr. 8, 1962 (div. 1967); 1 child, Linda S.; m Carol G. Malamud, Aug. 4, 1991. BA, U. Va., 1962, LLB, 1965. Bar: Va. 1965, U.S. Dist. Ct. D.C. 1972, U.S. Ct. Appeals (D.C. cir.) 1972, U.S. Ct. Appeals (2d cir.) 1975, U.S. Ct. Appeals (8th cir.) 1981, U.S. Ct. Appeals (7th cir.) 1982, U.S. Supreme Ct. 1980. Atty. ICC, Washington, 1965-67; ptnr. Denning & Wohlstetter, Washington, 1967—. Mem. Va. State Bar Assn., D.C. Bar Assn., Transp. Lawyers Assn., Assn. Transp. Practitioners. Republican. Jewish. Home: 10009 Colebrook Ave Potomac MD 20854-1808 Office: Denning & Wohlstetter 1700 K St NW Washington DC 20006-3817

GOLDMAN, WILLIAM, writer, scriptwriter; b. Chgo., Aug. 12, 1931; s. M. Clarence and Marion (Well) Goldman; m. Ilene Jones, Apr. 15, 1961; children: Jenny, Susanna. BA, Oberlin Coll., 1952; MA, Columbia U., 1956. Author: (novels) The Temple of Gold, 1957, Your Turn to Curtsy, My Turn to Bow, 1958, Soldier in the Rain, 1960, Boys and Girls Together, 1964, No Way to Treat a Lady, 1964, The Thing of It Is, 1967, Father's Day, 1971, The Princess Bride, 1973, Marathon Man, 1974, Wigger, 1974, Magic, 1976, Tinsel, 1979, Control, 1982, The Silent Gondoliers, 1983, The Color of Light, 1984, Heat, 1985, Brothers, 1987, (non-fiction) The Season: A Candid Look at Broadway, 1969, Adventures in the Screen Trade, 1983; author: (with Mike Lupica) Wait Until Next year, 1988, Hype and Glory, 1990, Four Screenplays, 1995, Five Screenplays, 1997, Which Lie Did I Tell, 2000; author: (essays) The Big Picture, 1999; author: (with James Goldman) (plays) Blood Sweat and Stanley Poole, 1961; author: (with James Goldman and John Kander) (musical) A Family Affair, 1962; author: (films) Masquerade, 1965, Harper, 1966, Butch Cassidy and the Sundance Kid, 1969 (Acad. award Best Original Screenplay, 1970), The Hot Rock, 1972, The Stepford Wives, 1974, The Great Waldo Pepper, 1975, Marathon Man, 1976, All the President's Men, 1976 (Acad. award Best Screenplay Adaptation, 1977), A Bridge Too Far, 1977, Magic, 1978, The Princess Bride, 1987, Heat, 1987, Misery, 1990, The Year of the Comet, 1992, Memoirs of an Invisible Man, 1992, Chaplin, 1992, Maverick, 1994, Ghost and the Darkness, 1996, Absolute Power, 1997, Hearts in Atlantis, 2001, Dreamcatcher, 2003. Recipient Laurel award for Lifetime Achievement in Screenwriting, 1983. Office: c/o William Morris 151 El Courino Dr Beverly Hills CA 90212-1804

GOLDMAN, WILLIAM SCOTT, lawyer; b. Far Rockaway, N.Y., July 31, 1966; s. Elliot and Karen G.; m. Catharine Hamerling BA, Oberlin Coll., 1988; JD, Dickinson Sch. Law, 1991; LLM, George Washington U., 1993. Bar: Pa., U.S. Ct. Appeals (fed. cir.), Ct. Internat. Trade. Mng. atty. Litman Law Offices, Ltd., Arlington, Va., 1992—. Contbr. articles to profl. jours. Mem. ABA, Am. Intellectual Property Law Assn., Fed. Circuit Bar Assn. Jewish. Avocations: sports, music, reading. Office: Litman Law Offices Ltd 3717 Columbia Pike Arlington VA 22204-4255 E-mail: litman@4patent.com.

GOLDMANN, JAMES ALLEN, healthcare consultant; b. Milw., Feb. 26, 1952; s. Allen Abraham and Ruth Lois (Kolbur) G.; m. Pamela Anne McCole, June 6, 1980; children: Michael, Elissa, Kerry. AB, Harvard Coll., 1974; MHA, Washington U., St. Louis, 1979. V.p. Riverside Meth. Hosp., Columbus, Ohio, 1980—85; COO Children's Med. Ctr., Dallas, 1986—92; cons. APM, Inc., N.Y.C., 1993—96; ptnr. Arthur Andersen, Dallas, 1996—2000, IBM, Dallas, 2001—. Bd. dirs. Hope Cottage, Dallas, 1989-93; scout leader Boy Scouts Am., Columbus and Grapevine, Tex., 1980-84, 92, 93. Fellow Am. Coll. Healthcare Execs. Office: 1507 Lyndon B Johnson Fwy Dallas TX 75234-6032 E-mail: goldmanj@us.ibm.com.

GOLDMANN, MORTON AARON, cardiologist, educator; b. Chgo., July 11, 1924; s. Harry Ascher and Frieda (Cohon) G.; m. Doris-Jane Tumpeer, July 18, 1951; children: Deborah, Jory, Erica, Leslie BS, U. Ill., 1943, MD, 1946. Diplomate Am. Bd. Internal Medicine. Intern Cook County Hosp., Chgo., 1946-47, resident physician, 1949-52, practice medicine specializing in internal medicine and cardiology Skokie, Ill., 1952—2003, trustee emeritus, 2003—; chief of medicine Rush North Shore Med. Ctr. (formerly Skokie Valley Hosp.), 1964-65, also trustee, 1968—2002, trustee emeritus, 2002—, pres. med. staff, 1968-69, attending physician, med. dir. heart sta. and cardiac rehab. unit, 1973-96, bd. dirs., 1970—; former attending physician Ill. Rsch. Hosp.; former assoc. prof. Abraham Lincoln Sch. Medicine, U. Ill., Chgo.; prof. Cook County Grad. Sch. Medicine. Pres. Heart Assn. North Cook County, 1978-81, North Suburban Assn. Health Resources, 1974-77 Contbr. numerous articles to profl. jours. Capt. M.C., AUS, 1947-49, PTO Fellow ACP, Inst. Medicine Chgo., Am. Coll. Cardiology; mem. AMA, Am. Soc. Internal Medicine, Am. Heart Assn., Ill. Med. Soc., Chgo. Med. Soc., Chgo. Heart Assn. (bd. govs., bd. dirs. 1978-87, bd. trustees 1979-83). Office: 636 Echo Ln Glenview IL 60025-5402

GOLDMAN-RAKIC, PATRICIA SHOER, neuroscience educator; b. Salem, Mass., Apr. 22, 1937; AB cum laude, Vassar Coll., 1959; PhD, UCLA, 1963; AM (hon.), Yale U., 1979. USPHS predoctoral fellow dept. psychology UCLA, 1961—63, USPhS postdoctoral fellow dept. psychiatry, 1963—64; rsch. assoc. dept. animal behavior Am. Mus. Natural History, N.Y.C., 1964—65; staff fellow sect. neuropsychology NIMH, Bethesda, Md., 1965—68, rsch. physiologist Lab. Neuropsychology, 1968—78, chief sect. devel. neurobiology, 1978—79; prof. neurosci. sect. neurobiology Yale U. Sch. Medicine, New Haven, 1979—2003, joint appointment dept. psychology, 1991—96, dir. grad. studies sect. neuroanatomy, 1981—86, acting chmn. sect. neurobiology, 1986—87. USPHS postdoctoral trainee dept. psychiatry NYU, N.Y.C., 1964—65; vis. scientist MIT, Cambridge, 1974—75; Edward Sacher lectr. Columbia U., 1992; Herbert Birch meml. lectr. Internat. Neuropsychobiology Soc., 1981; Plenary lectr. Union Swiss Socs. for Exptl. Biology, 1983; Sigma Xi lectr. Brown U., 1984, SUNY Downstate Med. Sch., Bklyn., 1988; Kendon Smith meml. lectr. U. N.C., 1985, Hal Robinson disting. lectr., 92; Bernard Sachs meml. lectr. Child Neurology Soc., Memphis, 1985; Frontiers of Sci. lectr. Am. Psychiat. Assn., 1988; Sally Harrington Goldwater lectr. Barrow Neurol. Inst., Phoenix, 1990; 4th Hillarp lectr. European Neurosci. Soc., 1990; Rushton lectr. Fla. State U., 1990; Lanier lectr. U. Ill., 1991; Jock Cleghorn meml. lectr. McMaster U., 1994; mem. sci. adv. bd. Ency. Neurosci., from 1994; mem. Nat. Adv. Mental Health Coun., from 1993, numerous others; participant sems., confs., symposia and workshops throughout the world. Editor-in-chief: Cerebral Cortex, mem. adv. bd. : Advances in Neurosci., Behavioral Brain Rsch., Behavioral Neurosci., Brain Rsch., Brain Rsch. Bull., Concepts in Neurosci., Devel. Brain Rsch., Devel. Neuropsychology, Devel. Psychobiology, Exptl. Neurology, Jour. Neurosci., Progress in Brain Rsch., Trends in Neurosci., Sci., Critical Revs. in Neurobiology, Biol. Psychiatry, Neuropsychopharmacology, Jour. Comparative and Physiol. Psychology. Recipient Lieber award, Nat. Alliance for Rsch. on Schizophrenia and Depression, 1991, award, Robert T. and Claire Pasarow Found., 1993, prize in neurosci., Fyssen Found., Paris, 1990, Alden Spencer award, Columbia U., 1982, Karl Spencer Lashley prize, Am. Philos. Soc., 1996; grantee NIMH, 1980—2000. Fellow: APA (Disting. Sci. Contbn. award 1991), AAAS (John P. McGovern award 1993), N.Y. Acad. Scis., Am. Psychopath. Assn.; mem.: NAS, Inst. Medicine, Am. Acad. Arts and Scis., Internat. Brain Rsch. Orgn., Internat. Neuropsychology Symposium, Am. Anat. Assn. (Krieg Cortical Discoverer award Cajal Club 1989), Internat. Soc. for Devel. Psychobiology, Soc. for Neurosci. (councilor 1984—88, Young Investigator Award selection com. 1985—87, pres. 1989—90). Home: New Haven, Conn. Died July 31, 2003.

GOLDMARK, PETER CARL, JR., publishing executive; b. N.Y.C., Dec. 2, 1940; s. Peter Carl and Frances Charlotte (Trainer) G.; Aliette Marie Misson, Nov. 7, 1964; children: Lara, Karin, Sandra. BA in Govt., Harvard Coll., 1962. Tchr. history Putney (Vt.) Sch., 1962-64; program analyst, then asst. to dep. dir. OEO, Washington, 1965-66; exec. asst. to dir. budget of N.Y.C., 1966-67; acting chief program planning unit, 1966-68; asst. dir. N.Y.C budget, 1968-70; exec. asst. to N.Y.C. mayor, 1970; sec. human svcs. Commonwealth of Mass., 1971-74; dir. budget State of N.Y., Albany, 1975-77; exec. dir. Port Authority of N.Y. & N.J., 1977-85; sr. v.p. Times Mirror Co., 1985-88; pres. Rockefeller Found., N.Y.C., 1988-97; chmn., CEO, Internat. Herald Tribune, Paris, 1998—2003. Dir. Knight-Ridder Co., 1991-98, Fin. Acctg. Found., 1998—, Lend Lease, 1999—, Whitehead Inst., 1999—. Overseer Harvard U., 1984-90. With USAR, 1965-70. Office: Internat Herald Tribune 6 bis rue des Graviers 92521 Neuilly Cedex France

GOLDMARK, PETER FRANCIS, banker; b. Budapest, Hungary, Nov. 27, 1946; came to U.S., 1964; s. Francis Martin Goldmark and Eva Magdolna (Balla) Sander; m. Cassandra K. Masson; children: Alexander, Nicolas. BS, Fairleigh Dickinson U., 1968; MBA, Columbia U., 1970. Asst. treas. Am. Express Bank, N.Y.C., 1970-74; dir. Coun. of the Ams., N.Y.C., 1974-76; group mgr. N.Y. Times, N.Y.C., 1976-82; v.p. Chase Manhattan Bank, N.Y.C., 1982-91; rep. Union Bancaire Privee, N.Y.C., 1991-95; exec. v.p. Inter-Nation Capital Mgmt. Corp., N.Y.C., 1997—; pres. Rockport Internat. Cons., N.Y.C., 1995—. Chmn., pres. The Ams. Found., N.Y.C., 1993—. Mem. Ams. Soc., Columbia U. Bus. Sch. Counseling Bd., Colombian-Am. Assn., N.Am. Chilean C. of C., Argentine-Am. Assn., European-Am. Assn., Venezuelan-Am. Assn. (dir., asst. treas. 1991—), Bolivarian Soc. U.S. (dir. 1992—). Democrat. Avocations: skiing, tennis, scuba diving. Office: 230 Park Ave Rm 2600 New York NY 10169-9415

GOLDNER, JOHN DARROL, retired pharmacist; b. Mpls., Aug. 13, 1927; s. thor H. and Laura B. (Allen) G.; m. Lois Jean Gustafson, Mar. 23, 1952; children: Alan P., David J. BS in Pharmacy, U. Minn., 1952. Registered pharmacist, Minn. Pharmacist Judges Pharmacy, Mpls., 1953-59, Doctor's Bldg. Pharmacy, Mpls., 1959-64, Hennepin County Med. Ctr., Mpls., 1964-67, asst. dir. pharmacy, 1967-70, dir. pharmacy, 1970-87; pharmacist Pilot City Health Ctr., Mpls., 1987-94; ret. Clin. asst. prof. Coll. Pharmacy, U. Minn., Mpls., 1981-87; adv. com. pharmacy tech. tng. 916 Area Vo-Tech Inst., White Bear Lake, Minn., 1980-87. Contbr. articles to profl. jours. With USN, 1945-47. Mem. Minn. Pharm. Assn. (bd. dirs.), Am. Pharm. Assn., Am. Soc. Hosp. Pharmacists, Minn. Soc. Hosp. Pharmacists (Hallie Bruce Meml. Lecture award 1981), Ctrl. Minn. Soc. Hosp. Pharmacists (pres. 1974-75). Avocations: model railroading, photography. Home: 2800 Townview Ave NE Minneapolis MN 55418-2475

GOLDNER, LEONARD HOWARD, lawyer; b. N.Y.C., June 18, 1947; s. Adolph and Florence (Cohen) G.; m. Jacqueline Slotnik, Apr. 1, 1969; children: Claudia Mara, Benjamin Micah. BA, U. Wis., 1969; JD, Harvard U., 1972. Bar: N.Y. 1974, U.S. Dist. Ct. (so. dist.) N.Y. 1974, U.S. Ct. Appeals (2d cir.) 1975. Law clk. U.S. Ct. Appeals (9th cir.) Honolulu, 1972-73; assoc. Simpson Thacher & Bartlett, N.Y.C., 1973-76, Shereff, Friedman, Hoffman & Goodman, N.Y.C., 1976-79, ptnr., 1979-90; sen. v.p., gen. counsel Symbol Techs., Inc., Holtsville, N.Y., 1990-2001, exec. v.p., gen. counsel, 2001—03. Trustee Soc. for Advancement of Judaism, N.Y.C., 1974-85; chmn. West End Synagogue, N.Y.C., 1985-87. Trustee West End Synagogue, N.Y.C., 1985-90, Reconstructionist Rabbinical Coll., Phila., 1988-2002, bd. govs. E-mail: goldner@symbol.com.

GOLDNER, SHELDON HERBERT, export-import company executive; b. Bklyn., Aug. 3, 1928; s. David and Esther (Maskowsky) G.; m. Lila Diane Silber, Aug. 14, 1954; children: Jonathan Shepard, Jeffrey Scott, Barbara Jill. BS in acctg., L.I. U., 1950. C.P.A., N.Y. Acct. S.H. Goldner & Co., N.Y.C., 1950-59; v.p. fin. Connell Rice & Sugar Co., Inc., Westfield, N.J., 1959-89, ret., 1989. Pres., trustee Temple Israel, Union, N.J. Served with U.S. Army Signal Corps, 1946-47, PTO. Mem. AICPA, N.Y. State Soc. CPAs, Halloween Yacht Club (Stamford, Conn.), Royal Veere (Netherlands) Yacht Club, Dartmouth Yacht Club (Devon, Eng.), Miles River Yacht Club (St. Michaels, Md.).

GOLDOFF, ANNA CARLSON, public administration educator; m. Barry Goldoff, June 2, 1968; children: David, William, Jacqueline. BA, Hunter Coll., 1969; PhD, CUNY, 1974. Asst. prof. pub. adminstrn. John Jay Coll. Criminal Justice, N.Y.C., 1974-80, assoc. prof. pub. adminstrn., 1980—. Mem. editl. bd. Public Adminstrn. & Mgmt.; an Interactive Jour., Internat. Jour. of Orgn. Theory & Behavior. Author, editor: The Essence of Decision Redux Crisis Decision Making, 1999; contbg. editor: Ency. Pub. Adminstrn., 1999—2002. Bd. dirs. St. Christopher's, Inc., N.Y.C., 1997—; elder Rye (N.Y.) Presbyn. Ch., 1994-97; trustee Rye (N.Y.) Presbyn. Ch., 2001-03. Mem.: Women's Coalition, Am. Soc. Pub. Adminstrn., Am. Polit. Sci. Assn. Democrat. Avocations: reading, swimming, walking.

GOLDREICH, PETER MARTIN, astrophysics and planetary physics educator; b. N.Y.C., July 14, 1939; s. Paul and Edith (Rosenfield) Goldreich; m. Susan Kroll, June 14, 1960; children: Eric, Daniel. BS in Physics, Cornell U., 1960, PhD in Physics, 1963. Instr. Cornell U., summers, 1961—63; post-doctoral fellow Cambridge U., 1963—64; asst. prof. astronomy and geophysics UCLA, 1964—66, assoc. prof., 1966; assoc. prof. planetary sci. and astronomy Calif. Inst. Tech., 1966—69, prof. planetary sci. and astronomy, 1969—, Lee DuBridge prof. astrophysics and planetary physics, 1981—. Named Calif. Scientist of Yr., 1981; recipient Chapman medal, Royal Astron. Soc., 1985, Gold medal, 1990, Nat. medal of Sci., 1995; fellow Woodrow Wilson hon., 1960—61, NSF, 1961—63, Sloan Found., 1968—70. Fellow: NAS, Am. Acad. Arts and Scis.; mem.: Am. Astron. Soc. (Henry Norris Russell lectr., Dick Brouwer award 1986, George P. Kuiper prize divsn. planetary sci. 1992). Office: Calif Inst Tech Msc 150-21 1200 E California Blvd Pasadena CA 91125-0001

GOLDRICH, STANLEY GILBERT, optometrist; b. N.Y.C., Sept. 22, 1937; s. Joseph and Doris (Stelzner) G. BA, Queens Coll., 1959, MA, 1965; PhD, CUNY, 1966; OD, Mass. Coll. Optometry, 1974. Lic. optometrist, N.Y., Calif. Rsch. assoc. U. Wis. Primate Ctr., Madison, 1965-67; asst. prof. Ohio State U., Columbus, 1967-72; assoc. clin. prof. SUNY Coll. Optometry, N.Y.C., 1974—. Cons. in field. Contbr. articles to profl. jours.; inventor in field. With USAR, 1960-65. NSF grantee, 1967. Fellow Am. Acad. Optometry; mem. Am. Psychol. Assn., Am. Optometric Assn., N.Y. State Optometric Assn. Jewish. Avocation: piano. Office: SUNY 33 W 42nd St New York NY 10036-8003 E-mail: sgoldrich@sunyopt.edu.

GOLDRING, NORMAN MAX, advertising executive; b. Chgo., June 22, 1937; s. Jack and Carolyn (Wolf) G.; m. Cynthia Lois Garland, Dec. 20, 1959; children: Jay Marshall, Diane. BS in Bus., Miami (Ohio) U., 1959; MBA, U. Chgo., 1963. Advt. account mgr. Edward H. Weiss & Co., Chgo., 1959-61; sr. v.p., dir. mktg. svcs. Stern, Walters & Simmons, Inc., Chgo., 1961-68; chmn. Goldring & Co., Inc., Chgo., 1968-89; pres., CEO CPM, Inc., 1969-93, chmn., 1994-99; pres. CPO Inc., 1994—. Dir. Creative Works, Inc., 1994-97; instr. mktg. and advt. mgmt. Roosevelt U., 1965-68. Mem. editl. bd. Jour. Media Planning; mem. editl. bd. advisors Response Mag., 2001—. Commr. Ridgeville Park Dist., Evanston, Ill., 1971-75, pres. 1974-75; bd. dirs., v.p. Mus. Broadcast Comm., 1983-92; bd. dirs. Chgo. Chamber Musicians 1988—, Chgo. Metro History Fair, 1990; bd. dirs. Lake Forest Grad. Sch. Mgmt., 2000—, mem. exec. com., 2002—; trustee Chgo. Assn. Dirs. Mktg. Ednl. Found., 2001—. Mem. Am. Mktg. Assn. (speaker), Advt. Coun. Inc. (Midwest adv. bd. 1983-90), Am. Mgmt. Assn., Direct Mktg. Assn. (mem. chmn., broadcast coun.), Chgo. Assn. Dirs. Mktg., Elec. Ret. Assn. Home: 855 Beverly Pl Lake Forest IL 60045-3901 Office: CPO Inc # 16 233 N Michigan Ave Chicago IL 60601-5519 E-mail: ngoldring@cpodirect.com.

GOLDSBOROUGH, ROBERT GERALD, publishing executive, author; b. Chgo., Oct. 3, 1937; s. Robert Vincent and Wilma (Janak) G.; m. Janet Elizabeth Moore, Jan. 15, 1966; children: Suzanne Joy, Robert Michael, Colleen Marie, Bonnie Laura. BS, Northwestern U., 1959, MS with honors, 1960. Reporter A.P., 1959, City News Bur., Chgo., 1959; with Chgo. Tribune, 1960-82, reporter neighborhood news sect., asst. editor Sunday mag. and TV sect., 1963-66, editor TV Week mag., 1966-67, asst. to features editor, 1967-71, asst. to editor, 1971-72, Sunday editor, 1972-75, editor Sunday mag., 1975-82; exec. editor Advt. Age Mag., Chgo., 1982-88, spl. projects dir., 1988-91; corp. projects editor Crain Communications, Chgo., 1991-96, spl. projects dir., 1997—. Author: Great Railroad Paintings, 1976, The Crain Adventure, 1992, Nero Wolfe Mysteries: Murder in E-Minor, 1986, Death on Deadline, 1987, The Bloodied Ivy, 1988, The Last Coincidence, 1989, Fade to Black, 1990, Silver Spire, 1992, The Missing Chapter, 1994, The Year Diz Came to Town, 2003. Served with AUS, 1961. Recipient Northwestern U. Alumni Svc. award, 2001. Mem. Arts Club. Presbyterian. Office: 360 N Michigan Ave Chicago IL 60601 E-mail: rgoldsborough@crain.com.

GOLDSCHEIN, STEVEN M. computer retail executive; BA, Mich. State U., 1968. CPA NY. Sr. audit mgr. Ernst & Young, N.Y.C.; corp. contr. Lambda Electronics Inc., Melville, N.Y., 1980, v.p. adminstrn., CFO; sr. v.p., CFO Systemax, Inc. (formerly Global DirectMail Corp.), Port Washington, N.Y., 1998—. Office: Systemax Inc 11 Harbor Park Dr Port Washington NY 11050

GOLDSCHMID, HARVEY JEROME, law educator; b. N.Y.C., May 6, 1940; s. Bernard and Rose (Braiker) G.; m. Mary Tait Seibert, Dec. 22, 1973; children: Charles Maxwell, Paul MacNeil, Joseph Tait. AB, Columbia U., 1962, JD, 1965. Bar: N.Y. 1965, U.S. Supreme Ct. 1970. Law clk. to judge 2d Circuit Ct. Appeals, N.Y.C., 1965-66; assoc. firm Debevoise & Plimpton, N.Y.C., 1966-70; asst. prof. law Columbia U., 1970-71, assoc. prof., 1971-73, prof., 1973-84, Dwight prof. law, 1984—, founding dir. Ctr. for Law and Econ. Studies, 1975-78; gen. counsel SEC, 1998-99, adv. to chmn., 2000, commr., 2002—; of counsel Weil, Gotshal & Manges, N.Y.C., 2000—02. Cons. in field to pub. and pvt. orgns.; mem. planning and program com. 2d Cir. Jud. Conf., 1982-85; reporter 2d Cir. Jud. Conf. Evaluation Com., 1980-82, 88-89; mem. legal adv. com. N.Y.S.E., 1997-98, chmn. subcom. on corp. governance. Author(with others) Cases and Materials on Trade Regulation, 1975, 4th edit., 1997; editor: (with others) Industrial Concentration: The New Learning, 1974, Business Disclosure: Government's Need to Know, 1979, The Impact of the Modern Corporation, 1984. Chmn. bd. advisors program on philanthropy and the law NYU Sch. Law, 1992-94; bd. dirs. Nat. Ctr. on Philanthropy and the Law, 1996—; nat. coun. Washington U. Sch. of Law, 1999—; bd. dirs. Greenwall Found., 1996—, vice chair, 1999-2002. Fellow Am. Bar Found.; mem. ABA (task force on lawyers polit. contbrns. 1997-98), Am. Law Inst. (reporter part IV, duty of care and the bus. judgment rule, corp. governance project 1980-93), N.Y. State Bar Assn., Assn. Bar City N.Y. (v.p. 1985-86, chmn. exec. com. 1984-85, chmn. com. on antitrust and trade regulation 1971-74, com. on the 2d century, chmn. com. on securities regulation 1992-95, chmn. audit com. 1988-96, chmn. com. on corp. takeover legislation 1985-86, 88-92, treas., mem. exec. com. 1996-98, chmn. nominating com. 2000-01), Assn. Am. Law Schs. (chmn. sect. antitrust and econ. regulation 1976-78), Am. Assn. Internat. Commn. Jurists (sec.-treas., bd. dirs. 1969-2002), Century Assn., Riverdale Yacht Club (bd. dirs. 1987-90), Phi Beta Kappa. Office: US SEC 450 Fifth St NW Washington DC 20549 E-mail: goldschmidh@sec.gov.

GOLDSCHMIDT, ARTHUR EDUARD, JR., history educator, author; b. Washington, Mar. 17, 1938; s. Arthur Eduard and Elizabeth (Wickenden) G.; m. Louise Robb, June 17, 1961; children: Stephen Robb, Paul William. AB, Colby Coll., Waterville, Maine, 1959; AM, Harvard U., 1961, PhD, 1968. Asst. prof. history Pa. State U., University Park, 1965-73, assoc. prof., 1974-89, prof. Middle East History, 1989-2000, prof. emeritus, 2000—. Vis. assoc. prof. middle east history Haifa U., Israel, 1973-74; vis. prof. Semester at Sea, 1987, 2001, vis. rsch. fellow Durham U., 1989, 90; acad. dean N.J. Scholars, Lawrenceville, 1985. Author: Concise History of the Middle East, 1979, 7th edit., 2002, Modern Egypt, 1988, The Memoirs and Diaries of Muhammad Farid: An Egyptian Nationalist Leader (1868-1919), 1992, Historical Dictionary of Egypt, 3d edit., 2003, Biographical Dictionary of Modern Egypt, 2000; contbr. AHA Guide to Historical Literature, 3d edit., 1995, American National Biography, 1999, Understanding the Contemporary Middle East, 2000; cons., contbr. The Encyclopedia of the Modern Middle East, 1996, Encarta On-Line Encyclopedia, 2000; editor: Articles on the Middle East, 1947-71, 1980. Trustee Unitarian-Universalist Fellowship, State College, 1977-80, 85-87, 2000—. Recipient AMOCO Tchg. award Pa. State U., 1981, Mentoring award Mid. East Studies Assn., 2000; Fulbright rsch. fellow, 1981-82; faculty fellow Am. Rsch. Ctr. Egypt, 1998. Mem. Middle East Studies Assn., Am. Rsch. Ctr. Egypt (bd. govs. 1989-92), Am. Hist. Assn., Ctrl. Pa. Torch Club (pres. 1993), Voice of Ctrl. Pa. (founding pres. 1993-97). Democrat. Avocations: cooking, reading. Home: 1173 Oneida St State College PA 16801-5938 E-mail: axg2@psu.edu.

GOLDSCHMIDT, CHARLES, advertising agency executive; b. N.Y.C., June 15, 1921; s. Harry and Adele (Safir) G.; m. Patricia Nevins, Jan. 17, 1951; children: Richard Walter, Jane, Peter. BA, NYU, 1941. Advt. copywriter Warner Bros. Pictures Co., 1946-48, Buchanan & Co., N.Y.C., 1948-49, Ray Austrian Assocs., N.Y.C., 1949-52; founder, ptnr. Daniel & Charles Inc., N.Y.C., 1952; chmn. bd. dirs. LCF&L, Inc., 1980—. Author fiction, play, articles. Served to lt. USNR, 1941-46. Mem. Beach Point Club (Mamaroneck, N.Y.), Phoenix Country Club. Democrat. Home: 710 The Cres Mamaroneck NY 10543-4531 Office: LCF&L Inc 260 Madison Ave New York NY 10016-2401

GOLDSCHMIDT, LYNN HARVEY, lawyer; b. Chgo., June 14, 1951; d. Arthur and Ida (Shirman) H.; m. Robert Allen Goldschmidt, Aug. 27, 1972; children: Elizabeth Anne, Carolyn Helene. BS with honors, U. Ill., 1973; JD magna cum laude, Northwestern U., 1976. Bar: Ill. 1976. Ptnr. Hopkins & Sutter, Chgo., 1976-2001, Foley & Lardner, Chgo., 2001—02; prin. D and G Cons. Group, 2002—. Articles editor Northwestern U. Law Rev. Mem. Airport Coun. Internat., N. Am., Order of Coif. Office: D&G Cons Grp 120 S LaSalle St Chicago IL 60603 E-mail: lhg@dg-cg.com.

GOLDSCHMIDT, PETER GRAHAM, physician executive, business development consultant; b. Cardiff, Wales, Feb. 18, 1945; came to U.S., 1970; s. Heinz Joachim Siefried and Marjorie (Sweet) G. DMS, U. Westminster, 1968; MB, BS, U. London, 1970; MPH, Johns Hopkins U., 1971, DPH, 1980. Rsch. assoc. Johns Hopkins U. Sch. Hygiene and Pub. Health, Balt., 1972-75; v.p., dir. Policy Rsch. Inc., Balt., 1974-81; dir. health svcs. R&D svc. VA, Washington, 1981-86; v.p., dir. Quality Standards in Medicine, Inc., Boston, 1986-90; pres. World Devel. Group, Inc., Bethesda, Md., 1986—. Bd. dirs. Quality Standards in Medicine, Inc., Boston, 1986-96; pres. Health Improvement Inst., Bethesda, 1991—, Med. Care Mgmt. Corp., Bethesda, 1992—, CGO, MCMC LLC, Bethesda, 2002—. Author: Quality Management in Health Care, 1995; contbr. numerous articles to profl. jours. Bd. dirs. Policy Rsch. Inst., Balt., 1978-87. Recipient various grants. Mem. AMA, APHA, Balt.-Washington Venture Group. Office: MCMC LLC 5272 River Rd Ste 650 Bethesda MD 20816-1448 E-mail: pgg@has.com.

GOLDSCHMIDT, ROBERT ALPHONSE, financial executive; b. Cin., July 3, 1937; s. Alphonse Francis and Lillian Mary (Ashbrock) G.; m. Karen Ann Koehnemann, June 10, 1961; children: Diane, Kristine, Linda, Mark, Erik. BA, U. Notre Dame, 1959, BSME, 1960; MS in Indsl. Mgmt., Purdue U., 1961. CPA; registered profl indsl. engr. Mgmt. cons. Touche Ross & Co., N.Y.C., 1961-66; mgr. planning and control Litton Med. Group, Des Plaines, Ill., 1966-68; v.p. fin. Bell TV, N.Y.C., 1968-70; pres., chief exec. officer Living Industries, Farmingdale, N.Y., 1971-72; asst. to pres. Gen. Instrument Corp., N.Y.C., 1972-73; v.p. ops. Jackson Communications, Dayton, Ohio, 1973-74; v.p., chief fin. officer Esterline Corp., Darien, Conn., 1974-87; v.p. fin. controls The Dyson-Kissner-Moran Corp., N.Y.C., 1987-93; CFO The Archdiocese of New York, 1994—2002. Treas. YMCA, Tarrytown, N.Y., 1980-82. Mem.: Sleepy Hollow Country (Scarborough, N.Y.) (treas. 1982-84). Republican. Roman Catholic. Home: 226 River Rd Briarcliff Manor NY 10510-2414

GOLDSCHMIDT, WALTER ROCHS, anthropologist, educator; b. San Antonio, Feb. 24, 1913; s. Hermann and Gretchen (Rochs) G.; m. Beatrice Lucia Gale, May 27, 1937 (dec.); children: Karl Gale, Mark Stefan. BA, U. Tex., 1933, MA, 1935; PhD, U. Calif. at Berkeley, 1942. Social scientist Bur. Agrl. Econs., 1940-46; mem. faculty UCLA, 1946—, prof. anthropology, 1956—, chmn. dept., 1964-69, prof. anthropology and psychiatry, 1970-83, prof. emeritus, 1983—. Vis. lectr. Stanford, summer 1945, U. Calif. at Berkeley, 1949, Harvard, 1950 Dir. radio program: Ways of Mankind, 1951-53, Culture and Ecology in E. Africa, 1960-68. Spl. editor: World of Man Series, Aldine Pub. Co., 1966-75. Author: Small Business and the Community, 1946, As You Sow, 1947, 2d edit., 1978, Nomlaki Ethnography, 1951, Ways to Justice, 1953, Man's Way, 1959, Exploring the Ways of Mankind, 1960, 3d edit., 1977, Comparative Functionalism, 1966, Sebei Law, 1967, Kambuya's Cattle, The Legacy of an African Herdsman, 1968, On Being an Anthropologist, 1970, Culture and Behavior of the Sebei, 1976, The Sebei: A Study in Cultural Adaptation, 1986; The Human Career: The Self in The Symbolic World, 1990; co-author: Haa Aaní, Our Land: Tlingit and Haida Land Rights and Use, 1998; editor: The U.S. and Africa, rev, 1963, French edit., 1965, The Anthropology of Franz Boas, 1959, (with H. Hoijer) The Social Anthropology of Latin America, 1970, The Uses of Anthropology, 1979, Anthropology and Public Policy: A Dialogue, 1986, Am. Anthropologist, 1956-59; founding editor: Ethos, 1972-79. Fulbright scholar U.K., 1953; grantee Social Sci. Rsch. Coun., 1953; grantee Wenner-Gren. Found., 1953; NSF postdoctoral fellow, 1964-65; fellow Center Advanced Study Behavioral Scis., 1964-65; sr. sci. fellow NIMH, 1970-75; disting. lectr. U. Indonesia, 1993. Fellow Am. Anthrop. Assn. (pres. 1975-76, Dist. Svc. award 1994), African Studies Assn. (founding, bd. dirs. 1957-60); mem. Southwestern Anthrop. Assn. (pres. 1950-51), Am. Ethnol. Soc. (pres. 1969-70), Phi Beta Kappa, Sigma Xi. Home: 978 N Norman Pl Los Angeles CA 90049-1535 E-mail: walterg@ucla.edu.

GOLDSCHMIDT, YADIN Y, science educator; b. Kfar-Saba, Israel, Aug. 25, 1949; s. Zvi and Zipora Goldschmidt; m. Lidush Youssefi, Aug. 4, 1975; children: Tirtza Giles (Goldschmidt), Ariel, Margalit Zipora. Ph. D., Hebrew U. of Jerusalem, Jerusalem, Israel, 1976—78; M.Sc., Weizmann Inst. of Sci., Rehovot, Israel, 1974—76; B.Sc., Hebrew U. of Jerusalem, Jerusalem, Israel, 1970—73. Prof. of physics U. of Pitts., Pittsburgh, Pa., 1992—, assoc. prof., 1986—92, asst. prof., 1982—86; asst. prof. (rsch.) Brown U., Providence, 1982—83, rsch. assoc., 1980—82; vis. scientist CEA- Saclay, Paris, France (incl. Monaco), 1978—80. Contbr. more than 70 articles to sci. jours. 1st sgt. Israeli Defence Force, 1967—70, Israel. Fellow Michael Vis. Professorship, Weizmann Inst. of Sci., 1996, Meyerhoff Vis. Professorship, 2000; grantee Reaserch in Materials Theory, NSF, 1983-1994, Rsch. in Materials Sci., US Dept. of Energy (DOE), 1997-present. Mem.: Am. Phys. Soc. Achievements include research in the physics of phase transitions. Avocations: reading, computers. Office: University of Pittsburgh Dept Physics & Astronomy Pittsburgh PA 15260 Office Fax: 412-624-9163. E-mail: yadin@pitt.edu.

GOLDSMITH, AARON CLAIR, retired federal government executive, dean; b. Kalamazoo, July 4, 1946; s. Richard Samuel and Vivian Jean (Davis) G.; m. Wilma June Long, July 19, 1969; children: Philip, Kristin, Karen. BA, Bob Jones U., Greenville, S.C., 1969; MBA, Embry-Riddle Aero. U., 1995. Cert. govt. fin. mgr. Intern Tank Automotive and Armaments Command, Warren, Mich., 1969-71; sys. analyst U.S. Army Gen. Material and Petroleum Ctr., New Cumberland, Pa., 1971-76, Depot Sys. Command, Chambersburg, Pa., 1976-79; logistician TACOM, Warren, 1979-84, chief, Abrams Tank br., 1984-89, chief, budget and policy br., 1989-91, chief, plans, policy and program divsn., 1991-93, dir., bus. and planning office, 1993-97; dean Sch. Applied Studies Bob Jones U., Greenville, SC, 1999—2002, dean Sch. Bus. Mgmt., 2002—. Advisor Faith Christian Sch., Clinton Twp., Mich., 1993-99, Calvary Christian Sch., Roseville, 1980-93. Deacon and trustee Faith Baptist Ch., Warren, Mich., 1995-99, Calvary Baptist Ch., Roseville, Mich., 1981-92; founding bd. edn. Tri-County Christian H.S., Mechanicsburg, Pa., 1971. Mem. Assn. U.S. Army, Am. Soc. Mil. Comptr., Bob Jones U. Alumni Assn. Baptist. Avocations: traveling, reading, golf. E-mail: gold19@juno.com., acg46@worldnet.att.net.

GOLDSMITH, BARBARA, writer, historian, journalist; d. Joseph I. and Evelyn (Cronson) Lubin; children: Andrew Goldsmith, Alice Elgart, John Goldsmith. BA, Wellesley Coll., 1958; DLitt (hon.), Syracuse U., 1980; LHD (hon.), Pace U., 1982; DLitt (hon.), Lake Forest Coll., 1996. Contbr. N.Y. Herald Tribune, Esquire Mag., 1958—64; founder, contbg. editor N.Y. Mag., 1968—; sr. editor Harpers Bazaar Mag., N.Y.C., 1970-74. Lectr. NYU, 1969, 75. Spl. writer TV documentaries and entertainments; author: (novel) The Straw Man, 1975; (non-fiction) Little Gloria . . . Happy at Last, 1980, Johnson v. Johnson, 1987, Other Powers: The Age of Suffrage, Spiritualism and the Scandalous Victoria Woodhull, 1998. Pres. Com. for Preservation and Access, 1990—95; mem. Pres.'s Commn. on Celebration of Women in Am. History, 1998—2001; mem. jr. coun. Mus. Modern Art, N.Y.C., 1951—73; mem. acquisitions com. Friends of Whitney Mus. Art, 1964—69; mem. pres.'s coun. Mus. City N.Y., 1970—; mem. exec. bd. PEN Am. Ctr., 1984—96; chmn. permanent paper com. PEN Freedom to Write Com., 1989—; founder Ctr. for Learning Disabilities, Albert Einstein Coll. Medicine; trustee N.Y. Pub. Libr., 1985—; mem. N.Y. Pub. Libr. Rsch. Librs., 1985—; gubernatorial appointee N.Y. State Coun. on Arts, 1990; founder Barbara Goldsmith/PEN Freedom to Write awards, Barbara Goldsmith/N.Y. Pub. Libr. Conservation and Preservation Divsns., Barbara Goldsmith/NYU Preservation Lab., Am. Acad. in Rome Barbara Goldsmith Rare Book Rm.; bd. dirs. permanent paper task force Nat. Libr. Medicine, 1989—; bd. dirs. Parks Coun. N.Y.C., 1965—82, Nat. Dance Inst., 1979—, Goldsmith Found., 1981—. Recipient Brandeis U. Library Trust award, 1980, Albert Einstein Spirit of Achievement award, 1988, Permanent Paper citation N.Y. Pub. Libr., Lit. Lions award N.Y. Pub. Libr., 1988, Pubs. 1st Ann. award Lit. Market Place, 1990, Rome medal Am. Acad. in Rome, Nat. Libr. Medicine Lit. award, 1991, Nat. Archives award, 1991, NYU Presdl. Citation award, 1993, Lifetime Achievement award Guild Hall Acad. Arts, 1999, Poets and Writers Lit. award, 1999, Presdl. citation for pub. svc., 2000. Mem. Authors Guild, Century Assn., Am. Acad. Arts and Scis., Guild Hall Acad. Arts (Lit. Achievement award 1999). Office: Janklow & Nesbit Attn Ms Lynn Nesbit 598 Madison Ave New York NY 10022-1614

GOLDSMITH, BILLY JOE, real estate broker, rancher; b. Blum, Tex., Nov. 6, 1933; s. John T. and Gladys Aileen (Curlee) G.; m. Jean Elizabeth Wendel, Oct. 20, 1962; 1 child, Anne. BS, Tex. A&M U., 1955. Asst., county agrl. agt. Harris County Tex. Extension Svc., Houston, 1957-64; mgr. Rice Coun.,

Houston, 1964-75, exec. v.p., 1975-95, ret., 1995; owner, broker real estate co. Houston, 1995—; owner Goldsmith Realty, Houston, Bill Goldsmith Agrl. Consulting. Arena dir. Houston Livestock Show and Rodeo, 1966-73; bd. dirs. Tex. Soc. to Prevent Blindness. With U.S. Army, 1955-57. Internat. Rice Festival honoree, 1992. Mem. Tex. Cattle Raisers Assn., Southwestern Cattle Raisers Assn., Nat. Cattlemen's Assn., Houston Livestock Show and Rodeo Rancher, Res. Officer Assn., Harris County Ext. Bd. Advisors. Home: 5826 Cheena Dr Houston TX 77096-5928

GOLDSMITH, BRAM, banker; b. Chgo., Feb. 22, 1923; s. Max L. and Bertha (Gittelsohn) G.; m. Elaine Maltz; children: Bruce, Russell. Student, Herzl Jr. Coll., 1940, U. Ill., 1941-42. Asst. v.p. Pioneer-Atlas Liquor Co., Chgo., 1945-47; pres. Winston Lumber and Supply Co., East Chicago, Ind., 1947-50; v.p. Medal Distilled Products, Inc., Beverly Hills, Calif., 1950-75; pres. Buckeye Realty and Mgmt. Corp., Beverly Hills, 1952-75; exec. v.p. Buckeye Constrn. Co., Inc., Beverly Hills, 1952-75; chmn. bd., CEO City Nat. Corp., Beverly Hills, 1975-95; CEO City Nat. Bank, 1975-96, chmn., 1975-95, CNC, 1995—. Mem., bd. dirs. L.A. Philharm. Assn.; bd. dirs. Cedars/Sinai Med. Ctr.; pres. Jewish Fedn. Coun. Greater L.A., 1969-70; nat. chmn. United Jewish Appeal, 1970-74; regional chmn. United Crusade, 1976; co-chmn. bd. dirs. NCCJ; chmn. Am. com. Weizman Inst. Sci. With signal corps U.S. Army, 1942-45. Mem. Masons, Hillcrest Country Club, Balboa Bay Club. Office: City Nat Corp 400 N Roxbury Dr Beverly Hills CA 90210

GOLDSMITH, CAROLINE L. arts executive; b. N.Y.C., Nov. 25, 1925; d. Reuben and Gladys (Garf) Steinholz; m. Mortimer M. Lerner, Dec. 1, 1946 (div. Nov., 1968); children: Lawrence, David; m. John F. Goldsmith, Dec. 1973. BA, Cornell U., 1946. Pres. dir. Gallery Passport Ltd., N.Y.C., 1960-66; sr. v.p. Ruder Finn Arts & Comm. Counselors, N.Y.C., 1966—; exec. dir. Arttable, Inc., N.Y.C., 1980-94. Mem. Cmty. Bd., N.Y.C., 1987-95. Mem.: Coll. Art Assn., Internat. Coun. Museums, Am. Fedn. Arts, Am. Assn. Museums, Internat. Women's Forum (bd. dirs.), The Century Assn., Smithsonian Inst. Democrat. Jewish. Avocations: theater, museums. Home: 375 W End Ave New York NY 10024-6568 Office: Ruder Finn Inc 301 E 57th St New York NY 10022-2900

GOLDSMITH, CATHY ELLEN, retired special education educator; b. NYC, Feb. 18, 1947; d. Eli D. and Gertrude A. G. BS, NYU, 1968, MA in Elem. Edn., 1971, MA in Ednl. Psychology, 1974. Cert. phys. handicapped, K-6 elem. edn. tchr., N.Y. 2d grade tchr. N.Y.C. Bd. Edn., 1968-69, tchr. learning disabled students (spl. edn.), 1969-86, tchr. emotionally disturbed learning disabled students, 1986-87, tchr. learning disabled students, 1987-88, tchr. trainable retarded students, 1988-2000, tchr. mixed disabilities class, 2000-01; ret., 2001. Represented in permanent collections Bobst Libr. NYU. Recipient Charles Oscar Maas Essay award in Am. History, 1968, Disting. Alumni Svc. award NYU, 1987. Mem. AAUW, Nat. Mus. Women in Arts, NYU Alumni Assn. (past rec. sec., v.p.), NYU Alumni Assn., NYU Alumnae Club (v.p.), Pi Lambda Theta (past pres., past historian). Home: 418 Beach 133d St Belle Harbor NY 11694-1416

GOLDSMITH, CLIFFORD HENRY, former tobacco company executive; b. Leipzig, Germany, Sept. 6, 1919; came to U.S., 1940, naturalized, 1943; s. Conrad and Elise (Stahl) G.; m. Katherine W. Kaynis; children: Corinne Elizabeth Goldsmith Dickinson (dec.), Audrey Jane Goldsmith Kubie, Alexandra Eve Goldsmith Fallon. Grad., Bradford (Eng.) U., 1939. Technologist, Glenside Mills Corp., Skaneateles, N.Y., 1940-41; supt. Falls Yarn Mills, Woonsocket, R.I., 1941-42, Aldon Spinning Mills, Talcotville, Conn., 1942-43; with Benson & Hedges Co., 1945-53, plant mgr., 1945-53; with Philip Morris, Inc., 1954-84, pres., 1978-83, vice chmn., 1983-84; now prin. Prendel Co. Chmn. emeritus Nat. Multiple Sclerosis Soc., FOJP Svc. Corp.; trustee Mt. Sinai Sch. Medicine, Mt. Sinai Hosp. & Med. Ctr.; vice chmn. Poly. U. With inf. U.S. Army, 1943—45. Mem. Textile Inst. (Manchester, Eng., assoc.), Commonwealth Club (Richmond), Univ. Club (N.Y.), Century Club (N.Y. Office: 900 Park Ave New York NY 10021-0231

GOLDSMITH, ELSA M. painter, graphic artist; b. N.Y.C., Jan. 26, 1920; BA, Parsons Sch. Fine & Applied Art; studied, N.Y.U.; studied lithography, Pratt Graphic Ctr.; etching with Ruth Leaf, painting with Betty Holiday. Advert artist Newsweek Mag., New York, 1940—41; indsl. designer Belle Kogan Assoc., New York, 1941—48; freelance artist book & mag. illustrating, New York, 1942—. Tchr. and owner Elsa Goldsmith's Studio, 1950—74, N. Shore Cmty. Art Ctr., Great Neck, NY, 1971—73, bd. dir., art coord., 1973—; painting tchr. Adult Edn. Sewanhake H.S., Floral Manor, NY, 1972—74; guest lectr. La Salle Coll., 1974; mem. Guild Hall Mus., Artists & Equity and L.I. Art Alliance, 1985; del. U.S. Com. Women Artists, 1994; lectr., demonstrator NOW, NY, 1970—80. Prin. works include Human Landscapes Collection, 1940— (Honors at London Art Museum, 1969, Gold Medal Honor for painting from Cannes Inst., 1969), 15 solo exhibits, 1972—73, 4 One-Woman Shows in N.Y., 1972—73, exhibitions include Retrospective 4, Old Bergen Art Guild, 1974, Silverpoint Exhibn., Port Washington Libr., 1975, Works on Paper Women Artists, Bklyn. Mus., 1975, 1985, Cayuga Mus., N.Y., 1983, Syosset Libr., N.Y., 1983, Retrospective 5, Huntington Libr., N.Y., 1989, Retrospective 6, E. Meadow Libr. Retrospective, 1990, 75th Anniversary Show of the LWV, Les Malamut Art Gallery, Union, N.J., 1990, Nat. Mus. Women in the Arts, Washington, 1994—95. Bd. mem. UN Internat. Womens Year Arts Festival, 1975—76. Named to Nat. Woman's Hall of Fame, 1994; recipient Eleanor Roosevelt award for Contbn. to Women in the Arts, 1973, Doris Krindel Award, 1974, Honored at Nassau County Mus. Art, N.Y., 1997. Mem.: Silvermine Guild Artists, Women in the Arts, Inc. (bd. mem. & bicentennial chmn. 1974—76, Susan Kahn award 1974), Internat. Art Assn., Nat. Assn. Women Artist (chairwoman 1994, 22 maj. awards 1972—73, Nat. Exhbn. Award 1993, Honors 1994). Achievements include promoting greater participation and organizing two shows for women artists in Bulgaria and Italy; arranging an exhibit for 75 women artists at the Palazzo Vecchio for the city of Florence, Italy in 1990; actively seeking and helping gain equal representation for women in museums and galleries in the 1950s and 1960s; painting Joan of Arc, 1994, featured on "20/20".

GOLDSMITH, ETHEL FRANK, medical social worker; b. Chgo., May 31, 1919; d. Theodore and Rose (Falk) Frank; m. Julian Royce Goldsmith, Sept. 4, 1940; children: Richard, Susan, John. BA, U. Chgo., 1940. Lic. social worker, Ill. Liaison worker psychiat. consultation service U. Chgo. Hosp., 1964-68; med. social worker Wyler Children's Hosp., Chgo., 1968-98. Treas. U. Chgo. Service League, 1958-62, chmn. camp Brueckner Farr Aux., 1966-72; pres. Bobs Roberts Hosp. Service Commn., 1962; bd. dirs. Richardson Wildlife Sanctuary, 1988-2000; mem. Field Mus. Women's Bd., 1966—; bd. dirs. Hyde Park Art Ctr., 1964-82, Chgo. Commons Assn., 1967-77, Alumni Assn. Sch. Social Service Adminstrn., 1976-80, Self Help Home for Aged, 1985-2000, U. Chgo. Svc. League, 2002—; vol. Chgo. Found. for Edn.; mem. womens bd. U. Chgo., 1999—. Recipient Alumni Citation Pub. Service, U. Chgo., 1972. Mem. Phi Beta Kappa. Home: 5631 S Blackstone Ave Chicago IL 60637-1827

GOLDSMITH, GARY L. advertising executive; b. Dallas, Aug. 24, 1954; s. Charles and Jennie (Levine) G. BFA, U. Tex., 1977, Art Ctr. Coll. Design, Los Angeles, 1980. Art dir. Doyle Dane Bernbach, N.Y.C., 1980-82, v.p., 1982-84, assoc. creative dir., 1984-85; exec. art. dir. Chiat/Day Inc., N.Y.C., 1985-86; chmn., creative dir. Goldsmith/Jeffrey, N.Y.C., 1987—; vice chmn. & exec. creative dir. Lowe Lintas & Partners Worldwide, N.Y.C. Instr. Sch. Visual Arts, N.Y.C., 1982-84. Recipient Clio award, 1981-88, One Show award The One Club, 1981-95, New York Art Dirs. Club award, 1981-95, Graphis Annual award, 1981-95, Andy award Advt. Club N.Y., 1981-95, Communication Arts mag. award, 1981-95, Bronze Lion award Cannes Film Festival, 1984, 86, Disting. Merit award Am. Inst. Graphic Arts, 1981-95. Jewish. Office: Lowe Lintas & Partners Worldwide 1114 Avenue Of The Americas New York NY 10036-7703 also: 885 2nd Ave Fl 2 New York NY 10017-2201

GOLDSMITH, HARRY SAWYER, surgeon, educator; b. Newton, Mass., Sept. 30, 1929; s. Leo and Dorothy Amy (Appleton) G.; m. Linda Perry, Dec. 8, 1961; children: John, Robert, Lynne. AB, Dartmouth, 1952; MD, Boston U., 1956; hon. degree in medicine, Shanghai Second Med. U., 1988, Xuzhou (China) Med. Coll., 1995. Intern Boston City Hosp., 1956-57, resident in surgery, 1957-61, Meml. Sloan Kettering Inst., N.Y.C., 1963-65, chief gastric and mixed tumor svc., 1965-70; Samuel D. Gross prof. surgery, chmn. dept. Jefferson Med. Coll., Phila., 1970-77; surgeon-in-chief Jefferson U. Hosp., 1970-77; disting. prof. surgery Jefferson Med. Coll., Phila., 1977; prof. surgery Dartmouth Coll. Med. Sch., Hanover, N.H., 1977-83; prof. surgery, adj. prof. neurosurgery Boston U. Sch. Medicine, 1983-95; clin. prof. surgery U. Nev., Reno, 1996—. Editor-in-chief: Goldsmith's Practice of Surgery, 1976-89; editor: The Omentum: Research and Clinical Applications, 1990, The Omentum: Application to Brain and Spinal Cord, 2000; contbr. articles to profl. jours. Capt. U.S. Army, 1961-63. Mem. ACS, Soc. Vascular Surgery, Brit. Assn. Surg. Oncology, Soc. for Surgery of Alimentary Tract, Internat. Surg. Soc., Ctrl. Surg. Assn., New England Surg. Soc. Address: PO Box 493 Glenbrook NV 89413-0493 Fax: (775) 749-5861. E-mail: hlgldsmith@aol.com.

GOLDSMITH, HOWARD, writer, consultant; b. N.Y.C., Aug. 24, 1945; s. Philip and Sophie (Feldman) G. BA with honors, CUNY, 1965; MA with honors, U. Mich., Ann Arbor, 1966. Research psychologist Mental Hygiene Clinic, Detroit, 1966-70; freelance writer Ency. Britannica Ednl. Corp., Chgo., 1970; writer, pvt. practice editorial cons. Flushing, N.Y., 1970—. Editorial cons. Mountain View Ctr. for Environ. Edn., U. Colo., Boulder, 1970-85. Author poetry, videos, plays, numerous short stories, books, novels including: The Whispering Sea, 1976, What Makes a Grumble Smile?, 1977, The Shadow and Other Strange Tales, 1977, Terror by Night, 1977, Spine-Chillers, 1978, Sooner Round the Corner, 1979, Invasion: 2200 A.D., 1979, The Ivy Plot, 1981, Three-Ring Inferno, 1982, Plaf Le Paresseux, 1982, Ninon, Miss Vison, 1982, Toufou Le Hibou, 1982, Fourtou Le Kangourou, 1982, The Tooth chicken, 1982, Mireille l'Abeille, 1982, Little Dog Lost, 1983, Stormy Day Together, 1983, The Sinister Circle, 1983, Shadow of Fear, 1983, Treasure Hunt, 1983, The Square, 1983, The Circle, 1983, The Contest, 1983, Welcome, Makoto!, 1983, Helpful Julio, 1984, The Secret of Success, 1984, Pedro's Puzzling Birthday, 1984, Rosa's Prank, 1984, A Day of Fun, 1984, The Rectangle, 1984, Kirby the Kangaroo, 1985, Ollie the Owl, 1985, The Twiddle Twins' Haunted House, 1985, Young Ghosts, 1985, Von Geistern Besessen, 1987, The Further Adventures of Batman, 1989, Visions of Fantasy, 1989, The Pig and the Witch, 1990, The Mind-Stalkers, 1990, Spooky Stories, 1990, Little Quack and Baby Duckling, 1991, The Proust Syndrome, 1992, The President's Train, 1993, Thomas Edison Had A Bright Idea, 1993, The Day My Dad and I Got Mugged, 1993, Evil Tales of Evil Things, 1993, The Christmas Star, 1994, The Curiosity Kid, 1994, Tales of the Batman, 1995, Dream Weavers, 1996, The Gooey Chewy Contest, 1997, The Twiddle Twins' Music Box Mystery, 1997, The Twiddle Twins' Amusement Park Mystery, 1998, Science Through Stories (series), 1998-99, The Twiddle Twins' Single Footprint Mystery, 1999, The Tooth Fairy Mystery, 1999, Roundabout the Rain, 2000, Three Bags of Chips, 2000, See It Fly!, 2000, Strike up the Band, 2000, Danger Zone, 2000, Thomas Edison to the Rescue!, 2003, Mark Twain at Work, 2003; contbg. editor: Children's Magic Window, 1987—. Fellow U.S. Pub. Health Svc., 1965; Rackham predoctoral fellow U. Mich., 1966; recipient Phi Sigma Sci. award, 1966. Mem. Poets and Writers, Sci. Fiction Writers of Am., Soc. Children's Book Writers and Illustrators, Phi Beta Kappa, Psi Chi, Sigma Xi, Phi Kappa Phi. Avocations: classical music, book collecting, chess, old movies. Home: 41-07 Bowne St Apt 6B Flushing NY 11355-5629

GOLDSMITH, HOWARD MICHAEL, lawyer; b. Atlantic City, Mar. 22, 1942; s. Leonard M. and Annette (Rothenberg) G.; m. Molly Hartman, Dec. 17, 1943; 1 child, Michael Stephen. BS in Bus., Rider Coll., 1965; JD, Dickinson Sch. Law, 1968. Bar: Pa. 1968, U.S. Dist. Ct. (ea. dist.) Pa. 1969, U.S. Supreme Ct. 1973, U.S. Ct. Claims 1980, U.S. Ct. Appeals (3d cir.) 1982, U.S. Ct. Appeals (fed. cir.) 1988. Prin. Howard M. Goldsmith, P.C., Phila., 1998—. Apptd. custody rules com., divorce code rev. com, support guidelines com. Phila. county Ct. Common Pleas; procedural rules com. Pa. Supreme Ct., 1997—2003; apptd. master pro tem to hear custody and support cases Phila. County; lectr. in field. Bd. dirs. Jewish Cmty. Ctr., Klein Br., press., 1987-90. Fellow Am. Acad. Matrimonial Lawyers (pres. Pa. chpt. 2002-03), Internat. Acad. Matrimonial Lawyers; mem. ABA (family law sect.), Pa. Bar Assn. (family law sect., chair 1997-98), Phila. Bar Assn. (chmn. 1987, past chmn. adoption com., commr. jud. selection and retention commn. 1987), Vidocq Soc., B'nai B'rith. Jewish. Office: 7716 Castor Ave Philadelphia PA 19152-3602

GOLDSMITH, JACK LANDMAN, former retail company executive; b. Memphis, Apr. 10, 1910; s. Fred and Aimee (Landman) G.; m. Dorothy Metzger, Feb. 9, 1960; children— Joan Goldsmith Marks, Jack Landman; stepchildren— Larry, Melvin. Grad., Memphis Law Sch.; student, Washington U., St. Louis, N.Y. U. Dir. First Nat. Bank, 1946-71; With Federated Dept. Stores, Inc., 1959—, v.p., 1961—; ret. chmn. bd., chmn. exec. com. Goldsmith's Dept. Store. Past dir. world trade adv. com. Dept. Commerce; mem. U.S. Trade Mission to Greece, 1957, to Austria, 1958; past pres. Cavendis Trading Corp., N.Y.C. Former trustee Brooks Art Gallery, Memphis; pres. Goldsmith Found.; past bd. dirs. Bapt. Hosp., Memphis; del. to Tenn. Constnl. Conv., 1953. Served to maj. USAR, 1931-41, U.S. Army, 1942-45. Mem. Nat. Retail Mchts. Coun. (past pres.), Tenn. Retail Mchts. Coun., Downtown Assn. (pres.). Clubs: Rotary (Memphis) (past dir.), One Hundred (Memphis). Home: 601 Putting Green Ln Longboat Key FL 34228-3523

GOLDSMITH, JANET JANE, retired pediatric nurse practitioner; b. creston, Iowa, Mar. 3, 1942; d. Paul William and Mary Lucille (Crow) Schafroth; m. Olin Russel Goldsmith, Aug. 31, 1963; children: Rodney, Scott, Kristen. Diploma, Iowa Meth. Hosp. Sch. Nursing, Des Moines, 1963; PNP, U. Iowa, 1982; BSN, Graceland U., Lamoni, Iowa, 1984. Cert. pediatric nurse practitioner. Staff nurse Rosary Hosp., Corning, Iowa, 1963-66, 71-72; sch. nurse Corning Commun. Schs., 1966-67; area adminstr., occupant protection program adminstr. Iowa Gov.'s Traffic Safety Bur., Des Moines, 1985—2002; ret., 2002. Clin. instr. Southwestern C.C., Creston, Iowa, 1970, adj. faculty, 1985-86; health/handicap coord. Matura-Head Start, Creston, 1973-81; pediatric devel. nurse Child Diagnostic and Planning Svc., Creston, 1975-81; pediatric nurse practitioner, physician's office, Lenox, Iowa, 1982-84, Otologic Med. Svcs., Iowa City, 1982-87, Taylor County Pub. Health, Bedford, Iowa, 1982-87, Heart and Hands, Des Moines, 2003—; cons. Hwy Safety Area, adv. bd. Iowa Ctr. for Agrl. Safety and Health; sexual assault nurse investigator, 2002; presenter, cons. in field. Author booklets, tng. video, articles, tng. curricula. Recipient Recognition of Accomplishment award Gov. of Iowa, 1989. Mem. Internat. Assn. Forensic Nurses, Iowa Pub. Health Assn. (exec. bd., legis. com.) Nat. Assn. Pediatric Nurse Assocs. and Practitioners (pub. rels. com.), Iowa Nurses Assn. (local treas., state policy com.), Iowa Assn. Nurse Practitioners (constn. and by-laws chmn., pres.), Iowa Traffic Control and Safety Assn. (bd. dirs., treas., sec., v.p., pres.). Methodist. Home: 1675 Walnut Woods Dr West Des Moines IA 50265-8511

GOLDSMITH, JEFF CHARLES, management consultant; b. Portland, Oreg., Oct. 31, 1948; children: Jason, Trevor, Amelia. BA, Reed Coll., 1970; PhD, U. Chgo., 1973. Dir. health planning, regulatory affairs U. Chgo. Med. Ctr., 1975-82; nat. advisor Ernst & Young, 1982-94; pres. Health Futures, Inc., 1982—; dir. Cerner Corp., 1999—, Essent Healthcare, 2000—; assoc. prof. med. edn. Sch. Medicine U. Va., 1997—. Lectr. U. Chgo. Grad. Sch. Bus., 1979—90; adv. Burrill Biotech. Capital Fund. Author: Can Hospitals Survive?, 1981; mem. editl. bd. Health Affairs, 1990 ; contbr. articles to profl. jours. including Harvard Bus. Rev., Jour. AMA, Health Affairs. Recipient Woodrow Wilson Nat. Fellowship, 1971. Avocations: skiing, audiophile, native american art, whitewater. E-mail: hfutures@healthfutures.net.

GOLDSMITH, JERRY, composer; b. L.A., Feb. 10, 1929; m. Carol Sheinkopf. Student, L.A. City Coll.; studies with, Jakob Gimpel, Mario Castelnuovo-Tedesco; MusD, Berklee Coll. Music, 1990. Composer: (radio scores) Romance, Suspense, CBS Radio, (TV scores) Twilight Zone, GE Theatre, Doctor Kildare, Gunsmoke, Climax, Playhouse 90, Studio One, Star Trek: Voyager (Emmy award, 1995), (film scores, partial list) (debut) Black Patch, 1956, Lonely are the Brave, 1961, Freud, 1962 (Acad. award nomination), The Stripper, 1962, Lilies of the Field, 1963, The Prize, 1963, Seven Days in May, 1963, In Harm's Way, 1964, The Man from UNCLE, 1965, Von Ryan's Express, 1965, A Patch of Blue, 1965 (Acad. award nomination), The Blue Max, 1965, Our Man Flint, 1965, Seconds, 1965, Stagecoach, 1965, The Sand Pebbles, 1966 (Acad. award nomination), In Like Flint, 1967, Planet of the Apes, 1968 (Acad. award nomination), The Ballad of Cable Hogue, 1969, Tora! Tora! Tora!, 1970, Patton, 1970 (Acad. award nomination), Wild Rovers, 1971, The Other, 1972, The Red Pony, 1972 (Emmy award), Papillon, 1973 (Acad. award nomination), QB VII, 1974 (Emmy award), Chinatown, 1974 (Acad. award nomination), The Reincarnation of Peter Proud, 1974, Logan's Run, 1975, The Wind and the Lion, 1976 (Acad. award nomination), The Omen, 1976 (Acad. award winner, Grammy award nomination, two N.B. nominations), Islands in the Stream, 1976, MacArthur, 1977, Coma, 1977, The Boys from Brazil, 1978 (Acad. award nomination), Damien-Omen II, 1978, Alien, 1979, Star Trek: The Motion Picture, 1979 (Acad. award nomination), Babe, 1980 (Emmy award), Masada, 1981 (Emmy award), The Final Conflict, 1981, Outland, 1981, Raggedy Man, 1981, Mrs. Brisby: The Secret of NIMH, 1982, Poltergeist, 1982 (Acad. award nomination, Edgar Allan Poe award), First Blood, 1982, Twilight Zone-The Movie, 1983, Psycho II, 1983, Under Fire, 1983 (Acad. award nomination), Gremlins, 1984 (Saturn award), Legend (European version), 1985, Explorers, 1985, Rambo: First Blood II, 1985, Poltergeist II: The Other Side, 1986, Hoosiers, 1986 (Acad. award nomination), Innerspace, 1987, Extreme Prejudice, 1987, Rambo III, 1988, Criminal Law, 1989, The 'Burbs, 1989, Leviathan, 1989, Star Trek V: The Final Frontier, 1989, Total Recall, 1990, Gremlins 2: The New Batch, 1990, The Russia House, 1990, Not Without My Daughter, 1991, Sleeping with the Enemy, 1991, Medicine Man, 1991, Love Field, 1992, Mom and Dad Save the World, 1992, Basic Instinct, 1992 (Acad. award nomination, Golden Globe nomination), Mr. Baseball, 1992, Forever Young, 1992, Matinee, 1992, The Vanishing, 1993, Dennis the Menace, 1993, Malice, 1993, Rudy, 1993, Six Degrees of Separation, 1993, Angie, 1994, Bad Girls, 1994, The Shadow, 1994, I.Q., 1994, The River Wild, 1994, First Knight, 1995, Congo, 1995, Powder, 1995, City Hall, 1995, Executive Decision, 1996, Chain Reaction, 1996, The Ghost and the Darkness, 1996, Star Trek: First Contact, 1996, Fierce Creatures, 1996, L.A. Confidential, 1997 (Acad. award nomination, Golden Globe nomination), Air Force One, 1997, The Edge, 1997, Deep Rising, 1997, U.S. Marshals, 1998, Mulan, 1998 (Acad. award nomination, Golden Globe nomination), Small Soldiers, 1998, Star Trek: Insurrection, 1998, The Mummy, 1999, The 13th Warrior, 1999, The Haunting, 1999, Hollow Man, 2000, Along Came a Spider, 2000, The Last Castle, 2001, The Sum of All Fears, 2002, Star Trek: Nemesis, 2002; debuted as a concert condr. with Christus Apollo, So. Calif. Chamber Symphony, 1969, guest condr. Royal Philharm. Orch., London, 1975, 1987, Glendale Symphony, 1975, USAF Band, 1976, 1983, Okla. Symphony Orch., 1983, San Diego Pops Orch., 1985, London Philharmonia, 1987, Pitts. Symphony, 1988, Ala. Symphony, 1988, Nat. Symphony, Washington, 1988, Indpls. Symphony, 1989, Ft. Worth Symphony, 1989, London Symphony, 1989, 1999, 2000, 2001, Utah Symphony, 1990, 1991, El Paso (Tex.) Symphony, 1990, Syracuse Symphony, 1990, Toronto (Ont., Can.) Symphony, 1990, Balt. Symphony, 1990, New World Symphony, Miami, Fla., 1991, 2000, Cin. Symphony, 1991, Memphis Symphony, 1992, Milw. Symphony, 1993, Detroit Symphony, 1993, 2000, Oulu (Finland) City Orch., 1993, Colo. Symphony, 1993, Madrid Symphony, 1993, BBC Concert Orch., Eng., 1994, San Diego Symphony Orch., 1994, Toledo Symphony, 1995, San Jose Symphony, 1997, Pasadena POPS Orch., 1997, N.Y. FILMharmonic Orch., 1998, Seville (Spain) Symphony, 1998, Kanagawa (Japan) Philharm. Orch., 1998, 2000, Royal Scottish Nat. Orch., 1999, Budapest Festival Orch., 1999, L.A. Philharm., 1999, Barcelona (Spain) Symphony, 1999, Monte Carlo Philharm., 2001, ballet scores include Othello, 1971, A Patch of Blue, 1970, Capricorn One, 1989, premier Music for Orch. with St. Louis Symphony, 1971—72. Recipient Max Steiner award, Nat. Film Soc., 1982, 1st ann. Richard Kirk award, BMI, 1987, Golden Score award, Am. Soc. Music Arrangers, 1990, Career Achievement award, Soc. for Preservation of Film Music, 1993, 1st Am. Music Legend award, Variety, 1995, 18 Acad. award nominations, 7 Emmy award nominations, 7 Grammy award nominations, 9 Golden Globe award nominations. Office: c/o Savitsky & Co 1901 Ave Of Stars Ste 1450 Los Angeles CA 90067-6087

GOLDSMITH, LEE SELIG, lawyer, physician; b. N.Y.C., Nov. 18, 1939; s. Isidore L. and Elsie (Friedman) G.; m. Arlene F. Applebaum, June 10, 1962; children: Ian Lance, Helena Ayn, Jordan Seth. BS with honors, N.Y. U., 1960, MD, 1964, LL.B., 1967. Bar: N.Y. 1968, N.J. 1974; cert. civil trial atty. 2000. Assoc. clk. Speiser, Shumate, Geoghan Krause & Rheingold, 1965-70; individual practice law, 1970-72; mem. firm Lea, Goldberg, Goldsmith & Spellen, N.Y.C., 1972-74; of counsel Newark, 1974-77; mem. firm Goldsmith, Cohen & Simon, 1976-77, Goldsmith & Cohen, 1977-80, Greenstone, Greenstone, Naishuler & Goldsmith, Newark, 1981, Goldsmith & Richman, P.C., N.Y.C., 1981-2000, Goldsmith & Richman, P.A., Englewood, N.J., 1981-2000. Adj. prof. law Fordham U., 1976-88 ; spl. counsel N.Y. State Senate health com., 1971; lectr. Practicing Law Inst.; chmn. Am. Bd. Law in Medicine, 1984-85. Author: Malpractice Made Easy, 1976, Hospital Liability Law, 1972, 2d edit. 1979; editor: Jour. Legal Medicine, 1978-81, Legal Aspects of Med. Practice, 1981—, Medical Malpractice, Guide to Medical Issues, 7 vols., 1986; contbr. articles to various publs. Fellow: NY Acad. Medicine, Am. Coll. Legal Medicine (bd. govs. 1982, pres.-elect 1986—87, pres. 1987—88, chmn. com. legis. rev.); mem.: ATLA (sec. NJ chpt. 1988—89, treas. 1989—89, 2d v.p. 1990—91, 1st v.p. 1991—92, pres. 1993—94, PAC bd. govs. 1996—2000, treas. NJ PAC 1996—, bd. govs. 2000—), AMA, NY Trial Lawyers Assn., Assn. Bar City NY (sec. sci. and law com. 1985—87), NY County Med. Soc., NY Med. Soc. Home: 1 Kelwynne Rd Scarsdale NY 10583-4507 Office: Goldsmith Richman & Harz LLP 747 3rd Ave New York NY 10017-2803 also: 140 Sylvan Ave Englewood Cliffs NJ 07632-2502 E-mail: lee@goldrich.com.

GOLDSMITH, LOWELL ALAN, medical educator; b. Bklyn., Mar. 29, 1938; s. Isidore Alexander and Ida (Kaplan) G.; m. Carol Amreich, June 11, 1960; children: Meredith, Eileen. AB, Columbia Coll., 1959; MD, SUNY, Bklyn., 1963; MPH, U. Rochester Sch. Medicine & Dentistry, 2002. Diplomate Am. Bd. Dermatology. Intern, then resident in medicine UCLA Med. Ctr., 1963-65; resident in dermatology Harvard Med. Sch., Boston, 1967-69; asst. prof. dermatology Harvard U. Med. Sch., Boston, 1970-73; asst. in dermatology Mass. Gen. Hosp., Boston, 1970-71, asst. dermatologist, 1971-73; assoc. prof. medicine Duke U. Med. Ctr., Durham, N.C., 1973-78, prof., 1978-81; James H. Sterner prof. dermatology Sch. Medicine and Dentistry, U. Rochester, N.Y., 1981-96, chief dermatology unit, 1981-87, acting chmn. dept. medicine, 1985-87, chmn. dept. dermatology, 1987-96; dean Sch. Medicine and Dentistry U. Rochester, NY, 1996-2000, dean emeritus, 2000—; prof. dermatology U. N.C., Chapel Hill, 2002—, clin. prof. epidemiology Sch. Pub. Health, 2002—. Mem. dermatology adv. com. FDA, 1983-87; chmn. Gordon Rsch. Cong. on Epithelial Differentiation and Keratiniazation, 1987, AAD-CDC Conf. on skin cancer prevention and edn., Washington, 1995; mem. gen. medicine A study sect. USPHS, NIH, 1988-92, chmn., 1990-92; mem. coun. NIAMS, NIH, 1996-99; chmn. med. adv. bd. Nat. Alopecia Areata Found., 1981-87, 90-2002, bd. dirs.; bd. dirs. Monroe Cmty. Hosp., Rochester, Ctr. for Alternatives in Animal Testing, Balt.; chmn. NIH Consensus Conf. on Diagnosis and Treatment of Early Melanoma, Bethesda, 1992. Author, editor: Biochemistry and Physiology of the Skin, 1983, 2d edit., 1991, Physiology, Biochemistry and Molecular Biology of the Skin, 1991, Differential Diagnosis of Skin Disease, 2d edit., 1996; mem. editl. bd. Archives Dermatology, 1981-92, Clinics in Dermatology, 1982-96, Seminars in Dermatology, 1991-96, Jour. Dermatological Sci., 1994—; mem. editl. bd. Jour. Investigative Dermatology, 1987-95, editor, 2002--, also numerous articles. With USPHS, 1965-67. Recipient Rsch. Career Devel. award USPHS, 1975-80; Macy Found. fellow, 1978-79. Mem. Assn. Am. Physicians, Am. Soc. Clin. Investigation, Am. Acad. Dermatology (bd. dirs., Presdl. citation 2003), Soc. Investigative Dermatology (bd. dirs., pres. 1994-95, Rothman Gold medal), Nat. Ichthyosis Found. (chmn. adv. bd. 1981-85), Assn. Profs. Dermatology (bd. dirs. 1984-87, pres. 1992-94), Am. Bd. Dermatology (bd. dirs. 1993-96), N.Y. State Soc. Dermatology (pres. 1985-89), Am. Dermatol. ASsn. (bd. dirs. 1996-2001, pres. 2002—, Buffalo-Rochester Dermatology Soc. (pres. 1987), Rochester Dermatology Soc., Rochester Acad. Medicine, Polish Dermatol. Assn. (hon.), Brit. Dermatology Assn. (hon.), Japanese Dermatology Assn. (hon.; DOHI lectr. 2003), Alpha Omega Alpha. Office: U NC Dept Dermatology 3100 Thurston-Bowles Bldg CB #7287 Chapel Hill NC 27599

GOLDSMITH, MELISSA URSULA DAWN, musicologist; d. John Hugh Parrott and Ursula Irene Anna Goldsmith. BA in Music and Biochemistry, Smith Coll., 1993, MA in Music, 1995; M Libr. and Info. Sci., La. State U., 1999, PhD in Music, Cert. of Advanced Studies in Libr. and Info. Sci., La. State U., 2002. Tchg. fellow and rsch. asst. music dept. and Werner Josten Music Libr. Smith Coll., Northampton, Mass., 1993—95; grad. tchg. asst. Sch. of Music/Coll. of Music and Dramatic Arts La. State U., Baton Rouge, 1995—99, grad. asst. Carter Ctr. for Music Resources, 1996—2002. Historian Grad. Libr. and Info. Sci. Student Assn. La. State U., Baton Rouge, 1999. Grantee, La. State U., 2000. Mem.: Delta Phi Alpha, Film Music Soc., Music Libr. Assn. (mem. local arrangements com.), Am. Musicological Soc. (chmn., moderator panel), Nature Conservancy, Nat. Arbor Day Found., Beta Phi Mu. Achievements

include Sheet Music Database at Louisiana State University's Carter Center for Music Resources. Avocations: film studies, tap dance, recorder performance, embroidery. Home: PO Box 1567 Santa Barbara CA 93102 Personal E-mail: mgolds2@lsu.edu.

GOLDSMITH, MERWIN, actor, theater director; b. Detroit, Aug. 7, 1937; s. Max Harold and Alice Flora (Singer) G.; m. Susan Leigh Benson, Mar. 1966 (div. 1969); m. Barbara Parry, July, 1996. BA in Theater, UCLA, 1960; student, Bristol Old Vic Theatre Sch., Bristol. Appeared in (stage prodns.) Auntie Mame, 1958, License to Murder, 1964, The Tempest, Trap for a Lonely Man, Phaedra, Gentlemen Prefer Blondes, 1965, Billy Budd, 1967, Fiddler on the Roof, 1968-69, Minnie's Boys, 1970, Much Ado About Nothing, Pal Joey, 1973, Last of the Red Hot Lovers, 1974, Hedda Gabler, 1975, Dirty Linen, 1977, Oklahoma!, 1978, Death of a Salesman, The Importance of Being Ernest, 1982, Hello Dolly!, 1983, La Boheme, 1984, The Taming of the Shrew, 1985, Hamlet, 1986, Me & My Girl, 1988, 89, Grand Hotel, The Musical, 1991, Merry Widow, 1991, Learned Ladies, 1991, Ain't Broadway Grand, 1993, The Little Prince, 1993, An Imaginary Life, 1993, Beau Jest, 1994, After-Play, 1995, By Jeeves, 1996, Loot, 2000, The Investigation, 2001, Bloomer Girl, 2001, The Pajama Game, 2001, Franklin of Philadelphia, 2002; (films) Shamus, 1972, Boardwalk, 1979, So Fine, 1981, Blue Heaven, 1984, Making Mr. Right, 1986, Cadillac Man, 1991, It Could Happen To You, 1993, Quiz Show, 1993, Rounders, 1998, The Hurricane, 1998, Company Man, 1999, Joe Gould's Secret, 1999, Au Plus Pres du Paradis, 2001; (TV) All My Children, Ryan's Hope, The Guiding Light, Search for Tomorrow, As the World Turns, Another World, Wide World of Mystery, The Connection, Law & Order; dir. Vanities, 1980. Served with USAFR. Nominated Best Actor in a Mus. award Variety Critics Poll, 1972, Best Supporting Actor in a Mus. award, 1973; nominee Best Actor Mus., Joseph Jefferson Awards, 1972. Mem.: NARAS (Grammy awards voter), SAG, AFTRA, Actors Equity Assn., The Century Assn., The Players Club. Avocations: photography, studying French and Hebrew. Office: Silver & Massetti & Szatmary Ltd 145 W 45th St New York NY 10036-4008

GOLDSMITH, MICHAEL ALLEN, oncologist, educator; b. Bronx, Jan. 28, 1946; s. Walter and Bertha (Tannenberg) G.; m. Judith Harriet Plaut, June 6, 1971; children: Sharon, Esther, Eva, Steven. BA, Yeshiva U., 1967; MD, Albert Einstein Coll. Medicine, 1971. Diplomate Am. Bd. Internal Medicine. Intern Bronx Mcpl. Hosp. Ctr., 1971-72; staff assoc. Nat. Cancer Inst., Bethesda, Md., 1972-74; resident in medicine Mt. Sinai Hosp., N.Y.C., 1974-75, fellow in neoplastic diseases, 1975-77, asst. clin. prof. medicine and neoplastic diseases, 1977—; attending physician Oncology Consultants, P.C., N.Y.C., 1977—. Assoc. editor Cancer Investigation. 2001—; reviewer Jour. AMA, 1988-90, New Eng. Jour. Medicine, 1995—. Contbr. articles to med. jours. Vice-pres. Congregation Orach Chaim, N.Y.C., 1978-83. Lt. comdr. USPHS, 1972-74. Fellow ACP; mem. Am. Soc. Clin. Oncology, Am. Assn. Cancer Rsch. Achievements include research in new anticancer drugs. Office: Oncology Cons PC 1045 5th Ave New York NY 10028-0138

GOLDSMITH, NANCY CARROL, business and health services management educator; b. Conemaugh, Pa., May 11, 1940; d. John and Mary (Appley) Stinich; m. Sidney Goldsmith, Apr. 2, 1966. RN, Temple U., 1961; Assoc. summa cum laude, C.C. Phila., 1984; BS in Health Care Mgmt. summa cum laude, Phila. Coll. Textiles and Sci., 1986; MA in Health Care Adminstrn. summa cum laude, Antioch U., Yellow Springs, Ohio, 1988; PhD in Health Svcs. and Hosp. Adminstrn. summa cum laude, Southwest U., New Orleans, 1990. Nurse, head nurse to med. surg. supr. Temple U. Hosp., Phila., 1961-67; nursing rsch. assoc. Smith Klein & French, Inc. and Ames Med. Co., Phila. and Elkhart, Ind., 1967-69; sr. nursing rsch. assoc. NIH, Washington, 1969-75; adminstrv. supr. nursing svcs. Rolling Hill Hosp. and Diagnostic Ctr., Elkins Park, Pa., 1975-87, lectr. legal aspects nursing, 1980-90, dir. cost containment strategies, 1987-89, lectr. in health svcs. mgmt., 1989—, asst. dir. nursing svcs., 1988-89, nursing svcs. dir., 1989-90; prof. health svcs. adminstrn. and svcs. Phila U., 1991—, prof. bus. mgmt., 1992—, mem. adv. bd. health and wellness programs, 1993—, advisor, counselor, 1997—. Prof. managed care in health svcs. adminstrn. Ea. Coll., St. Davids, Pa., 1996—; lectr. Sr. Edn. League, 1992—; lectr. healthcare fin. and health svcs. adminstrn. Pa. State U., 1994; lectr. health svcs. reform C.C. Phila., 1993—, Free Libr. Phila., 1994—; instr. med./surg. nursing Sch. Nursing, Temple U., 1964-67, chmn. ann. fundraising, 1978-86. Author 2 books. Inventor use of dextrostix in hypoglycemic range, 1972 (Rsch. award 1974); co-patentee multipurpose biopsy needle, 1972; mem. editl. bd. Phila. U. Newletter, 1993—. Recipient Mayor's Liberty Bell award City of Phila., 1978, Legion of Honor award Chapel of Four Chaplains, 1981, Capitol award Nat. Leadership Coun., 1991; named to Hall of Fame, Internat. Profl. and Bus. Women's Assn., 1994. Mem. Am. Hosp. Assn., Am. Mgmt. Assn., Temple U. Nurse's Alumni Assn. (bd. dirs., v.p. 1991-92, pres. 1993-94, dir. continuing edn. com. 1986—), Temple U. Gen. Alumni Assn. (bd. dirs. 1980-88, 93—, Disting. Svc. award 1984), Downtown Club Temple U., Phi Beta Kappa, Phi Theta Kappa (pres. Delta of Pa. chpt. 1991-94, Honors Hall of Fame 1991). Jewish. Avocations: tennis, golf, home computing. Office: Phila U School House Ln Henry Ave Philadelphia PA 19144

GOLDSMITH, PAUL FELIX, physics and astronomy educator; b. Washington, Nov. 5, 1948; s. Raymond William and Selma Evelyn (Fine) G.; m. Sheryl E. Reiss, June 5, 1988. AB, U. Calif., Berkeley, 1969, PhD., 1975. Mem. tech. staff AT&T Bell Labs., Holmdel, N.J., 1975-77; asst. prof. U. Mass., Amherst, 1977-82, assoc. prof., 1982-85, prof. physics and astronomy, 1985-92; prof. astronomy, dir. Nat. Astronomy and Ionosphere Ctr. Cornell U., Ithaca, NY, 1993—2002, James A. Weeks prof. phys. sci., 1999—. Cons. MIT Lincoln Lab., Lexington, Mass., 1977-80; v.p. R & D Millitech Corp., South Deerfield, Mass., 1983-92. Author: Quasioptical Systems, 1998; editor: Instrumentation and Techniques for Radio Astronomy, 1988; contbr. articles on radio astronomy and millimeter and submillimeter wavelength tech. to profl. jours. Fellow IEEE; mem. Microwave Theory Tech. Soc. of IEEE (mem. spkr.'s bur. 1989-90, Disting. lectr. 1992-93), Am. Astron. Soc. Office: Dept Astronomy Cornell University Space Sciences Building Ithaca NY 14853

GOLDSMITH, RICHARD ELSINGER, lawyer; b. L.A., Dec. 17, 1933; s. Nat and Ruth (Elsinger) G.; m. Antonia Elisabeth Kunz, Nov. 17, 1967; children: Ruth Elisabeth, Joan Margaret. BA, Harvard U., 1955, JD, 1958; LLM in Tax, NYU, 1965. Bar: Tex. 1958, U.S. Dist. Ct. (we. dist.) Tex. 1961, U.S. Tax Ct. 1967. Mem. Matthews & Branscomb (formerly Matthews, Nowlin, MacFarlane & Barrett), San Antonio, 1960—. Founder, chmn. San Antonio Area Found., 1964, pres., 76-79; pres. Cmty. Guidance Ctr., 1964, 80; pres. United Way San Antonio and Bexar County, 1970-71; co-founder, 1st pres. Half Way House of San Antonio; pres. Jewish Fedn., San Antonio, 1978-79; co-founder Combined Charities Investment Group, 1987, chmn., 1990--; co-founder, pres. Temple Beth-El Permanent Charities Found., 1988-2001; pres., San Antonio Food Bank, 2003—. Recipient Donated Legal Svcs. award bus. law section. Tex. Bar Assn. Office: Matthews & Branscomb 112 E Pecan St Ste 1100 San Antonio TX 78205-1516 E-mail: rgoldsmith@mattbran.com.

GOLDSMITH, ROBERT LEWIS, youth association magazine executive; b. N.Y.C., Jan. 9, 1928; s. Arthur and Elizabeth (Kohn) G.; m. Joan M. Hartman, 1976. BS, NYU, 1950. Advt. promotion mgr. Esquire, Inc., N.Y.C., 1952-53; advt. dir. Schine Hotels, N.Y.C., 1953; promotion dir. Dell Pub. Co., N.Y.C., 1953-58, Outdoor Life Mag., N.Y.C., 1958-65; assoc. dir. mag. div. Boy Scouts Am., N.Y.C., 1965-89, ret., 1989. N.Am. rep. Ea. Art Report, London, 1991—. Bd. dirs. Inst. Asian Studies, N.Y.C., 1981—, assoc. dir., 1989—, pres., 1995-99; mem. Friends of Asian Art, Met. Mus. Art, Oriental Art Coun. Bklyn. Mus., Indpls Mus. Art, life trustee. Mem. N.Y. Sales Execs. Club, Mktg. Comms. Execs. Assn., Am. Mktg. Assn., Asia Soc., Japan Soc., China Inst. Am., NYU Club (bd. govs., v.p. exec. com.). Office: 141 E 44th St New York NY 10017-4006 *The general purpose I have had in mind is to leave the world no worse a place than I found it, and to try in my own way to make improvements wherever possible. To help people, to teach them to help themselves, to combat ignorance, to give material and emotional support to those who need, to the extent that is possible... are all factors of great importance. I have tried to learn about a wide variety of subjects and to use that knowledge to make both my business life and my personal life more satisfying and more productive.*

GOLDSMITH, ROBIN JEAN, anesthesiologist; b. Dubuque, Iowa, Aug. 20, 1965; d. Robert Arthur and Karen Mary (Koelker) G.; m. Paul Cassian Utrie, Oct. 20, 1990; children: Cassian Andrew, Luke Paul, Marc Robert-John. BS, U. Notre Dame, 1987; MD, U. Wis., 1991; postgrad., U. Iowa, 1995-96. Diplomate Am. Bd. Anesthesiology. Fellow assoc. in obstetric anesthesia U. Iowa, Iowa City, 1995-96, assoc., 1996-97; staff anesthesiologist Appleton (Wis.) Med. Ctr., 1997—. Cons. ASA OB Anesthesia Task Force, 1997. Recipient Gertie Marx Rsch. award Soc. Obstetrical, Anesthesia and Perinatology., 1996-97. Avocations: tennis, aerobics, music, art, cycling. Home: 4400 N Knollwood Ln Appleton WI 54913-7662 Office: Appleton Med Ctr 1818 N Meade St Appleton WI 54911-3454 E-mail: rgoldnd@aol.com.

GOLDSMITH, STANLEY JOSEPH, nuclear medicine physician, educator; b. Bklyn., Aug. 17, 1937; s. Jack and Mae (Greenzweig) G.; m. Miriam Schulman, June 6, 1959; children: Ira, Arthur, Beth, Mark. BA, Columbia U., 1958; MD, SUNY, Bklyn., 1962. Diplomate Am. Bd. Internal Medicine, Am. Bd. Nuclear Medicine (bd. dirs. 1990-96, treas. 1995-96). Intern SUNY-Kings County Med. Ctr., Bklyn., 1962-63, resident, 1965-66, chief resident, 1966-67; fellow in endocrinology Mt. Sinai Hosp., N.Y.C., 1967-68, dir. physics nuclear medicine, 1973-92; clin. dir. nuclear medicine Meml. Sloan-Kettering Cancer Ctr., N.Y.C., 1992-95; dir. nuclear medicine N.Y. Hosp.-Cornell Med. Ctr., N.Y.C., 1995—. Rsch. assoc. radioisotope svc. Bronx (N.Y.) VA Hosp., 1968-69; dir. nuclear medicine, asst. dir. endocrine dept. Nassau County Med. Ctr., East Meadow, N.Y., 1969-73; asst. prof. medicine radiology SUNY-Stony Brook Health Sci. Ctr., 1971-73; asst. prof. medicine Mt. Sinai Sch. Medicine, 1973-76, assoc. prof., 1976-84, prof. clin. medicine, 1985-91, prof. radiology and medicine, 1991-92, Cornell U. Med. Coll., 1993—, prof. radiology, medicine; bd. dirs. Capintec, Inc., Ramsey, N.J.; rsch. collaborator Brookhaven Nat. Labs., Upton, N.Y., 1971-75; cons. nuclear medicine; cons. dept. health State of N.Y., 1973-77, Health Svcs. Adminstrn., N.Y.C., 1976; mem. radiopharm. adv. com. FDA, 1987-90, low level radioactive waste disposal site commn., N.Y., 1987-95. Assoc. editor Newline, 1984-93, Jour. Nuclear Medicine, editor-in-chief, 1993-98; mem. editl. bd. Am. Jour. Cardiology, 1978-82, European Jour. Nuclear Medicine, 1993-98, Cancer Biotherapy and Radiopharm., 1998—; reviewer Israeli Jour. Med. Scis., 1979, JAMA, 1983-92, Jour. Am. Coll. Cardiology, 1984-94, Jour. Nuclear Medicine, 1989-93, 99—. Capt. U.S. Army, 1963-65. Recipient Radiology Educator award, SUNY Downstate Alumni, 2001. Fellow Am. Coll. Cardiology, ACP, Am. Coll. Nuclear Physicians (chmn. nuclear med. tech. affairs, chmn. Washington oversight com.), N.Y. Acad. Sci.; mem. AAAS, Am. Fedn. Clin. Rsch., Am. Coll. Radiology, Endocrine Soc., N.Y. Acad. Medicine (pres-elect sect. on nuclear medicine 2002-), Radiol. Soc. N.Am., Soc. Nuclear Medicine (trustee 1982-84, pres.-elect 1984-85, prse. 1985-86, chmn. govt. rels. com. 1991-93, sec. Greater N.Y. chpt. 1975-78, pres. 1979-80, pres. therapy coun. 2001-2003, named Outstanding Educator, 2000). Home: 72 Ivy Way Port Washington NY 11050-3817 Office: NY Presbyn Hosp Weill Cornell Med Ctr 525 E 68th St New York NY 10021-4885 E-mail: sjg2002@med.cornell.edu.

GOLDSMITH, WILLIS JAY, lawyer; b. Paris, Feb. 21, 1947; arrived in U.S., 1949; s. Irving and Alice (Rosenfeld) Goldsmith; m. Marilynn Jacobson, Aug. 12, 1973; children: Andrew Edward, Helene Sara. AB, Brown U., 1969; JD, NYU, 1972. Bar: N.Y. 1973, U.S. Ct. Appeals (2d cir.) 1975, D.C. 1978, U.S. Ct. Appeals (4th cir.) 1979, U.S. Ct. Appeals (D.C. cir.) 1979, U.S. Supreme Ct. 1980, U.S. Ct. Appeals (6th cir.) 1985, U.S. Ct. Appeals (7th cir.) 1989, U.S. Ct. Appeals (3d cir.) 1991, U.S. Ct. Appeals (5th cir.) 1998. Atty. Dept. Labor, Washington, 1972-74; assoc. Guggenheimer & Untermyer, NYC, 1974-77, Seyfarth, Shaw, Fairweather & Geraldson, Washington, 1977-79, ptnr., 1979-83, Jones Day, Washington, 1983—, chmn. labor and employment law practice, 1991—. Adj. prof. law Georgetown U., 1988—91. Editor (contbg.): Employee Rels. Law Jour., 1983—91; editor: (assoc.) Occupl. Safety and Health Law; mem. editl. adv. bd. Benefits Law Jour., 1991—2002. Fellow, Coll. Labor and Employment Law, 1997—. Mem.: ABA (sec. labor and employment law com. on employee benefits, com. on occupl. safety and health), Nat. Adv. Com. on Ergonomics, D.C. Bar Assn., NYU Ctr. for Labor and Employment Law (bd. dirs.), Kenwood Golf and Country Club Bethesda, Met. Club Washington. Democrat. Jewish. Home: 6409 Elmwood Rd Chevy Chase MD 20815-6621 Office: Jones Day Reavis & Pogue 51 Louisiana Ave NW Washington DC 20001-2113 E-mail: wgoldsmith@jonesday.com.

GOLDSON, ALFRED LLOYD, oncologist, educator; BS, Hampton Inst., 1968; MD, Howard U., Washington, 1972. Diplomate Am. Bd. Therapeutic Radiology; med. lic. D.C.; cert. Ga. state med. bd. Resident in radiation therapy Howard U. Hosp., Washington, 1972-75; fellow Meml. Sloan-Kettering Cancer Ctr., N.Y.C., 1975-76; clin. instr. radiation therapy coll. medicine Howard U., 1976, from asst. prof. to assoc. prof., 1977-79, chmn. dept. radiotherapy, 1979—, prof., 1984. Clin. assoc. prof. radiation oncology coll. medicine Georgetown U., Washington, 1979; chmn. radiation therapy Greater Southeastern Cmty. Hosp., 1991; chmn. Howard U. Cancer Com., 1985—; interim dir. Howard U. Cancer Ctr., 1991, exec. com., 1979—; chmn. adv. bd. Howard U. Coll. Allied Health Scis. Radiation Therapy Tech., 1977—; appt. to Nat. Cancer Adv. Bd., 1994—. Contbr. articles to profl. jours. Chmn. D.C. Cancer Consortiu,; chmn. trial com. Nat. Cancer Inst., 1984-86, patient data query editl. bd., 1984-86; program com. nat. conf. Am. Cancer Soc., 1984, trustee, 1979—; mem. Nat. Cancer Adv. Bd., 1994—. Jr. Faculty Clin. fellow Am. Cancer Soc., 1977-79. Mem. Am. Soc. Therapeutic Radiology (scientific program com. 1982-85), Am. Coll. Radiology (com. radiotherapy rsch. and devel. 1982-85), Am. Soc. Clin. Onocology, Nat. Med. Assn., Radiologic Soc. North Am., Mid-Atlantic Soc. Radiation Onocologists, N.Y. Acad. Scis., Meml. Sloan-Kettering Radiation Therapy Dept. Alumni Assn. (pres. 1989). Home: 4015 28th Pl NW Washington DC 20008-3801 Office: Howard U Dept Radiotherapy 2041 Georgia Ave NW Dept Washington DC 20060-0002

GOLDSPIEL, ARNOLD NELSON, real estate executive; b. N.Y.C., Aug. 4, 1949; s. Julius and Minna (Nelson) G. BA in Econ., Rutgers U., 1971. Elec. data processing auditor Chubb and Son, Inc., Short Hills, N.J., 1972-74; audit coord., tech. support Merrill Lynch and Co., N.Y.C., 1974-76; sr. EDP auditor Hoffman-LaRoche, Inc., Nutley, N.J., 1976-78; sr. EDP auditor then EDP audit assoc. Mut. Benefit Life Ins. Co., Newark, 1978-82, asst. comptr. corp. data security, 1982-85; sr. EDP auditor Bristol-Myers Co., N.Y.C., 1985-88; sales rep. Century 21 Valerius Realty, Belleville, N.J., 1989-90, Century 21 Stanford Agy., Nutley, N.J., 1990—; sr. EDP auditor Securitas Security Svcs. USA, Inc. (formerly Pinkerton), 1994—2001, mgr. quality assurance and change mgmt., 2002—. Mem. Info. Mgmt. System com. IBM Share-Audit Project, 1980-81. Mem. citizens planning adv. com. Nutley Sch. Bd., 1978. Staff sgt. N.J. Air N.G., 1968-74. Mem. Info. Sys. Audit and Control Assn. (cert.), Inst. Internal Auditors, Nat. Assn. Realtors, United Assn. Realtors.

GOLDSTEIN, ABRAHAM SAMUEL, lawyer, educator; b. N.Y.C., July 27, 1925; s. Isidore and Yetta (Crystal) G.; m. Ruth Tessler, Aug. 31, 1947 (dec. Feb. 1989); children: William Ira, Marianne Susan; m. Sarah Feidelson, May 7, 1995. BBA, CCNY, 1946; LL.B., Yale U., 1949, MA (hon.), 1961, Cambridge (Eng.) U., 1964; LL.D. (hon.), N.Y. Law Sch., 1979, DePaul U., 1987. Bar: D.C. bar 1949. Law clk. to judge U.S. Ct. Appeals, 1949-51; partner firm Donohue & Kaufmann, Washington, 1951-56; mem. faculty Yale Law Sch., 1956—, prof. law, 1961—, dean, 1970-75, Sterling prof. law, 1975—. Vis. prof. law Stanford Law Sch., summer 1963; vis. fellow Inst. Criminology, fellow Christ's Coll. Cambridge U., 1964-65; faculty Salzburg Seminar in Am. Studies, 1969, Inst. on Social Sci. Methods on Legal Edn., U. Denver, 1970-72; vis. prof. Hebrew U., Jerusalem, 1976, UN Asia and Far East Inst. for Prevention Crime, Tokyo, 1983, Tel Aviv U., 1986; cons. Pres.'s Com. Law Enforcement, 1967; mem. Conn. Bd. of Parole, 1967-69, Conn. Commn. Revise Criminal Code, 1966-70; mem. of the Conn. Planning Com. on Criminal Adminstrn., 1967-71; sr. v.p. Am. Jewish Congress, 1977-84, mem. exec. com., 1977-89, gov. coun., 1989-94. Author: The Insanity Defense, 1967, The Passive Judiciary, 1981, (with L. Orland) Criminal Procedure, 1974, (with J. Goldstein) Crime, Law and Society, 1971; contbr. numerous articles and revs to profl. jours. Served with AUS, 1943- 46. Guggenheim fellow, 1964-65, 75-76, Am. Acad. Arts & Scis., 1975—. Office: Yale Law Sch PO Box 208215 New Haven CT 06520-8215

GOLDSTEIN, ALFRED GEORGE, retail and consumer products executive; b. N.Y.C., Sept. 22, 1932; s. Milton and Pauline M. G.; m. Hope D. Perry, July 5, 1959; children: Mark, Robert. AB, CCNY, 1953; MS, Columbia U., 1954. With Sears, Roebuck & Co., Chgo., 1956-79, v.p. mdse, group nat. mdse. mgr., 1976-79; sr. v.p. consumer bus. Am. Can Co., Greenwich, Conn., 1979-81, sr. v.p. waste recovery bus., 1981-82, exec. v.p. plastics packaging bus., 1982-83, pres. splty. retailing sector, 1983-87; pres. splty. merchandising and direct mktg. group, Sears Logistics Svc. Sears, Roebuck & Co., Chgo., 1987-93; pres., CEO AG Assocs., Chgo., 1993 —; bd. dirs. Sears Mdse. Group, Sears Can., Ltd. Former vice chmn., CEO, bd. dirs. Fingerhut Corp.; chmn. bd. dirs. Pickwick Internat.; chmn., CEO, Musicland Group; bd. dirs. Gander Mountain Corp., 1994. Exec. editor: Internat. Jour. Addictions, 1975-80. Trustee Archaeus Found., 1978—90; bd. dirs. United Negro Coll. Fund, 1991—, mem. exec. com., 1991—, vice chmn., 2001—; mem. mktg. com. bd. trustees Art Inst. Chgo., 1988—2002; mem. adv. bd. J.L. Kellogg Sch. Mgmt. Ctr. Study Ethical Issues in Bus., Northwestern U., 1992—2001, Goizueta Bus. Sch. Ctr. Leadership and Career Studies, Emory U., 1990—97, Ford Motor Co. Ctr. Global Leadership; mem. exec. com. Columbia U. Grad. Sch. Bus. Alumni Assn., 1980—86, Am. Can Co. Found.; bd. dirs. Art Americana, 1996. Mem. Am. Arbitration Assn. (arbitrator).

GOLDSTEIN, ALLAN LEONARD, biochemist, educator; b. Bronx, N.Y., Nov. 8, 1937; s. Morris and Miriam (Siegel) G.; m. Linda Jo Tish, Dec. 23, 1975; children: Jennifer Joy, Dawn Eden, Adam Lee. BS, Wagner Coll., 1959; MS, Rutgers U., 1961, PhD, 1964; DSc (hon.), Wagner Coll., 1997. Teaching asst. Rutgers U., New Brunswick, N.J., 1959-61; asst. instr. biology, 1961-63; instr. physiology, 1963-64; research fellow Albert Einstein Coll. Medicine, 1964-66, instr. biochemistry, 1966-67, asst. prof., 1967-71, asso. prof., 1971-72; prof., dir. div. biochemistry U. Tex. Med. Br., Galveston, 1972-78, acting dir. multidisciplinary research program in mental health, 1973-78; prof., chmn. dept. biochemistry and molecular biology George Washington U. Sch. Medicine, Washington, 1978—, pres., sci. dir. Inst. for Advanced Studies in Immunology and Aging, 1985-95; chmn. bd. Alpha 1 Biomeds., 1982-2000, RegeneRX Biopharms., Inc., 2000—. Cons. Syntex Rsch., 1972-74, Hoffmann-LaRoche, 1974-82; spl. cons. bd. sci. counselors Nat. Inst. Allergy and Infectious Diseases, 1975; mem. med. rsch. svc. rev. bd. in oncology VA, 1977-80; cons. mem. decisive network com. Biol. Response Modifiers program Div. Cancer Treatment, Nat. Cancer Inst., 1982-84; mem. sci. adv. com. to pres. Papanicolaou Cancer Rsch. Inst. Miami, Inc., 1981-84; mem. AIDS task force adv. com. Nat. Cancer Inst., 1983-84; mem. sci. bd. Alliance for Aging Rsch., 1986—; trustee Albert Sabin Vaccine Inst., 2000—. Discoverer (with Abraham White) Thymosins, hormones of thymus gland and HGP-30 a "core" based p17 AIDS Vaccine. Decorated chevalier des Palmes Academiques (France), comdr. Order Vasco Nuñez de Balboa; recipient Career Scientist award N.Y.C. Health Rsch. Coun., 1967, Alumni Achievement award Wagner Coll., 1974, Gordon Wilson medal Am. Clin. and Climatol Soc., 1976, Disting. Faculty Rsch. award U. Tex. Sch. Biomed. Scis., 1976, Van Dyke award in pharmacology Columbia Coll. Physicians and Surgeons, 1984; vis. prof. award Burroughs Wellcome Found., FASEB, 1986, Ferrnandez-Cruz award, 1989, Martin Rubin award Am. Coll. Advancement in Medicine, 1990, Michele Fodera Internat. prize for Biomed. Rsch., 1990. Mem. AAAS, Endocrine Soc., Am. Soc. Biol. Chemists and Molecular Biologists, Am. Assn. Immunologists, Internat. Soc. Immunopharmacology (coun. mem. 1985-94), Assn. Med. Sch. Chm. of Depts. Biochemistry, AAUP, Acad. Medicine of Washington, Toastmasters Internat. (pres. N.Y. chpt. 1971), Sigma Xi. Home: 800 25th St NW Apt 1005 Washington DC 20037-2207 Office: George Washington U Med Ctr Dept Biochemistry/Molecular Biology 2300 I St NW Washington DC 20037-2336

GOLDSTEIN, ALVIN, lawyer; b. N.Y.C., Nov. 21, 1929; s. Abraham and Florence (Bruckner) G.; m. Eleanor Kronish, Dec. 27, 1959; children— Eric, Michael, Eileen. BSS., Coll. City N.Y., 1950; LL.B., Bklyn. Law Sch., 1953, S.JD magna cum laude, 1960. Bar: N.Y. State 1953, U.S. Supreme Ct. Asso. firm Levine & Berman, N.Y.C., 1955-59, partner, 1963; practiced in N.Y.C., 1960-62; partner firm Berman, Paley, Goldstein, Kannry, N.Y.C., 1964—. Contbr. articles to profl. publs. Served with AUS, 1953-55. Mem. N.Y. State Bar Assn., Assn. Bar City of N.Y. Home: 1 Chester Ter Hastings On Hudson NY 10706-3907 Office: Berman Paley Goldstein & Kannry 500 5th Ave Fl 43 New York NY 10110-0375

GOLDSTEIN, ANNE BRENDA, law educator; b. N.Y.C., Mar. 4, 1949; d. Emanuel Valle and Frances Virginia (Dearborn) G.; life ptnr., Kathleen Bernadette Lachance. Student, Reed Coll., Portland, Oreg., 1966-68, 70; BA, Simon Fraser U., Burnaby, B.C., 1972; JD, Northeastern U., Boston, 1976. Bar: Mass. 1977. Assoc. Burnham, Stern and Shapiro, Boston, 1977, Stern and Shapiro, Boston, 1977-80, partner, 1980-84; asst. prof. Western N.E. Coll. Sch. of Law, Springfield, Mass., 1984-86, assoc. prof., 1986-88, prof., 1988—. Conf. co-chair SALT, 1992-93; chair AALS-Gay and Lesbian Issues, 1994; vis. prof. U. Conn. Sch. Law, 1995, U. Tex. Sch. Law, 1995. Author: Representing Lesbians, Tex J. Woman and the Law, 1992; contbr. articles to profl. jours. Mem. Mass. Gay and Lesbian Bar Assn. (bd. dirs. 1989-91). Avocation: gardening. Office: WNEC Sch of Law 1215 Wilbraham Rd Springfield MA 01119-2612 E-mail: agoldstein@law.wnec.edu.

GOLDSTEIN, ARTHUR LOUIS, water purification company executive; s. David and Henrietta (Frankfort) Goldstein; m. Vida F. Fishbach; children: Jonathan M., Susanne B., James A. BSChE, Rensselaer Poly. Inst., 1957; MSChE, U. Del., 1959; MBA, Harvard U., 1960. Chmn. Ionics, Inc., Watertown, Mass., 1971—2003, pres., CEO, 1990—. Bd. dirs. State St. Boston Corp., State St. Bank and Trust Co., Cabot Corp., Ptnrs. Healthcare Sys. Inc. Bd. dirs. Jobs for Mass., Inc.; trustee Calif. Inst. Tech., Mass. Gen. Physicians Orgn., Inc., Dana-Farber/Ptnrs. Cancer Care; co-chmn. Indsl. Rels. and Ventures com. Ptnrs. Healthcare Sys. Inc.; mem. Nat.Acad. Engring. and its Industry Adv. bd.; exec. com. CEOs for Fundamental Change in Edn., Inner-City Scholarship Fund; chmn. Mass. High Tech. Coun., 1985—87, bd. dirs., mem. exec. com.; past pres. Rensselaer Coun.; former mem. vis. com. Harvard Bus. sch., Harvard Sch. Pub. Health; mem. cardiovascular adv. coun. Harvard Environ. Health Coun. Mem.: Nat. acad. Engring. Achievements include patents for related to purification and processing of liquids. Office: Ionics Inc PO Box 9131 Watertown MA 02471-9131 also: 65 Grove St Watertown MA 02472-2826

GOLDSTEIN, AVRAM, pharmacology educator; b. N.Y.C., July 3, 1919; s. Israel and Bertha (Markowitz) Goldstein; m. Dora Benedict, Aug. 29, 1947; children: Margaret, Daniel, Joshua, Michael. AB, Harvard, 1940, MD, 1943. Intern Mt. Sinai Hosp., N.Y.C., 1944; successively instr., assoc., asst. prof. pharmacology Harvard U., 1947—55; prof. dept. pharmacology Stanford U., Palo Alto, Calif., 1955—89, exec. head dept., 1955—70, prof. emeritus, 1989—. Dir. Addiction Rsch. Found., Palo Alto, Calif., 1973—87. Author: Biostatistics, Principles of Drug Action, 1965, ADDICTION: From Biology to Drug Policy, 2001. Served from 1st lt. to capt., Med. Corps U.S. Army, 1944—46. Mem.: AAAS, Am. Soc. Biol. Chemists, Am. Soc. Pharmacology and Exptl. Therapeutics, Am. Acad. Arts and Scis., Inst. Medicine NAS. Office: Stanford U Sch Medicine Edwards Bldg Rm 354 300 Pasteur Dr Stanford CA 94305*

GOLDSTEIN, BARRY BRUCE, biologist, food company executive, lawyer; b. N.Y.C., Aug. 2, 1947; s. George and Pauline (Kolodner) G.; m. Jacqueline Barbara Aboulafia, Dec. 21, 1968; children: Joshua, Jessica. BA, Queens Coll., 1968; MA, CCNY, N.Y.C., 1974; PhD, CUNY, N.Y.C., 1980; JD, U. N.Mex., 1994. Microbiologist CPC Internat., Yonkers, NY, 1968—71; rsch. scientist U. Tex., Austin, 1977—80; v.p. SystemCulture Inc., Honolulu, 1980—83; bioenergy/aquaculture program mgr. N.Mex. Solar Energy Inst., Las Cruces, 1983—89; pres. Ancient Seas Aquaculture Inc., Roswell, N.Mex., 1989—92, Desert Seas Aquaculture Inc., Roswell, 1990—92, Hawaii Shellfish Co., Las Cruces, 1991—94; prin. mem. tech. staff Sandia Nat. Labs., Albuquerque, 1994—. Editl. bd. Natural Resources Jour.; contbr. articles to profl. jours. Recipient Nat. Energy Innovation award Dept. Energy, Washington, 1985; Grad. fellow CUNY, 1971, Jesse Smith Noyes fellow, 1975, Regents scholar SUNY, 1964. Mem. World Aquaculture Soc., N.Mex. State Bar Assn. Avocations: aquaculture, reading. E-mail: bgoldst@sandia.gov.

GOLDSTEIN, BERNARD, transportation and casino gaming company executive; b. Rock Island, Ill., Feb. 5, 1929; s. Morris and Fannie (Borenstein) G.; m. Irene Alter, Dec. 18, 1949; children: Jeffrey, Robert, Kathy, Richard. BA, U. Ill., 1949, LLB, 1951. Bar: Iowa 1951. With Alter Co., Bettendorf, Iowa, 1951—, chmn. bd., 1979—, Isle of Capri Casinos, Inc., Biloxi, Miss., 1992—, chmn. CEO, 1997—. Pres. Quad City Jewish Fedn., 1975. Named Top Performing Gaming CEO of the Yr., Am. Gaming Assn., 2001; recipient Ernst and Young Entrepreneur of the Yr. award, 1999, Rivers Hall of Fame

Achievement award, 1999, Simon Wiesenthal Nat. Cmty. award, Compass award, Passenger Vessel Assn., Outstanding Bus. Leader award, Jewish Fedn. South Palm Beach County, Jerusalem medal, State of Israel Bonds. Jewish.

GOLDSTEIN, BERNARD DAVID, physician, educator; b. Bronx, N.Y., Feb. 28, 1939; m. Russellyn Carruth, May 5, 1995; children: Lara, Ross. BS, U. Wis., 1958; MD, NYU, 1962. Diplomate Am. Bd. Toxicology, Am. Bd. Internal Medicine, Am. Bd. Hematology. Intern, asst. resident, resident 3d and 4th (NYU) med. divns. Bellevue Hosp., N.Y.C., 1962—65; faculty depts. environ. medicine and medicine NYU Med. Ctr., N.Y.C., 1968—80; attending physician Bellevue and Univ. Hosps., N.Y.C., 1968—80; prof., chmn. dept. environ. and cmty. medicine U. Medicine and Dentistry, N.J.-Robert Wood Johnson Med. Sch., Piscataway, 1980—, dir. grad. program in pub. health, 1982—89, dir. environ. and occupl. health scis. inst., 1985—; asst. adminstr. for R & D EPA, Washington, 1983—85; acting dean Sch. Pub. Health of N.J., Piscataway, 1998—99; dir. Nat. Inst. Environ. Health Scis. Ctr. of Excellence, 1988—94. Chmn. clean air sci. adv. com. EPA, 1982—83; toxicology study sect. NIH, 1980—84, chmn., 1982—84; bd. sci. dirs. Risk Sci. Inst., 1986—, nat. adv. environ. health effects coun., 1987—91; chmn. ad hoc com. on dioxin EPA, 1988—89, vice-chmn., chmn. sci. group on methodology for sci. evaluation chems., 1989—, chmn. working group on Air Quality Guidelines for Major Urban Air Pollutants, 1985; health rev. com., chmn. health rsch. com. Health Effects Inst., 1987—; bd. dirs. Internat. Life Sci. Inst., Roy F. Weston, Inc.; pres.-elect Soc. for Risk Analysis, 2002. Contbr. articles. Recipient Solomon Berson Med. Alumni Achievement award, NYU, Sullivan award, N.J. Pub. Health Assn., 20th Century Disting. Svc. award, Pa. State U., Disting. Achievement award, Soc. for Risk Analysis. Fellow: ACP, Am. Coll. Preventive Medicine; mem.: Am. Soc. Clin. Investigation, Inst. Medicine NAS. Achievements include research in in concept of biological markers in the field of risk assessment. Office: Office of the Dean Univ of Pitts 130 Desoto St Pittsburgh PA 15261

GOLDSTEIN, BRIAN ALAN, lawyer, physician; b. Bronx, N.Y., Oct. 24, 1959; s. Stanley Irving and Hortense G.; m. Eva Rubinstein, June 19, 1988; children: Ariel Petra, Adam Izak. MD, Ctr. Tech. U., Santo Domingo, 1980; JD magna cum laude, SUNY Buffalo, 1995. Diplomate Am. Bd. Surgery; bar: N.Y. 1996, U.S. Dist. Ct. (we. dist.) N.Y., U.S. Dist. Ct. (ea. dist.) Mich., 1997 (we. dist.) 1999, U. S. Dist. Ct. (no. dist.) Ohio 1999. Resident N.Y. Meth. Hosp., Bklyn., 1981-86; surgeon Hadassah Med. Ctr., Jerusalem, 1988-91; cardiothoracic surgeon Tygerburg Hosp., Capetown, South Africa, 1992; assoc. Michael Doran & Assocs., Buffalo, 1994—2002; ptnr. Cellino & Barnes, Buffalo, 2002—. Instr. surgery Hebrew U., Jerusalem, 1989-91, U. Stellenbosch, South Africa, 1992. Contbr. articles to profl. jours. Fellow Interam. Coll. Physicians and Surgeons; mem. ABA, Internat. Soc. Cardiothoracic Surgeons, Assn. Trial Lawyers Am., We. N.Y. Trial Lawyers Assn., N.Y. State Bar Assn., Erie County Bar Assn. (health law com. 1996). Office: Cellino & Barnes 17 Court St Buffalo NY 14202

GOLDSTEIN, BRUCE A. lawyer; b. Buffalo, May 19, 1945; s. Lew and Sally (Freedman) G.; m. Betsy S. Robins, May 30, 1968; children: Lisa, Dena. BS, SUNY, Buffalo, 1967; JD, U. Mich., 1972. Bar: N.Y. 1973, U.S. Dist. Ct. (we. dist.) N.Y. 1973, U.S. Claims Ct., U.S. Ct. Appeals (2d cir.), U.S. Supreme Ct. 1980. Asst. county atty. Erie County Atty.'s Office, Buffalo, 1973-75; asst. dist. atty. Eric County Dist. Atty., Buffalo, 1975-77; assoc. Lipsitz, Green et. al., Buffalo, 1977-80; ptnr. Serotte, Reich & Goldstein, Buffalo, 1980-85; sr. ptnr. Bouvier, O'Connor, Buffalo, 1985—. Assoc. prof., instr. law SUNY, Buffalo, 1987—. Author: Legal Rights of Persons with Disabilities: An Analysis of Federal Law, 1989—. Mem. Leadership Buffalo, N.Y. State Developmental Disabilities Planning Coun., Albany, 1986-94; bd. dirs. Alexander Graham Bell Assn. for the Deaf, pres., 1994-96. Named Citizen of the Yr., Buffalo News, 1989, Lifetime Membership award Nat. PTA, Brotherhood/Sisterhood award NCCJ, 1993. Mem. N.Y. State Bar Assn., Erie County Bar Assn. Home: 56 Fairlawn Rd Amherst NY 14226-3422 Office: Bouvier O'Connor 350 Main St 1400 Main Place Tower Buffalo NY 14202-3714 E-mail: bgoldste@bouvierlaw.com.

GOLDSTEIN, BURTON JACK, psychiatrist; b. Balt., Sept. 23, 1930; s. Hyman and Roz (Levin) G.; m. Linda Feuer, June 16, 1989; children: Howard, Herbert, Brian, Esther, Leonard, Mark. BS in Pharmacy, U. Md., 1953, MD, 1960. Diplomate Am. Bd. Psychiatry and Neurology (bd. examiner). Intern Jackson Meml. Hosp., Miami, Fla., 1960-61, NIMH fellow in psychiatry, 1961-63, chief resident, 1963-64; dir. div. clin. psychopharmacology, dept. psychiatry U. Miami, 1964-92, chief div. research, 1964-71, prof. pharmacology, 1973—, prof. psychiatry, 1973—, acting chmn. dept. psychiatry, 1983-85; prof. epidemiology, pub. health Sch. Medicine, 1999; sr. cons. in psychopharmacology Mt. Sinai Med. Ctr., Miami Beach, 1993—; dir. psychiat. consultation liaison svc. Mt. Sinai Hosp., Miami Beach, 1993—. Bd. advs. Fla. Mental Health Inst. U. South Fla.; cons. in psychiat. rsch. South Fla. State Hosp., West Hollywood; cons. indsl. security program Dept. Def.; cons. VA Psychiatry Svc., Miami; chmn. panel on neuropharmacologic drugs U.S. Pharmacopeial Conv., Inc., mem. exec. com.; mem. faculty Health Svcs. Ctr., U. Miami, 1996. Mem. editorial bd. Miami Medicine, Clin. Advancement in Treatment of Depression; contbr. chpts. to books, articles to profl. publs. Served to maj. AUS, 1953-62. Fellow Am. Psychiat. Assn. (life), Am. Coll. Psychiatrists, Am. Coll. Clin. Pharmacology, Am. Coll. Neuropsychopharmacology; mem. Fla. Med. Assn., Dade County Med. Assn., Royal Soc. Health, Am. Assn. Clin. Pharmacology and Chemotherapy, Am. Soc. Addiction Medicine, Collegium Internationale Neuropsychopharmacologium, South Fla. Psychiat. Soc. Office: 1800 NW 9th Ave Ste 420 Miami FL 33136-1131

GOLDSTEIN, CHARLES ARTHUR, lawyer; b. N.Y.C., Nov. 20, 1936; s. Murray and Evelyn V. Goldstein; m. Judith Stein, Sept. 29, 1962 (div. 1982); 1 child, Deborah Ruth; m. Carol Sager, Nov. 10, 1990 (div. 1995). AB, Columbia U., 1958; JD cum laude, Harvard U., 1961. Bar: N.Y. 1962. Law clk. U.S. Ct. Appeals (2d cir.), 1961-62; assoc. Fried, Frank, Harris, Shriver & Jacobson, N.Y.C., 1962-69; ptnr. Schulte Roth & Zabel, N.Y.C., 1969-79, Weil, Gotshal & Manges, N.Y.C., 1979-83, counsel, 1983-85; ptnr. Shea & Gould, N.Y.C., 1985-94, Sutherland, Asbill & Brennan, N.Y.C., 1994-95; counsel Squire, Sanders & Dempsey, N.Y.C., 1996-01; counsel to amb. Ronald S. Lauder, 2001—. Lectr. Columbia U. Law Sch. Gen. counsel to Citizens Budget Commn., 1980-87; mem. Temp. Commn. on City Fins., 1975-77; mem. Gov.'s Task Force on World Trade Ctr. Mem. Am. Coll. Real Estate Lawyers. Republican. Home: 220 E 65th St New York NY 10021-6620 Office: 767 Fifth Ave Ste 4200 New York NY 10153 E-mail: cgoldstein@rslmgmt.com.

GOLDSTEIN, DARRA JANE, language educator, editor; b. Lakewood, N.J., Apr. 28, 1951; d. Irving S. and Helen Haft Goldstein; m. Dean Adams Crawford, Aug. 23, 1980; 1 child, Leila Adams Crawford. BA, Vassar Coll., 1973; MA, Stanford U., 1976, PhD, 1983. Prof. Russian Williams Coll., Williamstown, Mass., 1983—; founding editor Gastronomica: The Jour. of Food and Culture, Berkeley, Calif., 2000—. Mem. acad. adv. coun. The Am. Coll. in Georgia; restaurant cons. Firebird, N.Y.C., 1996, Russian Tea Rm., N.Y.C., 1999—2000. Author: A la Russe: A Cookbook of Russian Hospitality, 1983, reissued as A Taste of Russia, 1985, 1991, 2d rev. edit., 1999, All About Love, 1985, Art for the Masses, 1985; author: (with Elizabeth Gaynor and Kari Haavisto) Russian Houses, 1991; author: The Georgian Feast: The Vibrant Culture and Savory Food of the Republic of Georgia, 1993, reprinted, 1999, Nikolai Zabolotsky: Play for Mortal Stakes, 1993, The Vegetarian Hearth: Recipes and Reflections for the Cold Season, 1996, reprinted as The Winter Vegetarian, 2000; author: (with Deborah Rothschild and Ellen Lupton) Graphic Design in the Mechanical Age, 1998; contbr. articles to profl. jours.; editor (with Jill Meredith): The World Opened Wide: 20th Century Russian Women Artists from the Collection of Thomas P. Whitney, 2001; series editor California Studies in Food and Culture, food editor Russian Life mag., mem. adv. bd. Finalist M.F.K. Fisher award, Les Dames d'Escoffier, 2002; recipient Sophie Coe Subsidiary prize in food history, The Oxford Symposium on Food History, 1997; Nat. Def. Fgn. Lang. fellow, 1975—77, Fulbright-Hays Doctoral Dissertation Abroad grantee, Slavic Inst., Stockholm U., 1980—81, rsch. grantee, Internat. Rsch. and Exchs. Bd., 1980—81, 1982—83, 1987, 1994, Mellon Found., 1984, 1997, Kennan Inst. for Advanced Russian Studies Rsch. fellow, 1986, rsch. fellow, Am. Coun. Learned Socs., 1987, coll. tchrs. fellow, NEH, 1999. Mem.: Internat. Assn. Culinary Profls., Am. Assn. for Advancement of Slavic Studies, Culinary Historians of Boston. Office: Williams Coll Weston Hall 995 Main St Williamstown MA 01267 Business E-Mail: darra.goldstein@williams.edu.

GOLDSTEIN, DAVID ARTHUR, biophysicist, educator; b. Rochester, N.Y., Nov. 8, 1934; s. Jacob David and Elizabeth Maude (Brown) G.; m. Marie Elaine Nardone, May 25, 1969; 1 child, David James. AB in Physics, Harvard U., 1956, MD, 1960. Rsch. fellow biophys. lab Harvard Med. Sch., Cambridge, Mass., 1960-62, rsch. assoc. biophys. lab., 1964-65; asst. prof. radiation biology and biophysics Rochester Sch. Med. and Dentistry, 1965-68, assoc. prof. biophysics, 1968-97, assoc. prof. biomath., 1969-74, assoc. prof. med. informatics, 1988—. Dir. Med. Ctr. Computing, U. Rochester Med. Sch., 1975-77, assoc. chmn. dept. radiation biology and biophysics, 1980-85, dir. divsn. med. informatics, 1988-98; cons. mathematician NIMH, Bethesda, Md., 1963-64. Contbr. articles to profl. jours. Treas. Stormers Soccer Club, Rochester, 1983-93; bd. dirs. Monroe County Girls Soccer League, Rochester, 1988-93. Surgeon, USPHS, 1963-64. Grantee AEC, NIH, NSF, ERDA, DOE, 1965-96. Mem. Biophys. Soc., N.Y. Acad. Scis. Home: 75 Deer Creek Rd Pittsford NY 14534-4147

GOLDSTEIN, DAVID BAIRD, energy program director, physicist; b. Cleve., June 29, 1951; s. Laurence and Gloria Reta (Baumgarten) G.; m. Julia Beth Vetromile, May 17, 1980; children: Elianna Louise, Abraham Micah. AB in Physics, U. Calif., Berkeley, 1973; PhD in Physics, U. Calif., 1978. Rsch. asst. Lawrence Berkeley (Calif.) Lab., 1975-78, staff scientist, 1978-80; sr. scientist, dir. energy program Natural Resources Def. Coun., San Francisco, 1980—. Sub-com. chair standing standards project com. 90.1 ASHRAE, Atlanta, 1983-96; vice-chmn. bd. Consortium for Energy Efficiency, Inc., Sacramento, 1991-93, 99-02, advisor, 1993-96; initiator and advisor Super Efficient Refrigerator Program, Inc., 1991-96. Contbr. articles to profl. jours. Recipient Champion of Energy Efficiency award Am. Coun. for an Energy Efficient Economy, 1988, 94; MacArthur Found. fellow, 2002. Fellow: Am. Phys. Soc. (Leo Szilard award 1998); mem.: Inst. Location Efficiency (treas. 1999—, bd. mem.), New Bldgs. Inst. (co-initiator, pres. 2000—), Inst. Market Transformation (chmn. 1995—, initiator, bd. mem.), Sigma Xi, Phi Beta Kappa. Jewish. Avocations: travel, hiking, music, photography. Home: 1240 Washington St San Francisco CA 94108-1041 Office: Natural Resources Def Coun 71 Stevenson St Ste 1825 San Francisco CA 94105-2964 E-mail: dgoldstein@nrdc.org.

GOLDSTEIN, DAVID MEYER, physician; b. Detroit, Apr. 26, 1955; s. Albert and Marge Goldstein; m. Kathryn Elizabeth Brown, Sept. 1, 1990; children: Nicole, Jessica. BSME, U. Mich., 1977, MS, 1979, MD, 1982. Diplomate Am. Bd. Phys. Medicine and Rehab., Am. Bd. Holistic Medicine. Mem. cons. staff West Penn Hosp., Pitts., 1996-2000; pvt. practice Pitts., 1994—; resident PM&R Rehab. Inst. of Chgo., 1982-85; cons. staff HealthSouth Harmarville Rehab. Hosp., Pitts., 1997-2000. Mem. Am. Holistic Med. Assn., Am. Coll. for Advancement in Medicine. Office: 9401 McKnight Rd Ste 301B Pittsburgh PA 15237-6000

GOLDSTEIN, DEBRA HOLLY, judge; b. Newark, Mar. 11, 1953; d. Aaron and Erica (Schreier) Green; m. Joel Ray Goldstein, Aug. 14, 1983; children: Stephen Michael, Jennifer Ann. BA, U. Mich., 1973; JD, Emory U., 1977. Bar: Ga. 1977, Mich. 1978, D.C. 1978, Ala. 1984. Tax analyst atty. Gen. Motors Corp., Detroit, 1977-78; trial atty. U.S. Dept. Labor, Birmingham, Ala., 1978-90; U.S. adminstrv. law judge office hearing and appeals Social Security Adminstrn., Birmingham, 1990—. New judge faculty U.S. adminstrv. law judges Social Security Adminstrn., 1991, 93—; co-chair Girl Scout Pluralism Think Tank, 1999. Mem. editl. bd. The Ala. Lawyer, 1994-99, The Addendum, 1995-99. Mem. United Way, Birmingham, mem. vis. allocation team, 1998—, mem. planning com., 2001—; mem. Birmingham Bus. and Profl. Women Fedn., mem. steering com., 1995—2000; leader Girl Scout Troop, 1992—; bd. dirs. Cahaba Girl Scout Coun., 1996—2002; mem. Leadership for Diversity Initative, 1995—96, Leadership Birmingham, 1997—98, Momentum, 2002—03; chmn. Success By 6 Blue Ribbon Adv. Com., 2003—; bd. dirs. Temple Emanu-El, 2000—03, YWCA, 2002—. Mem. ABA, Ga. Bar Assn., D.C. Bar Assn., Birmingham Bar Assn. (bd. dirs. women's sect. 1999—), Ala. Bar Assn., Zonta (co-pres. 1996-98), B'nai B'rith Women (chair S.E. region 1984-86, Women's Humanitarian award 1981), Hadassah (social action v.p. 2000-01). Jewish.

GOLDSTEIN, DONALD MAURICE, historian, educator; b. Dec. 15, 1932, s. Max A. and Jean M. Goldstein; m. Mariann Norma Zinck, Aug. 5, 1961; children: Tammie, Timmie, Tommie, Teri. BA, U. Md., 1954, MA, 1962; MS, Georgetown U., 1963; MPA, George Washington U., 1965; PhD, U. Denver, 1970; grad., War Coll., 1973, Air Command and Staff Coll., 1965. Commd. 2d. lt. USAF, 1955, advanced through grades to lt. col., 1972, comdr. missile site, 1958-59; staff officer US Strike Command, 1961-64; rsch. assoc. Airstaff Pentagon; assoc. prof. history USAF Acad., 1965-71, asst. track coach, 1965-71; ret., 1977; assoc. prof. history Troy State U., Ala., 1971-74; prof. aerospace studies U. Pitts., 1975-77, assoc. prof. pub. and internat. affairs, 1975-92, prof., 1993, dir. placement and alumni, 1977-85, assoc. dean, 1985-88. Author: Ennis C. Whithead Aerospace Commander, 1970, Adolph Hitler in the Perspective of the Am. Press, 1961, Adolph Hitler Administr. of a Society, 1965, (with others) Miracle at Midway, 1982, 2001, 3d edit., 2002, Target Tokyo: The Story of the Surge Spy Ring in Japan, 1984, 3d edit., 2001; collaborator: At Dawn We Slept: The Untold Story of Pearl Harbor, 1981, 3d edit., 2001, Pearl Harbor: The Verdict of History, 1985, 3d edit., 2001, December 7, 1941: The Day the Japanese Attacked Pearl Harbor, 1990, Fading Victory: The Diary of Matome Ugaki, 1991, The Way It Was: A Pictorial Hist.of Pearl Harbor, 1991, The Williwar War: The Arkansas Nat. Guard in World War II, 1992, The Pearl Harbor Paper, 1993, Classics in Internat. Affairs with Others, 1993, 2d edit., 1998, D Day: A Pictorial Hist., 1994, Nuts: The Battle of the Bulge, 1994, Security in Korea: War, Stalemate and Negotiation, 1994, Rain of Ruin: A Photographic Hist. of Hiroshima and Nagasaki, 1995, Amelia Earhart: A Biography, 1997, Vietnam: A Pictorial History, 1997, The Spanish American War: A Centennial Hist., 1998, The Korean War: The Story and Photographs, 2000, World War I: The Story and Photographs, 2002, God's Samurai: Lead Pilot at Pearl Harbor, 2003; asst. editor papers on fgn. policy for House Com. on Internat. Affairs, 1947-54; contbr. articles on def. policy and nat. security affairs to profl. jour. Decorated Soldiers medal, Meritorious Svc. medal with 2 oak leaf clusters, Joint Svc. Commendation medal, Air Force Commendation medal with oak leaf cluster. Mem. Am. Hist. Assn., Internat. Studies Assn., Am. Soc. Pub. Adminstr., Am. Polit. Sci. Assn., Air Force Assn., Toastmasters, Omicron Delta Kappa, Phi Kappa Phi, Phi Alpha Theta, Sigma Nu. Roman Catholic. Home: 2146 Meadowmont Dr Upper St Clair Pittsburgh PA 15241 Office: U Pitts Grad Sch Pub Int Affairs Dean's Office Forbes Complex 3J-11 Pittsburgh PA 15260

GOLDSTEIN, DORA BENEDICT, pharmacologist, educator; b. Milton, Mass., Apr. 25, 1922; d. George Wheeler and Marjory (Pierce) Benedict; m. Avram Goldstein, Aug. 29, 1947; children: Margaret E. Wallace, Daniel P., Joshua S., Michael B. Student, Bryn Mawr Coll., 1940-42, Stanford U., 1945; MD, Harvard U., 1949. Research assoc. Stanford U., 1955-70, sr. research assoc., 1970-74, adj. prof., 1974-78, prof. pharmacology, 1978-92, prof. pharmacology emerita, 1992—, co-dir. faculty mentoring program sch. medicine, 1994—2001. Author: Pharmacology of Alcohol, 1983; contbr. articles to sci. jours. Bd. dirs. Parents, Families and Friends of Lesbians and Gays. Mem. Research Soc. Alcoholism (pres. 1979-81, award for excellence), Am. Soc. Pharmacology and Exptl. Therapeutics, Am. Soc. Biol. Chemists, Internat. Soc. Biomed. Research on Alcoholism, Intersex Soc. of N. Am. (adv. bd.). E-mail: dody@stanford.edu.

GOLDSTEIN, DORIS MUELLER, librarian, researcher; b. Somerville, N.J., Mar. 11, 1942; d. Henry Frederick and Sophie (Lages) Mueller; m. Steven Morris Goldstein, July 4, 1971. BA, U. Nebr., 1964, MA, 1966; cert., Goethe U., Frankfurt, Fed. Republic Germany, 1966; MLS, U. Md., 1973. Vol., instr. Peace Corps, Addis Abeba, Ethiopia, 1966-68; cataloger Libr. of Congress, Washington, 1968-69; instr. Bowie (Md.) State Coll., 1969-72; libr. Kennedy Inst. of Ethics Georgetown U., Washington, 1973-81, dir. libr. and info. svcs., 1981—, dir. Nat. Reference Ctr. for Bioethics Lit., 1984—. Cons. dept. nursing George Mason U., Fairfax, Va., 1984-89; adj. faculty mem. in libr. sci. U. Md., 1990. Author: Bioethics: A Guide to Information Sources, 1982; editor Scope Note Series, 1985—; co-editor Bibliography of Bioethics, 2002-; contbr. articles to profl. jours. Mem. Phi Beta Kappa, Alpha Lambda Delta, Delta Phi Alpha, Beta Phi Mu. Office: Georgetown U Kennedy Inst Ethics Washington DC 20057-1212

GOLDSTEIN, E. ERNEST, lawyer, consultant; b. Pitts., Oct. 9, 1918; s. Nathan E. and Annie (Ginsberg) G.; m. Peggy Janet Rosenfeld, June 22, 1941 (dec. Aug. 2003); children: Susan M. Goldstein Lipsitch, Daniel F. AB cum laude, Amherst Coll., 1939; student, U. Chgo. Law Sch., 1940-42; LL.B., Georgetown U., 1947; S.JD, U. Wis., 1956. Bar: D.C. 1947, Tex. 1958, U.S. Supreme Ct. 1967, conseil juridique, France 1973-79. Pvt. practice, Washington, 1947; with Dept. Justice, also War Claims Commn., 1947-50; assoc. counsel crime com. U.S. Senate, 1950-51; gen. counsel antitrust subcom. jud. Ho. of Reps., 1951-52; restrictive trade practices specialist Office U.S. Spl. Rep., Paris; also U.S. rep. productivity and applied research com. OEEC, 1952-54; prof. law U. Tex., 1955-65; spl. asst. to Pres. U.S. Lyndon B. Johnson, 1967-69; counsel Coudert Freres, Paris, 1966-67, ptnr., 1969-79; cons. CBS, Inc., 1980-85; advisor Ransom Humanities Rsch. Ctr. U. Tex., 1995—2003; ret. Cons. on antitrust European coal and steel cmty., Luxembourg, 1956, on trade regulation Justice Sec., P.R., 1962; internat. law cons. Naval War Coll., 1962, 64; lectr. Inst. Advanced European Studies, U. Nice, France, 1967, Free U. Brussels, 1967, Europa Inst., Amsterdam, 1970; vis. prof. U. P.R. Law Sch., 1962; prof. Am. sem., Salzburg, Austria, 1963, 79; adj. prof. law U. Tex., 1993-95; chmn. Internat. Lawyers Ann. Conf. Mgmt. Ctr., Europe, 1971-79. Author: Patent, Trademark and Copyright Law, 1959, American Enterprise and Scandinavian Antitrust Law, 1962; contbr. author: LBJ: To Know Him Better, 1995, procs. of The Conference on Global Responsibility of Law Librarians, 1990; founder Tex. Internat. Law Jour., 1963, mem. adv. bd., 1983—. Membership chair Am. Vets. Com., Washington, 1946-47; chmn. S.W. regional adv. bd. Anti-Defamation League, 1964-65; bd. dirs. Am. C. of C. in France, 1970-79, Ctr. Internat. Formation Europèene, 1971—; trustee Leadership Enrichment Arts Program, 1996—; dir. Bus. Alliance for Vietnamese Edn., 1996—, chmn. adv. bd., 1994, co-chmn. adv. bd., 1995—; bd. govs. Am. Hosp. Paris, 1972-79, sec., 1974-79; chmn. fund raising Dem. Party Com. in France, 1973-77; mem. nat. com. Lyndon B. Johnson Meml. Grove, 1972-74; mem. nat. fin. coun. Dem. Nat. Com., 1975-77. With AUS, 1942-46. Decorated Legion of Merit; chevalier Légion d'Honneur, 1971; chevalier Ordre des Arts et des Lettres, 1981; recipient Carl Fulda Internat. Law award U. Tex., 1978; Medal of Honor, Am. C. of C., Paris, 1984, Carnegie Found. fellow, 1954-55, Ford. Found. Internat. Studies fellow, 1959, 60. Mem. Am. Club Paris (pres. 1976-78); Philos Soc. of Tex., Tex. Internat. Law Soc. (founder), Headliners Club, Austin Town and Gown Club, Order of Coif, Phi Delta Phi. Home: Cambridge Tower 1801 Lavaca St Apt 15F Austin TX 78701-1333

GOLDSTEIN, EDWARD DAVID, lawyer, former glass company executive; b. N.Y.C., July 12, 1927; s. Michael and Leah (Kirsh) G.; m. Rhoda Gordon, Apr. 18, 1950; children: Linda, Ellen, Ruth, Michael. BA, U. Mich., 1950, JD with distinction, 1952. Bar: Calif. 1952. Assoc. Orrick, Dahlquist, Herrington & Sutcliffe, San Francisco, 1952-54, Johnston & Johnston, San Francisco, 1954-56; with legal dept. Ohio Match Co., Hunt Foods & Industries, 1956-58; asst. gen. mgr., sales mgr. Glass Containers Corp., Fullerton, Calif., 1958-62, v.p., gen. mgr., 1962-68, pres., CEO, 1968-83. Chmn. bd. Knox Glass Co., Fairmount Glass Cos., 1967-68; gen. counsel FHP, Internat., FHP, Inc., 1985-87. Chmn. bd. trustees St. Jude Hosp., Fullerton, 1984-88. Served with USNR, 1945-46. Mem. ABA, State Bar Calif., Orange County Bar Assn., Nat. Health Lawyers Assn., Am. Arbitration Assn., Am. Coll. Legal Medicine (assoc.-in-law), Calif. Soc. Healthcare Attys. Home: 2230 Yucca Ave Fullerton CA 92835-3320 Office: 110 E Wilshire Ave STe 305 Fullerton CA 92832-1900 E-mail: edgatty@aol.com.

GOLDSTEIN, ELEANOR, artist, social worker; b. N.Y.C., May 2, 1935; d. Benjamin and Gertrude (Bober) Kronish; m. Alvin Goldstein, Dec. 27, 1959; children: Eric, Michael, Eileen. BA, Bennington (Vt.) Coll., 1957; MSW, Columbia U., 1981. Cert. social worker, N.Y. Asst. dir. Westchester Student Adv. Coalition, White Plains, N.Y., 1981-82, exec. dir., 1982-85; artist Hastings-on-the-Hudson, N.Y., 1985—. Exhibited in group shows at Mus. of Fine Arts, Springfield, Mass., 1989, Salmagundi Club, N.Y.C., 1989, 2000, Lever House Gallery, 1989, 1992, N.J. Bergen Mus. Arts, Paramus, 1991, Nat. Arts Club, N.Y.C., 1991, 1998, Hammond Mus., North Salem, N.Y., 1992, Pen and Brush Club, N.Y.C., 1992, Westbeth Gallery, 1994, Am. Embassy, Sanaa, Yemen, 1995—98, Sch. House Gallery, Croton Falls, N.Y., 1997—98, Cornell Med. Libr., 1998, Allen Shephard Gallery, N.Y.C., 2001, Art of the N.E., Silvermine Guild, New Canaan, Conn., 2002, Represented in permanent collections IBM, Pepisco, Pfizer & Co., The Cathedral of St. John the Devine, N.Y.C., Std. & Poor . Organizer Hastings Com. for Youth, Inc., 1976-79. Recipient Pastel Soc. Am. award, The Salmagundo Club Seascape award, 2000. Mem. N.Y. Artists Equity Assn., Pastel Soc. of Am. Home: 1 Chester Ter Hastings On Hudson NY 10706

GOLDSTEIN, ELLIOTT, lawyer, director; b. Atlanta, Oct. 23, 1915; s. Max Fullmore and Sarah Ray (London) G.; m. Harriet Weinberg, Oct. 24, 1942; children: Lillian, Ellen. Student, Ga. Sch. Tech., 1932-33; BS, U. Ga., 1936; LL.B., Yale U., 1939. Bar: Ga. 1938, D.C. 1977. Asso. firm Little, Powell, Reid & Goldstein, Atlanta, 1939-40; partner firm Powell, Goldstein, Frazer & Murphy, Atlanta, 1946-77, 80—, Washington, 1977-80. Spl. counsel com. on standards ofcl. conduct U.S. Ho. of Reps., 1978; mem. legal adv. com. N.Y. Stock Exchange, 1982-85. Author: Counselling the Board of Directors in its Structure, Functions and Compensation, 1985, Georgia Corporation Law and Practice, 1989; contbr. articles to profl. jours. Hon. v.p. Am. Jewish Com.; chmn. Atlanta Hist. Soc., 1990-94. Lt. col. F.A., U.S. Army, 1941-46, ETO. Decorated Bronze Star. Fellow ABA Found.; mem. ABA (chmn. com. corp. laws 1979-84, chmn. ad hoc com. ALI Corp. governance project 1982-86, mem. coun. sect. corp. banking and bus. law 1983-86, sr. del. ho. of dels. 1986-94), Am. Law Inst., Ga. Bar Assn., Atlanta Bar Assn., Lawyers Club Atlanta, Commerce Club, Standard Club. Democrat. Home: 2660 Peachtree Rd NW Atlanta GA 30305-3673 Office: Powell Goldstein Frazer & Murphy 191 Peachtree St NE Fl 16 Atlanta GA 30303-1740

GOLDSTEIN, EUGENE E. lawyer; b. Bklyn., Jan. 5, 1946; s. Lester R. and Hannah (Strauss) G.; m. Anita Lorraine Wolis, June 10, 1975; children—Michael Jonathan, Lawrence Evan. B.A., CCNY, 1967; J.D., Washington U., 1970. Bar: N.Y. 1971, U.S. Dist. Ct. (ea. dist.) N.Y. 1973, U.S. Dist. Ct. (so. dist.) N.Y. 1974, U.S. Ct. Appeals (2d cir.) 1975, U.S. Supreme Ct. 1982. Law clk. VISTA, Portland, Oreg., 1970-71; assoc. firm Forscher, Glassman & Elias, N.Y.C., 1971-76; sole practice, N.Y.C., 1976-78; mem. firm Newman, Aronson & Neumann, P.C., N.Y.C., 1978-88. Mem. Am. Immigration Lawyers Assn., ABA, N.Y. State Bar Assn., N.Y. County Lawyers Assn., FBA, Assn. Internat. Educators, Jewish, B'nai B'rith, Anti-Defamation League (exec. com. N.Y. regional bd.). Office: 150 Broadway Rm 1115 New York NY 10038-4302

GOLDSTEIN, FRANK ROBERT, lawyer; b. July 31, 1943; s. Morris Herman and Maxine (Herzfeld) G.; m. Phyllis Ellen Levy, Jan. 26, 1967; children: Matthew Alexander, Andrew Stephen. AB, Duke U., 1964; LLB, U. Md., 1967. Bar: Md. 1967, D.C. 1981, Mass. 1985. Clk. to chief justice U.S. Dist. Ct. Md., Balt., 1967—68; assoc. Piper & Marbury, Balt. and Washington, 1968—74, ptnr. Washington, 1974—88, Morgan, Lewis & Bockius LLP, Washington, 1989—96, Sidley Austin Brown & Wood LLP, Washington, 1997—. Bd. govs. Reconstructionist Rabbincal Coll., Wyncote, Pa. 1992-94; bd. dirs. Washington-Balt. Regional Assn., 1984-93, Al Marah Neighborhood Assn., Bethesda, Md., 1982-85, Paine Webber Mortgage Fin. Inc., Columbia, Md., 1987-93 Author: Mournful Numbers, 1995; co-author: District of Columbia Limited Liability Company Forms and Practice Manual, 1995. Pres. Meadowbrook Neighborhood Assn., Potomac, Md., 1990—93, Tidesfall Neighborhood Assn., Columbia, Md., 1972; bd. visitors U. Md. Sch. Law, Balt., 1992—2001; pres. Adat Shalom Reconstructionist Congregation, Bethesda, Md., 1982—85. Fellow Am. Bar Found.; mem. ABA, D.C. Bar Assn. (chmn. ptnr. com. 1985-86, treas. 1988-89), Mass. Bar Assn., Md. State Bar Assn. (chmn. ptnr. com. 1980-82, chmn. sect. legal edn. and admission to bar com. 1975, chmn. D.C. corp. code rev. project 1989-93), Order of Coif. Jewish. Home: 11516 Big Piney Way Potomac MD 20854-1365 Office: Sidley Austin Brown & Wood LLP 1501 K St NW Washington DC 20005 E-mail: fgoldstein@sidley.com.

GOLDSTEIN, FRED, accountant; b. N.Y.C., Aug. 24, 1924; s. Max and Mary (Frisch) G.; m. Roslyn Weissman, Dec. 24, 1953; children: Lori Beth, Barry Mark. BBA cum laude, CCNY, 1950; MBA, NYU, 1952. CPA. Ptnr. Wertheim & Co., N.Y.C., 1959—. Lectr. Found. Acctg. Edn., N.Y.C., 1986. Pres. South Park Civic Assn., Roslyn, 1962-63, Temple Sinai Brotherhood, Roslyn, 1979-80, of Temple Sinai, 1987-89; mem. exec. bd. N.Y. Fed. Union, N.Y. State chpt. Union of Am. Hebrew Congregations. With inf. U.S. Army, WWII. Decorated Bronze Star, Purple Heart. Mem. AICPA, N.Y. State Soc. CPAs, Jewish Chautauqua Soc. (life). Jewish. Home: 4 Woodcrest Dr Roslyn NY 11576-3028 Office: Wertheim & Co 1025 Old Country Rd Westbury NY 11590

GOLDSTEIN, GARY SANFORD, executive recruiter; b. Rochester, N.Y., Nov. 29, 1954; s. Perry Leon and Joyce Lorraine (Hoffman) G.; m. Lisa Ann Bernstein, Sept. 24, 1977 (div. 1980); m. Alicia de la Caridad Lazaro, Jan. 3, 1983 (div. 1992); children: Jessica Leigh, Vanessa Kyle; m. Jill Allyson Brooke, June 11, 1995; 1 child, Parker Leon. BS in Acctg., Canisius Coll., 1976; OPM, Harvard U. Acct. Arthur Andersen & Co., N.Y.C., 1976-79; mng. dir. A-L Assocs., N.Y.C., 1979-84; chmn., pres. The Whitney Group, N.Y.C., 1984—; chmn., CEO Headway Corp. Resources, 1992—2003; CEO Whitney Group LLC, N.Y.C., 2003—. Coun. mem. The Brookings Instn., Washington, 1990—; mem. bd. dirs. Rippowam Cisqa Sch., 1992—2000. Mem. Young Pres. Orgn. Avocations: horseback riding, tennis, collecting photorealistic art, basketball. Home: 161 Buxton Rd Bedford Hills NY 10507-2310 Office: Whitney Group LLC 850 3rd Ave New York NY 10022-6222 E-mail: ggoldstein@whitneygroup.com.

GOLDSTEIN, GERALD, research scientist; b. N.Y.C., Sept. 16, 1931; s. Eli and Lillian (Schneiderman) G.; m. Carolyn Shelly, June 13, 1975 (dec. Feb. 1988). BA, CCNY, 1953, MS in Edn., 1956; PhD, U. Kans, 1962. Licensed psychologist. Psychologist VA Hosp., Topeka, 1962-75; rsch. career scientist VA Med. Ctr., Pitts., 1975—; asst. prof., prof. psychiatry and psychology U. Pitts., 1975—. Cons. U. Pitts., 1977—. Co-author: Assessment of Brain Damage, 1970, Contemporary Approaches to Neuropsychological Assessment, 1986, Handbook of Psychological Assessment, 2000; author: A Clinician's Guide to Research Design, 1980. With U.S. Army, 1955-56. Grantee VA, NIH, 1973—. Fellow APA (div. pres. 1988-89), Am. Psychopath. Assn., Nat. Acad. Neuropsychology; mem. Internat. Neuropsychol. Soc. Democrat. Jewish. Avocations: travel, photography. Home: 300 Fox Chapel Rd Apt 513 Pittsburgh PA 15238-2327 Office: VA Med Ctr (151R) 7180 Highland Dr Pittsburgh PA 15206-1206

GOLDSTEIN, HENRY, philanthropic institutions consultant; b. NYC, Nov. 6, 1933; s. Morris and Frances (Sholdar) G.; children: Janet, Jonathan. BS in Journalism, NYU, 1954, postgrad., 1958-61. Campaign dir. United Cmty. Chest, Paterson, NJ, 1956-58, Greater NY Fund, NYC, 1958-64; with The Oram Group, Inc., NYC, 1964—, pres., CEO, 1978—. Adj. prof. Milano Grad. Sch. Mgmt. and Urban Policy, New Sch. U., NYC Co-author: Dear Friend: Mastering the Art of Direct Mail Fund Raising; columnist Chronicle of Philanthropy. Active scholarship awards com. Jackie Robinson Found.; bd. dir. Berkshire Theatre Festival, emeritus. With US Army, 1954-56. Mem. Assn. Fund Raising Profl., Pacific Inst. Cmty. Orgns., Women's Prison Assn. Office: 275 Madison Ave New York NY 10016-1101 E-mail: hankus@juno.com.

GOLDSTEIN, HOWARD BERNARD, investment banker, advertising and marketing executive; b. Bronx, N.Y., Dec. 4, 1943; s. Maurice and Matilda Goldstein; m. Susan Nadine Goldberg, June 25, 1967; children: Jill Alecya, Brett Adam. Student, Bernard Baruch/CCNY, 1962-63; BFA, Pratt Inst., 1970. Lic. ins. agt., N.Y., spl. tng. radiation detection, chemical, electrical and fire disaster, damage assessment specialist; lic. health and life ins. agt.; cert. for 1st responder hazardous materials ops., N.J. State Police/Bergen County Law and Pub. Safety Inst.; registered security broker. Art dir. Fairfax Advt. divsn. Ogilvy & Mather, Inc., N.Y.C., 1968-72; creative dir. Hoffman Advt., N.Y.C., 1972-80, Miller, Addison, Steele, Inc., N.Y.C., 1980-82; pres. Gould Advt., Cliffside Park, N.J., 1969—; br. officer, tax shelter coord. E.F. Hutton & Co., Inc., 1983-85; security broker, sr. v.p., mem. chmn.'s coun., dir.'s coun. Lehman Bros. Shearson Lehman Bros., Inc., 1985-94, mem. guided portfolio mgmt. program, 1985-94; securities broker, sr. v.p. Gruntal & Co., 1994—2002; securities broker, sr. v.p., health and life ins. agt. Ryan Beck & Co., 2003—. V.p. bd. dirs. Winston Tower 200, Condominium Assn.; mem. Internat. Assn. Fin. Planning, Inst. Cert. Fin. Planners, Coll. Cert. Fin. Planners, Denver Grad. Police & Fire Acad. of Bergen County, N.J., 1986; capt., team leader Dept. Justice Emergency Response to Terrorism, 2000; trainee Nat. Fire Acad., Fed. Emergency Mgmt. Agy.; spl. trainee radiation detection, chm., elec. and fire disaster; damage assessment specialist ARC, Bergen Crossroads chpt., 1998; terrorism cons. Ft. Lee Office of Emergency Mgmt., 2002—. Designed Seal for art svcs. for ARC, 1961; exhibited photo show Bronx Hist. Soc., N.Y.C., 1970, paintings Soc. of Illustrators show, 1971-72, numerous other shows; represented in permanent collection Smithsonian Inst. Fin. officer N.J. State Police Office of Emergency Mgmt., Cliffside Park, 1986; spl. police officer Cliffside Park Police Dept., N.J. State Police Benevolent Assn., 1986—, Montclair State Coll. World of Computers, 1981; mem. steering com. Coalition Bus., Labor and Cmty. Orgns. N.Y., 1992, mem. exec. com., chmn. fin., 1992—; bd. advisor to UN Nat. Com. for Habitat, 1993—; first Am. investment banker to coord. prt. bus. coun. meeting N.Y.C. with His Excellency Saparmurad A. Niyazov (1st elected pres. The Rep. of Turkismanistan, previously part of USSR) and cabinet of ministers, 1993; mem. Rep. Senatorial Inner Circle, 1992; mem. Graphic Artists Guild, 1976-80, Bronx County Hist. Soc., 1968-71, Cliffside Park Baseball Assn., 1979—, coach, 1981, 83; sponsor Project High Frontier, U.S. Govt., 1986, sustaining mem. Rep. Nat. Com., 1981—; preferred mem. U.S. Senatorial Club, 1984—; majority mem. Nat. Rep. Senatorial Com., 1984—; mem. Heritage Found., 1990—, Nat. Rep. Congrl. Com., 1984—, N.J. Rep. State Com., 1994—; capt., team leader emergency response to terrorism Dept. Justice, 2000; terrorism cons. Ft. Lee Office of Emergency Mgmt., 2002—. Sachs Art scholar, 1955; recipient medal for art svc. Youth Friends Assn., 1961, Ga. Pacific award, 1978, Scholastic Mixed media award Scholastic Mag., 1961. Mem. Citizens Against Govt. Waste, The City Club N.Y. (govt. ops. com.), Tenafly Rifle and Pistol Club Inc., Nat. Rifle Assn. Clubs: Fort Lee Racquetball. Lodges: Bnai Brith. Jewish. Address: 200 Winston Dr Cliffside Park NJ 07010-3235 E-mail: howard.goldstein@ryanbeck.com.

GOLDSTEIN, HOWARD SHELDON, lawyer; b. Apr. 22, 1952; s. Jerome Harold and Goldie Goldstein; m. Amy Ruth, 1980. BA, CUNY, 1974; JD, Bklyn. Law Sch., 1977. Bar: N.Y. 1978, U.S. Dist. Ct. (so. and ea. dists.) N.Y. 1978. Assoc. Loew & Cohen, Esquires, N.Y.C., 1976-82, ptnr., 1982-87, Cohen & Goldstein, N.Y.C., 1988—. Contbr. articles to profl. jours. Mem. N.Y. State Bar Assn. (family law com., legis. com.), N.Y. County Lawyers Assn., Nassau County Bar Assn., N.Y.C. Bar Assn. (legal referral svcs.). Republican. Jewish. Office: Cohen & Goldstein Esqs LLP 32 Broadway Rm 1700 New York NY 10004-1670 E-mail: cohengolds@aol.com.

GOLDSTEIN, HOWARD WARREN, lawyer; b. N.Y.C., Mar. 29, 1949; s. Murray and Claire (Millrod) G.; m. Wendy Jo Zacharius, Sept. 9, 1973; children: Lindsay Rebecca, Amanda Mikael, Justin Zacharius. BA, Northwestern U., 1970; JD, NYU, 1973. Bar: N.Y. 1974, U.S. Dist. Ct. (so. and ea. dists.) N.Y. 1974, U.S. Ct. Appeals (2d cir.) 1975, U.S. Ct. Appeals (10th cir.) 1984, U.S. Ct. Appeals (6th cir.) 1985, U.S. Ct. Appeals (3d cir.) 1997, U.S. Supreme Ct. 1984, U.S. Claims Ct. 1988. Law clk. to judge U.S. Dist. Ct. (ea. dist.) N.Y., 1973-74; assoc. Cravath, Swaine & Moore, N.Y.C., 1974-76; asst. U.S. atty. Office of U.S. Atty. (so. dist.) N.Y., N.Y.C., 1976-80; assoc. Mudge, Rose, Guthrie, Alexander & Ferdon, N.Y.C., 1980-81, ptnr., 1982-90, Fried, Frank, Harris, Shriver & Jacobson, N.Y.C., 1990—. Author: Grand Jury Practice, 1998; co-author: The Rights of Crime Victims, 1985, RICO: Civil and Criminal, Law and Strategy, 1989, Corporate Sentencing Guidelines, 1993. Mem. Fed. Bar Coun., Assn. of Bar of City of N.Y., Nat. Assn. Criminal Def. Lawyers, N.Y. Coun. Def. Lawyers, Order of Coif, Phi Beta Kappa. Jewish. Office: Fried Frank Harris Shriver & Jacobson One New York Plz New York NY 10004

GOLDSTEIN, ILENE JOY, allergist, immunologist; b. Bklyn., May 8, 1962; BA summa cum laude in Biology, Hofstra U., 1984; MD, SUNY, Bklyn., 1988. Diplomate Am. Bd. Pediats., Am. Bd. Allergy and Immunology. Intern in pediatrics Schneider Children's Hosp./L.I. Jewish Med. Ctr., New Hyde Park, N.Y., 1988-89, resident in pediatrics, 1989-91; fellow in adult and pediat. allergy/immunology Schneider Children's Hosp.-L.I. Jewish Med. Ctr., 1991-93. Fellow Am. Coll. Allergy Asthma and Immunology, Am. Acad. Pediatrics, N.Y. Soc. Allergy Asthma Immunology, L.I. Allergy Asthma Soc., Am. Acad. Allergy, Asthma & Immunology, Suffolk County Med. Soc., Suffolk County Pediatric Soc., L.I. Allergy Soc.; mem. AMA, Am. Med. Women's Assn., Phi Beta Kappa. Office: 158 E Main St Huntington NY 11743-2988

GOLDSTEIN, IRA J. lawyer; b. N.Y.C., Sept. 10, 1930; s. David and Anna Frances (Sherman) G.; m. Thelma R. Zucker, Apr. 11, 1954; children— Cindy, Roberta. A.B., CCNY, 1952; LL.B., N.Y.U., 1954. Bar: N.Y. 1956, Calif. 1965. Assoc., House, Grossman, Vorhaus & Hemley, N.Y.C., 1956-61; asst. gen. counsel Metromedia Inc., N.Y. and Calif., 1961-69, v.p., gen. counsel, 1982—; v.p., gen. counsel Reeves Telecom, N.Y.C., 1969-70; ptnr. Fine, Tofel, Saxl & Goldstein, N.Y.C., 1970-72, Moses & Singer, N.Y.C., 1972-82. Mem., Kings Point Civil Assn., 1980— . Served to cpl. U.S. Army, 1954-56. Mem. ABA, Trustee Copyright Soc., N.Y. State Bar Assn., Assn. Bar City N.Y. Office: Metromedia Inc 1 Harmon Plz Secaucus NJ 07094-2803

GOLDSTEIN, IRVING SOLOMON, chemistry educator, consultant; b. Bronx, N.Y., Aug. 20, 1921; s. Jacob and Jennie (Rathsprecher) G.; m. Helen Haft, Dec. 16, 1945; children: Ardath Ann, Darra Jane, Jared. BS in Chemistry, Rensselaer Poly. Inst., 1941; MS in Chemistry, Ill. Inst. Tech., 1944; PhD in Organic Chemistry, Harvard U., 1948. Teaching asst. Ill. Inst. Tech., Chgo., 1941-42; teaching fellow Harvard U., Cambridge, Mass., 1946-48; rsch. chemist N.Am. Rayon Corp., Elizabethton, Tenn., 1948-51; mgr. wood chemistry rsch. Koppers Co., Inc., Pitts., 1951-63; sr. rsch. scientist Nalco Chem. Co., Chgo., 1963-66; mgr. paper rsch. Continental Can Co., Chgo., 1966-68; prof. forest sci. Texas A&M U., College Station, 1968-71; prof., head wood and paper sci. dept. N.C. State U., Raleigh, 1971-78, prof. wood chemistry, 1978-92; prof. emeritus, 1992—. Editor: Wood Technology: Chemical Aspects, 1977, Organic Chemicals From Biomass, 1981, Composition and Structure of Wood, 1991; contbr. articles to profl. jours.; 15 inventions in field. Lt. USNR, 1942—46, ATO, PTO. Fellow Internat. Acad. Wood Sci.; mem. AAAS, Am. Chem. Soc. (chmn. cellulose div. 1982), Tech. Assn. Pulp and Paper Industry, Forest Products Rsch. Soc., Soc. Wood Sci. and Tech. E-mail: isgold@unity.ncsu.edu.

GOLDSTEIN, IRWIN JOSEPH, medical research executive; b. Newark, N.J., Sept. 8, 1929; 2 children. BA, Syracuse U., 1951; PhD in Biochemistry, U. Minn., 1956. Rsch. fellow, dept. agrl. biochemistry U. Minn., St. Paul, 1956-59; asst. prof., dept. biochemistry State U. N.Y., Buffalo, 1961-65; assoc. prof., dept. biological chemistry U. Mich., Ann Arbor, 1965-72, prof., dept. biological chemistry, 1972—, mem. comprehensive Cancer Ctr. Cons. Ann Arbor Community, 1968-71, Procter & Gamble Co., 1968-90; assoc. dean Rsch. and Grad. Studies U. Mich., 1986-98; mem. rsch com. Henry Ford Hosp., 1983—. Editorial bd.: Journal of Biological Chemistry, 1983-88, 1991-96, Plant Physiology, 1983-86, Carbohydrate Research, 1984-87, Glycoconjugate Journal, 1985-88, Archive Biochemistry and Biophysics, 1989-95. Rsch. bd. United Fund, Buffalo, N.Y., 1963-65; bd. dirs. Guild House U. Mich., 1975-80. Recipient Kaiser Permanente Pre Clinical Teaching award, 1980, Claude S. Hudson Carbohydrate Chemistry award Am. Chem. Soc., 1993; Guggenheim fellow, 1959-60, NIH fellow, 1960-61. Mem. Am. Heart Assn., Biochemical Soc., Chem. Soc., Am. Soc. Biological Chemists, Am. Chem. Soc., Soc. Complex Carbohydrates (exec. com. 1987—), Sigma Xi, Phi Lambda Upsilon. Achievements include research in carbohydrate-protein interactions; isolation, purification and characterization of lectins (carbohydrate-binding proteins); use of lectins to study cell-surface phenomena; studies on the structure and biosynthesis of glycoproteins; immunochemistry of carbohydrates. Address: U Mich Med Sch Dept Biol Chem 4320 Med Sci I 1301 Catherine St Ann Arbor MI 48109-0600

GOLDSTEIN, IRWIN MELVIN, lawyer; b. Bklyn., Oct. 17, 1944; s. Oscar D. Goldstein and Berdie (Grossman) Schames; m. Maxine B. Herzog, June 14, 1970; children: Oliver M., Evan D., Shawn M. BA, Bklyn. Coll., 1964; JD, St. John's U., Bklyn., 1967; LLM, NYU, 1968. Bar: N.Y. 1968, Fla. 1978. Ptnr. Reynolds, Richards, LaVenture, Hadley & Davis, N.Y.C., 1970-81; mgr. Ira Sarinsky & Co., P.C., N.Y.C., 1982-84, M. Sternlieb & Co., P.C., Hackensack, N.J., 1984-85; ptnr. McGladrey & Pullen, LLP (formerly Edward Issacs & Co.), N.Y.C., 1985—. Home: 96 Margaret Ave Lawrence NY 11559-1826 E-mail: Irwin_Goldstein@rsmi.com.

GOLDSTEIN, JACK, health science executive, microbiologist; b. N.Y.C., June 7, 1947; s. Arnold L. and Rachel (Vogel) G.; m. Laurie Ann Sacks, Aug. 28, 1969; 1 child, Justin T. BA, Rider Coll., Trenton, N.J., 1969; MS, St. John's U., Jamaica, N.Y., 1974, PhD, 1976. Diplomate Am. Bd. Med. Microbiology. Asst. dir. microbiology Queens Hosp. Ctr., Jamaica, 1976-81; dir. diagnostic labs. API div. Sherwood Med. Co., Plainview, N.Y., 1981-83; v.p. research and devel. MicroScan div. Baxter Travenol, Sacramento, 1983-86; group v.p. Ortho Diagnostic Systems Inc. div. Johnson & Johnson Co., Raritan, N.J., 1986-88; group v.p., gen. mgr. infectious disease bus. Ortho Diagnostic Systems, Inc. div. Johnson & Johnson Co., Raritan, N.J., 1988-92; exec. v.p. worldwide Ortho Diagnostic Sys. Inc. divsn. Johnson & Johnson Co., Raritan, N.J., 1992-93, pres. Ortho Diagnostic Sys. Inc. divsn., 1993-97; pres., CEO Applied Imaging Corp., Santa Clara, Calif., 1997-2001, chmn. bd., 2001—02; gen. ptnr. Windamere Venture Ptnrs., San Diego, 2001—02; pres. blood testing divsn. Chiron Corp., Emeryville, Calif., 2002—. Mem. exam. com. Am. Bd. Med. Microbiology, Washington, 1984-91. Mem. editl. bd. Jour. Clin. Microbiology, Wasington, 1983-91; contbr. articles to profl. jours. Mem. Am. Soc. Microbiology, Am. Soc. Clin. Chemistry, Beta Beta Beta. Avocations: reading, skiing. Office: Chiron Corp 4560 Horton St Emeryville CA 94608-2916

GOLDSTEIN, JEROME ARTHUR, mathematics educator; b. Pitts., Aug. 5, 1941; s. Morris and Henrietta (Vogel) G.; children: Maurice Roland, David Jonathan, Devra. BS, Carnegie-Mellon U., 1963, MS, 1964, PhD, 1967; S.MD (hon.), Internat. Boswell Inst., Loyola U., New Orleans, 1973. Mem. Inst. Advanced Study, Princeton, N.J., 1967-68; asst. prof. math. Tulane U., New Orleans, 1968-71, assoc. prof., 1971-75, prof., 1975-91; prof. Math. Sci. Rsch. Inst. U. Calif., Berkeley, 1990-91; prof. math. La. State U., Baton Rouge, 1992-96, U. Memphis, 1996—. Author: Semigroups of Linear Operators and Applications, 1985; editor: P.D.E. and Related Topics, 1975, Mathematics Applied to Science, 1988, Differential Equations in Biology, Physics and Engineering, 1991, Semigroups of Operators and Applications, 1993, Stochastic Processes and Functional Analysis, 1997, Applied Analysis, 1999, Semigroup Forum, 1982—, Applied and Computational Mathematics, 1983—, Differential and Integral Equations, 1988—, Electronic Jour. Differential Equations, 1992—, Advances in Differential Equations, 1995—, Communications in Applied Analysis, 1995—, Positivity, 1996—, Jour. Math. Analysis and Applications, 1998—, Jour. of Computational Analysis and Applications, 1998—, Internat. Jour. Differential Equations and Applications, 1999—, Jour. Evolution Equations, 2000—, Electronic Jour. Math. Phys. Sci., 2002-, others; contbr. articles to profl. jours. Recipient Faculty Excellence in Research award Coll. Arts and Scis., Tulane U., 1985; NSF grantee, 1968-96. Mem. Am. Math. Soc., Math. Assn. Am., Soc. Indsl. Applied Math., London Math. Soc. Soc. Math. Brazil, Edinburgh Math. Soc., Assn. Women in Math., Sigma Xi (Rsch. award 1972). Jewish. Office: U Memphis Dept Math Scis Memphis TN 38138

GOLDSTEIN, JEROME CHARLES, professional association executive, surgeon, otolaryngologist; b. Glens Falls, N.Y., Nov. 4, 1935; s. Morris and Estelle (Ginsburg) G.; m. Rochelle Jacobs; children: Harry Glenn, Bradley John, Brian Louis. AB, U. Rochester, 1957; MD, SUNY, Syracuse, 1963. Diplomate Am. Bd. Otolaryngology (bd. dirs. 1982-2000). Intern Phila. Gen. Hosp., 1963-64; resident in gen. surgery Bronx Mcpl. Hosp. Ctr., N.Y.C., 1964-65; resident in otolaryngology SUNY, Syracuse, 1965-68; asst. prof. Northwestern U. Med. Sch., Chgo., 1968-71; pvt. practice Glens Falls, N.Y., 1971-74; prof. surgery, head div. otolaryngology Albany (N.Y.) Med. Coll., 1974-83; exec. v.p. Am. Acad. Otolaryngology-Head and Neck Surgery, Washington, 1984-94, sr. exec. v.p., 1995-96, exec. v.p. emeritus, 1997-99. Otolaryngologist-in-chief Albany Med. Ctr. Hosp., 1974-83; prof. dept. otolaryngology, head and neck surgery Johns Hopkins Med. Sch., 1986—, Georgetown Med. Sch., 1990; pres. Centurions of Deafness Rsch. Found., N.Y.C., 1987-88. With USAFR, 1965-70. Fellow ACS, Royal Coll. Surgeons Edinburgh, Am. Acad. Facial, Plastic and Reconstructive Surgery, Triologic Soc., Am. Laryngol. Assn., Am. Soc. for Head and Neck Surgery (pres. 1982-83), Soc. Head and Neck Surgeons, Am. Neurotol. Soc. (hon.), Am. Bronchoesoph. Soc., Am. Head and Neck Soc., Nat. Assn. Physicians for the Environment (founding pres. 1993-95, pres. 1999-2000); mem. AMA, Am. Otol. Soc. (hon.), Internat. Fedn. Otorhino-Laryngol. Socs. (regional sec. for N.Am. 1985-2000), Coun. of Med. Specialty Socs. (pres. 1996), Pan Pacific Surg. Assn. (pres.-elect 2000—). Home and Office: 4119 Manchester Lake Dr Lake Worth FL 33467-8175 Fax: 561-649-9412. E-mail: JCGMD@aol.com.

GOLDSTEIN, JOEL, finance and statistics educator, researcher; b. N.Y.C., Mar. 29, 1938; s. Jack and Regina (Gross) G.; m. Marcia Rosen, Sept. 5, 1966; children: Jennifer Ann, Carol Lynn. BME, CCNY, 1967; MS, NYU, 1971; PhD, Polytech U., 1980. Analyst Allied Corp., N.Y.C., 1963-67; automation engr. Ebasco Svcs., N.Y.C., 1967-68; mgr. Bunker Ramo Corp., Trumbull, Conn., 1969-74; sr. analyst Getty Oil Co., N.Y.C., 1974-77; dir. Am. Express Co., N.Y.C., 1978-83; v.p. Citicorp, NA, N.Y.C., 1983-86; assoc. prof. Western Conn. State U., Danbury, 1987-96, prof. fin. and stats., 1997—. Coord. MBA program Ancell Sch. Bus., 1994-97. Author: (with R. Montague) Lotus 1-2-3 The Easy Way, 1989; contbr. articles to profl. jours. Mem. Internat. Assn. Fin. Engrs., INFORMS. Office: Western Conn State Univ 181 White St Danbury CT 06810-6826

GOLDSTEIN, JONATHAN AMOS, retired ancient history and classics educator; b. N.Y.C., July 19, 1929; s. David Aaron and Rose Frances (Berman) G.; m. Helen Charlotte Tunik, Feb. 1, 1959; children— Rise Belle, Rachel Sarah AB cum laude, Harvard U., 1950, AM, 1951; M of Hebrew Lit., Jewish Theol. Sem., 1955, D of Hebrew Letters (hon.), 1987; PhD, Columbia U., 1959. Instr. Columbia U., N.Y.C., 1960-62; prof. U. Iowa, 1962-97; ret., 1997. Author: The Letters of Demosthenes, 1968, I Maccabees, 1976, II Maccabees, 1983, Semites, Iranians, Greeks, and Romans, 1990, Peoples of an Almighty God, 2001. Pres. Congregation Agudas Achim, Iowa City, 1969-70 Fulbright scholar U.S. State Dept., Israel, 1959-60; sr. faculty fellow U. Iowa, 1984 Fellow Am. Acad. for Jewish Rsch.; mem. AAUP, Am. Philol. Assn., Assn. Ancient Historians, Archaeol. Inst. Am., Phi Beta Kappa. Democrat. Jewish. Avocations: singing, jewish community activities. Home: 312 Windsor Dr Iowa City IA 52245-6044 Office: U Iowa Dept History Schaeffer Hall Iowa City IA 52242

GOLDSTEIN, JOSEPH IRWIN, materials scientist, educator; b. Syracuse, N.Y., Jan. 6, 1939; s. Louis and Sylvia (Scharfeld) G.; m. Barbara Hammond, June 30, 1963; children: Steven, Anne. BS in Metallurgy, MIT, 1960, MS, 1962, ScD in Metallurgy, 1964. Instr. metallurgy dept. MIT, 1960-63; phys. metallurgist Smithsonian Astron. Obs., Cambridge, Mass., 1963-64; aerospace technologist NASA-Goddard Space Ctr., Greenbelt, Md., 1966-68; lectr. chem. engring. U. Md., 1966-68; asst. prof. metall. and materials sci. Lehigh U., Bethlehem, Pa., 1968-70, assoc. prof., 1970-75, prof., 1975-93, T.L. Diamond Disting. prof., 1976-79, assoc. v.p. rsch., 1979-83, v.p. rsch., 1983-90, R.D. Stout prof. materials sci. and engring., 1990-93; dean engring. U. Mass., Amherst, 1993—, disting. prof., 2003—. Author, editor 8 books; contbr. more than 200 articles to profl. jours. Recipient Nat. Environ. Rsch. Coun. award, Britain, 1974. Fellow Am. Soc. for Metals; mem. Microbeam Analysis Soc. (pres. 1977-78, Sci. award 1991, Svc. award 1984), Meteoritical Soc. (mem. coun. 1979-81, treas. 1995-99). Democrat. Jewish. Home: 49 Sheerman Ln Amherst MA 01002-1584 Office: U Mass Office of the Dean Coll of Engineering Amherst MA 01003

GOLDSTEIN, JOSEPH LEONARD, physician, medical educator, molecular genetics scientist; b. Sumter, S.C., Apr. 18, 1940; s. Isadore E. and Fannie A. Goldstein. BS, Washington and Lee U., 1962, DSc, 1986; MD, U. Tex., Dallas, 1966; DSc (hon.), U. Chgo., 1982, Rensselaer Poly. Inst., 1982, U. Paris, 1988, U. Buenos Aires, 1990; DSc (hon.), So. Meth. U., 1993, U. Miami, 1996; DSc (hon.), Rockefeller U., 2001. Intern, then resident in medicine Mass. Gen. Hosp., Boston, 1966—68; clin. assoc. NIH, 1968—70; fellow U. Wash., Seattle, 1970—72; faculty U. Tex. Southwestern Med. Ctr., Dallas, 1972—77, Paul J. Thomas prof. medicine, chmn. dept. molecular genetics, 1977—85, regental prof., 1985—. Harvey Soc. lectr., 1977; mem. sci. rev. bd. Howard Hughes Med. Inst., 1978—84, med. adv. bd., 1985—90, chmn. med. adv. bd., 1995—2002, trustee, 2002—, non-resident fellow Salk Inst., 1983—94; chmn. award jury Albert Lasker Med. Rsch., 1996—; mem. bd. sci. govs. Scripps Rsch. Inst., 1996—. Co-author: The Metabolic Basis of Inherited Disease, 5th edit., 1983. Trustee Rockefeller U., 1994—; mem. sci. adv. bd. Welch Found., 1986—; bd. dirs. Passano Found., 1985—. Recipient Heinrich-Wieland prize, 1974, Pfizer award in enzyme chemistry, ACS, 1976, Passano award, Johns Hopkins U., 1978, Gairdner Found. award, 1981, award in biol. and med. scis., NY Acad. Sci., 1981, Lita Annenberg Hazen award, 1982, Rsch. Achievement award, Am. Heart Assn., 1984, Louisa Gross Horwitz award, 1984, 3M Life Sci. award, 1984, Albert Lasker award in basic med. rsch., 1985, Nobel Prize in physiology or medicine, 1985, Trustees's medal, Mass. Gen. Hosp., 1986, US Nat. medal of sci., 1988, prize, Warren Alpert Found., 2000, prize in Medicine and Biomed. Rsch., Albany Med. Ctr., 2003. Mem.: Tex. Philos. Soc., Royal Soc. London (fgn. mem.), Inst. Medicine, Am. Philos. Soc., Am. Fedn. Clin. Rsch., Am. Soc. Biol. Chemists, Am. Acad. Arts and Scis., Am. Soc. Human Genetics (William Allan award 1985), Am. Soc. Clin. Investigation (pres. 1985—86), Assn. Am. Physicians, ACP (award 1986), NAS (coun. 1991—94, Lounsbery award 1979), Alpha Omega Alpha, Phi Beta Kappa. Home: 3831 Turtle Creek Blvd Apt 22B Dallas TX 75219-4538 Office: U Tex Southwestern Med Ctr 5323 Harry Hines Blvd Dallas TX 75390-9046 E-mail: jgolds@mednet.swmed.edu.

GOLDSTEIN, JOSHUA S, writer, educator; b. Boston, Dec. 27, 1952; s. Avram Goldstein, Dora B. Goldstein; m. Andra M. Rose; children: Solomon Goldstein-Rose, Ruth Goldstein-Rose. PhD, M.I.T., Cambridge, MA, 1982—86; BA with distinction, Stanford, Stanford, CA, 1970—81. NSF Graduate Fellow M.I.T., Cambridge, MA, 1983—86; Assistant/Associate Professor Univ. of Southern California, Los Angeles, CA, 1986—93; Professor of International Relations American University, Washington, 1993—. Author: (book) War and Gender: How Gender Shapes the War System and Vice Versa, 2001, International Relations, 2003, Long Cycles: Prosperity and War in the Modern Age, 1988, Three-Way Street: Strategic Reciprocity in World Politics, 1990. Founder and Chair Bosnia Support Committee, Washington, 1993—95. Office: Watson Inst International Studies Brown Univ Box 1970 Providence RI 02912 Fax: 413-256-6363. Personal E-mail: jg@joshuagoldstein.com. Business E-Mail: jg@joshuagoldstein.com.

GOLDSTEIN, JUDITH SHELLEY, reading and learning specialist; b. Bklyn., Mar. 5, 1935; d. Maurice and Mary (Goldstein) G. BA, Adelphi U., 1956; MA, Columbia U., 1957; EdD, Hofstra U., 1984. Cert. permanent tchr. in reading, spl. and elem. edn., N.Y. Early childhood tchr. N.Y.C. Sch. System, Bklyn., 1957-80; reading specialist Southampton (N.Y.) Unified Sch. Dist., 1981-87; spl. edn. tchr. Amagansett (N.Y.) Sch., 1987-88; mem. adj. faculty C.W. Post Campus, L.I. U., Brookville, N.Y., 1984-88, supr. clin. practice Southampton Campus, 1988-95. Exec. dir. nursery sch. Jewish Ctr. of Hamptons, East Hampton, N.Y., 1988-89; adj. assoc. prof. Southampton Campus L.I. U., 1989-94, Dowling Coll., 1990-92; chmn. edn. Hadassau, 2003-; adj. asst. prof. Suffolk County C.C., 1989-95, adj. assoc. prof. 1995—. Mem. Guild Hall, East Hampton, 1980—; v.p. edn. Hadassah, East Hampton, 1989-92, chmn. edn., 2003; chair Am. Affairs, 1993-96, Hadassah edn. chair 2002-03; tchr. religious ch. Jewish Ctr. of the Hamptons, 1990-98; vol. Bay St. Theatre, Sag Harbor, N.Y., Long House Res., East Hampton; mem., vol. Friends of Guild Hall, East Hampton. Mem. ASCD, AAUW (v.p. programming 1987-89, sec. 1993-99, 2003), Internat. Reading Assn. Democrat. Avocations: gardening, museums, theater. Home: 138 Windward Rd East Hampton NY 11937-3189

GOLDSTEIN, JULIUS LESTER, biomedical engineer, consultant; b. Bklyn., July 9, 1935; s. Benjamin and Dorothy (Steinberg) G.; m. Batya Abramson, June 17, 1962; children: Hillel N., Miriam D., Naama L., Avi D. BEE, Cooper Union, 1957; MEE, Poly. Inst. Bklyn., 1960; PhD, U. Rochester, 1965. Postdoctoral fellow Inst. for Perception Rsch., Eindhoven, Netherlands, 1965-66; rsch. assoc., Lab. Psychophysics Harvard U., Cambridge, Mass., 1966-68; asst. prof. elec. engring. MIT, Cambridge, Mass., 1968-71, assoc. prof. elec. engring., 1971-73; dir. biomed. engring. Tel Aviv U., Israel, 1973-76, chmn. dept. electronics, 1976-78, assoc. prof., 1973-82, prof. elec. engring., 1982-90; vis. prof. Johns Hopkins U., Balt., 1986-88; rsch. prof. Ctrl. Inst. for the Deaf, St. Louis, 1988-96; adj. prof. elec. engring. Washington U., St. Louis, 1996—, adj. prof. biomed. engring., 2001—. Pres. Israel Soc. for Med. and Biomed. Engrs., Tel Aviv, 1975-77; dir. biomed. engring. program Tel Aviv U., 1973-76;

cons. Digital Speech Systems, Tel Aviv, 1984-86, Models of Human Hearing, AT&T Bell Labs., Murray Hill, NJ, 1991-96; co-founder, pres. Hearing Emulations, LLC, 2000. Contrb. articles profl. jour. Achievements include the discovery and formulation of math models of basic principles of auditory signal processing, including nonlinear cochlear sound analysis, detection of signal peaks and intervals, central processing in pitch perception, hearing aids based on auditory models. Bd. dir. Epstein Hebrew Acad., Block Yeshiva HS, St. Louis, 1991-94, 98—; organizer, symposium chmn. Assn. for Rsch. in Otolaryngology 17th Midwinter meeting, 1994. NIH grantee MIT, 1972, Johns Hopkins U., 1986-88, U.S./Israel Binational Fund grantee, 1977-80, NIH-NIDCD grantee Ctrl. Inst. for the Deaf, 1990-95, NSF-IBN grantee Washington U., 1998-00, NIH-NIDCD SBIR grantee BECS Tech., 1999—. Fellow Acoustical Soc. Am., Collegium Oto-Rhino-Laryngologicum Amicitae Sacrum, 1980; mem. IEEE (sr.). Office: Hearing Emulations LLC 9479 Dielman Rock Island Dr Saint Louis MO 63132

GOLDSTEIN, KENNETH B. lawyer; b. Bklyn., Sept. 16, 1949; s. Nathan and Isabella (Solow) G. BA, Tulane U., 1973, JD, 1974; postdoctoral, Fordham U., 1979. Bar: N.Y. 1977, U.S. Dist. Ct. (so. and ea. dist.) N.Y. 1980, U.S. Ct. Appeals (D.C. cir.) 1981. Gen. mgr., v.p. Middletown (N.Y.) Window Cleaning Co., Inc., 1974; tchr. various schs., Middletown and Chester, N.Y., 1975-77; asst. sr. v.p., dir. mktg. Saks Fifth Ave, N.Y.C., 1977-79; sr. asst. dist. atty. Orange County, Goshen, N.Y., 1979-81; assoc. Zola & Zola, N.Y.C., 1981-83, Freedman, Weisbein & Samuelson P.C., Garden City, N.Y., 1983-85, Jaffe & Asher, N.Y.C., 1985-91, Raoul Lionel Felder P.C., N.Y.C., 1991—. Bd. dirs. Middletown Window Cleaning Co., Inc. Bd. dirs. New Orleans Jazz and Heritage Found., 1972-74, Jewish Family Svcs. Orange County, 2000—. Named one of Outstanding Young Men in Am., 1980. Mem. ABA, N.Y. State Bar Assn., Middletown Bar Assn., Orange County Bar Assn., Order of DeMolay. Republican. Jewish. Avocations: swimming, art, dance, opera. Home: 145 E 35th St Apt 2me New York NY 10016-4121 also: PO Box 3 Middletown NY 10940-0003 Office: Raoul Lionel Felder PC 437 Madison Ave New York NY 10022-7001

GOLDSTEIN, KENNETH F. entertainment executive, software publisher; b. Detroit, Mar. 10, 1962; s. Earl Goldstein and Sarita (Bow) Snow. BA in Philosophy and Theater, Yale U., 1984. Freelance writer, TV and film producer, L.A., 1984-89; writer, producer Cinemaware Corp., Westlake Village, Calif., 1989-91; designer, producer Philips Interactive Media, L.A., 1991-92; exec. publisher Carmen Sandiego series Broderbund Software, Inc., Novato, Calif., 1992-96, v.p. entertainment, gen. mgr. divsn. Red Orb Entertainment Myst, Riven Series, 1996-98, Journeyman Project series, Warlords series, 1996-98; sr. v.p., gen. mgr. Disney Online, 1998-2000; exec. v.p., mng. dir. Walt Disney Internet Group, 2000—. Author: (screenplays) 8, 1992-95; designer (software programs) Carmen Sandiego: Jr. Detective Edition, 1994 (Software Publs. Assn. award 1995), Reading Galaxy, 1994 (Family PC, Mac World awards 1996), In the 1st Degree, 1995 (Software Publs. Assn. award 1996); pub. Disney's Toontown Online, 2003, Blast, 1998-03, FamilyFun.com, 1999—03; Movies.com, 2002-03. Vol. Olive Crest Treatment Ctr., 1986, Free Arts for Abused Children, 1988; sec. bd. trustees Full Circle Programs, Marin County, Calif., 1992-98; trustee Hathaway Children & Family Svcs, 2002—; bd. advs. Mediascope, 2002—. Recipient Pub. Svc. awards, Olive Crest Treatment Ctrs., 1986, Free Arts for Abused Children, 1988; named one of Top 100 Multimedia Producers, Multimedia Producer Mag., 1995, Best of What's New in Computers, Electronics, Popular Sci. Mag., 1995, Upside Mag. Elite 100, Honorable Mention Digital Entertainment, 1998, Best of Festival award Internat. Web Awards, 2000, Web Mktg. Assn. Web Awards Best Game, Family Movie, Entertainment Sites award 2001, Modalis Rsch. Excellence award, 2001, Outstanding Achievement award Web Mktg. Assn., 2002, 03, Web Internet Visionary award, Best of the Web, 2001, All Star Software award Software Rev., 2003, People's Voice award kids' category Webby Awards, 2003. Mem. Writers Guild of Am. West, Acad. Interactive Arts and Scis (founding mem., bd. govs. L.A.), Yale Univ. Alumni (schs. com. 1988—), Computer Game Developers Assn. Avocations: skiing, health and fitness, reading lit. and non-fiction. Office: Disney Online 500 S Buena Vista St Burbank CA 91521-0001

GOLDSTEIN, LAURENCE ALAN, trade association executive; b. Milw., June 4, 1948; s. Henry David and Sylvia (Sadowsky) G.; m. Carolyn Frances Chamoy, Sept. 6, 1981; children: Justin Chamoy, Doran Alisa, Shira Kate. BA, U. Wis., Milw., 1970, MA, 1971. Assoc. dir. State of Israel Bonds, Milw., 1977-81; exec. dir. Wis. region Jewish Nat. Fund, Milw., 1981-84; ptnr. Chamoy Goldstein & Assocs., Milw. and Washington, 1984-93; dir. pub. rels. Nat. Aggregates Assn., Silver Spring, Md., 1993-97; mgr. Washington Gas, 1998—. Author: (periodical) Aggregates For Tomorrow: The Sand Gravel and Crushed Stone Industry, 1994, 50 Fascinating Facts About Aggregates, 1994; editor, reviser (periodicals) How to Plan and Conduct an Aggregates Industry Open House, 1993, The Year 2000 and You, 1999; producer and writer (video slide show) Aggregates: The Fundamental Resource For The Future, 1995. Bd. dirs. Jewish Nat. Fund of Nat. Capitol Region. Mem. Pub. Rels. Soc. Am. (accredited mem.), Am. Planning Assn., Urban Land Inst., Am. Soc. Landscape Architects, Masons, Shriners. Republican. Avocations: reading, music, historical research, family activities. E-mail: lgoldstein@washgas.com., marylandpr@aol.com.

GOLDSTEIN, LAURENCE EVAN, journalist; m. Veronika Horvath, Aug. 25, 2002; 1 child, Alec Stuart. Broadcast journalist Whitney Broadcasting, New Rochelle, NY, 1993—. Office: Whitney Broadcasting 1 Broadcast Forum New Rochelle NY 10801

GOLDSTEIN, LEONARD BARRY, dentist, educator; b. Seaford, N.Y., Feb. 6, 1944; s. Jacob Martin and Adele (Pelzner) G.; m. Phyllis Lynn Kerwin, June 25, 1967; children: Marcie Ilene, Sherri Elysse. Student, Ind. U., 1961-63; DDS, Case Western Reserve U., 1967; Cert. in Orthodontics, Dewey Sch. Orthodontics, N.Y.C., 1969; PhD in Electro-Medicine, City U., Los Angeles, 1988. Diplomate Am. Acad. of Pain Mgmt., Am. Bd. Forensic Medicine, Am. Bd. Forensic Dentistry. Gen. practice dentistry, Smithtown, N.Y., 1969—; attending orthodontist Abe Stark Philanthropies Dental Clinic, Bklyn., 1970-77; med. dir. TMJ Facial Pain Ctr. Southside Hosp., Bay Shore, N.Y. Guest prof. Dept. Phys. Edn. Queens Coll., N.Y., 1979—; guest lectr. Dept. Phys. Edn. Queensboro (N.Y.) C.C., 1980—; dir. dental svcs. Good Samaritan Profl. Svcs., St. James, N.Y., 1979—, v.p. med. bd., 1979—; attending dental staff St. John's Episc. Hosp., 1980—, Cmty. Hosp. Western Suffolk, 1980—; bd. dirs. L.I. Ctr. for Cranio-Facial Pain, Smithtown; med. dir. TMJ/Facial Pain Ctr., Southside Hosp.; dir. grad. program in forensic exam. Touro Coll. Sch. Health Scis., Bay Shore; chmn. Instnl. Review Bd., Touro Coll.; vice chmn. com. on scholarly rsch., Touro Coll. Sch. Health Scis. Contbr. articles to profl. jours. Served to capt. Dental Corps, U.S. Army, 1967-69. Recipient fellowship in removeable prosthetics U.S. Army Dental Corps, 1967. Fellow Acad. Stress and Chronic Disease, Acad. Gen. Dentistry, Am. Endodontic Soc., Internat. Coll. Dentists; mem. Am. Equilibration Soc., Am. Coll. Sports Medicine, Internat. Acad. Preventive Medicine, Cranial Acad. of Am. Osteopathic Soc., Am. Orthodontic Soc., Internat. Soc. Orthodontists, Am. Dental Soc., Cronio-Mandibular Study Club of N.Y., L.I. Gnathological Study Club, Northeastern Gnathological Soc. Office: Touro Coll Sch Health Scis 1700 Union Blvd Bay Shore NY 11706 E-mail: leonardg@touro.edu., ddsphd@erols.com.

GOLDSTEIN, LESLIE DEBORAH, library director; b. Boston, Feb. 20, 1958; d. Irving and Shirley Goldstein; m. Robert Goetz, Mar. 28, 1987 (div. Aug. 1992). BA, Brandeis U., 1980; MLS, Simmons Coll., 1989. Libr. asst. III Widener Libr., Harvard U., 1981—83, libr. asst. IV, 1983—84; libr. asst. V Francis Loeb Libr., Harvard U., 1985—87; project archivist Mass. Archives, Boston, Mass., 1989—91; slide libr. Art Inst. of Boston, 1991—96; dir., br. services N.Y. Inst. of Tech., 1996—. Contbr. articles; spkr. (conf. presentation) Ask ARCIS - Be Prepared: Disaster Planning and Recovery, L.A., 2001. Vol. Manhattan Island Found., 2002. Mem.: Art Libr. of North Am., Art Libr. of North Am., N.Y. Avocations: bicycling, gardening, swimming. Office: NY Institute of Technology P O Box 8000 Old Westbury NY 11568

GOLDSTEIN, LIONEL ALVIN, personal financial and investment advisor; b. Bklyn., Oct. 19, 1932; s. Alexander and Ruth (Spitzer) G.; m. Judy Calk, May 19, 1973; children: Alex Nolan, Sharon Anne. Student, So. Meth. U., 1965; MS, U. Dallas, Irving, Tex., 1977; cert. fin. planner, Coll. Fin. Planning, 1983. CPA, Tex.; CFP; cert. personal fin. specialist; accredited estate planner; accredited investment mgmt. cons. V.p. fin., treas. Arrow Industries, Inc, Carrollton, Tex., 1965-76; pres. Goldstein & Co., CPA, Dallas, 1976-87; prin., co-founder Quest Capital Mgmt., Inc., Dallas, 1987-89; owner, mgr. Goldstein & Assocs., Dallas, 1989—. Dir. MBA program fin. planning services U. Dallas Grad. Sch. Mgmt., 1985-88. Served with U.S. Army, 1951-53. Mem. AICPA, Nat. Assn. Accts. (internat. bd. standards and practices for cert. fin. planners, bd. examiners 1988), Inst. CFPs (pres. Dallas chpt. 1987-88, chmn. Dallas chpt. 1988-89), Inst. Investment Mgmt. Cons., North Tex. Estate Planning Coun. Republican. Jewish. Avocation: wood working. Home: 2627 Valley Creek Trl Mc Kinney TX 75070-4337 Office: PO Box 3127 Mc Kinney TX 75070-3314 E-mail: mcgoldy@juno.com.

GOLDSTEIN, LYNN MEG, language educator; d. Ira Murray Goldstein and Corinne Edith Sharcoff; m. Dennis Gary McCarthy, June 14, 1981; children: Daniel, Matthew. BA, SUNY, 1975; MA, U. Pitts., 1976; MEd, Tchrs. Coll. Columbia U., 1980, PhD, 1986. Asst. prof. Hunter Coll., N.Y.C., 1981—84; prof. ednl. linguistics Monterey Inst. Internat. Studies, Calif., 1986—. Chief reader test of written English Ednl. Testing Svc., 1990—; rules, resolutions com., nominating com. Am. Assn. Applied Linguistics. Editl. bd. Jour. Second Lang. Writing, 1992—; author various jour. articles and book chpts. Sch. site coun. Bay View Elem. Sch., Monterey, 1997—; v.p. gifted and talented edn. bd. Monterey Peninsula United Sch. Dist., 2001. Mem.: Newbury House (Disting. Rsch. award 1987), Am. Assn. Applied Linguists, TESOL (serials publ. com. 1999—). Achievements include research in second language acquisition/sociolinguistics and second language composition studies. Avocations: reading, travel, web design. Office: Monterey Inst Internat Studies 460 Pierce St Monterey CA 93940

GOLDSTEIN, M. ROBERT, lawyer, judge; b. N.Y.C., Nov. 18, 1927; s. Samuel and Dorothy (Kliban) G.; m. Susan Wallach, Nov. 17, 1932; children—Ellen Iris Goldstein Wasserson, Ivan. A.B., Pa. State U. 1947; J.D., NYU, 1949. Bar: N.Y. 1949, U.S. Dist. Ct. (so. and ea. dists.) N.Y. 1956, U.S. Supreme Ct. 1959, U.S. Ct. Appeals (2d cir.) 1969. Ptnr. Samuel Goldstein & Sons, N.Y.C., 1949—; judge Village Ct., Great Neck, N.Y., 1977-88. Columnist, Condemnation, Certiorari in N.Y. Law Jour., 1972—. Chmn. Great Neck Planning Bd., 1966-69, Great Neck Bd. Zoning and Appeals, 1969-73; trustee, dep. mayor Village of Great Neck, 1973-77; past pres. Couple's Club, Temple Beth El, Great Neck, United Community Fund, Great Neck; past bd. dirs. Men's Club, Temple Beth El. Mem. Assn. of Bar of City of N.Y., Nassau County Bar Assn., N.Y. County Lawyers' Assn. (chmn. real property com. 1979-84, sec. and bd. dirs. 1982—), Pi Lambda Phi (pres. nat. coun. 1970s, pres. endowment fund 1972—), Glen Head Country Club (N.Y., v.p. 1983-85), Boca West Club. Democrat. Jewish. Home: 13 Locust Cove Ln Great Neck NY 11024-1117 Office: Samuel Goldstein & Sons 30 Vesey St New York NY 10007-2914

GOLDSTEIN, MANFRED, retired consultant; b. Vienna, Jan. 30, 1927; came to U.S., 1939; naturalized, 1945; s. Isidore and Anna (Hahn) G.; m. Shirley Marie Lavine, Aug. 27, 1950 (dec. Feb. 2001); children: Cindy Marie, Lynn Alyse. Student, Manhattan Trade Ctr., 1947; E.E., Capitol Radio Engring. Inst., 1963; student, L.I. U., 1961, Indsl. Coll. Armed Forces, 1967-68. Sr. technician Bklyn. Radio, 1953-55, Budd Stanley, Inc., Long Island City, N.Y., 1955; lead engr. telephone equipment Precision Indsl. Design Newark, 1955-57, project engr., contrace adminstr., sales mgr. Leico, Inc., Syossett, N.Y., 1957-65, v.p., 1964-65; mgmt. and engring. cons., 1965-91; ret. Pres. Positive Cons. Inc., Bellmore, N.Y., 1967-86, Lake Luzerne, N.Y., 1986-91, 95—; owner Lake Luzerne (N.Y.) Seaplane Base, 1969—; tchr. intermediate computer courses Hadley-Luzerne Pub. Libr., Lake Luzerne, 2003—. Mem. small bus. adv. com. to Congressman Thomas J. Downey, 1977-91; mem. small bus. adv. council L.I. Assn. Commerce; founder NCMA L.I. Scholarship Fund; mem. Town of Lake Luzerne Zoning Bd. of Appeals, 2002--. Served with AUS, 1945-46. Fellow Nat. Contract Mgmt. Assn. (bd. dirs. L.I. chpt., v.p. 1983-85); mem. IEEE (sr.), Soc. Plastics Engrs., Am. Indsl. Preparedness Assn. (exec. bd. mgmt. div.), ABA (assoc.), Air Force Assn., Capitol Radio Engring. Inst. Alumni (sr.), Nat. Pilots Assn., Aircraft Owners and Pilots Assn., Internat. Platform Assn., Am. Legion, VFW. Inventor torpedo fire control cable and connector for Polaris, high pressure seals for Polaris submarine antennae. Home: 18 Bay Rd PO Box 11 Lake Luzerne NY 12846-0011

GOLDSTEIN, MARC, microsurgeon, urology and reproductive medicine educator, administrator; b. N.Y.C., Mar. 22, 1948; BS cum laude, CUNY, Bklyn., 1968; MD summa cum laude, SUNY, Bklyn., 1972. Diplomate Nat. Bd. Med. Examiners, Am. Bd. Urology. Surgical intern Columbia-Presbyn. Med. Ctr., N.Y.C., 1972-73, surgical resident, 1973-74; asst. instr., resident, chief resident dept. urology Downstate Med. Ctr. SUNY, Bklyn., 1977-80, asst. prof. urology dept. urology Downstate Med. Ctr., 1980-82; asst. attending surgeon Univ. Hosp., SUNY Downstate Med. Ctr., and Kings County Hosp. Ctr., Bklyn., 1980-82; fellow-in-residence Population Coun. Rockefeller U., N.Y.C., 1980-82, rsch. assoc., 1980-83; assoc. physician Rockefeller U. Hosp., N.Y.C., 1980-86, vis. assoc. physician, 1986-87; asst. attending surgeon urology N.Y. Hosp., N.Y.C., 1982-88; asst. prof. surgery Cornell U. Med. Ctr., N.Y.C., 1982-88; staff scientist Population Coun. Ctr. Biomed. Rsch., N.Y.C., 1982—; dir. divsn. male reproductive medicine and microsurgery, dept. urology N.Y. Hops.-Cornell Med. Ctr., N.Y.C., 1982—; assoc. attending surgeon N.Y. Hosp., N.Y.C., 1988-94; assoc. prof. surgery Cornell U. Med. Coll., N.Y.C., 1988-94; attending surgeon N.Y. Hosp., 1994—; prof. urology Cornell U. Med. Coll., N.Y.C., 1994—, prof. urology and reproductive medicine, 1999—, dir. ctr. for male reproductive medicine and microsurgery, 1982—, co-exec. dir. Cornell Inst. Reproductive Medicine, 1999—; surgeon-in-chief Inst. Reproductive Medicine Cornell Ctr., 2001—. Mem. adv. com. Assn. Voluntary Surgical Contraception, 1984—; participant concept clearance meeting NIH, 1989; mem. editorial bd. Microsugery, 1983—, Jour. of Andrology, 1991-93, Andrology Report, 1992—. Author: (with M. Feldberg) The Vasectomy Book: A Complete Guide to Decision Making, 1982, 2d edit., 1985, (with G. Berger, M. Fuerst) The Couples Guide to Fertility, 1989, 2d edit., 1995, 3d edit., 2001, (with Doubleday Co.) Surgery of Male Infertility, 1995, Atlas of the Urology Clinics: Surgery for Male Infertility, 1999; contbr. chpts. to books, articles to profl. jours.; patentee in field. Maj. USAF, 1974-77, USAFR, 1977-90. Honor scholar Downstate Med. Ctr., 1969; Summer Rsch. fellow Downstate Med. Ctr., 1969-70, Ferdinand C. Valentine fellow N.Y. Acad. Medicine, 1980-82; recipient Ferdinand C. Valentine Urology prize N.Y. Acad. Medicine and N.Y. sect. Am. Urological Assn., 1981, Best Movie award Am. Fertility Soc. and Can. Fertility and Andrology Soc., 1986, 96, Excellence in Video Prodn. award Video Urology, 1987, 90; commd. Ky. Col., Commonwealth of Ky., 1988. Fellow ACS; mem. AMA, Am. Soc. Andrology (mem. various coms.), Am. Fertility Soc., Am. Urological Assn. (scholar 1980-82, mem. various coms.), N.Y. County Med. Soc., Internat. Microsurgical Soc., Soc. Study Reproduction, Soc. Reproductive Surgeons (fellowship com. 1989—), Soc. for Male Reproduction and Urology (pres. 1996), Alpha Omega Alpha, N.Y. Rd. Runners Club (completed 18 N.Y.C. marathons), Brit. Mountaineering Coun. Office: NY Hosp-Cornell Med Ctr Dept Urology 525 E 68th St Dept Urology New York NY 10021-4885 E-mail: mgoldst@med.cornell.edu.

GOLDSTEIN, MARGARET ANN, biologist; b. Sinton, Tex., Mar. 13, 1939; d. Daniel Archibald and Sarah Elizabeth (Tegg) McNeill; m. Alexander Goldstein, Jr., Feb. 14, 1959; 1 child, David William. BA magna cum laude, Rice U., Houston, 1965; PhD, Rice U., 1969. Lab instr. biology Rice U., 1965-69; instr. biology U. Tex./M.D. Anderson Hosp., Houston, 1969-70; asst. prof. biology U. Tex., Houston, 1969-77; instr. cell biophysics and medicine Baylor Coll. Medicine, Houston, 1970-73, asst. prof. cell biophysics and medicine, 1973-77, asst. prof. medicine and cell biology, 1977-79, assoc. prof. medicine and molecular and cellular biology, 1979-89, prof. medicine and molecular and cellular biology, 1989—. Vis. fellow Clare Hall Cambridge U., Cambridge, U.K., 2001-02, life mem., 2002—; cons. NHLBI, NIH, 1986-94, NRC, 1996-2000; exec. com. basic scis. coun. Am. Heart Assn., Dallas, 1987-94, assembly del., 1995-98; biol. dir. Microscopy Soc. Am., 1990-92, chair internat. com., 1993-95, pres., 1995-96; liaison officer to AAAS/CAIP, 1990-95, resp. to AAAS bd., 1993-96. Contbr. articles to profl. jours. V.p., bd. dirs. Tex. Chamber Orch., Houston, 1982-86; bd. dirs. River Oaks Women's Breakfast Club, 1980-85, Houston Friends of Music, 1991—, Rice U. Shepherd Soc. Governing Coun., 1995—; mem. award com. YWCA Outstanding Houston Women, 1991-96; adv. bd. mem. Houston Grand Opera, 1995-96. Recipient Outstanding Houston Woman in Sci. and Tech. award YWCA, Houston, 1990, Order of Silver Thistle, Scottish Heritage Found., Houston, 1990, NASA Achievement award for Cosmos 2044, 1991, for Cosmos 2G, 1994, Women on the Move award, 2002; NIH grantee, 1974-98. Mem.: AAAS (affil. bd. consortium of affils. for internat. programs), Coun. Sci. Soc. Pres.'s (exec. bd. dirs. 1997), Assn. Women in Sci. (v.p. 1979—80), Am. Soc. Cell Biology, Tex. Soc. Electron Microscopy (pres. 1981—82, exec. coun. 1977—83), Microscopy Soc. Am. (biol. dir. 1990—92, pres. 1995—96), Clare Hall (life). Avocations: music, gardening, physical fitness. Office: Baylor College Medicine Dept Medicine Houston TX 77030-3498

GOLDSTEIN, MARGARET FRANKS, special education educator; b. Toledo, July 3, 1940; d. Ray E. and Esther R. (Drewicz) Franks; m. William D. Goldstein, July 30, 1961; children: Sheldon, Benjamin, Marshall, Rochelle. BS in Edn., Bowling Green (Ohio) State U., 1975; MEd, U. Toledo, 1984. Cert. spl. edn. and indsl. arts educator. Tchr. indsl. arts Toledo Pub. Schs., 1970-77, tchr. devel. handicapped/behavior disordered, 1980-86, tchr. devel. handicapped/transitional tchr., 1986—99, severe behavior disability career ladder tchr., 1987—2000, mem. state supt.'s spl. edn. adv. coun., 1988—, chair, 1999—. Mem. state supt.'s task force for preparing spl. educators Toledo Pub. Schs., 1986—. Mem. Am. Fedn. Tchrs. (conv. del.), Ohio Fedn. Tchrs. (exec. coun., publicity and svcs. com., elections com., chmn., conv. del.), Toledo Fedn. Tchrs. (bd. dirs.), NW Ohio Spl. Edn. Assn. Office: McTigue Jr HS 5537 Hill Ave Toledo OH 43615-4699

GOLDSTEIN, MARION ZUCKER, psychiatrist-clincian, educator, researcher; b. Berlin, Apr. 30, 1932; came to U.S., 1947; d. Julian Joseph and Gertrude (Feige) Zucker; m. May 28, 1962 (div. 1976); children: Lillian Rachel Goldstein Schapiro, Naomi Susannah. BS, Queens Coll., 1953; MS in Physiology, U. Ill., 1954; MD, Albert Einstein Coll. Medicine, 1959. Diplomate Am. Bd. Psychiatry and Neurology with added qualifications in Geriatric Psychiatry (BP N examiner, 1995). Intern Jewish Hosp. Bklyn., 1959-60; resident in psychiatry Hillside Hosp., Glen Oaks, N.Y., 1960-61, Western Psychiat. Inst. Clinic, Pitts., 1961-63; staff psychiatrist Haverford (Pa.) State Hosp., 1963-64; unit psychiatrist Devereaux Found., Devon, Pa., 1964-65; med. dir. day hosp., emergency rm., cons. St. Francis Gen. Hosp., Pitts., 1966-83; clin. assoc. prof. U. Buffalo, 1986-98, assoc. prof., 1998—2003, prof., 2003—. Dir. divsn. geriatric psychiatry Erie County Med. Ctr., Buffalo, 1986—; vis. psychiatrist Cassel Hosp., London, 1963; with student health svcs. U. Pitts., 1969-76; assoc. prof. U. Pitts., 1983-86; cons. in field; conducted seminars in field; chairperson in-svc. tng. com. St. Francis Gen. Hosp., 1969-71, tumor clinic com., 1973-77, rape mgmt. com., 1977-79, ER com. 1977-79, utilization com. 1977-83, quality assurance com. 1980-83, chmn. planning com. new psychiatric bldg., 1981-83; mem. various coms. U. Pitts., 1970-86, SUNY Buffalo, 1986—. Editor: Family Involvement in the Treatment of Schizophrenia, 1986, Clinical Practice Series: Family Involvement in the Treatment of the Frail Elderly, 1989, Selected Models of Practice in Geriatric Psychiatry, 1993; contbr. articles to jours., chpts. to books. Bd. dirs. Western N.Y. Alzheimer's Assn., Inc., 1987-94, chair adv. bd. 1987-94, adv. bd. 1994—. Grantee NIMH, 1989-94; recipient physician's recognition awards AMA, 1973, 76, 79, 82, 85, 88, 91-94, 97, 2000—. Fellow APA (disting. life, membership com. 1975-76, corr. mem. coun. aging 1985-92, task force on Alzheimer's disease 1986-88, chair task force on models of practice of geriatric psychiatry 1989-92, com. on family violence 1989-92, com. on access and effectiveness of psychiatric care for the elderly 1993-94, chair coun. on aging 1995-97, cons. 1998), Gerontol. Soc. Am., Am. Coll. Psychiatrists (membership com. 1994-97, awards com. 1997—, edn. award com. 2000—, bd. editors PIPE 2003—), Am. Geriatric Soc.; mem. Am. Assn. Geriatric Psychiatry (newsletter com. 1984-90, program com. 1984-95, APA booth com. 1984-86, bd. dirs. 1987-90, 95-98, ann. mtg. program com. 1988-89, geriatric psychiatry fellowship com. 1990-93, new jour. com. 1990-92, Gerontol. Soc. Am. liaison 1990-94, asst. editor jour. 1990-2002), Am. Soc. on Aging, Internat. Psychogeriatric Assn. (sci. program com. cons. 2003—), Assn. Women Psychiatrists (bd. dirs. 1987—, chair aging com. 1988—, v.p. 1991—, pres. 1993-95, exec. com. 1996-97). Office: Erie County Med Ctr 462 Grider St Buffalo NY 14215-3021 E-mail: mzg@buffalo.edu.

GOLDSTEIN, MARK ALLAN, pediatrician, adolescent medicine specialist; b. Washington, Jan. 8, 1947; s. Samuel and Jean (Epstein) G.; m. Myrna Chandler, Dec. 27, 1970; children: Brett Jonathan, Samantha Anne. BS, U. Md., 1968; MD, Georgetown U., 1972. Lic. physician, Mass. Intern in pediats. Boston City Hosp., 1972-73; resident in pediats. Mass. Gen. Hosp., Boston, 1975-77; fellow in adolescent and young adult medicine Children's Hosp., Boston, 1977-78; acad. practice and med. rsch. Cambridge, Mass.; chief adolescent divsn. Mass. Gen. Hosp., Boston, 2003—; chief pediats. and student health MIT, Cambridge, 1978—2003. Asst. clin. prof. pediats. Harvard Med Sch., Boston, 1990—. Author: Definitive Guide to Medical School Admission, 1996, 2d edit., 1998, Boys into Men: Staying Healthy Through the Teen Years, 2000, Controversies in the Practice of Medicine, 2001; co-author: Controversies in Food and Nutrition, 2002; editor: Our Baby: The First Year, 1997. Co-chair Presdl. Working Group on Dangerous Drinking, MIT, 1997—. Fellow Soc. for Adolescent Medicine, Am. Acad. Pediats.; mem. Mass. Med. Soc. (chmn. com. student health and sports medicine 1998—), New Eng. Pediat. Soc. Jewish. Avocation: historic preservation. Office: MIT 77 Massachusetts Ave Cambridge MA 02139-4307

GOLDSTEIN, MARK KINGSTON LEVIN, information technology executive, researcher; b. Burlington, Vt., Aug. 22, 1941; s. Harold Meyer Levin and Roberta (Butterfield) Goldstein; m. Kyoko Matsubara, Mar. 8, 1984; 1 child, Amanda Kellie. BS in Chemistry, U. Vt., 1964; PhD, U. Miami, Coral Gables, 1971. Pres. IBR, Inc., Coral Gables, Fla., 1970-74; group leader Brookhaven Nat. Lab., Upton, NY, 1974-77; sr. rschr. East-West Ctr., Honolulu, 1977-79; sr. tech. advisor JGC Corp., Tokyo, 1979-81; pres., chmn. bd. Quantum Group, Inc., La Jolla, Calif., 1981—; exec. dir. Magnatek, Inc., Brotas, Brazil, 1982—. Project leader proliferation and waste mgmt. policy study for Pres. Ford's sci. advisor. Fellow NSF, 1964, 1965. Mem.: AAAS, Am. Chem. Soc., Hawaii Yacht Club (Honolulu). Achievements include patents for biomimetic carbon monoxide sensors, carbon monoxide catalyst, fuel cell reform catalyst and sensors; thaser co-generators; supermitters; thermphotovolaics self powered gas appliance; photon control systems; gas safety valve; eyesafe laser radar; photon wedding; fuel cell reformer catalyst; superemissive light pipe. Home: 2248 Del Mar Heights Rd Del Mar CA 92014-3022 Office: Quantum Group Inc 7737 Kenamar Ct San Diego CA 92121-2425

GOLDSTEIN, MARSHA FEDER, tour company executive; b. Chgo., July 7, 1945; d. Charles S. and Geraldine (Shulman) Feder; m. Michael Warren Goldstein, Dec. 26, 1966; 1 child, Paul Goldstein. BA, Roosevelt U., 1967. Tchr. art Chgo. Pub. Schs., 1967-68; freelance artist Chgo., 1968-71; tchr. arch. Brandeis U., Northfield, Ill., 1974-80; tour guide My Kind of Town Tours, Highland Park, Ill., 1975-79, owner, 1979—. Owner Tours at the Mart, 1992-95; art cons. Randall Pub. Co., Inc., 1984—. Editor: Highland Park by Foot or Frame, 1980; contbr. to book in field. Chmn., commr. Highland Park Hist. Preservation Commn.; bd. dirs. Roosevelt U., Chgo., Art Encounter, Parisian Salon Concerts; charter mem. Nat. Mus. Women in the Arts; mayoral appt. Sister Cities Com., 1998; chmn. Paris Sister Cities, 2000; mem. devel. bd. The Feltre Sch.; mem. adv. bd., benefit chmn. Gene Siskel Film Ctr. Recipient Cert. of Completion, Chgo. Arch. Found., 1975; named Disting. Alumni of Yr. Roosevelt U., 1997. Mem.: Meeting Profls. Internat., Chgo. Conv. and Tourism Bd. (devel. com.), Women's Exec. Network, Nat. Assn. Women Bus. Owners (bd. dirs. Chgo. chpt., pres.), Assn. Destination Mgmt. Execs. (founder), Internat. Spl. Events Soc. (bd. dirs.), Brandeis U. Nat. Women (v.p. 1977—, bd. dirs.), The Auditorium Bldg. Soc. (chmn. 1994, founder), Union League Club (standing com.). Jewish. Office: My Kind of Town 1585 Tara Ln Lake Forest IL 60045-1221 E-mail: info@mykindoftown.net.

GOLDSTEIN, MARTIN BARNET, osteopathic physician, psychiatrist; b. N.Y.C., Jan. 9, 1933; s. Samuel Eli and Bessie Leah (Kurman) G.; m. Nov. 23, 1963. BS in Pharmacy, L.I. U., 1955; DO, Chgo. Coll. Osteo. Medicine, 1959. Diplomate Am. Osteo. Bd. Neuropsychiatry, Am. Bd. Sexology. Intern Met. Hosp., Phila., 1959-60; pvt. practice Phila., 1960—. Pres., chief exec. officer Neuro-Rsch. Inc., Phila., 1978-84, Lafayette Psychiat. Assocs., Whitemarsh, Pa., 1981-84; chmn. bd. dirs. Equibank Del., Wilmington, 1987-89; bd. dirs. Equimark, Pitts., 1985-89. Author: The Judgment of J.D., 1994; editor: Jour. Med. Aspects Human Sexuality, 1986—90; contbr. over 100 articles to med. jours. Mem. Penn Valley (Pa.) Civic Assn., 1966—. Fellow Am. Coll. Neuropsychiatrists, Am. Acad. Clin. Sexologists; mem. Am. Osteo. Assn. (editorial

referee Jour. 1966—), Am. Psychiat. Assn., Pa. Osteo. Med. Asssn., Phila. Osteo. Med. Assn., Philadelphia County Osteo. Soc. Republican. Jewish. Avocations: fishing, swimming, snorkeling, yachting, painting. Office: 2400 Chestnut St Apt 2506 Philadelphia PA 19103-4323

GOLDSTEIN, MARVIN NORMAN, physician; b. Balt., Aug. 10, 1940; s. Manuel Quezon and Sylvia (Wagenheim) G.; m. Athene Schiffmann, July 1, 1962; children: Joshua, Claire. AB summa cum laude, Western Md. Coll., 1960; MD, U. Md., 1964. Diplomate Am. Bd. Psychiatry and Neurology. Intern in internal medicine U. Chgo. Hosp., 1964-65; resident in neurology Strong Meml. Hosp., U. Rochester, N.Y., 1965-68, chief resident in neurology, 1967-68; asst. attending neurologist, instr. U. Md. Hosp., Balt., 1968-69, Johns Hopkins Hosp., Balt., 1969-70; asst. prof. neurology and anatomy U. Rochester Sch. Medicine and Dentistry, 1970-74, clin. asst. prof. neurology and anatomy, 1974-78, clin. assoc. prof. neurology and anatomy, 1978-97; sr. attending neurology The Genesee Hosp., Rochester, 1978—, dir. neurology unit, 1996—2001; clin. prof. neurology U. Rochester Sch. Medicine, 1997—. Instr. in neurology and anatomy U. Rochester Sch. Medicine and Dentistry, 1965-68, Sch. Medicine, Georgetown U., Washington, 1968-70; staff neurologist U.S. Naval Hosp., Bethesda, 1968-70; med. staff exec. com. The Genesee Hosp., Rochester, 1989-90. Contbr. articles to profl. jours. Bd. dirs. Rochester Area Multiple Sclerosis, Rochester, 1972-78: adult edn. com. Temple Beth El, Rochester, 1985-90. Lt. comdr. USNR, 1968-70. Grantee NIH, 1972-74; recipient Merit award Rochester Acad. Medicine, 2002. Fellow Am. Acad. Neurology, Royal Soc. Medicine; mem. AMA, Am. Epilepsy Soc., Am. Acad. Clin. Neurophysiology, Sigma Xi. Avocations: gardening, canoeing, model shipbuilding, fishing. Home: 20 Varinna Dr Rochester NY 14618-1508 Office: 2101 Lac de Ville Blvd Rochester NY 14618-

GOLDSTEIN, MARY KANE, physician; b. N.Y.C., Oct. 24, 1950; d. Edwin Patrick and Mary Kane; m. Yonkel Noah Goldstein, June 24, 1979; children: Keira, Gavi. Philosophy degree, Columbia U., 1973, MD, 1977; MS in Health Svcs. Rsch., Stanford U., 1994. Resident Duke U. Med. Ctr., Durham, N.C., 1977-80; asst. prof. medicine U. Calif., San Francisco, 1980-84; clin. instr. dept. family and cmty. preventive medicine Stanford U., 1984-85; staff physician Mid Peninsula Health Svc., Palo Alto, Calif., 1986-88; dir. grad. med. edn. divsn. gerontol. Stanford (Calif.) U., 1986-93, Agy. for Health Care Policy Rsch. fellow Sch. Medicine, 1991-94, asst. prof. medicine Med. Ctr. Line, 1996—99, assoc. prof. medicine Med. Ctr. Line, 1999—, Ctr. for Primary Care and Outcomes Rsch., 1998—, faculty fellow Inst. for Rsch. on Women and Gender, 2000—01; sect. chief for gen. internal medicine Palo Alto (Calif.) VA Med. Ctr., 1994-96, rsch. assoc. health svcs. R&D, 1996—2002; assoc. dir. clin. svcs. The VA Geriatric Rsch. Edn. and Clinical Ctr., Palo Alto, 1999—. Editor Computer Ctr. Pubs., N.Y.C., 1971-72; computer programmer Columbia U., N.Y.C., 1972-73; governing coun. evidence-based practice ctr. U. Calif., Stanford, 1998—. Author chpt. to book; contbr. articles to profl. jours. Recipient Clin. Practice Guildelines for Hypertension award, VA Health Svc. Rsch. & Devel., 1997, Practice Guidelines Multisite Study award, 2000, Intelligent Critiquing of Med. Records award, NIH/NLM, 2001, Disutility of Functional Limitations award NIH/NIA, 2001. Fellow: Am. Geriatrics Soc. (bd. dirs. 1997—2002). Office: VA Palo Alto Health Care Sys GRECC 182B 3801 Miranda Ave Palo Alto CA 94304-1207 E-mail: goldstein@stanford.edu.

GOLDSTEIN, MATTHEW, academic administrator; BBA in Stats. and Math., City Coll. CUNY, 1963; MS in Math. Stats., Rutgers U., 1965; PhD, U. Conn., 1970. Asst. prof. math. Eastern Conn. State U., 1969-70, Polytech. Inst. N.Y., 1971-75; assoc. prof., assoc. provost CUNY, 1976-78, prof. stats., mem. doctoral faculty, 1978-98, pres. Rsch. Found., 1982-90, acting vice chancellor acad. affairs, 1990-91, pres. Bernard M. Baruch Coll., 1991-98, apptd. chancellor, 1999—; pres. Adelphi U., 1998-99; mem. commn. leadership devel. Am. Coun. Edn., 1996—; mem. bd. overseers Albert Einstein Sch. Medicine, 1998—; mem. N.Y. State Commr.'s Adv. Coun. Higher Edn., 1998—; mem. bd. dirs. Lincoln Ctr. Inst. Arts in Edn., 1999—, New Plan Excel Realty Trust, Inc., 2000—. Part-time asst. prof. math. Cooper Union, 1970-71; nat. prominent statistician holding positions in math. and stats. Baruch Coll., CUNY Grad. Sch. and U. Ctr., Polytech. U. N.Y., Cooper Union, Ea. Conn. State U., U. Conn.; trustee Albert Einstein Sch. Medicine, 1998—, JP Morgan Funds, 2003--; trustee Bronx-Lebanon Hosp. Ctr., 1992—, chmn. strategic planning com., 1992—; ex-officio trustee Jean Cocteau Repertory, 1990—; mem. N.Y. adminstrv. com. Fleet Nat. Bank. Co-author: Discrete Discriminant Analysis, 1978, Intermediate Statistical Methods and Applications, 1983, Multivariate Analysis, 1984; contbr. articles for leading scholarly publs. in math. and stats. Mem. Jewish Cmty. Rels. Coun. of NY, 2000—; vol. United Way of N.Y.C., 2002—. Recipient Jewish Nat. Fund Tree Life award, Townsend Harris medal, Liberty award for Disting. Accomplishments in Field Edn., Lower East Side Multicultural Fest., 2001, Leadership in Edn. and Pub. Svc. award Italo-Am. Assn., 2002, Ellis Island medal of honor, 2002. Fellow N.Y. Acad. Scis.; mem. Lincoln Ctr. Inst. Arts in Edn. (bd. dirs.), Am. Coun. Edn.'s Commn. Leadership Devel., Gov. George E. Pataki's Adv. Com. for Rivers Inst., Senator Charles Schumer's Group of 35 Blue-Ribbon Task Force on Comml. Space, Am. Assn. State Colls. and Univs. (com. on policies and purposes), R & D Subcommittee Gov.'s Conf. Com. Sci. and Tech., Gov.-Elect George E. Pataki's Higher Edn. Transition Task Force, Adv. Coun. Econ. Info. and Rsch. N.Y. State Dept. Econ. Devel. N.Y. State Senate Higher Edn. Com.'s Adv. Com., Rsch. Policy Com. of Coun. on Rsch. and Tech. (bd. dirs.), N.Y.C. Partnership's Tech. Exec. Coun., Am. Statis. Assn. (pres. N.Y. chpt. 1981-83, nat. coun. 1981-83), Golden Key, Beta Gamma Sigma. Achievements include being the first graduate to lead the nation's most prominent urban public university, City College, Class of 1963. Office: CUNY 535 E 80th St New York NY 10021-0795

GOLDSTEIN, MELISSA ANNE, writer; b. Silver Spring, Md., Sept. 11, 1969; d. Larry Joel and Sandra Goldstein. BA in English, U. Pa., 1992, MLA concentration in relationship between medicine and lit., 1995. Rschr. with Dr. Renée Fox, sociology dept. U. Pa., Phila., 1990—91, Charlotte Newcombe intern with Dr. Renée Fox, sociology dept., 1991, 1993, 1994, Writing Across the U. fellow for medicine and lit. seminar, sociology dept., 1992, 1995; ind. writer, scholar, pub. spkr. Phila., 1995—. Guest spkr. U. Pa. Sch. Medicine, Phila., 1991, Phila., 2002; colloquium spkr. MLA program U. Pa., Phila., 1996; guest lectr. Quaker Mid. Sch., Horsham, Pa., 1998, Horsham, 2000; main spkr. 2000 Awareness Luncheon N.W. Fla. chpt. Lupus Found. Am., Pensacola, Fla., 2000; spkr. Cen. N.Y. chpt. Lupus Found. Am., Syracuse, NY, 2000; guest spkr. Everywoman Everywhere radio program, Syracuse, 2000; spkr. Alumni Vis. Series U. Pa., Kelly Writers House, Phila., 2001. Author: (book) Travels with the Wolf: A Story of Chronic Illness, 2000; contbr. essays, poetry and article to profl. publs. Vol. Lupus Found. Am., Phila., 1988—, Arthritis Found., Phila., 1988—, Am. Juvenile Arthritis Orgn., Phila., 1988—; founder Lupus Support Group, U. Pa., 1988. Mem.: Nat. Coalition of Ind. Scholars, Phi Beta Kappa, Philomathean Honor Soc. Democrat. Jewish. Avocations: traveling, swimming, attending ballets, jazz clubs, and modern dance performances. Home and Office: 1 Franklin Town Blvd Apt 2009 Philadelphia PA 19103

GOLDSTEIN, MELVYN C. anthropologist, educator; b. N.Y.C., Feb. 8, 1938; s. Harold and Rae (Binen) G.; 1 son, Andre. BA, U. Mich., 1959, MA, 1960; PhD, U. Wash., 1968. Asst. prof. Case Western Res. U., Cleve., 1968—71, assoc. prof., 1971—76, prof. anthropology, 1976—2002, chmn. dept. anthropology, 1976—2002, dir. ctr. rsch. on Tibet, 1987—, J.R. Harkness prof., 1991—. Author: Modern Spoken Tibetan, 1970, Modern Literary Tibetan: A Grammar and Reader, 1973, Tibetan English Dictionary of Modern Tibetan, 1975, Tibetan for Travellers and Beginners, 1980, English-Tibetan Dictionary of Modern Tibetan, 1984, Tibet Phrasebook, 1987, A History of Modern Tibet, 1913-1951: The Demise of the Lamist State, 1989, 2d edit., 1991, Nomads of Western Tibet, The Survival of a Way of Life, 1990, Essentials of Modern Literary Tibetan: A Reading Course and Reference Grammar, 1991, The Changing World of Mongolian Nomads, 1994, The Struggle for Modern Tibet: The Autobiography of Tashi Tsering, 1997, The Snow Lion and the Dragon: China, Tibet and the Dalai Lama, 1997, Buddhism in Contemporary Tibet: Religious Revival and Cultural Identity (with Matthew Kapstein), 1998, The New Tibetan-English Dictionary of Modern Tibetan, 2001; editor Jour. Cross-Cultural Gerontology; contbr. articles to profl. jours. Grantee Am. Council Learned Socs., 1973-74, NIH, 1976-77, 80-82, NEH, 1980-82, 84-85, 89-97, 2000-03, Dept. Edn., 1980-82, Smithsonian Instn., 1981-83, Nat. Geographic Soc., 1980-81, Nat. Inst. Child Health and Human Devel., 1981-83, NSF, 1982-83, Com. for Scholarly Exchange with People's Republic China, 1985-86, 87-88, Nat. Geog. Soc., 1986-88, 90, 91-93, 96-97, Dept. of Edn., 1986-87, 94-96, IREX, 1990-92, Henry Luce Found., 1997-2000, 2001—. Mem. Assn. Asian Studies, Am. Anthrop. Assn., Soc. Applied Anthropology, Soc. Med. Anthropology, Assn. for Anthropology and Gerontology. Home: 50 E 252d St Euclid OH 44132-3901 Office: Case Western Res Univ 241 Mather Memorial Cleveland OH 44106

GOLDSTEIN, MICHAEL, retail executive; Formerly exec. v.p., treas., CFO Toys R Us Inc., Rochelle Park, N.J., exec. v.p. fin. and adminstrn., vice chmn., CEO, chmn. bd., 1998—. Office: Toys R Us Inc 461 From Rd Paramus NJ 07652-3524*

GOLDSTEIN, MICHAEL AARON, finance educator; b. Winchester, Mass., Oct. 9, 1964; s. Norman and Sheila Judith G.; m. Joanne C. Pratt Nov. 27, 1999. BS, U. Pa., 1986, MBA, 1991, MA in Fin., 1992, PhD in Fin., 1993. Investment banker Merrill Lynch Capital, N.Y.C., 1986-88; rsch. assoc. WhartonSch, U. Pa., Phila., 1988-93; adviser Ministry of Privatization, Warsaw, 1990; asst. prof. U. Colo., Boulder, 1993-99; co-CEO JD.Com, 1999—2002; assoc. prof., Joseph Winn term chair Babson Coll., 2000—. Vis. economist NYSE, 1997-98; various appearances on CNN, PBS, N.Y. Times, Wall Street Jour., Boston Globe, CNNfn, News Hour with Jim Leher, BBC, others; bd. adv. Starwood Cons. Contbr. articles to profl. jours. incl. Jour. of Fin. Econs. Treas., CFO Boulder County Dems., Boulder, Colo., 1996-2000; contr. Boulder County Clinton/Gore, 1995-96; bd. dirs. Hillel of Colo., Denver, 1993-96, chair, Boulder, 1994-96; mem. adv. bd. Nasdaq. Recipient Tchg. award U. Colo., 1994-2000; GeeWax Terker fellow, 1988-91. Mem. Am. Fin. Assn., Fin. Mgmt. Assn., Phi Beta Kappa, Beta Gamma Sigma, Delta Sigma Pi. Democrat. Jewish. Avocations: skiing, hiking, travel, flying, running in N.Y.C. and Boston marathons. Office: Babson Coll Fin Dept Babson Park MA 02457-0310

GOLDSTEIN, MICHAEL B. lawyer; b. N.Y.C., Sept. 29, 1943; s. Isaac and Betty (Friedman) G.; m. Jinny M. Loewenthal, Dec. 18, 1966; 1 child, Eric Loren. BA in Govt., Cornell U., 1964; JD, NYU, 1967. Bar: N.Y. 1967, Ill. 1974, D.C 1978. Spl. asst., dep. mayor Office of Mayor, N.Y.C., 1965-66, asst. city adminstr., dir. univ. rels., 1969-72; dir. N.Y.C. Urban Corps, 1966-69; assoc. vice chancellor for urban and govtl. affairs, assoc. prof. urban scis. U. Ill., Chgo., 1972-78; mem. Dow, Lohnes & Albertson PLLC, Washington, 1978—. Practice leader Ednl. Inst. Rels.; chmn. task force on pub. policy Commn.on Higher Edn. and Adult Learner Am. Coun. on Edn.; mem. bd. advisors Stanford Forum for Coll. Financing. Contbr. articles to profl. texts and jours. Pres. Nat. Ctr. for Pub. Svc. Internship Programs, 1975-77; bd. dirs., officer Washington Ctr. Internships and Acad. Seminars, 1977—; bd. dirs. and gen. counsel Washington Ballet, 1978—; bd. dirs. Greater Washington Rsch. Ctr., 1982-96, Chgo. Urban Corps, 1972-75, Am. Assoc. Higher Edn., 1998—; trustee Fielding Inst., 1989-94, 98—; trustee, chmn. fin. com. Mt. Vernon Coll., 1991-96; dir. Am.-Russian Cultural Cooperation Found., 1995—; bd. visitors Mt. Vernon Coll., 1996-98; bd. dirs. Sta. WETA, 1997-99; mem. Friendship Fire Assocs., D.C. Fire Dept., 1985—. Wall St. Jour. Newspaper Fund fellow, 1963, Loeb fellow Harvard U., 1972. Mem. ABA (chmn. edn. law com. 1991-92), D.C. Bar Assn. (vice chair edn. task force 1999—), FBA (co-chmn. edn. grants com. 1985-86, 91-92), Nat. Assn. Coll. and Univ. Attys. (mem. ctrl. office com. 1986-88, vice chmn. pvt. bar com. 1989-90, chair continuing legal edn. com. 2001—), Nat. Soc. Internships and Exptl. Edn. (pres. 1972), Am. Assn. Higher Edn. (dir. 1997-2003). Democrat. Jewish. Office: Dow Lohnes & Albertson 1200 New Hampshire Ave NW Washington DC 20036-6802

GOLDSTEIN, MICHAEL GERALD, lawyer, director; b. St. Louis, Sept. 21, 1946; s. Joseph and Sara G. (Finkelstein) G.; m. Ilene Marcia Ballin, July 19, 1970; children: Stephen Eric, Rebecca Leigh. BA, Tulane U., 1968; JD, U. Mo., 1971; LLM in Taxation, Washington U., 1972. Bar: Mo. 1971, U.S. Dist. Ct. (ea. dist.) Mo. 1972, U.S. Tax Ct. 1972, U.S. Ct. Appeals (8th cir.) 1974, U.S. Supreme Ct. 1976. Atty. Morris A. Shenker, St. Louis, 1972-78; ptnr. Lashly, Caruthers, Baer & Hamel and predecessor, St. Louis, 1979-84, Suelthaus & Kaplan, P.C. and predecessors, St. Louis, 1974-91; ptnr., chmn. dept. tax & estate planning Husch & Eppenberger, 1991-99; pres., CEO 1st Fin. Resources, 1999—2001; sr. v.p. EPS Fin. Solutions Corp., 1999-2000; sr. v.p., gen. counsel The Benefits Group, Inc., 2001—; pres., COO Benefits Group Worldwide, 2003—. Adj. prof. tax law Washington U. Sch. Law, 1986-97; planning com. Mid-Am. Tax Confs., chmn. ALI/ABA Tax Seminar; lectr., author taxation field. Author: BNA Tax Mgmt. Portfolios, ABA The Insurance Counselor Books; contbr. articles to profl. jours. Bd. dirs. Jewish Family and Children's Svc. St. Louis, 1980—, pres., 1986-88; bd. dirs. Jewish Fedn. of St. Louis; trustee United Hebrew Temple, 1986-88; grad. Jwish Fedn. St. Louis Leadership Devel. Coun.; co-chmn. lawyers divsn. Jewish Fedn. St. Louis Campaign, 1981-82, Leadership St. Louis, 1988-89. Capt. USAR, 1970-78. Fellow Am. Coll. Tax Counsel, Am. Coll. Trust and Estate Counsel; mem. ABA (chmn. tax seminar, group editor newsletter for taxation sect.), Am. Law Inst., Mo. Bar Assn., Bar Assn. Met. St. Louis, St. Louis County Bar Assn. Home: 2011 Yacht Mischief Newport Beach CA 92660-6713 Office: 1875 Century Park East Ste 2100 Los Angeles CA 90067

GOLDSTEIN, MICHAEL L. neurologist; b. Chgo., June 14, 1945; s. Charles and Dorothy (Mack) G.; m. Barbara Joan Kaplan, June 18, 1967; children: Rachel, Elizabeth, Adam. AB, Princeton, 1966; MD, U. of Chgo., 1970. Intern Stanford U., 1970-71; resident in neurology Beth Israel Hosp., Boston, 1971-74; fellow in neurology Harvard U. Med. Sch., 1971-74; chief resident in neurology Children's Hosp., Boston, 1973-74; with Western Neurol. Assoc., Salt Lake City. Cons. Soc. Sec., Balt., 1990-91; bd. dirs., edn. comm. chmn. Rowland Hall, St. Marks Sch., Salt Lake City, 1986-92; examiner Am. Bd. Psychiatry and Neurology, 1987—; clin. assoc. prof. U. Utah Med. Sch., Salt Lake City, 1977—. Co-author: Managing Attention Disorders, 1990, Parent's Guide to ADD, 1993; co-producer: Educating Inattentive Children, 1992, It's Just Attention Disorder, 1993. Pres. synagogue, Salt Lake City, 1985-86. Fellow Am. Acad. Pediat., Am. Acad. Neurology (chair practice com, 1995-2000, treas. 2001—). Office: Western Neurol Assn 1151 E 3900 S Salt Lake City UT 84124-1216

GOLDSTEIN, MICHAEL LEWIS, investment strategist; b. Racine, Wis., May 25, 1955; s. Julius and Sylvia Goldstein. BBA, U. Wis., 1977; MBA, U. Mich., 1979. Mgr. Arthur Anderson, N.Y.C., 1979-84; sr. analyst Goldman Sachs, N.Y.C., 1984-86; investment strategist Sanford C. Bernstein, N.Y.C., 1986—2002; mng. ptnr. Empirical Rsch. Ptnrs. LLC, 2002—. Named to Institutional Investor All-Am. Rsch. team Institutional Investor mag., 1989-90, 93-2001. Office: Empirical Rsch Ptnrs LLC 477 Madison Ave New York NY 10022

GOLDSTEIN, MICHAEL SAUL, sociologist; b. N.Y.C., Aug. 1, 1944; s. Abraham J. and Rose G.; m. Laura Geller, Dec. 23, 1979 (div. May 1992); children: Joshua, Adam, Elana. BA, Queens Coll., Flushing, N.Y., 1965; MA, Brown U., Providence, 1967, PhD, 1971. Lectr. Brown U., Providence, 1970-71; asst. prof. Sch. Pub. Health, UCLA, 1971-78, assoc. prof., 1978-88, prof., 1988—, chair dept. community health, 1988-91. Author: The Health Movement, 1992; author, editor: 50 Simple Things You Can Do to Save Your Life, 1992. Mem. APHA, Am. Sociol. Assn. Soc. for Study Social Problems, Hastings Inst. Soc. Ethics and the Life Scis. Office: UCLA Sch Pub Health po bOX 95177 Los Angeles CA 90024

GOLDSTEIN, MILTON, art educator, printmaker, painter; b. Holyoke, Mass., Nov. 14, 1914; s. Jacob Bernard and Sarah (Peskin) G.; m. Mollie Brick. Student, Northeastern U., 1934-35, Art Students League, 1939-41, 46-49. Part-time instr. Art. Students League, N.Y.C., 1948-65; instr. graphics arts dept. Adelphi U., Garden City, N.Y., 1953-56, asst. prof., 1956-59, assoc. prof., 1959-65, prof., 1965-85, prof. emeritus, 1985. Represented in permanent collections Mus. Modern Art, Pila. Mus. Art, Met. Mus., Bklyn. Mus., Smithsonian Nat. Mus., Libr. Congress., Mil. Mus. of War Dept., Washington, U.S. Army Ctr. of Mil. History, Washington, and other pub. and pvt. collections in Am. and Europe; several one-man shows (nat. prizes and purchase awards); inventor color printing method for making color etchings. With U.S. Army, 1942-45. Guggenheim fellow, 1950. Fellow Royal Soc. Arts; mem. Soc. Am. Graphic Artists, Art Student League (life). Avocations: refinishing old furniture, fixing broken objects, sports. Home and Office: 56-16 219th St Flushing NY 11364-1918

GOLDSTEIN, MINDY SUE, biologist; b. N.Y.C., July 20, 1952; d. Seymour and Ida (Silver) Zibitt; m. Jerome Sidney Goldstein, Aug. 5, 1972; children: Ila Beth, Cori Anne. BS cum laude, NYU, 1974, MS, 1978, PhD, 1983; postgrad., SUNY, Stony Brook, 1983-85. Staff scientist Applied Genetics, Freeport, N.Y., 1985-87; dir. devel. svcs. Collaborative Labs., East Setauket, N.Y., 1987-95; dir. product devel. Lipo Chems., Paterson, N.J., 1995-99; dir. strategic tech. outreach Body & Bath Works, Reynoldsburg, Ohio, 1999-2001; exec. dir. biol. rsch. treatment materials dept. Estee Lauder Cos., Melville, NY, 2001—. Patentee absorbable bandage, cosmetic delivery system for salicylic acid. Mem. Am. Soc. for Cell Biology, AAAS, N.Y. Acad. Sci. Jewish. Avocations: ice skating, skiing. Office: Estee Lauder Cos 125 Pinelawn Rd Melville NY 11747 E-mail: icgymnasts@worldnet.att.net.

GOLDSTEIN, MORRIS, retired entertainment company executive; b. Pitts., Feb. 2, 1945; s. Irving and Clara (Caplan) G.; m. Diane Donna Davis, Aug. 21, 1966 (div. Nov. 1985); children: Jonathan, Julie; m. Kathy Evelyn Niemeier, July 7, 1990. BS, Carnegie Inst. Tech., 1967; MBA, U. Pa., 1979. Sales rep. computer divsn. RCA, Cherry Hill, N.J., 1968-70; sales mgr. Sedgwick Printout Sys., Princeton, N.J., 1970-76, pres., 1976-80; v.p. Courier-Jour. Louisville Times, 1980-81; mgr. bus. devel. Ziff-Davis Pub., N.Y.C., 1982-2000; pres. Information Access Corp. divsn., Foster City, Calif., 1982-2000; pres., COO Imagination Network Inc., Oakhurst, Calif., 1994; sr. v.p. Ziff-Davis Pub., Foster City, Calif., 1994; CEO Info. Access Co., A Thomson Corp. Co., Foster City, Calif., 1995-96, Thomson Tech. Ventures, San Mateo, Calif., 1997; pres., CEO Alliance Gaming Inc, Las Vegas, Nev., 1997-99; pres. entertainment bus. divsn. InnoVentry LLC, Las Vegas, 1999-2000; ret., 2000; exec. v.p. Global Cash Access, Las Vegas, 2001—03; prin., owner Nev. Slots and Supplies. Founder Nev. Slots and Supplies, Las Vegas, 2002. Dep mayor Mt. Laurel Twp., N.J., 1974-78. Home: 3581 E Maule Ave Las Vegas NV 89120-2918 Office: Global Cash Access 3525 E Post Rd Las Vegas NV 89120 also: Nevada Slots and Supplies 2245 N Green Valley Pkwy Ste 283 Henderson NV 89120

GOLDSTEIN, MORTON HILL, surgeon, educator; b. N.Y.C., Apr. 21, 1934; s. Abraham Arthur and Evelyn Goldstein; m. Deanna Gizella, Jan. 13, 1968; children: Robin, David, Peter. AB cum laude, Alfred U., 1955; MD, U. Chgo., 1959. Diplomate Am. Bd. Surgery, Am. Bd. Plastic Surgery. Intern U. Chgo. Clinics, 1959-60; resident SUNY, Syracuse, 1960-61, Columbia U., N.Y.C., 1961-63, Bklyn. Va Hosp., 1963-65, Montefiore-Albert Einstein Med. Ctr., Bronx, 1966-68; sr. attending surgeon St. Peters Med. Ctr., New Brunswick, N.J., 1968-96; attending surgeon Robert Wood Johnson U. Hosp., New Brunswick, 1968-99; surgeon pvt. practice, 1968-93; clin. assoc. prof. surgery U. Medicine & Dentistry N.J., Robert Wood Johnson Med. Sch., Piscataway, N.J., 1974-95. Contbr. articles to profl. jours. Vol. surgeon Health Vols. Overseas, St. Lucia St. Jude Hosp., 1989, 90, 91, Operation Smile Internat., Philipines, Kenya, 1992, 94, Interplast Internat., Nicaragua, 1995, Rio Vista Equipo Medico, Guatamala, 1996, Indian Svc. Hosps., N.Mex., Ben Gurion U., Soroka Med. Ctr., Israel. Capt. USAF Res., 1961-68. Recipient Disting. Svc. award U. Chgo., Divsn. Biol. Scis., 1999. Fellow ACS; mem. Am. Soc. of Plastic Surgeons, N.J. Soc. of Surgeons. Avocations: writing, traveling, reading, bicycling, correspondence. also: 23 Calimo Cir Santa Fe NM 87505-8916

GOLDSTEIN, MURRAY, health organization official; b. N.Y.C., Oct. 13, 1925; s. Israel and Yetta (Zeigen) G.; m. Sue Mary Michael, June 13, 1957; children: Patricia Sue Robertson, Barbara Jean Warner. BA, NYU, 1947; DO, Des Moines U., 1950; MPH, U. Calif., 1959; DSc (hon.), Kirksville Coll. Osteo. Medicine, 1970, U. New Eng., 1984, Ohio U., 1986, U. Osteo. Medicine and Health Scis., 1990, Mich. State U., 2000; LLD (hon.), N.Y. Inst. Tech., 1982; Dr. honoris causa, Med. Univ. Pecs, Hungary, 1985; LHD (hon.), Coll. Osteo. Medicine Pacific, 1988; Dr. honoris causa, Med. Sch. U. Lund, Sweden, 1994. Diplomate Am. Osteo. Bd. Preventive Medicine (sec.-treas. 1987-88, vice chmn. 1988-92). Rotating intern Still Coll. Osteo. Hosp., Des Moines, 1950-51, resident internal medicine, 1951-53; commd. corps USPHS, 1953, advanced through grades to asst. surgeon gen., 1980, ret., 1993; asst. to chief, then asst. chief, grants and tng. br., Nat. Heart Inst. NIH, Bethesda, Md., 1953-58, chief epidemiology and biometry tng. grant program, divsn. rsch. grants, 1956-58, asst. chief rsch. grants rev. br., divsn. rsch. grants, 1959-60; exec. sec. joint coun. subcom. cerebrovascular disease Nat. Inst. Neurol. Diseases and Stroke and Nat. Heart and Lung Inst., NIH, Bethesda, Md., 1961-67, 69-75; dir. extramural programs Nat. Inst. Neurol. and Communicative Disorders and Stroke, NIH, Bethesda, Md., 1961-76, dir. stroke and trauma program, 1976-78, dep. dir., 1978-81, acting dir., 1981-82, dir., 1982-93; pub. health trainee epidemiology Calif. State Dept. Pub. Health, Berkeley, 1958, acting chief sect. virus diseases ctrl. nervous system, Bur. Acute Communicable Disease, 1958; med. dir., COO, United Cerebral Palsy Rsch. and Edn. Found., Washington, 1993—, bd. dirs., 1972-93; clin. prof. neurol. medicine N.Y. Coll. Osteo. Medicine, 1977—; sr. lectr. dept. neurology Uniformed Svcs. U. Health Scis., 1986—; osteo. pioneer Des Moines U., 2000. Bd. dirs. Nat. Stroke Assn., Burke Rsch. Inst., Robarts Rsch. Inst.; adj. prof. pub. health Nova-Southeastern U., 1995—; chmn. Commd. Corps Adv. Com. to NIH dir., 1990-93, WHO Task Force on stroke and other vascular cerebral disorders, 1986-89; dir. WHO Neurosci. Collaborating Ctr., Bethesda, 1981-93; liaison, mem. sci. adv. bd. Kent Waldrep Nat. Paralysis Found., 1989-94; vis. prof. med. rsch. Semmelweis Med. U., Budapest, Hungary, 1975; vis. sci. sect. neurology Mayo Clinic and grad. sch., Rochester, Minn., 1967-68; vis. scholar Henry Ford Hosp., 1979-80; v.p. Eisenhower Inst. Stroke Rsch., 1975-88; cons. bur. rsch. Am. Osteo. Assn., 1990-99; mem. nat. adv. coun. Nat. Ctr. for Complimentary and Alternative Medicine/NIH, 2000—; lectr., cons. in field. Assoc. editor Stroke: A Journal of Cerebral Circulation, 1976-91, consulting editor, 1992—; mem. editl. bd. Osteo. Annals, 1973-85, 87-88, Internat. Jour. Neurology, 1980—, Jour. Neuroepidemiology, 1981-90, Hosp. and Community Psychiatry, 1980—, Alzheimer Disease: An Internat. Jour., 1985-93, Cerebralvascular and Brain Metabolism Revs., 1985-93; contbr. articles to profl. jours. Bd. dirs. Bapt. Home for Children and Adults, 1999—. With U.S. Army, 1943-45. Decorated DSM, Silver Star, Purple Heart; recipient USPHS Disting. Svc. medal with oak leaf cluster, Surgeon Gen.'s Exemplary Svc. medal, Surgeon Gen.'s medallion, Founders Day medal U. Osteo. Medicine and Health Scis., 1983, Patenge Pub. Svc. medal Mich. State U., 1987, Marjorie Guthrie award The Huntington's Disease Soc. Am., 1988, Burke award Buke Found., 1988, Spl. Leadership award United Cerebral Palsy Rsch. & Ednl. Found., 1989, Phillips Pubs. Svc. medal Ohio U., 1990, others; named Pioneer in Osteo. Medicine, Des Moines U., 2000. Fellow: Am. Acad. Neurology (mem. long range planning com. 1972—75, mem. manpower com. 1979—85, mem. neurology in govtl. svcs. and insts. com. 1979—85, chmn. 1981—83, 1981—83, mem. internat. affairs com. 1981—90, mem. com. govt. rels. 1983—85, ANA-AAN del. to World Fedn. Neurology 1983—85, mem. AAN com. on pub. comm. and legislation 1983—85, mem. ad hoc com. for soc. neurology liaison 1987—89, sr. advisor uniformed svcs. orgn. neurologists com. 1987—93, chmn. 1993—95, bd. dirs. 1993—); mem.: NIH Alumni Assn. (v.p. bd. dirs. 1999—), Am. Acad. Cerebral Palsy and Devel. Medicine, United Cerebral Palsy Assn. (interim dir. 1998). Avocations: gardening, golf, swimming. Home: 6210 Swords Way Bethesda MD 20817-3349 Office: United Cerebral Palsy Rsch & Ednl Found 1660 L St NW Ste 700 Washington DC 20036-5616

GOLDSTEIN, NEIL WARREN, filmmaker; b. Washington, June 3, 1950; s. Alfred Frank and Tillie Goldstein; m. Janice Posatery Burke, Mar. 28, 1981; 1 child, Evan Benjamin. BA, Washington U., St. Louis, 1972, MA, 1974. Dir. instl. tech. Childrens Hosp., L.A., 1975-82; chief exec. officer Corp. Disabilities and Telecommunication, L.A., 1982-88, chmn. East Coast chpt. Phila., 1988-92; pres. Neil Goldstein & Assocs., 1992—. Pres. Concept Works, Inc., L.A., 1980—82, Ctrl. Coast Cmty. TV, L.A., 1982; co-founder Lyme Project, Phila., 1988—92; vice chmn. Pub. Health Planning Group, Phila., 1988; instr. Montgomery County C.C., 1992—98, asst. prof., 2003—; instr. Drexel U., 1997—2001; comm. cons. U. of the Arts, Phila., 1998—99; instr., cons. Chestnut Hill Coll., 1998—; coord. comm. program Montgomery Cmty. C.C., 1999—. Dir., prodr. film festival Superfest, 1976-88 (CC Robinson award 1987); exec. prodr. TV spl. Superfest, 1982-89 (Emmy 1986, Gov. award 1989); dir., prodr. TV spl. Breaking Ground, 1987 (Gov. award 1988, Presdl. Commendation 1988, Emmy nominee), Amnesty KTLA-TV, 1988, Lyme Disease: In Our Own Backyard, N.J. Network, 1991, Shattered Lives: Composing an Identity After a Traumatic Brain Injury, 1994, Barriers, The Montgomery County Neighborhood Youth Corps, 1995 (Best H.S. Documentary, Tusculum Videofest, 1995, Best Practice, 1998, A Chance to Hear, 1998, Maddie's Story, 2002. Vol. Westside YMCA, West L.A., Calif., 1982—84; adv. com. Sch. Bd. Upper Moreland Twp., Calif., 1990—91; co-chair health issues

adv. com. Montgomery County, 1992; bd. dirs. Ranch Owners Assn., Tehachapi, Calif., 1984—88. Grantee Corp. Pub. Broadcasting, L.A., 1987, Am. Film Inst., 1988. Mem.: Acad. TV., Dirs. Guild, Soc. Motion Picture and TV Engrs. Avocations: reading, writing, walking, biking. Home: 1930 Cathedral Rd Huntingdon Valley PA 19006-5006 E-mail: ngoldste@mc3.edu.

GOLDSTEIN, NILES ELLIOT, rabbi, author; b. Chgo., Feb. 5, 1966; s. Melvin Joel and Lois Ann (Rakita) G. BA, U. Pa., 1988; MA in Hebrew Letters, Hebrew Union Coll., 1993. Ordained rabbi, 1994. Jewish educator Jewish Cmty. Ctr. of Staten Island, NY, 1994-95; asst. rabbi Temple Israel, New Rochelle, N.Y., 1995-97; Steinhardt fellow CLAL: The Nat. Jewish Ctr. for Learning and Leadership, N.Y.C., 1996-97, sr. fellow, 1997-98; prgm. officer/educator Jewish Life Network, N.Y.C., 1998-2000; founding rabbi The New Shul, N.Y.C., 1999—. Bd. dirs. Union of Couns., Washington, 1996—; mem. com. on interreligious affairs Union Am. Hebrew Congregations, 1993—, mem. liturgy com. Central Conf. of Am. Rabbis, 2000—; spkr., presenter in field. Author: Forests of the Night, 1996, Judaism and Spiritual Ethics, 1996, God at the Edge, 2000, Lost Souls, 2002; editor: Duties of the Soul, 1999, Spiritual Manifestos, 1999. Nat. Jewish chaplain Fed. Law Enforcement Officers Assn., 1994—; chaplain Drug Enforcement Adminstrn., N.Y.C., 1996—. 1st lt. USAR, 1991-97. Fellow Bd. Jewish Edn., 1994-96. Mem. Ctrl Conf. Am. Rabbis, N.Y. Bd. Rabbis, Shelley Soc. N.Y., Acad. Am. Poets, Assn. for Jewish Studies. Avocations: hiking, dogsledding, Karate. Home: 196 8th Ave Apt 8 Brooklyn NY 11215-2615

GOLDSTEIN, NORM, editor, writer; b. N.Y.C., Mar. 24, 1939; s. Michael David and Minna (Shaffer) G.; m. Ruth Weiss, Sept. 15, 1963 (div. 1975), m. Jeannette Reilly, Nov. 12, 1975; 1 child, Frank Parker. BA, Bklyn. Coll., 1959; MA, Pa. State U., 1961. Assoc. editor Ind. Film Jour., N.Y.C., 1960-61; writer, editor AP, Phila., 1963-66, N.Y.C., 1966-72, dir. ednl. svcs., 1972-84, editor, spl. editions, 1984-91, dir. spl. projects, 1991—. Author: John Wayne: A Tribute, 1979, Frank Sinatra: Ol' Blue Eyes, 1982, Henry Fonda, 1982, History of Television, 1991, Marshal: The Story of the U.S. Marshals, 1991, Kim Dae-Jung, 1998; editor: Footprints on the Moon, 1969, Seventy-Six, 1976, 444 Days, 1981, Eyewitness History of the Vietnam War, 1983, Moments in Time, 1984, Moments in Sports, 1985, Front Page, 1985, Moments in Space, 1986, World War II: A 50th Anniversary History, 1989; project dir.: 20th Century America: A Primary Source Collection From the Associated Press, 1995; editor AP Stylebook and Libel Manual, 1986—. With USAR. Avocation: softball. Home: 75 Henry St Brooklyn NY 11201 Office: Assoc Press 50 Rockefeller Plz Fl 5 New York NY 10020-1605

GOLDSTEIN, SIR NORMAN, dermatologist; b. Bklyn. July 14, 1934; s. Joseph H. and Bertha (Docteroff) G.; B.A., Columbia Coll., 1955; M.D., SUNY, 1959; m. Ramsay, Feb. 14, 1980; children: Richard, Heidi. Intern, Maimonides Hosp., N.Y.C., 1959-60; resident Skin and Cancer Hosp., 1960-61, Bellevue Hosp., 1961-62, NYU. Postgrad. Center, 1962-63 (all N.Y.C.); ptnr. Honolulu Med. Group, 1967-72; practice medicine specializing in dermatology, Honolulu, 1972—; clin. prof. dermatology U. Hawaii Sch. Medicine, 1973—; bd. dirs. Pacific Laser. Bd. dirs. Skin Cancer Found., 1979—; trustee Dermatol. Found., 1979-82, Hist. Hawaii Found., 1981-87; pres. Hawaii Theater Ctr., 1985-89, Hawaii Med. Libr., 1987; mem. Oahu Heritage Council, 1986-94. Served with U.S. Army, 1960-67. Recipient Henry Silver award Dermatol. Soc. Greater N.Y., 1963; Husik award NYU, 1963; Spl. award Acad. Dermatologia Hawaiiana, 1971, Outstanding Scientific Exhibit award Calif. Med. Assn., 1979, Special award for Exhibit Am. Urologic Assn., 1980, Svc. to Hawaii's Youth award Adult Friends for Youth, 1991, Nat. Cosmetic Tattoo Assn. award, 1993, Cmty. Svc. award Am. Acad. Dermatology, 1993; named Physician of Yr., Hawaii Med. Assn., 1993. Fellow ACP, Am. Acad. Dermatology (Silver award 1972), Am. Soc. Lasers Medicine & Surgery, Royal Soc. Medicine; mem. Internat. Soc. Tropical Dermatologists (Hist. and Culture award), Soc. Investigative Dermatologists, AAAS, Am. Soc. Photobiology, Internat. Soc. Cryosurgery, Am. Soc. Micropigmentation Surgery, Pacific and Asian Affairs Council, Navy League, Assn. Hawaii Artists, Biol. Photog. Assn., Health Sci. Communication Assn., Internat. Pigment Cell Soc., Am. Med. Writers Assn., Physicians Exchange of Hawaii (bd. dirs.), Am. Coll. Cryosurgery, Internat. Soc. Dermatol. Surgery, Am. Soc. Preventive Oncology, Soc. for Computer Medicine, Am. Assn. for Med. Systems and Info., Japan Am. Soc. Hawaii (bd. dirs.), Pacific Telecom Council, Hawaii State Med. Assn. (mem. public affairs com.), Hawaii Dermatol. Soc. (sec.-pres.), Hawaii Public Health Assn., Pacific Dermatol. Assn., Pacific Health Research Inst., Honolulu County Med. Soc. (gov.), Nat. Wildlife Fedn., C. of C., Preservation Action, Am. Coll. Sports Medicine, Rotary, Hemlock Soc. USA (med. bd.), Hawaii Govs. Blue Ribbon Panel on Living and Dying with Dignity, Ancient Gaelic Nobilitary Soc. (named Knight of the Niadh Nask, 1995), Outrigger Canoe Club, Plaza Club (pres. bd. dirs. 1990-92), Chancellor's Club, Oahu Country Club. Editor: Hawaii Med. Jour.; contbr. articles to profl. jours. Office: Tan Sing Bldg 1128 Smith St Honolulu HI 96817-5197

GOLDSTEIN, NORMAN RAY, international trading company executive, consultant; b. Chgo., Nov. 20, 1944; s. Max and Rose (Weiner) G.; m. Bonnie A. Brod, Aug. 31, 1969; children: Russell, Matthew, Jamie. AA, Wright Jr. Coll., 1965; BS in Fin., No. Ill. U., DeKalb, 1967; MS in Acctg. cum laude, Roosevelt U., 1986. Gen. bus. mgr. Greenstreet Corp., Whiting, Ind., 1967; wholesale credit mgr. Atlantic Richfield Co., Chgo., 1968-74; v.p. fin., treas. Barton Inc. (Barton Brands, Ltd.), Chgo., 1974-96; chmn., CEO Gold Internat., 1996—. Spl. master U.S. Dist. Ct., 1998; chmn. ABC Fin. Communications Forum, Chgo., 1987-88; v.p. Consort Corp., Chgo., 1971-80; spl. master U.S. Dist. Ct., 1998; adj. prof. fin. No. Ill. U., 2000-04, mem. adv. bd. dept. fin., 2003-; instr. Ctr. Profl. Edn., 1997—; spkr. in field. Contbg. author: Handbook of Cash Flow and Treasury Management, 1987; contbr. articles to profl. publs. Bd. dirs. Maine Twp. Jewish Congregation Shaare Emet, Des Plaines, 1986—, pres. 1989-91; mem. adv. bd. dept. fin. No. Ill. U., 2003—. Named Outstanding Credit Exec. of Yr., Nat. Assn. Credit Mgmt., 1987, Disting. Alumnus Coll. Bus. No. Ill. U., 1998, Outstanding Alumnus Dept. Fin., No. Ill. U., 2001. Fellow Nat. Inst. Credit; mem. Fin. Mgrs. Assn. Chgo. (treas. 1991-92), Treasury Mgmt. Assn. Chgo. (chmn. ednl. scholarship com. 1995-99, chmn. Windy City Summit Treasury Conf. 1999-2000, 2003—, bd. dirs. 2003—), Distillers Imports and Vintners (chmn. 1980-82), N.Y. Credit and Fin. Mgmt. Assn., Chgo. Midwest Credit Mgmt. Assn. (bd. dirs. 1984-87), Dept. Fin. Advisors Bd. No. Ill. U 2003-, No. Ill. U. Exec. Club (bd. dirs. 2003—).

GOLDSTEIN, NORTON MAURICE (GOLDY NORTON), public relations consultant; b. Cleve., Apr. 11, 1930; s. Jacob N. and Phyllis Ruth (Weinstein) G.; m. Judith Marcia Morris, Oct. 29, 1955; 1 child, Ann Dee. Reporter L.A. Daily News, 1952-54; writer, producer Cleve Hermann Radio-TV Sports, L.A., 1952-59; exec. v.p. Kennett Pub. Rels. Assocs., L.A., 1959-71; writer, producer Vin Scully Sports Program, L.A., 1959-64; owner, oper. Goldy Norton Pub. Rels., L.A., 1971—. Author: Official Frisbee Handbook, 1972. Founding dir. U.S. Acad. Decathlon, L.A., 1982. With U.S. Army, 1949-52, Korea. Named to Frisbee Hall of Fame, Internat. Frisbee Assn., Hancock, Mich., 1979. Mem. So. Calif. Sports Broadcasters Assn. (charter). Avocations: sports, reading, travel. Office: Goldy Norton Pub Rels 6200 Wilshire Blvd Ste 1112 Los Angeles CA 90048-5810

GOLDSTEIN, PAUL, lawyer, educator; b. Mount Vernon, N.Y., Jan. 14, 1943; s. Martin and Hannah Goldstein; m. Jan Thompson, Aug. 28, 1977. BA, Brandeis U., 1964; LL.B. Columbia U., 1967. Bar: N.Y. 1968, Calif. 1978. Asst. prof. law SUNY-Buffalo, 1967-69, assoc. prof., 1969-71, prof., 1972-75; vis. assoc. prof. Stanford U., Calif., 1972-73, prof. law, 1975—, Stella W. and Ira S. Lillick prof. law, 1985—; of counsel Morrison and Foerster, San Francisco, 1988—. Author: Changing the American Schoolbook--Law, Politics and Technology, 1978, Real Estate Transactions--Cases and Materials on Land Transfer, Development and Finance, 1980, 3d edit. (with G. Korngold), 1993, Real Property, 1984, Copyright, 4 vols., 2d edit., 1996, Copyright, Patent, Trademark and Related State Doctrines--Cases and Materials on the Law of Intellectual Property, 5th edit., 2002, Copyright's Highway: From Gutenberg to the Celestial Jukebox, 1995, revised edit., 2003, International Copyright Law, 2001, International Intellectual Property Law, 2001. Mem. Assn. Litteraire et Artistique Internationale, Copyright Soc. U.S.A. Office: Stanford U Law Sch Nathan Abbott Way Stanford CA 94305 E-mail: paulgold@stanford.edu.

GOLDSTEIN, PAUL H(ENRY), ophthalmologist, educator; b. Chgo., May 20, 1936; s. Alex and Leah (Swabsky) G.; m. Marilyn Gail Holtzman, Sept. 4, 1960; children: Todd, Jordan, Karen, Ross. BS, U. Ill., 1956; MD, U. Ill., Chgo., 1960. Diplomate Am. Bd. Ophthalmology. With basic and clin. sci. ophthalmology Harvard Med. Sch., 1961-62; intern Cook County Hosp., Chgo., 1960-61, resident, 1962-64; pvt. practice Milw., 1965—; asst. clin. prof. Med. Coll. of Wis., Milw., 1965—; chief of ophthalmology Sinai-Samaritan Med. Ctr., Milw., 1989-96. Mem. Milw. Ophthal. Soc. (pres. 1973), Alpha Omega Alpha. Avocations: tennis, golf. Office: Eye Physicians Assn Ste 170 2801 W Kinnickinnic River Pkwy 170 Milwaukee WI 53215-3678

GOLDSTEIN, PAUL ROBERT, management company executive, consultant; b. Indpls., May 13, 1928; s. Harry and Belle Witcovski Goldstein; m. Nancy L. Fink, Dec., 18, 1955 (div. May 1969); children: Lynne G. Throop, James H. BS, Ind. U., 1948; postgrad., NYU, 1948, Purdue U., 1954. Registered money mgr. SEC. Rsch. corr. Merrill, Lynch, Pierce, Fenner & Smith, N.Y.C., 1950, account exec. trainee, 1953; account exec. Merrill, Lynch, Pierce, Fenner & Reaves, Indpls., 1954—61, DuPont, Glore, Forgan, Indpls., 1961-73, Paine, Webber, Jackson & Curtis, Indpls., 1973-78; dep. assessor Marion County, Indpls., 1978-83; mgr. margin dept. C.L. McKinney & Co., L.A., 1985-86; CEO PRG Mgmt. Co., Indpls., 1987—. Columnist I.U. Daily Student, 1945-46. Commdr. post #114 Jewish War Vets., Indpls., 1994; regional adv. bd. Anti-Defamation League, Indpls., 1962-66; ward chairperson Dem. Cen. Com., Indpls., 1978-82; mem. vet. adv. bd. Roude Bush VA Hosp., 1996-98. Sgt. Corps. of Engrs., 1950-52, Korea. Recipient 50 Yr. Gold Cir., Sigma Alpha Mu, 1995. Mem. Am. Legion, Greater Indpls. Progress Com. (sec., profl. sports sub-com. 1966-68), B'nai B'rith (pres. lodge # 58 1961-62). Democrat. Jewish. Avocations: collecting art and rare books, tennis, golf. Home: 226 E 45th St Indianapolis IN 46205 Office: PRG Mgmt Co 226 E 45th St Indianapolis IN 46205

GOLDSTEIN, PEGGY R. sculptor; b. NYC, Jan. 16, 1921; d. Francis Mortimer and Ruth (Schram) Rosenfeld; m. E. Ernest Goldstein, June 22, 1941; children: Susan Lipsitch, Daniel Frank. AB, Smith Coll., 1941; student, Art Inst. Chgo., 1941-42, Corcoran Sch. Art, 1951-52, Acad. de la Grand Chaumière, Paris, 1952-53, Atelier 17, 1953, 66-67, Acad. de Peinture Orientale, 1973-75. Tchr. Anacostia Neighborhood Mus., Smithsonian Instn., Washington, 1967-68, Am. Coll., Paris, 1976-77. One woman shows include Creative Gallery, NYC, 1951, 53, Springfield Mus. Fine Arts, Mass., 1956, SW Tex. State Coll., San Marcos, 1960, Laguna Gloria, Austin, 1956, 61, Maison du Décor, Washington, 1968, Gottesman and Ptnrs., London, 1976, Galerie Lambert, Paris, 1970, 73, 77-78, Galerie de la Cathédrale, Fribourg, 1981, Galerie Cimaise, Lausanne, 1983, Galerie Cardas, Lausanne, 1983, Galerie Valentine, Bex, 1984, Galerie Farel, Aigle, 1982, 85, Le Vieux Bourg, Denges, 1987, Galerie Motte, Geneva, 1989, Animalart, Austin Tex., 1995, Waldorf Sch. Balt., 2000; exhibited in group shows at Salon de la Jeune Sculpture, 1961, 71-76, Salon de Mai, 1970, 72-73, 77, Galerie Horizon, 1978-2000, Galerie Picpus, Montreux, 1981, Biennale of Fedn. Internat. de la Médaille, 1983, 85, 87, Création 85, Montreux, 1986, France-Chine, Marseille, 1987, Gravure, Paris, 1987, Galerie Siret, Paris, 1987-88, U. Fribourg, 1988, La Fondation Taylor, Paris, 1990, Galerie Les Hirondelles, Coppet, 1990, Bibliothèque Nat., Paris, 1992, Austin Visual Arts Assn., 1999-2000, Waldorf Sch., Baltimore, 2000; US Info. Agy. exhbns. Latin Am.; represented in permanent collections Bibliothèque Nat., Paris, Nat. Archives, Washington, Musée Jenisch, Vevey, Bibliothèque Nat., Berne, L.B.J. Libr., Austin, Tex.; also pvt. collections; executed bronze sculpture Nat. Hdqrs. Am. Camping Assn., Ind., 2 bronze mural sculptures, Austin, sculpture Andrews Elem. Sch., Austin; designer 20 medals Adminstrn. des Monnaies et Médailles, Ministère de Fin., Paris, 1973-86; illustrator: At Home After 1840, 1965; author, calligrapher: Lóng is a Dragon: Chinese Writing for Children, 1990 (Gold award Parents Choice 1991); author, calligrapher, illustrator: Hu is a Tiger, An Introduction to Chinese Writing, 1995; contbr. articles to profl. jours. Recipient Sculpture prize Soc. Washington D.C. Artists, 1954, Small Sculpture award Ball State Tchrs. Coll., 1961, Prize UPFS Concours de Masque, 1977; Prèfecture de Paris grantee, 1971; nominated Outstanding Ptnr., Ptnrs. in Edn., Austin Adopt-a-Sch., 1995-96. Fellow Tex. Fine Art Assn., Austin Visual Arts Assn. Home: 1801 Lavaca St Apt 15F Austin TX 78701-1333 Fax: 512 474-6220.

GOLDSTEIN, PHYLLIS ANN, art historian, educator; b. Chgo., Apr. 27, 1926; d. Frederick and Belle Florence (Hirsch) Jacoby; m. Seymour Goldstein, Nov. 19, 1947 (dec. 1980); children: Arthur Bruce, Kathy Susan Goldstein Maultasch. BA, Hunter Coll., 1948; MA, Hofstra U., 1985. Tchr. home econs. Cin. Pub. Schs., 1948-50; nutrition instr. Brandeis U. Nat. Women's Com., Westbury, N.Y., 1975-78, instr. art history, 1984-91; lectr. art history Brandeis U./Nat. Women's Com., Westbury, N.Y., 1985-92; instr. art history Herricks Adult Cmty. Edn. Program, 1990-91. Camp counselor, troop leader Girl Scouts U.S., N.Y.C., Cin., 1942-51; cub leader Boy Scouts Am., Westbury, 1963-64; active Sisterhood of Temple Beth Avodah, Westbury, 1958-80, pres. 1964-65; active Sisterhood of Temple of Beth Am., Merrick, N.Y., 1980-91; life mem. Brandeis U. Nat. Women's Com., lectr. art history, 1992—, Meadowbrook chpt. pres., 1985-87, South Dade chpt., 1996-98, mem. Fla. regional bd., 1998-99; vol. Fairchild Tropical Gardens, 1994—. Mem. Williamsburg Mus., Mus. Art Ft. Lauderdale, Met. Mus. Art N.Y., Hadassah (life). Democrat. Avocations: sewing, swimming, needlework, quilting, travel.

GOLDSTEIN, RICHARD A. consumer products company executive; b. 1942; married. BBA, U. Mass.; LLB, Boston U.; LLM, Harvard U. Atty. Choate Hall & Stewart, 1968-70; spl. asst. to cabinet mem. U.S. Govt., Washington, 1970-73; assoc. Arnold & Porter, Washington, 1973-75; staff atty., asst. gen. counsel Lever Bros. Co., 1975-80, v.p. asst. to chmn., 1980-84; pres., CEO Unilever Can. Ltd., 1984; exec. v.p., COO Unilever U.S., N.Y.C., 1988, pres., CEO, 1989; chmn., CEO Unilever Can. Ltd., 1989-97; pres., CEO Unilever N.Am. Foods, 1996-00; pres. and CEO Unilever U.S. Inc., 1989—2000; chmn., chief exec. ofcr. Intl. Flavors & Fragrances, N.Y.C., 2000—. Office: IFF 521 W 57th St New York NY 10019

GOLDSTEIN, RICHARD JAY, mechanical engineer, educator; b. NYC, Mar. 27, 1928; s. Henry and Rose (Steierman) G.; m. Barbara Goldstein; children: Arthur Sander, Jonathan Jacob, Benjamin Samuel, Naomi Sarith. BME, Cornell U., 1948; MS in Mech. Engring., U. Minn., 1950, MS in Physics, 1951, PhD in Mech. Engring., 1959; DSc (hon.), Israel Inst. Tech., 1994; Dr. honoris causa, U. Lisbon, 1996; hon. doctorate, A.V. Luikov Heat and Mass Transfer Inst., Minsk, Belarus, 1997. Instr. U. Minn., Mpls., 1948-51, instr., rsch. fellow, 1956-58, mem. faculty, 1961—, prof. mech. engring., 1965—, head dept., 1977-97, James J. Ryan prof., 1989—, Regents' prof., 1990—; devel. rsch. engr. Oak Ridge Nat. Lab., 1951-54; sr. engr. Lockheed Aircraft, 1956; asst. prof. Brown U., 1959-61. Vis. prof. Technion, Israel, 1976, Imperial Coll., Eng., 1984; cons. in field, 1956—; chmn. Midwest U. Energy Consortium; chmn. Coun. Energy Engring. Rsch.; NSF sr. postdoctoral fellow, vis. prof. Cambridge (Eng.) U., 1971-72; Prince lectr., 1983, William Gurley lectr., 1988, Hawkins Meml. lectr., 1991; disting. lectr. Pa. State U., 1992; mem. acad. com. internat. bd. govs. Technion; hon. mem. sci. bd. A.V. Luikov Heat and Mass Transfer Inst., Minsk, 1997. Mem. editl. bd. Experiments in Fluids, Heat Transfer-Japanese Rsch., Heat Transfer-Soviet Rsch., Bull of the Internat. Centre for Heat and Mass Transfer, Internat. Archives of Heat and Mass Transfer; hon. editl. adv. bd. Internat. J. Heat and Mass Transfer, Internat. Comms. in Heat and Mass Transfer. 1st U.S. Army lt. AUS, 1954-55. Recipient NASA award for tech. innovation, 1977, MUEC Dist. Svc. award, 1986, NAE, 1985, George Taylor Alumni Soc. award, 1988, A.V. Lykov medal, 1990, Max Jakob Meml. award ASME/AICE, 1990, Nusselt-Reynolds prize, 1993, Dr. Scientiarum Honoris Causa award Technion-Israel Inst. Tech., 1994, Thermal Engring. Internat. award Japan Soc. Mech. Engring.; NATO fellow, Paris, 1960-61, Lady Davis fellow Technion, Israel, 1976. Fellow AAAS, ASME (hon., BEG v.p. 1984-88, sr. v.p. 1989-93, BOG 1993-97, pres. 1996-97, sr. v.p. COE 1988-92, Heat Transfer Meml. award 1978, Svc. award 1978, Centennial medal 1980, 50th anniv. award of heat transfer divsn. 1988, Dedicated Svc. award 2001, Long Term Mem. award 2002-03), Royal Acad. Engring. 1999 (fgn.), Am. Soc. Engring. Edn., Assembly for Internat. Heat Transfer Confs. (pres. 1986-90), Internat. Ctr. for Heat and Mass Transfer (exec. com. 1985—, chmn. 1992, pres. 1998-2002), Am. Phys. Soc., Japan Soc. Promotion of Sci., Royal Acad. Engring. (fgn.); mem. Am. Phys. Soc., Minn. Acad. Sci., Nat. Acad. Engring., Nat. Acad. Engring.-Mex. (corr. 1991), Golden Key Nat. Honor Soc., Sigma Xi, Tau Beta Pi, Pi Tau Sigma. Achievements include research in thermodynamics, fluid mechanics, heat transfer, optical measuring techniques. Home: 4241 Bassett Creek Dr Golden Valley MN 55422-4257 Office: U Minn Dept Mech Engring 111 Church St SE Minneapolis MN 55455-0150

GOLDSTEIN, ROBERT DAVID, plastic surgeon, educator; b. Nov. 5, 1951; BS, Wilkes U., 1973; MD, Pa. State U., 1977. Diplomate in plastic surgery and in hand surgery Am. Bd. Plastic Surgery. Resident in gen. surgery Montefiore Med. Ctr., Bronx, N.Y., 1977-82, resident in plastic and reconstructive surgery, 1982-84; dir. plastic surgery Weiler Hosp./Montefiore Med. Ctr., Bronx, 1989—; assoc. prof. plastic surgery Albert Einstein Coll. Medicine, Bronx, 1993—. Mem. ACS (pres. Bronx chpt. 1994-95). Office: 2425 Eastchester Rd Bronx NY 10469

GOLDSTEIN, SANDRA CARA, lawyer; b. Bklyn., May 12, 1964; BA, Barnard Coll., 1984; JD, NYU, 1987. Bar: N.Y. 1988. Office: Cravath Swaine & Moore LLP Worldwide Plz 825 8th Ave Fl 38 New York NY 10019-7475

GOLDSTEIN, SIDNEY, sociology educator, demographer; b. New London, Conn., Aug. 4, 1927; s. Max and Bella (Hoffman) G.; m. Alice Dreifuss, June 21, 1953; children; Beth Leah, David Louis, Brenda Ruth. BA, U. Conn., 1949, MA, 1951; PhD, U. Pa., 1953. Instr. sociology U. Pa., 1953-55; mem. faculty Brown U., Providence, 1955—, prof. sociology, 1960—, George Hazard Crooker prof., 1977—, prof. emeritus, 1993—, rsch. prof. population studies, 1997—, chmn. dept. sociology and anthropology, 1963-70, dir. Population Studies & Tng. Ctr., 1965-89. Demographic advisor Chulalongkorn U., Bangkok, 1968-69; cons. UN Econ. and Social Commn. for Asia and Pacific, 1971-72, 77-82, Nat. Ctr. Health Stats., 1970-77, Internat. Program Population Analysis, Smithsonian Instn., 1971-76; mem. U.S. Bur. Census Adv. Com., 1965-71, Rand Corp., 1975-83; mem. nat. com. rsch. 1980 census Social Sci. Rsch. Coun., 1981-88; mem. governing bur. Com. Internat. Cooperation in Nat. Rsch. Demography, 1981-98, treas., 1994-98; mem. com. on population Nat. Rsch. Coun., Nat. Acad. Scis., 1983-87; chmn. nat. tech. adv. com. Jewish population studies Coun. Jewish Fedns., 1984-95; co-chmn. internat. sci. com. 1990 census surveys world Jewry, Jerusalem, 1988-92. Author: Patterns of Mobility, 1910-1950, 1958, Consumption Patterns of the Aged, 1960, The Norristown Study: An Experiment in Interdisciplinary Research Training, 1961, (with K.B. Mayer) The First Two Years: Problems of Small Business Growth and Survival, 1961, Migration and Economic Development in Rhode Island, 1958, (with Calvin Goldscheider) Jewish Americans, 1968, URbanization in Thailand, 1947-1960, 1970, The Demography of Bangkok, 1972, (with V. Prachuabmoh and A. Goldstein) Urban-Rural Migration Differentials in Thailand, 1974, (with A. Speare and W. Frey) Residential Mobility, Migration and Metropolitan Change, 1975, Circulation in the Context of Total Mobility in Southeast Asia, 1978; editor: (with D.F. Sly) Basic Data Needed for the Study of Urbanization, 1975, The Measurement of Urbanization and the Projection of Urban Population, 1975, Patterns of Ubranization: Comparative Country Studies, 1977, (with wife) A Test of the Potential Use of Mulltiplicity in Research on Population Movement, 1979, Population Mobility in the People's Republic of China, 1985, Surveys of Migration in Developing Countries. A Methodological Review, 1981, Migration and Fertility in Peninsular Malaysia, 1983, Urbanization in China, 1985, (with wife) Migration in Thailand: A Twenty-Five Year Review, 1986, (with C. Goldscheider) The Jewish Community of Rhode Island: A Social and Demographic Survey, 1988, Comparative Migration Patterns to Shanghai and Bangkok, 1989, Urbanization in China, 1982-1987, The Role of Migration and Reclassification, 1990, (with wife and Zai Liang) Migration, Gender, and Labor Force in Hubei Province, 1985-90, (with wife) Permanent and Temporary Migration Differentials in China, 1991, Demographic Issues and Data Needs for Mega-City Research, 1994, The Impact of Temporary Migration on Urban Places, 1993, (with R. Neupert) Urbanization and Population Redistribution in Mongolia, 1994, (with wife) Jews on the Move, 1996, (with Gang Liu) Migrant-Non Migrant Fertility in Anhui China, 1996, (with Dang Anh) Internal Migration and Development in Vietnam, 1997, (with wife and Michael White) Migration Fertility and State Policy in Hubei Province, China, 1997, (with wife) Lithuanian Jewry, 1993: A Demographic and Sociocultural Profile, 1997, (with wife) Conservative Jewry in the United States: A Sociodemographic Profile, 1998,(with wife and Yanyi Djamba) Permanent and Temporary Migration During Periods of Economic Change: Vietnam and China Compared, 1999. Bd. dirs. Jewish Fedn. R.I., 1964-68, 78-82, 85—; bd. dirs. Bur. Jewish Edn., Providence, 1959-82, 94—, bd. dirs. area v.p., 1997—; bd. dirs. Coun. Jewish Fedns., 1987-94; v.p. JFRA. Recipient Disting. Svc. medal Chilalongkorn U., 1969, Disting. Silver medal Mahidol U., 1992, Disting. Leadership award Coun. Jewish. Fedns., 1992, Lifetime Achievement award Assn. Social Sci. Study of Jewry, 1992, sr. rsch. award NAS, 1983; Harrison fellow, 1953, Social Sci. Rsch. Coun. fellow, 1961-62, Guggenheom fellow, 1961-63, rsch. fellow Inst. Contemporary Jewry, Hebrew U. Jerusalem, 1969—, sr. fellow East-West Population Inst., Honolulu, 1976, 82, 90, fellow Inst. Advanced Study, Ind. U., 1995, vis. fellow Australian Nat. U., Canberra, 1977; scholar-in-residence Rockefeller Study Ctr., Bellagio, 1990, sr. vis. scholar Hebrew U., 990. Mem. Am. Sociol. Assn., Population Assn. Am. (pres. 1975-76), Assn. Jewish Demography and Stats. (dir.), Internat. Union Sci. Study Population (chair com. urbanization and population distbn. 1971-76), Assn. Sociol. Study Jewry, Phi Beta Kappa. Home: 95 Kiwanee Rd Warwick RI 02888-4040 Office: Brown U Sociology Dept 79 Waterman St Providence RI 02912-9079

GOLDSTEIN, SIDNEY, pharmaceutical scientist; b. Phila., Mar. 27, 1932; s. Israel and Gertrude (Stein) G.; m. Janice Levy, June 19, 1955; children: Rhonda, David, Nina. BSc in Pharmacy, Phila. Coll. Pharmacy & Sci., 1954, MSc in Pharmacy, 1955, DSc in Pharmacy, 1958. Cardiovascular unit head Eaton Labs, Norwich, N.Y., 1958-59; anti-inflammatory unit head Lederle Labs, Pearl River, N.Y., 1959-61; with Merrell Dow Rsch. Inst., Cin., 1961-93; v.p. global pharm. and analytical scis. Marion Merrell Dow Inc., Kansas City, Mo., 1991-93; v.p. sci. and tech. Duramed Pharm., Inc., Cin., 1994-98, v.p. bus. devel., sci. and tech., 1998—2002; chief sci. officer Prasco, LLC, Cin., 2002—. Adj. assoc. prof. U. Cin. Coll. Pharmacy, 1984-98, dean's adv. coun., 1998—; lectr. pharmacology Phila. Coll. Pharmacy, 1967-70, chair PQRI-drug product tech. com., 1997—; mem. So. Ohio Life Sci. Task Force, 1999-2001, GPhA sci. com., 2001—; mem. tech. validation adv. bd. Cinn. Children's Hosp., 2003—.. Contbr. articles to profl. jours. Bd. trustees Glen Manor Home for Aged, Cin., 1983-89. Recipient Award for Nicoderm, R&D Mag., 1992. Mem. Am. Assn. Pharm. Scientists, Am. Soc. Clin. Pharmacology and Therapeutics, Soc. Exptl. Biology and Medicine, Am. Soc. Pharmacology and Exptl. Therapeutics, B'nai B'rith (chpt. v.p. 1978). Home: 1125 Fort View Pl Cincinnati OH 45202-1713 Office: Prasco LLC 7155 Kemper Rd Cincinnati OH 45249 E-mail: s.goldstein@prascolabs.com.

GOLDSTEIN, STANLEY IRVING, podiatric surgeon, pharmacist; b. Bronx, N.Y., Oct. 1, 1925; s. Louis and Eva (Yollis) G.; children: Jerome Eric, Keith Stuart, Brian Allen. BS in Pharmacy, Fordham U., 1949; DPM, N.Y. Coll. Podiatric Med-Surg., 1952; student, Coll. Medicine and Surgery, Bologna, Italy, 1966-68. Pvt. practice, podiatric medicine and surgery, N.Y.C., 1957—; chief, dir. podiatry svcs. N.Y. State (Helen Hayes) Rehab. Hosp., Stony Point, N.Y., 1968—; lectr. on med. relaxation in practice to med. staff Seton Hall U. Coll. Medicine, 1969—. Asst. chief pharmacist George Nemeroff Pharmacy, 1951; chief pharmacist Dr. Berner's Pharmacy, Livingston, 1959; dir. podiatric svc. N.Y. State Rehab. Hosp., 1968; dir. podiatric svc. AFL/CIO, N.Y.C., White Plains, Boston, 1976; lectr. in field. Contbr. articles to profl. jours. Vol. N.Y. State Psychiatric Hosp., Orangburg Clinican, 1959; vol. podiatric medicine N.Y. State Rehab. Hosp., 1967, dir. pediatric med. and surg. svcs., 1998—. With USN, 1944-46. Mem. N.Y. State Podiatry Assn., Am. Podiatric and Med. Assn., World Health Orgn. (Eng.), Holocaust Mus., Jewish War Vets, Masons. Avocations: swimming, rifle, instructor nra. Office: 561 S Main St # Route304 New City NY 10956-2926

GOLDSTEIN, STANLEY PHILIP, engineering educator; b. Bklyn., Feb. 3, 1923; s. Max and Rose (Ahrenstein) G.; m. Wanda Rouse, June 6, 1949; children— Bruce, Richard. BS, U. Okla., 1949; MS, NYU, 1956; PhD in Astronautics, Poly. Inst. Bklyn., 1969. Engr. Vapor Recovery Systems Corp., Compton, Calif., 1950-52; project engr. Alderson Research Labs., N.Y.C., 1952-54; mem. faculty Hofstra U., Hempstead, N.Y., 1954—, prof. engring., 1957-84, prof. emeritus, 1984—, chmn. engring. sci. dept., 1956-68, 70-72, 80-83, dir. acad. computer center, 1970-72; assoc. dean Hofstra U. (Coll. Arts and Scis.), 1973-74, 77, assoc. provost for planning, budgeting and instl.

research, 1974-76. Pres. Techmark Enterprises, Inc.; Alcorn Combustion Co., N.Y.C. Transit Authority, Hofstra Internat. Trade & Devel. Corp.; dir. Collegiate Sci. and Tech. Entry Program Hofstra U., 1987-89 Served to 1st lt. USAAF, 1942-45, ETO. Decorated DFC, Air medal with four oak leaf clusters, French Normandy medal. Mem. Sigma Xi. Home: 18 Millers Ln Kingston NY 12401-4426 Office: Hofstra U Engring Dept Hempstead NY 11550

GOLDSTEIN, STEVEN, lawyer; b. St. Louis, Sept. 8, 1950; s. Alexander Julius and Dorothy Lea (Matier) G.; m. Laura Lou Staley, July 20, 1980. BS in Speech, Northwestern U., Evanston, Ill., 1972; JD, U. Mich., 1975. Bar: Mo. 1975. Prin. Goldstein & Pressman, P.C., St. Louis, 1993—. Mem. ABA, Mo. Bar Assn. (chmn. bankruptcy com. 1983-85), Bar Assn. of Met. St. Louis. Home: 712 Swarthmore Ln Saint Louis MO 63130-3618 Office: Goldstein & Pressman PC 121 Hunter Ave Ste 101 Saint Louis MO 63124-2082 E-mail: stg@goldsteinpressman.com.

GOLDSTEIN, STEVEN EDWARD, psychologist; b. Bronx, NY, Nov. 25, 1948; s. Maurice and Matilda (Weiss) Goldstein. BS in Psychology, CCNY, 1970, MS in Sch. Psychology, 1971; EdD in Sch. Psychology, U. No. Colo., 1977. Lic. psychologist Nev., cert. sch. psychologist N.Y., Calif. Tchr. N.Y.C. Pub. Schs., 1970-71, 72-73, tchr., counselor, 1974; extern in sch. psychology N. Shore Child Guidance, 1972; sch. psychologist Denver Pub. Schs., 1975; asst. prof. psychology Northeastern Okla. State U., Tahlequah, 1976-78; coord. inpatient, emergency svcs. Winnemucca (Nev.) Mental Health Ctr., 1978-80; residential dir. Desert Devel. Ctr., Las Vegas, Nev., 1980-82; sr. psychologist Las Vegas Mental Health Ctr., 1982-92; pvt. practice psychology Las Vegas, 1983—; sr. psychologist Desert Regional Ctr., 1992—. Participant NSF biofeedback seminar, 1977; presenter papers to profl. confs. Sec. grad. coun. CUNY, 1971; pres. grad. coun. CCNY, 1971. Mem.: APA (Nev. coord. office profl. practice 1987—88), So. Nev. Soc. Cert. Psychologists (pres. 1984—86), Nev. Soc. Tng. and Devel. (dir. 1982—83), Biofeedback Soc. Nev. (membership dir. 1982—90), Jewish Fedn. Las Vegas (bus. and profl. com. 1995—). Office: 1391 S Jones Blvd Las Vegas NV 89146-1200 also: 3180 W Sahara Ave Ste C-25 Las Vegas NV 89102-6073 Personal E-mail: goldsteinse@aol.com.

GOLDSTEIN, STEVEN HOWARD, podiatrist; b. Bklyn., Nov. 23, 1954; s. Arthur and Miriam Rosalyn (Gilden) G.; m. Susan Kobetz, June 15, 1980; children: Elyssa, Stacey. AAS in Med. Tech., SUNY, Farmingdale, 1974; BA, SUNY, Buffalo, 1976; DPM in Podiatric Medicine, Ohio Coll. Podiatric Medicine, 1980. Diplomate Am. Bd. Podiatric Surgery, Am. Bd. Disability Analysts. Resident in surgery Brent Gen. Hosp., Detroit, 1980-81; pvt. practice, Livingston, N.J., 1981—; mem. med. staff St. Barnabas Med. Ctr., Livingston, 1997—, Chitton Meml. Hosp., Pompton Plains, N.J. Mem. ambulatory surg. ctr. com.Chilton Meml. Hosp., Pompton Plains, N.J., 1994—. Contbr. articles to profl. jours. Fellow Am. Profl. Wound Care Assn. (bd. dirs. membership, chair); mem. Am. Diabetes Assn., Am. Coll. Sports Medicine, Am. Running and Fitness Assn. Avocations: photography, music, automobiles. Office: Family Footcare Livingston 349 E Northfield Rd Livingston NJ 07039-4802 E-mail: stevefootdrl@cs.com.

GOLDSTEIN, STUART ZANE, public affairs executive; b. Bklyn., Sept. 9, 1950; s. Murray and Bobbie (Sugarman) G.; m. Eritt Brauner, Nov. 2, 1980; children: Adam Matthew, Jessica Ronni. BA in English, Trenton State Coll., 1972; MA in Am. Govt., Rutgers U., 1976. Reporter Trenton Times, 1971-72; spl. asst. legis. affairs N.J. Dept. Pub. Advocate, Trenton, 1972-80; ombudsman N.J. Div. Motor Vehicles, Trenton, 1980-82; v.p., dir. customer communications chmns. office Citicorp, N.Y.C., 1982-87, v.p., dep. dir. nat. pub. affairs, 1987-89; dir. corp. communications Am. Express Co., N.Y.C., 1989-91; mng. dir. corp. commn. Nat. Security Clearing Corp., N.Y.C., 1991-99; mng. dir. corp. comms. Depository Trust and Clearing Corp., N.Y.C., 1999—. Pub. newspaper op-ed and mag. articles, 1975-94; author (with others) Practical Public Affairs in an Era of Change, 1996. Campaign coord. County Freeholder Campaign, Mercer County, N.J., 1974-76; mem. campaign staff 4th Dist. Congl. Seat, 1972, 74, 76; chmn. Citizens Coms. for Re-election Gov. Brendan Byrne, 1977. Named Grand Winner, Internat. Ann. Report Competition, 1999, Gold Winner, 1995, 98, 99, 2000, 01. Mem. Internat. Assn. Bus. Comm. (IABC), PRSA. Avocations: jogging, baseball, writing. Home: 23 Kristin Way Trenton NJ 08690-2441 Office: Depository Trust & Clearing Corp 55 Water St Fl 22 New York NY 10041-2299 E-mail: sgoldstein@dtcc.com.

GOLDSTEIN, SYDNEY RACHEL, photographer, writer, producer; b. San Francisco, Oct. 13, 1944; d. Edward William and Dorian Claire G.; m. Charles R. Breyer, Jan. 18, 1976; children: Katherine, Joseph. Grad. h.s., San Francisco. Photographer, writer, 1970—; prodr., founding exec. dir. City Arts & Lectures, Inc., San Francisco, 1981—; exec. prodr. City Arts & Lecturs, Radio Broadcasts, 1997—. Author: Earned Income, 2001. Adv. bd. Grants for the Arts, San Francisco Hotel Tax Fund, 1979-82. Recipient Koret Israel prize Koret Found., 1990. Democrat. Office: 2720 Pierce St San Francisco CA 94123 also: City Arts & Lectures Inc 1955 Sutter St San Francisco CA 94115

GOLDSTEIN, TAMARA BETH, musician; b. Tenafly, N.J., Dec. 20, 1961; d. Nathan and Beatrice Goldstein. MusB, Ind. U, 1984; MusM, Julliard Sch., 1987; Mus D, U Colo., 1996. Pianist Colo. Chamber Player, 1995, Ctrl. City Opera Co., Denver; vis. asst. prof. Met. State Coll. of Denver, 2000—02; instr. U of Colo., Boulder, 1997—98; staff Aspen (Colo.) Music Festival, Aspen, Colo.; vis. asst. prof. Met. State Coll. of Denver, Denver, 2002—. V.p. Colo. Chamber Players, 1997—. Mem.: Suzuki Assn. of Am. (assoc.), Denver Jusicians Assn./Am. Federation of Musicians (assoc.), Music Tchr. Nat. Assn. (assoc.), Pi Kappa Lambda Music Honors Soc. (hon.). Home: 263 Pearl St No 6 Boulder CO 80302

GOLDSTEIN, WALTER CARL, retired physician; b. N.Y.C., Jan. 23, 1927; s. Charles and Sadie (Fink) G.; m. Eleanore Monica Bugler, May 16, 1959; 1 child, Charles. BS, George Washington U., 1951; MD, U. Chgo., 1955. Diplomate Am. Bd. Internal Medicine, Nat. Bd. Med. Examiners. Intern Phila. Gen. Hosp., 1955-56; resident in internal medicine Cook County Hosp., 1956-58; sr. resident in internal medicine Bklyn. VA Med. Ctr., 1958-59; resident in internal medicine Cook County Hosp., 1956-58; sr. resident Bklyn. VA Hosp., 1958-59; resident in pathology Univ. Hosp., Balt., 1959-60; staff internist Lebanon (Pa.) VA Hosp., 1967-75; chief med. svc., clin. asst. prof. Wilkes-Barre (Pa.) VA Hosp., Hahnemann Med. Sch., 1976-87; internist Medigroup Ctr., Trenton, N.J., 1987-90; physician, med. dir. Interstate Blood and Plasma Ctr., Phila., 1991—. Fellow ACP.

GOLDSTEIN, WILLIAM A. investment counsel; b. Chgo., June 24, 1939; s. Jacob E. and Marion B. G.; m. Anne B. Goldstein, Aug. 19, 1962; chidlren: Deborah, Catherine. BS, Purdue U., 1962. Registered rep. Hornblower & Weeks-Hemphill Noyes, Chgo., 1962-70; exec. v.p. Burton J. Vincent-Chesley & Co., Chgo., 1970-83; chmn. Prescott Asset Mgmt., Prescott, Ball & Turben, Chgo., 1983-89; pres. Lodestar Investment Counsel LLC, Chgo., 1989—; dir. The Pvt. Bank, Chgo. Trustee Chgo. Symphony Orch., chmn. governing mems., 1997-99, vice chmn., treas.; bd. dirs. Grant Park Concert Soc., Chgo., 1995-97. Mem. Standard Club, Chgo. Yacht Club. Avocations: sailing, bicycling, golf, reading. Office: Lodestar Investment Counsel LLC 208 S Lasalle St Chicago IL 60604-1000

GOLDSTEIN, WILLIAM MARKS, lawyer; b. Phila., Aug. 28, 1935; s. David and Estelle (Marks) G.; m. Lilia E. Demchuk; 1 child, Laura; children by previous marriage: Adam, Benjamin, Daniel. AB, Princeton U., 1957; JD magna cum laude, Harvard U., 1960. Bar: Pa. 1961, D.C. 1977. Law clk. to judge U.S. Ct. Appeals, Phila., 1960-61; assoc. firm Morgan Lewis & Bockius, Phila., 1961-66, ptnr., 1967-75, 77-82, Drinker, Biddle & Reath LLP, Phila., 1982—; dep. asst. sec. for tax policy Dept. Treasury, Washington, 1975-76. Contbr. numerous articles on fed. taxation to law pubs. Mem. Democratic Party Com. Lower Merion, Pa., 1965-68; candidate for Sch. Bd. Lower Merion, 1965, for state legis., 1966. Mem. ABA, Pa. Bar Assn., Phila. Bar Assn., D.C. Bar Assn., Am. Law Inst., Am. Coll. Tax Counsel. Jewish. Home: 787 Trephanny Ln Wayne PA 19087-1931 Office: Drinker Biddle & Reath LLP 1 Logan Sq 18th & Cherry St Philadelphia PA 19103-6996 E-mail: Goldstwm@dbr.com.

GOLDSTEN, ROBERT EMANUEL, lawyer, investor; b. Charlottesville, Va., Oct. 8, 1916; s. Joseph and Rebecca S. (Shapero) B.; m. Janice F. Wasserman, Nov. 30, 1979; children by previous marriage: Douglas Kahn, Ina Lee. BS in Commerce, U. Va., 1937, LLB, 1940. Bar: Va. 1939, D.C. 1941. Ptnr. Goldsten Bros. Developers & Builders, Washington, 1941-72; pres. Gen. Mortgage Corp., Washington, 1948-66, Vero Beach (Fla.) Yacht Basin, Inc., 1957-71, Devel. Funding Corp., Washington, 1972-74; v.p. Allied Fin. Corp., Silver Spring, Md., 1950-58, World Wide Airlines, Burbank, Calif., 1960-62; pres., CEO McLean (Va.) Savs. & Loan Assn., 1977-80; dir. McLean Fin. Corp., 1981-87; chmn. U.S. Mortgage Credit Corp., 1983-87, Allied Protective Sys. Inc., 1981-88; pres. Gen. Funding Corp., Washington, 1998—. Vis. lectr. real estate mgmt. Am. U., 1950-57. Pres., Brotherhood, Washington Hebrew Congregation, 1955-56; treas., bd. dirs. Washington Area Coun. on Alcoholism and Drug Abuse, 1971-77, Carl G. Jung Fund of Washington, 1976-79; co-founder Washington Inst. Natural Medicine, 1998; mem. D.C. governing bd. Anti-Defamation League, 1997—. Recipient award for outstanding contbn. to success of Home Builders Met. Washington, 1966, Spl. Beautification award City of Alexandria, Va., Disting. Svc. award Washington Area Coun. Alcoholism and Drug Abuse, 1977. Mem. U. Va. Alumni Club Washington, Indian Spring Club, Woodmont Country Club, Tower Club, Boca Rio Golf Club, Univ. Club, B'nai B'rith, Georgetown Club. Democrat. Home and Office: #8 Harborage Isle Fort Lauderdale FL 33316-2303 also: 3134 Ellicott St NW Washington DC 20008-2025

GOLDSTENE, PAUL NORTON, writer, educator; b. Brooklyn, NY, Nov. 23, 1930; s. Lester G. and Anna G. Lewis; m. Ellen Patricia Fetterman Goldstene, Sept. 6, 1959; children: James Nathan, Claire Claudia, Beth Mirriam. BA, Wayne State U., Detroit, MI, 1957; MA, U. Ariz., Tucson, AZ, 1963, PhD, 1970. Profl. photographer Lawrence Studios, New York, NY, 1948—51, self-employed, Detroit, Mich., 1951—51, Gene Lester, Los Angeles, Calif., 1957—58; instr. U. Calif., Los Angeles, Calif., 1959—60, U. Ariz., Tuscon, 1960—64; prof. Idaho State U., Pocatello, Idaho, 1964—66, Calif. State U., Chico, Calif., 1966—70, U. Calif., Davis, Calif., 1971—71, Calif. State U., Sacramento, Calif., 1970—. Pub. opinion interviewer and supr. George Sieros Agy., Los Angeles, Calif., 1962—62; program leader, cmty. seminar Ford Found., Marysville, Calif., 1969—69; editor Chandler and Sharp, Novato, Calif., 1968—, Prentice-Hall, New York, NY, 1968—; jour. referee and article contbr. Am. Polit. Sci. Rev., Jour. of Econ. Issues. Contbr. articles to profl. jours.; author: The Collapse of Liberal Empire: Science and Revolution in the Twentieth Century, 1977, 2d edit., 1998, Democracy in America: Sardonic Speculations: Three Essays with a Postscript on Equal Opportunity, 1987, (book) The Bittersweet Century: Speculations on Modern Science and American Democracy, 1989, Revolution, American Style: The Nineteen-Sixties and Beyond, 1997. Mem. ACLU, 1983—2002, Union of Concerned Scientists, 1996—2002. Recipient Meritorious Performance - Tchg., Calif. State U., 1985,1986, 1988-1989, Outstanding Scholarly Achievement Award, 1994-1995; grantee Rsch. and Writing Grant, 1973,1974, 1982-1983, 1984, Rsch. Assigned Time grant, 1985—86; scholar Meritorious Performance Scholarship, 1985-1986,1988-1989. Mem.: Phi Alpha Theta (nat. history hon. 1963—2002), No. Polit. Sci. Assn. (bd. of counselors 1979—81). Avocations: photography, photograph collecting.

GOLDSTICK, THOMAS KARL, biomedical engineering educator; b. Toronto, Ont., Can., Aug. 21, 1934; came to U.S., 1955, naturalized. s. David and Iva Sarah (Kaplan) G.; m. Marcia Adrienne Jenkins, July 4, 1982. BS, MIT, 1957, MS, 1959; PhD, U. Calif., Berkeley, 1966, U. Calif., San Francisco, 1966-67. Asst. prof. Northwestern U., Evanston, Ill., 1967-71, assoc. prof. chem. engring. and biol. sci., 1971-81, prof. chem. engring., neurobiology and physiology, 1981-85, prof. chem. engring., biomed. engring., neurobiology and physiology, 1985-99, prof. emeritus, 1999—. Adj. prof. ophthalmology U. Ill., Chgo., 1981-91. Editor: Oxygen Transport to Tissue V, 1983, VII, 1985, X, 1988, XI, 1989, XII, 1990, XIII, 1992. Rsch. grantee NIH, 1968—; Spl. Rsch. fellow U. Calif., San Diego, LaJolla, 1971-73. Mem. Internat. Soc. Oxygen Transport to Tissue (sec. 1980-86, exec. com. 1986-93), Biomed. Engring. Soc. (bd. dirs. 1983-86, chmn. publs. bd. 1985-86). Home: 2025 Sherman Ave Apt 504 Evanston IL 60201-3269 Office: Chem Engring Dept Northwestern U Evanston IL 60208-3120 E-mail: t-goldstick@northwestern.edu.

GOLDSTINE, HERMAN HEINE, mathematician, association executive; b. Chgo., Sept. 13, 1913; s. Isaac Oscar and Bessie (Lipsey) Goldstine; m. Adele Katz, Sept. 15, 1941 (dec. 1964); children: Madlen, Jonathan; m. Ellen Watson, Jan. 8, 1966. BS, U. Chgo., 1933, MS, 1934, PhD, 1936; PhD honoris causa (hon.), U. Lund, Sweden, 1974; DSc (hon.), Amherst Coll., 1978, Adelphi U., 1978, Rutgers U., 1994. Rsch. asst. U. Chgo., 1937—37, instr., 1937—39, U. Mich., Ann Arbor, 1939—42, asst. prof., 1942—50; assoc. project dir. electronic computer project Inst. Advanced Study, Princeton, 1946—55, acting project dir., 1954—57, permanent mem., 1952—; dir. math. scis. dept. IBM Rsch., 1960—65; dir. sci. devel. IBM Data Processing Hdqrs., White Plains, 1965—67; cons. to dir. rsch. IBM, 1967—69, fellow, 1969—; exec. officer Am. Philos. Soc., Phila., 1984—97. Head electronic Numerical Integrator and Computer Project U.S. Army; officer in charge of sub-sta. Aberdeen Proving Grounds, U. Pa., 1942—46; cons. various govt. and mil. agys., 1946—84. Author: Author: The Computer from Pascal to vonNeumann, 1972, New and Full Moons 1001 B.C. to A.D. 1651, 1973, A History of Numerical Analysis from the 16th through the 19th century, 1977, A History of the Calculus of Variations from the 17th through the 19th Century, 1980; editor: Mathematical Papers of John I and James I Bernouilli, 1988, Die Streitschriften von Jacob und Johann Bernouilli, 1991. Bd. dirs. Nat. Constrn. Ctr., 1987—90; trustee Hampshire Coll., 1969—77, U. Pa. Press, 1985—; mem. adv. coun . history of sci. program Princeton U., 1982—87; mem. vis. com. phys. sci. divsn. U. Chgo., 1976—86; mem. com. Annenberg Rsch. Inst., 1987—91; bd. dirs. Glaucoma Svc. Found. to Prevent Blindness, 1989—. Lt. col. U.S. Army, World War II. Named to Hall of Fame, U.s. Army Ordnance Dept., 1997; recipient Alumni Achievement award, U. Chgo., 1975, Harry Goode award, Am. Fedn. Info. Processing Socs., 1979, Charter Pioneer award, IEEE, 1982, Nat. medal sci., U.S. Army, 1983, Outstanding Civilian medal, 1983, Disting. Svc. medal, 1996, Disting. Civilian Svc. medal, 1996, Herman Goldstine Fellowship in Math. Scis. IBM Rsch. renamed in honor, 1998. Mem.: NAS, Coll. Physicians Phila., Math. Assn. Am., Am. Acad. Arts and Scis., Am. Philos. Soc. (Ben Franklin medal), Am. Math. Soc., Union League, Century Assn., Phi Beta Kappa (book award in sci. 1973). Home: 56 Pasture Ln Bryn Mawr PA 19010-1764*

GOLDSTINE, STEPHEN JOSEPH, college administrator; b. San Francisco, Nov. 16, 1937; s. Edgar Nathan and Regina Thelma (Benno) G.; m. Emily Raechel Miller Keeler, Apr. 12, 1981; children: Rachel, Bettina, Simone Massimiliana Student, Calif. Sch. Fine Arts, 1951, 58; BA, U. Calif., Berkeley, 1961, postgrad. in philosophy, 1962-67. Teaching asst. rhetoric dept. U. Calif., Berkeley, 1963-66; asst. prof. St. Mary's Coll., Moraga, Calif., 1964-70, chmn. art dept., 1969-70; cons. Freeman & Gossage, San Francisco, 1967-69; dir. neighborhood arts program Art Commn. City and County San Francisco, 1970-77; exec. sec. Mayor's Interagency Com. for Arts, San Francisco, 1971-75; founding dir. Performing Arts for the Third Age, San Francisco, 1973; co-dir. Rockefeller Tng. Fellowships in Mus. Edn., San Francisco, 1975; pres. San Francisco Art Inst., 1977-86; dir. grad. programs Calif. Coll. Arts and Crafts, 1986—; visiting faculty San Francisco State U.; Dennis Leon prof. grad. studies Calif. Coll. Arts and Crafts, 2002—. Sr. cons. Daniel Solomon Architects and Planners, 1988; mem. chancellor's adv. bd. Univ. Art Mus., U. Calif., Berkeley, 1979—; exec. com., trustee San Francisco Arts Edn. Found., 1985—; mem. Oakland Cultural Affairs Commn., 2002—; mem. prominent orgns. panel Calif. Arts Coun., 1981, vice chmn., 1983, chmn., 1985-87; chmn. invited session Am. Philos. Assn. (Pacific divsn.), 1986, lectr. UCLA, 1976, Stanford U., 1966, Harvard U., 1976, 71; docent Lycee Internat. Franco-Am., 1993—. Editor: Western Round Table on Modern Art, 1993; co-prodr., co-dir. (film) Walz um die Wände hoch zu gehen, 1999. Conductor The Art Orch., Calif. Palace of the Legion of Honor, 1997. Democrat. Jewish. Home: 1331 Green St San Francisco CA 94109-1926 Office: Calif Coll Arts Crafts 1111 Eighth St San Francisco CA 94107-2206 E-mail: mrgoldstine@earthlink.net.

GOLDSTOCK, BARRY PHILIP, lawyer; b. Chgo., Sept. 10, 1941; s. George Arthur and Beatrice (Shapiro) G.; m. Eve-Ellen Schneider; children— Brian Steven, Michelle. B.A., UCLA, 1964, J.D., 1967. Bar: Calif. 1968, U.S. Dist. Ct. (ctrl. dist.) Calif. 1968, U.S. Supreme Ct. 1971; cert. family law specialist. Law clk. U.S. Dist. Ct. (ctrl. dist.) Calif., 1967-68; assoc. firm Epport & Delevie, L.A., 1968-69; ptnr. Stern & Goldstock, Newport Beach, Calif., 1969-88, Goldstock & Morris, Newport Beach, 1988-89; sole practice, 1989—. Pres. Lakewood Coordinating Council, 1972-74; chmn. bd. Helpline Youth Counseling, 1979-81. Named Man of Yr., Bellflower Jaycees, 1972; recipient commendation Los Angeles County Bd. Suprs., 1974. Mem. Los Angeles County Bar Assn., Orange County Bar Assn., Lions Internat. (dep. gov. dist. 1982-83, regional chair 1995-96). Democrat. Jewish. E=mail: bgoldstock@col.com. Office: 2 Park Plz Ste 300 Irvine CA 92614-8513

GOLDSTON, STEPHEN EUGENE, community psychologist, educator, consultant; b. N.Y.C., Apr. 19, 1931; s. Michael Louis and Molly Ruth (Rothenberg) G.; children— Beth Karen, Lisa Robin BA, NYU, 1952; MSPH, Columbia U., 1953, MA, 1957, EdD, 1958. Lectr., instr. Columbia U., N.Y.C., 1956-58; asst. to dir. Westchester County Cmty. Mental Health Bd., White Plains, N.Y., 1958-60; chief mental health edn. unit, dir. mental health consultation program N.Y.C. Cmty. Mental Health Bd., 1960-62; staff asst. to assoc. dir. extramural programs NIMH, Rockville, Md., 1962-63, tng. specialist pilot and spl. grants sect. Tng. and Manpower Resources br., 1963-65, tng. specialist exptl. and spl. tng. br., 1966-67, chief pub. health sect. exptl. and spl. tng. br., 1967-69, spl. asst. to dir. for preventive programs, 1967-71, coord. primary prevention program, 1972-80, chief primary prevention service programs, Div. Mental Health Service Program, 1980-81, dir. office of prevention, 1981-85; cons. in preventive psychiatry Neuropsychiat. Inst., UCLA, 1985-87; assoc. dir. UCLA Preventive Psychiatry Ctr., 1987-89, chair ann. nat. conf., 1987, 88; staff dir. Mayor's Citizen's Task Force on Cen. City East, Los Angeles, 1986-88; pres. Goldston & Assocs., Chgo., 1986—. Chmn. nat. conf. UCLA Preventive Psychiatry Ctr., 1987-88; coord. nat. conf. Mental Health in Pub. Health Tng., 1967-68; lectr. Bar-Ilan U. Sch. Soc. Work, Ramat Gan, Israel, 1996-98, 2000—, The Hebrew U. Sch. Soc. Work, Jerusalem, Israel, 1997-2000, 03; sr. editor NIMH Prevention Publ. Series, 1976-85; assoc. editor cons. Am. Assn. Applied and Preventive Psychology, 1991—. Mem. editl. bd. Jour. Preventive Psychiatry, Jour. Primary Prevention; contbr. articles to profl. jours. With U.S. Army, 1953-55, USPHS, 1957-85. Recipient Sustained High Quality Peformance award HEW, 1968, 72, 76; Superior Work Performance award HEW, 1970; Outstanding Contbn. to Prevention in Mental Health award Nat. Council Community Mental Health Ctrs., Washington, 1985 Fellow Am. Psychol. Assn. (Disting. Profl. Contbns. award 1984), Am Psychol. Soc. (charter mem.), Am. Pub. Health Assn. (chmn. com. on prevention mental health sect. 1974-77, Am. Assn. Applied and Preventive Psychology (founding). E-mail: goldston@netvision.net.il.

GOLDSTONE, JACK ANDREW, sociologist; b. San Francisco, Sept. 30, 1953; s. Jack Robert and Ursula (Weinberg) G.; m. Gina Belinda Saleman, Feb. 9, 1992; children: Alexander, Simone. AB, Harvard U., 1976, AM, 1979, PhD, 1981. Asst. prof. Northwestern U., Evanston, Ill., 1981-84, assoc. prof., 1984-88; prof. U. Calif., Davis, 1989—. Hazel prof. of pub. policy, Geroge Mason U., 2003—. Author: Revolution and Rebellion, 1991 (disting. pub. award Am. Sociol. Assn. 1993); editor: Encyclopedia of Political Revolutions, 1998. ACLS fellow, 1983-84, Ctr. for Advanced Studies fellow Stanford U., 1993-94. Mem. Am. Sociol. Assn., Sociol. Rsch. Assn. Office: U Calif Sociology Dept Davis CA 95616

GOLDSTONE, JEFFREY, physicist, educator; b. Manchester, Eng., Sept. 3, 1933; arrived in U.S., 1977; m. Roberta Gordon; 1 child, Andrew. BA, Cambridge (Eng.) U., 1954, PhD, 1958. Fellow Trinity Coll., Cambridge, 1956-60, 62-82, hon. fellow, 2000; lectr., reader U. Cambridge, England, 1961-76, MIT, Cambridge, Mass., 1977—, Cecil and Ida Green prof. physics, 1983—. Recipient Dannie Heineman prize, Am. Phys. Soc., 1981, Guthrie medal, Inst. Physics, 1983, Dirac prize, Internat. Ctr. Theoretical Physics, 1991. Mem.: Am. Acad. Arts and Scis., Royal Soc. Office: MIT 77 Massachusetts Ave # 6-313 Cambridge MA 02139-4307 E-mail: goldston@mit.edu.

GOLDSTONE, SANFORD, psychology educator; b. N.Y.C., July 17, 1926; s. Albert and Anna (Steckel) G.; children: Susan Beth, Arthur Craig, Nancy Lynn; stepchildren: Peter B., Anthony A., Jane P., Elisabeth W.; m. Lois Adams. BS, CCNY, 1947; PhD, Duke U., 1953. Intern Duke Sch. Medicine, 1949-51; chief clin. psychologist Duke Sch. Medicine (Psychiat. Out-Patient Clinic), 1951-54, lectr. psychology, 1953-54, asso. dept. psychiatry, 1953-54; asst. prof. to prof. psychiatry, chief psychologist, program dir. Baylor U. Coll. Medicine, 1955-67; prof., head div. psychology dept. psychiatry Cornell U. Med. Coll., 1967-79; prof. psychology field neurobiology Cornell U. Med. Coll. (Grad. Sch. Med. Scis.), 1969-79; prof., dir. clin. tng., dept. psychology U. Maine, Orono, 1979-86, prof. psychology emeritus, 1986—. Cons. VA Hosps., Durham, N.C., 1953-54, Houston, 1959-67, Temple, Tex., 1964-67, Montrose, N.Y., 1968-79, Togus, Maine, 1979-88; mem. profl. staff Eastern Maine Med. Center and; Bangor Mental Health Inst., 1980-86; trustee Miles Meml. Hosp., Damariscotta, Maine, 1990-99; cons. criminal law sect. Am. Bar Assn., 1967-69, Westchester County Probation Dept., 1968-71, Community Service Bur., N.Y. State Tng. Schs., 1969-75; head div. psychology Houston State Psychiat. Inst., 1958-67, acting bus. mgr., 1959-60, head div. crime and delinquency, 1966-67; clin. asso. prof. to clin. prof. U. Houston, 1958-67; dir. mental health services Harris County Probation Dept., Houston, 1963-67; cons. Silver Hill Found., 1974-81; psychologist-in-chief Payne Whitney Psychiat. Clinic, 1967-74, Westchester div. N.Y. Hosp., 1967-74; attending psychologist N.Y. Hosp., 1967-79; head, community cons. services outpatient dept. Payne Whitney Psychiat. Clinic, 1970-73; head community cons. services Westchester div. N.Y. Hosp.-Cornell Med. Center, 1973-75 Contbr. numerous articles to profl. jours. Served with USAAF, 1945. USPHS grantee, 1955-65, 79-86. Fellow APA (life); mem. Am. Psychopath. Assn. (life). Home: PO Box 282 East Boothbay ME 04544-0282 Office: U Maine Psychology Little Hall Orono ME 04469 E-mail: sanfordg@wiscasset.net., sanfordg@maine.edu.

GOLDSTONE, STEVEN F. consumer products company executive; b. N.Y.C., Jan. 30, 1946; s. Milton Harold and Beatrice (Chase) G.; m. Elizabeth Caravella; children: Elissa Eve, Margaret Chase, Douglas. BA, U. Pa., 1967; JD, NYU, 1970. Bar: N.Y. 1971, U.S. Dist. Ct. (so. dist.) N.Y. 1972, U.S. Ct. Appeals (2d cir.) 1971). Assoc. Davis, Polk & Wardwell, N.Y.C., 1970-78, ptnr., 1978-95; gen. counsel RJR Nabisco, Inc., 1995; chmn., CEO, bd. dirs. RJR Nabisco Inc., 1995-2000; also bd. dirs. Nabisco Holdings, Inc., 1997-2000; pvt. exec. Silver Spring Group, N.Y.C., 2000—. Office: Silver Spring Group 570 Lexington Ave Fl 37 New York NY 10022-6837

GOLDSTRAND, DENNIS JOSEPH, business and estate planning executive; b. Oakland, Calif., July 12, 1952; s. Joseph Nelson and Frances Marie (Royce) G.; m. Judy A. Goldstrand. BSBA, Calif. State U., Chico, 1975; CLU, Am. Coll., 1986, CFC, 1988. Accredited estate planner, Nat. Assn. Estate Planners Couns., registered investment advisor. Asst. mgr. Household Fin. Corp., San Leandro, Calif., 1975-76; registered rep. Equitable Fin. Svcs., San Francisco, 1976-79, dist. mgr., 1979-85; ptnr. Goldstrand & Small Ins. and Fin. Svcs., Stockton, Calif., 1986-89; owner Goldstrand Fin. & Ins. Svcs. (now Goldstrand Planning Group and Goldstrand Ins. Svcs.), Stockton, 1989—. Spkr. taxation course Law Sch. Humphreys Coll., 1997-2000; spkr. in field. Spkr. Calif. Assn. Life Underwriters, 1986, 95, 99, San Joaquin chpt. Calif. CPA Soc., 1997; contbr. articles to Life Ins. Selling mag., 1986, 88, 99; featured guest writer articles to Bus Jour. (San Joaquin and Stanislaus counties), Bldrs. Exch. of Stockton's Constrn. Weekly. Mem. Stockton Estate Planning Coun., bd. dirs. 1995-2000, pres. 1998-99, spkr., 1996, 97; past pres. United Way San Joaquin County Endowment Found., Inc., 1994, Keel Club; charter mem. planned giving com. U. of Pacific; assoc. mem. scholarship adv. coun. Bldr.'s Exch. of Stockton. Mem. Stockton Assn. Ins. and Fin. Advisors (pres. 1990-91, chair ethics com. 1993-94), Life Underwriter of Yr. 1994, Fin. Planning Assn., Soc. Fin. Svc. Profls. (formerly Soc. CLU ChFC, pres. Stockton chpt. 1989-90), Calif. Assn. Life Underwriters (trustee 1995-96), Million Dollar Round Table, Greater Stockton C. of C. (govt. rels. coun., bd. dirs.), Rotary, Brookside Country Club. Avocations: tennis, golf. Home: 4162 Pebble Beach Dr Stockton CA 95219-1912 Office: Goldstrand Planning Group 2800 W March Ln Ste 326 Stockton CA 95219-8202 E-mail: planning@goldstrand.com.

GOLDTHWAIT, CHRISTOPHER E. ambassador; b. Atlanta; BA, Am. U.; MPA, Harvard U. Joined U.S. Fgn. Agrl. Svc., agrl. attaché, 1978-82, agrl. counselor, 1982-86, various positions, then Gen. Sales Mgr., 1993-99, U.S. ambassador to Republic of Chad, 1999—. Office: US Embassy Ave Felix Ebou Box 413 N'Djamena Chad E-mail: goldthwaitce@state.gov.

GOLDWASSER, EDWIN LEO, physicist; b. N.Y.C., Mar. 9, 1919; s. I. Edwin and Edith (Goldstein) G.; m. Elizabeth Weiss, Oct. 27, 1940; children: Michael, John, Katherine, David, Richard. BA, Harvard U., 1940; PhD, U. Calif., Berkeley, 1950. Rsch. asst. and rsch. assoc. U. Calif., Berkeley, 1946-51; rsch. assoc., prof. physics U. Ill., Urbana, 1951-88; dep. dir. Fermi Nat. Accelerator Lab., Batavia, Ill., 1967-78; vice chancellor for rsch. U. Ill., Urbana, 1978-80, vice chancellor acad. affairs, 1979-86, acting dir. internat. programs, 1988-89, acting dir. Computer-based Edn. Rsch. Lab., 1989-92; assoc. dir. Superconducting Super Collider Cen. Design Group, Berkeley, 1986-88; disting. fellow Calif. Inst. Tech., 1993-94. Mem., chmn. Nat. Rsch. Coun. div. Phys. Scis., Washington, 1961-69; chmn. sci. policy com. Stanford (Calif.) Linear Accelerator Ctr., 1980-84; chmn. sci. and ednl. adv. com. U. Calif., Berkeley, 1986-92. Author: Optics, Waves, Atoms and Nuclei, 1965; contbr. articles to profl. jours. Westinghouse fellow, 1949-50; Guggenheim fellow, 1957-58; Fulbright fellow, 1957-58. Fellow: AAAS; mem.: Phi Kappa Phi, Xigma Xi, Phi Beta Kappa. Avocations: tennis, swimming, opera. Home: 612 W Delaware Ave Urbana IL 61801-4805 Office: U Ill Dept Physics 1110 W Green St Urbana IL 61801-9013 E-mail: egoldwas@uiuc.edu.

GOLDWASSER, EUGENE, biochemist, educator; b. N.Y.C., Oct. 14, 1922; s. Herman and Anna (Ackerman) G.; m. Florence Cohen, Dec. 22, 1949 (dec.); children— Thomas Alan, Matthew Laurence, James Herman; m. Deone Jackman, Feb. 15, 1986 BS, U. Chgo., 1943, PhD, 1950; ScD (hon.), N.Y. Med. Coll. Am. Cancer Soc. fellow U. Copenhagen, Denmark, 1950-52; rsch. assoc. U. Chgo., 1952-61, mem. faculty, 1962—, prof. biochemistry, 1963-91, prof. emeritus biochemistry and molecular biology, 1991—, chmn. com. on devel. biology., 1976-91, chmn. biochemistry and molecular biology, 1994-98. Served with AUS, 1944-46. Recipient Esther Langer medal for cancer rsch. Internat. Soc. Blood Purification, 1987, Simpson award Wayne State U., Lucerne award Fedn. European Physiol. Soc., Karl Landsteiner award Am. Assn. of Blood Banks; Guggenheim fellow Oxford (Eng.) U., 1966-67. Fellow AAAS, Am. Acad. Arts and Scis.; mem. Am. Soc. Biol. Chemists, Biochem. Soc., Internat. Soc. Exptl. Hematology, Am. Soc. Hematology, Sigma Xi. Achievements include purification of human erythropoietin; rsch. in biochemistry and red blood cell formation. Home: 5656 S Dorchester Ave Chicago IL 60637-1706 E-mail: egoldwas@midway.uchicago.edu.

GOLDWATER, WALTER EUGENE, psychiatrist, musician; b. N.Y.C., Aug. 27, 1944; s. Walter Delmar and Ethel (Libson) G.; m. Eva Ann Nosty, June 28, 1968; children: Daniel, Sharon. BA, Harvard U., 1966; MD, Columbia U., 1970; Cert., Boston Grad. Sch. Psychoanalysis, Brookline, Mass., 1987. Diplomate Am. Bd. Psychiatry and Neurology. Intern N.Y. Polyclinic Hosp., 1970-71; resident N.Y. State Pyschiat. Inst., 1971, 74-76; dir. alcoholism rehab. unit South Beach Psychiat. Ctr., N.Y.C., 1976-78; chief alcohol dependence treatment ctr. VA Med. Ctr., Northampton, Mass., 1978-80; staff psychiatrist River Valley Counseling Ctr., Holyoke, Mass., 1980-97; adj. faculty Boston Grad. Sch. Psychoanalysis, Brookline, Mass., 1987—. Cons. psychiatrist Mass.-Rehab. Commn., Holyoke, 1980—. Contbr. articles to Modern Psychoanalysis; leader internat. folk dance band Panharmonium, 1992—. Bd. dirs. The Common Sch., Amherst, Mass., 1981-87. Capt. U.S. Army, 1972-74. Mem. Nat. Assn. Advancement of Pschoanalysis (cert.), Soc. Modern Psychoanalysts. Office: 108 Russell St PO Box 236 Hadley MA 01035-0236

GOLECKI, ILAN, physicist, researcher, educator; b. Haifa, Israel; arrived in U.S., 1978; s. Moshe and Rebecca (Lazarovici) Golecki. BS cum laude in Physics, Technion, Israel Inst. Tech., Haifa, Israel, 1970, MS in Physics, 1974; PhD in Physics, U. Neuchâtel, Neuchâtel, Switzerland, 1978. Rsch. fellow Calif. Inst. Tech., Pasadena, Calif., 1978-79, vis. assoc., 1979-86; mem. tech. staff Rockwell Internat. Corp., Anaheim, Calif., 1979-85, Thousand Oaks, Calif., 1985-86; ind. cons. Thousand Oaks, Calif., 1986-87; sr. rsch. physicist Allied-Signal, Inc. (now Honeywell Internat., Inc.), Morristown, N.J., 1987-93, rsch. scientist, 1993-96, prin. scientist, 1997—. Organizer, chmn. of session on silicon-on-insulators, SPIE Conf., L.A., 1986; chem. vapor infiltration session co-chair ECS Conf., Paris, 1997; co-chair, organizer and procs. editor Engring. Found. Conf. on High-Temperature Electronics, San Diego, 1998; referee of jour. articles in field. Mem. steering com. Jour. Lightwave Tech.; contbr. more than 74 articles to sci. jours. and chpt. to book, including archival invited rev. papers. Mem. IEEE, Am. Vacuum Soc., Böhmische Phys. Soc., Electrochem. Soc., Materials Rsch. Soc., Am. Ceramic Soc. Achievements include 11 patents concerning the processing of silicon-on-sapphire; semiconductor circuit metallizations, SiC epitaxial growth by chemical vapor deposition; rapid densification of carbon-carbon composites by chemical vapor infiltration; in-situ densification monitor; carbon-carbon heat exchangers; oxidation protection of carbon-carbon; development of new silicon-on-insulator technologies; co-discovery of ion beam induced epitaxial regrowth effect in silicon; development of apparatus enabling ion channeling measurements at elevated pressure; research interests include growth and analytical characterization of thin films and coatings and densification of porous composites by chemical vapor deposition and infiltration; intelligent in-situ densification monitor; ion beam analysis by Rutherford backscattering and channeling; vacuum science and technology and apparatus design and fabrication. Home: 100 Vail Rd Apt N-5 Parsippany NJ 07054-1337 Office: Honeywell Internat Inc CTC-1 101 Columbia Rd Morristown NJ 07960-4658 E-mail: ilan_golecki@ieee.org.

GOLEMBESKI, JEROME JOHN, wire and cable company executive; b. Nanticoke, Pa., Mar. 16, 1931; s. Edward and Mary Ellen (Grozio) G.; m. June Beverly Chadwick, Aug. 9, 1958; children— Dale, Gary, Gregg, Cheryl, Kim. BS, U. Conn., 1957. Auditor Price Waterhouse & Co., Hartford, Conn., 1957-59; mem. controller's staff Insilco Corp., Meriden, Conn., 1959-86; Times Fiber Comm. Inc. Times Wire & Cable Co., Wallingford, Conn., 1959-86; contr., treas. Uniset Inc., Wallingford, 1986—. Served with USNR, 1949-53. Mem. Nat. Assn. Accountants (Cost Accounting award Hartford chpt.) Office: Uniset Inc 85 Legend Hill Rd Madison CT 06443-1879

GOLEMBIEWSKI, ROBERT THOMAS, educator, management consultant; b. Lawrenceville, N.J., July 2, 1932; s. John and Pauline Pelka Golembiewska; m. Margaret Hughes, Sept. 1, 1956; children: Alice, Hope, Geoffrey. AB, Princeton (N.J.) U., 1954; MA, Yale U., 1956, PhD, 1958; ScD (hon.), U. Lethbridge, Alb., Can. Instr. Princeton U., 1958-60; rsch. asst. prof. U. Ill., Champaign, 1960-63; vis. lectr. Yale U., New Haven, 1963-64; assoc. prof. U. Ga., Athens, 1968-71, rsch. prof., 1972—98, disting. rsch. prof., 1998—2002, disting. rsch. prof. emeritus, 2002—. Cons. in field. Author, editor over 70 books; contbr. over 800 articles to profl. publs. Named Ky. col. (hon.) State of Ky. Fellow Acad. of Mgmt., Nat. Acad. of Pub. Adminstrn. Avocations: fly-fishing, hunting, numismatics. Home: 145 Highland Dr Athens GA 30606-3211 Office: U Ga Baldwin Hall Athens GA 30602

GOLEMON, PATRICIA LYNN, education educator, writer; b. Nacogdoches, Texas, May 28, 1944; d. Robert Bruce and Catherine Hall (Blake) Golemon; m. Peter Williamson; children: Anna Garrett, Allison Skinner. BA Summa Cum Laude, U. Houston, Houston, 1974; MA, U.Houston, Houston, 1975, PhD, 1999. Asst. prof. U. Houston, Houston, 2001—; mgr. Blount Internat. Ltd., Montgomery, Ala., 1979—82; mgr. mktg. svc. Geosource, Inc., 1982—84; asst. gen. mgr. for com. Met. Transit Authority of Houston, Houston, 1984—88; v.p. mktg. Nat. Transit Svc., 1988—90; cons. Golemon Ventures, 1990—. Lectr. Am. Mktg. Assn., 1984—88. Author publ., papers and presentations. Recipient Award for short story written, Atlantic Monthly, 1973, first pl. award for transit advt., Am. Pub. Transit Assn., 1984—88, Houston Mktg. Person of the Yr., Am. Mktg. Assn., Houston, 1987, Silver Anvil Award, Pub. Rels. Soc. of Am.; grantee Outstanding Grad. Student, U. Houston, 1974—75, fellowship to attend Oxford U., U. Houston Eng. Dept., 1975, full funding of Faculty Devel. Award, U. Houston,Downtown, 2003. Mem.: Soc. of Tech. Communicators, Soc. for Intercultural Edn.,Tng., and Rsch., Nat. Coun. of Tchr. of Eng., IEEE, Assn. of U. Women, ATTW.

GOLEMON, RONALD KINNAN, lawyer; b. Atlanta, Tex., Nov. 22, 1938; s. William Layton and Avis (Bogle) G.; m. Jacqueline Alice Burst, Sept. 2, 1966; children: Donald Brent, Jennifer Alice. BS in Indsl. Mgmt. Engring., U. Okla., 1961; LLB, U. Tex., 1967. Bar: Tex. 1967, U.S. Ct. Appeals (5th cir.) 1970, U.S. Dist. Ct. (so. dist.) Tex. 1968, U.S. Dist. Ct. (we. dist.) Tex. 1981, U.S. Dist. Ct. (no. dist.) 1986. Engr. asst. Tex. Water Pollution Control Bd., Austin, 1964-67; assoc. Keys, Russell, Watson & Seaman, Corpus Christi, Tex., 1967-71, ptnr., 1971-73, Brown McCarroll, LLP (formerly Brown McCarroll & Oaks Hartline), Austin, 1973—; mng. ptnr. Brown McCarroll & Oaks Hartline, 1989-94. Contbg. author The Southwestern Legal Foundation, 40th Annual Institute on Oil and Gas Law and Taxation, 1989, The Southwestern Legal Foundation, 43rd Annual Institute on Oil and Gas Law and Taxation, 1992; contbr articles to profl. jours. Alt. mem. RCRA permit adv. com. U.S. EPA, 1983; mem. Gov.'s Hazardous Waste Task Force, 1984-85; v.p. St. Stephen's Sch. PTA, 1985-86, pres., 1986-87; mem. cmty. adv. bd. Ronald McDonald House, Austin, 1990—. Fellow Am. Bar Found.; mem. ABA (chmn. standing com. constnl. and by-laws 2001—, ho. dels. 2000—, mem. standing com. membership & liaison 1997-2000, mem. market rsch. task force 1995-96, chmn. sect. natural resources, energy and environ. law 1994-95, chmn.-elect 1993-94, vice-chmn. 1992-93, mem. coun. liaison environ. group 1989-91, chmn. air quality com. 1986-89, vice chmn. 1982-86), State Bar Tex. (chmn. environ. law sect. 1971-72), Tex. Mining and Reclamation Assn. (dir. 1988-2000), Travis County Bar Assn., U. Tex. Law Alumni Assn. (pres. 1984-85, mem. exec. bd. 1984-86), Tex. Corriente Cattle Assn. (bd. dirs. 2002). Avocations: ranching, hunting, skiing, golf. Office: Brown McCarroll LLP 111 Congress Ave Ste 1400 Austin TX 78701-4043 E-mail: kgolemon@mailbmc.com.

GOLER, MICHAEL DAVID, lawyer; b. Cleve., June 29, 1952; s. George G. and Harriet (Zellen) G.; children: Jonathan A. Jennifer S. BA in Classics (Greek), Union Coll., 1974; JD, Case We. Reserve U., 1977. Bar: Ohio 1977, U.S. Dist. Ct. Ohio 1977, U.S. Ct. Appeals (6th cir.) 1982. Assoc. Persky, Marken, Konigsberg & Shapiro, Cleve., 1977-81; assoc. counsel Cardinal Fed. Savings Bank, Cleve., 1981-84; assoc. Arter & Hadden, Cleve., 1984-86, Kohrman, Jackson & Krantz, Cleve., 1988-86, ptnr., 1988-94, Goodman Weiss Miller LLP, Cleve., 1994—. Fellow ABA (sect. real property probate and trust law, chmn. com. enforcement of creditor's rights and bankruptcy, 1991-95, vice chair, 1995-97, chair, 1997-2001, com. on econs., tech. and practice methods, mng. editor EDirt electronic newsletter 1999—, mem. coun. 2001—, liaison to ABA sect. law practice mgmt. sect. 1999—, liaison to ABA soc. pro bono com. 2001—); mem. Am. Coll. Mortgage Attys., Cleve. Bar Assn. (founder, chmn. environ. law sect. 1991-95, chmn. real estate sect. 1989-90). Avocations: music, golf, squash, bicycling, skiing. Office: Goodman Weiss Miller LLP 100 Erieview Plz Fl 27 Cleveland OH 44114-1824 Home: 12931 Shaker Blvd #301 Cleveland OH 44120 E-mail: goler@goodmanweissmiller.com.

GOLICK, TOBY, law educator, legal services administrator; b. Boston, Apr. 9, 1945; d. Albert David and Sara (Sharaf) G.; children: Benjamin Taylor, Samuel Taylor. BA, Columbia U., 1966, JD, 1969. Bar: N.Y. 1969. Mng. atty. Queens (N.Y.) Legal Svcs., 1969-70; atty. Columbia Ctr. on Social Welfare Policy, N.Y.C., 1970-71; sr. atty. Legal Svcs. for Elderly, N.Y.C., 1972-74, 76-85; clin. prof. Yeshiva U. Cardozo Law Sch., N.Y.C., 1985—; dir. Cardozo Bet Tzedek Legal Svcs., N.Y.C., 1985—. Recipient Eleanor Roosevelt award State of N.Y., 1986, Disting. Svc. award Brookdale Ctr. on Aging, N.Y.C., 1998. Mem. N.Y. State Bar Assn., Assn. Bar City N.Y. Home: 54 Morningside Dr New York NY 10025-1740 Office: Yeshiva U Cardozo Law Sch 55 5th Ave New York NY 10003-4301 E mail: tgolick@ymail.yu.edu.

GOLIGHTLY, DOUGLAS RAYMOND, artist; b. Milw., Feb. 13, 1931; s. William Bruce and Dorothy Agnes (Klein) G.; m. Patricia Anne Jelinek, June 20, 1959; children: Christine Marie Golightly Richter, William James. BS in Art, U. Wis., 1957, MS in Art, 1959, MFA, 1960. Instr. Layton Sch. Art, Milw., 1964-65. One-man shows Bradley Galleries, Milw., 1962, 66, 69, Wustum Mus. Art, Racine, Wis., 1968, Madison Art Ctr, Wis., 1968, Rahr Civic Ctr. and Pub. Mus., 1968, Manitowoc, Wis., Kenosha (Wis.) Pub. Mus., 1968, Hardy Gallery, Door County, Wis., 1969, Santa Cruz (Calif.) Art League, 1986-87, Sunset Cultural Ctr., Carmel, Calif., 1989, C.L. Clark Gallery, Bakersfield, Calif., 1993, Kings Art Ctr., Hanford, Calif., 1994; 2-person shows include Layton Sch. Art, Milw., 1965, Sanchez Art Ctr., 2002; 3-person show Sun Gallery, Hayward, Calif., 1985; exhibited in group shows Milw. Art Inst., 1950, 55, U. Wis. Meml. Libr., Madison, 1960, Milw. Art Ctr., 1960, 61, 66, 67, 68, Capitol Ct., Milw., 1961, 62, C.W. Post Coll., L.I., N.Y., 1962 (hon. mention), Nat. Arts Club, N.Y.C., 1962, Long Beach (N.Y.) Art Assn., 1962, Madison Gallery, N.Y.C., 1962, Lynn Kottler Galleries, N.Y.C., 1964, Marquette U., Milw., Wis., 1966, Wis. State Fair, Milw., 1967, Mus. Fine Art, Springfield, Mass., 1968, Las Vegas (Nev.) Art Roundup, 1968, Butler Inst. Am. Art, Youngstown, Ohio, 1972, Janacek Atelier, Madison, 1978, Milw. Symphony Showcase, 1980, Santa Cruz Art League, 1987-88, 2000-01, Gallery Imago, San Francisco, 1987, Tulare County Fair, Tulare, Calif., 1989-94 (3d prize for oil 1989, 1st and 2d prizes for oils 1990, 92, Best in Show award 1991, 1st prize for oil 1993, 94), Visions Gallery, Reedley, Calif., 1989, 93 (hon. mention 1993) Fanny Garver Gallery, Madison, Wis., 1989, 90, 91, C.L. Clark Galleries, 1990, 91, 92, Mus. Fine Arts, Mus. N.Mex., Santa Fe, 1991, La. State U., Baton Rouge, 1992, Northlight Gallery, West Los Angeles, Calif., 1994, Kings Art Ctr., Hanford, Calif., 1995-2002, Gallery 198, Three Rivers, Calif., 1999-2000, San Luis Obispo Art Ctr., Calif., 2000, 2001, 2002, 03, Carnegie Art Mus., Oxnard, Calif., 2000, 02, 03, Pacific Grove Art Ctr., Calif., 2000, 02, 03 Second City Coun., Long Beach, Calif., 2000-02, 40-Year Retrospective Exhibit, Wylie & May Louise Jones Gallery, Bakersfield Coll., Calif., 2000, Berkeley Art Ctr., 2001-03, San Francisco State U., 2001, Porterville Art Assn., Calif, 2001-03, Sanchez Art Ctr., Pacifica, Calif., 2001-02(Grand Prize co-winner 2001), Sun Gallery, Hayward, Calif., 2001, 2002, Orange County Ctr. Contemporary Art, Santa Ana, Calif., 2001, Bedford Gallery at the Dean Lesher Regional Ctr. for Arts, Walnut Creek, Calif., 2001, 03, San Jose Art League, 2002, Sebastopol (Calif.) Ctr. for the Arts, 2002, Nicolet Coll, Rhinelander, Wis., 2002, Armory Art Ctr., West Palm Beach, Fla., 2002, Artisans Gallery, Mill Valley, Calif., 2002, Palos Verdes (Calif.) Art Ctr., Racho Palos Verdes, Calif., 2003, Chris Vanderlei Gallery, Bakersfield, Calif., 2003, also others; represented in permanent collections Milw. Jour., Wis., Milw. Pub. Libr.; represented in pvt. collections C.L. Clark, Bakersfield, Calif., Ms. Jane Doud, Elm Grove, Wis., many others. With U.S. Army, 1953-55, Korea. Recipient purchase award Milw. Pub. Libr., 1961, Best in Show Award, Second City Coun., Long Beach, Calif., 2000, Third Place prize, Second City Coun., 2002. Mem. Berkeley Art Ctr., Elvehjem Mus. Art (Madison, Wis.), San Luis Obispo Art Ctr. Avocations: philosophy, theology, ethics, Hebrew, Greek and Arabic linguistics. Home: 1155 Brown Ave Porterville CA 93257-5803

GOLIGHTLY, JOHN WESLEY, music educator; b. Abilene, Tex., July 20, 1951; s. Norman Lee and Mildred Christine Golightly; m. Terry Ann White, Oct. 23, 1976; children: David, Paul, Amy. MusB, Hardin-Simmons U., 1973; MusM, Tex. Christian U., 1975; D in Musical Arts, Ohio State U., 1980. Pvt. piano tchr., Sacramento, 1975—76; min. of music Sylvan Oaks Christian Ch., Citrus Heights, Calif., 1981—89; prof. music Ky. Christian Coll., Grayson, 1989—. Pvt. piano technician, Grayson, 1989—; music discipline adv. Appalachian Coll. Assn., Berea, Ky., 2001—. Author: The Piano from 1800 to 1850, 1980. Com. chmn. Boy Scouts Am., Grayson, 1999—. Music Tech. grantee, Appalachian Coll. Assn., 1998. Mem.: Ky. Music Tchrs. Assn. (festival coord. 2001—03). Mem. Ch. Of Christ. Avocations: hiking, growing epiphyllum plants. Home: 623 Falls Ln Grayson KY 41143 Office: Ky Christian Coll 100 Academic Pkwy Grayson KY 41143-2205

GOLIN, ALVIN, public relations company executive; b. Chgo., June 19, 1929; s. Charles and Jeanette Golin; m. June Kerns, Aug. 25, 1961; children: Barry, Karen, Ellen. B.J., Roosevelt U., 1950. Publicity rep. MGM Pictures, N.Y.C., 1951—54; chmn. Golin/Harris Internat., Chgo., 1975—. Lectr. to numerous univs. Adv. Chgo. Coun. Boy Scouts Am., Nat. Multiple Sclerosis Soc., U. Tenn. Mem.: Pub. Club of Chgo., Pub. Rels. Soc. Am. Office: Golin/Harris International 111 E Wacker Dr Fl 10 Chicago IL 60601-4305

GOLINKIN, WEBSTER FOWLER, healthcare executive, media consultant; b. N.Y.C., Aug. 3, 1951; s. Joseph Webster and Ruth Forman (Fowler) G.; m. Allison Ann Willeford, Apr. 19, 1985; children: Joseph Webster, George Willeford. BA, Harvard U., 1973. Comms. project adminstr. IBM Corp., Armonk, N.Y., 1974-76; v.p. Geer, DuBois Advtg., N.Y.C., 1976-79, Reeves Comm. Corp., 1979-88; sr. v.p. Reeves Entertainment Group, 1986-88; pres. Reeves Corp. Svcs., N.Y.C., 1979-88; co-chmn., CEO, Am. Med. Comms., Inc., Houston, 1988-93; chmn., CEO, America's Health Network, Inc., Orlando, Fla., 1993-99; vice chmn., chief mktg. and sales officer Norwood Promotional Products Inc., Austin, Tex., 1999—2001; CEO, Interfit Health, Inc., Houston, 2001—. Bd. dirs. Meth. DeBakey Heart Ctr., Houston, 2000—. Mem. World Presidents' Orgn. Home: 5660 Longmont Dr Houston TX 77056-2345 Office: 8707 Katy Freeway Ste 200 Houston TX 77024

GOLINSKI, JAN VICTOR, history of science educator; b. London, Apr. 9, 1957; came to the U.S., 1990; s. Jerzy and Shelagh Golinski. BA, Cambridge (Eng.) U., 1979, MA, 1983; PhD, U. Leeds, Eng., 1984. Rsch. fellow Churchill Coll., Cambridge, 1986-90; asst. prof. U. N.H., Durham, 1990-94, assoc. prof., 1994-2000, prof., 2000—. Author: Science As Public Culture, 1992, Making Natural Knowledge, 1998; co-editor: The Sciences in Enlightened Europe, 1999. Postdoctoral fellow U. Wis., Madison, 1989. Mem. Am. Soc. for Eighteenth-Century Studies, Am. Hist. Assn., History Sci. Soc. (coun. mem. 1997-99), Brit. Soc. for History Sci. (sec. 1987-88). Office: U NH Dept History 20 College Rd Durham NH 03824 E-mail: jan.golinski@unh.edu.

GOLIS, PAUL ROBERT, lawyer; b. San Francisco, Sept. 25, 1954; BA with high distinction, Calif. State U., Long Beach, 1977; JD, Syracuse U., 1981. Bar: Fla. 1984, U.S. Dist. Ct. (so. dist.) Fla. 1985, U.S. Ct. Appeals (11th cir.) 2000. Assoc. Russell L. Forkey, P.A., Ft. Lauderdale, Fla., 1984-85, Josias & Goren, P.A., Ft. Lauderdale, 1985-88; sr. trial atty. State of Fla. Dept. Transp., Ft. Lauderdale, 1988-90; asst. county atty. Palm Beach County, West Palm Beach, Fla., 1990-91; assoc. Scott, Royce, Harris, Bryan & Hyland, Palm Beach Gardens, Fla., 1991-93, Watterson, Hyland & Klett, Palm Beach Gardens, 1993-98; pvt. practice, Boca Raton, Fla., 1998—. Featured spkr. on eminent domain issues Palm Beach County Bar Assn., West Palm Beach, 1993, West Palm Beach, 96, West Palm Beach, 99, West Palm Beach, 2001; on legal ethics Nat. Bus. Inst., West Palm Beach, 1999, West Palm Beach, 2001, on land use, 00; on eminent domain issues Fla. Bar, 2002; spl. master code enforcement issues Town of Hypoluxo, 2002—. Bd. dirs. Aid to Victims of Domestic Abuse, Inc., 1990-99, v.p., 1993-97, pres. 1997-99, mem. adv. bd., 1999-2001, aux. bd., 2002—; bd. dirs. Boca Raton Soc. for Disabled, Inc., 1999-2002, treas. 2001-02. Mem. ABA, Fla. Bar Assn. (eminent domain com. 1989—, vice chair 2002-03, chair 2003—), Palm Beach County Bar Assn. (vice chmn. environ., land use and eminent domain CLE com. 1993-95, chmn. 1995-99, mem. 2000—, jud. rels. com. 1996-99, professionalism com. 2001—). Office: 2000 Glades Rd Ste 306 Boca Raton FL 33431-8504 E-mail: Parogo@adelphia.net.

GOLITZ, LOREN EUGENE, dermatologist, pathologist, clinical administrator, educator; b. Apr. 7, 1941; s. Ross Winston and Helen Francis (Schupp) G.; m. Deborah Burd Frazier, June 18, 1966; children: Carrie Campbell, Matthew Ross. MD, U. Mo., Columbia, 1966. Diplomate Am. Bd. Dermatology, Nat. Bd. Med. Examiners. Intern USPHS Hosp., San Francisco, 1966-67, med. resident, 1967-69, resident in dermatology S.I., N.Y., 1969-71, dep. chief dermatology, 1972-73; vis. fellow dermatology Columbia-Presbyn. Med. Ctr., N.Y.C., 1971-72; asst. in dermatology Coll. Physicians Surgeons, Columbia, N.Y.C., 1972-73; vice-chmn. Residency Rev. Com. for Dermatology, 1983-85; assoc. prof. dermatology, pathology Med. Sch. U. Colo., Denver, 1974-88, prof., 1988-97, clin. prof. pathology, dermatology, 1997—. Chief dermatology Denver Gen. Hosp., 1974-97; med. dir. Ambulatory Care Ctr., Denver Gen. Hosp., 1991-97. Mem. editl. bd. Jour. Cutaneous Pathology, Jour. Am. Acad. Dermatology, Advances in Dermatology (editl. bd. Current Opinion in Dermatology); contbr. articles to med. jours. Fellow Royal Soc. Medicine; mem. AMA (residency rev. com. for dermatology 1982-89, dermatopathology test com. 1979-85), AAAS, Am. Soc. Dermatopathology (sec., treas. 1985-89, pres.-elect 1989, pres. 1990), Am. Acad. Dermatology (chmn. coun. on clin. and lab. svcs., coun. sci. assembly 1987-91, bd. dirs. 1987-91, chmn. joint dermatopathology com.), Soc. Pediat. Dermatology (pres. 1981), Soc. Investigative Dermatology, Pacific Dermatol. Assn. (exec. com. 1979-89, sec.-treas. 1984-87, pres. 1988), Noah Worcester Dermatol. Soc. (publs. com. 1980, membership com. 1989-90), Colo. Dermatol. Soc. (pres. 1978), Am. Bd. Dermatology Inc. (chmn. part II test com. 1989—, exec. com. 1993—, v.p. 1994, pres.-elect 1995, pres. 1996, dir. Emeritus, cons. to bd. 1997—), Colo. Med. Soc., Denver Med. Soc., Denver Soc. Dermatopathology, Am. Dermatol. Assn., Women's Dermatologic Soc., So. Med. Assn., Internat. Soc. Pediat. Dermatology, Am. Contact Dermatitis Soc., Am. Soc. Dermatologic Surgery, Physicians Who Care, Am. Bd. Med. Specialties (del.), N.Y. Acad. Scis., Brit. Assn. Dermatologists (hon.), Brazilian Soc. Dermatology (hon.), U. Mo. Med. Alumni Orgn. (bd. govs. 1993—). Home: 130 S Elm St Denver CO 80246-1131 Office: Dermatopathology Svc PO Box 6218 Denver CO 80206-0218

GOLKA, ANNA MARIA, musician, educator; d. Mieczyslaw Karczewski and Irena Karczewska; m. Jerzy Golka, Nov. 5, 1974; children: Adam Fryderyk children: Tomasz Jerzy, Karl Stanislaw. MusM, Gdansk Acad. of Music, Gdansk, 1971—76. Piano Performance And Pedagogy Gdansk Acad. of Music, 1976. Pres. of the Chopin soc. of Houston Chopin Soc. of Houston, Houston, 2000—, pres., 2000—. Pres. Chopin Soc. of Houston, Houston, 2000—. Dir.(educator): (organizing competitions, master classes) for example Chopin Lives-workshop, Youth Chopin Competitions (Houston Music Assn. -Tchr. of the Yr., 2003). Educator, advisor various Polish organizations, Houston, Tex., 1982—2003. Recipient Houston Music Teachers Ass. Tchr. of the Yr., 2003 and nomination to TMTA tchr. of the Yr. (Tex. Music Teachers Ass.), Houston Music Tchr. Assn., 2003. Achievements include development of Youth knowledge on live and music of Chopin. Office: Chopin Society of Houston 631 Houghton Katy TX 77450

GOLL, PAULETTE SUSAN, education educator; b. Cleve., June 5, 1947; d. Ferdinand Paul and Lillian Clarice (Mehalko) G. BA in English, Cleve. State U., 1969, MEd, 1974; MA in English, U. Bridgeport, Conn., 1979; PhD in English, Case Western Res. U., 1987. Cert. secondary tchr., English tchr., asst. supr., secondary prin., Ohio. Part-time instr. U. Bridgeport, 1978-79, Case Western Res. U., Cleve., 1985-87; tchr. English, Cleve. Pub. Schs., 1969—99, chmn. dept., coord. Ohio Proficiency Test, 1991—96; regional dir. Summer Inst. for Gifted Midwest Region, Granville, Ohio, 2000—02; lectr. Case Western Reserve U., Cleve., 2002—. Adj. instr. English Case Western Reserve U., Cleve. State U., 1999—2000; vis. assoc. prof. edn. Dickinson Coll., Carlisle, Pa., 2000; advisor Students Against Drunk Drivers, 1985—86; coord project success Lincoln West H.S., Cleve., 1987—90; ACT vis. tchr., 1999; external reviewer Bedford/St. Martins, 2003. Co-author: Shakespearean Comedies, 1985; external reviewer Reading Critically, Writing Well, textbook cons. textbook cons. McDougal Littel, 1999—2000, Bedford St. Martin, 2003. Mem. com. on human rels. Cleve. Partnerships, 1989-92; co-chmn. High Schs. for Future, 1985-86; liaison MetroHealth/Lincoln-West Partnership, 1989-92. Named Master Tchr., Martha Holden Jennings Found., 1988; recipient Congl. Commendation Mary Rose Oaker, 1988, Award of Excellence, Rotary, 1989, British Petroleum Tchr. of Year, 1997; NEH fellow, 1985, NEH Ind. Studies in Humanities fellow, 1993; Jennings scholar, 1985, 88. Mem. ASCD (presenter), Nat. Assn. Gifted (presenter 2001), North Ctrl. Assn. (chair vis. team 1991, 93), Phi Delta Kappa (v.p. programs 1993). Republican. Roman Catholic. Avocations: travel, music, needlepoint, writing fiction, camping. Home: 11366 Clarke Rd Columbia Station OH 44028-9626 Personal E-mail: psg3ecwru.edu

GOLL, STEPHEN E. telecommuncations executive; b. Independence, Kans., Oct. 11, 1948; s. Robert L. and Frances M. (Forslund) G.; m. Stella L. Adamson, Aug. 6, 1978; children: Sondra Goll Knaus, Stacy, Aaron Goll. AA, Independence (Kans.) C.C., 1968; BA, Pitts. State U., 1974; attended, U.S. Navy Schs., 1974—77, U.S. Army Schs., 1981—82; BS, DeVry Inst. Tech., 1989. Faculty asst., computer lab. monitor DeVry Inst. Tech., Kansas City, Mo., 1988-89; comms. specialist RDA/Logicon, Ft. Leavenworth, Kans., 1989-92; retail sales rep. Comp-USA, Overland Park, Kans., 1993; computer product specialist Best Buy, Lenexa, Kans., 1993-94; writer, photographer, columnist The Fog-Line, Bonner Springs, Kans., 1994-95. Tchr. Bonner Springs Elem. Sch. Contbr. to World's Best Short Stories; with Better Than Fair Players, Bonner Springs, Kans. RM2 USN, 1975-81, sgt. U.S. Army, 1981-85. Mem. DAV (life), VFW (life), Soc. for Creative Anachronisms, Internat. Soc. Poets (Disting. mem., Cert. of Achievemnt), Bardic Coll., Delta Psi Omega, Beta Phi Gamma, Kappa Alpha Mu. Libertarinan. Avocations: computers, reading.

GOLLANCE, ROBERT BARNETT, ophthalmologist; b. N.Y.C., Oct. 25, 1937; s. Harvey and Sarah (Chinitz) G.; m. Carmen Côté Gollance, Nov. 8, 1969; 1 child, Stephen Andrew. BA cum laude, Harvard Coll., 1958; MD, Columbia Coll., 1962. Diplomate Am. Bd. Ophthalmology, Nat. Bd. Med. Examiners. Intern in medicine NYU-Bellevue, 1962-63, resident and chief resident in ophthalmology, 1963-66; fellowship NIH, 1964-69; sec.-treas. Ophthalmology Assocs., Wayne, N.J., 1970-93; pres. Eye Assocs. of Wayne, 1993—; lectr. in ophthalmology Columbia U., N.Y.C., 1998-2001; adv. bd. for devel. UMDNJ, 2002—. Chmn. ophthalmology Chilton Meml. Hosp., Pompton Plains, N.J., 1987-89, pres. med. staff, 1991; mem. great hands adv. com. Becton Dickinson Corp., Franklin Lakes, N.J., 1990—; mem. adv. com. Bausch & Lomb Corp., Rochester, N.Y., 1980-83; mem. found. bd. Eye Inst. of the N.J. Med.-Dental Sch.; mem. faculty various courses on cataract surgery and lens implantation; cons. Pharmacia Corp. Clin. Rsch. Glaucoma Medications, 2002—. Contbr. articles to profl. jours. Chmn. parent's fund raising Loomis Chaffee Sch., Windsor, Conn., 1989-90. Capt. U.S. Army, 1966-68. Recipient Letter of Appreciation Korean Opthalomology Soc., 1967, Cath. Med. Ctr., 1967. Fellow ACS, Am. Soc. Cataract and Refractive Surgery, Am. Acad. Ophthalmology, European Soc. Cataract and Refractive Surgery. Office: Eye Assocs of Wayne 968 Hamburg Tpke Wayne NJ 07470-3225 E-mail: rbgollance@yahoo.com., rbgollance@njeyeinstitute.com.

GOLLATA, JAMES ANTHONY, library director, educator; b. Manitowoc, Wis., Aug. 18, 1945; s. Anthony Francis and Evelyn Marion (Terens) G.; children: Davis, Adrian. BS, U. Wis., 1969, MA, 1973. Libr. dir. Mt. Senario Coll., Ladysmith, Wis., 1974-87, U. Wis., Richland Center, 1987—. Pres. Wis. Ctr. for the Book, Madison, 1997-98, bd. dirs. Author numerous poems; contbr. articles to profl. jours. Mem. Wis. Libr. Assn. (newsletter editor 1986—, Literary award 1984-87, 96-99), Wis. Acad. Scis., Arts and Letters (chmn. Gordon MacQuarrie com. 1997). Avocations: music, art, book collecting, theater, acting. Home: 489 S Ira St Richland Center WI 53581-2617 Office: Univ Wis 1200 US Hwy 14 W Richland Center WI 53581-1316

GOLLEHER, GEORGE, food company executive; b. Bethesda, Md., Mar. 16, 1948; s. George M. and Ruby Louise (Beecher) Golleher; 1 child, Carly Lynn. BA, Calif. State U., Fullerton, 1970. Supr. acctg. J.C. Penney, Buena Park, Calif., 1970-72; sys. auditor Mayfair Markets, Los Angeles, 1973, v.p., CFO, 1982-83; contr. Fazio's, Los Angeles, 1974-78; group contr. Fisher Foods, Ohio, 1978-79; v.p. fin. Stater Bros. Markets, Colton, Calif., 1979-82; sr. v.p., CFO Boys Markets Inc., Los Angeles, 1983-95; CEO Ralph Grocery Co., Compton, Calif., 1995-99; pres., COO Fred Meyer Inc., Portland, Oreg., 1997-99; chmn. Farrs Supermarkets, Albuquerque, 2001—. Office: Farrs Supermarkets PO Box 1037 Placitas NM 87043-1037

GOLLIN, RITA KAPLAN, English literature educator; b. Bklyn., Jan. 22, 1928; d. Max and Sophie (Horowitz) Kaplan; m. Richard M. Gollin, Jan. 1, 1950; children: Kathryn Gollin Marshak, Michael, James. BA, Queens Coll., 1949; MA, U. Minn., 1950, PhD, 1967. Asst. prof. English U. Rochester, N.Y., 1955-67; from asst. prof. to prof. English SUNY, Geneseo, 1967-95, Disting. prof., 1995—2002, emeritus prof., 2002—. Lectr. in field. Author: Nathaniel Hawthorne and the Truth of Dreams, 1979, Portraits of Nathaniel Hawthorne: An Iconography, 1983, (with John Idol) Prophetic Pictures: Hawthorne's Knowledge and Uses of The Visual Arts, 1991, Annie Adam Fields: Woman of Letters, 2001-02; contbr. chpts. to books, articles to profl. jours. Recipient House of Seven Gables Hawthorne award, 1984; Grace Ellis Ford fellow, 1955, Huntington Libr. fellow, 1984, 88, NEH sr. fellow, 1984-85, Geneseo Found. grantee, various yrs., 1975—, NEH travel grantee, 1988-89, others. Mem. MLA (chair 19th Century Am. Lit. divsn.), Am. Lit. Assn., N.E. MLA (pres.), Nathaniel Hawthorne Soc. (pres.), Phi Beta Kappa. E-mail: gollin@aol.com.

GOLLIN, STUART ALLEN, accountant; b. Bronx, N.Y., Aug. 7, 1941; s. Samuel and Suggie (Schreiber) G.; m. Harriet Joy Friedlander, Aug. 16, 1964; children: Deborah Lynn, Mark David, Adam Douglas, Seth Craig. BBA, CCNY, 1963. CPA, N.Y., N.J. Ptnr., nat. dir. retailing Touche Ross & Co., Newark, 1963-80; ptnr., nat. dir. retailing, nat. dir. bankruptcy and insolvency, dir. litigation and ins. cons. svcs. Laventhol & Horwath, N.Y.C., 1980-90; ptnr. in charge bankrupty litig. support and ins. cons. David Berdon & Co., N.Y.C., 1990-92; v.p. insolvency Buccino & Assocs., N.Y.C., 1993-94; dir. litig. and appraisal svcs. J.H. Cohn & Co., N.Y.C., 1994-96; mng. dir. corp. transactions KPMG Peat Marwick, N.Y.C., 1996-97, Morrison & Gollin LLP, N.Y.C., 1998—. Bd. dirs. Dad's Club of Hartsdale, Mid-Westchester YM/YMHA; treas. Am. Liver Found.; bd. dirs. The Transplant Living Ctr.; pres. Scarsdale Sports Assn. Mem. AICPA, N.Y. State Soc. CPAs, Am. Bankruptcy Inst., Nat. Cert. Insolvency & Reorgn. Acct., N.J. Soc. CPAs (acctg. and auditing stds., rels. with bankers, rels. with fin. writers coms., rels. with credit unions, chmn. bankruptcy and involvency com., litig. support com.), Nat. Assn. Accts. (dir. Westchester chpt.), Turnaround Mgmt. Assocs., Nat. Retail Mchts. Assn., Nat. Mass Retailers Inst., N.J. Retail Mchts. Assn., Met. Retail Fin. Execs. Assn., White Plains Jaycees, Bergen County C. of C., Ardsley Swim Club (dir.), Ridgeway Country Club, Beta Alpha Psi. Home: 34 Benedict Rd Scarsdale NY 10583-7340

GOLLINGS, RUTH ERICKSON, community health nurse; b. Oakland, Calif., July 19, 1944; d. Merland Walter and Astrid Christine (Sundberg) Erickson; m. Richard Haworth Gollings, Jan. 15, 1977; children: Eric Haworth, Sara Joy. Diploma, Mounds Midway, 1965; BSN, U. Colo., 1967; cert., Multnomah Sch. of the Bible, 1969; MA in Nursing, U. Wash., 1976. RN, Calif. Instr. in nursing Mesa Coll., Grand Junction, Colo.; asst. prof. nursing Seattle Pacific U.; lectr. in nursing Calif. State U., L.A.; missionary nurse Bapt. Gen. Conf. Global Ch. Planting, Arlington Heights, Ill.

GOLLOB, HERMAN COHEN, retired publishing company, editor; b. Waco, Tex., July 7, 1930; s. Abe and Ruybe (Cohen) G.; m. Barbara Kowal, Apr. 9, 1961; children: Emily, Jared. BA, Tex. A & M U., 1951. Lit. agt. MCA, Beverly Hills, Calif., 1956-58, William Morris, N.Y.C., 1958-59; editor Little, Brown & Co., Boston, 1959-64, Atheneum Pubs., N.Y.C., 1964-68, v.p., editor-in-chief, 1971—; editor-in-chief Harper's Mag. Press, N.Y.C., 1968-71; v.p., editorial dir. The Literary Guild, N.Y.C., 1979-81; v.p., sr. editor Simon & Schuster, N.Y.C., 1981-86; sr. v.p., editor-in-chief Doubleday Pub. Co., 1986-90, editor-at-large, 1990-95; ret., 1995. Author: Me and Shakespeare, 2002. Served to lt. USAF, 1951-53. Home: 40 Frederick St Montclair NJ 07042-4106

GOLLOBIN, LEONARD PAUL, chemical engineer; b. N.Y.C., July 2, 1928; s. Morris and Jennie (Levine) G.; m. Charlotte Weissman, Jan. 21, 1951; children: Michael L., Susan D. Brown. BSChemE, CUNY, 1951; MS, Kans. State U., 1952; grad. mgmt. program, Harvard U., 1975. Design engr. Foster Wheeler Corp., N.Y.C., 1952-55; mfg. engr. Gen. Electric Co., Waterford, N.Y., 1955-58; program dir. ORI, Inc., Silver Spring, Md., 1958-63; chmn, chief exec. Presearch, Inc., Fairfax, Va., 1963—. U.S. del. NATO Indsl. Avd. Group, 1989, chmn., 1992-93, chmn. emeritus, 1994-95; bd. visitors Nat. Def. U., Washington, 1989-98. Bd. dirs. Cultural Alliance Greater Washington, 1980-88, northern Va. bd. Va. Opera, 2000-01; trustee Washington Opera, 1988-90. Recipient NSIA Adrm. Charles Weakley award, 1986, Meritorious Pub. Svc. award U.S. Dept. Navy, 1987, U.S. Marine Corps, 1989. Mem. Nat. Security Indsl. Assn. (exec. com. 1986—, chmn. antisubmarine warfare com. 1981-84, chmn. amphibious warfare com. 1986-89, chmn. environ. com. 1990-92, chmn. internat. com. 1991-93, vice chmn. exec. com. 1993, chmn. 1994, chmn. bd. trustees 1994-95), Nat. Def. Indsl. Assn. (chmn. fin. com. 1998—), Naval Undersea Warfare Found. Mus., Loudon Golf and Country Club (Purcellville, Va.). Home: 6710 Bradley Blvd Bethesda MD 20817-3045 Office: Presearch Inc 8500 Executive Park Ave Fairfax VA 22031-2223

GOLOBY, GEORGE WILLIAM, JR., environmental scientist, editor, ornithologist, aviculturist; b. Franklin, Ky., Mar. 21, 1949; s. George William Sr. and Katherine Jacqueline (Panchot) G.; m. Diane Grayson, Dec. 29, 1974; children: Amy Vanessa, George William III. BS in Wildlife Sci., Tex. A&M U., 1971. Zookeeper of birds Houston Zool. Gardens, 1971-72; warehouseman, driver Houston Ind. Sch. Dist., 1972-76; lab. mgr. Empak Inc., Houston, 1976-80; asst. sect. chief City of Houston Dept. Pub. Works, 1980-90; environ. quality specialist III City of Houston Dept. Pub. Works & Engring., 1990—. Founder, owner Penfeathers Tours, Houston, 1984—; instr. Houston Arboretum and Nature Ctr., 1999; instr. Tex. birding cert. Armand Bayou Nature Ctr., U. Houston, 1999—. Editor (newsletters) Water Environment Assn. Tex. (WEAT) Pipeline 1984-2001,(advtg. manager 2001-), Tex. Ornithol. Soc. Newsletter, 1989-99, Penfeathers Newsletter, 1986—, Panchot Paper, 1989-93, Houston Audubon Soc., 1977-80, The Naturalist, 1986-89; asst. editor (books) Houston, 1978, Encyclopedia of American Cities, 1979; advt. mgr. Tex. WET Mag., 2002—. Mem. Houston Proud, 1986, Cy-Fair Houston C. of C., 1986, Greater Houston Conv. and Vis. Bur., 1986-88. Mem. Water Environ. Assn. Tex. (com. chmn. 1984—), Tex. Water Utilites Assn., Houston Audubon Soc. (v.p. adminstrv. affairs 1986-89), Am. Birding Assn., Outdoor Nature Club, Parrot People Club (v.p. Houston chpt. 1985-86), Purple Martin Conservation Assn., Whooping Crane Conservation Assn., Tex. Nature Conservancy. Office: City Houston 4545 Groveway Dr Houston TX 77087-1122 E-mail: pfcompany@aol.com.

GOLODNER, JACK, labor association official; b. NYC, Nov. 2, 1931; s. Maurice S. and Regina (Gaber) G.; m. Linda Louise Fowler, June 14, 1964; children: Dean Dovid, Daniel Dimmick, Jonathan Wilmot. BS, Cornell U., 1953; JD, Yale U., 1958. Labor arbitrator, Washington, 1958-60; exec. asst. to U.S. Congressman Giaimo, 1960-62; cons. pub. affairs, 1962-80; exec. sec. Coun. AFL-CIO Unions for Profl. Employees, 1967-77; dir. dept. for profl. employees AFL-CIO, 1977-89, pres., 1989—2001. V.p. bd. trustees Ford's Theater, Washington, 1973-79, Actors Studio, NY, 1982-87; bd. dir. Nat. Theatre, 1978—; mem. gen. bd. Am. Coun. for the Arts, 1981-96; presdl. appointee Nat. Info. Infrastructure adv. coun., 1994-96; mem. adv. coun. nat. orgns. Corp. Pub. Broadcasting, 1973-79; mem. Labor Adv. Com. for Multilateral Trade Negotiations of Dept. of Labor, 1975-2002; mem. arts and humanities com. Pres.'s Commn. on Internat. Women's Year, 1975-76; mem. US del. UNESCO govtl. experts meeting, Paris, 1980; US del. to adv. com. on salaried and profl. workers Internat. Labor Orgn., 1981, 85, 94, US labor del. Plenary Internat. Labor Orgn. Conf., 1981, 82; chmn. labor del. tripartit meeting on salaried authors and inventors, 1987, Internat. Labor Orgn.; mem. coun. Cornell U., 1987-93; chmn., mem. adv. coun. Cornell Sch. of Indsl. and Labor Rels., 1980-88, 90-94, mem. outside rev. com., 1986-87; mem. US govt. delegation Diplomatic Conf. on Certain Copyright and Neighboring Rights Questions, World Intellectual Property Orgn., Geneva, 1996. Capt. USAF, 1953-55. Recipient William B. Groat award Cornell U., 1979 Mem. Indsl. Rels. Rsch. Assn. (exec. bd. 1993-96), Internat. Secretariat Arts, Mass Media and Entertainment Trade Unions (world v.p. 1987-93), Media and Entertainment Internat. (1st v.p. 1993-97), Nat. Policy Assn. (exec. com. New Am. Realities Program 1987-2003, co-chair nat. digital econ. opportunity com. 2000-2002), Phi Kappa Phi. Office: 1140 Conn Ave NW Washington DC 20036

GOLOMB, BEATRICE ALEXANDRA, physician, medical researcher; b. Pasadena, Calif., May 16, 1959; d. Solomon W. Golomb; m. Terrence Joseph Sejnowski, Mar. 24, 1990. BS in Physics summa cum laude, U. So. Calif., 1979; PhD in Biology, U. Calif. at San Diego, 1988, MD, 1989. Resident VA Hosp. West L.A., 1990-93, chief resident, 1993-94; Robert Wood Johnson clin. scholar UCLA,, 1994—96; mem. faculty medicine U. Calif., San Diego, 1998—, mem. faculty dept. psychology, 2001—, mem. faculty dept. family and preventive medicine, 2002—, prin. investigator statin study, 1999—; mem. staff dept. psychology U. So. Calif., 1998—. Sci. dir. rsch. adv. com. on gulf war illness Dept. VA, 2002—. Mem. Phi Kappa Phi. Office: U Calif San Diego Dept Medicine 0995 9500 Gilman Dr La Jolla CA 92093

GOLOMB, DAVID BELA, lawyer; b. Bklyn., Apr. 19, 1949; s. Maurice and Rita (Pick) G.; m. Lisa Ann Cutler, June 17, 1984. BA, Cornell U., 1970; JD, St. John's U., 1974. Bar: N.Y. 1975, U.S. Dist. Ct. (so. dist.) N.Y. 1977, U.S. Dist. Ct. (ea. dist.) N.Y. 1978, U.S. Ct. Appeals (2d cir.) 1979, U.S. Supreme Ct. 1979. Trial atty. N.Y.C. Legal Aid Soc., 1974-77; adminstr. N.Y.C. Office of Dep. Mayor, 1977-78; spl. asst. atty. gen. N.Y. State Office of Medicaid Fraud Control, 1978-80; trial atty. Fuchsberg and Fuchsberg, N.Y.C., 1980-83, Paul D. Rheingold, PC, N.Y.C., 1983-84; ptnr. Rheingold & Golomb PC, N.Y.C., 1984-87; pvt. practice N.Y.C., 1987—. Lectr. ABA Nat. Inst. on Med. Malpractice, 1985, Ross Labs. Ann. Roundtable on Pediats., 1986. Mem. ABA, ATLA (N.Y. state del. 1992-94, gov. 1994—, exec. com. 2000—), Am. Bd. Trial Advs., Am. Inn of Ct., N.Y. State Bar Assn., Assn. of Bar of City of N.Y. (tort litigation com.), N.Y. State Trial Lawyers Assn. (bd. dirs. 1990-92, parliamentarian 1992-93, treas. 1993-95, sec. 1995-96, 2d v.p. 1996-97, 1st v.p. 1997-98, pres.-elect 1998-99, pres. 1999-2000, immediate past pres. 2000-01, chmn. jud. screening com., chmn. med. malpractice com., mem. com. on state legis., co-chmn. seminars on malpractice), N.Y. County Lawyers Assn. Home: 40 Hampton Rd Scarsdale NY 10583-3025 Office: Law Office David B Golomb 230 Park Ave Ste 527 New York NY 10169-0005 E-mail: golomblaw@aol.com.

GOLOMB, FREDERICK MARTIN, surgeon, educator; b. N.Y.C., Dec. 18, 1924; s. Jacob J. and Hannah (Loewy) G.; m. Joan E. Schneider, Nov. 28, 1954; children: James Bradley, Susan Lynn. BS, Yale U., 1945; MD, U. Rochester, 1949. Diplomate: Am. Bd. Surgery. Intern Johns Hopkins Hosp., 1949-50; resident NYU Hosp., 1950-56; pvt. practice specializing in surg. oncology N.Y.C.; mem. staff NYU Med. Center, 1950—, dir. chemoimmunotherapy divsn. tumor svc. dept. surgery, 1967-96; attending surgeon Tisch Hosp.; vis. surgeon Bellevue Hosp.; mem. faculty NYU Sch. Medicine, 1956—, prof., clin. surgery, 1977—. Cons. N.Y.C. div. Am. Cancer Soc., 1968—; mem. clin. trials rev. com. Nat. Cancer Inst., 1976-79; chmn. melanoma com. Eastern Coop. Oncology Group, 1978-80; prin. investigator Central Oncology Group, 1969-77, exec. com., 1976-77; mem. met. med. com. Chemotherapy Found.; co-prin. investigator Ea. Coop. Oncology Group NYU, 1978-95. Contbr. articles to profl. jours. Served with M.C. AUS, 1953-54, Korea. Recipient John E. Sullivan award Beth Israel Med. Ctr., 1993. Fellow ACS; mem. AMA, Soc. Head and Neck Surgeons, Am. Assn. Cancer Rsch., Am. Soc. Clin. Oncology, N.Y. Cancer Soc. (pres. 1974-75), N.Y. Surg. Soc., N.Y. State Med. Soc., N.Y. County Med. Soc., Soc. Surg. Oncology, George Hoyt Whipple Soc., Brit. Assn. Surg. Oncology (editl. adv. panel 1980-85), Am. Alpine Club, Explorers Club, Sigma Xi. Office: 910 Fifth Ave New York NY 10021 E-mail: frederick.golomb@med.nyu.edu.

GOLOMB, GEORGE EDWIN, lawyer; b. Newark, Jan. 28, 1947; s. Max and Elizabeth G.; m. Cynthia Lifson, 1984. BA, Yale U., 1968; JD, U. Pa., 1972. Bar: N.Y. 1974, N.J. 1977, D.C. 1985, Md. 1985. Law clk. to judge U.S. Dist. Ct. (ea. dist.) N.Y., Bklyn., 1974-76; trial atty. civil div. U.S. Dept. Justice, Washington, 1980-84, 1980-84; pvt. practice Balt., 1986—. Contbr. articles to profl. jours.; co-author: Federal Trial Guide, Federal Evidence Practice Guide, 1989. Fellow, Hague Acad., 1971, Phelps Assn. fellow, 1967. Mem. Balt. City Bar Assn. (exec. com. mem. 1986-96, 1999-2000, 02—, sec. 2003—), Md. State Bar Assn. (bd. govs. 1995-97, 2000-02, labor and employment law, chmn. CLE com. 2002—, com. on professionalism 1997-2002), Md. Inst. for Continuing Profl. Edn. for Lawyers (trustee 2002—). Office: 111 S Calvert St Ste 2700 Baltimore MD 21202-6143 E-mail: goegle@erols.com.

GOLOMB, HARVEY MORRIS, oncologist, educator; b. Pitts., Feb. 13, 1943; s. Russell Austin and Dorothy (Simon) G.; m. Lynne Rooth, Dec. 28, 1965; children: Adam, Sara. BA, U. Chgo., 1964; MD, U. Pitts., 1968. Diplomate Am. Bd. Internal Medicine, Am. Bd. Med. Oncology. Intern Boston City Hosp., 1968-69; resident Johns Hopkins U., Balt., 1971-72, fellow, 1972-73, U. Chgo., 1973-75, asst. prof. dept. medicine, 1975-79, assoc. prof., 1979-83, prof., 1983—, chief sect. hematology/oncology, 1981-98, chmn. dept. medicine, 1998—. Chmn. subspecialty bd. med. oncology Am. Bd. Internal Medicine, 1991-95. Contbr. over 300 articles, papers to profl. publs.; co-editor: Lung Cancer, 1988. Capt. U.S. Army, 1971-73. Mem. Am. Soc. Hematology (bd. dirs. 1987-91), Am. Soc. Oncology (pres. elect 1989-90, pres. 1990-91). Office: U Chgo MC 6092 5841 S Maryland Ave Chicago IL 60637-1463 E-mail: hgolomb@medicine.bsd.uchicago.edu.

GOLOMB, HERBERT STANLEY, dermatologist; b. Sept. 6, 1933; m. Suzanne Nazer, Dec. 20, 1964; children: Meredith, Valerie. AB, U. Pa., 1955; MD, SUNY, Bklyn., 1960. Diplomate Am. Bd. Dermatology. Intern Ohio State U. Hosp., Columbus, 1960—61; resident in dermatology SUNY-Kings County Med. Ctr., 1961—62, NYU Skin and Cancer Unit and Bellevue Hosp., N.Y.C., 1962—64; pres. Falls Church (Va.) Med. Ctr., 1963—64; practice medicine specializing in dermatology Falls Church, 1964—66, 1968—; mem. staff George Washington U. Hosp., Fairfax (Va.) Hosp., Arlington (Va.) Hosp. Instr., then clin. assoc. prof. dermatology George Washington U. Sch. Medicine, 1964—; cons. USPHS Dermatology Clinic, 1964—66; chmn. Atlantic Dermatol. Conf., 1978. Fellow: Am. Acad. Dermatology; mem.: AMA, Va. Dermatol. Soc., DC Dermatol. Soc., Fairfax County Med. Soc., DC Med. Soc., Med. Soc. Va., Internat. Soc. Tropical Dermatology, Soc. Investigative Dermatology, Tuckahoe Swim and Tennis Club. Home: 1910 Woodgate Ln Mc Lean VA 22101-5441 Office: 6060 Arlington Blvd Falls Church VA 22044-2943 E-mail: SueHerb@erols.com.

GOLOMB, SOLOMON WOLF, mathematician, electrical engineer, educator, university official; b. Balt., May 31, 1932; s. Elhanan Hirsh and Minna (Nadel) G. AB, Johns Hopkins U., 1951; MA, Harvard U., 1953, PhD, 1957; postgrad., U. Oslo, 1955-56; DSc (hon.), Dubna Internat. U., Russia, 1995; DHL (hon.), Hebrew Union Coll., L.A., 1996. Mem. faculty Boston U., 1954-55, Harvard U., 1954-55, UCLA, 1957-61, Calif. Inst. Tech., 1960-62; sr. research engr. Jet Propulsion Lab., Pasadena, Calif., 1956-58, research group supr., 1958-60, asst. chief telecommunications research sect., 1960-63; assoc. prof. U. So. Calif., L.A., 1963-64, prof. elec. engring. and math., 1964—, vice provost for research, 1986-89, univ. prof., 1993—, dir. tech. Annenberg Ctr. for Comms., 1995-98, Viterbi prof. comms., 1997—. Cons. to govt. and industry Author: Digital Communications with Space Applications, 1964, 81, Polyominoes, 1965, rev. edit., 1994, Shift Register Sequences, 1967, 82, Basic Concepts in Information Theory and Coding, 1994; contbr. articles to profl. jours. Recipient Presdl. medal U. So. Calif., 1985, Lomonosov medal Russian Acad. Sci., 1994, Kapistsa medal Russian Acad. Natural Scis., 1995, Disting. Alumnus award Johns Hopkins U., 2000. Fellow IEEE (Shannon award Info. Theory Soc. 1995, Hamming medal 2000), AAAS, Am. Acad. Arts and Scis.; mem. NAS, NAE, AAUP, Internat. Sci. Radio Union, Russian Acad. Natural Scis. (fgn.), Am. Math. Soc., Math. Assn. Am., Soc. Indsl. and Applied Math., Golden Key, Phi Beta Kappa, Sigma Xi, Pi Delta Epsilon, Eta Kappa Nu, Phi Kappa Phi. Office: U So Calif Univ Park Dept Elec Engring Eeb 504A Los Angeles CA 90089-0001

GOLOMBEK, SERGIO GUSTAVO, pediatrician, neonatologist, educator; b. Buenos Aires, May 14, 1959; s. Jaime Y. Golombek and Luisa R. Grunin; m. Karin Friederwitzer, Jan. 11, 1991; children: Gabriel David, Alexander. MD, U. Buenos Aires, 1983. Tng. in peds., Argentina; intern R. Blank Meml. Hosp. for Children, Des Moines, 1991—92, resident in pediatrics, 1992—93; fellow in neonatal perinatal medicine Children's Mercy Hosp., Kansas City, Mo., 1993-96; asst. prof. pediatrics SUNY, Stony Brook, 1996-99, Westchester Med. Ctr./NY Med. Coll., Vallhalla, 1999—2003, assoc. prof. pediatrics, 2003—, attending neonatologist. Jewish. Avocation: tennis. Office: Westchester Med Ctr NY Med Coll Vallhalla NY 10595 Fax: 914-493-1488. E-mail: sgolombek@pol.net., sergio_golombek@nymc.edu.

GOLON, MARYANNE, photojournalist; Picture editor Time Mag., NY, NY, 1983—99; coord. photographic coverage of the Olympic Games for Time mag., 1984—; photography editor of the Gulf War for Time and Life mag., Dhahran and Saudi Arabia, 1991—92; dir. of Photog. US News and World Report, 1999—2002; picture editor Time Mag., NY, NY, 2002—. Recipient Afred Eisenstaedt Award, Mag. Photgraphy; fellow On the Jury of Visa Pour L[00b0]Image, Pepignand. Mem.: Eddie Adams Workshop (Bd. of dir.). Office: Time 315 W End Ave New York NY 10023*

GOLONDZINIER, THEODORE MATTHEW, civil engineer; b. L.A., Feb. 25, 1943; s. Constant and Anna Alice G.; m. Lily Delia Anderson, June 25, 1966; children: Lori Louise, Traci Elaine. BSE, UCLA, 1966; MS in Indsl. Engring., Tex. A&M U., 1970. Registered profl. engr., Ohio, civil engr., Calif. From plans and programs officer to dep. support group comdr. USAF, 1966-87; from acting supr. to supr. Rohr Industries, Riverside, Calif., 1987-89; planning assoc., acting divsn. chief County of San Bernardino, Calif., 1989-92, divsn. chief transp. and flood control dept., 1992—2000, asst. dir. ops., 2000—. Contbr. articles to profl. jours. Mem.: ASCE, NSPE (chpt. pres. 1992—93, state dir. 1993—95, state v.p. 1997—99, state chmn. profl. engrs. in govt. 1994—96, Outstanding Engr. Yr. 1993), Am. Pub. Works Assn. (bd. dirs. local chpt. 2002—), Inst. Indsl. Engrs., Phi Kappa Phi, Alpha Pi Mu. Avocations: camping, gardening, computer programming. Office: County of San Bernardino Dept Pub Works 825 E 3rd St San Bernardino CA 92415-0085

GOLOVERSIC, MARY CECELIA, writer; b. Ishpeming, Mich., Jan. 7, 1941; d. Clyde Edward and Myrtle Jane Brandt; m. James Patric Goloversic Sr., Apr. 25, 1964; children: James Jr., Timothy, David. BS, No. Mich. U., 1963, M, 1968. Tchr. NICE Sch. Dist., Ishpeming, Mich., 1963—67, 1969—70, substitue tchr., 1966—92. Author: Iron Heart, 2002, living on the Edge, 2002, Raging Fire, 2002. Treas. Boy Scouts, Ishpeming. Avocations: artwork, piano, organ, singing, travel, rock collecting, camping, antiques.

GOLPHIN, ELOUISE, writer, educator; b. Augusta, Ga., Aug. 4, 1950; d. Lewis R. Golphin and Ruby M. Adderley; life ptnr. Descombe Wells Gray; children: Lanita Brinson, Tavezia Williams-Dunson, John Williams, Sabrina Cater, Timothy Yarbrough(dec.), Romanieo, Rutherford Wilson. A in Gen. Studies, Ga. Mil. Jr. Coll., Ft. Gordon, 1984; BS, Brenau Profl. Coll., Gainesville, Ga., 1990. Author: Poetry for All Reasons, 1994, Poetry for All Reasons Book II, 1999, CHEMO: My Son's Struggle With Cancer, 1999, Read, It's Fun!, Poetry for All Reasons Book III, 2003. Mem.: NAACP, Zeta Phi Beta. Baptist. Avocations: writing, travel, reading. Home: 2686 Crosscreek Rd Hephzibah GA 30815-7600 Office: Poetry for All Reasons 2686 Crosscreek Rd Hephzibah GA 30815-7600 Home Fax: 707-796-8043; Office Fax: 706-796-8043. E-mail: weezyg4@bellsouth.net.

GOLSHANI, FOROUZAN, computer science and engineering educator; b. Mashhad, Iran, Oct. 27, 1953; came to U.S., 1984; s. Azizullah and Khadijeh (Momtaz) G.; m. Rezvanieh Mazloom, Apr. 7, 1984; children: Ashkahn Edward, Afsaneh Aimee, Andrew Arian. BS, Arya Mehr U. Tech., Tehran, 1976; MS, U. Warwick, Coventry, Eng., 1979, PhD, 1982. Project mgr. Gen. Sys., Tehran, 1976-78; rsch. fellow Imperial Coll., London, 1982-84; from asst. prof. to assoc. prof. Ariz. State U., Tempe, 1984-95, prof., 1995—. Bd. dirs. Active Image Recognition Corp.; cons. Bull Worldwide Info. Sys., Phoenix, Ariz., 1988-97, Honeywell, Mpls., 1993-96, Frost & Sullivan, London, 1995-97, Motorola, Phoenix, 1997—; gen. chair IEEE Internat. Conf. on Computers and Comm., 1989, IEEE Internat. Conf. on Data Engring., 1992, IEEE Internat. Conf. on Distibuted Computing Sys., 2001; program chair ACM Internat. Conf. on Info. and Knowledge Mgmt., 1997. Editor-in-chief: IEEE Multimedia, 2002—. Co-founder Corp. Enhancement Group, Phoenix, 1995, Roz Software Sys., Inc., Scottsdale, Ariz., 1997. Mem. IEEE (sr., Disting. Spkr. 1990-93, gen. chmn. internat. conf., 1989, 92, 2001, program chmn., 1997), Computer Sci. Accreditation Bd. (team chair 1995-2001), Corp. Enhancement Group Phoenix (co-founding). Baha'I. Achievements include 9 inventions in field. Office: Ariz State U Dept Computer Sci Tempe AZ 85287-5406

GOLTZ, MARK NEIL, environmental engineer; b. Bklyn., July 1, 1951; s. Seymour and Harriet (Champagne) G.; m. Mi Suk So, Feb. 14, 1977; children: Hugh, Eric. BSEE, Cornell U., 1972; MS in Sanitary Engring., U. Calif., Berkeley, 1973; PhD in Environ. Engr., Stanford U., 1986. Lic. profl. engr., diplomate, environ. engr. Commd. 2d lt. USAF, 1972, advanced through grades to lt. col., 1989, ret., 1993; assoc. prof. environ. engring. Air Force Inst. Tech., Wright-Patterson AFB, Ohio, 1986-93; acting assoc. prof. dept. civil engring. Stanford (Calif.) U., 1993-96; prof. Air Force Inst. Tech., Wright-Patterson AFB, Ohio, 1996—. Asst. dir. Western Region Hazardous Substance Rsch. Ctr., 1993-96; mem. sci. adv. com. Great Lakes/Mid-Atlantic Hazardous Substance Rsch. Ctr., 1996-2001. Contbr. articles to profl. jours. Mem. environ. adv. com. City of Beavercreek, 1997—. Recipient Air Force Mil. Engr. of Yr., NSPE, 1992, Air Force Sci. Achievement award USAF, 1987, Air Force Meritorious Svc. medal USAF, 1978, 82, 93; New Zealand Crown Inst. for Environ. Sci. and Rsch. internat. fellow, 2002. Mem. Soc. Am. Mil. Engrs. (bd. dirs. Kittyhawk Post 1990-93, edn. com. chmn., 2002—), Assn. Environ. Engring. and Sci. Profs., Am. Geophys. Union, Am. Acad. Environ. Engrs. Home: 7143 Hunters Crk Dayton OH 45459-3468 Office: Dept Sys and Engring Mgmt Air Force Inst Tech 2950 Hobson Way Bldg 640 Wright Patterson Afb OH 45433-7765 E-mail: mark.goltz@afit.edu., mngoltz@aol.com.

GOLTZ, ROBERT WILLIAM, physician, educator; b. St. Paul, Sept. 21, 1923; s. Edward Victor and Clare (O'Neill) G.; m. Patricia Ann Sweeney, Sept. 27, 1945; children: Leni, Paul Robert. BS, U. Minn., 1943, MD, 1945. Diplomate: Am. Bd. Dermatology (pres. 1975-76). Intern Ancker Hosp., St.

Paul, 1944-45; resident in dermatology Mpls. Gen. Hosp., 1945-46, 48-49, U. Minn. Hosp., 1949-50; practice medicine specializing in dermatology Mpls., 1950-65; clin. instr. U. Minn. Grad. Sch., 1950-58, clin. asst. prof., 1958-60, clin. assoc. prof., 1960-65, prof., head dept. dermatology, 1971-85; prof. medicine and dermatology U. Calif., San Diego, 1985—, acting chair divsn. dermatology, 1995-97; prof. dermatology, head div. dermatology U. Colo. Med. Sch., Denver, 1965-71. Former editorial bd.: Archives of Dermatology; editor: Dermatology Digest. Served from 1st lt. to capt., M.C. U.S. Army, 1946-48. Mem. Assn. Am. Physicians, Am. Dermatol. Assn. (dir. 1976-79, pres. 1985-86), Am. Soc. Dermatopathology (pres. 1981), Am. Dermatologic Soc. Allergy and Immunology (pres. 1981), AMA (chmn. sect. on dermatology 1973-75), Dermatology Found. (past dir.), Minn. Dermatol. Soc., Soc. Investigative Dermatology (pres. 1972-73, hon. 1988), Histochem. Soc., Am. Acad. Dermatology (pres. 1978-79, past dir.) (hon.), Brit. Assn. Dermatology (hon.), Chilean Dermatology Soc. (hon.), Colombian Dermatol. Soc. (corr. mem.), Can. Dermatol. Soc. (hon. mem.), German Dermatol. Soc. (hon.), Pacific Dermatol. Soc. (hon.-mem.), S. African Dermatol. Soc. (hon. mem.), N.Am. Clin. Dermatol. Soc., Assn. Profs. Dermatology (sec.-treas. 1970-72, pres. 1973-74), West Assn. Physicians. Home: 6097 Avenida Chamnez La Jolla CA 92037-7404 Office: U Calif San Diego Med Ctr Divsn Dermatology H-8420 200 W Arbor Dr San Diego CA 92103-1911

GOLTZMAN, DAVID, endocrinologist, educator, researcher; b. Montreal, Que., Can., Sept. 22, 1944; s. Jack and Lily (Roth) G.; m. Naomi Lyon, Dec. 29, 1968; children: Jonathan, Rebecca, Daniel. BSc, McGill U., 1966, MD, 1968. Diplomate Am. Bd. Internal Medicine, Am. Bd. Endocrinology and Metabolism. Med. intern Royal Victoria Hosp., Montreal, 1968-69; med. resident Columbia U. Coll. Physicians and Surgeons, N.Y.C., 1969-71; clin. and rsch. fellow in endocrinology Mass. Gen. Hosp., Boston, 1971-75; instr. medicine Harvard Med. Sch., Boston, 1974-75; asst. prof. medicine McGill U., Montreal, 1976-78, assoc. prof., 1978-83, prof., 1983—, chmn. physiology, 1988-93, dir. calcium rsch. lab., 1981—, hosmer prof. physiology, 1992-93, Massabki prof. medicine, 1994—; chmn. medicine, 1994—. Sr. physician dept. medicine Royal Victoria Hosp., 1987-94, physician-in-chief, 1994-98; physician-in chief, McGill U. Hlth. Ctr., 1998—; chmn. exptl. medicine com. Med. Rsch. Coun. Can., Ottawa, Ont., 1984-88; mem. gen. medicine B study sect., NIH, Bethesda, Md., 1987-91; active Exec. Med. Rsch. Coun. Can., 1993—. Author: (with others) Principles of Bone Biology, 2001, Primer of Metabolic Bone Disease and Disorders of Mineral Metabolism, 1996, 1989, Primer of Osteoporosis, 2000, Principles and Practice of Endocrinology and Metabolism, 2001; editl. bd. Endocrinology Jour., 1985-90, Jour. Bone Mineral rsch., 1985-90, Bone and Mineral, 1991-94, Osteoporosis Internat., 1991-94, Assoc. Edn. Bone, 1989-94; assoc. editor: Jur. Bone Mineral research, 1995—; contbr. numerous articles to profl. jours. Recipient Chercheur Boursier award Que. Med. Rsch. Coun., 1980-83, Scientist award Med. Rsch. Coun. Can., 1983-88, Andre Lichtwitz prize Nat. Inst. for Med. Rsch., France, 1987; named officer Order of Can., 2000—. Fellow Royal Coll. Physicians and Surgeons, Royal Soc. Canada; mem. Can. Soc. Endocrinology and Metabolism (pres. 1990-92), Am. Soc. for Bone and Mineral Rsch. (chmn. program com. 1989-90, pres. 1999-00), Am. Assn. Physicians, Endocrine Soc. (program com. 1989-91), Can. Soc. Clin. Investigation (councillor 1986-89, pres. 1998-99) Am. Soc. Clin. Investigation, Canadian Assn. Profs. of Medicine (pres. 1998-99). Avocations: classical music, gardening, tennis. Office: Royal Victoria Hosp 687 Pine Ave W Montreal QC Canada H3A 1A1 E-mail: david.goltzman@mcgill.ca.

GOLUB, LEWIS, supermarket company executive; b. 1931; BS, Mich. State U., 1953; LHD (hon.), SUNY--Empire State Coll., 1998. With Golub Corp., 1953—, v.p., 1963 71, exec. v.p., 1971-72, pres., treas., 1972-82, chmn. bd., 1982—, also chief exec. officer, dir. Bd. dirs. Taylor Made Co., CIES; mem. regional adv. bd. Chase Bank. Advisor MBA program Russell Sage Coll.; mem. adv. coun. grad. mgmt. inst. Union Coll.; bd. dirs. Empire State Coll. Found., Saratoga Performing Arts Ctr., Proctor's Theatre, Food Mktg. Inst., N.Y. State Bus. Coun.; active Found. SUNY. Served with U.S. Army. Recipient Marketer Exec.-Citizen award Sales and Mktg. Execs. Ea. N.Y., 1988, Disting. Citizen award SUNY, 1989, Dr. Norman D. Kathan Cmty. Svc. award YMCA, 1990, Tree of Life award Jewish Nat. Fund, 1992, Disting. Cmty. Svc. award Chinese Cmty., 1993, Cmty. Svc. award Inter-Faith Cmty. of Schenectady, 1993, Cmty. Svc. accolate Northeastern N.Y. chpt. Arthritis Found., 1993, Achievement award Am. Diabetes Assn., 1994, Disting. Citizen Laureate award U. Albany Found., 1994, John J. O'Connor Excellence in Leadership award United Way, 1995, Disting. Citizen award Boy Scouts Am., 1995, N.Y. State Chiefs of Police, 1995, Cmty. Svc. awar Office of Aging, 1996, Legends of the Industry award N.Y. State Food Mchts. Assn., 1996; named Man of Yr., Am. Jewish Com., 1981, Exec. of Yr., The Capital Dist. Bus. Rev., 1989, Humanitarian of Yr., Ctr. for Disabled, 1999; named to Hall of Fame, Capital Region Bus., 1997, Jr. Achievement, 1997; Paul Harris hon. fellow Rotary Internat., 1992. Office: Golub Corp 501 Duanesburg Rd Schenectady NY 12306-1092*

GOLUB, NEIL, supermarket chain executive; b. 1937; married. BA, Mich. State U., 1959; MS, Cornell U., 1961. With Golub Corp., Schenectady, N.Y., 1962—, asst. sec., 1967-72, v.p., 1972-77, exec. v.p., 1977-82, pres., COO, 1982—2000, pres., CEO, 2000—. Served with U.S. Army. Office: Golub Corp 501 Duanesburg Rd Schenectady NY 12306-1092*

GOLUB, SHARON BRAMSON, psychologist, educator; b. N.Y.C., Mar. 25, 1937; m. Leon M. Golub, June 1, 1958; children: Lawrence E., David B. Diploma, Mt. Sinai Hosp. Sch. Nursing, 1957; BS, Columbia U., 1959, MA, 1966; PhD, Fordham U., 1974. Head nurse Mt. Sinai Hosp., N.Y.C., 1957-59; contbg. editor RN Mag., Oradell, N.J., 1967-74; asst. prof. psychology Coll. New Rochelle, N.Y., 1974-79, assoc. prof., 1979-86, prof., 1986-98, prof. emeritus, 1998—, dir. women's studies, 1978-79, chmn. dept. psychology, 1979-82; pvt. practice individual and group psychotherapy Harrison, N.Y., 1976—. Adj. prof. psychiatry N.Y. Med. Coll., Valhalla, 1980-94. Editor: Menarche, 1983 (Assn. Women in Psychology Disting. Pub. award 1984, Book of Yr. award Am. Jour. Nursing 1984), Lifting the Curse of Menstruation, 1983, Health Care of the Female Adolescent, 1984, Health Needs of Women as They Age, 1984, PERIODS from Menarche to Menopause, 1992; (with Rita Jackaway Freedman) Psychology of Women: Resources for a Core Curriculum, 1987; editor Women and Health, 1982-86, mem. editorial bd., 1986—; mem. editorial bd. Psychology of Women Quar., 1989-2000. Grantee Nat. Libr. Medicine, 1983-84; NIH rsch. fellow, 1971-74. Fellow Am. Psychol. Assn. (chmn. task force on teaching psychology of women 1980-83), Am. Psychol. Soc.; mem. Soc. for Menstrual Cycle Rsch. (pres. 1981-83, bd. dirs. 1981-93), Assn. Women in Psychology, Westchester County Psychol. Assn. (pres. acad. divsn., Disting. Svc. award 2003), Phi Beta Kappa, Sigma Xi, Psi Chi. Office: Coll New Rochelle Dept Psychology New Rochelle NY 10805 E-mail: sharongol@aol.com.

GOLUBEVA, ANNA, mathematician, application developer; b. ST. Petersburg, Russia, Feb. 1, 1968; PhD in Math., St. Petersburg State U., 1993. Cert. SCJP for Java 2 Platform Sun Microsystems. Prof. St. Petersburg State U. of Telecom.; cons. St. Petersburg AeroSpace U., 2000—01; software developer Parametric Tech. Corp., Boston, 2001—. Scholar, St. Petersburg State U., 1985—92. Mem.: St. Petersburg Math. Soc.

GOLUBITSKY, MARTIN AARON, mathematician, educator; b. Phila., Apr. 5, 1945; s. Isaac and Rose (Sarvetnick) G.; m. Barbara Lee Keyfitz, May 30, 1976; children: Elizabeth Ann, Alexander. AB, AM, U. Pa., 1966; PhD, MIT, 1970. Vis. lectr. UCLA, 1970-71; lectr. MIT, Cambridge, 1971-73; asst. prof., then assoc. prof. Queens Coll., CUNY, N.Y.C., 1973-79; prof. math. Ariz. State U., Tempe, 1979-83, U. Houston, 1983—. Co-author: Stable Mappings and Their Singularities, 1978, Singularities and Groups in Bifurcation, vols. I and II, 1985, 88, Fearful Symmetry, 1992, Symmetry in Chaos, 1992, Linear Algebra and Differential Equations Using MATLAB, 1999, The Symmetry Perspective, 2002; editor-in-chief SIAM Jour. Applied Dynamic Systems, 2001—; mem. editl. bd. Dynamics and Differential Equations, 1990—, Jour. Nonlinear Sci., 1990—. Cullen prof. U. Houston, 1989. Fellow AAAS; mem. Am. Math Soc., Soc. Indsl. and Applied Math. (v.p. at large). Home: 6419 Sewanee St Houston TX 77005-3759 Office: Univ Houston Dept Math 4800 Calhoun Rd Houston TX 77204-3008 E-mail: mg@uh.edu.

GOLUBOCK, RHONA, lawyer; b. Suffern, NY, May 22, 1969; BA, Emory U., 1991; JD, Benjamin N. Cardozo Sch. Law, N.Y.C., 1994. Bar: N.Y. 1995, N.J. 1994. Atty. Instinct Records, N.Y.C., 1995-98; corp. cousnel Am. Softworks Corp., Darien, Conn., 1998—2000; assoc. gen. counsel Net2Phone, Newark, 2000—01; staff atty. Heineken USA Inc., 2002—. Vol., Dem. Party, N.Y.C., 1995-96, Jewish Home and Hosp. for the Aged, N.Y.C., 1996-98. Mem. ABA, N.Y. State Bar Assn., B'nai B'rith. Avocations: reading, sports.

GOLUSIN, MILLARD R. obstetrician and gynecologist; b. Detroit, Feb. 14, 1947; s. Raddie and Joan (Lalich) G.; m. Yvonne Marie Cronovich, Sept. 29, 1974; children: Milan, Marko, Matthew. BS with honors, Wayne State U., 1968, MS, 1970, MD, 1975. Diplomate Am. Bd. Obstetrics and Gynecology. Intern, then resident William Beaumont Hosp., Royal Oak, Mich., 1975-78; practice medicine specializing in obstetrics and gynecology Village Gynecologic and Obstetric Assocs., P.C., Southfield and Troy, Mich., 1978-92; pvt. practice specializing in obstetrics and gynecology Troy, Mich., 1992-98; assoc. Wilshire Obstetrics-Gynecol. Assocs. PC, Troy, 1998—. Mem. quality assurance com. William Beaumont Hosp., Royal Oak, Mich., 1979—, mem. gynecol. quality assurance com., 1993—; charter mem., pres. Preferred Ob-Gyn. Mgmt. Group L.L.C. Trustee, mem. credentials com. Preferred Provider Network, 2000; trustee United Beaumont Physicians Group, 1993—. Served with U.S. Army, 1969-71. Fellow ACOG; mem. Am. Soc. Reproductive Medicine, Mich. State Med. Soc., Am. Inst. Ultrasound Medicine, Serbian Singing Soc., Ravanica (musical dir. 1967—, pres. 1981-82). Republican. Serbian Eastern Orthodox. Avocations: music, golf. Office: Wilshire Obstetrics-Gynecol Assocs PC 4600 Investment Dr Ste 170 Troy MI 48098-6369

GOMBERG, EDITH S. LISANSKY, psychologist, educator; b. N.Y.C., Jan. 14, 1920; d. Barnet and Dorothy (Resnick) Silverglied; m. Henry Jacob Gomberg, June 24, 1967; children: Stephen, Judith, Eugene, Richard, Robert. MA, Columbia U., 1940; PhD, Yale U., 1949. Lectr., rsch. asst., rsch. assoc. Center Alcohol Studies, Yale U., New Haven, 1949-67; assoc. prof. dept. psychology U. P.R., 1968-71; prof. Sch. Social Work, U. Mich., Ann Arbor, 1974-90; prof. psychology, dept. psychiatry U. Mich., Ann Arbor, 1988-99, prof. emerita, 1999—. Author: Gender and Disordered Behavior, 1979, Alcohol, Science and Society Revisited, 1982, Current Issues in Alcohol/Drug Studies, 1989, Drugs and Human Behavior: A Sourcebook for the Helping Professions, 1991, Women and Substance Abuse, 1993, Alcohol and Aging, 1995, Alcohol Problems and Aging, 1998; contbr. chpts. to books, articles to profl. jours. Mem. Rep. Town Meeting, Hamden, Conn., 1964-65; mem. Blue Ribbon Study Commn. on Alcoholism and Aging, Nat. Council on Alcoholism, 1979-82; chmn. panel on prevention, study to assess sci. opportunities of alcohol-related research Inst. Medicine, Nat. Acad. Sci.; mem. alcohol psychosocial research rev. com. Nat. Inst. Alcohol Abuse and Alcoholism, 1981-82. Mary E. Ives fellow, 1944; AAUW Elizabeth Avery Colten fellow, 1955 Mem. Psychonomic Soc., Sociedad Interamericana de Psicología, Rsch. Soc. on Alcoholism, Sigma Xi. Jewish. Home: 430 Hillspur Rd Ann Arbor MI 48105-1049 Office: U Mich Addiction Rsch Ctr 400 E Eisenhower Pkwy Ann Arbor MI 48108-3318

GOMBERG, SYDELLE, dancer educator; m. Ralph Gomberg. Student, Met. Opera Ballet Sch.; studies with Pierre Vladimiroff, Anatole Oboukoff, Edward Caton, Anatole Vilzak, Vincenzo Celli, Margaret Craske. Dir. Boston Ballet Sch., until 1993; faculty mem. Boston Converatory of Music; resident master teacher Walnut Hill School, Natick, Mass., 1993-96; guest tchr., mem. adv. bd. Walnut Hill Sch., Natick, Mass., 1996—. Performed with Met. Opera Ballet, Radio City Ballet; soloist (Broadway play) Lute Song starring Mary Martin and the Late Yul Brynner. Founder dance dept. All Newton Music Sch., Walnut Hill Sch., 1971-85, apptd. dean arts, trustee, adv. bd. mem.; regional sec. Royal Acad. Dancing; mem. dance panel Mass. Coun. on the Arts and Humanities; chmn. spl. com. Dance Edn. Home: 93 Pilgrim Rd Concord MA 01742

GOMBOCZ, ERICH ALFRED, biochemist; b. Vienna, Aug. 29, 1951; came to U.S., 1990; s. Erich and Maria (Mayer) G.; m. Gisela M. Dorner, June 12, 1973 (div. Apr. 1992); 1 child, Manfred Alexander (dec.). Cert., T.U., Vienna, 1970-75. With Fed. Inst. for Food Analysis and Rsch., Vienna, 1975-90, head of sect. dept. biochem. analysis, 1980-90, contbr. Cen. Lab. Info. Mgmt. System, 1987-90; chmn. scientific adv. bd. LabIntelligence, Inc., Menlo Park, Calif., 1989-99, COO, v.p. R & D, 1989-99; chief sci. officer NucleoTech Corp., San Mateo, Calif., 1999-2000; chief sci. officer, chief tech. officer Biosentients, Inc., Emeryville, Calif., 2000—03; v.p., chief sci. officer IO Informatics, Inc., Emeryville, 2003—. Speaker and lectr. in field. Editor: Computers in Electrophoresis; contbr. articles to profl. jours.; patentee in field. Postdoctoral Rsch. award NIH, Bethesda, Md., 1985-86, 88. Mem. Internat. Assn. for Cereal Chemistry, Internat. Electrophoresis Soc., Am. Electrophoresis Soc., Am. Chem. Soc., N.Y. Acad. Scis., Microsoft Developers Network, Silicon Valley Computer Soc. Roman Catholic. Office: IO Informatics Inc 2000 St Ste 520 Emeryville CA 94608 E-mail: egombocz@ix.netcom.com.

GOMER, ROBERT, chemistry educator; b. Vienna, Mar. 24, 1924; m. Anne Olah, 1955; children: Richard, Maria. BA, Pomona Coll., 1944; PhD in Chemistry, U. Rochester, 1949; AEC fellow chemistry, Harvard, 1949-50. Instr. dept. chemistry James Franck Inst. U. Chgo., 1950-51; asst. prof., 1951-54, assoc. prof., 1954-58, prof., 1958-96, Carl William Eisendrath Disting. Service prof., 1984-96, prof. emeritus, 1996—. Dir. James Franck Inst. U. Chgo., 1977-83 Bd. dirs. Bull. Atomic Scientists, 1960-84. Served with AUS, 1944-46. Recipient Kendall award in surface chemistry Am. Chem. Soc., 1975, Davisson Germer prize Am. Phys. Soc., 1981, Medard W. Welch award Am. Vacuum Soc., 1989, Arthur W. Adamson award Am. Chem. Soc., 1996; Sloan fellow, 1958-62, Guggenheinm fellow, 1969-70; Bourke lectr. Eng., 1959. Mem. Leopoldina Acad. Scis., Nat. Acad. Scis., Am. Acad. Arts and Sci. Home: 4824 S Kimbark Ave Chicago IL 60615-1916 Office: 5640 S Ellis Ave Chicago IL 60637-1433 E-mail: r-gomer@uchicago.edu.

GOMERY, DOUGLAS, communications educator, writer; b. N.Y.C., Apr. 5, 1945; s. John Edgar and Julia (Halsted) G.; m. Marilyn L. Moon, Jan. 13, 1973. BS, Lehigh U., 1967; MA, U. Wis., 1970, PhD, 1975. Asst. prof. mass communication U. Wis., Milw., 1974-79, assoc. prof., 1980, U. Md., College Park, 1981-87, prof., 1987—. Sr. rschr. media studies project Woodrow Wilson Ctr. for Internat. Scholarship, Washington, 1988-92; vis. prof. Northwestern U., Evanston, Ill., 1980, U. Iowa, Iowa City, 1982, U. Utrecht, The Netherlands, 1990, 92; cons. Am. Film Inst., Washington, 1982-90. Author: High Sierra, 1979; author: (with Annette Michelson) The Art of Moving Shadows, 1989; author: (with Robert C. Allen) Film History: Theory and Practice, 1985; author: The Hollywood Studio System, 1986; author: (with Phil Cook and L.W. Lichty) American Media, 1988; author: Movie History: A Survey, 1991, Shared Pleasures, 1992 (Am. Theater Libr. Assn. Book award, 1992); author: (with Ben Compaine) Who Owns the Media, 2000 (AEJMC Picard prize award, 2001); author: The FCC's Newspaper-Broadcast Cross-Ownership Rule: An Analysis, 2002; editor: The Will Hays Papers, 1987, The Future of News, 1992; : Media in America, 1998; : mem. editl. bd.: Cinema Jour., 1983—92, Jour. Media Econs., 1989—, Jour. Film and Video, 1983—, contbg. editor: Screen, 1984—89, Iris, 1983—89, Jour. of Comm., 1995—; editor: Marquee, 1991; columnist: Am. Journalism Rev., 1995—, author more than 500 articles. Cons. Joint Com. on Landmarks Washington, 1983, 85, 86, 90, NEH, 1980—, Nat. Endowment Arts, 1980—, Md. State Hist. Preservation Office, 1988, Voice of Am., Nat. Gallery Art., Wis. Dept. Revenue, 1978; trustee Am. Film Inst., 1986-89. Mem. Theatre Hist. Soc. (chmn. Weiss award com. 1984-87, bd. dirs. 1987-89, Weiss prize 1988), Soc. Cinema Studies, Univ. Film and Video Assn. (editorial bd. jours. 1983-92), Broadcast Edn. Assn., Assn. for Edn. in Journalism and Mass Comm., Internat. Comm. Assn. Avocation: economics. Home: 4817 Drummond Ave Chevy Chase MD 20815-5428 Office: U Md Coll Journalism College Park MD 20742-0001 E-mail: dgomery@jmail.umd.edu.

GOMES, NORMAN VINCENT, retired industrial engineer; b. New Bedford, Mass., Nov. 7, 1914; s. John Vincent and Georgianna (Sylvia) G.; m. Carolyn Moore, June 6, 1942 (dec. Apr. 1983); m. Helen Groesbeck Kurzawa, Apr. 22, 1995. BS in Indsl. Engring. and Mgmt., Okla. State U., 1950; MBA in Mgmt., Xavier U., 1955. Asst. chief engr. Leschen divsn. H.K. Porter Co., St. Louis, 1950-52; staff mfg. cons. GE Co., Cin., 1952-57; lectr. indsl. mgmt. U. Cin., 1955-56; staff indsl. engr. Gen. Dynamics, Ft. Worth, 1957-60; chief ops. analysis Ryan Elecs., San Diego, 1960-64; sr. engr. Jet Propulsion Lab. Calif. Inst. Tech., Pasadena, 1964-67, mem. tech. staff, 1967, mgr. mgmt. sys., 1967-71; industry rep. and cons. U.S. Commn. Govt. Procurement, Washington, 1970-72; adminstrv. officer GSA, Washington, 1973-78, program dir., 1979. Vis. lectr. indsl. mgmt. Xavier U. Grad. Sch. Bus. Adminstrn., 1956-57; vis. lectr. mgmt. San Antonio Coll., 1982-85. Active Sierra Internat., v.p. membership San Antonio chpt., 1991-92, mem. Drug and Alcohol Adv. Coun., N.E. Ind. Sch. Dist., San Antonio, 1989-95. Maj. C.E. AUS, 1941-46. Decorated Army Commendation medal, Armed Svcs. Res. medal; recipient Apollo Achievement award, 1969, Outstanding Performance award GSA, 1974-75, 76, 77, 79. Mem. Am. Inst. Indsl. Engrs. (nat. chmn. prodn. control rsch. com. 1951-57, bd. dirs. Cin., Fort Worth, San Diego, L.A., San Antonio chpts. 1954-84, pres. Cin. chpt. 1956-57, pres. L.A. chpt. 1970-71, nat. dir. cmty. svcs. 1969-73), Ret. Officers Assn. U.S. (chpt. pres. 1968-69, recipient Nat. Pres. cert. Merit 1969), Nat. Security Indsl. Assn. (mgmt. systems subcom. 1967-69), Vis. Nurse Assn. San Antonio (mem. adv. coun. 1988-95), Freedoms Found. at Valley Forge (v.p. edn. and youth leadership programs San Antonio chpt. 1987-89), Pillars San Fernando Cathedral, Old Dartmouth Hist. Soc., Equestrian Order of Holy Sepulchre Jerusalem (knight comdr. with star), KC (4th deg.). Republican. Roman Catholic. Home: c/o Cravey 2103 A La Casa Dr Austin TX 78704 E-mail: h.k.gomes@aol.com.

GOMES, PETER JOHN, clergyman, educator; b. Boston, May 22, 1942; s. Peter L. and Orissa Josephine (White) G. AB, Bates Coll., Lewiston, Maine, 1965; STB (Rockefeller fellow 1967-68), Harvard U., 1968; DD (hon.), New Eng. Coll., 1974; LHD (hon.), Waynesburg Coll., 1978; HumD (hon.), Gordon Coll., 1985; LittD (hon.), Knox Coll., 1987; DD (hon.), U. South, 1989, Bates U., 1997; LHD (hon.), Duke U., 1997, U. Nebr., 1997. Ordained to ministry Am. Bapt. Ch., 1968. Instr. history, dir. freshmen exptl. program Tuskegee (Ala.) Inst., 1968-70; asst. minister, then acting minister Meml. Ch. Harvard U., 1970-74, minister Meml. Ch., 1974—, Plummer prof. Christian morals, 1974—. Nat. chaplain Am. Guild Organists, 1978-82; hon. fellow Emmanuel Coll., U. Cambridge, Eng., vis. prof. Duke U., Durham, N.C., 1993-94; Brecher lectr. Yale Divinity Sch., 1998. Author: Proclamation Series Commentaries, Lent, 1985, Proclamation Series Lent, 1995, History of Harvard Divinity School, 1992, Good Book, 1996, Sermons, 1998, Sundays at Harvard, 1995, 96, 97, 98; co-author: Books of the Pilgrims; editor: Parnassus, 1970, History of the Pilgrim Society, 1970; editor: Harvard Divinity School History, 1992; edtl. bd. Pulpit Digest. Trustee Bates Coll., 1973-78, 80-94, Pilgrim Soc., 1970—, pres. 1989, 93, Charity of Edward Hopkins, 1974—, Donation to Liberia, 1973—, Plimoth Plantation, 1977—, Roxbury Latin Sch., 1982—, Wellesley Coll., 1985—, Boston Found., 1985—, Plymouth Pub. Libr., 1985—; acting dir. W.E.B. DuBois Inst. for Afro-Am. History Harvard U., 1990—. Fellow Royal Soc. Arts; mem. Royal Soc. Ch. Music, Colonial Soc. Mass., Mass. Hist. Soc., Handel and Hayden Soc. (trustee), New Eng. Conservatory (trustee), Signet Soc. (pres.), Country Day Sch. Headmasters Assn. (hon.), Phi Beta Kappa. Clubs: Tavern. Office: Harvard U Meml Ch Cambridge MA 02138

GOMES, WAYNE REGINALD, academic administrator; b. Modesto, Calif., Nov. 15, 1938; s. Frank C. and Mary (Rogers) G.; m. Carol L. Gerlach, Sept. 2, 1964 (deceased); children: John Charles, Regina Carol. BS, Calif. Poly. State U., 1960; MS, Wash. State U., 1962; PhD, Purdue U., 1965. Asst. prof. dairy sci. Ohio State U., Columbus, 1965-69, assoc. prof. dairy sci., 1969-72, prof. dairy sci., 1972-81; prof., head dept. dairy sci. U. Ill., Urbana, 1981-85, prof., head dept. animal scis., 1985-89, acting dean Coll. Agr., 1988-89, dean, 1989-95; v.p. agr. and natural resources U. Calif. System, Oakland, 1995—. Fulbright prof. Zagreb U., Yugoslavia, 1974, vis. scholar Kyoto U., Japan, 1980; mem. bd. on agr. and natural resources NRC. Editor: The Testis, Vols. 1-4, 1970-77; contbr. over 100 articles to jours. and chpts. to books. Mem. Coun. for Agrl. Sci. and Tech., Am. Soc. of Animal Sci., Am. Dairy Sci. Assn., Soc. for Study of Reprodn., Endocrine Soc., others. Lodges: Rotary. Office: U Calif 1111 Franklin St Oakland CA 94607-5201

GOMEZ, CARLOS GUILLERMO, artist, educator, curator; b. Mexico City, Mex., May 3, 1952; s. Isidoro Gonzalez Dosal and Librada Cuellar Gómez; m. Guillermina Gómez, Aug. 4, 1976; children: Laura-Kristina, Fernando-Christo. BFA, Pan Am. U., 1977; MFA, Wash. State U., 1979. Instr. Tex. Southmost Coll., Brownsville, 1985—2003; prof. fine arts U. Tex., Brownsville, 1992—. Exhibited in more than 33 one-man shows, including La Pena Gallery Austin, 2003, Rio Grande Valley Mus., 2000, U. Tex. Brownsville, 2000, more than 100 group exhbns., including 79th Am. Ann. at Newport, R.I., Latin Spirit of the 80s, Houston, Art in Nature at Natural History Mus., Austin, Tex., Brownsville (Tex.) Hist. Mus., 2002, U. Tex. Brownsville, 2002, Boise State U., 2001, Wichita, Kans., 2001, Austin Mus. of Art, 1997 Grantee Gorgas Sci. Found., 1996. Mem. Museo Atzlan, South Tex. Inst. for the Arts, Mexic-Arte Mus., public collections: Hispan Rsch. Ctr., Arizona St. Un. Art Museum of S. Texas, Mexic-Arte Mus., U.S.D.I.F.W.S. Avocations: fishing, off-road driving. Office: U Tex 80 Ft Brown Brownsville TX 78520 E-mail: CGomez@utb1.utb.edu.

GOMEZ, DAVID FREDERICK, lawyer; b. LA, Nov. 19, 1940; s. Fred and Jennie (Fujier) G.; m. Kathleen Holt, Oct. 18, 1977. BA in Philosophy, St. Paul's Coll., Washington, 1965, MA in Theology, 1968; JD, U. So. Calif., 1974. Bar: Calif. 1975, US Dist. Ct. (cen. dist.) Calif. 1975, US Dist. Ct. (ea. dist.) Calif. 1977, Ariz. 1981, US Dist. Ct. Ariz. 1981, US Ct. Claims 1981, US Ct. Appeals (9th cir.) 1981, US Supreme Ct. 1981; ordained priest Roman Cath. Ch., 1969; law clk. Law clk./staff atty. Nat. Labor Rels. Bd., Los Angeles, Calif., 1974-75; ptnr. Gomez, Paz, Rodriguez & Sanora, Los Angeles, Calif., 1975-77, Garrett, Bourdette & Williams, San Francisco, 1977-80, Van O'Steen & Partners, Phoenix, 1981-85; pres. Gomez & Petitti, PC, Phoenix, 1985—. Faculty Practicing Law Inst., 1989; instr. contracts law Nat. Lawyers Guild, Peoples Coll. Law, 1975-76; mem. Missionary Soc. St. Paul the Apostle (Paulist Fathers), 1963-75; jud. oversight coun. ltd. jurisdiction Cts. Maricopa County, 2002—. Author: Somos Chicanos: Strangers in Our Own Land, 1973; co-author: Advanced Strategies in Employment Law, 1988, Arizona Employment Law Handbook, Vol. 2, 1995. Fellow: Ariz. Bar Found.; mem.: ABA, Ariz. State Bar Assn. (com. on rules of profl. conduct 1991—97, civil jury instrns. com. 1992—94, peer rev. com. 1992—2000, task force on future of the legal profession 1998—2001), Ariz. Employment Lawyers Assn. (bd. dirs. 1996—), Calif. State Bar Assn., Nat. Employment Lawyer's Assn., Los Abogados Hispanic Bar Assn., Maricopa County Bar Assn. Democrat. Office: 2525 E Camelback Rd Ste 860 Phoenix AZ 85016-4279 E-mail: dfg@gomezlaw.net.

GOMEZ, FRANCIS DEAN, corporate executive, former foreign service officer; b. Belle Fourche, SD, July 24, 1941; s. Frank Garcia and Mae Elizabeth (Larive) G.; m. Esperanza Narino, Sept. 30, 1966; children: Frank T., Laura E. BA, U. Wash., 1964; MS in Adminstrn., George Washington U., 1982; cert. in translation, NYU, 1995. With US Info. Agy, 1965; asst. cultural affairs officer Bogotá, Colombia, 1965-67, San José, Costa Rica, 1968-71; Caribbean desk officer, 1971-72; writer, editor West Hemisphere Newswire, 1972-73; mid-career fellow USIA, Princeton, NJ, 1973-74; pub. affairs officer Am. Embassy, Bamako, Mali, 1974-76, pub. affairs, 1976-78; chief fgn. service personnel USIA, Washington, 1978-80; dep. asst. sec. pub. affairs Dept. State, Washington, 1980-82; dir. fgn. press centers USIA, Washington, 1984—88; cons. pub. affairs Washington, 1986—2001; dir. pub. affairs Philip Morris Mgmt. Corp., NYC, 1988—; dir. media rels. and exec. outreach Altria Corp. Svcs., Inc., 2001—. Adj. faculty NYU, 1995—. Founder, pres. Hispanic Employees Coun., Dept. State, 1979-81; trustee WETA TV, Washington, 1983-86; bd. dir. Nat. Hispanic Scholarship Fund, 1991-94; pres. bd. dir. Pan Am. Devel. Found. Recipient Superior Honor award USIA, 1967, Meritorious Honor awards, 1976, 78, Annual Agy. EEO award, 1980; named Outstanding Young Men Am. US Jaycees, 1968, NYU Outstanding Svc. award, 2000. Mem. Am. Fgn. Svc. Assn., Nat. Assn. Hispanic Journalists, Nat. Press Club, Hispanic Coun. Internat. Rels., Princeton Club NY, Pi Alpha Alpha. Office: Altria Corp Svcs Inc 120 Park Ave 25th Flr New York NY 10017-5592

GOMEZ, LOUIS SALAZAR, college president; b. Santa Ana, Calif., Dec. 7, 1939; s. Louis Reza and Mary (Salazar) G.; m. Patricia Ann Aboytes, June 30, 1962; children: Louis Aboytes, Diana Maria, Ramon Reza. Student, Calif. State Poly. U., 1959-65; BA, Calif. State U., San Bernardino, 1971; MA, Calif. State U., 1975; EdD, U. So. Calif., L.A., 1987. Cert. tchr., counselor, adminstr., Calif. Tchr., counselor San Bernardino City Schs., 1971-76; human rels. coord. San Bernardino Valley Coll., 1976-78, counselor, 1978-82, coord. of counseling, 1982-87; asst. dean student svcs. Crafton Hills Coll., Yucaipa, Calif., 1987-89, dean student svcs., 1989-90, acting pres., 1990-92, pres., 1992—. Lectr. Calif. State U., San Bernardino, 1976-81, mem. adv. bd., 1987-95. Bd. dirs. Redlands YMCA, 1995—; pres. San Bernardino Regional Emergency Tng. Ctr. Joint

Power Authority, 1998—. Mem. San Bernardino Valley Coll. Faculty Assn. (treas. 1980-82), Faculty Assn. Calif. Community Colls., San Bernardino Community Coll. Dist. Mgmt. Assn., Kiwanis (pres. San Bernardino chpt. 1982). Democrat. Roman Catholic. Avocations: financial planning, photography, treasure hunting. Home: 10682 Berrywood Cir Yucaipa CA 92399-5924 Office: Crafton Hills Coll 11711 Sand Canyon Rd Yucaipa CA 92399-1742

GOMEZ, LUIS OSCAR, Asian and religious studies educator, clinical psychology educator; b. Guayanilla, P.R., Apr. 7, 1943; s. Manuel Gomez and Lucila Rodriguez; m. Ruth Cedenia Maldonado, Dec. 24, 1963; children: Luis Oscar, Jr., Miran Ruth. BA, U. P.R., 1963; PhD Asian Langs. and Lit., Yale U., 1967; MA in Clin. Psychology, U. Mich., 1991, PhD, 1998. Lic. clin. psychologist. Vis. asst. prof. U. P.R., Rio Piedras, 1967, lectr., 1969-70, assoc. prof., 1970-73; assoc. prof. dept. Asian langs. and cultures U. Mich., Ann Arbor, 1973-80, prof. Buddhist studies, prof. religious studies dept. Asian langs. and cultures, 1980—, chmn. dept., 1981-89, 2002—, prof. psychology dept. psychology, 1999—. Vis. asst. prof. U. Wash., Seattle, 1967-68; Evans-Wentz Disting. lectr. Stanford (Calif.) U., 1983, vis. prof., 1985; vis. prof. Otani U. Kyoto, Japan, 1991-94. Author: The Land of Bliss, 1996; co-editor: Barabudur, Problemas de Filosofia, Studies in the Literature of the Great Vehicle, 1989. Mem. Am. Psychol. Assn., Soc. for Sci. Study Religion, Am. Acad. Religion, Internat. Assn. Buddhist Studies (gen. sec. 1986-89), Assn. Asian Studies. Home: 3204 Lockridge Dr Ann Arbor MI 48108-1722 Office: U Mich Dept Asian Langs & Cultures 105 S State St Ann Arbor MI 48109-1285

GOMEZ, LYNNE MARIE, lawyer; b. Highland Park, Ill., May 9, 1952; d. John Ferdinand and Lucille Elizabeth (Devereaux) G.; m. William Joseph Coffey, Dec. 17, 1977; 1 child William Joseph Coffey III.. B.A., U. Tex.-Austin, 1972, M.A., 1974, J.D., 1977. Bar: Tex. 1977, U.S. Dist. Ct. (so. dist.) Tex. 1978, U.S. Ct. Appeals (5th Cir.) 1981, U.S. Dist. Ct. (we. dist.) Tex. 1984, U.S. Supreme Ct. 1983. Sole practice, Houston, 1978; staff atty. U.S. Dist. Ct., Houston, 1979-81; judicial clk. U.S. Dist. Judge, Houston, 1981-83; assoc. Blackburn, Gamble, & Henderson, Houston, 1983— ; adj. prof. law U. Houston, 1984— . Vol. March of Dimes, Houston, 1979-80, Am. Heart Assn., Houston, 1980-81, mem. com. to celebrate the Bicentennial of the Constn., dir. The Women's Advocacy Group, The Sheltering Arms, Houston, 1981— ; mem. The Met. Orgn., Houston, 1982— . Mem. ABA, State Bar Tex., Houston Young Lawyers' Assn. (chmn. courthouse visitation com. 1980-82), Am. Bus. Women's Assn. (sec. 1982-83, treas. 1983-84), Democrat. Roman Catholic. Office: Blackburn Gamble & Henderson 1900 West Loop S Ste 800 Houston TX 77027-3214

GOMEZ, MANUEL RODRIGUEZ, physician; b. Minaya, Spain, July 4, 1928; came to U.S., 1952, naturalized, 1961; s. Argimiro Rodriguez Herguedas and Isabel Gomez Torrente; m. Joan A. Stormer, Sept. 25, 1954; children: Christopher, Gregory, Douglas, Timothy. MD, U. Havana, Cuba, 1952; MS in Anatomy, U. Mich., 1956. Intern Michael Reese Hosp., 1952-53, asst. resident in pediatrics, 1953-54; resident in neurology U. Mich., 1954-56; fellow in pediatric neurology U. Chgo. Med. Sch., 1956-57; instr. neurology U. Buffalo Med. Sch., 1957-58, 59-60; clin. clk. neurology Inst. Neurology, U. London, 1958-59; asst. prof., then assoc. prof. neurology Wayne State U. Med. Sch., 1960-64; mem. faculty Mayo Med. Sch., Rochester, Minn., 1964—, prof. pediatric neurology, 1975—, emeritus prof. pediatric neurology, 1994—. Cons. pediatric neurology, head sect. Mayo Clinic, 1964-84, sr. cons. 1992—; vis. prof. King Faisal Hosp., Riyjadh, Saudia Arabia, 1994, Children's Hosp. Miami, 1995, Seville, Spain, 1995. Author: Tuberous Sclerosis, 1979, 2nd edit., 1988, 3d edit., 1999, Neurocutaneous Diseases, 1987; co-editor: Tuberous Sclerosis and Allied Disorders, 1991, Neurologia y Neuropsicologia Pediatrica, 1996; adv. bd. Brain and Devel., Pedriatrika. Recipient Ramón y Cajal award Academia Iberoamericana de Neuropediatría, 1995. Mem. Am. Acad. Neurology, Am. Neurol. Assn., Child Neurology Assn. (founder, former pres., Hower award 1989), N.Y. Acad. Scis., Philippine Pediatric Soc. (hon.), Sociedad Española de Neurologia (hon.), Sociedad Española de Neuropediatria (hon.), Assn. Research Nervous and Mental Disease, Orton-Dyslexia Soc. (adv. bd.), Am. Epilepsy Soc., Internat. Child Neurology Soc. (founder), Cen. Soc. Neurol. Research, Nat. Tuberous Sclerosis Assn. (hon. profl. advisor, Leadership award 1994), Sociedad Centroamericana de Neurologia y Neurociugia, Colombian Neurologic Soc. (hon.), Soc. Psiquiatría y Neurologia de Infancia y Adolescencia Chile (hon.), Costarican Neurol. Sci. Soc. (hon.), soc. Argentina de Neurologia Infantil (hon.). Home: 4225 Meadow Ridge Dr SW Rochester MN 55902-6640 Office: Mayo Clinic 200 1st St SW Rochester MN 55905-0001

GOMEZ, NANCY, engineer, architect; b. Cali, Colombia, S.Am., Aug. 18, 1953; came to U.S., 1979; d. Jorge Gomez and Concepcion Carvajal. BArch, U. del Valle, 1977; M in Constrn. Mgmt., Fla. Internat. U., 1996. Registered architect, Colombia. Project mgr. Fla. Dept. of Transport, Miami. Roman Catholic. Avocations: tennis, golf, swimming, biking, reading. Office: Fla Dept of Transp 1000 NW 111th Ave Miami FL 33172-6042

GOMEZ-JIMÉNEZ, CARLOS, science educator, microbiologist, geneticist; b. Mayagüez, P.R., Sept. 1, 1964; s. Carlos Gómez and Emma Jiménez. BS in Biology, U. P.R., Mayagüez, 1986, MS in Microbiology and Genetics, 1991; postgrad., Alliance Theol. Sem., P.R. Tchr. asst. U. P.R., Mayagüez, 1986-88, 91, biochemistry lab. technician, 1988; quality assurance analyst Microbiology and Cell Culture Lab. Ortho Biologics, Inc., Manatí, P.R., 1989-90; prof. Inter Am. U., Aguadilla, P.R., 1991-92, U. P.R., Aguadilla, 1992—, Inter Am. U., San Germán, P.R., ., 1992—; invited prof. Kaplan P.R. Ctr., 1997—; prof. Pontificis Universidad Catolica P.R., 2000—. Cons., advisor Academia Investigación Científica Maestros Estudiantes Talentosos-Inter Am. U., San Germán, P.R., 1992—, Young Scholars Program-NSF-Inter Am. U., San Germán, 1992—; cons. drug, alcohol, violence & HIV/AIDS Prevention programs U. P.R., Aguadilla, 1992—, dir. honor program, 1996—; mem. Nat. Collegiate Honors Coun., 1996—; bd. dirs. Assn. U. de Programas de Estudios de Honor de P.R.; invited prof. Kaplan P.R. Ctr., 1997—. Editor (newsletters) The Probe-Caribbean Soc. Biotech., Inc., 1994—, Biosfera-U. P.R.-Aguadilla, 1994—; contbr. articles to profl. jours. Co-founder Primera Iglesia Bautista de Leguísamo, Mayagüez, 1977—; first tenor Mayagüez Choir, 1994—. Mem. AAAS, Am. Soc. Microbiology, Caribbean Soc. Biotechnology (bd. dirs. 1994—), P.R. Soc. Microbiologists (bd. dirs. 1995—), P.R. Sci. Tchr. Assn., Assn. Para La Ciencia Y La Tech. de Alimentos de P.R., Biostudy I (hon., counselor, bd. dirs. 1997—), Asociacion Universitaria de Programes de Honor de P.R. (bd. dirs. 1997—), Bapt. Student Union (hon.), Beta Beta Beta (hon., Zeta Alpha chpt.). Baptist. Avocations: star trek fan, singing, book collecting, cooking. Home: PO Box 1595 Mayaguez PR 00681-1595 Office: U PR Aguadilla-Dept Nat Scis PO Box 250160 Aguadilla PR 00604-0160

GOMEZ-MARTINEZ, JOSÉ LUIS, Spanish language professional, researcher; b. Soria, Spain, June 1, 1943; came to U.S., 1967; s. José L. and Trinidad (Martinez) G.; m. Beatrice N. de Thibault, Oct. 10, 1967; children: José, Javier, Miguel. BA, Tchr.'s Coll., Bilbao, Spain, 1963; postgrad., Heidelberg U., Federal Republic of Germany, 1964-66; MA, Roosevelt U., 1969; PhD, U. Iowa, 1973. Instr. Union Español, Federal Republic of Germany, 1965-66, Luther Coll., Decorah, Iowa, 1969-70; asst. prof. Augustana Coll., Sioux Falls, S.D., 1972-74, U. Ga., Athens, 1974-78, assoc. prof., 1978-82, prof., 1982-89, rsch. prof., 1989—. Author: Américo Castro, 1975, Teoria del Ensayo, 1981, 2d edit., 1992, España 1991, Chile, 1987, Bolivia, 1988, Discurso Narrativo y Pensamiento de la Liberación, 1993, Más Allá de la posmodernidad, 1999, Hacia un Nuevo paradigma, 2001; editor Los Ensayistas, Athens, Ga., 1976-93, Anuario Bibliográfico, Athens, 1989-94; assoc. editor. 20th Century, Denver, 1986—; contbr. over 100 articles to profl. jours.; grantee NEH, 1983; fellow Guggenheim Meml. Found., 1984-85; recipient Albert-Crist-Janer award, 1988. Mem. Internat. Assn. Spanish Scholars, Am. Assn. Tchrs. of Spanish and Portuguese, Latin Am. Studies Assn., Soc. for Iberian and Latin Am. Thought (pres.), South Eastern Coun. Latin Am. Studies (Sturgis Leavitt prize 1989), Twentieth Century Spanish Assn. Am., Asociación de Hispanismo Filosófico. Office: U Ga Dept Romance Langs Athens GA 30602

GOMIS PORQUERAS, PEDRO, economics eduator; b. Barcelona, June 19, 1971; arrived in US, 1992; s. Joaquin Gomis Torne and Montserrat Porqueras Antonin. BS in physics (honors), U. Tex., 1994, MS in economics, 1998, PhD in economics, 2001. Rsch. asst. Fusion Rsch. Ctr., Austin, Tex., 1993—95; faculty Centro Militar Veterinaria, Madrid, 1995—96; tchr. asst. U. Tex., Austin, 1996—2001, rsch. asst., 1999; vis. scholar Fed. Res. Cleve., 2000; asst. prof. U. Miami, Coral Gables, Fla., 2001—. Author: (rsch.) various profl. jours., 2000—02. Grantee fellowship, U. Tex., 2000. Mem.: Am. Econ. Assn., Sigma Pi Sigma. Avocations: tennis, water polo. Office Fax: 305-284-2985.

GOMOLIN, IRVING HAROLD, medical educator; b. Montreal, Que., Can., Dec. 17, 1951; came to U.S., 1978; Diploma of collegial studies, McGill U., 1971, MD, 1976. Asst. dir. med. svcs. Hebrew Home & Hosp., Hartford, Conn., 1981-88, assoc. dir. med. svcs., 1988-90; med. dir. Gurwin Jewish Geriatric Ctr., Commack, 1990—2002; clin. prof. medicine SUNY, Stony Brook, 2000—; chief divsn. of geriatric medicine, clin. pharm. Winthrop U. Hosp., Mineola, 2002—. Mem. med. and sci. adv. bd. Alzheimer's Assn., L.I., 1994—. Contbr. numerous med. papers to profl. jours. Recipient Recognition of Innovation in Improving Health Care Quality Mgmt., Am. Coll. Physician Execs., 1993, Recognition of Innovation in Improving Health Care Cost Mgmt., Am. Coll. Physician Execs., 1993. Fellow ACP, Am. Geriatrics Soc., Am. Coll. Clin. Pharmacology, Royal Coll. Physicians and Surgeons of Can.; mem. N.Y. Med. Dirs. Assn. (bd. dirs. 1996—). Office: Winthrop U Hosp 222 Station Plz N Ste 518 Mineola NY 11501

GOMOLL, ALLEN WARREN, cardiovascular pharmacologist; b. Chgo., July 10, 1933; s. Herbert Fredrick and Sara Evelyn (Cowan) G.; m. Elaine L. Kirkpatrick, Sept. 17, 1955; children: Gary A., Lisa E. BS in Pharmacy, U. Ill., Chgo., 1955, MS, 1958, PhD, 1961. Instr. U. Ill. Coll. Medicine, Chgo., 1960-61, asst. prof., 1961-66; group leader Mead Johnson, Evansville, Ind., 1966-70, sect. leader, mgr., 1970-81; prin. rsch. scientist Bristol-Myers, Evansville, 1981-84, rsch. fellow Wallingford, Conn., 1984-90; sr. rsch. fellow Bristol-Myers Squibb, Princeton, 1990—2001. Reviewer Life Scis., 1973-2001, Jour. Med. Chemistry, 1975-2001, Circulation, 1989-2001; contbr. sci. articles to profl. jours. Fellow Am. Coll. Cardiology, Am. Heart Assn. Coun. Circulation and Basic Sci. Coun.; mem. Am. Soc. Pharmacology & Exptl. Therapy, Internat. Soc. Heart Rsch., Sigma Xi. E-mail: gomolla@rcn.com.

GOMORY, RALPH EDWARD, mathematician, manufacturing company executive, foundation executive; b. N.Y.C., N.Y., May 7, 1929; s. Andrew L. and Marian (Schellenberg) Gomory; m. Laura Dumper, 1954 (div. 1968); children: Andrew C., Susan S., Stephen H. BA, Williams Coll., 1950, ScD (hon.), 1973; postgrad., Kings Coll., 1950—51, Cambridge U., Eng., 1950—51; PhD Princeton U., 1954; LHD (hon.), Pace U., 1986; DSc (hon.), Poly. U., 1987, Syracuse U., 1989, Worcester Poly. U., 1989, Carnegie-Mellon U., 1989. Rsch. assoc. Princeton U., 1951—54, asst. prof. math., Higgins lectr., 1957—59; with IBM, Yorktown Heights, NY, 1959—86, dir. math. scis., rsch. div., 1965—67, dir. rsch., 1970—86, v.p., 1973—84, sr. v.p., 1985—89, sr. v.p. for sci. and tech., 1986—89, also mem. corp. mgmt. bd., 1983—89, dir. Asia Pacific Group, 1982—88; pres. Alfred P. Sloan Found., N.Y.C., 1989—. Mem. governing bd. NRC, 1980—83, 1980—, chmn. com. on mandatory retirement in higher edn., 1989—91; trustee Hampshire Coll., 1977—86, Alfred P. Sloan Found., 1988—89. With USN, 1954—57. Recipient Lanchester prize, Ops. Rsch. Soc. Am., 1964, Harry Goode Meml. award, Am. Fedn. Info. Processing Socs., 1984, John Von Neumann Theory prize, Ops. Rschl. Soc. Am. and Inst. Mgmt. Scis., 1984, IRI medal, Indsl. Rsch. Inst., 1985, Engring. Leadership Recognition award, IEEE, 1988, Arthur M. Bueche award, NAE, 1993; fellow IBM, 1964. Fellow: NAS (coun. 1977—78, 1980—83, 1997—, com. sci. engring. and pub. policy 1985—), Am. Acad. Arts and Scis., Econometric Soc.; mem.: IEEE (hon.), Am. Philos. Soc. (coun. 1986—92), Nat. Acad. Engring. (coun. 1986—92). Home: 260 Douglas Rd Chappaqua NY 10514-3100 Office: Alfred P Sloan Found 630 5th Ave Ste 2550 New York NY 10111-0100

GOMORY, TOMI, educator; b. Debrecen, Hungary, Nov. 9, 1947; s. Alex and Ilona Gomory; m. Francine Morris; children: Aniko, Rozsa. PhD, U. Calif., Berkeley, 1998. Author: (series of critical mental health articles) Programs of Assertive Community Treatment: A Critical Review, 1999. Recipient Freedom Project award, John Templeton Found., 2001. Independent. Avocations: road and trail biking, running. Office: Fla State U UCC2410 Tallahassee FL 32306-2570 Office Fax: 850-644-9750. Personal E-mail: tgomory@mailer.fsu.edu. Business E-Mail: tgomory@mailer.fsu.edu.

GOMPERS, JOSEPH ALAN, lawyer; b. Wheeling, W.Va., Jan. 21, 1924; s. William J. and Rose M. (Wilhelm) G.; m. Patricia Ann Nicholl, Mar. 27, 1951; children: Joseph, John, Ann, Patricia, Timothy, Thomas, James, Matthew, Edward, Mary, Eric. AB, Mount St. Mary's Coll., 1944; JD, U. Va., 1948. Bar: W.Va. 1948, U.S. Dist. Ct. (no. dist.) W.Va. 1948, U.S. Ct. Appeals (4th cir.) 1948. Sr. ptnr. Gompers, McCarthy & McClure, Wheeling, W.Va., 1948—; pros. atty. Ohio County W.Va., Wheeling, 1953—57. Mem. W.Va. House of Dels., 1951-52; fiduciary commr. Ohio County, W.Va., 1961-91. Bd. dirs. 12th St. Garage; past bd. dirs. Am. Legion Home Corp., Wheeling Post #1, past pres. Ohio Valley Indsl. and Bus. Devel. Corp., Boy Boy Scouts Am., W.Va. Alcohol Beverage Control Commn.; past mem. athletic com. Cen. Cath. High Sch.; pst mem. YMCA; dir. Oglebay Inst., 1963-69, pres., 1965-66; past mem. parish coun. St. Michael's Cath. Ch. Mem. Nat. Lawyers Assn., W.Va. Bar Assn., W.Va. State Bar Assn. (former mem. bd. govs.), Ohio County Bar Assn. (past pres.), Elks, K.C., Am. Legion, Kiwanis, Cave Club. Republican. Avocation: woodworking. Office: Gompers McCarthy & McClure 60 14th St Wheeling WV 26003-3430 E-mail: jagompers@lexquest.com.

GOMULKA, STANISLAW, economist, educator; b. Krezoly, Poland, Sept. 10, 1940; s. Wladyslaw and Zofia (Kucharzyk) G.; m. Joanna Majerczyk, Jan. 26, 1964; 1 child, Michael. MSc in Physics, Warsaw U., 1962, PhD in Econs., 1966. Asst. lectr. Warsaw U., 1962-65; research fellow Aarhus (Denmark) U., 1970; lectr., then sr. lectr. in econs. London Sch. Econs., 1970-87, reader in econs., 1987—. Fellow Netherlands Inst. advanced Study, Wassenaar, 1980-81; vis. prof. U. Pa., Phila., 1984-85; scholar Stanford (Calif.) U.-Hoover Inst., 1985; sr. fellow Columbia U.-Harriman Inst., N.Y.C., 1986, Harvard U., Russian Rsch. Ctr., 1989; cons. Internat. Monetary Fund, Washington, 1985, joint econ. com., U.S. Congress, Washington, 1988, European Econ. Commn., 1989-90; econ. adviser to Polish Govt., 1989-2002, adviser on econ. reform Russian Govt., 1991-92. Author: Inventive Activity, Diffusion and the Stages of Economic Growth, 1971, Growth, Innovation and Reform in Eastern Europe, 1986, 87, Theory of Technological Change and Economic Growth, 1990, Economic Reforms in the Socialist World, 1989, Polish Peradoxes, 1990, Emerging from Communism: Lessons from Russia, China and Eastern Europe, 1998. Mem. Royal Econ. Soc., European Econ. Soc. Home: 4 Woodfield Way London N11 2PH England Office: London Sch Econs Houghton St London WC2A 2AE England

GONANO, J. ROLAND, technology research and development manager; b. Winchester, Va., Jan. 21, 1939; s. Lezelle and Mary (Fuss) G.; m. Joyce Dove, Aug. 22, 1959; children: Gina Gonano Bickish, Dawn, John R. Jr. BS in Physics, W.Va. U., 1960; PhD in Physics, Duke U., 1966. Postdoctoral fellow U. Fla., Gainesville, 1966-68; physicist U.S. Nat. Bur. Standards, Washington, 1968-71, U.S. Army Belvoir R&D Ctr., Ft. Belvoir, Va., 1971-82; R&D mgr. U.S. Army Material Command, Alexandria, Va., 1982-85; R&D br. chief U.S. Army Lab. Command, Adelphi, Md., 1985-87; chief advanced concepts & tech. U.S. Army Rsch. Lab., Adelphi, 1987-92; dep. chief R&D integration U.S. Army Material Command, Alexandria, 1992-93; army tech. transfer mgr. U.S. Army Rsch. Lab., Adelphi, 1993-95; R&D mgmt. and tech. transfer consulting Gonano Tech. Portfolios, Clarksburg, Md., 1996—. Pres. F-G Farms, Hedgesville, W.Va., 1975—; lectr. dept. physics U. Md., 2001—; adj. instr. dept. math. Frederick C.C., 2001—. Recipient Bronze medal, Army Sci. Conf., 1974. Mem. AAAS, Am. Phys. Soc., Army Acquisition Corps, Sr. Scientists and Engrs., Sigma Xi, Sigma Pi Sigma. Office: 10401 Regina Ct Clarksburg MD 20871-8525

GONÇALVES, PITAGORAS L. music educator; b. Arapongas, PR, Brazil, Jan. 25, 1972; arrived in U.S., 1999; s. Clenison Batista and Soliman Jordão Gonçalves; m. Cléusia Carreira Gonçalves, Oct. 11, 1997. Diploma in piano performance, Villa-Lobos Conservatory, Campinas, Brazil, 1989; BA in music performance, Campinas (Brazil) State U., 1994; MusM, Pensacola (Fla.) Christian Coll., 2001. Faculty Carlos Gomes Conservatoire, Campinas, Brazil, 1995—99, Piox Conservatoire, Jundiai, Brazil, 1996—99; organist First Ind. Presbyn. Ch., São Paulo, Brazil, 1996—99; faculty Pensacola Christian Coll., 2001—. Mem.: Music Tchrs. Nat. Assn. Presbyn. Avocations: soccer, fishing, tennis. Home: 250 Brent Ln Pensacola FL 32503 Office: Pensacola Christian College 250 Brent Ln Pensacola FL 32503 E-mail: pcgon@wmconnect.com.

GONDEK, JULIANA, soprano soloist, music educator; b. Pasadena, Calif. BM in Voice, U. So. Calif., 1975, MM in Vocal Arts, 1977. Tchr. master classes Pacific Music Festival/Hong Kong Acad. for Performing Arts, Manhattan Sch. Music, USC, Rice U., U. Calif., Berkeley, U. Chgo., Butler U., Pepperdine U.; vis. prof. of vocal studies Juilliard Sch., Curtis Inst. Music, Mannes Coll. Music, U. Calif., L.A.; adjudicator Geneva Internat. Open Competition, Met. Open Auditions, Denver Lyric Opera Guild, NATS Career Award Auditions; tchr. master classes Shanghai Conservatory Music. Soprano soloist with opera co., music festivals and orchs. including Netherlands Opera, Scottish Opera, Edinburgh Festival, Gottingen and Halle Handel Festivals, Germany, Pacific Music Festival, Sapporo, Japan, Carnegie Hall, The Kennedy Ctr., Avignon Festival, Antibes Bel Canto Festival, Orch. de la Suisse Romande, German Radio Symphony, Munich Chamber Orch., Freiburger Barockorchester, Hong Kong Philharmonic, Netherlands Radio Symphony, Spanish Radio and Television Orch., L'Orchestre du Rhin, Teatro La Fenice (Venice), Teatro del Gran Liceo (Barcelona), San Francisco Symphony, N.Y. Philharm., St. Louis Symphony, Toronto Symphony, Montreal Symphony, Vancouver Symphony, Dallas Symphony, Seattle Symphony, Minn. Orch., Columbus Symphony, San Antonio Symphony, Kans. City Symphony, Charleston Symphony, San Diego Symphony, Rochester Philharmonic Buffalo Symphony, N.Y. Chamber Symphony, Philharmonia Baroque Orch., St. Luke's Chamber Orch., EOS Ensemble, Detroit Symphony, Milw. Symphony, Met. Opera, N.Y.C, San Francisco Opera, N.Y.C. Opera, Dallas Opera, Seattle Opera, Houstong Grand Opera, Miami Opera, St. Louis Opera, Utah Opera, Hawaii Opera, San Diego Opera, Balt. Opera, Baton Rouge Opera; soloist recordings Yoav Chamber Ensemble, 1982 (Yehudi Menuhin Found. prize), West Side Story, 1985, Die Zauberflöte, 1992, Ottone, 1992, Radamisto, 1993, Giustino, 1994, Ariodante, 1995 (Gramophone Mag. Record of Yr. award), Esther, 1999, Sung Dynasty, 2002 (named Gramophone Top 10 CDs of Yr. 2003), Karol Szymanowski, 2003; soloist performer premieres of musical compositions Kaddish Requiem, 1977, The Tenth Muse, 1986, Song of Majnun, 1992, Flower of the Mountain, 1993, Songs from the Sung Dynasty, 1993, A Quiet Place, 1984, Under the Double Moon, 1992, Dreamkeepers, 1996, Harvey Milk, 1994, 96, Hopper's Wife, 1997, The Noblest Game, 1999, Rosarium, 1999, Blood on the Dining Room Floor, 1999; film: Song of the Lark. Recipient Peter Pears prize Aldeburgh Snape-Maltings Sch. for Advanced Musical Study, 1977, gold medalist Geneva Internat. Singing Competition, Barcelona Internat. Singing Competition, Spain, 1983, 84; grantee Metropolitan Opera Ctr., 1979-84, William Sullivan Found., 1979-86, Martha Baird Rockefeller Found., 1980-84, Nat. Endowment for the Arts, 1989; named Young Artist of Yr. Musical Am./High Fidelity, 1984. Mem.: SAG, AFTRA, AM. Guild Musical Artists. Office: California Artists Mgmt 41 Sutter St Ste 420 San Francisco CA 94104 Fax: 818-753-0552.

GONDEK, MARY JANE (MARY JANE SUCHORSKI), property manager; b. Milw, May 19, 1958; d. Zigmund Alexander and Felicia Theodore (Staszewski) Suchorski; children from previous marriage: Amy Lynn Seamars, Joseph Alexander, Christine Ann. Student, S.W. Tech. Coll., 1989, 94, Internat. Correspondence Sch., 1995. Cert. nursing asst., CPR. Nursing asst. Lancaster Living Ctr., 1988-89, 95-96, Franciscan Villa Nursing Home, South Mil., Wis., 1990-92; home care provider Homeward Bound, Inc., Lancaster, 1994-95; dietary aide St. Joseph's Convent, Milw., 1995-96; on-site mgr. Meridian Group, Inc., Middleton, Wis., 1997-98; home care provider Supported Home Care Options, Inc., Wauwatosa, Wis., 1999, Anew Home Care Options, Wauwatosa, Wis., 1999—; nursing asst. Allis Care Ctr., West Allis, Wis., 1998, 99-2000, VA Med. Ctr., Milw., 2000—; rep. and beauty cons. Avon, 2002—; owner Mary's Treasured Gifts, 2002—. Democrat. Roman Catholic. Avocations: gardening, canning. Address: 1232 S 46th St Milwaukee WI 53214 Personal E-mail: mjgcna@yahoo.com.

GONDER, SHARON, special education educator; b. Princeton, Mo., Aug. 1, 1943; d. Raymond Dale and V. Juanita (Wharton) Hagan; m. Glen William Gonder, Oct. 18, 1985; 1 child, Patricia; stepchildren: Gil, Gailen, Gary, Geoffrey, Gregory, Douglas. BS in Edn., U. Mo., 1968, MEd in Spl. Edn., 1971; MEd in Counseling, Lincoln U., Jefferson City, Mo., 1978. Cert. elem. edn., behavioral disorders, learning disabilities, mentally handicapped, orthopedic handicapped, counseling, psychol. exam., adaptive phys. edn.. Instr. Mental Health Ctr., Columbia, Mo., 1969-71; diagnostician staffing coord. Non-Pub. By-Pass Program, Jefferson City, 1976-89; psychol. examiner Disabilities Determ. Dept. Elem. and Sec. Edn., Jefferson City, 1981-84; coord. Project Lift-Up Lincoln U., Jefferson City, 1984-86; diagnostician Metro Bus. Coll., Jefferson City, 1987-89; tchr., psychol. examiner Jefferson City Pub. Schs., 1968-97. Program cons. Lincoln U., Jefferson City, 1980-99, adj. prof., 1985-99; sec., spl. programming cons. Osage Bend Pub. Co., 1989—; bd. dirs. Ednl. Resources Info. Ctr.; cons. for establishing vol. programs, 2000—; developer policies for reporting child abuse/neglect for vols., 2002—; presenter workshops in field. Leader 4-H, Jefferson City, 1978-81; non-registered lobbyist Mo. State Tchrs. Assn., 1987-97; deacon, tchr. Sunday sch. First Christian Ch., 1985—, elder; mem. task force to establish area at risk programs Jefferson City C. of C., 1993-97. Named Mo. State Spl. Edn. Tchr. of Yr., Mo. Fedn. Coun. for Exceptional Children, 1991. Mem. Coun. for Exceptional Children (legis. chmn., sec.-treas., pres. subdivsns. learning disabilities and mentally retarded and pioneers 1988—, bd. rep. Mo. coun. 1973-88, state fedn. pres. 1984-86, internat. del. 1974, 85, non-registered lobbyist 1983—, profl. devel. standing com. internat. coun. 1997-2001, Internat. Spl. Edn. Tchr. of the Yr. 1992), Learning Disabilities Assn. (chpt. pres., exec. bd. dirs. 1975-91), Gen. Fedn. Women's Clubs (1st v.p.), Delta Kappa Gamma (spkr. nat. circuit 1991-99), author nat. publs. 1992—, bd. dirs. Ednl. Resource Info. Ctr. 1993-2000). Avocations: traveling, camping, crafts, gardening, volunteer tutoring. Office: Osage Bend Pub Co Inc 213 Belair Dr Jefferson City MO 65109-0703 E-mail: obpc@socket.net.

GONDOLESI, GABRIEL EDUARDO, transplant surgeon; b. Tandil, Buenos Aires, Argentina, Nov. 6, 1968; s. Carlos Eduardo Gondolesi and Marta Esther Bahi; m. Carolina Rumbo, May 15, 1998; children: Manuel children: Ignacio. MD, Facultad de Ciencias Medicas, Universidad Nacional de La Plata, La Plata, Buenos Aires, Argentina, 1987—92. Diplomate Buenos Aires, 1993. Chief resident on gen. surgery Surgery Svc., pavilion Finochietto of the Hosp. Interzonal de Agudos, La Plata, Argentina, 1993—97; fellow hepatobiliary surgery annd liver transplantation. Liver and Liver Transplant Unit at Fundación Favaloro, Buenos Aires, 1997—99; fellow multi-organ transplantation Recanati/Miller Transplantation Inst., N.Y.C., 1999—2001, asst. prof. pediatric and adult liver transplant, chief intestinal transplant, 2002. Contbr. chapters to books, scientific papers, articles to profl. jours. including Jour. Gastrointestinal Surgery, Transplantation, Transplant Proc, Liver Transplant. Recipient Gold Medal, Best med. student (9, 9/10 pints average qualifications at the end of the 6 years of med. sch.). Facultad de Ciencias Medicas. UNLP., 1986-1992, Rotary Club prize for performance in the med. field, La Plata's Rotary Club. Argentina, 1996. Mem.: Miembro de la Asociacion Argentina de Cirugia (assoc.), Am. Assn. of Transplant Surgeons (assoc.), Internat. Hepato-Bilio-Pancreatic Assn. (assoc.). Office: Recanati/Miller Transplantation Inst 19 E 98 St 6th Ff Ste A New York NY 10029 Office Fax: 212-996-9688. Personal E-mail: gegondolesi@yahoo.com. E-mail: gabriel.gondolesi@mountsinai.org.

GONDOLO, PAOLO, physicist; b. Monfalcone, Italy, Oct. 7, 1962; s. Emilio Gondolo and Gabriella D'Amore; m. Manuela Chetti, Oct. 14, 1989; children: Alessandro, Elisabeth Yvonne. Laurea in Physics, U. Trieste, Italy, 1986; PhD in Physics, UCLA, 1991. Postdoctoral fellow Uppsala (Sweden) U., 1991-93; postdoctoral rschr. U. Paris, 1993-95; rsch. asst. U. Oxford, Eng., 1995-96; vis. scientist U. Calif., Berkeley, 1996-97; rschr. Max-Planck Inst. Physics, Munich, 1997-2000; vis. asst. prof. Case Western Res. U., Cleve., 2000—03; asst. prof. U. Utah, Salt Lake City, 2003—. Contbr. numerous articles to profl. jours. Mem. Am. Phys. Soc., UCLA Alumni Assn. Achievements include research in methods to discover the nature of dark matter; contributions to first search for gravitational microlensing of unresolved extragalactic stars, to high-energy neutrino astronomy, to the dark energy problem. Office: U Utah 115 S 1400 E Rm 201 Salt Lake City UT 84112-0830 Fax: 801-581-6256. E-mail: paolo@physics.utah.edu.

GONE, JOSEPH PATRICK, psychologist, educator; b. Helena, Mont., Feb. 13, 1967; s. Joseph William Azure and Rowena Marie Gone, Sharon Lee Juelfs; m. Tiya Alicia Miles, Aug. 1, 1998. PhD, U. of Ill., Champaign, IL, 1993—2001; AB, Harvard Coll., Cambridge, MA, 1990—92; N.A., US Mil. Acad., West Point, NY, 1988—90. Asst. prof. U. Chgo., 2000—02, U. Mich.,

Ann Arbor, 2002—. Specialist U.S. Army, 1986—88, 2nd Cavalry, West Germany. Office: University of Michigan 2239 East Hall 525 East University Ann Arbor MI 48109-1109 E-mail: jgone@umich.edu.

GONG, HENRY, JR., physician, researcher; b. Tulare, Calif., May 23, 1947; s. Henry and Choy (Low) G.; m. Janice Wong; children: Gregory, Jaimee. BA, U. of the Pacific, 1969; MD, U. Calif., Davis, 1973. Diplomate Am. Bd. Internal Medicine, 1977, Pulmonary Disease subspecialty bd., 1980. Resident in medicine Boston U., 1973-75; fellow in pulmonary medicine UCLA Med. Ctr., 1975-77; asst. prof., then assoc. prof. Sch. Medicine UCLA, 1977-89, prof. medicine, 1989-93; assoc. chief pulmonary div. UCLA Med. Ctr., 1985-92; chief Environ. Health Svc. Rancho Los Amigos Med. Ctr., 1993—; prof. medicine U. So. Calif., 1993—, prof. preventive medicine, 1997—. Dir. Environ. Exposure Lab., UCLA, 1988-93; chmn. dept. medicine Rancho Los Amigos Med. Ctr., 1996—; mem. pub. health and socio-econs. task force South Coast Air Quality Mgmt. Dist., El Monte, Calif., 1989-90. Contbr. over 300 articles to rsch. publs., chpts. to books; editorial bd. Jour. Clin. Pharmacology, 1983-02, Am. Jour. Critical Care, 1992—, Arch Environ. Health, 2000—. Elder on session Pacific Palisades Presbyn. Ch., 1984-86, 89-91, 2003. Fellow Am. Coll. Chest Physicians (pres. Calif. chpt. 1991-92), Am. Coll. Clin. Pharmacology; mem. Am. Thoracic Soc., Am. Fedn. Clin. Rsch., Western Soc. Clin. Investigation, Phi Eta Sigma. Avocation: travel. Office: Environ Health Svc Rancho Los Amigos Med Ctr 7601 Imperial Hwy Downey CA 90242-3456

GONG, MAMIE POGGIO, elementary education educator; b. San Francisco, June 26, 1951; d. Louis and Mary Lee (Lum) G.; m. Andy Anthony Poggio. BA, U. Calif., Berkeley, 1973, postgrad., 1981-83, MEd, 1982. Tchr. Oakland (Calif.) Unified Sch. Dist., 1974-84, Palo Alto (Calif.) Unified Sch. Dist., 1984-91. Cons., writer Nat. Clearinghouse for Bilingual Edn., Washington, 1984; cons. ARC Assocs., Oakland, 1983; rsch. asst. dept. edn. Stanford U., 1987-89. Co-author: Promising Practices: A Teacher Resource, 1984. Recipient Kearney Found. award, 1969, others. Mem. Tchrs. English to Speakers Other Langs. (presenter 1990 conf.), Calif. Assn. Tchrs. English to Speakers Other Langs. Democrat. Office: Palo Alto Unified Sch Dist 25 Churchill Ave Palo Alto CA 94306-1099

GONG, SU, computer engineer; s. Shaoquan Su and Hanqiao Shi. PhD, Columbia U., 1994—2003. Chief software engr. NeXtorage Inc., N.Y.C., 2000—03. Recipient Best Paper Award, Elsevier Sci. Pub., 2001. Mem.: ACM. Office: Columbia University Dept of Computer Sci New York NY 10027 E-mail: gongsu@cs.columbia.edu.

GONG, XIAOYI, engineer; b. Beijing, Dec. 6, 1958; arrived in U.S., 1998; d. Run-Gang Gong and Jun-Shu Lin; m. Yuqing Justin Yang, Apr. 2, 1986; 1 child, Guan Yang. BSc, Northwestern Poly. U., Xian, China, 1982; MSc, Chengdu (China) U. Sci. and Tech., 1985, PhD, 1988. Rsch. fellow Chinese Acad. Scis., Guangzhou, China, 1988—95; postdoctoral rsch. fellow U. Leeds, England, 1991—92; prof. Guangdong U. Tech., Guangzhou, 1995; rsch. scientist CSIRO Molecular Sci., Melbourne, Australia, 1995—98; rsch. assoc. Pacific N W. Nat. Lab., Richland, Wash., 1998—2000; sr. staff engr. Conoco, Inc., Ponca City, Okla., 2000—. Contbr. articles to profl. jours. Named Youth Chemist, Chinese Chem. Soc., Beijing, 1990; named one of Ten Most Outstanding Women, Guangdong Province Govt., 1995; fellow, Brit. Coun., London, 1991. Mem.: AAAS, Am. Chem. Soc. Achievements include materials research and device development in electronic, biomedical and environmental applications; research in surface chemistry to develop new materials and new products. Avocations: travel, reading. Home: 2908 Rice St Ponca City OK 74604 Office: Conoco PhillipsI nc 1000 S Pine Ponca City OK 74602

GONG, YU, molecular biologist; b. Shanghai, Oct. 6, 1939; arrived in U.S., 1983; m. Shu Lin Hu; 1 child, Qin. BS, Fa Dan U., Shanghai, 1962; PhD, Shanghai First Med. U., 1967. Rsch. fellow Immunology Dept., Shanghai Cancer Inst., 1967—82; post doctoral trainee in molecular hematology Nat. Heart Lung and Blood Inst., NIH, Bethesda, Md., 1983—85; vis. fellow lab. chem. biology NIDDK/NIH, Bethesda, 1985—86; vis. assoc. lab. oral medicine NIDR/NIH, Bethesda, 1986—88; molecular biology scientist Pan-Data Systems, Inc., Rockville, Md., 1989—90; scientist HIR Inc., Concord, Calif., 1990—. Mem. editl. bd., cons. Shanghai Jour. Immunology, 1983—. Fellow: Soc. of Oncology/Chinese Med. Assn.; mem.: Chinese Biopharm. Assn. (Mid-Atlantic Region), Am. Soc. Microbiology. Achievements include invention of diagnostic array for virus infection; blood cell adhesion test for cancer; human ovarian cancer antigen; patent for infection disease invention. Avocations: gardening, travel, swimming. Home: 11484 Brundidge Ter Germantown MD 20876

GONGORA, EDUARDO, plastic surgeon; b. Baja, Calif., July 9, 1963; MD, U. Autonoma, Baja, Calif. Owner Clinica Genesis, Rosarito Baja, Calif. Office: PO Box 148 Chula Vista CA 91912-0148

GONICK, HARVEY CRAIG, nephrologist, educator; b. Winnipeg, Man., Can., Apr. 10, 1930; s. Joseph Wolfe and Rose (Chernick) G.; m. Gloria Granz, Dec. 16, 1967; children: Stefan, Teri, Julie, Suzanne. BS in Chemistry, UCLA, 1951; MD, U. Calif., San Francisco, 1955. Diplomate Am. Bd. Internal Medicine, Am. Bd. Nephrology. Intern Peter Bent Brigham Hosp., 1955-56; fellow in nephrology Mass. Meml. Hosp., 1956-57; fellow in nephrology, resident in internal medicine Wadsworth VA Hosp., Los Angeles, 1959-61, clin. investigator, 1961-64, chief metabolic balance unit, 1964-67; instr. medicine Sch. Medicine, UCLA, 1961-64, asst. prof., 1964-69, assoc. prof., 1969-72, adj. assoc. prof., 1972-76, adj. prof., 1976—, assoc. chief div. nephrology, 1965-72, co-dir. Bone and Stone Clinic, 1972-76, coordinator postgrad. nephrology edn., 1975-78; mem. staff St. John's Hosp., Santa Monica, Calif., Century City Hosp., L.A., med. dir. dialysis unit, 1972-79, chief medicine, 1978-79; mem. staff Cedars-Sinai Med. Ctr., L.A., dir. trace element lab., 1979-96, clin. chief nephrology, 1983-85, coord. renal tng., dir. hypertension rsch., 1996—; practice medicine specializing in nephrology Los Angeles, 1972-94. Co-founder, med. dir. Berkeley East Dialysis Unit, Santa Monica, 1971-75; co-founder, cons. Kidney Dialysis Care Units Inc., Lynwood, Calif., 1971-78; co-dir. Osteoporosis Prevention and Treatment Ctr., Santa Monica, 1987-93; mem. numerous adv. coms. to state and fed. agys., 1969-83. Contbr. articles to profl. jours.; editor: Current Nephrology, 1977-96. Served to capt. M.C., USAF, 1957-59. Fellow Charles Nelson Fund, Kaiser Found., NIH; recipient Oliver P. Douglas Meml. award Los Angeles County Heart Assn., 1959, Vis. Scientist award Deutscher Academischer Austauschendienst, 1978. Fellow ACP; mem. AMA, AAAS, Internat. Soc. Nephrology (organizing com. internat. cong. 1984), Am. Soc. Nephrology, European Dialysis and Transplant Assn., Soc. Exptl. Biology and Medicine, Calif. Med. Assn., Los Angeles County Med. Assn., Nat. Kidney Found. (active ann. conf. 1963-65, sec. nat. med. adv. coun. 1969-70, regional rep. and legis. com. nat. med. adv. coun. 1970-73, grantee 1963), So. Calif. Kidney Found. (chmn. sci. adv. coun. 1968-70, co-chmn. legis. com. 1970-73, bd. dirs. 1974-83, honoree 1979), Am. Soc. Bone and Mineral Rsch., Am. Coll. Toxicology, Soc. Toxicology, Am. Heart Assn. (renal sect. of coun. on circulation), Am. Fedn. Clin. Rsch., Western Soc. Clin. Rsch., Western Assn. Physicians, Phi Beta Kappa, Sigma Xi, Alpha Omega Alpha, Phi Eta Sigma, Alpha Mu Gamma, Phi Lambda Upsilon. Avocation: tennis. Office: Cedars Sinai Med Ctr Ste 475 W Tower 8700 Beverly Blvd Ste 475 Los Angeles CA 90048-1865

GONICK, PAUL, retired urologist; b. Bklyn., July 5, 1930; s. Benjamin and Yetta (Shedrofsky) G.; m. Angela M. Furlong, Mar. 24, 1963; children— Brian Michael, Peter Benjamin, Julia Nancy. BA, N.Y. U., 1951; MD, Yale U., 1955. Diplomate: Nat. Bd. Med. Examiners. Intern Albany (N.Y.) Hosp., 1955-56; resident VA Hosp. and U. Minn., Mpls., 1958-62; instr. urology Wayne State U., Detroit, 1964-65, asst. prof. urology, 1965; asst. clin. prof. urology Columbia U., N.Y.C., 1966-69; asso. prof. urology Hahnemann Med. Coll. and Hosp., Phila., 1969-74, prof. urology, 1974-95, dir. div. urology, 1969-80; practice medicine specializing in urology Phila., 1969-95; chief urology sect. VA Hosp., Dearborn, Mich., 1963-66, acting asso. chief staff for research and edn., 1964-65; jr. attending physician Detroit Receiving Hosp., 1964-65; chief urology sect. VA Hosp., Bronx, 1966-69; asst. urologist Presbyn. Hosp., N.Y.C., 1966-69, dir. div. urology Phila., 1992-95. Cons. urology Harlem Hosp., 1967-69, Radiol. Therapy Oncology Group, numerous hosps. Contbr. numerous articles to med jours. Served to capt. USAF, 1956-58. James Hudson Brown fellow, 1953 Fellow ACS; mem. AMA, Yale Med. Soc., Am. Urol. Assn., Vets. Urol. Assn. (treas. 1969), Soc. Univ. Urologists, Phila. Urol. Soc. (pres. 1994-95), Pa. Med. Soc., Philadelphia County Med. Soc., Phila. Acad. Surgery, Caducean Soc., Phi Beta Kappa, Mu Chi Sigma, Beta Lambda Sigma. Home: 341 Conshohocken State Rd Gladwyne PA 19035-1348 E-mail: paulgonick@aol.com.

GONICK, PETER B. lawyer; b. N.Y.C., Aug. 22, 1966; s. Paul and Angela Mary Gonick; m. Edie Anne Adams, Sept. 14, 1996; children, Elena Adams, Evan Adams. BS in Econ., U. Pa., 1988; JD, U. Wash., 1995. Bar: Wash. 1995, U.S. Dist. Ct. (we. dist.) Wash. 1998. Legal asst. Ballard Spahr Andrews & Ingersoll, Phila., 1988-89; law clk. justice Rosselle Pekelis Wash. State Supreme Ct., Olympia, 1995-96; staff atty. Pub. Defenders Assn., Seattle, 1996-97; assoc. McKay Chadwell, PLLC, Seattle, 1998—. Notes and comments editor Wash. Law Rev., 1995. Agrl. vol. U.S. Peace Corps, Mbeya II, Zaire, 1990-91; pro bono atty. N.W. Immigration Rights Project, Seattle, 1998. Recipient Judge Lawless Meml. award King County Judges, Seattle, 1993, Criminal Law and Contracts Law award Am. Jurisprudence, 1993. Mem. Wash. State Bar Assn., Wash. Assn. Criminal Def. Lawyers, King County Bar Assn., Delta Theta Phi. Avocations: hiking, running, literature. Office: McKay Chadwell PLLC 1601 One Union Sw 600 University Ave Seattle WA 98101

GONLIN, NANCY, archaeologist, educator; BS, Juniata Coll., 1982; MA, Pa. State U., 1985, PhD, 1993. Lectr. Pa. State U., University Park, 1988—91; asst. prof., part-time Kennesaw (Ga.) State U., 1993—96; lectr. to prof. archaeology Bellevue (Wash.) C.C., 1997—. Archaeol. cons. U. Maine Mixtec Project, Orono, 2002—; survey co-dir. Pa. State U. Proyecto Acatzingo-Tepeaca, University Park, 1995; archaeologist for Proyecto Archaeologico Copan Pa. State U., University Park, 1984—86; vis. scholar U. Ga., Athens. Co-author: Copan, The rise and fall of an ancient Maya kingdom, 2000; contbr. chapters to books;, co-editor books. Guest lectr. for 6th grade classes Crestwood Elem. Sch., Kent, Wash., 2002—. Fellow, Dumbarton Oaks/Harvard U., 1994. Mem.: Am. Anthrop. Assn., Soc. Am. Archaeology. Office: Bellevue Cmty Coll 3000 Landerholm Circle Bellevue WA 98007 Office Fax: 425-564-3108.

GONNERING, RUSSELL STEPHEN, ophthalmic plastic surgeon; b. Milw., Nov. 21, 1949; s. Russell Richard and Virginia Mary (Mlinar) G.; m. Sandra Lynne Brubaker, Aug. 6, 1971; children: Julie Kathleen, Stephen Russell, Scott Duncan. Student, U. Vienna, Austria, 1969-70; AB in History cum laude, Boston Coll., 1971; MD, Med. Coll. Wis., 1975. Diplomate Am. Bd. Ophthalmology; lic. physician, Wis. Intern St. Luke's Hosp., Milw., 1975-76; fellow in ophthalmic plastic and reconstructive surgery U. Wis., Madison, 1980-81, asst. clin. prof. dept. ophthalmology, 1981-92, assoc. clin. prof. dept. ophthalmology, 1992-96, clin. prof. dept. ophthalmology, 1996—, Kambara lectr., 1997; resident in ophthalmology Med. Coll. Wis., Milw., 1977-80, asst. clin. prof. dept. ophthalmology, 1985-2000, prof. ophthalmology, 2000—; ophthalmologist Children's Hosp. Wis., Milw., St. Luke's Hosp., Milw., chief ophthalmologist, 1983-94, 97-99, vice chief staff, 2000; pvt. practice Ophthalmic Plastic & Reconstructive Surgery, 1981-2000, Full-time acad. practice, 2000—; rsch. assoc. in corneal physiology Med. Coll. Wis., 1976-77; rsch. advisor to fellowship in ophthalmic plastic and reconstructive surgery U. Wis., Madison, 1983-2002. Author: (with others) Infections of the Eye and Ocular Adnexa, 1986, Oculoplastic, Orbital and Reconstructive Surgery, 1988, Oculoplastic and Orbital Emergencies, 1990, Ophthalmic Plastic, reconstructive and Orbital Surgery, 1997, Ophthalmic Surgery: Principles and Techniques, 1999; sect. editor: Principles and Practice of Ophthalmic Plastic and Reconstructive Surgery, 1995; contbr. numerous articles to profl. jours.; presenter in field. Recipient George K. Kambara award U. Wis., 1997, Wisdom Soc. Honor award, 1999. Fellow: ACS (coun. Wis. chpt. 1996—2000), Am. Soc. Ophthalmic Plastic and Reconstructive Surgery (editl. bd. 1987—99, edn. com. 1988—99, vice chmn. edn. com. 1995—97, chmn. edn. com. 1997—99, Marvin H. Quickert award 1982, Rsch. award 1982, Reeh Pathology award 1999), Am. Acad. Ophthalmology (basic and clin. sci. course com. 1986—92, chmn. 1988—92, Honor award 1990, Ruedemann lectr. 1994, Sr. Achievement award 2001); mem.: Milw. Surg. Soc., Nat. Soc. to Prevent Blindness (mem. adv. bd. Wis. chpt. 1987—88), Am. Soc. Ocularists (med. adv. bd. 1987—2001), Milw. Ophthalmol. Soc. (treas. 1989—90, sec. 1990—91, v.p. 1991—92, pres. 1992—93), Milw. Acad. Surgery, Milw. Acad. Medicine, Milw. County Med. Soc. (del. to state med. soc. 1987—90, bd. dirs. 1989—94, Dirs. citation 1994), Med. Soc. Wis., Assn. for Rsch. in Vision and Ophthalmology, Internat. Dacryology Soc., European Soc. Ophthalmic Plastic and Reconstructive Surgery, Internat. Soc. Orbital Disorders, Mensa. Avocations: sailing, skiing, tai kwon do, cycling. Office. Med College of Wisconsin Dept Ophthalmology 925 N 87th St Milwaukee WI 53226 E-mail: rsgonnering@hotmail.com.

GONSALVES, MARGARET LEBOY, elementary school educator; b. Paia, Maui, Hawaii, Feb. 10, 1935; d. John Algarin and Antonia (Leboy) G. BS in Edn., Marylhurst U., 1959; elem. tchr. cert., U. Hawaii, 1971. Cert. elem. tchr., Hawaii. Nurses' aide St. Vincent Hosp., Portland, Oreg., 1956; office clk. Bur. Med. Econs., Honolulu, 1959; tchr. State of Hawaii Dept. Edn., Honolulu, 1959—, Benjamin Park Sch., Kaneohe, Hawaii, 1966-92. Tchr. ESEA-Title I Chpt. I reading and math. fed. program, 1979-92, coord. Parker Sch. Chpt. 1 reading and math. program. Vol. Am. Cancer Soc., Honolulu, 1979, Am. Diabetes Assn., Honolulu, 1992; reporter Nat. Data Corp.-Price Waterhouse, Springfield, Va., 1991-2002. Mem. NEA, Internat. Reading Assn., Hawaii State Tchrs. Assn. (faculty rep. 1960-62, 87-89, Golden Heart cert., 2003), Sigma Delta Pi. Roman Catholic. Avocations: reading, sweepstakes, fishing, gardening, traveling. Home: 1328 Maalahi St Honolulu HI 96819-1727

GONSALVES, PATRICIA E. surgical nurse; b. N.Y.C., Oct. 28, 1943; d. John A. Gonsalves and Julia Rivera Brosa. Diploma in practical nursing, Caledonian Hosp., Bklyn., 1963; student, Cornell Med. Ctr., 1965-66, L.I. U., 1971, SUNY, L.I., 1988. Lic. practical nurse; cert. surg. technologist, preceptor, oper. rm., med. photographer. Lic. practical nurse Luth. Med. Ctr., Bklyn.; assoc. primary nurse, lic. practical nurse Maimonides Med. Ctr., Bklyn., LPN, surg. technologist, oper. rm. vascular surg. specialist, sr. tech. and neuro., 1980—. Contbr. articles to profl. jours. Guild del. Local 1199, Freedom of Health Choice; polit. Dem. endorser; lay min. Bay Ridge Christian Ctr., Bklyn. Mem.: NAACOG (Outstanding Leadership Recognition award), Found. for Advancement of Innovative Medicine, Nat. Ctr. Homeopathy, Assn. Surg. Technologists (pres. chpt. Metro 47 1994—96, nat. bd. dirs. 1993—94, apptd. mem. exam. rev. com. various awards 1992), Soc. Peripheral Vascular Nursing, Nat. Surg. Asst. Assn., Nat. Assn. Practical Nurse Edn. and Svc. Home: 814 57th St Apt 2A Brooklyn NY 11220-3631

GONSER, THOMAS HOWARD, lawyer, former bar association executive; b. Berkeley, Calif, May 8, 1938; s. William Adam and Alice Gertrude (Lease) G.; m. Stephanie Jane Griffiths, Nov. 27, 1960; children: Thomas Howard, Catherine Ruth. AA, U. Calif., Berkeley, 1958, BA in Polit. Sci., 1960, JD, 1965. Bar: Calif. 1965, Idaho 1970. Atty. S.P. Co., San Francisco, 1965-68; asst. gen. counsel Cascade Corp., Boise, Idaho, 1969-72, assoc. gen. counsel, 1972-81, asst. sec., 1972-81; exec. dir. ABA, Chgo., 1981-87, exec. v.p., COO, 1987, also bd. dir. Author: The Bar Foundation, 1979; editor, pub. RVers Online, 1996—. Served with US Army, 1960-62. Fellow Am. Bar Found.; mem. Internat. Bar Assn. (dep. sec. gen. 1982-86). Methodist. Office: T H Gonser & Associates 709 Cape Dr Friday Harbor WA 98250-9322

GONSHAK, ISABELLE LEE, nurse, civic worker; b. Newark, Apr. 4, 1932; d. Robert John and Clara Kate (Cooperman) McClelland; m. David M. Gonshak, Aug. 8, 1953; children: Evan J., Brett A., Kathryn Susan. RN, N.J. Nurse Newark City Hosp., 1953; tchr. Ideal Sch. for Nurse's Aides, Miami, Fla., 1972-74. Vocal soloist numerous TV and social affairs; photographer multiple media, multi-faceted subjects. Bd. dirs. Miami Beach Symphony, 1971—, pres., 1978-79; bd. dirs. South Fla. Symphony; life mem. Opera Guild Soc. Ft. Lauderdale; active Statue of Liberty Refinishing Com. Mem. Greater Miami Opera Assn., Hadassah (life). Jewish. Home: 1700 SW 72d Ave Plantation FL 33317-5037

GONSON, S. DONALD, lawyer; b. Buffalo, June 13, 1936; s. Samuel and Laura Rose (Greenspan) G.; m. Dorothy Rose, Aug. 28, 1960; children: Julia, Claudia AB, Columbia U., 1958; JD, Harvard U., 1961; postgrad., U. Bombay, India, 1961-62; cert., London (Eng.) Sch. Econs., 1957. Bar: Mass. 1962, N.Y. 1983. With Hale and Dorr, Boston, 1962—, sr. ptnr., 1972-2000, of counsel, 2000—. Co-chmn. Speech-Tech., N.Y.C., 1987; instr. in law Boston U., 1963-65, bd. trustees Boston Five Cents Savs. Bank, 1978-83, bd. advisors, 1983-88; adj. prof. internat. law Tufts U. Fletcher Sch. Law and Diplomacy, 1999—; lectr. Fin. Times (U.K.), Instnl. Investors, New Eng. Law Inst., Mass. Soc. CPA's. Chmn. Mass. Comty. Devel. Fin. Corp., 1976-82; pres. Cambridge Ctr. for Adult Edn., 1985-88; bd. dirs. Boston Psychoanalytic Soc. and Inst., 1994—. Fulbright scholar, 1961-62. Fellow Am. Bar Found.; mem. ABA, Internat. Bar Assn., Mass. Bar Assn., Boston Bar Assn. (chmn. internat. law sect. 1998-2001), Harvard Club. Home: 32 Hubbard Park Rd Cambridge MA 02138-4731 Office: Hale & Dorr LLP 60 State St Boston MA 02109-1816 E-mail: donald.gonson@haledorr.com.

GONTARZ, MICHAEL JOSEPH, school psychologist; b. Berwyn, Ill., June 20, 1959; s. Thaddeus M. and Gertrude (Szerlag) G.; m. Frances M. Lecheler, July 18, 1987; children: Danielle, Christian, Jonathan. BA in Psychology, U. Dallas, 1981; MSEd in Sch. Psychology, U. Wis., LaCrosse, 1984, Cert. Adv. Grad. Study, 1985; EdD, Indiana U. of Pa., 2002. Nat. Wis. cert. sch. psychologist; lic. pvt. practice sch. psychologist, Wis., 1988; lic. profl. counselor, Wis., 1996. Sch. psychologist D.C. Everest Area Schs., Schofield, Wis., 1986—; intern in Neuropsychology Med. Coll. Wis., 1996; pres., founder Psychol./Ednl. Cons., 2002—. Adv. bd. mem. Learning Disabilities Assn. Wis., Neceedah, 1997—; edn. adv. com. mem. Children of ADHD Assoc. Wis., Wausau, 1990-91; chair pupil svcs. self eval. D.C. Everest Area Schs., Schofield, 1994—. Pres. pastoral coun. St. Michael's Ch., Wausau, 1995-96, mem. religious edn. com., 1995-96, liturgical min., 1998—; mem. Christian Family Movement Diocese of LaCrosse, 1993—. Mem. Nat. Acad. Neuropsychology, Nat. Assn. Sch. Psychologists, Internat. Sch. Psychology Assn., Wis. Sch. Psychology Assn., Soc. Cath. Social Scientists, Cath. United for the Faith, Fellowship of Cath. Scholars, Cardinal Newman Soc., Coun. for Exceptional Children, Am. Psychological Assn. Roman Catholic. Avocations: photography, writing, reading, outdoor sports, traveling. Home: 4029 Carl St Wausau WI 54403-2287 Office: DC Everest Area Schs 6300 Alderson St Schofield WI 54476-3906 E-mail: mgontarz@dce.K12.wi.us.

GONTHIER, CHARLES DOHERTY, Canadian supreme court justice; b. Montreal, Que., Can., Aug. 1, 1928; s. Georges and Kathleen (Doherty) G.; m. Mariette Morin, June 17, 1961; children: Georges, François, Pierre, Jean-Charles, Yves. BA, Paris Coll. Stanislas, Montreal, 1947; BCL, McGill U., Montreal, 1951, LLD (hon.), 1990; DHC (hon.), U. Montreal, 2002. Queen's counsel, 1971. Atty. Hackett, Mulvena and Laverty, Montreal, 1952-57, Laing, Weldon, Courtois, Clarkson, Parsons, Gonthier & Tetrault (name now McCarthy & Tetrault), Montreal, 1957-74; judge Superior Ct. Que., Montreal, 1974-88, Que. Ct. Appeal, Montreal, 1988-89; puisne judge Supreme Ct. Can., Ottawa, Ont., 1989—. Sec. Montreal br. Can. Inst. Internat. Affairs, 1957-58; bd. dirs. Montreal Legal Aid Bur., 1959-69; pres. Jr. Bar Montreal, 1960-61; pres. jr. bar sect. Can. Bar Assn., 1961-62, sec. Que. div., 1963-64; bd. dirs. Montreal Bar, 1961-62; mem. Com. on Bldg. Contracts Que. Civil Code Rev., 1969-72; mem. com. on discipline Bar Que., 1973-74; chmn. Commn. for Nat. Judges, 1st World Conf. on Independence of Justice, Montreal, 1983; pres. Can. Inst. for Adminstrn. Justice, 1986-87; pres. Can. Judges Conf., 1988-89. Chmn. Assn. Anciens Coll. Stanislas, Montreal, 1954-55; hon. sec. Montreal Mus. Fine Arts, 1961-76; bd. dirs. McCord Mus. Can. History, Montreal, 1976-89; chmn. bd. Coll. Stanislas, Montreal, 1984-90; mem. Internat. Commn. Jurists, 1989. Decorated knight L'Ordre des Palmes académiques (France). Fellow Am. Coll. Trial Lawyers (hon.); mem. Univ. Club (Montreal). Roman Catholic. Office: Supreme Ct Can Wellington St Supreme Ct Bldg Ottawa ON Canada K1A 0J1

GONWA, THOMAS ARTHUR, nephrologist, transplant physician, educator; b. Chgo., Sept. 2, 1949; s. George Joseph and Darline (Sears) G.; m. Mary Alice Westrick, Sept. 28, 1974; children: Claire, Charlotte. BS, St. Joseph's Coll., 1971; MD, U. Ill., 1975. Diplomate Am. Bd. Internal Medicine, Am. Bd. Nephrology, Am. Bd. Critical Care Medicine. Resident Bowman Gray, Winston-Salem, N.C., 1975-78, renal fellow, 1978-80; postdoctoral rsch. fellow U. Calif., San Francisco, 1980-82, instr., 1982-83; asst. prof. U. Iowa, Iowa City, 1983-86; pvt. practice, Dallas, 1986-2001; assoc. dir. transplant Baylor U. Med. Ctr., Dallas, 1987-2001; med. dir. renal and pancreas transplant Mayo Clinic, Jacksonville, Fla., 2001—; prof. medicine Mayo Med. Sch., 2001—. Clin. assoc. prof. medicine U. Tex. Southwestern Med. Sch., 1993-2001. Assoc. editor Jour. Immunology, 1985-86; editl. bd. Transplantation, Graft, Clin. Transplantation; contbr. more than 150 articles to profl. jours. Recipient rsch. award VA, 1984. Fellow ACP; mem. Am. Soc. Transplant Physicians (sec., treas. 1990-93, pres. 1994-95, Upjohn award 1983), Am. Soc. Nephrology, Am. Assn. Immunologists, Transplantation Soc., Nat. Kidney Found. (head coun. transplantation 1998-99, bd. dirs. 1998-99, chmn. pub. policy com. 1999-2001). Office: Mayo Clinic Jacksonville Transplant Ctr 4203 Belfort Rd Ste 1101 Jacksonville FL 32216

GONZALES, ALBERTO R. federal official, former state supreme court justice, former secretary of state; b. San Antonio, Tex., Aug. 4, 1955; Student, U.S. Air Force Acad., 1975-77; BA, Rice U., 1979; JD, Harvard U., 1982. Bar: Tex. Ptnr. Vinson & Elkins, LLP, Houston, 1982-95; gen. counsel Gov. George W. Bush, 1995-97; sec. of state State of Tex., 1997-98; justice Supreme Ct of Texas, Austin, Tex., 1999—2000; gen. counsel to President George W. Bush, DC, 2001—. Trustee Tex. Bar Found., 1996—; mem. Tex. Jud. Dists. Bd., 1996-97; bd. dirs. United Way of Tex. Gulf Coast, 1993-94; pres. Leadership Houston, 1993-94; chair Commn. for Dist. Decentralization of Houston Ind. Sch. Dist., 1994; mem. com. on undergrad. admissions Rice U., 1994; chair Rep. Nat. Hispanic Assembly of Houston, 1992-94; pres. Houston Hispanic Forum, 1990-92; chair adv. com. Tex. Real Estae Ctr., 1989-90; bd. dirs. Big Bros. and sisters, Houston, 1985-91, Cath. Charities, Houston, 1989-93, others. Recipient Commitment to Leadership award United Way, 1993, Hispanic Salute award Houston Metro Ford Dealers, 1989, others; named one of Five Outstanding Young Texans, Tex. Jaycess, 1994, Outstanding Young Lawyer of Tex., Tex. Young Lawyers Assn., 1992. Mem. Houston Bar Assn., State Bar Tex. (bd. dirs. 1992-94). Republican. Office: Office of the General Council 1600 Pennsylvania Ave Washington DC 20500

GONZALES, DANIEL S. lawyer; b. San Antonio, Nov. 10, 1959; s. Sam and Mary Louise (Stewart) G.; m. Mary David McCauley, May 16, 1980 (div. 1983); m. Devon Elaine Cattell, Jan. 1, 1988 (div. 2001). BA, U. Notre Dame, 1981; JD, Stanford U., 1984. Bar: Calif. 1986, U.S. Dist. Ct. (no. dist.) Calif. 1986, U.S. Tax Ct. 1987, U.S. Ct. Appeals (9th cir.) 1988, U.S. Dist. Ct. (ea. dist.) Calif. 1990. Trivia game writer Axlon Games, Sunnyvale, Calif., 1984; legal writer Matthew Bender & Co., San Francisco, 1984—86; assoc. Carey & Carey, Palo Alto, Calif., 1986—96, Ferrari, Olsen, Ottoboni & Bebb, San Jose, Calif., 1996—97, Bryant, Clohan, Eller, Maines & Baruh, San Jose, 1997—2001, Eller & Assocs., San Jose, 2002—. Mng. editor Stanford Jour. Internat. Law, 1983-84. Candidate Menlo Park (Calif.) City Coun., 1988; bd. dirs. Page Mill YMCA, Palo Alto, 1993-99, YMCA of the Midpeninsula, 1999—, Project Match, San Jose, 1997—, pres., 1998-99, 2002-03; pres. Menlo Park Dispute Resolution Svc., 1994-95; backup guitarist, keyboardist for Beau Brummels 35th Anniversary Summer of Love Concert, San Francisco, 2002. U. Notre Dame scholar, 1977, Nat. Merit scholar, 1977, scholar Nat. Hispanic Scholarship Bd., 1980. Mem. ABA, San Mateo County La Raza Lawyers (pres. 1994), Santa Clara County Bar Assn. (chmn. minority access com. 1994, chmn. judiciary com. 1995), San Mateo County Bar Assn., Palo Alto Area Bar Assn. Democrat. Avocations: guitar, college football. Office: Eller & Assocs 60 S Market St Ste 1201 San Jose CA 95113

GONZALES, GREGORY, music educator; s. Federico and Ann Gonzales. Mus M, U. of Tex., 1997. Jazz and blues saxophonist, vocalist The Mighty Houserockers et. al., San Antonio, 1965—; woodwind instr. Judson Sch. Dist., Converse, Tex., 1993—2000; music instr. St. Philip's Coll., San Antonio, 2000—. Composer (musician): (saxophone quartet) D Sonata; composer: (song cycle for soprano, flute, and piano) Canciónes de Jiménez, (electronic composition) At the Weasel Jamboree. Mem.: Am. Fedn. of Musicians. Avocations: hiking, nature photography.

GONZALES, RICHARD JOSEPH, lawyer; b. Tucson, Mar. 5, 1950; s. Diego D. and Helen O. (Olivas) G.; children: Adrianne, Laura. BA, U. Ariz., 1972, JD, 1975. Bar: Ariz. 1976, U.S. Dist. Ct. Ariz. 1976, U.S. Ct. Appeals 1977, U.S. Supreme Ct. 1993. Asst. pub. defender Pima County Pub. Defenders Office, Tucson, 1976-77; dep. atty. criminal div. Pima County Atty.'s Office, Tucson, 1977-80; ptnr. Gonzales & Villarreal, P.C., Tucson, 1980-96, The Gonzales Law

Firm, Tucson, 1997—. Assoc. instr. bus. law Pima Community Coll.,Tucson, 1977, criminal law, 1978-80; judge pro tem Pima County Superior Ct., 1983—; magistrate City of South Tucson, 1982-85; spl. magistrate City of Tucson, 1982-85; comn. appellate ct. appointments, 1991-95; sr. coun. Coll. Master Advocates and Barristers, 2002. Mem. Tucson Tomorrow, 1984-89, Citizen's adv. coun. Sunnyside Sch. Dist., 1986-88; chmn. com. Udall for Congress 2d Congl. Dist., United Way Hispanic Leadership Devel. Program, 1984-86, vice-chmn., 1983-84, chmn., 1984-85; bd. dirs. Girls Club of Tucson, Inc., 1980-81, Teatro Carmen, Inc., 1981-84, Sunnyside Devilaides, Inc., 1982-83, Alcoholism Coun. Tucson, 1982-83, Crime Resisters, 1984-85, La Frontera Ctr., Inc., 1985-96, Crime Prevention League, 1985-87; gen. counsel U. Ariz. Hispanic Alumni; bd. dirs. U. Ariz. Law Coll. Assn., 1984-95, Am.-Israel Friendship League, 1990—, Tucson Internat. Mariachi Conf., 1990—. Named one of Outstanding Young Men of Am. U.S. Jaycee's, 1980; recipient Vol. of Yr. award United Way Greater Tucson, 1985, Cmty. Svc. award Ariz. Minority Bar Assn., 1992, Citizen Svc. award U. Ariz. Hispanic Alumni, 1995, League United Latin Am. Citizen's F.B.I. Community Svcs. Award, 1996, human betterment award Roots & Wings, Inc., 1996, Centennial Achievement award U. Arizona Alumni Assn., 1998, Noche De Las Estrellas Award, Sunnyside High Sch., 2000; honoree State Bar Arizona One Hundred Women & Minority Lawyers, 2001. Fellow Ariz. Bar Found.; mem. ABA, Ariz. Bar Assn., Pima County Bar Assn., Assn. Trial Lawyers Am., Ariz. Trial Lawyers Assn. (bd. dirs.), Nat. Orgn. on Legal Problems of Edn., Supreme Ct. Hist. Soc., Univ. Ariz. Alumni Assn. (bd. dirs. 1988-91), Tucson 30, Phi Delta Phi. Lodges: Optimists (Optimist of Yr. 1981). Democrat. Roman Catholic. Office: The Gonzales Law Firm 3501 N Campbell Ave Ste 104 Tucson AZ 85719-2032

GONZALES, RICHARD ROBERT, counselor; b. Palo Alto, Calif., Jan. 12, 1945; s. Pedro and Virginia (Ramos) G.; m. Jennifer Ayres; children: Lisa Dianne, Jeffrey Ayres. AA, Foothill Coll., 1966; BA, San Jose (Calif.) State U., 1969; MA, Calif. Poly. State U., San Luis Obispo, 1971; grad., Def. Info. Sch., Def. Equal Opportunity Mgmt. Inst. Lic. marriage family child counselor, Calif.; cert. counselor Nat. Bd. Cert. Counselors. Counselor student activities Calif. Poly. State U., San Luis Obispo, 1969-71, instr. ethnic studies, 1970-71; counselor Ohlone Coll., Fremont, Calif., 1971-72, coord. coll. readiness, 1971; counselor De Anza Coll., Cupertino, Calif., 1972-78, mem. cmty. spkrs. bur., 1975-78; counselor Foothill Coll., Los Altos Hills, Calif., 1978—, mem. cmty. spkrs. bur., 1978—. Instr. Def. Equal Opportunity Mgmt. Inst., 1984-96; mem. U. Calif. C.C. Counselor Adv. Com., 1998—. Mem. master plan com. Los Altos (Calif.) Sch. Dist., 1975-76; vol. worker, Chicano cmtys., Calif.; active mem. Woodside (Calif.) Recreation Commn. Commd. officer Calif. Army N.G., now ret. Adj. Gen. Corps, USAR. Masters and Johnson fellow. Mem. ACA, Am. Coll. Counseling Assn., Calif. Assn. Marriage and Family Therapists, Calif. C.C. Counselor Assn. (former pres.), Calif. Assn. Counseling and Devel. (former pres. Hispanic Caucus, former pres.), Calif. Assn. for Humanistic Edn. and Devel. (former pres.), Calif. Assn. for Multi-Cultural Counseling, Res. Officers Assn., La Raza Faculty Assn. Calif. C.C., Nat. Career Devel. Assn., Phi Delta Kappa, Chi Sigma Iota. Republican. E-mail: rrgincal@aol.com.

GONZALES, RON, mayor, former county supervisor; b. San Francisco; m. Alvina Gonzales; 3 children: Miranda, Rachel, Alejandra. BA in Community Studies, U. Calif., Santa Cruz. Formerly with Sunnyvale (Calif.) Sch. Dist., City of Santa Clara, Calif.; then human resource mgr. Hewlett-Packard Co.; market program mgmt. cons. state and local govts.; mem. city coun. City of Sunnyvale, 1979-87, mayor, 1982, 87; mem. bd. suprs. Santa Clara County, 1989-96; edn. program mgr. Hewlett Packard Co., 1996-98; mayor San Jose, Calif., 1999—. Bd. chair, 1993; bd. transit suprs. Santa Clara County, 1989—; bd. dirs. Joint Venture: Silicon Valley, The Role Model Program, Bay Area Biosci. Ctr., Am. Leadership Forum, Santa Clara County. Office: City Hall Office Mayor 801 N 1st St Rm 600 San Jose CA 95110-1704*

GONZALES, STEPHANIE, state official; b. Santa Fe, Aug. 12, 1950; 1 child, Adan Gonzales. Degree, Loretto Acad. for Girls. Office mgr. Jerry Wood & Assocs., 1973-86; dep. sec. of state Santa Fe, 1987-90; sec. of state, 1991-99; state dir. rural devel. U.S. Dept. of Agriculture, Albuquerque, 1999—; state liaison dept. energy Los Alamos Eviron. Mgmt. Site. Bd. dirs. N.Mex. Pub. Employees Retirement, N.Mex. State Convassing Bd., N.Mex. Commn. Pub. Records. Mem. exec. bd. N.Mex. AIDS Svc.; mem. Commn. White House Fellowships. Mem. Nat. Assn. Secs. State, United League United Latin Am. Citizens (women's coun.), Nat. Assn. Latin Elected and Appointed Ofcls. Office: Los Alamos Nat Lab PO Box 1663 Los Alamos NM 87545*

GONZALEZ, ANTONIO, academic administrator, mortgage company executive; b. Edinburg, Tex., Mar. 14, 1943; s. Manuel Gonzalez and Natalia Torres; m. Elma De Luna, Oct. 10, 1975; 1 child, Julissa Priscilla. BA, U. Md., Balt., 1971; MA, U. Tenn., 1973; JD, Miles Coll., 1979. Law clk. Crain Caton James & Oberwetter, Houston, 1979-81; instr. U. Houston, 1981-83, asst. dir., 1983-86; instr. Houston C.C., 1982—85, 1995, 2001—02; assoc. dir. No. Ill. U., Dekalb, 1986-88; adminstr. Prairie View (Tex.) A&M U., 1988—96; instr. Houston Internat. U., 1988-89, pres., CEO, 1989-90, Am. Fidelity Mortgage & Title Co., Houston, 1992-95; instr. North Harris Coll., Houston, 1994-95, Wharton County Jr. Coll., 1996—2002, Tomball Coll., 2001—02, Montgomery Coll., 2002—03, Tex. So. U., 2003. Mem. adv. com. Houston C.C., 1994-95. Editor: Mexican-American Musicians, 1987; mem. editl. bd. Jour. Minority Issues, 1993-94. Chair tng. and devel. LULAC Dist. 18, Houston, 1994-96; dir. Inst. Chicano Culture, Houston, 1995; mem. SER Jobs for Progress, Houston, 1994-96; Dem. candidate Tex. Ho. Reps. Dist. 130, 1994; mem. Tejano Ctr. for Cmty. Concerns. With USAF, 1966-70, Vietnam. Named Man of Yr. LULAC, Ill., 1987. Mem.: VFW, AAUP, Tex. Assn. Coll. and Univ. Student Pers. Adminstrs., Nat. Bar Assn., Tex. Fgn. Lang. Assn., Ala. Assn. Mortgage Brokers, Tex. C.C. Tchrs. Assn., Tex. Assn. Coll. Admissions Counselors, Tex. Assn. Chicanos in Higher Edn., Am. Hist. Assn., Air Force Assn., Am. Legion, Vietnam Vets. Assn., Delta Theta Phi, Phi Delta Kappa. Roman Catholic. Avocations: writing, research. Home: 16614 Dounreay Dr Houston TX 77084-3410 Office: Prairie View A&M U PO Box 188 Prairie View TX 77446 E-mail: Amerfid@aol.com.

GONZALEZ, ARTHUR PADILLA, artist, educator; b. Sacramento, July 22, 1954; s. John and Rita (Padilla) G.; m. Christine Carol Ciavarella, Feb. 11, 1988; stepchild, Nick Port. BA, Calif. State U., Sacramento, 1977, MA, 1979; MFA, U. Calif., Davis, 1981. Vis. artist La. State U., Baton Rouge, 1982-83, U. Ga., Athens, summer 1984, R.I. Sch. Design, Providence, 1985; asst. prof. U. Calif., Davis, 1985-86, Berkeley, 1987-88; vis. artist, instr. San Francisco Art Inst., 1990-91; assoc. prof. art Calif. Coll. Arts & Crafts, Oakland, 1991—. Mem. adv. bd. Calif. Craft Mus., San Francisco, 1994-95; juror Sacramento Met. Arts Commn., 1994-95. One-person shows include Sharpe Gallery, N.Y.C., 1984, 85, 86, 88, Phyllis Kind Gallery, N.Y.C., 1995, John Elder Gallery, N.Y.C., 1999, 2002. Recipient awards Nat. Endowment for Arts, 1982, 84, 86, 90, Virginia Groot award, 1997. Democrat. Avocation: polynesian dance. Home: 1713 Versailles Ave Alameda CA 94501-1650 Office: Calif Coll Arts & Crafts 5212 Broadway Oakland CA 94618-1426

GONZALEZ, ARTURO FRANCIS, JR., journalist; b. NYC, June 5, 1928; s. Arturo Francis Sr. and Katherine (Phippen) G.; m. Maureen Carroll; children: Martha, Peter, Ann. AB, Brown U., 1952. Promotion dir. Time-Life, N.Y.C. & London, 1952-57, 62-71, Reader's Digest, N.Y.C., 1957-61; creative dir. Asia Mag., Hong Kong, 1961-62; press officer UNHCR, Geneva, 1978-79; comm. dir. Internat. Herald Tribune, Paris & London, 1982-86. Contbr. over 3,000 articles to internat. mags. and newspapers. With USN, 1946-48, Panama. Mem. Soc. Am. Travel Writers (pres. 1996-97), Overseas Press Club, Soc. Profl. Journalists, Travel Journalists Guild (v.p. 1999), Am. Soc. Journalists and Authors, Internat. Food, Wine, Travel Writers Assn. E-mail: arkyg@aol.com.

GONZALEZ, CHARLES A. congressman; b. San Antonio, Tex., May 5, 1945; s. Henry B. and Bertha G.; m. Becky Whetstone; children: Leo Gonzalez, Benjamin and Casey Schmidt. BA in Govt., U. Tex., Austin, 1969; JD, St. Mary's Sch. Law, San Antonio, 1972. 5th grade tchr. Kindred Elem. Sch. So. San Antonio Sch. Dist.; pvt. practice San Antonio, 1972-82; mcpl. ct. judge; county ct. at law judge, 1983-87; dist. judge, 1989-97; mem. U.S. Congress from 20th Tex. dist., Washington, 1999—; mem. banking and fin. svcs. com, small bus. com. Appointed regional whip for the Dem. Caucus; elected v.p. freshman class for 106th Congress; as mem. of Congl. Hispanic Caucus, named chair of Census Task Force; co-chair Census Task Force for Dem. Caucus Bd. dirs. Arthritis Found., Literacy Coun., YMCA Metroboard, Camp Fire Girls, March of Dimes, Easter Seals. Democrat. Achievements include being recognized as one of the highest rated trial judges; responsible for introducing the latest in tech. into the courtroom and streamlining the dockets; earned reputation as ardent mediator. Office: 327 Cannon Ho Office Bldg Washington DC 20515-4320*

GONZALEZ, DIANA M. language educator; b. Spain, Dec. 21, 1964; MA, Columbia U., 1986; BA in Biology, Chemistry & Fine Arts, Bklyn. Coll., 1988; EdM, Columbia U.; postgrad., Fordham U., 2003—. TV anchorwoman World Television Cor., Whitestone, NY, 1972; theater asst. dir. Trinity Tabernacle Theatre Group, Bklyn., 1991; tutor Spanish lang. Tchg. Corps Program, Bklyn., 1992; tchr., governess Palermo, Italy, 1992; art instr. Chinese student Herald Summer Camp, NY, 1993; tchr. English Nanjing (China) Auditing Inst., 1993—94; tchr. English Nanjing Rwy. Med. Coll., 1994—95; liaison between sculptor and staff, tchr. English Tom Otterness Studio, Bklyn., 1996; tchr. Spanish NYU, N.Y.C., 1996; lang. instr. French, Italian and Spanish lang. divsn. Baruch Coll., N.Y.C., 1996; sci. chairperson Liberty H.S., 1996; instr. math. and English South Bronx Job Corps, 1997; art instr. for deaf and multiple handicapped J4 7 Sch. for the Deaf, 1998; itinerary lang. specialist of the hearing impaired Hearing Edn. Svcs., 1998—; tchr. Chinese culture and lang. N.Y.C. Police Dept. Dep. Commr., 1999—; note taker, transcriber of lectrs. for deaf students deaf edn. dept. Tchr.'s Coll., 2000—. Rep. Xunta Galicia, N.Y.C. Recipient Eleventh Inst. Children's Lit. award, Spanish Embassy, 1998; scholar Bd. Edn. scholar, Columbia U. Tchr.'s Coll., 1998. Achievements include speaking eight languages: Spanish, English, French, Italian, Cantonese, Mandarin, Am. Sign Language, German. Avocations: Chinese martial arts, dancing, ping pong, swimming, cartoon drawing. Address: Apt E-26 511 W 232 St Bronx NY 10463

GONZALEZ, DOMINGO, neurosurgeon; b. Buenos Aires, Sept. 15, 1939; s. Salvador Gonzalez and Concepcion Moles; m. Beth Henry, Dec. 15, 1980; children: Gustavo, Paola, Aimee. MD, U. Buenos Aires, 1964. Diplomate Am. Bd. Neurol. Surgeons. Resident in neurosurgery Wayne State U., 1966-72; neurosurgeon Knud-Hansen Meml. Hosp., St. Thomas, U.S. V.I., 1972-73, Timiken Mercy Hosp., Canton, Ohio, 1973-80, Massillon Cmty. Hosp., Ohio, 1973-80, Doctor's Hosp., Massillon, Ohio, 1973-80; chief neurosurgery Sanatorio Guemes, Buenos Aires, 1981-89, Swiss Med. Group, Buenos Aires, 1981-2000; pvt. practice Doctor's Hosp., 2001—, Cmty. Hosp., Massilion, 2001—. Mem. Am. Assn. Neurol. Surgeons, Ohio State Med. Soc., Colegio Argentino de Neurocirujanos. Avocation: woodworking. Office: 1455 Harrison Ave NW Canton OH 44708 Home: 1455 Harrison Ave NW Canton OH 44708-2621 Fax: 330-452-0779. E-mail: dgneuro@earthlink.net.

GONZALEZ, EMILIO BUSTAMANTE, rheumatologist, educator; b. Asuncion, Paraguay, Jan. 9, 1949; came to U.S., 1974; s. Emilio Gonzalez-Jovellanos and Clara (Bustamante) Gonzalez; m. Elizabeth Ferreira, Jan. 4, 1973; 1 child, Daniel. BS in Scis. and Humanities, C.A.L. Coll., Asuncion, 1972; MD summa cum laude, Nat. U., Asuncion, 1972. Diplomate Am. Bd. Internal Medicine, Am. Bd. Rheumatology, Am. Bd. Allergy and Immunology. Intern Univ. Hosp., Asuncion, 1973-74; resident Danbury (Conn.) Hosp., 1975-78; tchg. fellow in allergy and clin. immunology U. Pitts. Sch. Medicine/VA Med. Ctr., 1978-79; mem. staff allergy/clin. immunology Nat. Jewish Hosp. and U. Colo. Affiliated Hosps., Denver, 1979-80; mem. staff clin. immunology/rheumatology U. Tex. Med. Br., Galveston, 1980-81, clin. instr. dept. medicine, 1981-82, asst. prof. medicine, 1982-89, assoc. prof. medicine, 1989—; chief rheumatology svc. Grady Meml. Hosp./Emory U. Sch. Medicine, Atlanta, 1989—; attending physician rheumatology sect. med. svc. VA Med. Svc., Emory U., Decatur, Ga., 1989—; attending physician divsn. rheumatology Emory U. Hosp., Atlanta, 1989—; cons., part-time mem. divsn. rheumatology The Emory Clinic/Emory U., Atlanta, 1989—; dir. rheumatology Atlanta Med. Ctr., 1998—. Bd. dirs. Arthritis Found., Ga., sci. com., 1993—; presenter in field. Contbr. numerous articles to profl. jours.; nat. manuscript reviewer jours. in field. Fellow ACP, Am. Coll. Rheumatology; mem. AMA, Am. Acad. Allergy and Immunology, Ga. Rheumatism Soc. (program chmn. 1993-94), Ga. Soc. Rheumatology (pres. 1995-96), Sigma Xi. Office: Atlanta Med Ctr Box 423 303 Parkway Dr NE Atlanta GA 30312-1212 E-mail: egonzal@emory.edu., emilio.gonzalez@tenethealth.com.

GONZALEZ, EUGENE ROBERT, investment banker; s. Eugenio Tomas and Alice Marie (Macdonald) Gonzalez-Mandiola. *Father's family left San Sebastian, Spain for Chile during the early Colonial period, and were owners of the "Mariposa" ranch, a major agricultural and farming complex south of Santiago. He returned to Chile, to look after the family's interests, after completing his graduate studies at M.I.T. Mother moved from Boston to join husband in South America in the late 1920's where she founded, and served as principal, of an Anglo-American elementary school.* BA in Internat. Rels., Yale U., 1952; postgrad., Georgetown U., 1954; postgrad. sem. in advanced mgmt., Internat. Mgmt. Devel. Inst., Lausanne, Switzerland, 1967. Econ. officer Dept. Defense, Washington, 1954-57; project fin. officer Devel. Loan Fund (now AID), Washington, 1957-58; fin. mgr. RCA Internat., N.Y.C., 1958-61; fin. instns. specialist Interam. Devel. Bank, Washington, 1961-62, fin. officer, 1962-63, dep. regional rep. for Europe, 1964; exec. v.p. Adela Investment Co., Luxembourg, 1964-74; pres., chief exec. officer Adelatec Mgmt. Cons. Co., 1969-72; mng. dir. Adela Investment Co., 1974-75, pres., chief exec. officer, 1975-76; adviser, regional coordinator Ibero Am. Morgan Stanley Internat., N.Y.C., 1977-89; sr. v.p., head internat. pvt. banking Barclays Bank, N.Y.C., 1989-91; mng. dir. Kidder, Peabody & Co., N.Y.C., 1992-94; pres. Quasar Capital Corp., S.A., 1995—. *The ADELA Investment Company, a multi-national consortium of more than 100 leading international banks and corporations, was established to promote economic development through venture capital activities in Latin America. The ADELA Board of Directors consisted primarily of Chairmen or Presidents of the corporate shareholders. The ADELA group succeeded in developing close to 100 new joint ventures of foreign and local capital in twenty countries of the Region.* Author: International Sources of Financing, 1961. Served with U.S. Army, 1952-54. Mem. Nat. Com. on Am. Fgn. Policy, Internat. Assn. Fin. Planners, Am. Soc. Profl. Cons., Presidents Assn., Americas Soc., Spanish Inst., Met. Club (Washington), City Tavern Club (Washington), Brook Club (N.Y.C.), Racquet and Tennis Club (N.Y.C.), Yale Club (N.Y.C.), Pacific Union Club (San Francisco), Zeta Psi Soc. N.Am. Home: 165 E 66th St # 9K New York NY 10021-6132 E-mail: egonz88888@aol.com.

GONZALEZ, GABRIELA INES, physics educator; b. Cordoba, Argentina, Feb. 24, 1965; d. Pedro Arnaldo Gonzalez Bofill and Dora Luisa Trembinsky de Gonzalez; m. Jorge Alfredo Pullin, Oct. 7, 1988. Lic. in Physics, Cordoba Nat. U., 1988; MSc in Physics, Syracuse U., 1993, PhD in Physics, 1995. Asst. tchr. Manuel Belgrano H.S., Cordoba, 1983-85; tchg. asst. Cordoba Nat. U., 1985-89, Syracuse (N.Y.) U., 1990-93, rsch. asst., 1993-95; staff scientist Ctr. for Space Rsch., MIT, Cambridge, 1995-97; asst. prof. physics Pa. State U., University Park, 1997—2001, La. State U., Baton Rouge, 2001—. Mem. coun. Laser Interferometric Gravitational Wave Obs. project LIGO Sci. Collaboration, Pasadena, Calif., 1997—. Grantee NSF, 1998—. Mem. AAAS, m. Phys. Soc. (exec. com. topical group on gravitation), ACLU, Nat. Geog. Soc. Achievements include research in gravitational wave detection, associated with the Laser-Interferometer Gravitational-wave Observatory project. Office: La State U 202 Nicholson Hall Baton Rouge LA 70803 Fax: 225-578-0464. E-mail: gonzalez@lsu.edu.

GONZALEZ, GEORGE G. priest, pastor; b. Miami, Nov. 21, 1939; s. David and Anna G. BS in Philosopy, Loyola U., 1963, MDiv in Theology, 1968. Assoc. pastor Cath. Ch., Miami, 1967-70, San Antonio, 1970-75; chaplain U.S. Army, various locations, 1976-96; pastor Our Lady of Lourdes, Columbus, Ga., 1996-98, St. Mary's Americus, Midland, Ga., 1998—. Recipient medal of honor U.S. Army, 1996. Republican. Roman Catholic. Avocations: tennis, swimming, soccer, reading, jogging. Office: St Mary's Americus 332 S Lee St Americus GA 31709-3916

GONZALEZ, GUILLERMO ENRIQUE, diplomat; b. Córdoba, Argentina, Dec. 30, 1942; m. Adriana Posse; six children. Degree in Polit. and Social Scis. Joined Fgn. Svc. Argentine Republic, 1965, promoted to rank amb. extraordinary and plenipotentiary, 1993; from mem. office dir. gen. policy to amb. Ministry Fgn. Affairs, Buenos Aires, 1965—99; amb. Argentina to Switzerland Ministry of Fgn. Affairs, Bern, Switzerland, 2002—. Office: Embassy of Argentine Rep Jungfraustrasse 1 3005 Bern Switzerland Fax: 202-332-3171.

GONZALEZ, HECTOR HUGO, nurse, educator, consultant; b. Roma, Tex., Mar. 9, 1937; s. Amadeo Lorenzo and Carlotta (Trevino) G. BSN, Incarnate Word Coll., 1963; MSN, Cath. U. Am., 1966; PhD in Edn., U. Tex., 1974. RN, Tex. Staff nurse Santa Rosa Med. Ctr., San Antonio, 1962-65; asst. dir. nursing divsn. Incarnate Word Coll., San Antonio, 1968-72; prof., chmn. dept. nursing San Antonio Coll., 1972-92, dir. Ctr. for Assoc. Degree Edn. Rsch. and Svc., 1987-92, prof. and chmn. emeritus, 1993—. Cons. NIMH, 1973, FDA, 1989-93, mem. anesthesiology and respiratory devices panel, mem. dispute resolution panel, 2000—01; numerous ednl. instns. and hosps. in U.S., Mex., P.R., Kuwait; mem. Nat. Adv. Coun. on Alcohol Abuse and Alcoholism, 1976-80; mem. nat. adv. coun. nurses edn. and practice, 1992-96; mem. panel on nursing practice U.S. Pharmacopeia, 1985-2000. Contbr. articles to profl. jours.; peer reviewer Nursing Outlook, 1983, Advancing Clinical Care. Mem. legis. affairs adv. com. State Senator Glen Kothman, San Antonio, 1983; bd. dirs. Family Svcs. Assn. San Antonio; mem. multidisciplinary academic external com. U. Autonoma de Nuevo Leon, Mex., 1986-88. Capt. nurse corps U.S. Army, 1966-68. Recipient cert. of appreciation Citizens of Bexar County, San Antonio, 1970, Nat. Student Nurses Assn., 1977. Mem. ANA (mem. adv. bd. minority fellowship program 1976-80), Nat. Assn. Hispanic Nurses (pres. 1982-84, bd. dirs. 1995-97, CEO San Antonio chpt. 1998—, project dir. breast cancer tng. grant Am. Cancer Soc. and Nat. Assn. Hispanic Nurses 1992-96), Nat. League for Nursing (bd. dirs. 1973-81). Democrat. Roman Catholic. Home: 114 Magnolia Dr San Antonio TX 78212-3115 E-mail: hhgzz@cs.com.

GONZALEZ, IRMA ELSA, federal judge; b. 1948; BA, Stanford U., 1970; JD, U. Ariz., 1973. Law clk. to Hon. William C. Frey U.S. Dist. Ct. (Ariz. dist.), 1973-75; asst. U.S. atty. U.S. Attys. Office Ariz., 1975-79, U.S. Attys. Office (ctrl. dist.) Calif., 1979-81; trial atty. antitrust divsn. U.S. Dept. Justice, 1979; assoc. Seltzer Caplan Wilkins & McMahon, San Diego, 1981-84; judge U.S. Magistrate Ct. (so. dist.) Calif., 1984-91; ct. judge San Diego County Superior Ct., 1991-92; dist. judge U.S. Dist. Ct. (so. dist.) Calif., San Diego, 1992—. Adj. prof. U. San Diego, 1992; trustee Calif. Western Sch. Law; bd. visitors Sch. Law U. Ariz. Mem. Girl Scout Women's Adv. Cabinet. Mem. Lawyers' Club San Diego, Inns of Ct. Office: Edward J Schwartz US Courthouse 940 Front St Ste 5135 San Diego CA 92101-8911

GONZALEZ, JOE FRED, JR., mathematical statistician, educator; b. San Antonio, Tex., Jan. 16, 1947; s. Joe Fred Gonzalez, Sr. and Gloria Rodriquez Gonzalez; m. Patricia Vaive Gonzalez, July 15, 1987; children: Joe Fred III, Jennifer Melanie Day, Michele Yvette Frates, Francesca Joelle. BS in Math., St. Mary's U., 1965—70; MS in Stats., The George Wash. U., 1979—81. Math. statistician Office of Rsch. and Methodology, Nat. Ctr. for Health Stats., Hyattsville, Md., 1972—. Adj. asst. prof. Montgomery Coll., Rockville, Md., 1985—99, U. of Md. U. Coll., Coll. Pk., Md., 1990—; presenter Nat. Acad. Scis., Washington, 2002—03. Co-author (with Lester R. Curtin): (math. computer graph) The Bivariate Normal Distbn. (Rho=0.8) (Most Creative Use of Software, First Place-monochrome, 1986); co-author: (asa proceedings paper) Alternative Designs for the 1993 Nat. Mortality Followback Survey, Issues in Sampling Blacks and Hispanics in Sch.-Based Surveys, Sample Design for the 1988 Nat. Maternal and Infant Health Survey, Nonresponse and Noncoverage Analysis in the S.W. Component of the Hispanic Health and Nutrition Examination Survey, Smoothing Procedures for Life Tables Based on Small Numbers of Deaths, Estimation in the S.W. Component of the Hispanic Health and Nutrition Examination Survey, (conf. proceedings paper) Sample Design and Estimation Issues in the Hispanic Health and Nutrition Survey, 1982—84, (nchs series 1 report) Chap. 5: Sample Design and Estimation Procedures, (asa proceedings paper) Stratifying Primary Sampling Units with the SAS Cluster Procedure, (jour. article) Chpt. 2, Synthetic Estimation in Followback Surveys at the Nat. Ctr. for Health Stats., Indirect Estimators, (asa proceedings paper) Alternative Adjustments for Nonresponse in the Nat. Hosp. Discharge Survey, Optimum Recall Periods for Accidental Injury Data in the Nat. Health Interview Survey, (online modules) Modules for UMUC Online BMGT 230 Bus. Stats. Class, (asa proceedings paper) Methods to Improve the Precision of Health Stats. for Non-Hispanic Asians in the Nat. Health Interview Survey, Software for Tabular Data Protection, (tech. paper) Approximation of Relative Stand. Errors for Multi-Yr. Estimates in the NHIS, Effects of Design Assumptions on SUDAAN Variances for Estimates of Aggregates in the National Hospital Ambulatory Care Survey, (nchs series 2 report) 1988 Nat. Maternal and Infant Health Survey: Methods and Response Characteristics. National Center for Health Statistics, Vital and Health Statistics, Series 2, Number 125, 1998., (asa proceedings paper) Estimation in the 1988 Nat. Maternal and Infant Health Survey. Pres. Richard Montgomery H.S. Band Parents Orgn., Rockville, Md., 1984—85; swim team rep. Hungerford Stoneridge Swim Club, Rockville, pres., 1984—86. Recipient Cited with biosketch and photo in a textbook Advanced Math., Precalculus with Discrete Math. and Data Analysis, Houghton Mifflin Co., 1992; scholar LULAC Scholarship Award, League of United Latin Am. Citizens, 1965. Mem.: Wash. Statis. Soc. (assoc.), Am. Statis. Assn. (assoc.; chair, com. on minorities in stats. 1992—95), Math. Assn. of Am. (assoc.), Am. Statis. Assn. (assoc.; mem. asa adv. com. on continuing edn. 1999—2002). Office: Nat Ctr for Health Statistics 6525 Belcrest Rd Hyattsville MD 20782 Office Fax: 301-458-4031. E-mail: jgonzalez@cdc.gov.

GONZALEZ, JOHN M. educator; b. Harlingen, Tex., June 30, 1966; s. Juan H. and Matiana M. Gonzalez. AB, Princeton U., 1988; MA, Stanford U., 1991, PhD, 1998. Asst. prof. U. Mich., Ann Arbor, 1996—2002, U. Tex., Austin, 2002—. Andrew Mellon Found. doctoral fellow Stanford U., 1989, Ford Found. fellow, 1991, 2001; Pres.'s postdoctoral fellow U. Calif., Santa Cruz, 1995. Mem. MLA (del. 1991—), Nat. Assn. Chicano/a Studies, L.Am. Studies Assn., Am. Studies Assn. E-mail: gonzalez@alumni.princeton.edu.

GONZALEZ, JORGE ANTONIO, education educator; b. McAllen, Tex., Sept. 10, 1972; s. Jorge Gonzalez and Sonia Moya. PhD, Tex. A&M U., Coll. Sta., TX, 2001. Asst. prof. U. Wis., Milw., 2000—. Contbr. scientific papers to profl. jour. (promising young scholar rsch. excellence, 1999). Grantee GE Faculty for the Future, GE, 1995. Mem.: Acad. of Mgmt. Avocations: travel, photography. Office: Univ Wis Milw PO Box 742 Milwaukee WI 53201-0742 E-mail: jorgeg@uwm.edu.

GONZALEZ, JOSE ALEJANDRO, JR., federal judge; b. Tampa, Fla., Nov. 26, 1931; s. Jose A. and Luisa Secundina (Collia) G.; m. Frances Frierson, Aug. 22, 1956 (dec. Aug. 1981); children— Margaret Ann, Mary Frances; m. Mary Sue Copeland, Sept. 24, 1983 BA, U. Fla., 1952, JD, 1957; LLD, Nova Southeastern U., 1998. Bar: Fla. 1958, U.S. Dist. Ct. (so. dist.) Fla. 1959, U.S. Ct. Appeals 1959, U.S. Supreme Ct. 1963. Practice in, Ft. Lauderdale, 1958-64; claim rep. State Farm Mut., Lakeland, Fla., 1957-58; assoc. firm Watson, Hubert and Sousley, 1958-61, ptnr., 1961-64; asst. state atty. 15th Cir. Fla., 1961-64; cir. judge 17th Cir. Ft. Lauderdale, 1964-78, chief judge, 1969-70; assoc. judge 4th Dist. Ct. Appeals, West Palm Beach; U.S. dist. judge So. Dist. Fla., 1978—, sr. judge, 1996—. Bd. dirs. Arthritis Found., 1962-72; bd. dirs. Henderson Clinic Broward County, 1964-68, v.p., 1967-68. Served to 1st lt. AUS, 1952-54. Recipient Kupferman award Laymen's Nat. Bible Assn., 1991; named Broward County Outstanding Young Man, 1967, one of Fla.'s Five Outstanding Young Men, Fla. Jaycees, 1967, Broward Legal Exec. of Yr., 1978. Mem.: ABA, Broward County Bar, Fla. Bar Assn., Fed. Bar Assn., Am. Judicature Soc., Pittsfield Country Club, Kiwanian Club (pres. 1971—72), Fla. Blue Key, Lauderdale Yacht Club, Greenock Country Club, Ft. Lauderdale Jaycees (dir. 1960—61), Phi Alpha Delta, Sigma Chi (Significant Sig). Democrat. Office: US Dist Ct 205 US Courthouse 299 E Broward Blvd Fort Lauderdale FL 33301-1944 Home: Ste 205D 299 E Broward Blvd Fort Lauderdale FL 33301-1902

GONZALEZ, JUAN CARLOS, music educator, musician; b. Havana, Cuba, Jan. 18, 1966; arrived in U.S., 1969; s. Virgilio and Aida Rosa Gonzalez; m. Elizabeth Ann Dickson, Nov. 17, 1990; children: Adrian William, Anna Rosa. BFA, Fla. Atlantic U., 1989, MFA in Tchg., 1992. Cert. tchr. Fla. State Bd. Edn. Adj. faculty Palm Beach CC, 1990—, Fla. Atlantic U., 1992—94; music tchr. Palm Beach County Schools, 1994—2000, choral dir., 2000—. Pvt. classical guitar instr., Boynton Beach, 1990—; composer. Composer (recording artist):

(CD) Owls on the Ground, 1998; composer: (composition, performance piece) Clariones. Mem.: Fla. Vocal Assn., MENL. Avocations: scuba diving, golf. Office: Polo Park Middle School 11901 Lake Worth Rd Wellington FL 33437

GONZALEZ, JULIO JORGE, electrical engineering educator; b. Córdoba, Argentina, July 9, 1951; came to U.S., 1986; s. Hilmar Oscar and Rosa Elvira González; m. Mónica Susana González, July 8, 1980; children: María Jorgelina, Fernando David. BSEE, U. Mendoza, Argentina, 1976; MSEE, U. Birmingham, Eng., 1979; PhDEE, Colo. State U., 1991. Rsch. asst. Nat. Coun. for Technol. and Scientific Rsch., Mendoza, 1980-84; asst. prof. U. Mendoza, 1980-84; rsch. assoc. San Juan (Argentina) U., 1984-86; assoc. prof. Nat. Technol. U., Mendoza, 1984-86; asst. prof. Colo. State U., Fort Collins, 1991-93; vis. prof. Fachhochschule Regensburg, Germany, 1994; asst. prof. SUNY, New Paltz, 1993-98, assoc. prof., 1998—. Rsch. cons. ABB-ESAB Co., Fort Collins, 1991-93. Contbr. articles to profl. jours. Recipient SUNY Chancellor's award for excellence in tchg., 2001; scholar British Coun., 1978-79; fellow Orgn. of Am. States, 1986-88; Konrad Zuse prof. German Govt., 1994. Mem. IEEE (sr.), Am. Soc. of Engring. Edn., Tau Beta Pi, Eta Kappa Nu. Avocations: soccer coach, playing chess, playing classical guitar, singing. Office: SUNY at New Paltz Resnick Engring Hall Rm 213 75 S Manheim Blvd New Paltz NY 12561

GONZALEZ, LARRY JUSTIN, political scientist, educator; b. Munich, Aug. 19, 1954; arrived in U.S., 1956; m. Kimberlee Morgan Gonzalez, July 4, 1982; children: Dezerea Lee, Justin Daniel. AA, San Antonio Coll., 1977; BS, U. Houston, 1979, MA, 1985, PhD, 1994. Acct. Browning Ferris, Inc., Houston, 1979—85; asset risk analyst Southland Corp., Houston, 1985—88; prof. Houston C.C., 1988—; asst. prof. U. Houston, 1993—99. Co-dir. S.W. Coll. Svc. Learning Program, Houston, 1998—. Asst. scoutmaster Troop 1115 Boy Scouts Am., 2000—. Recipient Disting. Svc. award, Bedichek Faculty Found., 1992, Tchg. Excellence award, NISOD, 1999. Mem.: Southwestern Polit. Sci. Assn., Am. Polit. Sci. Assn. Avocations: fishing, dancing, camping, boating. Office: Houston CC Southwest 10141 Cash Rd Stafford TX 77477

GONZALEZ, MICHAEL JOHN, nutrition scientist, nutriologist; b. N.Y.C., July 5, 1962; s. R. Miguel and Daisy (Guzman) G.; m. Enid J. Bauza, Mar. 28, 1987; children: Michael John Jr., Michael Joseph. BS in Biology, Cath. U., 1983; MS in Cell Biology, Nova Coll., 1985; MNS in Nutrition and Biochemistry, U. P.R., 1986; NMD in Nutrition, John F Kennedy, 1988; DSc in Health Sci, Lafayette U., 1989; PhD in Tumor Biology, Mich. State U., 1993; postgrad. in geriatrics, U. P.R., 1993-95. Rsch. asst. dept. chemistry Cath. U., Ponce, P.R., 1982-83; lab. instr. dept. biology U. P.R., Mayaguez, 1983-85, rsch. asst. dept. biochemistry Rio Piedras, 1985-86; mem. dept. biology faculty Cath. U., Ponce, 1986-87; rsch. asst. dept. human nutrition Mich. State U., East Lansing, 1987-90, sci. instr. dept. Upward Bound, 1990-91, lab. instr., rsch. asst. dept. food sci. and pharmacology, 1991-93; asst. prof. U. P.R. Med. Sci., San Juan, 1993-96, assoc. prof., 1996—. Mem. faculty Sch. Pub. Health U. P.R. Med. Scis., 1989-93. Reviewer, contbr. articles to profl. jours. Fellow Am. Nutritional Med. Assn. (v.p. 1991—); mem. Am. Inst. Nutrition, Am. Assn. Cancer Rsch., Soc. for Exptl. Biology, N.Y. Acad. Sci., Am. Assn. Police, United Farmers. Democrat. Roman Catholic. Office: Univ PR Med Sci Sch of Pub Health B-456 PO Box 365067 San Juan PR 00936-5067 E-mail: mgonzalez@rcm.upr.edu.

GONZALEZ, RAQUEL MARIA, pharmacist; b. Veguitas, Oriente, Cuba, June 1, 1952; d. Ernesto Esteban and Evora Cristina (Ramirez) G. BS in Biology, Ga. Coll., 1974; BS in Pharmacy, Mercer U., 1977. Registered pharmacist, Ga., Fla., Tenn.; registered pharmacist cons., Fla. Staff pharmacist Cobb Gen. Hosp., Austell, Ga., 1978, VA Hosp., Nashville, 1978-79, Decatur, Ga., 1979-81, Lewisburg (Tenn.) Community Hosp., 1981-89; pharmacist Pharmacy Staffing Svcs. Inc., Brentwood, Tenn., 1989—; chief pharmacist Super D Drug Store # 50, Fayetteville, Tenn., 1989-93; chief of pharmacy Fred's Discount Pharmacy, Lewisburg, Tenn., 1993—. Relief pharmacist Farmer's Market Pharmacy (Kroger), Nashville, 1989—. Mem. Tenn. Pharmacist Assn., Ducks Unltd., Atlanta Ski Club. Republican. Roman Catholic. Avocations: piano, white water rafting, snow skiing, snorkeling, gardening. Home: RR 1 Box 35 Belfast TN 37019-9801 Office: Fred's Discount Pharmacy 1800 Mooresville Hwy Lewisburg TN 37091-2010

GONZALEZ, RENE, government executive; b. Nuevo Laredo, Mexico, May 9, 1967; s. Aurora Castaño and Rene Gonzalez. BBA, U. of Tex. at San Antonio, 1990. Cmty. devel. officer Laredo Nat. Bank, Tex., 1994—99; coord. Tex. Border Infrastructure Coalition, 1999—2000; state, fed. & internat. affairs dir. City of Laredo, Tex., 2000—. Pres. Leadership Laredo, Tex., 1997—98; chmn. Mi Laredo, 1998—2001; dir. Internat. Good Neighbor Coun., Laredo, 1998—99; bd. mem. Habitat for Humanity, Laredo, 1995—2000; bd. of dirs. Laredo C. of C., 1999—2003; treas. Terra Genesis Housing, Laredo, 2000 —03, chmn. Laredo Conv. & Visitor's Bur., 1999— 2000, dir., 1998—2002; internat. bd. of directors North Am. Internat. Trade Corridor Partnership, 2001—03. Mem.: Kiwanis Club of Laredo (pres. 1998—99). D-Conservative. Office: City of Laredo PO Box 440356 Laredo TX 78044-0356 Office Fax: 956-722-6247. Personal E-mail: hazel@lmtonline.com. E-mail: hazel@lmtonline.com.

GONZALEZ, RICARDO, surgeon, educator; b. Buenos Aires, June 26, 1943; s. Salvador Maria and Clyde Alcira (Prevettoni) G.; children: Diego Andres, Carlos Ricardo. BA, Coll. Nat. San Isidro, Buenos Aires, 1959; MD, U. Buenos Aires, 1965. Diplomate Am. Bd. Urology. Resident in surgery Hosp. Militar Cent., Buenos Aires, 1966-68; intern in surgery U. Minn., 1969-70, resident (med. fellow) in urologic surgery, 1970-74, from instr. to prof. urology, 1974-85, prof. urology, 1985-94, prof. pediat., 1993-94; chief, pediat. urology Children's Hosp. of Mich., Detroit, 1994; prof. urology Wayne State U., Detroit, 1995-99; prof. urology and pediat., chief pediat. urology divsn. U. Miami /Jackson Meml. Hosp., Fla., 1999—2002; dir. pediatric urology AI DuPont Hosp. for children, Wilmington, Del., 2002—; prof. urology Thomas Jefferson U., Phila., 2002—, pres., 2002. Pres. Pediat. Urology P.C., Detroit, 1995-2000; vis. prof. Harvard U., Cambridge, Mass., 1994, Johns Hopkins U., Balt., 1995, U. Washington, Seattle, 1995, U. Calif., San Francisco, 1996, Cornell U., NY, 1998, U. Montreal, 2000, Thomas Jefferson U., 2000, McGill U., 2000, U. Vienna, Austria, 2003, Chinese U. Hong Kong, 2003; presenter in field. Contbr. over 200 articles to profl. jours., over 50 chpts. to books; editor 2 books. Am. Acad. Pediat. fellow, 1981, Nat. Kidney Found. rsch. fellow 1974-76; co-prin. investigator USPHS cancer grant 1976-78. Fellow Am. Acad. Pediat. (mem. exec. sect. on urology com. 1995-98); mem. Am. Urologic Assn., Mex. Coll. Urology (hon.), Venezuelan Soc. for Spina Bifida, Argentine Confedn. Urology, Societé Internat. d'Urologie, Ibero-Am. Soc. Pediat. Urology (pres. 1995-98, Medal of Merit 2000), Soc. for Pediatric Urol. Surgeons (by invitation), European Soc. Paediat. Urology (hon.). Avocations: opera, music, language, reading, writing. Office: AI duPont Hosp for Children Dept Urology 1600 Rockland Rd Wilmington DE 19899 E-mail: rgonzale@nemours.org.

GONZALEZ, RICHARD THEODORE, photographer; b. Trona, Calif., Nov. 9, 1939; s. Alfonso Contreras and Mary (Duarte) G.; m. Gerry Price, Oct. 30, 1958 (div. 1972); children: Richard K., Debra G., Maria E., Felicia F.; m. Yolanda Quijano, Apr. 18, 1991; 1 child, Andrea. Degree in profl. still photography, N.Y. Inst. Photography, 1962. Photographer Kerr McGee Chem. Corp., Trona, 1962-86, San Bernadino, Calif., 1987-89; founder Gonzalez's Modeling Agy., Midwest City, Okla., 1996—. Newspaper photographer Trona Argonaut, 1962-86; freelance photographer, Trona, 1962-86. Democrat. Roman Catholic. Home: 769 NW 1st St Moore OK 73160-2329 Office: 700 S Air Depot Blvd Ste D-366 Midwest City OK 73110-4833

GONZALEZ, ROBERTO O. bishop; b. Elizabeth, N.J., June 2, 1950; Student, St. Joseph Seraphic Sem., Sienna Coll., Washington Theol. Union, Fordham U. Joined Franciscan Order, 1976, ordained priest Roman Cath. Ch., 1977. Titular bishop Ursona and aux. bishop, Boston, 1988-95; coadjutor bishop Diocese of Corpus Christi, 1995-97, bishop, 1997-2000; archbishop Archdiocese of San Juan, 1999—. Roman Catholic. Office: PO Box 9021967 San Juan PR 00902-1967

GONZALEZ, ROLANDO NOEL, secondary school educator, religion educator, photographer; b. Rio Grande City, Tex., Sept. 10, 1947; s. Ubaldo and Beulah (Gutierrez) G. BA, U. Tex., 1968; MA, Tex. A & I U., 1972. Cert. tchr. all scis., guidance and counseling. Tchr., head sci. dept. Roma (Tex.) Jr. High Sch., 1968-71; migrant/Title I counselor Roma Elem. and Roma Jr. High Sch., 1972-76; head sci. dept. Rio Grande High Sch., Rio Grande City, Tex., 1976-78; tchr., head sci. dept. Ringgold Jr. High Sch., Rio Grande City, 1982-83, Pharr-San Juan-Alamo High Sch., Pharr, Tex., 1986—; seminarian Diocese of Brownsville, San Antonio, 1979-82; pastoral asst. Our Lady, Queen of Angels Ch., La Joya, Tex., 1982-83; coord., lay ministries Brownsville Diocese, McAllen, Tex., 1983-85; lectr., tchr. on scripture Perpetual Help Ch., McAllen, 1986-88, Holy Spirit Ch., McAllen, 1989—; tchr. psychology South Tex. C.C., 2003—. Instr. history of chemistry U. Tex. Pan Am., Edinburg, 1990; wedding and portrait photographer, 1973—; psychology tchr., South Tex. C.C., 2003—. Contbr. articles to profl. jours. Tchr. scripture, lectr. Sts. Mary and Margaret Ch., Pharr, Tex., 1988, Sacred Heart Ch., Mercedes, Tex., 1990; tchr. scripture Holy Spirit Parish, McAllen, Tex., 1992—. Recipient Appreciation award Sacred Heart Ch., 1990, Tchr. of Yr. award Rio Grande Valley Sci. Assn., 1996-97, Holy Spirit Parish Vol. award, 2000. Home: 2800 W Iris Ave Mcallen TX 78501-6200 *Humans are so resilient and basically optimistic. I marvel at how humans reach for the stars even though they see around them a planet full of woes.*

GONZALEZ, ROSE A-NAVARRO, artist; b. Granada, Nicaragua, May 22, 1936; d. Manuel Navarro and Candelaria (Guerrero) Martinez; m. Simeon Gonzalez, Oct. 15, 1959. Diploma, Nat. Inst. Orient, Granada, Nicaragua, 1956, Sch. Art and Design, N.Y.C., 1964, Abbey Sch. N.Y., 1972; postgrad., Art Student's League, N.Y.C., 1972-73. Group exhbns. include Empire Savs. Bank, N.Y.C., 1973, Mus. City of N.Y., 1977, 82, Cayman Gallery, 1977, New Rochelle Gallery, 1978, Los Sures Gallery, 1978, Bklyn. Mus. Gallery, 1979, Louis Aborns Arts for Living Ctr., 1979, Studio 54, 1983, Keanne Mason Gallery, N.Y.C., 1983, Queen's Coll., 1984, St. Sabastian Parish Ctr., 1991, Latino Open-Air and Cultural Festival, N.Y.C., 1992, SUNY, 1992, Agora Gallery, N.Y.C., 1993, Progress Gallery, N.Y.C., 1993-94, 98, Dist. Coun. 37, N.Y.C., 1994, 95, New Rochelle Pub. Libr., 1996, Goya Gallery, N.Y.C., 1997, Colombian Consulate, N.Y.C., 1997, Aguilar Libr., N.Y.C., 1997, Oller Campeche Gallery, 1997, N.Y.C., Taller Romano Gallery, Madrid, 1998, N.E. Hispanic Cath. Ctr., N.Y.C., 1999, Dic St. Coun. 37, N.Y.C., 1999, Hispanic Cath. Ctr., N.Y.C., 2000, Consulate Domican Republic, 2000, Ctrl. Pk. Gallery, N.Y.C., 2001, Fundtion Gallery, N.Y.C., 2001, Consulate Ecuador, N.Y.C., 2001, Hostus Cool, N.Y.C., 2001, Sant Peter's Ch., N.Y.C., 2001, Golden Ctr., N.Y.C., 2001, Golden Ctr., N.Y.C., 2001, Centro Cutural Latino, N.Y.C., 2001, Mus. Paterson N.J., 2001. Mem. coun. Eisenhower Commn., Rep. Nat. Com., Washington, 1995. Recipient spl. prize Friends of Puerto Rico; Comision awarded Hispana Pro-Obra Ruben Dario, 1999; recipient Medal of Freedom, 1999, Outstanding Artist and Designer of the 20th Century medal, award Nicaraguan Consultate, N.Y.C., named Rep. N.Y. as Republican of Yr., 2001, Cuidad de Ange Les award N.Y., 2001. Mem. Lions Club Internat. (v.p. 1995—, Melvin Jones award 1993-94). Republican. Roman Catholic. Home: 1121 Morrison Ave Bronx NY 10472-4235

GONZALEZ, TONY, football player; b. Huntington Beach, California, Feb. 27, 1976; Attended, Univ. Calif. Tight end Kans. City Chiefs, 1997—. Two-time participant Pro Bowl; spokesperson Midwest Donor Organ Bank, U.S. Dept. Transp. Safety Campaign, Sch. Safety Hotline, Kans. Cons. (movie) Any Given Sunday, appeared (HBO episode) Arliss, 2000, host (TV series) KCTV-5, appeared Buckle Up: Football Is a Game, Your Life is Not. Founder Tony Gonzalez Found.; contbr. Shadow Buddies Program, Boys & Girls Clubs; donator Kans. City Boys & Girls Club, 1999. Recipient Mack Lee Hill award. Office: 1 Arrowhead Dr Kansas City MO 64129

GONZALEZ ARIAS, VICTOR HUGO, management executive, b. Guayaquil, Ecuador, July 12, 1955; s. Porfirio Alfredo and Ernestina Perpetua (Arias) G.; children: Victor Christopher, Andres Alfredo; m. Rosa Amalia Hernandez; 1 child, Victor Hugo Jr. BA in Econ. and Internat. Svcs., Cath. U., 1980; MBA, U. D.C., 1983. Utility specialist Water & Sewer Dept., Washington, 1981-83; pres., founder hispanic student assn. U. D.C., Washington, 1982-83; gen. mgr. Inter-High Connection Entrepreneurship Program, a tng. program on how to manage and operate a small bus., Washington, 1983—; v.p. Hispanic Festival, Washington, 1987-88; commr. for Columbia Heights Mayor's Office, Washington, 1987-88; ptnr. Victor H. Gonzalez & Assocs., Washington, 1994—. Mktg. cons. Small Bus. Administrn., Washington, 1981-82. Activist Hispanic Community Coalition, Washington, 1973—; mem. Coun. hispanic Agencies, Washington, 1976-81, Change, Inc., Washington, 1976-78, Latino Students Assn. Cath. U., Washington, 1976-78, pres. PTA Elem. Sch., 2001-03. Comm Anc, 2003-04. Mem. Nat. Soc. Accts., Tax Refund Express, Am. Mgmt. Assn., Nat. Soc. Tax Profls., Sheraton Internat. Democrat. Roman Catholic. Office: 5506 Kenilworth Ave Ste 100 Riverdale MD 20737-3123 E-mail: victorhgonzalez@hotmail.com.

GONZALEZ-BYRD, M. TERESA, physician assistant; b. Caracas, Venezuela, Dec. 7, 1970; came to U.S., 1984; d. Fernando Gonzalez and Leonor Filardo; m. Phllip B. Boyd Byrd III, May 30, 1998. BA in Health Sci., Mt. Vernon Coll., 1992; cert. physician assoc., Yale U., 1998. Cert. ACLS, MET, neonatal cardiac BLS. Physician asst. Advance Ob/Gyn, Vienna, Va.; emergency medicine physician asst. Yale New Haven Hosp., 1998—2001; internal medicine PA-C Trinity Clinic, Tyler, Tex., 2001—. Fellow Am. Acad. Physician Assts., Conn. Acad. Physician Assts. Avocations: painting, cooking, dancing. Home: 4910 Hallye Ln Tyler TX 75703

GONZALEZ-CRUSSI, FRANK, pathologist, author, essayist; b. Mexico City, Oct. 4, 1936; s. Pablo and Maria (Crussi) Gonzalez; m. Wei Hsueh, Oct. 7, 1978; children: Daniel, Francis, Xavier, Juliana. MD, Nat. Autonomous U. N. Mex., 1961. Am. Bd. Pathology. Asst. prof. Queen's U., Kingston, Canada, 1967-72, assoc. prof., 1972-73; prof. pathology Ind. U., Indpls., 1973-78; prof. pathology Northwestern U., Chgo., 1978-2000, prof. emeritus, 2001—; head labs. Children's Meml. Hosp., Chgo., 1986-2000. Author: Notes of an Anatomist, 1985, Three Forms of Sudden Death, 1986, On the Nature of Things Erotic, 1988, The Five Senses, 1989, The Day of the Dead, 1993, Suspended Animation, 1995, There is a World Elsewhere, 1998; author, editor: Nephroblastoma, 1984. Royal Coll. Physicians and Surgeons of Can.; mem. Author's Guild, Soc. Midland Authors, Soc. for Pediatric Pathology. Office: Children's Meml Hosp 2300 N Children's Plz Chicago IL 60614-3394 E-mail: fgcrussi@yahoo.com.

GONZALEZ DE LEON, FERNANDO, historian, educator; AB, Rutgers Coll., 1981; MA, U. Va., 1983; MA, PhD, Johns Hopkins U., 1991. Vis. asst. prof. SUNY, Purchase, 1990-91, Bard Coll., Annandale-on-Hudson, N.Y., 1991-92; asst. prof. Springfield (Mass.) Coll., 1992—97, assoc. prof., 1997—; Olin postdoctoral fellow Yale U., New Haven, 1995. Contbr. articles to profl. jours. Mem.: The Hist. Soc., Am. Hist. Assn., Soc. of spanish and Portugese Hist. Studies, Poe Studies Assn. Home: 128 Bay Rd PO Box 145 Hadley MA 01035 Office: Springfield Coll 263 Alden St Springfield MA 01109

GONZALEZ-DEL-VALLE, LUIS TOMAS, Spanish language educator; b. Nov. 19, 1946; BA in Spanish cum laude, Wilmington Coll.-U. N.C., Wilmington, 1968; MA in Spanish and Spanish-Am. Lits., U. Mass., 1972; Phd in Spanish and Spanish-Am. Lits. five coll. coop. program, Amherst Coll., Hampshire Coll., Mt. Holyoke Coll., Smith Coll., U. Mass., 1972. Asst. prof. modern langs. Kans. State U., 1972-75, assoc. prof. modern langs., 1975-77; assoc. prof. modern langs. and lits. U. Nebr., Lincoln, 1977-79, prof. modern langs. and lits., 1979-86; prof. Spanish and Portuguese U. Colo., Boulder, 1986—, chmn. dept. Spanish and Portuguese, 1986-98. Reading cons. South-Western Pub. Co., Inc., 1974, Eliseo Torres & Sons, 1974; dir. Ibero-Latin Am. Studies Ctr., 1987—; lectr. in field. Author: La nueva ficcion hispanoamericana a traves de M.A. Asturias y G. Garcia Marquez, 1972, La ficcion breve de Valle Inclán, 1990, El Canon: Reflexiones Sobre la Recepcion Literaria-Teatral, 1993, La canonización del Diablo: Baudelaire y la estética moderna en España, 2002, Bauelaire y la estetica moderna en Espana, 2002; co-author: Luis Romero, 1979; gen. editor Anales de la literatura española contemporánea, 1975—, Siglo xx/20th Century, 1985—; editor: Jour. Spanish Studies: 20th Century, 1972—80, Studies in 20th Century Lit., 1975—79, Annual Bibliography of Post-Civil War Spanish Fiction, 1977—82, Ecos de Cuba, 1997; co-editor: La generacion de 1898 ante España, 1997; contbr. articles, essays, book revs. to profl. jours. Recipient Postdoctoral Rsch. award Coun. for Internat. Exch. Scholars, 1984, 500th Rsch. Award Spanish Fgn. Ministry, 1992, Silver Medal of Honor Galician Govt., 2000; grantee Coun. on Rsch. and Creative Work, U. Colo., 1986-87, Com. for Ednl. & Cultural Affairs, U. Nebr.-Lincoln, Chancellor's Rsch. Initiation Fund, U. Nebr.-Lincoln, 1980-81, Rsch. Coun., U. Nebr.-Lincoln, 1978, 79; Sr. Faculty Summer Rsch. fellow Rsch. Coun., U. Nebr.-Lincoln, 1978, Woodrow Wilson Dissertation fellow, 1971-72, Univ. fellow U. Mass., 1968-69, 70-72, Grad. fellow, 1969-70. Mem.: MLA, Nebr. Fgn. Lang. Assn., Cervantes Soc. Am., Cir. de Cultura Panamericano (exec. coun. 1972), 20th Century Spanish Assn. (exec. sec. 1982—), Soc. Spanish and Spanish-Am. Studies (bd. dirs. 1975—), Am. Assn. Tchrs. Spanish and Portuguese (Excellence in Tchg. award Colo. chpt. 1996), Assn. Europea de Profesores de Espanol, Fgn. Lang. Adminstrs. of Colo., Assn. de Escritores y Artistas Espanoles (U.S. rep.), Assn. Colegial de Escritores (spl. rep. to U.S., v.p.), Spain's Pen Club (founding 1984), Conf. Editors of Learned Jours. (bd. dirs. 1987—), N.Am. Acad. Spanish Lang. (corr.), Castilian Assn. Writers (hon.), others, Phi Kappa Phi. Home: 1875 Del Rosa Ct Boulder CO 80304-1800 Office: U Colo Dept Spanish Portuguese Boulder CO 80309-0001

GONZALEZ ECHEVARRIA, AMELIA L. librarian, counselor; b. Santurce, P.R., June 22, 1950; d. Raul A. and Arminda (Echevarria) Gonzalez; m. Angel Sepulveda, Sept. 11, 1980 (div. 1982). BA, U. P.R., Rio Piedras, 1967, MLS, 1975, MA, 1989; EdD, Interam. U., San Juan, 1992—. Tchr. spl. edn. Colegio Bautista Carolina (P.R.), 1972-73; dist. supr. Youth Program of P.R., Carolina, 1973-75; libr. dir. New Hampshire Coll., San Juan, P.R., 1985-89, Municipality of San Juan, 1975—. Counselor Fundacion Sida P.R., San Juan, 1987—; mem. Asegrab, San Juan, 1984—, Pracde, San Juan, 1985—. Mem. coun. Mcpl. Assembly, Municipality of Carolina, 1972-75; sec. Democrat. Com. of Carolina, 1969-72; mem. Consejo Vecinal Seguridad, Isla Verde, Carolina, 1989—; asst. treas. Salon de la Fama Deporte, Carolina, 1984-86; bd. dirs. Condominium St. Tropez, pres. 1989—, sec. 1987-88; sec. Asociación Condominios de Isla Verde, P.R., 1989-92; mem. Vecinal Coun. for Security, 1989—; vol. AIDS Found. of P.R., 1987—, counselor, 1987—. Mem. ALA, Sociedad de Bibliotecarios, Federación Nacional Puertorriqueña de Análisis Transaccional Inc., Assn. de Ex-Alumnos de la Escuela Graduuada de Bibliotecología (sec. 1984-86), P.R. Assn. for Counselling and Devel. Baptist. Avocations: reading, theater and arts, traveling, sewing. Home: Cond St Tropez # 8K Carolina PR 00979-7108

GONZALEZ-HERMOSILLO, BRENDA, economist, researcher; b. Mexico City, Oct. 28, 1955; d. Jesus and Emilia (Gonzalez Watkins) G. BA in Econs., Inst. Tech. Autonomo de Mexico, Mexico City, 1979; MA in Econs., U. Western Ont., London, 1980, PhD in Econs., 1983. Rsch. asst. Bank of Mex., Mexico City, 1977; economist Banco Nacional de Mex., Mexico City, 1978, Min. of Fin., Mexico City, 1979, Bank of Montreal, Toronto, Ont., 1983-84, Bank of N.S., Toronto, 1985-89; sr. economist Bank of Can., Ottawa, Ont., 1989-94, Internat. Monetary Fund, Washington, 1994—. Contbr. articles to profl. jours. Recipient Govt. of Can. award to fgn. nationals, 1980-83; Inst. of Tech. scholar, 1976-78, U. Western Ont. scholar, 1979-80. Mem. Can. and Am. Econ. Assn. Achievements include research on financial crises, financial markets, monetary policy, medicare. Home: 4332 Leland St Chevy Chase MD 20815-6064 Office: Internat Monetary Fund 700 19th St NW Washington DC 20431-0001

GONZALEZ-LICEA, AUGUSTIN, pathologist, public health service officer; b. Mexico City, Sept. 27, 1936; arrived in U.S., 1981; s. Benjamin and Guadalupe (Licea) Gonzalez; m. Virginia Marcela Hernandez, Jan. 5, 1981; children: Monica Rosanne Gonzalez-Licea, Karla Gabriella Gonzalez-Licea. BS, Ctr. U. Mex., Mexico City, 1953; MD, Nat. Autonomous U. Mex. (UNAM), Mexico City, 1960. Diplomate Mex. Bd. Pathology. Intern in pathology UNAM Gen. Hosp., Mexico City, 1960-61, resident in pathology, 1961-64; fellow in pathology Johns Hopkins U., Balt., 1964-67; rschr., dept. scientific investigation Nat. Med. Ctr., Mexico City, 1969-80, head evaluation and control, Rsch. Programs Office, 1974-77, dir. Biomed. Rsch. Unit, 1978-80; med. dir., blood chemistry Miles Labs., Inc., Elkhart, Ind., 1981-89; dir. med. affairs Technicon Instruments, Inc., Tarrytown, N.Y., 1990-92; med. officer FDA, Rockville, Md., 1992—. Republican. Roman Catholic. Avocation: tennis. Office: FDA/ODE OIVD HFZ-440 2098 Gaither Rd Rockville MD 20850-4009 E-mail: alg@cdrh.fda.gov.

GONZALEZ-PITA, J. ALBERTO, lawyer; b. Havana, Cuba, Aug. 20, 1954; came to U.S., 1960; s. Benigno Jesus and Maria Modesta (Diaz) G.P.; m. Suzanne J. Martin, Apr. 7, 1984; children: Roberto Martin, Antonio Martin. AA, Miami-Dade Community Coll., 1973; BA, U. Miami, 1974, JD, Boston U., 1977. Bar: Fla. 1977, U.S. Dist. Ct. (so. dist.) Fla. 1977, U.S. Ct. Appeals (5th cir.) 1977, U.S. Ct. Appeals (11th cir.) 1981. Assoc. Walton, Lantaff, Schroeder & Carson, Miami, Fla., 1977-80, Patton & Kanner, Miami, 1980-82, ptnr., 1982-86, mng. ptnr., 1986-89; ptnr. McDermott, Will & Emery, Miami, 1989-91, White & Case, Miami, 1991-99. Chair Worldwide Privatization Practice Group; co-chair Latin Am. Practice Group; v.p., gen. couns., Bell South Internat., Inc., 1999—. Mem. Acad. for Community Edn., Miami, 1980-90; bd. dirs. Inst. Innovative Intervention, Miami, 1980-90; trustee St. Thomas U., Miami, 1991-96. Mem. ABA, Internat. Bar Assn., Inter-Am. Bar Assn., Internationale des Avocats, Cuban-Am. Bar Assn., Maritime Law Assn. U.S. Roman Catholic. Office: Bell South Internatl Inc 1100 Peachtree St NE Atlanta GA 30309-4501

GONZALEZ-SANCHEZ, ENRIQUE, economist; b. Concepcion del Oro, Zacatecas, Mex., May 28, 1959; s. Pablo and M. de la Luz (Sanchez) Gonzalez. B in Econs., U. Nuevo Leon, Monterrey, Mex., 1981; MA in Econs., U. Chgo., 1986; diploma, Studien Centrum Gerzensee, Switzerland, 1991, Internat. Monetary Fund, Washington, 1992, EU-Rio Group, Montevideo, Uruguay, 1994. Analyst Bank of Mex., Mexico City, 1982-84, specialist, 1986-88, chief economist, 1988-93, vice mgr. internat. economy, 1993-98, vice mgr., 2002—; asst. to exec. dir. Internat. Monetary Fund, Washington, 1998—2002. Contbr. articles to profl. publs. Recipient Disting. Pl. award Internat. Essay Contest Ludming von Mises, Mexico City, 1990. Fellow U. Chgo. Ex-Students in Mexico Soc. (founder). Avocation: swimming. Home: Lirios 232 Col La Florida 53160 Naucalpan, Edo. de Mexico Mexico Office: Banco de Mexico 5 de Mayo 20 4 piso 06059 Mexico DF Mexico E-mail: enrique20037@hotmail.com.

GONZALEZ-SCARANO, FRANCISCO ANTONIO, neurologist, virologist; b. Ponce, P.R., Mar. 23, 1950; s. Francisco and Genoveva (Scarano) Gonzalez-Hernandez; m. Barbara Jean Turner, June 23, 1979; children: Genevieve Carre, Stephanie Katharine, Lisa Frances. BA, Yale U., 1971; MD, Northwestern U., Chgo., 1975; MA (hon.), U. Pa., Phila., 1988. Diplomate Am. Bd. Neurology. Intern Hosp. U. Pa., 1975-76, resident in neurology, 1976-79, fellow U. Pa., Phila., 1979-82, NIMR, London, 1981-82; asst. prof. depts. neurology and microbiology U. Pa., Phila., 1982-88, assoc. prof., 1988-94, prof., 1994—. Vice-chair for rsch. neurology dept. U. Pa, 1998-99, chair 1999—; co-dir. Pa. Ctr. for HIV and AIDS, 1998—; chmn. bd. sci. counselors Nat. Inst. Neurol. Diseases and Stroke, Bethesda, Md., 1993-97. Assoc. editor Viral Pathogenesis, 1997; editl. bd. Jour. Neurovirology, 1996—, Virus Rsch., 1997—, AIDS, 1995-2002, GLIA, 1999—, Jour. Virology, 2000 –, Virology, 2003–. Bd. trustees Swarthmore Presbyn. Ch., 1997-2000. Harry Weaver scholar Multiple Sclerosis Soc., N.Y.C., 1982-87. Mem.: Am. Soc. Clin. Investigation, Am. Acad. Neurology (mem. sci. issues com. 1985—89, profl. and pub. issues com. 1987—93), Am. Neurol. Assn. (exec. coun. 2001—), Scroll & Key, John Morgan Soc, Penn Club, Alpha Omega Alpha. Presbyterian. Avocation: photography. Office: U Pa Dept Neurology Hosp U Pa 3 W Gates Bldg Philadelphia PA 19104-4283 E-mail: scarano@mail.med.upenn.edu.

GONZALEZ-STAWINSKI, GONZALO VINCENTE, surgeon, researcher; b. Santurce, P.R., Mar. 16, 1967; s. Gonzalo Arturo Gonzalez, Rafel I. Aponte (Stepfather) and Margarita Stawinski; m. Natalie Vallecillo, Nov. 6, 1999; 1 child, Julian Andres. BS, U. Sagrado Corazon, 1990; MD, Ponce Sch. Medicine, 1994; postgrad., Duke U., 2003—. Cert. Nat. Bd. Medicine, 1971. Jr. asst. surgery resident Grad. Hosp., Phila., 1996—97, Nemir surg. rsch. fellow, 1997—99; surg. rsch. fellow Duke U., Durham, NC, 1999—2000, sr. asst. surgery resident, 2000—02, chief resident gen. surgery, 2002—. Cons. Baxter Healthcare, Chgo., 1998—; co-prin. investigator dept. surgery Duke U., 2001—; cons. Genonntech, San Francisco, 2002—. Mem.: Am. Coll. Surgeons, Duke U. Health Related Mentor. Avocations: sailing, volleyball, baseball, softball. Office: Duke Univ Med Ctr Box 31177 Durham NC 27710 E-mail: gonza005@mc.duke.edu.

GONZALEZ-TORNERO, SERGIO, artist; b. Santiago, Chile, May 22, 1927; came to the U.S., 1962; s. Higinio and Rebecca (Tornero) Gonzalez; m. Maxine Adrienne Cullom, 1962; children: Katya, Alicia, Savina. Studies in, Chile, Brasil, U.S., France and Eng., 1959-62; student under S.W. Hayter, Atelier 17, Paris, 1959-62. Retrospective exhbn. Mus. Fine Arts, Santiago, Chile, 1993. Thousands of works in pub. and pvt. collections worldwide; one-man exhbns. of paintings based on native arts of the first nations of N.W. Coast of N.Am. at Haida Gwaii Mus., Qay'Llnagaay, Skidegate, B.C., 1996, The Gallery of Tribal Art, Vancouver, 1996, Mus. No. B.C. at Prince Rupert, 1997, Putnam Arts Coun., Mahopac, N.Y., 1999, Greenhill Invitationals, Yorktown, N.Y., 2000, Silvermine Galleries, New Canaan, Conn., 2001, Shelnutt Gallery, Rensselaer Polytechnic Inst., Troy, N.Y., 2001, The Studio, Armonk, N.Y., 2002; retrospective of 218 prints at Antiguo Asilo de Beneficencia, San Juan, 1998. Recipient UNESCO prize Internat. Bienial of Prints, Krakow, 1966, 1st prize X Bienial of Prints, L.Am. and the Caribbean, San Juan, P.R., 1993, 26 other prizes from nat. and internat. art orgns., 1960—; N.Y. State Coun. for the Arts fellow, 1987; grantee Adolph and Esther Gottlieb Found., N.Y., 1990. Mem. Soc. Am. Graphic Artists. Home and Office: 30 Highridge Rd Mahopac NY 10541-2165

GONZALEZ TRICOCHE, CYNTHIA MARIE, human resources specialist; b. Bayamon, Rio Piedras, Puerto Rico, Nov. 13, 1970; d. Mario González, Martina Tricoche; m. Michael Figgis; 1 child, Katie Liv Figgis. Student, Ind. U., Pa., 1990; B in Labor and Indsl. Rels., U. PR, 1994; postgrad., 2003—. Cert. Cert. Hospitality Supr. Hotel and Motel Assn. Home: 13301 SW 24th St Miramar FL 33027 Office: 3700 Lakeside Dr Miramar FL 33027

GONZALEZ-TRUJILLO, CÉSAR AUGUSTO, Chicano studies educator, writer; b. L.A., Jan. 17, 1931; s. José Andalón and Camerina (Trujillo) González; m. Bette L. Beattie, Aug. 30, 1969. BA, Gonzaga U., 1953, MA, Licentiate in Philosophy, 1954; MST, Licentiate in Sacred Theology, U. Santa Clara, 1961; postgrad., UCLA, 1962-65. Tchr. Instituto Regional Mex., Chihuahua, Mex., 1954-57; community devel. specialist Centro Laboral Méx., México D.F., Mex., 1965-68; supr. ABC Headstart East L.A., L.A., 1968-69; employment counselor Op. SER, San Diego, 1969-70; prof., founding chair dept. Chicano studies San Diego Mesa Coll., 1970-99, prof. emeritus, 1999—. Founding chairperson Raza Consortium, San Diego, 1971-72; cons. Chicano Fedn. San Diego, Inc., 1987-89. Author poetry, short fiction and criticism, 1976—. Mem. Ednl. Issues Coordinating Com., L.A., 1968-69; founding bd. dirs. Mex.-Am. Adv. Com. to Bd. of Edn., L.A., 1969; amb. Cancer Awareness Rsch. Tng. Fulbright-Hays fellow, Peru, 1982, NEH fellow, 1984; recipient Cmty. Svc. award Chicano Fedn. San Diego Inc., 1982, Teaching Excellence award Nat. Inst. Staff and Orgnl. Devel., 1993, Outstanding Tchr. San Diego Mesa Coll., 1985, 95, Editor's Choice award Poet Mag., 1993, Cesar Chavez Social Justice award, 1994, Latina Latino Indigenous People Coalition award, 1995; named Outstanding Tchr. and Scholar, Concilio of Chicano Studies for San Diego, Imperial Valley and Baja, Calif., 1990; Spl. Congl. recognition Congressman Bob Filner, 1995; AVID Writer of the Yr. award San Diego Imperial Counties, 1997, Premio Aztla'n, 2000. Mem. Am. Fedn. Tchrs., Centro Cultural De La Raza (past bd. dirs.), Poets and Writers, Asociación Internacional de Hispanistas, REDES en Accion. Democrat. Roman Catholic. Avocations: reading, travel. Office: San Diego Mesa Coll 7250 Mesa College Dr San Diego CA 92111-4902

GOO, ABRAHAM MEU SEN, retired aircraft company executive; b. Honolulu, May 21, 1925; s. Tai Chong and Lily En Wui (Dai) Goo; m. Shin Quon Wong, June 12, 1950; children: Marilynn, Steven, Beverly Cardinal. BSEE, U. Ill., 1951; postgrad., MIT, 1975. With Boeing Co., Seattle, 1951—73; mgr. B-1 avionics program, v.p., gen. mgr. aircraft armament divsn. Boeing Aerospace Co., Seattle, 1974—77; v.p. mil. sys., exec. v.p., pres. Boeing Mil. Airplane Co., Wichita, Kans., 1977—87; pres. Boeing Advanced Sys., Seattle, 1987—89. With USAAF, 1946—47. Recipient Chinese-Am. Engrs. and Scientists of So. Calif. Achievement award, Sci. and Engring., 1989, Pioneer award, Unmanned Vehicle Sys., 1989. Home: 18909 SE 282nd Ct Kent WA 98042-5458

GOOCH, ANTHONY CUSHING, lawyer; b. Amarillo, Tex., Dec. 3, 1937; s. Cornelius Skinner and Sidney Seale (Crawford) G.; m. Elizabeth Melissa Ivanoff, May 27, 1963 (div. Nov. 1983); children: Katherine C., Jennifer C. Gooch Avery, Melissa G., Andrew E.; m. Linda B. Klein, Nov. 7, 1987. BA, U. of South, 1959; diploma, Coll. of Europe, 1960; JD, NYU, 1963, M in Comparative Law, 1964. Bar: N.Y. 1963. Assoc. Cleary, Gottlieb, Steen & Hamilton, N.Y.C., Paris, Brussels, 1963-72, ptnr. Rio de Janeiro, 1973-78, N.Y.C., 1978-99, sr. counsel, 2000—; gen. counsel Internat. Inst. Rural Reconstruction, 2000—02, bd. trustees, 2002—. Co-author: Loan Agreement Documentation, 1982, 2d edit., 1991, Swap Apreement Documentation, 1987, 2d edit., 1988, Documentation for Derivatives, 1993, Credit Support Supplement, 1995, Cross-Product Risk Mgmt. Supplement, 2000, 4th edit., 2002, Documentation for Loans, Assignments and Participations, 1996; articles editor NYU Law Rev., 1962-63. Bd. trustees Internat. Inst. Rural Reconstrn., 2002—; v.p. planned giving Assoc. Alumni, U. of the South, Sewanee, Tenn. Mem. ABA, N.Y. State Bar Assn., Assn. Bar City N.Y., New York County Lawyers Assn. Episcopalian. Home: 7 Mine Hill Rd Redding CT 06896-2701 E-mail: agooch@cgsh.com., tonygooch@aol.com.

GOOCH, CAROL ANN, psychotherapist consultant; b. Meridian, Miss., Apr. 17, 1950; d. James Tackett and Chris M. Page; (div.); 1 child, Aaron Patrick Gooch. BS, Fla. State U., 1972, DS, 1975; MS, Troy State U., 1974. Lic. profl. counselor Tex., chem. dependency counselor Tex., marriage and family therapist Tex., cert. chem. dependency specialist Tex., compulsive gambling counselor Tex., tobacco addiction counselor ACP Tex., bereavement counselor. Tchr. Okaloosa Sch. Dist., Fort Walton, Fla., 1972-77; counselor USAF, Osan AFB, Korea, 1977-79; sch. counselor Tomball (Tex.) Sch. Dist., 1983-90; cons. Montgomery (Tex.) Sch. Dist., 1992—; psychotherapist pvt. practice, Houston, 1990—; dir. cmty. rels. Cypress Creek Hosp., 1998—. Cons. school systems, Houston, 1990—; coord. sr. program Forest Springs Hosp., Houston, 1993—, Cypress Creek Hosp., 1994—. Vol. cons. PTO, Woodlands, Tex., 1990. Named Outstanding H.S. Counselor, Tomball Ind. Sch. Dist., 1989, Diplomat of Yr. for Woodlands C. of C., 2002; named to Leadership Montgomery County; recipient fellowship, Fla. State U., Tallahassee, 1973, Nat. Disting. Svc. award, Ex Coun. U.S. Pubs., N.J., 1989. Mem.: NAFE, ASCD, ACA, AAUW, Am. Bus. Women's Assn., Tex. Mental Health Counselors Assn., Am. Mental Health Counselors Assn., Tex. Sch. Counselors Assn., Fla. State U. Alumni Assn., Kappa Delta Pi. Avocations: travel, dancing, boating. Home and Office: Carol A Gooch MS LPC PO Box 1308 Montgomery TX 77356-1308 E-mail: psychstages@aol.com.

GOOCH, JOHN CASEY, education educator, consultant; b. Lubbock, Tex., Dec. 5, 1971; s. Norman D. and Jenny Lynn Gooch. BS in History and English, Texas Tech. U., 1994; PhD, Tex. Tech. U., 1994—2002; M in Comm., Texas Tech. U., 1997. Cert. tchr. Tex. State Bd. Edn., 1994. Instr., dept. of eng. Tex. Tech. U., Lubbock, 1995—2002; asst. prof., dept. of eng. Lou Tech. U., Ruston, La., 2002—. Scholar 2002 Grad. Rsch. Scholarship, Tex. Tech U., 2002. Mem.: Assn. of Teachers of Tech. Writing (corr.). Independent. Protestant. Avocations: books, travel, theater/movies, music, arts. Home: 1019 Lee Ave Ruston LA 71270 Office: Dept of English Louisiana Tech U PO Box 3162 Ruston LA 71272-3162 Personal E-mail: jcgooch@cox-internet.com. E-mail: jgooch@latech.edu.

GOOCH, STANFORD RONDALL, Air Force Operations research analyst; b. Selmer, Tenn., Feb. 15, 1944; s. Tolbert Johnson and Eula Demillus (Wilson) G.; m. Linda Lee Hunt; 1 child, Aimee Marie. BS, Memphis State U., 1967; MA, Auburn U., 1980; BS, Bellevue U., 2000. Chief svcs. br. 7th Bomb Wing, Carswell AFB, Tex., 1967-68; arc light 4133 Bomb Wing, Anderson AFB, Guam, 1968; chief, main supr. 7th Bomb Wing, Carswell AFB, 1968-69, 305th Bomb Wing, Grissom AFB, Ind., 1969-70; mgt. comdr. staff ofcl. Strategic Air Command, Offutt AFB, Nebr., 1970-72; br. chief, svcs. br. 307th Maintenance Squadron, U. Tapao, Thailand, 1972-73; maj. comdr. program mgr. Strategic Air Command, Offutt AFB, 1973-79; air comdr. and staff col. Air U., Maxwell AFB, Ala., 1979-80; comdr. 10th equipment maintenance squadron RAF Alconbury, Eng., 1980-83; chief, sys. info. br. Def. Nuclear Agy., Alexandria, Va., 1983-86; mgr. nuclear weapon acquisitions Strategic Air Command, Offutt AFB, 1986-91, program analyst, 1991-92, U.S. Strategic Command, 1992-97, ops. rsch. analyst, 1997—. Mem. CINCSTRAT posture team U.S. Strategic Command, Offutt AFB, 1993—, mem. stockpile assessment team, 1996—; leader weapons team Plans & Policy Directorate, Offutt AFB, 1994—. Vol. Meals-on-Whells, Eastern Nebr. Office on Aging, 1992-93. Recipient Bronze Star medal USAF, 1973, Def. Meritorious Svc. medal Dept. of Def., 1986, USAF Meritorious Svc. medal (3) USAF, 1979, 83, 90, USAF Commendation medal (2), 1970, 72, Viet Nam Svc. medal w/4 Bronze stars USAF, 1973, Superior Performance awards (10) U.S. Strategic Commn, 1992-2001, Cert. of Recognitiion (3), U.S. Strategic Command, 1992, 93, 95, Performer of Yr. award, 1995, Exemplary Civilian Svc. award, 1995, Letter of Appreciation (2), 1993, 96, Meritorious Civilian Svc. award, 1998. Mem. Nat. Polit. Sci. Honor Soc. Republican. Avocations: reading, music. Home: 13701 S 22d Cir Bellevue NE 68123-4145 Office: USSTRATCOM/J533 901 SAC Blvd Ste 2E9 Offutt A F B NE 68113-5455

GOOD, ALLEN HOVEY, investment banker, real estate broker, business consultant; b. Boston, July 5, 1930; s. Herbert Shelley Good and Elizabeth (Hovey) Jack; m. Catherine Forrester Campbell, June 25, 1959 (div. June 1975); children: Alison Good Ross, Forrester Hovey; m. Joan Duffey Meyers, June 12, 1976; stepchildren: Robert Whitney Meyers Jr., Mary Meyers. AB in English, Bus. Adminstrn., U. Mass., 1955. Ea. region sales mgr. Sandpaper, Inc., Rockland, Mass., 1956-67; pres. A.H. Good Corp., Summit, N.J., 1967-75, Chemdyne, Inc., Summit, 1975-84; v.p. Mid-Atlantic Bus. Brokers, Florham Park, N.J., 1984-86; pres. Atlantic Nat. Acquisitions & Mergers, Inc., Short Hills, N.J., 1987—, Atlantic Nat. Mgmt. Cons., 1995—. Cons. Pfizer, Inc., N.Y.C., 1983; substitute instr. Fairleigh-Dickinson Grad. Sch., Madison, N.J., 1986, Soc. Colonial Wars, 1999—, Presdl. Roundtable, 2001; mem. Lic. Exec. Soc., Norwalk, Conn., 1988-89. Editor Newsletter Summit Tennis Club, 1977; patentee: skin lotion, 1982, skin cleanser, 1985. Mem. Rep. Club, Short Hills, N.J., 1957-59, N.J. Symphony Jr. Com., 1959-60; chmn. spl. projects, 1995—; mem. Images Exec. Com., 1995-2001, N.J. Ctr. for Visual Arts, Summit. Mem.: Short Hills Club. Avocations: tennis, sailing. Office: Atlantic Nat Acquisitions & Mergers Inc 15 Hobart Ave Short Hills NJ 07078-2026 E-mail: merging@comcast.net.

GOOD, DOUGLAS JAY, lawyer; b. Bklyn., Mar. 29, 1947; s. Sidney B. and Sophie (Mohel) G.; m. Lynda Edes, Feb. 25, 1979; 1 child, Sara. BA, Columbia U., 1967; JD, NYU, 1971. Bar: N.Y. 1972, U.S. Dist. Ct. (so. and ea. dists.) N.Y. 1973, U.S. Ct. Appeals (2d cir.) 1975, U.S. Supreme Ct. 1976, U.S. Ct. Appeals (11th cir.) 1989. Staff atty. Legal Aid Soc. Rockland County, Inc., New City, N.Y., 1972-73, dir., 1973-81; assoc. Ruskin, Moscou, Faltishchek, P.C., Mineola, NY, 1981-85, ptnr., 1985—, mng. ptnr., 1990-98. Adj. lectr. NYU Inst. for Paralegal Studies, N.Y.C., 1982-85; adj. asst. prof.; bd. dirs. Nassau/Suffolk Law Svcs. Com., Inc., 1986—, chairperson, 1987—; bd. dirs. Nassau Bar Tech. Ctr., Inc., 1995-2000, sec., 1995, vice chmn., 1996, pres. 1998. Mem.: ABA, Fed. Bar. Coun., Nassau County Bar Assn. (bd. dirs. 1996—99, adv. bd. We Care Fund 2000—, sec. 2001—02, treas. 2002—03, 2nd v.p. 2003—), N.Y. State Bar Assn. Jewish. Office: Ruskin Moscou Faltischek PC 190 EAB Plaza 15th Fl E Tower Uniondale NY 11556-0190

GOOD, GLENN EDWARD, psychologist, educator; b. Sacramento, Feb. 3, 1954; s. Robert Alfred and Jeanne (Ermel) G.; m. Laurie Beth Mintz, July 21, 1985; children: Jennifer Elyse, Allison Jean. BA, Univ. Calif., Davis, 1977; MS, U. Oreg., 1979; PhD, Ohio State U., 1987. Lic. psychologist, Calif., Mo. Clin. asst. prof. U. So. Calif., L.A., 1987-90; assoc. prof., dir. counseling psychology area U. Mo., Columbia, 1995—. Mem. State Com. of Psychologists. Editor: The New Handbook of Psychotherapy and Counseling With Men, 2001; contbr. chpts. to books. Mem. APA (past pres.), Soc. for Psychol. Study of Men and Masculinity. Avocations: biking, swimming. Office: U Mo ESCP 16 Hill Columbia MO 65211-2130

GOOD, IRVING JOHN, statistics educator, mathematician, philosopher of science; b. London, Dec. 9, 1916; arrived in US, 1967; s. Morris Edward and Sophia (Polikoff) G. ScD, Cambridge (Eng.) U., 1963; DSc, Oxford (Eng.) U., 1964. Scientific officer Fgn. Office, Bletchley, Eng., 1941-45; lectr. math. and electronic computing Manchester (Eng.) U., 1945-48; sr. prin. sci. officer Govt. Communications Hdqrs., Cheltenham, Eng., 1948-59; spl. merit dep. chief sci. officer Admiralty Rsch. Lab., Teddington, Middlesex, Eng., 1959-62; sr. rsch. fellow Trinity Coll., Oxford U. and Atlas Computer Lab., Didcot, Berkshire, Eng., 1964-67; Univ. disting. prof. stats, adj. prof. philosophy Va. Poly. Inst. and State U., Blacksburg, 1967—; prof. emeritus. Adj. prof. Ctr. Study of Sci. in Society; mem. comm. theory com. Ministry Supply, London, 1953-56; mem. comm. com. electronics rsch. com. Ministry Aviation, London, 1960-62; mem. rsch. sect. com. Royal Statis. Soc., London, 1965-67. Author: Probability and the Weighing of Evidence, 1950, The Estimation of Probabilities, 1965, Good Thinking, 1983; gen. editor: The Scientist Speculates, 1962 (also French and German translations); chpt. in The Codebreakers, 1994; also 5 chpts. in Festschriften; contbr. over 900 articles to profl. jours. Grantee NIH, 1970-89; recipient Smith's prize, Cambridge, Eng., 1940. Fellow Am. Acad. Arts and Scis., Va. Acad. Scis., Inst. Math. Stats., Am. Statis. Assn.; mem. IEEE Computer Soc. (Pioneer award 1998), Internat. Statis. Inst. (hon.), Internat. Order Merit. Home: 1309 Lynn Dr Blacksburg VA 24060-3001 Office: Va Poly Inst and State U Dept Stats Blacksburg VA 24061-0439

GOOD, JOSEPH COLE, JR., lawyer; b. Columbia, S.C., Sept. 18, 1945; s. Joseph Cole and Virginia (Williams) G.; m. Virginia St. Claire Craver, Apr. 5, 1969; children: Joseph III, Katharine. AB, Wofford Coll., 1967; JD, U. S.C., 1970. Bar: S.C., 1970. Asst. atty. gen. State of S.C., Columbia, 1970-73; atty. S.C. Electric & Gas Co., Columbia, 1973-83, dir. corp. and civic affairs Charleston, 1983-85; gen. counsel Med. U. S.C., Charleston, 1987—, faculty mem., 1988—. Lectr. S.C. Higher Edn. Assn. Pres. Charleston Navy League, 1987; exec. bd. Low Country Council Girl Scouts U.S.A., 1987. Mem. ABA, S.C. Bar Assn. (state chmn. lawyers caring about lawyers com. 1987), Edison Electric Inst., Charleston Hibernian Soc., Carolina Yacht Club, The Charleston Club. Presbyterian. Avocations: tennis, golf. Home: 883 Parrot Creek Way Charleston SC 29412-9055 Office: 171 Ashley Ave Charleston SC 29425-0001 E-mail: Goodj@musc.edu.

GOOD, LARRY IRWIN, physician, consultant; b. N.Y.C., Feb. 8, 1948; s. Samuel and Lillie (Sternlight) G.; m. Judy Chafetz, Aug. 16, 1969; children: Adam Eric, Lauren Elyse, Bryan Scott, Allison Jill. BA, Colgate U., 1969; MD, Med. U. of S.C., 1973. Diplomate Am. Bd. Internal Medicine, Am. Bd. Gastroenterology. Intern in medicine Teaching Hosp. Med. U. of S.C., 1973-74, resident in medicine Teaching Hosp., 1974-75, chief resident in medicine Teaching Hosp., 1975-76; fellow in gastroenterology U. Pa., 1976-78; with Hempstead (N.Y.) Gen. Hosp., 1978—, Nassau County Med. Ctr., East Meadow, N.Y., 1978—, South Nassau Communities Hosp., Oceanside, N.Y., 1978—, chief div. gastroenterology dept. medicine, 1989. Asst. prof. Sch. of Medicine, SUNY, Stony Brook, 1978; mem. health adv. bd. Hofstra Health Dome Uniondale, N.Y., 1983; with Lydia E. Hall Hosp., Freeport, N.Y., 1978-86, Mercy Hosp., Rockville Centre, N.Y., 1978-80. Contbr. articles to Am. Jour. Gastroenterology, The Papilla Vateri and its Diseases, Med. Times, New Eng. Jour. Medicine., Gastroenterology, Alpha Omega Alpha. Trustee, dir. Little Village Sch. & House, Garden City, N.Y., 1985—. Recipient Rsch. Svc. award NIH, 1977. Fellow Am. Coll. Gastroenterology; mem. AMA, ACP, L.I. Gastroenterologic Assn., Am. Gastroenterologic Assn. Jewish. Office: 229 7th St Ste 307 Garden City NY 11530-2913

GOOD, LAURANCE FREDERIC, medical foundation administrator; b. Wheeling, W.Va., Sept. 26, 1932; s. Sidney Samuel and Jeannette (Berg) G.; m. Barbara S. Mayer, Oct. 18, 1959; children: Philip (dec.), Jay, Paul, Jenny, Heidi. BA, Brown U., 1954; postgrad., U. Va., 1955. CLU, ChFC, cert. employee benefits specialist, health ins. assoc.; registered health underwriter, LUTCF. V.p., gen. mdse. mgr. L.S. Good & Co., Wheeling, 1961-80, exec. v.p., 1969-80, vice chmn., sec. bd., 1961-80; pres. Personal History Systems, Inc.; life underwriter Equitable Life Assurance Soc. Am., 1983-89; health and welfare cons. Mockenhaupt, Mockenhaupt, Cowden & Parks, 1989; employee benefit specialist, life underwriter Lincoln Fin. Svcs., Inc., Pitts., 1990; exec. dir. Wheeling Works, Inc., Wheeling, W.Va., 1993-95; dir. Office of Gift Planning Med. Park Found., Wheeling, W.Va., 1995—. Mem. Million Dollar Roundtable, 1985-86. Producer: Wheeling Rediscovered; Author: My Lifetime Book. Mem. bd. Wheeling Symphony Soc., 1964-67, 68-73; active Ohio Valley Indsl. & Bus. Devel. Corp., Wheeling, 1971; area chmn. Brown U. Alumni Program, 1954-88; Christmas seals chmn. Tb Assn. Ohio Valley, 1973; co-chmn. United Jewish Appeal, 1971-73; v.p., chmn. fin. com. Temple Shalom, 1986-89; co-founder Good Zoo in memory of eldest son, Philip; also pres. Good Zoo Friends, 1974-78; chmn. establishment com. Wheeling Devel. Conf.; bd. found. W. Liberty State Coll., 1971; creator Kraft-Good Archives; bd. dirs. Wheeling Hosp., 1972-87, hon. bd. dirs., 1988-96; bd. visitors Bethany Coll., 1972-77; trustee Oglebay Inst., 1972-90; mem. Estate Planning Coun. of Ohio Valley and Pitts.; co-chair Greater Wheeling/Bel-o-Mar Empowerment Zone/Enterprise Community Initiative, 1994; campaign dir. Toward the Next Century, Wheeling Hosp., 1998. With USN, 1955-57. Decorated South China Sea medal, Good Conduct medal; recipient Disting. West Virginian award, 1976. Fellow Life Tng. Underwriters Coun.; mem. Nat. Retail Mchts. Assn. (dir. merchandising div. 1966-71, del. conf. 1969), Am. Technion Soc. (trustee Pa. chpt. 1965), Ohio Valley Assn. Life Underwriters (pres. 1987), W.Va. Assn. Life Underwriters (regional dir. 1988). Office: Med Park Found Office Gift Planning One Medical Pk Wheeling WV 26003 Personal E-mail: lgood@wheelinghosp.com. E-mail: goodforyou@earthlink.net.

GOOD, LINDA LOU, elementary education educator; b. Zanesville, Ohio, May 30, 1941; d. John Robert and Alice Laura (Fulkerson) Moore; m. Larry Alvin Good, Jan. 11, 1964; children: Jason (dec.) Alicia and Tricia (twins), Amy Jo. BS in Elem. Edn., Ohio U., 1964. Tchr. West Muskingum Sch. Dist., 1962-64; 1st grade tchr. Bellevue, Ohio, 1964-68; 2nd grade tchr. Zanesville Sch. Sys., 1970—, head tchr., 1981—89. Head tchr. Munson Sch., Zanesville. Co-chmn. Zane Trace Commemoration; pres. Munson-Garfield Schs. PTA; mem. Trinity Presbyn. Ch. Scholar Jennings scholar, 1997—98. Mem. NEA, Ohio Edn. Assn., Zanesville Edn. Assn., Ea. Ohio Tchrs. Assn. Presbyterian.

GOOD, MARY LOWE (MRS. BILLY JEWEL GOOD), investment company executive, educator; b. Grapevine, Tex., June 20, 1931; d. John W. and Winnie (Mercer) Lowe; m. Billy Jewel Good, May 17, 1952; children: Billy, James. BS, Ark. State Tchrs. Coll., 1950; MS, U. Ark., 1953, PhD, 1955, LLD (hon.), 1979; DSc (hon.), U. Ill., Chgo., 1983, Clarkson U., 1984, Ea. Mich. U., 1986, Duke U., 1987; hon. degree, St. Mary's Coll., 1987, Kenyon Coll., 1988, Stevens Inst. Tech., 1989, Lehigh U., 1989, Northeastern Ill. U., 1989, U. S.C., 1989, N.J. Inst. Tech., 1989; hon. law degree, Newcomb Coll. of Tulane U., 1991; LLD (hon.), Coll. of William and Mary, 1992; DSc (hon.), Manhattan Coll., 1992, Ind. U., 1992, SUNY, Binghamton, 1994, Rensselaer Polytechnic Inst., 1994, Monmouth U., 1995, La. State U., 1995, Ill. Inst. Tech., 1997, Mich. State U., 1997, U. Mich., 1998; DEng (hon.), Mich. State U., 1997, U. Mich., 1998, Colo. Sch. Mines, 2000. Instr. Ark. State Tchrs. Coll., Conway, summer 1949, La. State U., Baton Rouge, 1954-56, asst. prof., 1956-58, assoc. prof. New Orleans, 1958-63, prof., 1963-80, Boyd prof. materials sci., divsn. engring. rsch. Baton Rouge, 1979-80; v.p., dir. rsch. UOP, Inc., Des Plaines, Ill., 1980-84; pres. Signal Rsch. Ctr. Inc., 1985-87; pres. engineered materials rsch. divsn Allied-Signal Inc., Des Plaines, Ill., 1986-88, sr. v.p.-tech. Morristown, N.J., 1988-93; under sec. of commerce for technology Dept. of Commerce, Washington, 1993-97; mng. mem. Venture Capital Investors LLC, Little Rock, 1997—; Donaghey Univ. prof., dean Coll. Info. Sci. & Systems Engr U. Ark., Little Rock, 1998—. Chmn. Pres.'s Com. for Nat. Medal Sci., 1979-82; adv. bd. NSF Chemistry Sect., 1972-76; com. medicinal chemistry NIH, 1972-76, Office of USAF Rsch., 1974-78, chemist divsn. Brookhaven and Oak Ridge Nat. Labs., 1973-83, chem. tech. divsn. Oak Ridge Nat. Lab., catalysis program Lawrence-Berkeley Lab.; catalysis program coll. engring. La. State U.; vice chair Nat. Sci. Bd., 1984, chair, 1988-90; bd. dirs. Biogen, IDEXX Labs., Delta Bank and Trust, bd. chem. sci. and tech., Nat. Rsch. Council, 2003-, Govt. U., industry roundtable, Nat. Rsch. Council, 2000-, Ark. Sci and Tech. Authority, 1998-, Dialoge Com, Am. Chem. Council, 2002-. Contbr. articles to profl. jours. Mem. Nat. Sci. Bd., 1980-91, chair, 1988-91; mem. Pres.' Coun. Advisors for Sci. and Tech., 1991-93. Recipient Agnes Faye Morgan rsch. award, 1969, Disting. Alumni citation U. Ark., 1973, Scientist of Yr. award Indsl. R&D mag., 1983, Delmer S. Fahrney medal Franklin Inst., 1988, N.J. Women of Achievement award Douglass Coll., Rutgers U., 1990, Indsl. Rsch. Inst. medal, 1991, Disting. Svc. award NSF, 1992, Roe award ASME, 1993, Gold medal SME, 1995, Earle Barnes award ACS, 1996, Priestley medal, 1997, UCLA Glenn T. Seaborg medal, 1996, Nat. Materials Advancement award Fedn. Materials Socs., 1996, Othmer medal award Chem. Heritage Found., 1998, Henry Michel award, Civil Engring. Rsch. Found., 1998, Heinz award for tech. The Economy and Employment, 2000; AEC tng. grantee, 1967, NSF Internat. travel grantee, 1968, NSF rsch. grantee, 1969-80, Albert Fox Demers award, 1992. Fellow AAAS (Abelson award 1999, pres. 2000, chmn. bd. dirs. 2001), Am. Inst. Chemistry (Gold medal 1983), Chem. Soc. London, Royal Soc. Chemistry (hon.); mem. NAE, Acad. Arts and Scis, Am. Philos. Soc., Swedish Acad. Engring., Am. Chem. Soc. (1st woman dir. 1971-74, regional dir. 1972-80, chmn. bd. 1978, 80, pres. 1987, Garvan medal 1973, Herty medal 1975, award Fla. sect. 1979, Charles Lathrop Parsons award 1991), Internat. Union Pure and Applied Chmistry (pres. inorganic div. 1980-85),Alliance for Sci. and Tech. Rsch. in Am. (chmn. bd. dirs. 2000—), Zonta (past pres. New Orleans club, chmn. dist. status of women com. and nominating com., chmn. internat. Amelia Earhart scholarship com. 1978-88, pres. internat. Found. 1988-93, mem. internat. bd. 1988-90), Rotary Internat., Phi Beta Kappa, Sigma Xi, Iota Sigma Pi (regional dir. 1967-93, hon. mem. 1983), Ark. Women's Forum. Home: 13824 Rivercrest Dr Little Rock AR 72212-1521 Office: Venture Capital Investors LLC 400 W Capitol Ave Ste 1845 Little Rock AR 72201-4857 also: U Ark at Little Rock Coll Info Sci/Sys Engring 2801 S University Ave Little Rock AR 72204-1000 E-mail: thegoods@aristotle.net., mlgood@ualr.edu.

GOOD, RICHARD STANDISH, geologist; b. West Chester, Pa., Sept. 18, 1928; s. Bernard Stafford Good and Marjorie Payne Johnson; m. Edith Read Brodhead, Oct. 15, 1966 (div. Aug. 1982); m. Marsha Wallace, Apr. 29, 2000. BS in Geology and Mineralogy, Pa. State U., 1950, MS in Geology, 1955. Cert. profl. geologist, Va. Chem. analyst Foote Mineral Co., Malvern, Pa., 1951; project engr. Aeroprojects, Inc., West Chester, Pa., 1952-53; rsch. asst. Pa. State U., State College, 1953-55; geologist Geo-Tech Devel. Co., Ltd., Toronto, Ont., Can., 1955-56, Hunting Tech Svcs., Ltd., London, 1957-58; cons., geologist San Francisco, 1958-60; chem. analyst Kawecki Chem. Co., Boyertown, Pa., 1960. Tchg. asst. Bryn Mawr Coll., Pa., 1962-64; geologist, head Geol. Lab, Va. Divsn. of Mineral Resources, Charlottesville, Va., 1966-91; collection mgr. rocks/fossil, Va. Museumont Naturaly History, 1992. Vol. Hospice, Charlottesville, 2001. Fellow NSF, Bryn Mawr, 1963-64. Fellow Assn. Exploration Geochemists; mem. Geol. Soc. Am., Soc. Mining Engrs., Va. Acad. Sci., AAAS, Sigma Xi. Avocations: writing, tennis, hiking, reading. Home: 63 Woodlake Dr Charlottesville VA 22901

GOOD, SHELDON FRED, realtor; b. Chgo., June 4, 1933; s. Joseph and Sylvia (Schwartz) G.; children: Steven, Todd; m. Susan Forman, Dec. 22, 1990. BBA, U. Ill., 1955. Sales mgr. Baird & Warner Real Estate, Chgo., 1957-65; chmn. Sheldon F. Good & Co. Realtors, Chgo., 1965—. Guest lectr. Northwestern U., U. Chgo., U. Calif., Wharton Grad. Sch., U. Pa., Stanford U., Vanderbilt U., U. Ill.; staff instr. Cen. YMCA City Coll., Chgo.; guest spkr. Wall St. Week UN, 1993; cons. in field. Chmn. United Settlement Appeal, Chgo., YMCA Edn. Libr. Drive, Chgo., Chgo. Jewish United Fund.; bd. dirs. Child, Inc.; pres. Gastrointestinal Rsch. Found., U. Chgo., 1979; chmn. Chgo. Assn. Realtors Hall of Fame, 1996-97; bd. dirs. U. Ill. Found., 1995-97. Served with AUS, 1955-57. Bd. dirs. Hundred Club of Ill., 1997—, Weizmann Inst. Sci., 2001-03; founder, life vice-chmn. Chgo. Assn. Realtors Edn. Found. Recipient Levi Eshkol Premier medal State Israel, 1967, Crown of a Good Name award Jewish Nat. Fund, 1972, Chgo. Realtor of Yr. award 1991; first recipient of Richard W. Dewees Meml. award 1998; named one of 10 outstanding young men Chgo., 1968, Chgo. Man of Yr., 1998, Illini of Yr. Chgo. Assn. Realtors, 1999, Achievement award U. Ill., 2000; inducted into Chgo. Assn. Realtors Hall of Fame, 2000. Mem. Chgo. Real Estate Bd. (treas., pres. 1988-89), Nat. Assn. Real Estate Bds., Nat. Assn. Realtors (chmn. nat. auction com. 1990, RTC task force), State of Ill. Internat. Real Estate Assn., Bryn Mawr Country Club (pres. 1986-87). Home: 180 E Pearson St Chicago IL 60611-2130 Office: 333 W Wacker Dr Chicago IL 60606-1220

GOOD, STEPHEN BOYD, librarian; b. Kingston, Ont., Canada, Apr. 4, 1961; s. Donald Boyd and Lin May Good; m. Sheila McRae Barbour; children: Liam, Anna, Phoebe, Chloe. BA, Trent U., Peterborough, Ont., Can., 1986; MLIS, Dalhousie U., Halifax, N.S., Can., 1991; LLB, Queen's U., Kingston, 1999. Collection devel. libr. Tex. Tech U., Lubbock, 2002—. Office: Texas Tech U 1802 Hartford Ave Lubbock TX 79409-0004 Office Fax: 806-742-1629. E-mail: stephen.good@ttu.edu.

GOOD, STEPHEN HANSCOM, academic administrator; b. Columbus, Nebr., July 19, 1942; s. William Stanley and Cleora Eleanor (Hanscom) G.; m. Judith Ann Schroetlin, Sept. 1, 1963; children: Jennifer, Catherine, William. BA with distinction, Nebr. Wesleyan U., 1964; MA, U. Pitts., 1965, PhD, 1972. English instr. U. Nebr., Lincoln, 1966-68; prof., chmn. dept. English, Mt. St. Mary's Coll., Emmitsburg, Md., 1968-79; v.p. for acad. affairs Westmar Coll., LeMars, Iowa, 1979-83, Drury U., Springfield, Mo., 1983—. Cons. Coun. Ind. Colls. Nat. Cons. Network, Washington, 1980—. Editor and introduction: The Virgin Unmask'e, 1975, A Treatise of the Hypochondriack and Hysterick Diseases, 1976, Free Thoughts on Religon, 1988. Mem. adminstrv. lay bd. Wesley United Meth. Ch., Springfield, 1983-88; mem. adv. bd. S.W. Mo. Assn. Talented and Gifted, Springfield, 1983-88; mem. Springfield Commn. on Excellence in Edn., 1983-85; pres. Ozarks Sci. and Engring. Fair Found., 1990-94; pres. coun. fin. and adminstrn. Mo. West Conf., United Meth. Ch., 1992-96, mem. gen. bd. for higher edn. and ministry, 1996—; bd. dirs. Sister Cities Assn., 1987-95, treas., 1991-95; bd. dirs. Sta. KOZK Pub. TV, 1991-95. Recipient Dean's award Coun. Ind. Colls., 1994. Mem. Am. Conf. Acd. Deans, Am. Assn. Higher Edn., Am. Soc. for 18th Century Studies (pres. Eastern Ctrl. Conf. 1976-77), Assn. N.W. Am. Colls. (v.p. coord. coun. 1999—), Higher Learning Commn. N.C. Assn. (cons./evaluator 1990—, mem. instnl. actions coun. 2003—). Home: 1134 W Highpoint St Springfield MO 65810-2522 Office: Drury U 900 N Benton Ave Springfield MO 65802-3712 E-mail: sgood@drury.edu.

GOOD, WALTER RAYMOND, investment executive; b. Oak Park, Ill., Sept. 9, 1924; s. Walter William and Elsie Sophia (Lussow) G.; m. Jean W. Stockman, Feb. 5, 1949; children: Elizabeth, Deborah, William. Ph.B., U. Chgo., 1947, MBA, 1949. Buyer fats and oils Procter and Gamble, Cin., 1949-52; security analyst, dir. research Brown Bros. Harriman, N.Y.C., 1952-70; exec. v.p., dir. Lionel D. Edie, N.Y.C., 1970-80; v.p. Continental Group Inc., Stamford, Conn., 1980-85; mng. ptnr. Actively Managed Universes, Darien, Conn., 1985-86; pres. Mellon Universe Mgmt. Group, Stamford, 1986-90; mng. ptnr. Capital Market Systems, Darien, 1990-98. Mem. investment adv. panel Pension Benefit Guaranty Corp., Washington, 1980-83; dir., mem. exec. com. Retirement Systems for Savs. Instns., N.Y.C., 1985-86; mem. investment adv. council N.Y.C. Retirement Funds, 1980-85; mem. Pension Execs. Conf., 1981-85, chmn., 1983, mem. fin. adv. panel The Aerospace Corp., 1986—. Author: (with D. Love) Managing Pension Assets: Pension Finance and Corporate Financial Goals, 1990, (with R. Hermansen and J. Meyer) Active Asset Allocation: Gaining Advantage in a Highly Efficient Stock Market, 1993, (with R. Hermansen) Index Your Way to Investment Success, 1998; mem. editl. bd. Fin. Analysts Jour., 1972-97. Served with USAAF, 1943-46. Recipient Graham and Dodd Scroll Fin. Analysts Fedn., 1979. Mem. Inst. Chartered Fin. Analysts (council examiners 1980-86), N.Y. Soc. Security Analysts, Stamford Soc. Investment of Analysts. E-mail: wrgg@msn.com.

GOOD, WILLIAM ALLEN, professional society executive; b. Oak Park, Ill., May 29, 1949; s. Fred Clifton and Dorothy Helen (Stockdale) G.; m. Julianne Doggett, Jan. 8, 1972 (div. Apr. 1980); m. Paulette Edith Gordon, Apr. 23, 1983 (div. Apr. 1991), m. Laura Elizabeth Wellbank, Sept. 25, 1993. MBA, U. Chgo., 1992. Supr. Dun & Bradstreet, Inc., Chgo., 1972-73; gen. mgr. Nat. Roofing Contractors Assn., Chgo., 1973-85, exec. v.p., Rosemont, Ill., 1987—; dir. mktg. Rand Devel. Corp., San Antonio, 1983-86; co-owner GT Communications, Inc., Dallas, 1985-87. Mem. Am. Soc. Assn. Execs. (cert.), Inst. for Orgn. Mgmt. (chmn. 1990-91), Chgo. Soc. Assn. Execs. (pres. 1996-97). Republican. Roman Catholic. Avocations: tennis, photography. Office: Nat Roofing Contractors Assn 10255 W Higgins Rd Rosemont IL 60018-5606 E-mail: bgood@nrca.net.

GOODACRE, CHARLES J. academic administrator; DDS, Loma Linda U., 1971; MSD, Ind. U., Indpls., 1974. Prof. Loma Linda U., dean, Sch. Dentistry, 2002—. Contbr. articles to profl. jours. Avocations: woodworking, sports, Lionel trains, off-road motorcylcing. Office: Loma Linda Univ Loma Linda CA 92350

GOODALE, ARTHUR WORTHINGTON, civil engineer, researcher; b. Dover, N.J., Aug. 19, 1912; s. Arthur Huston and Caroline W. (Worthington) G.; m. Winifred Bryant, Jan. 1, 1946; children: Sondra, Alan. BSCE, Newark Coll. Engring., 1937. Civil engr. Frederick Snare Corp., N.Y.C., 1946-49, Hardaway Contracting, Columbus, Ga., 1950-58; pvt. practice Dunedin, Fla., 1960-80; civil estimator Inter-Bay Marine Constrn., Largo, Fla., 1980—. Rsch. and structural cons., St. Petersburg, Fla., 1980—. Lt. USN, 1943-46, PTO. Mem. ASCE (life). Republican. Presbyterian. Achievements include investigations of various Fla. bridges and structures of poor construction; research in construction materials used in bridges. Home: 1753 San Mateo Dr Dunedin FL 34698-3718

GOODALE, DOUGLAS M, dean, educator; b. Cortland, Ny, Oct. 22, 1947; s. W Asher and Ruth E Goodale; m. Sandra J Pond, Aug. 30, 1969; children: Brian D, Eric W. AAS, SUNY at Cobleskill, Cobleskill, NY, 1967; BS, U. Del., Newark, DE, 1969; MS, SUNY Albany, Albany, NY, 1978; PhD, Pa. State U., State College, PA, 1983. Tchr. Oxford Acad., Oxford, NY, 1969—74; asst prof. SUNY Cobleskill, Cobleskill, NY, 1974—83; rsch. asst Penn State, University Park, Pa., 1981—83; assoc prof. SUNY Cobleskill, Cobleskill, NY, 1983—84, prof., 1984—99, dean-agriculture and natural resources, 1999—. Recipient Outstanding Edn. Award, NE Weed Sci. Assoc, 1999; fellow, Nat. Assn. of Colls. and Tchrs. of Agr., 1995. Mem.: NY State Agri-Business Assoc, NY State Agr. Soc., Nat. Assoc of Colleges and Teachers of Agr. R-Conservative. Methodist. Avocations: golf, home landscaping. Office: SUNY Cobleskill 100 Curtis-Mott Hall Cobleskill NY 12043 E-mail: goodaldm@cobleskill.edu.

GOODALE, JAMES CAMPBELL, lawyer, media executive, television producer/host; b. Cambridge, Mass., July 27, 1933; s. Robert Leonard and Eunice (Campbell) G.; m. Toni Krissel, May 3, 1964; children: Timothy Fuller, Ashley Krissel; foster child: Joseph Clayton Akiwenzie. Grad., Pomfret Sch., 1951; BA, Yale U., 1955; JD, U. Chgo., 1958. Bar: N.Y. 1960. Assoc. Lord, Day and Lord, N.Y.C., 1959-63; gen. atty. N.Y. Times Co., 1963-67, gen. counsel, 1967-72, sr. v.p., 1972-73, exec. v.p., 1973-79, vice-chmn., 1979-80; ptnr. Debevoise and Plimpton, 1980-93, founder, head media-comm. and intellectual property sect., 1980—96, mem. exec. com., 1981-84, of counsel, 1994-96; co-prodr., host Digital Age (formerly The Telecom. and Info. Revolution), 25 WYNE, N.Y.C., 1995—. With Cmty. Law Office, East Harlem, 1968-70; vis. lectr. Yale U. Law Sch., 1977-80; adj. prof. NYU Sch. Law, 1983-86, Fordham Law Sch., 1986—; affiliated scholar N.Y. Law Sch., 1995—; mem. N.Y. State Privacy and Security Com., 1976-79; 2nd cir. Commn. Reduction of Burdens and Costs in Civil Litigation, 1977-80; vice chmn. N.Y. State Jud. Commn. on Minorities, 1987-90, chmn., 1990-91, bd. dirs. com. to protect journalists, 1989—, chmn., 1989-94; mem. adv. bd. Comm. and the Law, 1980—; pres., owner Midtown Skating Corp., 1981-90; chmn. bd. Cable TV Law and Fin., 1981—; trustee N.Y.C. Citizens Budget Commn., 1990-98; advisor U.S. Supreme Ct. Jud. Conf. Com. on the Judiciary, 1980-89; chmn., founder PLI Comm. Law Seminar, 1972—; sec. N.Y. Observer, 1988-92, Paris Rev. Found., 2001-. Author: All About Cable, 1987; compilor, editor: The New York Times Company vs. U.S., 1971; bd. editors: Media Law Reporter (co-founder), Nat. Law Jour., 1983—; columnist nat. and N.Y. law jours.; contbr. articles on comms. law to profl. jours. Mem. rules com. Dem. Nat. Conv., 1988; chmn. N.Y. lawyer com. for Dukakis, 1988; former bd. dirs. N.Y. Times, N.Y. Times Neediest Cases Fund, N.Y. Times Found.; former trustee Pomfret Sch., Gunnery Sch., St. Bernard's Sch., Boys' Club N.Y., Salzburg Seminar, Fed. Bar Coun.; mem. vis. com. U. Chgo. Law Sch., 1977-80; bd. dirs. Human Rights Watch, 1994-96, Sky Rink Scholarship Fund, Inc., 1990-99, Citizens Pub. Utilities, 1996-99, Ice Theatre of N.Y., 1999—, Internat. Ctr. Journalists, 1998—. With AUS, 1958-59, Res., 1959-64. Named one of 200 Rising Leaders in U.S., Time mag., 1974, with 100 Most Influential Lawyers in U.S., Nat. Law Jour., 1991-97, one of Best Lawyers in Am., 1991-99; William Brinckerhoff Jackson scholar, 1954-55, Nat. Honor scholar U. Chgo. Law Sch., 1955-58. Fellow Inst. Judicial Adminstrn., N.Y. State Bar Assn. (chmn. spl. com. on pub. access to info. and proc. 1979-84, spl. com. on media law 1985-92); mem. N.Y.C. Bar Assn. (chmn. comm. law com. 1978-83, mem. corp. law com. 1977-81), ABA (governing bd. comm. law forum, commn. on pub. understanding about law 1979-82), Fed. Bar Coun. (trustee 1980-84), Columbia U. Seminars on Media and Society. Clubs: Yale (gov. 1964-67), Century Assn, Economic, St. Elmo, Elihu (gov. 1966-70), Washington Conn. (gov. 1972-78). Office: Debevoise & Plimpton 919 3rd Ave Fl 30 New York NY 10022-6225

GOODALE, MARK RYAN GABRIEL, social sciences educator, lawyer; b. Ft. Lee, Va., Sept. 28, 1967; s. William and Susan Goodale; m. Romana Iorga, Oct. 2, 1999; 1 child, Dara Leonarda Iorga. BA, UCLA, 1990; MSc, London Sch. Econs., 1991; JD, U. of the Pacific, Sacramento, Calif., 1994; LLM, U. Wis., 1998, PhD, 2001. Bar: (Calif.) 1994. Asst. prof. St. Olaf Coll., Northfield, Minn., 2000—01; Marjorie Shostak Disting. lectr. Emory U. Dept. Anthropology, Atlanta, 2001—03; asst. prof. conflict analysis and anthropology Inst. Conflict Analysis and Resolution George Mason U., Farifax, Va., 2003—; Fulbright scholar Romania, 2003—. Fellow Inst. Legal Studies, Madison, 1995—2000. Author: Practicing Ethnography in Law, 2002; contbr. articles to profl. jours. Fellow Rsch. fellow, Nat. Security Edn. Program, 1998—99, grantee Rsch. grant, NSF, 1998—99, Tchg. seminar grant, Nat. Endowment Humanities, 2001, Andrew W. Mellon Found., 2001; scholar Rsch. scholar, Orgn. Am. States, Bolivia, 1998, Van Calker scholar, Inst. suisse de droit comparé, Switzerland, 2000. Mem.: Assn. Polit. and Legal Anthropology, Soc. Latin Am. Anthropology, Law and Soc. Assn., Am. Anthropological Assn., California State Bar Assn. (life). Democrat. Office: Inst for Conflict Analysis and Resolution George Mason Univ 4260 Chain Bridge Rd Fairfax VA 22030 E-mail: mgoodale@gmu.edu.

GOODALE, RALPH E. Canadian government minister; b. Regina, Sask., Can., Oct. 5, 1949; s. Thomas Henry and Winnifred Claire (Myers) G.; m. Pamela Jean Kendel, Feb. 8, 1986. BA, U. Regina, 1971; LLB, U. Sask., 1972. M.P. from Assiniboia, Sask. Ho. of Commons, Ottawa, 1974-79; leader Sask. Liberal Party, 1981-88; mem. Legis. Assembly from provincial riding Assiniboia-Gravelbourg, Sask., 1986-88; corp. sec. Pioneer Life Ins. Co., 1989-90, Soveriegn Life Ins. Co., 1990-93; M.P. from Wascana Ho. of Commons, Ottawa, 1993—; min. Nat. Resources Can., Can. Wheat Bd., 1997—2002; also min. Agr. and Agri-Food Can., Ottawa, 1993-97; fed. interlocutor for Metis and Non-States Indians, 1997—; min. of state, leader of the govt. House of Commons, Ottawa, 2002, min. pub. works and govt. svcs., 2002—. Parliamentary sec. to Min. Transport, Min. Wheat Bd., Pres. Privy Coun., 1974-79. Active polit. coms. Mem. Law Soc. Sask. Lutheran. Office: 215-S Centre Block Ottawa ON Canada K1A 0A6

GOODALE, SEAN DOUGLAS, healthcare administrator, consultant; b. Muscatine, Iowa, Mar. 15, 1968; s. E. Gary and Joyce M. Goodale; m. Kimberly Kay Young, Sept. 7, 1991; children: Blake, Keaton. BS in Acctg., U. Kans., Lawrence, 1990, MBA, 2000. CPA, Kans., 1992. Acct., cons. Resnik's Bus. Consulting, Prairie Village, Kans., 1987-90, Koch & Koch, CPAs, Kansas City, Mo., 1991-92; supervising acct. Arthur Andersen & Co., Kansas City, Mo., 1992-94; CFO Physician Resources, Inc., Kansas City, Kans., 1994—. Sec.-treas., bd. dirs., Physician Resources, Inc., 2000-01; treas., bd. dir.s, Sigma Phi Epsilon Alumni Bd., Lawrence, 1994—. HCECU Bd., Kansas City, Kans., 1994—. Vice-chmn. Cmty. Covenant Ch., Shawnee, kans., 1991— Republican. Avocations: sports, youth mentoring, music. Home: 14712 Eby Overland Park KS 66221 Office: Comprehensive Profl Resources LLC Ste 500 9393 W 110th Overland Park KS 66210 Fax: 866-728-3450. E-mail: sdghnance@kc.rr.com.

GOODALE, TONI KRISSEL, development consultant; b. N.Y.C., May 26, 1941; d. Walter DuPont and Ricka Krissel; m. James Campbell Goodale, May 3, 1964; children: Timothy Fuller, Ashley Krissel, Clayton A. (Ward). AB cum laude, Smith Coll., 1963; student, U. Geneva, 1962-63; postgrad., Hunter Coll., 1964-65. Congl. intern Senator Keating U.S. Senate, Washington, 1963; broadcast analyst FCC, Washington, 1963-64; adminstrv. asst., dir. grant rsch. dept. Ford Found., N.Y.C., 1964-67, cons. pub. edn. dept., 1968-69; N.Y. rep. Smith Coll., N.Y.C., 1975-78, asst. dir. devel., 1978-79; pres. Goodale Assocs., N.Y.C., 1979-92, chmn., CEO, 1992—. Mem. NYC 2000 Millennium Coun.; vis. com. continuing edn. New Sch. Social; mem. bd. advs. First Women's Bank; bd. dirs. N.Y. Outward Bound., mem. exec. com., chmn. alumni com.; lectr., writer in field. Columnist Fund Raising Mgmt. Bd. dirs. N.Y. Pub. Libr.; bd. dirs., mem. exec. com. Pen Am. Ctr., chmn.; mem. Women's Fgn. Policy Group; mem. UNA Chmn. Coun.; lectr. U.S. Naval Acad.; mem. alumnae fund com. Smith Coll., v.p. class, chmn. 25th reunion, Women's Forum; univ. chmn.'s coun., trustee, alumnae fund chmn., mem. alumnae coun.; bd. dirs. Brearley Sch.; mem. exec. com. Parents' Assn., St. Bernard's Sch.; mem. benefit com. N.Y. Philharmonic; trustee, bd. govs. Churchill Sch.; co-chmn. spl. events com. Carnegie Hall, The Joffrey Ballet Opening Gala; chmn. Coro Benefit Dinners; trustee N.Y. Inst. Child Devel.; mem. women's divsn. Legal Aid Soc.; mem. N.Y. com. Joffrey Ballet; mem. benefit com. Grosvenor House; vice chmn. N.Y.C. Opera Benefit, Peir Ctr. Benefit; mem. com. Sch. Am. Ballet; active Women's Forum. Mem. Am. Coun. Arts (vice-chmn. bd., exec. com., chmn. nat. patrons commn., chair long range planning com.), Nat. Cultural Alliance (bd. dirs.), Am. Assn. Fund-Raising Counsel (bd. dirs. trust for philanthropy), Nat. Assn. Fund Raising Execs., Assn. Healthcare Philanthropy, Brearley Sch. Alumnae Assn., Smith Coll. Alumnae Assn., Cosmopolitan Club, Smith Club, Washington Club, Seventh Regiment Armory Club, Doubles Internat. Club, Women's Forum (Women's Leadership Forum select cir., transition team, NYC pub. adv.). E-mail: tkgassoc@aol.com.

GOODALL, LEONARD EDWIN, public administration educator; b. Warrensburg, Mo., Mar. 16, 1937; s. Leonard Burton and Eula (Johnson) G.; m. Lois Marie Stubblefield, Aug. 16, 1959; children: Karla, Karen, Greg. BA, Central Mo. State U., 1958; MA, U. Mo., 1960; PhD (Kendrick C. Babcock fellow), U. Ill., 1962; AA (hon.), Schoolcraft Coll., 1977. Asst. prof. polit. sci., asst. dir. Bur. Govt. Research, Ariz. State U., Tempe, 1962-65, bur. dir., 1965-67; assoc. prof. polit. sci., assoc. dean faculties U. Ill. at Chgo. Circle, 1968-69, vice chancellor, 1969-71; chancellor U. Mich., Dearborn, 1971-79; pres. U. Nev., Las Vegas, 1979-85, prof. mgmt. and pub. adminstrn., 1985—2000. Cons. Ariz. Acad., Phoenix, 1964-67; dir. Peace Corps tng. program for Chile, 1965; vice chmn. bd. Comml. Bank of Nev., 1993-98; chmn. bd. Colonial Bank Nev., 1998—. Contributing editor, Canadian Moneysaver, 1997—; Author: The American Metropolis: Its Governments and Politics, 1968, rev. edit., 1975, Gearing Arizona's Communities to Orderly Growth, 1965, State Politics and Higher Education, 1976, When Colleges Lobby States, 1987, Managing Your TIAA-CREF Retirement Accounts, 1990, The World Wide Investor, 1991, Nevada Government and Politics, 1996, Reinventing the System, 2001; editor: Urban Politics in the Southwest, 1967. Mem. univ. exec. com. United Fund, 1966-67; v.p. Met. Fund, Inc.; mem. Mich. Gov.'s Commn. Long Range Planning, 1973-75, Tempe Planning and Zoning Commn., 1965-67, New Detroit Com., 1972-79; mem. Wayne County (Mich.) Planning Commn., 1973-79, vice chmn., 1976-79; mem. exec. bd. Clark County chpt. NCCJ, 1979-86; bd. dirs. Nev. Devel. Authority, 1980-86, Boulder Dam coun. Boy Scouts Am., 1980-89; bd. dirs. Nev. Power Co. Consumer Adv. Coun., 1984-90, chmn., 1986-89. Served with AUS, 1959. Mem. Am. Polit. Sci. Assn., Am. Soc. Pub. Adminstrn. (chpt. pres. 1989-90), Western Govtl. Rsch. Assn. (exec. coun. 1966-68), Dearborn C. of C. (dir. 1974-79), Phi Sigma Epsilon, Phi Kappa Phi Found. (bd. dirs. 1994-96). Lodges: Rotary. Home: 6530 Darby Ave Las Vegas NV 89146-6518 Office: U Nev Dept Pub Adminstrn Las Vegas NV 89154 E-mail: patgoodall@aol.com.

GOODBERRY, DIANE JEAN (DIANE OBERKIRCHER), mathematics educator, tax accountant; b. Buffalo, June 24, 1950; d. Ralph Arthur and Muriel Carol (Glaeser) O.; m. Lawrence D. Goodberry, Sr. BS in Math. Edn., State Univ. Coll., Brockport, N.Y., 1972, MS in Ednl. Adminstrn., 1974; grad., Nat.Tax Tng. Sch., Monsey, N.Y., 2000. Cert. in secondary math. edn., N.Y. Uni-Pay clk. Marine Midland Bank, Buffalo, 1968-72; asst. registrar State Univ. Coll., Brockport, 1972-74; home instrn. tutor Clarence Ctrl. Sr. H.S., Sweet Home Sr. H.S., NY, 1974-75; part-time inst. Erie C.C., Buffalo, 1975-86; instr. math. Ednl. Testing Methods, Buffalo, 1984-90, Buffalo Pub. Sch. System, 1974—. Mem. curriculum devel. com. Buffalo Pub. Schs., 1988, 92—, yearbook advisor 1994—, math. intervention coord., 2002—; cooperating tchr. BRIET-U. Buffalo, 1990-96; owner Taxes by Diane; CEO, Larry's GrassRoots Landscaping Inc.; cons. Nat. Tax Tng. Sch., 1999—; AIS coord., Buffalo Pub. Sch. Sys., 2002—. Vol., World Univ. Games, Buffalo, 1993. Mem. AAUW, Nat. Assn. of Female Execs., Women Tchrs. Assn. (bd. dirs., v.p. 1993-94, pres. 1994-96, rec. sec. 1996-98, treas. 1998), Assn. Math. Tchrs. N.Y. State (conf. spkr.), Theodore Roosevelt Rough Riders, Nat. Coun. Math. (conf. spkr.), Assn. Curriculum Devel. and Supervision (Top 2000 scholar of 20th Century award, named one of 2000 Outstanding Scholars of 20th Century Winner in Math). Republican. Methodist. Avocations: crafts, reading, travel, sports. Home: 10644 Crump Rd Holland NY 14080-9303 Office: South Park HS 150 Southside Pkwy Buffalo NY 14220-1552

GOOD-BLACK, EDITH ELISSA (PEARL WILLIAMS), writer; b. Hollywood, Calif., Jan. 10, 1945; d. Jack Brian and Rose Marie (Miller) Good; m. Michael Lawrence Black, Dec. 18, 1986 (dec.). BA in English, Calif. State U., Northridge, 1974; student, UCLA and U. Calif., Berkeley, 1962-92. Explorer Mayan ruins, Mex., 1963; author, pub. Gull Press, L.A., 1990-95. Participant numerous dance, art, music, lit., math. and sci. classes; dancer Hajde Dance Troop, Berkeley, Calif., 1962-66. One-woman shows, L.A., 1962-95; singer, various venues, L.A., 1986-96; author: (pseudonym Pearl Williams) The Trickster of Tarzana, 1992, Short Stories, 1995, Mad in Craft, 1995, Missives, 1995, others; author numerous poems; CDs, radio and internet broadcasts. Fundraiser, del. to local convs. Dem. clubs, Calif. and Mex., 1962—; supporter mental health orgns., 1962—; participant Consciousness raising groups, del. local convs., fundraiser, canvasser, office worker, driver, participant W.E.B. DuBois Club, Congress Racial Equality, San Francisco, Berkeley, L.A., and Oakland, 1965, Peace in Alliance for Survival, Berkeley, Oakland, L.A., 1964-80, women's rights Westside Women's Ctr., Woman's Bldg., L.A., 1974-80, Environment in Earth Day, L.A., 1977, phys. and mental health VA, cons. book reviewer, tutor, Mental Health Assn., L.A., 1962—. Recipient achievement prize, Internat. Biographical Ctr., Cambridge, Eng., 2000. Mem. Mensa, Am. Soc. Composers, Authors, and Pubs., Plummer Park Writers, Westside Writers. Achievements include writing chosen by a jury of experts for inclusion in the permanent collecton of the Library of Congress. Home: 1470 S Robertson Blvd Apt B Los Angeles CA 90035-3402

GOODCHILD, ROSINA ANN, community health nurse; b. Streator, Ill., Nov. 28, 1963; d. David Floyd and Reita Mae (Keith) Allen; m. Robert Joseph Goodchild, June 4, 1988; children: Christopher Robert, Matthew James, Nathan Charles. AAS in Nursing, Ill. Valley Community Coll., 1984; BSN, Bradley U., 1988. RN, Ill. Camp nurse, counselor YMCA/CETA, Streator, 1983; pvt. duty nurse Streator, 1982-85; staff nurse emergency/trauma dept. St. James Hosp., Pontiac, Ill., 1984-88; charge nurse, preceptor ARC, Peoria, Ill., 1988-94; immunization nurse La Salle County Health Dept., Ottawa, Ill., 1992-94; ins. physicals nurse, ins. examiner nurse Am. Para Profl. Sys. Co., Peoria, Ill., 1999—; ins. phys. nurse, ins. examiner nurse Exam. Mgmt. Svcs., Inc. and Countrywide Paramed., 2002—. Nursing adv. com. Heart of Ill. Blood Svcs., ARC, 1985-88. Spl. events coord. Village of Grand Ridge, Ill., 1995—; feature and staff writer Round the Ridge, 1995—; youth choir dir., 1995—; local charter rep., troop com. chair, Tiger Cub coach, den leader, pack coord. Boy Scouts Am., 1998—, day camp mgmt. dir., 1999—, cubmaster, 2000—. Mem. ANA, Ill. Nurses Assn., Emergency Nurses Assn., Ottawa Jaycees (adminstrv. v.p. Ottawa chpt. 2002-03, pres. 2003—). Home: PO Box 233 400 Sylvan Ave Grand Ridge IL 61325-0233

GOODE, B. ERICH, sociologist, educator, retired criminologist; b. Austin, Tex., Sept. 21, 1938; s. William Josiah and Josephine Mary (Cannizzo) Goode; m. Alice N. Neufeld, Dec. 23, 1968 (div.); m. Barbara S. Weinstein, Mar. 23, 1984; children: Sarah Rachel, Lawrence Daniel. BA, Oberlin Coll., 1960; PhD, Columbia U., 1966. Asst. prof. NYU, N.Y.C., 1965-67; asst. prof. sociology SUNY, Stony Brook, 1967-70, assoc. prof., 1970-81, prof., 1981-2000; vis. prof. U. Md., College Park, 2000—03, ret., 2003. Vis. assoc. prof. U. N.C., Chapel Hill, 1977—2003; Lady Davis vis. prof. Hebrew U., Jerusalem, 1993. Author: (book) The Marijuana Smokers, 1970, Drugs in American Society, 1972, 1999, Deviant Behavior, 1978, 2001, Paranormal Beliefs, 2000, Deviance in Everyday Life, 2002. Recipient Chancellors award for excellence in tchg., SUNY, 1997; grantee, NIMH, 1968; Guggenheim fellow, 1975—76. Office: U Md Dept Criminal and Criminal Justice Le Frak Hall College Park MD 20742 E-mail: egoode2001@comcast.net.

GOODE, BARRY PAUL, lawyer; b. N.Y.C., Apr. 11, 1948; s. Hy and Charlotte (Langer) G.; m. Erica Tucker, Sept. 1, 1974; children: Adam, Aaron. AB magna cum laude, Kenyon Coll., 1969; JD cum laude, Harvard U., 1972. Bar: Mass. 1972, Calif. 1975, Hawaii 1995, U.S. Dist. Ct. Mass. 1972, U.S. Dist. Ct. (no. dist.) Calif. 1975, U.S. Dist. Ct. (ctrl. dist.) Calif. 1983, U.S. Dist. Ct. Hawaii 1995, U.S. Ct. Appeals (9th cir.) 1976, U.S. Ct. Appeals (6th cir.) 1999, U.S. Supreme Ct. 1986. Spl. asst. Sen Adlai E. Stevenson III, Washington, 1972-74; assoc. McCutchen, Doyle, Brown & Enersen, San Francisco, 1974-80, ptnr., 1980-2001; legal affairs sec. Gov. Gray Davis, 2001—. Co-author: Federal Litigation Guide, 1985. Advisor Gov.'s Com. to Review Water Law, San Francisco, 1979; bd. dirs. Stanford Pub. Interest Law Found., 1979-82; bd. dirs. Coro No. Calif., 1997—. Mem. San Francisco Bar Assn. (exec. com. environ. law sect. 1989-91), Am. Law Inst. Office: Gov Gray Davis State Capitol Sacramento CA 95814

GOODE, BOBBY CLAUDE, retired secondary education educator, writer; b. Celeste, Tex., Dec. 10, 1940; s. Claude Elmer and Clarice Edna G.; m. Jean Helen Ames, June 9, 1963; children: James Lonnie, Joel Dietrich, John Shalom. BS, MIT, 1963; MA, Andover Newton Sem., Newton Centre, Mass., 1968; MS, Rensselaer Poly. Inst., 1972. Cert. tchr. sci. and math. Tchr. math. Lawrence D. Bell High Sch., Hurst, Tex., 1966-67; tchr. physics and chemistry Grapevine (Tex.) High Sch., 1967-70; tchr. advanced physics, advanced chemistry, advanced biology South Plainfield (N.J.) High Sch., 1970-96, ret., 1996. Sci. tchr. Princeton (N.J.) U., 1983, Disting. Secondary Sch. Tchg. finalist, 1983. Author: (booklets) Lap Physics, 1973, Stars, Planets, People, 1980, Atoms and Molecules, 1980, Physics Problem Solutions, 1980. Mem. Civil Rights Commn., Piscataway, N.J., 1977, Sr. Citizens Housing Com., Piscataway, 1975; ch. sch. tchr. First Bapt. Ch. of New Market, 1970-96. Named Outstanding Sci. Tchr., Sigma Xi, 1986. Mem. NEA, N.J. Edn. Assn., Am. Assn. Physics Tchrs., Nat. Sci. Tchrs. Assn. (recipient Exemplary Secondary Sci. Tchr. Nat. award 1980). Democrat. Avocations: family, travel, writing, sports. Home: 129 Stonegate S Boerne TX 78006-3411 E-mail: bobgoode@gvtc.com.

GOODE, DAVID RONALD, transportation company executive; b. Vinton, Va., Jan. 13, 1941; s. Otto and Hessie M. (Maxey) G.; m. Susan Skiles, June 22, 1963; children: Christina, Martha. AB, Duke U., 1962; JD, Harvard U., 1965; LHD (hon.), Old Dominion U., 2003. With Norfolk & Western Ry., Roanoke, Va., 1965—82; chmn., pres., CEO Norfolk So. Corp., 1982—. Bd. dirs. Caterpillar, Inc., Delta Air Lines, Ga.-Pacific Corp., Tex. Instruments, Inc., Assn. Am. R.R., Bus. Comm. for Arts, Va. Econ. Devel. Partnership, Ctr. Energy and Economic Devel. Bd. trustees Gen. Douglas MacArthur Meml. Found., Va. Found. Ind. Colls.; bd. visitors Fuqua Sch. Bus., Duke U.; mem. Am. Soc. Corp. Execs., Northwestern U. Transp. Ctr., Bus. Adv. Coun., Bus. Roundtable, Coal Industry Adv. Bd.; Kennedy Ctr. Corp. Fund Bd.; Nat. Freight Transp. Assn. Mem. ABA, Va. State Bar Assn. Democrat. Presbyterian. Avocation: golf. Home: 7301 Woodway Ln Norfolk VA 23505-3149 Office: Norfolk So Corp 3 Commercial Pl Norfolk VA 23510-2191

GOODE, ERICA TUCKER, internist; b. Berkeley, Calif., Mar. 25, 1940; d. Howard Edwin and Mary Louise (Tucker) Sweeting; m. Bruce Tucker (div. 1971); m. Barry Paul Goode, Sept. 1, 1974; children: Adam Nathaniel, Aaron Benjamin. BS summa cum laude, U. Calif., Berkeley, 1962, MPH, 1967; MD, U. Calif., San Francisco, 1977. Diplomate Am. Bd. Internal Medicine. Chief dietitian Washington Hosp. Ctr., Washington, 1968; pub. health nutritionist Dept. Human Resources, Washington, 1969—73; intern Children's Hosp. (now Calif. Pacific Med. Ctr.), San Francisco, 1977—78, resident, 1978—80, chief med. resident internal medicine, 1979—80; pvt. practice internal medicine San Francisco, 1980—. Expert witness med.-legal issues, Calif., 1990—; lectr., tchr. med. house staff Calif. Pacific Med. Ctr. Hosp., 1982—; assoc. prof. medicine U. Calif., San Francisco, 1984—. Contbr. articles to profl. publs. Co-chair Physicians for Clinton, No. Calif., 1992, 96. Mem. ACP, Calif. Med. Assn., Calif. Soc. Internal Medicine, San Francisco Med. Soc., U. Calif. Alumni Assn. (del.), Alpha Omega Alpha (named Best Doctor's list 1998-2001). Office: CPMC Inst for Health & Healing Clinic 2300 California St Ste 200 San Francisco CA 94115-2754

GOODE, JANE KINNEY, artist; b. Mpls., July 22, 1919; d. Edwin Cyril and Irene Francis (Woodruff) Kinney; m. Howard Joseph Charles La Perriere, Oct. 15, 1948 (div. Aug. 1949); 1 child, Bonnie; m. Calvin Morris Goode, Oct. 17, 1959. Student, Terry Art Sch., Miami, Fla., 1941, Art Workshops, 1973—. Pvt.

sec. to col. U.S. Army Corps. of Engrs., Miami, 1942-45; mem. singing trio USO, 1945-48; staff mem. Little River Shopper, Miami, 1949-50; sales WTSP Radio Station and St. Petersburg Times, St. Petersburg, Fla., 1950-55; acct. exec. Adcraft Adv. Agy., Corpus Christi, Tex., 1955-74; exec. dir. Paisano Girl Scout Coun., Corpus Christi, Tex., 1974-86; artist Corpus Christi, Tex., 1986—. Mem. Pres. team to hire the Handicapped, 1962-63; mem. pub. rels. United Way, 1964; bd. dirs. Corpus Christi Press Club, 1960-61; pres. Corpus Christi Advt. Club, 1961-62; mem. and adv. mem. Mcpl. Arts Commn., Corpus Christi, 1987—; fin. com. YWCA, 1988-90; bd. dirs. Early Childhood Devel., 1988-91, Art Ctr. Corpus Christi, 1998—. Named Women of Yr. Advt. Club, 1961; recipient Thanks Badge award Paisano Girl Scout, 1979, The Silver Medal award Advertising Fedn., 2001; named one of 7 Women in Careers, YWCA, 2003. Mem. Art Mus. of Corpus Christs, Art Ctr. of Corpus Christi. Home: 437 Barracuda Pl Corpus Christi TX 78411-1521 Office: Goode Pastel Portraits 437 Barracuda Pl Corpus Christi TX 78411-1521

GOODE, JANET WEISS, elementary school educator; b. Chattanooga, Tenn., Sept. 3, 1935; d. Albert H. and Dorothy E. (Crandall) Weiss; m. Gene G. Goode, June 11, 1961; children: Jennifer E., Amy V. BS in Biology, Carson-Newman Coll., 1957; MA in Botany, Vanderbilt U., 1959; MEd, Lynchburg Coll., 1980. Cert. postgrad. profl. tchr., Va. Instr. gen. biology, botany, zoology, animal ecology Carson-Newman Coll., Tenn., 1959-61; tchr. biology, chemistry Salem Acad., Winston-Salem, N.C., 1961-64; tchr. chemistry Wade Hampton High Sch., Greenville, S.C., 1964-65; tchr. sci. Va. Treatment Ctr. for Children, Richmond, 1966; tchr. biology Quantico (Va.) H.S., 1969-70; pvt. tutor Madison Heights, Va., 1980-85, James River Day Sch. and Seven Hills Sch., Lynchburg, Va., 1980-85; reading specialist Title I reading program Monelison Mid. Sch., Madison Heights, 1985-93; reading specialist Amherst County Adult Basic Edn. Program, 1992-94, 95—; reading specialist Title I reading and Reading Recovery Pleasant View Elem. Sch., Monroe, Va., 1993-96, Madison Heights (Va.) Elem. Sch., 1996—. Vis. instr. U. Chattanooga, summer 1960; mem. learning disabilities del. to Russia and Lithuania, Citizen Amb. Program, 1993; mem. mentor tchr. program Amherst County Pub. Schs., 1999-2000. Editor: (newsletter) Topics for Title I, author: Can You Read a Baseball Card?; co-author: Transitional Intervention Program. Sponsor sch. lit. mag. Monelison Mid. Sch., Pleasant View Elem. Sch.; organist, newsletter editor for Ptnr. Ch. com. First Unitarian Ch.; mem. Friends of Libr., Madison Heights Br. Libr., helper ann. book sale. Recipient Reading Tchr. of the Year Piedmont Va. Area Reading Coun., 1993-94. Mem. NEA, Nat. Coun. Tchrs. of English, Va. Edn. Assn., Amherst Edn. Assn., Internat. Dyslexia Assn., Piedmont Area Reading Coun. (past newletter editor, past treas.), Va. State Reading Assn., Internat. Reading Assn., Lynchburg Stamp Club. E-mail: jwgoode@worldnet.att.net.

GOODE, JOHN MARTIN, manufacturing company executive; b. Chgo., Sept. 24, 1934; s. Robert C. and Alyce (Belz) G.; children: John Martin, Sue Ellen, James Edward, Leslie Maureen. B Commerce, DePaul U., 1960; MBA, U. Chgo., 1966; EdD, No. Ill. U., 1984. CPA, Ill.; CMA, Ill. Contr. farm equipment div. Allis Chalmers, Milw., 1966-69; v.p., contr. Maremont Corp., Chgo., 1969-73; sr. v.p. Whittakers Corp., Chgo., 1973-75; assoc. dean DePaul U., Chgo., 1976-78, asst. prof., 1975-80; sr. v.p. fin. and corp. planning J.I. Case Co., Racine, Wis., 1980-85; chmn. bd., chief exec. officer Prestolite Electric Inc., Toledo, 1986-91; dean Sch. Mgmt. and Bus. Nat. U., San Diego, 1991-93; investor, 1993—; chmn. bd. dirs., CEO K&W Products, LLC, Bloomington, Ind., 1996-2000. Chmn. bd. dirs., CEO, A.P. Labs, Inc., San Diego, Am. Innotek Inc., San Diego. Mem. San Diego Yacht club, Univ. Club, Del Mar Country Club. Home: 334 Genoa Springs Dr Genoa NV 89411-0668

GOODE, PAUL, psychologist, educator, consultant; b. Bklyn., Nov. 14, 1937; s. Arthur and Bertha (Rose) G.; m. Judith Granich, June 22, 1960; children: Lawrence J., Andrew P., Joshua S. BA in Psychology, Bklyn. Coll., 1959; MA in Sch. Psychology (rsch. asst.), Syracuse U., 1962; EdD in Sch. Psychology (doctoral fellow), Temple U., 1972. Unemployment ins. claims examiner N.Y. State Employment Svc., Cortland, 1961-62; sch. psychologist Steuben County Bd. Coop. Ednl. Svcs., Bath, N.Y., 1962-66, Camden (N.J.) Bd. Edn., 1966-67, Delaware County Bd. Sch. Dirs., Media, Pa., 1967-68, intern psychologist, 1968-69; sch. psychologist specialist Phila. Non-Pub. Elem. Schs., 1969-70; assocs. dir. clin. ednl. svcs. project King of Prussia (Pa.) Intermediate Unit #23, 1970-73; coord. suburban unit Nat. Regional Resource Ctr. of Pa., King of Prussia, 1971-74, assoc. dir., 1974-75; dir. Pa. Area Learning Resources Ctr., Doylestown, 1975-77; dir. IEP devel. program Bucks County (Pa.) Intermediate Unit #22, Doylestown, 1977-79, coord. fed. programs in spl. edn., 1979-81, acting dir. spl. edn., 1980-81, asst. exec. dir., dir. spl. edn., 1981-93; pvt. practice Melrose Park, Pa., 1993—. Vis. prof. U. de Antioquia, Colombia, 1964-65; part-time instr. Corning (N.Y.) C.C., 1965-66, Cabrini Coll., Radnor, Pa., 1972; instr. diagnosis of ednl. disabilities Pa. State U., Ogontz, 1972-84; adj. prof. faculty Temple U., Phila., 1988—. Assoc. editor : Archives, newsletter Nat. Regional Resource Ctr. Pa., 1970—72. Treas. Cub Scout Pack 190, 1970—80; mgr. Old York Rd. Little League, 1970—80. Recipient Alumni award Temple U., 1980. Fellow Pa. Psychol. Assn. (editor divsn. newsletter 1975-77, pres. sch. psychology divsn. 1978-79, pres. 1981-82); mem. APA (divsn. 16), Coun. Exceptional Children, Coun. Orgn. Edn. (pres. 1989-90), Pa. Assn. Sch. Adminstrs., Pa. Assn. Pupil Pers. Adminstrs., Phi Delta Kappa. Home and Office: 7610 Montgomery Ave Elkins Park PA 19027-2901 E-mail: pgoode3@comcast.net.

GOODE, RICHARD BENJAMIN, economist, educator; b. Ft. Worth, July 31, 1916; s. Flavius M. and Laura Nell (Carson) G.; m. Liesel Gottscho, June 23, 1943 (dec. May 2002). AB, Baylor U., 1937; MA, U. Ky., 1939; PhD, U. Wis., 1947. Economist U.S. Bur. Budget, 1941-45, Treasury Dept., 1945-47; asst. prof. econs. U. Chgo., 1947-51; with IMF, Washington, 1951-59, 65-81, dir. fiscal affairs dept., 1965-81; mem. staff Brookings Instn., Washington, 1959-65, guest scholar, 1981-87; professorial lectr. Sch. Advanced Internat. Studies, Johns Hopkins U., 1981-88. Cons. Treasury Dept., 1947-51, UN, 1950, World Bank, 1964. Author: The Corporation Income Tax, 1951; The Individual Income Tax, 1964, rev. edit., 1976; Government Finance in Developing Countries, 1984; Economic Assistance to Developing Countries through the IMF, 1985. Editor Nat. Tax Jour, 1948-51. Mem. Am. Econ. Assn., Royal Econ. Soc., Nat. Tax Assn. (Holland medal for contbns. to study and practice of pub. fin. 1997), Internat. Inst. Pub. Fin., Cosmos Club. Home: 5420 Connecticut Ave NW Washington DC 20015-2813

GOODE, STEPHEN HOGUE, publishing company executive; b. Charlotte, N.C., Dec. 25, 1924; s. Henry Grady and Marie Louella (Creamer) G.; m. Jean Cameron Advena, Oct. 16, 1953; children: Elizabeth Whitston Joane Downe, Polly Turpin Dulcinea Hogue. BA, U. Md., 1948; MA, U. Pa., 1954, PhD, 1958. Asst. prof. English Rensselaer Poly. Inst., 1958-59; asst. prof. Fairleigh Dickinson U., 1960-65; dir. libraries, asso. prof. English Russell Sage Coll., 1965-78; pres., chmn. bd. Whitston Pub. Co., Troy, N.Y., 1968-81, Turpin Book Corp., Troy, 1973-80; pres. Penkevill Pub. Co., Greenwood, Fla., 1982—. Dir. Trenowyth Pub. Co., Penkivil Book Co. Author: Index to Little Magazines, 1943-47, 1965, Index to Little Magazines, 1940-42, 1967, Index to Commonwealth Little Magazines, 1966-67, 68, plus, biennial, Index to American Little Magazines, 1920-39, 1969, 1900-1919, 1974; editor: Studies in 20th Century, 1968-75; founding editor Am. Humanities Index, 1978-82. Served with AUS, 1943-46, 49-52. Decorated Purple Heart, Bronze Star with oak leaf cluster. Mem. MLA, Am. Hist. Assn., Bibliog. Soc. (London), Bibliog. Soc. Am., Bibliog. Soc. U. Va., Index Soc. (London). Clubs: Grolier (N.Y.C.).

GOODE, VIRGIL H., JR., congressman; b. Richmond, Va., Oct. 17, 1946; m. Lucy D. Dodson; 1 child, Catherine S. BA, U. Richmond, 1969; JD, U. Va., 1973. Mem. Va. Senate, 1973-97, U.S. Congress from 5th Va. dist., 1997—; mem. appropriations com., subcoms. on military contruction, agr. and vet. admin. Recipient Outstanding Legis. Svc. award Va. State Sheriffs' Assn., Outstanding Svc. award Vol. Rescue Squads, 1994. Mem. Phi Beta Kappa, Omicron Delta Kappa, Lambda Chi Alpha, Phi Alpha Delta. Republican. Baptist. Office: Ho of Reps 1520 Longworth Ho Office Bldg Washington DC 20515-4605*

GOODELL, JOSEPH EDWARD, manufacturing executive; b. El Paso, Tex., Aug. 18, 1937; s. Joseph Edward and Grace Louise (Beck) g.; m. Margaret Rives, Aug. 12, 1961 (di. June 1978); children: Marian, Margaret Trout, Martha, Maryellen Olszyk; m. Mary Ellen Hager, Sept. 17, 1993. BSME, MIT, 1959; MBA, Harvard U., 1961. Project engr. Bechtel Corp., San Francisco, 1961-65; mfg. engr. Chase Brass and Copper Co., Cleve., 1965-67; adminstrv. mgr. Montpelier, Ohio, 1967-69, Waterbury, Conn., 1969-71; v.p., gen. mgr. Montpelier, 1971-76; group v.p. Chase Brass and Copper Co., Cleve., 1976-79, Pangborn div. Carborundum, Hagerstown, Md., 1979-81; v.p. planning Standard Oil Ind. Products, Cleve., 1981-82, sr. v.p., 1982-85; pres., chief exec. officer Am. Brass Co., Buffalo, N.Y., 1985-94; chmn. bd. West Tex. and Buffalo Steam Ship & Rwy. Co., N.Y., 1991—, Empire Steel Co., 2000—01. Bd. dirs. Nitto Metals, Tokyo, 1974-79, TWI Properties, El Paso, Tex., 1975-93, Tech. Devel. Corp., Buffalo, Tech. Bldg. Corp., Boston. Active Boy Scouts Am., Waterbury, Conn.; past chmn. Buffalo Health Care Coalition; vice chmn. Greater Buffalo Partnership; chmn. Horizons Waterfront Commn.; dir. Downtown Devel., Inc.; dir. Buffalo State Coll. Found.; trustee, past pres., past exec. dir. Buffalo Philharm. Orch.; chmn. planning com. Buffalo Expo Pan Am. 2001; former mem. bd. advisors Symphony Orch. Inst.; former v.p. Sheas Preservation Soc.; mem. Erie County Who Does What Commn.; former bd. dirs. Kenmore Mercy Hosp.; mem. Erie County Exec. transition Com.; bd. dirs. Kleinmans Music Hall. Recipient Spl. award Buffalo Philharm. Orch., 1999; named Citizen of Yr. Buffalo, 1996. Mem. Country Club of Buffalo, Buffalo Club, Wanaka Country Club. Home: 6746 Lake Shore Rd Derby NY 14047-9739

GOODELL, KATHY SUSAN, artist, educator; d. Herbert Sumner and Celestine Goodell; m. Ralph James Rogers, June 30, 1996. BFA, San Francisco Art Inst., 1969—71, MFA, 1972. Instr. Calif. Coll. of Arts and Crafts, San Francisco, 1974—77, San Francisco (Calif.) State U, 1978—81, The San Francisco Art Inst., 1978—80; lectr. U Calif., Davis, 1981—82; assoc. prof. Moore Coll. of Art and Design, Philadelphia, 1984—91; instr. sculpture The Sch. of Visual Arts, N.Y.C., 1986—; prof. painting, drawing SUNY, New Paltz, 1993—. Juror sculpture fellowship N.Y. Found. For The Arts, N.Y.C., 1995; juror Nat. Scholastic Award Nat. Scholastic Soc., N.Y.C., 1999; lectr.,workshops at various colls.,univs., film festivals. lectr. in field. Contbr. video, book, articles and reviews; cinematographer: ; one-woman shows include Queens Art Ctr., Queens,N.Y., 2000, Willoughby Sharp Gallery, N.Y.C., 2000, Calkins Gallery, Hofstra U, 1982, Gallery Paule Anglim, San Francisco,Calif., 1982, Atholl McBean Gallery, 1981, exhibited in group shows at The Chandler Gallery-Faculty Exhbn. SUNY, New Paltz N.Y., 2002, Paul Morris Gallery, N.Y.C., 2001, Wake Forest U., Winston-Salem, N.C., 2000, Nicolai Fine Art, N.Y.C., 1999, The Islip Mus., East Islip, N.Y., 1998, Satellite, AT, Long Island,N.Y., 1997, URBANGLASS, N.Y.C., 1996, The Boise Mus., Boise,Id., 1994, numeroust group shows at galleries and univs., 1977—, Represented in permanent collections DeSaisset Mus., Santa Clara,Calif., The Samuel Dorshy Mus., New Paltz,N.Y., Fortroyal Found., Fultonville,N.Y., Calif. Pacific Corp., San Francisco,Calif., The Oakland Mus., Oakland, Calif., The Albuquerque Mus., Albuquerque,N.M., The Inst. of Plastic Arts, Bucharest, Romania, The Ctr. for Visual Arts, Anchorage, AK. Recipient James D. Phelan Award, Internat. award to a Calif. born artist., James D. Phelan, 1983; grantee Fellowship, N.Y. Found. for the Arts, 1997, 1993, Pollock-Krasne Found. Grant In Sculpture, 1991, Artist In Residence, N.Y. Council for the Arts, 1985, Fellowship in Sculpture, Nat. Endowment for the Arts, 1983, 1979, Fulbright-Hays Fellowship - Romania, Fulbright-Hayes Foun. Mem.: Tribera Organ. of Artists, United Fed. of Tchrs. Home: 401 Washington St New York NY 10013 Office: SUNY 75 South Manheim Blvd New Paltz NY 12561

GOODELL, SOL, retired lawyer; b. St. Louis, Aug. 24, 1906; s. Abram and Jennie (Silverberg) G.; m. Beatrice Cholden, Feb. 24, 1946 (dec. Mar. 1998); children: Thomas C., Susan Jean. LLB, U. Tex., 1929. Bar: Tex. 1929. Asso. prof. law U. Tex. Law Sch., 1929-30; asso., then mem. firm Thompson & Knight, and predecessors, Dallas, 1930-76, of counsel, 1976—. Former chmn. bd. Greenhill Sch., Dallas; former trustee bd. devel. U. Tex., Dallas; former trustee, v.p. Excellence in Edn. Found.; former sec., trustee Goals for Dallas; former trustee Dallas Grand Opera Assn.; former pres. Found. for Callier Ctr. and Communication Disorders. Served to capt. AUS, 1942-46. Mem. ABA, Dallas Bar Assn., State Bar Tex. Jewish (trustee, past pres. temple). Home: 5927 Joyce Way Dallas TX 75225-1626 Office: 1700 Pacific Ave Ste 3300 Dallas TX 75201-4656

GOODEN, BENNY L. school system administrator; Supt. Ft. Smith (Ark.) Pub. Schs. State finalist Nat. Supt. Yr. award, 1993; recipient Phoebe Apperson Hearst Outstanding Educator award Nat. PTA, 1999. Office: Ft Smith Pub Schs 3205 Jenny Lind Rd Fort Smith AR 72901-7101

GOODEN, DWIGHT EUGENE, professional baseball player; b. Tampa, Fla., Nov. 16, 1964; s. Dan and Ella Mae Gooden; m. Monica Colleen Harris, Nov. 21, 1987. Pitcher minor league teams, Kingsport, Little Falls and Lynchburg, 1982—83, N.Y. Mets, Nat. League, 1984—96, Cleveland Indians, 1996—99, Tampa Bay Devilrays, St. Petersburg, Fla., 2000—. Named Pitcher of Yr., Carolina League, 1983, Rookie of Yr., Nat. League, 1984, Rookie Pitcher of Yr., 1984; named to All-Star Team, 1984—86; recipient, 1988, Cy Young award, 1985. Achievements include first major pitcher to record 200 strikeouts in each of first 3 seasons. Office: 1 Tropicana Dr Saint Petersburg FL 33705-1703

GOODEN, ERIC, government agency administrator, real estate agent; b. Balt., Apr. 20, 1974; s. Esau Gooden, Jr. and Shirley May Spell. BA Polit. Sci., Morgan State U., 1997, MA Internat. Studies, 2003. Cert. realtor Long and Foster Real Estate Inst., Md., 1998. Contact rep. IRS, Balt., 1998—2001; summer intern Diplomatic Security, Washington, 2001; dist. adjudicators officer INS, Balt., 2001—; real estate agt. Von Realty, Inc., Balt., 2001—. Fellow Morris Goldseker fellowship, Morgan State U., 1998—99; scholar Dacosta scholarship, 2000. Mem.: Balt. Coun. Fgn. Affairs, Psi Sigma Alpha. Avocations: studying Mandarin Chinese, traveling. Home: 2901 Presbury St Baltimore MD 21216-3522 Personal E-mail: eincognito4life@aol.com.

GOODENBERGER, DANIEL MARVIN, medical educator; b. McCook, Nebr., Apr. 24, 1948; s. Marvin Eugene and Mary Ellen (Marshall) G.; m. Janet Ann King, July 30, 1979; children: James Michael, Katherine Elizabeth. BS, U. Nebr., 1970; MD, Duke U., 1974. Diplomate Am. Bd. Internal Medicine, Am. Bd. Emergency Medicine (examiner 1983-95), Am. Bd. Pulmonary Disease, Am. Bd. Critical Care Medicine. Intern Peter Bent Brigham Hosp., Boston, 1974-75, resident in internal medicine, 1975-76; clin. assoc. Nat. Cancer Inst., Bethesda, Md., 1976-78; fellow pulmonary and critical care medicine Boston U. Med. Ctr., 1985-88; assoc. dir. emergency dept. Arlington (Va.) Hosp., 1979-82; edn. dir. emergency dept. Georgetown U. Hosp., Washington, 1982-85; dir. emergency svcs. U. Hosp., Boston, 1986-87; dir. pulmonary and critical care fellowship Washington U. Med. Schs., St. Louis, 1989-93; dir. pulmonary cons. svcs. Barnes Hosp., St. Louis, 1990-93, dir. internal medicine residency program, 1992—; assoc. prof. medicine Washington U., St. Louis, 1995-99; dir. divsn. med. edn. Washington U. Sch. Medicine, St. Louis, 1998—, prof. medicine, 1999—. Chief Wood-Moore Firm, Barnes-Jewish Hosp., 1996-2001. Editor Careers, 1996-98. Lt. comdr. USPHS, 1973-78. Winthrop Breon and Am. Coll. Chest Physicians scholar, 1987. Fellow ACP, Am. Coll. Chest Physicians; mem. AMA, Am. Thoracic Soc., Am. Clin. and Climatological Assn., Assn. Program Dirs. Internal Medicine (nominating and publs. com. 1991-98), St. Louis Met. Med. Soc. (councilor 1997-2000), Phi Beta Kappa, Alpha Omega Alpha. Methodist. Avocations: theatre, symphony music, travel, sailing. Home: 4355 Maryland Ave Saint Louis MO 63108-2737 Office: Washington U Sch Medicine Box 8121 660 S Euclid Ave Saint Louis MO 63110-1010

GOODENDAY, LUCY SHERMAN, physician, educator; b. N.Y.C., Oct. 2, 1937; d. Leo Daniel and Winnie Victoria (Bornstein) Sherman; m. Kenneth Benjamin Goodenday, Aug. 31, 1958. AB, Bryn Mawr Coll., 1959; MD, N.Y. Med. Coll., 1963. Diplomate cardiovasc. disease Am. Bd. Internal Medicine; cert. nuclear cardiology. Clin. instr. U. Calif., San Francisco, 1969-71, asst. clin. prof., 1971-75; asst. prof. medicine U. Mich., Ann Arbor, 1975-78; assoc. prof. med. Med. Coll. Ohio, Toledo, 1979—2003, prof. medicine, 2003—. Editor: Hypertension in the Community, 1971; author: (movie, booklet) Current Approach to the Hypertensive Patient, 1970, (tape) Pro and Con Views on Routine Exercise Testing, 1977, Nuclear Cardiology Interactive Learning System, 1996—; editor-in-chief Studies in Nuclear Cardiology, 2001—; contbr. articles to profl. jours. Trustee N.W. Ohio AHA, 1983—, mem. rsch. rev. bd., 1988—; trustee Ohio Valley affil. AHA, mem. exec. com., 1996—99. Fellow NIH, 1965-68, AAUW, 1968-69, Med. Coll. Ohio Tchg. Scholars Fellow, 2000; grantee VA, 1973-78, Am. Heart Assn., 1977-84, Warner Lambert, 1976, Nycomed Amersham, 2000-01. Mem. Am. Fedn. for Clin. Rsch., Am. Soc. Nuclear Medicine, Am. Soc. Nuclear Cardiology (founding mem.), Med. Rsch. Soc., Am. Coll. Cardiology. Mem. Soc. Of Friends. Avocation: horse breeding and training. Office: Med Coll of Ohio PO Box 10008 Toledo OH 43699-0008 E-mail: lgoodenday@mco.edu.

GOODENOUGH, ELIZABETH NOBLE, literature educator, child advocate; b. Detroit, May 12, 1947; d. Daniel Webster Goodenough and Margaret Brooks Van Dusen; m. James Gillespie Leaf, Aug. 14, 1976; children: James Munro Leaf, William Goodnough Leaf. BA, Smith Coll., 1969; MAT, Harvard U., 1971, PhD, 1982. Tchr., admissions officer Phillips Acad., Andover, Mass., 1972—74; asst. sr. tutor Eliot House, Harvard U., Cambridge, Mass., 1975—82, Allston Burr sr. tutor, 1982—88; lectr. English Harvard U., Cambridge, Mass., 1982—88; asst. prof. English Claremont (Calif.) McKenna Coll., 1988—93; vis. prof. English U. Mich., Ann Arbor, 1993—95; lectr., adj. prof. English U. Mich. Residential Coll., Sch. Edn., Ann Arbor, 1995—. Bd. dirs. Alliance for Childhood, College Park, Md., 2001—; adv. bd. Skillman Ctr. for Children, Detroit, 2000—; asst. editor Mich. Quar. Rev., Ann Arbor, 2000—; established The Child and the City series, Wayne State U. Press, series editor. Editor: Secret Spaces of Childhood, 2003; co-editor: (jour.) Lion and the Unicorn, 2000, Infant Tongues: Voice of the Child in Literature, 1994. Exhbn. curator Garden Club of Mich., Grosse Pointe, 1999; hunger kitchen vol. St. Clare's Episc. Hunger Coalition, Ann Arbor, 1993—; bd. dirs. Mich. Youth Mus., Detroit, 1997—. Fellow: Soc. for Values in Higher Edn.; mem.: U. Mich. Com. for Children, Children's Literature Assn. Democrat. Episcopalian. Avocations: yoga, squash, tennis, hiking. Office: U Mich Residential Coll East Quad Ann Arbor MI 98109-1245 Home: 2260 Pinegrove Ct Ann Arbor MI 48103 E-mail: lizgoode@umich.edu.

GOODENOUGH, JOHN BANNISTER, engineering educator, research physicist; b. Jena, Germany, July 25, 1922; came to U.S., 1922; parents Am. citizens. s. Erwin Ramsdell and Helen Meriam (Lewis) G.; m. Irene Johnston Wiseman, June 16, 1951. AB, Yale U., 1943; MS, U. Chgo., 1951, PhD, 1952; DHC (hon.), U. Bordeaux, France, 1967; MA (hon.), Oxford (Eng.) U., 1976; DHC U. Santiago de Compostela (hon.), 2002. Rsch. engr. Westinghouse Rsch. Corp., 1951-52; rsch. scientist, group leader Lincoln Lab., MIT, 1952-76; prof., head inorganic chem. lab. U. Oxford, Eng., 1976-86; centennial prof. engring. U. Tex., Austin, 1986—. Cons. numerous firms in U.K. and U.S.; trustee, fellow Neuroscis. Rsch. Program, 1962-76; Centenary lectr. Royal Soc. Chemistry, 1976; vis. Raman prof. Indian Inst. Sci., 1983; hon. prof. Northwestern U., Changchun, China, 1996, Jilin U., Shenyang, China, 1996. Author: Magnetism and the Chemical Bond, 1963, Les Oxydes des métaux de transition, 1973; assoc. editor Materials Rsch. Bull., 1966—, Jour. Solid State Chemistry, 1968—, Structure and Bonding, 1977—, Solid State Ionics, 1980—, Superconductor Sci. and Tech., 1987, Jour. Materials Chem., 1991—, Chem. of Materials, 1989-92; mem. exec. editorial bd. Jour. Applied Electrochemistry, 1982-89, European Jour. Solid State and Inorganic chemistry, 1992—, contbr. over 500 articles to profl. jours., 76 revs., chpts. to books. Capt. USAAF, 1942-48. Recipient Solid State Chemistry prize Chem. Soc. U.K., 1980, Sr. Rsch. award Am.Soc. for Engring. Edn., 1990; professorial fellow St. Catherine's Coll., Oxford U., 1976; recipient medal for disting. achievement U. Pa., 1996, John Bardeen award Minerals, Metals and Materials Soc., 1997, Olin Palladium award Electrochem. Soc., 1999, Japan prize, 2001. Fellow AAAS, Royal Soc. Chemistry, Am. Phys. Soc. (profl.), Indian Acad. Scis. (fgn. assoc.), Nat. Acad. Engring., Academie des Scis. L'Institut de France, Materials Rsch. Soc. (hon.); mem. Am. Chem. Soc., Materials Rsch. Soc. (Von Hippel award 1989), Japanese Phys. Soc., Ashmolean Club (Oxford), Skull and Bones, Phi Beta Kappa, Sigma Xi. Episcopalian. Home: 4311 Greystone Dr Austin TX 78731-1240 Office: U Tex ETC 9 102 Austin TX 78712-1063

GOODENOUGH, URSULA WILTSHIRE, cell biologist, researcher, educator; b. Queens Village, N.Y., Mar. 16, 1943; d. Erwin Ramsdell Goodenough and Evelyn (Wiltshire) Pitcher; m. Robert Paul Levine, Aug. 10, 1969 (div. 1980); children— Jason, Mathea; m. John Edward Heuser, July 29, 1980; children— Jessica, Thomas, James. Student Radcliffe Coll., 1960-61; B.A., Barnard Coll., N.Y.C., 1963; M.A., Columbia U., 1965; Ph.D., Harvard U., 1969. Asst. prof. biology Harvard U., 1971-76, assoc. prof., 1976-78; assoc. prof. Washington U., St. Louis, 1978-81, prof., 1981— ; mem. study sect. NIH, Bethesda, Md., 1977-81. Author: Genetics, 1974, 3d edit., 1984; contbr. articles to profl. jours. Grantee NIH, NSF. Mem. Am. Soc. Cell Biology (assoc. editor jour. 1978-81, pres. 1994-95). Democrat. Office: Washington U Dept Biology Saint Louis MO 63130 E-mail: ursula@biology.wustl.edu.

GOODENOUGH, WARD HUNT, anthropologist, educator; b. Cambridge, Mass., May 30, 1919; s. Erwin Ramsdell and Helen Miriam (Lewis) G.; m. Ruth Gallagher, Feb. 8, 1941, (dec. March 6, 2001); children: Hester G. Goodenough Gelber, Deborah L. Goodenough Gordon, Oliver R., Garrick G. Grad., Groton (Mass.) Sch., 1937; AB, Cornell U., 1940; PhD, Yale U., 1949. Instr. anthropology U. Wis., 1948-49; mem. faculty U. Pa., Phila., 1949—, prof. anthropology, 1962-89, university prof., 1980-89, emeritus univ. prof., 1989—, chmn. dept. anthropology, 1976-82. Vis. prof. Cornell U., Ithaca, N.Y., 1961-62, vis. lectr., summer 1950; vis. lectr. Swarthmore Coll., spring 1955, Bryn Mawr Coll., fall 1955, U. Hawaii, summer 1959, 75-77; vis. prof. U. Wis., Milw., summer 1967, Yale U., New Haven, spring 1969, Colo. Coll., spring 1979, U. Hawaii, 1982-83; anthrop. studies in Truk, 1947, 64-65, Gilbert Islands, 1951, New Guinea, 1951, 54; Pacific Sci. bd. Nat. Acad. Scis.-NRC, 1962-66; standing com. anthropology and social scis. Pacific Sci. Assn., 1962-66; cons. Office Sci. and Tech., 1961-62. Author: Property, Kin and Community on Truk, 1951, Cooperation in Change, 1963, Explorations in Cultural Anthropology, 1964, Description and Comparison in Cultural Anthropology, 1970, Culture, Language and Society, 1971, Trukese-English Dictionary, 1980, 90, Prehistoric Settlement of the Pacific, 1996, Under Heaven's Brow, 2002. Bd. dirs. Human Rels. Area Files, Inc., 1964-86, chmn., 1971-81; bd. dirs. East Rock Inst., 1986-98, sec., 1995-98. With AUS, 1941-45. Fellow Center Advanced Study Behavioral Scis., 1957-58; Guggenheim fellow, 1979-80; Fulbright lectr. St. Patrick's Coll., Ireland, 1987. Mem. NAS, AAAS (v.p., chmn. sect. H 1971, bd. dirs. 1972-75), Am. Philos. Soc., Am. Acad. Arts and Scis., Royal Anthrop. Inst., Am. Anthrop. Assn. (editor 1966-70, Disting. Svc. award 1986), Am. Ethnol. Soc. (pres. 1962), Soc. Applied Anthropology (pres. 1963, Malinowski award 1997), Linguistics Soc. Am., Inst. on Religion in an Age of Sci. (pres. 1987-89), Polynesian Soc., Assn. Social Anthropology in Oceania, Phi Beta Kappa, Sigma Xi, Phi Kappa Phi. Office: Univ Penn Univ Museum Philadelphia PA 19104-6398 E-mail: whgooden@sas.upenn.edu.

GOODENOW, ROBERT W. labor union administrator; Exec. dir. Nat. Hockey League Player's Assn., Toronto, ON, Canada. Office: Nat Hockey League Players Assn 777 Bay St Ste 2400 Toronto ON Canada M5G 2C8

GOODFELLOW, ROBIN IRENE, surgeon; b. Xenia, Ohio, Apr. 14, 1945; d. Willis Douglas and Irene Linna (Kirkland) G. BA summa cum laude, Western Res. U., Cleve., 1967; MD cum laude, Harvard U., 1971. Diplomate Am. Bd. Surgery. Intern, resident Peter Bent Brigham Hosp., Boston, 1971-76; staff surgeon Boston U., 1976-80, asst. prof. surgery, 1977-80; pvt. practice medicine specializing in surgery Jonesboro, La., 1980-81; practice medicine specializing in surgery Albion, Mich., 1984-87, Coldwater, Mich., 1987—. Bd. Overseers Case Western Res. U., 1977-82. AAUW fellow, 1970. Fellow ACS; mem. AMA, Phi Beta Kappa. Republican. Methodist.

GOODFRIEND, HERBERT JAY, lawyer; b. N.Y.C., Sept. 9, 1926; s. Sidney and Blanche (Prager) G.; m. Barbara Gottlieb, Oct. 12, 1952; children: Sandra, Beth Ann. AB, NYU, 1947, LLB, 1950, LLM in Taxation, 1953. Bar: N.Y. 1950, U.S. Dist. Ct. (so. dist.) N.Y. 1951, U.S. Dist. Ct. (ea. dist.) N.Y. 1982, U.S. Ct. Appeals (2nd cir.) 1953, U.S. Tax Ct. 1954. Assoc. Otterbourg, Steindler Houston & Rosen, N.Y.C., 1950—83, ptnr., 1983—86; counsel Summit, Solomon & Feldesman, 1986-93, Philips, Nizer, 1993—. Counsel N.Y. Bd. Trade, N.Y.C., 1981-87, bd. dirs., 1982-88; spl. master Supreme Ct. New York County, N.Y.C., 1977-79; vice chmn., bd. dirs. Jones Apparel Group, Inc., 1990-98., sec., 1990-2001. Columnist N.Y. Law Jour., 1977-79 Treas., dir. N.Y.C. Alliance Against Sexual Abuse, 2001—. With U.S. Army, 1945-46. Fellow Am. Bar Found., Coll. Law Practice Mgmt.; mem. ABA (chmn. econs. law practice sect. 1984-85, ho. of dels. 1994-97), N.Y. State Bar Assn. (chmn. com. on law office econ. and mgmt. 1983-85), N.Y. County Lawyers Assn. (com. on arbitration 1974-87), NYU Club (v.p. exec. com. 1976-80), Adelphi U. Inst. for Paralegal Tng. (adv. bd. 1976-96), Am. Apparel Mfg. Assn. (fin. mgmt.

com. 1980-2001), Tau Delta Phi (nat. pres. 1952-57). Avocations: golf, computers. Home: 176 E 71st St New York NY 10021-5159 Office: Phillips Nizer 666 Fifth Ave New York NY 10103 E-mail: hgoodfriend@pillipsnizer.com.

GOODHARTZ, GERALD, law librarian; b. N.Y.C., Oct. 23, 1938; s. Jack and Anna (Sperling) G.; m. Carol Scialli, Aug. 18, 1969; children: Joanna, Allison. BSCE, CCNY, 1961; MLS, U. So. Calif., 1970. Night reference asst. Assn. Bar of City of N.Y., 1956-61; libr. asst. Cravath, Swaine & Moore, N.Y.C., 1961-65; head libr. Rosenman, Colin, Freund, Lewis & Cohen, N.Y.C., 1965-69, Keatinge & Sterling, L.A., 1969-70, Kaye, Scholer, Fierman, Hays & Handler, N.Y.C., 1970-98; mgr. info. svcs. Broad and Cassel, Orlando, 1998-99; dir. libr. svcs. Brown Raysman Millstein Felder & Steiner LLP, N.Y.C., 1999—. Libr. planning cons. Olympic Towers, N.Y.C., 1975; lectr. in field. Mem. ABA, ALA, Am. Assn. Law Librs. (cert.), Law Libr. Assn. Greater N.Y., Assn. Law Librs. of Upstate N.Y., Spl. Librs. Assn., Am. Soc. Info. Scientists, Am. Mgmt. Assn., Assn. Info. Mgrs., Nat. Micrographics Assn. Office: Brown Raysman Millstein Felder & Steiner LLP 900 3rd Ave New York NY 10022

GOODHEART, EUGENE, English language educator; b. Bklyn., June 26, 1931; s. Samuel and Miriam G.; m. Patricia Somer, Aug. 13, 1960 (div. July 1973); children: Eric, Jessica; m. Joan Bamberger, July 8, 1977. BA, Columbia U., 1953, PhD in English and Comparative Lit., 1961; MA in English, U. Va., 1954; postgrad. (Fulbright fellow), Sorbonne, U. Paris, 1956-57. From instr. to asst. prof. English Bard Coll., 1958-62; asst. prof. U. Chgo., 1962-66; assoc. prof. Mt. Holyoke Coll., 1966-67; from assoc. prof. to prof. MIT, 1967-74; prof., chmn. dept. English Boston U., 1974-83; Edytha Macy Gross prof. emeritus humanities Brandeis U., 1983—2001, emeritus, 2001—. Vis. prof. Wesleyan U. Summer Sch., 1963-64, 66, 69; Gauss seminarist Princeton U., 1972. Author: The Utopian Vision of D.H. Lawrence, 1963, The Cult of the Ego, 1968, Culture and the Radical Conscience, 1973, The Failure of Criticism, 1978, The Skeptic Disposition in Contemporary Criticism, 1984, Pieces of Resistance, 1987, Desire and Its Discontents, 1991, The Reign of Ideology, 1996, Does Literary Studies Have a Future, 1999, Confessions of a Secular Jew, 2001. Fellow Am. Coun. Learned Socs., 1965-66, Guggenheim Found., 1970-71, NEH, 1980-81, Nat. Humanities Ctr., 1987—; resident Rockefeller Found., Bellagio. Mem. MLA, PEN. Home: 25 Barnard Ave Watertown MA 02472-3412 Office: Brandeis Univ Dept English Waltham MA 02454 E-mail: goodheart@brandeis.edu.

GOODHUE, MARY BRIER, lawyer, former state senator; b. London, 1921; naturalized, 1942; d. Ernest and Marion H. (Hawks) Brier; m. Francis A. Goodhue, Jr., May 15, 1948 (dec. Sept. 1990); 1 child, Francis A. III. BA, Vassar Coll., 1942; LLB, U. Mich., 1944. Bar: N.Y. 1945. Assoc. Root, Clark, Buckner & Ballantine, N.Y.C., 1945-48; asst. counsel N.Y. State Crime Commn., N.Y.C., 1951-53, Moreland Commn., N.Y.C., 1953-54; mem. firm Goodhue, Arons & Neary and predecessors, Mt. Kisco, 1955—. Mem. N.Y. State Assembly from 93d Dist., 1975-78, N.Y. State Senate, 1979-92. N.Y. del. Nat. Women's Conf., Houston, 1977. Mem. ABA, West Bar Assn., No. Westchester Bar Assn. Office: 126 Barker St Mount Kisco NY 10549-1502 also: Rock Gate Farm Rd Mount Kisco NY 10549

GOODHUE, PETER AMES, obstetrician and gynecologist, educator; b. Ft. Fairfield, Maine, Feb. 26, 1931; s. Lawrence and Zylpha (Ames) G.; m. Edith Ann Helfenstein, June 21, 1958; children: Lisa Grace, Scott Ames. BA, Amherst Coll., 1954; MD, U. Vt., 1958. Diplomate Am. Bd. Ob-Gyn. Intern Bellevue Hosp., N.Y.C., 1958-59; resident Yale-New Haven Med. Ctr., 1959-62; practice medicine specializing in ob-gyn. Stamford, Conn., 1964—. Assoc. clin. prof. ob-gyn. N.Y. Med. Coll., 1984—98; asst. clin. prof. ob-gyn. Columbia Presbyn. Hosp., 1999—. Contbr. articles to profl. jours. Served to capt. USAF, 1962-64. Recipient Carbee prize U. Vt., 1958. Fellow ACOG (chmn. Conn. sect. 1976, pres. Conn. sect. 1973-76), ACS, Am. Fertility Soc., Am. Soc. for Colposcopy and Cervical Pathology, Am. Assn. Gynecologic Laproscopists; mem. Conn. Med. Soc., Conn. Soc. Am. Bd. Obstetricians and Gynecologists (pres. 1973-76), Fairfield County Med. Soc., Fairfield County Gynecol. and Obstet. Soc., Stamford Med. Soc. (pres. 1989-90). Republican. Episcopalian. Office: Stamford Gynecology PC 70 Mill River St Stamford CT 06902-3725

GOODHUE, WILLIAM WALTER, JR., forensic pathologist, military officer, educator; b. St. Louis, Feb. 5, 1945; s. William W. and Rose Marie (Vahousek) Goodhue. BS cum laude, Georgetown U., 1966; MD, Cornell U., 1970. Diplomate Am. Bd. Pathology. Intern anatomic pathology N.Y. Hosp.-Cornell Med Ctr., N.Y.C., 1970-71, resident anatomic pathology, 1971-74; chief resident pediatric pathology Columbia-Presbyn. Med. Ctr., N.Y.C., 1974-75; resident clinical pathology Tripler Army Med. Ctr., Honolulu, 1976-78, chief pathology grad. med. edn., dir. electron microscopy, 1994-97, asst. chief dept. pathology and area lab. svcs., 1997-2001; first dep. med. examiner, de facto mayoral cabinet mem. City and County of Honolulu, 2001—. Chief dept. pathology U.S. Army Hosp., Ft. Campbell, Ky., 1978—80; chief dept. pathology, med. dir. Sch. Med. Tech., dir. pathology residency tng. Gorgas Army Hosp.; C.Z. and assoc. prof. med. tech. Panama Canal Coll., 1980—82; resident officer U.S. Army Command and Gen. Staff Coll., Ft. Leavenworth, Kans., 1982—83; divsn. surgeon 2d Inf. Divsn., 1983—84; dep. comdr. clin. svcs., chief dept. primary care and cmty. medicine, staff pathologist, acting comdr. Bayne-Jones Army Hosp., Ft. Polk, La., 1984—85; chief dept. pathology and are lab. svcs., dir. pathology residency tng. Dwight David Eisenhower Army Med. Ctr., Ft. Gordon, Ga., 1985—94; clin. assoc. prof. pathology Med. Coll. Ga., Augusta, 1986—94, Sch. Medicine U. Hawaii, Honolulu, 1997—; cons. in pathology Eisenhower Health Svc. Region to Comdg. Gen.; cons. ARC, 1978—80; rep. Alt. Army Med. Dept. Coll. Am. Pathologists Ho. of Dels., Am. Soc. Clin. Pathologist Adv. Coun., 1990—2001; mem. profl. adv. bd. Med. Lab. Observer, 1993—95; Army councillor-at-large Armed Forces Med. Lab. Scientists, 1993—2001; v.p. Land Bd. R.W. Meyer, Ltd. Assoc. editor: Hawaii Med. Jour., 2003—; contbr. articles to profl. jours. Col. M.C. U.S. Army, 1975—2001. Decorated Order Mil. Med. Merit; recipient Surgeon Gen.'s "A" designator med. splty. excellence, 1997; fellow Rsch., USPHS, 1971—74. Fellow: Coll. Am. Pathologists, Am. Soc. Investigative Pathology, Nat. Assn. Med. Examiners, Am. Soc. Clin. Pathologists (lab. accreditation insp. & accreditation program 1988—), Am. Acad. Forensic Scis.; mem.: AMA (Physicians Recognition award 1976, 1978, 1980, 1982, 1986, 1989, 1992, 1995, 1998, 2001), U.S.-Can. Acad. Pathology, Clin. Lab. Mgrs. Assn. (bd. dir. 1989—92), Alliance Française, Assn. U.S. Army, Soc. Armed Forces Med. Lab. Scientists, NY Acad. Sci., Hawaii Soc. Pathologists, Soc. Ultrastructural Pathology, Am. Assn. Blood Banks, Assn. Mil. Surgeons U.S., Med. Assn. Isthmian C.A. (v.p. 1980—81), Soc. Pediat. Pathology, Outrigger Canoe Club, Cornell Club NY. Republican. Roman Catholic. Home: 45-995 Wailele Rd # 52 Kaneohe HI 96744-3040 Office: Dept Medical Examiner 835 Iwilei Rd Honolulu HI 96817 E-mail: wwgjrmd@aol.com., wgoodhue@co.honolulu.hi.us.

GOODIN, JULIA C. forensic pathologist, state official, educator; b. Columbia, Ky., Mar. 10, 1957; d. Vitus Jack and Geneva Goodin. BS, Western Ky. U., 1979; MD, U. Ky., 1983. Diplomate Am. Bd. Clin. and Anatomic Pathology, Am. Bd. Forensic Pathology. Intern Vanderbilt U. Med. Ctr., Nashville, 1983, resident in anatomic and clin. pathology, 1984-87, fellow in forensic pathology Med. Examiner's Office, Balt., 1987-88; asst. med. examiner Office of Chief Med. Examiner, Balt., 1988-90; dep. chief med. examiner State of Tenn., 1990-94; asst. med. examiner Nashville, 1990-93; chief med. examiner, 1993-94; asst. med. investigator State of N.Mex., Albuquerque, 1994-96; asst. prof. U. N.Mex., Albuquerque, 1994-96; clin. assoc. prof. U. of South Ala. Sch. Medicine, 1996-99; state med. examiner Ala. Dept. Forensic Scis., Mobile, 1996-99; chief state med. examiner State of Iowa, Des Moines, 1999—. Clin. prof. U. Md. Med. Sch., Balt., 1988-90, Vanderbilt U. Med. Ctr., 1990-94. Capt. USNR, 1985—. Mem. Am. Acad. Forensic Sci., Assn. Mil. Surgeons of U.S., AMA. Avocations: long-distance running, weight lifting, photography, studying french. Home: 100 Market St Unit 414 Des Moines IA 50309-4765 Office: 321 E 12th St Des Moines IA 50319-0075

GOODINE, ISAAC THOMAS, development executive, educator; b. Hazeldean, N.B., Can., Apr. 11, 1932; s. Lewis Ambrose and Beatrice Ann (Babineau) G.; m. Sandra Jean Campbell, May 3, 1958 (div. 1981); children: Darlene Lynn, Sharon Ann, Catherine Elizabeth; m. Gloria Ann Whiting, Aug. 3, 1981; 1 child, Claudia Ann. BS, Mt. Allison U., Sackville, N.B., 1956, Cert. in Engring., 1957, BE, 1960. Instr. N.B. Inst. Tech., Moncton, 1961-65, vice prin., 1965-66, prin., 1966-70, Zambia Inst. Tech., Kitwe, 1970-72; dep. dir. Dept. Tech. Edn. and Vocat. Tng., Lusaka, Zambia, 1972-73; dir., 1973-74; policy analyst N.B. Community Coll., Fredericton, 1974-75; dir. Kenya Tech. Tch's. Coll., Nairobi, 1975-78; sr. tech. educator The World Bank, Washington, 1978-88; sr. devel. officer Can. Internat. Devel. Agy., 1988-91; dir. tech. edn. Colombo Plan Staff Coll., Manila, 1991-92; first sec. Can. High Commn., Barbados, 1992-94; mng. dir. Knowledge Devel. Inst., Barbados, 1994—96. Sec. Nat. Com. on Physics for Insts. Tech. in Can., 1955-58, Coordinating Com. on Tech. Tchr. Edn. for Ea. Africa, Nairobi, 1975-78; co-chmn. Working Party on Coun. for Higher Edn. in Zambia, Lusaka, 1973-74; bd. dirs. Greater Moncton Community Chest, 1968-69, Moncton Family YMCA, 1966-69, Colombo Plan Staff Coll. for Technician Edn., 1988-90. Mem. Internat. Vocat. Edn. and Tng. Assn., Am. Vocat. Assn., Can. Vocat. Assn., Royal Can. Armoured Corps Assn. Mem. United Ch. Lodge: Rotary (Moncton, Kitwe, Nairobi clubs). Address: 902, 27 Henderosn Ave Ottawa ON Canada K1N 7P3 E-mail: itgoodine@rogers.com.

GOODING, CHARLES ARTHUR, radiologist, physician, educator; b. Cleve., Feb. 28, 1936; s. Joseph J. and Florence G. (Pitt) G.; m. Gretchen Wagner, June 19, 1961; children: Gunnar, Justin, Britta. BA, Western Res. U., 1957; MD, Ohio State U., 1961. Intern Ohio State U. Hosp., 1961-62; resident in radiology Peter Bent Brigham Hosp., Children's Hosp. Med. Center, both Boston, 1963-65; rsch. fellow radiology Harvard Med. Sch., Boston, 1962, tchg. fellow, 1965-66; Harvard Med. Sch. fellow Hosp. for Sick Children, London, Karolinska Hosp., Stockholm, 1966; faculty U. Calif. Med. Center, San Francisco, 1967—, prof. radiology and pediatrics, 1976—, exec. vice-chmn. dept. radiology, 1974—2001. Pres. Radiology Rsch. and Edn. Found., 1973-96, Radiology Outreach Found., 1988-2002, pres. emeritus 2002—; hon. mem. faculty Francesco Maroquin U. Sch. Medicine, Guatemala City. Contbr. chpts. to books.; Editor: Pediatric Radiology, 1973—96; editor: Diagnostic Radiology, 1972-92; contbr. articles to profl. jours. Capt. M.C. USAR, 1967-68. Recipient Outstanding Alumni award Brigham Women's Hosp. Harvard Med. Sch., 1994, Disting. Alumnus award Ohio State U., 1986, Case Western Res. U., 1999, Beclere medal Internat. Soc. Radiology, 1998; named to Disting. Alumni Hall of Fame Cleve. Heights H.S., 1999, Top Pediat. Radiologist San Francisco mag., 2001. Fellow Am. Coll. Radiology, Coll. Radiologists (hon.), Royal Coll. Radiologists London (hon.), Armenian Radiol. Soc. (hon.); mem. Am. Roentgen Ray Soc., Assn. Univ. Radiologists, European Soc. Pediat. Radiologists (hon.), Pacific Coast Pediat. Radiologists Assn., Radiol. Soc. N.Am., Polish Radiology Soc. (hon.), Hungarian Radiology Soc. (hon.), San Francisco Med. Soc., Soc. Pediat. Radiology (v.p. 1994, pres. 1997 pres. SPR rsch. and edn. found. 1993-96, chmn., bd. dirs. 1998), Rocky Mountain Radiol. Soc. (hon.), Australian Soc. for Pediatric Imaging (hon.), Chinese Radiol. Soc. (hon.), Swiss Radiol. Soc. (hon.), Malaysian Radiol. Soc. (hon.), Vietnamese Radiol. Soc. (hon.), (French Soc. of Radiology (hon.), Indian Radiol. and Imaging Soc. (hon.), Radiol. Soc. of Pakistan (hon.), Indonesian Radiol. Soc. (hon.), Mongolian Nat. Radiol. Assn. (hon.), Nepal Radiol. Soc. (hon.), Armenian Med. Diagnostic Assn. (hon.), Brazilian Coll. Radiology (hon.), Cuban Radiol. Soc. (hon.), Indonesian Pediatric Radiol. Soc. (hon.). Office: U Calif Med Ctr Dept Radiology San Francisco CA 94143-0628 E-mail: charles.gooding@radiology.ucsf.edu.

GOODING, CHARLES THOMAS, psychology educator, retired college provost; b. Tampa, Fla., Nov. 18, 1931; s. Charles T. and Gladys (Bingman) G.; m. Shirley Ann Puckett, June 7, 1953, children: Steven Thomas, Carol Ann, David Lee, Mark Charles. BA, U. Fla., 1954, M.Ed., 1962, Ed.D., 1964; postgrad., U. Tampa, 1956-58. Tchr. Meml. Sch., Tampa, 1956-58; asst. prin., then prin. St. Mary's Sch., Tampa, 1958-62; grad. fellow U. Fla., Gainesville, 1962-63, instr., 1963-64; assoc. prof., then prof. SUNY, Oswego, 1964-79, prof. psychology, 1980-98, assoc. dean grad. studies, 1982-89, dean grad. studies and rsch., 1989-95, provost, v.p. for acad. affairs, 1995-98, emeritus, 1998—. Vis. prof. U. Liverpool, Eng., 1979-80; mem. SUNY Chancellor's Task Force on Tchr. Edn., 1984; grad. fellow U. Fla., Gainesville, 1962-63 Author: Learning Theories in Educational Practice, 1971; contbg. author: Florida Studies in the Helping Professions, 1969, Questioning and Discussion: A Multidisciplinary Study, 1988, Research Matters to the Science Teacher, 1992; contbr. articles to profl. jours. Bd. dirs. Oswego County unit Am. Cancer Soc., N.Y., 1972-74, 82-84; mem. commn. on ordination Episcopal Diocese Central N.Y., 1980-95; bd. trustees U. of South, 2002—; bd. dirs. Lancaster Career Devel. Ctr., 1984-95, Oswego Coll. Found., 1996—. Served to 1st lt. USAR, 1954-56. SUNY Rsch. Found. grantee, 1966, 69, 70; N.Y. State Dept. Edn. grantee, 1971-72, 88-94; NSF grantee, 1980-81, 85-88, 90-95. Mem. APA, Ea. Ednl. Rsch. Assn. (v.p. 1979-81, treas., dir. 1983-85, pres.-elect 1987-88, pres. 1989-91, editl. bd. 1991-2000), Am. Ednl. Rsch. Assn. (chair ednl. enterprises SIG, 1994-96). Avocations: antique and classic automobiles, jaguar sports cars specialist. Home: 603 Wild Pine Way Venice FL 34292-4618

GOODING, CUBA, JR., actor; b. Bronx, N.Y., Jan. 2, 1968; s. Cuba, Sr. and Shirley Gooding; m. Sara Gooding, 1994; 2 children. Films include: Coming to America, 1988, Sing, 1989, Boyz N the Hood, 1991, Gladiator, 1992, A Few Good Men, 1992, Hitz, 1992, Judgement Night, 1993, Lightning Jack, 1994, Losing Isaiah, 1995, Outbreak, 1995, Jerry Maguire, 1996 (Golden Globe nomination, Academy award for Best Supporting Actor, 1997), The Audition, 1996, As Good As It Gets, 1997, What Dreams May Come, 1998, A Murder of Crows, 1999, Instinct, 1999, Menof Honor, 2000 (NAACP Image award nominee), Pearl Harbor, 2001, Rat Race, 2001, In the Shadows, 2001, Snow Dogs, 2002, Boat Trip, 2002, Psychic, 2003, The Fighting Temptations, 2003; TV movies include: Kill or Be Killed, 1990, Murder with Motive: The Edmund Perry Story, 1992, Daybreak, 1993, Tuskegee Airmen, 1995 (NAACP Image award nominee); (TV appearances) MacGyver, Hill Street Blues, The Untouchables. Office: Rogers & Cowan 1888 Century Park E Ste 500 Los Angeles CA 90067-1709 also: Endeavor Talent Agy 9701 Wilshire Blvd Fl 10 Beverly Hills CA 90210*

GOODING, JUDSON, writer; b. Rochester, Minn., Oct. 12, 1926; s. Arthur Faitoute and Frances (Judson) G.; m. Françoise Ridoux, June 21, 1952; children: Amélie, Timothy. Grad. with honors, Yale U., 1948; diplome d'Études Françaises, U. Paris, 1950. Staff writer Dept. Army, Hdqrs. EUCOM, Germany, 1950-52; script writer Affiliated Film Producers, N.Y.C., 1952-53; news writer WCCO-CBS, Mpls., 1953; reporter Mpls. Tribune, 1953-57, Life mag., N.Y.C., 1957-60, fgn. corr. Paris, 1960-62, Time mag., Paris, 1962-65; chief of bur. Time-Life News Service, San Francisco, 1966-68; edn. editor Time mag., N.Y.C., 1968-69; assoc. editor Fortune mag., 1969-73; v.p. Urban Research Corp.; also editor Trend Report, Chgo., 1973-75; mng. partner Trend Analysis Assocs., 1975—; exec. editor Next Mag., N.Y.C., 1979-81, contbg. editor, 1981-82; counselor for pub. affairs U.S. Permanent Del. to UNESCO, 1982-84. Vis. lectr. in journalism U. Paris, Ecole Nationale d'Administration, also Togo, Kenya, Zaire, Senegal and Nigeria; writing cons. UN, Ford Found., Am. Assembly, also corps.; vis. lectr. in journalism, Barbados, Grenada, Dominica, Haiti and Martinique Author: The Job Revolution, 1972; contbr. to: American Dreams, The Environment, The Hippies, The Survival Equation, The Failure of Success; Contbr. articles to popular mags. and profl. jours. Bd. patrons Wilson Ctr., Faribault, Minn.; mem. program com. Internat. Found. for Cultural Cooperation, Courchevel, France; trustee Friends of John Jay Homestead, Walpole Hist. Soc., Walpole Pub. Libr. Served with USNR, 1944-46. Recipient 1st place award U. Mo. Sch. Journalism Penney-Mo., 1980, hon. certificate Program Mgmt. Devel. Harvard U. Grad. Sch., Disting. Alumnus award Middlesex Sch., 1994. Mem. Inst. Current World Affairs (elected), Common Cause, World Future Soc., Nat. Trust Hist. Preservation, Am. Soc. Journalists and Authors, Mensa. Clubs: Elizabethan (New Haven); Century Assn. (N.Y.C.), Yale (N.Y.C.); Bedford Bicycle Polo (founder, co-capt.); Polo de Paris, The Travellers (Paris). Office: Old North Main St PO Box 745 Walpole NH 03608-0745

GOODKIN, DEBORAH GAY, mutual funds administrator; b. Oceanside, N.Y., Dec. 8, 1951; d. Harold and Rose (Mostkoff) G.; m. Glenn Richard; children: Samuel Goodkin Richard, Sarah Goodkin Richard. BA, Syracuse U., 1972; M in Urban Planning, NYU, 1977. Planner Nassau-Suffolk Planning, Hauppauge, N.Y., 1972; asst. to treas. Nat. Assn. Savs. Banks, N.Y.C., 1973; planning aide Dept. City Planning, N.Y.C., 1973-79; planner, real property mgr. N.Y.C. Bd. Edn., 1979-81; dir. Capital Budget Bur., 1981-85; supervising mgmt. engr. Port Authority N.Y. & N.J., 1985-90, mgr. fin. sys., 1989-96; mutual funds ops. mgr. Tchrs. Ins. Annuity Assn., N.Y.C., 1997-99, tuition savs. program ops. mgr., 1999—2002; v.p. Citigroup Coll. Savs., 2002—. Cons. C Corp., L.A., 1983—. Author: (zoning law) Bay Ridge Zoning Dist., 1978; artist Show of Selected Works, Sireuil, France, 1983. Security cons. Dem. Nat. Com., N.Y.C., 1980; founder, pres. Allendale Opportunity and Enrichment Program. Recipient CEO Award of Excellence, 1987, 92. Mem. Women in Govt. (guest lectr. 1983), Syracuse U. Alumni Assn., NYU Alumni Assn. Office: Citigroup 300 1st Stamford Pl Stamford CT 06902

GOODKIN, MICHAEL JON, publishing company executive; b. N.Y.C., June 10, 1941; s. Harold and Rose (Mostkoff) G.; m. Helen Graham Fairbank, Oct. 1, 1971; children: Graham Laird, Nathalie Fairbank. BA, Harvard U., 1963; postgrad., U. Chgo., 1964. Trainee Random House, N.Y.C., 1964-65; asst. dir. Simulmatics, N.Y.C., 1966-67; account exec. World Book Ency., Inc., Chgo., 1967-70, rsch. dir., 1970-73, v.p. mktg., 1973-76, v.p., gen. mgr. mail order div., 1976-78, pres., chief operating officer, 1978-86, chmn., chief exec. officer, pres., dir., 1983; exec. v.p. World Book Inc., 1978-84, pres., 1984-86, sr. v.p., 1979-80; exec. v.p., corp. dir. mktg., dir. World Book Internat. Inc., 1983-84; dep. dir. World Book Pty. Ltd., Australia, 1983-86; pres. World Book Life Ins. Co., 1983; prin. Chgo. City Capital Group, 1987-91; chmn. Med. Holdings, Inc., Chgo., 1987-91; sr. v.p. mktg. internat. P.F. Collier, N.Y.C., 1992—94, pres., 1994—96; pres.-dir. KT holdings, 1996—99; mng. mem. Arlington Haven Partners LLC, 2000—. Bd. dirs. Chgo. Area Project; pres. aux. bd. Art Inst. Chgo., 1975-77, trustee, 1974-99; trustee Modern Poetry Assn., Latin Sch. Chgo., 1983-92, chmn. ednl. policy com., pres., 1990-92, mem. long range com., chmn. mktg. com., 1979-99; trustee DMA Edn. Found., 1983-94, mem. exec. com., 1988-94; mem. vis. com. visual arts U. Chgo., 1990-2002. With Army N.G., 1963-69. Mem. Direct Mktg. Assn. (internat. coun. steering com. 1983), Direct Selling Assn. (internat. com. 1982-86), Racquet Club, Harvard Club (N.Y.C.), Harvard Club (Boston).

GOODKIND, CONRAD GEORGE, lawyer; b. Arlington, Va., Aug. 8, 1944; s. Bernard Arthur and Sylvia (Lieber) G.; m. Sandra Timme, Aug. 27, 1966; children: Carley M., Adam B., Erica L., Anne G. BS, U. Wis., 1966, JD, 1969. Bar: Wis. 1969, U.S. Dist. Ct. (ea. and we. dists.) Wis. 1969. Assoc. Kivett & Kasdorf, Milw., 1969-71; counsel Citizens' Study Com. on Jud. Orgn., Madison, Wis., 1971-73; dep. commr. securities State of Wis., Madison, 1973-79; assoc. Quarles & Brady, Milw., 1979-81, ptnr., 1981—, mem. exec. com., 1983—. Adj. prof. securities law U. Wis. Law Sch., Madison, 1975-79, Marquette U. Law Sch., Milw., 1981-83; mem. Gov.'s Bus. Cts. Task Force, 1994-98, state regulation com. Nat. Assn. Securities Dealers, Inc., Washington, 1986-92; bd. dirs. Able Distbg. Corp., 1995-; bd. dirs., sec. Cade Industries, Inc., 1989-99; sec. Brady Corp., 1999—. Bd. dirs. Milw. Repertory Theatre, 1995-2001, exec. com. mem., 1997-2001. Mem. ABA (vice chmn. state regulation securities com. 1986-89, chmn. 1989-92, vice chmn. bus. law sect. com. on insts. and seminars 2001—), Wis. Bar Assn. (chmn. securities com., 1981-95, bd. dirs. sect. bus. law 1991-2001, vice chair sect. bus. law 1996-98, chair 1998-2000). Office: Quarles & Brady LLP 411 E Wisconsin Ave Ste 2550 Milwaukee WI 53202-4497 E-mail: cgg@quarles.com.

GOODLAD, JOHN INKSTER, education educator, writer; b. North Vancouver, B.C., Can., 1920; s. William James and Mary Goodlad; m. Evalene M. Pearson, Aug. 23, 1945; children: Stephen John, Mary Paula. Teaching certificate, Vancouver Normal Sch., 1939; BA, U. B.C., 1945, MA, 1946; PhD, U. Chgo., 1949; DPS (hon.), Brigham Young U., 1995; LHD (hon.), Nat. Coll. Edn., 1967, U. Louisville, 1968, So. Ill. U., 1982, Bank Street Coll. Edn., 1984, Niagara U., 1989, SUNY Coll. Brockport, 1991, Miami U., 1991, Linfield Coll., 1993, W.Va. U., 1998; LLD (hon.), Kent State U., 1974, Pepperdine U., 1976, Simon Fraser U., 1983, U. Man., 1992; DEd (hon.), Eastern Mich. U., 1982, U. Victoria, 1998; LittD (hon.), Montclair State U., 1992; PedD (hon.), Doane Coll., 1995; LHD (hon.), U. Nebr., Lincoln, 1999, U. So. Maine, 2001. Tchr. Surrey Schs., B.C., 1939-41, prin., 1941-42; dir. edn. Provincial Sch. For Boys, B.C., 1942-46; cons. curriculum Atlanta Area Tchr. Edn. Service, 1947 49; assoc. prof. Emory U., 1949-50; prof., dir. div. tchr. edn. Agnes Scott Coll. and Emory U., 1950-56; prof., dir. U. Chgo. Center Tchr. Edn., 1956-60; prof., dir. Univ. Elem. Sch. UCLA, 1960-85, dean Grad. Sch. Edn., 1967-83; prof. U. Wash., Seattle, 1985-91; prof. emeritus, 1991—; dir. Ctr. for Ednl. Renewal U. Wash., Seattle, 1986-2000; pres. Inst. for Ednl. Inquiry, Seattle, 1992—. Chmn. Coun. on Coop. Tchr. Edn., Am. Coun. Edn., 1959-62; dir. rsch. Inst. for Devel. of Ednl. Activities, 1966-82; mem. governing bd. UNESCO Inst. for Edn., 1971-79. Author: (with others) The Elementary School, 1956, Educational Leadership and the Elementary School Principal, 1956, (with Robert H. Anderson) The Nongraded Elementary School, 1959, rev. edit., 1963, reprinted, 1987, (with others) Computers and Information Systems in Education, 1966, Looking Behind the Classroom Door, 1970, rev. edit., 1974, Toward a Mankind School, 1974, The Conventional and the Alternative in Education, 1975, Curriculum Inquiry: The Study of Curriculum Practice, 1979, Planning and Organizing for Teaching, 1963, School Curriculum Reform, 1964, The Changing School Curriculum, 1966, School, Curriculum and the Individual, 1966, The Dynamics of Educational Change, 1975, Facing the Future, 1976, What Schools Are For, 1979, A Place Called School, 1983, Teachers for Our Nation's Schools, 1990, Educational Renewal: Better Teachers, Better Schools, 1994, In Praise of Education, 1997; author, editor: The Changing American School, 1966, (with Harold S. Shane) The Elementary School in the United States, 1973, (with M. Frances Klein and Jerrold M. Novotney) Early Schooling in the United States, 1973, (with Norma Feshback and Alvima Lombard) Early Schooling in England and Israel, 1973, (with Gary Fenstermacher) Individual Differences and the Common Curriculum, 1983, The Ecology of School Renewal, 1987, (with Kenneth A. Sirotnik) School-University Partnerships in Action, 1988, (with Pamela Keating) Access to Knowledge, 1990, (with others) The Moral Dimensions of Teaching, 1990, Places Where Teachers Are Taught, 1990, (with Thomas C. Lovitt) Integrating General and Special Education, 1992, (with Timothy J. McMannon) The Public Purpose of Education and Schooling, 1997, (with Roger Soder and Timothy J. McMannon) Developing Democratic Character in the Young, 2001; mem. bd. editors Sch. Rev, 1956-58, Jour. Tchr. Edn, 1958-60; contbg. editor Progressive Edn, 1955-58; mem. editorial adv. bd. Child's World, 1952-80; chmn. editorial adv. bd. New Standard Ency, 1953—; chmn. ednl. adv. bd. Ency. Brit. Ednl. Corp, 1966-69; contbr. chpts. to books, articles to profl. jours. Recipient Disting. Svc. medal Tchrs. Coll., Columbia U., 1983, Outstanding Book award Am. Ednl. Rsch. Assn., 1985, Disting. Contbns. to Ednl. Rsch. award 1993; named Faculty Rsch. Lectr. U. Wash., 1987-88, faculty of High Distinction, UCLA, 1987; Edward C. Pomeroy award, Amer. Assn. of Coll. for Teacher Edn., 1995, Disting. Svc. award Coun. Chief State Sch. Officials, 1997, Harold W. McGraw, Jr. Prize in Edn., 1999, Edn. Commn. State James Bryant Conant award, 2000, Brock Internat. prize in edn., 2002, N.Y. Acad. of Edn. medal, 2003. Fellow Internat. Inst. Arts and Letters; mem. Nat. Acad. Edn. (charter; sec.-treas.), Am. Ednl. Rsch. Assn. (past pres., award for Disting. Contbns. to Ednl. Rsch. 1993), Nat. Soc. Coll. Tchrs. Edn. (past pres.), Nat. Soc. for Study of Edn. (dir.), Am. Assn. Colls. for Tchr. Edn. (pres. 1989-90). Office: U Wash Coll Edn PO Box 353600 Seattle WA 98195-3600

GOODLATTE, ROBERT WILLIAM (BOB GOODLATTE), congressman, lawyer; b. Holyoke, Mass., Sept. 22, 1952; m. Maryellen Flaherty; children: Jennifer, Robert. BA, Bates Coll., 1974; JD, Washington & Lee U., 1977. Bar: Mass. 1977, Va. 1978, U.S. Ct. Appeals (4th cir.) 1981. Dist. mgr. Congressman M. Caldwell Butler U.S. Ho. of Reps., Washington, 1977-79; pvt. practice Roanoke, Va., 1979-81; ptnr. Bird, Kinder & Huffman, Roanoke, 1981-93; mem. 103d-108th Congresses from 6th Va. dist., Washington, 1993—, dep. majority whip, chmn. agriculture com., jud. com., ho. select com. on homeland security, co-chair of Congl. Internet Caucus, Rep. policy com., chmn. Ho. Rep. high tech working group, ho. Rep. cybersecurity task force, vice chmn. the cts., the Internet. and intellectual property subcom. Mem. bldg. better bds. adv. com. United Way of Roanoke Valley, Roanoke, 1988-92; chmn. Roanoke City Rep. Com., 1980-83, 6th Cong. Dist. Rep. Com., Va., 1983-88. Mem. Civitan (pres. Roanoke chpt. 1989-90). Republican. Avocations: tennis, travel, swimming, hiking. Office: US Ho of Reps 2240 Rayburn Hob Washington DC 20515-4606 E-mail: talk2bob@mail.house.gov.*

GOODLAW, EDWARD, retired optometrist; b. Denver, Colo., Jan. 4, 1913; AB in Optometry summa cum laude, U. Calif., 1934; DOS, L.A. Coll. Optometry, 1950. Lic. optometrist; diplomate in 3 specialties. With Mt. Sinai Hosp. (now Cedar-Sinai Hosp.), 1936—, chief of staff; pvt. practice optometry

L.A., 1934—96; ret., 1996. Contbr. over 50 articles to profl. jours.; patentee in field. Named Optometrist of Yr. Optometry Alumni Assn., 1979. Mem. Am. Acad. Optometry (Feinbloom award 1983, Vision Care award 1996), L.A. County Optometric Soc. (pres. 1950, Life Membership award 1997), Calif. State Optometric Soc., Am. Optometric Assn. (Disting. Svc. award 1983), Am. Acad. Of Optometry, Alumni Assn. of Sch. of Optometry at Berkeley (life), Alumni Assn. of So. Calif. Sch. of Optometry at Fullerton. Avocations: metal and woodworking, photography, walking, hiking, traveling. Home: 1136 S Plymouth Blvd Los Angeles CA 90019-6825

GOODLING, KIMBERLY HALL, language educator, consultant; b. Lancaster, Pa., Mar. 13, 1973; d. Denton F and Alice Steinruck Hall; MA, U. of Md., 1996—99; BA magna cum laude, Millersville U., 1992—95. Adj. instr. Harrisburg Area C.C., Lancaster, Pa., 1999—. Adv. Am. Cancer Soc., Lancaster, Pa., 2002. Mem.: Linguistic Soc. of Am., Modern Lang. Assn., Phi Kappa Phi, Phi Sigma Iota. Avocations: travel, reading, tennis, ice hockey. Home: 3016 Miller Rd Washington Boro PA 17582 Office: Harrisburg Area Cmty Coll 1641 Old Philadelphia Pike Lancaster PA 17602 Personal E-mail: ksgoodli@hacc.edu.

GOODLING, LAURI BOHANAN, documentation specialist; b. Jacksonville, Fla., Sept. 25, 1974; d. Marcus Wayne Bohanan and Judy Darlene (Higgins) Pike; m. Michael Levis Goodling, July 24, 1999. BA in English, Fla. State U., 1996; MA in Profl. Writing, Kennesaw State U., 1999. Sales assoc. Pitney Bowes, Atlanta, 1997—99; tchr. U. North Fla., Jacksonville, 1999—2000; editor Kidz Dayz Mag., Jacksonville, Fla., 2000; tech. writer SkillLearning.com, Atlanta, 2000; sr. documentation specialist, program mgr., content leader CD Group, Inc., Norcross, Ga., 2000—. Content cons. CD Group, Inc., Norcross, Ga. Author, editor (mag.) Kidz Dayz, 2000, (web site) KidzDayz.com, 2000; author: (mag.) Jacksonville Woman, 2000, (web site) SkillLearning.com, 2000. Vol. G.W. Bush for Pres., Atlanta, 2000. Mem.: Soc. for Tech. Communicators. Republican. Roman Catholic. Avocations: travel, reading, volunteering, writing. Home: 1258 Niles Ave Atlanta GA 30318 Office: CD Group Inc 5550 Triangle Pky Ste 200 Norcross GA 30092

GOODLING, WILLIAM F. former congressman; b. Loganville, Pa., Dec. 5, 1927; m. Hilda Wright; children: Todd, Jennifer. BS, U. Md.; MS, Western Md. Coll.; postgrad., Pa. State U. Various tchg. positions including prin. West York Area H.S.; supt. Spring Grove Area Schs.; supr. student tchrs. Pa. State U.; mem. 94th-106th Congresses from 19th Pa. Dist., 1975-2001; mem., bd. of dirs. Nat. Job Corps. Assoc. Chmn. com. on edn. and the workforce, mem. internat. rels. com. With Armed Forces, 1946-48. Mem. Lions. Republican. Methodist. Office: Nat Job Corps Assoc 1199 N Fairfax St Ste 702 Alexandria VA 22314

GOODMAN, ALFRED NELSON, lawyer; b. Jan. 21, 1945; s. Bernard R. and Mildred (Schlanger) Goodman. BS in Mech. and Aerospace Scis., U. Rochester, 1966; JD, Georgetown U., 1969. Bar: N.Y. 1970, D.C. 1971, U.S. Supreme Ct. 1974. Patent examiner U.S. Patent Office, Washington, 1969—71; assoc. Roylance, Abrams, Berdo & Goodman, LLP, Washington, 1971—74, ptnr., 1975—. Mem.: ABA, Bar Assn. D.C. (chmn. patent, trademark and copyright law sect. 1984—85, bd. dir. 1985—86), Am. Patent Law Assn. Home: 4948 Sentinel Dr Bethesda MD 20816-3556 Office: Roylance Abrams Berdo & Goodman LLP 1300 19th St NW Ste 600 Washington DC 20036-1649

GOODMAN, ALLEN CHARLES, economist, educator; b. Cleve., Oct. 28, 1947; s. Nathan and Pearl (Dorfman) Goodman; m. Janet Hankin, July 22, 1984; 1 child, Sara. AB, U. Mich., 1969; PhD, Yale U., 1976. Asst. prof. Lawrence U., Appleton, Wis., 1975-78; rsch. scientist Johns Hopkins U., Balt., 1978-86; economist HUD, Washington, 1985-86; assoc. prof. Wayne State U., Detroit, 1986-88, prof. econs., 1988—, chmn. dept., 1988-96. Author: (book) Changing Downtown, 1987, Economics of Housing Markets, 1989, Economics of Health and Health Care, 3d edit., 2001. Mem. Mayor's Coord. Coun. Criminal Justice, Balt., 1984—86. Fellow, Homer Hoyt Advanced Studies Inst., 2002—. Mem.: APHA, Am. Real Estate and Urban Econs. Assn., Am. Econs. Assn. Office: Wayne State U Dept Econs Detroit MI 48202

GOODMAN, ALVIN IRWIN, internist, nephrologist, educator; b. N.Y.C., July 12, 1929; s. Morris and Fanny (Rifkin) G.; m. Suzanna Elizabeth Gebhard; children: Nadine, Derek, Danielle, Leslie, Reva. BA, NYU, 1949; MD, U. Geneva, 1955. Diplomate Am. Bd. Internal Medicine, Am. Bd. Nephrology. Intern Jewish Hosp. Bklyn., 1956, resident in medicine, 1957—58; fellow in medicine Yale U. Sch. Medicine, New Haven, 1960—62, resident in medicine, 1962—63; dir. nephrology and renal ctr. Westchester County Med. Ctr., Valhalla, 1963—2000; prof. medicine, dir. nephrology N.Y. Med. Coll., Valhalla, 1975—2000, prof. med., 1963—. Dir. endstage renal disease program Bur. Quality Assurance, USPHS, Rockville, Md., 1974-75. Contbr. numerous articles to medl jours. Capt. M.C., U.S. Army, 1958-60. Recipient President's award Nat. Kidney Found., 1977, Cardinal Cook award N.Y. Med. Coll., 1986. Fellow ACP; mem. Am. Soc. Nephrology, Internat. Soc. Nephrology, Am. Soc. Transplant Physicians, N.Y. Soc. Nephrology (pres. 1980-81), Beta Lambda Sigma. Avocation: travel. Office: Westchester County Med Ctr NY Med Coll Valhalla NY 10595

GOODMAN, ALVIN S. engineering educator, consultant; b. N.Y.C., Mar. 14, 1925; s. Solomon and Dora Goodman; m. Nettie Leef Gilson, Sept. 9, 1951; children: Sandra, Lynn, Nancy, Sally. B of Civil Engring., CCNY, 1944; MSCE, Columbia U., 1948; PhD, NYU, 1966. Registered profl. engr. N.Y., Mass., Conn., N.C.; profl. hydrologist, AIH. Engr. Interstate Sanitation Commn., N.Y.C., 1950-51; project engr. Tippets-Abbett-McCarthy-Stratton, N.Y.C., 1951-62, staff cons. water resources, 1962-85; prof. civil engring. Northeastern U., Boston, 1962-69, NYU, N.Y.C., 1969-73, Poly. U., Bklyn., 1973—, head dept., 1985—90. Cons. engring. firms, ednl. instns., 1970—. Author: Principles of Water Resources Planning, 1984; contbr. articles to profl. jours., papers and reports to confs. 1st lt. C.E., U.S. Army, 1944-47; ETO. Fellow ASCE; mem. Am. Water Resources Assn., Am. Geophys. Union, Water Environ. Fedn., Am. Soc. Engring. Edn., Sigma Xi, Tau Beta Pi, Chi Epsilon. Office: Poly U Dept Civil Engring 6 Metrotech Ctr Brooklyn NY 11201-3840 E-mail: asgpoly@aol.com., agoodman@poly.edu.

GOODMAN, ANN PATON, lawyer; b. Winchester, Mass., Aug. 16, 1957; d. Thomas Paton and Sara Kriner Goodman; m. Donald Smith II, June 15, 1996. AB, Wellesley Coll., 1979; JD, Vanderbilt U., 1984. Bar: Ill. 1984, U.S. Dist. Ct. (no. dist.) Ill. 1984, U.S. Ct. Appeals (7th cir.) 1989, U.S. Supreme Ct. 1995. Assoc. Peterson, Ross, Schloerb & Seidel, Chgo., 1984-87, McCullough, Campbell & Lane, Chgo., 1987-93, ptnr., 1993—. V.p. Newberry Plz. Condo Assn., Chgo., 1992-2003; bd. dirs. Chgo. Wellesley Club, 1986-90. Mem. ABA, Internat. Aviation Women's Assn. (sec. 1998-2000), Chgo. Bar Assn., Fortnightly of Chgo. Avocations: travel, kayaking, bicycling. Office: McCullough Campbell & Lane 205 N Michigan Ave Ste 4100 Chicago IL 60601 E-mail: agoodman@mcandl.com.

GOODMAN, BARRY S. lawyer; b. Jersey City, June 7, 1951; s. Milton and Margaret Goodman; m. Emily J. Reynolds, Dec. 5, 1982. BA cum laude, Rutgers Coll., 1973; JD, Rutgers U., Newark, 1977. Bar: N.J., U.S. Dist. Ct. N.J., U.S. Ct. Appeals (3rd cir.), U.S. Supreme Ct. Jud. law clk. hon. Eugene L. Lora Superior Ct. N.J. Appellate Divsn., Hackensack, 1977-78; atty. Essex-Newark Legal Svcs., Orange, N.J., 1978-79, Crummy, Del Deo, Dolan & Purcell, Newark, 1979-84, Greenbaum, Rowe, Smith, Ravin, Davis & Himmel LLP, Woodbridge, N.J., 1984—. Author: (manual) New Jersey Students' Rights, 1977; mem. editl. bd. Rutgers Law Rev., 1976-77; contbr. articles to profl. jours. Vol. atty. Essex-Newark Legal Svcs., 1979-81; mem. Kinoy Fellowship Adv. Com., Newark, 1991-96; mem. 20th reunion conf. com. Rutgers Constnl. Litigation Clinic, Newark, 1991; co-chairperson Hunterdon County Dems. for Clinton Com., Flemington, N.J., 1992; mem. Hunterdon County Dem. Com., Flemington, 1994—, mem. exec. com., 1996-2000, 2002-; mem. funds allocation com. United Way Hunterdon County, Clinton, 1995—, agy. admissions com., 1996, trustee, 1997—, treas. 1998-99, exec. com., 1998—, spl. gifts com., 1998—, cmty. rels. com., 1998—, v.p., 1999-2001, pres., 2001-2003; mem. Hunterdon County Health and Human Svcs. Adv. Coun., Flemington, 1998-2000; trustee Hunterdon Health Care Sys., 2003—. Mem. ABA (litigation sect., antitrust sect.), Fed. Bar Assn. N.J., N.J. State Bar Assn. (civil trial sect., antitrust sect., real property and probate sect.), Trial Attys. N.J. (trustee 1996—), Middlesex County Bar Assn., Hunterdon County Bar Assn., Rutgers-Newark Sch. Law Alumni Assn. (annual reunion dinner com. 1992, co-chair 1999, annual spring dinner com. 1995-98, treas. 1999-2000, sec. 2000-01, v.p. 2001-2002, pres. elect 2002-2003, pres. 2003), IOLTA fund of the bar assn. of N.J. (trustee, 2003-), Phi Beta Kappa, Phi Kappa Phi. Office: Greenbaum Rowe Smith Ravin Davis & Himmel LLP 99 Wood Ave S Iselin NJ 08830-2715

GOODMAN, BERNARD, physics educator; b. Phila., June 14, 1923; s. Louis and Fannie (Solomon) G.; m. Joyce Janet Willoughby, Mar. 3, 1950; children—David Nathan, Jonathan Bernard, Mark William AB, U. Pa., 1943, PhD, 1955. Stress analyst Internat. Harvester Co., Chgo., 1947-52; research assoc. U. Mo., 1952, asst. prof. physics, 1954-58, assoc. prof., 1958-64, prof., 1964—; prof. physics U. Cin., 1965-93, prof. emeritus, 1993—. Vis. sci. Argonne Nat. Lab., 1956-57, 61-62, 65-66, 70, Brookhaven Nat. Lab., 1960, Bell Telephone Lab., 1967, Ohio U., 1969; Nordita guest prof. Inst. Theoretical Physics, Uppsala, Sweden, 1962-63, Gothenberg, Sweden, 1971-72; vis. prof. Inst. Theoretical Physics, Gothenberg, 1985. Guggenheim fellow, 1962-63, Gordon Godfrey fellow U. NSW, Sydney, Australia, 1990; Fulbright scholar Inst. Theoretical Physics, Trieste, Italy, 1979-80 Fellow Am. Phys. Soc.; mem. AAAS, Phi Beta Kappa, Sigma Xi Achievements include rsch. on condensed matter theory. Home: 3411 Cornell Pl Cincinnati OH 45220-1501 Office: U Cin Dept Physics Cincinnati OH 45221-0011 E-mail: goodman@physics.uc.edu.

GOODMAN, CHARLES SCHAFFNER, JR., food product executive, consultant; b. Phila., Nov. 15, 1949; s. Charles Schaffner Sr. and Dorothy Ruth (Irwin) G. BA, U. Pa., 1971. Warehouse and distb. mgr. Odyssey Records, Santa Cruz, Calif., 1974-75; mgr. Paradiso's, Santa Cruz, Calif., 1978-79; sales mgr. Mask Prodns., Chatsworth, Calif., 1980; regional sales mgr. Harmony Foods, Inc., Santa Cruz, 1981-83, nat. sales mgr., 1983-85, nat. sales mgr. foodsvc., 1985-88, v.p. foodsvc., 1988-90; owner, pres. Creative Mktg. Group, Soquel, Calif., 1990-97; nat. sales mgr. food svc. Galaxy Foods Inc., 1997—2001; nat. sales mgr. Silk Singles, White Wave Inc., 2001—02; nat. sales mgr. Quail Mountain Herbs, Watsonville, Calif., 2002—. Bd. dirs. Noema Software. Mem. No. Calif. Food Svc. Mktg. Assn., The Foodsters, Internat. Food Svc. Execs. Assn. Avocations: scuba diving, golf. Home: 4713 Soquel Creek Rd Soquel CA 95073-9657 Office: Creative Mktg Group PO Box 1736 Soquel CA 95073-1736 Address: PO Box 1736 Soquel CA 95073-1736

GOODMAN, COREY SCOTT, neurobiology educator, researcher, biotechnology company executive; b. Chgo., June 29, 1951; s. Arnold Harold and Florence (Friedman) G.; m. Marcia M. Barinaga, Dec. 8, 1984. BS, Stanford U., 1972; PhD, U. Calif., Berkeley, 1977. Postdoctoral fellow U. Calif., San Diego, 1979; asst. prof. dept. biol. scis. Stanford (Calif.) U., 1979-82, assoc. prof., 1982-87; prof. neurobiology and genetics U. Calif., Berkeley, 1987—. Evan Rauch prof. neurosci., 1999—2001; CEO, pres. Renovis Inc., 2001—. Investigator Howard Hughes Med. Inst., 1988—2001; dir. Helen Wills Neurosci. Inst., 1999—2001; chair bd. life sci. Nat. Rsch. Coun. Contbr. more than 200 articles to profl. jours. Pres. McKnight Found. Endowment Fund Neurosci. Recipient Charles Judson Herrick award, 1982, Alan T. Waterman award Nat. Sci. Bd., 1983, Javits Neurosci. Investigator award NIH, 1985, 92, NIH Merit award, 1985, Found. IPSEN Neuronal Plasticity prize, 1996, J. Allyn Taylor Internat. prize in medicine, 1996, Gairdner Found. Internat. award for achievement in med. sci., 1997, Ameritec Found. Basic Rsch. Toward Cure Paralysis prize, 1997, Wakeman award for rsch. in neuroscis., 1998, March-Of-Dimes Prize in Devel. Biology, 2001. Fellow Am. Acad. Arts and Scis.; mem. NAS, Am. Philos. Soc. Office: Renovis Inc 270 Littlefield Ave South San Francisco CA 94080 E-mail: goodman@renovis.com.

GOODMAN, DANIEL SOLOMON, real estate broker, consultant; b. New Bedford, Mass., June 16, 1932; s. George and Sarah Wollison Goodman. Student, Northeastern U., 1956—60. Lic. real estate broker Calif. Dental supply specialist L.D. Caulk Co., Balt., 1950—52; prodn. coord. Raytheon, Waltham, Mass., 1956—58; logistician Sylvania Electronic Systems, Waltham, Mass., 1958—63; pres. C. Jay Products, San Francisco, 1988—93; profl. actor, entertainer, 1940—; real estate broker, 1964—2000; cons. Vicor, Napa, Calif., 2001—. Freelance writer USA Table Tennis, Colorado Springs, Colo., 1956—2000; profl. model, 1972—; voice-over talent, 1972—. Author: I'll Take Spiked Mustard, 2002, I Like Your Shirt, 2003; creator, editor 2 quar. newsletters, actor TV commls. Sgt. U.S. Army, 1952—55. Avocations: tournament calibre table tennis, directing regional and national table tennis championships, sprint medalist freestyle swimming, poetry, writing lyrics.

GOODMAN, DAVID G. Japanese, comparative literature educator, writer; b. Racine, Wis., Feb. 12, 1946; BA, Yale U., 1969; PhD, Cornell U., 1982. Asst. prof. U. Kans., Lawrence, 1981-82; prof. U. Ill., Champaign, 1982—. Author: After Apocalypse, 1986, Japanese Drama and Culture, 1988, Hashiru (Running), 1989, Jews in the Japanese Mind, 1995, Angura: Posters of the Japanese Avant-Garde, 1999; editor, translator: Long Long Autumn Nights, 1989; editor, pub. Concerned Theatre Japan, 1969-73. Univ. scholar U. Ill., 1992; Fulbright fellow 1980, 90; NEH grantee, 1985, NEA, 1993; recipient Translation Ctr. award Columbia U., 1990. Office: U Ill 707 S Mathews Ave Ste 2090A Urbana IL 61801-3623 E-mail: dgoodman@uiuc.edu.

GOODMAN, DAVID WAYNE, research chemist, educator; b. Dec. 14, 1945; s. Henry G. and Anniebelle G.; m. Sandra Faye Hewitt, June 9, 1967; 1 child, Jac Hewitt. BS, Miss. Coll., 1968; PhD, U. Tex., 1974. NATO postdoctoral fellow Tech. Hochschule, Darmstadt, Fed. Republic of Germany, 1974-75; NRC postdoctoral fellow NBS, Washington, 1975-76, mem. rsch. staff, 1976-80, Sandia Labs., Albuquerque, 1980-85, head surface sci. divsn., 1985-88; prof. chemistry Tex. A&M U., College Station, 1988-94, head phys. and nuc. divsn., 1991-94, Welch prof., 1994—, Welch chair, 1998—, disting. prof., 2000. Lectr. Texas A&M U., 1987, U. Tex. 1990, Northwestern U., 1993, Am. Chemical Soc., 1993. Recipient Yarwood medal, 1994, Humboldt Rsch. award 1995, Giuseppe Parravano award, 2001, ACS Arthur W. Adamson award, 2002; Fulbright Disting. scholar, 2002; named Disting. Alumnus, Miss. Coll., 1992, Robert Burwell lectr. North Am. Catalysis Soc., 2003, 1997. Mem. Am. Chem. Soc. (treas. divsn. colloid and surface sci. 1980-83, v. chair 1983, chmn. 1984, Colloid or Surface Chemistry award 1993, Langmuir Disting. Lectr. award, 1991, Ipatieff prize 1983, Arthur W. Adamson award 2002), Am. Vacuum Soc. (mem. exec. council 1981, 85-87). Office: Tex A&M University Dept Chemistry PO Box 30012 College Station TX 77842-3012

GOODMAN, DIANE M. critical care nurse, geriatrics nurse; b. Ft. Wayne, Ind., Mar. 5, 1953; d. Carl R. and Lois J. Jackson. ADN, Parkview-Meth. Sch. Nursing, Ft. Wayne, Ind., 1974; BSN, Alverno Coll., 1998; postgrad., Marquette U. Cert. CCRN gerontology, ANCC. Nurse Lake Forest (Ill.) Hosp., Lake Forest, 1979—. Contbr. articles to profl. jours. Vol. Humane Shelter, Wis. Mem.: Sigma Theta Tau (Delta Gamma chpt.). Fax: 847-535-7827. E-mail: dgoodman@lakeforesthospital.com.

GOODMAN, DONALD C. university administrator; b. Chgo., Nov. 24, 1927; s. Alexander Goodman and Freda (Mermelstein) G.; m. Martha Huggins, July 3, 1968; children: Brian and Eric (twins), Michael and Susan (twins), Elaine, Alison; stepchildren: Bruce, Adam, Mitchell. BS, U. Ill., 1949, MS, 1950, PhD, 1954. Instr. U. Pa., 1954-56; mem. faculty U. Fla., 1956-68, prof., 1963-68, chmn. dept. anatomical scis., 1965-68; co-dir. Center Neurol. Sci., 1964-68; prof. anatomy, chmn. dept. SUNY Med. Center, Syracuse, 1968-82, dean Coll. Grad. Studies, 1973-82, interim dean med. scis., 1975-76, v.p. acad. affairs, 1975-78, v.p. research and acad. affairs, 1978-82; v.p. acad. affairs East Tenn. State U., 1982; dean health related professions SUNY-Syracuse Health Scis. Ctr., 1983-95, v.p. acad. affairs, 1983-86, provost, 1986-95, interim pres., 1992. Mem. interdisciplinary studies adv. coun. Fla. Gulf Coast U., 1997. Author books and articles; editor: Brain, Behavior and Evolution. Mem. study sect. NIH. Served with AUS, 1946-48. Recipient Annual Research award Fla. chpt. Sigma Xi; fellow award Assn. Schs. Allied Health Professions, 1993. Fellow Am. Soc. Allied Health Professions; mem. Am. Assn. Anatomists (exec. com. 1978-82), Nat. Coun. Univ. Rsch. Adminstrs., Soc. Neurosci., Am. Assn. Higher Edn., Sigma Xi. Home: 401 Via Esplanade Punta Gorda FL 33950-6400

GOODMAN, DONALD JOSEPH, dentist; b. Cleve., Aug. 14, 1922; s. Joseph Henry and Henrietta Inez (Mandel) G.; BS, Adelbert Coll., 1943; DDS, Case-Western Reserve U., 1945; m. Dora May Hirsh, Sept. 18, 1947; children: Lynda (Mrs. Barry Allen Levin), Keith, Bruce; m. Ruth Jeanette Weber, May 1, 1974. Pvt. practice dentistry, Cleve., 1949-86; lectr. in field. With Dental Corps, USNR, 1946-48. Mem. Am. Acad. Gen. Dentistry, ADA Ohio State Dental Assn., Cleve. Dental Soc., Fedn. Dentaire Internationale, Cleve. Council on World Affairs, Greater Cleve. Growth Assn., Council of Smaller Enterprises, Phi Sigma Delta, Zeta Beta Tau, Alpha Omega. Clubs: Masons (32 deg.), Shriners, Travelers' Century (Gold award, special award), Circumnavigators. Home: 29099 Shaker Blvd Pepper Pike OH 44124-5022

GOODMAN, ELIZABETH ANN, lawyer; b. Marquette, Mich., Aug. 11, 1950; d. Paul William and Pearl Marie Goodman; m. Herbert Charles Gardner, Sept. 24, 1977. Student, U. Munich, 1970-71; BA cum laude, Alma (Mich.) Coll., 1972; JD cum laude, U. Mich., 1977. Bar: Minn. 1978, Mich. 1978, U.S. Dist. Ct. Minn. 1979. Cert. real property law specialist, real property sect. Minn. Bar Assn. High sch. tchr. Onaway (Mich.) High Sch., 1973-74; assoc. Dorsey & Whitney LLP, Mpls., 1978-82; ptnr. Dorsey & Whitney, Mpls., 1983-99; v.p., chief gen. counsel Ryan Cos., 2000—. Mem. Am. Corp. Counsel Assn., Minn. Bar Assn., Hennepin County Bar Assn. Office: Ryan Cos 50 S 10th St Ste 300 Minneapolis MN 55403-2012

GOODMAN, ELLEN HOLTZ, journalist; b. Newton, Mass., Apr. 11, 1941; d. Jackson Jacob and Edith (Weinstein) Holtz; m. Robert Levey; 1 dau., Katherine Anne. BA cum laude, Radcliffe Coll., 1963; hon. degrees, Mt. Holyoke Coll., Amherst Coll., U. Pa., U. N.H. Researcher, reporter Newsweek Mag., 1963-65; feature writer Detroit Free Press, 1965-67; feature writer columnist Boston Globe, 1967-74, assoc. editor, 1986—2001; syndicated columnist Washington Post Writers Group, 1976—; radio commentator Spectrum, CBS, 1978-80, NBC, 1979-80; commentator NBC Today Show, 1979-81. Vis. prof. Stanford U., 1995. Author: Close to Home, 1979, Turning Points, 1979, At Large, 1981, Keeping in Touch, 1985, Making Sense, 1989, Value Judgments, 1993, (with Patricia O'Brien) I Know Just What You Mean, 2000. Trustee Radcliffe Coll.; judge Livingston Awards for Young Journalists, 1986—. Nieman fellow Harvard U., 1974, Lyndhurst fellow, 2000; named New Eng. Newspaper Woman of Year New Eng. Press Assn., 1968; recipient Catherine O'Brien award Stanley Home Products, 1971, Media award Mass. Commn. Status Women, 1974, Columnist of Year award New Eng. Women's Press Assn., 1975, Pulitzer Prize for Commentary, 1980, prize for column writing Am. Soc. Newspaper Editors, 1980, Hubert H. Humphrey Civil Rights award, 1988, William Allen White award 1995. Office: Globe Newspapers Co 135 Morrissey Blvd Dorchester MA 02125-3310 E-mail: ellengoodman@globe.com.

GOODMAN, ELLIOT RAYMOND, political scientist, educator; b. Indpls., Sept. 3, 1923; s. Lazure L. and Esther (Miller) G.; m. Norma B., Mar. 1, 1947; children— Laura Goodman Humphrey, Jordan, Roger. AB, Dartmouth Coll., 1948; MA and cert. Russian Inst., Columbia U., 1951, PhD, 1957; MA (hon.), Brown U., 1960. Ford teaching intern Brown U., Providence, 1955-56, instr., 1956-58, asst. prof., 1958-60, asso. prof., 1960-70, prof. polit. sci., 1970-87, prof. emeritus, 1987—. Author: The Soviet Design for a World State, 1960, The Fate of the Atlantic Community, 1975; contbr. numerous articles to profl. jours. Served with U.S. Army, 1943-46. Guggenheim fellow, 1962-63; NATO research fellow, 1962-63 Mem. Internat. Inst. Strategic Studies (London), Atlantic Council U.S. (politico-mil. com. 1971-74, acad. assoc. 1985—), New Eng. Polit. Sci. Assn., Am. Polit. Sci. Assn., Am. Assn. Advancement of Slavic Studies, Com. Atlantic Studies (N. Am. sect.) Home: 45 Amherst Rd Cranston RI 02920-6010 Office: Brown U Dept Polit Sci Providence RI 02912-0001

GOODMAN, ELLIOTT I(RVIN), retired lawyer; b. Mar. 28, 1934; s. Sidney W. and Jean (Strauss) G.; m. Sybil J. Shapiro, Dec. 25, 1957; children: Jessica, Paul, Jonathan. BS, Northwestern U., 1955, JD, 1958. Bar: Ill. 1958, U.S. Dist. Ct. (no. dist.) Ill. 1959; CPA, Ill. With Gottlieb & Schwartz, Chgo., 1959-90, ptnr., 1966-90, mng. ptnr., 1981-88; ptnr. D'Ancona and Pflaum, Chgo., 1990-95; exec. v.p. ATI Carriage House, Inc., Lombard, Ill., 1995-99. Permanent arbitrator Amalgamated Social Benefit Ins. Plan. Sec., bd. dirs. Ind. Basketball Players Assn., 1971-74, Abe Saperstein Found., Athletes for Better Edn. Found., 1975-79 Mem. Highland Park Housing Commn. (Ill.), 1980-87. Mem. ABA (labor law com. 1977-97, environ. law com. 1988-97), Chgo. Bar Assn. (past chmn. Am. citizenship com. 1967-69, mem. labor law com. 1971—, environ. law com. 1988-97), Human Resource Mgmt. Assn. Chgo., Lake Geneva Yacht Club. Home: 211 Rivershire Ln Apt 201 Lincolnshire IL 60069-3817 Office: ATI Carriage House Inc 1111 N Ridge Ave Lombard IL 60148-1212

GOODMAN, ERIK DAVID, engineering educator; b. Palo Alto, Calif., Feb. 14, 1944; s. Harold Orbeck and Shirley Mae (Lillie) G.; m. Denise Rowand Dyktor, Aug. 10, 1968 (div. 1976); m. Cheryl Diane Barris, Aug. 27, 1978; 1 child, David Richard. BS in Math., Mich. State U., 1966, MS in Systems Sci., 1968; PhD in Computer Communication Sci., U. Mich., 1972; Hon. Doctorate, Dneprodzerzhinsk State Tech U., Ukraine, 1996. Asst. prof. elec. engring. Mich. State U., East Lansing, 1972-77, assoc. prof. elec. engring., 1977-84, dir. case ctr. for computer aided engring. and mfg., 1983—2002, prof. elec. engring., dir., 1984—, prof. mech. engring., 1992—. Dir. Mich. State U. Mfg. Rsch. Consortium, 1993—; v.p. Red Cedar Tech., Inc., East Lansing, Mich., 1999-; pres. Tech. Gateway, Inc., East Lansing; cons. Chinese Computer Comms., Inc., Lansing, 1988—; gen. chair First Internat. Conf. on Evolutionary Computation and its Applications, Moscow, 1996, Seventh Internat Conf. on Genetic Algorithms, 1997, Genetic and Evolutionary Computation Conf., 2001; gen. co-chmn. Internat. Computer Graphics Conf., Detroit, 1986; adv. prof. Tongji U., Shanghai, China, 2002-. Author: (with others) SYSKIT: Linear Systems Toolkit, 1986; patentee in field. Academician, Internat. Informatization Acad. (Russia), 1993—. Mem. AIAA (chair rsch. and future dirs., subcom. CAD/CAM tech. com. 1987-89, Outstanding Svc. 1990), IEEE Computer Soc., Soc. Mfg. Engrs., Aircraft Owners and Pilots Assn., Acad. Engring. Scis. Ukraine, Internat. Soc. for Genetic and Evolutionary Computation (exec. com. 2001—, chair 2001-). Avocations: musician, tennis, studying chinese. Office: Mich State U Dept Elec & Computer Engring 2308M Engineering Bldg East Lansing MI 48824 E-mail: goodman@egr.msu.edu., e.goodman@redcedartech.com. *Evolutionary computation is now allowing huge advances in engineering design optimization and design automation of complex structures.*

GOODMAN, ERIKA, dancer, actress; b. Phila. d. A. Allan and Laura (Baylin) G. Student, Sch. of Am. Ballet, 1961-63; BA in Theatre and Dance, Empire State Coll., 1993; master classes, Princeton Ballet, 1994, Hartford Ballet Co., 1995, Va. Intermont Coll., 1995—. Mem. faculty Actors and Dirs. Lab., N.Y.C., 1979—; founding mem. ensemble theater co. The Barrow Group, N.Y.C., 1986—; mem. dance faculty CCNY, 1990. Mem. dance faculty CCNY, 1990; guest tchr. ballet Balettakademein, Stockholm, 1986, 89; instr. master classes Rutgers U., East Carolina U., 1989, Hofstra U., U. Kans., 1990, Harvard U., summer 1993, Cornell U., Skidmore Coll., Vassar Coll., 1992—, Conn. Coll.; vis. prof. ballet, head ballet dept. CCNY, 1992—, lectr. world arts, 1993—. Dancer N.Y.C. Ballet Co., 1964-65, prin. dancer Joffrey Ballet, N.Y.C., 1966-75; performer (with Barrow Group) Seymour in the Heart of Winter, Perry St. Theatre, N.Y.C., 1986, When You Comin' Back Red Rider, 1987, Feather Hat, Three Sisters, 1989; casting dir. (films) Hazing in Hell, Neon Red; dir. ballet rehearsal Ballet Hispanico. Richard Porter Leach fellow, 1992-93. *In my life as with my art, I have strived to achieve purity, truth and beauty— to preserve my integrity when it was challenged, and never to compromise the dictates of my heart.*

GOODMAN, ERNEST MONROE, military officer; b. Casper, Wyo., May 14, 1955; s. Gordon Lee and Georgia Lee (Lent) G.; m. Songkran Sana, Sept. 30, 1976 (div. Feb. 1995). BSEE, U. Okla., 1982; MBA in Mgmt., Cen. State U., Edmond, Okla., 1986; postgrad., Air Command and Staff Coll., Air U., Maxwell AFB, Ala., 2001. Registered profl. engr., Okla. Avionics technician USAF, N.D., Okla., and S.E. Asia, 1973-78, USAFR, Tinker AFB, Okla., 1978-83; project engr., mgr. engring. Okla. City Air Logistics Ctr., Tinker AFB, 1982-90, 90—; commd. 2nd lt. USAF, 1983, advanced through grades to lt. col.; engring. officer USAFR, Tinker AFB, 1983—. Mem. NSPE, Okla. Soc. Profl. Engrs., Air Force Assn., Res. Officers Assn. (pres. Okla. dept. 1999-2000), Tinker Mgmt. Assn. (pres. 1997-98), Toastmasters Internat. Democrat. Roman Catholic. Avocations: photography, fishing, hunting, hiking, jogging. Home: 1313 SW 22d St Moore OK 73170-7483 Office: USAF OC-ALC/MASKN Bldg 3220 Tinker AFB OK 73145

GOODMAN, GAIL BUSMAN, small business owner; b. N.Y.C., Feb. 8, 1953; d. Irving Laurence and Harriet (Topol) Busman; m. Laurence Goodman, June 17, 1979 (div. 1987). Student, Northwestern U., 1970-72; BS magna cum laude, Tufts U., 1975. Staff occupational therapist St. Joseph's Hosp., Yonkers, N.Y., 1975-77; sr. occupational therapist N.Y. Hosp., White Plains, 1977-79; chief occupational therapist Phelps Hosp., Tarrytown, N.Y., 1979-80; occupational therapy cons. Elmwood Manor Nursing Home, Nanuet, N.Y., 1982-83; from v.p. tng. to pres. Facelifters, Bklyn., 1981-86; pres. Visual Impact, Rye, N.Y., 1987—; owner, pres. ConsulTel, Inc., White Plains, N.Y., 1988—. Guest speaker Columbia U., N.Y.C., 1977, 78, 79, 82. Mem. Women in Sales (pres. Westchester chpt. 1989-91). Democrat. Jewish. Avocations: reading, movies, needlepoint, antique refinishing.

GOODMAN, GARY A. lawyer; b. N.Y.C., Mar. 8, 1948; s. Nathaniel and Edith (Rosen) G.; m. Susan Schachter, Aug. 13, 1972; children: Max, Jonah, William, Zachary, Holden. AB in History summa cum laude, Economics with honors, U. Rochester, 1970; JD, NYU, 1973. Bar: N.Y. 1974, U.S. Dist. Ct. (so. dist. and ea. dist.) N.Y. 1974, U.S. Dist. Ct. Guam, 1975, U.S. Ct. Appeals (2d cir.) 1975, Calif. 1996, Tex. 1996. Ptnr. Sonnenschein Nath & Rosenthal LLP, N.Y.C., 2002—. Contbr. numerous articles to profl. jours. Mem. bd. edn. Locust Valley (N.Y.) Ctrl. Sch. Dist., 1995-96, v.p., 1996-97, pres., 1997-98. Mem.: ABA (vice chmn. internat. investment in real estate com. 1983—90, chmn. Pacific Rim trans. subcom. real estate financing com. 1987—88), Comml. Mortgage Securities Assn., Assn. Fgn. Investors in Real Estate, Real Estate Bd., Internat. Coun. Shopping Ctrs. (task force environ. issues 1987—90, law com. 1991—94), Assn. Bar of City of N.Y. (uniform state laws com. 1978—80, real property law com. 1991—94, land use com. 1994—97, real property law com. 1997—2000), N.Y. State Bar Assn. (chmn. fgn. investment in U.S. real estate com. 1987—88). Office: Sonnenschein Nath & Rosenthal 1221 Ave of the Americas New York NY 10020 E-mail: ggoodman@sonnenschein.com.

GOODMAN, GARY ALAN, lawyer; b. Memphis, Nov. 27, 1947; s. Louis H. and Margie (Evensky) G.; m. Teresa E. Berry, July 2, 1987. AB, Cornell U., 1969; JD, Columbia U., 1972. Bar: N.Y., 1973, U.S. Dist. Ct. (so. dist.) N.Y. 1973, Ill. 1979, U.S. Dist. Ct. (no. dist.) Ill. 1979, U.S. Cir. Ct. (2d cir.), U.S. Cir. Ct. (7th cir). Assoc. Sullivan & Cromwell, N.Y.C., 1972-79; ptrn., gen. counsel Winston & Strawn, Chgo., 1979—. Bd. dirs. Lyric Opera Chgo., 1998—. Home: 219 E Lake Shore Dr Chicago IL 60611-1352 Office: Winston & Strawn 35 W Wacker Dr Ste 4200 Chicago IL 60601-1695

GOODMAN, GEORGE JEROME WALDO (ADAM SMITH), author, television journalist, editor; b. St. Louis, Aug. 10, 1930; s. Alexander Mark and Viola (Cremer) G.; m. Sallie Cullen Brophy, Oct. 6, 1961; children: Alexander Mark, Susannah Blake. AB magna cum laude, Harvard U., 1952; AB Rhodes scholar, Oxford (Eng.) U., 1952-54. Reporter Barron's, 1957; contbg. editor, assoc. editor Time and Fortune mags., 1958-60; portfolio mgr., v.p. Lincoln Fund, 1960-62; co-founder New York mag., 1967, contbg. editor, v.p., 1967-77; exec. editor, then cons. Esquire, 1978-81; 1st editor, exec. v.p., bd. dirs. Instl. Investor, 1967-72; chmn. Continental Fidelity Group, 1980—, also dir. Exec. v.p., dir. Instl. Investor Systems, 1969-72; dir. USAIR, Inc., 1978-99, Hyatt Hotels, 1977-81, Cambrex, Inc., 1981-2003, Providentia Ltd., Sweden, 1984-86; bd. dirs. New Eng. Life; lectr. Harvard Bus. Sch., Princeton; commentator NBC News, 1974, PBS, 1981—; creator, host, editor-in-chief Adam Smith's Money World, PBS, 1984-97; 1st U.S. pub. affairs TV broadcast in Russia, 1990—; host, editor-in-chief Adam Smith's Money Game, PBS, 1998-99; editl. chmn. N.J. Monthly, 1976-79; adv. com. publs. U.S. Tennis Assn., 1978-83; chmn. Adam Smith Global TV, 1997—. Screenwriter, L.A., 1962-65, screenplay The Wheeler Dealers; author: The Bubble Makers, 1955, A Time for Paris, 1957, Bascombe, The Fastest Hound Alive, 1958, A Killing in the Market, 1958, The Wheeler Dealers, 1959; under pseudonym Adam Smith: The Money Game, 1968 (#1 bestseller), Supermoney, 1971 (#1 bestseller), Powers of Mind, 1975, Paper Money, 1981, The Roaring 80's, 1988; mem. editl. bd. N.Y. Times, 1977; contbr. articles to profl. jours. Trustee Glassboro (N.J.) State Coll., 1967-71, co-chmn. presdl. selection com., 1968; trustee C.G. Jung Found., 1981-88; mem. adv. council econs. dept. Princeton U., 1970-89, chmn., 1975-77; rep. com. on shareholder responsibility Harvard U., 1971-74, mem. vis. com. psychology and social relations dept., 1974-80—, mem. vis. com. Middle East Inst.; mem. adv. council Sloan Fellowships, Princeton U., 1976-79, Ctr. for Internat. Studies, Princeton U., 1990—; trustee The Urban Inst., 1986-96, Found. for Child Devel., 1986-88. Served with AUS, 1954-56. Recipient G.M. Loeb award for disting. achievement bus. and fin. writing U. Conn., 1969, Media award for econ. understanding with TV documentary Amos Tuck Sch., Dartmouth Coll., 1978, Overseas Press award, 1996; Ind award Brown U., 1993; nominee 8 Emmy awards, 1985-97, winner Best Interview 1995, winner 3 Emmys, graphics, 1985-94, PBS Documentaries medal Hosuton Internat. Film Festival, Russia. Mem.: Assn. Harvard Alumni (bd. dirs. 1972—75), Authors Guild (bd. dirs. 1975—), Authors League Fund (v.p.), Coun. Fgn. Rels., Knickerbocker Club, Century Assn., Harvard Club. Office: Adam Smith Global TV 26 E 63rd St New York NY 10021-8030

GOODMAN, GERTRUDE AMELIA, civic worker; b. El Paso, Tex., Oct. 24, 1924; d. Karl Perry and Helen Sylvia (Pinkiert) G. BA, Mills Coll., 1945. Pres. El Paso chpt. Tex. Social Welfare Assn., 1963-65, bd. dirs. 1965-70, state bd. dirs., 1965-70; state bd. dirs. Pan-Am. Round Table, El Paso, 1966—, bd. dirs. 1970-71, sec., 1973-74, life mem.; founder, 1st chmn. El Paso Mus. Art Mem. Guild, 1962-68; bd. dirs. Mus. Art Assn., 1962-69, also v.p.; chmn. dir. El Paso C. of C. women's Dept., 1976-77; bd. dirs. Rio Grande Food Bank, 1988-94; bd. dirs. El Paso Pub. Libr., 1972-80, pres. bd. dirs., 1978-80; pres. El Paso County Hist. Soc., 1981-82, bd. dirs., 1986-92; mem. planning com. El Paso United Way, 1953—; mem. El Paso Mus. Art Bd. Coun.; pres. Las Comadres, 2000-01. Recipient Hall of Honor award El Paso County Hist. Soc., Nat. Human Rels. award NCCJ, 1981, numerous awards for civic vol. work. Avocations: tennis, travel, art, books. Home: 905 Cincinnati Ave El Paso TX 79902-2435

GOODMAN, GLENN DAVID, occupational therapist, educator; b. Canton, Ohio, Mar. 31, 1956; s. Paul W. and Marie Esther Goodman; m. Susan Mary Pierce; children: Paul, Elizabeth, Anna. PhD, Kent State U., 2000. Cert. occupl. therapy. Assoc. prof. Cleve. State U., 1992—2001, dir. occupl. therapy program, 2001—. Participant Distance Edn. in Health Scis. award, Ohio Bd. Regents, 2000. Co-author: (book chpt.) Preventing Occupational Dysfunction Secondary to Aging, in Occupational Therapy for Physical Dysfunction, 5th edit., Trombly, C. and Radomski, M. Eds., 2002; contbr. articles to profl. jours. Rsch. cons. Cleve. Clinic Found., 2000—02; bd. dirs. Arthritis Found., Cleve., 1983—90; Bd. dirs. Camp Gideon Evangel. Friends Ch., Ea. Region, Canton, 2000—02. Named Project Team participant, NSF, 1997—2001; recipient Internet II Implementation Projects award, 2001, Adaptive Computer Lab. and Equipment award, Ohio House Bill 790, 1995; fellow tchg. fellow, Cleve. State U., 1997. Mem.: Ohio Occupl. Therapy Assn. (chair edn. spl. interest sect. 1988—91, Continuing Edn. Award of Recognition 1991), Am. Occupl. Therapy Assn. Mem. Soc. Of Friends. Avocations: water and snow skiing, fishing, golf. Office: Cleve State U HS 103 2121 Euclid Ave Cleveland OH 44115 Office Fax: 216-687-9316 Personal E-mail: g.goodman@csuohio.edu. Business E-Mail: g.goodman@csuohio.edu.

GOODMAN, HAROLD S. lawyer; b. St. Louis, Aug. 17, 1937; s. David and Eva Katherine (Wasserman) G.; m. Karen K. Mauldin, Aug. 5, 1979; 1 child, James Richardson. AB, U. Mo., 1960; LLB, JD, Washington U., St. Louis, 1963. Bar: Mo. 1963. Assoc., ptnr. Bishop & Goodman, St. Louis, 1963—70; v.p., gen. counsel, sec. World Color Press, Inc., St. Louis, 1970-75; pvt. practice St. Louis, 1975-81; ptnr. Gallop, Johnson & Neuman, L.C., St. Louis, 1981—. Mem. St. Louis County CSC, 1976-80; trustee Cystic Fibrosis Found., 1971—2002, pres., 1975; mem. Mo.-St. Louis Met. Airport Authority, 1980-86; trustee-at-large Nat. Cystic Fibrosis Found., 1984-90; mem. Laumeier Sculpture Park, 1996—, chmn. bd. trustees, 2001—; mem. Cmty. in Partnership., 1986-88. Mem. ABA, Mo. Bar Assn., Bar Assn. St. Louis, Washington U. Law Alumni Assn. (pres. 1976-77), Zeta Beta Tau (pres. trustee corp. 1964-69), Phi Delta Phi. Home: 340 Falling Leaves Ct Saint Louis MO 63141-7405 Office: Gallop Johnson & Neuman LC 101 S Hanley Rd Ste 1600 Saint Louis MO 63105-3489 E-mail: hsgoodman@gjn.com.

GOODMAN, HERBERT IRWIN, petroleum company executive; b. Pitts., Mar. 11, 1923; s. Meyer Irwin and Bessie (Crossof) G.; m. Mary Katherine Schilken, Aug. 12, 1978; children: Michael Christopher, Anne Katheryn, Nancy Hjortshoj, Sara Elizabeth, Mary Elien. BS, U. Pitts., 1943; cert., U. Besancon, 1945; MBA, Harvard U., 1949, AM, 1950. Commd. officer U.S. Fgn. Svc., 1951; served in U.S. Embassy, Copenhagen, 1951-53, Vietnam, 1953-54, U.S. Fgn. Service, Kampuchea, 1954-55; intelligence rsch. officer Dept. State, 1956-57; with Gulf Oil Corp., 1957-84, coord. European sales, 1957 59; gen. mgr. Pacific Gulf Oil, Tokyo, 1960-64, coord. crude oil dept. Pitts., 1964-66, coord. Far East, 1966-70; pres. Gulf Oil Co. South Asia, Singapore, 1970-72, Gulf Oil Trading Co., Pitts., 1972-80, Gulf Trading and Transp. Co., Houston, 1980-84, GOTCO USA, Inc., Houston, 1984-87, SARMAR Corp., Houston, 1987—; bd. chmn. Applied Trading Sys., Houston, 1988-96, IQ Holdings, Inc., Houston, 1996—, pepex.net LLC, 2000—. Bd. dirs. Houston Livestock Show and Rodeo, Genesis Energy L.P.; adv. bd. Pacific Inst.; bd. chmn. Pepex-.netLLC, 2000—. Bd. dirs., chmn. internat. adv. bd. Tex. A&M U.; bd. dirs. U. Houston Coll. Bus., U. St. Thomas Sch. Bus. 1st lt. U.S. Army, 1943-46. Decorated Bronze Star; médaille de la Réconnaissance (France). Mem. Am. Petroleum Inst., Am. Mgmt. Assn., Coun. on Fgn. Rels., Assn. Asian Studies, Mid East Inst., Asia Soc. N.Y. (corp. coun.), Assn. Internat. Petroleum Negotiators, Harvard Club (N.Y.C.), Lakeside Country Club, Racquet Club, Univ. Club, Petroleum Club. Office: SARMAR Corp 16212 State Highway 249 Houston TX 77086-1014 E-mail: herbg@lqproducts.com., herbg@iaproducts.com.

GOODMAN, JEROME DAVID, psychiatrist; b. Chester, Pa., Oct. 23, 1933; s. William Henry and Amelia (Kopl) G.; m. Gail Ann Theis, Feb. 10, 1961; children: David Hammond, Douglas Andrew. BA, Swarthmore Coll., 1955; MD, U. Pa., 1959. Diplomate Am. Bd. Psychiatry and Neurology with subspecialty in child psychiatry. Asst. clin. prof. psychiatry coll. physicians and surgeons Columbia U., N.Y.C., 1964-75; pvt. practice Saddle River, N.J., 1968—. Author: Child Mental Status Examination, 1967, 2d edit., 1998; composer: Sonata for Violin and Piano, 1990, Six Cryptic Rhythms for Chamber Orch., 1992, Montségur Suite, 1993, Symphony # 2, 1994, Violin Concerto, 1995, Concerto for Clarinet, Violoncello and Orch., 1996, Dance Patterns: A Choreographic Poem for Orch., 1997, Stockbridge Overtones: Tone Poem for Orch., 1998, Saddle River Almanac: A Tone Poem for Orchestra, 2002, Saxophone Quartet, 2002; (soprano and piano) Two Elizabethan Lyrics for Soprano and Piano, 2003, Concert Piece for Piano Trio and Percussion, 2003. Capt. U.S. Army, 1966-68. Recipient Margaret Fairbanks Jory award, 1992. Jewish. Office: 45 W Saddle River Rd Saddle River NJ 07458-3016

GOODMAN, JERRY L(YNN), judge; b. Mangum, Okla., Apr. 17, 1939; s. A.O. and Viola Louise (Bogart) G.; m. Donna L. Rudy, Dec. 16, 1961; children: Courtney L., Polly K., Mallory E., Benjamin R. BA, U. Tulsa, 1961; JD, Georgetown U., 1964. Bar: Okla. 1964. Law clk. antitrust divsn. Dept. Justice, 1962-63; legis. asst. to U.S. Senator J. Howard Edmondson, 1963-64; assoc. David M. Thornton Atty.-at-Law, 1964-65; asst. city atty. City of Tulsa, Okla., 1965-68; ptnr. Owens & Goodman, Tulsa, 1968-70; gen. counsel OTASCO Stores, Tulsa, 1970-74, v.p., gen. counsel, 1974-85, chmn., CEO, 1985-89; spl. counsel Bank of Okla., 1989-90; pres., gen. counsel The Sigma Asset Mgmt. Group, Inc., 1991-92; sec. policy and mgmt., COO Office of Gov., State of Okla., Tulsa, 1992-94; judge Okla. Ct. Civil Appeals, Tulsa, 1994—. Bd. dirs. United Way, 1984—87; chmn., bd. trustees Univ. Ctr. at Tulsa, 1992. Served to lt. (j.g.) USNR, 1964—70. Mem.: ABA, Tulsa County Bar Assn. (v.p. 1971), Okla. Bar Assn., Okla. Jud. Conf. (pres. 2001), Tulsa C. of C. (chmn. 1988). Presbyterian. Home: 3417 E 87th St Tulsa OK 74137-2628 Office: Okla Ct Civil Appeals 601 State Office Bldg 440 S Houston Ave Tulsa OK 74127-8922 E-mail: jerry.goodman@oscn.net.

GOODMAN, JOE READ, utilities executive; b. Corsicana, Tex., Dec. 28, 1952; s. Joe Read and Betty LAne Goodman; m. Patricia Norman, June 1, 1996; children: Aaron Daniel Risinger, Rachel Marie Risinger. BS, U. Houston, 1988. Cert. pub. mgr. Tex., 2000. Gen. mgr. Galveston County Mcpl. Utility Dist. # 1, 1984—89; tech. cons. Cmty. Resources Group, Nashville, 1989—90; waste treatment supt. City of Galveston, Tex., 1990—93; city adminstr. City of Kountze, Tex., 1993; dir. pub. works City of Harker Heights, Tex., 1994; pub. works maintenance mgr. City of Houston, 1995—. Pres. Rice Belt Water Utility assn., Tex., 1985, Gulf Area Water Utility Dist., Tex., 2001. Disaster chmn. ARC, Galveston, Tex., 1986—87. Mem.: Tex. Water Utilities Assn. Baptist. Office: City of Houston 2700 Dalton Houston TX 77017 Personal E-mail: pjgoodman@houston.rr.com. E-mail: joe.goodman@cityofhouston.net.

GOODMAN, JOHN M. lawyer; b. N.Y.C., Oct. 31, 1947; s. Melvin D. and Margaret H. (Barnett) G.; children: Andrew, Nicholas. AB, Princeton U., 1969; JD, Harvard U., 1973. Bar: N.Y. 1974, U.S. Dist. Ct. (so. and ea. dists.) NY 1974, U.S. Ct. Appeals (2d cir.) 1975, D.C. 1984, U.S. Ct. Appeals (D.C. cir.) 1984. Assoc. Dewey, Ballantine, Bushby, Palmer & Wood, N.Y.C., 1973-83; gen. atty. Verizon, Washington, 1983— . Office: Verizon 1300 I St NW Washington DC 20005-3314

GOODMAN, JOHN M. construction executive; b. Omaha, Apr. 5, 1947; BS in Acctg., Calif. State U., Long Beach, 1970; JD, Pepperdine U., 1974. CPA, Calif.; cert. real estate broker, Calif.; cert. ins. agt., Calif.; lic. contractor, Calif. Sr. v.p., CEO, dir. Lewis Homes Mgmt. Corp., Upland, Calif. Office: Lewis Operating Corp PO Box 670 Upland CA 91785-0670

GOODMAN, JORDAN ELLIOT, journalist; b. N.Y.C., Sept. 13, 1954; s. Elliot Raymond and Norma (Bromberg) G.; m. Suzanne Kay Koblentz, June 20, 1981; 1 child, Jason Koblentz. Student, London Sch. Econ., 1974-75; BA, Amherst Coll., 1976; MA, Columbia U., 1977. Editor in chief Info Mag., N.Y.C., 1977-79; sr. reporter Money Mag., N.Y.C., 1979-92, Wall St. corr., 1992-97. Commentator Fin. News Network, N.Y.C., 1985—91, Mut. Broadcasting Sys., Washington, 1988—97, Marketplace Pub. Radio Internat., 1988—, Cable News Network, N.Y.C., 1989—90; regional dir. Soc. Profl. Journalists, Chgo., 1989—90; columnist onmoney.com, 2000—02, Moneyanswers.com, 2000—. Author: Dictionary of Finance and Investment Terms, 1986; : 6th edit., 2003, Barron's Finance and Investment Handbook, 1987, rev., 1991; : 6th edit., 2003, Dictionary of Business Terms, 1989, 1998, Everyone's Money Book series, 1993, rev. edit., 1997, 3rd edit., 2001, Reading Between the Lies, 2003, Everyone's Money Book, 2002. Mem. Common Cause, N.Y.C., 1985—. Mem. Mid-Atlantic Club, N.Y.C. Fin. Writers Assn., N.Y. Deadline Club (pres. 1986-87). Democrat. Jewish. Avocation: sailing. Home and Office: 84 Walworth Ave Scarsdale NY 10583-1139 E-mail: jordan.goodman@verizon.net.

GOODMAN, JOSEPH WILFRED, electrical engineering educator; b. Boston, Feb. 8, 1936; s. Joseph and Doris (Ryan) G.; m. Hon Mai Lam, Dec. 5, 1962; 1 dau., Michele Ann. BA, Harvard U., 1958, MS in E.E., Stanford U., 1960, PhD, 1963; DSc (hon.), U. Ala., 1996. Postdoctoral fellow Norwegian Def. Rsch. Establishment, Oslo, 1962-63; rsch. assoc. Stanford U., 1963-67, asst. prof., 1967-69, assoc. prof., 1969-72, prof. elec. engring., 1972-99; vis. prof. Univ. Paris XI, Orsay, France, 1973-74; dir. Info. Sys. Lab. Elec. Engring. Stanford U., 1981-83, chmn. dept. of elec. engring., 1988-96, William E. Ayer prof. elec. engring., 1988-99, sr. assoc. dean engring., 1996-98, acting dean engring., 1999, prof. emeritus, 2000—. Cons. to govt. and industry, 1965—; v.p. Internat. Comm. for Optics, 1985-87, pres., 1988-90, past pres., 1991-93. Author: Introduction to Fourier Optics, 1968, 2nd edit. 1996, Statistical Optics, 1985, (with R. Gray) Fourier Transforms: An Introduction for Engineers; editor: International Trends in Optics, 1991; contbr. articles to profl. jours. Recipient F.E. Terman award Am. Soc. Engring. Edn., 1971, Frederic Ives Medal, 1990, Optical Soc. Am., Ester Hoffman Beller award Optical Soc. of Am., 1995. Fellow AAAS, Optical Soc. Am. (dir. 1977-83, editor jour. 1978-83, Max Born award 1983, Frederick Ives award 1990, Esther Hoffman Beller medal 1995, v.p. 1990, pres.-elect 1991, pres. 1992, past pres. 1993), IEEE (edn. medal 1987), Soc. Photo-optical Instrumentation Engrs. (bd. govs. 1979-82, 88-90, Dennis Gabor award 1987), Am. Acad. Arts & Scis.; mem. NAE, Electromagnetics Acad. Home: 570 University Ter Los Altos CA 94022-3523 Office: Stanford U Dept Elec Engring Stanford CA 94305 E-mail: goodman@ee.stanford.edu.

GOODMAN, KAREN LACERTE, financial services executive; b. Mesa, Ariz., Nov. 9, 1946; d. Howard Lee and Margaret (Duncan) G.; m. Grant A. Lacerte, Feb. 1, 1964; children: Arthur Grant Jr., Arcel Leon Rene. Student, George Washington U., 1974-76. Prodn. mgr. Data Corp. of Am., Reston, Va., 1967-73; pres. Transco Leasing Co., Washington, 1974-78; sec., treas. to v.p. Certa Data Corp., Orlando, Fla., 1989—; pres. Fin. Rsch. Assocs., Inc., Orlando, 1979—. Cons. in field, 1979—; dir. statis. seminars in field. Editor, pub.: Financial Studies of the Small Business (annual publ.), 1976—. Mem. Am. Heart Assn., Winter Haven, Fla., MADD, 1985—. Mem. Greater Orlando C. of C. Republican. Home: 6759 Winterset Gardens Rd Winter Haven FL 33884-3154 Office: 203 Ave A NW Ste 202 Winter Haven FL 33881-4503

GOODMAN, KENNETH ALAN, secondary school educator; b. Ill., Mar. 20, 1971; BS, U. Ill., 1993; MusM, La. State U., 1999. Cert. tchr. Ill., 1993. Educator Roxana H.S., Ill., 1993—97, Sycamore H.S., 1999—. Trustee Wheaton Mcpl. Band, Ill. Mem.: NEA, Internat. Clarinet Assn., Music Educators Nat. Conf. Avocations: reading, travel, tennis, bicycling, swimming. Home: 1121 Golf Ct DeKalb IL 60115 Office: Sycamore High Sch Spartan Trail Sycamore IL 60178

GOODMAN, KENNETH JOEL, radiologist; b. N.Y.C., Oct. 3, 1946; s. Herman and Mina G.; m. Kathleen Christine Frappaolo, June 23, 1974; children: Eric, Laura. BA, CUNY, 1967; MD, U. Tex., San Antonio, 1972. Diplomate Am. Bd. Radiology. Intern in internal medicine Cornell Cooperating Hosp., N.Y.C., 1972-73, resident in internal medicine, 1973-74; resident in diagnostic radiology N.Y. Hosp.-Cornell U., N.Y.C., 1974-77, fellow in computered tomography and ultrasound, 1977-78; assoc. prof. radiology, chief divsn. diagnostic radiology SUNY, Stony Brook, 1979-87; dir. dept. radiology St. Francis Hosp., Roslyn, N.Y., 1988—. Pres. Physicians Diagnostic Imaging, Roslyn, 1988—. Contbr. over 15 articles to med. jours.; manuscript reviewer Radiology, 1985. Bd. dirs. Pt. Washington Staff Orgn., 1988—; trustee Village of Matinecock, N.Y., 1998—, dep. mayor, 1998—. Fellow Am. Coll. Radiology (councilor 2000); mem. N.Y. State Radiol. Soc. (del. 1996—). Avocations: scuba diving, skiing, mountaineering, photography, cycling. Office: Phys Diag Imaging PC 100 Port Washington Blvd Roslyn NY 11576-1353

GOODMAN, LEWIS ELTON, JR., lawyer; b. Lynchburg, Va., Jan. 27, 1936; s. Lewis Elton and Mary (Oliver) G.; m. Elizabeth Shumaker, July 10, 1960; children: William L., Lee E. JD, U. Richmond, 1973. Bar: Va. 1973, U.S. Dist. Ct. (we. dist.) Va. 1973, U.S. Ct. Appeals (4th cir.) 1979, U.S. Supreme Ct. 1986. Pvt. practice, Danville, Va., 1973—. Office: 520 Piney Forest Rd Danville VA 24540-3352

GOODMAN, LINDSEY ALAN, furniture manufacturing executive, architect; b. LA, Nov. 17, 1957; s. Ira and Wilma Carolyn (Sanders) G.; m. Joan Frances Radditz, July 7, 1990; children: Alexandra Isabelle, Andrew Nicholas. BA, UCLA, 1980; MArch, Calif. State Poly. U., Pomona, 1983. Registered architect. Project designer Bertram Berenson, Architect, Claremont, Calif., 1983; job capt. Architecture & Planning, San Rafael, Calif., 1985-86, Barry Archtl. Design Group, Santa Barbara, Calif., 1986-87; project architect Architects West, Santa Barbara, 1987-89; prin. L.A. Goodman, Architect, Santa Barbara, 1989-91; v.p. Homtomi Am., Inc. (formerly IWI/Internat.), Chino, Calif., 1992—2000, pres., 2000—, also bd. dirs. Bd. dirs. Homtomi Holdings, Inc.; ptnr. IWI/Capital Devel., Chino, 1991 ; bd. advisors Human Race, Inc., Santa Barbara, 1997-98. Author: (poem) The Camargue, 1987. Adv. coun. Santa Barbara Mus. Natural History, 1988-89, 95-96, trustee, 1989-95, v.p. bd. trustees, 96-98, pres., 1998-2001; patron Santa Barbara Civic Light Opera, 1992-2000. Recipient Richard J. Neutra Meml. award, 1983, . Mem.: NRCC Bus. Adv. Coun. (hon. chmn. 2003—), AIA, Young Pres.'s Orgn. Avocations: tennis, international travel, reading, attending musicals and plays. Office: Homtomi Am Inc 15044 La Palma Dr Chino CA 91710-9669

GOODMAN, LOUIS ALLAN, lawyer; b. Providence, Nov. 13, 1943; s. Jacob and Frieda (Feldman) G.; m. Phebe Silver, June 9, 1968; children: Jonathan J., Rebecca A. AB, Columbia U., 1965; MA, Harvard U., 1966, JD, 1969. Bar: N.Y. 1970, Mass. 1973. Assoc. Skadden, Arps, Slate, Meagher & Flom LLP, 1970—77, ptnr., 1978—. Home: 59 North St Newton MA 02460-1065 Office: Skadden, Arps, Slate, Meagher & Flom LLP 1 Beacon St Boston MA 02108-3107

GOODMAN, MARK, journalist, educator; B in Journalism with honors, U. Mo., 1982; JD, Duke U., 1985. Lectr. U. Md. Univ. Coll., College Park, 1987-88; exec. dir. Student Press Law Ctr., Washington, 1985—. Mem. faculty Inst. Study Ednl. Policy, U. Wash., Seattle, 1987; instr. summer journalism workshops Ball State U., Muncie, Ind., 1988, U. Iowa, Iowa City, 1991, 92, 93, 94, Mich. State U., East Lansing, 1991, 93; adj. guest lectr. Sch. Mass Comm., Bowling Green (Ohio) State U., 1990; mem. faculty coll. newspaper advisers seminar Poynter Inst. Media Studies, St. Petersburg, Fla., 1989, 90, 92; media law com. Coll. Media Advisers, Inc.; panelist Danforth Found., 1988, 89, Assn. Edn. in Journalism and Mass Comm., 1987, 88; guest lectr. Sch. Comm. Am. U., Washington, 1989, 90, 94. Contbr. articles to profl. jours. Recipient Golden Quill award Garden State Scholastic Press Assn., 1987, Disting. Svc. award Mich. Interscholastic Press Assn., 1987, Ind. Scholastic Journalism award Ball State U., 1988, Disting. Svc. award So. Interscholastic Press Assn., 1988, Presdl. citations Coll. Media Advisers, Inc., 1987, 88, 89, Disting. Svc. award Fla. C.C. Press Assn., 1989, Knight award, Earl English Scholastic Journalism award Mo. Interscholastic Press Assn./Mo. Journalism Edn. Assn., 1992, Cert. of Merit, Soc. Collegiate Journalists, 1989, Gold Key award Columbia U. Scholastic Press Assn., 1988, Carl Towley award Journalism Edn. Assn., 1992. Mem. Kappa Tau Alpha. Office: Student Press Law Ctr 1815 Fort Myer Dr Ste 900 Arlington VA 22209-1817 E-mail: director@splc.org.

GOODMAN, MARK N. lawyer; BA, Prescott Coll., 1973; JD summa cum laude, Calif. Western Sch. Law, 1977; LLM, U. Calif., Berkeley, 1978. Bar: Ariz. 1977, U.S. Dist. Ct. Ariz. 1978, U.S. Ct. Appeals (9th cir.) 1978, U.S. Supreme Ct. 1981. Practice Law Offices Mark N. Goodman, Prescott, Ariz., 1978-79, 81-82, Mark N. Goodman, Ltd., Prescott, 1983—88; ptnr. Alward and Goodman, Ltd., Prescott, 1979-81, Goodman Law Firm, P.C., Prescott, 1988—. Author: The Ninth Amendment, 1981; contbr. articles to profl. jours.; notes and comments editor Calif. Western Law Rev., 1976. Bd. dirs. Yavapai Symphony Assn., Prescott, 1981 84, N. Ariz. chpt. Alzheimer's Assn., 1995-97. Mem.: ATLA, ABA, Nat. Acad. Elder Law Attys., Yavapai County Bar Assn. (v.p. 1981—82), State Bar Ariz. (vice chmn. fee arbitration com. 1988—2002), Def. Rsch. Inst. Office: Goodman Law Firm PC PO Box 2489 Prescott AZ 86302-2489 E-mail: info@goodmanlaw.com.

GOODMAN, MARK PAUL, physician; b. N.Y.C., Mar. 6, 1967; s. Leonard Carl and Alice Belle (Barnum) G. BS in Biology cum laude, UCLA, 1989, MD, 1993. Diplomate Am. Bd. Internal Medicine. Resident physician UCLA Med. Ctr., 1993-96, internist, 1996—. Mem. risk mgmt. com., ethics com. UCLA Med. Ctr.; mem. morbidity and mortality com. UCLA Dept. Medicine. Author: The Physician in Sherlock Holmes: The Anatomy of a Legend, 1993 (Donald O'Malley award in med. history). Founder, 1st pres. UCLA Regents Scholar Soc., 1989, U. Calif. Regents scholar, U. Calif. Alumni scholar, L.A. County Med. Assn. scholar. Mem. AMA (nat. patient safety found., western steering com.), ACP, Los Angeles County Med. Assn., UCLA Med. Alumni Assn., Golden Key Honor Soc., Phi Eta Sigma. Avocations: nature, photography, music and the arts, travel, marine fish, skiing. Office: 435 N Roxbury Dr Ste 300 Beverly Hills CA 90210-5005

GOODMAN, MAX A. lawyer, educator; b. Chgo., May 24, 1924; s. Sam and Nettie (Abramowitz) G.; m. Marlyene Monkarsh, June 2, 1946; children: Jan M., Lauren A. Packard, Melanie Murez. AA, Herzl Jr. Coll., 1943; student, Northwestern U., 1946-47; JD, Loyola U., 1948; LLD (hon.), Southwestern U. Sch. Law, 2000. Bar: Calif. 1948; cert. family law specialist, 1980, 85, 90. Pvt. practice, L.A., 1948-53; ptnr. Goodman, Hirschberg & King, L.A., 1953-81; prof. Southwestern U. Sch. Law, L.A., 1966—. Lectr. Calif. Continuing Edn. of the Bar, 1971—90. Contbr. articles to profl. jours. Served to cpl. U.S. Army, 1943-45. Mem. ABA (chmn. law sch. curriculum com. family law sect. 1987-88, family law sect. 1987-88, 97-98), State Bar Calif. (del. conf. dels. 1972, 80-87, 91, exec. com. family law sect. 1981-85), Los Angeles County Bar Assn. (chmn. family law sect. 1971-72, editor family law handbook 1974-89). Avocation: contract bridge. Office: Southwestern U Sch Law 675 S Westmoreland Ave Los Angeles CA 90005-3905 Business E-Mail: mgoodman@swlaw.edu.

GOODMAN, MICHAEL B(ARRY), communications educator; b. Dallas, July 10, 1949; s. Harold A. and Dora (Einhorn) G.; m. Karen E. Kailenta, June 4, 1977; children: 1 stepchild, Craig Cook, 1 child, John David. BA, U. Tex., 1971; MA, SUNY, Stony Brook, 1972, PhD, 1979. Adj. instr. SUNY, Old Westbury, 1976-79; adj. asst. prof. N.Y. Inst. Tech., N.Y.C., 1976-82, N.Y.U., 1979-81; asst. prof. SUNY, Stony Brook, 1979-81, Northea. U., Boston, 1982-86; prof., dir. MA in Corp. Comm. program Fairleigh Dickinson U., Madison, NJ, 1986—2002; founder, dir. Corp. Comms. Inst., 1999—. Cons. in communications to numerous orgns. in U.S.; conducts seminars and workshops on written communication, 1979—; conf. chmn. Internat. Profl. Communication Conf., Phila., 1993, New Orleans, 1999; lectr. Moscow, 1992, U. Alaska, 1996; founder Ann. Conf. on Corp. Comm., 1988-98. Author: William S. Burroughs: An Annotated Bibliography, 1975, Contemporary Literary Censorship: The Case History of Burroughs Naked Lunch, 1981, Write to the Point: Effective Communication in the Workplace, 1984, William S. Burroughs: A Research Guide, 1990, Corporate Communication: Theory and Practice, 1994, Working in a Global Environment—Understanding, Communicating, and Managing Transnationally, 1995, Corporate Communications for Executives, 1998; contbr. articles and revs. to profl. jours., encys. and lit. mags.; assoc. editor Issues in Corp. Comm., IEEE Transactions on Profl. Comm., 1990-99; editl. bd. mem. N.J. Jour. Comm.; mem. editl. adv. bd. Corp. Comms. An Internat. Jour., 1999—; cons. reader for Coll. English. V.p. Friends Sem. PTA, N.Y.C., 1990-91. Named to Resident Faculty Nat. Faculty Excellence in Teaching English Program, Vassar Coll., 1984. Fellow Royal Soc. Encouragement Arts, Mfrs. & Commerce (London)Soc. Tech. Comm. (assoc.); mem. Profl. Comm. Soc. of IEEE (sr., mem. adminstrv. com., Alfred Goldsmith award 1994), MLA, Nat. Coun. Tchrs. of English, Am. Mgmt. Assn., Assn. for Bus. Comm., Authors Guild, Authors League. Avocations: hiking, skiing, running, cycling. Home: 28 W 38th St Apt 11W New York NY 10018-6287 Office: Fairleigh Dickinson U 285 Madison Ave Madison NJ 07940-1099

GOODMAN, MYRNA MARCIA, school nurse; b. Bklyn., Mar. 5, 1936; d. Louis and Anna R. (Bernowitz) Sheinberg; m. Stanley M. Goodman, June 30, 1957; children: Farrell Jay, Blayne Barrie, Devin Josh, Danica Janine. Diploma, L.I. Coll. Hosp., Bklyn., 1956; B in Elected Studies, Thomas More Coll., 1980; postgrad., Xavier U., 1984-86. Cert. sch. nurse, Ohio. Sch. nurse, supr. health and wellness svcs. L.I. Coll. Hosp., 1956-58; nurse, office mgr. Pediatric Assocs. of Fairfield (Ohio), Inc., 1962-72; nurse Fairfield City Sch. Dist., 1972-89, dir. health svcs., 1989-92, supr. health and wellness svcs., 1992-96, ret., 1996, sch. nurse Kindergarten Ctr., 1995. Sec. Fairfield City Safety Coun., 1987-90; mem. Intervention Team for At-Risk Students, 1987-90, 95-96, Del. to Study Sch. Health, Australia, 1989, Mentor Program at Fairfield West Elem. Sch., 2002-; keynote spkr. Ohio Comprehensive Sch. Health Conf., 1991; conf. spkr. Ohio Assn. Health, Phys. Edn., Recreation and Dance, 1990, Nat. Sch. Bds. Assn., 1993; mem. Butler Behavioral Health Svcs. Bd., 1997-2003, sec.-treas., 2002. Mem. adv. coun. on drug free schs. and cmty. Butler County Mental Health Assn., 1988; mentor Fairfield W. Elem. Sch., 2002; chmn. sch. site com. Am. Heart Assn., 1981—, coord. heart-at-work program, co-pres. Hamilton-Fairfield divsn., 1995, bd. dirs., chmn. employee wellness com., spkr. del. assembly Ohio affiliate, 1992, pres., 1995, mem. adv. com. for county practical nurse program, 1994-95; pres. Fairfield Tempo Club, 1976; com. mem. Fairfield Sister City Program; mem. Modern Music Masters, 1976; mem. adv. coun. Daytime Ctr. for Girls; bd. dirs. Greater Hamilton Safety Coun., 1988; mem. adv. com. Fairfield Pub. Presch.; chmn. adv. com. Fairfield Schs. Food Svc.; co-founder B'nai Tikvah Congregation, 1998, svc. chair, 1999—, mem. ritual and worship com., chair. Recipient Outstanding Svc. award Fairfield Cen. Sch., 1974, 77, 78, 89, Letters of Recognition for Outstanding Svc. to Fairfield Sch. Dist. Supt., 1980, 86, 89, 90, March of Dimes, Am. Lung Assn., 1980, Am. Heart Assn., 1988, 89, 90, Hall of Fame award Am. Heart Assn., 1992, co-recipient Cert. of Appreciation, Am. Heart Assn. Sch. Site Task Force, 1992. Mem. NEA, ASCD, Ohio Edn. Assn., Ohio Assn. Sch. Nurses (conf. speaker 1993), S.W. Ohio Sch. Nurses Assn. (sec. 1987-90), Am. Sch. Health Assn., Nat. Assn. Sch. Nurses, Parents and Tchrs. for Children, Ohio Assn. Secondary Sch. Adminstrs., Nat. Assn. Secondary Sch. Adminstrs., Butler County Ret. Tchrs. Assn., Ohio Ret. Tchrs. Assn. (life). Home: 5180 Suwannee Dr Fairfield OH 45014-2482

GOODMAN, N. JANE, small business owner, legal analyst; b. Monett, Mo., May 9, 1946; d. William F. and Audie L. (Stolle; m. Douglas L. Goodman, May 9, 1969; children: Kelly, Gregory, Kristi, Anthony, Richard. Student, Drury Coll., Springfield, Mo., 1969-70; AA summa cum laude, Crowder Coll., Neosho, Mo., 1997; BS summa cum laude, S.W. Mo. State U., 1999; JD, U. Tulsa, 2003; postgrad., U. Mo., 2003. Lic. real estate salesperson, Mo., notary public. Supr. Family Svcs., Aurora, Mo., 1972-87; exec. sec. Little Tikes Toy Co., Aurora, 1987-90, buyer, 1990-97; owner DJ's Catering, Aurora, 1997—; real estate salesperson Monett Realty, 1997—. Author: South American Travel, 1985. Area rep. Am. Intercultural Student Exch., Aurora, 1989—; treas. for state rep. polit. campaign. Mem. NAFE, Am. Purchasing Soc., Optimist Club (charter pres., lt. gov. Western Mo. dist. 1996—), Phi Theta Kappa, Lambda Pi Eta, Phi Alpha Delta, Golden Key Honor Soc. Avocations: travel, music, foreign languages, studying south american cultures, reading. Home: 519 W College St Aurora MO 65605-2833

GOODMAN, NORMAN, sociologist, researcher; b. NYC, Feb. 19, 1934; s. Jack Goodman and Hannah (Hoffman) Brodsky; m. Marilyn Goldberg, Dec. 26, 1954; children: Jack, Susan, Carolyn. BA, Bklyn. Coll., 1955; MA, NYU, 1961, PhD, 1963. Social investigator N.Y.C. Dept. of Welfare, Bklyn., 1957-58; instr. sociology Columbia U. Tchrs. Coll., N.Y.C., 1961-62; from lectr. to asst. prof. Queens Coll. CUNY, 1962-64; from asst. to assoc. prof. SUNY, Stony Brook, 1964-73, prof., chmn. sociology dept., 1973-89, 2000—, Disting. Teaching prof. sociology, 1986—, Disting. Svc. prof., 1990—. Reviewer proposals NSF, 1975-76, Social Scis. and Humanities Council of Can., 1981-86; reviewer manuscripts numerous pubs., N.Y.C., 1970—. Author: (with others) Personality and Decision Processes, 1962, (with others) Society Today, 3d edit., 1978, 4th edit., 1982; (with other) Marriage, Family and Intimate Relationships, 1980, (with other) Social Roles and Social Institutions, 1991, Introduction to Sociology, 1992, Marriage and the Family, 1993, (with other) Test Yourself in Introduction to Sociology, 1996, (with others) Extending Self-Esteem Theory and Research: Sociological and Psychological Currents, 2001. Served with U.S. Army, 1955-56. Mem. Am. Sociol. Assn., Eastern Sociol. Soc., Soc. for Study of Symbolic Interaction, Nat. Council on Family Relations. Jewish. Avocations: classical and operatic music, sports. Office: SUNY At Stony Brook Dept Sociology Stony Brook NY 11794-4356 E-mail: Norman.Goodman@sunysb.edu.

GOODMAN, NORMAN LOYAL, microbiologist, educator; b. Milburn, Okla., Sept. 29, 1931; s. James Loyal and Jocie Lee (Clemons) G .;m. Markita Marie Staton; children: James, Cathryn. BS, Southeastern State U., Durant, Okla., 1954; MS, U. Okla., 1960, PhD, 1965. Diplomate Am. Bd. Med. Microbiology, Am. Bd. bioanalysis. Microbiologist USPHS, Norman, Okla., 1962-68; asst. prof., dir. bacteriology lba. Med. U. S.C., Charleston, 1968-71; from assoc. prof. to prof. dept. pathology, dir. mycology U. Ky. Coll. Medicine, Lexington, 1971—. Cons. Bur. Lab. Svcs. S.C. Bd. Health, Columbia, 1969-71. Fellow: Am. Acad. Microbiology (bd. govs. 1983—86); mem.: South Ctrl. Assn. Clin. Microbiology (pres. 1992, bd.dirs. 1999—), Internat. Union Microbiol. Socs. (chmn. mycology divsn. 1982—86), Mycol. Soc. Am. (pres. 1982), Am. Soc. Microbiology (chmn. continuing edn. com. 1975—79, chmn. mycology divsn. 1976—77). Home: 2153 Lakeside Dr Lexington KY 40502-3073 Office: U Ky Coll Medicine 800 Rose St Lexington KY 40536-0001 E-mail: Nlgood01@pop.uky.edu.

GOODMAN, OSCAR BAYLIN, mayor, lawyer; b. Phila., July 26, 1939; s. A. Allan and Laura (Baylin) G.; m. Carolyn Goldmark, June 6, 1962; children: Oscar B. Jr., Ross C., Eric A., Cara Lee. BA, Haverford Coll., 1961; JD, U. Pa., 1964. Bar: Nev., U.S. Ct. Appeals. Ptnr. Goodman, Chesnoff and Keach, Las Vegas, 1965—; mayor City of Las Vegas, 1999—. Mem. Nat. Assn. Criminal Def. Lawyers (pres. 1983). Jewish. Office: Off of the Mayor 400 Stewart Ave Las Vegas NV 89101-2927 also: Goodman Chesnoff & Keach 520 S 4th St Las Vegas NV 89101-6524*

GOODMAN, PHYLLIS L. public relations executive; b. N.Y.C., Sept. 7, 1946; d. Bernard Jacob and Claire (Rosenberg) Goodman. BS, Cornell U., 1967. Ext. home economist Nassau County Ext. Svc., Mineola, N.Y., 1967-68; editl. asst. Funk & Wagnalls, N.Y.C., 1968-69; sr. v.p. Glick & Lorwin, Inc., N.Y.C., 1969-80, Sci. and Medicine, N.Y.C., 1980-82; v.p. Hill and Knowlton, Inc., N.Y.C., 1982-85; assoc. v.p. comm. and pub. affairs St. Luke's-Roosevelt Hosp. Ctr., N.Y.C., 1985-92; owner Goodman Pub. Rels., Albuquerque, 1993-95; v.p. corp. comm. Sun Healthcare Group, Inc., Albuquerque, 1995-2000; v.p. mktg. and comms. St. Vincent Hosp., Santa Fe, 2000-01; v.p. mktg. and comm. Cin. Children's Hosp. Med. Ctr., 2001—. Mem. com. pub. affairs Greater N.Y. Hosp. Assn., 1988-92. Bd. dirs. Chamber Music Albuquerque, 1998-2001. Mem. Am. Soc. Health Care Mktg. and Pub. Rels. (treas. N.Mex. chpt. 1993-94), Pub. Rels. Soc. Am. (accredited, pres. N.Mex. chpt. 1996), Healthcare Pub. Rels. and Mktg. Soc. Greater N.Y. (pres. 1990-91), Westside C. of C. N.Y.C. (bd. dirs. 1986-92), Pi Lambda Theta. Office: Cin Childrens Hosp MLC 9102 3333 Burnet Ave Cincinnati OH 45229

GOODMAN, REBECCA GRUVER, education educator, writer; b. St. Joseph, Mo., Nov. 3, 1931; d. Arthur Lester Gruver and Dana Theodore Brooks; m. Phil P. Goodman, June 17, 1972 (dec. June 1986). BA, Stanford U., 1954; MA, U. Calif., Berkeley, 1956, PhD, 1964. Full time lectr./prof. Hunter Coll., CUNY, 1961—73, part time adj. prof., 1973—97. Author: (history) Am. Nationalism 1783-1830, (history textbook) An Am. History, 1972—85, (book chapters) Ency. of U.S. Fgn. Rels., 1997. Mem.: Soc. for Historians of Am. Fgn. Rels., Orgn. of Am. Historians, Am. Hist. Assn. Avocations: baseball, theater.

GOODMAN, RICHARD SHALEM, lawyer, orthopedic surgeon; m. Jemi Horn; children: Lorraine, Carolyn Pianin, Deborah Lieb, Keith London, Evan London. BA, Alfred (N.Y.) U., 1955; MD, N.Y. U., 1960; JD, Touro Coll., 1987. Bar: N.Y. 1991, U.S. Ct. Claims 1995, U.S. Ct. Mil. Appeals 1995, U.S. Ct. Appeals 1995, U.S. Supreme Ct. 1995; lic. physician, N.Y., Calif.; diplomate Am. Bd. Orthopedic Surgery. Intern Ind. U. Med. Ctr., Indianapolis, 1960—61; asst. resident in gen. surgery Bronx Mcpl. Hosp. Ctr., 1961—62; resident in orthopedics N.Y.C. Med. Ctr. and various others, 1964—67; attending physician St. Catherine of Sienna Hosp. (formerly St. John's Episcopal Hosp.), Smithtown, NY, 1967—, pres. med. staff, 1978; attending physician Cmty. Hosp. Suffolk, Smithtown, 1967—96; cons. in orthop. LIJ Hosp., New Hyde Park, NY, 1996—; adjunct staff dept. Orthop. Surgery North Shore U. Med. Ctr., 2001—. Asst. prof. dept. anatomy SUNY, Stony Brook, 1971-88, Stonybrook Found. Pres. Marine Scis. Rsch. Ctr., 1984-87; pres. staff Community Hosp. of We. Suffolk, 1977-78; policy advisor Inst. Advancement Health Care Mgmt., U. Albany, SUNY, 1992—; cons. to numerous bus., govt. agys., and ins. cos.; presenter, speaker, and panelist in fields. Co-author: American Jurisprudence Proof of Facts, 3d series, vol. 2 Pelvic Injuries, 1988, Handling Soft Tissue Injury Cases: Medical Aspects, 1988, 2d edit., 1993, Preparing and Winning Medical Negligence Cases, 1989, 2d edit., 1994, Legal Medicine: Legal Dynamics of Medical Encounters, 2d edit., 1990; contbr. articles to med. and lega. jours., chapters to books; mem. editl. bd.: Orthopedics and Orthopedics Today, 1984—87, Med. Malpractice Prevention, bd. editl. cons.:. Trustee Alfred U., 1978-84; policy adv. Inst. Advancement Health Care Mgmt. U. Albany; nat. chmn. U. Albany Parents Fund, 1991-94; nat. chmn. U. Albany Parent's Fund, 1991-92; active Arthritis Found. Fellow: Am. Coll. Legal Med. (mem. policy and planning com., program chmn. annual meeting 1988—), Am. Acad. Orthoped. Surgeons; mem.: Pitts. Inst. Legal Med., Nat. Health Lawyers Assn., Assn. Bar City N.Y., Suffolk County Bar Assn., N.Y. Bar Assn., Am. Acad. Legal and Industrial Med. (bd. govs.), N.Y. State. Soc. Orthoped. Surgeons, Arthritis Found., PanAm. Med. Assn., Internat. Coll. Surgeons, N.Y. State Med. Soc., Suffolk County Med. Soc., Am. Rheumatism Assn., Am. Coll. Sports Med., Am. Soc. Law and Med., Ea. Orthoped. Assn., Am. Coll. Legal Medicine (chmn. exhibits com. ann. meeting 1989—90, mem. policy and planning com., mem. program com. ann. meeting 1989—90, co-chmn. exhibitor's com. 1993, mem. rsch. com. 1993, mem. com. to confer with com. Med. Soc. State N.Y. 1991—, mem. student awards com. 1993, chmn. computer bull. bd. sys. 1995, assoc. editor Communique and newsbriefs), Bach Aria Group (bd. dirs. 1970—88), NYU Bellevue Alumni Assn., Stony Brook Yacht Club, Mutton Town Golf Club, Univ. Club. Office: 285 E Main St Smithtown NY 11787 also: 70 Glen Cove Rd Roslyn Heights NY 11577 also: 743 Columbia Tpke East Greenbush NY 12061

GOODMAN, ROBERT LEE, nursing administrator; b. Sumter, SC, July 30, 1962; s. Helen Ragin Goodman; m. Deborah Jean Clark, Oct. 16, 1999; children: Janeen Goodman Malloy, Bionca Anne. Cert. nursing asst., Bremerton Tech. Sch., 1989; cert. in med. assistance, Eton Coll., 1999. Cert. med. asst., nursing asst. Nursing asst. Bremerton (Wash.) Convalescent Home, 1989—92, Harrison Meml. Hosp., Bremerton, 1993—95, Port Orchard (Wash.) Convalescent Home, Port Orchard, 1996—98; med. asst. Kitsap Pain Clinic, Bremerton, 1998—99; staff coord. Kindred Health Care Corp., Winston-Salem, NC, 1999—. Author: Born of Rags, 2002. With USN, 1980—85. Scholar, Eton Coll. Found., 1998. Avocations: bowling, singing, song writing, bird breeding, fish breeding.

GOODMAN, ROBERT MERRILL, United Nations executive, artist; b. Caldwell, N.J., Mar. 10, 1925; s. Emery Goodman and Pearl Tennesee (Loveman) Ross; m. Sonia Helene Bjelinki, Sept. 2, 1949; 1 child, Emery D. BA in History cum laude, Rutgers U., 1950; postgrad. in Art, Art Students League, 1950-51; postgrad. in Econs., New Sch., N.Y.C., 1955-56, Columbia U., 1957. Adminstrv. asst. Dept. Tech. Assistance, UN Secretariat, N.Y.C., 1951-61, program officer, tng. projects, 1961-80, chief fellowship and tng. svc., 1980-85, cons. tng. projects for developing countries, 1985—. Pres. UN Art Club, 1969-79. With USN, 1944-46. Recipient 1st prize in watercolor 13th Ann. Art Exhbn. for UNICEF, 1963, 1st prize in painting South Nassau Unitarian Ch., 1966, Appreciation award World Assn. Former UN Internes and Fellows, Inc., 1998. Mem. Natural Resources Def. Coun., So. Poverty Law Ctr., Assn. Former Internat. Civil Servants, Rutgers U. Alumni Assn. Avocations: painting, travel, sailing, handball, philosophy. Home: 13014 229th St Laurelton NY 11413-1837

GOODMAN, ROBERT STANLEY, management educator; s. Irwin Aaron and Virginia Rose Goodman; m. Roberta Lynn Louis, June 28, 1987; children: Shoshana Hannah, Evan Simcha. BS, U. Wis.; MA, U. Iowa; MBA, PHD, U. Minn., 1988. Exec. trainee, asst. cashier, asst. v.p. Nat. Bank Albany Park, Chgo., 1974—78; v.p. Deerbrook State Bank, Deerfield, Ill., 1978—80; v.p., sr. lending officer First Nat. Bank Waukegan, Ill., 1980—82; asst. prof. orgn. and mgmt. Syracuse (N.Y.) U., 1986—89; asst. prof. strategic mgmt. York U., Toronto, Canada, 1988—91; asst. prof. mgmt. U. Wis., Madison, 1991—95; asoc. prof. mgmt. Bentley Coll., Waltham, Mass., 1995—98; assoc. prof. mgmt. Northeastern Ill. U., Chgo., 1998—2000; assoc. prof. strategic mgmt. and internat. bus. Niagara (N.Y.) U., 2000—02; program dir., assoc. prof. bus. adminstrn. divsn. East-West U., Chgo., 2002—. Presenter in field. Co-author: Managing for Global Competitiveness: A Study Guide for BGS 3-004, 1998; editor: International Research in the Business Disciplines, Vol. 4, 2003; contbr. articles to profl. jours. Bd. dirs., mem. exec. com. Hist. Keyboard Soc., Milw., 1994—97. Fellow, U. Minn., Mpls., 1983—84; grantee, U. Minn. Strategic Mgmt. Rsch. Ctr., 1985, 1994, U. Minn. Grad. Sch., 1986, Syracuse U. Senate, 1987, Office Info. and Econ. Rsch., Fed. Home Loan Bank Bd., 1989, Ont. Ctr. for Internat. Bus./The Estonian Bus. Sch., 1990, York U., Toronto, 1991, U. Wis. Sch. Bus., 1992—93, U.S. Dept. Edn., Washington, 1996—99. Mem.: Internat. Assn. for Bus. and Soc. (charter), Strategic Mgmt. Soc., Acad. Mgmt., Internat. Cantorial Found., Univ. Club Chgo., Beta Gamma Sigma. Avocations: swimming, racquetball, reading, travel. Office: East-West Univ 816 S Michigan Ave Chicago IL 60605

GOODMAN, ROGER MARK, television director; b. Chgo., Apr. 28, 1945; s. David and Bette (Goldfinger) G.; m. Sharon Ann Dosh, July 5, 1975; children: Danielle Lynn, Gregory Michael. Student, Tarkio Coll. Prodn. assoc. WBKB, Chgo., 1964-65, ABC Sports, N.Y.C., 1965-68, assoc. dir., 1968-76, dir., 1976-80; dir. prodn. devel. ABC News and Sports, N.Y.C., 1980-85, dir. prodn. and design, 1985-95; sr. dir. ABC News, N.Y.C., 1996—; exec. dir. spl. projects ABC TV Network, N.Y.C., 1992—. Recipient 21 Emmy awards, Silver award Internat. Film and 3 Cine TV Festival, 1982, Gold award Internat. Film and TV Festival, 1983, Desi award, 1983, Creativity award, 1983, 85, Typographic Excellence award, 1984, Gold Baton Alfred I. DuPont Awards, 1985. Office: ABC News 47 W 66th St Fl 6 New York NY 10023-6201

GOODMAN, ROY MATZ, corporate president, chief executive officer, former state senator; b. NYC, Mar. 5, 1930; s. Bernard A. and Alice (Matz) G.; m. Barbara Christine Furrer, June 28, 1955; children: Claire Goodman Pellegrini Cloud, Leslie Alice, Randolph Bernard. BA cum laude, Harvard U., 1951, MBA with distinction, 1953; DHL (hon.), Pratt Inst., 1994; LLD (hon.), Baruch Coll. CUNY, 2002. Assoc. buying and new bus. dept. Kuhn, Loeb & Co. Investment Bankers, 1955-60; pres., dir. Drug Devel. Corp., Ex-Lax, Inc., Roycemore, Inc., 1962-71; mem. N.Y. State Senate, 1969—2002; pres., CEO UN Devel. Corp., N.Y.C., 2002—. Dep. majority leader for policy, chmn. investigations, taxation and govt. ops. com.; chmn. Senate spl. com. on arts and cultural affairs ; mem. Senate task forces on def. spending, AIDS, vandalism, religious desecration and bigotry, and econ. recovery and devel.; fin., rules, cities, edn., crime and correction and transp. coms., subcom. on libraries chmn. legis. com. on pub. pvt., coop., 1985-88; chmn. housing and urban devel. com., 1968-76; pres. Goodman Family Found.; adv. bd. M & T Bank Corp., 2000-, Chemical Bank, 1963-65; commr. fin., fin. adminstr. City of N.Y., 1966-68; mem. N.Y.C. Banking Commn., 1966-68; past trustee N.Y.C. Police Pension Fund, N.Y.C. Fire Dept. Pension Fund, 1966-68; mem. Mayor's Cabinet and Supercabinet, 1966-68, N.Y.C. Treasurer, 1966-68; Chmn. State Charter Revision Commn. for N.Y.C., 1972-76; adj. prof. pub. admin. Baruch Coll. CUNY, 1975; mem. Mayor Guiliani Transition Team, 1993, mem. Gov. Pataki Transition Team, 1994; mem. Bklyn. adv. bd. Chem. Bank N.Y. Trust Co., 1963-65. Bd. dirs. Citizens Com. N.Y.C.; trustee Dalton Schs.; past mem. bd. Brotherhood-In-Action; trustee Heart Rsch. Found.; exec. asst. to chmn. N.Y. State Assembly Jud. Com., 1963-64; asst. to atty. gen. State N.Y., 1960; pres. 9th A.D. Rep. Club, 1963-64; del. N.Y. State Rep. Convs., 1966-20024, del. Rep. Nat. Conv., 1968, 72, 76, 80, 84, 88, 92. 96, Presdl. Elector, 1984; chmn. N.Y. County Rep. Com., 1981-2002, treas., 1965; mem. N.Y. Rep. State Com., exec. com.; N.Y. State co-chmn. Bush-for-Pres. campaigns, 1988, 92, Bush-Quayle Nat. Fin. Com., 1988, 92; candidate for Mayor of N.Y.C., 1977; trustee Carnegie Hall Soc., Inc., Carnegie Hall Corp., past trustee Columbia Coll. Pharm. Scis., L.I. Coll. Hosp., N.Y. Com. Young Audiences, United Jewish Appeal, Tel Aviv U., Freedom House, Dalton Schs. Brotherhood-In-Action, Heart Rsch. Found.; presdl. appointee to Nat. Commn. Fine Arts, 1985-89, Nat. Endowment Arts Coun., 1989-96, trustee John F. Kennedy Ctr. for Performing Arts, 2002-; amb. arts NEA, 2000; fellow Met. Mus. Art; patron Met. Opera; sponsor N.Y. Philharm. Soc.; mem. Regents vis. com. N.Y. State Mus.; trustee Temple Emanu-El; past bd. dirs. Freedom House, Dalton Sch.; mem. N.Y. Com. for Young Audiences, Harvard Com. on Univ. Resources,; mem. com. Harvard U. Overseers visitors com. John F. Kennedy Sch. Govt.; grad. officer, Candidate Sch., Newport, R.I.; Lt. USNR, 1953-56, recipient Admiral's Meritorious Svc. Citation. Recipient Disting. Service award Jaycees, 1966, Mt. Scopus citation Hebrew U., Jerusalem, 1968, Scroll of Honor United Jewish Appeal, 1970, Kennedy Ctr. award for Disting. Leadership in Arts-in Edn., Nat. Arts Club Citation of Merit, City U., Medal of Merit, 1972, Man of Yr. award Brotherhood-in-Action, 1972, Humanitarian award Soc. for Prevention Cruelty to Children, 1976, citation for cmty. service Odyssey House, 1976, Our Town newspaper award for leadership in City Charter revision, 1976, Fiorello H. LaGuardia Meml. award, 1979-80, citation for outstanding service N.Y. Young Rep. Club, 1982, Disting. Alumni award Hunter Coll. Elem. Sch. Parents Assn., 1985, Service awards N.Y. Police Found. and N.Y. Fire Safety Found., 1986, Patriotic Service award U.S. Treasury Dept., N.Y. Governor's Arts Medal, 2002, Sutton Area Cmty. Svc. Award, 2002, WNYC Radio Arts Award, 2002, U.N. Delegations' Citizen of the World Award, 2002, Alliance of N.Y. Arts Org. Arts Advocate Award, 2002, City Club of N.Y. Disting. New Yorker Award, 2002, Internat. Coun. for Caring Communities Caring Citizen of the Humanities Award, 2003; named to honor scroll Columbia Assn. of N.Y.C. Police Dept., 1979, N.Y. State Rep. of Yr. Ripon Soc., 1972, Cmty. Activist award Lenox Hill Neighorhood Assn., Inc., 1995, Artists fellowship award, John LaFarge Meml. award for interracial justice, Local Hero award Stanley Isaacs Assn., Playwrights Horizon award, 1995, Gari Melchers Meml. medal, 1995, South Street Seaport Mus. award, 1995, Friend of the Arts award Town Hall Found., 1995, Legacy of Hope award N.Y. Foundling Home, Carnegie Hall, 1996, Margaret Sanger award Family Advs. N.Y., 1997; Statesman Father of Yr. award, 1984, named to Econ. Hon. Soc. St. John's U., 1991. Mem. Anti-Defamation League (bd. govs. N.Y.), Am. Young Pres.'s Orgn., Fin. Analysts Fedn., N.Y. Soc. Security Analysts, Council Fgn. Relations, Assn. Harvard Alumni (past dir.), Harvard Club (gov.), Century Assn., Century Country Club, Dutch Treat Club, Senate Club (pres.), Harvard Bus. Sch., City Club, Omicron Delta Epsilon (hon.). Home: 1035 5th Ave New York NY 10028-0135 Office: 2 UN Plaza 27th Fl New York NY 10017

GOODMAN, SAM RICHARD, electronics company executive; b. N.Y.C., May 23, 1930; s. Morris and Virginia (Gross) G.; m. Beatrice Bettencourt, Sept. 15, 1957; children: Mark Stuart, Stephen Manuel, Christopher Bettencourt. BBA, CCNY, 1951; MBA, NYU, 1957, PhD, 1968. Chief acct. John C. Valentine Co., N.Y.C., 1957-60; mgr. budgets and analysis Gen. Foods. Corp., White Plains, N.Y., 1960-63; budget dir. Crowell Collier Pub. Co., N.Y.C., 1963-64; v.p., chief fin. officer Nestle Co., Inc., White Plains, 1964; chief fin. officer Aileen, Inc., N.Y.C., 1973-74, Ampex Corp., 1974-76; exec. v.p. fin. and adminstrn. Baker & Taylor Co. div. W.R. Grace Co., N.Y.C., 1976-79, Magnuson Computer Systems, Inc., San Jose, Calif., 1979-81; v.p., chief fin. officer Datamac Computer Systems, Sunnyvale, Calif., 1981; pres. Nutritional Foods Inc., San Francisco, 1983-84; chmn., chief exec. officer CMX Corp., Santa Clara, Calif., 1984-88; dir., sr. v.p. Masstor Systems Corp., Santa Clara, 1988—; pvt. cons. Atherton, Calif., 1990—; sr. mgmt. cons. Durkee/Sharlit, 1991—; pres. Mayfair Packing Co., 1991—; mng. dir. Quincy Pacific Ptnrs., L.P., 1992—; pres., CEO Mayfair Packing Co., San Jose, Calif., 1991-94; pvt. cons. BMG Assocs., 1994—. Lectr. NYU Inst. Mgmt., 1965-67; asst. prof. mktg. Iona Coll. Grad. Sch. Adminstrn., 1967-69; prof. Golden Gate U., 1974—; prof. fin. and mktg. Pace U. Grad. Sch. Bus. Adminstrn., 1969-79. Author 7 books, including Controller's Handbook; contbr. articles to jours. Lt. (j.g.) USNR, 1951-55. Lt. jg USN, 1951—55. Decorated Korean Occupation Svc. medal Armed Forces Svc., Nat. Def. Svc. medal. Mem. Fin. Execs. Inst., Nat. Assn. Accts., Am. Statis. Assn., Am. Econs. Assn., Planning Execs. Inst., Am. Arbitration Assn., Turnaround Mgmt. Assn. Home and Office: 60 Shearer Dr Atherton CA 94027-3957 E-mail: bgoodman@cbnorcal.com.

GOODMAN, SAMUEL J. lawyer; b. East Chicago, Ind., Nov. 6, 1942; s. Max M. Goodman and Rosetta (Weinberg) Goodman Small; m. Nancy Marx, Oct. 5, 1968; children— Greer, Max. B.A., Purdue U., 1964; J.D., U. Mich., 1967. Bar: Ind. 1967, U.S. Dist. Ct. (no. and so. dists.) Ind. 1967. Assoc., then ptnr. firm Given, Dawson & Cappas, East Chicago, 1967-77; founding ptnr. firm Goldsmith, Goodman, Ball & Van Bokkelen, Highland, Ind., 1977— . Sec. Lake County Jud. Nominating Com., 1973— . Mem. Ind. Bar Assn. (chmn. family law sect. 1983—), Lake County Ind. Bar Assn. (bd. dirs. 1981—). Democrat. Jewish. Home: 6534 Forest Ave Hammond IN 46324-1016 Office: Goodman Ball et al 9013 Indianapolis Blvd Highland IN 46322-2502

GOODMAN, SEYMOUR EVAN, computer science and international studies educator, researcher, consultant; b. Chgo., June 19, 1943; s. Paul S. and Shirley (Young) G.; m. Diane Margot Samuel, Dec. 18, 1966; children: Richard Michael, Steven Neal. BS, Columbia U., 1965, MS, 1966; PhD, Calif. Inst. Tech., 1970. Asst. prof. applied math. U. Va., Charlottesville, 1970-75, assoc. prof. applied math. and computer sci., 1975-81; prof. mgmt. info. sys. U. Ariz., Tucson, 1981—; prof. Sam Nunn Sch. Internat. Affairs Coll. of Computing, Ga. Inst. of Tech., Atlanta, 1999—; co-dir. Ctr. Internat. Strategy Tech. and Policy, 2000—, Ga. Tech. Info. Security Ctr., 2000—. Vis. prof. pub. and internat. affairs, Princeton (N.J.) U., 1977-79, rsch. fellow, 1978-79; vis. scholar U. Chgo., 1979; mem. Mid. Ea. Ctr., 1992—; Carnegie Sci. fellow Ctr. Internat. Security and Arms Control, Stanford U., 1994-97; dir. program info. tech. and nat. security, 1996-98, dir. Consortium for Rsch. on Info. Security and Policy, Stanford U., 1998—, vis. prof. dept. engring. econ. sys. and ops. rsch., 1998-99; mem. adv. com. Internat. Trade Adminstrn., Dept. Commerce, 1979-82; mem. adv. com. Def. Sci. Bd., Dept. Def., 1981-84, Def. Intelligence Agy., 1983-87, NRC coms., 1985-92, Dept. State, 1987-89; chmn. NRC com. Internat. Devel. in Computer Sci. and Tech., 1987-88; chmn. computer tech.-subpanel NRC panel on Future Design and Implementation of U.S. Nat. Security Export Controls, 1989-91; cons. govtl. agys. Danforth Assoc., 1977-82; Sesquicentennial Assoc. State of Va., 1977. Editor: Technology and Transnational Political Issues, International Information Systems, 1991-93; adv. bd. PRIISM, 1995-97; adv. editor Jour. Global Info. Tech. Mgmt., 1997—; contbr. numerous articles to profl. jours. NSF grantee, 1978-79, 83, 2001-; numerous grant and rsch. contracts Office Tech. Assessment, U.S. Congress, MacArthur Found., 1979-81,

Los Alamos Nat. Lab., USAF, Battelle Meml. Labs., IBM, Nat. Coun. for Soviet and East European Rsch., Dept. Commerce, Dept. Def.; U.S. participant U.S.-USSR IREX program, 1988-96. Mem. Assn. for Computing Machinery (nat. lectr. 1981-82, com. computing and pub. policy 1981-83, 93—, contbg. editor Internat. Perspectives, Comms. 1991—), Am. Assn. for Advancement of Slavic Studies, Computer Soc. of IEEE (com. on pub. policy 1987-95), Highlands Forum. Office: Sam Nunn Sch Internat Affairs Coll Computing Ga Inst Tech 781 Marietta Ave NW Atlanta GA 30332-0610 E-mail: goodman@cc.gatech.edu.

GOODMAN, SHERRI WASSERMAN, lawyer; b. N.Y.C., Apr. 9, 1959; m. John B. Goodman, Aug. 8, 1987. BA, Amherst (Mass.) Coll., 1981; JD, MPP, Harvard U., 1987. Bar: Mass. 1988, D.C. 1990. Analyst Sci. Applications, Inc., McLean, Va., 1981-83; counsel Senate Armed Svcs. Com., Washington, 1987-90, assoc. Goodwin, Procter & Hoar, Boston, 1990-93, dep. under sec. for env. security Dept. Def., Washington, 1993-2000; sr. fellow Ctr. for Naval Analyses, Alexandria, Va., 2001—. Cons. Def. Nuclear Facilities Safety Bd., Washington, 1990-92. Author: The Neutron Bomb Controversy, 1983, Weapons Acquisition, 1988; contbr. articles to profl. jours. Mem. Coun. on Fgn. Rels. Office: The CNA Corp 4825 Mark Center Dr Alexandria VA 22311

GOODMAN, STANLEY, lawyer; b. Cin., June 16, 1931; s. Sol and Ethel (Barsman) G.; m. Diane Elaine Kassel, Apr. 15, 1956; children: Julie Lerner, Jeffrey Stephen, Richard Paul. BA, U. Cin., 1953, JD, 1955. Bar: Ohio 1955, Ky. 1976. Ptnr. Goodman & Goodman, Cin., 1955—. Dir. Winbco Tank Co., Ottumwa, Iowa; lectr. Ohio Bar Continuing Legal Edn. Series. Mem. ABA, Am. Health Lawyers Assn., Ohio State Bar Assn. (chair eminent domain com. 1997-2000), Ky. Bar Assn., Cin. Bar Assn., Bankers Club, Ridge Club. Jewish. Office: 123 E 4th St Cincinnati OH 45202-4003 E-mail: sgoodman@goodlaw.com.

GOODMAN, STANLEY LEONARD, advertising executive; b. N.Y.C., Jan. 21, 1920; s. Abraham and Leah (Fellman) G.; m. Anita Davis, Aug. 30, 1960; children— Patricia, Laurence; stepchildren— Marilyn Rice, Stuart Rice. BS in Econs, Wharton Sch. U. Pa., 1941; certificate electronics, U. Richmond, 1943. Asst. to pres. Decca Records, Inc., N.Y.C., 1941-56; v.p., mktg. dir. Grayson Robinson Stores, N.Y.C., 1956-61; club plan creative dir. Popular Mdse. Co., Inc., Passaic, N.J., 1961-62, dir. mktg., 1962-64; pres. Elliot, Goodman & Russell, Inc., advt., N.Y.C., 1964, EGR Travel Promotion, Inc., N.Y.C., 1969-80, EGR Mktg., Inc., N.Y.C., 1968-80, EGR Communications, Inc., Detroit, 1969-80; chmn. Consol. Tech. Industries, Northvale, N.J., 1987—. Pres., dir. EGR Communications, Inc., N.Y.C., 1968— ; dir. Pub. Service Mut. Ins. Co., N.Y.C.; Lectr. Am. Mgmt. Assn., 1964-82; instr. mktg. dept. Pace Coll.; chmn. Consolidated Tech. Industries, Inc., 1988—. Contbr. articles to sales mags. Bd. trustees Westchester Philharmonic Orch., 1996—, Union Am. Hebrew Congs., 1996—. Mem. Sales Promotion Execs. Assn. (Sales Promotion Man of Year N.Y. 1959), internat. pres. 1960-62, honored Stanley Goodman grant 1954—), Direct Mail Advt. Assn., Council Sales Promotion Agys. (pres. 1969-71), Am. Mktg. Assn., Hundred Million Club, Westchester Alumni Assn. U. Pa. (v.p. 1966—) Home: 46 Crosshill Rd Hartsdale NY 10530-3013

GOODMAN, STEPHEN MURRY, lawyer; b. Phila., Oct. 8, 1940; s. Edward and Jean (Landau) G.; m. Janis Freeman, Jan. 8, 1983; children: Carl, Rachel. BS cum laude, U. Pa., 1962, LLB magna cum laude, 1965. Bar: D.C. 1967, Pa. 1969. Law clerk to Hon. David Bazelon U.S. Ct. Appeals (D.C. cir.), Washington, 1965-66; law clk. to Hon. William J. Brennan Jr. U.S. Supreme Ct., Washington, 1966-67; ptnr. Goodman & Ewing, Phila., 1970-83, Wolf, Block, Schorr & Solis-Cohen, Phila., 1983-94, Morgan, Lewis & Bockius LLP. Mem. Order of Coif. Democrat. Jewish. Avocation: profl. jazz pianist. Office: Morgan Lewis & Bockius LLP 1701 Market St Philadelphia PA 19103-2903

GOODMAN, SYLVIA KLUMOK, volunteer; b. Moorhead, Miss., June 19, 1940; d. Sol Harry and Fannie Ida (Davidson) Klumok; m. Carl Gerald Goodman, June 5, 1960; children: Lisa Wynne Goodman Stone, Gary Steven, Jeffrey David. BS in Zoology with honors, Newcomb Coll., 1962; M in Zoology, Tulane U., 1963; postgrad., Harvard U., summer 1990. Tchr. Midway Jr. H.S., Shreveport, La., 1963-68; instr. biology La. State U., Shreveport, 1967-68; instr. physiology, asst. coord. plans La. State U. Med. Ctr., Shreveport, 1970-74. Chmn. bd. dirs. Goldring Woldenberg Inst. So. Jewish Life, 2000—. Mem. Shreveport Mayor's Women's Commn., 1986-90, C. of C. 100 Women of the Century; vice-chair La. State Mineral Bd., Baton Rouge, 1988-92; chmn. Food Project, Shreveport, 1990-92; chair beautification com. Shreveport Regional Airport, 1990-94, So. Jewish Inst., 2000—; chmn. bd. dirs. Goldring/Woldenberg Inst. So. Jewish Life, 2000—; bd. dirs. Sci-Port Discovery Ctr., Shreveport, 1990—, pres., 1993-95; bd. dirs. La. Endowment Humanities, 1996-99; pres. Shreveport Jewish Fedn., 1982-83; trustee Shreveport-Bossier Cmty. Found., chmn., 1993—; bd. dirs. Meadows Art Mus., 1991-97, vice chmn., 1995; bd. dirs. Red River Film Soc., 2003—, chair capital campaign, 2003; chancellor's adv. com. LSU-S, 1996—. Recipient Humanitarian award NCCJ, Humanitarian award Caddo Commn., 1991, Vol. Fundraiser award Nat. Fedn. Fundraising Execs., 1996, Angel award Blue Cross Blue Shield, 1998, award Point of Light Found., 1999, Friend of Edn. aard Caddo Assn. Educators, 2001; named Women Who Made a Difference Shreveport Celebration of Women Week, 1996, Best-Dressed Woman of No. La. Shreveport Times, 1998. Mem. Jr. League Shreveport (Sustainer of Yr. award 1995, Daily Point of Light 1999), Mensa, Phi Beta Kappa, Alpha Epsilon Phi. Jewish. Avocations: theater, piano, dance, taking courses, movies. Home: 409 Southfield Rd Shreveport LA 71106-2213 E-mail: gigigood@aol.com.

GOODMAN, WILLIAM BEEHLER, editor, literary agent; b. Bklyn., July 1, 1923; s. Philip Howard and Anne Louise (Landersman) G.; m. Lorraine Rappaport, Nov. 24, 1948; children: Jonas Robert, Sara Emily. BA, Washington Sq. Coll., NYU, 1948; MA, U. Mich., 1952. Editor coll. and trade Harcourt Brace Jovanovich Inc., N.Y.C., 1956-76; gen. editor Harvard Univ. Press, Cambridge, Mass., 1976-79; editorial dir. David R. Godine Pub., Inc., Boston, 1979-90, editor, lit. agt., 1990—. Tutor history and lit. Harvard U., 1953-54, lectr. in English, 1982-83, 84-85. Contbr.: essay Reading in the 1980's, 1983. Trustee Warner Library, Tarrytown, N.Y., 1973-75. Served with U.S. Army, 1943-44. Mem.: Harvard (N.Y.C.). Home: 26 Pickman Dr Bedford MA 01730-1005 E-mail: goodbill@comcast.net.

GOODMAN, WILLIAM CHARLES, economist, playwright; b. Washington, Aug. 11, 1953; s. Stanley and Elsie (Hoexter) Goodman; m. Barbara Gale Cohn, Apr. 20, 1997. BA, Ohio Wesleyan U., 1975. Social sci. rsch. analyst Bur. of Labor Stats., U.S. Dept. of Labor, Washington, 1975—. Playwright and prodr.: RE-SUR-REK; also one-act plays; contbr. articles to profl. pubs. Crisis hotline vol. The Help Ctr., College Park, Md., 1976—78. Achievements include design of multi-faceted automated method of checking survey responses for errors. Avocations: woodworking, tropical fishkeeping. Office: Bureau of Labor Statistics 2 Massachusetts Ave NE Ste 4860 Washington DC 20212 Office Fax: 202-691-6644. E-mail: goodman_w@bls.gov.

GOODMAN, WILLIAM FLOURNOY, III, lawyer; b. Aberdeen Miss., June 8, 1952; s. William Flournoy, Jr. and Edwina (McDuffie) G.; m. Tommie E. Goodman, July 19, 1992; children: William F. IV, Nancy Elizabeth. BA cum laude, Millsaps Coll., 1974; JD, U. Miss., 1977. Bar: Miss. 1977, U.S. Dist Ct. (so. and no. dists.) Miss. 1977, U.S. Ct. Appeals (5th cir.) 1977, U.S. Ct. Appeals (11th cir.) 1981. Assoc. Watkins & Eager PLLC, Jackson, Miss., 1977-81; ptnr., 1982—. Mem. ABA, Hinds County Bar Assn., Miss. Bar Assn., Miss. Def. Lawyers Assn., Def. Rsch. Inst., Internat. Assn. Def. Counsel, Omicron Delta Kappa. Methodist. Home: 1256 Belvoir Pl Jackson MS 39202-1205 Office: Watkins & Eager PO Box 650 Jackson MS 39205-0650

GOODMAN, WILLIAM RICHARD, insurance adjusting company executive; b. Staunton, Va., Sept. 19, 1930; s. Harry and Ruth (Meyer) G.; m. Alice Helene Katzenstein, June 13, 1954; children: Harvey, Laurie, Barry. BS, U. Md., 1952; JD, U. Balt., 1955. Cert. fellow profl. pub. adjuster, sr. profl. pub. adjuster. Pub. ins. adjuster, lawyer Goodman-Gable-Gould Co., Balt., 1952-73, v.p., 1973-85, pres., 1985-97, CEO, 1985—, chmn. bd., 1989—. Chmn. Baltimore County Indsl. Devel. Commn., 1967-69; mem. Met. Transit Authority, Balt., 1969-71, bd. rev. Dept. Transp., Md., 1971-76, Md. Racing Commn., 1984. Mem. Nat. Assn. Pub. Ins. Adjusters (dir., v.p., pres., chmn. bd. dirs., Disting. Svc. award 1987, Man of Yr. 1995, fellow in profession of pub. adjusting), B'nai B'rith (v.p. Menorah Lodge 1992-94, pres. 1996-98). Democrat. Jewish. Avocation: collecting toy trains and antique cars. Home: 7811 Park Heights Ave Baltimore MD 21208-4322 Office: Goodman-Gable-Gould Co Adjusters Internat 6 Reservoir Cir Ste 202 Baltimore MD 21208-7310

GOODNER, NORMAN WESLEY, governmental relations specialist; b. Fort Smith, Ark., Apr. 16, 1969; s. Charles E. and Sharron A. (Langston) G. BS in Pub. Adminstrn., U. Ark., 1990, student, 1991-92. Govt. rels. Auditor of State's Office, Little Rock, 1992—. Mem. Ark. State Dem. Com., 2002—. Bd. dirs. Scott County Friends of Libr., Waldron, Ark., 1988; asst. coord. Little Rock Town Hall Meeting On Africa, 1997; constituent liaison Ark. Senate Adv. Com., Waldron, 1983—; vol. Victims Svcs. Program, 2001. Recipient Capitol citation Ark. Sec. of State, 1986. Democrat. Methodist. Avocations: hiking, reading. Home: 2501 Riverfront Dr Apt A108 Little Rock AR 72202-1772 Office: Auditor States Office State Capitol Bldg Rm230 Little Rock AR 72201-1088

GOODNEY, PHILIP PAUL, surgeon, researcher; b. Worcester, Mass., Aug. 6, 1973; m. Amy Carfora, Jan. 29, 1973; 1 child, Eric James. Med. degree, U. of Conn., 1999. Lic. physician N.H. Resident in gen. surgery Dartmouth-Hitchcock Med. Ctr., Lebanon, NH, 1999—.

GOODNICK, PAUL JOEL, psychiatrist; b. Phila., Sept. 29, 1950; BA magna cum laude, U. Pa.; MD with honors, SUNY Downstate Med. Ctr., Bklyn. Diplomate Am. Bd. Psychiatry and Neurology. Resident Washington U., St. Louis, Columbia U., N.Y.C.; fellow Mt. Sinai Hosp., N.Y.C.; asst. prof. psychiatry Wayne State U., Detroit, 1980-81, U. Chgo., 1981-84, Columbia U., N.Y.C., 1984-87, U. Miami, Fla., 1987-89, clin. assoc. prof. psychiatry, 1989-90, assoc. prof., 1990-93, prof., 1993—2002, dir. mood disorders program, dept. psychiatry, 1989—2003; dir. clin. svc. Carrier Clinic, Belle Mead, NJ, 2003—. Dir. outpatient svcs. and affective disorders program Fair Oaks Hosp., Boca/Delray, Fla., 1987-90; cons. APA, 1991. Assoc. editor jour. Lithium, 1989-94; editor: Chronic Fatigue and Related Immune Deficiency Syndromes, 1993, Predictors of Response in Mood Disorders, 1996, Mania, 1998; editor Expert Opinion on Pharmacotherapy, 1999—, Annals of Clinical Psychiatry, 2000—, Expert Opinion on Drug Safety, 2001—, Mem. nat. adv. bd. Jerusalem Health Ctr. Recipient Clin. Excellence award N.Y. Alliance for Mentally Ill, 1987, SUNY Downstate award, 2001. Fellow Am. Psychopathol. Assn., Am. Psychiat. Assn., Internat. Soc. Affective Disorders; mem. AAAS, Soc. Biol. Psychiatry, N.Y. Acad. Sci., Am. Acad. Clin. Psychiatry, KP. Office: Carrier Clinic 252 Rte 601 POB 147 Belle Mead NJ 08550 E-mail: pgoodnick@aol.com.

GOODNIGHT, JAMES H. software company executive; b. Wilmington, N.C., Jan. 6, 1943; PhD in Statistics, N.C. State U., 1971. Faculty N.C. State U., 1972-76; pres. SAS Inst. Inc., Cary, N.C., 1976—. Adj. prof. N.C. State U., 1976—. Fellow Am. Statis. Assn. Office: SAS Inst Inc Attn Miranda Drake-Shaw Corp Commn Dept SAS Campus Dr Cary NC 27513 E-mail: software@sas.com.

GOODNIGHT, JIM, computer company executive; Grad., N.C. State U. Former instr. N.C. State U.; CEO SAS Am., Cary, NC, 1976—. Co-founder Cary Acad., 1996. Office: SAS Inst Inc 100 SAS Campus Dr Cary NC 27513-2414 Office Fax: 919-677-4444.

GOODPASTER, ANDREW JACKSON, retired army officer; b. Granite City, Ill., Feb. 12, 1915; s. Andrew Jackson and Teresa Mary (Mrovka) G.; m. Dorothy Dulaney Anderson, Aug. 28, 1939; children: Susan Dulaney, Anne Morgan. Student, McKendree Coll., 1931-33; BS, U.S. Mil. Acad., 1939; MS in Engring., MA, Princeton U., 1949, PhD in Internat. Rels., 1950. Commd. 2d lt., C.E. U.S. Army, 1939, advanced through grades to gen., 1968; comdg. officer 48th Engr. Combat Bn., World War II; strategic and policy staff duty War Dept. Gen. Staff, 1944-47; mem. Joint Adv. Study Com., 1950; spl. staff asst. SHAPE, 1950-54; dist. engr. C.E., 1954; def. liaison officer and staff sec. to Pres. U.S., 1954-61; asst. div. comdr. 3d Inf. Div., 1961; div. comdr. 8th Inf. Div., 1961-62; asst. to chmn. Joint Chiefs Staff, 1962-66; dir. Joint Staff, 1966-67; dir. spl. studies Office Chief of Staff U.S. Army, 1967; sr. U.S. Army mem. mil. staff com. UN, 1966-68; comdt. Nat. War Coll., 1967-68; mem. U.S. Del. Paris negotiations with N.Vietnam, 1968; dep. comdr. U.S. forces in Vietnam, 1968-69; comdr.-in-chief U.S. forces, Europe, supreme allied comdr., 1969-74; ret., 1974; recalled, 1977-81; supt. U.S. Mil. Acad., 1977-81, ret., 1981; chmn. Am. Battle Monuments Commn., 1985-90; pres. Inst. Def. Analyses, 1983-85, trustee, 1981-89. Sr. fellow security and strategic studies Woodrow Wilson Internat. Ctr. for Scholars, 1975-76; prof. govt. and internat. studies The Citadel, Charleston, S.C., 1976-77; chmn. adv. bd. Eisenhower Inst.; chmn. Atlantic Coun. of U.S., 1985-97; spl. cons. to Vice Pres. U.S., Commn. Orgn. Govt. for Conduct Fgn. Policy, 1975. Author: For the Common Defense, 1977. Chmn. George C. Marshall Found., 1993-2000; mem. numerous adv. groups on strategy, security, internat. affairs, mgmt. and orgn. Decorated U.S. Medal of Freedom, D.S.C., Def. D.S.M. with oak leaf cluster, Army D.S.M. with 3 oak leaf clusters, Navy D.S.M., Air Force D.S.M., Silver Star, Legion of Merit with oak leaf cluster, Purple Heart with oak leaf cluster; numerous fgn. decorations including; Italian Mil. Cross of Valor, Korean Order Mil. Merit, Vietnamese Cross Valor, Grand Cross Mil. Order Aviz Portugal, Grand Cordon Order Leopold Belgium, Grand Cross with Swords Order Orange-Nassau Netherlands, Grand Cross 1st class Order of Merit Fed. Republic Germany, Disting. Service medal Turkish Armed Forces, Disting. Pub. Service award Dept. Def.; recipient James Madison award Princeton U. Fellow Am. Acad. Arts Scis.; mem. Nat. Acad. Pub. Adminstrn., Coun. Fgn. Rels., Soc. Am. Mil. Engrs., Army and Navy Club, Sigma Xi, Phi Kappa Phi. Home: 6200 Oregon Ave NW Apt 345 Washington DC 20015-1542 Office: Eisenhower Inst 915 15th St NW Washington DC 20005 Fax: 202-628-4445.

GOODPASTURE, BRUCE, retired editor, publisher, social sciences educator; b. Roanoke, Va., Jan. 24, 1919; s. Charlie Hopkins and Leola Scott (Simmons) Goodpasture; m. Margaret Doss Black, Sept. 7, 1946; children: Ellen Goodpasture Everett, Emily Goodpasture Roosma. B in Journalism, U. Mo., 1947; MA in History, Georgetown U., 1964. Reporter Bristol (Va.) Herald-Courier, 1947—48; mag. editor Craddock-Ferry Shoe Corp., Lynchburg, Va., 1949—59; pub. Armed Svcs. Tech. Info. Agy., Arlington, Va., 1960—61; editor, pub. U.S. SBA, Washington, 1961—79; tchr. USDA Grad. Sch., Washington, 1977—. Dir. Nat. Assn. Govt. Comms., Washington, 1964—95; v.p. Internat. Coun. for Small Bus., Washington, 1970—85. Contbr. articles to profl. jours. Mem. Adv. Coun. for Adult Edn., Arlington County, 1970—75, Arlington Citizens Police Acad., 1999. Pharmacist mate 1st class USNR, 1942—45, PTO. Mem.: Am. Hist. Assn., Nat. Press Club. Democrat. Methodist. Avocations: hiking, reading, public speaking, travel. Home: 1957 N Vermont St Arlington VA 22207

GOODPASTURE, PHILIP HENRY, lawyer; b. Lisbon, Portugal, Sept. 16, 1960; s. Henry McKennie and Ellen Ingabor (Moller) G., m. Paige Everett Hargroves, June 25, 1994. BA with high distinction, U. Va., 1982, JD, 1985. Bar: Va. 1985, U.S. Dist. Ct. (ea. dist.) Va. 1985. Assoc. Christian & Barton and predecessor firm, Richmond, Va., 1985-92, ptnr., 1993—, vice-chmn. corp. team, 1994-97, mem. exec. com., 1998. Dir. Downtown Presents Inc., Richmond, 1993-2001, Va. League for Planned Parenthood, Richmond, 1989-95, Vol. Emergency Families for Children, Richmond, 1998-2000; dir. Parliament City of Richmond, 1997-98; mem. Leadership Metro Richmond, 1994; mem. Leadership Devel. Coun. ARC, 1995. Mem. Va. Bar Assn., Richmond Bar Assn. Office: Christian & Barton 909 E Main St Ste 1200 Richmond VA 23219-3013 E-mail: pgoodpasture@cblaw.com.

GOODRICH, EDWARD OLIN, surgeon, educator; b. New Haven, May 7, 1925; s. Edward Olin and Laura May (MacKay) G.; m. Gladys Patricia Murphy, July 1, 1950 (div. May, 1974); children: Edward, Timothy, Jonathan; m. Alfreda Leona Verratti, May 20, 1974 (dec. May, 1990); children: Alfred James, Claudia MacKay. Student, Yale U., 1943-44; MD, N.Y. Med. Coll., 1949. Diplomate Am. Bd. Surgery. Surg. intern Albany (N.Y.) Hosp., 1950, asst. resident in surgery, 1952—53; asst. resident in surgery and surg. rsch. Albany VA Hosp., 1953—56; resident in surgery Albany VA Hosp, 1956—57; attending surgeon St. Vincent Hosp., Santa Fe, 1959—81; asst. resident pathology Med. Coll. Ohio, Toledo, 1983—84; resident in phys. medicine and rehab. Hosp. U. Penn, Phila., 1984—85; pvt. gen. practice, Ardmore, Pa., 1984-85. Guest rschr. Health Rsch. Lab., Los Alamos, N.Mex., 1962-81; instr. in phys. medicine and rehab. U. Pa., 1987—. Founding trustee Santa Fe Prep. Sch. Col. M.C. USAR, 1949—83, ret. USAR, 1983. Decorated Silver Star. Fellow: ACS (mem. oper. rm. environ. com.); mem.: Am. Soc. for Bariatric Surgery (emeritus), Surg. Infection Soc., Internat. Surg. Soc., Southwestern Surg. Congress, LAm. Guild for Arts, Masons. Achievements include research in clean air, skin cell growth, liver transplantation, obesity, plutonium effects on liver. Home: 28 Simpson Rd Ardmore PA 19003-2211

GOODRICH, GEORGE HERBERT, judge; b. Charleston, W.Va., June 19, 1925; s. Edgar Jennings and Beulah Etta (Lenfest) G.; m. Nancy Ann Needham, Sept. 3, 1949; children: George Herbert, Craig N., Thomas A. BA, Williams Coll., 1949; LL.B., U. Va., 1952. Bar: D.C. 1953, Md. 1958. Gen. practice law, Washington, also, Md., 1953-69; asso. judge D.C. Superior Ct., 1969-91, sr. judge, 1991—; lectr. law Am. U., 1969-74 Pres. Homemakers Service, 1962-63; v.p. Hillcrest Children's Center, 1963-69; mem. community adv. com. Jr. League D.C., 1969-73; bd. dirs. ARC. Served with USNR, 1943-46. Mem. D.C. Bar Assn., Delta Psi. Clubs: Chevy Chase. Republican. Presbyterian. Home: 6003 Corbin Rd Bethesda MD 20816-3402 Office: DC Superior Ct 500 Indiana Ave NW Ste 1 Washington DC 20001-2131

GOODRICH, ISAAC, neurosurgeon, educator; b. Milledgeville, Ga., Sept. 19, 1939; s. Ellis and Frieda (Bergman) G.; m. Dianne L. Brittain, Aug. 28, 1965; children: Mindy Anne, Scott David, Jennifer Gale. AA, Ga. Mil. Coll., 1959; BS, U. Ga., 1961; MD, Med. Coll. Ga., 1964. Cert. Am. Bd. Neurol. Surgery. Intern Columbia-Presbyn. Med. Ctr., N.Y.C., 1964-65; resident in neurosurgery Yale-New Haven Med. Ctr., 1967-71; practice medicine specializing in neurosurgery New Haven, 1971—. Instr. neurosurgery, Yale U. Med. Sch., 1970-71, asst. clin. prof., 1978-86; assoc. clin. prof., 1986—; attending neurosurgeon Yale-New Haven Hosp., 1973—, Hosp. St. Raphael, 1971—; mem. courtesy staff Milford Hosp., 1986—; cons. staff Midstate Med. Ctr., 1986—, VA Hosp., West Haven, 1990—, Griffin Hosp., 1992-99, St. Mary's Hosp., 1995-99, courtesy staff, 1999—. Contbr. articles to profl. jours. Capt. U.S. Army, 1965-67. Decorated Bronze Star, Air Medal; recipient Disting. Alumni award Ga. Mil. Coll., 1980; named Hon. Citizen, Boys Town, Nebr., 1971. Fellow: ACS, Royal Soc. Medicine, Internat. Coll. Surgeons; mem.: AAAS, AMA (Physicians Recognition award for Continuing Med. Edn. 1969, 1972, 1975, 1978, 1981, 1985, 1988, 1991, 1994, 1997, 2000), N.Y. Acad. Scis., New Haven County Med. Assn. (pres. 1998—99), Conn. State Med. Soc. (v.p. 2000—01, pres.-elect 2001—02, pres. 2002—03), Conn. State Neurosurg. Soc. (pres. 2001—03), Am. Assn. Neurol. Surgeons, Soc. Med. Cons. to Armed Forces, Pan Pacific Surg. Assn., New Eng. Neurosurg. Soc. (pres. 1997—99), Congress Neurol. Surgeons, Veterans of Fgn. Wars, New Haven City Med. Assn. (pres. 1989—90), 28th Inf. Assn., Soc. 1st Inf. Divsn., Am. Legion. Jewish. Home: 264 Rimmon Rd Woodbridge CT 06525-1847 Office: 330 Orchard St Ste 316 New Haven CT 06511-4430

GOODRICH, JAMES WILLIAM, historian, association executive; b. Burlington, Iowa, Oct. 31, 1939; s. Martin Glenn and Marion Elizabeth (Prasse) G.; m. Linda Marlyse Andreoli, Aug. 31, 1963 (div. Aug. 1989); children: Anne Marlyse, Kimberly Ann. BS in Edn., Cen. Mo. State U., 1962; MA, U. Mo., 1964, PhD, 1974. Archivist Sec. of State, Mo., 1966; asst. then assoc. editor State Hist. Soc. Mo., Columbia, 1967-78, assoc. dir., 1978-85, dir., 1985—. Cons. USDA Soil Conservation Svc., Columbia, 1976, Mus. History and Sci., Kansas City, Mo., 1978, Mo. State Mus., 1989, Mo. Dept. Conservation, 1990, 91, 95, 97; mem. Mo. Hist. Records Adv. Bd., Jefferson City, 1985—, State Records Commn., Jefferson City, 1984—, Mo. Bd. Geographic Names, 1995–; dir. Western Hist. Manuscript Collection, 1985—; adj. prof. history U. Mo., Columbia, 1988—. Co-author: Historic Missouri, 1988; editor: Report on a Journey to North America, 1980; assoc. editor Mo. Hist. Rev., 1967-85, editor 1985—; co-editor: German-American Experience in Missouri, 1986; co-editor, contbr. Marking Missouri History, 1998; contbr. articles to profl. jours. Mem. Planning and Zoning Commn., Columbia, 1975-77; councilman City of Columbia, 1977-79, 79-81; chmn. city audit com., Columbia, 1981-88; v.p. Friends of Mo. St. Archives, 1989-94; mem. 13th Jud. Cir. Bar Rev. Com., 1991 97; bd. dirs. Mo. Mansion Preservation Inc., 1991—; bd. dirs. Boone County Cmty. Trust, 1992—; mem. exec. com. Mo. State U. Alumni Assn., 1988-92, pres. 1991; mem. 6th Regional Disciplinary Com. Mo. Judiciary, 1997—; mem. Mo. Lewis and Clark Bicentennial Com., 1997—. Mem. Orgn. Am. Historians, Western History Assn., Am. Assn. for State & Local History, Conservation Fedn. Mo., Ducks Unlimited, Mo. Mus. Assn., Mo. Press Assn., Wild Canid Survival and Rsch. Ctr. Avocations: decoy collecting, waterfowl hunting, orinthoscopy. Office: State Hist Soc Mo 1020 Lowry St Columbia MO 65201-7207

GOODRICH, JOHN BERNARD, lawyer, consultant; b. Spokane, Wash., Jan. 4, 1928; s. John Casey and Dorothy (Koll) G.; m. Therese H. Vollmer, June 14, 1952; children— Joseph B., Bernadette M., Andrew J., Philip M., Thomas A., Mary Elizabeth, Jennifer H., Rosanne M. JD, Gonzaga U., 1954. Bar: Wash, 1954, Ill. 1955. Indsl. traffic mgr. Pacific N.W. Alloys, Spokane, 1950-54; asst. to gen. counsel Cromium Mining & Smelting Corp., Chgo., 1954-56; with Monon R.R., 1956-69, atty., gen. solicitor, 1956-66, sec., 1957-69, treas., 1959-66, v.p. law, 1966-69; also dir.; sec.-treas. I.C.G.R.R., Chgo., 1970-79, sec., gen. atty., 1979-85; gen. counsel Ill. Devel. Fin. Authority, Chgo., 1985-92, spl. counsel, 1993; atty., cons. pvt. practice, Park Forest, Ill., 1994—. Mem. Park Forest Traffic and Safety Commn., 1963-66; mem. Park Forest Recreation Bd., 1966-77, chmn., 1969-70; trustee Village of Park Forest, 1977-80; mem. bd. Sch. Dist. 163, 1984-89; pres. South Cook Orgn. for Pub. Edn., 1988-89; conf. and meeting planner The Compassionate Friends, Inc., Oak Brook, Ill., 1991-94; bd. dirs. Park Forest Art Ctr., 1993-95, Ill. Philharm. Orch., 1994-98, treas., 1995-98; mem. adv. bd. Chgo. Self Help Ctr., 1993-94; bd. dirs. Ill Self Help Coalition, 1994-96; treas. Bereaved Parents of the U.S.A., 1995-2000, bd. dirs. 2000-2003, Tall Grass Arts Assn., 1999-2003; trustee Chgo. South Suburban Mass Transit Dist., 1996—, treas., 2000—. Inducted into Park Forest Hall of Fame, 1998. Mem. KC, The Parkforesters, Inc. (pres. 1998—, dir.), Kiwanis. Republican. Roman Catholic. Home and Office: 35 Cunningham Ln Park Forest IL 60466-2094

GOODRICH, JOHN M. conservation ecologist; b. Catskill, N.Y., Nov. 26, 1965; s. James H. and Marian Goodrich. PhD, U. of Wyo., Laramie, 1994. Conservation ecologist Wildlife Conservation Soc., Bronx, 1995—. Field coord. Siberian tiger project Wildlife Conservation Soc., Terney, Primorsky Krai, Russia, 1995—. Office: Wildlife Conservation Soc 2023 Stadium Dr Bozeman MT 59715 Office Fax: 406-522-9377.

GOODRICH, KENNETH PAUL, retired college dean; b. Elkhorn, Wis., 1933; s. Kenneth Potter and Helene (Keller) G.; m. Elaine L. Ashby, June 12, 1954; children— Laurel Lynn, David Kenneth, Paul Ashby, Karen Elaine. AB Oberlin Coll, 1955; MA, U. Ia., 1958, PhD, 1959. Mem. faculty U. Pa. Phila., 1959-63; lectr., project assoc. U. Wis., Madison, 1963-65; mem. faculty psychology Macalester Coll., St. Paul, 1965-73, chmn. dept. psychology, 1965-67, dean coll., 1967-69, dean and dir. ednl. resources, 1969-71, v.p. for acad. affairs and provost, 1971-73; dean Coll. Arts and Scis., prof. psychology Syracuse (N.Y.) U., 1973-78; provost Ohio Wesleyan U., Delaware, 1978-83; v.p. acad. affairs, dean of faculty Linfield Coll., McMinnville, Oreg., 1983-94, spl. asst. to pres. for instnl. rsch. and planning, 1994-95. Bd. dirs. Group Health Plan, Inc., St. Paul, 1970-73, Yamhill County (Oreg.) United Way, 1991-95, McMinnville Area Habitat for Humanity, 1993-95; vol. carpenter Greater Columbus Habitat for Humanity, 1995—.

GOODRICH, NORMA LORRE (MRS. JOHN H. HOWARD), French and comparative literature educator; b. Huntington, Vt., May 10, 1917; d. Charles Edmund and Edyth (Riggs) Falby; m. J.M.A. Lorre, Dec. 10, 1943 (div. June 1946); 1 son, Jean-Joseph; m. John Hereford Howard, Jan. 20, 1964. BS cum laude, U. Vt., 1938; postgrad. (U. Vt. fellow), U. Grenoble, France, 1938-39; PhD (Ellis fellow), Columbia U., 1965; LittD, U. Vt., 1993. Tchr. high schs., Vt., 1939-43, Bentley Sch., N.Y.C., 1943-47; owner dir. Am. Villa in Normandy, Trouville, France, 1947-53; tchr. Fieldston Sch., N.Y.C., 1954-63; asst. prof. French U. So. Calif., 1964-66, assoc. prof., 1966-71; dean faculty Scripps Coll., Claremont, Calif., 1971-72; prof. French and comparative lit. Claremont Colls., 1972, prof. emeritus, 1982—. Vis. scholar Calif. Luth. Coll., 1965, Isle of Man, U.K., 1986, Claremont McKenna Coll., 1986; vis. prof. John Carroll U., Cleve., 1987, Calif. State U., Long Beach, 1986, 87, 88, Cal Arts, Pasadena, 1989,

Calif. Poly. U., Pomona, 1992, Southwestern Coll., 1993, Riverside Bapt. Coll., 1994, Scripps Coll., Claremont, 1994; lectr. Arthurian Soc., Carlisle, Cumbria, Eng., 1994, 96, 97, Santa Anita (Calif.) Ch., 1995, Trinity Episc. Ch., Redlands, Calif., 1996. Author: Ancient Myths, 1959, rev. edit., 1977, 94, Medieval Myths, 1960, rev. edit., 1977, 94, Doctor and Maria Theresa, 1961, Myths of the Hero, 1961, Ways of Love, 1963, Charles of Orleans: A Study of Themes in His French and English Poetry, 1967, Giono: Master of Fictional Modes, 1973, Afterword for the Man Who Planted Trees (Jean Giono), 1985 (New Eng. Book award), London edit., 1989, King Arthur, 1986, 2d edit., 1989, Merlin, 1987, 2d edit., 1989, Il Mito della Tavola Rotonda (transl. of King Arthur), 1989, Le Roi Arthur, 1989, Die Ritter von Camelot, 1994, 95 (transl. of King Arthur), Castle Epstein (transl. of Alexander Dumas), 1989, Priestesses, 1989, Guinevere, 1991, The Holy Grail, 1992, Il Mito di Merlino, 1992 (transl. of Merlin), Heroines, 1993, Il Mito di Ginevra (transl. Guinevere), 1995; editor: Bullfinch Mythology, The Age of Fable, 1995, Bullfinch Mythology, The Age of Chivalry, 1995, Il Santo Graal, 1997, (boxed edit.) Hors Commerce, 1997; contbr. articles to internat. profl. jours.; guest appearances various TV and radio shows, Eng., 1986, 94, U.S., 1986-90, 93, 94. Mem. pub. rels. staff Worthington Corp., N.Y.C., 1953-54; bd. dirs. patron West End Opera Assn., 1973-74, program dir., 1975-76; guest lectr. Flower Festival, Arthuret Ch., Longtown, Cumbria, Eng., 1991, guest preacher, 1992. Recipient Good Citizen medal SAR, 1989, Martha Washington medal, 1992, Wallace award Am. Scottish Found., 1990; invested as Dame Knights Templar, Commandery of Nova Scotia, in the Rosslyn Chapel, Scotland, 1990; reinvested as Knight Templar, Dame and Officer with the rank of comdr. in Teampull of Sion, Edinburgh, Scotland, 1990, St. Mary's Cath., Edinburgh, Order of St. George, 1993, Mil. Order Fgn. Wars, 1994, Calif. Commandery medal, 1997. Fellow Soc. Antiquarians, Nat. Inst. Social Scis.; mem. Assn. Study of Dada and Surrealism (sec. 1970-72), Philol. Assn. Pacific Coast (nominating com. 1971-72), MLA (mem. del. assembly's election com. 1975), The Prehistoric Soc., Am. Assn. Tchrs. French, Medieval Assn. Pacific, Medieval Acad. Am., Nat. Soc. DAR (vice-regent 1996-97), Columbia U. Alumni Assn., Dante Soc., Pierport Morgan Libr., Clan MacArthur, Clan MacKay (hon.), 78th Fraser's Highlanders 2d Bn. of Foot Am. (lt.), Tordarroch Trust (Scotland and U.S.), Met. Opera Guild, Order of the Crown of Charlemagne in the U.S.A. (life), Phi Kappa Phi. Avocations: gymnastics, gardening, dressmaking, traveling in South Pacific, studying U.S. battle sites and prisons in South Pacific. Home: 620 Diablo Dr Claremont CA 91711-1616 *I believe in the creative power of certain individuals who, because of this power or gift, must be allowed by society to be alone, work alone, and alone to perfect their work. Our education must be more lenient to these individuals and more understanding of that individual who does not conform to the average.*

GOODRICH, THOMAS MICHAEL, engineering and construction executive, lawyer; b. Milan, Tenn., Apr. 28, 1945; s. Henry Calvin and Billie Grace (Walker) Goodrich; m. Gillian Comer White, Dec. 28, 1968; children: Michael, Braxton, Charles, Grace. BSCE, Tulane U., 1968; JD, U. Ala., 1971. Bar: Ala. 1971. Adminstrv. asst. Supreme Ct. Ala., Montgomery, 1971—72; various mgmt. positions BE & K, Inc., Birmingham, Ala., 1989—95, pres., CEO, 1995—, also bd. dirs. Bd. dirs. First Comml. Bank, Energen Corp., Birmingham. Bd. dirs. Birmingham Civil Rights Inst., Constrn. Industry Inst., Birmingham Area coun. Boy Scouts Am., U. Ala. Health System; trustee Nat. Bldg. Mus., Elsenhowen Exchg. Fellow. Capt. U.S. Army, 1970—72. Mem.: Constrn. Industry Roundtable, Assn. Builders and Contractors (pres. 1990), Ala. State Bar Assn., ABA, TAPPI. Avocation: hunting, jogging.. Office: B E & K Inc 2000 Internat Park Dr Birmingham AL 35243

GOODRIDGE, ALAN GARDNER, research biochemist, educator; b. Peabody, Mass., Apr. 2, 1937; s. Lester Elmer and Gertrude Edith (Gardner) G.; m. R. Ann Funderburk, Aug. 19, 1960; children— Alan Gardner Jr., Bryant C. BS in Biology, Tufts U., 1958; MS in Zoology, U. Mich., 1963, PhD in Zoology, 1964. Rsch. fellow dept. biochemistry Harvard Med. Sch., Boston, 1964-66; asst. prof. physiology U. Kans. Med. Ctr., Kansas City, 1966-68; assoc. prof. Banting and Best dept. med. rsch. U. Toronto, Ont., Can., 1968-76, prof. Banting and Best dept. med. rsch., 1976-77; prof. pharmacology and biochemistry Case Western Res. U., Cleve., 1977-87; prof., head dept. biochemistry U. Iowa, 1987-96; prof. biochemistry Ohio State U., 1996—, dean Coll. Biol. Scis., 1996-2001, exec. dean Colls. of Arts and Sci., 1999-2001. Assoc. editor Jour. Biol. Chemistry, 1990—, Ann. Rev. of Nutrition, 1994-99, Jour. Lipid Rsch., 1995-99; contbr. numerous articles to profl. jours. Served with USN, 1958-61 Grantee Med. Rsch. Coun. Can., 1968-77, NIH, 1966-68, 77-97, USDA 1986-90, 93-97; Josiah Macy Jr. faculty scholar, 1975-76. Mem. AAAS, Am. Soc. Biochemistry and Molecular Biology, Thyroid Assn. Home: 844 W Orange Rd Delaware OH 43015-7978 Office: Ohio State U Coll Biol Scis 484 W 12th Ave Columbus OH 43210-1214 E-mail: goodridge.4@osu.edu.

GOODRIDGE, ALLAN D. lawyer; b. Bucharest, Romania, June 12, 1936; s. Benjamin F. and Fanny M. (Weissman) G.; m. Lora, Sept. 12, 1965; children: Jeremy P., Andrew P. BA, Harvard U., 1957; JD, Columbia U., 1960. Bar: N.Y., U.S. Dist. Ct. (so. dist., ea. dist. N.Y.), U.S. Ct. Appeals (2d circuit). Assoc. Wickes, Riddell, Bloomer, Jacobi & McGuire, N.Y.C., 1960-64, Spitzer & Feldman, N.Y.C., 1965, Demov, Morris & Hammerling, N.Y.C., 1965-70, ptnr., 1970-85, Schnader, Harrison, Segal & Lewis, N.Y.C., 1985—. Mem. ABA, N.Y. Bar Assn. Clubs: Harvard (N.Y.C.). Home: 336 Central Park W New York NY 10025-7111 Office: Schnader Harrison Ste 3100 140 Broadway New York NY 10005 E-mail: agoodridge@shsl.com.

GOODRO, JULIE NICHOLS, music educator; b. Salt Lake City, Mar. 5, 1950; d. Ivan LeRoy and Elaine Cannon Nichols; m. Jerry Brighton Goodro, Dec. 10, 1971; children: Mark, Matthew, Peter, Benjamin, Michael. BA in Home Econ. Edn. with honors, U. Utah, 1972. Cert. child devel. assoc. Nat. Assn. Edn. Young Children, Suzuki piano tchr., tchr. Utah. Pvt. piano instr., Murray, Utah and Chino, Calif., 1968—2003; music specialist Va. Tanner Fine Arts Presch., U. Utah, Salt Lake City, 1992—; Kindermusik tchr. Mt. Tabor Luth. Ch., Salt Lake City, 2002; Kindermusik tchr. piano prep. dept. Weber State U., Ogden, Utah, 2001—. Youth leader Boy Scouts Am., 1975—. Recipient Silver Beaver award, Boy Scouts Am., 2002. Mem.: Early Childhood Music and Movement Assn., Suzuki Assn. Utah, Music Tchrs. Nat. Assn., Utah Music Tchrs. Assn. (mag. rep.), Orff-Schulwerk Assn. (sec. Utah chpt. 2000—, bd. dirs.). Republican. Mem. Lds Ch. Avocations: botany, languages, textile work, organ. Home: 892 Spring Clover Dr Salt Lake City UT 84123

GOODSELL, CHARLES TRUE, retired educator; b. July 23, 1932; BA, Kalamazoo Coll., 1954; MPA, Harvard U., 1958, MA, 1959, PhD, 1961. Asst. prof. U. P.R., Rio Piedras, 1961-64; prof. So. Ill. U., Carbondale, 1966-78; prof. pub. adminstrn. Va. Tech., Blacksburg, 1978—2002. Author: Administration of A Revolution, 1965, American Corporations and Peruvian Politics, 1974, The Social Meaning of Public Space, 1988, The Case for Bureaucracy, 1994, The American Statehouse, 2001. Recipient Waldo award for lifetime contbn. to lit. in pub. adminstrn., 2003. E-mail: goodsell@vt.edu.

GOODSON, CAROL FAYE, librarian; b. Detroit, Mar. 28, 1947; d. Norman Elwood and Wilma Mary (Harmon) G.; m. Lawrence J. Price, May 10, 1974 (div. 1977). BA, SUNY, Buffalo, 1970, MLS, 1972; MA, State U. West Ga., 1996. Libr. SUNY, Buffalo, 1970-72, St. Louis Pub. Libr., 1973-77; community sch. dir. St. Louis Bd. Edn., 1977-80; reference libr. Ga. Dept. Edn., Atlanta, 1981-84; head pub. svcs. Atlanta campus Mercer U., Chamblee, Ga., 1985; mem. Dominican Sisters of Nashville, 1985-90; asst. dir. Clayton County Libr. System, Jonesboro, Ga., 1990-91; coord. off-campus libr. svcs. State U. West Ga., Carrollton, 1991-96, head libr. access svcs., 1996—. State coord. Ga. Summer Reading Club, 1991; owner and moderator, ALA-PLAN listserv., FISC-L listserv and WOODY-L listserv. Author: The Complete Guide to Performance Standards for Library Personnel, 1997, Providing Library Services for Distance Education Students, 2001; editor: Ga. conf. AAUP Summary, 1996—98, Jour. Libr. Svcs. Distance Edn., 1997—; contbr. Pres. Tower/Literacy Vols. Am., Clayton County, 1991; with Leadership Clayton, 1990-91. Mem. ALA, Ga. Libr. Assn., Libr. Info. Tech. Assn. (program planning com. 1992-97, sec. 1993-95), Assn. Coll. Rsch. Librs. (clip notes com. 1992-96, extended campus libr. svcs. sect., comm. com. 1994-98), Libr. Adminstrn. and Mgmt. Assn., Beta Phi Mu, Phi Kappa Phi, Omicron Delta Kappa, Sigma Tau Delta. Avocations: genealogy, computers. Home: 210 Oak Ave Carrollton GA 30117-3726 Office: State U West Ga Ingram Libr 1500 Maple St Carrollton GA 30117-4233 Business E-Mail: cgoodson@westga.edu.

GOODSON, RAYMOND EUGENE, business educator, former automotive executive; b. Canton, N.C., Apr. 22, 1935; s. Lon R. and Ruby M. (Goodson); m. Susie Elisabeth Tweed, Aug. 10, 1957; children: Kathryn, Kenneth. AB, Duke U., 1957, BSME, 1959; MSME, Purdue U., 1961, PhD, 1963. Registered profl. engr., Ind. Mem. faculty Purdue U., West Lafayette, Ind., 1963-81; chief scientist U.S. Dept. Transp., Washington, 1973-75; dir. Interdisciplinary Inst., Purdue U., 1975-80, assoc. dean rsch., 1980-81; chmn. bd., CEO GLN, Inc., West Lafayette, 1971-81; v.p., gen. mgr. Hoover Universal, Ann Arbor, Mich., 1981-85; group v.p. Automotive Systems Group Johnson Controls, Inc., Milw., 1985-90; chmn. bd., CEO, Oshkosh (Wis.) Truck Corp., 1990-97; adj. prof. U. Mich. Sch. Bus. Adminstrn., Ann Arbor, 1998—; chmn., CEO, pres. Williams Controls, Portland, Oreg., 2002—. Bd. dirs. Am. Indsl. Ptnrs., San Francisco; chmn. CIS Corp., Dallas. Patentee in field; contbr. articles to tech. jours. Named Disting. Engring. Alumnus, Duke U., 1984, Purdue U., 1991. Fellow ASME. Republican. Presbyterian.

GOODSON, RICHARD CARLE, JR., chemist, consultant; b. Toledo, June 22, 1945; s. Richard Carle Goodson Sr. and Norma (Buehler) Robinson; m. Deborah Ann Hart, Mar. 29, 1969 (div. Feb. 1978); 1 child, Geoffrey Carle; m. Thelma Agnes Matthews, Nov. 22, 1978. BS in Chemistry, Union Coll., 1967; MS in Inorganic Chemistry, U. Conn., 1970. Dist. engr. Drew Chem. Corp., Boonton, N.J., 1972-74, product supr., 1974-75, regional tech. supr., 1975-76; chief chemist, tech. dir. Environ. Waste Removal, Waterbury, Conn., 1976-79; gen. mgr., dir. tech. lab. Conn. Treatment Corp., Bristol, Conn., 1979-82; pres., owner Goodson Assocs., Avon, Conn., 1982—; dir. ops., corp. dir. waste mgmt. and regulatory compliance Hampden Mathieu Chem. Co., Springfield, Mass., 1990-2000. Mem. Am. Chem. Soc. Republican. Avocations: boating, hiking, skiing, cycling. Home and Office: 2 Azalea Ct Farmington CT 06032-2037

GOODSPEED, BARBARA, artist; b. Sept. 1, 1919; d. George Daniel and Bernice (Lucas) G. Diploma, Stoneleigh Coll., 1939, Famous Artist Schs., Westport, Conn., 1955. Freelance photographer, N.Y.C., 1941-52; Christmas card designer Sherman, Conn., 1952-69; oil and watercolor, fine arts artist, 1969—. Forever Flowers, 1979; contbr. . Recipient Merit award Sheffield Arts League, 1979, 81, 83, others, named Artist of Yr., Art League of Harlem Valley, 1981. Fellow Am. Artists Profl. League (John Dole Meml. award, Parsons award 1991); mem. Salmagundi Club (Jane Peterson Meml. award, Samuel Shaw Meml. award 1997, Arthur Hill award 1998), Hudson Valley Art Assn. (bd. mem.), Acad. Artists, Nat. League Am. Pen Women, Allied Artist Am. (N.Y.C.), Butler Mus., Kent Art Assn. (trustee), Inc. (pres. 1970-72, 80-83, 85-88, 91-93, 97, 98, medal of Merit 1979, Grumbacher Gold medal 1989, 91, K.A.A. award 1995, 96, 97), Housatonic Art League (v.p., bd. dirs. 1977-83), Catharine Lorillard Wolfe Art Club (bd. dirs. 1990-93, 98-01, travel show 1996, Corp. award). Avocations: camping, crafts. Home: 11 Holiday Point Rd Sherman CT 06784-1624 E-mail: bgoodspeedb@aol.com.

GOODSTEIN, AARON E. federal magistrate judge; b. Sheboygan, Wis., Apr. 28, 1942; BA, U. Wis. Madison, 1964; JD, U. Wis., 1967. Bar: Wis. 1967, U.S. Dist. Ct. (ea. and we. dists.) Wis. 1967, U.S. Ct. Appeals (7th crct.) 1968. Law clk. to Hon. Myron L. Gordon U.S. Dist. Ct., Ea. Dist. Wis., 1967-68; shareholder Chernov, Croen & Goodstein, S.C., Milw., 1968-79; U.S. magistrate judge Ea. Dist. Wis., Milw., 1979-87, reapptd., 1987-95, 95—. Panelist Current Issues Relating to the Fourth, Fifth and Sixth Amendments, Jud. Conf. of 7th Cir., 1991; speaker fed. ct.'s class Marquette Law Sch., 1992; moderator probation and pretrial svcs. divsn. U.S. Cts., 1992; chair magistrate judges edn. com. Fed. Jud. Ctr., 1990-98, mem. magistrate judges com. of Jud. Conf. of U.S., 1993-99; adv. com. local rules and practice Ea. Dist. Wis., mem. adv. panel under Civil Justice Reform Act 1990; faculty mem. in field. Prodr: (video) Complaints, Warrants for Arrest and Search Warrants, 1992, Administrative Matters Pertaining to Magistrate Judges and Their Staff, 1993, Social Security: Process and Problems, Parts One and Two, 2000; mem. editl. adv. panel Handbook of Federal Civil Discovery and Disclosure, 1998; contbr. articles to profl. jours. Bd. dirs. Milw. Legal Aid Soc., 1974-79, Milw. Jewish Coun., 1977-79; pres. Milw. Forum, 1979-80, alumni mem.; pres. Congregation Shalom, 1990-92. Recipient Pro Bono award Gene and Ruth Posner Found., 1988. Mem. ABA (former chair magistrate judges com. Nat. Conf. Fed. Trial Judges), Fed. Magistrate Judges Assn. (pres.-elect), State Bar Wis. (pres. young lawyer's divsn. 1975-76, bd. govs. 1975-77), Milw. Bar Assn. (exec. bd. 1978-79, sec. 1979-82), U. of Wis. Law Sch. Alumni Assn. (bd. dirs. 1989-98), Order Coif, Phi Kappa Phi. Office: US Magistrate Judge 258 US Courthouse 517 E Wisconsin Ave Milwaukee WI 53202-4500

GOODSTEIN, BARNETT MAURICE, lawyer; b. Dallas, Oct. 1, 1921; s. Arthur Louis and Viola Esther (Levy) G.; m. Mira Brodsky, Jan. 26, 1947; children— Pamela Renee, Heather Ann, Robin Leslie. Student, Rice Inst., 1938-40; BA, MA, U. Tex., Austin, 1942; postgrad., U. Wis., 1949-51; JD, So. Meth. U., 1957. Bar: Tex. 1957, U.S. Dist. Ct. (no. dist.) Tex. 1963, U.S. Supreme Ct. 1971. Acting dir. case analysis Wage Stblzn. Bd., Dallas, 1951-53; practice of law Dallas, 1957—; pres. Goodstein & Starr, P.C., 1977-91, Goodstein, Starr & Pascoe, P.C., 1991—95; adminstrv. law judge City of Dallas, 1994—95; atty. pvt. practice, 1995—. Lectr. econs. So. Meth. U., Dallas, 1946-48, 51-60; lectr. Massey Realty Coll., Real Estate Inst., Dallas; labor arbitrator, 1953—; former permanent arbitrator City of San Antonio, Police Officers' Assn.; mem. permanent arbitration panel Tinker AFB, Okla., 1984-88, Am. Fedn. Govt. Employees, 1984-90, SW Bell Telephone, AT&T, CWA, IBEW, 1988—, FAA, 1993—, Nat. Assn. Air Traffic Specialists, 1994—, Ga. Pacific, 1994—, UPIU, 1994—, U.S. Customs and INS, 2001-, also various VA Med. Facilities, paper and copper industries, others; mem. permanent panel Dallas Area Rapid Transit Sys., 1988-90, 94-96; adminstrv. law judge City of Dallas, 1994-96. Hearing officer work suspensions appeals bd. City of Dallas, 1981-83; trustee Dallas County Sch. Bd., 1980—, v.p., 1990-91, 2003—; past trustee Temple Emanu-El; mem. legal representation com. Nat. Acad. Arbitrators, 1992-96, chmn. legal affairs com. 1997-99. Served with USAAF, 1942-46, China, 1945-46. Mem.: ABA, Am. Arbitration Assn. (Southwestern adv. coun. 1985—92), Indsl. Rels. Rsch. Assn. (pres. North Tex. chpt. 1985—86, neutral mem. bd. dirs. North Tex. chpt. 1990—92), Nat. Acad. Arbitrators (chmn. S.W. region 1987—88), Tex. Bar Assn. Home: 6427 Forest Creek Dr Dallas TX 75230-2814 Office: Law Offices of Barnett M Goodstein Ste 215J 4230 Lyndon B Johnson Fwy Dallas TX 75244-5816 E-mail: bgoodsteinb@aol.com.

GOODSTEIN, DAVID LOUIS, physics educator; b. Bklyn., Apr. 5, 1939; s. Sam and Claire (Axel) G.; m. Judith R. Koral, June 30, 1960; children: Marcia, Mark. BS, Bklyn. Coll., 1960; PhD, U. Wash., 1965. Research instr. U. Wash., Seattle, 1965-66; research fellow Calif. Inst. Tech., Pasadena, 1966-67, asst. prof., 1968-71, asso. prof., 1971-76, prof., 1976—, vice-provost, 1987—, Frank J. Gilloon disting. teaching and svc. prof., 1995—. Vis. scientist Frascati Nat. Lab., Italy, 1971— . Author: States of Matter, 1975, (with J. Goodstein) Feynman's Lost Lecture, 1996, Out of Gas, 2004; mem. editl. bd. Il Nuovo Cimento, 1987—; contbr. articles to profl. jours.; project dir., host physics TV course The Mechanical Universe. Bd. dirs. Calif. Coun. Sci. and Tech., 1989—, Sierra Monolithics; sci. adv. com. David and Lucille Packard Found., 1988—. NSF postdoctoral fellow, 1967-68; Sloan Found. fellow, 1969-71; recipient Oersted medal, 1999, John P. McGovern Sci. and Soc. award, 2000. Fellow AAAS; mem. Am. Phys. Soc., Am. Inst. Physics. Office: Calif Inst Tech Dept Physics Pasadena CA 91125-0001 E-mail: dg@caltech.edu.

GOODSTEIN, LES, newspaper publishing executive; Grad., SUNY. With The Daily News, N.Y.C., 1977—, v.p.-advertising, 1991—95, exec. v.p. assoc. pub., 1995—2000, pres., COO, 2000—. Office: The Daily News 450 W 33rd St Fl 3 New York NY 10001-2681*

GOODSTEIN, SANDERS ABRAHAM, scrap iron company executive; b. NYC, Oct. 3, 1918; s. Samuel G. and Katie (Lipson) G.; m. Rose Laro, June 28, 1942; children: Peter, Esther, Jack, Rachel. Student, Wayne State U., 1934-36; AB, U. Mich., 1938, MBA, 1939, JD, 1946; postgrad., Harvard, 1943. Bar: Mich., 1946. Sec. Laro Coal & Iron Co., Flint, Mich., 1946-60, pres., 1960—; owner, operator Paterson Mfg. Co., Flint, 1953-94. Gen. ptnr. Indianhead Co., Pontiac, Mich., 1955-70, pres., 1965-70; sec. Amatac Corp., Erie, Pa., unitl 1969; chmn. bd. Gen. Foundry & Mfg. Co., Flint, 1968—, pres., 1970-92; pres. Lacron Steel Co., Providence, 1975-80, ETL Corp., Flint, 1983-91, Can. Blending and Processing, Windsor, 1988-97; mem. corp. body Mich. Blue Shield, 1970-76. Served to lt. comdr. USNR, 1942-46. Mem. Fed. Bar Assn., Am. Bar Assn., Bar Mich., Am. Pub. Works Assn., Am. Foundrymen's Soc., Order of Coif, Beta Gamma Sigma, Phi Kappa Phi. Jewish. Home: 2602 Parkside Dr Flint MI 48503-4662 Office: PO Box 307 Flint MI 48501

GOODSTONE, EDWARD HAROLD, retired insurance company executive; b. N.Y.C., July 19, 1934; s. Abraham and Gladys (Lande) Goodstone; m. Harriet Jill Pearle, Oct. 16, 1955; children: Marjorie Faith, Michael Stuart. BA, CUNY, 1956; CLU, Coll. Life Underwriters, 1973. Agt. Penn. Mut. Ins. Co., N.Y.C., 1957-67, assoc. gen. agt., 1971-72; agy. mgr. Lincoln Nat. Life of N.Y., N.Y.C., 1967-71, 2d v.p., dir. advanced markets Pearl River, N.Y., 1972-75; v.p. U.S. Life Ins. Co., N.Y.C., 1975-78; sr. v.p. USLIFE Corp., N.Y.C., 1978-95, exec. v.p., 1984-90; nexec. v.p. U.S. Life Ins. Co. (now Am. Internat. Group), N.Y.C., 1990-95; ret., 1995.

GOODWICK, DAVID LEE, advertising executive; b. Beloit, Wis., Oct. 20, 1954; s. James Lee and Helen Maude (Alton) G.; m. Christie Wren Spencer, Apr. 18, 1981; children: Jesse David, Lindsey Leah, Jamie Christopher. BA in Polit. Sci., BA in Journalism, U. Wis.-Whitewater, 1976. Intern J. Walter Thompson, Chgo., 1975; advt. mgr. LRP, Inc., Lake Geneva, Wis., 1976; mktg. svcs. mgr. Mercury Marine, Fond du lac, Wis., 1976-77; advt. mgr. Johnson Outboards, Waukegan, Wis., 1977-79; advt. account mgr. GE Co., Fairfield, Conn., 1979-82; ptnr. Profl. Svcs. Assocs., Inc., Newtown, Conn., 1986-91, Hist. Property Preservations, ltd., Newtown, 1986-91; pres./owner Typ-Hi Printers, Newtown, 1989-92; v.p., ptnr. Best Homes Constrn. Co., Janesville, Wis., 1993-95; pres., owner Goodwick Assocs., Inc., Newtown, 1982-99; CEO, creative dir. The Leverage Mktg. Group, Newtown, 1999—; chmn. Goodwick/Liazon Co., Newtown, 1999—. Advisor Insight Assocs., Westport, Conn., 1984—; press sec. to Gov. Patrick Lucey of Wis., Madison, 1974; pres./owner Bandwick Prodns., Newtown, 1998—. Pub.: newspaper The Alternative, 1974—76. Co-prodr. Ox Ridge Charity Horse Show, Darien, Conn., 1984-86; chmn. comms. com. United Way, Danbury, Conn., 1987-88; bus. mem. Newtown H.S. Alliance, Ancell Sch. Bus., Western Conn. State U. Recipient Matty award of Excellence, Ad Club of Fairfield County, 1980, Best Ad of Issue award Industry Week, 1981, readership awards various mags., Most Significant Ads of the 20th Century award Indsl. Equipment News. Mem. Am. Entrepenurial Assn., Internat. Platform Assn. Avocations: musician, fishing. Home: 201 Hattertown Rd Newtown CT 06470-2451 Office: Leverage Mktg Group 117-119 S Main St Newtown CT 06470-2380 E-mail: david@leverage-marketing.com.

GOODWILLIE, EUGENE WILLIAM, JR., lawyer; b. Montclair, N.J., May 14, 1941; s. Eugene W. G. and Janet (Williams) G.; children: David Todd, Douglas Linn. BA, Williams Coll., 1963; LLB, JD, Columbia U., 1966. Bar: N.Y. 1966. Assoc. White & Case, N.Y.C., 1966-75, ptnr., 1975—. Stone scholar Columbia U., 1964-66; grantee Noble Found., 1963-65. Mem. ABA, Montclair Golf Club (pres. 1985-86), Phi Beta Kappa. Office: White & Case Bldg Ll 1155 Avenue Of The Americas New York NY 10036-2787

GOODWIN, ALFRED THEODORE, federal judge; b. Bellingham, Wash., June 29, 1923; s. Alonzo Theodore and Miriam Hazel (Williams) G.; m. Marjorie Elizabeth Major, Dec. 23, 1943 (div. 1948); 1 child, Michael Theodore; m. Mary Ellin Handelin, Dec. 23, 1949; children: Karl Alfred, Margaret Ellen, Sara Jane, James Paul. BA, U. Oreg., 1947; JD, 1951. Bar: Oreg. 1951. Newspaper reporter Eugene (Oreg.) Register-Guard, 1947—50; practiced in Eugene until, 1955; circuit judge Oreg. 2d. Jud. Dist., 1955—60; assoc. justice Oreg. Supreme Ct., 1960—69; judge U.S. Dist. Ct. Oreg., 1969—71, U.S. Ct. Appeals for (9th cir.), Pasadena, Calif., 1971—88, chief judge, 1988—91, sr. judge, 1991—. Editor: Oreg. Law Rev., 1950—51. Adv. bd. Eugene Salvation Army, 1956—60; chmn., 1959; Bd. dirs. Central Lane YMCA, Eugene, 1956—60, Salem (Oreg.) Art Assn., 1960—69. Capt., inf. AUS, 1942—46, ETO. Mem.: ABA (ho. of dels. 1986—87), Am. Law Inst., Am. Judicature Soc., Order of Coif, Alpha Tau Omega, Sigma Delta Chi, Phi Delta Phi. Republican. Office: US Ct Appeals 9th Cir PO Box 91510 125 S Grand Ave Pasadena CA 91105-1621

GOODWIN, ANDREW WIRT, II, radiologist; b. Oil City, Pa., Feb. 4, 1932; s. Frank Bert and Florence Bickford (Green) G.; m. Anita Faye Adkins, May 27, 1987; children: Andrew, Victoria, Mary Elizabeth, Mark H., Martha J., Lisa R. BA, Colgate U., 1953; MD, U. Mich., 1957. Diplomate Am. Bd. Radiology, Am. Bd. Nuclear Medicine. Intern Mary Hitchcock Meml. Hosp., Hanover, N.H., 1957-58; resident in radiology Mayo Clinic, Rochester, Minn., 1958-61, resident, 1958-61; radiologist Associated Radiologists, Inc., Charleston, W.Va., 1961-86, Radiol. Physicians Assn., Fairmont, W.Va., 1988—; pvt. practice. Republican. Episcopalian. Fax: (304) 926-0851. E-mail: agoodwinii@aol.com.

GOODWIN, BRUCE KESSELI, retired geology educator, researcher; b. Providence, Oct. 14, 1931; s. Thomas William and Lizetta Christina (Kesseli) G.; m. Joan Marilyn Horton, June 9, 1956; children: Stephen Bruce, Susan Joan, Jennifer Anne. AB, U. Pa., 1953; MS, Lehigh U., 1957, PhD, 1959. Grad. asst. Lehigh U., Bethlehem, Pa., 1956-59; geologist Vt. Geol. Survey, Burlington, 1956-58; instr. U. Pa., Phila., 1959-63; asst. prof. geology Coll. William and Mary, Williamsburg, Va., 1963-66, assoc. prof. geology, 1966-71, prof. geology, 1971-96, chmn. dept. geology, 1970-76, 82-88, 92-96; tchr. geology Math.-Sci. Ctr., Richmond, Va., 1968-70. With Va. Bd. Geology, 1982-88, chair, 1983; mem. Va. Geologic Mapping Adv. Com., 1993—. Contbr. articles to profl. jours. Pres. Lafayette Ednl. Fund, Inc., Williamsburg, Va., 1976-79, Lafayette High Sch. PTA, Williamsburg, Bruton Heights PTA, Williamsburg; mem. com. Va. Jr. Acad. Sci., 1971-73. Recipient Thomas Jefferson Teaching award Coll. William and Mary, 1971; cert. of merit Math.-Sci. Ctr. Fellow Geol. Soc. Am. (edn. com. 1994-96); mem. AAAS, Nat. Assn. Geology Tchrs. (pres. eastern sect. 1982), Va. Acad. Sci. (chmn. geology sect. 1970, 98), Am. Inst. Profl. Geologists (sec., treas. Va. sect. 1989, pres. Va. sect. 1990), St. Andrews Soc., Coun. on Undergrad. Rsch (geology councilor 1988-94), Kiwanis, Delta Upsilon, Sigma Xi. Republican. Presbyterian. Avocations: fishing, sailing, geology, travel, ballroom dancing. Home: 103 Wakerobin Rd Williamsburg VA 23185-4441

GOODWIN, CHARLES HUGH, technology education educator; b. Cortland, NY, Feb. 2, 1945; s. Arthur George and Elizabeth Sarah (Pratt) G.; m. Frances Margaret Dunkle, Aug. 18, 1967 (div. June 1979); 1 child, Chad Conlin; m. Barbara Louetta Milan, Aug. 16, 1980. BS, SUNY, Oswego, 1967, MS in Edn., 1973. Cert. tech. tchr. trainer, N.Y. Indsl. arts tchr. Worcester (N.Y.) Ctrl. Schs., 1967-69, Endicott (N.Y.) Ctrl. Schs., 1969-86, tech. edn. tchr., 1986—; chairperson tech. and mgmt. sci. dept. Union-Endicott (N.Y.) Ctrl. Schs., 1996—. Applied physics tchr. Broome C.C., Binghamton, N.Y., 1994—; curriculum writer N.Y. State Edn. Dept., Albany, 1983-88, test writer, evaluator, 1978—, tchr. trainer, 1986-92, sch. quality reviewer, 1992—; higher edn. com. N.Y. State Strategic Systemic Initiative, 1995; mem. Endicott Sch. Dist. Planning Team, 1992-03; N.Y. State Edn. Assn. adv. coun. chair, 2002-03. Contbr. articles to profl. publs. Merit badge counselor Boy Scouts Am., Endicott, 1984—; mem. com., planner Endicott Tech. Ctr., 1993—. Named N.Y. State Tech. Tchr. of Yr., Internat. Tech. Edn. Assn., 1986; named Disting. Alumnus, SUNY, Oswego, 1986; named to Elmira Southside H.S. Sports Hall of Fame, 1997; recipient Tech. in Edn. award 8 N.Y. County Tech. Rsch. Com., 1997, Outstanding Educator award N.Y. State Tech. Prep. Conf., 1998, 2003, Citizen of Yr. award N.Y. State Soc. Profl. Engrs., 1999. Mem.: N.Y. State Congress Parents and Tchrs. (hon. life), So. Tier Tech. Educators' Assn. (pres. 1974—75, Tchr. of Yr. 1984), Soc. Plastics Engrs. (pres. 1991—92, editor newsletter Perspective, Mem. of Yr. 1991—92, Past Pres. award 1992), N.Y. State Tech. Edn. Assn. (pres. 1992—93, polit. action chmn. 1991—96, authentic assessment chmn. 1994—, co-chair statewide adv. coun. 2002—03, Outstanding Svc. award 1996, Recognition award 2003), Epsilon Pi Tau. Avocations: running, hunting, woodworking, dancing. Home: 12 Tudor Dr Endicott NY 13760-4332 Office: Union-Endicott Ctrl Schs 1200 E Main St Endicott NY 13760-5220 E-mail: cgnystea@aol.com., cgoodwin@uegw.stier.org.

GOODWIN, CRAUFURD DAVID, economics educator; b. Montreal, Que., Can., May 23, 1934; came to U.S., 1962; s. George G. and Roma (Stewart) G.; m. Nancy Virginia Sanders, June 7, 1958. BA, McGill U., 1955; PhD, Duke U., 1958. Econ. research asst. Courtauld's Can., Ltd., 1955; lectr. econs. U. Windsor, Ont., 1958-59; exec. sec. Commonwealth Studies Center, Duke U., also; vis. asst. prof., 1959-60; hon. research fellow Australian Nat. U., 1960-61; asst. prof. econs. York U., Toronto, 1961-62; asst. prof. econs., asst. to provost Duke U., Durham, N.C., 1962-63, assoc. prof. econs., sec. to Univ., asst. to

provost, 1963-64, assoc. prof. econs., sec. Univ., asst. provost, 1964- 66, assoc. prof. econs., asst. provost, dir. internat. studies, 1966-68, prof. econs., vice provost for internat. studies, 1968-69, prof. econs., vice provost, dir. internat., 1969-72, prof. econs., 1971-74, James B. Duke prof. econs., 1974—, dean Grad. Sch., vice provost for research, 1980-86, acting chmn. dept. econs., 2002—03, interim chair Dept. Econs., 2002—03. Smuts vis. prof. Cambridge U., 1967-68; officer in charge European and internat. affairs Ford Found., 1971-76. Author: Canadian Economic Thought: The Political Economy of a Developing Nation 1814-1914, 1961, Economic Enquiry in Australia, 1966, The Image of Australia, 1974, (with M. Nacht) Absence of Decision, 1983, Fondness and Frustration, 1984, Decline and Renewal, 1986, Abroad and Beyond, 1988, Missing the Boat, 1991; editor: (with W.B. Hamilton and Kenneth Robinson) A Decade of the Commonwealth 1955-64, 1966, (with I.B. Holley) The Transfer of Ideas, 1968, (with R.D.C. Black and A.W. Coats) The Marginal Revolution in Economics, 1973, Exhortation and Controls, 1975, Energy Policy in Perspective, 1981, Economics and National Security, 1991, International Investment in Human Capital, 1993, (with Alan Smith, Ulrich Teichler, and Peggy Blumenthal) Academic Mobility in a Changing World: Regional and Global Trends, 1996, (with M. Nacht) Beyond Government, 1995, Talking to Themselves, 1995, Art and the Market, 1998, (with N. Demarchi) Economic Engagements with Art, 2000; editor: (jour.) History of Political Economy, 1969—, (series) Historical Perspectives on Modern Economics, 1981—. Guggenheim fellow, 1967-68 Home: PO Box 957 Hillsborough NC 27278-0957 E-mail: goodwin@econ.duke.edu.

GOODWIN, DORIS HELEN KEARNS, history educator, writer; b. Rockville Centre, N.Y., Jan. 4, 1943; d. Michael Alouisius and Helen Witt (Miller) Kearns; m. Richard Goodwin, 1975; three sons. BA magna cum laude, Colby Coll., 1964; PhD, Harvard U., 1968. Intern Dept. State, D.C., 1963, Ho. of Reps., D.C., 1965; rsch. assoc. U.S. Dept. Health, Edn., and Welfare, D.C., 1966; spl. asst. to Willard Wirtz U.S. Dept. Labor, D.C., 1967; spl. asst. to President Lyndon B. Johnson, 1968; asst. prof. Harvard U., Cambridge, 1969-71, assoc. prof. govt., 1972, historian. Spl. cons. to President Johnson, 1969-73; asst. dir. Inst. Politics, 1971—; hostess "What's the Big Idea", WGBH-TV, Boston, 1972; polit. analyst news desk, WBZ-TV, Boston, 1972; mem. Women's Polit. Caucus, Mass., 1972, Faculty Coun. Harvard U., 1971, Dem. Party Platform Com., 1972; trustee Wesleyan U., Colby Coll., Robert F. Kennedy Found. Author: Lyndon Johnson and the American Dream, 1976, The Fitzgeralds and the Kennedys: An American Saga, 1987, No Ordinary Time: Franklin and Eleanor Roosevelt-The Homefront in World War II, 1994 (Pulitzer Prize for history 1995); contbr.: Telling Lives: The Biographer's Art, 1979; forward: Mortal Friends: A Novel, 1992. Named Fulbright fellow, 1966, White House fellow, 1967. Mem. Am. Polit. Sci. Assn., Coun. Fgn. Relations, Women Involved, Group for Applied Psychoanalysis, Signet Soc., Phi Beta Kappa (outstanding young women of yr. award 1966), Phi Sigma Iota. Roman Catholic. Office: c/o Dori Lawson Soldier Creek Assoc PO Box 477 Rockport ME 04856

GOODWIN, EVERETT CARLTON, minister; b. L.A., July 28, 1944; s. Carlton Byron and Pauline (Freeman) G.; m. Jane Gray, Sept. 3, 1966; children: Elizabeth Jane, Leah Grace. BA in Polit. Sci., U. Chgo., 1966; MDiv, Andover Newton Theol. Sch., 1969; MA in History, Brown U., 1971, PhD, 1979. Ordained to ministry Am. Bapt. Chs. in U.S.A., 1971. Asst. chaplain Harvard U. No. Bapt. Edn. Soc., Cambridge, Mass., 1968—69, pastor Peoples Bapt. Ch., Cranston, RI, 1971—78, First Bapt. Ch., Meriden, Conn., 1978—81, First Bapt. Ch., Washington, 1981—94; chaplain The Flint Hill Sch., Oakton, Va., 1994—98; pastor Bapt. Fellowship of Met., Washington, 1995—2001; sr. min. Scarsdale (N.Y.) Cmty. Bapt. Ch., 1998—. Chmn. United Ministries in Higher Edn., R.I. State Coun. Chs., 1976-78; bd. dirs. Am. Bapt. Chs. R.I., Am. Bapt. Chs. Conn.; mem. exec. coun. D.C. Bapt. Conv., 1981—; mem. statements of concern com. Am. Bapt. Chs., 1993-97, chair 1995-97. Author: (book) The Magistracy Rediscovered, 1980, The New Hiscox Guide for Baptist Churches, 1995, Baptists in the Balance: The Tension Between Freedom and Responsibility, 1997, Down by the Riverside: A Brief History of Baptist Faith, 2002; contbr. ; revisions editor Diary of Isaac Backus, 1974. Mem. United Way S.E. New Eng., Providence, 1974-76, chmn. appeals com., 1977; trustee Cranston Pub. Libr., 1976-78; bd. dirs. Nat. Rainbow Coalition; vice chmn. No. Va. Youth Symphony Assn., 1992-98. Recipient Religious Leadership award Order Ea. Star, Providence, 1976; Brown U. fellow, 1971, Woodrow Wilson Found. fellow, 1971-73. Mem.: Am. Bapt. Mins. Assn., Westchester County Hist. Soc. (bd. dirs. 1999—), Am. Bapt. Hist. Soc. (v.p. 1993—2000), Bapt. World Alliance (program com. 1985—90, chair, budget and fin. com. 1990—95, history commn. 1995—), Inter-Ch. Club of D.C. (pres. 1988—90). Address: 5 Autenreith Rd Scarsdale NY 10583-4201 E-mail: ecgoodwin1@aol.com., godfrnd@aol.com. *The former structures of church and denomination are in decline. Now we come full circle to again value the significance of the individual as teacher and spiritual guide.*

GOODWIN, FREDERICK KING, psychiatrist; b. Cin., Apr. 21, 1936; s. Robert Clifford and Marion Cronin (Schmadel) G.; m. Rosemary Powers, Oct. 19, 1963; children: Kathleen Kelly, Frederick King, Daniel Clifford. BS, Georgetown U., 1958; philosophy fellow, St. Louis U., 1958-59, MD, 1963. Intern medicine and psychiatry SUNY, Syracuse, 1963-64; resident psychiatry U. N.C., Chapel Hill, 1964-65; commd. med. officer USPHS, 1965; clin. assoc. adult psychiatry br. NIMH, 1965-67; research fellow Lab. Biochemistry, Nat. Heart Inst., NIH, Bethesda, Md., 1967-68; chief sect. on psychiatry NIMH, Bethesda, 1968-73, chief clin. psychobiology br., 1977-81, sci. dir., 1981-88; apptd. by Pres. adminstr. Alcohol, Drug Abuse and Mental Health Adminstrn., Washington, 1988-92; pvt. practice Chevy Chase, Md., 1967—; dir. NIMH, Rockville, Md., 1992-94; dir. Ctr. on Neurosci. Med. Progress and Soc. George Washington U. Med. Ctr., Washington, 1994—. Faculty George Washington U. Sch. Medicine, Washington Sch. Psychiatry, Uniformed U. Sch. Health Scis.; vis. prof. U. Calif., Irvine, U. Wis., Boston U., U. So. Calif., Duke U.; cons. AMA Council on Drugs; AIDS coordinator Alcohol, Drug Abuse and Mental Health Adminstrn., 1986-90; participant pub. edn. programs on local and network television and radio. Author: (with K.R. Jamison) Manic-Depressive Illness, 1990 (Best Med. Book award 1990 Assn. Am. Pubsd.); editor in chief Psychiatry Research, 1979-97; mem. editorial bd. Archives of Gen. Psychiatry, 1978—, Psychopharmacology, 1976-79; contbr. articles to med. jours.; host (pub. radio program) The Infinite Mind, 1998— (EDI award for excellence in media, 1999). Mem. adv. bd. Max Planck Inst., Munich, W. Ger. Recipient Psychopharmacology Research prize Am. Psychol. Assn., 1970, Internat. Anna Monica prize for research in depression, 1971, Taylor Manor award, 1976, Adminstrs. award HEW, 1977, Superior Service award USPHS, 1980, Strecker award, 1983, Sr. Exec. Service Presdl. Meritorious Rank award, 1982, Disting. Rank award, 1986, Disting. Exec. Service award Sr. Exec. Assn. Profl. Devel. League, 1986, Best Tchr. in Am. Psychiatry award CME Inc., 1989, Svc. to Sci. award Nat. Assn. for Biomed. Rsch., 1990, Pub. Svc. award. Fed. Am. Socs. for Exptl. Biology, 1990, 1st recipient of Fawcett Humanitarian award NDMDA, 1990, McAlpin award NMHA, 1991, EDI award Easter Seal Soc., 1999, Nola Maddox Falcone prize, 1999; NIMH Spl. fellow, 1967-68. Fellow Am. Psychiat. Assn. (chmn. com. on protection of human subjects, task force on research tng., Hofheimer prize for research 1971, chmn. task force on future of psychiat. research), Am. Coll. Neuropsychopharmacology (chmn. com. on problems of public concern); mem. Inst. Medicine, Nat. Acad. Scis., AAAS, Am. Psychosomatic Soc., Soc. Biol. Psychiatry (A.E. Bennett award 1970), Am. Acad. Psychoanalysis, Soc. for Neuroscience, Psychiat. Rsch. Soc. (pres. 1998—), Washington Psychiat. Soc. Home: 5712 Warwick Pl Bethesda MD 20815-5502 Office: George Washington U Med Ctr Dept Psychiatry 2150 Pennsylvania Ave NW Washington DC 20037-3201 Office Fax: 202-741-2874. *Many aspects of one's innerself contribute to shaping a career, most, I suspect, evolving and changing along the way. For me, one characteristic stands out as unchanging - the capacity to derive genuine pleasure and a special sense of satisfaction from the successes and the growth of those whose careers you have helped - in a sense, your professional "children."*

GOODWIN, GEORGE EVANS, public relations executive; b. Atlanta, June 20, 1917; s. George and Carrie (Clark) G.; m. Lois Milstead, Nov. 2, 1940; children: Clark, Allen. AB with cert. in journalism, Washington and Lee U., 1939, HDL, 1997. Reporter Atlanta Georgian, 1939, Charleston (S.C.) News and Courier, 1940, Washington Times-Herald, 1940-41, Miami Daily News, 1941-42; staff writer Atlanta Jour., 1945-52; exec. dir. Central Atlanta Improvement Assn., 1952-54; v.p. First Nat. Bank of Atlanta, 1954-64; exec. v.p. Bell & Stanton, Inc., 1965-76; pres. Manning, Selvage & Lee, Atlanta, 1976-85, sr. counselor, 1985—. Exec. sec. Ga. Senatorial Transit Study Com., 1954 Chmn. Atlanta Bicentennial Commn., 1974-76; trustee emeritus Oglethorpe U.; life dir. Alliance Theater; elder Presbyn. Ch.; mem. Ga. Citizens Y2K Task Force, 1999-2000. Decorated Purple Heart, Navy Unit Commendation; recipient Pulitzer prize for local reporting, 1948, Pall Mall Big Story award, 1949, Sigma Delta Chi award for gen. reporting, 1948. Mem. SAR, Pub. Rels. Soc. Am., Rotary Internat., Delta Tau Delta, Soc. Profl. Journalists/Sigma Delta Chi (award for gen. reporting on vote fraud 1948), Omicron Delta Kappa. Home: 3302 Ivanhoe Dr NW Atlanta GA 30327-1528 Office: Manning Selvage & Lee Ste 400 1170 Peachtree St NE Atlanta GA 30309 E-mail: george.goodwin@mslpr.com.

GOODWIN, IRWIN, journalist, writer; b. Chgo., Aug. 19, 1929; s. Albert and Sarah Esther (Wallen) Goodwin; m. Mary Margaret Revell, Apr. 21, 1966 (div. 1986). AB, Roosevelt U., Chgo., 1948; MA, U. Mich., 1949. Reporter City News Bur., Chgo., 1949-50; reporter, asst. editor Newsweek, Chgo. and N.Y.C., 1952-58; dir. pub. info. Sci. Rsch. Assocs., Chgo., 1958-60; corr. Newsweek, London, 1960-70; Caribbean corr. Washington Post, San Juan, PR, 1970-72; corr. NBC News, 1970—72; spl. asst. to dir. Smithsonian Instn., Washington, 1972-73; sr. editor Nat. Acad. Scis., Washington, 1973-82; editor Washington bur. Physics Today, Washington, 1983-93, sr. editor Washington bur., 1993-2000; corr. Nature, 2000—. Co-author: Physics and Nuclear Arms Today, 1991; editor: Paying for America's Health Care, 1973, Energy and Environment: Collision of Crises, 1974; contbr. articles to profl. jours. Sgt. maj. U.S. Army, 1950-52. Recipient News Writing award Overseas Press Club, 1971, 72, Pub. Svc. Group Achievement award NASA, 1981. Mem. AAAS, Nat. Assn. Sci. Writers, Fedn. Am. Scientists, Fgn. Affairs Coun., D.C. Sci. Writers Assn., Nat. Press Club, Phi Beta Kappa. E-mail: irwingoodwin@aol.com.

GOODWIN, JAMES GORDON, JR., engineering educator, consultant, researcher; b. Walterboro, S.C., Dec. 14, 1945; BSCE, Clemson U., 1967; MSCE, Ga. Inst. Tech., 1968; PhD in Chem. Engring., U. Mich., 1976. Devel. engr. Fiber Industries, Inc., Greenville, S.C., 1967; instr. math. Nasson Coll., Springvale, Maine, 1968-69, US Peace Corps-Mid.-East Tech. U., Ankara, Turkey, 1969-70, US Peace Corps-U. Liberia, Monrovia, 1970-71; rsch. asst. dept. chem. engring. U. Mich., Ann Arbor, 1972-76; U.S.-France exch. scientist Inst. Catalysis Rsch., Villeurbanne, France, 1977-78; asst. prof. engring. U. S.C., Columbia, 1978-79; asst. prof. chem. engring. U. Pitts., 1979-83, assoc. prof., 1983-87, prof., 1987-90, William Kepler Whiteford prof. chem. engring., 1990-2000, dir. Chinese studies program Sch. Engring., 2000—. Guest prof. Inst. Chem. Physics, Tech. U. Vienna, 1987; cons. Gas-to-Oil, Inc., Pitts., 1986-89, Energy Internat., Pitts., 1991-2000, U.S. Dept. Justice, Washington, 1998-2000; co founder, dir., cons. Altamira Instruments, Inc., Pitts., 1984-94. Contbr. articles to profl. jours.; patentee in field of catalysis. Recipient award Pitts.-Cleve. Catalysis Soc., 1991. Mem. AIChE, Am. Chem. Soc., N.Am. Catalysis Soc. Office: Clemson U Dept Chem Engring Clemson SC 29634-0909 Fax: 864-656-0784. E-mail: james.goodwin@ces.clemson.edu.

GOODWIN, JAMES JEFFRIES, lawyer; b. San Juan, P.R., Aug. 24, 1949; s. David Badger and Elizabeth Ann (Ryan) G.; m. Mary Ann Schweikert, Nov. 29, 1981; 1 child, David Charles. B.A., U. Ky., 1971; M.P.A., Golden Gate U., 1977; J.D., U. Pacific, Sacramento, 1981. Bar: Calif. 1981, U.S. Dist. Ct. (ea. dist.) Calif. 1981, U.S. Ct. Appeals (9th cir.) 1983, U.S. Supreme Ct. 1984. Atty. Sacramento Pub. Defender's Office, 1980-82; sole practice, Sacramento, 1982— , legis. advocate Aircraft Owners and Pilots Assn., Washington, 1982— ; legal counsel Emergency Med. Services, Sacramento, 1984. Served to capt. U.S. Army, 1971-77. Mem. Assn. Trial Lawyers Am., Calif. Trial Lawyers Assn. Episcopalian. Office: 175 Stonington Way Folsom CA 95630-6811

GOODWIN, JEAN MCCLUNG, psychiatrist; b. Pueblo, Colo., Mar. 28, 1946; d. Paul Stanley and Geraldine (Smart) McClung; m. James Simeon Goodwin, Aug. 8, 1970; children: Laura (dec.), Amanda Harding Goodwin, Robert Caleb, Paul Joshua, Elizabeth Cronin Goodwin. BA in Anthropology summa cum laude, Radcliffe Coll., 1967; MD, Harvard U., 1971; MPH, UCLA, 1972. Diplomate Am. Bd. Psychiatry and Neurology, Am. Bd. Forensic Psychiatry; added qualifications in forensic psychiatry, psychoanalytic tng. Resident in psychiatry Georgetown U. Hosp., Washington, 1972-74, U. N.Mex. Sch. Medicine, 1974-76, asst. dir., dir. psychiat. residents tng., 1979-85; prof. Med. Coll. Wis., 1985-92, U. Tex. Med. Br., Galveston, 1992-98, prof. clin. psychiatry, 1998—; pvt. practice in gen. psychiatry, psychoanalysis. From instr. to assoc. prof. dept. psychiatry U. N.Mex. Sch. Medicine, 1976-85; cons. protective services Dept. Human Services, N.Mex., 1976-84; lectr. profl. groups; faculty Houston-Galveston Psychoanalytic Inst., 1999—. Author: Effects of High Altitude on Human Birth, 1969, Sexual Abuse: Incest Victims and Their Families, 1982, 2d edit., 1989, Rediscovering Childhood Trauma: Historical Casebook and Clinical Applications, 1993, Mischief and Mercy, 1993; co-author (with Reina Attias) Splintered Reflections: Images of the Body in Trauma, 1999; mem. editl. bd. Jour. Traumatic Stress, 1985-93, Dissociation, 1988-98, Psychotherapy Rev., 1998-2000, Trauma and Dissociation, 2000—; contbr. numerous articles on child abuse to profl. jours. Chmn. work group on child sexual abuse Surgeon Gen.'s Conf. on Violence and Pub. Health, Leesburg, Va., 1985; mem. adv. bd. Nat. Resource Ctr. on Child Sexual Abuse, 1989-96. Recipient Esther Haar award Am. Acad. Psychoanalysis, 1990, Cornelia Wilbur award Internat. Soc. for Study of Dissociation, 1994; Nat. Cen. Child Abuse and Neglect grantee, 1979-82, Nat. Inst. Aging grantee, 1980-85. Fellow Internat. Soc. Study Dissociation (exec. com. 1991-96), Am. Psychiat. Assn. (dist. br. treas., sec. N.Mex. br. 1980-82, exhibits and programs subcoms. 1985-91); mem. Am. Profl. Soc. on Sexual Abuse in Children (bd. dirs. 1986-90). Democrat. Roman Catholic. Office: 4925 Fort Crockett Blvd Apt 510 Galveston TX 77551-5949 Fax: 409-762-1163.

GOODWIN, JOHN ROBERT, lawyer, law educator, author; b. Morgantown, W.Va., Nov. 3, 1929; s. John Emory and Ruby Iona Goodwin; m. Betty Lou Wilson, June 2, 1952; children: John R., Elizabeth Ann Paugh, Mark Edward, Luke Jackson, Matthew Emory. BS, W.Va. U., 1952, LLB, 1964, JD, 1970. Bar: W.Va., U.S. Supreme Ct. Formerly city atty., county commr., spl. pros. atty.; then mayor City of Morgantown; prof. bus. law W.Va. U., Morgantown, 1964—80; prof. hotel and casino law U. Nev., Las Vegas, 1980—93, prof. emeritus, 1994—; pvt. practice, Morgantown, 1964— . Author: Legal Primer for Artists, Craftspersons, 1987, Hotel Law, Principles and Cases, 1987, Twenty Feet from Glory, 1970, Bus. Law, 3d edit., 1976, High Points of Legal History, 1982, Travel and Lodging Law, 1980, Desert Adventure, Gaming Control Law, 1985; editor Hotel and Casino Letter; past editor Bus. Law Rev., Bus. Law Letter. 1st lt. U.S. Army, Korean War. Named Outstanding West Virginian, State of W.Va.; named Hon. Gen. Gov. of W.Va., 1970. Democrat. Home: Casa Linda 48 5250 E Lake Mead Blvd Las Vegas NV 89156-6751 also: Goodwin Bldg 2d Fl Morgantown WV 26505

GOODWIN, MARTIN BRUNE, radiologist; b. Vancouver, B.C., Can., Aug. 8, 1921; came to U.S., 1948; m. Cathy Dennison, Mar. 7, 1980; 1 child, Suzanne; stepchildren: Chuck Glikas, Dianna; 1 child from previous marriage, Nancijane Goodwin Hilling. BSA in Agriculture, U. B.C., 1943, postgrad., 1943-44; MD, CM, McGill U. Med. Sch., Montreal, Can., 1948. Diplomate Am. Bd. Med. Examiners, lic. Med. Coun. Can.; cert. diagnostic and therapeutic radiology Am. Bd. Radiology; cert. Am. Bd. Nuclear Medicine. Intern Scott & White Hosp., Temple, Tex., 1948-49; fellow radiology Scott & White Clinic, 1949-52, mem. staff, 1952-53; instr. U. Tex., Galveston, 1952-53; radiologist Plains Regional Med. Ctr., Clovis, N.Mex., Portales, N.Mex., pres. med. staff; chief radiology De Baca Gen. Hosp., Ft. Sumner, N.Mex.; cons. Cannon AFB Hosp., Clovis; pvt. practice radiology Clovis, Portales, Ft. Sumner and Tucumcari, 1955— Adj. prof. health scis. Ea. N.Mex. U., 1976-77; adj. clin. prof. health scis. We. Mich. U., 1976-78 Apptd. N.Mex. Radiation Tech. Adv. Coun., N.Mex. Bd. Pub. Health; former chmn. N.Mex. Health and Social Svcs. Bd.; mem. Regional Health Planning Coun.; treas. Roosevelt County Rep. Ctrl. Com. Capt. U.S. Army M.C., 1953-55; Col. USAF M.C., 1975-79. Fellow AAAS, Am. Coll. Radiology, Am. Coll. Radiology (past councillor); mem. Am. Soc. Thoracic Radiologists (founder), Radiol. Soc. of N.Am. (past councillor), N.Mex. Med. Soc. (various coms., chmn. joint practice com., councillor bd. dirs.), N.Mex. Radiol. Soc. (past pres.), N.Mex. Thoracic Soc. (past pres.), N.Mex. Med. Review Assn. (bd. dirs. 1970-93), N.Mex. Med. Soc. Found. for Med. Care (bd. dirs. 1975—, former v.p., former treas.), County Med. Soc. (past pres., past v.p., past sec.), Clovis C. of C. (chmn. civic affairs com., bd. dirs.), Clovis Elks Lodge (past exalted ruler), Clovis Noonday Lions Club (past sec.). Republican. Presbyterian. Home: 505 E 18th St Portales NM 88130-9201

GOODWIN, NANCY LEE, corporate executive; b. Peoria, Ill., Aug. 11, 1940; d. Raymond Darrell and Mildred Louise (Brown) G. BA (Nat. Meth. scholar, Nat. Merit scholar), MacMurray Coll., 1961; MA, U. Colo., 1963; PhD, U. Ill., 1971. Tchr. Roosevelt Jr. High Sch., Peoria, 1961-62; counselor U. Ill., Urbana, 1963-66, staff assoc., asst. prof. edn. measurement Chgo., 1967-71; asst. v.p., assoc. prof. stats. Fla. Internat. U., Miami, 1971-78; pres. Greenfield (Mass.) Community Coll., 1978-82, Arapahoe Community Coll., Colo., from 1982; corp. owner MTF Enterprises; prof. Nat. U.; owner C.A.T.S. Inc., 1987—; corp. mgr. DRM Enterprises. Dir. Cons. Mid-Am. Computer Corp., First Chance Network U.S. Office Edn., 1972-78 Mem. Com. on Ill. Govt., Higher Edn. Task Force; mem. Vol. Action Center, Miami, 1972-78; active Girl Scouts U.S.A.; mem. Franklin/Hampshire Area Service Planning Team, 1978; incorporator Franklin County (Mass.) United Way, Farren Meml. Hosp.; adv. Franklin County Public Hosp.; bd. dirs. Women's Inst. Fla., Franklin County Arts Council, Franklin County Devel. Corp., Western Welcome Week, Inc.; bd. dirs., mem. fin. monitoring com. New Eng. Soy Dairy, 1980. Recipient Merit award Chgo. Tchrs. Assn., 1969; citation Girl Scouts U.S.A., 1973 Mem. NEA, Am. Assn. Higher Edn., Am. Ednl. Research Assn., Assn. Instl. Research, Centennial C. of C. (dir. 1983) Home: 5228 Del Rey Ave Las Vegas NV 89146-1414

GOODWIN, NEVA R. economist; b. N.Y.C., June 1, 1944; children: David Kaiser, Miranda Kaiser; m. Bruce Mazlish. BA, Harvard Coll., 1962; MPA, Kennedy Sch. of Govt., 1982; PhD, Boston U., 1987; BA (hon.), Coll. of the Atlantic, Bar Harbor, Maine, 1990. Dir. Program for Study of Sustainable Change and Devel. Tufts U., Medford, Mass., 1991-94, co-dir. Global Devel. And Environment Inst., 1994—. Author: Social Economics: An Alternative Theory, 1991; series editor: (6 books) Frontier Issues in Economic Thought, 1995; editor: As If the Future Mattered: Translating Social and Economic Theory into Human Behavior, 1996; editor jour. spl. issue World Devel., 1991. Trustee Winrock Internat. Inst. for Agrl. Devel., 1986—; mem. task force on population and consumption Pres.'s Coun. on Sustainable Devel., 1995; mem. adv. coun. Coll. of the Atlantic, 1996—; vice chair bd. Coll. of the Atlantic, Bar Harbor, 1981-90. Avocations: gardening, cooking, bicycling, hiking. Office: Tufts U G-DAE Fletcher Sch Medford MA 02155

GOODWIN, PHILLIP HUGH, hospital administrator; b. Paragould, Ark., Sept. 10, 1940; s. Ray H. and Helen L. (Griffin) G.; m. Pamela J. Davis, June 24, 1962; children: Philip Grey, Julie Ann. BA in Bus. and Econs., Hendrix Coll., 1962; M in Hosp. Adminstrn., Washington U., St. Louis, 1968; LLD (hon.), U. Charleston, 1995. Bus. mgr. Stuttgart (Ark.) Meml. Hosp., 1962-64; asst. adminstr. Union Meml. Hosp., El Dorado, Ark., 1964-67; adminstrv. asst. to assoc. adminstr. Hillcrest Med. Ctr., Tulsa, 1968-77, v.p., adminstr., chief operating officer, 1977-82; exec. v.p. Charleston (W.Va.) Area Med. Ctr., 1982-87, pres., chief exec. officer, 1987—2001; pres., CEO Camcare, Inc., Charleston, W.Va., 1998—, ret., 2001. Adj. faculty Wash. U., St. Louis, W.Va. U., Med. Coll. Va., W.Va. Coll. Grad. Studies; bd. dirs. Auther B. Hodges Nursing Home, Charleston, One Valley Bank N.A., Charleston, One Valley BanCorp of W.Va., frequent speaker ednl., profl. and bus. assns. Co-author: Time Management for Hospital Administrators; contbr. articles to profl. publs. Bd. dirs. Kanawha Hospice Inc., Charleston, 1987-89, W.Va. Bus. Roundtable, Wellness Coun. Am., Nat. Com. for Quality Health Care; vol. Mgmt. Assistance Program, Charleston, 1987-89, Nat. Inst. Chem. Studies, Charleston, 1988-91, Charleston Renisance Corp., Bus. and Industry Coun. of W.Va., Pvt. Industry Coun. of W.Va.; pres. Civitan Club, Tulsa, 1970. Fellow Am. Coll. healthcare Execs.; mem. W.Va. Hosp. Assn. (pres. 1987, 88), Am. Hosp. Assn. (ho. of dels. 1988—), Vol. Hosps. Am. (bd. dirs. 1978-82, bd. Wellness Coun. of Am. 1994), Charleston Ranaisance Soc., W.Va. C. of C., Charleston C. of C., Ducks Unltd., Berry Hill Country Club. Republican. Methodist. Avocations: hunting, golf, rafting, sports.

GOODWIN, RICHARD CHARLES, performing arts association administrator, actor; b. Cleve., Aug. 4, 1949; s. Ralph Wilbur and Genevieve Mary Goodwin; m. Kathleen Mary Reilly, Aug. 16, 1979 (div. Dec. 1985); 1 child, Erin Marie. BS in Edn., Ashland Coll., Ohio, 1971; MA in Theater, U. Akron, 1977; MFA in Acting, Wayne State U., 1979. Guest instr. Ashland Coll., 1972—73; tchr. speech and theatre Hillsdale H.S., Jeromesville, Ohio, 1973—74, Cloverleaf H.S., Lodi, Ohio, 1976—77; profl. actor, stuntman Hollywood, Calif., 1979—81; asst. prof. theater U. Wis., River Falls, 1981—84; prof. theater Ashland U., 1984—. Coll. liaison Ohio Ednl. Theatre Assn., Columbus, 1997—, Ohio Theatre Edn. Adv. Bd., Columbus, 1991—. Actor: (plays) Midsummer Night's Dream, 2001, How I Learned to Drive, 2003; dir.: (Am. premier) Whistle down the Wind, 1997, (world premier) Divide the Living Child, 2000. Dir. benefit performance Medina County Performing Arts Found., Medina, Ohio, 2001; site program dir. AIDS Meml. Quilt Exhibit, Ashland, Ohio, 1995; dir. all-Ohio prodn. Ohio Edn. Theatre Assn. Recipient Ashland Alumni Recognition award, Ashland Alumni Assn., 1986. Mem.: Ohio Ednl. Theatre Assn. (Hall of Fame 1997), Ohio Theatre Alliance (state chair 1997), Soc. of Am. Fight Dirs., Internat. Thespian Soc. (life). Congregationalist. Avocations: exercise, reading, sailing, theater. Office: Ashland Univ Dept Theatre 401 College Ave Ashland OH 44805

GOODWIN, RICHARD HALE, botany educator; b. Brookline, Mass., Dec. 14, 1910; s. Harry Manley and Mary Blanchard (Linder) G.; m. Esther Bemis, Oct. 12, 1936; children: Mary G. Wetzel, Richard H. Jr. AB, Harvard U., 1933, MA, 1934, PhD, 1937. Fellow Am.-Scandinavian Found., U. Copenhagen, 1937-38; instr. botany U. Rochester, N.Y., 1938-41, asst. prof., 1941-44; prof. Conn. Coll., New London, 1944-76, prof. emeritus, 1976—. Dir. conn. Arboretum, New London, 1944-65, 67-68; pres. Conservation and Rsch. Found., Boston, 1953-94; treas. Inst. Ecology, Washington, 1975-77. Co-author: Inland Wetlands of the U.S. Fellow AAAS, Am. Acad. Arts and Scis.; mem. Nat. Com. Plant Sci. Socs. (coord. 1961-62), Am. Inst. Biol. Scis. (governing bd. 1967-71), Nature Conservancy (pres. 1956-58, 64-66), Conservation and Rsch. Found. (pres. 1953-94), Am. Soc. Plant Biology, Ecol. Soc. Am., New Eng. Bot. Soc., Bot. Soc. Am., Torrey Bot. Club. Democrat. Unitarian-Universalist. Achievements include rsch. in plant morphogenesis, growth inhibitors, fluorescent constituents of plants, long range vegetation studies, effects of prescribed burning.

GOODWIN, ROBERT CRONIN, lawyer; b. Cleve., Mar. 17, 1941; s. Robert Clifford and Marion (Schmadel) G.; m. Judith Mary Baxter, June 7, 1968; children: Anne, Helen, Sharon, Katherine. AB, Fordham U., 1963; JD, Georgetown U., 1969. Bar: D.C. 1970, Md. 1990. Vol. Peace Corps, Thailand, 1964-65; asst. cmty. devel. advisor AID, Thailand, 1965-66; atty. advisor Office Gen. Coun., Dept. Commerce, 1969-74; dep. asst. gen. coun. internat. & resouce devel. programs Fed. Energy Adminstrn., Washington, 1974-77, asst. gen. coun. internat. conservation & resource devel., 1977; asst. gen. coun. internat. trade & emergency preparedness Dept. Energy, Washington, 1977-79; ptnr. Thompson, Hine & Flory, 1979-82; v.p., gen. coun. China Energy Ventures, Washington, 1982-86; ptnr. Goodwin & Soble, 1986-90; pvt. practice, 1990-92; exec. v.p., gen. coun., dir. Chindex Internat., Inc., 1992—; dir. Med. Adv. Sys., Inc., 1999—2002. Guest lectr. internat. petroleum contracts East China Petroleum Inst. Beijing, 1985; frequent lectr. on internat. contracts and Chineses legal and bus. issues; adj. assoc. prof. internat. mgmt. progam, U. Md., 1990—. Editor-in-chief Law and Policy in International Business, 1968-69; co-editor Legal Environ. for Fgn. Direct Investment in U.S., 1994; contbr. articles to profl. jours. Mem. bd. sch. bd., 1980-83. Recipient cert. of Merit Fed. Energy Adminstrn., 1974, cert. Spl. Acheivement, 1974, 76. Mem. ABA, D.C. Bar Assn., Thai-Am. Assn. (chmn. bus. com. 1991, pres. 1995), Nat. Coun. U.S. China Trade (chmn. legal com. 1987), Am. Corp. Counsel Assn., Md.-China Bus. Coun. (bd. dirs., v.p. 1999—). Home: 3710 Bradley Ln Chevy Chase MD 20815-4257 Office: 7201 Wisconsin Ave Ste 703 Bethesda MD 20814-4850

GOODWIN, ROLF ERVINE, lawyer; b. Bethlehem, Pennsylvania, May 2, 1956; s. Francis Black and Grethe Julie (Andresen) G.; m. Nancy Elsbeth (Sarstedt), Feb. 2, 1991. BA, Harvard U., 1978; JD, State U. N.Y., 1982. Bar: N.H., 1982. Assoc. Hamblett & Kerrigan P.A., Nashua, N.H., 1982-87; ptnr. Deasy & Dwyer P.A., Nashua, N.H., 1988-98, McLane Graf Raulerson & Middleton PA, 1998—. Pres., trustee Cmty. Music Sch., Nashua, 1984-95; trustee Nashua Symphony Assn., 1983-93; bd. dir. Harvard Pierian Found., Inc.,

Cambridge, Mass., 1990-2000, pres., 1993-97, life trustee, 2000; admissions chmn. Harvard-Radcliffe Club N.H., 1983—; bd. trustees United Way of Greater Nashua, 2002—. Mem. Nashua Bar Assn.; N.H. Bar Assn. (ethics com. 1987—, vice-chair 1993-97, chair 1997-2001, com. on revision of rules of profl. conduct); Greater Nashua C. of C. (chair parents and children together 1999—, leadership greater Nashua, edn. comm., local affairs comm.). Avocations: classical music, back country skiing, sailing, hiking, swimming. Office: McLane Graf Raulerson and Middleton Pa PO Box 328 900 Elm St Manchester NH 03106-0328

GOODWIN, SCOTT CRAIG, interventional radiologist; b. Gardena, Calif., July 15, 1957; s. Alfred Boree Goodwin and Dorothy Tena Curtis; m. Suzie May El-Saden, Aug. 7, 1993; children: Alexander Boree, Adam El-Saden. BS magna cum laude with dept. honors, UCLA, 1979; MD, Harvard U., 1984. Intern in internal medicine St. Luke's Hosps./Wash. U., St. Louis, 1984-85; resident in diagnostic radiology UCLA Med. Ctr., 1985-88, fellowship in cardiovascular and interventional radiology, 1988-89, vis. asst. prof. radiology, 1989, asst. prof. radiology, 1989-97, assoc. prof. radiology, 1997-2001, prof. radiology, 2001—, chief vascular, interventional radiology, 1994-2001; chief angiography and interventional radiology Daniel Freeman Hosp., Inglewood, Calif., 1989-91; vice chmn. imaging svcs. Irvine (Calif.) Med. Ctr., 1991-92; chmn., prof. radiology Wayne State U., Detroit, 2001—02; chmn. radiology Greater L.A. VA Med. Ctr., 2002—. Lectr. in field. Author: (with others) Uterine Artery Embolization for the Treatment of Uterine Leiomyomata, 1997; contbr. numerous articles to profl. jours. Recipient numerous rsch. grants. Office: Greater LA VA Med Ctr Wilshire and Sawtelle Los Angeles CA

GOODWIN, SHARON ANN, academic administrator; b. Little Rock, May 19, 1949; d. Jimmy Lee and Eddie DeLois (Cluck) G.; m. Mitchell Shayne Mick, May 4, 1968 (div. Mar. 1973); 1 child, Heather Michelle; m. Raymond Eugene Vaclavik, June 24, 1974 (div. Aug. 1982); 1 child, Tasha Rae Vaclavik. BA in Psychology, U. Houston-Clear Lake, 1980; MEd in Higher Edn. Adminstrn., U. Houston, 1990. Various clerical positions Gen. Telephone Co., Dickinson, Tex., 1969-80; state dir. Challenge, Inc., Oklahoma City, 1980-82; gen. mgr. Mr. Fix It, Houston, 1982-85; assoc. dir. admissions U. Houston, Tex., 1985-92; adminstr. Inst. for the Med. Humanities U. Tex. Med. Br., Galveston, 1992—. Contbr. poetry to World of Poetry Anthology, 1986, 87, 90, 91, Nat. Libr. of Poetry Anthology, 1997, SOL Mag., 1997-2000, Lucidity Jour., 1997, New Winds Jour., 1997, Galveston Writers Anthology 1998-99, Nat. Poetry Guild Anthology, 1998; author (poetry exhibited) Moody Med. Libr., UTMB, 2003. Mem. legis. com. Comm. Workers, Dickinson and Austin, 1975; mem. centennial choir U. Tex. Med. Br., Galveston, 1992—; vol. Dickens on the Strand, Galveston, 1993—. Recipient award of merit World of Poetry Anthology, 1986, 91, Golden Poet award, 1987, Silver Poet award, 1990, rd 1990, Golden Poet award, 1991, hon. mention SOL Mag., 1997, 98, 1st pl., 1998, 2d pl., 1998; named to Internat. Poetry Hall of Fame, 1997. Mem. AAUW, Assn. of Am. Med. Colls.-Group on Institutional Planning. Avocations: travel, music, sports, books, movies. Office: Univ Tex Med Br Inst for the Med Humanities 301 University Blvd Galveston TX 77555-1311 Home: PO Box 1346 League City TX 77574

GOODWIN, SUSAN ANN, academic administrator; b. Boston, June 9, 1944; d. Herbert Franklin and Elizabeth (Dunlap) G.; m. Michael L. Finson, June 20, 1968 (div. 1972); m. 2d Samuel Brackston Hinchey, Jan. 20, 1973. BA, Wellesley Coll., 1966; MA, Boston U., 1967; PhD, Tufts U., 1975. Assoc. prof. U. Lowell (now U. Mass. Lowell) 1977-78, spl. asst. to pres., 1977-78, dir. info. systems, 1978-80, acting dean rsch., dir. rsch. found., 1980-81, v.p. for adminstrn., 1981-84, v.p. adminstrn. and fin., 1984-91, vice chancellor adminstrn. and fin., 1991—. Bd. dir. Greater Lowell Workforce Investment Bd. Bd. dirs. Merrimack Valley United Fund, Lawrence, Mass., 1980-86. Office: U Mass Lowell MA 01854

GOODWIN, TODD, banker; b. Rochester, N.Y., Aug. 6, 1931; s. Philip Curtis and Ellen Laura (Todd) G.; m. Jacqueline Haswell, Nov. 27, 1987; children: Alexandra, Leslie, Ian (dec.), Elizabeth, Amanda. AB, Harvard Coll., 1954. With Bankers Trust, N.Y.C., 1954-57; banker White, Weld & Co., N.Y.C., 1957-78, Merrill Lynch, N.Y.C., 1978-84, Gibbons, Goodwin, Van Amerongen, N.Y.C., 1984—. Bd. dirs. Merrill Lynch Instnl. Funds, Boston. Home: 500 Captains Neck Ln Southampton NY 11968-5020 Office: Gibbons Goodwin Van Amerongen 600 Madison Ave New York NY 10022-1615

GOODWIN, W. JARRARD, otolaryngologist, educator; MD, Albany Med. Coll., 1972. Prof. dept. otolaryngology U. Miami, Fla., 1989—; dir. Sylvester Comprehensive Cancer Ctr. U. Miami Hosp. and Clinic, 1993—. Mem. Am. Acad. Otolaryngology/Head and Neck Surgery (Disting. Svc. award 1996), Am. Head and Neck Soc., Triologic Soc., Am. Soc. for Clin. Oncology, Am. Assn. for Cancer Rsch. Office: 1611 NW 12th Ave Miami FL 33136-1005 E-mail: jgoodwin@miami.edu.

GOODWIN, WILLIAM DEAN, consulting company executive; b. Independence, Kans., Aug. 3, 1937; s. William Brice and Rozella Delia (Lillibridge) G.; m. Jane Louise Varnum, Oct. 23, 1960 (div. 1973); children: Deborah Diane, Laura Louise; m. Linda Ann Booth, July 26, 1980; 1 child, William D. II. BS in Advt. and Bus., U. Kans., 1961. Editor Marshall County News, Marysville, Kans., 1961-63; dir. pub. relations U.S. Jaycees, Tulsa, 1963-67; account exec. Carl Byoir & Assocs., Chgo., 1967-68, Holder, Kennedy & Co., Nashville, 1968-70; press sec. U.S. Senator Bill Brock, Washington, 1970-74; exec. v.p. Nat. Energy Corp., Nashville, 1974-78, Tenn. Land & Exploration, Nashville, 1979-80; pres. Commerce Oil Co., Nashville, 1980-83; pvt. practice oil producer Crossville, Tenn., 1984-91; v.p. Tom Jackson & Assocs., Nashville, 1991-96; prin. Akins & Tombras, Nashville, 1996-97, Target Market Devel., Nashville, 1997—; pres. TMD Energy, 1999—, Cumberland Oil Producers Co., 2002—. Treas. Tenn. Oil Producers Polit. Action Com., Nashville, 1983-88. Editor-in-chief Future mag., 1966-67; editor Nat. Young Reps. mag., 1971-72, The Oilpatch newsletter, PLS News mag. Chmn. Davidson County Reps., Nashville, 1979; nominee Candidate for U.S. Congress 5th Dist. Tenn., 1978; cons. Nat. Rep. Senatorial Com., Washington, 1973; dir. publicity Com. to Reelect the Pres., 1972; vice chmn. Tenn. Commn. on Status of Women, 1979-80. Served with USN, 1956-57. Mem. Nat. Assn. Royalty Owners Assn. (life, bd. govs. 1986—, bd. dirs.), Tenn. Oil and Gas Assn. (exec. v.p. 1975-82, pres. 2000-2001, named Tenn. Oil Man of Yr. 1981), VFW, Nashville City Club, Downtown Kiwanis (pres.). Clubs: Lake Tansi (Crossville). Methodist. Home: 900 Hawthorne Ct Franklin TN 37069-4134 Office: One Brentwood Commons 750 Old Hickory Blvd Ste 285 Brentwood TN 37027-4509 E-mail: tmdbill@aol.com.

GOODWIN, WILLIAM MAXWELL, financial executive; b. Muncie, Ind., Oct. 13, 1939; s. Donald Dunkin and Beth Virginia (Maxwell) G.; m. LaDonna Sherry Erickson, June 9, 1962; children: Lauri Michelle, Lisa Dianne. AB, Ind. U., 1961, MBA, 1966. CPA, Ind. Staff acct., supr. Ernst & Whinney (now Ernst Whinney & Young), Indpls., 1966-72; contr. Lilly Endowment, Inc., Indpls., 1972-82, treas., sec., 1983-95, v.p. cmty. devel., 1996—. Advisor Sch. Bus., Ind. U., Bloomington, Ind., 1980-95; fin. advisor U.S. Gymnastic Fedn., Indpls., 1983-89; treas., dir. Nat. Gymnastics Found. Inc., Indpls., 1988-89. Contbr. articles to profl. jours. Treas., dir. Ind. Sports Corp., Indpls., 1979-88; dir. Youth Works, Inc., Indpls., 1977-85, Greater Indpls. Progress Com., 1996—; treas. Nat. Sports Festival, Indpls., 1982; treas., mem. exec. com. 1987 Pan Am. Games, Indpls.; chmn. AAU Sullivan Award Dinner, Indpls., 1983-94, mem. award selection com., 1993—. Capt. U.S. Army, 1962-64. Mem. AICPA, Ind. Assn. CPAs, Beta Gamma Sigma, Delta Phi Alpha. Republican. Methodist. Home: 3586 Inverness Blvd Carmel IN 46032-9380 Office: Lilly Endowment Inc PO Box 88068 Indianapolis IN 46208-0068 E-mail: goodwinb@lei.org.

GOODWYN, BETTY RUTH, librarian; b. Jasper, Ala., Oct. 7, 1930; d. Elzie Ervin and Nellie Virginia (Blackwell) O'Rear; m. Edward T. Goodwyn, Dec. 22, 1951. BA in English, Mt. Union Coll., 1962; MA in Edn., U. No. Ala., 1969; MLS, Geo. Peabody Coll., 1972; EdS, U. Ala., Birmingham, 1979; PhD, U. Ala., Tuscaloosa, 1984. Acting dir. publicity dept. Mt. Union Coll., Alliance, Ohio, 1958-60; tchr. English, dept. head Alliance (Ohio) City Schs., 1962-68; libr. Knoxville (Tenn.) City Schs., 1969-72; libr., dir. Mountain Brook High Sch. Libr., Birmingham, 1972-94. Bd. dirs. Friends of Ala. Librs., Birmingham. Author: (with others) Alabama St. Dept. of Education, 1978, 83, 84; town historian, editor The Village Voice. City mother for inc. of home area Village of Indian Springs, 1990. Mountain Brook City Schs. grantee, 1990, 93. Mem. ALA, NEA, Ala. Libr. Assn., Ala. Edn. Assn., Mountain Brook Edn. Assn., Beta Phi Mu, Phi Delta Kappa. Lutheran. Avocations: reading, photography, interior decorating, hiking.

GOODY, JOAN EDELMAN, architect; b. N.Y.C., Dec. 1, 1935; d. Beril and Sylvia (Feldman) Edelman; m. Marvin E. Goody, Dec. 18, 1960 (dec. 1980); m. Peter H. Davison, Aug. 11, 1984. BA, Cornell U., 1956; MArch, Harvard U., 1960. Registerd architect, Mass., Conn., Maine, Md., N.Y., R.I. Prin. Goody, Clancy & Assocs., Inc., Boston. Asst. prof., design critic Harvard U., Cambridge, Mass., 1973-80, Eliot Noyes vis. critic, 1985; faculty Mayors Inst. for Design, 1989—; lectr. in field. Mem. Boston Landmarks Commn., 1976-87; chair Boston Civic Design Commn.; bd. dirs. Historic Boston. Fellow AIA (hon. award 1980), Boston Soc. Architects (bd. dirs. 1983-85, design awards), Boston Archtl. Ctr. (hon.), Saturday Club, Tavern Club. Office: Goody Clancy & Assocs Inc 334 Boylston St Boston MA 02116-3866

GOODY, RICHARD MEAD, geophysicist; b. Welwyn-Garden-City, Eng., June 19, 1921; came to U.S., 1958, naturalized, 1966; s. Harold Earnest and Lilian (Rankine) G.; m. Elfriede Koch, Sept. 11, 1946; 1 dau., Brigid. PhD, Cambridge U., 1949; MA (hon.), Harvard U., 1958. With Brit. Civil Service, 1942-46; fellow St. John's Coll., Cambridge, 1950-53; reader London U., 1953-58; prof. div. applied scis. Harvard U., 1958-91; dir. Blue Hill Obs., 1958-70, Center for Earth and Planetary Physics, 1970-71. Disting. vis. scientist Jet Propulsion Lab., 1977—. Author: Physics of the Stratosphere, 1947, Atmospheric Radiation, 1964, rev. edit., 1989, Atmospheres, 1974, The Principles of Atmospheric Physics and Chemistry, 1995. Fellow Am. Geophys. Union (William Bowie medal 1998), Am. Meteorol. Soc. (hon., 50th Anniversary medal 1970, Cleveland Abbé award 1977); mem. Royal Meteorol. Soc. (Buchan prize 1955), Nat. Acad. Scis., Am. Philos. Soc. Home: 101 Cumloden Dr Falmouth MA 02540-1609

GOODYEAR, JOHN L. artist, educator; b. L.A., Oct. 22, 1930; s. Ronald R. and Lillian Lake G.; m. Anne Dixon, Dec. 12, 1953; children: Sarah Goodyear La Grange, Amy. B of Design, U. Mich., 1952, M of Design, 1954. Instr. U. Mich., Ann Arbor, 1956-62, U. Mass., Amherst, 1962-64; prof. Rutgers U., New Brunswick, N.J., 1964-97. Guest curator Rosenwald-Wolf Gallery, Phila. One-man shows include Amel Gallery, N.Y.C., 1964-66, Inhibodress Gallery, Sydney, Australia, 1972, MIT, Cambridge, 1976, N.J. State Mus., Trenton, 1981, Princeton Gallery Fine Arts, N.J., 1987, Pyramid Gallery, N.Y.C., 1989, Snyder Fine Art, N.Y.C., 1992, Frank Martin Gallery, Allentown, Pa., 1995, Michener Mus., Doylestown, Pa., 2000, Ericson Gallery, Phila., 2000, Ben Shahn Galleries Paterson U., Wayne, N.J., 2001; exhibited in group shows at Mus. Modern Art, N.Y.C., 1965, 72, Whitney Mus. Am. Art, N.Y.C., 1966, 68, Milw. Art Ctr., 1968, Chgo. Mus. Contemporary Art, 1968, Albright-Knox Gallery, Buffalo, 1968, MIT, 1973, Neuberger Mus, Purchase, N.Y., 1980, Atrium Gallery, Schenectady, 1985, Macedonian Ctr. for Contemporary Art, Thessalonika, Greece, 1987, Kunsthalle, Karlsruhe, West Germany, 1988, Henri Gallery, Washington, 1989, Amerikahaus, Cologne, 1990, Horodner-Romley Gallery, N.Y.C., 1992, Art Gallery of Hamilton, Can., 1994, N.J. State Mus., Trenton, 1996, Gallery at Bristol-Myers Squibb, Lawrenceville, N.J., 2001, Gary Snyder Fine Art, N.Y.C., 2002; represented in permanent collections Whitney Mus. Art, N.Y.C., Princeton U. Art Mus., Neuberger Mus., NYU, Nat. Mus. Am. Art, Smithsonian Instn., Mus. Modern Art, N.Y.C., Mus. des beaux arts de l'Ontario, Toronto, The Boca Raton Art Mus., Detroit Inst. of Arts, Spelman Coll., Atlanta, Met. Mus. Art, N.Y.C., Herbert F. Johnson Mus., Ithaca, N.Y., Solomon R. Guggenheim Mus., N.Y.C., British Mus., London, Bibliotecque Nat., Paris, Biblioteca di Gallery Nat. Modern Art, Rom. Mem. Am. Abstract Artists. Home: 167 Seabrook Rd Lambertville NJ 08530-2406 E-mail: jgoodyear@crusoe.net.

GOODYKOONTZ, CHARLES ALFRED, newspaper editor, retired; b. Radford, Va., Dec. 29, 1928; s. Charles A. and Claudine (Noell) G.; m. Jean Shirley Beasley, Sept. 17, 1955; 1 child, Charles Alfred III. Student, Emory and Henry Coll., 1946-48. Sports editor Radford News Jour., 1948-50; mem. staff Richmond (Va.) Times-Dispatch, 1952-81, mng. editor, 1969-81; v.p., exec. editor Richmond (Va.) Times-Dispatch and The Richmond News Leader, 1982-93, ret., 1993. Former chmn. Va. AP, UPI. Trustee Emory and Henry Coll., 1985-92; trustee, chmn. Trinity United Meth. Ch., Richmond, 1995-97; bd. govs. Va. Home for Boys, 1995-2001. With AUS, 1950-52. Recipient George Mason award for service to Va. journalism, 1973; inducted into Va. Comm. Hall of Fame, 1992. Mem. AP Mng. Editors Assn. (treas. 1988-90), Va. Press Assn. (bd. dirs. 1986-89, life), Soc. Profl. Journalists, Sigma Delta Chi (regional dir. 1971-74, nat. officer 1975-79, pres. 1978, Wells Key award 1982, pres. Found. 1985-87), Va. Inst. of Pastoral Care (bd. dirs. 1995-2000, 2001-, v.p. 1997-99). Home: 2127 Cedarfield Ln Richmond VA 23233

GOOGASIAN, GEORGE ARA, lawyer; b. Pontiac, Mich., Feb. 22, 1936; s. Peter and Lucy (Chobanian) G.; m. Phyllis Elaine Law, June 27, 1959; children— Karen Ann, Steven George, Dean Michael BA, U. Mich., 1958; JD, Northwestern U., 1961. Bar: Mich. 1961. Assoc. Marentay, Rouse, Selby, Fischer & Webber, Detroit, 1961-62; asst. U.S. Atty. U.S. Dept. Justice, Detroit, 1962-64; assoc. Howlett, Hartman & Beier, Pontiac and Bloomfield Hills, Mich., 1964-81; ptnr. Googasian Hopkins Hohauser & Forhan, Bloomfield Hills, Mich., 1981-96, The Googasian Firm, Bloomfield Hills, 1996—. Mem. bd. law examiners State of Mich., 1997—2002, pres., 2001—02. Author: Trial Advocacy Manual, 1984, West Groups Michigan Practice Torts, vols. 14 and 15, 2001. Pres. Oakland Parks Found., Pontiac, 1984-89; chmn. Oakland County Dem. party, Pontiac, 1964-70; state campaign chmn. U.S. Senator Philip A. Hart, Detroit, 1970; bd. dirs. Big Bros. Oakland County. 1968-73 Fellow Am. Bar Found., Am. Coll. Trial Lawyers, Internat. Acad. Trial Lawyers; mem. ABA (del. 1992-93, exec. coun. nat. conf. bar pres. 1993-96), ATLA, Am. Bd. Trial Advocates, State Bar Mich. (pres. elect 1991-92, pres. 1992—), Oakland County Bar Assn. (pres. 1985-86), Oakland Bar Found. (pres. 1990-92). Clubs: U. Mich. Club Greater Detroit. Presbyterian. Home: 3750 Orion Rd Oakland MI 48363-3029 Office: 6895 Telegraph Rd Bloomfield Hills MI 48301-3138

GOOKIN, THOMAS ALLEN JAUDON, civil engineer; b. Tulsa, Aug. 5, 1951; s. William Scudder and Mildred (Hartman) G.; m. Sandra Jean Andrews, July 23, 1983. BS with distinction, Ariz. State U., 1975. Registered profl. engr., Calif., Ariz., Nev., land surveyor Ariz., hydrologist. Civil engr., treas. Gookin Engrs. Ltd, Scottsdale, Ariz., 1968—. Chmn. adv. com. Ariz. State Bd. Tech. Registration Engring., 1984—. Recipient Spl. Recognition award Ariz. State Bd. Tech. Registration Engring., 1990. Mem. NSPE, Ariz. Soc. Profl. Engrs. (sec. Papago chpt. 1979-81, v.p. 1981-84, pres. 1984-85, named Young Engr. of Yr. 1979, Outstanding Engring. Project award 1988), Order Engr., Ariz. Congress on Surveying and Mapping, Am. Soc. Civil Engrs., Ariz. Water Works Assn., Tau Beta Pi, Delta Chi (Tempe chpt. treas. 1970-71, sec. 1970, v.p. 1971), Phi Kappa Delta (pres. 1971-73). Republican. Episcopalian. Achievements include co-author Globe Equity # 59 Call System. Avocations: disneyana, science fiction, computer gaming. Home: 10760 E Becker Ln Scottsdale AZ 85259-3868 Office: Gookin Engrs Ltd 4203 N Brown Ave Ste A Scottsdale AZ 85251-3946

GOOLDY, PATRICIA ALICE, retired elementary education educator; b. Indpls., Nov. 23, 1937; d. Harold Emanuel and Emma Irene (Wade) VanTreese; m. Walter Raymond Gooldy, May 4, 1968. BS, U. Indpls., 1959; MS, Butler U., 1963. Tchr. Franklin Twp. Cmty. Schs., Indpls., 1959-68, 72-99, USA Dep. Schs., Bad Kreuznach, Germany, 1969-72; ret., 1999. Owner Ye Olde Genealogie Shoppe, Indpls., 1972—; lectr. in field. Author: 21 Things I Wish I'd Found, 1984; editor: Indiana Wills to 1880: Index to Indiana Wills, 1987; co-editor: Indiana Manual For Gen, 1991, Illinois Manual For Gen, 1994. Mem. Franklin Twp. Hist. Soc. (founder), Ind. Geneal. Soc. (chartered). Office: Ye Olde Genealogie Shoppe PO Box 39128 Indianapolis IN 46239-0128 E-mail: yogs@iquest.net.

GOOLKASIAN, PAULA A. psychologist, educator; b. Methuen, Mass., Aug. 9, 1948; d. Paul K. and Sadie T. (Touma) G.; m. Francis C. Martin, July 29, 1978; 1 child, Christopher. BA, Emmanuel Coll., 1970; MS, Iowa State U., 1972, PhD, 1974. Asst. prof. U. N.C., Charlotte, 1974-79, assoc. prof., 1979-85, prof. psychology, 1985—, pres. faculty, 1989—. Cons. in field Contbr. articles to profl. jours. Nat. Def. Ednl. Act. fellow, 1971-74; grantee NSF, NIH, and numerous others. Mem. AAAS, APA, Am. Psychol. Soc., Psychonomics Soc., Soc. for Computers in Psychology (sec.-treas. 1989-91, pres. 1994), Sigma Xi, Phi Kappa Phi. Home: 20125 River Chase Dr Cornelius NC 28031-7175 Office: U NC Dept Psychology Charlotte NC 28223 E-mail: pagoolka@email.uncc.edu.

GOOLRICK, JOHN COLE, congressional staff member, writer, consultant; b. Fredericksburg, Va., July 7, 1935; s. John Tackett and Olive Elizabeth (Jones) G.; m. Alice Solone Rock, Mar. 26, 1960 (div. June 1992); 1 child, Lisa Cole. Student, U. Richmond, 1953-58. Polit. reporter, columnist Star, Fredericksburg, 1957-87; dist. rep. U.S. Congressman French Slaughter, Washington, 1987-91, U.S. Congressman George Allen, Washington, 1991-92, U.S. Congressman Herbert Bateman, Washington, 1993-2000, U.S. Congressman Jo Ann Davis, Washington, 2001—. Polit. columnist Va. newspapers. Mem. Va. Bd. Hist. Resources, Va. Bd. Mil. Affairs, Richmond, Mil. Adv. Coun., Richmond, Va. Charitable Gaming Bd. Mem. Nat. Assn. Uniformed Svcs., Va. Capital Corr. Assn. (co-founder), Elks, Pythians, Eagles, Am. Legion, Gen. Meade Soc. Phila., Three Stooges Fan Club. Republican. Avocations: history, travel. Home: Box 8283 Fredericksburg VA 22404 Office: 4500 Plank Rd Fredericksburg VA 22407 E-mail: JohnCGoolrick@aol.com.

GOOLRICK, ROBERT MASON, lawyer; b. Fredericksburg, Va., Mar. 25, 1934; s. John T. and Olive E. (Jones) G.; m. Audrey J. Dippo (div.); children: Stephanie M., Meade A. BA with distinction, U. Va., 1956, JD, 1959. BAr: Va. 1959, D.C. 1959, U.S. Dist. Ct. D.C. 1961, U.S. Ct. Appeals (D.C. cir.) 1961. Assoc. Steptoe & Johnson, Washington, 1959-65, ptnr., 1965-79; sole practice Alexandria, Va., 1979-83; cons. bus., oil and gas fin. Instr. U. Va. Law Sch. Author: Public Policy Toward Corporate Growth, 1978, Corporate Mergers and Acquisitions under Federal Securities Laws, 1978. Mem. ABA (corps. sect.), Jefferson Soc., Raven Soc., Order of Coif, Phi Beta Kappa. Home: 7462 Cross Gate Ln Alexandria VA 22315-4618 Office: PO Box 150672 Alexandria VA 22315-0672 E-mail: rmgoolrick@starpower.net.

GOOLSBY, ALLEN CUNNINGHAM, III, lawyer; b. Richmond, Va., Oct. 19, 1939; s. Allen C. Goolsby Jr. and Adelaide Rawles; m. Louanna Godwin. BA, Yale U., 1961; LLB, U. Va., 1968. Bar: Va., U.S. Dist. Ct. (ea. dist.) Va. Ptnr. Hunton & Williams, Richmond, Va., 1975—. Bd. dirs. Noland Co. Author: Virginia Corporation Law Practice, 1990, Goolsby on Virginia Corporations, 2002. Fellow Am. Bar Found., Va. Bar Found. Office: Hunton & Williams Riverfront Plz East Tower PO Box 1535 Richmond VA 23218-1535

GOOLSBY, CHARLES WILLIAM, artist, educator; b. Trenton, Mich., Sept. 11, 1958; s. William Lyman and Helen May (Richardson) G. BFA in Art, Radford U., 1980; MFA in Art, James Madison U., 1994. Art instr. Pulaski County H.S., Dublin, Va., 1980-87, Augusta County Schs., Fishersville, Va., 1987-88, Waynesboro (Va.) H.S., 1988-90; adj. instr. art Blue Ridge C.C., Weyers Cave, 1989-90; grad. tchg. asst. James Madison U., Harrisonburg, 1991-94; assoc. prof. art Emory & Henry Coll., Emory, 1994—. One-person shows include Danville (Va.) Mus. Fine Arts, 1986, James Madison U.,1 994, Washington and Lee U., Lexington, Va., 1991, Roanoke Coll., Salem, Va., 1992, Berea (Ky.) Coll., 1997, Ralston Fine Arts, Johnson City, Tenn., 1997, William King Regional Arts Ctr. Abingdon, Va., 1998, Spartanburg (S.C.) Mus. Art, 1998, Elon U., 2000; exhibited in group shows at Brevard Coll., N.C., Butler Inst. Am. Art, Youngstown, Ohio, Ctrl. Mo. State U., Warrensburg, Appalachian State U., Boone, N.C., Md. Fedn. Art, Annapolis, others; represented in collections at Appalachian State U., Blue Ridge C.C., Weyers Cave, Va., Roanoke County Courthouse, Salem, Va., Radford (Va.) U., Roanoke Times and World News. Fellow Va. Mus. Fine Arts, 1997, Marie Walsh Sharpe Art Found., 1989, Va. Ctr. for Creative Arts, 2002, Va. Ctr. for the Arts, 2002, others; Liquitex-Binney & Smith Inc. grantee, 1992. Mem. So. Graphics Coun., Coll. Art Assn. Avocations: bicycling, hiking, tennis.

GOOLSBY, DONALD ALLTON, water resources scientist; b. Pinehurst, N.C., Dec. 10, 1937; s. Allton Arras and Esther Belle Goolsby; m. Eddie Barbara Fletcher, Dec. 29, 1961; children: Gregory Allton, Kimberly Kay Adair. BS, Fla. State U., 1964. Analytical chemist U.S. Geol. Survey, Ocala, Fla., 1964—71, water quality specialist Tallahassee, 1971—76, staff chemist Reston, Va., 1976—79, regional water quality specialist Denver, 1980—90, chief midcontinent herbicide project Lakewood, Colo., 1991—96, sr. scientist gulf hypoxia assessment, 1997—2001, scientist emeritus, 2001—. Author: (book) Agrochemical Environmental Fate; contbr. chapters to books, articles to profl. jours. Recipient Meritorious Svc. award, U.S. Dept. Interior, 1988, Disting. Svc. award, 1999. Mem.: Estuarine Rsch. Fedn., Am. Geophysican Union (assoc.), Am. Water Resources Assn. (assoc.). Avocations: golf, travel, hiking, music. Office: US Geological Survey Mail Stop 406 Lakewood CO 80225

GOON, GILBERT, software consultant; b. N.Y.C., Oct. 7, 1946; s. Fook Mun and Nellie (Eng) G.; m. Susan R. Lishinsky, May 23, 1982; 1 stepchild, Deborah F. Rosenblum; 1 child, Michael Francis. BA, Princeton U., 1967; MA, Columbia U., 1972, MPH, 1975. Assoc. engr. Sperry Systems Mgmt., Great Neck, N.Y., 1972-75; sr. staff analyst Loral Electronic Systems, Yonkers, N.Y., 1975-81; cons. ITT Avionics Div., Nutley, N.J., 1981-86, Norden Sys., Norwalk, Conn., 1986; software mgr. BAE Systems, Yonkers, 1986—. Recipient BAE Sys. Engring. Bus. Area Leadership award, 2001; named Princeton U. chess champion, 1964-67, N.Y.C amateur chess champion, 1967. Mem. World Tae Kwon Do Assn. (3rd degree black belt), Harley Owners Group (charter mem. White Plains, N.Y. chpt.). Democrat. Lutheran. Avocations: Tae Kwon Do, motorcycling, contract bridge (life master). Office: BAE Systems 1 Ridge Hill Yonkers NY 10710 E-mail: gilbert.goon@baesystems.com.

GOOREY, NANCY JANE, dentist; b. Davenport, Iowa, May 8, 1922; d. Edgar Ray and Glenna Mae (Williams) Miller; m. Douglas B. Miller, Sept. 12, 1939 (div. 1951); children: Victoria Lee, Nickola Ellen, Douglas George, Melahna Marie; m. Louis Joseph Roseberry Goorey, Feb. 22, 1980. Student, Wooster (Ohio) Coll., 1939-40; DDS, Ohio State U., 1955. Cert. in gen. anesthesiology. Mem. faculty coll. dentistry Ohio State U., Columbus, 1955-86, dir., chmn. div. dental hygiene coll. dentistry, 1969-86, asst. dean coll. dentistry, 1975-86, mem. grad. faculty colls. dentistry and medicine, 1980-86, asst. dean, prof. emeritus colls. dentistry, 1986—. Moderator, prodn. chmn. Lifesavers 40 Prodns., 1981—; mem. task force on sch. based-linked oral health project Ohio Dept. Health, 1999—; mem. Franklin County Task Force on Access to Dental Care. Producer, video program Giving Your Mouth a Sporting Chance, 1990, video Operation TACTIC. Chmn. State Planning Com. for Health Edn. in Ohio, Columbus, 1976-77, 87-88, 95-97; founder Coun. on Health Info., Columbus, 1980, del., 1981-85, chmn., pres., 1985-86, chmn. prodn. com., 1986—, chmn. Capital Campaign; trustee Caring Dentists Found., Mayor's Drug Edn. and Prevention Program, Columbus, 1980—; mem. edn. com. Franklin County Rep. com., exec. com., 1993—; mem. human svcs. com. The Columbus Found.; pres. Worthington Arts Coun., 1998-2000. Recipient Vol. of Yr. award Columbus Health Dept., 1988-89, Dental Hygiene Nancy J. Goorey award Ohio State U., 1988, Drug Free Sch. Consortium award, 1996, Champion of Children's Oral Health award Ohio Dept. of Health Dental Divsn., 1997, Disting. Alumnus award Ohio State U. Coll. Dentistry, YWCA Women of Achievement award, 2000. Fellow: Internat. Coll. Dentists, Am. Soc. Dental Anesthesiology, Am. Coll. Dentists (chmn.-elect 1989—90, chmn. Columbus sect.); mem.: ADA (nat. consumer advisor 1975—78, coun. edn. and licensure 1997—), Cols. Med. Assoc. Mem. Sports Med. Comm., Ohio Dept. Health (sch. linked oral health project 1999), Ohio State Med. Assn. Alliance (chmn. state com. legis. affairs 1993—94, chmn. state health promotions com. 1994—95, v.p. 1995—97, pres.-elect 1997, pres. 1998), The Found. of the Acad. of Medicine (v.p. 1993—94), Columbus Dental Soc. (chmn. coun. on constn. and bilaws on jud. affairs 1989—, pres. bd. dirs. 1986—87, 1989—91, chmn. sports dentistry com. 1995—), Ohio Dental Assn. (cons. 1979—, mem. subcoun. on dentists concerned for dentists 1994—96, chmn. subcoun. chem. dependency, prin. investigator, chair smokeless tobacco rsch., Ohio Disting. Dentist 1983), Am. Assn. Dental Schs. (pres. 1972—77, v.p.), Caring Dentists Found. (trustee), The Columbus Found. (human svcs. com.), Acad. of Medicine Aux. (pres. 1992—93, 1996—97, chair mouthguard project), Ohio State U. Faculty and Profl. Womens Club (pres. 1971—72), Ohio State U. Starling Womens Club (pres. 1982—83), Omicron Kappa Upsilon. Republican. Episcopalian. Avocations: camping, travel, bridge, cooking, wine. Office: Ohio State U Coll Dentistry 305 W 12th Ave Columbus OH 43210-1267

GOORLEY, JOHN THEODORE, consulting chemist; b. Mar. 12, 1907; s. William H. and Emma (Ness) G.; m. Ethel L. Coleman, Nov. 27, 1935; children: John. ALice (Mrs. Harold A. Bread, Jr.), Robert, Richard. Chief control chemist Burroughs Wellcome & Co., Tuckahoe, N.Y., 1933-38; rsch. dir. Labs. Lex, Havanna, Cuba, 1939-42, Ben Venue Labs., Bedford, Ohio, 1946-48, Johnson & Johnson de Argentina, Buenos Aires, 1948-50; owner, dir. Labs. Goorley, Buenos Aires, 1950-55; prof. pharm. chemistry Ohio No. U., Ada, 1956-57; v.p., gen. mgr. Inland Alkaloid Co., Tipton, Ind., 1957-58; prof. pharm. chemistry N.E. La. U., Monroe, 1957-68; prof. pharmacognosy, 1968-72; chemist Labs. Finlay, S.A., San Pedro Sula, Honduras, 1974-76; prof. chemistry and pharmacy U. Nacional Autonoma de Honduras, Tegucigalpa, 1976; Fulbright prof. U. Honduras, 1966-67; cons. chemist, 1967—; exec. v.p. Enviro-Med. Labs., Ruston, La., 1978-82. Vis. prof. U. El Salvador, 1968. Active Little Theater, Monroe; rsch. in pharm. chemistry and biochemistry; contbr. articles to profl. jours.; patentee in field. Served to capt. AUS, 1942-46; lt. col. AUS, 1956-63. Col. staff govs., Ky., La. Mem. AAAS, Am. Pharm. Assn., Am. Chem. Soc., NY Acad. Scis., Sigma Xi, Rho Chi, Phi Delta Chi, Tau Kappa Epsilon. Achievements include being the first to isolate the antibiotic Bacitracin in pure form. Home: 3806 Gilbert Dr Apt B Shreveport LA 71104-5032

GOORLEY, JOHN TIMOTHY, nuclear engineer; b. Ft. Campbell, Ky., Apr. 13, 1974; s. John Thomas and Sherrie Goorley. BS in nuc. engring., Tex. A&M U., 1992—96; BS in radiol. health engring., Tex.A&M U., 1992—96; MS in nuc. engring., PhD in nuc. engring., MIT, 1996—2002. Technical staff Los Alamos Nat. Lab., N.Mex., 2002—. Scholar President's Endowed scholarship, Tex. A&M U., 1992—96. Mem.: Am. Nuc. Soc., Sigma Xi, Alpha Nu Sigma. Avocations: medieval studies, travel, fencing. Home: 601 West San Mateo #80 Santa Fe NM 87505 Personal E-mail: jgoorley@alum.mit.edu.

GOOS, ROGER DELMON, mycologist; b. Beaman, Iowa, Oct. 29, 1924; s. Gus and Georgiana Bertha (Witt) G.; m. Mary Lee Engel, Sept. 21, 1946; children: Marinda Lee, Suzanne Maurine. BA, U. Iowa, 1950, PhD, 1958. Mycologist United Fruit Co., Norwood, Mass., 1958-62; scientist USPHS, NIH, Bethesda, Md., 1962-64; curator of fungi Am. Type Culture Collection, Rockville, Md., 1964-68; assoc. researcher, vis. assoc. prof. botany U. Hawaii, Honolulu, 1968-70; assoc. prof. botany U. R.I., Kingston, 1970-72, chair dept. of botany, 1971-86, prof. botany, 1972-95, prof. emeritus, 1995—. Trustee Am. Type Culture Collection, Rockville, Md., 1977-82; vis. rschr. U. B.C., 1977, U. Hawaii, 1977, U. Exeter, U.K., 1984, Bishop Mus., 1990. Served with U.S. Army, 1944-46, 50-51. Decorated Bronze Star, Purple Heart, Combat Infantry badge; Indo-Am. fellow, U. Madras, India, 1981; Fulbright scholar U. Lisbon, 1993. Mem. Mycol. Soc. Am. (sec.-treas. 1980-83, v.p. 1983-84, pres.-elect 1984-85, pres. 1985-86), Bot. Soc. Am., Am. Soc. Microbiology, Am. Phytopath. Soc., Mycol. Soc. Japan, Brit. Mycol. Soc. Home: 4 Tanglewood Trl Narragansett RI 02882-1034 Office: U RI Ranger Hall Dept Biol Scis Kingston RI 02881 E-mail: Rgoos@uri.edu.

GOOTEE, JANE MARIE, lawyer; b. Jasper, Ind., July 5, 1953; d. Thomas H. and Anne M. (Dreifke) G. BA, Ind. U., 1974; JD cum laude, St. Louis U., 1977. Bar: Ind. 1977, Mo. 1978, Mich. 1980, Ohio 1983, U.S. Dist. Ct. (so. dist.) Ind. 1977, U.S. Dist. Ct. (ea. dist.) Mich. 1980, U.S. Ct. Appeals (7th cir.) 1978, U.S. Supreme Ct. 1980, U.S. Ct. Appeals (6th cir.) 1982, U.S. Ct. Appeals (4th cir.) 1986. Dep. atty. gen. Ind., Indpls., 1977-79; corp. atty. Dow Chem. Co., Midland, Mich., 1979-81, ea. div. counsel, 1981 84, sr. atty., 1984-86, Mich. div. counsel, 1986-90, Dow Europe sr. staff counsel, 1990-94, asst. gen. counsel fin. law, 1994-99, asst. gen. counsel litigation, 1999-2002, dep. dir. global ethics and compliance, 2003—; adv. com. Nat. Chamber Litigation Ctr. Environ. Law, 1985-90; chair Dow Epidemiology Instl. Rev. Bd., 1984-90; pro-bono def. Midland Cir. Ct., 1980-81. Bd. dirs. Big Sisters Midland, 1979-81, 84-86, Big Bros./Big Sisters Midland, 1986-90, also pres., 1988-89; exec. bd. Lake Huron Area coun. Boy Scouts Am., 1988-90, N.Y.C. YWCA Acad. of Women Achievers, 1988. Fellow Mich. State Bar Found; mem. ABA, Mo. Bar, Mich. Bar Assn. Home: 1303 Foxwood Dr Midland MI 48642 Office: Dow Legal Dept 2030 Dow Ctr Midland MI 48674 E-mail: jgootee@dow.com.

GOOTNICK, MARGERY FISCHBEIN, lawyer; b. Rochester, N.Y., Oct. 24, 1927; d. Morris R. and Regina (Kroll) Fischbein; m. Lester T. Gootnick, Mar. 1, 1952; children— Jonathon, David, Amy. B.A., Harvard U., 1949; J.D., Cornell U., 1952. Bar: N.Y. 1952. Assoc. Stone & Hoffenberg, Rochester, N.Y., 1952-55; sole practice, Rochester, 1968—; permanent arbitrator Am. Airlines and Assn. Profl. Flight Attendants, NW Airlines and Teamsters Local 2000, Presbyn. Hosp.-N.Y. State Nurses Assn., U. Rochester and U. Rochester Security Guards Union, numerous others; chmn. Fgn. Service Impasse Disputes Panel, Washington, 1983-97; apptd. fgn. svc. grievance bd. U.S. State Dept., 1997; mem. exec. com. N.Y. State Bar, 1998. Mem. Rep. Jud. Screening Com., Rochester, 1976—. Mem. ABA, Fed. Bar Assn., Nat. Acad. Arbitrators (v.p. 1992-94, chair membership com. 1988-91, exec. com. 1987, bd. govs. 1983-86), N.Y. State Bar Assn. (labor and employment sect. chair elect 1994—, exec. com. 1982—), Soc. Fed. Labor Rels. Profls. (1st v.p. 1993—), Am. Arbitration Assn. (upstate N.Y. labor adv. panel). Office e-mail: mornings@ix.netcom.com. Home and Office: 46 Knollwood Dr Rochester NY 14618-3513

GOOTT, ALAN F(RANKLIN), lawyer; b. Washington, Aug. 6, 1947; BA, George Washington U., 1969; JD cum laude, Harvard U., 1973. Bar: N.Y., 1974, U.S. Dist. Ct. (so., ea. dists.) N.Y. 1974, U.S. Ct. Appeals (2d cir) 1974. Assoc. Kaye Scholer LLP, N.Y.C., 1973-82, ptnr., 1982—. Office: Kaye Scholer LLP 425 Park Ave New York NY 10022-3506 E-mail: agoott@kayescholer.com.

GOOTT, DANIEL, government official, consultant; b. N.Y.C., Apr. 23, 1919; s. Hyman and Min (Novak) G.; m. Sylvia Blousman, Aug. 29, 1940; children: Alan F., Eugene M. BSS, CCNY, 1940; postgrad., Columbia U., 1940-41; diploma, Sch. Internat. Studies, Geneva, 1946. Assoc. chief labor rels. br. War Prodn. Bd., 1942-43; spl. asst. internat. labor affairs to under sec. state US Dept. State, Washington, 1955—60; dep. coord. internat. labor affairs Office Sec. State, Washington, 1961-62; 1st sec., labor attache Am. Embassy, Paris, 1962-65; chief spl. profl. affairs Office Dep. Undersec. of State for Adminstrn., Washington, 1965—. Labor and UN advisor Bur. European Affairs; mem. U.S. del. 7th spl. and 30th regular sessions UN Gen. Assembly, 1975; pvt. cons. internat. labor and bus. affairs, 1980. With AUS, 1943-46. Decorated Bronze Star. Mem. Am. Econ. Assn., Indsl. Rels. Rsch. Assn., Am. Fgn. Svc. Assn., Am. Acad. Polit. and Social Sci., Am. Club, mem. US Delegation to Annual Conferences of UN Spec. Agency, ILO, Geneva, Switzerland. Home: 15101 Interlachen Dr Apt 917 Silver Spring MD 20906-5620

GOOVAERTS, PIERRE ETIENNE, agriculture engineering educator; b. Charleroi, Hainaut, Belgium, June 12, 1964; s. Jacques and Bernadette (Philippe) G.; m. Nathalie Marthe Vandecan, Jul. 26, 1988; children: Maxime, Xavier. Degree in agrl. engring., Cath. U. Louvain, 1987, PhD in Agr., 1992. Rsch. asst. Nat. Fund for Sci. Rsch., 1988-92, sr. rsch. scientist, 1994-97; postdoctoral fellow Stanford (Calif.) U., 1993-94; asst. prof. U. Mich., Ann Arbor, 1997—2002; chief scientist Biomedware, Inc., Ann Arbor, 2002—. Pres. Pteestet, 2003—. Author: Geostatistics for Natural Resources Evaluation, 1997; contbr. articles to profl. jours. Lt. Belgian Air Force, 1987-88. Grantee Fulbright, 1993, NATO, 1994, Belgian Am. Ednl. Found., 1993; recipient Vistelius Rsch. award, 1999. Mem. Am. Coun. Geostatistics (mem. exec. com.), Internat. Assn. for Math. Geology, Internat. Assn. Soil Sci. (working group on peolometrics). Avocations: soccer, stamps. Home: 710 Ridgemont Ln Ann Arbor MI 48103-2655 Office: Biomedware Inc 516 N State St Ann Arbor MI 48109 Business E-Mail: goovaert@engin.umich.edu.

GOOZNER, MERRILL, journalist; b. N.Y.C., 1950; Degree in History, U. Cin., 1975; MS in Journalism, Columbia U., 1982. Journalist Hammond Times, Hammond, Ind., 1982—83, Crain's Chgo. Bus., 1983—87; bus. reporter, Tokyo bur. chief Chgo. Tribune, 1987—, chief Asia corr., 1991—95, nat. corr., 1995—98, chief econs. corr., 1998—2000. Vis. prof. sch. journalism NYU, N.Y.C., 2000—. Office: NYU Dept Journalims Washington Bur 10 Washington Pl New York NY 10003-6604

GOPALAKRISHNA, SRINATH, finance educator; PhD, Purdue U., 1988. Asst. prof. mktg. Pa. State U., University Park, 1988—96; assoc. prof. mktg. U. Mo., Columbia, 1996—. Mem.: Am. Mktg. Assn. Office: U Mo 434 Cornell Hall Columbia MO 65211 Office Fax: 573-884-0368. E-mail: srinath@missouri.edu.

GOPALAKRISHNAN, SHANTHI, technology educator; b. Chennai, Tamil Nadu, India, Dec. 14, 1961; d. Neela Gopalakrishnan; m. Anil Vijayan; children: Kavita Vijayan, Divya Vijayan. BA, Womens' Christian Coll., Chennai, India, 1981; MBA, Bajaj Inst., Bombay, India, 1983, Rutgers U., 1991, PhD, 1995. Assoc. prof. N.J. Inst. Tech., Newark, 1999—; from asst. prof. to assoc. prof. Fairleigh Dickinson U., Teaneck, NJ, 1994—99; asst. prof. Montclair State U., Upper Montclair, NJ, 1993—94. Recipient Best Empirical paper, Ea. Acad. Mgmt., 1995, Best Paper award, IEEE, 2001. Mem.: Acad. Mgmt. (Best Paper award TIM divsn. 1997). Hindu. Office: NJ Inst Tech Sch Mgmt Newark NJ 07102 Office Fax: 973-596-3074. Business E-Mail: gopalakr@adm.njit.edu.

GOPALAKRISHNAN, SURESH, computer engineer; b. Trichur, Kerala, India, May 14, 1973; arrived in U.S., 1997; s. Gopalakrishnan Venkateswaran and Lalitha Gopalakrishnan. B in Technology, Regional Engring. Coll. Calcutta, 1994; MS, Rutgers U., 2001. Sr. software engr. Tata Unisys Ltd., Bangalore, India, 1994—96; intern, grad. asst. C&C Labs, Princeton, NJ, 1997—99, Tacit Networks, South Plainfield, NJ, 2001—02, sr. software engr., 2003—. Tchg. asst., instr. Rutgers U., New Brunswick, NJ, 1997—2002; intern Bell Labs Lucent Technologies, Murray Hill, NJ, 2002. Contbr. Achievements include patents in field. Avocations: flying, cricket, music, reading, motorbikes. Office: Tacit Networks 4041 N Hadley Rd South Plainfield NJ 07080 Home: 10 Landing Ln #1A New Brunswick NJ 08901*

GOPHEN, MOSHE, research scientist; b. Kibbutz Afikim, Israel, Dec. 18, 1936; s. Itzchak and Sara (Sheinberger) G.; m. Eva Gophen, May 5, 1998; children from previous marriage: Michal, Yair, Ruth, Rachel. BSc, Hebrew U., Jerusalem, 1963, MSc, 1967, PhD, 1976. H.S. tchr., Beit-Yerach, Israel, 1963-69; sr. scientist Kinneret Limnological Lab., Tiberias, Israel, 1968—; lectr. Hebrew U., 1972 73, Haifa U., Oranim, Israel, 1973-78; sr. scientist Kinneret Limnological Lab., Tiberias, Israel, 1968—2001, dir., 1980-86; rsch. prof. U. Okla., Norman, 1992-94; ret., 2001. Sci. coord. Hula (Israel) Project, 1995—, chmn. Hula com., 1997—; sr. coord. Hula Project MIGAL Galilee Tech. Ctr., 2001—; prof. Tel-Hai (Israel) Coll., 1995—; cons. Ilopango Assn., San-Salvador, El-Salvador, 1995—, Lake Amatitlan Assn., Guatemala City, Guatamela, 1995-96. Author: Lake Kinneret, 1992 (Kinneret Authority award 1989); co-author: Scientific Basis for Water Resources Management, 1985, Large Lakes-Ecological Structure and Function, 1990 (Minerva award 1990), Guidelines of Lake Management, 1995 (Kinneret Lab. award 1995); contbr. articles to profl. jours. Edn. com. Karmiel mcplty., 1979; chmn. Ctrl. Com. for Labor Party, Karmiel, 1987-88; vol. Ecological Com., Karmiel, 1995—. Sgt. Israel mil., 1955-58. Eshkol Found. Water Rsch. fellow Israel Kinneret Inst., 1973, DAAD fellow, Germany, 1982, Minerva fellow, Germany, 1987-88. Mem. Internat. Assn. Limnology, Am. Soc. Limnology and Oceanography, Freshwater Biol. Assn. (life). Avocations: classical music, art, astronomy and universe sciences, nature. Home: Hativat Iftach St 73/1 20100 Karmiel Israel Office: MIGAL POB 90000 12100 Rosh-Pina Israel

GOPMAN, HOWARD Z. lawyer; b. Kansas City, Mo., Oct. 29, 1940; s. Norman S. and Rose E. G.; m. Carol Ann, Mar. 25, 1979; children: James, William. BS, U. Wis., 1962, JD, 1965, MBA, 1967. Cert. Wis. 1965, Ill. 1969, U.S. Dist. Ct. (no. dist.) Ill. 1969. Trial atty. FTC, Washington, 1967-69; assoc. Quinn, Jacobs & Barry, Chgo., 1969-71, Katz, Karacic & Mansfield, Chgo., 1971-73, Michaelson & Marder, Chgo., 1973-74; prin. Howard Z. Gopman & Assocs. Ltd., Skokie, Ill., 1974—. Pres., dir. Am. Realty & Mgmt., Ltd., Skokie, 1977—; comml. arbitrator Am. Arbitration Assn., Chgo., 1977—; arbitrator Nat. Assn. Securities Dealers, Inc., N.Y. Stock Exch., Inc., Nat. Futures Assn., Cir. Cts. Cook and Lake Counties, Ill., Nat. Arbitration Forum. Contbr. articles to profl. jours. Hearing officer Ill. Office Edn., Chgo., 1977—. Mem. ABA, Ill. State Bar Assn., Wis. Bar Assn. Office: 5225 Old Orchard Rd Ste 24B Skokie IL 60077-1027

GOPPELT, JOHN WALTER, physician, psychiatrist; b. Saginaw, Mich., Jan. 20, 1924; s. Paul Gustave and Marion LeRoy (Payne) G.; m. Martha Keller Rowland, Mar. 31, 1956; 1 child, Edmund H. S.B., MIT, 1949; MD, U. Pa., 1955. Diplomate Am. Bd. Psychiatry and Neurology. Intern Bryn Mawr Hosp., Pa., 1955—56, resident in psychiatry Inst. of Pa. Hosp., Phila., 1956-59; practice medicine, specializing in psychiatry Haverford, Pa., 1959—. Contbr. articles to profl. jours. Chmn. Drug and Alcohol Coun. Del. County, Media, Pa., 1979—83; committeeman Rep. Party, Haverford Twp., Pa., 1980. With U.S. Army, 1943—46. Recipient Legion of Honor award Chapel of Four Chaplains. Mem. AMA, Am. Psychiat. Assn., N.Y. Acad. Scis., Math. Assn. Am., Sigma Xi. Avocation: mathematics. Address: 369 Exeter Rd Haverford PA 19041-1084 E-mail: mgoppelt@yahoo.com.

GORA, DANIEL MARTIN, lawyer; b. Chgo., Oct. 27, 1969; s. Martin O. and Jacqueline K. (Lancaster) G. BS, No. Ill. U., 1992; JD, Hamline U., 1995; MBA, U. St. Thomas, Mpls., 1996, MSS, 1999. Bar: Minn. 1995, Ill. 1996. Assoc. Spence, Ricke & Thurmer, St. Paul, 1992-96; ptnr. Weatherman, Wolters & Gora, Roseville, Minn., 1995-97; counsel Carlson Cos. Inc., Mpls., 1998-99; info. tech. specialist, sr. cons. Pillsbury Co., 1999-2000; legal mgr. Thomson Legal & Regulatory Svcs., 2000—. Mem. faculty Minn. Sch. Bus., Oakdale, 1996—, Met. State U., Mpls., 1997—. Judge Am. Mock Trial Assn., Minn., 1994-99. Dean's Law scholar Hamline U., 1992, Ill. Gen. Assembly scholar, 1988. Mem. ABA, Minn. Bar Assn., Ill. Bar Assn., Chgo. Bar Assn., Acad. Polit. Sci., Golden Key Nat. Honor Soc., Phi Sigma Alpha. Avocations: golf, basketball, reading, theater. E-mail: goralaw@email.com., dan.gora@westgroup.com.

GORA, JOANN M. university chancellor; BA, Vassar Coll.; M in Sociology, D in Sociology, Rutgers U. Various adminstrv. positions univ.-level, 1980—; dean Coll. Arts and Scis., sr. dean Madison campus Fairleigh Dickinson U.; provost, v.p. for acad. affairs, prof. sociology Old Dominion U., Norfolk, Va., 1992-01; chancellor U. Mass., Boston, 2001—. Author: The New Female Criminal: Empirical Reality or Social Myth?; co-author: Emergency Squad Volunteers: Professionalism in Unpaid Work; contbr. numerous articles to profl. jours. Office: U Mass Office of Chancellor 100 Morrissey Blvd Boston MA 02125-3393 E-mail: joann.gora@umb.edu.

GORAL, JUDITH ANN, educator; b. Cleve., July 12, 1947; d. Chester and Elenore (Majka) C. BA, Cleve. State U., 1969; postgrad., Inst. Am., Guadalajara, Jalisco, Mex.; MAT, Marygrove Coll., 1998. Cert. Spanish, Eng. tchr., Ohio. Tchr. Spanish Wiley Mid. Schs., Cleveland Heights, Ohio; advanced courses coord. Inst. Cultural Mexicano Norteamericano de Jai, Guadalajara, tchr., bus.; tchr. Colegio Victoria, Guadalajara; tchr., Spanish Brecksville (Ohio) Sr. High Sch. Mem. Am. Assn. Tchrs. Spanish and Portuguese, MFs. Assn. Tchrs. Eng. to Speakers of Other Langs. (2d v.p. acad. programs and events 1985-86, pres. 1986-87), Ohio Fgn. Lang. Assn., Phi Beta Omicron. Office: Wiley Middle Sch 2155 Miramar Blvd University Heights OH 44118

GORALSKI, DONALD JOHN, public relations executive, counselor; b. Buffalo, Apr. 21, 1957; s. John Bernard and Irene (Kazmierczak) G. BA, Canisius Coll., 1980. Cmty. svc. rep. western N.Y. chpt. March of Dimes Birth Defects Found., Buffalo, 1981-82, pub. rels. dir. western N.Y. chpt., 1982-83, pub. rels. dir. no. Jersey chpt. Fairfield, N.J., 1983-84; pub. rels. dir. Ellis Singer, Greve, St. Paul, Minn., 1984-87, Buffalo, 1984-87; sr. pub. rels. officer Multidisciplinary Ctr. for Earthquake Engring. Rsch., Buffalo, 1987—. Guest lectr. U. Buffalo, Buffalo State Coll., Medaille Coll., 1984-88, 95, Canisius Coll., 1990, 95, 97, 99, 2000, 01. Mem. spl. events com. Am. Cancer Soc., Western N.Y. chpt., 1985—86; mem. mktg. subcom. St. Mary's Sch. for the Deaf, 1987; mentor Pub. Rels. Student Soc. of Am., Buffalo, 1989—91; mem. Allied Comm. Talent for Literacy, Buffalo, 1990—91; mem. meeting and event planners coun. Univ. at Buffalo, 1992; mem. comm. com. World Assn. Vet. Athletes 1995 Games, 1994—95; mem. Ad Coun. Western N.Y., 1995; mem. comm. com. Buffalo Alliance for Edn., 1993; mem. Mayor's Adv. Com. for a City Vision, Buffalo, 1994—95; trustee Turner/Carroll H.S., 1996—97; mem. Dr. Marilyn G.S. Watt scholarship com. Canisius Coll., 1997—, mem. May C. Randazzo Meml. scholarship com., 1997—; liaison State Employees Federated Appeal/United Way, 1998—; mem. comm. com. ARC Greater Buffalo chpt., 2000—. Mem. Pub. Rels. Soc. Am. (bd. dirs. Buffalo-Niagara chpt. 1987-91, pres.-elect 1992, pres. 1993, past pres. 1994-95, accredited, 1995, assembly del. 1997-2001, N.E. dist. sec./treas. 1999, N.E. dist. chair elect 2000, N.E. dist. chair 2001, N.E. dist. immediate past chair 2002, nat. nominating com. 2001, Cert. Recognition 1993, Nat. Chpt. Banner award Buffalo/Niagara chpt. 1993), Pub. Rels. Assn. Western N.Y. (treas. 1986-87, v.p. 1987-88, pres. 1989), Western N.Y. Pub. Rels. and Comm. (exec. steering com. 1987-90, 92-94, chmn. 1994). Avocations: golf, football, reading, current events, on-line computer networks/services. Home: 4284 Coventry Green Cir Williamsville NY 14221-7237 Office: Multidisciplinary Ctr Quake Engring Rsch U Buffalo Red Jacket Quad Buffalo NY 14261 E-mail: goralski@buffalo.edu.

GORBATY, MARTIN LEO, chemist, researcher; b. Bklyn., Nov. 17, 1942; s. Julius and Florence (Birnbach) G.; m. Dianne Morse, June 30, 1968; children: Howard M., Matthew J., Lisa R. BS in Chemistry with honors, CCNY, 1964; PhD in Organic Chemistry, Purdue U., 1969. Rsch. chemist Esso Agrl. Products Lab. Esso Rsch. and Engring. Co., Linden, NJ, 1969-70; sr. rsch. chemist Corp. Rsch. Lab., Exxon Rsch. and Engring. Co., Linden, 1970-73, sr. rsch. chemist Baytown (Tex.) R & D divsn., 1973-75, group head Corp. Rsch. Labs. Linden, 1975-78, lab. dir. corp. rsch., 1978-84; disting. rsch. assoc. Corp. Rsch.-Resource Chemistry Lab., ExxonMobil Rsch. and Engring. Co., Annandale, NJ, 1984—. Mem. internat. editorial bd. Fuel, 1983—; chmn. Gordon Conf. Fuel Sci., 1988. Editor 5 books on synthetic crudes and coal sci.; contbr. some 70 articles to profl. jours.; holder 50 patents. Recipient R.A. Glenn award Bituminous Coal Rsch., Inc., 1990, Disting. Alumnus award Sch. of Sci. Purdue U., 1993, Spl. Svc. award, Petroleum Chemistry, 2003. Mem. AAAS, Am. Chem. Soc. (chmn. divsn. petroleum chemistry 1983-84, program com. 1978—, councilor 1988-99, 2001—, divsn. fuel chemistry, adv. bd. ACS books 1984-87, editl. bd. Chemtech 1986-99, Henry H. Storch award 1993), N.Y. Acad. Scis., Soc. Sigma Xi, Phi Lambda Upsilon. Achievements include patents in field of coal and petroleum processing. Office: ExxonMobil Rsch & Engring Co PO Box 998 Annandale NJ 08801-0998

GORBMAN, CLAUDIA L. literature educator, researcher; b. Yonkers, NY, May 14, 1948; d. Aubrey and Genevieve Dorothy (Tapperman) Gorbman. MA French, Univ. of Wash., Seattle, Wash., 1972, PhD Romance Lang. & Lit., 1978. Asst. prof., comp. lit. Ind. Univ., Bloomington, Ind., 1978—85, assoc. lit., comp. lit., 1986—90; assoc. prof., lib. studies Univ. of Wash., Tacoma, 1990—96, prof. film studies, 1996—. Dir. Paris Film & Critical Studies Program, Paris, 1981—82. Author: (book) Unheard Melodies: Narrative Film Music, 1987; translator: (3 books by Michael Chion) Audio-Vision; The Voice in Cinema; 2001, 1994, 1999, 2001; co-editor: (book) Film Music II, 2003. Mem.: Film Music Soc., Modern Lang. Assoc., Soc. for Cinema & Media Studies. Achievements include first to pioneer in the study of film music. Home: 4402 S Ferdinand St Seattle WA 98118 Office: Univ of Wash 1900 Commerce St Tacoma WA 98402

GORBUNOVA, VERA, biologist; m. Andrei Seluanov, Dec. 13, 1989; children: Michael Seluanov, Moshe Seluanov. PhD, Weizmann Inst. of Sci., Israel, 1999. Postdoctoral assoc. McGill U., Montreal, Canada, 1999—2001, Baylor Coll. of Medicine, Houston, 2001—02, instr., 2002—. Fellow Short term EMBO fellowship, European molecular Biology Assn., 1997, Postdoctoral Fellowship, Nat. Cancer Inst. of Can., 1999—2001, Long term fellowship, Human Frontier of Sci. Orgn., 2001—. Achievements include research in Proposed a model for Ac transposition; Analysed the process of DNA repair by nonhomologous end joining in plants; discovery of Discovered that senescent human cells undergo necrosis instead of apoptosis in respose to genotoxic stress; Biochemical activity of a protein encoded by longevity gene Clk-1; research in Found that telomerase does not protect human cells from sterss-induced premature senescence; discovery of Discovered that excessive telomerase activity may induce senescence in human cells. Avocations: travel, hiking, camping, wildlife watching, dogs. Home: 4021 Woodshire Houston TX 77025 Office: Baylor Coll of Medicine One Baylor Plz Houston TX 77030 Office Fax: 713-796-9438. E-mail: gorbunov@bcm.tmc.edu.

GORBUNOVS, ANATOLIJS, engineer, construction specialist, politician; b. Ludza Distr., Republic of Latvia, 1942; married; 1 child. Diploma, Riga (Latvia) Poly. Inst., Latvia, 1970; grad., Acad. Social Scis., Moscow, 1978. Constructor on state farm Rural Design Inst., 1959-62; sec. Komsomol com. Riga Poly. Inst., 1969-70, sr. lectr., 1970-74; various offices Latvian Communist Party, 1974-88; presidium, chmn. presidium Supreme Coun. Latvia SSR, 1988-90, chmn., 1990-93, 5th Saeima Latvia, 1993-95; dep. 6th Saeima Latvia, 1995-96; min. environ. protection and regional devel. Ministry Environ. Protection, Riga, 1996-98, dep. prime min., chmn. Latvian-Russian Intergovtl. Commn., 1996-99; minister of transp. Ministry Transport, Riga, 1998—. Chmn. European Affairs Com; mem. Com. of Nat. Economy and Agriculture; mem. land com. 6th Saeima Republic Latvia, 1995-96. Served with Soviet Mil. Forces, 1962-65.

GORCHOW, BRUCE D. investment company executive; b. Mpls., Mar. 13, 1958; s. Neil Gorchow, Roslyn Gorchow; m. Marie L. Fioramonti; children: Grace Fioramonti-Gorchow, Sophia Fioramonti-Gorchow, Gabriel Fioramonti-Gorchow. BA, Haverford Coll., 1980; MBA, U. Pa., 1982. Investment mgr. TIAA/CREF, New York, NY, 1982—86; v.p. Equitable Capital Mgmt., Inc., 1987—91; exec. v.p. PPM Am., Inc., Chgo., 1991—2000; pres. PPM Am. Capital Ptnrs., LLC, 2000—. Bd. dirs. PPM Am., Inc.; bd. dir. Global Imaging Systems, Inc., Tampa, Fla., 1996—2002; bd. dirs. Elizabeth Arden Salon and Spa Holdings, Inc, Phoenix, Examination Mgmt. Svcs., Inc, Dallas; Director Tomah Products, Inc, Tomah, WI, 1997—99, Applied Process Solutions, Inc., Tulsa, OK, 1998—2000, Corvest Promotional Products, Miami, FL, 1999—. Mem.: U. Club Chgo., Phi Beta Kappa. Office: PPM Am Capital Ptnrs LLC 225 West Wacker Dr Ste 1200 Chicago IL 60606

GORDAN, CYNTHIA LEE, lawyer, textile company executive; b. Decatur, Ill., Apr. 4, 1947; d. Delbert R. and Jacqueline (McKinney) Smith; children: Rebecca, Elisabeth. A.B., Oberlin Coll., 1969; J.D., Boston U., 1975, LL.M. in Taxation, 1976. Bar: Mass. 1975, Ill. 1987. Assoc. counsel New Eng. Mut. Boston, 1976-80; assoc. counsel, asst. sec. Puritan Life Ins. Co., Providence, 1980-81, v.p., gen. counsel, sec., 1981-85, bd. dir.; mgr. ops. planning GE Capital, Stmaford, Conn., 1985-86; sr. assoc. Katten Muchin, Chgo., 1986-87; v.p., gen. counsel Quaker Fabric Corp., Fall River, Mass., 1988—. Mem. Am. Soc. CLU. Office: Quaker Fabric Corp 931 Grinnell St Fall River MA 02721-5215 Home: 31 Washington St Milton MA 02186-5720

GORDEN, PHILLIP, federal agency administrator; BA, Vanderbilt U., 1957, MD, 1961. Resident Yale U., New Haven; sr. investigator Nat. Inst. Diabetes, Digestive and Kidney Diseases, NIH, Bethesda, Md., 1966-86, dir., 1986-2000, clin. and cellular biology chief, 2001—. Office: Nat Inst Diabetes Digestive & Kidney Diseases Rm 85235A Bldg 10 Bethesda MD 20892-1770 Fax: 435-5873.*

GORDENKER, LEON, political sciences educator; b. Detroit, Oct. 7, 1923; s. Samuel and Anna (Posalsky) G.; m. Belia Emilie Strootman, Aug. 16, 1956 (dec. Apr. 1984); children: Robert Jan Mario, Hendrik Willem Paul, Emilie Elise Saskia. AB, U. Mich., 1943; student, Inst. d'Etudes Politiques, Paris, 1951-52; MA, Columbia U., 1954, PhD, 1958; postgrad., Acad. Internat. Law, Hague, The Netherlands, 1958. Journalist AP, 1943, Detroit Free Press, 1944-45; info. officer Nat. War Labor Bd., 1945; pub. info. officer UN, 1945-53; instr. Dartmouth Coll., 1956-58; mem. faculty Princeton U., 1958—, prof. politics, 1966-86, faculty assoc. Ctr. Internat. Studies, 1963—, prof. emeritus, 1986—, sr. rsch. polit. scientist, 1990-94; prof. Institut Universitaire de Hautes Internationales, Geneva, 1986-89, vis. prof., 1979-80; dir. Centre de Recherches sur les Institutions Internationales, Geneva, 1986-89. Vis. prof. Columbia U., 1961, 67, Makerere U., Uganda, 1969-70, U. Pa., 1971, 74, U. Witwatersrand, South Africa, 1976, Leiden U., 1984-85, 93, Erasmus U., 1985, CUNY, 1989, 90, 92, 95, Inst. Social Studies, The Hague, 1993-97. Author: The United Nations and the Peaceful Unification of Korea, 1959, The UN Secretary-General and the Maintenance of Peace, 1967, The United Nations in the International System, 1971, International Aid and National Decisions, 1976, The International Executive, 1978, (with W.P. Davison) Resolving Nationality

Conflicts, 1980, (with P.R. Baehr) The United Nations: Reality and Ideal, 1984, Refugees in International Politics, 1987, (with T.G. Weiss) Soldiers, Peacekeepers and Disasters, 1991, (with P.R. Baehr) The United Nations in the 1990s, 1992, 94, De Verenigde Naties: Werkelijkheid en Ideaal, 1992, 94, 96, (with Benjamin Rivlin) The Challenging Role of the UN Secretary-General, 1993, (with others) International Cooperation in Response to AIDS, 1995, (with T.G. Weiss) NGOs, The UN and Global Governance, 1996, (with P.R. Baehr) The United Nations at the End of the 1990s, 1999; mem. editl. bd. Acta Politica, Global Governance. Fellow The Netherlands Inst. Advanced Study, 1972-73, 96-97. Mem. Acad. Coun. on UN, Princeton Club of N.Y. Office: Princeton U Ctr Internat Studies Princeton NJ 08544-0001

GORDER, JENNIFER LEANN, special education educator; b. Spokane, Wash., Nov. 17, 1976; d. Donald James and Vicki Lee Gorder. BA, U. of Wash., 1995—98; MA, Whitworth Coll., 1998—99; PhD, Wash. State U., 2000—03. Tchg. Cert. Wash. State, 1999. Grant adminstr. Ea. Wash. U., Cheney, 2000—01; tchg. asst. Wash. State U., Pullman, 2001—02; adj. faculty Ea. Wash. U., Cheney, 2001—02; spl. edn. tchr./ dept. head Mukilteo Sch. Dist., Everett, Wash. Mem.: NEA, Rotoract Svc. Club, Alpha Xi Delta (philanthropy chair 1996—97). Independent. Presbyn. Avocations: swimming, crafts, reading, golf, scuba diving.

GORDEVITCH, IGOR, publishing company executive; b. Kaunas, Lithuania, Dec. 17, 1924; came to U.S., 1950, naturalized, 1955; s. Alexander Michael and Militsa (de Nikitin) G.; m. Margaret Boomer; children: Alexandra, Tatiana; m. Carin Roechling, Oct. 7, 1960. Ed., Institut Sillig, Vevey, Switzerland, 1937-39, Royal U., Rome, 1939-40. Sr. adminstrv. asst. Allied Mil. Govt., Europe, 1944-45; corr. N.Y. Herald Tribune, 1945-50; Washington bur. chief Vision Inc., N.Y.C., 1950-56, editor, 1957-64, CEO Latin Am. ops., 1964-67; pub., exec. v.p., dir. Vision Group of Cos., N.Y.C., 1967-76, pres., 1973-77; mng. dir., chmn. Vision/Europe, Paris, 1970-77; pres. Publi-Comms. Inc., N.Y.C., 1977-83; exec. v.p., dir. Gruner & Jahr USA, Inc., N.Y.C., 1979-83. Also pub. dir. GEO mag. 1979-81; pres. U.S. Investment Pub., 1983-89; pres. ECO Inc, 1990-96; dir. PHP Inst. Am., Inc.; edit. dir., pub. Impact 21 mag., 1996; pub. cons.; lectr. in field. Mem. Pan Am. Soc. U.S., Coun. of Ams., Akin Hall Assn., Knickerbocker Club (N.Y.C.), Coral Beach and Tennis Club (Bermuda), Nat. Press Club (Washington). Republican. Eastern Orthodox. Home: 790 Quaker Hill Rd Pawling NY 12564-1814 Office: 216 E 49th St New York NY 10017-1546 E-mail: gordevitch@aol.com.

GORDIMER, NADINE, author; b. Republic of South Africa, Nov. 20, 1923; d. Isidore and Nan (Myers) Gordimer; m. Reinhold Cassirer, Jan. 29, 1954; children: Oriane, Hugo. Ed., Convent Sch., Springs, Republic of South Africa. Author: (story collections) Face to Face, 1949, The Soft Voice of the Serpent, 1952, Six Feet of the Country, 1956, Friday's Footprint, 1960 (W.H. Smith and Son Literary award 1961), Not for Publication, 1965, Livingstone's Companions, 1971, Selected Stories, 1975, Some Monday for Sure, 1976, A Soldier's Embrace, 1980, Something Out There, 1984, Crimes of Conscience, 1991, Jump, 1991, Why Haven't You Written?, 1992; (polit. and lit. essays) The Essential Gesture, 1988, Three in a Bed, 1991, Living in Hope and History: Notes From Our Century, 1999; (literary criticism) The Black Interpreters, 1973, Writing & Being: Charles Eliot Norton Lectures, 1995; (essays) Living in Hope and History: Notes from Our Century, 1999; (novels) The Lying Days, 1953, A World of Strangers, 1958, Occasion for Loving, 1963, The Late Bourgeois World, 1966, A Guest of Honour, 1970 (James Tait Black Meml. prize 1973), The Conservationist, 1974 (Booker prize for fiction Eng. 1974), Burger's Daughter, 1979, July's People, 1981, A Sport of Nature, 1987, My Son's Story, 1991, None to Accompany Me, 1994, The House Gun, 1998, The Pickup, 2001, Loot, 2003; (other) On the Mines, 1973, Lifetimes Under Apartheid, 1986; editor: (with Lionel Abrahams) Southern African Writing Today, 1967. Decorated comdr. de l'Ordre des Arts et des Lettres (France), 1986; recipient Thomas Pringle award English Acad. South Africa, 1969, CNA award, 1974, 79, 81, 91, Grand Aigle d'Or, 1975, Disting. Svc. in Lit. Commonwealth award, 1981, MLA award, 1982, Nelly Sachs prize (Germany), 1985, Malaparte award (Italy), 1986, Bennett award, 1986, Internat. Premo Leui award, 2002, Mary McCarthy award, 2003; Benson medal, 1990, Nobel Prize for Literature, 1991; Neil Gunn fellow Scottish Arts Coun., 1981. Fellow Royal Soc. Lit.; mem. AAAS, Com. European Authors, Am. Acad. (hon.), Inst. Arts and Letters (hon.), PEN (v.p.).

GORDINIER, TERRI KLEIN, speech-language pathologist; b. Inglewood, Calif., Aug. 20, 1959; d. Jerome Lee Klein and Justina Dean (Woodard) Popp; m. Terry Lee Gordinier, July 23, 1988; children: Cory James, Collin William. MA, Ea. Mich. U., 1989; BS in Edn. cum laude, Columbus (Ga.) Coll., 1985. Cert. speech-lang. tchr., Mich. Instr. in sign lang. Main Post Office, Columbus, 1983-84, Columbus Coll., 1984-85; speech pathology intern Buena Vista (Ga.) Elem. Sch., 1985; tchr. speech-lang. impaired Burger devel. learning program Wayne County Program for Autistically Impaired, Garden City, Mich., 1986-90; speech lang. pathologist Mich. Sch. for the Deaf, Flint, 1991-94; instr. Ann Arbor Cmty. Edn. and Recreation, 1995—; speech lang. pathologist Ann Arbor Pub. Schs., 1997—. Asst. instr. swimming Listening Eyes Presch. for Deaf, Columbus, 1983-84; program coord., counselor Outdoor Freedon Camporee Ala. Soc. for Crippled Children and Adults, 1983-85; speech clinician Columbus Coll., 1982-85; asst. interpreter for deaf Packard Road Bapt. Ch., Ann Arbor, 1985-; teaching asst. Key Elem. Sch., Columbus, 1982-84; lectr. in field. Fellow Am. Speech-Lang.-Hearing Assn., Libr. of Spl. Edn. Pathology, Alliance for Speech Communication; mem. Communication Disorders Assn. (sec., treas. 1984-85), Communications Disorders Assn. Fall Conf. (exec. coun. rep. 1984-85), Ea. Mich. U.'s Fall Conf. (student rep. 1986-87), Mich. Speech Lang. Hearing Assn. Baptist. Avocations: swimming, sailing, white water canoeing, camping. Home: 5196 Sutton Rd Ann Arbor MI 48105-9538

GORDIS, DAVID MOSES, academic administrator, rabbi; b. N.Y.C., June 4, 1940; s. Robert and Fannie (Jacobson) G.; m. Felice Witztum, Sept. 3, 1962; children: Lisa, Elana. BA, Columbia U., 1960, MA, 1966; MHL, Jewish Theol. Sem., 1962, PhD, 1980. Ordained rabbi, 1964. Dean of students Tchrs. Inst., Jewish Theol. Sem., N.Y.C., 1966-72; exec. dir. Found. for Conservative Judaism, 1981-84; assoc. prof., v.p. U. of Judaism, L.A., 1972-84; v.p. Jewish Theol. Sem., N.Y.C., 1981-84; exec. v.p. Am. Jewish Com., N.Y.C., 1984-87; v.p. U. Judaism, L.A., 1988-92, dir. Wilstein Inst. of Jewish Policy Studies, 1988—, adj. assoc. prof. Talmud, 1988-92, dir. inst. rsch.; pres. Hebrew Coll., 1993—. Mem. editl. bd.: Tikkun. Pres., prof. rabbinics Hebrew Coll., 1993—; exec. com. Am. Found. for Polish-Jewish Studies, 1988—; trustee Am. Jewish Hist. Soc., 1993—, vice-chair Archives for Hist. Documentation, 1995—; chair United Synagogue Coun. on Jewish Edn., 1973-82. Mem. Rabbinical Assembly Am., Assn. Colls. of Jewish Studies. Avocation: cello. E-mail: dgordis@hebrewcollege.edu.

GORDIS, ENOCH, retired science administrator, internist; b. N.Y.C., Feb. 21, 1931; s. Robert and Fannie (Jacobson) Gordis. BA, Columbia U., 1950, MD, 1954. Fellow Dazian Found., N.Y.C., 1958—59; clin. fellow Mt. Sinai Hosp., N.Y.C., 1959, chief resident dept. medicine, 1960; assoc. prof. dept. medicine Mt. Sinai Sch. Medicine, N.Y.C., 1971—79, prof. medicine, 1979—; guest investigator Rockefeller U., N.Y.C., 1961—62, rsch. assoc., 1962—63, assoc. prof., 1965—71, prof. clin. medicine, 1971—; dir., mem. treatment prevention study sect. Nat. Inst. on Alcohol Abuse and Alcoholism, Rockville, Md., 1986—2002. Extensive pub. appearances in U.S. and abroad on topics related to alcoholism and addiction. Author (with others): Controversies in Clinical Care, 1981, Current Therapy in Gastroenterology and Liver Disease, 1986; manuscript reviewer: Annals Internal Medicine, Butterworth Inc., Clin. Textbook of Addictive Disorders, European Jour. Clin. Investigation, Jour. Clin. Investigation, Jour. Lipid Rsch., Jour. Studies in Alcohol, Med. Letter, others, assoc. editor: Alcoholism: Clin. and Exptl. Rsch., 1979—, mem. editl. bd.: U. Medicine and Dentistry of N.J., —, N.J. Med. Sch., —; contbr. articles, abstracts to profl. jours. Corr. Com. on Human Rights, 1988—89. Capt. M.C. U.S. Army, 1955—57. Fellow: ACP; mem.: Rsch. Soc. on Alcoholism, Inst. of Medicine of NAS (corr. com. human rights 1988—89), Am. Physiol. Soc., Am. Soc. Addiction Medicine, Am. Gastroent. Assn., Am. Fedn. for Clin. Rsch., Am. Coll. Neuropsychopharmacology, Adv. Group on Fellowships in Alcohol and Drug Abuse, Phi Beta Kappa, Sigma Xi.

GORDIS, LEON, physician; b. N.Y.C., July 19, 1934; s. Robert and Fannie (Jacobson) Gordis; m. Hadassah Cohen, June 14, 1955; children: Daniel, Elihu, Jonathan. BA, Columbia, 1954; BHL, Jewish Theol. Sem., 1954; MD, SUNY, 1958; MPH, Johns Hopkins U., 1966, DPH, 1968. Intern, then resident in pediat. Jewish Hosp., Bklyn., 1958—61; fellow in pediat. Sch. Medicine Johns Hopkins U., 1962—66, instr. Sch. Medicine, 1966—68, assoc. prof. epidemiology, Sch. Hygiene and Pub. Health, 1971—73; asst. med. dir. ambulatory care Sinai Hosp., Balt., 1966—68, chief dept. community medicine, 1968—69; prof. epidemiology Johns Hopkins, 1973—, chmn. dept. epidemiology, 1975—93; prof. pediat., 1992—; assoc. dean admissions & Acad. affairs Johns Hopkins Sch. Medicine, 1993—99. Vis. prof. med. ecology Hebrew U., Jerusalem, 1969—71. Served with USPHS, 1961—65. Fellow: AAAS, Am. Acad. Pediat.; mem.: APHA, Assn. Tchrs. Preventive Medicine, Am. Heart Assn., Soc. Pediatric Rsch., Am. Pediatric Soc., Am. Epidemiol. Soc. (pres. 1983—84), Soc. Epidemiologic Rsch. (pres. 1979—80), Inst. Medicine NAS. Home: 105 Swanhill Ct Baltimore MD 21208-1608 Office: 615 N Wolfe St Baltimore MD 21205-2103

GORDLY, AVEL LOUISE, state legislator, community activist; b. Portland, Oreg., Feb. 13, 1947; d. Fay Lee and Beatrice Bernice (Coleman) G.; 1 child, Tyrone Wayne Waters. BS in Adminstrn. of Justice, Portland State U., 1974; Grad. John F. Kennedy Sch. Govt., Harvard U., 1995; grad., U. Oreg. Pacific Program, 1998. Phone co. clk. Pacific West Bell, Portland, 1966-70, mgmt. trainee, 1969-70; work release counselor Oreg. Corrections Divsn., Portland, 1974-78, parole and probation officer, 1974-78; dir. youth svcs. Urban League of Portland, 1979-83; dir. So. Africa program Am. Friends Svc. Com., Portland, 1983-89, assoc. exec. sec., dir. Pacific N.W. region, 1987-90; freelance writer Portland Observer, Portland, 1988-90; program dir. Portland House of Umoja, 1991; mem. Oreg. Ho. of Reps., Portland, 1991-96, mem. joint ways and means com., adv. mem. appropriations com., rules and reorgn. com., low income housing com., energy policy rev. com., others; mem. Oreg. Senate from 10th dist., Salem, 1997—; mem. crime and corrections com., trades econ. devel. com. Oreg. Senate, 1997, mem. joint ways and means com. on pub. safety, 1997, mem. joint ways and means com. on edn., 1999. Mem. joint ways and means com. on edn., mem. gov. drug and violent crime policy bd., mem. Oreg. liquor control commn. task force, mem. sexual harrassement task force, mem. Hanford waste bd., mem. Gov.'s Commn. for Women, Gov.'s Drug and Violent Crime Policy Bd.; originator, producer, host Black Women's Forum, 1983-88; co-producer, rotating host N.E. Spectrum, 1983-88. Mem. corrections adv. com. Multnomah Cmty.; mem. adv. com. Oregonians Against Gun Violence; mem. Black Leadership Conf.; treas., bd. dirs. Black United Fund; co-founder, facilitator Unity Breakfast Com.; co-founder Sisterhood Luncheon; past project adv. bd. dirs. Nat. Orgn. Victims Assistance; past citizen chmn. Portland Police Bur.; past mem. coordinating com. Portland Future Focus Policy Com.; past coord. Cmty. Rescue Plan; past vice chmn. internat. affairs Black United Front; past sec. Urban League Portland, past vice chmn. and exec. com.; past adv. com. Black Ednl. Ctr.; past vice chmn. Desegregation Monitoring; also past adv. com., past chmn. curriculum com., founder African Am. Leg. Issues Roundtable; founder Black Women Gathering; other past orgn. coms.; elected state senate First African Am. Woman, 1996. Recipient Outstanding Cmty. Svc. award NAACP, 1986, Outstanding Women in Govt. award YWCA, 1991, Girl Scout-Cmty. Svc. award, 1991, N.W. Conf. of Black Studies-Outstanding Progressive Leadership in the African-Am. Cmty. award, 1986, Cmty. Svc. award Delta Sigma Theta, 1981, Joint Action in Cmty. Svc.-Vol. and Cmty. Svc. award, 1981, Quality of Life Photography award Pacific Power & Light Co., 1986, Am. Leadership Forum Sr. fellow, 1988, Equal Opportunity award, Urban League, 1996, Outstanding Alumni, 1996, PSU, Causa '98 En Defensa de la Comunidad award, 1997, Matrix award Assn. for Women in Comm., 1999, Pres.'s award Portland Oreg. Visitors Assn., 1999, Legacy award Black United Fund, 2000, Leadership award Albina Ministerial Alliance, 2000 Mem. NAACP. Avocations: reading group, mentoring, photography, walking.

GORDON, ALAN LEE, psychiatrist; b. N.Y.C., Nov. 26, 1936; s. Abe and Fan Gordon; m. Lois Goldfein; 1 child, Robert Michael. AB, Columbia Coll., 1957; MD, U. Wis., 1963. Resident Albert Einstein Coll. Medicine, N.Y.C., 1964-66, 68-69; dir. of aftercare Riverdale Mental Health Clinic, N.Y.C., 1969-78; clin. instr. Mt. Sinai Sch. of Medicine, N.Y.C., 1982-90; psychiatrist divsn. of post-institutional svcs. Human Resources Adminstrn.-City of N.Y., 1986—; psychiatrist Bowery Residence Com., CSS Program, N.Y.C., 1990—. Lectr. in field; TV, radio interviewer; spkr. in field. Author: American Chronicle: Six Decades in American Life, 1920-79, 1987, American Chronicle: Seven Decades of American Life 1920-89, 1990, Columbia Chronicles of American Life, 1960-92, 1995, American Chronicle: Year by Year through the Twentieth Century, 1999; contbr. poetry to various jours. and sci. jours. Capt. U.S. Army, 1966-68. Mem. Alpha Omega Alpha. Democrat. Jewish. Avocations: history, literature, sports. Office: 300 Central Park W New York NY 10024-1513

GORDON, ALICE JEANNETTE IRWIN, secondary and elementary education educator; b. Detroit, Mar. 18, 1934; d. Manley Elwood and Jeannette (Coffron) Irwin; m. Edgar George Gordon, Feb. 4, 1967; children: David Alexander, John Scott. BA in Elem. Edn., Mich. State U., 1956; MA in Child Devel., U. Mich., 1959, EdS in Ednl. Psychology, 1967, MA in Reading, 1990; postgrad., Western Mich. U., 1990-97. Cert. K-12 tchr., Mich.; cert. K-12 reading specialist. Elem. tchr. Detroit Pub. Schs., 1956-67, reading tchr., 1967-68; secondary tchr. English and reading Parchment Pub. Schs., 1989-94; secondary reading specialist Kalamazoo Pub. Schs., 1994-96; jr. high reading specialist South Middle Sch., Kalamazoo, 1996-99; tchr. Milwood Elem. Sch., Mich., 1999-2001; ret. Reading therapist Western Mich. U., Kalamazoo, 1992-97; participant Ednl. Leadership Acad., 1998-99; bd. dir. U. Mich. Coll. Edn. Mem. alumni bd. Mich. State U. Coll. Edn., 1992-96; chmn. Century Ball, Nazareth Coll., Kalamazoo, 1987; co-chmn. Evening of Nte, Kalamazoo Symphony, 1989; precinct del. Kalamazoo Rep. Com., 1989, 92, 96, 99—; mem. Mich. Adult Edn. Practitioner Inquiry Project, 1994, 95, 96; docent Kalamazoo Inst. Art, 2002; bd. mem. Ready to Read, 2002, Literacy Coun., 2002; bd. dirs. U. Mich. Coll. Edn., 2003—, alumni bd. Coll. Edn., 2003—; bd. dirs. Ready to Read, 1998-2003, Kalamazoo Literacy Coun., 2002—; mentor, tutor Cmty. in Schs. Americorps, 2002—03; docent Kalamazoo Inst. Arts, 2003. Recipient Crystal Apple award Mich. a., 1990, Excellence in Edn. grantee, 1997, Kalamazoo Pub. Edn. Found. grantee, 1997, 98, Arts Coun. Greater Kalamazoo mini-grantee, 1997, 2000, State Dept. Arts grantee, 1997, Kalamazoo Pub. Edn. Found., 1998; Third Coast Writing fellow, 1998; MLPP grantee, 2001. Mem. Internat. Reading Assn., Mich. Reading Assn., Homer Carter Reading Assn., P.E.O. (pres. 2003—), Jr. League, Lawyers Wives Aux. (bd. dirs. 2002—, pres. 2003—), Phi Delta Kappa (pres. 1998-01, bd. dirs. 2002—), Alpha Omega Pi, Delta Kappa Gamma (bd. dirs. 2002—). Presbyterian. Avocations: miniatures, antiques, reading, genealogy, public education. Home: 4339 Lakeside Dr Kalamazoo MI 49008-2802

GORDON, ALLEN BARRY, musician, composer; b. L.A., Mar. 12, 1950; s. Rubin and Florence Irene G.; m. Susan Sutwarti, Jan. 2, 1976. Studied piano with Antonio Iturioz; student, Santa Monica Coll., 1998. Master jazz pianist. Head pianist Filmex, 1979-81, Jonathan Club, 1989-91; freelance pianist. Instr. piano. Played televised banquet, Biltmore Hotel, Ted Kennedy (US senator), 1981, concert for Mikhail Gorbachev (former Russian Premier), Pheonix Hall Anaheim, 2000. Played concerts for sr. citizens; played concert at VA Hosp. Recipient Pub. Citation award, City of L.A. Mem. ASCAP. Democrat. Jewish. Avocations: playing and listening to music, reading biographies, teaching, coin collecting, baseball art. Home: 4140 Grand View Blvd Los Angeles CA 90066-5258

GORDON, ANITRA, librarian; b. Bklyn., July 10, 1936; d. Samuel Frank and Florence (Aronowitz) Sisholce; m. Jesse E. Gordon, Mar. 8, 1956; children: Scott, Jessani, Erica. BA, U. Wis., 1957; MA, Mont. State U., 1961; MA in Library Sci., U. Mich., 1970, PhD, 1985. Tchr. French Ann Arbor (Mich.) Pub. Schs., 1964-66; librarian Lincoln Consol. Schs., Ypsilanti, Mich., 1967—. Writer, cons. Sch. Libr. Mgmt. Notebook, 1991; supervising tchr. Ea. Mich. U., Ypsilanti, 1968-80, lectr., 1975-85; supervising tchr. U. Mich., Ann Arbor, 1968-80; workshop presenter various orgns., 1975—; editorial advisor Jour. Reading, 1974-75. Author, cons Sch. Libr. Mgmt. Notebook, 2d edit., 1991; contbr. articles and revs. to profl. publs. Recipient Disting. Achievement award Edpress, 1973. Mem. Mich. Assn. Media in Edn. (workshop presenter 1974—, bd. dirs. 1991—), Faculty Womens Book Club, Faculty Womens Garden Club, Beta Phi Mu. Democrat. Jewish. Avocations: photography, gardening, travel. Home: 1300 Chalmers Dr Ann Arbor MI 48104-4216 Office: Lincoln High Sch 7425 Willis Rd Ypsilanti MI 48197-8919

GORDON, ANNE KATHLEEN, editor; m. Phillip L. Berman. BA, U. Denver, 1979; postgrad., Columbia Grad. Sch. Journalism, 1983. Fin. writer Rocky Mountain Bus. Jour., Denver, 1981, Sun-Tattler, Hollywood, Fla., 1982-83, fin. editor, 1983; asst. bus. editor Ft. Lauderdale (Fla.) News, 1983-85; bus. editor The Denver Post, 1985-88, asst. mng. editor, 1988; news cons. Sta. KCNC-TV, Denver, 1988-89, assignment mgr., 1989-90; editor Jackson Hole News, 1990-92; editor Sunday Mag. The Plain Dealer, Cleve., 1993-99; arts and entertainment editor The Phila. Inquirer, 1999—, from assoc. mng. editor to dep. mng. editor arts and features, 2000—02, mng. editor, 2002—. Author: A Book of Saints, 1994. Recipient Best of Show award Colo. Press Assn., 1981, 86, Woman of Yr. award Broward County Bus. and Profl. Women's Assn., 1983, 1st Pl. Spot News award Colo. Associated Press, 1986, 1st Pl. Breaking News award Colo. Press Assn., 1986, Gen. Excellence award Wyo. Press Assn., 1991, Gen. Excellence award Nat. Newspaper Assn., 1992; Eisenhower fellow, 2000. Home: 149 Fairview Rd Narberth PA 19072-1330 Office: The Philadelphia Inquirer 400 N Broad St Philadelphia PA 19130-4015 E-mail: agordon@phillynews.com.

GORDON, ARNOLD MARK, lawyer; b. Norwich, Conn., Oct. 2, 1937; s. Barney and Rose (Bilsky) G.; m. Carolyn. BSBA, Wayne State U., Detroit, 1959, JD, 1962. Bar: Mich. 1962. With Gordon & Gordon P.C. and predecessor firms, Southfield, Mich.; arbitrator Am. Arbitration Assn., 1969—. Lectr. in field. Mem. Am. Coll. Trial Lawyers, State Bar Mich. (chmn. med.-legal com. 1976—, negligence sect. 1977-78, pub. negligence sect. bull.), Detroit Bar Assn. (co-chmn. trial advocacy program continguing legal edn. 1972—), Assn. Trial Lawyers Am. (exec. bd. Mich. 1967—), Mich., Detroit trial lawyers assns., Tau Epsilon Rho. Clubs: Masons. Office: Gordon & Gordon PC 17250 W 12 Mile Rd Ste 119 Southfield MI 48076-2663 E-mail: agordon404@aol.com.

GORDON, AUDREY KRAMEN, healthcare educator; b. Chgo., Nov. 18, 1935; d. Edward J. and Anne (Levin) Kramen; children: Bradley, Dale, Holly. BS with highest distinction, Northwestern U., 1965, MA, 1967, postgrad., 1971; MA, U. Chgo., 1970; PhD, U. Ill., Chgo., 1991. Cert. in clin. pastoral edn. Lectr. Northwestern U., Evanston, Ill., 1966-74; vis. asst. prof. Beloit (Wis.) Coll., 1974-75; research specialist U. Ill., Chgo., 1983-86, dir. continuing edn. Sch. Pub. Health, 1986-91, lectr. cmty. health scis., 1988-91, dir. coll. advancement Sch. Pub. Health, 1991-92, asst. prof., 1992—, sr. rsch. specialist Health Rsch. and Policy Ctr., 1992-2001, dir. instnl. rev. bd., 1998—, dir. human subjects rsch. Health Rsch. Policy Ctrs., 2001—; coord., counselor Jewish Hospice, Chgo., 1984-89. Lectr. Loyola U. Stritch Sch. Medicine, Maywood, Ill., 1982—90; pres. Rainbow Hospice Orgn., 1984—88, cons., 1988—92, rsch. cons., 2001—; project dir. S.E. Lake County Faith in Action Program, Highland Pk., 2003—. Co-author: (book) They Need to Know: How to Teach Children About Death, 1979; co-editor: Hospice and Cultural Diversity, 1995. Bd. dirs. AIDS Pastoral Care Network, 1999—2001. Recipient Merit award, Northwestern U. Alumni, 1993, Heart of Hospice award, Nat. Coun. Hospice Profls., 1997. Mem.: APHA, Nat. Hospice Orgn. (mem. ethics com. 1997—2000), Ill. Hospice Orgn. (pres. 1989—90, v.p. 1997—98), Ill. Pub. Health Assn., Delta Omega, Alpha Kappa Lambda, Alpha Sigma Lambda.

GORDON, BARON JACK, stockbroker; b. 1926; m. Ellin Bachrach, Aug. 20, 1954; children: Jonathan Ross, Rose Patricia, Alison. Midshipman, U.S. Naval Acad., 1946; BS, Lynchburg Coll., 1953. Asst. treas. Henry Montor Assocs., Inc., N.Y.C., 1956; v.p., sec. Propp & Co., Inc., N.Y.C., 1957-58; ptnr. Koerner, Gordon & Co., N.Y.C., 1959-62; sr. ptnr. Gordon, Kulman Perry, and predecessor firm, N.Y.C., 1962-71, pres., chmn. bd., 1971-74, Palison, Inc., White Plains, N.Y., 1974—; chmn. bd. Rojon, Inc., Williamsburg, Va., 1979—. Mem. N.Y. Stock Exch., White Plains, N.Y., 1974—. Mem. Harrison (N.Y.) Archtl. Rev. Bd., 1970-72, Harrison Planning Bd., 1975-77; bd. dirs. Montefiore Hosp. Assn., YM-YWHA, Lafayette Ednl. Fund, Inc., 1986-92; internat. adv. coun. Mus. of Am. Folk Art, 1990—; naval aide-de-camp to gov. State of Va., with rank of capt., 1989—98. Lt. USNR, 1953—55, U.S.S. Midway. Recipient Wisdom award of honor and eminent wisdom; fellow Wisdom Hall of Fame. Mem. Folk Art Soc. (bd. dirs. 1987-95, mem. nat. adv. bd. 1996—), U.S. Naval Acad. Alumni Assn. (life), Stock Exch. Luncheon Club (N.Y.C.), Buttonwood Club. Home: 113 Elizabeth Meriwether Williamsburg VA 23185-5107 Office: Drawer JG Williamsburg VA 23187

GORDON, BARTON JENNINGS (BART GORDON), congressman, lawyer; b. Murfreesboro, Tenn., Jan. 24, 1949; s. Robert Jennings and Margaret Louise (Barton) G.; m. Leslie Peyton, 1998. BS, Middle Tenn. State U., 1971; JD, U. Tenn., 1973. Bar: Tenn. 1974. Mem. U.S. Congress from 6th Tenn. dist., Washington, 1985—; mem. energy and commerce com.; mem. sci. com.; mem. energy and air quality, telecom, trade and consumer protection subcoms.; ranking mem. space and aeronautics subcom. Mem. Tenn. Democratic Exec. Com., 1974-83, exec. dir., 1979-81, chmn., 1981-83; bd. dirs. Middle Tenn. State U. Found.; chmn. Rutherford County United Givers Fund, Rutherford County Cancer Crusade Mem. Rutherford County C. of C. (bd. dirs.) Democrat. Methodist. Office: US Ho of Reps 2304 Rayburn Ho Office Bldg Washington DC 20515-0001*

GORDON, BASIL, mathematics educator; b. Balt., Dec. 23, 1932; s. Basil and Helen (Williams) G. MA, Johns Hopkins, 1953; PhD, Calif. Inst. Tech., 1956. Instr. Calif. Inst. Tech., 1956-57; asst. prof. math. U. Calif. at Los Angeles, 1959-63, assoc. prof., 1963-67, prof., 1967-93; prof. emeritus, 1993—. Editor: Pacific Jour. Mathematics, 1969-70, 72-73, Jour. Combinatorial Theory, 1970-2002, Ramanujan Jour., 1997—; contbr. articles to profl. jours. Served with AUS, 1957-59. Alfred P. Sloan fellow, 1962-64 Mem. Math. Assn. Am., Pi Mu Epsilon. Achievements include rsch. on number theory, combinatorics, group theory, and function theory. Home: 526 Palisades Ave Santa Monica CA 90402-2722 Office: 405 Hilgard Ave Los Angeles CA 90095-9000 E-mail: bg@math.ucla.edu.

GORDON, BENJAMIN DICHTER, medical executive, pediatrician; b. Bklyn., Mar. 4, 1927; s. Abraham S. and Selma F. (Dichter) G.; m. Ellen M. Nimaroff, June 10, 1951; children: Wendy, Marcy, Amanda. AB, Amherst Coll., 1947; MD, U. Md., 1951. Diplomate Am. Bd. of Pediatrics. Rotating intern Kings County Hosp., Bklyn., 1951-52, asst. resident in pediatrics, 1953-54, Maimonides Hosp., Bklyn., 1952-53; research fellow Irvington House, Irvington-on-Hudson, N.Y., 1954-55; practice medicine specializing in pediatrics Stratford & Bridgeport, Conn., 1955-73; assoc. attendant, emergency dept. Bridgeport Hosp., 1973-78; asst. dir. emergency dept. Danbury (Conn.) Hosp., 1978-82; clin. dir. Union Carbide Corp., Danbury, 1982-87; med. dir Chesebrough-Ponds, Inc., Trumbull, Conn., 1987-90. Asst. prof. occupational medicine Yale U.; chmn. Rheumatic Fever com. Conn. State Heart Assn.; cons. to cosmetic industry and product-testing labs.; attending occupl. med. clinic Milton (Mass.) Hosp., Jordan Hosp., Plymouth, Mass. Author: Practical Guide for New Parents, 1970; contbr. articles to profl. jours. Served with USNR, 1945-46. Fellow: Am. Coll. Occupl. and Environ. Medicine, Am. Acad. Pediats.; mem.: Barnstable Dist. Med. Soc. (com. on violence), Mass. Med. Soc., Occupl. Med. Assn. Conn. (pres. 1987—88), Fairfield County Med. Soc. (past chmn. pub. health com.), Conn. State Med. Soc. (past chmn. comty. pub. health), Williams Club (N.Y.C.). Jewish. Avocations: music, dance, skiing, reading, history, golf. Home: 14 Hillsea Rd Yarmouth Port MA 02675-1111 Fax: 508-375-0559.

GORDON, BERNARD M. computer company executive; b. 1927; Pres., CEO, chmn. Analogic Corp., Peabody, Mass., 1967-94, CEO, chmn., 1994—. Recipient Nat. Medal Tech., 1986, John Fulke Sr. Meml. award, 1993. Fellow IEEE (Leadership Recognition award 1992); mem. Nat. Acad. Engrs. Office: Analogic Corp 8 Centennial Dr # B-1 Peabody MA 01960-7987

GORDON, BETH N. real estate appraiser; b. Mobile, Ala., Jan. 30, 1951; d. Earl Cyrullus Noel and Julia Marie Turberville; m. Barry Evan Gordon, July 28, 1973; children: Leah Ashley, Robert Gray. B in Liberal Arts, U. Ala., 1973. Tchr. City of Opelika, Ala., 1973-75; mktg. staff IBM Corp., Ft. Lauderdale, Fla., 1976, mktg. mgr. Nashville, edn. mgr. Atlanta, segment mgr., cons., skills mgr.; appraiser Orange Beach, Ala., 2002—. Key contact Nat. Skills Std. Bd.,

Washington. Leader Girl Scouts Am., Atlanta; trainer Cobb County Schs., Marietta, Ga.; adminstrv. bd. mem. Mt. Bethel United Meth. Ch., Marietta; bd. mem. Sea Spray Condominiums, Pensacola, Fla.; active Gulf Shores United Meth. Ch.; v.p. Ono Island Assn. Republican. Avocations: diving, snow skiing, fishing, reading. Home: 32254 River Rd Orange Beach AL 36561-5708 E-mail: bethgordon@gulftel.com.

GORDON, BETTY L. health services administrator; b. Sayre, Pa., Apr. 4, 1947; d. Manley and Helen (Featherman) Rockman; m. Alan F. Gordon, Dec. 29, 1972. BSN, Russell Sage Coll., 1964; postgrad., Boston U., 1973-74; MPH in Health Svcs. Adminstrn., John Hopkins U., 1981. RN, Mass., N.Y. Gen. staff nurse Robert Packer Hosp., Sayre, Pa., 1968; staff nurse, team leader Vis. Nurse Assn. Allegheny County, Pa., 1968-71; nurse pub. health Vis. Nurse Assn. Boston, 1971; staff continuing care coord. Faulkner Hosp., Jamaica Plain, Mass., 1972-74; nurse pub. health, home health coord. Arlington County Dept. Human Resources, Va., 1974-78; dir. patient care svcs. Hospice Met. Denver, 1978-80; project site dir. long term care channeling demonstration City Balt., 1981-83; sr. v.p. clin. svcs. Kimberly Quality Care, Boston, 1983-94; v.p. Simione Ctrl., Inc., Westboro, Mass., 1994—2001; principal Simione Consultants, LLC, Westboro, Mass., 2001—. Home: 125 Coolidge Ave Apt 606 Watertown MA 02472-2875 Office: 176 E Main St # 8 Westborough MA 01581-3941 E-mail: bgordon@simioneconsultants.com.

GORDON, CAREY NATHANIEL, lawyer, federal agency administrator; b. Cleve., Mar. 11, 1950; s. Murray Byron and Pearl Miriam (Jackson) G.; m. Lois Elizabeth Bradshaw, Nov. 28, 1981. BA, Ohio State U., 1972; MA, U. London, 1973; postgrad., Cambridge (Eng.) U., 1973-74; JD, Cleve. State U., 1977. Bar: Ohio 1977, D.C. 1978, U.S. Supreme Ct. 1983. Assoc. Rippner Schwartz & Carlin, Cleve., 1977-80, ptnr., 1980-84; spl. advisor Atty. Gen.'s Chambers, Khartoum, Sudan, 1984-85; contract advisor U.S. Agy. for Internat. Devel., Khartoum, Cairo, Kinshasa, Islamabad, 1986-94, contracting officer Abidjan, Ivory Coast, 1995-97, Phnom Penh, Cambodia, 1997—. Vis. lectr. U. Khartoum, 1984-85. Bd. dirs., treas. Internat. Sch. of Phnom Penh, 2000—02. Mem. Fed. Bar Assn., Cleve. Bar Assn. Office: USAID Box 47 Am Embassy Bangkok Apo AR 96546

GORDON, COREY LEE, lawyer; b. Mpls., Aug. 22, 1956; s. Jack I. and LaVerne (Shedlov) G.; m. Ciel Schaeffer, Aug. 29, 1982; children: Jared Isaac, Lian Miriam. BA, Macalester Coll., 1976; JD cum laude, U. Minn., 1980. Bar: Minn. 1980, U.S. Dist. Ct. Minn. 1981, U.S. Ct. Appeals (8th cir.) 1983, U.S. Supreme Ct. 1983, Wis. 1987, U.S. Dist. Ct. (ea. and we. dists.) Wis. 1987, N.Y. 1991, U.S. Dist. Ct. (so. dist.) N.Y. 1991, U.S. Ct. Appeals (3d cir.) 1992, Ill. 1993, U.S. Dist. Ct. (no. dist.) Ill. 1995, Fla. 1995, U.S. Dist. Ct. (we., ea., and no. dists.) N.Y. 1999, U.S. Ct. Appeals (11th cir.) 1999, U.S. Ct. Appeals (7th cir.) 1999, U.S. Dist. Ct. (so. and ctrl. dists.) Ill. 1999, U.S. Ct. Appeals (2d cir.) 1999, U.S. Dist. Ct. (so. and no. dists.) Fla. 2000. Assoc. Fried, Frank, Harris, Shriver & Jacobson, N.Y.C., 1980-81; ptnr. Shapiro, Lavintman & Gordon P.A., Mpls., 1982-85; assoc. Robins, Zelle, Larson & Kaplan, St. Paul, 1986-88; ptnr. Robins, Kaplan, Miller & Ciresi, Mpls., 1989—2000; dep. atty. gen. State of Minn., St. Paul, 2001—02; counsel Blackwell, Igbanugo, P.A., Mpls., 2002—. Bd. dirs. Jewish Family and Children's Svc. of Mpls., 1992-96, Mpls. Fedn. for Jewish Svc., 1994-99, chair bd. dirs. Circus Juventas, 2002—, bd. dirs. Jewish Vocational Svc., 2002—. Treas. The H.H H. Fund, Minn., 1984—89; bd. dirs., sec.-treas. Minn. Humane Soc., 1985—86; active Dem. Farm Labor Party; trustee Bet Shalom Synagogue, 1992—93, v.p., 1993—97, pres., 1997—99, past pres., 1999—. Mem. ABA, ATLA (co-chair inadequate security litigation group 1992-95). Jewish. Avocations: folk music, scuba diving, photography. Home: 2640 Glenhurst Pl Minneapolis MN 55416-3957 Office: Blackwell Igbanugo Engen & Saffold Ste 250 3601 W 76th St Minneapolis MN 55435

GORDON, DAN, food service executive; Exec. v.p. Gordon Food Svc. Inc., Grand Rapids, Mich., 1989—91, pres., CEO, 1991—. Office: Gordon Food Svc Inc 333 5th St SW Grand Rapids MI 49501*

GORDON, DANIEL SETH, business executive, consultant; b. L.A., Aug. 7, 1945; s. William Franklin Payne and Patricia Jean Gordon. MBA, Calif. Western U., Santa Ana, 1972, PhD in Bus., 1974; PhD in Motivational Psychology, U. Stockton, Calif., 1984, DDiv, 1987; PhD in Mgmt., U. Stockton, 1989. Pres., founder World in Water Corp., L.A., 1969-71, Design Trust, L.A., 1971-73; gen. mgr. Arbitron Meter Svcs./Control Data Corp., Beltsville, Md., also L.A., 1973-75; mktg. mgr. Dickenson Comms. Inc., Huntington Beach, Calif., 1975-77; dir. devel. Six Star Cablevision, L.A., Chgo., N.Y.C., Detroit, Kansas City, 1977-81; pres. Evergreen Travel, Beverly Hills, Calif., 1981-93; CEO Nat. TV Network, Honolulu, Anchorage, Aspen, Cheyenne, L.A., 1988-95, Stepping Stone Co., 1991—. Bus. devel. cons. French Govt., Paris, Haiti, Tahiti, Morea, Bora Bora, 1973-94; mng. ptnr. Travel Royal, 1994—. Author: The First Retirement Community in America--Allensworth, California, 1965; also articles. Co-founder Nat. Libertarian Party, Denver, 1966, Santa Monica Mountains Nat. Park., L.A., 1976; founder Allensworth State Park, 1971, Wolf Preservation League, Calif. and N.D., 1998. Recipient Am. Mktg. award U.S. Mktg. Assn., 1987, Archtl. Restoration Merit award Archtl. Preservation League, 1989, Key to the City, Sydney, Australia, 1982. Mem. Calif. Rare Fruit Growers Assn., World Wolf Fedn. (pres. 1998—, Lifetime Achievement award), Travel Writers Am. (Lifetime Achievement award 1998), Bus. Devel. Assn. (pres. 1997-98, Lifetime Achievement award 1999). Avocations: nature study, photography, victorian home and garden restoration, ultralights. Home: 2156 Hewitt Ave Oroville CA 95966-5404 Office: 3440 Orange Ave Oroville CA 95966-3611 E-mail: drdangordon@hotmail.com.

GORDON, DAVID, playwright, director, choreographer; b. N.Y.C., July 14, 1936; m. Valda Setterfield; 1 child, Ain. Dir. Pick Up Performance Co., Inc., N.Y.C., 1978—. Playwright, dir. dance, theater, music prodn. The Mysteries and What's So Funny?, 1991; writer, dir. TV program (1992-93) and theatrical work (1996) Punch and Judy Get Divorced; co-writer, dir.: (with Ain Gordon) The Family Business, 1994-95; dir. Shlemiel The First, Am. Repertory Theater, 1994-95; dir., choreographer: The Firebugs, The Guthrie Theater, 1995; co-writer, dir. (with Ain Gordon) First Picture Show, 1999; dir.: Past/Forward with Mikhail Baryshnikov, 2000-01. Guggenheim fellow, 1981, 87. Office: Pick Up Performance Co 520 8th Ave Ste 303 New York NY 10018 E-mail: pickupperformance@earthlink.net.

GORDON, DAVID ELIOT, lawyer; b. Santa Monica, Calif., Mar. 8, 1949; s. Sam and Dee G.; m. Mary Debora Lane, Mar. 5, 1978. BA, Harvard U., 1969, JD, 1972. Bar: Calif. 1972. Ptnr. O'Melveny & Myers, L.A., 1980—. Adj. prof. Loyola Law Sch., 2000—. Founder, editor ERISA Litigation Reporter; contbr. articles on tax and employee benefits to profl. jours. Trustee Ctr. for Early Edn., 1997 . Fellow Los Angeles County Bar Found. (life, pres. 1984-85, bd. dirs. 1980-86); mem. ABA (employee benefits com. 1986—), Am. Coll. Tax Counsel, Los Angeles County Bar Assn. (tax sect., pres. 1990-91). Republican. Avocations: tennis, squash, racquetball. Office: O'Melveny & Myers 400 S Hope St Los Angeles CA 90071-2899

GORDON, DAVID JAMIESON, tenor; b. Phila, Pa, Dec. 7, 1947; s. David William and Lois Irene (Lukens) G. Student, Coll. of Wooster, 1965-68, McGill U., Montreal, Que., Can., 1968-70; student of Dale Moore, 1965—. Mem. faculty U. Calif., Berkeley, Sonoma State U. Debut with Lyric Opera Chgo., 1973; leading tenor Landestheater Linz (Austria), 1975-79; prin. roles with San Francisco Opera, Houston Grand Opera, Met. Opera, Hamburg Staatsoper, Washington Opera, Mostly Mozart Festival, Salzburg Festival; concert soloist with Bach Festivals: Carmel, Calif., Bethlehem, Pa., Festival Casals, Stuttgart, Tokyo, Buenos Aires, Eugene, Oreg., Boston Symphony, Berlin Philharm., Czech Philharmonic, Vienna Symphony, St. Louis Symphony, San Francisco Symphony, LA Philharm., Seattle Symphony, Phila. Orch., Cleve. Orch., Nat. Symphony Washington, Baltimore Symphony; appears in opera, concerts, chamber music, recitals throughout US and Europe as performer, lectr., and tchr.; specialist in music of J.S. Bach; performing artist for Delos, Dorian, Telarc, London Records, Decca Records, Smithsoniam Collection of Recs., RCA Red Seal, Nonesuch Records. Home: 105 Merion Terr Moraga CA 94556 E-mail: dgordon@spiritsound.com.

GORDON, DAVID ZEVI, retired lawyer; b. Bklyn., Mar. 2, 1943; s. Isidore and Yaffa S. (Stern) G.; m. Karen Baranker, Apr. 25, 1971; children: Ilana, Naomi. BA magna cum laude, Yeshiva U., 1964; JD cum laude, MBA, Columbia U., 1969. Bar: N.Y. 1970, U.S. Dist. Ct. (so. dist.) N.Y. 1973, U.S. Ct. Appeals (2d cir.) 1973. Assoc. Spear and Hill, N.Y.C., 1969-71; sr. assoc. LeBoeuf Lamb Leiby & McRae, N.Y.C., 1971-77; ptnr. Finley Kumble Heine & Underburg, N.Y.C., 1977-78, David Z. Gordon and Assocs., N.Y.C., 1978-81; mng. ptnr. Moroze Sherman Gordon & Gordon, P.C., N.Y.C., 1981-96. Trustee, exec. com. Stern Coll. for Women, 1990-96; co-chmn. United Jewish Appeal, Operation Exodus, 1991-96, Project Renewal, 1987-96, exec. com. Israel econ. devel.; chmn. Israel Bonds, Bronx, 1988-96; co-chmn. bd. dirs. Am. Com. for Shaare Zedek Med. Ctr., Jerusalem, 2000—. Recipient Heritage award Yeshiva U., 1988, Star of Peace and Hope award Israel Bonds, 2002, Cmty. Svc. award Shaare Zedek Med. Ctr. 2002. Mem. ABA, N.Y. State Bar Assn., N.Y.C. Bar Assn. (mem. com. condemnation and tax certiorari), Real Estate Tax Bar Assn. Democrat. E-mail: FLASHGORDON@peoplepc.com.

GORDON, DOLORES JOAN, retired emergency medical technician; b. Cicero, Ill., Mar. 21, 1935; d. Harry Lewis and Louise Eva Marie (Uxa) G.; m. Joseph Delbert Ebert, Mar. 29, 1968 (div. Aug. 1977); children: Mark Harry Louis, Gloria Louise Dolores. Student, Mundelein Coll., 1953—54; BA in Bus., Farington U.; MS in Emergency Med. Svc., Farington U. Distance Learning Online, DBA, 2003. Cert. EMT, Am. Coll. Surgeons. Floral designer, office mgr. E.T. Will Landscaping and Florist, Berwyn, Ill., 1964-67; co-owner, EMT Ebert's Ambulance Svc., Berwyn, 1968-76; with invoicing dept. Turner Mfg. Co., Chgo., 1957-58. Interview subject on ghosts and Resurrection Mary CNN, 1997. Author: A Nanny's Memoirs, 1994, re-released in assn. with Conservatory Am. Letters, 2000; co-author: God's Country, 1996, Let the Lions Roar, 1998; contbg. author (with Dale Kaczmarek) to Windy City Ghosts. Named Woman of Yr. Hon. Mention Morton Twp. Women's History Com., 1997. Mem. Betsy Ross Lodge (50-Yr. Recognition pin), St. Mary's H.S. Alumni Assn. Roman Catholic. Achievement: 1st woman in 5 states to become EMT cert. by ACS. Home: 6506 Pershing Rd Berwyn IL 60402-4046 E-mail: GordonDJM@aol.com.

GORDON, DOROTHY K. silversmith, goldsmith; b. Boston, May 7, 1919; d. Barney and Sarah M. Kazer; m. Benjamin Gordon, Mar. 27, 1949; children: Judith, Ellis, William. Student, Mus. Sch. Art, Boston, Cath. U., Montgomery Coll. Tchr. metalsmithing D.C. Dept. Recreation, USDA Grad. Sch.; lectr. in field. Exhibited in group shows at YWCA, Washington, Smithsonian Instn. and Nat. Housing Ctr., St. John's Episcopal Ch., McLean, Va., Jewish Cmty. Ctr., Rockville, Md., Temple Micah, Washington, Crafts of the Synagogue touring exhbn, Plum Gallery, Kensington, Md., 1987, Nat. Mus. Am. Jewish History, Phila., 1990, Target Gallery, Alexandria, Va., 1993, B'nai B'rith Klutznick Nat. Jewish Mus., Washington, 1997, Washington Hebrew Congregation, 1998, 2000, Goldman Gallery, Jewish Cmty. Ctr., Rockville, 1999, television series, HGTV Modern Masters, 2003. Mem.: Soc. Am. Silversmiths (artisan mem.), Am. Art League, Washington Guild Goldsmiths. Avocation: painting. Home: 2856 Davenport St NW Washington DC 20008

GORDON, DOUGLAS, artist; b. Glasgow, Scotland, 1966; Student, Glasgow Sch. Art, 1984—88, Slade Sch. Art, London, 1988—90. One-man shows include Mus. d'Art Moderne de la Ville de Paris, 1993, Tramway, Glasgow, 1993, Kunst-werke, Berlin, 1993, Lisson Gallery, London, 1994, Rooseum Espresso, Malmö, 1995, Ctr. Georges Pompidou, Paris, 1995, Van Abbe Mus., Eindhoven, 1995, The Agy., London, 1995, Kunstlerhaus, Stuttgart, 1995, Tate Gallery, London, 1996, Galerie Walchenturm, Zurich, 1996, Mus. Gegenwartskunst, 1996, Canberra Contemporary Art Space, 1996, Galleria Bonoma, Rome, 1996, Uppsala Konstmus, 1996, FRAC Languedoc-Roussillion, Montpelier, France, 1996, Deutsches Mus., Bonn, 1997, Kunstverein Hannover, 1997, Biennale de Lyon, 1997, Gandy Gallery, Prague, 1997, Gelerie Mot & Van den Boogaard, Brussels, 1997, Munster Skulptur Projekt, 1997, Galerie Micheline Swajcer, Antwerp, 1997, Bloom Gallery, Amsterdam, 1997, Galleri Nicolai Wallner, Copenhagen, 1997, others, exhibited in group shows at Hayward Gallery, London, 1996, Transmission Gallery, Glasgow, 1996, Soros Contemporary Art Gallery, Kiev, 1997, Southampton City Art Gallery, 1997, Ashiya City Mus. Art and History, 1998, Guggenheim Mus. SoHo, N.Y., 1998, numerous others. Recipient Turner prize, 1996, Premio 2000 award, Venice Biennale, 1997. Office: care Gagostan Gallery 136 Wooster St New York NY 10012-3112 Fax: 212-228-2878.

GORDON, EDGAR GEORGE, retired lawyer; b. Detroit, Feb. 27, 1924; s. Edgar George and Verna Florence (Hay) G.; m. Alice Irwin, Feb. 4, 1967; children: David A., J. Scott. AB, Princeton U., 1947; JD, Harvard U., 1950. Bar: Mich. 1951, U.S. Supreme Ct. 1953. Assoc. Poole, Warren & Littell, Detroit, 1950-54; ptnr. Poole, Warren, Littell & Gordon, Detroit, 1953-63; gen. counsel Hygrade Food Products Corp., Detroit, 1963-69, sec., 1966-69, v.p., 1968-69; v.p., sec. counsel City Nat. Bank of Detroit, 1969-81; v.p., sec., gen. counsel No. States Bancorp, 1970-81; v.p., sec., counsel First of Am. Bank Corp., Kalamazoo, 1981-84; also ptnr. Howard & Howard, Kalamazoo, 1981-2000; ret., 2000. Dir. First Citizens Bank, Troy, Mich., 1973-81, First Nat. Bank, Plymouth, Mich., 1974-81; pres., chmn. bd. First of Am. Mortgage Co., Kalamazoo, 1978-84. Commr. City of Kalamazoo, 1995-2001. Lt. (j.g.) USN, 1943-46. Mem. ABA, Mich. Bar Assn., Kalamazoo Bar Assn., Country Club of Detroit (Grosse Pointe, Mich.). Republican. Presbyterian. Home: 4339 Lakeside Dr Kalamazoo MI 49008-2802

GORDON, ELLA DEAN, health and nurse educator, women's health and orthopedic nurse; b. Chgo., Jan. 19, 1947; d. Ed and Mozelle (Jordan) Hall; m. Starling Alexander Gordon, Aug. 2, 1969; children: Gerald Alexander, Dana Rolean. Diploma, Grady Meml. Hosp., 1968; student, Ga. State U., 1969-75; BSN, Med. Coll. Ga., 1976; M in Health Sci., Armstrong State Coll., 1983. RN, Ga., Tex. Charge nurse pediatrics evenings Grady Meml. Hosp., Atlanta, 1968-71; staff nurse pediatrics Dr.'s Meml. Hosp., Atlanta, 1971; charge nurse Pediatricians Office, Decatur, Ga., 1971-72; staff nurse VA Hosp., Atlanta, 1972-76, nurse primary care med. ICU San Antonio, 1983; charge nurse, army nurse corps Eisenhower Army Med. Ctr., Ft. Gordon, Ga., 1976-79; staff nurse obstet. Noble Army Hosp., Ft. McClellan, Ala., 1984; instr. clin. nursing Jacksonville (Ala.) State Coll. Nursing, 1984-85; clin. nurse obstet. Gorgas Army Hosp., Republic of Panama, 1987-89; charge nurse oncology days Eisenhower Army Med. Ctr., Ft. Gordon, Ga., 1989-90; charge nurse obstet. Brooke Army Med. Ctr., Ft. Sam Houston, Tex., 1990-96; mem. labor & delivery Wilford Hall Air Force Med. Ctr., Lackland AFB, Tex., 1996; charge nurse orthopedics Brooke Army Med. Ctr., Ft. Sam Houston, Tex., 1996-99, health/nurse educator Health Promotion Ctr., 2000—. Cons. health edn. ETOWAH County Clinics, Gadsden, Ala, 1985; health educator Cardiovascular Coun. of Savannah, Ga., 1983, Parent/Child Devel. Svcs., Savannah, 1982. Contbr. articles to profl. jours. Instr. ARC, Ft. McClellan, 1985-86, chmn., vols., 1986-87. Capt. U.S. Army, 1976-79; col. USAR, 1991, ret., 1998. Named One of Outstanding Young Women in Am., 1979, 83. Mem. Ret. Army Nurse Corps Assn., Orthopaedic Nurses Assn., Officers Wives Club (publicity chmn. 1982-83), Sigma Theta Tau. Democrat. Avocations: cross-stitching, bowling, reading, ceramics. Home: 12810 El Marro St San Antonio TX 78233-5832 Office: Brooke Army Med Ctr Fort Sam Houston TX 78234 E-mail: satxella33@hotmail.com.

GORDON, ERLINE SCHECTER, educational administrator; b. El Paso, Tex., Apr. 7, 1956; d. Irving and Jean (Lapowski) Schecter; m. Bruce L. Gordon. BA in Elem. Edn., U. Ariz., Tucson, 1978; MEd, Lesley Coll., 1988; postgrad., Sul Ross State U., 1990. Cert. mid-mgmt., Tex. Tchr. Dept. Def. Dependent Schs., Iwakuni, Japan, 1980-83; elem. tchr. El Paso Ind. Sch. Dist., 1978-80, 83-85, tchr. computers, 1985-92, staff devel., 1992-96, asst. dir. tech. tng. programs, staff devel., 1996-97, facilitator region 1, 1997-2000, facilitator curriculum, instrn., & assessment, 2000-01, facilitator career and tech. edn. program, 2001—. Cons. Region XIX Edn. Svc. Ctr., El Paso, 1985-88, Norton Bros. Computer Ctr., El Paso, 1984-86, Ector County Ind. Sch. Dist., 1989-90. Chairperson Border Ednl. Tech. Conf., 1996-98. Mem. AAUW, ASCD, Tex. Computer Edn. Assn. (treas.1990-94, Area II dir. 1986-90, electronic editor 1994-95, scholarship chairperson 1996-97), Internat. Soc. for Tech. in Edn., Nat. Coun. Jewish Women, Alpha Epsilon Phi, Phi Delta Kappa. Avocations: needlework, computers, reading. Office: El Paso Ind Sch Dist 6531 Boeing Dr El Paso TX 79925-1008

GORDON, EVAN L. lawyer; b. N.Y.C., July 10, 1941; s. Myron P. and Henrietta (Lediger) Gordon. AB, Columbia U., 1963, LLB, 1966. Bar: N.Y. 1966, U.S. Dist. Ct. (so. and ea. dists.) N.Y. 1968, U.S. Dist. Ct. (no. and we. dists.) N.Y. 1985, U.S. Ct. Appeals (2nd cir.) 1967, U.S. Ct. Appeals (8th cir.) 1988, U.S. Ct. Appeals (11th cir.) 1986, U.S. Supreme Ct. 1976. Ptnr. Delson & Gordon, N.Y.C., 1968-78, Wofsey, Certilman et al, N.Y.C., 1978-85, Bangser & Weiss, N.Y.C., 1986-89; pvt. practice N.Y.C., 1990—. Contbg. author: The Law of Gray and Counterfeit Goods, 1987. Mem. corp. and security del. to Ea. Europe through People to People Internat., 1990. Mem. ABA (securities litigation com. 1977—), N.Y. State Bar Assn., Assn. of Bar of City of N.Y., Fed. Bar Council. Home: 400 E 56th St New York NY 10022-4147 Office: 230 Park Ave New York NY 10169-0005

GORDON, EZRA, architect, educator; b. Detroit, Apr. 5, 1921; s. Abraham and Rebecca (Reimer) G.; m. Jeanette Greenberg, Oct. 8, 1942; children: Cheryl P. Gordon Van Ausdal, Rana Gordon Oremland, Judith Gordon Eichhorn. Roosevelt Coll., 1946-48; BS in Architecture, U. Ill., 1951. Draftsman Pace Assos. Architects, 1951-53; sr. planner Chgo. Plan Commn., 1953-54; project architect Harry Weese & Assos., 1954-61; ptnr. Gordon-Levin & Assocs., Chgo., 1961-84, Gordon & Levin, Inc., Chgo., 1984-95; cons. Dept. Urban Renewal City Chgo., Council for Jewish Elderly, Chgo. Jewish Fedn. Prof. emeritus U. Ill.-Chgo. Sch. Architecture; former mem. Mayor's Adv. Coun. on Bldg. Code Amendments; master juror Nat. Coun. Archtl. Registration Bds. Works include Long-Kogan Office Bldg., 1957, 5401 Hyde Park Apt. Bldg., Chgo., 1962, South Commons, Chgo., 1968, The Commons Townhouse Devel., Chgo., 1968, Hyde Park West Apts., Chgo., 1969, IBM Office bldgs., Kalamazoo, 1969, Moline, Ill. 1970, Jefferson City, Mo., Omaha, 1971, Eastwood Tower Apts., Chgo., 1970, Wexler Pavilion and Siegel Inst., Michael Reese Hosp., Chgo., 1971, Arbor Trails Apts. and Townhouses, Park Forest, Ill., 1972, Kenmore Plaza Apts. Sr. Housing, Chgo., 1972, Kennaly Sq. Warehouse Apts., Chgo., 1972-74, Pontiac Office Bldg., Mich., 1972, Concourse Office Towers, Skokie, 1972, Belle Plaine Apts., Chgo., 1972, Newberry Plaza, Chgo., 1973, Greenwood Park Apts., Chgo., 1974, River Plaza, Chgo., 1976, Elm St. Plaza, Chgo., 1976, Dearborn Park, Twin Tower Apts., Chgo., 1979, Huron Plaza, Chgo., 1981, 400 E. Ohio Condominiums, Streeterville, Chgo., 1983, East Bank Club, Chgo., 1983, Dearborn-Elm Apts., Chgo., 1986-87; designer World Trade Ctr. Apts., Chgo., 1989, Lachman Montisorri Sch. for Hearing Impaired Children, Deerfield, Ill., 1990, Elm Street Apts., 1990, restoration of 1130 S. Michigan Ave., 1991, Chgo. Montessori Sch. for the Hearing Impaired, 1991, Love residence addition, Glencoe, Ill., 1991, Drs. Barak & Oremland offices, Skokie, Ill., 1991, Oral Rehab. Ctr., Skokie, 1992, residence addition, Glencoe, 1998. Former bd. dirs. Hyde Park-Kenwood Cmty. Conf., Astor St.-Lake Shore Dr. Assocs.; former v.p. Harper Ct. Found.; former trustee Chgo. Athenaeum Mus. Archtl. Art and Urban Studies; mem. Art Inst. Chgo., Mus. Sci. and Industry, Spertus Mus., Mus. Contemporary Art, Chgo. Hist. Soc.; mem. Landmarks Preservation Coun., Chgo. Archtl. Found., former v.p. 1300 Lake Shore Drive Condo Assn. Decorated Croix de Guerre with palm; recipient Honor award Dept. Housing and Urban Devel., 1967, Honor award AIA-Chgo. C. of C., 1967, award AIA-House & Home Mag., 1967, Distinguished Bldg. award AIA, 1957, 63, 69, 71, 73, 75, award City of Chgo. Beautification, 1969, 75, award of excellence Concrete Post Tensioning Inst., 1984, Silver Circle award for excellence in teaching U. Ill., Chgo., 1985 Fellow AIA (past bd. dir. Chgo. chpt.); mem. AIA, Labor Zionist Alliance, Am. Profs. for Peace in Middle East, Am. Jewish Congress, Chgo. Archtl. Found., Lambda Alpha. Clubs: Cliff Dwellers. Jewish.

GORDON, FLORENCE IRENE, graphic artist, illustrator; b. L.A., Oct. 22, 1928; d. Harry and Etta (Goldstein) Gronoff; widowed; 1 child. Student, Chounard Art Inst., L.A., Santa Monica City Coll.; BA, Art Ctr., L.A. Graphic artist Ned North Enterprises, L.A.; artist Hawaii Newspaper, Oahu; tech. illustrator Northrop-Aircraft, L.A., McDonnell Douglas, L.A. Exhibited in group shows. Art scholar Chounard Art Inst., 1950. Home: 5166 Sepulveda Blvd Apt 208 Culver City CA 90230-5235

GORDON, FRANK JEFFREY, medical educator; b. Washington, Dec. 5, 1948; married; 2 children. Attended, Case Western Reserve U., 1966-69; BS in Biology, N.Mex. State U., 1972, MA in Psychology, 1974; PhD in Biopsychology, U. Iowa, 1980, Interdisciplinary rsch. fellow U. Iowa, Iowa City, 1978 80, postdoctoral rsch. fellow Dept. Internal Medicine, 1980-81, rsch. scientist, 1981-82; asst. prof. Dept. Pharmacology Emory U. Sch. Medicine, Atlanta, 1982-88, assoc. prof., 1988—. Spkr. in field. Editl. bd. Am. Jour. Physiology, 1989-93. Mem. com. on risk factors Iowa Heart Assn., 1982. USPHS predoctoral fellow, 1978-80, post-doctoral fellow, 1980-82; rsch. starter grantee Pharm. Mfgs. Assn. Found., 1983-85. Fellow Coun. High Blood Pressure Rsch.; mem. Am. Physiol. Soc., Am. Soc. Pharmacology and Exptl. Therapeutics, Am. Heart Assn. (rsch. investigatorship Ga. affiliate 1987-88, AHA established investigator 1989-94), Soc. Neurosci., Sigma Xi. Achievements include research in brain and spinal cord regulation of peripheral cardiovascular systems in normal and pathological states. Office: Dept Pharmacology Rollins Rsch Ctr Rm 5011 Atlanta GA 30322-0001

GORDON, GARET MARK, cardiologist; b. Bklyn., Aug. 12, 1934; s. Sam and Nellie G.; m. Barbara Diesenhof, June 5, 1960; children: Meredith, Pamela, Sanford. BA, NYU, 1955; MD, SUNY, 1958; MBA, Columbia U., 1987. Intern Montefiore Med. Ctr., Bronx, 1958-59, resident, 1959-61, fellow in cardiology, 1961-62; cardiologist pvt. practice, Bronx, 1964-88; head cardiology Montefiore-Morrisania Affiliation, Bronx, 1966-76, Montefiore-NCB Affiliation, Bronx, 1976-88; dep. med. dir. Moses divsn. Montefiore Med. Ctr., Bronx, 1988-89, med. dir. Moses divsn., 1989-93, mem. cardiology faculty divsn. cardiology, 1993—, interim dir. noninvasive lab., 2001—. Pres. med. staff Montefiore Med. Ctr., 1993-95; assoc. prof. Albert Einstein Coll. Medicine, Bronx, 1988—. Capt. U.S. Army, 1962-64. Fellow Am. Coll. Cardiologists, Am. Coll. Physicians, Coun. Clin. Cardiology. Avocations: skiing, biking, reading history. Office: Montefiore Med Ctr 111 E 210th St Bronx NY 10467-2401 E-mail: ggordon@montefiore.org.

GORDON, GILBERT, chemist, educator; b. Chgo., Nov. 11, 1933; s. Walter and Catherine Gordon; m. Joyce Elaine Masura; children: Thomas, Lyndi. BS, Bradley U., 1955; PhD, Mich. State U., 1959. Postdoctoral research assoc. U. Chgo., 1959-60; asst. prof. U. Md., College Park, 1960-64, assoc. prof., 1964-67, prof., 1967; prof. chemistry U. Iowa, Iowa City, 1967-73; prof., chmn. dept. Miami U., Oxford, Ohio, 1973-84, Volwiler Disting. Research prof., 1984—. Mem. editl. bd. synthesis inorganic metal, organic chemistry; contbr. articles to chem. jours. Editor: catalysis kinetics sect. Chem. Abstracts, 1970—; editorial bd. synthesis inorganic metal, organic chemistry: catalysis kinetics sect. Ohio Jour. Sci, 1971— ; contbr. articles to chem. jours. Named Cin. Chemist of Yr., 1981 Mem.: Faraday Soc., Chem. Soc. London, Am. Chem. Soc., Internat. Ozone Assn. (pres. 2002, treas. 1998—2001, dir. 1995—), Phi Kappa Phi, Sigma Xi. Home: 190 Shadowy Hills Dr Oxford OH 45056-1441 Office: Miami U Dept Chemistry Oxford OH 45056 E-mail: gordong@muohio.edu. *My objectives have been to investigate meaningful areas of chemistry in an attempt to better understand chemical phenomena affecting our everyday lives (such as better and less expensive ways to purify drinking water), and to work diligently with students while helping to educate them to be better citizens and aware of the exciting potential of science.*

GORDON, GRANVILLE HOLLIS, church official; b. Picayune, Miss., Oct. 12, 1922; s. Thomas and Eugenia (Landrum) G.; m. Miriam C. Culpepper, Sept. 6, 1942; children: Tessa Eileen, Gerald Keith, Cathy Annette, Connie Jean, Donna Lynn. Student, Jacksonville Bapt. Coll. & Sem., 1950-52. Ordained to ministry Bapt. Ch., 1950. Pastor Friendship Bapt. Ch., Jewett, Tex., 1950-51, Little Flock Bapt. Ch., Jewett, 1950-51, Rural Shade Bapt., Kerens, Tex., 1951-52, Ogden Ave. Bapt., Mobile, Ala., 1952-54, Stanton Way Bapt., Mobile, 1954-58, Creston Hills Bapt., Jackson, Miss., 1958-65, 1st Bapt. Shady Grove, Laurel, Miss., 1965 74, Creston Hills Bapt., Jackson, Miss., 1974-84, Rolling Hills Bapt., Jacksonville, Fla., 1984-86, Temple Bapt. Ch., Lucedale, Miss., 1986-89, Highland Pk. Bapt., Hattiesburg, Miss., 1990-96, Shiloh Bapt. Church, Mt. Olive, Miss., 1996-98; Pastor Pear Orchard Bapt. Ch., Jackson, Miss., 1998—. With USAF, ETO. Mem. Miss. Bapt. Assn. (rec. clk. 1961-70), Bapt. Missionary Assn. (rec. clk. 1975-94). Baptist. Office: Baptist Missionary Assoc of Am 193 Old Canton Hills Dr Jackson MS 39211-3337

GORDON, HAROLD P. manufacturing executive; b. Montreal, Can., 1937; BA, Sir. George Williams U., 1961; B Civil Law, McGill U., 1964, B Comm, 1958. Atty. Stikeman Elliott, Montreal, Can., 1967-75, ptnr., 1975-95; vice-chmn. Hasbro, Inc., Pawtucket, R.I., 1995—. Apptd. Queen's Coun., Montreal, 1985. Bd. dirs. Alliance Comm. Can. Office: Hasbro Inc 1027 Newport Ave Pawtucket RI 02861-2539

GORDON, HARRISON J. lawyer; b. Newark, Aug. 21, 1950; s. Carl and Rose (Katz) G.; children by previous marriage: Caryn Rachel, Robert Jonathan. BS, U. Bridgeport, 1972; JD, U. Miami, 1975. Bar: N.J. 1976, D.C. 1995, N.Y., 1997, U.S. Dist. Ct. N.J. 1976, U.S. Supreme Ct. 1980. Sole practice, West Orange, N.J., 1976-78, Montclair, N.J., 1978-83; ptnr. Gordon & Gordon, West Orange, 1983-87, Gordon, Gordon & Haley, West Orange, 1987-90, Gordon & Gordon, PC, West Orange, 1990—. Adj. prof. Montclair State Coll., Upper Montclair, N.J., 1979. Recipient West Orange Cmty. Svc. award, 2001. Mem. N.J. State Bar Assn. (exec. com. young lawyers div. 1981-83), Assn. Trial Lawyers Am. (chmn. automobile and premises liability sect.), N.J. Trial Lawyers Assn. (bd. govs. 1987–, sec. 1990-91, treas. 1991-92, 3d v.p. 1992-93, 2d v.p. 1993-94, 1st v.p. 1994-95, pres.-elect 1995—, assoc. editor mag. 1987—, pres. 1996-97), Am. Arbitration Assn. (arbitrator), Soc. Bar and Gavel, Optimists Club (pres. 1981-82), Psi Chi, Phi Alpha Theta. Democrat. Office: Gordon & Gordon PC 80 Main St West Orange NJ 07052-5460

GORDON, HELEN HEIGHTSMAN, English language educator, writer, publisher; b. Salt Lake City, Sept. 7, 1932; d. Fred C. and Florence Isabel Heightsman; m. Norman C. Winn, Aug. 10, 1950 (div. Sept. 1972); children: Bruce Vernon Winn, Brent Terry Winn, Holly Winn Willner; m. Clifton Beverly Gordon, Feb. 17, 1974. Student, U. Utah, 1959-62; BA in English and Edn., Calif. State U., Sacramento, 1964, MA in English, 1967; EdD, Nova U., 1979. Cert. tchr., Calif.; lic. counselor, Calif. Stenographer, payroll clk. Associated Food Stores, Inc., Salt Lake City, 1951-59; part-time instr. in remedial English U. Utah, Salt Lake City, 1960-61; tchr. high sch. Rio Americano H.S., Sacramento, 1965-66; assoc. prof., counselor Porterville (Calif.) Coll., 1967-74; prof., counselor Bakersfield (Calif.) Coll., 1974-95; editor, tech. writer dept. computer engring. U. Calif., Santa Barbara, 1999—. Chair lang. arts divsn. Porterville Coll., 1971-74; coord. women's studies Bakersfield Coll., 1977-78, adminstrv. intern, 1982-83; dir. region V, English Coun. of Calif. Two Yr. Colls., 1990-92; articulation coord. Bakersfield Coll., 1992-93; pres., pub. Anacade Internat. Ednl. Books and Games, 1998—. Author: (textbook) From Copying to Creating, 2d edit., 1983, Developing College Writing, 1989, Wordforms, Book I & II, 2d edit., 1990, Interplay: Sentence Skills in Context, 1991, (novel) Voice of the Vanquished: The Story of the Slave Marina and Hernan Cortes, 1995 (memoirs) First Captured, Last Freed: Memoirs of a P.O.W. in World War II Guam and Japan, 1995; pub.: (game) Anagrabber, the Word Game for All Ages, 1998 (poetry book) Life, Love and Laughter, 1998, (game book) Anagrams, Anagrabber and Other Word Games, 1999, (poetry book) Love Lyrics in Light and Shadow, 1999, (humor book) Age is a Laughing Matter: How to Laugh Through the Second Half of Your Life, 1999. Founder, 1st pres. Writers of Kern, Bakersfield, 1993; guest mem. editl. bd. Bakersfield Californian Newspaper, 1988; past pres. Unitarian Fellowship of Kern County, Bakersfield, 1976-78. Calif. Fund for Instrn. grantee, 1978; U. Utah scholar, 1959-62. Mem. NEA, AAUW (pres. Santa Barbara chpt. 1997-98), Am. Assn. Women in Cmty. and Jr. Colls. (founder Bakersfield chpt., pres., program chair 1988-91), Nat. Coun. Tchrs. of English, Faculty Assn. Calif. Cmty. Coll., Text and Acad. Authors Assn. (charter, columnist Acad. Author 1996—), LWV (pres. Bakersfield chpt. 1981-83, 89-90), Calif. Writers Club, Pi Lambda Theta. Democrat. Avocations: poetry, personal computer, travel, bowling, theatre. Home: 3775 Modoc Rd Apt 135 Santa Barbara CA 93105-4462

GORDON, HOWARD LYON, advertising and marketing executive; b. Chgo., Oct. 8, 1930; s. Milton Arthur and Bess Z. (Ginsburg) G.; m. Lois Jean Kaufman, Aug. 21, 1955; children: Carolyn Ann, Leslie Meredith. BS, U. Ill., 1953; MS, Northwestern U., 1954, MBA, 1962. Mktg. rsch. mgr. Marsteller Inc.; advt. Chgo., 1960-64; v.p. mktg. services Marsteller Inc. and Burson Marsteller, Chgo., 1968-76; dir. client service Britt and Frerichs Inc., mktg. research and advt. cons., 1977-78, sr. v.p., 1978—, prin., 1979—, ptnr., 1986—; lectr. advt. and mktg. Northwestern U., 1963—. Vis. prof. Medill grad. studies in advt., 1981—; advt. prof. in residence No. Ill. U., DeKalb, 1974-76; lectr., seminar leader Am. Mgmt. Assn., 1965-72; adj. lectr. Ctr. Intellectual Property Law, The John Marshall Law Sch., 2000—; bd. dirs. Bus. Advt. Rsch. Coun., 1985—, chmn. life style rsch. com. Advt. Rsch. Found., 1991—; bd. dirs. Advt. Rsch. Found., Media Comm. Coun.; mem. alumni awards com. Medill Sch. Northwestern U., 1986, fund-raising com. Kellogg Grad. Sch. Northwestern U., 1986—; presenter 17th World Advt. Congress, Amsterdam, 1992; mem. publs. bd. U. Ill., 1997—. Author: Know The Buyer Better, 1991; co-author: Marketing Manager's Handbook, 3rd edit., 1994; contbr. articles to profl. publs. and mktg. texts. Regional chmn. Crusade of Mercy, Evanston, Ill., 1969; founding dir. Alumni Assn. Medill Sch., 1984—; adv. council athletic dept. Northwestern U., 1985—. With AUS, 1954-56. Recipient award Dept. Def., 1956, Alumni award Northwestern U., 1989. Mem. Am. Mktg. Assn. (dir., v.p. mktg. mgmt.), Northwestern U. Faculty, Kellogg Alumni Assn. (program com., exec. bd. dirs.), Direct Mktg. Assn., Assn. Consumer Rsch., Sigma Delta Chi. Office: 400 E Randolph Dr Chicago IL 60601-7329 E-mail: hgordon@grfiltd.com.

GORDON, JACK DAVID, foundation administrator, real estate company officer; b. Detroit, June 3, 1922; s. A. Louis and Henrietta (Rodgers) G.; m. Myra L. MacPherson; children: Andrew Louis, Deborah Mary, Jonathan Henry;stepchildren: Leah Siegel, Michael Siegel. BA, U. Mich., 1942. Engaged in real estate and ins. businesses, Miami Beach, Fla., 1946-52; founding dir., pres., chief mng. officer Washington Savs. & Loan Assn., Miami Beach, 1952-80, vice chmn. bd., 1980-81; founding dir. Jefferson Nat. Bank of Miami Beach, 1962-77, past chmn. exec. com.; dir. Inst. Pub. Policy and Citizenship Studies Fla. Internat. U., now the Jack D. Gordon Inst.; pres. The Hospice Found. of Am., Miami. Mem. Fla. Senate, 1972-92; housing fin. cons. Dept. State and; expert cons. UN Tech. Assistance Program in Costa Rica, Nicaragua, Panama, Ethiopia, Somali Republic, Nigeria, 1959-63; cons. to ROCAP, 1962-64, Eastern Nigerian Housing Corp., 1963; contract supr. AID Housing Guaranty Program in Latin Am., 1966-69; chmn. Miami Beach Housing Authority. 1947-56. Author: (with others) A Survey of New Home Financing Institutions in Latin America, 1969. Mem. Dade County Bd. Pub. Instrn., 1961-68. Served with AUS, 1943-46. Mem. Am. Jewish Congress, Am. Friends of Hebrew U., ACLU. Democrat. Office: 12000 Biscayne Blvd # 505 North Miami FL 33181 E-mail: senatorjack@att.net.

GORDON, JAMES POWER, optics scientist; b. N.Y.C., Mar. 20, 1928; BS, MIT, 1949; MA, Columbia U., 1951, PhD in Physics, 1955. Asst. physics dept. Columbia U., 1953-55; mem. tech. staff electronics rsch. AT&T Bell Labs., Holmdel, N.J., 1955-59, head quantum electronics rsch. dept. Murray Hill, N.J., 1959-80; sr. tech. staff cons. Lucent Technologies, Murray Hill, N.J., 1980—. Recipient Max Born award, 1991, Optical Soc. Am. Fellow Am. Phys. Soc., Optical Soc.; mem. IEEE (sr.), Nat. Acad. Engring., Nat. Acad. Scis. Achievements include demonstration of lot MASER, research in quantum electronics, interaction of electromagnetic waves with matter and soliton theory, communication theory. Office: Lucent Bell Labs Crawfords Corner Rd Holmdel NJ 07733

GORDON, JAMES S. lawyer, director; b. N.Y.C., Feb. 15, 1941; s. George S. and Sylvia A. (Wolfson) Gordon; m. Marica G. Gordon, Dec. 22, 1968 (dec.); children: Daniel, Sarah; m. Debbie S. Pase, June 15, 1996. BA with high honors, U. Fla., 1962; LLB, Yale U., 1965. Bar: Ill. 1965, Fla. 1966, U.S. Supreme Ct. 1974. Asst. prof. Ind. U. Sch. Law, Bloomington, 1967-68, assoc. prof., 1969; ptnr. Feiwell, Galper & Gordon, Chgo., 1970-72; pvt. practice Chgo., 1972-80; pres. James S. Gordon, Ltd., Chgo., 1981-93; chmn. Gordon, Glickman, Flesch, Woody & Rosenwein, Chgo., 1994—; dir. Mo. Metals, LLC. Editor: Yale Law Jour., 1963—65; contbr. articles to profl. jours. Ford Found. grantee, 1965—66. Mem.: Order of the Coif (exec. com.), Fla. Blue Key, Birchwood Club (Highland Park, Ill.), Lawyers Club Chgo., Phi Beta Kappa, Phi Alpha Delta. Office: 140 S Dearborn St Ste 404 Chicago IL 60603-5202 E-mail: jgordon@lawggf.com.

GORDON, JAMES SAMUEL, psychiatrist; b. N.Y.C., Oct. 12, 1941; s. Jules David and Cynthia (Hymanson) G. AB magna cum laude, Harvard U., 1962, MD, 1967. Diplomate Am. Bd. Psychiatry and Neurology. Tchg. fellow gen. edn. Harvard U., Cambridge, Mass., 1963-67; NIH rsch. fellow, tchg. asst. dept. pathology Cornell Med. Coll., N.Y.C., 1964-65; intern Mt. Zion Hosp., San Francisco, 1967-68; resident in psychiatry Albert Einstein Coll. Medicine, Bronx, N.Y., 1968-70, chief resident, clin. instr. psychiatry, 1970-71; research psychiatrist NIMH, Rockville, Md., 1971-82, cons. alternative forms of svc., 1974-82, dir. spl. study Pres.'s Commn. Mental Health, 1977-78; chief adolescent svcs. St. Elizabeth's Hosp., Washington, 1980-82; clin. prof. Georgetown U. Med. Sch., Washington, 1980—; dir. Ctr. for Mind-Body Medicine, Washington, 1991—. Chair program adv. coun. Office of Alternative Medicine NIH, 1994-97; sr. cons. L.Am. Youth Ctr., Washington, 1984—; mem. cancer adv. panel NIH, 1998—; chair White House Commn. on Complimentary and Alternative Medicine Policy, 2000—; vis. scholar Aurora Assocs., Washington, 1982-84; rsch. psychiatrist divsn. spl. mental health programs NIMH, 1980-82; med. cons. wellness program Walter Reed Army Med. Ctr., Washington, 1980-82; sr. cons. on adolescence divsn. child and adolescent svcs. St. Elizabeth's Hosp., Washington, 1979-80; Blanche Ittleson cons. Group for Advancement of Psychiatry, 1979; dir. spl. study on alternative svcs. Pres.' Commn. on Mental Health, 1977-78; vis. lectr. Cmty. Therapy Tng. Ctr., Washington, 1975, Cath. U. Am., Washington, 1974; lectr. in field. Author: The Golden Guru, 1987, Holistic Medicine, 1988, Transforming Medicine, 1996, Manifesto for a New Medicine, 1996, Comprehensive Cancer Care, 2000; editor: Health for the Whole Person (Med. Self Care Book award 1980), Mind, Body and Health: Towards and Integral Medicine, 1984; contbr. articles to profl. jours. Commdr. USPHS, 1971-82. Recipient award Ford Found., 1982. Fellow Am. Assn. Social Psychiatry; mem. Am. Psychiat. Assn., Am. Holistic Med. Assn. (founding mem. 1980, trustee 1980-86), Am. Assn. Med. Acupuncture (founding mem. 1987), Physicians for Social Responsibility (exec. com. 1984-86). Office: Ste 414 5225 Connecticut Ave NW Washington DC 20015-1845

GORDON, JEFF, race car driver; b. Pittsboro, Ind., Aug. 4, 1971; m. Brooke Sealy. Stock race car driver DuPont Chevrolet, 1993—. Named Maxx Race Cards ROokie of Yr., 1993, winner, NASCAR Winston Cup, 1994, 1997, Busch Clash, 1994, Winston Select Open, pole for Coca-Cola 600, 1994, Brickyard 400, 1994, 1998, Goodwrench 500, 1995, Purolator 500, 1995, Ford City 500, 1995, 1997, 1998, Pepsi 400, 1995, Slick 50 300, 1995, Mountain Dew So. 500, 1995, MNBA 500, 1995, Daytona 500, 1997, 1999, CMT 300, 1997, Bud at the Glen, 1997, 1998, Calif 500, 1997, 1999, Pocono 500, 1997, Coca-Cola 600, 1997, 1998, Goody's 500, 1997, Goodwrench 400, 1997, 1998, Pa. 500, 1998, Pepsi 400, Daytona, 1998, AC Delco 500, 1998, NAPA 500, 1998, Cracker Barrel 500, 1999, Save Mart/Kragen 350, 1998; named to McDonald's All-Star Team, 1994, 1995; recipient winner, Save Mart/Kragen 350, 1999, Frontier at the Glen, 1999, NAPA Autocave 500, 1999, UAW-GM 500, 1999, Die Hard 500, 2000. Achievements include 2d youngest Winston Cup Champion NASCAR ever at age 24. Office: NASCAR PO Box 2875 Daytona Beach FL 32120-2875 also: Jeff Gordon Nat Fan Club 514 E Route 66 Williams AZ 86046-2704 E-mail: JGFAN@Primenet.com.

GORDON, JEFFREY (JACK GORDON), lawyer; b. Boston, Sept. 6, 1964; BA, Tulane U., 1986, JD, 1989. Bar: Fla. 1990, U.S. Dist. Ct. (mid. dist.) Fla. 1995, cert.: (trial lawyer). Law clk. intern 1st dist. Ct. Appeal Fla., Tallahassee, 1989; spl. asst. pub. defender Dade County, Miami, Fla., 1990-92; cert. cir. ct. arbitrator Palm Beach County, West Palm Beach, Fla., 1990-92; ptnr. Maney & Gordon, P.A., Tampa, Fla., 1992—. Fellow Roscoe Pound Inst.; sr. counsel Am. Coll. Barristers. Teen ct. judge pro bono Hillsborough County, Tampa, 1992-98. Fellow Roscoe Pound Inst. Mem. ATLA, Acad. Fla. Trial Attys., Animal Legal Def. Fund, Hillsborough County Bar Trial Lawyers (lawyers sect.). Office: Maney & Gordon PA 101 E Kennedy Blvd Ste 3170 Tampa FL 33602-5151 E-mail: J.Gordon@ManeyGordon.com.

GORDON, JOHN A. career officer; BS in Physics with hons., U. Mo., 1968; MS, Naval Postgrad. Sch., 1970; MA in Bus. Adminstrn., New Mexico Highlands U., Las Vegas, 1972; Diploma, Squadron Officer Sch., 1975, Air Command and Staff Coll., 1978, Air War Coll., 1986. Commd. 2d lt. USAF, 1968, advanced through ranks to gen., 1997; various assignments to dir. opers. Hdqtrs. Air Force Space Command, Peterson AFB, Colo., 1994-95; spl. asst. to chief of staff Hdqtrs. USAF, Washington, 1995-96; assoc. dir. cen. intelligence for mil. support CIA, Washington, 1996-97, dep. dir. cen. intelligence, 1997-2000; undersec. of energy nuclear security, adminstr. Nat. Nuclear Security Adminstrn., Washington, 2000—01; dep. asst. to President George W. Bush, 2002—03; nat. dir., dep. nat. security advisor Nat. Security Coun., Washington, 2002; Homeland Security advisor, asst. to President George W. Bush, 2003—. Decorated Def. Disting. Svc. medal with oak leaf cluster, Def. Superior Svc. medal, Legion of Merit, Def. Meritorious Svc. medal, Meritorious Svc. medal with oak leaf cluster, Air Force Commendation medal. Mailing: 2nd Fl West Wing 1600 Penn Ave NW Washington DC 20500*

GORDON, JOHN BENNETT, lawyer; b. Des Moines, Nov. 21, 1947; s. Bennett and Mary (Adelman) G.; m. Joanne Dunbar Westgate, Jan. 17, 1976; children: Anne Dunbar, Bennett Westgate, Susan Julia. AB, Princeton U., 1969; JD, Harvard U., 1973. Bar: Minn. 1974, U.S. Dist. Ct. Minn. 1974, U.S. Ct. Appeals (8th cir.) 1974, U.S. Supreme Ct. 1985. Clerk U.S. Ct. Appeals (5th cir.), Newnan, Ga., 1973-74; assoc. law firm Faegre & Benson, Mpls., 1974-80, ptnr., 1981—. Mem. Minn. State Bar Assn., Hennepin County Bar Assn. (pres. 1985-86). Office: Faegre & Benson 90 S 7th St Ste 2200 Minneapolis MN 55402-3901 E-mail: jgordon@faegre.com.

GORDON, JOHN CHARLES, forestry educator; b. Nampa, Idaho, June 10, 1939; s. John Nicholas and Ada Elizabeth (Scheuermann) G.; m. Helka Lehtinen, Aug. 6, 1964; 1 child, Sean Nicholas. BS, Iowa State U., Ames, 1961, PhD, 1966; postgrad., U. Helsinki, Finland, 1961-62; MA (hon.), Yale U., New Haven, 1984; LHD (hon.), Unity Coll., 2000. Instr. forestry Iowa State U., Ames, 1965-66; plant physiologist U.S. Forest Service, Rhinelander, Wis., 1966-70; prof. forestry Iowa State U., Ames, 1970-77; prof., head dept. forest sci. Oreg. State U., Corvallis, 1977-83; prof., dean forestry and environ. studies Yale U., New Haven, 1983-92, 97-98, Pinchot prof. forestry and environ. studies, 1991—2001, acting dir. Inst. for Biospheric Studies, 1994-95, 96; founding ptnr. Interforest LLC, 1996—; chmn., mem. exec. com. Candlewood Timber Group, 1999—; Pinchot prof. emeritus Yale U., New Haven, 2001—. Chmn. Commn. on Rsch. and Resources Mgmt. in Nat. Pks., 1988—89, Nat. Commn. on Sci. and Sustainable Forestry, 2000—02, bd. dirs., 2000—; chmn. com. on forestry rsch. NAS, 1989—92; lectr. Syracuse U., 1990, Oreg. State U., 1993, U. Fla., 1994, U. Mont., 1998. Editor: Symbiotic Nitrogen Fixation, 1983; author (books) Agroforestry Research, 1991, Environmental Leadership, 1993, Ecosystems, 1998, Forests to Fight Poverty, 1999, Forest Certification, 1999; contbr. articles to profl. jours. Bd. dirs. Friends of Gray Towers, Milford, Pa., 1983-87, Yale U. Alumni Fund, 1985-92, Tropical Forest Found., 1991-94, Wintock Internat., 1993-95, Soc. for Protection N.H. Forests, 2001—; vis. com. Harvard U., 1985-92; pres. C.V. Riley Found., N.Y.C., 1985, 92-94, Conn. Fund for Environ., 1986-92; mem. rsch. adv. com. U.S. AID, 1988-92; co-chmn. 7th Am. Forest Congress, 1994-97. Fulbright scholar, 1961, 84; hon. sr. fellow U. Glasgow, Scotland, 1975-76; Green vis. prof. U. B.C., Vancouver, 1985; named Conservationist of the Yr., Pacific Rivers Coun., 1992; fellow Timothy Dwight Coll., Yale U.; disting. svc. award Am. Forests, 1996. Mem. Soc. Am. Foresters, Am. Forestry Assn. (Disting. Svc. award 1996), Sigma Xi (hon.), Phi Kappa Phi (hon.). Clubs: Yale (N.Y.C.), Morys (New Haven), Cosmos (Washington). Presbyterian. Avocations: hiking, fishing, writing short stories. Home: RR 3 Box 129A Plymouth NH 03264-9123 Office: Interforest LLC 175 N Main St Branford CT 06405 E-mail: johngordon@fcgnetworks.net.

GORDON, JOHN L., JR., historian, educator; b. Elizabethtown, Ky., July 14, 1942; s. John L. and Rose (Kemph) G.; m. Susan L. Cooper, Sept. 1963; 1 child, Sarah Elizabeth. AB History and Mathematics, Western Ky. U., 1963; MA, Vanderbilt U., 1965, PhD, 1972. From instr. to assoc. prof. history U. Richmond, Va., 1967-90, prof. history, 1990—, interim v.p., provost, 1983, interim dean faculty arts and scis., 1981-82, assoc. dean faculty arts and scis., 1980-87, dean grad. studies, 1980-87, chair dept. history, 1989—. Spkr. in field; rschr. in field, England, Ireland, Can. Contbr. numerous articles to profl. jours. Grantee Can. Studies Faculty Enrichment Program, 1987; Duke Alberta Rsch. fellow, 1984; faculty summer rsch. fellow, grantee U. Richmond, 1977, 88, 95. Mem. Am. Hist. Assn., Assn. Can. Studies in U.S., Can. Hist. Assn., Carolinas Symposium Brit. Studies, N.Am. Conf. Brit. Studies, S.E. Coun. Can. Studies (exec. com., pres. 1993-96), So. Conf. Brit. Studies (exec. coun., program chair 1993, 94), So. Hist. Assn., Omicron Delta Kappa, Phi Alpha Theta. Home: 4 Bostwick Ln Richmond VA 23226-3107 Office: U Richmond Ryland Hall Richmond VA 23173

GORDON, JOSEPH ELWELL, university official, educator; b. Deatsville, Ala., July 2, 1921; s. Joseph Elwell and Martha (Berry) G.; m. Doris Elizabeth Smith, June 5, 1948; children— Cecile Lizabeth, Joseph Elwell, Melissa Innes. AB, Birmingham-So. Coll., 1942; MS, Auburn U., 1949; PhD, U. Chgo., 1951. Tchr. math., Montgomery, Ala., 1946-48; instr. math. Auburn U., 1948-49; research asst. North Central Assn. Colls. and Secondary Schs., Chgo., 1949-51; program analyst Air U., Maxwell AFB, 1951-54; mem. faculty Tulane U., 1954—, asst. prof. edn., 1958—, assoc. dir. admissions, 1957-63, dean Coll. Arts and Scis., 1964-84, dir. found. rels., 1984-86, spl. asst. to v.p. devel., 1986-90, univ. historian, 1990-96, vice provost, 1996-97. Author (with Clarence Mohr): Tulane: The Emergence of a Modern University 1945-1980, 2001. Served to lt. USNR, 1942-46. Mem. Omicron Delta Kappa, Phi Delta Kappa, Pi Kappa Alpha. Democrat. Presbyterian. Home: 1108 Lowerline St New Orleans LA 70118-5205

GORDON, JOY, music educator; d. Morris and Dorothy; m. Bernard Gordon, Oct. 14, 1956 (div. Apr. 1975); children: Gordon, Howard. MusB, Am. U., 1971; EdM, Md. State U., 1990. Pvt. music tchr., 1939—. Tchr. Hebrew music Temple Beth Tikvah, Silver Spring, Md., 1961—63. Recipient medal in piano, Nassau Philharm. Soc., 1935. Mem.: Fla. State Music Tchrs. Assn., Md. State Music Tchrs. Assn., Music Tchrs. Nat. Assn. (nat. cert.). Jewish. Home: 12403 Vinton Terr Silver Spring MD 20906

GORDON, JUDITH, communications consultant, writer; b. Long Beach, Calif. d. Irwin Ernest and Susan (Perlman) G.; m. Lawrence Banka, May 1, 1977. BA, Oakland U., 1966; MS in Libr. Sci., Wayne State U., 1973. Researcher Detroit Inst. of Arts, 1968-69; libr. Detroit Pub. Libr., 1971-74; caseworker Wayne County Dept. Social Svcs., Detroit, 1974-77; advt. copywriter Hudson's Dept. Store, Detroit, 1979; mgr. The Poster Gallery, Detroit, 1980-81; mktg., corp. communications specialist Bank of Am., San Francisco, 1983-84, mgr., consumer pubs., 1984-86; prin. Active Voice, San Francisco, 1986—. *Judith Gordon brings a singular combination of capabilities to ACTIVE VOICE, a company she founded in 1986. Since then, she has provided editorial, project management, consulting, and marketing services to diverse clients worldwide. Gordon is the former manager of consumer publications at Bank of America where she directed an award-winning publications program within strict time and cost constraints. Among the publications were the bank's account disclosures, considered models of plain language. The name of Gordon's company reflects its key focus: to communicate clearly and compellingly to specialists and laypersons alike. Her company's primary emphasis is financial services, consumer information/education, and customer print and online materials that satisfy legal, compliance, and marketing objectives. For these efforts, Gordon has received frequent recognition.* Contbr. edit. The Artist's Mag., 1988-93; contbr. to book Flowers: Gary Bukovnik, Watercolors and Monotypes, Abrams, 1990. Vol. From the Heart, San Francisco, 1992, Bay Area Book Festival, San Francisco, 1990, 91, Aid & Comfort, San Francisco, 1987, Save Orch. Hall, Detroit, 1977-81, NOW sponsored abortion clinic project. Recipient award Merit. Soc. Consumer Affairs Profls. in Bus., 1986, Bay Area Best award Internat. Assn. Bus. Communicators, 1986, Internat. Galaxy awards, 1992, 95, 97, Internat. Mercury awards, 1995, Charles Schwab Excellence in Svc. award, 2000. Mem. AAUW, Nat. Writers Union, Editl. Freelancers Assn. Inc., Clarity, Achenbach Graphics Arts Coun., Women's Nat. Book Assn., Assn. for Women in Comms., Plain Lang. Assn., FIMA West (bd. dirs.), ZYZZYVA (bd. dirs.). Office: 899 Green St San Francisco CA 94133-3756 E-mail: activvduo@msn.com.

GORDON, JULIE PEYTON, foundation administrator; b. Jacksonville, Fla., June 21, 1940; d. Robert Benoist Shields and Bessie (Cavanaugh) Peyton; m. Robert James Gordon, June 22, 1963. BA, Boston U., 1963; MA, Harvard U., 1965, PhD, 1969. Asst. prof. English Ill. Inst. Tech., Chgo., 1968-75, assoc. prof., 1975-77, asst. dean students, 1975-78; asst. dean acad. affairs Northwestern U., Evanston, Ill., 1978-80, lectr. English, Univ. Coll., 1978—, assoc. dean Univ. Coll., 1980-85, sec. Econometric Soc., 1975—, exec. dir. Econometric Soc., 1985—. Mem. nat. adv. com. ALA, Chgo., 1983-86. Author: Seasons in the Contemporary American Family, 1984. Grantee NEH, 1971-73; project scholar NEH, 1983-86. Mem. Phi Beta Kappa. Avocation: writing fiction and poetry. Home: 202 Greenwood Evanston IL 60201-4714 Office: Northwestern U Dept Econs Econometric Soc Evanston IL 60208-2600

GORDON, KENNETH LEE, ophthalmologist; b. L.A., June 1, 1948; s. Arnold Jerome and Claire (Levine) G.; m. Debra Chernoff, June 18, 1978; children: Michael, Dara, David. BS, U. Oreg., 1970; MD, Tulane U., 1974. Diplomate Am. Bd. Ophthalmology (diplomate). Intern L.A. County/U. So. Calif. Med. Ctr., 1974-75, resident Doheny Eye Inst., 1976-79; pvt. practice Beverly Hills, Calif., 1979—. Chief ophthalmology Century City Hosp., L.A.; dir. Century City Eye Laser Ctr. Avocations: skiing, tennis, reading. Office: Century City Eye Med Group 2080 Century Park E Ste 800 Los Angeles CA 90067-2011 E-mail: klgordonmd@aol.com.

GORDON, LANA G. state representative; b. Kansas City, Mo., Aug. 20, 1950; m. Arnold Gordon; children: Jennifer, Stacey, Jaime. BS in Edn., U. Kans., 1971. Subst. tchr., Mo., 1971—72; tchr. Lee's Summit (Mo.) Pub. Sch., 1972—73; test adminstr. State of Kans., 1978—80; sec., treas. Cardinal Bldg. Svcs., 1997—2001; office gen. Cardinal DBA/BG Svc. Solution, 2002—; mem. Kans. Ho. of Reps., 2001—. Sec. citizens adv. coun. USD 501 Dist., 1982—85; bd. dirs. USD 501 Sch. Found., 1994—97, Vol. Ctr. Topeka, 1998—. Republican. Jewish. Office: 181-W State Capitol 300 SW 10th Ave Topeka KS 66612 Address: 5820 SW 27th St Topeka KS 66614*

GORDON, LARRY JEAN, education educator; b. Tipton, Okla., Oct. 16, 1926; s. Andrew J. and Deweylee (Stewart) G.; m. Nedra Callender, Aug. 26, 1950; children: Debra Gordon Dunlap, Kent, Gary. Student, U. Okla., 1943-44; BS, U. N.Mex., 1949, MS, 1951; MPH, U. Mich., 1954. High sch. sci. tchr., N.Mex., 1949-50; various positions N.Mex. Dept. Health, 1950-55; commd. officer USPHS, 1957—, advanced through grades to Dir. Grade (Navy capt.), dir. Albuquerque Environ. Health Dept., 1955-68, 82-86; dir. Environ. Improvement Agy., Santa Fe, 1968-73; adminstr. for health and environ. programs N.Mex. HHS Dept., Santa Fe, 1976-78; dir. N.Mex. Sci. Lab. System, Albuquerque, 1973-76; dep. sec. N.Mex. Health and Environ. Dept., Santa Fe, 1978-82, sec., 1987-88; vis. prof. pub. adminstrn. U. N.Mex., Albuquerque, 1988—, adj. prof. polit. sci., 1997—, sr. fellow Inst. for Pub. Policy, 1997—. Chmn. N.Mex. Water Quality Commn., 1971-73. Asst. editor Jour. Environ. Health, 1975-78; cons. editor Environ. News Digest, 1970-82; editl. cons. Jour. Pub. Health Policy, 1980-96, Underwriters Labs., 1996; contbr. over 240 articles to profl. jours. Recipient Samuel J. Crumbine award for Outstanding Devel. of Comprehensive Program for Environ. Sanitation, 1959 and 65, Sanitarians Disting. Service award Internat. Assn. Milk, Food, and Environ. Sanitarians, 1962, Outstanding Contrbn. award N.Mex. Assn. Pub. Health Sanitarians, 1967, Boss of Yr. award Santa Fe chpt. Nat. Secs. Assn., 1970, Walter F. Snyder award For Achievement in Environ. Quality, 1978, Commendation for Leadership in Health Care N.Mex. Hosp. Assn., 1981, N.Mex. Outstanding Pub. Svc. award, 1988, Zimmerman award U. N.Mex. Alumni, 1993, L.A. County Breslow award L.A. County Dept. Health Svcs., 1994, Outstanding Leadership in Environ. Adminstrn. award Am. Soc. for Pub. Adminstrn., 1994. Mem. APHA (exec. bd. 1975-82, pres. 1980-81, John J. Sippy Meml. award 1962, other coms., Sedgwick award 1987), Am. Acad. Sanitarians (founder, David Calvin Wagner Excellence award 1984), N.Mex. Pub. Health Assn. (past pres., Disting. Svc. award 1970, Spl. award, 1978, D.A. Larrazola award 1989), N.Mex. Environ. Health Assn., (past pres.), Am. Lung Assn. N.Mex. (bd. dirs. 1982-94, Clinton P. Anderson award for Outstanding Contbn. to Lung Health 1987), Nat. Accreditation Coun. Environ. Health Curricula, Nat. Audubon Soc. (pres. coun. 1982-86), U. Mich. Sch. Pub. Health Alumni Assn. (bd. govs. 1985-88, Outstanding Alumnus award 1995), Royal Soc. Promotion of Health, London (hon.), N.Mex. Soc. Pub. Adminstrn. (Disting. Pub. Adminstr. award 1996), Delta Omega, Phi Kappa Phi, Phi Sigma.

Republican. Avocations: fishing, boating, golf. Home: 1674 Tierra Del Rio NW Albuquerque NM 87107-3259 Office: Univ NMex Polit Sci Dept Albuquerque NM 87131-0001 E-mail: 1016Larry@msn.com.

GORDON, LAWRENCE ALLAN, accounting educator; b. Bklyn., Apr. 15, 1943; s. Seymour and Jessie (Killion) G.; m. Hedy Hellen Ambrozy, Nov. 23, 1968; children: Lauren Allison, Marc Elliot. BS, SUNY, Albany, 1966, MBA, 1967; PhD, Rensselaer Poly. Inst., 1973. Asst. prof. acctg. Clarkson Coll. Tech., 1971-72, McGill U., Montreal, Can., 1972-74, assoc. prof. acctg., 1974-76, U. Kans., Lawrence, 1976-79, prof. acctg., 1979-80, U. Md., College Park, 1980-81, Ernst & Young Alumni prof. managerial acctg. and info. assurance, 1981. Coord. PhD program in acctg. U. Md., 1980-96, dir. PhD program Coll. Bus. and Mgmt., 1996—, chairperson acctg. faculty, 1982-87, chairperson numerous univ. and profl. coms., 1972—; cons. IBM, 1984-91, U.S. Dept. Labor, 1985-87, U.S. Gen. Acctg. Office, 1978-84, N.Y. State Tchr.'s Retirement System, 1968-69; mgmt. acctg. cons./lectr. Dept. of Supplies and Svcs., Ottawa, Can., 1974-79; mem. audit staff Peat, Marwick, Mitchell & Co., N.Y.C., 1966; presenter in field. Co-editor Jour. Acctg. and Pub. Policy, 1982—; assoc. editor Jour. Bus. Fin. and Acctg., 1991—; editorial bd. mem. Acctg. Rev., 1981-82, Mgmt. Internat. Rev., 1982—, Contemporary Acctg. Rsch., 1984-92; ad-hoc reviewer Jour. Fin. and Quantitative Analysis, Acctg., Orgns. and Soc., Acctg. Rev., Jour. Bus. and Econ. Stats., author: (with others) Improving Capital Budgeting: A Decision Support System Approach, 1984, The Pricing Decision, 1981, others; author: Managerial Accounting: Concepts and Empirical Evidence, 2000 (5th edit.); author articles. Rsch. grantee U. Md. Coll. Bus. and Mgmt., 1980—, Am. Acctg. Assn., 1976, summer rsch. grantee U. Kans., 1977, grantee Arthur Andersen & Co., 1977, Nat. Assn. Accts. and the Soc. Mgmt. Accts., 1976-80, McGill U., 1975, 75-76, U. Western Ont., 1974, expense grantee for rsch. McGill U., 1973, grantee (with others) U.S. Dept. Labor, 1978-80. Mem. Am. Acctg. Assn., Am. Econ. Assn., Inst. Mgmt. Accts. Office: Robert H Smith Sch Bus U Md College Park College Park MD 20742-0001

GORDON, LEE DIANE, school librarian, educator; b. Lafayette, Ind., Oct. 30, 1948; d. Henry Charles and Leonora (Brower) G.; m. James J. Thomas, Aug. 27, 1977 (div. Feb. 1994); m. Daniel L. Weber, July 10, 1999. BA, Calif. State U., Long Beach, 1970; MEd, U. Nev., Las Vegas, 1980. Cert. tchr., Nev., Calif.; cert. libr., Nev. Tchr. Carmenita Jr. High Sch., Cerritos, Calif., 1971-77, Jim Bridger Jr. High Sch., North Las Vegas, Nev., 1977-79, libr., 1979-84, Eldorado High Sch., Las Vegas, 1984—2001. Sierra Vista H.S., Las Vegas, 2001—. Adj. faculty U. Nev.-Las Vegas, 1997—. Co-author: The Overworked Teacher's Bulletin Board Book, 1981; filmstrips, 1983; author: World Historical Fiction Guide for Young Adults, 1996; contbr. articles to profl. jours. Mem. Am. Assn. Sch. Librs. (affiliate del., various coms. 1987—; dir. Region VII 1999-2001), Nev. Assn. Sch. Librs. (chair 1987), Clark County Sch. Librs. Assn. (pres. 1987-88), Delta Kappa Gamma (Iota chpt. pres. 1990-92). Office: Sierra Vista High Sch 8100 W Robindale Rd Las Vegas NV 89113

GORDON, L(ELAND) JAMES, lawyer; b. Phila., Mar. 17, 1927; s. Leland James and Doris Mellor (Gilbert) G.; m. Jane Busby, June 10, 1950; children: James Douglas, Leslie Anne, John Scott. BA, Denison U., 1950; JD, Yale U., 1953. Bar: Ohio 1953, U.S. Dist. Ct. (so. dist.) Ohio 1957, U.S. Tax Ct. 1979, U.S. Supreme Ct. 1978, U.S. Ct. Appeals (6th dist.) 1992. Assoc. E. Clark Morrow, Newark, Ohio, 1953-60; ptnr. Morrow & Gordon, Newark, Ohio, 1960 67; sr. ptnr. Morrow, Gordon & Byrd, Newark, Ohio, 1967-98, of counsel, 1998—. Counsel Weakley Apts, Inc. Co., Newark. Pres. bd. edn., Granville Exempted Village, Ohio, 1969-79; pres. United Way of Licking County, Newark, 1972-74; pres. Granville Found., 1991-92. Served with USAF, 1945-47. Fellow Am. Coll. Trial Lawyers, Am. Bar Found., Ohio Bar Found., Am. Bd. Trial Advs. (adv.); mem. Ohio State Bar Assn. (chmn. negligence law com. 1986), Licking County Bar Assn. (pres. 1968), Mental Health Assn. Licking County (pres. 1986), Newark Area C. of C. (treas. 1983-84), Symposiarchs Club (pres. 1981-82), Masons, Kiwanis (pres. 1965), Rotary (pres. 1992-93). Democrat. Baptist. Home: 732 Mount Parnassus Dr Granville OH 43023-1444 Office: Morrow Gordon & Byrd 33 W Main St PO Box 4190 Newark OH 43058-4190 E-mail: Gorden@nextech.net.

GORDON, LEONARD, retired sociology educator; b. Detroit, Dec. 6, 1935; s. Abraham and Sarah (Rosen) G.; m. Rena Joyce Feigelman, Dec. 25, 1955; children: Susan Melinda, Matthew Seth, Melissa Gail. BA, Wayne State U., 1957; MA, U. Mich., 1958; PhD, Wayne State U., 1966. Instr. Wayne State U., Detroit, 1960-62; research dir. Jewish Community Council, Detroit, 1962-64; dir. Mich. area Am. Jewish Com., N.Y.C., 1964-67; asst. prof. Ariz. State U., Tempe, 1967-70, assoc. prof., 1970-77, prof., 1977 , chmn. dept. sociology, 1981-90, assoc. dean for acad. programs Coll. Liberal Arts and Scis., 1990-2001, rsch. prof., 2001—02, prof. emeritus, 2002—. Cons. OEO, Maricopa County, Ariz., 1968 Author: A City in Racial Crisis, 1971, Sociology and American Social Issues, 1978, (with A. Mayer) Urban Life and the Struggle To Be Human, 1979, (with R. Hardert, M. Laner and M. Reader) Confronting Social Problems, 1984, (with J. Hall and R. Melnick) Harmonizing Arizona's Ethnic and Cultural Diversity, 1992. Sec. Conf. on Religion and Race, Detroit, 1962-67; mem. exec. bd. dirs. Am. Jewish Com., Phoenix chpt., 1969-70. Grantee NSF, 1962, Rockefeller found., 1970, 84. Fellow Am. Sociol. Assn. (chair task force on current knowledge on hate/bias acts on coll. and univ. campuses 2000—); mem. AAUP, Pacific Sociol. Assn. (v.p. 1978-79, pres. 1980-81), Soc. Study Social Problems (chair C. Wright Mills award com. 1988, treas. 1989-96), Ariz. State U. Alumni Assn. (faculty dir. 1981-82). Democrat. Jewish. Home: 13660 E Columbine Dr Scottsdale AZ 85259-3753 Office: Ariz State U Dept Sociology Tempe AZ 85287

GORDON, LEONARD VICTOR, retired psychology educator; b. Montreal, Aug. 15, 1917; came to U.S., 1936, naturalized, 1938; s. Peter Z. and Bessie Victoria (Kirsch) G.; m. Katharine Ann Burton, Nov. 30, 1946; children: John Christopher (dec.), Jeffrey Burton. BA, UCLA, 1940; MA, Ohio State U., 1947, PhD, 1950. Instr. Ohio State U., Columbus, 1947-49, rsch. assoc., 1949-50; assoc. dir. office rsch. svcs. Boston U., 1950-51; vis. asst. prof. U. N.Mex., Albuquerque, 1951-52; divsn. dir. Naval Pers. Rsch. Activity, San Diego, 1952-62; lab chief U.S. Army Pers. Rsch. Office, Washington, 1962-66; prof. ednl. psychology and stats. SUNY, Albany, 1966-87, prof. emeritus, 1987—; pres. Intertest, Guilderland, N.Y. 1985—. Disting. vis. prof. Wilford Hall U.S. Air Force Med. Ctr., Lackland AFB, Tex., 1977-79; rsch. adv. com. Office of Edn., 1969-70; advisor European Test Publishers Group, 1992—; adv. com. Ednl. Psychologist, 1973-74; grant referee NIE, 1972-73, Can. Coun., 1975-77, NSF, 1977-78; external examiner U. West Indies, 1978-81, Patna U., 1969-75, India Inst. Tech., 1977-81; lectr., cons. in field. Author: (with Ross L. Mooney) Mooney Problem Check Lists, 1950, Gordon Personal Profile, 1953, (rev. edit. 1993), 1978, Gordon Personal Inventory, 1956, (rev. edit. 1993), 1978, Global edit., 1992, Survey of Interpersonal Values, 1960, (rev. edit.), 1976, Gordon Occupational Check List, 1963, (rev. edit.), 1981, Work Environment Preference Schedule, 1973, Measurement of Interpersonal Values, 1975, (with Akio Kikuchi) Social Psychology of Values, 1975, (rev. edit. with Akio Kikuchi), 1981, Survey of Personal Values, 1967, (rev. edit.), 1984, School Environment Preference Survey, 1978; mem. edit. bd. Jour. Applied Psychology, 1971 82; contbr. articles to profl. jours. Rsch. coord. Peace Corps, Washington, 1964-65; internat. steering com. Evaluation Rsch. Soc., 1976-77. With USAAC, 1941-44. Recipient Personal commendations Dir. of the Peace Corps, 1965, Sec. of the Army, 1965. Fellow Am. Psychol. Assn., AAAS; mem. Internat. Assn. Applied Psychology, Am. Ednl. Research Assn., Nat. Council Measurement in Edn., Author's Guild. Home: 385 Highland Dr Schenectady NY 12303-5727 Office: Intertest PO Box 27 Guilderland NY 12084-0027 E-mail: vgordon@nycap.rr.com.

GORDON, LINCOLN, political economist; b. N.Y.C., Sept. 10, 1913; s. Bernard and Dorothy (Lerned) G.; m. Allison Wright, June 25, 1937 (dec.); children: Anne, Robert W., Hugh, Amy. AB, Harvard, 1933; D. Phil. (Rhodes scholar), Oxford (Eng.) U., 1936; LL.D., Fairleigh Dickinson U., 1965, Columbia, 1967, Rutgers U., 1967, U. Md., 1968, Wash. Coll., 1968, U. Del., 1969; L.H.D., Loyola Coll., Balt., 1968. Instr., faculty instr. govt. Harvard, 1936-41, William Ziegler prof. internat. econ. relations, 1955-61; research technician water, energy resources U.S. Nat. Resources Planning Bd., Washington, 1939-1940; mem. staff requirements com. W.P.B., 1942-45, program vice chmn., 1945; dir. bur. reconversion priorities Civilian Prodn. Adminstrn., 1945-46; assoc. prof. bus. Harvard, 1946-47, prof. govt. and adminstrn., 1947-50; cons. U.S. Rep. UN AEC, 1946, Army and Navy Munitions Bd., Dept. of State, 1947, ECA, 1948; North Atlantic Council Com. of Three on non-mil. aspects of NATO, 1956; dir. program div. Office ECA, spl. rep. in Europe, 1949-50; econ. adviser to spl. asst. to President, 1950-51; asst. dir. Office of Mut. Security, 1951-52; chief Marshall Aid mission and minister econ. affairs in Am. Embassy in London, 1952-55; U.S. amb. Brazil, 1961-66; asst. sec. state for inter-Am. affairs, 1966-67; pres. Johns Hopkins, Balt., 1967-71; vis. prof. polit. economy Sch. Advanced Internat. Studies, Washington, 1971-72; fellow Woodrow Wilson Internat. Center for Scholars, 1972-75; sr. fellow Resources for Future, Washington, 1975-80; mem. sr. rev. panel CIA, 1980-82, nat. intelligence officer-at-large, 1982-83; guest scholar Brookings Instn., 1984—. Author: The Public Corporation in Great Britain, 1938; author: (with M. Fainsod) Government and the American Economy, 1941; author: rev. edit., 1948, 1959, Fuel and Power in Industrial Location and National Policy, Nat. Resources Planning Bd., 1942, Representation of the U.S. Abroad (in part), 1956, rev. edit., 1964; author: (with Engelbert L. Grommers) United States Manufacturing Investment in Brazil, 1961; author: A New Deal for Latin America, 1963, Growth Policies and the International Order, 1979; author: (with Joy Dunkerley and others) Energy Strategies for Developing Nations, 1981; author: (with J.F. Brown and others) Eroding Empire: Western Relations with Eastern Europe, 1987; author: (with T. Stanley) Integrating Economic and Security Factors in East-West Relations, 1988; author: Brazil's Second Chance En Route toward the First World, 2001; editor: International Stability and Progress: U.S. Interests and Instruments, 1957, From Marshall Plan to Global Interdependence, 1978. Bd. dirs. Atlantic Council U.S.; hon. trustee Com. for Econ. Devel. Decorated Grand Cross Order Quetzal Guatemala; Grand Cross Order Cruzeiro do Sul Brazil). Fellow Am. Acad. Arts and Scis.; mem. Am. Polit. Sci. Assn., Am. Econ. Assn., Coun. on Fgn. Rels., Internat. Inst. Strategic Studies, Royal Econ. Soc., Phi Beta Kappa, Cosmos Club Washington. Home: 3069 University Ter NW Washington DC 20016-3462

GORDON, LISA DIANE, psychologist; b. Lower Merion Twp., Pa., May 25, 1960; d. Robert Bruce and Elinor Cloud G. BS in Psychology, Ursinus Coll., 1982; MA in Clin. Psychology, West Chester U., 1984; PhD in Counseling Psychology, Pa. State U., 1992. Lic. psychologist; cert. sch. counselor, Pa. Psychology intern USN/Nat. Naval Med. Ctr., Bethesda, Md., 1987-88; clin. psychologist Naval Hosp. Orlando, Fla., 1988-90; psychologist Delphic Mental Health Assocs., York, Pa., 1990-92; staff psychologist Reading (Pa.) Rehab. Hosp., 1992-94; psychologist Berks Counseling Assocs., West Lawn, Pa., 1994-97, PrimeCare Med., Harrisburg, Pa., 1994—2002; predoctoral intern supr. Pa. Coll. Osteopathic Medicine, Phila., 2001—02; psychologist Del. County Neurobehavioral Unit Riddle Health Care Ctr., Media, Pa., 2002—. Practicum supr. Millersville (Pa.) U., 1992. Lt. USNR, 1987-90. Fellow Pa. Psychol. Assn.; mem. APA, Mensa, Psi Chi. Republican. Episcopalian. Avocations: singing, reading, swimming, crafts, boating. Home: 6130 Pond View Dr Birdsboro PA 19508 Office: Delaware County Neurobehav Unit Riddle Health Care Ctr Ste 2205 1088 W Baltimore Pike Media PA 19063 Fax: 610-892-7908. E-mail: starry5@ptdprolog.net.

GORDON, LOIS G. English language educator; b. Englewood, N.J. d. Irving David and Betty (Davis) Goldfein; m. Alan Lee Gordon, Nov. 13, 1961; 1 son, Robert Michael. BA (Nat. Merit scholar, Barbour scholar), U. Mich., 1960; postgrad., Columbia U., 1960-61; MA, U. Wis., 1962, PhD (Dissertation Completion fellow), 1966. Teaching asst. U. Wis., 1962-64; lectr. CCNY, 1964-66; asst. prof. U. Mo., Kansas City, 1966-68; asst. prof. English Fairleigh Dickinson U., Teaneck, N.J., 1968 71, assoc. prof., 1971-75, prof., 1975—, chmn. dept. English and comparative lit., 1982-90. Vis. exch. prof. Rutgers U., 1994; cons. U. Mo. Press, 1968-69, Doubleday Inc., 1974, Fairleigh Dickinson U. Press, 1975—, Prentice Hall, 1977—, Duke U. Press, 1986—, U. Wis. Press, Rutgers U. Press, Cambridge U. Press, Harper Collins, The New Yorker. Author: Stratagems To Uncover Nakedness: The Dramas of Harold Pinter, 1969, Donald Barthelme, 1981, Robert Coover: The Universal Fiction-Making Process, 1983, American Chronicle: Six Decades in American Life, 1920-79, 1987, Seven Decades in American Life, 1920-89, 1990, Harold Pinter: A Casebook, 1990, The Columbia Chronicles of American Life, 1910-1992, 1995, The World of Samuel Beckett, 1906-1946, 1996, Chinese edit., 2001, American Chronicle: Year by Year Through the Twentieth Century, 1999, Pinter at 70, 2001, Reading Godot, 2002; asst. editor Lit. and Psychology, 1968-71; contbr. book revs. to profl. jours. and newspapers. Research grantee U. Mo., 1968, Fairleigh Dickinson U., 1985, 89, 97, 2001. Mem. MLA, PEN, Internat. Bach Soc., Internat. League Human Rights, Authors Guild, Acad. Am. Poets, Harold Pinter Soc., Samuel Beckett Soc., U.S. Hist. Landmarks Commn. Jewish. Home: 300 Central Park W New York NY 10024-1513 Office: Fairleigh Dickinson U Dept English Teaneck NJ 07666 E-mail: loisgord@aol.com.

GORDON, LONNY JOSEPH, choreographer, dance and fine arts educator; b. Edinburg, Tex., Sept. 21, 1942; BFA, U. Tex., 1965; MFA, U. Wis., 1967; DFA, Nishikawa Sch. of Classical Japanese Dance, Tokyo, 1980. Dir. Kinetic Art Theater, N.Y.C., 1970, Tokyo, 1971-72; dir. modern dance Jacobs Pillow, Lee, Mass., 1970; dir. So. Repertory Dance Theater, So. Ill. U., Carbondale, 1972-76; artist-in-residence Smith Coll., Northampton, Mass., 1975; grad. dir. dance U. Wis., Madison, 1976-86, prof., 1985-91; prof., chmn. dance dept. U. Nev., Las Vegas, 1991-94, dir. devel. Performing Arts Ctr., 1994—. Choreographer numerous dance works including Fleetings, artist-in-residence; cons. and lectr. in dance and fine arts to numerous profl. dance cos. and ednl. instns. Contbr. articles to profl. jours. including Japan Modern Dance Quarterly, Okura Lantern, Dance Scope; columnist Capital Times, Asahi Evening News, Korean Times; subject of numerous books and profl. works in dance. One man exhbn. watercolor paintings, collage and mixed media works. Grantee numerous profl. and ednl. instns., fellow Fulbright-Hays, 1967-69, 83, NEA Choreographers, 1982-83, Japan Found. profl., 1979, Mobile Found., 1971-72, Nev. State Arts Coun., 1992, 93, 94, 95, 96, 97, 98. Mem. Asian Dance Assn. (bd. dirs.), Am. Coll. Dance Festival (bd. dirs. 1987—), Fulbright Alumni Assn., Ruth Page Dance Series (bd. dirs.). Avocations: painting, writing, swimming, bodybuilding, gardening. Office: U Nevada/Las Vegas Performing Arts Ctr 45005 Maryland Pkwy Las Vegas NV 89154 Home: 412 Park Way E Las Vegas NV 89106

GORDON, MALCOLM STEPHEN, biology educator; b. Bklyn., Nov. 13, 1933; s. Abraham and Rose (Walters) G.; m. Diane M. Kestin, Apr. 16, 1959 (div. Sept. 1973); 1 child, Dana Malcolm; m. Marjorie J. Weinzweig, Jan. 28, 1976 (dec. Mar. 1990); m. Carol A. Cowen, July 19, 1992. BA with high honors, Cornell U., 1954; PhD, Yale U., 1958. Instr. UCLA, 1958-60, asst. prof., 1960-65, assoc. prof., 1965-68, prof. biology, 1968—, dir. Inst. Evolutionary and Environ. Biology, 1971-76, chmn. interdept. com. Environ. Sci. Engring. Program, 1984-88; asst. dir. rsch. Nat. Fisheries Ctr. and Aquarium, U.S. Dept of Interior, Washington, 1968-69. Vis. prof. zoology Chinese U. Hong Kong, 1971-72; mem. panel on marine biology, panel on oceanography Pres.'s Sci. Adv. Com., 1965-66; mem. nat. adv com. R/V Alpha Helix, Scripps Inst. Oceanography, 1969-73; mem. com. on Latimeria, NAS, 1969-72; mem. tech. adv. com. Santa Monica Bay Restoration Project, EPA, 1988—; mem. tech. adv. group on milkfish reprodn. AID, 1984-92, chmn. Commn. on Comparative Physiology, Internat. Union Physiol. Sci., 1993—; co-founder Inst. of Environment, UCLA, 1997; vis. assoc. prof. bioengring. and aeronautics Calif. Inst. Tech., 2003--. Author coll. textbooks, technical books; mem. editorial bd. Fish Physiol. Biochem. Jour., 1986—, Jour. Exptl. Zool., 1990-93; contbr. articles to sci. jours. Active cmty. orgns. on environ., civil liberties. NSF fellow Yale U., 1954-57, Fulbright fellow U.K., 1957-58, Guggenheim fellow Italy and Denmark, 1961-62; Sr. Queen's fellow in marine sci. Australia, 1976; Irving-Scholander Meml. lectr., U. Alaska-Fairbanks, 2000. Fellow AAAS; mem. Am. Physiol. Soc. (mem. exec. com. pub. affairs 1989-92), Am. Soc. Ichthyologists and Herpetologists, Soc. Integrative Comparative Biology (chmn. divsn. ecology 1979-80, chmn. divsn. comparative biochem. physiology 1988-89), Soc. for Exptl. Biology. Home: 2801 Glendower Ave Los Angeles CA 90027-1118 Office: UCLA Dept Organismic Biology PO Box 951606 Los Angeles CA 90095-1606 E-mail: msgordon@ucla.edu.

GORDON, MARC STEWART, pharmacist, scientist; b. Cleve., June 13, 1958; s. Eugene and Eileen (Israel) G.; m. Diane Schmidt, Aug. 11, 1985; children: Evan, Emma. BS in Pharmacy, U. Mich., 1982. Registered pharmacist, Calif. Staff rschr. II, mgr. Syntex Rsch., Palo Alto, Calif., 1982-95; sr. scientist Inhale Therapeutic Systems, Palo Alto, Calif., 1995—2002. Contbr. numerous articles to profl. jours.; numerous patentee pharmaceuticals. Mem. Am. Assn. Pharm. Scientists, Am. Pharm. Assn., No. Calif. Pharm. Discussion Group, Rho Chi. Avocations: reading, hiking. Home: 1474 Samedra St Sunnyvale CA 94087-4054

GORDON, MARJORIE, lyric coloratura soprano, opera producer, teacher; b. N.Y.C. d. Theodore and Minnie (Glantz) Fishberg; m. Nathan Gordon; children: Maxine, Peter Jon. BA cum laude, Hunter Coll. Nat. cert. voice tchr. Prof. voice Duquesne U., 1957-59, Wayne State U., 1961-91, Nat. Music Camp, Interlochen, 1963-65, Meadowbrook Sch. Music, 1966-71, U. Mich., 1970, Mich. State U., 1971; soloist, tchr. Am. U.-Wolf Trap Program, Washington, 1973. Spl. edn. cons. Detroit Grand Opera Assn.; adj. prof. Oakland (Mich.) U.; pres., gen. dir. Piccolo Opera Co., Inc. Solo debut N.Y. Philharm. Symphony, 1950, soprano soloist, N.Y.C. Opera, 1955-57, Chautauqua Opera Co., 1949-61, Pitts. Opera, 1956; dir. Detroit Opera Theatre, 1960-72, Piccolo Opera Co., 1961—; soloist with orchs., opera cos., summer stock, on radio and TV; recitals U.S., Greece, Europe, Can., Israel; editor: Opera Study Guide, 1968—. Mem. music adv. panel Mich. Arts Coun.; mem. Palm Beach County Cultural Coun.; opera producer Blue Lake Fine Arts Camp, 1993—. Recipient resolution honoring 25th Anniversary Piccolo Opera Co., Mich. Senate; established voice scholarship in perpetuity Nat. Opera Assn. Mem.: AFTRA, Nat. Assn. Tchrs. Singing, Met. Opera Guild, Ctrl. Opera Svc., Nat. Opera Assn., Music Tchrs. Nat. Assn., Am. Guild Mus. Artists, Mich. Music Tchrs. Assn. (voice chmn. 1970—76), Fla. Music Tchrs. Assn., Boca Delray Music Soc., Broward County Music Club, Mu Phi Epsilon. Avocations: handcrafts, swimming, reading, sketching. Fax: 561-394-0520. E-mail: leejon51@msn.com.

GORDON, MARK, actor, theater director, theater educator; b. N.Y.C., May 19, 1926; s. Jacob and Sarah (Benin) G.; m. Barbara Glenn, Oct. 13, 1955; 1 child, Keith. Student, Theater Sch. Dramatic Arts, N.Y.C., 1946-47, Actors Lab., Los Angeles, 1947-50, Am. Theater Wing, N.Y.C., 1950-54, Drama Lab., 1954-55. Workshop dir., actor Compass Players, Chgo., 1955-56; ind. theatrical and film actor, 1955—; ind. theatrical dir., 1969—. Guest prof. theater Carnegie-Mellon Univ., Pitts., 1969-70, Columbia Univ., N.Y.C., 1970-71, High Sch. Performing Arts, N.Y.C., 1970-72, Finch Coll., N.Y.C.; head M.B.K. Prodns., N.Y.C., 1982—. Playwight: (with others) Glorious Age, 1975; actor numerous Broadway prodns. including Desire Under the Elms, Of Mice and Men, Mr. Roberts, The Devils, off-Broadway prodns. include The Iceman Cometh, The Man Who Never Died...Joe Hill, TV appearances include Mary Tyler Moore, Hawaii 5-O, Kojack, Dick Van Dyke, Ed, Law and Order; film appearances include Take the Money and Run, A New Leaf, Don't Drink the Water, Ninth Configuration; dir. Broadway prodn.: Before You Go (named Best Comedy Dir. on Broadway 1969), off-Broadway prodns. for Los Angeles Actors Theater, Carnegie Recital Hall, Playwrites Horizon, participating dir. Actors Studio; dir. numerous TV commls. Recipient numerous Andy awards, Clio nominations, Contribution to Comedy in Chgo. medal Univ. Chgo.; Rockefeller grantee Ctr. Opera of Mpls., 1963-64; scholar Am. Theater Wing. Mem. AAUP, AFTRA, Dirs. Guild Am., Screen Actors Guild, Actors Equity Assn., Nat. Acad. TV Arts and Scis., Soc. Stage Dirs. and Choreographers. Avocations: violin, scuba diving, photography. Office: MBK Prodns 323 W 83rd St New York NY 10024-4835 E-mail: mgord393@aol.com.

GORDON, MARK, II, film producer; b. 1957; Prodr. films including: Sawdust, 1988, Brothers in Arms, 1989, Opportunity Knocks, 1990, traces of Red, 1992, Fly by Night, 1993, Swing Kids, 1993, Speed, 1994, Trial by Jury, 1994, A Pyromaniac's Love Story, 1995, Broken Arrow, 1996, Hard Rain, 1998, Paulie, 1998, Saving Private Ryan, 1998, To the Moon, 1999, The Patriot, 2000, exec. prodr.: The Relic, 1997, Speed2: Cruise Control, 1997, The Jackal, 1997, A Simple Plan, 1998, Black Dog, 1998, Virus, 1999; TV movies include: Out of Step, 1983, One Too Many, 1983, How to be a Perfect Person in Just Three Days, 1983, War Between the Classes, 1985, Double Switch, 1987, Lightning Field, 1991, exec. prodr. TV: Love Kills, 1991, Past Tense, 1994, The Man Who Wouldn't Die, 1995, The Ripper, 1997; dir. TV: Good Time Harry, 1980, Children Remember the Holocaust (also prodr.), 1995. Winner Daytime Emmy award for outstanding children's spl. for War Between the Classes, 1985, Motion Picture Prodr. of the Yr. award for Saving Pvt. Ryan, 1999. Office: Mutual Film Co Raleigh Studios Clinton Bldg 650 N Bronson Ave Los Angeles CA 90004-1404*

GORDON, MARY CATHERINE, writer; b. L.I., N.Y., Dec. 8, 1949; d. David and Anna (Gagliano) G.; m. James Brain, 1974 (div.); m. Arthur Cash, 1979; children: Anna Gordon, David Dess Gordon. BA, Barnard Coll., 1971; MA, Syracuse U., 1973. Tchr. English Dutchess Community Coll., Poughkeepsie, N.Y., 1974-78, Amherst (Mass.) Coll., 1979-80, Barnard Coll., 1988—. Author: (novels) Final Payments, 1978, The Company of Women, 1981, Men and Angels,1985, The Other Side, 1989, The Rest of Life, 1993, Spending, 1998, (short stories) Temporary Shelter, 1987, Good Boys and Dead Girls and Other Essays, 1991, The Rest of Life: Three Novellas, 1993, The Shadow Man, 1996, Seeing Through Places, 2000, Joan of Arc, 2000. Guggenheim fellow; recipient Kafka prize for Fiction, 1979, 82, Lila Acheson Wallace Reader's digest award. Roman Catholic. Office: Barnard Coll Dept English 3009 Broadway New York NY 10027-6501 Agent: Sterling Lord Literistic 65 Bleecker St Fl 12 New York NY 10012-2420*

GORDON, MICHAEL MACKIN, lawyer; b. Boston, Apr. 15, 1950; s. Lawrence H. and Gladys (Mackin) G.; m. Linda Lowry, June 8, 1991; children: Alexandra, Harrison. AB, Vassar Coll., 1972; JD, Columbia U., 1976. Bar: N.Y. 1977, U.S. Dist. Ct. (so. and ea. dists. N.Y. 1977), D.C. 1980, U.S. Ct. Appeals (2d cir.) 1985, U.S. Supreme Ct. 1985, U.S. Claims Ct. 1991, U.S. Ct. Appeals (3d cir.) 1992, U.S. Dist. Ct. (no. dist.), Tex. 1993, U.S. Ct. Appeals (5th cir.) 1995, U.S. Dist. Ct. (ea. dist.) Tex. 1996, U.S. Dist. Ct. (no. dist. N.Y.) 1999. Assoc. Seward & Kissel, N.Y.C., 1977-79, Cadwalader, Wickersham & Taft, N.Y.C., 1979-85, ptnr., 1985—. Mem. ABA, N.Y. State Bar Assn., N.Y. County Lawyers Assn. Clubs: Vassar (N.Y.C.). Home: 12 W 72nd St New York NY 10023-4163 Office: Cadwalader Wickersham & Taft 100 Maiden Ln New York NY 10038-4818 E-mail: michael.gordon@cwt.com.

GORDON, MICHAEL ROBERT, lawyer, state legislator; b. Montgomery County, Md., July 5, 1947; s. Frank and Frances (Fox) G. BA, Towson State U., 1969; JD, Georgetown U., 1972. BAr: D.C. 1973, Md. 1973, U.S. Supreme Ct. 1980. Student tech. asst. Sec. of State, Annapolis, Md., 1969-70; adminstrv. and legis. aide State Senator U. Crawford, Annapolis, Md., 1971—72; mem. Md. Ho. of Dels., Annapolis, Md., 1983—, vice chair econs. com., 1995—2002, chair fiscal affairs and govt. ops. subcom., 1996—98, exec. com. alt., 1996—2003; ptnr. Ehrlich & Gordon, Rockville, Md., 1984—; chair Spending and Affordability Com., 2003—, Southern Legis. Conf., 1990—; chair subcom. on taxation Ways and Means Com., 2003—. Arbitrator Am. Arbitration Assn., 1975-79, Md. Med. Malpractice Commn., Balt., 1979—; gen. counsel Rockville Little Theater, 1974—. Pres. Rockville Civil Fedn., 1980-81, West End Citizens Assn., Rockville, 1979-80; mem. Rockville Alternative Cmty. Svc., 1981-83; mem. Rockville and Gaithersburg C. of C. Named Outstanding Young Dem. of Yr., Montgomery County Young Dems., 1973, Outstanding State-Eleced Ofcl., Md. Young Dems., 1986, Most Outstanding Legislator, 1985; recipient Disting. Svc. award, Md. Mcpl. League, 1983, 1984, 1988, 1991, 1998, award of achievement, 1985, 1986, 1989, 1992, 1993, 1995, 1999, 2000, 2001, 2002, 2003. Mem. ABA, Md. Bar Assn., Montgomery County Bar Assn. Office: Ehrlich & Gordon 416 Hungerford Dr Ste 330 Rockville MD 20850-4127 Address: Md Ho of Dels Lowe House Ofc Bldg Rm 403 84 College Ave Annapolis MD 21401-1991 E-mail: delgordon1@aol.com.

GORDON, MICHAEL WALLACE, law educator; b. May 4, 1935; s. Seery Clarence and Anne Catharine (Gregory) Gordon; m. Elsbeth Leimomi Kunzig, Mar. 15, 1958; children: Huntly Milne, Elsbeth Wallace. BS, U. Conn., 1957, JD, 1963; MA, Trinity Coll.; Diploma de Droit Compare, U. Strasbourg, France, 1973; Maestra en Derecho, Iberoamerica, Mex., 1982; auditor, L'Academie de Droit de la Haye, 1973, auditor, 1982. Bar: (Conn.) 1963. Assoc. Shipman & Goodwin, Hartford, Conn., 1963—66; asst. dean U. Conn. Law Sch. of Law, Hartford, 1966—68; prof. law U. Fla., Gainesville, 1968—94, Chesterfield Smith prof. law, 1994—. Vis. prof. U. Costa Rica, 1970, Duke U., 1984; Lyle T. Alverson vis. prof. George Washington U., 1986—87, U. Konstanz, 1995; Fulbright prof. U. Mex., U. Guatemala, U. Frankfort; Centennial prof. London Sch. Econs., 1992; John Stone prof. U. Ala., 1998; vis. lectr. U. Francisco Marroquin, Guatemala, Escuela Libre de Derecho, Mexico, 2000—03, U.

Bombay, U. Brasilia, Leiden U., Leuven U., U. Nairobi, Zagreb U., U. Nicaragua, U. Regensburg, U. Peking, Hong Kong U., U. Tamaulipas; external examiner U. Khartoum; of counsel Ogarrio y Diaz, Mex. City, 1976—; cons. govt. agys. Nigeria, Brazil, India, Mex., Yugoslavia, Paraguay, Panama, Oman, Sudan, Costa Rica; contbg. editor Lawyer of the Am.; mem. editl. bd. Syracuse Jour. Internat. Law and Commerce, Fla. Jour. Internat. Trade Law, UCLA Pacific Basin Jour.; lectr. Coun. Fgn. Rels., Brit. Inst. Internat. and Comparative Law. Author: Fla. Corp. Law (5 vols.), 1975, The Cuban Nationalizations-The Demise of Fgn. Pvt. Property, 1976, Multinat. Corps. Law-Mex., Ctrl. Am., Panama and the CACM (2 vols.), 1978, The Civil Code of Mex., 1978; author: (with Glendon and Osakwe) Comparative Legal Traditions, 1982, 1994, Comml., Bus. and Trade Laws of Mex., 1983, Fgn. State Immunity in Comml. Transactions., 1990; author: (with Folsom and Spanogle) Internat. Bus. Transactions, 1985, 1989, 1993, 1997, 2002, 2003, Handbook on NAFTA Dispute Settlement, 1999; author: (with Folsom and Lopez) Law of NAFTA, 2000; author: (with Baldwin, Brand and Epstein) Internat. Civil Litig., 2003. Lt. j.g. USNR, 1957—60. Presdl. scholar, U. Fla., 1977, scholar-in-residence, Bellagio Found., Italy. Mem.: Am. Assn. for Comparative Study of Law, Brit. Inst. Internat. and Comparative Law, Am. Fgn. Law Assn., Am. Soc. Internat. Law, Guatemala Bar Assn. (hon.), Mex. Acad. Pvt. Internat. and Comparative Law (hon.). Republican. Episcopalian. Office: Coll Law U Fla Gainesville FL 32611

GORDON, MILTON PAUL, biochemist, educator; b. St. Paul, Feb. 8, 1930; s. Abraham and Rebecca (Ryan) G.; m. Elaine Travis, Jan. 1, 1955; children—David, Karen, Nancy, Peter. BA summa cum laude, U. Minn., 1950; PhD, U. Ill., 1953. Upjohn Co. fellow U. Ill., 1950-51; Am. Cancer Inst. fellow Sloan-Kettering Inst. for Cancer Research, N.Y.C., 1953-55, research asst., 1955-57; lectr. Bklyn. Coll., 1955-57; asst. research biochemist Virus Lab., U. Calif. at Berkeley, 1957-59; mem. faculty U. Wash., Seattle, 1959—, prof., 1966—, acting chmn., 1984-85. Sec., treas. Pacific Slope Biochem. Conf., 1964-68, pres., 1968; vis. scholar Max Planck Inst., Tübingen, Fed. Republic Germany, 1975; sci. adv. bd. Ctr. forExcellence in Molecular Biology, Lahore, Pakistan; founding organizer Verdant Technologies.; mem. adv. bd. Calgene, Biolex, Caisson Labs., SynGene Biotech., Inc. Assoc. editor Biochemistry, 1960-91. Mem. Am. Chem. Soc., AAAS, Am. Soc. Biol. Chemists, Am. Acad. Microbiology. Rsch. and publs. on plant tumorogenesis and plant transformation, research on phytoremediation. Home: 7111 Linden Ave N Apt 404 Seattle WA 98103-5169 E-mail: miltong@u.washington.edu

GORDON, MORRIS AARON, medical mycologist, microbiologist; b. Waterbury, Conn., Apr. 3, 1920; s. Samuel and Anna (Rubinstein) G.; m. Ruth Kathryn McKee, May 22, 1945 (div. 1970); children: Barbara Jean, David Spencer, Sarah Elizabeth. BS, City Coll. N.Y., N.Y.C., 1940; MS, U. Chgo., 1942; PhD, Duke U., 1949. Diplomate Am. Bd. Microbiology; cert. lab. dir., N.Y. Lab. officer Regional Hosp., U.S. Army, Camp Blanding, Fla., 1945-46; mycologist Communicable Disease Ctr., Atlanta, 1949-54; biol. warfare specialist Chem. Corps Training Command, Fort McClellan, Ala., 1954-55; assoc. prof. microbiology Med. Coll. S.C., Charleston, 1955-59; sr. to prin. rsch. scientist, dir. mycology labs. N.Y. State Dept. Health, Albany, 1959-87, dir. clin. microbiology & mycology labs., 1983-87, dir. emeritus clin. microbiology and mycology labs., 1987—. Study sect. NIH, Washington, 1971-75; adv. com. Brown-Hazen Awards, N.Y.C., 1974-78; cons. VA Hosp., Albany, 1959-96; rsch. prof. Albany Med. Coll., 1975-90. Author: Laboratory Identification of Pathogenic Fungi, 1970; founder/editor Bull. Med. Mycol. Soc. Ams., 1976-94; contbr. articles to numerous profl. jours. Lt. comdr. USPHS, 1949-54. Recipient various rsch. grants NIH, teaching fellowship Duke U., 1947-49; Fulbright professor, 1978, Inter-Am. fellow La. State U., 1959. Mem. Med. Mycol. Soc. Ams. (pres. 1978-79, Benham award 1988), Internat. Soc. Human and Animal Mycology (v.p. 1982-85, Georg award 1991), Am. Soc. Microbiology (pres. mycology sect.), Phi Beta Kappa, Sigma Xi (pres. Albany chpt. 1972). Achievements include invention of latex test for cryptococcosis; initiation of diagnostic immunofluorescence for human fungal diseases; cultured pathogenic lipophilic yeasts; establishment of first presence in North America and first presence in humans of Dermatophilus infection. Address: 251 Springmoor Dr Raleigh NC 27615 E-mail: gordonmeyer@peoplepc.com.

GORDON, MURRAY BRUCE, endocrinologist; b. Niagara Falls, N.Y., Nov. 2, 1953; s. Irving and Molly (Kramer) G.; m. Donna Rudo, June 15, 1980; children: Aaron Joseph, Ellie Miriam, Abby Ilana. BS, Rensselaer Poly. Inst., 1977; MD, Albany Med. Coll., 1977. Diplomate Am. Bd. Internal Medicine, Am. Bd. Endocrinology and Metabolism. Resident in medicine Presbyn. U. Hosp., Pitts., 1977-80; rsch. fellow in medicine Brigham & Womens Hosp., Boston, 1980-82; clin. asst. prof. medicine U. Pitts. Sch. Medicine, 1982-90; asst. prof. medicine Med. Coll. Pa./ Hahnemann U., Pitts., 1988—95; assoc. prof. medicine Med. Coll. Pa./Hahnemann U., 1996—; assoc. prof. neurosurgery Med. Coll. Pa./Hahnemann U., 2000—; assoc. attending physician Allegheny Gen. Hosp., Pitts., 1982-89, sr. attending physician, 1989—, dir. divsn. endocrinology, 1995—; dir. Allegheny Neuroendocrinology Ctr., 2000—. Contbr. articles to profl. jours. Recipient Dean's Cert. for Outstanding Rsch., Albany Med. Coll., 1974, C.V. Mosby award for Outstanding Rsch., 1974, Dr. Glenn H. Leak Meml. award, 1975. Mem.: ACP, AMA, Growth Hormone Rsch. Soc., Am. Assn. Clin. Endocrinologists, Pituitary Soc., Am. Thyroid Assn., Endocrine Soc., Pa. Med. Soc., Alpha Omega Alpha. Jewish. Avocations: stamp collecting, talmud study, travel. Home: 150 Westland Dr Pittsburgh PA 15217-2539 Office: Divsn of Endocrinology 420 E North Ave Pittsburgh PA 15212-4746

GORDON, NICHOLAS, broadcasting executive; b. Chgo., Apr. 12, 1928; s. Jacques and Ruth (Janeway) G.; m. Gladys Sack, Apr. 10, 1950 (div. 1976); children: Catherine, Christopher, Susan; m. Julie E. Miles, Aug. 12, 1977. Ph.B., U. Chgo., 1946. Reporter City News Bur., Chgo., 1948; radio-TV analyst William Weintraub Agy., N.Y.C., 1949-50; dir. rsch. and sales planning Keystone Broadcasting Sys., N.Y.C., 1951-52; with NBC, 1953-74, mgr. rates and program evaluation, 1956-58, mgr. sales devel. NBC-TV Sales, 1959-60, dir. sales devel. NBC-TV Sales, 1960-63, account exec. TV sales, 1964-68, v.p. Ea. sales, 1968-70, v.p. radio network sales, 1970-74; pres. Keystone Broadcasting Sys., N.Y.C., 1974-85, chmn., 1985—. Vice chmn. Riverdale Cmty. Coun., 1968-71; mem. N.Y.C. Planning Bd., Riverdale, 1969-75, vice chmn., 1972-74; pres. Riverdale Cmty. Planning Assn., 1972-76; mem. vol. corps N.Y.C. Dept. Commerce, 1968-70; bd. dirs. Wave Hill Ctr. Environ. Studies, 1969-80, exec. v.p., 1970-80; mem. Bronx Democratic County Com., 1968; bd. dirs. Music Mountain, Inc., Falls Village, Conn., 1970—, pres., 1974— ; bd. dirs. Riverdale Neighborhood House, Bronx, N.Y., 1970-74, Bronx Coun. Arts, 1970-72, Phila. Orch. Media Inst., 1998—; trustee St. Hilda's and St. Hugh's Sch., 1965-76. Decorated chevalier l'Ordre des Arts et Lettres (France) Mem. Century Assn., Univ. Club, Explorers Club (N.Y.C.), Tavern Club, Cliff Dwellers Club (Chgo.), East India Club (London). Office: Keystone Broadcasting Syst PO Box 1739 Sharon CT 06069-1739 E-mail: ngordon@snet.net.

GORDON, NORMAN BOTNICK, psychology educator; b. N.Y.C., Feb. 12, 1921; s. Moses and Molvine (Botnick) G.; m. Diana Jean Drews, July 27, 1974; children: Jane Ellen, Judith Ann, Marc Daniel, Aaron Drew. BA, Bklyn. Coll., 1942; MA, New Sch. Social Research, 1951; PhD, NYU, 1957. Research psychologist U.S. Naval Tng. Device Ctr., Port Washington, N.Y., 1951-58; assoc. prof. psychology Yeshiva U., N.Y.C., 1959-68, prof., 1968-74; guest investigator Rockefeller U., N.Y.C., 1964-77; prin. rsch. scientist N.Y. State Office of Drug Abuse Svcs., 1974-77; prof. SUNYCO-Oswego, 1977—, chmn. dept. psychology, 1977-86, prof. emeritus, 1988—. Adj. prof. SUNY-Oswego, 1988-97, rsch. assoc., 1997—. Served with U.S. Army, 1942-46. Grantee USPHS, 1966-74, 64-67 Mem. APA, Eastern Psychol. Assn., Sigma Xi. Home: 900 County Route 20 Oswego NY 13126-5672 Office: SUNY Coll Dept Psychology Oswego NY 13126 E-mail: ngordon@oswego.edu.

GORDON, NORMAN JAMES, lawyer; b. Dec. 24, 1945; s. Meyer and Alice (Vetzner) G.; m. Cheryl Bisk, June 8, 1969; children: David Benjamin, Joshua. BA, U. Ill., 1967, JD, 1970. Bar: Ill. 1970, Tex. 1974, U.S. Dist. Ct. (we. dist.) Tex. 1974, U.S. Ct. Appeals (5th cir.) 1974, U.S. Supreme Ct. 1974. Asst. states atty. McLean County, Ill., 1970; assoc. Diamond, Rash, Gordon & Jackson P.C. (formerly Diamond, Rash, Leslie & Smith), El Paso, Tex., 1974-76; shareholder Diamond, Rash, Gordon & Jackson P.C., El Paso, Tex., 1976—. V.p. El Paso Jewish Cmty. Ctr., 1980-82, pres., 1983-86; sec. El Paso Jewish Fedn., 1986-88, v.p., 1988-94, pres., 1994-96; treas. Hospice of El Paso, 1982-83; bd. dirs. Congregation B'nai Zion, El Paso. Capt. JAGC, U.S. Army, 1970-74. Recipient New Leadership award Nat. Jewish Welfare Bd., 1982. Mem. ABA, Ill. Bar Assn., State Bar Tex., Tex. Bd. Legal Specialization (cert. civil trial law), Tex. Trial Lawyers Assn., El Paso Bar Assn., Rotary (El Paso). Office: 7th Fl 300 E Main Dr El Paso TX 79901-1372

GORDON, PAMELA ANN WENCE, pianist; b. Dayton, Ohio, Apr. 28, 1943; d. Arthur Elbert and Melva C. (Coleman) Wence (dec.); m. Clifford Elwood Gordon, Oct. 23, 1971. BS, Ind. State U., Terre Haute, 1966. Self-employed piano tchr., 1957—; round dance leader, 1973-98. Organist, Ctrl. Seventh Day Bapt. Ch., 1989—, choir dir. 2000—; Christmas carol pianist Williamsburg, Va., 2001--; mem. Greenbelt Astronomy Club, Md. Recipient Appreciation award Rock Eights, 1985. Mem. ROUNDALAB (charter mem., chair survey com. 1985-86, Maestro trophy 1998), Round Dance Tchrs. Assn. Greater D.C. Area (v.p.), Nat. Capital Area Sq. Dance Leaders Assn. (treas.), Washington Music Tchrs. Assn. (treas.). Avocations: camping, reading, caring for and playing with box turtles, indoor swimming, playing piano. Home: 219 Rainbow Dr # 11963 Livingston TX 77399-2019 E-mail: pcgordon@escapees.com.

GORDON, PAUL, retired dentist, artist; b. Phila., Jan. 22, 1936; s. Benjamin and Pearl (Kravitz) Gordon; m. Jeanette Epstein, Jan. 26, 1958 (dec. 1993). DDS, Temple U., 1960. Inventor dental device (Silver Circle award, 1971); Exhibited in group shows at Greater Del. Valley; author: (novels) Concrete Solution, 2001, (short stories) Van Gogh's Last Painting and Other Stories from the Edge. Violinist Savannah (Ga.) Symphony Orch., 1960—62. Lt. USN, 1960—62. Mem.: Phila. Art Mus., Portrait Soc. of Am. Jewish. Avocations: painting, violin, writing, inventing, teaching. Home: 616 Grand Ave Moorestown NJ 08057 Office: PO Box 210 590 S Lenola Rd Maple Shade NJ 08052-1602

GORDON, PAUL JOHN, management educator; b. N.Y.C., Oct. 14, 1921; s. Arthur L. and Georgiana (McDonough) G.; m. Mary Brigid Keany, Jan. 28, 1950; children: Brian Joseph, Peter Christopher, Martha Ann, Hugh John, Paul John. BBA, CCNY, 1945; MBA, Cornell U., 1949; PhD, Syracuse U., 1958. With Brooks Bros., N.Y.C., 1941-43, Lago Oil & Transp. Co., Ltd., Netherlands W. Indies, also Bayway Refinery, Linden, N.J. and Standard Oil Co. N.J., 1943-48; asst. prof. Cornell U., Ithaca, N.Y., 1949-54; prof., chmn. dept. mgmt. Sch. Bus. Duquesne U., Pitts., 1954-55; rsch. cons. Sloan-Kettering Meml. Ctr. for Cancer, N.Y.C., 1955-56; assoc. prof. bus. adminstrn., planning dir. grad. program hosp. adminstrn. Sch. Bus. Adminstrn. Emory U., Atlanta, 1956—59; assoc. prof. Grad. Sch. Bus. Ind. U., 1959-63, prof., chmn. dept. mgmt. adminstrv. studies Grad. Sch. Bus., 1963-67, prof. mgmt. Grad. Sch. Bus., 1963-89, chmn. adminstrv. and behavioral studies Grad. Sch. Bus., 1980-83, prof. emeritus mgmt. Grad. Sch. Bus., 1989—; disting. prof. mgmt. St. John's U., N.Y.C., 1990-93. Fulbright/FLAD chair in strategic mgmt. Tech. U. Lisbon, Portugal, 1997; chief U.S. Dept. State-Ford Found. party Ljubljana U., Yugoslavia, 1967; vis. prof. Trinity Coll., Dublin, 1967; vis. prof., Fulbright lectr. Instituto Post-Universitario Per Lo Studio Dell Organizazzione Aziendale, Turin, Italy, 1963; Fulbright lectr., cons. Nat. U. Republic Uruguay, 1970; disting. guest Systems Rsch. Inst., Polish Acad. Scis., 1980; vis. Fulbright prof. Helsinki Sch. Econs. and Bus. Adminstrn., Finland, 1990; mem. U.S. AID Mgmt. Edn. Reconnaissance Survey, India, also Pakistan, 1971; cons. IRS, 1956-63, Am. Coll. Hosp. Adminstrs., 1957—; with Inst. Higher Studies of Adminstrn., Caracas, Venezuela, 1973-79. Editor Acad. Mgmt. Jour, 1964-66, mem. editorial bd., 1961-75; editorial cons. adv. bd.: Bus. Horizons, Hosp. Adminstrn, W.B. Saunders Co.; contbr. articles to profl. jours. Mem. Cath. Commn. on Intellectual and Cultural Affairs, 1973—, chmn., 1980-81; chmn. UNESCO multi-nat. bus. conf. Ind. U., 1972; chmn. adv. screening com. in bus. mgmt. Coun. for Internat. Exch. of Scholars, Fulbright-Hays Program, 1979-80, 90-93, chmn., 1991-93; bd. dirs. Ind. Newman Found., 1971-82; mem. adv. bd. Abbey Press, St. Meinrad, Ind., 1991-95. Ford Found. grantee, 1963, 66, 70; IBM fellow, 1964. Fellow Acad. Mgmt. (v.p. program 1967, pres. 1969, Disting. Svc. award 1992), Internat. Acad. Mgmt., Am. Acad. Med. Adminstrs. (hon.); mem. Fulbright Assn. (life). Home: 1422 S Winfield Rd Bloomington IN 47401-6152 E-mail: pauljgordon@aol.com.

GORDON, PETER LOWELL, federal agency administrator; b. Powell, Wyo., Feb. 16, 1953; s. John Eric Gordon and Carol Mae (Peterson) Olson; m. Mitsuko Natsume, Sept. 18, 1993. BA in Polit. Sci., Criminal Justice, Calif. State U., L.A., 1975. Asst. cook Country Kitchen, LaCrosse, Wis., 1970-71; asst. mgr. Ky. Fried Chicken, Tujunga, Calif., 1975-76, Parasol Restaurant, Alhambra, Calif., 1976-77; border patrol agt. Immigration and Naturalization Svc., Dept. Justice, San Diego, 1977-80, immigration insp. Anchorage, 1980-83, immigration examiner L.A., 1983-87, legalization mgr. Laguna Niguel, Calif., 1987-90, asst. dir., 1990-98, dep. dist. dir. Anchorage, Ala., 1998-99, asst. regional dir. inspections Laguna Niguel, Calif., 1999—2003; asst. dir. immigration policy and programs, customs and border protection Dept. Homeland Security, Long Beach, Calif., 2003—. Co-developer (nat. data base) Legalization Adjustment Processing System, 1987 (Commr.'s award 1987); co-designer Calif. Svc. Ctr., 1989; co-author Calif. Svc. Ctr. Guidelines, 1989. Spkr. Am. Immigration Lawyers Assn., So. and Northern Calif. chpts.; contbr. Dedication and Everlasting Love to Animals. Republican. Lutheran. Avocations: coin and stamp collecting, baseball and softball, reading, hiking.

GORDON, REVA JO, retired librarian; b. Martinsville, Mo., Feb. 16, 1928; d. Earl G. and Claudia Olive (Goodwin) Kerns; m. Roland Gordon, Nov. 24, 1949; children: Gary Paul, Gloria Gay Gordon Zuber. BS, N.W. Mo. State U., 1949; postgrad., State U. Iowa, 1951; MA in Libr. Sci., U. Mich., 1970. Ordained elder and deacon Presbyn. Ch. Bus. tchr. LeRoy (Iowa) H.S., 1948; bus./English tchr. Malvern (Iowa) Consolidated Schs., 1949-51; English tchr. Flushing (Mich.) Cmty. Schs., 1959-64, libr., media dir., 1964-86, ret., 1986. Author: The Goodwins and Hensleys, 1990, Sammy's Red Shirt, 2003; contbr. articles to newspapers and mags. Mem. Mich. Assn. Retired Sch. Personnel (W. Genesee County chpt.), Flushing Hist. Soc., Flushing Book Club, Royal Quarter. Avocations: writing, lecturing. Home: PO Box 406 Flushing MI 48433-0406 E-mail: revajg@aol.com.

GORDON, RICHARD LEWIS, mineral economics educator; b. Portland, Maine, June 19, 1934; s. Benjamin M. and Sara I. Gordon; m. Nancy Ellen Helfand, June 8, 1958; children: David William, Benjamin Mark. AB, Dartmouth Coll., 1956; PhD, MIT, 1960. Econ. analyst Union Carbide Corp., 1960-64; asst. economist First Nat. City Bank, N.Y.C., 1964; mem. faculty Pa. State U., State College, 1964—, prof. mineral econs., 1970-96, prof. emeritus, 1996—. Shell lectr. on energy econs. Surrey (Eng.) U., 1981; bd. dirs. Ctr. for Energy and Mineral Policy, 1987-96; Micasu U. endowed fellow in mineral econs., 1990. Author: The Evolution of Energy Policy in Western Europe, 1970, U.S. Coal and Electric Power Industry, 1975, Coal in the U.S. Energy Market, 1978, An Economic Analysis of World Energy Problems, 1981, Reforming the Regulation of Electric Utilities, 1982, World Coal Economics, Policies and Prospects, 1987, Regulation and Economic Analysis: A Critique Over Two Centuries, 1994, Antitrust Abuse in the New Economy: The Microsoft Case, 2002. Recipient Scholars medal The Pa. State U., 1989; decorated officer with honors 1st class Decoration of Andres Bello, Venezuela, 1989. Mem. AIME (chmn. coun. econs. 1973 Mineral Econs. award), Internat. Assn. Energy Economists (Outstanding Contbn. award 1992), Am. Econ. Assn., Econometric Soc., Royal Econ. Soc. Jewish. Home: 214 Horizon Dr State College PA 16801-8616

GORDON, ROBBY, race car driver; b. Bellflower, Calif., Jan. 2, 1969; Racecar driver Junie Donlavey, 1991, Robert Yates Racing, Kranefuss-Haas, Dale Earnhardt Inc., Felix Sabates, 1996—98, Morgan-McClure Motorsports' Chevrolets, Richard Childress Racing, Welcome, NC, 2001—. Recipient 2d pl., Internat. Race of Champions, 1996—97. Avocations: boating, bicycling, motorcycling, water-skiing, go-karting. Office: c/o Richard Childress Racing PO Box 1189 Welcome NC 27374-1189

GORDON, ROBERT, utility company executive, lawyer; b. Price, Utah, Aug. 15, 1927; s. Harry N. and Sarah (Bontsik) G.; m. Rosanne Cline, Nov. 29, 1952; children— Steven, Cindy, Gary. LL.B., U. Utah, 1952. Bar: Utah 1953. Sole practice, Salt Lake City, 1953-66; atty. Utah Power & Light Co., Salt Lake City, 1966-80, asst. corp. sec., 1973-76, corp. sec., 1976-80, v.p., corp. sec., 1980—. Pres. United Cerebral Palsy of Utah, Salt Lake City, 1965; trustee Ballet West, Salt Lake City, 1982-86 . Served with USAF, 1945-46. Mem. Utah Taxpayers Assn. (dir. 1981—), Utah State Bar Assn. (chmn. Law Day com. Salt Lake City 1983, 84). Republican. Jewish. Club: Salt Lake Tennis (pres. 1979-81). Office: Utah Power & Light Co 1407 W North Temple Salt Lake City UT 84140-0002

GORDON, ROBERT EUGENE, lawyer; b. L.A., Sept. 20, 1932; s. Harry Maurice and Minnie (Shaffer); 1 child, Victor Marten. BA, UCLA, 1954; LLB, U. Calif., Berkeley, 1959, JD, 1960; cert., U. Hamburg, Fed. Republic Germany, 1960. Bar: Calif. 1960. Assoc. Lillick, Geary, McHose, Roethke & Myers, Los Angeles, 1960-64, Schoichet & Rifkind, Beverly Hills, Calif., 1964-67; ptnr. Baerwitz & Gordon, Beverly Hills, 1967-69, Ball, Hunt, Hart, Brown & Baerwitz, Beverly Hills, 1970-71; of counsel Jacobs, Sills & Coblentz, San Francisco, 1972-78; ptnr. Gordon & Hodge, San Francisco, 1978-81; pvt. practice San Francisco, 1981—89, Corte Madera, Calif., 1989—2002, Sausalito, Calif., 2002—. Adj. prof. entertainment law Hastings Coll. of Law, San Francisco, 1990-91, U. Calif., Berkeley, 1992. Served to 1st lt. U.S. Army, 1954-56. Mem. ABA (forum com. on entertainment and sports law), Los Angeles Copyright Soc. (bd. trustees 1970-71), Copyright Soc. of the USA. Avocations: cycling, skiing. Home: 35 Elaine Ave Mill Valley CA 94941-1014 Office: One Harbor Dr Ste 106 Sausalito CA 94965

GORDON, ROBERT JAMES, economics educator; b. Boston, Sept. 3, 1940; s. Robert Aaron and Margaret (Shaughnessy) G.; m. Julie S. Peyton, June 22, 1963. AB, Harvard U., 1962; MA, Oxford U., Eng., 1969; PhD, MIT, 1967. Asst. prof. econs. Harvard U., 1967-68; asst. prof. U. Chgo., 1968-73; prof. econs. Northwestern U., Evanston, Ill., 1973—, Stanley G. Harris prof. social scis., 1987—, chair econs. dept., 1992-96. Rsch. assoc. Nat. Bur. Econ Rsch., 1968—; mem. Brookings Panel Econ. Activity, 1970—; co-chmn. Internat. Seminar Macroecons., 1978-94; mem. exec. com. Conf. Rsch., Income and Wealth, 1978-83; mem. panel rev. productivity measures NAS, 1977-79; cons. bd. govs. Fed. Res. Sys., 1973-83. U.S. Dept. Treasury, 1967-80, U.S. Congl. Budget Office, 1996—, U.S. Bur. Econ. Analysis, 1999—; mem. Nat. Commn. on Consumer Price Index, 1995-97. Author: Macroeconomics, 1978, 9th edit., 2003, Milton Friedman's Monetary Framework, 1974, Challenges to Interdependent Economies, 1979, The American Business Cycle: Continuity and Change, 1986, The Measurement of Durable Goods Prices, 1990, International Volatility and Economic Growth, 1991, The Economics of New Goods, 1997; editor Jour. Polit. Economy, 1970-73. Recipient Lustrum prize Erasmus U., 1999; Marshall fellow, 1962-64; fellow Ford Found., 1966-67; grantee NSF, 1971—; fellow Guggenheim Meml. Found., 1980-81; rsch. fellow German Marshall Fund, 1985-86. Fellow AAAS, Econometric Soc. (treas. 1975—); mem. Am. Econ. Assn. (bd. editors 1975-77, mem. exec. com. 1981-83), Phi Beta Kappa Office: Northwestern U Dept Econs Evanston IL 60208-0001 E-mail: rjg@northwestern.edu.

GORDON, ROBERT M. lawyer; b. Chgo., July 17, 1953; s. Lloyd M. and Betty (Bernstein) G.; m. Alanna Barr, Apr. 16, 1978. AB, U. Ill., Chgo., 1974; JD, Northwestern U., 1983. Bar: Ill. 1983, U.S. Dist. Ct. (no. dist.) Ill. 1983, U.S. Tax Ct. 1985. Editor Argus Communications, Niles, Ill., 1975-78; assoc. editor Follett Pub. Co., Chgo., 1978-80; assoc. Wilson & McIlvaine, Chgo., 1983-87, Winston & Strawn, Chgo., 1987-89; mgr. U.S. tax planning BP Am. Inc. (formerly Amoco Corp.), Chgo., 1989—. Contbr. articles to profl. jours. Mem. ABA. Office: BP Am Inc 4101 Winfield Rd Warrenville IL 60555

GORDON, ROY GERALD, chemistry educator; b. Akron, Ohio, Jan. 11, 1940; s. Nathan Gold and Frances (Teitel) G.; m. Myra Sheila Miller, Dec. 24, 1961; children: Avra Karen, Emily Francine, Steven Eric. AB summa cum laude, Harvard, 1961, A.M. in Physics, 1962, PhD in Chem. Physics, 1964. Jr. fellow Soc. of Fellows, Harvard, 1964-66, mem. faculty, 1966—, prof., 1969—. Sloan Found. fellow, 1966-69, Einstein fellow, Israel, 1985. Fellow Am. Phys. Soc.; mem. Am. Chem. Soc. (award in pure chemistry 1972, Baekeland award 1979, Esselen award 1996) R & D award 1991, Faraday Soc., Union of Concerned Scientists, NAS, Am. Acad. Arts and Scis., Phi Beta Kappa, Sigma Xi. Achievements include inventions in solar energy, energy conservation and microelectronics, theoretical research discovering forms of forces between molecules, the way molecules collide with each other, motion of molecules in liquids and solids. Office: Harvard U Dept Chemistry 12 Oxford St Cambridge MA 02138-2902 E-mail: gordon@chemistry.harvard.edu.

GORDON, RUBY DANIELS, retired nursing educator, counselor; b. Camden, Ark., Dec. 28, 1927; d. Fred Jewell and Etta Matilda (Watson) Daniels; m. DeVore Basil Gordon, Sept. 1, 1946 (div. 1950); children: Sally Ann Gordon, Lynne Gordon. Diploma, St. Monica's Hosp., Phoenix, 1949; BS, Ariz. State U., 1959, MA, 1962, PhD, 1975. Instr. basic sci. St. Joseph Hosp. Sch. Nursing, Phoenix, 1962-67; chairperson dept. nursing Glendale C.C., Ariz., 1967-80; prof. Phoenix Coll., 1980-92; counselor Glendale C.C., 1993-98; ret., 1998.

GORDON, SANDY GALE COMBS, medical/surgical nurse, community health nurse; b. Lafollette, Tenn., Sept. 8, 1950; d. Wise and Edna Leona (Boshears) Combs; m. Ralph William Gordon, Aug. 30, 1975 (dec. Feb. 1998). Diploma, Middletown Hosp., 1971. RN, Ohio. Pub. health nurse Bur. Pub. Health, Middletown, Ohio, 1979-82; staff nurse Middletown Hosp., 1971-79. Named Internat. Women of Yr., 1994-95. Mem. Middletown Hosp. Alumni Assn. Home: 1107 Ellen Dr Middletown OH 45042-3341 E-mail: sgordon@erinet.com.

GORDON, SANFORD DANIEL, economics educator; b. Newark, June 23, 1924; s. Harry Louis and Beatrice (Safris) G.; m. Alice Lillian Pressman, May 27, 1948; children— Ellen Ann, Eric Alan. Student, Tulane U., 1942; BS magna cum laude, NYU, 1947, MA, 1948, PhD, 1953. Instr. econ. NYU, 1948-50; mem. faculty State U. Coll., Oneonta, N.Y., 1950—, prof. econs., 1957—, chmn. dept., 1960—; asst. vice chancellor for policy and planning State U. N.Y. Central Adminstrn., 1972-76, provost for policy analysis, 1976-79; exec. dir. N.Y. State Coun. on Econ. Edn., 1979-89; prof. econs. Russell Sage Coll., 1979-89. Adj. prof. econs. U. So. Fla., 1989-99; lectr. to elder hostels; econ. editor Kennikat Press., Inc., Port Washington, N.Y., 1970— ; cons. to govt., industry, banks, pub. schs., 1954— ; vis. prof. State U. N.Y., Buffalo, 1965, U. Miami, 1967. Author: (with J. Witchel) An Introduction to the American Economy, 1967, A Visual Analysis of the American Economy, 1968, (with G. Dawson) The American Economy, 1969, Introductory Economics, 1972, 7th edit., 1991; (with Conover and Ramstadder) Business Dynamics, 1982, 2d edit., 1988, The Economy of New York State, 1987, Basic Economic Principles, 1988, Economics U$A: A Resource Guide for Teachers, 1988, (with A. Stafford) Applying Economic Principles, 1994; lectr., writer: pub. TV series The American Economy, Conversations on Economic Issues, 1970— . Mem. Parks Commn., also Charter Revision Commn., Oneonta, 1957—; v.p. Oneonta Brotherhood, 1958; Dem. candidate for 13th Congl. Dist., Fla., for U.S. Ho. of Reps. Served to sgt. USAAF, 1942-44. Recipient Kazajian Found. award, 1967, Bessie B. Moore Service award, 1987. Mem. N.Y. Econ. Assn. (past pres.), AAUP (past pres. N.Y. conf.) Home: 7127 Fairway Bend Ln Sarasota FL 34243-3608 E-mail: Budalice@aol.com. *Success has less to do with innate ability than with self-confidence, motivation, and perhaps most important, resiliancy.*

GORDON, SARAH HERBERT, historian; b. Phila., Feb. 16, 1950; d. Edward Joseph and Patricia Dearborn (Jencks) G. AB in History with honors, Smith Coll., 1972; postgrad., Cambridge U., 1972—73; MA in Am. History, U. Chgo., 1974, PhD in Am. History, 1981. Rsch. asst. Prof. Lynn Lees, 1972, Prof. David Potts, 1973-75; rsch. historian Bicentennial Exhibit History Ill., 1976; rsch. asst. Edward James, 1977; lectr. Roosevelt U., Chgo., 1978; archivist Michael Reese Hosp., Chgo., 1978-80; archival cons. Mus. Sci. & Industry, Chgo., 1981; processing clk. U. Chgo. Archives, 1981; rsch. asst. Stanley Katz, 1987; mktg. asst. Gaylord Hosp., Wallingford, Conn., 1982-89; tchr. history Yeshiva of New Haven, 1989-94, 95—; spl. lectr. U. New Haven, 1991-94, 95-96; asst. prof. Quinnipiac Coll., Hamden, Conn., 1994-95, adj. lectr., 1989-97, adj. assoc. prof., 1998—. Author: All Our Lives, 1981, No Service Too Small, 1986, Passage to Union: How the Railroads Transformed American Life, 1829-1929, 1997; contbr. articles to profl. jours. Mem. North Haven Dem. Com., 1983-85, North Haven Conservation Commn., 1984-89. Mem.: Conn. Hist. Soc., Orgn. Am. Historians. Mem. Soc. Of Friends. Avocations: book collecting, gardening, hiking, swimming. Home: 127 Morse St Hamden CT 06517-3213 Office: Yeshiva of New Haven 765 Elm St New Haven CT 06511-4019

GORDON, SCOTT (HARRY SCOTT BUEHLMEIER), entertainer, actor; b. Dumont, N.J., Oct. 12, 1949; s. Harry Gordon and Florence Victoria (Bielawski) B.; m. Dian Mary Kenlon, Nov. 10, 1973. Grad. high sch., Mahwah, N.J. Pres. Scott Gordon Enterprises, Inc., Paramus, N.J., 1974—; performer, writer The Uncle Floyd Show, West Orange, N.J., 1976—, Gordon and Rogue, 1993—; ptnr. WWW.PlanetShowbiz.com, 1999—2001, www.GoofyParty-People.com; writer Burns and Hope at Madison Sq. Garden, N.Y.C., 1989. Audio cons. Playhouse on the Mall, Paramus, NJ, 1974; make-up cons. Ken's Costumes, Fair Lawn, NJ, 1976—94, SYSOP/Cons. Genie On-Line Svc., 1990—97; rec. artist Mercury Records; comedy team mem. Gordon and Rogue; mem. nominating com. MixMag. TEC Awards, 1998—. Author, editor (Profl. mag.) Psychicos, 1978-80; author (column) Vibrations, 1987; maker radio commls.; San Antonio Rose with Willie Nelson, B-52s, Labour of Lust, First Exposure; enbr. (radio programs) The Italian American Serenade, The Colavita Music Hall, Italian Melodies, Sunday Funnies; air personality Remember When, 1987-98, syndicates 1995; entertainer Nickelodeon Turkey TV, appeared on Broadway with Collinsport Players, 1995. Mem. AFTRA, Psychic Entertainers Assn. (bd. dirs. 1978-80, founder), Audio Engring. Soc., Circle Tri Corbies, The Radio Repertory Co. of Am. Avocations: musician (guitar, bass, drums), performing psychic. Office: Scott Gordon Enterprises Inc PO Box 791 Paramus NJ 07653-0791

GORDON, STEPHEN MAURICE, manufacturing company executive, rancher; b. Chgo., Aug. 20, 1942; s. Milton A. and Elinor (Loeff) G.; m. Helene Lindow, Feb. 11, 1978 (div. Mar. 1998); 2 children: Hallie Lindow, Lacey Edison; m. Marilee Ann Enright, Mar. 21, 1998. Student, Middlebury Coll., 1960-61; BA, U. Chgo., 1964; JD, N.Y. U., 1967; D.I.L., Cambridge (Eng.) U., 1968. Bar: N.Y. State 1968. Aide to Vice Pres. Hubert Humphrey, Democratic Nat. Com., Washington, 1968; assoc. firm Marshall, Bratter, Greene, Allison & Tucker, N.Y.C., 1968-70; sr. rsch. assoc. Halle & Stieglitz, Inc., N.Y.C., 1970-72, v.p., 1972-75, pres., 1975-79; pres., chief exec. officer Irvin Industries Inc., N.Y.C., 1979-89; pres. Diamond G Ranch Inc., Dubois, Wyo. Chmn. bd. dirs. Vincennes Steel Corp.; dir. Minerva Health; mem. vis. com. U. Chgo. Mem. Nat. Wildlife Art Mus. (dir., treas.), MacLean-Fogg (dir.), Am. Red Angus Assn., Young Pres.' Orgn., Beta Gamma Sigma, Psi Upsilon. Home: Diamond G Ranch Dunoir Rd Dubois WY 82513 Office: PO Box 25009 Jackson WY 83001-7000

GORDON, STEVE, real estate executive; b. Ottawa, Ont., Can., July 13, 1951; m. Laurie Gordon, 1973; children: Erin, Nina, Shanon, Alex, Aliza. BSc, U. Ottawa, 1973. Pres., CEO The Regional Group of Cos., Inc., Ottawa, Ont., Can., 1982—. Chmn. Regional Capital Properties; pres. Regional Realty Ltd., Gemini Capital Corp.; bd. govs. Ottawa Boys & Girls Club; active Jr. Achievement Can.; co-chair Counsellors of Real Estate, Can.; past exec. mem. Ottawa-Carleton Econ. Devel. Corp. Bd.; past chmn. Ottawa-Carleton Bd. Trade; past pres. Real Estate Inst. Can., Ea. Ont. chpt., Inst. Real Estate Property Mgmt., Ottawa, Housing & Urban Devel. Assn. Can., Ottawa; past nat. dir. Real Estate Inst. Can. Recipient Man of Yr. award HUDAC, 1984. Mem. Internat. Real Estate Inst., Am. Soc. Real Estate Counsellors, Inst. Real Estate Mgmt., Appraisal Inst. Can., Can. Home Builders Assn. (Presdl. award of honour), Assn. Ont. Land Economists, AF&AM, Rideau Club, Can. Club, Lambda Alpha Internat. Avocations: walking, swimming, mountain hiking. Office: The Regional Group of Cos Inc 200 Catherine St 6th Fl Ottawa ON Canada K2P 2K9

GORDON, STEWART LYNELL, musician, educator; b. Olathe, Kans., Aug. 28, 1930; s. Lynell Frank and Guanetta (Stewart) Gordon. Diploma, State Conservatory Music, 1951; BA, U.Kans., 1954, MA, 1955; D of Musical Arts, Eastman Sch., Rochester, N.Y., 1965. Asst. prof. music Wilmington (Ohio) Coll., 1957—60; from asst. prof. to assoc. prof. to prof. U. Md., Coll. Park, 1960—86, music dept. chair, 1979—86; v.p. for acad. affairs, provost Queens Coll., Flushing, NY, 1986—89; prof. keyboard studies U. So. Calif., L.A., 1989—, chair keyboard studies, dir undergrad. studies, 1996—. Adjudicator Gina Bachauer Internat. Piano competition, Canadian Music Competition finals, Gilmore Found. Nominating Com.; touring pianist Europe, 1955—60, N. Am., 1960—80, Middle East, 1968, Asia, 1977—79; founder, dir. Wm. Kapell Internat. Piano Competition, Md., 1970—85, Savannah On Stage Festival and Am. Trads. Competition, 1989—2002, Cultural Heritage and Great Gospel Competitions, Queens, NY, 1990—91. Author: (books) Etudes for Piano Teachers, Essays on the Teachers' Art, 1995, A History of Keyboard Music for the Piano and Its Forerunners, 1996; co-author (with others): The Well Tempered Keyboard Teacher 2d edit., 1999; composer several music theater works including:: Spirit of the Navy, 1955. Lt. j.g. USN, 1954—57. Recipient Danforth Tchr. Study grant, Danforth Found., 1963—64, Lifetime Achievement award, Md. Music Tchrs. Assn., 1983, Ramo Music Faculty award, U. So. Calif., 2001. Mem.: Calif. Music Tchrs. Assn., Nat. Music Tchrs. Assn. (adjudicator nat.music competition finals), Phi Kappa Phi, Phi Kappa Lambda, Phi Beta Kappa. Avocations: gardening, bull terriers, tropical fish, languages. Home: 775 E Mel Ave Palm Springs CA 92262-4832

GORDON, SYDNEY MICHAEL, research chemist; b. Pretoria, South Africa, Apr. 18, 1939; came to U.S., 1977; s. Cyril and Ida (Goldberg) G.; m. Patricia C. Hammerschlag, Sept. 1963 (div. Feb. 1982); children: Danielle, Anna K., Stephanie; m. Maria Hawryluk, Mar. 9, 1984; 1 child, Andrew M. BSc, U. Pretoria, 1959, MSc, 1962, DSc, 1964. Chief chemist Atomic Energy Bd., Pelindaba, South Africa, 1964-77; sci. advisor Ill. Inst. Tech. Rsch. Inst., Chgo., 1977-91; rsch. leader Battelle Meml. Inst., Columbus, Ohio, 1991—. Author: (with C.W. Spicer) Hazardous Air Pollutant Handbook, 2002; contbr. articles to profl. jours., chpts. to books. Mem. Am. Chem. Soc., Am. Soc. Mass Spectrometry, Internat. Soc. Exposure Analysis. Office: Battelle Meml Inst 505 King Ave Columbus OH 43201-2681

GORDON, WALTER KELLY, retired provost, English language educator; b. Bklyn., Jan. 25, 1930; s. William Benjamin and Grace Adele (Kelly) G.; m. Lydia Caroline Fruchtman, Aug. 29, 1959; 1 child, Karyn Gay. AB, Clark U., 1950; MA, U. Pa., 1956, PhD, 1961. Instr. Cedar Crest Coll., 1959-61; faculty Rutgers U., Camden, 1961-97, prof., dean coll., 1974-81, acad. dean, provost Camden campus, 1981-97; ret., 1997. Cons. Campbells Soup Co., 1976-94. Author: (with J.L. Sanderson) Exposition and the English Language, 1963, 2d edit., 1968, Literature in Critical Perspectives, 1969. Bd. dirs. Walt Whitman Internat. Poetry Center, 1974-77. Served to lt. USNR, 1951-56. Recipient Lindback award for disting. teaching, 1970 Home: 2803 Salem Dr Riverton NJ 08077-4027 Office: Rutgers U Camden Coll Arts & Scis 379 Armitage Hall Camden NJ 08102

GORDON, WILLIAM CHARLES, college administrator; m. Kathryn Gordon; children: Jason, Scott, Kate, Jonathan. Bachelor's degree, Master's degree, Wake Forest U.; PhD in Exptl. Psychology, Rutgers U. Asst. prof. psychology SUNY, Binghamton, 1973-78; tchr. psychology dept. U. N.Mex., Albuquerque, 1978, chair psychology dept., 1990, interim dean Coll. Arts and Scis., 1992, dean, 1993, provost, v.p. for acad. affairs, 1996, interim pres., 1998—; pres., 1999—2002; provost Wake Forest U., 2002. Office: Office of the Provost Wake Forest U 1834 Wake Forest Rd Winston Salem NC 27106

GORDON, WILLIAM EDMUND, JR., lawyer; b. Bryn Mawr, Pa., Aug. 9, 1948; s. William Edmund and Margaret Elizabeth (Bernstiel) G.; m. Mary Jo DeMatteo; 1 son, William Edmund III. B.S., Parsons Coll., 1971; J.D., S. Tex. Coll. Law, 1976. Bar: Tex. 1976, U.S. Dist. Ct. (so. dist.) Tex. 1976, U.S. Dist. Ct. (ea. dist. Pa.) 1978, U.S. Ct. Appeals (5th cir.) 1976, U.S. Dist. Ct. (ea. dist.) Tex. 1977. Assoc. firm Ryan & Marshall, Houston, 1976-77; asst. U.S. atty. Dept. Justice, Tyler, Tex., 1977-78, Phila., 1978-81; assoc. firm Curtin & Heefner, Morrisville, Pa., 1981-83; atty. E.I. du Pont de Nemours & Co., Wilmington, Del., 1984— ; instr. Atty. Gen.'s Advocacy Inst., Washington, 1979-80. Editor-in-chief S. Tex. Law Jour., 1975. E.E. Townes scholar S. Tex. Coll. Law, 1976. Mem. Pa. C. of C. (mem. truth and fairness in litigation com. 1984). Republican. Roman Catholic. Home: 20 Walnut Valley Rd Chadds Ford PA 19317-9434 Office: Legal Dept EI du Pont de Nemours & Co 1007 Market St Wilmington DE 19898

GORDON, WILLIAM EDWIN, physicist, engineer, educator, university official; b. Paterson, N.J., Jan. 8, 1918; s. William and Mary (Scott) G.; m. Elva Freile, June 22, 1941; children:Larry Scott, Nancy Lynn. BA, Montclair (N.J.) State Coll., 1939, MA, 1942; MS, NYU, 1946; PhD, Cornell U., Ithaca, N.Y., 1953. Registered profl. engr., Tex. Assoc. prof. Cornell U., 1953-59, prof., 1959-65; Walter R. Read prof. engring. Arecibo Ionospheric Obs., P.R., 1965; prof. elec. engring. and space physics and astronomy Rice U., Houston, 1966-86, dean engring. and sci., 1966-75, dean Sch. Natural Scis., 1975-80, provost, v.p. Sch. Natural Scis., 1980-86; fgn. sec. NAS, 1986-90. Conceived, directed design .and early operation of Arecibo Obs. and 1000 foot antenna, 1960-65 (named Milestone in Elec. Engring. and Landmark in Mech. Engring. 2001); chmn. bd. trustees Upper Atmosphere Rsch. Corp., 1971, 73-78, Univ. Corp. for Atmospheric Rsch., 1979-81, 86-89, 91-92; trustee Cornell U., 1976-80; mem. Arecibo Obs. Adv. Bd., 1977-80, 90-93. Bd. dirs. Taping for the Blind, Houston, 1994—. Capt. USAAF, 1942-46. Recipient Balth. Vander Pol award for disting. research in radio sci., 1966; 50th Anniversary medal Am. Meteorol. Soc., 1969, Arktowski medal, 1984, Arecibo Telescope award, 2001; Guggenheim fellow, 1972-73.. Fellow IEEE (chmn. profl. group on antennas and propagation 1964-65), Am. Geophys. Union; mem. AAAS, NAS, NAE, Am. Acad. Arts and Scis., Internat. Sci. Radio Union (v.p. 1975-81, pres. 1981-84, hon. pres. 1990—), Internat. Coun. Sci. Unions (v.p. 1988-93), Am. Meteorology Soc., Philos. Soc. Tex., Cosmos Club, Sigma Xi, Tau Beta Pi, Kappa Delta Pi, Sigma Kappa Nu, Phi Kappa Phi. Achievements include spl. rsch. radio scattering. E-mail: bgordon@spacsun.rice.edu.

GORDON, WILLIAM STOUT, lawyer; b. Liberty Center, Ind., Apr. 12, 1913; s. James Orin and Pearl Elizabeth (Stout) G.; m. Laura Kenner, Sept. 17, 1935; children: James Kenner, William Sumner. BS in Bus., Ind. U., 1934; JD with distinction, U. Mich., 1937. BAr: Ind. 1937, U.S. Dist. Ct. (no. dist.) Ind. 1937. Assoc. Slaymaker, Merrell, Locke, Indpls., 1937-42; spl. agt. FBI, 1942-45; ptnr. Gordon, Glenn, Miller, Bendall & Branham, Huntington, Ind., 1945—. Dir. Garrett Industries, Inc., Weaver Popcorn Co., Inc., Shuttleworth, Inc. Bd. dirs. Huntington YMCA Found., Huntington Coll. Found.; trustee Huntington Coll., 1971-80. Fellow Am. Coll. Trial Lawyers, Am. Bar Found., Ind. Bar Found.; mem. ABA, Ind. Satte Bar Assn. (pres. 1973-74), Am. Judicature Soc., Ft. Wayne Country Club, Oak Arbor Club (Vero Beach, Fla.), Masons Republican. Presbyterian. Home: 1510 Oak Harbor Blvd Apt 301 Vero Beach FL 32967-7360

GORDON, YEVGENIY I. mathematician, educator; b. Nizhnii Novgorod, Russia, Aug. 17, 1949; arrived in U.S., 1999; s. Israel I. Gordon and Nina A. Guber; m. Irina N. Ginzbourg, Nov. 5, 1968; 1 child, Igor Y. M in Math., Nizhnii Novgorod State U., 1971; PhD in Math. (hon.), Moscow State Pedagogical Inst., 1982; DSc in Physics and Math. (hon.), Novosibirsk (Russia) Inst. Math., 1994. Tchg. asst. Nizhmi Novgorod State U., 1971—78, from asst. to full prof., 1978—99; vis. prof. U. Ill., Champaign-Urbana, 1999—2001; asst. prof. Ea. Ill. U., Charleston, 2001—. Author: Non Stand Methods in Commutative Harmonic Analysis, 1977; co-author: Infinitesimal Analysis, 2002. Grantee, Russian Found. for Basic Rsch., Moscow, 1995—98, 1998—99. Mem.: Assn. for Symbolic Logic, Math. Assn. Am., Am. Math. Soc. Office: Ea Ill Univ Dept Math 600 Lincoln Ave Charleston IL 61920

GORDON-LOVE, SHAREL E. consumer products company executive, writer; b. Plainfield, N.J., Oct. 18, 1962; d. Ronald A. Gordon and Coretha Cobb; children: Khayree McCauley, Ronald Love, Sophia Love children: Alvin Love Jr. Author: (novels) When He Calls, 2002, Pentecostal. Avocations: writing, reading, softball, travel. Personal E-mail: slove@snet.net. Business E-Mail: slove@bdfusa.com.

GORDON-SEIFERT, CATHERINE ELIZABETH, musicologist, educator; b. Columbus, Ohio, Jan. 13, 1954; d. George D. and Virginia H. Gordon; m. Lewis Carl Seifert, Aug. 30, 1986; children: Andrew, Patrick. MusB, Bowling Green State U., 1976; MusM, Ind. U., 1981; PhD, U. Mich., 1994. Prof. music Boston Conservatory of Music, 1996—98; prof. Providence Coll., 1996—98, assoc. prof., 1998—. Freelance harpsichordist, Providence, 1989—. Contbr. essays to books. Fellow, Mortar Bd., 1986—87, U. Mich., 1986—87, Ctr. Nat. Rsch. Sci., Paris, 2001. Mem.: Coll. Music Soc., Soc. for 17t Century Music, Am. Musicol. Soc. Democrat. Congregational. Avocations: gardening, movies, cooking. Office: Providence Coll Dept Music Providence RI 02918 E-mail: cgordon@providence.edu.

GORDY, BERRY, entrepreneur, record company executive, motion picture executive; b. Detroit, Nov. 28, 1929; children from a previous marriage: Berry IV, Hazel Joy, Terry James, Kerry A., Sherry R., Kennedy W., Stefan K., Rhonda Ross-Kendrick. PhD of Music(hon.), Ea. Mich. U., 1971. Founder, chmn. bd. dirs. Motown Record Corp., 1961—; chmn. bd. dirs. The Gordy Co.; exec. prodr. motion pictures; chmn. bd. dirs. West Grand Media, 1998—; founder, chmn. bd. Jobete Music Co., Inc., 1997—. Dir.: (films) Mahogany, 1975; exec. prodr.: Lady Sings the Blues, 1972, Bingo Long Traveling All-Stars and Motor Kings, 1975, Berry Gordy's the Last Dragon, 1984; author: To Be Loved: The Music, the Magic, the Memories of Motown, 1994. Named star, Hollywood Walk of Fame, 1996; named to Minority Hall of Fame, Atlanta U. Sch. Bus. Adminstrn., 1981, Leading Entrepreneurs of Nation, Babson Coll., 1978, Rock and Roll Hall of Fame, 1988, Nat. Bus. Hall of Fame, Jr. Achievement, 1998; recipient Bus. Achievement award, Interracial Coun. for Bus. Opportunity, 1967, Golden Mike and MLK, Jr.'s Leadership award, NATRA, 1969, 2d Ann. Am. Music award for outstanding contbn. to music industry, 1975, Whitney M. Young Jr. award, L.A. Urban League, 1980, Trustees award, NARAS, 1991, 20th Century award, Black Radio Exclusive, 1993, Abe Olman Pub. award, Songwriters Hall of Fame, 1993, Livetime Achievement award, Black Bus. Assn., 1993, Generation award, Congl. Black Caucus Found., 1993, Am. Legend award, ASCAP Pop Music Awards, 1998, Lifetime Achievement award, NABOB, 1998, Legend award, BESLA, 1998, A.G. Gaston Lifetime Achievement award, Black Ent./Bank of Am., 2001, Wall St. Project Millennium award, Rainbow/Push, 2000, Legend award, Rainbow/Push Coalition, 2001; fellow Gordon Grand fellow, Yale U., 1985. Mem.: NAACP, Acad. Motion Picture Arts and Scis., BMI, Dirs. Guild Am. Office: West Grand Media LLC Ste 724 6255 W Sunset Blvd Los Angeles CA 90028-7412

GORE, ALBERT, JR., former Vice President of the United States; b. Washington, Mar. 31, 1948; s. Albert and Pauline (LaFon) G.; m. Mary Elizabeth Aitcheson, May 19, 1970; children: Karenna, Kristin, Sarah, Albert III. BA cum laude (Univ. scholar), Harvard U., 1969; postgrad., Grad. Sch. of Religion, Vanderbilt U., 1971-72, Law Sch., 1974-76. Investigative reporter, editorial writer The Tennessean, 1971-76; homebuilder and land developer Tanglewood Home Builders Co., 1971-76; livestock and tobacco farmer, from 1973; mem. 95th-98th Congresses from Tenn., 1977-85; U.S. senator from Tenn., 1985-93; v.p. served under Pres. Clinton U.S., 1993-2001; Dem. candidate for Pres., 2000; vice chmn. Metropolitan West Fin., Los Angeles, Calif., 2001—. Bd. dirs. Apple Computer Inc.; vis. prof. Columbia U. Sch. Journalism, 2001, Fisk U., Middle Tenn. State U., UCLA, 2001—. Author: Earth in the Balance: Ecology and the Human Spirit, 1992. Served with U.S. Army, 1969-71, Vietnam. Mem. Farm Bur., Tenn. Jaycees Clubs: Am. Legion, VFW. Democrat. Baptist.*

GORE, DAVID CURTISS, investor; b. Conway, S.C., Dec. 4, 1964; BS in Fin., U. S.C., 1986. Co-owner, v.p., software co. exec. Gem-Clarke Co., Inc., Columbia, SC, 1985—89; cons. Columbia, SC, 1989—95; exec. Tomlin & Co. Inc.; investor, investment banker and venture capital investor Columbia, SC, 1995—2001. Mem.: Lambda Chi Alpha (treas. 1984—85). Republican. Baptist. Office: PO Box 7304 Columbia SC 29202-7304

GORE, JAMES ARNOLD, biology educator, aquatic ecologist, hydrologist; b. Los Alamos, N.Mex., Sept. 3, 1949; s. Kenneth and Margaret Emma (Arnold) G.; m. Gertrude Morron, Aug. 21, 1971 (div. 1978); children: Sarah Elizabeth, James Matthew; m. Ellen Diane O'Quinn, Mar. 8, 1980 (div. 1994); 1 child, Erin Kathleen; m. Susan Carol Nichols, May 20, 2002. BA, U. Colo., 1971; MA, U. Mont., 1976, PhD, 1981. Rsch. aquatic biologist Wyo. Water Resources Res. Inst., Laramie, 1978-80; rsch. assoc. Tenn. Coop. Fisheries Res. Unit, Cookeville, Tenn., 1980-81; assoc. prof. U. Tulsa, 1981-90; prof., dir. Ctr. for Field Biology Austin Peay State U., Clarksville, Tenn., 1990-92; eminent scholar chair in environ. sci. Troy (Ala.) State U., 1992-94; dir. environ. protection The Conservancy SW Fla., Naples, Fla., 1994-96; prof., dir. environ. sci. grad. program Columbus (Ga.) State U., 1996—. Guest prof. Zoologishes Inst. U., Karlsruhe, Fed. Republic of Germany, 1985; rsch. ecologist Waterways Experiment Sta., Vicksburg, Miss., 1986-88; vis. prof. U. Cape Town, South Africa, 1989; mem. adv. bd. ecohydrology UNESCO Internat. Hydrol. Programme. Author and editor: The Restoration of Rivers and Streams, 1985, Alternatives in Regulated River Management, 1989. With USN, 1971-74, Vietnam. Fulbright scholar, South Africa, 1989. Mem. AAAS, Am. Inst. Biol. Scis., N.Am. Benthological Soc., South African Soc. Aquatic Scientists, N.Z. Limnological Soc. Achievements include research in hydraulic stream ecology and regulated river management. Office: Columbus State Univ Coll of Science Dept Environ Sci & Pub Heal Columbus GA 31907

GORE, RICHARD MICHAEL, radiologist; b. Chgo., July 1, 1953; s. George Joseph and Dorothy Jane (Freeman) G.; m. Margaret Dembo, Dec. 27, 1981; 3 children. BS, Northwestern U., Chgo., 1975; MD, Northwestern U., 1977. Diplomate Am. Bd. Radiology, Nat. Bd. Med. Examiners. Chief radiology resident Northwestern U., Chgo., 1980-81; clin. instr. U. Calif. Med. Ctr., San Francisco, 1981-82; asst. prof. radiology Northwestern U., Chgo., 1982-84, assoc. prof. radiology, 1984-90, prof. radiology, 1990—; attending radiologist Northwestern Meml. Hosp., Chgo., 1982-91, VA Lakeside Hosp., Chgo., 1983-91; sr. attending radiologist Evanston (Ill.) Hosp., 1992—. Vice-chmn. dept. radiology Evanston Northwe. Healthcare, 1995-2000. Editor: Textbook Gastrointestinal Radiology; mem. editl. bd Am. Jour. Roentgenology, The Radiologist; contbr. articles to profl. jours. Fellow ACP, Internat. Cancer Imaging Soc., Am. Coll. Radiology, Am. Coll. Angiology, Am. Coll. Gastroenterology, Royal Coll. Medicine; mem. AMA, Am. Coll. Physician Execs., European Soc. Radiology, European Soc. Gastrointestinal and Abdominal Radiology, Soc. Computed Body Tomography/Magnetic Resonance, Soc. Gastrointestinal Radiologists, Soc. Ultrasound in Medicine, Radiol. Soc. N.Am., Assn. Univ. Radiologists, Am. Roentgen Ray Soc., Brit. Inst. Radiology, Soc. Thoracic Radiology. Office: Evanston Hosp Dept Radiology Evanston IL 60201 E-mail: rmgore1953@aol.com.

GORE, ROBERT W. electronics executive; BSChemE, U. Del., 1959; PhD, U. Minn., 1963. Former pres., CEO W.L. Gore & Assocs., Newark, Del., 1976—, chmn. Mem.: NAE. Achievements include invention of Goretex. Office: W L Gore & Assocs 555 Paper Mill Rd Newark DE 19711*

GORE, STEVEN LOWELL, financial consultant; b. Paducah, Ky., June 22, 1953; BS in Acctg., David Lipscomb U., 1975. CPA Tenn., cert. treas. profl. Analyst fiscal svcs. King Faisal Hosp., Riyadh, Saudi Arabia, 1976—77; facility acct. Am. Retirement Corp., Nashville, 1983; staff auditor Hosp. Corp. of Am., Nashville, 1984—87; contr. Sumner Regional Med. Ctr., Gallatin, Tenn., 1987—2003; cons. Genetics Assocs., Nashville, 1998—; co-owner Genetics of Memphis; cons. Genetics Assn., Nashville, 2003—; co-owner Genetics of Memphis, Tenn. Vol. Margaret Maddox YMCA-East, Nashville, 1997—2000; active Friends of Warner Parks, Nashville, 1996—; poll ofcl. Metro-Davidson County Election Commn., Nashville, 1999. Recipient Appreciation Letter for Svc. United Way of Sumner County, 1997-2000. Mem.: Am. Math. Soc., Math Assn. Am., Nat. Space Soc., Population Reference Bur., World Future Soc., Planetary Soc., N.Y. Acad. of Sci., Am. Pub. Health Assn., Middle Tenn. Healthcare Exec. Assn., Healthcare Fin. Mgmt. Assn., Am. Chem. Soc., AAAS, Cheekwood. Avocations: playing golf, fishing, reading. Home and Office: S Gore Cons 1413 Clifton Ln Nashville TN 37215-1615 E-mail: stevengore@msn.com.

GORE, TIPPER (MARY ELIZABETH GORE), wife of the former vice president of the United States; b. Washington, Aug. 19, 1948; m. Albert Gore Jr., May 19, 1970; children: Karenna, Kristin, Sarah, Albert III. BA in Psychology, Boston U., 1970; MA in Psychology, Vanderbilt U., 1975. Freelance photographer. Mental health policy advisor to pres. Author: Raising PG Kids in an X-Rated Society, 1987, Picture This: A Visual Diary, 1996; co-prodr. (with Nat. Mental Health Assn.) Homeless in America: A Photographic Project. Cofounder Parents Music Resource Ctr., Arlington, Va., 1985; founder Tenn. Voices for Children, 1990; co-chair Am. Goes Back to Sch. Initiative, 1996—; chair Congl. Wives Task Force, 1978-79. Democrat. Office: 2100 West End Ave Nashville TN 37203*

GOREA, LUCIA-IOSEFINA, English educator, writer, poet; b. Oradea, Romania, Apr. 25, 1959; arrived in U.S., 1993; d. Joseph and Emilia Badea; m. Simion Liviu Gorea, Apr. 22, 1989; 1 child, Alex Raoul. MA in Philology, U. Bucharest, Romania, 1986; secondary degree, U. Bucharest, 1989; PhD in English, Atlantic Internat. U., Miami, Fla., 2002. Notary pub. Oreg. English tchr. Magherani H.S., Mures, Romania, 1986—89; English prof. U. Mures, Romania, 1989—92; 2d grade tchr. Columbia Acad., Portland, Oreg., 1998—2000; English instr. Marylhurst (Oreg.) U., 2000—01, Portland C.C., 2000—, tchr. ESL, 2000—, Mt. Hood C.C., Portland, 2000—. Founder, leader Poetry Around the World, Beaverton, Oreg. Contbr. poetry to Echoes of the Century, Eternal Portraits, America at the Millennium, Mirrors (Hon. Mention, 1999), Sunrise and Soft Mist (Editor's Choice award, 1999), Gresham Outlook. Recipient Pres.'s award for lit. excellence, Nat. Authors Registry, 2000, Internat. Poet of Merit award, Internat. Soc. Poets, 2001, Silver award, 2002, Outstanding Achievement in Poetry Silver Cup award, 2003, Bronze Medallion Commemorative award, 2003. Mem.: NEA, Internat. Libr. Poetry (Poet of Merit 2000), Oreg. Edn. Assn. Avocations: reading, writing, philosophy, performing arts, classical music, aquaerobics. Home: 6852SW 180th Ave Aloha OR 97007 Fax: 503-430-8642. E-mail: luciag_esl@yahoo.com.

GORECKI, JOHN PAUL, neurosurgeon, educator; b. Montreal, Que., Can., Jan. 24, 1960; came to U.S., 1990; s. Zbigniew and Irene (Warscewska) Gorecki; children: Mitchel, Alexis. MD, Queens U., Kingston, Can., 1983. Intern in surgery St. Michael's Hosp., Toronto, Ont., Can., 1983-84; resident U. Toronto, 1983-89; Botterel fellow in stereotactic and functional neurosurgery; asst. prof. U. Miss. Med. Ctr., Jackson, 1990-92; neurosurgeon St. Dominic, Jackson, 1992-94; asst. prof. Duke U., Durham, N.C., 1994—. Fellow Royal Coll. Physicians and Surgeons. Avocations: farming, aviation. Office: Wichita Surg Specialists Ste 200 818 N Emporia Wichita KS 67214-3788 E-mail: gorec001@hotmail.com

GORELICK, JAMIE SHONA, lawyer; b. N.Y.C., May 6, 1950; d. Leonard and Shirley (Fishman) G.; m. Richard E. Waldhorn, Sept. 28, 1975; children: Daniel H., Dana E. BA, Harvard U., 1972, JD, 1975. Bar: D.C. 1975, U.S. Dist. Ct. D.C. 1976, U.S. Tax Ct. 1976, U.S. Ct. Claims 1976, U.S. Ct. Appeals (D.C. cir.) 1976, U.S. Ct. Appeals (5th cir.) 1977, U.S. Supreme Ct. 1979, U.S. Ct. Appeals (Fed. cir.) 1982, U.S. Ct. Internat. Trade 1984, U.S. Dist. Ct. Md. 1985, U.S. Ct. Appeals (4th cir.) 1986, U.S. Ct. Appeals (3d. cir.) 1988. With Miller, Cassidy, Larroca & Lewin, Washington, 1975-79, 80-93; asst. to sec., counselor to dep. sec. U.S. Dept. Energy, 1979—80; gen. counsel Dept. Def., 1993—94; dep. atty. gen. Dept. Justice, Washington, 1994-97; vice chair Fannie Mae, Washington, 1997—2003; commr. Nat. Commn. on Terrorist Threats Upon the U.S., 2002—; ptnr. Wilmer, Cutler and Peckering, 2003—. Mem. chmn.'s adv. coun. U.S. Senate Jud. Com., 1988-93; tchr. Trial Advocacy Workshop Harvard Law Sch., Cambridge, Mass., 1982, 84; vice chair task force evaluation of audit investigative inspection components Dept. Def., 1979-80; mem. sec.'s transition team Dept. Energy, 1979; bd. dirs. Fannie Mae, United Technologies Corp., Schlumberger Ltd., Fannie Mae Found., John D. & Catherine T. MacArthur Found., D.C. Coll. Access, Am.'s Promise-Alliance for Youth, Nat. Park Found., Carnegie Endowment, 1989-93, Nat. Women's Law Ctr., 1991-93, Bazelon Ctr. Mental Health Law, Washington Legal Clinic for Homeless, Local Initiatives Support Corp., Nat. Legal Ctr. for the Pub. Interest; bd. overseers Harvard Coll.; mem. nat. security adv. panel CIA; mem. internat. security adv. panel, 1997—, mem. Pres.'s Intelligence Rev. Panel, 2001-2002; mem. threat reduction adv. com. Dept. of Def.; coun. mem. Am. Law Inst., D.C. Bar Found.; co-chair adv. com. Presdl. Commn. on Critical Infrastructure Protection, 1997-99; mem. Nat. Commn. Support Law Enforcement, Washington, 1995—; mem. Supreme Ct. Judicial Fellow. Selection Com. Mem. editl. bd. Corp. Criminal Liability Reporter, 1986-93, Destruction of Evidence, 1989; contbr. articles to profl. jours. Mem. bd. overseers Harvard Coll., 1989-93. Fellow Am. Bar Found.; mem. ABA (chair complex crimes litigation com. litigation sect. 1984-87, vice-chair complex crimes litigation com. 1983-84, Nat. Commn. to Support Law Enforcement, 1995—, sec. litigation sect. 1988-90, coun. mem. 1990-93, com. on profl. discipline, ho. of dels. 1991-93, 97—), D.C. Bar (pres. 1992-93, bd. govs. 1982-88, sec. bd. govs. 1981-92, bar found. advisors 1985-93, legal ethics com.), Womens Bar Assn., Am. Law Inst. (coun.), Coun. on Fgn. Rels. Office: Wilmer Cutler and Pickering 2445 M St NW Washington DC 20037

GORELICK, STEVEN MICHAEL, academic administrator, writer; b. LA, Sept. 26, 1951; s. Richard Henry and Betty Gorelick; m. Amy Susan Green; children: Jean-Marc William, Rebecca Ann, Molly Joanna. M.A., Columbia U., 1976, Ed.M., 1978; PhD, CUNY, 1995. Spl. asst. to pres. CUNY Grad. Ctr., N.Y.C., 1990—2000, v.p. instl. advancement, 2001—. Contbr. numerous essays and revs. to profl. jours. Recipient Candace Rogers award, Ea. Sociol. Soc., 1984, Gene Carte prize, Am. Soc. Criminology, 1985. Avocations: long distance cycling, 20th century European and American history. Office: CUNY Grad Ctr 365 5th Ave New York NY 10016 E-mail: sgorelick@gc.cuny.edu.

GOREN, STEVEN ELIOT, lawyer; b. Detroit, Apr. 9, 1960; s. Robert and Judith A. (Wise) G.; m. Eva Calmidis, Sept. 25, 1980; children: Robert C., Sophia J. BA with high distinction, U. Mich., 1981, JD cum laude, 1984. Bar: Mich. 1984, Ohio 2001, U.S. Dist. Ct. (ea. dist.) Mich. 1984. Atty. Dickinson, Wright, Moon, VanDusen & Freeman, Bloomfield Hills, Mich., 1984-86, pvt. practice, Birmingham, Mich., 1986—91. Adjunct prof. U. Detroit Law Sch., 1989-95; med. malpractice task force Mich. Trial lawyers, 1989; mem. litigation adv. com., Inst. Continuing Legal Edn. Contbr. articles to profl. jours. Precinct Del. Democratic Party, Beverly Hills, Mich., 1990-91. Mem.: Mich. Trial Lawyers Assn. (exec. bd. 2000—03). Office: 30400 Telegraph Rd Ste 470 Bingham Farms MI 48025-5818

GORENBERG, CHARLES LLOYD, financial services executive; b. Phila., Mar. 1, 1938; s. Abraham and Esther (Freedman) G.; m. Roslyn Grobman, May 22, 1960; children: David M., Kenneth M. BA, Franklin & Marshall Coll., 1960; MS, The Am. Coll., Bryn Mawr, Pa., 1981. Cert. Employee Benefit Specialist, CLU, ChFC. Sales assoc. Landis & Co., Phila., 1960-62; agt. Phoenix Mut. Life, Phila., 1962-64, supr., 1964-67; dir. tng. Rittenhouse Assocs., Phila., 1967-75; exec. v.p. Corp. Pension Actuaries, Phila., 1975-91; pres. Delta Fin. Group, Phila., 1991-97, Chaslyn Fin. Group, Marlton, N.J., 1997—. Co-editor: (book) Planning for Business Owners and Professionals, 1988; contbr. over 35 articles to mags. Mem. Internat. Soc. Cert. Employee Benefit Specialists, Am. Soc. CLUs and ChFCs (various offices), Am. Soc. Pension Actuaries. Avocation: golf. Office: Chaslyn Fin Group 1002 Lincoln Dr W Ste C Marlton NJ 08053-1531

GORENBERG, NORMAN BERNARD, aeronautical engineer, consultant, retired; b. St. Louis, May 18, 1923; s. Isadore and Ethel G.; m. Lucille Richmond, June 10, 1947; children: Judith Allyn Gorenberg Stein, Carol Ann Gorenberg, Gershom Gorenberg. BSME, Washington U., St. Louis, 1949. Registered profl. engr., Mo. Aero. engr. USAF Wright Air Devel. Ctr., Dayton, Ohio, 1949-51; aerodynamicist McDonnell Aircraft Corp., St. Louis, 1951-59; supervisory engr. Boeing Co., Vertol Div., Phila., 1959-62; R & D engr. Lockheed Corp., Burbank, Calif., 1962-89; vertical takeoff and landing aircraft cons. Dana Point, Calif., 1989-94; ret., 1994. Contbr. articles to profl. reports. With USAAF, 1943-46. Mem. AIAA, ASME, Am. Helicopter Soc. (chmn. St. Louis sect. 1955-56, nat. aerodyns. com. 1969-70, tech. dir. western region 1969-70), Nat. Mgmt. Assn. (life). Jewish.

GORENCE, PATRICIA JOSETTA, judge; b. Sheboygan, Wis., Mar. 6, 1943; d. Joseph and Antonia (Marinsheck) G.; m. John Michael Bach, July 11, 1969; children: Amy Jane, Mara Jo, J. Christopher Bach. BA, Marquette U., 1965, JD, 1977; MA, U. Wis., 1969. Bar: Wis. 1977, U.S. Dist. Ct. (ea. and we. dists.) Wis. 1977, U.S. Ct. Appeals (7th cir.) 1979, U.S. Supreme Ct. 1980. Asst. U.S. atty. U.S. Atty.'s Office, Milw., 1979-84, 1st asst. U.S. Atty., 1984-87, 89-91, U.S. Atty., 1987-88; dep. atty. gen. State of Wis. Dept. Justice, Madison, 1991-93; assoc. Ginbel, Reilly, Guerin & Brown, Milw., 1993-94; U.S. magistrate judge U.S. Dist. Ct. Wis., Milw., 1994—. Bd. dirs. U. Wis.-Milw. Slovenian Arts Coun., 1989—, treas., 1989—, Milw. Dance Theatre, 1993-98; bd. chair Bottomless Closet, 1999—. Recipient Spl. Commendation, U.S. Dept. Justice, 1986, IRS, 1988. Mem. ABA, Am. Law Inst., Nat. Assn. Women Judges, Fed. Magistrate Judges Assn. (cir. dir. 1997-2000), Milw. Bar Assn. (chair cmty. rels. com. 2000—, Prosecutor of Yr. 1990), State Bar Wis. (chair lawyer dispute resolution com. 1986—, chair professionalism com. 1988-2000, vice chair legal edn. commn. 1994-96, Pres. award 1995), 7th Cir. Bar Assn. (chair rules and practices com. 1991-95), Assn. for Women Lawyers, Profl. Dimensions (sec. 1998-2000, v.p. adminstrn. 2000-2002).

GORENSTEIN, DAVID G. chemistry and biochemistry educator; b. Oct. 6, 1945; s. Ben and Shirley (Adelberg) G.; m. Deborah H. Joseph, June 11, 1967; 1 child, Jennifer. BS in Chemistry, M.I.T., 1966; MA in Chemistry, Harvard U., 1967, PhD in Chemistry, 1969. Asst. prof. U. Ill., Chgo., 1969-73, assoc. prof., 1973-76, prof., 1976-85; prof. chemistry Purdue Univ., West Lafayette, Ind., 1985-94; dir. Purdue Biochem. MRI Lab., West Lafayette, Ind., 1985-94, NSF Nat. Biol. Facilities Ctr., West Lafayette, 1987-93, NMR and Structural Biology Cores, West Lafayette, 1988-94; dep. dir. NIH Designated AIDS Rsch. Ctr., West Lafayette, 1993-94; prof. human biol. chemistry and genetics U. Tex. Med. Sch., Galveston, 1994—; sr. investigator Sealy Ctr. Molecular Sci. U. Tex. Med. Br., Galveston, 1994—; dir. Nuclear Magnetic Resonance Ctr. U. Tex. Med. Br., Galveston, dir. Sealy Ctr. for Structural Biology, 1995—2002, dep. dir. NIEHS Ctr., 1996—, Charles Marc Pomerat Disting. Prof. of biology, 1997—, vice chmn. human biol. chem. genetics, 1999—2002, assoc. dean rsch., 2002—. Dir. Gulf Coast NMR Consortium; vis. assoc. prof. U. Wis., Madison, 1975; vis. prof. Oxford U., 1977-78, U. Calif., San Francisco, 1986; adj. prof. Biomed. Engring. U. Tex., Austin, 1996—; cons. Baxter Travenol, 1985-95, Merck and Co., 1988, Eli Lilly, 1987-89, Ill. Tool Works, 1973-85, Chronomatic Inc., 1973-85, U.S. Dept. of Labor, 1975, Continental Group, Inc., 1982-84, Abbott Corp., 2001- Abbott Diagnostics, 2002; active numerous univ. coms.; lectr. in field. Editor Bull. of Magnetic Resonance, 1982-99; mem. editorial bd. Magnetic Resonance Revs., 1983-93, Jour. Magnetic Resonance, 1992-99, Biophys. Jour., 1992-98; pub. abstracts; contbr. articles to profl. jours. Grantee: NSF, 1987-93, NIH, 1970—, Eli Lilly, 1988-94 and numerous others; tchg. fellow Harvard U., 1966-69, trainee summer fellow NSF, 1966, predoctoral fellow NIH, 1967-69, Alfred P. Sloan fellow 1975-79, Sr. Rsch. fellow Fulbright, 1977-78, Guggenheim fellow, 1986; recipient Internat. Lectr. award Fulbright, 1978. Fellow AAAS; mem. Am. Soc. for Biochemistry and Molecular Biology, Am. Chem. Soc. (program chmn. divsn. biol. chemistry 1985-87, vice chmn. Purdue sect. 1990-91, chmn. 1991-92), Biophys. Soc., Protein Soc., Sigma Xi, Phi Lambda Upsilon. Achievements include patents in process for Preparing Dithiophosphate Oligonucleotide Analogs via Nucleoside Thiophosphoramidite Intermediates and in vivo selection of aptamers; research in proteomics and applications of NMR spectroscopy and other physical techniques to biological systems, theoretical bio-organic chemistry, biomolecular design; cancer and anti-viral drugs development. Address: 3922 Crown Ridge Ct Houston TX 77059-3711 Office: U Tex Med Br Sch Medicine Galveston TX 77555-1157

GORENSTEIN, SAMUEL, retired mathematician, educator; s. Isidore and Bessie Gorenstein; m. Shirley Slotkin, July 3, 1948; children: Ethan Ezra, Gabriel William. PhD, N.Y. U., 1968. Sr. mathematician Sys. Devel. Corp., Paramus, NJ, 1959—63; mathematician advisor IBM, Armonk, NY, 1963—89. Adj. prof. Poly. Inst. N.Y., N.Y. U., N.Y.C., 1968—83. Contbr. articles. Vol. math tutor Union Settlement Cmty. Ctr., N.Y.C., 1997—2000. 2nd lt. navigator Army AC, 1943—45, European Theatre of Operations. Fellow, NASA, 1966. Mem.: Ops. Rsch. Soc. (chair constructed sci. sect. 1975—81). Achievements include development of constructed price index for total cost of computing systems. Personal E-mail: samgoren12@aol.com.

GORES, CHRISTOPHER MERREL, lawyer; b. N.Y.C., Aug. 27, 1943; s. Guido James and Mary (Callaway) G.; children: Ellen, Eugenia. AB, Princeton U., 1965; LLB, Columbia U., 1968. Bar: N.Y. 1968, Tex. 1973, U.S. Dist. Ct (no. dist.) Tex. 1977. Assoc. Akin, Gump, Strauss, Hauer & Feld, LLP, Dallas, 1973-79, ptnr., 1979—. Bd. dirs. Shakespeare Festival of Dallas, 1982-88. Lt. USNR, 1969-72. Office: Akin Gump Strauss Hauer & Feld LLP 1700 Pacific Ave Ste 4100 Dallas TX 75201-4675 E-mail: cgores@akingump.com.

GORES, THOMAS C. lawyer; b. Milw., Sept. 24, 1948; s. Kenneth W. and Carolyn (Camblin) G.; m. Ann P. Pacelli, June 13, 1970; children: Lauren, Jake, Kathryn. BA, U. Notre Dame, 1970, JD, 1973; LLM, U. Miami, 1977. Bar: Wash. 1973, U.S. Tax Ct. 1973. Assoc., then ptnr. Bogle & Gates, Seattle, 1973-78, ptnr., 1978-93, Gores & Blais, Seattle, 1993-2001, Perkins Coie LLP, 2001—. Fellow Am. Coll. Trust and Estate Counsel; mem. Wash. State Bar Assn., Seattle Estate Planning Coun. (pres.). Office: Perkins Coie Ste 4800 1420 5th Ave Seattle WA 98101 E-mail: tgores@goresblais.com.

GORES, TOM T. investment company executive; B, Mich. State U. Entrepreneur; CEO Platinum Equity, L.A., 1995—. Bd. dirs. St. Joseph's Hosp., L.A., UCLA Med. Ctr. Office: Platinum Equity 2049 Century Park E Ste 2700 Los Angeles CA 90906*

GORHAM, BRADFORD, lawyer; b. Providence, Mar. 7, 1935; s. Sayles and Ruth C. (Campbell) G.; m. Diann Gebow, Aug. 1, 1959; children: Christopher, Nicholas, Joshua, Jane, Nancy. Degree, Dartmouth Coll., 1957, Harvard U., 1964. Bar: R.I. 1964. Ptnr. Gorham & Gorham, Scituate, R.I., 1964—. State rep. R.I. State Ho. of Reps., Providence, 1969-70, 77-90; state senator R.I. State Senate, Providence, 1991-97. Capt. USMC, 1957-60. Named Legislator of Yr. Nat. Conf. State Legislatures, 1985, Outstanding Legislator Am. Legis. Exch. Coun., 1986. Republican. Home: 11 Cucumber Hill Rd Foster RI 02825-1211 Office: Gorham & Gorham 25 Danielson Pike Scituate RI 02857-1801

GORHAM, EVILLE, ecologist, biogeochemist; b. Halifax, N.S., Can., Oct. 15, 1925; s. Ralph Arthur and Shirley Agatha (Eville) G.; m. Ada Verne MacLeod, Sept. 29, 1948; children: Kerstin, Vivien, Jocelyn, James. BSc in Biology with distinction, Dalhousie U., 1945, MSc in Zoology, 1947, LLD (hon.), 1991; PhD in Botany, U. London, Eng., 1951; DSc (hon.), McGill U., 1993, U. Minn., 1999. Lectr. botany U. Coll., London, Eng., 1951-54; sr. sci. officer Freshwater Biol. Assn., Ambleside, Eng., 1954-58; lectr., asst. prof. botany U. Toronto, 1958-62; assoc. prof. botany U. Minn., Mpls., 1962-65, prof., 1966-75, head dept., 1967-71, prof. ecology, 1975-84, Regents' prof. ecology and botany, 1984-98, Regents' prof. emeritus, 1999—; prof., head dept. biology U. Calgary, Alta., Can., 1965-66. Mem. for Can., Internat. Commn. on Atmospheric Chemistry and Radioactivity, 1959-62; mem. vis. panel to rev. toxicology program NAS-NRC, 1974-75, mem. com. on inland aquatic ecosys. Water Sci. and Tech. Bd., 1994-96, mem. com. to evaluate indicators for monitoring aquatic and terrestrial environments Water Sci. and Tech. Bd., 1997-99, mem. com. on hydrologic sci. bd. on Atmospheric Scis. and Climate, 1998-99; mem. coordinating com. for sci. and tech. assessment environ. pollutants Environ. Studies Bd., 1975-78; mem. com. on med. and biologic effects of environ. pollutants Assembly Life Scis., 1976-77; mem. com. to recommend nat. program for assessing problem of atmospheric deposition (acid rain) President's Coun. on Environ. Quality, 1978; mem. com. on atmosphere and biosphere Bd. Agr. and Renewable Resources, 1979-81; mem. panel on environ. impact diesel impact study com. NAE-NRC, 1980-81; mem. U.S.-Can.-Mex. joint sci. com. on acid precipitation Environ. Studies Bd., NAS-NRC, Royal Soc. Can., Mex. Acad. Scis., 1981-84; mem. health and environ. rsch. adv. com. U.S. Dept. Energy, 1992-94; mem. Water Sci. and Tech. Bd. NAS-NRC, 1996-99; mem. coun. sci. advisors Marine Biol. Lab., Woods Hole, Mass., 1996-99. Mem. editl. bd. Ecology, 1965-67, Limnology and Oceanography, 1970-72, Conservation Biology, 1987-88, Ecol. Applications, 1989-92, Environ. Revs., 1992—; contbr. articles on limnology, ecology, and biogeochemistry to profl. jours. Bd. dirs. Acid Rain Found., 1982-87, sec.-treas. 1982-84 Recipient Regents' medal U. Minn., 1984, Benjamin Franklin medal in earth sci. Franklin Inst., Phila., 2000; Royal Soc. Can. rsch. fellow State Forest Rsch. Inst., Stockholm, Sweden, 1950-51; grantee NSF, AEC, NIH, ERDA, NASA, Dept. of Energy, NRC Can., Ont. Rsch. Found., Environment Can., Office Water Resources Rsch., Dept. Interior, Andrew W. Mellon Found., N.Y.C. Fellow AAAS, Royal Soc. Can., Am. Acad. Arts and Scis.; mem. NAS, Am. Soc. Limnology and Oceanography (G. Evelyn Hutchinson medal 1986), Ecol. Soc. Am., Internat. Assn. Theoretical and Applied Limnology, Soc. Wetland Scientists, Swedish Phytogeog. Soc. (hon.), Gown in Town Club. Home: 1933 E River Ter Minneapolis MN 55414-3673

GORHAM, RAMSAY L. state legislator, political organization administrator; b. Rocky Mount, N.C., July 11, 1951; BA, Converse Coll., S.C. Artist; mem. N. Mex. Senate, Dist. 10., Sante Fe, 1996—; mem. edn. com., mem. rules com.; chmn. Republican Party N.Mex., 2003—. Republican. Office: 805 Salamanca St NW Albuquerque NM 87107-5619*

GORHAM, WILLIAM, organization executive; b. N.Y.C., Dec. 14, 1930; s. Jack and Fay (Blank) G.; m. Gail Wiley Finsterbusch, 1973; children from previous marriage: Sarah, Nancy, Kim, Jennifer, Becky. Student, MIT, 1949-50; BA, Stanford U., 1952; LLD (hon.), Trinity Coll., 1996. Mem. rsch. staff RAND Corp., 1953-62; dep. asst. sec. def. U.S., 1962-65; asst. sec. health, edn. and welfare, 1965-68; co-chmn. (with Daniel Bell) Pres.'s Panel Social Indicators, 1967-68; chmn. Pres.'s Task Force on Child Devel., 1966; pres. Urban Inst., Washington, 1968-2000, pres. emeritus, life trustee, 2000—. Bd. dirs. Insituform Group Ltd., 1986-92, chmn., 1987-92; bd. dirs Insituform Techs., Inc., 1992-97; mem. Internat. Commn. on Edn. for 21st Century, Delors Commn., UNESCO, 1992-97; mem. U.S. adv. com. Internat. Inst. Applied Sys. Analysis, 1974-82; bd. dirs.-at-large Social Sci. Rsch. Coun. Editor: (with Nathan Glazer) The Urban Predicament, 1976; mem. bd. editors Policy Scis, 1969—, Jour. Policy Analysis and Mgmt., 1980—. Bd. dirs. Price Charities, 2000—, San Diego Revitalization Corp., 2002—. Recipient Disting. Civilian Svc. award U.S. Dept. Def., 1965. Mem. Nat. Acad. Pub. Adminstrn., Assn. Pub. Policy Analysis and Mgmt. (policy coun. 1979-85), Cosmos Club (Washington). Office: Urban Institute 2100 M St NW Washington DC 20037-1264

GORIN, ABBYE ALEXANDER, electronics researcher; b. Houston, Aug. 22, 1927; d. Albert Arthur and Sophie Pepper Alexander; m. Steve Gorin, Jan. 29, 1947; children: Polly, Robin Montz. BFA, U. Tex., 1947; MS, U. New Orleans, 1985; PhD, Va. Poly. Inst. and State U., 1989. Radio writer Sta. KVET, Austin, 1947-48; writer, layout artist Houston Chronicle, 1948-49; ptnr., head acctg. and advt. Plastic Engineered Products Inc., Metairie, La., 1962-81; rsch. assoc. U. New Orleans, 1985, Va. Poly. Inst. and State U., Blacksburg, 1986-88; acting curator Southeastern Archtl. Archive Tulane U., New Orleans, 1992-93. Co-founder, designer photog. archive, inventoried 1st 10,000 images Latin Am. Libr., Tulane U., New Orleans, 1979. Designer, photographer: (photographic book) Saint Louis Cemeteries of New Orleans, 1963; author, co-prodr.: (TV spls.) Angela Gregory, Master Sculptor, 1985, Samuel Wilson Jr., Dean of Architectural Preservation in New Orleans, 1986, A Walking Tour of St. Louis Cemeteries, No. 1 and 2, 1986, (e-books) Nathaniel Curtis, FAIA, My Life in Modern Architecture, 2002, The Rivergate (1968-1995) Architecture and Politics No Strangers In Pair-A-Dice, 2002; author: (books) A Guide to Photographic Collections in New Orleans, 1987, Conversations with Samuel Wilson Jr., 1991, Learning from Samuel Wilson Jr., 1992, Abraham Guillén Melgar: The Art of Documentary Photography, A Peruvian Son's Contribution to the World Data Base of Social Scientific Photography, 2001; prodr., contbg. writer: (TV spl.) Chinese Traditional Architecture, 1987; prodr., writer: (laser disc) A Visual Text: Architectural History, 1988; project dir., info. designer, contbg. writer e-books The Rivergate, 1968-95, Architecture and Politics, No Strangers in Pair-A-Dice, 2000; co-adaptor for e-book, co-editor, visual editor Nathaniel Curtis, My Life in Modern Architecture, 2001.; prodr., writer poster The Rise and Demise of the Rivergate Exhibition Center, 1968-1995, 2000; continuity writer radio scripts for books Nathaniel Curtis, FAIA, My Life in Modern Architecture, 2002, The Rivergate (1968-1995), Architecture and Politics No Strangers in Pair-A-Dice; co-prodr. (CD-ROM) Curtis and Rivergate E-books; prodr., dir., writer video The Pitot House on Bayou St. John, 1994; author (video) Remembering an historic moment in our recent past, 1995. Archtl. activist Friends of Rivergate, New Orleans, 1993-95. Unitarian Universalist. Avocations: travel, swimming, hiking.

GORIN, BARNEY FRANKLIN, spacecraft systems, propulsion and robotics engineer; b. San Antonio, Oct. 20, 1945; s. Maurice and Dorothy Gertrude (Gemberling) G.; m. Gloria Jean Theye, Aug., 1966 (div. Oct. 1978); 1 child, Jennifer Anne; m. Cynthia Ulrich, Feb. 8, 1980 (div. 1990); m. Janis Tabor, July 18, 1993; stepchildren: Garret Lawrence Kulp, John Frank Kulp, Christopher Tabor-Fritts. BSAE, Tri-State Coll., 1965; MSAE, U. Notre Dame, 1968; MBA, Canisius Coll., 1972. Project engr. Cornell Aero. Lab., Buffalo, N.Y., 1968-70; sec., treas. Janik Paving, Inc., Buffalo, 1971-76; v.p. Zack Construction Corp., Buffalo, 1977-80; project engr. Hamilton Standard Div. United Tech., Windsor Locks, Conn., 1980-84, Fairchild Space Co., Germantown, Md., 1984—95, Go Ventures, Inc., Gaithersburg, Md., 1996—. Inventor in field; contbr. articles to profl. jours. Fellow AIAA (assoc., liquid propulsion tech. com. 1985-89, 2002—, space automation and robitic tech. com. 1990-91, servicable spacecraft com. on standards 1988-90, standards tech. coun. 1991-93); mem. ASME. Republican. Avocations: flying, travel, collecting books. Home: 465 Golden Ash Mews Gaithersburg MD 20878-5642 Office: Go Ventures Inc Box 83549 Gaithersburg MD 20383

GORIN, RALPH EDGAR, software engineer, consultant; b. Boston, Dec. 24, 1948; s. William and Helaine Miriam (Falkson) G. BS, MS, Rensselaer Polytech. Inst., 1970; postgrad., Stanford (Calif.) U., 1970-72. Mem. tech. staff Sanders Assocs., Nashua, N.H., 1970, Stanford U., 1972-76, mem. mgmt., 1976-87, dir. acad. computing, 1987-91; tech. staff XKL LLC, Redmond, Wash., 1992—. Bd. dirs. Ibuki, Inc., Mountain View, Calif. Author: Introduction to DECsystem-20 Assembly Language, 1981. Treas. Tom Nolan for Congress, 1992; chair 45th Dist. Dems., 2001—. Achievements include invention of computer spelling check and correction system. Office: XKL LLC 8420 154th Ave NE Redmond WA 98052-3800

GORIN, ROBERT MURRAY, JR., history educator; b. Oct. 29, 1948; s. Robert Murray and Vivian Margaret (Schleider) Gorin. AB, MA, Xavier U., 1970; MS in Edn., Hofstra U., 1974; MA, Fordham U., 1978; PhD, St. Louis U., 1980; MS, Johns Hopkins U., 1992; postgrad., Yale U., Harvard U., Civil War Inst., Gettburg Coll., U. Calif., Berkeley, Oxford U. Cert. N.Y. State Edn. Dept. Tchr. social studies Bellmore-Merrick (N.Y.) Ctrl. H.S. Dist., 1974—77, 1978—83, Rockville Centre (N.Y.) Union Free Sch. Dist., 1977—78, Manhasset (N.Y.) Pub. Sch., 1983—. Adj. asst. prof. history Hofstra U., 1986—. Mem. N.Y. Pub. Libr. With USAR, 1968—69. Fellow, Robert A. Taft Inst. Govt., 1976, Soc. Values in Higher Edn. Mem.: Moral Edn. Assn., Nat. Coun History Edn. Assn. for Preservation of Civil War Sites, Civil War Soc., Soc. Civil War Historians, N.Y. Hist. Soc., N.Y. State Coun. Social Studies, L.I. Coun. Social Studies, Nat. Coun. Social Studies, Soc. History Edn., Ctr. for Study Presidency, Orgn. History Edn., Orgn. Am. Historians, So. Hist. Assn., Am. Hist. Assn., Am. Mus. Natural History, Civil War Round Table N.Y., Worcester Coll. Assocs., Am. Friends of Bodleian Libr., Taft Assocs., Friends of Nat. Pks. Gettysburg, Am. Friends of Rowley House, Oxford, Met. Mus. Art, Met. Opera Guild, ASCD, Phi Alpha Theta. Republican. Roman Catholic. Home: 51 Somerset Ave Garden City NY 11530-1145

GORING, DAVID ARTHUR INGHAM, chemical engineering educator, scientist; b. Toronto, Ont., Can., Nov. 26, 1920; s. George Ingham and Susan Edna (Jones) G.; m. Elizabeth Dodds Haswell, Aug. 24, 1948; children—James, Rosemary, Christopher. B.Sc., U. London, 1942; PhD, McGill U., 1949, Cambridge U., 1953. Scientist NRC, Halifax, N.S., Can., 1951-55; with PAPRICAN, Pointe Claire, Que., Can., 1955-85, dir. research, 1971-77, v.p. sci., 1977-83, v.p. acad., 1983-85; prof. U. Toronto, 1986—2002; retired. Research assoc. McGill U., 1955-69, sr. research assoc., 1969-86 Contbr. chpts. to books and articles to profl. jours. Patentee in field. Served as flying officer RAF, 1943-46 Recipient Le Sueur Meml. Lecture award Can. Sect. Soc. Chem. Industry, 1988, Notable Achievement award Internat. Symposium on Wood and Pulping Chemistry, 2001. Fellow Royal Soc. Can., Chem. Inst. Can., TAPPI (Gunnar Nicholson Gold medal 1986), Internat. Acad. Wood Sci.; mem. Can. Pulp and Paper Assn. (tech. sect., cert. appreciation 1986, John Bates Meml. Gold medal 1995), Am. Chem. Soc. (cellulose paper textile chemistry div., Anselm Payen award 1973). Anglican. Avocations: fishing, music. Home: 14 1/2 Ottawa St Toronto ON Canada M4T 2B6

GORINSON, STANLEY M. lawyer; b. Bklyn., May 30, 1945; s. Rubin and Lena (Shulman) G.; children: Ross Evan, Hunter Lloyd. BA cum laude, Bklyn. Coll., 1967; JD with honors, Rutgers U., 1973. Bar: N.Y. 1974, U.S. Dist. Ct. (so. dist.) N.Y. 1976, U.S. Ct. Appeals (2nd cir.) 1976, Md. 1984, D.C. 1984, U.S. Dist. Ct. D.C. 1984, U.S. Ct. Appeals (D.C. cir.) 1985, U.S. Dist. Ct. (ea. dist.) Mich. 1986, U.S. Ct. Appeals (6th cir.) 1988, U.S. Supreme Ct. 1979. Atty. judgments sect. U.S. Dept. Justice, Washington, 1973-76, asst. chief transp. sect., 1977-80, chief spl. regulated industries, 1980-84; assoc. Wachtell, Lipton, Rosen & Katz, N.Y.C., 1976-77; chief counsel Pres. Com. on Three Mile Island, Washington, 1979; ptnr. Pillsbury, Madison & Sutro, Washington, 1984-91, Winthrop, Stimson, Putnam & Roberts, Washington, 1991-93, Preston Gates Ellis & Rouvelas Meeds, Washington, 1993-2001, Kilpatrick Stockton LLP, Washington, 2001—. Contbg. author: Report on Regulatory Reform, 1985; also articles. Cons. NSF, Washington, 1982-83. Mem. ABA (bd. editors Antitrust Law Devels. 1984-87, chmn. comms. subcom. antitrust sect. 1985-88, chmn. criminal practice subcom. litigation sect. 1985-89, adminstrv. law sect., chmn. industry regulation com. antitrust sect. 1988-92, mem. edn. com. dispute resolution sect. 1994—), Fed. Comm. Bar Assn., N.Y. State Bar Assn. Office: Kilpatrick Stockton LLP 607 14th St NW Ste 900 Washington DC 20005 E-mail: sgorinson@kilpatrickstockton.com.

GORLIN, RENA ANN, writer; b. Bklyn., Dec. 27, 1957; d. Philip and Sylvia (Levy) G.; BA magna cum laude, Brandeis U., 1979; JD, Am. U., 1982. Legal editor and reporter U.S. Law Week, Washington, 1983-86; legal editor and reporter BNA's Patent, Trademark and Copyright Jour. Bur. Nat. Affairs, Inc., Washington, 1983, sr. copywriter, 1986-96, coord. copywriting, 1996—. Freelance editor and copywriter, Washington area, 1986—. Author: Codes of Professional Responsibility: Ethics Standards in Business, Health, and Law, 1986, 4th edit. 1999. Mem. law com. Anti-Defamation League B'nai Brith, Washington, 1980; vol. Big Sisters, Waltham, Mass., 1976-78; moot ct. judge Cath. U. Law Sch. competitions, Washington, 1985-95. Recipient 1st place award for direct mail campaign Info. Industry Assn. Mktg. Awards, 1995. Mem. Washington Ind. Writers, Am. Soc. for Bioethics and Humanities. Avocation: photography. Office: BNA Sales and Mktg Div 1231 25th St NW Washington DC 20037-1157 E-mail: rgorlin@bna.com.

GORLIN, ROBERT JAMES, medical educator, educator; b. Hudson, N.Y., Jan. 11, 1923; s. James Alter and Gladys Gretchen (Hallenbeck) G.; m. Marilyn Alpern, Aug. 24, 1952; children: Cathy, Jed. AB, Columbia U., 1943, postgrad. 1947-50; DDS, Washington U., St. Louis, 1947; MS, State U. Iowa, 1956; DSc (hon.), U. Athens, Greece, 1982, U. Thesallonike, 1993, U. Md., 1999, U. Minn., 2002. Oral pathologist VA Hosp., Bronx, N.Y., 1950-51; instr. dentistry Columbia U., N.Y.C., 1950-51; dental dir., pathologist Op. Blue Jay, Thule, Greenland, 1951-52; mem. exec. faculty, chmn. oral pathology and genetics Sch. Dentistry U. Minn., Mpls., 1956-90, assoc. prof. div. oral pathology Sch. Dentistry, 1956-58, prof. Sch. Dentistry, 1958-93, prof. pathology and dermatology Sch. Medicine, Sch. Dentistry, 1971-93, prof. pediatrics, ob-gyn, otolaryngology Sch. Medicine, 1973-93, Regents' prof. oral pathology, 1978-93; Fulbright exch. prof., Guggenheim fellow Royal Dental Coll., Copenhagen, 1961; 1st Lingamfelter lectr. dermatology U. Va., 1971; 1st Boyle lectr. Case Western Res. U. Med. Ctr., Cleve., 1972; vis. prof. UCLA-Harbor Gen. Hosp., 1972; asst. chief dental service Glenwood Hills Med. Ctr., 1959-61, chief, 1962-64, cons., 1969-73; Regents' prof. emeritis U of Minn. Sch. of Dentistry, Mpls, 1994-. Cons. oral pathology Mpls. VA Hosp., 1958—, Mt. Sinai Hosp., Mpls., 1958—91; cons. pediatrics Hennepin County Gen. Hosp., St. Paul's Children's Hosp., Ramsey County Gen. Hosp., Mpls. Children's Hosp., Gillette State Hosp. Crippled Children; mem. Minn. Adv. Bd. Human Genetics, 1959—73; Minn. mem. U.S. Congl. Liaison Com. for Dentistry, 1963—80, mem. Ctr. Histologic Nomenclature and Classification of Odontogenic Tumors and Allied Lesions WHO, 1966—80; mem. adv. com. periodontal disease and soft tissue study NIH, 1967—78, mem. dental sect., 1970—73; mem. adv. com. Nat. Found. Clin. Rsch., 1974—; vis. prof. Tel Aviv U., 1980, Sch. Dentistry Jerusalem, 1981; 2nd Edward Sheridan lectr., Dublin, 89; Windemere lectr. Brit. Paediatric Assn., 1990; founder, bd. dirs. Found. for Devel. and Med. Genetics, 1994; lectr. in field. Author: (with M. Cohen) Syndromes of the Head and Neck, 1964, 76, 90, 2001 (with R. Goodman) The Face in Genetic Disorders, 1970, 77, The Malformed Infant and Child, 1983, (with B. Konigsmark) Genetic and Metabolic Disorders, 1977, Hereditary Hearing Loss and Its Syndromes, 1995; co-contbr.: Computer Assisted Diagnosis in Pediatrics, 2d edit., 1971; editor (with H. Goldman) Thoma's Oral Pathology, 1970, Chromosomes and Human Cancer (J. Cervenka and B. Koulischer), 1972; editorial cons. Jour. Dental Rsch., Geriatrics, Archives of Oral Biology, Jour. Pediats., Pediats., Am. Jour. Diseases of Children, Syndrome Identification, Radiology; editor oral pathology Oral Surgery, Oral Medicine, Oral Pathology, Clin. Pediats.; assoc. editor Am. Jour. Human Genetics, 1970-73, Jour. Oral Pathology, 1972-83, Jour. Maxillofacial Surgery, 1973—, Cleft Palate Jour., 1976—, Clin. Pediat., 1985—; mem. bd. Excerpta Medica, 1976-80, Jour. Craniofacial Genetic Devel. Biology, 1980—, Jour. Clin. Dysmorphology, 1982-86, Gerodontics, 1984-86, Birth Defects Ency., 1986—, Dysmorphology Clin. Genetics, 1987—; cons. editor

Stedman's Med. Dictionary, 1959—; contbr. numerous articles to profl. jours. Bd. dirs. Minn. div. Am. Cancer Soc., 1959-60, mem. nat. clin. fellowship com., 1962-65. With U.S. Army, 1943-44; lt. USNR, 1953-55. Named Spinoza chair, U. Amsterdam, 1995, Disting. lectr., Am. Soc. Human Genetics, 2001, Royal Soc. Medicine, London, 2001; recipient Fredrick Birnberg Rsch. award, Columbia U., 1987, Lifetime Achievement award, March of Dimes, 1989, award, Am. Cleft Palate Assn., 1993, Norton Ross prize, ADA, 1995, Disting. Alumni award, Washington U., 1997, Goldhaber award, Harvard U., 1997, Premio Anni Verdi award, Spoleto, Italy, 1997; fellow, Columbia U., 1947—48, NIH, 1948—49, Nat. Insts. Dental Rsch., 1949—50. Fellow: Royal Soc. Surgeons of Eng., Royal Soc. Surgeons of Ireland, Am. Bd. Oral Pathology, Am. Acad. Oral Pathology (v.p. 1957—58, sec. 1958—64, v.p. 1964—65, pres. 1966—67, award 1993, diplomate), Am. Coll. Med. Genetics (hon.); mem.: ADA (cons. coun. dental edn. 1967—), Internat. Soc. Craniofacial Biology (bd. dirs. 1966—67, v.p. 1967—68, pres. 1969—70), Hollywood Acad. Medicine (hon.), Nat. Inst. Medicine NAS (sr.), Internat. Assn. Oral Pathology (hon.), Skeletal Dysplasia Soc. (hon.), Internat. Skeletal Soc., Royal Soc. Medicine London (Burrough Wellcome fellow 1991, R. Abercrombie award in med. genetics 1994, Disting. lectr. 2001), Am. Soc. Human Genetics (Disting. lectr. 2001), Minn. Soc. Pathologists, Internat. Assn. Dental Rsch. (sec. Minn. divsn. 1958—59, pres. 1959—60), Nat. Trust Medicine (sr.), Omicron Kappa Upsilon, Sigma Xi. Office: U Minn 16-206 Health Sci Unit A Minneapolis MN 55455 E-mail: gorli002@tc.umn.edu.

GORMAN, CHARLOTTE A. family and consumer sciences agent; b. Tuscaloosa, Ala., Apr. 12, 1945; d. Buster and Rosie Gorman; m. C. Curtis Trent, May 5, 1984. BS, Delta State U., 1970; MA, U. Tenn., 1973, Ball State U., 1977, EdD, 1978. Sci. tchr. West Boliver Elem. Sch., Rosedale, Miss., 1970—71; ext. home economist Miss. State U., Starkville, 1973—75; state ext. specialist U. Ark., Little Rock, 1978—84; pres. GT Assocs., Denton, Tex., 1985—93; ext. agt. U. Ark., Little Rock, 1993—97, Tex. A&M U. Sys., College Station, 1997—. Author: The Frugal Mind, 1990 (Book Club selection), The Frugal Mind rev. edit., 1998, The Little Book of Living Frugal, 2001; co-author: Speak for Yourself, 2002. Recipient Charlotte Gorman Day named in her honor, 1993. Mem.: Tex. Extension Assn. Family and Consumer Scis., Nat. Extension Assn. Family and Consumer Scis., Tex. Assn. Family and Consumer Scis., Am. Assn. Family and Consumer Scis., Cleburne C. of C. (program devel. com. 2001—03), Epsilon Sigma Phi. Avocations: garage sales, piano. Home: 708 Meadowview Cleburne TX 76033

GORMAN, CHRIS, lawyer; b. Frankfort, Ky., Jan. 22, 1943; m. Vicki Lynn Beekman; two sons. Grad., U. Ky. Bar: Ky., 1967. Former ptnr. Conliffe, Sandman, Gorman, and Sullivan, Louisville; former dir. civil divsn. Jefferson County Attys. Office; atty. gen. Ky., 1992-95; gen. counsel Taylor Bldg. Corp. Am., Louisville, 1996—; ptnr. Sheffer, Hutchinson, Kinney, Louisville, 1999—2002; atty. Conliffe, Sandman & Sullivan, 2002—. Office: Conliffe, Sandman & Sullivan 2000 Waterfront Plz 325 W Main St Louisville KY 40202 E-mail: cgorman999@aol.com

GORMAN, COLUM ALPHONSUS, retired endocrinologist; b. Mayobridge, No. Ireland, June 27, 1936; arrived in U.S., 1960; s. James and Mary (McCollum) Gorman; m. Una Elizabeth O'Neill, Feb. 9, 1961; children: Kevin, Paul, Fiona, Michael. MB, Bch, BAO, Queens U., Belfast, Ireland, 1959; PhD, U. Minn., 1968. Cons. endocrinology Mayo Clinic, Rochester, Minn., 1966—; from asst. prof. to assoc. prof. Mayo Grad. Sch. Medicine, Rochester, 1971—81, prof., 1981-89; chmn. div. endocrinology Mayo Clinic, Rochester, 1985-92, bd. govs., 1999—2000, acting chair dept. health scis. rsch., 2000—01; assoc. dir. for rsch. devel. Mayo Found., Rochester, 2003—. Cons. in field. Editor, author: book The Eye and Orbit in Thyroid Disease, 1984. Fellow: ACP; mem.: AAAS, Endocrine Soc., Am. Thyroid Assn. (sec. 1984—88, pres. 1995—96). Republican. Avocations: reading, cross country skiing, auto restoration. Home and Office: 2607 Merrihills Dr Rochester MN 55902-1168

GORMAN, GAYLA MARLENE OSBORNE, consumer affairs executive; b. Owenton, Ky., Aug. 9, 1956; d. Frederick Clay and Helen Beatrice (Mason) O. AAS, No. Ky. U., 1982, BS, 1986; cert. in Chinese Mandarin, Def. Lang. Inst., 1975. Pers. clk. Dept. Edn. State Ky., Frankfort, 1974; sec. Dept. Health, Edn., Welfare Nat. Inst. Occupational Safety Health, Cin., 1977-79; specialist sales promotion U.S. Postal Svc., Cin., 1980, coord. customer liaison, task force pub. image, account rep., 1986-87, with stamp distbn. task force, 1993—; reservation sale agt. Delta Airlines, 1987-89. Councilmember Florence City Coun., Ky. 1984-87; vol. Children's Home, Covington, 1982, 87. With USAF, 1974-76. Named to Hon. Order Ky. Cols. Mem. Disabled Am. Veterans, No. Ky. U. Alumni Assn., Nat. Assn. Postmasters U.S., Boone County Fraternal Order Police, Ky. Assn. Realtors, Nat. Bd. Realtors, Women in Mil. Svc. for Am. (charter). Clubs: Fraternal Order Police. Democrat. Baptist. Avocations: horseback riding, travel, organizing seminars. Home: 8395 Juniper Ln Florence KY 41042-9279

GORMAN, GERALD PATRICK, lawyer; b. Buffalo, Oct. 6, 1948; s. Gerald Joseph and Ellen Patricia (Lynch) G.; m. Julia Lucille Pericek, Aug. 21, 1971; children— Jonathan G., Jillian L., Jared P. BA in English, Canisius Coll., Buffalo, 1970; JD, SUNY-Buffalo, 1973. Bar: N.Y. 1974, U.S. Supreme Ct. 1978, U.S. Dist. Ct. (we. dist.) N.Y. 1980, U.S. Ct. Apls. (2d cir.). Asst. dist. atty. Erie County, Buffalo, 1974-77; ptnr. Manz & Gorman Buffalo, 1977-83, Lankes, Semple, Waible & Gorman, Buffalo, 1983— . Mem. ABA, N.Y. State Bar Assn., Am. Trial Lawyers Assn., Erie County Bar Assn. (Trial Lawyers award 1973). Democrat. Roman Catholic. Club: Young Am. Soccer (v.p. 1984—), Southtowns Exc. Office: Lankes Semple Waible & Gorman 350 Elmwood Ave Buffalo NY 14222-2204

GORMAN, GERALD WARNER, lawyer; b. North Kansas City, Mo., May 30, 1933; s. William Shelton and Bessie (Warner) G.; m. Anita Belle McPike, June 26, 1954; children: Guinevere Eve, Victoria Rose AB cum laude, Harvard U., 1954, LLB magna cum laude, 1956. Bar: Mo. 1956. Assoc. firm Dietrich, Tyler, Davis, Burrell & Dicus, Kansas City, 1956-62; ptnr. Dietrich, Davis, Dicus, Rowlands, Schmitt & Gorman, 1963-90; dir. Slagle, Bernard & Gorman, P.C., 1990—. Bd.dirs. Musser-Davis Land Co., Curry Investment Co. Bd. govs. Citizens Assn. Kansas City, 1962—; trustee Harvard/Radcliffe Club Kansas City Endowment Fund, chmn. bd. trustees, 1977-83; trustee Kansas City Mus., 1967-82; chmn. bd. trustees Avondale Meth. Ch., 1969-92; mem. Citizens Bond Com. of Kansas City, 1973-2000, chmn. 7th jud. cir. citizens com., 1982-84; chmn. Downtown Coun. Allis Plaza Reconstrn., 1983-85; bd. dirs. Spofford Home for Children, 1972-77, Clay County Econ. Devel. Commn., 1989-94, mem. exec. com., 1991-93, bd. dirs. Jackson County Hist. Soc. 2001—. With U.S. Army, 1956-58; capt. USAR, 1958-64. Mem. Lawyers Assn. Kansas City (exec. com. 1968-71), ABA, Mo. Bar Assn., Kansas City Bar Assn., Clay County Bar Assn., Harvard Law Sch. Assn. Mo. (pres. 1973), Harvard Club (pres. 1966), Univ. Club (bd. dirs. 1983-86, 88-93, pres. 1990-91), Kansas City Club (bd. dirs. 1993-97), 611 Club (bd. dirs. 1987-91, pres. 1990), Kansas City Country Club, Old Pike Country Club, River Club., Nat. Golf Club of Kansas City. Republican. Home: 917 NE Vivion Rd Kansas City MO 64118-5317 Office: 4600 Madison Ave Ste 600 Kansas City MO 64112-3031 E-mail: ggorman@sbg-law.com.

GORMAN, IDA NIEBAUER, HMO outsourcing company executive; b. Fairview, Pa., Dec. 7, 1949; d. Ferdinand Oscar and Julia Catherine (Bausch) Niebauer; children: Jennifer Lynn, Chad Michael. BA in Biology, Mercyhurst Coll., 1971; postgrad., Pa. State U., Hershey. Jr. rsch. technician dept. surgery M. S. Hershey (Pa.) Med. Ctr., 1971-73, rsch. technician, 1973-78, sr. rsch. pacemaker technician, 1978-83, rsch. technician dept. radiology, 1984, sr. rsch. technician, 1984-86, rsch. support asst. dept. radiology, 1986-89; monitoring/telemetry cons. Intermedics, Inc., Freeport, Tex., 1974-83; magnetic resonance tech., spectroscopist York (Pa.) Imaging Ctr., 1989-93; med. policy coord. Synertech, Inc., Harrisburg, Pa., 1994—. Author: (manual) Basic Index and Troubleshooting Guide to Cardiac Pacing, 1983, (manuscript) T2 Weighted Image Manipulation to Accent Pathology, 1991, (software) SPECTROSCOPY, 1992, Data Logic Tables, 1999; contbr. articles to profl. jours. Sec. St. Theresa Home/Sch. Assn., New Cumberland, Pa., 1987—89, lector, 1989—91, St. Joseph's Ch., Mechanicsburg, Pa., 1992—, bd. dirs. parish pastoral coun., 1999—2002, co-facilitator COMFORT zONE, 1999—; mem. leadership bd. div./separated group Diocese of Harrisburg, 2000—; CCD tchr. St. Joseph's Ch., Mechanicsburg, Pa., 2002—03. Scholar, Mercyhurst Coll., 1967—71. Mem.: AAAS, N.Y. Acad. Scis., Am. Chem. Soc., Nat. Assn. Female Execs. Roman Catholic. Avocations: boating, snow skiing, gardening, piano, sewing. Home: 621 Park Ave New Cumberland PA 17070-1725 E-mail: maybelle51@aol.com., igorman@synertechsystems.com.

GORMAN, JAMES CARVILL, pump manufacturing company executive; b. Mansfield, Ohio, Apr. 16, 1924; s. James Carville and Ruth (Barnes) G.; m. Marjorie Newcomer, Apr. 10, 1950; children: Jeff, Gayle. BS, Ohio State U., 1949. Sales engr. Gorman Rupp Co., Mansfield, Ohio, 1949-58, sales mgr., 1958-64, pres., 1964-89, chmn., CEO, 1989-99, chmn., 1999—. Pres. Manairco, Inc., 1952-85, chmn. bd., 1985—; chmn. Mansfield Airport Commn., 1954-2000; treas. EAA Aviation Found., Oshkosh, Wis., 1980—. Capt. USAAF, 1942-46. Mem. Constrn. Industry Mfrs. Assn. Episcopalian. Home: PO Box 2599 Mansfield OH 44906-0599 Office: Gorman Rupp 305 Bowman St Mansfield OH 44903-1600

GORMAN, JAMES EDWARD, lawyer; b. Summit, Ill., Nov. 11, 1930; s. James Edward and Mae Catherine (Jiracek) G.; m. Beverly Ann Fink; children: Gregory, Stephen, Robert, William Mudge, Ann, James, Mary. BA, St. Ambrose Coll., 1952; JD, U. Ill., 1955. Bar: Ill. 1956, U.S. Dist. Ct. (so. dist.) Ill. 1958, U.S. Ct. Appeals 1979, U.S. Supreme Ct. 1980. Assoc. Heyl, Royster, Voelker and Allen, Peoria, Ill., 1957-59, Bernard, Gorman, Davidson, Edwardsville, Granite City, Ill., 1959-61; ptnr. Reed, Armstrong, Gorman, Mudge & Morrissey, Edwardsville, Ill., 1961—. With U.S. Army, 1955-57. Mem.: ATLA, ABA (Ill. atty. disciplinary panel 1974—94), Ill. Def. Coun., Madison County Bar Assn., Ill. Trial Lawyers Assn., Am. Coll. Trial Lawyers, Ill. Bar Assn., KC. Roman Catholic. Office: Reed Armstrong Gorman Mudge & Morrissey PC 115 N Buchanan St Edwardsville IL 62025-1771

GORMAN, JOSEPH BATTERTON, elementary school educator; b. Washington, Apr. 20, 1975; s. Richard Barthen and Virginia Taul Gorman; m. Jennifer Lynn Ruggerrio, Nov. 2, 2002. BA in History, M Tchr., U. Va., 1998. Cert. tchr. Va. Tchr. 8th grade social studies Liberty Mid. Sch., Ashland, Va., 1998—, chmn. social studies dept., 2000—. Leader youth recreation Hanover County Dept. Recreation, Ashland, 2000—01; mem. social studies curriculum com. Hanover County Sch. Bd., Ashland, 2000—. Author: (book and CD) Conversations in History, 2003; featured: Channel 36 TV, Herald Progress newspaper; author: curriculum for Internet. Sponsor Geography Bee Nat. Geog. Soc., 2003—; conf. del. Nat. Coun. for Social Studies, 1996. Recipient cert. of appreciation, Va. Assn. Sch. Supts., 2002. Mem.: NEA, Va. Edn. Assn., Hanover Edn. Assn., Phi Alpha Theta, Kappa Delta Pi. Avocations: writing, drawing, reading, tennis, travel. Home: 8272 Tarragon Dr Mechanicsville VA 23111

GORMAN, JOSEPH GREGORY, JR., lawyer; b. Chgo., Sept. 27, 1939; s. Joseph Gregory Sr. and Genevieve C. (Smith) G.; m. Mary (Molly) O'Donovan, Mar. 23, 1968; children: Jennifer Ann Gorman Patton, Joseph Gregory III. BA, U. Calif., Berkeley, 1961; MBA, UCLA, 1963, JD, 1966. Bar: U.S. Dist. Ct. (cen. dist.) Calif. 1967, U.S. Ct. Appeals (9th cir.) 1967, U.S. Tax Ct. Assoc., ptnr. Sheppard, Mullin, Richter & Hampton LLP, L.A., 1966—. Chair death and gift tax com. Los Angeles County Bar Assn., chair probate & trust law sect., 1980-81; chair death and gift tax com. Calif. State Bar, 1976-77; co-founder U. So. Calif. Probate & Trust Conf., 1974—; mem. adv. bd. U. Miami Heckerling Inst. Estate Planning, 1978—. Contbr. articles to profl. jours. Served with USAR, Calif. NG, 1962-68. Fellow Am. Coll. Trust and Estate Counsel, Academician, The Internat. Acad. of Estate and Trust Law. Clubs: Annandale Golf (Pasadena); Jonathan (Los Angeles). Republican. Roman Catholic. Office: Sheppard Mullin Richter & Hampton LLP 333 S Hope St Fl 48 Los Angeles CA 90071-1448 E-mail: jgorman@sheppardmullin.com.

GORMAN, JOSEPH TOLLE, automotive parts manufacturing executive; b. Rising Sun, Ind., 1937; BA, Kent State U., 1959; LLB, Yale U., 1962. Assoc. Baker, Hostetler & Patterson, Cleve., 1962-67; with legal dept. TRW Inc., Cleve., 1968-69, asst. sec., 1969-70, sec., 1970-72, v.p. sr. counsel automotive worldwide ops., 1972-73, v.p., asst. gen. counsel, 1973-76, v.p., gen. counsel, 1976-80, acting head communications function, 1978, exec. v.p. indsl. and energy sector, 1980-84, exec. v.p., asst. pres., 1984-85, pres., CEO, 1985-88, chmn., CEO, 1988—, also bd. dirs. Bd. dirs. Aluminum Co. Am., Procter & Gamble Co.; mem. adv. bd. BP Am. Inc.; bd. dirs. U.S.-China Bus. Coun., bd. dirs.; mem. Bd. of The Prince of Wales Bus. Leaders Form; mem. hon. com. Fedn. Internat. des Soc. d'Ingenieurs des Tech. de l'Automobile; mem. Def. Industry Initiative Steering Com.; chmn. Internat. Trade and Investment Task Force; mem. strengthening of Am. Initiative Ctr. for Strategic and Internat. Studies; adv. com. Nat. Security Telecom.; mem. Conf. Bd., Bus. Coun., Trilateral Commn., Bus. Roundtable's Policy Com., Coun. on Fgn. Rels., Pres.'s Export Coun., Coun. on Competitiveness. Trustee New Ohio Inst., Cleve. Tomorrow, Mus. Arts Assn., Cleve. Inst. Art, United Way Svcs., Cleve. Clinic Found., Com. for Econ. Devel., com. for econ. devel. and the Malcolm Baldrige Nat. Quality Award Found.; mem. Ohio Gov.'s Edn. Mgmt. Coun., Kent State U. Found.; bd. mem. The New Am. Schs. Devel. Corp., The Bus.-Higher Edn. Forum, Civic Vision 2000 and Beyond. Recipient Japan Prime Minister's Trade award, 1994.

GORMAN, JOYCE J(OHANNA), lawyer; b. N.Y.C., Aug. 23, 1952; d. Peter J. and Jane M. (Kelly) G. Student, Williams Coll., 1972-73; BA, Smith Coll., 1974; JD with honors, U. Md., 1977. Bar: Md. 1977, D.C. 1988. Assoc. Miles & Stockbridge, Balt., 1977-84, ptnr., 1984-87, Washington, 1987-88, Ballard, Spahr, Andrews & Ingersoll, Washington, 1988-94, Piper & Marbury, Washington, 1994-98; spl. counsel Cadwalader, Wickersham & Taft LLP, Washington, 1998—. Bd. dirs. Va. Opera, 1994-98. Mem. Md. Bar Assn. (sec. corp. banking and bus. sect. 1983-84, vice chmn. 1984-85, chmn. 1985-86), Merchants Club (Balt. bd. dirs. 1980-87), City Club (Washington). Roman Catholic. Avocations: swimming, gourmet cooking, travel. Home: 9492 Lynnhall Pl Alexandria VA 22309-3064 Office: Cadwalader Wickersham & Taft LLP Ste 1100 1201 F St NW Washington DC 20004

GORMAN, KAREN MACHMER, optometric physician; b. Poughkeepsie, N.Y., June 4, 1955; d. James Andrew and Joan (Benton) Machmer; m. D.L. McCartney III, Aug. 16, 1976 (div. June 1982); m. N. David Gorman, Oct. 16, 1985; 1 stepchild, Danette Y. Gorman. BS in Optometry, U. Houston, 1976, OD, 1978; therapeutic pharm. lic., U. Mo., St. Louis, 1993. Diplomate Nat. Bd. Examiners Optometry; lic. optometrist, Colo., Mo., Tex. Pvt. practice, Dallas, 1978-83, 1984-85, Hurst, Tex., 1984-85, St. Joseph, Mo., 1986-2000; councilwoman, chmn. pub. safety com. City Coun., City of St. Joseph, 1997-98, chmn. landfill and water pollution com., 1998—; pvt. practice Maryville, Mo., 1999—. Charter mem. optometric adv. panel Pearle, Inc., 1991-93; lectr. on eyecare to community groups; free-lance journalist St. Joseph News-Press, Benson (N.C.) Rev., jazzreview.com, Jazz Amb. mag. Contbr. poetry to lit. jours. including Nat. Libr. of Poetry, Typo mag., Edge mag., articles to profl. jours. including St. Joseph News Press and Benson (N.C.) Review; lead actress (play) None Come Back Innocent, Robidoux Resident Theatre, St. Joseph, 1990, Hay Fever, 1991, The Best Man, 1992, Wedded But No Wife, 1993, Mousetrap, 1993, Diary of Anne Frank, 1994, Death and the Maiden, 1995, Veronica's Room, 1996, Plaza Suite, 1997, Dial M for Murder, 2000, The Laramie Project, 2002. Vol. Dallas Humane Soc., 1981, YWCA Women's Abuse Shelter; patron Robidoux Resident Theatre, St. Joseph, 1988-92, Ice House Theatre, St. Joseph, Kemper Albrecht Art Mus., St. Joseph, St. Joseph Animal Shelter; sponsor, coach, cheerleader and drill team Mo. Western State Coll., St. Joseph, 1985-86; legis. corr. Humane Soc. U.S., 1990-92; mem. Nat. Soc. Newspaper Columnists; mem. St. Joseph (Mo.) City Coun., 1997—, chmn. landfill and water pollution com, chmn. pub. safety com. Recipient Optometric Recognition awards Pearle, Inc., 1986-90; U. Houston scholar, 1972-76 Mem.: DAR (Pony Express chpt.), Nat. Assn. Newspaper Columnists, U. Houston Alumni Assn., St. Joseph Lit. Guild, Tau Sigma. Avocations: jazz concerts, reading, writing, poetry, piano. Office: 1404 S Main Maryville MO 64468 E-mail: eyeDrKim@aol.com.

GORMAN, LEON A. mail order company executive; b. Nashua, N.H., Dec. 20, 1934; Mdse. trainee Filene's of Boston, 1956; with L.L. Bean, Inc., Freeport, Maine, 1960—, v.p., treas., 1967, pres., 1967—2001, chmn. bd. dirs., 2001—. Dir. Central Maine Power Co., Depositors Corp., Carroll Reed Ski Shops. Mem. Alumni Coun. Bowdoin Coll.; bd. dirs. Pine Tree Coun. Boy Scouts Am.; trustee Hurrican Usland Outward Bound Sch.; corp. Maine Med. Ctr.; adv. trustee Maine Audubon Soc. Lt. USNR, 1957-60. Mem. C. of C. Greater Portland (dir.). Office: L L Bean Inc Casco St Freeport ME 04033-0001*

GORMAN, MARCIE SOTHERN, personal care industry franchise executive; b. Feb. 25, 1949; d. Jerry R. and Carole Edith (Frendel) Sothern; m. N. Scott Gorman, June 14, 1969 (div.); children: Michael Stephen, Mark Jason. AA, U. Fla., 1968; BS, Memphis State U., 1970. Tchr. Memphis City Sch. Sys., 1970-73; tng. dir. Weight Watchers Palm Beach County, Weight Watchers So. Ala., West Palm Beach, Fla., 1973-97; pres. Weight Watchers Franchise Assn., 1999—. Pres. Markel Enterprises, LLC (formerly Markel Ads, Inc.). Cubmaster Boy Scouts Am. Hon. lt. col. a.d.c. Ala. Militia; bd. dirs. Crossroads Program, Palm Beach C.C., 2001—, Communities in Schs., West Palm Beach, 2003—. Mem. NAFE, NOW, Women Am. ORT (program chmn. 1975), Weight Watchers Franchise Assn. (chair mktg. com., advt./mktg. coun., chairperson region IV bd. dirs., treas., 2d v.p. 1991, 1st v.p., region IV co-chair 1998-99, bd. dirs., nat. pres. 1999—), Exec. Women of Palm Beaches, Am. Bus. Women's Assn., Women's C.of C., Zonta. Office: Weight Watchers Office 2435 10th Ave N Lake Worth FL 33461-3128

GORMAN, MARCY, health care administrator; b. Manhattan, N.Y., June 21, 1949; d. Vincent James and Angelina (Pugliani) Mannino; m. Dominick Licata, Feb. 4, 1967 (div. Sept. 1976); children: Lisa, Vincent; m. David E. Gorman, June 26, 1988. AA, Suffolk Community Coll., 1976; BA, Dowling Coll., 1978; MPS, New Sch. for Social Rsch., 1989. Social worker Outreach Services YMCA, Bayshore, N.Y., 1978-79; counselor Women's Pavilion, Deer Park, N.Y., 1978-79, Bill Baird Inst., Hauppauge, N.Y., 1979-82, asst. adminstr., 1982-85, adminstr., 1985—. Lectr. various schs. Women's Health Care Issues; TV talk show guest Point of View, N.Y.C., 1987. Mem. Nat. Abortion Rights Action League, Fund For Feminist Majority, L.I. Pro-choice Coalition. Mem. NAFE, NOW. Democrat. Roman Catholic. Avocations: bicycling, writing. Office: Bill Baird Inst 1324 Motor Pkwy Islandia NY 11749-5262

GORMAN, MICHAEL JOSEPH, library director, educator; b. Witney, Oxfordshire, Eng., Mar. 6, 1941; came to U.S. 1977; s. Philip Denis and Alicia F. (Barrett) G.; m. Anne Gillett, Mar. 6, 1962 (div. 1992); children— Emma, Alice Student, Ealing Sch. Librarianship, 1964-66. Dir. gen. services dept. Univ. Library U. Ill., Urbana, 1977-88, acting univ. librarian, 1986-87; prof. library adminstrn. U. Ill., Urbana, 1977-88; vis. prof. U. Chgo. Library Sch., 1984, 86-88, U. Calif., Berkeley, 1989-91; dean libr. svcs. Calif. State U., Fresno, 1988—. Vis. lectr. U. Ill. Grad. Sch. Library Sci., Urbana, 1974-75; bibliog. cons. Brit. Library Planning Secretariat, 1972-74; head cataloguing Brit. Nat. Bibliography 1969-72. Author: A Study of the Rules for Entry and Headings in the Anglo-American Cataloguing Rules, 1967, 68, Format for Machine Readable Cataloguing of Motion Pictures, 1973, Concise AACR2, 1980, 3d edit., 1999, Technical Services Today and Tomorrow,1990, 2nd edit., 1998, Future Libraries (with Walt Crawford) 1995, Our Singular Strengths: Meditations for Librarians, 1998, Our Enduring Values, 2000, The Enduring Library, 2002; others, editor. Anglo-American Cataloguing Rules, 2d edit., 1978, rev., 1988, Catalogue and Index, 1973, Non Solus, 1981, Crossroads, 1986, Convergence, 1990; contbr. articles to profl. jours., chpts. to books Recipient Blackwell scholarship award, 1997. Fellow Brit. Libr. Assn.; mem. ALA (mem. coun. 1991-95, 2002—, mem. exec. bd. 2003—, Margaret Mann citation 1979, Melvil Dewey medal 1992, Highsmith award 2001), Libr. Info. and Tech. Assn. (mem.-at-large exec. bd. 1982-85, pres. 1999-2000). Office: Calif State U Henry Madden Libr 5200 N Barton Ave Fresno CA 93740-8014

GORMAN, MICHAEL STEPHEN, construction executive; b. Tulsa, Aug. 3, 1951; s. Lawrence Matthew and Mary Alice (Veith) G.; m. Sheryl Lane McGee, Feb. 19, 1972; children: Kelley Lane, Michael Ryan. Student, Colo. State U., 1970, 71. With McGee Constrn. Co., Denver, 1972-74, with sales and estimating dept., 1974-78, gen. mgr., 1978-80, pres., owner, 1980-91; pres. Wisor Group, Boulder, 1990—95; prin. TechKnowledge, 1996—. Cons., author, columnist in remodeling and custom home building; mortgage banker, ins. cons., 1995—; presenter seminars in field. Author: If I Sell You I Have a Job, If I Serve You I Create a Career, 1997; contbg. editor: Profl. Remodeling Mag., 1995—. Mem. Nat. Assn. Remodeling Industry (chmn. membership svcs. com. 1987-91, bd. dirs. 1982-91, regional v.p. 1987-89, nat. sec. 1990-91, Man of Yr. 1982, Regional Contractor of Yr. 1988). Avocations: running, sailing, skiing, pilot. Office: 3109 Grand Ave Ste 424 Coconut Grove FL 33133 E-mail: mgbok@aol.com.

GORMAN, ROBERT DENNIS, lawyer; b. Santa Fe, N.Mex., Nov. 3, 1955; s. Robert D. and Virginia M. Gorman; m. Cathy M. Sanchez, Sept. 9, 1978; children: Sarah, Lillian, Stephanie. BBA, U. N.Mex., 1977, JD, 1983. Bar: N.Mex. 1983, U.S. Dist. Ct. N.Mex. 1983, U.S. Tax Ct. 1983, U.S. Ct. Appeals (10th cir.) 1983, U.S. Ct. Claims 1993, U.S. Supreme Ct. 1993. CPA, N.Mex. Auditor, rsch. adminstr. N.Mex. State Auditor, Santa Fe, 1977-84; pvt. practice acctg., Santa Fe and Albuquerque, 1978-83; assoc. Eaves, Darling & Porter, Albuquerque, 1983-89; pvt. practice, Albuquerque, 1989—. Supervisory com. First Fin. Credit Union, Albuquerque, 1990-92; instr. bus. law U. Phoenix, 1991. Parish and fin. coun. mem. Holy Rosary Parish, Albuquerque, 1988—. Mem. ABA, AICPA, N.Mex. State Bar (dir. tax sect. 1984-95), N.Mex. Soc. CPAs (ethics com. 1998). Democrat. Roman Catholic. Avocations: skiing, running. Office: 1201 Lomas Blvd NW Albuquerque NM 87102-1893 E-mail: rgorman@nm.net.

GORMAN, ROBERT SAUL, architect; b. N.Y.C., June 28, 1933; s. Philip and Lillian (Weiss) G.; m. Judith Alice Albaum, July 2, 1965; children: Melissa, Sahsa William Shannon. BArch, MArch, Yale U., 1966. Apprentice to Frank Lloyd Wright, 1953-56; designer Eero Saarinen, Hamden, Conn., 1961-67; architect, planner Victor Gruen Assocs., N.Y.C., 1967-69; Juster/Pope, Architects, Shelburne Falls, Mass., 1977-78; arch. Robert Gorman Assocs., Architects, Planners, Solar Energy, Richmond, N.H., 1969-80; founder, prin. Rawson Place Architects, 1980-89, Green River Archs., 1989—. Cons. Bklyn. Coll., 1967-69. Served with AUS, 1956-58. Fellow Frank Lloyd Wright Found., 1953—. Mem. AIA (Design award 1972). Achievements include development of of many original solar applications in environmentally concerned architecture. Home: 48 Morningside Common Brattleboro VT 05301 Office: Green River Architects 93 Green River Rd Brattleboro VT 05301-9202 E-mail: robert@greenriverarchitects.com.

GORMAN, SUSAN E. toxicologist, consultant; b. St. Marys, Pa., June 30, 1965; d. Alice A. and William D. Gorman. BS in Pharmacy, Duquesne U., 1988; PharmD, U. Md., 1991. Diplomate Am. Bd. Applied Toxicology; lic. pharmacist Pa. State Bd. Pharmacy. Pharmacist Andrew Kaul Meml. Hosp., St. Marys, Pa., 1988—89; pharmacist, asst. mgr. CVS Drug Store, Johnsonburg, Pa., 1988—89; rsch. pharmacist Johns Hopkins/Behavioral Pharmacology Rsch. Unit, Balt., 1989—91; emergency medicine/toxicology resident U. Ill., Chgo., 1991—92; asst. prof. U. Ark. for Med. Scis., Little Rock, 1992—94; asst. dir. Ga. Poison Ctr., Atlanta, 1994—2000, specialist in poison info., 2000—; assoc. dir. for sci. CDC Nat. Pharm. Stockpile Program, Atlanta, 2000—. Toxicology cons. Ga. Poison Ctr., Atlanta, 2000—; mem. adj. faculty Mercer U. Coll. Pharmacy, Atlanta, 1998—, U. Ga. Coll. Pharmacy, Athens, 1999—. Contbr. articles to profl. jours. Recipient award, Schering Pharm. Corp, 1987, Rsch. award, Upjohn Pharm. Co., 1991, Spl. Act or Svc. award, USPHS/CDC/NCEH Office of Dir., 2000—01, CDC/ATSDR Program Ops. Honor award, Centers for Disease Control and Prevention, 2001; scholar, Duquesne U., 1983—88, Stackpole Carbon Co., 1983—87. Mem.: Am. Coll. Clin. Pharmacy, Am. Soc. Health Sys. Pharmacists, Am. Assn. Colls. Pharmacy, Am. Assn. Poison Control Ctrs., Am. Bd. Applied Toxicology (bd. of directors 2001—), Am. Acad. Clin. Toxicology, Zeta Tau Alpha (life). Achievements include research in pediatric acetaminophen ingestions and health care referrals; utility and interpretation of serum acetaminophen concentrations drawn within four hours of acute overdose; impact on patient outcomes by a pharmacy based clinical toxicology consult service; controversial issues in iron toxicity. Avocations: travel, reading, volleyball, movies, music. Office: Ctrs for Disease Control and Prevention 1600 Clifton Rd MS D-08 Atlanta GA 30333

GORMAN, WILLIAM DAVID, artist, graphic artist; b. Jersey City, June 27, 1925; s. William Daniel and Margaret (Johnson) G.; m. Janice Echols Gary, Feb. 9, 1957. Grad., Newark Sch. Fine and Indsl. Arts, 1949. Art evaluator N.J.

Council of Arts, 1975 Contbr. articles to art mags.; One-man shows, Jersey City Mus., 1962, Revel Gallery, N.Y.C., 1963, East Side Gallery, N.Y.C., 1970, Madison (N.J.) Library, 1975, Caldwell (N.J.) Coll., 1976, SUNY, Alfred, 1977, Martin (Tenn.) Arts Commn., 1978, Old Bank Gallery, Port Washington, N.Y., 1981, The Academy/N.J. State Dept. Edn., Edison, 1987; group shows include, Davenport (Iowa) Mcpl. Art Gallery, 1975, Canton (Ohio) Art Inst., 1971, NAD, 1971-81, Am. Acad. and Inst. Arts and Letters, N.Y.C., 1979, 80, Internat. Waters invitational traveling exhbn., Can., U.S., U.K., 1991-93, U.S./China/Australian Watermedia Exposition, Taiwan, 1994; represented in permanent collections, U.S. State Dept., NAD, N.Y.C., Newark Mus., Montclair (N.J.) Art Mus., Springfield (Mo.) Art Mus., Colorado Springs Fine Arts Center, Syracuse (N.Y.) U., Butler Inst. Am. Art, Ohio. Served with U.S. Army, 1943-44, ETO. Recipient Artist's Mag. award, 1991 Mem. Allied Artists Am. (v.p. 1975-78, pres. 1978-81, hon. life pres. 1983, dir. watercolor 1981-84, Gold medal of honor 1973, De Maree award, 1981, FitzGerald Meml. award, 1982, 91, Diana Kan award, 1983, Bainbridge award 1985, Silver medal of Honor, 1986, John Young-Hunter award 1989), Am. Watercolor Soc. (hon. mem., 1st v.p. 1981-86, pres. 1986-93, Emily Lowe meml. award 1984, Ogden Pleissner meml. award 1988, Four Winds medal 1989, Mary S. Litt medal 1992, Silver Medal of Honor award 1993), Audubon Artists (hon. life, exhbn. chmn. 1974-77, dir. 1977-80), Nat. Soc. Painters in Casein and Acrylic (Shiva award 1987), N.J. Water Color Soc. (pres. 1957-59, Grumbacher Silver medal 1982, Warga award 1983), Artists Fellowship, Am. Vets. Soc. Artists, Garden State Watercolor Soc. (award 1985), Hudson Artists (founder 1955), Jersey City Mus. Assn. (dir. 1953-60), NAD (NA full acadamician, Henry Ward Ranger Fund purchase awards 1965, 71), Old Bergen Art Guild (pres. and dir. 1962—), Salmagundi Club (hon.), Australian Watercolor Inst. (hon.), Mexican Watercolor Soc. (hon.). Home: 43 W 33rd St Bayonne NJ 07002-3907 also: Am Watercolor Soc 47 5th Ave New York NY 10003-4303

GORMLEY, DENNIS MICHAEL, research scholar; b. Meriden, Conn., Feb. 1, 1943; s. Lawrence Edward and Anna (Seitz) G.; m. Elizabeth Carol Festa, Aug. 12, 1967 (div. Sept. 1984); children: Douglas Lawrence, Jennifer Marie; m. Janet Lee Johnson, Mar. 23, 1985. BA, U. Conn., 1965, MA, 1966. Advanced through grades to 1st lt. U.S. Army; sr. specialist fed. civil svc. Army Materiel Command, Washington, 1969-72; chief fgn. intelligence U.S. Army Harry Diamond Labs, Washington, 1972-79; sr. v.p. Pacific-Sierra Rsch. Corp., Arlington, Va., 1979-99; pres. Blue Ridge Consulting Group, Inc., 1999—. Cons. Sci. Applications Internat. Corp., 1996—, Sandia Nat. Labs., Albuquerque, 1992—, Rand Corp., Santa Monica, Calif., 1987-90, 2000—, The Brookings Instn., Washington, 1973-75; govt. adv. com. chmn., mem. Dept. Def., Washington, 1983—; vis. scholar Geneva Ctr. for Security Policy, 1997—; sr. fellow Monterey Inst. for Internat. Studies, Ctr. for Nonproliferation Studies, 2003—. Author: Double Zero and Soviet Military Strategy, 1988, rev. paperback, 1990, Dealing with the threat of Cruise Missiles, 2001; co-author: Controlling the Spread of Land-Attack Cruise Missiles, 1995; contbr. articles, book revs. to profl. jours. and newspapers. Vol. home hospice work. 1st lt. U.S. Army, 1966-69. Rsch. assoc. Internat. Inst. for Strategic Studies, London, 1984, sr. fellow, 2000-02. Mem. AAAS, Internat. Inst. for Strategic Studies, Arms Control Assn., Nat. Liberal Club, London, Phi Alpha Theta. Avocations: fly fishing, marathons, bicyling, volunteer work. Home: 3514 Valley Dr Alexandria VA 22303 E-mail: dennis.gormley@miis.edu.

GORMLEY, ROBERT JOHN, publishing executive; writer; b. Lynn, Mass., Oct. 14, 1939; s. Ernest Raymond and Catherine Louise (Maitl) G.; m. Beatrice LeCount, Sept. 4, 1966; children: Catherine, Jennifer. BA, Williams Coll., 1961; MA, U. Calif. at Berkeley, 1964. With Wadsworth Inc., 1964-85; pres., pub. PWS Pubs. (encompassing various divs. Wadsworth, Inc.), Boston, 1980-85; pres. Duxbury Press, Boston, 1971-80; corp. v.p. Wadsworth, Boston, 1981-83, Ea. group v.p., 1983-85; exec. dir. Orbis Books, Maryknoll, N.Y., 1986-98; pub. Chatham House, N.Y.C., 1998-2001; ptnr. Seven Bridges Press, N.Y.C., 1998-2001; pub. Wiley/Jossey Bass Edn., 2001—; editor-in-chief Northeastern U. Press, 2002—. Bd. dirs. Mayflower Mental Health Assn.; trustee Duxbury Free Library; pres. Greater Boston Irish Children's Fund, Inc. Served with U.S. Army, 1964-69. Mem. Cath. Book Pubs. Assn. (pres.). Democrat. Roman Catholic. Home: 1775 Drift Rd Westport MA 02790-0299

GORMLEY, WILLIAM L. state legislator; b. Atlantic City, N.J., May 2, 1946; BA, Notre Dame U., 1968; JD, Villanova U., 1971. Bar: N.J. Ptnr. Gormley and Savio; elected mem. Atlantic County Bd. Freeholders, 1975; mem. N.J. Gen. Assembly, 1977-82; asst. minority leader, 1982; mem. N.J. Senate, 1982—, mem. senate jud. com. Founder Atlantic County Women's Abuse Ctr.; hon. trustee S. Jersey Regional Theatre. Served to capt. USMC, 1975. Named One of 10 Outstanding Young Citizens of N.J., N.J. Jaycees, 1981; recipient commendation award Jackson Twp. for efforts in assisting to supply a safe water supply to twp.; named Citizen of Yr., Holly Shores coun. Girl Scouts U.S., 1985; interracial award Tropicana Federated Charity Club, 1985. Mem. N.J. Bar Assn., Atlantic County Bar Assn., Marine Corps League. Office: Hamilton Mall Ste 108 Black Horse Pike Mays Landing NJ 08330*

GORN, ELLIOTT JACOB, historian, educator, writer; b. L.A, May 3, 1951; s. Max Gorn and Anne Frances Kline; 1 child, Jade Yee-Gorn. AB, U. Calif., Berkeley, 1973, MA, 1975; PhD, Yale U., 1983. Prof. U. Ala., Tuscaloosa, 1981-85, Miami U., Oxford, Ohio, 1985-98, Purdue U., West Lafayette, Ind., 1998, Brown U., Providence, 2003—. Author: The Manly Art, 1986, Mother Jones, 2001; co-author: A Brief History of American Sports, 1993; co-editor: Encyclopedia of American Social History, 1993 (Dartmouth cert. 1994). Harry Frank Guggenheim fellow, 1984-85, Stanford Humanities Ctr. fellow, 1988-89, Newberry Libr.-NEH fellow, 1992-93, John Simon Guggenheim Found. fellow, 1997-98. Office: Dept History Brown U Providence RI 02912

GORNBEIN, HENRY SEIDEL, lawyer; b. Detroit, May 27, 1943; s. Abe Siedel and Lillian (Westerman) G.; m. Debra Marilyn Gornbein, June 13, 1993; children: Jonathan David and Laurie Beth. B in Philosophy, Wayne State U., 1965; JD, U. Mich., 1968. Bar: Mich. 1968. Law clk. Wayne County Cir. Ct., Detroit, 1968-69; assoc. Gage & Brukoff, Southfield, Mich., 1969-70, Coleman, Goodman & Schifman, Southfield, 1970-71; ptnr. Bayer, Goren, Gornbein, Gropman & Kaplan, P.C., Southfield, 1979-81; sole practice and ptnr. in various entities, 1971-81; assoc. Baskin, Feldstein & Gornbein, Birmingham, Mich., 1982-85; pvt. practice Birmingham, 1985-95; ptnr. Bookholder, Bassett, Gornbein, Solomon & Cohen PLLC, 1995-98. Creator, host (cable TV show) Practical Law; pres. Am. Divorce Info. Network, Inc., pub. Divorce Online (internet). Home and Office: 4190 Telegraph Rd Ste 3000 Bloomfield Hills MI 48302-2082 E-mail: henry@divorceonline.com.

GORNEY, RODERIC, psychiatry educator; b. Grand Rapids, Mich., Aug. 13, 1924; s. Abraham Jacob Gorney and Edelaine (Roden) Harburg; m. Carol Ann Sobel, Apr. 13, 1986. BS, Stanford U., 1948, MD, 1949; PhD in Psychoanalysis, So. Calif. Psychoanalytic Inst., 1977. Diplomate Am. Bd. Psychiatry and Neurology. Pvt. practice psychiatry, San Francisco, 1952-62; asst. prof. UCLA, 1962-71, assoc. prof., 1971-73, prof. psychiatry, 1980—, dir. psychosocial adaptation and the future program, 1971—. Faculty So. Calif. Psychoanalytic Inst. Author: The Human Agenda, 1972. Served with USAF, 1943-46. Fellow AAAS, Acad. Psychoanalysis, Am. Psychoanalytic Assn., Internat. Psychoanalytic Assn., Am. Psychiatric Assn. (essay prize 1971), Group for Advancement of Psychiatry. Avocation: music. Office: UCLA Neuropsychiatric Inst 760 Westwood Plz Los Angeles CA 90095-8353 E-mail: preadapt@ucla.edu.

GORNISH, GERALD, lawyer; b. Phila., July 14, 1937; s. Edward H. and Sylvia (Elkan) G.; m. Rochelle Schildkraut, Mar. 5, 1961; children: Karen, Edward H. BA with honors, U. Pa., 1958; LLB, Harvard U., 1961. Bar: Pa. 1962. Pvt. practice, Phila., 1962-66; asst. city solicitor City of Phila., 1964-66; with Goodis, Greenfield, Henry, Shaiman & Levin, Phila., 1966-71; from dep. atty. gen. to atty. gen. Pa. Dept. Justice, 1971-78; with Wolf, Block, Schorr and Solis-Cohen, Phila., 1979—2003; chief counsel Pa. Pub. Sch. Employees' Retirement System, Harrisburg, 2003—. Atty. gen. State of Pa., 1978; dir. Office Civil Law, Pa. Dept. Justice, 1975-78; mem. Supreme Ct. Adv. Com. on Appellate Ct. Rules, 1974-85. Mem. ABA, Pa. Bar Assn. (coun. pub. utility law sect. 1984-86, vice-chmn. 1988, chmn. 1989), Phila. Bar Assn. (chmn. appellate cts. com. 1987, treas. campaign for qualified judges 1986-2003). Home: 511 Anthwyn Rd Merion Station PA 19066-1328 Office: Pub Sch Employees' RetirementSys 5 N Fifth St 5th Fl Harrisburg PA 17101 E-mail: ggornish@state.pa.us.

GOROG, WILLIAM FRANCIS, corporate executive; b. Warren, Ohio, Sept. 2, 1925; s. Frank and Margaret R. G.; m. Gretchen Elizabeth Meister, June 11, 1949; children: Robin, Jonathan, William Christopher, Lesley Anne, Jennifer, Peter. BS, U.S. Mil. Acad, 1949; MS, Ohio State U., 1951. Mktg. mgr. Bulova Watch Co., N.Y.C., 1954-55; exec. v.p. Data Corp., Dayton, Ohio, 1956-63, chmn., chief exec. officer, 1963-75; v.p. Mead Corp., Dayton, Ohio, 1972-75; dep. asst. to pres. The White House, Washington, 1975; exec. dir. White House Council on Internat. Econ. Policy, 1976; pres., chief exec. officer Mag. Pubs. Am., N.Y.C., 1982-87; chmn., chief exec. officer Arbor Internat., Vienna, Va., 1987-90; chmn., founder InteliData, Reston, Va., from 1990; chmn. Worldcorp, Herndon, Va., 1993-97. Bd. dirs. Nations Bank, C & S Sovran Corp., Verifone Inc., Fiskars, Helsinki, Finland, Chief Execs. Orgn. Chmn. adv. bd. Georgetown U. Grad. Sch. of Bus., 1982, chmn. Washington campus. Capt. USAF, 1949-53. Mem.: Bay Colony Club, Maroon Creek Club (Aspen, Colo.), Columbia Country Club (Chevy Chase, Md.). Republican. Roman Catholic. Home: Naples, Fla. Died July 2002.

GORON, MARA J. social studies educator, assistant principal; b. Jackson Heights, N.Y., Apr. 9, 1968; d. Stuart Platt and Joan (Arkin) Scolnick. BA, The George Washington U., 1990, MA, 1992; MEd, U. Md., 1995. Cert. secondary social studies and spl. edn. adminstrn. Resident asst., adminstr., supr. The George Washington U., Washington, 1989-92; tchr. religion Temple Sinai, Washington, 1990-96; peer tutoring coord. The George Washington U., 1991-92; adult edn. tchr. Montgomery County Pub., Rockville, Md., 1992; spl. edn. tchr. Alexandria (Va.) Pub. Schs., 1992, Prince Georges Pub. Schs., Upper Marlboro, Md., 1992-93; tutor Lab Sch. Washington, 1992—2002; spl. edn. tchr. Howard County Pub. Schs., Ellicott City, Md., 1993-96, social studies tchr., 1996-99; asst. prin. Centennial H.S., Ellicott City, 1999—2001; inaugural asst. prin. Reservoir H.S., 2001—02; asst. prin. Spanish River Cmty. H.S., Boca Raton, Fla., 2002—. Adviser Howard County Assn. Student Couns., 1997—99; pres. Howard County Coun. for Social Studies, 1997—99; adj. prof. Towson U., 1998, 99. Troop leader Girl Scouts of Am., 1994-95. Mem. ASCD, NAFE, Nat. Assn. Secondary Sch. Prins., Pi Kappa Phi, Omicron Delta Kappa. Avocations: walking, hiking, knitting, reading, going to movies. E-mail: goronm@palmbeach.k12.fl.us.

GORONKIN, HERBERT, physicist; b. Pitts., Jan. 9, 1936; s. Sander (Tammie) and Mae (Shulman) G.; children: David, Jeffrey, Michael; m. Pamela Louise Cooper, Oct. 4, 1980; children: Rebecca Louise, Theresa Louise, James David. BA, Temple U., 1961, MA, 1962, PhD, 1973. Physicist Internat. Resistance Co., Phila., 1963-65; sr. research physicist Honeywell Inc., Ft. Washington, Pa., 1965-66; sect. head Am. Electronic Labs., Colmar, Pa., 1966-69; project engr. Gen. Electric Co., Syracuse, N.Y., 1969-75; mgr. semiconductor ops. Varian Assocs., Beverly, Mass., 1975-77; from mgr. high speed devices to chief scientist Phoenix copr. rsch. labs. Motorola Inc., Phoenix, 1977-88, mgr. to dir. phys. rsch. lab., 1988-99; v.p. phys. rsch. labs. Phys. Scis. Rsch. Labs., Phoenix, 1999—2003, dir. rsch. activities in molecular electronics, spintronics, biotechnology and nanosci.; pres. Tech. Acceleration Assoc., 2003—. Chmn. Workshop on Compound Semicondr. Microwave Materials and Devices, 1984-86, Quantum Electronics, Quantum Functional Devices and Compound Semicondr. Devices, 1986, Advanced Hetrostructure Workshop, 1994; program chair Internat. Symposium on Compound Semicondrs., 1994, gen. chair, 1997; govering bd. Ctr. of Intergrated Nanosystems, 2003; bd. dirs. Zehacore, 2003. Contbr. articles to profl. jours., chpts. to books; patentee in field. Served with USAF, 1954-57. Recipient Motorola Disting. Innovator award, 1993, Motorola Master Innovator award, 1995, Motorola Dan Noble fellow, 1996; named IEEE Phoenix Sect. Sr. Engr. of Yr., 1993. Fellow IEEE (IEDM compound semiconductor tech. program com. 1983-86); mem. Am. Phys. Soc., Sigma Xi. Avocations: hiking, japanese, cooking. Home: 8641 S Willow Dr Tempe AZ 85284-2473 Office: Motorola Inc 7700 S River Pkwy Tempe AZ 85284-1806 E-mail: herb.goronkin@motorola.com.

GOROVITS, BORIS, analytical biochemist; PhD, Moscow State U., 1990. Rsch. instr., dept. biochemistry U. Tex., Health Sci. Ctr. at San Antonio, 1993—97; scientist Regeneron Pharm. Inc, Tarrytown, NY, 1997—2000; sr. rsch. scientist Wyeth Rsch., Pearl River, NY, 2000—. Mem.: AAPS. Home: 273 Treetop Cir Nanuet NY 10954 Office: Wyeth Research 401 N Middletown Pearl River NY 10965 Personal E-mail: bgorovits@yahoo.com.

GORR, LOUIS FREDERICK, investment consultant; b. North Platte, Nebr., Aug. 1, 1941; s. Ernest Frederick and Eileen Bethel (Green) G.; m. Madeleine Zangla, Dec. 12, 1967; 1 dau., Michaela. BA, U. Nebr., 1963, MA, 1967; postgrad., U. Md., 1972; MBA, U. Dallas, 1981; postgrad., So. Meth. U. Spl. asst. to dir. Nat. Mus. Am. History and Tech., Smithsonian Instn., Washington, 1969-73; dir. divsn. museums and historic preservation Fairfax (Va.) County Govt., 1973-77; dir. Dallas County (Tex.) Heritage Soc., 1977-79, Dallas Mus. Natural History, 1979-86, Dallas Aquarium, 1979-86; dep. dir. fin and adminstrn., treas. Winterthur (Del.) Mus. and Gardens, 1986-89; owner East End Devel. Corp., 1984-86; pres. Janus Mgmt. Advisors, 1985-86; exec. dir. Mus. of the Confederacy, Richmond, Va., 1989-92; investment cons. Branch Cabell & Co., Richmond, Va., 1993-96; fin. planner Lincoln fin. advs. Profl. Fin. Planning Corp., Richmond, Va., 1996-2000; pres. Harbor Fin. Advisors, LLC, Richmond, Va., 1996-2000; faculty, lectr. personal fin. Va. Cooperative Ext. Svc. Va. Poly. Inst. and State U., 2001—. Fin. counselor U.S. Army, 1999-2001, USN, 2000; real estate broker, Tex.; cons., lectr. mus. and mgmt. fields, 1970—; adj. prof. mus. studies U. Okla., 1982-93; mem. bd. commerce Dallas Nat. Bank, 1980-84; dir., mem. exam. and shareholder rels. coms. Fidelity Nat. Bank, 1985-86, advisory dir., 1986-88—; chmn. bd. commerce Republic Bank Dallas East, 1983-84. Contbr. articles to profl. jours.; columnist Inside Bus., 1995—. Pres. Fairfax Symphony Orch., 1976-77; bd. dirs. No. Va. Youth Symphony, 1975-77, Met. Washington Cultural Alliance, 1976, Prince George's County (Md.) Arts Council, 1973, Fairfax County Assn. Civic Orgns., 1976-77; bd. dirs. Cen. Va. Pub. Broadcasting, 1990-93; arts and culture adv. com. Dallas Ind. Sch. Dist., Leadership Dallas, 1983; leadership devel. trainer United Way, 1980-83; adv. bd. March of Dimes Found.; cmty. adv. bd. Med. Coll. Va., 1991-93. With USAF, 1963-64. Rsch. fellow Smithsonian Instn., 1971, Naval Inst. Mem. Am. Assn. Mus. (bd. dirs. 1982-83), Va. Assn. Mus. (bd. dirs. 1989-93), Tex. Assn. Mus. (pres. 1981-83, dir.), Assn. Sci. Mus. Dirs. (v.p. 1983), Dallas Bus. League, Dallas 40, Dallas C. of C., East Dallas C. of C., Leadership Dallas Alumni Assn., Bus. Workout Coun., Internat. Assn. Fin. Planning, Inst. CFPs, Internat. Assn. of Registered Fin. Cons., Masons (32 degree), Shriners, Sigma Iota Epsilon, Lambda Chi Alpha. Republican. Home and Office: 2310 E Marshall St Richmond VA 23223-7147

GORRIAZ, MARY ALICE, real estate broker; b. Mesa, Ariz., Aug. 5, 1953; d. Edward Lee and Evangeline Lauda (Gorraiz) Meeker; m. Michael David Izzo, Dec. 26, 1971 (div. 1999); children: Michael Wade, Clinton Jarred, Antoinette Marie. Student, Pioneer Coll., 1977, Yavapai Coll., 1984-93, 98—. Cert. broker, realtor, Ariz. Sales agt. Babbit Bros., Flagstaff, Ariz., 1970-76; owner Cottonwood (Ariz.) Tees, 1978-84; realtor Weston Realty, Cottonwood, 1985-86, Coldwell Banker Mabery Real Estate, Cottonwood, 1986-89; sales agent, assoc. broker The Glenarm Land Co., Cottonwood, 1989-97; office mgr., sec. Izzo & Sons Contracting, 1985-97, Wilhoit Water Co., 1991-93; sales assoc. Walmart, 1995-96, asst. regional commr. AYSO, 1996-97; broker, owner ISO Realty, 1997—; sec. Journey-Yavapai County Bd. Suprs. Dist. 3, 1999-2001; legal sec. Yavapai County Pub. Defenders Office, 2001—. Office mgr., sec. Gonzales & Sons Electric, 1996-97; para educator Mingus Union H.S., Cottonwood, 1997-99. Author: Current Customer Cook Book, 1984. Bd. dirs. cub scouts Boy Scouts Am., 1984, 87; bd. dirs. AYSO Soccer, Verde Valley, Ariz., 1984-87, 92-2000, purchaser, 1992-99, soccer coach tournament all girls' traveling team, 1993-95, 97, 98, also pub. dir., asst. regional commn., purchaser, publicity, 1996-2000; leader youth group, Cottonwood. Democrat. Roman Catholic. Avocations: fishing, hiking, sewing, hunting, travel. Home: 862 East Brook Hollow Dr Cottonwood AZ 86326 E-mail: mary.gorraiz@co.yavapai.az.us.

GORRIN, EUGENE, lawyer; b. Irvington, N.J., Apr. 22, 1956; s. Harry and Ruth (Goldberg) G. BA, Rutgers U., 1978; JD, George Washington U., 1981; LLM in Taxation, NYU, 1982. Bar: N.J. 1981, U.S. Dist. Ct. N.J. 1981, U.S. Tax Ct. 1982, U.S. Supreme Ct. 1985. Assoc. Ozzard, Rizzolo, Klein, Mauro & Savo, Somerville, NJ, 1982-83; Assoc. Levine, Furman & Davis, East Brunswick, NJ, 1984-88; ptnr. Cole, Schotz, Meisel, Forman & Leonard, P.A., Hackensack, NJ, 1988-98; v.p., corp. adv. specialist Family Office Group Merrill Lynch Trust Co., Pennington, NJ, 1999—2000, sr. trust officer, mgr. spl. assets real estate fiduciary svcs. group, 2001—. Contbr. articles to profl. pubs. Mem. ABA (taxation sect.), N.J. Bar Assn. (taxation sect.), Phi Alpha Delta. Home: 2607 Frederick Ter Union NJ 07083-5603 Office: Merrill Lynch Trust Co 1300 Merrill Lynch Dr Pennington NJ 08534 E-mail: eugene_gorrin@ml.com.

GORRY, G. ANTHONY, medical educator, educator; BSE, Yale U., 1962; MS, U. Calif., Berkeley, 1962; PhD in Computer Sci., MIT, 1967. From asst. prof. to assoc. prof. Sloan Sch. Mgmt., 1967—73, assoc. prof. computer sci., 1973—75; from assoc. prof. cmty. medicine to prof. health mgmt. Baylor Coll. Medicine, Houston, 1975—85, prof. divsn. neurosci., v.p. info. tech., 1986—89; dean tech., v.p. for info. tech. Rice U., Houston, 1989—, dir. Ctr. Tech. in Tchg. and Learning, dir. W.M. Keck Ctr. Computational Biology; adj. prof., dir. neurosci Baylor Coll. Medicine; prof. dept. computer sci. Rice U. Assoc. faculty Oper. Rsch. Ctr. MIT, 1971—75; lectr. dept. med. Tufts U. Sch. Medicine, 1971—75; adj. assoc. prof. math. sci. Rice U., 1975—78, adj. prof. dept. computer sci., 1985—; adj. prof. bus. and econ. Tex. Women's U., 1978—79; mem. com. Nat. Libr. Med., 1984—88; dir. W.M. Keck ctr. computer biology Baylor Coll. Med. and Rice U.; dir. evaluation rsch. group Nat. Heart and Blood Vessel Rsch. and Demonstration Ctr., 1975—82, dir. health mgmt. rsch., 1978—80; 1978-80; adj. prof. neurosci. and cmty. medicine Baylor Coll. Medicine. Fellow: Am. Coll. Med. Informatics; mem.: Inst. Med.-NAS. Office: Rice University PO Box 1892 Houston TX 77251-1892

GORSKE, ROBERT H. retired lawyer; b. Milw, Wis, June 8, 1932; s. Herman Albert and Lorraine (McDermott) G.; m. Antonette Dujick, Aug. 28, 1954; 1 child, Judith Mary (Mrs. Charles H. McMullen). Student, U. Wis., Milw., 1949-50; BA cum laude, Marquette U., 1953, JD magna cum laude, 1955, MS in Clin. Psychology, 1996; LLM (W.W. Cook fellow), U. Mich., 1959; student, Hague Acad. Internat. Law, The Netherlands, 1981. Bar: Wis. bar 1955, D.C. bar 1975, U.S. Supreme Ct. bar 1970; cert. Gerontology, Marquette U., 2002. Assoc. firm Quarles, Spence & Quarles, Milw., 1955-56, atty. Allis-Chalmers Mfg. Co., West Allis, Wis., 1956-62; instr. law U. Mich. Law Sch., Ann Arbor, Mich., 1958-59; lectr. law Marquette U. Law Sch., Milw., 1963; assoc. firm Quarles, Herriott & Clemons, Milw., 1962-64; atty. Wis. Electric Power Co., Milw., 1964-67, gen. counsel, 1967-94, v.p., 1970-72, 76-94, dir., 1991-94; mem. firm Quarles & Brady, Milw., 1972-76; gen. counsel Wis. Energy Corp., Milw., 1981-94. Tutor in psychiatry Med. Coll. Wis., 1995. Contbr. articles to profl. jours.; Editor-in-chief: Marquette Law Rev, 1954-55. Bd. dirs. Guadalupe Children's Med. Dental Clinic, Inc., Milw., 1976-86; bd. dirs. Milw. Urban League, 1991-94, treas., 1993-94; trustee Ronald McDonald House, Wauwatosa, Wis., 1987-94; trustee St. Mary's Parish, Elm Grove, Wis., 2003-. Mem. State Bar Wis., Edison Electric Inst. (vice chmn. legal com. 1975-77, chmn. 1977-79), Am. Arbitration Assn. (panelist comml. arbitrators 1985—), Ctr. for Pub. Resources (com. on alt. dispute resolution 1985-94, exec. com. 1991-94, panel disting. neutrals 1991-94).

GORSKI, JACK, biochemistry educator; b. Green Bay, Wis., Mar. 14, 1931; s. John R. and Martha (Kenney) G.; m. Harriet M. Fischer, Sept. 9, 1955; children: Michael, Jo Anne. Student, Calif. Poly. Coll., 1949-50; BS, U. Wis., 1953; postgrad., U. Utah, 1957; MS, Wash. State U., 1956, PhD, 1958. NIH postdoctoral fellow U. Wis., 1958-61; asst. prof., asso. prof. physiology U. Ill., Urbana, 1961-66, prof. physiology, 1967—, prof. biochemistry, 1969—; prof. biochemistry and animal scis. U. Wis., Madison, 1973—. Wis. Alumni Research Found. prof., 1985. NSF research fellow Princeton, 1966-67; mem. endocrinology study sect. NIH, 1966-70, molecular biology study sect., 1977-81; mem. biochemistry adv. com. Am. Cancer Soc., 1973-76, mem. personnel for research com., 1983— Contbr. articles to profl. jours. Recipient NIH Merit award, 1986. Fellow Am. Acad. Arts and Sci.; mem. NAS, Am. Soc. Biol. Chemists, Endocrine Soc. (Oppenheimer award 1971, Disting. Leadership award 1987, pres. 1990-91, F.C. Koch award 1995). Democrat. Unitarian Universalist. Office: U Wis Dept Biochemistry 433 Babcock Dr Madison WI 53706-1544

GORSKI, ROBERT ALEXANDER, chemist, consultant; b. Passaic, N.J., Nov. 24, 1922; s. Stephen T. and Wanda P. (Amlicke) G.; m. Helen Marie Thompson, Aug. 19, 1944; children: Robert J., Mary Ann B., Mark G., Stephen J., Paul F. BA in Sci., La Salle U., 1947; MS in Chemistry, U. Pa., 1948, PhD in Phys. Chemistry, 1951. Chemist DuPont, Wilmington, Del., 1951-53; rsch. chemist DuPont Freon Products Lab., Wilmington, Del., 1953-60, sr. rsch. chemist, 1960-70, rsch. assoc., 1970-78, tech. assoc., 1978-85; cons. DuPont Fluorochemicals Lab., Wilmington, Del., 1985-91; ret., 1991—. Author book chpt.; contbr. articles to profl. jours. With U.S. Army, 1943-46, ETO. Mem. Am. Chem. Soc., ASTM, Nat. Geog. Soc., KC, Sigma Xi. Republican. Roman Catholic. Achievements include patents for solvents, refrigeration, blowing agents for plastic foams and fire extinguishing. Avocations: sports, reading. Home: 735 Harvard Ln Newark DE 19711-3134

GORSLINE, STEPHEN PAUL, security specialist; b. Washington, Aug. 22, 1954; s. Robert William and Patricia Ann (Ketchum) G.; m. Kelly Kathleen Wade, Dec. 7, 2002. AAS in Criminal Justice, Coll. of Lake County, 1987; BS in Criminal Justice, Madonna U., 1998. Dir. safety ops. Thielenhaus Corp., Novi, Mich., 1998-99; with US Dept. of Def. Vol. Nat. Rep. Com., Washington, 1992. Staff sgt. USAF, 1977-82. Mem. Safety/Security Mgmt. Assn. (exec. dir. 1996-99), Fraternal Order Police. Roman Catholic. Avocations: collecting stamps, old coins and postcards. E-mail: stevegorsline@yahoo.com.

GORSUCH, EDWARD LEE, chancellor; Degree in Econ. and Cmty. Devel., U. Mo. Dir. Inst. Social and Econ. Rsch., 1976-94; dean Sch. Pub. Affairs U. Alaska, Anchorage, 1988-94, chancellor, 1994—. Bd. dirs. Commonwealth North; mem. adv. bd. Alaska Airlines Anchorage Cmty.; mem. civilian adv. bd. ALCOM; mem. Fiscal Policy Coun. Alaska. Office: U Alaska Anchorage Chancellor's Office 3211 Providence Dr Anchorage AK 99508-8060 E-mail: aychanc@uaa.alaska.edu.

GORSUCH, NEIL MCGILL, lawyer; b. Denver, Aug. 29, 1967; s. David Ronald Gorsuch and Anne McGill Burford; m. Marie Louise Burletson, June 22, 1996; children: Belinda Loveday, Emma Louise. BA with honors, Columbia U., 1988; JD cum laude, Harvard U., 1991; postgrad., Oxford (England) U., 1995. Bar: NY 1992, Co. 1994, D.C. 1997, U.S. Ct. Appeals (4th Cir.) 1997, U.S. Ct. Appeals (3rd Cir.) 1998, U.S. Supreme Ct. 1998, U.S. Ct. Appeals (6th Cir.) 2000, U.S. Dist Ct. (D.C.) 2001, U.S. Dist. Ct. (so. dist) N.Y. 2002. Law clk. to hon. David B. Sentelle US Ct. of Appeals (D.C. Cir.), Washington, 1991—92; law clk. to hon. Byron R. White and hon. Anthony M. Kennedy US Supreme Ct., Washington, 1993—94; assoc. Kellogg, Huber, Hansen, Todd & Evans, Washington, 1995—97, ptnr., 1998—. Contbr. articles to profl. jours. Recipient Marshall scholarship, U.K. Govt., 1992—95, Harry S. Truman scholarship, U.S. Govt., 1987—90. Mem.: ATLA, ABA, Phi Beta Kappa, John Carroll Soc., Trout Unltd., Westwood Country Club, Univ. Club. Avocations: skiing, fly fishing, tennis. Home: 1711 Wind Haven Way Vienna VA 22182 Office: Kellogg Huber Hansen Todd & Evans 1615 M Street NW Ste 400 Washington DC 20036 Office Fax: 202-326-7999. E-mail: ngorsuch@khhte.com.

GORT, MICHAEL, economics educator; b. Minsk, USSR, Sept. 30, 1923; came from China to U.S., 1937; m. Elizabeth Ann Mitchell, June 15, 1957; children: William Henry, Adam Michael. AB, Bklyn. Coll., CUNY, 1943; AM, Columbia U., 1951, PhD, 1954. Lectr. in econs. U. Calif., Berkeley, 1951-54; mem. research staff Nat. Bur. Econ. Research, N.Y.C., 1954-57; assoc. prof. fin. U. Chgo., 1957-62; cons. Dept. Commerce, Washington, 1962-63; prof. econs. SUNY, Buffalo, 1963—. Vis. prof. econs. Northwestern U., Evanston, Ill., 1967-68; sr. research staff mem. and dir. research program in indsl. orgn. Nat. Bur. Econ. Research, N.Y.C., 1971-75; pres. Michael Gort Assocs., Buffalo, 1977—. Author: Diversification and Integration in American Industry, 1962, Changes in the Size Standard of Business Firms, 1964; contbr. articles to profl. jours. Mem. adv. com. U.S. Bur. of the Census, 1994-2000. Social Sci. Rsch. Coun. fellow, 1950-51. Mem. Am. Econ. Assn. Home: 71 Smallwood Dr Buffalo NY 14226-4028 Office: SUNY Dept of Econs North Campus Buffalo NY 14260

GORTATOWSKI, MELVIN JEROME, retired chemist; b. Chgo., Oct. 30, 1925; s. Walter Harry and Anna Martha (Santowski) G. BS, U. Ill., 1950, PhD, 1956; MS, Wash. State U., 1952. Research instr. biochemistry U. Utah, Salt Lake City, 1955-58, research assoc. psychiatry, 1958-59, research instr. biochemistry, chemist VA Hosp., 1959-65; assoc. investigator, asst. rsch. prof. pediatrics, biochemistry U. So. Calif. Children's Hosp., Los Angeles, 1965-71; dir. bur. clin. chemistry Utah State Health Lab., Salt Lake City, 1971-87, safety officer, 1980-87. Contbr. articles to jours. Served with U.S. Army, 1944-46. Eastman Kodak fellow U. Ill., 1954. Mem. Am. Chem. Soc., Mineral Collectors Utah, Utah Numismatic Soc. (bd. dirs. 1976-77), Sigma Xi, Phi Lambda Upsilon. Roman Catholic. Avocations: photography, philatelics, music, mineral collecting, swimming. Home: 4045 Foubert Ave Salt Lake City UT 84124-3410

GORTON, NATHANIEL M. federal judge; b. 1938; m. Jodi Linnell; 3 children. AB, Dartmouth Coll., 1960; LLB, Columbia U., 1966. Bar: Mass. 1966, U.S. Dist. Ct. Mass. 1967, U.S. Ct. Appeals (5th cir.) 1975, U.S. Ct. Appeals (9th cir.) 1977, U.S. Ct. Appeals (1st cir.) 1979, U.S. Ct. Appeals (11th cir.) 1990. Assoc. Nutter, McClennen & Fish, Boston, 1966-69, Powers & Hall, P.C., Boston, 1970-74, ptnr., dir., 1975-92; judge U.S. Dist. Ct., Mass., 1992—. Trustee Buckingham Browne & Nichols Sch., Cambridge, Mass., 1984-93, chmn., 1989-93; mem. corp. New Eng. Home for Little Wanderers; mem. Wellesley Town Meeting, 1971-86; sr. warden All Saints Episcopal Ch., Brookline, Mass., 1975-80; apptd. Mass. Citizens Commn. on Gen. Ct., 1976; mem. com. Modern Legis., 1967-69; coach Wellesley Little League and Youth Hockey, 1983-87; bd. dirs. Rep. Club Mass., 1991-92; mem. fin. com. Citizens for Joe Malone, 1989-90; mem. Weld/Cellucci Com., 1989-90; program chmn. Boston chpt. Ripon Soc., 1967-68. (Lt. (j.g.) USNR, 1960-62. Mem. Boston Bar Assn. (law day classroom program, 1987-93, litigation, adminstrn. justice sect.). Avocations: hockey, tennis, skiing, sailing, mem. Boston Atoms Hockey N.Am.- (nat. finalist 1988, 91). Office: US Dist Ct 595 Main St Worcester MA 01608-2093

GORTON, SLADE, attorney, former senator; b. Chicago, Ill., Jan. 8, 1928; s. Thomas Slade and Ruth (Israel) Gorton; m. Sally Jean Clark, June 28, 1958; children: Tod, Sarah Jane, Rebecca Lynn. AB, Dartmouth Coll., 1950; LLB with honors, Columbia U., 1953. Bar: Wash. 1953. Assoc. law firm, Seattle, 1953—65; ptnr. law firm, 1965—69; atty. gen. State of Wash., Olympia, 1969—81; ptnr. Davis, Wright & Jones, Seattle, 1987—89; senator from Wash. U.S. Senate, 1981—87, 1989—2001; of counsel Preston, Gates & Ellis, Seattle and Washington, 2001—. Mem. Wash. Ho. of Reps., 1959—69, majority leader, 1967—69, nat. Rep. senatorial com., Indian affairs, budget com., appropriations com., commerce/sci. and transp. com., energy and natural resources com.; chmn. commerce, sci. and transp. subcom. on aviation, com. on appropriations subcom. on interior. Trustee, founding mem. Pacific Sci. Ctr., Seattle, 1977—78; mem. Pres.'s Consumer Adv. Coun., 1975—77, Wash. State Law and Justice Commn., 1969—80, chmn., 1969—76; mem. State Criminal Justice Tng. Commn., 1969—80, chmn., 1969—76. Served with U.S. Army, 1946—47, to 1st lt. USAF, 1953—56, col. (ret.) USAF. Mem.: ABA, Nat. Assn. Attys. Gen. (pres. 1976—77, Wyman award 1980), Wash. Bar Assn., Wash. Athletic Club (Seattle), Seattle Tennis Club, Phi Beta Kappa, Phi Delta Phi. Office: Preston Gates & Ellis LLP 701 5th Ave Ste 5000 Seattle WA 98104-7011

GORUM, JACQUELYNE W. dean, social work educator; b. Pitman, N.J., July 20, 1941; d. John Emerick and Evelyn Carnetta (Weekes) W.; m. Wendell J.L. Gorum, Nov. 24, 1964; children: W. Jay, Guy, Marc. MSW, U. Denver, 1965; postgrad., Pa. State U.; DSW, Howard U., 1983. Asst. prof. Sch. Social Work Howard U., Washington, 1980-84, dir. admissions, recruitment and fin. aid dir., undergrad., 1983-84; asst. prof. Sch. Social Work SUNY, Stony Brook, 1984-89; assoc. prof., dir. undergrad. programs Dept. Social Work Del. State U., Dover, 1989-91, dean Sch. Profl. Studies, 1991—. Active Del. Perinatal Bd., Dover, 1996—, Del. Health Care Commn., Dover, 1994—; liaison, mem. program bd. Leadership Alliance, 1991—. Recipient Beyond War award Peace Inst., 1987. Mem. Black Women in Higher Edn. (bd. dirs. 1997—, award 1993), Nat. Black Alcoholics and Addictions Coun. (exec. bd. dirs. 1991-2002), Coun. Social Work Edn. (site vis., Svc. award 1991), Pioneer Peace Corps Vol., Delta Sigma Theta (chair program and planning devel.). Avocations: travel, swimming, reading. Office: Del State U 1200 N Dupont Hwy Dover DE 19901-2202

GORUP, GREGORY JAMES, marketing executive; b. Kansas City, Kans., Mar. 27, 1948; s. Mike and Helen F. Gorup; m. Kathleen Susan Grogan, Apr. 12, 1986 (div.); children: Michael Thomas, Ryan Nicholas. BA in Econs., St. Benedict Coll., 1970; MBA, U. Pa., 1972. Market analyst product planning and devel. dept. Citibank, N.Y.C., 1972-73, market planning officer corp. product mgmt. divsn., 1973-74, product mgr. securities svcs., 1974-75; v.p., dir. product devel. Irving Trust Co., N.Y.C., 1975-80, mgr. product mgmt. dept., 1980-81; v.p. mktg. U.S. area Credit Suisse, 1981-84; sr. cons. Wesley, Brown and Bartle, N.Y.C., 1985-86; bank mktg. mgr. Digital Equipment Corp., N.Y.C., 1986-87; money mktg. mgr. Reuters N.Am., 1987-88; pres. Gorup Assocs., 1989-91; dist. v.p. Nat. Computer Sys., N.Y., 1991-94; regional mgr. Soc. Worldwide InterBank Fin. Telecomm., 1994-96, sr. regional mgr., 1996-98, mgr., 1998-2000, sr. mgr., 2000—01; dir. Rogue Wave Software, LSOS Div., Mamaroneck, NY, 2001—. Mem. Rep. Nat. Com., Nat. Rep. Senatorial Com., U.S. Shooting Team. Mem. NRA (life), West Point Soc. N.Y., Wharton Bus. Sch. Club, Princeton Club N.Y., Orienta Beach Club, Willow Wood Gun Club, Army "A" Club, U.S. Naval Inst., Naval League of the U.S., Air Force Assn. Roman Catholic. Home and Office: 910 Stuart Ave # 2-0 Mamaroneck NY 10543-4134 E-mail: ussocom1@aol.com.

GOSCIEWSKI, ROBERT LOUIS, logistician; b. Bristol, Pa., Mar. 10, 1957; s. Victor Stanley and Palma Mary Gosciewski; m. Maria Luisa Capasso, May 26, 1984; children: Diana Dawn, Kathryn Kelly. BA, U. Pa., 1979; prof. cert. Italian, Def. Lang. Inst., Monterey, Calif., 1981; MSBA, Boston U., 1985. Cert. profl. logistician Internat. Soc. Logistics Engrs., 3wizard 3com Corp. Instr. Big Bend C.C., Vicenza, Italy, 1984-85; cons. engring. Ingegneria Info. S.p.A., Turin, Italy, 1985-86; prodn. mgr. L.F. Lambert Spawn Co., Coatesville, Pa., 1986-89; computer systems analyst Army Legal Svcs. Agy., Falls Church, Va., 1989-92; treas. Valley Ctr. Corp., Parkesburg, Pa., 1989-90; mktg. cons. Conemar, Manassas, Va., 1989-92; computer specialist, engr. Office Dep. Chief of Staff, U.S. Army, Heidelberg, Germany, 1992-93; info. mgmt. officer Office Provost Marshal, HQUSAREUR, Mannheim, Germany, 1993-96; logistics automation specialist Logistics Automation Divsn., HQUSASETAF, Vicenza, Italy, 1996-98, chief logistics automation divsn., 1998 2000, 2002—; chief programs integration and execution, dir. combat devel. Combat Svc. Support, U.S. Army Combined Arms Support Commd., 2000—02; chief, LAD Logistics Automation Divsn. So. European Task Force, Vicenza, 2002—. Cons. Engring. Ingegneria Informatica S.p.A., Torino, Italy, 1985—86; internet working computer cons., local wide area networking svcs., 1993—98. Mem. West End Fire Co. No. 3, Coatesville, 1989. Capt. inf. U.S. Army, 1979—83. Mem.: Assn. U.S. Army, Internat. Soc. Logistics, Am. Econs. Assn., Beta Theta Pi. Roman Catholic. Avocations: gardening, critical thinking, travel, community service, golf. E-mail: gosciews@alumni.upenn.edu.

GOSDECK, THOMAS JOSEPH, lawyer; b. Buffalo, Oct. 10, 1951; s. Kermit Ronald and Mary Jane (O'Brien) G.; m. Catherine E. Schuth, July 31, 1982. BA, SUNY, 1973, JD, 1976. Bar: N.Y. 1979. Counsel environ. conservation com. N.Y. State Senate, Albany, 1980-82, counsel agr. com., 1982-85, counsel consumer protection com., 1985-88; ptnr. Newman, Kehoe et al., Lyons, N.Y., 1988-88, Steinhaus Assocs., Albany, 1988-90, DeGraff, Foy, Holt-Harris & Mealey, Albany, 1991-92, Hill & Gosdeck, Albany, 1993—. Counsel Webster (N.Y.) Republican Com., 1987-88. Recipient Teddi award Camp Good Day & Spl. Times, Rochester, N.Y., 1982. Mem. Brockport Coll. Found., Normanside Country Club, Ft. Orange Club. Roman Catholic. Avocations: golf, reading, travel, photography. Office: Hill & Gosdeck 99 Washington Ave Ste 400 Albany NY 12210-2823

GOSE, RICHARD VERNIE, lawyer; b. Hot Springs, S.D., Aug. 3, 1927; children: Beverly Marie, Donald Paul, Celeste Marlene. MS in Engring., Northwestern U., 1955; LLB, George Washington U., 1967, JD, 1968. Registered profl. engr., Wyo.; bar: N.Mex 1967, U.S. Supreme Ct. 1976, Wyo. 1979. Sr. aerodynamics engr. N.Am. Aviation, 1955—57; exec. asst. to U.S. Senator Hickey Washington, 1960—62; mgr. E. G. & G., Inc., Washington, 1964—66; asst. atty. gen. State of N.Mex, Santa Fe, 1967—70; pvt. practice Santa Fe, 1967—, Casper, Wyo., 1978—83, Prescott, 1989—. Ranch mgr., foreman, 1945—49; assoc. prof. engring. U. Wyo., 1957—60; owner, mgr. Gose & Assocs., Santa Fe, 1967—78; pres. Argosy Internat., Inc., 1994—. Mem. com. fgn. rels., Phoenix, 1980—; co-chmn. Wyo. Johnson for Pres., 1960, Henry Jackson for Pres., N.Mex., 1976. With U.S. Army, 1950—52. Mem.: Yavapai County Bar Assn., Wyo. Bar Assn., N.Mex Bar Assn., High Country Hounds, Masons, Sigma Tau, Pi Tau Sigma, Phi Delta Theta. Methodist. Achievements include conceived legislation for U.S. Congress forcing refinancing of farmers and ranchers. Home and Office: PO Box 3998 Prescott AZ 86302-3998

GOSE, WILLIAM CHRISTOPHER, retired chemist; b. Dante, Va., Oct. 8, 1940; s. Willie Gibson and Lillian Beatrice (Addington) G.; m. Mary Hildreth Gross, Dec. 31, 1974. BS in Chem. and Math., East Tenn. State U., 1976; MBA in Bus. Mgmt., U. Tenn., 1983. Chief lab. analyst Holston Def. Corp., Kingsport, Tenn., 1961-74; sr. technician Holston Def. Corp./Tenn. Eastman Co., Kingsport, 1974-78; rsch. chemist Tenn. Eastman Co., Kingsport, 1978-85; tech. rep. Eastman Chem. Products, Inc., Kingsport, 1985-94; prin. tech. rep. Eastman Chem. Co., Kingsport, 1994-98, ret., 1998. Contbr. papers to profl confs. including Schotland Conf., Houston, 1990, Polymer Conf., Lucerne, Switzerland, 1991. With USN, 1958-61. Mem. Soc. Plastics Engrs. (sr., author papers plastics recycle conf. Atlanta 1992, additives conf. Orlando, Fla. 1993), Am. Chem. Soc., Elks (exalted ruler 1991-93, state officer 1991-96, Merit award 1991-93), Optimist Internat. (pres. local chpt. 1993-94) Republican. Methodist. Achievements include 13 U.S. patents and multiple foreign patents for co-development of a methodology for preparation and application of polymer modifiers and additives to the surface of polymer substrates in aqueous medium. Address: PO Box 6604 Kingsport TN 37663-1604

GOSENDE, ROBERT ROSALINO, academic administrator; b. Springfield, Mass., June 22, 1936; s. Rosalino Sorribas and Jane Bilton (Nimmons) Gosende; m. Mary Elizabeth Cabana, Nov. 17, 1962. BA in History and Polit. Sci., Am. Internat. Coll., 1958, MA in History and Edn., 1961, DHL, 1991. Tchr. English, Spanish and history Valley Regional H.S., Deep River, Conn., 1960—61, East Longmeadow(Mass.) H.S., 1961—64; faculty mem. Sch. Edn. U. Mass., Amherst, 1964—66; asst. cultural affairs officer Am. Embassy, Tripoli, Libya, 1966—68, cultural affairs officer Mogadishu, Somalia, 1968—70, field program officer Pretoria, South Africa, 1970—71; dir. U.S. Info. Svc., Am. Consulate Gen., Cape Town, South Africa, 1971—74; cultural affairs officer Am. Embassy, Warsaw, 1974—78; fellow Ctr. for Internat. Affairs, Harvard U., 1978—79; dep. dir. Office Program Coordination and Devel., U.S. Info. Agy., Washington, 1979—81; dep. dir. African affairs U.S. Info. Agy., Washington, 1981—83; min.-counselor for pub. affairs Am. Embassy, Pretoria, South Africa, 1983—86; dep. assoc. dir. Bur. Ednl. and Cultural Affairs U.S. Info. Agy., Washington, 1986—89, dir. African Affias, 1989—92; diplomat in residence Inst. for the Study of Diplomacy, Sch. Fgn. Svc. Georgetown U., 1992; pres. spl. envoy for Somalia, 1992—93; sr. advisor to the asst. sec. of state for African affairs U.S. Dept. State, Washington, 1994; Edward R. Murrow prof. pub. diplomacy Tufts U., Fletcher Sch. Law and Diplomacy, 1994—96; min.-counselor for press and cultural affairs, dir. U.S. Info. Svc. in the Russian Fedn. Am. Embassy, Moscow, 1996—98; dir. Office Internat. Programs SUNY, 1999—2000, assoc. vice chancellor for internat. programs. Cons. internat. rels., 1998—. Vice chmn. Albany (N.Y.)/Tula Alliance, 1998—. Capt. U.S. Army, 1954—68. Recipient Disting. Svc. award, Am. Inst. Polish Culture, 1989, Palmes Academiques Republic of France, 2001. Fellow: Am. Fgn. Policy Assn.; mem.: Nat. Assn. Historic Preservation. Avocations: woodworking, carpentry, painting. Office: SUNY State University Plaza Albany NY 12246

GOSHAW, ALFRED T. physicist, educator; b. West Bend, Wis., Aug. 26, 1937; s. Percy Lewis Goshaw and Dorothy Gladis Thomas; m. Jene Montgomery, May 6, 1943; children: Christina, David. BSEE, U. Wis., 1959, MS in Physics, 1961, PhD in Physics, 1966. Instr. Princeton (N.J.) U., 1966—69; staff physicist CERN, Geneva, 1970—73; asst. prof. Duke U., Durham, NC, 1973—78, assoc. prof., 1978—84, prof., 1984—99, James B. Duke prof., 2000—. Co-spokesperson Collider Detector at Fermilab Collaboration, 1997—2003. Fellow: Am. Phys. Soc. Office: Duke Univ Physics Dept Durham NC 27708 Business E-Mail: goshaw@phy.duke.edu.

GOSLIN, GERALD HUGH, concert pianist, educator; b. Detroit, Jan. 7, 1947; s. Hugh Jennings and Helen Margaret (Senauit) Goslin. Student, Wayne State U., Detroit, 1966-69. Music tchr. Peralta Music, Farmington, Mich., 1965—80, Hammell Music, Livonia, 1980—83; prof. music Oakland CC, Farmington Hills, 1983—; host The Piano Hour Sta. WHND-AM, Oak Park, 1995; recitalist Allen, Rodgers and Baldwin Organs, Detroit, 1975—90; prof. voice, theory and piano Livonia Conservatory, 1998—. Judge Leontyne Price Vocal Competition, 1986—2003, Verdi Opera Assn. Vocal Competition, 1995—96. Block capt. Rogers Park Residents Assn., Redford, Mich., 1995—2002; choirmaster, organist Bushnell Congl. Ch., Detroit, 2000—. Mem.: Am. Guild Organists, Am. Choir Dir. Assn., Detroit Fedn. Musicians Local # 5. Home and Office: 22600 Middlebelt Rd C-10 Farmington Hills MI 48336-3672

GOSLIN, THOMAS B. career officer; BA in Polit. Sci., La. State U., 1970; grad., Officer Tng. Sch., 1970; student pilot tng., Columbus AFB, Miss., 1971-72; student, Squadron Officer Sch., 1974; MA in Guidance and Counseling, La. Tech U., 1975; student, Air Command and Staff Coll., 1975, Air War Coll., 1980, Armed Forces Staff Coll., 1981, Can. Nat. Def. Coll., 1988, Duke U., 1995. Commd. 2d lt. USAF, 1970, advanced through grades to brig. gen., 1996; forward air controller Tan Son Nhut Air Base, S. Vietnam, 1972-73; pilot, instr. pilot 71st Air Refueling Squadron, Barksdale AFB, La., 1973-76; air staff tng. officer, intelligence threat assessment Pentagon, Washington, 1976-77, various positions, 1993-94; pilot, instr. pilot, flight comdr. 62d Bomb Squadron, Barksdale AFB, 1977-80; stationed at Hdqs. USAF, Pentagon, Washington, 1981-84, 94-95, now dep. dir. programs, dep. chief staff plans and programs; fighter lead-in tng. Holloman AFB, N.Mex., 1984; pilot 162d Tactical Fighter Group Air NG, Tucson, 1984; various comdr. assignments, 1984-93; asst. dir. ops. Hdqs. Air Combat Command, Langley AFB, Va., 1995-96; comdr. 509th Bomb Wing, Whiteman AFB, Mo., 1996—. Decorated Legion of Merit, D.F.C. with oak leaf cluster, Air medal with seven oak leaf clusters, Rep. Vietnam Gallantry Cross.

GOSLINE, NORMAN ABBOT, real estate appraiser, consultant; b. Gardiner, Maine, Nov. 6, 1935; s. Arthur N. and Katherine R. (Wadsworth) G.; m. Shirlene Heath Hoch; children: M. Lee (dec.), Jeffrey C., Mark A; stepchildren: Jolene Hoch Collins, Ellen M. Hoch, William K. Hoch Jr. BA, U. Maine, 1957. Realtor A.C. Brooks & Co., 1959-60; prin. Gosline & Co., Gardiner, 1960—. Mem. faculty (part-time) U. Maine, Augusta, 1973-81; cons. in real estate to various agys. and firms of No. New Eng., 1965—; mem. real estate team visit to People's Republic of China, Citizen Amb. Program of People to People, 1995. Past mem. Gardiner Planning Bd. ambulance adv. com. Mem. Am. Inst. Real Estate Appraisers (pres. N.E. chpt. 1985), Soc. of Real Estate Appraisers (pres. Maine chpt. 1975-76, 81-82), Appraisal Inst. (dir. 1993-96), Nat. Assn. Realtors (bd. dirs. 1967), Maine Assn. Realtors (pres. 1967), Am. Soc. Real Estate Counselors, Kennebec Valley Bd. Realtors (pres. 1963-64, Realtor of Yr. 1967), Rotary (Paul Harris fellow), Shrine. Home: 87 W Hill Rd Gardiner ME 04345 1931 Office: PO Box 247 Gardiner ME 04345-0247

GOSPE, SIDNEY MALOCH, JR., child neurologist; b. San Francisco, Oct. 7, 1952; s. Sidney Maloch and Ruth Marie (Winger) G.; m. Mary Elizabeth Williams, Apr. 12, 1980; children: Sidney III, Jessica. BS, Stanford U., 1974, MS, 1975; PhD, Duke U., 1980, MD, 1981. Diplomate Am. Bd. Pediatrics, Am. Bd. Psychiatry and Neurology. Pediatric resident Baylor Coll. of Med., Houston, 1981-83, child neurology resident, 1983-86; asst. prof. Albany (N.Y.) Med. Coll., 1986-87, U. Calif., Davis, 1987-91, assoc. prof., 1991-97, prof., 1997-2000; Sarkowsky prof. child neurology U. Wash., Seattle, 2000—. Fellow Am. Acad. Pediatrics; mem. Am. Pediatric Soc., Am. Neurol. Assn., Am. Acad. Neurology, Child Neurology Soc., Soc. Pediat. Rsch., Alpha Omega Alpha. Democrat. Jewish. Office: Children's Hosp and Regional Med Ctr 5D-4 4800 Sand Point Way NE Seattle WA 98105 E-mail: sgospe@u.washington.edu.

GOSS, CYNTHIA LEE, tax specialist; b. Anderson, Ind., May 6, 1955; d. Ralph Samuel and Jacqueline Joyce LeMaster Ewell; m. George Gregory Goss, Sept. 17, 1977; 1 child, Cassandra Renee. Basic tax course H&R Block, Tenn. Receptionist Drs. Bridges Campbell & Woodall, Anderson, 1974-75; nurse's aide various orgns., Anderson, 1976-83; tax preparer, 1985-94; tax preparer, acct. Mayes & Assocs. Liberty Tax Svc., Chattanooga, 1995—2002; bank teller SunTrust Bank, Chattanooga, 2001—02. Tax instr. Liberty Tax Svc., Chattanooga, 1999—2002. Author: (poetry) Hearts Uplifted, 1997 (award winner Sure Truth, The Olive Garden and Lord Take Me), Internat. Libr. Poetry; composer: (song) You're Still Here, 1991, (ch. choruses) I Am the One, John 10:28, My Prayer, My Plea, David's Song; author numerous poems. Mem. Neighborhood Watch, Highland Park, Chattanooga, 1990-93; rep. for neighborhood Am. Cancer Soc., Highland Park, Chattanooga, 1991-93. Recipient poetry awards; named Guard Dir. of Yr., Awana Ch. Orgn., Rossville, Ga., 1999. Republican. Baptist. Avocations: sewing, writing and singing music, writing poetry, walking, church activities. Home: 1001 School St Apt 313 Elk River MN 55330 Personal E-mail: cindybritches@aol.com.

GOSS, GEORGIA BULMAN, freelance/self-employed translator; b. N.Y.C., Dec. 1, 1939; d. James Cornelius and Marian Bright (McLaughlin) Bulman; m. Douglas Keith Goss, Dec. 21, 1957; children: Kristin Anne, David. BA, U. Mich., 1961. Libr. High Altitude Obs., Boulder, Colo., 1963-64, U.S. Bur. Stds., Boulder, Colo., 1964-65, cons. editor Spanish lang. pilot's tng. manual, 1981-82; freelance translator, 1982—. Mem. U. Mich. Alumni Assn., Phi Sigma Iota. Republican. Episcopalian. Home: 9 Dayton Cir Fredericksburg VA 22406

GOSS, JAMES WALTER, oil company executive; b. Farmerville, La., Mar. 18, 1924; s. Walter Frank and Lovie (Hollis) G.; m. Mertie Henry, Jan. 1, 1953; children: James Walter, Kimberly. BS, La. State U., 1949. With Gen. Am. Oil Co. Tex., Dallas, 1949—, v.p. charge land dept., 1960—, exec. v.p., dir., mem. exec. com., 1970—, chief oper. officer, 1979-83; oil and gas cons., 1983—. Lt. comdr. USNR, 1943-46, Res., ret. Mem. Ind. Petroleum Assn. Am. (exec. com., past v.p.), Dallas (past pres., dir.), Assns. Petroleum Landmen, Midcontinent Oil and Gas Assn., Am. Petroleum Inst., Dallas Athletic, Petroleum, Brook Hollow Golf, Lambda Chi Alpha. Home: 3509 Centenary Ave Dallas TX 75225-5014 Office: Meadows Bldg Dallas TX 75206

GOSS, JAMES WILLIAM, lawyer; b. London, Ont., Can., Mar. 10, 1941; s. Joseph Allen and Virginia Ruth (Farrah) G.; m. Rita Meyer, Aug. 2, 1969; children: Anne Candace, Jennette Courtney. BBA, West Mich. U., 1966; MS, U. Ill., 1972; JD, Georgetown U., 1974. Bar: Mich. 1974, U.S. Dist. Ct. (ea. dist.) Mich. 1974, U.S. Ct. Appeals (6th cir.) 1974. Sr. acct. Price Waterhouse & Co., Washington, 1969-71; assoc. Miller, Canfield, Paddock & Stone, Detroit, 1974-82, James W. Goss P.C., Southfield, Mich., 1982-88; ptnr. Dean & Fulkerson, Troy, Mich., 1988-95, James W. Goss P.C., Grosse Pointe Farms, Mich., 1995—. Adj. lectr. U. Mich. Law, Ann Arbor, 1978-82. Bd. dirs. Old Newsboys Goodfellow Fund of Detroit, 1990—96, Adrian Coll., 1991—96; bd. dirs., v.p. Svc. to Older Citizens Soc., Grosse Pointe, Mich., 1997—2001; assoc., bd. govs., mem. exec. com. William L. Clements Libr. U. Mich., 1998—. Named Outstanding Goodfellow, Old Newsboys Goodfellows of Detroit, 1991; recipient Disting. Alumni award Western Mich. U., 1995. Mem. Georgetown U. Law Alumni Assn., Grosse Pointe Yacht Club, Georgetown Club of Mich., Commanderie de Bordeaux, Hundred Club, Rotary (Grosse Pointe Rotarian of Yr. 2000-01), Masons. Presbyterian. Avocations: philately, wine collecting, cartographic collecting. Home: 398 Rivard Blvd Grosse Pointe MI 48230-1629 Office: 230 Punch and Judy Bldg 21 Kercheval Ave Grosse Pointe MI 48236-3698 E-mail: jameswgoss@earthlink.net.

GOSS, JEROME ELDON, cardiologist; b. Dodge City, Kans., Nov. 30, 1935; s. Horton Maurice and Mary Alice (Mountain) G.; m. Lorraine Ann Sanchez, Apr. 20, 1986. BA, U. Kans., 1957; MD, Northwestern U., 1961. Diplomate Am. Bd. Internal Medicine, Am. Bd. Cardiology (fellow, bd. govs. 1981-84). Intern Met. Gen. Hosp., Cleve., 1961-62; resident in internal medicine Northwestern U. Med. Ctr., Chgo., 1962-64; fellow in cardiology U. Colo., Denver, 1964-66; asst. prof. medicine U. N.Mex., Albuquerque, 1968-70; pvt. practice N.Mex. Heart Clinic, Albuquerque, 1970—99, Presbyn. Med. Group, Albuquerque, 2000—02; with Presbyn. Heart Group, Albuquerque, 2003—. Bd. alumni counsellors Northwestern U. Med. Sch., 1977-89, nat. alumni bd., 1991-97; chief dept. medicine Presbyn. Hosp., Albuquerque, 1978-80, exec. com., 1980-82, dir. cardiac diagnostic svcs., 1970-96. Contbr. articles to profl. jours. Bd. dirs. Presbyn. Heart Inst., Ballet West N.Mex., N.Mex. Symphony Orch.; pres. Albuquerque Mus. Found., Corrales Hist. Soc., 2002—. Lt. comdr. USN, 1966-68. Nat. Heart Inst. research fellow, 1965-66; named one of Outstanding Young Men Am., Jaycees, 1970; recipient Alumni Service award Northwestern U. Med. Sch., 1986, Disting. Achievement award Albuquerque Mus. Found., 1997, Sr. Svc. award Presbyn. Healthcare Sys., 1999. Fellow ACP, ACC, Coun. Clin. Cardiology of Am. Heart Assn., Soc. Cardiac Angiography, Am. Soc. of Geriatric Cardiology; mem. Albuquerque-Bernalillo County Med. Soc. (sec. 1972, treas. 1975, v.p. 1980), Alpha Omega Alpha. Republican. Methodist. Office: High Resort Cardiology 4100 High Resort Blvd Rio Rancho NM 87124-2310 E-mail: jegoss@comcast.net.

GOSS, JOEL FRANCIS, writer; b. Pawnee, Okla., Nov. 15, 1955; s. William Richard and Mary Ann (Webb) G.; m. Cat Guthrie, 1992; 1 child, William Keaton Guthrie-Goss. BA, U. Tenn., 1985. Staff writer Sta. WDXB, Chattanooga, 1970-73, Sta. WGOW, Knoxville, Tenn., 1973-75; writer, dir. V.T. Films, Knoxville, 1974-76; writer Hi-Test Films, Knoxville, 1976; freelance writer N.Y.C., 1976-80; writer, mgr. Improvisation, Inc., N.Y.C., 1980-84; writer, producer CB Prodns., N.Y.C., 1984; mng. dir. Albuquerque '49, N.Y.C., 1983—; v.p. Buster Keaton Archive, N.Y.C., 1985—. Cons. Rohauer Films, London, 1985-88, Am. Theatre Wing, N.Y.C., 1987; film instr. Brown Sch., Knoxville, 1976; chmn. Film com., Knoxville, 1974-76. Author: Albuquerque '49, 1973; author: (with Michael Kaluta) The Shadow, 1992; author: Coils of Leviathan, 1993, (screenplays) The Prairie Traveler, 1986, Manhattan Underground, 1987, Bard of Broadway, 1988, Sandhogs, 1991, Battling Butler, 1991; author: (with Mike Rowe) Warm Toast, 1989; author: (with Eliot Camaren) Good Night Bassington, 2003; translator: (tng. manuals) Construzione Aeronaticle, 1973; co-screenwriter (with Raymond Rohauer), rschr. Buster Keaton-A Hard Act to Follow, 1987, writer Spectacular Days of Radio, 1990, (with Martin Connor) Madame Sherry, 1989, Cat Guthrie in Concert, 1992, The Rich Conaty Radio Show, 1992, (with others) The Rocketeer, The Shadow, 1994, The Shadow & the Mysterious 3, 1994, (with M. Kaluta and Gary Gianni) Hell's Heat Wave, 1994, Buster Keaton: Genius In Slapshoes, 1995, Cut To The Chase: Buster Keaton, 1995, The Sound of Buster Keaton, 1995, Complete Films of BK, A Satin Doll Christmas, 2000; restored dialog to film: with Bruce Goldstein The Donovan Affair (1929), 1992, Cliff Edwards--Fascinatin' Rhythm, 1996; author (with Cat Guthrie): A Day In The Life of a Mother & Wife, 2001. Vol. Nat. Music Theatre Network, N.Y.C., Washington, 1985, 87, Nat. Theatre Wing, N.Y.C., 1987, Muscular Dystrophy Assn., N.Y.C., 1987; signings for St. Jude's Children's Hosp., 1994. Grantee U. Tenn., 1975, CB Prodns., 1984. Mem. Buster Keaton Soc., CVPO Assn. Fax: 845-424-2454. E-mail: keatonguy@cs.com., joelgoss1@cs.com., joelgoss@compuserve.com.

GOSS, KAY COLLETT, data company executive; BA in Polit. Sci. and Pub. Adminstrn., U. Ark., 1963, MA in Polit. Sci. and Pub. Adminstrn., 1966; postgrad., W.Va. U., 1969-71, N.W. Mo. State U., 1964, San Diego State U., 1982, Harvard U., 1983, Am. U., 1998—2000. Cert. emergency mgr. Internat. Assn. Emergency Mgrs. Online instr. Western Washington U. and John Jay Coll. of CUNY, 2002—; instr. govt., polit. sci., geography, history and sociology Westark C.C., Ft. Smith, Ark., U. Ark., Fayetteville, Little Rock, adj. asst. prof. Ark. govt. and politics; adj. prof. Fla. Atlantic U. and Istanbul Tech. U.; legislative and administrv. asst. U. S. Ho. of Reps., Washington; chief dep. auditor of state of Ark., Little Rock, sr. asst. for intrgovtl. rels. Office of Gov.; assoc. dir. for preparedness Fed. Emergency Mgmt. Agy., Washington, 1994-2001; sr. advisor for emergency mgmt., homeland security and bus. continuity Electronic Data Sys. Corp. (EDS), Alexandria, Va., 2001—. Former project coord. Assn. Ark. Counties; chmn. Emergency Food and Shelter Nat. Bd.; mem. Pre.'s Interagy. Coun. on Women, Pre.'s Interagy. Coun. on Homeless, Nat Security Steering Group; co-chmn. Joint U.S.-Russian Com. on Emergencies, U.S. Interagy. Coordination Group for Counter Terrorism, 1996—98; mem. nat. adv. com. Natural Hazards Rsch. and Applications Info. Ctr., U. Colo., Boulder, 1994—2001; mem. project steering com. Vice Pres.'s Global Disaster Info. Network, 1995—2001; mem. nat. adv. coun. for emergency adminstrn. and mgmt. program Ark. Tech. U., Russellville, online instr. emergency mgmt., 2003—. Author: Wilbur D. Mills: The People's Congressman, The Arkansas Constitution: A Reference Guide, The City Manager Plan in Arkansas, Political Paradox: Constitutional Revision in Arkansas, Going to the

Grassroots: Governor Bill Clinton in Arkansas. Bd. dirs. Opera Co. Boston, Wilbur D. Mills Meml. Found., Wilbur D. Mills Treatment Ctr. for Alcoholism and Drug Abuse, Ark. Women's History Inst. Recipient Lifetime Achievement award Wilbur D. Mills Treatment Ctr. for Alcohol and Drug Abuse, 2000, Cmty. Svc. of Yr. award North Ark. Human Svcs., Inc., Ark. Mental Health Inst., 2000. Mem.: Ark. State Soc., Ark. Polit. Sci. Assn. (past pres.), Nat. Fallen Firefighters Meml., U.S. House Adminstrv. Assts. Alumni Assn., Harvard U. John F. Kennedy Sch. Govt. Alumni Assn. (former mem. exec. coun.). also: 13600 EDS Dr Herndon VA 21701 E-mail: kay.goss@eds.com., kaycgoss@hotmail.com.

GOSS, LAURENCE EDWARD, JR., geographer, educator; b. Greenfield, Mass., Dec. 9, 1944; s. Laurence Edward and Anna Louise (Oliver) G.; m. Sharon Margaret Ripp, June 9, 1968; children: Laura Marie, Peter Edward. AB, Dartmouth Coll., 1966; MA, U. Wash., 1969, PhD, 1973. Registered planner, Am. Inst. Cert. Planners. Adminstr., lectr. Dartmouth Coll., Hanover, N.H., 1970-71; asst. prof. SUNY, Oswego, 1971-76; asst. dir. Office of State Planning, Concord, N.H., 1976-86; project dir. Provan & Lorber, Inc., Contoocook, N.H., 1986-91; prin. No. Econ. Planners, Concord, 1991—; assoc. prof. Salem (Mass.) State Coll., 1996—2003, prof., 2003—. Pres. Frontiers of Knowledge Lyceum, Concord, 1996. Lead author: Garvins Falls Devel. Strategy for City of concord, N.H., 1996 (Tech. Merit award for Maine, N.H. and Vt. 1997 No. New Eng. chpt. Am. Planners Assn.). Recipient Letter of Commendation Nat. award HUD, Washington, 1986. Mem. Am. Planners Assn. (pres. no. New Eng. chpt. 1989-91, Profl. Planner of Yr. 1993, Project of Yr. award 1995), New Eng.-St. Lawrence Valley Geog. Soc. (bd. dirs. 1992-94), N.H. Planners Assn. (pres. 1982-83), N.H. Natural Resources Forum (treas. 1993-2000). Congregationalist. Office: Dept Geography Salem State Coll Salem MA 01970 E-mail: lgoss@salemstate.edu.

GOSS, MARTHA CLARK, consulting company executive; b. Glen Ridge, N.J., May 31, 1949; d. David Ormiston and Marion Jane (Drury) Clark; m. Richard Keith Dentel, Dec. 29, 1972 (dec. Feb. 1974); m. Joseph Coyle Briley, Mar. 25, 1978 (div. May 1993); children: Christopher Briley, Alexis Briley; m. David Charles Goss, June 18, 1994. AB, Brown U., 1971; MBA, Harvard U., 1978. CLU, ChFC. Trainee, credit analyst Chase Manhattan Bank, N.Y.C., 1972-74, asst. treas., 1974-76, 2d v.p., 1976, v.p., team leader, 1978-81; v.p. corp. fin. Prudential Ins. Co. Am., Newark, 1981-83, v.p., treas., 1983-88; pres., CFO Prudential Power Funding Assn., Newark, 1989-92; pres. Prudential Asset Mgmt. Co., Newark, 1992-94; sr. v.p., enterprise integrated control officer Prudential Ins. Co. Am., Newark, 1994-95; v.p., CFO Booz Allen and Hamilton Inc., Parsippany, N.J., 1995-99; ptnr., CFO, The Capital Market Co., N.Y.C., 1999-2001, Blagwell, Inc., 2001—. Bd. dirs. Foster Wheeler Corp., Clinton, N.J., IBJ Whitehall Bus. Credit Corp.; mem. met. regional bd. Chase Manhattan Bank, N.Y.C. Active Women's Campaign Fund, Washington, 1989—; trustee Ind. Coll. Fund N.J., 1984-96; trustee, treas. Brown U., 1987-98; trustee Stuart Country Day Sch. of Sacred Heart, 1989-95. Mem. Fin. Women's Assn., Com. of 200. Republican. Presbyterian. Avocations: skiing, travel, gardening, wine collection.

GOSS, MARY E. WEBER, sociology educator; b. Chgo., May 8, 1926; m. Albert E. Goss, 1945; 1 son, Charles. BA in Sociology with distinction (Univ. Merit scholar 1946-47, Chi Omega Sociology prize 1947), U. Iowa, 1947, MA, 1948; PhD (Gilder fellow 1951-52), Columbia U., 1959. Rsch. asst. U. Iowa, 1947-48, Amherst Coll., 1949; instr. Smith Coll., 1949-50, U. Mass., 1950-51, 55-56, adj. mem. grad. faculty, 1961-66; rsch. assoc. Bur. Applied Social Rsch., Columbia U., 1952-53; cons. sociology, mem. rsch. staff, rsch. coord. N.Y. Hosp.-Cornell U. Med. Center, N.Y.C., 1957-66; mem. faculty dept. medicine Cornell U. Med. Coll., 1959-72, prof. sociology in pub. health, 1973-92, prof. emerita, 1992—. Author: Physicians in Bureaucracy, 1980; also numerous articles; editor: Jour. Health and Social Behavior, 1976-78; co-editor: Comprehensive Medical Care and Teaching: A Report on the N.Y. Hospital-Cornell Medical Center Program, 1967; mem. editorial bd. profl. jours. Fellow APHA, N.Y. Acad. Medicine; mem. AAAS, AAUP, Am. Sociol. Assn., Assn. Tchrs. Preventive Medicine, Acad. Health Svcs. Rsch., Internat. Sociol. Assn., Ea. Sociol. Soc., Phi Beta Kappa, Sigma Xi. Home: 25 Hillcrest Drive Piscataway NJ 08854 Office: Weill Med Coll Cornell Univ Dept Pub Health 411 E 69th St New York NY 10021-5608

GOSS, PORTER J. congressman; b. Waterbury, Conn., Nov. 26, 1938; m. Mariel Robinson; children: Leslie, Chauncey, Mason, Gerrit. BA, Yale U., 1960. Clandestine svcs. officer CIA, 1962-71; co-founder Island Reporter, Sanibel, Fla., 1973; mayor City of Sanibel, 1975—77, 1982, coun. mem., 1974—80, 1981—82; commr. County of Lee, Fla., 1983—88, chmn., 1985—86; mem. U.S. Congress from 14th Fla. dist., 1988—; chmn. intelligence com.; mem. rules com.; mem. Select Com. on Homeland Security. Port commr. S.W. Fla. Regional Airport. Dir. Lee County Mental Health Ctr., J.N. "Ding" Darling Found.; dir. chmn. Sanibel-Captiva Conservation Found.; chmn. bd. Canterbury Sch.; mem. S.W. Fla. Mental Health Dist. Bd. Intelligence officer U.S. Army, 1960-62. Republican. Presbyterian. Office: US Ho of Reps 108 Cannon Ho Office Bldg Washington DC 20515-0001*

GOSS, RICHARD HENRY, lawyer; b. Worcester, Mass., Oct. 24, 1935; s. George Lee and Marion Bernadine (Henry) G.; children: Margaret Elizabeth, Richard Henry Eric, Emily Charlotte; m. Eleanor Kirsten Berg, Nov. 27, 1971. Student, Mich. State U., 1952-54; BA in Econs., Clark U., 1956; JD, Northwestern U., 1959. Bar: Ill. 1959, U.S. Supreme Ct. 1970. Asst. cashier Nat. Blvd. Bank of Chgo., 1959-61; v.p. Paul D. Speer & Assocs. Inc., Mcpl. Fin. Cons., Chgo., 1962-68; mng. ptnr. Chapman and Cutler, Attys. at Law, Chgo., 1968-95. Bd. dirs. Japan Am. Soc. Chgo., 1987-96, v.p., chmn. mem. com., 1988-90; chmn. bd. dirs. Brays Island Plantation Colony, Inc., 1995-97. Mem. Eastman (N.H.) Golf Club. Republican. Episcopalian. Avocations: hunting, skeet, sporting clays and trap shooting, travel, oriental studies. Home: 7 Par Brae Eastman Box 1316 Grantham NH 03753

GOSS, STEPHEN D. music educator, musician; b. Lancaster, Pa., July 26, 1970; s. Kenneth R and Beverly G Goss; m. Tanya M Tanya Wertz, Feb. 19, 1994; children: Ian Timothy Stephen, Hannah Elizabeth, Abigail Marie. B.S Music Edn., West Chester U., West Chester, PA, 1990—94. Educator Pa, 1994. Dir. of bands Ephrata Area Sch. Dist., Ephrata, Pa., 1998—; classroom music tchr. Ea. Lancaster County Sch. Dist., New Holland, Pa. Asst. dir. of ephrata h.s. marching band Ephrata Marching band, Ephrata, Pa., 17522, 1998—; dir. of ephrata high schol percussion ensemble Ephrata H.S., Ephrata, Pa., 17522, 1995—, percussion ensemble dir., 1998—; pvt. music tchr. STG Music Studios, Strasburg, Pa., 17579. Mem.: Percussive Arts Soc., MENC. Republican. Avocations: bicycling, hunting, skiing. Home: 113 N Decatur Str Strasburg PA 17579 Personal E-mail: drumtech@quixnet.net.

GOSS, THOMAS PIXTON, orthopaedic surgeon; b. Boston, Mar. 1, 1947; s. William Oscar and Catherine Jeanette (Van Dyke) G.; m. Joan Mary Maughan, May 19, 1979; children: Thomas William, Christine Anne, John Michael. AB, Dartmouth Coll., 1968; BMS, Dartmouth Med. Sch., 1969; MD, Harvard U., 1971. Diplomate Am. Bd. Orthop. Surgery. Surgical intern and resident Roosvelt Hosp., N.Y.C., 1971-73; orthop. resident Columbia-Presbyn. Hosp., N.Y.C., 1973-76, orthop. fellow, 1976-77; med. officer USN Regional Med. Ctr., Portsmouth, Va., 1977-79; attending orthop. surgeon U. Mass. Med. Ctr., Worcester, 1979—. Chief shoulder svc. dept. orthop. surgery, U. Mass. Med. Ctr., Worcester, 1979—; asst. prof. orthop. surgery, U. Mass. Med. Sch., Worcester, 1979-84, assoc. prof., 1984-89, prof., 1990—; cons., reviewer Jour. Bone and Joint Surgery, Jour. Shoulder and Elbow Surgery; presenter numerous local and regional presentations to gen. public, students, sci groups and some nat. and internat. profl. socs. Contbr. articles to profl. jours. Lt. cmmdr. USN, 1977-79. Fellow Am. Acad. Orthop. Surgeons; mem. Am. Orthopaedic Assn., Am. Shoulder and Elbow Surgeons, Orthop. Trauma Assn., New Eng. Orthop. Soc. (treas. 1995-2000, pres.-elect 2000-, pres. 2002-). Roman Catholic. Avocations: skiing, jogging, tennis. Office: U Mass Meml Health Care Dept Orthop Surgery 55 Lake Ave N Worcester MA 01655-0002 E-mail: gosst@ummhc.org.

GOSSAGE, ROZA, lawyer, educator; b. Landreis Celle Lohheide, Germany, Mar. 21, 1947; came to U.S., 1949; d. Abram and Lola (Strubel) Berlinski; m. David Jordan Gossage, Feb. 21, 1970; children: Brenda, Sara, Leah. BA, U. Ill., 1968; JD, DePaul Sch. Law, 1971. Bar: Ill. 1971, Fla. 1972, Mo. 1981, U.S. Dist. Ct. (no. dist.) Ill. 1971, U.S. Dist. Ct. (so. dist.) Ill. 1978, U.S. Ct. Appeals (7th cir.) 1972. Law clk. U.S. Dist. Ct. (no. dist.) Ill., Chgo., 1971-72; atty. State's Atty.'s Office of Cook County, Ill., 1972-74, State's Atty.'s Office of St. Clair County, Belleville, Ill., 1974-78, Hutnick & Gossage, Belleville, 1978—89; pvt. practice Belleville, 1990—. Atty. Commn. to Revise and Rewrite Pub. Aid Code of Ill., Springfield, 1978-80; atty. Village of Summerfield, Ill., 1983—89; arbitrator Better Bus. Bur., St. Louis, 1982—; lectr. in family law. Bd. dirs. YWCA, St. Clair County, Ill., 1981-89; co-chair continuing legal edn. Women's Lawyers of Greater St. Louis, 2001-2002. Mem. St. Clair County Bar Assn., Met. Women's Bar Assn. (bd. dirs. 1981—), Ill. Bar Assn., Mo. Bar Assn., Fla. Bar Assn., So. Ill. Network of Women, Ill. State Bar Assn. (family law sect. 2003, chair CLE, sexual orientation and gender identity com.). Office: 521 W Main St Ste 110 Belleville IL 62220-1535

GOSSAGE, WAYNE, library director, management consultant, entrepreneur, executive recruiter; b. Bellingham, Wash., June 13, 1926; s. Coy Dell and Sadie Fay (Campbell) G.; m. Grace Villella, July 3, 1950; children: Leslie Anne, Gordon. BS, U. Wash., 1947; MS, Columbia U., 1951, MA, 1969. Asst. head adult svcs. East Orange (N.J.) Pub. Libr., 1951-54; head adult svcs. Levittown (N.Y.) Pub. Libr., 1954-55; dir. Warner Libr., Tarrytown, N.Y., 1956-63; asst. libr. Tchrs. Coll., Columbia U., N.Y.C., 1964-67; dir. Bank St. Coll. Edn. Libr., N.Y.C., 1967-80; pres. Gossage Regan Assocs., Inc., N.Y.C., 1980-2000; chmn. Gossage Sager Assocs. LLC, N.Y.C., 2000—03; ret., 2003—. Libr. search cons. Gossage Regan Assocs., Inc., N.Y.C., 1980-2000, Gossage Sager Assocs., LLC, N.Y.C., 2000—. Contbr. articles to profl. jours. Vice pres. Hist. Soc. Tarrytown, 1960-61; trustee Harvard Libr., N.Y., 1978-2000; mem. alumni trustee nominating com. Columbia U., 1974-76; bd. advisors Pratt Inst. Sch. Info. and Libr. Sci., 1988-2001. With USNR, 1944-46. Coun. on Libr. Resources fellow, 1978-79; recipient Disting. Community Svc. award Tarrytown, 1962. Mem. ALA (notable books coun. 1961-62, ACRL bd. dirs. 1975-76, chmn. edn. and behavioral scis. sect. 1975-76, Ralph Shaw award for libr. lit. jury 1975-76, chmn. Wilson indexes com. 1978-81, Mudge citation com. 1985-87), N.Y. Libr. Assn. (v.p. resources and tech. svcs. sect. 1974-75, legis. com. 1974-75, pres. coll. and univ. librs. sect. 1978-79), N.Y. Libr. Club (pres. 1990-91), Spl. Libr. Assn. (chmn. div. social sci. 1975-76), Columbia U. Sch. Libr. Svcs. Alumni Assn. (sec.-treas. 1974-76, pres. 1977-78), Archons of Colophon (convenor 1989-90). Avocations: reading, writing, walking, travel. Office: Gossage Sager Assocs LLC 25 W 43d St New York NY 10036-7406 Mailing: 607 N Mesquite St Carlsbad NM 88220

GOSSARD, ARTHUR CHARLES, physicist, researcher; b. Ottawa, Ill., June 18, 1935; s. Arthur Paul and Mary Catherine (Lineberger) G.; m. Marsha Jean Palmer, Jan. 8, 1965; children: Girard Christopher, Elinore Suzanne. BA, Harvard U., 1956; PhD, U. Calif., Berkeley, 1960. Solid state physicist, disting. mem. tech. staff AT&T Bell Labs., Murray Hill, N.J., 1960-87; prof. materials and electrical and computer engring. U. Calif., Santa Barbara, 1987—. Author tech. papers magnetic resonance, magnetism, transition metals, molecular beam epitaxy, quantum structures, semiconductors. Sr. fellow Humboldt Found. Fellow IEEE, Am. Phys. Soc. (Oliver Buckley condensed matter physics prize 1984, James McGroddy prize for New Materials 2001); mem. NAS, Nat. Acad. of Engring. Office: U Calif Materials Dept Santa Barbara CA 93106 E-mail: gossard@engineering.ucsb.edu.

GOSSELIN, BENOIT JEAN, otolaryngologist, facial plastic surgeon, head and neck and reconstructive surgeon; b. Quebec City, Can., Oct. 24, 1962; BSc, U. Ottawa, 1983, BSc Hon, 1984, MD, 1988. Diplomate Am. Bd. Otolaryngology, Bd. of Facial Plastic & Reconstructive Surgery. Resident in otolaryngology U. Ottawa, 1989-93; fellow head and neck surgery U. Toronto, 1993-94; fellow in microvascular and facial plastic surgery Mercy Hosp. Pitts., 1994-95; asst. prof. surgery Dartmouth Coll., Hanover, N.H., 1995—; staff otolaryngology sect. Dartmouth-Hitchcock Med. Ctr., Lebanon, N.H., 1995—; staff otolaryngologist, head and neck surgeon VA Med. Ctr., White River Junction, Vt., 2002—. Fellow ACS, Royal Coll. Surgeons (Can.), Am. Soc. Head and Neck Surgery; mem. AMA, Am. Acad. Otolaryngology, Head and Neck Surgery, Am. Acad. Facial Plastics and Reconstructive Surgery, Am. Rhinologic Soc., Am. Soc. Univ. Otolaryngologists, Can. Soc. Otolaryngology, Head and Neck Surgery, Can. Med. Assn. Office: Dartmouth-Hitchcock Med Ctr Sect Otolaryngology One Medical Ctr Dr Lebanon NH 03755

GOSSELIN, TRACY KAREN, nursing administrator; b. Worcester, Mass., Dec. 21, 1970; d. Kenneth James and Karen Helen Gosselin; m. David Thompson Acomb, Sept. 5, 1998. BSN, Northeastern U., 1993; M of Nursing Sci., Duke U., 1997. Staff nurse Duke U. Med. Ctr., Durham, N.C., 1993-95, asst. nurse mgr., 1995-97, nurse mgr., 1998-2001; adminstrv. dir., 2001—. Spkr. MedImmune Inc., Gaithersburg, Md. Author: (book chpt.) A Nurse's Guide to Cancer Care, 2000; reviewer: Clin. Jour. of Oncology Nursing. Mem.: AOCN, Am. Coll. Surgeons Oncology Group, Triangle Oncology Nursing Soc. (sec. 1999—2001, pres.-elect 2001, pres. 2002), Oncology Nursing Soc. (contbg. editor monthly newsletter 1998—2002), Sigma Theta Tau. Avocations: cooking, reading. Office: Duke U Med Ctr Rm 005134 PO Box 3085 Durham NC 27710-0001 Fax: 919-684-3953. E-mail: gosse001@mc.duke.edu.

GOSSELS, CLAUS PETER ROLF, lawyer; b. Berlin, Aug. 11, 1930; came to U.S., 1941; s. Max and Charlotte (Lewy) G.; m. Nancy Lee Tuber, June 29, 1958; children: Lisa Rae, Amy Devra, Daniel Joshua. AB, Harvard U., 1951, LLB, 1954. Bar: Mass. 1955, U.S. Dist. Ct. Mass. 1957, U.S. Ct. Appeals (1st cir.) 1957, U.S. Supreme Ct. 1965. Assoc. Sullivan & Worcester, Boston, 1956-65; mem. Zelman, Gossels & Alexander, Boston, 1965-72, Weston, Patrick, Willard & Redding, Boston, 1972—. Master Superior Ct. Mass., 1984—; guardian ad litem, conservator Mass. Probate and Family Ct. Co-author, editor: Vetaher Libenu, 1980, Chadesh Yameynu, 1997. Moderator Town of Wayland, Mass., 1982—. With U.S. Army, 1954-56. Mem. Mass. Bar Assn., Boston Bar Assn., Mass. Moderators Assn., Mass. Acad. Trial Lawyers. Jewish. Avocations: reading, tennis, travel, gardening, theatre. Home: 32 Hampshire Rd Wayland MA 01778-1021 Office: Weston Patrick Willard & Redding 84 State St Boston MA 02109-2299

GOSSETT, ROBERT FRANCIS, JR., merchant banker; b. San Antonio, Tex., Nov. 19, 1943; s. Robert Francis and Anne Elizabeth (Donnell) G.; m. Pauline Washington Gillespie, June 27, 1964; children: Robert Francis III, Frank Morgan Gillespie. BA, U. Tex., 1964; JD, Georgetown U., 1967; MBA, U. Pa., 1969. Assoc., investment bank div. Merrill Lynche, Pierce, Fenner & Smith, N.Y.C., 1969-74; v.p. Oppenheimer Properties, Inc., N.Y.C., 1974-78; exec. v.p., dir. Loeb Rhoades Hornblower Capital Corp., N.Y.C., 1978-81; chmn. bd., pres. Vance Capital Corp., N.Y.C., 1981—. Gen. ptnr. First San Bernardio Assoc., Ltd., Long Beach, Calif., 1979—, First Riverside (Calif.) Assoc., 1980—, First Portland Assoc., Beaverton, Oreg., 1980—, Corp. Realty Income Fund I, Ltd., N.Y.C., 1986—, Vance, Teel & Co. Ltd., San Antonio, 1998—; chmn. bd. dirs. 1345 Realty Corp., N.Y.C., 1994—, Minn. Street Assoc., Inc., St. Paul, 1988—; gen. ptnr. Hoopes Assocs., Ltd., Rockport, Tex., 1989—, Teel Land and Cattle Co., LLC, Yancey, Tex., 1997—. Mem. bd. regents Georgetown U., 1993-99. Mem. Campfire Club, The Mashomack Preserve Club. Office: Vance Capital Corp 406 E 85th St New York NY 10028-6302

GOSSICK, LEE VAN, consultant, executive, retired air force officer; b. Meadville, Mo., Jan. 23, 1920; s. Clark and Myrtle (Staats) G.; m. Ruth Matter, Apr. 29, 1942; children: Roger V., Cynthia L. BS in Aero. Engring, MS, Ohio State U., 1951; grad., Air War Coll., 1959, Advanced Mgmt. Program, Harvard, 1961. Aviation cadet, 1941-42; commd. 2d lt. USAAF, 1942; advanced through grades to maj. gen. USAF, 1968; fighter pilot (87th Fighter Squadron), North Africa, 1942- 43; various R & D posts, 1951-64; comdr. Arnold Engring. Devel. Center, 1964-67; dep. for F-111 Aero. Systems div., Wright-Patterson AFB, Ohio, 1967-68; vice comdr. Aero. Systems Div., 1968-69, comdr., 1969-70; dep. chief staff systems Hdqrs. Air Force Systems Command, Andrews AFB, Md., 1970-71, chief of staff, 1971-73, ret., 1973; asst. dir. regulation AEC, Washington, 1973-74; exec. dir. ops. Nuclear Regulatory Commn., Washington, 1975-79; v.p., gen. mgr. Sverdrup Tech. Inc., Tullahoma, Tenn., 1980-89. Decorated D.S.M. with oak leaf cluster; Legion of Merit with oak leaf cluster; D.F.C.; Air medal with 9 oak leaf clusters; named Distinguished Alumnus Ohio State U., 1960, Centennial Achievement award, 1970; recipient Vandenberg trophy Arnold Air Soc., 1967, Distinguished Service award AEC, 1974 Fellow AIAA, Arnold Engring. Devel. Ctr. Home: 106 Blantonwood Dr Tullahoma TN 37388-5801

GOSSINGER, GARY THOMAS, physician, psychiatrist, educator; b. Detroit, Oct. 3, 1945; s. Frank J. and Florence (Bryan) G.; m. Ava Carp, June, 1975; children: Michelle, Lauren. BA, Albion (Mich.) Coll., 1967; MD, U. Mich., 1971. Diplomate Am. Bd. Psychiatry and Neurology. Intern Pacific Med. Ctr., San Francisco, 1971-72; resident U. Mich., Ann Arbor, 1972-75; chief psychiatrist N. Central Fla. Mental Health, Gainesville, Fla., 1975-79; attending physician Alachua Gen. Hosp., Gainesville, 1975—; clin. asst. prof. U. Fla., Gainesville, 1978—. Cons. VA, Lake City, Fla., 1982-88, St. John's ARC, St. Augustine, Fla., 1994-99; med. dir. Shands at Vista, Gainesville, 1994-99; attending physician Shands at Vista, 1987—. Mem. Coast Guard Aux., Gainesville, 1986-97; comdr. U.S. Power Squad, Gainesville, 1987-88. Recipient Cert. Appreciation Alachua Co., 1978. Mem. AMA, Am. Psychiatric Assn., Fla. Med. Assn., Fla. Psychiatric Assn., Gainesville Amateur Radio Soc. (pres. 1989-93). Avocations: flying scuba diving, amateur radio, boating. Office: 2830 NW 41st St Ste E Gainesville FL 32606-6667

GOSTIN, LAWRENCE O. lawyer, educator; b. Oct. 19, 1949; s. Joseph and Sylvia (Berkman) G.; m. Jean Catherine Allison, July 30, 1977; children: Bryn Gareth, Kieran Gavin. BA summa cum laude, SUNY, Brockport, 1971; LLD (hon.), SUNY; JD, Duke U., 1974. Bar: N.Y. 1981, Coun. Europe. Legal dir. Nat. Assn. Mental Health, London, 1975-82; vis. fellow U. Oxford Ctr. for Criminol. Rsch., 1982-83; gen. sec. Nat. Coun. Civil Liberties, London, 1983-85; sr. fellow in health law Harvard U. Sch. Pub. Health, 1985—. Vis. prof. social policy McMaster U., Hamilton, Ont., Can., 1978-79; exec. dir. Am. Soc. Law, Medicine, and Ethics, Boston, 1987-94; adj. assoc. prof. Sch. Pub. Health, Harvard U., 1988—, adj. prof., 1990—, lectr. Law Sch., 1990—; vis. prof. Georgetown U. Law Ctr., 1993-94, assoc. prof., 1994-95, prof., 1996—; prof. Johns Hopkins Sch. Hygiene and Pub. Health, 1994—; co-dir. Georgetown/Johns Hopkins Program on Law and Pub. Health; dir. CDC Collaborating Ctr. on Law and the Pub.'s Health; legis. coun. U.S. Senate Labor and Human Resources Com., Washington, 1987, 88; bd. dirs., nat. exec. com. Am. Civil Liberties Union, 1987—; assoc. dir. Harvard U. WHO Internat. Collaborating Ctr. on Health Legis., 1989— Western European editor Internat. Jour. Law and Psychiatry, London, 1978-81; editor in chief: Law Medicine & Health Care; exec. editor: Am. Jour. Law and Medicine; sect. editor Jour. AMA; editor: Secure Provision, 1985, AIDS and the Health Care System, 1990, Surrogate Motherhood: Politics and Privacy, 1990, Implementing the Americans with Disabilities Act, 1993; co-editor: Law, Science and Medicine, 2d edit., 1996; author: Human Rights and Public Health in the AIDS Pandemic, 1997, The Rights of Persons with HIV Disease, 1996, Mental Health Services: Law and Practice, 1986, Institutions Observed, 1986, Mental Health: Tribunal Procedure, 1984, 2d edit., 1992, A Human Condition, 1975, 2d vol., 1977, Civil Liberties in Conflict, 1988, Public Health Law: Power, Duty, Restraint, 2000, The AIDS Pandemic: Complacency, Injustice and Unfulfilled Expectations, 2003; editor Public Health law and Ethics: A Reader, 2002, The Human Rights of Persons with Intellectual Disabilities: Different But Equal, 2003. Legal affairs com. Internat. League Socs. for Mentally Handicapped, Brussels, 1980—; trustee Cobden Trust, London, 1983-85; chmn. Advocacy Alliance, London, 1981-84; sec. All Party Parliamentary Civil Liberties Group, London, 1984-85; bd. dirs. ACLU, 1986—, exec. com., 1988—; mem. com. experts drafting conventions on human experientation UN, Siracusa, Italy, 1980-82. Recipient Rosemary Deldridge Meml. award Nat. Consumer Coun. U.K., 1983; fellow Kennedy Inst. Ethics, 1994—, Fulbright fellow U. Oxford, 1974-75. Avocations: climbing, vegetable growing. Home: 10413 Masters Ter Potomac MD 20854-3862 Office: Georgetown U Law Ctr 600 New Jersey Ave NW Washington DC 20001-2075 E-mail: gostin@law.georgetown.edu.

GOTHARD, DONALD LEE, retired auto company executive; b. Madison, Wis., Dec. 2, 1934; s. William Henry and Lorraine Marie (Williams) G.; m. Doris Marie Lockhart, May 27, 1990; children from previous marriage: children: Donald Lee Jr., Ann Marie. BSEE, U. Notre Dame, 1956. Elec. engr. AC Spark Plug div. Milw. GM, 1956-62, systems engr. AC Electronics div., 1962-63, Oak Creek, Wis., 1963-67, sr. project engr., supr. Delco Electronics div. Bethpage, N.Y., 1967-71; systems engr., asst. mgr. engring. staff GM Tech. Ctr., Warren, Mich., 1971-75; asst. staff engr., then staff engr. Chevrolet Engring. div. Warren, 1975-82; chief engr. GM Truck & Bus. Engring., Pontiac, Mich., 1982-85, exec. engr. Auburn Hills and Troy, Mich., 1985-90; dir. rsch. and adminstrv. svcs. GM Rsch. and Environ. Activities Staff, Warren, 1990-92; exec. prototype, process engring. GM Design Ctr., GM Tech. Ctr., Warren, 1992-93; dir. quality and mfg. engrs. GM N.Am. Ops. N.Am. Tech. Ctr., Warren, 1993-96. Cons. United Technologies Automotive, 1996. Chmn. fin. com. adv. coun. Utica (Mich.) Cmty. Schs., 1975; mem. Shelby Twp (Mich.) Cable TV Coordinating Com., 1980; mem. engring. adv. coun. U. Notre Dame, 1988—, mem. minority engring. program adv. coun., 1994—; bd. dirs. Sci. Engring. Fair Met. Detroit, 1992-99; chmn. ch. fin. com., 1996-2003; judge, Internat. Sci. and Engring. Fair, 1996-2001. 1st lt. U.S. Army, 1956-58. Recipient Cert. of Commendation MIT, 1969, Apollo Achievement award NASA, 1969, Disting. Svc. award Utica Cmty. Schs., 1976, Cert. of Recognition Coun. of Engring. Deans of Historically Black Colls., Mobil Corp. and U.S. Black Engr. Mag., 1991; team leader, internat. land speed records with Pickup Truck, Internat. Motor Sports Assn./So. Calif. Timing Assn., 1989, U. Notre Dame Coll. of Engring. Honor award, 1994, Rev. Edward Williams Svc. award U. Notre Dame Black Alumni, 1994. Mem. Soc. Automotive Engrs. (excellence in oral presentation award 1987, Black Engr. of Yr. award for lifetime achievement-industry 1995), Black Alumni Assn. U. Notre Dame (coord.-at-large exec. bd. 1987-94). Avocations: photography, senior softball and volleyball, exercising. Home: 5510 Brookside Ln Washington MI 48094-2683

GOTHOLD, STUART EUGENE, school system administrator, educator; b. L.A., Sept. 20, 1935; s. Hubert Eugene and Adelaide Louise (Erickson) G.; m. Jane Ruth Soderberg, July 15, 1955; children: Jon Ernest, Susan Louise, Eric Arthur, Ruth Ann. BA, Whittier Coll., 1956, MA in Edn., 1961, LLD (hon.), 1988; EdD, U. So. Calif., 1974. Tchr. grades 1-9 El Rancho Sch. Dist., Pico Rivera, Calif., 1956-61, prin. jr. h.s., 1961-66; curriculum cons. L.A. County Office Edn., 1966-70; asst. supt. South Whittier (Calif.) Sch. Dist., 1970-72, supt., 1972-77; asst. supt. L.A. County Office Edn., Downey, 1977-78, chief dep. supt., 1978-79, supt., 1979-94; clin. prof. U. So. Calif., L.A., 1994—. Charter mem. Edn. Insights, Detroit, 1990—; bd. dirs. Fedco Found. Author: (book) Inquiry, 1970, Decisions-A Health Edn. Curriculum, 1971. Recipient Alumni Merit award USC, 1993, Alumni Achievement award Whittier Coll., 1986; named Dist. Educator Calif. State U., 1993. Republican. Roman Catholic. Avocations: tennis, choral singing, photography, hiking. Home: 10121 Pounds Ave Whittier CA 90603-1649 Office: U So Calif WPH 902 C Los Angeles CA 90089-0031 E-mail: gothold@usc.edu.

GOTKIN, MICHAEL STANLEY, lawyer, director; b. Washington, Aug. 15 1942; s. Charles and Florence (Rosenberg) G. m. Diana Rubin, Aug. 22, 1964 children: Lisa, Steven. AA, Montgomery C.C., 1962; BS, Columbia U., 1964 JD, Vanderbilt U., 1967. Bar: D.C. 1968, Tenn. 1973, Ill. 1997. Trial atty. Bur Restraint of Trade FTC, Washington, 1967-70; atty. H.J. Heinz Co., Pitts. 1970-73; ptnr. Moseley & Gotkin, Nashville, 1973; atty. K.F.C. Corp., Louisville, 1974-75; sr. v.p., gen. counsel Farley Candy Co., Chgo., 1975-98; ptnr Pullman and Gotkin, Northbrook, Ill., 1998—; also. bd. dirs. Mem. ABA, Am Corp. Counsel Assn. (past v.p., pres., bd. dirs. Chgo. chpt., pres. 1990-91), D.C Bar Assn., Tenn. Bar Assn., Montgomery C.C. Assn. (past pres.), Skokie C. o C. (past pres., dir.), Columbia U. Alumni Assn., Candy Prodn. Club, Vanderbil U. Alumni Assn., Spotsmans Country Club (Northbrook), B'nai Brith. Office 4820 Searle Pkwy Skokie IL 60077-2918

GOTLIEB, ALLAN E. former ambassador; b. Winnipeg, Man., Can., Feb. 28 1928; s. David Phillip and Sarah (Schiller) G.; m. Sondra Kaufman, Dec. 20 1955; children: Rebecca, Marcus, Rachel. BA, U. Calif., 1949; LL.B., Harvard U., 1954; MA, B.C.L. (Vinerian Law scholar), Oxford U., 1956. Bar: Eng 1956. Fellow Wadham Coll. and univ. lectr. in law Oxford U., 1954-56; joined Can. Dept. External Affairs, 1957; asst. under sec. for external affairs and lega adviser, 1967-68; dep. minister communications, 1968-73; dep. minister man power and immigration, 1973-76; chmn. Can. Employment and Immigration Commn., 1976-77; under sec. Dept. External Affairs, 1977-81; Can. ambassado

to U.S., Washington, 1981-89; chmn. Can. Coun., Ottawa, 1989-94. Vis. fellow All Souls Coll., Oxford, 1975-76; William Lyon Mackenzie King vis. prof. Harvard U., 1989, Claude Bissell vis. prof. U. Toronto, 1989; hon. fellow Wadham Coll., Oxford, Eng.; sr. fellow Massey Coll.; former gov. Internat. Devel. Rsch. Ctr., Nat. Film Bd.; former pub. Saturday Night Mag.; bd. dirs. Hollinger Inc., Davis and Henderson Income Trust; mem. adv. bd. Nestle Canada, Inc.; Can. advisor Julius Baer Investment Adv. (Canada) Ltd., The Carlyle Group, Washington; 1st asset mgmt., former hon. sec. Hollinger Internat. Adv. Bd.; N.Am. vice chmn. Trilateral Commn.; chmn. Donner Canadian Found., Ont. Heritage Found., Sotheby's Can.; sr. advisor Stikeman Elliott, Toronto; trustee Art Gallery Ont. Author: Disarmament and International Law, 1965, Canadian Treaty-Making, 1968, Impact of Technology on the Development of International Law, 1982, I'll Be With You In A Minute, Mr. Ambassador, 1991; editor: Human Rights, Federalism and Minorities, 1979; editor: Harvard Law Rev., 1950-51. Decorated companion Order of Can.; recipient outstanding achievement award Govt. of Can., 1983, Haas internat. award U. Calif. Bd. Regents, 1985, Woodrow Wilson Pub. Svc. award. Office: Commerce Court West PO Box 85 Ste 5300 Toronto ON Canada M5L 1B9

GOTLIEB, CALVIN CARL, computer scientist, educator; b. Toronto, Ont., Can., Mar. 27, 1921; s. Israel and Jennie G.; m. Phyllis Fay Bloom, June 12, 1949; children: Leo, Margaret, Jane. BA, U. Toronto, 1942, MA, 1944, PhD, 1947; D in Math. (hon.)., U. Waterloo, Can., 1968; D in Engring. (hon.), N.S. Tech. U., 1985; LLD (hon.), U. Toronto, 1996. Faculty U. Toronto, 1949—; dir. Inst. Computer Sci., 1962-70, chmn. dept. computer sci., 1964-67, prof. computer sci., 1962—, emeritus, 1986—. Pres. C.C. Gotlieb Cons. Ltd., 1978—; cons. info. scis. to various govts., internat. orgns., indsl. cos., 1969— ; McKay vis. prof. U. Calif., Berkeley, 1981; chmn. tech. com. 9 on relationship between computers and soc. Internat. Fedn. for Info. Processing, 1975-81 Author: (with J.N.P. Hume) High-Speed Data Processing, 1958, (with A. Borodin) Social Issues in Computing, 1973, (with L.R. Gotlieb) Data Types and Structures, 1978, Economics of Computers, 1985; editor, editor-in-chief, contbr. various Can., Netherlands, U.S. sci. jours. Recipient Silver Core award Internat. Fedn. of Info. Processing Socs., 1974, Auerbach award, 1994; rsch. grantee Nat. Sci. and Engring. Rsch. Coun. Can., 1955-90, C.M. Order of Can., 1996. Fellow: Assn. Computing Machinery (Pres.'s medal 2002), Brit. Computer Soc., Royal Soc. Can.; mem.: Can. Info. Processing Soc. (hon.), Nat. Yacht Club (Toronto), Faculty Club (U. Toronto). Jewish. Home: 19 Lower Village Gate PH 06 Toronto ON Canada M5P 3L9 Office: U Toronto Dept Computer Sci Toronto ON Canada M5S 3G4 E-mail: ccg@cs.toronto.edu.

GOTLIEB, EDWARD MARVIN, pediatrician; b. Decatur, Ga., Dec. 21, 1945; s. Sam and Dorothy (Schwartz) G.; m. Jaquelin Smith, June 25, 1970; children: Sarah Ruth, Aaron Franklin, David Jacob. AB, Duke U., 1967; MD, Vanderbilt U., 1971. Diplomate Am. Bd. Pediat. Intern in pediat. Va. Commonwealth U.-Med. Coll. Va., Richmond, 1971-72, resident in pediat., 1972-74; fellow in adolescent medicine U. Col. Sch. Medicine, Denver, 1975-76; med. dir. The Pediatric Ctr., Stone Mountain, Ga., 1976—, Hillside Hosp., Atlanta, 1986—. Dir. Inst. Adolescent Studies, Stone Mountain, 1978—; clin. assoc. Emory U. Sch. Nursing, Atlanta, 1978—; mem. Gov.'s Commn. on Adolescent Svcs., Atlanta, 1980-81; clin. prof. Ga. State U. Sch. Nursing, Atlanta, 1982—; clin. asst. prof. Emory U. Sch. Medicine, Atlanta, 1987-2000, Morehouse Sch. Medicine, Atlanta, 1998—; clin. assoc. prof. Emory U. Sch. Medicine, 2000—; adolescent medicine cons. DeKalb Bd. Health, Decatur, Ga., 1990-91; mem. tech. working group Nat. Immunization Program, Nat. Ctrs. for Disease Control Prevention, Atlanta, 2000—; cons. Comprehensive Adolescent Preventive Svcs., Ga. Dept. Human Resources, Atlanta, 1999-2000; bd. dirs. Atlanta-Fulton Commn. on Children and Youth, Atlanta. Editor: Practicing Adolescent Medicine, 1994. Cons. cyber playground Sci Trek Sci. and Tech. Mus., Atlanta, 1996; mem. Ahavath Achim Synagogue, Atlanta, 1987-2001; mem. Am. Jewish Hist. Soc., Waltham, Mass., 1973-2001; mem. Nat. Yiddish Book Ctr., Amherst, Mass., 1998-2001. Recipient Primary Care Achievement award Pew Health Professions Commn., 1998, Health-Care Heroes award Atlanta Bus. Chronicle, 2000. Fellow Am. Acad. Pediat. (chmn. com. on adolescence Ga. chpt. 1980-83, Ga. state coord. pediat. rsch. in office settings 1986—, com. on adolescence 1992-97, med. informatics cons. Coun. on Pediatric Practice 1996-98, chmn. task force on med. informatics 2001-02, chmn. policy group steering com. on clinical info. tech. 2002-, Pediat. Leadership Alliance award 2000), Soc. Adolescent Medicine (pres. Southeastern chpt. 1978-84, regional chpts. rep. 1983-84); mem. Med. Assn. Ga., Dekalb Med. Soc. Democrat. Jewish. Avocations: swimming, genealogy, computers. Office: The Pediatric Ctr 5405D Memorial Dr Stone Mountain GA 30083 Fax: 404-297-8753. E-mail: egotlie@emory.edu.

GOTLIEB, LAWRENCE BARRY, lawyer; b. L.A., July 24, 1948; s. Samuel and Sally (Friedman) G.; m. Virginia L. Moorman, Oct. 4, 1975; children: Shana E., Kenneth H., Rebecca J. AB, Dartmouth Coll., 1970; JD, Harvard U., 1973. Bar: Calif. 1973, D.C. 1984, N.Y. 1984, U.S. Supreme Ct. 1981. Asst. U.S. atty. Dept. Justice, L.A., 1978-82; asst. gen. counsel Distilled Spirits Coun., Washington, 1982-86; sr. counsel, v.p., asst. sec. First Interstate BanCorp, L.A., 1987-96; v.p. govt. and pub. affairs, assoc. corp. counsel KB Home Corp., 1996—. Dep. gen. counsel ind. commn. on Christopher Commn., 1991; instr. Atty. Gen.'s Advocacy Inst., Washington, 1981-86; pro tem judge L.A. Mcpl. Ct., 1991. Mem. Housing Mediation Bd., Pasadena, Calif., 1981-82, Calif. Citizens Compensation Commn., 2003—; bd. dirs. Juvenile Gang Prevention, L.A., 9174-77, pasadena Redistricting Commn., 1981-82; chmn. Calif. Workforce Investment Bd., 1999—; trustee Orthopaedic Hosp. Found., 1998—, Hugh O'Brian Youth Found., 1998-2000. Mem. ABA, State Bar Calif., D.C. Bar Assn., N.Y. State Bar Assn., Los Angeles County Bar Assn. (chmn. com. on professionalism, trustee 1995-97), Phi Beta Kappa. Jewish. E-mail: lgotlieb@kbhome.com.

GOTSCHLICH, EMIL CLAUS, physician; b. Bangkok, Jan. 17, 1935; arrived in U.S., 1950, naturalized, 1955; s. Emil Clemens and Magdalene (Holst) Gotschlich; m. Kathleen-Anne Haines, May 24, 1975; children: Emil Christopher, Hilda Christina, Emil Chandler, Emily Claire. BA, NYU, 1955, MD, 1959. Intern Bellevue Hosp., N.Y.C., 1959—60; mem. faculty Rockefeller U., N.Y.C., 1960—, prof. microbiology, 1978—, sr. physician, 1978—, prof., v.p. med. sci. Capt. med. corps U.S. Army, 1966—68. Recipient Squibb award, Am. Soc. Infectious Disease, 0197, Lasker award, Albert and Mary Lasker Found., 1978. Mem.: NAS, Am. Soc. Clin. Investigation, Am. Assn. Immunologists, Peripatetic Club, Alpha Omega Alpha, Sigma Xi. Office: Rockefeller U Dept Bacterial Pathogenesis & Immunology 1230 York Ave New York NY 10021-6399

GOTSHALL, CORDIA ANN, publishing company executive, distributing executive; b. Greenwood, Ark., Jan. 21, 1931; d. Harrison Wages and Mabel Magdalene (Boswell) Wages Moreland; m. Daniel W. Gotshall, Apr. 12, 1952. AA with honors, Foothill Jr. Coll., Los Altos Hills, Calif., 1966; BA magna cum laude, Humboldt State U., Arcata, Calif., 1969; student, Humboldt State U., 1969-71. Clk., typist Indentification Bur. Stanislaus County Sheriff's Office, Modesto, Calif., 1950-55; credit dept. mgr. Brizard's Dept. Store, Arcata, 1955-56; sec.-coord. City of Eureka (Calif.) Recreation Dept., 1956-60; seasonal aide State of Calif. Dept. Fish and Game, Palo Alto, 1961; owner, v.p. Sea Challengers Pub. Co., Monterey, Calif., 1976-83, pres., 1983—, v.p., 2001—. Co-editor (with Daniel W. Gotshall) Fishwatcher's Guide, 1977; U.S. rep. Moscow Internat. Book Fair, 1985; vol. Bayview Grammar Sch. Mem. Chi Sigma Epsilon. Avocations: reading, travel, hiking, nature studies, exploring. Office: 4 Sommerset Rise Monterey CA 93940-4112 E-mail: anngot@aol.com.

GOTSHALL, JAN DOYLE, financial planner; b. Pa., Nov. 5, 1942; d. Edward Albert and Rose M. (Leahy) Doyle; m. Ralph M. Gotshall Jr., Dec. 24, 1963; children: Rosemarie, Annmarie, Elizabeth Marie. AA, Neuman Coll., 1979; MSM, Am. Coll., Bryn Mawr, 1997. CFP; registered investment advisor. Co-founder Radnor Planning Assocs., Devon, Pa., 1979-82; fin. cons. Exeter Fin. Svcs. Co., Devon, 1982-85; owner, pres. GM Fin. Planners, Inc., Devon, 1985—. Minority-majority insp. Del. County Electorate, Broomall, Pa., 1973-83; mem. fin. bd. St. Pius X Ch., Broomall, 1988. Mem. Inst. CFP (CFP, pres. 1986-87, chmn. 1987-89), Internat. Assn. Fin. Planners (v.p. 1980-88, pres. 1991-92, chmn. 1992-93), Nat. Assn. Ins. Women (cert. profl. ins. woman 1985, bd. dirs. local chpt. 1980-82), Del County Estate Planning Coun. (exec. com. 1989-90, 96—, v.p. 1991-94, pres. 1994-96, dir. 1996-98). Republican. Avocations: reading, golf, tennis. Office: GM Fin Planners Inc 49 Chestnut Rd Paoli PA 19301-1502

GOTT, MARJORIE EDA CROSBY, conservationist, former educator; b. Louisville; d. Alva Baird and Nellie (Jones) Crosby; m. John Richard Gott, Jr., Mar. 12, 1946 (dec. Sept. 1993); 1 child, J. Richard III. AB in Math., U. Louisville, 1934; postgrad., U. Ky., 1938-42. Nationally accredited flower show judge, landscape design critic and judge. Underwriter Commonwealth Life Ins. Co., Louisville, 1934-37; tchr. English Hikes Sch., Buechel, Ky., 1937-43; civilian chief statis. control unit Materiel Command, Army Air Force, Dayton, Ohio, 1943-46; tchr. psychology Bapt. Hosp. and Gen. Hosp., Louisville, 1950-52. Dedicated Ky.'s Floral Clock to All Kentuckians Who Take Pride in the Beauty of Their State Commonwealth of Ky.,1961. Author: (booklet) How a Garden Club Beautifies a City, 1967. Pres. Young Women's Rep. Club of Louisville and Jefferson County, 1938-40; pres. Beautification League Louisville and Jefferson County, 1963-64; co-chair Keep Ky. Cleaner-Greener, 1963-68; bd. dirs. Scenic Ky., Inc., 1989—, Nat. Coun. State Garden Clubs, 1961-83. Recipient Conservation award of merit Commonwealth of Ky., 1963, Landscape Design Critics award Nat. Coun. State Garden Clubs, 1979. Mem. Woman's Club of Louisville (pres. 1973-75, hon. 1991—), Garden Club of Ky. (pres. 1961-63), Nat. Assn. Parliamentarians (founder, pres. Louisville unit 1961-63), Louisville Astron. Soc. (hon.). Presbyterian. Avocations: travel, bridge, cooking. Home: 136 Indian Hills Trl Louisville KY 40207-1541

GOTTESMAN, A(RTHUR) EDWARD, lawyer; b. Hillside, N.J., July 29, 1937; s. Joseph Jack Gottesman, Sadonia Herskowitz; m. Patricia Jo Matson; m. Allison Pierce Coudert (div.); children: Polly Moore, Catherine Coudert. BA, U.Chgo., 1954; LLB, Yale U., 1957. Bar: N.Y. 1959. Ptnr. Coudert Bros., London, 1963—70; sr. ptnr. Gottesman Jones & Partners, London, 1970—. Pres. Am. C. of C., London, 1981—83; chmn. Derby Internat. Corp., Luxembourg, 1986—98, Exeter Internat. Corp., Luxembourg, Prin. Healthcare Fin. Ltd., London. Dir. London Bach Orch., 1980—89; Member Yale University President's Council on International Activities, New Haven. Private US Army, 1960—61, Fort Dix, N.J. Mem.: Yale Club, Reform Club. Office: Centenary International Corporation 1120 Avenue of the Americas New York NY 10036 Personal E-mail: centenint@aol.com. Business E-Mail: gottesmanjones@aol.com.

GOTTESMAN, CHARLES R. music educator; b. Abington, Pa., Aug. 24, 1971; s. Charles and Beatrice Boston Gottesman; m. Lauren L Lopez, Dec. 22, 2001. MusB, Temple U., Philadelphia, PA. Cert. tchr. Pa., 1994. Music educator Sch. Dist. of Springfield Twp., Oreland, Pa., 1994—. Recipient Lloyd C. Clemmer PTA Citizenship award, Erdenheim Elem. Sch. PTA, 1999. Home: 500 Greenhill Rd Willow Grove PA 19090 Office: Springfield Twp HS 1801 E Paper Mill Rd Erdenheim PA 19038 Personal E-mail: chuck_gottesman@sdst.org.

GOTTESMAN, DAVID SANFORD, investment executive; b. N.Y.C., Apr. 26, 1926; s. Benjamin and Esther (Garfunkel) G.; m. Ruth Levy, Aug. 17, 1950; children: Robert, Alice, William. BA, Trinity Coll., 1948; MBA, Harvard U., 1950; LHD (hon.), Yeshiva U., 1988. Mng. ptnr. First Manhattan Co., N.Y.C., 1964—. Bd. dirs. Sequa Corp. Vice-chmn. and trustee Am. Mus. Natural History; trustee Mt. Sinai Hosp.; chmn. emeritus Yeshiva U., N.Y.C. Mem. N.Y. Soc. Security Analysts, The Century Assn., Econs. Club, Harmonie Club, Century Country Club. Office: First Manhattan Co 437 Madison Ave New York NY 10022-7001 E-mail: dgottesman@firstmanhattan.com.

GOTTESMAN, IRVING ISADORE, psychology educator; b. Cleve., Dec. 29, 1930; s. Bernard and Virginia (Weitzner) G.; m. Carol Applen, Dec. 23, 1970; children— Adam M., David B. BS, Ill. Inst. Tech., 1953; PhD, U. Minn., 1960. Diplomate in clin. psychology and psychol. assessment; lic. psychologist Calif., Va. Intern clin. psychology VA Hosp., Mpls., 1959-60; lectr. dept. social relations Harvard U., 1960-63; USPHS fellow in psychiat. genetics Inst. Psychiatry, London, 1963-64; assoc. prof. psychiat. & genetics, dept. psychiatry U. N.C., 1964-66; prof. dept. psychology, psychiatry and genetics U. Minn., 1966-80; prof. dept. psychiatry and genetics Washington U., St. Louis, 1980-85; Commonwealth prof. psychology U. Va., Charlottesville, 1985-94, Sherrell J. Aston prof. psychology, prof. clin. pediats., 1994-2001, prof. emeritus, 2001—; sr. fellow, Drs. Irving and Dorothy Bernstein prof. adult psychiatry U. Minn., 2001—. Cons. NIMH, Washington, 1975-79, 92-96, NIMH Nat. Plan for Schizophrenia, 1988-89; mem. Pres.'s Commn. on Huntington Disease, 1977; tng. cons. VA, Washington, 1968-85, 2001—; fellow Ctr. for Advanced Studies in the Behavioral Scis., Stanford, Calif., 1987-88; Inst. of Medicine Com. cons. Vietnam War Experience Study, 1987-88, Med. Follow-Up Agy., 2000—; NRC cons. Workshop on Schizophrenia, 1995-96; cons. human rights Equal Opportunities Commn., Hong Kong, 1999-2003; mem. Inst. Medicine Follow-up Agy., 2000—; chair twins com. Inst. Medicine, 2000—. Author: Schizophrenia and Genetics, 1972 (Hofheimer prize), Schizophrenia The Epigenetic Puzzle, 1982, Schizophrenia Genesis: The Origins of Madness, 1991 (transl. into Japanese and German, William James Book award, Phi Beta Kappa U. Va. Book award 1992), Schizophrenia and Genetic Risks, 1992, 3d edit., 1999, Schizophrenia and Manic Depressive Disorder: Biological Roots of Mental Illness Revealed by Study of Identical Twins, 1994, transl. into Japanese, 1998, Seminars in Psychiatric Genetics, 1994, 2d edit., 2004, Psychiatric Genetics and Genomics, 2002; editor: Man, Mind and Heredity, 1971, Vital Statistics, Demography and Schizophrenia, 1989. Served with USNR, 1949-53, 56-61; USN, 1953-56. Guggenheim fellow U. Copenhagen, 1972; recipient R. Thornton Wilson prize Ea. Psychiat. Rsch. Assn., 1965, Stanley Dean award Am. Coll. Psychiatrists, 1988, Eric Stromgren medal Danish Psychiat. Soc., 1991, Kurt Schneider prize, Bonn, 1992, Alexander Gralnick prize Am. Assn. Suicidology, 1992, Jonathan Logan award Nat. Alliance for Mentally Ill, 1995; David C. Wilson lectr. U. Va. Sch. Medicine, 1967, Lifetime Achievement award Internat. Soc. for Psychiat. Genetics, 1997; Parker lectr. Ohio State U. Sch. Medicine, 1983, 93, others. Fellow APA (Disting. Scientist award divsn. 12, sect. 3 1994, Disting. Sci. Contbns. award 2001), AAAS, Am. Psychopathol. Assn., Royal Coll. Psychiatrists (hon.), Am. Psychol. Soc. (human capital initiative task force for psychopathology rsch. agenda 1993-96); mem. Minn. Human Genetics League (v.p. 1969-71), Soc. Study Social Biology (v.p. 1976-80), Behavior Genetics Assn. (pres. 1976-77, T. Dobzhansky award 1990), Am. Soc. Human Genetics (editl. bd. 1967-72), Soc. Rsch. in Psychopathology (pres. 1993, Joseph Zubin award 2001), Japanese Soc. Biol. Psychiatry (spl. lecture award 2001), Inst. of Psychiatry (14th Eliot Slater Lectr., 2002). Home: 5823 Vernon Ln Edina MN 55436 E-mail: gotte003@umn.edu.

GOTTESMAN, MICHAEL MARC, biomedical researcher, researcher; b. Jersey City, N.J., Oct. 7, 1946; s. Jacob Joseph and Frieda (Shapiro) G.; m. Susan Kemelhor, Feb. 5, 1966; children: Daniel Eric, Rebecca Fran. AB, Harvard Coll., 1966; MD, Harvard Med. Sch., 1970. Diplomate Am. Bd. Internal Medicine. Med. intern then resident Peter Bent Brigham Hosp., Boston, 1970-71, 74-75; rsch. assoc. NIH, Bethesda, Md., 1971-74; asst. prof. Harvard Med. Sch., Boston, 1975-76; sr. investigator Nat. Cancer Inst., Bethesda, 1976-80, sect. head, 1980-90, lab. chief, 1990—. Acting dir. Nat. Ctr. for Human Genome Rsch., 1992-93, deputy dir. intramural rsch., 1994—. Author and editor: Molecular Cell Genetics, Molecular Genetics of Mammalian Cells, The Role of Proteases in Cancer. With USPHS, 1971—. Recipient Milken Family award for cancer rsch., 1990. Fellow AAAS; mem. Am. Soc. Biochemistry Molecular Biology, Genetics Soc. Am., Am. Soc. Cell Biology, Am. Assn. Cancer Rsch. (Richard and Hinda Rosenthal Found. award 1992). Achievements include rsch. on molecular basis of resistance to anti-cancer drugs. Office: Nat Cancer Inst Lab of Cell Biology Bdlg 37 Rm 1A09 37 Convent Dr MSC 4255 Bethesda MD 20892-0001

GOTTFELD, GUNTHER MAX, retired urban mass transit official, consultant; b. Berlin, June 13, 1934; came to U.S., 1941; s. William James and Charlotte Jeanette (Less) G.; m. Linda Stratton Keene, Oct. 26, 1969 (div. Jan. 1976); children: Deborah Charlotte, David William; m. Ann Richmond, July 13, 1985. BS, Shepherd Coll., 1958; MA, Am. U., 1960. Transp. planner Nat. Capital Trnasp. Agy., Washington, 1961-63; cons. Stockholm Transit Authority, 1963-64; fed. liaison officer Mass. Bay Transp. Authority, Boston, 1965-70; sr. transp. planner Md. Mass Transit Adminstrn., Balt., 1970-74, intergovtl. coordinator, 1974-94. Mem. Am. Pub. Transit Assn. (mem. legis. com. 1981—), Md. Mass Transit Adminstrn., Am. Rd. and Transp. Builders Assn. (mem. pub. transit council 1986-94, mem. legis. watch com. 1986-94), Internat. Union Pub. Transport (rail transit new starts com. 1992—). Democrat. Jewish. Avocations: european travel, cross-country skiing, hiking, classical music. Home: 5301 Hesperus Dr Columbia MD 21044-1808

GOTTFRIED, BENJAMIN FRANK, retired manufacturing executive; b. Phila., Apr. 13, 1939; s. Harry Nathan and Sylvia (Chernow) G.; m. Nancy L. Prunty, June 24, 1994; 1 child from previous marriage, Hal. Student, U. Md., 1973-74, 79-80, Cen. Tex. Coll., 1974-75. Enlisted U.S. Army, 1959; served as chief warrant officer U.S. Army C.E., 1959-79, ret., 1979; regional maintenance mgr. Avis Truck Leasing, Balt., 1979-82; svc. mgr. Hale Truck and Trailer Equipment, Marlton, N.J., 1982-85; sr. dir. svc. Iveco Trucks N.Am., Bensalem, Pa., 1985-95; ret., 1995. Author: (with others) Fleet Equipment, 1986, Transport Topics, 1987. Decorated Purple Heart, Bronze Star, Commendation Medal, Meritorious Svc. Medal, Cross of Gallantry, N.J. Meritorious Svc. medal. Mem. DAV (life), Vietnam Vets. Am. (life), Warrant Officers Assn., Hon. Order Ky. Cols., Fraternal Order Police, Mil. Order of The Purple Heart (life). Jewish. Avocations: remote control car racing, camping, pool, exercise. Home: 303 N Elmwood Rd Marlton NJ 08053-3307 E-mail: bfgottfr@aol.com.

GOTTFRIED, EUGENE LESLIE, physician, educator; b. Passaic, N.J., Feb. 26, 1929; s. David Robert and Rose (Chill) G.; m. Phyllis Doris Swain, Aug. 16, 1957. AB, Columbia U., 1950, MD, 1954. Cert. Nat. Bd. Med. Examiners, Am. Bd. Internal Medicine. Intern Presbyn. Hosp., N.Y.C., 1954-55, asst. resident in medicine, 1957-58; resident Bronx (N.Y.) Mcpl. Hosp. Ctr., 1958-59, fellow in medicine, 1959-60; asst. instr. medicine Albert Einstein Coll. Medicine Yeshiva U., N.Y.C., 1959-60, instr., 1960-61, assoc., 1961-65, asst. prof., 1965-69; assoc. prof. medicine Cornell U. Med. Coll., N.Y.C., 1969-81, assoc. prof. pathology, 1975-81; clin. prof. dept. lab. medicine U. Calif., San Francisco, 1981-93, prof., 1993-99, vice chmn. dept. lab. medicine, 1981-98, prof. emeritus, 1999—. Hosp. appointments include asst. vis. physician Bronx Mcpl. Hosp. Ctr., 1960-66, assoc. attending physician, 1966-69; assoc. attending physician N.Y. Hosp., N.Y.C., 1969-81, assoc. attending pathologist, 1975-81, dir. lab. clin. hematology, 1969-81; chief lab. medicine San Francisco Gen. Hosp. Med. Ctr., 1981-98, dir. clin. labs., 1981-98. Assoc. editor Jour. Lipid Research, 1971-72, 75-77; mem. editorial bd. Jour. Lipid Research, 1972-77. Dir. Rescue One Found., 1998—, Moraga-Orinda Fire Protection Dist., 2002—. Lt. comdr. USNR, 1955—57. Recipient Career Scientist award Health Research Council City of N.Y., 1964-72. Fellow ACP, Am. Soc. Hematology, Internat. Soc. Hematology, Acad. Clin. Lab. Physicians and Scientists; mem. Nat. Com. for Clin. Lab. Stds., Phi Beta Kappa, Alpha Omega Alpha. E-mail: gottfrie@labmed2.ucsf.edu.

GOTTFRIED, IRA SIDNEY, management consulting executive; b. Bronx, N.Y., Jan. 4, 1932; s. Louis and Augusta (Champagne) G.; m. Judith Claire Rosenberg, Sept. 19, 1954; children: Richard Alan, Glenn Steven, David Aaron. BBA, CCNY, 1953; MBA, U. So. Calif., 1959. Lic. airline transport pilot. Sales mgr. Kleerpak Plastics, North Hollywood, Calif., 1956-57; head sys. and procedures Hughes Aircraft Co., Culver City, Calif., 1957-60; mgr. corp. bus. sys. The Aerospace Corp., El Segundo, Calif., 1960-61, dir. adminstrn. Eldon Industries, Inc., Hawthorne, Calif., 1962; mgr. info. sys. Litton Industries, Inc., Woodland Hills, Calif., 1963-64; exec. v.p. Norris & Gottfried, Inc., L.A., 1964-69; pres. Gottfried Cons., Inc., L.A., 1970-85; exec. ptnr. PriceWaterhouseCoopers, LLP, L.A., 1985-88, ret., 1988. V.p. Cresap/Towers Perrin, 1988-90; pres., dir. Gottfried Cons. Internat. 1990—; vice chmn. ACME Inc., 1984-85; dir., mem. exec. com. Blue Cross of Calif., 1968-77. Contbr. articles to profl. jours. Bd. dirs. ARC, Westside Amateur Radio Club, Univ. Synagogue, 1986-92. With USNR, 1953-56. Recipient Pres.'s award United Hosp. Assn. Mem. Inst. Mgmt. Cons. (life), Am. Arbitration Assn., Assn. Info. Tech. Profls. (life), Alpha Phi Omega (life), Brentwood Country Club. Jewish. Avocations: amateur radio K6IRA, flying, model railroading, macramé. Home: 12118 La Casa Ln Los Angeles CA 90049-1530

GOTTFRIED, PAUL EDWARD, humanities educator, editor; b. N.Y.C., Nov. 21, 1941; s. Andrew Gottfried and Ruth Weiser; m. Diane Zelcer, June 15, 1969 (dec. Feb. 1994); children: Barbara Hollander, Joseph, Jonathan, Beth, Sara; m. Mary Zwir, May 12, 2000. BA, Yeshiva U., 1963; MS, Yale U., 1965, PhD, 1967. Grad. fellow Yale U., New Haven, 1965-66; asst. prof. history Case Western Res. U., Cleve., 1968-71; vis. asst. prof. history NYU, N.Y.C., 1971-72; chmn. history dept. Rockford (Ill.) Coll., 1974-86; sr. editor The World and I, Washington, 1986-93; prof. humanities Elizabethtown (Pa.) Coll., 1989—; editor-in-chief This World, 1992—. Author: The Conservative Movement, 1993, After Liberalism, 1999; contbr. articles to profl. jours. Recipient award NEH, 1969; Earhart fellow, 1970, 73, 77, 83, 88, Guggenheim fellow, 1984; NEH tchg. fellow U.S. Naval Acad., 1993. Mem. Neoclassical Reform Jewish Movement (organizer), Società Libera (assoc.). Avocations: jogging, tennis, gardening. Home: 327 College Ave Elizabethtown PA 17022-2414 E-mail: gottfrpe@etown.edu.

GOTTHEIMER, GEORGE MALCOLM, JR., insurance executive, educator; b. Orange, N.J., Mar. 26, 1933; s. George Malcolm Sr. and Rosalie Kahn Zugsmith; m. Patricia Ann Savarese, Apr. 30, 1966; children: Nancy Lorraine, Kerry Suzannne. BSBA, Edison State Coll., Princeton, N.J., 1978; MBA, St. John's U., N.Y.C., 1980; PhD, Calif. Coast U., 1983. Cert. assoc. in reinsurance. Sec. Am. Internat. Group, N.Y.C., 1958-66; pres. Reinsurance Agy. Mgmt. Corp., Bala Cynwyd, Pa., 1966-69; v.p. Occidental Life Ins. Co., Raleigh, N.C., 1969-72, Midland Ins. Co., N.Y.C., 1972-77; exec. v.p. John D. Ryan & Co. Inc., N.Y.C., 1977-82; v.p. Gen. Re Group, 1982-84; sr. v.p. Pro Re of Am., Inc., N.Y.C., 1984-86; pres. Kernan Assocs., Inc., Berkeley Heights, N.J., 1986—. Adj. asst. prof. ins., reinsurance mgmt. St. John's U., N.Y.C., 1972-80, adj. assoc. prof., 1980-97, assoc. prof., 1997—; adj. prof. Baruch Coll. CUNY. Contbr. articles to profl. jours. Research fellow Harry J. Loman Found., Malvern, Pa., 1982. Mem. Chartered Property Casualty Underwriters (cert. 1957, nat. dir. 1983-86, regional v.p. 1985-86, pres. N.Y. chpt. 1980-81, Eugene A. Toale Meml. award 1985), CLU's (cert. 1973). Home: 6 Oechsner Ct Berkeley Heights NJ 07922-1731 E-mail: ggottheimer@kernanassoc.com.

GOTTHELF, BETH, lawyer; b. Detroit, Mar. 24, 1958; BS in Pub. Adminstrn., Oakland U., 1980; JD, U. Detroit, 1985. Bar: Mich. 1986, U.S. Dist. Ct. (ea. dist.) Mich. 1986. Claims rep. Social Security Adminstrn., Pontiac, Mich., 1979-82; law clk. U.S. Atty.'s Office, Detroit, 1984-85; asst. prof. law Clermont-Ferrand U. de Droit, France, 1985-86; jud. law clk. Mich. Ct. Appeals, Detroit, 1986-87; assoc. Philip G. Tannian PC, Detroit, 1987—89, Honingman, Miller, Schwartz and Cohn, Detroit, 1989—91; from assoc. to shareholder Seyburn, Kahn, Ginn, Bess and Serlin PC, Southfield, Mich., 1991—2003; shareholder Butzel Long, Bloomfield Hills, Mich., 2003—. Bd. dirs. JVS, Inc. Bd. dirs., vice chair Nat. Multiple Sclerosis Soc., Detroit Area Comml. Bd. Realtors, S.E. Mich. Coun. Govts. (environ. policy adv. coun.), Greater Detroit C. of C. (chair task force on water and sewer issues); bd. dirs. U. Cancer Found. Mem. ABA (solid and hazardous waste com., chmn. water and wetlands, natural resources, energy and environ. law sect., mem. fed. adv. com. on storm water),Internat. Women's Forum, Am. Electroplaters and Surface Finishers Assn., Oakland County Bar Assn. (past chair environ. law sec.), Mich. State Bar Assn. (environ. law sect., past chair, coun. mem., program com., solid waste/hazardous waste/ins. com., superfund com., past sec., treas.). Jewish. Office: Butzel Long Ste 200 100 Bloomfield Hills Pkwy Bloomfield Hills MI 48304 E-mail: gotthelf@butzel.com.

GOTTHELF, ERIC, astrophysicist, research scientist; b. N.Y.C., N.Y., Oct. 24, 1956; PhD, Columbia U., 1992. Achievements include discovery of young X-ray pulsars; new astronomical object.

GOTTHOFFER, LANCE, lawyer; b. N.Y.C., June 23, 1949; s. Joel Sidney and Muriel (Diamond) G. BA, Monmouth Coll., 1971; JD, Georgetown U., 1974. Bar: N.Y. 1975, U.S. Dist. Ct. (so. dist.) N.Y. 1975, U.S. Ct. Appeals (2nd, 3rd, 5th, 6th and 9th cirs.) 1981, U.S. Ct. Internat. Trade 1986, U.S. Supreme Ct. 1987. Legal asst. Office of N.Y.C. Coun. Pres., N.Y.C., 1970-73; assoc. Mudge, Rose, Guthrie & Alexander, N.Y.C., 1974-77; ptnr. Marks & Murase, N.Y.C., 1977-94, Oppenheimer, Wolff & Donnelly, N.Y.C., 1994—2002, Reed

Smith, N.Y.C., 2003—. Guest lectr. Grad. Sch. Bus., Baruch Coll., N.Y.C.; speaker in field. Mem. ABA. Office: Reed Smith 599 Lexington Ave New York NY 10022 Home: 245 E 40th St New York NY 10016 E-mail: lgotthoffer@reedsmith.com.

GOTTIER, RICHARD CHALMERS, retired computer company executive; b. Columbus, Ohio, Oct. 12, 1918; s. Chalmers M. and Grace (Eisnaugle) G.; m. Mary S. Hiatt, Nov. 13, 1965; children: Barbara, Diane, Richard Chalmers, Penny. BS in Bus. Adminstrn, Ohio State U., 1939; postgrad., Northwestern U. Grad. Sch. Bus., 1969. Spl. agt. FBI, Washington, 1940-51; with RCA, Indpls., 1951-59; dir. Magnavox Co., Ft. Wayne, Ind., 1959-70; sr. v.p. Control Data Corp., Mpls., 1970-80; chmn., gen. ptnr. Minn. Seed Capital, Inc., 1980-97. Home: 4735 Sparrow Rd Minnetonka MN 55345-2438

GOTTLIEB, ALAN MERRIL, advertising, fundraising and broadcasting executive, writer; b. L.A., May 2, 1947; s. Seymour and Sherry (Schutz) G.; m. Julie Hoy Versnel, July 27, 1979; children: Amy Jean, Sarah Merril, Alexis Hope, Andrew Michael. Grad., Inst. on Comparative Political and Economic Sys. at Georgetown U., 1970; BS Nuc. Engring., U. Tenn., 1971. Press sec. Congressman John Duncan, Knoxville, Tenn., 1971; regional rep. Young Am. for Freedom, Seattle, 1972, nat. dir. Washington, 1971-72; nat. treas. Am. Conservative Union, Washington, 1971—, bd. dirs., 1974—; pres. Merril Assoc., 1974—. Chmn. Citizens Com. for Right to keep and Bear Arms, Bellevue, Wash., 1972—, exec. dir., 1973; pres. Ctr. Def. of Free Enterprise, Bellevue, 1976—, Second Amendment Found., Bellevue, 1974—, NoInternet-Tax.org, 2001—; pub. Gun Week, 1985—, The Gottlieb-Tartaro Report, 1995—; bd. dir. Nat. Pk. User Assn., 1988—; bd. dirs. Am. Polit. Action Com., 1988—; bd. dir. Coun. Nat. Policy, bd. gov., 1985—, Svc. Bur. Assn., pres., dir., 1974—, Chancellor Broadcasting, Inc., Las Vegas, 1990—93; pres. Sta. KBNP Radio, Portland, 1990—, Sta. KITZ Radio, Evergreen Radio Network, Seattle, 1990—93, Westnet Broadcasting Inc., Bellevue, 1990, Sta. KSBN Radio, Spokane, 1995—; chmn. Talk Am. Radio Networks, 1994—2001, Univ. Talk Network, 2002. Author: The Gun Owners Political Action Manual, 1976, The Rights of Gun Owners, 1981, rev. edit., 1991, The Gun Grabbers, 1988, Gun Rights Fact Book, 1989, Guns for Women, 1988, The Wise Use Agenda, 1989, Trashing the Economy, 1993, Thinks You Can Do To Defend Your Gun Rights, 1993, Alan Gottlieb's Celebrity Address Book, 1994, 2d edit., 2001, More Things You Can Do To Defend Your Gun Rights, 1995, Politically Correct guns, 1996, She Took a Village, 1998, Double Trouble, 2001, Gun Rights Affirmed, 2001. With U.S. Army, 1968-74. Recipient Good Citizenship award Citizens Home Protective Assn., Honolulu, 1978, Cicero award Nat. Assn. Federally Licensed Firearms Dealers, Fla., 1982, Second Amendment award Scope, 1983, 91, Outstanding Am. Handgunner award, Am. Handgunners Award found., Milwaukee, Wisc., 1984, Roy Rogers award, Nat. Antique Arms Collectors Assn., Reno, Nev., 1987, Golden Eagle award, Am. Fedn. Police, Washington, 1990. Mem. NRA. Republican. E-mail: alangottlieb@aol.com.

GOTTLIEB, ALICE BENDIX, medical educator; b. N.Y.C., July 24, 1952; d. Gerhard and Eva (Sternberger) Bendix; m. Allan Gottlieb, Jan. 7, 1972; children: David, Michael. BA, Brandeis U., 1973; PhD, The Rockefeller U., 1979; MD, Cornell U., 1980. Diplomate Am. Bd. Internal Medicine, Am. Bd. Dermatology, Am. Bd. Rheumatology; ACLS, BLS. Med. resident The N.Y. Hosp., 1980-82; rheumatic diseases fellow The Hosp. for Spl. Surgery, N.Y.C., 1982-84; asst. prof. The Rockefeller U., 1982-89, assoc. prof., 1989-93, physician, 1989—; dermatology resident N.Y. Hosp., 1990-93; assoc. med. dir. dermatology Internat. Clin. Rsch., Hoffmann-LaRoche Inc., 1993-94, group leader in dermatology, 1994; chief divsn. dermatology dept. medicine U. Medicine/Dentistry N.J.-Robert Wood Johnson Med. Sch., 1995-99, WH Conzen chair in clin. pharmacology, dir. clin. rsch. ctr., 1997—, prof. medicine, 1999—, prof. dept. molecular genetics and microbiology, 2000—. Adj. prof. The Rockefeller U., 1993—2000; info. broker NDA Expert Sys., 1994—95; spkr. in field. Assoc. editor : Jour. of Immunology, 1990—94, mem. editl. bd.: Bd. of Am. Clin. Dermatology; editor: Psoriasis Forum, dermatology sect. Clin. Immunology; mem. editl. bd.: Jour. of Cutaneous Medicine and Surgery, 2000—, Jour. Am. Acad. of Dermatology, 1993—, Jour. of European Acad. of Dermatology and Venereology, 1992—, jour. reviewer: New Eng. Jour. of Medicine, The Lancet, Jour. of Investigative Dermatology, Jour. of Am. Acad. Dermatology, Archieves of Dermatology, Jour. of Clin. Investigation, Jour. of Immunology, Jour. of Cuaneous Medicine and Surgery; contbr. Mem. exec. coun. Millburn Music Boosters, Millburn Knickers; vol. March of Dimes. Recipient Psoriasis Rsch. award, Am. Skin Assn., 2001. Mem. Am. Dermatol. Assn., Women's Dermatologic Soc. (bd. dirs. 2000—, chmn. networking com. 1999-2000, chmn. industry rev. task force 1998—), Nat. Psoriasis Found. (med. adv. bd. 1999—, med. advisor 1996—), Nat. Eczema Assn. (scientific adv. bd. 1998—), Noah Worcester Dermatological Soc., Soc. for Investigative Dermatology, Am. Acad. Dermatology, Assn. of Clin. Rsch. Profls., Am. Acad. Pham. Physicians, Am. Coll. Rheumaology, The Henry Kunkel Soc., N.J. Dermatologic Soc., Cancer Inst. of N.J., Gerontological Inst. of Robert Wood Johnson Med. Sch. Office: UMDNJ-Robert Wood Johnson Med Sch Clin Rsch Ctr 51 French St New Brunswick NJ 08901-0019

GOTTLIEB, ARNOLD NEAL, lawyer; b. Toledo, Ohio, Feb. 18, 1952; s. Elliott A. and Rose Gottlieb; children: Eli, Cydney. BBA, U. Cin., 1974; JD, U. Toledo, 1977. Bar: Ohio 1978. Pvt. practice, Toledo, Ohio, 1978—. Participating atty. AARP Legal Svcs. Network, Toledo, 1999—. Bd. dirs. Toledo Vol. Lawyers for Arts, 1980—; past pres. bd. dirs. Arts Commn. Greater Toledo, 1992-93, Darlington Home for Aged, Toledo, 1994-95; mem. Civilian Police Rev. Bd., Toledo. Mem. ABA, ATLA, Ohio State Bar Assn., Ohio Acad. Trial Lawyers, Ohio Assn. Criminal Def. Lawyers, Toledo Bar Assn. (mem. grievance com. 1998—), Maumee Valley Criminal Def. Lawyers Assn. (sec. 1998—). Office: 608 Madison Ste 1523 Toledo OH 43604

GOTTLIEB, DANIEL SETH, lawyer; b. Los Angeles, Sept. 19, 1954; s. Seymour and Blanche Joyce (Kaufman) G.; m. Marilynn Jeanne Payne, July 21, 1985; children: Gwendolyn Z., Rebecca Lucinda. BA summa cum laude, Columbia U., 1976; JD, Harvard U., 1980. Bar: Wash. 1980, U.S. Dist. Ct. (we. dist.) Wash. 1980. Assoc. Riddell, Williams, Bullitt & Walkinshaw, Seattle, 1980-86, ptnr., 1986-95; prin. Graham & James LLP/Riddell Williams P.S., Seattle, 1996-97; mem. Gottlieb, Fisher & Andrews, PLLC, Seattle, 1997—. Coord. S.E. Legal Clinic, Seattle, 1984-86. Mem. Seattle Fremont Adv. Com. Recipient Achievement award Seattle-King County Econ. Devel. Coun., 1990. Mem. ABA, Nat. Assn. Bond Lawyers, Wash. State Bar Assn., King County Bar Assn. (treas. 1993-95, 2d v.p. 1995-96, 1st v.p. 1996-97, pres. 1997-98, bd. dirs. young lawyers divsn. 1987-90, treas. 1987-88, vice-chmn. 1988-89, chmn. 1989-90, chmn. legal info. and referral clinics com. 1986-87, Helen Geisness award 2001), Wash. State Assn. Mcpl. Attys., Wash. Coun. Sch. Attys., Wash. State Soc. Hosp. Attys., Bainbridge Island-North Kitsap Jewish Chavurah (v.p. and sec. 1993-95). Jewish. Avocations: tuba, hiking, bicycling. Home: 4880 NE North Tolo Rd Bainbridge Island WA 98110-3461 Office: Gottlieb Fisher & Andrews PLLC 1325 Fourth Ave Ste 1200 Seattle WA 98101-2531 E-mail: dan@goandfish.com.

GOTTLIEB, ELAINE P. writer; b. N.Y.C., Dec. 18, 1954; d. Milton and Rosalie (Wasserman) G. BA, SUNY, Buffalo, 1977. Editor, interviewer WGBH-FM, Boston, 1979-80; project cons. State Dept. Edn., Boston, 1981-82; mktg. comms. specialist Dun & Bradstreet Software/McCormack & Dodge, Natick, Mass., 1983-91; freelance writer Cambridge, Mass., 1991—. Part-time freelance journalist, 1983—. Contbr. freelance articles to Boston Globe, Chgo. Tribune, Dallas Morning News, Hartford Courant, Nat. Bus. Equipment Weekly, Cleve. Plain Dealer, Healthgate.com, Harvard Bus. Sch. Bulletin, others. Organizer Women's Action for Nuclear Disarmament, Cambridge, 1982-83; campaign worker Cambridge Tenants Union, 1983—, Barney Frank Campaign, Boston, 1982; vol. Cambridge Recycling, 1989-90. Mem. Nat. Writers Union (exec. bd. 1991—, journalism coord. 1993-96, co-chair Boston Local 1996-97, chair 1998-2000). Avocations: reading, running, hiking, skiing. Home: 19 Shepard St Cambridge MA 02138-1729 E-mail: elainepg@cs.com.

GOTTLIEB, GIDON ALAIN GUY, law educator; b. Paris, Dec. 9, 1932; m. Antoinette Rozoy Countess de Roussy de Sales, May 12, 1965. LLB with honors, London Sch. Econs., 1954, Cambridge (Eng.) U., 1956, diploma in comparative law, 1958; LLM, Harvard U., 1957, SJD, 1962. Bar: Called to bar Lincoln Inn, London 1958. Lectr. govt. Dartmouth Coll., 1960-61; assoc. firm Shearman & Sterling, N.Y.C., 1962-65; mem. faculty N.Y. U. Law Sch., 1965-76; Leo Spitz prof. internat. law and diplomacy U. Chgo. Law Sch., 1976—. UN rep. Amnesty Internat., 1966-72; mem. founding com. World Assembly Human Rights, 1968; adv. bd. Internat. League Rights of Man; disting. vis. fellow Hoover Instn., Stanford, Calif., 1991-94, 97—. Author: The Logic of Choice: An Investigation of the Concepts of Rule and Rationality, 1968, Nation Against State, 1993. Fellow N.Y. Coun. on Fgn. Rels. (sr. fellow, dir., Middle East Peace Project 1988-94); mem. Am. Soc. Internat. Law, Century Assn. (N.Y.C.). Office: U Chgo Law Sch 1111 E 60th St Chicago IL 60637-2776

GOTTLIEB, GILBERT, psychobiologist, educator; b. Bklyn., Oct. 22, 1929; s. Leo and Sylvia Sherman; m. Nora Lee Willis, Feb. 28, 1961; children: Jonathan Brian, David Herschel (dec.), Aaron Lee, Marc Sherman. AB, U. Miami, 1955, MS, 1956; PhD, Duke U., 1960. Clin. psychologist Dorothea Dix Hosp., Raleigh, N.C., 1959-61; rsch. scientist N.C. Divsn. Mental Health, Raleigh, 1961-82; head dept. psychology U. N.C., Greensboro, 1982-86, Excellence Found. prof., 1982-95, mem. faculty Carolina consortium human devel. Chapel Hill, 1988—; rsch. prof. psychology U. N.C. Ctr. Devel. Sci., Chapel Hill, 1995—. Guest Czechoslovak Acad. Scis., 1967, USSR Acad. Scis., 1989; advisor German NSF, 1977; U.S. del. Internat. Ethological Congress com., 1977-83; exec. com. Ctr. for Devel. Sci., U. N.C., 1993—; vis. lectr. Inst. Child Devel., U. Minn., 1975; vis. scholar Ctr. Interdisciplinary Rsch., U. Bielefeld, Germany, 1977; disting. vis. prof. psychology dept. U. Colo., Boulder, 1985; vis. fellow The Neuroscis. Inst., San Diego, 1996; disting. vis. lectr. dept. psychology U. Alta., 1996, Clark U., 1999; cons. in field. Author: Development of Species Identification in Birds, 1971, Individual Development and Evolution: The Genesis of Novel Behavior, 1992, reprinted, 2002, Synthesizing Nature-Nurture: Prenatal Roots of Instinctive Behavior, 1997 (Eleanor Maccoby Book award Am. Psychol. Assn., 1998), Probabilistic Epigenesis and Evolution, 1999; editor: Behavioral Embryology, 1973, Aspects of Neurogenesis, 1974, Neural and Behavioral Specificity, 1976, Early Influences, 1978, Measurement of Audition and Vision in the First Year of Postnatal Life, 1985; assoc. editor: Jour. Comparative and Physiol. Psychology, 1974—80. Recipient Disting. Sci. Contbn. award for child devel., Soc. Rsch. Child Devel., 1997, Eleanor Maccoly award devel. psychology divsn., APA, 1998; grantee, Nat. Inst. Child Health and Human Devel., 1963—84, 1989—95, NIMH, 1962-63, 1993-2003, NSF, 1963, 1985—88, 2001—. Fellow: AAAS; mem.: Internat. Conf. Infant Studies, Internat. Soc. Devel. Psychobiology (pres. 1986—87). Home: 4908 Forestville Rd Raleigh NC 27616-9683 Office: U NC Ctr Devel Sci Chapel Hill NC 27599-8115

GOTTLIEB, HELEN, social worker, legal immigration consultant; b. Newark, June 17, 1922; d. Nathan and Dorothy (Scherer) Yeager; m. Albert E. Gottlieb, June 19, 1946 (dec. Jan. 1982); children: Daniel, Richard. BA, Montclair State U., Upper Montclair, N.J., 1943; MSW, Rutgers U., 1967. Lic. clin. social worker. Caseworker State Bd. Children's Guardians, Newark, 1943-45; social worker immigration and resettlement Jewish Family Svc. of MetroWest, 1945-90. Legal immigration cons., Springfield, N.J. and N.Y.C., 1990—. Mem. NASW, N.J. Assn. Jewish Communal Service (hon. trustee, Saul Schwarz Disting. Svc. award 1985). Avocation: violin. Home: 100 Stone Hill Rd Apt H3 Springfield NJ 07081-2125

GOTTLIEB, JAMES RUBEL, federal agency administrator, lawyer; b. N.Y.C., July 2, 1947; s. Robert J. Gottlieb and Mildred C. Blaufox; m. Roberta James, 1974; children: Zoe, Zachary. BA, Mich. State U., 1969; MA, NYU, 1970; JD, N.Y. Law Sch., 1974. Bar: N.Y. 1974, D.C. 1983. Trial asst. Fuchsberg & Fuchsberg, 1971-74, assoc., 1974-77; adminstrv. asst., legis. dir., counsel for rep. Ted Weiss U.S. House of Reps., 1977-83, staff dir., chief counsel Human Resources & Intergovt. Rels. Subcom., 1983-93; chief counsel, staff dir. Senate Com. on Vets. Affairs, Washington, 1993-94; minority chief counsel, staff dir. Senate Com. Vets. Affairs, Washington, 1995—2000; chief of staff Senator John D. Rockefeller IV, 2000—. Democrat. Office: Office of Sen John D Rockefeller IV 531 Hart Senate Office Washington DC 20510-4802

GOTTLIEB, JERROLD HOWARD, advertising executive; b. N.Y.C., Aug. 25, 1946; s. Saul and Sylvia (Siegel) G.; m. June L. Brownstein, June 18, 1978; children: Steven Andrew, Melissa Eve BA, Mich. State U., 1968; MBA, Am. U., 1969. Sales rep. Gen. Foods Corp., White Plains, N.Y., 1969-71; v.p., account mgr. J. Walter Thompson, N.Y.C., 1971-75; sr. product mgr. Gen. Foods Corp., White Plains, 1976-78; v.p., account mgr. Batten, Barton, Durstein & Osborn, N.Y.C., 1978-80; sr. v.p. N.Y.O., account dir. J. Walter Thompson, N.Y.C., 1980-82, sr. v.p. U.S.A., mng. dir., 1982-84, sr. v.p. U.S.A., worldwide mng. dir., 1984-87, sr. v.p. worldwide, dir. account mgmt., 1987-90; exec. v.p. Backer Spielvogel Bates Inc., N.Y.C., 1991-92, exec. v.p., mng. dir. office of chmn., 1992-94; pres. Lane Gottlieb Advt., N.Y.C., 1994-96; ptnr. McCaffery Ratner Gottlieb & Lane Inc., N.Y.C., 1997—. Bd. dirs. Advt. Hall of Fame, N.Y.C., U.J.A. Fedn. N.Y. Founder Washington Saturday Coll., 1969; chmn. Am. U. campus, Washington, 1969; mem. adv. coun. ARC, Washington, 1981-86; vice chmn. mktg. UJA Fedn., N.Y.C., 1987-91, chmn., 1992-96, bd. dirs., 1994-2001. Mem.: Metropolis Club (bd. govs., vice chmn. admissions com.). Home: 1095 Park Ave New York NY 10128-1154 Office: mng ptr McCaffery Ratner Gottlieb & Lane 370 Lexington Ave New York NY 10017-6503

GOTTLIEB, JONATHAN W. lawyer; b. Washington, June 24, 1959; s. Julius Judah and Charlotte (Papernick) G.; m. Deborah Jo Levine, June 28, 1987; children: Maya Lane, Seth Joseph. BA with honors, DePaul U., 1982; student, Am. U., 1984-85; JD, N.Y. Law Sch., 1985. Bar: Pa. 1986, D.C. 1989, U.S. Ct. Appeals (D.C. cir.) 1990. Trial atty. Fed. Energy Regulatory Commn., Washington, 1987-88; assoc. Wickwire, Gavin & Gibbs, Washington, 1988-89, Ballard Spahr Andrews & Ingersoll, Washington, 1990-92, Reid & Priest, Washington, 1992-94, ptnr., 1995-98, Thelen Reid & Priest, Washington, 1998-99, Baker & McKenzie, Washington, 1999—. Chmn. legal affairs task force Nat. Hydropower Assn., 1992-95; counsel Mid-Atlantic Ind. Power Producers; gen. counsel Power Markets Devel. Co. (PPL Global), 1995-96; adv. bd. Bradley Energy Internat., 1997—; acting gen. counsel Packard Bell NEC, Inc., 1998. Contbg. editor Project Fin. Monthly; editor Competitive Utility, 1993—. Donor mem. Corning Mus. Glass. Mem. Fed. Energy Bar Assn., Pa. Bar Assn., D.C. Bar Assn., Southeastern Energy Soc. Republican. Avocations: glass collecting, stained glass making, gardening. Home: 9317 W Parkhill Dr Bethesda MD 20814-3966 E-mail: jonathan.w.gottlieb@bakernet.com.

GOTTLIEB, JULIUS JUDAH, podiatrist; b. Jersey City, May 27, 1919; s. Joseph Uziel and Gussie (Farber) G.; m. Charlotte Papernik, Oct. 18, 1942; children: Sheldon, Cynthia, Lorinda, David, Jonathan. Student, NYU, 1938-39, Ill. Coll. Podiatric Medicine, 1940-42; DPM, Ohio Coll. Podiatric Medicine, 1943. Diplomate Am. Podiatric Med. Specialties Bd. Pvt. practice podiatric medicine, Washington, 1943-92; pres. Chevy Chase Profl. Cons., 1993-96. Past cons. Army Footwear Clinic. Co-inventor fiberglass foot prosthetics and plastic shoe lasts. Podiatry dir. Greater Washington Hebrew Home for the Aged, 1963; pres. Franklin Knolls Citizens Assn., 1963, Ridgefield Citizens Inc., 1994-96, 97—; chmn. com. Nat. Capital Area coun. Boy Scouts Am., 1969-73; pres. Active Retirees of Kehilat Shalom, 1996-98. Recipient Shofar award Boy Scouts Am. Fellow Acad. Ambulatory Foot Surgeons (region 8 sci. chmn. 1987-88); mem. Am. Podiatric Med. Assn. (life), Am. Pub. Health Assn., Am. Podiatric Circulatory Soc., Am. Bd. Foot Surgeons (founding diplomate), D.C. Podiatric Med. Soc. (past pres.), Am. Assn. Foot Specialists (past pres., Foot Specialist of the Yr. 1973), Am. Assn. Individual Investors, Am. Physicians Fellowship Inc. for Medicine in Israel, Columbia Heights Bus. Men's Assn. (past pres., Man of Yr. 1964), Parents Assn. U. Md. (co v.p. parents fund 1980-81, co-recipient Outstanding Svc. Award), B'nai B'rith. Republican. Jewish. Home: 15812 Ancient Oak Dr Darnestown MD 20878-2110

GOTTLIEB, LEONARD SOLOMON, pathology educator; b. Boston, May 26, 1927; s. Julius and Jeanette (Miller) G.; m. Dorothy Helen Apt, Mar. 23, 1952; children: Julie Ann, William Apt, Andrew Richard. AB cum laude, Bowdoin Coll., 1946; MD, Tufts U., 1950; MPH, Harvard U., 1969. Diplomate Am. Bd. Anatomic Pathology. Intern in surgery Boston City Hosp., 1950-51, resident Mallory Inst. Pathology, 1951-55; assoc. pathologist Mallory Inst. Pathology, Boston, 1957-66, assoc. dir., 1966-72, dir., 1972—2003; asst. chief pathology U.S. Naval Hosp., Chelsea, Mass., 1955-57; chief pathology dept. Boston U. Med. Ctr. Hosp., 1973-96; prof. pathology & lab. medicine Sch. Medicine Boston U., 1970—, chmn. dept., 1980—2003; dir. Mallory Inst. Pathology Found., 1980—; pathologist-in-chief divsn. pathology Boston City Hosp., 1994-96; pathologist-in-chief, divsn. pathology Boston Med. Ctr., 1996—2003. Lectr. Harvard Med. Sch., 1963-98; dir. student faculty exch. program Boston U. and Hebrew U., Hadassah Med. Sch., 1988—. Gen. editor Biopsy Pathology Series, Chapman and Hall, 1981-93, editor emeritus, 1993—; mem. editl. bd. Am. Jour. Surg. Pathology, 1981-2000, Judeo Med. Jour., 2002—; author or co-author approximately 180 publs. and abstracts and 14 book chpts. dealing primarily with exptl. and human diseases of the liver and gastrointestinal tract. Assoc. mem. bd. govs. Hebrew U. Jerusalem, 1991-95, mem. bd. govs., 1995—, mem. exec. com., 2001—; pres. New Eng. region Am. Friends of Hebrew U., 1989-97, 2000—, coun. trustees, 1992—, founder, 1991, trustee, 1994, guardian, 2000, mem. grants com., 1997—; mem. sci. adv. bd. Boston chpt. Israel Cancer Rsch. Fund, 1991-92; co-chair and chair Physicians divsn. Greater Boston chpt. State of Israel Bonds Cabinet, 1991-98; pres. Am. Physicians Fellowship for Medicine in Israel, 1990-93; class sec. 1977 Program for Health Sys. Mgmt., Harvard Bus. Sch., 1995-97. Lt. M.C. USNR, 1955-57, lt. comdr. res. ret. 1963. Recipient Stanley L. Robbins award for excellence in teaching, 1986, Jerusalem City of Peace award Boston chpt. State of Israel Bonds, 1992, Disting. Bowdoin Educator award, 1995, Torch of Learning award Am. Friends of The Hebrew U., 1997, Lion of Judah award State of Israel Bonds, 1998, Lifetime Achievement award The Hebrew U., 2000; named hon. mem. faculty medicine Hebrew U., 1987; James Bowdoin scholar, 1945, Bingham scholar, 1944-50; hon. fellow Hebrew U. Jerusalem, 2001. Mem. Am. Soc. for Investigative Pathology, Am. Assn. for Study of Liver Diseases, U.S.-Can. Acad. Pathology, Coll. Am. Pathologists, Am. Soc. Cell Biology, Am. Gastroenterol. Assn., Am. Soc. Clin. Pathologists, Am. Coll. Physician Execs., New Eng. Soc. Pathologists (pres. 1968-69), Mass. Med. Soc., Charles River Med. Soc., Assn. Pathology Chairs, N.Y. Acad. Sci., Torch of Jerusalem Soc. (founding mem.), Am. Friends Hebrew U., Alpha Omega Alpha (faculty mem.). Office: Mallory Inst Pathology 784 Massachusetts Ave Boston MA 02118-4130 E-mail: busmpath@bu.edu.

GOTTLIEB, MICHAEL NORMAN, internist, educator, health facility administrator; b. Bklyn., July 26, 1943; s. Louis and Grace Gottlieb; m. Anne A. Appelman, Dec. 25, 1965; children: Brian, Elizabeth. BA, SUNY, Binghamton, 1964; MD, SUNY, Bklyn., 1968. Diplomate Am. Bd. Internal Medicine. Intern Univ. Hosp. U. Calif., San Diego, 1968-69, resident Univ Hosp., 1969-71, clin, fellow in nephrology, 1971-72, 1971-72; rsch. fellow in medicine Harvard Med. Sch., Boston, 1972 73; spl. fellow Peter Bent Brigham Hosp. NIH, Boston, 1972-73; instr. in medicine Peter Bent Brigham Hosp., Harvard Med. Sch., Boston, 1974-77; asst. clin. prof. medicine Harvard Med. Sch., Boston, 1976—; ptnr. Commonwealth Nephrology Assn., Boston, 1977—; assoc. chair dept. medicine Metrowest Med. Ctr., Framingham, Mass., 1992-95, v.p. med. mgmt., 1995—. Assoc. in medicine Peter Bent Brigham Hosp., Boston, 1975—82; courtesy staff New Eng. Bapt. Hosp., Boston, 1975—2000; cons. staff Lynn (Mass.) Hosp., Union Hosp., 1976—85; asst. vis. physician Carney Hosp., Boston, 1977—; med. dir. West Suburban Artificial Kidney Ctr., Framingham, Mass., 1980—, The Kidney Ctr., Boston, 2001—, MetroWest Artificial Kidney Ctr., Waltham, Mass., 1990—, active staff, 1992—; assoc. physician Brigham and Women's Hosp., Boston, 1982—; courtesy staff Norwood (Mass.) Hosp., 1994—; bd. dirs. End Stage Renal Disease Network #1. Contbr. to med. textbooks, numerous articles to profl. jours. Mem. AMA, ACP, Am. Soc. Nephrology, Am. Soc. Artificial Internal Organs, Mass. Med. Soc., Am. Soc. Enteral and Parenteral Nutrition, Am. Coll. Physician Execs., Internat. Soc. Artificial Organs. Avocations: boating, sailing. Office: Metrowest Med Ctr 67 Union St Natick MA 01760-6056 E-mail: michael.gottlieb@mwmc.com.

GOTTLIEB, PAUL, publishing company executive; b. N.Y.C., Jan. 16, 1935; s. Vitaly Matthew and Liza (Rabinowitz) G.; m. Linda Ellen Salzman, June 19, 1960 (div. Nov. 1989); children: Nicholas, Andrew; m. Elisabeth Lohman Scharlatt, Jan. 27, 1990; 1 stepchild Nicholas T. Scharlatt. BA, Swarthmore Coll., 1956; LHD (hon.), SUNY, Purchase, 1999. Lit. agt. William Morris Agy., N.Y.C., 1956-57, 59-60; asst. to pres. Omni Products Corp., N.Y.C., 1960-62; with Am. Heritage Pub. Co. Inc., N.Y.C., 1962-75, pres., 1970-75; chmn. bd. Fulfillment Corp. Am.; pres. Paul Gottlieb Assos., Inc., 1975—, Thames and Hudson Inc., 1976-79; CEO, pres., vice-chmn, pub., editor-in-chief Harry N. Abrams, Inc., N.Y.C., 1980-2000; vice-chmn. La Martinière Groupe (parent co. Harry N. Abrams, Inc.), 2001—02; exec. dir. Aperture Found., 2002—. Chmn. Hermitage Interant. Merchandising, B.V., Amsterdam; bd. dirs. Tanya Corp.; cons. in field. Guide U.S. exhbns., Moscow, 1959, 1961; vice chmn. E. Harlem Coll. and Career Counseling Program, 1971—74; trustee Mus. Modern Art, Dalton Sch.; bd. dirs. Nat. Found. Depressive Illness, Pub. Ctr. for Cultural Resources, N.Y. Studio Sch. Drawing, Painting and Sculpture, Acad. Am. Poets, chmn., 2002, Hermitage Internat. Merchandising, B.V., Amsterdam, 2002. Decorated chevalier Ordre des Artes et Lettres (France). Mem. Assn. Am. Pubs., Coffee House Club, Century Assn. Home: 1 Fifth Ave New York NY 10003 Office: Aperture Found 20 E 23d St New York NY 10010 E-mail: pgottlieb@aperture.org.

GOTTLIEB, PAUL MITCHEL, lawyer; b. N.Y.C., Mar. 30, 1954; s. Henry Gottlieb and Thelma Ethel (Friedman) Miller; m. Helene Manya Roiter, Apr. 3, 1982; children: Jordan Seth, Zachary Michael. BA, Hobart Coll., 1976; JD, MBA, Washington U., St. Louis, 1980. Bar: Ill. 1980, U.S. Dist. Ct. (no. dist.) Ill. 1980, N.Y. 1988. Assoc. Rudnick & Wolfe, Chgo., 1980-81; ind. trader Chgo. Bd. of Trade, 1981—82; staff atty. Chgo. Merc. Exch., 1983-84, v.p. market regulation, 1984—87; commodity counsel Morgan Stanley and Co. Inc., N.Y.C., 1987-89; spl. counsel commodities, futures and derivative products Skadden, Arps, Slate, Meagher & Flom, N.Y.C., 1989-92; ptnr., chair derivative products practice group Seward & Kissel, N.Y.C., 1992-96; dir., sr. counsel structured products & commodities Union Bank of Switzerland, N.Y.C., 1996-98; sr. v.p., dep. gen. counsel PaineWebber Inc., N.Y.C., 1998—2000; exec. dir. UBS Warburg LLC, N.Y.C., 2000-01; mng. dir., COO RBC Dominion Securities Corp., N.Y.C., 2001—; sr. v.p. Royal Bank of Can., 2001—. Eisenhower fellow to New Zealand, 1992; adj. prof. Ctr. for Tech. & Fin. Svcs. Polytechnic U. Contbr. chpts. to books, articles to profl. jours. Mem.: Securities Industry Assn. (law and compliance divsn.), Chgo. Bd. Trade, Chgo. Mercantile Exch., N.Y. Stock Exch. Jewish. Avocations: coaching youth hockey and lacrosse, golf, skiing. Home: 11 Highpoint Pl West Windsor NJ 08550-5238 Office: RBC Dominion Securities Corp 1 Liberty Plz 165 Broadway New York NY 10006-1404

GOTTLIEB, RICHARD MATTHEW, psychiatrist, consultant; b. N.Y.C., Aug. 26, 1943; m. Josephine L. Wright; 2 children. BS (hon.), U. Chgo., 1965; MD, U. Chgo. Sch. Medicine, 1969. Lic. N.Y., Conn., Mass. Asst. dir. Outpatient Svcs. Bronx Mcpl. Hosp. Ctr., N.Y., 1973-1974; attending psychiatrist Montefiore Hosp. and Med. Ctr., 1977-82; asst. attending physician Montefiore Hosp. Ctr., 1974—; adjunct attending physician St. Luke's/Roosevelt Hosp. Ctr., 1990—; attending physician Dept. Psychiatry Bronx Mcpl. Hosp. Ctr., 1973-74; cons. Housatonic Mental Health Ctr., Lakeville, Conn., 1988—; psychiatric cons. The Marvelwood Sch., Cornwall, Conn., 1979—, The Salisbury Sch., Lakeville, Conn., 1986—, The Indian Mountain Sch., 1994—; consulting staff The Sharon (Conn.) Hosp., 1988—; assoc. clin. prof. The Albert Einstein Coll. of Medicine, Bronx, N.Y., 1996—; faculty The Psychoanalytic Inst. of the Sch. Medicine of N.Y. U., 1989—, The N.Y. Psychoanalytic Inst., 1991—. Sec. N.Y. Psychoanalytic Soc.; chmn. Scientific Program Com., N.Y. Psychoanalytic Soc., A.A. Brill award Lecture Com. N.Y. Psychoanalytic Soc.; nat. treas. Coun. for Advancement of Psychoanalytic Edn.; tng. and supervising psychoanalyst The Am. Psychoanalytic Assn., 2002; founding chmn. Berkshire Inst. for Psychoanalysis; keynote spkr. Ind. Schs. Health Assn., 1997. Contbr. numerous papers and presentations in field. Recipient Heinz Hartmann award N.Y. Psychoanalytic Inst., 1994. Mem. Am. Psychoanalytic Assn., N.Y. Psychoanalytic Soc., Psychoanalytic Assn. N.Y., Internat. Psychoanalytical Assn., Am. Soc. for Adolescent Psychiatry, N.Y. Soc. for Adolescent Psychiatry, N.Y. Psychoanalytic Inst. (Heinz Hartmann award com.). Home: 170 Fairchild Rd Sharon CT 06069-2440

GOTTLIEB, SYLMA R. music educator, performing arts educator; b. Phila., Pa., Sept. 12, 1922; d. Joseph Berr and Esther Kay (Rosenkrantz) Paperman; m. Robert Gottlieb, May 19, 1945; children: Nancy Carol, Roanne Kay, Aaron Michael. Music, Overbrook HS, Phila., Pa., 1941; pvt. piano, Florence Steinberg, Phila., Pa.; pvt. voice, Mrs. Mary Phillips Jenkin, Phila., Pa., Konrad Neuger. Music tchr. Pikesville Elem. Sch., Pikesville, NC, 1961—63; kindergarten tchr. Ft. Meade Sch., Ft. Meade, Md., 1963—66; piano tchr. Pvt., Bowie,

Md., 1964—93, voice tchr., 1964—; judge Nat. Guild of Piano Tchr., York, Pa., 1983, St. Louis, 1985, Hagerstown, Md., 1986, 1990, Freehold, NJ, 1991, Severna Pk., Md., 1993. Dir. Officers' Wives Club Chorale, Tyndall AF Base, Fla., 1954—57, Seymour Johnson AF Base, NC, 1960—63, Ft. Meade, Md., 1964—66. Bd. of dir. Bowie regional Arts Vision Assoc., Bowie, Md., 1998. Recipient Tchr. of the Yr., Rosa Ponselle Found., Goucher Coll./ Maryland, 1996, Appreciation and Dedication, Music Tchr. Assoc. of Bowie/ Bowie, Md., 1997. Mem.: Nat. Assoc. Tchr. of Singing, Music Tchr. Assoc. of Md., Music Tchr. Assoc. of Bowie (pres. 1970—72). Home: 12013 Tweed Lane Bowie MD 20715-2061

GOTTO, ANTONIO MARION, JR., internist, educator; b. Nashville, Tenn., Oct. 10, 1935; s. Antonio M. and Reather (Gray) Gotto; m. Anita Louise Safford, July 21, 1959; children: Jennifer, Gillian, Teresa. BA magna cum laude, Vanderbilt U., 1957, MD, 1965; DPhil, Oxford (Eng.) U., 1961; LLD (hon.), Abilene Christian U., 1979; MD (hon.), U. Bologna, 1982. Diplomate Am. Bd. Internal Medicine. Intern Mass. Gen. Hosp., Boston, 1965—66, resident, 1966—67; practice medicine specializing in internal medicine, 1967—; head molecular disease br. Nat. Heart and Lung Inst. NIH, Bethesda, Md., 1969—71; dir. and prin. investigator Lipid Research Clinic, Houston, 1971—77; prof. medicine, chief dir., arteriosclerosis and lipoprotein rsch. Baylor Coll. Medicine, Houston, 1971—96; dir., prin. investigator specialized center rsch in arteriosclerosis Nat. Heart, Lung and Blood Inst., 1971—96; dir., prin. investigator Spl. Ctr. Rsch. Arteriosclerosis Nat. Heart, Lung, and Blood Inst., 1971—96; J.S. Abercrombie prof. Baylor Coll. Medicine, 1976—96, Disting. Service prof., 1985—96; sci. dir. Meth. Hosp. and Baylor Nat. Rsch. and Demonstration Ctr., 1974—83, 1987—90; Bob and Vivian Smith prof. and chmn. dept. medicine Baylor Coll. Medicine, 1977—96; chief internal medicine svcs. The Meth. Hosp., 1977—96; dean Weill Med. Coll., Cornell U., 1997—; provost med. affairs Cornell U., 1997—. Hon. guest lectr. various med. socs., schs. and hosps., 1972—; mem. nat. diabetes adv. bd. HEW (now HHS), 1977—84; mem. steering com. Italian-Am. com. on cardiovascular disease NIH, 1978—; mem. adv. coun. Nat. Heart, Lung and Blood Inst., 1987—91; hon. prof. U. Buenos Aires, 1985. Author (with Michael E. DeBakey): The Living Heart, 1977; author: The Living Heart Diet, 1984, The New Living Heart Diet, 1996, The New Living Heart, 1997; editor: Current Atherosclerosis Reports, 1998—, Current Practice of Medicine, 1999—; co-editor: Atherosclerosis Rev. Series, 1976—92, Jour. Cardiovasc. Risk, 1994—; mem. editl. bd.: Jour. Biol. Chemistry, 1976—81, Advanced in Lipid Rsch., 1973—78, Am. Heart Jour., 1981—, Arteriosclerosis, 1981—89, Circulation Rsch., 1974—79, Cardiovascular Rsch. Ctr. Bull., 1972—; contbr. articles on biochem. and cardiovascular rsch. to profl. publs. Mem. sci. adv. bd. Fondation Cardiologique Princesse Liliane, Brussels, 1976—, Lorenzini Found., Milan, Fritz Thyssen Found., Cologne, Germany; mem. Mission of Houston Econ. Devel. Coun., 1985; walkathon chmn. Juvenile Diabetes Found., 1986. With USPHS, 1967—69. Decorated knight Order of Merit, Italy, Order of the Lion Finland; named hon. cons., Adm. Bristol Hosp., Istanbul, Turkey, Houston Internat. Exec. Yr., 1987; recipient Albert Weinstein award, 1965, Laurea ad Honorem, U. Bologna, Seale Harris award, So. Med. Assn., 1995; grantee, John A. Hartford Found., 1971—75. Fellow: Am. Coll. Cardiology; mem.: Am. Longevity Assn., Am. Assn. Rhodes Scholars, Am. Bd. Internal Medicine, Am. Heart Assn. (pres. 1983—84, past pres. 1984—86, Paul Ledbetter award for disting. svc., Paul Dudley White award for outstanding contbns., Gold Heart award 1989), Am. Diabetes Assn., Am. Soc. Biol. Chemists, Am. Assn. Physicians, Internat. Soc. Atherosclerosis (pres. 1985—, Achievement award 1982), So. Soc. Clin. Investigation, Am. Soc. Clin. Investigation (v.p. 1980—81), Inst. Medicine of NAS, River Oaks Country Club, Alpha Omega Alpha. Presbyterian. Home: 435 E 70th St Apt 31 J K New York NY 10021-5351 Office: Weill Med of Cornell U 1300 York Ave Rm F 105 New York NY 10021-4805

GOTTRON, FRANCIS ROBERT, III, small business owner; b. Youngstown, Ohio, Dec. 26, 1953; s. Francis R. Jr. and Norma J. (Giba) G.; m. Joyce L. Garling, Nov. 25, 1975. BSBA cum laude, Youngstown State U., 1978. With Commonwealth Land Title Youngstown, Inc., 1972-87, Lender's Svc., Inc., 1979—, Title Agy. Michaels, 1984—; examiner delinquent tax Mahoning County Prosecutor's Office, 1989—; owner, prin. Mahoning County Recorder's Office, Youngstown, 1978—; examiner Fed. Title Agy., 1982—; pres. M&G Title Search Inc. Appraiser Probate Ct., 1989—. Democrat. Lutheran. Avocations: fantasy baseball, camping, forestry, environment. Home: 9165 New Rd North Jackson OH 44451-9707 Office: PO Box 268 Youngstown OH 44501-0268 E-mail: f_gottron@yahoo.com.

GOTTS, ILENE KNABLE, lawyer; b. Phila., Nov. 25, 1959; d. Harry Lee and Ethel Beatrice (Teitelman) Knable; m. Michael D. Gotts, May 25, 1986; children: Isaac, Samuel. BA magna cum laude with hon., U. Md., 1980; JD cum laude, Georgetown U., 1984. Bar: D.C. 1984, N.Y., 1997, U.S. Dist. Ct. D.C. 1986, U.S. Ct. Appeals (D.C. cir.) 1985, U.S. Dist. Ct. Md. 1987, U.S. Ct. Appeals (fed. cir.) 1989, U.S. Supreme Ct. 1988. Staff atty. FTC, 1984-86; assoc. Foley & Lardner, Washington, 1986-92, ptnr., head legis./adminstrv. group, antitrust practice group, 1992-96; ptnr. Wachtell, Lipton, Rosen & Katz, N.Y.C., 1996—. Adj. prof. George Washington U. Law Ctr., 1995-96. Mem. editl. bd. The Practical Lawyer, 1994—; mem. editl. adv. bd. The Antitrust Counselor, 1995—; mem. adv. bd. Antitrust Trade and Regulatory Report, 2003-; contbr. articles to profl. jours. Mem. legal adv. bd. NOW Legal and Edn. Fund., 2001—. Recipient Sklar award U. Md., 1980; Mary Elizabeth Robey scholar. Mem.: NOW (legal adv. bd. 2001—), FBA (chair health care com. of antitrust sect. 1991—95, chair antitrust and trade regulation sec. 1995—97), ABA (health care com. antitrust sect. 1988—, consumer protection com. 1994—96, vice chair intellectual property com. 1994—97, vice chair Clayton Act com. 1997—98, chair 1998—2001, coun. 2001—, chair merger rev. task force 1998—, editor The Merger Rev. Process, 2d edit.), Internat. Bar Assn., N.Y. Women's Bar Assn., N.Y. State Bar Assn. (exec. com. antitrust law sect. 2000—), Washington Coun. Lawyers (exec. com. and bd. dirs. 1988—97, pres. 1994—95), Am. Law Inst., D.C. Bar (steering com., antitrust and trade regulation com. 1994—95), Phi Beta Kappa, Mortar Board, Phi Alpha Theta, Pi Sigma Alpha, Phi Kappa Phi. Democrat. Jewish. Office: Wachtell Lipton Rosen & Katz 51 W 52d St New York NY 10019 E-mail: ikgotts@wlrk.com.

GOTTSCHALK, ALEXANDER, radiologist, diagnostic radiology educator; b. Chgo., Mar. 23, 1932; s. Louis R. and Fruma (Kasden) G.; m. Jane Rosenbloom, Aug. 13, 1960; children: Rand, Karen, Amy. BA magna cum laude, Harvard U., 1954; MD, Washington U., St. Louis, 1958. Diplomate: Am. Bd. Radiology, Am. Bd. Nuclear Medicine. Intern U. Ill. Research and Edn. Hosps., Chgo., 1958-59; resident U. Chgo., 1959-62, asst. prof., 1964-66, assoc. prof., 1966-68, prof. radiology, 1968-74, chmn. dept. radiology, 1971-72; research assoc. Donner Lab., Lawrence Radiol. Lab., Calif., 1962-64; dir. Franklin McLean Meml. Research Hosp., 1967-74; prof. and dir. nuclear medicine Sch. Medicine Yale U., New Haven, 1974-77, acting chmn. radiology, 1980-81, vice-chmn. radiology, 1977-89; prof. radiology Mich. State U., East Lansing, 1990—. Contbr. chpts. to books, articles to publs. in field. Fleischner lectr., 1983 Fellow Am. Coll. Radiology, Am. Coll. Chest Physicians; mem. Radiol. Soc. N.Am. (2d v.p. 1977), Assn. Univ. Radiologists (pres. 1971), Soc. Nuclear Medicine (pres. 1974-75), Am. Roentgen Ray Soc., Fleischner Soc. (treas. 1978-83, pres. 1989-90), Phi Beta Kappa, Alpha Omega Alpha. Home: 4246 Van Atta Rd Okemos MI 48864-3137 Office: Radiology Bldg Rm 120 Mich State U East Lansing MI 48824-1303 E-mail: alex.gottschalk@radiology.msu.edu.

GOTTSCHALK, ALFRED, retired college chancellor, museum executive; b. Oberwesel, Germany, Mar. 7, 1930; came to U.S., 1939, naturalized, 1945; s. Max and Erna (Trum-Gerson) G.; m. Deanna Zeff, 1977; children by previous marriage: Marc Hillel, Rachel Lisa. AB, Bklyn. Coll., 1952; MA with honors, Hebrew Union Coll.-Jewish Inst. Religion, 1957; PhD, U. So. Calif., 1965, STD (hon.), 1968, LLD (hon.), 1976, U. Cin., 1976, Xavier U., 1981, Mt. St. Joseph Coll., 1995, No. Ky. U., 1996; DHL (hon.), U. Judaism, 1971, Jewish Theol. Sem., 1986, Bklyn. Coll., 1991, Trinity Coll., 1996; LittD (hon.), Dropsie U., 1974, St. Thomas Inst., 1982; D Religious Edn. (hon.), Loyola-Marymount U., 1977; DD (hon.), NYU, 1985. Ordained rabbi, 1957. Dir. Hebrew Union Coll., Jewish Inst. Religion, L.A., 1957-59, dean, 1959-71, prof. Bible and Jewish intellectual history, 1965—, pres., 1971-95, chancellor, 1996—2000, chancellor emeritus, disting. prof. emeritus of Jewish Intellectual History, 1995—; pres. Mus. of Jewish Heritage, N.Y.C., 1999—2001. Hon. fellow Hebrew U., Jerusalem, 1972, Oxford Ctr. for Hebrew and Jewish Studies, 1994. Author: Your Future as a Rabbi-A Calling that Counts, 1967, (translator) Hesed in the Bible, 1967, The Man Must be the Message, 1968, Jewish Ecumenism and Jewish Survival, 1968, Ahad Ha-Am, Maimonides and Spinoza, 1969, Ahad Ha-Am as Bible Critic, 1971, A Jubilee of the Spirit, 1972, Israel and the Diaspora: A New Look, 1974, Limits of Ecumenicity, 1979, Israel and Reform Judaism: A Zionist Perspective, 1979, Ahad Ha-Am and Leopold Zunz: Two Perspectives on the Wissenschaft Des Judentums, 1980, Hebrew Union College and Its Impact on World Progressive Judaism, 1980, Diaspora Zionism: Achievements and Problems, 1980, What Ecumenism Means to a Jew, 1981, Introduction: Religion in a Post-Holocaust World, 1982, Problematics in the Future of American Jewish Community, 1982, Introduction to the American Synagogue in the Nineteenth Century, 1982, A Strategy for Non-Orthodox Judaism in Israel, 1982, Our problems and Our Future: Jews and America, 1983, From the Kingdom of Night to the Kingdom of God: Jewish Christian Relations and the Search for Religious Authenticity after the Holocaust, 1983, The Making of a Contemporary Reform Rabbi, 1984, Is Yom Kippur Obsolete?, 1985, Ahad Ha-am: Confronting the Plight of Judaism, 1987, To Learn and To Teach, Your Future as a Rabbi, 1988, Preface to Gezer V: The Field I Caves, 1988, The American Reform Rabbinate Retrospect and Prospect, A Personal View, 1988, The German Pogrom of November 1938 and the Reaction of American Jewry, 1988, Building Unity in Diversity 1989, Ahad Ha'am and the Jewish National Spirit (Hebrew), 1992; contbr. to Studies in Jewish Bibliography, History, and Literature, 1971, The Yom Kippur War: Israel and the Jewish People, 1974, The Image of Man in Genesis and the Ancient Near East, 1976, The Public Function of the Jewish Scholar, 1978, The Reform Movement and Israel: A New Perspective, 1978, The Use of Reason in Maimonides--An Evaluation by Ahad Ha-Am, 1993, Reform Judaism of the New Millenium: A Challenge, 2001, Israel and America: Beyond Survival and Philanthropy, 2000; also numerous articles to profl. jours. Mem. Pres. Johnson's Com. on EEO, 1964-66, Gov.'s Poverty Support Corps Program, 1964-66, Pres.'s Commn. on Holocaust, 1979, U.S. Holocaust Meml. Coun., 1980-92, 96-01 (exec. com., 1980-87, 96—, chmn. edn. com., 1986-88, chmn. acad. com., 1988-96, com. on conscience, 1996—); chmn. N.Am. Assoc. Internat. Ctr. Univ. Teaching of Jewish Civilization, 1982-93; bd. trustees Am. Sch. Oriental Rsch., Albright Inst. Archaeol. Rsch., 1972-95; sr. fellow Mus. of Jewish Heritage, N.Y.C., 2001—; bd. govs. Oxford Ctr. for Hebrew and Jewish Studies, 1995—; bd. trustees Mus. Jewish Heritage, N.Y.C., 2001-; exec. com. Nat. Underground Railroad Freedom Ctr., 1997-2000, Nat. Adv. Bd., Nat. Underground Freedom Ctr., 1996—; mem. coun. World Union Jewish Studies, 1997. Recipient award for contbns. to edn. L.A. City Coun., 1971, Human Relations award Am. Jewish Com., 1971, Tower of David award for cultural contbn. to Israel and Am., 1972, Gold medallion Jewish Nat. Fund, 1972, Alumnus of Yr. award Bklyn. Coll., 1972, Myrtle Wreath award Hadassah, 1977, Brandeis award Z.O.A., 1977, Nat. Brotherhood award NCCJ, 1979, Alfred Gottschalk Chair in Communal Svc. HUC, 1979, Jerusalem City of Peace award 1988, Defender of Jerusalem award honoree, 1990, Isaac M. Wise award, 1991, Heritage award Jewish Club of 1933, 1991, Nat. award NCCJ, 1994, Shanghai Acad. Social Scis. award, 1994, others, Xavier Medallion, Xavier U., 1996, Elie Wiesel Holocaust Rememberance award, State of Israel bonds, 2001; grantee State Dept./Smithsonian Instn., 1963, 67.; honoree Assn. Hebrew Union Coll., 1996; recipient Award Svc. to City, Cin. City Council, 2001. Mem. AAUP, NEA, Union Am. Hebrew Congregations and Ctrl. Conf. Am. Rabbis (exec. com., bd. govs. Hebrew Union Coll.), Soc. Study Religion, Am. Acad. Religion, Soc. Bibl. Lit. and Exegesis, Internat. Conf. Jewish Communal Svc., Israel Exploration Soc., So. Calif. Assn. Liberal Rabbis (past pres.), So. Calif. Jewish Hist. Soc. (hon. pres.), World Union Jewish Studies (internat. coun.), World Union Progressive Judaism (gov. bd.), Coun. for Initiatives in Jewish Edn. (bd. dirs.). Office: Hebrew Union Coll Jewish Inst of Religion One W 4th St New York NY 10012-1186 *I value the need for the individual to feel unique and for the collective to remain hospitable to diversity. I believe in unity without uniformity and in humanity's capacity to redeem himself.*

GOTTSCHALK, CHARLES M. international energy consultant; b. Bochum, Germany, Feb. 2, 1928; emigrated to U.S., 1941, naturalized, 1949; s. Josef and Elsbeth Gottschalk; m. Marianne Ida Besser, Dec. 24, 1948; children: Diane Linda, Leslie Anne. B Engring. Scis., Cleve. State U., 1950; MA, Pa. State U., 1951; MLS, Catholic U., 1966. Research analyst Library of Congress, 1951-54, phys. sci. adminstr., head reference sect., sci. and tech. div., 1956-62, chief stack and reader div., 1962, head systems identification and analysis sect., 1962-63; instrumentation physicist Nat. Bur. Standards, 1954-56; information systems specialist Atomic Energy Commn., 1963-66, dir. libraries, 1966-69; sr. officer Internat. Atomic Energy Agy., Vienna, Austria, 1969-74, Energy Research and Devel. Adminstrn., Washington, 1974-77, Dept. Energy, 1977-79; sr. ofcl. UNESCO, Paris, 1979-88, cons., expert, 1988-94, CMG Internat. Energy Consultancy, Paris and Washington, 1994—. Liaison officer/registrar Internat. Tech. U., London and Paris, 1989-93; liaison officer World Fedn. Engring. Orgns., London and Paris, 1995-96; lectr. Dept. Agr. Grad. Sch., 1964-66; cons. Arctic Inst. N.Am., 1954-59; rsch. asst. Ohio State U., 1958-59; exec. sec. oper. com. Fed. Coun. Sci. and Tech. Com. on Sci. and Tech. Info., 1965, exec. sec. panel edn. and tng., 1965-66, mem. panel info. scis. and tech., 1966-68, mem. nuclear cross sect. adv. group, 1965-69; mem. com. on terminology World Energy Conf., 1980-96. Author articles, monographs. Served with AUS, 1946-47; Served with USMCR, 1947-51. NSF grantee, 1961-62. Mem. World Energy Coun., Assn. Energy Engrs., Diplomatic and Consular Officers Ret., Mensa, Beta Phi Mu.

GOTTSCHALK, FRANK KLAUS, real estate company executive; b. Berlin, Jan. 25, 1932; came to U.S. 1947, naturalized 1953; s. Richard and Grete Johanna (Singer) G.; m. Ellen Ruth Meinhardt, June 16, 1957. Student N.Y. Inst. Banking & Fin., N.Y.C., 1952-53, NYU, 1955-56. Lic. comml. real estate broker. Trainee, investment securities Newborg & Co. mem. N.Y. Stock Exchange, N.Y.C., 1951-52; fin. analyst Bendix Luitweiler & Co. Investment Bankers, N.Y.C., 1952-53; assoc. broker, v.p., dir. Peter F. Pasbjerg & Co., Inc., Mortgage Bankers, Newark, N.J., 1955-62; v.p., dir. Baldwin Bros., Inc. Real Estate Investors, Erie, Pa., 1962—; pres., treas., dir. The Baldwin-Gottschalk Group, Investment Real Estate, asst. mgmt. cons., Erie, Pa., Charleston, W.Va., 1994—; pres. Baldwin-Gottschalk, Inc. Real Estate and Mortgage Financing, N.Y.C., Erie, Charleston, 1962—; pres., treas., dir. Baldwin Gottschalk Properties, Erie, 1967—, Balgot Realty Corp., Erie, 1963—, Balgot Bldg. Corp., Erie, 1967—; pres. The Kanawha Realty Investment Group, Investment Real Estate, Charleston, Erie, 1990—; pres., treas., dir. Kanawha Realty & Devel. Corp., Charleston, 1959—, Associated Properties Holdings, Inc., Charleston, 1962—; pres. Assoc. Properties Holdings Pension Trust, Charleston, W. Va., 1982—; pres., dir. APH Securities, Charleston, W. Va., 1990—; trustee Assoc. Properties Holding Retirement Trust, Charleston, 1982—; mng. ptnr. Kanawha-Monarch Holdings, Erie, 1980—, Balgot-Kanawha Holdings, Erie, Pa., 1994—. Trustee, Erie Philharm., 1971-90; corporator Gannon U., 1980—. Served with U.S. Army, 1953-55, ETO. Mem. Internat. Real Estate Inst., Erie Club, Aviation Country Club Erie, Addison Reserve Country Club, Delray Bch., Fla. Office: Baldwin Gottschalk Inc 5 W 10th St Erie PA 16501-1492

GOTTSCHALK, JOHN E. newspaper publishing executive; b. 1943; Pub. Sidney (Nebr.) Newspaper, 1966-74; with Omaha World Herald Co., 1975—, pres., CEO, 1989—. Bd. dir. Creighton U. Council chmn. Boy Scouts of America, 1994—95, regional pres., 1996—97; bd. of dirs. Omaha Symphony Assn., 1999—. Recipient Citizen of the Year award, Boy Scouts of America, 1998, Outstanding Svc. Profession award, U. Nebr. Alumni, 1998. Mem.: Omaha Performing Arts Soc. (chmn. 2003—). Office: Omaha-World Herald Co World-Herald Sq Omaha NE 68102-1138*

GOTTSCHALK, SISTER MARY THERESE, nun, hospital administrator; b. Doellwang, Germany, June 21, 1931; arrived in U.S., 1953, naturalized, 1959; d. John and Sabina (Dietz) G. BS in Pharmacy, Creighton U., 1960; M.H.A., St. Louis U., 1970; DHL (hon.), U. Okla., 2001. Joined Sisters of the Sorrowful Mother, Roman Catholic Ch, 1952. Dir. pharmacy St. Mary's Hosp., Roswell, N.Mex., 1960-68, chief exec. officer, 1972-74; asst. adminstr. St. John Med. Ctr., Tulsa, 1970-72, pres., CEO, 1974-99, St. John Health Sys., Tulsa, 1982—; pres. Marian Health Sys., Tulsa, 1989—. Vol. ARC, United Way. Fellow: Am. Coll. Hosp. Adminstrs.; mem.: Cath. Health Assn. (bd. dirs. 1995—2001), Tulsa C. of C., Okla. Conf. Cath. Hosps. (past pres.), Tulsa Hosp. Coun., Okla. Hosp. Assn. (pres. 1984), Am. Hosp. Assn. (ho. of dels., regional policy bd.). Office: St John Med Ctr 1923 S Utica Ave Tulsa OK 74104-6502

GOTTSCHALK, SIMON, sociologist, educator; b. Brussels, Dec. 5, 1959; arrived in US, 1983; s. Marcel and Sarah (Bursztein) Gottschalk; m. Krystyna Dabrowska, June 21, 1996. BA in Sociology and English, U. Haifa, Israel, 1982; MA in Sociology, U. Houston, 1985; PhD, U. Calif., Santa Barbara, 1992. Lectr. U. Calif., Santa Barbara, 1985—91; asst. prof. U. Nev., Las Vegas, 1992—98, assoc. prof., 1998—. Dir. cultural studies U. Nev., Las Vegas, 1996—. Co-author: Pathology and the Postmodern, 2000, Social Science and Fiction, 2000; contbr. articles to profl. jours. Fellow, U. Calif., 1985—91; scholar, 1985—91. Avocations: music, hiking, yoga, writing. Office: Univ Nev 4505 Maryland Pkwy Las Vegas NV 89154 Office Fax: 702-895-5480. Business E-Mail: karma@nevada.edu.

GOTTSCHALK, STEPHEN ELMER, lawyer; b. Rochester, Minn., Oct. 9, 1947; s. Elmer H. and Ruth F. (Thurley) G.; m. Lorilyn J. Dopp, Feb. 14, 1970; children: Andrew Stephen, Stephanie Beth, Lorissa Christine, Michael Donald. BS, Valparaiso U., 1969, JD, 1972. Bar: Minn. 1972, U.S. Dist. Ct. (Minn.) 1972. Jud. clk. Minn. Supreme Ct., St. Paul, 1972-73; assoc. Dorsey & Whitney, Minn., 1973-78, ptnr., 1979—, dept. head employee benefits dept., 1986-91, 98—. Adj. prof. employee benefits Sch. Law U. Minn. Mem. pres. adv. coun., Valparaiso U., 1983—; bd. dirs. Twin Cities Habitat for Humanity, Inc. Recipient Svc. award Valparaiso Alumni Assn., 1986. Mem. Midwest Pension Conf. Avocation: squash. Home: 4339 Fremont Ave S Minneapolis MN 55409-1720 Office: Dorsey & Whitney 50 S 6th St Ste 1500 Minneapolis MN 55402-1498 E-mail: gottschalk.steve@dorseylaw.com.

GOTTSCHALK, THOMAS A. lawyer; b. Decatur, Ind., July 5, 1942; s. John Simson and Edith (Liechty) G.; m. Barbara J. Risen, Aug. 28, 1965; children: Deborah, Diane. AB, Earlham Coll., 1964; JD, U. Chgo., 1967. Bar: Ill. 1967, D.C. 1986, U.S. Supreme Ct. Assoc. Kirkland & Ellis, Chgo., 1967-73, ptnr., 1973-94; sr. v.p., gen. counsel Gen. Motors Corp., Detroit, 1994—2001, exec. v.p., 2001—. Trustee Earlham Coll., Richmond, Ind., 1972—, chmn., 1985-91. Mem. ABA (mem. litigation, antitrust and criminal law sects.), D.C. Bar Assn., Chgo. Coun. of Lawyers, Conf. Bd. Coun. of Chief Legal Officers; mem. bd. of trustees, Am. Univ., Wash., D.C. Office: Gen Motors Corp 300 Renaissance Ctr Detroit MI 48265-0001

GOTTSCHALK, WALTER HELBIG, mathematician, educator; b. Lynchburg, Va., Nov. 3, 1918; s. Carl and Lula (Helbig) G.; m. Margaret Hemsworth, Aug. 27, 1952; children: Heather, Steven. BS, U. Va., 1939, MA, 1942, PhD in Math, 1944; MA (hon.), Wesleyan U., Middletown, Conn., 1964. From instr. to prof. math. U. Pa., 1944-63, chmn. dept., 1955-58; prof. math. Wesleyan U., 1963-82, prof. emeritus, 1982—, chmn. dept., 1964-69, 70-71. Mem. Inst. Advanced Study, Princeton, 1947-48; research assoc. Yale U., 1960-61 Author: (with G.A. Hedlund) Topological Dynamics, 1955; Mem. editorial bd.: Math. Systems Theory, 1967-75; Contbr. articles to profl. jours. Mem. Am. Math. Soc. (asso. editor proc. 1954-56, assoc. sec. for East 1971-76), Math. Assn. Am., Soc. Indsl. and Applied Math., AAUP, Phi Beta Kappa, Sigma Xi. Democrat. Unitarian Universalist. Home: 500 Angell St Apt 414 Providence RI 02906-4491

GOTTSCHALL, EDWARD MAURICE, graphic arts company executive; b. N.Y.C., Dec. 28, 1915; s. Myer and Stephanie (Kraus) G.; m. Lee Beatrice Natale, Feb. 6, 1943 (dec. 1984); 1 child, Robert J.; m. Alice J. Wise, Jan. 20, 1985. BS, CCNY, 1937; MS, Columbia U. Sch. of Journalism, 1938. Mng. editor Graphic Arts Prodn. Yearbook, Colton Press, 1937-51; editor Art Direction, 1952-69; sr. editor Popular Merchandising Co., Passaic, N.J., 1964-67; co-pub., editorial dir. Advt. Trade Publs., Inc., 1967-69; exec. dir. Am. Inst. Graphic Arts, N.Y.C., 1969-75; exec. v.p. Internat. Typeface Corp., N.Y.C., 1975-86, vice chmn., 1986-90; editor U & lc, 1981-89, cons. editor, 1990—. V.p. Design Processing Internat., Inc., 1977-85; U.S. rep. Assn. Typographique Internat., 1978-89, chmn. world conf. on typographic communication, 1988; lectr. Pratt Inst. Evening Art Sch., 1947-64, N.Y. U., 1955-64 Author: (with F.C. Rodewald) Commercial Art as a Business, 3d edit., 1972; Author: Vision '80s, 1980, Graphic Communication '80s, 1981, Typographic Communications Today, 1988, reprinted 1992; co-editor: Advertising Directions, vols. 1-4, 1960-64, Editor Typographic i, 1969-79; cons. editor: Graphic Arts Manual, 1973-80; contbr. essay to Contemporary Masterworks, 1992. Served with Signall Corps. U.S. Army, 1943-44, USAAF, 1944-45, ETO. Mem. Type Dirs. Club (past pres., Spl. award 1963), N.Y. Club of Printing House Craftsmen (Fellowship award 1993), Phi Delta Pi. Clubs: Masons. Home: 63 Highland Ave Eastchester NY 10709-3627 *Knowledge is never enough. One must be able to evaluate, to judge, to have taste, and to make decisions.*

GOTTSCHALL, JOAN B. judge; b. Oak Ridge, Tenn., Apr. 23, 1947; d. Herbert A. and Elaine (Reichbaum) G. BA cum laude, Smith Coll., Mass., 1969; JD, Stanford Univ., Calif., 1973. Bar: Ill. 1973. Assoc. Jenner & Block, 1973-76, 78-81, ptnr., 1981-82; staff atty. Fed. Defender Program, 1976-78, Univ. of Chgo., Office of Legal Counsel, 1983-84; magistrate judge U.S. Dist. Ct. (no. dist.) Ill., Chgo., 1984—96, judge, 1996—2002. Mem. vis. com., past chair Divinity Sch., U. Chgo., 1984—97. Bd. dirs. Constl. Rights Found. Chgo., Martin Marty Ctr., U. Chgo. Div. Sch. Mem.: Divinity Sch. (vis. com.), Women's Bar Assn. Ill., Chgo. Bar Assn., Am. Bar Assn. Office: Everett McKinley Dirksen Bldg 219 S Dearborn St Ste 1978 Chicago IL 60604-1877

GOTTSTEIN, BARNARD JACOB, retail and wholesale food company executive, real estate executive; b. Des Moines, Dec. 30, 1925; s. Jacob B. and Anna (Jacobs) G.; children: Sandra, James, Ruth Anne, David, Robert; m. Rachel Landau, July, 1986. BA in Econs. and Bus., U. Wash., 1949; LLD (hon.), U. Alaska, Fairbanks, 1991. Pres. J.B. Gottstein & Co., Anchorage, 1953-90; chmn. bd. Carr-Gottstein Inc., Anchorage, 1974-90; ret., 1990—. Dir. United Bank Alaska, Anchorage, 1975-86. Commr. Alaska State Human Rights Commn., 1963-68; del. Dem. Nat. Conv., 1964, 68, 76, 88, 92; committeeman Dem. Nat. Com., 1976-80; v.p. State Bd. Edn., Alaska, 1983-87, pres., 1987-91. Served with USAF, 1944-45. Jewish. Office: Carr Gottstein Properties 550 W 7th Ave Ste 1540 Anchorage AK 99501-3567

GOTTWALD, FLOYD DEWEY, JR., chemical company executive; b. Richmond, Va., July 29, 1922; s. Floyd Dewey and Anne (Cobb) G.; m. Elisabeth Morris Shelton, Mar. 22, 1947; children: William M., James T., John D. BS, Va. Mil. Inst., 1943; MS, U. Richmond, 1951. With Albemarle Paper Co., Richmond, 1943-62, sec., 1956-57, v.p., sec., 1957-62, pres., 1962; exec. v.p. Ethyl Corp., Richmond, 1962-64, vice chmn., 1964-68, chmn., 1968-94, CEO, 1970-92, chmn. exec. com., 1970-94, vice chmn., 1994-96. Bd. dirs. Tredegar Industries, Inc.; vice-chmn. Albemarle Corp. Past bd. dirs. Nat. Petroleum Coun.; trustee U. Richmond; mem. River Rd. Bapt. Ch.; past trustee V.M.I. Found., Inc.; mem. bd. visitors Coll. William and Mary, 1993-97; pres. bd. trustees Va. Mus. Fine Arts, 1994-96. Decorated Bronze Star, Purple Heart. Mem. NAM (former bd. dirs.), Am. Petroleum Inst. (bd. dirs.), Am. Chem. Coun. (bd. dirs.), Internat. Game Fish Assn. (trustee 1992—), Alfalfa Club, Country Club Va., Commonwealth Club. Office: Albemarle Corp PO Box 1335 Richmond VA 23218-1335

GOTWALS, CHARLES PLACE, JR., lawyer; b. Muskogee, Okla., May 19, 1917; s. Charles Place and Anna M. (Koehler) G.; m. Mary Frances Brownlee, Jan. 31, 1948 (dec. Mar. 1982); children: Charles William, James Robert, Frances Ann, Virginia Hunt; m. Marion Miller, Jan. 6, 1984. AB, U. Okla., 1938, JD, 1940. Bar: Okla. 1940. Pvt. practice, Tulsa, 1940—; ptnr. Gable & Gotwals, until 1990; of counsel, 1990—. Sr. warden Trinity Episcopal Ch., Tulsa, 1984-87, also former vestryman and jr. warden. Served to maj. AUS, 1942-46, ETO. Decorated Bronze Star Mem. ABA, Tulsa County Bar Assn. (sec. 1949), Okla. Bar Assn., Am. Judicature Soc., Order of Coif, Phi Beta Kappa, Phi Delta Phi, Beta Theta Pi. Clubs: Kiwanian (pres. 1961), Tulsa, Summit. Office: 1100 Oneok Plz 100 W 5th St Tulsa OK 74103-4240

GOTWAY, MICHAEL B. radiologist, health facility administrator; b. Springfield, Ill., July 23, 1966; s. Clement Alonzo and Patricia Louise Gotway; m. Mary Pat Jacobson, June 13, 1998. MD, U. Ill., Chgo., 1989. Cert. Am. Bd. of Radiology. Physician U. of Calif., San Francisco, 1994—, program dir. diagnostic radiology, 2001—. Dir. fellowship program, body imaging San Francisco Gen. Hosp., U. Calif., 2001—; radiology resident edn. and tng. U. Calif., 2000—02. Achievements include research in AIDS imaging, lung transplant imaging, interstitial lung disease, imaging for pulmonary embolism.

Office: U Calif San Francisco Rm 1X 55A Box 1325 1001 Potrero Ave San Francisco CA 94110 Home Fax: 415-206-4004; Office Fax: 415-206-4004. Personal E-mail: michael.gotway@radiology.ucsf.edu. E-mail: michael.gotway@radiology.ucsf.edu.

GOUDARZI, BEHNAM MALEK, physician; b. Abadan, Iran, Sept. 12, 1966; came to US, 1997; s. Nosrat and Mahin (Mohamadnejad) M.; m. Rozita Rouzbeh, Sept. 2, 1993. MD, Tehran U. Med. Sci., 1991. Diplomate Am. Bd. Internal Medicine & pulmonary disease. Instr. anatomy Anatomy Hall, Tehran U., 1986-87; translator and editor med. books Esharat Publ., Tehran, 1990-96; resident in internal medicine Nassau Univ. Med. Ctr., East Meadow, NY, 1997-2000; pulmonary critical care fellow Albert Einstein Coll. Medicine, Bronx, NY, 2000—. Editor: Maxillofacial Trauma, 1993; translator 2 books; contbr. articles to profl. jour. Mem. ACP, ACCP, SCCM. Avocations: swimming, playing se'tar. Office: Montefiore Hosp Pulmonary Divsn 111 E 210th St Bronx NY 10467 E-mail: bmgoudarzi@hotmail.com.

GOUDY, JAMES JOSEPH RALPH, electronics executive, educator; b. Bloomfield, Iowa, Nov. 3, 1952; s. Charles Jacob and Marjorie Ethel (Morten) G.; m. Diane Marie Guenther, Nov. 24, 1978; children: Megan Joanne, Monica Victoria, Mitchell Thaddeus. BS, Wayne State Coll., 1976; AAS, Indian Hills C.C., Ottumwa, Iowa, 1978; MA, N.E. Mo. State U., 1980; BA, Iowa Wesleyan Coll., 1986. Cert. sr. engring. technician Nat. Inst. Certification Engring. Technicians. Sr. electronic comm. cons. ANR Pipeline Co., Fairfield, Iowa, 1978—, instr. high tech., 1987—, sr. electronics technician Birmingham, Iowa, 1991—; owner Advanced Tech. Cons., 1993—. Temp. instr. Wayne (Nebr.) State Coll., 1976-77; instr. VA program Indian Hills C.C., Ottumwa, 1978, mem. high tech. programs adv. com., 1992—; instr. Iowa Wesleyan Coll., Mt. Pleasant, 1986. Bd. dirs. Wapello County Agrl. Fair, Eldon, 1988—, Ottumwa Area Translator Sys.; participant Nat. Runners Health Study, U. Calif. Mem. Radio Club Am., Masons, Shriners, Order Ea. Star, Toastmasters, Optimists. Avocations: amateur radio, running. Home: 702 S 32nd St Fairfield IA 52556-4704 Office: ANR Pipeline Co PO Box 9 Birmingham IA 52535-0009

GOUGELMAN, PAUL REINA, lawyer; b. Chgo., Mar. 16, 1951; s. Paul Reina Gougelman and Jayne Bohus. BA, Fla. Internat. U., Miami, 1975; JD, Nova Law Sch., Ft. Lauderdale, 1980. Bar: Fla. 1981, U.S. Ct. Appeals (11th cir.) 1981, US. Dist. Ct. (mid. dist.) Fla. 1983. Atty. 1st Dist. Ct. Appeals, Tallahassee, 1980-83; ptnr. Holland & Knight LLP, Melbourne, Fla., 1996-99; city atty. Indialantic, Fla., 1989—, Melbourne Beach, Fla., 1990—, Melbourne, Fla., 1996—, Cocoa Beach, Fla., 1998-99. Spl. counsel for land use and growth mgmt. City of Maitland, 1984-88; spl. counsel for code enforcement bd. City of Longwood, Fla., 1985-87; cons. growth mgmt. City of Lake Mary, Fla., 1985-87; gov.'s appointee East Ctrl. Fla. Regional Planning Coun., 1986-98; mem. Seminole County Charter Adv. Com., 1987-88; gen. counsel City of Cocoa Redevel. Agy., 1990-99, Brevard Met. Planning Orgn., 1993—, Space Coast League of Cities, 1991—; gen. coun., adv. coun. Fla. Met. Planning Orgn., 1994—. With Orange County Bar Task Force, 1985, Brevard County Planning and Zoning Bd., 1989-92, chmn., 1991-92; chmn. Brevard County Charter Com., 1993-94; chmn. bd. dirs. Harbor City Vol. Ambulance Squad, 1994-97. Mem. ABA, Fla. Bar (local govt. law sect., elected exec. coun. environ. and land use law sect.). Republican. Presbyterian. Office: City of Melbourne 900 E Strawbridge Ave Melbourne FL 32901-4739

GOUGH, CAROLYN HARLEY, library director; b. Paterson, N.J., Sept. 23, 1922; d. Frank Ellsworth and Mabel (Harrison) Harley; m. George Harrison Gough, Sept. 21, 1944; children: Deborah Ann Gough Bornholdt, Douglas Alan. BA, Coll. William and Mary, 1943; MLS, Drexel U., 1966. Rsch. asst. Young and Rubicam, Inc., N.Y.C., 1943-44; libr. dir., asst. prof. Cabrini Coll., Radnor, Pa., 1966-81; chmn. Palm Beach County Libr. Bd., 1984-86. Mem. resources study com. Tredyffrin Twp. Libr., 1964-65; docent Henry Morrison Flagler Mus., 1982-92. Mem. AAUP, DAR (Palm Beach chpt.), Tri-State Coll. Libr. Coop. (v.p. 1973-74, pres. 1974-75), Assn. Coll. and Rsch. Librs. (dir. 1978-81), Questers, Inc. (1st nat. v.p. 1964-66), Atlantis Golf Club, Atlantis Women's Club (co-pres. 1982-83), Sir Robert Boyle Soc., Beta Phi Mu, Kappa Delta. Republican. Episcopalian. Home: 458 S Country Club Dr Lake Worth FL 33462

GOUGH, CLARENCE RAY, retired designer, educator; b. Denton County, Tex, Dec. 7, 1919; s. Herman Lang and Gertrude (Page) G.; m. Georgia Belle Leach, Feb. 7, 1975. BS in Art, U. North Tex., Denton, 1940, MS in Art, 1941; BArch, Ill. Inst. Tech., 1950. Art tchr. Edinburg Ind. Sch. Dist., Tex., 1941; interior designer Contemporary House, Dallas, 1950; environ. designer Gough Assoc., Denton, 1951-90; prof. U. North Tex., Denton, 1951-88. Juror Nat. Coun. Interior Design Qualifications, 1983-88; chmn. accreditation com. Found. Interior Design Rsch., 1985-90. Illustrator Modern Dance for the Youth of Am., 1944, photographer (exhibitions) Visual Arts Ctr., Denton, 2001; exhibitions include photography No. Tex. area Art League Exhbn., 2003. Exhbn. chmn. U. North. Tex., Denton, 1950-63; curator exhbns. Greater Denton Arts Coun., 1997-98. Lt. USNR, 1942-46, PTO. Recipient Career Educator award Am. Soc. Interior Designers, 1993, Dallas, Svc. award Gov. Conf. on the Arts, Denton, 1990; Internat. Artist award, North Tex. Area Art League, 2003. Avocations: photography, collecting art. Home: 1813 Willowwood St Denton TX 76205-6992

GOUGH, DENIS IAN, geophysics educator; b. Port Elizabeth, Cape, South Africa, June 20, 1922; came to Can., 1966; s. Frederick William and Ivy Catherine (Hingle) G.; m. Winifred Irving Nelson, June 2, 1945; children—Catherine Veronica, Stephen William Cyprian B.Sc., Rhodes U., Grahamstown, Republic of South Africa, 1943, M.Sc., 1947, D.Sc. (hon.), 1990; PhD, U. Witwatersrand, Johannesburg, Republic of South Africa, 1953. Research officer Nat. Phys. Lab., Johannesburg, S. Africa, 1947, sr. research officer; lectr. Univ. Coll. Rhodesia, Salisbury, 1958, sr. lectr.; assoc. prof. geophysics Southwest Ctr. for Advanced Studies, Dallas, 1964-66; prof. geophysics U. Alta., Edmonton, Can., 1966-87, prof. emeritus, 1987—, dir. Inst. Earth and Planetary Physics, 1975-80. Contbr. numerous articles to profl. jours. Royal Soc. Can. fellow, 1972 Fellow Royal Astron. Soc. (Chapman medal 1988), Am. Geophys. Union; Geol. Assn. Can.; mem. Can. Geophys. Union (past pres., J. Tuzo Wilson medal 1983), Internat. Assn. Geomagnetism and Aeronomy (pres. 1983-87), S. African Geophys. Assn. (Rudolf Krahmann medal 1989). Avocations: reading, music, poetry. Office: Univ Alta Dept Physics Edmonton AB Canada T6G 2J1 E-mail: iangough@incentre.net.

GOUGH, EUGENE V. vocational education educator; b. Salt Lake City, Apr. 3, 1931; s. Frank and Veneda Carrie (Stewart) G.; m. Penny Diane Fry, Dec. 28, 1956; children: Liane, Loren Jay, Noel Dion. BA, San Jose State U., 1959; M of Indsl. Edn., Brigham Young U., 1979; postgrad., U. Utah, 1962-80. Cert. secondary edn. tchr., vocat. edn./drafting and carpentry, Utah, Calif. Tchr., dept. chmn. Mapusaga High Sch., Tutuila, Am. Samoa, 1959-62, Butte Valley High Sch., Dorris, Calif., 1962-64; tchr. Skyline High Sch., Salt Lake City, 1966-67, Bonneville Jr. High Sch., Salt Lake City, 1967-70; tchr., co-op edn. coord. Cottonwood High Sch., Salt Lake City, 1970-81; tchr., dept. chmn. Taylorsville High Sch., Salt Lake City, 1981-91. Dist. Boy Scout exec., Snake River Coun., Boy Scouts Am., Twin Falls, Idaho, 1962-64. Sgt. U.S. Army, 1953-55. Named Vocat. Tchr. of Yr., Granite Sch. Dist., Salt Lake City, 1987. Mem. NEA, Am. Vocat. Assn., Utah Edn. Assn., Granite Edn. Assn., Vocat. Indsl. Clubs of Am. (advisor 1970-91). Republican. Mem. Lds Ch. Avocations: woodworking, landscaping, gardening, fly fishing. Home: 6227 S 1200 E Salt Lake City UT 84121-1921

GOUGH, JOHN FRANCIS, lawyer; b. Phila., Nov. 28, 1934; s. John Joseph and Honora Veronica (Garrity) G.; m. Natalie Smith, Mar. 8, 1984; children: David, Robert, J. Joseph II, Richard, Jonathan, Kristin. AB cum laude, St. Joseph's U., 1957; JD, Yale Law Sch., 1960. Bar: Pa. 1961, N.J. 1994, U.S. Dist. Ct. (ea. dist.) Pa. 1961, U.S. Ct. Appeals (3d cir.) 1966, U.S. Supreme Ct. 1967. Assoc. Erskine, Barbieri & Sheer, Phila., 1960-65, White and Williams, Phila., 1965-68, ptnr., 1968-80, Toll, Ebby & Gough, Phila., 1980-87; ptnr., chmn. corp. dept. Abrahams & Loewenstein, Phila., 1987-88; ptnr. Hoyle, Morris & Kerr, Phila., 1988-92, Montgomery, Mccracken, Walker & Rhoads, LLP, Phila., 1992-98, co-chair bus. bankruptcy sect., 1998; ptnr. Hoyle, Morris & Kerr LLP, Phila., 1998-2000; of counsel Montgomery, McCracken, Walker & Rhoads, LLP, Phila., 2000—. Exec. com. Ea. Dist Bankruptcy Conf., 1989—; faculty co-chmn. and lectr. Temple Grad. Sch. Law C.L.E. Program, 1989-92; lectr. U. Pa. Grad. Sch., Temple Law Sch., 1990—. Author course materials for profl. and ednl. orgns. Pres. Highfield Sch. PTA, Plymouth, Pa., 1966-68, Greene Towne Montessori Sch., Phila., 1979-80; mem. exec. com., sec. Schuylkill River Devel. Corp., 2000—; chmn. Tidal Schuylkill River Master Plan Task Force; treas. Rittenhouse Savoy Owners Assn. Mem. ABA, Am. Law Inst., Phila. Bar Assn. (pres. Jr. Bar Assn. 1964-65), Hosp. Attys. S.E. Pa. (pres. 1977-79), Am. Bankruptcy Inst. (bd. cert. in bus. bankruptcy), Yale Club Phila. Avocations: tennis, gardening, fitness. Office: Montgomery, McCracken, Walker & Rhoads, LLP 123 South Broad Street Philadelphia PA 19109 Fax: 215-772-7620. E-mail: jgough@mmwr.com.

GOUGH, SAMUEL NATHANAEL, JR., fund-raising executive; b. Washington, Aug. 25, 1939; s. Samuel Nathanael Sr. and Ruth E. Matthews Gough; m. Betty Ann Rhone, July 13, 1940; 1 child, Sean Nathan. BS, Howard U., 1962. Cert. fund-raising exec. Dir. devel. Howard U., Washington, 1967-90; cons. Washington, 1990-97; prin. The AFRAM Group, Washington, 1997—. Chair dist. II Coun. for Advancement and Support Edn., Washington, 1986-88. Contbg. author: Cultivating Diversity in Fundraising, 2002, New Directions in Fundraising: Diversity in the Fundraising Profession, 2001; contbr. articles to profl. jours. Staff Peace Corps.; chair bd. dirs. Friendship House, Inc., Washington, 1987-90, USO of Washington, 1979-80; bd. dirs. Nat. Ctr. on Black Philanthropy, The Washington Project, A Rsch. and Leadership Devel. Project. Capt. U.S. Army, 1963-65. Recipient Exceptional Achievement award Coun. for Achievement; named Outstanding Fund Raising Profls. Nat. Soc. of Fund Raising Execs., 1993. Mem. Assn. of Fund Raising Officers, Inc. (founder). Home: 1323 Underwood St NW Washington DC 20012-2925 Office: The AFRAM Group 1207 Kennedy St NW Washington DC 20011

GOUGH, WILLIAM CABOT, engineer; b. Jersey City, Aug. 22, 1930; s. William Lincoln and Lillian May (Mansmann) G.; m. Marion Louise McConnell, Apr. 27, 1957; children: Barbara Louise, William Scott. BS in Engring., Priceton U., 1952, MA in Engring., 1953; postgrad., Harvard U., 1966-67. Registered prof. engr., Calif. Adminstr. engr. Civilian Power Program AEC, Washington, 1953-55, indsl. info. officer, 1958-60, tech. asst. for systems, plans and programs, div. controlled thermonuclear rsch., 1960-74; project engr. nuclear aircraft program USN, Washington, 1955-58; program mgr. fusion power Electric Power Rsch. Inst., Palo Alto, Calif., 1974-77; sr. DOE/EPRI energy porgram coord., tech. dir. Office Program Assessment and Integration U.S. Dept. of Energy, San Francisco and Palo Alto, 1977-81; dir. DOE Site Office Stanford Linear Accelerator Ctr. Stanford (Calif.) U., 1981-88; ret., 1988, co-founder, pres. Found. for Mind-Being Rsch., Los Altos, Calif., 1980, chmn. bd. dirs., 2001—. Bd. dirs. Sage Seminars, Inc., San Francisco, 1984-88, MERU Found., San Anselmo, Calif., 1988-93; mem. bd. advisors Bonny Found., Salina, Kans., 1990—; mem. physics of humanity coun. Inst. Heart Math., Boulder Creek, Calif., 1993—. Contbr. articles and chpts. to tech. jours. and texts. Lt. (j.g.) USN, 1955-58. Mem. AAAS, Am. Nuclear Soc., N.Y. Acad. Sci., Fedn. Am. Scientists, Soc. for Sci. Exploration, Internat. Soc. Study of Subtle Energies and Energy Medicine (jour. adv. bd. 1990—, program chair ann. conf. 1996), World Future Soc., Common Cause, UN Assn., Sci. and Med. Network. Achievements include being co-inventor of the Fusion Torch concept; initiated and directed independent program of fusion power research for utility industry; developed first organized effort to evaluate technoloty problems confronting fusion; research on the relationship between science and consciousness. Home and Office: 442 Knoll Dr Los Altos CA 94024-4731 E-mail: wgough@pacbell.net.

GOUGHER, RONALD LEE, foreign language educator and administrator; b. Allentown, Pa., July 27, 1939; s. Samuel Franklin and Beatrice Dorothy (Shanaberger) G.; 1 child, Robert. BA, Muhlenberg Coll., 1961; MA, Lehigh U., 1964; postgrad., Albright Coll., 1962, Stanford U., 1963, Harvard U., 1964, U. Pa., 1964-75; advanced cert., Goethe Inst., Munich, 1969. Chmn. fgn. lang. dept. Parkland H.S., Allentown, Pa., 1961-65; tchr. German Moravian Sem. for Girls, 1965-69; instr. German Lehigh U., 1965-69; assoc. prof. German West Chester (Pa.) U., 1969—, coord. German studies, 1972-2001, dir. internat. edn., 1974-83, chmn. dept. fgn. langs., 1977-96, campus dir. Expt. in Internat. Living, 1972-92, coord. German studies, 1972—. Treas. Pa. Consortium Internat. Edn., 1978-83, pres., 1983-86, World Learning Inc., 1992—; coord.-chairperson Assn. Depts. Fgn. Langs., State Sys. Higher Edn., Pa., 1984-88, del. First Joint Conf. Chinese and Am. Edn. Great Hall of People, Beijing, 1992; citizen amb. Linguistics del. to China, 1991, 92, lectr. in field, cons. Franklin Mint, 1992—; cons., program dir. Chester Conty Intermediate Unit; guest lectr. Ufa, Ivanova, Russia, 1993, Czestochowa, Poland, Ufa, Russia, Sendai, Japan, Jurmala, Riga, Valmiera, Latvia, 1994-96, Kaunus, Lithuania, 1995; participant Hungarian Parliament Sessions, Budapest, 1994; dir. Am.-European studies program, West Chester U. and Soros Found., Latvia, Lithuania, Czech Republic, Slovakia, Hungary, Romania, Yugoslavia, Bulgaria, Croatia, Slovenia, Macedonia, 1994, Moldova, 1995, Estonia, 1996, Albania, Bosnia, Kyrgystan, Mongolia, 1997—, Kazakhstan, 1998—, Azerbaijan, 1999, Kosovo, 2001-02, Georgia, 2003; dir. Internat. Sch.-U. Partnership Program, West Chester U. and Chester County Intermediate Unit, 1988—. Co-editor, Individualization Fgn. Lang. Learning in Am., 1970-75; author numerous publs. in German lang. and lit., individualizing instrn. in fgn. langs. Bd. dirs. Peters Valley Crafts Ctr., U.S. Info. Agy., 1988-95; active Congress-Bundestag Youth Exch. Program, 1988-96, Citizen Amb. Program, China, 1991, 92. Fulbright travel grantee, 1963, 69, Soros Found., 1990-94; travel and study grantee, Finland and Leningrad, USSR, 1990; travel grantee to Poland, Slovakia, Romania, 1991-92, Russia, 1993, 95, Bulgaria, Slovenia, 1994, Kagoshima, Japan and Taipei, Taiwan, 1996, Croatia, Latvia, Lithuania, Slovenia, 1996, Hungary, Bulgaria, Macedonia, 1999, Mongolia, 1999; Fed. Fgn. Lang. Assistance Act grantee, 1992-96, dir. Internat. Sch.-U. Ptnrs. program Chester County Intermediate Unit and West Chester U., 1991-97, Soros Found. grantee internat. program devel. Latvia, Lithuania, Czech Republic, Slovakia, Hungary, Slovenia, Yugoslavia, Romania, Bulgaria, Macedonia, Moldova, Estonia, Mongolia, Kyrgystan, Bosnia, Albania, 1994—; Open Soc. grantee, 1994-2003, others; recipient Chapel of Four Chaplains award, 1981. Mem. Am. Assn. Tchrs. German, Am. Coun. Tchg. Fgn. Langs., N.E. Conf. Tchg. Fgn. Langs., Internat. Platform Assn., Smithsonian Instn., Ruffed Grouse Soc., Trout Unlimited, Ducks Unlimited. Republican. Lutheran. Home: 3309 Windsor Ln Thorndale PA 19372-1038 Office: West Chester U Dept Fgn Langs West Chester PA 19380

GOUGHNOUR, ROY ROBERT, civil engineer, consultant; b. Canton, Ohio, May 10, 1928; s. Roy George and Doris Belle (Malone) G.; m. Marilynn Ruth Knoll, Sept. 20, 1948 (div. Mar. 1968); children: Robert Lee, Steven David, Mekyla Ann Goughnour Hart; m. Mary Rosetta Strahan, June 28, 1968. BS, Mich. State U., 1961, MS, 1965, PhD, 1967. Registered profl. engr., Mich. Vice pres. A.C. Aukerman Co., Jackson, Mich., 1958-64; assoc. prof. No. Ariz. U., Flagstaff, 1967-68, Mich. State U., East Lansing, 1968-72; v.p. Aukerman-Goughnour Co., Jackson, 1972-76; pres. Strahan Mfg. Co., Tampa, Fla., 1976-77; v.p. R & D, Vibroflotation Found. Co., Pitts., 1976-86; exec. v.p. GeoSystems, Inc., Sterling, Va., 1986-89; v.p. Geotechnics Am., Inc., Peachtree City, Ga., 1989—2000; mgr. engring. Nilex Corp., Centennial, Colo., 2000—. Cons. Hubbell, Roth & Clark, Bloomfield Hills, Mich., 1989-91, Tensar Corp., Morrow, Ga., 1989-91. Contbr. articles to profl. jours.; patentee slipform and ground improvement fields. Rsch. grantee NSF, 1969, Fed. Hwy. Assn., 1980. Mem. ASCE (assoc.), Internat. Soc. Soil Mechanics and Found. Engring., SE Asian Geotech. Soc. Republican. Avocations: hunting, target shooting. Home: 705 Duff Rd NE Leesburg VA 20176-4907 Office: Nilex Corp 15171 E Fremont Dr Centennial CO 80112

GOUIN, SERGE, corporate executive; b. Montreal, Mar. 6, 1943; came to U.S., 1984; s. Jean-Marie and Mariette (Champoux) G.; m. Ginette DuPuy, Aug. 22, 1964 (div.); children: Sophie, Philippe, Simon. BA, U. Western Ont., 1966, BBA, 1965, MBA, 1966. Mgmt. cons. Currie, Cooper & Lybrand, Montreal, 1968-73; gen. mgr. Nat. Cablevision Ltd., Montreal, 1973-76; exec. v.p. Can. Devel. Corp., Toronto, Ont., Can., 1976-83; chmn. Savin Corp., Stamford, Conn., 1983-86, also bd. dirs.; pres., CEO TéLé-Métropole Inc., 1987-91, chmn. bd., 1991-96; pres., COO Le Groupe Vidéotron Ltée, 1991-96; pres. Sofimon Inc., Outremont, Que., 1997; adv. dir. Citigroveitigron & Global Markets Con., Inc., Montreal, 1998—. Lead dir. Cott Beverages Ltd.; bd. dirs. Cossette Comm. Group, Montreal, Onex Corp., Toronto, Astral Comms., Montreal, Siemens Can. Inc., Toronto; chmn. Quebecor Media Inc., Montreal; bd. dirs. TVA Group, Montreal; chmn. Videotron Ltd., Montreal. Mem. Mt. Royal Club (Montreal), Quail Ridge Country Club (Boynton Beach, Fla.). Roman Catholic. Avocations: hunting, cross country skiing, golfing. Home: 740 Pratt Outremont QC Canada H2V 2T6 Office: Ste 2450 630 René Levesque Blvd W Montreal QC Canada H3B 1S6 Business E-Mail: serge.gouin@citigroup.com.

GOUIN, WARNER PETER, information technology specialist; b. International Falls, Minn., Sept. 14, 1954; s. Joseph Andre and Rose Marie (Grandaw) G.; m. Judith Ann Nelson, Aug. 25, 1979; 1 child, Nicole Renee. AA, Rainy River Community Coll., 1974; BS Mgmt., St. Cloud State U., 1979; BSEE, N.D. State U., 1985, MS in Indsl. Engring. and Mgmt., 1987. Cert. sys. integrator; cert. prodn. and inventory control mgr. Purchasing/prodn. contr. Plastech Rsch., Inc., Rush City, Minn., 1979-80; inventory supr. Aero Sys. Engring., St. Paul, 1980-81; grad. asst. N.D. State U., 1985-87; elec. engr. Marvin Windows, Warroad, Minn., 1987-93, sys. integrator MIS dept., 1993-95, sys. engr., automation sys. acquisition, sr. project engr., 1995-97; sales rep. Digi-Key Corp., Thief River Falls, Minn., 1997; info. tech. specialist 3 Mnn. Correctional Facility, Shakopee, 1997—. Trainer process reengring. Total Quality Mgmt., Warroad, Minn., 1992-95. Scoutmaster Boy Scouts Am., Warroad, 1989-91. Mem. Office Automation Soc. Internat. (editor 1989-90), Soc. Mfg. Engrs. Avocations: computer integrated mfg. rsch., fishing, hunting, walking, guitar. Office: State of Minn Minn Correctional Facility 1010 6th Ave W Shakopee MN 55379-2213 E-mail: thegouina@aol.com.

GOULART, JANELL ANN, elementary education educator; b. Merced, Calif., July 29, 1936; d. James Riddoch and Rowena Janell (Futrell) Mitchell; m. Frank Goulart, May 19, 1956; children: Robert, Frank, Sharon. BA, Fresno (Calif.) State U., 1972, postgrad., Fresno Pacific Coll., Irvine U. Cert. elem. sci. tchr., Calif.; cert. Calif. Assn. for Gifted. Tchr. Royal Oaks Sch., Visalia, Calif., 1972—; sci. staff developer, K-12 alliance staff developer Calif. Sci. Implementation Network, Irvine, Calif., 1989-2001. Trainer Calif. Learning Assessment System state testing; sci. and math mentor for Visalia Unified Sch. Dist. Mem. Nat. Sci. Tchrs. Assn., Calif. Sci. Tchrs. Assn., Ctrl. Calif. Sci. Tchrs. Assn., Tulare County Reading Coun., Kappa Delta Pi. Home: 1546 River Way Dr Visalia CA 93291-9212 Office: Royal Oaks Sch 1323 S Clover St Visalia CA 93277-4299

GOULAZIAN, PETER ROBERT, retired broadcasting executive; b. N.Y.C., Apr. 17, 1939; s. G.B. and Alice Goulazian; m. Mary C. Holland, Dec. 19, 1965; children: Cindy Anne, Peter Robert. BA, Columbia U., 1962. With media and programming dept. Dancer-Fitzgerald-Sample, Inc., N.Y.C., 1963-67; v.p., mktg. dir. Katz Communications, Inc., N.Y.C., 1967-79, v.p. broadcasting, 1980-81; pres. Continental TV div., 1981-84, pres. TV group, 1985-91; pres., CEO Katz Media Corp., 1992-94. Bd. dirs. The TV Bur., Seltel, Inc., Cable Media Corp., Katz Internat., Petry Media Corp. Trustee Standardbred Retirement Found. Mem. Varsity "C" Club, N.Y. Athletic Club, Nantucket Anglers Club, Columbia U. Club. Home: PO Box 404 Woodstock VT 05091

GOULD, ALAN BRANT, academic administrator; b. Aug. 2, 1938; m. Mary Nell; children: Adam, Charles, Christopher. BA in History cum laude, Marshall U., 1961, MA in History, 1962; PhD in Am. History, W.Va. U., 1969. Grad. instr., dept. history W.Va. U., Morgantown, 1962-65; instr., dept. history D.C. Tchrs. Coll., 1965-66; asst. prof. history No. Va. Community Coll., 1966-69; prof., dept. history Marshall U., Huntington, W.Va., 1969—, sr. v.p., 1988-89, provost, 1989-92, interim pres., 1990-91, v.p. for acad. affairs, 1991-94, dean Coll. Liberal Arts, 1980-88, acting v.p. acad. affairs, 1984-86, asst. to pres. for spl. projects, 1986, chmn. dept. history, 1977-80, asst. to v.p. acad. affairs, 1976-77, coord. Regents BA degree program, 1976-80, 86-94; exec. dir. John Deaver Drinko Acad., 1994—. Adj. prof. history W.Va. Coll. Grad. Studies, 1976-86; lectr. Ohio U., Ironton, 1970-74; vis. lectr. for Project Newgate, Fed. Youth Correction Inst., Summit, Ky., fall 1970. Contbr. articles to hist. jours, also conf. papers. Chmn. Cabell County Hist. Landmark Commn., 1983-92; trustee Huntington Mus. Art, 1983-93, chmn. edn. com., mem. exec. com.; pres. River Cities Cultural Coun., 1985-91; bd. dirs. W.Va. Humanities Coun., 1986-90, v.p., 1989-91, pres., 1991-94, W.Va. Coalways, Inc., 1987—; mem. Mayor of Huntington's Main St. Project, 1987-92, Marshall U. Rsch. Corp., 1988, mem., 1982-86; mem. W.Va. Antiquities Commn., 1975-77, Cabell County Commn. on Crime, Delinquency and Corrections, 1982-86, statewide steering com. Ideas That Built Am., 1985-86, Carter G. Woodson Meml. Commn., 1986—; mem. steering com. Ethics W.Va. Program, 1983-84, chmn. Great Books Program; mem. affirmative action bd. City of Huntington, 1989-91, mem. Cabell County (W.Va.) hist. landmark commn., 1989-91, 94—; trustee W. Va. Ednl. Found., Inc., 1993-2001; mem. W.Va. Libr. Commn., 1997—. Inducted into Huntington East High Sch. Hall of Fame, Class of 1986, City of Huntington (W.Va.) Wall of Fame, 1997; recipient Charles Daugherty Humanities award W.Va. Humanities Coun., 1996. Mem. Am. Hist. Assn. (com. on status of history in schs. 1974-76), Orgn. Am. Historians (state rep.), W.Va. Hist. Assn. (sec. 1974, v.p. 1975, pres. 1976), W.Va. Assn. Acad. Deans (mem. exec. bd. 1982-86). W.Va. Bd. Regents (univ. rep., acad. affairs adv. com. 1984-86), Soc. Yeager Scholars (steering com. 1986-87), W.Va. Humanities Ctr. (exec. com. 1987—), Gamma Theta Upsilon, Omicron Delta Kappa, Phi Alpha Theta, Phi Eta Sigma, Pi Sigma Alpha. Avocations: tennis, travel. Office: Marshall U John Deaver Drinko Acad One John Marshall Dr Huntington WV 25755-0003

GOULD, ALVIN R. international business executive; b. Seattle, May 16, 1922; s. Charlie I. and Laura (Klos) G.; m. Ruth Nelson, May 25, 1946; children: Stephen Charles, Jon Patrick. Grad. pub. schs. Mem. engring. dept. Pacific Car & Foundry Co., Renton, Wash., 1943-45, asst. mgr. indsl. sales, 1945-48, mgr. indsl. sales, 1948-55, gen. sales mgr., 1956-60, Peterbilt Motors Co., Newark, Calif., 1961-64; v.p., dir., gen. sales mgr. Honolulu Iron Works Co., 1964-66, exec. v.p., dir., chief operating officer, 1966, pres., dir., chief exec. officer, 1968—71; group pres. Food Equipment Group Ward Foods Inc., N.Y.C., 1970-71; v.p. merchandising Dillingham Corp., Honolulu, 1972-73, v.p. mining and merchandising, 1973-75, group v.p., exec. mgmt. com. mining and merchandising; pres. Truck Center Corp., Seattle, 1976-90, co-owner, sec.-treas., 1991-95; pvt. practice in personal investments, 1996—. Mem. nat. export expansion Council Dept. Commerce, 1969-74, chmn. regional export expansion council, 1969-74; mem. Western Regional Export Council; chmn. Honolulu Export Council, 1975-77; Chmn. bd. trustees Hawaii Pacific Coll., 1973-77; bd. dirs. Center for Internat. Bus. Mem. Hawaii C. of C. (chmn. trade com. 1968-69), Hawaii World Trade Assn. (mem. exec. com. 1968-69), Hawaii Assn. Industries (v.p., dir. 1975-76), Navy League (dir.), Rotary Club, Outrigger Canoe Club, Rainier Club. Home: 8464 W Mercer Way Mercer Island WA 98040-5633

GOULD, ARTHUR PAUL, investment banker; b. N.Y.C., May 9, 1917; s. I.V. and Manya (Ostrow) G.; m. Julia Cooper, Jan. 23, 1948; children: David, Andrew, Victoria. BS, NYU, 1938; cert. (hon.), Harvard U., 1942. Mktg. rep. Talon, Inc., 1940-42; asst. gen. sales mgr. Philco Corp., 1948-51; gen. mgr., founder spl. products divsn. Bulova Watch Co., 1951-58; pres. Golden Shield Corp. (subsidiary of Gen. Telephone & Electronics Corp.), 1959-67; pres. corp. devel. divsn. Laidlaw & Co. Inc., 1967-73; v.p., stockholder, dir. Laidlaw & Co., 1967-73; pres. Arthur P. Gould & Co., 1973—. Bd. dirs. Cityscape Fin. Corp. Chmn. Yale U. Alumni Fund parents com.; dir. Yale Alumni Fund. Lt. comdr. USN, 1942-46. Mem. NYU Club (bd. govs.), AM Radio Relay League. Office: Arthur P Gould & Co 1 Wilshire Dr Lake Success NY 11020-1420

GOULD, BERNARD HOWARD, insurance agent; b. N.Y.C., Oct. 2, 1929; s. Abraham Lincoln Goldberg and Helen Stern; m. Louise Grayson Gould, Jan. 27, 1971; children: Sharon Miller, Amy Spector, Scott. BS in Journalism, U. Ill., 1951. Reporter, photographer Syracuse (NY) Post Std., 1953—55; staff reporter, writer AP, Columbus, Ohio, 1956—63, NYC, 1956—69; writer Nat. Enquirer, Lantana, Fla., 1970—75; writer, reporter Globe Mag., W. Palm Beach, Fla., 1975—78; agt. Equitable Life Assurance, Ft. Lauderdale, Fla., 1978—89; rep. Gould Ins. Svcs., Tamarac, Fla., 1989—. Cpl. U.S. Army, 1951—53. Mem.: Key Club, Sigma Delta Chi. Democrat. Jewish. Home: 9201 NW 61st St Tamarac FL 33321 Office: Gould Ins Svcs 9201 NW 61st St Tamarac FL 33321 Office Fax: 954-726-2132. E-mail: lbgouldfla@aol.com.

GOULD, BONNIE M(ARINCIC), realtor; b. Cleve., Sept. 3, 1947; d. Edward Louis and Frances (Dee (Pavlovich) Marincic. Student, John Carroll U. Asst. prodn. mgr. Nelson Stern Advt., Cleve., 1966-73; sec. acctg. S. James Dubin & Assocs., Eastlake, Ohio, 1976-78; sec., atty. James Todoroff, Andrews &

Todoroff, Eastlake, 1977-78; realtor sales Century 21-Baur, Euclid, Ohio, 1978-82; relocations dir., mgr. Century 21, Euclid, 1979-82; realtor assoc., relocation dir. Century 21-Malone, Inc., Willowick, Ohio, 1982-83, Century 21-William T. Byrne, Cleve., 1983-84, Smythe, Cramer Co., Euclid, 1984-86; sr. v.p., treas., corp. mgr. Acacia Realty Profls. Inc., 1986-98; pres., treas., interior design coord. Acacia Design and Trade Profls. Inc. Gen. Contractors, 1990—; pres., CEO Acacia Design Fine Homes and Properties, 1999—. Mem. Realtors Polit. Action Com., Cleve., 1981—; vice chmn. local taxation and legislation com. Cleve. Area Bd. Realtors, 1983-84, vice chmn. polit. affairs, 1987—, chmn. home and flower 1986, mem. enlarged legis. com., 1986-97, internat. rules and fin. com., 1993-95, chmn. 1995; sec., trustee Euclid Gateway Found., 1987—. Recipient Disting. Svc. award Cleve. Bd. Realtors, 1983-87, 96, Woman of Yr. award 1990. Mem. Cleve. Bd. Realtors (dir. 1984-86, 93—, 2d v.p. 1994, treas. 1995, gov. No.Ohio multiple listings svc. 1992—, contract and fin. com., 1992—), Ohio Assn. Realtors (trustee 1981-97), Nat. Assn. Realtors Women's Coun. of Realtors (treas. Cleve. chpt. 1986-87, v.p. 1987-88, pres. 1989, chmn. nominating com. 1990, Woman of Yr. 1990), Lake and Geague Area Assn. Realtors (fin. com. 2001--, 2d v.p. 2003--), North East Roundtable (sec. 1980, chair 1981), Euclid C. of C. (trustee), Wickliffe C. of C. Republican. Roman Catholic. Office: Acacia Design Fine Homes & Properties 293 E 266th St Cleveland OH 44132-1552 E-mail: acaciadsgn@aol.com., acaciarelo@aol.com.

GOULD, DAVID, lawyer; b. L.A., Feb. 19, 1940; s. Erwin and Beatrice (Altman) G.; m. Bonnie Becker, Feb. 12, 1967; children: Julie M., Michael. AB, U. Calif., L.A., 1962; LLB, U. Calif., Berkeley, 1965. Bar: Calif. 1965, U.S. Dist. Ct. (cen., so., ea. and no. dists.) Calif. 1966, U.S. Ct. Appeals (9th cir.) 1967, U.S. Supreme Ct. 1995. Dep. atty. gen. Calif. Dept. of Justice, L.A., 1965-68; assoc. Loeb & Loeb, L.A., 1968-73, Danning, Gill, Gould, Diamond & Spector, L.A., 1974-76, ptnr., 1976-92, McDermott, Will & Emery, L.A., 1992—. Adj. assoc. prof. Southwestern U. Sch. of Law, L.A., 1978-80; adj. prof. Pepperdine U. Sch. of Law, Malibu, Calif., 1982. Co-author: Local Bankruptcy Practice Manual for the Central District of California, 2d edit., 1990—. Fellow: Am. Coll. Bankruptcy; mem.: L.A. Bankruptcy Forum (bd. trustees 1989, sec. 1990—, pres. 1993—94), lawyer rep. ctrl. dist. Calif. to 9th cir. jud. conf.), Calif. Bankruptcy Forum, L.A. County Bar Assn. (fed. cts. com. 1987—, treas. 1998—99, sec. 1999—), Calif. Bar Assn. (debtor/creditor rels. and bankruptcy com. 1984—87, chair 1987—88, advisor 1988—89, uniform comml. code com. 1988—92, bankruptcy cons. gorup bd. legal specialization 1989—93), ABA (bus. bankruptcy com. sect. on bus. law 1982—, vice chair rules subcom. 1986—92, chair 1992—). Avocation: trap and skeet shooting. Office: McDermott Will & Emery 2049 Century Park E Ste 3400 Los Angeles CA 90067-3208

GOULD, DONALD EVERETT, retired chemical company executive, consultant; b. Concord, N.H., May 19, 1932; s. Everett Luther and Gladys (Wilcox) G.; m. Marilyn Bachelder, June 13, 1953; children: Barbara, Allen, Douglas. BS in Chem. Engring., U. N.H., 1954; postgrad., Rutgers U., 1955-59. Devel. chem. engr. plastics divsn. Union Carbide Co., Bound Brook, N.J., 1954-59, tech. svc. engr. Bound Brook and Wayne, N.J., 1959-64, mgr. tech. svc. indsl. bag dept. Wayne, 1964-66, mgr. tech. svcs. indsl. fabricated products dept., 1966-67, mktg., mgr. indsl. bags, 1967-69, sr. packaging engr., 1969-72, mgr. packaging, 1972-74, mgr. distbn. safegy and regulations, 1974-79, staff engr. packaging, 1980-85, sr. staff engr. packaging, labeling, 1985-91, prin. engr. packaging, labeling and regulations, 1991-94, cons., 1994—. Contbg. author Encyclopedia of Engineering Materials and Processes; contbr. articles profl. jours. Chmn. Andover Planning Bd., NH, 2001—. Mem. Inst. Packaging Profls. (vice chmn. films, foils and laminations com. 1962-64, chmn. 1964-66, sect. leader bottle containers, chmn. bag com. 1975-78, 85-88, exec. com. chem. packaging 1985-94, hon. life mem. 1992), Am. Soc. Quality Control (hon., life), Chem. Mfrs. Assn. (chmn. distbn. work group), Am. Coun. Chem. Labeling, Andover Hist. Soc. (treas.), Alpha Chi Sigma, Alpha Gamma Rho. Home: PO Box 231 21 Lawrence St East Andover NH 03231-0231 Office: River Rd PO Box 670 Bound Brook NJ 08805-0670

GOULD, DOROTHY MAE, executive secretary, soprano; b. Bridgeport, Conn., Sept. 9, 1927; d. Clifford Alexander and Mary Irene Hedin; m. John Colquitt Gould, Nov. 26, 1958; children: Natalie Mary, Clifford Gardner, Andrew Woodhouse. BA in English Lit. and Creative Writing, U. Mont., 1997; studied voice with Estelle Liebling, Julliard, 1959—63, studied voice with Bernard Taylor, 1943; scholar, New Eng. Conservatory. Legal sec. Thompson Knight, Dallas, White, McElroy, Dallas, Gibbons, Tucker, Smith, McEwen, Coxer and Taub, Tampa, Fla., Curtis, Trevethan & Gerety, Bridgeport, Conn., Music Corp. Am., N.Y.C., NY; sec. GE Co., Bridgeport, Columbia Artists Mgmt., N.Y.C., AMF, Greenwich, Conn.; soprano USO, Conn., 1944—45, Tampa Opera, 2002—; oratorio singer, soloist soprano N.Y., Conn., Fla. Finalist Barnum Festival Jenny Lind contest, 1948, Stamford Advocate, Greenwich Times contest, 1985—86. Home: 13871 N 91st Ln Peoria AZ 85381

GOULD, EDWARD WARD, lawyer; b. Warwick, R.I., Jan. 3, 1957; s. Whitney and Shirley (Willis) G.; m. Lynn Frances O'Rourke, May 30, 1981; children: Kathryn, Andrew, Matthew, Kelly. AB, Brown U., 1979; JD, Boston U., 1982. Bar: Maine 1982, U.S. Dist. Ct. Maine 1982, U.S. Ct. Appeals (1st cir.) 1985. With Gross, Minsky & Mogul, P.A., Bangor, Maine, 1982—. Pres. Bangor Area Vis. Nurses, 1998—. Bd. dirs. Penobscot Area Housing Devel. Corp., Bangor, 1986—; YMCA, Bangor, 1998—. Mem. Penobscot County Bar Assn. (pres. 2001), Am. Bd. Trial Lawyers (pres. 2001-02 Maine chpt.), Maine Trial Lawyers Assn. Office: Gross Minsky & Mogul 23 Water St Ste 400 Bangor ME 04401-6372

GOULD, GERALD G. electrical engineer; b. Budapest, Hungary, Nov. 17, 1913; arrived in U.S., 1921; m. Jeanette Beiss Gould, Mar. 12, 1941; children: James, Mark, Jane. BS, N.Y. City Coll., 1935; MS, Purdue U., 1936. Registered profl. engr., Fla. Engr. Porcelain Products Inc., Parkersburg, W.Va., 1936—40, N.Y. Subway Sys., N.Y.C., 1940—42, Naval Ordnance Lab. and Bur. of Ordnance, USN, Washington, 1946—55; tech. dir. Naval Underwater Ordnance Sta., Newport, RI, 1955—72, Naval Coastal Sys. Ctr., Panama City, Fla., 1972—81; pres. Gerald Gould Assocs., Panama City, 1981—. Participant naval studies bd. NAS, 1990. Comdr. USN, 1942—46. Recipient Radm Parsons award, Navy League U.S., 1975, Superior Svc. award, USN, 1981, Hall of Fame award, Naval Coastal Sys. Ctr., 2001. Fellow: IEEE. Home: 2329 Magnolia Dr Panama City FL 32408-7006

GOULD, GLENN HUNTING, marketing professional, consultant; b. Martinsburg, W.Va., June 15, 1949; s. Glenn Hunting Sr. and Margaret Alice (Otto) G.; m. Marilyn Kay Jones, July 12, 1953; 2 children: Courtney Lynn, Angela Pace. BA in Sociology, W.Va. U., 1973, MS in Indsl. Relations, 1974. Mgr. human resources Hillenbrand Ind., Batesville, Ind., 1979-81; mgr. human resources, MIAD div. Bausch & Lomb, Balt., 1981-82; dir. human resources Universal Security Inst., Balt., 1982-83; chief exec. officer MKJ Mktg., Largo, Fla., 1983—. Bd. dirs. Pitts. Inst. Mortuary Soc.; cons. Colombian Fin. Group, 1995-2000, Wilbert Inc. Contbg. author: Successful Funeral Service Practice, 1987. Served as sgt. USAF, 1967-71, Vietnam. Named one of Outstanding Young Men Am., 1980. Mem. Soc. Human Resource Mgmt. (cert. sr. profl.), Alpha Kappa Delta. Presbyterian. Avocations: antiques, reading, skiing, golf. Office: 1501B Belcher Rd S Largo FL 33771-4505

GOULD, HARRY EDWARD, JR., paper company executive; b. N.Y.C., Sept. 24, 1938; s. Harry Edward and Lucille (Quartucy) Gould; m. Barbara Clement, Apr. 26, 1975; children: Harry Edward III, Katharine Elizabeth. Student, Oxford U., 1958; BA cum laude, Colgate U., 1960; postgrad., Harvard Bus. Sch., 1960—61; MBA, Columbia U., 1964. Assoc. in corp. fin. dept. Goldman, Sachs & Co., N.Y.C., 1961—62; exec. asst. to sr. v.p. ops. Universal Am., N.Y.C., 1964—65; sec., treas. Young Spring & Wire Corp., Detroit, 1965—67, exec. v.p., COO, 1967—69, also bd. dirs.; v.p. adminstrn. and fin. Universal Am. Corp., 1968—69; mem. exec. com., v.p., sec.-treas. Daybrook-Ottawa Corp., Bowling Green, Ohio, 1967—69; dir., mem. exec. com. Am. Med. Ins. Co., N.Y.C., 1966—74; chmn., pres., CEO Gould Paper Corp., N.Y.C., 1969—, also chmn. bd. dirs.; chmn. bd., dir. Vrisimo Mfg., Inc., Ceres, 1974—; chmn. bd. Lewis & Gould Paper Co., Inc., Northfield, Ill., 1975—78; chmn., pres., CEO Signature Comm. Ltd., L.A. and N.Y.C., 1986—; chmn. bd. Legion Paper West Corp., Commerce, Calif., 1997—. Chmn. bd. dirs. Samuel Porritt & Co., East Peoria, Ill., Ingalls Mfg., Inc., Ceres, Calif., McNair Mfg., Inc., Chico, Calif., Hawthorne Paper Co., Kalamazoo, Weiss Mfg., Inc., Chico; bd. dirs. Reinhold Gould GmbH, Hamburg, Germany; ltd. ptnr. Hardy & Co., N.Y.C., 1973—78; chmn. exec. com., bd. dirs. Richard Lewis Paper Corp., Northfield, Ill., 1992—97; bd. dirs., mem. environ. and health and safety com. Domtar, Inc., Montreal, 1995—. Co-chmn. Pacesetters com. Boy Scouts Am., 1966—69; participant as U.S. Pres.'s rep. UN E-W Trade Devel. Commn., 1967; mem. nat. coun. Colgate U., 1973—76, trustee, mem. budget, devel., fin. and student affairs coms., 1976—82; mem. exec. com., chmn. export expansion subcom., mem. export promotion subcom. U.S. Pres.'s Export Coun., 1979—82; nat. trustee, mem. exec. com. Nat. Symphony Orch., Washington, 1978—; mem. N.Y. Gov.'s Task Force on N.Y. State Cultural Life and Arts, 1975—; pres. Harry E. Gould Found., N.Y.C., 1971—; mem. bd. govs. Actors Studio Drama Sch. of New Sch. U., 1995—; mem. exec. br. Acad. Motion Picture Arts and Scis., 1985—; trustee Riverdale Country Sch., 1990—98; mem. Dem. Nat. Fin. Coun., 1974—78, also vice chmn. exec. com., chmn. budget and audit coms.; treas. N.Y. State Dem. Com., 1976—77; mem. mayor's citizens com. Dem. Nat. Conv., 1976; bd. dirs. United Cerebral Palsy Rsch. and Ednl. Found., 1976—, Nat. Multiple Sclerosis Soc., 1977—, N.Y.C. Housing Corp., 1977—, USO of Met. N.Y., 1981—; trustee Housing N.Y. Corp., 1986—, vice chmn., 1987—; bd. dirs., chmn. exec. com. Cinema Group, Inc., L.A., 1979—86, chmn., pres., 1982—86; bd. dirs. Residential Mortgage Ins. Corp., 1992—. Mem.: Fin. Execs. Inst., Am. Mgmt. Assn. (trustee, audit com. 1997—), Young Pres. Orgn., Paper Distbn. Coun. (chmn. 1993—94), Paper Mchts. Assn. N.Y. (dir. 1972—84), Nat. Paper Trade Alliance (dir., mem. printing paper com. 1973—74), Marco Polo Club (NYC), Harvard Bus. Sch. Club, Pres.'s N.Y. Club (co-chmn. assocs. divsn. 1964—68), Paper Club N.Y., City Athletic Club, Friars Club, Les Ambassadeurs (London), Harvard Club, Rockrimmon Country Club (Stamford, Conn.), Friars Club, Phi Kappa Tau. Office: Gould Paper Corp 11 Madison Ave Fl 14 New York NY 10010-3629 *In business the most difficult problem to resolve is blending the profit goals with the dignity of human relations. In the long run, it is probably best to forego some of the profits in order to successfully meld the economic and human sides of business.*

GOULD, HOWARD RICHARD, retired physician; b. N.Y.C., May 21, 1931; m. Barbara Ann Paretti, Oct. 6, 1956; children: Susan, Carolyn, Richard, Joanne, Anthony, MaryJean, Eileen, Laura, Margaret. Student, Fordham U., 1949-52; MD, SUNY, 1956. Diplomate Am. Bd. Radiology (examiner oral exams. 1979), Am. Bd. Nuclear Medicine, Nat. Bd. Med. Examiners. Resident in radiology St. Vincent's Hosp., N.Y.C., 1957-60, assoc. dir., 1974-79; chief radiology 811th Med. Group, Loring AFB, Maine, 1960-62, USAF Hosp., Wiesbaden, Germany, 1962-65; radiologist St. Vincent's Hosp., N.Y.C., 1965-79; dir. diagnostic radiology Clin. Sci. Ctr. U. Wis., Madison, 1979-84, U. Tenn. Med. Ctr., Knoxville, 1984-95, sr. radiologist, 1995-99, prof. radiology, 1984-99, prof. emeritus, 2000—. Clin. asst. prof. N.J. Coll. Med., 1965-69; clin. assoc. prof. NYU Sch. Med., N.Y.C., 1969-79; prof. radiology U. Wis., Madison, 1979-84; sec. v.p., pres. elect, pres. med. staff St. Vincent's Hosp., 1969-76; chief staff elect, chief staff U. Tenn. Med. Ctr., 1993, 94; sec. N.Y. Celtic Med. Soc., N.Y.C., 1969-73. Author various book chpts.; contbr. articles to profl. jours. Maj. USAF, 1957-65. Fellow Am. Coll. Radiology; mem. AMA, Radiol. Soc. N.Am., Am. Coll. Radiology, N.Y. Roentgen Soc. (sec., v.p., pres. 1971-78), Assn. Univ Radiologists, Am. Roentgen Ray Soc., Alpha Omega Alpha. Roman Catholic. Avocations: reading, woodworking, radio control flying.

GOULD, JAMES L. biology educator; b. Tulsa, July 31, 1945; s. James L. and Doris Mae (Frazier) G.; m. Carol Holly Grant, June 6, 1970; children: Grant Frazier, Clare Holly. BS, Calif. Inst. Tech., 1970; PhD, Rockefeller U., 1975. Asst. prof. Princeton (N.J.) U., 1975-80, assoc. prof., 1980-84, prof. biology, 1984—. Author: Ethology, 1982, Biological Science, rev. edit., 1996, The Honey Bee, 1988, Sexual Selection, 1989, The Animal Mind, 1994, Biostats Basics, 2001; contbr. more than 100 articles to profl. jours. With U.S. Army, 1967-68. Guggenheim Found. fellow, 1987, AAAS fellow, 1988, Animal Behavior Soc. fellow, 1992; grantee NSF, 1976, 79, 82, 85, NIH, 1976, Nat. Geogrphic Soc., 1984; named Prof. of Yr. Carnegie Found. N.J., 1996, Tchr. of Yr. Animal Behavior Soc., 1997. Presbyterian. Achievements include research in animal behavior. Office: Princeton U Dept Ecol Evol Biology Princeton NJ 08544-0001 E-mail: gould@princeton.edu.

GOULD, JOHN PHILIP, economist, educator; b. Chgo., Jan. 19, 1939; s. John Philip and Lillian Gould; children: John Philip III, Jeffrey Hayes; m. Kathleen A. Carpenter. BS with highest distinction, Northwestern U., 1960; MBA, U. Chgo., 1963, PhD, 1966. Faculty U. Chgo., 1965—, prof. econs., 1974—, disting. service prof. econs., 1984—, dean Grad. Sch. Bus., 1983-93, v.p. planning, 1988—91; Steven G. Rothmeier prof., disting. svc. prof. econs., 1996—; exec. v.p. Lexecon Inc., Chgo., 1994—; pres. Cardean, Chgo., 1999—2001. Vis. prof. Nat. Taiwan U., 1978; spl. asst. econ. affairs to sec. labor, 1969-70; spl. asst. to dir. Office Mgmt. and Budget, 1970; past chmn. econ. policy adv. com. Dept. Labor; bd. dirs. DFA Investment Dimensions Group, Harbor Capital Advisors, First Prairie Funds, 1985-96; chmn. Pegasus Funds, 1996-99, Milw. Mutual, 1997—, Unext.com, 1999—. Author: (with E. Lazear) Microeconomic Theory, 6th edit, 1989; contbg. author: Microeconomic Foundations of Employment and Inflation Theory, 1970; editor: Jour. of Bus., 1976-83, Jour. Fin. Econs., 1976-83, Jour. Accounting and Econs., 1978-81; contbr. articles to profl. jours. Bd. dirs. United Way/Crusade of Mercy, 1986-91, Lookingglass Theatre Co., 1994-96. Recipient Wall St. Jour. award, 1960, Am. Marketing Assn. award, 1960; Earhart Found. fellow. Mem. Am. Econs. Assn., Econometric Soc. (chmn. local arrangements 1968), Econ. Club of Chgo., Comml. Club of Chgo., Beta Gamma Sigma. Home: 100 E Huron St Apt 2105 Chicago IL 60611-5903 Office: U Chgo Grad Sch Bus 1101 E 58th St Chicago IL 60637-1511

GOULD, JULIAN SAUL, lawyer; b. L.A., Apr. 15, 1924; s. David H. and Jeanette (Palm) G.; m. Norma Patricia Gould; 1 child, Paul Julian. Student, U. So. Calif., 1946-48; JD, Southwestern U., L.A., 1950. Bar: Calif. 1950. Lawyer in pvt. practice, L.A., 1950—. Named Alumnus of Yr., Southwestern U., 1972. Mem. Hollywood Bar Assn. (pres. 1978), Am. Legion (comdr. 24th Dist. 1960), Southwestern U. Alumni Assn. (pres. 1972), Masons (32 deg., Shriners. Democrat. Office: 6381 Hollywood Blvd Ste 605 Hollywood CA 90028-6325

GOULD, LILIAN, writer; b. Phila., Apr. 19, 1920; d. Reuben Barr and Lilian Valentine (Scott) Seidel; m. Irving Gould, Nov. 16, 1944; children: Mark, Scott, Paul, John. Student, U. Pa., Charles Morris Price Sch. of Advt. and Journalism, Phila. Copywriter, mgr. advt. agys., Phila. Author: Our Living Past, 1969, Jeremy and the Gorillas, 1977 (award 1977); freelance journalist mags. and newspapers. Mem. Authors Guild, Phila. Children's Reading Roundtable, Phila. Writers Orgn., Soc. of Children's Book Writers and Illustrators. Home: 772 Newtown Rd Villanova PA 19085-1121

GOULD, MARTHA BERNICE, retired librarian; b. Claremont, NH, Oct. 8, 1931; d. Sigmund and Gertrude Heller; m. Arthur Gould, July 29, 1960; children: Leslie, Stephen. BA in Edn., U. Mich., 1953; MS in Library Sci., Simmons Coll., 1956; cert., U. Denver Library Sch. Community Analysis Research Inst., 1978. Childrens librarian N.Y. Pub. Libr., 1956-58; adminstr. library services act demonstration regional library project Pawhuska, Okla., 1958-59; cons. N.Mex. State Libr., 1959-60; childrens librarian then sr. childrens librarian Los Angeles Pub. Libr., 1960-72; acctg. dir. pub. srvices, reference librarian Nev. State Libr., 1972-74; pub. services librarian Washoe County (Nev.) Libr., 1974-79, asst. county librarian, 1979-84, county librarian, 1984-94; ret., 1994. Cons. Nev. State Libr. and Archives, 1996—; part-time lectr. libr. adminstrn. U. Nev.; acting dir. Nev. Ctr. for the Book; chair, Presdl. appointee Nat. Commn. in Librs. & Info. Sci., 2000—03; mem. adv. coun. Nev. Coun. on Librs. and Literacy, 2001—; mem. adv. bd. Fleischmann Planetarium, 1999—. Co-editor: Nevada Women's History Project Annotated Bibliography, 1999; contbr. articles to jours. Exec. dir. Kids Voting/USA, Nev., 1996; treas. United Jewish Appeals, 1981; bd. dirs. Temple Sinai, Planned Parenthood, 1996-97, Truckee Meadows Habitat for Humanity, 1995-98; trustee RSVP, North Nevadans for ERA; No. Nev. chmn. Gov.'s Conf. on Libr., 1990; bd. dirs. Campaign for Choice, No. Nev. Food Bank, Nev. Women's Fund (Hall of Fame award 1989); mem. No. Nev. NCCJ, Washoe County Quality Life Task Force, 1992—, Washoe County Elections Taskforce, 1999—; bd. dirs. KUNR Pub. Radio, 1999—, chair bd. dirs., 2000—; chair Nat. Commn. Librs. & Info. Sci., 2000-03; chair Sierra (Nev.) Cmty. Access TV; presdl. appointee vice-chair Nat. Commn. on Librs. and Info. Sci., 1993-2000, chair, 2000-03; adv. bd. Partnership Librs. Washoe County, Fleischmann Planetarium, 2003—; co-chair social studies curriculum adv. task force Washoe County Sch. Dist.; mem. Nev. Women's History Project Bd.; chair Downtown River Corridor Com., 1995-97; vice chair Dem. Party Washoe County; v.p. Nev. Diabetes Assn. for Children and Adults, 1998-2002, pres., 2002-03; chair devel. com. Planned Parenthood, 2002—; bd. dirs. Washoe Libr. Found.; mem. adv. Adv. Coun. on Edn./to the Holocaust, 2000—; chair Washoe County Dem. Women's Club, 2003—. Recipient Nev. State Libr. Letter of Commendation, 1973, Washoe County Bd. Commrs. Resolution of Appreciation, 1978, ACLU of Nev. Civil Libertarian of Yr. 1988, Freedom's Sake award AAUW, 1989, Leadership in Literacy award Sierra chpt. Internat. Reading Assn., 1992, Woman of Distinction award 1992, Nev. Libr. Assn. Libr. of Yr., 1993. Mem. ALA (bd. dirs., intellectual freedom roundtable 1977-79, intellectual freedom com. 1979-83, coun. 1983-86), ACLU (bd. dirs. Civil Libertarian of Yr. Nev. chpt. 1988, chair gov.'s conf. for women 1989), Nev. Libr. Assn. (chmn. pub. info. com. 1972-73, intellectual freedom com. 1975-78, govt. rels. com. 1978-79, v.p., pres.-elect 1980, pres. 1981, Spl. Citation 1978, 87, Libr. of Yr. 1993), Nev. Diabetes Assn. for Children and Adults (pres. 2002—). E-mail: mgould@powernet.net.

GOULD, MARY CHRISTA, small business owner; b. Chattanooga, Tenn., Dec. 20, 1977; d. Wallace Harry and Sandra Gayle Gould; 1 child, Christian Charles. Co-owner Creative Minds Pub., Chattanooga, 1999—; proprieter True Worship Music, Chattanooga, 2000—; rep. A&R Fresh On Delivery Records, Chattanooga, 2000—. Composer: (songs) Fields of Life, 2000; author: Poems From the Heart, 2001. Mem.: ASCAP, BMI. Avocation: Avocations: public speaking against domestic violence, singing, writing, reading. Home: 1005 S Highland Park Ave Chattanooga TN 37404-4216

GOULD, PHILLIP, engineer; b. N.Y.C., Feb. 19, 1940; s. Isaac and Blanche (Handler) Gould; m. Elizabeth West Ratigan, Nov. 29, 1980; children: David Elliot, Jessica Ann. BSME, CCNY, 1961; MS, MIT, 1963, ScD, 1965. Asst. prof. mech. engring. MIT, Cambridge, 1965-67; mem. staff Inst. for Def. Analyses, Alexandria, Va., asst. dir., 1984—. Dir. Def. Sci. Study Group, 1998—. Fellow, Ford Found., 1965. Fellow: AAAS; mem.: Am. Soc. Engring. Edn., Inst. for Ops. Rsch. and Mgmt. Sci., N.Y. Acad. Scis., Washington Congregation for Secular Humanistic Judaism (pres.), Soc. for Humanistic Judaism (pres.), Sigma Xi. Home: 4590 Indian Rock Ter NW Washington DC 20007-2567 Office: Inst Def Analyses 4850 Mark Ctr Dr Alexandria VA 22311-1882 E-mail: pgould@alum.mit.edu.

GOULD, PHILLIP LOUIS, civil engineering educator, consultant; b. Chgo., May 24, 1937; m. Deborah Paula Rothholtz, Feb. 5, 1961; children: Elizabeth, Nathan, Rebecca, Joshua. BS, U. Ill., 1959, MS, 1960; PhD, Northwestern U., 1966. Structural designer Skidmore, Owings & Merrill, Chgo., 1960-63; prin. structural engr. Westenhoff & Novick, Chgo., 1963-64; NASA trainee Northwestern U., Evanston, Ill., 1964-66; asst. prof. civil engring. Washington U., St. Louis, 1966-68, assoc. prof., 1968-74, prof., 1974—, chmn. dept. civil engring., 1978-98, Harold D. Jolly prof. civil engring., 1981—. Vis. prof. Ruhr U., Fed. Republic Germany, 1974-75, U. Sydney, Australia, 1981, Shanghai Inst. Tech., Peoples Republic of China, 1986; dir. Earthquake Engring. Rsch. Inst., exec. coun. Internat. Assn. for Shell and Spatial Structures, pres. Great Lakes chpt. and New Madrid chpt. Earthquake Engring. Rsch. Inst. Author: Static Analysis of Shells: A Unified Development of Surface Structures, 1977, Introduction to Linear Elasticity, 1984, Finite Element Analysis of Shells of Revolution, 1985, Analysis of Shells and Plates, 1987, 2d edit., 1999; co-author: Dynamic Response of Structures to Wind and Earthquake Loading, 1980; co-editor: Environmental Forces on Engineering Structures, 1979, Natural Draught Cooling Towers, 1985; editor: Engineering Structures, 1979—. Dir. Earthquake Engring. Rsch. Inst., 1993—95; vice chmn. Mo. Seismic Safety Commn., 1998—99, chmn., 2000—01; St. Louis regional dir. Mid-Am. Earthquake Ctr. Recipient Sr. Scientist award Alexander von Humboldt Found., Fed. Republic Germany, 1974-75 Fellow ASCE (bd. dirs. St. Louis sect. 1985-87, Otto Nutli award); mem. Am. Soc. Engring. Edn., Internat. Assn. Shell Structures, Structural Engrs. Assn. Ill., Mo. Soc. Profl. Engrs. (Outstanding Engr. in Edn. award), Civil Engring. Alumni Assn. U. Ill., Urbana-Champaign (Disting. Alumnus award). Home: 102 Lake Frst Saint Louis MO 63117-1303 Office: Washington U Dept Civil Engring PO Box 1130 Saint Louis MO 63188-1130 E-mail: pgoul@seas.wustl.edu.

GOULD, RODNEY ELLIOTT, lawyer, university dean, educator; b. Boston, June 3, 1943; s. Samuel H. and Sylvia (Gerrish) G.; m. Nancy Lund, Sept. 10, 1968; children: Jody R., Amy L. Student, London Sch. Econs., 1963-64; AB, Colby Coll., 1965; JD, Columbia U., 1968. Bar: D.C. 1969, N.Y. 1969, Mass. 1975, Pa. 2001, U.S. Dist. Ct. (so. dist.) N.Y. 1969, U.S. Dist. Ct. D.C. 1969, U.S. Ct. Appeals (2d cir.) 1969, U.S. Ct. Appeals (D.C. cir.) 1970, U.S. Dist. Ct. Mass. 1975, U.s. Ct. Appeals (3d and 8th cirs.) 1981, U.S. Ct. Appeals (1st cir.) 1989, U.S. Supreme Ct. 1989, U.S. Ct. Appeals (6th cir.) 1990, U.S. Ct. Appeals (4th cir.) 1998. Law clk. to judge U.S. Dist. Ct. for So. Dist. N.Y., 1968-69; assoc. Covington & Burling, Washington, 1969-75, Rosenman Colin Freund Lewis & Cohen, N.Y.C., 1979-82; assoc. dir. FTC, Boston, 1975-78; antitrust counsel Digital Equipment Co., Maynard, Mass., 1983-84; gen. counsel Internat. Weekends, Boston, 1985-86; ptnr. Rubin Hay & Gould, Framingham, Mass., 1986—. Adj. prof. Law Sch., Western New Eng. U., Springfield, Mass., 1980-82, Northeastern U., Boston, 1983—, Boston U., 1985—; lectr. in field. Editor Columbia Law Rev., 1967-68. Bd. dirs. Mass. Aububon Soc., 1996—. Mem. ABA, Mass. Bar Assn., N.Y. Bar Assn., D.C. Bar Assn., Phi Beta Kappa. Home: 84 Gordon Rd Newton MA 02468-1617 Office: Rubin Hay & Gould 205 Newbury St Framingham MA 01701-4581

GOULD, RONALD MURRAY, federal judge; b. St. Louis, Oct. 17, 1946; s. Harry H. and Sylvia C. (Sadofsky) Gould; m. Suzanne H. Goldblatt, Dec. 1, 1968; children: Daniel, Rebecca. BS in Econs., U. Pa., 1968; JD, U. Mich., 1973. Bar: Wash. 1975, U.S. Dist. Ct. (we. dist.) Wash. 1976, U.S. Ct. Appeals (9th cir.) 1980, U.S. Supreme Ct. 1981, U.S. Dist. Ct. (ea. dist.) Wash. 1982, U.S. Ct. Appeals (fed. cir.) 1986. Law clk. to hon. Wade H. McCree Jr. U.S. Ct. Appeals (6th cir.), Detroit, 1973—74; law clk. to hon. justice Potter Stewart U.S. Supreme Ct., Washington, 1974—75; assoc. Perkins Coie, Seattle, 1975—80, ptnr., 1981—99; judge U.S. Ct. Appeals (9th cir.), Seattle, 1999—. Editor-in-chief: Mich. Law Rev., 1972—73; editor: Washington Civil Procedure Deskbook, 1981. Exec. bd. chief Seattle coun. Boy Scouts Am., 1984—; bd. dirs. econ. devel. coun. Seattle and King County, 1991—94; citizens cabinet mem. Gov. Mike Lowry, Seattle, 1993—96; bd. trustees Bellevue CC, 1993—99; mem. cmty. rels. coun. Jewish Fedn. of Greater Seattle, 1985—88. Fellow: ABA (antitrust sect., litig. sect.); mem.: King County Bar Assn. (Disting. Svc. award 1987), Wash. State Bar Assn. (bd. govs. 1988—91, pres. 1994—95), 9th Jud. Cir. Hist. Soc. (bd. dirs. 1994—), Supreme Ct. Hist. Soc. Jewish. Avocations: reading, chess. Office: US Courthouse 1200 6th Ave Fl 21 Seattle WA 98101-3123*

GOULD, SUSAN EILEEN, social worker, elementary school educator; b. New Brunswick, N.J., Sept. 2, 1959; d. Samuel and Marion (Louis) Naar; m. Brian Jay Gould, Apr. 10, 1983; children: Leah, Lauren. BA in Sociology, U. Hartford, 1981; BSW, St. Joseph's Coll., West Hartford, Conn., 1981; MSW, Rutgers U., 1982; elem. edn. tchr. cert., Rider U., 2001. Caseworker Big Bros./Big Sisters, Houston, 1982; social worker Millhill Child & Family Devel. Ctr., Trenton, N.J., 1983, Cath. Welfare Bur., Trenton, 1983-86, Richard Hall Community Mental Health Ctr., Bridgewater, N.J., 1986-87, Family Svc. Assn. Middlesex County, Old Bridge, N.J., 1987-88, CPC Mental Health Svcs., Morganville, N.J., 1989-90, Princeton (N.J.) YWCA-Interim Homes, 1990-92; with HIP/Rutgers Health Plan, 1992-94, Corner House, Princeton, N.J., 1994-96; social worker Magnitude LLC, Plainsboro, N.J., 1996, Nat. Coun. Alcoholism & Drug Dependence, East Brunswick, NJ, 1996—2001; 4th grade tchr. Lawrence Twp. Pub. Schs., Lawrenceville, NJ, 2002—. Mem. NASW, Crohn's and Colitis Found. Am. Avocations: bicycling, singing, swimming. Home: 7 Mifflin Ct Plainsboro NJ 08536-2331 E-mail: suelcsw@comcast.net.

GOULD, TAFFY, Internet company executive, real estate executive; b. Miami, Fla., Apr. 14, 1942; d. Emil J. and Estelle F. Gould; m. Bernard Arthur Beber, Apr. 5, 1964 (div. Jan. 1975); children: Karen B. Futernick, J. Gregory Beber. BA, Smith Coll., 1963. Cert. real estate broker, Fla. Pres. Housing Engrs. Fla., Inc., Miami, 1977—; chmn. e-Med. Edn., LLC, Fla., 1999—; chmn. coun. Oceania U. Medicine; vice chmn. Non-Invasive Monitoring Sys., Inc. Lectr. Potomac Spkrs. Bur., Washington, 1993-98. Author: South Africa: Land of

Hope, 1989, White Woman Witchdoctor, 1993 (Best Seller 1994); co-author: Create Your Own Future, 1996; newspaper columnist Miami Today, 1983-88, Miami Today, Miami Herald; radio talk host WINZ, Miami, 1986-88. Mem. nat. com. Zionist Orgn. Am., N.Y., 1995—; bd. dirs. Alexander Muss H.S. in Israel, Miami, 1995—, Cen. Agy. for Jewish Edn.; dir. U. Miami, Miami Hot Glass, Coral Gables, Fla., 1998—; governing coun. Fla. Philharmonic Orch., 1998—. Recipient Humanitarian and Arts award Internat. Bolivarian Soc., Miami, 1994, City of the Future award City of Ariel, Israel, 1999, Louis Brandeis award Zionist Orgn. Am., N.Y., 2000. Avocations: classical music, reading. Home: 10 Edgewater Dr Apt 14F Coral Gables FL 33133-6968 Fax: (305) 668-3298. E-mail: taffyg@bellsouth.net.

GOULD, THOMAS DENTON, lawyer; b. Elmira, N.Y., Oct. 29, 1950; BS, Pa. State U., 1972, JD, 1982. Bar: Pa. 1982, U.S. Supreme Ct. 1991. Pvt. practice, Shiremanstown, Pa., 1990—. Chmn. Shiremanstown Parks and Recreation, 1996—, 2000, pres. neighborhood dispute settlement com. Mem.: ATLA, ABA, Cumberland County Bar Assn., Dauphin County Bar Assn., Pa. Bar Assn. Office: Law Offices of Thomas D Gould 2 E Main St Shiremanstown PA 17011-6309

GOULD, WILLIAM BENJAMIN, IV, lawyer, educator, federal agency administrator; b. 1936; AB, U. R.I., 1958; LLB, Cornell U., 1961; postgrad., London Sch. Econs., 1962—63; LLD (hon.), U. R.I., 1986, D.C. Sch. Law, 1995, Stetson U., 1996, Capital U., 1997, Rutgers U., 1998. Bar: Mich. 1962. Asst. gen. counsel UAW, AFL-CIO, Detroit, 1961—62; atty. NLRB, Washington, 1963—65; assoc. Battle, Fowler, Stokes & Kheel, N.Y.C., 1965—68; prof. Wayne State U., Detroit, 1968—71, Stanford (Calif.) U. Law Sch., 1972—, Charles A. Beardsley prof. law. Chmn. Nat. Labor Rels. Bd., Washington, 1994—98, Coun. Adminstrv. Conf. U.S., Washington, 1994—95; vis. prof. Harvard U., 1971—72; overseas fellow and vis. prof. Churchill Coll., Cambridge, England, 1975; vis. scholar U. Tokyo, 1975, 78; Fulbright-Hays Disting. lectr. Kyoto Am. Studies Summer Seminar; Charles A. Beardsley prof. Stanford Law Sch., 1984; vis. fellow Australian Nat. U. Faculty of Law, 1985; vis. prof. European U. Inst., Florence, Italy, 1988, U. Witwatersrand, Johannesburg, 1991; lectr. Am. and fgn. indsl. rels., labor law U.S., Europe, Japan, S.E. Asia, Africa, Eastern Europe. Fellow, Rockefeller Found., 1975, Guggenheim, 1978. Mem.: ABA (sec. labor and employment law sect.), Internat. Soc. for Labor Law and Social Security (exec. com. U.S. nat. br.), Nat. Acad. Arbitrators. Office: National Labor Relations Board Crown Quadrangle #310 Stanford CA 94305

GOULDEN, JOSEPH CHESLEY, author; b. Marshall, Tex., May 23, 1934; s. Joe C. and Lecta M. (Everitt) G.; m. Leslie Cantrell Smith, 1979; children by previous marriage: Joseph C., Jim Craig. Student, U. Tex., 1952-56. Reporter Marshall News Messenger, 1956, Dallas News, 1958-61, Phila. Inquirer, 1961-68. Dir. media analysis Accuracy in Media, 1989-98. Books include The Curtis Caper, 1965, Monopoly, 1968, Truth Is the First Casualty, 1969, The Money Givers, 1971, Meany, 1972, The Superlawyers, 1972, The Benchwarmers, 1974, The Best Years, 1976, The Million Dollar Lawyers, 1978, Korea: The Untold Story of the War, 1982, Jerry Wurf: Labor's Last Angry Man, 1982, The Death Merchant, 1984, (as Henry S.A. Becket) The Dictionary of Espionage, 1986, Fit to Print: A.M. Rosenthal and His Times, 1988; author: (with Paul Dickson) There Are Alligators in Our Sewers, 1983, (with Paul Dickson) Myth-Informed, 1993, (with Reed Irvine and Cliff Kincaid) The News Manipulators, 1993; editor: books include Mencken's Last Campaign, 1976. Served with U.S. Army, 1956-58. Mem.: Assn. Former Intelligence Officers, Washington Ind. Writers, Tex. Inst. Letters, H.L. Mencken Soc., Cosmos Club, Phi Kappa Tau. Home: 1534 29th St NW Washington DC 20007-3060 Office: Brandt & Hochman 1501 Broadway New York NY 10036-5601 Address: # 206 The Henlopen Rehoboth Beach DE 19971 E-mail: josephg894@aol.com.

GOULDER, CAROLJEAN HEMPSTEAD, retired psychologist, consultant; b. Houston, Minn., Apr. 9, 1933; d. Orson George and Jean Helen (Lischer) Hempstead; m. L. Lynton Goulder, Jr., May 26, 1956 (div. 1978); children: Jean Virginia, David Thomas, Ann Rachel; m. John T. Blake, Apr. 12, 1986. BS, Hamline U., 1956; CAGS, R.I. Coll., 1975, MA in Sch. Psychology, 1972; postgrad., Nova U., 1977-78. Cert. sch. psychologist, R.I. Dept. head, instr. Highsmith Hosp., Fayetteville, N.C., 1956-57; instr. nursing New Eng. Deaconess Hosp., Boston, 1957-58; dir. psychol. svcs. Burrillville Sch. Dept., Harrisville, R.I., 1972-79, sch. psychologist, 1972—2000; cons. Norton (Mass.) Schs., 2001—01; retired psychologist; embroidery quilting educator, 1992—. Coord. presch. handicapped, 1985-86; lectr. pediatric problems Sturdy Meml. Hosp., Attleboro, Mass., 1970-72; cons. Wheeler Sch., Providence, 1970-73. Chmn. 2d Congl. Ch. Sch., Attleboro, Mass., 1962-65, mem. religious edn. com., kindergarten com. and choir, 1965; active 1st Unitarian Ch., Providence, 1982-86. Mem.: APA (assoc.), Nat. Assn. Sch. Psychology (cert.), R.I. Sch. Psychologists Assn. Avocations: creative cooking, quilting, crewel embroidery, nature study, concerts. Office: 6 Dail Drive Providence RI 02911

GOULDER, DIANE KESSLER, lawyer; b. Columbus, Ohio, Apr. 27, 1950; d. Berry Lester and Shirley Lorraine (Goldstein) Kessler; m. Sidney A. Cohen, June 12, 2003; children: Jeremy, Joel, Anna Lisa. BA, Ohio State U., 1972; JD, Cornell U., 1975. Bar: Ohio 1975. Assoc. Mayer Terakedis & Weed, Columbus, 1975-76, Mayer, Terakedis & Blue Co. L.P.A., Columbus, 1976-79; pvt. practice Worthington, Ohio, 1979-85; prin. Martin, Eichenberger & Baxter Co., L.P.A., 1985-87, Martin & Eichenberger Co., L.P.A., 1987-89; ptnr. Porter, Wright, Morris & Arthur, 1989—; of counsel James J. Tansey & Assocs., Washington, 1984-85. Active Twig 173, Women's Aux. of Children's Hosp., Worthington, 1980-85; trustee Goodwill Rehab. Ctr., 1993-01, immediate past chair. Fellow Ohio State Bar Found.; mem. ABA (adj. mem. taxation com. 1979—), Ohio State Bar Assn., Ohio Women's Bar Assn., Columbus Bar Assn. (employee benefits com. 1984—), Women Lawyers Franklin County, Mortar Bd. Office: Porter Wright Morris & Arthur 41 S High St Ste 2800 Columbus OH 43215-6194 E-mail: dgoulder@porterwright.com.

GOULDEY, GLENN CHARLES, manufacturing company executive; b. N.Y.C., July 28, 1952; s. George Howard and Jeannette Ruth Williamson; m. Leslie Jeanne Ruth, Oct. 2, 1982; children: Jeremy Charles, Nicholas Glenn, Alexander James George. BS in Bus., Coll. N.J., 1976; postgrad., Portland State U., 1980; MBA, Rider U., 1981; postgrad., Dartmouth Coll., 1994-95. Cert. in purchasing mgmt., cert. in prodn. and inventory control. Sr. planner Eaton Corp., Flemington, N.J., 1975-77, pricing mgr., distbn., 1977-79, inventory control mgr., 1979-80, materials mgr., purchasing Beaverton, Oreg., 1980-81, mfg. and materials mgr., 1981-83, mktg. and materials mgr., 1983-87, plant and gen. mgr., 1987-88, v.p. sales and mktg. Carol Stream, Ill., 1988-89, mgr. ops. divsn., 1989-93, gen. bus. mgr., 1993-95, pres., gen. mgr. Lectron Products divsn. Rochester Hills, Mich., 1995-99, v.p., gen. mgr. Actuator Sensor Divsn., 2000—01; v.p. technology, planning strategy IT Eaton Automotive Group Worldwide, Rochester Hills, Mich., 2001—. Patentee in field. Mem. bd. advisors Oakland U. Bus. Sch., Mich. Colls. Found., Albion Coll.-Gerstacker Inst.; bd. dirs., chair Rochester Cmty. Schs. Found.; asst. coach lacrosse Rochester Hills United H.S. Mem. Am. Prodn. Inventory Control Soc., Nat. Youth Sports Coaches Assn. (cert.), Soc. Automotive Engrs. Internat. Republican. Lutheran. Office: Eaton Corp 1400 S Livernois Rd Rochester MI 48307-3362 E-mail: GlennGouldey@eaton.com.

GOULDIN, DAVID MILLEN, lawyer; b. Binghamton, N.Y., Mar. 8, 1941; s. Paul C. and Virginia M. Gouldin; m. Deborah A. Gouldin, Aug. 20, 1966; children: Robert, Michael, Lauryn, Derek. AB, Princeton U., 1963; JD, Cornell U., 1966. Bar: N.Y., U.S. Dist. Ct. N.Y. Ptnr. Levene, Gouldin & Thompson, LLP, Binghamton, 1966—. Mem. N.Y. State Bd. Law Examiners, 1999—. Author: (with others) Commercial Litigation in New York Courts, 1995. Chmn. Broome County (N.Y.) Arena, 1981; chmn. Broome County Health Fair, 1986-87; gen. chmn. ministry endowment campaign Broome County Coun. Chs., 1986-87; pres. United Way Broome County, 1982-84; mem. United Way N.Y. State, 1985-99, chmn., 1991-92; chancellor Wyo. conf. United Meth. Ch., 1987—; bd. dirs. Roberson Ctr. for Arts, 1983-89, United Health Svcs. Hosps., 1990-2002; bd. dirs. Broome County Urban League, 1994-2000, sec., 1995-2000; trustee Wyo. Sem., 1973-88, Millie S. Gaffney and Adelaide S. Gaffney Found., 1996—; trustee Edwin A. Link and Marion C. Link Found., 1989—, chmn., 1993—. Recipient Sertoma Svc. to Mankind Dist. award, 1988, Disting. Citizens award Baden-Powell coun. Boy Scouts Am., 1996; named to Sect. Four Hall of Fame, 1978, Outstanding Young Men of Am., 1974, Sect. IV Hall of Fame, 1978; named Man of Yr. Post 80 Am. Legion Hall of Fame, 1989. Mem. N.Y. State Bar Assn. (chmn. TICL sect. 1992, Root-Stimson award 1987, John Leach award 1999), Broome County Bar Assn. (pres. 1989), Fedn. Bar 6th Dist. (pres. 1974), Rotary. Republican. Home: 85 Highland Ave Binghamton NY 13905-4039 Office: PO Box F1706 Binghamton NY 13902-0106 E-mail: dgouldin@binghamtonlaw.com.

GOULDIN, FREDERICK CASKEY, mechanical and aerospace engineering professor; b. Washington, July 4, 1943; s. James Daniel Colman and Jane (Caskey) G.; m. Elizabeth Fairfax MacRae, Sept. 3, 1966; children: Ann Caskey, Cary Fairfax. BS in Engring., Princeton (N.J.) U., 1965, PhD, 1970. Asst. prof. Cornell U., Ithaca, N.Y., 1970-75, assoc. prof., 1975-85, prof., 1985—. Mem. rsch. staff Sandia Nat. Labs., Livermore, Calif., 1976-77; assoc. dir. mech. and aerospace engring. Cornell U., 1982-85, 98-2002, dir. combustion simulation lab., 1989-93; vis. fellow Cambridge (Eng.) U., 1985-86; poste rouge Ctr. Nat. de la Recherche Scientifique, Orléans, France, 1993; cons. GE Corp., Schenectady, N.Y., GM Corp., Warren, Mich., Sandia Nat. Labs., Corning (N.Y.) Glass, Reaction Engring. Internat., Salt Lake City. Contbr. articles to profl. jours. Mem. vestry St. John's Episcopal Ch., Ithaca, 1979-82, treas., 1974-76; bd. dirs. United Way Tompkins County, Ithaca, 1981-85. Guggenheim Jet Propulsion fellow Princeton U., 1968. Fellow AIAA (assoc.); mem. ASME, Soc. Automotive Engrs. (Teetor award 1971), Combustion Inst. (mem. exec. com. ea. sect. 1989-2001, program chair 1989-91, paper chair 1991-92, sect. chair 1997-99), Ithaca Yacht Club (commodore 1988-89, chmn. bd. dirs. 1989-90), Rotary (pres. 1994-95), Pi Tau Sigma. Avocations: sailing, skiing, hiking, photography. Office: Cornell U Upson Hall Ithaca NY 14853

GOULDIN, JUDITH ANN, nuclear medicine physician; b. Binghamton, N.Y., Nov. 20, 1947; d. Paul C. and Virginia E. (Millen) G.; m. Anthony M. Parente, May 15, 1982. AB, U. Mich., 1968; MD, Hahnemann U., 1972. Resident in internal medicine Mayo Grad. Sch. Medicine, Rochester, Minn., 1972-75; resident in nuclear medicine Stanford (Calif.) U. Hosps., 1975-77; med. dir. nuclear medicine Williamsport (Pa.) Hosp. and Med. Ctr., 1977—. Mem.: AMA, Lycoming County Med. Soc. (pres. 1994), Pa. Med. Soc., Soc. Nuclear Medicine. Office: Williamsport Hosp & Med Ctr 777 Rural Ave Williamsport PA 17701-3198

GOULDING, NORA See CLARK, SUSAN

GOULDTHORPE, KENNETH ALFRED PERCIVAL, publisher, state official; b. Jan. 7, 1928; came to U.S., 1951, naturalized, 1956; s. Alfred Edward and Frances Elizabeth Finch (Callow) G.; m. Judith Marion Cutts, Aug. 9, 1975; children: Amanda Frances, Timothy Graham Cutts. Student, U. Westminster, 1948-49; diploma, City and Guilds of London, 1949; student, Washington, 1951-52. Staff photographer Kentish Mercury, London, 1949-50, St. Louis Post-Dispatch, 1951-55, picture editor, 1955-57; nat. and fgn. corr. Life mag., Time, Inc., N.Y.C., 1957-61, Paris Bur., 1961-65, regional editor Australia-New Zealand, 1966-68, editl. dir. Latin Am., 1969-70; editor Signature mag., N.Y.C., 1970-73; mng. editor Penthouse mag., N.Y.C., 1973-76, pub. cons., 1976-79; editor, exec. pub. Adventure Travel mag., Seattle, 1979-80; sr. ptnr. Pacific Pub. Assocs., Seattle, 1979-80; editor, pub. Washington mag., 1984-89; vice-chmn. Evergreen Pub Co., 1984-89; dir. tourism State of Wash., 1989-91. Pub., cons., writer, 1991—; bd. dirs. Grand Fir Pub. Corp., Pacific Pub. Assocs., Seattle; tchr. design, editl. techniques Parsons Sch. Design, N.Y.C.; lectr., contbr. elem. schs. lit. progs. Author: Design for Music, 1998, Seafood Secrets of the Pacific Northwest, 2002; contbr. articles, photographs to nat. mags., books by Life mag. With Royal Navy, 1946-48. Decorated Naval Medal and bar; recipient awards of excellence Nat. Press Photographers Assn., AP and UP, 1951-57, Pres.'s medal Ea. Wash. U., 1986; certs. excellence Am. Inst. Graphic Arts, 1971, 72, 73, Comm. Arts, 1980, 81, 84; Spl. award N.Y. Soc. Pubs. Designers, 1980; nominated for Pulitzer Prize for coverage of Andrea Doria disaster, 1956. Mem. Regional Pubs. Assn. (v.p., pres., Best Typography award 1985, Best Spl. Issue 1989), Western Pubs. Assn. (Best Consumer Mag. award, Best Travel Mag. awards 1980, Best Regional and State Mag. award 1985, 86, 88, Best New Publ. award 1985, Best Column award 1985, Best Signed Essay 1986, 87, Best Four-Color Layout 1985, Best Four Color Design), City and Regional Mag. Assn. (William Allen White Bronze awards), Time/Life Alumni Soc., Assn. Washington Gens. (gen. of state 1995, bd. dirs.), Sigma Delta Chi. Episcopalian. Home: 3049 NW Esplanade Seattle WA 98117-2624 E-mail: kgouldthorpe@aol.net.

GOULET, CHARLES RYAN, retired insurance company executive; b. Fond du Lac, Wis., Oct. 13, 1927; s. Charles N. and Irene (Ryan) G.; m. Jeanne Comfort, Aug. 18, 1951; 1 child, Christopher Robert. BA, Beloit Coll., 1951; MBA, U. Chgo., 1953. Adminstrv. resident Jefferson-Hillman Hosp., Birmingham, Ala., 1952-53; adminstrv. asst., asst. supt. Cleve. City Hosp., 1953-55; asst. prof. U. Pitts., 1955-58; asso. dir. Johns Hopkins Hosp., 1958-62; dir. U. Chgo. Hosps. and Clinics, 1962-69; prof. hosp. adminstrn. U. Chgo., 1962-69, assoc. dir. program in hosp. adminstrn., 1962-69; prin. Cresap, McCormick and Paget, Inc.; mgmt. cons., Chgo., 1969-71; v.p. Blue Cross-Blue Shield, Chgo., 1971-75, exec. v.p., 1975-88; vice chmn., dir. H.M.O. Ill. Inc., 1980-88; exec. sec. Assn. U. Programs in Hosp. Adminstrn., 1962-65, pres. Chgo. Hosp. Council, 1968; pres. HMO Ill., Inc., 1976-82. Treas. Ill. Hosp. Assn., 1969; mem. exec. com. Council Teaching Hosps., Assn. Am. Med. Colls., 1966-69 Mem. adv. coun. Kellogg Found., 1965-67; bd. dirs. Hyde Park Dept. YMCA, 1966-68, Coop. Blood Replacement Plan, Home for destitute Crippled Children, 1965-69, Chgo. Home for Incurables, 1966-69, Harvard-St. George Sch. Chgo., 1968-72, Hosp. Planning Coun. Met. Chgo., 1968-69, Comprehensive Health Planning, Chgo., 1968-71, Ill. Regional Med. Program, 1967-69, Am. Blood Commn., 1976-89, v.p., 1978-83, Geneva (Ill.) Cmty. Chest, 1990, 93-96, pres., 1975-76; mem. governing commn. Cook County Hosp., 1969-70; mem. Ill. Health Fin. Authority, 1979-82, Ill. Health Care Cost Containment Com., 1984-96; trustee Alexian Bros. Med. Ctr., Elk Grove Village, Ill., 1993-94; bd. govs. Alexian Bros. Health Sys., 1995—; dir. Alexian Bros. Health Providers, 1996—. 1st lt. Med. Adminstrn. Corps AUS, 1946-47. Recipient Bachmeyer award U. Chgo., 1953; Disting. Service award Beloit Coll., 1976 Fellow Am. Coll. Hosp. Adminstrs.; mem. Am. Hosp. Assn., Phi Kappa Psi, Skyline Club (Chgo.), Big Foot Country Club (Fontana, Wis.), Quadrangle Club (Chgo.), Oasis Country Club (Palm Desert, Calif.).

GOULET, DENIS ANDRÉ, development ethicist, writer; b. Fall River, Mass., May 27, 1931; s. Fernand Joseph and Lumena (Bouchard) G.; m. Ana Maria Reynaldo, Nov. 21, 1964; children: Andrea, Sinane. BA in Philosophy, St. Paul's Coll., Washington, 1954, MA in Philosophy, 1956; MA in Social Planning, Institut de Recherche et de Formation en Vue du Développement, Paris, 1960; PhD in Polit. Sci., U. São Paulo, Brazil, 1963. Laborer, France, Spain, Algeria, 1956-59; planning advisor AID, Recife, Brazil, 1964-65; vis. prof. U. Sask., Regina, Can., 1965-66; assoc. prof. Ind. U., Bloomington, 1966-68; vis. fellow Ctr. for Study of Dem. Instns., Santa Barbara, Calif., 1969; fellow Ctr. for Study Devel. & Social Change, Cambridge, Mass., 1970-74; vis. prof. U. Calif., San Diego, 1969-70; sr. fellow Ctr. for Study Devel. and Social Change, Cambridge, Mass., 1970-74; vis. fellow Overseas Devel. Coun./OAS, Washington, 1974-76; sr. fellow Overseas Devel. Coun., Washington, 1976-79; O'Neill chair in edn. for justice, dept. econs. U. Notre Dame, Ind., 1979—2002, O'Neill chair emeritus, 2002—; faculty fellow Kellogg Inst. for Internat. Study, Kroc Inst. for Internat. Peace Studies. Vis. prof. U. Warsaw, Poland, 1989-90. Author: The Cruel Choice, 1971, The Uncertain Promise, 1977, Mexico: Development Strategies for the Future, 1983, Incentives for Development: The Key to Equity, 1989, Development Ethics: A Guide to Theory and Practice, 1995. Exec. bd. Internat. Dev. Ethics Assn.; editl. bd. Jour. of Health and Population in Developing Countries; internat. adv. coun. TODA Inst. for Global Peace and Policy Rsch.; internat. adv. bd. Internat. Centre for Islamic Political Economy. Decorated chevalier Odre Nat. du Cèdre (Lebanon), 1960; OAS grantee, 1961-62, Fulbright grantee, 1986; recipient Reinhold Niebuhr award U. Notre Dame, 1988. Democrat. Roman Catholic. Avocations: racquetball, piano. Home: 825 Ashland Ave South Bend IN 46616-1307 Office: U Notre Dame Dept Econs Notre Dame IN 46556-5677

GOULET, ROBERT GERARD, singer, actor; b. Lawrence, Mass., Nov. 26, 1933; s. Joseph and Jeannette (Gauthier) G.; m. Louise Longmore, 1956 (div.); 1 child, Nicolette; m. Carol Lawrence, 1963 (div.); children: Christopher, Michael; m. Vera Chochrovska Novak, 1982. Student, Royal Conservatory Music, Toronto, Ont. Made Broadway debut in Camelot, 1960; numerous stage appearances including: Carousel, 1955, Finian's Rainbow, 1956, Gentlemen Prefer Blondes, 1956, The Pajama Game, 1957, The Beggar's Opera, 1958, Bell's Are Ringing, 1959, Meet Me in St. Louis, 1960, The Happy Time, 1968 (Tony award); (Broadway plays) I Do I Do, 1970, Carousel, 1979, On a Clear Day, 1980, Kiss Me Kate, 1981, South Pacific, 1986-88, Fantasticks, 1990, Camelot as King Arthur, 1990, 92-94; (nat. tour and Broadway) South Pacific, 1995, Moon Over Buffalo, 1996, Man of La Mancha, 1996-97; star in ABC-TV series Blue Light, 1966; numerous TV spls. and guest TV appearances including The Big Valley, 1967, Police Story, 1970, Mission Impossible, 1972, Police Woman, 1975, Cannon, 1976, The Dream Merchants, 1980, Matt Houston, 1983, Glitter, 1984, Murder, She Wrote, 1985, Finder of Lost Love, 1985, Mr. Belvedere, 1986, 88, 89, 90, (CBS pilot) Make My Day, 1991, In the Heat of the Night, 1992, Based on a Untrue Story, 1992, Burke's Law, 1994, Get Smart, 1994, ESPN Coll. Basketball Commls., 1995-97; star films Honeymoon Hotel, 1964, I'd Rather Be Rich, 1964, I Deal in Danger, 1966, Underground, 1970, Atlantic City, 1981, Beetlejuice, 1988, Scrooged, 1989, Naked Gun II 1/2, 1991, Mr. Wrong, 1996, (voice) Toy Story 2, 1999, The Last Producer, 2000, G-Men From Hell, 2000; has recorded over 60 albums. Recipient numerous awards including World Theatre award, Tony award, Grammy award Best New Artist, 1962, Grammy award Gold Album for My Love Forgive Me, 1964. Fellow (hon.) Toronto Royal Conservatory Music. Fellow Royal Conservatory Music (hon.). Office: Rogo & Rove Inc 3110 Monte Rosa Ave Las Vegas NV 89120-3040

GOULETAS, EVANGELINE, investment executive; m. Hugh L. Carey, 1981. MA in Math, Northeastern Ill. State Coll. Formerly mem. faculty dept. Chgo. Bd. Edn.; prin. Am. Invsco Corp., Chgo., 1969—; ptnr. Electronic Realty Assns., IMB (Internat. Mcht. Banking), N.Y.C., 1969—. Formerly trustee DePaul U.; trustee Chgo. City Library, Com. for Thalassemia Concern; chairperson Combined Cardiac Research Women's Found., U. Chgo., N.Y. State Watch Com.; mem. exec. bd. Chgo. City Ballet, N.Y.C. Meals-On-Wheels, LaGuardia Community Coll. Recipient Great Am. award B'nai B'rith, 1977, Businesswoman of Yr. award Soc. of the Little Flower, 1979, Exec. Businesswoman of the Yr. Internat. Orgn. of Women Execs., 1980, Tree of Life Honor, Jewish Nat. Fund, 1981, Myrtle Wreath award, Nassau County Hadassah, 1981, Paedia award DePaul U., 1982, Eleanor Roosevelt Humanities award, State of Israel Bonds, 1983, humanitarian award Assn. for Children with Retarded Mental Devel., 1985, Woman of Distinction Pan Euboean Soc. of Am., 1985; two residences named in her honor Fedn. of P.R. Orgns., Bronx, United Cerebral Palsy, Staten Island; Evangeline Gouletas-Carey Leadership award presented annually in her name by LaGuardia Community Coll. of CUNY. Mem. Nat. Assn. Realtors, Inst. Real Estate Mgmt., Pres.'s Assn. of Am. Mgmt. Assn. Greek Orthodox.

GOULIANOS, KONSTANTIN, physics educator; b. Thessaloniki, Greece, Nov. 9, 1935; came to U.S., 1958, naturalized, 1967; s. Achilles and Olga (Nakopoulou) G. Student U. Thessaloniki, 1953—58; PhD, Columbia U., 1963. Research assoc. Columbia U., N.Y.C., 1963-64; instr. physics Princeton U., N.J., 1964-67, asst. prof., 1967-71; assoc. prof. physics Rockefeller U., N.Y.C., 1971-81, prof., 1981—. Patentee electronic device of analysis of radioactivitively labeled gel electrophoretograms Fulbright scholar, 1958-59 Home: 11 W 69th St Apt 4A New York NY 10023-4700 Office: Rockefeller U Lab Expt High-Energy Physics 1230 York Ave New York NY 10021-6399

GOULIAS, KONSTADINOS G. director; b. Athens, Greece, Jan. 27, 1959; m. Elizabeth L. Morrison. MSCE, U. Mich., 1987; PhD in Engring., U. Calif., 1991. Dir. Ctr. Intelligent Transp. Systems, University Park, Pa., 1997—2003, Mid-Atlantic Univs. Transp. Ctr., 2002. Author: Transportation Systems Planning. Chair com., task force Transp. Rsch. Bd., Washington, 1997—2003. Achievements include research in A regional activity-based microsimulation model called centre SIM; A demographic microsimulation model called DEMOS; 80+ Articles On Research Of Travel Behavior. Home: 201 Transp Rsch Bldg - PTI University Park PA 16802 Office: Pa State U Civil and Environ Engring 212 Sackett Bldg University Park PA 16802 Home Fax: 814-865-3039; Office Fax: 814-865-3039. Personal E-mail: goulias@psu.edu. E-mail: goulias@psu.edu.

GOULIMIS, JANET THERESA, human resources professional; b. Jackson Heights, N.Y., May 9, 1967; d. William C. and Ruth G. (Knabbe) W.; m. John G. Goulimis. Secretarial cert., Wood Sch., N.Y.C., 1986; BA in Bus. Mgmt., Marymount Manhattan Coll., 1997. Sec. Am. Home Products, N.Y.C., 1985-86; clk. typist KPMG Peat Marwick, N.Y.C., 1986-87, exec. sec., 1987-89, Ernst and Young, N.Y.C., 1989-91; sr. sec. Chase Manhattan Bank, N.A., N.Y.C., 1991-93, human resources specialist, 1993—2001; human resources assoc. Anti-Defamation League, N.Y.C., 2002—. Night coord. Blessed Sacrament Shelter Program, 1989-96. Mem. Soc. Human Resource Mgmt., Blessed Sacrament Alumni Assn. (treas. 1991-92). Democrat. Avocations: stamp collecting, music trivia, reading. E-mail: jgoulimis@msn.com.

GOUMNEROVA, LILIANA CHRISTOVA, physician, neurosurgeon, educator; b. Jakarta, Indonesia, Sept. 27, 1956; came to U.S., 1988; d. Christo Todorov and Jeanne Dimitrova (Petkova) G. BSc, Faculty of Medicine, Sofia, Bulgaria, 1977; MD, U. Toronto, 1980. Intern U. Toronto, 1980-81; resident in neurosurgery U. Ottawa, Can., 1981-86; fellow in pediatric neurosurgery Hosp. Sick Children, Toronto, 1987-88, assoc. staff neurosurgeon, 1987-88; assoc. staff surgeon Ottawa (Can.) Civic Hosp., 1986-87; Dana fellow in neurosurgery U. Pa., Phila., 1988-90; assoc. in neurosurgery Children's Hosp., Boston, 1990—, dir. clin. pediat. neurosurg. oncology, 1999—; assoc. in neurosurgery Brigham & Women's Hosp., Boston, 1990—; cons. neurosurgeon Dana Farber Cancer Inst., Boston, 1990—, dir. clin. pediat. neurosurg. oncology; asst. prof. surgery Sch. Medicine Harvard U., Boston, 1990—. Mem. Am. Assn. Neurol. Surgeons (Young Investigator award 1996). Office: Childrens Hosp 300 Longwood Ave Boston MA 02115-5737

GOUNARIDOU, KIKI, higher education educator; PhD, U. Calif., Davis, 1992. Prof. U. Pitts., 1992-99, Smith Coll., Northampton, Mass., 1999—. Office: Smith College Theater Dept Northampton MA 01063-0001 Fax: 413-585-3229. E-mail: kgounari@email.smith.edu.

GOUNLEY, DENNIS JOSEPH, lawyer; b. Jan. 29, 1950; s. George Gerard and Elizabeth Mary (Maggioncalda) G.; m. Martha Ann Zatezalo, Sept. 25, 1976. BA, St. Joseph's Coll., Phila., 1971; JD, Dickinson Sch. Law, 1974. Bar: Pa. 1974, U.S. Dist. Ct. (we. dist.) Pa. 1995, U.S. Ct. Appeals (3d cir.) 1976, U.S. Supreme Ct. 1977. Pvt. practice, Greensburg, Pa., 1974-83, 90—; ptnr. Gounley & O'Halloran, Greensburg, 1984-90. Westmoreland County mental health rev. officer, 1991—. Coun. mem. Franklin Towne Condominium Assn., Murrysville, Pa., 1976-79. Mem. Pa. Bar Assn., Westmoreland Bar Assn., Murrysville-Export Rotary Club (pres. 1999-00). Republican. Roman Catholic. Home: 3590 N Hills Rd Murrysville PA 15668-1438 Office: 15 E Otterman St Greensburg PA 15601-2543

GOUREVITCH, JACQUELINE, artist; b. Paris, Oct. 28, 1933; came to U.S., 1940; d. Henry and Sophie (Eliasberg) Herrmann; m. Victor Gourevitch, June 18, 1954; children: Marc, Philip. BA, U. Chgo., 1954; student, Black Mountain (N.C.) Coll., 1950, Art Inst. Chgo., 1955-57. Vis. artist Wesleyan U., Middletown, Conn., 1967-71, Hartford (Conn.) Art Sch., 1973-78; vis. artist, lectr. U. Calif., Berkeley, 1974, Vassar Coll., Poughkeepsie, N.Y., 1977; prof. painting and drawing Wesleyan U., 1978-89; adj. faculty Cooper Union, N.Y.C., 1989-92; vis. prof. Mt. Holyoke Coll., South Hadley, Mass., 1995. Solo exhbns. at Eleanor Rigelhaupt Gallery, Boston, 1967, 69, Tibor DeNagy, N.Y.C., 1971, 72, 73, Wadsworth Atheneum, Matrix Gallery, Hartford, 1975, Gallery Marina Dinkler, Berlin, 1988, New Britain Mus. Am. Art, New Britain, Conn., 1994, Paesaggio Gallery, West Hartford, Conn., 1993, 96, 99, DFN Gallery, N.Y.C., 2000, 02; represented in pub. collections at Wadsworth Atheneum, Menil Collection, Houston, De Cordova Mus., Lincoln., Mass., U.Calif., Berkeley, Yale U. Art Gallery, Conn. NEA grantee, 1976; Conn. Commn. on Arts grantee, 1983; Tamarind Inst. fellow, 1973. Home: 120 Duane St New York NY 10007-1113

GOURLEY, DICK R. college dean; b. Franklin, Ky., Dec. 26, 1944; m. Greta Ann Kimbrough, Dec. 7, 1968; 1 child, Kristin Marie. BS in Pharmacy, U. Tenn., 1969, D of Pharmacy, 1970. Lic. pharmacist Tenn. Asst. prof. clin. pharmacy Mercer U., Atlanta, 1970-72, prof., dean., 1984-89, Coll. Pharmacy,

U. Tenn., Memphis, 1989—; asst. prof., chmn. dept. pharmacy practice U. Nebr., Omaha, 1972-73, assoc. prof., chmn., 1973-81, prof. chmn., 1981-84. Vis. prof. U. Sydney, Australia, 1978; vis. tutor Ctrl. Inst. Tech., Upper Hutt, New Zealand, 1978; bd. dirs. Internat. Fedn. for Pharmacy Edn., MERTT, Accredo, Inc.; cons. Eli Lilly Co., 1983-85, Australian Nat. Health and Med. Rsch. Coun., 1982—, Lancaster County Bd. Lancaster Manor Nursing Home, 1981-82, Nebr. State Dept. Pub. Instns., 1976-84, Family Health Care, Inc., Omaha, 1975-84, Tri-County Meml. Hosp., Lexington, Nebr., 1975-76, Pharmacy and Therapeutics Com. Luth. Med. Ctr., Omaha, 1975, Henderson-Floyd Drugs and Shannondale Nursing Home, Knoxville, Tenn., 1971-72, Drs. Meml. Hosp. Atlanta, 1971-72, Ga. Narcotic Treatment Program, 1971-72, Grady Meml. Hosp., Atlanta, 1971-72, and numerous others; active Bd. Pharm Specialists, 1993—, vice chmn., 1994, chair 1995, 96, 97). Author: (with J. McHan) Laboratory Manual for Introductory Pharmacy, Physical Pharmacy and Pharmacy Technology, 1971; (with others) Practicing Pharmacist Handbook: Guidlines for the Establishment of High Blood Pressure Control Services by the Practicing Pharmacist, 1977, various chpts. in Pharmacy Technicians' Manual, 1988, Applied Therapeutics for Clinical Pharmacists, 1983, Clinical Pharmacy and Therapeutics, 1982, Pharmaceutics and Pharmacy Practice, 1981, Sourcebook on Clinical Pharmacy, 1980, Clinical Pharmacy and Therapeutics, 1979, Handbook of Non-Prescription Drugs, 1979, Handbook for Institutional Pharmacy Practice, 1979; editor: A Study Guide for the PCAT Examination, 1983, 3d edit., 1998; co-editor: Clinical Pharmacy and Therapeutics, 4th edit., 1988, 5th edit., 1992, Textbook of Therapeutics: Drug and Disease Management, 6th edit., 1996, 7th edit., 2000; mem. editorial bds. Topics in Hosp. Mgmt., Clin. Rsch. Practices and Drug Regulatory Affairs, World Pharmacy Sci., Am. Jour. Managed Care; published audio-visual ednl. materials; contbr. articles to profl. jours. Chmn. UNMC Coll. Pharmacy United Way Campaign, 1979-81; judge Greater Nebr. Sci. and Engring. Fair, 1973-79. Grantee Eli Lilly and Co., 1996, 97, 98, U. Nebr-Lincoln, 1979, HEW, 1976-80, Area Health Edn. Ctr., 1974, 73, Robert Wood Johnson Found., 1973-76, Novartis, 1994, 95, 96, 97, 98, Schering Plough, 1997, SKB, 1997, Roche, 1997; fellow Internat. Ctr. for Pharmacy Edn. and Rsch., 1988, U. Nebr., 1978. Mem. Am. Coun. Pharm. Edn. (mem. site team), Am. Soc. Hosp., Pharmacists (chmn., vice chmn. ASHP-ANA Joint Com., 1977-79, bd. dirs. 1981-84, del. Ho. Delegates, 1977, 78, 82, 83, 84, bd. liaison Coun. on Legal and Pub. Affairs, 1983-84, Coun. Edn. and Manpower 1982-83, Coun. Organizational Affairs, 1981-82, mem. several other coms.), Am. Assn. Colls. of Pharmacy (chmn. Sect. Teachers of Clin. Instrn. 1977-79, chmn. Coun. of Sects. 1995 —, chmn. Standing Rules of Procedure Com., 1974-76, mem. several other coms.), Am. Pharm. Assn. (del. Ho. Delegates, 1977, 88-94), Nebr. Soc. Hosp. Pharmacists (chmn. Program Com. 1979-81, co-chmn. 1976-77, Spl. Svc. to Hosp. Pharmacy award 1984), Ga. Pharmaceutical Assn., Greater Omaha Pharmacists Assn. (bd. dirs. 1974-77), Nebr. Pharmacists Assn., Tenn. Pharmacists Assn., Internat. Found. for Pharmacy Edn. (pres. 1992—), Fedn. Internat. Pharm., Soc. Hosp. Pharmacists Australia, Pan Pacific Found. (program coord. II Conf. 1979-82, III Conf. 1982—, IV Conf. 1987, chmn. V Conf. exec. v.p. 1982-92), Blue Lodge, Shriners, Phi Delta Chi (v.p. collegiate affairs 1973-78), Rho Chi (counselor region V 1976-78). Office: U Tenn Coll Pharmacy 847 Monroe Ave Memphis TN 38103-4901 E-mail: dgourley@bellsouth.net., dgourley@utmem.edu.

GOURLEY, EVERETT HAYNIE, educator; b. Hammond, Ind., Apr. 14, 1952; m. Cheryl Maureen McGuire, Sept. 25, 1974 (dec. Oct. 1978); m. Sandra Jean Lentz, Dec. 28, 1990. AA, Delta Coll., 1972; BS, Ea. Mich. U., 1974, MA, 1978. Instr. English Dowagiac (Mich.) Schs., 1975—; counselor Madison Ctr., Mishawaka, Ind., 1981-89. Adj. instr. speech Southwestern Mich. Coll., Dowagiac, 1979-81, Lake Mich. Coll., Benton Harbor, 1982-87, adj. instr. interpersonal theory Notre Dame U., South Bend, Ind., 1983-91; advisor interpersonal studies Lake Mich Coll., 1985-88, Purdue U., Westville, Ind., 1986-88; cons. in field. Author of poems. Founder strides for life Am. Cancer Soc., Southwestern Mich., 1978-87. Mem. Nat. Coun. Tchrs. English, Nat. Coun. Tchrs. Speech, Bay Striders Running Club (dir., pres.). Taoist. Avocations: ultra marathons, writing. Home: 5318 Brandy Ave Kalamazoo MI 49009-9585 Office: Dowagiac Union Schs 701 Ptairie Ronde Dowagiac MI 49047 E-mail: hayniegourley@hotmail.com.

GOURLEY, FRANK ARNETT, JR., engineering educator; b. Danville, Va., June 24, 1940; s. Frank Arnett and Georgia Davis (Bousman) G.; m. Mary Joyce Pass, June 17, 1967 (div. 1997); children: Elizabeth, F. Austin; m. Joy Genene Spangler, May 28, 2000. BSME, Va. Poly. Inst. & State U., 1962; MS in Tech. Edn., N.C. State U., 1970, EdD in Occupl. Edn., 1984. Profl. engr., N.C. Instr. engring. Va. Poly. Inst. & State U., Danville, 1962-65; rsch. asst. N.C. State U., Raleigh, 1965-66; asst. dir. engring. tech. programs N.C. Dept. C.C.'s, Raleigh, 1966-80; from coord. tech. devel. to sr. safety engr. Carolina Power & Light Co., Raleigh, 1980-90; dir. divsn. engring. tech. W.Va. U. Inst. Technology, Montgomery, 1990—. Bd. dirs. Kanawha Valley Mining Inst., Charleston, W.Va.; commr. Tech. Accreditation Commn. Accreditation Bd. Engring. Tech., 1995-2000. Author: Engineering Technology: An ASEE History, 1995, Directory of Engineering Technology Institutes and Programs, 1995; contbr. articles to profl. jours. Mem. ASME (chair com. on tech. accreditation 2000-01), Am. Soc. Engring. Edn. (numerous offices), Rotary. Avocations: music, crafts, skiing, canoeing, travel. Office: WVa U Inst Technology 218 Davis Hall Montgomery WV 25136

GOURLEY, GRETA ANN KIMBROUGH, pharmaceutical sciences educator; b. Oak Ridge, Tenn., July 23, 1946; m. Dick R. Gourley, Dec. 7, 1968; 1 child, Kristin Marie. RN, East Tenn. Bapt. Hosp. Sch. Nursing, 1967; BSN magna cum laude, U. Nebr., 1975, MSN in Cmty. Health Nursing summa cum laude, 1979, PhD in Adult Edn./Cmty. & Human Resources summa cum laude, 1983; postgrad., Mercer U., 1987-89; PharmD with highest honors, U. Tenn., 1993. Lic. nurse Tenn., Ga., Nebr.; lic. pharmacist Tenn. Staff nurse med. surg. unit East Tenn. Bapt. Hosp., Knoxville, 1967—68; staff nurse in med.-surg. and coronary care Bapt. Meml. Hosp., Memphis, 1968-70; instr. med. surg. nursing in cardiac and intensive care Ga. Bapt. Hosp. Sch. Nursing, Atlanta, 1971-72; drug studies unit nurse Nebr. Psychiat. Inst., Omaha, 1972-73; instr. cmty. health nursing Midland Luth. Sch. Nursing, Fremont, Nebr., 1979-81; rsch. asst. in health svcs. adminstrn. U. Nebr. Hosp. and Clinic, Omaha, 1981-82; asst. prof. cmty. health nursing U. Nebr. Coll. Nursing, Omaha, 1982-84; assoc. prof. cmty. health nursing Mercer U. Sch. Nursing, Atlanta, 1985—87; intern in pharmacy Germantown (Tenn.) Bapt. Hosp., 1990-91; resident in geriatric pharmacy VA Med. Ctr., Memphis, 1993-94; asst. prof. dept. pharmacy practice and pharmacoecons. U. Tenn. Coll. Pharmacy, Memphis, 1994—95, assoc. prof. dept. pharmacy practice and pharmacoecons., 1996—98, dir. ednl. experience program, 1998—2001, dir. grad. program in health sci. adminstrn., 2001—. Bd. dirs., profl. adv. com. Vis. Nurses Assn., Inc., Memphis, 1996—; pub. edn. com., state coalition bd. Tenn. Diabetes Prevention and Control Program, 1996—; cons. panel on diabetes Bayer Pharm. Co., 1997—; diabetes panel Aventis Pharms., 2001—; lectr. in field. Contbr. chpts. to gooks, articles to profl. jours. Nursing scholar East Tenn. Bapt. Hosp., 1966 Mem. ANA, Am. Pharm. Assn., Am. Soc. Hosp. Pharmacists, Am. Coll. Clin. Pharmacists, Am. Assn. Colls. Pharmacy, Tenn. Pharmacists Assn. (profl. affairs com. 1996-97), MidSouth Coll. Clin. Pharmacy, Sigma Theta Tau, Rho Chi. Office: U Tenn Coll Pharmacy 847 Monroe Ave Memphis TN 38163-0001

GOURLEY, JAMES LELAND, editor, publishing executive; b. Mounds, Okla., Jan. 29, 1919; s. Samuel O. and Lodema (Scott) G.; m. Vicki Graham Clark, Nov. 24, 1976; children: James Leland II, Janna Lynn Rousey, Kelly Clark, Brandon Clark. BA in Liberal Studies, U. Okla., 1963. Editor, pub., pres. Daily Free-Lance, Henryetta, Okla., 1946-73; pub., editor-in-chief Oklahoma City Friday, 1974—; CEO Nichols Hills Pub. Co., 1974—; pres. Suburban Graphics, Inc., 1991-93. Pres. Central Okla. Newspaper Group, 1987, 90, 93, 96, 98, 99, 2000—; pres. Sta. KHEN, KHEN-FM, Henryetta, 1955-63; pres. Hugo (Okla.) Daily News, 1953-63; chief of staff gov. Okla., 1959-63; chmn., pres. State Capitol Bank, 1962-69; v.p. sta. KXOJ Sapulpa, 1972-75; treas. Sta. KJEM-FM, Oklahoma City, 1962-67. Mem. Pres. Nat. Pub. Advisory Com. to Sec. Commerce, 1963-66; exec. dir. Gov's Comm. Higher Edn., 1960-61; Dem. candidate for gov. Okla., 1966. Dist. chmn. Boy Scouts Am., 1963-65; bd. dirs. So. Regional Edn. Bd., 1959-67, Okla. Symphony Soc., 1976-88, Oklahoma City Crimestoppers, 1982—, Salvation Army, Oklahoma City, 1985-87, Okla. Goodwill Industries, 1989-91; mem. Gov.'s Reform Com., 1984; bd. trustees Okla. City Univ., 1993—; bd. dirs. Okla. City Edn. Round Table, 1992—. Maj. AUS, 1942-46, ETO. Recipient Best Okla. Small Daily newspaper awards, 1949-58, 69-72, Best Large City Weekly newspaper awards, 1977-80, 83-85, 87-91, 94-95, 97, 98; inducted into Okla. Journalism Hall of Fame, 1980. Mem. UP Internat. Editors Okla. (pres. 1958-59), Okla. Disciples of Christ Laymen (pres. 1964-65), Suburban Newspapers Am. (dir. 1980-89), Nat. Newspaper Assn., Okla. Press Assn. (pres. 1988-89, treas. 1991-93), Oklahoma City C. of C. (dir. 1975—), Henryetta C. of C. (pres. 1955), Oklahoma City Golf and Country Club (bd. dirs. 1991-95), Econ. Club Okla., Oklahoma City Com. of 100, Rotary (pres. Oklahoma City club 1992-93), Mil. Order of World Wars, The Ret. Officers Assn., Pi Kappa Alpha. Republican. Home: 6435 Grandmark Dr Oklahoma City OK 73116-6535 Office: 10801 Quail Plaza Dr Oklahoma City OK 73120-3123 E-mail: lgourley@okcfriday.com.

GOURLEY, JAMES WALTER, III, airport executive; b. L.A., Jan. 8, 1941; s. James Walter and Eleanor Mae (Kanel) G.; children: Jennifer Lane, Matthew James; m. Dana C. Matthews, Dec. 20, 1986; stepchildren: Lance, Wendee. AA, Fullerton Coll., 1960; BS in Geology cum laude, U. Redlands, 1962; MS in Earth Scis., U. So. Calif., 1971; Exec. Mgmt. Program, Pa. State U., 1989. Cert. profl. geologist, Calif. Petroleum engr., geologist Standard Oil Calif., La Habra, 1964-72; supr. energy planning, mgr. energy resources So. Calif. Gas Co., L.A., 1972-80, mgr. supply forecasting, 1980-82, mgr. underground storage, 1982-86, mgr. pub. affairs planning, 1986-89, mgr. West Valley divsn., 1989-92, mgr. Inland Empire Region, 1992-98; exec. dir. Inland Valley Devel. Agy./San Bernardino Airport Authority, 1998-00; econ. devel. and transportation cons., 2001—. Adj. prof. U. Redlands, 2003—. Bd. mem. Inland Empire Econ. Partnership, 1992—, chmn., 1997; adv. bd. Sch. Bus. and Mgmt., U. Redlands, 2000—; adj. faculty, 2003—; bd. dirs. Cmty. Water and Sewer Dist., 2001—. Republican. Home: PO Box 5301 Blue Jay CA 92317-5301 Fax: 909-337-7618. E-mail: arrow.head2@verizon.net.

GOURLEY, VICKI CLARK, publishing executive; b. Lawton, Okla., Aug. 31, 1946; d. Tom L. Graham and Mary Helen McKenzie; m. Jerry Allan Clark, Aug. 23, 1965 (div. Sept. 1974); children: Kelly Brett, Brandon Graham; m. James Leland Gourley, Nov. 24, 1976. Student, Okla. State U., 1963-66, 71-73. Adminstrv. asst. Anaheim (Calif.) H.S. Dist., 1966-71; mng. editor Oklahoma City Friday, 1974-76, exec. editor, 1976—; pres. Nichols Hills Pub. Co., Oklahoma City, 1976-99, chmn., 1999—. Cons. Suburban Graphics, Inc., Oklahoma City, 1990-98, Ctrl. Okla. Newspaper Group, Oklahoma City, 1980—; com. chmn. Suburban Newspaper Am., Chgo., 1993-95. Photographer Crossing America, 1994. Pres. The Christmas Connection, 1986-90, Cmty. Literacy Ctr., Oklahoma City, 1991-94; commr. Govs. Literacy Commn., Oklahoma City, 1991 99, Nichols Hills (Okla.) Park Bd., 1995-99; bd. mem. Oklahoma Symphony Soc., Oklahoma City, 1990-92, The Village (Okla.) CrimeStoppers, 1990-98; co-chmn. Nichols Hills Employees Scholarship Fund Program, 1997—, Okla. State U. Bring Dreams to Life Drive, Stillwater, 1999-2000. Recipient Golden Rule award J.C. Penney Co., Oklahoma City, 1992, Humanitarian award Nat. Conf. Christians and Jews, Oklahoma City, 1997, Lt. Govs. Media awad Cmty. Literacy Ctr., Oklahoma City, 1992; named Exec. Woman of Yr., High Noon Club, Oklahoma City U., 2000, Woman Vol. Yr., Byliners Club, Oklahoma City, 1993, Woman Vol. Yr., Girl Scouts Am., Oklahoma City, 1997. Mem. Nat. Newspaper Assn., Okla. Press Assn. (conv. chmn. 1991-92), Soc. for Profl. Journalists, Rotary Anns Oklahoma City (pres. 1987-88), Delta Delta Delta. Republican. Methodist. Avocations: traveling, reading, scuba diving. Home: 6435 Grandmark Dr Nichols Hills OK 73116 Office: Oklahoma City Friday PO Box 20340 Oklahoma City OK 73156 also: Nichols Hills Pub Co PO Box 20340 Oklahoma City OK 73156-0340 E-mail: vcgfriday@aol.com.

GOURVITZ, ELLIOT HOWARD, lawyer; b. Lewiston, Pa., Sept. 21, 1945; s. Louis and Irene (Brass) Gourvitz; m. Bonnie S. Hirsch; children: Evan, Amy, Ross, Ari. BA, Rutgers U., 1966, JD, 1969. Bar: N.J. 1969, N.Y. 1985, U.S. Dist. Ct. N.J. 1969, U.S. Dist. Ct. (ea. dist.) Wis. 1985, U.S. Ct. Appeals 93d cir.) 1972, U.S. Ct. Appeals (2d, 4th, 5th, 7th, 8th, 9th, 10th, and fed. cirs.) 1982, U.S. Tax Ct. 1970, U.S. Ct. Claims 1970, U.S. Ct. Internat. Trade 1985, U.S. Supreme Ct. 1973, cert.: N.J. (matrimonial atty.). Pvt. practice, Springfield. Chmn., Early Settlement Panel of Union County, NJ; panelist Essex and Middlesex Counties. Contbr. articles to profl. jours. Named Man of Yr., United Cerebral Palsy League Union County, 1980. Fellow: Internat. Acad. Matrimonial Lawyers, Am. Acad. Matrimonial Attys. (pres. N.J.); mem.: N.Y. State Bar Assn., N.J. Bar Assn., Am. Coll. Trial Lawyers (diplomate).

GOUSE, S. WILLIAM, JR., engineering executive, scientist; b. Utica, N.Y., Dec. 15, 1931; s. S. William and Charlotte Virginia G.; m. Jacqueline Ann McLaughlin, Aug. 6, 1955; children: Linda Ellen, S. William III. S.B., S.M., Mass. Inst. Tech., 1954, Sc.D., 1958. Instr. mech. engring. MIT, 1956-57, asst. prof., 1957-61, 62-65, assoc. prof., 1965-67, lectr., 1967-68; prof. mech. engring., prin. rsch. engr. Transp. Rsch. Inst., Carnegie-Mellon U., 1967-69; staff mem. Office Sci. and Tech. of Exec. Office of the Pres., Washington, 1969-70; assoc. dean Carnegie Inst. Tech. and Sch. Urban and Pub. Affairs Carnegie-Mellon U., 1971-73, dir. Environ. Studies Inst., 1971-73, adj. prof. engring. and pub. policy, 1980-90; dir. Office R&D, sci. advisor to sec. U.S. Dept. Interior, 1973-75; acting dir. Office Coal Rsch., 1974-75; dep. asst. adminstr. fossil energy ERDA, 1975-77; chief scientist MITRE Corp., 1977-79, v.p., 1979-80, v.p., gen. mgr. Ctr. for Civil Systems, 1980-84, sr. v.p., gen. mgr. Ctr. for Civil Systems, 1984-90, 1990-92, sr. v.p., 1992-94; mng. dir. Energy Sys. and Tech., 1994—. Cons. and mem. panels various industry and govt. agys. including U.S. Dept. Commerce, U.S. Office Sci. and Tech., NSF; mem. rsch. adv. com. Electric Power Rsch. Inst., 1973-76; chmn. rev. adv. bd. on coal liquefaction Internat. Energy Agy., Paris, 1981-82; mem. energy engring. bd. NRC, 1985-88; U.S. rep. to com. energy conservation in indsl. processes World Energy Conf., 1984-89; mem. com. on environ. and energy aspects of waste handling World Energy Coun., vice chmn. com. on efficient use of energy utilization using high tech.; mem. adv. bd. Aspen Inst. Humanistic Studies Com. Pub. Policy Issues Energy and Resources, 1982-95; internat. adv. bd. World Energy Coun.; dir. Colshire Group, 1997; tech. advisor AB Volvo, 1996-2000; tech. adv. bd. Earth First Techs., 2002—; assoc. dir. Aspen Inst., 1996. Editorial bd. Internat. Jour. Environ. Studies, 1971-81; editor-in-chief Energy Systems and Policy, 1973-93; assoc. editor Energy Sources, 1994-2001; contbr. to books, profl. jours., and congl. testimony. Mem. vis. com. mech. engring. dept. MIT, 1978-85. Served with ordnance AUS, 1961-62. Visking Corp. fellow, 1954-55; GE W. Rice Jr. fellow, 1955-56; recipient Ralph Teetor award Soc. Automotive Engrs., 1966; Sir A.L. Mudslior lectr in tech. Al Alagappa Chettiar Coll. Tech., U. Madras, 1969; Disting lectr. mech. engring. Pa. State U., 1980; recipient Outstanding Svc. award No. Area Environ. Coun., Allegheny County, Pa., 1973, Meritorious Svc. award ERDA, 1976, 60th Lord Melchett Medal Lectr. Inst. Energy London, 1994. Fellow ASME, AIAA (assoc.); mem. AAAS, SAE, U.S. Energy Assn. (bd. dirs. 1987-88, 91-92, audit com. 1992—), Internat. Com. Coal Rsch., Cosmos Club, Explorers Club, Tower Club. E-mail: swgjmg@alum.mit.edu.

GOUTERMAN, MARTIN PAUL, chemistry educator; b. Phila., Dec. 26, 1931; s. Bernard and Melba (Buxbaum) G.; 1 child, Mikaelin BlueSpruce. BA, U. Chgo., 1951, MS, 1955, PhD in Physics (NSF Predoctoral fellow), 1958. Faculty Harvard U., Cambridge, Mass., 1958-66, postdoctoral fellow to asst. prof. chemistry dept.; mem. faculty U. Wash., Seattle, 1966—, prof. chemistry, 1968-99, prof. emeritus, 2000—. Fellow Am. Inst. Physics; mem. Am. Chem. Soc., Sigma Xi. Achievements include research and publications in spectroscopy and quantum chemistry of porphyrins and their use as luminescence sensors for biomedical and aeronautical application, in particular pressure sensitive paint; developed BS degree program in biochemistry and a chemistry minors program. Office: U Wash Chemistry Box 351700 Seattle WA 98195-1700

GOUTMAN, LOIS CLAIR, retired drama educator; b. Clairton, Pa., Apr. 14, 1923; m. Dolya Goutman, Mar. 10, 1947; children: Andrew, Christopher, Thomas. BFA in Drama, Carnegie-Mellon U., 1944. Tchr., head drama dept. Baldwin Sch., Bryn Mawr, Pa.; ret. Dir. St. Thomas Players, Circle Theatre, L.A., Carnegie Tech. Drama Sch.; asst. dir. Actors' Lab., L.A., Arlington Films; presenter workshops in field; instr. theatre studies program Rosemont Coll. Forum, Pa. Appeared in various theatrical prodns., including The Tempest; writer, performer of one woman play Edith Wharton; dir. play reading group of srs. Surrey Sr. Svcs., Berwyn, Pa. Stanford U. fellow, Nat. Theatre Conf. alt. fellow, 1947; recipient Olmsted prize Williams Coll., Williamstown, Mass., 1992; holder first Rosamond Cross Chair in Teaching, The Baldwin Sch., 1991; teaching chair endowed in her honor Baldwin Sch. Mem. Am. Edn. Theatre Assn., Am. Alliance for Theatre and Edn., Theatre Edn. Assn., Actors' Equity. Avocations: theatre, concerts, reading, art exhibitions. Home: 314 Williams Rd Bryn Mawr PA 19010-1214

GOUVERNET, GERARD RAOUL, language educator; b. Aigues Vives, Gard, Sept. 19, 1939; s. Raoul Mariyos Gouvernet and Andrée Rose Pinol; m. Suzanne d'Autremont Gouvernet, Mar. 30, 1968; 1 child, Philippe. PhD, Harvard U., 1978. Prof. dept. fgn. lang. SUNY, Geneseo, 1982—. Author: (book) Le Valet chez Molière et ses successeurs, 1985; co-author: Homage to Paul Benichou, 1994, Dictionnaire Analytique du Théâtre, 1998. Avocations: reading, tennis, Pétanque. Home: 61 Pelham Rd Rochester NY 14610 Office: SUNY College Dept Fgn Lang 1 College Cir Geneseo NY 14454-1401 E-mail: gouverne@genesco.edu.

GOUWENS, KENNETH VELD, history educator; b. Niles, Mich., May 28, 1959; s. Robert Veld and Joyce Moore Gouwens; m. Joan Ellen Meznar, May 11, 1996. BA in History with distinction, Duke U., 1981; MA in History, Stanford U., 1986, PhD in History and Humanities, 1991. Asst. prof. U. S.C., Columbia, 1991-98; asst. prof. dept. history U. Conn., Storrs, 1998-2000, assoc. prof., 2000—. Vis. asst. prof. dept. history U. Calif., Santa Barbara, 1996-97. Fulbright fellow, Rome, 1987—88, short-term fellow, The Newberry Libr., 1993, 1999, Andrew W. Mellon fellow, Harvard U. Ctr. Renaissance Studies, Florence, Italy, 1997—98, Phyllis G. Gordan fellow, Am. Acad. Rome, 2002—03. Mem.: Am. Cath. Hist. Assn., Soc. for Reformation Rsch., New Eng. Renaissance Conf. (pres. 1999—), Renaissance Soc. Am. (exec. com. 1997—2000). Avocations: playing jazz flugelhorn, swimming. Office: Dept History U-103 U Conn 241 Glenbrook Rd Storrs CT 06269-2103 E-mail: clement.7@uconn.edu.

GOVAN, GLADYS VERNITA MOSLEY, retired critical care and medical/surgical nurse; b. Tyler, Tex., July 24, 1918; d. Stacy Thomas and Lucy Victoria (Whitmill) Mosley; m. Osby David Govan, July 20, 1938; children Orbrenett K. (Govan) Carter, Diana Lynn (Govan) Mosley. Student, East Los Angeles Coll., Montebello, Calif., 1951; lic. vocat. nurse, Calif. Hosp. Med. Ctr., L.A., 1953; cert., Western States IV Assn., L.A., 1978. Lic. vocat. nurse, Calif.; cert. in EKG. Intravenous therapist Calif. Hosp. Med. Ctr., cardiac monitor, nurse; ret. Past pres. PTA, also hon. mem., 1963-2000; charter mem. Nat. Rep. Presdl. Task Force.

GOVE, SAMUEL KIMBALL, political science educator; b. Walpole, Mass., Dec. 27, 1923; Student, Mass. State Coll., 1941-43; BS in Econs, U. Mass., 1947; MA in Polit. Sci, Syracuse U., 1951. Research asst. govt. and pub. affairs U. Ill., 1950-51, research asso., 1951-54, mem. faculty, 1954—, prof. polit. sci., 1966-89, prof. emeritus, 1989—, dir. Inst. Govt. and Pub. Affairs, 1967-85, dir. emeritus, 1987—. Staff asst. Nat. Assn. Assessing Officers, 1949; mem. rsch. staff Ill. Commn. Study State Govt., 1950—51; staff fellow Nat. Mcpl. League, 1955—56; exec. asst. Ill. Auditor Pub. Accounts, 1957; program coord. Ill. Legis. Staff Intern Program, 1962—70; mem. com. financing higher edn. Ill. Master Plan Higher Edn., 1963; mem. Ill. Commn. Orgn. Gen. Assembly, 1965—69, 1970—73, Ill. Commn. State Govt., 1965—67; cons. elections ABC, 1964, 66, 68; chmn. Champaign (Ill.) County Econ. Opportunity Coun., 1966—67; state legis. rsch. fellow Am. Polit. Sci. Assn., 1966—68; cons. Am. Council Edn., 1966—67; sec. Local Govts. Commn., 1967—69; staff dir. Ill. Constn. Study Commn., 1968—69; exec. sec. Gov. Ill. Constn. Research Group, 1969—70; mem. Ill. Constn. Study Commn., 1969—70; chmn. Citizens Task Force on Constl. Implementation, 1970—71; mem. Gov. Elect's Task Force on Transition, 1972, 1991—92; adv. coun. Ill. Dept. Local Govt. Affairs, 1969—79, Gov.'s Human Resources, 1991—93, Ill. Commn. on Regulatory Rev., 1994—98, Ill. Bd. Higher Edn., 1998—, Ill. Issues Bd., 1974, chmn. bd. dirs., 1974—93. Lt. j.g. USNR, 1943—46. Fellow Nat. Acad. Pub. Adminstrn.; mem. AAUP (past chpt. pres., mem. nat. com. R 1969-75, 78-84, nat. coun. 1978-80), Am. Polit Sci. Assn., Am. Soc. Pub. Adminstrn. (past chpt. chmn.; chmn. univs. govtl. rsch. conf. 1969-71), Govtl. Rsch. Assn. (dir. 1969-71), Ill. Hist. Soc., Midwest Polit. Sci. Assn. (v.p. 1978-80), Nat. Mcpl. League (council 1972-80, 81-84, 85), Nat Civic League (coun. advisors 1987-89), Cosmos Club. Home: 2006 Bruce Dr Urbana IL 61801-6419 Office: 1007 W Nevada St Urbana IL 61801-3812 E-mail: s.govc@uiuc.edu.

GOVE, WALTER R. sociology educator; b. June 8, 1938; married; 2 children. BS, SUNY, Syracuse, 1960; MA in Sociology, U. Wash., 1967, PhD in Sociology, 1968. From asst. prof. to assoc. prof. Vanderbilt U., Nashville, 1968-75, prof. sociology, 1975—, dir. grad. studies, 1985-86. Dir. NIMH Grad. Tng. Program, 1972-76; organizer confs., symposia in field; participant profl. confs., presenter in field. Author: (with Michael Geerken) At Home and at Work: The Family's Allocation of Labor, 1983; (with Michael Hughes) Household Crowding: Social and Structural Determinants of Its Effects, 1983; editor: Deviance and Mental Illness, 1982, co-editor: Labelling Deviant Behavior: Evaluating a Perspective, 1975, 2 edit., 1980, The Fundamental Connection Between Nature and Nurture, 1982, A Feminist Perspective in the Academy, 1983; adv. editor Social Forces, 1971-74; cons. editor Am. Jour. Sociology, 1974-76, Women and Politics, 1978-86; assoc. editor Social Sci. Rsch., 1974—, Social Psychology Quarterly, 1978-80, Jour. Health and Social Behavior, 1981-83, 97—, Jour. Family Issues, 1984-92; contbr. articles to profl., non-profl. jours., book revs. Recipient Reuben Hill award Nat. Coun. Family Rels., 1979; grantee PHS, 1963-65, 71-76, 79-82, NSF, 1973-77, 93, Dept. Justice, 1984-85, Okla. Dept. Corrections, 1993-94, Ethel Mae Wilson Found., 1980-81, Shell Found., 1974, others. Fellow: AAAS; mem.: So. Sociol. Soc. (pres.-elect 1992—93, pres. 1993—94, exec. coun., program com. 1986), Am. Sociol. Assn. (liaison com. to AAAS 1990—94, Leo Reeder award for disting. svc. to med. sociology 2003), Am. Soc. Criminology, Sociology Rsch. Assn., Soc. Study of Social Problems (Outstanding Scholarship and Svc. to Psychiat. Sociology award 1989). Avocations: numerous first ascents as mountaineer, primarily in alaska. Office: Vanderbilt U PO Box 1811 Nashville TN 37235-1811 E-mail: walter.r.gove@vanderbilt.edu.

GOVER, ALAN SHORE, lawyer; b. Lyons, N.Y., Sept. 5, 1948; s. Norman Marvin and Beatrice L. (Shore) Gover; m. Ellen Rae Ross, Dec. 4, 1976; children: Maxwell Ross, Mary Trace. AB, Tufts U., 1970; JD, Georgetown U., 1973. Bar: Tex. 1973, U.S. Dist. Ct. (so. dist.) Tex. 1974, U.S. Ct. Appeals (5th cir.) 1974, U.S. Dist. Ct. (we. dist.) Tex. 1976, U.S. Supreme Ct. 1976, U.S. Dist. Ct. Appeals (DC cir.) 1977, U.S. Ct. Appeals (2d cir.) 1979, DC 1980, U.S. Ct. Appeals (8th, 9th and 11th cirs.) 1981, U.S. Dist. Ct. (no. dist.) Tex. 1988, U.S. Dist. Ct. (ea. dist.) Tex. 1990. Assoc. Baker & Botts, Houston, 1973-80, ptnr., 1981-85, Weil, Gotshal & Manges, Houston, 1985—2001, Dewey Ballantine LLP, Houston, 2001—. Co-author: (book) The Texas Nonjudicial Foreclosure Process, 1990; editor, chmn. editl. bd. P. L. I. Oil and Gas and Bankruptcy Laws, 1985. Trustee Houston Ballet, 1986, 2003—, v.p., 1993—96; chmn. ann. fund St. John's Sch., Houston, 1993—95, trustee, 1996—, Retina Rsch. Found., Houston, 1996—; chmn. East Downtown Mgmt. Dist., Houston, 2000—; v.p. Congregation Beth Israel, Houston, 1996—2001, pres., 2001—. Fellow: Tex. Bar Found.; mem.: ABA, N.Y. Athletic Club, Coronado Club, The Argyle (San Antonio). Jewish. Office: Dewey Ballantine LLP 700 Louisiana St Ste 1900 Houston TX 77002

GOVER, RAYMOND LEWIS, retired newspaper executive; b. Somerset, Ky., Dec. 5, 1927; s. Raymond Bolen and Leslie Fay (Silvers) G.; m. Frieda Jane McGill, July 27, 1957; children: Janine Gover Park, Mark H., Janet L., Matthew R. BA, U. Mich., Ann Arbor, 1951; PhD (hon.), Shippensburg U., 1996. Reporter Port Huron Times, Mich., 1951-54; reporter, asst. city editor, city editor The Jour., Flint, Mich., 1954-70, editor, 1976-78; editor, pub. The News, Saginaw, Mich., 1970-76, 78-81; pub. The Patriot News, Harrisburg, Pa., 1981-97; pres. Patriot News Co., Harrisburg, 1997-2001. Bd. dirs. Hershey Trust Co. Bd. dirs. Ctrl. Pa. Hospice, 2000-01, YMCA, Harrisburg, 1984-90, Harrisburg Symphony Orch., Milton Hershey Sch.; v.p. Tri-County United Way, Harrisburg; bd. adv. Pa. State U., Harrisburg; trustee. v.p. Pa. Newspaper Pubs. Found., Pine St. Presbyn. Ch., Harrisburg, Greater Harrisburg Found. Mem. Newspaper Assn. Am., Pa. Newspaper Assn. (bd. dirs. 1987—, pres. 1990-91), Am. Soc. Newspaper Editors, Mich. Press Assn. (bd. dirs. 1978-81), Soc. Profl. Journalists, West Shore Country Club (mem. bd. govs. 1991-95), Tuesday Club, Masons. Avocations: golf, fishing, hunting. Home: 905 Grandon Way Mechanicsburg PA 17050-9171 Office: Patriot-News Co PO Box 2265 812 Market St Harrisburg PA 17101-2827 E-mail: gover@pnco.com., gover@epix.net.

GOVERN, FRANK STANLEY, health facility administrator, consultant, healthcare educator, writer; b. Plainfield, NJ, May 18, 1951; s. Fred John and Jane Louise (Schweitzer) Govern; m. Patricia Loretta Hermanns, Aug. 19, 1972; children: Jason, Heather. AAS, Middlesex County Coll., 1973; BA, Salem State Coll., 1979; MAS, Johns Hopkins U., 1981; PhD in law, policy, and soc., Northeastern U., 1997. Asst. adminstrn. Circle Terrace Hosp., Alexandria, Va., 1981-84; CEO Tyrone (Pa.) Hosp., 1984—85; pres., CEO Charles River Hosp., Wellesley, Mass., 1985—86; COO Joint Ctr. Radiation Therapy, Boston, 1986—98; dep. dir. radiation oncology scis. program, chief oncology outreach, radiation rsch. Nat. Cancer Inst., Bethesda, Md., 1998—. Sr. instr. Northeastern U., Boston, 1986—98; instr. Harvard Med. Sch., Boston, 1986—98. Author: U.S. Health Policy and Problem Definition: A Policy Process Adrift, 2000; contbr. chapters to books, articles to profl. jours. Founder, pres. Cmty. for Ednl. Excellence, Beverly, Mass., 1991. Capt. USAF, 1974—76. Avocations: cycling, reading, writing, skiing. Home: 11908 Bristol Manor Ct North Bethesda MD 20852-5804 Office: NCI Exec Plz N 6130 Exec Blvd Ste 6020 Bethesda MD 20892

GOVETT, BRETT CHRISTOPHER, lawyer; b. Corpus Christi, Tex., May 17, 1965; s. Raymond Weston and Martha Lenora (Barton) G.; m. Cynthia Lynn Rowell, June 5, 1993. BA in Chemistry cum laude, The Citadel, 1987; JD cum laude, Tex. Tech U., 1990. Bar: Tex. 1990, U.S. Ct. Appeals (5th cir.) 1990, U.S. Dist. Ct. (so. dist.) Tex. 1990, U.S. Dist. Ct. (no. dist.) Tex. 1991, U.S. Supreme Ct. 1998; cert. civil trial law, Tex. bd. legal specialization; reg. U.S. Patent and Trademan. Jud. clk. for Judge Reynaldo G. Garza U.S. Ct. Appeals (5th cir.), Brownsville, Tex., 1990-91; assoc. Fulbright & Jaworski L.L.P., Dallas, 1991-98, ptnr., 1999—. Note editor Tex. Tech. Law Rev., 1989-90, contbr. articles. Mem. ABA, Tex. Bar Assn., Dallas Bar Assn.,, Am. Inn. of Ct. (barrister Patrick Higginbothom), Order of Coif. Office: Fulbright & Jaworski LLP 2200 Ross Ave Ste 2800 Dallas TX 75201-2784 E-mail: bgovett@fulbright.com.

GOVIC, RUDOLF, structural engineer; b. Sibenik, Croatia, May 21, 1971; came to the U.S., 1976; s. Joso and Volga (Tanfara) G. B in Engring., Stevens Inst. Tech., 1994, M in Engring., 1996. Engr.-in-tng., N.J. Summer mgmt. intern Port Authority N.Y. and N.J., Newark, 1995; project engr. Paul Beck Assocs., P.A., Fairfield, N.J., 1996—. Engring. technician U.S. Army Corps Engrs., 1991. Mem. ASCE (assoc.), Am. Concrete Inst. Roman Catholic. Avocations: stamp collecting, swimming, coin collecting, aviation. Office: Paul Beck Assocs 12 Kulick Rd Fairfield NJ 07004-3308

GOVIL, MANISH KUMAR, customer service administrator; s. Yogendra Kumar and Usha Govil; m. Kermin Gandhi, Apr. 18, 2000; 1 child, Mishika. B of Tech., Indian Inst. of Tech., India, 1995; MS, U. of Md., 1997, PhD, 1999. Cons. i2 Technologies, Parsipanny, NJ, 1998—2000, product mgr. Cambridge, 2000—01, customer success mgr. Dallas, 2001—. Author: (book) Supply Chain Design and Mgmt.: Strategic and Tactical Perspectives, (dissertation) Integrating Product Design and Production: Designing for Time-to-Market; contbr. jour. paper, conf. paper. Fellow Grad. Sch. Fellowship, U. of Md., 1995—98. Mem.: Soc. of Mfg. Engrs., Student Chpt. 66 (activities chair 1996—98), ASME (assoc.), Omicron Delta Kappa, Phi Kappa Phi, Student Senate, IIT Kanpur (senator 1993—95, chief election officer 1994—95, parliamentarian 1994—95), Student's Coun. of India, U. of Md. (pres. 1996—98). Achievements include research in New design methodology, design for Time-to-Market. Office: i2 Technologies 11701 Luna Rd Dallas TX 75234

GOVIL, NARENDRA KUMAR, mathematics educator; b. Aligarh, India, Jan. 5, 1940; arrived in U.S., 1983; s. Panna Lal and Kamla Devi (Agrawal) G.; m. Urmila Agrawal, Feb. 1, 1964; children: Sanjay, Sandeep. BSc, Agra (India) U., 1957; MSc, Aligarh (India) U., 1959; PhD, U. Montreal, Que., Can., 1968. Lectr. Concordia U., Montreal, 1967-68, asst. prof., 1968-70, Indian Inst. Tech., New Delhi, 1970-78, assoc. prof., 1978-80, prof., 1980-85; assoc. prof. Auburn (Ala.) U., 1985-86, prof., 1986—. Vis. scientist Dalhousie U., Halifax, Canada, 1980; vis. prof. U. Alberta, Edmonton, Canada, 1981, Auburn U., 1983—85; mem. exec. com. Forum Interdisciplinary Math, Delhi, 1989—91; reviewer Math. Reviews; mem. editl. bd. Archives of Inequalities and Applications, Internat. Jour. Math. and Math. Sci., Internat. Jour. Nonlinear Differential Equations, Pan-Am. Math. Jour., 1994—98, Jour. Inequalities and Applications, 2000—02. Co-editor 2 books; contbr. articles. Mem. exec. India Cultural Assn. East Ala., Auburn, 1986, 96-97. Fellow: Nat. Acad. Scis. India (life); mem.: Indian Math Soc. (life), India Cultural Assn. East Ala. (pres. Auburn 1991). Avocations: music, reading. Home: 523 Owens Rd Auburn AL 36830-2513 Office: Auburn Univ Dept Math Auburn AL 36849 E-mail: govilnk@auburn.edu.

GOVINDJEE, biophysics, biochemistry, and biology educator; b. Allahabad, India, Oct. 24, 1933; came to U.S., 1956, naturalized, 1972; s. Vishveshwar Prasad and Savitri Devi Asthana; m. Rajni Varma, Oct. 24, 1957; children: Anita Govindjee, Sanjay Govindjee. BSc, U. Allahabad, 1952, MSc, 1954; PhD, U. Ill., 1960. Lectr. botany U. Allahabad, 1954-56; grad. fellow U. Ill., Urbana, 1956-58, research asst., 1958-60, USPHS postdoctoral trainee biophysics, 1960-61, mem. faculty, 1961—, assoc. prof. botany and biophysics, 1965-69, prof. biophysics and plant biology, 1969-99, disting. lectr. Sch. Life Scis., 1978, emeritus prof. biophysics, plant biology and biochemistry, 1999—. Author (with E. Rabinowitch): Photosynthesis, 1969; editor: Bioenergetics of Photosynthesis, 1975, Photosynthesis: Energy Conversion by Plants and Bacteria Carbon Assimilation and Plant Productivity, 2 vols., 1982 (Russian transl. 1987); co-editor: The Oxygen Evolving System of Photosynthesis, 1983, Light Emission by Plants and Bacteria, 1986, Excitation Energy and Electron Transfer in Photosynthesis, 1989, Molecular Biology of Photosynthesis, 1989, Photosynthesis: From Photoreactions to Productivity, 1993, Concepts in Photobiology: Photosynthesis and Photomorphogenesis, 1999; editor Hist. Corner: Photosynthesis Rsch., 1989—; guest editor spl. issue Biophys. Jour., 1972, Photochemistry and Photobiology, 1978, Photosynthesis Research, 1993, 96, 2002-04; editor-in-chief Photosynthesis Rsch., 1985-88; series editor: Advances in Photosynthesis and Respiration, vol. 1, 1994, vol. 2, 1995, vols. 3, 4 and 5, 1996, vols. 6 and 7, 1998, vol. 8, 1999, vol. 9, 2000, vols. 10 and 11, 2001, vol. 12, 2002, vol. 13, 2003; contbr. articles to profl. jour., also Sci. Am. Fulbright scholar, 1956-61, 96-97. Fellow AAAS, NAS (India); mem. Am. Soc. Plant Biologists, Biophys. Soc. Am., Am. Soc. Photobiology (coun. 1976, pres. 1981), Internat. Photosynthesis Soc. (exec. com., publ. com. 1995-01), Sigma Xi (emeritus). Home: 2401 Boudreau Dr Urbana IL 61801-6655 E-mail: gov@uiuc.edu.

GOW, LINDA YVONNE CARIGNAN CHERWIN, travel executive; b. Plymouth, N.H., Dec. 15, 1948; d. Roger and Alice Mary (Theriault) Carignan; m. James T. Gow Jr., Aug. 29, 1987 (dec.); 1 child, Alison. Student, Rivier Coll., 1966-68, Whittemore Sch. Bus., 1976-79. Asst. mgr. Travel New Horizons, Peterborough, N.H., 1972-76; mgr. Garnsey Bros. Travel, Sanford, Maine, 1976-77; gen. mgr. R-W Travel, Dover, NH, 1977—84; pres., owner The Travel Pro, Somersworth, N.H., 1984—. Owner Cruise Quarters, Somersworth, 1988—. Sponsor Internat. Children's Festival, Somersworth, 1985—; mem. Gov.'s Pvt. Industry Council, 1987, 88. The Travel Pro named Bus. of Yr., Somerworth C. of C., 2001. Mem. Am. Retail Travel Agts. Assn., Cruise Lines Internat. Assn., Rochester C. of C., Somersworth C. of C., Seacoast Widowed Persons Assn. (bd. dirs. 2000—), Rotary Internat. (Somersworth chpt.). Office: The Travel Pro 394 High St Somersworth NH 03878-1420

GOWA, ANDREW, real estate investor, lawyer; b. N.Y.C., Nov. 6, 1949; s. Everett M. and Louise (Friedman) G.; m. Robin P. Lincoln May 21, 1995; children: Catherine J., Jon T., Timothy M., Melissa Lincoln, Jennifer Lincoln. AB magna cum laude, Tufts U., 1971; JD, U. Pa., 1974. Bar: Pa. 1974, N.Y. 1982. From assoc. to ptnr. Blank, Rome, Comisky & McCauley, Phila., 1974-84; sr. v.p North Atlantic Investment Corp., Phila., 1984-85; pres., chief exec. officer First Equity Devel. Corp., West Chester, Pa., 1984-90; ptnr. Schnader Harrison Segal & Lewis LLP, Phila., 1990—2002; chmn. Gowa Lincoln, PC, Phila., 2002—. Bd. dirs. Equitrust Real Estate Corp., West Chester; developer Brampton Chase, Malvern, Pa., 1988-89; faculty Grad. Builders Inst. Pa. State U., State Coll., 1987-90; faculty Pa. Bar Inst., 1991—; chmn. Allegheny Cardiovascular Inst., 1997, Likoff Cardiovascular Inst., 1995-97. Mem. Tufts U. Alumni Coun., Medford, Mass., 1982—; bd. overseers Tufts U., Medford, 1988-93; bd. dirs. Kaiserman Ctr. Jewish Community Ctrs. Phila, 1982-88. Recipient Disting. Service medal Tufts U., 1982. Mem. Pa. Bar Assn. (ho. dels. 1983-87), Phila. Bar Assn. (bd. govs. 1985, chmn. real estate sect. 1985, exec. com. real estate sect. 1983-89), Am. Coll. Real Estate Laywers, Internat. Coun. Shopping Ctrs. Avocations: amateur radio, cooking. Office: Gowa Lincoln PC 1525 Locust St Ste 1000 Philadelphia PA 19102 Fax: 215-320-9006. E-mail: andy@gowalaw.com.

GOWANS, SIR JAMES LEARMONTH, science administrator, immunologist; b. Sheffield, Eng., May 7, 1924; s. John Gowans and Selma Ljung; m. Moyra Leatham, July 28, 1956; children: William, Jenny, Lucy. MB, BS, U. London, 1947; MA, DPhil, Oxford U., 1953; ScD (hon.), Yale U., 1966; DSc (hon.), U. Chgo., 1971, U. Birmingham, Eng., 1978, U. Rochester, 1987; MD (hon.), U. Edinburgh, Scotland, 1979, U. Sheffield, Eng.; DM (hon.), U. Southampton, Eng., 1987; LLD, U. Glasgow, Scotland, 1988. Rsch. prof. sch. pathology Oxford U., Eng., 1962-77, dir. med. rsch. coun. cellular immunology unit, 1963-77; sec., CEO U.K. Med. Rsch. Coun., 1977-87; cons. WHO Global Program on AIDS, Geneva, Switzerland, 1987-88; rsch. programs adv. com. Nat. Multiple Sclerosis Soc., N.Y.C., 1988-90; sec.-gen. Human Frontier Scis. Program, Strasbourg, France, 1989-93. Chmn. European Med. Rsch. Coun., 1985-87; mem. governing coun. Internat. Agy. for Rsch. on Cancer, Lyon, France, 1980-87; mem. awards assembly GM Cancer Rsch. Found., N.Y.C., 1988-92; dir. European Iniativie for Communicators of Sci., Munich, Germany, 1995-99, Charing Cross Sunley Rsch. Ctr., London, 1989-91. Contbr. articles on cellular immunology to profl. jours. Recipient Gairdner Found. award, 1968, Paul Ehrlich prize, 1974, Feldberg award, 1979, Wolf prize in medicine, 1980, Medawar prize, 1990. Fellow Royal Soc. (Royal Medal 1976); mem. NAS (fgn. assoc.), Am. Assn. Immunologists (hon.), Am. Assn. Anatomists (hon.). Avocations: music, gardening, old books. Home: 75 Cumnor Hill Oxford OX2 9HX England Fax: (44) 1865-865548.

GOWDY, FRANKLIN BROCKWAY, lawyer; b. Burlington, Iowa, Dec. 27, 1945; s. Franklin Kamm and Dorothy Faye (Brockway) G.; m. Jennifer June McKenrick, Nov. 27, 1982; stepchildren: Jeffrey F. Hammond, Tracy Lawrence, Jonathan R. Hammond, Julie E. Rawls. BA in Polit. Sci., Stanford U., 1967; JD, U. Calif., Berkeley, 1970. Bar: U.S. Dist. Ct. (no. dist.) Calif. 1971, U.S. Ct. Appeals (9th cir.) 1971, U.S. Supreme Ct. 1979, U.S. Dist. Ct. (cen. dist.) Calif. 1984. Assoc. Brobeck, Phleger & Harrison, San Francisco, 1971-78, ptnr., 1978—. Fellow Am. Coll. Trial Lawyers; mem. ABA, Calif. Bar Assn., San Francisco Bar Assn., Assn. Bus. Trial Lawyers (bd. govs.). Home: 3428 Shangrila Rd Lafayette CA 94549-2423 Office: Morgan Lewis Bockius LLP Spear St Tower 1 Market Plz San Francisco CA 94105-1420 E-mail: fgowdy@brobeck.com.

GOWEN, LEO FRANCIS, artist; b. St. Louis, Jan. 29, 1948; s. Leo Francis Gowen and Louise Barbara (Gizinski) Gowel. Student St. Benedicts Coll., St Benedict Coll, Atchison, Kans., 1966—68; student, Tex. A&M Ext. U., Bryan and College Station, Tex., 1972—82. Orthopedic orderly DePaul Hosp., St. Louis, 1967—68; dental lab technician U.S. Army, San Antonio, 1969—70, med. lab technician U.s. and Europe, 1970—72; stationary engr. City of Houston, 1972—84; surveyor various orgns., Houston, 1985—96; freelance artist, 1970—. Spec. 4 U.S. Army, 1968—72. Recipient Laureate in poetry, 2002. Roman Catholic. Avocations: chess, dioramas, garden art. Home and Office: AH & I 23 East Rose Saint Louis MO 63119

GOWEN, THOMAS LEO, JR., lawyer; b. Phila., June 22, 1949; s. Thomas L. and Jacqueline Gowen; m. Michele F. Charrier, Sept. 25, 1971; children: Christopher, Jonathan. BA, Haverford Coll., 1971; JD, Villanova U., 1977. Bar: Pa. 1977, U.S. Dist. (ea. dist.) Pa. 1977. Securities analyst Continental Bank, Phila., 1971-74; ptnr. Caiola, Caiola & Gowen, Norristown, Pa., 1977—97, Murphy, Oliver, Caiola & Gowen, 1997—2003, Oliver, Caiola & Gowen LLC, 2002—; counsel, dir. Arthur Ashe Tennis and Edn. Found., Phila., 2002—. V.p., counsel Phila. Tennis Patrons, 1977—; bd. dirs. WHRC Radio Corp., Haverford, Pa., 1990-94, Phila. Internat. Tennis Corp.; chmn. Comcast U.S. Indoor Tennis Tournament, Phila., 1991-96; mem. faculty Nat. Coll. Advocacy, 1987—, lectr.faculty product liabilities, law and practice, Pa. Trial Lawyers, 2002, Developments in Traumatic Brain Injury Litigation, Assn. Trial Lawyers Am., NJ, 2001. Contbr. articles to profl. jours. Fellow Nat. Coll. Advocates; mem. Montgomery County Bar Assn. (continuing legal edn. com.), Assn. Trial Lawyers Am. (exchange com. 1985-86), Pa. Trial Lawyers Assn. (chmn. headtrauma seminar 1986, bd. govs. 2000—, lectr. product liability 2002, gov. 2000-), Nat. Jr. Tennis League of Phila. (pres. 1980-83, 87-95, vice-chmn. bd. dirs. 1983-87), Phila. Tennis Assn. (Seymour Coren award 1976), Phila. Sports Congress (World Cup Soccer com. 1991—), Pa. Supreme Ct. Bd. (chmn. special hearing com. 1994-2000). Home: 36 Glenbrook Rd Ardmore PA 19003-1025 Office: Oliver Caiola and Gowen LLC 2500 DeKalb Pike Norristown PA 19401-4828 E-mail: tgowen@injury-law.com.

GOWENS, WALTER, II, financial and business services executive; b. Tampa, Fla., Sept. 30, 1954; s. Walter and Bessie (Bridges) G. BS, Ariz. State U., 1975; MBA, Ind. U., 1977. CFP; registered investment advisor. Fin. analyst Am. Can Co., Greenwich, Conn., 1977-79; cons. Norman Jaspan Assocs., N.Y.C., 1979; pvt. cons. practice N.Y.C., 1979-80; mgr. fin. reporting YMCA Greater N.Y.C., 1980-81; sr. fin. analyst Met. Transp. Authority, N.Y.C., 1981-83; pres. Prudential Vanguard Cos., Inc., N.Y.C., 1983—. Portfolio mgr., lic. stockbroker, lic. ins. broker, N.Y.C., 1986—; former contbg. pers. fin. advisor to online expert svcs. incl. Allexperts.com. and Infomarkets.com. Founder, editor Prudential Vanguard Tax & Investment newsletter, 1986-89. Recipient Entrepreneurial Skills award C.A. C. of C., 1987; Consortium Grad. Study fellow, 1975. Mem. Nat. Soc. Tax Profls., Fin. Planning Assn., Nat. Soc. Accts., Nat. Notary Assn., Am. Assn. Individual Investors. Avocations: attending N.Y.C. theaters, tennis, exploring N.Y.C. Office: Prudential Vanguard Cos Inc 1501 Broadway Ste 1607 New York NY 10036-5601 E-mail: pruvan1@prudentialvanguard.net.

GOWER, DANA W. financial consultant; b. Skowhegan, Maine, Oct. 17, 1956; s. Roger L. and Shirley P. Gower; m. Amy C. Gair, July 1, 1990; children: Erin, Katie, Danielle, Reid, Hannah. AS in Resource Econs., U. Maine, 1978, BS in Fin., 1980; MBA in Fin., Rollins Coll., Winter Park, Fla., 1982. Cert. compensation profl. Am. Compensation Assn., mediator Wake County, N.C., master trainer Achieve Global. Benefits coord. Cooper Industries, Inc., Houston, 1982—83, supr. group ins., 1983—85, mgr. employee relations power tools divsn. Lexington, SC, 1985—87, pers. mgr. Belden divsn. Essex Junction, Vt., 1987—89, employee relations rep. Raleigh, NC, 1989—91; divsn. mgr. human resources Cooper Industries, Raleigh, NC, 1991—99; fin. cons. AXA Advisors, Raleigh, 1999—. Presenter in field. Co-author: The Career and Financial Power Book, 0202. Coord. United Way, 1985—99; active Boy Scouts Am., Cary, NC; nominating com. Bald Head Island Assn., NC, 2002—. Mem.: Rotary, K.C. Republican. Roman Catholic. Office: AXA Advisors 3201 Beechleaf Ct Raleigh NC 27511

GOWIN, RICHARD BRYAN, lawyer; b. Louisville, Oct. 16, 1969; s. Charles R. and Sherrin M. Gowin; m. Lisa M. Gowin, Dec. 19, 1998. BS, U. Ky., 1992, JD, 1996. Bar: Ky. 1997. Law clk. U.S. Army Corps Engrs., Louisville, 1992, Ky. Local Governance Project, Lexington, Ky., 1993-96; atty. Hoge & Assocs., Louisville, 1997—2002; pvt. practice Louisville, 2002. Mem. ABA, Ky. Bar Assn., Louisville Bar Assn. (family law sect.). Home: 3226 Eagle Pass Louisville KY 40213-1273 Office: Bryan Gowin Atty at Law Ste 506 Legal Arts Bldg 200 S 7th St Louisville KY 40202

GOYAK, ELIZABETH FAIRBAIRN, retired public relations executive; b. Chgo., Oct. 7, 1922; d. Lewis Howard and Berenice Marie (Bowers) Fairbairn; m. Edward Anthony Goyak, May 20, 1951. BEd, So. Ill. U., 1943; MA, No. Ill. U., 1979. Reporter Internat. News Svc., Chgo., 1945-49, Chgo. Tribune, 1949-52; writer Gardner & Jones, Chgo., 1954-59, Aaron Cushman & Assocs., Chgo., 1959-60; v.p. Daniel J. Edelman, Chgo., 1960-76; mgr. pub. rels. Stone Container Corp., Chgo., 1976-82; pres. pub. rels. Firm Chgo. Connection, Matteson, Ill., 1982-98. Dir. pub. rels. Ill. Dem. Women for Adlai Stevenson, 1952; founder, pres. bd. dirs. Matteson Pub. Libr., 1958-87; chmn. Matteson Bicentennial Commn., 1973-76. Mem. Pub. Rels. Soc. Am. (accredited, Silver anvil award 1975), Publicity Club Chgo. (sec., bd. dirs. 1964-76, Golden Trumpet award 1965, 66, 75), Chgo. Press Vets. Mem. United Ch. Christ. Home: 9200 Lalique Ln Apt 1503 Fort Myers FL 33919-7408

GOYAL, RAVINDRA KUMAR, physician; b. Nasirabad, India, Nov. 24, 1949; came to U.S., 1974; s. Santulal and Ramjyoti (Airan) G.; m. Damyanti, Feb. 12, 1952; children: Rishi, Rajeev, Raghav. MBBS, SMS Med. Coll., Jaipur, India, 1972. Diplomate Am. Bd. Internal & Pulmonary Medicine, Am. Bd. Critical Care Medicine. Intern Kingsbrook Jewish Med. Ctr., Bklyn., 1974-75, resident, 1975-77; pulmonary fellow Queens Hosp. Ctr./L.I. Jewish Hillside Med. Ctr., Jamaica, N.Y., 1977-79; mem. staff Kingsbrook Med. Ctr., Bklyn., 1982-85; with Brookdale U., Bklyn., 1995—; med. dir. respiratory therapy dept., chief pulmonary medicine N.Y. Cmty. Hosp. V.p. Hindu Ctr., Flushing, N.Y., 1997. Fellow Am. Coll. Chest Physicians. Avocation: skiing. Home: 51 Larch Dr New Hyde Park NY 11040-2327 Office: 1640 Ocean Ave Brooklyn NY 11230-4963 E-mail: rgoyalmd@hotmail.com.

GOYAN, JERE EDWIN, business executive, former university dean; b. Oakland, Calif., Aug. 3, 1930; s. Gerald H. and Lucille (Johnson) G.; m. Patricia B. Mesirow, Aug. 24, 1952 (div.); children: Pamela, Terrence H., Andrea; m. Linda Lloyd Hart, Mar. 25, 1988. BS, U. Calif. Sch. Pharmacy, 1952, PhD, 1957. Asst. prof. pharmacy U. Mich., 1956-61, assoc. prof., 1961-63; assoc. prof. pharmacy and pharm. chemistry U. Calif. at San Francisco, 1963-65, prof., 1965-79, 81-92; assoc. dean Sch. Pharmacy, 1966-67, dean, 1967-79, 81-92; pres., COO Alteon, Inc., Ramsey, N.J., 1993-99; pres. Goyan & Hart Assocs., 1999—. Commr. FDA/HHS, 1979-81 Fellow AAAS; mem. Inst. Medicine of NAS, N.Y. Acad. Scis., Am. Pharm. Assn., Acad. Pharm. Scis., Am. Assn. Pharm. Scientists (pres. 1990), Calif. Pharm. Assn., Am. Assn. Colls. Pharmacy (pres. 1978-79), Sigma Xi, Rho Chi, Phi Lambda Upsilon. Office: SciClone Pharmaceuticals Inc 901 Mariner Island Blvd San Mateo CA 94404 E-mail: jgoyan@aol.com.

GOYER, ROBERT ANDREW, pathology educator; b. Hartford, Conn., June 2, 1927; s. Andrew R. and Cecelia P. (Castonquay) G.; m. Mary Ellen Wilke, Feb. 4, 1955; children— Barbara, John, Peter, Ellen. BS, Holy Cross Coll., 1950; MD, St. Louis U., 1955. Diplomate: Am. Bd. Pathology. Intern St. Francis Hosp., Hartford, 1955-56; resident in pathology St. Louis U. Hosps., 1956-60; practice medicine specializing in pathology St. Louis, 1956-65; instr. pathology St. Louis U., 1960-62, asst. prof., 1962-65, Sch. Medicine, U. N.C., Chapel Hill, 1965-68, assoc. prof., 1968-71, prof. pathology, 1971-74, adj. prof. pathology, 1979-87; clin. pathologist Cardinal Glennon Meml. Hosp. for Children, St. Louis, 1961-62, dir. labs., 1962-64; staff pathologist N.C. Meml. Hosp., Chapel Hill, 1965-74; chief pathology U. Hosp., London, Ont., Can., 1974-79; prof. pathology Health Scis. Centre, U. Western Ont., Can., 1974-79 87-92, prof. emeritus, 1992—; dept. dir. Nat. Inst. Environ. Health Scis., Research Triangle Park, N.C., 1979-87; pvt. cons. health effects, toxic metals Chapel Hill, N.C., 1992—. Nat. assoc. Nat. Acads.; mem. com. WHO/IPCS, NAS, NRC. Contbr. articles to profl. jours.; mem. editorial bd. Yearbook Pathology, 1979-88, AMA Archives of Pathology, 1973-82. Served with USN, 1945-47. Nat. Found. fellow, 1959-60 Mem. Coll. Am. Pathology, Am. Assn. Pathologists, Internat. Acad. Pathology, Soc. Exptl. Biology and Medicine. Roman Catholic. Achievements include rsch. in exptl. pathology and metal toxicology. Office: 6405 Huntingridge Rd Chapel Hill NC 27517 E-mail: robert_goyer@msn.com.

GOYER, ROBERT STANTON, communication educator; b. Kokomo, Ind., Oct. 7, 1923; s. Clarence V. and Genevieve M. (Sober) G.; m. Patricia Ann Stutz, Aug. 12, 1950; children: Karen, Susan, Linda, Amy. BA, DePauw U., 1948; MA, Miami U., Oxford, Ohio, 1950; PhD, Ohio State U., 1955. Instr. Miami U., Oxford, 1949-51; instr., then asst. prof. Ohio State U., Columbus, 1955-58, rsch. assoc., cons. rsch. found., 1956-63; from asst. to assoc. to prof. Purdue U., Lafayette, Ind., 1958-66; prof. Ohio U., Athens, 1966-81, dir. ctr. communication studies, 1966-74, 79-81, assoc. dean grad. coll., 1978, dean grad. coll., acting dir. rsch., 1979, acting assoc. provost grad. and rsch. programs, 1979, prof. emeritus, 1981—; prof., chmn. dept. communication Ariz. State U., Tempe, 1981-89, prof., 1989-94, prof. emeritus, 1994—. Cons. in field. Author books; contbr. articles to profl. jours. 1st lt. U.S. Army, 1943-46, 52-53. Decorated Bronze Star. Fellow AAAS, Internat. Comm. Assn.; mem. APA, Nat. Comm. Assn. Presbyterian. Home: 517 W Summit Pl Chandler AZ 85225-7799

GOYER, VIRGINIA L. accountant; b. Troy, N.Y., July 19, 1942; d. Clarence Archie and Edna Alice (Toussaint) G.; m. James Cobb Stewart, May 17, 1986. BS, Rochester Inst. Tech., 1975, MBA, 1976. Tax mgr. Deloitte Haskins & Sells, Rochester, N.Y., 1976-82; pres. Lamanna & Goyer, PC, CPAs, Rochester, 1982-89; owner Goyer & Assocs., CPAs, Rochester, 1989-93; pres. Virginia L. Goyer, CPA, P.C., Rochester, 1993—. Mem. adv. bd. Salvation Army, Rochester, 1985-88, Rochester Inst. Tech. Deferred Giving, 1988-89; mem. bd. Nat. Women's Hall of Fame, 1993-98; bd. dirs., treas. Friends of Women's Rights Nat. Park Inc., 2000—. Mem. AICPA (nat. coun. 1995-98), Fla. Inst. CPAs, N.Y. State Inst. CPAs (bd. dirs. 1990-93, v.p. 1994-95, 1st woman pres. Rochester chpt. 1988-89), Rochester Women's Network, Nat. Assn. Women Bus. Owners (bd. dirs. 1992-93), Estate Planning Coun. (bd. dirs. 1987-89), NOW, Century Club Rochester (bd. dirs., fin. chair 2001—). Office: 354 Westminster Rd Rochester NY 14607-3233

GOYNE, CHRISTOPHER PAUL, aerospace scientist, educator; s. Phillip James and Mary Josephine Goyne. B in Mech. Engring. with honors, U. Queensland, Australia, 1991, PhD, 1999. Rsch. assoc. U. Va., Charlottesville, 1998—99, 2000—01, aerospace rsch. scientist, 2002—03, rsch. asst. prof., 2003—; postdoctoral scholar U. Queensland, Brisbane, 1999. Contbr. articles to profl. jours. Mem.: AIAA (reviewer AIAA Jour. and Jour. Propulsion and Power 2002—). Achievements include patents pending for reducing skin friction drag; development of advanced instrumentation and diagnostics for experiments in the areas of high speed aerodynamics and high speed propulsion (scramjet engines); research in supersonic combustion, hypersonic aerodynamics and boundary layer flows. Office: U Va 570 Edgemont Rd PO Box 400248 Charlottesville VA 22904

GOZANI, TSAHI, nuclear physicist; b. Tel Aviv, Nov. 25, 1934; came to U.S., 1965; s. Arieh and Rivcca Gozani; m. Adit Soffer, Oct. 14, 1958; children: Mor, Shai Nachum, Or Pinchas, Tal. BSc, Technion-Israel Inst. Tech., Haifa, 1956, MSc, 1958; DSc, Swiss Fed. Inst. Tech. (ETH), Zurich, Switzerland, 1962. Registered profl. nuclear engr., Calif.; accredited nuclear material mgr. Rsch. physicist Israel Atomic Energy Commn., Beer-Sheva, 1962-65; rsch. assoc. nuclear engring. dept. Rensselaer Poly. Inst., Troy, N.Y., 1965-66; sr. staff scientist General-Atomic & IRT, San Diego, 1966-70, 71-75; prof. applied physics Tel Aviv U., 1971; chief scientist, divsn. mgr. SAIC, Palo Alto and Sunnyvale, Calif., 1975-84, v.p., chief scientist Sunnyvale, 1984-87, corp. v.p. Santa Clara, Calif., 1987-93, sr. v.p., 1993-97; pres., CEO Ancore Corp., Santa Clara, 1997—2002; pres. Ancore, an OSI Sys. Co., 2002. Lady Davis vis. prof. Technion-Israel Inst. Tech., 1983-84; bd. dirs. Radiation Sci. Inst., San Jose State U. Author: Active Non-Destructive Assay of Nuclear Materials, 1981; co-author: Handbook of Nuclear Safeguards Measurement Methods, 1983; contbr. over 200 articles to profl. jours. Recipient 1989 Laurel award Aviation Week Jour., R&D 100 award, 1988, Most Innovative New Products. Fellow Am. Nuclear Soc.; mem. Am. Phys. Soc., Inst. Nuclear Materials. Achievements include patents for explosive detection system, explosive detection system using an artificial neural system, multi sensor explosive detection system, composite cavity structure for an explosive detection system, apparatus and method for detecting contraband using fast neutron activation, contraband detection system using direct imaging pulsed fast neutrons; invention of method to measure nuclear reactor's reactivity. Office: Ancore Corp 2950 Patrick Henry Dr Santa Clara CA 95054-1813 E-mail: tsahi@ancore.com.

GOZON, JOZSEF STEPHAN, engineering educator; b. Öcsény, Hungary, Nov. 16, 1933; came to U.S., 1979; s. Jozsef and Erzsebet (Grof) G.; m. Jolan Szabo, May 10, 1958 (dec. 1972); m. Julianna Teleki, Nov. 18, 1972; children: Eszter Julianna, Peter Richard. BS, Coll. Mining, Sopron, Hungary, 1958; D of Tech., Tech. U., Miskolc, Hungary, 1967; PhD in Mining, Mining Inst. Moscow, 1967; PhD in Tech. Sci., Acad. Scis., Budapest, Hungary, 1967. Registered profl. engr. Asst. lectr. Tech. U., Miskolc, 1958-60, lectr., 1964-69, assoc. prof., 1969-73, 75-79, Coll. Petroleum and Mining, Tripoli, Libya, 1973-75; assoc. prof. mining engring. Ohio State U., Columbus, 1979-82, prof., 1982—; rsch. fellow Geothermal Lab., Miskolc, 1960-64; pres. Mining Tech. and Measurement Inc., Columbus, 1985-95; v.p. GCK Corp., 1991—. Mem. adj. faculty Kennedy-Western U., Thousand Oaks, Calif., 1995-2000—; cons. in field.

Author: Use of Geothermal Energy, 1965, Mining Machines, 1968; editor Internat. Jour. Surface Mining, 1987-90. Active Forest Park Civic Assn., Columbus, 1980-95; bd. dirs. Ohio Hungary Sister State Support Found., 1996—. Mem. Am. Soc. Mining Engrs., Hungarian Soc. Mining Engrs. (vice chmn. 1977-79), Am. Soc. Engring. Edn. Roman Catholic. Avocations: travel, gardening, photography. Home: 3246 Foxcroft Dr Lewis Center OH 43035-9338 Office: Ohio State Univ Dept Civil Engring 2070 Neil Ave Columbus OH 43210-1226 E-mail: gozon.1@osu.edu.

GOZONSKY, EDWIN O. O. investment broker; b. Laconia, N.H., Mar. 31, 1930; s. Archie and Ida G.; m. Dorothy Adelson, Feb. 28, 1965; children: Judith, Diane. BA, Yale U., 1952; MBA, Harvard U., 1954. With Eastman Dillon, Union Securities (merged with Paine Webber 1980), Boston, 1959—, v.p. Boston office, 1971—; pres. Variable Annuities Provide Personal Security, 1979—. Lectr. in retirement income, sales variable annuities, bonds, 1979—; mem. investment coms. Maine and R.I. Founds.; mem. compliance com. New Eng., Nat. Assn. Securities Dealers, 1994-96. With U.S. Army, 1954-56. Mem. Bulldog Soc. (provisional dir.), Harvard Bus. Sch. Alumni (class sec. 1988—). Home: 118 Irving Ave Providence RI 02906-4510 Office: UBS/Paine Webber 265 Franklin St Fl 13 Boston MA 02110-3196

GOZUM, MARVIN ENRIQUEZ, internist; b. Phila., Jan. 01; s. Filemon Tizon and Teresita Ver G. BS in Biology, Ateneo de Manila, The Philippines, 1980; MD, Fatima Coll. of Medicine, The Philippines, 1984. Intern The Bklyn.-Caledonian Hosp. div. Downstate Med. Ctr., N.Y., 1984-85, resident in internal medicine, 1985-87; attending physician Thomas Jefferson U. Hosp., Phila., 1987—; clin. instr. Jefferson Med. Coll., Phila., 1987-89, rsch. assoc. Ctr. for Rsch., 1989—, clin. asst. prof. medicine, 1989—, chief med. informatics div. internal medicine, 1989—; med. cons. Wills Eye Hosp., Phila., 1987—, chief med. cons., 1990—. Adv. bd. computers in medicine com. Thomas Jefferson U. Hosp., 1987—; adv. bd. computer com. Wills Eye Hosp., 1987; adv. bd. curriculum devel. com. Thomas Jefferson U., Phila., 1988; adv. bd. Continuing Med. Edn. Com. Internal Medicine, 1991—. Developer: (computer programs) Diagnosticon Computer Assisted Diagnosis, 1982, Fluid/Electrolyte Calculator, 1984, Preoperative Evaluation, 1987; co-developer: (computer program) VACAD Image Processor, 1987. Named to Osteoporosis Project, Health Sci. Inst., 1990. Mem. AAAS, Am. Med. Informatics Assn., Soc. Gen. Internal Medicine. Achievements include development of computer assisted preoperative evaluation, automated report generation for preoperative evaluations, automated medical diagnosis, pocket intensive care calculator. Office: Jefferson Med Coll 1025 Walnut St Philadelphia PA 19107-5001

GRAB, FREDERICK CHARLES, lawyer; b. N.Y.C., Aug. 1, 1946; s. Daniel Justin and Elizabeth (Kam) G. BS in Aerospace Enging., Polytech U. N.Y., 1967; JD, U. So. Calif., 1977. Bar: Calif. 1978, U.S. Dist. Ct. (cen. dist.) Calif. 1978, U.S. Supreme Ct. 1988, U.S. Ct. Appeals (9th cir.) 1989. Deputy atty. gen. Calif. Atty. Gen., L.A., 1977-2000. Polit. journalist: Washington Times; contbr. articles to profl. jours. Polit. activist. Avocations: playwright, author, composer, musican.

GRABAR, OLEG, retired art educator; b. Strasbourg, France, Nov. 3, 1929; came to U.S., 1948, naturalized, 1960; s. Andre and Julie (Ivanova) G.; m. Terry Ann Harris, June 9, 1951; children— Nicolas Howard, Anne Louise. BA magna cum laude, Harvard, 1950; licence d'Histoire, U. Paris, 1950; PhD, Princeton, 1955; D (hon.), U. Mich. Instr. U. Mich., 1954-55, asst. prof., 1955-59, asso. prof., 1959-64, prof., 1964-69; dir. Am. Sch. of Oriental Research, Jerusalem, Jordan, 1960-61; v.p. Am. Sch. of Oriental Rsch., Jerusalem, 1968-75; prof. fine arts Harvard U., 1969-81; Aga Khan prof. Islamic art Harvard, 1981-90; with sch. hist. studies Inst. For Advanced Study, Princeton, 1990-99; ret., 1999. Dir. Mich.-Harvard U. excavations in Syria, 1964-71. Author: Coinage of Tulunide, 1957, Islamic Architecture and Its Decoration, 1967, Sasanian Silver, 1967, The Formation of Islamic Art, 1973, The Alhambra, 1978, City in the Desert, 1978, Epic Images, 1982, Illustrations of the Maqamat, 1984, Islamic Art, 1987, Great Mosque of Isfahan, 1989, The Mediation of Ornament, 1992, The Shape of the Holy, 1996, La Peinture Persane, 1999, Mostly Miniatures, 2000, Islamic Art and Architecture, 660-1250, 2001; editor: Ars Orientalis, 1957—71, Muquarnas, 1983—92; contbr. Mem. Coll. Art Assn. (dir. 1968-72), Archeol. Inst. Am., Mediaeval Acad. Am., German Archeol. Inst., Middle Eastern Studies Assn., Am. Acad. Arts and Scis., Am. Philosophy Soc., Brit. Acad. (hon.), Austrian Acad. (hon.), Acad. INscriptions et Belles-Lettres (Paris). Home: 43 Maxwell Ln Princeton NJ 08540-4931 Office: Inst for Advanced Study Princeton NJ 08540 E-mail: grabar@ias.edu.

GRABÉ, CHRISTOPHER K. architectural firm executive; Prin. Davis & Grabé; ptnr. Davis Brody Bond, 1979—. Office: Davis Brody Bond LLP 315 Hudson St 9th Fl New York NY 10013 Fax: 212-633-4762.*

GRABENSTEIN, JOHN DOUGLAS, pharmacist, army officer; b. Cumberland, Md., Aug. 12, 1957; s. Herman J. and Irene R. (Ley) G.; m. Laurie Ann Sandquist, Oct. 16, 1982; children: Emily C., Andrea L., Erica K., Peter C. BS in Pharmacy, Duquesne U., Pitts., 1980; EdM with honors, Boston U., 1988; MS in Pharmacy Adminstrn., U. N.C., Chapel Hill, 1991, PhD in Epidemiology, 1999. CPH pharmacist. Commd. officer U.S. Army, 1975, advanced through grades to col., 1979—; supr. satellite pharmacies Walter Reed Army Med. Ctr., Washington, 1981-83, chief allergen extract lab., 1983-85; chief pharmacy svc. U.S. Army Hosp., Bremerhaven, 1986-89; resident in pharmacy practice and pharm. care Fitzsimons Army Med. Ctr., Aurora, Colo., 1991-92; chief human subjects protection U.S. Army Clin. Investigation Regulatory Office, Ft. Sam Houston, 1992-96; dep. dir. mil. vaccine program Army Surgeon Gen.'s Office, Falls Church, Va., 1999—. Pharmacy rep. influenza and pneumococcal action group Nat. Coalition on Adult Immunization, 1991-99; clin. adv. Inst. Safe Medication Practices, 1995—; mem. adv. bd. Immunization Action Coalition and Hepatitis B Coalition, 1997—. Author: ImmunoFacts: Vaccines and Immunologic Drugs, 1993 (named Best New Health Sci. Books of 1993, Doody's Rating Svc.), 2002, Phi Delta Chi: A Tradition of Leaders in Pharmacy, 1995, Pocket ImmunoFacts: Vaccines and Immunologics, 1997, 98, 2000, 02, Immunization Delivery: A Complete Guide, 1997, Pharmacy-Based Immunization Delivery: A National Certificate Training Program, 1997, 98, 99, 2000, 02; author: (with others) American Hospital Formulary Service-Drug Information, 1987, 88, American Society of Hospital Pharmacists, 1987, 88, Sterile Dosage Forms: Their Preparation and Clinical Application, 3rd edit., 1987, 4th edit., 1994, Nurses Drug Facts, 1996, Guidelines for Pharmacy-Based Immunization Advocacy, 1997; editor, prin. author The Communicator of Phi Delta Chi Pharmacy Frat., 1985-95, Booster Shots, 1994-2001; editor Allergy-Clinical Immunology Specialist Training Manual, 3rd edit., 1984, 4th edit., 1985, Leader-Development Seminar: Facilitator Guide and Participant Syllabus, 1989-92, ImmunoGuide: Response to Disaster, 1993, 3rd edit., 1999; mem. editl. bd. Hosp. Pharmacy, 1990-2002, DRUGDEX Info. Sys., 1992-98, Drug Facts and Comparisons, 1993—, ISMP Medication Safety Alert, 1997—, Needle Tips and Hepatitis B News, 1997—; contbg. editor Jour. Am. Pharm. Assn., 1998—; moderator electronic bull. bd., Internet website; reviewer various pubs.; referee numerous profl. jours.; contbr. articles to profl. jours.; presenter in field. Chmn. student-faculty-parent senate Bishop Walsh H.S., Cumberland, Md., 1974-75. Recipient Student Pub. Affairs award Am. Assn. Colls. Pharmacy, 1978, Eli Lilly award for outstanding scholastic and profl. achievement and leadership, 1980, Pharmacy Rsch. award U.S. Army, 1991, Career Achievement award We. Md. Cath. Schs., 1997, Duquesne U. Alumni Achievement award, 1998, Pinnacle award Health Care Quality Alliance, 1998, Du Mez Lectr. award U. Md., 1999, Pharmacy Practice Rsch. award Am. Soc. Health-Sys. Pharmacists, 2002; named Model Mayor of Cumberland, Model City Coun. Bishop Walsh H.S., 1975; named one of Outstanding Young Men in Am., 1980, 96. Fellow Nat. Cath. Pharmacists Guild, Am. Pharm. Assn. (mem. acad. pharmacy practice and mgmt., judge student patient counseling competition 1986, mem. strategic and tactical analysis team on pharmacy payment reform 1995-99, dir. immunication delivery ednl. program 1996—); mem. Fedn. Internat. Pharmaceutique, Christian Pharmacists Fedn. Internat., Assn. Mil. Surgeons of U.S., Am. Soc. Health-Sys. Pharmacists, Soc. Infectious Disease Pharmacists, Phi Delta Chi (nat. grand pres. 1995-99, dir. pharmacy leadership and edn. inst. 1996—, nat. collegiate v.p. 1983-85, nat. v.p. comm. 1985-95, leader devel. seminars 1989-92), Delta Omega, Rho Chi, Phi Lambda Sigma. Roman Catholic. Avocations: reading, history. Office: Mil Vaccine Agy US Army Med Command 5111 Leesburg Pike Ste 401 Falls Church VA 22041-3206

GRABER, GLENN C. medical educator, educational consultant; b. Knoxville, Tenn., June 2, 1942; s. George Garnel and Virginia Fort Graber; m. M. Caroline Rigsby, Aug. 1, 1964; 1 child, Rosalie Caroline;1 child, Janna Graber Werner. PhD, U. of Mich., Ann Arbor, MI, 1964—72; BA, U. of Ky., Lexington, KY, 1960—64. Prof. of philosophy U. of Tenn., Knoxville, Tenn., 1968—; prof. of medicine U. of Tenn. Grad. Sch. of Medicine, Knoxville, Tenn., 1978—. Author (principal author): (monograph) Ethical Analysis of Clin. Medicine; editor (co-editor): (textbook) Bioethics; author (principal author): (monograph) Theory and Practice in Med. Ethics; author: (secondary author) Euthanasia - Toward an Ethical Social Policy; author: (essays in prof. journals,) 42 essays; dir.: (26 PhD dissertations), (16 MA theses) applied ethics. Mem., ethics com. United Network for Organ Sharing, Richmond, Va., 1993—95; adv. com., code of med. ethics online curriculum (CMEOC) AMA, Chgo., 2000—01; adv. bd. Tenn. Donor Services, Knoxville, Tenn., 1987—2002; cons. to Hosp. ethics com. St. Mary's Med. Ctr., Knoxville, Tenn., 1984—2002. Recipient, Phi Beta Kappa, 1963, Lindsay Young Professorship, U. of Tenn., 1980-1981, Chancellor's Citation for Extraordinary Svc. to the U., 1979; fellow Woodrow Wilson Fellowship, Woodrow Wilson Fellowship Found., 1964-1965, fellowship for postdoctoral clin. residency at The U. of Tenn. Ctr. for the Health Sciences, Inst. for Human Values in Medicine, 1976. Mem.: Assn. for Practical and Profl. Ethics, Am. Soc. for Bioethics and Humanities, Am. Philos. Assn. Episcopal. Achievements include first to developed Graduate Concentration in Medical Ethics within graduate program in Philosophy at the University of Tennessee; established the Center for Applied and Professional Ethics at the University of Tennessee. Home: 7325 Toxaway Drive Knoxville TN 37909-3130 Office: The Univ of Tennessee 801 McClung Tower Knoxville TN 37996-0480 E mail: ggraber@utk.edu.

GRABER, HARRY LEE, internist; b. Auburn, Ind., Aug. 23, 1931; s. Benjamin and Anna (Leichty) G.; m. Roberta M. Schertz, Dec. 22, 1957; children: Cheryl Lynn, Rhonda Sue, Rodney Curtis, Charles LeVan. BS in Elem. Edn., Goshen Coll., 1954; MD, St. Louis U., 1964. Diplomate Am. Bd. Internal Medicine; cert elem. sch. tchr. Elem. sch. tchr. Bur. Indian Affairs, Tuba City, Ariz., 1954-56, South Bend (Ind.) City Schs., 1956-59; med. intern, resident Akron (Ohio) Med. Ctr., 1964-69; internist Mary Rutan Hosp., Bellefontaine, Ohio, 1969-74, non-invasive cardiologist, 1979-91; fellow in cardiology Ohio State U., Columbus, 1974-79, asst. clin. prof., 1989—; med. dir. Mary Rutan Hosp., 1990-99. Clin. rschr. cardiomyopathy Divsn. Cardiology Ohio State U., Columbus, 1974—. Contbr. articles to profl. jours. Mem. West Liberty-Salem Schs. Bd., 1980-87, Logan County Bd. of Health, Bellefontaine, Ohio, 1994—; Sunday sch. tchr. Bethel Mennonite Ch., West Liberty, Ohio, 1994—. Named Intern of Yr. Akron Gen. Hosp., 1965, Citizen of Yr., Kiwanis of Logan County, Bellefontaine, Ohio, 1996. Fellow Am. Coll. Cardiology; mem. AMA, Ohio State Med. Assn. Republican. Avocations: gardening, growing and grafting fruit trees, golf, family, fishing. Home: 314 Road 191 West Liberty OH 43357 Office: Mary Rutan Hosp 205 E Palmer Rd Bellefontaine OH 43311-2281

GRABER, RICHARD WILLIAM, lawyer, political organization worker; b. Lakewood, Ohio, July 31, 1956; s. Richard Allen and Lynn Carol (Hurschman) G.; m. Alexandria Ahlquist Richardson, Apr. 28, 1984; children: Scott Bailey, Erik Richard. AB magna cum laude, Duke U., 1978; JD, Boston U., 1981. Bar: Wis. 1981. Mem. Reinhart Boerner Van Deuren Norris & Rieselbach, S.C., Milw., Wis., 1981—. Bd. dirs. Crane Mfg. & Svc. Corp., Cudahy, Wis. Mem. bd. of governors, Wis. Patient Compensation Fund, 1988-97; chmn. fin. com. Wis. Rep. Party, 1993-97, chmn., 1999—; mem. exec. com. North Shore Rep. Club, Milw., 1988—, Reps. of Wis., 1991; mem. Am. Coun. Young Polit. Leaders, 1990; candidate for Wis. Assembly, 1990; chmn. Kasten for Senate com. 1993; mem. bd. of appeals, Village of Shorewood, 1991—, mem. bd. of trustees of the Medical College of Wis., 1997—. Mem. Rotary (pres. Milw. 1988-89, Paul Harris fellow 1990). Avocations: politics, softball, basketball. Home: 2726 E Shorewood Blvd Milwaukee WI 53211-2458 Office: Reinhart Boerner Van Deuren Norris & Rieselbach 1000 N Water St PO Box 92900 Milwaukee WI 53202-0900 E-mail: rgraber@reinhartlaw.com., rgraber@wisgop.org.*

GRABER, SAMUEL DAVID, environmental and water resources engineer, consultant; b. N.Y.C., Jan. 12, 1942; s. Sam Mandel Graber and Maud Alice Larson; m. Arlene Jenkins Graber, June 19, 1965; children: Steven David, Brian Earl, Keven Lee, Allen Eben. BSME, U. Miami, 1963; SMME, MIT, 1965, CE, 1966. Profl. engring., N.Y., 1970, Ma., 1975. Project engr. Camp Dresser & McKee Inc, Boston, 1966—67, dir. hydraulic svcs., 1969—74; wastewater tech. dir. Metcalf & Eddy Inc, Boston, 1974—77; cons. engr. Stoughton, Mass., 1977—. Scout leader Boy Scouts Am., Stoughton, 1976—, scoutmaster, 1980—94. Capt. U.S. Army, 1967—69, Panama. Recipient Eagle Scout, Boy Scouts Am., 1954. Mem.: ASME, ASCE (urban drainge stds. com. 1993—, Samuel A. Greeley award 1969, J.C. Stevens award 1972), Water Environment Fedn., Tau Beta Pi. Independent. Unitarian Universalist. Avocations: reading, history, genealogy, fishing, travel.

GRABER, SUSAN P. federal judge; b. Oklahoma City, July 5, 1949; d. Julius A. and Bertha (Fenyves) Graber; m. William June, May 3, 1981; 1 child, Rachel June-Graber. BA, Wellesley Coll., 1969; JD, Yale U., 1972. Bar: N.Mex. 1972, Ohio 1977, Oreg. 1978. Asst. atty. gen. Bur. of Revenue, Santa Fe, 1972—74; assoc. Jones Gallegos Snead & Wertheim, Santa Fe, 1974—75, Taft Stettinius & Hollister, Cin., 1975—78; assoc., then ptnr. Stoel Rives Boley Jones & Grey, Portland, Oreg., 1978—88; judge, then presiding judge Oreg. Ct. Appeals, Salem, 1988—90; assoc. justice Oreg. Supreme Ct., Salem, 1990—98; judge U.S. Ct. Appeals (9th cir.), Portland, 1998—. Mem. Gov.'s Adv. Coun. on Legal Svcs., 1979—88; mem. bd. visitors Sch. Law, U. Oreg., 1986—93; bd. dirs. U.S. Dist. Ct. of Oreg. Hist. Soc., 1985—, Oreg. Law Found., 1990—91. Mem.: Am. Inns of Ct. (master), Oreg. Appellate Judges Assn. (sec.-treas. 1990—91, vice chair 1991—92, chair 1992—93), Oreg. Jud. Conf. (edn. com. 1988—91, program chair 1990), Ninth Cir. Jud. Conf. (chair exec. com. 1987—88), Oreg. State Bar (jud. adminstrn. com. 1985—87, pro bono com. 1988—90), Phi Beta Kappa. Mailing: US Ct Appeals 9th Cir PO Box 193939 San Francisco CA 94119-3939 Office: US Ct Appeals 9th Cir 95 Seventh St San Francisco CA 94119*

GRABER, THOMAS M. orthodontist, researcher; b. St. Louis, May 27, 1917; Diplomate Am. Bd. Orthodontics. DMD, Washington U., St. Louis, 1940, MS in Dentistry, Northwestern U., 1946, PhD in Anatomy, 1950; Doctorate (hon.), U. Gothenberg, 1989; DSc (hon.), Washington U., 1991, U. Mich., 1994, U. Kunming, 1996. Diplomate Am. Bd. Orthodontics (Recognition award 1990, Dewel award, 1992). Mem. faculty Northwestern U. Dental Sch., 1946-58, assoc. prof. orthodontics, 1954-58; dir. research Northwestern U. Dental Sch. (cleft lip and palate Inst.), 1947-58, assoc. attending orthodontist Children's Meml. Hosp., Chgo., 1951-58; vis. lectr. U. Mich. Dental Sch., 1958-67; dir. Kenilworth Research Found., Ill., 1967—; prof. orthodontics Zoller Dental Clinic; pediatrics research assoc. prof. anthropology and anatomy U. Chgo., 1969-81, assoc. prof. plastic and reconstructive surgery, 1980-82; research scientist ADA Research Inst., Chgo., 1980-90; dir. G.V. Black Inst. for Continuing Edn., 1967—; vis. prof. U. Mich., 1984-94; clin. prof. orthodontics U. Ill. Coll. Dentistry, Chgo., 1994—. Northcroft lectr., Birmingham, Eng., 1989; cons. in field. Author textbooks, articles; editor-in-chief Am. Jour. Orthodontics, 1985-2000, World Jour Orthodontics, 2000—. Served as capt. Dental Corps AUS, 1941-45. Decorated Japanese Order of the Sacred Treasure; recipient Alumni Merit award Northwestern U., 1977; named Disting. Alumnus Washington U., 1980; NIH grantee, 1954, 56-60, 76, 77, 79, 80, 85, 86. Fellow Royal Coll. Surgeons (Eng.), Am. Coll. of Dentists, Internat. Coll. of Dentists; mem. Am. Dental Soc., Ill. Dental Soc., Am. Assn. Orthodontist (gen. chmn. 1960, 77, 80, founding mem., chmn. coun. on orthodontic edn. and audio visual com. 1962, 67, gen. chmn. jour. 1977, trustee, Grieve Meml. award 1964, 84, Disting. Service award 1970, Ketcham award 1975, Salzmann award 1979, 75th Anniversary citation 1990, Mershon award 1989, Horace Hayden award 1991, Jarabak Internat. Teaching and Rsch. award 1994, Heritage award 1998, 99), Internat. Assn. Research (chmn. Chgo. sect. 1973-74), Chgo. Orthodontists Assn. (pres. 1961-62), European Orthodontists Soc.(hon.life mem. 2002), Ill. Orthodontists Soc. (pres. 1969-70, Outstanding Tchg. award 1999), Angle Soc. (pres. 1968), Japan Orthodontists Soc., World Fedn. Orthodontists (hon., Millenium award 2000), Ill. Soc. Orthodontists, SAR. Republican. Presbyterian. Home: 2895 Sheridan Pl Evanston IL 60201-1725 Office: U Ill Coll Dentistry MC842 801 S Paulina St # Mc842 Chicago IL 60612-7210 E-mail: tgraber@uic.edu., tmgraber@attbi.com.

GRABER, WILLIAM RAYMOND, pharmaceutical executive; b. Vancouver, Wash., Apr. 10, 1943; s. R. Archie and Josephine N. (Martin) G.; m. Mary Lynn McArthur, June 19, 1965; children: Kristine, Kathleen, Timothy. BA in Math., Wash. State U., 1965. Fin. mgr. GE, 1965-91; contr. The Mead Corp., Dayton, Ohio, 1991—; CFO, sr. v.p. McKesson HBOC, San Francisco, 2000—. Avocations: golf, jogging. Home: 145 Las Vegas Rd Orinda CA 94563-1954

GRABINER, SANDY, mathematics educator; b. N.Y.C., Dec. 15, 1939; s. Morris and Anna (Present) G.; m. Judith Victor, June 14, 1964; children: David, Rebecca. BA, Rice U., 1960; AM, Harvard U., 1961, PhD, 1967. Instr. MIT, Cambridge, 1967-69; asst. prof. Claremont Grad. Sch., Calif., 1969-74; assoc. prof. math. Pomona Coll., Claremont, 1974-82, prof., 1982—. Editl. bd. Carus Monographs, 1990-93; contbr. articles to profl. jours. Mem. Math. Assn. Am. (program chmn. 1984-85), Am. Math. Soc., London Math. Soc., AAAS. Office: Pomona Coll Dept Maths 610 N College Ave Dept Maths Claremont CA 91711-4411

GRABNER, GEORGE JOHN, manufacturing executive; b. Muskogee, Okla., Aug. 25, 1918; s. George and Helen (Leitch) G.; m. Martha Ebright, Oct. 2, 1993; children: George John, Jan, Heidi, John, Thomas. BA, Western Res. U., 1939; postgrad., Harvard Grad. Sch. Bus. Adminstrn., 1940. CPA, Ohio. Asst. mgr. Ernst & Ernst (CPAs), Cleve., 1946-57; v.p., dir. Cyrus Eaton Interests, 1957-58; fin. v.p., treas. Weatherhead Co., Cleve., 1958-63, exec. v.p., 1963-65, pres., dir., 1965-70, Weatherhead Co. Can., Ltd., 1966-70, LPG Leasing Corp., Cleve., 1958-70; pres., chief exec. officer Lamson & Sessions Co., 1970-78, chmn. bd., 1978-84, chmn. exec. com., 1985-90, CEO, 1990; ret., 1990. Trustee 1st Union Realty, 1967-91; bd. dirs. Cardinal Fastener and Specialty Co., Cardinal Am. Corp. Chmn. bd. Greater Cleve. Growth Assn., 1966-69; chmn. Cleve. Devel. Found., 1966-69, Fin. Supervisory Commn. of City of Cleve., 1980-88; trustee S.A. Horvitz Testamentary Trust, WLD Trust, 1988—, WRH Trust, 1988—, LJR Trust, 1988—; life trustee Univ. Sch., 1970—. 1st lt. USAAF, 1942-45. Mem. Ohio Soc. CPAs, Am. Ordinance Assn. (past pres., dir.), Union Club, Pepper Pike Country Club, Hole in the Wall Club, The Everglades Club, The Ocean Club, The Little Club. Home: 6830 N Ocean Blvd #8 Ocean Ridge FL 33435

GRABOIS, NEIL ROBERT, foundation administrator, former college president; b. N.Y.C., Dec. 11, 1935; s. Lazarus Lawrence and Florence (Graber) G.; m. Miriam Blau, Aug. 19, 1956; children: Adam, Daniel. BA, Swarthmore Coll., 1957; MA, U. Pa., 1959, PhD, 1963; LLD (hon.), Williams Coll., 1988, LHD (hon.), Colgate U., 1999. Asst. instr. math. U. Pa., Phila., 1957-61; instr. math. Lafayette Coll., Easton, Pa., 1961-63; mem. faculty Williams Coll., Williamstown, Mass., 1963-88, prof. math., 1972-88, dean coll., dean faculty, then provost, 1970-80, chmn. dept. math. scis., 1981-83, provost, 1983-88; pres. Colgate U., Hamilton, N.Y., 1988-99; v.p. for strategic planning, program coord. Carnegie Corp. N.Y., N.Y.C., 1999—. Treas. Roper Ctr., Storrs, Conn., 1979-88. Co-author: Linear Algebra and Multivariable Calculus, 1970. Chmn. edn. subcom. Gov.'s Task Force for No. Berkshires, North Adams, Mass., 1985-87; trustee Swarthmore Coll., 1991—, L.I.U., 2002—. Mem. Am. Math. Soc., Math. Assn. Am. (vis. lectr. 1971), AAAS, N.Y. Acad. Scis. Democrat. Avocations: squash, tennis, clarinet, recorder. Office: Carnegie Corp NY 437 Madison Ave New York NY 10022-7001 E-mail: nrg@carnegie.org. *Without the support of our fellows, there can be no success; without understanding, and compassion, ideas have shape but may lead only into darkness; without honesty and clarity, and a willingness to hear the other side, tactics may succeed but the right path will be lost; no person sees the whole truth but the leader can help us find our way.*

GRABOW, RAYMOND JOHN, mayor, lawyer; b. Cleve., Jan. 27, 1932; s. Joseph Stanley and Frances (Kalata) G.; m. Margaret Jean Knoll, Nov. 27, 1969; children: Rachel Jean, Ryan Joseph. BSBA, Kent State U., 1953; JD, Western Res. U., 1958. Bar: Ohio 1958. Counsel No. Ohio Petroleum Retailers Assn., Cleve., 1965-78; counsel, trustee Alliance of Poles Fed. Credit Union, 1972; also gen. counsel Alliance of Poles of Am., Parma Polish Am. League; councilman City of Warrensville Heights (Ohio), 1962-68, mayor, 1968-98. Sec. Space Comfort Co., S.S.K., Inc.; fed. panelist U.S. Dist. Ct.; active Dem. Exec. Com. Cuyahoga County, 1966—98, precinct com., 1966—80; trustee Brentwood Hosp., Nat. League Cities, Brentwood Found.; bd. govs. Meridia Southpoint Hosp., 1996—99. Mem. Ohio Jud. Conf. (life), Ohio State Bar Assn., Cuyahoga County Bar Assn., Cleve. Bar Assn., U.S. Conf. of Mayors, Am. Legion, PLAV Vets, Cleve. Soc., Warrensville Heights C. of C. (trustee 1989-98), Ohio Assn. Pub. Safety Dirs., Ohio Mcpl. League, Mcpl. Treas. Assn., Order of Alhambra, Fraternal Order of Eagles, West Harbor Lagoons Assn. (pres.). Home: 10545 Cambridge Cir Cleveland OH 44133- Office: 5005 Rockside Rd Cleveland OH 44131-2194 Business E-Mail: rjggf@juno.com.

GRABOW, STEPHEN HARRIS, architecture educator; b. Bklyn., Jan. 15, 1943; s. Philip and Ida (England) G.; 1 child, Nicole Elizabeth. BArch., U. Mich., 1965; MArch., Pratt Inst., 1966; postgrad., U. Calif.-Berkeley, 1966-67; PhD, U. Wash., 1973. Architect-planner U.S. Peace Corps, Tunisia, 1967-69; regional planning cons. Teheran, Iran, 1969; asst. prof. architecture U. Ariz., 1969-70; teaching assoc. U. Wash., 1970-72; lectr. town and regional planning Duncan of Jordanstone Coll. Art, U. Dundee, Scotland, 1972-73; asst. prof. architecture and urban design U. Kans.-Lawrence, 1973-76, assoc. prof., 1976-82, prof., 1982—, dir. architecture, 1979-82, 83-86; vis. fellow U. Calif.-Berkeley, 1977; research and design cons. Design Build Architects, Lawrence; bd. dirs. Assn. Collegiate Schs. Architecture, 1982-87. Vis. lectr. Royal Danish Acad. Fine Arts, Copenhagen, 1987-88. Author: Christopher Alexander and the Search for a New Paradigm in Architecture, 1983; mem. editorial bd.: Jour. Archtl. Edn., 1982-84. Recipient award Nat. Endowment for Arts, 1974, citation for excellence in design rsch. NEA, 1980, Biennial Svc. award Denmark's Internat. Studies Program, 1997, Bradley Tchg. award in architecture U. Kans., 1998; Fulbright Scholar award, 1987-88; NEH fellow, 1976-77. Mem. Nat. Archtl. Research Council (appointee 1986-87). Home: 1518 Crossgate Dr Lawrence KS 66047-3504 Office: U Kans Sch Architecture & Urban Design 1465 Jayhawk Blvd Lawrence KS 66045-7614 E-mail: sgrabow@ku.edu.

GRABOWSKI, JOHN JOSEPH, education educator, researcher; b. Cleveland, Ohio, Jan 15, 1949; s. Ben Joseph Grabowski and Frances Joanne Wolfe; m. Diane Louise Ewart. BA, Case Western Res. U., 1967—71, MA, 1971—73, PhD, 1973—77. Curator of manuscripts Western Res. Hist. Soc., Cleve., 1985—94; assoc. prof. Case Western Res. U., Cleve., 1999—; dir. of rsch. Western Res. Hist. Soc., Cleve., 1994—. Editor: (book) Encyclopedia of Cleveland History; author: Sports in Cleveland: An Illustrated History, 1992; managing editor (book) Dictionary of Cleveland Biography, 1996, co-editor Cleveland: A Tradition of Reform, 1986. Mem. of bd. Hist. Associates of Case Western Res. U., Cleve., 2000; pres. NE Ohio Chpt. of the Fulbright Assn., Cleve. Fulbright Sr. Lectureship, Bilkent U., Ankara, Turkey, Fulbright Commn., 1996—97. Mem.: Soc. of Am. Archivists, Orgn. of Am. Historians, Am. Hist. Assn. Avocation: travel. Office: Case Western Reserve University 10900 Euclid Ave - Mather House 309 Cleveland OH 44106

GRABOWSKI, MICHAEL JOSEPH, financial executive; b. Milw., Dec. 17, 1961; s. Joseph Casmir and Cecile (Bendyk) G.; m. Denise Marie Krauske, Oct. 19, 1991. BBA in Fin., U. Wis., Milw., 1984; MBA, Keller Grad. Sch. Mgmt., Chgo., 1991. Customer acct. rep. Ford Motor Credit, Milw., 1984-85; fin. planner Capital Concepts Corp., Milw., 1984-87; pres. Michael Properties, Milw., 1987—; corp. controller Leo Lieberman, Inc., Milw., 1991-92; CFO Advance Cleaning Products, Milw., 1992-93; pres., acct., fin. adv. Insight Acctg. and Fin. Cons., Inc., Milw., 1987—. Author: (newsletter) Your Money Management, 1987. Mem. Nat. Assn. Enrolled Agts., Nat. Assn. Tac Practitioners, Nat. Soc. Pub. Accts., Milw. Apt. Assn., St. Alphonsus Athletic Assn. (bd. dirs.). Avocation: athletic activities. Office: Insight Acctg & Fin Cons Inc 4712 W Forest Home Ave Milwaukee WI 53219-4716

GRABOWSKI, WOJCIECH W. physicist, researcher; b. Warsaw, June 20, 1955; s. Janusz Grabowski and Alicja Grabowska; m. Elzbieta M. Wroblewska; children: Magda Grabowska, Dorota Grabowska. MSc in Physics(hon.), U. Warsaw, 1981; PhD, Polish Acad. Scis., 1987. Rsch. fellow Inst. Geophysics Polish Acad. Scis., Warsaw, 1985—87; scientist Nat. Ctr. Atmospheric Rsch., Boulder, Colo., 1987—. Contbr. articles to profl. jours. Mem.: Am. Meteorol. Soc. Office: Nat Ctr Atmospheric Rsch PO Box 3000 Boulder CO 80301-3000 Office Fax: 303-497-8181.

GRACE, ELLEN MARIA, attorney; b. N.Y.C. BS in Acctg., Pa. State U., University Park, 1989; MBA, U. Ill., Urbana-Champaign, 1992; JD, Ind. U., Bloomington, 1994. Cert. CPA, Ind., Bar: Ind. 1994, Pa. 1997. Staff acct. audit Price Waterhouse, Morristown, N.J., 1989-90; teaching asst. U. Ill., Urbana-Champaign, 1991-92; sr. tax specialist KPMG Peat Marwick LLP, Indpls., 1994-95, sr. cons. personal fin. planning Phila., 1995-96, sr. cons. corp. transactions svcs., 1996-97; adj. prof. N.H. Coll., Ceiba, P.R., 1997-98; counsel GE, Lynchburg, Va., 1998-99, asst. dir. advanced mktg., atty., 1999-2001, sourcing atty. Schenectady, N.Y., 2001—. Assoc. Fed. Comms. Law Jour., Bloomington, Ind., 1993-94. Author: Privacy vs. Convenience: The Benefits and Drawbacks of Tax System Modernization, 1994. Pres. MBA Assn., Urbana-Champaign, 1991-92. Recipient award, GE, 1999, 2000, 2001. Avocations: private pilot, classical pianist. E-mail address. Office: GE 1 River Rd Bldg 5-2 East Schenectady NY 12345 Fax: 804-948-5396. E-mail: maria.grace@corporate.ge.com.

GRACE, JAMES MARTIN, JR., lawyer; b. Columbus, Ohio, Sept. 6, 1967; s. James Martin and Letitia Jean (Stively) G.; m. Michèle Lee Sirna, June 22, 1991. BA, U. Notre Dame, 1989; JD cum laude, U. Houston, 1992. Bar: Tex. Law clk. to Hon. Samuel B. Kent U.S. Dist. Ct. (so. dist.) Tex., Galveston, 1992-93; assoc. Baker Botts, LLP, Houston, 1993-2000; sr. counsel Enron N.Am. Corp., Houston, 2000-2001; mgr. Enron Wholesale Svcs., Houston, 2001—02; dir. Tex. state affairs Ctr. Point Energy Inc., Houston, 2002—. Author tchr.'s guide: Copyright Law, 1992. Adv. coun. Local Initiatives Support Corp.; pres. R Club PAC, 1998-99, co-chair Young Profls. for Aspiring Youth, 2000-02. Mem.: Greater Heights Area C. of C. (bd. dirs. 2002—), Houston Law Rev. Alumni Assn. (dir.), Houston Bar Assn., State Bar Tex., U. Notre Dame Alumni Assn. (treas. Class of '89), Notre Dame Club Houston (bd. dirs.), Houston Jaycees (dir. edn. 1993—94, legal counsel 1994, Outstanding Leadership award 1993, Silver Key award 1994), Order of the Barons, Phi Delta Phi. Republican. Roman Catholic. Avocations: soccer, football, reading. Office: Ctr Point Energy Inc 1111 Louisiana St Houston TX 77002 E-mail: jim.m.grace@centerpointenergy.com.

GRACE, JASON ROY, advertising agency executive; b. N.Y.C., Dec. 5, 1936; s. Jack and Mitzi (Goldstick) G.; m. Marcia Jean Bell, May 16, 1966; children: Jessica Bell, Nicholas Bell. Student, Cooper Union, 1955-56, 58-62. Art dir. Benton & Bowles Inc., N.Y.C., 1962-63, Grey Advt., N.Y.C., 1963-64; sr. v.p., creative mgmt. supr. Doyle Dane Bernbach Inc., N.Y.C., 1964-72; creative dir., exec. v.p. Gilbert, Grace & Stark, N.Y.C., 1972-75, Doyle Dane Bernbach Inc., 1975-79, exec. v.p., exec. creative dir., from 1979, vice chmn., 1981-86, chmn. bd. U.S., exec. creative dir., from 1986; chmn. bd. Grace and Rothschild. Film dir., 1970— Elected art dirs. Hall of Fame, 1986—; trustee Cooper Union, 1987—; bd. dirs. Nat. Mus. Am. History, Smithsonian Inst., 1988—. With U.S. Army, 1956-58. Recipient 8 Andy awards Advt. Club N.Y., 28 Clio awards Am. Film Festival, 5 Gold Lion awards, 3 Silver Lion awards Cannes Film Festival, 9 Gold medals Art Dirs. Club, Best TV Comml. of Last 20 Yrs. award; recipient Internat. Broadcasting award, 1980, St. Gaudens medal Cooper Union Alumni Assn., Grand Masters Lifetime Achievement award N.Y.C. Tech. Coll., 2002; 6 comml̃s. named in Clio Hall of Fame, Outstanding Alumnus Sch. Art and Design, 1987; 4 commls. placed in permanent collection Mus. Modern Art; elected to Creative Hall of Fame, The One Club, 1994, 97; 2 commls. in Advtg. Age's 50 Best TV Commls. of All Time, 3 of Top 6 in TV Guide's List of Best 50 Commls. of All Time. Home: New York, NY. Died Feb. 26, 2003.

GRACE, JOHN EUGENE, business forms company executive; b. Dundee, Ill., Nov. 22, 1931; s. Arnold Victor and Louise Joan (Boncosky) G.; m. Janice Rae Fohey, June 30, 1956; children: Gregory Alan, Michael Brian, Michele Marie. BS in Bus. Adminstrn. with high honors, U. Ill., 1958; MSBA in Fin., No. Ill. U., 1976. Gen. acctg. mgr. Elgin Watch Co., Ill., 1958-60; corp. controller Newell Cos., Freeport, Ill., 1960-68; controller jewelry div. Josten's, Inc., Owatonna, Minn., 1968-71; v.p. fin., chief fin. officer, asst. sec. Duplex Products Inc., Sycamore, Ill., 1971-87, cons., 1987-97. Cons. in field Active local United Fund, Little League, YMCA. Served with USAF, 1951-53. Mem. Fin. Execs. Inst. (past pres., dir. Fox-Rock chpt.), IMA (past dir.), Adminstrv. Mgmt. Soc. (past dir.), Jaycees, C. of C., Beta Alpha Psi. Clubs: Elks. Republican. Methodist. Home and Office: 405 Timber Ln Palm Harbor FL 34683-3737

GRACE, JOHN JOSEPH, retired priest; b. Chgo., Jan. 20, 1924; s. John Joseph and Mary Hamilton Grace. MA, St. Mary of Lake Sem., 1946, Licentiate of Sacred Theology, 1950. Ordained priest Roman Cath. Ch. Visitation asst. pastor, Chgo., 1950—60; asst. pastor St. Mary Ch., Des Plaines, Ill., 1960—65, Old St. Patrick Ch., Chgo., 1965—69; pastor St. Ludmilla, Chgo., 1969—83, St. Tarcissus, Chgo., 1983—2001; ret., 2001. Helper Cath. Charities, Chgo., 1970—. Home: St Benedict Home # 27 6930 W Touhy Ave Niles IL 60714

GRACE, JOHN ROSS, chemical engineering educator; b. London, Ont., Can., June 8, 1943; s. Archibald John and Mary Kathleen (Disney) G.; m. Sherrill Elizabeth Perley, Dec. 20, 1964; children— Elizabeth, Malcolm. B.E.Sc., U. Western Ont., 1965; PhD, Cambridge (Eng.) U., 1968. From asst. prof. to prof. chem. engring. McGill U., Montreal, Que., 1968-79; sr. research engr. Surveyor Nenniger & Chenevert Inc., 1974-75; prof. chem. engring. U. B.C., Vancouver, 1979—, head dept. chem. engrin., 1979-87, dean faculty grad. studies, 1990-96, prof. chem. and biol. engring., 2000—, Can. rsch. chair, 2001—; pres., CEO Membrane Reactor Techs. Ltd., 1998—2003. Cons. in field. Co-author: Bubbles, Drops and Particles, 1978; co-editor: Fluidization, 1980, Fluidization VI, 1989, Circulating Fluidized Beds, 1997, Circulating Fluidized Bed Technology VII, 2002; editor: Chem. Engring. Sci., 1984—90; contbr. articles to profl. jours. NRC sr. indsl. fellow; Athlone fellow; Can. Coun. Killam Res. fellow, 1999. Fellow Royal Soc. Can., Can. Acad. Engring., Chem. Inst. Can. (v.p. 1994-95, pres. 1995-96); mem. Can. Soc. Chem. Engring. (pres. 1989-90, Erco award, R.S. Jane award), Assn. Profl. Engrs. B.C., Instn. Chem. Engrs. Office: 2216 Main Mall Vancouver BC Canada V6T 1Z4 E-mail: jgrace@chml.ubc.ca.

GRACE, JOHN WILLIAM, electrical company executive; b. May 29, 1921; s. Joseph and Ruth Margaret (Bailey) G.; m. Ruth Delores Schroeder, Nov. 25, 1950; children: Martha, Joan, Nancy, John William. Student, Am. TV Inst. Tech., 1950; BEE, Drexel U., 1960. Technician missiles and surface radar divsn. RCA, Moorestown, NJ, 1950—53, design engr., 1953—56, project engr., 1960—66; mgr. engring. and sci. exec. EG & G, Inc., Las Vegas, Nev., 1966-73, mgr. bus. devel. operational test and evaluation Albuquerque, 1973-77, engring. mgr. instrumentation divsn. Idaho Falls, Idaho, 1977-79, mgr. sys. project office, 1979, mgr. instrumentation program office, 1979-82, mgr. engring. spl. products divsn. Las Vegas, 1982-84, dir. tech. resources, 1984-91; ret., 1991. Patentee contradirectional waveguide coupler. E-mail: rudieabq@aol.com. Active Boy Scouts Am., 1969-71; pres. Episcopalian couples retreat, 1969-70. With USNR, 1941-45. Mem. IEEE, Instrumentation Soc. Am. (dir. sci. instrumentation and rsch. divsn.), Assn. Old Crows, Am. Legion (post adj. vice commdr. 1950). Home: 8311 Loma Del Norte Dr NE Albuquerque NM 87109-4901 Office: EG&G Spl Projects Divsn PO Box 93747 Las Vegas NV 89193-3747 E-mail: rudieabq@aol.com.

GRACE, JULIANNE ALICE, investor relations firm executive; b. Riverdale, N.Y., Oct. 29, 1937; d. Arthur Edward and Julia May (McCarthy) Thompson; m. Daniel Vincent Grace, July 2, 1960; children: Daniel Vincent III, Deirdre Elizabeth Beck. BA, Marymount Manhattan Coll., 1959; MA, Fordham U., 1960. Dir. admissions Marymount Manhattan Coll., N.Y.C., 1966-72; mgr. human resources The Perkin-Elmer Corp., Norwalk, Conn., 1972-78, dir. human resources, 1978-81, asst. sr. v.p. semiconductor equipment, 1981-83, asst. pres., 1983-85, v.p., asst. to chief exec. officer, 1985-86, v.p. adminstrn., 1986-90, v.p. corp. rels., 1990-95; pres. The Jagcom Group, New Canaan, Conn., 1995—. Bd. dirs. Norwalk and Wilton chpts. ARC, 1975—85, Metropool, 1991—98; pres., bd. dirs. Waveny (Conn.) Care Ctr., 1998—; bd. dirs. Waveny Network; trustee Norwalk YMCA, 1986—94; active Norwalk C.C. Found., 1986—90, Fairfield 2000; mem. corp. cabinet U. Conn. Downstate Initiative, 1995—98, mem. adv. com., lectr. exec. edn. program U. Conn., 1996—2001. Fellow Woodrow Wilson Nat. Found., 1959—60. Mem.: Fairfield Pub. Rels. Assn., Nat. Investor Rels. Inst. (sr. exec. roundtable), Econ. Soc. Conn., Saugatuck Harbor Yacht Club (bd. govs., flag officer fleet capt.), Wolfpit Running Club, Sports Car Club Am. Home and Office: 54 Louises Ln New Canaan CT 06840-2120

GRACE, MARCELLUS, pharmacy educator, university dean; b. Selma, Ala., Oct. 17, 1947; s. Capp and Mary (Davis) G.; m. Laura Dunn, Sept. 8, 1973; children: K'Chebe M., Syreeta L., Marcellus Jr. BS in Pharmacy, Xavier U. La., 1971; MS in Hosp. Pharmacy, U. Minn., 1975, PhD in Pharmacy Adminstrn., 1976. Registered pharmacist, La., Ohio, Calif., Minn., D.C. Hosp. pharmacy resident USPHS Hosp., Balt., 1971-72, staff pharmacist Boston, 1972-73, Thrifty Drug Stores, L.A., 1973; asst. dir. pharmacy Bethesda Hosps., Cin., 1975; dir. pharmacy svcs. Tulane U. Med. Ctr., New Orleans, 1976-77; assoc. prof., asst. dean Howard U., Washington, 1979-82; asst. prof. clin. pharmacy Xavier U. La., New Orleans, 1976-78, dean, 1983-99, prof. pharmacy adminstrn., 1983—. Mem. adv. coun. Nat. Heart Lung and Blood Inst., NIH, Bethesda, 1990-93; mem. Walgreens Pharmacy adv. coun., 1993-97; chair pharmacy panel Peer Health Professionscommn., 1991-92; bd. dirs. New Orleans Regional Med. Complex, 1993-98, Ernest N. Morial Asthma and Respiratory Disease Ctr., 1995—, La. Cancer and Lung Trust Fund, 1995-98, Alton Ochsner Med. Found., 1996—. Contbr. articles and abstracts to profl. jours. Recipient Bowl of Hygeia award, 1998, Wendell T. Hill award Assn. Black Hosp. Pharmacists, 2000. Mem. Am. Assn. Colls. Pharmacy (bd. dirs. 1992-94), N.Y. Acad. Scis., Assn., Rho Chi. Democrat. Baptist. Avocations: automobile restoration, flying. Office: Xavier U La Coll Pharmacy 7325 Palmetto St New Orleans LA 70125-1056

GRACE, MARCIA BELL, advertising executive; b. Pitts., July 29, 1937; d. Daniel Henry and Gertrude Margaret (Loew) Bell; m. Roy Grace, May 16, 1966; children: Jessica Bell, Nicholas Bell. AB, Harvard U., 1959. V.p., assoc. creative dir. Doyle Dane Bernbach, N.Y.C., 1964-77; sr. v.p., creative dir. Wells, Rich, Greene, Inc., N.Y.C., 1977-85, exec. v.p., creative dir., 1986-90; cons. Marcia Grace & Co., N.Y.C., 1990—. Represented in permanent collection Mus. Modern Art. Recipient 1st Pl. ANDY award Advt. Club N.Y., 1968, 70, 72, 75, 1st Pl. Gold award The One Show, 1973, 78, Hall of Fame award The Clio Show, N.Y.C., 1982, 86. Avocations: horseback riding, gardening.

GRACE, MICHAEL JUDD, immunologist; b. Chambley, France, Oct. 20, 1957; came to U.S., 1958; s. Judd Harper and Laura Belle (Davidson) G.; m. Jo Ann Fox, June 2, 1979; children: Christina Marie, Stephanie Ann, David Michael. BS, U. Nebr., 1979, PhD, 1984. Scientist Procter and Gamble Corp., Cin., 1984-88; sr. scientist Schering-Plough Corp., Bloomfield, N.J., 1988-90; prin. scientist Schering Plough Rsch. Inst., Kenilworth, N.J., 1990-93, sr. prin. scientist, 1993-96, fellow, 1996—. Adv. bd. chept. chemistry U. Nebr., Lincoln, 1991—. Contbr. over 60 articles in cytokine biology and gene therapy to profl. pubs.; patentee in cytokines as human therapeutics. Miessner Minerva grantee U. Nebr., 1976; Avery fellow U. Nebr., 1979. Mem. Am. Soc. Microbiologists, Reticuloendothelial Soc., N.Y. Acad. Scis., Phi Lambda Upsilon. Achievements include patent for method for increasing numbers of neutrophils and for treating wounds with IL-4, patent for method for increasing and activating monocytes and neutrophils and for inducing maturation of myeloid cells with IL-5, patent for stimulating response to pneumoccocal vaccine in the elderly with IL-10. Home: 1 Buckalew Ct Hamilton NJ 08610-1227 E-mail: michael.grace@spcorp.com.

GRACE, THOMAS LEE, health facility administrator, emergency nurse practitioner; b. Huntingdon, Pa., Mar. 29, 1955; s. Robert Leroy and Mary Elizabeth (Isenberg) Grace; m. Renee Lee Ramsey, Oct. 20, 1979; children: Elliott, Amanda. ASN, Robert Morris Coll., 1978; diploma in nursing, Sewickley (Pa.) Valley Hosp., 1979; BSN, LaRoche Coll., 1984; M in Pub. Mgmt., Carnegie Mellon U., 1985; PhD in Mgmt., Cambridge State U., 1999. RN Pa. Staff nurse orthop. dept. McKeesport (Pa.) Hosp., 1979-80; staff nurse emergency rm. Allegheny Gen. Hosp., Pitts., 1980-81; flight nurse Life-Flight-Allegheny Gen. Hosp., Pitts., 1981-85; chief flight nurse Aries-Fairfax Hosp., Falls Church, Va., 1985-86; coord. emergency svcs. Fairfax Hosp., Falls Church, 1986-87; flight program dir. Pennstar U. Pa. Med. Ctr., Phila., 1987-91; asst. adminstr. Hosp. of U. Pa., Phila., 1991-96; dir. safety mgmt. U. Pa. Health Sys., 1996-2000, dir. corp. support svcs., 2000—02, dir. AVP safety programs, 2002—. Contbr. articles to profl. jours. Mem. Huntingdon Vol. Fire Dept., 1972—, Valley Ambulance Authority, Corapolis, Pa., 1977—79; del. Ctrl. Dist. Fireman's Assn., Tyrone, Pa., 1983—; scoutmaster Sewickley Math. Ch. troop Boy Scouts Am., 1978—79; mem. bioterrorism hosp. adv. com. Pa. Dept. Heatlh, 2001—; mem. emergency preparedness task force Delaware Valley Healthcare Coun., 2001—; citizen rep. Upper Merion Twp. (Pa.) Emergency Svc. Bd., 1994—97; bd. dirs., citizen rep. Lafayette Ambulance Svc., King of Prussia, Pa., 1996—, treas., 1998—99, pres., 2000—02. With U.S. Army, 1973—76. Mem.: Am. Phys. Plant Adminstrs., Nat. Flight Nurses Assn. (past pres.), Nat. Fire Protection Assn., Am. Legion. Democrat. Achievements include invention of crico ventillation device. Avocations: fishing, skiing. Home: 594 Forest Rd Wayne PA 19087-2322 E-mail: tgrace@uphs.upenn.edu.

GRACE, WESLEY GEE, JR., engineer; b. Jackson, Tenn., Mar. 14, 1945; s. Wesley G. Sr. and Serena H. (Herriman) G.; m. Brenda P. Poff; l child, James Wesley. BS in Civil Engring., U. Tenn., 1967; MA in Urban Geography, Memphis State U., 1972. Registered profl. engr., Tenn., Miss., Ala.; lic. real estate broker, Tenn. Draftsman City of Jackson, 1964-66, city planner, 1969-72; engring. tech. TVA, 1966-67; urban planner Harland Bartholomew & Assoc., Memphis, 1967-69; dir. planning Urban Cons., Montgomery, Ala., 1972-73; v.p. Gregory-Grace & Assoc., Inc., Memphis, 1973-77; pres. Grace & Assoc., Inc., Memphis, 1977-86, chmn., 1986—. Bd. dirs. Kevin Wright, Inc., Memphis, Mid-South Surveying & Mapping, Inc., Memphis, Asbestos Cons., Inc., Memphis, Profl. Devel. Seminar, Inc. Author numerous urban and regional planning studies; adviser to video Bartlett Feels So Good, 1987 (state and regional awards). Advisor Shelby County Sheriff's Dept., Memphis, 1987—, spl. dep., 1987; trustee Tenn. Engring. Found., Nashville, 1986; bd. dirs. Ctr. City Fin. Corp., Memphis. Mem. Cons. Engrs. Memphis (v.p. 1979-80, pres. 1980-81, Engr. of Yr. award 1982), Am. Coun. Cons. Engrs., Home Builders Assn. Memphis (mem. coun. 1985-86), Cons. Engrs. Tenn., Rotary (bd. dirs. Bartlett, Tenn. club 1991-92), Bartlett C. of C. (bd. dirs. 1986, v.p. 1987), Summitt Club, Crescent Club, Wimbelton Sportsplex. Republican. Baptist. Avocations: flying, golf, snow skiing, reading. Office: PDS Inc PO Box 341143 Memphis TN 38184-1143

GRACE, WILLIAM PERSHING, petroleum geologist, real estate developer; b. Mineral Point, Mo., Sept. 19, 1920; s. William Francis and Bertha Luciel (Nephew) Grace; m. Jeannette Marie Grace, Mar. 28, 1942 (dec.); children: Joyce Medaris, Pamela, Sonia Scott, Patricia Lawser. Student, Corpus Christi U., 1946-47; B in Geology, Tex. Tech. U., 1947-50; student (GRI), U. Colo. Extension, 1968-69. Capt. USAF, 1940-46; regional geologist Anderson-Prichard Oil Corp., San Antonio, Tex., 1950-62; real estate broker Grace Reality, Aurora, Colo., 1963-66; pres. Kimberley Homes, Construction, Aurora, 1966-72; pres., broker Grace-Scott-Cooper Corp., Aurora, 1972—. Pres. Friends of the Aurora Pub. Libr., 1967, trustee mem., 1978, chmn. Adams County Rep. Party, 1970—72; mem. vocat. edn. coun. Sch. Dist. 28J, 1989—. Named Colorado of Yr., Colo. State Libr. Assn., 1988. Mem.: Sixty Five Roses Found., Aurora C. of C. (dir. 1966—68, Man of Yr. 1980), Aurora Bd. Realtors (treas. 1979, Realtor of Yr. 1980), Colo. State Friends and Trustees Assn., Colo. Assn. Realtors, Rocky Mountain Assn. Petroleum Geologists, Nat. Assn. Realtors, Am. Assn. Petroleum Geologists (del., House of Dels. 1961—62), Aurora Kiwainis (internat. del. in Nice, France 1993, lt. gov. Rocky Mountain divsn. 1992, sec. 1965, pres. 1972), Denver Petroleum Club, Sigma Gamma Epsilon. Lutheran. Avocations: geologic exploration, flying, golf, skiing, travel. Home: PO Box 440755 Aurora CO 80044-0755

GRACE-CRUM, PHYLLIS VENETIA, military officer; b. Phila., Jan. 16, 1957; d. Philip Dean, Doris Eleanor Dean-Hagood; m. H. Ellis, Apr. 14, 2001. BS, Lincoln U., Oxford, Pa., 1979. Petroleum platoon leader 590th Combat Support and Combat Svcs. Support Co., Zebra Base, Saudi Arabia, 1991—91; chief billeting and housing Hdqrs. and Hdqrs. Co., 1st Area Support Group, Damman, Saudi Arabia, 1991—91; exec. officer Hdqrs. and Hdqrs. Co., 22nd Support Ctr., Dammam, Saudi Arabia, 1991—92; supply and svcs. platoon leader 226th Supply and Svcs. Co., Fort Stewart, Ga., 1992—93, platoon leader Ft. Stewart, Ga., 1992—93; with 632nd Maintenance Co. 87th Corps Support Bn., Ft. Stewart, Ga., 1993—94, asst. supply and svcs. officer, 1995—96; U.S. Army Recruiting Co. comdr. Pitts. Recruiting Bn., 1st Recruiting Brigade, 1996—99; co. comdr. 183rd Maintenance Co., 68th Corps Support Battalion, 43rd Area Support Group, Ft. Carson, Colo., 1999; logistics ops. officer 3/345th Regiment, 4th Brigade, 87th DIV (Tng. Support Divsn.), Forest Park, Ga., 2000—. Environ. health specialist Ft. Devens, 1986—88. Contbr. The Logistician, 1996. Decorated Army Achievement medal U.S. Army, Army Commendation medal, Nat. Def. medal, Joint Meritorious Unit award, Meritorious Svc. medal. Mem.: Am. Legion, Alpha Kappa Delta, Delta Sigma Theta. Avocations: horseback riding, ballroom dancing, reading, weightlifting. Home: 2812 Waterford Club Dr Lithia Springs GA 30122 Office: 3/345th CS/CSS TS Bn Bldg 207B 4653 N First St Forest Park GA 30297-5000 Personal E-mail: phylliscrum@hotmail.com.

GRACEFFA, JOHN PHILIP, lawyer; b. Boston, Aug. 4, 1953; s. Anthony Joseph and Ruth Elizabeth (Nudd) G.; m. Elaine Marie Margeson, June 17, 1978; 1 child, Victoria Rose. BA magna cum laude, Ea. Nazarene Coll., Quincy, Mass., 1975; JD cum laude, Suffolk U., 1979. Bar: Mass. 1979, U.S. Dist. Ct. Mass. 1980, U.S. Ct. Appeals (1st cir.) 1981, R.I. 1994, U.S. Supreme Ct. 1994, U.S. Dist. Ct. R.I. 1995; CPCU. Asst. atty. gen. Mass. Office of the Atty. Gen., Boston, 1979-84; lawyer Gallagher and Gallagher, P.C., Boston, 1984-89, mgr. first-party litigation, 1990-95; lawyer Morrison, Mahoney & Miller, Boston and Providence, Mass., 1995—. Former mem. adj. faculty Northea. U. Sch. Continuing Edn., Boston, 1994-95. Contbr. articles to profl. jours. Spl. asst. atty. gen. Office of the Atty. Gen., Boston, 1992. Mem. FBA, Mass. Bar Assn., R.I. Bar Assn., Hingham Yacht Club. Avocations: yacht cruising and racing, bicycling, reading, skiing, travel. Office: Morrison Mahoney & Miller 250 Summer St Fl 1 Boston MA 02210-1181

GRACEY, DOUGLAS ROBERT, physician, physiologist, educator; b. Fort Dodge, Iowa, Aug. 7, 1936; s. Warren Robert and Aleta Mary (Thompson) G.; m. Edith Ann Haas, Dec. 23, 1961; children— Laura, Douglas Robert BA, Coe Coll., 1958; MD, Northwestern U., 1962; MS, U. Minn., 1968. Diplomate Am. Bd. Internal Medicine. Intern Cook County Hosp., Chgo., 1962-63; resident Mayo Grad. Sch. Medicine, 1963-66, 68-69; asst. prof. medicine Northwestern U. Med. Sch., 1969-75; assoc. prof. medicine Mayo Med. Sch., Rochester, Minn., 1975-83, prof., 1983—, vice chmn. pulmonary div., 1982-87; vice chmn. for practice dept. medicine Mayo Clinic, Rochester, 1983-93, dir. critical care medicine div., 1985-89, chmn. revenue systems com., chmn. divsn. pulmonary and critical care medicine. Author: (with W.W. Addington) Tuberculosis, 1972, Flying Lessons, Ambulances and orther Air Force Vignettes, 2000; editor: Pulmonary Diseases in the Adult, 1981; contbr. articles to profl. jours. Trustee Coe Coll., 1976-92. Served to capt. M.C., USAF, 1966-68 Am. Thoracic Soc. tng. fellow, 1968-69 Fellow ACP, Am. Coll. Chest Physicians, AMA. Lodges: Masons, Shriners. Republican. Office: Mayo Clinic Chmn Div Pulmonary & Critical Care Med Rochester MN 55901

GRACEY, JAMES STEELE, corporate director, retired coast guard officer, consultant; b. Newton, Mass., Aug. 24, 1927; s. Ernest James and Edna Alicia (Steele) G.; m. Dorcas Randall Neal, June 15, 1949; children: Kevin S., Cheryl A., Pamela R. BS, U.S. Coast Guard Acad., 1949; MBA, Harvard U., 1956. Commd. ensign USCG, 1949, advanced through grades to adm.; comptroller 2d Coast Guard Dist., St. Louis, 1962-65; dep. Governors' Island (N.Y.) project and Coast Guard Base, 1965-69; chief programs div. Chief of Staff's Office, Washington, 1969-74; chief of staff 5th Coast Guard Dist., Portsmouth, Va., 1974; comdr. 9th Coast Guard Dist., Cleve., 1974-77; chief of staff Coast Guard Hqtrs., Washington, 1977-78; comdr. Coast Guard Pacific Area and 12th Coast Guard Dist., San Francisco, 1978-81, Coast Guard Atlantic Area and 3d Coast Guard Dist., N.Y.C., 1981-82; commandant of USCG, Washington, 1982-86; sr. fellow Inst. for Higher Def. Studies, Capstone, 1986—2001. Chmn. Fed. Exec. Bd. Cleve., 1976-77; coord. regional emegency transp. Fed. Region IX, 1978-81; bd. dirs. Marine Spill Response Corp., chmn. audit com.; bd. dirs. Maguire Group, Inc., Maguire Group Conn., Inc., chmn., 1993-98; advisor New Sulzer Diesel Group, 1991-95; cons. Mitre Corp., 1987-92; vis. lectr. Nat. Def. U., Navy, Air and Army war colls., Fgn. Svc. Inst., Presdl. Classroom, Sloane Fellows, MIT, Kennedy Sch. Govt., Harvard U., 1982-86; bd. mgrs. Am. Bur. Shipping, 1982-86; bd. dirs. Nat. Cargo Bur., 1981-86; leader U.S. del. to Internat. Maritime Orgn., UN Assembly, 1983, 85; bd. visitors Mich. Maritime Acad. Mem. world bd. govs. USO, 1982-91; trustee Calvary United Meth. Ch., chmn. ch. coun., 1998-2001. Decorated Legion of Merit with gold star, D.S.M. with gold star; named Bay Stater of Yr., Maritime Man of Yr., San Diego NL Man of the Yr.; recipient Michelob Schooner award, San Francisco Honor medal. Mem. Ret. Officers Assn. (bd. dirs. 1986-92), Coast Guard Found. (bd. dirs. 1982—), Navy League, Nat. Mil. Family Assn. (advisor 1986-2002), Assn. for Rescue at Sea (bd. dirs., vice chmn. 1988-97, chmn. 1997-2003), Army-Navy Country Club. Home and Office: 1411 21st St S Arlington VA 22202-1507

GRACIAS, MAURICE, economist; b. Nairobi, Kenya, July 16, 1923; came to U.S., 1969, naturalized, 1975; s. John Ludgero and Olga Rosalina (Themudo) G.; m. Angela Coutinho, Aug. 22, 1954; children: Loretta, Belinda, Marina. BA, U. Internat. Studies, Geneva, 1962; postgrad., Inst. Transport, London, 1956. Asst. to controller East African Rys. and Harbours, Nairobi, 1948-63; contr. East African Rd. Svcs., Nairobi, 1963-65; chief auditor U.S. State Dept., Africa, 1965-69, Econ. Devel. Orgn., San Francisco, 1970-71; sr. acct. Coopers & Lybrand CPAs, Oakland, Calif., 1969; corp. audit mgr. Blue Cross, Oakland, 1971-80; owner, pres. Gracias & Assocs., Oakland, 1976—. Bd. dirs. Land Title Ins. Co., Oakland, 1986-88; pres. Internat. Investment Assocs., Oakland, 1976—; cons. Asian Devel. Bank, UN, 1976-2001, coord. econ. devel. funding projects with UN, World Bank, European Econ. Commn., White House Conf. on Small Bus., 1979, 86-96; keynote speaker internat. conventions, 1988, 90. Contbr. articles to newspaper pubs. Active local Roman Cath. Ch., community affairs; founder Goan Inst., San Francisco, pres., 1975-78. Named Outstanding Immigrant to U.S., Calif. State Legislature, 1978; Royal Econ. Soc. fellow, Eng., 1964-68. Republican. Avocations: sports, international cricket and field hockey, field hockey selection for Kenya in Melbourne Olympic games 1956.

GRACIN, HANK, lawyer; b. Massapequa Park, N.Y., Jan. 27, 1957; s. Bernard Tobias and Ada (Rosenberg) G.; m. Marisol L. Perez, Sept. 9, 1990. BA with honors, SUNY, Binghamton, 1978; JD cum laude, NYU, 1981. Bar: N.Y. 1982, U.S. Dist. Ct. (so. dist.) N.Y. 1982. Assoc. Sullivan & Cromwell, N.Y.C., 1981-83, Schulte Roth & Zabel, N.Y.C., 1983-86, Fulbright Jaworski & Reavis McGrath, N.Y.C., 1986-90; corp. counsel Computer Assocs. Internat., Inc., 1990-94; ptnr. Lehman & Eilen, 1994—. Editor: Private Placements and Restricted Securities, 1981. Mem. Nassau County Bar Assn., Order of Coif (NYU chpt.). Avocations: bicycling, reading, piano. Office: Lehman & Eilen Ste 505 50 Charles Lindbergh Blvd Uniondale NY 11553-3612 E-mail: HGracin@Lehmaneilen.com.

GRACY, DAVID BERGEN, II, archivist, information science educator, writer; b. Austin, Tex., Oct. 25, 1941; married; 3 children. BA, U. Tex., Austin, 1963, MA, 1966; PhD in History, Tex. Tech. U., 1971. Cert. archivist. Archivist S.W. Collection Tex. Tech. U., 1966-71; from asst. prof. to assoc. prof. urban life Ga. State U., 1971-77; archivist So. Labor Archives, 1971-77; dir. Tex. State Archives, 1977-86; Gov. Bill Daniel prof. in archival enterprise U. Tex., Austin, 1986—, assoc. dean Grad. Sch. of Libr. and Info. Sci., 1991-95; interim dir. preservation and conservation studies program U. Tex. Grad. Sch. Libr. and Info. Sci.; dir. Ctr. for the Cultural Record, 2000—. Gen. ptnr. David B. Gracy II & Assocs., 1989—; adj. prof. history De Kalb C.C., 1973—74; vis. prof. archival enterprise San Jose State U., 2001, U. Ariz., 2003; instr. Ga. Archives Inst., Grad. Sch. Libr. and Info. Sci. U. Tex., Austin, Modern Archives Inst. Nat. Archives of U.S., Rare Books Sch. Columbia U., Soc. Am. Archivists, S.W. Archivists, Spl. Librs. Assn., Tex. State Libr., Trinity U., U.S. Info. Agy. for U. Philippines, Presdl. Commn. on Culture and Arts, Univ. Republic, Uruguay, Utah State Archives, Western Archives Inst.; cons. N.Mex. State Archives and Libr. Bldg. project, 1994—98, Nat. Episc. Ch. Archives, 1978, Oral Roberts U., 1978, Archives Civil Rights, M.L. King Ctr., Atlanta, 1976—81, Am. Heritage Ctr. U. Wyo., 1988—89, San Antonio Pub. Libr., 1988, Nat. Assn. for Preservation and Perpetuation of Storytelling, Jonesborough, Tenn., 1988—89,

King Ranch, Kingsville, Tex., 1987; coord. Tex. Hist. Records Adv. Bd., 1979—86; mem. Ga. Hist. Records Adv. Bd., 1976, Nat. Hist. Publs. and Rec. Commn., 1980—85; lectr. U. Tex., Austin, 1980—81, sr. lectr., 1982—86. Author: Littlefield Lands: Colonization on the Texas Plains, 1912-1920, 1968, Archives and Manuscripts: Arrangement and Description, 1977, It's Your Heritage: The Archives of Texas, 1977, An Introduction to Archives and Manuscripts, 1981, Moses Austin: His Life, 1987; co-author: Ships of the Texas Navy, 1979; bibliography advisor The New Handbook of Texas, 1988-94; mem. editl. bd. Libraries and Culture, 1985—, Am. Archivist, 1976-79; founder, editor Ga. Archive (subsequently Provenance), 1972-76; contbr. to Reflections of Western Historians, 1969; assoc. editor Tex. Mil. History, 1962-88; editl. asst. Southwestern Hist. Quar., 1963-66; contbr. articles to profl. jours. Bd. dirs. Nat. Archives Episcopal Ch., 1986—98, vice chair, 1995—98; bd. dirs. Task Force on Preservation Edn., Commn. on Preservation and Access, 1989—90, mem., 1991—97; chmn. task force on archives Summerlee Comm. on Tex. History, 1989—93, Tex. Preservation Task Force, 1988—90; sec. Coun. on Libr. and Info. Resources, 1997—2000. Named Disting. Alumnus Dept. History Tex. Tech. U., 1987; recipient award of merit Am. Assn. for State and Local History, 1969, Disting. Svc. award Organized Labor and Workmen's Circle, Atlanta, 1976, Cert. Merit Soc. Ga. Archivists, 1976, Soc. S.W. Archivists, 1978, Tex. Excellence in Teaching award Grad. Sch. Libr. and Info. Sci. U. Tex. at Austin, 1987, San Jacinto award, 1993. Fellow: Tex. State Hist. Assn., Tex. State Geneal. Soc., Soc. Am. Archivists (v.p., pres. 1982—84, award of merit 1975); mem.: Soc. Ga. Archivists (pres. 1972—74, cert. merit 1976), Acad. Cert. Archivists (bd. regents 1990—93, v.p., pres. 1999—2000), Pan Am. Inst. Geography and History (U.S. rep. archives com. 1982—97), Assn. Records Mgrs. and Adminstrs. (pres. Austin chpt. 1980—81, cert. award 1981), Internat. Coun. Archives (editor Edn. and Devel. News 1989—96, listmaster sect. archival edn. and tng. listserv. 1996—2002, v.p. sect. on archival edn. and tng.), Am. Assn. State and Local History (award of merit 1968), Tex. Bar Hist. Found. Office: U Tex Sch of Info Austin TX 78712-0390 E-mail: gracyiis@hotmail.com., gracy@ischool.utexas.edu.

GRAD, BONNIE LEE, art historian, educator; b. N.Y.C., June 1, 1949; d. Julius and Sue (Roberts) Grad; m. Gary Wolf, June 21, 1980; children: Alexander, Theodore. BA cum laude, Cornell U., 1971; PhD, U. Va., 1977. Art instr. Cin. Art Mus., 1967, 68; tchg. asst. U. Va., Charlottesville, 1973-74; collections asst., graphic arts collection Princeton (N.J.) Univ. Libr., 1976-77; asst. prof. art history Clark U., Worcester, Mass., 1977-83, assoc. prof., 1983—. Bd. dirs. New Eng. Fulbright Assn., 1997—, v.p. 1998-2000; grant reviewer Nat. Endowment for Humanities, 1997; reviewer The Bunting Inst., 1991; vis. scholar Pollock-Krasner Home and Studies Ctr., 1994, 97. Curator exhbns. including The Princeton U. Graphic Arts Collection, Worcester Arts Mus., Nat. Gallery of Art, Simmons Coll., Rose Art Mus.; author: Milton Avery Monotypes, 1977, Milton Avery, 1981, Robert Richenburg, 1993; co-author: Visions of City and Country, 1982; contbr. articles to profl. jours. Mem. Weston (Mass.) Arts Coun., 1988-94. Fulbright-Hays grantee, 1974-75, Nat. Endowment for Humanities grantee, 1980 83, Mellon grantee, 1984-87, Higgins grantee, 1989-95, 98, 99, Richard A. Florsheim Art Fund grantee, 1993-94, Seymour N. Logan fellow, 1992-94. Mem. Mass. Fulbright Assn. (bd. dirs. ea. chpt. 1997—, v.p. 1998-99). Office: 950 Main St Worcester MA 01610-1400 E-mail: bonniegrad@aol.com.

GRAD, FRANK PAUL, law educator, lawyer; b. Vienna, May 2, 1924; came to U.S., 1939, naturalized, 1943; s. Morris and Clara Sophie (Scher) G.; m. Lisa Szilagyi, Dec. 6, 1946; children: David Anthony, Catharine Ann. BA magna cum laude, Bklyn. Coll., 1947; LLB, Columbia U., 1949. Bar: N.Y. 1949. Assoc. in law Columbia U. Law Sch., N.Y.C., 1949-50, asst. dir. Legis. Drafting Research Fund, 1953-55, assoc. dir., 1956-68, dir., 1969-95, faculty, 1954-69, prof., 1969—, Joseph P. Chamberlain prof. legis., 1982-95, Joseph P. Chamberlain prof. emeritus legis. and spl. lectr., 1995—; legal adv. com. U.S. Council Environ. Quality, 1970-73; mem. N.Y. Deptl. Com. Ct. Adminstrn., Appellate Div., 1st Dept., 1970-74; counsel N.Y. State Spl. Adv. Panel Med. Malpractice, 1975; legal counsel Nat. Mcpl. League, 1967-88. Cons. in field; reporter U.S. Superfund Study group, 1981-82; dir. rsch. N.Y.C. Charter Revision Commn., 1982-83, N.Y. State-City Commn. on Integrity in Govt., 1986. Author: Public Health Law Manual, 1st edit., 1965, 2d rev. edit., 1990, The Drafting of State Constitutions, 1963, Environmental law: Sources and Problems, 3d edit., 1985, 4th edit. (with Joel Mintz), 2000, Treatise on Environmental Law, 8 vols., 1973—; co-author other legal reports; contbr. articles to profl. jours.; draftsman mcpl. codes and state legislation. With AUS, 1943-46. 10th Horace E. Read Meml. lectr. Dalhousie Law Sch., 1984. Mem. ABA, APHA, Assn. of Bar of City of N.Y., N.Y. Bar Assn., Am. Law Inst., Am. Soc. Law and Medicine, World Conservation Union (commn. on environ. law 1991—), Human Genome Orgn., Internat. Coun. Environ. Law, N.Y. Soc. Med. Jurisprudence. Office: Columbia U Sch Law 435 W 116th St New York NY 10027-7297 E-mail: fgrad@law.columbia.edu.

GRADDICK, CHARLES ALLEN, lawyer; b. Mobile, Ala., Dec. 10, 1944; s. Julian and Elvera (Smith) G.; m. Corinne Whiting, Aug. 19, 1966; children: Charles Allen, Herndon Whiting, Corinne. JD, Cumberland Sch. Law, 1970. Bar: Ala. 1970. Clk. Ala. Supreme Ct., 1970; asst. dist. atty. County of Mobile, Ala., 1971-75, dist. atty., 1975-79; atty. gen. State of Ala., Montgomery, 1979-87; ptnr. Thorton, Farish and Gaunt, Montgomery, 1987-89, Anderson, Graddick and Nabors, P.C., Montgomery, 1989-90; dist. atty. Montgomery County, Montgomery County, Ala., 1991-93; ptnr. Graddick & Belser, P.C., Montgomery and Mobile, 1992-99, Sims, Graddick & Dodson, Mobile, 2000—. Served with USNG, 1969-96. Named Outstanding Young Man of Mobile, Mobile Jaycees, 1976, State Conservationist of Yr., Ala. Wildlife Fedn.; recipient cert. appreciation Ala. Peace Officers, 1978, Appreciation award Optimists, 1978. Mem. ABA, ATLA, Ala. Bar Assn., Mobile Bar Assn., Montgomery Bar Assn., Ala. Trial Lawyers Assn., Ala. Dist. Attys. Assn., Nat. Dist. Attys. Assn., Nat. Assn. Attys. Gen. Republican. Episcopalian. Office: Sims Graddick & Dodson 205 Saint Emanuel St Mobile AL 36602-3009 E-mail: cag@simsgraddick.com.

GRADER, PATRICIA ALISON LANDE, editor; b. L.A., Mar. 23, 1960; d. Frederick and Irma Rose (Davidson) L.; m. Scott P. Grader, Feb. 11, 1995; 1 child, Louisa Frances Duo. Student, Washington U., St. Louis, 1977-79; BA with high distinction, U. Calif., San Diego, 1982. Editl. asst. Crown Pubs., N.Y.C., 1982-83; asst. editor St. Martin's Press, N.Y.C., 1983-84; editor Atheneum Pubs., N.Y.C., 1984-87; v.p., sr. editor Simon & Schuster, Inc., N.Y.C., 1987-91; v.p., dir. IMG-The Julian Bach Literary Agy., N.Y.C., 1992-95; exec. editor William Morrow, N.Y.C., 1995—. Mentor internship program Simon & Schuster, 1991; mem. adminstrv. com. IMG, 1992-95; speaker in field. Mem. Pi Beta Phi. Office: William Morrow 10 E 53d St New York NY 10022

GRADER, SCOTT PAUL, lawyer; b. Bklyn., June 25, 1956; s. Jack and Bernice Grader; m. Patricia Lande, Feb. 11, 1995; one child, Louisa Frances Duo. BA with honors, CUNY, 1977; JD with honors, Rutgers U., 1980; LLM, U. London, 1983. Bar: N.Y. 1981. Asst. gen. counsel N.Y.C. Office of Econ. Devel., 1981-82; assoc. Cahill, Gordon & Reindel, N.Y.C., 1984-86, Paul, Weiss, Rifkind, Wharton & Garrison, N.Y.C., 1986-97, counsel, 1998—. Assoc. editor Rutgers-Camden Law Rev., 1978-80. Hague Acad. Internat. scholar, The Hague, The Netherlands, 1983. Mem. Assn. of Bar of City of N.Y. Home: 670 W End Ave Apt 14C New York NY 10025-7328 Office: Paul Weiss Rifkind Wharton & Garrison 1285 Ave of the Ams New York NY 10019 E-mail: sgrader@paulweiss.com.

GRADINGER, GILBERT PAUL, plastic surgeon; b. Waterloo, Iowa, 1930; MD, Wash. U., 1956. Diplomate Am. Bd. Plastic Surgery . Intern U. Calif. Hosp., San Francisco, 1956—57, resident in surgery, 1957—59, chief resident in plastic surgery, 1960—61; resident in plastic surgery Franklin Hosp., San Francisco, 1959—60; plastic surgeon Peninsula Hosp. Med. Ctr., Burlingame, Calif.; clin. prof. plastic surgery U. Calif., San Francisco, prof. plastic surgery. Sec.-treas. Am. Bd. Plastic Surgery, 1993, chmn., 94. Fellow: ACS; mem.: Calif. Soc. Plastic Surgeons, Am. Soc. Plastic Surgery, Am. Assn. Plastic Surgeons. Office: Ste 420 2330 Post St San Francisco CA 94115-3000 E-mail: gilg800@RCN.com.

GRADO, ANGELO JOHN, artist; b. N.Y.C., Feb. 17, 1922; s. Pasquale and Rose (Valenti) G.; m. Justine Barbara Johnson, June 26, 1943; children: Barbara, Paul, John, Frank, Richard. Student, Art Students League, Nat. Acad. Design, Frank Reilley Sch. Art. Comml. artist N.Y. Jour.-Am., N.Y.C., 1946-52; art dir. Harrison Publs., N.Y.C., 1952-55; art dir., owner advt. agy. Angelo John Assocs., N.Y.C., 1955-70; artist oils and pastels, 1970—. Tchr. Nat. Art League, N.Y., Naples Art League, Von Lebig Art Ctr., Naples, Fla.; lectr., Europe and U.S. Author: Mastering the Craft of Painting, 1985. Served with USAAF, 1943-46. Recipient 80 nat. awards, 1957—; recipient Best in Show-Newington award, 1980 Mem.: Am. Watercolor Soc., Pastel Soc. Am. (elected master pastelist, $1000 Mrs. Pearl Kalikow award 2001), Hudson Valley Art Assn. (Best Portrait award 1994), Am. Artists Profl. League (pres. N.Y. 1977—88, pres. emeritus 1988—), Salmagundi Club. Home: 641 46th St Brooklyn NY 11220-1410

GRADOVILLE, ROBERT THOMAS, lawyer; b. Des Moines, May 16, 1946; BA, Loras Coll., 1968; MBA, Ind. U., 1970; JD, Duke U., 1973; LLM in Taxation, NYU, 1976. Bar: N.Y. 1975, Conn. 1979. Mgr. Coopers & Lybrand, N.Y.C., 1974-78; assoc. Bergman, Horowitz & Reynolds, New Haven, 1978-81; mem. Kleban, Samor, Perles, etc., Southport, Conn., 1981-92, DeSarbo, Reichert & Gradoville, P.C., North Haven, Conn., 1992-2000, Reichert & Gradoville, P.C., North Haven, Conn., 2000—. Pres. Farmington Canal Rail to Trail Assn., 1991. Recipient Silver medal N.C. CPA, 1973. Mem. ABA (tax sect.), AICPA, Conn. Bar Assn. (tax sect.), Conn. Soc. CPAs (mem. fed. tax. com. 1984-95, mem. personal fin. planning com. 1996—, mem. employee benefit plan com. 1998—, Disting. Author award 1990), High Lane Club (pres. 1995-96). Office: Reichert & Gradoville PC 127 Washington Ave East North Haven CT 06473 E-mail: robertgradoville@reichertgradoville.com.

GRADWOHL, DAVID MAYER, anthropology educator; b. Lincoln, Nebr., Jan. 22, 1934; s. Bernard Sam and Elaine (Mayer) G.; m. Hanna Rosenberg, Dec. 29, 1957; children: Steven Ernst, Jane Mayer Nash, Kathryn Mayer Flaminio. BA in Anthropology and Geology, Nebr. U., 1955; postgrad., Edinburgh (Scotland) U., 1955-56; PhD in Anthropology, Harvard U., 1967. Instr. anthropology Iowa State U., Ames, 1962-66, asst. prof., 1966-67, assoc. prof., 1967-72, coord. anthropology, 1968-75, chair Am. Indian studies program, 1981-85, prof. anthropology, 1972—; asst site supr. Winchester (Eng.) Excavations Com., 1965. Advisor Nat. Register Hist. Sites, Des Moines, 1969-88, Office of State Archaeologist, Iowa City, 1983—; commr. Ames Hist. Preservation Commn., 1988-91. Co-author: The Worlds Between Two Rivers, 1987, 2d edit., 2000, Exploring Buried Buxton, 1990; co-author (audio visual programs) Iowa's Indian Heritage, 1972, Blacks and Whites in Buxton, 1986, Outside In: African American History in Iowa, 1838-2000, 2001. With U.S. Army, 1957-59. Fulbright fellow U.S. Ednl. Commn., Edinburgh, 1956, Touro Nat. Heritage Trust fellow, 1997-98; recipient Faculty Citation, Iowa State Alumni Assn., Ames, 1980, Charles Irby Disting. Svc. award Nat. Assn. Ethnic Studies, 1990, Career Achievement award for undergrad. tchg. AMOCO, 1992, Alumni Achievement award U. Nebr., 2001; Touro Nat. Heritage Trust fellow, 1997-98. Fellow Am. Anthropol. Assn., Assn. Iowa Archaeologists (chair 1977-78), Nebr. Assn. Profl. Archaeologists; mem. Soc. Am. Archaeology, Soc. Hist. Archaeology, Nebr. Jewish Hist. Soc., Nebr. State Hist. Soc., Plains Anthropol. Soc. (bd. dirs. 1969-72, 87-90, Disting. Svc. award 1998), Nat. Assn. Ethnic Studies (mem. editorial bd. 1987—), Iowa Archaeol. Soc. (mem. editl. bd. 1992—, Keyes Orr Disting. Svc. award 1997), Iowa Jewish Hist. Soc. (co-founder, bd. dirs. 1996—). Democrat. Jewish. Avocations: hiking, mountain climbing, music. Home: 2003 Ashmore Dr Ames IA 50014-7804 Office: Iowa State U Dept Anthropology Ames IA 50011-0001 E-mail: gradwohl@iastate.edu.

GRADY, BRENDA JAYNE, small business owner, business consultant, instructor; b. Syracuse, NY, Oct. 14, 1953; d. John Luther and Betty Jane (Hartinger) G. Grad., cert. computer programming/sys., Control Data Inst., Syracuse, 1972; AS in Bus. with highest honors, Onondaga C.C., Syracuse, 1979; BS in Acctg. summa cum laude, Ithaca Coll., 1981; MBA with honors, Simmons Coll., 1995. Payroll and accounts receivable specialist Marine Midland Svc., Syracuse, NY, 1972-74; supr. night ops. Automatic Data Processing, Syracuse, NY, 1974-77; spl. projects Paul Jeffrey Co., Syracuse, NY, 1977-79; sr. auditor and info. systems cons. Peat Marwick Mitchell, Syracuse, NY, 1981-84; fin. controls analyst United Tech. Carrier Corp., Syracuse, NY, 1984-85; contr. Giffen Svc. Co. subs. United Tech. Carrier Corp., Phoenix, 1985; sr. bus. analyst United Tech. Carrier Corp., Syracuse, NY, 1985-87, sr. project leader, 1987-89, mgr. systems group, 1989-93; owner, bus. cons., instr., author Bus. Growth Consulting, Dewitt, NY, 1992—; owner, pub. Syracuse Planner, 2000—. Bd. dir., vol. Jr. Achievement. Scholar Emerson Fund, 1979, 80, Am. Soc. Women Accts., 1979, Forster Edn. Found., 1980, Ithaca Coll., 1980, Simmons Coll. Grad. Sch. Mgmt., 1994;Women in Bus., 2001; Great Syracuse Chamber of Volunteer of the Yr., 2002. Mem. AICPA, ASTD, NY State Soc. CPAs, Greater Syracuse C. of C. (past chair tng. and edn. com., past chair needs assessment com., cmty. amb., leadership coun.), SCORE (past mktg. chair, vol. bus. counselor), Women Bus. Owners Connection (sec.), CNY Futurists Soc., Inst. Mgmt. Acct., Corp. Vol. Coun. (v.p.), Internat. Spl. Events Soc. (vice chmn.) Avocations: travel, crafts, reading, gardening. Home and Office: 307 Deforest Rd Dewitt NY 13214-2002

GRADY, C.P. LESLIE, JR., engineering educator; b. Des Arc, Ark., June 25, 1938; s. C. P. Leslie and Edith Claude (Booth) G.; m. Joni Jean Kellough, June 9, 1961; children: Ross Alan, Megan Suzanne. BA in Engring., Rice Inst., 1960; BSCE, Rice U., 1961, MS, 1963; PhD, Okla. State U., 1969. Registered profl. engr., Tex. Rsch. fellow Rice U., Houston, 1961-63, Okla. State U., Stillwater, 1965-68; asst. prof. Purdue U., West Lafayette, Ind., 1968-72, assoc. prof., 1972-79, prof., 1979-81, asst. dean Grad. Sch., 1980-81; prof. engring. Clemson (S.C.) U., 1981-83, R.A. Bowen prof., 1983—2003; prof. emeritus. Cons. CH2M-Hill, Atlanta and Charlotte, N.C., 1988—. Co-author: Biological Wastewater Treatment: Theory and Application, 1980, Biological Wastewater Treatment, 1999; contbr. articles to profl. jours. 1st lt. Med. Svc. Corp U.S. Army, 1963-65. Recipient Simon W. Freese award ASCE, 1989. Fellow: Am. Acad. Microbiology; mem.: Internat. Water Assn., Assn. Environ. and Engring. and Sci. Profs., Water Environ. Fedn. (editor Water Environ. Rsch. 1989—95, Harrison Prescott Eddy medal 2002). Democrat. Unitarian Universalist. Achievements include development of a variety of respirometric techniques for determining the biodegradation kinetics of synthetic organic chemicals; first recognition of the importance of soluble microbial products in biological process performance. Home: 103 Long View Ct Pickens SC 29671 Office: Clemson U Environ Engring and Sci Rich Environ Rsch Lab Clemson SC 29634-0001

GRADY, FRANCIS XAVIER, lawyer; b. Cleve., Nov. 17, 1957; s. John J. and Mary Veronica (Carey) G.; m. Donita Marie Labas. BS in Internat. Politics magna cum laude, Georgetown U., 1980; cert. advanced European studies, Coll. Europe, 1981; JD, Ohio State U., 1984. Bar: Ohio 1984, D.C. 1985. Atty. FDIC, Washington, 1984 86; assoc. Muldoon, Murphy & Faucette, Washington, 1986-87, Hahn, Loeser & Parks, Cleve., 1987-90; of counsel Seeley, Savidge & Aussem, Cleve., 1990-94; ptnr. Grady & Assocs., Cleve., 1994—. Author: The New CRA: A Practical Guide to Compliance, 1997; contbr. articles to profl. jours. Mem. Am.'s Cmty. Bankers. Roman Catholic. Office: Grady & Assocs 20950 Center Ridge Rd Rocky River OH 44116-4307

GRADY, GREGORY, lawyer, banker; b. Takoma Park, Md., Oct. 10, 1945; s. Francis Joseph Grady and Deane (McGehee) Black; m. Carol Love Harrison, Feb. 25, 1978; children: Olivia Love, Blake McGregor, Harrison Edwards. Diploma, Bullis Sch., 1964; BA in Econs., U. Va., 1969; JD, Tulane U., 1972. Bar: D.C. 1973, U.S. Ct. Appeals (D.C. cir.) 1973, U.S. Ct. Appeals (4th cir.) 1975, U.S. Supreme Ct. 1976, U.S. Ct. Appeals (5th cir.) 1977, U.S. Ct. Appeals (10th cir.) 1979, U.S. Ct. Appeals (11th cir.) 1981, U.S. Ct. Appeals (6th cir.) 1982, U.S. Dist. Ct. 1988. Staff atty., supervisory atty. FPC, Washington, 1972-74; assoc. Littman, Richter, Wright & Talisman, P.C., Washington, 1974-79; mem. Wright & Talisman, P.C., Washington, 1979—, pres., chmn. bd. dirs., chmn. exec. com., 1997-98, mng. mem., 1999—. Bd. dirs. Bank of Franklin, Miss., D.R. McGehee Ins. Agy., Inc., Miss. Mem. Energy Bar Assn., D.C. Bar Assn., The Federalist Soc., Congl. Country Club. Republican. Episcopalian. Home: 666 Live Oak Dr Mc Lean VA 22101-1569 Office: Wright & Talisman PC 1200 G St NW Ste 600 Washington DC 20005-3838

GRADY, JANET LAURA, nurse, educator; b. Monessen, Pa., Aug. 17, 1952; d. George and Delma (Picchiarini) Bindi; m. Kevin Patrick Grady, Apr. 30, 1976; children: Erika, Kevin, Christopher. Cert., U. Rouen, France, 1973; BA in Edn., U. Pitts., 1974; BSN, St. Francis Coll., 1986; MSN, U. Pitts., 1989, DrPH, 2000. Cert. profl. Pa. Dept. Edn. Tchr. Cen. Cambria Sch. Dist., Ebensburg, Pa., 1974-80, Richland Sch. Dist., Johnstown, Pa., 1981-83; staff nurse Meml. Hosp., Johnstown, 1986-87; faculty and course coord. Conemaugh Sch. Nursing, Johnstown, 1987-93; faculty Sch. of Nursing U. Pitts., Johnstown, Pa., 1993-2000; hosp. adminstr, v.p. Windber (Pa.) Med. Ctr., 2000—02; assoc. prof. nursing, chmn. divsn. Mt. Aloysius Coll., Cresson, Pa., 2002—. Adj. faculty Sch. Nursing U. Pitts., 2001—; guest lectr. Conemaugh Outpatient Diabetes Edn. Program, Johnstown, 1989-99. Active St. Benedict Edn. Coun., Johnstown, 1992-96; radio reader for the blind, 1995—. Scholar St. Francis Coll., 1986. Mem.: Pa. Colls. Assoc. Degree Nursing, Pa. Higher Edn. Nursing Schs. Assn., Nat. League Nursing, Pa. Pub. Health Assn., U. Pitts. Johnstown Women's Assn. (exec. bd. 1990—, v.p. 1998—, pres. 2000—02), St. Francis Coll. Alumni Assn., U. Pitts. Sch. Nursing Alumni Assn., Delta Epsilon Sigma, Sigma Theta Tau. Avocation: family activities. Home: 139 Peggy Ln Johnstown PA 15904-1242 Office: Mt Aloysius Coll 7373 Admiral Peary Hwy Cresson PA 16630 E-mail: jgrady@mtaloy.edu.

GRADY, JOYCE (MARIAN JOYCE GRADY), psychotherapist, consultant; b. Riverside, N.J., Sept. 27, 1930; d. David and Agnes Marian (Conroy) Lawber; children: Andrea, Christine; m. James F. Moller, June 11, 1983. BA in Clin. Psychology, U. Penna, 1951; M in Social Work, certificate in alcohol studies, Rutgers U., New Brunswick, N.J., 1968; certificate in psychotherapy, Inst. Psychoanalytic Psychotherapy, 1973. Lic. clin. social worker, N.J. Caseworker Upward Bound Program, Rutgers U., New Brunswick, summer 1966; psychiat. social work supr., chief psychiat. social worker Roosevelt Hosp., Edison, N.J., 1968-92, in-svc. educator in nursing and social work, 1972-92, support group caregiver, 1970-92; nursing home cons. Abbot Manor Nursing Home, Plainfield, N.J., 1984-92; pvt. practice psychotherapy, Highland Park, N.J., 1975—. Adj. prof., field instr. grad. sch. social work Rutgers U., New Brunswick, 1970-92; guest lectr. depression and geriatrics Rutgers Sch. Social Work, New Brunswick, 1975-92; cmty. lectr. dying, aging, loss, and depression in long term care; outreach cons. personal assistance and homebound elderly, Middlesex County, N.J., 1975-78; mem. adv. bd., chmn. Middlesex County Adv. Coun. Aging, North Brunswick, N.J., 1973-95. Contbr. papers, panelist in field. Advocate, Middlesex County Adv. Coun. on Aging, North Brunswick, 1970-92; mem. Cmty. Outreach Adv. Coun.; participant seminars svc. providers, Middlesex County, N.J., 1995. Mem.: NASW (guest panel mem., guest spkr. psychotherapy confs.), Rutgers Club, Penn Club N.Y.C. Avocations: writing, decorating, music, computers, gardening. Office: 12 N 4th Ave Highland Park NJ 08904-2736

GRADY, KEVIN E. lawyer; b. Charlotte, N.C., Jan. 19, 1948; s. Thomas F. and Rosemary (Loughran) G.; m. Mary Beth O'Brien, Dec. 27, 1975; children: Martin E., Donald F. BA, Vanderbilt U., 1969; JD, Harvard U., 1974. Bar: Ga. 1974, U.S. Dist. Ct. (no. dist.) Ga. 1975, U.S. Ct. Appeals (11th cir.) 1981, U.S. Supreme Ct. 1990. Assoc. Jones, Bird & Howell, Atlanta, 1974-76; trial atty. Antitrust divsn. U.S. Dept. Justice, Atlanta, 1976-77; ptnr. Alston & Bird, Atlanta, 1977—. Editor: Georgia Hospital Law Manual, 1997. Mem. bd. trust Vanderbilt U., 1995-97; hon. consul gen. of Sri Lanka to Georgia, 2000—. Recipient Top Hat award St. Vincent de Paul Soc., 1995. Mem. ABA (chair antitrust sect. 2003-), Ga. Acad. Healthcare Attys. (pres. 1997-98), Am. Health Lawyers Assn. (vice chair antitrust program 1992-99, chair 1999—), Am. Counsel Assn. (dir. 1991-2000, pres. 1995), State Bar Ga. (health law sect., chair 1999-2000). Democrat. Roman Catholic. Avocations: running, reading. Office: Alston & Bird 1201 W Peachtree St NW Ste 4200 Atlanta GA 30309-3449

GRADY, LEE TIMOTHY, pharmaceutical chemist; b. Chgo., Mar. 21, 1937; s. Thomas Aloysius and Lentella Kathryn (Eibel) G.; m. Ann Marie Gill, Aug. 8, 1964; children: Patricia Ann, Meghan Elizabeth. BS in Pharmacy with high honors, U. Ill., 1959, PhD in Chemistry, 1963. Registered pharmacist, Ill., Va., Md. Analyst CIA, Langley, Va., 1963—65; sr. rsch. pharmacologist Merck Inst. Therapeutic Rsch., West Point, Pa., 1965-68; dir. drug standards lab. Am. Pharm. Assn. Found., Washington, 1968-74; dir. drug rsch. and testing lab. U.S. Pharmacopeia, Rockville, Md., 1975-78, v.p., dir. stds. devel., dir. drug stds., 1979-99, v.p. dir. emeritus, 2000—. Mem. expert coms. WHO, Geneva, 1980-87; temp. advisor Pan Am. Health Orgn., Washington, 1984; observer Internat. Conf. Harmonization, 1990-2000; mem. Pharmacopeial Discussion group, U.S., Japan, Europe, 1989-2000. Contbr. articles to sci. jours.; sci. editor U.S. Pharmacopeia National Formulary, 1980-2000. Docent Nat. Mus. Am. History, 2000—; vol. Nat. Park Svc. Recipient rsch. award Am. Soc. Hosp. Pharmacists, 1982. Fellow AAAS, Am. Assn. Pharm. Scientists; mem. Am. Pharm. Assn. (J.L. Powers rsch. achievement award 1990), Am. Chem. Soc., Cath. Acad. Scis. (U.S.), Order of Holy Sepulchre, Rho Chi, Phi Kappa Phi. Roman Catholic. Avocations: swimming, hiking. E-mail: l.t.grady@worldnet.att.net.

GRADY, MAUREEN FRANCES, lawyer; b. N.Y.C., Oct. 6, 1960; d. Frank J. and Pauline (Laberge) G. BA, Manhattan Coll., 1982; JD, Georgetown U., 1985. Bar: N.Y. 1986, U.S. Dist. Ct. (so. and ea. dists.) N.Y. 1987, U.S. Ct. Appeals (2d cir.) 1990. Assoc. Griffin, Scully & Savona, N.Y.C., 1985-87, Morris & Duffy, N.Y.C., 1987-88, Summit, Rovins & Feldesman, N.Y.C., 1988-89; asst. gen. counsel N.Y.C. Transit Authority, 1989-92; trial atty. Fireman's Fund Ins. Co., N.Y.C., 1992-97; sr. assoc. DeCicco Gibbons & McNamara, P.C., N.Y.C., 1998-99; assoc. Kral Clerkin Redmond Ryan Perry & Girvan, N.Y.C., 1999-2000, Schwartzapfel Novick Truhowsky & Marcus, P.C., 2000-2001. Asst. vice pres. Am. Arbitration Assn., 2001—, N.Y. state EMT, 2000-. Recipient Bur. Nat. Affairs award, 1985. Mem. Assn. Bar City N.Y. (young lawyers com. 1987-90, constrn. law com. 1991-92, spl. com. on alcoholism and substance abuse 1994-97, sec. spl. com. on alcoholism and substance abuse 1995-97, product liability com. 1995-98, lesbian, gay, transgender rights com. 2001—, chair 2003—, mem. spl. task force on women in the cts., 2003-), Phi Beta Kappa, Epsilon Sigma Pi, Phi Alpha Theta. E-mail: GradyM@adr.org.

GRADY, PATRICIA A. health institute director, researcher; Diploma in nursing, St. Francis Hosp. Sch. Nursing, 1964; BSN, Georgetown U., 1967; MS, U. Md., 1968, PhD, 1977, D of Pub. Svc. (hon.), 1996; cert. in sr. mgrs. in govt., John F. Kennedy sch. Govt., Cambridge, 1994. Instr. Sch. Nursing Washington Hosp. Ctr., 1966-67; from instr. to rsch. asst. prof. Sch. Nursing U. Md., Bethesda, 1968-88, rsch. assoc., 1976-77; health sci. administrator Nat. Inst. Neurol. Disorders and Stroke NIH, Bethesda, 1988-92, asst. dir. Nat. Inst. Neurol. Disorders and Stroke, 1992-93, acting dir., dep. dir. Nat. Inst. Neurol. Disorders and Stroke, 1993-94, dep. dir. Nat. Inst. Neurol. Disorders and Stroke, 1994-95, dir. Nat. Inst. Nursing Rsch., 1995—. Cons., spkr., presenter in field. Ad hoc reviewer SCIENCE; reviewer Physiol. Measurement in Nursing; reviewer, editor all sci. statements, press releases, policy statements, manuscripts, and confl. corr. Nat. Insts. Neurol. Disorders and Stroke; mem. editl. bd. STROKE; contbr. articles to profl. jours., chpts. to books. NIH fellow, 1973-76; NIN(C)DS grantee, 1976-88; recipient Sol Greenberg award for leadership ability and clin. excellence St. Francis Hosp., 1964, Rozella M. Schlottfeld Disting. Lecture award Case Western Reserve U., 1996. Fellow Am. Acad. Nursing, Am. Heart Assn. (excellence in nursing lectr. award 1995); mem. AAAS, ANA, Am. Lung Assn., Am. Soc. Profl. and Exec. Women, Am. Acad. Neurology (lectr. 1993-95), Am. Neurol. Assn., Soc. Neurosci., N.Y. Acad. Scis., Neurotrauma Soc., Sigma Theta Tau (award 1966). Office: Nat Inst Nursing Rsch NIH 31 Center Dr Bldg 31 Bethesda MD 20892-0001 Fax: (301) 594-3405.

GRADY, SEAN MICHAEL, writer; b. Palo Alto, Calif., Oct. 3, 1965; s. Michael Wilmont and Naomi Jane (Gladstone) G. BA, U. So. Calif., 1988. Bus. writer Daily Press, Victorville, Calif., 1988-89; bus. editor The Olympian, Olympia, Wash., 1989-90; freelance writer, 1990-98, 2000—; writer, asst. editor Custom Pub. Group, Reno Gazette-Jour., 1998-2000. Instrnl. asst. Truckee Meadows C.C., Reno, 1992, part-time instr., 1993. Author: Plate Tectonics: Earth's Shifting Crust, 1991, Ships: Crossing the World's Oceans, 1992, The Importance of Marie Curie, 1992, Submarines: Probing the Ocean Depths, 1994, Illiteracy, 1994, Explosives: Devices of Controlled Destruction, 1995,

Virtual Reality: Computers Mimic the Physical World, 1998, Virtual Reality: Simulating and Enhancing the World with Computers, 2003. Home and Office: 1555 Ridgeview Dr Apt 229 Reno NV 89509-6245

GRADY, WAYNE J. government official; b. Halifax, N.S., Can., Dec. 15, 1943; s. Joseph Myles and Helen Virginia (McNeil) G. B.Comm., St. Mary's U., Halifax, 1973; MHA, U. Alta., Edmonton, 1975. Cons. Health Commn., Halifax, 1975-78; asst. to dep. minister Dept. of Health, Halifax, 1978-87, dep. minister health, 1987-91; dep. minister Dept. of the Environment, Halifax, 1991-96, ret., 1996. Roman Catholic. Home: Site 8 Box 48 RR 1 Waverley NS Canada B0N 2SO E-mail: wgrady@hfx.eastlink.ca.

GRAEBNER, JAMES HERBERT, transportation executive; b. New Castle, Pa., Aug. 5, 1940; s. Herbert Conrad and Mildred Elizabeth (Fessel) Graebner; children: Karla Elizabeth, Michael Conrad, James Conrad, David Fessel, Mildred Ann. BA, Valparaiso U., 1962; MBA, Case Western Res. U., 1970. Assoc. W. C. Gilman & Co., Inc., Cleve., 1967-71; with Regional Transp. Dist., Denver, 1971-75; gen. mgr. R.I. Pub. Transit Authority, Providence, 1975-78; dir. Santa Clara County Transp. Agy., Calif., 1978-84; dir. product devel. UTDC, 1984-86; pres. Lomarado Group, Denver, 1986—. Vis. prof. Northeastern U., 1979; COO Transit Constrn. Authority, Denver, 1987—89; v.p. San Jose Hist. Trolley Corp.; guest lectr. numerous univs. Bd. dirs. Denver Rail Heritage Soc. Mem.: Regional Transit Assn. Bay Area (LoDo dist. bd. dirs. 1999—, pres. 2002), Calif. Assn. Publicly Owned Transit Sys. (vice chmn. 1984), Am. Pub. Transit Assn. (pres. 1983—84). Lutheran. E-mail: carbarn@aol.com.

GRAEBNER, NORMAN ARTHUR, history educator; b. Kingman, Kans., Oct. 19, 1915; s. Rudolph William and Helen (Brauer) G.; m. Laura Edna Baum, Aug. 30, 1941; m. Jane Shannon, Jan. 3, 1998. BS, Milw. State Tchrs. Coll., 1939; MA, U. Okla., 1940; PhD, U. Chgo., 1949; Litt.D., Albright Coll., 1976; MA, Oxford (Eng.) U., 1978; D.H.L., U. Pitts., 1981, Valparaiso U., 1981, Eastern Ill. U., 1986, U. Wis., Milw., 1997, Averett U., 2003; D of Pedagogy, Marshall U., 1993. Asst. prof. Okla. Coll. for Women, 1942-43, 46-47; from asst. prof. to prof. Iowa State Coll., 1948-56; prof. history U. Ill., Urbana 1956-67 chmn. dept. history, 1961-63; Edward R. Stettinius prof. modern Am. history U. Va., 1967-82, Randolph P. Compton prof., Miller Ctr. Pub. Affairs, 1982—. Vis. prof. Stanford U., 1952-53, summers 1959, 72, U. Colo., summer 1968, Concordia Tchrs. Coll., summer 1971, U.S. Mil. Acad., West Point, N.Y., 1981-82, Beloit Coll., spring 1987, Va. Mil. Inst., fall 1987, Coll. of William and Mary, spring 1988, Marshall U., spring 1989; Commonwealth Fund lectr. U. Coll., London, 1958; Fulbright lectr. U. Queensland, Brisbane, Australia, 1963, U. Sydney, Australia, 1983, U. Heidelberg, Germany, 1998-99; disting. vis. prof. history Pa. State U., 1975-76; Harmsworth prof. Am. history Oxford U., 1978-79; Phi Beta Kappa vis. scholar, 1981-82; Thomas Jefferson vis. scholar Downing Coll., Cambridge U., 1985; disting. vis. prof. Nat. War Coll., 1994-95. Author: Empire on the Pacific, 1955, The New Isolationism, 1956, Cold War Diplomacy, 1962, rev. edit., 1977, The Age of Global Power, 1979, America As a World Power: A Realist Appraisal from Wilson to Reagan, 1984, Foundations of American Foreign Policy: A Realist Appraisal from Franklin to McKinley, 1985, A Twentieth-Century Odyssey: Memoir of a Life in Academe, 2002; co-author: A History of the United States, 2 vols, 1970, A History of the American People, 1970, 2d edit., 1975, Recent United States History, 1972; Editor: The Enduring Lincoln, 1959, Politics and the Crisis of 1860, 1961, An Uncertain Tradition: American Secretaries of State in the Twentieth Century, 1961, The Cold War: A Conflict of Ideology and Power, 1963, rev. edit., 1976, Ideas and Diplomacy, 1964, Manifest Destiny, 1968, Nationalism and Communism in Asia: The American Response, 1977, Freedom in America: A 200-Year Perspective, 1977, American Diplomatic History before 1900, 1978; Traditions and Values: American Diplomacy, 1790-1865, 1985, 1865-1945, 1985; The National Security: Its Theory and Practice, 1945-1960, 1986; contbr. articles to hist. jours. Dir. bicentennial program Pa. State U., 1975-76. Served to 1st lt. U.S. Army, 1943-46. Recipient Thomas Jefferson award U. Va., 1985. Mem. Am., So. hist. assns., Orgn. Am. Historians, Soc. Am. Historians, Soc. Historians Am., Fgn. Rels. (pres. 1972), Am. Acad. Arts and Scis., Mass. Hist. Soc., Phi Beta Kappa. Home: 11 Ednam Vlg Charlottesville VA 22903-4636 *One should never demand more of society than society can grant to all without suffering chaos or disintegration.*

GRAEDEL, THOMAS ELDON, industrial ecology educator, researcher; b. Portland, Oreg., Aug. 23, 1938; s. Philip Edward and Helen Beatrice (Peterson) G.; m. Susannah Grace Ketchum, July 23, 1966; children: Laura, Martha. BSChemE, Wash. State U., 1960; MA in Physics, Kent State U., 1964; MS in Astronomy, U. Mich., 1967, PhD in Astronomy, 1969. Tech. staff Bell Labs., Murray Hill, N.J., 1969-84; disting. mem. tech. staff AT&T Bell Labs., Murray Hill, N.J., 1984-96; prof. indsl. ecology Yale U., 1997—. Bd. dirs. Am. Inst. Physics; exec. com. Bd. Atmospheric Scis. and Climate Nat. Rsch. Coun., 1989—93; convener Global Emission Inventory Project Internat. Global Atmospheric Chem. Programme; chmn. Chem. Rsch. Applied to World Needs Poster Session, NAS panel to rev. U.S. High Speed Civil Transport Rsch. Program, 1993; bd. advisors Bowers Medals of the Franklin Inst., Phila.; mem. NAS Panel to Rev. the FY 1991 U.S. Global Change Rsch. Program; commr. Commn. on Geoscis., Environment and Resources, NRC, 1997—2001; chmn. NAS commn. Grand Challenges in Environ. Scis., 2000, NAS Commn. Rev. U.S. Climate Change Sci. Program, 2002. Author: Chemical Compounds in the Atmosphere, 1978; co-author: Atmospheric Chemical Compounds: Sources, Occurrence and Bioassay, 1986, Atmospheric Change: An Earth System Perspective, 1993, Industrial Ecology, 1995, 2d edit., 2002, Atmosphere, Climate and Change, 1995, Design for Environment, 1996, Industrial Ecology and Automobile, 1997, Streamlined Life Cycle Assessment, 1998, Atmospheric Corrosion, 2000; assoc. editor Atmospheric Environment, 1979—82, Rev. of Geophysics, 1987—91, Jour. Geophys. Rsch., 1989—92; author/co-author: more than 250 tech. papers and articles for profl. jours. Chmn. Environ. Commn., Mendham, N.J., 1971-74; ruling elder First Presbyn. Ch., Mendham, 1989-91. Capt. Armed Svcs., 1960-62. Fellow: AAAS, Am. Geophys. Union; mem.: Am. Chem. Soc., Conn. Acad. of Sci. and Engring., Nat. Acad. Engring. (elected). Presbyterian. Achievements include patents for composition useful for detecting H2S and for protection of devices; research on sulfur chemistry in lower atmosphere, on trends in atmospheric "greenhouse" gases, on atmospheric compounds, on chemistry in atmospheric droplets, on effects of atmosphere on materials, on the formation of copper patinas in the atmosphere, on the implications of trends in atmospheric composition, and on theoretical and practical foundations of industrial ecology. Office: Yale U Sch Forestry Envir Studies 205 Prospect St New Haven CT 06511-2106

GRAEF, LUTHER WILLIAM, civil engineer; b. Milw., Aug. 14, 1931; s. John and Pearl (Luther) G.; m. Lorraine Linnerud, Sept. 18, 1954; children: Ronald, Sharon, Gerald. BCE, Marquette U., 1952; MCE, U. Wis., 1961. Registered prof. engr., Wis., Colo. Engr. C.W. Yoder & Assocs. cons. engrs., Milw., 1956-61; ptnr. Graef Anhalt Schloemer, cons. engrs., Milw., 1961-67; chmn. bd. Graef Anhalt Schloemer Assocs., Inc., Milw., 1978—96. Mem. accreditation bd. for engring. and tech., 1989-95. Active boy Scouts Am.; chmn. bd. assessment City of Milw., 1962-89; bd. dirs. Luther Manor. 1st lt. AUS, 1953-56. Named Disting. Marquette U. Alumnus, 1982, Wis. Profl. Engr. of Yr., 1983. Mem. ASCE (sect. pres. 1968, nat. bd. dirs. 1989-92, nat. v.p. 1993-95, nat. pres. 1997-98), Am. Assn. Engring. Soc. (vice chmn. 2000, chmn. 2001), NSPE, Wis. Soc. Profl. Engrs., Cons. Engrs. Coun. Wis. (pres. 1973-75), Engrs. Scientist Milw. (pres. 1975), World Fedn. Orgns. (exec. coun. 2001-02), World Fedn. Socs. (U.S. rep. 2002. Home: 8503 Country Club Dr Franklin WI 53132-2710 Office: Graef Anhalt Schloemer 125 S 84th St Ste 401 Milwaukee WI 53214-1470

GRAEFF, ALAN S. health association executive; BS in Distributed Scis., Am. U. Chief Clin. Ctr. info. sys. dept. NIH, 1995-98, CIO, 1998—. Office: NIH Ctr for Info Tech 10401 Fernwood Rd Bethesda MD 20817

GRAEFF, DAVID WAYNE, maintenance executive, consultant; b. West Reading, Pa., Oct. 24, 1946; s. Wayne Samuel and Sara (Spohn) G.; m. Linda Ruth Lohrke, Aug. 17, 1968; children— Hether, Rebecca, Matthew. BSM.E., Ind. Inst. Tech., 1969. Lic. in sewage treatment plant and waterworks, Pa. Maintenance engr. Central Soya, Decatur, Ind., 1969-71; mfg. engr. Nat. Seal div. Fed. Mogul, Van Wert, Ohio, 1971-73; facilities engr. Kawecki Berylco div. Cabot, Van Wert, Ohio, 1973-76; plant engr. Willson Products div. E.S.B., Reading, 1976-78; facilities and environ. health/safety mgr. Brush-Wellman Inc., Reading, 1978—98, maintenance mgr., 1998—2002; project engr. Engring. Solutions, Inc., Exton, Pa., 2002—03; plant engr. Rahns Specialty Metals Inc., Pa., 2002—. Maintenance cons. Maintenance Inc., Fleetwood, Pa., 1976—. Vice comr. USCG Aux., Reading, 1983-84, cert. marine examiner, 1982—, info. system officer, 1984; mem. Local Emergency Planning Commn., 1999—. Mem. AICE, NRA, Soc. Mfg. Engrs., Am. Water Works Assn., Am. Inst. Plant Engrs., Am. Assn. Energy Engrs., Am. Chem. Soc., Environ. Engrs. & Mgrs. Inst., Pa. Soc. Profl. Engrs., Wire Assn. Internat., Local Emergency Planning Commn., Ducks Unltd., Moose, Theta Xi. Republican. Lutheran. Avocations: boating, woodworking. Home: 815 N Forest St Fleetwood PA 19522-1021 Office: Rahns Specialty Metals Inc Route 113 70 Rahns Rd Rahns PA 19426

GRAESSLEY, WILLIAM WALTER, retired chemical engineering educator; b. Muskegon, Mich., Sept. 10, 1933; s. William Walter and Mary Iva (Isler) G.; m. Helen Lorraine Carlsen, June 13, 1953; children: Kathryn Lorraine, William W., Laurie Jo. BS, BS in Engring, U. Mich., 1956, MS in Engring, 1957, PhD, 1960. With Air Reduction Co., 1959-63, group leader, 1962-63; mem. faculty Northwestern U., Evanston, Ill., 1963-82, assoc. prof. chem. engring. and materials sci., 1966-70, prof., 1970-81, Walter P. Murphy prof., 1981-82, asst. dir. Materials Research Ctr., 1968-69; sr. sci. advisor Exxon Research and Engring. Co., 1982-87; prof. chem. engring. Princeton U., 1987-98. Sr. vis. fellow Cambridge U., 1979-80; disting. lectr. various univs. Asst. editor Trans. Soc. Rheology, 1969-75; mem. editorial adv. bd. Jour. Polymer Sci., 1979-2000, Rubber Revs., 1981-85, Macromolecules, 1983-85; contbr. articles to profl. jours. NSF fellow, 1956-59; Bingham medalist Soc. Rheology. Fellow Am. Phys. Soc. (exec. com., div. high polymer physics 1975-78, high polymer physics prize awardee); mem. Soc. Rheology (exec. com. 1971-73), Am. Inst. Chem. Engrs., Am. Chem. Soc., Nat. Acad. of Engring. Achievements include rsch. in synthetic polymers. E-mail: graessle@princeton.edu.

GRAF, ALAN B., JR., transportation executive; b. Evansville, Ind., 1953; BS, MBA, Ind. U. With FedEx Corp., Memphis, 1980—, exec. v.p., CFO, 1996—. Office: FedEx Corp 842 S Shady Grove Rd Memphis TN 38120

GRAF, ARNOLD HAROLD, employee benefits executive, financial planner; b. Buffalo, Oct. 30, 1930; s. John Edward and Rose Ruth (Tyman) G.; m. Joan Nensel, Sept. 1, 1956 (div. Apr. 1980); children: Jenny, David, Laurie, Paul, Ellen, Amy; m. Rita Mary DiFlorio, Aug. 3, 1981; stepchildren: Patricia, William, Kathleen, Stephan. Student, Rutgers U., 1955-58; BS in Econs., U. Pa., Phila., 1968; postgrad., Command-Gen. Staff Coll., 1966; MA in Internat. Rels., Army War Coll., 1973-75; JD, Weidner U., 1985. CLU, CFP ChFC. Commd. 2d lt. U.S. Army, 1952, advanced through grades to col., 1975, served in Korea, served in Vietnam, ret., 1983; shift supr. Campbell Soup Co., Camden, N.J., 1956-57; pers. dir. Container Corp. of Am., Phila., Oaks, Pa., 1957-59; special agt. Provident Mut. Life Ins. Co., Phila., 1959-60; dist. and regional mgr. Franklin Life Ins. Co., Phila., 1960-68; field mktg. dir. Nat. Liberty Corp., Frazier, Pa., 1968-70; regional mgr. Southland Life Ins. Co., King of Prussia, Pa., 1970-72; sr. supt. agys. Ins. Co. N.Am., Phila., 1972-75; career gen. agt. Aetna Life Ins. Co., Phila., 1975-80; pres. Nebsco Fin. Svcs. Inc./Nebsco Mortgage Profs. Ltd., Newtown Square, Pa., 1980—. Mortgage banker, 1995—, HUD/FHA Mortgages, 2000—. Contbr. articles to profl. jours. Dir. sch. bd. Marple/Newtown Sch. Dist., 1995-2000. Paul Harris fellow Rotary Found., 1988, fellow Guntaker Found., 1990; recipient Humanitarian award Chapel of Four Chaplains, 1996. Mem. Pa. Assn. Ins./Fin. Advisors (dir. 2000—), Rotary Internat. (pres. Newton Sq. club 1987-88, R.I. dist. gov. 1990-91, chair dist. 7450 Rotary found. 2000—), Masons (32 degree), Del. County Assn. Life Underwriters (pres.), Serra Internat. (gov. dist. 28 1996-98, trustee found. 1998-2000). Republican. Roman Catholic. Avocations: bowling, golf, walking, reading. Home: 4107 Meadow Ln Newtown Square PA 19073-1611 E-mail: agraf@rcn.com.

GRAF, EDWARD DUTTON, grouting consultant; b. L.A., Dec. 31, 1924; s. John Edward and Florence Claire (Dutton) Graf; m. Verna M. Greenfield (div.); children: Teri, Thomas, Eric; m. Joyce Main, Sept. 12, 1981. BSc, UCLA, 1948. Field engr., estimator Bechtel Corp., 1950-52; engr., estimator EMSCO San Francisco, 1952-55; founder, owner, pres. Pressure Grout Co., Foster City, Calif., 1955-86; ind. cons. in pressure grouting, 1986—. Guest lectr. civil engring. Stanford (Calif.) U., U. Calif., Berkeley, UCLA, Ga. Inst. Tech., Purdue U., Northwestern U., others. Contbr. articles to profl. jours. Lt. USNR. Fellow: Am. Concrete Inst. (past chmn. com. geotech. cement grouting); mem.: ASCE (past chmn. nat. com. grouting, past pres. San Francisco br., Martin S. Kapp Found. Engring. award 1990, Grouting Greats 2003), Structural Engrs. Assn. Calif., Assn. Engring. Geologists, Soc. Mining Engrs., Internat. Soc. Rock Mechanics Commn. Rock Grouting. Home and Office: 182 Lumahai St Honolulu HI 96825-2102

GRAF, ERVIN DONALD, municipal official; b. Crow Rock, Mont., Mar. 9, 1930; s. Emanuel and Lydia (Bitz) G.; m. Carolyn Sue Robinson, Mar. 15, 1956 (div. 1958); m. Eleanor Mahlein, Apr. 13, 1959 (dec. Oct. 1990); children: Debra, Belinda, Corrina, Melanie (dec.), Ervin Jr. (dec.). Enlisted U.S. Army, 1948; served two tours of duty in Vietnam; ret. U.S. Army, 1972; with office and maintenance staff Greenfields Irrigation Dist., Fairfield, Mont., 1972-77, sec. to Bd. Commrs., 1977-95; ret., 1995. Decorated Bronze star with oak leaf cluster. Mem. Am. Legion (all offices Post #80 and Dist. 8 incl. dist. comdr.). Democrat. Lutheran. Avocations: bowling, coin collecting, fishing, camping. Home: 211-6St N Box 565 Fairfield MT 59436-0565

GRAF, HANS, conductor; b. Austria, Feb. 15, 1949; m. Margarita Graf; 1 child, Anna. Studied with Franco Ferrera and Arvid Jansons. Music dir. Mozarteum Orch., Salzburg, Austria, 1984-94, Calgary Philharm. Orch., 1995—2003, Orch. Nat. de Bordeaux-Aquitaine and Opera de Bordeaux, France, 1998—, Houston Symphony, 2000—01. Guest condr. Vienna Symphony, Vienna Philharm., Orchestre Nat. de France, Leningrad Philharm., Pitts. Symphony, Boston Symphony. Recipient Chevalier de l'Ordre de la Legion d'Honneur, French Govt., 2002. Avocation: fine wine. Office: Houston Symphony 615 Louisiana St Suite 102 Houston TX 77002

GRAF, KARL ROCKWELL, nuclear engineer; b. San Diego, Apr. 19, 1940; s. Frederic August and Beatrice (Rockwell) G.; m. Nancy Ann Scott, June 9, 1962; children: Robin Elizabeth, Scott Frederic. BS, U. S. Naval Acad., 1962. Submarine officer USN, 1962-84; comdg. officer USS George Bancroft, 1978—82; dep. comdr. readiness and tng. officer Submarine Squadron One, USN, Pearl Harbor, Hawaii, 1982—84; sr. mgmt. cons. Advanced Sci. and Tech. Assn., Solana Beach, Calif., 1984; dir. nuclear support Ill. Power Co., Decatur, 1985, dir. ops. monitoring, 1986-89, dir. quality assurance, 1990-92, dir. engring. projects, 1992-94, leader life cycle mgmt., 1994-2000; dir. adminstrn. St. Paul's Luth. Ch., Decatur, Ill., 2000—. Founder life cycle mgmt. program Clinton Nuclear Power Sta. Author: Monitoring Manual, 1986. Exec. dir. St. John's Luth. Ch., 1995-97; chmn. zoning bd. Village of Forsyth, Ill., 1988-96, chmn. long-range plan com., 1989-92, mem. long range plan task force, 1999-2002. Mem. Am. Nuclear Soc., U.S. Submarine League, Ret. Officers Assn. Achievements include the development and implementation of an innovative monitoring program at Illinois Power Company's Clinton Nuclear Power Station to monitor, evaluate and trend such things as individual responsibility and professionalism and develop actions to improve performance standards relating to the nuclear reactor, steam turbine and electrical generating systems. Home: 736 Weaver Rd Forsyth IL 62535-9777 Office: St Pauls Luth Ch 352 W Wood St Decatur IL 62522-3197 E-mail: stpaulskarl@aol.com. *To determine the right thing to do, and then to really do what is right is a formula that not only defines our integrity, but helps us to avoid many of the pitfalls that can be so destructive to success and meaningful relationships in all aspects of our lives.*

GRAF, MARJORIE BECK, sales and marketing executive; b. Hartford, Conn., May 25, 1956; d. Louis A. and Etta (Pasternack) B. Grad. high sch., West Hartford, Conn., 1974; diploma, Conn. Stenographic Inst., 1976. Assoc. Howard Gustafson Reporting Svc., Middletown, Conn., 1976-77; owner Marjorie R. Beck Reporting Svc., Cromwell, 1977-79; adminstrv. asst. Entertainment and Sports Programming Network, Bristol, Conn., 1979-82; sales sec. Sta. WVIT-TV Viacom Internat., West Hartford, 1982-84; account exec. Sta. WTIC-TV Chase Communications, Hartford, 1984-86; sr. account exec. Sta. WHCT-TV Astroline Communications, Hartford, 1986-88; exec. v.p. Career Media Network, Farmington, Conn., 1988-89; pres. MRB Media Svcs., Inc., East Wallingford, Vt., 1989—. Exec. producer For Your Leisure; founder Bus. Introduction Video Network; cons. Nikken Wellness. Avocations: swimming, reading, helicopter flying. Office: MRB Media Svcs Inc 1843 Vt Rte 155 East Wallingford VT 05742-9734 E-mail: mrb@mrbmedia.com.

GRAF, PETER GUSTAV, accountant, lawyer; b. Vienna, June 19, 1936; came to U.S. 1940, naturalized, 1945; m. Rosalie Greenbaum, Apr. 6, 1963; 1 child, Paul Evan BS in Econs., U. Pa., 1957; LLB, NYU, 1960, LLM, 1962. Bar: N.Y. 1960; CPA, N.Y. Tax acct. J.K. Lasser & Co., N.Y.C., 1961-62; with Joseph Graf & Co., N.Y.C., 1962-66, ptnr., 1966—. V.p., founder, dir. AGS Computers Inc., N.J., 1967—; ptnr., founder, treas., dir. Nardin Gallery, Inc., Somers, N.Y.; founder Cable Sys. USA Assocs., W.Va., Pa., Ohio, USA Mobile Commn., Inc., Cellular USA Inc., USA Ventures Ltd., MDchoice.com., 1999, Tongue Sys.; chmn. Phonetel Technologies, Inc., 1995-99. Mem. AICPA, N.Y. State Soc. CPA, N.Y. State Bar Assn. Home: 87 Holly Pl Briarcliff Manor NY 10510-2107 Office: Graf Repetti & Co 1114 Avenue Of The Americas New York NY 10036-7703

GRAF, ROBERT ARLAN, retired financial services executive; b. Bethlehem, Pa., Dec. 8, 1933; s. Rudolph Bernard and Edith May (Crossman) G.; m. Bernice Irene Garman, Dec. 21, 1957; 1 child, R. Mark. AB, U. Pa., 1955; JD, Temple U., 1958. Bar: Mass. 1963. Mgr. annuities The Paul Revere Life Ins. Co., Worcester, Mass., 1960-68; v.p. mass coverage adminstrn. Bankers Security Life Ins. Soc., Washington, 1968; regional dir. group pension Participating Annuity Life Ins. Co., McLean, Va., 1968-69; pres. LNC Equity Sales Corp., Ft. Wayne, Ind., 1969-84; 2d v.p. Lincoln Nat. Corp., Ft. Wayne, Ind., 1969-84; sr. v.p. personal fin. services mktg. and tng. The No. Trust, Chgo., 1984-86; sr. v.p. Kemper Fin. Services Inc., Kemper Investors Life Ins. Co., Chgo., 1986-90; pres. Investors Brokerage Svcs., Inc., Chgo., 1987-90; v.p. fin. instns. div. Rollins Splty. Group, Chgo., 1990-91; nat. sales dir. fin. instns. Paul Revere Ins. Group, Worcester, Mass., 1991-99; ret., 1999. Vol. Boy Scouts Am., Ft. Wayne, Sci. Ctrl., Ft. Wayne, St. Francis U., Ft. Wayne; vol. fundraiser United Way, Ft. Wayne, 1982-83, Fine Arts Found., Ft. Wayne, 1984. Served with USMC, 1958-60. Mem. Life Ins. Mktg. and Rsch. Assn. (chmn. investment products com. 1981-83, mem. mktg. through supplemental distbn. systems com.), Nat. Assn. Securities Dealers (prin.), Chgo. Bar Assn. (employee benefits com., fin. svcs. com., ins. com.), Bank Mktg. Assn., Fin. Instns. Ins. Assn., Assn. of Banks in Ins., Three Rivers Gem and Mineral Soc. Ft. Wayne, Met. Club Chgo., Chgo. Shell Club, Masons, Delta Tau Delta, Phi Delta Phi. Presbyterian. Avocations: collecting specimen seashells, tennis, reading, collecting fossils.

GRAF, SHERYL SUSAN, lawyer; b. Auburn, Wash., Feb. 23, 1959; d. Lawrence S. and Joyce May Graf; widowed, 1983; m. Gerald Cox, Feb. 14, 1987. AA, Grossmont Coll., El Cajon, Calif., 1977; JD, Thomas Jefferson Sch. Law, San Diego, 1994. Bar: Calif. 1995, U.S. Dist. Ct. (so. dist.) Calif. 1995, U.S. Supreme Ct. 1999. Exec. adminstr. Anacomp, Inc., San Diego, 1980-91; lawyer Law Offices of Sheryl S. Graf, El Cajon, Calif., 1995—. Contbr. articles to law revs. Mem. San Diego County Bar Assn. (chair solo and small firm sect. 1996-97), Calif. Attys. for Criminal Justice, Foothills Bar Assn. (bd. dirs. 2000-03), Calif. Women Lawyers, Lawyers Club East County (bd. dirs. 1997—, pres. 1999-01), Delta Theta Phi. Avocation: skiing. Office: 275 E Douglas Ave Ste 115 El Cajon CA 92020-4548

GRAF, TRUMAN FREDERICK, agricultural economist, educator; b. New Holstein, Wis., Sept. 18, 1922; s. Herbert and Rose (Sell) G.; m. Sylvia Ann Thompson, Sept. 6, 1947; children: Eric Kindley, Siri Lynne, Peter Truman. BS, U. Wis., 1947, MS, 1949, PhD, 1953. Mktg. specialist, coop. agt. USDA and U. Wis., 1948-50; instr. agrl. econs. U. Wis., Madison, 1951-53, asst. prof., 1953-56, assoc. prof., 1956-61, prof., 1961-85, prof. emeritus, 1985—. Expert witness, 1982—; mem. Gov.'s Com. on Wis. Dairy Mktg.; mem. 3-man team to make mktg. analysis in Nigeria, USDA, 1962, made U.S. milk mktg. study, 1971; made mktg. analyses in 13 Carribbean countries, 1964; made mktg. analysis U. Wis., Mex., 1965; made mktg. analyses U.S. Ednl. Found., Finland, 1970, Rumanian Ministry Edn., U.S. Dept. State, Rumania, USSR, 1976, France, 1981, Russia, 1992, Ukraine, 1992, 98, Bulgaria, 1992, 93, Hungary, 1993, Poland, 1993, Zimbabwe, Africa, 1994, Ukraine, 1998; rschr. for internat. agrl. mktg. agys., Kazakhstan, 1999, Uganda, 2000, U.S. Treasury Dept., Cuba, 2002, Armenia, 2003, U. Tchg. on Internat. Trade., 1963-93. Contbr. articles to profl. jours. Active Cub Scouts; bd. dirs. Univ. Houses Assn., 1955-56, Univ. Hill Farm Assn., 1958-59, Univ. Hill Farm Swim Club, 1959-60, Oakwood Retirement Homes, 1992-2001. Recipient Uhlman award Chgo. Bd. Trade, 1952, recipient Man of Yr. award World Dairy Expn., 1976, Disting. Svc. award U. Wis. Extension, 1981, Coop. Builder award Fedn. Coops., 1982, Internat. Trade Spl. award Gov. Wis., 1983. Mem. AARP (econ. security adv. com.), Am. Agrl. Econs. Assn. (Published Rsch. award 1974), Am. Mktg. Assn., Madison Naval Res. Assn. (pres. 1968-72), Am. Econ. Assn., Hist. Soc., United Dairy Industries Assn. (adv. com.), Wis. Fedn. Coops., Lakeshore Federated Dairy Coop., Wis. Ret. Educators Assn. (bd. dirs.), Wis. Coalition of Annuitants (vice chair), Civil War Club, Kiwanis (pres. Golden K). Lutheran. Achievements include applied rsch. study for dairy firms, orgns. state ed. regulatory agys. and agrl. bus. firms. Home: 9117 Whitestone Dr Apt 105 Middleton WI 53562-2385 Office: U Wis Dept of Agr Dept Agriculture Madison WI 53706

GRAF, WILLIAM J. entrepreneur; b. Phila., July 16, 1948; s. William J. and Margaret (Plenskofski) G.; m. Cecilia Ann Vogt, Sept. 18, 1971; children: David William, Paul. BA, Temple U., 1969. Agt. Mutual of N.Y., Phila., 1972-74; owner William J. Graf & Assocs., Phila., 1974-76; v.p. Nat. Equity Life Ins. Co., N.Mex., 1976-78, Pa. Physician Plan, Media, Pa., 1982-86; pres., CEO Graco Triad Group, Phila., 1986-90, Sales Success Inst., Phila., 1986-90, Graco Ins. Group, Bensalem, Pa., 1990—, Worldwide Mktg. Sys., Bensalem, 1995—; CEO, Internat. Comm. Network, Bensalem, 1997—; CEO Worldwide Fin. Svcs., Inc., Phila., 1999—, Eagle Publ. Co., Phila., 1999—, Aline Group Inc., Phila., 1999—2000, Sterling & Locke Inc., 2000. Instr. Life Assn. Tng. Coun., Washington, 1991-92; exec. dir. Nat. Assn. Master Athletes; founder, pub. Master Athlete Mag., 1993—. Author: Goals - The Dynamics of Life, 1989, Seven Steps to Successful Selling, 1994, Honesty, The Last Virtue, 1995, Cold Market Wealth, 2000; contbr. articles to profl. jours. 2nd lt. U.S. Army, 1969-71. Mem. Metro. Life Million Dollar Club, Nat. Assn. Life Underwriters (Million Dollar Round Table, Nat. Quality award 1972), Life Underwriters Tng. Coun., Pa. Assn. Life Underwriters, Buck County Estate Planning, Coun., Nat. Assn. Profl. Salespersons (pres. 1982), Phila. Masters Track Assn., Buck County Paces (pres. 1990-92), U.S. Track and Field Assn., Internat. Platform Assn. Republican. Roman Catholic. Home: 3968 Bainbridge Ct Bensalem PA 19020-4817 E-mail: rmasterone@mailexcel.com.

GRAFE, WARREN BLAIR, broadcast executive; b. N.Y.C., June 22, 1954; s. Warren Edward and Maree Lee Grafe; m. Pamela Arden Rearick, Mar. 8, 1980 (div. Nov. 1982). Student, Kendall Coll., 1974-75, U. Wis., Platteville, 1975-76; BA, Ind. U., 1979. Sales rep. Sta. WGTC-FM, Bloomington, Ind., 1979-84, account exec., coop. cord., 1980-84; nat. sales rep. Stas. WTTS-WGTC, Bloomington, 1984; sales rep. Sta. KLFF-KMZK, Phoenix, 1985; account exec. Rita Sanders Advt. and Pub. Rels. Agy., Tempe, Ariz., 1985, Am. Cable TV, Phoenix, 1985-86, Dimension Media Svcs., Phoenix, 1986-89, Greater Phoenix Interconnect, 1989-95, CableRep/Phoenix, 1995-99, CableRep/Ariz., Phoenix, 1999—2001; nat. sales mgr., rep. QWEST Choice TV and Cable Am, CableWest, Phoenix, 2001—. Named a Finalist for Nat. Sales Award, Cable TV Advt. Bur., 1999; named one of Cable's Best Top Ten Cable Advt. Sales Reps. in Country, Cable Avails, 1995; recipient Nat. Sales award, Cable TV Advt. Bur., 1986, 1987, 1991, 1994, 1996, 1998, 2000, $5 Million Career Sales award, 1997, $10 Million Career Sales award, 1999. Mem.: Mensa (Ariz.) C. of C., Chandler (Ariz.) C. of C., Tempe C. of C. (amb. 1986). Home: 9616 N 26th Pl Phoenix AZ 85028-4708 Office: CableWest 300 W Osborn # 105 Phoenix AZ 85013

GRAFF, CARLEEN, music educator; b. Bloomington, Ill., Oct. 24, 1946; BME, Ill. Wesleyan Univ., Bloomington, Ill., 1968; MA piano performance, Univ. Denver, Colo., 1970; ArtsD piano performance, Univ. No. Colo., Greeley, Co., 1984. Cert. master tchr. Music Tchr. Nat. Assn., 1985. Elem. & H.S. music tchr. Lamar/Granada Pub. Sch., Colo., 1970—72; tchr. piano Ind. State Univ., Terre Haute, Ind., 1972—73; prof. music Plymouth State Coll., Plymouth, NH, 1973—. Coord. of piano studies Plymouth State U., 1973—; founder, dir. Summer Piano Ensemble Plymouth State Coll., 1993—, 20th Piano festival Plymouth State U., 1999—. Performer: (soloist) Baroque through 20th Music,

1968—, (chamber pianist) Baroque through 20th Music, 1973—, (soloist with orchestra) Concertos, 1975—99. Mem.: Music Tchrs. Assn. (chair 1993—99, ea. divsn. pres. 2000—02, bd. mem. 2002—, Tchr. of the Yr. 1993). Office: Plymouth State U Dept Music Plymouth NH 03264

GRAFF, GEORGE LEONARD, lawyer; b. Bklyn., Sept. 6, 1940; s. Charles M. and Nettie (Starr) G.; m. Judith S. Udell, Apr. 20, 1963; children: David, Peter, Matthew. AB, Columbia U., 1962, LLB magna cum laude, 1967. Bar: N.Y. 1967, U.S. Dist. Ct. (so., ea. and no. dists.) N.Y. 1970, U.S. Ct. Appeals (2d, 3rd, 9th and Fed. cirs.) 1975, U.S. Ct. Claims, 1980, U.S. Supreme Ct. 1985. Law clk. to Hon. Stanley H. Fuld N.Y. Ct. Appeals, Albany, 1967-70; assoc. Nickerson, Kramer, Lowenstein, Nessen & Kamin, N.Y.C., 1970-74; member Milgrim, Thomajan & Lee, P.C., N.Y.C., 1974-92; ptnr. Paul, Hastings, Janofsky & Walker, N.Y.C., 1992—. Lt. comdr. USNR, 1962-64. Mem. ABA (advisor to drafting com. uniform computer info. transactions act 1994-2003, sci. and tech. sect. 1999-2003, mem. coun.), Assn. of Bar of City of N.Y. (chmn. state legislation com. 1973-75), Intellectual Property Owners Am. (vice chair amicus com.). Home: 112 Holly Pl Briarcliff Manor NY 10510-2107 Office: Paul Hastings Janofsky & Walker 75 E 55th St New York NY 10022

GRAFF, GEORGE STEPHEN, aerospace company executive; b. N.Y.C., Mar. 16, 1917; s. George Russell and Marjory Eleanor (Dolan) G.; m. Mary Rita Shaughnessy, Oct. 3, 1942 (dec.); children: Mary Ann, George Stephen, James Russell, Thomas Gerald, Maureen Rita; m. Marjory V. Kassabaum, Apr. 4, 1987; stepchildren: Douglas George, Ann Denise, Karen Jane. AB cum laude, DeSales Coll., Toledo, 1939; B.Aero. Engring., U. Detroit, 1942. Draftsman Continental Aviation & Engring. Corp., Detroit, 1940-42; with McDonnell Aircraft Co., 1942-82, dir. system tech., 1961-64, v.p. engring. tech., 1964-68, v.p. engring., 1968-70, exec. v.p., 1970-71, pres., 1971-82, also dir.; v.p. McDonnell Douglas Corp., 1971-82, mem. exec. com., 1974-87, also bd. dirs. Mem. subcom. stability and control NACA, 1951-56; mem. subcom. aerodynamic stability and control NASA, 1956-58, com. missile and spacecraft aerodynamics, 1959-61, com. aircraft aerodynamics, 1964-65, chmn. aircraft aerodynamics com., 1965-67, mem. research and tech. adv. com. on aeros., 1967-71 Mem. industry com. Parks Coll., St. Louis, 1950-58; chmn. bd. trustees Fontbonne Coll., 1977-87; bd. dirs. Jr. Achievement of Mississippi Valley, Inc. Recipient trophy for design excellence Continental Aviation and Engring. Corp., 1942; Outstanding Engring. Alumnus of Yr. award U. Detroit, 1973 Fellow AIAA (regional dir., chmn. com. aircraft design 1964-67, fellow grade com. 1975-76); mem. Nat. Acad. Engring., Tau Beta Pi. Home: 750 S Hanley Rd #38 Saint Louis MO 63105 E-mail: graffgsgxp67@aol.com.

GRAFF, HENRY FRANKLIN, historian, educator; b. NYC, Aug. 11, 1921; s. Samuel F. and Florence Babette (Morris) G.; m. Edith Krantz, June 16, 1946; children: Iris Joan (Mrs. Andrew R. Morse), Ellen Toby (Mrs. Martin A. Fox). BSS magna cum laude, Coll. City N.Y., 1941; MA, Columbia, 1942, PhD, 1949. Fellow history Coll. City N.Y., 1941-42, tutor history, 1946; lectr. history Columbia U., N.Y.C., 1946-47, instr. to asso. prof., 1946-61, prof. history, 1961-91, prof. emeritus, 1991—, chmn. dept. history, 1961-64; sr. fellow Freedom Forum Media Studies Ctr., N.Y.C., 1991-92; disting. lectr. Med. Sch. Columbia U., N.Y.C., 1992. Lectr. Vassar Coll., 1953; chmn. advanced placement com. Am. History Coll. Entrance Exam. Bd., 1959-63; presdl. appointee Nat. Hist. Publs. Commn., 1965-71; mem. hist. adv. com. to sec. Air Force, 1972-80; acad. cons. Gen. Learning Corp., Time-Life Books; cons. editor Alfred A. Knopf, Inc.; hist. adviser to CBS for Bicentennial TV Series The American Parade, 1973-76, Presdl. Portraits, 1987-88; disting. spkr. U.S. Air Force Acad., 1980; hist. adviser to ABC for TV series Our World, 1986-87, 20th Century Project, 1993-99; presdl. appointee J.F.K. Assassination Records Rev. Bd., 1993-98; humanities lectr. Med. Sch. Yale U., 1993; Richard W. Cooper lectr. Phi Beta Kappa Assocs., 1996. Author: Bluejackets with Perry in Japan, 1952; author: (with Jacques Barzun) The Modern Researcher, 1962; author: (with Clifford Lord) American Themes, 1963; author: (with John A. Krout) The Adventure of the American People, 3d edit., 1973; author: The Free and the Brave, 4th edit., 1980, Thomas Jefferson, 1968, American Imperialism and the Philippine Insurrection, 1969, The Tuesday Cabinet, 1970; author: (with Paul J. Bohannan) The Call of Freedom, 1978; author: The Promise of Democracy, 1978, This Great Nation, 1983, The Presidents: A Reference History, 1984, 2d edit., 1996, paperback, 1997, 3d edit., 2002, America: The Glorious Republic, 1985, rev. edit., 1990, Grover Cleveland, 2002; cons. editor Life's History of the United States, 1963—64; contbr. articles to profl. jours. 1st lt. AUS, 1942-46. Recipient citation War Dept., Townsend Harris medal CCNY, 1966, Mark Van Doren award Columbia U., 1981, Gt. Tchr. award Columbia U., 1982, Kidger award New Eng. History Tchrs. Assn., 1990; Am. Coun. Learned Socs. fellow, 1942, Presdl. medal George Washington U., 1997, James Madison award ALA, 1999, Disting. Author award Westchester C.C. Found., 2000. Mem. Orgn. Am. Historians, Am. Hist. Assn., Coun. Fgn. Rels., Author's Guild, P.E.N., Soc. Am. Historians, Soc. Historians Am. Fgn. Rels., Mass. Hist. Soc. (corr.), Century Assn. (N.Y.C.), Sunningdale Country Club, Phi Beta Kappa (former pres. Gamma chpt.), Phi Beta Assocs. (hon.). Home: 47 Andrea Ln Scarsdale NY 10583-3115

GRAFF, PAT STUEVER, secondary education educator; b. Tulsa, Mar. 24, 1955; d. Joseph H., Sr. and Joann (Schneider) Stuever; m. Mark A. Rumsey; children: Earl, Jr., Jeremy. BS in Secondary Edn., Okla. State U., 1976; postgrad., U. N.M., 1976-87. Cert. tchr. lang. arts, social studies, journalism, French, N.Mex. Substitute tchr. Albuquerque Pub. Schs., 1976-78; tchr. Cleveland Mid. Sch., Albuquerque, 1978-86, La Cueva H.S., Albuquerque, 1986—, co-chair English dept., 1996—, chair sch. restructuring coun., 1999-2001. Adviser award winning lit. mag. El Tesoro, sch. newspapers The Edition, Huellas del Oso; instr. journalism workshops, N.Mex. Press Assn., Ind. U., Bloomington, Nat. Scholastic Press, Mpls., Kans. State U., Manhattan, Interscholastic Press League, Austin, Tex., St. Mary's U., San Antonio, Ala. Scholastic Press Assn., Wash.; keynote spkr. at numerous confs. in Ohio, Ind., Kans., S.C., Utah, La., Okla., Ala., N.Mex., Tex., Wash., Idaho, and N.Y.; reviewer of lang. and textbooks for several cos.; instr. Dial-A-Tchr., N.Mex., 1991—; textook evaluator Holt Pub., Inc., 1991; nat. bd. cert. tchr. adolescent/young adult English lang. arts, 2001—; mem. N.Mex. Network of Nat. Bd. Cert. Tchrs., 2002—; bd. dirs. N.Mex. Coun. for the Social Studies, 1999—, chair state conf., 2001, state pres., 2002-03. Comm. coord. ABC Tchrs. Fed. 2003- rep. 2001- Author: Journalism Text, 1983; contbg. author: Communication Skills Resource Text, 1987, Classroom Publishing/Literacy, 1992; contbr. articles to profl. jours. Troop leader Girl Scouts U.S., 1979—90, coord. various programs, asst. program com. chmn. Chaparral Coun., 1988—89, chmn. adult recognition task force, 1991—96, bd. dirs., 1991—98; active PTA Gov. Bent Elem. Sch., 1983—86, v.p., 1985—86, Osuna Elem. Sch., 1986—92, N.Mex. PTA, 1994—2000; pub. various children's lit. mags., 1987—; pub. parent's newsletter, 1986—; newsletter layout editor Albuquerque Youth Soccer Orgn., 1985—88; active YMCA youth and govt. model legis.; faculty advisor La Cueva del., 1986—2002, press corps advisor, 1987—2001, asst. state dir., 2001—; asst. den. leader Boy Scouts Am., 1987—88, den leader, 1988—91; mem. N.Mex. Coun. for Social Studies, 1998—2003, state bd. dirs., 1998—, state pres., 2002—03. Recipient Innovative Teaching award Bus. Week mag., 1990, Svc. commendatin Coll. Edn. Alumni Assn., Okla. State U., 1990, Alumni Recognition award, 1993, Mem. Yr. Svc. award Bernalillo County Coun. Internat. Reading Assn., Thanks to Tchrs. award Apple Computers, 1990, Spl. Recognition Albuquerque C. of C., 1992; named Spotlighted Mem. Phi Delta Kappa, 1990, Spl. Recognition Advisor Dow Jones Newspaper Fund, 1990, Nat. H.S. Journalism Tchr. of Yr., 1995, Disting. Advisor, 1991, U.S. West Tchr. Yr. finalist, 1991, N.Mex. Pubs. Adviser of Yr., 1991, N.Mex. State Tchr. of Yr., 1993, finalist Nat. Tchr. Yr., 1993, finalist Am. Tchr. Awards, Disney, 1998; named USA Today All-Am. Tchr., 1999; grantee Phi Delta Kappa 1989, 91, Geraldine R. Dodge Found., 1990, 92, 95-97, Learn and Serve Am., 1999. Mem.: AAUW (chpt. newsletter editor 1995—2001, local v.p. 1997—99, state program v.p. 1997—99, state media chair 2000—), ASCD (editor newsletter 1991—92, focus on excellence awards com. 1992—94, state bd. dirs. 2002—; Focus on Excellence award 1990), N Mex. Coun. for Social Studies (mem. bd. 1999—, state vice- pres 2001—02, pres. 2002—03), N. Mex. World Class Tchr. Network (state vice-pres. 2002—), N.Mex. Goals 2000 (panel mem. 1994—97), Quill & Scroll (adv. La Cueva chpt. 1986—, judge nat. newspaper rating contest 1988—97), Albuquerque Press Women (v.p. 1994, pres. 1995, Communicator of Achievement award 1993), N.Mex. Press Women (state scholarship chair 1994, publicity chair 1995—96, state treas. 1996—98, state v.p. 1998—99), N.Mex. Scholastic Press Assn. (state v.p. 1985—89, coord. workshop 1986, editor newsletter 1986—89, asst. chair state conf. 1988, 1989, state bd. dirs. 1991—2000, state v.p. 1992—95), N.Mex. Coun. Tchrs. English (regional coord. Albuquerque 1983—86, chair state confs. 1985—87, editl. bd. N.Mex. English Jour. 1986—88, state pres. 1987—88, chair facilities for Fall conf. 1988—93, chair English Humanities expo com. 1988—99, adv. mgr. 1989—90, editor N.Mex. English Jour. 1999—, Svc. award 1989, Outstanding H.S. English Tchr. N.Mex. 1991), Journalism Edn. Assn., Journalism Edn. Assn. (judge nat. contests 1988—, mem. nat. cert. bd. 1989—99, presenter nat. convs. 1989—, cert. journalism educator 1990, nat. bd. 1991—2002), Nat. Fedn. Press Women, Nat. Sch. Pub. Rels. Assn. (issues seminar planning com. 1990, master journalism educator 1991, chair 1991, nat. conf. chmn. 1997—99, Zia chpt., contest winner 1991—94, Pres.'s award 1993), Nat. Coun. Tchrs. English (nat. chair com. English Tchrs. and Pubs. 1988—91, standing com. affiliates 1991—94, nat. chair 1995—98, Secondary Sect. Com. 1999—, nat. exec. com. 2001—, chair English Humanities expo com. 2001—, nat. chair assembly for advisors of student pubs., regional rep. Tex., La., N.Mex.), Nat. Alliance High Schs. (tchr. rep. 1997—2000), Nat. Assn. Secondary Sch. Prins. (Breaking Ranks tchr. rep.), Phi Delta Kappa (pres. U. N.Mex. br. 2002—), Delta Kappa Gamma, Pi Lambda Theta (Ethel Mary Moore award Outstanding Educator 1993). Roman Catholic. Avocations: soccer, running, hiking, travel, skiing. Home: 8101 Krim Dr NE Albuquerque NM 87109-5223 Office: La Cueva H S 7801 Wilshire Ave NE Albuquerque NM 87122-2807 Fax: 505-797-2250. E-mail: pgraff@aol.com.

GRAFF, ROBERT ALAN, computer consultant; b. Detroit, Nov. 13, 1953; s. Jack and Irene Bertha (Horowitz) G.; m. Karen Elaine Morgan, Dec. 21, 1985; 1 child, David. BS in Physics, Wayne State U., 1976, MS in Computer Engring., 1981. Office automation specialist Burroughs Corp., Detroit, 1977-78; optical engr. Energy Conversion Devices Co., Troy, Mich., 1978-80; ind. contract programmer Southfield, Mich., 1981; sr. programmer/analyst Comprehensive Health Planning Coun. Southeastern Mich., Detroit, 1981-86; pres., computer cons. Data Concepts, Bloomfield Hills, Mich., 1983—. Adj. instr. Walsh Coll., 1987-93, Davenport U. (formerly Detroit Coll. Bus.), 1990—; instr. U. Detroit, 1994—, Marygrove Coll., 1997-98, Baker Coll., 1999—. Contbr. articles for devel. custom software for acctg. oriented micro computer applications, network analysis and database design adminstrn.; custom tng. on software products; topical computer topics. Mem. IEEE, Assn. Computing Machinery. Democrat. Jewish. Office: Data Concepts 984 S Reading Rd Bloomfield Hills MI 48304-2044 E-mail: sales@rdataconcepts.com.

GRAFFAM, WARD IRVING, lawyer; b. Portland, Maine, Sept. 2, 1940; s. Irving Hall and Mary Earl (Williams) G.; m. Linda Lewsen, June 10, 1967; children: Ward Jr., Kristen, Jerome. Bar: Maine 1967, U.S. Dist. Ct. Maine 1967. Lawyer Unum Life Ins. Co., Portland, 1968-70, assoc. counsel, 1970-75, counsel, 1975-80, v.p. ltd. products, 1980-83, v.p. employee benefits mktg., 1983-85, v.p. reins ops., 1985-86, v.p. flexible benefits, 1986, v.p., counsel, 1986-88, v.p. internat. ops., 1988-90; chmn. NEL Britannica Life Assurance, 1990-92; pres., mng. dir. Unum European Holding Co. Ltd. (London), 1990-97; chmn. Unum, Ltd., 1990—95; sr. v.p. internat. ops. Unum European Holding Co. Ltd. (London), 1992-97; COO, Young Am. America's Cup Syndicate, 1997-98; co-owner Wayfarer Marine Corp., Camden, Maine, 1997-2000. Bd. dirs. Camden Nat. Corp., Acadia Trust, Montalvo Corp., J. Weston Walch, Me. Employers Mutual Ins. Co., N.E. Health; chmn. Unum Ltd., U.K., 1992-95; chmn. bd. dirs. Maine Internat. Trade Ctr., 1995-99, Waldron Group of Cos., 2002—; vice chmn. bd. dirs. Maine World Trade, Internat. Ins. Coun., Found. for Blood Rsch.; chmn. ACLI Internat. Life Ins. Co.; mem. bd. visitors U. Maine Law Sch. Author: (with others) The Mutual Company, 1971; editor-in-chief U. Maine Law Rev., 1966-67. Chmn. bd. South Portland HUD, 1973-75; mem. Gov.'s Coun. on Alcohol and Drug Abuse, Augusta, Maine, 1980-82; bd. dirs. Cumberland unit Am. Cancer Soc., Portland, 1976-78, Vis. Nurses Assn., Portland, 1971-72, YMCA, Portland, 1984-89; bd. dirs. Maine World Affairs Coun., Maine Maritime Mus.; mem. Gov.'s Internat. Adv. Bd., 1995-96; treas., bd. dirs. Maine Maritime Acad., 1997—. Recipient 1st Place award Moot Ct. Competition U. Maine Sch. Law, Dist. Alumni award. Mem. ABA, Am. Corp. Counsel Assn., Maine State Bar Assn., Cumberland Bar Assn. (award), Portland Country Club, Portland Yacht Club (commodore 1983-84), Masons. Home: 29 Orchard St Portland ME 04102-3613 Office: Graffam & Assocs 29 Orchard St Portland ME 04102

GRAFFEO, MARY THÉRÈSE, music educator, performer; b. Mineola, N.Y., Jan. 20, 1949; d. Michael Joseph and Florence Marie (Lonette) G. BA in Music Edn., Adelphi U., 1972; MusM in Vocal Performance, Kent State U., 1982. Cert. music tchr. N.Y. Tchr., therapist Nassau County Bd. Coop. Ednl. Svcs., Westbury, NY, 1972-85; tchr. music, developer curricula Great Neck (N.Y.) Pub. Schs., 1985-87; tchr. music Syosset (N.Y.) Pub. Schs., 1987-88, 89-90, Jericho (N.Y.) Pub. Schs., 1988-89; tchr. music, developer creative programs Lawrence (N.Y.) Pub. Schs., 1990-92; tchr. music Herricks Pub. Schs., New Hyde Park, N.Y., 1992-93, Hempstead (N.Y.) Pub. Schs., 1993—. Music dir. summer programs Friends Acad., Locust Valley, N.Y., 1989-95. Author: Creative Enrichment Programs/America: The First 300 Years in Song, 1990, (curriculum) Music for the Trainable Mentally Retarded, 1973, Music for the Early Childhood Center of Hempstead Public Schools, 2002; co-author: The Remediation of Learning Discrepancies Through Music, 1980; composer: (mus. play) Red Riding Hood's Day, 1993, The Bell of Atri, The Children's Song, 1995. Cultural adv. bd. Lawrence Pub. Schs., 1990-92, Hempstead Pub. Schs., 1993—; founding mem. United We Stand Am., Dallas, 1992-93. Scholar Adelphi U., 1968-72, Blossom Festival Sch., Kent, Ohio, 1978-79. Mem. NEA, Am. Fedn. Tchrs., Music Educators Nat. Conf., N.Y. State United Tchrs., N.Y. State Sch. Music Assn., Nassau Music Educators Assn. Democrat. Roman Catholic. Avocations: aviculture, needlework, travel, photography, concerts. Home: 18 Osborne Ln Greenvale NY 11548-1140 Office: Early Childhood Ctr 436 Front St Hempstead NY 11550-4212 E-mail: mgraffeo@optonline.net.

GRAFFEO, VICTORIA A. state appeals court judge; b. Rockville Centre, NY, Apr. 13, 1952; m. Edward E. Winders. BA, SUNY, Oneonta, 1974; JD Albany Law Sch., Union U., 1977. Pvt. practice, 1978—82; asst. counsel N.Y. State Div. Alcoholism and Alcohol Abuse, 1982—84; counsel to minority leader pro tempore Kemp Hannon N.Y. State Assembly, 1984—89, chief counsel to minority leader Clarence D. Rappleyea Jr., 1989—94; solicitor gen. State of NY, 1995—96; judge NY State Supreme Ct. (3d jud. dist.), 1996—98; assoc. justice Appellate div., 3d dept., 1998—2000; assoc. judge N.Y. Ct. Appeals, 2000—. Office: 20 Eagle St Albany NY 12207

GRAFFIUS, RICHARD STEWART, II, middle school educator; b. Punxsutawney, Pa., May 27, 1948; s. Richard S. and Adeline L. (Piquet) G.; m. Rose M. Ingham, Apr. 13, 1974; children: Alissa, Lindsay, Emily. BS in Elem. Edn., Ind. U. Pa., 1970; MEd in Ednl. Adminstrn., Pa. State U., 1975, EdD in Ednl. Adminstrn., 1993. Cert. elem. tchr., elem. and secondary prin., supt., Pa. Sci. tchr. Punxsutawney (Pa.) Area Middle Sch., 1970—. Author (coloring book) The Official Punxsutawney Phil Coloring Book, 1978. Councilman, v.p. Borough of Punxsutawney, 1981-85; consistory mem. St. Peter's United Ch. of Christ, Punxsutawney, 1993-96. Mem. NEA, ASCD, Pa. State Edn. Assn., Punxsutawney Area Ednl. Assn. Avocations: skiing, hunting, fishing, antique and classic car restoration. Home: 136 Wayne Rd Punxsutawney PA 15767

GRAFFMAN, GARY, pianist, music educator; b. N.Y.C., Oct. 14, 1928; s. Vladimir and Nadia (Margolin) G.; m. Naomi Helfman, Dec. 5, 1952. Student, Curtis Inst. Music, 1936-46, Columbia U., 1947-48; studied with Vladimir Horowitz, Rudolf Serkin, Isabelle Vengerova; MusD (hon.), Trinity Coll., 1986, Juilliard Sch., 1993, Moravian Coll., 1995, St. Josephs U., 1996, Univ. Pa., 1997, New Eng. Conservatory Music, 2003. Dir. Curtis Inst. Music, Phila., 1986-95, pres., dir., 1995—. Soloist debut, Phila. Orch, 1947; first tours U.S., 1951, S.Am., 1955, Europe, 1956, Asia-Australia, 1958, South Africa, 1961; solo appearances with N.Y. Philharmonic, Boston, Chgo., Cleve., San Francisco, Los Angeles, London, Cape Town symphony orchs., Philharmonia London, Halle Orch. of Manchester, Royal Liverpool, Berlin, Lisbon, Oslo, Warsaw philharmonic orchs., Johannesburg, Sydney, Melbourne orchs., others; rec. artist with N.Y., Phila., Boston, Cleve., Chgo., San Francisco orchs., also solo recs.; author: I Really Should Be Practicing, 1981. Fulbright scholar, 1950; Ford Found. fellow, 1962; recipient Rachmaninoff Fund. spl. award, 1948, Leventritt award, 1949, Pa. Gov. Excellence in Arts award, 1991. Office: Curtis Inst Music Office of Director 1726 Locust St Philadelphia PA 19103-6187 also: ICM Artists Ltd 40 W 57th St Fl 16 New York NY 10019-4001

GRAFSTEIN, JOEL M. lawyer; b. N.Y.C., May 27, 1948; s. Max G. and Elaine (Weisner) G.; m. Andree M. Clement, Aug. 4, 1974; 1 son, Michael Louis. BS, U. Bridgeport, 1970; JD, N.Y. Law Sch., 1973; LLM, NYU, 1974. Bar: N.Y. 1973, Conn. 1973, U.S. Dist. Ct. Conn. 1973, U.S. Tax Ct. 1973. Assoc. Rome & Case, Bloomfield, Conn., 1974-82, Albrecht, Zelman, Hartford, Conn., 1982-83; ptnr. Lublin, Wolfe, Kantor & Silver, East Hartford, Conn., 1984—1989. Author: Connecticut Collection Law 1982, 83; Connecticut Foreclosure Law, 1984, 87; Bankruptcy: A Primer, 1984, 2d edit., 1987; The Connecticut Unfair Trade Practices Act, 1986, Problem Loans in Connecticut, 1988, Connecticut Forclosure Law, 2001, Chmn. Republican Town Com., Barkhamstead, Conn., 1980-82; region chmn. Disaster Relief Com., Hartford, 1978-83. Mem. ABA, Conn. Bar Assn. (exec. com. 1978-83), Hartford County Bar Assn. Club: Lions (treas. 1976-80) (Bloomfield, Conn.). Home: 20 Pond Rd Canton CT 06019-2623 Office: Grafstein & Assoc 10 Melrose Dr Farmington CT 06034

GRAFTON, ANTHONY THOMAS, history educator; b. New Haven, May 21, 1950; s. Samuel and Edith (Kingstone) G.; m. Louise Erlich, May 13, 1972; children: Samuel David, Anna Temma Rachel. BA, U. Chgo., 1971, MA, 1972, PhD, 1975. Instr. Cornell U., Ithaca, N.Y., 1974-75; from asst. prof. to assoc. prof. Princeton (N.J.) U., 1975-85, prof., 1985—, Andrew Mellon prof., 1988-93, Dodge prof. of history, 1993-2000, Henry Putnam prof., 2000—. Meyer Schapiro lectr. Columbia U., 1996-97; exhibit curator N.Y. Pub. Libr., N.Y.C., 1992, Libr. of Congress, Washington, 1993. Author: Joseph Scaliger, 1983-93, Defenders of the Text, 1991, New Worlds, Ancient Texts, 1992, The Footnote: A Curious History, 1997, Commerce with the Classics, 1997, Cardano's Cosmos, 1999, Leon Battista Alberti, 2000, Bring Out Your Dead, 2001. Recipient L.A. Times prize for history, 1993, Balzan prize for History of Humanities, 2002; Danforth fellow, 1971-75, Guggenheim fellow, 1988-89, Fairchild fellow Calif. Tech. Inst., 1988-89, Behrman fellow Princeton U., 1994-95. Mem. Am. Philos. Soc., Brit. Acad., Berlin-Brandenburgische Akad. der Wissenschaften (corr.). Democrat. Jewish. Avocations: walking, reading. Office: Princeton U Dickinson Hall History Dept Hl Princeton NJ 08544-0001

GRAFTON, EDNA FISHER, writer; b. Memphis, May 24; d. Ollie Fred and Alberta Louise Fisher. BS, U. Wis.; postgrad., U. Memphis, Memhis Theol. Sem.; PhD in Religion (hon.), Tenn. Sch. Religion, Memphis, 1998. Author: (book) Poems of the Beyonder, 1995, My Walk with God, 1996, Black Woman Why Are You Here, 2000, Nuture For Baptist Churches, 2002. Mem. Sarah Brown YWCA, Memphis; sec. Memphis Dist. Assn.; mem. exec. bd. Sun Sch. Pub. Bd., Nashville. Named one of Ten Best Dressed Women, City of Memphis Women, 1994; recipient Keys to the City and County, Mayors of City and County, Memphis, 1998, Unsung Heroes award, Memphis Dist. Assn., 2003. Mem.: Zeta Phi Beta (asst. sec. 1984—90). Democrat. Baptist. Avocations: writing, reading, singing. Home: 826 Alida Ave Memphis TN 38106-6732

GRAFTON, SUE, novelist; b. Louisville, Apr. 24, 1940; d. Cornelius Warren and Vivian Boisseau (Harnsberger) G.; children: Leslie, Jay, Jamie; m. Steven Humphrey, Oct. 1, 1978. BA, U. Louisville, 1961. Lectr. L.A. City Coll., Long Beach (Calif.) City Coll., U. Dayton (Ohio) Writers Conf., Midwest Writers Conf., Canton, Ohio, Calif. Luth. Coll., Thousand Oaks, Santa Barbara (Calif.) Writers Conf., L.A. Valley Coll., Antioch Writers Conf., Yellow Springs, Ohio, S.W. Writers Conf., Albuquerque, Smithsonian Campus on the Mall, Washington, and others. Author: (novels) Keziah Dane, 1967, The Lolly-Madona War, 1969, "A" is for Alibi, 1982 (Mysterious Stranger award 1982-83), "B" is for Burglar, 1985 (Shamus award 1986, Anthony award 1987), "C" is for Corpse, 1986, "D" is for Deadbeat, 1987, "E" is for Evidence, 1988 (Doubleday Mystery Guild award 1989), "F" is for Fugitive, 1989 (Doubleday Mystery Guild award 1990, The Falcon award 1990), "G" is for Gumshoe, 1990 (Doubleday Mystery Guild award 1991, Anthony award 1991, Shamus award 1991), "H" is for Homicide, 1991 (Doubleday Mystery Guild award 1992), "I" is for Innocent, 1992 (Doubleday Mystery Guild award 1992, Mystery Scene Am. Mystery award 1993), Kinsey and Me, 1992, "J" is for Judgement, 1994, "K" is for Killer, 1994 (Shamus award 1994), "L" is For Lawless, 1995, "M" is For Malice, 1996, "N" is for Noose, 1998, "O" is for Outlaw, 1999, "P" is for Peril, 2001, Q is for Quarry, 2002; editor: Writing Mysteries, 1992; author short fiction, short stories, screenplay, teleplay TV episodes. Mem. Writers Guild Am. West, Mystery Writers Am. Inc. (pres. 1994), Private Eye Writers Assn. (pres. 1989-90), Crime Writers Assn. Address: Penguin/Putnam 375 Hudson St New York NY 10014-3672*

GRAGER, STEVEN P. investment consultant; b. Everett, Wash., July 18, 1964; s. Clara A. Grager; m. Courtney A. Van Detta, June 27, 1987; children: Emma, Camille. BA in Mktg. magna cum laude, Seattle Pacific U., 1986; MBA in Fin., U. Chgo., 1991. CLU, ChFC, CFP. Fin. cons. H.D. Vest Fin. Svcs., Irving, Tex., 1987-89; mktg. dir. Mut. of N.Y., San Francisco, 1991-92, fin. planner Bellevue, Wash., 1992-94; regional v.p. Pacific Life, Seattle, 1994-98; v.p. PaineWebber, San Francisco, 1998-99; CEO Capital Advisers Group, Danville, Calif., 2000—. Investment advisor Steven P. Grager & Assocs., Seattle, 1992-96. Co-chmn. Giving Something Back, Chgo., 1989-91; v.p. Toastmasters, Chgo., 1990-91. Arthur Andersen scholar Seattle Pacific U., 1984; Student Activities grantee U. Chgo., 1990. Mem. Nat. Assn. Ins. Fin. Advisors, Am. Soc. CLU, Am. Assn. Individual Investors, Commonwealth Club San Francisco, Fin. Planning Assn. (bd. dirs. East Bay chpt.), No. Calif. Planned Giving Coun., East Bay Estate Planning Coun. Republican. Presbyterian. Avocations: skiing, travel. Office: 370 Diablo Rd Ste 207 Danville CA 94526 E-mail: steve.grager@capitaladvisors.com.

GRAGG, KARL LAWRENCE, lawyer; b. Watertown, N.Y., Sept. 25, 1946; s. Karl Lawrence and Pauline (Sykes) G.; m. Maureen Gilluly, Dec. 13, 1975; children: Meaghan Christina, Erika Lawrence, Jenny Camille. BS, Fla. State U., 1968; JD, U. Fla., 1974, LLM in Taxation, 1975. Bar: Fla. 1975, U.S Dist. Ct. (so. dist.) Fla., U.S. Tax Ct., U.S. Ct. Appeals (5th cir.). Assoc. Mershon, Sawyer, Johnson, Dunwoody & Cole, Miami, Fla., 1975-80, ptnr., 1980-82, Gunster, Yoakley, Criser & Stewart, Palm Beach, Fla., 1982 84, Walker Ellis Gragg & Deaktor, Miami, 1984-86, White & Case, LLP, Miami, 1987—. Adj. prof. law U. Miami, 1978-89; mem. tax com. Fla. Ho. of Reps., Tallahassee, 1983. Contbr. articles to U. Fla. Law Rev. Vol. Miami United Way, 1977-80. Mem. ABA (taxation sect.), Nat. Assn. State Bar (chmn. 1986), Am. Coll. Tax Counsel, Fla. Bar Assn. (tax sect., chmn. tax sect. 1991, chmn. coun. of sect.), Nat. Assn. Indsl. and Office Parks (bd. dirs. 1989-91), Ctr. for Health Techs., Inc. (bd. dirs. 1992-98), Japan Soc. South Fla. (bd. dirs. 1990-98). Office: White & Case LLP 200 S Biscayne Blvd Ste 4900 Miami FL 33131-2352

GRAGLIA, LINO ANTHONY, lawyer, educator; b. Bklyn., Jan. 22, 1930; s. Pasquale and Antoinette (Romeo) G.; m. F. Carolyn Pennington, July 17, 1954; children: Donna, Carol, Laura. BA, CCNY, 1952; LLB, Columbia U., 1954. Bar: N.Y. 1954, D.C. 1957, Tex. 1980, U.S. Supreme Ct. Atty. U.S. Dept. Justice, Washington, 1954-57; pvt. practice law Washington and N.Y.C., 1957-66; prof. law U. Tex., Austin, 1966—. Author: Disaster by Decree: The Supreme Court Decisions on Race and the Schools, 1976. Recipient George Washington medal Freedoms Foundation at Valley Forge, 1989. Republican. Avocations: tennis, biking, hiking, billiards. Office: U Tex Sch Law 727 E 26th St Austin TX 78705-3224 E-mail: lgraglia@mail.law.utexas.edu.

GRAHAM, AARON RICHARD, school superintendent; b. St. Petersburg, Fla., Apr. 4, 1944; s. Willie and Willie Mae (George) G.; m. Janet Lorraine Wilkins, June 21, 1969; children: Andrea Yvonne, Aaron Richard II. AA, St. Petersburg Jr. Coll., 1965; BS, N.C. Cen. U., 1967; MS in Edn., Akron U., 1969; EdD, Fordham U., 1990; Grad., Nat. Bus. Leadership Inst., 1995. Cert. prin., sch. adminstr., N.J. Sci. tchr. Nat. Tchr. Corps, Akron, Ohio, 1967-69, Akron Pub. Schs., 1969-71; biology tchr. Palisades Park (N.J.) Pub. Schs., 1973-77; program coord. N.J. Dept. Edn., Bergen County, 1977-83, ednl. planner, 1983-89; asst. dir. curriculum and instrn. Bergen County Tech. Schs., Hackensack, 1989-91; asst. prof. adminstrn., curriculum and instrn. New Jersey City U., 1991—92; dist. project dir. curriculum and instrn. Bergen County Tech. Sch., 1992-96. Mem. adv. com. Acad. Advancement of Teaching and Mgmt., Edison, N.J., 1991-94; presenter U. Coun. for Ednl. Adminstrn., Scottsdale, Ariz., 1989. Trustee Teaneck (N.J.) Libr. Bd., 1983-96; mem. Human Rels. Coalition Bergen County, 1987-95, v.p., 1991-93; bd. dirs. Bergen Community Coll. Found., 1994-96; bd. trustees Bergen Cmty. Coll., 1996—; mem. bd. edn. Bergen County Tech. Schs., 1996—, Bergen County Spl. Svcs., 1996—. Mem. ASCD, N.J. Staff Devel. Coun., Am. Assn. of Sch. Adminstrations, Nat. Staff

Devel. Coun., N.J. Coun. of Edn., Urban League (bd. dirs. 1982-96, Svc. award 1987, 97, Adolph Holmes award 1999, Child Assault Prevention award 2000, Congressional Citation for Outstanding Leadership, 2002, Bergen County Leadership award 2003), Phi Delta Kappa. Avocations: reading, travel, sports. Home: 86 Church St Teaneck NJ 07666-4932

GRAHAM, ALAN MORRISON, surgeon; b. Perth, Scotland, Mar. 23, 1953; m. Michiko P. Graham; children: George A., Mie I, Fraser S., Queen's U., Kingston, Ont., 1973-75, MD, 1979. Diplomate Am. Bd. Surgery, Am. Bd. Gen. Surgery and Vascular Surgery. Internship Kingston Gen. Hosp. Queen's U., 1979—80; residency Royal Victoria Hosp. McGill U., 1980—84; fellowship U. Chgo., 1984—85; asst. prof. dept. surgery Royal Victoria Hosp., 1985-91, McGill U., 1985—91, assoc. prof., 1991—92; assoc. prof. dept. surgery Royal Victoria Hosp., 1991—92; prof., chief div. vascular surgery Robert Wood Johnson Med. Sch., 1992—, program dir. vascular fellowship program, 1992—, Ruth and Norman Rosenberg chair in vascular surgery, 2002—, 2003—. Author numerous book chapters; contbr. articles to profl. jours. Recipient Edgar Forrester scholarship, 1977, W.W. Near scholarship, 1977, Alice Pierce Waddington scholarship, 1977, Prof. prize in Surgery, 1979, Neil Currie Polson Meml. prize, 1979, Outstanding Tchr. award U. Chgo., 1985, E.J. Wylie Travelling fellowship, 1989, numerous grants. Fellow ACS, Royal Coll. Physicians and Surgeons; mem. Soc. Univ. Surgeons, Soc. Vascular Surgery, Ea. Vascular Soc., Can. Assn. Gen. Surgeons, Assn. Acad. Surgeons, Assn. Internat. Vascular Surgery, Can. Soc. Vascular Surgery, Peripheral Vascular Surgery Soc., Internat. Soc. Cardiovascular Surgery, Soc. Clin. Vascular Surgery, Phoenix Alliance, Inc., Vascular Soc. N.J. (pres.), Internat. Fedn. Surg. Colls., Soc. of Surgeons of N.J. Office: Robert Wood Johnson Med Sch 1 Robert Wood Johnson Pl New Brunswick NJ 08901-1928

GRAHAM, ALBERT DARLINGTON, JR., educational administrator; b. Camden, N.J., July 28, 1948; s. Albert Darlington and Betty Jane (Belancin) g.; m. Susan K. Tomarchio, July 30, 1994; children: Jason Carl, Jayme Lynn. BS cum laude, Union Coll., Barbourville, Ky., 1970, MA, 1973; EdM, Johns Hopkins U., 1977; EdD, Calif. Western U., 1980; MA, Rowan U., 1991; PhD, LaSalle U., 1992. Cert. supt., prin., supr., sch. bus. adminstr., secondary social studies tchr., in student personnel svcs., N.J. Tchr. social studies Penns Grove (N.J.) Mid. Sch., 1970-82, coord. career edn., 1974-75, chmn. social studies dept., 1978-82; athletic dir. Penns Grove H.S., Carneys Point, N.J., 1983-85, coord. gifted and talented program, 1986-87, dir. guidance, vice prin. in charge curriculum, fin.-instrn., 1982-92, dir. spl. projects, 1992—, dir. early childhood and fed./state programs, 2001—. Adj. prof. Sch. Law Wilmington Coll., 2002—, LaSalle U., 2002—. Mem. Carneys Point Twp., 1979-84, 91—; mayor Carneys Point Twp., 1992, 96, 99, 2000; mem. Salem County (N.J.) Bd. Chosen Freeholders, 1985-87, N.J. Gov.'s Coun. on Phys. Fitness and Sports, 1986—; chmn. Carneys Point Sewerage Authority, 1981-85, 91—; pres. Salem County Selective Svc. Bd., 1982-2002; pres. Salem County Assn. Local Govt., 1983-84, Village Arms Sr. Citizens Complex, Carneys Point, 1984—; pres. Carneys Point Rep. Club, 1981-84; trustee Salem C.C., 1987-91, Union Coll., 1992—. Recipient Gov. James D. Black Sr. award for acad. excellence, Balckwell Meml. award in polit. sci., medal for excellence in ednl. adminstrn., Disting. Cmty. Svc. award Carneys Point Twp. Com., 1983, Disting. Leadership award Salem County Assn. Local Govt., 1986, Salem County recognition award Salem County Bd. Chosen Freholders, 1987, Citizen of Yr. Penns Grove VFW, 1993; named to Personal Achievement Hall of Fame, Penns Grove H.S., 1994, Educators Hall of Fame, Union Coll., 1998, Selective Svc. medal, 2002. Mem. ASCD, N.J. Pins. and Suprs. Assn. (svc. and leadership award 1984), N.J. League Municipalities (svc. and leadership award 1984), South Jersey Assn. Freeholders (svc. and leadership award 1985), Penns Grove High Sch. Alumni Assn. (treas. 1975—, Selective Svc. medal 2002, Personal Achievement Hall of Fame 1994), Penns Grove Exch. Club (pres. Penns Grove 1984-85, Exchangite of Yr. 1984, Cmty. Svc. award 1985), Masons (32d degree), Elks (leading knight Penns Grove 1986-87), Mensa, Phi Delta Kappa, Iota Sigma Nu, Gamma Beta Phi, Phi Delta Gamma. Roman Catholic. Avocations: reading, sports, coin collecting, working on 1929 mercedes. Home: 58 N Norman Ave Carneys Point NJ 08069-1546 Office: Penns Grove-Carneys Point Sch Dist Adminstrv Offices 100 Iona Ave Penns Grove NJ 08069-1322 E-mail: agraham@pennsgrove.k12.nj.us.

GRAHAM, ANNA REGINA, pathologist, educator; b. Phila., Nov. 1, 1947; d. Eugene Nelson and Anna Beatrice (McGovern) Chadwick; m. Larry L. Graham, June 29, 1973; 1 child, Jason. BS in Chemistry, Ariz. State U., 1969, BS in Zoology, 1970; MD, U. Ariz., 1974. Diplomate Am. Bd. Pathology. With Coll. Medicine U. Ariz., Tucson, 1974—, asst. prof. pathology, 1978-84, assoc. prof. pathology, 1984-90, prof. Pathology, 1990—. Fellow Am. Soc. Clin. Pathologists (bd. dirs. Chgo. chpt. 1993—, sec. 1995-99, v.p. 1999-2000, pres.-elect 2000-2001, pres. 2001-02), Internat. Acad. Pathology, Internat. Acad. Telemedicine, Coll. Am. Pathologists; mem. AMA (alt. del. Chgo. chpt. 1992-99, del. Chgo. chpt. 1999—), Ariz. Soc. Pathologists (pres. Phoenix chpt. 1989-91), Ariz. Med. Assn. (treas. Phoenix chpt. 1995-97). Republican. Baptist. Avocations: motorcycles, piano, choir. Office: Ariz Health Scis Ctr Dept Pathology Tucson AZ 85724-5108

GRAHAM, B. ALASDAIR, government official; b. Dominion, N.S., Can., May 21, 1929; m. Jean Elizabeth MacDonald, 1952; 10 children. BA, St. Francis Xavier U. Apptd. to Senate, Ottawa, 1972; dep. leader Govt. of Senate, Ottawa, 1995-97, leader, 1997—. Office: Senate of Canada Rm 279-S Parliament Hill Centre Blk Ottawa ON Canada K1A 0A4*

GRAHAM, BRENDA J. nurse; b. Savannah, Ga., July 30, 1944; d. Herman James and Dotha Lee Johnson; 1 child, La Trelle Denise Jackson. AAS, Bronx Community Coll., 1971; BS, Savannah State Coll., 1987; MEd, U. Ga., 1993. Cert. RN, Ga., N.Y., S.C. Retired staff nurse Athens (Ga.) Regional Med. Ctr./Hosp.; lead tchr. nursing instrn. South Coll., Savannah; dir. of nursing Pleasantview Nursing Home, Metter, Ga.; collection supr. Am. Red Cross, Savannah; program coord. Savannah (Ga.) State Coll.; retired, 1993. Facilitator Athens Sickle Cell Support Group.

GRAHAM, BRUCE S. dean, educator; b. Windsor, Ont., Can. ;, naturalized, U.S. m. Linda Graham; children: Todd, Beth. Student, U. Windsor, 1966; DDS, U. Toronto, 1970; MS, cert. in prosthodontics, Ohio State U., 1974; MEd, Dalhousie U., 1989. Assoc. dean acad. affairs Dalhousie U., Halifax, Canada; dean U. Detroit-Mercy Sch. Dentistry, 1992—2000, U. Ill. Chgo., 2000—. Spkr. in field. Office: 801 South Paulina Chicago IL 60612

GRAHAM, CHARLES, research psychologist; b. Atlantic City, N.J., Nov. 21, 1937; s. Charles Leroy and Margery (Kaplan) G.; m. Sally Jones, Dec. 8, 1962 (div. Apr. 1974); children: Ronna, Christopher, Glen; m. Mary R. Cook, May 18, 1996; 1 child, Sheri J. BS, U. Md., 1966; MS, Pa. State U., 1968, PhD, 1970. Rsch. assoc. Inst. Pa. Hosp., Phila., 1970-74; instr., lectr. dept. psychiatry U. Pa., Phila., 1970-74; sr. exptl. psychologist Midwest Rsch. Inst., Kansas City, 1974-78, prin. exptl. psychologist, 1979-94, sr. advisor for life scis., 1994—, prin. advisor for life scis., 1998—. Mgr. Bioelectromagnetics Rsch. Program, 1998—; tech. review panel Dept. of Energy, EPA, NIH, WHO, Internat. Commn. on Non-Ionizing Radiation Protection. With U.S. Army, 1960-62. NIH grantee, 1975-2000. Mem. Am. Psychol. Assn., Soc. Psychophysiol. Rsch., Claude Bernard Soc., Bioelectromagnetics, Sigma Xi. Avocations: travel, photography, gardening. Office: Midwest Rsch Inst 425 Volker Blvd Kansas City MO 64110-2299 E-mail: cmg@planetkc.com., cgraham@mriresearch.org.

GRAHAM, CHARLES JOHN, university educator, former university president; b. Peru, Ill., May 29, 1929; s. John William and Pauline (Powell) G.; m. Florence Yvonne Ure, Sept. 2, 1951; children: John Charles, James Spencer, David Powell. AB, U. Ill., 1950, MA, 1951, PhD, 1955. Mgmt. intern Navy Dept., 1953-54; contract negotiator Bur. Ships, 1954; from instr. to prof. polit. sci. Wis. State U., River Falls, 1954-63, chmn. dept. social scis., 1962-63; vis. lectr. U. Wis., summer 1957, U. Ill., summer 1959; legislative asst. to Senator Proxmire, 1960-61; dean Coll. Art and Scis., Wis. State U., Whitewater, 1963-70, asst. to pres. for fed. programs, 1965-68, acting chmn. dept. polit. sci., 1970-71; pres. St. Cloud (Minn.) State U., 1971-81, Hamline U., St. Paul, 1981-87; sr. v.p. Minn. Pvt. Coll. Council/Fund, 1987-88; interim pres. Met. State U., St. Paul, 1988-89; disting. svc. prof. Minn. State U. System, 1989-95; pres. emeritus Hamline U.; St. Cloud, State U. Mem. faculty Augsburg Coll. of the Third Age, 1998—. Bd. dirs., Minn. Inst. for Talented Youth; bd. dirs. Indianhead coun. Boy Scouts Am. Recipient Alumni Achievement award U. Ill., 1995, Spurgeon award St. Paul United Way, 2000; James W. Garner fellow polit. sci., 1951-52, 52-53 Mem.: Rotary, Phi Kappa Phi, Phi Beta Kappa. Methodist. Home: 1675 Ridgewood Ln S Saint Paul MN 55113-5625

GRAHAM, CHARLES PASSMORE, retired army officer; b. Seward, Alaska, Dec. 19, 1927; s. Thomas Phillip and Lynnie Ethel (Passmore) G.; m. Alice Ann Chandler, Nov. 20, 1954; children: Susan Kay, Edwin C., Richard C. BS, U.S. Mil. Acad., 1950; MS in Engring, U. Mich., 1957. C. Commd. 2d lt. U.S. Army, 1950, advanced through grades to lt. gen., 1977; dir. force programs and structure, office of dep. chief of staff for ops. Hdqrs. Dept. Army Washington, 1975-77; comdg. gen. 2d Armored Div. Ft. Hood, Tex., 1977-80; dep. chief of staff for ops. Hdqrs. U.S. Army Forces Command Ft. McPherson, Ga., 1980-81; chief of staff Hdqrs. U.S. Army Forces Command, 1981-83; comdg. gen. 2d U.S. Army, 1983-85; mgmt. cons., 1985—. Mediator Justice Ctr. of Atlanta, 1993—. Exec. dir. Ga. Internat. Cultural Exch., Inc., prodr. of fine arts and cultural exhbns., 1994-95. Decorated D.S.M., Legion of Merit, Bronze Star, Purple Heart. Mem. Assn. U.S. Army, Armor Assn., Assn. Grads U.S. Mil. Acad., Assn. Grads Army War Coll., 2d Armored Divsn. Assn. Lodges: Kiwanis. Presbyterian. Home: 134 Warbler Way Georgetown TX 78628-4804 *Guided by the principle of "Duty, Honor, Country" learned as a cadet at West Point, my goal was to do my very best in every assignment I was given, remembering that what was best for the United States, best for the U.S. Army, and best for the American soldier was the proper solution to each problem. With that goal, success would come naturally.*

GRAHAM, CHRISTOPHER FRANCIS, lawyer; b. Darby, Pa., June 21, 1957; s. Thomas Francis Graham and Margaret Veronica Kerr. Student, London U., 1978-79; BS in Bus. Adminstrn. magna cum laude, Georgetown U., 1979; JD, Pa. U., 1982. Bar: Hawaii 1997, U.S. Dist. Ct. (so. and ea. dist.) N.Y. 1983, U.S. Ct. Appeals (2d and 5th cirs.) 1991, U.S. Tax Ct. 1987, U.S. Supreme Ct. 1991. Assoc. Weil Gotshal & Manges, N.Y.C., 1982-84, Cadwalader Wickersham & Taft, N.Y.C., 1984-89; ptnr. Thacher Proffitt & Wood, N.Y.C., 1989—, mem. exec. com., 1997—. Mem. bd. advisors, adj. prof. St. John's U. Sch. Law. Trustee Georgetown Dean's Coun., Washington, 1986-91; co-chmn. Save Our Aging Religious, N.Y.C., 1994-2002; head coach Eastchester (N.Y.) Youth Soccer, 1996-2002. Mem. ABA, Am. Bankruptcy Inst. (chmn. real estate com. 1996-2001, dir. law sch. medal program 1997—, bd. dirs. 2001-, co-chmn. law sch. com. 2002-), Alpha Sigma Nu.

GRAHAM, CLAXTON A. business systems analyst; b. Charlotte, N.C., Mar. 31, 1970; s. Howard and Alberta M. Graham; m. Sherri J. Gordon, Apr. 10, 2000. BA in Comm., N.C. State U., 1992. Radiotelephone operator's lic. FCC. Adminstrv. asst. Southland Comm., Charlotte, 1993—94; document processor First Union Corp., Charlotte, 1994—98; bus. analyst Wachovia Corp., Charlotte, 1998—. Bd. dirs. Charlotte Mecklenburg Pub. Access Corp. Secondary edn. tour guide Levine Mus. New South, Charlotte, 2001—02; moderator Gaston Invitational High-Q Acad. Tournament Gaston County Schs., Gastonia, NC, 1997—; moderator Charlotte-Area High-Q Acad. Tournament, 1994—97; cons. Junior Achievement, Charlotte, 2000—02. Avocations: writing, trivia, bowling, sports, video games.

GRAHAM, DANIEL ROBERT (BOB GRAHAM), senator, former governor; b. Coral Gables, Flor., Nov. 9, 1936; m. Adele Khoury; children: Gwendolyn Patricia, Glynn Adele, Arva Suzanne, Kendall Elizabeth. BA, U. Fla., 1959; LLB, Harvard U., 1962. Atty.; cattle and dairy farmer; real estate developer; mem. Fla. Ho. of Reps., 1966-70, Fla. Senate, 1970-78; gov. State of Fla., Tallahassee, 1978-86; U.S. senator from Fla. Washington, 1986—. Chmn. Edn. Commn. of the States, 1980-81, Caribbean/Central Am. Action, 1980-81, U.S. intergovtl. adv. council on edn.; mem. So. Growth Policies Bd., chmn., 1982-83; chmn. So. Govs.' Assn.; chmn. com. trade and fgn. affairs Nat. Govs.' Assn.; energy & natural resources, environ. & pub. works com., fin. com., VA affairs/intelligence com., senate Dem. steering & coord. com.; ranking mem. long-term growth, debt and deficit reduction com., com. on fin., 1997—; mem. com. environment and pub. works, ranking mem. clean air, wetlands, pvt. property and nuc. safety com., 1995—; mem. com. energy and natural resources, ranking mem. energy rsch., devel., prodn. and regulation subcom., 1997—. Active 4-H Youth Found., Nat. Commn. on Reform Secondary Edn., Nat. Found. Improvement Edn., Nat. Com. for Citizens in Edn., Sr. Centers of Dade County, Fla.; chmn. So. Regional Edn. Bd., 1979-81 Named one of 5 Most Outstanding Young Men in Fla. Fla. Jaycees, 1971; recipient Allen Morris award for outstanding 1st term mem. senate, 1972, Allen Morris award for most valuable mem. senate, 1973, Allen Morris award for 2d most effective senator, 1976 Mem. Fla. Bar Assn. Democrat. Mem. United Ch. Of Christ. Office: US Senate 524 Hart Bldg Washington DC 20510-0001*

GRAHAM, DAVID BOLDEN, food products executive; b. Miami Beach, Fla., Feb. 10, 1927; s. Robert Cabel and Bertha Eugenia (Hack) G.; m. Stuart Hill Smith, Sept. 1, 1956; children: Bird, Ellen, Darnall, Lamar, Lyle, Gerard, Barbara, David Bolden. Student, Colegio de San Bartolome, Bogota, Colombia, 1946; BS, Georgetown U., 1949; postgrad., Harvard Bus. Sch., 1950. Chmn. Graham Farms, Inc., Washington, Ind., 1950-99, Graham Cheese Corp., Washington, 1950-99; sec. Bal Harbour Square, Fla., 1956-57, Graham Bros., Inc., Washington, 1950-72. Dir. German Am. Bancorp. Contbr. articles on agr., transp., early fur traders to various publs. Past pres. Washington Planning Commn., Regional Planning Commn.; past bd. dirs. Hist. Landmarks Found., Ind.; mem. revolving fund com., mem. rural preservation com.; past mem. Ind. Agrl. Adv. Coun.; past mem. adv. coun. Bur. Water and Mineral Resources; past mem. Natural Resources Commn.; dir. Ind. Regional Hwy. Coalition; v.p. I-69 Mid-Continent Hwy. Coalition; past pres. Nat. Turkey Fedn.; mem. Olympic Yachting Staff, 1996; active Coast Guard Aux., Lic. Master Great Lakes or Inland Waters, FCC Marine Radio Lic. Lt. col. USAF Res., 1949-77. Mem. Columbia Club (Indpls.), Rotary (hon., past pres., Paul Harris fellow), Atlantic Cruising Club, Inland Yacht Club, Elks, Soc. of Children's Book Writers, N.Am. Fishing Club (life). Republican. Roman Catholic. Home and Office: Graham Farms PO Box 391 Washington IN 47501-0391

GRAHAM, DAVID BROWNING, lawyer; b. Wildwood, N.J., Dec. 20, 1942; s. William Browning and Mary Graham; m. Linda Lea Beasley, Feb. 20, 1971; children: Owen, Mary. BS, La. U., 1966, JD, 1969. Bar: La. 1969, D.C. 1972, U.S. Ct. Appeals (D.C. cir.) 1974, Ill. 1980, Ohio 1999. Atty. U.S. EPA, Washington, 1972-73; corp. counsel Nat. Rural Elec. Coop. Assn., Washington, 1973-77; dir. office hearing and appeals U.S. Dept. Interior, Arlington, Va., 1977-79; dep. gen. counsel Velsicol Chem. Corp., Chgo., 1979-84; ptnr. Freedman, Levy, Kroll & Simonds, Washington, 1984-89, Kaye, Scholer, Fierman, Hays & Handler, Washington, 1989-92, Howrey & Simon, Washington, 1992-98, Baker & Hostetler, Cleve., 1998—2003, Kaufman & Canoles, Williamsburg, Va., 2003—. Mem. bd. advisors Toxics Law Reporter, Washington, 1987—, Chem. Waste Litigation Reporter, Washington, 1986—. Co-author: Emergency Response: Is Your Company Ready?, 2002, New Approaches to Environmental Law and Agency Regulation: The Daubert Litigation Approach, 2000; contbr. articles to profl. jours. Mem. ABA (former officer sect. environ., energy & environ. law), D.C. Bar Assn., Ohio Bar Assn., Cleve. Bar Assn. Presbyterian. Avocations: running, skiing. Office: Kaufman & Canoles 1200 Old Colony Ln Williamsburg VA 23188

GRAHAM, DAVID G. preventive medicine physician, psychiatrist; b. Nov. 17, 1949; s. Thomas and Catherine G.; m. Katherine A. Graham; children: Brigitte, John. BA magna cum laude, Walsh U., 1971; MD, U. Puerto Rico, 1980; MPH, Columbia U., 1985. Diplomate Am. Bd. Preventive Medicine, Am. Bd. Clin. Psychiatry. Intern, then resident in psychiatry SUNY, Stony Brook, 1980-84, resident in preventive medicine, 1984-86, asst. prof. preventive medicine, 1985—; attending physician VA Med. Ctr., Northport, N.Y., 1985—; dir. pub. health Suffolk County (N.Y.) Dept. Health Svcs., 1986—. Author: Medieval Minds, 1985, Profiles in Protest, 1987, Statistics, 1987, Mental Status Manual, 1989. Fellow Am. Coll. Preventive Medicine; mem. APHA, Am. Psychiatric Assn., Am. Assn. Pub. Health Physicians, Alumni Assn. Columbia U. Avocations: gardening, antiques, tennis, reading, outdoor recreation.

GRAHAM, DAVID RICHARD, orthopedic surgeon; b. Detroit, May 15, 1940; s. Lewis J. and Elberta Y. Graham; m. Dorothy T. Young, June 11, 1966; children: Rebecca, Jeffrey. BA cum laude, Harvard U., 1962; MD, U. Rochester, 1966. Diplomate Am. Bd. Orthop. Surgery. Intern Highland Hosp., Rochester, NY, 1966—67, resident in surgery, 1967—68; resident in orthopaedic surgery Henry Ford Hosp., Detroit, 1970—72; orthopaedic surgeon Elmira (N.Y.) Orthopaedic Assocs., P.C., 1972—2001; pres. Elmira (N.Y.) Orthop. Assocs., P.C., 1992—2001. Pres. Arnot Ogden Med. Staff, Elmira, 1990; clin. assoc. Sch. Medicine & Dentistry U. Rochester, 1992—. Lt. comdr. U.S. Navy, 1968-70. Fellow Am. Coll. Surgeons, Am. Acad. Orthop. Surgeons; mem. AMA, Med. Soc. State N.Y., Ea. Orthop. Assn., Am. Coll. Sports Medicine, Chemung County Med. Soc. (pres. 1993-94), Elmira Torch Club (pres. 1990). Republican. Presbyterian. Home and Office: 690 W Clinton St Elmira NY 14905-2226

GRAHAM, DAVID YATES, gastroenterologist; b. Balboa, Panama, Dec. 24, 1940; came to U.S., 1941; s. Harry Edward and Helen Graham; m. Janet Susan Butel, Mar. 31, 1967; children: Kathleen, David. BS, U. Notre Dame, 1963; MD with honors, Baylor U., 1966. Diplomate Am. Bd. Internal Medicine, Am. Bd. Gastroenterology. Intern Ban Taub Gen. Hosp., VA Hosp., Houston, 1966-67; resident internal medicine Baylor Affiliated Hosps., Houston, 1969-71, fellow gastroenterology, 1972-73; from asst. prof. to prof. medicine Baylor Coll. Medicine, Houston, 1973—, chief gastroenterology sect. VA Med. Ctr., 1976—, from assoc. prof. to prof. virology, 1981-89, prof. molecular virology, 1989—; chief gastroenterology sect. Meth. Hosp., Houston, 1988—. Dir. gastroenterology fellowship program Ben Taub Gen. Hosp., Houston, 1975-80, 88—; chief div. digestive disease dept. medicine Baylor Coll. Medicine, Houston, 1988—; planning com. 10th World Congresses of Gastroenterology, 1991-94; advisor to Japanese Rsch. Soc. for Helicobacter pyloria Related Gastroduodenal Diseases, 1995; editor-in-chief of jour. Helicobacter. Contbr. 60 chpts. in 28 books, numerous articles to profl. jours. With U.S. Army, 1967-69. Recipient Joseph B. Kirsner award Am. Gastroenterology Assn., 1994, Michael E. DeBakey, M.D. award for Excellence in Rsch., 1994, Janssen award for Special Achievement in Gastroenterology, 1995, Frank Brown Berry prize in Fed. Medicine, 2000. Fellow Am. Coll. Physicians, Am. Coll. Gastroenterology (Henry Baker Lecture award 1983, pres. 1990-91), Infectious Diseases Soc. Am.; mem. Am. Gastroent. Assn., Am. Soc. Gastrointestinal Endoscopy, Tex. Soc. for Gastrointestinal Endoscopy, Houston Gastroent. Soc., Gastrointestinal Rsch. Group, Alpha Omega Alpha. Office: Vet Affairs Med Ctr 2002 Holcombe Blvd Houston TX 77030-4211 also: Baylor Coll of Medicine Dept of Medicine One Baylor Plaza Houston TX 77030-3498 E-mail: dgraham@bcm.tmc.edu.

GRAHAM, DENIS DAVID, marriage and family therapist, educational consultant; b. Santa Rosa, Calif., Oct. 21, 1941; s. Elbert Eldon and Mildred Bethana (Dyson) G.; m. Margaret Katherine Coughlan, Aug. 31, 1968; children: Kathleen Ann, Todd Cameron (dec.). BS in Edn., U. Nev., 1964, MEd, 1973, MA, 1982. Cert. for ednl. pers.; lic. marriage and family therapist, Nev. Tchr. vocat. bus. edn. Earl Wooster H.S., Reno, 1964-66, chmn. dept. bus. edn., 1966-67; stare supr. bus. and office edn. Nev. Dept. Edn., Carson City, 1967-70, adminstr. vocat. edn. field svcs., 1970-74, asst. dir., 1974-78, vocat. edn. cons., 1978-85; edn. curriculum specialist Washoe County Sch. Dist., Reno, 1985-89, curriculum coord., 1989-94, ret., 1994; pres. Midpoint Inc., 1995—. Marriage and family counselor Severance & Assocs., Carson City, 1983-85, Mountain Psychiat. Assocs., 1985-87; mem. tng. and youth employment coun. S.W. Regional Lab. for Ednl. R&D, Los Alamitos, Calif., 1982, mem. career edn. coun., 1980-81. Editor Coun. of Chief State Sch. Officers' Report: Staffing the Nation's Schools: A National Emergency, 1984; contbr. articles to profl. jours. Bd. dirs. U. Nev.-Reno Campus Christian Assn., 1988-90, 97-99; mem. adv. com. Truckee Meadows C.C., Reno, 1988-94; mem. Gov.'s Crime Prevention Com., Carson City, 1979-83, Atty. Gen.'s Anti-Shoplifting Com., Carson City, 1974-78, Gov.'s Devel. Disabilities Planning Coun., Carson City, 1977-79; bd. dirs. Jr. Achievement No. Nev., 1989-92, sec., mem. exec. com., 1990-91; bd. dirs. Friends of the Coll. of Edn., U. Nev., Reno, 1995-99. Recipient award for svc. Bus. Edn. Assn. No. Nev., 1973, Svc. award YMCA, 1962, 63, Helping Hand award Procter R. Hug H.S., 1993-94. Mem. ACA, Am. Vocat. Assn., Nat. Assn. Vocat. Edn. Spl. Needs Pers. (Outstanding Svc. award Region V 1982), Am. Assn. Marriage and Family Therapy, Nev. Vocat. Assn. (Outstanding Svc. award 1991, Bill Trabert Meml. award Excellence in Occup. Edn. 1994), Internat. Assn. Marriage and Family Counselors, U. Nev. Reno Alumni Assn. (exec. com. 1971-75), Phi Delta Kappa, Phi Kappa Phi. Democrat. Methodist. Home: 3056 Bramble Dr Reno NV 89509-6901 Office: PO Box 33034 Reno NV 89533-3034 E-mail: denisg2348@aol.com.

GRAHAM, DERRICK W. state representative, educator; b. June 9, 1958; MA Polit. Sci., Ohio State Univ.; BA Hist. and Polit. Sci., Ky. State Univ. State Rep. House of Rep., Dist. 57, Ky., 2002—. Mem. Local and State Gov., Ed. Mem.: Frankfort Salvation Army (Adv. Bd.), Frankfort Comm. Ctr. (Bd. of Dir.), Greenhill Cemetary (Bd.), St. John A.M.E. (Trustee Bd.), Ky YMCA Youth Assoc. (Bd. of Dir.). Democrat. Methodist A.M.E. Office: Capitol Capitol Annex, Rm 451-E Frankfort KY 40601*

GRAHAM, DIANE E. newspaper editor; b. Gary, Ind., June 29, 1953; d. William M. and Mary Jane (Shreve) Graham; m. Daniel Kevin Miller, Oct. 18, 1986. B, Drake U., 1974. Reporter Des Moines Tribune, 1974—78, Des Moines Register, 1978—84, bus. editor, 1984—86, dep. mng. editor, 1986—95, mng. editor, 1995—. Pres. Iowa Freedom of Info. Coun., Des Moines, 1992—93; chair adv. bd. Drake U. Sch. Journalism, Des Moines, 1995—. Recipient Davenport fellow for bus./econ. reporting, U. Mo., 1983. Avocations: playing pipe organ, gardening. Office: Des Moines Register 715 Locust St Des Moines IA 50309-3767

GRAHAM, DON BALLEW, literature educator, writer; b. Lucas, Tex., Jan. 30, 1940; s. Willie and Mrytle Joyce (Ballew) G.; m. Betsy Anne Berry, 1991. BA (high honors), North Tex. State U., Denton, 1962, MA, 1964; PhD, U. Tex., 1971. Asst. prof. U. Pa., Phila., 1971-76; instr. S.W. Tex. State U., San Marcos, 1965-1969; prof. U. Tex., 1976-1985, J. Frank Dobie Regents Prof.of Am. and English lit., 1985—. Author: No Name on the Bullet: A Biography of Audie Murphy, 1989; (criticism) Texas: A Literary Portrait, 1986, The Fiction of Frank Norris: The Aesthetic Context, 1978, Kings of Texas: The 150-year Saga of an American Ranching Empire, 2003; (cinema history) Cowboys and Cadillacs: How Hollywood Looks at Texas, 1983; editor: (anthology) South by Southwest: 24 Stories from Modern Texas, 1985; (criticism) The Texas Literary Tradition: Fiction Folklore History, 1983, Critical Essays on Frank Norris, 1978, Lone Star Literature; From the Red River to the Rio Grande, 2003; (film criticism) Western Movies, 1979. Mem. Tex. Inst. of Letters. Avocations: travel, writing. Office: University of Texas Calhoun Hall Austin TX 78712

GRAHAM, DONALD EDWARD, publishing company executive; b. Balt., Apr. 22, 1945; s. Philip L. and Katharine (Meyer) Graham; m. Mary L. Wissler, Jan. 7, 1967. BA, Harvard U., 1966. Patrolman Washington Metro. Police Dept., 1969—70; formerly with Newsweek mag.; with The Washington Post, 1971—, asst. mng. editor sports, 1974—75, asst. gen. mgr., 1975—76, exec. v.p., gen. mgr., 1976—79, pub., 1979—2000; pres. The Washington Post Co., 1991—93, CEO, 1991—, chmn., 1993—; CEO The Washington Post Newspaper, 1993—2000, chmn., 1993—. Dir. Washington Post Co. Trustee Fed. City Coun., 1976. With U.S. Army, 1966—68. Mem.: Am. Antiquarian Soc. Office: Washington Post 1150 15th St NW Washington DC 20071-0002*

GRAHAM, DONALD HOUSTON, JR., real estate developer; b. Oakland, Calif., June 14, 1914; s. Donald Houston and Martha Ford (Earl) G.; m. Ynez Pattiani, Apr. 6, 1940; children: Pattiann Earl Graham Smith, Donald Houston III; m. Kathryn Bowling, Oct. 8, 1993. BA, U. Calif., Berkeley, 1936; postgrad., Harvard Grad. Sch. Bus., Cambridge, Mass., 1942-43; grad., Command and Gen. Staff Sch., Ft. Leavenworth, Kans., 1943. Lic. real estate broker, Hawaii, mortgage broker, Hawaii. Bond salesman Dean Witter & Co., L.A., 1936-38; bond trader First Boston Corp., San Francisco, 1938-40; chmn., chief exec. officer Dillingham Land Corp., Honolulu, 1945-72; pres. D. H. Graham Co., Ltd., Honolulu, 1972—; gen. ptnr. Graham, Murata, Russell. Trustee MassMut. Mortgage and Real Estate Investors, Springfield, Mass., 1964-85. Contbr. articles to trade and profl. mags. Mem. bd. dirs. Bank of Honolulu, 1968-88; mem. adv. bd. Salvation Army, Honolulu, 1955—. Lt. col. U.S. Army., 1940-45, PTO. Mem. Internat. Coun. Shopping Ctrs. (past pres., trustee, cert. shopping ctr. mgr.), Am. Soc. Real Estate Counsellors (cert. counselor real estate), Inst. Real Estate Mgmt. (cert. property mgr.). Republican. Episcopalian. Avocations: library especially 1st editions of pacific voyages, chinese antique collecting. Office: D H Graham Co Ltd 345 Queen St Ste 400 Honolulu HI 96813-4707

GRAHAM, DONALD JAMES, food technologist; b. York, N.Y., Sept. 24, 1932; s. Howard Alexander Graham and Naomi Irene (Fletcher) Graham Horgan; m. Dorothy Jane Schroeder, Jan. 1, 1965; children: Christopher Howard, Jonathan Edward. AAS, N.Y. State Agrl. Tech. Inst., 1952; BS with honors, Mich. State U., 1958, MS, 1959; postgrad., Oreg. State U., 1959-62. Cert. quality control sanitarian Am. Inst. Baking. Profit planning dir. Green Giant Co., LeSueur, Minn., 1962-67; dir. tech. svc. Green Giant of Can., Windsor, Ont., 1967-77; dir. quality assurance William Underwood Co., Westwood, Mass., 1977-83; internat. tech. dir. Pet, Inc., St. Louis, 1983-87; sr. food technologist, food sanitation cons., lectr., fellow Sverdrup Corp., St. Louis, 1988-99; pres. Graham Sanitary Design Consulting, Ltd., Chesterfield, Mo., 1999—. Faculty, com. mem. Food Processors Inst., Washington, 1980-92. Contbr. articles to tech. publs. Troop com. chmn. Boy Scouts Am., Medfield, Mass., 1979-82, treas., Chesterfield, Mo., 1984-89; mem. Minn. Rep. Com., 1965-67. Sgt. U.S. Army, 1952-54, Korea. Mem. Inst. Food Technologists, Internat. Assn. for Food Protection, Inst. Thermal Processing Specialists (bd. dirs. 1980-82), Mo. Food Processors Assn. (bd. dirs. 1992—, pres. 1994, 95, 96, exec. v.p. 1997—), Am. Soc. Quality Control, Alpha Zeta (chancellor Kedzie chpt. 1957-58). Avocations: photography, videotaping, genealogy. Home: 14318 Aitken Hill Ct Chesterfield MO 63017-2820 Office: Graham Sanitary Design Cons 14318 Aitken Hill Ct Chesterfield MO 63017-2820 E-mail: grahamdj@prodigy.net.

GRAHAM, DONALD LYNN, federal judge; b. Salisbury, N.C., Dec. 15, 1948; s. Ernest Jethro and Mildred (Donald) G.; m. Brenda Joyce Savage, Sept. 27, 1969; 1 child, Sherrian Lynne. BA magna cum laude, W.Va. State Coll., 1971; JD, Ohio State U., 1974. Bar: Ohio 1974, U.S. Ct. Mil. Appeals, 1974, Fla. 1980, U.S. Dist. Ct. (so. dist.) Fla. 1980, Supreme Ct. 1980, U.S. Ct. Appeals (5th and 11th cirs.) 1981. Asst. U.S. atty. U.S. Dist. Ct. (so. dist.) Fla., Miami, 1979-84; ptnr. Raskin & Graham, Miami, 1984-91; judge U.S. Dist. Ct. (so. dist.) Fla., Miami, 1991—. Instr. U. Md., Hanau, Fed. Republic Germany, 1977-78, Embry Riddle U., Homestead, Fla., 1978-79. Maj., asst. staff judge adv. U.S. Army, 1974-79. Recipient Arthur S. Fleming award Washington Jaycees, 1982, Superior Performance award U.S. Dept. Justice; named one of Outstanding Young Men of Am., 1984. Mem. Assn. Trial Lawyers Am., Nat. Bar Assn., Fed. Bar Assn. (so. Fla. pres. 1984-85, treas. 1982-83), Fla. Bar Assn., N.Y. Bar Assn., Ohio Bar Assn., NAACP, Alpha Phi Alpha. Democrat. Baptist. Avocations: fishing, reading. Office: US Courthouse 99 NE 4th St Rm 1155 Miami FL 33132-2138

GRAHAM, DONALD R. epidemiologist; b. Springfield, Ill., Feb. 25, 1949; s. Hugh and Edith Graham; m. Patricia Graham; children: Louis, Edith, Hugh, Donald, Sarah, Maureen. BS, Notre Dame U., 1970; MD, Wash. U., St. Louis, 1974. Diplomate Am. Bd. Internal Medicine, Am. Bd. Infectious Diseases. Med. intern, resident Jewish Hosp. St. Louis, 1974—77; fellow, infectious diseases Washington U. Sch. Medicine, 1977—80; epidemic intelligence svc. officer Ctr. Disease Control, Atlanta, 1978—80; chief, divsn. infectious diseases Springfield Clinic, Ill., 1980—. Cons. med. epidemiologist City of Springfield. Contbr. articles to profl. jours., chpts. to books. Pres. Mental Health Ctr. Ctrl. Ill., Springfield, 1984—86; bd. mem. St. John's Hosp., 2000—. With USPHS, 1978—80. Fellow: ACP, Infectious Disease Soc. Am. Home: 1901 S Glenwood Springfield IL 62704 Office: Springfield Clinic 1025 S 7th St Springfield IL 62703 Office Fax: 217 528-7593. E-mail: infectn@springfieldclinic.com.

GRAHAM, DOROTHY H. education educator; b. Alamo, Ga., Oct. 24, 1949; d. George Ray Graham and Beth Evans Harbin; m. Charles Martin Wingo, Mar. 22, 1986; 1 child, Charles Wesley Graham Wingo. AB, Mercer U., Macon, Ga., 1971; MA, U. Ga., 1977; PhD, Ga. State U., 1985. Registered neutral Ga. Office of Dispute Resolution. Tchr. Wheeler County H.S., Alamo, 1972, Forsyth County H.S., Cumming, Ga., 1974—75; prof. and dir. ombuds office Kennesaw State U., Ga., 1977—. Mem. governance coun. Chamblee Charter H.S., Ga., 2002—. Mem.: AAUP (treas. Ga. conf. 1998—2001, pres. Ga. conf. 2001—03), Univ. and Coll. Ombuds Assn. (bd. dirs. 2002—). Avocations: reading, boating, swimming, film analysis. Office: Kennesaw State Univ 1000 Chastain Rd #2701 Kennesaw GA 30144

GRAHAM, DOROTHY RUTH, software engineering consultant; b. Grand Rapids, Mich., June 11, 1944; d. Anthony Andrew and Ruth A. (Brink) Hoekema; m. Roger Graham, Aug. 16, 1969; children: Sarah Anne, James Stephen. Student, U. Coll., London, 1965-66; BA in Math., Calvin Coll., 1967; MS in Math., Purdue U., 1969. ATMS Bell Labs., Whippany, N.J., 1970-72; software engr. Ferranti Computer Systems, Manchester, Eng., 1973-79; sr. cons. The Nat. Computing Ctr., Manchester, 1979-80; cons. Cheadle Hulme, Eng., 1980-88; mng. dir. Grove Software Engring. Cons., Macclesfield, Eng., 1988—. Program chair 1st European internat. conf. on software testing analysis and rev. Eurostar '93; mem. adv. bd. internat. confs. testing computer software, 1992—. Author: The Cast Report: Computer Aided Software Testing, 1991, further edits.; author: (with Tom Glib) Software Inspection, 1993; author: (with Mark Fewster) Software Test Automation, 1999; mem. editl. rev. bd. Software Testing and Quality Engring., contbr. articles to profl. jours. Recipient The European Software Testing Excellence award IBM, Barcellona, 1999. Mem.: Brit. Computer Soc. (founding mem. software testing bd. info. sys. exam. bd. 1996—). Mem. Ch. Eng. Avocation: choral and madrigal singing. Home: Grove House 40 Ryles Pk Rd SK11 8AH Macclesfield England Office: Grove Cons Grove House 40 Ryles Pk Rd Macclesfield SK11 8AH England

GRAHAM, DOUGLASS OF MONTROSE, museum curator, banker, artist, poet; b. Budapest, Hungary, July 6, 1924; came to U.S., 1959, naturalized, 1965; s. Hugh Merton and Ellen Charlotte (Baroness Podmaniczky) G.; children: Robert, Christopher, Anabel, Isis. MBA, N.Y. Inst. Fin., 1961. Ptnr. Mitchell, Hutchins & Co., N.Y.C., William D. Witter Inc., N.Y.C., 1959-72; founder, chmn. bd. trustees The Turner Mus., Denver, 1973—; pres. Internat. Bank Holdings Ltd., 1979-95. Bd. dirs. Turner Soc. London, patron H.R.H. The Prince of Wales, 1978—. Author: Turner's Cosmic Optimism, 1990, Turner's Angels, 1991, Turner's Rainbows, 1992, Turner's Children--So Much Love, 1993, Turner's Powerful Allegories, 1994, Ascendent Turner, 2002, Triple Turner Treat, 2003. Life mem. St. Andrew's Soc. Colo. Served in Ctrl.-European Underground Army and with M.I., Brit. Army, 1942-60. Cited as founder of one of Am.'s 99 Finest Museums, 1989, founder of first virtual art mus. in the world, 2001; recipient Papal Blessing, Pope John 23. Mem.: DAV (life). Achievements include founding of The (J.M.W.) Turner Museum and of the first virtual art museum in the world. Mailing: PO Box 18133 Sarasota FL 34276-1133 Personal E-mail: turnermuseum@comcast.com. Business E-Mail: turnermuseum@turnermuseum.org. *Personal philosophy: We are on this planet to do the will of God...during our journey here we come to realize what the ultimate truth is...we are all brothers and sisters...the children of a loving Father of limitless resources.*

GRAHAM, FRANCES KEESLER (MRS. DAVID TREDWAY GRAHAM), psychologist, educator; b. Canastota, N.Y., Aug. 1, 1918; d. Clyde C. and Norma (Van Surdam) Keesler; m. David Tredway Graham, June 14, 1941; children: Norma, Andrew, Mary. BA, Pa. State U., 1938; PhD, Yale U., 1942; DSc (hon.), U. Wis., 1996. Acting dir. St. Louis Psychiat. Clinic, 1942-44; instr. Barnard Coll., 1948-51; research assoc. Sch. Medicine, Washington U., St. Louis, 1942-48, 53-57, U. Wis., Madison, 1957-64, asso. prof. pediatrics and psychology, 1964-68, prof., 1968-86, Hilldale research prof., 1980-86; prof. U. Del., Newark, 1986-89, prof. emerita, 1989—. Disting. faculty lectr., U. Del., Newark, 1989; cons. Nat. Inst. Neurol. Diseases and Blindness perinatal research br.; mem. exptl. psychology research review com. NIMH, 1970-74, NRC, 1971-74; mem. bd. sci. counselors NIMH, 1977-81, chmn., 1979-81; mem. Pres.'s Commn. for Study of Ethical Problems in Medicine and Biomed. and Behavioral Research, 1980-82 Mem. editorial bd. Jour. Exptl. Child Psychology, 1964-67, Child Devel., 1966-68, Jour. Exptl. Psychology, 1968-73, Psychophysiology, 1968-73; contbr. articles to profl. jours. Recipient Rsch. Scientist award NIMH, 1964-89, Disting. Alumna award Pa. State U., 1983, Wilbur L. Cross medal Yale U., 1992, Gold medal Am. Psychol. Found., 1995. Fellow AAAS (chmn. sect. psychology 1979, mem. nominations com. 1992-95), APA (coun. 1975-77, pres. div. physiol. and comparative psychology 1978-79, G. Stanley Hall award 1982, Disting. Scientist award 1990); mem. NAS, Am. Psychol. Soc. (William James fellow 1990), Soc. Rsch. Child Devel. (council 1965-71; pres. 1975-77, Disting. Sci. Contbns. award 1991), Soc. Psychophysiol. Rsch. (dir. 1968-71, 72-75, pres. 1973-74, Disting. Contbns. award 1981), Soc. Exptl. Psychologists, Soc. Neurosci., Fedn. Behavioral Psychol. and Cognitive Scis. (exec. com. 1991-94), Psychonomic Soc., Acoustical Soc. Am., Internat. Soc. Devel. Psychobiology, Phi Beta Kappa, Sigma Xi. Home: 311 Dove Dr Newark DE 19713-1211 E-mail: fkgraham@udel.edu.

GRAHAM, GEORGE ADAMS, political scientist, emeritus educator; b. Cambridge, N.Y., Dec. 23, 1904; s. Andrew Allen and Anna Katherine (Adams) G.; m. Rosanna Grace Webster, Aug. 20, 1930 (dec. Mar. 17, 1985); children: Andrew Allen (dec. Sept. 13, 2001), Lora Katherine Graham Lunt, Mary Margaret Graham Jenne; m. Elisabeth Childs Rowse, June 25, 1986. AB, Monmouth Coll., 1926, LL.D., 1959; A.M., U. Ill., 1927, PhD, 1930; LL.D., Nova U., 1985. Instr. Monmouth Coll., 1927-28; asst. U. Ill., 1929-30; faculty Princeton, 1930-58, instr., 1930-31, asst. prof., 1931-39, asso. prof., 1939-45, prof., 1945-58, chmn. dept. politics, 1946-49, 52-55; dir. govtl. studies Brookings Inst., 1958-67; exec. dir. Nat. Acad. Pub. Adminstrn., 1967-72, sr. social scientist, 1972-73; prof. pub. adminstrn. Nova U., Ft. Lauderdale, Fla., 1974-85, prof. emeritus, 1985—. Mem. staff Detroit Bur. Govt. Research, 1929-30; with U.S. Bur. Budget, 1942-46, as adminstrn. cons., 1942-43, chief war supply sect., 1943-45; sec. Com. on Records War Adminstrn., 1944-45; chief Govt. Orgn. Br. and asst. chief Div. Adminstrv. mgmt., 1945; cons., 1945-46; chmn. com. on Indian Affairs, Hoover Commn. on Orgn. Exec. Br. Govt., 1948, staff dir., task force on personnel and civil service, 1953-54; cons. Senate subcom. Ethics in Govt., 1951; dir. pub. affairs program Ford Found., 1956-57. Author: books including Education for Public Administration, 1941, (with Henry Reining) Regulatory Administration, 1943; Morality in American Politics, 1952, America's Capacity to Govern, 1960. Mem. Nat. Acad. Pub. Adminstrn., Theta Chi. Clubs: Cosmos. Presbyterian. Home: 120 Kenan St Chapel Hill NC 27516-2528

GRAHAM, GEORGE ANDREW, JR., psychologist, consultant; b. Bakersfield, Calif., Dec. 7, 1930; s. George Andrew Graham and Mary Pearl Sandidge; m. Patricia Anne Phillips, June 19, 1953; children: G. Andrew III, Ronald Glen, Holly Anne Meikle. BA, U. Redlands, 1952; BD, Andover Newtown Theol. Sch., 1956; MA, Boston U., 1956; M in Sacred Theology, Union Theol. Sch., N.Y.C., 1957; postgrad., U. Chgo., 1957-60, 69-70; PhD, Marquette U., 1974. Lic. psychologist, Wis. Min. young adults Old S. Ch., Boston, 1952-55; min. youth 1st Bapt. Ch., Mt. Vernon, NY, 1955—57, min., chaplain Iowa City, 1960-63; lab sch. psychologist U. Chgo., 1957-60; chaplain U. Redlands, Calif., 1963-70; assoc. McGinley & Co., Milw., 1970-73; asst. v.p. personnel divsn. 1st Wis. (became Firstar, then US Bank), Milw., 1973-75, dir. employment and devel., 1975-77, v.p., 1977-81, 1st v.p., 1981-85, dir. employment, counseling, devel. and tng., 1985-88; 1st v.p. Firstar Corp., 1988-92; pres. Graham Consulting, Waukesha, Wis., 1992—. Adj. prof. U. Wis., Milw., 1978-88. Pres. Wis. chpt. Leukemia Soc. Am., Wis. Epilepsy Assn., Lad Lake; bd. dirs. Wis. Sch. Profl. Psychology, Wis. Conservatory Music, Wis. Coun. Econ. Edn.; personnel com. ARC; chmn. pers. com. United Way, Milw.; exec. com. Potawatomi Area coun. Boy Scouts Am. Recipient Silver Beaver award Boy Scouts Am., 1988. Mem. Am. Psychol. Assn., Soc. Indls. and Orgnl. Psychologists, Human Resource Planning Soc., Univ. Club Milw. Republican. Home and Office: N8W30095 Woodcrest Dr Waukesha WI 53188 E-mail: g1207@msn.com.

GRAHAM, GEORGE J., JR., political scientist, educator; b. Dayton, Ohio, Nov. 12, 1938; s. George J. and Mary Elizabeth (McBride) G.; m. Scarlett Gower, Sept. 10, 1966 (div. 1991); 1 child, Carmen Michelle. BA in History, Wabash Coll., 1960; PhD, Ind. U., 1965. Instr. Vanderbilt U., Nashville, 1963-64, asst. prof., 1965-71, assoc. prof., 1971-77, prof. polit. sci., 1977—, assoc. dean, 1986-88, 97-00, chair dept. polit. sci., 1988-92. Series editor Chatham (N.J.) House Pub., 1978—; Fulbright John Marshall chair Budapest U. of Econ. Studies, 1995-96. Author: Methodological Foundations, 1971; author, editor: Post-Behavioral Era, 1972, Founding Principles, 1977; contbr. articles to profl. jours. Chair Mt. Juliet (Tenn.) Sewer Commn., 1985-86; sec. Zoning Commn., Mt. Juliet, 1988-89. Guggenheim fellow, 1973-74, NEH fellow New Haven Nat. Humanities Inst., 1976-77; Fulbright John Marshall chair in Budapest, Hungary, 1995-96. Mem. Am. Polit. Sci. Assn. (founder Found. Polit. Theory sect. 1975—), So. Polit. Sci. Assn. (mem. coun. 1987-90), Midwest Polit. Sci. Assn., Internat. Polit. Sci. Assn., Com. Conceptual Analysis (chair). Avocations: painting, guitar, travel, bicycling. Office: Vanderbilt U PO Box 1814-B Nashville TN 37235-1814 Business E-Mail: grahamgj@trvax.vanderiblt.edu.

GRAHAM, GLORIA FLIPPEN, dermatologist; b. Durham, N.C., Mar. 3, 1935; d. James Meigs and Ida Mae (Boyd) F.; m. Douglas Graham (div.); 1 child, Wayne Meigs, m. James Herbert Graham, July 29, 1989. BS, Wake Forest U., 1957; MD, Bowman-Gray Sch. Medicine, 1961. Diplomate Am. Bd. Dermatology. Intern Sch. Medicine Vanderbilt U., 1961-62; resident, dermatology U. Va. Med. Ctr., Charlottesville, 1962-65; pvt. practice Columbia, S.C., 1965-66; attending physician Crystal Coast Dermatology Svcs., P.A., Morehead City, N.C., 2000; physician, owner Wilson (N.C.) Dermatology Clinic, 1966-94; physician, pres. Grahams Dermatology Svcs., Morehead City, N.C., 1992-2000; attending physician Crystal Coast Dermatology Svcs., P.A., Moorehead City, N.C., 2000—. Cons. Carteret Gen. Hosp., Morehead City, 1986-2000; clin. attending prof. Bowman Gray Sch. Medicine, Winston-Salem, N.C., 1991-2000; adj. clin. prof. U. N.C. Sch. Medicine, Chapel Hill, 1995-2001; assoc. prof. dermatology Wake Forest U. Med. Sch., 2001—. Co-exhibitor: Two Hereditary Osseocutaneous Syndromes, Acad. Dermatology, 1965 (Silver award), So. Med. Assn. Exhibit Hereditary Acrokeratotic Poikiloderma, 1970 (Third Place award). Named Woman of Yr., Women's Residence Coun. Wake Forest U., 1982, Practitioner of Yr., Dermatology Found., 1998; recipient Fox award mentoring in dermatology, Am. Acad. Dermatology, 2003. Mem.: Internat. Soc. Cryosurgery (v.p.), Women's Dermatologic Soc. (pres. 1997—98, Rose Hirschler award 2001), Am. Dermatologic Assn. (elect), Am. Acad. Dermatology (bd. dirs. 1991—96, audit com. 1996—2000, ethics com. 1996—2001, nominating com. 2002—, chair nominating com. 2003, Fox award 2003), N.Am. Clin. Dermatologic Soc. (bd. dirs. 1995—), World Congress Dermatology (co-chmn. cryosurgical symposium 1997, 2001), Wake Forest U. Sch. Medicine Alumni Assn. (bd. dirs.). Avocations: travel, fishing. Home: 305 Cutty Sark Rd Winston Salem NC 27103 E-mail: ggraham@wfubmc.edu., ggfgraham@aol.com.

GRAHAM, H. DEVON, III, otolaryngologist, plastic surgeon; b. Stuttgartt, Germany, Mar. 14, 1958; (parents Am. citizens); s. Homer Devon Jr. and Bettie Mae (Caldwell) G.; m. Constance Sentilles; children: Homer Devon IV, Ian Alexander. BS in Chemistry and Biology, Wash. and Lee U., 1980; MD, La. State U., 1984. Diplomate Am. Bd. Otolaryngology, Am. Bd. Facial Plastic & Reconstructive Surgery. Resident Ochsner Med. Found., 1984-86; resident in otolaryngology-head & neck surgery Tulane U. Med. Sch., New Orleans, 1986-89; fellow Am. Acad. Facial Plastic and Reconstructive Surgery, Miami, Chgo., 1989-90; asst. clin. instr. dept. otolaryngology-head & neck surgery U. Ill. Coll. Medicine, Chgo., 1990; active staff Ochsner Found. Hosp., New Orleans, Charity Hosp., New Orleans, Med. Ctr. La., New Orleans. Presenter in field. Contbr. articles to profl. jours. Vol. United Way; active carnival orgns. Fellow ACS, Am. Acad. Otolaryngology-Head and Neck Surgery, Am. Acad. Facial Plastic and Reconstructive Surgery (com. mem., exec. com., bd. dirs., mem. found. bd.); mem. AMA, Am. Soc. Liposuction Surgery, So. Med. Assn., La. State Med. Soc., Orleans Parish Med. Soc., Greater New Orleans Soc. Otolaryngology-Head and Neck Surgery, Rotary, Audobon Zoo Soc. Avocations: hunting, fishing, golf. Office: Oschsner Ctr Cosmetic Surg 1514 Jefferson Hwy New Orleans LA 70121-2429

GRAHAM, HAROLD STEVEN, lawyer; b. Kansas City, Mo., Feb. 1, 1950, s. Martie Sydney and Elsie Helen (Bradford) G.; m. Deborah Ruth Glick, Apr. 8, 1973; children: Elizabeth, Jonathan, Joshua, Lauren. BS, U. Wis., 1972; JD, U. Chgo., 1976. Bar: Mo. 1976. Assoc. Lathrop, Koontz & Norquist, Kansas City, 1976-81; mem. Lathrop & Norquist, L.C., Kansas City, 1982-95, Lathrop & Gage L.C., Kansas City, 1996—. Active Kansas City Tomorrow Alumni Assn. Year X; bd. dirs. Hyman Brand Hebrew Acad., Kansas City, 1985-99, Beth Shalom Synagogue, Kansas City, 1983-88, Jewish Cmty. Campus, 1992-98. Mem. ABA (sect. on real property and trust law, sect. on bus. law), Assn. for Corporate Growth, Mo. Bar Assn. (property law com.), Kansas City Met. Bar Assn., Assn. for Corp. Growth (Kansas City chpt.). Avocations: tennis, running. Office: Lathrop & Gage LC 2345 Grand Blvd Ste 2600 Kansas City MO 64108-2617

GRAHAM, HEATHER, actress; b. Milw., Jan. 29, 1970; Motion picture actress. Films include License to Drive, 1988, Drugstore Cowboy, 1989, I Love You to Death, 1990, Guilty as Charged, 1991, Diggstown, 1992, 6 Degrees of Separation, 1993, Don't Do It, 1994, Swingers, 1996, Boogie Nights, 1997 (MTV movie award 1998), Scream 2, 1997, Austin Powers: The Spy Who Shagged Me, 1999, Bowfinger, 1999, Kiss & Tell, 2000, Sidewalks of New York, 2001, From Hell, 2001, Killing Me Softly, 2002, The Guru, 2002, Alien Love Triangle, 2002, Hope Springs, 2003; T.V. series include Twin Peaks, 1990, 92. Recipient ShoWest award for Female Star of Tomorrow, 1999. Office: Creative Artists Agency 9830 Wilshire Blvd Beverly Hills CA 90211

GRAHAM, HOWARD LEE, SR., financial services company executive; b. Monroe, Mich., May 26, 1942; s. Carl Lee and Myrtle Leota (Manis) G.; m. Bobbie Jo Hamilton; children: Kimber Lee, Howard Lee Jr., Jacquelyn Leota, John-Nathan Howard. Grad., Dake Bible Sch., Atlanta, 1960-62; student, Cen. Bible Coll., Springfield, Mo., 1964-67; grad., Internat. Sem., 1993, DD, 1996. Debit agt. Met. Life Ins. Co., Colorado Springs, Colo., 1963-64, agt. Allen Park, Mich., 1964-67, 68; agy. mgr. Preferred Risk Life Ins. Co., Allen Park, 1968-72; agy. owner Howard Graham Ins. Agy., Taylor, Mich., 1972-85; spl. agt., rep. Prudential Ins. Co., Cleve., 1985-89; regional mgr. Primerica Fin. Svcs., Abingdon, Va., 1995—; pres. Graham & Graham Canvas Shoppe, Inc., 1976-95, CEO, 1995—. Pres. Graham Enterprises, Cleve., 1985—; CEO Graham & Graham Canvas Shoppe, Inc., 1976; nat. and regional sales leader Preferred Risk Ins. Co., Des Moines, 1969-72. Life mem. Full Gospel Bus. Men's Fellow, Detroit, 1963-85, officer, 1974-80, officer, Cleve., 1985—; active Gideons Internat., Cleve., 1963—; pres. Truth Alive, Inc., 1988—; Bible tchr., missionary. Named Central Region Agt. of Yr., 1985; admitted to Million Dollar Round Table, 1985, Hall of Honor, 1986. Mem. Indsl. Fabrics Assn. Internat., Am. Coll., Nat. Assn. Life Underwriters, Internat. Platform Assn. Republican. Mem. Pentecostal Ch. Avocations: sports, bible research. Office: PO Box 1805 Abingdon VA 24212-1805 Home: 9650 Loblolly Pine Cir Orlando FL 32827-6837

GRAHAM, HOWARD BARRETT, publishing company executive; b. Boston, Dec. 7, 1929; s. Robert M. and Belle (Brown) G.; m. Rita J. Mahony; children: Ronni M., Erica. BA, Syracuse U., 1951. Gen. mgr. sch. supply div., sales mgr. edni. div. Milton Bradley Co., Springfield, Mass., 1954-63; gen. mgr. jr. book div. McGraw-Hill Co., 1964-69; pres., dir. Franklin Watts Inc., N.Y.C., 1970-87; also chmn. bd. Franklin Watts Ltd.; sr. v.p. mktg/product devel., dir. Grolier, Inc., 1983-89, exec. v.p., 1988-89; pres. Grolier Internat., 1986-89; chmn., chief exec. officer Graham Internat. Pub. and Rsch., Inc., 1989—; ptnr. SMG Assocs., 1990; dir., v.p. The Millbrook Press, 1990-96, chmn. bd. dirs., 1997—; pres., CEO Chambers Kingfisher Graham, Publishers Inc., 1994-96. Mem. adv. bd. Internat. Exec. Svc., 1994-98. Served with USAF, 1951-53. Mem. Mensa, Save the Children (adv. bd. mem. 1994-98). Home: PO Box 77 Sagaponack NY 11962-0077 Office: 27 Main St # A Southampton NY 11968-4808 E-mail: gipr2@aol.com., howardgraham@millbrookpress.net.

GRAHAM, JAMES HERBERT, dermatologist; b. Calexico, Calif., Apr. 25, 1921; s. August K. and Esther (Choudoin) G.; m. Anna Kathryn Luiken, June 30, 1950 (dec. May 1987); children: James Herbert, John A., Angela Joann; m. Gloria Boyd Flippin, July 29, 1989. Student, Brawley Jr. Coll., 1941-42; AB, Emory U., 1945; MD, Med. Coll. Ala., 1949. Diplomate: Am. Bd. Dermatology (dir. 1977-87, v.p. 1985-86, pres. 1986-87, Disting. Service medal 1987); diplomate in dermatopathology Am. Bd. Dermatology and Am. Bd. Pathology. Intern Jefferson-Hillman Hosp., Birmingham, Ala., 1949-50; resident in dermatology VA Center and UCLA Med. Center, 1953-56; clin. asst. instr. in medicine UCLA, 1954-56; Osborne fellow and NRC fellow in dermal pathology Armed Forces Inst. Pathology, Washington, 1956-58, vis. scientist, 1958-69, chmn. dept. dermatopathology, 1980-88; registrar Registry of Dermatopathology, Armed Forces Inst. Pathology, 1980-88, also program dir. dermatopathology, 1979-88; program dir. dermatopathology Walter Reed Army Med. Center, Washington, 1979-88; asst. prof. dermatology and pathology Temple U., 1958-61, assoc. prof., 1961-65, prof. dermatology, 1965-69, assoc. prof. pathology, 1965-67, prof. pathology, 1967-69; prof. medicine, chief div. dermatology, prof. pathology, dir. sect. dermal pathology and histochemistry U. Calif., Irvine, 1969-78; chief dermatology U. Calif. Med. Ctr., Irvine, 1977-78; prof. emeritus Coll. Medicine, U. Calif., 1978—; head sect. dermatology Orange County (Calif.) Med. Center, 1969-73; cons. dermatology VA Hosp., Long Beach, Calif., 1969-73, chief dermatology sect., 1973-78, acting chief med. service, 1976; cons. dermatology, dermal pathology Regional Naval Med. Center, San Diego, 1969-82, Long Beach, 1969-78, Camp Pendleton, Calif., 1972-78, Meml. Hosp. Med. Center, Long Beach, 1972-86, Fairview State Hosp., Costa Mesa, Calif., 1969-78; cons. for career devel. for rev. clin. investigator applications VA Central Office, Washington, 1973-78; Disting. Eminent physician VA physician and dentist-in-residence program, 1980-88; mem. organizational com. Am. Registry Pathology, Armed Forces Inst. Pathology, Washington, 1976-77, mem. exec. com., 1977-78; prof. dermatology, clin. prof. pathology Uniformed Services U. of Health Scis., Bethesda, Md., 1979-88, prof. emeritus, 1989—; program dir. dermatopathology Naval Hosp. and Scripps Clin. and Rsch. Found., San Diego, 1991-94; head divsn. dermatopathology, dept. pathology Scripps Clinic and Rsch. Found., LaJolla, Calif., 1988-94, ret., 1994. Sr. author: Dermal Pathology, 1972; contbr. articles to profl. publs. Served with M.C. USNR, 1949-53. Named Disting. Alumnus, Med. Coll. Ala., 1994; recipient ASDP 3d ann. Walter R. Nickel Award for Excellence in Teaching of Dermatopathology, Hilton La Jolla (Calif.) Torrey Pines Hotel, 1999. Mem. AMA (accreditation coun. for grad. med. edn., 1977-87, residency rev. com. for dermatology 1977-87, chmn. 1984-87, cert. of merit 1960), Soc. Investigative Dermatology (life), U.S. and Can. Acad. Pathology (life), Am. Soc. Investigative Pathology (life, emeritus mem. 1995), Am. Dermatol. Assn. (essay award 1958, v.p. 1986-87), Am. Soc. Dermatopathology (pres. 1975-76, Founder's award 1990, rep. to bd. of mem. Am. Registry Pathology 1988-92), Dermatopathology Club (pres. 1980-81), Assn. Mil. Dermatologists (life), Am. Acad. Dermatology (life, dir. 1974-77, 82, v.p. 1980-81, rep. to bd. mems. Am. Registry Pathology 1977-78, hon. mem. San Francisco 2000), N.Am. Clin. Dermatologic Soc. (hon.), 1973, Pa. Acad. Dermatology, Pacific Dermatol. Assn. (dir. 1972-75, hon. mem. 1981), Dermatology Found. (Leader's Soc. and Annenberg Circle), Washington Dermatol. Soc. (spl. hon.), Phila. Dermatol. Soc. (pres. 1967-68, hon mem. 1994), San Diego Dermatol. Soc., Cutaneous Therapy Soc., Alpha Omega Alpha, Cosmos Club. *I have achieved far more than I dreamed possible but it could only happen in America. Being generally optimistic, enthusiastic and persistent has resulted in my serving society in a positive way.*

GRAHAM, JAN, former state attorney general; b. Salt Lake City; BS in Psychology, Clark U., Worcester, Mass., 1973; MS in Psychology, U. Utah, 1977, JD, 1980. Bar: Utah. Ptnr. Jones, Waldo, Holbrook & McDonough, Salt Lake City, 1979—89; soliciter gen. Utah Atty. Gen.'s Office, Salt Lake City, 1989—93; atty. gen. State of Utah, 1993—2000. Adj. prof. law U. Utah Law Sch.; bar commr. Utah State Bar, 1991; master of bench Utah Inns Ct. VII; mem. Utah Commn. on Justice in 21st Century, bd. dirs. Jones, Waldo, Holbrook & McDonough; bd. trustees, pres. Coll. Law U. Utah. Fin. devel. chair YWCA; chair Ctrl. Bus. Improvement Dist.; mem. Salt Lake City Olympic Bid Com. 1988 Games. Named Woman Lawyer of Yr., Utah, 1987. Mem.: Women Lawyers Utah (co-founder, mem. exec. com.), Am. Arbitration Assn. (nat. panel arbitrators). Democrat.

GRAHAM, JEWEL FREEMAN, social worker, lawyer, educator; b. Springfield, Ohio, May 3, 1925; d. Robert Lee and Lula Belle Freeman; m. Paul N. Graham, Aug. 8, 1953; children: Robert, Nathan. BA, Fisk U., 1946; student, Howard U., 1946-47; MS in Social Svc. Adminstrn., Case Western Res. U., 1953; JD, U. Dayton, 1979; LHD (hon.), Meadville-Lombard Theol. Sch., 1991. Bar: Ohio; cert. social worker. Assoc. dir. teenage program dept. YWCA, Grand Rapids, Mich., 1947-50, coord. met. teenage program Detroit, 1953-56; dir. program for interracial edn. Antioch Coll., Yellow Springs, Ohio, 1964-69, from asst. prof. to prof., 1969-92, prof. emeritus, 1992—. Mem. Ohio Commn. on Dispute Resolution and Conflict Mgmt., 1990-92. Mem. exec. com. World YWCA, Geneva, 1975-83, 87—, pres., 1983; bd. dirs. YWCA of the U.S.A., 1970-89, pres., 1979-85; bd. dirs. Antioch U., 1994-96. Named to Greene County Women's Hall of Fame, 1982, Ohio Women's Hall of Fame, 1988; named 1 of 10 Outstanding Women of Miami Valley, 1987; recipient Ambassador award YWCA of the U.S.A., 1993. Mem. ABA, Nat. Assn. of Social

Workers (charter), Nat. Coun. of Negro Women (life), Alpha Kappa Alpha. Democrat. Unitarian Universalist. Avocations: bicycling, swimming, walking, needlework. Office: Antioch Coll Livermore 51 Yellow Springs OH 45387 E-mail: jewelg@aol.com.

GRAHAM, JOHN BORDEN, pathologist, writer, educator; b. Goldsboro, N.C., Jan. 26, 1918; s. Ernest Heap and Mary (Borden) G.; m. Ruby Barrett, Mar. 23, 1943; children: Charles Barrett, Virginia Borden, Thomas Wentworth. BS, Davidson Coll., 1938, D.Sc. (hon.), 1984; MD, Cornell U., 1942. Asst. Cornell U., 1943-44; medical corps U.S. Army, 1944-46; mem. faculty U. N.C., Chapel Hill, 1946—, Alumni Disting. prof. pathology, 1966—, chmn. genetics curriculum, 1963-85, assoc. dean medicine for basic scis., 1968-70, coordinator interdisciplinary grad. programs in biology, 1968—, dir. hemostasis program, 1974-87. Vis. prof. haematology St. Thomas's Hosp. Med. Sch., London, 1972; vis. prof. Teikyo U. Med. Sch., Tokyo, 1976; mem. selection com. NIH research career awards, 1959-62; genetics tng. com. USPHS, 1962-66, chmn., 1967-71; mem. genetic basis of disease com. Nat. Inst. Gen. Med. Scis., 1977-80; mem. pathology test com. Nat. Bd. Med. Examiners, 1963-67; mem. research adv. com. U. Colo. Inst. Behavioral Genetics, 1967-71; mem. Internat. Com. Haemostasis and Thrombosis, 1963-67; chmn. bd. U. N.C. Population Program, 1964-67; sec. policy bd. Carolina Population Center, 1972-78; cons. Environ. Health Center, USPHS, WHO, Bolt, Beranek & Newman, Inc.; mem. med. and sci. adv. council Nat. Hemophilia Found., 1972-76; hon. cons. in genetics Margaret Pyke Centre, London, 1972— Author: Sand in the Gears, 1992, 2d edit., 1998, How It Was, 1896-1973, 1996, Coping with Old Age: An Odyssey, 1998, Southeastern Cookery, 2000, Memories and Reflections, 2002; mem. editl. bd.: NC Med. Jour., 1949—66, Am. Jour. Human Genetics, 1958—61, Soc. Exptl. Biology and Medicine, 1959—62, Human Genetics Abstracts, 1962—72, Haemostasis, 1975—80, Christian Scholar, 1958—60. Recipient O. Max Gardner award U. N.C., 1968, Disting. Svc. award U. N.C. Med. Sch., 1992; Markle scholar in med. sci., 1949-54. Mem. AMA, AAAS, Elisha Mitchell Sci. Soc. (pres. 1963), AAUP, Soc. Exptl. Biology and Medicine, Am. Soc. Exptl. Pathology, Assn. Univ. Pathologists, Am. Assn. Pathologists and Bacteriologists, Am. Soc. Human Genetics (sec. 1964-67, pres. 1972), Genetics Soc. Am., Internat. Soc. Hematology, Am. Inst. Biol. Sci., Royal Soc. Medicine (London), Med. Soc. N.C., Mayflower Soc., Cosmos Club, Sigma Xi. Democrat. Presbyterian. Achievements include publs. on blood clotting, inherited diseases in humans including x-linked vitamin D resistant richets, human population dynamics, medical history; co-discoverer blood coagulant Factor X (Stuart factor). Home: 108 Glendale Dr Chapel Hill NC 27514-5910

GRAHAM, JOHN DALBY, public relations executive; b. Maryville, Mo., Aug. 24, 1937; s. Kyle T. and Irma Irene (Dalby) Graham; m. Linda Mills Graham, Dec. 21, 1996; children: Katherine Elizabeth, David Landon. B.J., U. Mo., 1959. Editor Hallmark Cards, Inc., Kans. City, Mo., 1959—62; dir. pub. rels. St. Louis Met. YMCA, 1962—66; chmn., chief exec. officer Fleishman-Hillard, Inc., St. Louis, 1966—; chmn. Fleishman-Hillard Europe. Bd. dirs. Fleishman-Hillard/U.K. Ltd. Trustee St. Louis U.; mem. exec. bd. St. Louis Area Coun. Boy Scouts Am. Capt. U.S. Army, 1959—66. Fellow: Pub. Rels. Soc. Am.; mem.: Arthur Page Soc., Round Table, Nat. Investors Rels. Inst., Internat. Pub. Rels. Assn., Log Cabin Club. Home: PO Box 8797 Saint Louis MO 63101-8797 Office: Fleishman Hillard Inc 200 N Broadway Saint Louis MO 63102-2796

GRAHAM, JOHN DAVID, public health educator; b. Pitts., Oct. 3, 1956; s. Thomas Carlisle and Irene Olive (Wallace) G.; m. Susan Patricia Woerner; children— Jennifer, Kathryn. B.A. in Politics and Econs., Wake Forest U., 1978; M.A. in Pub. Affairs, Duke U., 1980; Ph.D. in Pub. Policy Analysis, Carnegie-Mellon U., 1983. Budget examiner Office of Mgmt. and Budget, Washington, 1979; staff assoc. Nat. Acad. Scis., Washington, 1980; vis. scholar Brookings Instn., Washington, 1982-83; prof. policy and decision scis., Harvard U., Boston, 1985—; dep. chmn. dept. of health policy and mgmt. The Harvard Sch. of Public Health, 1987-93; dir. Harvard Ctr. for Risk Analysis, 1989—; dir. Harvard Injury Control Ctr., 1990—; cons. Health Effects Inst., Cambridge, Mass., 1985—, Nat. Acad. Scis., 1979-81. Contbr. articles to profl. jours; author 4 books. Republican committeeman, Mt. Lebanon, Pitts., 1984-85. Named Outstanding Debator, Nat. Debate Tournament, 1978; Recipient Outstanding Svc. award Surgeon Gen. U.S., 1991. Mem. Soc. for Risk Analysis (pres.), Am. Econ. Assn., Assn. Pub. Policy Analysis and Mgmt. (Saltzman award 1984), Omicron Delta Kappa. Presbyterian. Avocations: golf; bridge; tennis. Office: Exec Off of the Pres Info and Regulatory Affairs EEOB, 17th & Pennsylvania Ave NW Washington DC 20503

GRAHAM, JOHN H., IV, health science association administrator; BA, Franklin and Marshall Coll., 1971. Mem. Valley Forge coun. Boy Scouts Am., 1971—79; exec. dir. Am. Diabetes Assn., Phila., 1979—83, dir. devel. divsn. N.Y.C., 1983—85, asst. exec. v.p. Alexandria, Va., 1985—88, dep. exec. v.p., 1988—90, CEO, 1990—. Mem.: Combined Health Appeal, Independent Sector, Greater Washington Soc. Assn. Execs., Nat. Health Coun., Am. Soc. Assn. Execs. Office: Am Diabetes Assn 1701 N Beauregard St Alexandria VA 22311-1717

GRAHAM, JOHN HAMILTON, II, professional athletics manager; b. Waynesboro, Va., Mar. 30, 1960; s. John Hamilton and Joan (Clay) G. BA in Polit. Sci., Christopher Newport Coll., 1983; DD, Am. Fellowship, 1986. Notary pub.: Va., Ga. Dir. pub. rels. Peninsula Pilots (minor league affiliate Phila. Phillies), Hampton, Va., 1977-79, dir. broadcasting and pub. rels., 1979-81, asst. gen. mgr., 1981-85; v.p., gen. mgr. Peninsula White Sox (minor league affiliate Chgo. White Sox), Hampton, 1985-87; gen. mgr. Auburn (N.Y.) Astros Baseball Club, 1988-92; pres. Sports of the Peninsula, Hampton, 1992-94; customer svc. specialist Airborne Express, Atlanta, 1994-96; sr. agt., night ops. mgr. Airborne Express Internat., College Park, Ga., 1996—2001; chmn. Peninsula Pro Baseball Hall of Fame, Hampton, Va., 1993; pres. Graham Web Wizard; pres., CEO Field of Dreams Cmtys.; gen. ptnr., gen. mgr. Blackstone. Vice-chmn. Rep. Nat. Com., 1981, Rep. Party Va., Hampton, 1982-92; election bd., election ofcl. Commonwealth of Va., Hampton, 1985-95; notary pub. Commonwealth of Va., Richmond, 1988—; mem. Carolina League Champion peninsula Pilots, 1977, 80, 97, Confederate Meml. Soc., Va. Air and Space Mus., Va. Living Mus., Nat. Rifle Assn., Va. Sheriffs Inst., Smithsonian Assn., Republican Presdl. Task Force, Sons of Confederate Soldiers, Republican Party Platform Planning Com., Spl. Olympics, Nat. Republican Senatorial Com., Presdl. Trust; pres. Virtual U.S. Polit. Simulation. Named Broadcaster of Yr. Carolina League, Hampton, Va., 1980, 81, 85, 87, Exec. of Yr. N.Y. Penn League, Auburn, 1991; named to Peninsula Pro Baseball Hall of Fame, 1992, Hampton Rds. Baseball Hall of Fame, 1994, Auburn Baseball Hall of Fame, 1993; recipient Bill Dancy award Phila. Phillies, 1987. Mem. NRA, Nat. Assn. Writers and Broadcasters, Assn. Profl. Ballplayers Am. (life), Probaseball Execs. Assn. (pres.), Baseball USA, Smithsonian Instn., Nature Conservancy, Mus. of the Confederacy, Va. Air and Space Ctr., Va. Living Mus., Vietnam Vets. Meml. Fund, Va. Sheriffs Inst., Pro Baseball Broadcasters USA (pres.), Major League Baseball Alumni Assn., Minor League Baseball Alumni Assn., Players Alumni Assn., First Family of Va., USA Freedom Corps, Moose, Am. Legion, Baseball USA, Baseball Club, Va. League, Notary. Avocations: tennis, art. E-mail: John@johnhamHongraham.us.

GRAHAM, JOHN JOSEPH, lawyer, economics educator; b. New Haven, Sept. 12, 1920; s. Hugh Munson and Alice W. (Cummings) G. BA in Econs., Yale U., 1942, MA, 1943; JD, Boston Coll., 1946; MA, Boston U., 1949; DHL (hon.), Am. Coll. Greece, 1997. Bar: Mass. 1946, U.S. Dist. Ct. Mass. 1947, U.S. Dist. Ct. Conn. 1949, U.S. Cir. Ct. Appeals (1st cir.) 1947, U.S. Cir. Ct. Appeals (2d cir.) 1953, U.S. Supreme Ct. 1952. Pvt. practice, Boston, 1946—; asst. commerce counsel New Haven R.R., 1947-49; atty. Rwy. Express Agy., Northeastern U.S., 1949-53; arbitrator Fed. Med. and Conciliation Svc. Am. Arbitration Assn., N.Y.C. and Washington, 1953—. Lectr. in econs. Northeastern U. Grad. Sch. Bus. Adminstrn., Boston, 1953-68; vis. prof. econs. Am. Coll. of Greece, Athens, 1981—. Spl. asst. atty. gen. Commonwealth of Mass., 1961; pres. Mass. Consumer Assn., 1961; fin. trustee Met. Transit Authority, Boston, 1957-61; commr. State Dept. Pub. Utilities, Mass., 1957. Yale Labor-Mgmt. Inst. fellow, 1948. Mem. World Peace Through Law Ctr. (founding mem.), Nat. Economists Club (founding mem.), Acad. Polit. Sci. (life), Am. Econ. Assn., Mansfield Law Soc. U.K., Fed. Bar Assn., Yale Club. Roman Catholic. Home and Office: PO Box 1962 Boston MA 02105-1962

GRAHAM, JOHN ROBERT, JR., financial executive; b. Chgo., Oct. 11, 1930; s. John Robert and Grace Beatrice (Strangeman) G.; m. Bettina Abigail Hoffman, Sept. 6, 1958 (div. June 1975); children: Jonathan, Karl; m. Beverly Criley, Dec. 31, 1975. BS, U.S. Mcht. Marine Acad., 1952; MBA, Harvard U., 1959. Ship officer Moore-McCormack Lines, N.Y.C., 1952-53, 55-58; asst. v.p., loan officer Hartford (Conn.) Nat. Bank, 1959-67; asst. treas. Heublein, Inc., Hartford, 1967-68, treas., 1968-74; sr. v.p. fin. and adminstrn. Sikorsky Aircraft Co., Stratford, Conn., 1974-80; v.p. fin., CFO Planning Rsch. Corp., Washington, 1980-82; v.p., CFO Uniroyal Inc., Middlebury, Conn., 1982-88, Uniroyal Holding, Inc., Waterbury, Conn., 1982-88, also bd. dirs.; v.p. fin., CFO, treas., dir. Healthware Corp., Seattle, 1989-92. Bd. dirs. Uniroyal Goodrich Tire Co., Akron, Ohio, U.S. Mcht. Marine Acad. Found.; trustee CDU Holding, Inc. Liquidating Trust, N.Y.C., 1986—. Co-author: Nonwoven Textiles-An Unbiased Appraisal, 1959. Corporator Middlesex Hosp., Middletown, Conn., 1964-85; v.p., treas. Conn. Valley YMCA, Deep River, 1962-64; pres. Essex (Conn.) Bus. Assn., 1964-65; bd. dirs. U.S. Mcht. Marine Acad. Found., 1987—. Lt. (j.g.) USNR, 1953-55, PTO, Korea. Mem. Harvard Club (N.Y.C.), Masons. Avocations: sailing, skiing. Home: 1806 Bellevue Way NE Bellevue WA 98004

GRAHAM, JOHN WALLACE, pathologist; MD, McGill U., Montreal, Que., Can., 1960. Diplomate Am. Bd. Pathology. Intern L.A. County-U. So. Calif. Med. Ctr., 1960-61; resident in pathology U. Oreg. Health Sci. Ctr., Portland, 1961-63, V.A. Med. Ctr. West Los Angeles, 1963-65; fellow in forensic pathology Office Med. Examiner, Balt., 1965-66, dep. med. examiner L.A., 1966-67, chief div. forensic medicine, 1968, 1983-84, asst. med. examiner Dallas, 1975-78, dep. chief med. examiner Calgary, Alt., Can., 1984-86; dir. Calif. Toxicology Service Inc., L.A., 1969-75; chief med. examiner State of Utah, Salt Lake City, 1978-83. Asst. clin. prof. pathology, U. So. Calif., 1970-75, U. Tex. Southwestern Med. Sch., 1975-78; assoc. clin. prof. U. Utah, 1979-84, U. Calgary, 1986-88. Fellow Am. Acad. Forensic Scis., Coll. Am. Pathologists. Home: 1571 Tomahawk Dr Salt Lake City UT 84103-4228

GRAHAM, JORIE, writer, educator; b. N.Y.C., May 9, 1951; d. Curtis Bell and Beverly (Stoll) Pepper; m. James Galvin. BFA, NYU, 1973; MFA, U. Iowa, 1978. Asst. prof. Murray (Ky.) State U., 1978-79, Humboldt State U., Arcata, Calif., 1979-81; instr. Columbia U., N.Y.C., 1981-83; mem. staff U. Iowa, Iowa City, 1983—, prof. English, dir. poetry workshop, 1999—. Poetry editor Crazy Horse, 1978-81, chancellor Acad. Am. Poets, 1997; Boylston chair Harvard U 1998-2002. Author: Hybrids of Plants and of Ghosts, 1980 (Great Lakes Colls. Assn. award 1981), Erosion, 1983, The End of Beauty, 1987, Region of Unlikeness, 1991, Materialism, 1993, The Dream of the Unified Field: Selected Poems 1974-94, 1995, The Errancy, 1997, Swarm, 1999; editor: Earth Took of Earth: 100 Great Poems of the English Language, 1996; editor: (with David Lehman) The Best American Poetry 1990, 1990, Never: Poems, 2002. Recipient Am. Acad. Poets award, 1977, Young Poet prize Poetry Northwest, 1980, Pushcart prize, 1980, 82, American Poetry Review prize, 1982, Pulitzer prize in poetry, 1996, Lavan award Acad. Am. Poets, 1991, Martin Zaubel award Acad. and Inst. of Arts and Letters, 1992; Bunting fellow Radcliff Inst., 1982, Guggenheim fellow, 1983, John D. and Catherine T. MacArthur Found. fellow, 1990; grantee Ingram-Merrill Found., 1981. Office: Harvard U English Dept Barker Cntr 12 Quincey St Cambridge MA 02138*

GRAHAM, K(ATHLEEN) M. (K. M. GRAHAM), artist; b. Hamilton, Ont., Can., Sept. 13, 1913; d. Charles and G. Blanche (Leitch) Howitt; m. J. Wallace Graham, Dec. 17, 1938; children: John Wallace, Janet Howitt. BA, U. Toronto, Ont., 1936. (one-woman shows) Carmen Lamanna Gallery, Toronto, 1967, Trinity Coll., U. Toronto, 1968, Founders Coll., York U., Toronto, 1970, Pollock Gallery, Toronto, 1971,73,75, Art Gallery Coburg, Ont., 1973, City Hall, Toronto, 1974, David Mirvish Gallery Gallery, Toronto, 1976, Klonaridis, Inc., Toronto, 1978, Watson-Willour Gallery, Houston, 1980, Downstairs Gallery, Edmonton, Alta., 1980, 82, Lillian Heidenberg Gallery, N.Y.C., 1981,86, Klonaridis, Inc., Toronto, 1981-85, 87, 88, 90, ELCA London Gallery, Montreal, Que., Can., 1983, MacDonald-Stewart Art Centre, Guelph, Ont., 1984, Glenbow Mus., Calgary, 1984, Concordia Gallery, Montreal, 1984, Hart House Gallery, Toronto, 1985, Lillian Heidenberg Gallery, N.Y.C., 1986, Klondaridis Inc., Toronto, 1985, 87, 88, 90, 91, Feheley Fine Arts, Toronto, 1989, Douglas Udell Gallery, Vancouver, 1993, Meml. Art Gallery, St. Johns, N.F., 1994, Beaverbrook Gallery, Fredericton, N.B., 1994, Costin and Klintworth, Toronto, Ont., 1994, 95, The Art Gallery of Ont., 1997, The Moore Gallery, Toronto, 2000, 2001, (group shows) Montreal Mus. Fine Arts, 1976, Hirshborn Mus., Washington, 1977, Edmonton (Alta., Can.) Art Gallery, 1977, Norman MacKenzie Art Gallery, Regina, Sask., Can., 1977, David Mirvish Gallery, Toronto, Watson De Nagy Gallery, Houston, Galerie Wentzel, Hamburg, Fed. Republic Germany, Beaverbrook Gallery, Fredericton, N.B., Associated Am. Artists, N.Y.C., 1986, 88, Elca London, Montreal, 1987, Klondaris Inc., Toronto, 1987, 91, Douglas Udell Gallery, Vancouver, 1987, Associated Am. Artists, N.Y.C., 1988, Feheley Fine Art, Toronto, 1989, (travelling shows) CanadaxTen, 1974, The Can. Canvas, 1975-76, Changing Visions, 1976-77, The Shell Canada Collection, 1977, The Fauve Heritage, 1997, 14 Canadians Hirschborn Mus., Washington, 1977, Certain Traditions, 1978, 79, Bolduc Fournier Graham, 1981, The Heritage of Jack Bush, 1981-82, Selections from the Westburne Collection, 1982-83, (permanent collections) Nat. Gallery Can., Ottawa, Edmonton Art Gallery, Art Gallery Ont., Art Gallery Hamilton, Ont., MacDonald-Stewart Art Gallery, Guelph, Ont., Toronto City Hall, The Brit. Mus., London, Art Gallery Vancouver, Agnes Etherington Art Centre, Kingston, Ont., Can., Musee d'Art Contemporarin Montreal, Beaverbrook Art Gallery, Frederickton, N.B., Art Gallery Nfld.and Labrador, Art Gallery, Peterborough, Ont., Robert McLaughlin Gallery, Oshawa, Ont., Kitchener Waterloo Art Gallery, McMichael Can. Art Gallery, Hart House Art Gallery, Toronto, also numerous corp. collections. Trinity Coll. fellow, U. Toronto, 1988. Mem. Royal Can. Acad.

GRAHAM, KENNETH ALBERT, lawyer; b. Bridgeport, Conn., Aug. 15, 1948; s. Albert Charles and Rosemary (Farrell) Graham. BA, U. Bridgeport, 1971; MA, Northeastern U., 1974; JD, Suffolk U., 1977. Bar: Conn. 1977, US Dist. Ct./Conn. 1979, US Ct. Appeals (2d cir.) 1980, US Supreme Ct. 1981. Sole practice, Stratford, Conn., 1977—78; asst. clk. Conn. Superior Ct., Norwich, 1978; staff atty. Conn. Dept. Consumer Protection, Hartford, 1978—81; assoc. prof. history Sacred Heart U., 1979—; asst. atty. gen. Conn. Atty. Gen. Office, Harford, 1981—2003; atty. trial referee Conn. Superior Ct., 2003—. Served U.S. Army, 1970—73. Mem.: Am. Hist. Assn., New Eng. Hist. Assn., Stratford Hist. Soc., Conn. Bar Assn. (exec. com. adminstrv. law sect. 1983—92, exec. com. consumer law sect. 1978—84), Bridgeport Bar Assn., ABA, Stratford Tennis Assn., Phi Alpha Theta, Delta Theta Phi (vice dean 1976 1976—77, scholarship key 1976). Home: 155 Butternut Ln Stratford CT 06614-2457 Office: Conn Atty Gens Office 1115 Main St Ste 604 Bridgeport CT 06604-4406 E-mail: kenneth.graham@po.state.ct.us.

GRAHAM, KENNETH ROBERT, psychologist, educator; b. Phila., June 5, 1943; s. Edgar and Margit (Leafgreen) Graham; m. Michele Carolyn Monroe, Aug. 10, 1968; children: Mark Andrew, Richard Alan. BA, U. Pa., 1964; PhD, Stanford U., 1969. Lic. psychologist, Pa. Asst. prof. Muhlenberg Coll., Allentown, Pa., 1970-77, assoc. prof., 1977-84, prof., 1984-99, emeritus prof., 1999—, head psychology dept., 1984-93; rsch. psychologist Unit for Exptl. Psychiatry Inst. of Pa. Hosp., Phila., 1969-70; adj. asst. prof. U. Pa., Phila., 1969-70. Cons. smoking cessation various hosps., 1985-1999. Author: (text) Psychological Research, 1977; asst. editor Am. Jour. Clin. Hypnosis, 1974-95; contbr. over 30 articles to profl. and sci. jours. Bd. dirs., pres. Lehigh Valley Child Care, Allentown, 1979-85; advisor Pathways (Conf. of Chs.), Allentown, 1989-98, N.E. Pa. Synod Luth. Ch. in Am., Wescosville, Pa., 1989-93. Mem. APA (pres. divsn. psychol. hypnosis 1980-81), European Soc. Hypnosis in Psychotherapy and Psychosomatic Medicine, Kiwanis (pres. Allentown chpt. 1991-92, lt. gov. Pa. dist. 1994-95). Democrat. Avocations: swimming, collecting glass paperweights and signatures of 19th century explorers. Office: Muhlenberg Coll Psychology Dept Allentown PA 18104 E-mail: krg6543@aol.com.

GRAHAM, KENT HILL, philanthropist, museum guide; b. Winston-Salem, N.C., May 16, 1937; d. Charles Gideon and Nancy Critz (O'Hanlon) Hill; m. William Thomas Graham, Feb. 1, 1958; children: William Thomas, Ashton Cannon. Student, Duke U., 1955-58, U. Hawaii, 1958. Chmn. of vols., sec., sec. to exec. bd. Forsyth County chpt. ARC, asst. to nat. chmn. vols. Am. Nat. Red Cross, Washington; bd. dirs. Centenary United Meth. Ch. Day Care Ctr.; bd. dirs. Am. Cancer Soc., Forsyth County, Little Theatre, Child Guidance Clinic, Carolina Ballet, 1996-97, Wake County Libr., 1996-99, Forsyth County Libr., 1970-77, chmn., 1975-77; Rep. candidate for alderman West Ward, Winston-Salem, 1965; vice chmn. N.C. Battleship Commn., 1973-77; bd. dirs. Winston-Salem Debutante Com., 1984-86, pres., 1985, nominating chmn., 1986; mem. exec. bd. Historic Winston, Inc.; trustee N.C. Sch. Arts, 1986-87; mem. N.C. Sentencing and Policy Adv. Com., 1990-93, Celebration N.C. Fin. Com. Capt. N.C. Naval Militia. Mem. Jr. League Nat. Fedn. Rep. Women, Order of the Long Leaf Pine, Twin City Garden Club (treas., 1st v.p., pres.), Garden Club Am. (zone VIII, bull. editor 1975-77, vice chmn. 1977-80, nominating com. 1979-80, water conservation coord. 1980-83), Bahia Vista Club (bd. dirs. 1995-2000). Avocations: horseback riding, travel, historic preservation, collecting early southern antiques. E-mail: kgraham553.aol.com. Home: 3421 Williamsborough Ct Raleigh NC 27609-6368

GRAHAM, KIRSTEN RAE, computer scientist, educator; b. Inglewood, Calif., July 20, 1946; d. Ray Selmer and Ella Louise (Carter) Newbury. BS, U. Wis., Oshkosh, 1971; MS, U. Colo., 1980; postgrad., Army War Coll., 1987; EdD in Adult and Higher Edn., EdD, Mont. State U., 1998. Cert. flight instr. FAA. Chief info. svc. Mont. State Dept. Labor and Industry, Helena; dir., personal property and bus. lic. div. County of Fairfax, Va.; analyst officer U.S. Army Pentagon, Washington; battalion commdr. U.S. Army, Frankfurt, Germany, assoc. prof. West Point, NY; tchr. computer tech. Helena Coll. Tech., U. Mont., chmn. computer electronics tech. dept., 2002—03. Adj. prof. Western Mont. Coll., U. Mont.; del. People-to-People Women Computer Sci. Profls. program, China; coord. 1st statewide program for instrs. new to 2-yr. coll. sys.; faculty practitioner U. Phoenix; faculty fellow for svc. learning Mont. Campus Compact, 1999—2000, mentoring fellow, 2001—03. Del. to China Citizen's Amb. Program, 1993. Lt. U.S. Army, 1964—88. Faculty fellow, Mont. Campus Compact, 1999—2000, Mentoring fellow, 2001—02. Mem.: Am. Fedn. Tchrs., Assn. Computing Machinery.

GRAHAM, LANIER, art historian, curator, cultural planner; b. Shawnee, Okla., Mar. 6, 1940; s. Floyd and Martha Graham; m. Gloria K. Smith; 1 child, Jennifer R. Ulrich. BA in Internat. Polit. & Cultural Rels., Am. U., 1963; MA in Art History, Columbia U., 1966. Planner cultural instns., 1965—; assoc. curator architecture and design Mus. Modern Art, N.Y.C., 1965-70; curator of paintings and sculpture, renaissance to modern Fine Arts Mus., San Francisco, 1970-76; curator Cultural Resource Mgmt. Ctr., San Francisco, 1976-83; curator of prints and books Australian Nat. Gallery, Canberra, 1984-87; curator of paintings, sculpture and prints, renaissance to modern Norton Simon Mus. Art, Pasadena, Calif., 1987-91; dir. Art Info. Ctr. - An Info. Svc., Northbank, Calif., 1991-97, Univ. Art Gallery, Calif. State U., Hayward, 1998—. Art history lectr., religious studies, mus. studies educator U. Calif., Berkeley, John F. Kennedy U., Calif. Inst. Asian Studies, Naropa Inst., Boulder, Humboldt State U., Arcata, Calif. State U., Hayward, 1977—. Author: Leonardo's Book Illustrations, 1961, Botticelli's Dante, 1963, Mies van der Rohe Drawings, 1966, The Architecture of Louis I. Kahn, 1966, Chess Sets, 1968, Hector Guimard, 1970, Three Centuries of American Painting, 1971, Three Centuries of French Art, vol. 1, 1973, vol. 2, 1975, Claude Monet, 1974, Brother Sun & Sister Moon: Alchemical Symbols in Traditional and Modern Art, 1979, Illustrated Books of Henri Matisse, 1979, Leonardo & the Androgyne: Nonduality in World Art, 1980, Decades of Light: Early Modern French Painting, 1980, The Spontaneous Gesture: Prints and Books of the Abstract Expressionist Era, 1987, Vincent Van Gogh: Painter, Printmaker, Collector, 1990, The Prints of Willem de Kooning: A Catalogue Raisonné, vol. 1, 1991, Impossible Realities: Marcel Duchamp and the Surrealist Tradition, 1991, Sacred Visions: A Survey of World Art and Architecture, vol. 1, 1991, vol. 2, 1992, The Double Serpent: Symbol of Transformation in World Art, 1993, Rhythms and Reverberations: Multicultural Art in the United States and its Development from the Tribal World, 1993, Solidity and Infinity: The Symbolism of the Circle and Square in World Architecture, 1995, Goddesses in Art, 1997, Life, Death and Laughter: The Art of Masami Teraoka, 1998, The Art of the Book: The Modern Livre d'Artiste, 1999, Duchamp and Androgyny: Art, Gender, and Metaphysics, 2003; collections of poetry include Nature Poems, 1958, The Sin of 100 Debts, 1967, Heavy Light: Haiku on the Theme of Modern Physics & Ancient Wisdom, 1978, Electro-Magnetism: Poems on the Theme of Complementarity, 1982, Fragments of Feelings: Selected Poems, 1994, Undulations of Eternity: Collected Poems, 1994; gen. editor: The Rainbow Book: Color...from Ancient to Modern Times, 1975, 76, rev. edit., 1979, Rodin Graphics: A Catalogue Raisonné, 1975, American Art from the Collection of Mr. and Mrs. John D. Rockefeller 3d, 1976, Giorgione & the Experts: A Documentary Exhibition of the Three Ages of Man & the Process of Authentication, 1993, 94, Leonardo's Light in the Last Supper and Christ among the Doctors, 1995; co-author Code of Ethics for Australian Assn. Mus., 1970-87; author studies in renaissance and modern art from Impressionism to Contemporary Art; rsch. in relationships between modern and traditional art, particularly symbols of the sacred; editor BOA: Bull. of Archives of Art Info. Ctr., 1960—, Renaissance Studies, 1963—, Muse: Newsletter of Visual Edn. and Cultural Planning, 1969—, Bi-Singularity: Double Images of Nonduality in World Art, 1979—, Leonardo Studies, 1980—, Sacred Spaces: World Architecture & Symbolism, 1976—, Poësis: A Rev. of Poetry by Artists, 1987-93, Iconography of Infinity: Essays on Art and Philosophy, 1992—; planner various cultural instns. including Internat. Study Ctr., N.Y.C., Mus. Modern Art, Greenwich Village Hist. Preservation Dist., N.Y.C., Fine Arts Mus., San Francisco, Urban Planning Think Tank, San Francisco, Exploratorium, San Francisco, Bay Area Conservation Ctr., San Francisco, Archives Am. Art, San Francisco, Ft. Mason Ctr., San Francisco, Headlands Ctr. Arts, Golden Gate Nat. Recreation Area, Nat. Pk. Svc., Sausalito, Yerba Buena Ctr. Arts, San Francisco, J. Paul Getty Mus., Malibu, Louvre Mus., Paris, Morris Graves Art Mus., Eureka, Calif. Indian Mus. and Cultural Ctr., Golden Gate Nat. Recreation Area, Nat. Park Svc., San Francisco. Mem. Soc. of Archtl. Historians, Nat. Soc. of Lit. and the Arts, World Print Coun. (adv. com. we. region), Archives of Am. Art, Smithsonian Instn., Internat. Soc. Poets., Inst. for Aesthetic Devel. Avocations: printmaking, poetry, publishing private press editions.

GRAHAM, LAURIE, editor, writer; b. Evanston, Ill., Nov. 22, 1941; d. Thomas Harlin and Mary Elisabeth (Stoner) Graham; m. George McKay Schieffelin, Dec. 12, 1980 (dec. Jan. 1988); m. Robert Dale Shearer, Apr. 6, 1994 (dec. Nov. 2002). Student, Mt. Holyoke Coll., 1959-61; BA, U. Colo., 1963. Editor Charles Scribner's Sons, N.Y.C., 1969-87. Originator, co-project dir. The Greater Pitts. Poem Chase, 2001. Author: Rebuilding the House, 1990, Singing the City, 1998; mem. editl. bd. Creative Nonfiction, 1994—, (press series) Emerging Writers in Creative Nonfiction, Duquesne U., 1994—; contbg. author: Pittsburgh Sports, 2000, Creative Nonfiction, 2003. Mem. PEN, N.Y. Jr. League, Colony Club. Home: 1000 Grandview Ave Pittsburgh PA 15211-1362

GRAHAM, LEROY CULLEN, retired electrical engineer; b. Meeker, Colo., Dec. 14, 1926; s. Roy Cullen Graham and Gertrude Margaret Metzger; m. Carolyn Roberta Clark, Sept. 2, 1949 (dec. Sept. 1985); m. Joan Margaret Tweedy; children: Patricia, James, Constance, Robert. BSEE with honors, U. Colo., 1950; MS, Stevens Inst. Tech., 1956. Mem. tech. staff Bell Telephone Labs, Murray Hill, NJ, 1950—56; sr. engr. Goodyear Aerospace Corp., Litchfield Park, Ariz., 1956—66, head, 1966—76, mgr. engring., 1976—89; dir. engring. Loral Corp., 1989; cons. Phoenix, 1989—96; ret., 1996. Panelist Naval Studies Bd., Nat. Acad. Sci., San Diego, 1979—80, USAF Space Command, 1982, NASA Experiment Selection, Langley AFB, Va., 1978. Contbg. author Manual of Photogrammetry, 1966; contbr. Vestryman All Saints Episc. Ch., Phoenix, mem. visioning com. With USN, 1944—46. Fellow: IEEE (sect. chair, awards chair 1963, treas. 1960, named Outstanding Engr. Phoenix sect. 1964); mem.: Kappa Kappa Psi, Eta Kappa Nu, Tau Beta Pi. Republican. Episcopalian. Achievements include patents for on airborne radar interferometer technique. Avocations: computer applications, gardening, music, photography. Home: 5 E Butler Dr Phoenix AZ 85020-3521

GRAHAM, LESTER LYNN, radio journalist; b. Carlinville, Ill., Aug. 16, 1960; s. Lyndal L. and Betty L. (Cottingham) G.; m. Evelyn Elaine Epperson, Aug. 4, 1979; children: Joshua Nathanael, Alayna Renee. AAS, Lewis & Clark Coll., 1985. News dir. Metroplex Comm. Sta. WBGZ, Alton, Ill., 1985; news dir. Midwest Comm. Stas. WPMB and WKRV, Vandalia, Ill., 1986-87; news dir. Seith-Serafin Comm. Stas. WSDR and WSSQ, Sterling, Ill., 1987-88; news dir. No. Ill. U. Stas. WNIU and WNIJ, Rockford, Ill., 1988-94; news dir. U. of Mo.-St. Louis Stas. KWMU, 1994-98; sr. editor Great Lakes Radio Consortium,

Mich. Radio U. Mich., 1998—. Trainer environ. journalism USIA, South Africa, Malawi, Swaziland, Lesotho, 1999. Co-writer, co-prodr. (radio documentary) Whistle-Stops: The 1948 Presidential Campaign, 1998; editor (revised) Pronunciation Guide for Illinois Place Names, 1998. Recipient Nat. Individual Achievement award UPI 1990, John Stewart Meml. Broadcasting award Lewis and Clark Coll., 1985, Alumnus Yr. award, 1997; fellow environ. journalism program Great Lakes Issues, Mich. State U., 1999, Environ. Issues program, Nat. Press Found., Washington, 2001, Insts. of Journalism and Natural Resources-Great Waters Inst., 2002. Mem. Pub. Radio News Dirs. Inc. (Nat. Spot News Coverage award 1990, 1994, Nat. Use of Medium award 1991, Nat. Documentary award 1996, bd. dirs., large staff rep. 1996-97), Radio and TV News Dirs. Assn. (Edward R. Murrow award, Network, Use of Sound 2002), Ill. News Broadcasters Assn. (v.p. 1996-97, bd. dirs. 1991-96, pres. 1997-98), Lewis and Clark Radio Adv. (bd. dirs.). Soc. Profl. Journalists (v.p. St. Louis chpt. 1996), Soc. Environ. Journalists. Avocation: Illinois history. Home and Office: 7828 Bramblewood Dr 1B Lansing MI 48917 E-mail: graham@glrc.org.

GRAHAM, LINDSEY O. senator; b. Pickens County, S.C., July 9, 1955; s. E. J. and Millie Graham. BA in Psychology, U. S.C., 1977, JD, 1981. Area def. counsel Shaw AFB, 1982-84; cir. trial counsel USAF Europe, 1984-88; asst. county atty. County of Oconee, S.C., 1988-92; pvt. practice, 1988-94; city atty., 1990-94; mem. S.C. Ho. of Reps., 1992—95, U.S. Congress from 3d S.C. dist., 1995—2001; mem. edn. and workforce com., armed svcs. com., jud. com.; U.S. senator from S.C., 2002—. With USAF, 1990, Desert Shield/Desert Storm. Lt. col. Air Force Reserves. Republican. Office: US Senate Washington DC 20510*

GRAHAM, LOREN RAYMOND, historian, educator; b. Hymera, Ind., June 29, 1933; s. Ross Raymond and Hazel Mae (McClanahan) G.; m. Patricia Parks Albjerg, Sept. 6, 1955; 1 child, Marguerite Elizabeth. BS, Purdue U., 1955, D.Letters (h.c.), 1986; MA, Columbia U., 1960, PhD, 1964; postgrad., Moscow U., 1960-61. Gandy-dancer Pa. R.R., 1950-51; research chem. engr. Dow Chem. Co., 1955; lectr. dept. history Ind. U., 1963-64, asst. prof., 1965-66; vis. asst. prof. dept. public law and govt. Columbia U., 1965-66, assoc. prof., dept. history, 1967-72, prof., 1972-78, adj. prof., 1978-89; mem. Russian Inst., 1966-78; assoc., mem. exec. com. Davis Ctr. for Russian and Eurasian Studies/Harvard U., 1980—; acting dir. Davis Ctr. for Russian Studies/Harvard U., 1995-96; vis. prof. dept. history of sci. Harvard U., 1985-99; prof. MIT, 1978—. Vis. scholar U. Chgo., 1991-92; mem. adv. bd. Internat. Sci. Found., 1992-96; mem. adv. coun. U.S. Civilian R&D Found., 2002--. Author: The Soviet Academy of Sciences and The Communist Party, 1967, Science and Philosophy in the Soviet Union, 1972, Between Science and Values, 1981, Sci. Philosophy and Human Behavior in the Soviet Union, 1987, Science in Russia and the Soviet Union: A Short History, 1993, The Ghost of the Executed Engineer: Technology and the Fall of the Soviet Union, 1993, A Face in the Rock: Tale of a Grand Island Chippewa, 1995, What Have We Learned About Science and Technology From the Russian Experience?, 1998; editor (with others) Functions and Uses of Disciplinary History, 1983, (with R. Stites) Red Star: The First Bolshevik Science Utopia, 1983, Science and the Soviet Social Order, 1990; contbr. numerous articles to profl. jours.; narrator, cons. Nova TV, 1987. Trustee European U., St. Petersburg, Russia, 2000—. Nat. Lighthouse Mus., 1997—. Served with USN, 1955-58. Recipient Gross award Saginaw Valley State U., 2003; Woodrow Wilson fellow, 1958-59; Danforth fellow, 1958-63; Fulbright Hayes fellow, 1966; Guggenheim fellow, 1969-70; Rockefeller fellow, 1976-77; Smithsonian Instn. fellow, 1981-82. Fellow AAAS, Am. Acad. Arts and Scis., Am. Philos. Soc.; mem. Acad. Natural Scis. (fgn.; Moscow), Acad. Humanitarian Scis. (fgn.; Moscow), Am. Hist. Assn., Am. Assn. Advancement of Slavic Studies, History of Sci. Soc. (Sarton medal 1996), Soc. History of Tech., Soc. Social Study of Sci., MIch. Hist. Soc. (Follo award 2000). Home: 7 Francis Ave Cambridge MA 02138-2009 Office: MIT E51-163 77 Massachusetts Ave Cambridge MA 02139-4307 E-mail: lrg@mit.edu.

GRAHAM, NORMA VAN SURDAM, psychologist, educator; b. St. Louis, Aug. 8, 1944; d. David Tredway and Frances Keesler G.; m. Wayne Allen Wickelgren, 1979; children: Peter W.G., Kirsten G.W., Jeanette G.W.[ ]BS in Math., Stanford U., 1966; PhD in Psychology, U. Pa., 1970. From asst. prof. to prof. Columbia U., N.Y.C., 1972-82, prof., 1982—. Author: Visual Pattern Analyzers, 1989. Fellow APA, Optical Soc. Am.; mem. AAAS, NAS.

GRAHAM, OTIS LIVINGSTON, JR., history educator; b. Little Rock, Ark., June 24, 1935; s. Otis Livingstone and Lois (Patterson) G.; m. Ann Zemke, Sept. 5, 1959 (div. 1981); children— Ann Kathryn Lakin, Wade Livingston; m. Delores Yochum, Apr. 24, 1982 BA, Yale U., New Haven, 1957; MA, Columbia U., N.Y.C., 1961, PhD, 1966. Asst. prof. history Mt. Vernon Coll, Washington, 1962-64, Calif. State U., Hayward, 1965-66; prof. history U. Calif., Santa Barbara, 1966-80, 89-95; disting. univ. prof. history U. N.C., Chapel Hill, NC, 1980-89, disting. vis. prof. Wilmington, 1995—. Mem. editl. bd. U. Calif. Press, 1991-95; disting. Fulbright lectr. U. Bologna, 2002. Author: An Encore for Reform: The Old Progressives and the New Deal, 1967; The Great Campaigns: Reform and War in America 1900-1928, 1971; The New Deal: The Critical Issues, 1971; Toward a Planned Society: From Roosevelt to Nixon, 1977, Losing Ground: The Industrial Policy Debate, 1992, A Limited Bounty: The U.S. Since World War II, 1996; editor The Pub. Historian, 1989-97; contbr. chpts. to books, articles to profl. jours. Chair policy bd. Ctr. for Immigration Studies. Served with USMC, 1957-60. Am. Philos. Soc. grantee, 1966; NEH sr. fellow, 1972; Guggenheim fellow, 1977; Woodrow Wilson Internat. Ctr. for Scholars fellow, 1983; recipient Robert Kelley award Nat. Coun. Pub. History, 1999. Fellow Soc. Am. Historians, Ctr. for Advanced Study in the Behavioral Scis.; mem. Am. Hist. Assn., Orgn. Am. Historians (program chmn. 1977, nominating bd. 1993-95), Ctr. Study Democratic Instns. (assoc. 1975—, program dir. 1976-79), Fedn. Am. Immigration Reform (nat. bd. dirs. 1978-2001), NEH, Woodrow Wilson Ctr., Soc. Am. Historians (chmn. Parkman prize com. 1974, 80). Avocation: sailing. Office: U NC 601 S College Rd Wilmington NC 28403-3297 E-mail: graham@history.ucsb.edu.

GRAHAM, PAMELA SMITH, artist, distributing company executive; b. Winona, Miss., Jan. 18, 1944; d. Douglas LaRue and Dorothy Jean (Hefty) Smith; m. Robert William Graham, Mar. 6, 1965 (div. 1974); children: Jennifer Courtney, Eric Douglas; m. Thomas Paul Harley, Dec. 4, 1976 (div. 2000). Student, U. Colo., 1962-65, U. Cin., 1974-76. Profl. artist, craft tchr., 1968—; property mgmt. and investor, 1972-77; acct., word processor Borden Chem. Co. divsn.. Borden, Inc., Cin., 1974-78; owner, pres. Hargram Enterprises, Cin., 1977-81; owner Sagebrush Studio, 1985—, Graham & Harley Enterprises, 1981-99; art tchr., dean of ceremonial art Coll. of Transformative Wisdom, 1999—; webpage designer dept. pharmacy U. Colo. Hosp., 1998-2000. Tchr.; cons. County committeewoman Bergen County, N.J., 1972, clk. of session, 1975-79, conv. chmn., 1981; campaign chmn. United Appeal, 1977; lifeline telephone counselor Suicide Hotline, 1985-90; coord. program svcs. and victim advisor Abusive Men Exploring New Directions, 1986-91; art tchr., dean ceremonial art Coll. of Transformative Wisdom, 1999—. One woman shows include U. Colo. Health Scis. Ctr. Denison Libr., 1992—, Jefferson County Nature Ctr., 1990, Mt. Vernon Country Club, 1998-99, Colo. Symphony, 1998; exhibited in group shows at Colo. Audubon Soc., 1989, Evergreen Artists Assn. Fine Arts Fair, 1988-95, River Sage, 1989, Evergreen Naturalists Audubon Soc., 1988-91, Foothills Art Ctr., 1989, 93, Gilpin County Arts Assn., 1989-94, Glenwood Springs Art Guild, 1989-90, Hilton Head Art League, 1999; featured in Spree mag., 1989, Weekend Arts sect. Denver Post, 1998; included in Ency. of Living Artists, 11th edit., 1999; represented in permanent collections at Univ. Hosp., AMEND, U. Colo. Health Scis. Ctr. Chancellor's Office, U. Colo. at Boulder Wardenburg Health Ctr., Willis Corroon Corp., Dean Witter Reynolds, Inc., others. Recipient awards for art exhibits including People's Choice award Evergreen Artists Assn. Mem. NAFE, Profl. Artists Assn., Nat. Assn. Fine Artists, Denver Art Mus., Denver Mus. Nature and Sci., Mus. Modern Art N.Y., United Sales Leaders Assn., Nat. Mus. Women in Arts, Colo. Artists Assn., Evergreen Artists Assn. (bd. dirs., pres. 1990-91, People's Choice award 1993), Hilton Head Art League, Ocean Journey Aquariaum, Colo. Calligraphers Guild, Gilpin County Arts Assn., Continental Divide Trail Alliance, Friends of Denver Pub. Libr. Assn., Foothills Art Ctr., Assn. Humanistic Psychology, Mt. Vernon Country Club, Queen City Racquet Club, Alpha Gamma Chi, Kappa Kappa Gamma. Studio: Sagebrush Studio 818 Logan St # 903 Denver CO 80203-3123 E-mail: sagebrushstudio@yahoo.com., graham@sagebrushstudios.com.

GRAHAM, PARKER LEE, II, information executive; b. Shelby, Ohio, Aug. 6, 1957; s. Parker Lee, Sr. and Shelvy Jean (Schwall) G.; m. Renee Marie MacCartney, Sept. 4, 1976 (div. 1995); children: Tella Marie, Kami Nicole; m. Kathy Lynn Jackson, July 18, 1999; 1 child, Tiffanye Adelia. Grad. high sch., Shelby. Parts insp. Essex Wire, Lexington, Ohio, 1974-76; supr. shipping dept. Supreme Distbr., Detroit, 1978-79; driver Everrett Delivery Service, Detroit, 1979-81; field supr. Wesco Energy Systems, Warren, Mich., 1981-82; mgr. shipping Kemar Inc., Sterling Heights, Mich., 1982-84; pres., chief exec. officer Metro Cartage Co., Romulus, Mich., also bd. dirs., 1984-90; salesman Swad Chevrolet, Columbus, Ohio, 1991-92; computer systems mgr. MBA Mktg. Corp. dba "Just for Feet", Dublin, Ohio, 1992-93; customer edn. specialist CAM Data Systems, Inc., Fountain Valley, Calif., 1993-96; sys. adminstr. Donatos Pizza, Inc., Columbus, 1996-97; sys. engr. CAM Data Sys., Inc., Fountain Valley, Calif., 1997-99; MIS dir. Petland Inc., Chillicothe, Ohio, 1999—. E-mail: pgraham@petland.com.

GRAHAM, PATRICIA ALBJERG, education educator; b. Lafayette, Ind., Feb. 9, 1935; d. Victor L. and Marguerite (Hall) Albjerg; m. Loren R. Graham, Sept. 6, 1955; 1 child, Marguerite Elizabeth. BS, Purdue U., 1955, MS, 1957, DLett (hon.), 1980; PhD, Columbia U., 1964; MA (hon.), Harvard U., 1974; DHL (hon.), Manhattanville Coll., 1976; LLD (hon.), Beloit Coll., 1977, Clark U., 1978; DPA (hon.), Suffolk U., 1978, Ind. U., 1980; DLitt (hon.), St. Norbert Coll., 1980; DH (hon.), Emmanuel Coll., 1983; DHL (hon.), No. Mich. U., 1987, York Coll. of Pa., 1989, Kenyon Coll., 1991, Bank St. Coll. Edn., 1993; LLD (hon.), Radcliffe Coll., 1994, Salem State Coll., 1998. Tchr. high sch., Norfolk, Va., 1955-56, 57-58, N.Y.C., 1958-60; lectr., asst. prof. Ind. U., 1964-66; asst. prof. history of edn. Barnard Coll. and Columbia Tchrs. Coll., N.Y.C., 1965-68, assoc. prof., 1968-72, prof., 1972-74; dean Radcliffe Inst., 1974-77; also v.p. Radcliffe Coll., Cambridge, Mass., 1976-77; prof. Harvard U., Cambridge, Mass., 1974-79, Warren prof., 1979—2001, Warren Rsch. prof., 2001—; dean Grad. Sch. Edn., 1982-91; pres. Spencer Found., Chgo., 1991-2000. Author: Progressive Education: From Arcady to Academe, 1967, Community and Class in American Education: 1865-1918, 1974, S.O.S. Sustain Our Schools, 1992. Bd. dirs. Dalton Sch., 1973-76, Josiah Macy, Jr. Found., 1976-77, 79—; trustee Beloit Coll., 1976-77, 79-82, Northwestern Mut. Life, 1980—, Found. for Teaching Econs., 1980-87; bd. dirs. Spencer Found., 1983-2000, Johnson Found., 1983-2001, Hitachi Found., 1985—, Carnegie Found. for Advancement of Tchg., 1984-92, Ctrl. European U., Budapest, 2002—, Apache, 2002—. Mem.: AAAS (coun. 1993—96, v.p. 1998—2001), Ctr. for Advanced Study in the Behavioral Scis. (bd. dirs. 2001—), Am. Philos. Soc., Am. Hist. Assn. (v.p. 1985—89), Nat. Acad. Edn. (pres. 1984—89), Sci. Rsch. Assocs. (dir. 1980—89), Phi Beta Kappa. Episcopalian. Office: Harvard U Grad Sch Edn Cambridge MA 02138

GRAHAM, PATRICIA KELSEY, music educator, writer, composer; b. Hollywood, Calif., Sept. 25, 1940; d. William Frank and Ida Mae (Feinauer) Kelsey; m. G. Robert Graham; children: Loralee, Andrea, Scott, Brett, Matt, Melinda. BSc, Brigham Young U., Provo, UT, 1962; EdM, U. Utah, Salt Lake City, 1982. Tchr. Red Granite Sch. Dist., Salt Lake City, 1962—65; freelance piano tchr., 1962—; tchr. music, Kindermusik U. UT, 1993—; music tchr. Global Artways, 2000—. Columnist The Friend Mag., Salt Lake City, 1981—89; lectr. ch. music workshop Brigham Young U., 1983—90; accompanist Crossroads Chorale Ensemble, Salt Lake City, 1997—. Author (and composer): (children'songs) Sing Out!, 1978, The Children's Songbook LDS Ch., 1989; author: A Children's Songbook Companion, 1995. Mem. steering com. Children's Treehouse Mus., 1999—; lectr. World-Wide Orgn. of Women, Salt Lake City, 1996—99; bd. mem. Gen. Primary, LDS Ch., Salt Lake City, 1980—89, music chair, 1984—89; bd. mem. World-Wide Orgn. of Women, Salt Lake City, 1996—99. Recipient First Pl. children's music, UT Composer's Guild, 1979, 1982, Outstanding Accompanist, Sacra Dulce Chorus, 1994. Mem.: UT Music Tchrs. Assn., Nat. Fedn. of Music Clubs, UT Fedn. of Music Clubs. Republican. Mem. Lds Ch. Avocations: comml. art, sewing, reading. Home: 2027 Keller Ln Salt Lake City UT 84109-2904

GRAHAM, PHILIP L., JR., lawyer; b. N.Y.C., 1943; BA, Harvard U., 1965, JD, 1968. Bar: N.Y. 1971. Mem. Sullivan & Cromwell, N.Y.C. Office: Sullivan & Cromwell 125 Broad St Fl 28 New York NY 10004-2489

GRAHAM, R(ICHARD) NEWELL, soft drink bottling company executive; b. Union City, Tenn., June 15, 1947; s. Hardy Moore and Cola Lee (Poindexter) G.; m. Bettie Rene Young, Dec. 28, 1968; children: Richard, Stanford. BA, U. Miss., 1969. Operating ptnr., chief exec. officer Union City Coca-Cola Bottling Co., 1972—; sec., treas. C.C. Coin Caterers Corp., Union City, 1972-93, pres., 1993—, ReelFoot Ordnance Inc., 1996—. Bd. dirs. First State Bank, Union City, Meridian (Miss.) Coca-Cola Bottling Co. Pres. Union City Arts Coun., 1978-79; mem. devel. com. U. Tenn., Martin, 1980-95, vice chmn. devel. coun., 1990-93; treas. St. James Episcopal Ch., Union City, 1987—. With USN, 1969-72. Recipient Project of Yr. award Tenn. Jaycees, Nashville, 1974, Friend of Edn. award Obion County Schs., Union City, 1980. Mem. Assn. Coca-Cola Bottlers Tenn. (pres. 1989-91), Tenn. Soft Drink Assn. (bd. dirs. 1985—), Obion County C. of C. (bd. dirs. 1989-93), Union City Jaycees (pres. 1975, Outstanding Young Man award 1976), Chaine des Rotisseurs (chavalier 1989—), Union City Rotary Club (Paul Harris fellow 1999). Republican. Avocations: wine, food, hunting, military weapons, gardening. Office: Union City Coca-Cola Bottling Co 1915 E Reelfoot Ave Union City TN 38261-6007

GRAHAM, ROBERT, medical association executive; b. Pueblo, Colo., Feb. 15, 1943; married. AB, Earlham Coll., 1965; MD, U. Kans., 1970. Asst. adminstr. agy. goals Health Svc. & Mental Health Admn. Dept. Health Edn. & Welfare, Washington, 1970—73; resident in family practice Bapt. Meml. Hosp., 1974—75; asst. dir. divsn. edn. Am. Acad. Family Physicians, Kansas City, Mo., 1973—76; dep. dir. Bur. Health Manpower, Health Resources Adminstrn. Dept. Health Edn. & Welfare, 1976—78, dep. adminstr., 1978—79; profl. staff mem. subcom. health & sci. rsch. Comty. Labor & Human Resources, U.S. Senate, 1979—80; acting adminstr. health resources adminstrn. Dept. Health & Human Svc., 1981—82, adminstr., 1982—85; exec. v.p. Am. Acad. Family Physicians, Kansas City, Mo., 1985—2001; dir. Agency for Healthcare Research and Quality, Ctr. for Practice and Technology Assessment, 2001—. Mem. staff Program Health Mgmt. Baylor Coll. Medicine, 1976; exec. sec. Grad. Med. Edn. Nat. Adv. Com., 1978—79; bd. dirs. Alliance for Health Referendum, 1994—. Sun Valley Forum Nat. Health. Contbr. articles. Mem.: AMA, Am. Soc. Assn. Execs., Am. Assn. Med. Soc. Execs., Am. Acad. Med. Dirs., Am. Acad. Family Physicians, Assn. Am. Med. Colls., Inst. Medicine of NAS (exec. v.p., CEO 1985—2000). Office: Agency for Healthcare Research and Quality 6010 Executive Blvd, Ste 300 Rockville MD 20852

GRAHAM, ROBERT ALBERT, research physicist; b. Dallas, Feb. 11, 1931; s. John Mark and Eleanor Ball (Evans) G.; m. Lettie Barbara Umphres, Sept. 1, 1951; children: Stephanie Ann Graham Farrow, Mark Lee, Stuart Russell; m. Nell Heard Griffin, Apr. 6, 1996. AA, Allen Jr. Coll., 1951; BS in Civil Engring., U. Tex., 1954, MS in Engring. Mechanics, 1958; DSc in Materials Sci. and Engring., by spl. invitation, Tokyo Inst. Tech., 1990. Rsch. engr. S.W. Rsch. Inst., San Antonio, 1956-57; staff mem. Sandia Labs., Albuquerque, 1958-83; disting. mem. tech. staff Sandia Nat. Labs., Albuquerque, 1983-96; dir. rsch. Tome Group, 1996—. Adviser NAS, Washington, 1982—, Ctr. for Explosives Tech. Rsch., Socorro, N.Mex., 1983-88, U. N.Mex., Albuquerque, 1988—. Editor: Proc. 1981 Shock Conference, Proc. 1983 Shock Conference, N.Mex. Genealogist, 1974—75, High Pressure Exptl. Processing of Ceramic Trans. Tech., 1987; author: Solids Under High Pressure Shock Compression: Mechanics, Physics and Chemistry, 1993; editor (mng.): Shock Waves, an Inter-Jour., 1991—96; editor: (in-chief) Springer-Verlag book series on Shock Compression of Condensed Matter, 1988—96; contbr. articles to profl. jours.; patentee in field. Vice pres. Amigos de las Ams., Albuquerque, 1968 70; host family Am. Field Service, Albuquerque, 1969. 1st lt. U.S. Army, 1954-56. Recipient Excellence award Dept. Energy, 1983, G.B. Sawyer Meml. award Sawyer Rsch. Products, 1984, Am. Phys. Soc. Shock Compression Sci. award, 1993. Fellow: AAAS, Am. Phys. Soc.; mem.: IEEE (life), Phi Theta Kappa, Chi Epsilon, Tau Beta Pi. Home and Office: 608 Cenizo Blvd Uvalde TX 78801-4009

GRAHAM, ROBERT CLARE, III, lawyer; b. Albuquerque, Mar. 24, 1955; s. Robert C. Jr. and Helen (Hoagland) G.; children: Jennifer, Jessica, Kourtney, Kate. BA, DePauw U., 1977; JD magna cum laude, Pepperdine U., 1980. Bar: Mo. 1980, Ill. 1981, U.S. Dist. Ct. (ea. dist.) Mo. 1981. Assoc. Shephard, Sandberg & Phoenix, St. Louis, 1980-82, Suelthaus & Kaplan, PC and predecessors, St. Louis, 1982-91, Armstrong Teasdale, LLP, St. Louis, 1991—. Chmn. Kirkwood (Mo.) Greentree Festival, 1985. Named one of Outstanding Young Men in Am. Jaycees, 1981; recipient Outstanding Service to the Community of Kirkwood award. Mem. ABA, Ill. Bar Assn., Mo. Bar Assn., Bar Assn. Met. St. Louis, St. Louis County Bar Assn. Republican. Presbyterian. Office: Armstrong Teasdale LLP 1 Metropolitan Sq Ste 2600 Saint Louis MO 63102-2740 E-mail: rgraham@armstrongteasdale.com.

GRAHAM, ROGER JOHN, photography and journalism educator; b. Phila., Feb. 16; s. William K. and Peggy E. (Owens) G.; divorced; children: John Roger, Robb Curt; m. Debbie Kenyon, Dec. 28, 1991. AA, Los Angeles Valley Coll., 1961; BA, Calif. State U., Fresno, 1962, MA, 1967; postgrad, UCLA, 1976. Cert. in elem., jr. high, high sch., cmty. coll., counseling and adminstrn. Tchr. Riverdale (Calif.) Sch., 1963, Raisin City (Calif.) Sch., 1964; tchr., counselor Calif. State Prison, Jamestown, 1966; tchr. trainer UCLA's Western Ctr. War on Poverty, 1967; chmn. media arts dept. Los Angeles Valley Coll., Van Nuys, Calif., 1968—, prof. emeritus, 1999—. Vis. prof. Pepperdine U., Malibu, Calif., 1976, Calif. Luth. Coll., Thousand Oaks, 1973, South Africa, 1997; vis. prof. Chapman U., Orange, Calif., 1996, GAIN prof., 1998; del. Calif. Fedn. Tchrs. Conv., 1997; dir. Photography Seminar, Spain, summer 1990. Author: Observations on the Mass Media, 1976, Our Lives in Bits and Pieces, 1998, Patchwork of Life, 2001, L.A. to Philly - Looking Back, 2002; co-author: We Remember WW II, 2003; author: (jour.) Jr. Coll. Jour., 1972; photo illustrator: The San Fernando Valley, 1980, display advertiser: Turlock (Calif.) jour., 1962, Fresno Guide, 1963; contbr. articles to profl. jours. Mem. Tom Hayden's Com. for Schs., Santa Monica, Calif., 1984; pres. Pacific Palisades Dem. Club, 1992; rep. to 41st assembly dist. Calif. Dem. Party State Ctrl. Com., 1993, sec. srs. caucus, 1993—. With USN, 1957. NEH scholar 1981; recipient Mayor's Outstanding Citizen award Los Angeles Mayor's Office, 1974, Extraordinary Service award UCLA, 1971; named one of Outstanding Young Men Am., 1971. Mem. C.C. Journalism Assn. (nat. pres. 1978—, Nat. Dedication Journalism award 1972-76), Journalism Assn. C.C. (pres. Calif. sect. 1972—), Calif. Srs. Caucus (state sec. 1993—), L.A. Profs. Club, Dem. Club Pacific Palisades (pres. 1992-93), Patrons Assn. (bd. dirs. 2000—), L.A. Valley Coll. Retirees Assn. (Outstanding Alumnus award 1999, pres. 1999), Am. Legion (sgt. at arms 1986—, Palisades chpt. adminstrv. officer 1996—), Patrons Assn. (bd. dirs. 2000), Sons of the Desert, SR, Sigma Delta Xi, Phi Delta Kappa, Pi Lambda Theta. Avocation: hiking. Home: 7878 Naylor Ave Los Angeles CA 90045-2909 Office: Los Angeles Valley Coll 5800 Fulton Ave Van Nuys CA 91401-4062

GRAHAM, RONALD LEWIS, mathematician; b. Taft, Calif., Oct. 31, 1935; s. Leo Lewis and Margaret Jane (Anderson) G.; children: Cheryl, Marc. Student, U. Chgo., 1951-54; BS, U. Alaska, 1958; MA, U. Calif., Berkeley, 1961, PhD, 1962; LLD (hon.), Western Mich. U., 1984; DSc, St. Olaf Coll., 1985, U. Alaska, 1988. Mem. tech. staff Bell Labs., Murray Hill, N.J., 1962—, head dept. discrete math., 1968—, dir. Math. Scis. Rsch. Ctr., 1983—, adj. dir. rsch., info. scis. divsn., 1987-95; prof. Rutgers U., 1987—; chief scientist AT&T Labs. Rsch., Florham Park, N.J., 1996-98; Jacobs Endowed chair computer and info. sci. U. Calif. San Diego, 1999—. Regents' prof. UCLA, 1975; vis. prof. computer sci. Stanford U., 1979, 81, Princeton (N.J.) U., 1987, 89; Irwin and Joan Jacobs prof. computer sci. U. Calif. San Diego, La Jolla, 1998—. Author: Ramsey Theory, 1980, Concrete Mathematics, 1989, Erdös on Graphs, 1998. Served with USAF, 1955 59. Recipient Polya prize, 1975; Euler prize, 1993, named Scientist of Yr. World Book Encyclopedia, 1981; scholar Ford Found., 1958, Fairchild Found. Disting. scholar Calif. Inst. Tech., 1983; fellow NSF, 1961, Woodrow Wilson Found., 1962. Fellow AAAS, N.Y. Acad. Scis., Assn. Computing Machinery; mem. NAS (treas. 1996—), Am. Math. Soc. (pres. 1993-94), Math. Assn. Am. (pres.-elect 2002—), Soc. Indsl. and Applied Math., Am. Acad. Arts and Scis., Internat. Jugglers Assn. (past pres.). Office: U Calif San Diego CSE La Jolla CA 92093-0114

GRAHAM, ROSALIND CARLIES, nursing educator; b. Tillery, N.C., Dec. 28, 1945; d. June Carlies and Katie (Mason) Williams; m. William Albert Graham, Jan. 1, 1971 (div. 1976); 1 child, Kenya Patrice. Diploma, Harlem Hosp. Sch. Nursing, 1967; BSN, L.I. U., 1971, postgrad., 2001—. RN Harlem Hosp. Sch. of Nursing N.Y. State Edn. Dept., N.Y.C., 1967—; staff nurse Harlem and Cumberland, N.Y.C. and Bklyn., 1967—; supr. nursing emergency rm. Cumberland Hosp., Bklyn., 1973—, HN clinician, 1976-77; supr. ICU and recovery rm. Harlem Hosp., N.Y.C., 1977-79; staff nurse gynecology, then surgery Queens Hosp. Ctr., Bklyn., 1981-83, asst. head nurse, then surg. ICU, 1983—96; instr., nurse supr. Ridgewood-Bushwick Sr. Citizen Home Care Coun., Inc., 1985-93; field supr. C.A.B.S. Home Attendant Agy., 1993—95; supr. nursing svcs. Brownsville Family Multi Svc. Ctr., 1994—95; clin. instr. Medgar Evers Coll., Bklyn., 1996-98. Paralegal nurse cons. program, L.I. U., 1999-2000. Sec. to bd. trustees and nurses' unit Calvary Bapt. Ch., Jamaica, N.Y., 1998—, corr. sec., Walter S. Pinn Meml. Com. 1995—. Lt. col. U.S. Army Nurse Corps Res., 1977-97, ret. Recipient Cert. of Appreciation Comdr. in Chief, 1997. Mem. AARP, Ret. Officer Assn. (chpt. bd. dirs. 1996-99), Harlem Hosp. Sch. Nursing Alumni Assn. (corr. sec. 1998—), Sigma Beta Delta. Republican. Baptist. Avocations: reading, sewing, computer literate, volunteer work in church, public health issues. Home: c/o Katie Williams 815 Hicks St Apt 3E Brooklyn NY 11231-2441

GRAHAM, SALLY JO, information technology executive, marketing professional; b. Davenport, Iowa, Nov. 29, 1969; d. Katherine Marie Rich and William Gordon Cole; m. Don Emerson Graham, July 25, 1992; children: Justin Joseph, Hunter Emerson. Student, DePaul U., Harvard U. E-commerce cons. BeFree Inc./Looksmart/L90/CBSTV, Chgo., 1997—2002; v.p. e-commerce strategy, owner Deep River Media Inc, Davenport, 2002—. V.p. mktg. AIP, Chgo., 2000—01. Chair Chgo. Internet Mktg. Assn., 1999—2001. Served with USN, 1987—89. Mem.: Chgo. Software Assn. (assoc.). Office: Deep River Media Inc 4931 Torrey Pines Davenport IA 52807 Fax: 563-359-8668. E-mail: grahams50@yahool.com.

GRAHAM, SAM DIXON, urologist; b. Norton, Va., Nov. 5, 1920; s. Sam G. and Ruth Cleveland Flanary; m. Jane Warwick O'Neill, Mar. 28, 1946; children: Sam D. Jr., Gordon Craig, Richard Warwick, Sallie Trigg. MD, U. Va., 1946. Intern U.S. Naval Hosp., Phila., 1946-47, chief of rehab. and phys. medicine, 1947-49; resident urology U. Va., Charlottesville, 1950-53; chief urology Kings Daus. Hosp., Staunton, Va., 1953-85. Clin. prof. urology U. Va. Med. Sch., Charlottesville, 1982-89; cons. in field. Co-author: (chpt.) Physical Medicine and Rehabilitation Approaches in Spinal Cord Injury, 1979; contbr. articles to profl. jours. Bd. trustees Mary Baldwin Coll., Staunton; mayor Town of Staunton; chmn. bd. Planters Bank & Trust, Staunton. Lt. USNR, 1942-49. Recipient U.S. Predl. Citation for care of handicapped, 1967. Mem. Am. Urol. Assn. (pres. 1979-80). Episcopalian. Avocation: golf. Home: 10010 Cedarfield Ct Richmond VA 23233-1935

GRAHAM, SAXON (LLOYD GRAHAM), epidemiology educator; b. Buffalo, Jan. 14, 1922; s. Lloyd S. and Kathryn (Graser) G.; m. Caroline Lee Morgan, June 19, 1948; children: Robin Porter, Saxon Parker, Morgan Graser. BA, Amherst Coll., 1943; MA, Yale U., 1949, PhD, 1951; DSc (hon.), SUNY, Buffalo, 1996. Asst. prof. Chatham Coll., Pitts., 1951-53; asst. prof. biostats. U. Pitts., 1953-56; from asst. prof. to prof. epidemiology dept. sociology and dept. social and preventive medicine SUNY, Buffalo, 1957—, chmn. dept. social and preventive medicine, 1981-91, prof. emeritus, 1992—; assoc. to prin. cancer rsch. scientist Roswell Pk. Cancer Inst., Buffalo, 1956-65, prof. SUNY div., 1967—. Mem. epidemiology and disease control sect. NIH, Bethesda, Md., 1966-70; cons. WHO, Switzerland, 1965-66; dir. demographic studies, Kabul, Afghanistan, 1970-74; chmn. adv. com. to study long-term effects of plutonium Los Alamos (N.Mex.) Nat. Lab., 1976-86; mem. coun. advisors divsn. cancer rsch., resources and ctrs. Nat. Cancer Inst., Bethesda, 1973-77, mem. bd. sci. councillor divsn. cancer prevention and control, 1982-86; mem. sci. coun. Internat. Agy. Rsch. on Cancer, Lyon, France, 1986-90. Author: American Culture, 1957; contbr. numerous articles to profl. jours. Spl. agt. Counter Intelligence Corps, U.S. Army, 1943-46, PTO. Nat. Cancer Inst. grantee, 1969-91. Fellow APHA, Am. Coll. Epidemiology, Am. Sociol. Assn.; mem. Soc. Epidemiologic Rsch. (pres. 1987-88), Am. Epidemiol. Soc., Planned Parenthood, Nat. Abortion Rights League, Orchard Park Country Club, Concord Ski Club (Ellicottville, N.Y.), Scriptores (Buffalo). Republican. Avocations:

piano, oil painting, alpine skiing, golf. Home: 32 Stonehenge Rd Orchard Park NY 14127 Office: SUNY Dept Social & Preventive Medicine 270 Farber Hall Buffalo NY 14214-8001 E-mail: saxon.graham@verizon.net.

GRAHAM, SELDON BAIN, JR., lawyer, engineer; b. Franklin, Tex., Apr. 14, 1926; s. Seldon Bain and Lillian Emma (Struwe) G.; m. Patricia Gene Noah, Feb. 14, 1953; children: Seldon Bain (dec.), Kyle, Laurie. BS, U.S. Mil. Acad., 1951; JD, U. Tex., 1970. Registered profl. engr., Tex. Bar: Tex. 1970, U.S. Dist. Ct. (so. dist.) Tex. 1980, U.S. Ct. Appeals (5th cir.) 1983; cert. in oil, gas and mineral law Tex. Bd. Legal Specialization, 1986-2001. Commd. 2d lt. U.S. Army, 1946, advanced through grades to col., 1979; with Office of Dep. Chief of Staff for Pers., 1979, ret., 1979. Area reservoir engr. ARCO, Okla., 1954-60; div. regulatory engr. Mobil Oil Co., Corpus Christi, 1961-67; counsel Exxon Co. USA, Houston, 1970-85. Decorated Legion of Merit. Mem. Soc. Petroleum Engrs. Methodist. Home and Office: 4713 Palisade Dr Austin TX 78731-4516

GRAHAM, STANLEY BELDING, retired secondary school educator, writer; b. Indpls., May 17, 1928; s. Luther Marion Graham and Ida Belding Graham-Appleby; m. Elizabeth Menges Ramirez-Graham, Sept. 12, 1992; m. Cynthia Ann Davis, Apr. 12, 1962 (dec. Aug. 1991); 2 children. BA, Ohio State U., 1954; MA, Wesleyan U., Middletown, Conn., 1968. Cert. tchr. State of Ohio, 1974. Tchr. Kingsville Sr. H.S., 1955—63, Medina Sr. H.S., 1964—90. Author: (novels) Country Zoo: The Perils of a First-Year Teacher, 1998, Meditations of a Great Lakes Sailor, 2001, (biography) Portrait of a Lady: A Biography, 2001, (novels) The Next Train to Chicago, 2002. Sgt. U.S. Army, 1946—49. Recipient numerous stipends for summer sci. insts., U. Vt., Fordham U., U. Redlands, Boston Coll., Kent State, NSF, 1959—84. Mem.: Ohio Ret. Tchrs. Assn. (life). Avocations: photography, carpentry, swimming, travel, writing novels and biographies. Home: 10 Bradley Ct Medina OH 44256 E-mail: sgraham101@aol.com.

GRAHAM, STEPHEN MICHAEL, lawyer; b. Houston, May 1, 1951; s. Frederick Mitchell and Lillian Louise (Miller) G.; m. Joanne Marie Sealock, Aug. 24, 1974; children: Aimee Elizabeth, Joseph Sealock, Jessica Anne. BS, Iowa State U., 1973; JD, Yale U., 1976. Bar: Wash. 1977. Assoc. Perkins Coie, Seattle, 1976-83, ptnr., 1983-2000, Orrick, Herrington & Sutcliffe LLP, Seattle, 2000—. Bd. dirs. Wash. Spl. Olympics, Seattle, 1979—83, pres., 1982—83; trustee Friends of the Children of King County, 2002—; mem. Seattle Fair Campaign Practices Commn., 1982—88; mem. exec. com. Cornish Coll. Arts, 1989—91, trustee, 1994—96, Seattle Repertory Theatre, 1993—95, Seattle Children's Theatre, 1996—98, mem. exec. com., 1997—98; trustee Fred Hutchinson Cancer Rsch. Ctr., 1999—2003; mem. bd. exec. com. Lawyers WSA, 2002—; trustee Arboretum Found., 1994—96; mem. Seattle Bd. Ethics, 1982—88, chmn., 1983—88; mem. exec. com. Sch. Law Yale U., 1988—92, 1993—97; bd. dirs. Wash. Biotech. and Biomed. Assn., 1996—, mem. exec. com., 1997—. Mem.: Wash. State Bar Assn., ABA, Rainier Club, Wash. Athletic Club. Episcopalian. Office: Orrick Herrington & Sutcliffe Ste 900 719 Second Ave Seattle WA 98104-7063

GRAHAM, STEVEN ANTHONY, writer; b. Portland, Oreg. M in Theol. Studies, George Fox U., 2002; postgrad., Portland State U., 2002—. Pvt. profl. mime, ny, USSR, 1978—2002; martial arts instr. Portland, 1983—84; acting instr. Troutman Modeling Agy., Portland, 1984—86, ABC-Kids, Portland, 1984—86; profl. model Nike, Glamour, N.Y.C., 1984—89; profl. actor Pub. Theater, CBS, ABC, N.Y.C., 1984—90; acting instr. The Acting Co., Portland, 1985—86, The Weist-Barron Acting Sch., New York, NY, 1986—87; profl. actor Fox TV among others, L.A., 1990—97; tchg. asst. Bibl. Hebrew George Fox U., Portland, 2000—01, tchg. asst. Koine Greek, 2001—02, rsch. asst. Author: (novels) Tell of His Glory: Growing up Penguin-Style, Hit It Again, (screenplays) BT, The Odds are in my favor: An Adaptation of Elijah on Mount Carmel, (plays) Compromise, never!...well, probably. An Adaptation of the Gospel of Jude, The Wizard of Uz: An Adaptation of the Book of Job, Trials: An Adaptation of the Gospel to the Philippians, Manasseh in Scripture and Tradition: An Analysis of Ancient Sources and the Development of the Manasseh Tradition; contbr. articles to profl. publs. Developed and oversaw youth ministry Willamette Valley Weslyan Ch., Wilsonville, Oreg., 1998—99; youth counselor Kansas City (Kans.) Youth For Christ, 1996—97. Grantee Richter Rsch. grantee, George Fox U., 2001. Mem.: Soc. Bibl. Lit. (corr.).

GRAHAM, SUSAN LOIS, computer science educator, consultant; b. Cleve, Sept. 16, 1942; m., 1971 AB in Math., Harvard U., 1964; MS, Stanford U., 1966, PhD in Computer Sci., 1971. Assoc. research scientist, adj. asst. prof. computer sci. Courant Inst. Math. Sci., NYU, 1969-71; asst. prof. computer sci. U. Calif., Berkeley, 1971-76, assoc. prof., 1976-81, prof. computer sci., 1981—. Vis. scientist Stanford U., 1981; mem. adv. com. div. computer and computation rsch. NSF, 1987-92, mem. program for sci. and tech. ctrs., 1987-91; mem. vis. com. for elec. engrng. and computer sci. MIT, 1989—; mem. vis. com. for engrng. and applied sci. Calif. Inst. Tech., 1994—; mem. vis. com. for applied scis. Harvard U., 1995—; mem. commn. on phys. sci., math. and applications NRC, 1992-95; mem. President's Com. on Nat. Medal Sci., 1994-96. Co-editor Communications, 1975-79; editor Transactions on Programming Languages and Systems, 1978-92. NSF grantee Fellow AAAS, Assn. for Computing Machinnery, Am. Acad. Arts and Sci.; mem. IEEE, NAE. Office: U Calif-Berkeley Computer Sci Div EECS 771 Soda Hall 1776 Berkeley CA 94720-1776

GRAHAM, SUSETTE RYAN, retired English educator; b. Plattsburgh, N.Y., Aug. 31, 1929; d. Andrew Warren Ryan and Lillian Grace MacDougall; m. James H. Graham, July 1, 1950; children: Marguerite, Andrea, James Jr., Martha, Amy, Matthew. BA, Wellesley Coll., 1950; MA, U. Rochester, 1967, PhD, 1987. Prof. English Nazareth Coll., Rochester, N.Y., 1963-93, prof. emerita, 1993; ret. Contbr. articles, revs. to profl. jours. Fulbright sr. lectr., Poland, 1992-93. Mem. AAUW, MLA, Am. Acad. Poets. Democrat. Avocations: travel, reading, genealogical research. Home: 10 Arbor Ct Fairport NY 14450-1602 also: 603 Pipers Ln Surfside Beach SC 29575-5846 E-mail: jamesgraham@sc.rr.com.

GRAHAM, SYLVIA ANGELENIA, wholesale distributor, retail buyer; b. Charlotte, N.C., Mar. 27, 1950; d. John Wesley and Willie Myrl (Ray) White; m. James Peter Cleveland Fisher, Apr. 23, 1967 (div. Sept. 1972); 1 child, Wesley James Fisher; m. Harold Walker Graham, Sept. 14, 1972 (dec. June 1994); 1 child, Angelique Jane Graham. Cert., Naval Reserve Force Detachment Mgmt. Sch., 1985; air cargo specialist cert., Air U., 1987. Store owner Naval Air Terminal/Naval Transp. Support Unit, Norfolk, Va., 1985—; fleet liaison technician Naval Material Transp. Orgn., Norfolk, 1988-93; passenger svc. rep. Naval Transp. Support Unit Naval Material Transport Orgn., Norfolk, Va., 1996—; distbr. Blair Divsn. of Merchants, Lynchburg, Va., 1988—, Mason Shoe Co., Chippewa Falls, Wis., 1988—, mem. dealer adv. bd., 1997—; driver Greater Charlotte Transp. Co., 1988—, Watkins Products, Winona, Minn., 1992—, Citizens Def. Products, St. Joseph, Mo., 1993—; dealer Creative Card Co.ducts, Chgo., 1995—, Home Showcase Products, Lynchburg, 1995—; driver Carolina Transp., Charlotte, 2000—; distbr. Navy Leader Tng. Unit, Little Creek, Va., 2002. Jewelry dealer Merlite Industries, N.Y.C., 1994; dealer Creative Cards, Chgo., 1995—; mem. Nat. Safety Coun., Charlotte, 1988—, "C" team Watkins Products, Lincoln, Nebr., 1992—; sec. Popular Club Plan, Dayton, N.J., 1990—; pub. Citizens Def. Products, 1993—; sponsor The Paralyzed Vets. Am., Wilton, N.H., 1994—; mem. RBC Ministries, Grand Rapids, Mich., 1998—. Crusader Cancer Ctr. for Detection and Preventin Drive, Seattle, 1991—; block chmn. Easter Seal Soc., 1988—; census taker Census 2000, Charlotte, 2000—; active ARC. With USN, 1991, Persian Gulf; USNR, 1992, Somalian Relief Effort; USN, 1993-94. Named Top Dealer, Home Showcase Products, Lynchburg, Va. Mem. NAFE, Am. Assn. Ret. Persons, Nat. Enlisted Res. Assn., Naval Enlisted Res. Assn., First Class Petty Office Assn., Nat. Pk. and Conservation Assn., Nat. Trust Hist. Preservation, Direct Selling Assn., Navy League of the U.S., Libr. of Congress Assocs., Nature Conservancy, Nat. Audubon Soc., N.C. Sheriffs Assn. (hon. citizen mem. 2000-03), Handyman Club Am. (ofcl.). mem. Am. Red Cross United Response Citizen Corps, 2003. Employer Support of the Gaurd and Res., 2003. Democrat. Pentecostal. Avocations: stamp collecting, reading, bicycling, dancing, painting. Home: PO Box 16066 Charlotte NC 28297-6066

GRAHAM, SYLVIA SWORDS, secondary school educator, retired; b. Atlanta, Nov. 15, 1935; d. Metz Jona and Christine (Gurley) Swords; m. Thomas A. Graham, Nov. 29, 1958 (div. 1970). BA, Mary Washington Coll., Fredericksburg, Va., 1957; MEd, W. Ga. Coll., Carrollton, 1980; SEd, W. Ga. Coll., 1981; postgrad., Coll. William and Mary, 1964-67. Tchr. Atlanta pub. schs., 1957-58, Newark County pub. schs., Newark, Calif., 1960-61; tchr. history Virginia Beach (Va.) pub. schs., 1964-75, Paulding County pub. schs., Dallas, Ga., 1976-97, ret., 1997. Tour dir. Paulding High Sch. trips, Far East, 1985, USSR, 1989, Australia, 1988-89. County chmn. Rep. Party, 1987-89, county chmn. for re-election of Newt Gingrich, 1982; mem. Gingrich edn. com., 1983, 88; 1st vice chmn. 6th Congl. Dist., 1989-90, chmn. 1989-90; chmn. 7th Congl. Dist., 1992-95; del. Nat. Rep. Conv., 1992. Named Star Tchr., Paulding County C. of C., Dallas, Ga., 1989, 97. Mem. Dallas Woman's Club (pres. 1982-84, 1st v.p. 1986-88, pub. affairs chmn. 1986—, treas. for Civic Ctr. fund 1984—), Phi Kappa Phi. Republican. Baptist. Avocations: travel, reading, piano, bridge. E-mail: maxitaxi2@earthlink.net.

GRAHAM, THOMAS, JR., lawyer; b. Louisville, Oct. 9, 1933; s. Thomas and Charlotte (Henriques) G.; m. Clover Nicholas, Aug. 10, 1968 (div. Dec. 1982); children: Elizabeth Malcolm, Thomas Lawrence, Clover Chace; m. Christine Coffey Ryan, Sept. 26, 1983; stepchildren: Thomas Coffey Ryan, Mary Christine Ryan. AB, Princeton U., 1955; postgrad., L'institute des Sciences Politiques, 1955-56; JD, Harvard U., 1961. Bar: Ky. 1961, D.C. 1963, N.Y. 1966. Law clk. U.S. Cir. Ct. Appeals (D.C. cir.), 1961-62; chief counsel U.S. Ho. Reps. Com. on Banking and Currency, Washington, 1962-63; counsel to compt. of currency Treasury Dept., Washington, 1963-64; assoc. Wyatt, Grafton & Sloss, Louisville, 1964-66, Shearman & Sterling, N.Y.C., 1966-69; lawyer Office of Sec. USAF, Washington, 1969-70; asst. gen. counsel U.S. Arms Control and Disarmament Agy., Washington, 1970-73, dep. gen. counsel, 1973-77, gen. counsel, 1977-81, 83-94, dir. Congl. rels. and pub. affairs, 1981-83, acting dir., 1993, acting dep. dir., 1993-94; spl. rep. of Pres. (amb.) Arms Control, Non-Proliferation and Disarmament, 1994-97; ret., 1997. Legal advisor U.S. SALT II del., Geneva, 1974-79; legal advisor U.S. del. to rev. conf. Nonproliferation Treaty, Geneva, 1980; sr. arms control advisor U.S. del. to negotiations on Intermediate Range Nuclear Forces, 1981-82; legal advisor U.S. del. to Conf. Disarmament, Geneva, 1985; legal advisor U.S. del. to negotiation on nuc. and space arms, Geneva, 1985-88, U.S. del. to ABM Treaty Rev. Conf., Geneva, 1988; sr. arms control advisor, legal advisor U.S. del. Conventional Armed Forces in Europe negotiation, 1989-90; legal advisor U.S. del. START Negotiation, 1991, START II Negotiation, 1992; chmn. U.S. del. ABM Treaty rev. conf., 1993, U.S. rep. Nonproliferation Treaty Ext. Conf., 1993-95; chmn. U.S. Del. Conventional Armed Forces Europe rev. com., 1996; chmn. bd. dirs. Mex. Energy Corp., 1997—; lectr. U. Va. Law Sch., 1984-91; adj. prof. Georgetown U. Law Ctr., 1991-93, Georgetown Sch. Fgn. Svc., 1991-94, Stanford U., 1999-; U. Washington, 2002-; pres. Lawyers Alliance for World Security, Washington, 1997-2002, chmn. bd. dirs., 2002-, spl. counsel Morgan, Lewis and Bockius, Washington, 2002-; bd. dirs. Thorium Power Inc.; sr. cons. Eisenhower Inst., Washington, 2002-. Author: Disarmament Sketches, Thirty Years of Arms Control and International Law, 2002, Cornerstones of Security, Arms Control Treaties in the Modern Era, 2003. Spl. asst. to chmn. United Citizens for Nixon-Agnew, Washington, 1968. With U.S. Army, 1956-58, 1st lt. U.S. Army Res., 1958-61. Mem. ABA (chmn. com. on arms control 1986-94), D.C. Bar Assn., N.Y. State Bar Assn., Ky. Bar Assn., Coun. on Fgn. Rels., Chevy Chase Club, Cosmos Club, Met. Club, Louisville Country Club, Ausable Club. Republican. Episcopalian. Avocations: tennis, golf, skiing, hiking. Home: 7609 Glenbrook Rd Bethesda MD 20814 Office: Morgan Lewis & Bockius 1111 Pennsylvania Ave NW Washington DC 20004

GRAHAM, THOMAS HILD, neurologist; b. Abington, Pa., Nov. 6, 1953; s. John Harry and Mary Louise (Hild) G.; m. Susan Mae Houpt; children: Lauren, Nathaniel, Jeremy. BS in Biology, Ursinus Coll., 1974; MD, Pa. State U., 1978. Bd. cert. neurology Am. Bd. Psychiatry and Neurology; bd. cert. electrodiagnostic medicine Am. Bd. Electrodiagnostic Medicine, added qualifications in clin. neurophysiology Am. Bd. Psychiatry and Neurology. Intern in medicine Hosp. of U. of Pa., Phila., 1978-79, resident in neurology, 1979-82, fellow in neurology, 1982-83; neurologist Neurology Cons., Bryn Mawr, Pa., 1983-89, ptnr., neurologist, 1989—; chief divsn. neurology Bryn Mawr Hosp., 1994-98; system chief neurology divsn. Main Line Health Hosps., 1998—. Clin. asst. prof. neurology U. Pa. Med. Coll., Phila., 1983—; attending neurologist Bryn Mawr Hosp. and Paoli Meml. Hosp., 1983—, Phoenixville (Pa.) Hosp., 1983—; cons. neurologist courtesy staff Chester County Hosp., West Chester, Pa., 1995—. Author book chpts. in field of neurology; contbg. editor med. periodical; contbr. articles, abstracts to neurologic jours. Recipient Nat. Rsch. Svc. award Pub. Health Svc., 1982; Hammond Meml. scholar Hershey Med. Coll., 1977. Fellow Am. Acad. Neurology, Stroke Coun. of Am. Heart Assn.; mem. Pa. Med. Soc., Chester County Med. Soc., Phila. Neurol. Soc. Schwenkfelder. Avocation: music. Office: Neurology Cons Ste 106 Bryn Mawr Med Bldg 875 County Line Rd Bryn Mawr PA 19010-3113

GRAHAM, THOMAS PEGRAM, JR., pediatric cardiologist; b. Charlotte, N.C., Mar. 1, 1937; s. Thomas P. and Margaret (Martin) G.; m. Carol Ann Noggle, June 1, 1960; children: Bethany, Brent, Brooke. AB, Duke U., 1959, MD, 1963. Diplomate Am. Bd. Pediatrics. Resident in pediatrics Children's Hosp., Boston, 1963-65; research assoc. Nat. Heart Inst., Bethesda, Md., 1965-67; fellow in pediatric cardilolgy Duke U., Durham, N.C., 1967-69, asst. prof. pediatrics, 1969-71; dir. pediatric cardiology, prof. pediatrics Vanderbilt U., Nashville, 1971—, vice chmn. pediat. dept., 1989—. Contbr. articles to profl. jours. Fellow Am. Acad. Pediatrics (exec. com. 1972-74), Am. Coll. Cardiology (chmn. pediatric cardiology subcom. 1979-86, bd. trust 1996—), Am. Heart Assn. (chmn. council on cardiovascular disease in the young 1981-83) Presbyterian. Office: Vanderbilt Med Ctr Div Ped & Cardiology D2220 Med Ctr N Nashville TN 37232-0001 also: 21st S At Garland Ave S Nashville TN 37232-0001

GRAHAM, THOMAS RICHARD, lawyer; b. Shelbyville, Ind., Nov. 23, 1942; s. Kermit A. and Esther L. (Thompson) G.; m. Rosemond Eve Toner, June 12, 1965; children: Rachel Graham Cody, Thomas Ian. BA, Ind. U., 1965; JD, Harvard U., 1968. Bar: D.C. 1970, U.S. Supreme Ct. 1973. Exec. asst. to pres. Ford Motor de Venezuela, Caracas, 1968-70; vis. prof. law U. Catolica Andres Bello, Caracas, 1968-70; legal officer UN, Geneva, 1970-73; dep. gen. counsel Office U.S. Trade Rep., Washington, 1974-79; vis. prof. U. N.C., Chapel Hill, 1979-80; assoc. Patton, Boggs & Blow, Washington, 1980-81; counsel, ptnr. Kilpatrick & Cody, Washington, 1981-85; ptnr. Skadden, Arps, Slate, Meagher & Flom, Washington, 1985-2000, King & Spalding, Washington, 2000—. Adj. prof. law Georgetown U., Washington, 1977-85, 95-98; vis. fellow Brookings Instn., Washington, 1978-79; sr. assoc. Carnegie Endowment, Washington, 1979-80. Co-editor: Managing Trade Relations in the 1980's, 1983, Trade and Environment, 1982; contbr. articles to profl. jours. Chief advisor on internat. trade John Glenn Presdl. Campaign, 1984. Mem. ABA (chmn. subcom. exports 1985-89), Am. Soc. Internat. Law (chmn. internat. econ. law sect. 1981-83). Avocations: history, sports. Home: 6115 33rd St NW Washington DC 20015-2403 Office: King & Spalding Ste 1000 1730 Pennsylvania Ave NW Washington DC 20006-4706

GRAHAM, TONI, writer; b. San Francisco, June 24, 1945; d. Joseph Foster and Maxine E. (Johnson) Avila; m. J. Richard Graham, Nov. 23, 1972 (div. 1987); 1 child, Salvatore Z. Graham. BA, New Coll. Calif., Calif., 1989; MA in English, San Francisco State U., 1992, MFA in creative writing, 1995. Lectr. creative writing San Francisco State U., 1992; asst. prof. English Okla. State U., 2000—; fiction editor The Cimarron Rev.; lectr. creative writing San Francisco U., 1998. Lectr., U. Calif., Santa Cruz, 1995-97, Chabot Coll., 1996-97, Dominican Coll., 1996-97, Santa Clara U., 1997-98, Chico State U., 1999—; vis. fiction writer, 1999-2000. Author: The Daiquiri Girls, 1998; contbr. short fiction to mags., including Am. Fiction, Five Fingers Rev., Miss. Rev., Ascent, Clockwatch Rev., Miss. Mud, Worcester Rev., Beloit Fiction, Meridian, River City, Green Mountain Rev., Chiron Rev., Other Voices. Bd. dirs. O'Collegian newspaper Okla. State U. Harrold scholar, 1986; recipient, Calif. Short Story Competition Award, 1987, Herbert Wilner Meml. Award short story, 1994; story, Shadow Boxing cited in Pushcart Prize XIV-Best of the Small Presses, 1989; recipient,Associated Writing Programs Fiction award,1997. Mem. MLA Assoc. Writing Programs, Hemingway Soc., Golden Key Honor Soc., PEN, Am. Culture Assn. Office: Okla State U English Dept Stillwater OK 74078-0001

GRAHAM, TONY RANDALL, anesthesiologist; b. Nashville, Apr. 18, 1961; m. Frances Higgins, Mar 23, 1985; children: Mary Elizabeth, Daniel. BA, U. Tenn., 1983, MD, 1987. Diplomate Am. Bd. Anesthesiology. Resident U. S.C. Sch. Medicine, Columbia, 1990-93; anesthesiologist Sangamon Associated Anesthesiologists, Springfield, Ill., 1993-95, Holston Anesthesia Assocs., Kingsport, Tenn., 1995—2002, Anesthesiology Svcs. of Anderson, 2002—. Mem. Soc. Cardiovascular Anesthesiologists. Office: Anesthesia Svcs of Anderson 300-C E Greenville St Anderson SC 29620 E-mail: tonygraham@charter.net.

GRAHAM, WARREN KENYON, counselor; b. Queens, NY, Nov. 23, 1971; s. Warren Lee Graham and Ruth Ann Howard; m. Jennifer Gabrielle Baker, Jan. 8, 1995; children: Ashanti Maliq, Jordan Tyler. BA, SUNY, Old Westbury, 2003. Cert. domestic violence counselor Nat. Assn. Forensic Counselors, 2003; Notary Public NY, 1995. Criminal justice liaison Human Svcs. Ctrs., Inc., Elmhurst, NY, 2001—02; intern Nassau County Dept. Drug and Alcohol Abuse, East Meadow, NY, 2002; criminal ct. liaison Choices Mental Health Ctr., LI, 2002. Cons. Ashanti Pub. Co., Inc., Uniondale, NY, 1995—. Author: Indigo Soul: Collage of Life & Love, (poetry) It is a sin (Best Poetry of Yr., 2002), Dust of Time (Editor's Choice award, 2001), Eternity (Editor's Choice award, 2000), Spanish Fly (Best Poets of 2001, 2001), Everyday (Poetry's Elite, 2000). Recipient Semester Honors, SUNY Old Westbury Coll., 2002, 1997, Silver Svc. Star, Chase Manhattan Bank, 1994, 1995 (2), 1996, 1997. Mem.: APA (assoc.), Am. Soc. Notaries (assoc.), Assn. Black Psychologists (assoc.). Achievements include patents pending for virtual reality substance abuse disorders database. Personal E-mail: mr_psychmajor@yahoo.com.

GRAHAM, WARREN KIRKLAND, dentist; b. Albuquerque, July 22, 1938; s. Warren Reno and Alice Barbara (Eller) G.; m. Nancy Lou White, Apr. 2, 1966; children: John Warren, Jason Kirkland. BS, U. N.Mex., 1960; DDS, Baylor U., 1964. Pvt. practice dentistry, Albuquerque, 1965-89; dental dir. Farmington Cmty. Health Ctr., 1989—; corp. dental dir. Presbyn. Med. Svcs., 1994—; adj. asst. prof. Coll. Dentistry, Baylor U., 1995—; adj. asst. prof. dental programs U. N.Mex., 1996-2000, U. Mo. Dental Sch., Kansas City, 2000—. Mem. N.Mex. Bd. Dental Health Care, 1997-2002, chmn., 2000-02; bd. dirs., examiner Western Regional Exam Bd., 1998-2002; implementor area sr. citizens' dental program, 1985. Bd. dirs. N.Mex. Coun. on Smoking and Health, 1969-71; mem. N.Mex. Medicaid Adv. Bd., 1972-77, Mid Rio Grande Health Planning Coun., 1972-76; chmn. N.Mex. Health Sys. Agy. Subarea Coun., Dist. II, 1977-78. Capt. USAF, 1964-65. Fellow Am. Coll. Dentists, Acad. Gen. Dentistry (pres. Albuquerque chpt. 1970), Pierre Fouchard Acad., mem. ADA, N.Mex. Acad. Gen. Dentistry (pres. 1990-91), N.Mex. Dental Assn. (sec.-treas. 1982-86, v.p. 1986-87, pres. 1988-89), Albuquerque Dist. Dental Soc. (pres. 1976), Am. Assn. Pub. Health Dentistry, Nat. Network Oral Health Access, Am. Assn. Dental Examiners, Sigma Chi, Delta Sigma Delta. Republican. Mem. Lds Ch. Office: Presbyn Med Svcs Farmington Cmty Health Ctr PO Box 3239 Farmington NM 87499-3239

GRAHAM, WILLIAM ALBERT, religion educator, history educator; b. Raleigh, NC, Aug. 16, 1943; s. William Albert and Evelyn (Powell) G.; m. Barbara Stecconi, Aug. 26, 1983; 1 child, Powell Louis. Student, U. Goettingen, Fed. Republic Germany, 1964-65; BA summa cum laude, U. N.C., 1966; AM, Harvard U., 1970, PhD, 1973. Lectr. Islamic religion Harvard U., Cambridge, Mass., 1973-74, asst. prof., 1974-79, Allston Burr sr. tutor, 1975-77, assoc. prof., 1979-81, sr. lectr. history of religion, 1981-85, prof. history of religion and Islamic studies, 1985—2001, chmn. Study of Religion, 1987-90, Murray A. Albertson prof. Middle Eastern studies, 2001—, dir. Ctr. for Middle Eastern Studies, 1990-96, chmn. Near Eastern Langs. and Civilizations, 1997—2002; master Currier House Harvard Coll., 1991—; dean and John Lord O'Brian prof. divinity Harvard Div. Sch., 2002—. Chmn. Coun. on Grad. Studies in Religion, 1993-96; vis. lectr. Friedrich-Wilhelms U., Bonn, 1982-83. Author: Divine Word and Prophetic Word in Early Islam, 1977 (Am. Coun. Learned Socs. book prize 1978), Beyond the Written Word, 1987, 93; co-author: Heritage of World Civilizations, 1986, 6th edit., 2003, Three Faiths, One God, 2002; co-editor: Islamfiche: Readings from Islamic Primary Sources, 1987; mem. editl. bd. jours. and ency.; contbr. articles to profl. jours. Woodrow Wilson Found. grad. fellow Harvard U., 1966-67, Danforth Found. grad. fellow Harvard U., 1966-73, John Simon Guggenheim Found. fellow, Germany, India, 1982-83, Alexander von Humboldt Found. fellow, Germany, 1982-83, IRCICA quinquinial award for excellence in rsch. Islamic Studies, Orgn. of the Islamic Conf., 2000; Keller vis. Scholar in religion, HighPoint U., 2001. Mem. Am. Soc. for Study of Religion, Am. Acad. Religion, Middle East Studies Assn., Am. Oriental Soc., Am. Alpine Club, Phi Beta Kappa. Democrat. Avocation: tech. mountaineering. Home: 44 Francis Ave Cambridge MA 02138 Office: Harvard Divinity Sch 45 Francis Ave Cambridge MA 02138

GRAHAM, WILLIAM B. pharmaceutical company executive; b. Chgo., July 14, 1911; s. William and Elizabeth (Burden) G.; m. Edna Kanaley, June 15, 1940 (dec.); children: William J., Elizabeth Anne, Margaret, Robert B.; m. Catherine Van Duzer, July 23, 1984. SB cum laude, U. Chgo., 1932, JD cum laude, 1936; LLD, Carthage Coll., 1974, Lake Forest Coll., 1983; LLD (hon.), U. Ill., 1988; LHD, St. Xavier Coll. and Nat. Coll. Edn., 1983; LHD (hon.), Barat Coll., 1997, DePaul U., 1998. Bar: Ill. 1936. Patent lawyer Dyrenforth, Lee, Chritton & Wiles, 1936-40; mem. Dawson & Ooms, 1940-45; v.p., mgr. Baxter Internat., Inc., Deerfield, Ill., 1945-53, pres., 1953-71, CEO, 1960-80, chmn. bd., 1980-85, sr. chmn., 1989-95, chmn. emeritus, 1995—. Prof., chair Weizmann Inst. Sci., Rehoboth, Israel, 1978; lectr. U. Chgo., 1981-82. Chmn. bd. dirs. Lyric Opera Chgo.; bd. dirs. Big Shoulders, Wendy Will Care Fedn., Chgo. Hort. Soc.; trustee Orchestral Assn., U. Chgo., Evanston (Ill.) Hosp.; past pres. Cmty. Fund of Chgo. Recipient V.I.P. award Lewis Found., 1963, Disting. Citizen award Ill. St. Andrew Soc., 1974, Decision Maker of Yr. award Am. Statis. Assn., 1974, Marketer of Yr. award AMA, 1976, Found. award Kidney Found., 1981, Chicagoan of Yr. award Chgo. Boys Club, 1981, Bus. Statesman of Yr. award Harvard Bus. Sch. Club Chgo., 1983, Achievement award Med. Tech. Svcs., 1983, Disting. Fellows award Internat. Ctr. for Artificial Organs and Transplantations, 1982, Chgo. Civic award DePaul U., 1986, Internat. Visitors Golden Medallion award U. Ill., 1988, Chgo. medal U. Chgo., 1992, Laureate award Lincoln Acad. Ill., 1992, Lyric Opera Carol Fox award, 1992, Good Scout award N.E. Coun. Boy Scouts Am., 1993, Making History award Chgo. Hist. Soc., 1996; recognized for pioneering work Health Industry Mfrs. Assn., 1981; inducted Jr. Achievement Chgo. Bus. Hall of Fame, 1986, Modern Healthcare Hall of Fame, 1994, Art Alliance Legend award Dreihaus Found., 2000. Mem. Am. Pharm. Mfrs. Assn. (past pres.), Ill. Mfrs. Assn. (past pres.), Pharm. Mfrs. Assn. (past chmn., award for spl. distinction leadership 1981), Chgo. Club (past pres.), Commonwealth Club, Comml. Club, Indian Hill Club, Casino Club, Old Elm Club, Seminole Club, Everglades Club, Bath and Tennis Club, Links Club, Phi Beta Kappa, Sigma Xi, Phi Delta Phi. Home: 40 Devonshire Ln Kenilworth IL 60043-1205 Office: Baxter Internat Inc 1 Baxter Pkwy Deerfield IL 60015-4625

GRAHAM, WILLIAM EDGAR, JR., lawyer, retired utility company executive; b. Jackson Springs, N.C., Dec. 31, 1929; s. William Edgar and Minnie Blanch (Autry) G.; children: William McLaurin, John McMillan, Sally Faircloth. AB, U. N.C., 1952, JD with honors, 1956. Bar: N.C. bar. Law clk. U.S. Ct. Appeals 4th Circuit, 1956-57; individual practice law Charlotte, N.C., 1957-69; judge N.C. Ct. Appeals, 1969-73; sr. v.p., gen. counsel Carolina Power & Light Co., Raleigh, N.C., 1973-81, exec. v.p., 1981-85, vice chmn., 1985-93; counsel Hunton & Williams, 1994—. Served with USAF, 1952-54. Mem. ABA, N.C. Bar Assn., Wake County Bar Assn. Presbyterian. Home: 510-508 Glenwood Ave Raleigh NC 27603 Office: Hunton & Williams PO Box 109 Raleigh NC 27602-0109 E-mail: dgraham@hunton.com.

GRAHAM, WILLIAM FRANKLIN (WILLIAM FRANKLIN GRAHAM), evangelist; b. Charlotte, N.C., Nov. 7, 1918; s. William Franklin and Morrow (Coffey) G.; m. Ruth McCue Bell, Aug. 13, 1943; children: Virginia Leftwich, Anne Morrow, Ruth Bell, William Franklin, Nelson Edman. BA, Wheaton Coll. (Ill.), 1943; ThB, Fla. Bible Inst., Tampa, 1940; ThB numerous hon. degrees, including, Houghton (N.Y.) Coll., Baylor U., The Citadel, William Jewell Coll. Ordained to ministry So. Baptist Conv., 1939; minister First Bapt. Ch., Western Springs, Ill., 1943-45; 1st v.p. Youth for Christ, Internat., 1945-50; pres. Northwestern Coll., Mpls., 1947-52; founder World Wide Pictures, Inc., Burbank, Calif.; worldwide evangelistic campaigns, 1949—; speaker weekly Hour of Decision radio program, 1950—; also periodic Crusade Telecasts; founder Billy Graham Evangelistic Assn.; hon. chmn. Lausanne Congress

World Evangelization, 1974. Author: Peace with God, 1953, World Aflame, 1965, The Jesus Generation, 1971, Angels: God's Secret Agents, 1975, How To Be Born Again, 1977, The Holy Spirit, 1978, Till Armageddon, 1981, A Biblical Standard for Evangelists, 1984, Approaching Hoofbeats, 1983, Unto the Hills, 1986, Facing Death and The Life After, 1987, Answers to Life's Problems, 1988, Hope for the Troubled Heart, 1991, Storm Warning, 1992, (autobiography) Just As I Am, 1997, Hope for Each Day, 2002; also writer of daily newspaper column. Recipient numerous awards, including Bernard Baruch award, 1955, Humane Order of African Redemption, 1960, Gold award George Washington Carver Meml. Inst., 1964, Horatio Alger award, 1965, Internat. Brotherhood award NCCJ, 1971, Sylvanus Thayer award Assn. Grads. U.S. Mil. Acad., 1972, Franciscan Internat. award, 1972, Man of South award, 1975, Liberty Bell award, 1975, Templeton prize for Progress in Religion, 1982, Presdl. Medal of Freedom, 1983, William Booth award Salvation Army, 1989, Congl. Gold Medal, 1996; Freedom award Ronald Reagan Presdl. Found., 2000, Hon. Knight Comdr. Order British Empire, 2001. Baptist. Office: Billy Graham Evangelistic Assn PO Box 9313 Minneapolis MN 55440-9313

GRAHAM, WILLIAM HENRY, lawyer; b. Newark, Jan. 6, 1946; s. Robert and Ruth Ellen (McElroy) G.; m. Lorraine Majeski, Mar. 23, 1969; 1 child, Allison. BA, Ohio State U., 1968; JD, Rutgers U., 1973; LLM in Corp. Law, NYU, 1978, LLM in Trade Regulation Law, 1980. Law clk. Connell Foley & Geiser, Roseland, N.J., 1971-73, atty., 1973-77, Bethlehem (Pa.) Steel Corp., 1977-79, sr. atty., 1979-81, gen. atty., 1981-85, asst. gen. counsel, 1985-89, asst. gen. counsel, asst. sec., 1989-92, gen. counsel, 1992-95, v.p., gen. counsel, sec., 1995-2000, sr. v.p., gen. counsel, sec., 2000—. Bd. dirs. Atlantic Legal Found., N.Y.C., 1986—; bd. mem. Pa. Civil Justice Coalition, Harrisburg, Pa., 1987—; chmn. Pa. Task Force on Product Liability, Harrisburg, 1989—. 1st lt. U.S. Army, 1969-71, Vietnam. Mem. ABA, N.J. Bar Assn., Pa. Bar Assn., Trial Attys. N.J., Am. Iron and Steel Inst., Assn. Gen. Counsel. Lutheran. Office: Bethlehem Steel Corp 1170 8th Ave Bethlehem PA 18016-7600 E-mail: william.graham@bethsteel.com.

GRAHAM, WILLIAM PIERSON, investment banker, entrepreneur; b. East St. Louis, Ill., Feb. 19, 1935; s. William Schley and Opal Elizabeth (Gray) G.; m. Margaret Newton McDowell, Sept. 30, 1961; children: Lisa, Heather, Jennifer. BS, U. Ill., 1956. With IBM Corp., 1956-69, asst. to pres., 1967-68, dir. mktg. comml. industries data processing div., 1968-69; exec. v.p. EDP Tech., Inc., Washington, 1969-71, pres., CEO, 1971-73; pres. Washington Profl. Group, 1973-81; pres. SRC Corps. Equisource Source Corps; mng. dir. Pierce Investment Banking, Inc. Dir., mem. exec. com. Cornerstone R.E.I.T., 1993-96; chmn. bd. Paradigm Integration Corp., Empowernet, Inc. Asst. for domestic programs White House, Washington, 1966-67; chmn. bd. dirs. Congl. Mgmt. Found.; mem. fgn. service profl. devel. rev. group Dept. State, 1976; mem. U.S. Adv. Com. Vocat. Edn., 1968-69, U.S. Fed. Adv. Com. Employment Security, 1968-71, Com. for Excellence in Govt.; panel cons. Edn. Profl. Devel. Act, HEW, 1969-71; del. German Am. Forum, Bonn, Berlin, 1975; chmn. parents assn. Sidwell Friends Sch., Washington, 1976-78; vice chmn. fin. adv. com. Nat. Com. for Effective Congress, 1976-77. Served with AUS, 1957. White House fellow, 1966-67. Mem. White House Fellows Assn. (pres. Assn. and Found. 1973-74). Home and Office: 3238 O St NW Washington DC 20007-2842

GRAHAM, WILLIAM THOMAS, lawyer; b. Waynesboro, Va., Oct. 24, 1933; s. James Monroe and Margaret Virginia (Goodwin) G.; m. Kent Hill, Feb. 1, 1958; children: Ashton Cannon, William Thomas Jr. AB in Econs., Duke U., 1956; JD, U. Va., 1962. Bar: N.C. 1962, Va. 1962, D.C. 1970, U.S. Supreme Ct. 1970. Assoc. Craige, Brawley and predecessor firms, Winston-Salem, N.C., 1962-64; ptnr. Craige, Brawley, Horton & Graham, Winston-Salem, 1965-69; asst. gen. counsel HUD, Washington, 1969-70; ptnr. Billings & Graham, Winston-Salem, 1971-75; judge N.C. Superior Ct., 1975-79; pvt. practice Winston-Salem, 1981-87; commr. of banks State of N.C., Raleigh, 1987-95; counsel Patton Boggs, LLP, Raleigh, 1995-98; pvt. practice William T. Graham Law Office, Raleigh, 1999—. Chmn. Forsyth County Reps., Winston-Salem, 1966-69, 73-75, George Bush for Pres., N.C., 1988. With U.S. Army, 1957-58. Mem. Old Town Club. Methodist. Avocation: travel. Home: 3421 Williamsborough Ct Raleigh NC 27609-6368 E-mail: wtggtw@aol.com.

GRAHM, CHARLES MORTON, retired sales executive; b. Orting, Wash., Aug. 15, 1914; s. Ralph R. and Jane Ethel (Morton) G. BBA, U. Miami, 1947-50. Sales agt., supr. Pan Am. World Airways, Miami, Fla., 1946-77, ret., 1977. With USMCR, 1943-45, PTO. Decorated two Purple Hearts, USMC. Mem. DAV (life). Republican. Avocations: fishing, cutting gemstones. Home: 1280 W 29th St Hialeah FL 33012-5527

GRAHMANN, CHARLES V. bishop; b. Halletsville, Tex., July 15, 1931; Student, Assumption-St. John's Sem., Tex. Ordained priest Roman Cath. Ch., 1956. Ordained titular bishop Equilium and aux., San Antonio, 1981—82; 1st bishop Victoria, Tex., 1982—89; coadjutor biship Dallas, 1990; bishop Diocese of Dallas, 1990—. Office: Diocese of Dallas Chancery Office PO Box 190507 Dallas TX 75219-0507*

GRAHN, BARBARA ASCHER, retired publishing executive; b. Chgo., Mar. 26, 1929; d. Harry L. and Eleanor (Simon) Ascher; m. Robert D. Grahn, Dec. 23, 1952; children: Susan Grahn Gantz, Nancy Lee, Wendy Grahn O'Brien. BA, Miami U., Oxford, Ohio, 1950. Promotion dir. George Williams Coll., Chgo., 1950-52; sales mgr. Chatham Mfg., Chgo., 1952-54; research asst. Standard Rate and Data Service, Skokie, Ill., 1968-70, adminstr. editorial services, 1970-75, asst. editor, 1975-77, editor Wilmette, Ill., 1977-87; assoc. pub. Std. Rate and Data Svc., Wilmette, Ill., 1987-95, quality assurance mgr., 1995—2002; ret., 2002. Pres. Cmty. Club of Jewish Women, Skokie, 1958-60; bd. dirs., treas. North Shore Towers Condo Assn., Skokie, 1986-90, 93-99, 2002-. Mem. NAFE, Chgo. Ad Club, Alpha Epsilon Phi. Avocations: choreography, swimming, spending time with grandchildren, travel.

GRAINEY, PHILIP J. lawyer; b. Helena, Mont., Apr. 6, 1950; s. Bernard and Elizabeth (Roche) G.; m. Marilyn Rose Marron, Aug. 12, 1972; children: Heather Lynn, Kate Elizabeth, Brennin Patrick. BA in Psychology, U. Mont., 1972, JD, 1975. Bar: Mont., U.S. Dist. Ct. Mont. Ptnr. French & Grainey, Ronan, Mont., 1975-81, French, Grainey & Duckworth, Ronan, Mont., 1981-85, French, Mercer, Grainey & Duckworth, Ronan and Polson, Mont., 1985-86, French, Mercer & Grainey, Ronan and Polson, Mont., 1986-95; French, Mercer, Grainey & O'Neill, 1995-2001; French & Grainey, 2001—. Lawyer St. Luke Cmty. Hosp., Ronan, 1976—, chmn. bd., 1982-86; atty. City of Ronan, 1980-84, City of Polson, Mont., 1986-94; mem. adv. commn. on rules of civil procedure Mont. Supreme Ct., 1999—. Bd. dirs. Big Bros. and Sisters, Ronan, 1979-82; mem. Ronan Vol. Fire Dept., 1978-84. Mem. Mont. Bar Assn., Ronan C. of C. (pres.), Mission Mountain Country Club (bd. dirs. 1982-2001). Avocations: golf, music, tennis, hunting, fishing. Office: French & Grainey 324 Main St SW Ronan MT 59864-2707 E-mail: fmgolaw@ronan.net.

GRAINGER, MARY MAXON, civic volunteer; b. Arlington, Va., Apr. 14, 1957; d. Fred J. and Grace A. (Ziel) Maxon; m. Bradley R. Grainger, Aug. 18, 1979; children: Aileen, Maura, Erin. BS, Cornell U., 1979, MPS, 1987. Dir. pub. rels. Cazenovia (N.Y.) Coll., 1979-80; assoc. dir. admissions Cornell U., Ithaca, N.Y., 1980-85. V.p. Cornell Class of 1979, 1984-99, reunion chair, 1999—. Mem. devel. and mktg./pub. rels. com. Sciencenter, 1993-2000, mem. Gala com., 1996-2001; mem. comms. com. 1st Congl. Ch., 1985—; pres. Cayuga Heights PTA, 2001-02; newsletter editor Ithaca H.S. PTA, 2001—; leader Girl Scouts, 1991—; chair equity com. Boynton Mid. Sch. PTA, 1997-2001, chmn. comms. com., 2003—; adv. Cayuga Heights Sch., literary mag., 1996-2002; bd. dirs. Cornell Alumni Fedn., Ithaca Pub. Edn. Initiative; coun. rep. Ithaca PTA, 1996—; mem. Cornell Coun., 2003—. Mem. AAUW (chair ednl. equity Ithaca br., event coord. Sister to Sister, 2000—), Tompkins Girls Hockey Assn. (v.p. bd. dirs.). Home: 421 Highland Rd Ithaca NY 14850-2215 Fax: 607-257-0483. E-mail: mmgithaca@aol.com.

GRAINGER, NESSA, artist; b. Atlantic City, Sept. 15, 1934; d. Barnet and Pauline (Gittelman) Posner; m. Murray Grainger; children: Richard Greenbaum, Margie Friedman. BFA, Phila. Mus. Sch., 1955; postgrad., Tyler Sch. Art, Phila., 1959—60, Pa. Acad. Art, 1962—64. Artist in residence Lafayette Coll., Easton, Pa., 2003. One-woman shows include Douglas Coll., N.J., 1990, The Interchurch Ctr., N.Y.C., 1992, Elliott Mus., Stuart, Fla., 1993, Ocean County Artists Guild, 1994, Warner-Lambert Corp. Hdqrs., Morris Plains, N.J., 1996, Van Eck Global Gallery, N.Y.C., 1998, Somerset Art Assn., N.J., 1998, Pen and Brush, Inc., NYC, 2000, Louisa Melrose Gallery, NJ, 2001; exhibited in group shows at Am. Watercolor Soc. Ann. Exhbn., 1995, Pen and Brush Club, N.Y.C., 2000, San Diego Watercolor Soc., 1997, NAD, 1981, 1992, 96, Calif. Watercolor Soc., 1998, Watercolor Soc. Ala., Adirondacks Nat. Exhbn., Old Forge, N.Y., 1998, Pa. Watercolor Soc. at Bucknell U., Lewisburg, Pa., 1998, Nat. Watercolor Soc. Okla., 1998, 99, Kilpatrick Galleries, Oklahoma City, 1998-99, Freyberger Gallery Pa. State U., 2002 (Purchase prize); represented in permanent collections Nat. Gallery of Art Libr., Washington, Mus. Modern Art Libr., N.Y.C., Newark Mus., Bergen Mus. Arts and Scis., N.J., Elliott Mus., Zhejiang Provincial Mus., Hangzhow, China, Victoria & Albert Mus. Libr., London, Freyberger Gallery, Pa. State U.. Recipient Best Landscape award, 1986, Nicholas Reale award, 1993—, 1st prize Essex Watercolor Soc., award of merit Perkins Art Ctr., 1987, 1st prize for abstract watercolor Miniature Art Soc. N.J., 1988, Catherine Wolfe Gold Medal of Honor award, 1994, Calendar award Pa. Watercolor Soc., 1995, Merit award Balt. Watercolor Soc., 1996, Merit award La. Watercolor Soc., 1996, award Ga. Watercolor Soc., 1998, Purchase prize, 2002; named to Signature Mem. group Am. Watercolor Soc., 2000. Mem. Am. Watercolor Soc. (signature mem.), Nat. Assn. Women Artists (pres. 1989-91, medal of honor 1973, Molly M. Canaday award 1997, Kopet award), N.J. Watercolor Soc. (pres. 1982-84, silver medal of honor 1985, Forbes award 1985, ODS award 1987, Mitzuki Kovacs award 1988, Henry Gasser award 1996, Avery and Nina Johnson award 1997, Orthodiagnostics award 1992), Phila. Watercolor Club (Village Art award 1995), Knickerbocker Artists (silver medal of honor 1992), Allied Artists Am. (Henry Grasser Meml. award 1993, Mary Low Fitzgerald award 1996), Audubon Artists (v.p. watermedia 1988, Koffler award 1987, Silver medal 1989, Elsie Ject Key award 1993, Liquitex award 1995, Dale Meyers Honor medal 1996), Am. Soc. Contemporary Artists (Doris Kreindler award), Soc. Exptl. Artists, Rocky Mountain Watercolor Soc., 1997— (Strathmore paper award), Pen and Brush Club, 1999, Phila. Watercolor Club (Dana meml. award 2000), Catherine Lorillard Wolfe Art Club (Edgar Whitney Meml. award 2001). Home: 5513 Jaclyn Ln Bethlehem PA 18017-9057 E-mail: nessa.grainger@att.net.

GRALA, JANE M. securities firm executive; b. Phila. d. Stanley Frank and Anna Stephanie Grala. BS, Rutgers U., Camden, 1976; MBA, Winthrop U., 1979; postgrad., Am. Mgmt. Assn., N.Y.C., 1980-82, Am. Inst. Real Estate Appraisers, Chgo., 1985. Mgr. acctg. dept. NDI Engring. Co., Pennsauken, N.J., 1968-72, project mgr., 1972-76; rep. sales Am. Cyanamid, Wayne, N.J., 1976-80; dist. mgr. Am. Appraisal Assocs., Phila., 1980-86; assoc. v.p. investments Prudential Securities Incorporated, Clearwater, Fla., 1986—. Adj. prof. fin. area Tampa (Fla.) Coll., 1995. Mem. Nat. Assn. Accts. (dir. advt. So. Jersey chpt. 1983-86), Assn. MBA Execs., Bus and Profl. Women's Assn., Nat. Assn. for Female Execs., Chi Delta, Phi Chi Theta. Republican. Avocation: archeology. Office: Prudential Securities Inc 28100 Us Highway 19 N Ste 100 Clearwater FL 33761-2660

GRALAPP, MARCELEE GAYL, librarian; b. Winfield, Kans., Nov. 2, 1931; d. Benjamin Harry and Lelia Iris (Compton) G. BA, Kans. State Tchrs. Coll., 1952; MA, U. Denver, 1963. Children's libr. Hutchinson (Kans.) Pub. Libr., 1952-57, Lawrence (Kans.) Pub. Libr., 1957-59; assoc. libr. Boulder (Colo.) Pub. Libr., 1959-66, libr. dir., 1966—. Vis. faculty U. Denver, 1965-66, 67, Kans. State Tchrs. Coll., Emporia, 1965. Chmn. state plan for libr. devel. Librs.-Colo., 1974; city staff liaison Boulder Arts Commn., 1979—; bd. dirs. Boulder Ctr. for Visual Arts, 1975-79. Named Woman of Yr., Boulder Bus. and Profl. Women, 1997; recipient Gov.'s award, Colo. Coun. on Arts and Humanities, 1981, Boulder Spunky Woman award, 2001, Pacetter award for arts and entertainment, Daily Camera, 2003. Mem. ALA, Colo. Libr. Assn. (Lifetime Achievement award 1992), Delta Kappa Gamma. Democrat. Home: 3080 15th St Boulder CO 80304-2614 Office: Boulder Pub Libr PO Drawer H 1000 Canyon Blvd Boulder CO 80302-5120 E-mail: gralappm@ci.boulder.co.us.

GRALEN, DONALD JOHN, lawyer; b. Oak Park, Ill., Mar. 18, 1933; s. Oliver Edwin and Rosalie Marie (Buskens) G.; m. Jane Walsh, Dec. 29, 1956; children: Alana, Mark, Paul, Ann, Sarah. BS, Loyola U., Chgo., 1956; JD with honors, Loyola U., 1957. Bar: Ill. 1958. Assoc. Sidley & Austin, Chgo., 1959-65, ptnr., 1966-94, counsel, 1994-99. Co-author chpts. in books. Trustee Village of LaGrange, Ill., 1973-77; chmn. LaGrange Zoning Bd., 1971-73, LaGrange Econ. Devel. Com., 1982, Cmty. Meml. Found., 1995—; bd. dirs. Carson Pirie Scott Found., Chgo., 1980-89, Jr. Achievement, 1978-88, Met. Housing and Planning Coun., 1982-89, Cmty. Family Svc. and Mental Health Assn., 1983-87, Chgo. Youth Conservation Corps, 1988-92, LaGrange Meml. Found., 1990-95, YMCA Met. Chgo., 1990—. 1st lt. U.S. Army, 1957-59. Mem. Ill. Bar Assn., Univ. Club, Big Foot Country Club. Home: 42 Durham Ct Burr Ridge IL 60527-7938 Office: Sidley & Austin 1 S First National Plz Chicago IL 60603-2000 E-mail: dgralen@aol.com.

GRALLA, EUGENE, natural gas company executive; b. N.Y.C., May 3, 1924; s. Jacob and Anna Ruth (Kleiman) G.; m. Beverly Dorman, Apr. 7, 1946; children: Rhona Gralla Spilka, Steven Stuart. BS, U.S. Naval Acad., 1945; MBA, Harvard U., 1947. Commd. ensign USN, 1945, advanced through grades to comdr., 1961; served sea duty, 1947-49, 54-56; control officer (Naval Supply Depot, Guantanamo Bay), Cuba, 1959-61; with (Office Asst. Sec. Def. for Installations and Logistics), 1961-64; ret., 1966; dir. data systems planning Trans World Airlines, N.Y.C., 1966-68; corp. dir. mgmt. info. systems Internat. Paper Co., N.Y.C., 1968; v.p. electronic data processing Columbia Gas System Service Corp., Wilmington, Del., 1969-73; sr. v.p. Columbia Gas Distbn. Cos., Columbus, Ohio, 1973-86, pres., 1986-89, ret., 1989. Mem. Harvard Bus. Sch. Club, Palm Beach Club, Ret. Officers Assn., Masons. Home: 7641 La Corniche Cir Boca Raton FL 33433-6007 E-mail: bevandgene@aol.com.

GRALLA, LAWRENCE, publishing company executive; b. Bronx, N.Y., June 24, 1930; s. Meyer and Julia (Barnett) G.; m. Yvette Glickenstein, Dec. 24, 1952; children— Adele, Heidi. BS, CCNY, 1951. V.p. Nationwide Trade News Service, N.Y.C., 1951-55; pres. Gralla Publs., N.Y.C., 1955-87, exec. cons., 1987-2001; founding pub. Kitchen Bus., 1955, Bank Systems & Equipment, 1964, Multi-Housing News, 1966, Meeting News, 1977, Comml. Property News, 1988. Pres. Woodlands Community Temple, White Plains, N.Y., 1979-81. Recipient Govt. Israel Spl. Trade award 1980, Townsend Harris medal CCNY, 2002; named to Comm. Alumni Hall of Fame C.C.N.Y., 2000. Jewish.

GRALLA, MILTON, publisher; b. Bklyn., Jan. 28, 1928; s. Meyer and Julia (Barnett) G.; m. Shirley Edelson, Aug. 31, 1950; children— Edward, Karen, Dennis. BA in Journalism, CCNY, 1948; LHD (hon.), Yeshiva U., 1991. News reporter, 1948-51; co-founder nat. bus. news agy., 1951-55; co-founder, exec. v.p. Gralla Pubs., N.Y.C., 1955-93. Adj. prof. journalism NYU, Ramapo Coll., Yeshiva U., 1989—; del. leader Reawakening 1990-91, Moscow, 1990. Author: How Good Guys Grow Rich, 1995. Candidate for Congress, N.J., 1974; chmn. Israel Salute parade, 1993-94. Recipient major awards (trade) Govt. of Israel, (community service) Brandeis U., United Jewish Appeal, Orgn. Rehab. Through Tng., NCCJ, medal of honor Ellis Island. Mem. Friars Club, 24 Karat Club. Republican. Jewish.

GRAMBOW, RICHARD F. construction engineer, consultant; b. N.Y.C., July 20, 1916; s. Charles H. and Mary (Rohr) G.; m. Dreda V. Grambow, Dec. 17, 1955; children: Richard F. Jr., David G., Steven C. BS in Marine Engring. and Naval Arch., Webb Inst. Naval Arch., 1937. Assoc. naval arch. Dept. Navy, N.Y., 1938-42; chief engr., naval arch. Marinship Corp., Sausalito, Calif., 1942-46; exec. engr. Bechtel Corp., San Francisco, 1946-48, chief engr. Indsl. Divsn. L.A., 1948-54, chief project coord., mgr. Internat. Divsn. San Francisco, 1954-62; project mgr. Bechtel/W.K.E., Johannesburg, 1962-66; mgr. ops. Internat. Power, Indsl., and Mining Divsn. Bechtel Corp., San Francisco, 1966-68, v.p. for Internat. Mining and Metals Divsn., 1968-72, v.p. for comml. bldg. and land ops., 1972-76, ret., 1976-78, cons., 1978—. V.p. Bechtel Corp., Bechtel Internat. Ltd., Bechtel Pacific Corp., Pacific Bechtel Corp., Bechtel Panama, Bechtel Internat. Corp., Bechtel Nuclear Corp.; archtl. projects in Korea, Thailand, Australia, The Philippines, Malaysia, Japan, Sweden, South Africa, Mauretania, Eng., France, Spain, Zambia, Argentina, Brazil, Can., Pakistan, among others. Mem. planning commn. City Govt., Sausalito, Calif., 1958-61; mem. Sr. Citizens Adv. Group, San Juan County, 1977-80. Mem. Soc. Naval Archs. and Marine Engrs. (life). Avocations: photography, computer sciences. Home: 1052 East Ave Napa CA 94559-2147 E-mail: dickgram@prodigy.net.

GRAMES-LYRA, JUDITH ELLEN, retired artist, building plans examiner; b. Inglewood, Calif, Feb. 7, 1938; d. Glover Victor and Dorothy Margaret (Burton-Bellingham) Hendrickson and Carolyne Marie Carrick Hendrickson (stepmother); children: Nansea Ellen Ryan, Amber Jeanne Shelley-Harris, Carolyn Jane Angel Longmire, Susan Elaine Gomez, Robert Derek Shallenberger; m. Jon Robert Lyra, Feb. 14, 1997. Cert in journalism, Newspaper Inst. Am., N.Y.C., 1960; AA, Santa Barbara City Coll., 1971; BA, U. Calif., Santa Barbara, 1978, cert. in teaching, 1979. Cert. bldg. inspector, plumbing inspector, Calif. Editor, reporter, photographer Goleta Valley Sun Newspaper, Santa Barbara, 1968-71; editor, team asst. Bur. of Ednl. Rsch. Devel., Santa Barbara, 1971; bus. writer, graphics cons. Santa Barbara, 1971-77; art and prodn. dir. Bedell Advt. Selling Improvement Corp., Santa Barbara, 1979-81; secondary sch. tchr. Coalinga Unified Sch. Dist., Calif., 1981-83; bldg. insp. aide Santa Barbara County, Lompoc, 1983-88, from bldg. engring. inspector I to III, 1988-99, asst. plans examiner, 1999—2003. Exhibited in group shows at Foley's Frameworks and Interiors, 1984, Grossman Gallery, 1984, 98, Lompoc Valley Art Assn., 1984— (numerous awards including Best of Show 1985, 1st place 1984, 94, 2002, 2d place 1984, 86, 88, 96, 97, 99, 3d place 1987, 89, 97, Hon. Mention 1986, 90, 91, 97, 99, 2001), Brushes and Blues Invitational, 1998; featured artist Harvest Arts Festival, 1989, Cypress Gallery, 1994; contbr. poetry to anthologies. Mem. disaster response team Calif. Bldg. Ofcl., 1992-2003; exec. bd. dir. Lompoc Mural Soc., 1991—. Delta Kappa Gamma scholar. Mem. NOW, Nat. Abortion Rights Action League, Nat. Mus. of Women in the Arts (charter), Internat. Conf. Bldg. Ofcl., Engr. and Tech. Assn., Lompoc Valley Art Assn. (bd. mem.), Toastmasters Internat. (Outstanding Speaker awards 1991-93). Avocations: painting, stained glass, home improvement activities, illustrating note cards, writing children's stories.

GRAMM, WARREN STANLEY, economics educator; b. Seattle, Sept. 23, 1920; s. Paul Francis and Genevieve Hazel (Barnecut) G.; m. Marilyn Lorraine Post, June 25, 1949; children: Karen, Christie, Randolph. BA, U. Wash., 1944, MA, 1948; PhD, U. Calif., Berkeley, 1955. Asst. prof. Econs. U. Calif., Davis, 1955-63; assoc. prof. Econs. Alaska Meth. U., Anchorage, 1963-65; prof. Econs. Wash. State U., Pullman, 1965-91, prof. emeritus, 1991—. Contbr. articles profl. jours. Mem. Am. Econs. Assn., Assn. for Evolutionary Econs., History of Econs. Soc. Home: 1455 NW Kenny Dr Pullman WA 99163-3722 Office: Wash State U Dept Econs Pullman WA 99164-0001

GRAMM, WILLIAM PHILIP (PHIL GRAMM), former senator, economist; b. Fort Benning, Ga., July 8, 1942; s. Kenneth Marsh and Florence (Scroggins) G.; m. Wendy Lee, Nov. 2, 1970; children: Marshall Kenneth, Jefferson Philip. BA, U. Ga., 1964, PhD, 1967. Mem. faculty dept. econs. Tex. A&M U., College Station, 1967-78, prof., 1973-78; ptnr. Gramm & Assocs., 1971-78; mem. 96th-98th Congresses from 6th Tex. Dist.; U.S. senator from Tex., 1985—2002; vice chmn., mng. dir. UBS Warburg, 2002—. Chmn. Banking, Housing, and Urban Affairs Com., Fin. Com., Budget Com.; chmn. Nat. Rep. Senatorial Com., 1991-95; chmn. Senate Steering Com. Contbr. articles to profl. jours., periodicals. Republican. Episcopalian. Office: UBS Warburg 299 Park Ave New York NY 10171*

GRAMMER, JOHN COLQUITTE, cardiologist; b. Brenham, Tex., June 20, 1925; Student, Tex. A&M U., 1942-44; MD, U. Tex., 1947. Diplomate Am. Bd. Internal Medicine, Am. Bd. Cardiovascular Diseases. Intern Ft. Worth City-County Hosp., 1947-48; resident internal medicine Kansas City (Mo.) Gen. Hosp., 1948-51, U. Pa. Hosp., Phila., 1953-54; fellow cardiology Scripps Clin. Rsch. Found., 1966-67; dir. cardiac care unit St. Paul Med. Ctr., Dallas, 1967-97; clin. assoc. prof. internal medicine U. Tex. S.W.; pvt. practice. Med. author, lectr., filmmaker. Fellow ACP, Am. Coll. Cardiology, Am. Coll. Chest Physicians. Office: 3602 N Versailles Ave Dallas TX 75209-6230

GRAMMER, KELSEY, actor; b. St. Thomas, V.I., Feb. 21, 1955; s. Allen and Sally Grammer. Studied, Juilliard Sch., N.Y.C. Actor (films) Toy Story 2 (voice), 1999, 15 Minutes, 1999, New Jersey Turnpikes, 1999, Standing on Fishes, 1999, The Real Howard Spitz, 1998, Down Periscope, 1996, (voice) Anastasia, 1997, (TV series) Cheers, 1984-93, Frasier, 1993— (Best New Comedy award Viewers Quality TV, Favorite Male in New TV Series award 20th Ann. People's Choice Awards, Lead Actor Emmy award - Comedy Series, 1994, 1995, 98, Best Actor in TV Series Golden Globe award 1996, 2000, other awards), 15 Minutes, 2001; appeared in (Off-Broadway prodns.) Plenty, A Month in the Country, Sunday in the Park with George, Quartermaine's Terms, (Broadway prodns.) Macbeth, Othello, TV appearances include Kate and Allie (premiere episode), Wings, Tracy Ullman Show, The Simpsons, mini-series include Kennedy, 1983, George Washington, 1984, Crossings, 1986; TV movies include Dance 'til Dawn, 1988, Beyond Suspicion, 1993, (also exec. prodr.) The Innocent, 1994, London Suite, 1996, The Pentagon Wars, The Sports Pages, 2001; exec. prodr. (TV series) Fired Up, 1997; voice (video) Bartok the Magnificent, 1999, (TV) Animal Farm, 1999, The Hand Behind the Mouse: The Ub Iwerks Story, 1999; guest appearance Stark Raving Mad, 1999. Recipient SAG award, 2000. Office: The Artists Agency Ste 301 1180 S Beverly Dr Los Angeles CA 90035-1154

GRAMMIG, ROBERT JAMES, lawyer; b. Oceanside, Calif., June 15, 1956; s. Richard Adolf and Mary Elizabeth (Spisak) G.; m. Laurel Jean Lenfestey, Aug. 10, 1996; children: Clare Marie, James Richard. BA, MA, U. Pa., 1978; JD, Harvard U., 1981. Bar: Fla. 1982, D.C. 1986, U.S. Dist. Ct. (mid. dist.) Fla. 1982, U.S. Ct. Appeals (11th and 5th cirs.) 1982, U.S. Supreme Ct. 1985. Law clk. to Hon. Thomas A. Clark U.S. Ct. Appeals (5th and 11th cirs.), Atlanta, 1981-82; assoc. Holland & Knight, Tampa, Fla., 1982-88, ptnr., 1989—. Bd. dirs. Child Abuse Coun., Tampa, 1993-97; mem. Leadership Tampa, 1994-95; Sec. Tampa Bay Internat. Trade Coun., 1994, vice chmn., 1995. Mem. Tampa Bay Coun. on Fgn. Rels., German Am. C. of C., U.S.-Austrian C. of C., Phi Beta Kappa. Republican. Roman Catholic. Home: 21 Bahama Cir Tampa FL 33606-3317 Office: 100 N Tampa St Ste 4102 Tampa FL 33602-4322

GRAMPP, WILLIAM DYER, economist, educator; b. Columbus, Ohio, Aug. 22, 1914; children: Wendy P., Heather M., Christopher W. AB, U. Akron, 1936; A.M., U. Chgo., 1942, PhD, 1944; student, Columbia U., 1941. Mem. editorial staff Akron Times-Press, 1937-38, Press Wireless, Paris, 1938, Chgo. Tribune, London, 1939; instr. Adelphi Coll., 1942; vice consul econ. sect. Am. embassy, Rome, 1944-45; asst. prof. econs. Elmhurst Coll., 1942-44; asst. prof., then prof. econs. Coll. Commerce, DePaul U., 1945-46; mem. faculty Coll. Bus. Adminstrn., U. Ill., 1947—, prof. econs., 1957-80, prof. emeritus, 1980—. Vis. prof. Lake Forest (Ill.) Coll., UCLA, Ind. U., CCNY, U. Wis., U. Chgo. 1980-2001, Wake Forest U., U. Minn.; vis. scholar Hoover Instn. Author: The Manchester School of Economics, 1960, Economic Liberalism, 1965, Pricing the Priceless: Art, Artists, and Economics, 1989; editor, (with E.T. Weiler) Economic Policy, 3d edit, 1961; mem. editorial bd. History of Polit. Economy, 1972-81, Rivista Internazionale di Scienze Economiche e Commerciali, 1985—; contbr. to profl. jours. and gen. interest periodicals. Mem. Am. Econ. Assn., Midwest Econs. Assn. (pres. 1972-73), History of Econs. Soc. (pres. 1980-81) Home: 5426 S Ridgewood Ct Chicago IL 60615-5347

GRAMS, DIANE M. artist, educator; b. South Bend, Ind., Dec. 9, 1957; d. Ralph Richard Grams and Dorothy Gertrude Walters; m. Timothy D. Lace, Mar. 2, 1990. BA in Painting, Ind. U., 1981; MA in Sociology, Loyola U., Chgo., 2001, postgrad., 2002—. Free-lance designer, art dir., Chgo., 1982—88; membership dir. Chgo. Artists Coalition, 1987—92; exec. dir. The Peace Mus., Chgo., 1992—98; rsch. asst. Loyola U., Chgo., 1998—2000, part-time faculty, 2000—02; adj. faculty DePaul U., Chgo., 2001—; rschr. D. Grams Cons., Chgo., 1998—. Grant writer Guild Complex, Chgo., 1998—2001; cons. in rsch., fundraising and program evaluation for founds., 1998—; lectr. in field. Editor: (book) Poetry for Peace, 1996; author: A Prayer in No Man's Land, 1993; one-woman shows include Chgo. Dramatists' Workshop, Chgo., 1989, Artemisia Gallery, 1992—93, exhibited in group shows at Arbutus Gallery, Bloomington, Ind., 1979—80, Contemporary Art Workshop, Chgo., 1982, Chgo. Artists Return to Ragdale, Lake Forest, Ill., 1985, No. Ill. U. Gallery, Chgo., 1988, Upstart Gallery, 1988, A.R.C. Gallery, 1989, Beacon St. Gallery, 1989, Northeastern Ill. U. Gallery/North Rivery Cmty. Gallery, 1989, Lannon

Gallery, 1989, R.H. Love Gallery, 1990, 1992, Holstein Park Firehouse, 1990, North Lakeside Cultural Ctr., 1991, Hyde Park Art Ctr., 1991, Artemisia, 1991—93, Centro Colombo Americano, Medellin, Colombia, 1992, Suburban Fine Arts Ctr., Highland Park, Ill., 1994, Painted Bride, Phila., 1995, Inclusion Art Gallery, Chgo., 2002; contbr. ; Represented in permanent collections Circa Restaurant, Musikantow Cons. and Mgmt., pvt. individuals. Recipient Civil Liberties award, ACLU of Chgo., 1989; fellow Schmitt fellow, Schmitt Found. and Loyola U.-Chgo., 2002—03; grantee Rsch. grantee, R.H. Driehaus Found. and C.T. MacArthur Found., 2001, Artist ghrantee, Art Matters Found., N.Y.C., 1992; scholar Merit scholar, Loyola U. Chgo., 1998—2002; One of 100 Women Making a Difference in Chgo., Today's Chgo. Women, 1990. Mem.: Coll. Art Assn., Chgo. Artists Coalition, Am. Assn. Mus., Am. Sociol. Assn.

GRAMS, RODNEY D. former senator, former congressman; b. 1948; Student, Anoka-Ramsey Jr. Coll., Brown Inst., Minneapolis, Minn., Carroll Coll., Helena, Mont. Engring. cons. Orr-Schelen Mayeron & Assoc., Mpls.; anchor, producer Sta. KFBB-TV, Great Falls, Mont., Sta. WSAU-TV, Wausau, Wis., Sta. WIFR-TV, Rockford, Ill., Sta. KMSP-TV, Mpls.; mem. 103d Congress from 6th Minn. Dist., 1993-94; U.S. Senator from Minn., 1995—2001. Pres., CEO Sun Ridge Builders. Republican.

GRAMS, THEODORE CARL WILLIAM, librarian, educator; b. Portland, Oreg., Sept. 29, 1918; s. Theodore Albert and Emma Elise (Boehne) G. BA, U. Wash., 1947; postgrad., Harvard Law Sch., 1947-48; MS in LS, U. So. Calif., 1951. Land title asst. U.S. Bonneville Power Adminstrn., Portland, 1939-45, acct., 1948-50, libr., 1951-52; head cataloger, lectr. Portland State U. Libr., 1952-59, dir. processing svcs., 1960-83, prof., 1969-87, prof. emeritus, 1988—. Pres. Portland Area Spl. Librs., 1954-55; panelist on impact new tech. on info. scis. Am. Soc. Info. Sci., 1974, panelist on Libr. Congress svcs., 1976. Author: Textbook Classification, 1968; editor: Procs. 4th Am. Soc. Info. Scis. Midyear Meeting, 1975, Spl. Collections in the Librs. of the Pacific N.W., 1979, Disaster Preparedness and Recovery, 1983, Technical Services: The Decade Ahead, 1983. Panelist on cmty. action N.W. Luth. Welfare Assn. Conf., 1969; mem. adv. coun. Area Agy. on Aging, 1974-75; commr. City-County Commn. Aging, Portland-Multnomah County, 1975-80; bd. dirs. Hub-Cmty. Action Program, Portland, 1967-70, Project ABLE, 1972-74. HEW Inst. fellow, 1968-69. Mem. ALA, Beta Phi Mu. Lutheran. Home: 6653 E Carondelet Dr Tucson AZ 85710-2150

GRAMSTORFF, JEANNE B. retired farmer; b. Floydada, Tex., June 23, 1930; d. David Stephen Battey and Ruth Asbury Pitts; m. John C. Gramstorff, Feb. 14, 1951 (dec. Feb. 1993); children: Susan G. Gramstorff Fetzer, John C. BA, Tex. Tech U., 1951. Cert. tchr. Tex. Tchr. Perryton (Tex.) Mid. and HS's, 1951-66; farmer Gramstorff & Son, Farnsworth, Tex., 1951-2000; ret., 2000. Bd. dirs. Perryton Nat. Bank. Trustee, officer Perry Meml. Libr., Perryton, 1956—, pres., 2000—03; mem., officer Tex. Panhandle Libr. Sys. Coun., Amarillo, 1978—, chairperson, 2001—02; bd. dirs. Lydia Patterson Inst., 1993—2000; sec. Acocrd Agr., Inc., Farnsworth, 1995—; historian, v.p., pres. N.W. Tex. United Meth. Women; bd. dirs. N.W. Tex. Conf. United Meth. Ch., 1976—, dist. mission chair, 1996—. Avocations: reading, needlepoint. Home: PO Box 250 Farnsworth TX 79033-0250

GRANADE, FRED KING, lawyer; b. Mobile, Ala., Mar. 3, 1950; s. Joe C. and Lucille (Williams) G.; m. Callie Virginia Smith, Oct. 9, 1976; children: Taylor Rives, Milton Smith, Joseph Kee. BA, Auburn U., 1972; JD, Washington and Lee U., 1975. Bar: Ala. 1975, Fla. 1976, U.S. Dist. Ct. (so. and mid. dists.) Ala., 1977, U.S. Supreme Ct. 1979, U.S. Ct. Appeals (5th and 11th cirs.) 1981. Law clk. Ala. Ct. of Criminal Appeals, Montgomery, 1975-76; ptnr. Stone, Granade & Crosby P.C., Bay Minette, Daphne, Ala., 1986—. Bd. dirs. First Community Bank, Chatom, Ala., S.W. Bancshares, Mt. Vernon, Ala. Bd. dirs. Historic Blakeley Authority, Ala., 1983-85, North Baldwin Hosp., North Baldwin County Health Care Authority; mem. adv. bd. North Baldwin Infirmary; chmn. profl. div. North Baldwin United Fund, Bay Minette, 1987. Fellow Am. Bar Found.; mem. ABA, Ala. Bar Assn., Fla. Bar Assn., Baldwin County Bar Assn., Omicron Delta Kappa. Presbyterian. Office: Stone Granade & Crosby 34 N Pine St Bay Minette AL 36507-3202 E-mail: FKG@SGClaw.com.

GRANADOS, FRANCISCO D. physician; b. Camargo, Chihauhua, Mex., Aug. 10, 1942; s. Granados Francisco, Elizabeth Pineda; children from previous marriage: Elizabeth, Martha Elena, Liliana, Daniela, Margarita. Grad., Sch. of Med., Chihauha, Mex., 1968. Gen. practice Instituto Mexicano del Seuro Social, Chihauha, Mexico; dir. clinic Instituto Mexicano del Seguro Social, Chihauha, Mexico, dir. gen. hosp. Tamaulipas, Mexico, external consult chief Delicias, Mexico, gen. practice Camargo, Mexico; ret. Author: (books) Carbohydrate Tolerance Index, 2000, Jehovah's Sons: Knowing Jehovah, Allah, Adonai, 2003. Home: 73(Harvard St NW Washington DC 20001

GRANAT, RICHARD STUART, lawyer, educator; b. N.Y.C., Nov. 11, 1940; s. George and Judith G.; m. Nancy Ruth Wruble, Dec. 23, 1962; children: Lisa, Hilary, Peter, David. BA, Lehigh U., 1962; JD (Harlan Fiske Stone scholar), Columbia U., 1965. Bar: Md. 1966, D.C. 1977. Asst. counsel U.S. OEO, Washington, 1965-67, dir. housing programs, 1967-78; asst. dir. Model Cities Agy. Office of Mayor, Balt., 1968-69; dir. Cmty. Planning and Evaluation Inst., Balt., 1970-71; pres. Univ. Rsch. Corp. Mgmt. Svcs. Corp., Balt., 1970-77; pvt. practice Washington and Md., 1969—. Pres. Automated Lagal Systems, Inc., Phila., 1984—89; dir. MA in Legal Studies Program, Antioch Sch. Law, 1979—83; pres., chmn. bd. Ctr. for Legal Studies, Washington, 1979—89; chmn. bd. dirs. Ctr. Sch., Rockville, Md.; pres. Inst. Paralegal Tng., Inc., Phila., 1982—89, The Phila. Inst., 1987—89, Inst. for Employee Benefits Tng., 1986—89, The Inst. for Law and Tech., Phila., 1990—92, Interactive Legal Media, Inc., 1992—96; instr. Rutgers Sch. Law, Camden, NJ, 1992—94, Sch. Lang., U. Balt., 1995—; adj. prof. Sch. Law, U. Md., 1994—, dir. Ctr. for Law Practice Tech., 1994—, dir. Peoples Law Libr., 1996—2000, dir. Ctr. for On-Line Mediation, Inc., 1996—2000; pres. The Granat Group, LLC, Am. Law On Line, Inc., 2001—. Mem. ABA, Md. Bar Assn., D.C. Bar Assn. Home: 320 Morgause Pl N Baltimore MD 21208-1430 Office: 9141 Reisterstown Rd Owings Mills MD 21117 E-mail: richard@granat.com.

GRANATA, ATTILIO VINCENT, medical educator, physician executive; b. New Haven, June 29, 1953; s. Attilio Clemente and Rose Marie (Petrillo) G.; m. Claudia Dinan, Oct. 27, 1984; children: Vincent Matthew, Christopher Joseph, Timothy Daniel, Elizabeth Catherine. BS magna cum laude, Yale U., 1974, MD, 1977; MBA, U. Pa., 1994. Diplomate Am Bd. Internal Medicine. Intern Stanford U. Med. Ctr., Palo Alto, Calif., 1977-78, resident internal medicine, 1978-90; attending physician VA Med. Ctr., West Haven, Conn., 1980-82, Hosp. of St. Raphael, New Haven, 1982-84; dir. med. ambulatory care Bridgeport (Conn.) Hosp., 1984-92, med. dir. quality mgmt., 1992-95; med. dir. med. mgmt., sr. regional med. dir. Oxford Health Plans, Trumbull, Conn., 1995—2000; health econs. cons., 2000—; med. dir. Norwalk (Conn.) Cmty. Health Ctr., 2003—. Cons. health econs. quality of care, tech. assessment, 2000—; clin. instr. dept. medicine Yale U. Sch. Medicine, New Haven, 1980—81, asst. clin. prof., 1981—87, assoc. clin. prof., 1987—; physician advisor Conn. Peer Rev. Orgn., Middletown, 1988—95; mem. com. on quality assessment Conn. Hosp. Assn., Wallingford, 1992—95; mem. adv. coun. Boston Healthcare, 1997—. Contbr. articles to profl. jours.; mem. editl. bd. Jour. Care Mgmt., 1995—; reviewer Annals of Internal Medicine, 1997—. Bd. dirs. South Ctrl. Conn. chpt. ARC, 1970-72, S.W. Cmty. Health Ctr., Bridgeport, Conn., 1984-89; v.p. bd. trustees St. Thomas More Chapel, Yale U., 1997—. Palmer scholar Wharton, 1994; recipient Innovation in Med. Mgmt. award Am. Coll. Physician Execs., 1995, Rodney T. West Literary Achievement award, 1999. Fellow ACP (chmn. health and pub. policy com. Conn. chpt. 1994-96), Soc. Med. Decision Making, Soc. Gen. Internal Medicine, Alpha Omega Alpha. Roman Catholic. Avocations: piano, opera, magic. Home: 130 Wild Rose Rd Orange CT 06477-1837 E-mail: agranata01@snet.net.

GRANATO, CAROL ANNE, writer; b. Phila., May 2, 1946; d. Leo Joseph De Stephanis and Margaret McLean; m. Robert Natale Granato, June 20, 1964; children: Robert Anthony, Stephen. Clk. typist Reliance Ins., Phila., 1963-65; receptionist Phila. Coll. Art, 1984-85; nursing office asst. Meth. Hosp., Phila., 1987; freelance writer, editor Garnet Pub., Phila., 1999—. Author, editor: The Universe and Beyond, 1999; contbr. poems to lit. jours. Asst. dir. Edward Rendell for Mayor, Phila., 1988, 92. Democrat. Roman Catholic. Avocations: paranormal research, gardening, cooking, educational reading. Home: 2506 S 18th St Philadelphia PA 19145-3701 Office: Garnet Pub PO Box 11955 Philadelphia PA 19145 E-mail: garnet1945@aol.com.

GRANATSTEIN, JACK LAWRENCE, history educator; b. Toronto, May 21, 1939; s. S. Benjamin and Shirley (Geller) G.; m. Mary Elaine Hitchcock, 1961; children: Carole, Michael (dec.) BA, Royal Mil. Coll., Kingston, Ont., 1961; MA, U. Toronto, 1962; PhD, Duke U., 1966; DLitt (hon.), Meml. U., 1993; LLD (hon.), U. Calgary, 1994, Ryerson Polytech. U., 1999, U. We. Ont., 2000, McMaster U., 2000. Historian Dept. Nat. Def., Ottawa, Ont., 1965-66; prof. history York U., 1966-95, Disting. rsch. prof. history emeritus, 1995—; Rowell Jackman fellow Canadian Inst. of Internat. Affairs, 1995-98; commr. Spl. Commn. on the Restructuring of the Can. Forces Reserves, 1995; CEO, dir. Can. War Mus., 1998-2000; chair Coun. for Can. Security in 21st Century, 2001—. Author: Politics of Survival, 1967, Canada's War, 1975, Broken Promises, 1977, Ties That Bind, 1977, American Dollars-Canadian Prosperity, 1978, A Man of Influence, 1981, The Ottawa Men, 1982, Twentieth Century Canada, 1983, The Great Brain Robbery, 1984, Canada 1957-67, 1986, Sacred Trust? Brian Mulroney and the Conservatives in Power, 1986, The Collins Dictionary of Canadian History, 1988, Marching to Armageddon, 1989, How Britain's Weakness Forced Canada into the Arms of the United States, 1989, A Nation Forged in Fire, 1989, Pirouette: Pierre Trudeau and Canadian Foreign Policy, 1990, Mutual Hostages: Canadians and Japanese in the Second World War, 1990, Spy Wars, Espionage and Canada from Gouzenko to Glasnost, 1990, For Better or Worse: Canada and the U.S. to the 1990's, War and Peacekeeping, 1991, English Canada Speaks Out, 1991, Oxford Dictionary of Canadian Military History, 1992, The Generals: The Canadian Army's Senior Commanders in the Second World War, 1993, Empire to Umpire: Canada and the World to the 1990's, 1994, The Good Fight: Canadians and World War II, 1995, Victory 1945: Canadians From War to Peace, 1995, Yankee Go Home? Canadians and Anti-Americanism, 1997, The Canadian 100, 1997, Petrified Campus: The Crisis of Canada's Universities, 1997, The Veterans Charter and Post World War II Canada, 1998, Who Killed Canadian History?, 1998, Trudeau's Shadow, 1998, Prime Ministers, 1999, Our Century, 2000, Canada's Army, 2002, First Drafts, 2002. Bd. govs. Royal Mil. Coll., 1996—. Served to lt. Can. Army, 1956-66. Recipient Tyrrell medal for Can. history, 1992, J.W. Dafoe prize, 1993, medal for biography U. B.C., 1993, Vimy award Conf. Def. Assns. Inst., 1996; Killam rsch. fellow Can. Coun., 1982-84, 91-93; rsch. grantee Can. Dept. External Affairs, 1978-80, Can. Dept. Nat. Def., 1987-88, Social Sci. and Humanities Rsch. Coun. Can., 1978-79, 82-84, 85-89, 91-97; named officer Order of Can., 1997. Fellow Royal Soc. Can. Home: 53 Marlborough Ave Toronto ON Canada M5R 1X5 E-mail: jgranatstein@sympatico.ca.

GRANATSTEIN, VICTOR LAWRENCE, electrical engineer, educator; b. Toronto, Feb. 8, 1935; s. Charles Samuel and Bella (Godfrey) G.; m. Bethie Mills, Sept. 4, 1955; children: Rebecca Miriam, Abraham Solomon, Annie Sara Khaya. BS, Columbia U., 1960, MS, 1961, PhD, 1963. Rsch. staff physicist Bell Tel. Labs., Murray Hill, N.J., 1964-72; head high power electromagnetic radiation br. Naval Rsch. Lab., Washington, 1972-83; prof. elec. engring. U. Md., College Park, 1983—, acting dir. Inst. for Plasma Rsch., 1986-88, dir., 1988-98. Vis. lectr. Hebrew U., Jerusalem, 1969—70; vis. prof. Tel Aviv U., 1994, 2003; cons. BDM Corp., McLean, Va., 1981—83, Sci. Applications Corp., McLean, 1983—, Omega-P Inc., New Haven, 1983—2000, Pulse Scis. Inc., San Leandro, 1985—88, Jet Propulsion Lab., Pasadena, 1987—91, Mission Res. Corp., Newington, Va., 2001—. Editor: Wave Heating and Current Drive in Magnetic Plasmas, 1985, High Power Microwaves, 1987, Applications of High Power Microwaves, 1994; contbr. articles to profl. jours.; patentee microwave devices. Pres. Bethesda-Chevy Chase Jewish Cmty. Group, 1983—84. Recipient R.D. Conrad award Sec. Navy, 1981, Superior Civilian Svc. award Office Naval Rsch., 1980, E.O. Hulbert award Naval Rsch. Lab., 1980, Robert L. Woods award Sec. Def., 1998; Fulbright sr. scholar, 1993-94, Fullbright sr. specialist, 2003. Fellow IEEE (life, vice chmn. plasma sci. com. 1984-85, Plasma Sci. and Applications award 1991), Am. Phys. Soc. Democrat. Avocations: folk dancing, swimming. Home: 13508 Rippling Brook Dr Silver Spring MD 20906-3177 Office: U Md Inst Rsch in Electronics and Applied Physics College Park MD 20742-3511 E-mail: vlg@glue.umd.edu.

GRANBERG, KURT, state legislator, lawyer; b. Breese, Ill., June 16, 1953; s. Marnen George and Agnes Mary (Vahlkamp) G. BS, U. Ill., Chgo., 1975; postgrad., Ill. Inst. Tech., 1980. Bar: Ill. 1980, U.S. Dist. Ct. (so. dist.) Ill. 1983. Legis. intern Ill. Ho. Reps., Springfield, 1975-76, mem. staff, 1975-77; assoc. James Donnewald Law Office, Breese, 1980-83; asst. pub. defender Clinton County, Ill., 1981-83; ptnr. Donnewald & Granberg, Breese, 1983—; spl. asst. atty. gen. State of Ill., Breese, 1983—; registered lobbyist Breese, 1984—; mem. Ill. Ho. Reps., 1986—; asst. Dem. majority leader. Mem. fin. com. Ill. Inst. Tech.-Chgo. Kent. Sch. Law, 1979-80. Dem. precinct committeeman, Carlyle, Ill., 1982-84; mem. Clinton County Bd., Carlyle, 1984—, Carlyle Lake Adv. Com.; bd. dirs. Ctrl. Comprehensive Mental Health Ctr., Centralia, Ill., 1984—. Mem. ABA, Ill. Bar Assn., Clinton County Bar Assn., Jaycees, Carlyle Bus. and Profl. Assn., K.C., Optimists. Roman Catholic. Home: 17918 Oakwood Dr Carlyle IL 62231-2918 Office: Ill Ho of Reps 300 E Capitol Ave Springfield IL 62701-1710*

GRANBERRY, EDWIN PHILLIPS, JR., safety engineer, consultant; b. Orange, N.J., Aug. 20, 1926; s. Edwin Phillips Sr. and Mabel (Leflar) G.; m. Joanne Park, June 15, 1991; children: Melissa, Edwin Phillips III, James, Jennifer, Claudia. BS, Rollins Coll., 1950; MBA, Embry Riddle Aero. U., 1985. Cert. profl. chemist. Weapons sys. engr. Martin Co., Orlando, Fla., 1958-62; supt. indsl. safety Guided Missiles Range divsn. Pan Am. World Airways, Cape Canaveral, Fla., 1962-72; mgr. indsl. hygiene/safety engring. Pratt & Whitney Aircraft, West Palm Beach, Fla., 1972-88; mgr. indsl. and sys. safety engring. Chem. Sys. divsn. United Tech. Corp., San Jose, Calif., 1988-89; pres. Granberry & Assocs. Inc., Winter Park, Fla., 1989—. Adj. faculty Valencia C.C., Orlando; mem. Fla. State Toxic Substances Adv. Coun., 1984-88, Fla. State Emergency Response Commn., 1988, Fla. Divsn. Safety Customer Adv. Coun.; mem. restoration adv. bd. U.S. Naval Tng. Sta., Orlando, 1996—. Scoutmaster Boy Scouts Am., 1946-74, dist. chmn. Wekiwa dist. Ctrl. Fla. coun., 1946-74, also coun. commr. Served with USNR, 1944-54, PTO. Recipient Silver Beaver award Boy Scouts Am., 1960. Fellow Am. Inst. Chemists; mem. ASTM, Welding Soc., Am. Chem. Soc., Am. Bd. Forensic Examiners, Am. Nat. Stds. Inst., Nat. Fire Protection Assn., Rollins Coll. Alumni Assn. (bd. dirs. 1958-61), Am. Soc. Safety Engrs. (chmn. Gold Coast chpt. 1979-90, pres. 1981-84, regional v.p. 1984-88, 94—, v.p. divsns. 1988-90, adminstr. environ. divsn. 1992—, nat. bd. dirs. 1984-90, 94—), Am. Soc. Safety Engrs. Found. (chmn. 1997—, Saftey Profl. of Yr. Fla., Ga., P.R. chpts., 1985, Saftey Profl of Yr. divs., 1991, Saftey Profl. of Yr. Environ. Divsn. 1995-96), Safety Coun. Palm Beach County (pres. 1981-82, chmn. bd. 1983, treas. 1984). Home: 521 Langholm Dr Winter Park FL 32789-5251 Office: Granberry & Assocs Inc 2431 Aloma Ave Ste 276 Winter Park FL 32792-2566

GRAND, CINDY, foundation director; BA in Humanities, Menlo Coll., 1989. V.p., CFO Richard Grand Found., San Francisco, 1987—. Bd. trustees Menlo Coll., Atherton, 1995—98. Mem.: AAUW.

GRAND, MARCIA, civic worker; b. N.Y.C., Aug. 9, 1933; d. Irving and Dorothy (Miller) Kosta; m. Richard Grand, Jan. 27, 1952. Student, U. Ariz., 1950-52, 59-60. Docent, coord., docent trainer Tucson Mus. Art, 1965-71; bd. dirs., 1972-79; chmn. edn. com., 1975-79; v.p., sec. Richard Grand Found., 1966-80; pres., 1980—. Bd. dirs., sec. U. Ariz. Found., 1979-80, v.p., 1986-87, chmn. exec. com., 1986-87; mem. spl. com. office of chair U. Ariz., 1987-92; bd. dirs. Tucson Airport Authority, Greenfield Schs., 1977-82; bd. fellows Ctr. Creative Photography, 1984-98, chmn., 1993-98, mem.-at-large, bd. dirs. Tucson Mus. Art League, 1977-78; bd. trustees San Francisco Art Inst., 1995-2003. Nominated for YWCA Woman on the Move award, 1982; recipient Cmty. Svc. award Mortar Bd., 1978, Disting. Citizen award U. Ariz. Coll. Fine Arts, 1979. Office: 127 W Franklin St Tucson AZ 85701-1020 E-mail: rg@rgrand.com.

GRANDE, THOMAS ROBERT, lawyer; b. Providence, Dec. 27, 1952; s. Albert and Gloria (Palmieri) G. Student, U. Copenhagen, 1975; BA in Govt., Bates Coll., Lewiston, Maine, 1976; JD, U. Hawaii, 1985. Bar: Hawaii, 1985, U.S. Dist. Ct. Hawaii 1985, U.S. Ct. Appeals (9th cir.) 1985. Exec. dir. Common Cause Hawaii, Honolulu, 1979-82; law clk. to chief justice Federated States Micronesia Supreme Ct., Pohnpei, Caroline Islands, 1985; ptnr. Davis Levin Livingston Grande, Honolulu, 1985—. Contbr. articles to profl. jours. Vista Vol. Waimanalo Coun. Community Orgns., 1978; candidate for nat. governing bd. Common Cause, Washington, 1983; vol. ACLU, Honolulu, 1983-84; organizer Com. to Keep Waimanalo Rural, 1984; bd. dirs. Hawaii's Thousand Friends, Honolulu, 1987, Hawaii Lawyers Care, 1988. Recipient Outstanding Contbn. to the Delivery of Legal Svcs. award Hawaii Lawyers Care, 1994. Mem. ABA (sec. litig., chair state law subcom. of com. on class actions, editor-in-chief ABA Survey of State Class Action Law), ATLA (co-chair Qui Tam Litigation Group), Hawaii Bar Assn. (chmn. lawyer referral com. 1991-94), Consumer Lawyers Hawaii (mem. bd. govs. 1993—, parliamentarian 1993-94, sec. 1994-95, v.p. 1995-96), Am. Inns of Ct. (barrister 1989-90). Avocations: hiking, reading, martial arts, gardening. Office: 400 Davis Levin Livingston Grande 851 Fort St Honolulu HI 96813 Fax: 808545-7802. E-mail: tgrande@davislevin.com.

GRANDI, ATTILIO, engineering consultant; b. La Spezia, Italy, Sept. 24, 1929; s. Luigi and Egle (Canese) G.; m. Maria Teresa Berti, Apr. 23, 1962; 1 child, Giovanni. Maturita scientifica, Liceo Scientifico Pacinotti, La Spezia, 1949; univ. degree in aero. engring., U. Pisa (Italy), 1958. Project engr. S.p.A. Piaggio, Pontedera, Italy, 1959-60, Termomeccanica Italiana, La Spezia, 1960-71, tech. mgr., 1971-85, rsch. and mktg. mgr., 1985-88; cons. hydraulic machinery refrigeration and marine propulsive systems, 1988—. Patentee in field. Mem. Italian Standard Hydraulic Machinery, N.Y. Acad. Scis. Roman Catholic. Avocations: mathematics, old languages, fishing.

GRANDIN, TEMPLE, industrial designer, science educator; b. Boston, Aug. 29, 1947; d. Richard McCurdy and Eustacia (Cutler) G. BA in Psychology, Franklin Pierce Coll., 1970; MS in Animal Sci., Arizona State U., 1975; PhD in Animal Sci., U. Ill., Urbana, 1989; D (hon.), McGill U., 1999. Livestock editor Ariz. Farmer Ranchman, Phoenix, 1973-78; equipment designer Corral Industries, Phoenix, 1974-75; ind. cons. Grandin Livestock Systems, Urbana, 1975-90, Fort Collins, Colo., 1990—; lectr., asst. prof. animal sci. dept. Colo. State U., Fort Collins, 1990—. Chmn. handing com. Livestock Conservation Inst., Madison, Wis., 1976—; surveyor USDA. Author: Emergence Labelled Autistic, 1986, Recommended Animal Handling Guidelines for Meat Packers, 1991, Livestock Handling and Transport, 1993, 2nd edit., 2000, Thinking in Pictures, 1995, Genetics and the Behavior of Domestic Animals, 1998, Beef Cattle Behavior Handling and Facilities Design, 2000; contbg. editor Meat and Poultry mag., 1987-98; contbr. articles to profl. jours.; patentee in field. Named One of Processing Stars of 1990 Nat. Provisioner, 1990, Woman of Yr. in Svc. to Agr. Progressive Farmer, 1999; recipient Meritorious Svcs. award Livestock Conservation, Madison, Wis., 1986, Disting. Alumni award Franklin Pierce Coll., 1989, Industry Innovators award Meat Mktg. and Tech. Mag., 1994, Brownlee award for internat. leadership in sci. publ. promoting respect for animals Animal Welfare Found. of Canada, 1995, Harry Roswell award Scientists Ctr. for Animal Welfare, 1995, Humane Ethics in Action award Geraldine R. Dodge Found., 1998, Forbes award Nat. Meat Assn., 1998, Founders award Am. Soc. Prevention Cruelty Animals, 1999, Humane award Am. Vet. Med. Assn., 1999, Joseph Wood Krutch award, Humane Soc. of U.S., 2001, Knowlton Innovation award in Meat Mktg. and Tech. Mag., 2001, 2002, Animal Welfare award, Brit. Soc. Animal Sci. and Royal Soc. Prevention Cruelty to Animals, 2002. Mem. Autism Soc. Am. (bd. dirs. 1988—, Trammel Crow award 1989), Am. Soc. Animal Sci. (Animal Mgmt. award 1995, Disting. Svc. award We. sect. 2003), Am. Soc. Agrl. Cons. (bd. dirs. 1981-83), Am. Soc. Agrl. Engrs., Am. Meat Inst. (supplier mem., Industry Advancement award 1995), Am. Registry of Profl. Animal Scis. Republican. Episcopalian. Achievements include design of stockyards and humane restraint equipment for major meat packing companies in the U.S., Canada and Australia; development of an objective scoring system used for monitoring animal welfare in slaughter plants. Home: Grandin Livestock Systems 2918 Silverplume Dr Apt C3 Fort Collins CO 80526-2402 Office: Colo State U Animal Sci Dept Fort Collins CO 80523-0001

GRANDIZIO, LENORE, social worker; b. N.Y.C., Apr. 20, 1952; d. Louis and Angelina (Prez de Garcia) G.; m. Lenny Mars Rothbart; 1 child, Angelica M. BA, SUNY, Geneseo, 1973; MSSW, Columbia U., 1978. Cert. social worker, N.Y.; cert. child psychiatry and child guidance; diplomate clin. social work. Assoc. staff mem. Child, Adolescent and Family Clinic Postgrad. Ctr. for Mental Health, N.Y.C., 1981-83, assoc. staff mem. Adult Clinic, 1984-87; social worker East Harlem Consultation Svc., N.Y.C., 1983-84; sr. worker Jewish Bd. Family and Children's Svcs., Bklyn., 1984-85; sch. social worker N.Y.C. Bd. Edn., 1985—. Co-chair regional staff devel. com. N.Y.C. Bd. Edn., 1996-98; presenter in field, N.Y.C., 1995-97. Mem. NAFE, NASW. Home: 229 W 105th St Apt 53 New York NY 10025-3918

GRANDMAISON, J. JOSEPH, federal agency administrator; b. Nashua, N.H., May 19, 1943; s. Oscar N. and Irene P. (Bouchard) G. BA, Burdett Coll., 1963. Campaign dir. Dukakis for Gov., Boston, 1973-74; dir. fed. state relations Commonwealth of Mass., Washington, 1975—; Dem. candidate U.S. Ho. of Reps., 1976; fellow John F. Kennedy Inst. Politics Harvard U., 1976—; fed. co-chmn. New Eng. Regional Commn., Washington, 1977-81; econ. devel. and polit. cons. Augusta, Maine, 1981—93; v.p. Weil & Howe, Augusta, 1983—93; commentator, polit. analyst Sta. WMUR-TV, Manchester, 1986—; dir. U.S. Trade and Devel. Agy., Washington, 1993—2001. Adj. prof. Boston U. Coll. Communications; co-host Focus N.H., 1987-90; bd. dirs. U.S. Export-Import Bank. Mem. bd. aldermen, Nashua, NH, 1970—71; chair N.H. Dem. Party, 1987—90; dem. nominee Gov. of N.H., 1990. Democrat. Roman Catholic. Office: US Export Import Bank Bd of Dir 811 Vermont Ave NW Washington DC 20571-0001 Office Fax: 202-565-3533.

GRAND-MAITRE, JEAN, performing company executive; b. Hull, Quebec; Studied at, York U., Montreal's L'Ecole superieure de danse du Quebec, 1983—86. Ind. choreographer Can. and Europe, 1990—2002; artistic dir. Alberta Ballet, 2002—. Danced with Theatre Ballet of Can., 1987—89, Les Ballets de Montreal Eddy Toussaint, 1990, Ballet British Columbia, 1991; artist in residence Bayerisches Staatsballet, 1998—99, Nat. Norwegian Ballet, 1999—2000. Major commissions include La Veglia degli Angeli, Teatro all Scala, Milan, 1995, Exilium, Stuggart Ballet, 1997, Eja Mater, Paris Opera Ballet, 1997, Ecclesia and Emma B., Bavarian State Ballet, Munich, 1998, 1999, Liaisons Dangereuses, Nat. Ballet of Norway, 2000, Frames of Mind, Hartford Ballet, 1995, Ancient Airs and Uroboros, 1996, 1999, Romeo and Juliet, Dance Conneticut, 2000, The Winter Room, Ballet BC, 1995, Boy Wonder, 1996, Tema Celeste, 2000, La Memoire de l'eau, Les Grand Ballets Canadiens, 1997. Nominee Dora Mavor Moore award. Office: Alberta Ballet Nat Christie Ctr 141-18 Ave South West Calgary AL T2S 0B8 Canada

GRANDONE-LLORENTE, MARIA ELISA, dean, consultant; b. Ponce, P.R., June 14, 1973; d. Roberto Grandone and Maria Antonia Cruz; m. Rafael Angel Llorente. B in Psychology, Pontifical Cath. U., Ponce, 1995; M in Founds. on Adult and Continuing Edn., Kans. State U., 1997, PhD in Founds. on Adult and Continuing Edn., 2001. Sr. coord. McNair Program, Manhattan, Kans.; ESL coord. Kans. State U., Manhattan; dir. internat. rels., dean students Concordia U., Irvine, Calif., 2001—. Cons./rschr. Dept. Water and Power, L.A.; cons. in field. Com. mem. Diversity Concordia, Calif., 2001—; bd. dirs. edn. Hispanic Chamber, Calif., 2002, Preparing for a Degree, Calif., 2003. Mem.: AESA, NASPA, Hispanic Assn. Colls. and Univs., Assn. Coll. Pers. Office: Concordia Univ Irvine 1530 Concordia West Irvine CA 92612

GRANDSTRAND, RUTH HELENA, retired community health and gerontology nurse; b. Shafer, Minn., Jan. 28, 1916; d. Gustav Furman and Edna Gertrude (Paulson) Hawkinson; m. Clifford J. Grandstrand, Aug. 28, 1943; children: Mark Clifford, Lois Ruth, Gail Louise (dec.) Diploma, Bethesda Sch. Nursing, St. Paul, 1937; postgrad., U. Minn., 1938-39. Cert. in hospice mgmt. Surg. nursing supr. Asbury Hosp., Mpls., 1939-41; instr. nursing arts Bethesda Hosp., 1941-43; dir. insvc. edn. Margaret S. Parmly Residence, Chisago City, Minn., 1977-85; home care nurse Meml. Enterprises, Freeport, Ill., 1985-94; ret., 1994. Home care nurse, Freeport. Vol. Ret. Sr. Vol. Program. 2d lt. Army Nurse Corps, 1941-43. Mem. Minn. Nurses Assn., Ill. Nurses Assn.

GRANER, EVAN, academic administrator; s. Theresa DeLong and Gerald Graner. BA, Concordia Coll., 1999. Admissions counselor Ill. Inst. Tech., Chgo., 2000; acad. advisor DePaul U., Coll. Commerce, Chgo., 2000—02, asst. dir. undergrad. programs, 2003—. Presenter at confs. Judge Evanston H.S. Speech Team, Ill., 2000—03. Mem.: Nat. Assn. Student Pers. Adminstrs., Nat. Acad. Advising Assn., Assn. Internat. Educators. Avocation: travel. Office: DePaul Univ Coll Commerce 1 East Jackson Blvd Ste 8500 Chicago IL 60657 E-mail: egraner@depaul.edu.

GRANGAARD, DANIEL ROBERT, psychologist; b. Fond du Lac, Wis., Jan. 7, 1950; s. Lawrence Robert and Dorothy Ruth (Giove) G.; m. Becky Anne Byas, June 16, 1979; children: Dawn Michelle, Scott Robert. BA, Baylor U., 1972, MS, 1974, EdD, 1976. Lic. psychologist; lic. specialist in sch. psychology. Teaching fellow Baylor U., Waco, Tex., 1974-76; assoc. sch. psychologist Edn. Svc. Ctr. Region XII, 1976-77; sch. psychologist Austin Ind. Sch. Dist., 1977-85; dir. testing, internship tng. Minirth-Meier Tunnell & Wilson Clinic, 1989-94; pvt. practice, 1985—89, 1994—2000. Psychologist Genesis unit Shoal Creek Hosp., Austin, 1987—92, 1994—95; cons. psychologist Charter Hosp., Austin, 1984—94, United Cerebral Palsy Assn., 1992—98, Genesis Behavioral Health Clinic, Austin, 1994—95, Austin Child Guidance Ctr., 1995—96; instr. psychology Austin C.C., 1995—, coll. assoc. student svcs., 2001—; adj. prof. psychology St. Edwards U., 1997—2001. Author: psychology textbook supplements; contbr. chpts. to books, articles to profl. jours.; webpage designer Austin C.C., 1999—. Westcreek rep. Austin Neighborhood Coun., 1980; coach YMCA Little League Baseball, 1995-99; dir. counseling First Evangel. Free Ch., Austin, 1994-95, elder, 1993-96. Mem. APA, Soc. for Tchg. of Psychology, Tex. C.C. Tchrs. Assn. Republican. Mem. Evangelical Free Ch. Avocations: golf, basketball, model railroading, fly fishing. Office: Austin CC Rio Grande Campus 1212 Rio Grande St Austin TX 78701-1710 E-mail: dgran@austincc.edu.

GRANGE, GEORGE ROBERT, II, lawyer; b. Alexandria, Va., Apr. 14, 1947; s. George Robert and Lucille (Bell) G.; m. Kathy McPeek, Aug. 21, 1971; children: Steven, John, George Robert III, Sarah Ruth, Peter Mark. BA with honors, U. Va., 1969; postgrad., Yale U., 1970-71; JD, Harvard U., 1974. Bar: Mass. 1975, D.C. 1975, U.S. Supreme Ct. 1980, U.S. Dist. Ct. D.C. 1984, U.S. Ct. Appeals (D.C. cir.) 1984, U.S. Ct. Appeals (fed. cir.) 1988, U.S. Claims Ct. 1989. Assoc. Zuggert, Scott & Rasenberger, Washington, 1975-77; prin. Gammon & Grange, Washington, 1977—. CEO Dialogs, 1990—. Bd. dirs. Evang. Coun. for Fin. Accountability, Washington, 1980-88, Christian Mgmt. Assn., 1988-91. Mem. Christian Legal Soc. (nat. bd. dirs. 1983-91), D.C. Bar Assn., Va. Bar Assn., Nat. Bar Assn., Phi Beta Kappa. Republican. E-mail: GRG@GandGLaw.com.

GRANGE, MARY JANE, writer, adult nurse practitioner; b. Sheridan, Wyoming, July 13, 1946; d. Edward Marshall Hartman, Sr. and Virgina Belle (Coffman) Hartman; m. Joseph Edwin Grange, Feb. 29, 1936; children: Richard, Debbie, Cindy, David, Joseph, Sherry, Jeff, Cheryl;1 child, Pamela. AS, Sheridan Jr. Coll., Sheridan, WY., 1968; BS Nursing, U. Wyo., Laramie, WY., 1970; grad. ICU course, L.D.S. Hosp., Salt Lake City, UT., 1980. Student nurse Dr. Gerdd Smith, Cheyenne, Wyo.; supr. UT. State Hosp., Provo, Utah; staff RN UT. Valley Hosp., Provo, Utah, Dr. Allen Thomas, Salt Lake City, L.D.S. Hosp., Salt Lake City. Author: The Medicine Wheel for Step Parents, 2000, So You are Tired of Being a Lame Duck, 2001, The Nurse and the Prophet, 2001. Sec. Wasatch Beekeepers Assn., Salt Lake City, 1992 ; amateur radio operator UARC, Salt Lake City, 1999—.

GRANGE-MAASOUMI, LYNETTE DANIELLE, community health nurse, educator; b. Camrose, Alta., Can., May 14, 1967; arrived in U.S., 1986; d. Gordon Dale and Danielda (Fair) Grange; m. Esfandiar Maasoumi, Oct. 23, 1999; 1 child, Maya Amitis Maasoumi. ASN, Pacific Union Coll., Angwin, Calif., 1988, BSN, 1989; MSN, U. So. Calif., 1995. RN Tex., Calif., cert. family nurse practitioner, childbirth educator, profl. health svc. credential, Calif., cert. pub. health nurse, Calif., Sch. Audiometrist, Calif., scoliosis, vision and hearing screening, Tex. Charge nurse, fl. nurse Glendale (Calif.) Adventist Med. Ctr., 1988-91, Lamaze instr., 1990-94; sch. nurse L.A. Unified Sch. Dist., 1992-94, family nurse practitioner, 1994-96, resource nurse practitioner, 1996-99; clin. instr. women's health and cmty. health Tex. Woman's U., Dallas, 1999—. Vol. health counselor Glendale Adventist Med. Ctr., 1990. Alexander Rutherford scholar, 1984, Leavey scholar, 1993—95. Mem.: Attention Deficit Disorder Assn. (so. region), Tex. Assn. Sch. Nurses, Am. Acad. Nurse Practitioners, Sigma Theta Tau. Office: Tex Woman s Univ Coll Nursing 1810 Inwood Rd Dallas TX 75235-7299

GRANGER, CARL V. physician, educator; b. Bklyn., Nov. 26, 1928; s. Carl Victor and Marie Henson Granger; m. Helen Bolden (div. 1983); m. Joanne Champion (dec. 1994); m. Eloise Morrow, Sept. 1, 1995; children: Glenn, Marilyn. BA, Dartmouth Coll., 1948; MD, NYU, 1952. Bd. cert. in phys. medicine and rehab. Intern Nassau County Med. Ctr., Hempstead, N.Y., 1952-53; resident in phys. medicine and rehab. Walter Reed Army Med. Ctr., Washington, 1955-58; asst. prof. Yale U., New Haven, 1961-68; prof., chmn. Tufts U., Boston, 1968-76; prof. Brown U., Providence, 1977-83, U. Buffalo, 1983—, prof., chmn. rehab. medicine, 1998-2001. Contbr. articles to profl. jours. Maj. U.S. Army, 1954-61. Mem. Alpha Kappa Phi. Office: Uniform Data Sys Med Rehab Ste 300 270 Northpointe Pkwy Amherst NY 14228 E-mail: CGranger@udsmr.org.

GRANGER, CLIVE WILLIAM JOHN, economist, educator; b. Swansea, Wales, Sept. 4, 1934; came to U.S., 1974. s. Edward John and Evelyn Agnes (Hessey) G.; m. Patricia Ann Loveland, May 14, 1960; children: Mark, Claire. BA, U. Nottingham, Eng., 1955; PhD in Stats., U. Nottingham, 1959, DSc, 1992, Carlos III, Madrid, 1997; D. Econ. (hon.), Stockholm Sch. Econs., 1998; DSc (hon.), Loughborough U., 2002. Lectr. in maths. U. Nottingham, 1956—64; prof. stats., 1964—74; prof. econs. U. Calif., San Diego, 1976—2002; chancellor's assoc. chair, 1994—2002; ret., 2003. Author: Forecasting Stock Markets, 1970; editor: Commodity Markets, 1973. Fellow Harkness Fund, 1959-60, Econometric Soc., 1973, Guggenheim Found., 1988. Fellow: Am. Econ. Soc. (Disting.), Am. Acad. Arts and Scis., Brit. Acad. (corr.). Avocations: hiking, swimming, travel, reading. Office: U Calif San Diego Econs Dept D-008 La Jolla CA 92093

GRANGER, HARVEY, JR., retired manufacturing company executive; b. Savannah, Ga., Sept. 9, 1928; s. Harvey and Marion (Rauers) G.; m. Barbara Brandt, Sept. 8, 1951; children: Harvey, Matthew Brandt, Barbara James. B in Indsl. Engring., Ga. Inst. Tech, 1951. Indsl. engr. Union Camp Paper Co., Savannah, 1950-56, Great Dane Trailers, Savannah, 1956-61, plant mgr., 1961-71, v.p. mfg., 1971-78, exec. v.p., chief operating officer, 1978-84, pres., chief exec. officer, 1984-91; cons. Savannah, 1992-96; ret., 1996. City adv. bd. dirs. Nations Bank, Savannah, 1979-95. Mem. adv. bd. Sch. Engring. Ga. Inst. Tech., 1985-91; mem. bd. trustees St. Joseph's Hosp., Savannah, 1988-97, vice-chmn. 1995, chmn. 1996-97; chmn. bd. trustees St. Joseph's-Candler Health Sys., Savannah, 1997-2000, vice chmn., 2000—03; dir. vol. trustees Not-For-Profit Hosps., Washington, 1995—2003, mem. exec. com., 1997, sec., 1998, vice chmn., 1999—2003. With USN, 1945-47. Mem. Truck Trailer Mfrs. Assn. (chmn. 1986-87). Clubs: Oglethorpe (Savannah) (pres. 1984-85), Savannah Golf. Avocations: golf, fishing. Home: 405 Coveview Dr Savannah GA 31406-3204

GRANGER, KAY, congresswoman; b. Greenville, Tex., Jan. 18, 1943; children: John Dean, Chelsea, Brandon. BS, Tex. Wesleyan U., 1965, DHL. Mem. zoning com. City of Ft. Worth, 1981—89; mem. pvt. industry coun., 1988-89; councilwoman City of Ft. Worth, 1989-91, mayor, 1991-95; mem. 105th-108th Congress from 12th Tex. dist., 1997—; owner G&R Ins. Agy., Ft. Worth. Owner Kay Granger & Assocs. Recipient Woman of Yr. award, 1987, Bus. and Profl. Woman award, 1987; named Exec. of Yr., Ft. Worth Bus. Hall of Fame, 1999; inductee Tex. Women's Hall of Fame, 1999. Mem. Am. Planning Assn., Internat. Sister Cities Assn., Women's Policy Forum (bd. dirs.), East Ft. Worth Bus. and Profl. Assn. (bd. dirs.), Ft. Worth Bus. and Estate Planning Coun., Meadowbrook Bus. and Profl. Womens Assn., East Ft. Worth C. of C. (vice chmn.). Republican. Methodist.*

GRANGER, LUC ANDRE, university dean, psychologist; b. St. Jean, Que., Can., Apr. 8, 1944; s. Andrew and Georgette (Lacasse) G. BA, U. Montreal, 1962, B.Sc., 1964, L.P.S., 1966, PhD, 1969. Asst. prof. psychology U. Montreal, 1969-73, assoc. prof., 1973-79, prof., 1979—, head dept., 1979-83, 90—, assoc. dean, 1983-87. Author: Apprentissage et Therapie, 1972, La Therapie Behaviorale, 1976, La Communication dans le Couple, 1979. Postdoctoral fellow U. Lille, France, 1969 Mem. Can. Psychol. Assn. (sec.-treas. 1982-85, pres. 1992-95), Corp. des Psychologues (treas. 1974-78, pres. 1986-90). Office: U Montreal Dept Psychology CP 6128 Succa Centre Ville Montreal QC Canada H3C 3J7 E-mail: luc.granger@umontreal.ca.

GRANGER, PHILIP RICHARD, minister; b. Detroit, June 19, 1943; s. Myrl Richard and Alvirta May (Kling) G.; m. Karen Elizabeth Draper, Feb. 20, 1965 (div. 1972); children: Mark, Leslie; m. Susan Kay Alderfer, Mar. 4, 1973; children: Randall, Candace. AA, Jackson Jr. Coll., 1963; BA, MBA, Mich. State U., 1965, 67; MDiv, No. Bapt. Theol. Sem., Lombard, Ill., 1978; D of Ministry, Oral Roberts U., 1986. Ordained deacon United Meth. Ch., 1977, ordained elder, 1980; CPA, Mich. Audit staff, cons. Ernst & Ernst, Detroit, 1967-71; mem. contrs. staff Assocs. Corp., South Bend, Ind., 1971-73; v.p., contr. 1st Fed. Savs. and Loan, Chgo., 1973-76; pastor Mokena (Ill.) United Meth. Ch., 1976-82; dir. fin. No. Ind. Conf. United Meth. Ch., Marion, 1982-86; sr. pastor St. Lukes United Meth. Ch., Kokomo, Ind., 1986-89, Trinity United Meth. Ch., Huntington, Ind., 1989-94; dist. supt. Kokomo (Ind.) Dist. United Meth. Ch., 1994-99; sr. pastor Coll. Ave. United Meth. Ch., Muncie, Ind., 1999—2001; pres., CEO Mission Soc. United Meths., 2001—. Mem. adj. faculty Huntington Coll., 1990-94; new life missioner Gen. Bd. Discipleship, Nashville, 1980—; past chmn. bd. dirs. Good News, Wilmore, Ky., Samaritan Ctr., Inc., Huntington, Found. for Mission and Ministry, Inc., Marion; del. gen .conf. United Meth. Ch., 1988, 92, 96, 2000; bd. dirs. gen. bd. Ch. & Soc., Washington. Author: Discernment Planning, 1986. Founding mem. Tri-Village Crisis Intervention Ctr., Mokena, 1978-81; treas. Village of Mokena, 1978-82; bd. dirs. Mental Health Assn. Ill., Chgo., 1974-75. Mem. Am. Assn. Christian Counselors, Rotary Internat., Delta Sigma Pi, Beta Gamma Sigma, Beta Alpha Psi. Avocations: reading, travel, personal computers. Office: Mission Soc United Meths 6234 Crooked Creek Rd Norcross GA 30092 Home: 228 Brookcliff Dr Sugar Hill GA 30518-8197 E-mail: pgranger@msum.org. *To experience life requires more than experiencing the simple joys and pleasures that life provides. To really experience life is to experience the Christian community of caring and sharing that only occurs when we are truly one in Christ.*

GRANGER, ROBERT ALAN, mechanical and aerospace engineering educator; b. Evanston, Ill., Aug. 7, 1928; s. Robert Alan and Kathleen (Buehr) G.; m. Ruth Nickerson, Oct. 7, 1951; children: Eric Carl, Erin Alyson. BA, Pomona Coll., 1955; MS, Drexel Inst. Tech., 1959; PhD, U. Md., 1970. Sr. rsch. scientist Martin Co., Balt., 1955-60; prin. engr. Boeing Co., Renton, Wash., 1975; prof. mech. and aerospace engring. U.S. Naval Acad., Annapolis, Md., 1960-98, discipline dir., 1972-75; ret., 1998. Prof. emeritus U.S. Naval Acad., Annapolis, 2001; adj. prof. LSC Coll., 1999, lectr., U. Cambridge (Eng.), 2000—; fellow (hon.) Cambridge (England) U., 1991; pub., CEO Sci. Archives, Inc., 1997; sci. contbr. editor Daily Sun newspaper, 1999; cons. NASA, Boeing Co.; vis. prof. U. Petroleum and Minerals, Saudi Arabia, 1977-79, U. Zurich, Switzerland, 1978, Yale U., 1989; dir. Vortex Dynamics Symposium von Karman Inst., Brussels, Belgium; dir., prin. lectr. Introduction to Wing Flutter Symposium, 1991. Author: Fluid Mechanics, 1985, Unified Method of Aeroelasticity, 1986, Experiments in Fluid Mechanics, 1986, Design of Spacecraft, 1988, Introduction to the Flutter of Winged Aircraft, 1992, Experiments in Heat Transfer and Thermodynamics, 1994, Fluid Mechanics, 1994, Life on Mars, 1997; contbr. over 650 tech. papers to profl. publs. Served with U.S. Army, 1950-52, Korea. Ford Found. fellow, 1965; recipient USN Meritorious Civilian award, 1996, Euler Math. prize, 1999. Hon. mem. Inst. Modern Physics (Athens, Greece); mem. AIAA, Kappa Mu Epsilon, Alpha Gamma Sigma. Republican. Avocations: composing, mountain climbing, writing, tennis, swimming. Home: 31 Hickory Head Hammock Lady Lake FL 32159-8868 E-mail: rgranger@thevillages.net.

GRANHOLM, JENNIFER MULHERN, governor; b. Vancouver, B.C., Can., Feb. 5, 1959; arrived in U.S., 1962; d. Civtor Ivar and Shirley Alfreda (Dowden) Granholm; m. Daniel Granholm Mulhern, May 23, 1986; children: Kathryn, Cecelia, Jack. BA, U. Calif., Berkeley, 1984; JD, Harvard U., 1987. Bar: Mich. 1987, U.S. Dist. Ct. (ea. dist.) Mich. 1987, U.S. Ct. Appeals (6th cir.) 1987. Jud. law clk. 6th Cir Ct. Appeals, Detroit, 1987—88; exec. asst. Wayne County Exec., Detroit, 1988—89; asst. U.S. atty. Dept. Justice, Detroit, 1990—94; corp. counsel Wayne County, Detroit, 1994—98; atty. gen. State of Mich., 1999—2002, gov., 2003—. Gen. counsel Detroit/Wayne County Stadium Authority, 1996—98. Contbr. articles to profl. jours. Commr. Great Lakes Commn.; mem. bd. Cyberstate.org YWCA. Mem.: Inc. Soc. Irish Lawyers, Women's Law Assn., Detroit Bar Assn. Democrat. Roman Catholic. Avocations: running, family, laughing. Office: Gov Office PO Box 30013 Lansing MI 48909*

GRANIK, RUSSELL T. sports association executive; m. Joyce Granik; children: Daniel, Erynn. Grad. magna cum laude, Dartmouth Coll., 1969; law degree cum laude, Harvard U., 1973. With Breed, Abbott & Morgan, N.Y.C.; staff atty. NBA, 1976-78, asst. gen. counsel, 1978-80, gen. counsel, 1980-84, exec. v.p., 1984-90, dep. commr., 1990—. V.p. USA Basketball, 1989-96, pres. 1996—. Trustee, mem. exec. com. Naismith Meml. Basketball Hall of Fame. Office: Nat Basketball Assn Olympic Tower 645 5th Ave Fl 15 New York NY 10022-5910*

GRANIK, VLADIMIR, mechanics researcher, educator; b. USSR, May 16, 1934; came to US, 1991; naturalized, 1996; m. Galina Gaevskaya, Apr. 28, 1957; children: Yuri, Tanya. BS summa cum laude, Civil Engring. Inst., Odessa, USSR, 1957; PhD, Ctrl. Rsch. Inst. Concrete, Moscow, 1967; Assoc. Prof. Strength of Materials, Higher Exam. Bd. USSR, Moscow, 1970, D Tech. Scis., 1990. Rsch. engr. Ctrl. Rsch. Inst. Structural Mechanics, Moscow, 1957-66; assoc. prof. Civil Engring. Inst., Odessa, 1966-69; assoc. prof. structural mechanics Mil. Engring. Acad., Odessa, 1969-72, prof. continuum mechanics, 1972-88; prof. strength of materials Maritime Engring. Inst., Odessa, 1988-91; rsch. fellow in continuum mechanics U. Calif., Berkeley, 1991-93, rsch. assoc. continuum mechanics, 1993-97, prof. cons. strength of materials and structural mechanics, 1997—. Head optimization theory dept. Rsch. Inst. Automation, Odessa, 1985-88; founder Doublet Mechanics. Co-author, co-editor: Advances in Doublet Mechanics, 1997; contbr. articles to profl. jours.; assoc. mem., reviewer Jour. Structural Mechanics and Structure Design, 1981-91. Recipient First Prize Queueing Theory Application award Ministry Def., Moscow, 1976, Academician Gadolin medal Ministry Def., 1984. Achievements include rsch. in doublet mechanics; microstructural mechanics of granular media; stochastic dynamics of granular flows in tall shells (silos); revision of infinitesimal theory of plasticity and yield criteria; stochastic dynamics of supply and demand in a single market; a new theory of osmotic pressures in non-electrolytic solutions of any concentration. Home: 615 W 7th St Apt 205 Antioch CA 94509-1675

GRANIRER, EDMOND ERNEST, mathematician, educator; b. Constanza, Romania, Feb. 19, 1935; s. Jacob G. M.Sc., Hebrew U., Jerusalem, 1959, PhD, 1962. Mem. faculty dept. math. U. Ill., 1962-64, Cornell U., 1964-65, U. B.C., Vancouver, 1965-66, 67—, prof. math., 1970-97, prof. emeritus, 1997—; faculty U. Montreal, 1966-67. Contbr. articles to profl. jours. Grantee NSERC, 1996. Fellow Royal Soc. Can.; mem. Can. Math. Soc., Am. Math. Soc. Office: U BC Dept Math Vancouver BC Canada V6T 1Z2

GRANN, PHYLLIS, former publisher, editor; b. London, Sept. 2, 1937; d. Solomon and Louisa (Bois-Smith) Eitingon; m. Victor Grann, Sept. 28, 1962; children: Alison, David, Edward. BA cum laude, Barnard Coll., 1958. Sec. Doubleday Pubs., N.Y.C., 1958-60; editor William Morrow Inc., N.Y.C., 1960-62, David McKay Co., N.Y.C., 1962-70, Simon & Schuster Inc., N.Y.C., 1970, v.p., 1976; pres., pub. G. P. Putnam's & Sons., N.Y.C., 1976-86; pres. Penguin Putnam, Inc., N.Y.C., 1986-96, CEO, 1987-96, chmn., 1997—2001; vice chmn. Random House, 2002.

GRANNATT, MILTON HENDERSON, III, economist; b. Morristown, N.J., July 20, 1946; s. Milton H. Grannatt, Jr. and Helene B. Grannatt; m. Patricia Schenck, Aug. 1, 1970; children: Theodore Milton, Robert Charles. Industry economist bldg. econs. sect. Nat. Bur. Stds., Washington, 1972—73; economist Chase Manhattan Bank, N.Y.C., 1973—78; dir. industry econs. W.R. Grace & Co., N.Y.C., 1978—79; mgr. econ. and mktg. analysis Lex Svc., Inc., N.Y.C., 1979—82, planning mgr., 1982—84, v.p. planning, supplier devel., 1984—85; v.p. planning Lex Electronics, N.Y.C., 1986—89; v.p. fin. Sterling Drug, Inc., N.Y.C., 1989—94; v.p., licensing Novartis Pharms. Corp., East Hanover, NJ, 1994—. Adj. asst. prof. Rider Coll.; adj. prof. Coll. of N.J. Contbr. articles and revs. to profl. jours.; co-editor: Economics of Tall Buildings, 1981. Mem. Juvenile Conf. Coun., Mercer County, NJ, 1975—. Officer USAR, 1972. Mem.: Licensing Execs. Soc., N.Y. Assn. Bus. Economists, Nat. Assn. Bus. Economists, Planning Forum, Am. Econ. Assn., Trenton Country Club, Alpha Kappa Psi, Omicron Delta Epsilon, Beta Gamma Sigma. Republican. Presbyterian. Home: 4 Pineknoll Dr Lawrenceville NJ 08648-3138

GRANNIS, JOSEPH M. power plant operator; b. Fargo, N.D., Nov. 15, 1962; s. James F. Grannis and Shirley A. Piatz; m. Dawn M. Lang, June 14, 1985; children: Amber D., Tiffany J. Grad., Stanton Pub. Sch., 1981. Worker United Power Assn., Stanton, N.D., 1982-84; plant operator United Power Assn. (now Great River Energy), Stanton, 1985—. Mem. city coun., City of Stanton, 1987—, pres. city coun., 1995—, mayor, 1999-2001, sch. bd., 1990-92. Avocations: reading, hunting, woodworking. Home: PO Box 291 Stanton ND 58571-0291

GRANOF, MICHAEL H. accounting educator; b. N.Y.C., June 16, 1942; s. David H. and Diana (Simon) G.; m. Dena Gloria Hirsch, Aug. 27, 1972; children: Leah, Joshua AB, Hamilton Coll., 1963; MBA, Columbia U., 1965; PhD, U. Mich., 1972. CPA, Tex. Sr. acct. Coopers & Lybrand, N.Y.C., 1966-68; asst. prof. to prof. acctg. U. Tex., Austin, 1972-84, Ernst & Young disting. centennial prof., chmn. acctg. dept., 1984-88. Mem. Nat. Council on Govtl. Acctg., 1982-84, Govtl. Acctg. Standards Adv. Council, Norwalk, Conn., 1984-90; Fulbright prof. Council for Internat. Exchange Scholars, Hebrew U., Jerusalem, 1978-79; vis. prof. U. Tel Aviv, 1981. Author: How To Cost Your Labor Contract, 1973, Financial Accounting: Principles and Issues, 1977, 4th edit., 1990, Accounting for Managers and Investors, 1983, 2d edit., 1993, Government and Not-for-Profit Accounting, 1998, 2d edit, 2001 Core Concepts in Government and Not-for -Profit Accounting, 2003; co-editor: Government Accounting and Auditing Update, 1989-97. Co-pres. Congregation Agudas Achim; treas. Austin Area Urban League. With USCG, 1965-66 Erskine fellow U. Canterbury, Christchurch, N.Z., 1983 Mem. AICPAs (com. on govt. acctg. and auditing), Am. Acctg. Assn. (chmn. pub. sector sect. 1981-82), Tex. Soc. CPAs (chmn. govt. acctg. standards com.), Govt. Fin. Officers Assn., Assn. Govt. Accts. Jewish. Home: 7310 Valburn Dr Austin TX 78731-1146 Office: U Tex Dept Acctg CBA 4M 202 Austin TX 78712 E-mail: michael.granof@bus.utexas.edu.

GRANOFF, BARRY, mathematician, educator; b. Jersey City, N.J., June 30, 1938; s. Herbert and Dorothy (Gottlieb) Granoff; m. Betty Joan Kuhn, Jan. 8, 1989; 1 child, Molly Yande Granoff-Kuhn. BS, Fairleigh Dickinson U., 1960; MS, PhD, N.Y. U., 1965. Assoc. rsch. scientist Courant Inst. Math. Sci., N.Y. U., 1965—66; assoc. prof. math. Boston U., 1966—. Assoc. prof. math. Harvard U., 1984—2001. Contbr. articles. Grad. fellow, Courant Inst. Math. Sci., N.Y. U., 1960—62, NSF, 1962—65. Avocations: woodworking, gardening. Home: 1401 Walnut St Newton MA 02461 Office: Boston Univ 111 Cummington St Boston MA 02215 E-mail: bg@bu.edu.

GRANOFF, DAN MARTIN, research scientist; b. N.Y.C., Jan. 22, 1944; s. N. Henry and Jeannette (Trum) G.; m. Alice B. Baghdassarian, Feb. 15, 1971 (div May 1986); children: Jeffrey, Jonathan. AB, Johns Hopkins U., 1965, MD, 1968. Diplomate Am. Bd. Pediat. Pediatric resident Johns Hopkins Hosp., Balt., 1969-71, infectious disease fellow Case Western Res. U., Cleve., 1973-75; asst. chief pediat. Valley Med. Ctr., Fresno, Calif., 1975-79; asst. clin. prof. pediat. U. Calif., San Francisco, 1977-79; assoc. prof. pediat. E. Carolina U., Greenville, NC, 1979-80, Washington U. Sch. Medicine, St. Louis, 1980-85, prof. pediat. and assoc. prof. molecular microbiology, 1985-93; dir. Divsn. Infectious Diseases St. Louis Children's Hosp., 1980-93; exec. dir. Clin. Rsch., Chiron Corp., Emeryville, Calif., 1993-95; v.p. Sci. Affairs, Chiron Vaccines, Emeryville, 1995-98. Rsch. scientist Children's Hosp. Oakland Rsch. Inst., Oakland, Calif., 1993-98, sr. rsch. scientist, 1998—; cons. WHO, 1999—. Editor: (book) Development and Clinical Uses of Haemophilus b Conjugate Vaccines, 1994, (jour.) Pediatric Rsch., 1989-92; contbr. numerous articles to profl. jours.; patentee in field. Maj. USAF, 1971-73. Grantee in bacterial immunology Nat. Inst. Allergy, Immunology and Infectious Diseases, NIH, Washington, 1980—97, in bacterial immunology Nat. Inst. Allergy, Immunology and Infecious Diseases, 2000—. Fellow Infectious Diseases Soc. of Am., Am. Acad. Pediatrics (mem. infectious disease com. 1991-93); mem. Am. Soc. Clin. Investigation (emeritus), Soc. for Pediatric Rsch. (emeritus), Am. Pediatrics Soc., Am. Soc. Microbiology (mem. organizing com. Intersci. conf. on antimicrobial agts. and chemotherapy 1998-2000). Office: Childrens Hosp Oakland Rsch Inst 5700 Martin Luther King Jr Way Oakland CA 94609-1673 E-mail: dgranoff@chori.org.

GRANOFF, GAIL PATRICIA, lawyer; b. Phila., July 25, 1952; d. Jerome Claymont and Jean (Kessler) G.; m. Stanley B. Edelstein; children: Jessica, Jonathan. AB, Temple U., 1973; JD, U. Pa., 1976. Bar: Pa. 1976, U.S. Dist. Ct. (ea. dist.) Pa. 1977, U.S. Ct. Appeals (3d cir.) 1977, U.S. Supreme Ct. 1981. Law clk. to Judge Kalodner U.S. Ct. Appeals (3d cir.), Phila., 1976-77; assoc. Pepper Hamilton & Scheetz, Phila., 1977-84; counsel Rohm and Haas Co., Phila., 1984-86, sr. counsel, 1987-90, corp. sec., sr. counsel, 1990-93, asst. gen. counsel and corp. sec., 1993—. Mem. ABA (chair Reporting Cos. Under the '34 Act, Fed. Securities Com., Bus. Law sect. 1995—), Phila. Bar Assn. (exec. young lawyers sect. 1983-86, sec. 1984-86, commn. on jud. selection and retention investigative divsn. 1985-95, exec. com. bus. law sect. 1998—), Am. Corp. Counsel Assn. Office: Rohm & Haas Co 100 Independence Mall W Philadelphia PA 19106-2399

GRANOFF, GARY CHARLES, lawyer, investment company executive; b. N.Y.C., Feb. 2, 1948; s. N. Henry and Jeannette (Trum) G.; m. Leslie Barbara Resnick, Dec. 21, 1969; children: Stephen, Robert, Joshua. BBA in Acctg., George Washington U., 1970, JD with honors, 1973. Bar: N.Y. 1974, Fla. 1974, U.S. Dist. Ct. (so. dist.) N.Y. 1976. Assoc. Dreyer & Traub, N.Y.C., 1973-75; ptnr. Ezon, Langberg & Granoff, N.Y.C., 1975-78, Granoff & Walker, N.Y.C., 1982-92, Granoff, Walker & Forlenza PC, N.Y.C., 1993—; pvt. practice N.Y.C., 1978-81; pres., also bd. dirs. Elk Assocs. Funding Corp., N.Y.C., 1979—, GCG Assocs., Inc., N.Y.C., 1982—; pres., dir. Gemini Capital Corp., 1996—; pres., chmn. Ameritrans Capital Corp., 1999—. Atty. del. to U.S.-China Joint Session on Trade, Investment and Econ. Law, Beijing, 1987; dean's adv. bd. George Washington U. Law Sch., 1993—. Campaign vol. Mondale for Pres., N.Y.C., 1984; fundraiser Robert Garcia for Congress, Dem. Senatorial Campaign Com., N.Y.C., 1987—88; active N.Y. Lawyers for Dukakis Com., 1988; chmn. N.Y.C. chpt. George Washington U. Nat. Law Ctr. Leadership Gifts Com., 1998 ; trustee George Washington U., 1998—2003, Parker Jewish Inst. for Health Care and Rehab., 2001—; chmn. fin. com. George Washington U., 2001—02. Recipient Jacob Burns award George Washngton U. Law Sch., 1998. Mem. ABA, N.Y. State Bar Assn., Fla. Bar Assn., Assn. Bar City N.Y., People to People Internat., Nat. Assn. Investment Cos. (legis com.), George Washington U. Alumni Assn. (chmn. N.Y.C. chpt., bd. dirs. law sch. alumni assn., alumni com. 21 century, trustee), North Shore Country Club (chmn. legal com., bd. govs. 1994-96, 98-2001, chmn. admissions com. 1999-2001). Avocations: golf, tennis, skiing. Office: Granoff Walker & Forlenza 747 3rd Ave Fl 4 New York NY 10017-2803

GRANROSE, CHERLYN SUE, psychology educator, researcher; b. Dearborn, Mich., Nov. 23, 1942; d. Lawrence Hilmer and Margaret Elizabeth (Gleason) Skromme; m. John Thomas Granrose, Apr. 14, 1963 (div. Dec. 1973); children: Karen Lynn, Kathleen Diane(dec.), Jonathon Lawrence. BS in Zoology, U. Mich., 1964, MS in Zoology, 1966; MS in Counseling Edn., Kans. State U., 1977; PhD in Psychology, Rutgers U., 1981. Rsch. asst. zoology U. Mich., Ann Arbor, 1966; adj. instr. biology U. Ga., Athens, 1967-72; biology instr. Kans. State U., Manhattan, 1974-78; psychology instr. Rutgers U., Newark, 1980; rsch. asst. AT&T, N.J., 1979-81; from asst. to assoc. prof. human resource adminstrn. Temple U., Phila., 1981-93; assoc. prof. mgmt. Clarkson U., Potsdam, N.Y., 1989; prof. psychology Claremont (Calif.) Grad. Sch., 1993-2000; dir. grad. edn. Berry Coll., Rome, Ga., 2000—02, prof. mgmt., 2000—. Cons. Development Dimensions Internat., Pitts., 1982-89, Phila.

Suburban Water, 1986-90, A&P/SuperFresh Foods, Phila., 1982-84. Author: The Careers of Business Managers in East Asia, 1997; co-author: Science, Sex and Society, 1979, Job Saving Strategies, Worker Ownership and Quality of Work Life, 1989, Work-Family Role Choices for Women in their 20s and 30s, 1996; editor: Cross-Cultural Work Groups, 1997, Careers of Business Managers in East Asia, 1997; contbr. articles to profl. jours. Mem. adminstrv. bd. First United Meth. Ch. of Germantown, Phila., 1986-88, LWV, Athens, Ga., 1966-72. Fulbright fellow, South Korea, Taiwan, 1988, Singapore, 1991, China, 1997, 98, Radcliffe fellow H. Murray Ctr., 1991, Rackham fellow U. Mich., 1965-66, Danforth Found. fellow, 1968-72. Mem. Am. Psychol. Soc., Soc. Indsl. Orgn. Psychologists, Assn. Internat. Bus., Acad. Mgmt. (divsn. bd. dirs. 1982-94), Phi Kappa Phi, Sigma Xi. Democrat. Avocations: scuba diving, poetry, folk music. Office: Berry Coll Campbell Sch Bus Rome GA 30149-5024 E-mail: cgranrose@berry.edu.

GRANSTEIN, RICHARD DAVID, dermatologist; b. Detroit, July 24, 1952; s. Harry and Estella Leah Granstein; m. Ilene Siegal, Nov. 24, 1985; children: Justin, Alicia. SB, MIT, 1974; MD, UCLA, 1978. Diplomate Nat. Bd. Med. Examiners, Am. Bd. Dermatology. Intern Harbor-UCLA Med. Ctr., Torrance, 1978-79; resident in dermatology Mass. Gen. Hosp., Boston, 1979-81, rsch. fellow, 1982-84, NCI-Frederick (Md.) Cancer Rsch. Facility, 1981-82; asst. prof. dermatology Harvard Med. Sch., Boston, 1984-90, assoc. prof. dermatology, 1990-96; dermatologist-in-chief N.Y. Presbyn. Hosp., N.Y.C., 1995—; chmn., prof. dermatology Weill Med. Coll., Cornell U., N.Y.C., 1995—. Cons. Connetics Corp., Palo Alto, Calif., 1995—98, Zeneca, Wilmington, Del., 1999—2000; sci. adv. bd. AGI Dermatics, Freeport, NY, 1998—. Editor: Mechanisms of Immune Regulation, 1994. Fellow Am. Acad. Dermatology, N.Y. Acad. Medicine, N.Y. Dermatol. Soc.; mem. Soc. Investigative Dermatology (bd. dirs. 1995-2000), Am. Soc. Clin. Investigation, Alpha Omega Alpha. Avocations: skiing, tennis. Office: Weil Med Coll Cornell U 1300 York Ave Rm F-342 New York NY 10021-4805 E-mail: rdgranst@med.cornell.edu.

GRANSTROM, MARVIN LEROY, civil and sanitary engineering educator; b. Anaconda, Mont., Sept. 25, 1920; s. Carl August and Alida Sophia (Eckstrom) G.; m. Ruth Maybelle Olsen, Jan. 1, 1944; children— David Marvin, Kay Ruth, Chris Carl. BS, Morningside Coll., 1942; BS in Civil Engring, Iowa State Coll., 1943; MS in San. Engring, Harvard, 1947, PhD, 1955. Engring. aide Soil Conservation Service, Whiting, Iowa, 1939; cons. engr. Sioux Falls, S.D., 1946; instr. civil and san. engring. Case Inst. Tech., 1947-49; assoc. prof. san. engring. U. N.C., 1949-58; prof. civil engring. Rutgers U., New Brunswick, N.J., 1958-83, prof. emeritus, 1983; research participant Oak Ridge Nat. Labs., 1954; cons. Nat. Engring. Sch., Lima, Peru, 1955-57, WHO, 1966—. Cons. in hydrology, 1970— Author articles in field. Served with USMCR, 1943-46. Research grantee N.C., 1953; Research grantee NIH, 1954-58; Research grantee NSF, 1954-63; Research grantee Army Chem. Center, 1961-64; Research grantee surgeon gen. U.S. Army, 1962; Research grantee Office Water Resources Research, Dept. Interior, 1965-76; Research grantee N.J. Dept. Environ. Protection, 1957— ; fellow Nat. Found., 1946-47; fellow USPHS, 1952-53 Mem. Am. Chem. Soc., ASCE, Am. Water Works Assn., Am. Water Resources Assn., Am. Acad. Environ. Engrs., Tau Beta Pi, Sigma Xi, Delta Omega, Chi Epsilon. Home: Apt 347 620 Hwy 35 S Middletown NJ 07748

GRANT, ALAN J. business executive, educator; b. Chgo., Dec. 18, 1925; s. Hugo Bernard and May (Gardner) G.; m. Margaret Stewart, Dec. 21, 1946; children: Pamela Rose, Deborah May, Bruce David. BSEE, Ill. Inst. Tech., 1946, MSEE, 1948; EdD, U. San Diego, 1992. Instr. elec. engring. Ill. Inst. Tech., Chgo., 1946-49; with N.Am. Aviation, Inc. (Autonetics), Anaheim, Calif., 1949-64, v.p., gen. mgr. computer and data systems div., 1962-64; pres. Lockheed Electronics Co. div. Lockheed Aircraft Corp., Plainfield, N.J., 1965-69; also v.p. parent co.; exec. v.p. Aerojet-Gen. Corp., El Monte, Calif., 1970-74; chmn., pres. Wavecom Industries, Sunnyvale, Calif., 1974-78, Primark Corp., San Mateo, Calif., 1975-80; chmn., chief exec. officer Internat. Rotex, Inc., Reno, Nev., 1980-86; dir. UNC Resources Inc, Falls Church, Va., 1974-81; chmn. Atasi Corp., San Jose, Calif., 1982-85; gen. ptnr. EMC Venture Ptnrs., San Diego, 1984-86; pres. Grant Venture Mgmt. Co., Coronado, Calif., 1986-96; chmn. Am. Innovision, San Diego, 1986-92, SalePoint Systems Corp., San Diego, 1987-92. Adj. prof. managerial scis. U. Nev., Reno, 1979—84; mgmt. San Diego State U., 1986—90; pres. Corp. Mgmt. Assocs., 1996—; adj. prof., dir. Ctr. for Entrepreneurship, Calif. State U., Long Beach, 1999—2001; adj. prof. entrepreneurship Calif. State U., Hayward, 2001—. Paul T. Babson prof. entrepreneurship Babson Coll., Babson Park, Mass., 1992-94. Mem. Am. Electronics Assn. (chmn. 1973, dir. 1970-74). Office: Corp Mgmt Assocs 778 Wimbledon Ln Livermore CA 94551-1750 E-mail: agrant105@comcast.net.

GRANT, ALEXANDER MARSHALL, ballet director; b. Wellington, New Zealand, Feb. 22, 1925; s. Alexander Gibb and Eleather May (Marshall) G. Ed., Wellington Coll.; scholarship student, Sadler's Wells Sch., London, 1946-46. Mem. Sadler's Wells Ballet (now Royal Ballet), London, 1946-76, prin. dancer, 1950-76, co-dir. Ballet for All touring co., 1970-71, dir., 1971-76; artistic dir. Nat. Ballet Can., 1976-83, ret. Judge internat. ballet competitions, Jackson, Miss., Moscow, Varna, Bulgaria, Helsinki, Paris, Budapest, Hungary. Prin. dancer London Festival Ballet (now English Nat. Ballet), 1985-91; guest artist Royal Ballet, Joffrey Ballet, English Nat. Ballet; numerous leading roles on stage, also in film Tales of Beatrice Potter, others; staged La Fille Mal Gardeé, various cities, 1988—. Decorated comdr. Brit. Empire.

GRANT, ALFRED DAVID, orthopaedic surgeon, educator; b. N.Y.C., June 12, 1933; s. Charles Meyer and Lillie (Eigen) G.; m. Ellen M. Michels, Apr. 16, 1961; children: Susan, Michele, Laura. BA, Emory U., 1952; MD, Chgo. Medical, 1957. Cert. Nat. Bd. Medical Examiners. Intern 4th surg. divsn. Bellevue Hosp, N.Y., 1957-58; resident gen. surgery Montefiore Hosp, Bronx, N.Y., 1958-59; resident orthopaedic surgery Hosp. for Joint Diseases/Orthopaedic Inst., N.Y., 1959-62; instr., prosecutor gross anatomy Chgo. Medical Sch., 1954-57; assoc. orthopaedic surgery Tulane Medical Sch., 1962-64; pvt. practice orthopaedic surgery, 1964—; with Hosp. Joint Diseases/Orthopaedic Inst., N.Y.C., 1964—, emeritus chief neuromuscular sect. dept. orthopaedics, 1973—, emeritus med. dir. first chance child devel. sch., 1974—, med. dir. Muscular Dystrophy clinic, 1974—, emeritus dir. ctr. neuromuscular and devel. disorders, 1979—97, assoc. dir. orthopaedic surgery, 1982—; clin. asst. prof. orthopaedic surgery Albert Einstein Coll., 1970-79; asst. prof. orthopaedic surgery Mt. Sinai Sch. of Medicine, 1981—; clin. prof. orthopedic surgery NYU Sch. Medicine, 1987-95; clin. prof., 1995—. Vis. surgeon Boston Children's Hosp., 1989, Shriner's Hosp., Springfield, Mass., 1989; asst. attending Montefiore Hosp., 1964—66, Morrisania Hosp., Bronx, NY, 1964—66, Albert Einstein Coll. Hosp., 1969—73; chief orthopaedic surgery United Hosp., Port Chester, NY, 1964—81, cons., 1981—; orthopaedic cons. St. Vincent's Hosp. Westchester Divsn., 1966—, Rye Psychiat. Hosp., 1968—83, Staten Island (N.Y.) Devel. Ctr., 1976—89, Osborne Meml. Home, Rye, 1973—89; attending orthopaedist Rose Kennedy Ctr. Human Devel. and Retardation, Bronx, 1970—73; attending orthopaedics and birth defects clinic Albert Einstein Coll. Hosp., 1969—93; dept. surgery, orthopaedics sect. Beth Israel Hosp., NY, 1979—98. Edit. bd. Bulletin Hosp. Joint Diseases/Orthopaedic Inst.; lectr., presenter numerous courses, papers, symposia in field, U.S., Eur.; contbr. articles, chpts. profl. jours. Bd. trustees United Cerebral Palsy of Westchester, 1982—. HEW grant, 1974-77. Fellow N.Y. Acad. Medicine; mem. AMA, Am. Bd. Orthopaedic Surgery (examiner 1984—), N.Y. Med. Soc., Am. Soc. Surgery Foot and Ankle, Am. Ortho. Assn., Am. Acad. Orthopaedic Surgery (rehab. com. 1984-87), Am. Coll. Surgeons (trauma com. Westchester chpt. 1973-76), Am. Acad. Cerebral Palsy and Devel. Medicine (credential's com. 1987—, sci. program com., 1986-88, rsch. and awards com., 1995—), Pediatric Orthopaedic Club of N.Y. (pres. 1988-89, sec. 1986-87, pres.-elect 1987-88), N.Y. County Med. Soc., Internat. Soc. Prosthetics and Orthotics, N.Y. State Soc. Orthopaedic Surgeons, Pediatric Orthopaedic Soc. No. Am., No. Am. Assn. Study and Application of Methods of Ilizarov, Israel Ortho. Assn. (hon.). Office: Hosp Joint Diseases Orthopaedic Inst 301 E 17th St New York NY 10003-3804

GRANT, ANJALI, architectural firm executive; b. N.Y.C., Jan. 15, 1969; d. Douglas McQueen and Swadesh Sachdeva Grant; m. Daniel Gregg Miller, June 29, 2002. BA, U. Chgo., 1990; MArch, U. Wash., 1996. Project mgr. Walter Schacht Arch., Seattle, 1997—98; designer Jambhekar Strauss PC, N.Y.C., 1998—99; assoc. Mitchell Kurtz Arch. PC, N.Y.C., 1999—2003. Contbr. articles. Recipient Seattle AIA Honor award, 1997.

GRANT, ARTHUR GORDON, JR., lawyer, educator; b. New Orleans, May 16, 1945; s. Arthur Gordon and Martha (McCutchon) G.; children: Arthur Gordon III, Kathryn S., Douglas M. BA, U. N.C., 1967; JD, Tulane U., 1970. Bar: La. 1970, U.S. Ct. Appeals (5th cir.) 1970, U.S. Dist. Ct. (ea. and mid. dists.) La. 1970, U.S. Dist. Ct. (we. dist.) La. 1970, U.S. Ct. Appeals (11th cir.) 1981, U.S. Supreme Ct. 1990, U.S. Dist. Ct. (so. dist.) Tex. 1998. Assoc. Montgomery, Barnett, Brown, Read, Hammond & Mintz, New Orleans, 1970-73, ptnr., 1973—. Admiralty and maritime law instr. U. New Orleans Sch. Naval Architecture, 1990—; bd. dirs. Am. Boat and Yacht Coun., 1990-98, 2002-. Author: Recreational Craft, Jurisdiction, Claims and Coverage, 1989; contbg. author: Recreational Boating Law, 1992, Benedict on Admiralty, Vol. 8, 7th edit., 1995. Fellow La. Bar Found.; mem. Fed. Bar Assn., Navy League of U.S., La. Bar Assn., Soc. Naval Architects and Marine Engrs., Maritime Law Assn. U.S. (vice chmn. recreational boating com. 1990-94, vice chmn. Hull and P&I ins. com.), Bar Assn. 5th Fed. Cir., Southeastern Admiralty Law Inst.(bd. dirs. 2002—), So. Yacht Club, Propellor Club Port, New Orleans. Episcopalian. Avocations: hunting, fishing, boating, civil war history. Office: Montgomery Barnett Brown Read Hammond & Mintz 3200 Energy Ctr New Orleans LA 70163 E-mail: ggrant@monbar.com.

GRANT, BARBARA HURWITZ, educator; b. Ottawa, Ont., Can., Mar. 12, 1955; d. Jan Krosst and Helen Ruth Hurwitz; children: Reilly Morgan, Alexander Maxim. AB, Yale U., 1977, MA, 1978, MPhil, 1979, PhD, 1983. Post-doctoral fellow Wesleyan U., Middletown, Conn., 1983—84; asst. prof. RISD, Providence, 1984—88; rschr. and editor Mid. English Dictionary U. Mich., Ann Arbor, 1991—93; vis. scholar dept. nr. ea. studies Cornell U., Ithaca, NY, 1994—96, curator law rare books Law Libr., 1995—96; faculty Commonwealth Sch., Boston, 1997—. Chmn. Yale Medieval Consortium, New Haven, 1980; chmn. Liberal Arts Lecture Series RISD, Providence, 1984—85, mem. com. on dyslexia policy, 1985, mem. admissions com., 86; mem. Yale Alumni Schs. Com., Boston, 1996—97; dir. Commonwealth Sch. Libr., Boston, 1999—. Robert C. Bates Traveling fellow, Yale U., 1976, Marshall Bidwell fellow, 1977—78, Yale U. fellow, 1978—80, Mary Miller fellow, 1981, Post-doctoral fellow, 1986—87, Hughes Faculty Project grantee, Commonwealth Sch., 2002—03. Mem.: Medieval Acad. Am., Phi Beta Kappa. Avocations: swimming, bicycling, travel. Office: Commonwealth School 151 Commonwealth Ave Boston MA 02116 E-mail: bgrant@commschool.org.

GRANT, BETTYE, writer; b. Flora, Miss., Jan. 13, 1957; d. Mike Connor Thaggard and Ruthie Mae Magee Smoot. AS, Mary Holmes Coll., 1977; BS, Jackson State U., 1983. Author: Rachel's Tears, 2002. Democrat. Avocations: singing, song writing, hiking, bicycling. Office: A Writers Dream Prodn PO Box 31516 Jackson MS 39286

GRANT, CARL N. communications and sales executive; b. Sharon, Pa., July 10, 1939; s. Carl and Hedwig Theresa Nothhaft; m. Carol Ann Pasacic, June 12, 1965; children: Carl, Kevin, Heather Lee. BA, Kent State U., 1963, MA, 1966; PhD, Ohio State U., 1972. With various radio, TV stas., Ohio and Mich., 1962-67; asst. news dir. Sta. WLWC-TV, Columbus, Ohio, 1967-69; news and pub. affairs dir. Sta. WKBS-TV, Phila., 1969-72; exec. staff dir., nat. com. employer support and guard Dept. Def., Washington, 1972-73; dir. Pres. Com. on White House Fellows, Washington, 1973-74; dir. news and pub. affairs Kaiser Broadcasting Corp., Washington, 1974; assoc. dir. and editor Def. Manpower Commn., Washington, 1974-76; dir. pub. affairs Gen. Svcs. Adminstrn., Washington, 1976-77; sr. v.p., exec. counselor to pres. U.S. C. of C., Washington, 1977—. Brig. gen. Army Nat. Guard, ret. 1999. Recipient Investigative Reporting award AP, 1968, 69, Emmy award nomination NATAS, 1968, George Washington medal Freedoms Found., 1989, William Taylor Disting. Alumnus award Kent State U., 1991, Legion of Merit award, 1994. Avocations: running, weight training, golf, cycling. Office: US C of C 1615 H St NW Washington DC 20062-0001

GRANT, CYNTHIA D. writer; b. Brockton, Mass., Nov. 23, 1950; d. Robert Cheyne and Jacqueline Ann (Ford) G.; m. Daniel Heatley; 1 child: Morgan; m. Erik Neel; 1 child, Forest. Author: Joshua Fortune, 1980 (Woodward Park Sch. annual book award 1981), Summer Home, 1981, Big Time, 1982, Hard Love, 1983, Kumquat May, I'll Always Love You, 1986, Phoenix Rising, 1989 (Mich. Libr. Assn. Young Adult Caucus best book of yr. 1990, PEN/Norma Klein award 1991, Detroit Pub. Libr. Author Day award 1992), Keep Laughing, 1991, Shadow Man, 1992, Uncle Vampire, 1993 (ALA best books for young adults list 1994), Mary Wolf, 1995, The White Horse, 1998, The Cannibals, Starring Tiffany Spratt, 2002. Recipient Book of Distinction award Hungry Mind Review, 1993, 94. Mem.: PEN (Norma Klein award 1991), Soc. Children's Book Writers and Illustrators. Avocations: reading, volunteer work, Cloverstock. Home: PO Box 95 Cloverdale CA 95425-0095 Office: Writers House LLC 21 W 26th St New York NY 10010

GRANT, DANIEL HOWARD, author; b. Westport, Conn., Sept. 5, 1954; s. Howard Alexander and Marjorie Grant; m. Alexandra Louise Chesner, Oct. 28, 1984; children: Sarah, Emma. BA, Northwestern U., 1976. Asst. dir. Found. for Cmty. of Artists, N.Y.C., 1976-84; art critic Newsday, Melville, L.I., N.Y., 1980-84, Comml.-Appeal, Memphis, 1984-86; artists' advisor Amherst, Mass., 1986—; prof. Greenfield (Mass.) C.C., 1992—. Lectr. in field. Author: The Business of Being an Artist, 1991, How to Start and Succeed as an Artist, 1993, The Artist's Resource Handbook, 1994, The Writer's Resource Handbook, 1997, The Fine Artist's Career Guide, 1998, The Artist's Guide to Making It in New York, 2001. Chmn. Amherst Cultural Coun., 1992-94, Amherst Pub. Arts Com., 1998—. Home and Office: 19 Summer St Amherst MA 01002-1121 E-mail: danhg@aol.com.

GRANT, DANIEL ROSS, retired academic administrator; b. Little Rock, Aug. 18, 1923; s. James Richard and Gracie (Sowers) Grant; m. Betty Jo Oliver, June 17, 1947; children: Carolyn, Shirley, Ross. BA, Ouachita Bapt. U., 1945; MA, U. Ala., 1946; PhD, Northwestern U., 1948. Asst. prof. polit. sci. Vanderbilt U., 1948-54, assoc. prof., 1954-63, prof., 1963-70, dir. Urban and Regional Devel. Ctr., 1968-70; pres. Ouachita Bapt. U., Akadelphia, Ark., 1970-88, pres. emeritus, 1988—. Assoc. dir. Harris County Home Rule Commn., Houston, 1957; vis. prof. mcpl. govt. and planning Thammasat U., Bangkok, 1958—59; cons. U.S. Adv. Commn. Intergovernmental Rels., 1962—67; mem. adv. com. federalism and met. govt. Nat. Com. Econ. Devel., 1969—73. Author (with others): (book) Plan of Metropolitan Government for Nashville and Davidson County, 1956, Metropolitan Surveys: A Digest, 1958, The States and Metropolis, 1968, Government and Politics: An Introduction to Political Science, rev. edit., 1971; author: The Christian and Politics, 1968; author: (with Lloyd Omdahl) State and Local Government in America, 6th edit., 1993. Chmn. Coop. Svcs. Internat. Edn. (name now Consortium Global Edn.), 1987—88, cons., 1988—90, pres., 1990—98; active So. Bapt. Found., 1959—60, Ark. Bapt. Found., 1991—97, vice chmn., 1995—96, chmn., 1996—97; mem. regional rev. panel Harry S Truman Scholarship Found., 1982—96, chmn., 1984—96; active Ark. Postsecondary Edn. Planning Commn., 1980—89; mem. Ark. Higher Edn. Coordinating Bd., 1997—, vice chmn., 2002—; mem. commn. religious liberty and human rights Bapt. Worldwide Alliance, 1971—75, vice chmn., 1985—90; mem. edn. commn. So. Bapt. Conv., 1973—80, chmn., 1978—80; 1st v.p. Ark. Bapt. State Conv., 1989—91. Mem.: Am. Soc. Pub. Adminstrn., So. Polit. Sci. Assn., Am. Polit. Sci. Assn., Arkadelphia C. of C. (bd. dirs. 2000—02), Rotary (pres. 1986—87). Home: 4 Glendale Pl Arkadelphia AR 71923-3529 Office: Ouachita Bapt Univ PO Box 3636 Arkadelphia AR 71998-3636 E-mail: dangrant@iocc.com.

GRANT, DAVID JAMES WILLIAM, pharmacy educator; b. Walsall, Eng., Mar. 26, 1937; came to U.S., 1988; s. James and Attie Hilda May (Stringer) G. BA in Chemistry with 1st class honors, Oxford U., Eng., 1961, MA, DPhil in Phys. Chemistry, 1963, DSc in Phys. Sci., 1990. Lectr. chemistry U. Coll. of Sierra Leone, Freetown, 1963-65; lectr. then sr. lectr. pharm. chemistry U. Nottingham, Eng., 1965-81; prof. phys. pharmacy Sch. Pharmacy, U. Toronto, Ont., Can., 1981-88, assoc. dean grad. studies and rsch., 1984-87; endowed prof. pharmaceutics Coll. Pharmacy, U. Minn., Mpls., 1988—. Bd. dirs. Hosokawa Micron Internat., Inc., 1998-2001; mem. grants com. for pharm. sci. Med. Rsch. Coun. Can., Ottawa, 1983-87; mem. com. on health rsch. Ont. Univs., Toronto, 1985-87; vis. prof. Med. Rsch. Coun. Can.; mem. stds. expert com. for excipients: test methods for U.S. Pharmacopeia, 1991—; cons. to numerous chem. and pharm. cos. Co-author: Physical Chemistry for Students of Pharmacy and Biology, 1977, Solubility Behavior of Organic Compounds, 1990; mem. editl. bd. Jour. Pharm. Scis., 1990-93, assoc. editor, 1994—; mem. editl. adv. bd. Pharm. Devel. and Tech., 1995—, Kona, 1996—, AAPS Pharm. Sci., 1999—; contbr. more than 200 articles to sci. jours Lt. Brit. Army, 1955-57. Recipient Rsch. award Leverhulme Found., U.K., 1969, Pharmaceutics award of excellence PhRMA Found., 1999; grantee rsch. couns. and indsl. cos., U.K., Can., U.S. Fellow Royal Soc. Chemistry, Am. Assn. Pharm. Scientists (sustaining charter mem. 1986—), AAAS, Internat. Union Pure and Applied Chemistry; mem. Am. Inst. Chem. Engrs., Am. Pharm. Assn., Am. Chem. Soc., Am. Assn. Coll. Pharmacy. Achievements include showing how small amounts of additives or impurities modify the physical properties of crystalline drugs and excipients; development of crystal engineering of pharmaceutical substances. Office: U Minn Dept Pharmaceutics Weaver-Densford Hall 308 Harvard St SE Minneapolis MN 55455-0343

GRANT, DENNIS, newspaper publishing executive; Dir. advt. Chgo. Tribune. Office: Chgo Tribune Co 435 N Michigan Ave Chicago IL 60611-4066

GRANT, DONALD MARCUS, alcohol policy specialist; b. Inverness, U.K., Sept. 21, 1945; came to U.S., 1994; s. George Henry Grant and Kathleen Mary Gilchrist; m. Anne Elizabeth Stephens, 1967 (div. 1987); m. Courtney Mireille O'Connor, Feb. 15, 1992; children: Rachel, Josie, Marika, Kasya. BA, Cambridge (U.K.) U., 1967, DES, 1968, MA, 1970. Dir. Alcohol Edn. Ctr., London, 1973-83; sr. scientist WHO, Geneva, Switzerland, 1984-94; pres. Internat. Ctr. for Alcohol Policies, Washington, 1994—. Author, editor 20 books and contbr. numerous articles to profl. jours.; author (as Tom Gilchrist): Committed Agent, 1985. Democrat. Avocations: cross country skiing, fiction, travel. Home: 2506 Cliffbourne Pl NW Washington DC 20009-1512 Office: ICAP 1519 New Hampshire Ave NW Washington DC 20036-1203 E-mail: mgrant@icap.org.

GRANT, EDWIN RANDOLPH, retail and manufacturing executive; b. Stoneham, Mass., Oct. 6, 1943; s. Lauris Levi and Dorothy Hall (Lewis) G.; m. Ruth Louise Kennedy, June 24, 1967; children: Randolph T., George C. BFA, Denison U., 1966; MBA, Syracuse U., 1969. Trainee Sears, Roebuck & Co., Springfield, Mass., 1968-69; asst. to pres. Kennedy Bros., Inc., Vergennes, Vt., 1969-70, v.p., 1970-72, exec. v.p., 1972-74, pres., treas., 1974—; dir., corp. sec. Porter Med. Ctr., Inc., 1999—. Chair Porter Health Sys., Inc. subs. Porter Med. Ctr., Inc., Middlebury, Vt., 1996-2002; ptnr. Vergennes (Vt.) Shopping Ctr., 1974-82; exec. bd. Chittenden Trust Co., Vergennes, 1980-94; bd. dirs. Middlebury (Vt.) Inn, 1989—; chmn. bd. Burlington Coll., Vt., 1983-85; devel., founder Kennedy Bros. Factory Marketplace, Vergennes, 1987; commr. Commn. on Status of Women, 1984-85, Vt. Com. chmn. Cub Scout Pack 539, 1987—96; mem. com. Boy Scout Troop 539, 1991—2000, chair, 1997—2000; active Boy Scouts Am., Vergennes; bd. dirs. Addison County (Vt.) Career Devel. Ctr., 1994—97, Friends of Vergennes Opera House, 1995—, pres., 2000—02, chair, 2000—. Recipient Bus. of Yr. award Addison Area C. of C., 1990. Mem. Vergennes Area C. of C. (pres. 1976-81), Vt. State C. of C. (bd. dirs. 1977-78), Addison C. of C. (bd. dirs. 1975-76, 86-93), Lake Champlain C. of C. (bd. dirs. 1977-81), Vt. Retail Assn., Vt. Attractions Assn. (pres. 1978-80), Green Mountain Transp. Club (pres. 1976-77), Lake Champlain Yacht Club (bd. govs. 1989-94), Rotary. Home and Office: 11 N Main St Vergennes VT 05491

GRANT, H. ROGER, history educator; b. Ottumwa, Iowa, Nov. 28, 1943; s. Harry Roger Grant and J. Marcella (Dinsmore) Dearinger; m. Martha Farrington, June 12, 1966; 1 child, Julia Dinsmore. BA, Simpson Coll., 1966; MA, U. Mo., 1967, PhD, 1970; LHD (hon.), Simpson Coll., 2003. Asst. prof. to prof. history U. Akron, Ohio, 1970-96; prof. history Clemson (S.C.) U., 1996—, chair dept. history, 1996—2001. Author 22 books, including: The Corn Belt Route: A History of the Chicago Great Western Railway, 1984 (Railroad History Book award), Spirit Fruit: A Gentle Utopia, 1988, Living in the Depot: The Two-Story Railroad Station, 1993, Erie Lackawanna: Death of an American Railroad, 1938-1992, 1994, The North Western: A History of the Chicago and North Western Railway System, 1996 (Railroad History Book award), Ohio on the Move: A Transportation History of Ohio, 2000; contbr. over 150 articles to profl. jours., chpts. to books. Democrat. Home: 123 Hickory Ridge Rd Central SC 29630-9461 Office: Clemson U Dept History Hardin Hall 226 Clemson SC 29634-0527 E-mail: ggrant@clemson.edu.

GRANT, HUGH, biotechnology company executive; b. Mar. 1958; BS in Molecular Biology and Agrl. Zoology with honors, Glasgow U., Scotland; MS, Edinburgh U., Scotland; MBA, Internat. Mgmt. Ctr., Buckingham, Eng. Co-pres. agrl. sector Pharmacia Corp., 1998; v.p., COO Monsanto Co., 2000; pres., COO Monstanto Co., 2000, exec. v.p., COO, 2000—. Mem. exec. com. Microedit Summit Campaign; mem. internat. adv. bd. Scottish Enterprise. Bd. govs. United Way St. Louis. Mem.: Internat. Policy Coun. on Agr., Food and Trade. Address: 800 N Lindbergh Blvd Saint Louis MO 63167*

GRANT, IGOR, psychiatrist; b. Mar. 26, 1942; MD, U. of BC, Canada, 1966—66. Medical Council Licentiate of the Med. Coun. of Can., 1967, lic. Calif., 1970, cert. Specialist Royal Coll. of Physicians and Surgeons,Can., 1971, Am. Bd. of Psychiatry and Neurology (Psychiatry), 1972. Intern U. Pa. Hosp., Phila., 1966—67; resident in psychiatry U. Pa., Phila., 1967—71; psychiatry educator U. Calif., San Diego, 1972—; staff psychiatrist Veterans Affairs San Diego Healthcare Sys., San Diego, 1972—; chmn. core course in social and behavioral scis. U. Calif. Sch. Medicine, San Diego, 1975—; psychiatry exec. Ambulatory Care Psychiatry, Veterans Affairs San Diego Healthcare Sys., 1976—; adj. educator dept. psychology San Diego State U., 1986—; dir., San Diego HIV Neurobehavioral Rsch. Ctr., 1989—, Calif. Neuro AIDS Tissue Network, 1998—; program project dir. Neuro AIDS: Effects of Methamphetamine, 1999—; dir. Ctr. for Medicinal Cannabis Rsch., 2000—. Psychiatry educator U. Pa., 1970—71; staff psychiatrist Hosp. of the U. of Pa, 1971—72; asst. psychiatry educator U. Calif., San Diego, 1972—78; health clinic exec. Mental Health Clinic Veterans Adminstrn. Hosp., San Diego, 1972—74; dir. Curtis W. Gifford Mental Health Clinic Dept. Psychiatry U. Calif., San Diego, 1974—76; med. exec. Consultation-Liaison Svc. Vetrans Adminstrn. Med. Ctr., San Diego, 1976—80; assoc. educator U. Calif., San Diego, 1978—80; psychiatry asst. Veterans Adminstrn. Med. Ctr., San Diego, 1982—88; vice chmn. UCSD Dept. Psychiatry, 1984—88. Contbr. articles to profl. jours. Recipient CIBA Prize Psychiatry, U. BC Sch. Medicine, 1966, Outstanding Scholastic Achievement, Alma Mater Soc. U. of BC, 1966, Profl. achievement, dedication, and scholar, U. of Pa., 1971. Fellow: Collegium Internationale Neuropsychopharmacologium, West Coast Coll. of Biol. Psychiatry, Am. Psychiat. Assn., Royal Coll. of Physicians and Surgeons of Can.; mem.: Internat. Neuropsychological soc., A.O.A., Am. Bd. of Psychiatry and Neurology (assoc.). Office: University of California San Diego La Jolla San Diego CA 92093-0680 Office Fax: 858-534-7723. E-mail: igrant@ucsd.edu.

GRANT, ISABELLA HORTON, retired judge; b. L.A., Sept. 24, 1924; d. John Daniel and Hannabelle (Horton) Grant. BA, Swarthmore Coll., 1944; MA, UCLA, 1946; JD, Columbia U., 1950; LLD (hon.), Molloy Coll., 1976. Jr. profl. asst. OSS, Washington, 1944-45; economist Inst. Indsl. Rels., UCLA, 1946-47, Office Price Stblzn., L.A., 1951-52; ptnr. Livingston, Grant, Stone & Kay, San Francisco, 1953-79; judge Mcpl. Ct., San Francisco, 1979-82, Superior Ct., San Francisco, 1982-97; ret., 1997. Bd. dirs. Kid's Turn, Pocket Opera. Fellow ABA; mem. Am. Arbitration Assn., San Francisco Ethics Commn. (chair 1999), San Francisco Bar Assn. (bd. dirs. 1978-79), Acad. Matrimonial Lawyers (pres. No. Calif. chpt. 1976), Assn. Family and Conciliation Cts. (pres. Calif. chpt. 1987-89), Nat. Coll. Probate Judges (William W. Treat award 2000), Queen's Bench (pres. 1964), Calif. Tennis Club, Phi Beta Kappa. E-mail: ihortongrant@cs.com.

GRANT, JAMES COLIN, banker; b. N.S., Can., Jan. 24, 1937; s. Jack Danial and Isabel G.; m. Sonia Chicorli, July 3, 1965; 1 dau., Allison Lee-Anne. Student, St. Francis Xavier U., 1954-57, Dal/Tech., 1957-59. Engr. Dept. Transport, Fed. Govt., 1959-65; mgr. tech. support Gulf Oil Ltd., Toronto and Montreal, 1965-69; mgr. tech. design Royal Bank of Can., Montreal, 1969-72, dir. ops., 1972-75, asst. gen. mgr. systems, 1975-79, v.p. systems, 1979-81, v.p. strategic planning, retail banking, 1981-84, sr. v.p. ops. and systems, 1984-87, exec. v.p. ops. and systems, 1987-88, exec. v.p. systems and tech., 1988-92;

pres. C.G. James & Assocs., Internat. Adv. Svcs., 1992—. Mem. sectorial adv. group on internat. trade Govt. of Can.; bd. dirs. Rogers, AT&T Wirless Mobile Comm. Inc., ORI Inc., Electrans (U.K.); mem. exec. coun. info. mgmt. and tech. G.A.O. U.S. Govt. Bd. dirs. Tech. U. N.S., 1974-78. Recipient award for achievement in mng. info. tech. Carnegie Mellon U. Grad. Sch. Indsl. Adminstrn./Am. Mgmt. Systems Inc., 1989, Quality System award C.I.O. Mag., 1991, Pres. award contbn. telecomm. in Can. Canadian Telecomm. Alliance, 1992, Can. Info. Productivity award ORI, Inc. Mem. Order Profl. Engrs. Ont., Can. Info. Processing Soc. (Outstanding Achievement in Information Processing award 1993), Internat. C. of C. (Can. del., commn. on computing, telecommunications and info. policies)

GRANT, JANETT ULRICA, medical/surgical nurse; b. Mavis Bank, St. Andrew, Jamaica, Jan. 15, 1956; came to U.S., 1990; d. John Edgerton and Daisy Ann (Sterling) Welsh; m. Aurnandy Alfanso Grant, Nov. 25, 1978; children: Avril, Adrian, Christophe. Grad., Kingston (Jamaica) Sch. Nursing, 1978, diploma in midwifery, 1988; BSN, N.J. City U., 1998. RN, N.J.; cert. med.-surg. nurse. Mem. staff med. surg. nursing Isaac Barrant Hosp., St. Thomas, Jamaica, 1978-79, Kingston Pub. Hosp., 1979-87, acting sister supr., 1988-90; mem. staff med. surg. nursing Newark Beth Israel Med. Ctr., 1990—, team leader Med.-Surg. Unit, 1995—97. Alt. unit rep. Coun. Nursing Practice, Newark Beth Israel Med. Ctr., 1994; pain resource nurse, 1996—. Mem. planning com. Salvation Army Basic Sch., Kingston, 1988-90. Mem. N.J. State Nurses Assn., Jamaica Nurses Assn. (N.J. chpt.). Methodist. Avocations: reading, sewing, cooking, gardening, craft work.

GRANT, JOAN JULIEN, artist, poet; b. Cornwall, Ont., Can., Apr. 15, 1934; d. John Duncan Julien and Winnifred Josephine McCormick; m. Douglas MacDougal Grant, Sept. 24, 1955; children: Stephen John, Ann Elizabeth, Abigail Jennifer, David King. AA, West L.A. C.C., 1975; BFA, Otis Art Inst., 1977, MFA, 1979. Instr. Plymouth (N.H.) State Coll., 1998. With works in nat. and internat. pvt. collections; author, editor: Terrestis, 1995, Flight of the Muse, 2002. Mem. CLCC Citizens for a Livable Culver City, 1998-2000. Avocations: reading, book discussion groups, walking, hiking. Home: 4274 LeBourget Ave Culver City CA 90232

GRANT, JOHN HALLORAN, lawyer; b. Aug. 15, 1950; s. Clarence John and Virginia Louise (Dwinnell) Grant; m. Mary Elizabeth Davy; children: Elizabeth Ann, Virginia Marie. BA, U. Mont., 1972; JD, Gonzaga U., 1977. Bar: Mont. 1977, U.S. Dist. Ct. Mont. 1977, U.S. Supreme Ct. 1982. Shareholder Jackson Murdo, Grant & McFarland, P.C., Helena, Mont., 1977—. Office: Jackson Murdo Grant & McFarland PC 203 N Ewing St Helena MT 59601-4202

GRANT, JOHN THOMAS, retired state supreme court justice; b. Omaha, Oct. 25, 1920; s. Thomas J. and Mary Elizabeth (Smith) G.; m. Marian Louise Saner, Dec. 27, 1947 (dec. 1995); children: Martha Grant Bruckner, John P., Susan J., Joseph W., Timothy K.; m. Zella Forehead, June 7, 1997. LLB, JD, Creighton U., 1950. Bar: Nebr. 1950. Sole practice law, Omaha, 1950-74; judge State Dist. Ct., Omaha, 1974-83; justice Nebr. Supreme Ct., Lincoln, 1983-92. Served with Signal Corps, U.S. Army, 1942-45, PTO Home: 912 S 118th Plz Omaha NE 68154-3404

GRANT, JOSEPH MOORMAN, finance executive; b. San Antonio, Oct. 30, 1938; s. George William and Mary Christian (Moorman) G.; m. Sheila Ann Peterson, Aug. 26, 1961; children: Mary Elizabeth, Steven Clay. BBA, So. Meth. U., 1960; MBA, U. Tex., 1961, PhD, 1970. Banking officer Citibank, N.Y.C., 1961-65; sr. v.p., economist Tex. Commerce Bank (N.A.) also Tex. Commerce Bancshares, Houston, 1970-73; pres., dir. Tex. Commerce Bank, Austin, 1974-75; chmn., CEO Tex. Am. Bankshares/Ft. Worth, 1986-89; pres. Tex. Am. Bank/Ft. Worth, 1976-89, chmn., CEO, 1983-89; exec. v.p., CFO Electronic Data Systems, Dallas, 1990-98; chmn., CEO Tex. Capital Bancshares, 1998—. Bd. dirs. Wingate Ptnrs. Author: (with Lawrence L. Crum) The Development of State-Chartered Banking in Texas, 1978, The Great Texas Banking Crash, 1996. Trustee Tex. Christian U., 1989-94, So. Meth. U., 1980-89; chmn. adv. coun. Coll. Bus. Adminstrn. Found., U. Tex., Austin; trustee Dallas County C.C.; bd. dirs. North Tex. Commn., 1976-86, chmn., 1981-82; trustee Paul Quinn Coll., 1995-98; bd. dirs. Communities Found. Tex., KERA. Recipient Man of Yr. award Anti-Defamation League B'nai B'rith, 1988, Banker of the Year award Am. Banker, 2001; named to Disting. Alumni, U. Tex. at Austin, Coll. Bus. Adminstrn., 1982, Hall of Fame U. Tex. Coll. Bus. Adminstrn., Austin, 1999, Am. Banker, 2001, Ernst & Young's Entrepeneur of Yr. fin. svs., 2002, Dallas Citizen's Coun., 2002. Mem. Ft. Worth C. of C. (past chmn.), Young Pres. Orgn. (bd. dirs. 1980-89, internat. pres. 1987-88, exec. com.), Blue Key, World Presidents Ogrn., Exch. Club, Sigma Alpha Epsilon. Episcopalian. Home: 4305 Overhill Dallas TX 75205

GRANT, KAY LALLIER, early childhood education educator; b. Leavenworth, Kans., Oct. 22, 1951; d. Leon Ernest and Retha Pearl (Poos) Lallier; m. Cary Benson Grant, Aug. 12, 1972; children: Shannon, Ryan. BA in Psychology, Human Devel. & Family Life, U. Kans., 1973; MA in Spl. Edn., U. Tulsa, 1982; EdD in Curriculum & Instrn., Okla. State U., 1990. Cert. early childhood and spl. edn.-mental retardation tchr. Kindergarten tchr. Muskogee (Okla.) Day Nursery, 1973; presch. tchr. Children's House Montessori Sch., Muskogee, 1974; kindergarten tchr. Haskell (Okla.) Pub. Schs., 1974-75; dir., tchr. presch. for handicapped Muskogee Pub. Schs., 1975-78; dir. child care ctr. Muskogee Gen. Hosp., 1982-84; instr. early childhood edn., field svc. coord. Northeastern State U., Tahlequah, Okla., 1985-88, program chair early childhood edn., 1988—92, asst. prof. early childhood Coll. of Edn., 1990—92; dir. early childhood edn. Muskogee Pub. Schs., 1992—99; asst. dean coll. edn. Northeastern State U., 1999—2001, interim dean, 2001—03, dean, 2003—. Reviewer Music and Child Devel., 1988, Total Learning: Curriculum for Young Child, 1987, The Boy Who Would Be a Helicopter, 1990; contbr. articles to profl. jours. Elder Bethany Presbyn. Ch., Muskogee, 1991—99. Recipient scholarship award Okla. Assn. on Children Under Six, 1988, Faculty Rsch. grant Northeastern State U., 1989. Mem. Okla. Assn. Childhood Edn. Internat. (pres. 1991-1999), Nat. Assn. Edn. Young Children, Okla. Assn. Early Childhood Tchr. Educators, So. Early Childhood Assn., Okla. Inst. Child Advocacy (bd. dirs. 1999-2001), Internat. Reading Assn., Phi Delta Kappa, Delta Kappa Gamma, Kappa Delta Phi, Okla. Assoc. Colls. Edn. Office: Northeastern State U Coll Edn Tahlequah OK 74464 E-mail: grantk1@nsuok.edu.

GRANT, LEONARD TYDINGS, clergyman; b. Lakewood, N.J., May 8, 1930; s. Allaire Harrison and Edith Dorothy (MacEntee) Grant; m. Nancy Elisabeth MacKerell, June 21, 1958; children: Scott Alexander, Elisabeth Tydings, Constance Allaire. BA, Rutgers U., 1952; BD, Princeton Theol. Sem., 1955; STM, Temple U., 1958; PhD, U. Edinburgh, 1961; LHD (hon.), Elmira Coll., 1987. Ordained Presbyn. Ch. U.S.A., 1955. Pastor 4th Presbyn. Ch., Camden, N.J., 1955-58, Meml. Presbyn. Ch., Wenonah, N.J., 1961-65; instr. Rutgers U., 1956-58; lectr. Conwell Sch. Theology, Phila., 1962-65; prof. history Indpls. Univ., 1965-76; grad. dean Indpls. U., 1966-76, acad. dean, 1974-76; pres. Elmira (N.Y.) Coll., 1976-87; pres. emeritus, 1987—; pres. Independent Coll. Fund N.Y., 1987-95; interim assoc. pastor Presbyn. Ch., Westfield, NJ, 1995-97; assoc. pastor Ctrl. Presbyn. Ch., Summit, NJ, 1997—2002, dir. planned giving, 2003—. Author: Prayers and Devotions of Richard Baxter, 1965; contbr. Former mem. adv. com. Am. Inst. Banking, Arnot-Ogden Hosp., Coun. Ind. Coll., Ind. Coll. Fund N.Y.; former mem. adv. com. Sullivan Trail Coun. Boy Scouts Am.; former mem. adv. com. Coun. Elizabeth Presbytery, Found. for Ind. Higher Edn.; trustee Elizabeth Presbytery. Mem.: Princeton Club N.Y.C., Rotary, Phi Delta Kappa, Phi Alpha Theta, Alpha Sigma Lambda. Presbyterian.

GRANT, LINDA HESS, educator; b. Cin., Aug. 17, 1949; d. Guy Cleveland and Mildred Moore Hess; m. James Benjamin Grant, Oct. 21, 1972; children: Mirrin Elizabeth, Lindsey Ann. BS in Speech Pathology, U. Cin., 1971, MA in Audiology, 1972. Clin. audiologist Mercy Hosp., Hamilton, Ohio, 1972-73; ednl. audiologist Davison Sch., Atlanta, 1973-77; ESL faculty Ga. Inst. Tech., Lang. Inst., Atlanta, 1979-96; asst. dir., faculty ESL program Emory U., Atlanta, 1998—. Adj. faculty applied linguistics grad. program Ga. State U., 1994—; cons. in field. Author: Well Said, 1993, (chpt.) Material Writer's Handbook, 1995. Chmn. bd. Bond Cmty. Fed. Credit Union, Atlanta, 1983—84; Olympic torchbearer, 2001; v.p. Candler Park Neighborhood Orgn., Atlanta, 1979—80; sec. Fernbank PTA, Atlanta, 1987—88; founding bd. dirs. Inman Park Parent Coop. Presch., Atlanta, 1974—84. Recipient Lee Foshay award, Cin. Speech and Hearing Ctr., 1971. Mem. Ga. Tchrs. English to Spkrs. of Other Langs. (newsletter editor 1986-87, v.p. 1987-89, Profl. Svc. award 1989, 92), Southeast Regional Tchrs. English to Spkrs. of Other Langs. (conf. chair 1991), Internat. Tchrs. English to Spkrs. of Other Langs. (chair interest sect. 2000), Phi Beta Kappa. Avocations: reading, writing, travel, gardening. E-mail: lgrant@hsrd.emory.edu.

GRANT, M. DUNCAN, lawyer; b. Madison, Wis., Apr. 22, 1950; s. David Evans and Margaret Jane (Bloomfield) G.; m. Marcia Joan Cox, Sept. 18, 1970 (div. Dec. 1975); 1 child, Thomas David; m. Margaret Ann MacDonald, Mar. 24, 1990 (div. Jan. 1995); m. Victoria Lynn Nichols, Oct. 14, 2000. AB, Princeton U., 1972; JD, U. Pa., 1975. Bar: Pa. 1975, Del. 1991, U.S. Dist. Ct. (ea. dist.) Pa. 1976, U.S. Ct. Appeals (3d cir.) 1977, U.S. Supreme Ct. 1980, U.S. Dist. Ct. (Del.) 1992, U.S. Ct. Appeals (10th cir.) 1986, U.S. Ct. Appeals (11th cir.) 1996, U.S. Ct. Appeals (fed. cir.) 2002. Law clk. to judge U.S. Ct. Appeals (3d cir.), Phila., 1975-76; assoc. Pepper Hamilton LLP, Phila., 1976-83, ptnr., 1983—. Ed. in chief U. Penn Law Review. Am. fellow Salzburg Seminar, 1986. Mem. ABA, Pa. Bar Assn., Phila. Bar Assn., Del. State Bar Assn. Democrat. Avocations: baseball, wine, golf. Home: 415 Gate Ln Philadelphia PA 19119-2815 Office: Pepper Hamilton LLP 3000 Two Logan Sq 18th & Arch Sts Philadelphia PA 19103-1083 E-mail: grantm@pepperlaw.com.

GRANT, MARILYNN PATTERSON, secondary educator; b. Washington, Oct. 26, 1952; d. Rossie Lee and Mattie (Pringle) Patterson; m. David Michael Grant, Oct. 11, 1980; children; Karissa Joy, Jared David Michael. BA in History, U. Rochester, 1975, MS in Edn., 1982, postgrad; Cert. advanced studies, SUNY, Brockport, 1987. Cert. tchr., sch. adminstr., supr., N.Y. Jr. high coord. Rochester (N.Y.) City Sch. Dist., 1980-81, team tchr., 1981-83, skills cluster tchr., 1983-85, jr. high tchr., 1985-86, alternative to suspension, 1986-87, 89-90, dean of students, 1987-88, curriculum coord., 1988-89, acting house adminstr., 1990-91, social studies tchr., 1991—96, dir. of social Studies & multicultral edn., 1996—2002; prin. Joseph C. Wilson HS, Rochester, 2002—. Bd. dirs., allocations com. Rochester Monroe County Youth Bd., 1990-92; active Mt. Olivet Bapt. Ch., 1990—. Named one of Outstanding Young Women Am., 1984; recipient Volunteerism award Mayor of Rochester, 1991, Jack & Jill of Rochester Disting. Mother, 2000-01, RCSD Staff excellance award, 2001. Mem. Christian Visitor's Com. (chmn. 1990—), Rochester Urban League Guild (v.p. 1982-83), Jack & Jill of Am. (corr. sec. 1991-92, group leader 1992-93), Zeta Phi Beta (pres. 1985-87, parliamentarian 1985-87), Kappa Delta Pi. Democrat. Avocations: event planning, singing, drama, reading, writing. Home: 227 Genesee Park Blvd Rochester NY 14619-2459

GRANT, MARTHA F. social worker; b. Syracuse, N.Y., Feb. 21, 1943; d. George Lawson and Elizabeth (Russell) Farrington; m. H. Roger Grant, June 12, 1966; 1 child, Julia Dinsmore. BA, Stetson U., 1965; MS in Social Work, U. Mo., 1969. Lic. ind. social worker, Ohio, master social worker, S.C.; lic. med. social worker, S.C. Program asst. Office of Econ. Opportunity/Office for Interagency Rels., Washington, 1965-66; caseworker I Cath. Svc. League of Akron, 1970-72; contractor, adoption investigator Summit County Probate Ct., Akron, 1980—94; home health social worker Olsten Kimberly Quality Care, 1994—96, 1998—; med. social worker OMH Hospice of the Foothills, Seneca, SC. Mem.: LWV, NASW, Oconee County Svc. Assn., SC Gerontol. Soc. Home: 123 Hickory Ridge Rd Central SC 29630-9461 Office: OMH Hospice of Foothills 390 Keowee School Rd Seneca SC 29672

GRANT, MERRILL THEODORE, producer; b. N.Y.C., July 9, 1932; s. Samuel and Rae (Renko) G.; m. Barbara Rosner, May 21, 1961; children: Andrea, Jonathan Samuel. BBA, CCNY, 1953; MS, Columbia U., 1954. V.p., dir. programming Benton & Bowles, N.Y.C., 1957-70; sr. v.p., dir. radio and TV Grey Advt., N.Y.C., 1970-72; v.p. Viacom Internat., N.Y.C., 1972-74; pres. Don Kirshner Prodns., N.Y.C., 1974-78, Grant Case McGrath, N.Y.C., 1978-79, Grant-Reeves Entertainment, N.Y.C., 1979-85; chmn., CEO Reeves Entertainment, N.Y.C., 1985-93. Served with AUS, 1954-56.

GRANT, MERWIN DARWIN, lawyer; b. Safford, Ariz., May 7, 1944; s. Darwin Dewey and Erma (Whiting) G.; m. Charlotte Richey, June 27, 1969; children: Brandon, Taggart, Christian, Brittany. BA in Econs., Brigham Young U., 1968; JD, Duke U., 1971. Bar: Ariz. 1971, U.S. Dist. Ct. Ariz., U.S. Dist. Ct. (we. dist.) Tex., U.S. Ct. Appeals (5th, 7th, 8th, 9th and 10th cirs.), U.S. Tax Ct., U.S. Supreme Ct. Pres. Merwin D. Grant, P.C., Phoenix, 1977—; ptnr. Beus, Gilbert & Morrill, Phoenix, 1984—93; pres. Grant Williams P.C., Phoenix, 1994—. Guest condr. Phoenix Symphony Orch., 1989. Bd. dirs. Grand Canyon coun. Boy Scouts Am., Phoenix, 1974-76, Maricopa Hosp., Health Sys. Bd., 1997—, Ariz. Motorsports Charitable Found.; pres., bd. dirs. Golden Gate Settlement, Phoenix, 1975-80, 84-88, Phoenix Internat. Raceway Charities, Ariz. Acad. Decathalon Assn., exec. com., 1999-2002; charter mem. Rep. Presl. Task Force, Washington, 1984—; vice chmn. Ariz. Joint County Tobacco Revenue Use and Security Charitable Trust, 2000—; mem. Ariz. Joint House/Senate Ad Hoc Com. on Health Care Dists., 2001; chmn. Citizens' Task Force, Maricopa County Hosp., 2002—. Fellow Ariz. Bar Found.; mem. ABA (litigation sect.), Assn. Trial Lawyers Am., Kiwanis (bd. dirs. Phoenix chpt. 1972-79). Office: Grant Williams PC 3200 N Central Ave Ste 2400 Phoenix AZ 85012 E-mail: grant@phxlaw.com.

GRANT, MICHAEL ERNEST, educational administrator, institutional management educator; b. L.A., June 6, 1952; s. Ernest Grant and Shirley Ruth (George) G. BA in Spanish, Calif. State U., Long Beach, 1974, MA in Edn. Adminstrn., 1978; EdD, Pepperdine U., 1984. Cert. elem., secondary, and community coll. tchr., bilingual and cross-cultural edn., adminstr. Tchr. kindergarten through adult edn. Long Beach Unified Sch. Dist., 1975-83, tchr. 5th grade, 1975, tchr. 6th grade, 1975-76, bilingual multicultural specialist, 1976-78, tchr. 6th, 7th and 8th grades, 1978-79, mgmt. program specialist, 1979-80, adminstr., program specialist, 1980-81, vice prin., 1981-83; asst. prof. tchr. edn. Calif. State U., San Bernardino, 1986-88, prin. dir. IMPACT/TEACH, assoc. prof. ednl. psychology and adminstrn. Long Beach, 1988-91; pres., founder Mykulphone-An Empowerment Through Edn. Project, Beverly Hills, 1991—; Spanish instr. Calif. Disting. Sch., Beverly Hills, 1993—. Asst. part-time instr. tchr. edn. Grad. Sch. Edn., Calif. State U., Long Beach, 1983-86; pres., CEO Mykulphone, Real Estate Developer, 999—; lectr. in field. Exec. prodr., dancer, singer, songwriter (animated music video) The Flashy Dancer, 2003; contbr. articles to profl. jours. Pepperdine U. scholar, 1983-84; Calif. State U. grantee, 1988-89, 89-90, 89-91. Mem. NEA, Assn. Calif. Sch. Adminstrs., Nat. Assn. Tchr. Educators, Nat. Coun. States In-Svc. Edn., Nat. Black Congress Faculty, Calif. Faculty Assn., Calif. State Intersegmental Coordination Coun., Calif. Black Faculty and Staff Assn., Calif. Assn. Tchr. Educators, Calif. Edn. Rsch. Assn., Intersegmental Coordinating Coun. Democrat. Baptist. Avocations: shotokon karate (black belt), acting, dancing, singing, songwriting. Home and Office: No 1220 270 N Canon Dr Beverly Hills CA 90210-9999

GRANT, MICHAEL PETER, electrical engineer; b. Oshkosh, Wis., Feb. 26, 1936; s. Robert J. and Ione (Michelson) G.; m. Mary Susan Corcoran, Sept. 2, 1961; children: James, Steven, Laura. BS, Purdue U., 1957, MS, 1958, PhD, 1964. With Westinghouse Research Labs., Pitts., summers 1953-57; mem. tech. staff Aerospace Corp., El Segundo, Calif., 1961; instr. elec. engring. Purdue U., West Lafayette, Ind., 1958-64; sr. engr. Combustion Engring. Corp., Columbus, Ohio, 1964-67, mgr. advanced devel. and control systems, 1967-72, mgr. control and info. scis. div., 1972-74, asst. gen. mgr. indsl. systems div., 1974-76, mgr. system design, 1976-87; v.p., chief scientist SynGenics Corp., Columbus, 1987—; dir. Nat. Ctr. for Mfg. Scis., Ann Arbor, MIch., 1987-95. Contbr. articles to profl. jours.; holder 8 patents in field of automation. Mem. IEEE, Sigma Xi, Eta Kappa Nu, Pi Mu Epsilon, Tau Beta Pi Home: 4461 Sussex Dr Columbus OH 43220-3857

GRANT, MICHELE BYRD, educator; b. Kansas City, Mo., Oct. 30, 1926; d. Ernest Louis and Violetta (Wallace) Byrd. B.S., Lincoln U., 1952; M.S. in Sci. Edn., U. Ill., 1955, advanced cert., 1964. Tchr., Unit 4, Champaign, Ill., 1956-66; tchr. sci. St. Louis Pub. Schs., 1966—, dept. head, 1978—, Mo. Outstanding Biology Tchrs. program dir., 1974— ; participant NSF Summer Inst., CCNY, 1968-69; instr. Webster Coll. Upward Bound Program, 1969-70; judge Monsanto-St. Louis Post Dispatch Sci. Fair, 1970— . Developer, edn. dir. Adventures in Medicine and Sci., 1992; coord., co-develpper Vashon Interdisciplinary Project for Edn. Reform, 1999-2000. Mem. Cath. Sch. Bd., St. Louis, 1982-83; mem. life aux. Barnes Hosp., 1968— ; trustee Meml. and Planned Funeral Soc., 1980. Recipient Mo. Outstanding Biology Tchr. award, Nat. Biology Tchrs. Assn., 1974, One of 50 Nationwide Unsung Heroes award Newsweek, 1987, Excellence in Leadership award Lincoln U., 1987, Newsweek Mag. Unsung Hero Satte Mo., 1987, Monsanto Sci. Tchg. award, 2001; named STARS Tchr., Solutia-NSF, 1999. Mem. ASCD, Nat. Sci. Tchrs. Assn., Nat. Assn. Biology Tchrs., Biology Tchrs. Assn., Mo. Sci. Tchrs. Assn., Mo. Acad. Sci., Alpha Kappa Alpha, Kappa Delta Pi. Roman Catholic. Office: 3405 Bell Ave Saint Louis MO 63106-1604

GRANT, NEWELL M. real estate investment manager; b. Denver, Nov. 2, 1941; s. Edwin Hendrie and Mary Belle (McIntyre) G.; m. Judith G. Wilson, June 19, 1971; children: Margaret, James, Newell, Caroline. BA, Dartmouth Coll., 1964; postgrad, U. Pa., 1967-68. Assoc. Kidder Peabody Realty, N.Y.C., 1969-74; ptnr. Borden, Danielson & Grant, Denver, 1975; cons. N.M. Grant & Co., Denver, 1976-78; ptnr. Grant Mgmt. Co., Denver, 1978—. Gen. ptnr. Grant Properties, Denver, 1977-93; chmn. bd. Colo. Nat. Bank Southwest, Littleton, 1983-89; Inc., 1991—. Pres. bd. trustees Denver Botanic Gardens, 1976—; pres. Denver Botanic Garden Endowment Inc., 1991—; active Gov.'s Task Force for Efficiency and Economy in Colo. State Govt., Denver, 1976; mem. Dartmouth Alumni Coun., 2002—; bd. dirs. Colo. World of Golf, 1990. Served to 1st lt. U.S. Army, 1965-66. Mem. Urban Land Inst. (assoc.)., Garden of the Gods (Colorado Springs). Democrat. Episcopalian. Avocations: hunting, gardening, reading. Home: 1325 Cherryville Rd Littleton CO 80121-1221

GRANT, PATRICK ALEXANDER, lawyer, association administrator; b. Denver, Nov. 14, 1945; s. Edwin Hendrie and Mary Belle (McIntyre) G.; m. Carla Clyde Yancey, Aug. 16, 1975; children: Mary Cameron, Sara Mansur, Alexis Hendrie. BA with honors, Colgate U., 1967; MBA, Denver U., 1973; JD, Drake U., 1976. Bar: Colo. 1977. Law clk. to Judge Donald P. Smith, Jr. Colo. Ct. Appeals, Denver, 1976-77; assoc. Grant, McHendrie, Haines & Crouse, PC, Denver, 1977-83, ptnr., v.p., 1984-91, also bd. dirs.; state rep. Colo. Gen. Assembly, Denver, 1984-92, vice-chmn. fin. com., 1987-88, chmn. audit com., 1989-90, chmn. judiciary com., 1988-92, chmn. legal svcs. com., 1988-89. Mem. Colo. Coun. Elected Ofcls. for Soviet Jewry, Denver, 1985-92, Colo. Spl. Task Force Tort Liability and Ins., Denver, 1985, Local U.S. Bank Bd.; bd. dirs. Colo. Sports Hall of Fame, 1992-98, Colo. State U. Livestock Leader Coun. Kent Denver Leadership Fund, 1996-97, upper sch. chmn. parents divsn.; mem. Denver Cmty. Mental Health Commn., 1985-86; mem. exec. coun., planning com. St. Joseph Hosp., Denver, 1985-88; mem. Denver Bd. for Developmentally Disabled, 1987-88; vestryman, jr. warden St. Barnabas Parish, Denver, 1979-84; adv. com. Nat. Ctr. Preventive Law, 1987-90; bd. dirs. Colo. Jud. Inst., 1990-96, bd. govs. Colo. State U. system, 2001—; exec. bd. Parents Assn., Gettsyburg (Pa.) Coll., 1997-2001, chmn. parents fund, 2000-01, nat. campaign steering com. Gettysburg Coll., 2000-01, Colgate U. (N.Y.) Soc. of Families steering com.; exec. bd. Denver coun. Boy Scouts Am., scout show chmn., 1997-99; mem. Colo. Rev'd Statutes Adv. Group, Roundup Riders of Rockies, 1989—; mem. bd. govs. Colo. State U. Sys., 2001—. Bd. dirs. Assoc. Rodeo Coms., Gates Found. fellow John F. Kennedy Sch. Govt. Harvard U., 1985, Toll Fellow Coun. of State Govts., 1987; recipient Outstanding Alumni award Kent Denver Country Day Sch., 1986, Colo. Wildlife Fedn. Appreciation award, 1987, Disting. Svc. to Higher Edn. award U. Denver, 1988, Bus. Legis. of Yr., award Colo. Pub. Affairs Coun., 1989, Outstanding Achievement award EPA, 1989, award of honor Hist. Denver, 1989, Stephen H. Hart award Colo. Hist. Soc., 1990, Spl. Recognition award AIA; named one of Outstanding Young Men in Am., U.S. Jaycees, 1980, Legislator of Yr. Associated Builders and Contractors, 1991, Gen. Heritage award for Former Legislator, 1997, mem. Grant Family Recipient, Citizen of West, 2000, UCHSC Chancellor Soc. Lunch honoree, 2002 Mem. Colo. Med. Soc. Found. (bd. dirs., pres. 1997-99, pres. emeritus 1999—), Western Stock Show Assn. (exec. com., bd. dirs. 1984—, exec. v.p., CEO 1990-91, pres., CEO 1991—), Metro Denver C. of C. (chmn. econ. devel. coun. 1995-96, co-chmn. pub. affairs coun. 1999-2000, co-chmn. entrepeneurship coun. 2001-02), Assn. Rodeo Coms. (bd. dirs. 2000—). Republican. Episcopalian. Avocations: wood chopping, horseback riding. Home: 3777 S Dahlia St Englewood CO 80110-4215 Office: 4655 Humboldt St Denver CO 80216-2818

GRANT, PAUL BERNARD, industrial relations educator, arbitrator; b. Chgo., Mar. 18, 1931; s. Paul B. and Catherine (Flyke) G.; m. Madeleine Grant, Aug. 15, 1959 (dec. Nov. 2000); children: Maura, Elizabeth, Paul, Francis, Timothy. BS, Loyola U., Chgo., 1952; MS, Inst. Indsl. Rels., Chgo., 1954. Asst. prof. Loyola U., Chgo., 1959-89, assoc. prof. indsl. rels., 1989-96, asst. v.p., 1977-85, dir. employee rels., 1967-76, sec. retirement com., 1967-95; expert witness Employment Matters, Chgo., 1993—; prof. emeritus Loyola U., Chgo., 1996—. Labor arbitrator Am. Arbitration Assn., Chgo., 1972—, Fed. Mediation Conciliation Svc., Washington, 1976—, Ill. Labor Rels. Bd., Chgo., 1984—, Ill. Ednl. Labor Rels. Bd., Chgo., 1987—, Nat. Mediation Bd., Chgo., Washington, 1988—, Social Security Adminstrn., 2002—; mediator Ctr. for Employment Dispute Resolution, 1993—; U.S. arbitrator, del. N.Am. Agreement on Labor Cooperation, 1993—; expert witness employment and civil rights. Author: Cutting Health Care Costs, 1987. Sgt. U.S. Army, 1954-56. Mem. Am. Arbitration Assn., Assn. for Conflict Resolution, Indsl. Rels. Rsch. Assn., Am. Legion, Ill. Labor History Soc. Roman Catholic. Avocation: history. Home and Office: 3300 W Rance Ter Lincolnwood IL 60712-3831

GRANT, RAYMOND THOMAS, arts administrator; b. Yonkers, N.Y., Nov. 1, 1957; s. Kieran J. and Rita B. (Benedek) G.; m. Susan Mary McLoughlin, Nov. 6, 1993; children: Kieran John, Stephen Thomas. B of Music Edn., U. Kans., 1980; MA in Arts Adminstrn., NYU, 1984. Cert. music edn. tchr. Intern John F. Kennedy Ctr. for the Performing Arts, Washington, 1980; band dir. Lawrence (Kans.) Pub. Schs., 1980—81; dir. spl. projects 92nd St. YM-YWHA, N.Y.C., 1983—85; gen. mgr. Am. Symphony Orch., N.Y.C., 1985—91; pres. Raymond T. Grant, Ltd., 1989—93; dir. Tisch Ctr. for the Arts of the 92d St. Y, N.Y.C., 1991—92; mgr. program devel. performing arts and film The Disney Inst., Celebration, Fla., 1993—96; programming cons. Walt Disney Attractions, Inc., 1996—98; mng. dir. arts and culture Salt Lake Organizing Com. for Olympic Winter Games of 2002, 1998—2003; artistic dir. 2002 Cultural Olympiad; exec. dir. Sundance, 2003—. Guest lectr., spkr. King's Coll., NYU, N.Y.C., 1990, The Hartt Sch., U. Hartford, U. No. Iowa, Ind. U., 1997, The Sch. of the Art Inst. of Chgo., 1998, Va. Tech., 1998, U. Utah, 2000; mem. adv. com. Carnegie Hall Profl. Tng. Workshops, 1990-91; programming cons. Imperial Tombs of China Exhbn., Orlando (Fla.) Mus. Art, 1997—. Contbr. articles. Bd. dirs. North Fork Preservation Alliance, 2003—, Kans. Alliance for Arts Edn., Lawrence, 1981, Concerts for Young People, Lawrence, 1981, Negro Spiritual Scholarship Found., Orlando, Fla., 1997-2001; mem. adv. bd. N.Y. Youth Symphony, 1986; panel mem. presenting and commissioning program, challenge grant program NEA, 1993, site visitor presenting and commissioning program, 1994; mem. music orgn. panel divsn. cultural affairs Fla. Dept. State, 1994, 95, 96; facilitator, mem. panel Martin Luther King, Jr. Forum, Diocese of Orlando, Orlando Mus. Art, 1997, 98. Power Found. scholar U. Kans., 1979; Stella Wolcott Aten grantee U. Kans., 1978, Scholarship Found. grantee, N.Y.C., 1980. Mem. Rocky Mountain Elk Found., Blue Mountain Sportsman Ctr., Ducks Unltd. Roman Catholic. Office: Sundance RR3 Box A-1 Sundance UT 84604 Home: 2188 Wilson Ave Salt Lake City UT 84108-3022 E-mail: rtgrant@sundance-utah.com.

GRANT, RICHARD EARL, retired medical and legal consultant; b. Spokane, Wash., Aug. 27, 1935; s. Conrad Morrison and Sylva Celeste (Sims) G.; m. Susan Kimberly Hawkins, Mar. 17, 1979; children: Paaqua A., Camber Do'otsie O. BSc cum laude, U. Wash., 1961; MEd, Whitworth Coll., 1974; PhD, Wash. State U., 1980. Cert. ins. rehab. specialist; cert. case mgr. Supr. nursing Providence Hosp., Seattle, 1970-72; asst. prof. nursing Wash. State U., Spokane, 1972-78; dir. nursing Winslow (Ariz.) Meml. Hosp., 1978-79; adminstr. psychiat. nursing Ariz. State Hosp., Phoenix, 1979-80; asst. prof. Ariz. State U., Tempe, 1980-83; assoc. prof. Linfield Coll., Portland, Oreg., 1983-86, Intercollegiate Ctr. for Nursing Edn., Spokane, 1986-88; sr. med. care coord. Fortis Corp., Spokane, 1988-92; med. svcs. cons. CorVel Corp., Spokane, 1992-94; owner Richard Grant & Assoc., Spokane, 1995-99; med./voc. case mgr. Genex Svcs., Seattle, 1999—2003; ret., 2003. Cons. Ariz. State Hosp., 1980-82, Pres.'s Commn., Washington, 1981-83, U. No. Colo., Greely, 1985-86; area med. svcs. cons., 1992—. Author: The God-Man-God Book, 1976, Publications of the Membership (Conaa), 1983, 4th rev. edit., 1988, Predetermined Careplan Handbook-Nursing, 1988, Duhikya: The Hopi Healer, 1996; contbr. articles to profl. jours. Judge Student Space Shuttle Project, Portland,

1983, N.W. Sci. Expo, Portland, 1983. With U.S. Army, 1953-56. Grantee NIMH, U. Wash., 1961; named one of top Hopi Scholars, Hopi Tribe, Second Mesa, Ariz., 1981. Mem. AAAS, Nat. League for Nursing, Wash. League for Nursing (v.p. 1988-90), Coun. on Nursing and Anthropology (editor 1982-90), N.Y. Acad. Scis., Case Mgmt. Soc. Am., Sigma Theta Tau. Avocations: painting, scuba diving. E-mail: dr.regrant@comcast.net.

GRANT, ROBERT, state representative; b. Clovis, N.Mex., Nov. 28, 1948; m. Lynn Grant; 1 child. AA, Labette C.C. Owner Idle-A-While, Inc.; mem. Kans. Ho. of Reps., 1992—93, 1997—. Mayor, Cherokee. Mem.: Am. Legion, K. of C., Fraternal Order Eagles. Democrat. Roman Catholic. Office: 273-W State Capitol 300 SW 10th Ave Topeka KS 66612 Address: 407 W Magnolia Cherokee KS 66724*

GRANT, ROBERT MCQUEEN, humanities educator; b. Evanston, Ill., Nov. 25, 1917; s. Frederick Clifton and Helen McQueen (Hardie) G.; m. Margaret Huntington Horton, Dec. 21, 1940; children: Douglas McQueen, Peter Williams, Susan Hardie, James Frederick. AB, Northwestern U., 1938; postgrad., Episcopal Theol. Sch., 1938-39, Columbia U., 1939-40; BD, Union Theol. Sem., 1941; STM, Harvard U., 1942, ThD, 1944; DD, Seabury-Western Theol. Sem., 1969, U. Glasgow, 1979; LHD, Kalamazoo Coll., 1979; DD, Ch. Div. Sch. Pacific, 1992. Ordained to ministry Episcopal Ch., 1942. Minister St. James Ch., South Groveland, Mass., 1942-44; instr. to prof. N.T. U. of South, 1944-53, acting dean, 1947; vis. lectr. U. Chgo., 1945, research assoc., 1952-53, assoc. prof., 1953-58, prof., 1958-87, emeritus, 1988—, Carl Darling Buck prof. humanities, 1973-87, Carl Darling Buck prof. emeritus, 1988—. Vis. lectr. Vanderbilt U., 1945-47, Seabury-Western Theol. Sem., 1954-55, 89, Augustinianum (Rome), 1990; lectr. Am. Council Learned Socs., 1957-58; vis. prof. Yale U., 1964-65, Fla. State U., 1989. Author: Second-Century Christianity, 1946, 2d edit., 2003, The Bible in the Church, 1948, rev. edit. (with David Tracy), 1984, Miracle and Natural Law, 1952, The Sword and the Cross, 1955, The Letter and the Spirit, 1957, Gnosticism and Early Christianity, 1959, 63, Gnosticism: An Anthology, 1961, The Earliest Lives of Jesus, 1961, Historical Introduction to the New Testament, 1963, The Apostolic Fathers, vol. I, 1964, vol. II (with H. H. Graham), 1965, vol. IV, 1966, U-Boats Destroyed 1914-1918, 1964, 2002, The Formation of the New Testament, 1965, History of Early Christian Literature (revision from E. J. Goodspeed), 1966, The Early Christian Doctrine of God, 1966, After the New Testament, 1967, U-Boat Intelligence 1914-1918, 1969, 2002, Augustus to Constantine, 1970, Theophilus of Antioch Ad Autolycum, 1970, Early Christianity and Society, 1977, Eusebius as Church Historian, 1980, Christian Beginnings: Apocalypse to History, 1983, Gods and the One God, 1986, Greek Apologists of the Second Century, 1988, Jesus after the Gospels, 1989, Heresy and Criticism, 1993, Irenaeus of Lyons, 1997; author: (with D. N. Freedman) The Secret Sayings of Jesus, 1960, (with G. Menzies) Joseph's Bible Notes, Hypomnestikon, 1996, Early Christians and Animals, 1999, Paul in the Roman World, 2001, U-Boat Hunters, 2003; assoc. editor Vigiliae Christianae. Fulbright research prof. U. Leiden, 1950-51; Guggenheim fellow, 1950, 54, 59. Fellow Am. Acad. Arts and Scis.; mem. Soc. Bibl. Lit. (pres. 1959), Am. Soc. Ch. History (pres. 1970, co-editor 1962-87), Chgo. Soc. Bibl. Research (pres. 1963-64, editor 1956-61), Phi Beta Kappa. Home: 5807 Dorchester Ave 11E Chicago IL 60637

GRANT, ROBERT NATHAN, lawyer; b. Newburgh, N.Y., Mar. 7, 1930; s. Henry and Helen (Berkowitz) Grusky; m. Barbara Weil, Feb. 10, 1952; children— Susan, Elizabeth Grant Ellerton, Nancy Grant Gray. BA, Yale U., 1951; LLB, Harvard U., 1956. Bar: Ill. 1956, N.Y. 1990; registered fgn. lawyer, U.K. Assoc. Sonnenschein Nath & Rosenthal, Chgo., 1956-65; ptnr. Sonnenschein, Nath & Rosenthal, Chgo., 1965—. Sec. UNR Industries, Inc., Chgo., 1979-90; sec. San Diego Padres Prof. Baseball Team, 1974-78. Contbr. articles to profl. jours. Trustee The Nature Conservancy-Ill., 1978—88; pres. Legal Aid Soc. Ill., 1988—94, Winnetka (Ill.) Pub. Schs. Found., 1995—98; bd. dirs. Winnetka Pub. Schs. Found.; pres. Winnetka Cmty. House, 2000—01, Winnetka Bd. Edn., 1980—81, mem., 1974—81, Winnetka Planning Commn., 1975—77, New Trier Twp. Caucus, 1974; bd. dirs. United Charities, 1984—94, mem. legal aid com., 1982—, vice chmn., 1986—87, chmn., 1987—94; bd. dirs. New Trier HS Ednl. Found., 2001—, chmn. 1st lt. USAF, 1951—53. Recipient William H. Avery award for 10 yrs. svc. as chmn. Legal Aid Soc., 1994. Mem. ABA (vice-chmn. commercial leasing com.), Scholarship and Guidance Assn. (bd. dirs. 1968-92, pres. 1979-83), Harvard Law Sch. Spl. Gifts, Yale Alumni Recruiting Com., Standard Club, Yale Club (N.Y.C.), Phi Beta Kappa. Avocations: tennis, jogging, travel, reading. Home: 1165 Hamptondale Ave Winnetka IL 60093-1811 Office: Sonnenschein Nath & Rosenthal 233 S Wacker Dr Ste 8000 Chicago IL 60606-6491 E-mail: rgrant@sonnenschein.com.

GRANT, ROBERT ULYSSES, retired manufacturing company executive; b. Laramie, Wyo., Sept. 19, 1929; s. Guy Reid and Martha Clotilda (Krehmke) G.; m. Patricia Anne Towle, Feb. 12, 1955; children— Elizabeth, Sheila, Guy, Wilson, Mary BS in Civil Engring., U. Wyo., 1951; MBA, Harvard U., 1957. Fin. analyst, dir. acquisition analysis, v.p. mgmt. services, sr. v.p. corp. devel. Lear Siegler, Inc., Santa Monica, Calif., 1964-87. Served to lt. USNR, 1952-55 Mem.: Jonathan (Los Angeles), Masons. Democrat. Lutheran. Avocations: sailing; jogging. Home: 6549 Via Lorenzo Palos Verdes Peninsula CA 90275-6571

GRANT, RUSSELL PORTER, JR., lawyer, petroleum land man; b. Ft. Sill, Okla., Nov. 5, 1943; s. Russell Porter and Jimmie (Bell) G.; m. Janice Rae Lockley, Nov. 19, 1966; 1 child, Russell Porter III. BS, U.S. Mil. Acad., 1966; JD, U. Miss., 1974. Bar: Miss. 1974, U.S. Dist. Ct. (no. dist.) Miss. 1974, U.S. Ct. Appeals (5th cir.) 1980, U.S. Dist. Ct. (so. dist.) Miss. 1992. Ptnr. Patterson & Patterson, Aberdeen, Miss., 1974-80; petroleum landman Aberdeen, 1980-81; ops. landman Hughes & Hughes Oil and Gas, Jackson, Miss., 1981-84; mgr. gas contracts Hughes Ea. Petroleum, Ltd., Jackson, 1984-88; corp. counsel Hughes Ea. Petroleum, Inc., Jackson, 1988-89; pvt. practice Jackson, 1989-90, 91; assoc. Overstreet & Kuykendall, Jackson, 1990-91; ptnr. McKibben, Grant & Assocs., Jackson, 1991-95; pvt. practice Jackson, 1995-2000; petroleum landman, 2000—. Mem. legal com. Interstate Oil and Gas Compact Commn., Oklahoma City, 1992—; speaker Oil and Gas Inst., U. Ala., 1990, natural gas seminar Miss. Natural Gas Assn., 1986. Co-chair exec. com. Monroe County Rep. Party, Aberdeen, 1980; pres. Aberdeen Exch. Club, 1978-79; mem. Monroe County (Miss.) Port Authority, 1979-80. Capt. U.S. Army, 1966-72. Named Outstanding Com. Chair, Aberdeen C. of C., 1979. Mem. Miss. Oil and Gas Lawyers (pres. 1986-87), Miss. Assn. Petroleum Landmen (v.p. 1987-88, pres. 1994-95), Miss. Bar (chmn. natural resources sect. 1988-89), Am. Assn. Profl. Landmen (cert. profl. landman), The Federalist Soc., Nat. Lawyers Assn. Episcopalian. Avocations: art, architecture, gardening, music, history. Home and Office: 1818 Aztec Dr Jackson MS 39211-6503 E-mail: grantjr@unidial.com.

GRANT, SANDRA LYNN, family practice nurse practitioner; b. Lubbock, Tex., Oct. 16, 1959; children: Chelsea, Stephanie, Chance, Rachael. Cert. vocat. nursing, Frank Phillips Coll., 1980; BSN, Tex. Tech U., 1995; MSN, Tex. Tech. U. Health Sci. Ctr., 2003. RN, Tex.; lic. vocat. nurse, Tex. Nurse aide Dumas (Tex.) Meml. Home, 1978-79, lic. vocat. nurse, 1980-81, K.W. Pieratt, M.D., Dumas, 1981-82; LPN Pawnee (Okla.) Mcpl. Hosp., 1982-84; LPN, child birth educator Dr. James P. Riemer, Pawnee, 1984-88; lic. vocat. nurse (med.-surg.) Meth. Hosp., Lubbock, 1988-91, lic. vocat. nurse (cardiac telemetry), 1991-94; RN supr. home health divsn. South Plains Cmty. Action Assn., 1995; program dir./coord. Alternative Home Health Svcs., Lubbock, Tex., 1995-98; CBA/PHC/FC program dir. Essential Home Health, Lubbock, 1998-99; dir. CBA/PHC program Interim Health Care, Lubbock, 1999—2001; lead nurse Outreach Health Svcs., Lubbock, 2001—02; field supr. Essential Home Health, Lubbock, 2002—03; family nurse practitioner Dr. Rodney T. Franklin MD, Lubbock, 2003—. Mem. NAFE, Tex. Nurse Practitioners Assn., Am. Assn. Nurse Practitioners, South Plains Nurse Practitioner Assn., Sigma Theta Tau. Avocations: guitar playing, sewing, camping, water-skiing, song writing.

GRANT, SONIA VIVIENNE, secondary school educator; b. Spanish Town, Jamaica, Jan. 27, 1947; arrived in US, 1967; d. Alfred Constantine and Mavis Adassah Jones; m. Gaffel Fritz Grant, June 23, 1968 (div. Dec. 15, 1989); children: Gaffel Sean, Nadique Tamika, Cynette Sonja. BA in Econs., Queens Coll., Flushing, N.Y., 1975; MS, Long Is. U., Bklyn., 2000—. Cert. tchr. N.Y. Author: A Client's Point of View, 2001. Achievements include invention of grapha-phonic-bar. Home: 531 W 152nd St Apt 1 D New York NY 10031

GRANT, STEPHEN ALLEN, lawyer; b. N.Y.C., Nov. 4, 1938; s. Benton H. and Irene A. Grant; m. Anne. K. Bagley, Feb. 11, 1961 (div. Nov. 1975); children: Stephen, Katharine, Michael; m. Anne-Marie Laignel, Dec. 8, 1975; children: Natalie, Elizabeth, Alexandra. AB, Yale U., 1960; LLB, Columbia U., 1965. Bar: N.Y. 1965, U.S. Supreme Ct. 1969. Law clk. to judge U.S. Ct. Appeals (2d cir.), N.Y.C., 1965-66; assoc. Sullivan & Cromwell, N.Y.C., 1966-73, ptnr., 1973—2002. Mem. Japan-U.S. Friendship Commn., U.S.-Japan Conf. on Cultural and Ednl. Interchange, 1989-92. Lt. (j.g.) USNR, 1960-62. Mem. ABA, N.Y. State Bar Assn., Assn. of Bar of City of N.Y., Coun. Fgn. Rels. Clubs: Down Town, Links. Office: 200 E 66th St Ste C2103 New York NY 10021-9187

GRANT, SUSAN IRENE, lawyer; b. N.Y.C., Apr. 27, 1953; d. Walter Arnold and Beatrice L. (Thalheimer) G.; m. Brian A. King, June 24, 1990; 1 child, Alexander Grant King. BA, NYU, 1974; JD, Columbia U., 1977. Bar: N.Y. 1978, U.S. Dist. Ct. (so. and ea. dists.) N.Y. 1978. Assoc. Law Offices of Rita Eredics, Esq., Flushing, NY, 1977-78; staff atty. The Dreyfus Corp., N.Y.C., 1978-85; asst. gen. counsel Prudential-Bache Securities Inc., N.Y.C., 1985-89, asst. v.p., 1986-89; asst. gen. counsel, assoc. v.p. Prudential Mut. Fund Mgmt., Inc., N.Y.C., 1987-89; asst. counsel First Investors Corp., N.Y.C., 1989-94; sr. counsel, chief compliance officer Royce & Assocs., N.Y.C., 1994-96; sr. atty. Van Eck Assocs. Corp., N.Y.C., 1996-98, Weil, Gotshal & Manges LLP, N.Y.C., 1998—2002; pvt. practice Forest Hills, NY, 2002—. Mem. ABA, N.Y. State Bar Assn., Bar Assn. City N.Y. Home: 11045 Queens Blvd Forest Hills NY 11375-5501 Office: 110-45 Queens Blvd Forest Hills NY 11375-5501 Fax: 718-268-6569. E-mail: bakfinguru@aol.com.

GRANT, SYDNEY R. education educator, consultant; b. N.Y.C., Feb. 3, 1926; s. Herman S. and Ethel H. G.; m. Margarita Henderson, Sept. 4, 1951. BS in Edn. cum laude, CCNY, 1950; MA in Spanish Letters, Nat. U. Mex., Mexico City, 1951; EdD, Columbia U. Tchrs. Coll., 1961. Cert. tchr., N.Y.; cert. gen. supr., N.J., Wash. Program asst. Sch. Gen. Studies CCNY, 1951-52, instr. Spanish Sch. Gen. Studies evening program, 1952-64; tchr. Spanish and common brs., cons. The P.R. study N.Y.C. Bd. Edn., 1952-60; dir. of instrn. K 12 Verona (N.J.) Pub. Schs., 1961 64; assoc. chief of party, assoc. prof. Columbia U. Tchrs. Coll., US./AID contract team, Lima, Peru, 1964-68; assoc. supt. for curriculum Bellevue (Wash.) Pub. Schs., 1968-69; dir. office internat. edn. Coll. Edn. Fla. State U., Tallahassee, 1969-72, assoc. prof., dir. Ctr. for Ednl. Tech., 1972-75, assoc. dean for grad. studies Coll. Edn., 1975-78, prof. Coll. Edn., 1972—, prof., head dept. ednl. founds. and policy studies, 1986-89, prof. internat.-intercultural devel. edn., 1979-85, prof. emeritus, 1994—. Cons. U.S./AID, UN Devel. Program, UNESCO, Fundacion Natura, Fla. State U., Latin Am., S.E. Asia, Africa, 1969-90; sr. resident tech. adv. Min. Edn. and Culture for Fla. State U. in Windhoek, Namibia, 1991-93. Cpl. U.S. Army, 1944-46, ETO. Recipient Esso award Esso Standard Oil Co., 1960, Palmas Magisteriales Peruvian Ministry of Edn., 1967, Pres.'s Teaching award Fla. State U., 1978; Downer scholar CCNY, 1950. Mem. Nat. Soc. for Study Edn., Comparative and Internat. Edn. Soc., Common Cause, Amnesty Internat. Avocations: short wave radio, reading. Office: 1503 Belleau Wood Dr Tallahassee FL 32308-0911

GRANT, VERNE EDWIN, biology educator; b. San Francisco, Oct. 17, 1917; s. Edwin and Bessie (Swallow) G.; m. Alva Day, June 12, 1946 (div. Aug. 1959); children: Joyce Grant Mixon, Brian, Brenda Grant Aley; m. Karen Alt, Nov. 3, 1960. AB, U. Calif., Berkeley, 1940, PhD, 1949. Teaching asst. botany U. Calif., Berkeley, 1946-49; NRC fellow Carnegie Inst., Stanford, Calif., 1949-50; geneticist Rancho Santa Ana Bot. Garden, Claremont, Calif., 1950-67; asst. prof. Claremont Grad. Sch., 1951-53, assoc. prof., 1953-57, prof., 1957-67; prof. biology Inst. Life Sci., Tex. A&M U., College Station, 1967-68; prof., dir. Boyce Thompson Southwestern Arboretum U. Ariz., Superior, 1968-70; prof. botany U. Tex., Austin, 1970-87, prof. emeritus, 1987—. Author: Natural History of the Phlox Family, 1959, The Origin of Adaptations, 1963, The Architecture of the Germplasm, 1964, (with Karen Grant) Flower Pollination in the Phlox Family, 1965, (with Karen Grant) Hummingbirds and Their Flowers, 1968, Plant Speciation, 1971, 2d edit., 1981, Genetics of Flowering Plants, 1975, Organismic Evolution, 1977, The Evolutionary Process, 1985, 2d edit., 1991, The Edward Grant Family and Related Families in Massachusetts, Rhode Island, Pennsylvania, and California, 1997; mem. editorial bd. Ency. Americana, 1955-64, Brittonia, 1957-62, Evolution, 1960-62, Am. Naturalist, 1964-67, Biologisches Zentralblatt, 1974-97; contbr. numerous articles to profl. jours. Recipient Sci. award Phi Beta Kappa, 1964 Fellow Am. Acad. Arts and Scis.; mem. NAS, Soc. for Study of Evolution (pres. 1968), Bot. Soc. Am. (cert. of merit 1971), Internat. Soc. Plant Taxonomists, Am. Soc. Plant Taxonomists. Home: 2811 W Fresco Dr Austin TX 78731-5028 Office: U Tex Sect Integrative Biology Austin TX 78712

GRANT, WALTER MATTHEWS, lawyer, corporate executive; b. Winchester, Ky., Mar. 30, 1945; s. Raymond Russell and Mary Mitchell (Rees) G.; m. Ann Carol Straus, Aug. 5, 1967; children— Walter Matthews II, Jean Ann, Raymond Russell II. ABJ, U. Ky., Lexington, 1967; JD, Vanderbilt U., 1971. Bar: Ga. 1971, Tenn. 1992. Assoc. Alston & Bird, Atlanta, 1971-76, ptnr., 1976-83; v.p., gen. counsel, sec. Contel Corp., Atlanta, 1983-91; sr. v.p., gen. counsel Smith & Nephew N.Am., Memphis, 1991-93; sr. v.p., gen. counsel, sec. The Actava Group Inc., Atlanta, 1993-96, Bruno's Supermarkets, Inc., Birmingham, Ala., 1996—2002. Bd. dirs. SCB Computer Tech., Inc., Memphis, Hat Shack, Inc., Atlanta. Editor in chief Vanderbilt Law Rev., 1970-71, Ga. State Bar Jour., 1979-82 Baptist. Home: 23 Rose Gate Dr NE Atlanta GA 30342-4161 E-mail: donhoff@homerelay.net.

GRANT, WILLIAM DAVIS, medical educator, dean; BS, U. Rio Grande, 1967; MEd, The Am. U., 1972; EdD, U. So. Calif., 1977. Asst. prof. family medicine U. Okla., Oklahoma City, 1982-87; adj. prof. marriage and family therapy Syracuse (N.Y.) U., 1995—; asst. prof. New Sch. for Social Rsch., N.Y.C., 1996—; prof. family medicine SUNY Health Sci. Ctr., Syracuse, 1987—, assoc. dean grad. med. edn., 1997—. Founding dir. Ctr. for Evidence Based Practice, SUNY Health Sci. Ctr., Syracuse, 1997-98. Pres. bd. dirs. McKenzie Inst., Syracuse, 1992-95; mem. internat. bd. dirs. McKenzie Internat., Waikanae, New Zealand, 1992-95. Recipient Excellence in Rsch. Edn. award South-Ctr. Rsch. Consortium, San Antonio; named Outstanding Alumnus U. Rio Grande. Fellow Royal Statis. Soc.; mem. Am. Coll. Legal Medicine (assoc.), World Orgn. Family Drs. Office: SUNY Health Sci Ctr at Syracuse 750 E Adams St Syracuse NY 13210-2306

GRANT, WILLIAM FREDERICK, geneticist, educator; b. Hamilton, Ont., Can., Oct. 20, 1924; s. William Aitken and Myrtle Irene (Taylor) Grant; m. Phyllis Kemp Harshaw, July 23, 1949; 1 child, William Taylor. BA, McMaster U., Hamilton, 1947, MA, 1949; PhD, U. Va., Charlottesville, 1953; DSc (hon.), McMaster U., 2000. Botanist, geneticist under Colombo Plan to Dept. Agr., Malaysia, 1953-55; asst. prof. McGill U., Montreal, Que., 1955-61, assoc. prof., 1961-66, prof. depts. plant sci. and biology, 1967-90, prof. emeritus, 1990—. Mem joint WHO and Int Program Chemical Safety Collaborative Study on Short Term Tests for Genotoxicity and Carcinogenicity, 1984—94; environ contaminants adv comt Ministers Environ and Nat health and Welfare, Ottawa, Ont, Canada, 1978—86; co-dir workshop higher plant mutagen bioassays UN Environ Program Quingao Ocean Univ, China, 1995. Editor: Lotus Newsletter, 1970—85, Can Jour Genetics and Cytology, 1974—82; mem ed bd: Mutation Research, 1978—85, Plant Species Biol, 1985—92, Revista Internacional de Contaminacion Ambiental, 1991—; editor (hon ed): Plant Species Biol, 1993—. Named award of Excellence, Grant- Moens, 2003; named to Alumni Gallery, McMaster Univ, 1996; recipient Andrew Fleming Award, 1953, Gov Gen Silver Medal commemorating 25th Ann Accession of H M Queen Elizabeth to Throne, 1977, Distinguished Alumni/Alumnae Scholar Award, McMaster Univ, 1990; fellow Blandy Research, 1950—53. Fellow: AAAS, Royal Soc Can, Linnean Soc London; mem.: Biol Coun Can (treas 1974—78), Soc Study Evolution (vpres 1972), Am Soc Plant Taxonomists, Int Orgn Plant Biosystematists (life; pres 1981—86), Can Botany Asn (George Lawson Medal 1989), Environ Mutagen Soc, Genetics Soc Can (pres 1975, archivist 1984—, Predsl Citation 1991), Sigma Xi (chpt pres 1975). Home: 43 St Andrews Rd Baie d'Urfe QC Canada H9X 2T9 Office: McGill U Macdonald campus Box 4000 Dept Plant Sci Sainte-Anne-de-Bellevue QC Canada H9X 3V9 E-mail: william.grant@mcgill.ca.

GRANT, WILLIAM WEST, III, banker; b. N.Y.C., May 9, 1932; s. William West and Katherine O'Connor (Neelands) G.; m. Rhondda Lowery, Dec. 3, 1955. BA, Yale U., 1954; postgrad., NYU Grad. Sch. Bus., 1958, Columbia U. Grad. Sch. Bus., 1968, Harvard U. Grad. Sch. Bus., 1971. With Bankers Trust Co., N.Y.C., 1954-58, br. credit adminstr., 1957-58; with Colo. Nat. Bank, Denver, 1958-93, pres., 1975-86, chmn. bd., 1986-93. Chmn. bd. Colo. Capital Advisors, 1989-94; bd. dirs. Barrett Resources Corp. Episc. Ch. Found.; Nat. Trust for Hist. Preservation; trustee Gates Family Found., Denver, Rocky Mountain Nat. Park Assocs., Denver, Midwest Rsch. Inst., Kansas City; bd. dirs. Mountain State Employers Coun. Mem. Met. Denver C. of C. Clubs: Denver Country, Denver. Episcopalian. Home: 545 Race St Denver CO 80206-4122

GRANT BRUCE, DARLENE CAMILLE, lawyer; b. Jackson Heights, N.Y., Apr. 25, 1959; d. Leonard DaCosta and Lucille Eleanor Grant; m. Raymond Lloyd Bruce, Nov. 30, 1996. BA, Brandeis U., 1981; JD, Georgetown U., 1986. Bar: N.Y. 1987, U.S. Dist. Ct. (ea. dist.) N.Y., U.S. Ct. Appeals (3d cir.) 1990, U.S. Ct. Appeals (D.C. cir.) 1996, U.S. Supreme Ct. 1999; cert. tng., Nat. Inst. Corrections. Jud. clk., Judge Mary Johnson Lowe U.S. Dist. Ct. N.Y., 1986-87, 1984; jud. clk., Judge Paul Webber Superior Ct., Washington, 1985; assoc. Cullen & Dykman, Garden City, N.Y., 1986-87, Law Offic Lee H. Bostic, Queens Village, N.Y., 1987-89; asst. atty. gen. V.I. Dept. Justice, Solicitor Gen. divsn., U.S. V.I., 1989-94; asst. gen. counsel Coun. for D.C., Office of Gen. Counsel, 1994; gen. counsel for prison litigation Nat. Coun. on Crime and Delinquency, Washington, 1994-98; spl. master U.S. Dist. Ct. V.I., 1996-99; assoc. counsel N.Y. State Assembly, Albany, 1998-99; gen. counsel Berkshire Farm Ctr. and Svcs. Youth, Canaan, NY, 1999—. Instr. Charles Hamilton Houston Inst., Georgetown U. Law Ctr., Washington, 1994. Chair Brandeis U. alumni admissions coun., 1990-99; chair St. Thomas Interagy. Coun. on Homeless, 1992-94; legal advisor V.I. Inst. Performing Arts, 1993-94; bd. trustees, Corona-East Elmhurst Civic Assn., 1987-89. Recipient awards Nat. Assn. Atty. Gens. appellate advocacy program, Am. Trial Lawyers Assn. Mem. ABA, Nat. Bar Assn., Am. Correctional Assn. (legal affairs com. 1997—), N.Y. State Bar Assn., Met. Black Bar Assn. (bd. dirs. 1997—), Macon B. Allen Bar Assn., D.C. Bar Assn., V.I. Bar Assn., Phi Delta Phi, Delta Sigma Theta, Inc. (legal advisor 1992-94, v.p. 1990-92). Office: Berkshire Farm Ctr & Svcs for Youth 13640 Rte 22 Canaan NY 10030-2429

GRANTE, JULLIAN IRVING, criminal justice consultant; b. Washington, Oct. 18, 1950; s. Mamie Elmara Landis; m. Jo Draper; children: Jamil Patricia, Dusan Arthur. BBA, U. Md., 1972; M in Spl. Edn., So. Ill. U., Carbondale, 1976. Sr. ptnr. J. Irving & Draper, Spotsylvania, Va. Testified before U.S. Congress subcom. hearing on youth empowerment; apptd. advisor release rev. com. Dept. Juvenile Justice, State of Va., 1995—, past mem. Criminal Justices Svcs. Bd.; developer program The Broken Classroom: A Dialogue on Youth and Community Violence-Problems and Solutions, 1999; spkr. in field. Named Vol. of Yr. D.C. Pub. Schs., 1988; recipient award Nat. Capitol Area Region, 1990, Recognition for Volunteerism in Edn., White House Points of Light, 1992, Finalist Kellogg Nat. Fellowship Program Group XIII, 1993, finalist Entrepreneur of Yr., Washington Post Inc. Mag., 1995, 96. Mem. Phi Delta Kappa. Office: 535 Mount Pleasant Dr Locust Grove VA 22508-5208 E-mail: jgrante2@aol.com.

GRANTHAM, CHARLES EDWARD, broadcast engineer; b. Andalusia, Ala., Mar. 15, 1950; s. J.C. and Geraldine (Brooks) G.; m. Sandra J. Mosley, Mar. 9, 1973; 1 child, Christopher Charles. Student, Enterprise State Jr. Coll., 1968-69; AA, Lurleen B. Wallace Coll., 1979; M in Elec. Engring., U. Devonshire, 2000. Sales engr., draftsman S.E. Ala. Gas Co., Andalusia, 1968-70; asst. mgr., engr. Sta. WAAO, Andalusia, 1972-78; engr. Ala. Public TV, WDIQ-TV, Dozier, Ala.; also chief technician Sta. WAAO, Andalusia, 1978—80; South Ala. microwave engr. APTV, 1980-93, asst. dir. broadcast ops., 1993-2000, dir. broadcast ops., 2000—. Notary pub., Ala.; bd. dirs. Carolina Vol. Fire Dept., sec./treas., 1985-91; pres. Andalusia Men's Ch. Softball, 1985-86; youth dir. Cedar Grove Ch., 1987-89, deacon, 1993—; pres. Andalusia High Sch. Band Boosters, 1990-91; coach Andalusia Little League, 1982-83; active Lt. Govs. Commn. on Youth and Violence, 1995-96. Sgt. inf. U.S. Army, 1970-72. Named Civitan Outstanding Young Am., 1967. Mem. IEEE, I.S.C.E.T., S.M.P.T.E., Assn. Cert. NABER Technicians (sr. mem.), N.A.R.T.E. (master endorsement), Internat. Soc. Cert. Electronic Technicians, Am. Film Inst., Nat. Ednl. TV Assn. (vice chair engring. coun. 2002--), NRA, Ala. State Employees Assn. (bd. dirs., pres. local chpt. 1991-99), Country Music Assn., Nat. Assn. Bus. and Ednl. Radio, Soc. Broadcast Engrs. (chmn. Montgomery chpt. 2000-02), Country Music Disc Jockey Assn., Rotary Club, Phi Theta Kappa. Mem. Ch. of Christ. Home: 13627 Pond Creek Rd Andalusia AL 36420 Office: 2112 11th Ave S Birmingham AL 35205 E-mail: grantham@alaweb.com.

GRANTHAM, DONALD JAMES, chemical engineer, educator, author; b. Grantham, N.C., Aug. 1, 1916; s. James Clarence and Nannie (Rose) G.; children: David S., Philip L. BA in Chemistry, U. N.C., 1939. Radio announcer, 1940-42; radio programmer, sta. gen. mgr., 1946-50; founder, pres. Grantham Coll. of Engring., L.A., 1951-90; with Grantham Edn. Corp., Grantham edn. CEO, 1992—. Home and Office: 3015 Lautenberg Ln Willow Spring NC 27592-8622

GRANTHAM, JOSEPH MICHAEL, JR., hotel executive, management/marketing consultant; b. Smithfield, N.C., Aug. 23, 1947; s. Joseph Michael and Anne Laurie (Hare) G.; m. Wilsie Moss Hartman, Nov. 3, 1973 (div. 1982); children: Molly Meade, Joseph Michael III; m. Jean Marie Scully, 1986; children: William Warner, Stewart Michael. Student, Oak Ridge Mil. Inst., 1965-66, East Tenn. State U., 1966-70. Cert. Lic. real estate broker N.C. With Grand Hotel, Mackinac Island, Mich., 1966-78, v.p. sales, 1973-74, V.P., mgr., 1974-78; dir. resort ops., gen. mgr. Pinehurst (N.C.) Hotel and Country Club, 1978-80; pres., chmn. bd. Ind. Fin. Investments, Pinehurst, 1980—. Pres., chmn. bd. Carolina Hotels, Inc., 1982—; pres., chmn. Asset Mgmt. & Mktg., Inc., 1986—, superior ct. cert. mediator, 2003-. Vice chmn. No. Mich. Conv. and Visitors Bur., Mackinac Island; commr. scouting Boy Scouts Am., Pinehurst, 1978—; bd. dirs., mem. exec. com., chair legal and risk mgmt. com. Sandhills Hospice Inc. With USNG, 1970-76. Mem. Mackinac Island C. of C. (dir. 1976-79), Mich. Lodging Assn. (dir. 1976-79), Meeting Planners Internat., Hotel Sales Mgmt. Assn. Internat., Am. Hotel and Motor Hotel Assn., N.C. Restaurant Assn., N.C. Hotel and Motel Assn., Nat. Tour Brokers Assn., Chgo. Assn. Execs., N.C. Innkeepers Assn. (dir. 1978-80), travel Coun. of N.C. (dir. 1978-80), Pinehurst Bus. Guild (bd. dirs., pres. 1986), Turnaround Mgmt. Assn., Sandhills Area c. of C. (dir. 1984—), Kappa Alpha, Shriners (bd. dirs. Moore County chpt. 1982—, pres. 1986—), Masons. Methodist. Home and Office: 95 Gray Fox Run Pinehurst NC 28374

GRANTHAM, NAN L. music educator, writer; b. Lawrenceburg, Tenn., June 21, 1936; d. William Lewis and Bernadine (Giles) Laurence; m. Kerry J. Grantham, July 27, 1957; children: James Laurence, Kerryl Ann Frank. BS in Music Edn., Miss. Coll., Clinton, 1957; M in Music, U. Miss., Clinton, 1972. Tchr. Pub. Schs., Fulfurrias, Tex., 1957—61; private /class piano tchr. Garland, Tex., 1961—69, Jackson, Miss., 1961—73; music assoc., pianist Broadmoor Bapt. Ch., Jackson, Miss., 1971—91; music assoc. Miss. Bapt. Conv. Bd., Jackson, 1973—75; music assoc 1st Bapt. Ch., Bossier City, La., 1991—96, 2d Bapt. Ch., Houston, 1996—2000; curriculum writer, clinician Lifeway So. Bapt. Conv., 1973—. Conf. leader Bapt. chs. and schs., United States, 1973—; asst. dir. Houston Children's Choit, 1997—2002. Author: (Books) Developing Tone Matching and Singing Skills, 1982, Leading and Accompanying Children's Singing, (book series) The Language of Music Set 1, 1988, The Language of Music Set 2, 1989, The Language of Music Set 3, 1990; composer: (songs for children, anthems) over 100. Dir. Mass Piano Concerts, Jackson, Miss., 1971—79; leader of numerous ch. music groups Performances at Nursing Homes, Hosps. etc., 1964—2002. Named Alumni of Yr., Miss. Coll. Music, 2001; recipient Order of the Golden Arrow, Miss. Coll., 1993, Editors Choice award Ch. Music Dept., So. Bapt. Conv., 1993. Mem.: Nat. Choristers Guild, Choristers Guild, Houston, Nat. Music Tchrs. Assn., Tex. Music Tchrs. Assn., Ky. Music Tchrs. Assn., Nat. Guild Piano Tchrs. (adjudicator 1982—).

Republican. Baptist. Achievements include invited workshop leader nationwide in both secular and religious music education; clinician for childens' music festivals. Avocations: gardening, sewing, grandchildren. Home: 4122 Weston Dr Fulshear TX 77441 Fax: 281-346-2400. E-mail: nan.grantham@pdg.net.

GRANTHAM, RICHARD ROBERT, financial consultant; b. Ogden, Utah, July 25, 1927; s. Arthur and Dorothy (Taylor) G.; m. Charlotte Blackwood, Aug. 10, 1951; children: Robert Arthur, Scott Ford, Ann Margaret, Susan Marie. BS magna cum laude, Claremont Men's Coll., 1950. C.P.A., Calif. Acct., Price Waterhouse & Co., Los Angeles, 1950-57; asst. controller Cyprus Mines Corp., Los Angeles, 1957-64, div. controller, 1964-65, budget dir., 1965-72, v.p., treas., 1972-74, sr. v.p., treas., 1975-79, sr. v.p., controller, 1979-81; controller Amoco Minerals Co., Denver, 1980-81; sr. v.p., treas. Trust Co. of the West, L.A., 1982-88; sec., treas. TCW Convertible Securities Fund, Inc., 1986-89; mng. dir. Trust Co. of the West, L.A., 1989, cons. on oil and gas matters, 1989-92; sr. ptnr., chief adminstrv. officer TCW Realty Advisors, 1989-95; cons. earthquake repair and ins. matters Westmark Realty Advisors, 1995-99; fin. cons. San Marino, Calif., 1999—. Lectr. in field. Trustee Claremont McKenna Coll., 1953-54, 65-68, 74—, vice chmn., 1976-96; dir. Pasadena (Calif.) Symphony Assn., 1995—, v.p. finance 1996-99, exec. v.p., 1999-2000, pres., 2000-2002. Mem. AICPA, San Marino Men's Republic Club (pres. 1967), Calif. Soc. CPAs, Claremont Men's Coll. Alumni Assn. (pres. 1953-54), Republican Assocs. Clubs: California, Valley Hunt. Home: 1660 Oak Grove Ave San Marino CA 91108-1109 Fax: (626) 585-1682. E-mail: grichardgrantham@cs.com.

GRANTS, VALDIS, engineering manager; b. Liepaja, Latvia, Mar. 5, 1942; came to U.S., 1949, naturalized, 1955; s. Karlis Valdemars and Meta Mudite (Greenvalds) G.; m. Yvette Marie Guhl, June 18, 1966; children: Kristine Marie, Carl Raymond. BS in Sci. Engring., U. Mich., 1964, BS in Engring. Maths., 1965, MS in Elec. Engring., 1967. Rsch. engr. U. Mich., Ann Arbor, 1965-70; sr. design engr. Info. Instrn., Inc., Ann Arbor, 1970-71, Allen-Bradley Co., Highland Heights, Ohio, 1971-76, engring. supr., 1976-77, engr. mgr., 1977-95; mgr. product safety Rockwell Automation, Mayfield Heights, Ohio, 1995. Patentee in field. Mem. IEEE, Am. Soc. for Quality, Tau Beta Pi, Eta Kappa Nu, Phi Kappa Phi. Avocations: astronomy, photography, personal computers, jogging, reading. Office: Rockwell Automation 1 Allen-Bradley Dr Mayfield Heights OH 44124-6118 E-mail: vgrants@ra.rockwell.com., val-yvette.grants@prodigy.net.

GRAPER, MARY CASPERS, librarian; b. Olivia, Minn., Apr. 26, 1957; d. Donald W. and Druzella A. Caspers; m. David F. Graper, July 26, 1996. BA in Psychology and Speech, Luther Coll., Decorah, Iowa, 1979; MA in Comms., U. Iowa, 1980; MLS, U. Ariz., 1985. Reference libr. S.D. State U., Brookings, 1985-98, acquisitions libr., 1998—. Author: South Dakota Periodicals Index, 1988, 93, South Dakota Farm and Home Research Index, 1978-1994, 1995, others; editor: Hilton M. Briggs Library: Handbook for Faculty, 1992. Mem. AAUW, ALA, S.D. Libr. Assn. (pres.-elect, S.D. Libr. of Yr. 2002), Mountain Plains Libr. Assn., Bet Phi Mu. Lutheran. Office: SD State U Hm Briggs Libr Brookings SD 57007-0001

GRAPER, WILLIAM EARL, state agency administrator; b. Schenectady, N.Y., Mar. 23, 1945; s. Earl E. and F. Shirley (Peterson) G.; m. Melanie M. Filion, Aug. 14, 1976 (dec. Feb. 1993); 1 child: Christopher E.; m. Sandra Bauer, Feb. 18, 1995; 1 stepchild, Ryan P. Reece. BA in Geography, Middlebury Coll.; MA in Geography, U. Vt. Various staff positions N.Y. State Dept. Econ. Devel., Albany, 1970-78, dir. commerce devel. team, 1978-83, dir. tech. svcs., 1983-86, dir. regional econ. devel., 1986-96; dir. east coast office Kans. Dept. Commerce and Housing, Scotia, N.Y., 1996—. Pres. Nat. Assn. State Devel. Agys., Washington, 1994-96, exec. com. 1991-96. Office: Kans Dept Commerce East Coast Office 352 Mohawk Ave Scotia NY 12302-1823 E-mail: kansas@capital.net.

GRAPIN, JACQUELINE G. economist; b. Paris, Dec. 15, 1942; came to U.S., 1985; d. Jean and Raymonde (Ledru) G.; m. Michel Le Goc, June 4, 1971; children: Claire, Julien. Degree, Institut d'Etudes Politiques, Paris, 1966; Degree in Law, U. Paris, 1967; Auditeur, Inst. des Hautes Etudes de Def. Nat., Paris, 1980. Staff writer LeMonde, Paris, 1967-81; dir.-gen. Interavia Pub. Group, Geneva, 1982-86; pres. The European Inst., Washington, 1989—; assoc. prof. Am. U. Econ. corr. Le Figaro, Washington, 1987—; prof. Inst. d'Etudes Politiques, Paris, 1974-77. Author: Guerre Civile Mondiale, 1977, Radioscopie des Etats-Unis, 1980, Fortress America, 1984, Pacific America, 1987, Transatlantic Interoperability in Defense Industries, 2002; pub. European Affairs; contbr. articles to profl. jours. Trustee Aspen Inst. for Humanistic Studies, N.Y.C., 1981—96; bd. dirs. French Am. C. of C., Washington, Internat. Action Against Hunger. Recipient Prix Vauban Inst. des Hautes-Etudes, Paris, 1977, Officer in Order of Legion of Honor, 2001. Mem.: Swiss Coc. of French Legion of Honor, Internat. Inst. Strategic Studies, Cosmos Club, Nat. Press Club, Pen Club. Home: 4745 Massachusetts Ave NW Washington DC 20016-2345 Office: The European Inst 5225 Wisconsin Ave NW Ste 200 Washington DC 20015-2014

GRASER, ALFRED J. airport terminal executive, director; Dep. dir. Port Authority NY, Jamaica, 2000—01; gen. mgr. John F. Kennedy Internat. Airport, Jamaica, 2001—. Mem.: Am. Assn. Airport Exec. (pres. NE chpt. 2002—). Office: JFK Internat Airport Bldg 14 Jamaica NY 11430*

GRASER, BERNICE ERCKERT, elementary school principal, educational consultant, psychologist; b. Buffalo, May 5, 1933; d. George Snead Sr. and Ada Louise (Sheasley) Erckert; m. Stanley Richard Graser, May 8, 1953; children: Deberah Dawn Walvoord Rogers. BA magna cum laude, Coll. Gordon & Barrington, 1963; MA, R.I. Coll., 1965; postgrad., Boston U., 1969-71. Cert. elem., pre-sch.-high sch. handicapped tchr.; cert. spl. edn. adminstr.; cert. sch. psychologist. Spl. edn. instr. United Coll. Gordon (Mass.) & Barrington; prin. Pleasant View Sch. for Handicapped Children, Providence; spl. edn. supr. Meeting Street Sch., East Providence; prin. Wm. D'Abate Meml. Elem. Sch., Providence. Established State Model Child Opportunity Zone at Wm. D'Abate Sch.; cons. on ednl. reform; spkr. on critical ednl. issues; presenter workshops and confs.; cons. and lectr. in field. Producer TV broadcast Internat. Celebrations of Cultures; contbr. articles to profl. jours. Named Sch. Adminstr. of Yr., State of R.I., 1993; grantee: U.S. Govt. Dept. Edn.1971—, 1991-93; Very Spl. Arts, State of R.I., 1985-87. Avocations: world travel, photography, videography, business economics, volunteer church work. Home: 45 Clarke Rd Barrington RI 02806-4037

GRASKEMPER, JOSEPH PETER, dentist; b. Cleve., Oct. 18, 1951; s. Joseph George and Ruth Helen (Hasek) G.; m. Tara Hammond, Mar. 17, 1984; children: Joseph William, Gena Claire, Paige Alexandra. BS, Xavier U., Cin., 1973; postgrad., Case Western Res. U., 1973-74; DDS, Ohio State U., 1977; JD, Thomas Jefferson Coll. Law, San Diego, 1987. Assoc. Univ. Towne Dental Group, San Diego, 1979-80; v.p., ptnr. Sorrento Valley Ceramic Arts, San Diego, 1980-82, Univ. Towne Dental Group, San Diego, 1980-84, pres., sole owner, 1984-96, The Bellport Village Dentist, 1997—; asst. clin. prof. advances edn. gen. dentistry Stonybrook Sch. Dental Medicine. Bd. dirs. Franklin County Crippled Children's Dental Program, 1976-77; v.p. Encinitas Town Council, 1981; bd. govs. Mary Haven Ctr. of Hope, 1998—. Lt. USN, 1977-79 Recipient Fellowship, Internat. Congress or Oral Implantology. Fellow Am. Endodontic Soc., Acad. Gen. Dentistry, Am. Soc. Osseointegration; mem. ADA, N.Y. State Dental Soc., Kiwanis Club Patchogue, Bellport C. of C., Patchogue C. of C. Republican. Roman Catholic. Office: 7 Bellport Ln Bellport NY 11713

GRASS, ALEXANDER, retail company executive; b. Scranton, Pa., Aug. 3, 1927; s. Louis and Rose (Breman) G.; m. Lois Lehrman, July 30, 1950; children: Linda Jane, Martin L., Roger L., Elizabeth Ann; m. Louise B. Gurkoff, Apr. 26, 1974. LLB, U. Fla., 1949; D (hon.), Hebrew U., 2000, Doctorate (hon.) of Philosphy, 2000. Bar: Fla. 1949, Pa. 1953. Pvt. practice, Miami Beach, Fla., 1949-51; v.p. Rite Aid Corp., Shiremanstown, Pa., 1952-66, pres., 1966-69, 77-89, chmn., chief exec. officer, 1969-95, chmn. exec. com., 1995-99; chmn., CEO Super Rite Foods, Inc., 1983-95. Chmn. bd. govs. Hebrew U. of Jerusalem, 1996-99. Mem. nat. exec. com. United Jewish Appeal, 1968-79, nat. vice chmn., 1970-79, gen. chmn., 1984-86, chmn. bd. trustees, 1986-88, mem. bd. trustees, 1988-99; pres. Harrisburg (Pa.) Jewish Fedn., 1970-72; chmn. Israel Edn. Fund, 1975-78; bd. dirs. Pa. Right to Work Found., 1972-74, Harrisburg Hosp., 1977-81; vice chmn. Harrisburg Hosp., 1988-95; bd. dirs. Pinnacle Health Sys., 1995-2001; mem. Pa. Coun. Arts, 1982; bd. dirs. Keystone State Games, 1982-92, Israel Ctr. Social and Econ. Studies, 1983; trustee Jerusalem Inst. Mgmt., 1983; mem. exec. com. Jewish Agy. for Israel, 1984-88, bd. govs. 1984-90, chmn. bd. govs., 1999—; treas. United Israel Appeal, 1986-90. With USNR, 1945-46. Recipient Disting. Alumnus award U. Fla., 1992, Nat. Scopus award Hebrew U., 1993, Americanism award Anti Defamation League, 1995. Mem. Nat. Am. Wholesale Grocers Assn. (bd. dirs. 1971-73), Nat. Assn. Chain Drug Stores (bd. dirs. 1972-95, chmn. 1985 86, Nat. Achievement award 1995). Jewish (dir. temple). Office: Grass Cos 1000 N Front St Ste 503 Wormleysburg PA 17043-1043 E-mail: agrass2140@aol.com.

GRASSELLI, MARGARET MORGAN, curator; b. Worcester, Mass., Mar. 1, 1951; d. Paul Shepard and Anne Piersol (Murray) Morgan; m. Nicholas Eugene Grasselli, May 24, 1981; children: James, Juliana, Anne Regina. AB magna cum laude, Radcliffe Coll., 1973; AM in Fine Arts, Harvard U., 1977, PhD, 1987. Curatorial asst. drawing dept. Fogg Art Mus., Cambridge, Mass., 1974-75, curatorial asst. print dept., 1977-78; asst. curator prints and drawings Nat. Gallery of Art, Washington, 1984-89, curator of Old Master Drawings, 1989—. Tutor fine arts dept. Harvard U., Cambridge, Mass., 1977; guest curator exhbn. Nat. Gallery of Art, Washington, 1980-84; professorial lectr. Georgetown U., Washington, 1988. Author: (exhbn. catalogs) Eighteenth-Century Drawings from the Collection of Mrs. Gertrude Laughlin Chanler, 1982; co-author: (exhbn. catalogs) Renaissance and Baroque Drawings from the Collection of John and Alice Steiner, 1977, Old Master Drawings and Bronzes from the Cottonian Collection, 1979, Watteau 1684-1721, 1984-85, Master Drawings from the Armand Hammer Collection, An Inaugural Celebration, 1989, Art for the Nation, Gifts in Honor of the 50th Anniversary of the National Gallery of Art, 1991, Dürer to Diebenkorn: Recent Acquisitions of Art on Paper, 1992, Drawings from the O'Neal Collection, 1993, The Touch of the Artist: Master Drawings from the Woodner Collections, 1995, Mastery and Elegance: Two Centuries of French Drawings from the Collection of Jeffrey E. Horvitz, 1998, The Drawings of Annibale Carracci, 1999; mem. editl. bd. Master Drawings, 1994—; contbr. articles to profl. jours. Agnes Mongan Travelling fellow Harvard U., 1978-79, Samuel H. Kress Pre-doctoral fellow Samuel H. Kress Found., 1979-80, Ailsa Mellon Bruce Curatorial fellow Ctr. for Advanced Study in Visual Arts, 1989-90. Mem. Print Coun. Am. (bd. dirs. 1993-96). Office: Nat Gallery of Art 4th & Constitution Ave NW Washington DC 20565-0001

GRASSER, GEORGE ROBERT, lawyer, real estate consultant; b. Staten Island, N.Y., Oct. 21, 1939; s. George J. and Anita F. (Spinetta) G.; m. Cecelia Frizziola, July 13, 1968; children: Mark, Eric. BBA, Iona Coll., 1960; JD, Fordham U., 1964. Asst. office mgr. Chgo. Title Ins. Co., N.Y.C., 1966-67, assoc., then ptnr. Moot & Sprague, Buffalo, 1967-75; ptnr. Willig, Grasser & Sheffer, Williamsville, N.Y., 1975-77; prin. Albrecht, Maguire, Heffern & Gregg, Buffalo, 1977-85, Law Offices of George R. Grasser, Buffalo, 1985-87; ptnr. Phillips, Lytle, Hitchcock, Blaine & Huber, LLP, Buffalo, 1987—2002; prin. Grasser & Assocs., LLC, Buffalo, 2002—. Adv. bd. Ticor Title Guarantee Co., Buffalo, 1981—, Friends of Sch. Architecture & Urban Planning SUNYAB, 1999-, Daemen Coll. Ctr. Sustainable Communities and Civic Engagement, 2002-. Author: Property Taxes and Homeowners Associations, 1980, 94, 95, 2002; contbg. author: Condominium Development, 1990; bd. editors N.Y. Land Report, Albany, 1980-83; contbr. articles to profl. jours. Pres. Ptnrs. for Livable Western N.Y., 2001—; mem. bd. advisors Friends of Sch. of Architecture and Urban Planning, SUNY at Buffalo, 1999—, Daemen Coll. Ctr. for Sustainable Cmtys. and Civic Engagement, 2002—. Mem. AIA (Cmty. Svc. award 2001), N.Y. State Bar Assn. (condominium and coop. com. 1978—, co-chmn. 1990-96, unlicensed practice of real estate law com. 1999—, co-chmn. 1999-2002), N.Y. State Builders Assn. (trustee legal def. fund 1987-2000, dir. 1989-2000), Erie County Environ. Mgmt. Coun. (Friend of Environment award 2002), Erie County Bar Assn. (chmn. real estate com. 1978-82), Niagara Frontier Builders Assn. (bd. dirs. 1978-80, 89-99, sec. 1980-81, v.p. 1981, Svc. award 1977-98), Cmty. Assns. Inst. (trustee 1988-90, Svc. award 1986), Coll. Cmty. Assn. Lawyers (bd. govs. 1996-99), Buffalo Niagara Partnership (Pres.'s award 2000). Roman Catholic. Office: Grasser & Assocs LLC 11 Summer Street Buffalo NY 14209 E-mail: ggrasser@irdprojectmanagers.com.

GRASSERBAUER, DORIS, computer scientist, educator; Diplom-Ingenieurin, Vienna U. Tech., 2003. Hardware and software engr. Andronic Gmbh, Vienna, 1991—95; dir. of the multimedia ctr. sch. edn. City Coll. NY, 2001—. Personal E-mail: doris@dograba.com.

GRASSEY, THOMAS BRANDT, humanities educator; b. Columbus, Ohio, Apr. 5, 1945; s. Henry Alfred and Margaret Coughlin Grassey. BA in history, Villanova(Pa.) U., 1967; MA in philosophy, U. Chgo., 1971, PhD in philosophy, 1983. Asst. prof. philosophy Villanova U., 1980—82; vis. prof. philosophy U. San Diego, 1982—83; coord. profl. ethics courses San Jose (Calif.) State U., 1983—86; dir. intelligence studies program U.S. Naval Postgraduate Sch., Montery, Calif., 1987—93; editor Naval College Review U.S. Naval War Coll., Newport, RI, 1993—2002, J.B. Stockdale prof. of leadership and ethics, 2002—. Capt. USNR, 1967—93. Grantee fellowship in ethics, Carnegie Coun., 1994, fellowship in history, NEH, 1992, fellowship in law, 1982. Mem.: Am. Philosophical Assn., U.S. Naval Inst. Roman Catholic. Office: Naval War College 686 Cushing Rd Newport RI 02841-1207 Business E-Mail: grasseyt@nwc.navy.mil.

GRASSHOFF, ALEX, writer, producer, director; b. Boston; Student, Tufts Coll., U. So. Calif. Writer, producer, dir.: TV series Rockford Files, CHiPs, Nightstalker. Recipient Acad. award nomination for Really Big Family, 1966; recipient Acad. award nomination for Journey to the Outer Limits, 1974, Acad. award for documentary Young Americans, 1968, Emmy award for Journey to the Outer Limits, 1974, Emmy award for The Wave, 1982 Office: 7845 Torreyson Dr West Hollywood CA 90046-1228

GRASSI, JAMES EDWARD, Christian ministry executive director; b. Oakland, Calif., Nov. 19, 1943; s. Dante Carlos and Mae Johanna (Condon) G.; m. Mary Louise Etter, Apr. 10, 1965; children: Daniel James, Thomas William. BS in Recreation Adminstrn., Calif. State U., Hayward, 1966; MPA, Calif. State U., 1971. Ordained to ministry Evangelical Ch.,1992. Recreation supr. Oakland (Calif.) Pks. & Recreation, 1964-66; adminstr., dept. head East Bay Regional Pk. Dist., Oakland, 1966-76; dep. town mgr. Town of Moraga, Calif., 1976-86; exec. dir. Let's Go Fishing & FOCAS Ministries, 1986—. Dir. Calif. Recreational Fisheries Coun., Sacramento, 1968-74; trustee Christian Heritage Coll. Bd., El Cajon, Calif., 1989-91; nat. spkr. on bldg. strong families. Author: (booklet) Ultimate Fishing Challenge, 1990, (books) Promising Waters, 1996, also audio cassette, 1998, Heaven on Earth, 1997, In Pursuit of the Prize, 1998 (Silver Angel award Excellence in Media, 1998), The Ultimate Hunt, 2000, Crunch Time, 2002, (tract) Anchoring Your Lives in Christ, 1990; co-host TV program Fishing Tales, 1988—91; contbr. articles to profl. jours.; freelance writer, photographer and videographer on outdoor sports. Bd. dirs. Rotary Internat., 1976—86, YMCA, Hayward, 1977—80. Recipient Legis. Resolution Appreciation and Accomodation, Disting. Employee award Moraga Town Counsel, 1986, Presdl. plaque Calif. Pks. & Recreation Soc., 1980, Faith & Freedom award Religious Heritage Am., 1996. Mem. U.S. Trout Farmers Aquaculture Assn., Nat. Assn. Evangs., Outdoor Writers Assn. Am., Safari Club Internat. Republican. Evangelical. Avocations: fishing, boating, water skiing, writing, hunting. Home: 815 S Madison Rd Post Falls ID 83854-9458 Office: Lets Go Fishing PO Box 3303 Post Falls ID 83877-3303

GRASSI, JOSEPH F. lawyer, mediator, arbitrator; b. N.Y.C., Dec. 6, 1949; BA, Queens Coll., 1970; JD, NYU, 1974. Bar: NY 1974, U.S. Dist. Ct. (so. and ea. dists.) NY 1977, U.S. Ct. Appeals (2d cir.) 1975, U.S. Claims Ct. 1996. Law asst. appellate divsn., 2d judicial dept. Supreme Ct. State of N.Y., 1975-76; assoc. Milbank, Tweed, Hadley & McCloy, N.Y.C., 1976-79; asst. corp. counsel Corp. Counsel of N.Y.C., 1979-83; pvt. practice N.Y.C., 1983—. Mem. ABA, N.Y. County Lawyers' Assn., N.Y. Bldg. Congress. Office: 275 Madison Ave Rm 900 New York NY 10016-0601

GRASSI, LOUIS C. accountant; b. Bklyn., Sept. 25, 1955; s. Salvatore R. and Lena (Cestone) G.; divorced; 1 child, Alessandra. BBA, Queens Coll., 1977. CPA, N.Y. Staff acct. Pustorino, Puglisi & Co., N.Y.C., 1977-79; sr. acct. Peat Marwick Mitchell & Co., N.Y.C., 1979-81; mng. ptnr. Grassi & Co., Westbury, NY, 1981-87; pres., CEO, Biscotti, Grassi & Co., Valley Stream, N.Y., 1987-95; mng. ptnr. Grassi & Co. CPAs P.C., Lake Success, N.Y., 1995—. Chmn. bd. EAC, Inc., Mineola, N.Y., 1987-96; bd. dirs. CPA Mut. Ins. Co., Flushing Savs. Bank; frequent speaker to profl. and trade groups. Editor Jour. of Constrn. Acctg. and Taxation, 1991-98; mem. editl. bd. The CPA Jour., 1999—, CPA Mng. Ptnr. Report; contbr. articles to profl. jours. Mem. N.Y. State Soc. CPAs (exec. bd.), Constn. Fin. Mgmt. Assn. (bd. dirs. 1989—), Profl. Liability Commn. (chmn. 1990—), North Hills Country Club (bd. dirs.), Strathmore Vandervilt Country Club (past pres.), Young Pres. Orgn. Republican. Roman Catholic. Avocations: golf, music, collecting wine. Office: Grassi & Co 2001 Marcus Ave New Hyde Park NY 11042-1011

GRASSIA, THOMAS CHARLES, lawyer, writer; b. Westfield, Mass., Aug. 26, 1946; s. Thomas C. and Assunta (Abatiell) G.; m. Judith Chace Cranshaw, Aug. 15, 1970; children: Susan C., Joseph C. BA, Boston U., 1968; JD, Suffolk U., 1974. Bar: Mass. 1974, U.S. Dist. Ct. Mass. 1976, U.S. Supreme Ct. 1980. Asst. v.p. Plymouth Rubber Co., Canton, Mass., 1969-71; ptnr. P.T.S. Computer Svcs., Waltham, Mass., 1971-81, D'Angio & Grassia, Waltham, 1974-85, Grassia & Assocs., P.A., Natick, Mass., 1985—98, Grassia, Murphy & Whitney, P.A., Natick, 1998—2002, Grassia, Murphy & Lupan, P.A., Natick, 2002—. Agt. Lawyers Title Ins. Co., First Am. Title Ins. Co., Fidelity Nat. Title Ins. Co., Stewart Title Ins. Co.; bd. dirs. many regional corps; pres., treas., bd. dirs. Lender's Title & Abstract Co., Ltd., Natick. Author: Campfires, 2000; contbr. articles to profl. publs., lectr. on law, pub. interest subjects. Mem. Bd. Health, Sherborn, Mass., 1976-81, Bd. Selectmen, Sherborn, 1981-85; trustee Leonard Morse Hosp., Natick, 1981-84; mem. Met. Boston Hosp. Coun., Burlington, Mass., 1983-84; mem., team leader Sherborn Fire and Rescue Dept., 1974—; former mem. Sherborn Sch. Bd. Long Planning com., Sherborn Police Chief Selection com., Sherborn Emergency Med. Com. Mem. ABA, Mass. Bar Assn., Mass. Conveyances Assn., Am. Arbitration Assn. (comml. arbitration bd.), New Eng. Helicopter Pilots Assn. (past pres., chmn. bd. dirs.). Home: PO Box 178 Sherborn MA 01770-0178 Office: Grassia Murphy & Lupan PA 5 Commonwealth Rd Natick MA 01760-1526 E-mail: tgrassia@gmllaw.com.

GRASSL, WOLFGANG, adult education educator; b. Graz, Austria, May 15, 1955; s. Johann and Irene Grassl; m. Rebecca Cathleen Proefrock. MA, Diplomatic Acad., 1985; PhD, U. of Graz, 1979. Jr. rsch. fellow Oxford U., 1979—82; sec. gen. (CEO) Austrian Hotel Assn., Vienna, 1985—90; gen. mgr. Horwath & Horwath Unternehmensberatung GmbH, Vienna, 1990—92; pres. Tourconsult Unternehmensberatung GmbH, Vienna, 1992—96; vis. prof. of mktg. U. of Applied Sciences, Heide, Germany, 1995—96; prof. of mgmt. Mona Sch. of Bus., U. of the WI, Kingston, Jamaica, 1996—98; assoc. prof. of mktg. Hillsdale Coll., Mich., 1998—. Cons. Consultorium, Hillsdale, Mich., 1999. Author: (book) Austrian Economics, 1986. Pres. Mich. Assn. of Scholars, 1999—2001; mem., bd. of scholars Mackinac Ctr. for Pub. Policy, Midland, Mich., 2000; gen. mgr. (chmn.) Liberales Forum, Vienna, 1993—94. Mem.: Acad. of Mktg. Sci., Am. Mktg. Assn. Avocations: travel, classical music, literature. Office: Hillsdale Coll 33 E College St Hillsdale MI 49242

GRASSLE, JUDITH PAYNE, marine biology educator; b. Brisbane, Australia, Dec. 4, 1936; came to U.S., 1960; d. Thomas Basil and Helena (Ripley) Payne; m. John Frederick Grassle, Nov. 21, 1964, 1 child, John Thomas. BSc, U. Queensland, Brisbane, 1958, BSc with 1st class honours, 1960; PhD, Duke U., 1968. Rsch. asst. Duke U., Durham, N.C., 1960-67; rsch. assoc. U. Queensland, 1968-69, Marine Biol. Lab., Woods Hole, Mass., 1970, ind. investigator, 1972-85, sr. scientist, 1986-89; prof. marine biology Rutgers U., New Brunswick, N.J., 1989—. Fellow AAAS. Home: 113 Cleveland Ln Princeton NJ 08540-3051 Office: Rutgers U Inst Marine and Coastal Sci 71 Dudley Rd New Brunswick NJ 08901-8521

GRASSLEY, CHARLES ERNEST, senator; b. New Hartford, Iowa, Sept. 17, 1933; s. Louis Arthur and Ruth (Corwin) G.; m. Barbara Ann Speicher; children: Lee, Wendy, Robin, Michele, Jay. BA, U. No. Iowa, 1955, MA, 1956; postgrad., U. Iowa, 1957-58. Farmer; instr. polit. sci. Drake U., 1962, Charles City Community Coll., 1967-68; mem. Iowa Ho. of Reps., 1959-75, U.S. Ho. Rep. 94th-96th Congresses from 3d Iowa Dist.; senator from Iowa U.S. Senate, Washington, 1980—; chmn. Senate Fin. Com., Washington, 2001—. Mem. Am. Farm Bur., Iowa Hist. Soc., Masons, Pi Gamma Mu, Kappa Delta Pi. Republican. Baptist. Office: US Senate 135 Hart Senate Bldg Washington DC 20510-0001*

GRASSO, JAMES ANTHONY, public relations executive, educator; b. Providence, Jan. 12, 1954; s. Eleanor Marie (D'Angelo) Grasso; m. Kimberly I. Maher, Sept. 14, 1986. BS in Pub. Communication cum laude, Boston U., 1976, MS in Pub. Relations, 1983. Land and pub. relations rep. Algonquin Gas Transmission Co., Boston, 1978-83, asst. mgr., 1983-85, mgr. land, pub. relations, govt. relations, 1985-94, dir. pub. & govt. rels., 1994-97; v.p. pub. & govt. affairs, investor rels. Providence (R.I.) Energy Corp./Providence Gas Co., 1998—99; v.p. pub. and govt. affairs New England divsn. So. Union Co., 1999—2000; pres., CEO Grasso Assocs., LLC, Needham, Mass., 2001—. Mem. adj. faculty Coll. Communications, Boston U., 1987-98. Bd. dirs. Beth Israel Deaconness Med. Ctr., Neeham, Mass., Ctrl. RI Devel. Corp., New Eng. Coun., New Eng. Can. Bus. Coun., Narragansett Coun. Boy Scouts Am., Ctrl. R.I. Devel. Corp.; mem. exec. com. New Eng. Can. Bus. Coun., Nat. Conf. for Cmty. and Justice. Mem. Pub. Rels. Soc. Am., New Eng.-Can. Bus. Council, Capitol Hill Club, New Eng. Gas Assn., New Eng. Gov.'s Conf., Greater Providence C. of C., Greater Boston C. of C. Roman Catholic. Office: Grasso Assocs LLC 17 Avery Sq Needham MA 02494 Fax: 781-455-0229. E-mail: jgrasso@grassoassociates.net.

GRASSO, MARY ANN, theater association executive; b. Rome, N.Y., Nov. 3, 1952; d. Vincent and Rose Mary (Pupa) Grasso. BA in Art History, U. Calif., Riverside, 1973; MLS, U. Oreg., 1974. Dir. Warner Rsch. Collection, Burbank, Calif., 1975-84; mgr. CBS TV/Docudrama, Hollywood, Calif., 1984-88; v.p., exec. dir. Nat. Assn. Theatre Owners, North Hollywood, Calif., 1988—. Instr. theatre arts UCLA, 1980-85, Am. Film Inst., L.A., 1985-88. Screen credits: The Scarlet O'Hara Wars, This Year's Blonde, The Silent Lovers, A Bunnies Tale, Embassy. Apptd. commr. Burbank Heritage Commn. Recipient Friend award, Tripod Sch., 1999, Stace award, Dolby, 2002. Mem.: Found. of the Motion Picture Pioneers, Acad. Motion Picture Arts and Scis., Retinitis Pigmentosa Internat. (The Vision award 1996), Bus. and Profl. Women's Assn. (Woman of Achievement award 1983), Phi Beta Kappa. Democrat. Avocations: traditional music and dance, environmental activities, tennis, yoga. Office: Nat Assn Theatre Owners 4605 Lankershim Blvd Ste 340 North Hollywood CA 91602-1875

GRASSO, RICHARD A. stock exchange executive; D in Comml. Sci.(hon.), Pace U., NYU; cert. advanced mgmt., Harvard U., 1985; JD (hon.), Fordham U., Pepperdine U. Graziadio Sch. Bus., LaSalle U. Mem. staff N.Y. Stock Exch., 1968-73, dir. listing and mktg., 1973-77, v.p. corp. svcs., 1977-81, sr. v.p. corp. svcs., 1981-83, exec. v.p. mktg. group, 1983-86, exec. v.p. capital markets, 1986-88; pres., chief operating officer N.Y. Stock Exchange, 1988-93, exec. vice-chmn., pres., 1993-95, chmn., CEO, 1995—2003. Overseer ops. N.Y. Future Exchange; coord. Depository Trust Co., Nat. Securities Clearing Corp.; bd. dirs. Securities Industry Automation Corp. Past chmn. bd. trustees Jr. Achievement N.Y; trustee Securities Industry Found. Econ. Edn., N.Y.C. Police Found., Inc., YMCA Greater N.Y.; bd. dirs. Nat. Italian Am. Found., Police Found., Washington, Centurion Found., Lower Manhattan Development Corp., Twin Towers Fund; metro N.Y. regional chmn. U.S. Olympic Com.; chmn. N.Y.C. Columbus Quincentennial Commn., 1992; hon. chmn. Friends of Statue of Liberty Nat. Monument/Ellis Island Found. Served U.S. Army, 1966—68. Recipient Humanitarian of Yr. award Tomorrows Children's Fund, Spl. Achievement award Nat. Italian Am. Found., Ellis Island medal of honor Nat. Ethnic Coalition of Orgs., Good Scout award Greater N.Y. Couns. Boy Scouts Am., Brotherhood award NCCJ; named Man of Yr., Cath. Big Brothers, 1994.*

GRASTORF, JEAN ELIZABETH HANCOCK, artist, educator; b. Rochester, N.Y., Oct. 24, 1934; d. Jack and Marjorie Cecelia Hancock; m. C. William Grastorf Jr., June 25, 1955; 1 child, Jean Marie (Mrs. Robert Wilhelm Jr.). AAS in Art and Design, Rochester Inst. Tech., 1955. Exhbn. juror Alaska Watercolor Soc., Ala. Watercolor Soc., Iowa Watercolor Soc., Miss. Watercolor Soc., Hawaii Watercolor Soc., Mont. Watercolor Soc., Ga. Wateercolor Soc., North-

west Watercolor Soc.; awards juror Am. Watercolor Soc. Contbr. art to (Maxine Masterfield) Painting in Harmony with Nature, 1990, (Rachel Wolf) Splash 3, 1994, Splash 4, 1996, Splash 5, 1998, Splash 8, 2004, (Chris Unwin) The Artistic Touch, 1994, Artistic Touch 2, 1996, Artistic Touch 3, (Betty Lou Schlemm an Larry Webster) Best of Watercolor 1995 Best of Watercolor 1997, (Betty Lou Schlemm) Best of Watercolor Figures, 1996, Best of Watercolor Abstracts, 1996, (M. Stephen Doherty) Watercolor - Easy Solutions Color Mixing, 1998, (Nita Leland) Exploring Color, rev. edit., 1998, (Christopher Willard) Watercolor Mixing the 12-Hue Method, 2000, (Mary Todd Beam) Celebrating Your Creative Self, 2001; contbr. art to mag. Bd. dir. The Arts Ctr., St. Petersburg, Fla., 1989-93; vol. Jones Meml. Hosp. Aux., Wellsville, NY, 1968-80, pres., 1978. Recipient Ellen Nelson Meml. award Watercolor West, Brea, Calif., 1990, Claggett-Rey Gallery, 1994, Strathmore award 1996, Founders award 1998, Daler Rowney award, 1998. Mem. Am. Watercolor Soc. (signature, dir. 2000-02, Elsie and David Wu Ject-Key award 2000, jury of awards 2002), Nat. Watercolor Soc. (signature, 1st award 1997, Robert E. Wood award 1999), Rocky Mount Nat. Water Media Soc. (signature, Clagett-Rey award 1994, Excellence award 1996, Founders award 1998), So. Watercolor Soc. (signature, 1st award 1996), Midwest Watercolor Soc. (signature, Award fo Excellence 1994, Founders' award 1998, Canson award 2002), Ga. Watercolor Soc. (signature), Fla. Watercolor Soc. (signature, 2d v.p. 1989, 1st v.p. 1990, Dick Blick award and award of merit 1988, Winsor & Newton award 1992, Cheap Joe award 1994, Jack Richeson award 1995, Alan Chiara award 1998, 2002, Dr. and Mrs. Chen Merit award 1999). Avocations: reading, travel. Home and Office: 6049 4th Ave N Saint Petersburg FL 33710-7824 E-mail: cwgfl@aol.com.

GRATALO, JOHN, JR., mortgage banker, business owner; b. Sommerville, N.J., May 2, 1963; s. John and Anna Mae (Tylka) Gratalo. BS in Fin., DePaul U. Banker Sears Mortgage Corp., Libertyville, Ill., 1987—94; sr. loan officer Lincoln Home, Bloomingdale, Ill., 1994—99, United Banc, Northbrook, Ill., 1999—. Owner The Cichild Hideout, Northbrook, Ill.; load officer First Chgo. Mortgage, 1994—. Mem.: Philipino-Am. C. of C. (officer 1996—). Roman Catholic. Avocation: rare exotic tropical fish. Office: Cichlid Inc 1108 Whitfield Rd Northbrook IL 60062-3947

GRATCH, SERGE, mechanical engineering educator; b. Monte San Pietro, Italy, May 2, 1921; s. Isaak F. and Tatiana (Dermaner) G.; m. Rosemary Delay, June 30, 1951; children: Susan, Mary, Lucia, Karen, Elizabeth, Ann, Barbara, Amy, Ellen, Thomas Charles. BSChemE, U. Pa., 1943, MS, ME, 1945, PhD, ME, 1950. Instr., U. Pa., 1943-45, asst. prof., 1945-50, assoc. prof., 1950-51; rsch. scientist Rohm & Haas Co., Phila., 1951-59; assoc. prof. mech. engring. Northwestern U., Evanston, Ill., 1959-61; supr. processes and devices Ford Motor Co., Dearborn, Mich., 1961-62, mgr. chem. processes and devices, 1963-69, asst. dir. engring. sci., 1969-72, dir. chem. sci. lab., 1972-85, dir. vehicles and component rsch. lab., 1985-86; prof. mech. engring. GMI Inst., Flint, Mich., 1986-96; prof. emeritus Kettering U. (formerly GMI Inst.), Flint, 1999—. Mem. adv. bd. Coll. Engring. U. Iowa, 1969-73, Coll. Engring. U. Detroit, 1971-88; adv. bd. dept. mech. engring. U. Pa., 1973-88; chmn. air pollution rsch. adv. com. Coord. Rsch. Coun., 1983-85; mem. Nat. Alcohol Fuels Commn., 1979-81. Regional editor Internat. Jour. Fracture, 1965-91; contbr. articles to profl. jours. Mem. ASME (hon., past v.p. rsch., past pres., John Fritz medal 1992, Internal Combustion Engine award 1999), NAE, AAAS, Am. Soc. Engring. Edn., Am. Chem. Soc., Engring. Soc. Detroit (past pres.), Soc. Automotive Engrs. (chmn. lubricant rev. bd. 1982-83), Sigma Xi, Tau Beta Pi, Sigma Tau. Roman Catholic. Home: 32475 Bingham Rd Bingham Farms MI 48025-2427 E-mail: sgratch112358MI@comcast.net.

GRATIOT, ROBERT B.R. artist, director; b. Carmel, Calif., Jan. 17, 1947; s. John Hempstead and Ruth Rhodes Gratiot; m. Ann Elizabeth Gast, June 11, 1971 (div. Feb. 28, 1973). BA, U. Pacific, Stockton, CA, 1968; MA, Denver U., Denver, CO, 1973. Pvt. practice, Denver, Colo., 1973—. Art educator Art Students League, Denver, 1997—. One-man shows include Calif. State U., Bakersfield, Sangre de Cristo Center, Pueblo, Colo., Goddard Art Ctr., Ardmone, Okla. Participant Art In Embassies Program U.S. State Dept., Harare, Zimbabwe, 1992. Recipient First Prize, Curtis Sch. All Colo. Show, 1999, Foothills Colo. Open, 1999. Mem.: Spark Gallery Denver (dir. 2001—03). Avocations: reading, bicycle riding, crosswords, crosswords, crosswords. Home: 925 Saint Paul Street Denver CO 80206 Personal E-mail: robgratiot@aol.com.

GRATKE, FRED EDWARD, lawyer; b. Chgo., Apr. 27, 1938; s. Paul Frederick and Conice May (Devol) G. B.S., U. Wis.-Milw., 1960; LL.B., U. Wis.-Madison, 1962. Bar: Wis. 1962, N.J. 1972. Investigator Office of Insp. Gen., Dept. Agrl., Chgo., 1962-65; atty. IRS, Phila., 1965— . Served with USNG, 1956-62. Recipient High Performance award IRS, 1975. Mem. ABA, Wis. Bar Assn., N.J. Bar Assn. Democrat. Unitarian. Clubs: Toastmasters (Independence Sq. 1983—) (treas. 1983-86, pres. 1986—) (asst. gov. Dist. 38 1984-85, gov. 1985-86, lt. gov. Div. C 1986—), IRS Golf League (treas. 1977, 86—, pres. 1978, 84-85). Home: 10102 Delaire Landing Rd Philadelphia PA 19114-5124 Office: IRS 600 Arch St Ste 1507A Philadelphia PA 19106-1612

GRATTAN, GEORGE GILMER, IV, lawyer; b. Harrisonburg, Va., Nov. 13, 1933; s. George Gilmer III and Elizabeth (Conover) G.; m. Martha Townes, Aug. 27, 1955; children: Rebecca, Kathleen, G. Stuart, David. BA, U. Va., 1955, JD, 1960. Bar: Va. 1960. Ptnr. Christian & Barton, Richmond, Va., 1960-74; gen. counsel U. Va., Charlottesville, 1974-88. Former pres. Big Bros. Richmond; former bd. dirs. Big Bros. Am. Served as 1st lt. U.S. Army, 1955-57. Fellow Va. Law Found., Am. Bar Found., Va. Bar Assn. (pres. 1984-85), SPEBSQSA Inc. (barbershop quartet and chorus). Presbyterian. Home and Office: 5250 Advance Mills Rd Earlysville VA 22936-1830

GRATTAN, PATRICIA ELIZABETH, retired art gallery director; b. Sault Ste. Marie, Ont., Can., Sept. 19, 1944; d. David Andrew and Virginia (Graham) G.; m. Ian Bowmer, June 29, 1968. BA with honours, U. Western Ont., London, 1966; BFA, Concordia U., Montreal, 1974; grad., Mus. Mgmt. Inst., Berkeley, Calif., 1995. Exhbns. coord. Art Gallery, Meml. U. Nfld., St. John's, 1978-80, acting curator, head visual and performing arts, 1980-81; acting chief curator Nfld. Mus., Govt. Nfld. and Labrador, St. John's, 1981-82; curator Art Gallery, Meml. U. Nfld., St. John's, 1982-88, dir., 1988-94; exec. dir. Art Gallery Nfld. and Labrador, St. John's, 1994—2003. Chmn. adv. com. Art Purchase Program, Govt. Nfld. and Labrador, 1984-89; mem. The Can. Coun., 1995-98. Author: (exhbn. catalogues) 25 Years of Art in Newfoundland, 1986, Flights of Fancy: Yard Art in Newfoundland, 1983, David Blackwood: Prints' 1960-1985, 1986, Pam Hall: The Coil, 1994. Bd. dirs. Resource Ctr. for Arts, St. John's, 1981-82, Arts Atlantic Mag., 1982-95, Anna Templeton Ctr., St. John's, 1997-99; treas. St. Michael's Printshop, 1985-87; mem. Provincial Govt. Spl. Anniversaries and Celebrations Com., 1987-89, Lakecrest Ind. Sch., 1998-2000. Mem. Can. Mus. Assn. (nat. councillor 1987-89), Can. Art Mus. dirs. Orgn. (pres. 1993-95). Office: Art Gallery Nfld-Labrador PO Box 4200 Saint John's NF Canada A1C 5S7 E-mail: pgrattan@mun.ca.

GRATTON, PATRICK JOHN FRANCIS, oil company executive; b. Denver, Aug. 28, 1933; s. Patrick Henry and Lorene Jean (Johnson) G.; m Jean Marie McKinney, June 10, 1955; children: Sara, Vivian, Patrick, Lizabeth (dec.). BS in Geology, U. N.Mex., 1955, MS in Geology, 1958. Geologist Westvaco Mineral Devel. Corp., Grants, N.Mex., 1955; mining engr. Utah Internat., Denver, 1956; geologist Shell Oil Co., Roswell, N.Mex. and Tyler, Tex., 1957-62; adminstrv. asst. Delhi-Taylor Oil Corp., Dallas, 1962-64; exploration mgr., ptnr. Eugene E. Nearburg, Dallas, 1965-70; ind. geologist Dallas, 1970—; pres. Patrick J.F. Gratton, Inc., Dallas, 1976—. Contbr. articles to profl. jours. Bd. dir. U. N.Mex. Found., 1992-2000. bd. dir. Caswell Silver Found, 1984-89, 1995-2003, With USCG, 1951-53, US Army, 1956-57. Named Disting. Alumnus in Geology, U. N.Mex., 1989; recipient Diplomacy and Innovation Spl. award, Assn. Engring. Geologists, 1991. Mem. Am. Assn. Petroleum Geologists, pres. elect 2003-04,(hon., v.p. S.W. sect. 1976-77, del. 1978-81, 91—, chair ho. of del. 1996-97, hon. mem. ho. of dels. 2000 pres. elect 2003—, pres. profl. affairs 1989-90, hon. life mem. profl. affairs 1993, adv. bd. divsn. environ. geoscientists 1993-96, Disting. Svc. award 1998), Soc. Ind. Profl. Earth Scientists (v.p. 1976-77, pres. 1977-78, Outstanding Svc. award 1990, hon. mem. 1998), Tex. Ind. Producers and Royalty Owners Assn. (exec. com. 1985-97, 99—), Dallas Geol. Soc. (hon. life 1999, Pub. Svc. award 1985, Profl. Svc. award 1992, Outstanding Svc. award 2002), Petroleum Club Dallas, Explorers Club (Tex. chpt. chmn. 1987-88), NY Athletic Club. Roman Catholic. Office: 3232 McKinney Ave # LB54 Dallas TX 75204-2429 E-mail: pjfginc@aol.com.

GRATTON, ROBERT, diversified financial services company executive; b. Montreal, Que., Can., Oct. 23, 1943; s. Bernard and Judith (Dufour) G.; m. Nicole Marcil, Aug. 1966; 3 children. LLL, U. Montreal; LLM, London Sch. Econs. & Polit. Sci.; MBA, Harvard U. Bar: Que. 1967. Asst. to Hon. Paul Gérin-Lajoie, Quebec City; with Credit Foncier, COO, pres., CEO; chmn., pres., CEO Montreal Trust; pres., CEO, bd. dirs. Power Fin. Corp., 1989—; bd. dirs. The Can. Life Assurance Co., Can. Life Fin. Corp. Chmn. Great-West Life & Annuity, U.S.; chmn., bd. dirs. Investors Group, Inc., Great-West Life, London Ins. Group, London Life Assurance Co., The Can. Life Assurance co., Can. Life Fin. Corp.; bd. dirs. Power Corp. Can., Power Fin. Corp., Pargesa Holding S.A. Mem. Mt. Royal Club, St.-James's Club, St.-Denis Club. Office: Power Fin Corp 751 Victoria Sq Montreal QC Canada H2Y 2J3

GRATWICK, JOHN, management consulting executive, writer, consultant; b. Langley, Eng., Mar. 2, 1923; emigrated to Can., 1956, naturalized, 1970; s. Ernest Frank and Doris Hilda (Shepherd) G.; m. Dorothy Shirley Vincent, Aug., 1945 (div. 1957); children: Jane Mary, Paul Vincent; m. Gwendoline Johnston, Mar. 23, 1957; 1 son, Adrian. Cert. in Physics, London U., 1942, B.Sc., 1948. Chmn. Transp. Devel. Agy., Montreal, 1970-72; v.p. research and devel. Canadian Nat., Montreal, 1972-76, corp. v.p., 1980-82; pres. CN Marine, Montreal, 1976-80; prof. Sch. Bus. Adminstrn. Dalhousie U., Halifax, NS, 1983-87, dir. Can. Marine Transp. Ctr., 1983-86, exec. dir. Internat. Inst. Transp. & Ocean Policy Studies, 1986-88; chmn. Halifax Industries Ltd., 1978-84; pres. Gratwick Hickling Inc., 1985-98; dir. Oceans Inst. Can., 1989-91. Bd. dirs. Hickling Corp., Ottawa; bd. dirs. CPCS Transcom Ltd.; chmn. Ctr. for Marine Vessel Design and Rsch., Tech. U. N.S., 1989-91; chmn. Halifax-Dartmouth Port Devel. Commn., 1991-96. Gov. Mt. St. Vincent U., 1989-98; mem. Nat. Transp. Act Rev. Commn., 1992-93. Recipient Achievement award Nat. Transp. Week, 1990. Fellow Royal Statis. Soc., Chartered Inst. of Transport; mem. Can. Operational Rsch. Soc. (pres. 1969-70), Can. Transp. Rsch. Forum (hon. life mem., pres. 1971-72), Internat. Fedn. Operational Rsch. Socs. (v.p. 1977-79). Home: 984 Bellevue Ave Halifax NS Canada B3H 3L7 Fax: 902-422-6215. E-mail: johngrat@hfx.eastlink.ca.

GRAU, JOHN MICHAEL, trade association executive; b. St. Joseph, Mich., May 22, 1952; s. Otto R. and Esther P. (Spitzer) G.; m. Gayle Luedeman, May 7, 1983 (div. Nov. 1996); m. Kristine Sweeney, Aug. 30, 1997; 1 child, Brendan Sweeney. BBA, U. Mich., 1974. Realty specialist HUD, Washington, 1974-75; field rep. Nat. Elec. Contractors Assn., San Mateo, Calif., 1975-76, chpt. mgr., Milw. chpt., 1976-85, asst. exec. v.p., Bethesda, Md., 1985-86, exec. v.p., CEO, 1986—. Chmn., trustee Nat. Elec. Benefit Fund, Washington, 1986-2002; co-chmn. Coun. Indsl. Rels., Washington, 1986—; bd. mem. Plan for Settlement Jurisdictional Disputes in Constrn. Industry, Washington, 1986—; co-chmn. Nat. Joint Apprenticeship and Tng. Com. for Elec. Industry, Washington, 1986—; trustee Associated Specialty Contractors, Washington, 1987—. V.p. Elec. Contracting Found., Bethesda, 1989—, vice chmn., 1999—; bd. dir. Underwriters Lab., Northbrook, Il., 2000, Nat. Elec. Safety Found., Rosslyn, Va., 1996—, treas., 1996-98, 2001-; trustee Nat. Labor-Mgmt. Coop. Com., Washington, 1997—. Fellow Acad. Elec. Contracting (bd. dirs. 1986—); mem. Am. Soc. Assn. Execs. (key industries assn. com. 1987—, chmn. 2003—), Am. Soc. Assn. Execs. Found. (bd. dirs. 2001—), Internat. Assn. Elec. Contractors (assoc. bd. dirs. 1993—), US C. of C. (Com. of 100 1990—). Lutheran. Home: 4805 Jamestown Rd Bethesda MD 20816-2710 Office: Nat Elec Contractors Assn 3 Bethesda Metro Ctr Ste 1100 Bethesda MD 20814-6302 E-mail: jmg@necanet.org.

GRAU, MARCY BEINISH, real estate broker, former investment banker; b. Bklyn., Aug. 7, 1950; d. Joseph Beinish and Gloria (Rosenbaum) Bennett; m. Bennett Grau, Nov. 19, 1978; 3 children. AB with high honors, U. Mich., 1971; postgrad., Columbia U., 1972, N.Y. Inst. Fin., 1973. Asst. to chmn. Bancroft Convertible Fund, N.Y.C., 1973-75; precious metals trader J. Aron & Co., N.Y.C., 1975-81, mgr. metals mktg., 1981-83; v.p. Goldman, Sachs & Co/J. Aron, N.Y.C., 1983-88; investment banking cons. N.Y.C., 1988-90; real estate broker Fox Residential Group, 1998-99, Stribling & Assoc., N.Y.C., 1999—. Editor Precious Metals Rev. and Outlook, 1980—; contbr. article to profl. jours. Vol. worker pediatrics dept. Lenox Hill Hosp., N.Y.C., 1978-79; asst. The Holiday Project, The Hunger Project, N.Y.C., 1978-83; vol. Yorkville Common Pantry, N.Y.C., 1984; tutor Yorkville Neighborhodd Assn., N.Y.C., 1984; assoc. Child Devel. Ctr., N.Y.C.; trustee Congregation B'nai Jeshurun, 1989—, pres., 1991-94, chair, 1994-97; trustee Ethical Fieldston Fund, 1994-2000. Mem. Phi Beta Kappa. Avocations: interior design, fashion, cooking, piano. Home: 300 West End Ave New York NY 10023-8156 Office: 924 Madison Ave New York NY 10021-3577 E-mail: marcyg300@aol.com.

GRAU, SHIRLEY ANN (MRS. JAMES KERN FEIBLEMAN), writer; b. New Orleans, July 8, 1929; d. Adolph and Katherine (Onion) G.; m. James Kern Feibleman, Aug. 4, 1955; children: Ian, James, Nora Miranda, William, Katherine. BA, Tulane U., 1950. Author: (short stories) The Black Prince and Other Stories, 1955, The Hard Blue Sky, 1958, The House on Coliseum Street, 1961, The Keepers of the House, 1964 (Pulitzer prize for fiction 1965), The Condor Passes, 1971, The Wind Shifting West and Other Stories, 1973, Evidence of Love, 1977, Nine Women, 1986, Roadwalkers, 1994; writer publs. including Holiday, New Yorker, New World Writing, Mademoiselle, Saturday Evening Post, Atlantic, The Reporter, 1954—. Mem. Phi Beta Kappa. Office: PO Box 9058 Metairie LA 70055-9058 E-mail: s.grau@worldnet.att.net.

GRAUBARD, JOHN J(OSEPH), lawyer; b. N.Y.C., Aug. 19, 1944; s. David J. and Florence (Pearl) G.; m. Myra L. Lubitz, June 10, 1967; children: Naomi, Michael. AB, N.Y. U., 1965; JD, Yale U., 1968. Bar: N.Y. 1968, U.S. Dist. Ct. (so. and ea. dists.) N.Y. 1970, U.S. Ct. Appeals (2d cir.) 1970, Conn. 1972, U.S. Supreme Ct. 1972, U.S. Dist. Ct. Conn. 1973, U.S. Dist. Ct. N.D. N.Y., 1995, U.S. Dist. Ct. W.D. N.Y. 1998, U.S. Tax Ct. 1982, U.S. Ct. Appeals (1st cir.) 1990, U.S. Ct. Appeals (3d cir.) 1997. Atty. opinions and appeal div. Port Authority N.Y. and N.J., 1968-72; assoc. firm Wofsey, Rosen, Kweskin & Kusiansky, Stamford, Conn., 1972-78; ptnr. firm Graubard and Graubard, Stamford, 1978-86; regional atty. Fed. Deposit Ins. Corp., 1987-89, litigation counsel, 1990-97; atty. Securities & Exch. Commn., N.Y.C., 1997—. Mem. Personnel Bd. of Appeals, City of Stamford, 1982-87. Mem. ABA. E-mail: graubard@scc.gov.

GRAUBARD, SEYMOUR, lawyer; b. N.Y.C., Mar. 8, 1911; s. John and Edna (Kiesler) G.; m. Blanche Kazon, Aug. 24, 1941; 1 child, Katherine (Mrs. William Calvin). AB, Columbia U., 1931, LL.B., 1933. Bar: N.Y. 1933. Legislative asst. to bd. aldermen, N.Y.C., 1934-35; ptnr. Joseph D. McGoldrick, N.Y.C., 1936-37; law sec. to comptroller N.Y.C., 1937-41; sec. to justice Supreme Ct. N.Y. County, 1942, 45-46; practice in N.Y.C., 1949-75; counsel Graubard & Miller, 1975—. Lectr. municipal govt. N.Y. U., New Sch. Social Research, 1938-40 Co-author: Building Regulation in New York City, 1944. Mem. N.Y.C. Commn. Govtl. Operations, 1959-61, Coordinating Council Criminal Justice, 1967-70; Nat. chmn. Anti-Defamation League, B'nai B'rith, 1970-76; pres. ADL Found., 1976-80; chmn. bd. dirs. Fund for N.Y.C., to, 1978; bd. dirs. Palm Beach Civic Assn., 1996—. Served to maj. U.S. Army, 1942-45. Mem. Assn. Bar City N.Y. (past chmn. com. city cts.), N.Y. State Bar Assn., N.Y. County Lawyers Assn. Clubs: City (trustee past pres.), Harmonie (N.Y.C.). Home: 2784 S Ocean Blvd Palm Beach FL 33480-5506

GRAUBARD, STEPHEN RICHARDS, history educator, editor; b. N.Y.C., Dec. 5, 1924; s. Harry and Rose (Polk) G.; m. Margaret Cavendish-Bentinck Georgiades, Aug. 5, 1978; stepsons: William J. Georgiades, David C. Georgiades. AB, George Washington U., 1945; AM, Harvard U., 1946, PhD, 1951; DHL, Providence Coll., 1971, Suffolk U., 1984, Union Coll., 1987; DLitt, U. Vt., 1990. Instr. history and gen. edn. Harvard U., 1952-55, asst. prof., 1955-60, lectr., 1960-63, exec. sec. com. on gen. edn., 1952-59, research assoc. in internat. affairs, 1963-65; vis. prof. history Brown U., 1965-66, prof. history, 1966-94, prof. history emeritus, 1994—; mng. editor Daedalus, 1960-61, editor, 1961-2000; asst. editor Confluence, 1952-55; dir. studies Assembly on Univ. Goals and Governance, 1969-75. Author: British Labour and the Russian Revolution, 1956, Burke, Disraeli and Churchill: The Politics of Perseverance, 1961, Kissinger, Portrait of a Mind, 1973, Mr. Bush's War: Adventures in the Politics of Illusion, 1992; editor: (with G. Holton) Excellence and Leadership in a Democracy, 1962, A New Europe?, 1964, (with G. Ballotti) The Embattled University, 1970 (with F. Gilbert) Historical Studies Today, 1972, (with S.N. Eisenstadt) Intellectuals and Tradition, 1973, (with F. Cavazza) Il Caso Italiano, 1974, A New America?, 1979, Generations, 1979, The State, 1980, Reading in the 1980s, 1983, Australia: The Daedalus Symposium, 1985, Art and Science, 1987, The Artificial Intelligence Debate, 1989, In Search of Canada, 1990, Living with Aids, 1990, Showa: The Japan of Hirohito (with Carol Gluck), 1992, The Research University in a Time of Discontent (with Jonathan R. Cole and Elinor G. Barber), 1994, (with Daniel Bell) Toward the Year 2000, 1997, A New Europe for and Old, 1998. Served with AUS, 1943. Social Sci. Research Council fellow, 1948-50, Acad. fellow Carnegie Corp., 1999—. Fellow Am. Acad. Arts and Scis. (editor 1963—2000), Council on Fgn. Relations, Mass. Hist. Soc. Clubs: Century, Signet. Home: 21 B Carlyle Square London SW36EY England E-mail: stephengraubard@aol.com.

GRAUER, DOUGLAS DALE, civil engineer; b. Marysville, Kans., June 27, 1956; s. Norman Wayne and Ruth Ann (Schwindaman) G.; m. Bette Lynn Bohnenblust, Aug. 16, 1980; children: Diana Kathryn, Laura Jaclyn. Student, Baker U., 1976; BSCE, Kans. State U., 1979. Registered profl. engr., Iowa, Kans., Nebr., Okla. Pipeline engr. Cities Service Pipeline Co., Shreveport, La., 1979-80; products terminal engr. Cities Service Co., Braintree, Mass., 1980-81, project engr. Tulsa, 1981-83; staff engr. Cities Service Oil and Gas Corp., Tulsa, 1983-85; asst. products pipeline and terminal supt. Nat. Coop. Refinery Assn., Blue Rapids, Kans., 1985-90, supt. products pipeline and terminal, 1990—. Mem. ASCE, NSPE, Kans. Soc. Profl. Engrs., Nat. Assn. Corrosion Engrs., Chi Epsilon. Republican. Avocations: golf, fishing, woodworking. Home: 1321 Ranch Rd Mcpherson KS 67460-2313 Office: Nat Coop Refinery Assn PO Box 1404 Mcpherson KS 67460-1404

GRAUER, GAY MEREDITH (SHERRARD GRAUER), artist; b. Toronto, Ont., Can., Feb. 20, 1939; d. Albert Edward and Shirley (Woodward) G.; m. John Keith-King, Feb. 12, 1971; children: Callum, Jonathan, Max. Student, Wellesley Coll., 1956-60, Ecole du Louvre, Paris, 1958-59; BFA, San Francisco Art Inst., 1964. One-woman shows include Mary Frazee Gallery, West Vancouver, Can., 1964, Bau-Xi Gallery, 1965, 67, 68, 70, 75, 76, 80, 83, 85, 87, 89, 90, 92, 97, 2001, Loyola Bonsecours Ctr., Montreal, Can., 1968, Jerrold Morris Gallery, Toronto, 1969, Surrey (B.C.) Art Gallery, 1980, Women in Focus Gallery, Vancouver, 1987, Art Gallery of the So. Okanagan, 1987, Churchill Coll., Cambridge, Eng., 2001; group exhbns. include Can. Group Painters, 1965-68, Montreal Mus. Fine Arts and Can. Pavilion Expo, 1978, Nine out of Ten Hamilton Art Gallery, 1973, Nat. Gallery Can, 1975, B.C. Prov. Coll., 1978-79, Vancouver Art Gallery, 1986, 2001, Charles H. Scott Gallery, Vancouver, 1985, ARTROPOLIS, Vancouver, 1993, Art Gallery of Greater Victoria, B.C., 2001; commns. include World Wide Internat. Travel Office, Vancouver, 1969, U. B.C., 1972, Dept. Pub. Works Ottawa, 1976, Can. Tng. Inst., 1978, Foreshore Projects, Vancouver, 1990, 2001; represented in various pub. and pvt. collections include Vancouver Art Gallery, Can. Coun. Art Bank, Musée d'Art Contemporain, Montreal, Nat. Gallery Can. Trustee Vancouver Art Gallery, 1974-76, hon. sec., 1975-76; founding bd. mem. Arts, Scis. and Tech. Ctr., Vancouver, 1980-83. Mem. Royal Can. Acad. Arts, Can. Artists' Rep./Front des Artistes Canadiens, Can. Conf. Arts, Royal Vancouver Yacht Club. Avocation: reading. Address: 106 8828 Heather St Vancouver BC Canada V6P 3S8

GRAUL, FAYE ANNE, lobbyist; b. Newton, Mass., July 29, 1954; d. Paul Francis and Grace Marie Gorman; m. Clifford Scott Graul, Apr. 12, 1997. BA, Trinity Coll., 1976; MA, Am. U., 1990. U.S. area v.p. govt. rels. Dow Corning Corp., Washington, 1980—. Bd. dirs. Pub. Affairs Coun., 1992--. Mem. Lawyers for Civil Justice (bd. dirs. 1999—), Women in Govt. Rels. (bd. dirs. 1984-88), Soc. for Womens Health Rsch. (adv. coun. 1997—2003), Univ. Club, Capitol Hill Club. Avocations: golfing, reading, traveling. Office: Dow Corning Corp 7105 Park Point Ct Fairfax Station VA 22039-2944

GRAULE, RAYMOND (SIEGFRIED), metallurgical engineer; b. Phila., Feb. 7, 1932; s. Oscar P. and Elizabeth Keim (Merkle) G.; m. Beatrice D. Miller, Sept. 4, 1954 (div. Nov. 1982); children: Melissa, Jon; m. Marlys Ann Sunkle, Sept. 21, 1985 (div. Jan. 1995); children: Troy, Tara, Tiffany. BSChemE, N.J. Inst. Tech., Newark, 1955; MS in Metallurgy, Stevens Inst. of Tech., Hoboken, N.J., 1961. Process engr. Wilbur B. Driver Co., Newark, 1954-62; supr. of prod. engring. G.T.E. Corp., Newark, 1962-77; engring. mgr. Amax Corp., Parsippany, N.J., 1977-84; specialist Carpenter Tech. Corp., Orangeburg, SC, 1984—2003; cons. metallurgist RSG Electronic Alloy Practice, LLC, 2003—. Cons., RSG Electronic Alloys Practice, Orangeburg, 2003—; adj. instr. Essex County Coll., Newark, 1979-81, Orangeburg Calhoun Tech. Coll., 1984-87. County committeeman Rep. Party, Parsippany, 1965-81; advisor Bd. of Edn., 1969-73. With U.S. Army, 1956-58. Mem. Rep. Club (Parsippany), Goodyear Blimp Club, Exptl. Aviation Assn., Orangeburg Pilots Assn. Avocations: woodworking, flying, boating. Home: 433 Gue Rd NW Orangeburg SC 29115-4128 Office: Carpenter Splty Wire Products PO Box 1467 144 Old Elloree Rd Orangeburg SC 29115-8461

GRAULTY, ROBERT THOMAS, engineer, consultant; b. Troy, N.Y., July 22, 1928; s. Thomas Joseph and Elsie (Connor) Graulty; m. Jacqueline Anne Shields, Feb. 18, 1950; children: Kevin, James, Mark, Karen, Dianne, Daniel, John. BS, U.S. Merchant Marine Acad., Kings Point, N.Y., 1949; diploma, Westinghouse Mgmt. Program, U. Pitts., 1959. Registered profl. engr., Pa., 68, S.C., 86. Diesel engr. Am. Locomotive Co., Schenectady, NY, 1949—55; nuc. engr. Westinghouse Bettis Lab., Pitts., 1955—69, mgr., reactor engring., 1969—73, mgr., core mfg., 1977—82; spl. assignment to Adm. H.G. Rickover U.S. Navy, Naval Reactors Br., 1973—77; mgr., fuel mfg. Westinghouse Elec. Corp., Columbia, SC, 1982—86; cons. Columbia, SC, 1986—. Instr. Midlands Tech. Coll., Columbia, SC, 2002—. Author: (design manual) Shock and Vibration Design, 1966. Midshipman USNR, 1945—49, Atlantic. Mem.: Soc. Mfg. Engrs. (sr.). Achievements include patents in field. Home: 109 Miles Rd Columbia SC 29223

GRAUSAM, JEFFREY LEONARD, lawyer; b. Newark, Sept. 21, 1943; s. John G. and Angela G.; m. Anne Jenks Boynton, Dec. 20, 1969; children: Daniel Carpenter, Elizabeth Wiley. BA, Wesleyan U., 1965; JD, U. Chgo., 1968; LLM in Taxation, NYU, 1975. Bar: Calif. 1969, N.Y. 1970, U.S. Supreme Ct. 1981. Law clk. to chief justice Roger J. Traynor Supreme Ct., State of Calif., San Francisco, 1968-69; assoc. Debevoise, Plimpton, Lyons & Gates, N.Y.C., 1969-75; officer, mem. firm Tuttle & Taylor, Inc., L.A., 1975-89; ptnr. Morgan, Lewis & Bockius, LLP, L.A., 1989—. Editor-in-chief law rev. U. Chgo., 1967-68. Dir. Libr. Found. L.A., 1993-98, 99—. Mem. L.A. County Bar Assn. (exec. com. taxation sect. 1994-95), Order of Coif. Avocation: cycling. Office: Morgan Lewis & Bockius LLP 300 S Grand Ave Fl 22 Los Angeles CA 90071-3109

GRAUSMAN, PHILIP, sculptor; b. N.Y.C., July 16, 1935; 1 child, David. Student, Sch. Painting and Sculpture, Skowhegan, Maine, 1956-57; BA cum laude, Syracuse U., 1957; student, Art Students' League, 1959; MFA, Cranbrook Acad. Art, 1959. Critic of archtl. drawing Grad. Sch. Architecture, Yale U., New Haven, 1974—. Instr. design Cooper Union, 1965-67; instr. design and drawing Pratt Inst., 1965-69; artist-in-residence Dartmouth Coll., 1972; instr. sculpture and drawing Skowhegan Sch. Painting and Sculpture, 1973; vis. asst. prof. art Yale U., 1974-76. Solo exhbns. include Frederik Meijer Gardens and Sculpture Park, Grand Rapids, Mich., 2001, Ice Gallery, N.Y.C., 1998, Borgenicht Gallery, N.Y.C., 1966, 74, 79, Alpha Gallery, Boston, 1968, 75, Dartmouth Coll., Hanover, N.H., 1972, U. Conn., 1976, Pa. State U., 1977, Washington Art Assn., Washington Depot, Conn., 1978, 82, Robert Schoelkopf Gallery, N.Y.C., 1983, 87, Babcock Galleries, N.Y.C., 1993; exhibited in group shows at The Aldrich Mus., Whitney Mus. Am. Art, Am. Acad. in Rome, Nat. Acad. Design, Art OMI Internat. Arts Ctr., Ohio State U., Boston Coliseum, Wadsworth Atheneum, Chgo. Arts Club, Fine Arts Mus. San Diego, U. N.C., Paris/N.Y./Kent Gallery, Kent, Conn., numerous others; represented in collections at Vassar Coll., U. Mich., U. Mass., U. Conn., Newark Mus., Met. Mus. Art, Jewish Mus., N.Y.C., De Cordova Mus. Art, Lincoln, Mass., Cornell U., Bklyn. Mus., Rose Art Mus./Brandeis U., Balt. Mus. Art, Akron Art Mus., others. Recipient Gold medal of honor in sculpture Audubon Artists, 1956, Alfred G.B. Steel Meml. prize Pa. Acad. Fine Aarts, 1962, Solon H. Borglum

award Silvermine Guild, Conn., 1980, Albert Jacobson Meml. award Silvermine Guild, 1984, Alex Ettel award, Nat. Acad. of Design, 1998, others; Huntington Hartford fellow, 1957, Louis Comfort Tiffany Found. grantee, 1959, Nat. Inst. Arts and Letters grantee, 1961, Prix de Rome fellow, 1962-65. Fellow Am. Acad. in Rome; mem. NAD (Dessie Greer prize 1981, Gold medal in sculpture 1988, cert. of merit in sculpture 1993. Office: Yale U Sch of Architecture New Haven CT 06520

GRAVE DE PERALTA, ARMANDO RENE, venture capitalist; b. New Orleans, Nov. 8, 1914; s. Pedro Grave de Peralta and Gloria Adele Dow; m. Marcia Houston Grave de Peralta (div.); m. Rosalba Roca Grave de Peralta; children: Armando Jr., Frederic, William Adams, Rene, Marcello. Student, Columbia U., 1945—48. Exec. v.p. Thor Eckert and Co., N.Y.C., 1936—61; pres. Peralta Shipping Corp., N.Y.C., 1961—90. Author: The Space Between, 1998, Tu, 1998, Lay Down Your Song, 1998, We Were Such Fools, 2000, Of Passion and Remorse, 2001, Tears of Remembrance, 2001. Cpl. U.S. Army, 1942—44. Avocations: writing, coin and stamp collecting, swimming. Home: 9882 La Jolla Farms Rd La Jolla CA 92037 Office: Peralta Shipping Corp 9882 La Jolla Farms Rd La Jolla CA 92037

GRAVELLE, JANE GIBSON, economist; b. Sandersville, Ga., May 22, 1947; d. Allen J. and Doris O. (Peavy) Gibson; m. Clark G. Gravelle, Nov. 1, 1969 (dec. July 1985); 1 child, Jennifer Colleen. BA, U. Ga., 1968, MA, 1969; MPhil, George Washington U., 1980, PhD, 1981. Rsch. asst. Congl. rsch. svc. Libr. of Congress, Washington, 1969-71, economist, 1971-88, sr. specialist econ. policy, 1988—. Vis. economist Dept. of Labor, Washington, 1977, Treasury Dept., 1989-90, prof., Boston U., 1988; cons. NSF, 1984, Am. Assn. Ret. Persons, 1988. Contbr. numerous articles to profl. jours. Named Nat. Def. Edn. Act fellow U. Ga., 1968-69. Mem. Am. Econ. Assn., Nat. Tax Assn. (2d v.p., editl. bd. Jour. 1984—, 2d v.p. 2003), Phi Beta Kappa, Phi Kappi Phi. Methodist. Home: 8023 Garlot Dr Annandale VA 22003-1309 Office: Libr Congress Congl Rsch Svc 101 Independence Ave SE Washington DC 20540-7470 E-mail: jgravelle@crs.loc.gov.

GRAVER, JACK EDWARD, mathematics educator; b. Cin., Apr. 13, 1935; s. Harold John and Rose Lucille (Miller) G.; m. Yana Regina Hanus, June 3, 1961; children: Juliet Rose, Yana-Maria, Paul Christopher. BA in Math., Miami U., Oxford, Ohio, 1958; MA in Math., Ind. U., 1961, PhD in Math., 1964. Instr. Ind. U., Bloomington, 1964; John Wesley Young Rsch. instr. Dartmouth Coll., Hanover, N.H., 1964-66; asst. prof. math. Syracuse (N.Y.) U., 1966-69, assoc. prof., 1969-76; vis. prof. U. Nottingham (Eng.), 1971-72; prof. math. Syracuse U., 1976—, chmn. dept. math., 1979-82. Co-author: (books) (with M. Watkins) Combinatorics with Emphasis on Graph Theory, 1977, Locally Finite, Planar, Edge-Transitive Graphs, 1997, (with J. Baglivo) Incidence and Symmetry in Design and Architecture, 1982, (with B. and H. Servatius) Combinatorial Rigidity, 1993, Counting on Frameworks, 2001; contbr. articles to profl. jours. With USN, 1953-55. Fellow Inst. Combinatories and its Applications; mem. Soc. Indsl. and Applied Math., Nat. Coun. Tchrs. of Math., Assn. Math. Tchrs. N.Y. State, Math. Assn. Am. (bd. govs. 1985-88, Seaway sect. chair 1995-97), Am. Math. Soc. Home: 871 Livingston Ave Syracuse NY 13210-2935 Office: Syracuse Univ Dept Math Syracuse NY 13244-1150 E-mail: jegraver@syr.edu.

GRAVER, LAWRENCE STANLEY, English language professional; b. N.Y.C., Dec. 6, 1931; s. Louis and Rose (Pearlstein) G.; m. Suzanne Levy, Jan 28, 1960; children— Ruth, Elizabeth. BA, CCNY, 1954; MA, U. Calif., Berkeley, 1959, PhD, 1961. Asst. prof. English UCLA, 1961-64; asst. prof. English, Williams Coll., Williamstown, Mass., 1964-67; assoc. prof. English Williams Coll., 1967-72, prof. English, 1972—; William R. Kenan, Jr. prof. English, Williams Coll., 1977-81, John H. Roberts prof., 1981-97, Roberts prof. emeritus, 1997—. Author: Conrad's Short Fiction, 1969, Carson McCullers, 1969; editor: Mastering the Film, 1977, Samuel Beckett, 1979, (Landmarks of World Lit. series) Waiting for Godot, 1989, An Obsession With Anne Frank: Meyer Levin and the Diary, 1995; asst. editor: Columbia Companion to the Twentieth Century American Short Story, 2001. Served with U.S. Army, 1954-56. Nat. Endowment for Humanities fellow, 1980-81 Mem. MLA, AAUP. Democrat. Home: 117 Forest Rd Williamstown MA 01267-2028 Office: Williams Coll Dept English Williamstown MA 01267 E-mail: lgraver@williams.edu.

GRAVER, MARY KATHRYN, medical, surgical nurse; b. Rehrersburg, Pa., Nov. 8, 1934; d. Levi B. and Emma A. (Sensenig) Gibbel; m. C. W. Graver, June 27, 1959; children: Elizabeth Ann, Craig Warren, Timothy John, Kathryn Renate. RN, Coatesville (Pa.) Sch. Nursing, 1956; BA, Eastern Coll., St. Davids, Pa., 1994. Staff nurse pediatrics unit Phila. Gen. Hosp., 1956; staff nurse med./surg. unit Coatesville Hosp., 1957; staff nurse maternal and med./surg. units Ephrata (Pa.) Hosp., 1958-59; staff/clinic nurse Bryn Mawr (Pa.) Hosp., 1976-93, vol., 2001—.

GRAVES, BENJAMIN BARNES, business administration educator; b. Jones County, Miss., Nov. 5, 1920; s. Thomas Cannon and Velma (Barnes) G.; m. Hazeline Wood, May 25, 1946; children— Benjamin Barnes, Janis Elizabeth, Cynthia Wood. BA, U. Miss., 1942; MBA, Harvard, 1947; PhD, La. State U., 1961; LL.D., U. Ala., 1970. Staff and supervisory positions Exxon Co., 1947-60; spl. lectr. Coll. Bus. Adminstrn., La. State U., 1959-60, asst. prof., 1960-62; assoc. prof. U. Va., 1962-64; Milner prof. indsl. econs. U. Miss., 1964-65; pres. Millsaps Coll., Jackson, Miss., 1965-70; prof. bus. adminstrn. U. Ala. in Huntsville, 1970-90, pres., 1970-79, prof. emeritus, 1990—. Guest lectr. Mid-South Exec. Devel. Program, La. State U., 1962-68, also asso. dir. program, 1961-62; guest lectr. mgmt. program Natural Resources Mgrs., Pa. State U., 1962-72, Va.-Md. Sch. Banking, U. Va., 1962-73; vis. prof. bus. adminstrn. U. N.C. at Charlotte, 1976-77 Author articles in field. Pres. Miss. Found. Ind. Colls., 1967-68; mem. com. human investigation U. Miss. Sch. Medicine, 1964-70; v.p. Miss. Jr.-Sr. Coll. Conf., 1968-69; pres. Miss. Assn. Colls., 1969-70; mem. exec. com. Ind. Coll. Funds Am.; mem. adv. com. Am. Council on Edn.'s Inst. for Coll. and U. Adminstrs.; mem. Am. Assn. Schs. and Colls. univ. pres.'s del. to People's Republic of China, 1975, Republic of China, 1976; Pres. Huntsville Research Park Adv. Bd., 1973; Mem. exec. bd. Andrew Jackson council Boy Scouts Am., 1966— ; bd. dirs. Jackson Symphony Assn., 1965-70, mem. pres.'s coun. U. Ala., Huntsville. Served to lt. (s.g.) USNR, 1942-46. Recipient Humanitarian of Yr. award The Arthritis Found. of Ala., 1999, Mem. Acad. Mgmt., Am. Mktg. Assn., Southwestern Social Sci. Assn., So. Econ. Assn., A.I.M. (pres.'s council), Jackson C. of C., Pi Kappa Alpha (mem. centennial com. 100), Phi Kappa Phi, Omicron Delta Kappa, Rotary (Paul Harris fellow; Vocat. Excellence award 2001). Clubs: Rotarian (dir. Huntsville 1973). Methodist. Home: 354 Inverness Dr SW Huntsville AL 35802-4516

GRAVES, BRUCE, lawyer, director; b. Oct. 5, 1939; s. Forrest J and Lillian (Kurtz) Graves; m. Jeanne M. Rooney; children: Gwendolyn Sue, Daniel Curtis, Brian Patrick. BS, U. Omaha, 1961; JD cum laude, U. Nebr.-Lincoln, 1964. Bar: Iowa 1964, Nebr. 1964, U.S. dist. Ct. (so. dist.) Iowa 1964, U.S. Dist. Ct. Nebr. 1964, U.S. Ct. Claims 1964, U.S. Ct. Appeals (8th cir.) 1968, U.S. Ct. Appeals (fed. cir.) 1991, U.S. Tax Ct. 1968, U.S. Supreme Ct. 1972. Bd. dir., West Des Moines Devel. Corp. Contbr. articles to law revs., mags. Dir. West Des Moines Sch. Bd., 1967—76, Polk-Des Moines Taxpayers Assn., 1982—84. Named Citizen of Yr., West Des Moines, 1983. Mem.: Polk County Bar Assn., Nebr. Bar Assn., Iowa Bar Assn. (bd. govs. 1994—98, pres. 2000—01), ABA (subcom. on litigation, com. on ins. cos. 1982—), Des Moines Club (past pres., dir.), Des Moines C. of C., Sigma Phi Epsilon, Omicron Delta Kappa, Order of Coif. Republican. Office: 601 Locust St Suite 1100 Two Ruan Ctr Des Moines IA 50309

GRAVES, ERNEST, JR., retired army officer, engineer; b. N.Y.C., July 6, 1924; s. Ernest and Lucy (Birnie) G.; m. Nancy Herbert Barclay, May 12, 1951; children: Ralph Henry, Robert Barclay, William Hooper, Emily Birnie. BS, U.S. Mil. Acad., 1944; PhD, M.I.T., 1951; postgrad., Engr. Sch., Ft. Belvoir, Va., 1954-55, Command and Gen. Staff Coll., Ft. Leavenworth, Kans., 1957-58, Army War Coll., Carlisle Barracks, Pa., 1964-65, Harvard Bus. Sch., 1968. Commd. 2d lt. U.S. Army, 1944, advanced through grades to lt. gen., 1978, ret., 1981; with (SHAPE), Paris, 1951-54, (Army Package Power Reactor), Ft. Belvoir, 1955-57; comdr. (44th Engr. Constrn. Bn.), Korea, 1958-59; dir. (Army Nuclear Cratering Group, Lawrence Radiation Lab.), Livermore, Cal., 1962-64; exec. to sec. army Washington, 1967-68; comdr. (34th Engr. Group), Vietnam, 1968-69; div. engr. (U.S. Army Engr. Div., N. Central), Chgo., 1970-73; asst. gen. mgr. for mil. application U.S. AEC, Washington, 1973-75; dir. civil works Office Chief Engrs., Washington, 1975-77, dep. chief engr., 1977-78; dir. Def. Security Assistance Agy., Washington, 1978-81; sr. advisor Ctr. for Strategic and Internat. Studies, Washington, 1982-99. Contbr. articles to profl. jours. Decorated D.S.M., Legion of Merit, Bronze Star, Air medal. Mem. Soc. Am. Mil. Engrs. Home: 2328 S Nash St Arlington VA 22202-1548

GRAVES, GAIL MARVEL, language educator; b. Fargo, ND, Apr. 14, 1940; d. M.F. Marvell and Gladys Pearl (Swenson) Peterson; m. John Paul Graves, Jr., Nov. 12, 1966 (div. Dec. 1994); children: Kevin Erik, Kristen Erika, Karron Elizabeth, Kia Elisa, Kelly Erin. BA in French and Spanish, St. Olaf Coll., 1962; certificate in Linguistics, U. Besancon, France, 1964; MA in French, Northwestern U., 1966; MA in Tchg. ESL, Hunter Coll., 1996. Instr. French North Ctrl. Coll., Naperville, Ill., 1965—66; tchr. Evanston (Ill.) Twp. H.S., 1966—67; lang. immersion programmer CUNY, N.Y.C., 1996—98, Rassias method tchr. trainer, 1998—2003, prof. French, ESL, 1999—, reading specialist, 2000—; prof. ESL Kings Coll., N.Y.C., 2000—01. Bi-lingual exec. asst. UN, N.Y.C., NY, 1994—95, chair South Africa com., 1994—95. V.p. Young Am. Freedom, Rockford, Ill., 1968—69. Mem.: Tchrs. English to Spkrs. Other Langs., Am. Assn. Tchr. French. Republican. Presbyterian. Avocations: theater, travel, singing, swimming, reading. Home: 161 W 61st St # 10 F New York NY 10023 Office: Baruch Coll CUNY One Bernard Baruch Way New York NY 10010

GRAVES, H. BRICE, retired lawyer; b. Charlottesville, Va., Sept. 1, 1912; BS, U. Va., 1932, MS, 1933, PhD, LL.B., 1938. Bar: N.Y. 1940, Va. 1949. Assoc. Cravath, Swaine & Moore, N.Y.C., 1938-42, 45-48; ptnr. Hunton & Williams, Richmond, Va., from 1949. Planning com. U. Va. Ann. Tax Conf., 1971-82, trustee emeritus, 1989—; lectr. in field Contbr. articles to profl. jours. Mem. Richmond Bar Assn., Va. Bar Assn. (chmn. taxation com. 1971-73), ABA (chmn. com. exempt orgns. tax sect. 1963-65, com. mem. 1975-77), Am. Law Inst., Richmond Estate Planning Council, Am. Coll. Tax Counsel Home: 10,000 Cedarfield Ct Cottage 20 Richmond VA 23233 Office: Hunton & Williams PO Box 1535 Richmond VA 23218-1535

GRAVES, JAMES E. state supreme court justice, educator; BA in Sociology, Millsaps Coll.; JD, MPA, Syracuse U. Pvt. practice; head Human Svcs. Dept. atty. gen.'s office, chief legal counsel Miss. Dept. Human Svcs.; spl. asst. atty. gen. Ctrl. Miss. Legal Svcs., staff atty.; dir. divsn. child support enforcement Miss. Dept. Human Svcs.; cir. ct. judge 7th Cir. Dist., 1991—2001; justice Miss. Supreme Ct., 2001—. Instr. trial advocacy Harvard Law Sch., 1998, 99, 2000; adj. prof. media and civil rights law Jackson State U. Active pub. sch. activities; coach student mock trial teams. Named Parent of Yr., 2000—01; recipient Judge of Yr. award, Nat. Conf. Black Lawyers, 1992, Disting. Jurist award, Nat. Bar Assn., 1996, Innovation award, Hinds County Bar Assn., 2000. Office: PO Box 249 Jackson MS 39205*

GRAVES, JERRELL LOREN, demographic studies researcher; b. Humansville, Mo., Feb. 10; s. Loren Silas and Edith Lucille (Childress) G. AA, San Jose City Coll., 1986. Lic. gen. contractor, Calif. Farm laborer Guy McDaniel, Bolivar, Mo., 1952-54; laborer Standard Milk Co., Bolivar, 1952-55; constrn. worker Local Union # 676, Springfield, Mo., 1957-59; wood worker Bolivar Wood Products, 1959-61; rschr. life cycles and coop. living, coord. S.W. Dem. Studies, Half Way, Mo., 1961—. Instr. hatha yoga San Jose City Coll., 1973. Coord. Caring and Sharing, San Jose, 1977-81, San Jose Coop., Inc., 1985-87; vol. Getting out the Vote Friends of John Vasconselles, San Jose, 1980. Mem. ACLU, UN Assn. U.S.A., World Federalists Assn., Common Cause, Greenpeace, World Watch, World Future Soc., Self-Realization Fellowship, Internat. Platform Assn., Rosicrucian. Avocations: studying mysticism and metaphysics, swimming, yoga. Home and Office: SW Demographic Studies 4282 Hwy P Half Way MO 65663-9133

GRAVES, JO ANN, state legislator; b. Jan. 3, 1951; m. Bill Graves; children: Barrett, Daniel, Whitney. BS in Bus. Adminstrn., U. N.C., 1977. Mem. Tenn. Senate 100th Gen. Assembly, 1996—, speaker pro. tem. Mem. Gallatin City Coun.; active First United Meth. Ch., Meals on Wheels; trustee Ind. Sch.; curriculum chair Pub. and Pvt. Sch. Mem. Rotary Club, C. of C. Democrat. Office: 6 Legislative Plaza Nashville TN 37243-0218 E-mail: sen.joann.graves@legislature.state.tn.us.*

GRAVES, JOHN WILLIAM, historian; b. Little Rock, June 25, 1942; s. William A. and Mabel (Morehart) G. BA in History, U. Ark., 1964, MA, 1967; PhD in History, U. Va., 1978. Grad. tchg. asst. U. Ark., 1965-66; instr. history U.S.W. La., LaFayette, 1966-68; rsch. asst. U. Va., Charlottesville, 1971-72; instr. history S.W. Tex. State U., San Marcos, 1972-77; coll. assistance migrant program, freshman studies coord., basic skills specialist, lectr. St. Edward's U., Austin, Tex., 1979—85; assoc. prof. then prof. history Henderson State U., Arkadelphia, Ark., 1985—, chmn. dept. social scis., 2002—. Rep. Liberal Arts Faculty Senate, 1987-88 Author: Town and Country: Race Relations in an Urban-Rural Context, Arkansas, 1865-1905, 1990 (Arkansiana award Ark. Libr. Assn. 1991, Commendation award Am. Assn. for Study of State and Local History 1993); contbr. articles to profl. jours. Bd. dirs. Soc. for Preservation of Mosaic Templars of Am. Bldg., Hillcrest Residents Assn., Little Rock, Black History Adv. Com. State of Ark.; adv. bd. dept. Ark. heritage Mosaic Templars Am. Ctr.; rep. Coalition of LIttle Rock Neighborhoods. Recipient Disting. Svc. award Henderson State U., 1999-2000, Disting. Rsch. award Henderson State U., 2001-2002; Meml. fellow Ark. History Commn., 1965, Philip Francis DuPont fellow U. Va., 1969-71. Mem. AAUP (pres. chpt. 1999-2001), So. Hist. Assn., Ark. Hist. Assn. (v.p. 1987-92, pres. 1992-96), Ark. History Coun. (Ark. sec. of state), Audubon Soc. (pres. Bastrop County Tex. 1985), Defenders of Wildlife, Environ. Def. Fund, Ark. Nature Conservancy, Nat. Trust for Hist. Preservation, Hist. Preservation Alliance Ark., Quapaw Qtr. Assn., Student Sen. U. Ark. (grad. sch. rep. 1965-66), Tau Kappa Epsilon (pres. 1964), Phi Alpha Theta. Home: 5218 G St Little Rock AR 72205-3517 Office: Henderson State U Dept History Arkadelphia AR 71999-0001 Fax: (870) 230-5144. E-mail: johnwgrav@aol.com., gravesj@hsu.edu.

GRAVES, JOHN WILLIAM, state supreme court justice; b. Paducah, Ky., Oct. 17, 1935; m. Mary Ann Breivo; children: James Anthony, Kevin Andrew. BS, U. Notre Dame, 1957; postgrad., U. Louisville, 1957-58; JD, U. Ky., 1963. Bar: Ky. 1963. Dist. judge, 1984-88; circuit ct. judge McCracken Cir., 1989-95; justice Ky. Supreme Ct., 1995—. Col. U.S. Army Res. Decorated Army Commendation medal, Army Meritorious Svc. medal. Office: Kentuky Supreme Court 222 Kentuky Avenue, PO Box 993 Paducah KY 42003*

GRAVES, KAREN LEE, counselor; b. Twin Falls, Idaho, Dec. 9, 1948; d. Isaac Mason and Agnes Popplewell; m. Frederick Ray Graves, Apr. 2, 1987 (dec. Dec. 2001). BA, Idaho State U., 1971; MEd, Coll. of Idaho, 1978. Cert. tchr. secondary edn., english 7-12, vocat. home econs. 7-12, pupil pers. svcs. K-12, Idaho. Tchr. Filer (Idaho) Sch. Dist., 1971-74, 76-80, Twin Falls (Idaho) Sch. Dist., 1974-76; counselor Mountain Home (Idaho) Sch. Dist., 1980—, dept. chairperson, dir. Mem. NEA, ACA, ASCD, Am. Sch. Counseling Assn., Idaho Counseling Assn., Idaho Sch. Counseling Assn., Idaho Edn. Assn., Idaho Affiliation Supervision and Curriculum Devel., Mountain Home Edn. Assn. Avocations: painting ceramics, crafting, stamping, reading, crossword puzzles. Home: 1105 Maple Dr Mountain Home ID 83647-2027 Office: Mountain Home H S 300 S 11th E Mountain Home ID 83647-3235 E-mail: graves_kp@sd193.k12.id.us.

GRAVES, KATHRYN LOUISE, dermatologist; b. Kansas City, Kans., Mar. 9, 1949; d. Jack Clair and Ruth Marjory (Prentice) Schroll; m. Jeffery Jackson Graves, Mar. 31, 1973; children: Jeffery Justin, Jonathon Tyler, Kathryn Camille. BA, U. Kans., 1971; MD, U. Kans., Kansas City, 1974. Diplomate Am. Bd. Dermatology. Intern St. Lukes Hosp., Kansas City, 1975-76, resident in internal medicine, 1976; resident dermatology Sch. Medicine U. Kans., Kansas City, 1976-79; dermatologist Hutchinson (Kans.) Clinic P.A., 1979—; mem. med. staff Hutchinson Hosp., 1979—. Fellow Am. Acad. Dermatology; mem. AMA, Kans. Dermatology Soc., Kans. Med. Assn., Hutchinson C. of C., Gamma Phi Beta (standards chair 1973—). Republican. Methodist. Avocations: reading, walking, golf, jetskiing. Home: 130 Hyde Park Dr Hutchinson KS 67502-2840 Office: Hutchinson Clinic 2101 N Waldron St Hutchinson KS 67502-1197

GRAVES, KENNETH MARTIN, architect; b. Beaumont, Tex., July 6, 1943; s. Ernest Leroy and Margaret Louise (Hillyer) G.; m. Patricia Edwards, Aug. 26, 1965 (div. 1978); m. Anne Brown, Jan. 26, 1991; 1 stepchild, Elizabeth Crutchfield Okamura. BArch, Okla. State U., 1967. Lic. architect, Tex., Okla., Mo., Fla., Ga., Ala., Tenn. Architect, designer Ford, Powell & Carson, San Antonio, 1969-73; architect, ptnr. Tuggle & Graves, San Antonio, 1973-87; prin. Kenneth Martin Graves Architect, San Antonio, 1988-2000, Thorn & Graves, San Antonio, 2001—. Restoration architect: Alamo Plaza, 1976, Reuter Bldg., 1980, The Commerce Bldg., 1982, Staacke-Stevens, 1983-84, Charles Ct., 1983-85, Gunn Acura Dealership Bldg. (Metal Bldg. Design award 1990), Alfred Giles House (Conservation Soc. award 1992); residence design pub. in Architectural Digest, 1981; guest house design pub. in Tex. Homes, 1984; contbr. articles to mags. Bd. dirs. San Antonio Soc. Performing Arts, 1982-84, Friends of McNay, San Antonio, 1983-85, Gallery of McNay, San Antonio, 1984-91, San Antonio Art League, 1991-97; mem. adv. bd. Winston Sch., 1988-90; trustee S.W. Craft Ctr., 1987-90, pres. bd trustees San Antonio Art League, 1997-97; lay reader St. Luke's Episc. Ch. Vestry, 1989-91, jr. warden, 1989, sr. warden, 1990; trustee St. Luke's Episc. Sch., 1989-90; chmn. bishop's com. for bldg. Diocese of West Tex., 1990-91, 97—. Served to 1st lt. U.S. Army, 1967-69. Mem. AIA, Tex. Soc. Architects, Rotary. Republican. Avocations: oil painting, collecting primitive antiques, travel. Home: 120 Devine Rd San Antonio TX 78212-2522 Office: 215 Broadway St San Antonio TX 78205-1923 E-mail: kgraves@thorngravesaia.com.

GRAVES, LORRAINE ELIZABETH, dancer, educator, coach; b. Norfolk, Va., Oct. 5, 1957; d. Thomas Edward and Mildred Fayette (Odom) G. BS, Ind. U., 1978. Dancer, Regisseuse Dance Theatre of Harlem, N.Y.C., 1978—, ballet mistress, 1980—, prin. dancer, 1980, artistic asst., 1998—. Artistic advisor Va. Ballet Theatre, 1997—; tchr./coach Dance Theatre of Harlem, 1998-99, 2001, guest ballet mistress, 2001—; guest tchr. N.C. Sch. of Arts, Winston-Salem, 1987, 93, Gov.'s Sch. for Arts, U. Richmond, 1990—, Carlton Johnson Acad. of Dance, 1991-95, Okla. Summer Arts Inst., 1993-94, The Flint Sch. Performing Arts, Flint Youth Ballet, 2001--, Dance Theatre of Harlem, Kennedy Ctr. Residency Program, 1993-95, 98--, Worcester Sch. Performing Arts, 1997, Greenville Ballet, 2001; resident guest tchr. Gov.'s Sch. for Arts, Norfolk, Va., 1988-91, mem. faculty, 1996—; guest tchr. Worcester Sch. Performing Arts, 1997; resident guest tchr. S.C. Gov.'s Sch. for Arts, 1995-97; guest tchr. Va. Ballet Theatre, 1996—, artistic advisor, 1998—; guest tchr. Va. Sch. for the Arts, 1997—; educator, judge Dance Olympus, 1997—; judge Internat. Dance Challenge, 1998—; guest faculty Mid-States Regional Dance Festival, 1999; mem. faculty SERBA Festival, Roanoke, Va., 2003. Dancer Dance Theatre of Harlem as Princess of Unreal Beauty in live TV prodn. of Firebird, 1982, as Myrta, Queen of the Willis in NBC prodn. of Creole Giselle, 1987, performed at White House, 1981, also at the closing ceremonies of the 1984 Olympics, toured with Dance Theatre of Harlem, USSR, 1988, South Africa, 1992, guest artist Young People's Concert series, N.Y. Philharm., 1988, Detroit Symphony, 1989, River City Ballet, Memphis, 1991, 1992, N.W. Fla. Ballet, 1994, prin. dancer Va. Ballet Theatre, Norfolk, 1996—, Dance Theatre of Harlem, 1999, guest ballet mistress, 1999—, regisseuse Dance Theatre of Harlem, 1989—96. Fellow Am. Guild Mus. Artists. Episcopalian. Avocations: modeling, teaching younger dancers.

GRAVES, MAUREEN ANN, self esteem and spirituality consultant; b. Sioux City, Iowa, July 10, 1946; d. Jack Milford and Elizabeth Mildred (St. George) Dryden; m. Thomas Darrel Graves, Oct. 9, 1965; children: Michael James, Lorrie Michelle. Grad. 1-yr. program, Gestalt Inst. Iowa, 1980. Cert. profl. asst., U. S.D.; cert. hypnotherapist, The Wellness Inst., Seattle. Counselor Siouxland Coun. on Alcoholism and Drug Abuse, Sioux City, 1979-81; counselor, co-founder New Hope Alcohol and Addiction Ctr., South Sioux City, Nebr., 1981-98; Reiki practitioner, 1997—. Cons. St. Luke Hosp. Addiction Ctr., Sioux City, 1987—; trainer Va. Satir-Internat. Tng. Inst., Crested Butte, Colo., 1988-89. Vol. co-facilitator Siouxland Coun. on Alcoholism and Drug Abuse, Sioux City, 1976-79; exec. team couple World Wide Marriage Encounter, N.E. Nebr., 1979-82; trainer Va. Satir-Internat. Tng. Inst., Crested Butte, Colo., 1992; co-leader Satir Family Camp, 1992-03; active Avanta Faculty Governing Coun., 1994-03. Mem. Avanta Network, Moscow Inst. for Profl. Devel. of Psychologists and Social Workers (founding). Roman Catholic. Avocation: reiki master. Home and Office: 1814 N 155th Ave Omaha NE 68154-4123

GRAVES, MICHAEL, architect, educator; b. Indpls., July 9, 1934; s. Thomas Browning and Erma Sanderson (Lowe) Graves; children from previous marriage: Sarah Browning, Adam Daimhinstepchildren: Anne Gilbert, Liza Gilbert. BS in Architecture, U. Cin., 1958, DFA (hon.), 1982; MArch, Harvard U., 1959; postgrad. (Acad. fellow), Am. Acad. in Rome, 1960—62; PhD (hon.), U. Cin., 1982; LHD (hon.), Boston U., 1984; HHD (hon.), Savannah Coll. Art and Design, 1986; DFA (hon.), RISD, 1990, N.J. Inst. Tech., 1991; LHD (hon.), Rutgers U., 1994, U. Colo., 1995; PhD (hon.), Internat. Fine Arts Coll., 1996, Pratt Inst., 1996, Drexel U., 2000. Lectr. architecture Princeton (N.J.) U., 1962—67, assoc. prof., 1967—72, Schirmer prof. architecture, 1972—2001, emeritus, 2001—; pres. Michael Graves & Assocs., Princeton, 1964—. Arch. in residence Am. Acad. in Rome, 1979. Exhibited in group shows including Mus. Modern Art, N.Y.C., 1967, 68, 75, 78, 79, 80, 81, 84, Cooper-Hewitt Mus., 1976, 78, 79, 80, 82, 85, 87, Triennale, Milan, Italy, 1973, 85, Roma Interrotta, Rome, 1978, Venice Biennale, Italy, 1980, Met. Mus. Art, 1985, 86, 87, Emory U. Mus. Art and Archaeology, Atlanta, 1985, Denver (Colo.) Art Mus., 2002; one-man shows include U. So. Calif., 1981, No. Ill. U., 1982, Inst. for Architecture and Urban Studies, N.Y.C., 1982, Colby Coll., Maine, 1982, Moore Coll. Art, Phila., 1983, Fla. Internat. U., Miami, 1983, Pa. State U., University Park, 1984, Royal Inst. Brit. Archs., Heinz Gallery, London, 1984, Wadsworth Athenaeum, Hartford, Conn., 1984, Carleton Coll., Northfield, Minn., 1986, W.Va. U., 1986, Hamilton Coll., Clinton, NY, 1987, Archivolto Gallery, Milan, Italy, 1987, U. Va., Charlottesville, 1987, U. Md., College Park, 1988, Duke U. Mus. Art, Durham, NC, 1988, Butler Inst. Art, Youngstown, Ohio, 1989, 1989, Deutsches Architekturmuseum, Frankfurt, German Dem. Republic, 1989, Washington Design Ctr., 1989, Syracuse U. Sch. Architecture, 1990, Kunstemes Hus, Oslo, 1990, Mikimoto Hall, Tokyo, 1992, Pitts. Cultural Trust, 1993, Richard Stockton Coll., 1993, Clark County Libr., 1994, Thessaloniki Design Mus., Greece, 1996, The Min. Bldg., Seoul, Korea, 1996, Princeton Arts Coun., 1996, 99, U. Conn. Aronoff Ctr. Design and Art, 1996, NJ Sch. Arch., NJ Inst. Tech., 2000; prin. works include Hanselmann House, 1967 (AIA Nat. Honor award, 1975), Newark (NJ) Mus., 1968, Rockefeller House, 1969 (Progressive Architecture Design award, 1970), Gunwyn Ventures Office, 1971 (AIA Nat. Honor award, 1979), Snyderman House, 1972, Crooks House, 1976 (Progressive Architecture Design award, 1977), Schulman House, 1976, (AIA Nat. Honor award, 1982), Fargo-Moorhead Cultural Ctr., 1977-79 (Progressive Architecture Design award, 1978), Plocek House, 1978 (Progressive Architecture Design award, 1979), pvt. residence in Green Brook, NJ, 1978 (Progressive Architecture Design award, 1980), Sunar showrooms N.Y.C., 1979, 81 (Interiors award, 1981), Chgo., 1979, Houston, 1980, LA, 1980, London, 1985, Loveladies Beach House, 1979 (Progressive Architecture Design award, 1979) Environ. Edn. Ctr., 1980 (Progressive Architecture award, 1983), Portland (Oreg.) Bldg., 1980 (AIA Nat. Honor award, 1983), San Juan Capistrano Pub. Libr., Calif., 1980 (AIA Nat. Honor award, 1985), Newark Mus. Master Plan and Renovation, 1982 (AIA Nat. Honor award, 1992), Human Bldg., Louisville, 1982 (Interiors award, 1985, AIA NAt. Honor award, 1987), Emory U. Mus. Art and Archaeology, 1982 (Interiors award 1985, AIA Nat. Honor award, 1987), Riverbend Music Ctr., 1983, Whitney Mus. Am. art, N.Y.C., 1984, Diane Von Furstenburg Boutique, 1984, Clos Pegase Winery, Calif., 1984 (AIA Nat. Honor award, 1990), Sotheby's Tower, N.Y.C., 1985, Warehouse Renovation (Graves House), 1985 (Progressive Architecture Design award, 1978), Aventine Devel., La Jolla, Calif., 1985, Shiseido Health Club, Tokyo, 1985, Disney Co. Corp. Office Bldg., Burbank, Calif., 1985, Crown Am. Hdqs., Johnston, Pa., 1985, Walt Disney World Dolphin and Walt Disney World Swan hotels, Fla., 1986 (Progressive Architecture award, 1989), Youngston (Ohio) Hist. Ctr. Industry and Labor, 1986 (Progressive Architecture Design award, 1987), 10 Peachtree Pl., Atlanta, 1987, Henry House, Rhinebeck, NY, 1987 (Progressive ARchitecture award, 1989), U. Va. Arts. and Scis. Bldg., Charlottesville, 1987, Portside Dist. Condominium Tower, Yokohama, Japan, 1987, Momochi Dist. Apt. Bldg., Fukuoka, Japan, 1987, Metropolis Master Plan

LA, 1988, stores and galleries for Lenox, Tysons Corner, Va., 1988, Palm Beach, 1988, N.Y.C., 1988, Mpls., 1988, Costa Mesa, 1989, Frankfurt, 1989, Phila., 1989, Nashville, 1989, Midousuji Minami Office Bldg., Osaka, 1988, Tajima Office Bldg., Tokyo, 1988, Hotel NY, 1988, Euro Disneyland, France, 1988, Inst. for Theoretical Physics, U. Calif., Santa Barbara, 1989, Detroit Inst. of Arts Master Plan, 1989, Indpls. Art Ctr., 1989, Emory U. Mus. Art and Archaeology Addition, 1989, Fukuoka Internat. Office Project, 1990, Kasumi Group Rsch. and Tng. Ctr., Tsukaba City, Japan, 1990, Clark County Libr., Las Vegas, 1990, U. Cin. Sci. and Engring. Rsch. Ctr., 1990, Richard Stockton Coll. Arts and Scis. Bldg., Pomoma, NJ, 1991, Denver Ctrl. Libr., 1991 (AIA-NJ Design award, 1992, 95, AIA Nat. Honor award for Interior Architecture, 1998, AIA and Am. Libr. Assn. Excellence award, 2001), Astrid Park Plz. Hotel and Bus. Ctr., Antwerp, Belgium, 1992, Thomson Consumer Electronics Hdqs., Indpls., 1992 (AIA-NJ Design award, 1994), Rome Reborn Vatican Exhibit, Libr. Congress, 1992 (Casebook award Print Mag., 1993), Pitts. Cultural Trust Theater and Office Bldg., 1992, Taiwan Mus. Pre-History, Taipei, 1993 (AIA-NJ Design award, 1994), Archdiocesan Ctr., Newark, 1993, Internat. Fin. Corp. Hdqs., Washington, 1993 (AIA-NJ Design award, 1997), 1500 Ocean Dr. Condominiums, Miami, 1994, Del. River Port Authority Hdqs., Camden, NJ, 1994 (AIA-NJ Design award, 1998), St. Martin's Coll. Libr., Lacey, Wash., 1994, Topeka (Kans.) and Shawnee County Pub. Libr., 1995, Miramar Hotel, Egypt, 1995 (AIA-NJ Design award, 1996), NJ Inst. Tech. Residence Hall, 1995, Jiang-to Blvd. Master Plan, Xiamen, China, 1995, Alexandria (Va.) Ctrl. Libr., 1996, U.S. Courthouse Annex, Washington, 1996, Life Mag. Dream House, 1996, Lake Hills country Club, Seoul, Korea, 1996, World Trade Exch., Manila, 1996, new residence Hall, Drexel U., Phila., 1997, Miele Appliances Americas Hdqs. Bldg., Princeton, 1997 (AIA-NJ Design award, 2002), NovaCare Sports Training Facility, 1997 (AIA-NJ Design award, 2002), El Gourna Golf Villas, Egypt, 1997 (AIA-NJ Design award, 2002), French Inst. Libr, N.Y.C., 1997, Hyatt Regency Taba Heights Hotel, Egypt, 1997, St. Mary's Ch., Rockledge, Fla., 1998, Rice U. Master Plan, Houston, 1998, The Impala Bldg., N.Y.C., 1998, Wash. Monument Restoration Scaffolding, 1998 (AIA-NJ Design award, 1998), Rolex Watch Technicum training and Svc. Ctr., Lancaster county, Pa., 1999, Theater Square: Pitts. Cultural Trust Svc. Ctr., 1999, Mus. Shenandoah Valley, Winchester, Va., 1999, 425 Fifth Ave. Tower, N.Y.C., 2000, Mahler IV Mixed-Use Bldg., Amsterdam, 2000, Fed. Res. Bank Dallas: Houston Br., 2000, Famillr-Tsukishima Bldg., Tokyo, 2000, U.S. Embassy, Seoul, 2000, Dept. Transp. Hdqs., Washington, 2001, Detroit Inst. Arts, 2001, St. Coletta's Sch., Washington, 2002, NJ City U. Arts and Scis. Bldg., 2002, Nat. Automobile Mus., The Netherlands, 2003, U.S. Courthouse, Nashville, 2003; designer furniture, artifacts, textiles, and consumer products, V'Soske, 1979-80, Sunar, 1980-83, Alessi, 1981—Baldinger Archtl. Lighting, 1983—, Swid Powell, 1985—, Steuben, 1986—, Munari, 1986—Tajima, 1987-88, WMF, 1987—, Atelier Internat., 1987—Vorwerk, 1987—, Lenox Inc., 1988—, Markuse Corp., 1989—, Dunbar Furniture, 1989—, Arkitektura, 1989—, Moeller Internat. Design, 1992—, Target Stores, 1997—, Glen Eden Wool Carpet, 2002—, Delta Faucets, 2003—; monographs include: Five Architects, 1972, Michael Graves, Academy Editions, 1979, Michael Graves: Buildings and Projects 1966-1981, 1981, Michael Graves: Buildings and Projects 1982-1989, 1990, Michael Graves: Buildings and Projects 1990-1994, 1995, The Master Architect Series III: Michael Graves: Selected and Current Works, 1999, Michael Graves:Buildings and Projects 1995-2002, 2003. Named Designer Yr., Interiors, 1981; recipient Arnold W. Brunner Meml. prize in Architect., 1981, 61 awards, N.J. Soc. Architects, Euster award, 1984, Ind. Arts award, 1984, Henry Hering Meml. medal, Am. Sculpture Soc., 1986, profile Best Architects and Designers Working Today, Architectural Digest, 1990, 1995, 2000, Nat. Medal Arts, Nat. Endowment Arts, 1999, Frank Annuzio award, 2001, AIA Gold medal, Sigma Tau Delta, 2003. Fellow: AIA (Gold medal, 2001); mem.: N.Y. Sch. Interior Design (bd. trustees), Mus. Arts and Design (bd. trustees), Am. Acad. in Rome (bd. trustees, Rome prize 1960—62), Am. Acad. Arts and Letters. Office: Michael Graves & Assoc 341 Nassau St Princeton NJ 08540 also: Michael Graves & Assocs 560 Broadway Ste 401 New York NY 10012 Office Fax: 609-924-1795. E-mail: info@michaelgraves.com.

GRAVES, MICHAEL KENNETH, nurse anesthetist; b. Fresno, Calif., Jan. 11, 1959; s. Robert Eugene and Bettyelou (Seagraves) Graves; m. Malgorzata Andrzejewska, Nov. 15, 1996; children: Jovahnna Kathleen, Marek Aleksander. AS in Respiratory Care, Fresno City Coll., 1981; BSN, Calif. State U., Bakersfield, 1988; MSN, Calif. State U., Long Beach, 1991; cert. RN anesthetist, Kaiser Permanente Med. Ctr., L.A., 1991. RN, Calif., N.C.; cert. ACLS instr.; registered respiratory therapist. Respiratory therapist St. Agnes Med. Ctr., Fresno, 1980-84; asst. dir. respiratory care Kern Med. Ctr., Bakersfield, 1984-86; critical care nurse San Joaquin Community Hosp., Bakersfield, 1986-89; resident in anesthesia Kaiser Permanente Med. Ctr., L.A., 1989-91, staff anesthetist Panorama City, Calif., 1991—, lectr. L.A., 1989—. Guest lectr. NC Assn. Nurse Anesthetists, 2000—02, dist. IV ednl. coord., 2001; pres. Graves Anesthesia Svcs. Inc., 2002—. Contbr. articles to nursing jours. Mem. Eagle Scout bd. rev. Verdugo Hills Coun., 1991—, Webelo den leader, 1991; mem. med. staff Nat. Boy Scout Jamboree, Ft. A.P. Hill, Va., 1985, 89, 93; mem. med. staff World Boy Scout Jamboree, Holland, 1995. Served to lt. USNR, 1990—. Recipient Vigil Honor-Order of Arrow, Boy Scouts Am., 1978. Mem. Am. Assn. Nurse Anesthetists, Calif. Assn. Nurse Anesthetists, Assn. Mil. Surgeons U.S., Anesthesia Patient Safety Found., Polish Scout Assn., Nat. Eagle Scout Assn., Sigma Theta Tau, Alpha Phi Omega. Republican. Avocations: backpacking, wildlife photography, scouting activities.

GRAVES, PATRICK LEE, lawyer; b. Pasadena, Calif., Sept. 16, 1945; s. James Edward and Virginia (Dudley) G.; children: Carrie Kathleen, Michael Patrick. AS, Citrus Jr. Coll., Glendora, Calif., 1969; BS, Calif. State Polytechnic U., 1973; BS in Law, Western State U., 1973, JD, 1975. Bar: Calif. 1975, U.S. Dist. Ct. (cen. dist.) Calif. 1976, U.S. Ct. Appeals (9th cir.) 1978, U.S. Supreme Ct. 1980. Assoc. Lynberg & Watkins, Los Angeles, 1975-80, ptnr., 1981-93, Graves & King, Irvine, Calif., 1993—. Settlement officer Los Angeles Superior Ct., 1988—, arbitrator, 1981—; arbitrator San Bernardino Superior Ct., 1990—; mediator L.A. Superior Ct., 1993—, Riverside Superior Ct., 1996—, AAA-Inland Empire, 1996—. Judge pro tem L.A. Superior Ct., 1992—. Sustaining mem. Rep. Nat. Com., Washington, 1979—; mem. Nat. Rep. Congl. Com., 1980—. Mem. ABA, San Bernardino County Bar Assn., Assn. So. Calif. Def. Counsel (chmn. 1988, bd. dirs. 1996—), Def. Rsch. Inst., Upland (Calif.) C. of C. Avocations: flyfishing, golf. Home: 32302 Alipaz St 246 San Juan Capistrano CA 92672 Office: Graves & King 30448 Rancho Viejo Rd Ste 200 San Juan Capistrano CA 92675

GRAVES, PAUL MATTHEW, secondary school educator, choir director; b. Oklahoma City, Oct. 19, 1971; s. Paul S. Graves and Mary Ann Huneke, Steve Huneke (Stepfather) and Vicki Graves(Stepmother); m. Denice W. Murphy, Feb. 8, 1997; 1 child, McKenzie. MusB Edn., Southwestern Okla. State U., 1995. Music asst. Sequoyah Mid. Sch., Edmond, Okla., 1995—96; music tchr., choir Independence Mid. Sch., Yukon, Okla., 1996—97, Yukon (Okla.) Pub. Schools, 1996—97; pianist First Bapt. Ch., Edmond, Okla., 1997—; music tchr., choir Edmond (Okla.) Meml. H.S., 1997—. Mem.: Okla. Music Educators Assn., Music Educators Nat. Conf., Okla. Choral Dirs. Assn., Am. Choral Dirs. Assn., Ctrl. Okla. Choral Dirs. Assn. (pres. 1997—2000). Baptist. Avocations: NASCAR racing, jet skiing, spending time with family. Home: 14000 Jeffrey Dr Edmond OK 73013 Office: Edmond Meml High Sch 1000 E 15 Edmond OK 73013 Office Fax: 405-340-2856. E-mail: paul_graves@edmond.k12.ok.us.

GRAVES, RAY REYNOLDS, retired judge; b. Tuscumbia, Ala., Jan. 10, 1946; s. Isaac and Olga Ernestine (Wilder) Graves; children: Claire Elise, Reynolds Douglass. BA, Trinity Coll., Hartford, Conn., 1967; JD, Wayne State U., 1970. Bar: Mich. 1971, U.S. Dist. Ct. (ea. dist.) Mich. 1971, U.S. Ct. Appeals (6th cir.) 1972, U.S. Supreme Ct. 1976, D.C. 1977. Defender Legal Aid and Defender Assn., Detroit, 1970-71; assoc. Liberson, Fink, Feiler, Crystal & Burdick, 1971-72, Patmon, Young & Kirk, 1972-73; ptnr. Lewis, White, Clay & Graves, 1974-81; mem. legal dept. Detroit Edison Co., 1981; judge U.S. Bankruptcy Ct., Ea. Dist. Mich., Detroit, 1982-2002; chief judge U.S. Bankruptcy Ct., 1991-95; prin. BBK, Ltd., Southfield, Mich., 2002—. Mem. U.S. ct. com. State Bar Mich. Trustee Mich. Opera Theatre, 1986—88; vestry Christ Ch. Episcopal, Grosse Pointe, Mich., 1994—97; del Diocesan Conv. Episcopal Ch., Mich., 1997; bd. dirs. Mich. Cancer Found. Fellow: Am. Coll. Bankruptcy; mem.: D.C. Bar Assn., Detroit Bar Assn., Wolverine Bar Assn., Assn. Black Judges Mich., World Peace Through Law Conf., World Assn. Judges, Nat. Conf. Bakruptcy Jduges (bd. govs. 1984—88), Iota Boulè (Sire Archon 1999—2001), Sigma Pi Phi, Delta Kappa Epsilon. Episcopalian. Office: BBK Ltd 300 Galleria Officentre # 103 Southfield MI 48034 Office Fax: 248-603-8374. Business E-Mail: rgraves@e-bbk.com.

GRAVES, ROBERT JOHN, industrial engineering educator; b. Buffalo, Sept. 25, 1945; s. Paul Frederick and Ann (Mayer) G.; m. Virginia Jane Burry, June 8, 1968; children: Peter F., Anna K., Christopher J. BS Indsl. Engring., Syracuse U., 1967; MS Indsl. Engring., SUNY, Buffalo, 1969, PhD, 1974. Instr. indsl. engring. SUNY, Buffalo, 1973-74; asst. prof. sch. indsl. and sys. engring. Ga. Tech., Atlanta, 1974-79; assoc. prof. indsl. engring. U. Mass., Amherst, 1979-80, prof. indsl. engring., 1988-91, Rensselaer Poly. Inst., Troy, NY, 1991—2003; Krehbiel chaired prof. engring. Thayer Sch. Engring. Dartmouth Coll., 2003—; program dir. Agile Mfg. Rsch. Inst., 1994—. Pres. Coll. Industry Coun. on Material Handling Edn., Charlotte, N.C., 1990-92. Editor: Material Handling of the 90's, 1991, Progress in Material Handling Research, 1992; U.S. editor Internat. Jour. Prodn. Planning and Control, 1992-99; contbr. articles to profl. jours. Mem. sch. com. Town of Pelham, Mass., 1985-86, mem. planning bd., 1987-95. Recipient David Baker Outstanding Rsch. award IIE, 1997; grantee Mass. Ctrs. Excellence Corp., 1987-90, NSF, 1989-91, NSF/ATT 1994-99, MHI's Reed Apple award, 2002. Fellow Soc. Mfg. Engrs., Inst. Indsl. Engrs. (sr., faculty divsn. rsch. chair 1980-81, program chair 1981-82, editor newsletter 1990-91, dir. divsn. 1991-92, Spl. Citation award 1985) Achievements include research in flexible assembly systems scheduling, printed circuit board assembly, electronics agile manufacturing. Office: Dartmouth Coll Thayer Sch Engring 8000 Cummings Hall Hanover NH 03755-8000 E-mail: graver@rpi.edu.

GRAVES, RUTH PARKER, educational executive, educator; b. Port Arthur, Tex., Oct. 19, 1934; d. Thomas B. and Eunice Parker; m. Glenn R. Graves, Aug. 8, 1956; 1 child, Christopher. BA, Baylor U., 1956; MA, U. Tex., 1961; postgrad., George Washington U., 1963-64. Migrant labor advisor Tex. State AFL-CIO, Austin, 1959-61; pub. info. officer Pres.'s Com. on EEO, Washington, 1961-63; tchg. fellow George Washington U., Washington, 1963-64; labor desk coord. Dem. Nat. Conv., Washington, 1965-67; program analyst U.S. OEO, Washington, 1965-67, dir. migrant divsn., 1967-72; pres. emerita Reading is Fundamental, Inc., Washington, 1998. Nat. adv. coun. Ctr. for the Book, Libr. of Congress, 1977-97; adv. bd. Kidwave Radio Network, Phila., 1990-97; bd. advisors Ednl. Pub. Group, 1994-97; faculty Salzburg Seminar, 1998—; lectr. in field. Mem. editl. bd. Child Mag., N.Y.C., 1989-97; adv. coun. Ednl. Pub. Group, 1994-97; editor: The RIF Guide to Encouraging Young Readers, 1987; contbr. articles to profl. jours. Recipient William A. Jump award, U.S. Govt., 1971, Jeremiah Ludington Literacy Leadership award Ednl. Paperback Assn., 1982, Manhattan Literacy Coun. award, 1986, Internat. Reading Assn. Literacy award, 1987, As They Grow award Parents Mag., 1991; named Bookwoman of the Yr. Woman's Nat. Book Assn., 1987. Avocations: reading, theater, design and production of craft items.

GRAVES, SAMUEL B. congressman, former state legislator; b. Fairfax, MO, Nov. 7, 1963; BS, Univ. Missouri-Columbia. State rep. Dist. 4 Mo. Gen. State Assembly, 1993-94, state senator Dist. 12, 1995-2001; mem. U.S. Congress from 6th Mo. dist., 2001—. Mem.: Transp. & Infrastructure Com., Small Bus. Com., Agriculture Com., U.S. Congress from 6th Mo. dist. Office: US Ho Reps 1513 Longworth Ho Office Bldg Washington DC 20515-2506 also: Dist Office 113 Blue Jay Dr Ste 200 Liberty MO 64068*

GRAVES, SID FOSTER, JR., retired library and museum director; b. Memphis, May 11, 1946; s. Sidney Foster and Sarah Susan (Peterson) G.; m. Laura Charjean Laughlin; 1 child from previous marriage, Martha Abigail. BA, Millsaps Coll., Jackson, Miss., 1968; MA, U. Miss., Oxford, 1971; MLS, Peabody Coll., 1973. Archtl. reporter Dodge div. McGraw Hill, Jackson, 1968-69; instr. English U. Miss., 1968-72; dir. South Miss. Regional Libr., Columbia, 1973-76; exec. dir. Carnegie Pub. Libr./Delta Blues Mus., Clarksdale, Miss., 1976-95; ret., 1995. Guest lectr. U. Ala. Grad. Sch. Libr. Scis., Tuscaloosa, 1979; mem. Miss. Humanities Coun., 1988—, project dir., 1983, Miss. Libr. Com., Jackson, 1983 Chmn. Tennessee Williams Festival Com., 1992, 93. Recipient Keeping the Blues Alive in Edn. award Blues Found. Memphis, 1987, Keeping the Blues Alive in Hist. Preservation, 1989, Early Wright award Sunflower River Blues Assn., 1993, Gov.'s Arts award for Career in the Arts, 1996. Mem. ALA (Notable Books Coun. 1990-94), Miss. Mus. Assn. (pres. 1985), Miss. Libr. Assn. (pres. 1989, Outstanding Achievement award 1980, Past Pres.'s award 1976), Governor's award for lifetime career in the arts, 1996. E-mail: sidfgraves@webtv.net.

GRAVES, THOMAS BROWNING, investment banker; b. Indpls., Feb. 1, 1932; s. Thomas Browning and Erma Sanderson (Lowe) G.; m. Betty Lee MacLeod, June 12, 1954; children: Russell Evan, Bruce Ryan, Jill Graves, Jeffrey Hall. BS, Ind. U., 1954; M in Pub. Adminstrn., Harvard U., 1975. Asst. v.p. Penn Cen. Corp., Phila., 1968-72, Union Pacific R.R., Omaha, 1972-77; v.p. fin. and adminstrn. Union Pacific Corp., Omaha, 1977-84; exec. dir. Merrill Lynch, N.Y.C., 1984-85; pres. Pvt. Capital Ptnrs., Inc., N.Y.C., 1985—; CEO Consumer Credit & Debt Counseling, Vineland, N.J., 1995-98. Trustee-in-bankruptcy U.S. Dept. of Justice, Newark,, 1991—, cons. Credit Budget Counseling, Marmora, N.J., 1998—. Maj. U.S. Army, 1955-57, 61-62. Mem. Greate Bay Golf Club (Somers Point, N.J.), Somers Point Yachting & Sportman Assn., Somers Point, NJ. Home: 120 E Wilmont Ave Somers Point NJ 08244-2736 Office: Consumer Credit & Budget Counseling 299 S Shore Rd Marmora NJ 08223-1210

GRAVES, THOMAS VINCENT, sculptor; b. Marblehead, Mass., Jan. 22, 1954; s. Robert G. and Nancy (Simpson) G.; children: Suddha, Varsha, Sara, Dina, Vincent. Commd. to sculpt a bust of Pope John Paul II for Vatican Art Collection, Rome, 1987, drawing to commemorate the Columbus Quincentennial, Kent, Washington, 35-foot monumental outdoor sculpture/Palace of Gold, Limestone, W.Va., 1991, six-foot outdoor sculpture, Valley Brook Meml. Garden, Moundsville, W.Va., 1989, Sitting Jesus/life-size statue, New Vrindaban Community, Moundsville, 1988, others; pub. collections of work include Vatican Art Collection, Vatican City, 1992, City of Kent Art Collection, 1992; exhbns. include: Radha Murlidar Temple, N.Y.C., 2002, The Sanctuary, N.Y.C., 1998-2002, Lynn Arts Coun., Mass., 1997, Mass. Coll. of Art, Boston, 1996, The State House, Boston, 1995, The Copley Soc. of Boston, 1994, Marblehead Arts Assn. Arts in Bloom, Mass., 1994, Marblehead Festival of the Arts, 1994, Grand Mondnock Arts Coun., Keene, N.H., 1994, numerous others. Home: 25 1st Ave Apt 2W New York NY 10003-9459 E-mail: somaart@juno.com.

GRAVES, WALLACE BILLINGSLEY, retired university executive; b. Ft-.Worth, Feb. 10, 1922; s. Ellery George and Edith (Billingsley) G.; m. Barbara Jeanne Abey, Nov. 20, 1943; children: David W., Emily Graves Mc Donald, John R., Julie Graves Williams. BA, U. Okla., 1943; MA, Tex. Christian U., 1947; PhD, U. Tex., 1953; LLD (hon.), Ind. State U., 1970, Valparaiso U., 1972; LHD (hon.), Morningside Coll., 1971, U. Evansville, 1989. Teaching fellow Tex. Christian U., Ft. Worth, 1946-47, U. Tex., Austin, 1947-50; prof. polit. sci. DePauw U., Greencastle, Ind., 1950-58; Armstrong prof. govt., dean of men Tex. Wesleyan Coll., Ft. Worth, 1958-63, asst. to pres., 1963-65; acad. v.p. U. Pacific, Stockton, Calif., 1965-67; pres. U. Evansville, Ind., 1967-87, chancellor, 1986-89, pres. emeritus, 1989—. Vis. prof. Butler U., summer 1956; bd. dirs. Citizens Nat. Bank, Evansville, Herrburger Brooks P.L.C., Nottingham, Eng. Author: The United Nations, Great Britain and the British Non-Self Governing Territories, 1954, The One Semester Course in International Relations, 1956, Harlaxton College: The Camelot of Academe, 1990; contbr. articles to profl. jours. Mem. exec. bd. Tarrant County chpt. ARC, 1960-65, chmn. home svc. com.; chmn. ARC of Southwestern Ind., 1994—; midwest region com. ARC, 2000-02; bd. dirs. Ft. Worth Assn. Retarded Children, 1963-65; mem. Met. Ft. Worth Devel. Coordinating Com., World Affairs Coun., Chgo. and Stockton, adv. bd. Supplementary Edn. Ctr., Stockton; v.p. Buffalo Trace coun. Boy Scouts Am., Evansville, 1968, exec. bd., 1968-74, adv. coun, 1974—; bd. dirs. Jr. Achievement Inc., Evansville, 1968-73; mem. commn. ecumenical affairs United Meth. Ch., Evansville, 1968-72, univ. senate, 1972-76, Ind. area study commn., 1972-74; bd. dirs. Evansville Day Sch., 1967-76; mem. Ind. State Scholarship Commn., 1969-77, adv. bd. St. Mary's Med. Ctr., Evansville, 1970—, Evansville's Future Inc., 1967—, pres., 1974-77; bd. dirs. Ind. Health Careers Inc., 1974-75; mem. Govs. Adv. Com. Pub. Health, 1971-72; bd. dirs. Leadership Evansville, 1975-71, Evansville Mus., 1978—, Lincolnland Hist. Trust, 1978—; pres. Beethoven Found., Indpls., 1980-88; mem. organizing com. Pan Am. Games, 1987; bd. dirs. Sta. WNIN Pub. TV, Evansville, 1973—, chmn. bd., 1982-84. With U.S. Army, 1943. Recipient Best Tchr. award DePauw U., 1954, medal of honor U. Evansville, 1977, medal of merit Govt. Thailand, 1984, medal of honofr DAR, 1999; Wallace B. Graves Day named in his honor Office Mayor City Evansville, 1977; rsch. scholar U. Tex., 1947; Ford Found. fellow, summer 1951, 55; Paul Harris (Rotary) fellow, 1995. Mem. AAUP, Am. Assn. Acad. Deans, Am. Coll. Pub. Relations Assn., Am. Polit. Sci. Assn., Ind. Colls. and Univs. Ind. Inc. (pres. 1970-71, 76-77), North Cen. Assn. Colls. and Secondary Schs. (cons., investigator), Am. Assn. Pres. Ind. Colls. and Univs. (exec. com. 1969-70), Am. Assn. Colls. (various coms.), Associated Colls. Ind. (pres. 1972-74), Carl Duisberg Soc. (pres. Am. assn. 1973-74), Internat. Assn. Univ. Pres. (bd. dirs. N.Am. council 1975-87), Ind. Consortium Computer and High Tech. Edn., Ft. Worth C. of C. (chmn. econ. edn. com. 1963-64), Gold Key, Blue Key, Phi Kappa Phi, Phi Mu Alpha, Alpha Sigma Lambda, Pi Sigma Alpha, Sigma Nu. Clubs: Knife and Fork (pres. 1964-65) (Ft. Worth); Commonwealth (San Francisco); Columbia (Indpls.); Petroleum; Evansville Country, Kennel (Evansville). Lodges: Rotary (pres. Ft. club 1964-65).

GRAVES, WILLIAM PRESTON, governor; b. Salina, Kans., Jan. 9, 1953; s. William Henry and Helen (Mayo) G.; m. Linda Richey, Apr. 1990; 1 child, Katie. BBA, Kans. Wesleyan U., Salina, 1975; postgrad., U. Kans., 1978-79. Dep. asst. sec. of state State of Kans., Topeka, 1980-85, asst. sec. of state, 1985-87, sec. of state, 1987-95, gov., 1995—2003. Former mem. Competitiveness Policy Coun. Mem. Kans. Cavalry; trustee Kans. Wesleyan U., 1987—; bd. trustes Sunflower State Games, Harry S. Truman Scholarship Found., 2003—. Named Outstanding Young Alumnus, Kans. Wesleyan U., Salina, 1975, Outstanding Young Kansan, Salina Jaycees, 1986, Kans. Jaycees, 1986, Outstanding Kans. Citizen, Jayhawk area BSA, 2002; named to Athletic Hall of Fame, Kans. Wesleyan U., Salina, 1986. Mem. Kans. C. of C. and Industry. Republican. Methodist. Avocations: running, reading, traveling.*

GRAVES-ROMAN, PATRICIA ANN, educator, researcher, writer; b. Jan. 8, 1959; d. Frank X. Graves and Grace Elizabeth Flowers; m. Roman, Aug. 24, 2000; children: Chassie, Willow, O'Her, Karen, Britten;children: Denise Genname, Sarhrona, Baby Shamon. AAS in Humanity of Arts, Passaic County C.C., 1987, MA in Eng. & Lit., Fairleigh Dickinson U., 1994; degree (hon.), U. London, 1989. Asst. dir. William Jefferson Clinton Sch., N.Y.C., 1997—2001; prof. Fairleigh Dickinson U., Teaneck, NJ, 2001—. Rschr. Sen. Frank R. Lautenberg, Washington. Author: Blood on The Dagger, 1998, Secrets, 1998. Mem.: Sheriff Soc. U.S.A. Home: 56 Park Ave Paterson NJ 07501 Office: Oval Office of George Bush Jr Pennsylvania Ave Washington DC 20002

GRAVING, RICHARD JOHN, law educator; b. Duluth, Minn., Aug. 24, 1929; s. Lawrence Richard and Laura Magdalene (Loucks) G.; m. Florence Sara Semel; children: Daniel, Sarah. BA, U. Minn., 1950; JD, Harvard U., 1953; postgrad., Nat. U. Mex., 1964-66. Bar: Minn. 1953, N.Y. 1956, U.S. Dist. Ct. (so. dist.) N.Y. 1956, Pa. 1968, U.S. Dist. Ct. (we. dist.) Pa. 1968, Tex. 1982, U.S. Dist. Ct. (so. dist.) Tex. 1982. Assoc. Reid & Priest, N.Y.C., 1955-61, Mexico City, 1961-66; v.p. Am. & Fgn. Power Co., Inc., Mexico City, 1966-68; atty. Gulf Oil Corp., Pitts., 1968-69, Madrid, 1969-73, London, 1973-80, Houston, 1980—82; pvt. practice London, 1982—84; prof. law South Tex. Coll., Houston, 1983—; prof. Bush Grad. Sch.. Tex. A&M U., Coll. Sta., 2001—. With U.S. Army, 1953-55. Mem. Am. Soc. Internat. Law. Home: 8515 Ariel St Houston TX 77074-2806 Office: 1303 San Jacinto St Houston TX 77002-7000

GRAVITZ, HERBERT L. clinical psychologist, writer; b. Washington, Aug. 18, 1942; s. Phillip Benjamin and Sophie (Korin) G.; m. Leslie Ann Gravitz; children: Brian Eric, Aaron David, Jason Michael. BS, U. Md., 1964; MA, U. Tenn., Knoxville, 1966, PhD, 1969. Diplomate Am. Bd. Forensic Examiners; lic. clin. psychologist; bd. cert. in Illness Trauma, diplomate in Psychotherapy, Am. Acad. of Experts in Traumatic Stress. Asst. dir. Counseling Ctr., U. Calif., Santa Barbara, 1972-74, counseling program dir., 1979-80, coord. tng., 1980-81; cons. psychologist Psychiat. Emergency Team, Santa Barbara, 1980-81, Sanctuary House, Inc., Santa Barbara, 1980-82; core faculty Suzanne Somers Inst., Palm Springs, Calif., 1989—93; ind. practice clin. psychology, Santa Barbara, 1979—. Asst. prof. psychology U. Windsor, Ont., Can., 1969-72. Author: Recovery: A Guide for Adult Children of Alcoholics, 1985, Genesis: Recovery from Childhood Traumas, 1988, Obsessive Compulsive Disorder: New Help for the Family, 1998, Words that Heal: More for the Family, 2003, Mental Illness and the Family: Unlocking the Doors to Triumph, 2003. Fellow Am. Acad. Experts in Traumatic Stress; mem. Calif. State Psychol. Assn. Avocations: music, writing, meditation, stamps. Office: 2020 Alameda Padre Serra Santa Barbara CA 93103-1756 E-mail: Gravitz@aol.com.

GRAW, LEROY HARRY, purchasing and contract management company executive; b. Dupree, S.Dak., Jan. 10, 1942; s. Harry Fred and Luella (Eichmann) G.; m. Kyong Hee Yuk, Sept. 25, 1969 (div. Feb. 1979); 1 child, Natasha; m. Anat Harari, July 3, 1981; children: Byron, Karen. BS, U.S. Mil. Acad., 1964; M Commerce, U. Richmond, 1974; EdD, U. So. Calif., 1980. Govt. contracting officer worldwide, 1971-88; mgr. govt. contracts Fluor Corp., Dallas, 1988-89; mgr. contracts Superconducting Super Collider, Dallas, 1989-95; dir. contract adminstnr. Los Angeles County MTA, L.A., 1995-96; pres. Internat. Resource Mgmt. Assocs., Upland, Calif., 1996—. Ccons., Dallas, 1991-95; adj. prof. U. Dallas, 1990-95, U. Calif., Riverside, 1996—, UCLA, Westwood, 1996—, Keller Grad. Sch., 1997—. Author: Service Purchasing, 1994, Cost/Price Analysis, 1994; editor: Global Purchasing, 1990; contbr. articles to profl. jours. Dist. commr. Boy Scouts Am., Portland, Oreg., 1987, mem. troop com. troop 608, La Crescenta, 1997. Capt. U.S. Army, 1964-70, Vietnam. Recipient dist. award of merit Boy Scouts Am., Honolulu, 1985. Fellow Nat. Contract Mgmt. Assn. (cert., chpt. pres. 1997—); mem. Nat. Assn. Purchasing Mgmt. (cert., nat. officer 1992—). Avocations: skiing, hiking, camping, chess. Home and Office: 1667 N Vallejo Way Upland CA 91784-1934

GRAY, ALFRED ORREN, retired journalism educator; b. Sun Prairie, Wis., Sept. 8, 1914; s. Charles Orren and Amelia Katherine (Schadel) G.; m. Nicolin Jane Plank, Sept. 5, 1947; children— Robin, Richard BA, U. Wis.-Madison, 1939, MA, 1941. Reporter-correspondent-intern U. Wis.-Madison and Medford newspapers, 1937-39; free-lance writer, 1938-41, 51-57; intelligence investigator U.S. Ordnance Dept., Ravenna, Ohio, 1941-42; hist. editor, chief writer U.S. Ordnance Service, ETO, Paris and Frankfurt, Germany, 1944-46; asst. prof. journalism Whitworth Coll., Spokane, Wash., 1946-48, assoc. prof., 1948-56, head dept. journalism, adviser student publs., 1946-80, prof., 1956-80, prof. emeritus, 1980—, chmn. div. bus. and communications arts, 1958-66, chmn. div. applied arts, 1978-79; rschr. writer Spokane, 1980—; dir. Whitworth News Bur., 1952-58. Prin. researcher, writer 12 hist. and ednl. projects. Author: The History of U.S. Ordnance Service in the European Theater of Operations, 1942-46, Not by Might, 1965, Eight Generations From Gondelsheim: A Genealogical Study, 1980; co-author: Many Lamps, One Light: A Centennial History, 1984; editor: The Synod Story, 1953-55; mem. editl. adv. bd. Whitworth Today mag., 1989-90; contbr. articles to newspapers, mags., jours.; reader Am. Presbyns.: The Jour. of Presbyn. History, 1992-94. Scoutmaster Troop 9, Four Lakes Coun., Boy Scouts Am., Madison, Wis., 1937-41; chmn. Pinewood Addition Archtl. Com., Spokane, 1956— ; dir. Inland Empire Publs. Clinic, Spokane, 1959-74; mem. ho. of dels. Greater Spokane Council of Chs., 1968-71; judge Goodwill Worker of Yr. awards Goodwill Industries Spokane County, 1972; vice-moderator Synod Wash.-Alaska, Presbyn. Ch. (U.S.A.), 1966-67; bd. dirs. Presbyn. Hist. Soc., 1984-90, 91-94, exec. com., 1986-90, chmn. hist. sites com., 1986-90; mem. Am. Bd. Mission Heritage Comm. for Sesquicentennial of Whitman Mission, 1986; elder Spokane 1st Presbyn. Ch., 1962—, clk. of session, 1984-86, mem. Inland Empire Presbytery Com. for Bicentennial of Gen. Assembly, 1988-89; mem. com. justice and peacemaking Presbytery of the Inland Northwest, 1988-95; mem. Care and Equipping of Congregations Com., 1995-2000; Dem. precinct official, Spokane, 1988-92. Served with AUS, 1942-46. Decorated Bronze Star and Army Commendation medals; recipient citation Nat. Coun. Coll. Publ. Advisers, 1967, Outstanding Teaching of Journalism award Whitworth Coll. Alumni Assn., 1972; named Disting. Newspaper Adviser in U.S. among colleges and univs., Nat. Coun. Coll. Publ. Advisers, 1979. Mem. Assn. for Edn. in Journalism and Mass Comms., Ea. Wash. Hist. Soc., Coll. Media Advisors (hon.), N.Am. Mycol.

Assn., U. Wis. Alumni Assn. Half Century Club, Phi Beta Kappa (pres. profl. chpt. 1949-50, 67-68, 70-71), Sigma Delta Chi, Phi Eta Sigma. Democrat. Avocations: genealogy, travel. Home: 101 E Hawthorne Rd B-8 Spokane WA 99218

GRAY, ALLAN P. chemist, health and environmental consultant; b. N.Y.C., May 14, 1922; s. Philip P. and Matilda J. (Freiberg) G.; m. Carol Leon, Nov. 26, 1947 (dec. Nov. 1986); 1 child, Stefanie. AB in Chemistry, Cornell U., 1943; AM in Organic Chemistry, Columbia U., 1947, PhD in Organic Chemistry, 1950; postdoctoral fellow, U. Chgo., 1950-51. Dir. chem. rsch. Neisler Labs., Decatur, Ill., 1951-66; sect. mgr. Neisler Labs. subsidiary Union Carbide, Tarrytown, N.Y., 1966-69; assoc. prof. U. Vt., Burlington, 1969-73; program mgr., sci. advisor Ill. Inst. Tech. Rsch. Inst., Chgo., 1973-79; program mgr. Dynamac Corp., Rockville, Md., 1979-82, mgr. health and environ. scis. dept., 1982-89, chief scientist environ. scis. and mgmt. div., 1989-90; cons. health and environ. hazard assessment chemicals pvt. practice, Silver Spring, Md., 1990—. Adj. prof. dept. pharmacology Georgetown U., Washington, 1987—; mem. grants rev. com. NIH; mem. nat. contract rev. com. Nat. Inst. on Drug Abuse, Nat. Cancer Inst.; presenter in field; invited lectr. Contbr. numerous articles to profl. publs.; holder 30 patents in chem. field. Served with U.S. Army, 1944-46. Fellow AAAS; mem. N.Y. Acad. Scis., Am. Chem. Soc. (chmn. local sect. 1955, 57, chmn.long range planning com. Divsn. Medicinal Chemistry 1974, 75, vice chmn. Divsn. 1974, 75, chmn 1976). Home and Office: 14809 Pennfield Cir # 303 Silver Spring MD 20906 E-mail: AGray15424@aol.com.

GRAY, ALLEN (ERNEST BUNGAARD), radio executive; b. Council Bluffs, Iowa, Nov. 13, 1920; s. Jeppe and Martha (Petersen) Bundgaard; m. Mary Lee Burden; children: Bruce Burden, Kurt Jepson, Robert Lee. BA in Speech and Radio Broadcasting, U. Iowa, 1943. Announcer Sta. KFAB, Omaha, 1947-50; dir. Housewives Protective League Sta. WCCO (CBS), Mpls., 1951-58, Sta. WCBS, N.Y.C., 1959-63; owner Food Brockerage Co., Mpls., 1963-71; freelance broadcaster, creator Coffee Breaks various stas., Mpls., 1971-77; owner Advt. Agy., Mpls., 1978-84; owner, founder, chmn. bd. Lakes Broadcasting Group, Sta. KLKS-FM, Breezy Point, Minn., 1984—. Author: The Lore of Uncle Fogy, 1971; creator, dir.: (cassette) Uncle Fogy's Bird Calls, 1974, (album) Nature's Choir, 1979. Founder Uncle Fogy Conservation Found., Mpls., 1973, hon. chmn. for life, 1983—. 1st lt. inf. U.S. Army, 1943—46, ETO. Recipient Minn. Pioneer Broadcaster of Yr. award Minn. Broadcasters Assn., 1997; inducted into Pavek Mus. Broadcasters Hall of Fame, 2001. Avocation: outdoor activities. Home: PO Box 300 Pequot Lakes MN 56172-0300 Office: Sta KLKS-FM PO Box 300 Pequot Lakes MN 56472-0300

GRAY, ANTHONY ROLLIN, retired finance company executive; b. Des Moines, Nov. 26, 1939; s. James W. and Pauline (Frink) G.; m. Janet Eicher, June 26, 1971 (div. Mar. 1987); m. Barbara Lacey Whittaker, June 14, 1991. BA, Grinnell Coll., 1961; MS, U. Iowa, 1963. Securities analyst Lincoln Nat. Life Ins. Co., Ft. Wayne, Ind., 1966—69; dir. rsch. 1st Wis. Trust, Milw., 1969—71; chief investment officer Oak Park (Ill.) Trust, 1971—74; asst. v.p. Union Ctrl. Life Ins. Co., Cin., 1974—79; dir. rsch. Sun Banks, Orlando, Fla., 1979—85; past pres. Sun Bank Capital Mgmt. Co., Orlando, past chmn. bd., CEO, 1985—2000; ret., 2002. Founder, ptnr. Graybeard Capital LLC, 2002—. Capt. USPHS, 1963-66. Avocations: biking, golf. Office: Sun Bank Capital Mgmt PO Box 3786 Orlando FL 32802-3786

GRAY, BARBARA BRONSON, nurse, foundation administrator, writer, public relations executive; b. Van Nuys, Calif., June 3, 1955; d. Gerald M. and Jane Marie (Strauss) Bronson; m. Thomas Stephen Gray, Aug. 27, 1977; children: Jonathan Thomas, Katherine Marie. BS, UCLA, 1977, M in Nursing, 1981. RN, Calif. Staff nurse Valley Presbyn. Hosp., Van Nuys, Calif., 1977—80; asst. adminstr. Calif. Med. Ctr., L.A., 1981—84; freelance writer Agoura, 1984—96; exec. dir. Nurseweek, 1995—96, editor-in-chief, 1996—99; mng. editor WebMD Corp., Atlanta, 1999—2000; sr. mgr. found. and cmty. affairs Amgen, 2000—02, assoc. dir. corp. comm., 2002—. Cons. St. John's Hosp. and Health Ctr., Santa Monica, Calif., 1986-90, Los Robles Regional Med. Ctr., Thousand Oaks, Calif., 1993-95; lectr. UCLA Sch. Nursing, 1991-98, asst. clin. prof., 1998—. Author: 120 Years of Medicine in Los Angeles County, 1991; contbr. articles to jours., mags. and newspapers; syndicated by L.A. Times Syndicate. Mem. City of Thousand Oaks Mayor's Bus. Roundtable, 2001—02; Bishop's com. Ch. of the Epiphany, Oak Park, Calif., 2002—; bd. dirs. New West Symphony, 2001—, Ventura County Econ. Devel. Assn., Conejo/Las Virgenes Futures Found., 2001—02, Sr. Concerns, 2001—02. Recipient Outstanding Achievement award Perinatal Network, Santa Clara County, Calif., 1994, named Writer of Yr. Nurseweek, 1991; Kellogg fellow, 1979-81. Mem. Nat. Assn. Sci. Writers, Am. Orgn. Nurse Execs., Assn. Calif. Nurse Leaders (bd. dirs. 1999-2001, Leadership award 1999), Valley Industry Commerce Assn. (bd. dirs. 2000-2002), Westlake/Thousand Oaks C. of C. (bd. dirs. 2001-2002), Sigma Theta Tau (Cert. of Appreciation 1994, Internat. Media award 1995). Republican. Episcopalian. Avocations: swimming, hiking, kayaking. E-mail: bbgray@sbcglobal.net.

GRAY, BARBARA MAY, artist; b. N.Y.C., Apr. 29, 1934; d. Samuel David and Sadie Blum Ampolsey; m. Edward Gray, Aug. 29, 1954; children: Karen, Douglas. BA, CUNY, 1955; postgrad., Art Student League, 1965; MA, NYU, 1996. Graphics design Fred Kessler Collectors, N.Y.C., 1955; draftsman J. Rowland AIA, Kinston, N.C., 1955-57; art instr. Strathmore Sch., Matawan, N.J., 1963; instr. Guild of Creative Art, New Shrewsbury, N.J., 1965-66; art tchr. St. Mary's Town and Country Sch., London, 1967-68; lectr. Ctrl. Sch. of Art, London, 1975; art instr. Norwalk (Conn.) C.C., 1985-86, 95. Founder, dir. Westport (Conn.) Ctr. for Arts, 1984-86; cons. Colorful Art Gallery, Stamford, Conn., 1988-95. Creator Haiga-Haiku, 1982; collaborator (catalog) Five, 1979, Inner Eye, 1975; exhibns. in three cities in Europe; invited artist-in-residence Atelier A, Apricale, Italy, 1998. Mem. Y's Women, Westport, Conn., 1997-99. Recipient Best in Graphics Fairfield U. Gallery, 1988. Mem. AAUW, Art/Place Gallery, Soc. of Am. Graphic Artists. Avocations: theatre, dining out, bicycling, writing poetry. E-mail: egray1@optonline.net.

GRAY, BRADFORD HITCH, health policy researcher; b. Greenwich, Conn., Dec. 31, 1942; s. John Bradford and Joyce (Hitch) G.; m. Anne Morgan, Aug. 6, 1966 (div. 1980); children: Carrie Elizabeth, Joshua Bradford; m. Helen Darling, Jan. 15, 1983. BS, Okla. State U., 1964; PhD, Yale U., 1973. Asst. prof. U. N.C., Chapel Hill, 1971-74; staff sociologist Nat. Commn. for the Protection of Human Subjects of Rsch., Washington, 1975-77; study dir. Inst. of Medicine NAS, Washington, 1977-88; prof. pub. health Yale Sch. Medicine, New Haven, 1989-96; exec. dir. Program on Non Profit Orgns, Yale U., New Haven, 1989-96, dir. Inst. for Social and Policy Studies, 1992-96; dir. divsn. health and sci. policy N.Y. Acad. Medicine, N.Y.C., 1996—. Author: Human Subjects in Medical Experimentation, 1975, The Profit Motive and Patient Care, 1991; editor: New Health Care for Profit, 1983, For-Profit Enterprise in Health Care, 1986. Grantee Lilly Endowment, Indpls., 1990, Ford Found., N.Y., 1989, Rockefeller Bros. Fund, N.Y., 1989, Robert Wood Johnson Found., 1989, 93, 96, Commonwealth Fund, 1997. Mem.: Inst. of Medicine, Grolier Club, Yale Club of N.Y. Home: 93 Buttery Rd New Canaan CT 06840-5002 Office: 2500 Virginia Ave NW #407-S Washington DC 20037

GRAY, C. MICHAEL, food products executive; With Kroger Co., Pocahontas Foods USA (subs. Performance Food Group Co.), 1975—95, pres., 1992—95; COO Performance Food Group Co., 1995—2001, pres., 1995—, CEO, 2001—. Office: 12500 W Creek Pkwy Richmond VA 23238*

GRAY, CARLOS GIBSON, restaurateur, agricultural products supplier, entertainer, producer; b. Shelbyville, Ind., Sept. 5, 1937; s. Gibson Tull and Edna Frances (Wicker) G.; m. Elizabeth Vivian Stickrod, Aug. 30, 1959 (div. 1971); children: Carla Elizabeth Christine Gray Stokes, Zarrell Thomas Gibson Gray; m. Carolyn June Breeden, 1971. BSEE, Purdue U., 1960. Cert. secondary tchr., Ind. Math. tchr. Reynolds (Ind.) High Sch., 1960-61, Jefferson High Sch., Lafayette, Ind., 1961-63, Warren Ctrl. High Sch., Indpls., 1963-64; systems engr. IBM, Indpls., 1964-67, mktg. rep., 1967-69; asst. v.p., data processing mgr. Aero Mayflower Transit Co., Indpls., 1969-74; asst. v.p. application devel. Ind. Nat. Bank, Indpls., 1974-76; co-owner Gray's Seed, Inc., Fairland, Ind., 1976—; owner Boggstown Inn and Cabaret-TDCC, Corp., Boggstown, Ind., 1984-99; co-owner Jacray Corp., 1994-98, Branson Stage Theatre Corp., 1996-97; owner, dir. Ind. Receptive Co., 1998—2002. Data processing cons. Meth. Hosp., Indpls., 1968, Ford Motor Corp., Dearborn, Mich., 1967, Army, Naval Class of Indsl. Coll. Nat. Security, Indpls., 1967. Ragtime music video and audio cassettes This is Boggstown, 1986; prodr., dir. Ragtime Lil & Banjo-Banjo, Branson, Mo., 1994-97. Active Hoosier Internat. Ragtime Soc. (developed home for preservation and promotion of Am.'s ragtime music), Boggstown, 1986, U.S. C.G. Aux., 2003. Mem. Fretted Instrument Guild Am., Exptl. Aircraft Assn., Purdue Pilots, Inc. (pres. 1959-60). Avocations: multi-engine, instrument rated pilot, scuba diving, entertaining. Home: 2410 Palo Duro Blvd Herons Glen North Fort Myers FL 33917 E-mail: carlos@swfla.rr.com.

GRAY, CAROL HICKSON, chemical engineer; b. Atlanta, Jan. 3, 1958; d.Ronald Allen and Charlotte Patricia (Blitch) Hickson; m. Randy Lee Gray, June 25, 1983; children: Amanda Christine, Stephanie Lee, Jamie Noel. BSChemE, Ga. Inst. Tech., 1979. Process engr. Air Products and Chems., Inc., Calvert City, Ky., 1979-83, sr. process engr., 1983-86, sr. prodn. engr., 1986-87, prin. prodn. engr., 1987-89, engring. supr. Pasadena, Tex., 1990-92, lead engr. Calvert City, Ky., 1992-93, area supr., 1993-95; area supt. Westvaco Corp., Wickliffe, Ky., 1996—. Mem. NAFE, Internat. Platform Assn. Avocations: bicycling, photography. Office: Westvaco Corp 2025 Beech Grove Rd Wickliffe KY 42087-9010

GRAY, CHARLES AUGUSTUS, banker; b. Syracuse, N.Y., Sept. 16, 1928; s. Charles William and Elizabeth Marie (Koch) G. Cert., Am. Inst. Banking, 1958, Sch. Bank Adminstrn., 1961. Cert. internal auditor. With Mchts. Nat. Bank & Trust Co. of Syracuse, 1946-77, auditor, 1959-77, v.p., 1970-77; N.Y. State dir. Bank Adminstrn. Inst., 1970-72; regional auditor cen. N.Y. region Irving Bank Corp., 1977-82, v.p. cen. N.Y. region, 1982-89. Author: A History of Brantingham, 2000. Treas. Upper N.Y. Synod, Luth. Ch. in Am., 1966-87, Upstate N.Y. Synod, Evang. Luth. Ch. in Am., 1988-2002, Meml. Masonic Temple Corp., 1996—, Luth. Found. Upstate N.Y., 1977-78, bd. dirs., 1980—; pres. Interfrat. Alumni Coun., Syracuse U., 1980-83; treas. N.Y. State Coun. Deliberation, 1997—. Mem. Bank Adminstrn. Inst. (pres. central N.Y. chpt. 1970-72), Inst. Internal Auditors (treas. cen. N.Y. chpt. 1974-76, pres. 1985-86), Lions (pres. local club 1973-75), Masons, Shriners. Republican. Home and Office: 1321 Westmoreland Ave Syracuse NY 13210-3436

GRAY, CHARLES ELMER, lawyer, rancher, investor; b. Elvins, Mo., July 23, 1919; s. Grover P. and Martha Elizabeth (Sullivan) G.; m. Beulah Henrich Gray, July 4, 1942; children— Karen Lee, Cecilia Jean, Bette Sue, Marsha Dawn. Student, Flat River Jr. Coll., 1937-38, U. Hawaii, 1940-41; LL.B., Washington U., St. Louis, 1947. Bar: Mo. 1947. Pvt. practice, St. Louis, 1947—; ptnr. Gray and Ritter. Gen. counsel, dir. United Mo. Bank, St Louis; mem. Mo. Appellate Jud. Commn.; mem. rules com. Supreme Ct. Mo., 1970-81 Served to capt. USAF, 1939-45. Fellow Internat. Acad. Trial Lawyers (dir.), Am. Coll. Trial Lawyers, Internat. Soc. Barristers (state chmn., dir.); mem. ABA, Mo. Bar Assn., St. Louis Bar Assn., Lawyers Assn. St. Louis (v.p. 1954, bd. govs., Honor award 1977), Harbour Ridge Yacht Club (commodore 1991-92), Phi Delta Phi. Home: PO Box 709 Farmington MO 63640-0709 Office: Gateway One on the Mall 701 Market St Fl 8 Saint Louis MO 63101-1850 also: Apt 312 4800 Highway A1A Vero Beach FL 32963 E-mail: Cgray34957@aol.com.

GRAY, CHARLES ROBERT, lawyer; b. Kirksville, Mo., Aug. 22, 1952; s. George Devon and Bettie Louise (McCormick) G.; m. Dana Elizabeth Kehr, June 1, 1974; children: Jennifer, Jessica, Marcus, Gregory, Victoria. BS, N.E. Mo. State U., 1974; JD, U. Mo., Kansas City, 1978. Bar: Mo. 1978, Va. 1993, U.S. Dist. Ct. (we. dist.) Mo. 1978, U.S. Ct. Appeals (fed. cir.) 1992, U.S. Ct. Appeals (4th cir.) 1995, U.S. Supreme Ct. 1981; cert. mediator; cert. hearing officer Va. Supereme Ct., 1997. Pvt. practice, Parkville, Mo., 1978-81; asst. pub. defender 5th Judicial Cir. Ct. Mo., St. Joseph, 1978-79; pub. defender 6th Judicial Cir. Ct. Mo., Platte City, 1981; asst. dist. counsel Army Corps of Engrs., Kansas City, 1981-82, Vicksburg, Miss., 1982-83; chief counsel space shuttle, MX missile U.S. Army, Vandenberg AFB, Calif., 1983-85, chief counsel troop support agy. Ft. Lee, Va., 1985-87; fraud counsel Def. Gen. Supply Ctr. Dept. of Def., Richmond, Va., 1987-93; pvt. practice, Chester, Va., 1993-99; asst. atty. gen. Atty. Gen.'s Office State of Va., 1999—; owner Pvt. Jud. Svcs., Inc., Chester, 1993—. Adj. prof. St. Leo Coll., Ft. Lee, 1986-91, John Tyler Coll., Chester, Va., 1994—; mem. dispute resolution coun. VA, 2002, mem. adv. oversite panel. Mem. Selective Svc. Draft Bd., Brookfield, Mo., 1972-74; pres. Old Towne Parkville Assn., 1979-81, Chester (Va.) Youth Sports Boosters, 1989-91; den leader Boy Scouts Am., Chester, 1991—. Victor Wilson honor scholar, 1977; recipient Am. Jurisprudence award Coop-Bancroft-Whitney, 1989. Mem. ATLA, Am. Arbitration Assn. (mem. nat. panel arbitrators 1994—, mem. govt. disputes panel 1995—, mem. constrn. panel 1995—, mem. comml. panel 1995—), Def. Rsch. Inst. (approved mem. panel on mediation and arbitration), Mo. Bar Assn., Va. Bar Assn., Va. Trial Lawyers Assn. Methodist. Avocations: coaching youth sports, cub scouts, softball, tennis, basketball. Home: 3813 Terjo Ln Chester VA 23831-1839 Office: Pres Presiding Ofcl PO Box 34386 Chester VA 23834 E-mail: cgray@oag.state.va.us.

GRAY, CLARENCE JONES, foreign language educator, dean emeritus; b. June 21, 1908; s. Clarence J. Sr. and Elsie (Megill) G.; m. Jane Love Little, Aug. 25, 1934 (dec. June 1998); children: Frances Gray Adams (dec. Nov. 1997), Kenneth Stewart. BA, U. Richmond, 1933; MA, Columbia U., 1934; postgrad., Centro de Estudios Historicos, Madrid, summer 1935; EdD, U. Va., 1962; LLD, U. Richmond, 1979. Underwriter Aetna Life and Casualty, 1925-30; instr. Spanish Columbia U., 1934-38; gen. sec., mem. exec. council Instituto de las Espanas en los Estados Unidos, 1934-39; instr., sec. dept. Romance langs. Queens Coll., N.Y.C., 1938-46; (on mil. leave 1943-46); dean students U. Richmond, Va., 1946-68, assoc. prof. modern langs., 1946-62, prof., 1962-79, emeritus, 1979—, dean adminstrv. svcs., 1968-73, exec. asst. to pres., 1971-79, dean adminstrn., 1973-79, emeritus, 1979—, spl. cons. to pres., 1979-91, spl. cons. to chancellor, 1991—. Editor bull., 1968-74, moderator U. Richmond-WRNL Radio Scholarship Quiz program, mem. bd. Univ. Assos. Cons., Commn. on Coll., So. Assn. Coll. and Schs. Trustee Inst. Mediterranean Studies. Contbr. articles to profl. jours. Served from lt. to lt. comdr., USNR, 1943-46. Recipient Nat. Alumni award for disting. svc. U. Richmond. Mem. MLA, NEA, Am. Assn. Tchrs. Spanish, Am. Assn. for Higher Edn., Newcomen Soc. N. Am., Inst. Internat. Edn. (cert. meritorious svc.), English-Speaking Union, Legion of Honor, Order of De Molay, Country Club of Va., Colonnade Club, Masons, Rotary, Phi Beta Kappa (Epsilon chpt. sec. emeritus, historian), Phi Delta Kappa, Kappa Delta Pi, Omicron Delta Kappa (nat. sec. gen. council 1966-72, Disting. Svc. key 1968, nat. chmn. scholarship awards 1972-78), Alpha Psi Omega, Phi Gamma Delta (award for disting. and exceptional svc.), Alpha Phi Omega, Phi Beta Kappa Assocs. (life).

GRAY, CLAYLAND BOYDEN, lawyer; b. Winston-Salem, N.C., Feb. 6, 1943; s. Gordon and Jane (Craige) G. JD with high honors, U. N.C., 1968; BA in History magna cum laude, Harvard U., 1964. Bar: D.C. 1970, N.C. Law clk. to chief justice Earl Warren, 1968; assoc. Wilmer, Cutler & Pickering, 1969, partner, 1976-81; counsel and dep. chief of staff to Vice Pres. George Bush, Washington, 1981 85, counsellor, 1985-89; counsel to the Pres., 1989-93; ptnr. Wilmer, Cutler & Pickering, Washington, 1993—. Chmn. Citizens for a Sound Economy, 1993—, Summit Comms., Inc., Atlanta, 1982-89. Mem. com. to visit coll. and com. on univ. devel., Harvard U.; pres. trustees St. Mark's Sch. With USMC, 1964-70. Mem. ABA (chmn. adminstrv. law and regulatory practice sect. 2001-02), D.C. Bar Assn., N.C. Bar Assn., Fed. Bar Assn., Met. Club, Chevy Chase Club, Alibi Club. Republican. Episcopalian. Home: 1534 28th St NW Washington DC 20007-3058 Office: Wilmer Cutler & Pickering 2445 M St NW Ste 500 Washington DC 20037-1487

GRAY, DAHLI, accounting educator and administrator; b. Grand Junction, Colo., Dec. 28, 1948; d. Forrest Walter and Mary (Crockett) G.; 1 child, Kimberly. BS, Ea. Oreg. State U., 1971; MBA, Portland (Oreg.) State U., 1976; D of Bus. Adminstrn., George Washington U., 1984. Instr. acctg. Portland State U., 1976-79, George Mason U., Fairfax, Va., 1980, George Washington U., Washington, 1981-82; asst. prof. Oreg. State U., Corvallis, 1983-86; rsch. fellow U. Notre Dame, South Bend, Ind., 1986-88; assoc. prof. Am. U., Washington, 1988-90; chair, Walpert, Smullian & Blumenthal prof. Towson (Md.) State U., 1990-92; chair Morgan State U., Balt., 1992-97, prof. acctg., 1997-2000, Wilson Coll., Chambersberg, Pa., 2000-2001, U. Md. Univ. Coll., Adelphi, 2001—03, Strayer U., 2000—. Contbr. articles to profl. jours. Named Tchr. of Yr., Alpha Lambda Delta, 1986; Peat Marwick Mitchell & Co. fellow, 1986-88. Mem. Internat. Assn. Acctg. Research and Edn., Am. Inst. CPA's, Nat. Assn. Accts. (Andrew Barr award 1982, 84, Cert. Merit 1982), Am. Acctg. Assn., Inst. Cert. Mgmt. Accts. Democrat. Home: 45 Timonium Rd Lutherville Timonium MD 21093-1206 E-mail: dhelmi@polaris.umuc.edu.

GRAY, DARLENE AGNES, nurse; b. Prince Frederick, Md., June 10, 1957; d. Reynold Jerome Gray and Ellen (Madaglene) Cooke. AA, Charles County Community Coll., 1988; student, U. Md., Balt., 1982. RN; cert. med. asst. Secretarial aide U. Md. Ea. Shore, Princess Anne, Md., 1979-82; med. surg. technician Calvert Meml. Hosp., Prince Frederick, Md., 1982—; nurse Home-call, Prince George, Md., 1985-88, night supr., 1988—, health care giver, 1996—. Mem. NAACP, Alpha Kappa Alpha, Alpha Beta Kappa. Avocations: poetry, writing.

GRAY, DAVID LAWRENCE, retired air force officer; b. Portland, Oreg., Aug. 19, 1930; s. Thomas Graham and Helen Lee (Brown) G.; m. Nelda Joyce Ryan, Nov. 17, 1951 (dec. June 1987); children: David Scott, Vicki Lynn Gray Copeland, Steven Mark; m. Patricia F. Umstead, Mar. 22, 1991. BS, U. Colo., 1958; MBA, George Washington U., 1962. Registered rep. United Services Planning Assn. & Ind. Research Agy., Montgomery, Ala., 1982-83, dist. agt. Charleston, S.C., 1983-86; exec. dir. Air Force Assn., Arlington, Va., 1986-87. Host: TV talk show Def. Issues, 1982-83 Exec. dir. Air War Coll. Found., 1992-94. Maj. gen. USAF, 1951-82; Korea, Vietnam. Mem. Air Force Assn. (pres. Charleston chpt. 1985-86, nat. exec. dir. 1986-87), Daedallians. Republican. Avocations: golf, boating. E-mail: dgray3@cfl.rr.com.

GRAY, DEBORAH MARY, wine importer; b. Sydney, N.S.W., Australia, Feb. 4, 1952; came to U.S., 1973; d. Anthony Eric and Mary Patricia (O'Mullane) Gray. Student, St. Petersburg Jr. Coll., 1973-85, Eckerd Coll., 1988-90. Fin. counselor Wuesthoff Meml. Hosp., Rockledge, Fla., 1973-75; admintrv. dir. Dresden & Ticktin, MDs, P.A., St. Petersburg, Fla., 1976-80; exec. dir., v.p. Am. Med. Mgmt., Inc., Clearwater, Fla., 1980-90; pres., dir. All Women's Health Ctr., Inc., various locations, Fla., 1980-90, Lakeland Women's Health Ctr., Fla., 1980-90, Ft. Myers Women's Health Ctr., Fla., 1980-90, Nat. Women's Health Svcs., Inc., Clearwater, Fla., 1983-90, Women's Ob-Gyn. Ctr. Countryside, Inc., 1984-90, D.M.S. of Ft. Myers, Inc., 1985-90; treas., v.p., dir. Birthing Mgmt. Inc., 1985-90; healthcare cons., 1990-92; N.Am. mgr. Cowra Wines, Australia, 1991-95; owner, sole proprietor The Australian Wine Connection, Carlsbad, Calif., 1992—; bd. dirs. Australian Trade Commn., N.Y., 1996—. Dir. Alternative Human Svcs., 1979; dir. Perinatal Ctr. Ga. Bapt. Med. Ctr., 1990-92. Mem. bd. agy. that facilitates hard to place children adoptions One Ch. One Child, 1990-94.

GRAY, DON, artist; b. San Francisco, June 16, 1935; s. Leslie George and Mildred Marie (Koester) G.; m. Jessie Benton Evans, Oct. 13, 1960. BA in Art, Ariz. State U., 1957; MA in Art, U. Iowa, 1962. Prof. artist and poet, N.Y.C., NY, 1962—68, Florida, NY, 1968—88, Scottsdale, Ariz., 1988—; assoc. prof. art Pace U., Briarcliff, N.Y., 1981-85; asst. prof. art Ladycliff Coll., Highland Falls, N.Y., 1971-81. Prodr., moderator Artist and Critic Manhattan Cable TV, 1975—95; participant TV programs comparing Rembrandt/Van Gogh self portraits, evalns. of 19th and 20th century art. Art critic Art World mag., 1982—88, Ashes Art Newspaper, Phoenix, 1992—95; exhibitions include many galleries and univs., N.Y., Ariz., N.Mex.; author: poems. Grantee Inst. for Urban Resources, N.Y., 1981. Mem. Coll. Art Assn. Home and Office: 8711 E Pinnacle Peak Rd # 223 Scottsdale AZ 85255-3517 E-mail: grayevans@msn.com.

GRAY, DONALD DWIGHT, civil engineering educator; b. New Orleans, July 1, 1946; s. Edward Morris and Jeanne (Saucier) G.; m. Kay Ann Hess, June 1, 1968; children: Donald Douglas, Benjamin David, Michael Joseph. BSE in Mech. Engring., Tulane U., 1968; MSE, Purdue U., 1969, PhD, 1974. Registerd profl. engr., Ind. Rsch. assoc. Oak Ridge (Tenn.) Nat. Lab., 1974—76; asst. prof. civil engring. Purdue U., West Lafayette, Ind., 1976—83; assoc. prof. civil and environ. engring. W.Va. U., Morgantown, 1983—2003, prof. civil and environ. engring., 2003—. Cons. Office of Energy Related Inventions Nat. Inst. Stds. and Tech., Gaithersburg, Md., 1987-89; part-time sr. scientist Ecodynamics Rsch. Assocs. Inc., Albuquerque, 1993. Author: A First Course in Fluid Mechanics for Civil Engineers, 2000. Co-founder, bd. dirs. Matrix Lifeline Greater Lafayette (Ind.), 1978-80; mem. Citizen's Adv. Com. on Bd. Policy Revision, West Lafayette Sch. Corp., 1978-79. Mem. ASCE, Assn. Groundwater Scientists and Engrs., Am. Geophys. Union, Nat. Assn. Scholars, Sigma Xi, Tau Beta Pi, Chi Epsilon (hon.). Office: WVa U Dept Civil/Environ Engring PO Box 6103 Morgantown WV 26506-6103

GRAY, DONALD MELVIN, molecular and cell biology educator; b. Milton, Pa., Apr. 4, 1938; s. Harry Seal and Edith Sophia (Larrison) G.; m. Carla Christine Winlund, Sept. 10, 1970. BA, Susquehanna U., 1960; MS, Yale U., 1963, PhD, 1967. Postdoctoral fellow U. Calif., Berkeley, 1967-70; asst. prof. molecular and cell biology U. Tex. at Dallas, Richardson, 1970-76, assoc. prof., 1976-83, prof., 1983—; program head, 1989-95. Contbr. articles to profl. jours. Fogarty Sr. Internat. fellow European Molecular Biology Lab., Heidelberg, Fed. Republic of Germany, 1977-78; NIH grantee U. Tex. at Dallas, 1972-93, NSF grantee, 1994-98, Welch Found. grantee, 1972—. Fellow AAAS; mem. Am. Chem. Soc., Biophys. Soc. Office: Univ Tex at Dallas Molecular and Cell Biology PO Box 830688 Richardson TX 75083-0688

GRAY, DOROTHY LOUISE ALLMAN POLLET, librarian; b. Billings, Mont., Dec. 17, 1945; d. Lee F. and Ruth H. (Behner) Allman; m. Michael Haslam Gray, Aug. 11, 1980; children: M. Alexander, Timothy Haslam. BA, U. Colo., 1969; MSLS, Syracuse U., 1972. Reference libr., bibliographer Libr. of Congress Div. Blind and Physically Handicapped, Washington, 1972-75; reference specialist Libr. of Congress Gen. Reference and Bibliography Div., Washington, 1975-77; ednl. liaison officer nat. programs Libr. of Congress, Washington, 1977-82; rsch. assoc. Nat. Commn. on Librs. and Info. Sci., Washington, 1982-88; info. ctr. mgr. Nat. Assn. Inveterate and Obdurate Politicos, Arlington, Va., 1988-92; libr. dir. Nat. Sch. Bds. Assn., Alexandria, Va., 1992—. Editor: Sign Systems for Libraries, 1979; editor Leads, the newsletter of Internat. Rels. Roundtable, ALA, 1979-82; cons. editor: The Bowker Annual of Library and Book Trade Information, 1986-88. Recipient Superior Svc. award Libr. of Congress, Washington, 1981. Mem. ALA, CEC, Spl. Librs. Assn. Avocations: music, calligraphy. Office: Nat Sch Bds Assn 1680 Duke St Ste 100 Alexandria VA 22314-3455

GRAY, DUNCAN MONTGOMERY, JR., retired bishop; b. Canton, Miss., Sept. 21, 1926; s. Duncan Montgomery and Isabel (McCrady) G.; m. Ruth Miller Spivey, Feb. 9, 1948; children: Duncan Montgomery, Anne Gray Finley, Lloyd Spivey, Catherine Gray Clark. B.E.E., Tulane U., 1948; M.Div., U. South, 1953, D.D. (hon.), 1972. Ordained priest Episcopal Ch., 1953, bishop, 1974; priest-in-charge Calvary Ch., Cleveland, Miss. and Grace Ch., Rosedale, Miss., 1953-57, Holy Innocents Ch., Como, Miss., 1957-60; rector St. Peter's Ch., Oxford, Miss., 1957-65, St. Paul's Ch., Meridian, Miss., 1965-74; bishop coadjutor Diocese of Miss., Jackson, 1974, bishop, 1974-93. Chmn. Standing Commn. on Constn. and Canons of Gen. Conv. of Episc. Ch., 1977-83, House of Bishops' Com. Canons, 1975 89; pres. Province IV Episc. Ch., 1984-88, chmn. com. on rules, 1989-93; mem. advice council to the Presiding Bishop, 1984-88; vice chmn, Bd. Archives Episc. Ch. Contbr. articles in field to religious publs. Chmn. bd. trustees All Saints Episc. Sch., Vicksburg, 1975-77; trustee U. South, Sewanee, Tenn., 1974-97, regent, 1981-87, chancellor, 1991-97; chmn. Miss. Religious Leadership Conf., 1977-79, So. Regional Council, 1967-73; mem. Miss. Mental Health Assn., 1968-73; bd. dirs. Miss. Council on Human Relations, 1962-93, pres., 1963-67; mem. Miss. Adv. Com. to U.S. Commn. on Civil Rights, 1975-90. Recipient Nat. Speaker of Year award Tau Kappa Alpha, 1962 Episcopalian. Home: 3775 Old Canton Rd Jackson MS 39216-3519

GRAY, D'WAYNE, retired marine corps officer; b. Navarro County, Tex., Apr. 9, 1931; s. Henry Oliver and Myrtle Daisy (Lee) G.; m. Mary Joan Sobieck, Oct. 11, 1955; children: Stephen D'Wayne, Elizabeth Joan Gray Hendrickson, Theresa Mary Gray Croghan. Student, N. Tex. Agrl. Coll., 1948-49; BA, U. Tex., 1952; MS in Internat. Affairs, George Washington U., 1971; postgrad., Naval War Coll., 1970-71, Harvard U., 1980. Commd. 2d lt. USMC, 1952, advanced through grades to lt. gen., 1983; combat svc. Korea, 1953, 1965, 71-72; asst. div. comdr. 1st Marine Div., 1977-79; dir. plans Hdqrs. Washington,

1979-80; dir. ops. Hdqrs., 1980-81; dir. personnel mgmt. Hdqrs., 1981-83; chief of staff Hdqrs., 1983-85; comdg. gen. Fleet Marine Force, Pacific; comdr. Marine Corps Bases, Pacific, Camp H.M. Smith, Hawaii, 1985-87; ret., 1987; ind. cons., 1987-89; exec. dir. Montgomery County Revenue Authority, Rockville, Md., 1989-90; undersec. veterans affairs for benefits Dept. Vet. Affairs, Washington, 1990-93. Chmn. bd. dirs. TROA EdPlus, Inc., Alexandria, Va., 2000—; del. Inter-Am. Def. Bd., 1980; bd. dirs. U.S. Naval Inst., 1980-85; mem. bd. govs. Uniformed Svcs. Benefit Assn. Kansas City, 1982-83, 85-88; mem. sec. of state's Adv. Panel on Overseas Security, 1984-85. Chmn. editorial bd., U.S. Naval Inst., 1980-83. Mem. maritime policy study group Ctr. for Strategic and Internat. Studies, Georgetown U., 1981-85. Decorated D.S.M., Legion of Merit with gold star and V, Bronze Star medal with V., Meritorious Svc. medal with gold star, Air medal with bronze numeral 5, Joint Svc. Commendation medal with V, Navy Commendation medal with V. Mem. Marine Corps Assn., U.S. Naval Inst., Marine Corps Heritage Found., Marine Corps Scholarship Found., Mil. Officers Assn. Am., Ret. Officers Assn. (bd. dirs. 1994-2000, 1st vice chmn. 1998-2000), Cath. War Vets. Roman Catholic. Home: 3423 Barger Dr Falls Church VA 22044-1202 *The military way of life is not for everyone. But, to those for whom it is right, it offers an unequalled opportunity for both personal adventure and service to one's fellow Americans. I wish I could do it all again!.*

GRAY, ELIZABETH VAN DOREN, lawyer; b. Columbia, S.C., Jan. 3, 1949; d. Robert Lawson and Elizabeth Dacus (Gaines) Van Doren; m. James Cranston Gray, Jr., Apr. 30, 1982; children: James Cranston III, Elizabeth Gaines. BA in Internat. Studies, U. S.C., 1970, JD cum laude, 1976; student, St. Mary's Coll., Raleigh, N.C., 1966-67. Bar: S.C. 1977, U.S. Dist. Ct. S.C. 1977, U.S. Ct. Appeals (4th cir.) 1980, U.S. Ct. Appeals (6th cir.) 1989, U.S. Supreme Ct. 1998. Assoc. McNair Law Firm, PA, Columbia, 1977-82, shareholder, 1982-87; ptnr. Glenn Irvin Murphy Gray & Stepp, Columbia, 1987—2000; now ptnr. Sowell Gray Stepp & Lafitte, LLC, Columbia. Contbr. articles to profl. jours. Mem. ABA, Am. Coll. Trial Lawyers, John Belton O'Neal Inn of Ct., S.C. Bar (pres. 2001-02), S.C. Women Lawyers Assn. (bd. dirs. 1995-99, sec. 1997-98), Richland County Bar Assn. Episcopalian. Office: Sowell Gray Stepp & Lafitte LLC PO Box 11449 Columbia SC 29211 Home: 8 Mahalo Ln Columbia SC 29204-3380

GRAY, FESTUS GAIL, electrical engineer, educator, researcher; b. Moundsville, W.Va., Aug. 16, 1943; s. Festus P. and Elsie V. (Rine) G.; m. Caryl Evelyn Anderson, Aug. 24, 1968; children: David, Andrew, Daniel. BSEE, W.Va. U., 1965, MSEE, 1967; PhD, U. Mich., 1971. Instr. W.Va. U., Morgantown, 1966-67; asst. prof. Va. Poly. Inst. and State U., Blacksburg, 1971-77, assoc. prof., 1977-82, prof., 1983—. Vis. scientist Rsch. Triangle Inst., N.C., 1984-85; faculty fellow NASA, 1975; cons. Inland Motors, Radford, Va., 1980, Rsch. Triangle Inst., 1987—; researcher Rome Air Devel. Ctr., N.Y., 1980-81, Naval Surface Weapons Ctr., Dahlgren, Va., 1982-83, Army Rsch. Office, 1983-86, NSF, 1991-93, 98-2001, ARPA, 1993-96, Wright-Patterson AFB, 1995-99; publs. chmn. Internat. Symposium on Fault Tolerant Computing, Ann Arbor, Mich., 1985. Co-author: Structured Logic Design with VHDL, 1993, VHDL Representation and Synthesis, 2d edit., 2000; contbr. articles to sci. jours. Assoc. treas. Northside Presbyn. Ch., Blacksburg, 1986—, bd. deacons, 1980-83; coach S.W. Va. Soccer Assn., Blacksburg, 1980-86; asst. scoutmaster Boy Scouts Am., 1990—. Grantee NSF, Office Naval Rsch., NASA, Adv. Rsch. Projects Agy; Teaching fellow U. Mich., 1967-70. Mem. IEEE (chpt. chmn. 1979-80), Computer Soc. IEEE, Sigma Xi. Democrat. Achievements include research on fault tolerance, diagnosis, testing and reliability issues for VLSI, distributed and multiprocessor computer architectures, modeling and synthesis with VHOL, modeling and design with hardware description languages. Home: 304 Fincastle Dr Blacksburg VA 24060-5036 Office: Va Poly Inst and State U Blacksburg VA 24061-0111

GRAY, FRANCES BOONE, minister; b. Miami, Fla., Aug. 23, 1939; d. Roy and Willie Artis Boone; m. Joel A. Gray, Apr. 17, 1959 (dec. Nov. 2002); children: Linda Lamarsh, Joel A., Frances S. AA, Miami Dade Jr. Coll., Miami, 1959; BS, U. Miami, 1965; MDiv, Jacksonville Theol. Sem., Jacksonville, Fla., 1995; PhD, Jacksonville Theol. Sem., 1999. RN 1965. Nurse Jackson Meml. Hosp., Miami, 1954—65, Mt. Sinai Hosp., Miami, 1965—70, Miami Heart Hosp., 1970—77; minister Temple Missionary Bapt. Ch., Miami, 1988—95; pastor Jesus Christ Unltd. Ministry, Miami, 1995—. Tchr. Lindsey Hopkins Sch., Miami, 1966—67. Bd. dirs. United Way, Miami; asst. sec. SCIC, Miami, 1984—90; mem. NAACP. With USPHS, 1970—75. Mem.: Order Eastern Star (worthy matron 1981—88). Democrat. Avocations: reading, sewing, swimming, singing. Home: 1510 NW 114th St Miami FL 33167

GRAY, FRANCINE DU PLESSIX, author; b. Warsaw; came to U.S., 1941, naturalized, 1952; d. Bertrand Jochaud and Tatiana (Iacovleff) du Plessix; m. Cleve Gray, Apr. 23, 1957; children: Thaddeus Ives, Luke Alexander. BA, Barnard Coll., 1952; Litt.D. (hon.), CUNY, Oberlin Coll., U. Santa Clara, St. Mary's Coll., U. Hartford. Annenberg fellow Brown U., 1997. Disting. vis. prof. CCNY, 1975; vis. lectr. Yale U., New Haven, 1981-82; Ferris prof. Princeton U., 1986; Disting. vis. prof. Vassar Coll., 1999. Author: Divine Disobedience: Profiles in Catholic Radicalism, 1970 (Nat. Cath. Book award), Hawaii: The Sugar-Coated Fortress, 1972, Lovers and Tyrants, 1976, World Without End, 1981, October Blood, 1985, Adam & Eve and the City, 1987, Soviet Women: Walking the Tightrope, 1989, Rage and Fire: A Life of Louise Colet, 1994, At Home with the Marquis de Sade: A Life, 1998, Simone Weil, 2001. Guggenheim Found. fellow, 1991-92. Mem. Am. P.E.N., Am. Acad. Arts and Letters. Democrat. Roman Catholic.

GRAY, FRANK TRUAN, lawyer; b. Prince Frederick, Md., Oct. 22, 1920; s. John B. and Aimèe Atlee (Truan) Gray; m. Sally A. Jackson, Dec. 31, 1976; children: John W., Edward A., Philip L., Theodora R. AB, Princeton U., 1942; student, Cambridge (Eng.) U., 1945; LL.B., Harvard U., 1948. Bar: Md. 1949. Assoc. firm Piper & Marbury, Balt., 1948-56, ptnr., 1957-90. Asst. atty. gen. State of Md., 1955—56; pres. Balt. Estate Planning Coun., 1975—76. Editor: Harvard Law Rev., 1947—48. Pres. Citizen's Planning and Housing Assn., Balt., 1960—62; bd. dirs. Balt. Neighborhoods, Inc., 1959—85, Balt. Bar Found., 1985—93; trustee Provident Hosp., Inc., 1961—74, Leonard and Helen R. Stulman Charitable Found., 1991—. Fellow: Md. Bar Found., Am. Bar Found. (chmn. Md. 1993—98); mem.: ABA, Balt. Bar Assn., Md. Bar Assn., Am. Law Inst. Office: Piper Rudnick LLP 111 S Calvert St Ste 1950 Baltimore MD 21202-6193

GRAY, FREDERICK THOMAS, JR., ('RICK GRAY), actor, educator, playwright; b. Hopewell, Va., Mar. 22, 1951; s. Frederick Thomas and Evelyn (Helms) Johnson Gray. BA with distinction, U. Va., 1972, JD, 1975, MEd, 1990, postgrad., 1991-94, U. Richmond, 1981-82. Bar: Va. 1976. Law clk. Williams, Mullen & Christian, Richmond, Va., 1975-76, assoc., 1976-78; sec. Commonwealth of Va., Richmond, 1978-81; high sch. tchr., 1982—89, 1999—2000, 2002—; asst. prin., 1991—92. Appeared in TV series In the Heat of the Night, profl. stage prodns. My Fair Lady, Macbeth, To Kill a Mockingbird, also others. Mem. Va. Democratic state ctrl. com., 2001—. Mem. SAG, Raven Soc. (U. Va.), Actor's Equity Assn. Address: 4701 Bermuda Hundred Rd Chester VA 23836-3257 E-mail: deinikes@yahoo.com.

GRAY, GAVIN CAMPBELL, II, computer information engineer; Student, U. Wis., Milw., 1966-71. Programmer, analyst Equitable Variable Life Ins., Farmingdale, N.Y., 1975-77; analyst, programmer Atty.'s Title Svcs., Orlando, Fla., 1977-78; systems analyst Cert. Grocers, Ocala, Fla., 1978-80; supr. R & D, Clay Electric Coop., Keystone Heights, Fla., 1980-86; mgr. info. svcs. Coldwell Banker Relocation Svcs., Mission Viejo, Calif., 1986-96; knowledge mgr. Oracle Corp., San Diego, 1996-99; dir. C-bridge Internet Solutions, Cambridge, Mass., 1999—2002, The Gray Domain, 2003—. Mem. Guide Internat. Bus. Rules Stds. Project, 1994—, Am. Nat. Stds. Inst. Accredited Stds. Com. X12, 1994-96, Asymetrix Corp. Adv. Coun. Author: IBM GIS Usage for IMS/DLI, 1979; developer software Map-Paint for CICS, methodology Path Evaluation Method (PEM), TRANS-FLOW Programming, Tier Diagramming Method; contbr. articles to profl. jours. Mem. IEEE, Project Mgmt. Inst., Assn. Computing Machinery, Data Adminstrn. Mgmt. Assn. Internat., Data Warehousing Inst., Math. Assn. Am., Internat. Platform Assn., IEEE Computer Soc., IEEE Engring. Mgmt. Soc., N.Y. Acad. Scis., Am. Mus. Natural History, Zool. Soc. San Diego, Apics, Am. Mensa Ltd., Nat. Eagle Scout Assn., Intertel.

GRAY, GEORGE, mural painter; b. Harrisburg, Pa., Dec. 23, 1907; s. George Zacharias and Anna Margaret (Barger) G. Ed., Harrisburg Tech. H.S., Phila., 1927-30, Acad. Fine Arts, Wilmington, Del., 1931-33, Art Students League, N.Y.C., Howard Pyle Sch. Illustration, Wilmington. Designer stage scenery, N.Y.C., 1926; invited to sketch scenes of army life in various forts and camps; tchr. anatomy and figure constrn. while attending art classes, Phila., Wilmington, later staff artist, U.S. Inf. Jour., U.S. Cav. Jour., Washington, N.Y. Nat. Guardsmen, Pa. N.G. Mag., mural painter patron, Gen. J. Leslie Kincaid, pres., Am. Hotels Corp., N.Y.C., 1934—; murals exhibited in hotels throughout U.S., including MacArthur of Battan, Hotel Jefferson-Clinton, Syracuse, N.Y.; Gen. George Rogers Clark, Louisville; 3 murals Hist. L.I, Suffolk County Savs. and Loan Bank, Babylon, L.I., Pony Express Nat. Meml. Mus., St. Joseph, Mo.; mural painting Brooklyn Bridge, Seamen's Ch. Inst., N.Y.C.; hist. picture map, Hotel Huntington, L.I., portraits and paintings in pvt. collections, U.S. and abroad; mil. artist, Engring. Bd., Ft. Belvoir, Va., combat artist, U.S. Coast Guard Hdqrs., Washington, originator, chmn., Navy Art Cooperation and Liaison Com. of Salmagundi Club. Founder, chmn. Coast Guard Art Program Salmagundi Club. Recipient Meritorious Pub. Svc. citation Dept. Navy, 1964; Louis E. Seley NACAL award, 1970; medal of honor Salmagundi Club, 1973; George Gray award U.S. Coast Guard, 1983 Life fellow Royal Soc. Arts (London); mem. Soc. Illustrators, Am. Mil. Inst., Am. Soc. Marine Artists, Co. Mil. Collectors and Historians, Nat. Soc. Mural Painters, Am. Vets. Soc. Artists, Am. Artists Profl. League, Nat. Hist. Soc. (founding mem.), Assn. Mil. Surgeons U.S., Navy League U.S. (Commodore Club), U.S. Naval Inst., Armed Forces Mgmt. Inst., Artists Fellowship, Arts Club (Washington), Salmagundi Club of N.Y. (originator, chmn. COGAP, Coast Guard art program of club) Address: Salmagundi Club 47 5th Ave New York NY 10003-4303

GRAY, GEORGE TRUMON, test development professional; b. Indpls., June 1, 1946; s. Trumon Lloyd and Helen Louise (McClain) G.; m. Beverly Diane Liebenow, Aug. 24, 1974; children: Elizabeth Diane, Steven Trumon. B in Music Edn., Ind. U., 1968, MS in Edn., 1969, EdD, 1973. Asst. prof. Tenn. Tech. U., Cookeville, 1973-75; coord. Office of Curriculum, Devel. and Evaluation Rush U., Chgo., 1976-80, dir. Office of Curriculum, Devel. and Evaluation, 1980-92; program assoc. health programs dept. Profl. Devel. Svcs. ACT, Iowa City, 1993-94; asst. dir. Health Programs Dept., PDS, ACT, Iowa City, 1994-99, dir., 1999—. R & D com. bd. registry Am. Soc. Clin. Pathologists, Chgo., 1985-91, computer adaptive testing com., 1988-93. Contbr. articles to profl. jours. Mem. Nat. Coun. Measurement in Edn., Am. Ednl. Rsch. Assn. Presbyterian. Office: ACT Inc 2201 N Dodge St Iowa City IA 52243-0001 E-mail: george.gray@act.org.

GRAY, GORDON L. communications educator; b. Hampton, Iowa, May 18, 1924; s. Leroy Ernest and Arianna (Oldham) G.; m. Barbara Ann Smith, Feb. 5, 1949; children: David Gordon, Jonathan William. BA, Cornell Coll., 1948; MA, Northwestern U., 1951, PhD, 1957. Radio announcer and newsman, 1948-50; broadcast coordinator NBC-TV, Chgo, 1951; instr. to asso. prof. television and radio Mich. State U., 1953-67; prof. communications Temple U., Phila., 1967-96, prof. emeritus, 1996—, chmn. dept. radio, TV, and Film, 1967-74, 78-82, 1994-95. Program assoc. Ednl. TV and Radio Ctr., Ann Arbor, Mich., 1956-57. Served to staff sgt. AUS, 1943-46. Fulbright scholar Inst. Edn. U. Leeds, U.K., 1965-66

GRAY, GWEN CASH, real estate broker; b. Cowpens, S.C., Oct. 24, 1943; d. Woodrow C. and Marie (Hamrick) Cash; m. Charles H. Gray, Oct. 24, 1987 ; children: Dianne Marie Young, Teena Michele Bulman. BS, Limestone Coll., Gaffney, S.C., 1984. Real estate sales rep., owner and broker-in-charge Southers Real Estate, Spartanburg, S.C. Bd. dirs. Bank of Am.; lectr. in field. Contbr. articles to profl. jours. Advisor S.C. Peach Festival, Gaffney, 1977—, Clemson U. Extension Svc., 1987—. Named Woman of Yr. Bus. and Profl. Women, 1979, Woman of Yr. S.C. Rural Electric Coop., 1984, Career Woman of Yr. Breakfast Club Spartanburg Bus. and Profl. Club, 1997. Mem. Am. Farm Bur., Nat. Bd. Realtors, S.C. Farm Bur., S.C. Bd. Realtors, Spartanburg Bd. Realtors (pres. 1998, Realtor of Yr. 1997), S.C. Hort. Soc. (bd. dirs.), S.C. Assn. Agr. Agts. (Friend of Extension award 1986), Spartanburg Multiple Listing Svc. Baptist. Republican. Avocations: reading, tech. coll. teaching. Office: Southers Real Estate 223 E Blackstock Rd Spartanburg SC 29301-2633 E-mail: GwenGray@teleplex.net.

GRAY, HANNA HOLBORN, history educator; b. Heidelberg, Germany, Oct. 25, 1930; d. Hajo and Annemarie (Bettmann) Holborn; m. Charles Montgomery Gray, June 19, 1954. AB, Bryn Mawr Coll., 1950; PhD, Harvard U., 1957; MA, Yale U., 1971, LLD, 1978; LittD (hon.), St. Lawrence U., 1974, Oxford (Eng.) U., 1979; LLD (hon.), Dickinson Coll., 1979, U. Notre Dame, 1980, Marquette U., 1984; LittD (hon.), Washington U., 1974; HHD (hon.), St. Mary's Coll., 1974; LHD (hon.), Grinnell (Iowa) Coll., 1974, Lawrence U., 1974, Denison U., 1974, Wheaton Coll., 1976, Marlboro Coll., 1979, Rikkyo (Japan) U., 1979, Roosevelt U., 1980, Knox Coll., 1980, Coe Coll., 1981, Thomas Jefferson U., 1981, Duke U., 1982, New Sch. for Social Research, 1982, Clark U., 1982, Brandeis U., 1983, Colgate U., 1983, Wayne State U., 1984, Miami U., Oxford, Ohio, 1984, So. Meth. U., 1984, CUNY, 1985, U. Denver, 1985, Am. Coll. Greece, 1986, Muskingum Coll., 1987, Rush Presbyn. St. Lukes Med. Ctr., 1987, NYU, 1988, Rosemont Coll., 1988, Claremont U. Ctr. Grad Sch., 1989, Moravian Coll., 1991, Rensselaer Poly. Inst., 1991, Coll. William and Mary, 1991, Centre Coll., 1991, Macalester Coll., 1993, McGill U., 1993, Ind. U., 1994, Med. U. of S.C., 1994; LLD (hon.), Union Coll., 1975, Regis Coll., 1976, Dartmouth Coll., 1978, Trinity Coll., 1978, U. Bridgeport, 1978, Dickinson Coll., 1979, Brown U., 1979, Wittenburg U., 1979, Dickinson Coll., 1979, U. Rochester, 1980, U. Notre Dame, 1980, U. So. Calif., 1980, U. Mich., 1981, Princeton U., 1982, Georgetown U., 1983, Marquette U., 1984, W.Va. Wesleyan U., 1985, Hamilton Coll., 1985, Smith Coll., 1986, U. Miami, 1986, Columbia U., 1987, NYU, 1988, Rosemont Coll., 1988, U. Toronto, Can., 1991; LDH, LHD, Haverford Coll., 1995; LDH (hon.), Tulane U., 1995; LLD, LLD, Harvard U., 1995; LHD (hon.), McGill U., 1993, Macalester Coll., 1993, Ind. U., 1994, Med. U. S.C., 1994, Haverford Coll., 1995, Tulane U., 1995; LLD (hon.), Harvard U., 1995, U. Chgo., 1996. Instr. Bryn Mawr Coll., 1953—54; tchg. fellow Harvard, 1955—57, instr., 1957—59, asst. prof., 1959—60, vis. lectr., 1963—64; asst. prof. U. Chgo., 1961—64, assoc. prof., 1964—72; dean, prof. Northwestern U., Evanston, Ill., 1972—74; provost, prof. history Yale U., 1974—78, acting pres., 1977—78; pres. U. Chgo., 1978—83, prof. dept. history, 1978—, Harry Pratt Judson disting. svc. prof. history, 1994—. Fellow Ctr. for Advanced Study in Behavioral Scis., 1966—67, vis. scholar, 1970—71; vis. prof. U. Calif., Berkeley, Calif., 1970—71. Co-editor (with Charles Gray): Jour. Modern History, 1965—70; contbr. articles to profl. jours. Mem. Nat. Coun.on Humanities, 1972—78; trustee Yale Corp., 1971—74; mem. bd. regents The Smithsonian Instn.; former chmn. bd. Andrew W. Mellon Found.; chmn. bd. Howard Hughes Med. Inst., Marlboro Sch. Music. Named Grosse Verdienstkreuz, Germany; recipient Grad. medal, Radcliffe Coll., 1976, Yale medal, 1978, Medal of Liberty award, 1986, Medal of Freedom, 1991, Frontrunner award, Sara Lee, 1991, Laureate Lincoln Acad. Ill., 1988, Charles Frankel prize, 1993, Centennial medal, Harvard U., 1994, Disting. Svc. award in edn., Inst. Internat. Edn., 1994, Medal of Distinction, Barnard Coll., 2000; fellow Newberry Libr., 1960—61, St. Anne's Coll., Oxford U., 1978—; scholar Fulbright scholar, 1950—51. Fellow: Am. Acad. Arts and Scis.; mem.: Coun. Fgn. Rels. N.Y., Coun. Fgn. Rels. Chgo., Nat. Acad. Edn., Am. Philos. Soc. (Jefferson medal 1993), Renaissance Soc. Am., Phi Beta Kappa (vis. scholar 1971—72). Office: U Chgo Dept History 1126 E 59th St Chicago IL 60637-1580 Business E-Mail: h-gray@uchicago.edu.

GRAY, HARRY BARKUS, chemistry educator; b. Woodburn, Ky., Nov. 14, 1935; s. Barkus and Ruby (Hopper) Gray; m. Shirley Barnes, June 2, 1957; children: Victoria Lynn, Andrew Thomas, Noah Harry Barkus. BS, Western Ky. U., 1957; PhD, Northwestern U., 1960, DSc (hon.), 1984, U. Chgo., 1987, U. Rochester, 1987, U. Paul Sabatier, 1991, U. Göteborg, 1991, U. Firenze, 1993, Columbia U., 1994, Bowling Green State U., 1994, Ill. Wesleyan, 1995, Oberlin Coll., 1996, U. Ariz., 1997, Carleton U., 2001, U. SC, 2003. Postdoctoral fellow U. Copenhagen, 1960—61; faculty Columbia U., 1961—66, prof., 1965—66; prof. chemistry Calif. Inst. Tech., Pasadena, 1966—, now Arnold O. Beckman prof. chemistry and founding dir. Beckman Inst. Vis. prof. Rockefeller U., Harvard U., U. Iowa, Pa. State U., Yeshiva U., U. Copenhagen, U. Witwatersrand, Johannesburg, South Africa, U. Canterbury, Christchurch, New Zealand, U. Hong Kong; George Eastman prof. Oxford (Eng.) U., 1997—98; cons. govt., industry; Kistiakowsky lectr. Harvard U., 1999. Author: Electrons and Chemical Bonding, 1965, Molecular Orbital Theory, 1965, Ligand Substitution Processes, 1966, Basic Principles of Chemistry, 1967, Chemical Dynamics, 1968, Chemical Principles, 1970, Models in Chemical Science, 1971, Chemical Bonds, 1973, Chemical Structure and Bonding, 1980, Molecular Electronic Structures, 1980, Braving the Elements, 1995. Named Calif. Scientist of Yr., 1988, Achievement Rewards for Coll. Scis. Man of Sci., 1990; recipient Franklin Meml. award, Stanford U., 1967, Fresenius award, Phi Lambda Upsilon, 1970, Shoemaker award, U. Louisville, 1970, award for excellence in tchg., Mfg. Chemists Assn., 1972, Centenary medal, Royal Soc. Chemistry, 1985, Nat. medal of Sci., 1986, Alfred Bader Bioinorganic Chemistry award, 1990, Gold medal, Am. Inst. Chemists, 1990, Linderstrom-Lang prize, 1992, Priestly award, Dickinson Coll., 1991, Chandler medal, Columbia U., 1999, Harvey prize, Technion Israel Inst. Tech., 2000; fellow Guggenheim, 1972—73; scholar Phi Beta Kappa, 1973—74. Fellow: AAAS; mem.: NAS (Nichols medal 2003, award in chem. scis. 2003), Royal Danish Acad. Scis. and Letters, Am. Philos. Soc., Royal Soc. (London), Royal Swedish Acad., Am. Chem. Soc. (award pure chemistry 1970, Harrison Howe award 1972, award inorganic chemistry 1978, Remsen Meml. award 1979, Tolman medal 1979, award for disting. svc. in advancement of inorganic chemistry 1984, Pauling medal 1986, Priestley medal 1991, Willard Gibbs medal 1992), Phi Lambda Upsilon, Alpha Chi Sigma. Home: 1415 E California Blvd Pasadena CA 91106-4101 Office: Calif Inst Tech 139-74 1200 E California Blvd Pasadena CA 91125-0001

GRAY, HARRY JOSHUA, electrical engineer, educator; b. St. Louis, June 24, 1924; s. Harry Joshua and Mary Margaret (Davis) G.; m. Cecilia M. McNulty, Apr. 23, 1949; children— Margaret, Cecilia, Kathleen (dec.), Mary. Student, Lehigh U., 1941-43; BSEE, U. Pa., 1944, PhD, 1953. Registered profl. engr., Pa. Instr. The Moore Sch. Elec. Engring., U. Pa., Phila., 1947-51, assoc., 1951-53, asst. prof., 1953-54, assoc. prof., 1957-64, prof. elec. engring. and computer and info. sci., 1964-89, prof. emeritus elec. engring., 1989—. Mem. ENIAC staff, 1947; with Remington Rand Univac, Phila., 1954-57; cons. in field; bd. dirs. Pa. Research Assocs., Inc., 1963 Contbr. articles to profl. jours.; author: Digital Computer Engineering, 1963, High Speed Digital Circuits and Memories, 1976; patentee in field. Served with USN, 1943-46. Grantee U.S. Army Electronics Command, 1966-69, NSF, 1966-68, NIMH, 1971-73, Burroughs Corp., 1973-75; medalist ENIAC, 50th Anniv., 1997. Mem. IEEE (IEEE Profl. Groups, life mem. EMC group), Sigma Xi, Tau Beta Pi, Eta Kappa Nu, Pi Mu Epsilon, Phi Eta Sigma. E-mail: grayhj@dca.net.

GRAY, HAZEL IRENE, retired special education educator, counselor, consultant; b. Van Nuys, Calif., July 2, 1921; d. Charles Clayton Cramer and Ida Mae (Leffler); m. Reed A. Gray; children: Mildred Lorene, Paul Charles; m. Neil Chapin Smith (dec.). BA, San Jose (Calif.) State Coll., 1964, MA, 1968; EdD, U. So. Calif., LA, 1977. Itinerant tchr. hearing impaired Santa Cruz County Office of Edn., 1964—66; resource specialist Santa Cruz Pub. Schools, 1966—68; psychologist Santa Cruz County Office of Edn., 1968—71; psychologist, cons. and parent counselor Project Idea, San Jose, 1971—72; dir. spl. edn. Live Oaks schs. Santa Cruz County Office of Edn., 1972—74; cons. Calif. State Dept. of Edn., Sacramento, 1975—76; adminstr. San Jose City Coll., 1976—78; dir. pupil pers. Campbell Union Sch. Dist., Calif., 1978; pvt. practice marriage counseling, 1971—. Cons. Catholic Pre-Sch., LA; lectr. Calif. State U, San Jose, U. Calif., Santa Clara, Santa Cruz; with Med. Info. Svcs. Co-author: (book) Behavior Modification, 1971. Mem. rescue Calif. Coast Guard, 1971—76; rev. applicants marriage family and child counseling licenses Calif. State Dept. of Licensing, Sacramento. Mem.: San Jose Movie TC Club, Camera Club. Republican. Mem. Lds Ch. Avocations: travel, photography, grandchildren.

GRAY, HELEN THERESA GOTT, religion editor; b. Jersey City, July 2, 1942; d. William E. and Cynthia B. (Williams) Gott; m. David L. Gray, Aug. 15, 1976; 1 child, David Lee Jr. BA, Syracuse U., 1963; M in Internat. Affairs, Columbia U., 1965. Editor religion sect. The Kansas City (Mo.) Star, 1971—; owner Pub. Co. and Christian Bookstore. Tchr. Bible sch. Pleasant Green Bapt. Ch., Kansas City, Kans., 1975—, counselor, 1978—. Co-author, editor several books; contbr. articles. Recipient writing award Valley Forge Freedom Found., 1967-97; John Hay Whitney Found. grantee, 1963-64; named 100 Most Influential African Ams. in Greater Kansas City. Mem. Religion Newswriters Assn., Kansas City Assn. Black Journalists (life achievement award 1998). Baptist. Office: The Kansas City Star 1729 Grand Blvd Kansas City MO 64108-1458 E-mail: hgray@kcstar.com.

GRAY, HERBERT ESER (THE RIGHT HONOURABLE HERBERT GRAY), former federal official; b. Windsor, Ont., Can., May 25, 1931; s. Harry and Fannie Gray; m. Sharon Sholzberg, July 23, 1967; children: Jonathan, Elizabeth Anne. Student, Kennedy Coll. Inst., Windsor; postgrad., McGill U. Grad. Sch. Commerce, Que., Osgoode Hall Law Sch., Toronto. Mem. Ho. of Commons for Windsor W., Ottawa, Canada, 1962—2002. Chmn. standing com. on fin., trade and econ. affairs Ho. of Commons, Ottawa, 1966—68, served as parliamentary sec. to Min. of Fin., 1968—69, named min. without portfolio, 1969, min. of nat. revenue, 1970—72, min. of consumer and corp. affairs, 1972—74, min. of industry, trade and commerce, 1980—82, min. regional econ. expansion, 1982—84, pres. of Treasury Bd., 1982—84, opposition ho. leader, 1984—90, dep. leader opposition, 1989—90, leader opposition, 1990, fin. critic off. opposition, 1991—93, leader gov. Ho. of Commons, solicitor gen. of Can., 1993—97; dep. prime min. Canada, Ottawa, 1997—2002; min. Millennium Bur. Can., Ottawa, 1998—2002; chair Can. section Internat. Joint Commn., 2002—. Apptd. spl. rep. Indian residential schs. Office of Indian Residential Schs. Resolution of Can., Ottawa, 2000—; mem. Can. dels. to various internat. confs. on econ. and other matters; del. IMF and World Bank, 1967, 1969, 1970; co-chmn. Can. del. OECD Ministerial, 1970; leader Can. del. Commonwealth Fin. Mins., 1970. Mem.: Jaycees (pres. Windsor sect. 1961—62), Richelieu Club, Rotary (hon.), B'nai B'rith Lodge. Office: Internat Joint Commn 234 Laurier Ave West 22nd fl Ottawa ON Canada K1P 6K6

GRAY, INA TURNER, fraternal organization administrator; b. Eagleville, Mo., July 25, 1926; d. Farris T. and Teloir (Anderson) Turner; m. Wallace G. Gray Jr., Dec. 18, 1948; children: Toni Jo, Tara Joy. BS with high honors, Cen. Meth. Coll., 1948; MA, Scarritt Coll., 1952; postgrad., U. Hawaii, 1969. Tchr. Rutherford-Met. Sch. Bus., Dallas, 1948-49; dir. Christian edn. 1st Meth. Ch., Lawton, Okla., 1953-54, Winfield, Kans., 1957-58; dir. religious life Southwestern Coll., Winfield, 1958-59; dir. commn. on archives and history Kans. West Conf., Winfield, 1960-78; exec. dir. Pi Gamma Mu, Winfield, 1976-96. English tchr. JoGakuin Jr. High, Hiroshima, Japan, 1971-72, Kitakyushu U., Japan, 1997-98. Mem. editorial bd. Fire on the Prairie, 1961-69; mem. editorial and pub. coms. The Lure of Kansas, 1990. Mem. Assn. Coll. Honor Socs. (del. 1986-96), Commn. Archives and History (local Ch. History award 1982—), Kans. State Assn. Parliamentarians (v.p. Walnut Valley unit 1991-92, 99-2000), Faculty Dames (pres. 1981-82). Republican. Avocations: travel, historical research, Japanese flower arranging. Home: 1701 Winfield Ave Winfield KS 67156-1919 E-mail: gray@sckans.edu.

GRAY, J. R. state representative; b. Eddyville, Ky, July 17, 1938; m. Yvonne Gray; 2 children. Grad., Am. Sch., Chgo., Ill.; Journeyman Machinist Apprenticeship, 1963; diploma, Lyon County HS, 1956. State Rep. House of Rep., Dist. 6, 1996—; pres. Gray Consulting, Inc., 1988—; lobbyist, cons., 1988—94; Rels. State Rep. Gov. and Labor Mgmt., 1976—89; dir. Bus. Rep. IAM & AW (AFL-CIO), 1967—86. Mem. Econ. Devel. & Tourism, Energy; chair Labor & Industry; mem. Local Gov., Veterans Affairs. Mem.: Dem. Party Exec. Comm., Marshall County Dem. Party, Ky. Ctrl. Comm. Democrat. Christian. Office: Capitol Capitol Annex Rm 324D Frankfort KY 40601 also: Dist 3188 Mayfield Hwy Benton KY 42025*

GRAY, JAMES, English literature educator; b. Montrose, Scotland, May 11, 1923; s. James and Matilda (Smythe) G.; m. Pamela Doris Knight, July 26, 1947; 1 child, Caroline Gordon MA, U. Aberdeen, 1946; BA with honours, U. Oxford, Eng., 1948, MA, 1951; PhD, U. Montreal, 1970. Prof. English Bishops U., Lennoxville, Que., Can., 1948-72, chmn. humanities div., 1971-72; prof., chmn. dept. English Dalhousie U., Halifax, N.S., 1972-75, dean Faculty Arts and Sci., 1975-80, Thomas McCulloch prof. English, 1980-88, prof. emeritus, 1988—. Mem. Humanities Rsch. Coun. Can.; vis. prof. Queen's U., Kingston, Ont., 1955, 70, U. B.C., 1958, Acadia U., 1991. Author: The Sermons of Samuel Johnson: A Study, 1972, Dr. Johnson's French, 1986, Miracles in the 18th

Century, 2002, Dr. Johnson's Oxford, 2003; co-editor: The Religious Writings of Samuel Johnson, 1978; mem. editl. bd. Yale U. Press edit. Works of Samuel Johnson, The Age of Johnson; contbr. articles to profl. jours. Served with Brit. and Indian Armies, 1942-46. Recipient Queen Elizabeth II Coronation medal, Jubilee medal. Fellow Royal Soc. Arts, Royal Soc. Can.; mem. Can. Inst. Internat. Affairs (br. pres.), MLA, English Inst., Am. Assn. for Eighteenth Century Studies, Can. Assn. for Eighteenth Century Studies, Internat. Assn. for Eighteenth Century Studies, Assn. Can. Univ. Tchrs. English (pres. 1982-84), Humanities Assn. Can. (past pres.) Mem. Liberal Party. Presbyterian. Club: University Faculty. Home: Ward MTN RR 2 3856 Prospect Rd Kentville NS Canada B4N 3V8 Office: Dalhousie U Dept English Halifax NS Canada B3H 3J5 E-mail: jgray000@ns.sympatico.ca.

GRAY, JAMES GORDON, JR., speech educator; b. Bedford, Va., Oct. 3, 1945; s. James and Cova Iris (Dooley) G. BA, U. Richmond, 1969; MA, Am. U., 1976. Prof. speech comm. Montgomery Coll., Germantown, Md., 1986—. Author: Technical Presentations, 1986, Managing Corporate Image, 1986, The Winning Image, 1993. Republican. Episcopalian. Avocations: astronomy, writing. Home: 7510 Old Chester Rd Bethesda MD 20817-6163

GRAY, JAMES H., JR., music educator; b. Columbus, Ohio, June 8, 1962; m. Elizabeth C. Dinkeloo, July 15, 1990; children: Sarah E., Larina C., Kelsey E. MusB in Edn., Ea. Ky. U., 1985. Dir. Band and Orch. Dublin Scioto H.S., Dublin, Ohio, 1995—; dir. band Davis Mid. Sch., Dublin, 1988—95. Mem.: Music Educators Nat. Conf. Republican. Office: Dublin Scioto High School 4000 Hard Rd Dublin OH 43016

GRAY, JAMES L. investment company executive; b. Jackson, Mich., Apr. 10, 1948; s. Biscoe LaFayette, Jr. and Margaret Anne (Hurley) G.; M. Mary Elizabeth Gaynon, Mar. 2, 1968 (div. July 1978); 1 child, Bennett Lee; m. Christine J. Smith, July 16, 1994. BA in History, U. Wis., 1972, MA in History, 1974, MA in Libr. Sci., 1975; MBA, Am. Grad. Sch. of Internat. Mgmt., Glendale, Ariz., 1977; JD, So. Tex. Coll. Law Texas A&M U., Houston, Tex., 1986. Trust officer Southwest Fla. Banks, Inc., Fort Myers, Fla., 1977-80; assoc. nat. trust examiner U.S. Treasury Dept./Comptroller of the Currency, Washington, 1980-82; asst. v.p. First City Nat. Bank of Houston, 1982-88; sr. v.p., mgr. trust divsn. First Nat. Bank in Albuquerque, 1988-92; chief operating officer MFR, Inc., N.Y.C., 1992-94; 1st v.p. Concord Holding Corp., N.Y.C., 1994-95; sr. v.p. Schroder Fund Advisors, N.Y.C., 1995-99; v.p. Schroder Capital Mgmt./Internat. Inc.; sr. v.p. Brandywine Asset Mgmt., Inc., Wilmington, Del., 1999-2000; mng. dir. Scudder pvt. investment counsel Deutsche Investment Mgmt., N.Y.C., 2000—. Bd. dirs. N.Mex. Estate Planning Coun., Albuquerque, 1989-92. Author: The Southwest Securities Transfer Association Reference Manual, 1985. Bd. dirs. Presbyn. Healthcare Found., Albuquerque, 1990-92, N.Mex. Repertory Theater, Albuquerque, 1989-92. Mem. SR, SAR (treas. N.Y. treas. 1997—), Union Club/N.Y., West Side Tennis Club, River Club. Episcopalian. Avocations: tennis, swimming, golf, gardening, history. Home: 240 E 47th St Apt 31E New York NY 10017-2138 also: 59 Pheasant Close W Southampton NY 11968-3062 Office: Scudder Investments Inc 345 Park Ave New York NY 10154 E-mail: james.gray@db.com.

GRAY, JAMES LARRY, international business executive; b. Southmayd, Tex., Dec. 17, 1932; s. Cecil Lawray and Coquese Adeline (Coe) G. Student, Tex. Tech. U., 1954, So. Meth. U., 1956; MBA, Pepperdine U., 1978. Sales engr. Simplex Wire & Cable, Cambridge, Mass., 1958-63; pres. Integral Corp., Dallas, 1963-97, Cern Internat. Corp., 1997—; CEO Zylec Corp., 2000—. Served with U.S. Army, 1956-58. Mem. IEEE, Sigma Alpha Epsilon. Clubs: Toastmasters (pres. 1966-67), Jaycees (v.p. 1969-70). Republican. Office: 3535A Routh St Dallas TX 75219-4731

GRAY, JAMES PATRICK, business executive, consultant, educator; b. Yonkers, N.Y., Oct. 27, 1958; s. James and Joan Frances (Saverese) G.; m. Lucy Marie Simoncic, July 26, 1985. BIE, Cleve. State U., 1982; MBA, Case Western Reserve U., 1987. Indsl. engr., project mgr. TRW, Inc., Cleve., 1980-87; gen. mgr. Ajax Mfg., Cleve., 1988-92; prin. J. P. Gray & Assocs., Chesterland, Ohio, 1991—; v.p. bus. devel. The Mentor Group, Mentor, Ohio, 1993—95; dir., mgmt. cons. SMR & Co. Bus. Svcs., Mayfield Village, Ohio, 1996-2001; COO Jet Inc., Cleve., 2001—02; dir. performance improvement DKW Value Recovery, LLC, Cleve., 2002—. Advisor Cleve. Coun. Smaller Enterprises, 1987—; contbr. Penton Pub., Cleve., 1992-98; adj. prof. engring. Lakeland C.C., Kirtland, 1993—; bd. dirs. Cardinal Cmty. Credit Union, Mentor. Mem. fin. com. Kirtland Sch. Mem. Inst. Indsl. Engr. (sr.), Am. Soc. for Quality (cert.), Inst. Mgmt. Cons., Turnaround Mgmt. Assn. (treas. Cleve. chpt.). Office: 26th Fl BP Tower 200 Public Sq Cleveland OH 44114 E-mail: jgray@dkwvaluerecovery.com.

GRAY, JAN CHARLES, lawyer, business owner; b. Des Moines, June 15, 1947; s. Charles Donald and Mary C. Gray; 1 child, Charles Jan. BA in Econs., U. Calif., Berkeley, 1969; MBA, Pepperdine U., 1986; JD, Harvard U., 1972. Bar: Calif. 1972, D.C. 1974, Wyo. 1992. Law clk. Kindel & Anderson, L.A., 1971-72; assoc. Halstead, Baker & Sterling, L.A., 1972-75; sr. v.p., gen. counsel and sec. Ralphs Grocery Co., L.A., 1975-97; pres. Am. Presidents Resorts, Custer, S.D., Casper/Glenrock, Wyo., 1983—; owner Big Bear (Calif.) Cabins-Lakeside, 1988—; pres. Mt. Rushmore Broadcasting, Inc., 1991—; owner Sta. KGOS/KERM, Torrington, Wyo., 1993—, Sta. KRAL/KIQZ, Rawlins, Wyo., 1995—, Sta. KZMX, Hot Springs, S.D., 1993—, Sta. KFCR, Custer, S.D., 1992—, Sta. KQLT-FM, Casper, Wyo., 1994—, Sta. KASS-FM, Casper, 1995—, Sta. KVOC-AM, Casper, 1997—, KAWK-FM, Rapid City, S.D., 1997—, KHOC, Casper, Wyo., 1998—, Mt. Rushmore Farm Horse Racing, 1999—. Judge pro tem L.A. Mcpl. Ct., 1977-85; instr. bus. UCLA, 1976-85, Pepperdine MBA Program, 1983-85; arbitrator Am. Arbitration Assn., 1977-97; media spokesman So. Calif. Grocers Assn., 1979-90, Calif. Grocers Assn., 1979-97, Calif. Retailers Assn., 1979-97; real estate broker, Calif., 1973—. Contbg. author: Life or Death, Who Controls?, 1976; contbr. articles to profl. jours. Trustee South Bay U. Coll. Law, 1978-79, mem. bd. visitors Southwestern U. Sch. Law, 1983—; mem. L.A. County Pvt. Industry Coun., 1982-96, exec. com. 1984-88, chmn. econ. devel. task force, 1986-89, chmn. mktg. com. 1991-93; mem. L.A. County Martin Luther King, Jr. Gen. Hosp. Authority, 1984—; mem. L.A. County Aviation Commn, 1986-92, chmn., 1990-91; L.A. Police Crime Prevention Adv. Coun., 1986—; Angelus Plaza Adv. Bd., 1983-85; bd. dirs. RecyCAL of So. Calif., 1983-89; trustee Santa Monica Hosp. Found., 1986-91, adv. bd., 1991—; mem. L.A. County Dem. Cen. Com., 1980-90, L.A. City Employees' Retirement System Commn., 1993—; del. Dem. Nat. Conv., 1980. Recipient So. Calif. Grocers Assn. award for outstanding contbn. to food industry, 1982, appreciation award for No on 11 Campaign, Calif./Nev. Soft Drink Assn., 1983; Tyler Price Meml. award Mex.-Am. Grocers Assn., 1995, Radio Affiliate of Yr.-Classic Rock ABC, 1998. Mem.: Casper Country Club, Petroleum Club, L.A. Athletic Club, Harvard Club of So. Calif., Ephebian Soc. L.A., U. Calif. Alumni Assn., Town Hall L.A., So. Calif. Bus. Assn. (bd. dirs. 1981—99, mem. exec. com. 1982—99, sec. 1986—91, chair 1991—98), Food Mktg. Inst. (govt. rels. com. 1977—97, chmn.lawyers, economists 1993—95, benefits coun. 1993—97), Calif. Retailers Assn. (supermarket com.), L.A. World Affairs Coun., L.A. Pub. Affairs Officers Assn., San Fernando Valley Bar Assn. (chmn. real property sect. 1975—77), L.A. County Bar Assn. (exec. com. corp. law depts. sect. 0179—, exec. com. barristers sect. 1974—75, exec. com. corp. law depts. sect. 1974—76, exec. com. barristers sect. 1979—81, chmn. 1989—90, trustee 1991—93, jud. evaluation com. 1993—, nominating com. 1994), Calif. Bar Assn., ABA, Phi Beta Kappa. Home: 2793 Creston Dr Los Angeles CA 90068-2209 Office: PO Box 2515 Casper WY 82602-2515

GRAY, JANET D. piano teacher, organist; b. Jackson, Miss., Aug. 7, 1936; d. Homer Bowman Davis and Velma Mary Hughes; m. Herman Lafayette Gray, June 22, 1957; children: Linda Carol Wofford, Mary Ellen Donaldson, Glen Davis(dec.), David Eugene. BS, Miss. State Coll. for Women, 1957. Lic. tchr. Tchr. English, speech Memphis City Schs., 1957-58; sec. 1st United Meth. Ch., Corinth, Miss., 1958-61; sec., bookkeeper Chism, Jones & Gray, CPAs, Corinth, 1959-62; piano tchr. Corinth, 1959—. Adjudicator Fedn. Music Clubs, 1980—, Germantown Piano Tchrs., Germantown, Tenn., 1985—; pianist, asst. organist 1st UMC. Founder Corinth Piano Tchrs. Forum, Children's Elem. Choir, 1968; dir., organizer Wesley Choir, 1972, Alethia Youth Choir, 1985; pres., v.p., treas. com. Nat. Assn. Jr. Aux., Greenville, Miss., 1977—87, Corinth Jr. Aux., 1965—75; chmn. Corinth Libr. Commn., 1985—95, neighborhood chmn., coun. com. Prairie Girl Scout Coun., Tupelo, Miss., 1982—90. Named Outstanding Citizen, Corinth Jr. Aux., 1994. Mem.: Corinth Music Club, Miss. Fedn. Music Clubs (v.p. 1996—98), NE Miss. Mus. Assn. (bd. dirs., treas. 1985—), Miss. Music Tchrs. Assn. (editor 1998—2002, treas. 2002—, v.p.), Nat. Guild Piano Tchrs. (adjudicator 1975—), Nat. Music Tchrs. Assn. Avocations: tennis, photography. Home: 4176 Harper Rd Corinth MS 38834-2908

GRAY, JOHN LEONARD, retired lawyer; b. N.Y.C., Feb. 14, 1924; s. James E. and Edna M. Gray; m. Margaret S. Gray, Aug. 23, 1947 (div. Jan. 1976); children: Linda S., James S.; m. Elizabeth Z. Gray, Apr. 24, 1976. BChE, Pratt Inst., N.Y.C., 1943; JD, Albany Law Sch., 1948. Bar: N.Y. 1951, Ohio 1951. Patent counsel, gen. counsel Battelle Meml. Inst., Columbus, Ohio, 1949-72; ptnr. Kegler Brown Hill & Ritter, Columbus, 1972-89, of counsel, 1989—. V.p. Battelle Devel. Corp., Scientific Advances Inc. Lt. (j.g.) USN, 1943-46, PTO, ATO. Mem.: Navy League (bd. dirs. 1990—2002), Ohio C. of C. (bd. dirs., exec. com. 1994—), Rotary (pres. 1994—95). E-mail: grayjl@keglerbrown.com.

GRAY, JOHN WALKER, mathematician, educator; b. St. Paul, Oct. 3, 1931; s. Clarence Walker and Helen (Ewald) G.; m. Eva Maria Wirth, Dec. 30, 1957; children— Stephen, Theodore, Elisabeth. BA, Swarthmore Coll., 1953; PhD, Stanford U., 1957. Temp. mem. Inst. for Advanced Study, Princeton, N.J., 1957-59; Ritt instr. Columbia U., 1959-62; asst. prof. math. U. Ill., Urbana, 1962-64, asso. prof., 1964-66, prof., 1966—, dir. grad. studies, 1995—2000, prof. emeritus, 2000—. Organizer Category Theory Session, Oberwolfach, Germany, 1971, 72, 73, 75, 77, 79 Contbr. to: Springer Lecture Notes in Mathematics, 1974. NSF sr. fellow, 1966-67; Fulbright-Hays sr. lectr., 1975-76 Mem. Am. Math. Soc., AAAS. Home: 303 W Michigan Ave Urbana IL 61801-4945 Office: U Ill Dept Math Urbana IL 61801

GRAY, JUDITH A. retired school librarian, educator; b. Pitts., Nov. 30, 1942; d. John and Helen Ondich; m. N. Gordon Gray, June 13, 1964; 1 child, Ameena. BS in Edn., Indiana U. Pa., 1963; MLS, U. Pitts., 1964. Cert. sch. libr., pub. libr., secondary tchr. English, N.Y. Peace Corps vol., libr. Tanzanian Nat. Libr., 1964-67; reference libr. Syracuse U., 1967; sch. libr. H.W. Smith Jr. H.S., Syracuse, N.Y., 1967-69; substitute tchr. Syracuse City Sch. Dist., 1971-72; sch. libr. Nottingham H.S., Syracuse, 1972—2001. Pres. coun. Good Shepherd Luth. Ch., Fayetteville, N.Y., 1988-89. Mem. Peoples Choice award for photography N.Y. State Fair, 1987. Mem. ALA, N.Y. Libr. Assn. (bd. dirs. sch. libr. media sect. 1988-92, pres. 1992-93), Am. Assn. Sch. Librs. (nat. guidelines revision com. 1995-98), Librs. Unltd. (sec. 1998-2000, pres. 2000-01), Syracuse Tchrs. Assn. (chair elections com. 1974-2001), Monday Evening Club (historian 1996—). Avocations: gardening, hiking and camping, knitting, photography, traveling. Home: 302 Pleasant St Manlius NY 13104-1816

GRAY, KAREN KAY, counselor; b. Tulsa, Okla., Aug. 5, 1957; d. Bobby Ray Phillipe and Ruth Marie Kay. BS in Mktg. & Econ., Okla. State U., 1979, MS in Recreation Adminstrn., 1980. Cert. drug and alcohol profl. counselor Okla.; therapeutic recreation specialist Nat. Coun. for Therapeutic Recreation Cert., internat. cert. alcohol and drug counselor. Recreation therapist Rader Children's Ctr., Sand Springs, Okla., 1981—89, St. John Med. Ctr., Tulsa, Okla., 1989—. Mem. adv. bd. Tulsa C. C., Tulsa, 1999—; bd. mem. Therapeutic Recreation Symposium of S.W., chmn., 1997—99. Mem. Gov.'s Adv. Coun. on Homeless, Okla. City, Okla., 2000—; precinct chmn. Rep. Party, Tulsa, 2000—. Mem.: LWV (mem. mental health com. 2000—, spkrs. bureau 2000—, bd. dirs. 2002—, edn. com. 2002—), Mental Health Assn. (edn. com. 1998—). Republican. Mem. United Ch. Of Christ. Avocations: reading, tennis, soccer, yardwork. Home: 1452 N Evanston Ave Tulsa OK 74110-4814 Office: St John Medical Ctr 1923 S Utica Ave Tulsa OK 74104 Fax: 918-744-3505.

GRAY, KARLA MARIE, state supreme court chief justice; b. May 10, 1947; BA, MA in African History, Western Mich. U.; JD, Hastings Coll. of Law, San Francisco, 1976. Bar: Mont. 1976, Calif. 1977. Law clk. to Hon. W. D. Murray U.S. Dist. Ct., 1976-77; staff atty. Atlantic Richfield Co., 1977-81; pvt. practice law Butte, Mont., 1981-84; staff atty., legis. lobbyist Mont. Power Co., Butte, 1984-91; justice Supreme Ct. Mont., Helena, 1991-2000, chief justice, 2000—. Mem. Mont. Supreme Ct. Gender Fairness Task Force. Fellow Am. Bar Found., Am. Judicature Soc., Internat. Women's Forum; mem. State Bar Mont., Silver Bow County Bar Assn. (past pres.), Nat. Assn. Women Judges. Avocations: travel, reading, piano, family genealogy, cross-country skiing. Office: Supreme Ct Mont PO Box 203001 Helena MT 59620-3001*

GRAY, KATHERINE, marriage, family and child therapist, writer, educator; b. L.A., July 6, 1941; d. Edward David and Marjorie Ross; m. Daniel C. Gray, Feb. 5, 1965; children: Michael, Lisa. BA, Calif. State U., Sacramento, 1983; MS in Edn. Cons. and Counseling, MS in Sch. Counseling, Calif. State U., 1987, EdD in Counseling Psychology, 1997. Lic. MFCT. Instr. Shasta Coll., Redding, Calif., 1965-69; owner Water Ojai (Calif.) Valley Chapel, 1971-77, Lipp & Sullivan, Marysville, Calif., 1978—. Instr. Yuba Coll., 1988—; pres. Interagy. Coun., 1988—; cons. and organizer various cmty. outreach programs in edn. Contbr. articles to profl. jours. and newspapers. County coord., bd. dirs. Am. Cancer Soc., Marysville, 1980—; mem. exec. com., bd. dirs., com. chairperson Gateway Projects, Yuba City, Calif., 1980—; bd. dirs. Mercy Guild, Yuba City, 1980—, Easter Seals; past bd. dirs., com. chairperson Campfire, Inc., Yuba City and Morro Bay, Calif., 1979-80; past pres. Ojai Valley-Oxnard Symphony Orch. Assn., Ventura County, Calif., 1975; Sacramento focus program coord. 4-H, Yuba and Sutter Counties, 1985—; exec. officer, bd. dirs. Gateway Projects, 1985-87; pres. Interagy. Coun. of Yuba and Sutter Counties, 1988—. Recipient, Presdl. Awd. for Outstanding Performance and Contribution of Svc., awds. granted for svc. on bd. and as an ofcr. on grad. stud. counc. and numerous univ. coms., Lipp & Sullivan. Mem. Calif. Funeral Dirs. Assn. (mem. legis. bd. com., edn., ethics and mem. bd. com.), Calif. Assn. for Counseling and Devel., Sacramento Area Gifted Assn., Children's Home Soc. (chpt. bd. sec.), Soroptimists (officer, bd. dirs.), Rainbow for Girls (pres., bd. dirs. 1985-87). Avocations: music, art, travel, historical studies. Home: PO Box 611 Yuba City CA 95992-0611 Office: PO Box 148 629 D St Marysville CA 95901-5527

GRAY, KATHLEEN ANN, lawyer; b. Reading, Pa., May 16, 1947; d. Sebastian and Helen Mary)Zajac) Vespico; m. George A. Gray, Oct. 22, 1966 (dec. 1968). BSBA, Drexel U., 1971, MBA, 1978; JD, Wake Forest U., 1977. Bar: Pa. 1977. Computer programmer Ednl. Testing Svc., Princeton, N.J., 1971-73, dir. EDP tng., 1973-74; assoc. Barley, Snyder, Cooper & Barber, Lancaster, Pa., 1977-83; ptnr. Barley, Snyder, Senft & Cohen, Lancaster, Pa., 1983—. Mem. Wake Forest Law Rev., 1975-77. Bd. dirs. Hist. Preservation Trust of Lancaster County, 1978-88, v.p., 1984; sec. bd. dirs. Lancaster Integrated Specialized Transp. Sys., 1981-85; bd. dirs. Am. Lung Assn. of Lancaster and Berks Counties, 1982-99, v.p., 1987-90, pres., 1994-96; bd. dirs. Leadership Lancaster, 1983-92, Lancaster Pub. Libr., 1987-90, Am. Lung Assn. Pa., 1993-98; sec. bd. dirs. Found. Lancaster Chamber, 1985-96, v.p., 1997-98, pres., 1999-2000; chmn. Lancaster County Parks and Open Space Funding Task Force, 1989-90. Mem. ABA, Nat. Assn. Bond Lawyers, Pa. Bar Assn., Pa. Assn. Bond Lawyers (bd. dirs., sec. 1988-94), Lancaster County Bar Assn., Jr. League of Lancaster (sustaining). Republican. Office: Barley Snyder Senft & Cohen 126 E King St Lancaster PA 17602-2832

GRAY, LILLIA ANN, lawyer; b. Miami, Fla., Aug. 18, 1955; d. Elbert Lewis and Lillia Irene (Aschiero) G. AA, Miami-Dade Community Coll., 1976; BA summa cum laude, Cen. Wesleyan Coll., 1979; JD, U. S.C., 1984. Bar: S.C., Ga. Shareholder Cooper, Coffas, Moore and Gray, P.A. Life mem. Girl Scouts of Am. Mem. Ga. State Bar Assn., Comml. Law League, S.C. Bar Assn., S.C. Bankruptcy Law Assn., S.C. Women Lawyers Assn., Fed. Bar Assn.

GRAY, LORETTA, language educator; b. Rochester, Minn., Dec. 28, 1959; d. Maynard H. Gray and Gessner Catherine; m. Robert Schnelle, June 22, 1985; 1 child, Erik. BA, Coll. of St. Catherine, St. Paul, 1982; MA in Tchg., Sch. for Internat. Tng., 1983; MA, Middlebury Coll., 1990; PhD, Boston U., 1993. Instr. U. So. Calif., Madrid, 1983—84, Putney (Vt.) Sch., 1991—93; tchr. Edward Devotion Sch., Brookline, Mass., 1984—85, Waterville Valley (NH) Acad., 1985—87; lectr. Clemson (SC) U., 1987—89, Sch. for Internat. Tng., Brattleboro, Vt., 1991—92; prof. English Ctrl. Wash. U., Ellensburg, 1992—. Cons. in field. Author: Idiomatic English, 2000, The Writer's Harbrace Hendbook, 2003. Mem. City of Ellensburg Environ. Commn., 1995—99; vol. Kittitas Environ. Edn. Network, Kittitas County, Wash., 1999—. Mellon grad. fellow, Literacias Inst., Newton, Mass., 1991. Mem.: Tchrs. of English to Spkrs. of Other Langs., Nat. Coun. Tchrs. of English (Affiliate Jour. award 1998), Assembly for Tchg. of English Grammar. Achievements include research in revival of grammar teaching in the English curriculum. Avocations: mountaineering, nature study, travel, music. Office: Ctrl Wash U Dept English 8th Ave Ellensburg WA 98926 E-mail: grayl@cwu.edu.

GRAY, LORI ANN, psychologist, researcher, educator; b. Saginaw, Mich., Apr. 15, 1972; d. Gary James Gray and Mae Gray Diane. B.Mus. Arts in Trumpet Performance, BA in Psychology, U. Mich., 1995; MA in Counseling Psychology, Western Mich. U., 1998; PhD in Counseling Psychology, Mich. State U., 2003. Cert. clin. hypnotherapist; lic. holistic healthcare worker. Instr. Mich. State U., East Lansing, 1998—2002, Western Mich. U., Kalamazoo, 1998—, doctoral intern, 2002—. Adj. lectr. music U. Mich., Flint. U. Mich. Music scholar, 1990, Mich. Tchrs. Assn. scholar, 1990, Mich. Competetive scholar, State of Mich. Dept. Edu., 1991—93, Grad. Student scholar, Western Mich. U., 1998—99, Grad. fellow, Mich. State U., 1998—99, The Milt Cudney Meml. scholar, Western Mich. U., 2002—03.

GRAY, MARVIN LEE, JR., lawyer; b. Pitts., May 9, 1945; s. Marvin L. and Frances (Stringfellow) G.; m. Jill Miller, Aug. 14, 1971; children: Elizabeth Ann, Carolyn Jill. AB, Princeton U., 1966; JD magna cum laude, Harvard U., 1969. Bar: Wash. 1973, U.S. Supreme Ct. 1977, Alaska 1984. Law clk. to judge U.S. Ct. Appeals, N.Y.C., 1969-70; law clk. to justice U.S. Supreme Ct., Washington, 1970-71; asst. U.S. atty. U.S. Dept. Justice, Seattle, 1973-76; ptnr. Davis Wright Tremaine, Seattle, 1976—, mng. ptnr., 1985-88. Staff counsel Rockefeller Commn. on CIA Activities in U.S., Washington, 1974; lectr. trial practice U. Wash. Law Sch., Seattle, 1979-80. Lay reader Episcopal Ch. of Ascension, Seattle, 1982-94. Capt. USAF, 1971-73. Fellow Am. Coll. Trial Lawyers; mem. ABA, Am. Law Inst. Office: Davis Wright Tremaine 1501 4th Ave Ste 2600 Seattle WA 98101-1688

GRAY, MARY JANE, obstetrician gynecologist; b. Columbus, Ohio, June 13, 1924; BA, Swarthmore Coll., 1945; MD, Wash. U., 1949; DS, Columbia U., 1954. Diplomate Am. Bd. Ob-Gyn. Intern Barnes Hosp., St. Louis, 1949-50; resident in ob-gyn. Presbyn. Hosp., N.Y.C., 1950-56; fellow Columbia U., 1953—54, instr., 1956-60; asst. prof. ob-gyn. Coll. Medicine U. Vermont, 1960-63, assoc. prof., 1963-69, prof., 1969-76; adj. prof. U. N.C., 1976-85, prof., asst. dean Coll. Medicine, 1985-90, prof. emeritus ob-gyn., 1990—. Mem. AMA, Am. Coll. Ob-Gyn., Soc. Gynecol. Investigation.

GRAY, MARY WHEAT, statistician, lawyer; b. Hastings, Nebr., 1939; d. Neil C. and Lillie W. (Alves) Wheat; m. Alfred Gray, Aug. 20, 1964. AB summa cum laude, Hastings Coll., 1959; postgrad., J.W. Goethe U., Frankfurt, Fed. Republic Germany, 1959-60; MA, U. Kans., 1962, PhD, 1964; JD summa cum laude, Am. U., 1979; LLD (hon.), U. Nebr., 1993; LHD (hon.), Hastings Coll., 1996. Bar: D.C. 1979, U.S. Supreme Ct. 1983, U.S. Dist. Ct., D.C. 1980. Physicist Nat. Bur. Standards, Washington, summers 1959-63, asst. instr. U. Kans., Lawrence, 1963-64; instr. dept. math. U. Calif., Berkeley, 1965; asst. prof. Calif. State U., Hayward, 1965-67, assoc. prof., 1967 68; assoc. prof. dept. math., stats. and computer sci. Am. U., 1968-71, prof., 1971—, chmn. dept., 1977-79, 80-81, 83—; statis. cons. for govt. agys., univs. and pvt. firms, 1976—. Author: A Radical Approach to Algebra, 1970; Calculus with Finite Mathematics for Social Sciences, 1972; contbr. numerous articles to profl. jours. Nat. treas., dir. Women's Equity Action League, from 1981, pres., from 1982; bd. dirs. treas. ACLU, Montgomery County, Md.; mem. adv. com. D.C. Dept. Employment Services, 1983—; dir. Amnesty Internat. USA, 1985—, treas., 1988-93, chair, 1993—; mem. Commn. on Coll. Retirement, 1984-86; bd. dirs. Am.-Middle East Edn. Found., 1983—, chair, 1998—. Recipient U.S. Presdl. award for excellence in sci., engring. and math. mentoring, 2001; Fulbright grantee, 1959-60; NSF fellow, 1963-64, NDEA fellow, 1960-63 Fellow AAAS (chmn. com. on women, com. on investments, com. on sci. freedom and responsibility, Lifetime Mentoring award 1995); mem. AAUP (regional counsel 1984—, com. on acad. freedom 1978—, dir. Legal Def. Fund 1974-78, bd. dirs. Exxon Project on Salary Discrimination 1974-76, com. on status of women 1972-78, Georgina Smith award), Am. Math. Soc. (v.p. 1976-78, coun. 1973-78), Amnesty Internat. (internat. treas. 1995-2001, chair USA 1993-95), Conf. Bd. Math. Scis. (chmn. com. on affirmative action 1977-78), Math. Assn. Am. (chmn. com. on sch. lectrs. 1973-75, vis. lectr. 1974—), Assn. for Women in Math (founding pres. 1971-74, exec. com. 1974-80, gen. counsel 1980—), D.C. Bar Assn., ABA, Am. Soc. Internat. Law, London Math. Soc., Societe de Mathematique de France, Brit. Soc. History of Math., Can. Soc. History of Math., Assn. Computing Machinery, N.Y. Acad. Scis., Am. Statis. Assn., Phi Beta Kappa, Sigma Xi, Phi Kappa Phi, Alpha Chi, Pi Mu Epsilon. Home: 6807 Connecticut Ave Chevy Chase MD 20815-4937 Office: Am U Math & Stats Dept Washington DC 20016 E-mail: mgray@american.edu.

GRAY, MYLES MCCLURE, retired insurance company executive; b. Lansing, Mich., Aug. 28, 1932; s. Carlyle Avery and Lucile (Meitz) G.; m. Marilyn Ida Osberg, Feb. 14, 1953; children: Kathleen (Mrs. Mark Abraham), David, Patricia. BBA with distinction, U. Mich., 1954. Div. mgr. Nat. Life & Accident Ins. Co., Nashville, 1954-58; from asst. actuary to exec. v.p., actuary United Benefit Life Ins. Co., Omaha, 1958-67; v.p., actuary Gen. Reins. Life Corp., N.Y.C., 1967-69, Cal. Western States Life Ins. Co., Sacramento, 1969-74; v.p. Alexander & Alexander, N.Y.C., 1974-75, Nat. Life & Accident Ins. Co., Nashville, 1975-81, NLT Corp., Nashville, 1981-83; sr. v.p., chief actuary Life Investors, Inc., Cedar Rapids, Iowa, 1983-86; v.p. Cal Farm Life Ins. Co., Sacramento, 1986-96; ret., 1996. Cons. in field. Docent Calif. State Railroad Mus., 1996—. Fellow Soc. Actuaries (sec., mem. exec. com. 1977-80, bd. govs. 1977-83); mem. Am. Acad. Actuaries (bd. dirs. 1986-87), Alpha Kappa Psi, Phi Kappa Phi, Beta Gamma Sigma. Republican. Home: 11454 Mother Lode Cir Gold River CA 95670-3042

GRAY, NANCY ANN OLIVER, college administrator; b. Dallas, Apr. 23, 1951; d. Howard Ross and Joan (Dawkins) Oliver; m. David Nelson Maxson, Oct. 5, 1985; children by previous marriage: Paul, Jeff, Scott. BA, Vanderbilt U. (hon.), 1973; MEd, North Tex. State U., 1975; postgrad., Vanderbilt U., 1976-79; PhD (hon.), Presbyterian Coll., 2002. Cert. fund raising exec. Tchr. Highland Park High Sch., Dallas, 1973-75; chmn. drama dept. Harpeth Hall Sch., Nashville, 1975-77; assoc. dir. devel. Vanderbilt U., Nashville, 1977-78, assist. dean students, 1978-80; dir. spl. gifts U. Louisville, 1982-86; dir. major gifts Oberlin (Ohio) Coll., 1986-90; dir. capital programs The Lawrenceville (N.J.) Sch., 1990-91; v.p. devel. and univ. rels. Rider U., Lawrenceville, 1991-98; v.p. sem. rels. Princeton (N.J.) Theol. Sem., 1998-99; pres. Converse Coll., Spartanburg, S.C., 1999—. Trustee Princeton Theol. Sem., 2000—, Spartanburg Day Sch., 2000-2002, Vanderbilt U., Nashville, 1973-77; bd. dirs. Brevard Music Ctr., 1999—; mem. governing bd. Wye Faculty Seminar, 2000—. Home: 488 Connecticut Ave Spartanburg SC 29302-2158 Office: Converse Coll 580 E Main St Spartanburg SC 29302-1931 E-mail: nancy.gray@converse.edu.

GRAY, NEIL HAROLD, healthcare marketing executive; b. Bklyn., July 9, 1952; s. Gerald Alfred and Romina (Barkann) G.; m. Karen Marie Woltman, May 28, 1978; children: Benjamin Jordan, Jonathan Milton, Katherine Landin. AB in History, Lafayette Coll., 1974. Promotion mgr. John Wiley & Sons, N.Y.C., 1974-79; mgr. advt. promotion and direct mail mktg. Holt, Rinehart & Winston divsn. CBS, Inc., N.Y.C., 1979-81; mktg. mgr. Med. Econs. Co., Oradell, N.J., 1981-84; dir. mktg. health professions divsn. McGraw-Hill, N.Y.C., 1984; dir. mktg. Human Rels. Media, Inc., Pleasantville, N.Y., 1984-86, St. Barnabas Med. Ctr., Livingston, N.J., 1986-87; assoc. Interspectrum Group, Advt. and Comm., Bridgewater, Millburn and Lincroft, N.J., 1987; v.p. program planning and devel. Health Learning Sys., Inc., Little Falls, N.J., 1988-91, v.p. sales and mktg., 1991-95; v.p. account mgmt. Physicians World Comm. Group, Secaucus, N.J., 1995-96; sr. v.p., mng. dir. Torre Lazur Healthcare Group, Parsippany, N.J., 1996-99; sr. v.p. strategy and commercial devel. Advanced Clin. Comms., Inc., Lambertville, NJ, 1999—2001; mng. ptnr. Healthcare Trends and Strategies, LLC, Bridgewater, NJ, 1999—2002; exec. v.p. global mktg. and strategy Wolters Kluwer Health-Pharma Solutions divsn., Parsippany, 2002—. Mem. profl./sci./tech. pub.'s mktg. com. Assn. Am. Pubs., N.Y.C., 1981-83. Sec. bd. mgrs. Briarcliff Woods Condominiums, Ossining, N.Y., 1981; coach Bridgewater In-Town Soccer; bd. dirs. Bridgewater Soccer Assn., 1990-96. Mem. Am. Mktg. Assn., Am. Coll. Healthcare Mktg., Acad. for Health

Svcs. Mktg., Lafayette Coll. Alumni Assn. (admissions rep.), Am. Jour. Nursing Co. (bd. dirs. 1990—, fin. com. chair, exec. com.). Avocations: racquet sports, canoeing, gardening, music, cooking. Office: Wolters Kluwer Health Pharma Solutions Divsn 4 Gatehall Dr Parsippany NJ 07054 E-mail: graysters@aol.com.

GRAY, ORVILLE, lawyer, retired judge; b. Great Falls, Mont., Aug. 12, 1920; s. Agustus H. and Ida (Wocasek) G.; m. Harriet Welsh, Oct. 28, 1946; children— Randall H., Jeffrey L. B.A., U. Mont., 1942, LL.B., 1946. Bar: Mont 1942, U.S. Dist. Ct. Mont. 1947, U.S. Supreme Ct. 1964. Dep. county atty. Cascade County, Mont., 1950-54; U.S. bankruptcy judge Dist. of Mont., Great Falls, 1955-84; sr. ptnr. James, Gray & McCafferty, Great Falls, 1977— . Mem. Dist. 1 Sch. Bd., Great Falls, 1961-70. Served to capt., inf. U.S. Army, 1942-46, ETO. Decorated Bronze Star medal, Purple Heart. Mem. Sigma Alpha Epsilon. Club: Rotary. Office: James Gray & McCafferty PO Box 2885 Great Falls MT 59403

GRAY, OSCAR SHALOM, lawyer; b. N.Y.C., Oct. 18, 1926; BA, Yale U., 1948, JD, 1951. Bar: Md. 1951, D.C. 1952, U.S. Supreme Ct. 1952. Atty.-adviser legal adviser's office U.S. Dept. State, Washington, 1951-57; sec. Nuclear Materials and Equipment Corp., Apollo, Pa., 1957-64, treas., 1957-67, v.p., 1964-71, dir., 1964-67; spl. counsel Presdl. Task Force on Communications Policy, Washington, 1967-68; cons. U.S. Dept. Transp., Washington, 1967-68, acting dir. office environ. impact, 1968-70; sole practice Washington, 1970—, Balt., 1971—. Adj. prof., professorial lectr. Law Ctr. Georgetown U., Washington, 1970-71; lectr. Cath. U. Am., Washington, 1970-71; assoc. prof. U. Md., Balt., 1971-74, prof., 1974-93, Jacob A. France prof. of torts, 1993-96, prof. emeritus, 1996—; vis. prof. U. Tenn., 1977. Author: Cases and Materials on Environmental Law, 1970, 2d edit., 1973, supplements, 1974, 1975, 1977; author: (with F. Harper and F. James Jr.) The Law of Torts, 2d edit., 1986; author: 3d edit., vol. 1, 1996; author: (with H. Shulman and F. James Jr.) Cases and Materials on the Law of Torts(with D. Gifford) 4th edit., 2003; contbr. articles to profl. legal jours. Mem.: ABA, D.C. Fedn. of Civic Assns. (parliamentarian 1991—99, 2000—03), D.C. Bar Assn., Am. Law Inst. (adviser Restatement of the Law, Third, Torts: Products Liability), Selden Soc. (state correspondent Md.), Phi Beta Kappa, Order of Coif. Office: 500 W Baltimore St Baltimore MD 21201-1602

GRAY, PATRICIA JOYCE, legal administration; b. Carlsbad, N.Mex., Feb. 5, 1951; d. Owen Corbett and Bobby Jo (Jones) G.; m. Patrick A. Edwards, Oct. 29, 1981 (div. June 1990). Student, U. Nev., Las Vegas, 1974-77. Receptionist, clk. Nationwide Fin., Las Vegas, 1969-70; dep. clk. U.S. Bankruptcy Ct. for Dist. Nev., Las Vegas, 1970-74, chief dep. clk., 1974-75, chief clk., 1975-79, clk. of ct., 1979—. Mem. bankruptcy work measurement subcom. of com. on adminstrn. bankruptcy system Jud. Conf. U.S., 1989-91; mem. tng. and edn. com. U.S. Bankruptcy Cts. Adminstrv. Office U.S. Cts., 1990-91; mem. Bankruptcy Work Measurement subcom. of Clerk's adv. com. Adminstrv. Office U.S. Cts., 1992-93, local rules subcom. Dist. Nev., 1991—. Mem. Space and Facilities Ad Hoc Task Force on Personnel of Adminstrv. Office of U.S. Cts., 1994-95, 9th Cir. Task Force on Race, Religious, and Ethnic Fairness, 1994-97; mem. bd. dirs. of Clark County, Nev. chpt. ARC, 1994-98. Mem. Nat. Conf. Bankruptcy Clks., Fed. Ct. Clks. Assn. Rebublican. Avocations: reading, pottery, gardening. Office: US Bankruptcy Ct Lloyd D George US Courthouse 333 Las Vegas Blvd S Las Vegas NV 89101-5833

GRAY, PAUL BRYAN, lawyer, historian, arbitrator; b. L.A., Apr. 10, 1938; s. Sylvester Bryan and Alice Esther (Flick) G.; m. Dorothy Jo Knorpp, Aug. 13, 1963 (div. May 1977); children: Christopher, Mark; m. Felipa Rios, July 31, 1987. JD, Hastings Coll. Law, U. Calif., San Francisco, 1968. Assoc. Unthoff, Gomez Vega and Unthoff, Mexico City, 1968-70; pvt. practice, South El Monte, Calif., 1970-93, Claremont, Calif., 1993—. Judge pro tem Mcpl. Ct. L.A., 1975—; arbitrator Superior Ct. L.A., 1990—. Author: Forster v. Pico: The Struggle for the Rancho Santa Margarita, 1997. Reader The Huntington Libr., San Marino, Calif., 1985—. Office: 250 W 1st St Ste 318 Claremont CA 91711-4740

GRAY, PAUL EDWARD, academic official; b. Newark, Feb. 7, 1932; s. Kenneth Frank and Florence (Gilleo) G.; m. Priscilla Wilson King, June 18, 1955; children: Virginia Wilson, Amy Brewer, Andrew King, Louise Meyer. SB, MIT, 1954, SM, 1955; Sc.D., Mass. Inst. Tech., 1960. Mem. faculty MIT, 1960-71, 90—, Class of 1922 prof. elec. engring., 1968-71, dean Sch. Engring., 1970-71, chancellor, 1971-80, pres., 1980-90; mem. MIT Corp., 1971—, chmn., 1990-97. Dir. Boeing Co., Seattle. Trustee Wheaton Coll., Norton, Mass., 1971-97, trustee emeritus 1997—, chmn. bd. trustees, 1976-87. 1st lt. AUS, 1955-57. Fellow IEEE (life, publs. bd. 1969-70), Am. Acad. Arts and Scis.; mem. NAE (treas. 1994-01), AAAS, Mex. Nat. Acad. Engring. (corr.), Sigma Xi, Eta Kappa Nu, Tau Beta Pi, Phi Sigma Kappa. Mem. United Ch. Christ Office: MIT Dept Elec Engring 77 Massachusetts Ave Cambridge MA 02139-4307

GRAY, PAUL WESLEY, university dean; b. Cicero, Ill., Jan. 30, 1947; s. Harry B. and Audrey (Tong) G.; m. Rachel E. Boehr, June 3, 1967; children: John M., Janel E., Robert B. BA, Faith Baptist Bible Coll., Ankeny, Tex., 1970; ThM, Dallas Theol. Sem., 1975; MS in Libr. Sci., East Tex. State U., 1977, EdD, 1980; MA, Tex. Woman's U., 1989. Dorm dir. Buckner Baptist Benevolences, Dallas, 1971-75; dir. community living residence IV Dallas County Mental Health/Mental Retardation, Dallas, 1975-78; cataloger W. Walworth Harrison Pub. Libr., Greenville, Tex., 1978-81; v.p. Golden Triangle Christian Acad., Garland, Tex., 1979-83; dir. libr. LeTourneau U., Longview, Tex., 1983-88; dean computer svc. and univ. libr. Azusa (Calif.) Pacific U., 1989—. Mem. ALA, Calif. Libr. Assn., So. Calif. Area Theol. Libr. Assn., Foothill Libr. Consortium. Republican. Baptist. Office: Azusa Pacific U 901 E Alosta Ave Azusa CA 91702-2769

GRAY, PETER FREDERICK, software engineer, educator; b. Belmont, U.K., July 12, 1962; s. Norman and Barbara Dorothy Gray; m. Gema Maria Escudero, Dec. 1, 1995; 1 child, Jacob James. Asst. v.p., devel. cons. State St. Corp., Boston, 1996—; adj. lectr. Northeastern U., Boston, 2001—02; robotics software engr. New Micros, Inc., Dallas, 2002—. Mem.: IEEE, AAUP, Nat. Writers Union. Avocations: martial arts, travel, science. Office: New Micros Inc 1601 Chalk Hill Rd Dallas TX 75212 Personal E-mail: petegray@ieee.org.

GRAY, PHENESSA ANTOINETTE, not-for-profit developer; b. Warrington, Fla., Dec. 31, 1974; d. Carlond Ann Gray; 1 child, Hannah. AA in Liberal Studies, BA in English Lit., Fla. State U., 1996; MSLS, Clark Atlanta U., 2000. Accelerated acad. educator Landmark Mid. Sch., Jacksonville, Fla., 1996—97; site rep. technician BellSouth Corp. Libr., Atlanta, 1997—98, corp. resource mgr., 1998; rsch. analyst Atlanta Bus. Chronicle, 1998—99; prospect rsch. mgr. SE divsn. Am. Cancer Soc., Atlanta, 1999—2002; prospect rsch. analyst Children's Healthcare of Altanta, 2002—. Author: (poetry) Sanctuary, 1997 (Homer Diamond award, 1998), (book) My Soul's Surrender, 2000; actor: (play) The Journey, 2000. Mem.: ALA, Assn. Profl. Rschrs. for Advancement, Spl. Libr. Assn., Alpha Kappa Alpha. Democrat. Avocations: poetry, art, cooking/baking, Scrabble, martial arts. Office: Childrens Healthcare of Atlanta 1687 Tullie Cir Atlanta GA 30329

GRAY, PHILIP HOWARD, former psychologist, writer; b. Cape Rosier, Maine, July 4, 1926; s. Asa and Bernice (Lawrence) G.; m. Iris McKinney, Dec. 31, 1954; children: Cindelyn Gray Eberts, Howard. MA, U. Chgo., 1958; PhD, U. Wash., 1960. Asst. prof. dept. psychology Mont. State U., Bozeman, 1960—65, assoc. prof., 1965—75, prof., 1975—92; ret., 1992. Vis. prof. U. Man., Winnipeg, Can., 1968-70, U. N.H., 1965, U. Mont., 1967, 74, Tufts U., 1968, U. Conn., 1971; pres. Mont. Psychol. Assn., 1968-70 (helped write Mont. licensing law for psychologists); chmn. Mont. Bd. Psychologist Examiners, 1972-74; spkr. sci. and geneal. meetings on ancestry of U.S. presidents; presenter, instr. grad. course on serial killers and the psychopathology of murder; founder Badger Press of Mont., 1998. Organizer folk art exhbns. Mont. and Maine, 1972-79; author: The Comparative Analysis of Behavior, 1966, (with F.L. Ruch and N. Warren) Working with Psychology, 1963, A Directory of Eskimo Artists in Sculpture and Prints, 1974, The Science That Lost Its Mind, 1985, Penobscot Pioneers vol. 1, 1992, vol. 2, 1992, vol. 3, 1993, vol. 4, 1994, vol. 5, 1995, vol. 6, 1996, Mean Streets and Dark Deeds: The He-Man's Guide to Mysteries, 1998, Ghoulies and Ghosties and Long-leggety Beasties: Imprinting Theory Linking Serial Killers, Child Assassins, Molesters, Homosexuality, Feminism and Day Care, 1998, Egoteria of a Psychologist: Poetry, Letters, Memos from Nether Montana, 2001; contbr. numerous articles on behavior to psychol. jours.; contbr. poetry to lit. jours. With U.S. Army, 1944—46. Decorated EAME medal Ctrl. Europe and Rhineland Campaigns, Victory medal WWII; recipient numerous rsch. grants. Fellow: APA, AAAS, Internat. Soc. Rsch. on Aggression, Am. Psychol. Soc.; mem.: SAR (trustee 1989, v.p. Sourdough chpt. 1990, pres. 1991—2002, v.p. gen. intermountain dist. 1997—98, pres. state soc. 1998—99, trustee 2001—03, v.p. gen. intermountain dist. 2003—), NRA (life), Order of the Crown of Charlemagne, Gallatin County Geneal. Soc. (charter, pres. 1991—93), Nat. Geneal. Soc., New Eng. Hist. Geneal. Soc., Deer Isle-Stonington Hist. Soc., Flagon and Trencher, Order Descs. Colonial Physicians and Chirugiens, Internat. Soc. Human Ethology, Descs. Illegitimate Sons and Daus. of Kings of Britain, Bozeman Rifle and Pistol Club. Republican. Avocations: collecting folk art, first and signed editions of novels, pistol shooting. Home: 1207 S Black Ave Bozeman MT 59715-5633 E-mail: phgray@mcn.net. *We are human to the extent that we have bondings and the more bondings we have the more human we are. These attachments include familial bonding (imprinting), friendship bonding, marital bonding, ethnic-religious bonding, possession and goal bondings, and bonding to the land and ocean. My life's work is the study of these bondings and I am thereby more firmly connected to the human race.*

GRAY, PHYLLIS, educational administrator; b. Chgo., Apr. 5, 1951; d. Walter James and Alma Everlyn (Berry) G. BA in Edn., Luther Coll., 1973; MA in Speech, U. No. Iowa, 1984. Permanent tchg. cert., Iowa. Tchr. 7th grade Waterloo (Iowa) Comty. Schs., 1973-77; acad. coord. Luther Coll. Upward Bound, Decorah, Iowa, 1977-79, asst. dir., 1979-86, dir., 1986—, interim dir. ednl. talent search, 1999. Mem. AAUW (treas. 1998), Mid-Am. Assn. Ednl. Opportunity Program Pers. (pres. elect 1995-96, pres. 1996-98), devel. chair 1993-95, TRIO achievers chair 1997-98, pres. Iowa chpt. 1992-93, bd. dirs. Iowa chpt. 1986-95, scholarship chair, bd. dirs. 1998-99), Nat. Coun. Ednl. Opportunity Assns. (bd. dirs. 1995-98). Democrat. Lutheran. Avocations: sewing, cooking, reading, crafts. Office: Luther Coll Upward Bound 700 College Dr Decorah IA 52101-1045

GRAY, PHYLLIS ANNE, librarian; b. Boston, Jan. 2, 1926; d. George Joseph and Eleanor (Morrison) G. PhB, Barry Coll., 1947, MBA, 1979; MS in LS, Cath. U. Am., 1950. Librarian U.S. Air Force Base, Miami, Fla., 1952-53; asst. librarian Brockway Meml. Library, Miami Shores, Fla., 1953-55; head librarian North Miami Pub. Library, 1955-59; supervising librarian Santa Clara County Library, San Jose, Calif., 1959-61; library dir. City of Commerce (Calif.) Pub. Library, 1961-68; adminstrv. librarian Miami Dade Pub. Library, 1969-76; library dir. Miami Beach (Fla.) Pub. Library, 1978-86; dir. Surf-Bal Bay Pub. Library, Surfside, Fla., 1987-91. Democrat. Roman Catholic. Councilwoman Bal Harbour Village, 1979-83; treas. Women in Govt. Service, 1981-86, pres., 1988-89. Mem. ALA, Barry U. Alumni Assn., Fla. Pub. Library Assn. Clubs: Pilot (rec. sec. 1981-82, pres. 1982-83). Democrat. Roman Catholic. Home: 575 Oakmount Pl #2925 Las Vegas NV 89109-1472

GRAY, R. BENTON, lawyer; b. Cleve., July 5, 1951; s. Roland Benton and Esther (Lockwood) G.; m. Kathleen Maloney, Aug. 9, 1998; children: John David, Michael Stuart, Kerry Shea, Daniel Benton. BA, Kenyon Coll., 1973; MA, U. Rochester, 1976; JD, Duke U., 1983. Bar: Ohio, 1983, U.S. Dist. Ct. (no. dist.) Ohio 1986, U.S. Ct. Appeals (6th cir.) 1986, U.S. Ct. Appeals (7th cir.) 1997. Assoc. Thompson, Hine and Flory, Cleve., 1983-92; ptnr. Thompson Hine & Flory LLP, Cleve., 1993-98. Contbr. articles, treatise to profl. jours. Chmn., vice chmn., mem. Citizens Adv. Com., Cleve., 1984-86. Mem. Ohio Bar Assn., Cleve. Bar Assn. (mem. cert. grievance com.). Office: R Benton Gray & Co Midland Bldg Ste 1650 101 W Prospect Ave Cleveland OH 44115-1093

GRAY, RANDALL JOSHUA, law librarian; b. Santa Monica, Calif., Sept. 30, 1949; s. Joshua and Eunice M. (Serr) G.; BA in English, San Fernando Valley State Coll., 1972; MLS, UCLA, 1974, cert. of specialization in law librarianship, 1974; m. Roberta Christine Johnsen, June 15, 1973. Intern, L.A. County Law Libr., 1973-74; asst. libr. O'Melveny & Myers, L.A., 1974-76; law libr. Adams, Duque & Hazeltine, L.A., 1976-82, dir. info. svcs., 1982-84; sales rep. Callaghan & Co. Law and Tax Publs., 1984-85; mgr. info. svcs. Haight, Brown & Bonesteel, L.A., 1986—; instr. Inst. Pvt. Law Librs., Biltmore Hotel, L.A., 1980, UCLA Extension, 1980, Practising Law Inst., 1981; participant Calif. State Colls. Internat. Studies Program, Uppsala, Sweden, 1971; chmn. 10th Ann. Inst. on Calif. Law, 1982. Mem. Am. Assn. Law Libr., So. Calif. Assn. Law Librs. (chmn. cons. com. 1980, v.p. 1981-82, pres. 1982-83), UCLA Grad. Sch. Libr. and Info. Sci. Students Assn. (pres. 1973-74). Author: Effective Administration: Better Decisions through Information, 1981. Home: 521 Ramona Ave Sierra Madre CA 91024-2230 Office: Haight Brown & Bonesteel 6080 Center Dr Ste 800 Los Angeles CA 90045-1574

GRAY, RICHARD, art dealer, consultant, holding company executive; b. Chgo., Dec. 30, 1928; s. Edward and Pearl B. Gray; m. Mary Kay Lackritz, Mar. 28, 1953; children— Paul, Jennifer, Harry Student, U. Ill., 1951. Pres. The Grayline Co., 1952-63; sec.-treas. The Edward Gray Corp., 1952-63; prin., dir. GrayCor, 1963—; dir. The Richard Gray Gallery, Chgo. and N.Y.C., 1963—. Lectr., juror, panelist Guggenheim Mus., N.Y.C., Art. Inst. Chgo., Harvard U., U. Ill., Mich. State U., Milw. Art Mus., New Sch. for Social Research, N.Y., Met. Mus., N.Y.C., Colloquium-The Getty Mus., U. Chgo., Seattle Art Mus.; mem. art adv. panel U.S. Internal Revenue Svc. Contbr. articles to Chgo. Tribune, Chgo. Daily News, Crain's Chgo. Bus., Chgo. Mag., Collector Investor Mag. Bd. dirs. Sta. WFMT-FM, 1992-98, Ill. Humanities Coun.; trustee, vice chmn. WTTW Channel 11—Chgo. Pub. TV; bd. dirs. Goodman Theatre, Chgo.; trustee Chgo. Symphony Orch.; former chair bd. Chgo. Internat. Theater Festival; adv. com. Smithsonian Inst.; bd. dirs. Old Masters Soc., Art Inst. Chgo.; mem. steering com. Friends of the Libraries, Art Inst Chgo.; mem. capital devel. bd. State of Ill., pub. arts adv. com., former mem. selection com. Gov.'s Awards for Arts; former mem. nat. adv. bd. Ohio State U. Wexner Ctr. for Visual Arts; pres. Art Dealers Assn. Am.; former pres. Chgo. Art Dealers Assn.; former chmn. Navy Pier Task Force, City of Chgo., 1986-88; mem. vis. com. U. Chgo. Humanities Div., chmn., bd. govs. Alfred Smart Mus. U. Chgo.; vice-chmn., bd. dirs. Chgo. Humanities Festival. Mem. Chgo. Pub. Schs. Alumni Assn. (former chmn. bd. dirs.), Chgo. Coun. Fgn. Rels. (Chgo. com.), Chgo. Club, Quadrangle Club, Arts Club of Chgo. Achievements include specializing in contemporary, modern and impressionist masters. Office: Richard Gray Gallery 875 N Michigan Ave Ste 2503 Chicago IL 60611-1876 also: 1018 Madison Ave New York NY E-mail: rgray@richardgraygallery.com.

GRAY, RICHARD ALEXANDER, JR., retired chemical company executive; b. Pitts., Apr. 28, 1927; s. Richard Alexander and Margaret Katheryn Gray; m. Lucia I. Long, Sept. 8, 1956; children: Richard Alexander III, James W. Midshipman, U.S. Mcht. Marine Acad., 1945-47; BA, Princeton U., 1950; LL.B., Harvard U., 1954; postgrad., Univ. Coll., Southampton, Eng., 1949. Bar: Pa. bar 1955, U.S. Supreme Ct. bar 1975. Asso. firm Reed Smith Shaw & McClay, Pitts., 1954-62; with Air Products and Chems., Inc., Allentown, Pa., 1962-90, asst. gen. counsel, 1976-78, corp. sec., 1978-90, assoc. gen. counsel, 1980-84, v.p., 1984-90. Trustee Kutztown (Pa.) U., 1988-96, chmn., 1995-96; mem. bd. regents Mercersburg (Pa.) Acad., 1968-82. Trustee First Presbyn. Ch. of Allentown. Served to lt. (j.g.) USNR, 1950-51. Mem. ABA, Am. Soc. Corp. Secs. (bd. dirs. 1985-89), Lehigh Country Club (bd. govs. 1993-96).

GRAY, RICHARD ARDEN, retired transportation executive; b. Ft. Bragg, Calif., Oct. 29, 1935; s. Arden Howard and Marion Florence (Coolidge) G.; m. Roberta Jeanne Montna, Feb. 5, 1955; children: Mark Alan, Laura Ann, Deborah Marie, Lisa Lynn. AA, Yuba Coll., 1955; BA, Calif. State U., 1957. Cert. coll. instr., Calif. Dep. sheriff Yuba County Sheriffs Dept., Marysville, Calif., 1957; traffic officer Calif. Hwy. Patrol, Ventura, 1958—60, Yuba City, 1961—68, sgt. field ops. officer Gardena, 1969—71, lt. exec. officer Van Nuys, 1972—76, lt. area comdr. Chico, 1977—88; wholesale, retail distbr. Dick Gray Enterprises, Chico, 1989—94, 1995—2000; rschr. alternative cancer treatments, 2000—; property developer, 2000—. Instr. Yuba Coll., Marysville, 1965-67, Calif. fish and game hunter safety program, Chico, 1982-86; profl. driver, transporter motor homes, 1989-2000. Chmn. citizen rev. com. United Way of Butte County, Chico, 1984 (outstanding achievement 1984-86), fundraising campaign chmn. 1986, pres. bd. dirs. 1985; pres., bd. dirs. No. Calif. Counties Exch. Club Child Abuse Prevention Ctr., Chico, 1987-91; mem. Ronald Reagan Presdl. Found., 2001—, Nat. Law Enforcement Mus., 2002—. With USNR, 1953-61. Recipient Individual Excellence Outstanding Cmty. Svc. award United Way Butte and Glenn Counties, 1994-95. Mem. Calif. Hwy. Patrolmen Assn., Mt. Vernon Ladies Assn., US Golf Assn., Oxford Club (dirs. cir. 1998—), Heritage Found. Leader's Club, RV Club, Elks (honors 1988, pres. 1988-89), Breakfast Exch. Club (pres., bd. dirs. 1980-81), Exch. Club Greater Chico (sponsor 1983). Republican. Avocations: traveling in recreational vehicle, tennis, golf.

GRAY, RICHARD MOSS, retired college president; b. Washington, Jan. 25, 1924; s. Wilbur Leslie and Betty Marie (Grey) G.; m. Catherine Claire Hammond, Oct. 17, 1943; children: Janice Lynn Gray Armstrong, Nancy Hammond Gray Schultz. BA, Bucknell U., 1942; MDiv summa cum laude, San Francisco Theol. Sem., 1961; PhD, U. Calif., Berkeley, 1972; doctorate degree (hon.), World Coll. West, 1988. Writer, creative dir. N.W. Ayer & Son, Phila., 1942-58; univ. pastor Portland State U., Oreg., 1961-68; founder, pres. World Coll. West, Petaluma, Calif., 1973-88, pres. emeritus, 1988—. Bd. dirs. World Centre, San Francisco, Life Plan Ctr.; founder Presidio World Coll., 1992—. Author poetry Advent, 1989. Bd. dirs. Citizens Found. Marin, San Rafael, Calif., 1988—, Marin Ednl. Found.; ruling elder Presbyn. Ch. U.S.A. Named Disting. Alumnus of Yr. San Francisco Theol. Sem., 1988, Marin Citizen of Yr. Citizens Found., 1988; recipient Svc. to Humanity award Bucknell U., 1992. Mem. Phi Beta Kappa. Avocations: song-writing, poetry.

GRAY, R(OBERT) J(AMES), JR., printmaker, editor; b. Stratton, Maine, June 9, 1956; s. Robert James and Carol Mae (Cox) Gray. BA in Fine Arts/Studio, Salem State Coll., Mass., 1989; student, Montserrart Sch. Visual Art, Beverly, Mass., 1974, Montserrart Sch. Visual Art, 1980—87, North Shore C.C., Beverly, 1983, Mass. Coll. Art, Boston, 1976—78. With Original Irregular newspaper, Kingfield, Maine, 1994—, editor, 2000—. Tchr. studio art Carrabassett Valley Acad., 1997—98. Exhibitions include Ritzo and Royall Gallery, Kingfield, Maine, 1998—99, Impressions: Contemporary Prints, Mesa Contemporary Arts, Ariz., 2000, Silvermine Guild Galleries, New Canaan, Conn., 2000, U. Wis., Parkside, 2001, Laband Art Gallery, L.A., 2001, Boston Printmakers, 808 Gallery, 2001, Creede Arts Coun., Colo., 2001—02, The Fredericksburg Ctr. for Creative Arts, Va., 2001, The Washington Printmakers' Gallery, 2001, Hopper House Art Ctr., Nyack, N.Y., 2001, Lahti City Art Mus., Finland, 2001, Purdue U. Galleries, West Lafayette, Ind., 2001—02, Sumei Multidisciplinary Arts Ctr., Newark, 2002, Burpee Mus. Natural History, Rockford, Ill., 2002, Arts in the Capitol, Augusta, ME, 2003, Stadler Gallery, Kingfield, ME, 2003. Home: 130 Main St Stratton ME 04982-0296 E-mail: rjgrayjr@tds.com.

GRAY, ROBERT JOSEPH, lawyer; b. Oak Park, Ill., Feb. 15, 1966; s. Donald Frank and Jane Gray; m. Danalee Jacobson, Sept. 2, 1995; 1 child, Parker Robert. BA, U. Ill., 1988; JD, Marquette U., 1991. Bar: Wis. 1991, U.S. Dist. Ct. (ea. and we. dists.) Wis. 1991; bd. cert. civil trial specialist NBTA. Assoc. Jerome A Maeder Law Office, Wausau, Wis., 1991—. Mem. ABA, ATLA, Wis. Bar Assn., Marathon County Bar Assn., Phi Alpha Delta. Office: Jerome A Maeder Law Office 602 Jackson St Wausau WI 54403-5549 E-mail: lawyer@maederlaw.com.

GRAY, ROBERT M(OLTEN), electrical engineering educator; b. San Diego, Nov. 1, 1943; s. Augustine Heard and Elizabeth DuBois (Jordan) G.; m. Arlene Frances Ericson; children: Timothy M., Lori A. BS, MS, MIT, 1966; PhD, U. So. Calif., 1969. Elec. engr. U.S. Naval Ordinance Lab., White Oak, Md., 1963-65, Jet Propulsion Lab., Pasadena, Calif., summers 1966, 67; asst. prof. elec. engring. Stanford (Calif.) U., 1969-75, assoc. prof., 1975-80, prof., 1980—, dir. Info. Systems Lab., 1984-87, vice chair dept. elec. engring., 1993—. Author: Probability, Random Processes and Ergodic Properties, 1988, Source Coding Theory, 1990, Entropy and Information Theory, 1990; co-author: Random Processes, 1986, Vector Quantization and Signal Compression, 1992, Fourier Transforms, 1995; contbr. articles to profl. jours. Fireman La Honda (Calif.) Vol. Fire Brigade, 1970-80, pres., 1971-72; coach Am. Youth Soccer Orgn., La Honda, 1971-78, commr., 1976-78. Japan Soc. for Promotion Sci. fellow, 1981, Guggenheim fellow, 1982, NATO/CNR fellow, 1990. Fellow IEEE (Centennial medal 1984, 3d Millennium medal 2000), Inst. Math. Stats.; mem. Info. Theory Soc. IEEE (assoc. editor Trans. 1977-80, editor in chief 1980-83, paper prize 1976, Golden Jubilee award for technol. achievement 1998), Signal Processing Soc. IEEE (sr. award 1983, soc. award 1993, program co-chmn. 1997 Internat. Conf. on Image Processing, Tech. Achievement award 1998, Presdl. Mentoring award 2002, Disting. Alumni award U. S.C., 2003). Avocations: maritime and gilded age history, hiking, computers. Home: PO Box 160 La Honda CA 94020-0160 Office: Stanford U Dept Elec Engring Stanford CA 94305 E-mail: rmgray@stanford.edu.

GRAY, ROBERT STEELE, publishing executive, editor, writer; b. Beaumont, Tex., Oct. 6, 1923; s. Fred and Ruth Louise (Lewelling) G.; m. Nellie Frances McGuinness, July 3, 1945; children: Robert Steele, Laura, Ruth Ellen (Mrs. Sommy L. Ham). BS, U. Houston, 1954. Newscaster Sta. KPRC-AM, Houston, 1947; news dir. Sta. KNUZ, Houston, 1948-49; reporter Citizens Papers, Houston, 1950; newsfilm dir. Sta. KPRC-TV, 1951-56; writer Houston Post, 1956-60; founder, pub. editor Cordovan Corp., Houston, 1960—, chmn. bd., 1982—; pub. Cordovan Bus. Jours., Houston, 1971; co-founder Golfer Mags., Inc., 1984—. Author: Survivor, 1998, also author and co-author 5 books on horses and horse tng. 2nd lt. USMCR, 1942-46, to 1st lt. 1951-52, Korea. Mem. Soc. Profl. Journalists. Office: 31715 Cottonwood Ln Magnolia TX 77355

GRAY, ROLAND WILLIAM, pediatrician; b. Nashville, Feb. 10, 1947; s. William Thurman and Margaret Helen (Miller) G.; m. Gloria Diane Gray, Mar. 14, 1969; children: Roland, Jr., Camilla, Andrew. BA, Vanderbilt U., 1969; MD, U. Tenn., 1972. Diplomate Am. Bd. Pediat. Asst. prof. U. Fla., Gainesville, 1976-78; pediatrician Children's Clinic Donelson, Nashville, 1978—. Med. dir., addictionist Koala Ctr., Nashville; clin. instr. pediat. Vanderbilt U., Nashville; med. dir. Physicians Health Program, Tenn. Med. Found., 2002. Bd. dirs. Recovery Residence, Nashville. Named Tenn. Vol. Hero, 2001. Mem. AMA, Am. Acad. Pediatrics, Am. Bd. Pediatrics, Am. Soc. Addiction Medicine,Tenn. Med. Assn., Fla. Med. Assn. Episcopalian. Avocations: gardening, fishing.

GRAY, SARAH VIRGINIA, retired librarian; b. Durham, N.C., Oct. 1, 1934; d. Irving Emory and Virginia Rose (Gearhart) G. AB in History, Duke U., 1956; MLS, U. N.C., 1964. Asst. to curator of manuscript Duke U. Library, Durham, N.C., 1956-58; asst. supr. res. reading rm. U. N.C., Chapel Hill, 1959-61, supr. reserve reading room, 1961-64; exchange librarian U. Exeter, England, 1968; periodicals librarian Coll. of William & Mary, Williamsburg, Va., 1964-81; circulation librarian Williamsburg Regional Library, 1981-85; systems adminstr. Colonial Williamsburg Found., Williamsburg, 1988—2001; ret., 2001. Author: Index to Commonwealth Little Magazines, 2 vols., 1976-79, 1 vol. 1980-82, 1 vol., 1983-84, 85. Sec. Lord Chamberlain Soc. Va. Shakespeare Festival, Williamsburg, 1987—. Democrat. Presbyterian. Avocations: historical cooking, antiques, travel, indexing. Home: 405 Tyler St Williamsburg VA 23185-4214

GRAY, SHEILA HAFTER, psychiatrist, psychoanalyst; b. NYC, Oct. 19, 1930; MD, Harvard U., 1958. cert. Washington Psychoanalytic Inst., 1969. Intern St. Elizabeths Hosp., Washington, 1958-59; resident McLean Hosp., Belmont, Mass., 1959-61; clin. and rsch. fellow Mass. Gen. Hosp., Boston, Mass., 1961-62; staff psychiatrist Chestnut Lodge, Inc., Rockville, Md., 1962-64; practice medicine, specializing in psychiatry and psychoanalysis Washington, 1964—; clin. asst. prof. psychiatry U. Md. Sch. Medicine, Balt., 1968-75, clin. assoc. prof., 1975-83, clin. prof., 1983-96; instr. Washington Psychoanalytic Inst., 1971-75, tchg. analyst, 1975-96, Balt.-Washington Inst. for Psychoanalysis, 1996—; clin. prof. psychiatry Uniformed Svcs. U. Health Scis., 1997-99, adj. prof. psychiatry, 1999—. Staff U. Md. Hosp., Balt., 1970-96; physician mem. Commn. on Mental Health, Superior Ct. of D.C., 1972-98; bd. govs. Nat. Capital Reciprocal Ins. Co., 1981-98; treas. NCRIC Physicians Orgn., 1994-97; cons. Walter Reed Army Med. Ctr., Washington, 1983—. Active Mayor's Adv. Com. on Mental Health Svcs. Reorgn., Washington, 1984; adv. panel Mayor's Environ. Design Awards Program, 1988-89; exec. com. D.C. Fedn. Civic Assns., 1984—, asst. rec. sec., 1985, rec. sec., 1986-88, 2d v.p., 1989-90, pres., 1991-92, del.-at-large, 1993—; v.p. programs Women's Equity Action League Met. D.C., 1986; commr. D.C. Adv. Neighborhood Commn., 1986-88; mem. Met. Washington Coun. of Govt.'s Partnership for

Regional Excellence, 1992—; trustee Accreditation Coun. for Psychoanalytic Edn., Inc., 2002—. Fellow: Am. Psychiat. Assn. (chair com. quality assurance and improvement, Coun. on Econ. Affairs, 1996—97); mem.: Washington Psychoanalytic Soc. (chmn. bd. dirs. psychoanalytic clinic and councillor ex officio 1987—90), Med. Soc. D.C. (exec. bd. 1982, ho. dels. 1992—97), Washington Psychiatric Soc. (councillor 1981—83), Am. Acad. Psychoanalysis (trustee 1996—99, pres.-elect 1999—2000, pres. 2000—01, editl. bd. jour. 2002—), Am. Psychoanalytic Assn. (diplomate Bd. Profl. Stds.), Palisades Citizens Assn. (bd. dirs. 1980—, treas. 1983—84, pres. 1984—86). Office: PO Box 40612 Palisades Sta Washington DC 20016

GRAY, SIMON JAMES HOLLIDAY, writer, educator; b. Oct. 21, 1936; s. James Davidson Gray and Barbara Cecelia Mary (Holliday) Davidson; m. Beryl Mary Kevern, 1965 (div. 1997); 2 children; m. Victoria Rothschild, 1997. Student, Westminister Sch., Dalhousie U., Halifax, N.S.; MA, U. Cambridge. Supr. English U. B.C., 1960-63. Sr. instr., 1963-64; lectr. Queen Mary Coll., U. London, 1965-84. Author: (novels) Colmain, 1963, Simple People, 1965, Little Portia, 1967, A Comeback for Stark, 1968, Breaking Hearts, 1997, (non-fiction) An Unnatural Pursuit and Other Pieces, 1985, How's That For Telling 'Em Fat Lady, 1988, Fat Chance, 1995, Enter a Fox, 2001, (plays) Wise Child, 1968, Sleeping Dog, 1968, Dutch Uncle, 1969, The Idiot, 1971, Spoiled, 1971, Butley, 1971 (Evening Std. award), Otherwise Engaged, 1975 (Best Play, N.Y. Drama Critics Cir., Evening Std. award), Plaintiffs and Defendants, 1975, Two Sundays, 1975, Dog Days, 1976, Molly, 1977, The Rear Column, 1978, Close of Play, 1979, Quartermaine's Terms, 1981, Tartuffe, 1982, Chapter 17, 1982, The Common Pursuit, 1984, Plays One, 1986, Melon, 1987, Hidden Laughter, 1991, The Holy Terror, 1992, Cell Mates, 1995, Simply Disconnected, 1996, Life Support, 1997, Just the Three of Us, 1997, The Late Middle Classes, 1999, Japes, 2000, (TV movies) After Pilkington, 1987, Quartermaine's Terms, 1987, Old Flames, 1990, They Never Slept, 1991, The Common Pursuit, 1992, Running Late, 1992, Unnatural Pursuits, 1993, Femme Fatale, 1993, (film) A Month in the Country, (radio plays) The Holy Terror (rev.), 1989, The Rector's Daughter, 1992, With a Nod and a Bow, 1993, Suffer the Little Children, 1993. Mem. Dramatists Guild. Office: care Judy Daish Assocs 2 St Charles Place London W10 6EG England

GRAY, THOMAS STEPHEN, journalist, writer; b. Burbank, Calif., Aug. 22, 1950; s. Thomas Edgar and Lily Irene (Ax) G.; m. Barbara Ellen Bronson, Aug. 27, 1977; children: Jonathan Thomas, Katherine Marie. BA, Stanford U., 1972; MA in English, UCLA, 1976. Tchg. assoc. UCLA, 1976-77; reporter L.A. Daily News, 1977-79, editl. writer, 1979-84, editl. page editor, 1984-95; sr. editor Investor's Bus. Daily, L.A., 1995-98; v.p. and account group mgr. Investor Rels. Internat., 2003—. Bd. dirs. Calif. Luth. U. Cmty. Leaders Assn. Author: Teach Yourself Investing Online, 1999, Investing Online for Dummies—Quick Reference, 2000, Online Investing Bible, 2001. Mem. bd. dirs. Calif. Luth. Univ. Cmty. Leaders Assn. Recipient 1st Place award Editl. Writing Greater L.A. Press Club, 1988, Inland Daily Press Assn., 1993. E-mail: tsgray@sbcglobal.net.

GRAY, VELMA LEVAN, medical surgical nurse; b. Estherville, Iowa, Jan. 23, 1921; d. Lynn Curtis and Hartte Elizabeth (Partello) LeVan; m. William Walter Gray, Nov. 3, 1945 (dec. June 1988); children: Patricia Ann, Larry Dean. Diploma, Kahler Sch. of Nursing, Rochester, Minn., 1944; BS, L.A. State Coll., 1961, MA in Health Safety, Calif. State Coll., 1970. Cert. CPR instr. Asst. supr. emergency rm. Kahler Corp. Metro Hosp., Rochester, Minn., 1944; nurse USN, 1944-46; staff nurse, supr. Hollywood (Calif.) Presbyn. Hosp., 1946-47, charge nurse, 1947-53, asst. dir. nursing, 1953-58; dir. nursing Hollywood/Presbyn. Hosp., Hollywood, Calif., 1966; instr., lectr. assoc. prof. Pasadena (Calif.) Jr. Coll., 1966-92, asst. prof., 1971, prof., 1978-92, prof. emeritus, 1992—. Republican. Presbyterian. Avocations: gardening, art, quilting, jewelry making. Home: 2635 Sea Pine Ln La Crescenta CA 91214-1443

GRAY, VIRGINIA HICKMAN, political science educator; b. Camden, Ark., June 10, 1945; d. George Leonard and Ethel Massengale (Bell) Hickman; 1 child, Brian Charles. BA with honors, Hendrix Coll., 1967; MA, Washington U., St. Louis, 1969, PhD, 1972. Asst. prof. polit. sci. U. Ky., Lexington, 1971-73; from asst. prof. to assoc. prof. U. Minn., Mpls., 1973-83, prof., 1983-2000, chairperson dept. polit. sci., 1985-88; Winston Disting. prof. polit. sci. U. N.C., Chapel Hill, 2001—. Guest scholar Brookings Inst., Washington, 1977-78; vis. prof. U. Oslo, 1985, Nankai U., 1988, U. B.C., 1992, U. N.C., 1993-94; NSF vis. prof. for women, 1993-94. Co-author: The Organizational Politics of Criminal Justice, 1980, Feminism and the New Right, 1983, Politics in the American States, 1983, 7th edit., 1999, American States and Cities, 1991, 2d edit., 1997, The Population Ecology of Interest Representation, 1996, Minnesota Politics and Government, 1999. Bd. dirs. Health Ptnrs. Inc., 1992-2001, chair, 1999-2001. Fellow Woodrow Wilson Found., 1970, NDEA, 1969-70; grantee Swedish Bicentennial Found., 1985; recipient rsch. assistantship NSF, 1968-69, rsch. grant NSF, 1997-2001; scholar in residence Rockefeller Ctr., Bellagio, Italy; Investigator award Robert Wood Johnson Found., 2003-2005. Mem. Am. Polit. Sci. Assn. (coun. 1990-92), Midwest Polit. Sci. Assn. (coun. 1984-86, v.p. 1997-99, pres. 2003-2004), Policy Studies Orgn. (coun. 1977-79), So. Polit. Sci. Assn., Western Polit. Sci. Assn. Democrat. Unitarian Universalist. Home: 2 Heather Ct Chapel Hill NC 27517 Office: U NC Dept Polit Sci CB 3265 Hamilton Hall Chapel Hill NC 27599-3265 E-mail: vagray@email.unc.edu.

GRAY, WALTER P., III, archivist, consultant; b. San Francisco, Aug. 8, 1952; s. Walter Patton II and Elsie Josephine (Stroop) G.; m. Mary Amanda Helmich, May 23, 1980. BA in History, Calif. State U., Sacramento, 1976. Rschr. Calif. State R.R. Mus., Sacramento, 1977-80, curator, 1980-81, 85-90, archivist, 1981-85, mus. dir., 1990-98; Calif. state archivist, 1998—. Cons. in field, 1976—. Contbr. articles to profl. jours. Buddhist. Avocations: woodworking, antique automobiles, photography. Office: California State Archives 1020 O St Sacramento CA 95814-5704 E-mail: wgray@ss.ca.gov.

GRAY, WILLIAM CAMPBELL, lawyer; b. North Wilkesboro, N.C., Mar. 3, 1951; BA, U. N.C., 1973; JD, Wake Forest U., 1976. Bar: N.C., U.S. Dist. Ct. (we. and mid. dists.) N.C., U.S. Ct. Appeals (4th, 5th and 11th cirs.), U.S. Supreme Ct. Ptnr. Cunningham & Gray, Wilkesboro, N.C., 1976—. Bar: N.C., 1976, U.S. Dist. Ct. (we. dist.) N.C., 1977, (mid. dist.) N.C., 1977, U.S. Supreme Ct., 1980, U.S. Ct. Appeals (4th cir.) 1978, (5th cir.) 1981, (11th cir.) 1981; chmn. 23d Jud. Bar Candidate Com., 1991—. Rep. Town of Wilkesboro, 1988—. Mem. 23d Jud. Bar Assn. (pres. 1987), Wilkes County Bar Assn. (pres. 1985), Elks, local country club. Democrat. Methodist. Office: Cunningham & Gray PO Box 520 Wilkesboro NC 28697-0520

GRAY, WILLIAM H., III, association executive, former congressman; b. Baton Rouge, Aug. 20, 1941; m. Andrea Dash, Apr. 17, 1971; children— William H. IV, Justin Yates, Andrew Dash. BA, Franklin and Marshall Coll., 1963; M.Div., Drew Theol. Sem., Madison, N.J., 1966; Th.M., Princeton Theol. Sem., 1970; postgrad., U. Pa., 1965, Temple U., 1966, Oxford U., 1967. Ordained to ministry Baptist Ch.; asst. minister Bright Hope Baptist Ch., Phila., 1963-64; dir. 1st Baptist Ch., Montclair, N.J., 1964-65; co-pastor, sr. minister Union Baptist Ch., Montclair, 1966-72; asst. prof., dir. St. Peter's Coll., Jersey City, 1970-74; sr. minister Bright Hope Baptist Ch., 1972—; lectr. Jersey City State Coll., 1968, Rutgers U., 1971, Montclair State Coll., 1970-72; mem. 96th-101st Congresses from 2d Dist. Pa.; House Majority Whip; pres., CEO United Negro Coll. Fund, N.Y.C., 1991—. Chmn. house budget com., 1985; mem. house appropriations com. Congl. Black Caucus, Nat. Economic Commn.; vice chmn. Dem. Leadership Coun.; envoy to Haiti, 1994. Trexler Found. scholar, 1962; Rockefeller Protestant fellow, 1965 Mem. Phila. Pastor's Conf., Phila. Baptist Assn., Progressive Nat. Baptist Assn., Am. Baptist Conv., Alpha Phi Alpha. Clubs: Frontier Internat. Lodges: Masons, Elks. Democrat. Office: United Negro Coll Fund PO Box 10444 8260 Willow Oaks Corporate Dr Fairfax VA 22031-4513

GRAY, WILLIAM OXLEY, retired lawyer; b. Iowa Falls, Iowa, Nov. 23, 1914; s. Clarence O. and Hazel (Oxley) G.; m. Mary Florence Comstock, Oct. 19, 1940; children: William Scott, John Steven, Mary Ellen Gray Hart, James C. B.A., Coe Coll., 1936; J.D., U. Iowa, 1938. Bar: Iowa 1938, U.S. Dist. Ct. (no. and so. dists.) Iowa 1938. Ptnr. Silliman & Gray, Cedar Rapids, Iowa, 1938-42; spl. agt. FBI, 1942-46; ptnr. Silliman, Gray & Stapleton, Cedar Rapids, 1946-85, Gray, Stefani & Mitvalsky, 1986-91; dir. Brenton Bank & Trust Co., Cedar Rapids. Chmn. Iowa Hwy. Commn., 1969-73; chmn. bd. trustees Coe Coll., Cedar Rapids, 1964-84. Mem. ABA, Iowa State Bar Assn., Linn County Bar Assn., Ex-Agts. FBI (pres. 1970-71), Cedar Rapids C. of C. (bd. dirs. 1968). Republican. Congregationalist. Club: Union League (Chgo.). Lodge: Masons. Office: Gray Stefani & Mitvalsky 200 American Bldg Cedar Rapids IA 52401

GRAYBEAL, BARBARA, editor, writer; b. Mountain City, Tenn., Sept. 21, 1935; d. Claude Harold and Ruby Lucille (Hodge) G.; m. Lewis N. Kremer, June 7, 1958 (div.); m. Charles L. Ring, May 8, 1982(div.). BA magna cum laude, Marietta Coll., 1957; grad. Pub. Procedures Course, Radcliffe Coll., 1957. With New Yorker mag., N.Y.C., 1957-58; assoc. editor Saturday Evening Post, Phila., 1958-62, Voter Registration in Mississippi, 1964, Episc. mag., Phila., 1962-69; asst. editor Luth. mag., Phila., 1971-72; instr. journalism Temple U., Phila., 1972-81; founding editor CGA World mag., 1980-82, sr. editor, 1982-83. Editor, writer: Fast and Fresh (by Julie Dannanbaum), 1981, The CGA Cookbook, 1984; editl. cons. Good Ideas for Decorating; contbr. articles, photographs and poetry to various publs. Mem. com. interpretation and promotion, dept. overseas missions Nat. Coun. Chs., 1966-68; mem. Phila. Dem. Com., 1968; bd. dirs., sec. Friends of Free Libr. Phila.; bd. dirs. N.C. Sch. Arts, The Assocs. of N.C. Sch. Arts, 1983-86; lay reader Episc. Ch.; vol. 1964 Miss. Freedom summer, Registration Project, Hattiesburg, Miss. Mem. AAUW (pres. br.), Women in Comms. (v.p. chpt.), Marietta Coll. Alumni Assn., Internat. Platform Assn., Phi Beta Kappa, Sigma Delta Chi, Alpha Xi Delta. Address: 1525 Woods Rd Apt 106 Winston Salem NC 27106-3135

GRAYBEAL, JACK DANIEL, chemist, educator; b. Detroit, May 16, 1930; s. Paul Herman and Polly Dale (McClintic) G.; m. Evelyn Alice Nicolai, June 13, 1954; children: Daniel Lee, David Eugene, Dale Kevin. BS in Chemistry, W.Va. U., 1951; MS in Chemistry, U. Wis., 1953, PhD in Chemistry, 1955. Mem. tech. staff Bell Telephone Labs., Holmdel, N.J., 1955-57; asst. prof. chemistry W.Va. U., Morgantown, 1957-63, assoc. prof., 1963-68; assoc. prof. chemistry Va. Poly. Inst. and State U., Blacksburg, 1968-69, prof., 1969-97, assoc. head dept., 1975-95, prof. emeritus, 1997—. Author: Molecular Spectroscopy, 1988; contbr. articles to profl. jours. Mem. Am. Chem. Soc., Am. Phys. Soc., Sigma Xi, Phi Lambda Upsilon (nat. editor 1981-87, nat. sec. 1987-96, nat. pres. 1996-2002, nat. historian 2002—). Home: 312 Apperson Dr Blacksburg VA 24060-3641 E-mail: graybealea@aol.com.

GRAYBILL, DAVID WESLEY, chamber of commerce executive; b. Council Bluffs, Iowa, Apr. 8, 1949; s. John Donald and Dorothy Lorraine (King) G.; m. Kortney Loraine Steinbeck, Aug. 17, 1974; 1 child, Darcy Lorraine. BA in Journalism, U. Iowa, 1971; MA in Mgmt. and Leadership Studies, City U., 1999. Cert. econ. developer, Chamber exec. Adminstrv. asst. Iowa City C. of C., 1972-74; exec. v.p. Brighton (Colo.) C. of C., 1974-77; pres. Fremont (Nebr.) C. of C., 1977-83; pres., chief exec. officer Tacoma-Pierce County C. of C., 1983—. Pres. Nebr. C. of C. Execs., 1981-82; treas. NE Nebr. Econ. Devel. Dist., 1980-83. Presiding elder Tacoma (Wash.) Cmty. of Christ; charter mem. Gov.'s Small Bus. Improvement Com., Wash., 1984—86. Recipient Barr Quality Mentor award, U. of Puget Sound, 2001, Leadership award, U. Wash., 2002. Mem. Am. Econ. Devel. Coun. (bd. dirs. 1985-87), Am. C. of C. (bd. dirs. 1990-94), Wash. C. of C. Execs. (pres. 1988-89, bd. dirs. 1988-90, 98-2002), Rotary (bd. dirs. Tacoma 1985-87). Office: Tacoma Pierce County C of C PO Box 1933 Tacoma WA 98401-1933

GRAYBILL, RUTH ANN, social worker; b. Hershey, Pa., Dec. 28, 1947; d. Franklin Nissley and Edna Ruth (Bennetch) G. BA in Sociology, Geneva Coll., 1969; MSW, Rutgers U., 1976; postgrad., Rosemead Sch. Psychology, 1988—. Lic. social worker. Staff social worker Bethany Christian Svcs., Grand Rapids, Mich., 1976-80; counselor Focus on Family, Pomona, Calif., 1985-88; psychology instr. Rosemead Sch. Psychology, La Mirada, Calif., 1984—; clin. social worker Biola Counseling Ctr., La Mirada, 1980—. Supr. psychology grad students Rosemead Sch. Psychology, La Mirada, 1986—; cons. in field. Women's leader, Bible study tchr. Ch. on The Way, Van Nuys, Calif., 1981-87. Mem. NASW, Christian Assn. for Psychol. Studies, N.Am. Assn. Christian in Social Work. Avocations: flower arranging, swimming, bicycling, crafts. Home: 743 Arroues Dr Fullerton CA 92835-1924 Office: Biola Counseling Ctr 13800 Biola Ave La Mirada CA 90639-0002

GRAY-BUSSARD, DOLLY H. energy company executive; b. Wilmington, Del., July 29, 1943; d. Henry Odell and Dorothy (Knotts) Gray; m. Robert William Bussard, Mar. 17, 1981; stepchildren: Elise Bright, William Bussard, Robert L. Bussard, Virginia B. Barausky. BA in History and English Lit., U. Calif., San Diego, 1984; MA in History, Georgetown U., 1990. Coord. Orgn. Human Devel., San Diego, 1977-78; owner, prin. Hello Dolly, La Jolla, Calif., 1978-80; ptnr. Linda Chester Lit. Agy., La Jolla, 1978-80; owner, pres. Unicorn Literary Agy., La Jolla, 1980-85; pres., chmn. bd. Energy/Matter Conversion Corp., San Diego, Calif., 1988—. Vis. lectr. writers' confs. U. Calif., San Diego, 1979-81. Co-author: The Best of San Diego, 1981. Mem. adv. bd. Women's Voices; mem. Artists Cir.; mem. nat. coun. Aspen Santa Fe Ballet; bd. dirs. Found. Santa Fe C.C.; mem. Santa Fe Chamber Music Festival. Mem. NAFE, Am. Hist. Assn., Phi Alpha Theta. Episcopalian. Avocations: book collecting, skiing, mountain climbing. Office: EMC2 Ste 103 9705 Carroll Center Rd San Diego CA 92126-6505

GRAYDON, FRANK DRAKE, retired accounting educator, university administrator; b. Ovalo, Tex., Feb. 11, 1921; s. Alonzo Otis and Jennie Lewis (Drake) G.; m. Mary Elizabeth Galt, June 16, 1943; children: Geoffrey Galt, David Drake. BBA, Tex. Tech. Coll., 1941; MBA, Northwestern U., 1943. CPA, Tex. Pub. acct. David Himmelblau & Co., Chgo., 1942-44; lectr. in acctg. Northwestern U., Chgo., 1942-44; instr. acctg. Tex. Tech. Coll., 1944-45; chief acct. U. Houston, 1945-46; asst. prof. acctg. U. Tex., 1946-50; with fin. statement sect. Ctrl. Contrs. Office Ford Motor Co., Dearborn, Mich., 1950-51; budget examiner Agys. of Higher Edn., Legis. Budget Bd., Austin, Tex., 1951-55; fin. planning staff Temp. Commn. on Higher Edn., Austin, 1954-55; budget dir. and prof. acctg. U. Tex. Sys., Austin, 1955-90, spl. counsel budget and fin., Office of the Chancellor, 1990-93, budget dir. emeritus, 1993—; prof. acctg. emeritus U. Tex., Austin, 1993—. Mem. AICPA. Home: 8158 Ceberry Dr Austin TX 78759-8743 Office: Univ Tex Sys 601 Colorado St Austin TX 78701-2904

GRAYESKI, MARY LYNN, chemist, consultant; BS in Chemistry, Kings Coll., 1974; PhD in Analytical Chemistry, U. N.H., 1982. Tchg., rsch. asst. U. N.H., Durham, 1979-82; asst. prof. Seton Hall U., S. Orange, N.J., 1982-87, assoc. prof., 1987-93, chair chemistry dept., 1991-93; program officer Rsch. Corp., Tucson, 1993—2002. Mem. govning. bd. Fa Analytical Symposium, N.J., 1985-93. Contbr. over 30 articles to profl. jours. Vol. ACTION/VISTA, Midland, Tex., 1975; vol. recruiter ACTION, San Francisco, 1976; vol. ACTION/Peach Corps, Ghana, 1977-78; judge Internat. Sci. and Engring. Fair, 1996. Mem. Am. Chem. Soc., Delta Epsilon Sigma.

GRAYHACK, JOHN THOMAS, urologist, educator; b. Kankakee, Ill., Aug. 21, 1923; s. John and Marie (Keckich) G.; m. Elizabeth Houlchin, June 3, 1950; children: Elizabeth, Anne Marie, Linda Jean, John, William. BS, U. Chgo., 1945, MD, 1947. Diplomate Am. Bd. Urology. Intern medicine Billings Hosp., Chgo., 1947; intern gen. surgery Johns Hopkins Hosp., 1947-48, asst. resident, 1948-49, fellow urology, 1949-50, asst. resident, 1950-52; resident urology, 1952-53; dir. Kretschmer Lab., Northwestern U. Med. Sch., 1956-75, prof. urology, 1963—, chmn. dept., 1961-90. Cons. VA Rsch. Hosp. Editor Year Book of Urology, 1963-78; editor Jour. Urology, 1985-94. Served to capt. USAF, 1954-56. Recipient Outstanding Achievement award USAF, Ferdinand C. Valentine award N.Y. Acad. Medicine, Disting. Svc. award U. Chgo., 1978, Pioneer award Internat. Symposium Biology Prostate Growth, 1998; fellow Am. Cancer Soc., 1949-50, Damon Runyon Fund, 1953-54, Johns Hopkins Soc. Scholars. Mem. AMA, Ill., Chgo. med. socs., Am. Assn. Genitourinary Surgeons (Barringer medal, Keyes medal), Am. Urology Assn. (Hugh H. Young award, Fuller award, Mary Hugh and Russell Scott award, Ramon Guiteras award 1994), Soc. Urol. Oncology (Huggins medal 2002), Chgo. Urology Soc. (John T. Grayhack lectr.), Endocrine Soc., Clin. Soc. Genitourinary Surgeons, Am. Surg. Assn., Soc. Univ. Urologists, Nephrology Soc., Phi Beta Kappa, Alpha Omega Alpha. Home: 95 N Park Rd La Grange IL 60525-5938 Office: Northwestern Meml Hosp Superior St Fairbanks Ct Chicago IL 60611

GRAY-NIX, ELIZABETH WHITWELL, occupational therapist; b. Milton, Mass., Apr. 9, 1956; d. Roland and Susan (Brooks) Gray; m. Ronald Harding Nix; 1 child, Roger Harrison Nix. BS, Syracuse U., N.Y., 1978. Registered occupl. therapist. From occupl. therapist to clin. supr. Walter E. Fernald State Sch., Waltham, Mass., 1978-97; dir. occupl. therapy The Fernald Ctr., 1997—. Trustee Mass. Jaycees Charitable Trust, Mansfield, 1983-91; dir.-at-large South End Hist. Soc., Boston, 1983-85, fundraising dir., 1985-87; alumni rep. Beaver country Day Sch., Brookline, 1974-99, alumni sec., 1988-94. Recipient Baystater award #060, Mass. Jaycees, 1984, Armbruster Keyman award, 1981, Merit award, Maddak, Inc., 1991, 96, Jaycee Internat. Senatorship award, 1992, Mass. State Employee Svc. award, 1998, Paul Duhamel Svc. award, 2000. Mem. Mass. Occupational Therapists Assn., State Employed Occupational Therapists Assn. (union rep.), Am. Occupational Therapists Assn., World Fedn. Occupational Therapists, Mass. Nurses Assn.(bd. dirs. 2002), Jaycees Internat. (Mass. sec., pres. Riverside chpt. 1983, mem. coun. Newton chpt. 1979-82, state sec. 1994-95), Boston Ctr. for Arts (mem. coun. 1979-84). Home: 90 Pelham Island Rd Sudbury MA 01776-3132 Office: The Fernald Ctr 200 Trapelo Rd Ste 1 Waltham MA 02452-6302

GRAYSHAW, JAMES RAYMOND, judge; b. Cleve., Apr. 3, 1948; s. Thomas J. and Bettie Lee Grayshaw; m. Susan Hancher, Oct. 15, 1980; 1 child, John H. BA, L.I. U., Bklyn., 1970; JD, Bklyn. Law Sch., 1975. Legal asst. Cadwalader, Wickersham & Taft, N.Y.C., 1975-77; law asst. Civil Ct., City N.Y., 1977-80; sr. law asst. Supreme Ct., State N.Y., 1980-82; judge housing part Civil Ct., City N.Y., 1983—. Judge advocate Cmty. Advocacy Ctr., N.Y.C., 1996. Sgt. U.S. Army, 1970-72. Mem. Queens Bar Assn., Protestant Lawyers N.Y.C. (dir. 1980—), Vietnam Vets. Am., 16th Inf. Reg. Assn., Masons, Sovereign Mil. Order of Temple of Jerusalem. Democrat. Episcopalian. Home: 21107 28th Ave Bayside NY 11360-2508 Office: Civil Ct City NY 89-17 Sutphin Blvd Jamaica NY 11435 E-mail: jgrayshaw@aol.com., jgraysha@courts.state.ny.us.

GRAYSMITH, ROBERT, political cartoonist, author; b. Pensacola, Fla., Sept. 17, 1942; s. Robert Gray and Frances Jane (Scott) Smith; m. Melanie Krakower, Oct. 15, 1975 (div. Sept. 1980); children— David Martin, Aaron Vincent, Margot Alexandra. BA, Calif. Coll. Arts and Crafts, 1965. Polit. cartoonist: Oakland (Calif.) Tribune, 1964-65, Stockton (Calif.) Record, 1965-68, San Francisco Chronicle, 1968-83 ; author: (non-fiction) Zodiac, 1986,Trailside, 1986, The Sleeping Lady, 1990, The Murder of Bob Crane, 1993, Unabomber: A Desire to Kill, 1997, The Bell-Tower, A True Detective Story of Gas-lit SanFrancisco, 1999, Ghost Fleet, 1999, Zodiac Unmasked, 2002, (motion pictured adapted from The Murder of Bob Crane) Auto-Focus, 2002, Amerithrax: The Hunt for the Anthrax Killer, 2003; illustrator (children's book by Penny Wallace) I Didn't Know What to Get You, 1993. Recipient 2d place Fgn. Press Awards 1973, World Population Contest 1976. Democrat. Presbyterian. Office: San Francisco Chronicle 901 Mission St San Francisco CA 94103-2905

GRAYSON, ALBERT KIRK, Near Eastern studies educator; b. Windsor, Ont., Can., Apr. 1, 1935; s. Albert Kirk and Helen (Smith) Grayson'; m. Eunice Marie Service, Aug. 3, 1956; children: Vera Lorraine, Sally Frances. BA, U. Toronto, Ont., 1955; MA, U. Toronto, 1958; postgrad., U. Vienna, Austria, 1959-60; PhD, Johns Hopkins U., 1962. Research asst. Chgo. Assyrian Dictionary Oriental Inst., Chgo., 1962-63; asst. prof. history Temple U., Phila., 1963-64; asst. prof. Near Eastern studies U. Toronto, 1964-67, assoc. prof., 1967-72, prof., 1972-2000, prof. emeritus, 2000—. Dir. Royal Inscriptions of Mesopotamia project, 1981—; vis. lectr. U. Pa., Phila., 1963-64; spl. asst. dept. Western Asiatic Antiquities Brit. Mus., London, intermittently, 1967-76; invited lectr. various univs., mus., U.S., Germany, Iraq, Eng., Austria, Italy Author: Assyrian Royal Inscriptions vol. I, 1972, Assyrian Royal Inscriptions vol. II, 1976, Assyrian and Babylonian Chronicles, 1975, Babylonian Historical-Literary Texts, 1975, Assyrian Rulers of the Third and Second Millennia, B.C. 1987, Assyrian Rulers of the Early First Millennium BC I-II, 1991-96; contbr. chpts. to books. Can. Council fellow, 1959-61; Samuel S. Fels Fund fellow, 1961-62; Social Scis. and Humanities Research Council Can. editorial grantee, 1981— Fellow Royal Soc. Can. (hon. sec. 1989-92); mem. Soc. Mesopotamian Studies (pres. 1980-92), Fondation Assyriologique Georges Dossin (Belgium), Oriental Club Toronto (sec. 1969-70, pres. 1979-80), Rencontre Assyriologique Internationale (sessional chmn. Berlin 1978, Vienna 1980, Leiden, Netherlands 1983), Am. Oriental Soc. (sec. Midwest br. 1965-68). Mem. Anglican Ch. of Canada. Office: U Toronto Near and Middle East Studies 4 Bancroft Ave Toronto ON Canada M5S 1A1

GRAYSON, CHARLES JACKSON, JR., research association executive; b. Ft. Necessity, La., Oct. 8, 1923; s. Charles Jackson and Daphne (DeGraffenreid) G.; m. Carla O'Dell, Dec. 11, 1982; children: Christopher Jackson, Michael Wiley, Randall Charles, Daniel Jackson. BBA, Tulane U., 1944; MBA, U. Pa., 1947; D.BA, Harvard, 1959. C.P.A., La. Instr., then asst. prof. Sch. Bus. Adminstrn., Tulane U., 1947-55, assoc. prof., 1959-63; assoc. dean Sch. Bus. Adminstrn., Tulane U. (Sch. Bus. Adminstrn.), 1961-63, dean, prof., 1963-68; dean Sch. Bus. Adminstrn., So. Meth. U., 1968-75, prof., 1968-75; chmn., founder Am. Productivity and Quality Ctr., Houston, 1975—. Chmn. Price Commn., Washington, 1971-73; vis. prof. Grad. Sch. Bus., Stanford, spring 1967; prof. IMEDE (Mgmt. Devel. Program), Switzerland, 1963-64; spl. agt. FBI, Washington, 1950-52; partner James E. O'Neill & Assocs., New Orleans, 1952-53. Reporter: New Orleans Item, 1949-50; author: Decisions Under Uncertainty: Drilling Decisions by Oil and Gas Operators, 1960, Confessions of a Price Controller, 1974, American Business: A Two-Minute Warning, 1988, 1988; co-author: (with Carla O'Dell) If We Only Knew What We Konw, 1998; contbr. articles to profl. publs. Served with USNR, 1943-46. Mem. Beta Gamma Sigma, Delta Tau Delta. Home: 123 N Post Oak Ln Houston TX 77024-7715

GRAYSON, DAVID S. paper company executive; b. Binghamton, N.Y., Oct. 16, 1943; s. Milton M. and Helen A. (Oretskin) G.; m. Wendy W. Grayson (div. June 1986); children: Natalie, Marc, Dana. BS, Coll. Forestry, Syracuse, N.Y., 1965; MS, Rensselaer Poly., 1967. Various positions Riegel Paper div. James River Co., Milford, N.J., 1967-80; sales mgr. Kerwin Paper, Appleton, Wis., 1980-81; pres., founder Am. Fine Paper, Appleton, 1981—. Jewish. Office: Am Fine Paper PO Box 2638 Appleton WI 54912-2638

GRAYSON, EDWARD DAVIS, lawyer, manufacturing company executive; b. Davenport, Iowa, June 20, 1938; s. Charles F. and Isabelle (Davis) G.; m. Alice Ann McLaughlin; children: Alice Anne, Maureen Isabelle, Edward Davis Jr. BA, U. Iowa, 1960, LLB, 1964. Bar: Iowa 1964, Mass. 1967. Atty. Goodwin, Procter & Hoar, Boston, 1967-74; sr. v.p., gen. counsel Wang Labs., Inc., Lowell, Mass., 1974-92; v.p., gen. counsel Honeywell, Inc., Mpls., 1992—99. Trustee U. Lowell, Mass., 1981-87, chmn. bd. trustees, 1982-85, 87; dir. Bus. Econs. Edn. Found., 1992—. Capt. USAF, 1964-67. Mem. ABA (com. corp. law depts.), Mass. Bar Assn. (bd. dels. 1977-80), Greater Mpls. C. of C. (dir. 1992—).*

GRAYSON, MARK, organization executive; b. Akron, Ohio, June 15, 1957; s. Thomas David G. and Suzanne Marie (Miller) Rowins; m. Sarah Richardson Houghton, Dec. 3, 1988; children: William Parker, Philip Houghton. BA cum laude, Harvard U., 1979; MBA, Columbia U., 1987. Asst. acct. exec. AC&R Advtsg., Inc., N.Y.C., 1981-83; acct. exec. North Castle Pntrs., Greenwich, Conn., 1983-85; tv packaging agent, v.p. internat. t.v. Triad Artists, Inc., L.A., 1987-92; pres., dir. Rabbit Ears Prodns., Inc., Rowayton, Conn., 1992-96; prin. Graybark Enterprises, Norwalk, Conn., 1996-98; CEO, exec. dir. All Kinds of Minds, Chapel Hill, NC, 1998—. Contbr. articles to profl. jours. Mem. The Fly Club, Beta Gamma Sigma. Office: All Kinds of Minds PO Box 3580- Chapel Hill NC 27515

GRAYSON, RICHARD ANDREW, aerospace engineer; b. Silver Spring, Md., Aug. 5, 1966; s. Benson Lee and Helen Marie (Donovan) G. BS in Aerospace Engring., U. Va., 1988; MBA, U. Ga., 1995, PhD in Fin., 2001. Engr. Army Rsch. Lab., Aberdeen Proving Ground, Md., 1989-95; engr., rschr. Terry Coll. Bus./U. Ga., Athens, 1995-99; vis. prof. fin. U. Del., Newark, 1999-2000, U. Ga., Athens, 2001—; asst. prof. Loyola Coll. Md., Balt., 2001—, asst. prof. fin., 2001—. Mem. Joint Tech. Coordinating Group Air Sys., Wright-Patterson AFB, Ohio, 1990-95; leader PATRIOT Assessment Team, Riyadh, Saudi Arabia, 1991-92. Advisor youth group Episcopal Ch., McLean, Va., 1988-94. Recipient comdr.'s award for civilian svc. Dept. Army, 1991. Mem. Am. Helicopter Soc., Internat. Platform Assn., Source Selection Evaluation bd., Army LHX helicopter. Achievements include leader of on-site investigations in

Saudi Arabia and at Ballistic Rsch. Lab, to assist in evaluating PATRIOT lethality against SCUD-B tactical ballistic missiles fired in Operation Desert Storm; performed AH-64 and UH-60 crew station vulnerability tests. Home: 3811 Canterbury Rd Apt 1011 Baltimore MD 21218 Office: Dept Fin Loyola Coll Med Baltimore MD 21210

GRAYSON, ROBERT LARRY, mining engineering educator, mining executive; b. Balt., Jan. 17, 1947; s. Charles Clinton and Nora Elizabeth (Burchette) Grayson; m. Karen Sue Miller, Nov. 16, 1966 (div. July 1971); 1 child, Jeffrey Robert; m. Maxine Louise Maurin, Mar. 24, 1972; children: David Michael, Jennifer Renee. BA in Math., California (Pa.) U., 1974; BS in Mining, W.Va. U., 1978, MS in Mining, 1981, PhD in Mining Engrng., 1986. Registered profl. engr., Pa., W.Va., Mo., cert. mine foreman, Pa. Prodn. foreman, engr. Nemacolin (Pa.) Mines Corp., 1975-81; group chief engr. J&L Steel Corp., Pitts., 1981-82, supt. Nemacolin Coal Mine, 1982-84; from grad. asst. to asst. prof. W.Va. U., Morgantown, 1984-89, assoc. prof., 1989-91, prof. mining engrng., dean Coll. Mineral & Energy Resources, 1991-95; prof. mining engrng. U. Mo., Rolla, 1996-97, chair dept. mining engrng., 2000—; assoc. dir. mining Nat. Inst. for Occupl. Safety and Health, Ctr. for Disease Control and Prevention, Washington, 1997-2000. Cons. to law firms and mining cos., 1984—. Co-editor: Use of Computers in Coal, 1987, 1990, 1996; contbr. . Pres. parish coun. St. Mary Ch., Crucible, Pa., 1988—91. With USAF, 1965—72. Recipient Profl. Excellence award, California U. Pa., 1992, Alice Hamilton award in phys. sci., NIOSH, 1998, Highest Degree of Safety award, ISMSP, 2001. Mem.: AIME, NSPE, Ill. Mining Inst., Internat. Soc. Mine Safety Profls. (bd. dirs.), Soc. Mining Engrs. (Disting. Mem. award, Henry Krumb lectr.), Pitts. Coal Mining Inst. Am. (bd. dirs. 1989—96), Nat. Safety Coun., W.Va. Coal Mining Inst. (sec. 1991—96), Soc. Mining, Metallurgy and Exploration (various offices, bd. dirs., Disting. Mem. award 2002), St. Louis Coal Club. Republican. Roman Catholic. Avocations: golf, racquetball, horseshoes, computers, math problems. Home: 802 Lariat Ln Rolla MO 65401 Office: UMR Dept Mining Engrng 226 McNutt Hall 1870 Miner Cir Rolla MO 65409-0450 E-mail: graysonl@umr.edu.

GRAYSON KURZWEIL, BETTE RITA, lawyer; b. Newark, July 10, 1947; d. Sidney and Joan (Rosenman) G.; m. Stanley Noah Kruzweil, Aug. 17, 1975; children: Jeremy, Cynthia. BA, NYU, 1969; JD, Bklyn. Law Sch., 1977. Bar: N.J. 1977. Pvt. practice, Union and Springfield, N.J., 1977—. Former real estate counsel City of Plainfield, N.J.; former spl. real estate counsel City of Orange; former rev. atty. for State Bank South Orange, N.J.; chairperson Fee Arbitration Com. Union County, N.J.; mem. adv. bd. Crown Bank, 1998—; rev. atty. First Americano. V.p. Millburn (N.J.) Hadassah, 1985-87, mem. steering com. for planned gifts, 1996-99; trustee Internat. Youth Orgn., 1997—; treas. Millburn Hoopsters, 1997-99. Recipient Trust Bklyn. Law Sch., 1974, Woman of Excellence award Union County, 1998. Mem. Women Lawyers Union County (pres. 1990-92, v.p. 1988-90, sec. 1983-84, treas. 1986-88). Democrat. Office: 140 Mountain Ave Springfield NJ 07081-1725

GRAYSTON, J. THOMAS, medical and public health educator; b. Wichita, Kans., Sept. 6, 1924; s. Jesse T. and Luzia B. (Thomas) Grayston; m. M. Nan Bryant, June 7, 1980; children: Susan, Jesse, David. Student, Carleton Coll., 1942—43; BS, U. Chgo., 1947, MD, 1948, MS, 1952. Diplomate Am. Bd. Internal Medicine, Am. Bd. Preventive Medicine. Intern Albany (N.Y.) Med. Sch., 1948—49; Seymour Coman fellow preventive medicine U. Chgo., 1949—50, asst. resident medicine, 1950—51; epidemiologist epidemic intelligence svc. USPHS, U. Kans. Med. Ctr., 1951—53; chief resident medicine U. Chgo., 1953—54, instr. medicine, 1953—55; fellow Nat. Found. Infantile Paralysis, 1954—56; asst. prof. medicine U. Chgo., 1955—60, assoc. prof., 1960; chief divsn. microbiology and epidemiology U.S. Naval Med. Rsch. Unit 2, Taipei, Taiwan, 1957—60, cons., 1960—79; prof. preventive medicine, chmn. dept. U. Wash. Sch. Medicine, 1960—70, founding dean Sch. Pub. Health and Community Medicine, 1970—71, v.p. for health scis., 1971—83, prof. dept. epidemiology, 1970—, adj. prof. pathobiology, 1982—; mem. exec. com. Regional Primate Rsch. Ctr., 1964—70, research affiliate, 1967—70; attending physician medicine Univ. Hosp., Seattle, 1960—70. Assoc. mem. commn. acute respiratory diseases Armed Forces Epidemiol. Bd., 1962—65; rsch. and engrng. adv. panel biology and medicine Dept. Def., 1963—67; sci. group trachoma rsch. WHO, 1963, expert adv. panel on Trachoma, 1970—88; virology and rickettsiology study sect. NIH, 1963—67, chmn. exec. com., nat. adv. council on health professions edn, 1972—75; internat. centers com. Nat. Inst. Allergy and Infectious Diseases, 1967—71. Contbr. articles to profl. jours. Fellow: Am. Pub. Health Assn. (governing bd. 1978—80), Am. Coll. Preventive Medicine (v.p. gen. preventive medicine 1970—71, regent 1971—74); mem.: Western Soc. Clin. Rsch., Western Assn. Physicians, Inst. Medicine NAS, Soc. Exptl. Biology and Medicine, Internat. Epidemiol. Assn., Infectious Diseases Soc., Assn. Tchrs. Preventive Medicine, Assn. Acad. Health Centers (dir. 1975—80, pres. 1978—79), Am. Soc. Tropical Medicine and Hygiene, Am. Soc. Clin. Investigation, Am. Soc. Microbiology, Am. Fedn. Clin. Rsch., Am. Epidemiol. Soc. (pres. 1982—83), Am. Assn. Physicians, Am. Assn. Immunologists. Office: U Washington Dept Epidemiology Ms 357236 Seattle WA 98195-0001

GRAZER, BRIAN, film company executive; Co-chair Imagine Films Entertainment. Prodr. films including: Night Shift, 1982, Splash, 1984, Real Genius, 1985, Spies Like Us (with George Folsey Jr.), 1985, Armed & Dangerous (with James Keach), 1986, Like Father, Like Son (with David Valdes, 1987, Parenthood, 1989, Cry Baby (with Jim Abrahams, 1990, Kindergarten Cop (with Ivan Reitman), 1990, Closet Land (with Ron Howard), 1991, The Doors (with Nicholas Clainos & Mario Kassar), 1991, Backdraft (with Raffaella DeLaurentiis), 1991, My Girl, 1991, Far and Away (with Ron Howard), 1992, Boomerang (with Warrington Hudlin), 1992, Housesitter, 1992, CB4 (with Sean Daniel), 1993, For Love or Money, 1993, The Paper (with Frederick Zollo), 1994, My Girl 2, 1994, Greedy, 1994, The Cowboy Way, 1994, Apollo 13 (with Ron Howard), 1995 (Acad. Award Nom. Best Picture, 1996), Sgt. Bilko, 1996, Ransom, 1996, Bowfinger, 1999, Beyond the Mat, 1999, Curious George, 2000, Nutty Professor II: The Klumps, 2000, How the Grinch Stole Christmas, 2000, Wonderland (TV series), 2000. Office: Imagine Films Entertainment 9465 Wilshire Blvd Fl 7 Beverly Hills CA 90212-2606

GRAZIANI, LEONARD JOSEPH, pediatric neurologist, researcher; b. Phila., Nov. 17, 1929; m. Amelia Honeyford, June 29, 1956; children: Paul, Amy, Virginia, David. BA, LaSalle Coll., Phila., 1951; MD, Jefferson Med. Coll., Phila., 1955. Diplomate Am. Bd. Pediatrics, Am. Bd. Psychiatry and Neurology. Intern Valley Forge Army Hosp., Pa., 1956; resident Brooke Army Hosp., San Antonio, 1959; chief pediatric svc. Ireland Army Hosp., Ft. Knox, Ky., 1960-61; neurology fellow Bronx Mcpl. Hosp. Ctr., N.Y., 1961-64; interdisciplinary fellow Albert Einstein Coll. Medicine, Bronx, N.Y., 1964-66, asst. prof. pediatrics and neurology, 1964-68; career scientist Health Rsch. Coun., N.Y.C., 1967-68; attending pediatrician, neurologist Thomas Jefferson U. Hosp., Phila., 1968—; chief div. pediatric neurology dept. pediatrics Jefferson Med. Coll., Thomas Jefferson U., Phila., 1974-99, vice chair dept. pediatrics, 1988-96, prof. pediatrics, neurology, 1968—. Cons. neurologist The Woods Schs., Langhorne, Pa., 1968—, Children's Rehab. Hosp., Phila.; cons. pediatrician Wills Eye Hosp., Phila.; staff cons. Wilmington (Del.) Med. Ctr.; staff E.I. duPont Inst., Wilmington, 1984—. Contbr. articles to profl. jours. Capt. U.S. Army, 1955-61. Fellow Am. Acad. Neurology, Am. Acad. Pediatrics; mem. Am. Pediatric Soc., Soc. Pediatric Rsch., Child Neurology Soc., Alpha Omega Alpha, Sigma Xi. Office: Jefferson Med Coll 1025 Walnut St Rm 700 Philadelphia PA 19107-5001 E-mail: lgrazi9361@aol.com.

GRAZIANO, CATHERINE ELIZABETH, state legislator, retired nursing educator; b. Providence, Dec. 2, 1931; d. William J. and Catherine E. (Keegan) Hawkins; m. Louis W. Graziano, Oct. 9, 1954; children: Mary Lou, William F., Catherine E., Paul, Carol. BS, Salve Regina Coll., Newport, R.I., 1953, MS, 1984, Boston Coll., 1965; PhD, Pacific Western U., 1988. Instr. nursing Salve Regina U., 1953-66, asst. prof., 1966-74, assoc. prof., 1974-82, prof., 1982-97, chair dept. nursing, 1974-93, ret., 1997; staff-charge nurse St. Joseph's Hosp., Providence, 1953-93, part-time faculty, 1960, 65; mem. R.I. Senate, Dist. 5, Providence, 1992—2002. Mem. R.I. Bd. Nurse Registration and Edn., 1970-79, pres., 1977-79; charter mem., sec. R.I. Health, Sci. and Edn. Council, 1972-78; adj. asst. prof. Coll. Nursing U. R.I., 1986-2000; mem. R.I. Senate, Providence, 1992-2002, chairperson health, edn. and welfare com., 2001-02. Active local and nat. senatorial campaigns. Named Outstanding RI Pro-Life Legislator, 2001; recipient Regina medal, Salve Regina U., 1997, Bishop's award, 2001. Mem. ANA, R.I. Nurses Assn. (pres. 1969-71, 73-75), Women Educators (charter), Nursing Leadership Coun. R.I. (charter, chair 1981-82, sec. 1982—), Nat. League Nursing (accreditation site visitor 1990-96), Sigma Theta Tau. Roman Catholic. Home: 42 Rowley St Providence RI 02909-5521

GRAZIANO, CRAIG FRANK, lawyer; b. Des Moines, Dec. 7, 1950; s. Charles Dominic and Corrine Rose (Comito) G. BA summa cum laude, Macalester Coll., 1973; JD with honors, Drake U., 1975. Bar: Iowa 1976, U.S. Dist. Ct. (no. and so. dists.) Iowa 1978, U.S. Ct. Appeals (8th cir.) 1977, U.S. Supreme Ct. 1988. Law clk. to Hon. M. D. Van Oosterhout U.S. Ct. Appeals (8th cir.), Sioux City, Iowa, 1976-78; pvt. practice Dickinson, Mackaman, Tyler & Hagen, PC, Des Moines, 1978-98; with Office of Consumer Advocate, Iowa Dept. Justice, Des Moines, 1999—. Mem. Gov.'s Task Force on Quality and Efficiency in Govt., 1999—2000. Mem. Iowa Bar Assn. (chair specialization com. 1993-96, chair adminstrv. law sect. 1996-99), Order of Coif, Phi Beta Kappa. Home: 500 44th St Des Moines IA 50312-2408 Office: 310 Maple St Des Moines IA 50319-0063 E-mail: craig.graziano@mchsi.com, cgraziano@mail.oca.state.ia.us.

GRAZIANO, JOHN MICHAEL, music educator; b. NYC, May 7, 1938; s. John and Anna Graziano; m. Roberta K Kochanczyk, Mar. 23, 1963; children: Laura Beth, Paul David. BS, NYU, 1959; BA, CUNY, 1964; MusM, Yale U., 1966, MPh, PhD, Yale U., 1969. Prof. CUNY, N.Y.C., 1967—. Editor: American Music, 1985—88; contbr. articles to profl. jours. (Richard Hill award for the best bibliog. article, 1994, Lowens award for Best article on Am. Music in 2000, 2002). Co-dir. Music in Gotham, N.Y.C. Cpl. U.S. Army, 1960—61. Recipient Composition award, NEA, 1986; grantee, 1986, 2002—; scholar Rockefeller scholar, NY Pub. Libr., 1987. Mem.: Soc. for Am. Music (v.p. 1995—99), Am. Musicological Soc. Home: 146 18 32 Avenue Flushing NY 11354 Office: Graduate Center City University of NY 365 Fifth Avenue New York NY 10036 Home Fax: same no.. Personal E-mail: jgraziano@ccny.cuny.edu.

GRAZIANO, RONALD ANTHONY, lawyer; b. N.Y.C., Aug. 13, 1948; s. Charles and Anna (DiPasquale) G.; m. Helen Ann McFadden, Aug. 4, 1973. B.A. in Polit. Sci., Fordham U., 1970; J.D., Rutgers-Camden Sch. Law, 1973. Bar: N.Y. 1974, N.J. 1974, U.S. Dist. Ct. N.J. 1974, U.S. Ct. Appeals (2d and 3d cirs.) 1975, U.S. Ct. Appeals (D.C. cir.) 1978, U.S. Supreme Ct. 1979; cert. civil trial atty Supreme Ct. of N.J. Law clk. to presiding judge U.S. Dist. Ct., N.J., 1973-74; assoc. Tomar, Parks, Seliger, Simonoff & Adourian, Haddonfield, N.J., 1974-79, ptnr., 1979— . Assoc. editor Rutgers-Camden Law Jour., 1972-73. Bd. dirs. Camden Regional Legal Services, 1977-80; mem. Planning Bd., Mount Laurel, N.J., 1981, 83, 84; councilman Mount Laurel Twp., 1981-83, mayor, 1984. Mem. Rutgers-Camden Law Sch. Alumni Assn. (chancellor 1976-77), Am. Arbitration Assn. (nat. panel 1979—), Camden County Bar Assn., N.J. State Bar Assn., ABA, Assn. Trial Lawyers Am. (exec. com. N.J. chpt. 1975). Democrat. Roman Catholic. Office: Tomar Parks Seliger Simonoff Adourian& O'Brien 41 S Haddon Ave Haddonfield NJ 08033-1800

GRAZIER, DIANA LYNN, community health nurse, medical/surgical nurse, writer; b. Washington, Oct. 17, 1958; d. Leroy Bone and Carol Lee Griswold; m. James Edward Grazier, Aug. 5, 1989; m. Merrill Kendrick Williams, Sept. 11, 1976 (div. June 1989); 1 child, Carmen Jennetta Williams. Diploma, Rockford Area Vocat. Ctr., 1976; BS in Health Arts, U. St. Francis, 1999. Rn, Ill., 1985. Nurse Sycamore Mcpl. Hosp., Ill., 1977—85, Valley Hosp., Las Vegas, 1985—86; charge nurse El-Jen Convalescent Ctr., Las Vegas, 1987—91; head nurse, asst. dir. nursing Vegas Valley Convalescent Hosp., 1991—95; case mgr. Sierra Health Svcs., Las Vegas, 1996—99; charge nurse La Paz Regional Hosp., Parker, Ariz., 1999—2000; pub. health nurse La Paz County Health Dept., 2001—; dir. nursing La Paz Clin. Health Dept., 2003—. Author: The Price of Fame, 2001, One Last Dance, 2002, The Heart of Hidden Secrets, 2003. Recipient Best Poets of 2002, Internat. Libr. of Poets, 2002. Avocations: writing, reading, crocheting, piano. Office: La Paz County Health Dept 1112 Joshua Ave Ste 206 Parker AZ 85344 Home Fax: 928-505-3283. Personal E-mail: jeg91dlg@citlink.net.

GREANEY, JOHN M. state supreme court justice; b. Westfield, Mass., Apr. 8, 1939; s. Patrick Joseph and Margaret Irene (Fitzgerald) G.; m. Susan H. Greaney, Nov. 23, 1967. 1 child, Jessica S. BA summa cum laude, Holly Cross Coll., 1960; JD, NYU, 1963; LLD (hon.), Westfield State Coll., 1967, Western New England Coll., 1969; LLD, New England Law Sch., 1991. Bar: Mass., Supreme Judicial Ct., U.S. Dist. Ct., U.S. Supreme Ct. Ptnr. Ely & King, Springfield, Mass., 1963-73; presiding judge Hampden County Housing Ct., Springfield, Mass., 1973-75; assoc. judge Mass. Superior Ct., Boston, 1975-76; assoc. justice Mass. Appeals Ct., Boston, 1976-84, 1976-84, chief justice, 1984-89; assoc. justice Mass. Supreme Judicial Ct., Boston, 1989—. Former faculty mem. Western New England Law Sch., Westfield State Coll.; co-chair. Supreme Judicial Ct's Gender Bias Study Commn; mem. bd. Tribunes WGBY-Channel #57. Former assoc. editor Mass. Law Review. Trustee, dir. Westfield Atheneum, participant Child and Family Svcs. Program. Fellow Am. Bar Found.; mem. ABA (litigation, judicial adminstrn. section), Hampden County Bar Assn.(former mem. exec. com., grievance com., treas.), Mass. Bar Assn.(former chmn. Young Lawyers section, bd. delegates, exec. com., grievance com., legal svc. to the poor com.,(current) civil litigation, criminal law sections), Am. Law Inst. Avocations: competitive running, reading. Office: 1 Beacon St 3rd Fl Boston MA 02108-1701*

GREASER, CONSTANCE UDEAN, automotive industry executive; b. Jan. 18, 1938; d. Lloyd Edward and Udean Greaser. BA, San Diego State Coll., 1959; postgrad., U. Copenhagen Grad. Sch. Fgn., 1963, Georgetown U. Sch. Fgn. Svc., 1967; MA, U. So. Calif., 1968; exec. MBA, UCLA, 1981. Advt., publicity mgr. Crofton Co., San Diego, 1959-62; supr. Mercury Publs., Fullerton, Calif., 1962-64; supr. engrng. support svcs. divsn. Arcata Data Mgmt., Hawthorne, Calif., 1964-67; mgr. computerized typesetting dept. Continental Graphics, L.A., 1967-70; v.p., editl. dir. Sage Publs., Inc., Beverly Hills, Calif., 1970-74; head publs. RAND Corp., Santa Monica, Calif., 1974-90; mgr. svc. comms. Am. Honda Motors Co., Torrance, Calif., 1990—2002; ret., 2001. Co-author: Quick Writer-Build Your Own Word Procesing Users Guide, 1983, Quick Writer-Word Processing Center Operations Manual, 1984; editor: Urban Research News, 1971-74; mng. editor: Comparative Polit. Studies, 1971-74; contbr. articles to various jours. Mem. nat. com. Million Minutes of Peace Appeal, 1986, Nat. Info. Stds. Orgn., 1987-93, nat. com. Global Cooperation for Better World, 1988. Recipient Berber award Graphic Arts Tech. Found., 1989. Mem. Women in Bus. (pres. 1977-78), Graphic Comm. Assn. (bd. dirs. 1994-99), Soc. for Scholarly Pubs. (nat. bd. dirs.), Women in Comm., Soc. Tech. Comm.

GREASER, MARION LEWIS, science educator; b. Vinton, Iowa, Feb. 10, 1942; s. Lewis Levi and Elisabeth (Sage) G.; m. Marilyn Sue Pfister, June 12, 1965; children— Suzanne, Scott BS, Iowa State U., 1964; MS, U. Wis., 1967, PhD, 1969. Postdoctoral fellow Boston Biomed. Research Inst., 1968-71; asst. prof. sci. U. Wis., Madison, 1971-73, assoc. prof., 1973-77, prof., 1977—. Contbr. articles to profl. jours. Recipient Outstanding Researcher award Am. Heart Assn.-Wis., 1985 Mem. AAAS, Am. Soc. Biochem. Molecular Biology, Biophys. Soc., Inst. Food Technologists, Am. Meat Sci. Assn. (Disting. Research award 1981), Am. Soc. Animal Sci. (Meat Rsch. award 2000). Home: 2374 Branch St Middleton WI 53562-2809 Office: U Wis Muscle Biology Lab 1805 Linden Dr W Madison WI 53706-1110 E-mail: mgreaser@ansci.wisc.edu.

GREASON, ARTHUR LEROY, JR., retired university administrator; b. Newport, R.I., Sept. 13, 1922; s. Arthur LeRoy and Pauline (Brown) G.; m. Pauline Schaaf, Dec. 29, 1945; children— Randall Mark, Katherine, Douglas Bradford. BA, Wesleyan U., Middletown, Conn., 1945; MA, Harvard U., 1947, PhD, 1954; LittD (hon.), Wesleyan U., 1987; LHD (hon.), Colby Coll., 1989, Bowdoin Coll., 1990, Bates Coll., 1990, U. Maine, 1992. Asst. to dean Wesleyan U., 1945-46; teaching fellow English Harvard, 1948-52; mem. faculty Bowdoin Coll., 1952-90, assoc. prof. English, 1961-66, prof., 1966-90, dean students, 1962-66, dean of coll., 1966-75, acting pres., 1981, pres., 1981-90. Trustee Portland Stage Co., 1991-97, Westbrook Coll., 1992-96, Maine Hist. Soc., 1994-97, U. New England, 1996—, Maine Bd. Bar Examiners, 1997—, DLF Charitable Found., 1997—. Kent fellow Soc. Religion Higher Edn., 1946 Mem. Maine Bar Assn. (fee arbitration commn. 1997-2002), Phi Beta Kappa. Congregationalist. Home: 20 Birch Meadow Brunswick ME 04011-2955

GREASON, MURRAY CROSSLEY, JR., lawyer; b. Wake Forest, N.C., Dec. 12, 1936; s. Murray Crossley and Evelyn Elizabeth (Hackney) G.; m. Joan Millicent Wilder. BS magna cum laude, Wake Forest U., 1959, JD magna cum laude, 1962. Bar: N.C. 1962. Assoc. firm Womble Carlyle Sandridge & Rice, PLLC, Winston-Salem, N.C., 1965-70; mem. firm Womble Carlyle Sandridge & Rice, Winston-Salem, N.C., 1970—; mng. ptnr. firm Womble Carlyle Sandridge & Rice, PLLC, Winston-Salem, 1988-96. Vis. lectr. Wake Forest U., 1972-74. Pres. Winston-Salem Estate Planning Coun., 1973; trustee Denmark Loan Fund, scholarships to Wake Forest U.; bd. visitors Wake Forest Law Sch., 1983—, chmn. 1994-2000; trustee Wake Forest U., 1990, vice chmn., 1997-2002, chmn., 2003—; chmn. N.W. N.C. chpt. ARC, 1996; chmn. bd. United Way Forsyth County, 1995; mem. Commn. on Ministry Episcopalian Diocese N.C., 1983-93; bd. dirs. Winston-Salem Alliance, 2000—, Idealliance, 1998—, Wake Forest U. Health Scis., 2000—. Capt. JAG, AUS, 1962-65. Fellow Am. Coll. Tax Coun.; mem. ABA, N.C. Bar Assn., Forsyth County Bar Assn. (pres. 1986-87), Winston-Salem C. of C. (bd. dirs., vice chmn. 2001, chmn. 2002), Wake Forest U. Alumni Assn. (pres. 1973), Forsyth Country Club, Phi Beta Kappa, Omicron Delta Kappa. Episcopalian. Home: 745 Arbor Rd Winston Salem NC 27104-2209 Office: Womble Carlyle Sandridge PLLC PO Box 84 Winston Salem NC 27102-0084 E-mail: mgreason@wcsr.com.

GREAT, DON CHARLES, composer, music company executive; b. Medford, Oreg., Mar. 11, 1951; s. Donald Charles Sr. and Anna Marie (Huff) G.; m. Andrea Louise Gerber, Oct. 31, 1970. Student, UCLA, 1975-76, 83-86, Dick Grove Sch. Music, 1983-87. Freelance songwriter Metro-Goldwyn-Mayer Records, 20th Century Records, Bell Records, L.A., 1968—; pres. Don Great Music, Inc., L.A., 1972—. Composer music for TV shows and feature films including Dead Zone (USA), The Crow, District (CBS), Gilmore Girls (Warner), Judging Amy (CBS, Leap Years (Showtime), Who's the Boss? (ABC), 227 (NBC), The Jeffersons (CBS), Gimme a Break (NBC), A Different World (NBC), Facts of Life (NBC), Unsolved Mysteries (NBC), Amen (NBC), Freddie's Nightmares (Lorimar-Warner Bros. TV), Saved By the Bell (NBC Disney), One Day at a Time (CBS), Married With Children (Fox/Columbia Pictures), Small Wonder (Fox TV), 1978—, Different Strokes (NBC), BJ and the Bear (NBC), Silverspoons (NBC), Sheriff Lobo (NBC), Incredible Hulk (CBS), Sanford (NBC), Real People (NBC), Crimetime After Primetime (CBS), The Promised Land (CBS), Candid Camera, Tales From the Crypt, In Living Color (Fox-TV), Laugh-In, Baby Races, Walker: Texas Ranger (CBS), Sex And The City (HBO), Girl Interrupted (Columbia Pictures), The Visitor (Fox), Thelma and Louise, The X-Men 2 (20th Century Fox), The Hulk (Universal Pictures), Shanghai Knights (Touchstone Pictures); composer music score Pres. Reagen Libr. Video, Pres. Carter Presdl. Libr. CD-ROM, 1994. Mem. Broadcast Music, Inc. (Best Music Score of Yr. award 1986, named TV Composer of Yr. 1986). Avocations: playing piano, going for sunday drives. E-mail: dgreatmxx@aol.com.

GREATBATCH, WILSON, biomedical engineer; b. Buffalo, Sept. 6, 1919; married; 5 children. BEE, Cornell U., 1950; MSEE, U. Buffalo, 1957; ScD (hon.), Houghton Coll., 1971, SUNY, Buffalo, 1984, Clarkson U., 1987, Roberts Wesleyan Coll., 1988, D'Youville Coll., 2002. Project engr. Cornell Aeronaut Lab. Inc., 1950—52; asst. prof. elec. engring. U. Buffalo, 1952—57; mgr. electronics div. Taber Instrument Corp., 1957—60; v.p. Mennen Greatbatch Electronics Inc., 1962—78. Adj. prof. elec. engring. SUNY, Buffalo, 1981—; adj. prof. engring. Cornell U., Ithaca, NY, 1989—; adj. prof. physical scis. Houghton (N.Y.) Coll., 1978—; adj. prof. phys. scis. Kingston U., Niagara Falls, Ont., Canada, 2001—. Contbr. over 100 articles to sci. jours.; holder over 320 U.S. and fgn. patents. Named Paul Harris fellow, Rotary Internat., 1993; named to, Am. Inventors Hall of Fame, 1986, U.S. Space Tech. Hall of Fame, 1993, Sci. and Engring. Hall of Fame, 1997; recipient Holley medal, ASME, 1986, Chancellor Morton medal, U. Buffalo, 1990, disting. svc. award, NSPE, 1984, Pacemaker award, Prince Rainier of Monaco, 1988, Nat. Medal of Tech., Pres. Bush, 1990, Vladimir Karapetoff award, Eta Kappa Nu, 1992, Washington award, Western Engring. Soc., Chgo., 1995, Lemelson/MIT Career Achievement award, 1996. Fellow: ASME, IEEE, AAAS, N.Y. Acad. Scis., Am. Inst. Med. and Biol. Engring. (founder), Am. Soc. Angiology, Am. Coll. Cardiology, Royal Soc. Health; mem.: NAE (Russ prize 2001), Assn. Advancement Med. Instrumentation (Laufman award 1982), Eta Kappa Nu., Tau Beta Pi, Sigma Xi. Achievements include invention of implantable cardiac pacemaker; research in implantable power supplies for medical uses, biomass energy, genetic engineering. Home: 5935 Davison Rd Akron NY 14001-9457 Office: Greatbatch Enterprise Inc 10510 Main St Clarence NY 14031-1621

GREAVER, HARRY, artist; b. L.A., Oct. 30, 1929; s. Harry Jones and Lucy Catherine (Coons) G.; m. Hanne Synnestvedt Nielsen, Nov. 30, 1955; children— Peter, Paul, Lotte. BFA, U. Kans., 1951, MFA, 1952. Assoc. prof. art U. Maine, Orono, 1955-66; exec. dir. Kalamazoo Inst. Arts, 1966-78; dir. Greaver Gallery, Cannon Beach, Oreg., 1978—. Mem. visual com. Mich. Coun. Arts, 1976-78. One-man exhbns. include Baker U., Baldwin, Kans., 1955, U. Maine, Orono, 1958, 59, Pacific U., 1985; group exhbns. include U. Utah Mus. Fine Arts, 1972-73, Purdue U., 1977, Drawings/U.S.A, St. Paul, 1963, San Diego Mus., 1971, Rathbun Gallery, Portland, Oreg., 1988; 10-yr. print retrospective Cannon Beach Arts Assn., 1989, 20-yr. retrospective, 1998, 25 yr. Anniversary exhibit. Mem. adv. bd. Haystack Ctr. for the Arts, Cannon Beach, 1988-91. Recipient Purchase award Nat. Endowment Arts, 1971; grantee U. Maine, 1962-64 Mem. Cannon Beach Arts Assn., 1986-88. Address: PO Box 120 Cannon Beach OR 97110-0120

GREAVER, JOANNE HUTCHINS, mathematics educator, author; b. Louisville, Aug. 9, 1939; d. Alphonso Victor and Mary Louise (Sage) Hutchins; 1 child, Mary Elizabeth. BS in Chemistry, U. Louisville, 1961, MEd, 1971; MAT in Math., Purdue U., 1973. Cert. tchr. Pres. Math Mentors Inc., 1962—. Part-time faculty Bellarmine Coll., Louisville, 1982-2002, U. Louisville, 1985—; project reviewer NSF, 1983—; advisor Council on Higher Edn., Frankfort, Ky., 1983-86; active regional and nat. summit on assessment in math., 1991, state task force on math., assessment adv. com., Nat. Assessment Ednl. Progress standards com.; charter mem. Commonwealth Tchrs. Inst., 1984—; mem. Nat. Forum for Excellence in Edn., Indpls., 1983; metric edn. leader Fed. Metric Project, Louisville, 1979-82; mem. Ky. Ednl. Reform Task Force, Assessment Com., Nat. Framework, Nat. Assessment Ednl. Progress Rev. Com.; lectr. in field. Author: (workbook) Down Algebra Alley, 1984; co-author curriculum guides. Named Outstanding Citizen, SAR, 1984; named to Hon. Order Ky. Cols.; recipient Presdl. award for excellence in math. tchg., 1983; grantee, NSF, 1983, Louisville Cmty. Found., 1984—86. Mem. Greater Louisville Coun. Tchrs. of Math. (pres. 1977-78, 94-95, Outstanding Educator award 1987), Nat. Coun. Tchrs. of Math. (reviewer 1981—), Ky. Coun. Tchrs. of Math. (pres. 1990-91, Jefferson County Tchr. of Yr. award 1985), Math. Assn. Am., Kappa Delta Pi, Delta Kappa Gamma, Zeta Tau Alpha. Republican. Presbyterian. Avocations: tropical fish, gardening, handicrafts, travel, tennis. Home: 11513 Tazwell Dr Louisville KY 40241 E-mail: jogreaver@aol.com.

GREAVES, ALISON ASH, retired physician; b. Evanston, Ill., Dec. 15, 1928; d. William Henry and Edythe E. Tower Ash; m. Robert George Greaves, June 9, 1962; children: Edmund, Cordelia Ann. B in Philosophy, Northwestern U., 1953; MD, U. Ill., 1962, MPH, 1974. Diplomate Am. Bd. Pediats. Med. technologist Northwestern U. Med. Sch., Chgo., 1949-51, G.D. Searle, Skokie, Ill., 1951-53, Evanston Hosp., 1953-56, Aramco, Saudi Arabia, 1956-58; pediatrician Chgo. Bd. Health, 1966-67; med. dir. Infant Welfare Soc. Chgo., 1967-73; physician Northwestern U. Student Svc., Evanston, 1974-85, Cook County Hosp. Employee Health Svc., Chgo., 1986-92. Organizer cropwalk Christ the King Episcopal Ch., Sturgeon Bay, Wis., 1995, 96; reading buddy Sunset Elem. Pub. Sch., Sturgeon Bay, 1997—; singer Door County Peninsula Chamber Singers, 1993—, So. Germany, Austria, 1998; active Cornell Lab. Ornithology Project Feeder Watch, 1998—; co-leader book discussion group Sturgeon Bay Pub. Libr. Fellow Am. Acad. Pediats.; mem. AMA, LWV, AAUW, Chgo. Med. Soc., Wis. State Med. Soc., Med. Soc. Door Kewaunee County, Alpha Omega Alpha. Home: 806 Memorial Dr Sturgeon Bay WI 54235-2661 E-mail: agreaves@charter.net.

GREAVES, JOHN ALLEN, lawyer; b. Kansas City, Mo., Feb. 18, 1948; s. John Allen Greaves and Nancy Lee (Farmer) Greaves-Meltzer; m. Sharon Louise Peace Ventura, Dec. 23, 1967 (div. Mar. 1971); 1 child, Karen Christine Greaves Calogne; m. Jerri Lynn Crawford, Sept. 5, 1981. BA in Polit. Sci., U. Mo., 1976; MPA, JD with honors, Drake U., 1992. Bar: Iowa 1992, U.S. Dist.

Ct. (so. dist.) Iowa 1992, Calif. 1994, U.S. Dist. Ct. (no. and ctrl. dists.) Calif. 1994, U.S. Dist. Ct. (so. and ea. dists.) Calif. 1995, U.S. Dist. Ct. N.Mex. 1995, U.S. Ct. Appeals (9th cir.) 1995, U.S. Dist. Ct. (no. dist.) N.Y. 1996, U.S. Dist. Ct. S.C. 1995, U.S. Ct. Appeals (4th and 10th cirs.) 1996, U.S. Dist. Ct. (no. dist.) Ill. 2000, D.C. 2001, U.S. Dist. Ct. (so. and ea. dists.) N.Y. 2002; lic. airline transport pilot. Pres., CEO VIPilot Svcs., Inc., Kansas City, 1980-83; pilot Air Illinois, Carbondale, Ill., 1983-84, Wright Airlines, Cleve., 1983-84, ComAir Airlines, Cin., 1984-88; jud. law clk. to Hon. Arthur E. Gamble Iowa Dist. Ct., Des Moines, 1990-91; pvt. practice Des Moines, 1992—94; shareholder Baum, Hedlund, Aristei, Guilford & Schiavo, L.A., 1994—. Mem. plaintiffs' steering com. Atlantic S.E. Airlines crash, Carrollton, Ga., 1995, Singapore Airlines crash, Taipei, Taiwan, 2000, MDL-1448 Am. Airlines 587 crash, Belle Harbor (Queens), N.Y., 2001; mem. plaintiffs' exec. com. Sept. 11, 2001 Tort Litig.; lectr. in field. Recipient Safety award, Nat. Air Disaster Found., 2002. Mem. ABA (mem. forum on air and space com.), ATLA, Air Line Pilots Assn. (coun. 37, chmn. contract adminstrn. com. 1985-87, Disting. Svc. award), Lawyer/Pilot Bar Assn., State Bar Calif., State Bar Iowa, Iowa Trial Lawyers Assn., Inn Ct., Delta Theta Phi. Avocations: aviation, snow and water skiing, boating and sailing, tennis, golf. Home: 3664 May St Los Angeles CA 90066-3606 Office: Baum Hedlund Aristei Guilford & Schiavo 12100 Wilshire Blvd Ste 950 Los Angeles CA 90025-7107 E-mail: jgreaves@baumhedlundlaw.com.

GREAVES, WILLIAM WALTER, preventive medicine physician, educator; b. Collinsville, Ill., Dec. 31, 1949; s. Robert Jesse and Evelyn Greaves; m. Kathleen Sarah Stokes, Sept. 20, 1981; children: Ian, Spencer, Malcolm. BS, U. Ill., 1971; MD, U. Ill., Chgo., 1975; MS in Pub. Health, U. Utah, 1980. Diplomate Am. Bd. Preventive Medicine in Occupl. Medicine, Pub. Health and Gen. Preventive Medicine. Resident in preventive medicine/family practice U. Utah, Salt Lake City, 1977-80, fellow in occupl. medicine, 1980-81; asst. prof. Med. Coll. Wis., Milw., 1981-87, assoc. prof., 1987—, dir. MPH degree programs, 1986—, acting chair dept. preventive medicine, 1988—94, 1997—98, chair dept. preventive medicine, 1998—2002, dir. Divsn. of Pub. Health, 2002—. Mem. bd. sci. advisors Am. Coun. for Sci. and Health, Washington, 1994—; mem. Coun. on Edn. for Pub. Health, 1993-98, mem. bd. councilors, then treas. and mem. adminstrv. com., 1996-98; mem. accreditation rev. com. Accreditation Coun. for Continuing Med. Edn., as rep. of Am. Bd. Med. Spltys., 1992-97; chmn. certification com. Am. Bd. Preventive Medicine, rep. to Am. Bd. Med. Spltys. Editor, author: Pearls in Occupl. Medicine, 1996, Project in Occupl. Medicine: M.P.H. Study Guide, 1995; mem. editl. bd. OEM Report, Boston, 1986—; contbr. numerous chpts. to books and study guides. Lay mem. Dist. 2 Bd. of Attys. Profl. Responsibility, Milw., Supreme Ct. of Wis., 1989-94; Flying Eagle mem. Boy Scouts Am., Milw., 1996—. Grantee Nat. Fund for Med. Edn., 1983, Pub. Health Svc., Human Resources Svcs. Adminstrn., 1983, Ctrs. for Disease Control and Prevention, 2000—. Fellow: Am. Coll. Preventive Medicine (exec. com. occupl. medicine regent 1993—97), Am. Coll. Occupl. and Environ. Medicine (exec. com. 1995—99, pres. 1998—99); mem.: AMA, Med. Soc. Milwaukee County (pres. 1995—96), Am. Coll. Physician Execs., Ctrl. States Occupl. Medicine Assn. (pres. 1996—97), Assn. Tchrs. Preventive Medicine (pres. 2000—02), Wis. Med. Soc., Am. Bd. Preventive Medicine. Office: Medical College of Wis Divsn Pub Health 8701 Watertown Plank Rd Milwaukee WI 53226-4801

GREAVES, WILLIAM WEBSTER, chemist, patent analyst, community liaison; b. Queenstown, Md., Jan. 10, 1951; s. William Emory and Mary Elizabeth (Wood) G. BS in Chemistry, Bucknell U., 1973; PhD in Inorganic Chemistry, Iowa State U., 1978. Tech. publ. editor Standard Oil of Ind., Naperville, Ill., 1978-81, rsch. info. scientist, 1981-84; assoc. editor Science mag., Washington, 1984-86; supr. chem. data systems SK&F Labs., Upper Merion, Pa., 1986-88; sr. patent searcher Abbott Labs., Abbott Park, Ill., 1988-90; patent analyst Amoco Corp., Chgo., 1990-99; sr. staff chemist ExxonMobil Rsch. and Engring. Co., 1999—2002. Dir., cmty. liaison Chgo. Adv. Coun. on Gay and Lesbian Issues, 2000—. Contbr. articles to profl. publs.; contbr. revs. to Lambda Book Report. Active Frontrunners Chgo., 1988—, sec., 1991, v.p., 1992, pres., 1993, past pres., 1994, Proud to Run com., 1996-99; active D.C. Front Runners, 1984—; mem. Chgo. Adv. Coun. on Gay and Lesbian Issues, 1994-99; Chgo. coord. track and field and marathon events Gay Games, N.Y.C., 1994; mem. Honorary bd. for Chgo. 2006. Mem. AAAS, Am. Chem. Soc. (sec. chem. info. divsn. 1994-96, edn. com. Chgo. chpt. 1981-84, mgr. Chgo. chpt. student symposium 1982), Soc. Tech. Comm. (sr., sec. Chgo. chpt. 1983), USA Track and Field, Chgo. Area Runners Assn., Stockton (N.J.) Runners Club, Sigma Xi. Republican. Roman Catholic.

GREBB, MICHAEL D. military officer, systems analyst; b. Webster, Mass., Feb. 20, 1950; s. Max G. and Jean A. (Ansorge) G.; m. Janet Meiburger, June 27, 1981 (div. 1997); children: Kevin, David. BS, USAF Acad., 1972; MA, Ind. U., 1973; JD, Georgetown U., 1985. Commd. 2d lt. USAF, 1972, advanced through grades to maj., 1984; systems analyst, asst. program mgr., program mgr. Betac Corp., Alexandria, Va., 1986—, dir. ISR architectures; col. Office Sec. Def. Nat. Security Agy., Ft. Meade, Md., 2000—. Col. USAFR, 1994—. Mem. Air Force Assn. (v.p. scholarships Steele chpt. 1994—), D.C. Bar Assn., Nat. Mil. Intelligence Assn. (v.p. reserve affairs). E-mail: MDgrebb@fggm.osis.gov.

GREBEL, LAWRENCE BOVARD, lawyer; b. St. Louis, Jan. 7, 1951; s. Clement Bovard and Jean Estelle (Schrieber) G.; children: David, Mark, Benjamin. BA, St. Louis U., 1973, JD, 1977. Bar: Mo. 1977, Ill. 1978, U.S. Dist. Ct. (ea. dist.) Mo. 1977. Mem. Moser, Marsalek, Carpenter, Cleary, Jaeckel, Keaney & Brown, St. Louis, 1977-80, Brown & James PC, St. Louis, 1980—. Mem. Internat. Assn. Def. Counsel, Assn. Def. Trial Attys., Mo. Bar Assn. (treas. 1981, sec. 1982, chmn. 1984), St. Louis Met. Bar Assn., Def. Rsch. Inst., Lawyers Assn. St. Louis. Roman Catholic. Home: 8822 Ryegate Saint Louis MO 63127 Office: Brown & James PC 1010 Market St 20th Fl Saint Louis MO 63101-2000 E-mail: lgrebel@bjpc.com.

GREBOW, EDWARD, media company executive; b. Lakewood, N.J., July 17, 1949; s. Benjamin and Ruth (Blume) G.; m. Cynthia Miller, Feb. 23, 1985. BBA, George Washington U., 1971; postgrad., George Washington, 1972. V.p. Morgan Guaranty Trust Co., N.Y.C., 1972-80, J.P. Morgan & Co., Inc., N.Y.C., 1980-85; exec. v.p. Bowery Savs. Bank, N.Y.C., 1985-88; sr. v.p. CBS, Inc., N.Y.C., 1988-94, exec. v.p., 1994-95; pres. Tele-TV Sys., Reston, Va., 1995-97; pres., CEO, Chyron Corp., Melville, N.Y., 1997-99; pres. Sony Electronics Broadcast and Profl. Co., 1999—2002; dep. pres. Sony Electronics, Inc., 2000—02; pres. Met. TV Alliance, 2002—. Acting pres., Ullico, Inc.; chmn. Morgan Data Svcs. Inc., Wilmington, Del., 1981-84; pres. J.P. Morgan Lease Funding Corp., N.Y.C., 1982-84; bd. dirs. CBS Studio Ctr. Inc., Panavision, Inc. Bd. dirs., treas. Theater Devel. Fund, George Washington U., Ave of Americas Assn., Delaware Valley Opera, Am. Film Inst.; mem. N.Y. Hosp. Rev. and Planning Coun. Mem. Nat. Assn. Bank Cost and Mgmt. Acctg. Avocations: deep sea fishing, computer programming. Home: 1136 Fifth Ave New York NY 10128-0122 Office: Met TV Alliance 157 Columbus Ave New York NY 10023 E-mail: edward.grebow@abc.com.

GREBSTEIN, SHELDON NORMAN, university administrator; b. Providence, Feb. 1, 1928; s. Sigmund and Sylvia (Skotkin) G.; m. Phyllis Strumar, Sept. 6, 1953; children: Jason Lyle, Gary Wade. BA cum laude, U. So. Calif., 1949; MA, Columbia U., 1950; PhD, Mich. State U., 1954. Instr. then asst. prof. English U. Ky., 1953-62; asst. prof. U. South Fla., 1962-63; mem. faculty SUNY, Binghamton, 1963-81, prof. English, 1968-81, asst. to pres., 1974-75; dean arts and scis. Harpur Coll., 1975-81; pres. SUNY, Purchase, 1981-93, univ. prof. of lit., 1993-95; dir. edn. Westchester Holocaust Edn. Ctr., 1995—. Fulbright-Hays lectr. U. Rouen, France, 1968-69; vis. lectr. Caen U., Hull U., and Edinburgh U., 1969. Author: Sinclair Lewis, 1962, John O'Hara, 1966, Hemingway's Craft, 1973; Editor: Monkey Trial, 1960, Perspectives in Contemporary Criticism, 1968, Studies in For Whom The Bell Tolls, 1971; editorial cons. univ. presses, publishers.; Contbr. articles to profl. jours. E-mail: whc@bestweb.net.

GRECH, CHRISTOPHER ALAN, lawyer, consultant; b. Richmond, Va., Oct. 5, 1960; s. George Alfred and Stella Mary Grech. BS in Mktg. and Mgmt., Fordham U., 1982; JD, Calif. Western Sch. of Law, San Diego, 1985. Bar: N.J. 1987, U.S. Dist. Ct. N.J. 1987, Md. 1993, D.C. 1994, N.Y. 1995. Solo practitioner, Hackensack, N.J., 1988-94, Berlin, Md., 1994—. Mem. ABA, City of Balt. Bar Assn., Bergen County Bar Assn., Internat. Law Soc., Md. Trial Lawyers Assn., Worcester County Bar Assn., Ocean Pines Yacht Club, Ocean Pines Country Club, KC, Phi Alpha Delta. Avocations: fishing, tennis, boating, jogging, bicycling. Home: PO Box 236 Showell MD 21862-0236

GRECHANIK, JEFFREY, military officer; s. Walter and Cynthia Grechanik; m. Connie Lana Remaley. BS in Engring. Scis., USAF Acad., 1978; MS Strategic and Tactical Scis., Air Force Inst. of Tech., 1987. Commd. 2d lt. USAF, 1978, advanced through grades to lt. col.; instr. weapon systems officer 20th Tactical Fighter Wing, 79th Tactical Fighter Squadron, Royal Air Force Upper Heyford, England, 1979—82, 27th Tactical Fighter Wing, 524th Tactical Fighter Tng. Squadron, Cannon Air Force Base, N.Mex., 1982—85; ops. analyst Air Force Wargaming Ctr., Maxwell Air Force Base, Ala., 1987—90; chief, current ops. 20th Fighter Wing, 20th Ops. Support Squadron, Royal Air Force Upper Heyford, England, 1990—93; dep. chief, treaty plans and policy Hdqs. Air Force, Plans Directorate, Washington, 1993—94; student, internat. tng. course in security policy and arms control Geneva Ctr. for Security Policy, Geneva, 1994—95; nuc. policy planner Joint Chiefs of Staff, Plans and Policy Directorate, Washington, 1995—98; prof. George C. Marshall European Ctr. for Security Policy, Garmisch-Partenkirchen, Germany, 1998—99; chief, airborne systems basing Air Combat Command, Plans and Programs Directorate, Langley Air Force Base, Va., 1999—2003; systems analyst Air Combat Command, Requirements Directorate, Langley AFB, Va., 2003—. Decorated DFC, Air medal. Mem.: Mil. Ops. Rsch. Soc., Inst. for Ops. Rsch. and Mgmt. Scis. Republican. Avocations: modeling and simulation, cycling, skiing, swimming.

GRECICH, DARYL GEORGE, marketing communications executive; b. Beaver Falls, Pa., Mar. 26, 1966; s. George William and Patricia Joan (Scassa) G. BA, U. Pitts., 1988, MA Public and Internat. Affairs, 1991. Dir. publs. and mktg. Inst. for the Study of Diplomacy, Georgetown U., Washington, 1992—95; dir. comm. Inst. for a Drug-Free Workplace, Washington, 1995—98; mktg. comm. mgr. Data Warehousing Inst., Washington, 1998—2000; v.p. mktg. and comms. Idealliance, Washington, 2000—01; dir. mktg. and comms. Internat. Trademark Assn., N.Y.C., 2002—. Recipient Wolves Club scholar, 1984. Mem. Delta Tau Delta Fraternity. Avocations: skiing, literature, raquetball, running, history. Office: Internat Trademark Assn 1133 Ave of Ams Fl 33 New York NY 10036 Home: Apt 3E 308 Mott St New York NY 10012-2814 E-mail: dgrecich@inta.org.

GRECO, ALBERT NICHOLAS, communications educator, educator; b. Trenton, N.J., June 15, 1945; s. Albert Charles and Nellie Marie G.; m. Elaine Anne Rovegno, Aug. 10, 1968; children: Albert, Timothy, John, Robert. BA, Duquesne U., 1967, MA, 1969; EdD, NYU, 1982. Teaching grad. asst. Duquesne U., 1967-68; tchr. Dwight-Englewood (N.J.) Sch., 1968-79, chmn. dept., 1970-73, dir. testing, 1973-75, prin. summer sch., 1970-78, prin. H.S., 1975-78, dir. devel., 1978-79; exec. dir. Met. Lithographers Assn., N.Y.C., 1979-83; dir. Ctr. for Graphic Communications Mgmt. and Tech. NYU, 1982-85; assoc. prof., assoc. dean Gallatin Sch. of Individualized Study, 1985-92, dir pub. studies, 1992-95; clin. assoc. prof. NYU Mgmt. Inst. and Ctr. for Pub., 1995-96; assoc. prof. comm. & media mgmt., grad. sch. bus. adminstrn. Fordham U., 1996—2003, prof., 2003—. Adj. instr. Bergen C.C., 1970-78, NYU, 1980-83; clin. assoc. prof. NYU Sch. Edn., 1982-85; exec. dir. Lithographic Industry Scholarship, Edn. and Devel. Fund., 1982-83; sr. advisor Jour. Advt. Rsch., 2001-. Author: Business Journalism: Management Notes and Cases, 1988, Advertising Management and the Business Publishing Industry, 1991, The Book Publishing Industry, 1997, The Media and Entertainment Industries, 2000, Access for All: Closing the Book Gap for Children in Early Education, 2001; editor: NYU Press Bus. mag. pub. series; editor-in-chief: Allyn & Bacon Series in Mass Communications, 10 vols., The Media and Entertainment Industry, 1999; co-editor: Editorial Excellence; assoc. editor: Jour. Media Econs., 2001—02; editl. bd. Jour. Media Econs., 2000—, Pub. Rsch. Quar., 1994—97; contbr. articles to profl. jours.; sr. adv. Jour. Advertising Rsch., 2001—. Bd. dirs. Book Industry Study Group, 1990-92. Recipient Cert. of Recognition Edn. Coun. of Graphic Arts Industry, 1985, Friedmman award N.Y.C. H.S. Graphic Comm. Arts, 1998, Svc. to Industry award The Navigators, 1998. Mem.: Assn.Am. Publs., Assn. Edn. in Journalism and Mass Comm. (head media mgmt. and econs divsn. 2000—01), Book Industry Study Group, Phi Alpha Theta. Roman Catholic. Home: 183 S Queen St Bergenfield NJ 07621-2636 Office: Fordham U Dept Comm and Media Mgmt 113 W 60th St New York NY 10023-7484

GRECO, CHRISTOPHER JON, musician, composer, educator; b. Inglewood, Calif., July 19, 1959; s. Donald Rudolph and Sharon Marie Greco; m. Yvette Marcia Ybarra, Dec. 26, 1995. MusB, Calif. State U., LA, 1990—93, MA in Composition, 1993—95. Free-lance performer/rec. artist- woodwinds, LA, 1982—; leader of ensembles (duo, trio, quartet, quintet, sextet), 1985—; composer Am. Soc. of Composers, Authors and Publishers, 1988—, pub. (pleiadian music), 1995—; rec. artist (composer/woodwinds) GWSFourwinds Records, Pasadena, 1995—; writer (new music column) Saxophone Jour., Medfield, Mass., 2002—. Composer: (compact disc) Trane of Thought, Pleiadian Call/Music for Trio; musician: Well You Needn't/Standards. Recipient Highly Recommended Performances, LA Weekly, 1990, 1991, 1992, 1993, 1994, 1996, Julius Hemphill Composition Award, Jazz Composers Alliance, 2001, Critics' Choice Performance, LA Reader, 1994, 1995, 1996, Recommended Performance, LA Times, 1997, Highly Recommended CD Rev., Jazz Jour. Internat., London U.K., 1996. Mem.: The Coll. Music Soc., Music Teachers Nat. Assn., Am. Soc. of Composers, Authors and Publishers (Plus award 2002, 2003), Am. Music Ctr. Avocations: walking, gardening. Office Fax: 626-440-9313. E-mail: c.j.greco@worldnet.att.net.

GRECO, GUY BENJAMIN, lawyer; b. Glen Ridge, N.J., May 28, 1951; s. Benjamin Francis and Dorothy Ann (Smith) G.; m. Marietta Suzanne D'Oro, June 16, 1973 (div. 1984); m. Pamela Ann Beckham McGuire, Feb. 2, 1993. BA, Rutgers U., 1973, JD, 1976. Bar: N.J. 1976, Oreg. 1977, U.S. Dist. Ct. N.J. 1976, Oreg. 1977, U.S. Supreme Ct. 1984. Assoc. Litchfield, Macpherson & Carstens, Newport, Oreg., 1977—81; ptnr. Greco & Escobar, Newport, 1981—89; pvt. practice Newport, 1989—. Chmn. Lincoln County Red Cross, Newport, 1979; pres. Oreg. Coast Coun. for the Arts, 1988-89. Mem. ABA, Oreg. Bar Assn., Lincoln County Bar Assn., Oreg. State Bar (counsel 1985, spl. task force on legal technicians 1991-92, legal assts. com. 1989-92, unlawful practice of law com. 1992-95, disciplinary bd. 1993-99, legal ethics com. 1995-98, client security fund com., 1998-2002, uniform criminal jury instrn. com. 2003—, local profl. responsibility com. 1985-88, 2003—). Democrat. Office: PO Box 1070 Newport OR 97365-0081 E-mail: greco@pioneer.net.

GRECO, RALPH STEVEN, surgeon, researcher, medical educator; b. N.Y.C., May 25, 1942; s. Charles Mario and Lydia Antoinette (Barone) G.; m. Irene Leonor Wapnir, Feb. 23, 1991; children: Justin Michael, Eric Matthew, Ilana Rose. BS, Fordham U., 1964; MD, Yale U., 1968. Surgery intern and resident Yale U., New Haven, 1968—73, instr., 1972—73; asst. prof. Rutgers Med. Sch., Piscataway, NJ, 1975-79, assoc. prof., 1979-83; chief gen. surgery Robert Wood Johnson Med. Sch., New Brunswick, 1982—2000, prof., 1983-2000; chief of surgery Robert Wood Johnson Univ. Hosp. U. Medicine & Dentistry of N.J., New Brunswick, 1997-2000; J & J prof., chief divsn. gen. surgery, dir. surg. tng. Stanford U. Sch. Medicine, 2000—. Cons. Nat. Heart, Lung and Blood Inst.-NSF, Bethesda, Md., 1991. Contbr. articles to profl. jours. Maj. U.S. Army, 1973-75. NHLBI grantee, 1980-84. Fellow Am. Surg. Assn.; mem. Soc. Univ. Surgeons. Achievements include research in antibiotic bonding, treatment of prosthetic infection and nanobiology; patents in field. Home: 773 Frenchman's Rd Stanford CA 94305 Office: Stanford U Sch Medicine 300 Pasteur Dr Stanford CA 94305 E-mail: grecors@stanford.edu.

GREDEN, JOHN FRANCIS, psychiatrist, educator; b. Winona, Minn., July 24, 1942; m. Renee Mary Kalmes; children: Daniel John, Sarah Renee, Leigh Raymond. BS, U. Minn., 1965, MD, 1967. Diplomate Am. Bd. Psychiatry and Neurology. Assoc. dir. psychiat. research Walter Reed Army Med. Ctr., Washington, 1972-74; asst. prof. dept. psychiatry U. Mich., Ann Arbor, 1974-77, assoc. prof., 1977-81, dir. clin. studies unit for affective disorders, 1980-85, prof., 1981—, chmn., sr. rsch. scientist, 1985—, chmn. faculty group practice, 1996—98, exec. dir. Depression Ctr., 2001—. Editor 3 books; contbr. more than 200 articles to profl. jours., more than 30 chpts. to books. Served to maj. U.S. Army, 1969-74. Recipient A.E. Bennett research award Cen. Neuropsychiat. Found., 1974, Nolan D.C. Lewis Vis. Scholar award Carrier Found., 1982. Fellow Am. Psychiat. Assn. (chair coun. on rsch. 2000—); mem. AAAS, Soc. Biol. Psychiatry (past pres., co-editor-in-chief Jour. Psychiatry Rsch. 1984-2000), Am. Coll. Neuropsychopharmacology (coun. 2001—, Psychiat. Rsch. Soc. (past pres.). Office: U Mich Med Ctr Dept Psychiatry 1500 E Medical Center Dr Ann Arbor MI 48109-0005

GREEFKES, ROLAND CORNELIS, artist; b. The Hague, Netherlands, May 27, 1941; s. Cornelis Greefkes and Marie Johanna Veltman; m. Charlotte Zoe Walker, Feb. 13, 1988; m. Helen Clair Frederick, Nov. 12, 1977 (div. May 13, 1984). HBS-B, The Hague Montessori Lyceum, 1956—62; Bachelor, U. of Toronto, 1963—68. Chem. Engr., Assn. of Profl. Engineers of Ont., 1969. Chem. engr. Goodyear Tire & Rubber Co., Toronto, Canada, 1968—71; ind. studies and travel Self Employed, India, 1972—77, artist in stained glass, 1977—79, art restoration and gilding Balt., 1980—83; artist in wrought iron Aesthetica, Gilbertsville, NY, 1986—. Exhibitions include Nat. Gallery Art, Washington, 1980, gilding, Capitol Bldg., 1981, wrought iron gate, for Blythe Danner and Bruce Paltrow, Sun and Moon Gates for Yoko Ono, Paradise Gate for Sara Douglass, Australia (Featured in Garden Design Mag., 2003), sculpture, Dithyramb, State U. at Oneonta, firescreens, for Bette Midler. Buddhist. Avocations: travel, nature. Home: PO Box 14 Gilbertsville NY 13776 Personal E-mail: rolandg@citlink.net.

GREEHEY, WILLIAM EUGENE, energy company executive; b. Ft. Dodge, Iowa, 1936; married. BBA, St. Mary's U., San Antonio, 1960. Auditor Price Waterhouse & Co., 1960-61; sr. auditor Humble Oil and Refining Co., 1961-63; sr. v.p. fin. Coastal Corp. (and predecessor), 1963-74; with Valero Energy Corp. (formerly Coastal States Gas Producing Co.), San Antonio, 1974—, pres., chief exec. officer, 1979-83, chmn. bd., 1983—, also chmn., chief exec. officer numerous subsidiaries. Office: Valero Energy Corp PO Box 500 San Antonio TX 78292-0500

GREEK, DAROLD I. lawyer; b. Kunkle, Ohio, Mar. 30, 1909; s. Albert F. and Iva (Shaffer) G.; m. Catherine Johnson, Oct. 12, 1935 (dec. 1962); 1 child, Darold I (dec.); m. Elizabeth Tracy Ridgley, Sept. 18, 1970 (dec. May 1972); stepchildren— Thomas B., David Ridgley; m. Nadine Berry Weisheimer Bivens, Dec. 23, 1976; stepchildren— Richard A. Weisheimer, Jon B. Weisheimer. Student, Bowling Green State U., 1926-28; LL.B., Ohio State U., 1932. Bar: Ohio 1932. Treas., Williams County, Ohio, 1932-33; atty. Ohio Dept. Taxation, 1934-36; practiced in Columbus, 1937-89; ptnr. George, Greek, King, McMahon & McConnaughey (and predecessors), 1937-79; of counsel Baker & Hostetler, 1979-89. Mem. Ohio Bar Assn., Columbus Bar Assn. (pres. 1966-67), The Golf Club, Naples Yacht Club, Hole in the Wall Golf Club. Presbyterian. Home: 6635 Lake of Woods Pt Galena OH 43021 also: 2901 Gulf Shore Blvd N Naples FL 34103-3937 Office: 65 E State St Columbus OH 43215-4213

GREELEY, ANDREW MORAN, sociologist, author; b. Oak Park, Ill., Feb. 5, 1928; s. Andrew T. and Grace G. AB, St. Mary of Lake Sem., 1950, STL, 1954; MA, U. Chgo., 1961, PhD, 1962; LHD (hon.), Bowling Green State U., 1986, No. Mich., 1993; HHD (hon.), St. Louis U., 1991; LHD, LLD, Ariz. State U., 1998; LHD (hon.), U. San Francisco, 2002, Bard Coll., 2002; LLD (hon.), Nat. U. Ireland, Galway, 2003. Ordained priest Roman Cath. Ch., 1954. Asst. pastor Ch. of Christ the King, Chgo., 1954-64; sr. study dir. Nat. Opinion Rsch. Ctr., Chgo., 1962-68; dir. Ctr. for Study Am. Pluralism, from 1973; lectr. sociology U. Chgo., 1963-72; prof. sociology U. Ariz., Tucson, from 1978, now adj. prof.; prof. social sci. U. Chgo., 1991—. Cons. Hazen Found. Commn. Columnist Daily Southtown; guest columnist Chgo. Sun Times, 1985—; Author: The Church and the Suburbs, 1959, Strangers in the House, 1961, Religion and Career, 1963, (with Peter H. Rossi) Education of Catholic Americans, 1966, Changing Catholic College, 1967, Come Blow Your Mind With Me, 1971, Life for a Wanderer: A New Look at Christian Spirituality, 1971, The Denominational Society: A Sociological Approach to Religion in America, 1972, Priests in the United States: Reflections on A Survey, 1972, That Most Distressful Nation, 1972, New Agenda, 1973, Jesus Myth, 1971, Unsecular Man, 1974, Ethnicity in the United States: A Preliminary Reconnaissance, 1974, Ecstasy: A Way of Knowing, 1974, Building Coalitions: American Politics in the 1970's, 1974, Sexual Intimacy, 1975, Denomination Society, 1975, The Great Mysteries: An Essential Catechism, 1976, The Communal Catholic: A Personal Manifesto, 1976, Death and Beyond, 1976, The American Catholic: A Social Portrait, 1977, The Making of the Popes, 1978, 79, The Magic Cup: An Irish Legend, 1979, Women I've Met, 1979, Why Can't They Be Like Us?, 1980, Death In April, 1980, The Cardinal Sins, 1981, Religion: A Secular Theory, 1982, Thy Brother's Wife, 1982, Ascent Into Hell, 1983, Lord of the Dance, 1984, Virgin & Martyr, 1985, Piece of My Mind on Just About Everything, 1985, Happy are the Meek, 1985, The Magic Cup, 1985, God Game, 1986, Happy Are the Clean of Heart, 1986, Confessions of a Parish Priest, 1986, Patience of a Saint, 1987, Rite of Spring, 1987, Angels of September, 1986, Happy Are Those Who Thirst For Justice, 1987, The Final Planet, 1987, Angel Fire, 1988, (photography) Andrew Greeley's Chicago, 1989, Love Song, 1989, St. Valentine's Night, 1989, The Bible and Us, 1990, The short stories All About Women, 1990, (photography) The Irish, 1990, The Catholic Myth: The Behavior and Beliefs of American Catholics, 1990, The Cardinal Virtues, 1990, Faithful Attraction: Discovering Intimacy, Love, and Fidelity in American Marriage, 1991, The Search for Maggie Ward, 1991, An Occasion of Sin, 1991, Happy Are the Merciful, 1992, Wages of Sin, 1992, Fall from Grace, 1993, Sacraments of Love: A Prayer Journal, 1994, Irish Gold, 1994, Happy are the Poor Spirit, 1994, Happy are Those Who Mourn, 1995, Angel Light: An Old-Fashioned Love Story, 1995, Windows: A Prayer Journal, 1995, Religion as Poetry, 1995, Sociology and Religion, 1995, White Smoke, 1996, Irish Lace, 1996, Happy Are The Oppressed, 1996, (with J. Neusner) Common Ground: A Priest and a Rabbi Read Scripture Together, 1996, Summer at the Lake, 1997, Star Bright!, 1997, The Bishop at Sea, 1997, I Hope You're Listening, God: A Prayer Journal, 1997, Irish Whiskey, 1998, Contract with an Angel, 1998, The Bishop and the Three Kings, 1998, A Mid-Winter's Tale, 1998, Furthermore! Memories of a Parish Priest, 1999, 2000, The Bishop and the Missing L Train, 2000, Christmas Wedding, 2000, Irish Love, 2001, The Bishop and the Begger Girl of St. Germain, 2001, September Song, 2001, Irish Stew, 2002, The Bishop in the West Wing, 2002, (with Mary Durkin) The Book of Love, 2002, The Bishop Goes to The University, 2003; (with Chilton, Green, and Neusner) Forging a Common Future, 1996, The Catholic Imagination, 2000, (with Albert Bergesen) God in the Movies, 2000, My Love: A Prayer Journal, 2001, Letters to a Loving God, 2002, Second Spring, 2003, Religion in Europe at the End of the Second Millennium, 2003; contbr. articles to profl. jours. Recipient Cath. Press Assn. award for best book for young people, 1965, Thomas Alva Edison award for radio broadcast, 1962, C. Albert Kobb award Nat. Cath. Edn. Assn., 1977, Mark Twain award Soc. Study Midwestern Lit., 1987, Popular Culture award Ctr. Study of Popular Culture, 1988, Freedom to Read award Friends Chgo. Pub. Libr., 1989, U.S. Cath. award, 1993, Ill. Outstanding Citizen award Coll. Lake County, 1993, Quigley Disting. Alumni award, 1997; named to Top 100 Irish Ams. Irish Am. Mag, 1992, named Irish Am. of Century Irish Am. Mag., 1999. Mem. Am. Sociol. Assn., Soc. for Sci. Study Religion, Religious Research Assn.

GREELEY, JENNIFER ANN, military officer, educator; d. Horace; children: Travis, Tyler. AA, Chaminate U., Honolulu, 1992; BA in sociology, U. Okla., Norman, 1995; EdM, U. R.I., Kingston, 1999; M Human Rels., U. Okla., 2003. Lt. USN, 1985—; yearbook editor U. Okla. NROTC, Norman, 1993—95; adminstrn. officer dept. head sch. surface warfare USN, Newport, RI, 1996—99, officer recruit trng. command Great Lakes, Ill., 1999—2002; adj. prof. Coll. of Lake County, Grayslake, 2001; transp. dir. military sealift command USN, Yokohama, Japan, 2002, officer in charge naval support facility Kamiseya, 2002—03, navy recruiting dist. Chgo. Ft. Sheridan, Ill., 2003—; adj. prof. Coll. Lake County, 2003—. Chmn. civilian adv. bd. Salvation Army, Waukegan, Ill., 2002—, mem., 2003—; mem. spl. events com. Highland Pk. C. of C., Ill., 2000—; bd. mem. civilian adv. bd. Salvation Army, Newport, RI, 1997—99, Sunday soup kitchen organizer, 1997—99. Ex-officio mem. human rels. Commn. Highland Park, Ill., 2003—. Named a Cited Vol., USO, Honolulu, 1991; recipient Community Spirit award, Combined Fed. Campaign United Way, 2001. Mem.: Women Officer Prof. Assn., Am. Assn. Pub. Adminstrn., Am. Assn. of U. Profs., City Club of Chgo., Kappa Delta Pi. Achievements include founding local branch of Drug Edn. for Youth in Atsugi, Japan, community outreach programs. Avocations: travel, writing.

GREELEY, SEAN MCGOVERN, sales executive; b. New Brunswick, N.J., Nov. 8, 1961; s. Horace James and Patricia Louise (McGovern) Greeley Jr.; m. Kristin Lindefjeld; children: Elisabeth Lindefjeld, Anna Barlinn, John Lindefjeld, James Barlinn. BSBA, Monmouth U., 1983, MBA, 1994. With Dean Witter Reynolds, N.Y.C., 1983-85; acct. exec. U.S. Trust Co., N.Y.C., 1985-87, fin. officer, 1987-90, asst. v.p., 1990-95; v.p. fin. instn. sales JP Morgan Chase, N.Y.C., 1995—. Bd. dirs., treas. Rumson Run. Mem. Tau Kappa Epsilon (pres., bd. dirs. 1984-90, cons. bd. fin. 1986-90). Republican. Avocations: running (N.Y.C. Marathon, Jersey Shore marathon), U.S. history, golf. Home: 14 North St Rumson NJ 07760-1610 Office: JP Morgan Chase 4 New York Plz Fl 2 New York NY 10004-2413 E-mail: Sean.Greeley@jpmorgan.com.

GREEN, AHMAN, football player; b. Omaha, Nebr., Feb. 16, 1977; Running back Green Bay Packers, 2000—, Seattle Seahawks, 1998—2000. Office: Green Bay Packers PO Box 10628 Green Bay WI 54307-0628

GREEN, ALVIN, lawyer, consultant; b. Elgin, Ill., Mar. 13, 1931; s. Samuel and Rose (Brustein) G.; m. Miriam E. Blau, June 13, 1954 (dec.); children: Andrew, Marie, Jennifer. BA, U. Mich., 1953, MA, 1954; LLB, Harvard U., 1957. Bar: N.Y., Ill. Atty. Eastern Air Lines, Inc., N.Y.C., 1957-65; asst. to gen. counsel C.I.T. Corp., N.Y.C., 1965-70, gen. counsel, 1970-72; v.p. Condren, Walker & Co., N.Y.C., 1972-75; v.p., gen. counsel, sec. Seatrain Lines, Inc., N.Y.C., 1975-81, exec. v.p., co-CEO, sr. counsel, 1981-90; exec. v.p. Seatrain Tankers Inc., 1987-90, Bay Tankers Inc., 1981-90, Bay Ocean Mgmt. Inc., Englewood Cliffs, NJ, 1990—95. NASD arbitrator; ptnr. Seham, Seham Meltz & Petersen; cons. in field. Bd. dirs. Inst. for Child, Adolescent and Family Studies, N.Y.C. Woodrow Wilson fellow, 1953-54. Mem. ABA, Assn. of Bar of City of N.Y. (mem. com. on aeronautics), Am. Bur. Shipping, Harvard Club (N.Y.C.), Phi Beta Kappa, Phi Kappa Phi. Home: 145 E 48th St New York NY 10017 Office: 145 E 48th St 5F New York NY 10017 E-mail: green_alvin@hotmail.com.

GREEN, ANDREW WILSON, lawyer; b. Harrisburg, Pa., May 17, 1923; s. M. Edwin and Gladys (Wilson) G.; m. Betty M. Wilson, Nov. 23, 1977. Student, Princeton U., 1940-43; BS, NYU, 1944; JD, Dickinson Law Sch., 1948; MBA, U. Pa., 1963, PhD, 1968; diploma, U. Amsterdam, 1967. Bar: Pa. 1950, D.C. 1950. Legal asst. Pa. Utility Commn., 1949-51; pvt. practice Harrisburg, 1951-61; asst. atty. gen. State of Pa., 1965-66; research assoc. Inst. Strategic and Internat. Studies, Belgium, 1968-70; prof. bus. adminstrn. West Chester U., Pa., 1970-92; prof. Del. Law Sch., Wilmington, 1973-81; pvt. practice West Chester, Pa., 1987—. Solicitor Coatesville (Pa.) Sch. Dist., 1988-91; mem. Reagan Transition Team, 1980-81 Author: Political Integration by Jurisprudence, 1969. Served as capt. USAAF, 1943-46. Pennfield fellow, 1966-67 Mem. Cercle Galouis (Brussels), Gremio Literario (Lisbon). Home: 6 Ivy Rock Rd West Chester PA 19382-8148 Office: PO Box 654 West Chester PA 19381-0654

GREEN, ANGEL YVONNE, literature educator; b. N.Y.C., Oct. 24, 1955; d. Henry Arthur Moss and Lillie Vera Harris; m. Joseph Cecil Green, Nov. 18, 1975 (div. Feb. 1979); 1 child, Gabriel Veran. Baccalaureate English, U. R.I., 1986, Masters English, 1997, PhD English, 2001; Baccalaureate Psychology, Coll. Continuing Edn./U. R.I., Providence, 1995. On-call police matron Newport and Jamestown Police Depts., RI, 1986—95; tchg. asst. U. R.I., Kingston, 1995—2000, fellow Grad. Sch., 2000—01, adj. faculty, 2001—. Vol. Literacy Vol. Am., Newport, RI, 1995—2002; enrichment instr. Talent Devel., U. R.I., Kingston, 1996—2002. Author short stories. Bd. mem. Wahid, Newport, 1986—90, First Step Newport County, Newport, 1990—95. With USN, 1973, with USNR, 1976—98. Recipient MLK Scholarship award, Providence Pub. Schs., 1995—98. Mem.: MLA, NAACP, Mensa. Home: 21-E Rolling Green Rd Newport RI 02840 Office: Univ RI English Dept Independence Hall Upper College Rd Kingston RI 02881

GREEN, ASA NORMAN, university president; b. Mars Hill, Maine, July 22, 1929; s. Clayton John and Annie Glenna (Shaw) G.; m. Elizabeth Jean Zirkelbach Ross, May 27, 1965; 1 son, Stephen Richard Ross. AB cum laude, Bates Coll., Lewiston, Maine, 1951; MA, U. Ala., 1955; LL.D., Jacksonville (Ala.) U., 1975. Research dir. Ala. League Municipalities, Montgomery, 1955-57; city mgr. Mountain Brook, Ala., 1957-65; exec. sec. Ala. Assn. Ins. Agts., 1965-66; dir. devel. Birmingham-So. Coll., 1966-71; dir. devel. and communications Dickinson Coll., Carlisle, Pa., 1971-73; pres. Livingston (Ala.) U., 1973-93; pres. emeritus Livingston U., 1993—. Cons. NCAA Pres.'s Commn., 1993—99; instr. polit. sci. U. Ala. Ext. Ctr., Montgomery and Birmingham, 1955—57, 1958—60. Author: Revenue for Alabama Cities, 1956. Dir. U. South Ala. Found., 1997—. Served with CIC U.S. Army, 1952—54. Grad. fellow So. Regional Tng. Program in Pub. Adminstrn., 1951 Mem.: Phi Beta Kappa. Democrat. Methodist. Office: PO Box 1620 Livingston AL 35470-1620

GREEN, BARBARA, communications educator; b. Hinsdale, Ill., May 26, 1950; d. Roger J. and Lois L. (Froehlich) Green; m. Richard A. Webb, Sept. 8, 1984; 1 child, Claire Catherine. BA, Drake U., Des Moines, 1972; MA, So. Ill. U., 1979, U. Chgo., 1998. Tech. writer Dial Fin. Corp., Des Moines, 1972-74; faculty St. Lawrence Coll., Kingston, Ont., Can., 1977-78; tech. writer Can. Dept. Def., Ottawa, Ont., 1978-79; copy editor Deltak Inc., Oak Brook, Ill., 1980-81; tng. cons., course designer Willowbrook, Ill., 1981-86; instr. composition and newswriting George Williams Coll., Downers Grove, Ill., 1983-85; instr. composition, tech. writing Benedictine U., Lisle, Ill., 1987-88, 91, Aurora (Ill.) U., 1988-90; weekly columnist Lisle Sun, 1993—; instr. writing Coll. of DuPage, Glen Ellyn, Ill., 1980-97, instr. composition, poetry, tech., creative and memoir writing, 2001—; tech. writer Lucent Technologies, Naperville, Ill., 1997, tng. mgr., 1998—99. Author, editor: (video) Peg Lehman Show, 1988; editor Rivulets 14, 2002, Rivulets 15, 2003; author numerous poems, short stories. Mem. No. Ill. Newspaper Assn., Naperville Writers Group. E-mail: barbara.l.green@worldnet.att.net.

GREEN, BARBARA MARIE, publisher, journalist, poet; b. N.Y.C., Mar. 21, 1928; d. James Matthew and Mae (McCarter) G. BA, CCNY, 1951, MA, 1955; ABD, NYU, 1978. Adminstr., tchr. English, 1952-82; tchr. English Newtown High Sch., Elmhurst, Queens, N.Y., 1961; asst. prin. Jr. High Sch. 142, Queens, N.Y., 1963; founder, pub. The "Creative" Record, Virginia Beach, Va., 1988-92. Keynote speaker; pres. Bar 'JaMae Comm. Inc. Founder, publisher The Good News, East Elmhurst, N.Y., 1985-88; author: (book of poetry) Love Pain Hope, 1990, More Poetic Thoughts, 1993, Dreams and Memories, 1996, Spirit, 1997; contbr. poetry to publs. Ch. and cmty. reporter N.Y. Voice; mem. libr. action com. Corona (N.Y.)-East Elmhurst, Inc.; mem. Langston Hughes Cmty. Libr. and Cultural Ctr., Corona, Harpers Ferry Hist. Assn., Va. Symphony League; mem. Crispus Attucks Theater Restoration Com., Norfolk. Recipient Profl. award Nat. Assn. Negro Bus. and Profl. Women's Club Inc., 1964, Trophy "Career Woman of Yr.", County Line Guild of Career Women, 1967, Cert. of Appreciation Women's Equality Action League, 1978, First Lynnhaven Bapt. Ch., Virginia Beach, Va., 1982, Cert. of merit City of N.Y., 1982, Community Svc. award Arlene of N.Y., 1990, N.Y. State Resolution commemorating the "Good" News, 1985, participation award Coalition of 100 Black Women, Valuable Service citation Phi Delta Kappa, cert. of appreciation Houston C.C., 1998, plaque U.S. Army and USAF N.G. Bur., Ageless Hero for Creativity award Blue Cross/Blue Shield, 1998; named Star Among Stars, 1991, Keeper of the Flame, 1997, Hampton Roads Poet Laureate, 2002; named to African-Am. Biographies Hall of Fame, Atlanta, 1994; elected to Hunter Coll. Alumni Hall of Fame, 1997; named poet laureate-in-residence First Lynnhaven Bapt. Ch., Virginia Beach, Va., 1996—, Hampton Roads Poets Laureate, New Jour.-Guide Newspaper, 2002. Mem. Am. Bus. Women's Assn. (Elizabeth River Charter chpt.), Nat. Assn. Negro Musicians (life; bd. dirs. Chgo. 1984-91, ea. region dir. 1990-91), Harpers Ferry Hist. Assn., Poetry Soc. Va., Nat. Assn. Black Journalists, Zonta Internat., Va. Fedn. Bus. and Profl. Women's Clubs (corr. sec. 1992, 1st v.p. 1993, pres. 1993, chair coastal region pub. rels. com. state level 1994-95), N.Y.C. Ret. Suprs. Assn., Phi Delta Kappa, Alpha Kappa Alpha. Baptist. Office: PO Box 15442 Chesapeake VA 23328-5442 Fax: 757-482-7016.

GREEN, BARBARA R. artist; b. N.Y.C., Nov. 7, 1942; d. Morris and Irene Edith Korr; m. Francis Eugene Green, Feb. 14, 1980. BS, NYU, 1964; MFA, Inst. Allende, San Miguel de Allende, Mex., 1974. Tchr. N.Y.C. Sch. Sys., 1964—73, 1975—76, 1982—84; chromiste Eleanor Ettinger Publisher, N.Y.C., 1976—82; tchr. Greene Correctional Facility, Russel Sage Coll., 1986—88. Recipient Silver Crown, Columbia U., 1985; grantee, Meml. Found. for Jewish Culture, 2000. Mem.: Greene County Coun. of the Arts, Woodstock Artists Assn. Home: 10 Rte 23A Catskill NY 12414

GREEN, BARBARA STRAWN, psychotherapist; b. Cleve., May 31, 1938; d. Charles Everard and Dorothy Haring (Strawn) G. BA, Pa. State U., 1960; MS, Columbia U., 1962; postgrad. in psychotherapy and psychoanalysis, Postgrad. Ctr. for Mental Health, N.Y.C., 1975. Cert. social worker, N.Y.; lic. social worker, Pa.; cert. Rutgers Summer Sch. Alcoholism Studies, 1982. Social worker VA, N.Y.C., 1962-66; sr. psychiat. social worker in child psychiat. Downstate Med. Ctr., Bklyn., 1966-71; staff therapist Inst. for Contemporary Psychotherapy, N.Y.C., 1971-73; social worker Lower East Side Service Ctr., N.Y.C., 1975-77; intake coordinator alcoholism program Postgrad. Ctr. for Mental Health, N.Y.C., 1981-82; program coordinator Bowery Residents Com., N.Y.C., 1984-86; pvt. practice psychotherapy N.Y.C., 1973—, Dingmans Ferry, Pa., 1994-2000. Sec. alcoholism com. N.Y.C. chpt. NASW, 1987-89. Author: Jogging the Mind, 1995. Participant N.Y.C. Marathon, 1991, 92. Mem. Social Workers Helping Social Workers (chmn. 1982-84). Avocations: pottery, travel. Office: 108 1/2 E 37th St New York NY 10016

GREEN, BENJAMIN W. poet; b. San Bernardino, Calif., July 17, 1956; s. Wayne Allen Green and Dorothy Joan Norton; m. Anita Punla, Sept. 24, 1993; 1 child, She'Ifa Zera Punla-Green. BA, Humboldt State U., 1984. poet, cons. Pacific Union Sch., Arcata, Calif., 1992—, Great Valley Writing Project, Turlock, Calif., 1998—. Author: Beyond Roses Are Red, Violets Are Blue, 1996, Sound of Fish Dreaming, 1996. Artist mem. Ferndale (Calif.) Arts Coop, 1993—. Home: 3415 Patricks Point Dr # 3 Trinidad CA 95570

GREEN, BENNETT DONALD, biotechnologist; b. N.Y.C., Nov. 24, 1950; s. John Jerome and Leona Pearl (Gillman) G.; m. Deborah Lynn Stephen, Dec. 23, 1972; children: Rebecca Lynn, John Stephen, Sara Elizabeth. BS, Rensselear Poly. Inst., 1972, MS, 1974; Exec. MBA, Claremont Grad. Sch., 1988. Cert. quality engr. Am. Soc. Quality. Sr. mfg. analyst internat. div. Bristol Myers, Syracuse, N.Y., 1974-77; sect. mgr. sterilization Baxter-Travenol Labs., Deerfield, Ill., 1977-78, quality control supr., 1978-82, quality assurance plant mgr. Hyland Therapeutics div., 1982-85; dir. quality assurance NeoRx Corp., Seattle 1985-87; dir. Genzyme Corp., Cambridge, Mass., 1987-91, v.p. quality, 1991-95, v.p. quality affairs and tech. svcs., 1996-97, sr. v.p., 1997—. Mem. Am. Soc. for Quality, Parenteral Drug Assn. Avocations: horses, golf.

GREEN, BERT FRANKLIN, JR., psychologist; b. Honesdale, Pa., Nov. 5, 1927; s. Bert Franklin and Emily May (Brown) G.; m. Hasseltine Beck Robinson, Apr. 29, 1961 (div. 1974); children: Malcolm, Edward. AB, Yale, 1949; MA, Princeton, 1950, PhD, 1951. Mem. psychology group Lincoln Lab., Mass. Inst. Tech., 1951-62, leader, 1958-62; cons. RAND Corp., 1961; prof. psychology Carnegie Inst. Tech., Pitts., 1962-69, head psychology dept., 1962-67; prof. psychology Johns Hopkins, Balt., 1969-98, prof. emeritus, 1998—. Author: Digital Computers in Research, 1963. Mem. Am. Psychol. Assn., Am. Statis. Assn., Psychometric Soc., Am. Edn. Rsch. Assn. Home: 311 Eastway Ct Baltimore MD 21212-4710 Personal E-mail: bfgreen@verizon.net. Business E-Mail: bfgreen@jhu.edu.

GREEN, BETH INGBER, intuitive practitioner, counselor, author, composer, spiritual educator; b. NYC, Feb. 28, 1945; d. Frank and Lillian Ingber. BA, Bklyn. Coll., 1970; MA, UCLA, 1978. Cert. in intuitive consulting, counseling, tchg. and learning, body and kinetic intervention. Spiritual dir. and founder The Stream, Calif., 1980—86; intuitive practitioner, counselor, cons. and tchr., founder The Stream Spiritual Orgn., 1980—; ptnr., co-founder The Healing Partnership, Ramona, Calif., 1986—90, LA, 1986—90; spiritual dir. and founder The Triple Eye Found., Ramona, Calif., 1990—93; spiritual dir. The Stream, Fallbrook, Calif. Spiritual activist, co-founder Rising Mountains Setting Suns, Ramona, Calif., 1993—95; co-founder Spiritual Activist Movement, LA and Ramona, 1993—95; owner Treehouse Music, Rising Mountain Press. Author: The Autobiography of Mary Magdalene, 1988, Sacred Union: The Healing of God, 2002, Living with Reality: Nine Platforms for Becoming Ourselves, (spoken tapes) The Healing of God, Loving Ourselves, God and Others, The Alienation of Love, Spirituality: The Last Block to Freedom, (CDs) The Gift of Peace, A Soul's Journey through Darkness and Light, (videotapes) Breaking the "I" Barrier; originator Giving the Gift of Peace, 2002. West Coast coord. Wages for Housework Campaign, L.A., 1974—78.

GREEN, BETTY NIELSEN, education educator, consultant; b. Copenhagen, Apr. 30, 1937; came to U.S., 1979; d. Alfred Christian Josef and Lilly Nielsen; m. Philip Irving Green, Apr. 16, 1962; children: Ruth, Erik, Nils. AA in Fgn. Lang., Daytona Beach C.C., 1981; BA in Liberal Arts, U. Ctrl. Fla., 1986; MS in TESOL, Nova Southeastern U., 1988; EdD in Curriculum and Instrn., U. Ctrl. Fla., 1994. Cert. tchr., Fla.; cert. TESOL trainer, Fla. Tchr. TESOL, program mgr. English Lang. Inst. Daytona Beach C.C., Fla., 1986-91; tchr. TESOL, fgn. lang. specialist Volusia County Schs., Daytona Beach, 1991—; tchr. trainer, facilitator Nova Southeastern U., Ft. Lauderdale, Fla., 1991—. Cons. TESOL, Ormond Beach, Fla., 1991; adj. faculty, Daytona Beach, 1997—; chair Fla. Consortium of Multilingual-Multicultural Edn., 2001--. Author, editor Teaching Assistant Manual, 1987; editor Unitarian Universalist Soc. newsletter, 1987—, religious editl. dir., 1996—; eidtor Fla. Fgn. Lang. Assn. Newsletter. Pres. Unitarian Universalists, Ormond Beach, 1982-84, N.E. Cluster Unitarian Universalists, Volusia, 1982-86; pres., v.p. S.E. Unitarian Universalists Sem. Inst., Blacksburg, Va., 1985-89. Mem. TESOL, Sunshine State TESOL (mem.-at-large 1999—, 2d v.p., 1st v.p., pres. 2003—), N.E. Fla. TESOL (pres. 1995—, editor newsletter 1998—), ASCD, Nat. Coun. Tchrs. of English, Fla. Fgn. Lang. Assn. (membership bd., editor 2002—), Fgn. Lang. Adminstrn. and Mgmt. Edn. (sec. 1995-97, pres. 1998), Fla. Assn. Bilingual Edn. Suprs. (sec. 1995), Fla. Consortium on Multicultural Edn. (chair), Phi Kappa Phi, Kappa Delta Pi, Pi Delta Kappa. Democrat. Avocations: foreign languages, research on second language and multi-cultural educations, music, travel. Home: 771 W River Oak Dr Ormond Beach FL 32174-4641 Office: Volusia County Schs 729 Loomis Ave Daytona Beach FL 32114-4723 E-mail: drtesol@philgreen.org., drtesol@philgreen.org.

GREEN, BEVERLY JEAN, nurse; b. Ithaca, N.Y., Aug. 6, 1955; d. Arthur W. Sr. and Edna M. (Pearson) G. Diploma, Arnot-Ogden Sch. Nursing, 1977. RN, S.C.; cert. ACLS, CEN, trauma nursing care course, pediat. advanced life support. Staff RN Arnot Ogden Meml. Hosp., Elmira, N.Y., 1977-88; staff nurse Loris (S.C.) Comty. Hosp., 1988-94; staff RN, supr. Columbia-Brunswick Hosp., Supply, N.C., 1988—. Mem. Emergency Nurses Assn. Avocations: reading, sewing, gardening. Home: 2140 Adams Cir Little River SC 29566-9111

GREEN, CARIN MARGRETA, art educator; b. Burbank, Calif., Mar. 30, 1948; d. Grover Neils and Hester Miriam (Johnson) Christensen; m. Peter Morris Green. BA, San Jose State Coll., 1971; MA, U. Texas, 1975; PhD, U. Va., 1991. Asst. prof. to assoc. prof. of classics U. Iowa, Iowa City, 1991—. Contbr. articles various profl. publications. Mem.: Am. Philological Assn., Cedar Rapids Museum of Art, Archaeological Inst. of Am., Iowas City Soc. (sec. 2000—), Classical Assn. of the Midwest and South (exe. bd. mem. 2002—). Avocations: travel, gardening. Home: 1268 Chamberlain Dr Iowa City IA 52240 Office: U Iowa Dept of Classics Schaeffer Hall 208 Iowa City IA 52242 E-mail: carin-green@uiowa.edu.

GREEN, CAROL H. lawyer, educator, journalist; b. Seattle, Feb. 18, 1944; BA in History/Journalism summa cum laude, La. Tech. U., 1965; MSL, Yale U., 1977; JD, U. Denver, 1979. Reporter Shreveport (La.) Times, 1965-66, Guam Daily News, 1966-67; city editor Pacific Jour., Agana, Guam, 1967-68, reporter, editl. writer, 1968-76, legal affairs reporter, 1977-79; asst. editor editl. page Denver Post, 1979-81, house counsel, 1980-83, labor rels. mgr., 1981-83; assoc. Holme Roberts & Owen, 1983-85; v.p. human resources and legal affairs Denver Post, 1985-87, mgr. circulation, 1988-90; gen. mgr. Distbn. Systems Am., Inc., 1990-92; dir. labor rels. Newsday, 1992-95, dir. comm. & labor rels., 1996-97; v.p. Weber Mgmt. Cons., 1997-98; v.p. human resources and labor rels. Denver Post, 1998—2000; v.p. human resources Denver Newspaper Agy., 2000—. 1985 speaker for USIA, India, Egypt; mem. Mailers Tech. Adv. Com. to Postmaster Gen., 1991-92. Recipient McWilliams award for juvenile justice, Denver, 1971, award for interpretive reporting Denver Newspaper Guild, 1979. Mem.: ABA, Soc. Human Resources Mgmt., Colo. and Internat. Women's Forum, Denver Bar Assn. (co-chair jud. selection and benefits com. 1982—85, 2nd v.p. 1986), Newspaper Assn. Am. (mem. human resources and labor rels. com.), Colo. Bar Assn. (bd. govs. 1985—87, chair BAR-press com. 1980), Leadership Denver. Episcopalian.

GREEN, CAROLE L. lawyer; b. Queens, N.Y., Mar. 17, 1959; d. Gerald Harry and Mary (Clark) G. AB cum laude with distinction, Dartmouth Coll., 1980; JD, Harvard Law Sch., 1983. Bar: N.Y. Congl. aide to rep. John Conyers U.S. House of Reps., Washington, 1980; assoc. real estate Kaye Scholer LLP, NY, 1983—85, Bingham McCuthen LLP, N.Y., 1985-87; gen. counsel Petrie Stores Corp., Secaucus, N.J., 1987-88; assoc. counsel Mfrs. Hanover Trust Co. (now JP Morgan Chase Bank), N.Y., 1988-91; v.p., asst. gen. counsel Chem. Bank (now JP Morgan Chase Bank), N.Y., 1991-96; contract atty. N.Y.C., 1996—. Mem.: ABA, Met. Black Bar Assn., Practicing Attys. for Law Students, Inc. (founding mem. 1986—95), Assn. Bar City N.Y., N.Y. State Bar Assn., Black Alumni of Dartmouth Assn. Avocations: travel, swimming, jazz, cinema.

GREEN, CATHERINE C. foreign language educator; b. Inchon, Korea, Feb. 13, 1962; parents Am. citizens; d. Ronald J. and Jean S. Carson; m. Nathaniel C. Green, June 16, 1985 (div. Dec. 1995). BS in French, Murray (Ky.) State U., 1985; MA in Fgn. Lang. Edn., U. Louisville, 1988, postgrad., 1991. Tchr. French and German Jefferson County Pub. Schs., Louisville, 1985—. Mem. Atherton budget Com., Louisville, 1991—. Vol. adult and continuing edn., Louisville, 1996-98. Recipient Ashland Oil Tchrs. Achievement award, 1995, 97, 98, 99; JCPS/U. Louisville Collaborative Ventures grantee, 1996-98. Mem.: Am. Assn. Tchrs. French. Avocations: snorkeling, reading, travel. Home: 3906 Longview Rd Louisville KY 40299-3367 Office: Atherton HS 3000 Dundee Rd Louisville KY 40205-2448 E-mail: cgreen1@jefferson.k12.ky.us.

GREEN, CATHERINE COOPER, artist; b. Bozeman, Mont., Oct. 2, 1948; d. David Lawrence and Mary Francis Cooper; m. Timothy Haskell Green, June 14, 1970. BFA, Temple U., 1970. Art tchr. Rumford (Maine) Sch. System, 1970-72, Newburyport (Mass.) Sch. System, 1972-86; instr. Divsn. of Continuing Edn., U. N.H., Durham, 1979-89; artist Stratham, N.H., 1989—. Illustrator Yankee Mag., 1985; exhibited in group shows at Westfield Art Festival, 1993 (1st prize in graphics), Stamford Art Festival, 1993 (1st prize in graphics), On the Green Art Show, 1994, 95 (1st prize in graphics), Nat. Print Biennial, 1996, Nat. Print Competition Artlink, Ft. Wayne, 1997, 98, 2000, 01, 02, Calif. State U., 1997, 2002, Works on and of Paper, U. West Fla., 2000. Recipient Yankee Print award Yankee Mag., 1983. Mem. Exeter League of N.H. Craftsmen Jury (chair 1989-95), League of N.H. Craftsmen (mem. stds. com. 1988—, print jury mem. 1989—, v.p. bd. trustees), N.H. Art Assn. Avocations: sailing, racquetball, organic gardening, tai chi, cooking. Home: 128 Bunker Hill Ave Stratham NH 03885-2411 E-mail: info@catherinegreenart.net.

GREEN, CHARLES ADAM, retired education educator, psychologist; b. Detroit, Mich., Oct. 17, 1927; s. Fred Green and Charlena Cragwall; m. Marilyn Anderson Anderson, Aug. 22, 1987; m. Mildred Saphronia Wilson, Jan. 4, 1957 (div. May 23, 1975); children: Iris Denise Diop, Robin Charles. BA, U. of Mich., 1952; MEd, Wayne State U., 1957, PhD, 1974. Diplomate Am. Coll. Forensic Examiners; lic. psychologist Mich. Tchr. Detroit Bd. of Edn., 1954—58; dir. of spl. edn. Northville (Mich.) State Hosp., 1958—62; sch. psychologist Detroit Bd. of Edn., 1962—68, rsch. assoc., 1968—2001. Pres. Met. Cmty. Housing Devel. Orgn., Detroit, 1995—. Contbr. articles to profl. jours. Chmn., Thunder Bird dist. Boys Scouts of Am., Detroit, 1973—75; chairperson The Westsider Orgn., Detroit, 2000—03; bd. chmn. Highland Park (Mich.) YMCA, 1981—85. Pvt. USAF, 1945—46. Recipient Ability is Ageless award, Operation Able of Mich. Fellow: Am. Assn. on Mental Deficiency; mem.: APA, Phi Delta Kappa. Liberal. Avocations: boating, photography, travel, writing. Home: 398 Lodge Dr Detroit MI 48214 Personal E-mail: marilyn.green6@gte.net.

GREEN, CLIFFORD SCOTT, federal judge; b. Phila., Apr. 2, 1923; s. Robert Lewis and Alice (Robinson) G.; m. Carole Green. BS, Temple U., 1948, JD, 1951. Bar: Pa. 1952. Pvt. practice law, Phila., 1952-64; dep. atty. gen. State of Pa., 1954; judge County Ct., Phila., 1964-68, Ct. Common Pleas, 1968-71, U.S. Dist. Ct. for Eastern Dist. Pa., Phila., 1971-88, sr. judge, 1988—. Former lectr. in law Temple U. Former bd. dirs. Children's Aid Soc. of Pa.; former bd. mgrs. Children's Hosp., Phila.; trustee Temple U. Served with USAAF, 1943-46. Recipient Judge William Hastie award NAACP Legal Def. Fund, 1985, awards for cmty. service Women's Christian Alliance, Health and Welfare Council, awards for cmty. service Opportunities Industrialization Ctr., J. Austin Norris Barrister's award, 1988, Temple Law Alumni Assn. award 1994, Justice Thurgood Marshall Meml. award Nat. Bar Assn., 1994, gen. alumni award Temple U., 1999, Spirit of Excellence award ABA. Mem. Sigma Pi Phi. Presbyterian. Office: US Courthouse Independence Mall W #15613 601 Market St Philadelphia PA 19106-1713

GREEN, DAN, publishing company executive; b. Passaic, N.J., Sept. 28, 1935; s. Harold and Bessie (Roslow) G.; m. Jane Oliphant, Sept. 20, 1959; children—Matthew Kenan, Simon Pom. BA, Syracuse (N.Y.) U., 1956. Publicity dir. Dover Press, 1957-58, Sta. WNAC-TV, 1958-59, Bobbs-Merrill Co., 1959-62; with Simon & Schuster Inc., 1962-85, assoc. publisher, 1976-80, v.p., pub., 1980-84, pres. trade pub. group, 1984-85; founder, pub. Kenan Press, 1979-80; chief exec. officer Wheatland Pub., N.Y.C., 1985-89; pub. Weidenfeld & Nicolson N.Y., 1985-89; chief exec. officer Grove Press, Inc., N.Y.C., 1985-89; pres. Kenan Books, N.Y.C., 1989—. Pres. Pom Literary Agy., 1989. Office: Pom Inc 611 Broadway Rm 907B New York NY 10012-2608

GREEN, DAVID, manufacturing company executive; b. Chgo., Mar. 22, 1922; s. Harry B. and Carrie (Scheinbaum) G.; m. Mary I. Winton, June 15, 1951; children: Sara Edmond, Howard Benjamin, Jonathan Winton. BA in Econs., U. Chgo., 1942, MA in Social Scis., 1949. Mgr. Toy Co., Chgo., 1946-54; founder, chmn., pres. Quartet Mfg. Co., Skokie, Ill., 1954-90, chmn., prin. officer, 1990-97. Pres. Colleague, Inc., Booneville, Miss., 1967-87; chmn. bd. and cons. DG Group, Chgo., 1977—. Pres.'s circle Chgo. Botanic Garden; playwright's circle Stratford Festival; founder dir. circle Steppenwolf Theatre Co.; chmn. Winnetka (Ill.) Caucus, 1971; chmn. Ill. state Dan Walker for Gov., 1972, 1976; governing mem. Chgo. Symphony Orch., Art Inst. Chgo.; spl. cons. to White House-Trade Expansion Act Washington, 1962; spl. asst. to Gov. for intergovtl. relations, 1973—77; mem. pres.'s coun., vis. com. social scis. U. Chgo., mem. vis. com. on the coll. and student activities. Served with U.S. Army, 1942—45, PTO. Recipient 1st Non-Smoking Office Bldg. award Skokie Clean Air Coalition, 1987; named Office Products Divsn. Man of Yr., Richard Karasik Humanitarian award, UJA, 1997, Alumni Svc. citation U. Chgo., 2002, 1st Green Gargoyle award for Outstanding Achievement, U. Chgo., 2002, Writers' Theatre Founder's award, 2003; named Alumni Emeritus chair U. Chgo., 2002. Mem. Bus. Products Industry Assn., Office Products Wholesale Assn. (Office Product Mfr. of Yr. award 1989, 93, 94), Chgo. Soc. of Clubs, Metropolitan (Chgo.), Bay Colony (Naples, Fla.). Home: 311 Woodley Rd Winnetka IL 60093-3740 Office: 650 Dundee Rd Ste 456 Northbrook IL 60062-2758 also: 8171 Bay Colony Dr Naples FL 34108-7561

GREEN, DAVID HENRY, manufacturing company executive; b. Worcester, Mass., Feb. 8, 1921; s. Herbert H. and Florence (Knapp) G.; m. Betty Jeppson, June 23, 1951; children: Anne L., Susan E., David Henry, Charles J., Sarah C. BA, Wesleyan U., Middletown, Conn., 1942; MBA, Harvard, 1943. Asst. treas. Valley Bank & Trust Co., Springfield, Mass., 1946-51; sr. v.p. Worcester County Nat. bank, 1952-65, New Eng. Mchts. Nat. Bank (now Fleet Bank), Boston, 1965-73; chmn. L.G. Balfour Co., Attleboro, Mass., 1973-87. Dir. L.G. Balfour Co. Trustee New Eng. Aquarium, Worcester Found. Exptl. Biology; hon. trustee Concord Acad.; bd. dirs. Bristol County Devel. Council, Attleboro Scholarship Found.; bd. assos. Wheaton Coll. Served as capt. AUS, 1943-46. Home: 207 Old Concord Rd Lincoln MA 01773-3602

GREEN, DAVID WILLIAM, chemist, educator; b. Hudson, Mich., Nov. 19, 1942; s. Francis Harger and Dorotha Louise (Onweller) G.; m. Mary Sarah McCullough, July 8, 1967; children: Laura, Brenda, Mark, Brian, William. BA, Albion Coll., 1964; PhD, U. Calif., Berkeley, 1968; MBA, U. Chgo., 1985. Instr. U. Calif., Berkeley, 1968; rsch. assoc. U. Chgo., 1968-71; asst. prof. Albion (Mich.) Coll., 1971-75; chemist Argonne (Ill.) Nat. Lab., 1975-82, mgr.

analytical chemistry, 1982—2001; prof. chemistry Coll. DuPage, Glen Ellyn, Ill., 1991-93. Vis. prof. chemistry Albion Coll., 2001—. Editor Mng. the Modern Lab, 1995—, mem. editl. bd., 1994—. Pres. Dist. 58 Bd. Edn., Downers Grove, Ill., 1976-79. Mem. Analytical Lab. Mgrs. Assn. (pres. 1986-87, treas. 1989). Home: 602 Bidwell Albion MI 49224- Office: Putnam Hall Albion College Albion MI 49224- E-mail: dwgreen@albion.edu.

GREEN, DENNIS, professional football coach; b. Harrisburg, Pa., Feb. 17, 1949; BS, U. Iowa, 1971. Asst. coach U. Iowa, 1972, 74-76, U. Dayton, 1973, Stanford U., 1977-78, 80, San Francisco 49ers, 1979; head coach Northwestern U., 1981-85; asst. coach San Francisco 49ers, 1986-88; head coach Stanford U., 1989-91, Minn. Vikings, 1992—2002. Office: Minnesota Vikings 9520 Viking Dr Eden Prairie MN 55344-3898

GREEN, DENNIS JOSEPH, lawyer; b. Milw., Sept. 28, 1941; m. Janet McQueen; children: Karla Pope, Cheryl Ashley, Deborah. BS in Mgmt., U. Ill., 1963, JD, 1968. Bar: Ill. 1968, Mo. 1968. Atty. Monsanto Co., St. Louis, 1968-75, asst. co. counsel, 1975-76, counsel, 1976-79; gen. counsel, sec. Fisher Controls Internat. Inc., Clayton, Mo., 1979-85, v.p., gen. counsel, sec., 1985-93; v.p., assoc. gen. counsel Emerson Electric Co., St. Louis, 1992—. 1st lt. U.S. Army, 1963-65. Office: Emerson Electric Co PO Box 4100 8000 W Florissant Ave Saint Louis MO 63136-1494 E-mail: dennis.green@emrsn.com.

GREEN, DETROY EDWARD, retired dean; b. Zalma, Mo., Mar. 26, 1930; s. Charley Edward and Cora Lorene Green; m. Marilyn Jereleen Ward, Aug. 3, 1951; children: Angela, Mona, Detroy II, Alan, Lori. BS, U. of Mo., Columbia, MO, 1954, MS, 1961, PhD, 1965. Asst. prof. Iowa State U., Ames, Iowa, 1964—66, assoc. prof., 1966—68, prof., 1968—89, assoc. dean, 1989—95. Contbr. articles to profl. jours. Fellow: Am. Soc. of Agron. Democrat. United Methodist. Avocations: fishing, hunting, reading. Home: 1801 20th Street J11 Ames IA 50010

GREEN, DON WESLEY, chemical and petroleum engineering educator; b. Tulsa, July 8, 1932; s. Earl Leslie and Erma Pansy (Brackins) G.; m. Patricia Louise Polston, Nov. 26, 1954; children: Guy Leslie, Don Michael, Charles Patrick. BS in Petroleum Engring., U. Tulsa, 1955; MSChemE, U. Okla., 1959, PhD in Chem. Engring., 1963. Rsch. scientist Continental Oil Co., Ponca City, Okla., 1962-64; asst. to assoc. prof. U. Kans., Lawrence, 1964-71, prof. chem. and petroleum engring., 1971-82, chmn. dept. chem. and petroleum engring., 1970-74, 96-200, co-dir. Tertiary Oil Recovery project, 1974—, Conger-Gabel Disting. prof., 1982-95, Deane E. Ackers Disting. prof., 1995—. Faculty rep. to NCAA. Editor: Perry's Chemical Engineers' Handbook, 1984, 1997; co-author: Enhanced Oil Recovery, 1998; contbr. articles to profl. jours. 1st lt. USAF, 1955-57. Fellow Am. Inst. Chem. Engrs.; mem. Soc. Petroleum Engrs. (Disting. Achievement award 1983, chmn. edn. and accreditation com. 1980-81, Disting. mem. 1986, Disting. lectr. 1986). Democrat. Avocations: handball, baseball, mountain hiking. Home: 1020 Sunset Dr Lawrence KS 66044-4546 Office: U Kans Dept Chem & Petroleum Engring 4008 Learned Hall Lawrence KS 66045-7526 E-mail: dgreen@ku.edu.

GREEN, DONALD HUGH, lawyer; b. Elizabeth, N.J., May 16, 1929; s. Mortimer Jordan and Edna (Reinherz) G.; m. Carol Margaret Medsger, Sept. 20, 1960; children: Michael, Margaret, Matthew, Mark. AB, Syracuse U., 1951; LLB, Harvard U., 1954. Bar: Fla. 1956, N.Y. 1957, D.C. 1960. Atty. Office of Legal Counsel, U.S. Dept. Justice, Washington, 1958-60, atty. civil div., 1960-61; assoc. Bergson & Borkland, Washington, 1961-65; ptnr. Fisher, Sharlitt, Gelband & Green, Washington, 1965-66, Wald, Harkrader & Ross, Washington, 1966-87; vice chmn. exec. com. mng. ptnr. Pepper, Hamilton LLP, Washington, 1987—, mem. exec. com., mng. ptnr. DC office, 1995—2000. Mem. faculty curriculum com. Legal Edn. Inst., U.S. Dept. Justice, Washington, 1985-92; lectr. Georgetown Law Ctr., Washington, 1981—, various symposia D.C. Bar; adj. prof. Georgetown Law Ctr., 1992-03; appointed defense adv. com. on women in the svcs. Sec. of Defense, 1999, exec. com. 1999-01. Contbr. articles to profl. jours. Mem., chmn. trustees Cedar Ln. Unitarian Ch., Bethesda, 1972-75. Col. USMCR, 1954-85. Decorated Legion of Merit. Mem. ABA, Internat. Assn. Women Judges (mem. bd. mng. trustees 2002—), Fed. Bar Assn., Am. Arbitration Assn., Dev. Rsch. Inst., Joint Svcs. Com. on Profl. Ethics, Nat. Panel Arbitrators, Fed. Am. Inn of Ct. (pres. 1994-95). Democrat. Avocations: painting, sailing, tennis. Home: 5610 Wisconsin Ave Apt 18A Chevy Chase MD 20815-4415 Office: Pepper Hamilton LLP Hamilton Sq 600 14th St NW Washington DC 20005-2008 E-mail: greendh@pepperlaw.com.

GREEN, DONALD PHILIP, education educator; b. Chgo., June 23, 1961; s. Burton and Isabel (Engelhardt) G.; m. Ann Gerken, June 18, 1989; children: Aaron, Rachel. BA in Polit. Sci., UCLA, 1983; MA in Polit. Sci., U. Calif., Berkeley, 1984, PhD, 1988. From asst. to assoc. prof. dept. polit. sci. Yale U., New Haven, 1989-94, prof., 1994—, dir. Instn. for Social and Policy Studies, 1996—, A. Whitney Giswold chair, 2001. Author: Pathologies of Rational Choice Theory, 1994; contbr. articles to profl. jours.; inventor abstract strategy games. Recipient Nat. Young Investigator award NSF, 1993—. Office: Yale Univ 124 Prospect St New Haven CT 06511-3741

GREEN, DOUGLAS ALVIN, retired library director; b. Gilmer, Tex., Feb. 17, 1925; s. Arthur Elmer and Evelena (Loyless) G.; m. Clovis Wayne Elwell, Dec. 15, 1945; 1 child, Danis (dec.). BA, U. N. Tex., 1950; MA, E. Tex. State U., 1951; MS, La. State U., 1968; EdD, E. Tex. State U., 1980. Chief bibliographer U. Ark. Gen. Libr., Fayetteville, 1963-67; libr. dir. Bee County Coll., Beeville, Tex., 1968-73; chmn. learning resources Richland Community Coll., Decatur, Ill., 1973-75; libr. dir. Laredo (Tex.) State U., 1975-76, Ambassador Coll., Big Sandy, Tex., 1976-77, Pasadena, 1977-78, U. Cen. Ark., Conway, 1981-84; ret., Ark. State U., Beebe, 1990. Author: An Index to Collected Essays on Educational Media and Technology, 1982; contbg. author: The Smaller Academic Library - A Management Handbook, 1988. With USNR, 1943-46. HEA Title II scholar, 1967-68. Avocations: piano, organ, keyboards, fishing, antique autos. Home: 3414 Lee St Tyler TX 75702-1628

GREEN, EDWARD ANTHONY, museum director; b. Milw., Apr. 20, 1922; s. Edward Eli and Elizabeth Mary (Hofmeister) G.; m. Dorinne May Traulsen, June 20, 1953; children: Erika Linden, Jeremy Jonathon. BS in Art Edn., MS in Applied Art, U. Wis., 1951; MFA in Fine Arts with honors, U. Wis., Milw., 1966; student, Layton Sch. Art, 1953. Archtl. designer Wilbur Lumber Co., West Allis, Wis., 1940-42; playground dir. Milw. Recreation Dept., 1947-49; art dir. Milw. Pub. Mus., 1951-84; landmarks commr. City of Milw., 1959-80, art commr., 1959-84; dir. mus. Mitchell Gallery Flight, Milw., 1984—. Art instr. U. Wis., Milw., 1955-69, 84, Whitnall Park, Greendale, Wis., 1966-79, Cardinal Stritch U., Fox Point, Wis., 1975-90, Mt. Mary Coll., 1997; art instr., lectr. Alverno Coll., 1998; mus. cons. Roger Williams Park Nat. Hist. Mus., Providence, 1982, Mus. Architecture, Quincy, Ill., 1984, Milw. Children's Mus., 1991—, Great Lakes Naval Tng. Ctr., North Chicago, Ill., 1991—, USCG Mus., New London, Conn., 1993—, others; careers lectr. Kiwanis, Milw., 1969—, Alverno Coll., 1980; lectr. U. Wis., Milw., 1992—; bd. dirs. Great Lakes Future Resource Ctr., U. Wis. Milw. Alumni Trustees, 1995—. Designer: Bapt. Mission Ch., Bamenda, Cameroon, (books) Masks of the Northwest Coast, 1966, Iroquois Masks, 1969, Mambila, 1972; co-author: Popular Culture in Museums, 1981; works included in state and nat. exhbns., also pvt. and pub. collections. Bd. dirs. Retired Sr. Vol. Program, 1996. With USCG, 1942-46; served convoy duty in North Atlantic. Recipient European Mus. Study award U. Wis., 1959, Urban Planning award Ford Found., 1969, One of 85 Outstanding Milwaukeens Milw. Mag., 1984, Lifework award Milw. Art Commn., 1985. Mem. USCG Aux. (life, comdr. 1976), Milw. Art Mus., Wis. Painters and Sculptors (pres. 1951-54), Jackson Park Assn., Longfield Shores Assn. (pres. 1976), Phi Kappa Phi. Roman Catholic. Avocations: collecting toy trains and britain's toy soldiers, softball, sailing, painting. Home: 3173 S 31st St Milwaukee WI 53215-4319 Office: Mitchell Gallery of Flight 5300 S Howell Ave Milwaukee WI 53207-6156

GREEN, EDWARD CROCKER, research scientist; b. Washington, Nov. 29, 1944; s. Marshall and Lispenard Seabury (Crocker) G.; m. K. Shannon McCaffray, Sept. 22, 1967 (div. 1977); 1 child, Timothy A.; m. M. Sue McLaughlin, Apr. 24, 1990. BA, George Washington U., 1967; MA, Northwestern U., 1968; PhD, Cath. U. Am., 1974; postgrad., Vanderbilt U., 1978-79. Asst. prof. W.Va. U., Morgantown, 1976-78; pvt. practice devel. cons. various orgns., Washington, 1979—; mgr. internat. programs John Short & Assocs., Columbia, Md., 1986-88; social scientist Acad. for Ednl. Devel., Swaziland, 1981—84; personal svcs. contractor U.S. AID, Swaziland, 1984—85; advisor Mozambique Govt., 1994—95; mgr., rschr. The Futures Group, Washington, 1988-89; sr. rsch. fellow in internat. health Harvard U., Cambridge, Mass., 2001—02, sr. rsch. scientist Sch. Pub. Health, 2002—. Social scientist Acad. for Ednl. Devel., Swaziland, 1981-84; personal svcs. contractor U.S. AID, Swaziland, 1984-85; advisor Mozambique Govt., 1994-95. Author: Planning Psychiatric Services for Southern Africa, 1979, Practicing Development Anthropology, 1986, AIDS and STDs in Africa, 1994, Indigenous Healers and The African State, 1996, Indigenous Theories of Contagious Disease, 1999; mem. editl. bd. Jour. Alternative and Complementary Medicine; contbr. over 95 articles to profl. jours. Bd. dirs. Bonobo Conservaation Initiative. Recipient Mozambique Govt. award for health rsch., 1992, Praxis award Washington Assn. Profl. Anthropologists, 1982, 83; NIMH postdoctoral fellow, 1978-79; Sigma Xi rsch. grantee, 1971; Takmi fellow Harvard U., 2001-02. Mem. Am. Anthrop. Assn., Soc. Applied Anthropology; mem. N.Y. Acad. Scis., Soc. Med. Anthropology, Global Initiative Traditional Sys. Health (bd. dirs.), World Population Soc. (bd. dirs.). Avocation: folk music. Home and Office: 2807 38th St NW Washington DC 20007-1341

GREEN, EDWARD FRANCIS, manufacturing executive; b. Malden, Mass., Sept. 5, 1952; s. John Patrick and Mary Eleanor (Cahill) G.; m. Eugenia Bonita Tolla, Oct. 13, 1974; 1 child, Tanya Celeste. BS, Northeastern U., 1977; MBA, Babson Coll., 1983; advanced cert. mgmt. studies, Boston U., 1986. Supr. machine shop GE Power Generation, Lynn, Mass., 1974-77; mfg. and quality engr. GE Lighting, Lexington, Ky., 1977-78; buyer GE Motors, Springfield, Mo., 1978-79; mgr. machine shop ops. GE Aircraft Engines, Lynn, Mass., 1979-84, mgr. quality and tech. planning, 1984-86, mgr. purchased material quality, 1986-88, mgr. prodn. and inventory control, 1988-89, engine program mgr., 1989-91; mfg. program mgr. GE Aerospace, Pittsfield, Mass., 1991-92; dir. mfg. Rome (N.Y.) Cable Corp., 1992-94; plant mgr. Chicago Pneumatic Tool Co., Utica, N.Y., 1994-96, Emerson Power Transmissions-Rollway Bearing, Syracuse, N.Y., 1996-2001; v.p., gen. mgr. GE-Garrett Aviation Svcs., Islip, N.Y., 2001—. Active Boy Scouts Am., Oneida County, N.Y., 1993-2001. Mem. GE Apprentice Alumni Assn., Mfrs. Assn. Ctrl. N.Y. (bd. dirs. factory mgmt. coun. 1992-2001), KC (4th deg.), Crystal Cmty. Club (treas. 1979-80), L.I. Bus. Aviation Assn., Shoreham Country Club. Republican. Roman Catholic. Avocations: sport fishing, home remodeling, automobile restoration, skiing, golf. Office: Garrett Aviation Svcs 2221 Smithtown Ave Ronkonkoma NY 11779-7387 Home: 11 Ashley Ln Shoreham NY 11786-1400 E-mail: ed.green@ae.ge.com.

GREEN, EDWARD THOMAS, JR., education educator; b. Oxford, N.J., Apr. 19, 1921; s. Edward Thomas and Euphemia (Lanterman) G.; m. Margaret Evelyn Tuttle, Jan. 30, 1944; children: Marsha, Margaret, Barbara. BS cum laude, Ithaca Coll., 1942; MS, Syracuse U., 1947, EdD, 1965. Music instr. high sch., Palmyra, N.Y., 1942-50; dir. guidance, vice-prin., 1946-50; prin. Palmyra-Macedon Ctrl. Sch., 1950-54; supervising prin. New Berlin (N.Y.) Ctrl. Sch., 1954-58, Rondout Valley Ctrl. Sch., Accord, N.Y., also supt. schs., 1958-66; supt. schs. Oneida (NY) City Schs., 1966-77; prof. edn. Ga. So. U., Statesboro, 1977-87, prof. emeritus, 1987—. Pres. Mid-Hudson Sch. Study Coun., New Paltz, N.Y., 1960; vice chmn. CHE-MAD-HER-ON, Inc.; area sec. Ctrl. Sch. Study; mem. exec. com. Catskill Study on Small Sch. Design; v.p. N.Y. State Tchrs. Retirement Bd.; v.p. Rip Van Winkle coun. Boy Scouts Am., 1964-66, v.p., then pres. Madison County coun., chmn. Madison Dist., pres. Iroquois coun.; pres. Palmyra Betterment Club 1952; mem. Ulster County Cmty. Action Program; past pres. Ithaca Coll. Alumni Coun. Served with AUS, 1942-46, ETO. Mem. N.Y. State Sch. Dist. Adminstrs. (pres.), Am. Assn. Sch. Adminstrs., Assn. for Supervision and Curriculum Devel., Nat. Sch. Pub. Rels. Assn., Nat. Assn. Secondary Sch. Prins., Nat. Assn. Elem. Sch. Prins., Ga. Assn. Ednl. Leaders, So. Assn. Colls. and Schs. (Ga. sec. com. 1991-95), Ga. Accrediting Commn., Nat. Orgn. for Legal Problems in Edn., Masons, Shriners, Rotary Internat., Lions Club, Phi Delta Kappa (chpt. pres., area coord.), Phi Mu Alpha. Republican. Presbyterian. Home: 301 Bella Vista Dr Ithaca NY 14850-5774

GREEN, ELBERT P. retired university official; b. Laneview, Va., June 9, 1935; s. James H. and Levallia C. (DeLeaver) G.; m. Mary M. Green, July 6, 1961; children: Mark B., Marsha B. BS, Va. State Coll., 1957; BD, Felix Adler Meml. U., Chapel Hill, N.C., 1969; MS in Edn., Troy State U., Montgomery, Ala., 1988; MBph, Am. Bible Sch., Kansas City, Kans., 1968; PhD, S.W. U., New Orleans, 1991. Cert. tchr., Ala., cert. hypnotherapist; ordained minister. 2d lt. U.S. Army, 1958, advanced through grades to maj., ret., 1979; dir. jr. ROTC, Indianola (Miss.) City Schs., Macon County (Ala.) Schs.; dir. residence hall Tuskegee (Ala.) U. Author: Poetry Is Soul, 1988, Poetry Is Gold, 1982, The Light of the World Is Poetry, 1995; contbr. articles to newspapers. Inductee Internat. Poetry Hall of Fame, 1997, Who Is Who of Contemporary Achievers Hall of Fame, 1997, Phi Beta Sigma Hall of Fame, 1999, Am. Biographical Inst. Hall of Fame, 2002. Mem. Internat. Soc. of Poets, Profl. Educators Orgn., Am. Legion, Lions Internat., Scabbard and Blade, Phi Beta Sigma, Phi Delta Kappa, Gamma Beta Phi. Home: 2910 W Martin L King Hwy Tuskegee AL 36083

GREEN, ELEANOR MYERS, veterinarian, educator; b. Phila., Feb. 10, 1948; d. Wade Cooper and Eleanor Ruth (McWherter) Myers; children: George Ashby Jr., Stacy Elizabeth, William Wade. Student, U. South Fla., 1965-67, U. Fla., 1967-69; DVM, Auburn U., 1973. Diplomate Am. Coll. Vet. Internal Medicine, Am. Bd. Vet. Practitioners (pres. 1993-95, past pres. 1995-96). Ptnrship, owner Guntown (Miss.) Vet. Clinic, 1973-76; asst. prof. Miss. State U., Starkville, 1976-84; assoc. prof. U. Mo., Columbia, 1984-91; prof. U. Tenn., Knoxville, 1991-96; prof., chair dept. U. Fla., Gainesville, 1996—. Named Disting. Practitioner Nat. Acads. of Practice. Mem. Am. Assn. Equine Practitioners (bd. dirs. 1997-99), Fla. Vet. Med. Assn., Am. Vet. Med. Assn., Internat. Soc. Vet. Perinatology, Am. Assn. Vet. Clinicians (Faculty Achievement award 1999, pres. 1995-96, past pres. 1996-97), Nat. Acad.'s Practice (Disting. Practitioner 1998—), Fla. Thoroughbred Owners and Breeders Assn., Fla. Quarter Horse Assn. (bd. dirs.), Rotary Internat. Presbyterian. Avocations: horseback riding, tennis, painting. Office: U Fla Coll Vet Medicine Dept Large Animal Clin Scis Gainesville FL 32610-0136 E-mail: greene@mail.vetmed.ufl.edu.

GREEN, FRANCIS EUGENE, artist, educator; b. San Diego, Apr. 3, 1946; s. Charles Green, Jr. and Lois Lavonne (Simmerman) Adelman; m. Bonnie Weigle, Oct. 8, 1966 (div. Apr. 1979); m. Barbara Korr, Feb. 14, 1980. AA in Painting, San Diego Mesa Jr. Coll., 1968; BA in Painting, San Diego State U., 1971; MFA, Temple U., 1973. Dept. head printmaking Instituto Allende, San Miguel de Allende, 1972-75; master printer Atelier Ettinger, N.Y.C., 1975-79; cons. fine art editions N.Y.C., 1979-84; vocat. comml. arts instr. Greene Correctional Facility, Coxsackie, 1984—; represented by Pierce Galleries, Inc., Nantucket, Mass., Deborah Davis Fine Art, Hudson, NY. Instr. Olana State Hist. Site, Hudson, N.Y., 1990-2000, Columbia/Greene C.C., Hudson, 1996-97. Exhibits in N.Y., N.J. and Conn. Democrat. Jewish. Home: #10 Rte 23A Catskill NY 12414

GREEN, FRANCIS WILLIAM, investment consultant, former missile scientist; b. Locust Grove, Okla., Mar. 17, 1920; s. Noel Francis and Mary (Lincoln) G.; m. Alma J. Ellison, Aug. 26, 1950 (dec. Sept. 1970); children: Sharmon, Rhonda; m. Susan G. Mathis, July 14, 1973 (div. July 1979). BS, Phoenix U., 1955; MS in Elec. Engring., Minerva U., Milan, Italy, 1959; MS in Engring., West Coast U., L.A., 1965. With USN Guided Missile Program, 1945-49; design and electronic project engr. Falcon missile program Hughes Aircraft Co., Culver City, Calif., 1949-55; sr. electronic engr. Atlas missile program Convair Astronautics, San Diego, 1955-59; sr. engr. Polaris missile program Nortronics divsn. Northrop, Anaheim, Calif., 1959-60; chief, supr. electronic engring. data sys. br. Tech. Support divsn. Rocket Propulsion Lab., USAF, Edwards AFB, Calif., 1960-67, dep. chief tech. support divsn., 1967-69; tech. advisor Air Force Missile Devel. Ctr., Holloman AFB, N.Mex., 1969-70, 6585 TestGroup, Air Force Spl. Weapons Ctr, Holloman AFB, 1970-78; pvt. investment cons., 1978—. Bd. examiners U.S. CSC; mem. Pres.'s Missile Site Labor Rels. Com.; cons. advanced computer and data processing tech. and systems engring.; mem. USAF Civilian Policy Bd. and Range Comdrs. Coun.; maj. gen., comdr. 2d brigade N.Mex. State Milit. Forces; comdr. N.Mex. State Mil. Forces, 1989-99, maj. gen. ret. Contbr. articles to profl. jours. Served as pilot, asst. engring. officer USAAF, 1941-47. Fellow AIAA; mem. IEEE (sr.), Nat. Assn. Flight Instrs., Res. Officers Assn. U.S. Home and Office: 2345 Apache Ln Alamogordo NM 88310-4851

GREEN, FRANK EARL, civil engineer; b. Joplin, Mo., Nov. 24, 1931; s. Lloyd Cuthbertson and Gladys Alberta (Kennedy) G.; m. Joan Imogene (Wheeler)July 25, 1953; children: Kevin Joe, Keely Sue Green LaNoue. BS in Math., S.W. Mo. State U., 1953; BSCE, Kans. State U., 1958. Registered profl. engr., Mo., land surveyor, Mo. Hwy. designer Mo. Hwy. and Transp. Dept., Kansas City, 1958-61, sr. hwy. designer, 1962-65, dist. hwy. design engr., 1966-96; retired, 1996. Usher, mem. Grandview (Mo.) United Meth. Ch., 1970—. With Army Corps. of Engrs., 1953-55. Mem. ASCE (life, bd. dirs. Kansas City sect. 1987-91, sec.-treas. and pres.-elect 1992, pres. 1993), Nat. Soc. Profl. Engrs. (life), Mo. Soc. Profl. Engrs. (bd. dirs. Western chpt. 1985-91). Republican. Home: 5608 E 100th Ter Kansas City MO 64137-1312

GREEN, FRANKLIN PASCO, music educator; b. Atlanta, Ga., Nov. 25, 1951; s. Franklin Pasco and Pearl Altman Green; m. Rachel McCallum, Sept. 1, 1973; children: Rachel Elizabeth, Franklin Carter. MusB magna cum laude, U. Ga., 1973, MusD, 2000; MusM, So. Bapt. Theol. Sem., 1975. Cert. tchr. Ga., 2000. Min. music Centerville Bapt. Ch., Chesapeake, Va., 1976—82, First Bapt. Ch., Decatur, Ga., 1982—88; instr. Ga. Coll. and State U., Milledgeville, Ga., 1995—96; choral dir. McIntosh HS, Peachtree City, Ga., 1996—. Recipient Selected for Masterclass performance with Samuel Sanders and Charles Wadsworth, Sch. of Music, U. of Ga., 1991; scholar, U. of Ga., 1991—92. Mem.: Phi Mu Alpha Sinfonia, Am. Choral Dirs. Assn. (condr.), Pi Kappa Lambda. Home: 34 Cobblestone Cove Sharpsburg GA 30277 Office: McIntosh High School 201 Walt Banks Road Peachtree City GA Office Fax: 770-631-3278. Personal E-mail: green.frank@fcboe.org. E-mail: green.frank@fcboe.org.

GREEN, GENE, congressman; b. Houston, Oct. 17, 1947; s. Garland B. and Evelyn (Clark) G.; m. Helen Lois Albers; children: Angela, Christopher. BS in Bus. Adminstrn., U. Houston, 1971; student, Bates Coll., Sch. of Law. Mgr. printing co.; atty.; mem. Tex. Ho. of Reps., 1973-85, Tex. Senate, 1985-92, U.S. Congress from 29th Tex. dist., 1993—; mem. energy and commerce com., standards of official conduct com., ethics com. Recipient Outstanding Legis. award Houston Park Police Assn., Appreciation award Dem. Nat. Com., Appreciation award Harris County Sheriff's Deputy Assn., Legis. Support award AFL-CIO, Support award Tex. Dem. Party. Mem. Baytown C. of C., Tex. Hist. Soc., Coastal Conservation Assn. Democrat. Methodist. Office: US House of Reps 2335 Rayburn Ho Office Bldg Washington DC 20515-4329 also: 11811 I-10 East Ste 430 Houston TX 77029*

GREEN, GEORGE JOSEPH, publishing executive; b. N.Y.C., May 6, 1938; s. Monroe and Ruth (Gast) G.; m. Wilma H. Jordan. BA, Yale U., 1960. Trainee advt. dept. Burlington Industries, N.Y.C., 1961-62; with The New Yorker Mag., 1962-84, salesman retail advt. N.Y.C. div., 1962-64, salesman advt. Atlanta div., 1964-66, salesman advt. N.Y.C. div., 1966-67, asst. treas., 1967-71, dir. circulation, v.p., 1971-75, pres., 1975-84; exec. v.p. Hearst Mags., N.Y.C., 1984—; pres. Hearst Mags. Internat., N.Y.C., 1989—. Bd. dirs. Nat. Magazine Co. Served with USAR, 1960-65. Mem. Mag. Publs. Assn. (bd. dirs.). Office: Hearst Mags 959 8th Ave New York NY 10019-3795

GREEN, GEORGE N. historian, educator; b. Rockdale, Tex., Apr. 27, 1939; s. Malcolm Alexander and Elizabeth Hughes Green; m. Penelope Smith Green, 1966 (div. 1970); m. Kathryn Park Green, May 20, 1972; children: Valerie Elizabeth, Deanna Park. BA in History, U. Tex., 1961; MA in History, Fla. State U., 1962, Doctorate in History, 1966. Instr. Fla. State U., Tallahassee, 1964—65, Tex. Woman's U., Denton, 1965—66, U. Tex., Arlington, 1966—67, asst. prof., 1967—71, assoc. prof., 1972—81, full prof., 1981—. Co-founder Tex. Labor and Polit. Archives U. Tex. Arlington Libr., 1967; vis. asst. prof. Tex. Tech. U., Lubbock, 1972; field agt. Tex. Labor Movement Found., Austin, 1991—; fellow Ctr. for Greater S.W. Studies, Arlington, 1991—; lectr. in field. Author: The Establishment in Texas Politics, 1979; contbr. articles to profl. jours. Chmn. 12th senatorial dist. Dem. Party, Tarrant County, Tex., 1980; del. 12th senatorial dist. Dem. Party Mini-Conf., 1978—. Recipient Best Article of the Yr. award, East Tex. Hist. Quarterly, Nacogdoches, 1988; Nat. Def. fellow, Fla. State U., Tallahassee, 1961—64. Fellow: Tex. State Hist. Assn. (life, mem. fellows com. 1989—93, pres. 2003—); mem.: Southwestern Labor History Assn. (bd. mem. 1970—). Avocations: softball, tennis. Home: 140 Varsity Cir Arlington TX 76013 Office: Univ Tex Arlington History Dept Box 19529 Arlington TX 76019

GREEN, GERALD, editor, consultant; b. Wilkes Barre, Pa., Mar. 3, 1923; s. Samuel and Esther G.; m. Bernice L. Green; children: Gail Green, Jeffrey Green. AS, Bucknell U. Jr. Coll., Wilkes-Barre, Pa., 1942; student, George Washington U., 1948-58. Engr. Bur. Ships, Washington, 1943-56; supr. elec. engr. Naval Air Systems Command, Arlington, Va., 1956-74; cons. Gerald Green Cons., Falls Church, Va., 1974-98; Washington editor Horizon House Publs., Falls Church, Va., 1975-98; editor-in-chief Elec. Warfare Digest, Springfield, Va., 1980-90, Green News Svc., 1998—. Internat. speaker, U.S., U.K., France, Japan, and Israel, 1998—; conf. moderator, U.S., England, and France, 1998—. Pres. Bailey's Sch., Falls Church, Va., 1973-74, Glasgow Int. Sch., Falls Church, Va., 1974-75. Mem. AOC Elec. Def. Assn. Avocation: painting. Home and Office: Apt 401 7408 Spring Village Dr Springfield VA 22150-4491

GREEN, GERALD B. state legislator; Freeholder Union County; assemblyman dist. 22 N.J. State Assembly. Chmn. fin. Union County Freehold, 1991, chair bd. dirs., 1990. Pvt. industry coun. Union County Coll. Bd. Sch. Estimate. Mem. Union County Police Chiefs Assn. Office: 17 Watchung Ave Plainfield NJ 07060-1228

GREEN, GERARD LEO, priest, educator; b. Batavia, N.Y., July 27, 1928; s. George Leo and Marian (Powers) G. BS, Mt. St. Mary's Coll., 1952; MA, St. Bonaventure U., 1958; postgrad., U. Notre Dame, summers 1961-62, U. Buffalo, 1965-66; EdM, SUNY, 1968. ordained priest Roman Catholic Ch., 1956. Lab technician Eastman Kodak Co., 1947-48; chemist Xerox Co., 1952; parish asst. Diocese Buffalo, 1956-59; instr. chemistry Bishop Turner H.S., Buffalo, 1959-74, dir. sci., 1959-70, 72-74; adminstr. Our Lady of the Rosary Parish, Wilson, N.Y., 1968, St. Barnabas Parish and Sch. Depew, N.Y., 1973-75, pastor, 1976-90; prelate of honor, 1984; mem., supr., leader tng. team, 1979-90; pastor Sts. Peter and Paul Parish, Hamburg, N.Y., 1990-99; rector pro tem St. Joseph's Cathedral, Buffalo, 2001. Mem. sci. curriculum com. Dept. Edn. Diocese Buffalo, 1960-70, chmn. diocesan chemistry textbook evaluation com., 1961-70, mem. diocesan pastoral coun. for handicapped, 1976-82, sec. 1978-79, diocesan regional coord., 1979-80, mem. diocesan fin. com., 1984-94, diocesan priests coun., 1990-99, 2003—, mem. diocesan coll. of consultors, 1994-99; active Diocesan Cons. Parish Computers, 1983-98, Diocesan Bd. Priests Retirement, 1985-91, 99—, Diocesan Cemetary Bd., 1994—, Sch. Bd. St. Francis H.S., 1992-98; diocesan bd. dirs. for TV prodn. 1986-94; chaplain Hyview Fire Co., 1976-81, Cheektowaga Police PBA, 1976-90, West End Fire Co., 1977-90, Depew Village Fire Co., 1980-88. Contbr. articles to profl. publs. Mem. Western N.Y. Sci. Congress Com., 1960-74, sec., 1968, co-chmn. 1969, chmn. 1972-73, state chmn. 1970; mem. gen. chemistry exam. com. N.Y. State Edn. Dept., 1970-73; mem. Maryvale Schs. Planning Bd., 1977-79; cons. sci. facilities in secondary schs.; mem. local IUE-AFL-CIO Scholarship Fund Com., 1968-71; mem. dist. com. Boy Scouts Am., Buffalo, 1957-74; bd. dirs. Tifft (Conservation) Farm, 1978-82, Hamburg Meals on Wheels, 1999-00; active Nat. Cath. Cemetary Conf., N.Y. State Fire Chaplains. With AUS, 1946-47. Recipient Disting. Svc. award in sci. edn., 1975, Justice and Charity award First Cath. Charities, 1999, Cure of ARS award Outstanding Priest, 1999, Eagle Scout. Mem. Sci. Tchrs. Assn., N.Y. (dir. 1971-73), Nat. Cath. Edn. Assn., Order of Arrow, KC 4th degree past grand knight). Address: 9686 Oak Grove Dr Angola NY 14006-8904 E-mail: msgrgreen@hotmail.com.

GREEN, GRANT S., JR., federal agency administrator; b. Seattle, June 16, 1938; s. Grant S. and Eveleth (Solberg) G.; m. Virginia Dondy; children: Kelley, Shelley, Tana. BA, U. Ark., 1960; MS, George Washington U., 1978. Commd. 2d lt. U.S. Army, 1961, advanced through grades to col., ret., 1983; various mgmt. positions Sears World Trade, Washington, 1983-86; spl. asst. to pres. for

nat. security affairs NSC, Washington, 1986-87; asst. sec. def. Office Sec. Def., Washington, 1987-88; v.p. IPAC, Washington; chmn. & pres. GMD Solutions; under sec. for mgmt. U.S. Dept. State, Washington, 2001—. Cons. Carlyle Group, Washington, 1988—; mem. bd. USO, Nat. Def. Univ., 1987—. Decorated Bronze Star, DFC, DDSM, DSSM, others; recipient Disting. Pub. Svc. award Dept. of Def., several fgn. awards. Mem. World Affairs Coun., Ctr. for Excellence in Govt., Assn. U.S. Army, Army Aviation Assn., Ret. Officers Assn., Am. Legion. Republican. Avocations: antique cars, boating, golf, skiing. Office: US Dept State Management 2201 C St NW Washington DC 20520-7207

GREEN, HARLAND NORTON, lawyer, accountant; b. Los Angeles, Feb. 14, 1930; s. William and Lena (Schwimer) G.; m. Melva Nudelman, Dec. 20, 1953. BS in Acctg., UCLA, 1951, JD, 1953; LLM in Taxation, U. S.C., 1962. Bar: Calif. 1955, U.S. Supreme Ct. 1963. Accountant J. Arthur Greenfield & Co., CPA's, Los Angeles, 1956-58; assoc. atty. Rosenthal & Green and predecessors, Beverly Hills, Calif., 1958-61, ptnr., 1961-68; pvt. practice Beverly Hills, 1969-72; pres. Harland N. Green, P.C., Beverly Hills, 1972—. Contbr. articles to UCLA Law Rev. Vice chmn., bd. trustees So. Calif. chpt. Nat. Multiple Sclerosis Soc.; elder Ahavat Zion Messianic Synagogue. Named an Outstanding Trustee So. Calif. chpt. Multiple Sclerosis Soc., 1966, Most Valuable Trustee, 1976. Mem. ABA, Calif. Bar Assn., Beverly Hills Bar Assn., Assn. Attys.-CPA's Los Angeles Copyright Soc., Order of Coif, Phi Beta Kappa, Beta Gamma Sigma.

GREEN, HAROLD DANIEL, dentist; b. Scranton, Pa., Feb. 4, 1934; s. Harold Charles and Viola Mildred (Brown) G.; m. Cornelia Ann Ellis, Aug. 1, 1959; children: Scott Alan, Mary Ann. BA, Beloit Coll. (Wis.), 1956; DDS, Northwestern U., 1960. Gen. practice dentistry, Beloit, Wis., 1964—. Dir. Beloit Savs. Bank, chmn. trust com., 1989—; mem loan com. Blackhawk State Bank, mem. fin. com., 1993. Contbr. articles to profl. jours. Active Wis. div. Am. Cancer Soc., 1964-75; 1st pres., co-organizer Citizen's Council Against Crime, Beloit; past officer, chmn. membership Beloit YMCA; pres. Beloit Brewers, chmn. bd., 1982-2002, class A midwest league affiliate of Milw. Brewers baseball team, 1986-87; chmn. Student Achievers Program, Wis., No. Ill.; mem. adv. bd. Salvation Army; chmn. Beloiters for Coun.-Mgr., 1989; stateline chmn. Student Achiever Program, 1988, 93; bd. dirs. Greater Beloit Found., 1989—; chmating com. Greater Beloit Community Trust, Inc., 1991,93; chmn. adminstrv. bd., chmn. Council of Ministries, First United Methodist Ch., Beloit, pastor parish rels., 1995 ; chmn. ann. dinner, bd. dirs., nominating com., fundraising, pub. speakers Beloit Crime Stoppers, 1993—, chmn., 1995-96; chmn. facilities study com. Sch. Dist. Beloit, 1991—; chmn. Eagle Scout bd. rev. Sinnisippi coun. Boy Scouts Am., 1995-96; vice chair spkrs. bur. Beloit Sports Hall of Fame, 1998-99, chmn., 1999. Recipient award for creativity in dentistry Johnson & Johnson Co., 1970; 3 citations for Cmty. Svc. United Givers Fund, 1970-75; Disting. Svc. citation Greater Beloit Assn. Commerce; named to Rock County Hall of Honor, 2000 Fellow Acad. Gen. Dentistry, Internat. Coll. Dentists. (Wis. editor), Am. Acad. Dental Practice Adminstrn. (past chmn. profl. liaison; mem. ADA (chmn. council on dental practice 1982-84), Wis. Dental Assn. (pres. 1979-80, trustee 1968-74), Wis. Dental Assn. Found., Rock County Dental Soc. (pres. 1976), Wis. Council of Professions (bd. dirs. 1974-80, pres. 1973-75), Chgo. Dental Soc., Greater Milw. Dental Assn., Fedn. Dentaire Internationale, Pierre Fauchard Acad., Am. Acad. History of Dentistry, Lions (beloit programs, 1993—, past pres.), Delta Sigma Delta. Avocations: cycling, golf, basketball, running, fishing. Home: 2207 Collingswood Dr Beloit WI 53511-2332 Office: 419 Pleasant St Beloit WI 53511-6249

GREEN, HAROLD MARTIN, social science writer; b. Bronx, Feb. 26, 1939; s. Sam and Rose Teitebaum Green. BA, Adelphi U., 1962; MA, New Sch. Social Rsch., 1966. Instr. sociology Wilkes Coll., Wilkes-Barre, Pa., 1966—69; freelance writer, 2000—. Lectr. in field. Contbr. articles to profl. jours. Mem.: Am. Acad. Polit. Sci., Alpha Phi Sigma, Phi Sigma Tau, Phi Tau Alpha, Sigma Xi, Psi Chi, Phi Alpha Theta, Alpha Kappa Delta, Pi Gamma Mu. Jewish. Home: 350 Chestnut St Liberty NY 12754-1403

GREEN, HARRY WESTERN, II, geology-geophysics educator; b. Orange, N.J., Mar. 13, 1940; s. Harry Buetel and Mabel (Hendrickson) G.; children from previous marriage: Mark, Stephen, Carolyn, Jennifer; m. Maria Manuela Marques Martins, May 15, 1975; children: Alice, Miguel, Maria. AB in Geology with honors, UCLA, 1963, MS in Geology and Geophysics, 1967, PhD in Geology and Geophysics with distinction, 1968. Postdoctoral research assoc. materials sci. Case Western Res. U., Cleve., 1968-70; asst. prof. geology U. Calif., Davis, 1970-74, assoc. prof., 1974-80, prof., 1980-92, chmn. dept., 1984-88, prof. geology and geophysics Riverside, 1993-99, disting. prof. geology and geophysics, 1999—, dir. Inst. Geophysics and Planetary Physics, 1993-95, 2001, dir. analytical electron microscopy facility, 1994—2000, vice chancellor for rsch., 1995-2000, dir. ctrl. facility advanced microscopy and microanalysis, 2000—. Exch. scientist U. Nantes, France, 1973, vis. prof., 1978-79; vis. prof. Monash U., Melbourne, Australia, 1984; specialist advisor World Bank Program, China U. of Geoscis., Wuhan, 1988; adj. sr. rsch. scientist Lamont-Doherty Earth Obs., Columbia U., 1989-95, Vetlesen vis. prof., 1991-92; expert advisor geophysics rev. panel NSF, 1991-94; co-founder Gordon Conf. on Rock Deformation, 1995, chmn. 2d conf., 1997; hon. faculty China U. Geoscis., Wuhan, 1998—; vis. scientist Carnegie Inst. Washington, 2000—, Abelson lectr., 2000, faculty rsch. lectr., U.C. Riverside, 2002-03. Contbr. articles to books and profl. jours. Grantee NSF, 1969—, Dept. Energy, 1988-94. Fellow AAAS, Mineral Soc. Am., Am. Geophys. Union (N.L. Bowen award 1994, Francis Birch lectr. 1995); mem. Materials Rsch. Soc., Cosmos Club (Washington), Sigma Xi. Achievements include discovery of a new mechanism of deep earthquakes and exhumation of rocks from great depth in subduction zones. Office: U Calif Inst Geophysics & Planetar Physics Riverside CA 92521-0001 E-mail: harry.green@ucr.edu.

GREEN, HENRY LEONARD, physician; b. Detroit, Apr. 9, 1931; s. Albert and Fanya (Newman) G.; m. Loretta Laurie Teplitz; children: Toby, Jennifer, Cheryl, Joseph. BA with distinction, U. Mich., 1951, MD, 1955. Cert. Am. Bd. Internal Medicine in internal medicine and cardiology. Intern Detroit Receiving Hosp., 1955-56; resident internal medicine Henry Ford Hosp., Detroit, 1956-59, resident cardiology, 1959-61; pvt. practice Framingham Hills, Mich., 1963—; dir. cardiac care unit surveillance project, 1969-74; attending physician Providence Hosp., Southfield, 1963—. Clin. assoc. prof. Wayne State U. Sch. Medicine, Detroit; attending physician William Beaumont Hosp., 1995; mem. adv. and exec. coms. Inter-Soc. Commn. for Heart Disease Resources, N.Y.C., 1968-84. Author various med. software programs; contbr. articles to med. jours.; author various oral presentations nat. and local med. meetings. Lt. comdr. USN, 1961-63. Recipient Grand award Mich. Hosp. Assn., Detroit, 1973. Fellow ACP, Am. Coll. Cardiology; mem. Am. Heart Assn., Phi Beta Kappa, Alpha Omega Alpha. Avocations: computers, photography, electronics, swimming. Office: Ste 220 30055 Northwestern Hwy Farmington Hills MI 48334 E-mail: dochlgreen@yahoo.com.

GREEN, HOLCOMBE TUCKER, JR., investment executive; b. Atlanta, Sept. 29, 1939; s. Holcombe Tucker and Mary Katharine (Woltz) G.; m. Nancy Reade Hall, June 18, 1966. AB, Yale U., 1961; LLB, U. Va., 1967; D of Bus. Adminstrn. (hon.), Piedmont Coll., 1995. Bar: Ga. 1967. Assoc. firm Hansell & Post, Atlanta, 1967-70, mem. firm, 1970-87, mgmt. com., 1980-87; CEO Green Capital Investors L.P., Atlanta, 1987—; chmn., CEO WestPoint Stevens, Inc., 1992—2003. Bd. dirs. Vytech Industries, Inc., Access Integrated Networks, Inc., Cumulus Media, Inc.; bd. dirs., chmn. Rhodes, Inc., 1988-96, chmn. HBO & Co., 1990-98. Trustee Atlanta Bot. Garden, 1976-92, pres., 1982-84, The Taft Sch., 1987-00, Woodruff Arts Ctr., 1990-98; vice chmn. Investments, 1992-98, Atlanta Hist. Soc., 1993-96, Atlanta Ballet, 1987-89; fellow Yale Corp., 1999—, chmn. Yale Devel. Bd., 1998—; bd. dirs. art gallery, 1992—; active Leadership Atlanta, 1974-75; hon. Swedish consul, State of Ga., 1988-96. Served to lt. (j.g.) U.S. Navy, 1961-64. Mem. Raven Soc. of Va., Order of Coif, Royal Order of Polar Star, Piedmont Driving Club, Capital City Club, Nine O'Clocks Club, Wade Hampton Club, Homosassa Fishing Club, The Chatooga Club, Doubles Club, Ocean Forest Golf Club. Democrat. Presbyterian. Home: 4295 Club Dr Atlanta GA 30319

GREEN, HOWARD ALAN, management consultant, educator; b. L.A., Aug. 31, 1938; s. Jack Oscar and Bertha Edith (Blumenthal) G.; m. Joyce Sheila Linn, May 13, 1962; children: Kenneth Ira, Michael Lewis. BA, Lehigh U., 1960; JD, NYU, 1968. With IBM, N.Y.C., 1965-67, Keydata Corp., Watertown, Mass., 1967-74, Xerox Computer Svcs., L.A., 1977-80; mgmt. cons. Coopers & Lybrand, L.A., 1980-2000; founder, CEO Capital Programs, Inc., 2000—. Adj. assoc. prof. Iona Coll., New Rochelle, N.Y, 1979-87. With USMC, 1960. Mem. Am. Prodn. and Inventory Control Soc., Inst. Mgmt. Cons. (cert.), Assn. systems Mgmt. (cert. systems profl.), Project Mgmt. Inst.

GREEN, JACK PETER, retired pharmacology educator, medical scientist; b. N.Y.C., Oct. 4, 1925; s. Maurice and Tillie (Herman) G.; m. Arlyne Genevieve Frank, Oct. 25, 1958. BS, Pa. State U., 1947, MS, 1949; PhD, Yale, 1951, MD, 1957; postgrad., Poly. Inst., Copenhagen, 1953-55, Inst. de Biologie Physico-Chimique, Paris, 1964-65. Vis. scientist Poly. Inst., Copenhagen, 1953-55, Inst. de Biologie Physico-Chimique, Paris, 1964-65; asst. prof. Yale, 1957-61, asso. prof., 1961-66, Cornell U. Med. Coll., 1966-68; prof., chmn. dept. pharmacology Mt. Sinai Sch. Medicine, 1968—98. Mem. research grant rev. com. USPHS; mem. N.Y.C. Health Research Council, Dysautonomia Found., Irma T. Hirsch Trust. Contbr. articles profl. jours.; Mem. editorial bds. profl. jours. Recipient Claude Bernard Vis. Professorship U. Montreal, 1966 Mem. N.Y. Acad. Sci., Am. Chem. Soc., Am. Soc. Biol. Chemists, Soc. Drug Research, N.Y. Acad. Medicine, Harvey Soc., A.A.A.S., Am. Soc. Pharmacology and Exptl. Therapeutics, Internat. Soc. Quantum Biology, Am. Coll. Neuropsychopharmacology, Am. Soc. Neurochemistry, Soc. for Neurosci., Sigma Xi, Alpha Omega Alpha, Phi Lambda Upsilon, Gamma Sigma Delta. Home: 1212 5th Ave New York NY 10029-5218 Office: Mt Sinai Sch Medicine Dept Pharmacology Fifth Ave at 100th St New York NY 10029

GREEN, JAMES FRANCIS, lawyer, consultant; b. Pittsfield, Mass., Oct. 1, 1948; s. Earl Levi and Frances Eleanor (Walshi) G.; m. Eileen Mary Kelly, July 31, 1971; childen: Michael Walshe, Maura Kelly, Kelsey Kathryn. BA, St. Anselm Coll., 1970; JD, Suffolk U., 1973. Bar: Mass 1973, U.S. Dist. Ct. Mass. 1874, U.S. Ct. Appeals (D.C. cir.) 1975, U.S. Dist. Ct. D.C. 1975, U.S. Supreme Ct. 1977, U.S. Ct. Appeals (4th cir.) 1978. Rsch. counsel Joint Com. on Jud. Reform of Joint Jud. Com. of Gen. Ct. Commonwealth of Mass., Boston, 1973-74; ptnr. Drucas, Edgerton & Green, Salem, Mass., 1974; gen. ptnr. Ashcraft & Gerel, Washington, 1975—; mem. Herman, Mathis, Casey, Kitchens and Gerel. Presdl. appointment Nat. Ad Hoc Com. on Disability. Mem. Mass. Bar Assn., Boston Bar Assn., Fed. Bar Assn. (bd. dirs. Washington chpt. 1985-86, internat. law com.), Bar Assn. D.C., D.C. Bar Assn., ABA (torts and ins. practice law sects., vice chmn. nat. com. on liaison with the jud. adminstrn.), Assn. Trial Lawyers Am. (sect. chmn. nat. com. workers compensation 1989-90), Am. Soc. Law and Medicine. Democrat. Roman Catholic. Home: 6522 Heather Brook Ct Mc Lean VA 22101-1607 Office: Ashcraft & Gerel 2000 L St NW Ste 400 Washington DC 20036

GREEN, JAMES LEITZE, surgeon; b. Jacksonville, Ill., 1938; Diploma, Ill. Coll., 1961; MD, U. Ill., 1965. Intern St. Louis County Hosp., Clayton, Mo., 1965-66, resident, 1966-67, Akron City Hosp., 1969-72; with Passavant Hosp., Jacksonville, Ill., 1972—. Mem. AMA, Am. Coll. Surgeons, Am. Coll. Sports Medicine. Office: 1606 W Lafayette Ave Jacksonville IL 62650-3707

GREEN, JAMES MATTHEW, anesthesiologist; b. Pitts., Dec. 7, 1960; m. Evelyn Angela Payne, July 6, 1985; children: Nicole, Kaitlin, Nathaniel. BS in Biochemistry, U. Pitts., 1983, MD, 1987. Diplomate Am. Bd. Anesthesiology with subspecialty in pain mgmt. Intern in internal medicine Allegheny Gen. Hosp., Pitts., 1987-88; resident in anesthesiology, critical care medicine Univ. Health Ctr. Pitts., 1988-91; asst. prof. anesthesia and critical care U. Pitts., 1991-95; staff anesthesiologist, dir. pain mgmt. VA Med. Ctr., Pitts., 1991-95, dir. pain svcs., coord. med. and dental student anesthesia, 1992-95; staff anesthesiologist Assoc. Anesthesiologists of Johnstown, Pa., 1995—. Contbr. articles to profl. jours. Recipient Dr. Leroy Harris award Dept. Anesthesiology, Pitts., 1995. Mem. Am. Soc. Anesthesiology, Pa. Soc. Anesthesiology, Pa. Med. Soc., Cambria County Med. Soc. Office: Assoc Anesthesiologists of Johnstown 1086 Franklin St Johnstown PA 15905-4305

GREEN, JAMES R. historian, educator, historian, researcher; b. Oak Park, Ill., Nov. 4, 1944; s. Gerald R. and Mary Kaye Green; m. Janet Grogan, Oct. 16, 1988; 1 child, Nicholas. BA, Northwestern U., 1966; PhD, Yale U., 1972. Asst. prof. history Brandeis U., Waltham, Mass., 1970—77; from assoc. to full prof. U. Mass., Boston, 1977—. Lectr. history Warwick U., Coventry, England, 1975—76; sr. lectr. U. Genoa, Italy, 1998; series rschr. Blackside Films Inc., Boston, 1991—92; mem. cmty. adv. bd. WGBH, Boston, 1993—94. Author: Grass-Roots Socialism, 1978, The World of the Worker, 1980, Taking History to Heart, 2000. Named Fulbright sr. lectr., Fulbright Found., Washington, 1998; Woodrow Wilson fellow, Woodrow Wilson Found., Washington, 1966—68. Mem.: Labor and Working Class History Soc. (v.p., pres.-elect 2001—). Office: Univ Mass Boston 1000 Morrissey Blvd Boston MA 02125

GREEN, JAMES SAMUEL, lawyer; b. Berwick, Pa., May 24, 1947; m. Carla Eyer; children: Jennifer, Emily, James Samuel Jr., Jared. AB, Princeton U., 1969; JD, Villanova U., 1972. Bar: Del. 1972, Pa. 1973, U.S. Dist. Ct. Del. 1973, U.S. Ct. Appeals (3d cir.) 1981, 2003, U.S. Supreme Ct. 1990. Assoc. Connolly, Bove, Lodge & Hutz, Wilmington, Del., 1972-74, ptnr., 1977-90; dep. atty. gen. State of Del., Wilmington, 1975-76; ptnr. Duane Morris & Heckscher, Wilmington, 1990-99, Seitz, Van Ogtrop & Green, P.A., Wilmington, 1999—. Bd. dirs. David Wellborn Found.; del. Bd. Unauthorized Practice of Law, chmn., 1994—99. Fellow Am. Coll. of Trial Lawyers; mem. ABA, Am. Bd. Trial Advocates (nat. bd. dirs. 1991-2000), Del. Bar Assn. (treas. 1980-81, chmn. litigation sect. 1988-91), Ivy Club (Princeton), Wilmington Country Club, Princeton Club NY. Home: 2603 W 17th St Wilmington DE 19806-1108 Office: Seitz Van Ogtrop & Green PA PO Box 68 Wilmington DE 19899-0068 E-mail: jgreen@svglaw.com.

GREEN, JAMES WYCHE, sociologist, anthropologist, psychotherapist; b. Alton, Va., Aug. 5, 1915; s. William Ivey and Mary (Crowder) G.; m. Pearl O'Neal Cornett, Mar. 2, 1940 (dec. 1982); 1 child, Margaret Lydia.; m. Arlene Borkenhagen, Mar. 26, 1983. BS with honors, Va. Poly. Inst., 1938, MS, 1939; postgrad., Duke U., 1947-48; PhD, U. N.C., 1953; postgrad., Sch. Advanced Internat. Studies, Johns Hopkins U., 1959. Research fellow Va. Poly. Inst., 1938-39; research field supr. Va. Expt. Sta., 1939; asst. specialist program planning N.C. State Coll. Extension Service, 1939-42; v.p. Greever's, Inc., 1946; tchr. high sch., farm operator, 1946-47; asst. prof. rural sociology N.C. State Coll., 1949-54; from asso. chief to chief community devel. adv. to Govt. of Pakistan, Karachi, 1954-59; prof. rural sociology dept. Cornell U., Ithaca, N.Y., 1960; community devel. adviser to Govt. of So. Rhodesia, AID, 1960-64; chief community devel., local govt. adviser to Govt. of Peru, 1964-67; chief urban community devel. adviser to Govt. of Panama, 1967-69; prof., chmn. dept. sociology and anthropology U. N.C., Charlotte, 1969-70; chief methodology div. Bur. Tech. Assistance, AID, Washington, 1970-74; sociologist/anthropologist cons. AID, Washington, 1974-75, contractor, 1975; pvt. practice cons., 1975—. Author: Integrative Meditation: Towards Unity of Mind/Body/Spirit, 1994, And It Was Never Dull: A Memoir, 2003, Publications and Writings of James Wyche Green, 27 vols., 2003; author monographs; contbr. chpts. to books and articles to profl. jours. Served from 1st lt. to capt. AUS, 1942-46; lt. col. Res. ret. 1975. Decorated Croix de Guerre with Silver Star France; Croix de Guerre with Palm Belgium; Bronze Star with cluster; named Outstanding Alumnus Hargrave Mil. Acad., 1979 Fellow Am. Anthrop. Assn., AAAS, Soc. Applied Anthropology; mem. Res. Officers Assn., Public Citizen, ACLU, Common Cause, Amnesty Internat., Omicron Delta Kappa, Alpha Zeta, Phi Kappa Phi. Democrat. Lutheran. Home and Office: 6430 Lily Dhu Ln Falls Church VA 22044-1409 *I have found few joys in life which are as deep and lasting as "cracking a culture," i.e. understanding how it really works, and then using that understanding for its people's good as they see the good.*

GREEN, JEFF, race car driver; b. Ownesboro, Ky., Sept. 6, 1962; m. Michelle Green. Racecar driver Richard Childress Racing, Welcome, NC, 2001—. Named champion, NASCAR Busch Series, 2000. Avocations: hunting, radio control cars. Office: Richard Childress Racing PO Box 1189 Welcome NC 27374-1189

GREEN, JEFFREY C. lawyer; b. Newark, July 6, 1941; s. Albert and Mildred (Rosenberg) G.; m. Iris Landow, Aug. 23, 1964; children: Michelle, Marlene. BA, Rutgers U., 1963, JD, 1966; postgrad., Nat. Coll. State Judiciary, Reno, 1974-75. Bar: N.J. 1966, U.S. Dist. Ct. N.J. 1966. Law clk. to judge N.J. Superior Ct., Middlesex County Ct., New Brunswick, 1966-67; assoc. Toolan, Romond & Burgess, Perth Amboy, N.J., 1967-68; ptnr. Green & Green and predecessors, Somerset, N.J., 1968—. Prosecutor Franklin Twp. Mcpl. Ct., Somerset, 1969-70, mcpl. judge, 1970-76, 97—; judge Millstone (N.J.) Mcpl. Ct., 1970-76, Manville (N.J.) Mcpl. Ct., 1972-73; atty. Cranbury (N.J.) Bd. Adjustment, 1978—. Legal counsel Temple Beth El, Somerset, 1974—; bd. dirs. Middlesex County Legal Svcs. Corp., New Brunswick, 1983—. Named Man of Yr., Temple Beth El, 1984; recipient Pro Bono Achievement award Middlesex County Legal Svcs. Corp., 1985, 87. Mem. N.J. State Bar Assn. (trustee 1997-2003, Gen. Practitioner of Yr. award 1997), Middlesex County Bar Assn. (pres. 1985-86), Middlesex County Bar Found. (trustee 1990—, pres. 1994-95), Franklin Twp. Jaycees (pres. 1970-71), Lions Club. Democrat. Home: 3 Denise Ct Somerset NJ 08873-2834 Office: Green & Green PO Box 5321 Somerset NJ 08875-5321

GREEN, JEROME GEORGE, federal government official; b. Bklyn., June 20, 1929; s. Samuel N. and Esther (Deiber) G.; m. Marie Charlotte Roder, Aug. 2, 1952; children— Karen Ann, Paul Jonathan. BS magna cum laude, Bklyn. Coll., 1950; MD, Albany Med. Coll., 1954. Intern Albany (N.Y.) Hosp., 1954-55; mem. staff br. grants and tng. Nat. Heart Inst., NIH, Bethesda, Md., 1955-57, assoc. dir. extramural rsch. and tng., 1965-72; resident USPHS Hosp., San Francisco, 1957-59; spl. fellow in cardiopulmonary rsch. Cardiovascular Research Inst., U. Calif., San Francisco, 1959-60; rsch. divsn. Cleve. Clinic, 1960-65; dir. divsn. extramural affairs Nat. Heart, Lung and Blood Inst., 1972-85; dir. divsn. rsch. grants NIH, Bethesda, 1986-95; asst. surgeon gen. USPHS, 1988-95; ret., 1995. Fellow Am. Coll. Cardiology, Am. Heart Assn.; mem. Phi Beta Kappa, Alpha Omega Alpha. Home: 8304 Loring Dr Bethesda MD 20817-3150

GREEN, JERRY, writer; b. Oxford, Miss., Apr. 21, 1954; s. Lorienzer and Chireline Green; m. Sharron Jackson, 1973 (div. 1976); 1 child, Angela; m. Maudie Green, Sept. 3, 1983. Prodr., mgr. Basement Club Prodns., South Bend, Ind., 2000—. Author: Poetry and the People - Teaching of Poetry, 1983, Poetry Stage Act and Show - Stage Act Poetry, 1987, Base American Poet - Teaching of American Poetry, 1996, Poetry 2000 - Modern Applications of Poetry, 1998. Sgt. USAF, 1973—76. Mem.: Acad. Am. Poets, Internat. Soc. Poets (Poet of Merit 1991), Urban Poets Soc., Am. Legion. Republican. Baptist. Avocations: music composition acoustic guitar, writing children's stories. Home and Office: 509 birdsell St South Bend IN 46628

GREEN, JERRY HOWARD, investment banker; b. Kansas City, Mo., June 10, 1930; s. Howard Jay and Selma (Stein) G.; m. Betsy Bozarth, July 18, 1981. BA, Yale U., 1952. Pres. Union Chevrolet, 1955-69, Union Securities, Inc., Kansas City, 1969—, Union Bancshares, Inc., Kansas City, 1969-76; chmn. Union Bank, Kansas City, 1976—, Budget Rent-A-Car Mo., Inc., 1961—, Budget Rent-A-Car Memphis, Inc., Budget Rent-A-Car, Wichita, Kans.; pres. Pembroke Bancshares, Kansas City, 1983—. Chmn. Union Broadcasting, Inc., Union Sports Broadcasting, (KCTE-AM) and (WHB-AM), Inc.; bd. dirs. Century City Artists Corp., L.A. Bd. dirs. Jackson County Pension Plan Com.; bd. dirs., chmn. bd. Mo. Higher Edn. Loan Authority, 1987—; chmn. bd. Mo. Valley Bancshares, Mountain Grove, Mo.; chmn. Yale Class of 1952 Reunion Gift. 1st lt. USAF, 1952-55. Mem. Am. Bankers Assn., Yale Alumni Assn. (bd. dirs.), Kansas City Club, Oakwood Country Club, Saddle and Sirloin Club, University Club. Republican. Office: Union Bank 12th And Wyandotte Kansas City MO 64105

GREEN, JERSEY MICHAEL-LEE, lawyer; b. Washington, Feb. 29, 1952; m. Jonelle Sue Burke, May 12, 1988. BA in criminology, U. Md., 1976; JD, Syracuse U., 1983. Bar: Colo. 1983, U.S. Dist. Ct. Colo. 1983, U.S. Ct. Appeals (10th cir.) 1983, U.S. Tax Ct. 1983, U.S. Ct. Appeals (9th cir.) 1987, U.S. Supreme Ct. 1988, U.S. Ct. Appeals (2d cir.) 1990, U.S. Dist. Ct. Ariz. 1994. Atty. Wagner & Waller, P.C., Denver, 1983-86, Waller, Mark & Allen, P.C., Denver, 1986-89, Orten & Hindman P.C., Denver, 1989-90, Elrod, Katz, Preeo, Look, Moison & Silverman, P.C., Denver, 1990-97, Preeo, Silverman & Green, P.C., Denver, 1998-99, Preeo, Silverman, Green & Egle, P.C., Denver, 1999—. Mem. exec. com. staff Lawyers for Romer, Denver, 1986; precinct committeeman, 1989-92. Recipient Syracuse (N.Y.) Def. Group scholarship, 1982. Mem. Assn. Trial Lawyers Am., Colo. Trial Lawyers Assn., Arapahoe County Bar Assn., Syracuse U. Alumni Assn. (pres. Colo. 1987-89). Democrat. Avocations: mountaineering, skiing, running. Office: Preeo Silverman Green & Eagle PC 1401 17th St Ste 800 Denver CO 80202-1246 E-mail: Jersey@preeosilv.com.

GREEN, JOHN LAFAYETTE, JR., education executive; b. Trenton, N.J., Apr. 3, 1929; m. Harriet Hardin Hill, Nov. 8, 1962; 1 child, John Lafayette III BA, Miss. State U., 1955; MEd, Wayne State U., 1971; PhD, Rensselaer Poly. Inst., 1974. Asst. to treas. Internat. Paper Co., 1955-57; mem. faculty U. Calif., Berkeley, 1957-65; v.p. U. Ga., Athens, 1965-71, Rensselaer Poly. Inst., Troy, N.Y., 1971-76; exec. v.p. U. Miami, 1976-80; sr. v.p. U. Houston, 1980-81; pres. Washburn U., Topeka, Kans., 1981-88; exec. dir. Assn. Collegiate Bus. Schs. and Programs, Overland Park, 1988-95. Pres., chmn. bd. dirs. Strategic Planning/Mgmt. Assocs., Inc., Overland Park, Kans., 1981—; CEO Internat. Assembly for Collegiate Bus. Edn., Overland Park, 1997—; past. pres. Kansas City and Topeka chpts. Planning Forum. Author: Budgeting, 1967, (with others) Cost Accounting, 1969, Administrative Data Processing, 1970, Strategic Planning, 1980, Strategic Planning: A System for Businesses, 1986, A Strategic Planning System for Higher Education, 1987, Strategy Development and Implementation for Banks, 1988, co-author: Outcomes Assessment in Higher Education Linked to Strategic Planning and Budgeting, 1997, Outcomes Assessment in Higher Education, 2002. Bd. dirs. Boy Scouts Am., Topeka, 1983-85. With U.S. Army 1951-53 Recipient Disting. Kansan of Yr. in Pub. Adminstrn. award Topeka Capital Jour., 1984, Kans. Pub. Adminstr. of Yr. award Am. Soc. Pub. Adminstrn., 1984, Disting. Exec. award Mktg. Exec. Kans., 1984, Edn. Leader's Hall of Fame award, 1995. Mem. AAUP, Conf. Bd., Am. Mgmt. Assn., Fin. Execs. Inst., Demographics Inst., Masons, Shriners, Royal Order of Jesters, Phi Delta Kappa, Beta Alpha Psi, Phi Kappa Phi, Pi Kappa Alpha, Delta Sigma Pi. Republican. Presbyterian. (elder, deacon). Avocations: golf, tennis. Home: 12568 Farley Overland Park KS 66213-2526 Office: PO Box 25217 Shawnee Mission KS 66225-5217

GREEN, JOHNNIE D. government agency administrator, finance educator; b. Malvern, Ark., Feb. 5, 1961; s. Edward and Edessia Green. AAS, Vincennes U., 1998; BBA, Ark. Bapt. Coll., 1999; MBA, Webster Univ., 1999, MA in internat. bus. and finance, 2000. Admin., finance and personnel specialist U.S. Army, 1981—84; asst. branch mgr. Twin City Bank, North Little Rock, Ark., 1984—94; asst. v.p., loan officer Bank of Malvern, Ark., 1994—95; comml. loan officer U.S. SBA, Little Rock, 1995—. Adj. prof. Vincennes U., North Little Rock, Ark., 2000—; CEO, chmn. Ark. Cmty. Recreational Svcs.; adj. prof. Webster Univ., Memphis, 2000—, Embry Riddle Aeronautical Univ. Little Rock AFB, Jacksonville, Ark., 2001—, Central Baptist Coll., Conway, Ark., 2001—, Philander Smith Coll., Little Rock, 2002—, Nova Southeastern Univ., Ft. Lauderdale, Fla., 2003—. Past pres. Malvern Stella Smith Boys and Girls Club; bd. dirs. Teen Promise, Inc.; CEO, chmn. Ark. Community Rec. Svcs. E-5 N.G. U.S. Army, 1987—2002. Recipient Cert. of Appreciation, Arkansas Nat. Guard, 2002, Meritorious Svc. Medal, U.S., 2002, Cert. of Svc. Award, Ark. Guard Bureau, 2002, Commendation Medal, State of Ark., 2002. Mem.: Financial Mgmt. Assn. Internat., Nat. Assn. Urban Bankers, Acad. Mgmt., Non-Commn. Officers Assn., ACLU, NAACP, Little Rock Club. Home: 507 Maurice Dr Malvern AR 72104 Office: US SBA 2120 Riverfront Dr Ste 100 Little Rock AR 72202

GREEN, JONATHAN DAVID, music educator, composer, conductor; b. Batavia, NY, Apr. 26, 1964; s. Gary Martin and Justine Elaine (Ferguson) G.; m. Lynn Marie Buck, Apr. 23, 1988. MusB, SUNY, Fredonia, 1985; MusM, U. Mass., 1987; D Musical Arts, U. N.C., Greensboro, 1992. Music libr. Bennington (Vt.) Coll., 1987-88; vis. asst. prof. Hampden-Sydney (Va.) Coll., 1988-89; co-condr. Greensboro Symphony Youth Orch., 1990-93; asst. prof. music Elon Coll., N.C., 1991-96; assoc. prof. music, chmn. Sweet Briar Coll., 1996—2002, assoc. dean, 2002—03, assoc. dean and v.p. for acad. affairs, 2003—. Adjudicator Festival, Richmond, Va., 1992—; condr. Lee County Orch., 1995-96. Author: A Conductor's Guide to Choral Orchestral Music, vols. I and II, 1994, 98, A Bio-Bibliography of Carl Ruggles, 1995, A Conductor's Guide to the Choral-Orchestral Works of J.S. Bach, 2000, A Conductor's Guide to the Choral-Orchestral Works of Mozart and Haydn, 2002; composer 40 songs, 6

symphonies, also others; editor Jour. of the Conductors Guild, 2001—. Crandall scholar Chautauqua Instn., 1982; Ornest fellow U. Mass., 1985-87, Excellence fellow U. N.C., 1989-92. Mem. ASCAP (mem. standard panel awards 1997—), Condrs. Guild (bd. dirs.), Am. Symphony Orch. League, Am. Choral Dirs. Assn., Am. Music Ctr., Phi Mu Alpha Sinfonia (sustaining). Avocations: hiking, cooking, travel. Office: Sweet Briar Coll Office of Dean Sweet Briar VA 24595 Home: 118 Madison St Lynchburg VA 24504 E-mail: jgreen@sbc.edu.

GREEN, JOSEPH BARNET, neurologist, educator; b. Phila., Aug. 2, 1928; s. Charles and Bella (Hurwitz) B.; married; children: Charna Alice Green Evans, Robert I. BS, St. Joseph's Coll., Phila., 1950; MD, Jefferson Med. Coll., Phila., 1954. Intern Wilkes Barre (Pa.) Gen. Hosp., 1954-55; resident in neurology Georgetown U. Med. Center, 1955-58; asst. neurologist Pa. Hosp., Phila., 1960-64; asst. prof., then prof. neurology Ind. U. Med. Sch., 1964-72; prof. neurology and pediatrics, chmn. dept. neurology Med. Coll. Ga., Augusta, 1972-82; prof., chmn. dept. psychiatry and neurology Tulane U. Sch. Medicine, New Orleans, 1982-87, prof. neurology, clin. prof. pediatrics, 1986-87; dir. neurology VA Cen. Office, Washington, 1987-88; chmn. dept. med. and surg. neurology Tex. Tech U. Health Scis. Ctr., Lubbock, 1988-94; prof. neurology Tex. Tech U Health Scis. Ctr., Lubbock, 1993-94; dir. rehab. rsch. Hines (Ill.) VA Med. Ctr., 1994-98; prof. neurology Loyola U. Stritch Sch. Medicine, Maywood, Ill., 1994-98; attending staff physician, rsch. investigator Spinal Cord Injury Unit, Memphis VA Med. Ctr., 1998—; prof. neurology U. Tenn. Coll. Medicine, 1998—. Mem. profl. adv. bd. Assn. Children with Learning Disabilities, Ga. chpt. Nat. Multiple Sclerosis Soc.; dir. NIH project Ga. Comprehensive Epilepsy Program, 1976; Fulbright lectr., Denmark, 1969; cons. VA Med. Ctr., Augusta. Author articles in field. Served with M.C. USNR, 1958-60. Fogarty Internat. Research fellow Israel, 1981 Mem. AMA, Am. Acad. Neurology, Child Neurology Soc., Am. Neurol. Assn., Am. EEG Soc., Am. Epilepsy Soc. (sec. 1972), Assn. U. Profs. Neurology (v.p. 1981) Clubs: B'nai B'rith. Democrat. Jewish. Office: Memphis VA Med Center 1030 Jefferson Ave Memphis TN 38104-2127 E-mail: joseph.green@med.va.gov.

GREEN, JOSHUA, III, retired banker; b. Seattle, June 30, 1936; s. Joshua, Jr. and Elaine (Brygger) G.; m. Pamela K. Pemberton, Nov. 1, 1974; children: Joshua IV, Jennifer Elaine, Paige Courtney. BA in English, Harvard U., 1958. With Peoples Nat. Bank Wash., Seattle, 1960-88, exec. v.p., 1972-75, pres., 1975—, chief exec. officer, 1977-78, chmn. bd., 1979-88, U.S. Bank Washington (merger PeoplesBank and Old Nat. Bank), 1988-96; chmn., CEO Joshua Green Corp., Seattle, 1996—. Bd. dirs., chmn., CEO, Joshua Green Corp., Safeco, Port Blakely Tree Farms, Virginia Mason Hosp. Found., Virginia Mason Hosp. Rsch. Pres. Joshua Green Found.; trustee Downtown Seattle Assn., Corp.Coun. for the Arts. Mem. Pacific Sci. Lenter, U. Club, Rainier Club, Seattle Tennis Club, Wash. Athletic Club. Home: 414 McGilvra Blvd E Seattle WA 98112-2308 Office: Joshua Green Corp 1425 4th Ave Ste 420 Seattle WA 98101-2218

GREEN, JOYCE, book publishing company executive; b. Taylorville, Ill., Oct. 22, 1928; d. Lynn and Vivian Coke (Richardson) Reinerd; m. Warren H. Green, Oct. 8, 1960. AA, Christian Coll., 1946; BS, MacMurray Coll., 1948. Pres. Warren H. Green, Inc., St. Louis, 1992—; editor Affirmative Action Register, 1977—; pres. InterContinental Industries, Inc., 1980—; chief exec. officer Pubs. Svc. Ctr. Mem. St. Louis C. of C., Jr. League Club, Media Club, Mo. Athletic Club. Home (Winter): 10000 Ocean Blvd Apt 90 Jensen Beach FL 34957 Office: 8356 Olive Blvd Saint Louis MO 63132-2814 Home (Summer): 12120 Hibler Dr St. Louis MO 63141 E-mail: JRG1036@aol.com.

GREEN, JOYCE HENS, federal judge; b. N.Y.C., Nov. 13, 1928; d. James S. and Hedy (Bucher) Hens; m. Samuel Green, Sept. 25, 1965 (dec.); children: Michael Timothy, June Heather, James Harry. BA, U. Md., 1949; JD, George Washington U., 1951, LLD, 1994. Practice law, Washington, 1951-68, Arlington, Va., 1956-68; ptnr. Green & Green, 1966-68; assoc. judge Superior Ct., D.C., 1968-79; judge U.S. Dist. Ct. for D.C., 1979—; judge presiding U.S. Fgn. Intelligence Surveillance Ct., 1988-95. Bd. advisors George Washington U. Law Sch., 1991-2001; jud. br. com. Jud. Conf. U.S., 1995-2001. Co-author: Dissolution of Marriage, 1986, supplements, 1987-89, Marriage and Family Law Agreements, 1985, supplements, 1986-89. Chair Task Force on Gender, Race and Ethnic Bias for the D.C. Cir. Recipient Alumni Achievement award George Washington U., 1975, Profl. Achievement award, 1978, Outstanding Contbn. to Equal Rights award Women's Legal Def. Fund, 1976, hon. doctor of Laws George Washington U., 1994, U.S. Dept. Justice Edmund J. Randolph award, 1995. Fellow Am. Bar Found.; ABA (jud. adminstrn. divsn., chair nat. conf. fed. trial judges 1997-98), Fed. Judges Assn., Nat. Assn. Women Judges, Va. Bar, Bar Assn. D.C. (jud. honoree of Yr. 1994), D.C. Bar, D.C. Women's Bar Assn., (pres. 1960-62, woman lawyer of yr. 1979), Exec. Women in Govt. (chmn. 1977), Woman's Forum of Washington D.C. Office: US Dist Ct E Barrett Prettyman US Courthouse 333 Constitution Ave NW Washington DC 20001-2802

GREEN, KENNETH NORTON, law educator; b. Chgo., Mar. 18, 1938; s. Martin and Sarah (Owens) G.; m. Joan Nemer, Oct. 17, 1968 (div. July 1974); 1 child, Joey. AA, Wright Jr. Coll., 1960; BA, Calif. State U., Los Angeles, 1963; postgrad. Southwestern U., 1965-67; JD, U. San Fernando Valley, 1968; Cert. (hon. teaching) Los Angeles Unified Sch. Dist., 1979. Bar: Calif. 1970, U.S. Dist. Ct. (cen. dist.) Calif. 1970, U.S. Supreme Ct. 1973. Tchr. Los Angeles, Calif., 1964-70; dep. pub. defender Los Angeles County, Calif., 1970-73, 75— ; ptnr. Green & Pirosh, Los Angeles, 1973-75; chief pub. defender, 1989; instr. Paralegal dept. U. Calif., Los Angeles, 1975— ; judge pro tem Los Angeles Mcpl. Ct., 1978. Contbr. articles to legal pubs. Ex officio mem. Prison Preventers, Calif. Dept. of Parole; mayor's com. Project Heavy; bd. dirs. City of Hope; Vista Del Mar; legal adv. panel Jewish Family Service; vol. atty for indigents UCLA Law Sch.; vol. in Parole Program, com. chmn. Research Prejudice-Pvt. Clubs (Disting. Service award 1971). Served with U.S. Army, 1957-58, Korea. Mem. Pub. Defender Assn. (dir. 1971-74, chief wage negotiator 1973-75) ABA, Los Angeles County Bar Assn. (vice chmn. drug abuse 1975, exec. com. criminal justice 1977). Democrat. Jewish. Lodge: Justice (bd. dirs. 1971-72). Office: Pub Defender Los Angeles County 210 W Temple St Los Angeles CA 90012-3210

GREEN, KEVIN PATRICK, career officer; b. Aug. 28, 1949; m. Kate Donohue; 3 children. Grad., U.S. Naval Acad., 1971; MS, Naval Postgrad. Sch., 1977; Grad., Nat. War Coll., 1992. Ensign USN, 1971, advanced through grades to rear adm., 1996; assigned to frigate USS Voge (DE 1047), 1971-74; weapons officer USS Richard L. Page (FFG 5), 1978-80; ops. officer USS Preble (DDG 46), 1980-82; exec. officer USS Dahlgren (DDG 43), 1984-85; comdr. USS Taylor (FFG 50), 1989-91; comdr. destroyer squadron twenty-three, 1994-95; duty in spl. ops. br. Atlantic fleet hqrs., 1982-84; instr. combat sys., tactics prospective comdg. officer course, 1985-88; mil. asst. office of Sec. of Def., 1992-94; dir. surface officer disbn. divsn. bur. naval personnel, 1995-97; comdr. Naval Tng. Ctr., Great Lakes, Ill., 1996-98, Cruiser-Destroyer Group Three, 1998-99, U.S. Naval Forces So. Command, 1999—. Decorated Legion of Merit. Office: Rear Adm USN COMUSNAVSO PSC 813 Box 2 Fpo AA 34099-6004 E-mail: greenk@navstarr.navy.mil.

GREEN, LARRY ALTON, physician, educator; b. Ardmore, Okla., Mar. 27, 1948; s. Thomas Alton and Mary Lou (Gauntt) Green; m. Margaret Joyce Ball, Mar. 27, 1971; children: Nathaniel, Katherine. BA, U. Okla., 1969; MD, Baylor Coll. Medicine, Houston, 1973. Diplomate Am. Bd. Family Practice. Intern then resident U. Rochester, Highland Hosp., NY, 1973—76; asst. prof. U. Colo., Denver, 1972—82, assoc. prof., 1982—85, prof., 1985—, chmn. dept., 1985—99, Woodward-Chisholm chair, 1989—99, dir. AAFP Ctr. for Policy Studies in Family Practice and Primary Care, 1998—. Vis. prof. various univrs., U.S., New Zealand, U.K., Republic of South Africa, 1982—; dir. residency Mercy Med. Ctr., Denver, 1980—85; founding pres. Ambulatory Sentinel Practice Network, Denver. Contbr. articles. Elder Presbyn. Ch., Denver. With USPHS, 1976—77. Grantee, USPHS, 1978—, Kellogg Found., 1982—87. Mem.: Inst. of Medicine 0f NAS, . Tchrs. Family Medicine, Am. Acad. Family Physicians, N.Am. Primary Care Rsch. Group (bd. dirs. 1989—93, pres. 1997—), Assn. Depts. Family Medicine (pres. 1987—89). Avocation: fly fishing. also: Ctr Policy Studies Family Practice & Primary Care 2023 Massachusetts Ave NW Washington DC 20036-1011 Office: PO Box 6508 Aurora CO 80045-0508

GREEN, LAURA LORRAINE, foundation administrator; b. Denver, Nov. 23, 1924; d. Jack Wayne and Anna Laura (Cheney) Skiles; m. James Edward Green, Aug. 12, 1945 (dec. 1987); 1 child, Sharon Lee Payne. Grad. high sch., Santa Monica, Calif. Payroll Hanson Glove Factory, Milw., 1943-45; credit interviewer Broadway Dept. Store Orgn., Anaheim, Calif., 1956-57; sect. divsn. mgr. Hughes Aircraft Co., Fullerton, Calif., 1957-61; sec., payroll J.T. Murphy Carpet Co., San Jose, Calif.; owner 49er Trailer Ranch/RV & Mobile Home Park, Columbia, Calif., 1963-70, dir. adminstr. Sheriffs Aux. Vols., Tucson, 1988-92; retired. Mem. Ariz. County Attys. and Sheriffs Assn., Order of Ea. Star, Fraternal Order Police. Democrat. Methodist. Avocation: collecting stamps and antiques.

GREEN, LEON, JR., mechanical engineer; b. Austin, Tex., Aug. 13, 1922; s. Leon and Notra (Anderson) G.; m. Eleanor Broome Samuels, Apr. 14, 1951; children: John Anderson, Emily Broome, Charles Leon. BS in Physics, Calif. Inst. Tech., 1944, MS in Mech. Engring, 1947, PhD, 1950. With N.Am. Aviation, Inc., 1949-51, Aerojet-Gen. Corp., 1951-59, Aeronutronic div. Ford Motor Co., 1959-62; chief scientist Lockheed Propulsion Co., 1962-64; sci. dir. research and tech. div. Air Force Systems Command, Washington, 1964-67; dir. planning Washington area Lockheed Aircraft Corp., 1967-70; exec. sec. Def. Sci. Bd., Dept. Def., 1970-73; sr. staff engr. applied physics lab. Johns Hopkins U.; also cons. AEC, 1973-74; mem. tech. staff Mitre Corp., McLean, Va., 1974-77; cons. Gen. Atomic Co., 1977-80; pres. Energy Conversion Alternatives, Ltd., Washington, 1980-88, cons., 1988-93; v.p. Clean Coal Coalition, Inc., 1983-86. Adj. prof. mech. and aerospace engring. W.Va. U., 1989-93. Contbr. articles to profl. jours. Mem. ASME, AAAS, Climate Inst. Home: 24055 Paseo Del Lago Laguna Woods CA 92653-2678

GREEN, LINDA GAIL, retired international healthcare and management consultant, nurse educator; b. Kalamazoo, Nov. 29, 1951; d. Jesse Floyd and Mattie Dean (Fulcher) G. BS in Nursing, Fla. State U., Tallahassee, 1974; postgrad., Nova U., Ft. Lauderdale, Fla. Staff nurse med./surg. unit St. Mary's Hosp., West Palm Beach, Fla., 1974, staff nurse coronary care, 1974-75, relief charge nurse ICU, 1975-76, asst. nursing care coord. post anesthesia recovery rm., 1976-78, insvc. instr., 1978-81, asst. dir. staff devel. and edn., 1981-83; dir. insvc. H.H. Raulerson Hosp., Okeechobee, Fla., 1983-84; adminstr. Med. Personnel Pool, Palm Beach, Fla., 1984-90; regional exec. healthcare divsn. Interim Svcs., Inc. (formerly Pers. Pool of Am., an H&R Block Co.), Ft. Lauderdale, 1990-93; pres. L.G.I. Consulting/Cmty. Health Educator, West Palm Beach, 1993—2000. Dir. edn. svcs., nurse educator Intracoastal Health Svcs., Inc., Good Samaritan Med. Ctr., St. Mary's Med. Ctr., West Palm Beach, Fla., 1998-2000; spkr. in field. Author: Sexual Harassment in Home Healthcare, 1993. Past bd. dirs. Vinceremos Therapeutic Riding Ctr., Inc. for Physically and Mentally Challenged, 1990-95; chair Helen K. Persson Endowment Scholarship, 1999-2000; mem. Palm Beach County Workshop Devel. Bus. Partnership Coun., 1999. Mem. ANA, AHA (heart walk industry leader 1994, 95), Fla. Nurses Assn., Palm Beach County Health Educators (past sec.), Palm Beach County Patient Educators (pres. 1989, Leadership and Spirit awards 1989), Royal Palm Beach Bus. Assn., Palms West C. of C. (v.p. 1987-88, Dedicated and Outstanding Svc. award 1989, Cert. of Appreciation 1986, 87), Zonta Internat. (pres. 1994-95, past v.p. Palms West chpt., del. to internat. conf., Hong Kong, 1992).

GREEN, LISA CANNON, online editor; b. Marshall, Ky., May 7, 1962; d. Walter L. and Phyllis (Jones) Cannon; m. Bob Dale Green, May 31, 1980; children: Emily, Ethan. BA in Journalism and English, Murray State U., 1983. With The Post-Intelligencer, Paris, Tenn., 1983-84, The Jackson (Tenn.) Sun, 1984-90, The Tennessean, Nashville, 1990—. Office: The Tennessean 1100 Broadway Nashville TN 37203-3134 E-mail: lgreen@tennessean.com.

GREEN, LISA R. journalist; b. Evanston, Ill., Nov. 2, 1964; d. Albert W. and Elease (Wesbrooks) G. BJ, Eastern Ill. U., Charleston, 1986. Rochelle bur. chief Register Star, 1986-88, regional reporter, 1988-90, asst. metro editor, 1990-91, city editor, 1991-93; loaner USA Today, Arlington, Va., 1995; asst. bus. editor Rockford (Ill.) Register Star, 1993-2000; bus. editor Fort Wayne (Ind.) Jour. Gazette, 2000—. Former editor New Zion Gazette, New Zion Bapt. Ch. Chair Black Achievers Steering Com., 1997-98; active Greater Progressive Bapt. Ch., Ft. Wayne, Ind. Mem. Nat. Assn. Black Journalists. Baptist. Avocation: reading. Home: 5010 Madiera Dr Apt C Fort Wayne IN 46815-7350

GREEN, LLOYD M. lawyer; b. Bklyn., June 21, 1959; s. Jack and Pearl Green; m. Julia Rubin, Feb. 7, 1999. AB magna cum laude, Columbia U., 1981; JD, Cornell U., 1984. Counsel to dir. rsch. Bush-Quayle '88, Washington, 1988; counsel to the dir. policy Office of the Pres.-Elect, Washington, 1988—89; counselor to asst. atty gen. civil divsn. U.S. Dept. Justice, Washington, 1990-92; of counsel Otterbourg, Steindler, Houston & Rosen, PC, N.Y.C., 1992—; corr. Talk Radio News, 2003. Alt. del. Rep. Nat. Conv., New Orleans, 1988. Mem.: Phi Beta Kappa. Office: Otterbourg Steindler Houston & Rosen 230 Park Ave New York NY 10169

GREEN, LOUIS HARRY, retired surgeon; b. Houston, Jan. 21, 1923; MD, U. Tex. Med. Br., 1947. Diplomate Am. Bd. Surgery. Intern D.C. Gen. Hosp., Washington, 1947-48; resident in surgery Meml. Hosp., Houston, 1948-49, Houston VA Hosp., 1951-54, Baylor Affiliated Hosps., Houston, emeritus clin. assoc. prof.; emeritus staff Meth., St. Luke's Episcopal, Tex. Children's, Hermann Hosps. Named Disting. Alumnus U. Houston, Great Texan Chron's and Colitis Found. Am., 1975. Fellow: ACS; mem.: AMA, Houston Surg. Soc. (pres. 1991—92). E-mail: louis@300kbps.com.

GREEN, MAE MAERA, artist; b. N.Y.C., Sept. 14, 1930; d. Phillip and Clara (Donnenfeld) Rabach; m. Sam Green, Feb. 1, 1953; children: Michelle, Tracy, Dori, Marshall. Student, Art Student League, 1947, Pratt Inst., 1951. Exhibited at Perspective Gallery, N.Y.C., 1949, State Mus. Art Gallery, Santa Fe, N Mex., 1958, 59, 60, 72 (award), U. N.Mex. Jonson Gallery, 1972 (award), Malvina Miller Gallery, San Francisco, 1972, Meridian Gallery, Albuquerque, 1979; represented in permanent collections at Mus. of Albuquerque, City Albuquerque 1% for the Arts, Aetna Life Ins. Co., Mass., Temple Albert, Albuquerque. Recipient award Nat. Design Wallpaper/Fabric, 1950. Avocations: reading, travel, walking, gardening. Home: 1521 Sagebrush Trl SE Albuquerque NM 87123-4489

GREEN, MARK ANDREW, congressman, lawyer; b. Boston, June 1, 1960; s. Jeremy Raleigh and Elizabeth Pamela (Roome) G.; m. Susan Keske, Aug. 5, 1985; children: Rachel Eve Libinu, Anna Faith Kitali, Alexander Mark Amutavi. BA, U. Wis., Eau Claire, 1983; JD, U. Wis., Madison, 1987. Bar: Wis. 1987. Tchr., intern World Teach Project, Kakamega, Kenya, 1987-88; of counsel Godfrey & Kahn, S.C., Green Bay, Wis., 1989-98; mem. Wis. Assembly, Madison, 1992-98, chmn. assembly majority caucus, chmn. assembly jud. com., 1994-98; state chmn. Am. Legis. Exch. Coun.; mem. U.S. Congress from 8th Wis. dist., 1999—; mem. fin. svcs. com., judiciary com. Legal counsel Rep. Assembly Campaign Com., Madison, 1993—. Chmn. mcpl. affairs Brown County Taxpayers Assn., Green Bay, 1990-92; chmn. Brown County Rep. Party, 1991-92; bd. dirs. Nat. R.R. Mus., Green Bay, 1992—; chmn. resolutions com. Wis. Rep. Conv., Milw., 1993. Recipient Wis. award Ind. Bus. Assn., 1996; named Wis. Outstanding Legislator of 1995, Wis. Builders Assn., Healthcare Leader of Wis., State Med. Soc., 1996; scholar U. Wis., Eau Claire, 1982. Mem. ABA, Wis. Bar Assn., Am. Legis. Exch. Coun., Nat. Conf. State Legislators, Brown County Home Builders Assn., Kiwanis. Republican. Office: Ho of Reps 1218 Longworth Ho Office Bldg Washington DC 20515-4908*

GREEN, MARTIN LINCOLN, financial analyst, consultant; b. Des Plaines, Ill., Feb. 22, 1940; s. Martin Lincoln and Madelyne Mae (Larson) G.; m. Carolyn Elizabeth Johnson, Jan. 19, 1968; children: Peter Cranston, Edward Reavy. BA in Econs., Lawrence U., 1963; MBA, U. Chgo., 1977. News asst. N.Y. Times, N.Y.C., 1963-64; reporter Sheffield (England) Telegraph, 1964-66, Balt. Sun, 1966—67; sales rep. 3M Co., Chgo., 1967—70; stockbroker Bache & Co., Chgo., 1970-71; sales mgr. Xerox Corp., Chgo., 1971-77, mgr. strategic planning Rochester, N.Y., 1977-81; dir. sales, mktg. Bausch & Lomb, Inc., Rochester, N.Y., 1981-84, v.p. sales, mktg., 1984-87; v.p. strategic planning Cambridge Instruments, Buffalo, 1987-88, pres. ophthalmic inst. divsn., 1988-90, Leica, Inc., Buffalo, 1990-97; pres. The Thornell Inst., Pittsford, NY, 1998—2002; ret., 2002. Republican. Avocations: investing, walking, reading, weight lifting, writing. Home: 16 Forest Knoll Pittsford NY 14534-3602

GREEN, MAURICE, molecular biologist, virologist, educator; b. N.Y.C., May 5, 1926; s. David and Bessie (Lipschitz) G.; m. Marilyn Glick, Aug. 20, 1950; children: Michael Richard, Wendy Allison Green Lee, Eric Douglas BS in Chemistry, U. Mich., 1949; MS in Biochemistry and Chemistry, U. Wis.-Madison, 1952, PhD in Biochemistry and Chemistry, 1954. Instr. biochemistry U. Pa. Med. Sch., Phila., 1955-56; asst. prof. St. Louis U. Health Scis. Ctr., 1956-60, assoc. prof., 1960-63, prof. microbiology, 1963-77; prof., chmn. Inst. for Molecular Virology, 1964—. Office: St Louis U Health Sci Ctr Inst for Molecular Virology 3681 Park Ave Saint Louis MO 63110-2511

GREEN, MAURICE RICHARD, neuropsychiatrist; b. Chgo., Oct. 28, 1922; divorced; children: Melissa, Suzanne, Constance. BS, Northwestern U., 1942; BM, Northwestern U. Med. Sch., 1945, MD, 1946; cert. in Psychoanalytic Tng., William Alanson White Inst., N.Y.C., 1954. Diplomate Am. Bd. Psychiatry and Neurology. Intern Passavant Hosp., Chgo., 1945-46; resident in psychiatry Bronx (N.Y.) VA Hosp., 1948-51; cons. psychiatrist Brookwood Hall, East Islip, L.I., N.Y., 1955-58; staff psychiatrist Psychiatric Clinic Ct. Spl. Sessions, 1956-60; cons. psychiatrist Bleuler Psychotherapy Ctr., Queens, N.Y., 1956-68; rsch. psychiatrist, mem. psychiat. epidemiology sect. William Alanson White Inst., N.Y.C., 1968-72; attending geriat. psychiatrist Albert Einstein Med. Sch., 1974-76; attending child and adolescent psychiatry Harlem Hosp. of Columbia Presbyn. Med. Ctr., N.Y.C., 1974-75; med. dir. geriat. and family psychiatry Lincoln Hosp., 1974-76; chief psychiatrist Family Ct. Svcs. divsn. South Beach Psychiat. Ctr., S.I., N.Y., 1976-80; sr. attending psychiatrist Columbia-Presbyn. at St. Luke's-Roosevelt Hosp., N.Y.C., 1978—; cons. psychiatrist Liaison-Consultation Svc. NYU Med. Ctr., N.Y.C., 1985-86; psychiatrist spl. evaluation and treatment unit Rockland Psychiat. Ctr., 1985-87. Mem. faculty William Alanson White Inst., N.Y.C., 1957—; cons. Goddard Coll., 1961-68; assoc. attending psychiatrist Bellevue Hosp., 1962-85, presently attending physician; supervisory and tng. analyst William Alanson White Inst., 1962—; clin. prof. psychiatry NYU Med. Sch., 1964—; mem. med. bd. Roosevelt Hosp., 1965-76; prin. investigator Diamox-Thiamine Research Unit Nathan S. Kline Research Inst., 1987; project dir. Brain Chemistry of Schizophrenia at Nathan Kline Inst., 1988-93; med. dir. Neurologic Sys., Inc., 1987; presidium Inst. for Brain Function Rsch., Inc., 1987; mem. Treatment Innovations Task Force-Soc. for Traumatic Stress Studies, 1987. Author: Interpersonal Psychoanalysis: Selected Papers of Clara Thompson, 1971, Psicoanalisi interpersonale, 1972, L'Esperiencze Prelogica, 1972, Violence and the Family, 1980; (with Edward S. Tauber) Prelogical Experience, 1959; assoc. editor Contemporary Psychoanalysis jour., 1968-80; contbr. articles to profl. jours. Project dir. Nathan Kline Rsch. Inst., 1988—. Fellow: N.Y. Acad. Medicine, Am. Acad. Child and Adolescent Psychiatry (com. on hospitalization of children, nat. legis. network 1982—86), Am. Psychiat. Assn. (com. on aging N.Y. Dist. br.), Am. Orthopsychiat. Assn. (publs. com. Anniversary Vol. 1968—71); mem.: Am. Assn. Geriat. Psychiatry, Internat. Soc. Psychoneuroendocrinology, Am. Assn. Psychosocial Rehab., Soc. Biol. Psychiatry, Nat. Assn. Patients Rights and Advocacy, Physicians for Social Responsibility, William Alanson White Psychoanalytic Soc., N.Y. Soc. Clin. Psychiatry, N.Y. Coun. Child Psychiatry. Home and Office: 275 Central Park W Apt 15 D New York NY 10024-3058 E-mail: munsongreen@mindspring.com. *We are all much more simply human than otherwise; what enhances our individual humanity will also enhance the common humanity of those around us.*

GREEN, MAY CLAYMAN, early childhood educator and administrator; b. Bklyn., Apr. 8, 1923; d. Joseph and Anna (Steinger) Clayman; m. Jerome E. Bloom, Oct. 14, 1945 (div. May 1963); children: Jeffrey Clayman Bloom, Claudia J. Segal; m. Milton Green, May 10, 1963; stepchildren: Carol R. Green, Peter A. Green. BA, Adelphi U., 1944; MA, NYU, 1956; postgrad., C.W. Post Coll./Long Island U., 1978. Rsch. asst. Winston Pub. Co., Phila., 1953-55; various positions Roslyn (N.Y.) Jr. H.S., 1956-80; adminstrv. asst. to dir. Afro-Am. affairs NYU, 1971-72; owner, exec. adminstr. New Horizons Country Day Sch., Palm Harbor, Fla., 1984-96; pres. New Horizons Edn. Cons. Firm, Palm Harbor, 1996—; bus. mgr. Curves For Women, Chantilly, Va., 2000—, Middleburg, Va., 2002. Mem. adv. bd. St. Petersburg Jr. Coll., Tarpon Springs, Fla., 1992; pres. New Horizons Edn. Found., Palm Harbor, 1992, New Horizons in Learning-Child Care Mgmt., Tarpon Springs, 1983-88, New Horizons Rsch. Cons., New Horizons Rsch. Divsn., 2003—; validator Nat. Acad. for Early Childhood Programs; mem. adv. bd. Cmty. Sch., Tarpon Springs, 1982-85; bd. dirs. Rexall Showcase Internat., Prentice Health Care; mgr. Curves for Women, 2002; rsch. dir. to author, 2003—. Pres. L.I. Riding for the Handicapped, Brookville, N.Y., 1978-80; audience devel. Fla. Orch., Tampa, 1995; mem. adv. com. Heritage Hall, Leesburg, Va., 1998—; mem. adv. bd. Fla. Symphony, 1995—; bd. dirs. North Suncoast Fla. Symphony, 1995-96; mem. Christmas in April, 1999-2000; chairperson Middleburg Point to Point Race Com., 2003. Recipient svc. appreciation awards Nassau County Children's Mus., 1960, Nassau County Girl Scouts, 1961, Inst. Afro-Am. Affaris, NYU, 1979, Jenkins Meml. award N.Y. State PTA, 1980, Pres.'s award Hempstead Child Care Ctr., 1962. Mem. ASCD, Nat. Tchrs. Assn., Roslyn Tchrs. (Ret.) Assn., Nat. Assn. for Edn. of Young Children, Middleburg Hunting Club. Avocations: travel, reading, knitting, water aerobics, theatre and music. Office: New Horizons Edn Consulting Firm # 1122 19385 Cypress Ridge Ter Lansdowne VA 20176-5171 E-mail: mayc45@aol.com.

GREEN, MICHAEL JEFFREY, retired psychologist, consultant, administrator; b. Boston, July 9, 1942; s. Bernard and Ruth (Paretsky) G. BSBA, Babson Coll., 1964; JD, Boston U., 1967; MEd, Boston Coll., 1970; PhD in Psychology, U. St. Moritz, London, 1998. Asst. athletic dir. Babson Coll., Babson Park, Mass., 1966-68; dir. student activities Bryant & Stratton Jr. Coll., Boston, 1968-69; dir. West Campus, Boston U., 1969-72; clin. dir. Brockton (Mass.) Area Drug Program, 1972-74; psychologist, adminstr. Brockton Multi Svc., 1974-78; dir., psychologist Family Counseling Assocs., Taunton, Mass., 1978—. Dir. youth programs Vol. of Am., Boston, 1993—94, dir. of ops., 1994—97, COO, 1997—2001; bd. dirs. Mass. Coun. Family Mediation, Boston, 1984—90, Cmty. Choice Behavioral health Network, Boston, 1997—2000; cons. Bridgewater Schs., Mass., 1984—89, Bristol-Plymouth Voke, 1985—94; with Vols. Am., 1991—93; clin. dir. The Road Back, 1989—90, dir., 1990—; mem. Mass. Profl. Recovery Program Adv. Bd., 2000—. Mem. Zoning Bd. Appeals, Middleboro, 1983—89, town mgr. selection com., Middleboro, 1985; exec. dir. New Eng. Intercoll. Soccer League, Boston, 1967—72; water safety instr.-trainer ARC, Boston, 1966—85; pres. Friends of Middleboro Pub. Libr., 1985—87, 1988—90, v.p., 1990—93, bd. dirs., 1987—92, Cmty. Choice, 1995—. Mem. Mass. Bar Assn. (tchg. faculty 1986), Nat. Assn. Group Psychotherapy, Am. Psychotherapy Assn. (diplomate), N.E. Group Psychotherapy Assn. Democrat. Jewish. Avocations: gardening, reading, writing professional articles. Home and Office: PO Box 310 Middleboro MA 02346-0310 E-mail: jeff1942@comcast.net.

GREEN, MORRIS, physician, educator; b. Indpls., May 27, 1922; s. Coleman and Rebecca (Oleinick) Green; m. Janice Barber Gorton, Mar. 11, 1955; children: David Schuster, Alan Coleman, Carolyn Ann, Susan Elaine, Marcia Ruth, Sylvia Rebecca. AB, Ind. U., 1942, MD, 1944. Intern Ind. Med. Ctr., 1945; resident pediat. U. Ill. Rsch. and Ednl. Hosps., 1947—49; instr. pediat. U. Ill. Coll. Medicine, 1949—52; asst. prof. Yale Sch. Medicine, 1952—57; faculty Ind. U. Sch. Medicine, Indpls., 1957—, Perry W. Lesh prof. pediat., 1963—; chmn. dept. pediat., physician-in-chief James Whitcomb Riley Hosp. for Children, Indpls., 1967—88. Commr. health State of Ind., 1990—91. Author: Pediatric Diagnosis, 6th edit., 1998; co-editor: Ambulatory Pediatrics, 1968, 5th edit., 1999, Bright Futures, 2d edit., 2000; mem. editl. bd.: Pediat. Rev., Contemporary Pediat., Current Problems Pediat., Jour. Devel. Behavioral Pediat., Jour. Ambulatory Pediat. Assn., Social Work in Health Care, nat. adviser: Children Today. Served to capt. M.C. U.S. Army, 1945—47. Recipient George Armstrong award in ambulatory pediat., 1971, C. Anderson Aldrich award in child devel., 1982, Irving S. Cutter award, Phi Rho Sigma, 1984, Ross award for pediat. edn., 1985, Simon Wile award, Am. Acad. Child and Adolescent Psychiatry, 1990, Joseph W. St. Geme award, Fedn. Pediat. Orgns., 1992, Disting. Career award, Ambulatory Pediat. Assn., 1996. Mem.: AMA (Abraham Jacobi award 1990), Soc. Rsch. Child Devel., Inst. Medicine, Am. Orthopsychiat. Assn., Am. Acad. Pediat. (Abraham Jacobi award 1990), Am.

Fedn. Clin. Rsch., Soc. Pediatric Rsch., Am. Pediatric Soc., Alpha Omega Alpha, Sigma Xi, Phi Beta Kappa. Home: 1840 Brewster Rd Indianapolis IN 46260-1561 Office: 702 Barnhill Dr Indianapolis IN 46202-5128

GREEN, NANCY LOUGHRIDGE, newspaper executive; b. Lexington, Ky., Jan. 19, 1942; d. William S. and Nancy O. (Green) Loughridge. BA in Journalism, U. Ky., 1964, postgrad., 1968; MA in Journalism, Ball State U., 1971; postgrad., U. Minn., 1968; EdD, Nova Southeastern U., 2003. Tchr. English, publs. adv. Clark County H.S., Winchester, Ky., 1965-66, Pleasure Ridge Park H.S., Louisville, 1966-67, Clarksville (Ind.) H.S., 1967-68, Charleston (W.Va.) H.S., 1968-69; asst. publs., pub. info. specialist W.Va. Dept. Edn., Charleston, 1969-70; tchr. journalism, publs. dir. Elmhurst H.S., Ft. Wayne, Ind., 1970-71; adviser student publs. U. Ky., Lexington, 1971-82; gen. mgr. student publs. U. Tex., Austin, 1982-85; pres., pub. Palladium-Item, Richmond, Ind., 1985-89, News-Leader, Springfield, Mo., 1989-92; asst. to pres. newspaper divsn. Gannett Co., Inc., Washington, 1992-94; exec. dir. advancement Clayton State Coll., Morrow, Ga., 1994-96; v.p. advancement Clayton Coll. & State U., Morrow, Ga., 1996-99; v.p. comm. Ga. GLOBE U. Sys., 1999-2000; dir. circulation/distbn., sales & mktg. Lee Enterprises, Davenport, Iowa, 2000—02; v.p. circulation LEE Enterprises, 2002—. Dir. urban journalism program Harte-Hanks, 1984, various Louisville and Lexington newspaper pubs., 1976-82; pres. Media Cons., Inc., Lexington, 1980; sec. Kernel Press, Inc., 1971-82. Contbr. articles to profl. jours. Bd. dirs. Studen Press Law Ctr., 1975—, Richmond Cmty. Devel. Corp., 1987-89, United Way of the Ozarks, 1990-92, ARC, 1990-92, Springfield Arts Coun., 1990-91, Bus. Devel. Corp., 1991-92, Bus. Edn. Alliance, 1991-92, Caring Found., 1991-92, Cox Hosp. Bd., 1990-92, Springfield Schs. Found., 1991-92, Jr. League, Lexington, 1980-82, Manchester Ctr., 1978-82, pres., 1979-82; chmn. Greater Richmond Progress Com., 1986-87, bd. dirs., 1986-89; pres. Leadership Wayne County, 1986-87, bd. dirs. 1985-89; adv. bd. Ind. U. East, 1985-89, Richmond C. of C., 1987-89, Ind. Humanities Coun., 1988-89, Youth Comm. Bd., 1988-92, Opera Theatre No. Va., 1992-94, Atlanta chpt. AIWF, 1995. Recipient Coll. Media Advisers First Amendment award, 1987, Disting. Svc. award Assn. Edn. Journalism and Mass Comm., 1989; named to Ball State Journalism Hall of Fame, 1988, Coll. Media Advisers Hall of Fame, 1994. Mem. Student Press Law Ctr. (bd. dirs. 1975—, pres. 1985-87, 94-96, v.p. 1992-94), Assoc. Collegiate Press, Journalism Edn. Assn. (Carl Towley award 1988), Nat. Coun. Coll. Publs. Advs. (pres. 1979-83, Disting. Newspaper Adv. 1976, Disting. Bus. Adviser 1984), Columbia Scholastic Press Assn. (Gold Key 1980), So. Interscholastic Press Assn. (Disting. Svc. award 1983), Nat. Scholastic Press Assn. (Pioneer award 1982, diversity com. 1992-, circulation fedn. bd. 2002-, postal com. 2001-), Soc. Profl. Journalists, Internat. Newspaper Mktg. Assn. N. Am. (bd. dir., 2002—), Newspaper Assn. of Am. Circulation Fedn. (postal com., 2001—, leadership adv. group, 2002—, diversity subcom., 1991—), Clayton County C. of C. (adv. bd. 1995-99, internat. com. chmn. 1996-98). E-mail: nancy.green@lee.net. *An opportunity each day to make the best of every situation to help others, your community, your profession and employees to be successful.*

GREEN, NORMAN HARRY, lawyer; b. L.A., Nov. 11, 1952; s. Leonard L. and Lily (Merecki) G.; m. Rachel Rubin, Oct. 19, 1980; children: Andrew S., L. Stephen. AB, U. Calif., Irvine, 1974; JD, UCLA, 1979. Bar: Calif. 1979; cert. specialist taxation U.S. Tax Ct. Tax auditor IRS, San Francisco, 1974-76; customs officer U.S. Customs Svc., L.A., 1977; tax acct. Arthur Andersen & Co., L.A., 1979-80; lawyer Barclay & Moskatel, Beverly Hills, Calif., 1980-84; ptnr., tax lawyer Irsfeld, Irsfeld & Younger, Glendale, Calif., 1984—. Dir., gen. counsel June Ebensteiner Hospice Found., Calabasas, Calif., 1990—. Mem. Glendale Bar Assn., L.A. County Bar Assn. (chmn. arbitration com. 1995-97), Glendale C. of C. (chmn. legis. action com. 1986-89), Kiwanis (Hollywood sec. 1990-93, pres. 1993-94). Avocations: hiking, gourmet cooking, singing. Office: Irsfeld Irsfeld & Younger LLP 100 W Broadway Ste 900 Glendale CA 91210-1296 E-mail: nhg@iiylaw.com.

GREEN, NORMAN KENNETH, retired oil industry executive, former naval officer; b. Columbus, Ind., July 1, 1924; s. Otto and Bernice Escalene (Snyder) G.; m. Mary Ann McCarthy, Mar. 12, 1949; children: David Bruce, Norman K., Penny Ann, Michael Anthony, Patricia Elizabeth. BS, U.S. Naval Acad., 1947; MS, Naval Postgrad. Sch., 1959. Joined U.S. Navy, 1943, advanced through grades to rear adm., 1974; comdg. officer USS St. Louis, 1970-72; comdg. officer USS Ticonderoga, 1972-73; capt. aviation assignment officer Bur. Naval Personnel, 1973-74; comdr. Sea Based ASW Wings Atlantic Fleet, 1974-77; comdr. Carrier Group 6 and Carrier Strike Force, 1977-79; dep. dir. command and control Office Chief Naval Ops., Navy Dept. Washington, 1979-80; ret., 1980; sr. v.p. Charter Co., Jacksonville, Fla., 1980-87. Mem. Com. of 100, Jacksonville, Fla., 1974-77; mem. exec. bd. United Way, 1974-77. Decorated Def. Superior Service medal, Legion of Merit.; recipient Brotherhood award NCCJ, 1979 Mem. Jacksonville C. of C. (bd. govs. 1974-77, 83-86) Clubs: Army-Navy, Ponte Vedra, Marsh Landing Country. Methodist. Home: 550 Granada Ter Ponte Vedra Beach FL 32082-2304

GREEN, NORMAN MARSTON, JR., minister; b. Oakland, Calif., June 27, 1932; s. Norman Marston and Gladys Marian (Meads) G.; m. Dolores Antoinette Taylor, June 27, 1953; children: Russell Norman, Cynthia Louise, Sharon Marie, Deona Lynn. BA, U. Calif., Berkeley, 1954; BD, Berkeley Bapt. Div. Sch., 1957; postgrad., U. Chgo., 1957-59; DMin, Ea. Bapt. Theol. Sem., Phila., 1982. Ordained to ministry Am. Baptist Ch., 1957. Pastor Grace Bapt. Ch., Downers Grove, Ill., 1959-62; field rep. Am. Bapt. Home Mission Soc., Valley Forge, Pa., 1962-66, field dir., 1966-76; dir. office planning resources Am. Bapt. Nat. Ministries, Valley Forge, Pa., 1977-95. Rec. clk. Cen. Bapt. Ch., Wayne, Pa., 1986-90, treas., 1990-96, bookkeeper, 1997—, treas., 2002-; sec.-treas. Assn. Statisticians of Am. Religious Bodies, 1987-94; championship statistician Masters Long Distance Running com. U.S.A. Track and Field, 1988—, sec., 1997-2001, chair, 2002—. Joint author: Local Church Planning Manual, 1977, Key Steps in Local Church Planning, 1980, Churches and Church Membership in the United States 1990, 1992. Insp. elections Tredyffrin Twp., Berwyn, Pa., 1976-81; U.S. del. World Assn. Vet. Athletes, 1988-2001; bd. dirs., sec. Springdell Village Homeowners Assn., 1994-98; mgr. USA Track & Field Masters Hall Fame, 1997—. Recipient Otto T. Essig award U.S.A. Track and Field, 1990; named Male Athlete of Yr. age 50-54, 1982-87, age 55-59, 1987-91, age 60-64, 1993-95, age 65-69, 1997; inducted into U.S.A. Track and Field Masters Hall of Fame, 1996, Mid-Atlantic Assn. Long Distance Runner of the Yr., 1982-90, 94-95, 98, Lifetime Achievement award, 1999. Mem. Am. Bapt. Ministers Coun., Phila. Masters Track and Field Assn. (life), Mid-Atlantic Assn. U.S.A. Track and Field (v.p. 1988-96, coord. grand prix 1991—, treas. 1997-98, membership chair 1997-98, sec. 1999—, membership processor 2000—), Am. Running and Fitness Assn. (pres. 1991-94), Rd. Runners Club Am. (inducted to hall of fame 1992). Democrat. Avocations: long-distance running, reading. Home: 407 Freedom Blvd Coatesville PA 19320-1559 E-mail: runrnorm@aol.com.

GREEN, PATRICIA PATAKY, school system administrator, consultant; b. NYC, June 18, 1949; d. William J. and Theresa M. (DiGianni) P.; m. Stephen I. Green, Dec. 7, 1975. BS, U. Md., 1971, MEd, 1977, PhD, 1994. Tchr. Prince George's County Pub. Sch., Md., 1971-83; elem. instrnl. adminstrv. specialist Thomas Stone Sch., Mt. Ranier, Md., 1984-85, Glenridge Sch., Lanham, Md., 1984, Greenbelt Ctr. Sch., Md., 1983-84, Prince George's County Pub. Schs., 1985-91; prin. Columbia Pk. Sch., Landover, Md., 1985-91; asst. supt. Prince George's County Pub. Sch., 1991-95, assoc. supt., chief divsn. adminstr., 1995-99, assoc. supt. for pupil svc., 1999—2001, acting dep. supt. for instrn., 2000—02, fellow Broad Ctr. Supt., Bd. Found., 2002; supt. sch. North Allegheny Sch. Dist., Pitts., 2002—. Exec. dir. North Allegheny Found.; cons. nationwide sch. systems; presenter in field. Featured in numerous mag. and on TV shows; contbr. articles to profl. jour. Apptd. commr. Prince George's Commn. for Children, Youth and Families; bd. dir. Prince George's County Cmty. in Sch., 1998—2002; trustee North Allegheny Found., 2002, exec. dir., 2002—03. Recipient Nat. Sch. Recognition award US Dept. Edn., 1988, Outstanding Adminstr. award Prince George's County C. of C., 1990, Outstanding Rsch. award Md. Assn. Supervision and Curriculum Devel., 1995, Outstanding Educator award Prince George's County, 1983, Spotlight on Prevention award Md. State Atty. Gen., 1998, Disting. Achievement award North Allegheny Sch. Dist., 2002. Mem. NAESP (Excellence of Achievement award 1988), ASCD, NEA, Am. Ednl. Rsch. Assn., Phi Kappa Phi. Kappa Delta Pi. Avocations: landscape gardening, photography, reading, writing, bicycling. E-mail: pgreen@northallegheny.org.

GREEN, PAUL ALLAN, scientist, engineer, educator; b. Phila., May 28, 1950; s. Leonard Arthur and Sylvia Ruth (Reuben) G. BSME, Drexel U., 1972; MSE, U. Mich., 1974, MA in Psychology, PhD, U. Mich., 1979. Occupational safety and health engr. Sterling Lighting div. Scovill, summers 1972-73; tchg. and rsch. asst. Trans Dept. Psychology/Indsl. Ops. Engring. U. Mich. Transp. Rsch., Ann Arbor, 1972-79; lectr. dept. psychology U. Mich. Transp. Rsch. Inst., 1980, lectr. dept. indsl. and ops. engring., 1980-82, adj. asst. prof. dept. indsl. and ops. engring., 1982—, asst. rsch. scientist Human Factors divsn., 1982-93, assoc. rsch. scientist Human Factors divsn., 1988-97, sr. rsch. scienstist Human Factors divsn., 1998—. Adj. assoc. prof. Dept. Indsl. and Ops. Engring. U. Mich., 1993—. Contbr. numerous articles to profl. jours. Phila. Naval Shipyard trainee, 1967-72; NSF fellow, 1972-73; Nat. Inst. Occupational Safety and Health fellow, 1974, others. Fellow Ergonomics Soc.; mem. SAE, Human Factors and Ergonomics Soc. (sec. treas. elect), ITS Am. Jewish. Avocations: volleyball, running, sailing, contra dancing. Home: 1615 Harbal Dr Ann Arbor MI 48105-1815 Office: Univ of Mich Transp Rsch Inst 2901 Baxter Rd Ann Arbor MI 48109-2150

GREEN, PAUL ELIOT, JR., optical communications consultant; b. Durham, N.C., Jan. 14, 1924; s. Paul Eliot and Elizabeth Atkinson (Lay) G.; m. Dorrit L. Gegan, Oct. 30, 1948; children: Dorrit Green Rodemeyer, Nancy E., Judith Green Godin, Paul M., Gordon M. AB, U. N.C., 1943; MS, N.C. State U., 1948; ScD, MIT, 1953. Group leader MIT Lincoln Lab., Lexington, 1951-69; sr. mgr. rsch. divsn. IBM, Yorktown Heights, N.Y., 1969-97; dir. optical networking tech. Tellabs, Hawthorne, N.Y., 1997-2000. Mem. radio engring. adv. com. USIA, 1984-93; panel on survivable communications NRC, 1982-89. Author: Fiber Optic Networks, 1992; co-editor: Computer Communications, 1974; editor: Computer Network Architectures and Protocols, 1982, Network Interconnection and Protocol Conversion, 1988. Served to lt. comdr. USNR, 1943-60; ret. Named Disting. Engring. Alumnus N.C. State U., 1983; recipient Data Comm. award Assn. Computing Machinery, SIGCOM, 1994. Fellow: IEEE (chmn. info. theory group 1960, pres. Comm. Soc. 1992—93, Aerospace Pioneer award 1981, E.H. Armstrong award 1989, Simon Ramo medal 1991); mem.. NAE, Russian Popov Soc. (hon.). Home: 35 Roseholm Pl Mount Kisco NY 10549-4619 E-mail: pegreen@earthlink.net.

GREEN, PAUL JOHN, independent critic; b. Seattle, July 27, 1936; s. Howard William and Ruth Yeo G. BA in French, Seattle Pacific Coll., 1957; MA in English Lit., U. Wash., 1958; M of Libr. Sci., U. Calif., Berkeley, 1968; PhD in Lit. Studies, Wash. State U., 1981. Teaching asst. English U. Wash., Seattle, 1963-66; instr. English Ctrl. Wash. U., Ellensburg, 1966-67; rsch. asst. U. Calif., Berkeley, 1967-68; asst. serial libr. U. Oreg., Eugene, 1968-69; teaching asst. English Wash. State U., Pullman, 1974-76; ind. critic various, Oreg., 1981—. Author: The Life of Jack Gray: An Education in Living and in Love, 1991, rev. and expanded edit., 2002, Previously Unpublished Literary Reviews, 1997-1999, 2001, Previously Unpublished Literary Essays, 1992-2000, 2001, Collected Writings on the Fictionof Franz Kafka, 2003, Eighteenth Century Salad with Italian Dressing: Swift-Voltaire, Fielding-Manzoni and Reviews Franco-Italian and Italian, 2003, From Russia With Love and a Literary Potpourri, 2003; contbr. articles to profl. jours. With USNR, 1953-65. Mem. Am. Comp. Lit. Assn. Modern Lang. Assn., London Diplomatic Acad. Avocations: reading, writing, research. Home: 825 Washington #20 Eugene OR 97401-2845

GREEN, PETER MORRIS, classics educator, writer, translator; b. London, Dec. 22, 1924; came to U.S., 1971; s. Arthur and Olive Emily (Slaughter) G.; m. Lalage Isobel Pulvertaft, July 28, 1951 (div.); children: Timothy Michael Bourke, Nicholas Paul, Sarah Francesca; m. Carin Margreta Christensen, July 18, 1975. BA, Cambridge U., 1950, MA, PhD, Cambridge U., 1954. Dir. studies in classics Selwyn Coll., Cambridge, Eng., 1952-53; freelance writer, journalist, translator, London, 1954-63; lectr. Greek history and lit. Coll. Yr. in Athens, 1966-71; prof. classics U. Tex., Austin, 1971-97, James R. Dougherty Centennial prof., 1982-97, prof. emeritus, 1997—. Vis. prof. classics UCLA, 1976; vis. prof. history U. Iowa, 1997-98, adj. prof. classics, 1998—; vis. prof. history, Athens, 1999; Mellon chair in humanities Tulane U., 1986; vis. fellow, writer-in-residence Hellenic studies program Princeton U., fall semester, 2001. Fiction critic: Daily Telegraph, London, 1954-63; sr. cons. editor: Hodder & Stoughton Ltd., London, 1959-63; cons.: (Odyssey project) Nat. Radio Theatre, Chgo., 1980-81; author: The Sword of Pleasure, 1957 (Heinemann award for Lit. 1957), The Laughter of Aphrodite, 1965, Armada from Athens, 1970, The Shadow of the Parthenon, 1972, Alexander of Macedon 356-323 BC: A Historical Biography, 1974, 2d edit., 1991, Classical Bearings, 1989, ed edit., 1998, Alexander to Actium: The Historical Evolution of the Hellenistic Age, 1990, rev. edit., 1993, The Greco-Persian Wars, 1996; translator, editor: Juvenal, The Sixteen Satires, 1967, 3d edit., 1998, Ovid: The Erotic Poems, 1982, Yannis Ritsos: The Fourth Dimension, 1993, Hellenistic History and Culture, 1993, Ovid: The Poems of Exile, 1994, Apollonios Rhodios, The Argonautika, 1997; editor-in-chief Syllecta Classica, 1999—. Served to sgt. RAF, 1943-47. NEH fellow, 1983-84; Craven scholar Cambridge U., 1950; Obermann Ctr. for Advanced Rsch. fellow U. Iowa, 1997; recipient 1st prize Nat. Poetry Libr., 1997. Fellow Royal Soc. Lit. (council 1959-63); mem. Soc. for Promotion of Hellenic Studies (U.K.), Classical Assn. (U.K.), Am. Philol. Assn., Archaeol. Inst. Am., Mem. Liberal Party. Club: Savile (London). Office: Dept Classics U Iowa Iowa City IA 52242 E-mail: peter-green-1@uiowa.edu. *Prime aims, then, now always; to have maximum possible time for writing, travel, sport, relationships; to avoid any job that threatens my solitude or independence; to shun mature opinions; to go on, forever if possible, finding every day exciting, new, a fresh challenge, mentally and physically; to love and be loved always, to write all the books I have in me, and be healthy in mind and body until I die, preferably at well over the century, in Greece.*

GREEN, RACHAEL PAULETTE, librarian; b. Shreveport, La., Nov. 28, 1953; d. Harold Dayton and Carolyn Francis (Sholars) G. BA in English, La. Tech U., 1975; M in Libr. and Info. Sci., La. State U., 1986; MA in Indsl. and Orgnl. Psychology, La. Tech. U., 1993. Libr. Shreve Meml. Libr., Shreveport, 1976-78, 79-89; dept. clk. ct. Fed. Ct. House, Shreveport, 1978-79; asst. libr. La. State U., Shreveport, 1989-96; mem. acad. calendar com., 1989-90, 92; mem. Noel Meml. Libr. faculty com., mem. environ. com. La. State U., Shreveport, 1991—, mem. bldgs. and grounds com., 1991—, mem. faculty senate, 1996-97, mem. faculty R&D com., 1995-97, faculty senate exec. com., 1997, assoc. libr., 1996—, mem. student affairs com., 1999-2000, chair student affairs com., 2001—02, mem. policy and pers. com., 2002—. Author: The Argument of the Eye: A Select Bibliography of the Pre-Raphaelite Movement 1848-1914, 1995; reviewer Nat. Productivity Rev., 1994-97, 99-2000, Am. Reference Books Annual, 1995—, Libr. and Info. Sci. Ann., 1999—, Jour. Organizational Excellence, 2000—. Contbg. mem. Dem. Nat. Com., 1990—. Mem. ALA (reference and adult svcs. divsn., govt. documents round table, libr. instruction round table), APA (tchg. of psychology sect.), So. States Comm. Assn., Assn. Coll. Rsch. Libraries. Democrat. Methodist. Avocations: gardening, reading. Office: 1 University Pl Shreveport LA 71115-2301 E-mail: rgreen@pilot.lsu.edu.

GREEN, RICHARD, research scientist, consultant; b. Vienna, Mar. 28, 1928; arrived in U.S., 1948; s. Emil and Irene Green; children from previous marriage: Michael David, Howard Jody. AB, Syracuse (NY) U., 1950; MS, Syracuse (NY)U., 1951; MBA, Rutgers U., Newark, NJ, 1960. Chemist H.D. Justi and S., Phila., 1952—55; scientist Congoleum- Nairn, Kearny, NJ, 1957—60; sr. scientist Tenneco Chem., Piscataway, NJ, 1960—67; cons. engr.; sr. scientist, group leader Johnson and Johnson, New Brunswick, NJ, 1967—2001; ret., 2001; ind. cons. Richard Green Cons., Livingston, NJ, 2001—. With U.S. Army, 1955—57. Achievements include patents in field of orthop.(12) with Johnson and Johnson. Mailing: 120 E Cedar St Livingston NJ 07039-4015

GREEN, RICHARD ALAN, lawyer; b. Springfield, Mass., Apr. 25, 1926; s. Herman and Emma (Rudnick) G.; m. Lorna H. Paul, Sept. 6, 1957; children: Charles C., Thomas F. AB cum laude, Harvard U., 1947, LL.B., 1952. Bar: N.Y. 1954, D.C. 1975, Md. 1987. Assoc. Steinberg & Patterson, N.Y.C., 1954-57; asst. U.S. atty. So. Dist. N.Y., 1957-59; 1st asst. counsel N.Y. State Commn. Investigation, 1960; individual practice law N.Y.C., 1961-64; dir. ABA Project on Standards for Criminal Justice, 1964-73; dep. dir. Nat. Commn. on Reform of Fed. Criminal Laws, 1967-71; lectr. U. Va. Sch. Law, 1971; dep. dir. Fed. Jud. Center, Washington, 1971-74; partner Rowley and Green, Washington, 1974-80, Stohlman, Beuchert, Egan & Smith, Washington, 1981-2000. Served with USN, 1944-46. Mem. ABA, Am. Law Inst., D.C. Bar Assn., Assn. of Bar of City of N.Y., Harvard (N.Y.C.) Club. Home: 1050 N Stuart St Apt 714 Arlington VA 22201-5749

GREEN, RICHARD BERTRAM, sculptor; b. Barrie, Ont., Can., Apr. 18, 1946; s. Lawrence Bertram and Vera Valdee (Bell) G.; m. Hilary Joan McDougall, July 27, 1979. Assoc., Ont. Coll. Art, 1969. Dir. Richard Green Gallery, Barrie, 1972-76; sculptor Ricahrd Green, Barrie, Bracebridge, 1972—; originator, benevolent dictator Muskoka Autumn Studio Tour, Bracebridge, 1979-83; pres. Richard Green Design Ltd., Lanexa, Va., 1991-99, Richard Green Sculpture Studio, Corrales, N.Mex., 1999—2001. Works in permanent collections of Coldwell Banker and numerous pvt. collections in 27 countries. Bd. dirs. Visual Arts Ont., Toronto, 1978-80. Mem. Sculptor Soc. of Can. (exec. 1974-84), Internat. Sculpture Ctr., Fine Arts League of Cary, Triangle Artists Guild, Cary Visual Arts, Rotary. Republican. Avocations: boating, motorcycling. Home and Office: 418 Warren Ave Cary NC 27511-4044 E-mail: richardgreensculpture@msn.com.

GREEN, RICHARD CALVIN, JR., electric power and gas industry executive; b. Kansas City, Mo., May 6, 1954; s. Richard C. and Ann (Gableman) G.; m. Nancy Jean Risk, Aug. 6, 1977; children: Allison Thompt, Ashley Jean, Richard Calvin III. BSBA, So. Methodist U., 1976. With Mo. Pub. Service, Kansas City, 1976-85, exec. v.p., 1982-85; pres., chief exec. officer UtiliCorp United Inc., Kansas City, 1985-89, pres., chmn. bd., from 1989, CEO, 1985—2002, chmn., 1989—. Bd. dirs. Midwest Rsch. Inst., The BHA Group, Inc., Urban Inst. Washington.

GREEN, RICHARD JAMES, federal agency administrator, aerospace engineer; b. Newark, Apr. 15, 1928; s. John and Alice Margaret (Murdoch) G.; m. Patricia Agnes Higgins, Oct. 7, 1957; children; John, Alice, Richard, Patricia. BS in Biology, Holy Cross Coll., 1949; MS in Physics, Fordham U., 1955; grad. advanced mgmt. program, Harvard U., 1977. Engr. Pratt & Whitney Aircraft, E. Hartford, Conn., 1955-57; R & D engr. Mobil Oil, Paulsboro, N.J., 1957-61; exec. tech. asst. NASA, Washington, 1962-66, mgr. Apollo Lunar Surface Expt. Program, 1966-70; exec. asst. NSF, Washington, 1970-72, dep. asst. dir. rsch. applications, 1972-79, asst. dir. Sci., Tech., and Internat. Affairs Directorate, 1982-89, dir. rsch. facilities office, 1989-91; assoc. dir. (Presdl. appointee) FEMA, Washington, 1979-81; pres. Green Assocs. Science, Tech. and Internat. Cons., Washington, 1996—. Chmn., vice chmn. U.S.-Israel Binat. Sci. Found., Washington, Jerusalem, 1982-90; sr. tech. advisor Tech. Adminstrn., U.S. Dept. Commerce, 1991-92; rsch. prof., dir. spl. projects Colo. Sch. Mines, Golden, 1991-94; dir. spl. programs U. Wyo., Laramie, 1994-95; spl. asst. U. Md. Sys. Adminstrn., 1995-96. Organizer, pres. Penn-Branch Citizen's Assn., Washington, 1963-70; com. chmn. Boy Scouts Am., Washington, 1969-76. Maj. USAF, 1950-54, 1961-62. Recipient Exceptional Sci. Achievement medal NASA, 1969, Commendation award AEC, 1970, Meritorious Svc. award NSF, 1974, U.S. Presdl. Meritorious Svc. award, 1986 Mem. AAAS, Cosmos Club. Roman Catholic.

GREEN, RICHARD JOHN, architect; b. Painesville, Ohio, Mar. 14, 1944; s. Robert Franklin and Hazel (Ruble) G.; m. Judith Marie Ellen Niemi, Aug. 25, 1965 (div. 1985); children: Kevin Ward, Tyler Andrew. BArch with honors, N.C. STate U., 1968. Registered architect, Mass., Calif., Pa., Ill., Ind., R.I., N.H., N.C., Nev., Conn., Minn., Tenn., S.C., N.Y., Mich., Singapore. Project designer The Stubbins Assocs., Inc., Cambridge, Mass., 1968-74, assoc., 1974-77, v.p. deisgn, 1977-83, pres., COO, 1983-92, chmn., pres., 1992—2003. Vis. instr. Calif. State Poly. U., Pomona, 1980—84; vis. lectr. Nat. U. Mex., Mexico City, 1981; instr. Boston Archtl. Ctr., 1971—72, 1975—76; thesis advisor Harvard U., Cambridge, 1981—82; part-time adj. faculty dept. arch. N.C. State U., 1998; adj. prof. arch. U. Hawaii, 1998—. Drawings, projects and photographs pub. in books. Bd. dirs. Sch. Design Found., N.C. State U. Fellow AIA (internat. com., corr. mem., com. design and urban design and planning, Cert. Merit 1968, Rotch Travelling scholar 1972); mem. Boston Soc. Architects, AIA Mass., Nat. Coun. Archtl. Registration Bds., Archtl. League N.Y., Corinthian Yacht Club. Avocations: athletics, travel, sailing, Tae Kwon Do. Home: 22 Oak St Marblehead MA 01945-1947 Office: The Stubbins Assocs Inc 1030 Massachusetts Ave Cambridge MA 02138-5388

GREEN, RICHARD M. academic administrator, internist; b. Chgo., Jan. 28, 1960; s. Henry and Reva Green; m. Marianne M. Green. MD, Duke U., 1986. Diplomate ABIM, 1993. Chief, divsn. gastroenterology Chgo. VAMC-Lakeside Divsn.; chief, divsn. hepatology Northwestern U. Feinberg Sch. Medicine, 2002—. Grantee, NIH, 2000—02. Office: Northwestern U Divsn Hepatology Searle 10-544 303 E Chicago Ave Chicago IL 60611

GREEN, RIVA LEE, social worker, minister; b. Denmark, S.C., May 18, 1953; d. Rious and Elizzillia (Banks) G.; m. George E. Collins, June 19, 1974 (div. June 1985); children: Corey E., Kevin L., Monique N. AAS, Cumberland County Coll., Vineland, N.J., 1992. Ordained to ministry Jamison Sch. Ministry, Phila., 1995. Caseworker Salem County Women's Svcs., Salem, N.J., 1992-97; family non-violence training U.S. Army, Ft. Dix, N.J., 1995—; family svc. specialist III State of N.J. Divsn. Youth and Family Svcs., Camden, 1997—. Pastor Strings of Faith ministry, Seabrook, N.J. Active NAACP (area coord. Bridgeton, N.J., 1995, 1st v.p. Cumberland County, 1995—); adv. bd. Maple Garden Tenant Assn., 1991-93; natural leader Martin Luther King Academy, 1995—; mem. C.O.R.E. Mem. C.O.R.E. Home: 32 Tower Ln Willingboro NJ 08046-4114

GREEN, ROBERT BAILEY, insurance executive, retired; b. Wilmington, Del., Apr. 18, 1932; s. Walter Johnson and Helen (Braddock) G.; m. Phyllis Hartman, Aug. 15, 1959; children: Sharon Buell, Bruce Green. BSBA, U. Del., 1954. CLU. Field supr., asst. mgr. The Travelers Ins. Co., Wilmington, N.Y.C., 1956-63; mgr. health ins. sales The Guardian Life Ins. Co. Am., N.Y.C., San Francisco, 1963-68; dir. agencies Maccabees Mut. Life Ins. Co., Southfield, Mich., 1968-75; mktg. v.p. Wis. Life Ins. Co., Madison, 1975-82; brokerage v.p. Ctrl. Life Assurance Co., Des Moines, 1982-84; sr. v.p. First Farwest Life Ins. Cos., Portland, Oreg., 1984-90, ret., 1990. 1st lt. U.S. Army, 1954-56. Avocations: walking, reading, travel.

GREEN, ROBERT EDWARD, JR., physicist, educator; b. Clifton Forge, Va., Jan. 17, 1932; s. Robert Edward and Hazle Hall (Smith) G.; m. Sydney Sue Truitt, Feb. 1, 1962; children: Kirsten Adair, Heather Scott. BS, Coll. William and Mary, 1953; PhD, Brown U., 1959; postgrad., Aachen (Germany) Technische Hochschule, 1959-60. Physicist underwater explosions rsch. divsn. Norfolk Naval Shipyard, Va., 1959; asst. prof. mechanics Johns Hopkins U., Balt., 1960-65, assoc. prof., 1965-70, prof., 1970—, chmn. mechanics dept., 1970-72, chmn. mechanics and materials sci. dept., 1972-73, chmn. civil engring./materials sci. and engring. dept., 1979-82, chmn. materials sci. and engring. dept., 1982-85, 91-93, dir. ctr. for nondestructive evaluation, 1985—2002. Ford Found. resident sr. engr. RCA, Lancaster, Pa., 1966-67; cons. U.S. Army Ballistic Research Labs., Aberdeen Proving Ground, Md., 1973-74; physicist Ctr. for Materials Sci., U.S. Nat. Bur. Standards, Washington, 1974-81; program mgr. Def. Advanced Research Projects Agy., 1981-82; mem. nat. materials adv. bd. Author: Ultrasonic Investigation of Mechanical Properties (Treatise on Materials Science and Technology, vol. 3), 1973; co-editor 11 books; also articles. Fulbright grantee. Mem. ASM Internat., Am. Phys. Soc., Acoustical Soc. Am., Met. Soc. AIME, Am. Soc. Nondestructive Testing, Soc. for the Advancement of Material and Process Engring., Materials Rsch. Soc., Sigma Xi, Tau Beta Pi, Alpha Sigma Mu, Sigma Nu. Methodist. Achievements include research in recovery, recrystallization, elasticity, plasticity, crystal growth and orientation, X-ray diffraction, electro-optical systems, linear and non-linear elastic wave propagation, light-sound interactions, high-power ultrasonics, ultrasonic attenuation, dislocation damping, fatigue, acoustic emission, non-destructive testing, polymers, biomaterials, synchrotron radiation, composites, sensors and process control. Office: Johns Hopkins U Materials Sci and Engring Dept 3400 N Charles St Baltimore MD 21218-2689 E-mail: robert.green@jhu.edu.

GREEN, ROBERT FREDERICK, physician, photographer; b. Newark, N.J., Oct. 13, 1923; s. Robert Aloysious (Green) and Sarah Wallington Schenck; m. June 20, 1960 (div.); children: Robert Daniel, Daniel Richard. BS, Seton Hall

Coll., 1948; MD, SUNY, Bklyn., 1952. Diplomate Am. Bd. Psychiatry and Neurology, Nat. Bd. Med. Examiners. Intern Bklyn. Hosp., 1952-53; resident Peter Bent Brigham Hosp., Boston, 1953-54, Worcester (Mass.) State Hosp., 1954-57; asst. in psychiatry Tufts U., 1955-57; pvt. practice psychiatry Worcester, 1957-61, Ft. Wayne, Ind., 1961-82; chief mental hygiene clinic VA Med. Ctr., Ft. Wayne, 1982, chief of staff, 1983-88; med. dir. Grant-Blackford Mental Hygiene Clinic, Marion, Ind., 1988-94; cons. psychiatry-comprehensive health Salt Lake City, 1994—. Psychiatry cons. VA Med. Ctr., Ft. Wayne, 1961-82, Ft. Wayne Occupational Health Ctr., 1984-95; cons. disability determination sect. Dept. Vocat. Rehab., State of Ind., 1961-94; teaching cons. Ind. Acad. Gen. Practice, 1971-75; med. dir. Evansville (Ind.) Hosp., 1996-99; cons. Prisod Health Svcs., 1999—. Presenter weekly live TV segment Coping, 1980-81; contbr. articles to profl. jours.; photography published in The Rangefinder, Petersons Photographica, Modern Photography, Popular Photography, Darkroom, Camera 35, the Photo, Spec, Wall Street Jour.; numerous commissions by individuals, art galleries, museums and corps. Cpl. USAF, 1943-46. Fellow Acad. Psychosomatic Medicine; mem. AAAS, Pan Am. Med Assn. (diplomate, life mem.), Ind. State Med. Assn., N.Y. Acad. Sci., Vanderburgh County Med. Soc. Home: 1330 Tall Timbers Dr Evansville IN 47725-8672 E-mail: gallery614@aol.com.

GREEN, ROBERT K. energy executive; BS in Engring., Princeton U.; JD, Vanderbilt U. Atty. Blackwell, Sanders, Matheny, Weary & Lombardi, Kansas City, 1987-88; asst. divsn. counsel Mo. Pub. Svc. divsn. UtiliCorp United, divsn. counsel Mo. Pub. Svc. divsn., v.p. adminstrn. Mo. Pub. Svc. divsn., sr. v.p. ops. Mo. Pub. Svc. divsn., pres. Mo. Pub. Svc. divsn., 1991—; exec. v.p., bd.d irs. UtiliCorp, Kansas City, Mo., 1993-96, pres., COO, 1996—2002; pres., CEO Aquila (formerly UtiliCorp), 2002—. Bd. dirs. United Mo. Bank, CompGeeks.com.; chmn. United Energy, Melbourne, Australia, 1995, UnitedNetworks, Auckland, New Zealand, 1998, Aquila Energy, 1999. Chmn. Initiative for Competitive Inner City, Kansas City. Mem. ABA, Mo. Bar Assn., Kansas City Met. Bar Assn. Office: UtiliCorp United 20 W 9th St Kansas City MO 64105-1704

GREEN, ROBERT S. lawyer; b. Newark, Feb. 9, 1927; s. Mortimer J. and Edna Vera (Reinherz) G.; m. Estelle Rothenberg, Jan. 29, 1961; children—Peter, Sara AB, Cornell U., 1948; JD, Columbia U., 1953. Bars: N.Y. 1954, Fla. 1957, D.C. 1959. Law clk. Cir. Judge Harold R. Medina, 1953-54; ptnr. Brennan, London & Buttenweiser, N.Y.C., 1963-70, Green, Sharpless & Greenstein, N.Y.C., 1971-80, Nixon, Peabody LLP, N.Y.C., 1981-94; counsel Pepper Hamilton LLP, N.Y.C., 1995-99, Wollmuth Maher & Deutsch, 2000—. Contbr. articles to profl. jours. Founder, trustee Citizens for Clean Air, 1964-68; trustee William Alanson White Inst., N.Y.C., 1968-89 ; advisor U.S. Senator Robert F. Kennedy, 1966-68. Served with USNR, 1945-46, PTO Mem. Am. Law Inst. Democrat. Jewish. Avocations: sailing, travel. Home: 90 Riverside Dr New York NY 10024-5306 E-mail: rgreen@wmd-law.com.

GREEN, ROBERT SCOTT, biotechnology company executive; b. N.Y.C., Aug. 7, 1953; s. Morris and Sophie (Weinstock) G.; m. Jill Susan Bolhack, June 24, 1979; children: Melissa, Meredith. BA, CUNY, 1974; JD, Fordham U., N.Y.C., 1977. Bar: N.Y. 1978, D.C. 1979. Assoc. Paul, Weiss, Rifkind, Wharton & Garrison, N.Y.C., 1979-87; v.p. Kaplan Capital Mgmt. Inc., N.Y.C., 1987-89; pres., bd. dirs. Integrated Biomolecule Corp., Tucson, 1992—. Mng. dir. Fusion Assocs., Ltd., Tucson, 1990-92; bd. dirs. Hearing Innovations Inc., Tucson, 1990-2001. Contbr. articles to profl. jours. Mem. N.Y. State Bar Assn. Office: Integrated Biomolecule Corp 9030 S Rita Rd Ste 100 Tucson AZ 85747-9102 E-mail: rsgreen@integratedbiomolecule.com.

GREEN, RONALD MICHAEL, ethics and religious studies educator; b. N.Y.C., Dec. 16, 1942; s. Daniel David and Beatrice (Friedlander) G.; m. Mary Jean Matthews, June 25, 1965; children— Julie Elisabeth, Matthew Daniel AB, Brown U., 1964; PhD, Harvard U., 1973. Instr. Dartmouth Coll., Hanover, NH, 1969-73, asst. prof., 1973-79, assoc. prof., 1979-85, John Phillips prof. of religion, 1985-98, chmn. dept. religion, 1980—83, 1985, 2000—, adj. prof. Amos Tuck Sch. Bus. Adminstrn., 1985-92, Cohen prof., 1998—. Vis. assoc. prof. Stanford U., Calif., 1984-85; adj. prof. dept. cmty. medicine Dartmouth Med. Sch., 1980—; dir. Dartmouth Ethics Inst., 1993—, Office of Genome Ethics Nat. Human Genome Rsch. Inst. NIH, 1996-97; human embryo rsch. panel NIH, 1994; chmn. ethics adv. bd. Advanced Cell Tech. Author: Population Growth and Justice, 1975, Religious Reason, 1978, Religion and Moral Reason, 1988, Kierkegaard and Kant, 1992, The Ethical Manager, 1994, The Human Embryo Research Debates, 2001; assoc. editor Jour. Religious Ethics, 1973-91, mem. editorial bd., 1991—; mem. editorial bd. Jour. Am. Acad. Religion, 1985-91. Kent fellow, 1965-69; recipient Fulbright award, 1964-65, Dartmouth Disting. Teaching award, 1978 Mem. Am. Acad. Religion (sec. 1995—), Soc. Christian Ethics (bd. dirs., v.p. 1997-98, pres. 1998-99), Soc. Bus. Ethics, Am. Soc. for Study Religion. Jewish. Office: Dartmouth Coll Dept Religion Hanover NH 03755 E-mail: ronald.m.green@dartmouth.edu. *I continue to believe in the ideals of the enlightenment: that human beings can use their reason to expand opportunity, freedom and community.*

GREEN, RUTHANN, marketing and management consultant; b. Streator, Ill., July 14, 1935; d. John Joseph and Edna Marie (Peters) G. BS in Edn., U. Ill., 1957. Elem. tchr. Jefferson Sch., Davenport, Iowa, 1957-59; tchr. Hinsdale (Ill.) Jr. High Sch., 1959-62; ednl. cons. Harcourt Brace & World, Chgo., 1962-63; exec. sec. Everpure, Inc., Oakbrook, Ill., 1963-68; ednl. cons. Houghton Mifflin Co., Europe, 1968-69, 1969-77, sr. mktg. mgr. Boston, 1977-87; v.p., nat. sales mgr. Riverside Pub. Co., Chgo., 1987-89; v.p., dir. mktg. McDougal, Littell & Co., Evanston, Ill., 1990-92; v.p., gen. mgr. Open Court Pub. Co., Chgo., 1992-94; pres. Peters & Green, Inc. Seminars & Bus. Devel., Chgo., 1994—. Author: WSIL: Why Should I Listen, 1987, 93, A Gadfield Memoir, 1995. Bd. dirs. Ritchie Tower Condo Assn. Recipient Svc. award Am. Arbitration Assn., 1987, Golden Reel of Excellence Internat. TV Assn., 1983. Mem. Am. Mktg. Assn., Nat. Assn. Women Bus. Owners, Internat. Reading Assn., People for Am. Way, Common Cause, Am. Arbitration Assn., Urban Gateways (bd. dirs.). Avocations: reading, fitness activities, travel, art. Home and Office: 1310 N Ritchie Ct Apt 21A Chicago IL 60610-8405 E-mail: petersgreen@att.net, rgreen3@att.net.

GREEN, SETH, actor; b. Phila., Feb. 8, 1974; Actor: (TV series) Tales from the Darkside, 1984, Amazing Stories, 1985, Spensere: For Hire, 1985, The Facts of Life, 1979, Free Spirit, 1989, Mr. Belvedere, 1985, Evening Shade, 1990, Life Goes On, 1989, The Wonder Years, 1988, Batman: The Animated Series, 1988, Beverly Hills, 90210, 1990; (TV films) The X-Files, 1993, SeaQuest DSV, 1993, Weird Science, 1994, Step by Step, 1991, Something So Right, 1996, Pearl, 1996, Mad About You, 1992, The Drew Carey Show, 1995, Cybil, 1995, Angel, 1991, Mad TV, 1995; actor, actor: (TV series) Buffy the Vampire Slayer, 1999, Whatever Happened to Robot Jones?, 2002, Jimmy Kimmel Live, 2003, That '70s Show, 1998, Punk'd, 2003, (films) The Hotel New Hampshire, 1984, Billions for Boris, 1984; (TV films) I Want to Go Home, 1985; (films) Charlie's Christmas Secret, 1985, Willy/Milly, 1986, Radio days, 1987, Can't Buy Me Love, 1987; (TV series) The Comic Strip, 1987, Action Family, 1987; (films) Big Business, 1988; (TV series) Divided We Stand, 1988; (films) My Stepmother Is An Alien, 1988, Pump Up the Volume, 1990; (TV series) It, 1990; (films) Missing Parents, 1990; (TV series) Our Shining Moment, 1991; (films) Good & Evil, 1991, Arcade, 1993, Airborne, 1993; (TV series) The Day My Parents Ran Away, 1993; (films) Ticks, 1993, The Double O Kid, 1993; (TV series) The Byrds of Paradise, 1994; (films) Notes from Underground, 1995, White Man's Burden, 1995; (TV series) Real Ghosts, 1995; (films) To Gillian on Her 37th Birthday, 1996; (TV series) Temporarily Yours, 1997; (films) Boys Life 2, 1997, Austin Powers: International Man of Mystery, 1997, Nunzio's Second Cousin, 1997; (films) Can't Hardly Wait, 1998, Enemy of the State, 1998, Batman Beyond, 1997, Family Guy, 1999; (films) Stonebrook, 1999, Idle Hands, 1999, Austin Powers: The Spy Who Shagged Me, 1999; (TV series) Batman Beyond: The Movie, 1999, 100 Deeds for Eddie McDowd, 1999; (films) Diary of a Mad Freshman, 2000, The Trumpet of the Swan, 2001, The Attic Expeditions, 2001, Josie and the Pussycats, 2001, America's Sweetheart, 2001, Rat Race, 2001, Knockaround Guys, 2001, Rock Star 101, 2001; (TV series) Greg the Bunny, 2002; (films) Austin Powers in Goldmember, 2002, Party Monster, 2003, The Italian Job, 2003. Office: United Talent Agy 9560 Wilshire Blvd Beverly Hills CA 90212*

GREEN, SHARON JORDAN, interior decorator; b. Mansfield, Ohio, Dec. 14, 1948; d. Garnet and L. Wynell (Baxley) Fraley; m. Trice Leroy Jordan Jr., Mar. 30, 1968 (dec. 1973); children: Trice Leroy III, Caerin Danielle, Christopher Robin; m. Joe Leonard Green, Mar. 13, 1978. Student, Ohio State U., 1966-67, 75-76, U. St. Thomas, 2001, Rice U., 2000—. Typist FBI, Washington, 1968; ward clk. Means Hall, Ohio State U. Hosp., Columbus, 1970; x-ray clk. Riverside Hosp., Columbus, 1971; contr., owner T&D Mold & Die, Houston, 1988—; interior decorator, franchise owner Decorating Den, Houston, 1989-91; owner T&D Interior Decorator, Houston, 1992—; custom window designer The Great Indoors, 2001—. Tchr. aide Bedford Sch., Mansfield, Ohio, 1976-77, Yeager Sch., 1981-82; pres. N.W. Welcome Wagon, Houston, 1980-81, Welcome Club, El Paso, 1986-87; active North Houston Symphony, 1992—, North Houston Performing Arts, 1993—, Mus. Fine Arts, Houston, 1993—, Edn. and Design Resource Network, 1993—, The Wellington Soc. for Arts, 1994, Jr. Forum, 1995, Rep. Nat. Com., 1995—, The Heritage Soc., 1999—; vol. Harris County Juvenile Probation Dept., 1996; chmn. N.W. Houston Symphony Student Competition, 1998-99, founding mem. The Centrum Arts League, 1998-99, mem. Ptnrs. of the Woodlands Arts Ctr., 1998-99, mem. The Shepard Sch. Music, Rice U., 1998—, Heritage Soc., Houston. Mem. United Daus. of Confederacy. Home: 15114 Marlebone Ct Houston TX 77069

GREEN, SHAWN, baseball player; b. Des Plaines, Ill., Nov. 10, 1972; Right field L.A. Dodgers, 2000—, Toronto Blue Jays, 1993—99. Office: LA Dodgers Dodge Stadium 1000 Elysian Park Ave Los Angeles CA 90012-1199

GREEN, SHIRLEY MOORE, retired public affairs and communications executive; b. Graham, Tex., Dec. 21, 1933; d. N. Edgar and Cora Day (Morrow) Moore; m. Paul M. Green, Aug. 26, 1967 (div. 1981); children: Ruth Lynn, Tracy Moore Anderson. Student, Midwestern U., Wichita Falls, Tex., 1952; BBA, U. Tex., 1956. Staff asst. Rep. Party, Austin, Tex., 1965-67; press asst. Bob Price U.S. Rep., Washington, 1967; coordinator Tex. and Ark. Bush for Pres. Campaign, Houston, 1979-80; dep. press sec. V.p. Bush, Washington, 1980-85, acting press sec., 1983; dir. pub. affairs NASA, Washington, 1985-86, dep. assoc. adminstr. communications, 1987-89; spl. asst. to the Pres. White House, Washington, 1989-92, dep. asst. to Pres., 1992; dir. Pres. Bush Transition Office, Washington, 1993; dir. program support Internat. Rep. Inst., Washington, 1993-96; dir. corr. and constituent svcs. Gov. George W. Bush, Austin, 1996-2001; dir. comm. svcs. Atty Gen. John Cornyn, 2001—03. Local chmn. Jim Baker for Atty. Gen., 1978, Pres. Ford Com., San Antonio, 1976; trustee S.W. Found. Forum, San Antonio, 1974-78; bd. dirs. Child Welfare Bd. Bexar County, 1975-79. Recipient Exceptional Svc. medal NASA, 1989. Mem.: Tex. Fedn. Rep. Women (editor Partyline mag. 1969—72, one of 10 Outstanding Rep. Women Tex. 1979). Presbyterian. Avocations: reading, traveling. Home: 1513 W 30th St Austin TX 78703-1403

GREEN, THEREASA ELLEN, elementary education educator; b. Wichita, Kans., Nov. 22, 1945; d. Ralph Elwood and Wilma Arleen (Ambler) Becker; m. Gary Joseph Fox, May 27, 1964 (dec. Dec. 1975); children: Angela Ellen, Tamara Jo; m. Bruce Green, Aug. 21, 1977 (div. 1993); 1 child, Christian Todd. BS Edn., McPherson Coll., 1968; M Elem. Edn., Wichita State U., 1987, Reading Specialist, 1990; cert. in Adminstrn., Kans. State U., 2001. Cert. tchr. elem. edn., Kans. Elem. tchr. Unified Sch Dist. 308, Hutchinson, Kans., 1969-70, 1970-72, 1972-78, 1978—; lead tchr. Unified Sch. Dist. Allen Elem., Hutchinson, 1994-98; McCandless reading specialist, 1998—2001; prin. Fairfield West Elem., Sylvia, Kans., 2001—. Cons./presenter Attention Deficit Disorder Orgn. for Parents of ADHD Children, 1994, 99; tchr. summer sch., Hutchinson, mem. curriculum coms, other coms.; ct. apptd. spl. child advocate, Reno County Kans. Cts. Author curriculum for Farm Skills for City Kids, 1986. Asst. chmn. Christian Bus. Women, Hutchinson, 1970-71; Christian edn. dir. First Christian Ch., Hutchinson, 1972-78; dir. children's ministries First Ch. of Nazarene, Hutchinson, 1993-94; Kans. self-propelled camping dir. Nat. Camper/Hikers Assn., 1978-90. Excellence grantee Southwestern Bell Telephone Co., Topeka, Kans., 1991-94; recipient scholarship Performance Learning Systems Project TEACH, 1993, others. Mem. ASCD, AAUW, Kans. Assn. Tchrs. USA Math., Internat. Reading Assn., Performance Learning Systems, Kans. Reading Assn. (sec. Reno county chpt. 1996-98), Elem. Adminstrs. of Kans., Ark Valley Reading Assn. (sec. 1996-97, 97-98, v.p. 1999—), others. Nazarene. Avocations: skiing, collecting cows and foxes, travel, working with children. Home: 602 Eldorado Dr Hutchinson KS 67502-8416 E-mail: egreen@usd310.k12.ks.us.

GREEN, THOMAS GEORGE, retired architect; b. Ackley, Iowa, July 12, 1931; s. Thomas Chalmers and Marie Angeline (Dentel) G. BA, U. Chgo., 1951, B.D., 1955; M.Arch., Yale U., 1959. Ordained to ministry United Ch. of Christ, 1955. With Architects Collaborative, 1959-65, assoc., 1964-65; ptnr. Benjamin Thompson & Assocs., architects, Cambridge, Mass., 1966-80; assoc. Wallace, Floyd, Assocs., Architects, Boston, 1981-88; commd. minister United Ch. Bd. of Homeland Ministries, 1962-69, mem. archtl. adv. panel, 1979—; prin. Benjamin Thompson & Assocs., Cambridge, Mass., 1988—2001. Vis. critic Harvard Grad. Sch. Deisgn, 1981, Yale Sch. Architecture, 1983-84 Prin. works include Greylock Residential Houses, Williams Coll., high sch., Bennington, Vt., Design Rsch. Bldg., Harvard Sch. Edn. Libr., Cambridge, music bldg. Amherst Coll., Berkshire Community Coll., Pittsfield Mass., Soldiers Field Park, Harvard U., Faneuil Hall Markets, Boston, Inter-Continental Hotels, Abu Dhabi, Al Ain, Cairo, Trinitarian Ch., Scituate, Mass., United Ch., Norwell, Mass., Custom House Docks, Dublin, Ireland, Harumi Waterfront, Tokyo, Spitalfields Market Redevel., London, Navy Pier Expn. Ctr., Chgo., J.F. Kennedy Performing Arts Ctr. Masterplan, Washington, Abasto Marketplace, Buenos Aires. Mem. Boston Zoning Commn., 1975-85, Boston Landmarks Commn., 1996—. Eliel Saarinen Traveling fellow Yale U., 1959 Fellow AIA.

GREEN, THORNTON GEORGE, software engineer; b. Ephrata, Wash., Oct. 14, 1970; BSE in Computer Systems Engring., Ariz. State U., 1993, MS in Computer Sci., 1995, PhD in Computer Sci., 1999, Rsch. asst. Ariz. State U., 1997-99, Lockheed Martin Astronautics, 2000—. Author: (computer software) GeoPad, 1996-01. Mem. Ariz. State U. Alumni Assn., Upsilon Pi Epsilon, Phi Kappa Phi, Tau Beta Pi. Avocations: painting, bicycling.

GREEN, TRACY V. financial consultant, management consultant; b. Harlem, NY, Dec. 11, 1970; d. William Elliott Green and Sharon R. Davis; m. Claude H. Boutin, Sept. 21, 1996; 1 child, Jackson M. Boutin. BA in polit. sci., Morgan State U., Md., 1992; MPA, John Jay Coll. of Criminal Justice, NYC, 1994. Cert. in fin. planning, St. John's U. NY, 1998. Tchr. August Aichhorn Residential Treatment Ctr., NY, 1992—93; sr. budget analyst Mayor's Office of Mgmt. and Budget, NYC, 1994—96; grants mgr. Grants Adminstrn. & Devel. Dept. of Health, NYC, 1996—99; cons. Accenture, NYC, 1999—2001; mgr./cons. Watson Rice, LLP, NYC, 2001—02; asst. dep. commr. Human Resources Adminstrn., NYC, 2002—. Author: (book) Twilight Moods, 2001. Avocations: sports, music, travel, writing, reading. E-mail: tgdiva@juno.com.

GREEN, TRENT JASON, football player; b. Cedar Rapids, Iowa, July 9, 1970; m. Julie Green; children: T.J., Derek Green. Degree in Bus., Ind. U. Football player San Diego Chargers, 1993, Washington Redskins, 1995—99, St. Louis Rams, 1999—2001, Kans. City Chiefs, 2001—. Established Trent Green Family Found., 1999; supporter Star Bright Rm. at Kans. Children's Mercy Hosp. Avocations: basketball, golf, hunting, fishing. Office: 1 Arrowhead Dr Kansas City MO 64129 Office Fax: 816-923-4719.

GREEN, WILLIAM, archaeologist; b. Chgo., May 30, 1953; s. David and Lillian (Kerdeman) G. AB, Grinnell Coll., 1974; MA, U. Wis., 1977, PhD, 1987. Staff archaeologist State Hist. Soc. of Wis., Madison, 1978-86; asst. prof. archaeology Western Ill. U., Macomb, 1980, 81; state archaeologist U. Iowa, Iowa City, 1988-2001, adj. asst. prof. anthropology, 1988-94, adj. assoc. prof. anthropology, 1994-2001; dir. Logan Mus. Anthropology, Beloit (Wis.) Coll., 2001—, adj. prof. anthropology, 2001—. Editor jour. The Wis. Archaeologist, 1983-88; editor: Midcontinental Jour. Archaeology, 1998-02; contbr. articles and revs. to profl. jours. Chair Johnson County Hist. Preservation Commn., Iowa, 1991-93. Grantee NSF, 1990-91, State Hist. Soc. Iowa, Leopold Ctr. for Sustainable Agr., Iowa Acad. Sci., 1988-91, 95. Fellow Am. Anthropol. Assn., Midwest Arch. Conf., Inc. (pres. 2002-). Jewish. Office: Logan Mus Anthropology Beloit Coll Beloit WI 53511

GREEN, WILLIAM H., JR., chemical engineer, educator; b. Phila., Apr. 11, 1963; s. William H. Green, Sr. and Marita Green; m. Amanda Cheetham Green, Aug. 10, 1985; children: John Emmanuel, Paul Romero, David Merton. BA with highest honors, Swarthmore Coll., 1983; PhD in Phys. Chemistry, U. Calif., Berkeley, 1988. Postdoctoral rsch. fellow Cambridge (Eng.) U., 1989—90, U. Pa., Phila., 1991; prin. investigator Exxon Rsch. and Engring., Annandale, NJ, 1991—97; asst. prof. MIT, Cambridge, Mass., 1997—2003, assoc. prof., 2003—. The Darwin Rsch. fellow Cambridge U., Darwin Coll., 1989—90. Assoc. editor: Internat. Jour. Chem. Kinetics, 2003—; contbr. articles to profl. jours. Town meeting rep. Precinct 7, Belmont, Mass., 1999—. Recipient Career award, NSF, 1999; postdoctoral fellow in chemistry, 1989, postdoctoral fellow in sci. and engring., NSF/NATO, 1989. Roman Catholic. Office: MIT Dept Chem Engring 77 Mass Ave Rm 66-270 Cambridge MA 02139

GREEN, WILLIAM PORTER, lawyer; b. Jacksonville, Ill., Mar. 19, 1920; s. Hugh Parker and Clara Belle (Hopper) G.; m. Rose Marie Hall, Oct. 1, 1944; children: Hugh Michael, Robert Alan, Richard William. BA, Ill. Coll., 1941; JD, Northwestern U., Evanston, Ill., 1947. Bar: Ill. 1947, Calif. 1948, U.S. Dist. Ct. (so. dist.) Tex. 1986, U.S. Ct. Customs and Patent Appeals, U.S. Patent and Trademark Office 1948, U.S. Ct. Appeals (fed. cir.) 1982, U.S. Ct. Appeals (5th and 9th cir.), U.S. Supreme Ct. 1948, U.S. Dist. Ct. (cen. dist.) Calif. 1949, (so. dist.) Tex.1986. Pvt. practice, L.A., 1947—; mem. Wills, Green & Mueth, L.A., 1974-83; of counsel Nilsson, Robbins, Dalgarn, Berliner, Carson & Wurst, L.A., 1984-91; of counsel Nilsson, Wurst & Green L.A., 1992—. Del. Calif. State Bar Conv., 1982—, chmn., 1986. Bd. editors Ill. Law Rev., 1946; patentee in field. Mem. L.A. world Affairs Coun., 1975—; deacon local Presbyn. Ch., 1961-63. Mem. ABA, Calif. State Bar, Am. Intellectual Property Law Assn., L.A. Patent Law Assn. (past. sec.-treas., mem. bd. govs.), Lawyers Club L.A. (past treas., past sec., mem. bd. govs., pres. 1985-86), Los Angeles County Bar Assn. (trustee 1986-87), Am. Legion (past post comdr.), Northwestern U. Alumni Club So. Calif., Big Ten Club So. Calif., Town Hall Calif. Club, PGA West Golf Club (La Quinta, Calif.), Phi Beta Kappa, Phi Delta Phi, Phi Alpha. Republican. Home: 3570 Lombardy Rd Pasadena CA 91107-5627 Office: 707 Wilshire Blvd Ste 3200 Los Angeles CA 90017-3514 E-mail: wpgreen@aol.com.

GREEN, WILLIE HAROLD, mathematician, physicist; b. Miami, Fla., Oct. 5, 1940; s. Marion and Addie (Butler) G.; m. Juanita Hall, June 4, 1966; children: Kendra Y., Katrice N. BS, U. Miami, 1967, MA, 1972; cert., USAF, 1973, 74. Electronic technician AT&T, Dade County, Fla., 1965-66; postal clk. U.S. Postal Svc., Dade County, 1966-67; mathematician Dade County Sch. Bd., 1967-72, Ann Arbor (Mich.) Sch. Bd., 1972-73, NASA/KSC, Fla., 1974-84, Applications Projects, Dade County and Brevard, Fla., 1974-87, 87—. Author: Statistics A Survey, 1984, Complex Mathematical Physics, 1988, Radiation & Exponential Decay, 1989. Mem. Cocoa (Fla.) Rockledge Civic League, 1984. With U.S. Army, 1963-67. Mem. Am. Math. Soc., Math. Assn. Am., Nat. Coun. Tchrs. Math., NAACP, Alpha Phi Alpha (dean of pledges 1981-82, cert. 1982). Democrat. Avocations: reading, tv, basketball, computer enthusiast. Home and Office: PO Box 248878 Coral Gables FL 33124-8878

GREENAGEL, DEBRA, travel agency executive; b. Beach, N.D., Aug. 13; d. Robert W. and Lucille (Booke) Taylor; m. David K. Greenagel, Sept. 11, 1976; children: Jessica, Jack. BA, Moorhead State U., 1972. Hostess Braniff Airlines, Dallas, 1973-82; acct. mgr. Talent Tree, Englewood, Colo., 1983-88; v.p. sales Corp. Travel Svcs., Englewood, 1988-91, Camelot Travel Svcs., Englewood, 1991-98; v.p. travel sales T6 Worldwide, Englewood, 1998-2000; v.p. sales and bus. devel. Rocky Mountain divsn. Navigant Internat. Mem. adv. bd. Nat. Car Rental, Mpls., 1996—, United Airlines Career Sch., Denver, 1996—. Vol. Kempe Ctr. for Battered and Abused Children, 1993-95. Mem. Nat. Bus. Execs. (pres. 1990-91), Am. Soc. Assn. Execs., Jr. League Denver, South Metro C. of C., Rocky Mountain Bus. Travel (pres. 2000—), Gamma Phi Beta. Avocations: golf, reading, cooking, walking, travel. Office: Navigant Internat 10731 E Easter Ave Ste 100 Englewood CO 80112 E-mail: dj.greenagel@rm.navigant.com.

GREENAN, THOMAS J. lawyer; b. Great Falls, Mont., July 13, 1933; s. Phil G. and Ada E. (Collins) G.; m. Helen Louise Shepard, June 1, 1957; children: Gregory, Kathleen, Timothy, Maureen, Daniel. Grad., Gonzaga U., 1955, JD, 1957. Bar: Wash. 1957, U.S. Dist. Ct. (we. dist.) Wash. 1959, U.S. Ct. Appeals (9th cir.) 1961, U.S. Supreme Ct. 1970. Asst. atty. gen. State of Washington, 1957-60, 62-63; assoc. Ferguson & Burdell (subsequently Schwabe, Williamson, Ferguson & Burdell), Seattle, 1963-68; ptnr. Ferguson & Burdell, Seattle, 1968-95, Gordon, Thomas, Honeywell, Malanca, Peterson & Daheim, Seattle, 1995—. Lectr. on antitrust and civil practice and procedure. Trustee Gonzaga U., Spokane, Wash., 1984—, chmn., 1991-92. Fellow Am. Coll. Trial Lawyers (regent 1990-93, sec. 1993-95); mem. ABA, Wash. State Bar Assn. (chmn. antitrust sect. 1980-81, chmn. disciplinary bd. 1983-84, chmn. character and fitness com. 1991-92), Seattle-King County Bar Assn., Fed. Bar Assn. (pres. we. dist. Wash. 1982-83), Am. Judicature Soc., Wash. Athletic Club, Broadmoor Golf Club (Seattle; pres. 1988-89), KC. Democrat. Roman Catholic. Office: Gordon Thomas Honeywell Malanca Peterson & Daheim 600 University St Ste 210O Seattle WA 98101-1176

GREENAWALT, PEGGY FREED TOMARKIN, advertising executive; b. Cleve., Apr. 27, 1942; d. Bernard H. and Gyta Elinor (Arsham) Freed; m. Gary Tomarkin, Aug. 7, 1966 (div. 1981); children: Craig William, Eric Lawrence; m. William Sloan Greenawalt, Oct. 31, 1987. BS, Simmons Coll., 1964. Asst. account exec. Howard Marks/Norman, Craig & Kummel, Inc., N.Y.C., 1964-66; account exec. Shaw Bros. Advt. Co., N.Y.C., 1966-67; copywriter Claire Advt. Co., N.Y.C., 1967; ptnr. Copywriters Coop., Hartsdale, N.Y., 1970-73; copy chief Howard Marks Advt., N.Y.C., 1973-80; sr. copywriter Wunderman, Ricotta & Kline, N.Y.C., 1980-82; v.p., assoc. creative dir. Ayer-Direct (N.W. Ayer), N.Y.C., 1982-84; sr. v.p. creative dir. D'Arcy Direct (D'Arcy MacManus & Masius), N.Y.C., 1984-86; pres. Tomarkin/Greenawalt, Inc., N.Y.C., 1986—. Judge Echo Awards, Caples Awards, Fin. Comm. Soc. Awards. Author: Kiss, The Real Story, 1980. Dem. dist. leader. Mem. Direct Mktg. Assn., Women in Comms., Direct Mktg. Club N.Y., Westchester Assn. Women Bus. Owners (past pres.). Office: 24 Lewis Ave Hartsdale NY 10530 E-mail: pegdirect@aol.com.

GREENAWALT, ROBERT KENT, lawyer, law educator; b. Bklyn., June 25, 1936; s. Kenneth William and Martha (Sloan) G.; m. Sanja Milic, July 14, 1968 (dec. Nov. 1988); children: Robert Milic, Alexander Kent Anton, Andrei Milenko Kenneth; m. Elaine Pagels, June 1995; children: Sarah Pagels, David. AB with honors, Swarthmore Coll., 1958; Ph.B.; Keasbey fellow, Oxford (Eng.) U., 1960; LL.B.; Kent scholar, Columbia U., 1963. Bar: N.Y. 1963. Law clk. to Justice Harlan, U.S. Supreme Ct., 1963-64; spl. asst. AID, Washington, 1964-65; mem. faculty Columbia U. Law Sch., 1965—, prof. law, 1969—, Cardozo prof., 1979—, Univ. prof., 1990—. Dep. solicitor gen. U.S., 1971-72; assoc. dir. N.Y. Inst. Legal Edn., 1969; vis. prof. Stanford U. Law Sch., 1970, Northwestern U. Law Sch., 1983, Marshall-Wythe Sch. Law, 1985, N.Y.U. Law Sch., 1989-90; atty. Lawyers Com. Civil Rights, 1965, trustee, 1992; mem. staff Task Force Law Enforcement N.Y.C., 1965; vis. fellow All Souls Coll. Oxford (Eng.) U., 1979 Co-author: The Sectarian College and The Public Purse, 1970; author: Legal Protections of Privacy, 1976, Discrimination and Reverse Discrimination, 1983, Conflicts of Law and Morality, 1987, Religious Convictions and Political Choice, 1988, Speech, Crime and the Uses of Language, 1989, Law and Objectivity, 1992, Private Consciences and Public Reasons, 1995, Fighting Words, 1995, Statutory Interpretation: Twenty Questions, 1999; editor in chief Columbia U. Law Rev., 1962-63; contbr. articles to legal jours. Recipient Ivy award Swarthmore Coll., 1958; fellow Am. Council Learned Soc., 1972-73. Fellow Am. Acad. Arts and Scis.; mem. Am. Philos. Soc., Am. Law Inst., Am. Soc. Polit. and Legal Philosophy (pres. 1992-93). Office: Columbia U Law Sch 435 W 116th St New York NY 10027-7201

GREENAWALT, WILLIAM SLOAN, lawyer; b. Bklyn., Mar. 4, 1934; s. Kenneth William and Martha Frances (Sloan) G.; m. Jane DeLano Plunkett, Aug. 17, 1957 (div. May 1986); m. Peggy Ellen Freed Tomarkin, Oct. 31, 1987; children: John DeLano, David Sloan, Katherine Downs. AB, Cornell U., 1956; LLB, Yale U., 1961. Bar: N.Y. 1962, U.S. Dist. Ct. (so and ea. dists.) N.Y. 1962, U.S. Ct. Apls. (2d cir.) 1962, U.S. Supreme Ct. 1966. Assoc. Sullivan & Cromwell, N.Y.C., 1961-65; N.E. regional legal svcs. dir. U.S. Office Econ. Opportunity, N.Y.C., 1965-68; assoc. Rogers & Wells, N.Y.C., 1968-69, ptnr.,

1969-77, sr. ptnr., 1977-81, Halperin, Shivitz, Eisenberg, Schneider & Greenawalt, N.Y.C., 1981-86, Eisenberg Honig Fogler Greenawalt & Davis, N.Y.C., 1986-91, Bangser Klein Rocca & Blum, N.Y.C., 1991-93, Loselle Greenawalt Kaplan Blair & Adler, N.Y.C., 1993-97, Loselle Greenawalt Kaplan & Blair, N.Y.C., 1997-99, Meyer Greenawalt Taub & Wild, LLP, N.Y.C., 1999-2001; pvt. practice N.Y.C., 2001—. Lectr. in field. Bd. editors: Yale Law Jour., 1959-61; contbr. articles in field to profl. jours. Chmn. bd. dirs. Applied Resources, Inc., N.Y.C., 1968-70; chmn. Cmty. Aid Employment of Ex-Offenders, Westchester, N.Y., 1971; pres. Westchester Legal Svcs., 1971-74, bd. dirs., 1975-91; mem. N.Y. State Gov.'s Task Force on Elem. and Secondary Edn., 1974-75; mem. Pres. Carter's Task Force on Criminal Justice, 1976; adv. coun. N.Y. State Senate Dems., 1978—; asst. and acting treas. N.Y. State Dem. Party, 1990-96, vice chair, 1996-2000, 9th jud. dist. rep. 2002—, state com., 1974—, exec. com. 1990-2000, 02—; chair Greenburgh Dem. Party, 1997-2002; mem. Greenburgh Recreation Commn., 1976-83, Dem. Statewide Spl. Commn. on Polit. Ethics, 1986-87, Statewide Spl. Commn. on Election Law and Campaign Spending Reform, 1989-95; pres. Westchester Crime Victims Assistance Agy., 1981-82; commr. Taconic State Pks., Recreation and Hist. Preservation Commn., 1984-96, chmn., 1989-96; vice chmn. N.Y. State Coun. on Pks., Recreation and Hist. Preservation, 1989-94; moderator Scarsdale Congl. Ch., 1988-90; mem. Westchester County Parks, Recreation and Conservation Bd., 1998—, vice chmn., 1999—; mem. Westchester County Execs. Transition Team on Planning, 1997. Lt. comdr. USN, 1956-58, with Res., 1961-68. Fellow N.Y. Bar Found.; mem. ABA, Am. Arbitration Assn. (mem. panel comml. arbitrators 1977—), N.Y. State Bar Assn. (chmn. com. on availability of legal svcs. 1968-70, chmn. action unit 3 1979-81, chmn. spl. commn. on alternatives to jud. resolution of disputes 1981-85), Assn. of Bar of City of N.Y., Nat. Legal Aid and Defenders Assn., Sphinx Head, Aleph Samach, County Tennis Club Westchester (Scarsdale, N.Y., pres. 1979-80), Yale Club, Phi Alpha Delta, Chi Psi. Democrat. Congregationalist. Home: 24 Lewis Ave Hartsdale NY 10530 Office: Law Offices William S Greenawalt 230 Park Ave Ste 2525 New York NY 10169-0199 E-mail: wsgreenawalt@aol.com.

GREENAWAY, JOSEPH ANTHONY, JR., judge; b. London, Nov. 16, 1957; came to U.S., 1959; s. Joseph Anthony Sr. and Brucel May (Lynch) G.; m. Veronica Blake, May 24, 1981; children: Joseph Anthony III, Samantha Blake. BA in History, Columbia U., 1978; JD, Harvard U., 1981. Law clk. to Hon. Vincent L. Broderick U.S. Dist. Ct. (so. dist.) N.Y., N.Y.C., 1982-83; lawyer Kramer, Levin, Nessen, Kamin & Frankel, N.Y.C., 1981-82, 83-85; chief narcotics divsn., asst. U.S. atty. Dept. Justice, Newark, 1985-90; in-house counsel Johnson & Johnson, New Brunswick, N.J., 1990-96; dist. judge U.S. Dist. Ct., Newark, 1996—; adj. prof. Rutgers Law Sch., 2002—. Weintraub lectr. Rutgers U. Law Sch., 1998. Presenter in field. Past sec. Columbia U. Alumni Assn., bd. dirs., N.Y.C.; bd. dirs. Columbia U. Nat. Coun.; chair Columbia Coll. Black Alumni Coun. Named Minority Achiever of Yr. East Orange YMCA, 1997; recipient proclamation Newark City Coun., 1990, medal of excellence Columbia U., 1997. John Jay award Columbia U., 2003; Earl Warren Legal scholar. Mem. ABA, Nat. Bar Assn., Garden State Bar Assn., Fed. Judges Assn., Am. Corp. Counsel Assn. (Disting. Svc. award 1997), Columbia Coll. Alumni Assn. Avocation: golf. Office: Martin Luther King Jr Fed Bldg PO Box 999 Newark NJ 07101-0999

GREENBACKER, JOHN EVERETT, retired lawyer and naval officer; b. Meriden, Conn., Oct. 4, 1917; s. Charles and Isabel Alice Francis G.; m. Carolyn Robertson Perrow, July 25, 1942; children: Susan Oller, John E. Jr., Florence Arnold, Christopher F. Student, U. Conn., 1935-36; BS, U.S. Naval Acad., 1940; JD, Georgetown U., 1949, LLM, 1969; MA, U.S. Naval War Coll., George Washington U., 1964. Bar: D.C. 1949, Md. 1970, Va. 1976, U.S. Dist. Ct. (we. dist.) Va. 1979. Commd. ensign U.S. Navy, 1940, advanced through grades to capt., 1960, comdg. officer subchaser, 1942-43, comdg. officer destroyer escorts, 1943-46, comdg. officer destroyer, 1955-57, comdg. officer attack transport, 1962-63, comdr. destroyer div. 262, 1961-62, comdr. destroyer squadron 6, 1965-66, ret., 1969; sr. atty. legal dept. Balt. Gas & Electric Co., 1969-72, mem. finance dept., 1972-74, treas., 1974-76; practice law Halifax, Va., 1976-94; estate planning cons., 1994—. Home: 4185 Grubby Rd Halifax VA 24558-2425

GREENBAUM, FRED, historian, educator; b. Bklyn., Nov. 6, 1930; s. David and Rose Greenbaum; m. Ann T. Corsini, May 3, 1954; children: Jonathan, Theodore. BA, Bklyn. Coll., 1952; AM, U. Wis., 1953; PhD, Columbia U., 1962. Lectr. Bklyn. Coll., 1957—60, Queens Coll., Flushing, NY, 1960—61; asst. prof. history Queens Borough C.C., Bayside, NY, 1962—64, assoc. prof. history, 1965—70, prof. history, 1971—2000, prof. history emeritus, 2001—. Del. Profl. Staff Congress Am. Fedn. Tchrs., NY, 1975—2000; mem. exec. com. faculty senate City U., N.Y.C., 1975—2000; Profl. Staff Congress chpt. chair Queens Borough C.C., N.Y.C., 1975—2001. Author: Fighting Progress: Edward P. Costiean, 1971, Robert Marion La Follette, 1975, Men Against Myths: The Progressive Response, 2000. County committeeman Nassau County Dem. Party, Garden City, NY, 1970—90, candidate N.Y. State Senate, 1984, 1986. With U.S. Army, 1953—54. Avocations: theater, camping, swimming. Home: 180 West End Ave #21M New York NY 10023

GREENBAUM, JAMES RICHARD, liquor distributing company executive, real estate developer; b. Cleve., July 3, 1933; s. Harold and Miriam (Lion) G.; m. Peggy Strauss, Jan. 29, 1955; children: Robert Strauss, James R., Clifford Harold. BA, Tulane U., 1955. V.p. Strauss Distbrs., Ark., 1961—. Bd. dirs. S&D Realty, Little Rock. Bd. dirs. Jewish Fedn. Palm Springs, Betty Ford Ctr., Rancho Mirage, Calif. Lt. U.S. Army, 1955-57. Mem. Beaver Creek Club (Colo.), Tamarisk Club (Rancho Mirage, Calif.), Country Club of Rockies (Vail, Colo.), Club at Morningside (Rancho Mirage), Tamarisk Country Club, Zeta Beta Tau. Jewish (past pres., bd. dirs. temple). Office: 1 Hawkeye Pk 69844 US Highway 111 Ste H Rancho Mirage CA 92270-2849

GREENBAUM, JEFFREY ALAN, lawyer; b. Ft. Benning, Ga., Feb. 9, 1968; s. Thomas L. and Rosalie (Montag) Greenbaum. BA summa cum laude, Brandeis U., Waltham, Mass., 1990; JD, Columbia U., N.Y.C., 1993. Bar: NY 1994, U.S. Dist. Ct. (so. and ea. dists.) NY 1995. Assoc. Paul, Weiss, Rifkind, Wharton & Garrison, N.Y.C., 1993-97, Frankfurt, Kurnit, Klein & Selz, N.Y.C., 1997-2000, ptnr., 2001—. Harlan Fiske Stone scholar Columbia U., N.Y.C., 1991-93. Mem. ABA (consumer protection com.), Assn. Bar of City of N.Y. (chair com. on consumer affairs), Phi Beta Kappa. Office: Frankfurt Kurnit Klein & Selz 488 Madison Ave Fl 9 New York NY 10022-5754

GREENBAUM, MAURICE COLEMAN, lawyer; b. Detroit, Apr. 3, 1918; s. Henry and Eva (Klayman) G.; m. Beatrice Wiener, June 28, 1942. BA, Wayne State U., 1938; JD, U. Mich., 1941; LLM, NYU, 1947. Bar: Mich. 1941, N.Y. 1947, Conn. 1948. Assoc. Herman H. Copelon, New Haven, 1948—50, Greenbaum, Wolff & Ernst, N.Y.C., 1950—54, ptnr., 1955—82, Katten, Muchin, Zavis & Rosenman (formerly Rosenman & Colin, LLP), N.Y.C., 1982—91, counsel, 1991—. Mem. vis. com. U. Miami Sch. Marine and Atmospheric Sci.; mem. adv. com. Great Neck Sr. Citizen Ctr.; mem. adv. com. Helen Merrill Fund; bd. dirs. Humanity in Action, Rosenstiel Found., Mandeville Found., World Rehab. Fund. Co-author: Estate Tax Techniques; grad. editor Tax Law Rev., 1946-47. Village Justice, Kings Point, N.Y., 1985—; assoc. trustee North Shore U. Hosp., Manhasset, N.Y.; bd. trustees N.Y. Found., 1967-83. Served to maj. U.S. Army, 1941-45. Democrat. Jewish. Home: 24 Cow Ln Kings Point NY 11024-1517 Office: Katten Muchin Zavis and Rosemman & Rosenman 575 Madison Ave 11th Fl New York NY 10022-2585

GREENBAUM, SHELDON MARC, lawyer; b. Bklyn., July 1, 1950; s. Emil and Edith (Greenbaum) G.; m. Susan M. Weisberg, May 27, 1971; children—Diana, Elizabeth. B.S. magna cum laude, NYU, 1971, J.D., 1974. Bar: N.Y. 1975, U.S. Dist. Ct. (so. and ea. dists.) N.Y. 1975, U.S. Ct. Appeals (2d cir.) 1975, U.S.Ct. Appeals (fed. cir.) 1987, U.S. Ct. Internat. Trade 1986, U.S. Supreme Ct. 1978. Law clk. Parker, Chapin, Flattau & Klimpl, N.Y.C., 1968-70; litigation atty., 1974-77; acct. Berkowitz & Brody, N.Y.C., 1971-72; asst. controller WaSko Gold Products Corp., N.Y.C., 1972-73; litigation atty. Hess, Segall, Guterman, Pelz & Steiner, N.Y.C., 1978-81; ptnr. Goldman and Greenbaum, P.C., N.Y.C., 1981-84, Goldman, Greenbaum & Milner, P.C., N.Y.C., 1984-86, Goldman & Greenbaum, P.C., N.Y.C., 1986—; adj. asst. prof. law Grad. Sch. Bus. Adminstrn. and Coll. Bus. and Pub. Adminstrn., NYU, 1978-83. Mem. bd. appeals Village of Port Washington North, N.Y., 1980-88, chmn., 1989—. Served with USAR, 1970-76. Mem. ABA, N.Y. State Bar Assn., Assn. Bar City NY. Home: 89 Radcliff Ave Port Washington NY 11050-1616 Office: Goldman & Greenbaum PC 60 E 42nd St New York NY 10165-0006 E-mail: shellyegg@aol.com.

GREENBAUM, STUART I. economist, educator; b. N.Y.C., Oct. 7, 1936; s. Sam and Bertha (Freimark) G.; m. Margaret E. Wache, July 29, 1964; children: Regina Gail, Nathan Carl. BS, NYU, 1959; PhD, Johns Hopkins U., 1964. Fin. economist Fed. Res. Bank of Kansas City, Mo., 1962-66; sr. economist Office of the Comptroller of the Currency, Washington, 1966-67; assoc. prof. econs. U. Ky., Lexington, 1968-74, prof., 1974-76, chmn. dept. econs., 1975-76; vis. prof. fin. Kellogg Grad. Sch. Mgmt., Northwestern U., Evanston, Ill., 1974-75, prof. fin., 1976-78, Harold L. Stuart prof. banking and fin., 1978-83, Norman Strunk disting. prof. fin. instns., 1983-95, dir. Banking Research Ctr., 1976-95, assoc. dean for acad. affairs, 1988-92; dean John M. Olin Sch. of Bus. Washington U., St. Louis, 1995—, Bank of Am. prof. mgrl. leadership, John M. Olin Sch. bus., 2000—. Cons. Fed. Res. Bank Chgo., 1994-95; mem. Fed. Savs. and Loan Adv. Coun., 1986-89; vis. prof. banking and fin. Leon Recanati Grad. Sch. Bus. Adminstrn., Tel Aviv (Israel) U., 1980-81. Assoc. editor Nat. Banking Rev., 1966-67, So. Econ. Jour., 1977-79, Jour. Fin., 1977-83, Jour. Banking and Fin., 1980-92, Jour. Fin. Rsch., 1981-87, Fin. Rev., 1985-89, Managerial and Decision Econs., 1989-94, Jour. Econs., Mgmt. and Strategy, 1991-95; founding and mng. editor Jour. Fin. Intermediation, 1989-96. With U.S. Army, 1958-64. Mem. Am. Econ. Assn., Am. Fin. Assn. Office: Washington U Campus Box 1133 One Brookings Dr Saint Louis MO 63130-4899 E-mail: greenbaum@olin.wwtl.edu.

GREENBERG, AARON ROSMARIN, public relations executive; b. Bklyn., July 5, 1932; s. J. George and Etta (Rosmarin) G.; m. Felice Barmash, June 29, 1958; children: Beth Susan, Marc David. BA in Journalism, Emory U., 1954; MS in Journalism, Columbia U., 1955; postgrad., NYU, 1964-65. Editor Fairchild Pubs., N.Y.C., 1955-56; account exec. Ruder & Finn, Inc., N.Y.C., 1958-61, dir. research, 1963-72; dir. pub. Yeshiva U., N.Y.C., 1961-62; dir. research Am. Stock Exchange, N.Y.C., 1972; v.p. William G. Hetherington & Co., Newark, 1973-78; pres. Livingston (N.J.) Pub. Relations, Inc., 1978—. Instr. Fairleigh-Dickinson U., Madison, N.J., 1980-81; sports corr. West Essex Tribune, Livington, N.J., 1981-92. Contbg. editor Book of Knowledge, Ency. Britannica. Mem. adv. commn. on Cable TV, Livingston, 1978-81, adv. commn. on energy, Livingston, 1981-83, adv. commn. transp., Livingston, 1983-85; chmn. adv. council parks & recreation, Livingston, 1985—. Served to sgt. U.S. Army, 1956-58. Mem. Livingston C. of C. (dir.). Jewish. Avocation: high school and amateur sports officiating. Office: Livingston Pub Rels Inc PO Box 82 Livingston NJ 07039-0082

GREENBERG, ALBERT, art director; b. N.Y.C., Mar. 15, 1924; s. Samuel David and Mary (Miller) G.; m. Marilyn Hoffner, May 29, 1949; children: Doren Roe, Peter Cooper. BFA, Cooper Union, 1948. Art editor Gentry, Am. Fabric Mags., N.Y.C., 1951-56; art dir. Gentlemen's Quar. Mag., Esquire, Inc., N.Y.C., 1956-70; sales promotion art dir. Lampert Agy., N.Y.C., 1970-71; v.p., sales promotion art dir. Wells Rich Greene Inc., N.Y.C., 1971-83; chmn. dept. comms. design Parsons Sch. Design, N.Y.C., 1983-94. Tchr. Pratt Inst., 1964-65, 73-74, Cooper Union, 1967-68, Finch Coll., 1973-75, Manhattanville Coll., 1974-75, Parsons Sch. Design, 1975-82. Contbg. editor: Typographic Directions, 1964, Advertising Directions, Photography, 1962, Advertising Directions, Visual Advertising, 1961. Trustee Cooper Union, 1979-82. Served with USAAF, 1943-45, ETO. Decorated air medal with silver oak leaf cluster; recipient more than 100 profl. awards, including Gold Medal, Art Dirs. Club, 1979, Pres.'s citation for profl. achievement Cooper Union, 1982; named Alumnus of Yr., Cooper Union, 1968. Mem. Art Dirs. Club N.Y. (designer 43d ann.), Cooper Union Alumni Coun. (1st v.p. 1970-71, pres. 1971-73).

GREENBERG, ALLAN, advertising and marketing research consultant; b. N.Y.C., Dec. 8, 1917; s. Solomon and Rose (Honik) G.; m. Rosalie Katz, Nov. 7, 1943; children— Barbara L. Gutman, Roy J. BS, CCNY, 1942; postgrad., U. Wis., 1944, New Sch. for Social Research, 1946-54. Assoc. Psychol. Corp., N.Y.C., 1937-38; research analyst Serutan, Inc., Jersey City, 1939-41; research mgr./asst. dir. research Grey Advt., Inc., N.Y.C., 1948-55; sr. v.p., dir. research and planning Doyle Dane Bernbach, Inc., N.Y.C., 1955-74; research cons. to advt. agys. and mfrs., 1974—. Former chmn. tech. rsch. com. Advt. Rsch. Found.; former pres. joint coun. Empire Blue Cross/Blue Shield-HMO. Author: (with Mary Joan Glynn) A Study of Young People; booklet, 1966; contbr. articles to profl. jours. Former pres. mems. coun. Cmty. Health Program Queens-Nassau; mem. Profls. and Execs. in Retirement Group at Hofstra U. With AUS, 1942-45. Mem.: B'nai Zion (past mem. nat. exec. bd.; past pres. L.I. region). Home and Office: 5333 Zelzah Ave Apt 140 Encino CA 91316-2207 E-mail: agreen3102@aol.com.

GREENBERG, ARLINE FRANCINE, artist, photographer; b. N.Y.C. m. Sidney Greenberg. BA, Hunter Coll.; postgrad., NYU; AS, Parson Sch. Design, Pratt Inst. Ind. practice cons. firm in jewelry and design; v.p. Reliable Textile Co., N.Y.C.; fashion dir. Burlington Klopman Fabrics, N.Y.C., 1988-92. Guest lectr. AWED and F.I.T. Contbr. fashion articles to newspapers. Recipient Medal in Fine Arts; scholar NYU. Mem.: Citizens Union, Opera Guild, Smithsonian, Met. Mus. Art, Preservation Soc., Victorian Soc. N.Y.C. Avocations: travel, art, architecture, opera, music. Home: 555 Kappock St Apt 15D Bronx NY 10463-6458

GREENBERG, ARTHUR, dean, chemist; b. Bklyn., Sept. 27, 1946; s. Murray and Bella Eta Greenberg; m. Susan Joan Covici; children: David, Rachel. PhD, Princeton U., 1971. From asst. to assoc. prof. Frostburg (Md.) State Coll., 1972—77; from asst. to assoc. to full prof. N.J. Inst. Tech., Newark, 1977—89; prof. Rutgers U., New Brunswick, NJ, 1989—94; prof., chemistry chair U. N.C., Charlotte, 1994—2000; dean, prof. chemistry U. N.H., Durham, 2000—. Editor Structural Chemistry, N.Y.C., 1989—. Author: (book) Strained Organic Molecules, 1978, A Chemical History Tour, 2000, The Art of Chemistry, 2003. Capt. Med. Svc. Corps USAR, 1972—81. Mem.: Am. Chem. Soc. Office: U NH Kingsbury Hall Durham NH 03824 Office Fax: 603-862-2486. Business E-Mail: art.greenberg@unh.edu.

GREENBERG, BARBARA LEVENSON, literature educator, poet; b. Boston, Aug. 27, 1932; d. Louis B Levenson, Esther Harrison Levenson; m. Harold L Greenberg; children: David A, Russell S. BA, Wellesley Coll., 1953; MA, Simmons Coll., 1973. Faculty MFA writing program Goddard Coll., Plainfield, Vt., 1976—80; faculty, mem. adv. bd. Warren Wilson MFA Program for Writers, Swannanoah, NC, 1981—83; faculty writing program MIT, Cambridge, Mass., 1988—90; sr. lectr. Suffolk U., Boston, 1998—2000; affiliated scholar Brandeis U. Women's Studies Rsch. Ctr., Waltham, 2000—. Author: (poems) The Spoils of August, 1974, The Never Not Sonnets, 1989, What Nell Knows, 1997, (short stories) Fire Drills, 1982.

GREENBERG, BARRY MICHAEL, talent executive; b. Bklyn., Nov. 9, 1951; s. Aaron Herbert and Alice Rhoda (Strauss) G.; m. Susan Kay Greenberg, Feb. 19, 1990; 1 child, Samuel Jacob; 1 child by previous marriage: Seth Grahame-Smith. BA, Antioch U. Dir. B'nai B'rith, Phila., 1976-80; acting dir. Jewish Nat. Fund, L.A., 1980-81; chmn. Celebrity Connection, L.A., 1981—. Co-founder Beverly Hills Air Force Co.; adj. faculty U. So. Calif. Annenberg Sch. Journalism. Emeritus mem. Air Force adv. bd. USAF; Wilshire cmty. police adv. bd. L.A. Police Dept.; fin. co-chair, past chair Cmty.-Police Adv. Bd. Summit; 50th Anniversary of WWII com. U.S. Dept. Def.; pub. safety steering com. L.A. 4th Councilmanic Dist.; exec. bd. CDC Bus. Responds to AIDS program; co-founder Windsor Watch; adv. bd. Windsor Sq. Assn.; charter past pres. entertainment industry unit B'nai B'rith; past pres. Temple Israel of Hollywood Men's Club, v.p.; bd. mgrs. Hollywood-Wilshire YMCA; treas. Fuller Av. Sr. Housing. Recipient Chief of Chaplains Meritorious Svc. award, USAF. Mem. Def. Orientation Conf. Assn., Air Force Pub. Affairs Alumni Assn. Jewish. Avocations: pilot, music. Office: Celebrity Connection 4311 Wilshire Blvd # 300 Los Angeles CA 90010-3713 E-mail: info@celebconn.com.

GREENBERG, BERNARD, entomologist, educator; b. N.Y.C., Apr. 24, 1922; s. Isidore and Rose (Gordon) G.; m. Barbara Muriel Dickler, Sept. 1, 1949; children: Gary, Linda, Deborah, Daniel. BA, Bklyn. Coll., 1944; MA, U. Kans., 1951, PhD, 1954. Asst. prof. biology U. Ill. Med. Center, Chgo., 1954-61, assoc. prof., 1961-66, prof. Geophys. Scis., 1966-90, prof. emeritus, 1990—. Vis. sci. Istituto Superiore di Sanitá, Rome, 1960-61, Fulbright-Hays sr. research scholar, 1967-68; vis. sci. Instituto de Salubridad y Enfermedades Tropicales, Mexico City, 1962, 63; cons. in field; cons., expert witness in forensic entomology; pres. Bioconcern; nat. lectr. Sigma Xi Hon. Sci. Rsch. Soc., 1996—. Author: Flies and Disease, vol. 1, 1971, Flies and Disease, vol. 2, 1973, Entomology and the Law: Flies as Forensic Indicators, 2002; contbr. articles. Pvt. USAF, 1944—46. NSF grantee, 1959-60, 79-81; NIH grantee, 1960-67; U.S. Army Med. Research and Devel. Command grantee, 1966-72, 85; Electric Power Research Inst. grantee, 1976-85; Office Naval Research grantee, 1977-78. Fellow AAAS; mem. Entomol. Soc. Am., Chgo. Acad. Sci. (sci. gov. 1981—), Home: 1463 E 55th Pl Chicago IL 60637-1875 Office: Dept Biol Scis M/C 066 U Ill Chgo Chicago IL 60607 E-mail: bugaboo@uic.edu.

GREENBERG, BRADLEY SANDER, communications educator; b. Toledo, Aug. 3, 1934; s. Abraham and Florence (Cohen) G.; m. Delight Thompson, June 7, 1959; children: Beth, Shawn, Debra. BA in Journalism; Univ. scholar, Bowling Green State U., 1956; MS in Journalism; Univ. fellow, U. Wis., 1957, PhD in Mass Communication, 1961. Postdoctoral fellow Mass. Comms. Rsch. Ctr., 1960-61; research asso. Inst. Communication Research, Stanford U., 1961-64; asst. prof. Mich. State U., East Lansing, 1964-66, assoc. prof., 1966-71, prof. dept. communication, 1971—, Univ. Disting. prof., 1990, chmn. dept., 1977-84, prof. telecommunication, 1975—, chmn. dept., 1984-90. Vis. prof. U. Ga., Athens, 1999, U. Calif., Berkeley, 1992; fellow Ctrs. Disease Control and Prevention, Atlanta, 1999; sr. fellow East-West Ctr., Comms. Inst., Honolulu, 1978-79, 81; rsch. fellow Ind. Broadcasting Authority, London, 1985-86; cons. Pres.'s Commn. on Causes and Prevention Violence, 1968-69, Surgeon Gen.'s Sci. Adv. Com. on TV and Social Behavior, 1970-72, 82. Author: The Kennedy Assassination and the American Public: Social Communication in Crisis, 1965, Use of Mass Media by the Urban Poor, 1970, Life on Television, 1980, Mexican Americans and the Mass Media, 1983, Cableviewing, 1988, Teletext in the U.K., 1988, Mass Media, Sex and the Adolescent, 1993, Desert Storm and the Mass Media, 1993, The Alphabet Soup of TV Ratings, 2001, Communication and Terrorism, 2003. Served to maj. U.S. Army Res., 1973. Recipient Chancellors award for disting. svc. in journalism U. Wis., 1978, disting. faculty award Mich. State U., 1979; named to Journalism Hall of Fame Bowling Green State U., 1980; rsch. grantee NIH, NSF, USPHS, Carnegie Corp., Hoso Bunka Found., Nat. Assn. Broadcasters. Fellow Internat. Comm. Assn. (pres. 1994-95); mem. Assn. for Edn. in Journalism, Phi Kappa Phi (pres. 1993-94). Home: 350 Winterberry Ln Okemos MI 48864-4166 Office: Mich State U Dept Telecommunication 477 Communication Arts Sci East Lansing MI 48824-1212 E-mail: bradg@msu.edu.

GREENBERG, BYRON STANLEY, newspaper and business executive, consultant; b. Bklyn., June 17, 1919; s. Albert and Bertha (Getleson) G.; m. Helena Marks, Feb. 10, 1946; children: David, Eric, Randy. Student, Bklyn. Coll., 1936-41. Circulation mgr. N.Y. Post, 1956-62, circulation dir., 1962-63, bus. mgr., 1963-72, gen. mgr., COO, 1973-79; sec., dir. N.Y. Post Corp., 1966-75, treas., dir., 1975-76, v.p., 1976-81. V.p., dir. Leisure Systems, Inc., 1978-80; pres., chief exec. officer, dir. Games Mgmt. Services, Inc., 1979-80 Bd. dirs. 92d St YMHA, 1970-71, Friars Nat. Found., 1981-82. Served with AUS, 1942-45. Mem. Friars Club. Home and Office: 2560 S Grade Rd Alpine CA 91901-3612

GREENBERG, CAROLYN PHYLLIS, anesthesiologist, educator; b. San Francisco, July 7, 1941; AB, Stanford U., 1962; MD, U. Calif., San Francisco, 1966. Diplomate Am. Bd. Anesthesiology. Rotating intern L.A. County Hosp., 1966-67; resident in anesthesiology Presbyn. Hosp., N.Y.C., 1967-69, vis. fellow in anesthesiology, 1969-70, asst. attending anesthesiologist, 1971-90, assoc. attending anesthesiologist, 1990-99, med. dir. ambulatory surgery, 1986-96, attending anesthesiologist, 1999; asst. attending anesthesiologist N.Y. Hosp., 1970-71; attending anesthesiologist N.Y. Presbyn. Hosp., 1999—. Instr. anesthesiology Cornell Med. Sch., 1970—71; assoc. anesthesiology Columbia U., N.Y.C., 1971—74, asst. prof. clin. anesthesiology, 1974—90, assoc. prof. clin. anesthesiology, 1990—99, prof. clin. anesthesiology, 1999; clin. prof. emerita anesthesiology Cornell Med. Sch., 1999—, prof. emerita, 1999. Contbr. book chpts., articles to profl. jours. Mem. Am. Soc. Anesthesiologists, N.Y. State Soc. Anesthesiologists (Media award 1992), Med. Soc. N.Y., Soc. Ambulatory Anesthesia (treas. 1994-98, 2nd v.p. 1998-99, 1st v.p. 1999, Ambulatory Anesthesia Rsch. Found. award 1992), Malignant Hyperthermia Assn. of U.S. (hotline cons. 1983-99, partnership award 1996). Jewish. Avocations: swimming, reading, piano, travel. E-mail: agfbogie@aol.com.

GREENBERG, DANIEL, electronics rental company executive; b. Mpls., May 14, 1941; s. Mayer and Ruth G.; m. Susan L. Steinhauser, Oct. 19, 1985. BA, Reed Coll., 1962; JD, U. Chgo., 1965. Staff atty. State of Calif. Dept. Water Resources, 1965-67; various positions, then pres., ceo Telecor, Inc., 1967-79; with Electro Rent Corp., Van Nuys, Calif., 1973—, chmn., chief exec. officer, 1979—. Former mem. U.S./Mex. Counsultive Group. Trustee Reed Coll., chmn., 2002--; trustee Nat. Pub. Radio Found.; former mem. visiting com. U. Chgo. Law Sch.; former mem. adv. com. Dept. Commerce, Fgn. Comml. Svc. Mem. Am. Bus. Conf. (charter, past bd. dirs.), Earthjustice(chmn. 1991-94), Bus. Execs. for Nat. Security. Office: Electro Rent Corp 6060 Sepulveda Blvd Van Nuys CA 91411-2512

GREENBERG, DANIEL HERBERT, lawyer; b. N.Y.C., Dec. 30, 1919; s. Moses Bernard and Sadye (Saltzman) G.; m. Jane Marian Frank, Jan. 22, 1943 (div. Apr. 1964); 1 child, Stanley Frank (dec.); m. Patricia Joy Williams, Aug. 29, 1964 (div. Jan. 1975); children: Dale Jeremy, Jason Bernard, Andrea Elizabeth, Nicole Victoria. BA, U. Wis., 1941; JD, Columbia U., 1947. Bar: N.Y. 1947, U.S. Supreme Ct. 1953, D.C. 1957. Asst. U.S. atty. U.S. Dept. Justice, N.Y.C., 1949-53; pvt. practice, N.Y.C., 1953—; spl. commr. in admiralty U.S. Dist. Ct. (so. dist.) N.Y., 1959-64. Guest lectr. in trial practice Columbia Law Sch., 1965-66. Lt. col. USAF and Res., 1941-79, World War II, Korea. Decorated Disting. Flying Cross, Air medal with three clusters, eight battle stars, Disting. Unit citation with one cluster, Cert. of Valor, 15th Air Force, Italy, 1944. Democrat. Jewish. Home: 77 Renchy St Fairfield CT 06430-4129 Office: 36 W 44th St Ste 1206 New York NY 10036-8102

GREENBERG, DANIEL LAWRENCE, lawyer; b. Bklyn., Oct. 14, 1945; s. Irving and Beatrice (Rabinowitz) G.; m. Karen R. Nelson, Apr. 4, 1987; children: Ilana Nelson-Greenberg, Mara Nelson-Greenberg. BA, Bklyn. Coll., 1966; JD, Columbia U., 1969; Hon. Fellow, U. Pa. Law Sch., 1996. Elem. tchr. N.Y.C. Pub. Sch. 208, 1969-71; atty. MFY Legal Svcs., N.Y.C., 1971-73, mng. atty., 1973-87; dir. clin. edn. Harvard U. Law Sch., Cambridge, Mass., 1987-94; pres./atty.-in-chief The Legal Aid Soc., N.Y.C., 1994—. Bd. visitors CUNY Law Sch., Queens, 1989—, Columbia Law Sch., 1995—, Boston Coll. Law Sch., 1996—; Sibley lectr. U. Ga. Sch. Law, 1999. Contbr. guest editls. N.Y. Times, Daily News, 1989-97. Mem bd. advisors The Workplace Project, Hempstead, N.Y., 1995—, Programs on the Legal Profession of the Open Soc. Inst., 1997-2000, Stein ethics program, Fordham Law Sch., 1996—; mem. selection panel Root-Tilden Project NYU Law Sch., 1997. Recipient First Ann. Pub. Interest Honoree award Columbia U. Law Sch., 1991, Disting. Pub. Interest Lawyer in Residence award Touro Coll. Sch. of Law, 1998, Emory Buckner award for pub. svc. Fed. Bar Coun. 2002. Mem. Nat. Lawyers Guild (pres. NYC chpt. 1985-87, Ann. award 2001), Assn. of the Bar of the City of N.Y., N.Y. County Lawyers, N.Y. State Bar Assn. Dem. Jewish. Home: 38 Montgomery Pl Brooklyn NY 11215-2324 Office: Legal Aid Soc 1 Battery Park Plaza New York NY E-mail: dgreenberg@legal-aid.org.

GREENBERG, DAVID, columnist, historian, educator; b. Boston, Aug. 8, 1968; s. Robert Sidney and Maida Jablon Greenberg; m. Suzanne Nossel, Nov. 9, 2003. BA in History, Yale U., 1990; MA in History, Columbia U., 1996, MPhil in History, 1998, PhD in History, 2001. Asst./collaborator Bob Woodward/Wash. Post, Wash., DC, 1991—94; mng. editor The New Rep., Wash., DC, 1994—95, acting editor, 1996; culture editor Slate Mag., NYC, 1996—98, columnist, 1998—. Vis. asst. prof., dept. of history Columbia U., 2001—02; vis. scholar Am. Acad. of Arts & Sci., 2002—03. Author: (book) Nixon's Shadow: The History of an Image, 2003; asst.: book The Agenda: Inside the Clinton White House, 1994; contbr. numerous articles and reviews for popular scholarly pubs. Recipient Whiting prize, Mrs. Giles R. Whiting

Found., 2000; grantee de Karman fellowship, Josephine de Karman Found. Mem.: Orgn. of Am. Historians, Coun. of Fgn. Rels., Am. Hist. Assn. Democrat. Jewish. Office: Am Acad of Arts & Sci 136 Irving St Cambridge MA 02138

GREENBERG, DAVID BERNARD, chemical engineering educator; b. Norfolk, Va., Nov. 2, 1928; s. Abraham David and Ida (Frenkil) G.; m. Helen Muriel Levine, Aug. 15, 1959 (div. Aug. 1980); children: Lisa, Jan, Jill BS in Chem. Engring., Carnegie Inst. Tech., 1952; MS in Chem. Engring., Johns Hopkins U., 1959; PhD, La. State U., 1964. Registered profl. engr., La. Process engr. U.S. Indsl. Chem. Co., Balt., 1952-55; project engr. FMC Corp., Balt., 1955-56; asst. prof. U.S. Naval Acad., Annapolis, Md., 1958-61; from instr. to prof. La. State U., Baton Rouge, 1961-74; prof. chem. engring. U. Cin., 1974—, head dept., 1974-81. Program dir. engring. divsn. NSF, Washington, 1972-73, chem. and thermal scis. divsn., 1989-90; sr. scientist Chem. Sys. Lab., Dept. Army, Edgewood, Md., 1981-83; cons. Burk & Assocs., New Orleans, 1970-78. Contbr. numerous articles on chem. engring. to profl. jours. Mem. Cin. Mayor's Energy Task Force, 1981— . Served to lt. USNR, 1947-52 Esso research fellow, 1964-65, NSF fellow, 1961 Fellow Am. Soc. for Laser Medicine and Surgery; mem. Am. Inst. Chem. Engrs., Am. Chem. Soc., Am. Soc. for Engring. Edn., Sigma Xi, Tau Beta Pi, Phi Lambda Upsilon. Jewish. Home: 8547 Wyoming Club Dr Cincinnati OH 45215-4243 Office: Univ Cin Dept Chem Engring PO Box 210012 Cincinnati OH 45221-0171 E-mail: David.Greenberg@uc.edu.

GREENBERG, DOUGLAS STUART, history educator; b. Jersey City, Jan. 11, 1947; s. Charles and Birdy (Neuman) G.; m. Margee G. Michaels, June 21, 1970. BA, Rutgers U., 1969; MA, Cornell U., 1971, PhD, 1974. Asst. prof. history Lawrence U., 1973-78; lectr. Princeton U., 1978-82, prof. history, 1978-86, assoc. dean faculty, 1982—. Educator; b. Jersey City, Jan. 11, 1947; s. Charles and Birdy (Neuman) G.; m. Margee G. Michaels, June 21, 1970. BA, Rutgers U., 1969; MA, Cornell U., 1971, PhD, 1974. Asst. prof. history Lawrence U., 1973-78; lectr. Princeton U., 1978-82, assoc. dean faculty, 1982—, prof. history, 1978-86; vis. prof. Rutgers U., 1987-93; v.p. Am. Council Learned Socs., N.Y.C., 1986-93; pres. and dir. Chgo. Hist. Soc., 1993—. Guggenheim fellow, 1979; Nat. Endowment Humanities fellow, 1976; Huntington Library fellow, 1980; recipient N.Y. State Hist. Assn. Manuscript award, 1974. Mem. Am. Soc. Legal History, Am. Hist. Assn., Orgn. Am. Historians, ACLU, Am. Assn. Mus., Nat. Coun. Pub. History, Am. Assn. State and Local History. Author: Crime and Law Enforcement in Colony of New York, 1691-1776, 1976; Co-author: The American People: A History, 1981; co-editor: Colonial America: Essays Political and Social Development, 1993, Constitutionalism and Democracy, 1993, The Life of Learning, 1994; contbr. articles to profl. jours., chpts. to books. Author: Crime and Law Enforcement in Colony of New York, 1691-1776, 1976; co-author: The American People: A History, 1981; co-editor: colonial America: Essays Political and Social Development, 1993, Constitutionalism and Democracy, 1993, The Life of Learning, 1994; contbr. articles to profl. jours., chpts. to books. Pres., dir. Chgo. Hist. Soc., 1993-2000; pres., CEO Survivors of the Shoah Visual History Found., 2000—. Guggenheim fellow, 1979, Nat. Endowment Humanities fellow, 1976, Huntington Libr. fellow, 1980; recipeint Manuscript award N.Y. State Hist. Assn., 1974. Mem. ACLU, Am. Soc. Legal History, Am. Hist. Assn., Orgn. Am. Historians, Am. Assn. Mus., Nat. Coun. Pub. History, Am. Assn. State and Local History. Address: Survivors of th Shoah Visual History Found PO Box 3168 Los Angeles CA 90078 E-mail: doug@vhf.org.

GREENBERG, EDWARD SEYMOUR, political science educator, writer; b. Phila., July 1, 1942; s. Samuel and Yetta (Kaplan) G.; m. Martha Ann Baker, Dec. 24, 1964; children: Joshua, Nathaniel. BA, Miami (Ohio) U., 1964, MA, 1965; PhD, U. Wis., 1969. Asst. prof. polit. sci. Stanford (Calif.) U., 1968-72; assoc. prof. Ind. U., Bloomington, 1972-73; prof. U. Colo., Boulder, 1973—, dir. research program polit. and econ. change Inst. Behavioral Sci., 1980—, chair dept. polit. sci., 1985-88. Author: Serving the Few, 1974, Understanding Modern Government, 1979, Capitalism and the American Political Ideal, 1985, The American Political System, 1989, Workplace Democracy, 1986 (Dean's Writing award Social Scis. 1987), The Struggle for Democracy, 1993, 95, 97, 99, 2001, 03, brief edit., 1996, 99, 2001, 02; contbr. articles to profl. jours. Recipient fellowship In Recognition of Disting. Tchg., 1968, Jeffrey Pressman award Policy Studies Assn.; grantee Russell Sage Found., 1968, U. Wis., 1968, NSF, 1976, 82, 85, NIH, 1991-94, 96-2001. Mem. Internat. Polit. Sci. Assn., Am. Polit. Sci. Assn., Western Polit. Sci. Assn. (mem. exec. bd. 1986-89). Avocations: skiing, reading, bicycling, travel. Home: 755 11th St Boulder CO 80302-7512 Office: U Colo Inst Behavioral Sci PO Box 487 Boulder CO 80309-0487 E-mail: edward.greenberg@colorado.edu.

GREENBERG, ELINOR MILLER, university official, consultant; b. Bklyn., Nov. 13, 1932; d. Ray and Susan (Weiss) Miller; m. Manuel Greenberg, Dec. 26, 1955; children: Andrea, Julie, Michael. BA, Mt. Holyoke Coll., 1953; MA, U. Wis.-Madison, 1954; EdD, U. No. Colo., 1981; LittD (hon.), St. Mary-of-the-Woods, Ind., 1983; LHD (hon.), Profl. Sch. Psychology, Calif., 1987. Speech pathologist, faculty mem. Arapahoe Inst. for Cmty. Devel., Littleton, Colo., 1954—69, exec. dir., 1969—71; founding dir. Univ. without Walls, Loretto Heights Coll., Denver, 1971—79, asst. acad. dean, 1982—84, asst. to pres., 1984—85; regional exec. officer Coun. for Adult and Experiential Learning, Chgo., 1979—91; founding exec. dir. US West Comm.-CWA, Pathways to the Future, 1986—91; rsch. assoc. Inst. for Rsch. on Adults in Higher Edn., U. Md., U. Coll., 1991; exec. dir. project leadership, 1986—. Project dir. Healthcare Seminars, Colo. Rural New Economy Initiative, 2000-02; pres., CEO EMG and Assocs.; sr. cons. US West Found., No. Telecom, Rose Found., Cogeoinfo., 1992-96; cons. Western Interstate Commn. on Higher Edn., 2003—; founding regional coord. Mountain and Plains Partnership, 1996-2002; adminstr. Visible Human Project-Undergrad. Edit., U. Colo. Health Scis. Ctr., 2002—; cons. NEON Project, Western Interstate Commn. for Higher Edn., 2003—; cons. in field. Co-editor, contbr.: Educating Learners of All Ages, 1980; co-author: Designing Undergraduate Education, 1981, Widening Ripples, 1986, Leading Effectively, 1987, In Our Fifties: Voices of Men and Women Reinventing Their Lives, 1993, MAPP Online Voices, 2000; editor, contbr.: New Partnerships: Higher Education and the Nonprofit Sector, 1982, Enhancing Leadership, 1989, Liberal Education Journal, 1992, Seven MAPP Studies, 2002; author: Weaving: The Fabric of a Woman's Life, 1991, Journey for Justice, 1994; guest editor Liberal Edn., 1992; gen. editor Seven MAPP Studies, 2002; feature writer Colo. Woman News, 1993-96, Women's Bus. News, 1995-96; contbr. Sculpting The Learning Organization, 1993; contbr. articles to profl. jours. Bd. dirs., exec. com. Anti Defamation League of B'nai B'rith, Denver, 1981-99, chair women's leadership com., 1991-93, bd. dirs., 1985-95; mem. Colo. State Bd. for C.C. and Occupational Edn., 1981-86, vice-chair, 1984-85; bd. dirs. Internat. Women's Forum, 1986-88, Internat. Women's Forum Leadership Found., 1991-95, Griffith Ctr., Golden, Colo., 1982-86, Colo. Bd. Continuing Legal and Jud. Edn., 1984-96; pres. Women's Forum of Colo., 1986; v.p. Women's Forum Colo. Found., 1987; adv. bd. Anchor Ctr. Blind Child, Colo. Coalition Prevention Nuclear War, Mile Hi Girl Scouts, Nat. Conf. on Edn. for Women's Devel.; cmty. adv. bd. Colo. Woman News; adv. com. Colo. Pvt. Occupl. Sch., 1990-98, Colo. Cmty. Incentive Fund; co-chair Gov.'s Women's Econ. Devel. Taskforce, Women's Econ. Devel. Coun., 1988-96; bd. visitors U. Hosp., U. Colo., 1990-91, gov. apptd. Colo. Math., Sci. and Tech. Commn., chair, 1991-93, co-telecom. adv. commn. TAC 14, chair, 1993-95; founding steering com. Colo. Women's Leadership Coalition, 1988-96; mem. interdisciplinary telecomm. program, exec. bd. U. Colo., 1992—; U.S. Dept. of Edn., mem. Tech. Panels, 1991—, mem. Expert Panel on Lifelong Learning, 1999—, Western AHEC Reg. Learning System, chair, coursework com., 1998; bd. dirs. Colo. Rural Tech. Program, 1996-2000, Housing for All/Metro Denver Fair Housing Ctr., 1999-2003, chair, 2002-03; chair Colo. Coalition for the Advancement of Telehealth, 2002—; co-chair Colo. Coun. on Telehealth, 2003—; mem. UPT Task Force on Telehealth. Named Citizen of Yr., Omega Psi Phi, Denver, 1966, Woman of Decade Littleton Ind. Newspapers, 1970; grantee W. K. Kellogg Found., 1982, Weyerhaeuser Found., 1986, Fund for Improvement of Post Secondary Edn., 1977, 80, Robert Wood Johnson Found., 1997-2002; recipient Sesquicentennial award Mt. Holyoke Coll. Alumni Assn., 1987, Minoru Yasui Cmty. Vol. award, 1991, Women of Excellence award Colo. Women's Leadership Coalition, 1996, Founding Mothers award, 1997, Woman of Dist., Mile High Girl Scouts, 1997, Martin Luther King Disting. Svc. award to Little Coun. for Human Rels., Arapahoe C.C., 2003, Arthur and Bea Branscombe Meml. award Housing for All: The Metro Denver Fair Housing Ctr., 2003. Mem. Am. Assn. for Higher Edn., Assn. for Experiential Edn. (editl. bd. 1978-80), Am. Speech, Lang. and Hearing Assn., Colo. Rural Devel. Coun., Nat. Conf. Women's Devel. Edn., Kappa Delta Pi. Democrat. Jewish. Home: 6725 S Adams Way Littleton CO 80122-1801 E-mail: ellie.greenberg@uchsc.edu.

GREENBERG, EVA MUELLER, librarian; b. Vienna, July 19, 1929; came to U.S., 1939; d. Paul and Greta (Scheuer) Mueller; m. Nathan Abraham Greenberg, June 22, 1952; children: David Stephen, Judith Helen, Lisa Pauline. AB, Harvard/Radcliffe Coll., 1951; MLS, Kent State U., 1975. Head reference McIntire Libr., Zanesville, Ohio, 1978; with Lorain (Ohio) Pub. Libr., 1978-81; head reference Elyria (Ohio) Pub. Libr., 1981-82; reference libr. adult svcs. Cuyahoga County Pub. Libr., Strongsville, Ohio, 1983-89; head adult svcs. Oberlin (Ohio) Pub. Libr., 1989—. Contbr. articles to profl. jours. Grantee Ohio Humanities Coun. for Pub. Programs; named Libr. of Yr., Ohio Support Svcs., 2000. Mem. ALA, Ohio Libr. Assn. (coord. community info. task force). Home: 34 S Cedar St Oberlin OH 44074-1520 Office: Oberlin Pub Libr 65 S Main St Oberlin OH 44074-1673

GREENBERG, GARY HOWARD, lawyer; b. N.Y.C., Mar. 2, 1948; s. Leo and Elizabeth P. (Weissman) G.; m. Sherri Snyder, June 21, 1987; children: Benjamin, Laura, Nicholas. BA, Johns Hopkins U., 1970; JD, N.Y.U., 1974. Bar: N.Y. 1975, U.S. Dist. Ct. (so. dist.) N.Y. 1975, U.S. Dist. Ct. (ea. dist.) N.Y. 1975, U.S. Ct. Appeals (2nd cir.) 1984. Assoc. Orans, Elsen & Lupert, N.Y.C., 1975—83, ptnr., 1983—2002; of counsel Vinson & Elkins LLP, N.Y.C., 2002—. Instr. trial acad. direct and cross exam. skills N.Y. County Lawyers' Assn.-Nat. Inst. of Trial Advocacy, 1995. Mem. ABA, Assn. of Bar of City of N.Y. (mem. com. on fed. legis. 1983-86), N.Y. State Bar Assn., N.Y. County Lawyers' Assn. (chair appellate cts. com. 1996-99). Office: Vinson & Elkins LLP 666 Fifth Ave New York NY 10103-0040

GREENBERG, GARY NORMAN, internist, occupational medicine physician; b. Detroit, Aug. 18, 1953; s. Ronald Lee and Tenny (Schlafer) G.; m. Marcia R. Gottfried, July 3, 1977; children: Samuel, Andrew. Student, U. Mich., 1971-73; BS, MD, Northwestern U., 1978; MPH, U. N.C., 1984. Diplomate Am. Bd. Internal Medicine, Am. Bd. Occupational and Preventive Medicine. Resident internal medicine U. Hosp., Cleve., 1978-82; fellow occupl. medicine Duke U. Med. Ctr., 1982-84; physician, chmn. internal medicine, health ctr. dir. Cigna Healthplan South Fla., Tampa, 1984-87; asst. clin. prof. Duke Occupl. and Environ. Medicine, Durham, N.C., 1987—; primary care medicine Duke Family Medicine, Durham, 1998—. Office: Duke Occupl and Environ Medicine Duke Med Ctr PO Box 3886 Durham NC 27710 E-mail: gary.greenberg@duke.edu.

GREENBERG, GERALD STEPHEN, lawyer; b. Phila., July 27, 1951; s. Bernard and Elaine Alice (Shapiro) G.; m. Pamela Sue Meyers, Aug. 24, 1975; children: David Stuart, Allison Brooke. BA, Dickinson Coll., 1973; JD, Harvard U., 1976. Bar: N.Y. 1977, U.S. Dist. Ct. (so. dist.) N.Y. 1977, Ohio 1988. Assoc. Kaye, Scholer, Fierman, Hays & Handler, N.Y.C., 1976-86; atty. Exxon Corp., N.Y.C., 1986 87; assoc. Taft, Stettinius & Hollister LLP, Cin., 1987-89; ptnr. Taft, Stettinius & Hollister, Cin., 1990—. Mem. ABA, Assn. of Bar of City of N.Y., Cin. Bar Assn. Office: 1800 Firstar Tower 425 Walnut St Cincinnati OH 45202-3923 E-mail: greenberg@taftlaw.com.

GREENBERG, HAROLD, legal educator; b. Phila., Jan. 19, 1938; s. George and Sarah (Elkins) G. Teaching cert. Gratz. Coll., Phila., 1957; A.B. summa cum laude, Temple U., 1959; J.D. magna cum laude U. Pa., 1962. Bar: Pa. 1963, U.S. Ct. Appeals (3d cir.) 1964, Ind. 1979. Law clk. Supreme Ct. of Pa., Phila. and Erie, 1963-64. Assoc., then ptnr. firm Cohen, Shapiro, Polisher, Shiekman & Cohen, Phila., 1964-77; assoc. prof. law Ind. U., Indpls., 1977-88, prof., 1988—2003, prof. emeritus, 2003—. Vis. prof. Fla. Coastal U., 2003, U. Ill., Chgo., Ill., 2003. Author: Rights and Remedies Under U.C.C. Article 2, 1987. Mem. ABA, Ind. Bar Assn., Indpls. Bar Assn. Democrat. Jewish. Office: Sch Law Ind U 530 W New York St Indianapolis IN 46202

GREENBERG, HARRY SETH, neurologist, educator; b. Bklyn, Sept. 28, 1946; s. Milton and Bertha (Bernstein) G.; m. Anne Ferris, Sept. 2, 1989. BA, Cornell U., 1968; MD, SUNY, 1973. Diplomate Am. Bd. Psychiatry and Neurology; lic. physician, Calif., Mich., NY. Intern medicine Upstate Med. Ctr., SUNY, Syracuse, 1973-74; resident neurology Stanford U. Med. Sch., Calif., 1974-77; fellow neuro-oncology Meml. Sloan-Kettering Cancer Ctr., NYC, 1977-79; fellow neurology N.Y. Hosp., Cornell U., NYC, 1978-79; asst. prof. neurology U. Mich., Ann Arbor, 1979 85, assoc. prof neurology, 1985-91; dir. neuro-oncology program U. Mich. Cancer Ctr., 1987—2001; prof. U. Mich., Ann Arbor, 1991—, neurology prof. surgery sect. neurosurgery, 1991—; part time pvt. practice Vail Co., 2002. Part-time pvt. practice neurology, Vail, Colo., 2002—; cons. U. Mich. Neurofibromatosis Ctr., 1985-94, VA Med. Ctr., Ann Arbor, 1980-2001, vis. prof., 1990-95, DepoCyt adv. bd., 1997; spkr. various confs. throughout US, Europe, Japan. Editl. bd., reviewer Annals of Neurology, 1982-2001, Neurology, 1984—, Cancer Treatment Reports, 1984-2001, Jour. Neuro-Oncology, 1985-2001, Jour. Clin. Oncology, 1985—, NY State Jour. Medicine, 1986—, Neurosurgery, 1988-2001, Molecular Medicine, 1995, Epilepsia, 1995, Cancer, 1995, Neuro-Oncology, 1997—, Neurology Network Commentary, 1994-2001; assoc. editor Neurobase, 1993—; adv. bd. Hypertext Neurological Knowledgebase, 1997; contbr. articles to profl. jour., chpt. to books. Bd. dir. U. Mich. Slusser Gallery, Ann Arbor, 1987-92; bd. dir. Ann Arbor Art Assn., 1990-95; v.p. bd. dir., 1993. Henry Viets scholar Nat. Myasthenia Gravis Found., 1970—; grantee NIH, Nat. Cancer Inst., U. Mich. Cancer Ctr. Support, 1988—, NIH, 1988—, NIH, Nat. Cancer Inst., 1992—, NIH, 1992. Fellow Am. Acad. Neurology; mem. Am. Fedn. Clin. Rsch., Am. Neurol. Assn. (membership adv. com. 1995), Am. Soc. Clin. Oncology, Am. Soc. Neurol. Investigation (Midwest councilor 1980-86), S.W. Oncology Group, Mich. Neurol. Assn. (program chmn. 1979-86, v.p. 1993-95, pres. 1995-97), Am. Assn. Neurosurgeons/Congress Neurol. Surgeons (joint tumor sect.), Mich. Cancer Ctr. (program dir. neuro-oncology), NY Acad. Sci., Am. Brain Tumor Assn. (sci. adv. bd. 1994—). Avocations: running, tennis, golf, skiing, biking. Home: 2611 Wylie Rd Dexter MI 48130-9781 Office: U Mich Dept Neurology 1914/0316 Taubman Ann Arbor MI 48109

GREENBERG, HENRY MORTON, physician, educator; b. N.Y.C., Oct. 5, 1940; s. David and Flora (Budnick) G.; m. Barbara Helene Brown, June 20, 1965; children: Lisa, Jeffrey Oliver. BA, U. Pa., 1961; MD, Tufts U., 1965. Intern St. Elizabeth Hosp., Boston, 1965-66; resident St. Lukes Hosp., N.Y.C., 1968-70; fellow in cardiology Roosevelt Hosp., N.Y.C., 1970-72, dir. CCU, 1972-79; dir. coronary care unit Roosevelt site St. Lukes Roosevelt Hosp., N.Y.C., 1979—; from instr. to assoc. clin. prof. of medicine Columbia U. Coll. Physicians & Surgeons, N.Y.C., 1972-87, assoc. prof. clin. medicine, 1987—. Editor: Sudden Coronary Death, 1982, Clinical Aspects of Life Threatening Arrhythmias, 1984, Beyond the Crisis: Preserving the Capacity for Excellence in Health Care and Medical Science, 1994; contbr. articles to profl. jours. With USPHS, 1966-68, Peace Corps physician, Cameroon, West Africa. Fellow ACP, Am. Coll. Cardiology, Am. Heart Assn. (coun. clin. cardiology), N.Y. Acad. Scis. (bd. govs. 1991-99, pres. 1994-95, chmn. 1995-96). Office: St Lukes Roosevelt Hosp 428 W 59th St 1000 10th Ave New York NY 10019-1192

GREENBERG, HINDA FEIGE, library director; b. Bayreuth, Germany, Feb. 26, 1947; arrived in U.S., 1951; d. Samuel Leon and Sima (Schampagnere) F.; m. Joseph Lawrence, July 6, 1968; children: David Micah, Jacob Alexander. BA, Temple U., 1969; MLS, Rutgers U., 1981; PhD, Drexel U., 1999. Assoc. librarian Ednl. Testing Svc., Princeton, NJ, 1981-86; dir. info. ctr. Carnegie Found., Princeton, 1986-97, Robert Wood Johnson Found., Princeton, 1997—. Pres.-elect Consortium of Found. Librs. Avocation: travel.

GREENBERG, IRA ARTHUR, psychologist; b. Bklyn., June 26, 1924; s. Philip and Minnie (S.) G.; m. Martha Estella Cantrell, 1949 (div. 1950); m. Judith Linda Burgard-Rials, 1952 (div. 1954); m. Monita Ruth Nibörod, 1961 (div. 1965). Grad. Scouts and Raiders Sch., US Naval Amphibious Tng. Base, Ft. Pierce, Fla., 1944; BA in Journalism, U. Okla., 1949; MA in English, U. So. Calif., 1962; MS in Counseling, Calif. State U., L.A., 1963; PhD in Psychology, Claremont (Calif.) Grad. Sch., 1967; Grad., Marine Corps Inst.'s Command and Staff Coll., 1992. Editor Ft. Riley (Kans.) Guidon, 1950-51; copy editor, reporter Columbus (Ga.) Enquirer, 1951-55; reporter Louisville Courier-Jour., 1955-56, L.A. Times, 1956-62; free-lance writer L.A., Montclair, Camarillo, Calif., 1960-69, 76—. Counselor Claremont Coll. Psychol. Clinic and Counseling Ctr., 1964-65; lectr. psychology Chapman Coll., Orange, Calif., 1965-66; psychologist Camarillo State Hosp., 1967-69, supervising psychologist, 1969-73, part-time clin. psychologist, 1973-93; part-time asst. prof. edn. San Fernando Valley State Coll., Northridge, Calif., 1967-69, lectr. psychodrama, social welfare U. Calif. Extension Divsn., Santa Barbara, 1968-69; vis. prof. edn. U. Nev., Reno, 1977—; vol. psychologist Free Clinic, L.A., 1968-70; staff dir. Calif. Inst. Psychodrama, 1969-71; tng. cons. Topanga Ctr. for Human Devel., 1970-75, bd. dirs., 1971-74, faculty Calif. Sch. Profl. Psychology, 1970-80; founder, exec. dir. Behavioral Studies Inst., mgmt. cons., L.A., 1970—; pvt. practice cons. in psychology, psychodrama, hypnosis, 1970—; founder, exec. dir. Psychodrama Ctr. for L.A., Inc., 1971—, Group Hypnosis Ctr., L.A., 1976—; prodr., host TV talk show Crime and Pub. Safety, Adelpial, Channel 77, 1983—. Author: Psychodrama and Audience Attitude Change, 1968; editor (author): Psychodrama: Theory and Therapy, 1974, Group Hypnotherapy and Hypnodrama, 1977, The Hebrew National Orphan Home: Memories of Orphanage Life, 2001. Vol. humane officer State of Calif., 1979-89; res. officer L.A. Police Dept., 1980-86; bd. dirs. Humane Educators Coun., 1982-86; mem. Nat. Coun. Employer Support of Guard and Res., 1998—. With AUS 78th inf. divsn., 1943, army specialized tng. program, 1944, 11th engr. combat battalion XXI corps 7th Army, ETO, 1944-46; USAR, 1950-51, sgt. 1st class; capt. Calif. State Mil. Res., 1986-93, maj., 1993-2000; lt. col. U.S. Svc. Command, 2000-02; col. Emergency Disaster Assistance Corps, 2002—. Fellow Am. Soc. Clin. Hypnosis, Am. Soc. Group Psychotherapy and Psychodrama; mem. Am. Psychol. Assn., Calif. Psychol. Assn., L.A. County Psychol. Assn., So. Calif. Soc. Clin. Hypnosis (pres. 1977-78), Group Psychotherapy Assn. So. Calif. (pres. 1987-88), So. Calif. Psychotherapy Affiliation (dir. 1976-85), Am. Soc. Psychical Rsch., Assn. Rsch. and Enlightenment, Peace Officers Assn., L.A. County, Acad. TV Arts and Scis., Nat. Acad. Cable Programming, UDT/SEAL Assn., Navy Amphibious Scouts and Raiders Assn., 11th Engr. Combat Battalion Assn., 78th Infantry Divsn. Assn., VFW, Am. Legion, Jewish War Vets., State Def. Forces Assn. Am., State Def. Forces Assn. Calif., Mensa, Am. Zionist Fedn., NRA, Calif. Rifle and Pistol Assn., SW Pistol League, Animal Protection Inst. Am., L.A. SPCA, Hebrew Nat. Orphan Home Alumni Assn., Sigma Delta Chi. Clubs: Sierra, Greater L.A. Press; B'nai B'rith; Beverly Hills Gun. Office: BSI & Group Hypnosis Ctr 8939 S Sepulveda Blvd Ste 318 Los Angeles CA 90045-3605

GREENBERG, IRA GEORGE, lawyer; b. N.Y.C., May 8, 1946; s. Julius M. and Florence Greenberg; m. Linda Sharon Padell, Apr. 29, 1979; children: Amanda, Glenn. AB, Harvard U., 1968, JD, 1971. Bar: N.Y. 1972, D.C. 1980. Asst. to gen. counsel Office of Sec. of Army, Washington, 1971-74; assoc. Dewey Ballantine, N.Y.C., 1974-81, Summit Solomon & Feldesman and predecessor firms, N.Y.C., 1981-83, ptnr., 1983-92, Edwards & Angell LLP, N.Y.C., 1992—. Capt. U.S. Army, 1971-74. Mem. ABA, Assn. Bar City N.Y. Democrat. Office: Edwards & Angell LLP 750 Lexington Ave Fl 12 New York NY 10022-1253 E-mail: igreenberg@EdwardsAngell.com.

GREENBERG, JACK, lawyer, law educator; b. N.Y.C., Dec. 22, 1924; s. Max and Bertha (Rosenberg) G.; m. Sema Ann Tanzer, 1950 (div. 1970); children: Josiah, David, Sarah, Ezra; m. Deborah M. Cole, 1970; children: Suzanne, William Cole. AB, Columbia U., 1945, LLB, 1948, LLD, 1984, Morgan State Coll., Central State Coll., 1965, Lincoln U., 1977, John Jay Coll. Criminal Justice, 1983, De Paul U., 1994. Bar: N.Y. 1949. Rsch. asst. N.Y. State Law Revision Commn., 1949; asst. counsel NAACP Legal Def. and Ednl. Fund, 1949-61, dir.-counsel, 1961-84; argued in sch. segregation, sit-in, employment discrimination, poverty, capital punishment, other cases before U.S. Supreme Ct.; adj. prof. Columbia U. Law Sch., 1970-84, prof., vice-dean, 1984-89; dean Columbia Coll., 1989-93; prof. Columbia U. Law Sch., 1993—. Cons. Ctr. Applied Legal Studies, U. Witwatersrand, 1978; vis. lectr. Yale U. Law Sch., 1971; vis. prof. CCNY, 1977, Tokyo U., 1993-94, 99, St. Louis U. Law Sch., 1994, Lewis and Clark Law Sch., 1994-98, Princeton U., 1995, U. Munich, 1998; lectr. Harvard U. Law Sch., 1983, Shikes fellow, 1981; disting. lectr. humanities Columbia Coll. Physicians and Surgeons, 1998, U. Nurenberg-Erlangen, 1999. Author: (with H. Hill) Citizens Guide to Desegregation, 1955, Race Relations and American Law, 1959, Judicial Process and Social Change, 1976, (with James Vorenberg) Dean Cuisine or the Liberated Man's Guide to Fine Cooking, 1990, Crusaders in the Courts, 1994; contbg. author: Race, Sex and Religious Discrimination in International Law, 1981; contbr. articles to profl. jours. Bd. dirs. N.Y.C. Legal Aid Soc., Internat. League for Human Rights, Mex.-Am. Legal Def. Fund, 1968-75, Asian Am. Legal Def. Fund, 1980—, Human Rights Watch, 1978-98, NAACP Legal Def. and Ednl. Fund. Co-recipient Grenville Clark prize, 1978; hon. fellow U. Pa. Law Sch., 1975. Fellow AAAS, Am. Coll. Trial Lawyers; mem. ABA (commn. to study FTC, adv. com. to spl. com. on crime prevention, sect. on individual rights and responsibilities, Silver Gavel award, Thurgood Marshall prize, Presdl. Citizens medal 2001), N.Y. State Bar Assn. (exec. dir. spl. com. study state antitrust laws 1956), Am. Law Inst., Bar Assn. City N.Y. (Cardozo lectr. 1973) Adminstrv. Conf. U.S. Home: 118 Riverside Dr New York NY 10024-3708 Office: Columbia Law Sch 435 W 116th St New York NY 10027-7297

GREENBERG, JACK M. food products executive; b. 1942; s. Edith S. Scher; m. Donna Greenberg; children: David, Ilyse, Allison. BSc in Acctg., DePaul U., Chgo., 1964, JD, 1968. CPA Ill.; bar:. With Arthur Young & Co., 1964-82; chief fin. officer, exec. v.p. McDonald's Corp., Oakbrook, Ill., 1982—, vice chmn., chief fin. officer Oak Brook, Ill., CFO, exec. v.p., 1982, vice chmn., CFO, 1992, bd. dirs., pres. and CEO, 1997—99, chmn., CEO, 1999—. Bd. dirs. Abbott Labs, Harcourt Gen., Boston. Bd. dirs. DePaul U., IIT, Kent Coll. Law. Mem.: AICPA, Ill. Inst. Cert. Pub. Accts. Office: McDonald's Corp 1 McDonalds Plz Oak Brook IL 60523-1911

GREENBERG, JACOB, biochemist, educator, consultant; b. Haifa, Israel, Mar. 10, 1929; came to U.S., 1961; s. Shlomo and Temima (Angelovitch) G.; m. Esther Kahana, May 19, 1957; children: Abraham, Daphne. PhD, Hebrew U., Jerusalem, 1958. Assoc. rsch. biochemist biochem. dept. NYU, 1962-67, assoc. rsch. scientist Sch. Medicine, 1969-71; assoc. rsch. scientist Mt. Sinai Med. Sch., N.Y.C., 1967-68; asst. prof. N.Y. Med. Coll., 1972-76; dir. R&D quality assurance Advanced Biofactures, N.Y.C., 1971-83; dir. R&D Protos, N.Y.C., 1983—. Cons. Columbia U., N.Y.C., 1965-67. Contbr. articles to profl. jours. Mem. White House Inner Cir., Washington, 1984-93, Autistic Soc. NIH fellow, 1961-62, grantee, 1972-76. Mem. AAUP, Internat. Congress Biochemistry, Am. Chem. Soc. (grantee 1967), N.Y. Acad. Scis. Avocations: swimming, chess, writing. Office: Protos Co 13016 Francis Lewis Blvd Jamaica NY 11413-1841

GREENBERG, JEFFREY W. professional services company executive; b. 1952; With Am. Internat. Group, 17 yrs, exev. v.p. in-charge domestic brokerage ins. group, 4 yrs; mgr. comml. aviation and aerospace ins. group Marsh & McLennan Cos., N.Y.C., from 1976; chmn. Marsh & McLennan Capital, Inc. subs. Marsh & McLennan Cos., N.Y.C., 1995—; pres., CEO Marsh & McLennan Cos., N.Y.C., 1999—, chmn., 2000—, also bd. dirs. Office: Marsh & McLennan Cos Inc 1166 Ave of Americas New York NY 10036-2774

GREENBERG, JERROLD SELIG, health education educator; b. N.Y.C., Jan. 19, 1942; s. David and Bess G.; m. Karen Lider, Aug. 29, 1970; children: Todd, Keri. BS, CCNY, 1964, MS, 1965; EdD, Syracuse U., 1969. Tchr. N.Y.C. and Syracuse Pub. Sch. Dists., 1964-67; instr. Syracuse U., 1968-69; asst. prof. Boston U., 1969-71; prof. health edn. SUNY, Buffalo, 1971-79; prof. pub. and cmty. health U. Md., 1979—. Presenter in field. Author: Health Through Discovery, 1980, Student Centered Health Instruction: A Humanistic Approach, 1978, Health Through Discovery, 1983, 1986, 1989, Sexuality Education: Theory and Practice, 1981, 1988, 1994, Comprehensive Stress Management, 1983, Comprehensive Stress Management, 7th edit., 2002, Sexuality: Insights and Issues, 1986, 1989, 1993, Physical Fitness: A Wellness Approach, 1986, 1989, Stress and Sexuality, 1987, Health Education: Learner-Centered Instructional Strategies, 1989, 1995, 1998, Coping With Stress: A Personal Guide, 1990, The College Student's Health Self-Care Diary, 1991, Exploring Health, 1992, Your Personal Stress Profile and Activity Workbook, 1992, 1996, 2002, The Health Education Ethics Book, 1992, The Caregiver's Guide, 1994, Holt Health, 1994, Holt Health, 2d edit., 1999, Physical Fitness and Wellness, 1995, Physical Fitness and Wellness, 2d edit., 1998, Wellness: Creating a Life of Health and Fitness, 1997, The Code of Ethics for the Health Education Profession, 2001, Service Learning in Health Education, 2000, Dimensions of

Human Sexuality, 2002. With U.S. Army, 1967. Grantee Western N.Y. chpt. Am. Heart Assn., 1977-78; Research Found. of SUNY, 1979-80, Met. Life Found., 1985-86, Consumer Health Found., 2003. Fellow AAHPERD (Alliance scholar), Am. Sch. Health Assn. (Disting. Svc. award), mem. APHA, Am. Assn. for Health Edn. (Presdl. citation, Profl. Svc. to Health Edn. award, Scholar award), Soc. Pub. Health Edn., Eta Sigma Gamma (finalist Thomas Ehrlich Faculty award). Jewish. Home: 9412 Reach Rd Rockville MD 20854-2852 E-mail: jg56@umail.umd.edu.

GREENBERG, JONATHAN, neurosurgeon; b. Fall River, Mass., Nov. 6, 1950; s. Paul and Thelma Faith (Bernstein) G.; children: Ilana, Nathaniel; m. Myriam Garzon, May 5, 1991; children: Danielle, Gabrielle, Samantha. BA, Columbia U., 1971, MD, JD, Columbia U., 1977. Diplomate Am. Bd. Neurological Surgery. Intern Johns Hopkins Hosp., Balt., 1977-78, resident in gen. surgery, 1978-79; resident in neurosurgery Med. Ctr. NYU, N.Y.C., 1979-84; attending neurosurgeon Md. Inst. Emergency Med. Svcs. System, Balt., 1985-87; clin. instr., asst. prof. U. Md. Sch. Medicine, Balt., 1985-87; asst. prof. U. Miami (Fla.) Sch. Medicine, 1987-93; chief neurtrauma svcs. Jackson Meml. Hosp., Miami, 1987-92, med. co-dir. neurosurg. ICU, 1987-92; mem. surg. teaching faculty Orlando Regional Healthcare System, 1993, chmn. dept. neurol. surgery, 1996-99, vice chmn., 2000—01, chmn. dept. neurol. surgery, 2001—, Winter Park (Fla.) Meml. Hosp., 1998-99. Editor: Handbook of Head and Spine Trauma, 1993; contbr. chpts. to books, article to profl. publ. Mem. Dade Country Trauma Adv. Com., Miami, 1989-93. Mem. ACS, Congress Neurol. Surgeons, Soc. Critical Care Medicine, Am. Assn. Neurol. Surgeons. Republican. Jewish. Avocations: piano, chess, swimming.

GREENBERG, JUDITH ANN, real estate developer; b. Pitts., July 8, 1951; d. Jack Zachary and Mary Adele (Chayet) G.; m. Manny Schechter, Feb. 18, 1990. BBA, SUNY, Binghamton, 1972. Account exec. Wells, Rich, Greene, N.Y.C., 1972-73, Weltin Advt., Atlanta, 1973-74, Grey Advt., N.Y.C., 1974-76; account supr. N. W. Ayer, N.Y.C., 1976-82; mng. dir. Core Resource (Far East) Ltd., Hong Kong, 1982-92; pres. Elysse of Key West (Fla.) Inc., 1993—, Elysse Investments of Key West Inc., 1995—, Key West MJM Investments Inc., 1996—; pres., gen. mgr. Hollywood (Fla.) Hotels Mgmt. Inc., 1996—; pres. Hollywood Realty Investors Inc., 1997—, 130 Duval St Inc., Key West, 1998—, Planet of Key West Inc., 1998—, Jungle Paradise of Key West, Inc., 1999—, MJM Realty Investors, Aventura, Fla., 2001—, Jungle Paradise of Nev., LLC, 2003—. Pres. Beit Edmund J. Safra Synagogue Sisterhood, 2003—. Mem. Downtown Hollywood Bus. Assn. (v.p. 1996-2001). Jewish.

GREENBERG, LARRIE WARREN, pediatrician; b. Toledo, July 15, 1940; s. Leonard and Lillian (Webne) G.; m. Joyce Godofsky; children: Abby, Jeffrey. BS, U. Toledo, 1961; MD, Ohio State U., 1965. Intern Buffalo (N.Y.) Children's Hosp., 1965-66; resident Columbus (Ohio) Children's Hosp., 1966-68, chief resident, 1968-69; chief pediat. Kimbrough Army Hosp., Ft. Meade, Md., 1969-71, Alyn Orthop. Hosp., Jerusalem, 1971-72; asst. prof. Johns Hopkins U., Balt., 1972-73; dir. pediat. edn. Holy Cross Hosp., Silver Spring, Md., 1974-78; dir. med. edn. Children's Hosp. Nat. Med. Ctr., Washington, 1978-2000, pres. med. staff, 1988-90; dir. Creative Med. Edn., Rockville, 2000—; internal cons. faculty devel. George Washington U. Sch. Medicine. Cons. faculty devel. George Washington U. Sch. of Medicine; owner Creative Med. Edn. Contbr. chpts. to med. texts; contbr. articles to med. jours. Bd. dirs. United Jewish Appeal Greater Washington, 1974-96. Maj. U.S. Army, 1969-71. Recipient Gold T award U. Toledo Alumni Assn., 1995, Ray Helfer award for Outstanding Rsch. in Med. Edn., Ambulatory Pediat. Assn., 1996, 97. Fellow Am. Acad. Pediat.; mem. Am. Pediat. Soc., Assn. Am. Med. Colls. (rsch. med. edn. com. 1990—, chmn. N.E. group on edn1. affairs 1993), Ambulatory Pediat. Assn. (bd. dirs. 1988-91), Am. Ednl. Rsch. Assn., Coun. on Med. Student Edn. in Pediat. (pres. 1994-96), U. Toledo Alumni Assn. (award coun. on med. student edn. in pediats.) Avocations: gardening, sports, jazz. Fax: 301 983-5616. E-mail: Larrie_greenberg@hotmail.com.

GREENBERG, LENORE, public relations professional; b. Flushing, N.Y. d. Jack and Frances Orenstein. BA, Hofstra U.; MS, SUNY. Dir .pub. rels. Bloomingdale's, Short Hills, N.J., 1977-78; dir. comms. N.J. Sch. Bds. Assn., Trenton, 1978-82; dir pub. info. N.J. State Dept. Edn., Trenton, 1982-90; assoc. exec. dir. Nat. Sch. Pub. Rels. Assn., Arlington, Va., 1990-91; pres. Lenore Greenberg & Assocs., Inc., 1991—. Adj. prof. pub. rels. Rutgers U. Freelance feature writer N.Y. Times. Mem. bd. assocs. McCarter Theatre, Princeton, N.J.; mem. Franklin Twp. Zoning Bd. Adjustment; mem. Franklin Twp. Human Rels. Commn.; chair Somerset County LWV; instr. Bus. Vols. for the Arts. Recipient award Am. Soc. Assn. Execs., award Women in Comms., award Internat. Assn. Bus. Communicators; Gold Medallion awrd Nat. Sch. Pub. Rels. Assn. Mem. Pub. Rels. Soc. Am. (accredited; pres. N.J. State chpt., nat. nominating and accreditation coms., Silver Anvil award), Nat. Health/Edn. Consortium. Home and Office: 30971 Carrara Rd Laguna Niguel CA 92677-2757

GREENBERG, LON RICHARD, energy company executive, lawyer; b. N.Y.C., Sept. 4, 1950; s. Ralph Austin and Miriam (Kenner) G.; m. Bonnie Small, June 25, 1972; children: Jody B. Scott B., Daniel A. BS, U. Pa., 1972; JD, Villanova U., 1975; postgrad., Harvard U., Boston, 1994. Bar: Pa. 1975. Law clk. to Hon. J. Sydney Hoffman, Superior Ct. Pa., Phila., 1975-76; assoc. Morgan, Lewis & Bockius, Phila., 1976-80; corp. devel. counsel UGI Corp., Valley Forge, Pa., 1980-82, corp. sec., 1982-87, v.p., gen. counsel, 1983-87, v.p. legal and corp. devel., 1987-89, sr. v.p. legal and corp. devel., 1989-94, pres., 1994-95, pres., CEO, 1995-96, chmn., pres., CEO, 1996—, also bd. dirs. Bd. dirs. AmeriGas Propane, Inc., chmn., CEO, 1996—; bd. dirs. Am. Gas Assn., World LP Gas Assn.; former mem. bd. dirs. Mellon PSFS, Phila. Bd. dirs., mem. fin. com., chmn. investment com., nominating com. Reading Is Fundamental, Washington, 1995—; mem. policy com., treas. Pa. Bus. Roundtable, Harrisburg, 1995—; bd. trustees Chestnut Hill Healthcare; former mem. nat. indsl. adv. coun. Industrialization Ctrs. Am.; former mem. task force com. United Way Leadership Giving Southeastern Pa., Phila.; mem., coach Chestnut Hill Fathers Club, Phila.; adv. bd. Ea. Pa. chpt. Arthritis Found.; bd. dir. Greater Phila. (Pa.) C. of C., CEO Coun. on Growth. Recipient Good Samaritan award N.W. Victim Svcs., 1994, Disting. Svc. award Chestnut Hill Cmty. Assn., 1994. Mem.: ABA, Pa. Bar Assn. Avocations: swimming, tennis, golf, family activities. Office: UGI Corp 460 N Gulph Rd King Of Prussia PA 19406

GREENBERG, MARC LELAND, education educator; b. LA, Nov. 9, 1961; s. Howard A. and Suzanne (Blau) G.; m. Marta Pirnat-Greenberg, July 6, 1988; children: Benjamin C., Lea H. BA, UCLA, 1983; MA, U. Chgo., 1984; PhD, U. Calif., L.A., 1990. Asst. prof. U. Kans., Lawrence, 1990-95, assoc. prof., 1995-2001, chmn. Slavic dept., 2000—, prof., 2001—. Author: A Historical Phonology of the Slovene Language, 2000; N.Am. editor Slovenski jezik/Slovene Linguistic Studies jour., Ljubljana, Slovenia, Lawrence, Kans., 1997—; contbr. articles to profl. jours. Humanities Rsch. fellow Hall Ctr., U. Kans., Lawrence, 1994; Univ. Tchrs.' fellow NEH, Washington, 1993; Tchg. fellow Am. Coun. Learned Soc., Washington, 1990; rsch. fellow Fulbright-Hayes, Washington, 1988-89; Zahvala/Gratitude award Govt. of Rep. Slovenia, Ljubljana, 1992. Mem. Soc. Slovene Studies (exec. coun. 1994-97), Am. Assn. Advancement Slavic Studies, Am. Assn. Tchrs. Slavic and East European Langs. (Best Book in Slavic Linguistics 2002), East European Anthropology Group, Assn. Study Nationalities, Phi Beta Kappa. Home: 4209 Wheat State St Lawrence KS 66049-3585 Office: U Kans Slavic Dept 1445 Jayhawk Blvd Rm 2133 Lawrence KS 66045-7590 E-mail: mlg@ku.edu.

GREENBERG, MARVIN, retired music educator; b. N.Y.C., June 24, 1936; s. Samuel and Rae (Sherry) G. BS cum laude, NYU, 1957; MA, Columbia U., 1958, EdD, 1962. Tchr. elem. schs., N.Y.C., 1957-63; prof. music edn. U. Hawaii, Honolulu, 1963-93, prof. emeritus, ret., 1993. Rsch. cons. Ctr. for Early Childhood Rsch., 1969-71; edn. adminstr. Model Cities project for disadvantaged children Family Svcs. Ctr., Honolulu, 1971-72. Author: Teaching Music in the Elementary School: Guide for ETV Programs, 1966, Preschool Music Curriculum, 1970, Music Handbook for the Elementary School, 1972, Staff Training in Child Care in Hawaii, 1975, Your Child Needs Music, 1979, Teachers' Guides Honolulu Symphony Children's Concerts, 1980-93; contbr. over 100 articles to profl. jours. Cons. western region Volt Tech. Svcs., Head Start Program, 1969-71; Head Start worker, 1972-75; Child Devel. Assoc. Consortium rep., 1975—. Recipient several fed. and state grants for ednl. rsch. and curriculum projects. Mem. Hawaii Music Educators Assn., Music Educators Nat. Conf., Soc. Rsch. in Music Edn., Coun. Rsch. Music Edn.

GREENBERG, MAURICE RAYMOND, insurance company executive; b. N.Y.C., May 4, 1925; s. Jacob and Ada (Rheingold) G.; m. Corinne Phyllis Zuckerman, Nov. 12, 1950; children: Jeffrey W., Evan G., L. Scott, Cathleen J. Pre-law cert., U. Miami, Fla., 1948; LLB, N.Y. Law Sch., 1950, also JD (hon.); JD (hon.), New Eng. Sch. Law, 1970, Bryant Coll., Middlebury Coll., Brown U., Pace U. Bar: N.Y. 1953. With Continental Casualty Co., 1952-60; joined Am. Internat. Group Inc., N.Y.C., 1960—, pres. subs. Am. Home Assurance Co., 1962-67, pres., CEO, 1967—, chmn. bd., CEO, 1989—. Mem. Bus. Roundtable, pres.'s adv. com. Trade Policy and Negotiations; vice-chmn. Ctr. for Strategic and Internat. Studies; chmn. U.S.-China Bus. Coun.; vice-chmn. Coun. on Fgn. Rels.; founding chmn. U.S.-Philippine Bus. Com.; chmn. emeritus NYH, 1995; bd. govs. N.Y. Hosp. Bd. govs. N.Y. Hosp.; mem. Pres.'s adv. com. on trade negotiations Ctr. for Strategic and Internat. Studies, mem. bus. roundtable. Capt. U.S. Army, ETO, Korea. Decorated Bronze Star. Mem. N.Y. Bar Assn., The Asia Soc. (chmn.), Police Athletic League, City Athletic Club, Sky Club, India House, Lotos Club, Harmonie Club, Georgetown Club (Washington). Office: Am Internat Group Inc 70 Pine St New York NY 10270-0002

GREENBERG, MICHAEL RICHARD, urban studies and community health educator; b. N.Y.C., Aug. 22, 1943; s. Sidney Saul and Mildred (Saletra) Greenberg; m. Gwendolyn Barker, Jan. 19, 1978; children: Seana Pappas, Heather Wilkerson, Joshua Suggs, Alexandra Greenberg. BA, CUNY, 1965; MA, Columbia U., 1966, PhD, 1969. Asst. prof. Columbia U., N.Y.C., 1969-71; assoc. prof. Rutgers U., New Brunswick, N.J., 1971-73, prof., 1973-78, disting. prof., 1978-82, prof. urban studies and community health, 1982—, assoc. dean faculty, 2000—. Co-dir. pub. health N.J. Grad. Progam in Pub. Health, New Brunswick, 1983—. Author: Urbanization and Cancer Mortality, 1983, Public Health and the Environment, 1988, Environmental Risk and the Press, 1989 (award 1988), Environmental Reporter's Handbook (award 1989), Environmentally Devastated Neighborhoods, 1996, Restoring America's Neighborhoods, 1999. Recipient Spl. Merit award, EPA, 1977, Dennis Sullivan award, Pub. Health Assn., 2001. Mem. APHA, Soc. for Epidemiol. Rsch., Assn. of Am. Geographers (Disting. Scholars award 1997), Soc. for Risk Analysis. Avocation: walking. Office: Rutgers U Dept Urban Studies Civic Sq Bldg 33 Livingston Ave Ste 100 New Brunswick NJ 08901-1900 E-mail: mrg@rci.rutgers.edu.

GREENBERG, MICHAEL RICHARD, family practice physician; b. Bound Brook, N.J., Oct. 20, 1945; s. Edward R. and Helen Regina Greenberg. MD, George Washington U., 1969; MBA, U. Pa., 1987. Diplomate Am. Bd. Family Practice, Am. Bd. Med. Mgmt. Surg. intern York (Pa.) Hosp., 1969-70; CEO Clinton Assoc. Physicians and Surgeons, Lock Haven, Pa., 1971-86; v.p. Geisinger Med. Ctr., Danville, Pa., 1986-94; CEO Clinton Med. Assocs., Mill Hall, Pa., 1994—. Clin. prof. and med. dir. Lock Haven U., 1995—; chief of staff Lock Haven Hosp., 1996—. Med. dir. Clinton County Prison, Lock Haven, 1994—. Major, U.S. Army, 1970-80. Fellow Am. Acad. Family Practice. Avocations: flying, skiing, scuba diving, travel, music. Home: PO Box 751 Lock Haven PA 17745-0751 Office: Clinton Med Assocs 7133 Nittany Valley Dr Mill Hall PA 17751-9013 E-mail: mgreenbe@lhup.edu.

GREENBERG, MILTON, political scientist, educator; b. Bklyn., Feb. 20, 1927; s. Samuel and Fannie (Schnell) G.; m. Sonia B. Brown, June 20, 1948; children: Anne Greenberg Bookin, Nancy R. BA, Bklyn. Coll., 1949; MA, U. Wis., 1950, PhD (univ. scholar), 1955; LLD (hon.), Am. U., 1993. Instr. polit. sci. U. Tenn., Knoxville, 1952-55; from asst. prof. to prof. Western Mich. U., Kalamazoo, 1955-64, chmn. polit. sci. dept., 1965-69; dean Coll. Arts and Scis., Ill. State U., Normal, 1969-72; v.p. acad. affairs, dean faculties Roosevelt U., Chgo., 1972-80; provost, v.p. acad. affairs Am. U., Washington, 1980-93, prof. govt., 1980-97, interim pres., provost, 1990-91, prof. emeritus, 1997—. Rsch. assoc. Cleve. Met. Svcs. Commn., 1957; cons. Citizens for Mich. (constl. reform movement), 1960; cons. Supreme Ct. Hist. Soc., 1997—, Coun. for Higher Edn. Accreditation, 1997—. Author: (companion book to PBS show) The GI Bill: The Law That Changed America, 1997, (with J.C. Plano) The American Political Dictionary, 1962, 11th edit., 2002; (with others) The Poltical Science Dictionary, 1973; contbr. to Collier's Yearbook, 1959-93, Chronicle of Higher Education Career Network, 1999-; mem. editl. bd. Ednl. Record, 1985-97, guest editor, 1994; cons. editor ASHE-ERIC Higher Edn. Reports, 1986-90; contbr. articles to profl. jours. and newspapers. Mem. Mich. Gov.'s Commn. on Legis. Apportionment, 1962, Kalamazoo Community Rels. Bd., 1964-65; mem. bd. dirs. Combined Health Appeal of Nat. Capital Area, 1982-93, v.p., 1983-85, pres., 1986-88. Social Sci. Rsch. Coun. grantee, 1959, 61. Mem. Am. Polit. Sci. Assn., Midwest Polit. Sci. Assn. (exec. coun. 1972-75), Mid. States Assn. Colls. and Schs. (cons.-evaluator 1983-97), Law and Soc. Assn., AAUP, Am. Assn. Higher Edn. (vis. scholar 1994), North Ctrl. Assn. Colls. and Schs. (commn. on instns. higher edn. 1975-80, exec. bd. 1979-80, cons.-evaluator 1975-80), Nat. Coun. Chief Acad. Officers, Am. Coun. on Edn. (exec.com. 1983-85, chmn. 1985). Office: Am U 4400 Massachusetts Ave NW Washington DC 20016-8022

GREENBERG, MORTON IRA, federal judge; b. Philadelphia, Pa., Mar. 20, 1933; s. Harry Arnold and Pauline (Hofkin) Greenberg; m. Barbara-Ann Kissel, May 29, 1987; children from previous marriage: Elizabeth, Suzanne, Lawrence. AB, U. Pa., 1954; LLB, Yale U., 1957. Bar: N.J. 1958, U.S. Dist. Ct. N.J. 1958, U.S. Ct. Appeals (3d cir.) 1972, U.S. Supreme Ct. 1973. Law clk.office of atty. gen. State of N.J., Trenton, NJ, 1957—58, dep. atty. gen., 1958—60, asst. atty. gen., 1971—73; pvt. practice Cape May, 1960—71; judge law div. Superior Ct. N.J., New Brunswick, 1973—76, judge chancery and gen. equity divs. Trenton, 1976—80, judge appellate div., 1980—87; judge U.S. Ct. Appeals (3d cir.), Trenton and Phila., 1987—. Office: US Ct Appeals US Courthouse 402 E State St Ste 7050 Trenton NJ 08608-1507

GREENBERG, MORTON PAUL, lawyer, consultant, life settlement broker; b. Fall River, Mass., June 2, 1946; s. Harry and Sylvia Shirley (Davis) Greenberg; m. Louise Beryl Schindler, Jan. 24, 1970; 1 child, Alexis Lynn. BSBA, NYU, 1968; JD, Bklyn. Law Sch., 1971. Bar: N.Y. 1972; CLU Am. Coll., 1975. Atty. Hanner, Fitzmaurice & Onorato, N.Y.C., 1971—72; dir., counsel, cons. on advanced underwriting The Mfrs. Life Ins. Co., Toronto, 1972—98; mng. gen. agt. for life settlements Viaticus, Inc., Chgo., 1999—2001; prin. life settlement broker Parker, Co., 1998—. Mem. sales ideas com. Million Dollar Roundtable, Chgo., 1982—83, 4th ann. George M. Graves meml. lectr., 1991; mem. adv. bd. Keeping Current, 1999—; spkr. on law, tax, life settlements, and advanced underwriting various profl. groups. Contbr. articles to profl. jours.; author: (tech. jour.) ManuBriefs. Mem.: ABA, Soc. Fin. Svcs. Profls., Nat. Assn. Ins. and Fin. Advisors, Internat. Platform Assn., Assn. for Advanced Life Underwriting (mem. bus. ins. and estate planning steering com. 1989—93), N.Y. State Bar Assn., Stern Sch. Bus. Alumni Assn., NYU Alumni Assn. Office: PO Box 183 7617 E Sunrise Trail Parker CO 80134-6915

GREENBERG, MYRON SILVER, lawyer; b. L.A., Oct. 17, 1945; s. Earl W. and Geri (Silver) G.; m. Shlomit Gross; children: David, Amy, Sophie, Benjamin. BSBA, UCLA, 1967; JD, 1970. Bar: Calif., 1971, U.S. Dist. Ct. (middle dist.) Calif. 1971, U.S. Tax Ct. 1977; cert. splst. in taxation law bd. legal specialization State Bar Calif.; CPA, Calif. Staff acct. Touche Ross & Co., L.A., 1970-71; assoc. Kaplan, Livingston, Goodwin, Berkowitz, & Selvin, Beverly Hills, Calif., 1971-74; ptnr. Steefel, Levitt, & Weiss, 1975—82, Myron S. Greenberg, a Profl. Corp., Larkspur, Calif., 1982—. Professorial lectr. tax. Golden Gate U.; instr. U. Calif., Berkeley, 2002-. Author: California Attorney's Guide to Professional Corporations, 1977, 79; bd. editors UCLA Law Rev., 1969-70. Mem. San Anselmo Planning Commn., 1976-77; mem. adv. bd. cert. program personal fin. planning U. Calif., Berkeley, 1991—; bd. dirs. Marin County Estate Planning Coun., 2001—, v.p. 2003. Mem.: ABA, AHA (bd. dirs. Marin county chpt. 1984—90, pres. 1988—89), Calif. Bd. Legal Specialization (mem. tax commn. 1998—2001, chmn. 2001, bd. dirs.), Real Estate Tax Inst. Calif. Cont. Edn. Bar (planning com.), Marin County (Calif.) Bar Assn. (bd. dirs. 1994—2001, pres. 1999), L.A. County Bar Assn., Larkspur C. of C. (bd. dirs. 1985—87). Democrat. Jewish. Office: # 205 700 Larkspur Landing Cir Larkspur CA 94939-1711 E-mail: msg@eplaw.com.

GREENBERG, NATHAN, accountant; b. Worcester, Mass., May 17, 1919; s. Samuel and Ida (Katz) G.; m. Mimi Aaron, Mar. 12, 1950 (dec.); children: Henry Aaron, Ruthanne; m. Barbara Rudnick, Feb. 9, 1979. BS in Bus. Adminstrn, Boston U., 1942. CPA, Mass. With IRS, 1945-47; v.p. finance, dir. Gt. Am. Plastics Co., Worcester, Mass., 1948-68, Gt. Am. Chem. Corp., Fitchburg, Mass., 1968-80; founder Greenberg, Rosenblatt, Kull & Bitsoli, P.C., Worcester, 1958—. Bd. dirs. Xsirius, Inc., Kleinert's, Inc. Trustee Nathan and Barbara Greenberg Charitable Trust, Jewish Home for Aged, Jewish Community Center, Jewish Fedn. Served with AUS, 1942-45, ETO. Decorated Bronze Star. Fellow AICPA, Mass. Soc. CPA's, Fla. Soc. CPA's, Controllers Inst. Am.; mem. Mu Sigma. Home: 85 Aylesbury Rd Worcester MA 01609-1217 Office: The Day Bldg 306 Main St Worcester MA 01608-1550

GREENBERG, PAUL, editor; b. Shreveport, La., Jan. 21, 1937; s. Ben and Sarah (Ackerman) G.; m. Carolyn Levy, Dec. 6, 1964; children: Daniel, Ruth Elizabeth. B. Journalism, U. Mo., 1958, MA in History, 1959; student, Columbia Grad. Sch., 1960-62; LittD, Rhodes Coll., 1995. Lectr. Am. history Hunter Coll., 1962; editorial page editor Pine Bluff (Ark.) Comml., 1962-66, 67-92; syndicated columnist, 1970—; editorial page editor Ark. Dem. Gazette, Little Rock, 1992—. Editorial writer Chgo. Daily News, 1966-67; adj. faculty in history U. Ark., Pine Bluff, 1978-82, vis. Fulbright fellow, 1985, mem. faculty in journalism, U. Ark., 1991. Author: Resonant Lives, 1991, Entirely Personal, 1992, No Surprises, 1996. Served to capt. U.S. Army, 1969. Recipient Grenville Clark award for best editorial, 1964, Pulitzer prize editorial writing, 1969, award Nat. Newspaper Assn., 1968, U. Mo. Sch. Journalism award, 1983, Walker Stone award for editorial writing, 1985, 86; Pulitzer Prize finalist for editorial writing, 1986; H.L. Mencken Writing award, 1987; William Allen White Journalism award U. Kans., 1988, Green Eyeshade award, 1997; Katie award Dallas Press Club, 1999, 2000. Jewish. Office: Arkansas Democrat Gazette Capitol at Scott Little Rock AR 72202

GREENBERG, PHILIP B. symphony orchestra conductor and music director; Asst. condr. Detroit Symphony, 4 yrs.; resident condr. Phoenix Symphony; music dir., condr. Fresno (Calif.) Philharm., Savannah (Ga.) Symphony, 1984—. Founder Kuhlman Changer Orch., Wachovia Chamber Orch., Branigar Chamber Orch. series, Black Heritage concert, Pops series. Gave first pub. violin concert at age 15; numerous appearances as guest condr. throughout world, including New Zealand Symphony, Spain and Portugal, Moscow State Orch., Danish Radio Orch., Austin, El Paso and Va. symphonys, Colo. Music Festival, N.H. Music Festival; made Asian debut with Beijing Broadcasting Symphony. Recipient 1st prize and orch. prize Nicolai Malko Conducting Competition, Copenhagen. Office: Savannah Symphony Orch PO Box 9505 225 Abercorn St Savannah GA 31401 Fax: 912-234-1450.

GREENBERG, RAYMOND SETH, academic administrator, educator; b. Chapel Hill, N.C., Aug. 10, 1955; s. Bernard George and Ruth Esther (Marck) G.; m. Leah Daniella Dacus, Oct. 23, 1988. BA with highest honors, U. N.C., 1976, PhD, 1983; MD, Duke U., 1979; MPH, Harvard U., 1980; DMS (hon.), The Citadel, 2001; DS (hon.), Simpson Coll., 2002. Asst. prof. sch. medicine Emory U., Atlanta, 1983-86, assoc. prof., 1986-90, dep. dir. Winship Cancer Ctr., 1985-90, chair epidemiology/ biostat., 1988-90, prof., dean sch. pub. health, 1990-95; v.p. for acad. affairs, provost Med. U. S.C., Charleston, 1995-99, pres., 2000—. Chair preventive medicine Nat. Bd. Med. Examiners, Phila., 1991-93; chair epidemiology study sect. NIH, Bethesda, Md., 1992-94; bd. sci. counselors Nat. Inst. for Dental and Craniofacial Rsch., Bethesda, 1994-99, mem. blue ribbon panel on rsch. tng. and career devel., 1999; chair adv. coun. Prudential Ctr. for Health Care Rsch., Atlanta, 1994-96; chair Harvard Adv. Com. on Electromagnetic Fields and Human Health, Boston, 1994-98; adv. com. on rsch. and med. grants, Am. Cancer Soc., Atlanta, 1994-96; breast and cervical cancer early detection and control adv. com., Ctrs. for Disease Control and Prevention, Atlanta, 1996-2000; adv. com. on agrl. health risks, Harvard Ctr. for Risk Analysis, Boston, 1996-99; clin. adv. bd. Deloitte and Touche Healthcare Consulting Group, 1997-99; chair sci. adv. panel 3M Corp., 1998—. Author: Medical Epidemiology, 1993, 2d edit., 1996, 3d edit., 2001, Epidemiologia Medica, 1995, 2nd edit., 1998; contbr. articles to profl. jours. Bd. dirs. Ga. divsn. Am. Cancer Soc., 1987-93, Carolina Art Assn., 1996-98, Trident United Way, 1999-2002. Fellow Am. Coll. Epidemiology (pres. 1990-91); mem. APHA, Am. Epidemiology Soc. Democrat. Jewish. Office: Med Univ SC Rm 200 A PO Box 250001 171 Ashley Ave Charleston SC 29425-0001

GREENBERG, RITA MOFFETT, special education educator, consultant; b. May 29, 1945; d. Joseph and Rita Marie (Clifford) Moffett; m. Morris Greenberg, Aug. 8, 1971. BA in Early Childhood Edn., Elem. Edn., Paterson State Coll., 1967; M in Spl. Edn., Learning Disabilities, William Paterson Coll. (formerly Paterson State Coll.), 1988. Cert. early childhood tchr., N.J., elem. tchr., N.J., spl. edn./learning disabilities tchr., N.J., supr. Tchr. learning disabilities, cons. child study team Waldwick (N.J.) Bd. of Edn., 1990—. Adj. on-site supr. William Paterson Coll., Wayne, N.J., 1987-90, adj. grad. extern in learning disabilities, summer 1991, 92, 97, adj. undergrad. in spl. edn., 1992-93, guest lectr., 1994; cons. Bergen County Dept. Youth and Family Guidance, 1994. Contbr. articles to profl. jours. Mem. N.J. Assn. Learning Cons. (chairperson membership com. 1990-92), Coun. for Exceptional Children (divsn. learning disabilities, Professionally Recognized Spl. Educator in Edn. Diagnosis 2001), Waldwick Edn. Assn., Orton Dyslexia Soc., N.J. Edn. Assn., Kappa Delta Pi. Avocations: baking, travel. Home: 2077 Center Ave Apt 18B Fort Lee NJ 07024-4904 Office: Waldwick Bd of Edn Spl Svcs 155 Summit Ave Waldwick NJ 07463-2133

GREENBERG, ROBERT JAY, law educator; b. N.Y.C., Nov. 22, 1959; s. Murray Louis and Jeanette (Adams) G.; m. Dafna Rena Fuerst, June 29, 1993; children: Ashira Esther, Aliza Gila, Leora Adina. BA, Yeshiva U., 1981, JD, 1984, LLM, 2000. Bar: N.Y. 1986, U.S. Dist. Ct. N.Y. (ea. and so. dists.) 1986, U.S. Supreme Ct. 1989, U.S. Ct. Appeals (2d cir.) 1998, N.J. 2000, U.S. Dist. Ct. N.Y. (no. and we. dists.) 2000, U.S. Dist. Ct. N.J. 2000, D.C. 2001, U.S. Ct. Appeals (fed. cir.) 2001, Conn. 2001, U.S. Ct. of Internat. Trade 2002, Wyo. 2003; lic. real estate broker N.Y., notary public N.Y., N.J. Asst. to judge N.Y.C. Civil Ct., Bklyn., 1982; assoc. Simon, Meyrowitz, Meyrowitz and Schlussel, N.Y.C., 1983-86; instr. Bruriah High Sch. for Girls, Elizabeth, N.J., 1985-87; lectr. Nat. Acad. for Paralegal Studies, Mahwah, N.J., 1987-88; sr. legal editor Matthew Bender and Co., Inc., N.Y.C., 1987-94. Adj. asst. prof. bus. law Yeshiva U., N.Y.C., 1994-98, asst. prof., 1998—; lectr. NYU Inst. Paralegal Studies, N.Y.C., 1994-2000, adj. assoc. prof., 2001—; instr. dept. paralegal studies Queens College CUNY, 1994—. Asst. to author: Judaism and Vegetarianism, Judaism and Global Survival. Lectr. in Jewish law Young Israel of Staten Island, 1976—93, Congregation Beth Yehuda, Staten Island, 1980—93, Young Israel of Forest Hills, Queens, 1993—2003, Queens Jewish Ctr., 2000—03, Congregation Ohr Moshe, Queens, 2003—. Recipient Disting. Svc. award Congregation Beth Yehuda, 1988, Outstanding Svc. award, 1991. Mem.: ABA, Acad. of Legal Studies in Bus., N.Y. County Lawyers Assn., N.Y. State Bar Assn. Democrat. Office: 75-27 171st St Fresh Meadows NY 11366-1416

GREENBERG, RONALD DAVID, lawyer, law educator; b. San Antonio, Sept. 9, 1939; s. Benjamin and Sylvia (Ghetlzer) G. BS, U. Tex., 1957; MBA, Harvard U., 1961, JD, 1964. Bar: N.Y., 1966, U.S. Dist. Ct. (ea. and so. dists.) N.Y. 1970, U.S. Ct. Appeals (2d cir.) 1975, U.S. Supreme Ct. 1975. Engring. lab. instr. U. Tex., 1957; engr. Redstone Arsenal, Army Ballistic Missile Agy., 1957; engr., bus. analyst Exxon Corp., N.Y.C., 1957-64; rsch. asst. Harvard Bus. Sch.; with Smithsonian Astrophys. Observatory and Ednl. Testing Svc., N.J., 1961-62; atty., engr. Allied Corp., N.Y.C., 1964-67; assoc. Arthur, Dry, Kalish, Taylor & Wood, N.Y.C., 1967-69, Valicenti, Leighton, Reid & Pine, N.Y.C., 1969-70; instr. faculty Columbia U., N.Y.C., 1972-81, adj. prof. bus. law and taxation, 1970-71, 82-98; of counsel Delson & Gordon, N.Y.C., 1973-87; sole practitioner Harrison, N.Y., 1988—. Lectr., cons. AICPA, Inst. Internal Auditors, New Haven C. of C., Citibank, Mfrs. Hanover Trust Co., Harcourt, Brace, Jovanovich, Inc., Prudential-Bache, Drexel, Burnham & Lambert, E.F. Hutton; vol. instr. vol. income tax program, Columbia U., N.Y.C., 1991-92; vis. prof. Stanford U., Palo Alto, Calif., 1978, Harvard U., Boston, 1981. Author: Business Income Tax Materials, 1994; (with others) Business Organizations: Corporations, General Practice in New York, 1998, Business/Corporate Law and Practice, 3d edit., 2001; editor: The Compleat Lawyer, 1985-88, Tax Lawyer, 1982-95; editor in chief N.Y. Internat. Law Rev., 1988-91, chair adv. bd., 1992—; editor in chief Internat. Law Practicum, 1987-91; contbr. chpts. to books, articles to profl. jours. Cons. coun. City of N.Y., 1971-72, Manhattan C.C., 1974-76. Lt. USNR, 1957-59. Recipient Outstanding Prof. award Columbia U. Grad. Sch. Bus., 1973, MIT Fellowship Mech. Engring. Dept., 1959, Harvard U., Teagle Found., 1959-61; grantee Ford Found., 1977, Columbia U. Ctr. Internat. Studies, Sch. Internat. Pub. Affairs, 1992, Columbia Bus. Sch.,

1976, 92, 93, 94. Mem. AAAS, ABA (chmn. com. on taxation gen. practice sect. 1978-83, chmn. com. on corp. banking and bus. law. gen. practice sect. 1985-87, moderator, chair profl. edn. programs 1986, 87), ASME, NSPE, N.Y. State Bar Assn. (gen. practice sect., chmn. tax law com. 1983-92, chmn. bus. law com. 1985-88, internat. law & practice sect., chmn. pubs. com. 1988-91, coord. study com. on med. malpractice legislation, 1980-82), Assn. Bar City N.Y., N.Y. Acad. Scis., Mensa, Tau Beta Pi, Pi Tau Sigma, Phi Eta Sigma, Am. Assn. for the Advancement of Sci. E-mail: rdgreenberg@hotmail.com.

GREENBERG, SAMUEL I. psychiatrist, psychoanalyst; b. Bklyn., July 4, 1912; s. Harry and Gitel Greenberg; children: Deborah A., Benjamin D., Jennifer. AB with distinction, George Washington U., 1932; MD, U. Chgo./Rush, 1936. Diplomate Am. Bd. Psychiatry and Neurology. Pvt. practice psychiatry, N.Y.C. and Miami, Fla., 1948-80; assoc. vis. prof. Med. Coll. U. Fla., Gainesville, 1980-85, clin. prof. psychiatry, 1997—. Cons. VA Med. Ctr., Gainesville, 1987—; vis. prof. U. Fla. Med. Coll., Gainesville, 1987-90. Author: Neurosis, 1971, Euthanasia and Assisted Suicide, 1997, Technique Psychotherapy, 1998. Lt. col. Med. Corps U.S. Army, 1941-46. Fellow Am. Psychiat. Assn.; mem. Fla. Psychiat. Assn., So. Fla. Psychiat. Assn. (pres. 1969-80). Address: 2715 NW 21st St Gainesville FL 32605-2936

GREENBERG, SHELDON BURT, plastic and reconstructive surgeon; b. Bklyn., July 8, 1948; s. Morris and Lillian (Liss) G.; m. Andrea R. Levy, Feb. 10, 1991; children: Matthew, Joshua. BS, Muhlenberg Coll., 1970; MD, Chgo. Med. Sch., 1974. Diplomate Am. Bd. Otolaryngology, Plastic Surgery. Resident in surgery Lenox Hill Hosp., N.Y.C., 1974-75; resident in otolaryngology Met. Hosp., Manhattan Eye and Ear Hosp., N.Y.C., 1978; resident in plastic surgery Akron (Ohio) City Hosp., 1978-80, fellow in hand surgery, 1980; pvt. practice Norwalk, Conn., 1981—; chief, plastic surgery Norwalk Hosp., 1996—. Fellow Am. Coll. Surgeons, Am. Soc. Plastic Surgeons; mem. Conn. Med. Soc., Fairfield County Med. Soc., Fairfield Men's Club. Republican. Jewish. Avocations: tennis, american history, gardening. Office: 40 Cross St Norwalk CT 06851-4647

GREENBERG, STEPHEN MICHAEL, lawyer, business executive; b. Passaic, N.J., July 27, 1944; s. Joseph Louis and Bess S. (Stein) G.; m. Sandra Lafer, Sept. 1, 1967; children: Seth, Sindy, Scott. BA, Washington (Pa.) Jefferson Coll., 1965; JD with honors, George Washington U., 1968. Bar: U.S. Dist. Ct. N.J. 1968, U.S. Ct. Appeals (3d cir.) 1968, U.S. Dist. Ct. (no. dist.) Ind. 1972, N.Y. 1983. Exec. asst. U.S. atty. N.J. Justice Dept., Newark, 1970-71; ptnr. Robinson, Wayne & Greenberg, Newark, 1971-82; gen. ptnr. Lafer Mgmt. Corp., N.Y.C., 1989—; ptnr. Hellring, Lindeman, Goldstein, Siegel, Stern & Greenberg, Newark, 1983-90; chmn. bd. dirs., sec. Flex Holding Co., N.Y.C., 1985-88; chmn. bd. dirs., acting chief exec. officer Graphic Scanning Corp., Teaneck, N.J., 1986-88; ptnr. Stern & Greenberg, Roseland, N.J., 1990—; CEO, vice chmn. Netzphone, Inc., 2000—. Bd. dirs. Switchco, Inc., Teaneck, Israel Investors Corp., N.Y.C.; chmn. bd. dirs. Time and Space Processing Inc., Santa Clara, Calif., bd. dirs. Winstar. Nat. vice chmn. United Jewish Appeal, N.Y.C., 1986—; v.p. Am. Friends of Hebrew U., N.Y.C., 1986-89; apptd. to Op. Independence by Prime Minister of Israel, Jerusalem and N.Y., 1986—. Recipient Lehman Leadership award United Jewish Appeal, 1984. Mem. ABA, N.J. Bar Assn. (Outstanding Profl. Achievement award 1986). Democrat. Home: 616 S Orange Ave Maplewood NJ 07040-1047 Office: Net2Phone Inc 520 Broad St Newark NJ 07102

GREENBERG, STEPHEN ROBERT, retired pathology educator; b. Omaha, May 5, 1927; s. Nathan Henry and Ruth (Levey) G.; m. Constance Bettine, June 4, 1952; children: Andrew Eugene, Nathan Henry. BS, St. Louis U., 1951, MS, 1952, PhD in Pathology, 1954. Asst. in pathology Clarkson Hosp., Omaha, 1954-55; instr. pathology Chgo. Med. Sch., 1955-57, assoc. in pathology, 1957-62, asst. prof., 1962-69, assoc. prof. pathology, 1969-93. Lectr. Cook County Grad. Sch. Medicine, Chgo., 1973-83. Contbr. over 150 articles to profl. jours. Forensic Scis. Found. grantee, 1988-91. Fellow Inst. of Medicine of Chgo.; mem. Am. Soc. Clin. Pathologists, Am. Acad. Forensic Scis., Am. Assn. Clin. Anatomists, Internat. Acad. Pathology, Masons (33 deg.). Republican. Jewish. Fax: 708-748-1262.

GREENBERG, STEVEN M. physician; b. N.Y.C., N.Y., June 26, 1956; s. Nathan and Jean Greenberg; m. Elizabeth Anne Altanasio, June 6, 1999; children: Aaron, Adam, Lauren. BS, SUNY, 1977; MD, Albany Med. Coll., 1983. Lic. N.Y., 1984, cert. diplomate Nat. Bd. Med. Examiners, 1983, Am. Bd. Internal Medicine, 1986, Am. Bd. Internal Medicine Subspecialty in Cardiovasc. Disease, 1989. Intern, resident internal medicine Bronx Med. Hosp. and Hosp. of Albert Einstein Coll. of Medicine, 1983—86; dir. clin. evaluation unit Weiler Hosp. of Albert Einstein Coll. of Medicine, Bronx, 1986, asst. attending physician, 1986; rsch. fellow cardiology Albert Einstein Coll. of Medicine, Bronx, 1986—87; asst. attending physician Queens Hosp. Ctr., 1986—89, Bronx Mcpl. Hosp. Ctr., 1986—90; fellow cardiology Mt. Sinai Hosp., N.Y.C., 1987—90, attending physician, 1989—90, St. Francis Hosp., Roslyn, NY, 1990—, coord., pacemaker ctr., 1991, dir. CCU, 1994—. Co-author articles in numerous profl. jours. Fellow: Am. Coll. Physicians, Am. Coll. Cardiology. Avocations: kayaking, coin collecting. Office: St Francis Hosp 100 Pt Washington Blvd Roslyn NY 11576 Fax: 516-562-6646.

GREENBERG, STEVEN MOREY, lawyer; b. Jersey City, Apr. 9, 1949; s. Joseph and Rhoda (Weisenfeld) Greenberg. AB cum laude, Syracuse U., 1971; JD, U. Pa., 1974. Bar: N.J. 1974, U.S. Dist. Ct. N.J. 1974, N.Y. 1980, U.S. Dist. Ct. (so. and ea. dists.) N.Y. 1986, U.S. Ct. Appeals (3d cir.) 1987, U.S. Ct. Fed. Claims 1989. Assoc. Carpenter, Bennett & Morrissey, Newark, 1974-77, Cole, Berman & Belsky, Rochelle Park, NJ, 1977-79; pvt. practice Hackensack, NJ, 1979-94; atty. Bergenfield (N.J.) Rent Leveling Bd., 1985-89, 92-93, 99, Bergenfield Planning Bd., 1993-96; ptnr. Greenberg & Marmorstein, Hackensack, 1994-97, Greenberg & Lanz, Hackensack, 1997—. Numerous offices Jewish Ctr. Teaneck, NJ, 1978—97, United Jewish Appeal Fedn., Bergen County, North Hudson, 1997—; pres. Jewish Inst. Bioethics, N.Y.C., 1998—; trustee Jewish Assn. Devel. Disabilities, 1999—, Jewish Family Svc. Inc., Bergen County, 1986—96, Bergen County HS Jewish Studies, 2000—; mem. Jewish Cmty. Rels. Coun. Bergen County and North Hudson, 1986—93, 1999—; trustee Assn. Jewish Fedns., NJ, 2002—03, mem. exec./ops. com., 2002; numerous offices Jewish Home, Rockleigh, NJ, 1999—, Jewish Home Found. N. Jersey, Inc., NJ, 2003—; dir. Union Traditional Judaism, 1993—97; numerous offices Jewish Home and Rehab. Ctr., Jersey City, River Vale, NJ, 1982—; mem. N.J. regional adv. bd. Anti-Defamation League, 1989—, mem. exec. com., 1989- ; mem. N.J. Leadership Think Tank The Allen and Joan Bildner Ctr. Study of Jewish Life Rutgers U., 2001—. Recipient Second Century award, Jewish Theol. Sem. Am., 1988, Cmty. Svc. award, Friends Lubavitch, 1997, award, Jewish Ctr. Teaneck, 1997, Ma'ayanot Yeshiva HS Girls, 2001, Americanism award, Anti-Defamation League, 2003. Mem.: ABA, Assn. Transp. Practitioners, N.Y. State Bar Assn., Bergen County Bar Assn., N.J. Bar Assn., Pi Sigma Alpha, Phi Kappa Phi. Home: 96 Westminster Ave Bergenfield NJ 07621-3916 Office: 2 University Plz Hackensack NJ 07601-6202 E-mail: smg@greenberglanz.com.

GREENBERG, STEWART GARY, lawyer; b. Flushing, N.Y., Feb. 2, 1955; s. Herman Leo and Constance Ann G.; m. Wendy L., Dec. 25, 1976; children: Melissa, Jonathan, Jennifer, Michael. BA, NYU, 1976; JD, U. Miami, 1979. Bar: Fla. 1979, N.Y. 1986. Assoc. Rizzo & Koltun, Miami, Fla., 1976-83; ptnr. Koltun & Greenberg, Miami, Fla., 1983-93; atty. pvt. practice, Miami, Fla., 1993—. CEO, dir. Upscale Techs., Inc., Miami, 1996-97. Pres. Bet Shira Congregation, Miami, 1990-91, v.p., 1984-90; bd. dirs. Jewish Adoption & Foster Care Options, Sunrise, Fla., 1998—. Mem. Assn. Trial Lawyers Am., Acad. Fla. Trial Lawyers, Dade County Trial Lawyers Assn. Avocations: golf, sailing, fishing. Office: 11440 N Kendall Dr Ste 400 Miami FL 33176-1025

GREENBERG, WILLIAM MICHAEL, psychiatrist; b. Bklyn., Oct. 19, 1946; s. Benjamin Greenberg and Marilyn (Berger) Hamberg; m. Wendy Faith Megerman, June 14, 1992. BA, Queens Coll., 1968; postgrad., U. Medicine & Dentistry N.J., 1974-76; MD, Albert Einstein Coll. Medicine, 1978. Diplomate Am. Bd. Psychiatry and Neurology, Am. Bd. Geriatric Psychiatry, Am. Bd. Forensic Psychiatry, Am. Bd. Addiction Psychiatry, cert. clin. psychopharmacology. Computer programmer Western Electric Co., N.Y.C., 1970-73; rsch. asst. Bklyn. Jewish Hosp., 1973-74; resident in psychiatry Bronx (N.Y.) Mcpl. Hosp. Ctr., 1978-83, house staff pres., 1981-82; acting med. dir. Met. Ctr. for Mental Health, N.Y.C., 1983; staff psychiatrist Bronx Psychiat. Ctr., 1983-84; dir. psychiatry clinic North Cen. Bronx Hosp., 1984-88; psychiatrist, cons. Montefiore Mental Health Svcs. at Rikers Island, East Elmhurst, N.Y., 1985-86; pvt. practice Bronx, 1985-88; chief psychiatrist, attending staff mem. Bergen Pines County Hosp. (now Bergen Regional Med. Ctr.), Paramus, N.J., 1988-96, dir. of psychiat. rsch., 1993-2000, interim med. dir. psychiatry, 1996-98, dir. psychiatry residency tng. program, 1997-2000, mem. spkr.'s bur., 1988-2000, chmn. instnl. rev. bd., 1996-2000; dir. outpatient rsch. ctr. Nat. Kline Inst., Orangeburg, NJ, 2001—; pvt practice NJ, 1997—. Asst clin prof Albert Einstein Col Med, Bronx, NY, 1988—90; vis asst prof Med Col Pa, 1990—94, adj asst prof, 1994—2000; adj. assoc. prof. Drexel U. Coll. Medicine, 2000—; adj. assoc. prof. environ. medicine NYU Sch. Medicine, 2001—; prin investigator clin drug trials. Editor: NJ Psychiatrist, 2001—; asst. editor: Cmty. Psychiatrist, 1985—89, mem. editl. bd.: Einstein Quar. Jour. Biology and Medicine, 1987—2000; contbr. articles to profl. jours. Union rep Comt Interns and Residents, New York, NY, 1979—81; speaker's bur Physicians for Social Responsibility, New York, NY, 1982—84. Recipient Bergen Pines Psychiat Residency Teaching Award, 1991, Psychiatrist Recognition Award, NJ Alliance for Mentally Ill, 1996, scholar Rock Sleyster Mem, AMA, 1977. Mem.: APHA, AAAS, N.J. Psychiat. Soc. (pres. 1998—99, pres.-elect 2003—), Assn. Advancement Philosophy and Psychiatry, Am. Assn. Cmty. Psychiatrists, Am. Psychiat. Assn. Avocations: analytic philosophy, meditation, computers, photography. Office: Nathan S Kline Inst Psychiatry Outpatient Rsch Orangeburg NY 10962

GREENBERGER, ALAN, architectural firm executive; BS in Architecture, Rensselaer Polytechnic Inst., 1973, B in Architecture (cum laude), 1974. Cert. NCARB, Pa., Calif., Va., D.C. Ptnr. Mitchell/Giurgola Architects, 1986—, assoc., 1981—86, with, 1974—81; ptnr. MGA Ptnrs., 1990—. Project ptnr. Wharton Sch. of Bus. Feasibility Study, U. of Pa., 1992, E.O. Bull Theater Renovation, West Chester U., Pa., 1994, New Meml. Hall, Grove City Coll., Pa., 1994, Swarthmore Coll., Intercultural Ctr. Study, 1999, Temple U., Tyler Sch. of Art Masterplan, Phila., 2000, Drexel U., Coll. of Design Arts Masterplan, Phila., 2000, Terra Bldg., U. of the Arts, Phila., 2000, student residence, U. of the Arts, Phila., 2000, Theater/Neal Marshall Edn. Ctr., Ind. U., Bloomington, 2002, Space Utilization Plan, U. of the Arts, Phila., 1998. Chmn. R/UDAT Cmty. Rels. Com., 1990; bd. mem. The Found. for Architecture, 1998—, Old City Spcl. Svcs. Dist., 1999—. Mem.: AIA (pres. Phila. chpt. 1992, chmn. Balt. design awards jury 1993, chmn. Phila. chpt. independance mall task force 1996), Phila. Found. for Architecture, Am. Inst. of Architects Phila. Chpt. Office: MGA Ptnrs Architects 234 Market St Philadelphia PA 19106 Fax: 215-923-4258.*

GREENBERGER, ELLEN, psychologist, educator; b. N.Y.C., Nov. 19, 1935; d. Edward Michael and Vera (Brisk) Silver; m. Michael Burton, Aug. 26, 1979; children by previous marriage— Kari Edwards, David Silver. BA, Vassar Coll., 1956; MA, Harvard U., 1959, PhD, 1961. Instr. Wellesley (Mass.) Coll., 1961—67; sr. rsch. scientist Johns Hopkins U., Balt., 1967-76; prof. psychology and social behavior U. Calif., Irvine, 1976—. Author: (with others) When Teenagers Work, 1986; contbr. articles to profl. jours. USPHS fellow, 1956-59; Margaret Floy Washburn fellow, 1956-58; Ford Found. grantee, 1979-81; Spencer Found. grantee, 1979 81, 87, 88-91. Fellow APA, Am. Psychol. Soc.; mem. Soc. Rsch. in Child Devel., Soc. Rsch. on Adolescent Devel. Office: U Calif 3340 Social Ecology II Irvine CA 92697-7085 E-mail: egreenbe@uci.edu.

GREENBERGER, HOWARD LEROY, lawyer, educator; b. Pitts., July 16, 1929; s. Abraham Harry and Alice (Levine) G.; m. Bette Jo Bergad, June 15, 1959. BS magna cum laude, U. Pitts., 1951; JD cum laude, NYU, 1954; diploma in law (Fulbright scholar), Oxford (Eng.) U., 1955. Bar: Pa. 1955, D.C. 1954, N.Y. 1969, U.S. Supreme Ct. 1964. Law clk. U.S. Ct. Appeals (3d cir.), 1958-60; assoc. Kaufman & Kaufman, Pitts., 1960-61; assoc. prof. law NYU, 1961-65, prof., 1965—2001, prof. emeritus, 2001—; assoc. dean NYU Sch. Law, 1968-72; dean and dir. Practising Law Inst., 1972-75; senator NYU, 1994—. Cons. in field.; v.p. Nat. Ctr. Para-Legal Tng.; pres. Early Am. Industries Assn., 1979-82; chmn. Commn. on Fgn. Grad. Study, AALS. Author: (with G. Cole) The Meriden Experiment, 1973; Study of the Quality of Continuing Legal Education in the U.S. 1980; contbr. articles to legal publs.; chmn. editorial bd. Jour. Legal Edn, 1974-77. Pres. N.Y.C. chpt. Am. Jewish Com., 1977-79, nat. bd. govs., 1979-85; vice chmn., gen. counsel Coalition to Free Soviet Jews, 1977—; trustee Law Ctr. Found., 1973-91, Am. Friends of Hebrew U. Jerusalem, 1986—; chair New Amsterdam dist. Boy Scouts Am., 1990—, Ctr. on Social Welfare Policy and Law, 1991—, Blaustein Inst. on Human Rights, 1992—. Capt. JAGC, U.S. Army, 1955-58. Recipient Alumni Meritorious Svc. award NYU, 1977, Stanley Isaacs award Am. Jewish Com., 1982, Gt. Tchr. award NYU, 1993, Friendship award Govt. of Germany, 1988, Robert B. McKay Disting. Svc. award N.Y.U. Sch. of Law, 1997, Great Tchr. award 1999; Root-Tilden grantee NYU, 1954. Fellow Am. Bar Found.; mem. ABA, Assn. of Bar of City of N.Y., N.Y. County Lawyers Assn. (bd. dirs. 1990—), Am. Law Inst., Assn. Am. Law Schs., NYU Club (pres. 1981-83, Masons, Sojourners, Order of Coif, Phi Epsilon Pi. Democrat. Jewish. Home: 4 Washington Square Vlg Apt 16 New York NY 10012-1936 Office: NYU Sch Law Vand Hall 40 Washington Sq S New York NY 10012-1005

GREENBERGER, I. MICHAEL, lawyer; b. Scranton, Pa., Oct. 30, 1945; s. David and Betty (Kabatchnick) G.; m. Marcia Devins, July 19, 1969; children: Sarah Devins, Anne Devins AB, Lafayette Coll., 1967; JD, U. Pa., 1970. Bar: D.C. 1971, U.S. Dist. Ct. D.C. 1971, U.S. Ct. Appeals (D.C. cir.) 1971, U.S. Supreme Ct. 1975. Law clk. to Judge Carl McGowan U.S. Ct. Appeals for D.C. Circuit, Washington, 1970-71; legis. asst. to U.S. Congresswoman Elizabeth Holtzman, 1972-73; atty., advisor Office of Criminal Justice, Office U.S. Atty. Gen., 1973; assoc. Shea & Gardner, Washington, 1973-77, ptnr., 1977-97; dir. divsn. of trading and markets U.S. Commodity Futures Trading Commn., 1997-99; counselor to U.S. Atty. Gen., 1999, prin. dep. assoc., atty. gen., 1999-2001; vis. prof. U. Md. Law Sch., 2001—02, prof., 2002—; dir. U. Md. Ctr. for Health and Homeland Security, Md., 2002—. Bd. govs. D.C. Bar, 1995—98, com. on legal ethics, 1993—95; mem. D.C. Cir. Adv. Com. on Procedures, 1983—89; mem. steering com D.C. Pro Bono Partnership, 1994—97, Lafayette Coll. Leadership Coun., 1994—99; mediator office of cir. exec. U.S. Cts. for D.C., 1989—; mem. D.C. Cir. Jud. Conf., 1983—; legal cons. Software Engring. Inst. Carnegie-Mellon U., Pitts., 1986—87; mem. steering com. Pres.'s Working Group on Fin. Markets, 1997—99; mem. hedge fund task force Internat. Orgn. Secs. Commrs., 1999. Editor-in-chief U. Pa. Law Rev., 1969-70; contbr. articles to profl. jours. Bd. dirs. Washington Legal Clinic for the Homeless, 1993-98, Am. Rivers, 1993-98, sec., 1995-98; bd. dirs. MIT Enterprise Forum Washington, 1984-87, Advanced Tech. Assn. Md., 1985-87, D.C. Prisoners' Legal Svc. Project, 1997-98. Fellow: Am. Bar Found.; mem.: ABA (chair criminal justice com. 2003—, mem.individual rights and responsibilities sector 2003—), Am. Law Inst., Phi Beta Kappa. Address: 2757 Brandywine St NW Washington DC 20008-1041 E-mail: mgreenberger@law.umaryland.edu.

GREENBERGER, MARTIN, biotechnologist, information scientist, educator; b. Elizabeth, N.J., Nov. 30, 1931; s. David and Sidelle (Jonas) G.; m. Ellen Danica Silver, Feb. 2, 1959 (div. June 1974); children: Kari Edwards, David Silver; m. Liz Attardo, Dec. 11, 1982; children: Beth Jonit, Jonah Ben, Jilly Sal. AB, Harvard U., 1955, AM, 1956, PhD, 1958. Teaching fellow, resident adviser, staff mem. Computation Lab., Harvard U., Cambridge, 1954-58; mgr. applied sci. Cambridge IBM, 1956-58; asst. prof. mgmt. Mass. Inst. Tech., Cambridge, 1958-61, assoc. prof., 1961-67, prof., chmn. computer sci., dir. info. processing Johns Hopkins U., Balt., 1967-72; prof. math. scis., sr. research assoc. Center for Met. Planning and Research, 1972-75, prof. math. scis., 1978-82; IBM chair in tech. and info. systems UCLA Anderson Grad. Sch. Mgmt., 1982—; dir. UCLA Ctr. Digital Media, 1995-2000; pres. Council for Tech. and the Individual, 1985—; sr. fellow Milken Inst., 1999—. Mgr. systems program Electric Power Research Inst., Palo Alto, Calif., 1976-77; Isaac Taylor vis. prof. Technion-Israel Inst. Tech., Haifa, 1978-79; vis. prof. Internat. Energy Program, Grad. Sch. Bus., Stanford U., 1980, MIT Media Lab., 1988-89, Harvard U., 2001; computer sci. and engring. bd. NAS, 1970-72; chmn. COSATI rev. group NSF, 1971-72; evaluation com. Internat. Inst. for Applied Systems Analysis, Laxenburg, Austria, 1980; adv. panels, Office Tech. Assessment, GAO, U.S. Congress; adv. com. Getty Info. Inst.; cons. IBM, AT&T, CBS, Rand Corp., Morgan Guaranty, Arthur D. Little, TRW, Munger Tolles, Bolt, Beranek & Newman, Brookings Inst., Resources for Future, Electric Power Rsch. Inst., Atlantic Richfield, Rockwell Internat., Security Pacific Corp., John F. Kennedy Sch. of Govt. Harvard U., Bell Atlantic Corp., Sony Corp., Applied Minds, Mitchell Silberberg and Knupp, Am. Online, Kirkland and Ellis, Vertex Pharmaceuticals. Author: (with Orcutt, Korbel and Rivlin) Microanalysis of Socioeconomic Systems: A Simulation Study, 1961; (with Jones, Morris and Ness) On-Line Computation and Simulation: The OPS-3 System, 1965; (with Crenson and Crissey) Models in the Policy Process: Public Decision Making in the Computer Era, 1976; (with Brewer, Hogan and Russell) Caught Unawares: The Energy Decade in Retrospect, 1983; editor: Management and The Computer of the Future, 1962, republished as Computers and the World of the Future, 1964; Computers, Communications, and the Public Interest, 1971; (with Aronofsky, McKenney and Massy) Networks for Research and Education, 1973; Electronic Publishing Plus: Media for a Technological Future, 1985, Technologies for the 21st Century, Vol. 1, On Multimedia, 1990, Vol. 3, Multimedia in Review, 1992, Vol. 5, Content and Communication, 1994, Vol. 7, Scaling Up, 1996. Mem. overseers' vis. com. Harvard U., 1975-81; founder and mem. working groups Energy Modeling Forum, Stanford U., 1978-81; mem. adv. com. Nat. Center Analysis of Energy Systems Brookhaven Nat. Lab., 1976-80, chmn., 1977; mem. rev. com. Energy and Environment div. Lawrence Berkeley Lab., 1983, applied sci. div., 1986-88; chmn. forum on electronic pub. Washington program Annenberg, 1983-84; co-founder ICC Forum, 1985; chmn. CTI Roundtable, 1990-99; trustee Educom, Princeton, N.J., 1969-73, chmn. council, 1969-70. With USAF, 1952-54, USAFR, 1954-60. NSF fellow, 1955-56; Guggenheim fellow U. Calif., Berkeley, 1965-66. Fellow: AAAS (v.p., chmn. sect. T 1973—75); mem.: Sigma Xi, Phi Beta Kappa. Office: UCLA Anderson Grad Sch Mgmt Los Angeles CA 90095-1481 E-mail: mg@ucla.edu.

GREENBERGER, NORTON JERALD, physician; b. Cleve., Sept. 13, 1933; m. Joan Narcus, Aug. 10, 1964; children: Sharon, Rachel, Wendy. AB, Yale U., 1955; MD, Western Res. U., 1959. Diplomate: Am. Bd. Internal Medicine (sec.-treas. 1980-82). Intern Univ. Hosps., Cleve., 1959-60, resident internal medicine, 1960-62; USPHS fellow in gastroenterology Harvard U., 1962-65, Mass. Gen. Hosp., Boston, 1962-65; with Ohio State U., Columbus, 1965-72, dir. div. gastroenterology, 1967-72, prof., 1971-72; prof., chmn. dept. medicine U. Kans., Kansas City, 1972-2000, sr. assoc. dean acad. affairs, 2000—02; clin. prof. medicine Harvard Med. Sch., 2002—. Mem. Nat. Bd. Med. Examiners, 1971-75; mem. gen. medicine study sect. A, NIH, 1973-76 Author: Gastrointestinal Disorders: A Pathophysiologic Approach, 1976, rev. edit., 1989,Medical Book of Lists, 5th edit., 1998, History Taking and Physical Examination: Essentials and Clinical Correlates, 1992; co-editor gastroent. sect. Yearbook of Medicine, 1969-98; editor Yearbook of Digestive Diseases, 1984-98; contbr. articles to med. jours. Recipient Outstanding Teaching award House Staff Dept. Medicine Ohio State U., 1970-71, Outstanding Teaching award Kans. U. Med. Sch. Class of 1978, Outstanding Med. Educator, 1984, 85, 90, 91, 98, 99. Fellow ACP (editorial com. gastoenterology sect. 1975-77, regent 1984-92, chmn. bd. regents 1988-89, pres. 1990-91, Disting. Tchg. award 2001); mem. Am. Fedn. Clin. Rsch. (pres. Midwestern sect. 1973-74), Ctrl. Soc. Clin. Rsch. (councillor 1975, pres. 1979-80), Midwestern Gut Club, Am. Gastroent. Assn. (pres.-elect 1983-84, pres. 1984-85, Disting. Educator award 1995), Am. Soc. Clin. Investigation, Am. Soc. Pharmacology and Exptl. Therapeutics, Assn. Am. Physicians, Assn. Profs. Medicine (pres. 1986-87, Williams award 2000), Phi Beta Kappa, Sigma Xi, Alpha Omega Alpha. Office: Brigham & Womens Hosp Boston MA 02115

GREENBLATT, DAVID J. pharmacologist, educator; b. Boston, Apr. 8, 1945; s. Milton and Gertrude A. (Rogers) G.; m. Lisa L. von Moltke, Nov. 29, 1991. BA, Amherst Coll., 1966; MD, Harvard Med. Sch., 1970. Diplomate Am. Bd. Clin. Pharmacology. Intern in medicine Montefiore Hosp., Bronx, N.Y., 1970-71; resident in medicine Harvard Med. Svc. Boston City Hosp., 1971-72; fellow clin. pharmacology Mass. Gen. Hosp., Boston, 1972-74, mem. staff clin. pharmacology unit, 1974-76, chief clin. pharmacology unit, 1976-79; dir. clin. pharmacology program Tufts-New England Med. Ctr., Boston, 1979—; prof. pharmacology/exptl. therapeutics, psychiatry, medicine, anesthesia Sch. Medicine, Tufts U., Boston, 1979—; chmn. dept. pharmacology and exptl. therapeutics Sch. Medicine, Tufts U., Boston, 1994—, Louis Lasagna chair in pharmacology and exptl. therapeutics, 1997—. Author, co-author 11 books; contbr. over 660 articles to profl. jours. Recipient T. George Bidder award UCLA, 1988. Fellow Am. Coll. Clin. Pharmacology (bd. regents 1987-91, McKeen-Cattell award 1985, Disting. Svc. award 2001, pres.-elect 1994-96, pres. 1996-98, Dist. Investigator award 2002); mem. Am. Soc. Clin. Pharmacology and Therapeutics (bd. dirs. 1983-85, Rawls-Palmer award 1980), Am. Soc. Clin. Investigation, Am. Coll. Neuropsychopharmacology. Avocation: baseball. Office: Tufts U Sch Medicine 136 Harrison Ave Boston MA 02111-1817 E-mail: dj.greenblatt@tufts.edu.

GREENBLATT, DEANA CHARLENE, elementary education educator; b. Chgo., Mar. 13, 1948; d. Walter and Betty (Lamasky) Beisel; BEd., Chgo. State U., 1969; MA in Guidance and Counseling, Roosevelt U., 1973; m. Mark Greenblatt, June 22, 1975. Tchr., counselor Chgo. Pub. Schs., 1969-75, City Colls. of Chgo. GED-TV, 1976; tchr. Columbus (Ohio) Pub. Schs., 1976-86; tchr. Chgo. Pub. Schs., 1993—; participant learning exchange, Chgo. Active B'nai B'rith; vol. Right-to-Read, Columbus; mem. Community Learning Exchange, Acad. Yr. in U.S.A. Com. Counselor, 1989—. Columbus. Cert. tchr. K-9, Ill., Ohio; cert. personnel guidance, Ill., Ohio; cert. Chgo. Bd. Edn. Mem. Am. Personnel and Guidance Assn., Internat. Platform Assn., B'nai B'rith Women Club (chpt. v.p.). Democrat. Home: 3820 W Touhy Ave Lincolnwood IL 60712-1026

GREENBLATT, FRED HAROLD, data processing consultant; b. N.Y.C., Aug. 24, 1938; s. Harry Joseph and Rose (Rosen) G.; m. Marsha R. Mechaneck, Nov. 30, 1963; 1 child, Jay S. BS in Edn., CCNY, 1960; postgrad., Baruch Sch. Bus., 1961-63. Sr. analyst Grosset & Dunlap, N.Y.C., 1969-73; asst. v.p. info. sys. GNY Ins., East Brunswick, N.J., 1973-79; cons. J.P. Sedlak Assocs., N.Y.C., 1979-80; adminstr. stds. and data ITT, N.Y.C., 1980-81; dir. sys. programs Reed, Roberts Assocs., Mitchell Field, N.Y., 1981-83; pres. Data Design, Holliswood, N.Y., 1983—; cons. MIS Tek Mate Ltd., 1986—. Affiliated cons. ADR, Princeton, N.J., 1985—; affiliated software cons. Software A.G., Reston, Va., 1986—. Served with U.S. Army, 1960-61. Mem. Data Processing Mgmt. Assn. (reviewer 1984, 85, cert. achievement 1984), IEEE (assoc.), N.Y. Personal Computer Club, Soc. Profl. Mgmt. Cons. (assoc.), Assn. Computing Machinery, Personal Engring. Computer Users Soc., Internat. Platform, Assn., B'nai B'rith. Republican. Avocations: golf, tennis, micro-processors, gardening. Home and Office: 19814 Epsom Crse Hollis NY 11423-1302 E-mail: postmaster@tek.mate.net.

GREENBLATT, HELLEN CHAYA, immunologist, microbiologist; b. Frankfurt au Main, Germany; came to U.S., 1948; d. Gedaljie and Sara (Glass) Greenblatt. BA, CCNY, 1968; MS, U. Okla., 1971; PhD, SUNY Downstate Med. Ctr., Bklyn., 1977. Microbiologist Walter Reed Army Inst., Washington, 1978-80; sr. rsch. immunoparasitologist Merck Sharp & Dohme, Rahway, N.J., 1980-81; assoc. Albert Einstein Coll. Medicine, Bronx, N.Y., 1981-84; dir. rsch. and devel. Clin. Scis. Inc., Whippany, N.J., 1984-86, dir. new bus. and sci. devel., 1986-88; sr. devel. virology E.I. DuPont, Wilmington, Del., 1988-90; mng. dir. M-CAP Techs. Internat./DCV, Wilmington, 1990-93; tech. rep. BTR Separations, Wilmington, 1993-94; v.p. R & D, DCV Biol. Scis., Wilmington, 1994-97; v.p. devel. Life Scis. divsn. DCV BioNutrition, Wilmington, 1997-2000; v.p. Legacy USA, Melbourne, Fla., 1999—2002; exec. v.p. Legacy for Life, 2002—. Numerous internat. and domestic tech. presentations in field. Contbr. chpt. to book, numerous articles to profl. jours. Bd. dirs. Interfaith Housing of Del., 1993-97; tutor Lit. Vols. Am., 1992-97. Recipient Outstanding Young Woman award Competitive Resident Rsch. Coun., Washington, 1978; grantee NRC, 1978-80; fellow NRC. Mem.: Am. Acad. Anti-Aging Medicine, Del. Acad. Medicine. Achievements include patents for gastroprotective, anti-inflammatory and anti-diarrheal properties of immune egg; foremost authority on applications of hyperimmune egg in humans and pets. Office: PO Box 5941 Wilmington DE 19808-0314 E-mail: hgreenblatt@legacyforlife.net.

GREENBLATT, MAURICE THEODORE, transportation executive; b. Vineland, N.J., Oct. 2, 1928; s. Benjamin and Emma (Pollock) Greenblatt; m. Joan Tobye Bailinger, Apr. 8, 1951; children: David, Daniel. Student, Bucknell U., 1945-48. Pres. Ware's Van and Storage Co., Inc., Vineland, 1958—; chmn., CEO United Van Lines, Inc. (UniGroup), Fenton, Mo., 1984—2001, chmn. emeritus, 2001—.*

GREENBLATT, MIRIAM, writer, editor, educator; b. Berlin; d. Gregory and Shifra (Zemach) Baraks; m. Howard Greenblatt (div.). BA magna cum laude, Hunter Coll.; postgrad., U. Chgo. Editor Am. People's Ency., Chgo., 1957-58, Scott Foresman & Co., Chgo., 1958-62; pres. Creative Textbooks, Chgo., 1972—. Tchr. New Trier (Ill.) HS, 1978—81. Author (with Chu): (book) The Story of China, 1968; author: (with Cuban) Japan, 1971; author: The History of Itasca, 1976; author: (with others) The American People, 1986; author: James Knox Polk, 1988, Franklin Delano Roosevelt, 1989, John Quincy Adams, 1990; author: (with Welty) The Human Expression, 1992; author: Cambodia, 1995; author: (with Jordan and Bowes) The Americans, 1996; author: Hatshepsut and Ancient Egypt, 2000, Alexander the Great and Ancient Greece, 2000, Augustus and Imperial Rome, 2000, Peter the Great and Tsarist Russia, 2000; author: (with Lemmo) Human Heritage, 2001; author: Genghis Khan and the Mongol Empire, 2002, Elizabeth I and Tudor England, 2002, The War of 1812, 2003, Iran, 2003, Charlemagne and the Early Middle Ages, 2003, Suleyman the Magnificent and the Ottoman Empire, 2003, Lorenzo de Medici and Renaissance Italy, 2003, Afghanistan, 2003; editl. cons. Peoples and Cultures Series, 1976—78, subject area cons. World Geography and Cultures, 1994; contbg. editor: (book) A World History, 1979. Mem. nat. exec. coun. Am. Jewish Com., 1980—84, v.p. Chgo chpt., 1977—79; treas. Glencoe Youth Svcs., 1981—83. Mem.: Cliff Dwellers, Nat. Assn. Scholars. Jewish. Address: 2754 Roslyn Ln Highland Park IL 60035-1408

GREENBLATT, MORTON HAROLD, retired assistant attorney general; b. Waterbury, Conn., Oct. 31, 1916; s. Samuel F. and Dorothy K. (Katz) G.; m. Evelyn Lipman, Oct. 26, 1947; children: Sarah Beth, Ruth, David. BA, Yale U., 1937; LLB, Harvard U., 1940. Bar: Conn. 1941, U.S. Dist. Ct. Conn. 1947, U.S. Supreme Ct. 1961, U.S. Ct. Appeals (7th cir.) 1971. Pvt. practice, Waterbury, Conn., 1941, 46-47; v.p., of counsel Ellmore Silver Co., Meriden, Conn., 1946-61, pvt. practice Meriden, 1961-67; asst. pros. atty. 7th Cir. Ct., Meriden, 1962-66; asst. corp. counsel City of Meriden, 1966-81; asst. atty. gen. State of Conn., Hartford, 1982-86; of counsel Pomeranz, Drayton and Stolnich, Hartford, 1986-96; ret., 1996. Sec. Meriden Planning Commn., 1953-55; pres. Meriden Bd. Edn., 1959-61; active Temple B'nai Abraham, 1946-85, pres., 1977-79; chmn. Solid Waste Mgmt. Commn. Branford, 1986-92, rep. policy bd. South Cen. Conn. Regional Water Dist., 1988-92; bd. assessment appeals Branford, 1987-91, 97—. Maj. USAAF, 1942-46. Mem. Meriden-Wallingford Bar Assn., Conn. Bar Assn., Am. Arbitration Assn., Conn. Assn. Mcpl. Attys. (treas.), New Haven County Bar Assn. Jewish. Home: 55 Canterbury Rd Hamden CT 06514-2016

GREENBLATT, RAY HARRIS, lawyer; b. Milw., June 29, 1931; s. Charles and Ethel (Harris) G.; m. Betty Goldsmith, July 11, 1955 (dec. Mar. 1967); children: Walter, Robert, Edward; m. Helen Judith Pick, Mar. 29, 1969 (div. Dec. 1969). BS in Econs., U. Pa., 1953; JD magna cum laude, Harvard U., 1956. Bar: Ill. 1956. Assoc. Mayer, Brown, Rowe & Maw, 1956-64, ptnr., 1965-94. Arbitrator, mediator Am. Arbitration Assn., 1970-96; hearing officer Ill. State Banking Bd., 1989; lectr. Sch. for Bankers U. Wis., Madison, 1964, 73, Ill. Inst. Continuing Legal Edn., 1973. Contbr. articles to profl. jours. Pres. Winnetka (Ill.) Bd. Edn., 1974-75, mem. 1969-74; vol. tchr. economics, poetry and debate, Providence-St. Mel Sch., Chgo., 1994-98. Mem. ABA, Chgo. Literary Club (pres. 2000-2001), Cliff Dwellers Club, Lake Shore Country Club. Jewish. Home: 1003 Westmoor Rd Winnetka IL 60093-1855 E-mail: rayofsunsh@aol.com.

GREENBLATT, SAMUEL HAROLD, neurosurgeon; b. Potsdam, N.Y., May 16, 1939; s. Louis and Rose Leah (Clopman) G.; m. Judith R. Shapiro, June 23, 1963; children: Rachel, Daniel, Miriam. BA, Cornell U., 1961, MD, 1966; MA, Johns Hopkins U., 1964; MA (hon.), Brown U., 1991. Diplomate Am. Bd. Neurol. Surgery, Nat. Bd. Med. Examiners. Intern Boston City Hosp., 1966-67; resident in neurology Boston VA Hosp., 1967-68; resident in neurol. surgery Dartmouth Med. Sch. Affiliated Hosps., Hanover, NH, 1970-74; asst. attending neurol. surgeon Bronx Mcpl. Hosp. Ctr., Hosp. Albert Einstein Coll., Bronx, 1974-77, Montefiore Hosp. Med. Ctr., Bronx, 1974-77; clin. asst. in neurol. surgery St. Barnabas Hosp., Bronx, 1975, rsch. asst. in neurol. surgery, 1976-77; staff neurosurgeon Med. Coll. of Ohio Hosp., Toledo, 1977-89; assoc. staff neurosurgeon Mercy Hosp., Toledo, 1977-80, courtesy staff neurosurgeon, 1980-89; chief neurosurgery Meml. Hosp. of R.I., Pawtucket, 1989—; active staff neurosurgeon R.I. Hosp., Providence, 1989—; cons. staff neurosurgeon Sturdy Meml. Hosp., 1991—; neurosurgery cons. VA Hosp., Providence, 1993-96. Instr. neurol. surgery Albert Einstein Coll. Medicine, 1974—77; asst. prof. of neurol. surgery, asst. prof. surgery Med. Coll. Ohio, 1977—80, assoc. prof. of neurol. surgery, assoc. prof. surgery, 1980—89, acting chmn. dept. neurol. surgery, 1986; assoc. prof. clin. neurosci. (neurosurgery) Brown U., 1989—98, prof. clin. neurosci. (neurosurgery), 1998—, asst. chmn. program in neurosurgery, prof. neurosci., 1999—; alternate del. R.I. Joint Coun. of State Neurosurg. Socs., 1994—; sec.-treas. Neurosurg. Found., Inc., 1993—2001, v.p., 2001—, bd. trustees, 1993—. Sect. editor: Neurosurgery, Jour. of the History of the Neuroscis. With reserve USAF, 1968—70. Tiffany Blake fellowship Hitchcock Found. Fellow: ACS; mem.: Internat. Soc. for the History of the Neurosci. (steering com. for founding the soc. 1995, treas. 1995—98, pres.-elect 1998—99, pres. 1999—2000), R.I. Med. Soc. Coun., Pawtucket Med. Assn., New Eng. Neurosurg. Soc., R.I. Neurosurg. Soc. (sec.-treas. 1993, pres. 1993—97), Am. Assn. of Neurol. Surgeons (sect. on the history of neurol. surgery, chmn. 1991—93), Congress of Neurol. Surgeons, Am. Assn. for the History of Medicine (clinician historian group 1994—), History of Sci. Soc. Office: Brown U Neurosurgery Memorial Hosp Pawtucket RI 02860 E-mail: Samuel_Greenblatt@Brown.edu.

GREENBLATT, STEPHEN J. English language educator; b. Cambridge, Mass., Nov. 7, 1943; s. Harry J. and Mollie (Brown) G.; m. Ramie Targoff; children: Joshua, Aaron, Harry. BA, Yale U., 1964, M. in Philosophy, 1968, PhD, 1969; BA, Cambridge U., England, 1966, MA, 1969. Prof. English U. Calif., Berkeley, 1969-97, Harvard U., 1997—. Vis. prof. Peking U., Beijing, 1982, U. Bologna, Italy, 1988, U. Chgo., 1989, U. Trieste, 1991, U. Florence, 1992, 96, Ecole des Hautes Etudes, Paris, 1989, Harvard U., Cambridge, Mass., 1990, 94, Wissenschaftskolleg zu Berlin, 1996-97, Kyoto U., 1998, U. Torino, 1998, Queen Mary and Westfield Coll., U. London, 1999. Author: Three Modern Satirists: Waugh, Orwell, and Huxley, 1965 (Lloyd Mifflin prize 1964), Sir Walter Raleigh, 1973, Renaissance Self-Fashioning, 1980, Shakespearean Negotiations, 1988, Learning to Curse, 1990, Marvelous Possessions, 1991; editor: Allegory and Representation, 1981, Power of Forms, 1982, Representing the English Renaissance, 1988, Redrawing the Boundaries of Literary Study in English, 1992, New World Encounters, 1993; gen editor: The Norton Shakespeare, 1997, The Norton Anthology of English Literature, 7th edit., 1999, Practicing New Historicism, 2000, Was ist Literaturgeschicte, 2000, Hamlet in Purgatory, 2001; co-editor: The 16th Century in Norton Anthology of English Literature, 1999. Recipient Porter prize, 1969, Brit. Coun. prize, 1981; Fulbright scholar, 1964-66, Woodrow Wilson scholar, 1966; Guggenheim fellow, 1975, 83, Mellon Disting. Humanist award, 2002, Erasmus Inst. prize, 2002. Fellow Am. Acad. Arts and Scis. Office: Harvard U Dept of English Cambridge MA 02138 E-mail: greenbl@fas.harvard.edu.

GREENBURG, DAN, author; b. Chgo., June 20, 1936; s. Samuel and Leah (Rozalsky) G.; m. Nora Ephron, Apr. 9, 1967 (div.); m. Suzanne O'Malley, June 28, 1980 (div.); m. Judith Wilson, Oct. 17, 1998. BFA, U. Ill., 1958; MFA, UCLA, 1960. Copywriter Lansdale Co., Los Angeles, 1960-61, Carson Roberts Advt., Los Angeles, 1961-62; mng. editor Eros mag., N.Y.C., 1962-63; copywriter Papert, Koenig, Lois (advt.), N.Y.C., 1963-65; freelance writer N.Y.C., 1965—. Author: How to Be a Jewish Mother, 1964, Kiss My Firm but Pliant Lips, 1965, How to Make Yourself Miserable, 1966, Chewsday: A Sex Novel, 1968, Jumbo the Boy and Arnold the Elephant, 1969, 89, Philly, 1969, Porno-Graphics, 1969, Scoring: A Sexual Memoir, 1972, Something's There: My Adventures in the Occult, 1976, Love Kills, 1978, What Do Women Want?, 1982; (with Suzanne O'Malley) How to Avoid Love and Marriage, 1983, True Adventures, 1985, Confessions of a Pregnant Father, 1986, How to Make Yourself Miserable for the Rest of the Century, 1987, The Nanny, 1987, Exes, 1990, The Guardian, 1990, The Bed Who Ran Away From Home, 1991, Young Santa, 1991, Great Grandpa's in the Litter Box, 1996, A Ghost Named Wanda, 1996, Through the Medicine Cabinet, 1996, Zap! I'm a Mind-Reader, 1996, Moses Supposes, 1997, Dr. Jekyll, Orthodontist, 1997, I'm Out of My Body, Please Leave a Message, 1997, My Son, the Time Traveler, 1997, Never Trust a Cat Who Wears Earrings, 1997, The Volcano Goddess Will See You Now, 1997, Bozo the Clone, 1997, How to Speak Dolphin in Three Easy Lessons, 1997, Now You See Me, Now You Don't, 1998, The Misfortune Cookie, 1998, Elvis the Turnip and Me, 1998, Hang a Left at Venus, 1999, Evil Queen Tut and the Great Ant Pyramids, 1999, Yikes! Grandma's a Teenager, 1999, How I Fixed the Year 1000 Problem, 1999, The Boy Who Cried Bigfoot, 2000, The Day I Went from Bad to Verse, 2000, Don't Count on Dracula, 2000, This Body Isn't Big Enough for Both of Us, 2000, Greenish Eggs and Dinosaurs, 2001, My Grandma, Major League Slugger, 2001, How I Became a Superhero, 2001, The Day Everything Tasted Like Broccoli, 2001, Invasion from the Planet of the Cows, 2001, Maximum Girl Unmasked, 2002, Attack of the Soggy Underwater People, 2002, Trapped in the Museum of Unnatural History, 2002, Me and My Mummy, 2002, Meet Super Sid, Crime-Fighting Kid, 2002, My Teacher Ate My Homework, 2002, If You Tell a Lie, Your Butt Will Grow, 2002, The Worst Bully in the Entire Universe, 2003, Just Add Water and Scream, 2003, It's Itchcraft, 2003; (films) I Could Never Have Sex with Any Man Who Has So Little Regard for My Husband, 1973, Private Lessons, 1981; (with Suzanne O'Malley) Private School, 1983, The Guardian, 1990; (plays) Arf, 1969, The Great Airplane Snatch, 1969; contbr. to Broadway revue Oh, Calcutta, 1969. Recipient Silver Key award Advt. Writers Assn., N.Y.C., 1964, Playboy Humor award, 1964, 72, 76. Mem. Dramatists Guild, Authors Guild Am., AFTRA, Screen Actors Guild, Writers Guild Am., Mystery Writers Am.

GREEN-DORSEY, JEAN AUDREY, information technology executive; b. Cleve., Oct. 27, 1940; d. Sydney Howard and Bennie Irene (Blake) Green; m. William R. Dorsey, Nov. 1, 1980. BA, L.I. U., 1962. With IBM, N.Y.C., 1966-72; mktg. mgr. office automation Olivetti, N.Y.C., 1972-80; dep. dir. N.Y.C Mgmt. Info. Sys., 1981-85; computer sys. mgr. Inter-agy. Task Force, N.Y.C., 1985-86; pres. Inst. Mgmt. Devel., N.Y.C., 1986—. Dir. PolySoft Systems Inc.; sr. cons. Inst. Mgmt. Devel., 1980—; exec. prod., host Management Matters, 1998—; founder Managementmatters.org, Inc., 2000; adv. editor Hearst Pubs., 1981—, Today's Office, 1986—, others; lectr. in field; bd. dirs. Nat. Inst. Mgmt.; bd. dirs., tech. advisor Am. Inst. Urban Psychol. Studies, 1996—. Bd. dirs. Fair Harbor Com. Assn., 1981—; co-dir. Westgate Tenants Assn., co-chair legal com., 1998—, chair, 1999; leader Citizen Amb. Program People to People office automation del. to People's Rep. China, 1988; mem. exec. bd. Cmty. Bd. #7. Recipient WESTY award for cmty. bldg., 2003. Mem. Assn. Computing Machinery, Assn. Info. Sys. Profls. (pres. N.Y.C. chpt., leader sci. and technology del. to People's Rep. China 1988). Clubs: Soroptomists Internat., The Club at N.Y. World Trade Ctr. Office: Managementmatters org Inc Westgate 160 W 91st New York NY 10025 E-mail: dorsey@managementmatters.org.

GREENE, ADDISON KENT, lawyer, accountant; b. Cardston, Alta., Can., Dec. 23, 1941; s. Addison Allen and Amy (Shipley) G.; m. Janice Hanks, Aug. 30, 1967; children: Lisa, Tiffany, Tyler, Darin. BS in Acctg., Brigham Young U., 1968; JD, U. Utah, 1973. Bar: Utah 1973, Nev. 1974, U.S. Tax Ct. 1979. Staff acct. Seidman and Seidman, Las Vegas, Nev., 1968-69, Peat Marwick Mitchell, Los Angeles, 1969-70; atty. Clark Greene & Assocs., Ltd., Las Vegas, 1973—. Instr. Nev. Bar Rev., Las Vegas, 1975-78; bd. dirs. Cumorah Credit Union. Mem. Citizen's for Responsible Gov't, Las Vegas, 1979—; asst. dist. com. mem. Boy Scouts Am., Las Vegas, 1985—. Mem. ABA, Utah Bar Assn., Nev. Bar Assn., Nev. Soc. CPA's (assoc.), Am. Assn., Pension Actuaries (assoc.). Republican. Mem. Lds Ch. Avocations: golf, snow skiing. Office: Clark Greene & Assocs Ltd 3770 Howard Hughes Pkwy Ste 195 Las Vegas NV 89109-0976

GREENE, ADELE S. management consultant; b. Newark; d. Adolph and Sara (Schubert) Shuminer; m. Alan Greene (div.); 1 child, Joshua. Student, Juilliard Sch. Music, 1942-44, NYU, 1942-44, New Sch. Social Research, 1944-47; diploma in mgmt., Harvard Bus. Sch., 1978. Account exec. Ruder and Finn Inc., N.Y.C., 1964-66, sr. assoc., 1966-68, v.p., 1968-72, sr. v.p., 1972-76; v.p. pub. affairs Corp. Pub. Broadcasting, Washington, 1976-78; pres., CEO TV Program Group, Washington, 1978-80; pres. Greene and Assocs., N.Y.C., 1981—. Exec. dir. Am. Friends of Brit. Mus., 1994—; instr. pub. relations and community affairs, NYU 1974-76; bd. dirs. Sci. Program Group, Washington 1976-81; treas., bd. dirs. Coliseum Park Apts. Co-author: Teen-Age Leadership, 1971. Advisor The Acting Co., Understudies, N.Y.C., 1987—; pres., CEO Am. Craft Coun., 1980-81, trustee, 1976-81; bd. dirs. Union Settlement, N.Y.C., 1987-90; trustee Duke Ellington Sch. Arts, Washington, 1977-81, Inst. for Cancer Prevention, 2002—. Mem. Pub. Relations Soc. Am. (silver anvil award 1971), Nat. Assn. Edn. Broadcasters, Am. Women Radio and TV. Home and Office: 30 W 60th St New York NY 10023-7902

GREENE, ALAN GUYER, retired radiologist; b. N.Y.C., May 11, 1935; s. Herman Stuart And Edna Betty (Jaffe) G.; m. Roberta Greene, June 7, 1959 (div. May, 1983); children: Judy Beth, David Sandler, Deborah Ruth; m. Susan Joffe, July 18, 1991. MD, SUNY, Syracuse, 1960. Diplomate Am. Bd. Radiology, Am. Bd. Nuclear Radiology. Intern SUNY Med. Ctr., Syracuse, 1960-61; resident in radiology Peter B. Brigham Hosp., Boston, 1961-64; pvt. practice radiology Boston, 1965-90. Jr. Radiology assoc. Peter Bent Brigham Hosp, Boston, 1964; hosp. appt. FaulknerHosp. Jamaica Plain, Mass., 1967-90; asst. clin. prof. Tufts U. Fellow Am. Coll. Radiology; mem. Am. Coll. Nuclear Physicians, Am. Coll. Radiologists, Am. Roentgen Ray Soc., New Eng. Roentgen Ray Soc., Soc. Nuclear Medicine. E-mail: alanggreene@comcast.net.

GREENE, ALBERT LAWRENCE, healthcare executive; b. N.Y.C., Dec. 10, 1949; s. Leonard and Anne (Birnbaum) G.; m. Jo Linda Anderson, Sept. 3, 1972; children: Stacy, Jeremy. BA, Ithaca Coll., 1971; MHA, U. Mich., 1973. Adminstrv. asst. Harper Hosp., Detroit, 1973-74, asst. adminstr., 1974-77, assoc. adminstr., 1977-80; adminstr. Grace Hosp., Detroit, 1980-84, Harper Hosp., Detroit, 1984-87; pres., CEO Sinai Samaritan Med. Ctr., Milw., 1988-90, Alta Bates Med. Ctr., Berkeley, Calif., 1990-98; CEO Sutter Health East Bay Svc. Area, Berkeley, Calif., 1998-99, HealthCtrl., Emeryville, Calif., 1999—2001, Queen of Angels Hollywood Presbyn. Med. Ctr., L.A., 2002—. Bd. dirs. Sierra Health Svcs., QuadraMed Corp.; chmn. Calif. Assn. Hosps. and Health Sys., 1998. Trustee Huron Valley Hosp., Milford, Mich., 1984-87. Mem.: Am. Coll. Healthcare Execs., World Pres. Orgn., City Ctr. Club, Braemar Country Club. Avocations: tennis, golf. Home: 25948 Wellington Ct Calabasas CA 91302 Office: Queen of Angels Hollywood Presbyn Med Ctr 1300 N Vermont Ave Los Angeles CA 90027

GREENE, ALVIN, service company executive, management consultant; b. Aug. 26, 1932; s. Samuel David and Yetta Kroff Greene; m. Louise Sokol, Nov. 11, 1977; children: Sharon, Aaron, Ami, Ann, Daniel. BA, Stanford U., 1954, MBA, 1959. Asst. to pres. Narmco Industries, Inc., San Diego, 1959—62; adminstrv. mgr., mgr. mktg. Whittaker Corp., L.A., 1962—67; sr. v.p. Cordura Corp., L.A., 1966—75; chmn. bd. Sharon-Sage, Inc., L.A., 1975—79; exec. v.p., COO Republic Distbrs., Inc., Carson, Calif., 1979—81, also dir.; COO Mermel, Jacobs & Ellsworth, 1981—87, 1987—; pres. SCI Cons., Inc. Bd. dirs. Sharon-Sage Inc., True Data Corp.; vis. prof. Am. Grad. Sch. Bus., Phoenix, 1977—81. Chmn. bd. commrs. Housing Authority City of L.A., 1983—88; tchr., mentor Anderson Grad. Sch. Bus., UCLA, 2002—; bd. dirs. Spl. Olympics, 2003. 1st lt. U.S. Army, 1955—57. Mem.: Bradley Group, Safety Helmet Mfrs. Assn., Direct Mail Assn. Fax: 310-459-6489. Business E-Mail: sciconsultants@aol.com.

GREENE, AMY POWERS, human resources specialist; b. Miami, Fla., Mar. 3, 1970; d. Frederic Carl and Colleen Ann Powers; m. Jerry Kevin Greene, Nov. 7, 1998. BA in English, N.C. State U., 1992, MA in English, 1998. Benefits mgr. News and Observer Pub. Co., Raleigh, NC, 1993—2000; mgr. benefits adminstrn. GlaxoSmithKline, Research Triangle Park, NC, 2000—01, mgr. human resources svc. delivery and comm., 2001—02, mgr. human resources svc. delivery, 2002—, mgr. human resources strategy and measurement, 2002—. Mentor Cities in Schs., Raleigh, 1999—2000. Mem.: Nat. Assn. Female Exec., Soc. Human Resources Mgmt. Avocations: sculpting, painting. Office: GlaxoSmithKline PO Box 13398 5 Moore Dr Research Triangle Park NC 27709

GREENE, ANNIE LUCILLE, artist, retired art educator; b. Waycross, Ga. d. Henry William and Ella Mae (Hall) Tarver; m. Oliver Nathaniel Greene; children: Zinta LaRecia Greene Perkins, Oliver N. Greene, Jr. BS, Albany State Coll., 1954; MA, NYU, 1961. Art tchr. Thomasville (Ga.) Sch. Sys., 1954—55, Troup County Sch. Sys., LaGrange, Ga., 1955—89; ret., 1989. Apptd. mem. Ga. Humanities Coun., 2002—. 34 one-woman art shows, 1976—, 112 group exhbns., 1962— (numerous awards). Past mem. Neighborhood Housing Svcs. Pub. Rels. com.; Grand Marshall Sweet Land of Liberty July 4th Parade, LaGrange, 2001; pianist St. Paul African Meth. Episcopal Ch. and McGhee Chapel African Meth. Episcopal Ch., Hogansville, Ga., trustee, chmn. stewardship and fin. commn.; bd. dirs. March of Dimes, 1991—; bd. mem. Keep Troup Beautiful, 1997—2001; past bd. dirs. LaGrange Meml. Libr. Named one of Gracious Ladies of Ga., 1998; recipient Outstanding Svc., St. Paul A.M.C. Ch., 2000, Ch. Citizen of Yr. award, McGhee Chapel A.M.E. Ch., 1999. Mem.: LaGrange Symphony Guild, LaGrange Artist Guild, Chattahoochee Valley Art Mus. (past bd. mem.), Troup Ret. Tchrs. Assn. (past sect.), The Links, Inc. (Outstanding Svc. award 1987, parliamentarian 1999—2001, Presdl. award 2001, LaGrange chpt., Outstanding Svc. award 1987, Presdl. award 2001), Delta Sigma Theta (pres. 1991—93, LaGrange Alumnae chpt. Presdl. awards 1993—97, pres. 1995—97, Annie B. Singleton award 2000, fund raiser chair 2001—03, LaGrange Alumnae chpt. Presdl. awards 1993—97, Annie B. Singleton award 2000, numerous other awards). Avocations: music, crafts, reading, photography, travel. Home: 712 Pyracantha Dr Lagrange GA 30241

GREENE, ARTHUR M. lawyer; b. NYC, Aug. 6, 1936; s. William B. and Hazel C. Greene; children: Stephanie Bosworth, Andrea Swan. BSc, Cornell U., 1958; LLB, N.Y. Law Sch., 1966. Bar: N.Y. 1967, Fla. 1995, U.S. Dist. Ct. (no. dist.) N.Y. 1975, U.S. Ct. Appeals (2nd cir.) 1971, U.S. Supreme Ct. 1995. House counsel Transamerica Ins. Co., Syracuse, N.Y., 1967-69, Empire Mut. Ins. Co., Syracuse, 1969-78; pvt. practice Syracuse, 1978-82; ptnr. Greene & Reid, Syracuse, 1982—. Co-author: Service of Process: Manual for the Attorney, 1984, Handling The Plaintiff's Personal Injury Case, 1989, New York Lawyer's Deskbook: Preparing for and Litigating the Plaintiff's Personal Injury Case in New York, 2001. Mem. Onondaga County Bar Assn. (chmn. ins. com. 1976-83, bd. dirs. 1979-86, chmn. lawyers ref. com. 1986-93). Avocations: sailing, bicycling, kayaking, running, roller blading. Office: Greene & Reid 173 Intrepid Ln Syracuse NY 13205-2538 E-mail: agreene@greenereid.com.

GREENE, BARRY, music educator, writer; b. Las Vegas, July 31, 1961; s. Howard and Sandra Greene; m. Sara E. Dizney, July 20, 1995; children: Mitchell Warren, Samuel Robert. M in Jazz Composition, U. South Fla., 1995. Prof. jazz studies U. North Fla., Jacksonville, 1995—. Author: (jazz instructional text) Solo Jazz Guitar Method, (guitar text) Master Anthology of Jazz Guitar Solos Vol. 2; composer: more than 5 large ensemble works, over 75 guitar ensemble music works, (CD) Sojourner; musician: over a dozen CDs. Recipient Disting. Performance award, Notre Dame Jazz Competition, 1984; Emerging Artist grantee, Hillsborough County Arts Soc., 1991. Mem.: Internat. Assn. Jazz Educators. Office: U North Fla 4567 St Johns Bluff Rd Jacksonville FL 32224 Home Fax: 904-620-2865. Personal E-mail: bgreene@unf.edu.

GREENE, BERNARD HAROLD, lawyer; b. Bklyn., Sept. 21, 1925; s. Max and Clara (Pasweg) G.; m. Magda C. Schwartz, Sept. 19, 1948; children: Michael, Edith, Susan, Jonathan, David. BBA magna cum laude, CCNY, 1948; LLB cum laude, Yale U., 1951. Bar: N.Y. 1952. Assoc. Paul, Weiss, Rifkind, Wharton & Garrison, N.Y.C., 1951-60, ptnr., 1960-94, of counsel, 1995—. Vis. lectr. Yale Law Sch., New Haven, 1972-78, 81-83; adj. prof. N.Y. Law Sch., N.Y.C., 1985-88. Chmn. deferred giving and estate planning com. Community Svc. Soc., N.Y.C., 1975-82. 1st lt. U.S. Army, 1943-47. Mem. Assn. Bar City N.Y. (mem. surrogate's ct. com. 1958-61) Home: 153 Union St Montclair NJ 07042-2102 Office: Paul Weiss Rifkind Wharton & Garrison Rm 200 1285 Avenue of the Americas New York NY 10019-6065

GREENE, C. MICHAEL, art association administrator; Pres., CEO NARAS, Santa Monica, Calif. Office: NARAS 3402 Pico Blvd Santa Monica CA 90405-2118

GREENE, DARLENE, elementary education educator; b. Hampton, Ark, Aug. 13, 1958; d. James Earnest Moore and Alma Lee Moore-Penny; m. Roderick Wendell, Mar. 19, 1994; children: Zachary Nathanael Greene. BSW, U. Ark., Pine Bluff, 1982; elem. edn. cert., So. Ark. U., 1992. Elem. tchr. McNeil Pub. Sch., Ark., 1991-92, Stephens Pub. Sch., Ark., 1992; first grade tchr. Fairview Elem. Sch., Camden, Ark., 1993—; second grade tchr. Ivory Primary, 2002—. Mem. Ark. Reading Coun., Camden. Democrat. Methodist. Avocations: reading, traveling, interior decorating, directing children activities. Home: 3125 Hwy 376 S Camden AR 71701 Office: Ivory Primary Schs 575 Jefferson Dr Camden AR 71701

GREENE, DAVID BECKWITH, music educator; b. Milford, Del., Jan. 28, 1939; s. David Beckwith and Edwena (Lambert) G.; m. Judith Cleveland Semple, June 30, 1962 (div. July 1988); children: Paul David, Thomas Gavin. BA, Harvard U., 1960; BD, Princeton Theol. Sem., 1963; PhD, Yale U., 1966. Prof. music Wabash Coll., Crawfordsville, Ind., 1966-88, N.C. State U., Raleigh, 1988—. Head divsn. multidisciplinary studies, chmn. arts adv. com. Coll. Bd., N.Y.C., 1982-87. Author: (monographs) Temporal Processes in Beethoven's Music, 1982, Mahler, Consciousness and Temporality, 1984, Nativity Art and the Incarnation, 1986, Listening to Strauss Operas: The Audience's Multiple Standpoints, 1991; also articles. Democrat. Presbyterian. Avocation: gardening. Home: 2827 Mayview Rd Raleigh NC 27607-4142 Office: NC State U PO Box 7107 Raleigh NC 27695-7107 Fax: 919-515-1828. E-mail: david_greene@ncsu.edu.

GREENE, DAVID LLOYD, transportation researcher; b. N.Y.C., Nov. 18, 1949; s. Donald and Alice (Lloyd) G.; m. Janet Margaret Lane, Jan. 2, 1971; children: Jennifer, Michael. BA, Columbia U., 1971; MA, U. Oreg., 1973; PhD, Johns Hopkins U., 1978. Rsch. assoc. Oak Ridge (Tenn.) Nat. Lab., 1977-80, leader transp. energy group, 1980-82, rsch. staff mem., 1982-84, sr. rsch. staff mem. I, 1984-87, head transp. rsch. sect., 1987-88; sr. rsch. analyst Office of Policy Integration U.S. Dept. of Energy (on assignment Oak Ridge Nat. Lab.), Washington, 1988-89, sr. rsch. staff mem. II, mgr. energy policy rsch. programs Ctr. for Transp. Analysis Oak Ridge, 1989-99; corp. fellow Oak Ridge Nat. Lab., 1999—. Bd. advisors Eno Transp. Found., 2003; mem. numerous coms. transp. rsch. bd. Nat. Rsch. Coun., 1982—, mem. emeritus Comm. on Trans. and Energy. Author: (with others) Transportation and Energy, The Full Costs and Benefits of Transportation, Transportation and Global Climate Change; editor-in-chief Jour. Transp. and Stats., 1997-2001; mem. editl. bd. MacMillan Encyclopedia Energy, Energy Policy, Transp. Quarterly, Transp. Rsch.; contbr. over 150 articles to profl. jours. Recipient UT-Batelle award Excellence in Sci., 2001, Disting. Svc. cert. Transp. Rsch. Bd., 1989, 93, Tech. Achievement award Oak Ridge Nat. Lab. 1985, 86, 91, 96, 99, 2001, Pyke Johnson award NAS, 1984, Johns Hopkins U. grad. fellowship, 1976-77, Ford Found. fellowship, 1973-75, Columbia U. faculty scholar, 1967-71, N.Y. State Regents scholar, 1967-71. Mem.: Internat. Assn. Energy Econ., Assn. Am. Geographers (Energy Specialty Group Paper award 1986). Achievements include research in vehicle stock modeling of transportation energy use, techniques for analyzing trends in transportation energy use, understanding the effects of fuel economy regulation, quantification of efficiency rebound effect on motor vehicle use, contributions to estimating the costs and benefits and technological potential for vehicle fuel economy improvement and mitigating transportation greenhouse gas emissions, and estimation of the economic costs of oil dependence. Office: Oak Ridge Nat Lab NTRC 2360 Cherahala Blvd Knoxville TN 37831

GREENE, DONALD RICHARD, dermatologist, educator; b. Buffalo, Aug. 20, 1947; s. Norman Sanborn and Helen Jean (Second) Powers; m. JoAnne D'Amico, Mar. 5, 1982; children: Patrick Ryan, Claire Elizabeth. BA, SUNY, Buffalo, 1970, MD, 1974. Diplomate Am. Bd. Dermatology. Intern Buffalo Gen. Hosp., 1974-75; resident Hosp. of U. Pa., Phila., 1975-76, Yale-New Haven Hosp., 1976-79, chief resident, 1978-79; clin. instr. Yale U. Sch. Medicine, New Haven, 1979-82, clin. asst. prof., 1982—. Attending physician Yale-New Haven Hosp., Hosp. St. Raphael, 1979— ; med. bd. Branford (Conn.) Health Care Ctr., 1983—. Grantee, Am. Cancer Soc., 1972. Fellow Am. Acad. Dermatology; mem. AMA, Conn. State Med. Soc. (pres. dermatology sect.

1984-85), New Haven County Med. Assn., New Haven City Med. Assn., New England Dermatologic Soc., N.Y. Acad. Sci., Assn. of Attendings at Yale U. Sch. Medicine, Mensa, Yale Club New Haven, Penn Club N.Y., Madison Winter Club, Mory's Assn. Episcopalian.

GREENE, DOUGLAS EDWARD, hotel executive; BA, U. Maine, 1973. Pres. Ocean Hospitalities, Inc., Portsmouth, N.H. Office: Ocean Hospitalities Inc Bldg 1 Ste 300 1000 Market St Portsmouth NH 03801-3358

GREENE, EDWARD ALLEN, retired public affairs executive; b. Waco, Tex., May 25, 1926; s. James Floyd and Marie Louise (DuPré) G.; m. Elizabeth Ann Love, Oct. 11, 1952; children: Edward Allen Jr., Deborah Ann Greene Lord, Judith Love Greene Murray, Philip James. BA, George Washington U., 1950. Reporter Washington Evening Star, 1950-52; asst. pub. rels. Assn. Gen. Contractors Am., Washington, 1952-58; pub. affairs asst. Am. Waterways Operators, Washington, 1958-60; pub. info. specialist USPHS, Washington, 1960-61; pub. affairs office interim dep. U.S. Army C.E., Washington, 1961 91. Author: D-Day: The Greatest Invasion, 1969. V.p. Park View Citizens Assn., 1968, pres., 1969-70, 85-86, 93-94; vol., chief pub. rels. officer ARC Walter Reed Hosp., Silver Spring, 1999-2002. Recipient U.S. Army Engrs. Comdrs. award for civilian svc., 1991. Mem. Contrsn. Writers Assn. (pres. 1977-78, Silver Hard Hat award 1989). Republican. Roman Catholic. Avocations: swimming, travel, bridge, music, eleven grandchildren. Home: 3226 Park View Rd Chevy Chase MD 20815-5644 E-mail: edgreene72713.2613@compuserve.com.

GREENE, EDWARD FORBES, chemistry educator; b. N.Y.C., Dec. 29, 1922; s. Roger Sherman and Kate (Brown) G.; m. Hildegarde Forbes, June 11, 1949; children: Susan Curtis, Judith Elizabeth, David Forbes, Roger Cobb. AB, Harvard U., 1943, A.M., 1947, PhD, 1949. Jr. research chemist Shell Oil Co., Wood River, Ill., 1943-44; mem. staff Los Alamos Sci. Lab., 1949; research assoc. Brown U., Providence, 1949-51, instr., 1952-53, asst. prof. chemistry, 1953-57, assoc. prof., 1957-63, prof., 1963-92, dept. chmn., 1980-83, Jesse H. and Louisa D. Sharpe Metcalf prof. chemistry, 1985-92; prof. emeritus, 1993—. Vis. prof. Tougaloo (Miss.) Coll., 1965; resident visitor Bell Labs., Murray Hill, N.J., 1976-77 Co-author: (with J.P. Toennies) Chemical Reactions in Shock Waves, 1964. Served with USN, 1944-46. NSF fellow, 1959-60, 66-67 Fellow Am. Phys. Soc.; mem. Am. Chem. Soc. Home: 229 Medway St Apt 105 Providence RI 02906-5300 E-mail: Edward_Greene@Brown.edu.

GREENE, ELINORE ASCHAH, speech and drama professional, writer; b. Springfield, Mass., Oct. 14, 1928; d. Harry Joshua and Esther Gertrude (Cohen) Ziff; m. Kermit Greene, June 29, 1947; children: Clifford M., Laura L., William L. B of Lit. Interpretation, Emerson Coll., Boston, 1949. Dramatic interpreter Margaret E. Richardson Lect. Agy., Boston, 1950s, Flora Frame Lect. Bureau, Boston, 1960s; speech tchr. Academie Moderne, Boston, early 1970s, pvt. practice, Newton, MA, 1975-87, speech cons., 1985-89; writer, dir. Newton, 1989—. Presenter in field; voice-overs radio, TV, indsl. Author: (children's stories) AIM, Lollipops, Happiness, The Communique, Players, 1970—80, (poetry) Creative Urge, Dark Starr, Dreams; reviewer books: ; contbr. Brandeis women's com. and aid to speech therapy Emerson Coll. Mem. Aid to Speech Therapy Found. (pres. 1970s, bd. dirs. 1960s, Advocate Rose award 1975), Mass. Comm. of Boston, Am. Fedn. Theatre-Radio-TV Assns., Nat. Writers Orgn. (sr. mem.), Orgn. for Rehab. through Tng. (life), Hadassah. Avocations: family, music, composing greeting cards, reading, theater.

GREENE, ELIZABETH IVORY, real estate company official; b. N.Y.C., Jan. 17, 1929; d. Percy Van Eman Ivory and Elizabeth (Schofield) Post Price; m. James Benno Greene Jr. (dec.); children: Elizabeth Tylawsky, James Benno III, Edgar Charles Ivory. BA, Bennington Coll., 1952. Sculptor Hansen Lamps, N.Y.C., 1952-57; real estate agent Ely-Cruikshank Co., N.Y.C., 1968-70; prin. Greene Realty Ltd., N.Y.C., 1970—, Apocalyptic Holdings Ltd., N.Y.C., 1972—. Bd. dirs. Bus. Improvement Dist. Greenwich Village, N.Y.C.; trustee City & County Sch., N.Y.C.; mem. Rep. Nat. Com., 1996. Bennington (Vt.) Coll. scholar, 1949-52. Mem. Small Property Owners Action Network (founder, pres. 1983—), Nat. Ctr. Neighborhood Enterprise, Village Visiting Neighbors (bd. dirs. 1987-89), DAR (John Jay chpt.), Greenwich Village C. of C. (bd. dirs.), Assn. Village Homeowners, N.Y. Mycological Soc. Avocation: gardening. Home and Office: Small Property Owners Action Network SPAN 82 Washington Pl Apt 3A New York NY 10011-9113 Fax: 212-989-7366.

GREENE, ERNEST RINALDO, JR., anesthesiologist, chemical engineer; b. Mobile, Ala., Jan. 26, 1941; s. Ernest Rinaldo and Dorris Rolinha (Lassiter) G.; m. Lois Ellen Laura Zullig, Sept. 23, 1967; children: Laura Rolinha, Ernest Rinaldo III, Ellen Victoria, Max McKeen. BA, Rice U., 1962, BS, 1963; MA, Princeton U., 1966, PhD, 1968; MD, Washington U., St. Louis, 1981. Diplomate Am. Bd. Anesthesiology; diplomate, Nat. Bd. Med. Examiners; registered profl. engr., Ala. Tenured asst. prof. engring. U. Ala., Birmingham, 1970-84, asst. prof. anesthesiology, 1986-88; chief anesthesiology Cooper Green Hosp., Birmingham, 1986-90, VA Med. Ctr., Birmingham, 1987-90; assoc. prof. anesthesiology U. Ala., Birmingham, 1988-90; chief anesthesiology Vaughan Regional Med. Ctr., Selma, Ala., 1990-92; adjunct assoc. prof. biomed. engring. U. Ala., Birmingham, 1990—; founder, CEO Hivex, Inc.; with AnesCare, Phenix City, Ala., 1994-98; anesthesiologist clin. svcs. E. A. Mangieri, PC, Northport, Ala., 1998-2000; anesthesiologist Michael Pesce and Assocs., Birmingham, 2000—; co-founder Aesthetic Laser Clinic, Tuscaloosa, Ala., 2000—, Southside Anesthesia Assoc., P.C., Birmingham, 2001—, Decatur Anesthesiology Assocs., LLC, 2003—. Reviewer (bioengring.) NSF, Washington, 1981-90; guest reviewer Anesthesiology (jour.), Phila., 1988-90; co-founder Aesthetic Laser Clin., Tuscaloosa, Ala., 2000—. Author: Homogenous Enzyme Kinetics, 1984, Immobilized Enzyme Kinetics, 1984; (with others) New Anesthetic Agents, Devices and Monitoring Techniques, 1984, Pain Management of AIDS Patients, 1991. Mem.: SAR, Sigma Tau, The Huguenot Soc. S.C. (founding chartered mem.), Gen. Soc. of War of 1812, Soc. Colonial Wars, S.R., Huguenot Soc. S.C., Internat. Anesthesia Rsch. Soc., Am. Soc. Anesthesiologists, AIChE, The Summit Club, Phi Lambda Upsilon, Tau Beta Pi, Sigma Xi (assoc.). Republican. Methodist. Office: PO Box 43858 Birmingham AL 35243-0858

GREENE, FRANK EDWARD WADE, writer, philanthropy adviser; b. Syracuse, N.Y., Jan. 17, 1933; s. Melville Hart Greene and Nan Wade Pearson; m. Susanne Cavanagh, Apr. 1, 1966; children: Nathanael Wade, Jennifer Robin. AB, Princeton U., 1956; MS, Columbia U., 1962. Reporter Hartford Courant, Conn., 1956-57; writer Look Mag., N.Y.C., 1958-59; editor Am. Heritage, N.Y.C., 1962-64, Newsweek, N.Y.C., 1964-69, Saturday Rev., San Francisco, 1972-73; writer, editor Commn. Pvt. Philanthropy and Pub. Needs, Washington, 1975-76; editor N.Y. Times Mag., N.Y.C., 1976-77; philanthropy adviser Rockefeller Family and Assocs., N.Y.C., 1979—. Bd. dirs. Environ. Media Svcs., Washington. Author: Disarmament, Challenge of Civilization, 1966, Giving in America, 1976 Liaison Pres.'s Coun. Sustainable Devel., Washington, 1993—95; mem. Coun. Fgn. Rels., 1994—, League Conservation Voters, Washington, 1995—; trustee Whitehead Found., N.Y.C., 1999—, Beldon Fund, N.Y.C., 2000—, Nantucket Sustainable Devel. Corp., 2000—, Nantucket Land Coun., 2001—. With U.S. Army, 1953—55, Korea. Recipient Eleanor Roosevelt Peace award Peace Action, 1997; Profl. Journalism fellow Stanford U., 1967-68, Alicia Patterson fellow Alica Patterson Found., 1977-78. Mem. Century Assn. Office: Rockefeller Family and Assocs 30 Rockefeller Plz New York NY 10112

GREENE, FRANK SULLIVAN, JR., investment management executive; b. Washington, Oct. 19, 1938; s. Frank S. Sr. and Irma O. Greene; m. Phyllis Davison, Jan. 1958 (dec. 1984); children: Angela, Frank, Ronald; m. Carolyn W. Greene, Sept. 1990. BS, Washington U., St. Louis, 1961; MS, Purdue U., 1962; PhD, U. Santa Clara, Calif., 1970. Part-time lectr. Washington U., Howard U., Am. U., 1959-65; pres., dir. Tech. Devel. Corp., Arlington, Tex., 1985-92; pres. Zero One Systems Inc. (formerly Tech. Devel. of Calif.), Santa Clara, Calif., 1971-87, Zero One Systems Group subs. Sterling Software Inc., 1987-89. Asst. chmn., lectr. Stanford U., 1972—74; mng. mem. New Vista Capital, LLC, Palo Alto, Calif., 1993—; pres. Networked Picture Sys. Inc., 1989—91, chmn., 1991—94; bd. dirs. Reach Comms., Compliance Coach, Bridgestream. Author two indsl. textbooks; also articles; patentee in field. Bd. dirs. NCCJ, Santa Clara, 1980—, NAACP, San Jose chpt., 1986-89, Am. Musical Theatre of San Jose, 1995—; bd. regents Santa Clara U., 1983-90, trustee, 1990-2000; mem. adv. bd. Urban League, Santa Clara County, 1986-89, East Side Union High Sch., 1985-88. Capt. USAF, 1961-65. Mem IEEE, IEEE Computer Soc. (governing bd. 1973-75), Assn. Black Mfrs. (bd. dirs. 1974-80), Am. Electric Assn. (indsl. adv. bd. 1975-76), Fairchild Rsch. and Devel. (tech. staff 1965-71), Bay Area Purchasing Coun. (bd. dirs. 1978-84), Security Affairs Support Assn. (bd. dirs. 1980-83), Sigma Xi, Eta Kappa Nu, Sigma Pi Phi.

GREENE, FREDERICK D., II, chemistry educator; b. Glen Ridge, N.J., July 9, 1927; s. Phillips Foster and Ruth (Altman) G.; m. Theodora Elizabeth Whatmough, June 5, 1953; children— Alan, Carol, Elizabeth, Phillips. Grad., Phillips Andover Acad., 1944; BA, Amherst Coll., 1949, D.Sc. (hon.), 1969; PhD, Harvard, 1952. Research assoc. U. Calif., Los Angeles, 1952-53; instr. dept. chemistry Mass. Inst. Tech., Cambridge, 1953-55, asst. prof., 1955-58; assoc. prof. MIT, 1958-62, prof., 1962-95; prof. emeritus, 1995—. Editor-in-chief: Jour. Organic Chemistry, 1962-88; contbr. articles to sci. jours. Served with USNR, 1945-46. Alfred P. Sloan fellow, 1958-62; NSF Sr. Postdoctoral fellow, 1965-66 Fellow AAAS; mem. Am. Chem. Soc., Royal Soc. Chem. (U.K.), Am. Acad. Arts and Scis., Phi Beta Kappa. Office: Mass Inst Tech Dept Chemistry 77 Massachusetts Ave Cambridge MA 02139-4301

GREENE, FREDERICK LESLIE, surgeon, educator; b. Norfolk, Va., Dec. 18, 1944; s. William Joseph and Theresa Davis Greene; m. Donna W. Greene, June 21, 1970; children: Stephanie, Adam. BA, U. Va., 1966, MD, 1970. Diplomate Am. Bd. Surgery. Prof. surgery U. S.C., Columbia, 1980-97; clin. prof. surgery U. N.C., Chapel Hill, 1997—; chmn. dept. surgery Carolinas Med. Ctr., Charlotte, N.C., 1997—. Author: Endoscopic Surgery, 1994. Lt. comdr. USN, 1976-78. Mem. ACS (gov. 1995), Soc. Surg. Oncology, Am. Surg. Assn. Office: Carolinas Med Ctr PO Box 32861 Charlotte NC 28232-2861 E-mail: Frederick.Greene@Carolinashealthcare.org.

GREENE, GERALD R. pediatrician; MD, U. So. Calif., 1966; MPH, Johns Hopkins U., 1971. Rotating intern U. So. Calif., 1966-67; with USPHS, 1967-69; resident in pediatrics Johns Hopkins U., 1969-70, 1971-72; fellow in infectious diseases U.So. Calif., 1972-74; mem. faculty U. Calif., Irvine, 1974-88; chmn. dept. pediatrics San Bernardino (Calif.) County Med. Ctr., 1988-98, Arrowhead Regional Med. Ctr., Colton, Calif., 1998—. Office: Arrowhead Regional Med Ctr 400 N Pepper Ave Colton CA 92324-1801

GREENE, GLADSTONE FITZPATRICK, educator, consultant; b. Liverpool, Corentyne, Guyana, Dec. 17, 1944; s. Gosnel Greene and Victoria Gibbs; m. Fleur Bonita Ainsworth; children: Karon, Kevin. BA, U. Guyana, Turkeyen, 1973; MSc in Econs., Cardiff Bus. Sch., Wales, 1987; PhD, Columbia Pacific U., 2000. Cert. respiratory asst., med. billing; trained class 1 grade 1 tchr.'s cert. Graduate Teacher Ministry of Education, Georgetown, Guyana, 1967—76; Education Officer Guyana Defence Force, Georgetown, Guyana, 1976—79; Principal Kuru Kuru College, Georgetown, Guyana, 1980—87; Lecturer University of Guyana, Turkeyen, Guyana, 1987—90; Resource Project Teacher New York City Board Of Education, Brooklyn, 1990—2002. Mgmt. cons. Guyana Mgmt. Inst., Georgetown, 1988—90. Contbr. poetry to anthologies. Faculty rep. Faculty of Edn., Guyana, Georgetown, 1974—75; pres. student coun. Tchrs.' Tng. Coll., Georgetown, 1965—66. Capt. Tng. Corps, 1976—79, Timehri, Guyana. Recipient Cert. Merit, 2001, 2002. Mem.: Am. Mgmt. Assn., Caribbean Mgmt. Devel. Assn. Office: Erasmus Hall Campus Bus and Tech 911 Flatbush Ave Brooklyn NY 11206 Personal E-mail: saggaboy2000@yahoo.com.

GREENE, HANS, facilities administrator; BFA in Ceramics, Ohio State U., 1979; M in Energy Resources, U. Pitts., 1996. Dir. facilities Pitts. Ctr. Arts, 1996—98; energy mgr., utility budget adminstr. Drexel U., Phila., 1998—. Mem.: Assn. Energy Engrs. (cert.). Achievements include music copyrights. Office: Drexel Univ 3330 Market 16-103 Philadelphia PA 19104 E-mail: h.greene@drexel.edu.

GREENE, HERBERT BRUCE, lawyer, investor; b. N.Y.C., Apr. 13, 1934; s. Joseph Lester and Shirley (Kasen) G.; m. Judith Jean Metricks, Dec. 31, 1958; children: Pamela S., Scott L. AB, Harvard U., 1955; JD, Columbia U., 1958. Bar: N.Y. 1959, Conn. 1975. Asst. U.S. atty So. Dist. N.Y., Dept. Justice, N.Y.C., 1958-61; assoc. Kaye, Scholer, Fierman, Hays & Handler, N.Y.C., 1961-66; asst. to gen. counsel CIT Fin. Corp., N.Y.C., 1966-67; group gen. counsel Xerox Corp., Rochester, N.Y., 1967-68, v.p. adminstrn., 1968-71; sr. v.p. Xerox Edn. Group, Stamford, Conn., 1971-75; v.p., gen. counsel, sec. Lone Star Industries, Inc., Greenwich, Conn., 1976-79, sr. v.p., asst. to chmn., 1979-82; chmn., CEO Earle and Greene & Co., Westport, 1982-96, Portland, Oreg., 1997—. Mem. Phi Delta Phi. Republican. Home: 4233 SW Redondo Ave Portland OR 97239 Office: Herbert B Greene & Co 4233 W Redondo Ave Portland OR 97239

GREENE, IRA S. lawyer; b. N.Y.C., Nov. 21, 1946; s. Melvin and Syd (Semmelman) G.; m. Robin Colin, Dec. 29, 1973; children: Jessica, Alexander. BA, Syracuse U., 1968; postgrad., U. Buffalo, 1968-69; JD, N.Y. U., 1971. Bar: N.Y. 1972, U.S. Dist. Ct. (so. and ea. dists.) N.Y. 1972, U.S. Ct. Appeals (2d cir.) 1974. Counsel Gainsburg, Gottlieb, Levitan & Cole, N.Y.C., 1982—84; ptnr. Gainsburg, Gottlieb, Levitan, Greene & Cole, N.Y.C., 1984—86, Gainsburg, Greene & Hirsch, Purchase, NY, 1986—91, Squadron, Ellenoff, Plesent & Sheinfeld, N.Y.C., 1991—2002, Hogan & Hartson, N.Y.C., 2002—. Lectr. in field. Mem. Assn. Comml. Fin. Attys., Bank Lawyers Conf., Bankruptcy Lawyers Bar Assn., Assn. of Bar of City of N.Y. Office: Hogan & Hartson LLP 875 Third Ave New York NY 10022

GREENE, JAMES S., III, school administrator; b. Harlan, Ky., Nov. 10, 1943; s. James S. Jr. and Elizabeth (Howard) G.; m. Glenda Hollors, Feb. 2, 1968; children: Laurel Elizabeth, Amy Janine, James McKeehan. Postgrad., U. N.C., 1961-62; BS in Edn. French and History, U. Wis., 1965; MA in Edn., Union Coll., Barbourville, Ky., 1973; PhD in Edn., Ohio State U., 1982. Cert. tchr. secondary edn., sch. adminstrn. and supervision, Ky. Tchr. French and History Harlan H.S., 1965-83; supr. instrn. Harlan Ind. Sch. Dist., 1983—. Adj. instr. history S.E. Cmty. Coll., Cumberland, Ky., 1977-83; humanities scholar multimedia project The Lynch Legacy Project, 1987. Reviewer The History Tchr., 1973-83; contbr. (book): The Kentucky Ency., 1992. Bd. dirs. Southeastern Ky. Spl. Edn. Coop., Harlan, 1983-88; mem. adv. coun. Stokely Inst. for Liberal Arts Edn., U. Tenn., Knoxville, 1982-89; trustee Pine Mountain (Ky.) Settlement Sch., 1989—; coord. Harlan Christian Arts Festival, 1973, 76; mem. Ky. Bicentennial Commn., Frankfort, 1988-93; pres. bd. dirs. Romance of the Hills Corp., Harlan, 1992-93; elder First Presbyn. Ch., Harlan, 1968-73, 80-83, 90-95, 97-2003, organist, 1982—; mem. Ky. State Hist. Records Adv. Bd., 1996—. Recipient Award for Outstanding Contbns. to Math. Edn., Ky. Coun. Tchrs. Math., 1992; Humanities scholar So. Mountains Settlement Symposium, 1999-2000. Avocation: composing and choral arranging. Office: Harlan Ind Sch Dist 420 E Central St Harlan KY 40831-2372 E-mail: jgreene@harlan-ind.k12.ky.us.

GREENE, JANE, health educator; b. L.A., Apr. 14, 1954; d. Ben Louis and Julie Eisen Cohen; m. Russell Edward Greene, Jan. 3, 1981; children: Rachael, Lisa, Joshua. Student, UCLA, 1971-75, MSN, 1981-83; BSN, Calif. State U., Long Beach, 1978. Cert. pediat. nurse practitioner. Dietitian's asst. Century City Hosp., L.A., 1972-76; nurses aide Long Beach (Calif.) Cmty. Hosp., 1976-78; charge nurse oncology dept. Children's Hosp. Orange County, Orange, Calif., 1978-80; staff nurse Children's Hosp. Boston, 1980-81, Cedars Sinai Med. Ctr., L.A., 1981-83; pediat. instr. Washburn U. Sch. Nursing, Topeka, 1983-85; mem. fitness staff Popeyes Cardiofitness, Topeka, 1988-90; phys. edn. instr., tchr. Topeka Collegiate Sch., 1991—94; tchr. Pediatrics PA, 1990—96, nurse practitioner, 1990-96; teen health instr. Topeka Collegiate Sch., 1996—2001. Girls varsity basketball coach Bellflower (Calif.) H.S., 1975, 76; basketball boach Topeka Collegiate Sch., 1995-97, volleyball coach, 1996-98. Candidate for Kans. Legislature, 1994; asst. coach Woman's Jr. Nat. AAU, 1997; v.p. Temple Beth Sholom, 1997-99, pres., 1999; asst. varsity basketball and softball Tarbut V'Topah Sch., 2001. Named to U.S. Olympic Festival Team, Amateur Racquetball Assn., 1993; Allstate Ins. scholar, 1977-78, Auxilary of Garfield Hosp. nursing scholar, 1977-78. Mem. Nat. Assn. Pediat. Nurse Practitioners, Kans. Nurses Assn., Am. Amateur Racquetball Assn. (Kans. Women's Open State Champion 11 yrs.). Democrat. Jewish. Avocations: racquetball, tennis, jogging, biking, skiing. Home: 6800 SW Aylesbury Rd Topeka KS 66610-1442

GREENE, JOHN CLIFFORD, dentist, former university dean; b. Ashland, Ky., July 19, 1926; s. G. Norman and Ella R. Greene; m. Gwen Rustin, Nov. 17, 1957; children: Alan, Lisa, Laura. AA, Ashland Jr. Coll., 1947; student, Marshall Coll., 1948; D.MD, U. Louisville, 1952, Sc.D. (hon.), 1980; M.P.H., U. Calif., Berkeley, 1961; Sc.D. (hon.), U. Ky., 1972, Boston U., 1975. Diplomate Am. Bd. Dental Pub. Health. Intern USPHS Hosp., Chgo., 1952-53, staff San Francisco, 1953-54; asst. regional dental cons. Region IX, San Francisco, 1954-56; asst. to chief dental officer USPHS, Washington, 1958-60; chief epidemiology program Dental Health Center, 1961-66; dep. dir. Div. Dental Health, 1966-70, acting dir., 1970, dir., 1970-73; acting dir. Bur. Health Resources Devel., 1973-74, dir., 1974-75; chief dental officer USPHS, 1974-81, dep. surgeon gen., 1978-81; with Epidemic Intelligence Service, Communicable Disease Center, Altanta and Kansas City, Mo., 1956-57; epidemiology and biometry br. Nat. Inst. Dental Research, NIH, Bethesda, Md., 1957-58; prof. and dean sch. dentistry U. Calif., San Francisco, 1981-94; prof. and dean emeritus, 1994—. Spl. cons. WHO, India, 1957; mem. adv. com. rsch. women's health NIH, Bethesda, Md., 1995—97. Contbr. With USN, 1945—46. Recipient citation, Sch. Grad. Dentistry Boston U., 1971, U. of the Pacific, 1977, Meritorious and Disting. Svc. awards, HEW, 1972, 1975, Outstanding Alumnus award, U. Louisville, 1980, award of merit, FDI, 1978, Alumnus of Yr. award, U. Calif. Sch. Pub. Health, Berkeley, 1984, John W. Knutson award, APHA, 1997, U. Calif. San Francisco medal, 1999, Disting. Svc. award, Am. Dental Edn. Assn., 2001, Bill Tuttle award, 2002. Fellow: Am. Coll. Dentists, Internat. Coll. Dentists; mem.: ADA, Inst. of Medicine of NAS, Am. Assn. Pub. Health Dentistry (Disting. Svc. award 1996), Am. Assn. Dental Schs. (former v.p., chair coun. of deans), Am. Assn. Pub. Health Dentists, Am. Assn. Dental Rsch. (past pres.), Internat. Assn. Dental Rsch. (past pres.), San Francisco Dental Soc., Calif. Dental Assn., Delta Omega, Omicron Kappa Upsilon. Home: 103 Peacock Dr San Rafael CA 94901-1551

GREENE, JOHN COLTON, retired history educator; b. Indpls., Mar. 5, 1917; s. Edward Martin and Helen (Carter) G.; m. Ellen Wiemann Greene, Nov. 3, 1945; children: Ruth, Ned, John David. BA, U. S.D., 1938, DHL (hon.), 1986; MA, Harvard U., 1939, PhD, 1952. Instr. U. Chgo., 1948-52; asst. prof. U. Wis., Madison, 1952-56; from assoc. prof. to prof. Iowa State U., Ames, 1956-62; vis. prof. U. Calif., Berkeley, 1962-63; prof. U. Kans., Lawrence, 1963-67, U. Conn., Storrs, 1967-87, prof. emeritus, 1987—. Author: The Death of Adam, 1959, Darwin and the Modern World View, 1961, Science, Ideology and World View, 1981, American Science in Age of Jefferson, 1984, Debating Darwin: Adventures of a Scholar, 1999. Capt. U.S. Army, 1942-46. Jr. fellow Harvard U., 1941-42, 46-48, Guggenheim fellow, 1966-67, Am. Antiquarian Soc. fellow, 1983—; vis. scholar Cambridge U., 1974. Mem. AAUP, History of Sci. Soc. (sec. 1960-70, pres. 1975-77, George Sarton medal 2002), Midwest Junto History of Sci. (pres. 1961-62), Internat. Acad. History of Sci. (corr.). Democrat. Episcopalian. Avocation: singing.

GREENE, JOHN JOSEPH, lawyer; b. Marshall, Tex., Mar. 19, 1946; s. William Henry and Camille Anne Greene. BA, U. Houston, 1969, MA, 1974; JD, South Tex. Coll., 1978. Bar: Tex. 1978, U.S. Supreme Ct. 1982. Asst. atty. City of Amarillo, Tex., 1978-79, Harris County, Tex., 1979-83; pvt. practice, 1983—; city atty. City of Conroe (Tex.), 1983-89; sr. asst. city atty. City of Austin (Tex.), 1990—. Capt. USAR, 1969-76. Decorated Bronze Star, Air Medal. Roman Catholic. Office: 114 W 7th St Ste 400 Austin TX 78701-3008

GREENE, JOHN THOMAS, judge; b. Salt Lake City, Nov. 28, 1929; s. John Thomas and Mary Agnes (Hindley) G.; m. Dorothy Kay Buchanan, Mar. 31, 1955; children: Thomas Buchanan Greene, John Buchanan Greene, Mary Kay Greene Platt. BA in Polit. Sci., U. Utah, 1952, JD, 1955. Bar: Utah 1955, U.S. Dist. Ct. (10th cir.) 1955, U.S. Supreme Ct. 1966. Pvt. practice, Salt Lake City, 1955-57; asst. U.S. atty., 1957-59; ptnr. Marr, Wilkins & Cannon (and successor firms), Salt Lake City, 1959-75; ptnr., pres., chmn. bd. dirs. Greene, Callister & Nebeker, Salt Lake City, 1975-85; judge U.S. Dist. Ct., Salt Lake City, 1985—. Author: (manual) American Mining Law, 1960; contbr. articles to profl. jours. Chmn. Salt Lake City Cmty. Coun., 1970-75, Utah State Bldg. Authority, Salt Lake City, 1980-85; Regent Utah State Bd. Higher Edn., Salt Lake City, 1982-86. Recipient Order of Coif U. Utah, 1955, Merit of Honor award, 1994, Utah Fed. Bar Disting. Svc. award, 1997. Fellow ABA Found. (life); ABA ho. of dels. 1972-92, bd. govs. 1987-91; mem. Dist. Judges Assn. (pres. 10th cir. 1998-2000), Utah Bar Assn. (pres. 1971-72, Judge of Yr. award 1995), Am. Law Inst. (life, panelist and lectr. 1980-85, advisor 1986-98); Phi Beta Kappa. Mem. Lds Ch. Avocations: travel, reading, tennis. Office: US Dist Ct 350 S Main St Ste 447 Salt Lake City UT 84101-2180 E-mail: JTGJR@hotmail.com., Thomas_Greene@utd.uscourts.gov.

GREENE, JULE BLOUNTE, lawyer; b. Dublin, Ga., Aug. 15, 1922; s. Jule B. and Bette (O'Neal) G.; m. George Williams, Aug. 22, 1952; children: James Herschel, Bradley O'Neal. AB, Mercer U., 1949, LL.B., 1950. Bar: Ga. 1950, U.S. Supreme Ct. 1960. Atty. SEC, Atlanta, 1950-53, Washington, 1956-58, atty.-in-charge Miami, Fla., 1958-69, regional adminstr. Atlanta, 1969-82; regional counsel Nat. Assn. Securities Dealers, Atlanta, 1982-90; pvt. practice law Macon and Waycross, Ga., 1953-56, Dublin, Ga., 1990—. Former mem. Atlanta Fed. Exec. Bd., Interagy. Bd. U.S. Civil Service Examiners; former v.p., dir. Peachtree Fed. Credit Union.; former treas., dir. Mental Health Assn. Met. Atlanta. Served with A.C. AUS, 1942-46. Recipient award for exemplary achievement in pub. adminstrn. William A. Jump Meml. Found., 1958 Mem. Fed. Bar Assn. (pres. South Fla. chpt. 1961), Ga. Bar Assn., Rotary, Kappa Alpha. Methodist. Home: 507 Woods Ave Dublin GA 31021-3542 E-mail: juleg@aol.com.

GREENE, KAY C. psychologist, author; b. Yankton, S.D., July 10, 1939; d. Fred Orin and Evelyn Irene (Sundy) Green. B.Mus. in Edn., U. Nebr., 1962; MA in Psychology, New Sch. Social Rsch., 1980, PhD in Clin. Psychology, 1983. Lic. psychologist, Md., N.Y., D.C.; ordained deacon Fifth Ave. Presbyn. Ch., N.Y.C., 1997. With Gulf States Utilities, Beaumont, Tex., 1963-64, Tatham, Laird & Kudner, N.Y.C., 1965-66; mgmt. cons. John Wiersma Cons., Washington, 1966; adv. coord. Sullivan Stauffer Colwell & Bayles, N.Y.C., 1966-67; acting supr., ticket agt., svc. rep. Am. Airlines, N.Y.C., 1967; exec. sec. to v.p./chief engr. WPIX-TV, N.Y.C., 1967-71, adminstrv. asst. to news chief, 1971-72; office mgr. Lawrence Letter Svc., N.Y.C., 1973-78; clin. psychologist in pvt. practice N.Y.C., 1985—; regional trainer APA HOPE (HIV) Project, 1992—. Tchr. music, English, spl. edn. MacArthur Jr. H.S., Beaumont, 1964-65; student music tchr. U. Nebr. Exptl. H.S., Lincoln, 1961-62; lectr. in field; condr. seminars in field; appeared on Donahue, Good Morning New York, Kelly and Co., Survival into the 21st Century, Turning Inward; radio shows include The Alan Colmes Show, WABC, N.Y., Alan Colmes, WPIX, N.Y., Open Session, Ben Reese, WNYE, N.Y., From Head to Heart, WXLO, N.Y., Foundation Focus, WNEW, N.Y., Wellness Workshop, WNWK FM, N.Y., others; founder, pres. Bridge of Change; sr. rep. UN Hdqrs. for World Fedn. Mental Health, 1990-95, organizer various confs., keynote spkr. various internat. confs. past staff therapist/sr. staff psychologist Fifth Ave. Ctr. for Counseling and Psychotherapy, N.Y.C.; rep. UN Hdqrs. for Internat. Coun. of Psychologists, 1996-2000; adj. asst. prof. St. Francis Coll., Bklyn. Coll., 1997-98; vis. assoc. prof. Lincoln Ctr. Fordham U., N.Y.C., 1997-98, adj. assoc. prof., 1998, adj. prof., 1998—; adj. assoc. prof. Pace U., N.Y.C., 1999-, adj. assoc. prof. John Jay Coll. Criminal Justice, N.Y.C., 2002—; vice chair NGO/DPI exec. com. UN Hdqs., 1998-2000, chair, 2000-2001; interim exec. dir. Millennium NGO Forum UN Hdqrs., 1998-99. Contbr. articles to profl. jours. Named Internat. Woman of the Yr. in recognition of svcs. to mental health Internat. Biog. Centre, 1993-94; recipient Disting. Leadership award Internat. Directory of Disting. Leadership. Mem. APA (Nat. AIDS task force 1988—, fellow internat. divsn. 52 1999), AFTRA, Authors Guild, Authors League, Internat. Coun. of Psychologists (sec.-gen. 1997-2000, rep. UN hdqrs. 1996-2000), Internat. Platform Assn., C.G. Jung Found. for Analytical Psychology, N.Y. Acad. Sci., N.Y. State Psychol. Assn. (pres.-elect acad. divsn. 1999, pres. acad. divsn. 2001), Screen Actors Guild, Soc. for Psychol. Study of Social Issues, World Assn. for Psychosocial Rehab. (rep. UN Hdqs. 1998-2000), World Fedn. Mental Health, Sigma Alpha Iota (Kappa chpt.), Pi Kappa Lambda, Psi Chi. Avocations: piano, photography, pets, painting, cooking. Home and Office: 30 Waterside Plz Apt 13E New York NY 10010-2630

GREENE, KELLY ELIZABETH, medical educator; b. Denver, Oct. 10, 1960; d. Robert Emmett and Charlotte Sophie Greene; m. Offner; children: Patrick Offner, Sean Offner, Robert Offner. BA, Carroll Coll., Helena, MT,

1979—83; MD, WA U, St. Louis, MO, 1983—87. Cert. Pulmonary and Critical Care specialist 1994. Assoc. prof. of med. Nat. Jewish Med. and Rsch. Ctr./ U of CO Health Sci. Ctr., Denver, 1996—. Med. dir. Prof. Ed., Nat. Jewish, Denver, 2000—02. Author. Chairperson Clin. Needs Comm., Denver, 2001—03, CO Asthma Coalition, Denver, 2001—03, Am. Lung Assoc., Denver, 2001—03. Recipient K08, Nat. Inst. of Health, 1996—2001, R01, 2002—06; fellow fellowship, Parker B. Fellowship/ Parker B. Found., 1993—96; grantee Cystic Fibrosis Rsch., Cystic Fibrosis Found., 1996—2003. Mem.: Am. Thoracic Soc., Am. Coll. of Chest Phys. Achievements include research in Continuous NIH funding for work on surfactant protein molecules as innate modulators of lung inflammation; Surfactant Proteins as Biomarkers in ARDS. Office: Nat Jewish Med and Rsch Cen 1400 Jackson St Denver CO 80220 Home: 363 Bellaire St Denver CO 80220

GREENE, LAURA HELEN, physicist; b. Cleve., June 12, 1952; d. Sam and Frances (Kain) G.; children: Max Greene Giannetta, Leo Greene Giannetta. BS cum laude in Physics, Ohio State U., 1974, MS in Physics, 1978; MS in Exptl. Physics, Cornell U., 1980, PhD in Physics, 1984. Mem. tech. staff Hughes Aircraft Co., Torrance, Calif., 1974-75; teaching asst. Ohio State U., Columbus, 1975-76, rsch. asst., 1976-77; teaching asst. Cornell U., Ithaca, N.Y., 1977-79, rsch. asst., 1979-83; postdoctoral mem. tech. staff Bellcore (formerly Bell Labs.), Red Bank, N.J., 1983-85, Murray Hill, N.J., 1983-85, mem. tech. staff Red Bank, N.J., 1985-92; prof. dept. physics U. Ill., Urbana, 1992—, Swanlund endowed chair, 2000, Ctr. for Advanced Study resident assoc., 2000—. Beckman assoc. Ctr. Advanced Study U Ill. at Urbana-Champaign, 1996-97, mem. provost's com. on sexual harassment edn., 1999-2000, mem. physics adv. com., 1999—; mem. McMillan award com. 1994-96, chair, 1995-97; co-chair Gordon Rsch. Conf., 1996, chair, 1998; mem.-at-large Com. Gordon Rsch. Confs., 1999—, mem. schedule and selection com.; mem. Basic Energy Scis. Adv. Com., 2000; interim and founding bd. trustee Inst. for Complex and Adaptive Materials, Los Alamos and U. Calif.; mem. various rev. panels and workshops NSF and Dept. Energy; presenter in field; resident assoc. ctr. for advanced study U. Ill., Urbana, Ill., 2000-2001; review panel Can. Inst. Advanced Rsch., Superconductivity Review, 2002; mem. provost com. sexual harrassment edn. U. Ill., 1999-2001, oversight com. for vice chancellor rsch., U. Ill., 2001-2002, Sloan Found. Selection Com. for Physics, 2001—; adv. com. Sec. of Energy Bill Richardson, 2000—; chair external rev. panel, mem. bd. trustees Ctr. Integrated Nahotechnologies Nat. Lab., Los Alamos Nat. Lab., Sandia Nat. Lab. Contbr. over 200 articles to profl. jours.; presenter over 150 domestic and internat. invited talks. Mem. selection com. in physics Sloan Found. Recipient Beckman award U. Ill. Campus Rsch. Bd., 1993, E.O. Lawrence award Dept. Energy, 1999, 2001; rsch. grantee NSF, 1991—, ONR, 1995—, Dept. Energy, 1995—. Fellow AAAS (electorate nominating com. of sect. B physics 2000—, chmn. nominating com. for physics, 2001-02), Am. Acad. Arts and Scis., Am. Phys. Soc. (gen. councilor 1992—, congl. fellow screening com. 1993, exec. bd. 1995—, com. on coms. 1995—, chair 1997, search com. The Phys. Rev. 1996, nominating com. divsn. condensed matter physics 1998—, Maria Goeppert-Mayer award 1994, Centennial Spkr. 1997); mem. Materials Rsch. Soc. (symposium chair 1992), Am. Assn. Physics Tchrs., Internat. Union Pure and Applied Physicists (commr., U.S. liaison com. 1996—, U.S. del. to Low-Temperature Physics Commn. 1996—), Phi Kappa Phi. Avocations: children, physics, working out, music. Office: U Ill Loomis Lab Physics 1110 W Green St Urbana IL 61801-9013 E-mail: lhg@uiuc.edu.

GREENE, LAURENCE WHITRIDGE, JR., surgical educator; b. Denver, Jan. 18, 1924; s. Laurence Whitridge Sr. and Freda (Schmitt) G.; m. Frances Steger, Sept. 16, 1950 (dec. Dec. 1977); children: Charlotte Greene Kerr, Mary Whitridge Greene, Laurence Whitridge III; m. Nancy Kay Bennett, Dec. 7, 1984. BA, Colo. Coll., 1945; MD, U. Colo., 1947; postgrad., U. Chgo., 1948-50. Diplomate Am. Bd. of Surgery. Intern St. Lukes Hosp., Denver, 1947-48; sr. intern in ob./gyn. U. Chgo. Lying-In Hosp., 1948-49; surg. resident U. Cin. Gen. Hosp., 1952-55, sr. surg. resident, 1955-57, chief surgery resident, 1957-58; clin. surgery asst. Sch. of Medicine U. Colo., Denver, 1958-61, clin. instr. Sch. of Medicine, 1961-67, asst. clin. prof. Sch. of Medicine, 1967-75, assoc. clin. prof. Sch. of Medicine, 1975-87, clin. prof. Sch. of Medicine, 1987—. Adj. prof. zoology and physiology U. Wyo., Laramie, 1970-80; mem. staff Ivinson Meml. Hosp., Laramie, 1958—; chmn. Wyo chpt. Com. on Trauma, 1973-89; tchr., mem. adv. staff U. Colo. Med. Sch., Denver, 1958-83; mem. advisor, surgeon U. Wyo. Athletics, Laramie, 1975-80, Wyo. Hwy. Patrol, 1950—. Contbr. numerous articles to profl. jours. Lt. M.C. (s.g.) USN, 1950-52, Korea. Fellow ACS; mem. Am. Assn. for Surgery of Trauma, Southwestern Surgery Congress, Western Surg. Assn., Mont Reed Soc., Masons, Shriners, Sigma Xi. Republican. Episcopalian. Avocations: golf, sports, hunting, fishing.

GREENE, LEONARD MICHAEL, aerospace manufacturing executive, institute executive; b. N.Y.C., June 8, 1918; s. Max and Lyn (Furman) G.; m. Beverly Kaufman, June 27, 1943 (div. 1957); children: Randall Ashley, Bonnie LeVar, Laurie Baldwin; m. Phyllis Saks, June 8, 1958 (dec. Oct. 1965); children: Douglas, Charles, Donald (dec.), Stephen, Terry; m. Joyce Teck, Jan. 2, 1967; stepchildren: Jeffrey Meller, William Meller, Gary Meller, Amy Meller Gerbe. BS in Engring., CCNY, 1937, MS in Engring., 1939; postgrad., Guggenheim Sch. Aeronautics, NYU; D in Civil Law (hon.), Pace U., 1977. Rsch. chemist Rubber & Asbestos Corp., New Jersey, 1938-41; aerodynamicist, engring. test pilot Grumman Aircraft Corp., L.I., N.Y., 1941-45; pres. Safe Flight Instrument Corp., White Plains, N.Y., 1946—. Pres., founder Sound-Titles, Inc., 1989; bd. dirs. Nationwide Ins. Author: Free Enterprise Without Poverty, 1981, The National Tax Rebate: A New America With Less Government, 1998, Inventorship: The Art of Innovation, 2001, (monographs) A Plan for a Nat. Demogrant Fianced by a Value-Added Tax, The Medical Costs Recovery Program. Mem. adv. bd. Martha's Vineyard Hosp.; pres., founder Inst. for SocioEcon. Studies, 1970; v.p., co-founder Corp. Angel Network, White Plains, 1981—; mem. spl. com. on income maintenance and council on trends and perspectives U.S. C. of C., 1975-76; bd. dirs. Blythedale Children's Hosp., Urban League Westchester Inc., Nationwide Ins.; chmn. Income Assistance/Community Devel. Program of Westchester Council of Social Agys.; pres., founder Fair Share Found., Inc.; mem. income maintenance com. Community Svc. Soc.; mem. work group on welfare reform Task Force on N.Y.C. Fiscal Crisis; mem. Westchester Coordinating Coun. on Handicapped; mem. Conf. Bd.'s Econ. Forum, 1979. Recipient Air Safety award Flight Safety Found., 1949, 81, Pilot Safety award Nat. Bus. Aircraft Assn., 1961, Employer Merit award Pres.'s Com. on Employment of Handicapped, Albert Gallatin award for Civic Leadership, Flight Safety Found award for Meritorious Svc., Disting. Svc. award Human Rights Commn. of White Plains, 1976, Medallion award Found. for Westchester C.C., 1988, U.S. EPA, Region I Spl. Act award, 1989, Meritorious Svc. to Aviation award Nat. Bus. Aircraft Assn., 1996, AlliedSignal Bendix trophy for aviation safety Flight Safety Found., 1999, Carrels award Outstanding Achievement Elecs. Aviation Week & Space Tech., 1999, Laureate award for lifetime achievement as a pioneer in flight safety, performance and innovation Aviation Week & Space Tech., 2001; nominated N.Y. State Employer of Yr; cited by N.Y. Gov.'s Com. to Employ Handicapped, 1966; commendation from sec. dept. HEW, private sector initiative commendation Pres. of U.S.; inducted into Nat. Inventors Hall of Fame, 1991. Fellow AIAA (assoc.); mem. Soc. Exptl. Test Pilots (life), Nat. Aviation Assn., Internat. 12 Meter Assn. (voting), Edgartown Yacht Club, N.Y. Yacht Club, Sheldrake Yacht Club (Mamaroneck, N.Y.), Royal Hamilton Amateur Dinghy Club (Bermuda), Quaker Ridge Golf Club (Scarsdale, N.Y.), Alpha Beta Gamma. Achievements include co-founding Courageous Sailing Ctr., Inc., Boston, to which donated 12-meter yacht Courageous IV, winner America's Cup, 1974, 77. Home: 6 Hickory Rd Scarsdale NY 10583-3016 Office: Safe Flight Instrument Corp 20 New King St White Plains NY 10604-1204

GREENE, LILIANE, French language and literature educator, editor; b. Salonica, Greece, Oct. 10, 1928; came to U.S., 1941; d. Maurice and Daisy (Kohn) Massarano; m. Thomas McLernon Greene, May 20, 1950; children: Philip James, Christopher George, Francis Richard BA, Hunter Coll., 1948; MA, Columbia U., 1949; PhD, Yale U., 1969. Asst. in instrn. French Yale U., New Haven, 1964-65, instr., 1967-68, lectr., mng. editor Yale French Studies, 1980-94 (ret.); instr. Conn. Coll., New London, 1968-69, asst. prof., 1970-75. Contbr. articles to profl. jours. Fullbright fellow, 1949-50. Mem. MLA, Am. Assn. Tchrs. French, Ctr. Ind. Study (founding mem., pres. 1978-79, bd. dirs. 1977-89), Conn. Acad. of Arts and Scis. Democrat. Avocations: travel, theater. Home: 125 Livingston St New Haven CT 06511-2428

GREENE, LYNNE JEANNETTE, fashion designer; b. Albany, N.Y., Aug. 27, 1938; d. Zebulon Stevens and Helen Matilde (Maier) Robbins; m. Stanley E. Greene, Jan. 31, 1962 (dec. June 27, 1987); 1 child, Stuart Nathaniel; m. Michael Alan Karlan, Sept. 29, 1991. Student, Goucher Coll., 1956-57; BA with honors, Parsons Sch. Design, 1960. Asst. designer Haymaker Sportswear (David Crystal), N.Y.C., 1959-61; designer Craig Craely Sportswear and Dresses, N.Y.C., 1961-63, Flair Lingerie, N.Y.C., 1964-66; designer, owner Kaleidoscope Lingerie, N.Y.C., 1966-67; head designer Contessa/Monique/Fisher Lingerie, N.Y.C., 1967-71; creative dir. Eye of the Peacock Sportswear, N.J., 1968-72; head designer, owner Lynne Greene Designs Retail, Montclair, N.J., 1972-74; designer, pres. Little Greene Apples Inc., Montville, N.J., 1971—; designer, dir. mktg. Lady Lynne Lingerie, Guy Laroche Lingerie, N.Y.C. and Paris, 1973-93, Paris, 1973—93, Val Mode by Lynne Greene, N.Y.C., 1993-97; v.p. design and merchandising The Intapp Group/Go Figure, N.Y.C., 1997-99; pres. Vital Advantage LLC, 1999—, owner, 1999—. Lingerie critic Pratt Inst., 1984—. Patentee in field; illustrator books, pamphlets in fashion and packaging fields; comml. artist and illustrator Home & Office Design. Active participant Montville Soccer Assn, 1972-88, fund drives for Am. Heart Assn., Cancer Inc., March of Dimes. Recipient Humanitarian award, Polar Bear Project, Nikken Inc., 2003, honors in field. Mem. The Fashion Group, Kiwanis, 200 Club N.J. Republican. Unitarian Universalist. Avocations: sketching, portraiture, cooking, sewing, painting. E-mail: maklynne@optonline.net.

GREENE, MAURICE, Olympic athlete, track and field athlete; b. Kansas City, Kans., July 23, 1974; Defeated Carl Lewis Tex. Relays, 1995; 3 Gold Medals World Championships, Seville, 1999; 2 Gold Medals Sydney, 2000; gold medalist 100m and 4x100m, 2000; U.S. indoor 60m champ, 2001; world indoor 60m champion, 1999; placed 1st at Home Depot invitational outdoors, 2003; placed 1st in Athens, 2002; placed 1st in Monaco, 2002; won3rd US 100m title, 2002; ranked #3 in the world (#2 in US) T&FN, 2002. Recipient USATF's Visa Humanitarian of the Yr. award, 2001, Jesse Owens award, 1999. Holder record time Grand Prix meet, Athens, 1999, world's fastest man, Sydney, 2000; became first man to win both 100 and 200 meter races at World Championship, 1999. Office: USA Track and Field Team One RCA Dome Ste 140 Indianapolis IN 46225

GREENE, MELINDA JEAN, retail maintenance analyst; b. Warren, Pa., Jan. 15, 1963; d. Nancy Louise Stanko, Gerald Paul Stanko (Stepfather). BA, Malone Coll., 1999. Customer svc. Blair Corp., Warren, Pa., 1980—92; retail clerk BP Products N.Am. Inc., Wexford, Pa., 1992—95, asst. maintenance and constrn., 1995—96, maintenance asst. Warrensville, Ohio, 1996—98, account svc. rep. Cuyahoga Heights, Ohio, 1998—2000, retail maintenance analyst Alpharetta, Ga., 2000—. Protestant. Home: 2752 Ashleigh Ln Alpharetta GA 30004 Office: BP Products NAm Inc 2475 Northwinds Pkwy Ste 400 Alpharetta GA 30004 Office Fax: 770-576-3282. Personal E-mail: greenemj@bp.com.

GREENE, MONICA LYNN BANKS, recreational therapist, director; b. Washington, Sept. 24, 1963; d. John Thomas and Pricilla (Sneed) Banks; m. Edward Ray Greene, Sept. 12, 1991. BS in Microbiology and Therapeutic Recreation, Howard U., 1986; MBA, U. Md. Cert. therapeutic recreation specialist, activity cons. Therapeutic recreation specialist Dept. Human Svcs., Washington, 1986-91; dir. activities, vols., transp. Independence Ct. Hyattsville, Md., 1991-93; dir. therapeutic activity svcs. Asbury Meth. Village, Gaithersburg, Md., 1993—; dir. therapeutic activities and vol. svcs. Presdl. Woods Health Care Ctr., Adelphi, Md.; owner, pres. Excell Eldercare Mgmt., Inc.; asst. adminstr. St. Thomas More Nursing & Rehab. Ctr., Hyattsville, Md.; exec. dir. Morningside HOuse of St. Charles, Waldorf, Ind., 2003—. Democrat. Baptist. Avocations: swimming, reading, needlework, quilting. E-mail: edmonicaathome@msn.com.

GREENE, NATALIE CONSTANCE, protective services official; b. Ft. Benning, Ga., Nov. 26, 1960; d. Wilbur Murray and Vernel Jeanette (Smalls) G. BS in Phys. Edn., East Stroudsburg U., 1983; AAS in Gen. Bus., Mercer County C.C., 1989, AS in Criminal Justice, 1998; AS in Allied Health Sci., Coll. of Air Force, 1997. Mil. pay clk. Dept. Def.-U.S. Army, Trenton, N.J., 1984-85, Dept. Def.-USAF, McGuire AFB, N.J., 1985-86; spl. police officer Willingboro (N.J.) Police Dept., 1986-90; budget asst. Dept. Def., West Trenton, N.J., 1986-88; edn. planner, budget officer Dept. Edn., Edison, N.J., 1988-89; mcht. svcs. clk. Chem. Bank, Cherry Hill, N.J., 1989-90; transit police officer Southeastern Pa. Transp. Authority, Phila., 1990-97; victim support adv. and investigator dept. pub. safety. Drexel U., Phila., 1997-99; info. tech. trainer, computer support specialist Cath. Charities, Trenton, 2002—. Master sgt. USAFR, 1980—. Recipient Desert Shield/Storm award, 1992, Cert. of Appreciation, CAP, 1991, Willingboro Twp., 1991, Morton Elem. Sch., 1991, Outstanding Young Women of N.J., 1989. Mem. NAFE, VFW, Air Force Sgts. Assn., Fraternal Order Police, Noncommd. Officers Acad. Grad. Assn. Baptist. Avocations: volleyball, tennis, track, swimming, piano. Home: 132 Crestview Dr Willingboro NJ 08046-3538

GREENE, NATHANAEL WADE, environmental scientist; b. N.Y.C., Mar. 12, 1969; s. Frank Edward Wade and Susanne Cavanagh Greene; m. Sara Duffy, Apr. 23, 1970. BA in Pub. Policy, Brown U., Providence, 1992; MS in Energy and Resources, U. Calif., Berkeley, 1996. Rsch. assoc. Natural Resources Def. Coun., N.Y.C., 1992—94, staff policy analyst, 1996—2001, sr. policy analyst, 2001—; rsch. assoc. Lawrence Berkeley Nat. Lab, Berkeley, 1995—96. Bd. dirs. Slide Ranch, Muir Beach, Calif., 1995—96. Office: Natural Resources Defense Council 40 W 20th St New York NY 10011

GREENE, RICHARD H. journalist, multimedia producer; b. Milford, Conn., Aug. 12, 1955; s. Eugene Harold and Bebe (Bender) G.; m. Katherine Barrett, Feb. 21, 1982; children: Benjamin, Sandra. BS in Journalism, Northwestern U., 1977. Rschr. Forbes mag., N.Y.C., 1977-79, reporter, 1979-81, staff writer, 1981-82, assoc. editor, 1982-84, contbg. editor, 1984-89; freelance writer N.Y.C., 1984—; pres. Barrett & Greene, N.Y.C., 1996—. Adv. bd. Govtl. Acctg. Stds. Bd.; spkr. in field. Author (with Katherine Barrett): The Man Behind the Magic, 1991, Frankly My Dear..., 1996, Powering Up, 2000, Inside the Dream, 2001; spl. projects editor Governing mag.; co-prodr. Walt Disney biographical CD-ROM; co-prodr., writer TV documentary Walt: The Man Behind the Myth; contbr. articles to mags., including Fin. World, Glamour, Ladies' Home Jour., Reader's Digest, Redbook, Working Woman, others. Curator Walt Disney Family On-line Mus. Named one of ten best articles of yr., Forbes' Media Guide, 1993; recipient Amos Tuck award, Dartmouth Coll., 1978, award for excellence in fin. journalism, N.Y. Soc. CPAs, 1984, 1991, cert. of merit, 1987, Children's Choice award, Internat. Reading Assn., 1992, Folio Editl. Excellence award, 2002. Home and Office: 25 Waterside Plz Apt GG New York NY 10010-2621 E-mail: greenebarrett@cs.com.

GREENE, RICHARD THADDEUS, bank executive; b. Charleston, S.C., July 18, 1918; s. Richard and Martha (Black) G.; m. Virginia L. Lea; children: Cheryll Y., Richard I. Jr. BS, Hampton U., 1938; D in Comml. Scis. (hon.), St. Johns U., 1992. Asst. treas. Citizen's & Southern Bank & Trust Co., Phila., 1938-41; rep., bus. mgr. Assoc. Pubs., Inc., N.Y.C., 1945-58; nat. advt. rep., sec./bus. mgr. Interstate United Newspapers, N.Y.C., 1958-60; exec. asst. to pres. Carver Fed. Savs. Bank, N.Y.C., 1960, mgr. Bklyn. office, 1961, asst. sec., mgr. Bklyn. office, 1961-63, asst. v.p., mgr. Bklyn. office, 1963-66, v.p., mgr. Bklyn. office, 1966-68, exec. v.p., 1968, pres., dir., 1969-95. Bd. dirs. finance com. HUDC, Fin. Svcs. Corp., Harlem Urban Devel. Corp., N.Y.C. Partnership Inc., Thrift Assns. Svc. Corp., Fed. Home Loan Bank N.Y.; bd. advisors Black Enterprise. Former bd. dirs. Am. Savs. & Loan League, Inc., Queens Coun. on the Arts, Uptown C. of C., United Way of Tri-State, N.Y. Urban League, Inc.; trustee George E. Meares Meml. Scholarship Fund; former trustee Citizen's Budget Commn., N.Y.C.; Bd. dirs., chmn. fin. com. Apollo Theatre Found.; elder Westminster Presbyn. Ch. Maj. U.S. Army, 1941-45. Recipient Outstanding Citizen award N.Y. Recorder, Citizenship award Bklyn. HOme for the Aged, Achievement award for contbn. to community Cornerstone Bapt. Ch., Bklyn., Black Bank Pres. award Westminster Presbyn. Ch., Jamaica, N.Y., Citation of Appreciation award Abyssinian Bapt. Ch., N.Y.C., Professionalism & Excellence in Banking award Urban Bankers Coalition Inc., Banking award Harlem Commonwealth Coun., Booker T. Washington award N.Y. Hampton Alumni Club Inc. Mem. N.Y. League of Savs. Insts. (legis. com.), Harlem Bus. Alliance, Nat. Freedom Day Assn., One Hundred Black Men Inc., N.Y. Hampton Alumni Club, Omega Psi Phi (Man of Yr. award, Citizen of Yr.), Sigma Pi Phi.

GREENE, ROBERT ALLAN, former university administrator; b. Boston, Nov. 6, 1931; s. Merrill Francis and Alice Josephine (Anderson) G.; m. Mary E. Mahoney, July 20, 1957; children— Robert, Merrill, Helen, Priscilla. BA, Boston Coll., 1953, MA, 1954; PhD, Harvard U., 1961. Lectr. dept. English Univ. Coll., U. Toronto, Ont., Can., 1958-61, asst. prof., 1962-65, assoc. prof., 1966-69, prof., 1969-80; dean U. Toronto Faculty of Arts and Sci., 1972-77; Leverhulme vis. lectr. Durham (Eng.) U., 1962-63; vice-chancellor for acad. affairs, provost U. Mass., Boston, 1980-87. Editor: (With H.R. MacCallum) Nathaniel Culverwell's Discourse of the Light of Nature, 1652, 1971, 2002. Home: 19 Centre St Apt 5 Cambridge MA 02139-2112 Office: U Mass Harbor Campus Boston MA 02125 E-mail: robert.greene@umb.edu.

GREENE, ROBERT MICHAEL, lawyer; b. Buffalo, Jan. 14, 1945; s. Gerald Henry and Dorothy Louise (Doll) G.; m. Catherine Ellen Ostanski, Sept. 28, 1974; children: Amy, Megan, Timothy, Daniel. BA, Canisius Coll., 1966; JD, U. Notre Dame, 1969; LLM, NYU, 1971. Bar: N.Y. 1970, U.S. Dist. Ct. (we. dist.) N.Y. 1970, U.S. Ct. Appeals (2d cir.) 1970. Atty. VISTA, N.Y.C., 1969-71; assoc. Phillips, Lytle, Hitchcock, Blaine & Huber, LLP, Buffalo, 1971-75, ptnr., 1976-81, mng. ptnr., 1982-95, CEO, 1982—2003. Del. White House Conf. on Small Bus., 1986; bd. dirs. Cello Pack Corp., Gioia Mgmt., Inc. Author: Managing Partner 101: A Primer on Law Firm Leadership, 1990, Making Partner, A Guide for Law Firm Associates, 1992; co-author: Summary of Land Use Regulation in the State of New York and State Land Use Programs, 1974; editor: The Quality Pursuit: Assuring Standards in the Practice of Law, 1989; bd. editors Law Practice Mgmt. mag., 1989-93, articles editor, 1992-93. Trustee Canisius Coll., 1971-77, 92-2000, chmn. 1993-97; chmn. Shea's Ctr. for Performing Arts, Buffalo, 1981-85; pres. Zool. Soc. of Buffalo, 1987-92; chmn. Buffalo Philharm. Orch., 1997-99; pres. bd. Cath. Edn. Diocese of Buffalo, 1987-97; trustee Western N.Y. Pub. Broadcasting Assn., 1984—, chmn. 1993-96; Greater Buffalo Devel. Found., 1992-93; bd. dirs. Greater Buffalo Partnership, 1993-2000, sec. 1996-2000; trustee Buffalo Philharm. Orch. Found., 2001—, chmn., 2003—; trustee Found. of Diocese of Buffalo, 2000—, Zool. Soc. Buffalo Found., 1999—, WNED Found., 2001—; bd. dirs. Albright-Knox Art Gallery, 2000—. Recipient LaSalle award Canisius Coll., 1980, Bd. Regents Dist. Citizens Achievement award, 1987, Disting. Alumni award 1991, Signum Fidei award St. Joseph's Collegiate Inst., 1990, Golden Marquee award Shea's Buffalo Theatre, 1984, Theodore Roosevelt Exemplary Citizen award, 1993, Person of Yr. award Notre Dame Club of Buffalo, 1994, Brotherhood award Nat. Conf., 1997, Chmn.'s award Buffalo Niagara Partnership, 1999, Humanitarian award Niagara Luth. Health Found., 2000, Caritas award St. Joseph Hosp. Found., 2003. Mem. N.Y. State Bar Assn., Erie County Bar Assn., U. Notre Dame Law Assn. (bd. dirs. 1988—, pres. 2003—), Buffalo Club (bd. dirs. 1997-2000), Cherry Hill Club. Democrat. Roman Catholic. Office: Phillips Lytle Hitchcock Blaine & Huber LLP 3400 HSBC Ctr Buffalo NY 14203-2887 Fax: 716-852-6100. E-mail: rgreene@phillipslytle.com.

GREENE, ROBERT WILLIAM, journalism educator, media consultant; b. Jamaica, N.Y., July 12, 1929; s. Francis McLaughlin and Mary Virginia (Clancy) G.; m. Kathleen A. Greene, Jan. 28, 1951; children: Robert William, Lea Marie (dec.). Student, Fordham U., 1947-50. Reporter Jersey Jour., 1949-50; sr. investigator N.Y.C. Anti-Crime Com., 1950-55; reporter Newsday, Garden City, N.Y., 1955, leader investigative team, 1967-73, sr. editor, 1970-92, Long Island editor, 1972-78, asst. mng. editor, 1978-93; ret., 1993; Disting. Stessin prof., chair dept. journalism and mass media studies Hofstra U., 2001—. Staff investigator U.S. Senate Select Com. on Unfair Practices in Labor/Mgmt. Field, 1957; dir. Ariz. Project, 1976-77; pres., CEO Greene Assocs.; lectr. in field; journalism program coord. SUNY, Stony Brook, 1986-95. Author: Naked Came the Stranger, 1969, The Heroin Trail, 1973, The Sting Man, 1981. Chmn. publicity Smithtown Tercentenary, 1967; founding mem., bd. dirs. Suffolk County Happy Landings Fund; bd. visitors Inst. on Polit. Journalism Georgetown U.; bd. dirs. Smithtown Hist. Soc., Mus. at Stony Brook, Cleary Sch. for Deaf; founder, former pres. L.I. Press Club; founder St. Anthony's Gridiron Club; mem. Pres.' Coun. Xavier H.S.; chmn. Mollenhoff Journalism Award Comn. Named Hon. mem. Class of 1996, U. Md. Coll. Journalism, Hon. Alumnus, Hofstra U., 1999, Tchr. of Yr., 2000, hon. pres., Norwegian Investigative Reporters, Oslo, 1991; named to, L.I. Hall of Fame, 1991; recipient George Polk award, L.I. U, Peter Zenger award, U. Ariz., James Wright Brown award, Gold Medal Pulitzer prize, 1970, 1974, Mo. medal for disting. svc. to Am. journalism, 1979, Front Page award, 1982, Edgar award, Mystery Writers Am., 1982, Disting. Achievement award, Fordham U. Grad. Sch. Edn., 1994, Pres.'s medal, Hofstra U., 2001. Fellow Soc. Profl. Journalists; mem. Investigative Reporters and Editors Group (pres. 1976-77, chmn. exec. bd.), Assn. Edn. Journalism & Mass Comms., Radio & TV News Dirs.'s Assn. Clubs: Hofstra Univ. Club, L.I. Press (pres. 1976). Republican. Roman Catholic. Office: 4 Ardmore Pl Kings Park NY 11754-4002 also: Hofstra U Dept Journalism Rm 121 Dempster Hall 111 Hofstra U Hempstead NY 11550-1090 E-mail: RGreene455@aol.com., jrnrwg@hofstra.edu.

GREENE, ROGER LEWIS, social studies educator; b. Cin., May 29, 1962; s. Ford Chamus Greene and Dorothy Katherine Stout. AA, Clermont Coll., 1989; BA, U. Cin., 1992; MA, Ohio State U., 1994. Cert. social studies tchr., Ohio. Social studies tchr. Amelia Mid. Sch., Cin., 1994-95, Delhi Jr. High Sch., Cin., 1996-99, Oak Hills H.S., Cin., 1999—2000, Western Brown H.S., Mt. Orab, Ohio, 2000—02; edml. cons., owner Impact Ednl. Svcs., Cin., 2000—. Mock trial adv., 2000-202 Mem. Phi Delta Kappa. Avocation: coaching high school football and track. Home: 366 S Andrews Dr Cincinnati OH 45245

GREENE, ROLAND, literature educator; BA, Brown U., 1979; PhD, Princeton U., 1985. Past positions at Harvard U., Princeton U., Oreg. U., dir. program comparative lit; prof. Eng. Stanford U., 2001—, chair divsn. lit., cultures and langs., 2001—02. Author: Post-Petrarchism: Origins and Innovations of the Western Lyric Sequence, 1991, Unrequited Conquests: Love and Empire in the Colonial Americas, 1999; editor (with Elizabeth Fowler): The Project of Prose in Early Modern Europe and the New World, 1997. Fellow, Am. Coun. Learned Soc., NEH, Danforth Found., and others. Mem.: Modern Lang. Assn. (exec. coun.), Internat. Spenser Soc. (pres.). Office: Stanford Univ English Dept 450 Serra Mall Stanford CA 94305-2087 Office Fax: 650-725-0755. E-mail: rgreene@stanford.edu.

GREENE, STEPHEN CRAIG, lawyer; b. Watertown, NY, Apr. 27, 1946; s. Harold Adelbert and Mildred Esther (Baker) G.; m. Nancy Jean Adams, Mar. 28, 1965; children: Kathryn, Stephen, Hilary. AB, Syracuse U., 1967, JD, 1970. Bar: NY 1971, US Tax Ct., 1977. Asst. to pres. SUNY, Oswego, NY, 1970-73; assoc. firm Leyden E. Brown, Oswego, NY, 1973-75; ptnr. Brown and Greene, 1976-81; pvt. practice law, 1981—. Bd. dir. Found. Corp. Legal Studies, Inc., 1968-70, United Way of Oswego County, Inc., 1985-88, Campbell's Point Assn., 1994-96, Oswego Hosp., 1981-2000, mem. exec. com., 1985-2000, pres., 1996-98; pres. Oswego Health, Inc., 1997-pres.; town atty. Oswego, 1972—; counsel Oswego County Bd. Realtors, 1978—; mem. Oswego County Rep. com., 1974-85, counsel, 1980-83; gen. counsel Express Abstract Co., 1992-95. Recipient Inst. Counsel, 1970. Mem. ABA, NY Bar Assn., Oswego County Bar Assn., Greater Oswego C. of C. (bd. dir. 1980-87), Oswego Country Club (counsel 1977-81), Masons, Shriners, Phi Delta Phi. Home: PO Box 115 611 W 1st St Oswego NY 13126-4137 Office: PO Box 60 85 W Bridge St Oswego NY 13126-2011

GREENE, THEODORE PHINNEY, historian, educator; b. N.Y.C., May 20, 1921; children: 3. BA, Amherst Coll., 1943; MA, Columbia U., 1948. Lectr. Am. history Columbia U., 1950-52; from asst. prof. to assoc. prof. history Amherst Coll, Mass., 1952-57; prof. history Amherst Coll., Mass., 1973-88, Winthrop H. Smith prof. history, prof. emeritus, 1988—. Editor: American Imperialism in 1898, 1955, Wilson at Versailles and Roger Williams and the Massachusetts Magistrates, 1962; author: American Heroes: The Changing Models of Success in American Magazines, 1970. Mem. Am. Hist. Assn., Am. Studies Assn. Office: Amherst Coll Dept History Amherst MA 01002

GREENE, THOMAS HARDY, architect; b. Washington, Apr. 19, 1948; s. Thomas Elbert and Marie Dabney (Sitton) G.; m. Linda Louise Weaver, June 16, 1978. Student, Montgomery Coll., 1966-68, 72-73; BArch cum laude, U. Md., 1979. Registered arch., D.C., Md., Tex., Wis., Va., Mass., N.Y., Fla., Conn., Calif., Okla., Pa., N.C.; cert. NCARB. Archtl. designer, technologist Clifton B. White, Silver Spring, Md., 1965, Cohen, Haft & Assocs., Silver Spring, Md., 1966-69, 70-72, Sullivan, Clark, Almy & Savage, Bethesda, Md.,

1973; archtl. model builder Roger Lewis & Assocs., Washington, 1974-75; archtl. designer Thomas H. Greene Design, Chevy Chase, Md., 1976; designer, technologist David M. Schwarz Archtl. Svcs., Washington, 1976-78; architect, chmn. bd. dirs. David M. Schwarz Archtl. Svcs., Inc., Washington, 1978—; ptnr. David M. Schwarz & Ptnrs., Washington, 1990—. Bd. dirs. Glen Briar Condominium Owners' Assn., Silver Spring, 1982, pres., 1983. Recipient U. Md. Divsn. Arts and Humanities cert. scholarship, 1977. Mem. AIA, Bldg. Ofcls. and Code Adminstrs. Internat., Nat. Fire Protection Assn., So. Bldg. Code Congress Internat., Nat. Trust Hist. Preservation, Amnesty Internat., U. Md. Alumni Assn., Phi Kappa Phi. Avocations: travel, photography, t'ai chi chuan, reading. Home: 2304 Ashboro Dr Chevy Chase MD 20815-3048 Office: David M Schwarz Archtl Svcs Inc 1707 L St NW Ste 400 Washington DC 20036 E-mail: thg@dmsas.com.

GREENE, THOMASINA TALLEY, concert pianist, educator; b. Nashville, June 29, 1913; d. Thomas Washington and Ellen Elizabeth (Roberts) Talley; m. Lorenzo Johnston, Dec. 19, 1942 (dec. 1988); 1 child, Lorenzo Thomas. BA, Fisk U., 1929; diploma in music, Julliard Sch. of Music, 1932; EdD, Columbia U., 1942. Head music dept. St. Phillips Jr. Coll., San Antonio, 1933-34; supr. music dept. Columbia (Mo.) Pub. Schs., 1932-33, Sam Houston Coll., Austin, Tex., summer 1934; head music dept. N.C. State U., Durham, 1934-39; part-time dir. art dept. Lincoln U., Jefferson City, Mo., summer 1942, part-time prof. music, 1943-45; dir. Greene Sch. of Music, Jefferson City, 1942-89. With music program Sta. KRCG-TV, Jefferson City, 1966-81. Mem. exec. bd. Jefferson City Community Concert Assn., 1967-71; dir. project upbeat grant Md. Coun. Arts, 1978-79. Named Woman of Achievement for Jefferson City, 1963; recipient Disting. Svc. award 2d Bapt. Ch., Jefferson City, 1978, 89; fellow Julliard Sch. Music, 1929-32, Rockefeller Found., 1939-42. Mem. Nat. Soc. Lit. and Arts, Nat. Music Tchrs. Assn., Mo. Music Tchrs. Assn., Area Music Tchrs. Assn., Modern Priscilla Art and Charity Club, AAUW (bd. dirs. Jefferson City chpt., Woman of Yr. award 1963), Alpha Kappa Alpha (Regional Disting. Svc. award 1965), Kappa Delta Pi, Pi Lambda Theta. Episcopalian. Avocations: painting, china, card games, exercise. Died June 3, 2003.

GREENE, TIMOTHY GEDDES, lawyer; b. Lewiston, Idaho, May 12, 1939; s. George and Norma (Geddes) G.; m. Patricia Apcar, Sept. 13, 1969; children: Andrew Apcar, Jonathan Apcar. BA cum laude, U. Idaho, 1961; LLB, George Washington U., 1965. Bar: D.C., 1966, Tex., 1990, 97. Exec v.p., gen. counsel Sallie Mae, Washington, 1965—69; exec. asst. to the chmn. SEC, Washington, 1969—71; spl. asst. to gen. counsel U.S. Treasury Dept., Washington, 1971—73; sec. U.S. Emergency Loan Guarantee Bd., Washington, 1971—73; exec. v.p., gen. counsel Student Loan Mktg. Assn. Sallie Mae, Washington, 1973—79; prin. Eggers & Greene, Dallas, 1979—90, Stuart Mill Capital, Inc., Arlington, Va., 1997—. Bd. dirs. Wolf Trap Found. for the Performing Arts, Vienna, Va., 1991-97, NCCJ, 1993-98. Ford Found. fellow Brown U. Grad. Sch. Econs., 1961-62. Republican. Mem. Lds Ch. Avocations: sports, golf, tennis. Home: 1026 Wallen Rd Moscow ID 83843

GREENE, TIMOTHY JAMES, industrial engineering educator; b. Lafayette, Ind., Oct. 18, 1952; s. James H. and Barbara H. (Holt) G.; m. Nancy E. Van Kuren, Nov. 16, 1996. BS in Aero. and Astron. Engring., Purdue U., 1975, MS in Indsl. Engring., 1977, PhD, 1980. Instr., rsch. asst. sch. indsl. engring. Purdue U., West Lafayette, Ind., 1975-80; asst. prof. indsl. engring. Va. Tech., Blacksburg, 1980-85, assoc. prof. indsl. engring., 1985-91, asst. head dept. indsl. engring., 1986-91; prof., head dept. indsl. engring. and mgmt. Okla. State U., Stillwater, 1991-96, assoc. dean for rsch. Coll. Engring., Arch. and Tech., 1995-99; dean coll. engring. U. Ala., Tuscaloosa, 2000—. Contbr. 5 chpts. to books, over 30 articles to profl. jours. Fellow Inst. Indsl. Engrs. (trustee 1991-99, sr. v.p. tech. ops. 1994-96, sr. profl. devel. 1992-94, Outstanding Young Indsl. Engr. 1987, pres. elect 1996-97, pres., 1997-98, past pres. 1998-99), Soc. Mfg. Engrs. (Outstanding Young Mfg. Engr. 1986); mem. Am. Soc. Engring. Educators. Home: 1626 Teal Cir Tuscaloosa AL 35405

GREENE, TRISTAN DORIAN, state agency administrator; b. New Orleans, Feb. 22, 1969; s. Richard Carl Greene and Cheryl Jean Arceneaux. BA, U. New Orleans, 1990, MA, 1992, MS in Urban Studies, 1993. Spl. asst. for rsch. Ark. Dept. Edn., Little Rock, 1993—; spl. advisor to atty. gen. Ark. Atty. Gen.'s Office, Little Rock, 1993—. Chmn. bd. dirs. NestEGG Prodns., New Orleans, 1996—2001. Author: (Book) How Does Arkansas Fund Its Schools?, 2000, (Monograph) Performance-Based Program Budgeting: A Government Worker's Guide to the Process, 1999. Mem. Nat. Edn. Stats. Adv. Com., Washington, 1996—99; bd. dirs. Storer Boone Theater Awards, New Orleans, 1992—98. Mem.: Am. Edn. Rsch. Assn., Am. Soc. Internat. Law, Am. Edn. Fin. Assn., Am. Polit. Sci. Assn., Am. Acad. Polit. Sci., Peace Sci. Soc., Internat. Studies Assn. Roman Catholic. Avocations: chess, golf, classical guitar, theater, travel. Office: Ark Dept Edn 323 Center St Ste 200 Little Rock AR 72201 Office Fax: 501-682-2591. Business E-Mail: TristanG@ag.state.ar.us.

GREENE, WARREN, advertising executive; m. Judye Greene. BFA, Auburn U. Creative dir. Doyle, Dane, Bernbach, Hong Kong, Grey Advt., J. Walter Thompson, Compton; Wiliam-Esty, Tinker, Cambell & Ewald, McDonald & Little; CEO Adair-Greene, Inc. Office: 200 Tech Ctr 1575 Northside Dr NW Atlanta GA 30318-4235 Fax: (404) 351-1495. E-mail: info@adair-green.com.

GREENE, WARREN W. anesthesiologist; b. Santa Monica, Calif., Sept. 12, 1912; BA, U. So. Calif., 1935; BM, U. Health Scis./Chgo. Med. Sc., 1940, MD, 1941. Diplomate Am. Bd. Anesthesiology. Intern Elmhurst Meml. Hosp., 1940-41; resident Wadsworth VA Hosp., L.A., 1949-50; mem. hon. staff St. John's Hosp., Santa Monica, Calif., 1972—. Fellow Am. Coll. Anesthesiologists; mem. AMA, Calif. Med. Assn., Calif. Soc. Anesthesiology, L.A. County Med. Assn. Home: 1224 Seafarer St Ventura CA 93001

GREENE, WENDY SEGAL, special education educator; b. New Rochelle, N.Y., Jan. 9, 1929; d. Louis Peter and Anna Henrietta (Kahan) Segal; m. Charles Edward Smith (div. 1952); m. Richard M. Greene Jr. (div. 1967); children: Christopher S., Kerry William, Karen Beth Greene Olson; m. Richard M. Greene Sr., Aug. 29, 1985 (dec. 1986). Student, Olivet Coll., 1946-48, Santa Monica Coll., 1967-70; BA in Child Devel., Calif. State U., Los Angeles, 1973, MA in Elem. Edn., 1975. Cert. tchr., Calif.; cert. Specially Designed Acad. Instrn. in English, 1999. Counselor Camp Watitoh, Becket, Mass., 1946-49; asst. tchr. Outdoor Play Group, New Rochelle, 1946-58; edn. sec. pediatrics Syracuse (N.Y.) Meml. Hosp., 1952-53; with St. John's Hosp., Santa Monica, Calif., 1962-63; head tchr. Head Start, L.A., 1966-77; tchr. spl. edn. L.A. Unified Sch. Dist., 1977—, Salvin Spl. Edn. Ctr., L.A., 1976—85, Perez Spl. Edn. Ctr., L.A., 1986-. Instr. mktg. rsch. for motivational rsch. Anderson-McConnell Agy., 1966; mentor tchr. L.A. Unified Sch. Dist., 1992-99; mem. adv. com. for spl. edn. Tustin Unified Sch. Dist. Comty., 1994—. Contbr. to house organ of St. John's Hosp.; co-editor of newspaper for Salvin Sch., L.A.; contbg. reporter El Aquilar (The Eagle), Perez. Mem. LEARN Coun., Perez, 1996—; mem. cmty. adv. com. spl. edn. Tustin Unified Sch. Dist., 1994—; bd. dirs. Tustin Area Coun. for Fine Arts, 2002—; bd. dirs. Richland Ave. Youth House, L.A., 1960-63, Emotional Health Assn., L.A., 1961-66, Richland Ave. Sch. PTA, 1959-63. Mem.: AAUW, United Tchrs. L.A., Olivet Coll. Alumni Assn., Celebration of Life Singers, Cmty. Singers Tustin, Westside Singers (L.A.), Kappa Delta Pi. Jewish. Avocations: music, writing, theater, travel, family. Home: 14291 Prospect Ave Tustin CA 92780-2316

GREENE, WILLIAM CASWELL, investment company executive; b. Dover, Mass., June 5, 1933; s. Whitney Eastman Greene and Maude Victoria Larsson; m. Davis Crane, Nov. 27, 1954 (div. 1983); children: William, Bruce, Josephine, Winnie, Leo, Amy; m. Catherine Radzewicz, Jan. 16, 1988; children: Whitney, Jill, Jeffrey. AB, Princeton (N.J.) U., 1954; MBA, Babson Coll., 1956; postgrad., Harvard Bus. Sch., 1956-57; cert., Hague Acad. of Internat. Law, The Netherlands, 1953. CPA, Mass. Rsch. assoc. Harvard Bus. Sch., Boston, 1957-59; auditor, cons. Coopers & Lybrand, Boston, 1959-65; ptnr. Greene & Vecchi, Wellesley, Mass., 1965-80, Greene and Co., Natick, Mass., 1980-87; prin. Lost Nation Mgmt., Lancaster, N.H., 1987—; ptnr. Natick Investments, 1965—. Trustee VAR Estates and Trusts; bd. dirs. VAR Corps., Mass., N.H.; lectr. Mgmt. Growth Inst., Wellesley, 1965-88. Author: Cases in Cost Administration, 1963, Stories for Kids, 2000; co-author: Small Business Workbook, 1975. Chmn. Dover Sch. Com., 1964-70; state committeeman 2nd Norfolk Dist., Mass., 1966-68; trustee town funds Northumberland, 1994—; bd. dirs. Mass. Gen. Hosp., 1985-91. Recipient Svc. award Small Bus. Assn. of N.E., 1981, Hist. Preservation award Town of Natick, 1980. Mem. New Bedford Yacht Club, Harvard Faculty Club, Country Club of Hilton Head. Republican. Episcopalian. Avocations: cattle and timber, sailing, carpentry, tennis, gardening. Home: Lost Nation Rd Lancaster NH 03584 Office: Greene & Co 70 Star of the Sea Dr South Dartmouth MA 02748

GREENE, WILLIAM HARRIS, hospital administrator; b. N.Y.C., July 23, 1943; s. Barnett Alan and Lee A. Greene; m. Beverly Kerish, Dec. 26, 1966; children: Ilyssa Kendra Frey, David Jonathan, Lauren Alexandra. BA, Yale U., 1964; MD, SUNY, Bklyn., 1968. Diplomate Am. Bd. Internal medicine with subspecialties in med. oncology and infectious diseases. Resident in internal medicine Yale-New Haven Hosp., 1968-70; clin. assoc. Balt. Cancer Rsch. Ctr./NCI/NIH, 1970-73; fellow in inflammatory disease Yale Sch. Medicine, 1973-75, asst. prof. medicine, 1975-80, assoc. prof. medicine, 1980-85; hosp. epidemiologist, dir. infection control Yale-New Haven Hosp., 1980-85; assoc. prof. clin. medicine SUNY-Stony Brook Sch. Medicine, 1985—, assoc. chief divsn. infectious diseases, 1996-99; assoc. med. dir. for quality mgmt. Univ. Hosp. at Stony Brook, 1995—, assoc. dir. for regulatory and med. affairs, 2000—, acting med. dir., 2000—01. Mem. infection control adv. com. N.Y. State Dept. Health, Albany, 1993—; N.Y. state liaison Soc. Healthcare Epidemiologists of Am., Washington, 1993—99, mem. fin. adv. com., 1997—; mem. clin. evaluative scis. coun. Univ. Healthcare Consortium, Chgo., 1998—. Contbr. articles to profl. jours., chpts. to books; mem. editl. bd. Infections in Medicine, 1988—. Lt. comdr. USPHS, 1970-75. Fellow Infectious Diseases Soc. of Am.; mem. Am. Soc. for Microbiology, Soc. of Healthcare Epidemiologists of Am. (chmn. nominating com. 1993, chmn. state liaison subcom. 1996-99), Am. Coll. Physician Execs, Alpha Omega Alpha. Avocations: ballet, travel. Office: SUNY-Stony Brook HSC L5-087 Stony Brook NY 11794-8500 E-mail: wgreene@notes.cc.sunysb.edu.

GREENEBAUM, LEONARD CHARLES, retired lawyer; b. Langgoens, Germany, Feb. 6, 1934; came to U.S. 1937, naturalized, 1952; s. Norbert and Henny Lisa (Greenbaum) G.; m. Barbara Rosendorf, Feb. 10, 1957; children: Beth Lynn, Cathy Sue, Steven I. *Immigrated to America with parents in 1937 under sponsorship of great uncle, Charles Greenebaum, owner of Young Men's Shop, a prominent men's store, in Richmond, Virginia. Shortly thereafter, sister Regina was born and grandmother Bertha followed family as well. Beth married Jeff Sirota (owner if Eastern Auto Co.) have Alex and Eli, and practices art therapy in Kingston, PA. Cathy married Matt Borten (an independent film producer) have Holden and Yardley and is a practicing attorney in Bethesda, MD. Steve married Christine Regan (business consultant) have Megan and Amanda and is "on air" radio personality in New Orleans, LA.* BS cum laude in Commerce, Washington and Lee U., 1956, JD cum laude, 1959. Bar: D.C. 1959, Va. 1959, Md. 1965. Atty. Sachs, Greenebaum & Tayler and predecessor firms, Washington, 1959-64, ptnr., 1964-75, mng. ptnr., 1975-90; ptnr., D.C. coord. litigation Baker & Hostetler, Washington, 1990-95, firmwide litigation group chair, 1996-2000, ret., 2001. Arbitrator Am. Arbitration Assn., Washington, 1975-2000; mem. Washington and Lee U. Law Coun. *Represented clients in Watergate, Pentagate and Irangate, with recognition in illegal campaign contributions, illegal foreign payments and other notable matters. Selected to appear in 1965 Edition of America's outstanding young men and received Presidential Sports Award for Golf in 1973. Received special recognition for services as president of Wild Dunes Ocean Club Condominiums (Isle of Palms, SC) in March 2003. Also selected as charter member of District of Columbia Chapter of American Board of Trial Advocates (1993) and selected by his peers to be included in Best Lawyers in America (2001-2002). Serves as director if Cold War Submarine Memorial Foundation completing construction in 2003 of memorial honoring those who served from Charleston Harbor.* Chmn. bd. Davis Meml. Goodwill Industries, Washington, 1979-82; bd. dirs. Coun. for Ct. Excellence. Capt. U.S. Army, 1957. Recipient Svc. to Handicapped People award Davis Meml. Goodwill Industries, 1982. Fellow: Am. Bar. Found. (life); mem.: Md. Bar Assn., D.C. Bar Assn., Isle of Palms, Wild Dunes Country Club, Country Club of Charleston, Bethesda (Md.) Country Club. Jewish. Fax: 843-406-8777.

GREENE LLOYD, NANCY ELLEN, retired infosystems specialist, physicist; b. Worcester, Mass., Nov. 4, 1947; d. William Arthur Greene II and Dorothy Goddard (Fuller) Greene; m. Stephen C. Lloyd, July 25, 1992; 11 foster children children: Ellen Dorothy, Gwyneth Tegan. BS in Physics, Ohio State U., 1969, MS in Physics, 1971. Instr. physics U. Colo., Colorado Springs, 1971-73; physics programmer U. N.Mex., Albuquerque, 1973-76; data analyst Los Alamos (N.Mex.) Nat. Lab., 1975-77, programmer, 1977-78, mem. tech. staff controlled thermonuclear reaction divsn., 1978-81, mem. tech. staff Accelerator Tech. div., 1981-84, mem. tech. staff adminstrv. data processing divsn., 1984-85, mem. tech. staff dynamic experimentation divsn., 1985-94, staff mem. supr., 1989-90, acting sect. leader, 1990-91, acting dep. divsn. leader, 1992, chief ops. explosives tech. and applications divsn., 1992-94, mem. tech. staff environ., safety, and health divsn. Instl. Affairs Office, 1994-97, with Environ., Safety and Health Divsn. Office, 1997-98, leader info. mgmt. team, 1997-98, mem. tech. staff info. mgmt. program, 1998—2002; ret., 2002. Speaker in field. Vol. Los Alamos Schs., 1980—88, Fountain Valley Sch., Colo., 1990—91; coord. nursery Christian Ch. Los Alamos, 1997—2000; foster parent State of N.Mex., 1998—; co-mgr. God's Pantry food bank, 1998—; children's ch. tchr. Christian Ch. Los Alamos, 1999—; liaison Hope Pregnancy Ctr.; Bldg. Blocks mentor Family Strengths Network, 2001—; vol. Calvary Christian Sch., 2002—; mentor Family Strengths Bldg. Blocks Network, 2001—; pres. Los Alamos Foster Parent Assn., 2002—; chair Los Alamos Rio Arriba Foster Parent Assn., 2002—. Nat. Merit scholar, Mich. State U., 1965, Nat. Defense Edn. Act Title IV fellow, Ohio State U., 1969. Mem. N.Mex. Digital Equipment Computer Users Soc. (exec. com. 1984-87, 88-90, registration chair computer conf. 1984-87, vice-chair 1988-89, publicity 1989-90), Nat. and N.Mex. Foster Parent Assn., N.Mex. Network for Women in Sci. and Engring., VAX Computer Local Users Group (chmn. 1981-82, sec. 1989-92), N.Mex. Square and Round Dance Assn. (dist. co-chair 1996-97). Avocations: reading, walking, dancing, foster children. E-mail: nancy.lloyd@covad.net.

GREENER, ANTHONY, telecommunications industry executive; b. 1940; Dir. Reed Internat., 1990-98, Reed Elsevier, 1993-98; chmn. Guinness plc, 1993—97, Diageo plc, 1997-2000, U. Industry Ltd., London, 2000—, Robert Mondavi, 2000—; dep. chmn. Brit. Telecom, 2001—. Chmn. Qualifications and Curriculum Auth., 2002—. Chmn. Qualifications and Curriculum Authority, London. Office: Ufi Ltd 88 Kingsway Holborn London WC2B 6AA England

GREENER, RALPH BERTRAM, lawyer; b. Rahway, N.J., Sept. 23, 1940; s. Ralph Bertram and Mary Ellen (Esch) G.; m. Jean Elizabeth Wilson, Mar. 21, 1964; children: Eric Wilson, Erin Hope, Nicholas Christian. BA, Wheaton Coll., 1962; JD, Duke U., 1968. Bar: Minn. 1969, U.S. Dist. Ct. 1969, U.S. Tax Ct. 1988. With Fredrikson & Byron P.A., Mpls., 1969—. Chmn. Minn. Lawyers Mutual Ins. Co., Mpls. 1981—; pres. Nat. Assn. of Bar-Related Ins. Cos., 1989-90. 1st Lt. USMCR, 1962-65. Recipient award of profl. excellence Minn. State Bar Assn., 1993. Mem. Rotary Club (pres. Mpls. 2002-03). Home: 1018 W Minnehaha Pky Minneapolis MN 55419-1161 Office: Fredrikson & Byron PA 4000 Pillsbury Ctr 200 S 6th St Minneapolis MN 55402-1425 E-mail: rgreener@fredlaw.com.

GREENERT, JONATHAN W. career officer; BS in Ocean Engring., U.S. Naval Acad., 1975. Commd. ensign USN, advanced through ranks to rear adm.; commdg. officer USS Honolulu, 1991-93; various assignments to comdr. Submarine Squadron Eleven/COMSUBPAC Rep West Coast, 1996-97; chief of staff for comdr. Seventh Fleet, Yokosuka, Japan, 1997-98; comdr.-in-chief U.S. Pacific Command Rep. to Guam, No. Marian Islands/Micronesia, 1998-99; comdr. U.S. Naval Forces, Marianas, 1998-99. Decorated Defense Superior Svc. medal, Legion of Merit (4 times), Meritorious Svc. medal (2 times), Navy Commendation medal (4 times), others. Office: Dir Ops Divsn Navy Comptroller Dept Navy Washington DC 20350-0001 E-mail: greenert.jonathan@hq.navy.mil.

GREENFIELD, BRUCE HAROLD, lawyer, banker; b. Phila., Mar. 12, 1917; s. William I. and Bertha (Kauffman) G.; m. Adele Gersh, Sept. 18, 1955; children: Gregory Richard, Elizabeth Susan, Margaret Alison. BA, Duke U., 1938; JD, Yale U., 1941. Bar: Pa. 1941. Atty. Office Tax Legis. Counsel, Treasury Dept., 1941-48; partner firm Folz, Bard, Kamsler, Goodis & Greenfield, Phila., 1949-53; v.p. Bankers Securities Corp., Phila., 1953-59, exec. v.p., 1959-70, pres., 1970-82; v.p., treas., dir. Sta. WSMB, Inc., New Orleans, 1957-82. Pres., bd. dirs. Albert M. Greenfield & Co., Inc., until, 1982; lectr. NYU, Tulane U., Am. U. Tax Insts. Contbg. author: Taxes mag. Trustee Albert M. Greenfield Found.; bd. dirs., Phila., Am. Jewish Com., Girl Scouts U.S.A., 1978-87. Served to maj. USAAF, 1942-46. Mem. Phi Beta Kappa. Democrat. Home: 1598 Landings Terrace Sarasota FL 34231-3215 Office: 1845 Walnut St Ste 800 Philadelphia PA 19103-4711

GREENFIELD, ESTER FRANCES, lawyer; b. Chgo., July 4, 1951; d. Aaron Arthur and Lea (Brody) Greenfield. BA, U. Chgo., 1973; JD, U. Ill., 1976. Bar: Ill. 1976, Wash. 1978, U.S. Dist. Ct. (no. dist.) Ill. 1976, U.S. Dist. Ct. (we. dist.) Wash. 1978. Law clk. U.S. Dist. Ct. Ill., Chgo., 1976-78; assoc. MacDonald, Hoague & Bayless, Seattle, 1978-83, dir., 1983—, mng. dir., 1993. Cooperating atty. ACLU, Seattle, 1982-86, Northwest Women's Law Ctr., Seattle, 1982-90; adj. prof. U. Puget Sound Law Sch., 1986-88. Sr. editor Am. Immigration Lawyers Assn., Immigration and Nationality Law Handbook. Pres. New Beginnings Shelter for Battered Women, Seattle, 1982-83; mem. Seattle Human Rights Commn., 1986-90. Recipient Gov.;s Disting. Vol. award Wash., 1983. Mem. Am. Immigration Lawyers Assn. (chmn. Wash. state chpt. 1986-87), Wash. State Bar Assn., Seattle-King County Bar Assn. Democrat. Home: 5955 49th Ave SW Seattle WA 98136-1526 Office: MacDonald Hoague & Bayless 705 2nd Ave Ste 1500 Seattle WA 98104-1796

GREENFIELD, GEORGE B. radiologist; b. N.Y.C., May 4, 1928; s. Jacob and Rose (Wolf) G.; m. Barbara Anne O'Driscoll, Mar. 3, 1956; children: Edward James, Sheelagh Anne. BA, NYU, 1949; MD, State U. Utrecht, Netherlands, 1956. Diplomate: Am. Bd. Radiology, Am. Bd. Nuclear Medicine. Intern Bridgeport (Conn.) Hosp., 1956-57; resident radiology Presbyn.-St. Lukes Hosp., Chgo., 1957-60; practice medicine, specializing in radiology Chgo., 1960—; radiologist Cook County Hosp., 1961-66, asst. dir. diagnostic radiology, 1966-69, assoc. prof. radiology U. Ill., 1966-69; prof., chmn. dept. radiology Chgo. Med. Sch., 1969-74, Mt. Sinai Hosp. Med. Center, 1969-89, pres. med. staff, 1983-85; prof. diagnostic radiology Rush Med. Coll., 1975-87; prof. radiology Cook County Grad. Sch. Medicine., Chgo. Med. Sch., 1987-89, vice chmn. dept. radiology, 1988-89; prof. radiology U. S.Fla., Tampa, 1989—. Attending radiologist H. Lee Moffitt Cancer Ctr. and Rsch. Inst., Tampa. Author: Radiology of Bone Diseases, 5th edit., 1990; sr. author: A Manual of Radiographic Positioning, 1973, Computers in Radiology, 1985, Imaging of Bone Tumors, 1995 Imaging of Arthritis, 2001; contbr. articles to profl. jours. Trustee Mt. Sinai Hosp., 1986-89. Served with U.S. Army, 1951. Fellow Am. Coll. Radiology; mem. AMA, AAAS, Chgo. Med. Soc., Chgo. Roentgen Soc., Am. Roentgen Ray Soc., Radiol. Soc. N.Am., Inst. Medicine Chgo., Internat. Skeletal Soc., Soc. Skeletal Radiology, Sigma Xi. Office: Moffitt Cancer Ctr & Rsch Inst PO Box 17 Tampa FL 33601-0017 E-mail: greenfield@moffitt.usf.edu.

GREENFIELD, GORDON KRAUS, software company executive; b. Phila., June 16, 1915; s. Albert Monroe and Edna Kraus (Paine) G.; m. Harriet F. Copelin, Feb. 6, 1945; children: Juliet Greenfield Six, Gordon Kraus, Faith Greenfield Lewis, Hope, James Donald. AB, Princeton U., 1937; D Musical Arts (hon.), Manhattan Sch. Music, 1994. Pres., dir. City Splty. Stores, N.Y.C., 1953-60, Am. Corp., N.Y.C., 1960-64, Franchard Corp., N.Y.C., 1965-68; pres. Autocue, Inc., N.Y.C., 1966-99; ret., 1999. Trustee Manhattan Sch. Music; bd. dirs. Opera Orch. of N.Y. Lt. USNR, 1940-45. Mem. Met. Opera Club. Clubs: University (N.Y.C.). Home: 2114 Devonshire Way Palm Beach Gardens FL 33418 also: 57 Cobb Hill Rd Hartland VT 05048 Mailing: PO Box 1174 New York NY 10159-1124

GREENFIELD, JAMES M. retired fund raiser; b. Hornell, N.Y., Feb. 12, 1936; s. James M. and Vera E. (Alger) G.; m. Diane Roberts, Aug., 1962 (div. 1973); children: Eryn J., Janine L.; m. Karen G. Gabrielson, Nov. 24, 1984. BA, U. Calif., Riverside, 1958. Exec. dir. U. Calif. Alumni Assn., Riverside, 1962-67; dir. corp. rels. Calif. Inst. Tech., Pasadena, 1967-72; dir. devel. Claremont (Calif.) U. Ctr., 1972-73; dir. spl. projects Childrens Hosp. Med. Ctr., Boston, 1973-76; dir. devel. Univ. Hosp., Boston, 1976-81, New Eng. Bapt. Hosp., Boston, 1981-85; dir. fund devel. Cleve. Clinic Found., 1985-87; sr. v.p. resource devel. Hoag Meml. Hosp. Presbyn., Newport Beach, Calif., 1987-2001. Author: Fund-Raising: Evaluating and Managing the Fund Development Process, 1991, 2d edit., 1999, Fund-Raising Fundamentals: A Guide to Annual Giving for Professionals and Volunteers, 1994, 2d edit., 2002, Fund-Raising Cost Effectiveness: A Self-Assessment Workbook, 1996; editor: The Nonprofit Handbook: Fund Raising, 3d edit., 2001. Cons. mem. bd. govs., Ctr. on Philanthropy, Ind. U., 1999—. With USNR, 1959-62. Mem. Assn for Healthcare Philanthropy (bd. dirs., Harold J. Seymour award 1993), Assn. Fundraising Profls. (bd. dirs. 1979-88, bd. dirs. Found. 1982-2001, Profl. Fund-Raiser of Yr. award Orange County chpt. 1994, Outstanding Fund Raising Exec. 2000). Democrat. Avocations: writing, backpacking, fly fishing. E-mail: fundrazer@cox.net.

GREENFIELD, JAMES ROBERT, lawyer; b. Phila., Mar. 31, 1926; s. Milton and Katherine E. (Rosenberg) G.; m. Phyllis Chaplowe, Aug. 17, 1947 (dec. May 1978); m. Joyce MacDonald Koehler, Mar. 22, 1980. BS, Bates Coll., 1947; JD, Yale U., 1950. Bar: Conn. 1950, U.S. Dist. Ct. Conn. 1951, U.S. Ct. Appeals (2d cir.) 1966, U.S. Supreme Ct. 1959. Atty. Chaplowe & Greenfield, 1950-54, Markle & Greenfield, New Haven, 1954-58; sr. ptnr. Lander, Greenfield & Krick, New Haven, 1958-80, Greenfield, Krick & Jacobs, New Haven, 1980-90, Greenfield & Murphy, New Haven, 1990-98; of counsel Tyler Cooper & Alcorn, New Haven, 1998—. Lectr. U. Conn. Law Sch., 1966-67, 71-72, 75-76 Mem. editorial bd. Conn. Bar Jour, 1963-77. Pres. New Haven Symphony, 1976-78, Conn. Bar Found., 1976-77; bd. dirs. Nat. Jud. Coll., 1978-84. With USNR, 1944-46. Fellow Am. Bar Found. (state chmn. 1985-90); mem. ABA (state del. 1975-78, bd. govs. 1978-81, ho. of dels. 1972-83, spl. com. on goverance 1983-84, chmn. various coms.), Conn. Bar Assn. (pres. 1973-74, Disting. Profl. Svc. award 1989), Judicature Soc. (bd. dirs. 1983-87, 2002-), Am. Law Inst., Am. Acad. Matrimonial Lawyers (pres. Conn. chpt. 1993-94), Internat. Acad. Matrimonial Lawyers, New Haven County Bar Assn. (pres. 1969-70, Lifetime Achievment award 1993, Conn. Law Tribune Svc. to the Profn. award 2002), Yale Law Sch. Assn. (sec. 1977-80), Quinnipiack Club, Mory's. Office: Tyler Cooper & Alcorn 205 Church St New Haven CT 06510-1805 E-mail: greenfield@tylercooper.com.

GREENFIELD, JEFF (HENRY JEFF GREENFIELD), news analyst; b. N.Y.C., June 10, 1943; s. Benjamin and Helen Evelyn (Greenwald) G.; m. Carrie Carmichael, May 11, 1968 (div. 1993); children: Casey Carmichael, David Carmichael; m. Karen Gannett, 1993 (div. 1997); m. Dena Sklar, June 21, 2002. BA with honors, U. Wis., 1964; LLB cum laude, Yale U., 1967. Legis. aide to Senator Robert F. Kennedy, Washington, 1967-68; speechwriter to Mayor John V. Lindsay, N.Y.C., 1968-70; polit. cons. Garth Assocs., Inc., N.Y.C., 1970-76; media critic CBS News, N.Y.C., 1979-83; polit. media analyst ABC News, N.Y.C., 1983-97; sr. analyst, co-anchor The World Today, CNN & Time CNN, N.Y.C., 1998—. Lectr. Royce-Carlton Agency, N.Y.C., 1980; columnist Universal Press Syndicate, 1981-96, Time Mag., 1996—. Co-author: The Advance Man, 1971, A Populist Manifesto, 1972; author: No Peace, No Place, 1973, The World's Greatest Team, 1975, TV--The First 50 Years, 1977, Playing to Win, 1980, The Real Campaign, 1982, The People's Choice 1995, Oh, Waiter-One Order of Crow, 2001. Recipient Emmy award NATAS, 1986, 91, 93, 99. Office: CNN 5 Penn Plz Fl 21 New York NY 10001-1878

GREENFIELD, JOHN CHARLES, bio-organic chemist; b. Dayton, Ohio, 1945; s. Ivan Ralph and Mildred Louise (House) G.; m. Liga Miervaldis, aug. 2, 1980; children: John Hollen, Mark Richard. BS cum laude, Ohio U., 1967; PhD, U. Ill., 1974. Instr. sci. area h.s., Dayton, 1968-71; grad. rsch. asst. U. Ill., 1971-74; postdoctoral rsch. fellow Swiss Fed. Inst. Tech., Zurich, 1975-76; rsch. chemist infectious diseases rsch. Upjohn Co., Kalamazoo, 1976-82, sr. rsch. scientist drug metabolism rsch., 1982-93; sr. project mgr. Upjohn Labs., Kalamazoo, 1993-95, Pharmacia & Upjohn Inc., Kalamazoo, 1995-96; acquisitions review specialist, bus. devel. Pharmacia and Upjohn, Inc., Kalamazoo, 1996-98, clin. monitor, U.S. market co. med. affairs, 1998-2000; dir. global med. svcs. Pharmacia Inc., Kalamazoo, 2000—03, Pfizer, Inc., Kalamazoo, 2003—. Contbr. articles to sci. jours.; patentee in field. Adult leader Boy Scouts Am. Am.-Swiss Found. for Sci. Exchange fellow, 1975; NSF-NATO postdoctoral fellow, 1975-76 Mem. AAAS, Am. Chem. Soc. (chmn. Kalamazoo sect. 1994, Disting. Svc. award 1996), N.Y. Acad. Scis., Am. Assn. Pharm. Scientists,

Am. Assn. Microbiology, Drug Info. Assn., Am. Soc. Hematology, Sigma Xi, Phi Eta Sigma, Blue Key, Phi Lambda Upsilon, Delta Tau Delta. Achievements include identification, evaluation, and management of worldwide research and development projects for new pharmaceutical agents. Home: 6695 E E Ave Richland MI 49083-9471 Office: Pharmacia Inc 7000 Portage Rd Kalamazoo MI 49001-0199

GREENFIELD, JOSEPH CHOLMONDELEY, JR., physician, educator; b. Atlanta, July 20, 1931; s. Joseph Cholmondeley and Agnes (Game) Greenfield; m. Mary Ruth Fordham, Aug. 13, 1955; children: Mary Agnes, Ruth Ann, Susan Lee. AB in History, Emory U., 1954, MD, 1956. Intern, resident in medicine Duke Med. Ctr., Durham, NC, 1956—59; clin. assoc. NIH, USPHS, 1959—62; mem. staff Vets. Affairs Med. Ctr., 1962—, Duke Med. Ctr., 1962—2001; dir. heart sta. Vets. Affairs Med. Ctr., Durham, 1962—; asst. prof. medicine Duke Med. Ctr., Durham, NC, 1962—65, assoc. prof. medicine, 1965—70, prof. medicine, 1970—, dir. heart sta., 1972—2001; mem. cardiovasc. and pulmonary study sect. NIH, USPHS, 1974—78, chmn., 1975—78, mem. cardiovasc. rev. com., 1980—84, chmn., 1983—84; James B. Duke disting. prof. Duke Med. Ctr., Durham, NC, 1981—, chief cardiovasc. divsn., 1981—89, chmn. dept. medicine, 1983—95. Author: A Quail Hunter's Odyssey, 2003; contbr. numerous articles profl. jours. Fellow: ACP, Am. Coll. Cardiology (disting. sci. award 1985); mem.: NRA (life), Inst. Medicine, Assn. Am. Physicians, Am. Physiol. Soc., Am. Soc. Clin. Investigation, Sons Confederate Vets., Safari Club Internat., Kappa Alpha, Alpha Omega Alpha, Phi Beta Kappa. Methodist. Home: 1212 Virginia Ave Durham NC 27705-3264 Office: Duke U Med Ctr PO Box 3246 Durham NC 27715-3246

GREENFIELD, LAZAR JOHN, surgeon, educator; b. Houston, Dec. 14, 1934; s. Robert G. and Betty B. (Greenfield) Heath; m. Sharon Dee Bishkin, Aug. 29, 1956; children: John, Julie, Jeff. Student, Rice U., 1951-54; MD, Baylor U., 1958. Diplomate: Am. Bd. Surgery (dir. 1976-82), Am. Bd. Thoracic Surgery, cert. gen. vascular surgery, 1991. Intern Johns Hopkins Hosp., Balt., 1958-59, resident, 1961-66; chief surgery VA Hosp., Oklahoma City, 1966-74; prof. dept. surgery U. Okla. Med. Center, 1971-74; Stuart McGuire prof., chmn. dept. surgery Med. Coll. Va., Richmond, 1974-87; F.A. Coller prof., chmn. dept of surgery U. Mich., 1987—2002; CEO U. Mich. Health System, 2002—03; exec. v.p. med. affairs U. Mich. Med. Sch., 2002—03. Mem. surgery A study sect. NIH. Author: Surgery in the Aged, 1975; editor-in-chief Surgery, Scientific Principles and Practice, 1993; editor Complications in Surgery and Trauma, 1983, 2d edit., 1990; contbr. to profl. publs. Served with USPHS, 1959-61. Thomas R. Franklin scholar, 1952; John and Mary Markle scholar in med. sci., 1968-73 Mem. Inst. of Medicine of NAS, Am. Surg. Assn., Am. Assn. Thoracic Surgery, Assn. Acad. Surgery, Soc. Univ. Surgeons, Phi Delta Epsilon. Home: 505 E Huron St Ann Arbor MI 48104-1573 Office: U Mich Med Sch 201 Taubman Ctr Ann Arbor MI 48109-0346

GREENFIELD, LEE, state legislator; b. Bklyn., July 29, 1941; s. Solomen and Edith (Herschman) G.; m. Marcia Greenfield, Nov. 25, 1965. BS in Physics, Purdue U., West Lafayette, Ind., 1963; postgrad., U. Minn., 1963-73. Instr. applied math. U. Minn., Mpls., 1964-73; prin. asst. Hennepin County and Health Cmty. Initiatives Dept., Mpls., 1975-77; mgmt. analyst Office of Planning & Devel., Hennepin County, Mpls., 1977; rep. Minn. Ho. of Reps., St. Paul, 1979-2000; prin. adminstrv. asst. Hennepin County Health and Cmty. Initiatives Dept., 2001—. Mem. steering com. Reforming State Group, N.Y.C., 1993, chmn., 1994-96. Bd. dirs. Twin City Cmty. Program for Affordable Health Care, Mpls., 1982-84, Arthritis Found., Mpls., 1988-90, Freeport West, Mpls., 1982—, Ams. for Dem. Action, Mpls., 1979—, v.p., 1976-78. Recipient Dwight V. Dixon award Mental Health Assn. Minn., 1994. Mem. Mental Health Assn. Minn. (Disting. Svc. award 1987), Planned Parenthood of Minn. (Pub. Svc. award 1993). Dfl. Jewish. Office: Hennepin County Health Policy Ctr A-1702 Government Center Minneapolis MN 55487-0172 E-mail: lee.greenfield@co.hennepin.mn.us.

GREENFIELD, LINDA SUE, nursing educator; b. Dover, Del., Aug. 5, 1950; d. Norman Raymond and Eleanor Henrietta (Harmon) Connell; m. Douglas Herman Greenfield, Dec. 27, 1976; children: Leah, Paige. BSN, Cath. U., 1972; MSN cum laude, Boston U., 1977; student, Met. Hosp. Sch. Nurse Anesthetists, 1979—81; postgrad., Coll. New Rochelle, 1986-88; PhD, Adelphi U., 1998. RN, N.Y. Staff nurse emergency rm. and ICU Washington Hosp. Ctr., 1974-75; operating rm. nurse Mass. Eye & Ear, Boston, 1975; ICU nurse Peter Bent Brigham Hosp., Boston, 1975-76; surg. nurse practitioner Kingsbrook Jewish Hosp., Bklyn., 1976-79; cert. registered nurse anesthetist Brookdale Hosp., Bklyn., 1981-92, Winthrop U. Hosp., Mineola, N.Y., 1992-94; adj. prof. Adelphi U., Garden City, N.Y., 1995-99; adj. prof. nursing N.Y. Inst. Tech., Old Westbury, 1998-99; clin. supr. Midtown Ctr. Complementary Care, N.Y.C., 1999-2000; clin specialist St. Francis Hosp., Roslyn, N.Y., 2000-01; asst. prof. nursing Adelphi U., 2001—. Bd. officer Manhasset Newcomers, N.Y., 1988-90; bd. dirs. Friends of Manhasset Libr., N.Y., 1990-94; mem. Make a Wish Found., Port Washington, N.Y., 1990—. Lt. U.S. Army, 1970-74. Mem.: ANA, Nat. Assn. U. Women, Nat. Assn. for Holistic Nurses, Nat. Assn. Homeopathy, Noetic Soc., Sch. Cmty. Assn., Am. Assn. Nurse Anesthetists, Sigma Theta Tau. Avocations: skiing, sailing, dancing.

GREENFIELD, MICHAEL A. federal agency administrator; b. New Rochelle, NY, 1943; M Engring. Mgmt., Cath. U., 1987; PhD in Metallurgy and Material Sci., NYU, 1971. Head joining tech. sect. Air Force Materials Lab., Dayton, Ohio, 1971—76; materials liaison officer, tech. dir. European Office Aerospace R&D, London, 1976—79; program mgr. materials Office Aeronautics and Space Tech. NASA, 1987—93, dir. systems assessment divsn. Office of Safety and Mission Assurance, 1993—2002, dep. assoc. adminstr., assoc. dep. adminstr. tech. headquarters, 2003—. Office: NASA Hdqrs Mail Code ADT 300 E St SW Washington DC 20546

GREENFIELD, MICHAEL C. lawyer; b. Chgo., May 4, 1934; BA, U. Ill., 1955; JD, Northwestern U., 1957. Bar: Ill. 1957, Ind. 1982, U.S. Suprmee Ct. 1974. Asst. states atty. Cook County, Ill., 1957-58; ptnr. Asher, Gittler & Greenfield, Ltd., Chgo., 1959—, Asher, Gittler, Greenfield & D'Alba, Ltd., Chgo. Mem. inquiry bd. Ill. Supreme Ct. Disciplinary Commn., 1973-77, mem. hearing bd., 1978-94, 97—, vice chmn., 1984, chmn., 1985, mem. oversight comm., 1995-96. Mem. ABA, Ill. Bar Assn., Chgo. Bar Assn., Internat. Found. Employee Benefit Plans (bd. dirs. 1977-80, 85-88, 92-94). Office: Asher Gittler Greenfield & D'Alba Ltd 200 W Jackson Blvd Ste 1900 Chicago Il. 60606-4397 E-mail: mcg@ulaw.com.

GREENFIELD, NORMAN SAMUEL, psychologist, educator; b. N.Y.C., June 2, 1923; s. Max and Dorothy (Hertz) G.; m. Marjorie Hanson Klein, May 17, 1969; children— Ellen Beth, Jennifer Ann, Susan Emery. BA, NYU, 1948; MA, U. Calif., Berkeley, 1951, PhD, 1953. Fellow med. psychology Langley Porter Clinic, U. Calif. Med. Center, 1949-50; VA Mental Health Clinic trainee San Francisco, 1950-53; instr. clin. psychology U. Oreg. Med. Sch., 1953-54; from asst. prof. to prof. psychiatry U. Wis. Med. Sch. at, Madison, 1954—; assoc. dir. Wis. Psychiat. Inst., U. Wis. Center for Health Scis., 1961-74. Emeritus prof. psychiatry, 1991—. Co-editor: The New Hospital Psychiatry, Handbook of Psychophysiology, Psychoanalysis and Current Biological Thought (with others); contbr. articles to profl. jours. Served with USAAF, 1943-46. Mem. AAUP, Am. Psychol. Assn., Soc. Psychophysiol. Rsch., Am. Psychosomatic Soc. Office: U Wis Psychiat Inst 6001 Research Park Blvd Madison WI 53719-1176 E-mail: ngreen5921@aol.com.

GREENFIELD, ROBERT KAUFFMAN, retired lawyer; b. Phila., Mar. 30, 1915; s. William I. and Bertha (Kauffman) G.; m. Louise Rose Stern, June 20, 1937; children: Linda Greenfield Baldwin, Mary Greenfield Davenport, William Stern, James Robert. AB, Swarthmore Coll., 1936; JD, Harvard U., 1939; LHD (hon.), Pa. Coll. Podiatric Medicine, 1990. Bar: Pa. 1939. Pvt. practice, Phila., 1939-87; with firm Goodis, Greenfield, Henry & Edelstein (and predecessors), 1939-77; of counsel Montgomery, McCracken, Walker & Rhoads, 1977-87; ret. Chmn. bd. Phila. Theatre Co., 1983-85. Bd. dirs. Conv. and Tourist Bur., Phila., 1942-84; commr., v.p. Phila. Fellowship Commn., 1965-74; pres. Jewish Comty. Rels. Coun., 1962-65; chmn. bd. Moss Rehab. Hosp., 1974-77; pres. Alexis Rosenberg Found., 1983-91; fin. chmn. Inst. Contemporary Art, 1974-83; exec. com. Coun. Performing Arts, 1964-70; v.p. Nat. Comty. Rels. Adv. Coun., 1965-68; pres. Phila. chpt. Am. Jewish Com., 1966-68; trustee Pa. Coll. Podiatric Medicine, 1967-91, chmn., 1989-90; pres. Goldsmith-Greenfield Found., 1991—; dir. Asolo Theatre Co., 1997-2002, v.p. 1999-2001. Mem. Landings Racquet Club (pres. 1994-96), Phi Beta Kappa. Home: 1650 Landings Blvd Sarasota FL 34231-3223

GREENFIELD, SANFORD RAYMOND, architect; b. N.Y.C., Feb. 3, 1926; s. Harry Leon and Dorothy (Shaefer) G.; m. Stella Berger, Oct. 12, 1952; children— Lise, Daniel, Stefanie. Student, Mich. State Coll. Liberal Arts, 1946-48; B.Arch., M.I.T., 1952, M.Arch., 1954; postgrad., New Sch. Social Research, N.Y.C., 1953, L'Inst. d'Urbanisme, Paris, 1954-55; Ed.M., Harvard U., 1975. Faculty Sch. Architecture and Planning, M.I.T., 1955-57; with Samuel Glaser, Boston, 1958-60; ptnr. Carroll & Greenfield (architects), Boston, 1960-73; dir. edn. Boston Archtl. Ctr. Sch. Architecture, 1967-75; research mgr. AIA Research Corp., 1975-76; cons. Sanford R. Greenfield & Asso., Boston; chmn. dept. architecture Iowa State U., Ames, 1976-81; dean Sch. Architecture, N.J. Inst. Tech., 1981-91, prof. architecture emeritus, 2001—. Lectr. Inst. Urban Design, Krakow (Poland) Politechnika, 1978; dir. edn. Boston Archtl. Ctr.; cons. ednl. planning; lectr. Mass. Coll. Art; mem. task force on edn. and tng. for internat. constrn. Bldg. Rsch. Bd. NRC, 1987; examiner archtl. registration exam. in design, 1984, 85, 86, 87, 90. Editor: Architecture and the Computer, 1964, Forces Shaping the Role of The Architect, 1966, Systems, 1968; contbr. articles to profl. jours.; Important works include Library St. John's Sem. Mem. 5-Presidents' Task Force on Edn., 1972-73; chmn. Nat. Adv. Coun. Continuing Edn., 1972-73; mem. adv. bd. Ctr. for Study of Profl. Edn., U. Cin., 1992—. Served with USNR, 1944-46. Recipient Centennial Educator award Boston Archtl. Ctr., 1989; Fulbright scholar, 1954-55; Nat. Endowment for Arts grantee, 1978; Sch. of Architecture Libr. Coll. named in his honor, N.J. Inst. Tech., 1996. Fellow AIA (bd. dirs. AIA/ACSA rsch. coun. 1989-91); mem. Iowa Assn. Architects, Assn. Collegiate Schs. Architecture (v.p. 1972-73, pres. 1973-74, also dir.), N.J. Soc. Architects (bd. dirs. 1982-91), Boston Archtl. Ctr. Task Force Limits of Growth, 2002.

GREENFIELD, SEYMOUR STEPHEN, mechanical engineer; b. Bklyn., July 9, 1922; s. Herman and Yetta (Silfen) G.; m. Eleanor Levy, Oct. 30, 1949 (dec. 1987); children: Meryl Joy, Bruce Howard; m. Judith A. Abrams, 1990. Student, N.Y. U., 1939-40; B.Mech. Engring., Poly. Inst. N.Y., 1943. Registered profl. engr. Calif., Conn., Mass., N.J., N.Y., La., Tex., Ohio. Engr. Percival R. Moses Assos., N.Y.C., 1946-47; sr. engr. and assoc. Parsons, Brinckerhoff, Quade & Douglas, N.Y.C., 1947-64, ptnr., 1964—, chmn. bd., 1979-90, chmn. emeritus, 1990—. Adviser Manhattan Coll., N.Y.C., 1974—; mem. devel. coun. Tex. A&M Sch. Architecture, 1981; chmn. coun. on transp. Ctr. for Transp. Policy and Mgmt., NYU. Bd. dirs. N.Y. chpt. March of Dimes, 1989. Served to lt. USNR, 1944-46. Recipient Engring. News Record Citation for Outstanding Contbns. to Constrn. Industry, 1982, Moles award, 1993, Golden Eagle award Soc. Am. Mil. Engrs., 1997; named Transp. Man of Yr., March of Dimes, 1982. Fellow Poltechnic Univ. of N.Y.; mem. Soc. Am. Mil. Engrs. (nat. pres. 1977, dir. 1975—, pres. N.Y.C. post 1974-75), Nat. Acad. Engring. Bldg. Research (mem. adv. bd. 1972—), N.Y. C. of C. and Industry (vice chmn. Transp. Council 1973—), N.Y. State Soc. Profl. Engrs., ASME, Am. Soc. Heating, Refrigerating and Air Conditioning Engrs., Moles (pres. 1986, trustee, chmn. coun. on transportation, N.Y.C.). Home: 1600 Parker Ave Fort Lee NJ 07024-7050 Office: Parsons Brinckerhoff Inc 1 Penn Plz Fl 2 New York NY 10119-0021

GREENFIELD, VAL SHEA, ophthalmologist; b. N.Y.C., Apr. 20, 1932; s. Frank Lynne and Helen (Meyers) G. Student, Brown U., 1948-49, 50-51, St. John's U., 1949; BA cum laude, Bklyn. Coll., 1952; MD, Yale U., 1956. Diplomate Am. Bd. Ophthalmology; lic. physician, pa., N.Y., N.J. Intern Walter Reed Army Hosp., Washington, 1956-57; asst. chief U.S. Army Dispensary, Phila., 1957-59, chief, 1959-60; postgrad. preceptorship in ophthal. under co-chief ophthal. Presbyn.-U. Pa. Med. Ctr., Phila., 1963-66; practice medicine specializing in obstetrics Phila., Riverside, N.J., 1960-63; practice medicine specializing in ophthalmology Phila., 1966—. Assoc. dir., lectr. in neuro-ophthalmology Hahnemann U., Phila., 1978—, from asst. prof. to assoc. prof. ophthalmology Sch. Medicine, 1977-88; assoc. clin. prof. Robert Wood Johnson Med. Sch.-N.J. U. Medicine and Dentistry, 1988—; attending surgeon in ophthalmology Frankford and Rolling Hills Hosps., Phila., 1970—; lectr. Bibl. topics U.S., Israel, Europe, New Zealand, USSR; guest speaker TV stas. and clubs; speaker, Gideons Internat. Gospel Soc. Internat., 2001. Contbr. articles to profl. jours., chpts. to textbooks. Mem. bd. deacons Cmty. Ch., Mt. Laurel Chapel and Fellowship, 1970—; bd. dirs. Hebrew Christian Outreach of Ch. of Our Lord Jesus Christ, 1958—; elected to Gideons Internat. Bible Distribution and LEctr. Soc.; spkr. ann. meeting G.I. Gospel Soc. Internat., 2001. Served to capt. M.C., U.S. Army, 1955-60. Inducted into Chapel of 4 Chaplains, Temple U., 1981; inducted Hon. Brave Cherokee Indians by Chief Rising Sun, Chief and High Priest of N.Am. and S.Am. Indian Tribes and Couns., 1947; recipient AMA Physicians Recognition award in med. edn., tri-annually, 1974—. Fellow ACS, ACP, Am. Geriatrics Soc., Phila. Coll. Physicians; mem. AMA, Pa. Med. Soc., Phila. County Med. Soc., Am. Acad. Ophthalmology, N.Y. State Ophthal. Soc., Pa. Acad. Ophthalmology, Pan-Am. Soc. Ophthalmology, Soc. Contemporary Ophthalmology, Christian Med. Soc., Am. Soc. Cataract and Refracture Surgery, Internat. Platform Soc., Am. Judeo-Christian Fellowship, Alpha Kappa Kappa. Avocations: book collecting, bible lectures and writings. *In over forty years of studying and applying the principles of medicine to my patients, I have seen the devastating toll that anger, hatred, fear, doubt, anguish, inordinate lust and jealousy have taken on men's and women's bodies and souls. I continually advise my patients that conventional medicines and therapies alone cannot heal or cure these "spiritual diseases". I add to my therapeutic armamentarium the concepts of the Ten Commandments and the Sermon on the Mount, which I suggest that my patients apply to their daily lives. The happiest moments in my professional life have been when I observe the salubrious effects that faith, hope and love have upon my patients' afflictions. Jesus, the Annointed One of God, prophetically called "The Mighty God, the Everlasting Father, the Prince of Peace", summed up His whole religion, which I heartily recommend to my patients, colleagues, friends, as well as to myself, as follows: "Thou shalt love The Lord thy God with all thy heart and with all thy soul and with all thy mind. Thou shalt love thy neighbor as thyself. On these two commandments hang all the law and Prophets." Unless mankind in general, and each and every man and woman in particular, appropriate and follow these commandments, then we will face the dire consequences that are already evolving worldwide: the scourges of war, pestilence and famine.*

GREENGARD, PAUL, neuroscientist; b. N.Y.C., Dec. 11, 1925; married; 3 children. AB, Hamilton Coll., 1948; PhD, Johns Hopkins U., 1953. NSF fellow in neurochemistry U. London (Eng.)Inst. Psychiatry, 1953—54; Nat. Found. Infantile Paralysis fellow U. Cambridge (Eng.) Molteno Inst., 1954—55; Paraplegia Found. fellow Nat. Inst. Med. Rsch., England, 1955—56; fellow Nat. Inst. Neurological Diseases and Blindness, 1956—58; dir. biochemistry dept. Ciba-Geigy Rsch. Labs., 1958—67; prof. pharmacology and psychiatry Yale U. Sch. Medicine, New Haven, 1968—83; Andrew D. White prof.-at-large Cornell U., Ithaca, NY, 1981—87; Vincent Astor prof. Rockefeller U., N.Y.C., 1983—. Vis. scientist Nat. Heart Inst., 1958—59; vis. assoc. prof. Albert Einstein Coll. Medicine, 1961—68, vis. prof., 1968—83, Vanderbilt U., 1967—68; Harvey Soc. lectr., 1980; lectr. in field. Recipient Dickson prize and medal in medicine, U. Pitts., 1977, Ciba-Geigy Drew award, 1979, Biol. and Med. Scis. award, N.Y. Acad. Scis., 1980, 3M Life Scis. award, Fedn. Am. Socs. Exptl. Biology, 1987, Bristol-Myers award for disting. achievement in neurosci. rsch., 1989, Goodman and Gilman award in receptor pharmacology, 1992, Karl Spencer Lashley prize, Am. Philos. Soc., 1993, Biochem. Soc. Thudichum medal, 1996, Charles A. Dana Found. award for pioneering achievements in health, 1997, Met. Life Found. award for excellence in sci. and tech., 1999, Nobel prize, 2000. Mem.: NAS (award in neurosis. 1991), Nat. Alliance for Rsch. on Schizophrenia and Depression (Lieber prize Outstanding Achievement Schizophrenia Rsch. 1996), Soc. for Neurosci. (Grass lectr. 1986, Gerard prize 1994), Am. Acad. Arts and Scis., Am. Neurol. Assn. (hon.). Office: Rockefeller U 1230 York Ave New York NY 10021-6399*

GREENGUS, SAMUEL, academic administrator, religion educator; b. Chgo., Mar. 11, 1936; s. Eugene and Thelma (Romirowsky) G.; m. Lesha Bellows, Apr. 30, 1957; children: Deana, Rachel, Judith. Student, Hebrew Theol. Coll., Chgo., 1950-58; MA, U. Chgo., 1959, PhD, 1963. Prof. semitic langs. Hebrew Union Coll.-Jewish Inst. Religion, Cin., 1963-89, Julian Morgenstern prof. bible and near eastern lit., 1989—, dean rabbinic sch., 1979-84, dean Cin. campus, 1985-87, dean sch. grad. studies, 1985-90, dean faculty, 1987-98, v.p. for Acad. affairs, 1990-96. Vis. lectr. U. of Dayton, Ohio, 1964-69, Leo Baeck Coll., London, 1976-77; area supr. Tel Gezer Excavation, Israel, 1966-67; mem. bd. editors Hebrew Union Coll. Ann. Author: Old Babylonian Tablets from Ishchali and Vicinity, 1979, Studies in Ishchali Documents, 1986; mem. bd. editors Zeitschrift fur Altorientalische und Biblische Rechtsgeschichte; contbr. articles to profl. jours. Mem. Cin. Community Hebrew Schs. Bd., 1970-75; mem. vis. com. Sch. for Creative and Performing Arts, Cin., 1980-82; chmn. acad. officers, Greater Cin. Consortium Colls. and Univs., 1984-85, mem. exec. com., 1989-96. Am. Council Learned Socs. fellow, 1970-71, Am. Assn. Theol. Schs. fellow, 1976-77. Mem. Am. Oriental Soc., Assn. Jewish Studies, Soc. Bibl. Lit., Phi Beta Kappa. Jewish. Office: Hebrew Union Coll Jewish Inst Religion 3101 Clifton Ave Cincinnati OH 45220-2404

GREENHALGH, TERRY LAMONT, marketing executive; b. Cin., Sept. 29, 1950; s. Frederick Olsen and Julia Ann (Gamble) G.; m. Erin J. Morgan, May 1992 (div. Feb. 1997); 1 child, Shannon Ann. AS in TV Prodn., Hillsborough Community Coll., Tampa, Fla., 1975; AA in Liberal Arts, Hillsborough Community Coll., 1978; BA in Pub. Rels., U. South Fla., 1981. Sports writer, reporter The Tampa (Fla.) Tribune Co., 1979-81; promotion dir. Palmer Communications, Inc., Naples, Fla., 1981-84; pres., chief exec. officer Grand Mktg. & Pub. Relations, Tampa, 1984-88; mktg. mgr. Modern Talking Picture Svc., Inc., St. Petersburg, 1988-91; gen. mgr. Europa Cruise Corp., Ft. Myers Beach, Fla., 1991-93; sales and mktg. rep. Continental Airlines, Tampa, Fla., 1993-94; v.p. mktg. and devel. Fla. Spl. Olympics, Inc., Tampa, 1994-96; mktg. specialist CBS Radio, St. Petersburg, Fla., 1997; dir. devel. The Astronauts Meml. Found., Kennedy Space Ctr., Fla., 1997-2000, Sun n'Fun Fly in Found., 2000—. Author: (history trivia game) Tampa Tycoon, 1985 (Addy 1986), (wine trivia game) The Wine Connoisseur, 1986 (Addy award 1987). With U.S. Army, 1970-72. Avocations: reading, fitness, snow skiing, water sports, travel writing. Home: PO Box 261616 Tampa FL 33685-1616 E-mail: TGinspace@aol.com.

GREENHAM, DAVID, theater administrator; b. Rochester, N.Y., Nov. 28, 1960; s. William and Catherine Greenham; m. Jeri Pitcher, May 17, 1989; 1 child, Zachary. BFA, Syracuse U., 1983. Producing dir. Brown's Head Repertory Theater, Monson, Maine, 1985-90; cmty. arts cons. Maine Arts Commn., Augusta, 1990-93; cmty. devel. adminstr. Town of Dexter, Maine, 1993-95; exec. dir. River Tree Arts, Kennebunk, Maine, 1995-97; mng. dir. Theater at Monmouth, Maine, 1997-2001, producing dir., 2001—. Cons. Maine Arts Sponsors Assn., Augusta, 1992-97; theater instr., Sr. Coll., U. Maine, Augusta. Mem. . Maine State Quar.Commn., 2002. Home: PO Box 634 Readfield ME 04355 Office: Theater At Monmouth PO Box 385 Monmouth ME 04259 Fax: (207) 933-2952. E-mail: tamoffice@Theateratmonmouth.org.

GREENHAW, HAROLD WAYNE, writer; b. Sheffield, Ala., Feb. 17, 1940; s. Harold and Myrtie Lee Greenhaw; m. Sally Maddox, Aug. 26, 1972. BS in English, U. of Ala., 1966; Nieman Fellowship, Harvard U., 1973. Editor, pub. Ala. Mag., Montgomery, 1982—86; dir. State Bur. of Tourism, Montgomery, Ala., 1993—94. Author: (novel) The Golfer (Hector award for Outstanding Journalism, 1990), King of Country, Beyond the Night, The Long Journey, (screenplay), (fiction collection) The Spider's Web, Tombigbee and other stories, (non-fiction books) Alabama on my Mind, The Making of a Hero: Lt. William Calley and the My Lai Massacre, Watch out for George Wallace, Elephants in the Cottonfields: Ronald Reagan and the New Republican South, Flying High: Inside Big-Time Drug Smuggling, My Heart is in the Earth: True Stories of Alabama and Mexico, Montogomery: The River City, (play) Rose: A Southern Lady; The Spirit Tree. Sec. Ala. Humanities Found., Birmingham, 2000—03. Mem.: Author's Guild. Democrat. Avocation: traveling to Mexico. Home: San Miguel de Allende Mexico Office: PR Assocs Inc PO Drawer 6161 Montgomery AL 36106 Personal E-mail: wgreenhaw@mindspring.com.

GREENHILL, H. GAYLON, retired academic administrator; Chancellor U. Wis., Whitewater, 1991-99, chancellor emeritus, 1999—. Address: PO Box 507 Whitewater WI 53190-0507 E-mail: greenhig@mail.uww.edu.

GREENHILL, JOE ROBERT, former chief justice state supreme court, lawyer; b. Houston, July 14, 1914; s. Joe R. Jr. and Violet (Stanuell) G.; m. Martha Shuford, June 15, 1940; children: Joe IV, William D. BBA, BA, U. Tex., 1936, LLB, 1939; LLD (hon.), So. Meth. U., 1977. Briefing atty. for chief justice Alexander Tex. Supreme Ct., Austin, 1941, 46; 1st asst. atty. gen. Tex. Austin, 1947-50; co-founder Graves, Dougherty & Greenhill, Austin, 1950-57; justice Supreme Ct. of Tex., Austin, 1957-72, chief justice, 1972-82; of counsel Baker & Botts, Austin, 1982—. Co-incorporator Tex. Ctr. for Professionalism and Ethics, Austin, 1991—; pres. elect Conf. Chief Justices and Nat. Ctr. for State Courts, Williamsburg, Va., 1982. Editor Tex. Law Rev., 1937-39 (Outstanding Ex-Editor 1975). Lt. USNR, 1942-46, PTO. Named Disting. Alumnus U. Tex., 1974, Disting. Alumnus U. Tex. Law Sch., 1977, Disting. Alumnus U. Tex. Coll. Bus. Adminstrn., 1974. Fellow Tex. Bar Found. (life, Outstanding 50 yr. lawyer 1989, exec. dir. 1984—), Am. Bar Found. (life); mem. Masons (33 degree). Office: Baker & Botts 98 San Jacinto Blvd Ste 1600 Austin TX 78701-4078

GREENHILL, ROBERT FOSTER, investment banker; b. Mpls., June 20, 1936; s. J. Raymond and Mary (Foster) G.; m. Mary Gayle Gussett, Sept. 13, 1958; children: Sarah B., Robert Foster, Mary B. AB, Yale U., 1958; MBA, Harvard U., 1962. Assoc. Morgan Stanley & Co., Inc., N.Y.C., 1962-70, mng. dir., 1970-93, pres., 1991-93; chmn., chief exec. officer Smith Barney Shearson, Inc., N.Y.C., 1993-96, Greenhill & Co., LLC, N.Y.C., 1996-. Trustee Am. Enterprise Inst. Served to lt. (j.g.) USNR, 1960-62. Mem. Ausable Club (Keene Valley, N.Y.), Field Club, Links Club, River Club. Clubs: Ausable (Keene Valley, N.Y.); Field (Greenwich); Links; River (N.Y.C.). Office: Greenhill & Co LLC 300 Park Ave New York NY 10022

GREENHOUSE, LINDA JOYCE, journalist; b. N.Y.C., Jan. 9, 1947; d. Herman Robert and Dorothy Eleanor (Greenlick) Greenhouse; m. Eugene R. Fidell, Jan. 1, 1981; 1 child, Hannah Margalit Fidell. BA, Radcliffe Coll., 1968; M of Studies in Law, Yale U., 1978; D.H.L. (hon.) (hon.), Brown U., 1991; LLD (hon.) (hon.), Colgate U., 1993, Northeastern U., 1997, CUNY, 1997. Asst. to James Reston The N.Y. Times, N.Y.C., 1968 -69, met. reporter, 1970—74, state polit. reporter, 1974—77, supreme ct. corr. Washington, 1978—85, 1988—, congl. corr., 1986—88. Adv. com. Schlesinger Libr. on the History of Women in Am., Radcliffe Coll., 1995—2002; mem. Schlesinger Libr. Coun., 2003—; bd. dirs. Yale Law Sch. Fund, New Haven, 1984—91. Recipient Pulitzer prize in journalism for beat reporting, 1998, Carey McWilliams award, Am. Polit. Sci. Assn., 2002, Henry J. Friendly medal, Am. Law Inst., 2002, Golden Pen award, Legal Writing Inst., 2002. Fellow: Am. Acad. Arts and Scis.; mem.: Women's Forum of Washington (v.p. 2003—), Yale Law Assn. (exec. com. 1993—97), Am. Law Inst. (hon.), Am. Philos. Soc., Harvard Club of Washington (bd. dirs. 1989—92). Office: The NY Times 1627 I St NW Washington DC 20006-4007 E-mail: ligree@nytimes.com.

GREENHUT, DEBORAH SCHNEIDER, management consultant; b. Yonkers, N.Y., Nov. 14, 1951; d. Howard and Virginia (Kelly) Schneider; m. Victor A. Greenhut, June 12, 1977; children: Adam, Nathan. AB, Middlebury Coll., 1973; MA, Rutgers U., 1977, MPhil, 1979, PhD, 1985. Priority cons., East Brunswick, N.J., 1988-90; cmty. edn. faculty Raritan Valley C.C., Somerville, N.J., 1989-91; cons. Inst. for Mgmt. and Tech. Devel., Edison, N.J., 1988-92. Nationwide speaker Dun and Bradstreet, Bus. Edn. Svcs., 1990-2001. Pub. Feminine Rhetorical Culture, 1988; author works on communications skills, computer tng., customer rels., video tng. program. Mem. Dramatists Guild of Am., Princeton Rsch. Forum, Phi Beta Kappa.

GREENHUT, MELVIN LEONARD, economist, educator; b. NYC, Mar. 10, 1921; s. Ab and Lillian (Frudman) G.; m. Elmara Margaret Griffith, Mar. 24, 1944; children: Margaret Lee, Pamela Jo, John Griffith, Patricia Lynn. PhD, Washington U., 1951. Prof. econ. various univ., 1948-62; prof., head dept. econ. Tex. A&M U., Coll. Sta., 1966-69, disting. prof. econ., 1969—, alumni disting. prof. econ., 1980-85, Abell Prof. Liberal Arts, disting. prof. econ., 1986—, Abell Prof. Liberal Arts, disting. prof. econ. emeritus, 1992—, chmn. disting. prof., 1988-89. Vis. prof., lectr. in field. Co-author (with John Greenhut): (book) Sci. and God, 2002, Our Teleological Econ. World, 2002; author: 19 books; contbr. articles to profl. jour. Mem. nat. econ. policy com. and econ. adv. coun.

US C. of C., 1960-63. Maj. US Army. Mem. Am. Econ. Assn., So. Econ. Assn. (past v.p.), Regional Sci. Assn. (councillor), Royal Econ. Soc., Econometric Soc., Delta Chi, Omicron Delta Gamma. Lutheran. Home: 5814 Constellation Cir Rockwall TX 75032-5770 Office: Tex A&M U Dept Econs College Station TX 77843-0001

GREENKORN, ROBERT ALBERT, chemical engineering educator; b. Oshkosh, Wis., Oct. 12, 1928; s. Frederick John and Sophie (Phillips) G.; m. Rosemary Drexler, Aug. 16, 1952; children: David Michael, Eileen Anne, Susan Marie, Nancy Joanne. Student, Oshkosh State Coll., 1951-52; BS, U. Wis., 1954, MS, 1955, PhD, 1957. Postdoctoral fellow Norwegian Tech. Inst., 1957-58; rsch. engr. Jersey Prodn. Rsch. Co., Tulsa, 1958-63; lectr. U. Tulsa, 1958-63; assoc. prof. theoretical and applied mechanics Marquette U., Milw., 1963-65; assoc. prof. chem. engring. Purdue U., Lafayette, Ind., 1965-67, prof., head chem. engring. dept., 1967-72, asst. dean engring., 1972-76, assoc. dean engring., dir. engring. expt. sta., 1976-80, v.p., assoc. provost, 1980-86; v.p. programs Purdue Rsch. Found., 1980-94, v.p. rsch., 1986-92, v.p. rsch., dean grad. sch., 1993-94, spl. asst. to the pres., 1994-2000, v.p. spl. programs, 1994-2000, R. Games Slayter disting. prof. chem. engring., 1995-2000, R. Games Slayter disting. prof. emeritus chem. engring., 2000—. Rsch. coord. Ind. Clean Mfg. and Safe Materials Inst., 1994-2000; dir. Tech. Assistance Program, 1996-2000. Author: (with D.P. Kessler) Transfer Operations, 1972, (with K.C. Chao) Thermodynamics of Fluids: An Introduction to Equilibrium Theory, 1975, (with D.P. Kessler) Modeling and Data Analysis for Engineers and Scientists, 1980, Flow Phenomena in Porous Media, 1983, Momentum, Heat and Mass Transfer Fundamentals (with D.P. Kessler), 1999; contbr. articles to profl. jours. Served with USN, 1946-51. Decorated D.F.C., Air medal with two oak leaf clusters; recipient Fellow Members awd., Am. Soc. for Engineering Education, 1992. Fellow AIChE, Am. Soc. Engring. Edn.; mem. AAAS, Soc. Petroleum Engrs., Am. Chem. Soc., Am. Geophys. Union, Sigma Xi, Phi Eta Sigma, Tau Beta Pi, Phi Gamma Delta. Roman Catholic. Achievements include patents in field. Home: 151 Knox Dr West Lafayette IN 47906-2147

GREENLAND, LEO, advertising executive; b. N.Y.C., Mar. 4, 1920; s. Jack and Ida (Abrams) G.; m. Rita Levine, June 29, 1955; children— Seth, Andrew. Student, New Sch. for Social Research, 1945—47. Pres. Sherwood Prodns., 1949-52; exec. various advt. agys., 1952-59; pres. Smith/Greenland Co., Inc., N.Y.C., 1959—, chmn., chief exec. officer, 1974—. Guest lectr. Fordham U. Sch. Communication Arts, 1967—, Cornell Sch. Hotel Mgmt., NYU. Nat. commr. Anti-Defamation League, chmn. radio-TV dept.; bd. dirs., pres. Friars Found.; trustee ADL Found., hon. vice-chmn.; hon. chief N.Y.C. Fire Dept.; mem. adv. bd. bus. coun. UN; mem. Am. Forces Info. Svc. Task Force; bd. dirs. Nat. Libr. Mus., Phila., Am. Interfaith Inst. Served with AUS, 1943-46. Mem. Am. Advt. Agys. (bd. govs. N.Y.), Nat. Advt. Rev. Bd., Am. Mgmt. Assn. (lectr. 1969—), Am. Arbitration Assn., Nat. Businessmen's Coun., Fgn. Policy Assn. Interracial Businessmen's Coun., Ea. Frosted Foods Assn. (pres. 1965-67, bd. dirs.), Chief Execs. Orgn., Met. Pres. Orgn., Sales Execs. Club N.Y., Newcomer Soc. N.Am., Def. Orientation Conf. Assn., Am. Forces Info. Svc. Task Force, Young Presidents Orgn., World Bus. Coun., Sierra Club, Econs. Club, Gilda's Club (founding mem.), Rockrimmon Country Club, Friars Club (pres. found.), Palm Beach Round Table. Home: PO Box 806 Bedford NY 10506 0806 Office: Smith/Greenland Inc 1056 5th Ave # 10A New York NY 10028-0112

GREENLAND, SANDER, education educator; b. Chgo., Ill., Jan. 16, 1951; s. Harold and Lorraine Greenland; m. Morgan Elizabeth Stewart, May 1984 (div. 1988); 1 child, David. AB and MA math, Univ. Calif., Berkeley, 1974; MS Pub. Health, Univ. Calif., L.A., 1976, DPH, 1978. Charted statistician Royal Statis. Soc., 1993. Statistician UCLA Sch. of Pub. Health, L.A., 1975—78; asst. prof. Harvard Sch. of Pub. Health, Boston, 1978—79; prof. UCLA Sch. of Pub. Health, L.A., 1979—. Adv. bd. Am. Coun. Sci. and Health, N.Y., 1994—; assoc. editor Statistics Medicine, 1984—. Co-author: Modern Epidmiology, 1998; contbr. articles of 250 to profl. jour. Mem.: Am. Inst. Assn., Soc. for Epidemiologic Rsch., Royal Statis. Soc. Office: Univ Calif Ctr for Health Sci Los Angeles CA 90095-1772

GREENLAW, ROGER LEE, interior designer; b. New London, Conn., Oct. 12, 1936; s. Kenneth Nelson and Lyndell Lee (Stinson) G; children: Carol Jennifer, Roger Lee. BFA, Syracuse U., 1958. Interior designer Cannell & Chaffin, 1958-59, William C. Wagner, Arch., L.A., 1959-60, Gen. Fireproofing Co., L.A., 1960-62, K-S Wilshire, Inc., L.A., 1963-64; dir. interior design Calif. Desk Co., L.A., 1967-67; sr. interior designer Bechtel Corp., L.A., 1967-70; sr. interior designer, project mgr. Daniel, Mann, Johnson & Mendehall, L.A., 1970-72, Morganelli-Heumann & Assocs., L.A., 1972-73; owner, prin. Greenlaw Design Assocs., Glendale, Calif., 1973—96, Greenlaw Interior Planning & Design, 1996—. Lectr. UCLA; mem. adv. curriculum com. Mt. San Antonio Coll., Walnut, Calif., Fashion Inst. Design, L.A.; bd. dirs. Calif. Legis. Conf. Interior Design, treas., 1992-94, v.p., 1990-92, pres., 1994-98. Past scoutmaster Verdugo coun. Boy Scouts Am.; pres. bd. dirs. Unity Ch., La Crescenta, Calif., 1989-91. Mem. ASID (treas. Pasadena chpt. 1983-84, 1st v.p. 1985, pres. 1986-87, chmn. So. Calif. regional conf. 1985, nat. dir. 1987-89, nat. com. legis., nat com. jury for catalog award, spkr. ho. dels., nat. bd. dirs., medallist award, regional v.p., nat. chair ethics com., nat. exec. com., v.p., treas. 1992 Calif. legis. conf. interior design, chmn. stds. task force, pres. 1994-98), Glendale C. of C. (bd. dirs. 1998), Adm. Farragut Acad. Alumni Assn., Kiwanis (bd. dirs.), Delta Upsilon. Republican. Office: 2155 Verdugo Blvd Montrose CA 91020-1628 Home: Apt 4 1145 Willow Bend Cir Colorado Springs CO 80918-7035 E-mail: greenlawdesign@msn.com.

GREENLEAF, ERIC ANDREW, marketing educator, researcher; b. N.Y.C., May 30, 1956; s. William and Ellen Greenleaf; m. Vicki Gail Morwitz, June 6, 1999. BS summa cum laude, U. N.H., 1977; MBA, Columbia U., 1981, PhD, 1985. Asst. prof. mktg. Yale U. Sch. Mgmt., New Haven, 1985-88; assoc. prof. mktg. Stern Sch. Bus. NYU, N.Y.C., 1988—. Vis. asst. prof. mktg. Columbia U. Grad. Sch. Bus., N.Y.C., 1992-93, Wharton Sch., U. Pa., 1996; vis. scholar Haas Sch. Bus., U. Calif., Berkeley, 2000. Contbr. articles to profl. jours. (Mktg. Sci. Inst. Behavioral Pricing award 1994). Mem. Assn. Consumer Rsch., Inst. Ops. Rsch. and Mgmt., Soc. Consumer Psychology, Phi Beta Kappa, Beta Gamma Sigma. Office: NYU Stern Sch Bus 44 W 4th St New York NY 10012 E mail: egreenle@stern.nyu.edu.

GREENLEAF, JOHN EDWARD, research physiologist; b. Joliet, Ill., Sept. 18, 1932; s. John Simon and Julia Clara (Flint) G.; m. Carol Lou Johnson, Aug. 28, 1960. MA, N.Mex. Highlands U., 1956; BA in Phys. Edn., U. Ill., 1955, MS, 1962, PhD in Physiol., 1963. Tchg. asst. N.Mex. Highlands U., Las Vegas, Nev., 1955-56; engring. draftsman Allis-Chalmers Mfg. Co., Springfield, Ill., 1956-57; tchg. asst. in phys. edn. U. Ill., Urbana, 1957-58, rsch. asst. in phys. edn., 1958-59, tchg. asst. in human anatomy and physiology, 1959-62; summer fellow NSF, 1962; pre-doctoral fellow NIH, 1962-63; rsch. physiologist Space Scis. Directorate, NASA, Ames Rsch. Ctr., Moffett Field, Calif., 1963—66; rsch. physiologist Space Scis. directorate NASA/Ames Rsch. Ctr., Moffett Field, Calif., 1967—2002; postdoctoral fellowship Karolinska Inst., Stockholm, 1966-67. Adj. prof. biology dept. San Francisco State U., 1988-2002; adj. prof. dept. exercise sci. U. Calif., Davis, 1996-01; adj. prof. dept. human performance San Jose State U., 2002—; Japan Soc. for Promotion of Sci. vis. prof. Kyoto Prefectural U. Medicine, 1997; mem. internat. adv. bd. Medicina Sportiva. Mem. editorial bd. Jour. Applied Physiology, 1989-99, Med. Sci. Sports Exercise, 2000-02; contbr. articles to profl. jours. Pub. dir. N.Mex. Highlands U. Found., 1999—. Served with U.S. Army, 1952-53. Recipient Disting. Alumni award N.Mex. Highlands U., 1990, Disting. Alumni award dept. molecular and integrative physiology U. Ill., 1998, Am. Coll. Sports Medicine Citation award, 1999, Internat. Cannes and Nestle Water Inst. prize water and medicine, 2003; exch. fellow NAS, 1973-74, 77, 89, NIH, 1980. Fellow AIAA (assoc.), Am. Coll. Sports Medicine (trustee 1984-87), Aerospace Med. Assn. (Harold Ellingson award 1981-82, Eric Liljencrantz award 1990); mem. Am. Physiol. Soc. (mem. com. on coms. 1984-87, long range planning com. 1987-90, internat. physiol. com. 1997-00), Polish Soc. Sports Medicine (hon.), Shooting Sports Rsch. Coun. (internat. shooters devel. fund 1984), Sigma Xi. Achievements include patents in field. Home: 12391 Farr Ranch Ct Saratoga CA 95070-6527

GREENLEAF, STEWART JOHN, state legislator; b. Phila., Oct. 4, 1939; s. Stewart William and Belford Denner G.; m. Cecilia Agnus Finley, 1973. BA, U. Pa., 1961; JD, U. Toledo, 1966. Asst. dist. atty. Montgomery County Dist. Attys. Office, 1969-76; mem. Pa. Ho. of Reps., 1976-78, Pa. State Senate, Dist. 12, 1979—. Commr. Upper Moreland Twp., 1971-75. Recipient Humanitarian award Humane Soc. U.S.-MidAtlantic region, Guardian of Small Bus. award Nat. Fedn. Ind. Bus., 1989-90; named Citizen of Yr., Willow Grove C. of C., Ukrainian Cultural Ctr., 1990. Presbyterian. Home: 27 York Rd Willow Grove PA 19090-3419 Office: Senate Box 203012 19 East Wing Harrisburg PA 17120

GREENLEAF, WALTER FRANKLIN, lawyer; b. Griffin, Ga., Sept. 21, 1946; BA, Mich. State U., 1968; MA, U. N.C., 1970; JD, U. Ala., 1973. Law clk. U.S. Dist. Ct., Birmingham, Ala., 1973-74; assoc. Sirote, Permutt, et al., Birmingham, Ala., 1975-76; assoc., then ptnr. Welbaum Guernsey, Hingston, Greenleaf & Gregory, LLP, Miami, Fla., 1976—. Home: 417 Madeira Ave Miami FL 33134-4234 Office: Welbaum Guernsey Hingston Greenleaf & Gregory LLP 901 Ponce De Leon Blvd Miami FL 33134-3073 Business E-Mail: fgreenleaf@welbaum.com.

GREENLER, ROBERT GEORGE, physics educator, researcher; b. Kenton, Ohio, Oct. 24, 1929; s. Dallas George and Ruth Edna (Mallett) G.; m. Barbara Stacy, May 30, 1954; children: Leland S., Karen R., Robin A. BS in Physics, U. Rochester, 1951; PhD in Physics, Johns Hopkins U., 1957. Research scientist Allis-Chalmers Mfg. Co., Milw., 1957-62; assoc. prof. physics U. Wis., Milw., 1962-67, prof., 1967-91, adj. prof., 1991-98, prof. emeritus, 1998—. Sr. vis. fellow U. East Anglia, Norwich, Eng., 1971-72; traveling lectr. Optical Soc. Am., 1973-74; lectr. Coop. Edn. Program, Malaysia, 1990-91; organizer pub. outreach program Sci. Bag; prodr. 25 edn!. videos; did field rsch. on optical atmospheric effects at U.S. Antarctic Rsch. Station, South Pole, 1976-77, 97-98, 98-99. Author: Rainbows, Halos and Glories, 1980, Chasing the Rainbow: Recurrences in the Life of a Scientist, 2000; contbr. 80 articles to profl. jours. Sr. Fulbright scholar Fritz Haber Inst. of Max Planck Soc., West Berlin, 1983; grantee NSF, Petroleum Research Fund, Am. Chem. Soc. Fellow AAAS, Optical Soc. Am. (v.p. 1985, pres.-elect 1986, pres. 1987, 1st Esther Hoffman Beller award 1993); mem. Am. Assn. Physics Tchrs. (Milikan Lectr. award 1988). Achievements include research in surface science, infrared spectroscopy of adsorbed molecules, meteorological optics, iridescent colors in biological systems. Home: 6225 Mineral Point Rd Madison WI 53705 Office: U Wis Milw Dept Physics PO Box 413 Milwaukee WI 53201-0413 E-mail: greenler@uwm.edu.

GREENLEY, BEVERLY JANE, lawyer, educator; b. Cleve., Sept. 24, 1947; d. Gaylord H. and Joan C. (Gurklis) G. BA, Principia Coll., 1969, JD, U. Mo., 1976; LLM, Washington U., 1981. Bar: Mo. 1976, Ill. 1977, U.S. Tax Ct. 1979. Ptnr. McCarter & Greenley, St. Louis, 1976-81, McCarter, Snyder & Greenley, St. Louis, 1981-85; assoc. prof. law Stetson U. Coll. Law, St. Petersburg, Fla., 1981-85; ptnr. Gage & Tucker, St. Louis, 1985-87, Husch, Eppenberger, Donohue, Cornfeld & Jenkins, St. Louis, 1987-90, McCarter & Greenley, St. Louis, 1990—. Estate planning lectr. for CLE programs, 1997—; estate planning expert witness, 2000—. Co-author: Missouri Lawyer's Guide, 1984. Mem. Mo. Bar Assn., Ill. Bar Assn. Office: 1 Metropolitan Sq Ste 2100 Saint Louis MO 63102-2797 E-mail: bgreenley@mccartergreenley.com.

GREENLICK, MERWYN RONALD, health services researcher; b. Detroit, Mich, Mar. 12, 1935; s. Emanuel and Fay Greenlick; m. Harriet Greenlick, Aug. 19, 1956; children: Phyllis, Michael;1 child, Vicki. BS, Wayne State U., 1957; MS, U. Mich., 1961, PhD, 1967. Pharmacist, Detroit, 1957—60; spl. instr., instr. pharmacy adminstrn. Coll. Pharmacy Wayne State U., 1958—62; dir. of research n.w. region Kaiser-Permanente, Portland, Oreg., 1964—95; v.p. (rsch.) Kaiser Found. Hosp., 1981—95; sr. fellow Ctr. for Advanced Study in the Behavioral Sci., Stanford, Calif., 1995—96; adj. prof. sociology and social work Portland State U., 1965—; clin. prof. preventive medicine and pub. health Oreg. Health Sci. U., 1971—89, prof., acting chair preventive medicine and pub. health, 1990—93, prof., chair preventive medicine and pub. health, 1993—2000, emeritus prof., 2000—. Mem. Gov.'s Commn. on Health Care, 1988; cons. Gov.'s Health Manpower Coun.; mem. Oreg. State House of Reps., 2003—. Pres. Jewish Edn. Assn., Portland, 1976—78; bd. dirs. Washington County Cmty. Action Orgn., 1966—70; Jewish Fedn., 1975—79. Recipient USPHS trainee award, 1962—63, 1963—64. Fellow: APHA, Inst. Medicine NAS; mem.: AAAS, Oregon House of Rep. (mem. (HD33) 2003), N.W. Health Found. (bd. dir. 1997—), Assn. Health Svc. Rsch. (Disting. fellow, Pres.'s award 1995). Jewish. Home: 712 NW Spring Ave Portland OR 97229-6913 Office: Oreg Health Svcs U CB 669 3181 SW Sam Jackson Park Rd Portland OR 97201-3011

GREENLY, COLIN, artist; b. London, Jan. 21, 1928; came to U.S., 1939, naturalized, 1948; s. Arthur John and Caroline Matilda (Fantini) G.; m. Laurie Ann Zadek, May 8, 1976; 1 child, Katharine Lydia Caro Herman. AB, Harvard Coll., 1948; student, Columbia U. Sch. Painting and Sculpture, 1951-53; attended Grad. Sch. Fine Arts, Am. U., 1956. Dir. art Madeira Sch., Greenway, Va., 1955-68; Dana prof. fine arts Colgate U., 1972-73; vis. artist numerous colls., univs. One-man shows Corcoran Gallery of Art, Washington, 1968, Royal Marks Gallery, N.Y.C., 1968, 70, Everson Mus., Syracuse, N.Y., 1971, Andrew Dickson White Mus. (now Herbert F. Johnson Mus.), Cornell U., 1972, Picker Gallery, Colgate U., 1973, Finch Coll. Mus., N.Y.C., 1974; group shows include Mus. Modern Art, N.Y.C., 1953, 73, De Cordova Mus., Lincoln, Mass., 1965, Des Moines Art Ctr., 1967, Nat. Collection Fine Arts, Washington, 1968, Krannert Art Mus., Champaign, Ill., 1969, 74, Emmerich Gallery Downtown, N.Y.C., 1972, John Weber Gallery, N.Y.C., 1975, Whitney Mus. Am. Art, N.Y.C., 1978, N.Y. State Mus., Albany, 1981; represented in permanent collections Albright Knox Art Gallery, Buffalo, Corcoran Gallery Art, Des Moines Art Ctr., Everson Mus., High Mus. Art, Atlanta, Mus. Modern Art, N.Y.C., Phila. Mus. Art, Nat. Gallery Art, Washington, Nat. Collection Fine Arts (now Smithsonain Am. Art Mus.), Washington, Herbert F. Johnson Mus., Ithaca, N.Y.; restoration and contemporary adaptation of Hulse Barn, Campbell Hall, N.Y.; contbr. works of art, videos, photographs to CDROM Images of the Whole, 1998; contbr. articles to profl. jours. Grantee Nat. Endowment for Arts, 1967, Com. for Visual Arts, 1974, Creative Artists Pub. Svc. Program, 1972, 78, N.Y. State Coun. on Arts, 1993; named winner nat. competition playground sculpture Art in Am. and Corcoran Gallery Sch. Art, 1967. Mem. Media Alliance N.Y.C., Nat. Audobon Soc., Nature Conservancy, Wilderness Soc., Nat. Trust for Hist. Preservation, Sierra Club. Achievements include incorporating the characteristics of a circle and a square into a single image, thereby discovering an effective visual symbol for the concepts of transition and change, 1964; Intangible Sculpture. Address: 487 Hulsetown Rd Campbell Hall NY 10916-3201 E-mail: greenly@leaningpost.com. *Developing one's abilities may require a measure of commitment and excellence, but committing excellence to indiscriminate ends is artless. The synthesis of life and art is art.*

GREEN MACIAS, ROSARIO, ambassador; Former sec. fgn. rels. Govt. Mex., Mexico City, 1990-98, min. fgn. affairs, 1998—2000; ambassador to Argentina, 2001—. Office: Calle Arcos No 1650 Belgrand 1426 Buenos Aires Argentina

GREENMAN, DAVID LEWIS, retired physiologist and toxicologist; b. Williamston, Mich., Jan. 19, 1934; s. Asa J. and Lucy B. (Hoover) G.; m. Jessie E. Blackman, Aug. 10, 1956; children: Karen, Martha. BA, Asbury Coll., 1956; MS, Purdue U., 1959, PhD, 1962. Asst. prof., rsch. assoc. Johns Hopkins U., Balt., 1964-70; pharmacologist FDA, Washington, 1970, EPA, Washington, 1970-72; rsch. pharmacologist Nat. Ctr. for Toxicol. Rsch., FDA, Jefferson, Ark., 1972-76, rsch. physiologist, 1976-94; cons. in toxicology and physiology, North Little Rock, Ark., 1994—2002. Chmn. precautionary labelling com. Assn. Am. Pest Control Operators, Washington, 1971-72; mem. adv. bd. Handbook Endocrinology, CRC Press, Inc., Boca Raton, Fla., 1981; FDA cons. Nigerian FDA, Lagos, 1982; chmn. Institutional Animal Care and Use Com., 1990-92. Contbr. articles to Steroids, Endocrinology, Lab. Animal Sci., Jour. Nat. Cancer Inst., Jour. Toxicological Environ. Health. Chmn. Old York Community Coun., Balt., 1967-68; del. NE Community Orgn., Balt., 1969-70; vol. mission svc. corps South Bapt. Conv., Ark. Bapt. State vol. prayer coord., 1995-2001. Recipient Group FDA award Merit, 1980, Spl. Svc. award FDA, 1988, FDA Disting. Career Svc. award, 1994; fellow NSF, 1959-62, Nat. Cancer Inst., 1963-64; rsch. grantee NIH, 1965-70. Baptist. Achievements include demonstration of importance of kinetics of RNA precursor distribution in interpreting the effect of hormones on radiolabeling of RNA, of impact that rack shelf level has on body weight gain, food consumption, retinal degeneration and neoplasm frequency in laboratory mice; first identification of a mouse strain that develops thyroid neoplasm in response to diethystilbestrol and has a tendency toward a higher frequency in females than males as is true in humans. E-mail: dnj@aristotle.net.

GREENMAN, FREDERICK F., JR., lawyer; b. N.Y.C., Feb. 22, 1933; s. Frederick F. and Mildred G.; m. Angela Lancieri; children: Paul Rudolph, Jodi La Bourene. BA, Harvard U., 1954, LLB, 1961, LLM, 1963. Bar: N.Y. 1962. Assoc. Hays, Sklar & Herzberg, N.Y.C., 1962-66; asst. U.S. atty. So. Dist. N.Y., N.Y.C., 1966-69; assoc. Linden and Deutsch, N.Y.C., 1969-70; ptnr. Deutsch Klagsbrun & Blasband (and predecessor firm), 1971-2001. Legal advisor Am. Adoption Congress. Mem. Assn. Bar City N.Y., N.Y. State Bar Assn. Jewish. Office: 641 Lexington Ave New York NY 10022-4503 E-mail: FFGreenman@aol.com.

GREENMAN, JANE FRIEDLIEB, lawyer, human resources specialist; b. N.Y.C., Sept. 9, 1950; d. Morton Jerome and Isabelle Irene (Bisgyer) F.; m. Charles P. Greenman, Nov. 23, 1975; children: Margot, Jaclyn, Danielle. BS, Cornell U., 1972; JD, NYU, 1975, LLM in Labor Law, 1981. Bar: N.Y. 1976. Assoc. Wolf Haldenstein, N.Y.C., 1975-79; faculty NYU Law Sch., 1979-81, Bklyn. Law Sch., 1981—82; assoc., counsel Hughes Hubbard & Reed, N.Y.C., 1982-91, ptnr., chair employee benefits dept., 1991-96; v.p., dep. gen. coun. human resources Honeywell Internat., Inc., Morristown, NJ, 1996—2003; v.p. compensation, benefits and labor rels. Tyco Internat., N.Y.C., 2003—. Bd. dirs. Corinthian Comm., N.Y.C., N.J. Women's Fund, Am. Benefits Counsel; vice chair bd. dirs. ERISA Industy com., N.J. Women's 300; adj. prof. Bklyn. Law Sch., 1982-92, 95, Hofstra U. Mem. Temple Sinai of Summit. Mem. ABA, N.Y.C. Bar Assn., N.Y. State Bar Assn., Pres.'s Coun. Cornell Women. Jewish. Office: Tyco Internat (US) Inc 9 Roszel Rd Princeton NJ 08540

GREENOUGH, WILLIAM BATES, III, medical educator; b. Providence, Jan. 3, 1932; s. William Bates Jr. and Dorothy Garrison (Rand) G.; m. Jane Cheney Woodruff, Aug. 14, 1954 (dec. 1964); children: William Beckley, Kate, Thomas Clark, Elisabeth Bates; m. Quaneta Ahmed, 1965; 1 child, Zarin Farah Naz. BA magna cum laude, Amherst Coll., 1953; MD cum laude, Harvard U., 1957. Intern, asst. resident Columbia U. Coll. Physicians and Surgeons, N.Y.C., 1957-59; sr. rsch. fellow Mary Imogene Bassett Hosp., Cooperstown, N.Y., 1959-61; sr. resident Peter Bent Brigham Hosp., Boston, 1961-62; staff assoc. Nat. Heart Inst. Cholera Rsch. Lab., Dhaka, Bangladesh, 1962-65; chief infectious diseases div. Johns Hopkins U. Sch. Medicine, Balt., 1970-76, dir. Robert Wood Johnson Clin. Scholars Program, 1974-77, prof. medicine, 1983—, prof. internat. health sch. pub. health, 1985—; dir. Internat. Ctr. for Diarrhoeal Disease Rsch., Dhaka, Bangladesh, 1979-85; mem. geriatric medicine div. Johns Hopkins U., 1985—. Cons. infectious diseases Perry Point VA Hosp., 1972-77, Internat. Rescue Com., N.Y.C., 1971-72; mem. bacteriology and mycology study sect. NIH, 1972-76, chmn., 1974-76; mem. ad hoc study group on enteric disease Walter Reed Army Inst. Rsch., 1975-77; pres. Bangladesh Info. Ctr., Washington, 1971-84; mem. adv. coun. Bangladesh Found., Chgo., 1972; active Md. Gov.'s Commn. on Phys. Fitness and Marathon Commn., 1971-77; pres., chmn. bd., trustee Internat. Child Health Found., Columbia, Md., 1985-95, pres., 1998 ; chmn. Internat. Ctr. for Diarrhoeal Disease Rsch., Bangladesh Endowment Fund, 1997—; cons. Cera Products Inc., 1993-. Editor Infection and Immunity, 1975-78, Topics in Infectious Disease, 1976—, Jour. Diarrhoeal Disease Rsch., 1983-85, 93-2000; internat. advisor Kuwait Med. Jour., Jour. of Health Population and Nutrition, 2000--; author monographs; contbr. articles and revs. to med. jours., chpts. to books; patentee in field. Sr. surgeon USPHS, 1962-67. Recipient Internat. Prize in Medicine, King Faisal Found., 1984, Maurice Pate prize UNICEF, 1984, recognized for svc. to children, 1983; Howard Florey Meml. lectr. U. Adelaide, 2001. Fellow: ACP, AAAS, Infectious Diseases Soc. Am. (mem. internat. affairs com. 2000—03); mem.: Bangladesh Med. Soc., Am. Soc. Microbiology, Bangladesh Assn. for Advancement Scis., Am. Geriatric Soc., Am. Soc. for Clin. Investigation, Assn. Am. Physicians. Moslem. Home: 1300 Hollins Ln Baltimore MD 21209-2237 Office: Johns Hopkins Geriatrics Ctr 5505 Hopkins Bayview Cir Baltimore MD 21224-6822 E-mail: wgreenou@hotmail.com. *"Assuredly The Creation of The Heavens And The earth Is a greater matter Than The creation of man: Yet most men understand not."*

GREENOUGH, WILLIAM TALLANT, psychobiologist, educator; b. Seattle, Oct. 11, 1944; s. Harrison and Maryon C. (Whitten) G.; 1 dau., Jennifer Anne. BA, U. Oreg., 1964; MA, UCLA, 1966, PhD, 1969. Instr. U. Ill., Urbana-Champaign, 1968-69, asst. prof., 1969-73, assoc. prof., 1973-77, chair neural and behavioral biology program, 1977-87, prof. psychology, psychiatry, cell and structural biology, 1978—; assoc. dir. Beckman Inst. for Advanced Sci. and Tech., 1987-91; prof. U. Ill. Ctr. Advanced Study, 1997—, Swanlund prof. psychology, psychiatry, cell biology, bioeng., 1998—; dir. neurosci. program U. Ill., 1999—2001, dir. Ctr. Advanced Study, 2000—. Vis. prof. psychobiology U. Calif., Irvine, 1972; vis. prof. psychology U. Wash., 1975-76; program chmn. Winter Conf. on Brain Rsch., 1984-85, conf. chair, 1994-95; panel mem. integrative neural sys. NSF, 1987-91; dir. NSF Ctr. of Neurobiology of Learning and Memory, 1989-94; v.p., exec. com. Forum on Rsch. Mgmt., Fed. Behavioral, Psychol. and Cognitive Sci., 1991-93; mem. sci. adv. bd. Am. Psychol. Assn. Sci. Directorate; mem. NSF Biol. Sci. Directorate Adv. Com. Editor: (with R.N. Walsh) Environments as Therapy for Brain Dysfunction, 1976, (with J.M. Juraska) Developmental Neuropsychobiology, 1987; co-editor jour. Neurobiol. Learning and Memory, 1984—; contbr. numerous articles to profl. jour. Recipient William Rosen award for rsch. Nat. Fragile X Found., 1998; Cattell Found. fellow, 1975-76; USPHS and NSF grantee, 1969— ; U. Ill. sr. scholar, 1985-88. Fellow AAAS (chair sect. I, Psychology 2001-02), Soc. for Rsch. into child dev. (SRCD) disting. Sci. contrib. award, 2003; APA (Disting. Sci. Contbn. award 1999), Am. Psychol. Soc. (William James Fellow award, 1998), Soc. Exptl. Psychology; mem. NAS, Soc. Neurosci. (councilor 1990-94, treas.-elect 2003), Soc. Devel. Neurosci., Soc. Devel. Psychobiology (bd. dir. 1977-80), Sigma Xi. Achievements include rsch. interests in morphological plasticity of cerebellum, experience and learning-based synapse formation, molecular mechanisms of mental retardation, and plasticity of glial cells. Home: 1919 Melrose Dr Apt C Champaign IL 61820-2013 Office: U Ill Beckman Inst 405 N Mathews Ave Urbana IL 61801-2325 E-mail: wgreenou@psych.uiuc.edu.

GREENSPAHN, BRUCE ROBERT, cardiologist; b. Chgo., Apr. 13, 1949; s. Irwin and Lorna Greenspahn; m. Gail Ann Goldenberg, June 18, 1972; children: Scott, Geoffrey, Rory, Deena. BS, U. Ill., 1971; MD, U. Ill., Chgo., 1975. Diplomate internal medicine, cardiovasc. disease, interventional cardiology. Med. resident U. Ill., Chgo., 1975—78, chief med. resident, 1978—79; fellow cardiology U. Chgo., 1979—81, clin. asst. prof., 1981 95; assoc. dir. Cardiac Cath Lab Luth. Gen. Hosp., Park Ridge, Ill., 1985—; pres. The Ctr. for Advanced Cardiology, Park Ridge, 1986—. Fellow: Soc. for Cardiac Angiography and Intervention (angioplasty com. 1992—2003), Am. Coll. Cardiology (chmn. rapid response team, Govs. Commendation award 2000). Office: The Ctr for Advanced Cardiology 1875 W Dempster Park Ridge IL 60068

GREENSPAN, ALAN, central banker, economist; b. N.Y.C., Mar. 6, 1926; s. Herman Herbert Greenspan and Rose Goldsmith. BS summa cum laude, NYU, 1948, MA, 1950, PhD, 1977; hon. (hon.), Harvard, Yale, Notre Dame, Wake Forest, Colgate U. Pres., CEO Townsend-Greenspan and Co., Inc., N.Y.C., 1954-74, 77-87; cons. Council Econ. Advisers, 1970-74, chmn., 1974-77; cons. Congressional Budget Office, 1977-87; mem. Pres.'s Econ. Policy Adv. Bd., 1981-87; chmn. Nat. Commn. on Social Security Reform, 1981-83; mem. Task Force on Econ. Growth, 1969, Pres.'s Fgn. Intelligence Adv. Bd., 1983-85; commn. on an All-Vol. Armed Force, 1969-70; commn. on Fin. Structure and Regulation, 1970-71; sr. adviser panel on econ. activity Brookings Instn., 1970-74, 77-87; corp. dir. Aluminum Co. of Am., Automatic Data Processing, Inc., Capital Cities/ABC, Inc., General Foods, Inc., J.P. Morgan & Co., Inc., Morgan Guarant Trust Co. of N.Y., Mobil Corp., The Pittston Co.; chmn. bd. govs. Fed. Res. System, 1987—. Mem. bd. economists Time mag., 1971-74, 77-87. Bd. overseers Hoover Instn. on War, Revolution and Peace, 1973-74, 77-87. Decorated comdr. Legion of Honor, France; named Hon. Knight Comdr. of Brit. Empire, 2002; recipient John P. Madden medal, 1975, Pub. Svc. Achievement award, 1976, William Butler Meml. award, 1977. Fellow: Am. Statis. Assn., Nat. Assn. Bus. Economists (past pres.); mem.: Econ. Club of NY (vice chmn., trustee), Harmonie Club, Hillcrest Country Club. Office: Federal Reserve System Office of Chmn 20th & C St NW Washington DC 20551-0001

GREENSPAN, DANIEL S. molecular biologist, educator; b. Jersey City, Aug. 31, 1951; s. Aaron and Doris Greenspan; m. Leslie Herman, June 27, 1999; 1 child, Ilana Rina. BA, NYU, 1974, MS, 1978, PhD, 1981. Postdoctoral fellow dept. human genetics Yale U., New Haven, 1981-84, rsch. scientist, mem. faculty, 1984-86; asst. prof. pathology and lab. medicine U. Wis., Madison, 1986-92, assoc. prof., 1992-97, prof., 1997—, vice chair for rsch., 2003—, mem. Comprehensive Cancer Ctr., 1996—, mem. Cardiovascular Ctr., 1999—, vice chair rsch., 2003—. Affiliate Waisman Ctr. for Human Devel. and Devel. Disabilities, 2003—. Contbr. articles to profl. jours. Arthritis Found. fellow, 1984-87; prin. investigator NIH. Mem. Am. Soc. Biochemistry and Molecular Biology, Am. Soc. Microbiology, Am. Soc. Human Genetics, N.Y. Acad. Scis., Sigma Xi. Office: U Wis Dept Pathology 1300 University Ave Madison WI 53706-1509

GREENSPAN, DEBORAH, dental educator; 2nd BDS, U. London, 1960, BDS, 1964, DSc, 1991; fellow in Dental Surgery (hon.), Royal Coll. Surgeons, Edinburgh, 1994; LDS, Royal Coll. Surgeons, Eng., 1964; ScD (hon.), Georgetown U., 1990. Registered dental practioner, U.K.; diplomate Am. Bd. Oral Medicine. Vis. lectr. oral medicine U. Calif., San Francisco, 1976-83, asst. clin. prof., 1983-85, assoc. clin. prof., 1985-89, clin. prof., 1989-96, prof. clin. oral medicine, 1996—. Lectr. in oral biology, U. Calif., San Francisco, 1972, clin. dir. Oral AIDS Ctr., 1987—, active Sch. Dentistry coms. including admissions com., 1985—, chair task force on infection control, 1987—; cons. Joint FDI/WHO Working Group on AIDS, 1989—, EEC, 1990, WHO, 1990, 91, Dept. Health State Calif., 1991, others; ad hoc reviews Epidemiology and Disease Control Sect. Div. Rsch. Grants NIH, 1987—; mem. programs adv. com. Nat. Inst. Dental Rsch., 1989—, mem. spl. ad hoc tech. rev. panel, 1991, mem. panel Fed. Drug Adminstrn., 1991-94; other svc. to govtl. agys.; participant numerous sci. and profl. workshops, meetings, and continuing edn. courses, numerous radio, TV, and press interviews concerning AIDS and infection control in dentistry. Author: (with J.S. Greenspan, Pindborg, and Schiødt), AIDS and the Dental Team, 1986 (transl. German, French, Italian, Spanish, Japanese), AIDS and the Mouth, 1990, (with others) San Francisco General Hospital AIDS Knowledge Base, 1986, Dermatologic Clinics, 5th edit., 1987, Infectious Disease Clinics of North America, 2nd. edit., 1988, Oral Manifestations of AIDS, 1988, Contemporary Periodontics, 1989, Opportunistic Infections in AIDS Patients, 1990, AIDS Clinical Review, 1990, Oral Manifestations of Systemic Disease, 1990, others; mem. editl. bd. rev. Jour. Am. Coll. Dentists, 1991; mem. editl. bd. Oral Diseases, 1999; ad hoc referee Jour. Oral Pathology, 1983—, Cancer, 1985—, Jour. Acad. Gen. Dentistry, 1986—, European Jour. Cancer & Clin. Oncology, 1986, Archives of Dermatology, 1988—, Jour. AMA, 1988—, AIDS, 1991; contbr. numerous articles to profl. jours. Mem. dental subcom. of profl. edn. com. Calif. div. Am. Cancer Soc., 1982-90, profl. health care providers task force, 1991. Nat. Cancer Inst. fellow, 1978-79, Am. Coll. Dentists fellow, 1988; recipient Woman of Distinction award, London, 1986, Commendation cert. Asst. Sec. for Health, 1989; named Seymour J. Kreshover lectr. Nat. Inst. Dental Rsch., 1989, Hon. Lectr. United Med. and Dental Schs. of Guys and St. Thomas Hosps., U. London, 1991. Fellow AAAS, Royal Soc. Medicine, Royal Coll. Surgeons; mem. ADA (vis. lectr. speaker's bur. 1988—, cons. coun. on dental therapeutics 1988—, mem. coun. sci. affairs 1999—), Am. Assn. Dental Rsch. (session chair 1986-87, constitution com. 1988-91, chair 1990-91, pres. San Francisco sect. 1990—, treas. 1992—), Am. Acad. Oral Pathology, Am. Soc. Microbiology, Am. Assn. Women Dentists, Am. Acad. Oral Medicine, Am. Assn. Dental Schs., Internat. Assn. Dental Rsch. (pres. exptl. pathology group 1989-90, other coms. and offices), Internat. Assn. Oral Pathologists, Calif. Dental Assn., San Francisco Dental Soc., Internat. AIDS Soc., Inst. of Medicine. Achievements include rsch. on oral candidiasis in HIV infection, on HIV-associated salivary gland disease, on oral hairy leukoplakia, and on the prevalence of HIV-associated gingivitis and periodontitis in HIV-infected patients. Office: U Calif Sch Dentistry Dept Stomatology S 612 513 Parnassus Ave Box 0422 San Francisco CA 94143-0422

GREENSPAN, DONALD, mathematician, educator; b. N.Y.C., Jan. 24, 1928; BS, NYU, 1948; MS, U. Wis., 1949; PhD, U. Md., 1956. Instr. U. Md., 1948-56; research engr. Hughes Aircraft Co., 1956-57; asst. prof. Purdue U., 1957-61, asso. prof., 1961-62; permanent mem. U. Wis. Math. Research Center, Madison, 1962-68; prof. computer scis., cons. to U. Wis. Computing Center, 1965-78; prof. math. U. Tex., 1978—. Lectr. Am. Math. Assn., 1963-64, U. Mich. Summer Conf., 1964; referee NRC, NSF. Author: Theory and Solution of Ordinary Differential Equations, 1960, Introduction to Partial Differential Equations, 1961, 2d edit., 2000, Introductory Numerical Analysis of Elliptic Boundary Value Problems, 1965, Introduction to Calculus, 1968, Lectures on the Numerical Solutions of Linear, Singular, and Nonlinear Differential Equations, 1968, Introduction to Numerical Analysis and Application, 1970, Discrete Models, 1973, Discrete Numerical Methods in Physics and Engineering, 1974, Arithmetic Applied Mathematics, 1980, Computer-Oriented Mathematical Physics, 1981, (with U. Bulgarelli and V. Casulli) Pressure Methods for the Numerical Solution of Free Surface Fluid Flow, 1984, (with V. Casulli) Numerical Analysis for Applied Mathematics, Science and Engineering, 1988, Quasimolecular Modelling, 1991, Particle Modeling, 1997, A Science Handbook for Musicians, Entrepreneurs and Candidates for Public Office, 2002; editor: Numerical Solutions of Nonlinear Differential Equations, 1966, (with Pal Rosza) Numerical Methods, 1988, 2d rev. edit., 1991; editl. bd. Jour. Computers and Math. with Applications, Systems Analysis-Modelling-Simulation, CDC Handbook of Fluid Dynamics; contbr. articles to profl. jours. Active Common Cause, NAACP. Mem. ACLU, Am. Math. Soc., Am. Phys. Soc., Assn. Computing Machinery, Ams. for Dem. Action. Office: U Tex Math Dept Arlington TX 76019-0001 E-mail: greenspan@uta.edu.

GREENSPAN, FRANCIS S. physician; b. Perth Amboy, N.J., Mar. 16, 1920; s. Philip and Francis (Davidson) G.; m. Bonnie Jean Fisher, Oct. 25, 1945; children: Richard L., Robert H., Susan L. BA, Cornell U., 1940, MD, 1943. Diplomate: Am. Bd. Internal Medicine. Mem. endocrinology staff U. Calif.-San Francisco; chief endocrinology Stanford (Calif.) Hosp., 1949-59; chief thyroid clinic U. Calif. Med. Ctr., San Francisco, 1959—; practice medicine specializing in endocrinology San Francisco; now clin. prof. medicine and radiology U. Calif. Med. Ctr.; chief staff U. Calif. Hosps. and Clinics, San Francisco, 1976-78. Editor: Textbook of Endocrinology; contbr. articles to med. jours. Served with USNR, 1944-45. Mem. San Francisco Med. Soc., Calif. Med. Assn., AMA, Endocrine Soc., Am. Thyroid Assn., Western Soc. Clin. Research, Western Assn. Physicians, Calif. Acad. Medicine. Office: U Calif Med Ctr 350 Parnassus Ave Ste 609 San Francisco CA 94117-3608

GREENSPAN, HARVEY PHILIP, applied mathematician, educator; b. N.Y.C., Feb. 22, 1933; s. Louis and Jessie (Scholnick) G.; m. Mirian Gordon, Sept. 6, 1953; children— Elizabeth, Judith. BS, CCNY, 1953; MS, Harvard U., 1954, PhD, 1956; D Tech. (hon.), Royal Inst. Tech., Stockholm, 1991. Asst. prof. applied math. Harvard, 1957-60; faculty MIT, Cambridge, 1960—, prof. applied math., 1964—2002, prof. emeritus, 2002—. Author: Theory of Rotating Fluids, 1968, Calculus: An Introduction to Applied Mathematics, 1973; editor: Studies in Applied Mathematics, 1969; patentee centrifugal spectrometer. Home: 15 Chatham Cir Brookline MA 02446-5410 Office: Mass Inst Tech 77 Massachusetts Ave Cambridge MA 02139-4301 E-mail: hpg@math.mit.edu.

GREENSPAN, JAY SCOTT See ALEXANDER, JASON

GREENSPAN, JEFFREY DOV, lawyer; b. Chgo., July 19, 1954; s. Philip and Sylvia (Haberman) G.; m. Eleanor Helen Goldman, Aug. 28, 1983. BS in Econs., U. Ill., Urbana, 1976; JD, Ill. Inst. Tech., 1979. Bar: Ill. 1979, U.S. Dist. Ct. (no. dist.) Ill. 1979, U.S. Ct. Appeals (7th cir.) 1979. Atty. Govs. Office Consumer Services, Chgo., 1978-80; asst. pub. defender Cook County Pub. Defenders Office, Chgo., 1980-81; asst. corp. counsel Village of Skokie, Chgo., 1981-91; of counsel Fioretti & Des Jardins, Chgo., 1990-91; with Ancel, Glink, Diamond, Cope & Bush, P.C., Chgo., 1991-99, Fioretti & Des Jardins, Chgo., 1999-2001; gen. counsel, dir. land acquisition CorLands, Chgo., 2001—. Sec., treas. Polit. Cons., Inc., Skokie, 1984—. Author polit. computer software Master Campaigner, 1984. Mem. Niles (Ill.) Twp. Dem. Orgn., 1976—; chmn. Niles Twp. Com. on Youth, 1982-85, TRY-Citizens for Drug Awareness, Niles, 1983-84; mem. Centereast Bd. Authority, 1998—; bd. dirs. Niles Twp. H.S., 1999—. Mem. Chgo. Bar Assn. (chmn. devel. of law com. 1990-91, chmn. local govt. law com. 1992-93). Home: 9445 Keeler Ave Skokie IL 60076-1442 Office: 25 E Washington St Ste 1650 Chicago IL 60602-1805 E-mail: jgreenspan@corlands.org.

GREENSPAN, LEON JOSEPH, lawyer; b. Phila., Feb. 10, 1932; s. Joseph and Minerva (Podolsky) G.; m. Irene Gordon, Nov. 2, 1958; children: Marjorie, David, Michael, Lisa. AB, Temple U., 1955, JD, 1958. Bar: N.Y. 1959, N.J. 1985, Fla. 1985, Pa. 1986, Conn. 1991, U.S. Tax Ct. 1973, U.S. Supreme Ct. 1969. Pvt. practice law, White Plains, N.Y., 1959-64; ptnr. Greenspan and Aurnou, White Plains, 1964-77, Greenspan, Jaffe & Rosenblatt, White Plains, 1987-91, Greenspan & Greenspan, White Plains, 1992—. Counsel Brown, Boston; lectr. Fla. Bar CLER Program, 1991, 92, 99; atty. Tarrytown (N.Y.) Housing Authority. Pres. Hebrew Inst., White Plains; vice chmn. ann. dinner NCCJ. Recipient Pres.'s award Union Orthodox Synagogues, 1982, Owl Club award Temple Univ., 2001; honoree Hebrew Inst., White Plains, 1983. Mem. ABA, N.J. Bar Assn., Fla. Bar Assn., Westchester County Bar Assn., White Plains Bar Assn., N.Y. State Trial Lawyers Assn., Criminal Cts. Bar Assn. Westchester County, N.J. Bar Assn. Home: 14 Pinebrook Dr White Plains NY 10605-4713 Office: Greenspan & Greenspan 150 Grand St 6th Fl White Plains NY 10601-4400

GREENSPAN, MICHAEL EVAN, lawyer; b. White Plains, N.Y., Jan. 18, 1967; s. Leon Joseph and Irene (Gordon) G.; m. Diane Gloria Blum, July 2, 1989; children: Daniel, Marc, Julia. BA magna cum laude, Temple U., 1988, JD, 1991. Bar: N.Y. 1992, U.S. Dist. Ct. (so. and ea. dists.) N.Y. 1992, U.S. Dist. Ct. Conn. 1992, U.S. Ct. Appeals (2d cir.) 1993, U.S. Ct. Appeals (11th cir.) 1996. Assoc. Greenspan, Jaffe & Rosenblatt, White Plains, 1991-92; ptnr. Greenspan & Greenspan, White Plains, 1992—. Mem. com. civil practice laws and rules State Bar N.Y.; Temple U. del. Symposium on the Presidency, Washington, 1987. Mem. exec. com. Loucks Track & Field Games, White Plains, 1991—. Recipient Lewis F. Powell Jr. medallion Am. Coll. Trial Lawyers Assn., 1991, James J. Manderino award Phila. Trial Lawyers Assn., 1991. Mem. ATLA, N.Y. Trial Lawyers Assn., Barristers Soc., N.Y. State Bar Assn., Westchester County Bar Assn., White Plains Bar Assn., Westchester Track and Field and Cross-Country Ofcls. Orgn., Golden Key, Order of Omega, Phi Beta Kappa, Pi Sigma Alpha, Phi Alpha Theta, Delta Tau Delta. Republican. Jewish. Avocations: officiating high school track and field, race walking, basketball. Office: Greenspan & Greenspan 150 Grand St White Plains NY 10601-4821 E-mail: GandGEsqs@aol.com.

GREENSPAN-MARGOLIS, JUNE E. psychiatrist; b. N.Y.C., June 28, 1934; d. Benjamin Robert and Theresa (Cooperstein) Edelman; divorced; 1 child, Alisa Greenspan; m. Gerald J. Margolis. AB, Bryn Mawr Coll., 1955; MD, Med. Coll. Pa., 1959; grad., Inst Phila Assn Psychoanalysis, Bala Cynwyd, 1975. Intern Albert Einstein Med. Ctr., Phila., 1959-60; pvt. practice medicine specializing in pediatrics Cinnaminson, N.J., 1961-67; psychiat. resident Hahnemann Med. Coll., Phila., 1967-71; practice medicine specializing in adult and child psychiatry, psychoanalysis Jenkintown, Pa., 1971—. Instr. U. Pa. Sch. Medicine, Phila., 1975—77, clin. assoc., 1977—81, clin. asst. prof., 1981—86, clin. assoc. prof., 1986—; tng. and supervisory analyst Phila. Ctr. for Psychoanalysis, Bala Cynwyd, Pa., 1986—. Fellow Am. Coll. Psychoanalysts, Am. Psychiat. Assn.; mem. AMA, Am. Psychoanalytic Assn. (cert. adult and child psychoanalysis), Am. Acad. Child Psychiatry, Ctr. for Advanced Psychoanalytic Studies (Princeton). Office: The Pavilion Ste 434 261 Old York Rd Jenkintown PA 19046

GREENSPON, ARNOLD JACK, cardiologist, cardiac electrophysiologist; b. Phila., July 8, 1949; s. Samuel E. and Harriet (Kalos) G.; m. Patricia Lynn Kapps, Dec. 18, 1977; children: Dana Ashley, Brian Bradley. BA, Johns Hopkins U., 1971; MD, U. Pa., 1975. Diplomate Am. Bd. Internal Medicine, Am. Bd. Cardiovascular Disease, Am. Bd. Cardiac Electrophysiology. Resident in internal medicine Wayne State U., Detroit, 1975-78; fellow cardiology Ohio State U., Columbus, 1978-80; asst. prof. medicine Thomas Jefferson U., Phila., 1980-86, dir. cardiac electrophysiology, 1980—, assoc. prof. medicine, 1986-92, clin. prof. medicine, 1992—, dir. cardiology tng. program, 1984—, assoc. dir. divsn. cardiology, 1995—. Editor: Contemporary Management of Ventricular Arrhythmias, 1992; contbr. articles to profl. jours. Fellow Am. Coll. Cardiology, Am. Coll. Physicians; mem. N.Am. Soc. Pacing and Electrophysiology, Phi Beta Kappa. Jewish. Achievements include patent in method and apparatus for high frequency catheter ablation. Office: Jefferson Med Coll 925 Chestnut St Mezzanine Philadelphia PA 19107-5001

GREENSPON, BURTON EDWARD, lawyer; b. Hartford, Conn., Dec. 9, 1946; s. Bernard and Anne (Mitnick) G.; m. Donna Carol Wallins, June 4, 1971; children— Amy Susan, Marc Jeffrey. B.A. with honors, U. Conn., 1969; J.D., U. Va., 1972. Bar: Conn. 1972, U.S. Dist. Ct. Conn. 1974, N.Y. 1980. Sole practice, Hartford, 1973-74; asst. house counsel Sanitas Service Corp., Bethany, Conn., 1974-75; counsel Delaware North Cos., Inc., Buffalo, 1976-82, asst. gen. counsel, 1982-86; v.p., gen. counsel Synder Corp., 1986—; guest lectr. dept. communications SUNY-Buffalo, summer 1981. Mem. communal services commn. Jewish Fedn. Buffalo, 1983-85, mem. planning and allocation com. and young men's cabinet, 1985-86. Served to capt. USAR, 1972-79. Mem. Niagara Frontier Corp. Counsel Assn., Alpha Epsilon Pi, Phi Alpha Delta. Home: 419 Wood Acres Dr East Amherst NY 14051-1669 Office: Snyder Corp 6 Fountain Plz # Plazalv Buffalo NY 14202-2211

GREENSPON, ROBERT ALAN, lawyer; b. Hartford, Conn., Apr. 17, 1947; s. George Arthur and Shirley Jean (Shelton) G.; m. Claire Alice Stone, Aug. 21, 1971; children: Colin Haynes, Alison Shelton. AB, Franklin and Marshall, 1969; JD, Columbia U., 1972. Bar: Conn. 1973, N.Y. 1998, U.S. Dist. Conn. 1973, U.S. Ct. Appeals (2d cir.) 1983. Assoc. Robinson & Cole, Hartford, Conn., 1972-78, ptnr., 1978-81, Stamford, Conn., 1981-86; sr. v.p., gen. counsel Guinness Peat Aviation Corp., Stamford, N.Y.C., N.Y.C., Shannon, Ireland, 1985-92; ptnr. Latham & Watkins, N.Y.C., 1992—. Contbr. articles to profl. jours. Mem. ABA (comml. fin. services, aircraft fin.), Conn. Bar Assn., N.Y. State Bar Assn., Internat. Bar Assn., Southwestern Legal Found. (bd. advisors internat. and comparative law ctr.). Home: 49 Old Farm Rd Darien CT 06820-6119 Office: Latham & Watkins 885 3rd Ave Fl 10 New York NY 10022-4834

GREENSPOON, IRMA NAIMAN, business executive; b. Washington, Oct. 18, 1920; d. Harry H. and Ada Marie (Himmelfarb) Naiman; m. Benjamin Greenspoon, July 10, 1960; children: Laurence, Julie. AB, George Washington U., 1942. Lic. tour guide, Washington, 1970-84; pres., CEO Guide Svc. of Washington, 1984-89. Bd. dirs. Washington Conv. and Visitors Assn., 1984-89, Am. Diabetes Assn., Washington, 1966-80; pres. Park View Citizens Assn., Chevy Chase, Md., 1986; Juvenile Ct. Com. Montgomery County, Md., 1999—. Democrat. Jewish. Home: 3223 Park View Rd Chevy Chase MD 20815-5643 E-mail: birma01@comcast.net.

GREENSTEIN, ABRAHAM JACOB, mortgage company executive, accountant; b. Munich, Fed. Republic of Germany, May 5, 1949; came to U.S., 1950; s. Morris and Bella (Yeger) G.; m. Ruth Sanik, June 5, 1974; children: Pinchus, Yisroel, Shlomo. BS in Acctg., Bklyn. Coll., 1972. Sr. auditor State Comptrollers Office, N.Y.C., 1972-75; asst. dir. Office of Spl. Dep. Comptroller, N.Y.C., 1978-82; sr. v.p. fin. N.Y.C. Housing Devel. Corp., 1983-88, exec. v.p., 1988-98. Treas. Housing Assistance Corp., N.Y.C., 1985-98, Residential Mortgage Ins. Co., N.Y.C., 1993-98; exec. v.p., chief oper. officer Housing for N.Y. Corp., N.Y.C., 1986-93, pres., 1993-98; v.p. Greystone & Co., N.Y.C., 1998—. Trustee Congregation Chasdi Gur, Bklyn., 1982-87 Mem. Am. Mgmt. Assn., Govt. Fin. Officers Assn., Council of State Housing Agys., Mortgage Bankers Assn. Jewish. Avocations: swimming, tennis. Office: Greystone & Co 60th Fl 152 W 57th St Fl 60 New York NY 10019-3310

GREENSTEIN, FRED IRWIN, political science educator; b. N.Y.C., Sept. 1, 1930; s. Arthur Aaron and Rose (Goldstein) G.; m. Barbara Elferink, July 14, 1957; children: Michael, Amy, Jessica. BA, Antioch Coll., 1953; MA, Yale U., 1956, PhD, 1960. Instr. Yale U., New Haven, 1959-62, vis. prof., 1965-68; mem. faculty Wesleyan U., Middletown, Conn., 1963-73, prof. polit. sci., 1966-73; Henry Luce prof. politics, law and society Princeton U., 1973-81, prof. politics, 1973—2000, prof. emeritus, 2000—. Vis. prof. U. Essex, Eng., 1968-69, 91. Author: The American Party System and the American People, 1970, Children and Politics, 2d edit., 1969, Personality and Politics, 2d edit., 1975; co-author: (with R.E. Lane and J.D. Barber) Introduction to Political Analysis, 2 edit., 1965, (with M. Lerner) A Source Book for the Study of Personality and Politics, 1971, (with N.W. Polsby) The Handbook of Political Science, 8 vols., (with R. Wolfinger and M. Shapiro) Dynamics and American Politics, 1976, (with L. Berman and A. Felzenberg) The Evolution of the Modern Presidency: A Bibliographical Review, 1977; author: The Hidden-Hand Presidency: Eisenhower as Leader, 1982, The Reagan Presidency: An Early Appraisal, 1983, Leadership in the Modern Presidency, 1988, How Presidents Test Reality: Decisions on Vietnam, 1954 and 1965, 1989, The Presidential Difference: Leadership Style from FDR to Clinton, 2000. Served with AUS, 1953-55. Fellow Ctr. Advanced Study Behavioral Scis., 1964-65; NSF sr. postdoctoral fellow, 1968-69 Fellow Am. Acad. Arts And Scis.; mem. Am. Polit. Sci. Assn. (editorial bd. 1968-72, sec. 1976-77), Internat. Soc. Polit. Psychology (pres. 1996-97). Home: 340 Jefferson Rd Princeton NJ 08540-3475 Office: Princeton Univ Dept Politics Princeton NJ 08544-0001

GREENSTEIN, GARY, periodontist, dental educator; b. Nyc, Ny, Feb. 2, 1947; s. Sidney and Anne Greenstein; m. Helene Cohen, Nov. 13, 1951; children: Benjamin, Jaclyn;1 child, Michele Gold. BA, Queens Coll., New York City, 1964—68; DDS, NYU Coll. of Dentistry, New York City, 1968—72; Periodontal Certification, Eastman Dental Ctr., Rochester, New York, 1978—80; MS, U. of Rochester, Rochester, New York, 1980—81. Periodontal Certification Eastman Dental Ctr., 1980, Board Diplomate Am. Acad. of Periodontology, 1993. Clin. prof., periodontology UMDNJ, Dept. of Periodontology, Newark, 1993—; pvt. practice Dr. Gary Greenstein, Freehold, NJ, 1983—; chief of periodontics Monmouth Med. Ctr., Long Branch, NJ, 1990—97. Cons. US Army Dental Corp, Ft. Gordon, Ga., 1988—; trustee Am. Acad. of Periodontology, Chgo., 1993—99, sci., rsch. and therapy com., 1992—2002. Author: (contributions to periodontal literature) 95 Publications, Jour. of Periodontology, Jour. of Am. Dental Assoc., Compendium of Continuing Ed. in Dentistry, Internat. Jour. of Restorative Dentistry and Periodontics. Maj. US Army, 1972—78, Kans., South Korea, New Jersey. Decorated Cert. of Achievement for Meritorious Svc. US Army, Army Commendation Medal; recipient Gies Award, Am. Acad. of Periodontology, 1997, Fellowship Award, 2000, Hirschfeld Meml. Award, NE Soc. of Periodontists, 2000. Mem.: NJ. Soc. of Periodontists (licentiate), NE Soc. of Periodontists (licentiate), ADA (licentiate), Am. Acad. of Periodontology (licentiate; trustee 1993—99). R-Consevative. Jewish. Achievements include research in Periodontal Therapy; Over 100 Guest Lectures. Avocations: tennis, rafting, mountain biking. Office: Dr Gary Greenstein 900 West Main Street Freehold NJ 07728 Office Fax: 732 700 7790. Personal E-mail: ggperio@aol.com.

GREENSTEIN, JEFFREY IAN, neurologist; b. Durban, South Africa, July 27, 1947; s. Joseph and Miriam (Shamos) G. MD, U. Cape Town, S. Africa, 1971. Diplomate Am. Bd. Neurology and Psychiatry. Asst. to assoc. prof. neurology Temple U. Sch. Med., Phila., 1983-89, prof., 1989—2002, chmn. neurology, 1989—2000; pres. Multiple Sclerosis Inst., 2002—. Mem. AAAS, Am. Acad. Neurology, N.Y. Acad. Sci., Nat. Multiple Sclerosis Soc. (chmn. profl. adv. com. Phila. 1992-95, bd. of trustees, Del. Valley Chpt. 1996-). Office: Multiple Sclerosis Inst 1740 South St Ste 401 Philadelphia PA 19146-2246

GREENSTEIN, LINDA R. assemblywoman; b. June 7, 1950; BA in Psychology, Vassar Coll.; MA in Psychology, Johns Hopkins U.; JD in Law, Georgetown U. Assemblywoman N.J. Gen. Assembly, 2000—; asst. majority leader, 2002—. Mem. West Windsor-Plainsboro Reg. Bd. of Edn., 1992—94, Plainsboro Twp. Com., 1995—2000. Democrat. Office: 7 Ctr Dr Ste 2 Monroe NJ 08831-1565 Fax: 609-395-9032. E-mail: AswGreenstein@njleg.org.*

GREENSTEIN, MERLE EDWARD, import and export company executive; b. Portland, Oreg., June 22, 1937; s. Sol and Tillie Germaine (Schnitzer) G.; m. Nasi Jenab; children: Todd Aaron, Boback Emad, Lela Emad. BA, Reed Coll., 1959. Pres. Acme Trading and Supply Co., Portland, 1963-82; chmn. MMI Group, Portland, 1982-91, Internat. Devel. Assocs., Portland, 1991—. Com. mem. ISRI, Washington, 1987-89; mem. dist. export coun. U.S. Dept. Commerce, 1980—, mem. first USA trade Missions to Vietnam, 1996; mem. Ariz. regional export coun. Trade Mission to Ea. Europe. Chmn. fin. Portland Opera, 1966, Anne Frank exhibit, Portland, Anne Frank Exhibit Return, 2001, Oreg. Holocaust Mem.; bd. dirs. Met. YMCA, 1964-67, Metro. Family Svc., Jewish Welfare Fedn., Oreg. Youth Leadership Sem.; del. to China, State of Oreg. Ofcl. Trade Mission, 1979; chmn. Western Internat. Trade Group, 1981-82; mem. State of Oreg. Korea Commn., 1985-90, State of Oreg. Internat. Trade Adv. Com.; joint chmn. bldg. campaign Oreg. Mus. Sci. and Industry; bd. dirs. Waverly Children's Home; mem. Food Bank Relocation Com.; property task force com. Oreg. Food Bank, capital campaign cabinet; treas. AJC; active Oreg. Mentoring Group; devel. com. Alzheimer's Assn. Oreg., Oreg. Uniting Group Discussions; joint chmn. State of Oreg. YMCA Youth Legislature; mem. coll. scholarship com. IPAO; mem. Oreg. Uniting Group Discussions. Recipient President's E for Export, U.S. Dept. Commerce, 1969; named Citizen of the Week, City of Portland, 1953. Mem. Rolls Royce Owners Club (London), Multnomah Athletic Club Portland, City Club, Masons, Shriners. Avocations: skiing, antique autos, Arabian horses. Office: Internat Devel Assocs 6731 NE 47th Ave Portland OR 97218-1205 E-mail: merlenasi@yahoo.com.

GREENSTEIN, RICHARD HENRY, lawyer; b. Newark, June 29, 1946; s. Jacob Harold and Florence G.; m. Irene Beth Polishuk, July 4, 1973; children: Suzanne Beth, Jonathan Henry. AB, Rutgers Coll., 1968; JD, Boston U., 1971. Bar: N.J. 1971, U.S. Dist. Ct. N.J. 1971, U.S. Supreme Ct. 1985. Law clk. Superior Ct. N.J., Elizabeth, 1971-72; asst. county prosecutor Union County Prosecutor, Elizabeth, 1972-74; assoc. atty. Mandel, Wysoker, Sherman, et al, Perth Amboy, N.J., 1974-77, Fox and Fox, Newark, 1977-83; ptnr. Kein, Pollatschek & Greenstein, Union, N.J., 1983—. Atty. Young Astronauts N.J. Inc., 1989—; mem. ethics com. Supreme Ct. Dist. N.J., 1991-95. Lighting dir. Wash. Sch. PTA Show, Westfield, N.J., 1985-94. Mem. Exchange Club Union (pres.-elect, dir. 1983—). Jewish. Avocations: skiing, hiking, reading. Home: 743 Saint Marks Ave Westfield NJ 07090-2035 Office: Kein Pollatschek & Greenstein 2042 Morris Ave Union NJ 07083-6028

GREENSTEIN, ROBERT, retired radiologist; b. Phila., Jan. 1, 1933; s. Abraham Greenstein; m. Maxine Trushinsky, July 20, 1959; children: David, Amy Greenstein Baynash, Daniel S., Joshua K. MD, Temple U., 1957. Intern Michael Reese Hosp., Chgo., 1957-58, resident in radiology, 1958-60, 62-63; radiol. assoc. St. Francis Hosp., Evanston, Ill., 1966, Weiss Meml. Hosp., Chgo., 1965-66, Bklyn. Jewish Hosp., 1963-65; clin. prof. radiology SUNY, Bklyn., 1993; chief radiology USMC MacDonald Army Hosp., Ft. Eustis, Va.; clin. asst. prof. radiology U. Ill. Coll. Medicine, 1993—2001, ret., 2001; clin. instr. radiology Stritch Sch. Medicine, Loyola U., 1966-93. Clin. prof. radiology Chgo. Coll. Osteo. Medicine. Fellow Am. Coll. Radiologists (cert.); mem. AMA, Am. Inst. Ultrasound Medicine, Am. Roentgen Ray Soc., Radiol. Soc. N.Am., SRU, Alpha Omega Alpha.

GREENSTEIN, RUTH LOUISE, research institute executive, lawyer; b. N.Y.C., Mar. 28, 1946; d. Milton and Beatrice (Zutty) G.; m. David Seidman, May 19, 1972. BA, Harvard U., 1966; MA, Yale U., 1968; JD, George Washington U., 1980. Bar: D.C. 1980. Fgn. service info. officer USIA, Washington and Tehran, Iran, 1968-70; adminstrv. asst. Export-Import Bank U.S., Washington, 1971-72; asst. dean Woodrow Wilson Sch. Pub. and Internat. Affairs, Princeton U., 1972-75; budget examiner U.S. Office Mgmt. and Budget, Washington, 1975-79; budget coordinator U.S. Internat. Devel. Coop. Agy., 1979-81; dep. gen. counsel NSF, 1981-84; treas., then v.p. and gen. counsel Genex Corp., Gaithersburg, Md., 1984-90; v.p. fin. and adminstrn., gen. counsel Inst. for Def. Analyses, Alexandria, Va., 1990—. Mem. acad. adv. panel to tech. transfer intelligence com. CIA, 1983-90; mem. def. trade adv. group U.S. Dept. State, 1994-96; mem. com. for protection of human subjects ARC, 1996—; dir. VSA arts, 1998—, PLATO Learning Inc., 2002--. Mem. NAS (panel on future design and implementation of nat. security export controls 1989-91), AAAS (com. on sci. freedom and responsibility 1987-93), D.C. Bar Assn. Home: 2737 Devonshire Pl NW Apt 511 Washington DC 20008-3458 Office: Inst for Def Analyses 4850 Mark Center Dr Alexandria VA 22311-1882 E-mail: rgreenst@ida.org.

GREENWALD, ALFRED EMANUEL, retired cosmetic surgeon; b. New Brunswick, N.J., Feb. 25, 1920; s. Louis and Ethel (Weiss) G.; m. Leatrice Joy Fleishman, June 15, 1947 (div. June 1995); children: Melvin Alan, Bryna Jane. Student, George Washington U., 1938-40; BA, NYU, 1942, MS in Chemistry, 1943; MD, N.Y. Med. Coll., 1947, postgrad., 1950-51. Diplomate Am. Bd. Surgery, Am. Bd. Cosmetic Surgery, Nat. Bd. Med. Examiners. Rotating intern Newark Beth Israel Hosp., NJ, 1947-48; surg. intern Flower and Fifth Avenue

Hosps., N.Y.C., 1948-49; resident in surgery Hackensack (N.J.) Hosp., 1949-50, Martland Med. Ctr.-Univ. Hosp., Newark, 1951-54; gen. practice medicine Hackensack, 1950-51; pvt. practice surgery, Paramus, N.J., 1954, New Brunswick, N.J., 1957-92; ret., 1992. Examining physician 1 N.Y. State Workers' Compensation Bd., Bklyn., 1994-95; former staff mem. Middlesex Same Day Surg. Ctr., Robert Wood Johnson Univ. Hosp., St. Peter's Univ. Hosp., Meml. Med. Ctr. South Amboy, N.J., Surgicare Ctrl. Jersey. Author: The Aging Face, 1985; contbr. articles to med. jours. Capt. M.C., U.S. Army, 1955-57. Mem. AMA, Am. Assn. Cosmetic Surgeons, Am. Soc. Cosmetic Surgeons, Am. Acad. Cosmetic Surgery, Pan Am. Med. Assn., Internat. Coll. Surgeons, Internat. Soc. Cosmetic, Plastic and Reconstructive Surgery, Internat. Acad. Cosmetic Surgery, French Soc. Esthetic Surgery, Med. Soc. N.J., N.J. Soc. Cosmetic Surgery, Phila. Soc. Facial Plastic Surgeons, Middlesex County Med. Soc., Am. Physicians Fellowship for Israel Med. Assn., Med. Amateur Radio Coun. (founder 1965, treas. 1986-00, conf. chmn. 1984), Princeton Personal Computer Users Group. Jewish. Achievements include pioneer work on high cheek bones, malar augmentation and the lip lift cheilopexy for cheiloptosis. Home: Ten Llewellyn Pl New Brunswick NJ 08901-3027 E-mail: ALFREDGR@aol.com.

GREENWALD, ANDREW ERIC, lawyer; b. N.Y.C., May 31, 1942; s. Harold and Lillian G.; m. Paula S., Aug. 20, 1967; children: Brooke Ellen, Karen Michelle. BS, U. Wis., 1964; JD, Georgetown U., 1967. Bar: D.C. 1968, Md. 1969, U.S. Ct. Appeals Md. 1969. Lawyer Nat. Labor Rels. Bd., Washington, 1967-68; asst. corp. counsel D.C. Govt., 1968-69; shareholder Joseph, Greenwald & Laake PA, Greenbelt, Md., 1969—. Past mem. dept. family and cmty. devel. U. Md. Contbr. articles to profl. jours. Active adv. com. Georgetown U. Continuing Legal Edn., 1991, Georgetown U. Law Ctr. Alumni Bd., 1995. Mem. ATLA (chmn. tort sect. 1985), ABA, Nat. Inst. Trial Advocacy, Am. Bd. Profl. Liability Attys., Am. Bd. Trial Advocates, William B. Bryant Inn, Am. Inns of Ct. Office: Joseph Greenwald & Laake PA 6404 Ivy Ln Ste 400 Greenbelt MD 20770-1407

GREENWALD, BURTON JAY, investment company executive, financial consultant; b. N.Y.C., Dec. 6, 1929; s. Max and Nettie (Jay) G.; m. Geraldine Bernstein, May 26, 1957; children: Ileana, Melissa, Matthew. BS, U. Pa., 1951. Asst. to pres. A.J. Wood & Co., Phila., 1955-57; dir. pub. rels. Nat. Securities & Rsch. Corp., N.Y.C., 1957-61, v.p. dealer rels., 1961-71, v.p. mktg., 1971-81, pres. underwriting div., 1981-85; pres., dir. Merit Group Mutual Funds, Sav/Vest Securities Corp., 1986; exec. v.p. L.F. Rothschild Fund Mgmt. Inc., L.F. Rothschild Managed Trust, 1987-88; prin. B.J. Greenwald Assocs., Fin. Svc. Cons., Phila., 1988—. Bd. dirs. mut. series funds Nat. Securities & Rsch. Corp., Franklin Mutual Series Funds, FTI Group of Funds, Fiduciary Trust Global Fund, Fiduciary Emerging Markets Bond Fund PLC, Fiduciary Internat. Ireland Ltd.; pres. Nat. Securities Tax Exempt Bonds Inc., Calif. Tax Exempt Bonds, Inc.; bd. govs., chmn. pub. info. and edn. com. Investment Co. Inst., Washington, 1979-85. Trustee Franklin Managed Trust and Franklin Value Investors Trust. Lt. USNR, 1951-54. Lt. USNR, 1951—54. Mem. Chequessett Yacht and Country Club, Bnai B'rith. Jewish. Home and Office: 2009 Spruce St Philadelphia PA 19103-5623 E-mail: bgreenwald@aol.com.

GREENWALD, CAROL SCHIRO, professional services marketing research executive; b. Phila., Mar. 2, 1939; d. Sidney L. and Adele R. (Rosenheim) Schiro; children: David Bruce, William Michael. BA cum laude, Smith Coll., 1961; MA, Hunter Coll., 1965; PhD in Polit. Sci., CUNY, 1972. Instr. polit. sci. Queen's Coll., CUNY, 1970-73; asst. dir. Evaluation N.Y.C. Adminstrv. Decentralization Project, 1971-73; asst. prof. Richmond Coll., CUNY, 1973-76, Bklyn. Coll., CUNY, 1976-77; research assoc. Bunting Inst., Radcliffe Coll., 1977-79; project dir. Jobs in the 1980s Pub. Agenda Found., N.Y.C., 1979-81; assoc. dir. Grant Thornton acctg. firm, 1984-86; sr. mgr. Seidman and Seidman, 1986-87; market research mgr. KPMG Peat Marwick, 1988-90; cons., 1990-91, 2002—; mktg. dir. Haight, Gardner, Poor & Havens, 1991-92; dir. comm. Richard A. Eisner & Co., LLP, 1993-97; dir. mktg. Hamilton, HMC divsn. Kurt Salmon Assoc., 1997—, Whitman Breed Abbott & Morgan LLP, 1998-2000; cons. MarketForce, a divsn. of Hildebrandt, Internat., 2002; pvt. practice, 2002—. Author: Group Power: Lobbying and Public Policy, 1977; mem. editl. bd. Mktg. Rev., 1997—; contbr. articles on polit. sci. to profl. jours. Lilly Found. fellow Mem. Am. Mktg. Assn. (chair profl. devel. leadership coun. 1995—, mem. edtl. bd. 1996—), Common Cause (chmn. N.Y. 1981-83, nat. dir. 1978 81), Westchester Women in Comm. (treas. 1993-95). Home: 688 Forest Ave Larchmont NY 10538-1535 E-mail: greenwaldcarol@hotmail.com.

GREENWALD, EDWARD SAMUEL, physician; b. New Rochelle, N.Y., May 13, 1928; s. Irving and Belle Elizabeth (Jacobson) G.; m. Edith Deborah Aaronson, Dec. 4, 1949; children: David, Daniel, Joel, Joshua. BA, Amherst Coll., 1948; MD, NYU, 1952. Intern Kings County Hosp., Bklyn., 1952-53; resident in internal medicine Montefiore Med. Ctr., Bronx, N.Y., 1955-56, Bronx Mcpl. Hosp. Ctr., 1956-57; Am. Cancer Soc. fellow Montefiore Hosp., Bronx, 1957-58; attending physician dept. oncology Montefiore Med. Ctr., 1978—; prof. dept. medicine (Oncology) Albert Einstein Coll. Medicine, Bronx, 1982—. Prin. investigator Ea. Coop. Oncology grant Montefiore Med. Ctr., Bronx, N.Y., 1978-92. Capt. USAF, 1953-55. Fellow ACP; mem. Am. Soc. Clin. Oncology, Am. Assn. for Cancer Rsch., Phi Beta Kappa. Democrat. Jewish. Home: 39 Disbrow Cir New Rochelle NY 10804-2503 Office: Montefiore Hosp Dept Oncology 111 E 210th St Bronx NY 10467-2490

GREENWALD, GILBERT SAUL, physiologist; b. N.Y.C., June 24, 1927; s. Morris M. and Celia G.; m. Pola Gorsky, Sept. 9, 1950; children: Susan Greenwald Waxman, Elizabeth Greenwald Jordan, Douglas. AB with honors, U. Calif., Berkeley, 1949, PhD in Zoology, 1954. Postdoctoral fellow dept. embryology USPHS Carnegie Inst. Washington, 1954-56; instr., then asst. prof. anatomy U. Wash. Med. Sch., Seattle, 1956-61; mem. faculty U. Kans. Med. Ctr., Kansas City, 1961-96, disting. prof. physiology, 1977-96, univ. disting. prof., 1995, disting. prof. emeritus, 1996—, chmn. dept. physiology, 1977-93, prof. ob-gyn., 1977-93, prof. anatomy, ob-gyn., 1965-77, rsch. prof. in human reprodn., 1961-77. Mem. reproductive biology study sect. NIH, 1966-70, mem. population rsch. adv. com., 1967-71; mem. regulatory biol. panel NSF, 1984-86 Editor Biology of Reprodn., 1974-77. With USNR, 1944-45. Recipient Higuchi Biomed. Sci. award U. Kans., 1984; USPHS fellow Carnegie Instn., 1954-56. Mem. AAAS, Soc. Study of Reprodn. (pres. 1971, Disting. Svc. award 1988, Carl Hartman award 1993), Endocrine Soc., Brit. Soc. Study Fertility, Am. Physiol. Soc., Soc. Exptl. Biology and Medicine (councillor 1991-95), Sigma Xi. Office: U Kans Med Ctr 39th and Rainbow Blvd Kansas City KS 66103 E-mail: ggreenwa@kumc.edu.

GREENWALD, JOHN DOYLE, lawyer; b. N.Y.C., July 27, 1945; s. Joseph Adolph and Virginia (Doyle) G.; m. Maria Teresa Tarujo de Almeida, Dec. 23, 1972; children— Nicholas, Fransisco, Katherine. A.B., U. N.C., 1967; J.D., Columbia U., 1972. Bar: N.Y. 1973. Assoc. Sullivan & Cromwell, N.Y.C., 1972-74; dep. gen. counsel Office of U.S. Trade Rep., 1974-80; dep. asst. sec. commerce for import adminstrn., 1980-81; counsel Verner, Liipfert, Bernhard & McPherson, 1981-83; ptnr. Wilmer, Cutler & Pickering, Washington, 1983— ; adj. prof. law Georgetown U. Sch. Law, 1981— . Office: Wilmer Cutler & Pickering 1666 K St NW Washington DC 20006-2803

GREENWALD, JOHN EDWARD, newspaper and magazine writer, editor and executive, painter; b. N.Y.C., Oct. 28, 1942; s. Herbert and Carrie (Weisberg) G.; m. Rita Lynn Lipman, May 16, 1987. BA, Syracuse U., 1963. Copy boy N.Y. Post, N.Y.C., 1963-64; assoc. editor Air Force Times, Washington, 1967-70; editor The Times Mag., Washington, 1970-80; editorial dir. Jour. Newspapers, Inc. (Fairfax Jour., Arlington Jour., Alexandria Jour., Prince George's Jour., Prince William Jour., Montgomery Jour.), Springfield, Va., 1980-90; editor Am. Legion Mag., Indpls., 1991-94; asst. mng. editor/Sunday & Spl. Projects The Sun, Lowell, Mass., 1994-98; entertainment columnist Waterbury (Conn.) Republican-Am., 2000—; free-lance writer, 1999—; art critic Lowell (Mass.) Sun, 2002—. Film reviewer Times Jour. Co., Springfield, Va., 1967-85. Exhibitions include include Nude 2002, Lexington (Ky.) Art League, La Boniche, Whistler House Mus. of Art, 2002, Higher Ground, 2003. Served with U.S. Army, 1964-67 E-mail: johnedit@bigfoot.com.

GREENWALD, MARC LEHRER, colon and rectal surgeon; b. N.Y.C., Feb. 28, 1959; s. Richard M. and Joyce S. (Lehrer) G.; m. Yvette Olstein, Mar. 21, 1991; children: Samuel, Julia, Lily. BA with distinction, Cornell U., 1981; MD, Albert Einstein Coll. Med., 1985. Diplomate Am. Bd. Surgery, Am. Bd. Colon and Rectal Surgery. Intern, resident Montefiore Med. Ctr., Albert Einstein Coll. Medicine, 1985-90; fellow in colon and rectal surgery St. Francis Hosp., U. Conn., 1990-91; colon and rectal surgeon North Shore Surgical Specialists, Great Neck, N.Y., 1991—; attending surgeon North Shore U. Hosp., Manhasset, N.Y., 1991—, Long Island Jewish Hosp., New Hyde Park, N.Y., 1993—, Winthrop U. Hosp., Mineola, N.Y., 1992—; clin. instr. surgery Cornell U., N.Y.C., 1993—; pres. med. staff North Shore Univ. Hosp., 2000-2001. Pres. N.Y. Med. Staff Leadership Coun., 2002. Contbr. chpts. to books: Problems in General Surgery, 1992, (textbook) Fundamentals of Anorectal Surgery, 1992, also to profl. jours. Fellow ACS, Am. Soc. Colon and Rectal Surgeons, N.Y. Soc. Colon and Rectal Surgeons; mem. AMA, Am. Soc. Am. Gastrointestinal Endoscopic Surgeons, Phi Beta Kappa. Office: North Shore Surg Specialist 310 E Shore Rd Great Neck NY 11023-2432

GREENWALD, MARTIN, publishing company executive; b. Bronx, N.Y., Apr. 25, 1942; s. David and Jean (Kaufman) G.; m. Irma Heldman; children: Karen Sue, Craig Mitchell. AB, Lafayette Coll., 1963; MBA, Columbia U., 1965. Mgr. acquisition planning, fin. analyst Macmillan Inc., N.Y.C., 1965-69, bus. mgr., trade div., 1970-72; new bus. devel. analyst Holt div. CBS, N.Y.C., 1969-70; v.p., gen. mgr. Hagstrom Co. Inc., N.Y.C., 1972-76; pres. Paddington Press, N.Y.C., 1976-80; dir. mktg. Facts On File, Inc., 1980-82, v.p. mktg., 1982-88, sr. v.p., 1988-90, pub., exec. v.p., 1990-95; pres. Martin Greenwald Assocs., Inc., N.Y.C., 1995-96; exec. dir. The Pub. Strategists, Bronxville, N.Y., 1996—, Krugosvet Encyclopedia, Moscow, 1996—; pub. mgr. Open Soc. Inst., 1998—. Author: Maps on File, 1981, Historical Maps on File, 1984 V.p. Green Acres Libr. Bd., Hempstead, NY, 1976—80, Green Acres Civic Assn., 1976—89; mem. Nassau County (N.Y.) Rep. Com., 1973—80; bd. dirs. Non-Profit Found. for the Support of Cultural, Ednl. and New Info. Techs.-Russia, 1999—, Internat. Debate Edn. Assocs., 2001—. Mem. Assn. Am. Pubs., Canadian Booksellers Assn., Internat. Debate Edn. Assn., N.Y. Road Runners Club. Jewish. Home: 275 Central Park W New York NY 10024-3015 Office: The Publishing Strategists 29 Palmer Pl Leonia NJ 07605 also: Open Soc Inst 400 W 59th St New York NY 10019 E-mail: mgaig@aol.com.

GREENWALD, PETER, physician, government medical research director; b. Newburgh, N.Y., Nov. 7, 1936; s. Louis and Pearl (Reingold) G.; m. Harriet Reif, Sept. 6, 1968; children— Rebecca, Laura, Daniel BA, Colgate U., 1957; MD, SUNY Coll. Medicine, 1961, MPH, Harvard U., 1967, DrPH, 1974. Intern Los Angeles County Hosp., 1961-62; resident in internal medicine Boston City Hosp., 1964-66; asst. in medicine Peter Bent Brigham Hosp., 1967-68; mem. epidemiology and disease control study sect. NIH, 1974-78; mem. N.Y. State Gov.'s Breast Task Force, 1976-78; with N.Y. State Dept. Health, Albany, 1968-81, dir., 1968-76, dir. epidemiology, 1976-81; prof. medicine Albany Med. Coll., 1976-81; attending physician Albany Med. Ctr. Hosp., 1968-81; adj. prof. biomed. engrng. Rensselaer Poly. Inst., Troy, N.Y., 1976-81; assoc. scientist Sloan-Kettering Inst. for Cancer Research, N.Y.C., 1977-81; dir. div. cancer prevention Nat. Cancer Inst., NIH, Bethesda, Md., 1981-97, 98—. Mem. VA Merit Rev. Bd. Med. Oncology, Washington, 1972-74 Editor-in-chief Jour. Nat. Cancer Inst., 1981-87; contbr. articles to profl. jours. Rear adm. USPHS, 1962 61, 81—. Recipient Disting. Svc. award N.Y. State Dept. Health, 1975; Redway medal and award for med. writing N.Y. State Jour. Medicine, 1977, N.Y. State Gov.'s Citationfor pub. health achievement, 1981, PHS commendation 1983, 88, Disting. Svc. medal, 1993, Disting. Svc. award, Am. Cancer Soc., 1997, Outstanding Rsch. award Am. Inst. Cancer Rsch., 1997, Pub. Svc. award Cancer Treatment and Rsch. Found., 1997 ; named to SUNY Honor Roll of Disting. Grads., 1997. Fellow ACP, Am. Coll. Preventive Medicine, APHA (epidemiology sect. chmn. 1981); mem. AMA, Am. Assn. Cancer Rsch. (DeWitt Goodman lectr. 1998), Am. Soc. Clin. Oncology, Am. Coll. Epidemiology (bd. dirs. 1981-82), Am. Soc. Preventive Oncology (Disting. Achievement award 1998), Am. Inst. Nutrition, Internat. Epidemiology Soc., Nat. Acad. Scis. (food and nutrition bd. 1982-88). Office: NIH/NCI Divsn Cancer Prevention EPN/2040 6130 Exec Blvd Bethesda MD 20892-7309

GREENWALD, RICHARD ALAN, history educator; s. Richard Patrick and Rosalie Greenwald; m. Debbie A. Gotti-Greenwald. BA, CUNY, 1987; MPhil, NYU, 1995, PhD, 1998. Asst. prof. history SUNY, Morrisville, 1995—99, SUNY-Orange, Middletown, 1999—2000, U.S. Merchant Marine Acad., Kings Point, NY, 2000—. Cons. Ednl. Testing Svc., Princeton, NY, 1995—2000, Gotham Ctr. N.Y.C. History, 2002—; spkr. N.Y. Humanities Coun., N.Y.C., 2002—. Author: Bargaining for Industrial Democracy, 2003; editor: Sweatshop USA, 2003. Fellow, CUNY Labor Mgmt. Ctr., 1990—94; tchg. fellow, NYU, 1990—95, Lubin fellow, FDR Libr., Hyde Park, N.Y., 1995. Democrat. Roman Catholic. Office: US Merchant Marine Acad Dept Humanities Kings Point NY 11024

GREENWALD, ROBERT, public relations executive; b. N.Y.C., Jan. 14, 1927; s. Louis and Rebecca (Shapiro) G.; m. Genevieve Kushnir, Apr. 15, 1957 (div. 1960); m. Dorothy Pearl Brand, Apr. 19, 1963; children: Liza, Mark. BA, NYU, 1949, postgrad., 1951-54; postgrad, Columbia U., 1950, New Sch., 1950-51. Account exec. Ruder & Finn, Inc., N.Y.C., 1954—, sr. assoc., 1955-56, v.p., 1957-65; sr. v.p. Ruder, Finn & Rotman, Inc., N.Y.C., 1965-79; exec. v.p. Ruder, Finn & Rotman Inc., N.Y.C., 1980-83, sr. counsel, 1983-85; vice-chmn. Makovsky & Co. Inc., N.Y.C., 1987—; pvt. quality control cons. N.Y.C., 1994—. Author: (with Dorothy Brand) Learning To Live with The Love of Your Life, 1979. Chmn. pub. relations com. UNICEF, N.Y.C., 1976-82, dir., 1976-82, mem. nat. adv. com., 1983-97, mem. nominating com., 1983-87; bd. dirs. Jewish Family Services, N.Y.C., 1972-75. Served with U.S. Army, 1945-46, ETO. Recipient Silver Anvil award Pub. Relations Soc. Am., 1955, 73, 81; recipient Paul B. Zucker award Ruder & Finn Inc., 1976, 82 Democrat. Jewish. Home: 88 Fairview Ave Verona NJ 07044-1315

GREENWALD, SHEILA ELLEN, writer, illustrator; b. N.Y.C., May 26, 1934; d. Julius and Florence (Friedman) Greenwald; m. George E. Green, Feb. 18, 1960; children: Samuel Green, Benjamin Green. BA, Sarah Lawrence Coll., 1956. Author over 24 children's books, including Give Us a Great Big Smile Rosy Cole, 1980, Valentine Rosy, 1984, Rosy Cole's Great American Guilt Club, 1987, Write on Rosy, 1988, Rosy's Romance, 1989, Here's Hermione, 1991, The Mariah Delary Author of the Month Club, 1990, Rosy Cole Discovers America, 1992, My Fabulous NewLife, 1993, Rosy Cole, She Walks in Beauty, 1994, Rosy Cole: She Grows and Graduates, 1997, Stucksville, 2000, Mariah Delany Lending Library Disaster (The Mariah Delany Author of The Month Club 1999), Stucksville, 2001, The Hot Day reissued as Silver Mountain, 2002, Rosy Cole's Worst Ever, Best Yet Tour of New York City, 2003. Mem. PEN, Authors League. Jewish. Office: Melanie Kroupa Books Ferrar Straus & Geroux 19 Union Sq W New York NY 10003 and: Orchard/Scholastic Inc 555 Broadway New York NY 10012

GREENWALT, TIBOR JACK, physician, educator; b. Budapest, Hungary, Jan. 23, 1914; arrived in U.S., 1920, naturalized, 1943; s. Bela and Irene (Foldes) Greenwalt; m. Shirley Johnson, Aug. 6, 1960 (dec. Sept. 1970); 1 child, Peter H.; m. Pia Glas, Feb. 27, 1971 (dec. July 1996). BA summa cum laude, MD, NYU, 1937. Diplomate Am. Bd. Internal Medicine. Intern pathology and bacteriology Mt. Sinai Hosp., N.Y.C., 1937—38; rotating intern Kings County Hosp., Bklyn., 1938—40; resident medicine Montefiore Hosp., N.Y.C., 1940—41; research asso. New Eng. Med. Center, Boston, 1941—42; med. dir. Milw. Blood Center, 1947—66; faculty medicine Marquette U. Sch. Medicine, 1948—66, prof. medicine, 1963—66, cons. hematology VA Hosp., Wood, Wis., 1946—66, Milw. County Gen. Hosp., 1948—66; dir. blood program ARC, 1967—78, sr. sci. adviser blood program, 1978—79; clin. prof. medicine George Washington U. Sch. Medicine, 1967—79; prof. medicine U. Cin. Med. Center, 1979—84, prof. emeritus medicine and pathology, 1984—; dir. Hoxworth Blood Center, 1979—87, dir. research, 1987—. Chmn. com. blood and transfusion problems NAS-NRC, 1963—66; mem. hematology study sect. NIH, 1960—63, chmn., 1970—72; vis. prof., spkr. throughout U.S., 1960—; mem. Med. Rsch. Srv. Merit Rev. Bd. for Hematology, VA, 1981—83; mem. blood diseases and resources adv. com. Nat. Heart, Lung and Blood Inst., 1983—87, adv. coun., 1986—90, coordinating com. Nat. Blood Resources Edn. Program, adv. com. Office of Prevention Edn. and Control, 1987—91. Author (with others): Hemolytic Syndromes, 1942; author: (with Shirley Greenwalt) Coagulation and Transfusion in Clinical Medicine, 1965; editor (with Graham A. Jamieson): The Red Cell Membrane, 1969; editor: Formation and Destruction of Blood Cells, 1970, Glycoproteins of Plasma and Membranes, 1971, The Human Red Cell in Vitro, 1974, Transmissible Disease and Blood Transfusion, 1974, Trace Proteins of Plasma, 1976, The Granuloctye, 1977, Blood Substitutes and Plasma Expanders, 1978, The Blood Platelet in Transfusion Therapy, 1978, Methods in Hematology: Blood Transfusion, 1988, History of International Society of Blood Transfusion, 2000; editor, contbr.: Immunogenetics, 1967, editor-in-chief: Transfusion, 1960—66, assoc. editor:, 1966—86, mem. editl. bd.: Gen. Prins. of Blood Transfusion, 1962—83, Vox Sanguinis, 1956—76, Haematologia, 1968—90, Blood, 1979—84; contbr. articles to profl. lit. Maj. M.C. U.S. Army, 1942—46. Recipient Gold medal, Caduceus Soc., NYU, 1933, Jr. Achievement award for outstanding contbn. sci., 1958, 1st Charles R. Drew award, ARC, Washington, 1981, Disting. Citizen's award, Allied Vets. Coun., 1963, award pioneer blood group rsch., Ctr. for Immunology, SUNY, Buffalo, 1976, Witebsky lectureship, 1994, Albion O. Bernstein award, Med. Soc. State N.Y., 1997. Fellow: AAAS, N.Y. Acad. Scis.; mem.: ACP, Am. Soc. Human Genetics, Soc. Exptl. Biology and Medicine, Am. Assn. Immunologists, Am. Soc. Hematology (treas. 1963—67), Ohio Sci. Roundtable, Internat. Soc. Haemostasis and Thrombosis (life), Inst. Medicine (sr.), Ctrl. Soc. Clin. Rsch., Am. Soc. Clin. Pathologists, Internat. Soc. Blood Transfusion (pres. 1966—72, historian 1975—96), Internat. Soc. Hematology, Am. Assn. Blood Banks (v.p. 1959—60, med. dir. ctrl. file rare donors 1960—66, 50th anniversary com., John Elliot award 1966, Grove-Rasmussen award 1988, Bernard Fantus medal 1993, Tibor J. Greenwalt lectr. 1997—), Cosmos Club, Alpha Omega Alpha, Sigma Xi. Home: 2444 Madison Rd #1501 Cincinnati OH 45208-1228 Office: Hoxworth Blood Ctr 3130 Highland Ave Cincinnati OH 45267-0001 E-mail: tjgreenwalt@aol.com.

GREENWAY, HUGH DAVIDS SCOTT, journalist; b. Boston, May 8, 1935; s. James Cowen and Helen Livingston (Scott) G.; m. Joy Beverly Brooks, June 11, 1960; children— Julia Livingston, Alice Lauder, Sarah Davids. BA, Yale U., 1958; postgrad., Oxford U., Eng., 1960-62. Corr. Time mag., London, 1962-63, Washington, 1963-64, Boston, 1964-66, Saigon, 1967-68, Bangkok, 1968-70, UN, N.Y.C., 1970-72; corr. Washington Post, Hong Kong, 1973-76, Jerusalem, 1976-78; assoc. editor for nat. and fgn. news Boston Globe, 1978-91, sr. assoc. editor, 1991-93, editl. page editor, 1994-2000, fgn. affairs columnist, 2000—. Trustee, Woods Hole (Mass.) Oceanographic Inst.; bd. dirs. Internat. Press Inst., Vienna. Served with USNR, 1958-60. Nieman fellow Harvard U., 1971-72 Mem.: Coun. on Fgn. Rels., Am. Soc. Newspaper Editors. Home: 634 Charles River St Needham MA 02492-1031 E-mail: greenway@globe.com.

GREENWAY, JOAN M. dean; b. Adelaide, South Australia, Australia; d. John Francis Matthew and Ida Gladys Wilding; m. Elliott D. Full, Feb. 9, 1997; m. Ian MacKinnon Disher, Aug. 30, 1944 (dec. Mar. 16, 1957); children: Carolyn Wilding Whitting, Susan MacIntosh Miller, Jamie Sutherland MacDonald. BA, U. Colo., Boulder, CO, 1968, MA, 1969, PhD, 1970. TV journalist NEWS Ltd., South Australia, Australia, 1957—62, Australian Broadcasting Commn., Australia, 1962—66; asst. prof. Regis Coll., Denver, 1969—71; prof. and chmn. Calif. State U., Pomona, Calif., 1971—76; dean Continuing Edn. Calif. State U., Pomona, Calif., 1976—88. Spl. adv. children Superior Ct. LA County, Los Angeles, Calif., 1993—97. Recipient Disting. Prof. Am., Wash., D.C., 1975. Mem.: Phi Beta Kappa Colo. Chpt. Home Fax: 949-240-0545.

GREENWELL, ARNOLD, associate editor, photographer; b. Tokyo, Mar. 3, 1956; came to U.S., 1958; s. Charles Warren Greenwell and Miyoko (Takahashi) Wallace. AS cum laude, Lees-McRae Coll., 1976; BA, U. N.C., 1979. Research technician dept. zoology U. N.C., Chapel Hill, 1977-79; research technician Howard Hughes Med. Inst., Durham, N.C., 1979-80; biol. lab. technician Nat. Inst. Environ. Health Scis., Research Triangle Park, N.C., 1980-84, research biologist, 1984-2000; tech. info. specialist, 2000—; assoc. editor, photographer Eviron. Health Perspectives, 2000—. Pvt. pilot, 1982—; free-lance photographer, 1977—. Mem. editl. adv. bd. The Southern Aviator, 1993-95; contbr. articles to profl. jours.; pub. numerous photographs in aviation pubs., calendars, mus. exhbns. Mem.: Nat. Inst. Environ. Health Scis. Camera Club (v.p. 1981—83, sec. 1987—94), Nat. Press Photographers Assn., Exptl. Aircraft Assn., Aircraft Owners and Pilots Assn., Wings of Carolina Flying Club, Phi Theta Kappa. Republican. Avocations: flying, hunting, fishing, photography. Home: 6211 Dawn Dr Hurdle Mills NC 27541 Office: Nat Inst Environ Health Scis PO Box 12233 Research Triangle Park NC 27709 E-mail: greenwe1@niehs.nih.gov.

GREENWELL, RAYMOND N. mathematician, educator, writer; b. Alhambra, Calif., Apr. 14, 1953; s. Robert N. and Katherine M. Greenwell; m. Karla Harby, June 10, 1978. BA, Univ. San Diego, 1974; PhD, Mich. State U., 1979. Asst. prof. math. Albion (Mich.) Coll., 1979—83; prof. math. Hofstra U., Hempstead, NY, 1983—. Author: (mathematics textbook) Finite Mathematics and Calculus with Applications; contbr. articles to profl. jours. Trip leader Sierra Club Inner City Outings, N.Y.C., 1986—2002. Mem.: Math. Assn. Am. (gov. met. N.Y. sect. 2002—05). Home: 264 National Blvd Long Beach NY 11561 Office: Dept of Mathematics 103 Hofstra University Hempstead NY 11549 Office Fax: 516-463-6596. E-mail: matrng@hofstra.edu.

GREENWELL, RONALD EVERETT, communications executive; b. Louisville, Oct. 28, 1938; s. Woodrow M. and Christine (Comer) Gossett G.; m. Diane J. Greenwell, Mar. 18, 1967; children: Wendy, Robin. With Motorola Inc., Schaumburg, Ill., 1962-94, sr. v.p., gen. mgr. communications internat. group, 1986-94; pres. Motorola Communications Internat. Inc., Schaumburg, Ill., 1986-94, ret., 1994. Bd. dirs. Meso Fuel Inc. Bd. dirs. East Mountain Sch. Found.; former bd. dirs. NC Ctr. for World Langs. and Culture. Home: 30 Canyon Ridge Dr Sandia Park NM 87047-8506

GREENWOOD, AUDREY GATES, librarian; b. Buffalo, Mar. 27, 1917; d. Marc Herbert and Genevieve Cecelia (Naab) Gates; BA, D'Youville Coll., 1939; BS in Library Sci., Cath. U. Am., 1940, MA, 1944; m. Clayton Edward Greenwood, Sept. 2, 1944; children— Mary Ellen, Nancy Jane, Susan Jean. Head librarian Gonzaga High Sch., Washington, 1940-45, Southeastern U. Evening Sch., 1941-45; reference librarian Cath. U. Am., evenings 1942-43; librarian St. Joseph's Collegiate Inst., Buffalo, 1945-46; head librarian Canisius High Sch., Buffalo, 1949-50, head librarian Eden (N.Y.) Central Schs., 1950-83, coordinator state and fed. funds, 1969-83, dir. adult edn., 1973-83. Recipient Frederica Hollinter award, 2002. Mem. Eden Tchrs. Assn. (past pres.), Erie County Ednl. Assn. (past v.p.), NEA, N.Y. State Tchrs. Assn., N.Y. State United Tchrs. (state del. 1992—, legis. chmn. Western zone, chmn. retirees of western N.Y. 1984-88, pres. retirees of western N.Y. 1989-96, mem. ROC com. 1985-88, mem. editl. bd. The Active N.Y. State United Tchrs. Retiree, pres. coun. II 1997—, mem. Commn. 100, retiree del. 1992—), N.Y. State Retired Tchrs. Assn. (pres. Southtowns chpt. 1987—, legis. commn. 1987—, historian western zone 1988-97, del. 1991—), Am. Fedn. Tchrs. (nat. del. 1984--), Sch. Librarians Assn. Western N.Y. (past pres.), N.Y. Educators Assn., Delta Kappa Gamma. (state legis. chmn., state fin. com. 1991—), Beta Zeta (v.p. 1986-89, pres. 1989-95). Democrat. Roman Catholic. Home: 5595 Armor Duells Rd Orchard Park NY 14127-3121

GREENWOOD, DANN EDWARD, lawyer; b. Dickinson, N.D., Sept. 21, 1952; s. Lawrence E. and Joyce E. (Henley) G.; m. Debra K. Ableidinger, June 15, 1975; children: Jay, Lindsey, Paige. BSBA magna cum laude, U. N.D., 1974, JD, 1977. Bar: N.D. 1977, U.S. Dist. Ct. N.D. 1980. Ptnr. Greenwood, Greenwood & Greenwood and predecessor firms, Dickinson, 1977-98, Greenwood & Ramsey PLLP, 1998—. Mem. N.D. Supreme Ct. Disciplinary Bd., 1983-89, Northern Lights Boy Scouts Council, Dickinson, 1985—; bd. dirs. Legal Assistance N.D., Bismarck, 1980-86. Mem. N.D. Bar Assn. (pres. 1998-99), Stark-Dunn County Bar Assn., N.D. Trial Lawyers Assn. (sec. 1983-84, treas. 1984-85, v.p. 1985-86, pres. 1987-88), Kiwanis, Masons, Shriners, Elks. Lutheran. Home: PO Box 688 Dickinson ND 58602-0688 E-mail: shadyln@ndsupernet.com, grlawdg@ndsupernet.com.

GREENWOOD, FRANK, information scientist, educator; b. Rio de Janeiro, Mar. 6, 1924; came to U.S., 1935; s. Heman Charles and Evelyn (Heyns) G.; m. Mary Mallas, Oct. 24, 1972; children: Margaret, Ernest, Nicholas. BA, Bucknell U., 1950; MBA, U. So. Calif., 1959; PhD, UCLA, 1963; hon. doctorate, Commonwealth Open U. Brit. VI, 1999. Cert. systems profl., project mgmt. profl. Various positions The Tex. Co., U.S., Africa and Can., 1950-60; assoc. prof. U. Ga., Athens, 1961-65; chmn. dept. computer sys. Ohio U., Athens, 1966-76; dir. computer ctr. U. Mont., Missoula, 1977-84; prof. mgmt. info. sys. Southea. Mass. U. (now U. Mass.), North Dartmouth, 1985-89, Ctrl. Mich. U., Mt. Pleasant, 1990-93; pres. Greenwood & Assocs., Ltd., Bloomfield Hills,

Mich., 1993. Instr. on-line clases Jones Internat. U., Englewood, Colo., Gatlin Ednl. Svcs., Ft. Worth, Tex. Author: Casebook for Management and Business Policy: A Systems Approach, 1968, Managing the Systems Analysis Function, 1968; (with Nicolai Siemens and C.H. Marting Jr.) Operations Research: Planning, Operating and Information Systems, 1973; (with Mary Greenwood) Information Resources in the Office Tomorrow, 1980, Profitable Small Business Computing, 1982, Office Technology: Principles of Automation, 1984, Business Telecommuncations: Data Communications in the Information Age, 1988, Introduction to Computer-Integrated Manufacturing, 1990, How to Raise Office Productivity, 1991, Meeting the Challenges of Project Management: A Primer, 1998; columnist: Computerworld mag., 1972-73, The Daily Record, 1982-83, (with Mary Greenwood) Herald News, 1986, The Beacon, 1986, Morning Sun, 1990-93; contbr. monographs, articles to profl. jours. and chpts. to books. Sgt. AUS, 1943-45. UCLA Alumni scholar, 1961; Ford Found. fellow, 1962-63. Mem. Wamsutta Club (New Bedford, Mass.). Greek Orthodox. Avocation: exercise. Home and Office: 7426 Deep Run Apt 1322 Bloomfield Hills MI 48301-3844 E-mail: fgreenw617@aol.com. *Do what you believe you should (and not what others do). Put your trust in your own capacity to provide products/services others need (and don't seek security as a "corporate slave"). Mental and physical health are the key to all else.*

GREENWOOD, HARRIET LOIS, environmental banker, researcher; b. Detroit, Oct. 4, 1950; d. Samuel H. and Elizabeth Ann (Bode) G.; m. Michael E. Carlson, Aug. 23, 1981 (div. Sept. 1986); m. Eric J. Halbeisen, Sept. 5, 1987; 1 child, Robin Faith. BA in Biology, Antioch Coll., 1972; MS in Tchg., Antioch Coll. New Eng., 1975; postgrad., U. Mich., 1985-87. Dir. environ. studies Swanson Environ., Southfield, Mich., 1978-80; project mgr. ESEI, Ecol. Scis., Detroit, 1981-82; pres. Greenwood & Assocs., Detroit, 1982-83; mgr. environ. studies Environ. Rsch. Group, Ann Arbor, Mich., 1983-85; environ. policy specialist Clayton Environ., Southfield, 1985-91; pres. Environ. Tng. Svcs., Detroit, 1991-93; asst. v.p. Comerica Bank, 1993—. Part-time instr. Wayne State U., 1992—; rec. clk. Detroit Friends Meeting, 1985-88; bd. dirs. Friends Sch. Detroit, 1987-89. U. Mich. fellow, 1985-86. Mem.: S.E. Mich. Sustainable Bus. Forum, Mich. Bankers Assn. (environ. com.), Mich. Assn. Environ. Profls., East Mich. Environ. Action Coun., Environ. Bankers Assn., Nat. Trust Real Estate Assn. Mem. Soc. Of Friends. Avocations: english country dancing, cross country skiing. Office: Comerica Bank Trust Real Estate-3228 PO Box 75000 Detroit MI 48275-3228

GREENWOOD, HELEN MAXINE, retired office manager, executive assistant; b. Hoopeston, Ill., Oct. 20, 1916; d. Lloyd Earle and Eugenia Blanche (Evans) Gladding; m. James Condon, 1940 (div. 1957); children: Yvonne Condon Brosius, Marguita Condon Brown, Vivienne Condon Sargeant; m. James Raymond Greenwood, Sept. 11, 1970. BS in Journalism, U. Ill., 1938. Mem. display advt. staff Moline (Ill.) Daily Dispatch, 1938-41, book rev. columnist, 1939-41; legal sec. Moyer and Hiebert, Wichita, Kans., 1961-65; exec. sec. Learjet Corp., Wichita, 1965-70; adminstr. Camp Tapawingo, Alexandria, Va., 1971-73; exec. asst. Aerospace Cons., Green Valley, Ariz., 1985-98. Co-author: Stunt Flying in the Movies, 1982 (award Aviation Space Writers Assn. 1983); editor various publs. Life mem. pres. coun. U. Ill.; vol. Am. Red Cross, Wichita Art Mus. Bronze Tablet scholar U. Ill. Mem. AAUW (hon. life mem., pres. Wichita Branch, 1962-64, Svc. award 1988), Green Valley Women's Club, Aero Club Ariz., Ariz. Hist. Soc., Tubac Hist. Soc. Avocations: music, travel, hiking, reading, historical research. Home and Office: 435 E El Valle Green Valley AZ 85614-2924

GREENWOOD, JAMES CHARLES, congressman; b. Philadelphia, Pa., May 4, 1951; s. James Charles and Alice Mary (Gibson) G.; m. Jane Christina Paugh, Oct. 6, 1984; children: Robert, Andrew (dec.), Laura, Kathryn. BA, Dickinson Coll., 1973. Head house parent The Woods Schs., Langhorne, Pa., 1974-76; campaign mgr. Renninger for Congress, Doylestown, Pa., 1976; caseworker Bucks County Children and Youth Agy., Doylestown, 1977-80; mem. Pa. Ho. Reps., Harrisburg, 1981-86, Pa. Senate, Harrisburg, 1987-92, U.S. Congress from 8th Pa. dist., Washington, 1993—. Mem. Energy and Commerce com.; subcom. on Fin. and Hazardous Materials, Health and the Environ.; mem. Com. on Edn. and Workforce, Early Childhood, Youth and Families subcom., Postsecondary Edn., Tng. and Life-Long Learning. Bd. dirs. Bucks County Coun. on Alcoholism, The Woods Sch., Parents Anonymous Pa.; hon. bd. dirs. Bucks County Assn. for Retarded Citizens, Big Bros./Big Sisters Bucks County, Friends of the Farmstead, Inc.; mem. adv. bd. Today, Inc., About Face U.S.A. Mem. League Women Voters, Sierra Club, Lions Club. Republican. Office: US House of Reps 2436 Rayburn House Off Bldg Washington DC 20515-0001 : 69 East Oakland Avenue Doylestown PA 18901*

GREENWOOD, JANET KAE DALY, psychologist, educational administrator, marketing professional; b. Goldsboro, N.C., Dec. 9, 1943; d. Fulton Benton and Kelminy Ethel Esther (Ball) Daly; 1 child, Gerald Thompson. AA, Peace Coll., 1963; BS in English and Psychology, East Carolina U., 1965, MEd in Counseling, 1967; postgrad., N.C. State U., 1967-69, U. London, 1969; PhD in Counseling and Higher Ednl. Adminstrn., Fla. State U., 1972. Tchr. English Kinston (N.C.) City Schs., 1965-66, Goldsboro City Schs., 1966-67; counselor and psychometrist primary and secondary schs. County of Wake, N.C., 1967-69; coord. Am. Inst. for Fgn. Study, 1969; supr. student tours in Eng., France, Switzerland, Italy, and Capri, 1969; counselor Fla. State U., Tallahassee, 1969-72; asst. dir. counseling Rutgers U., New Brunswick, N.J., 1972-73, cons. to v.p. for student svcs., 1973-74, lectr. in counseling psychology, 1972-74; coord. and assoc. prof. counselor edn. U. Cin., 1974-77, adviser to grad. students, 1974-77, vice provost student affairs, 1977-81; pres. Longwood Coll., Farmville, Va., 1981-87, U. Bridgeport, Conn., 1987-92; cons., ptnr., dir. Heidrick & Struggles, Washington, 1992-2000; v.p. A.T. Kearney, Inc., 2000—. Guidance cons. South Plainfield Pub. Schs., 1973-76; adviser Parents without Ptnrs., 1976; bd. dirs. Hydraulic Co.; mem. Gov.'s Partnership To Prevent Substance Abuse in the Workforce, mem. audit com. and cmty. and govt. rels. com. Contbr. articles to profl. jours. Mem. Gov.'s Ad Hoc Edn. Com. on Tchr. Edn. and Counselor Edn., State of Ohio, 1975; mem. state planning commn. Nat. Identification of Women Project; chair Twin Rivers Tenants Rights Assn., 1972-74; bd. dirs. Bridgeport Hosp., Bridgeport Bus. Coun.; mem. adv. com. Bridgeport Pub. Edn. Fund; bd. dirs. Conn. Ballet Theatre, chair South End streeting com; mem. mgmt. adv. com. City of Bridgeport; mem. adv. com. United Way Tri-State; chair South End Partnership Com; mem. The Schiavone Steering Com./Downtown Bridgeport Project, YWCA Bd., Champion/United Way, United Way Community Human Svcs. Planning Coun., Bridgeport Symphony Bd., Bridgeport Opera Bd., Bridgeport Area Coll./Univ. Consortium, Conn. Conf. Ind. Colls., The Newcomen Soc. of U.S., The United Way Ea. Fairfield County; mem. adv. bd. Sacred Heart/St. Anthony Sch., Roosevelt Sch; mem. ct. com. Regional Plan Assn. Fairfield 2000; bd. dirs. Conn. Ballet Theatre; chair The Bridgeport Regional Bus. Coun. Brass Ring Task Force on Leadership; bd. govs. Fairfield County Study; mem. hon. bd. dirs. Conn. Earth Day 20, Inc.; chair L.I. Sound Western Regional Coun.; founding mem. L.I. Sound Assembly; mem. membership com., campus partnership subcom. Drugs Don't Work program, 1989-91. Recipient Spl. award Black Arts Festival, Meritorious Svc. award Am. Assn. State Colls. and Univs. Mem. AAUP, Am. Coll. Pers. Assn. (editor and chair media bd. 1975—), Am. Pers. and Guidance Assn., Cin. Pers. and Guidance Assn., Ohio Psychol. Assn., Cin. Psychol. Assn., Organizational Behavior Assn., Am. Sch. Counselors Assn., Ohio Sch. Counselors Assn., Assn. for Women Faculty, Ohio Counselor Edn. and Supervision Assn., Kappa Delta Pi.

GREENWOOD, JOHN E. stock brokerage executive; b. Gas City, Ind., May 15, 1922; s. Elmer Middleton and Lenora Cassinda (Reynolds) G.; m. Valerie Louise Komanich, Dec. 26, 1947. Student, W.Va. U., 1940-42, Cornell U., 1942-43; BSBA, U. Mo., 1949. Registered rep. N.Y. Stock Exchange. Stockbroker Newhard, Cook & Co., Inc., St. Louis, 1949-50, Alton, Ill., 1950-89, resident mgr., 1977-88, v.p. St. Louis and Alton, 1984-89; v.p. investments Newhard, Cook/Advest, Inc., 1989-92, Longrow Securities, Inc., St. Louis, also Alton, Ill., 1992-96; v.p. Alton Securities Group, Inc., 1996—. Founder Midcoast Aviation Svcs., Inc., St. Louis, 1957, bd. dirs., 1970-78. Editor: Alton Rotary Historical Building Survey, 1972; contbr. articles and book revs. to hist. publs. Campaign chmn. March of Dimes, Alton, 1957; chmn., bd. dirs. Hayner Pub. Libr., Alton, 1964-77; chmn. Alton Hist. Commn., 1972-74; founder, bd. dirs. 8th Air Force Meml. Mus. Found., Inc., pres., 1985-86, 86-97, chmn., CEO, 1998—; governing trustee Air Force Hist. Found., 1986—; trustee Am. Airpower Heritage Found., 1987-89; bd. dirs. Am. Air Mus. in Britain, 1992—, Imperial War Mus. 1st lt. USAAF, 1942-45, ETO. Decorated Air medal with four oak leaf clusters. Mem. 8th Air Force Hist. Soc. (founder, bd. dirs., pres. 1982-83), Army and Navy Club (Washington), Lockhaven Country Club, Rotary (bd. dirs., treas. Alton 1960—, President's award for outstanding svc. 1965), Air Force Assn., VFW, Friends of U.S. Air Force Mus., Retired Officers Assn., Greater Alton Growth Assn., Air Crew Assn. (Gt. Britain), Sigma Chi. Republican. Methodist. Avocations: aviation research, photography, golf, travel. Home: 607 State St Alton IL 62002-6141 Office: Alton Securities Group 2410 State St PO Box 160 Alton IL 62002-0160

GREENWOOD, LAWRENCE GEORGE, banker; b. Briercrest, Sask., Can., June 16, 1921; s. Goerge Tuckfield and Mildred Jane (Clifford) G.; m. Margaret Purser, June 28, 1947 (dec.). Grad., Regina Central Collegiate, 1938; LLD (hon.), Queens U., Ont., 1980. With Cn. Bank Commerce, Regina, Sask., 1938—, merged to form Can. Imperial Bank Commerce, 1961; pres. Can. Imperial Bank Commerce, Toronto, 1968-71, vice chmn., Toronto and Montreal, 1971-76; dir. emeritus Can. Imperial Bank of Commerce, Toronto. Mem. Nat. Trust for Scotland; hon. trustee Hosp. for Sick Children, Toronto. Served with RCAF, 1941-45. Mem.: York. Home: 7 Tudor Gate Willowdale ON Canada M2L 1N3 Office: PO Box 63 Commerce Ct N Ste 2601 Toronto ON Canada M5L 1B9

GREENWOOD, MARK LAWRENCE, lawyer; b. Fargo, N.D., Sept. 14, 1951; s. Lawrence Edward and Joyce Eleanor (Henley) G.; m. Linda Marie Heck, June 5, 1973; children: Dawn Malinda, Jonn Scott, Geoff Michael. BBA, Dickinson State U., 1973; JD, U. N.D., 1976. Bar: N.D. 1976, U.S. Dist. Ct. N.D. 1976. Ptnr. Greenwood Law Offices, Dickinson, N.D., 1976-79, Greenwood, Greenwood & Greenwood, Dickinson, 1979-91, Greenwood, Greenwood, Greenwood, Selinger and Ramsey, P.C., Dickinson, 1991-98; pvt. practice Mark Greenwood Law Office, Dickinson, 1998—. Chmn. Dist. 37 Dem. NPL, Dickinson, 1988-92, treas., 1986-88. Mem. Nat. Assn. Criminal Def. Lawyers, N.D. Trial Lawyers Assn., SW Jud. Dist. Bar Assn. (sec. 1983-84, pres. 1984-86, N.D. Bar Assn. (bd. govs. 1984-86), Dickinson Lodge 32 A.F. & A.M. (master 1984), El Zagel Temple Shrine, El Zagel Frontiersmen (pres. 1985), Dickinson Jaycees (sec. 1976). Methodist. Avocations: firearms and bow hunting, camping, reading. Office: PO Box 327 Dickinson ND 58602-0327 E-mail: mlglaw@ndsupernet.com.

GREENWOOD, NAOMI, social worker; b. Phila., Feb. 12, 1941; d. David Nisan and Emma (Morgenstern) Greenwood; m. Burton S. Kolko, June 17, 1962 (div. 1993); children: David Joseph, Joshua Howard; m. Thomas E. Dahl, Jan. 2, 1999. BA in Sociology with honors, U. Pa., 1962; MSW, Smith Coll., 1964. Cert. Am. Bd. Examiners of Clin. Social Work; lic. clin. social worker. Clin. social worker St. Elizabeths Hosp., Washington, 1964-69; social worker children's unit Psychiat. Inst., Washington, 1972-76, assoc. dir. social work, 1976-79; acting dir., summer, 1979; pvt. practice clin. social work, 1979-84; co-founder, ptnr. North Bethesda Assocs., 1984-86; founder The Bethesda Group, 1993. Cons. Community Psychiat. Clinic, Wheaton, Md., 1980-83, Gaithersburg, Md., 1983-85; provisional vice chmn. Precinct 7-14, Montgomery County, Md., 1982-84. Fellow Am. Orthopsychiat. Assn.; mem. Nat. Assn. Social Workers, Greater Wash. Soc. Clin. Social Workers, Hadassah Club. Democrat. Jewish. Home: 8313 Beech Tree Rd Bethesda MD 20817-2934 Office: Wyngate Med Park 5654 Shields Dr Bethesda MD 20817-3574

GREENWOOD, TED RONALD IVAN, foundation administrator; b. Toronto, Ont., Can., Dec. 30, 1944; came to U.S., 1967; s. Saul Harry and Ada (Cohen) G.; m. Catherine Drury Crigler, Sept. 6, 1970; children: Daniel Aaron, Benjamin Norris. BSc, U. Toronto, 1967; SM, MIT, 1970, PhD, 1973. Postdoctoral fellow Ctr. for Internat. Studies MIT, Cambridge, Mass., 1973-74, from asst. to assoc. prof. polit. sci. dept., 1974-84; from rsch. fellow to rsch. assoc. program for sci./internat. affairs Harvard U., Cambridge, 1973-77; sr. policy analyst Office of Sci. and Tech. Policy Exec. Office of the Pres., Washington, 1977-79; assoc. prof. polit. sci. dept. Columbia U., N.Y.C., 1984-90, dir. internat. security policy program Sch. Internat. and Pub. Affairs, 1990-92; program officer Alfred P. SLoan Found, N.Y.C., 1992-98, program dir., 1998—. Cons. Energy Resources Co., 1975, Office of Tech. Assessment, U.S. Congress, 1976-77, State Planning Coun. on Radioactive Waste Mgmt., 1980-81, U.S. Nuclear Regulatory Commn., 1981, Pacific-Sierra Rsch. Corp., 1985-93, Inst. Nat. Security Studies, Nat. Def. U., 1988-93; editor Westview Press. Author: Making the MIRV: A Study of Defense Decision-Making, 1975, Knowledge and Discretion in Government Regulation, 1984, (monograph) Reconnaissance Survelliance and Arms Control, 1972; contbr. articles to profl. jours. including Sci., Tech. and Human Values, Arms Control Today, Global Affairs, Sci. Am. Pres. Common Cents, N.Y.C., 1995—99; vice chair Jewish comty. rels. coun. UJA Fedn. Bergen County and North Hudson, NJ, 1998—2000, chair Jewish comty. rels. coun., 2000—02; v.p. Temple Emeth, Teaneck, NJ, 1987—92, pres., 1992—95; v.p. Bergen Acad. Reform Judaism, Paramus, NJ, 1987—89, pres., 1989—92. Woodrow Wilson fellow, 1967-78; recipient James Loudon Gold medal U. Toronto, 1967. Office: Alfred P Sloan Found 630 5th Ave Rm 2550 New York NY 10111-0100

GREENWOOD, VIRGINIA MAXINE MCLEOD, real estate executive, broker; b. Ballinger, Tex., Mar. 3, 1930; d. Vernie L. and Alma (Simpson) McLeod; m. Lester Greenwood, Apr. 21, 1951 (div. May 1985), children: Virginia Leslie Pattison, Randal Lester, Sheree Lou Stiles. Student, Draughn's Bus. Sch., Wichita Falls, 1948-49; completed real estate courses, Grad. Realtors Inst., 1972. Cert. residential specialist; cert. buyer rep. Sr. real estate specialist, real estate agt. C. V. Perry Co., Columbus, Ohio, 1967-69; real estate agt. Montague, Miller and Co., Charlottesville, Va., 1970-74; sales mgr. Great Eastern Mgmt. Corp., Charlottesville, 1974-75; real estate broker Greenwood Realty Ltd., Charlottesville, 1975-93; sr. assoc. broker Coldwell Banker-Bailey Realty Co., Charlottesville, 1993-98; assoc. broker Real Estate III, Charlottesville, 1998—. Mem. Monticello Area Cmty. Action Agy. adv. bd., 1988-92, Albemarle (Va.) County Rep. com., 1974-76; Albemarle County Housing adv. com., 1991-92, 94—, Thomas Jefferson Planning Dist. Housing adv. com., 1991-92; mem. Albemarle Housing Coalition, 1989-96. Mem. Nat. Assn. Realtors, Va. Assn. Realtors (bd. dirs. 1985-92), Charlottesville Area Assn. of Realtors (sec. 1983-84, bd. dirs. 1983-91, 2d v.p. 1988, 1st v.p. 1989, pres. 1990) Avocations: reading, gardening, genealogy. Office: Real Estate III PO Box 8186 Charlottesville VA 22906-8186 E-mail: jennyg@charlottesville.net.

GREENWOOD, WILLIAM WARREN, journalist; b. Richmond, Va., Mar. 28, 1942; s. William Rogers and Gloria Vivian (Brown) Warren; m. Marsha Ann Sheppard, Dec. 21, 1968; 1 child, Kelly. Student, Fla. State U., 1960-63; BA, Am. U., 1970. Announcer Sta. WZRO, Jacksonville Beach, Fla., 1956-60; newscaster Sta. WMBR, Jacksonville, Fla., 1960-64, Sta. WPDQ, Jacksonville, 1964-66, Sta. WWDC, Washington, 1966-67; dir. pub. affairs Nat. Ednl. Radio, Washington, 1967-68; news corr. U.P.I., Washington, 1968-70; corr. MBS, Washington, 1970-74, v.p. news, 1974-76; news corr. Sta. WCBS-TV, N.Y.C., 1976-79, ABC News, N.Y.C., 1979, White House corr. Washington, 1980-81, Washington corr., 1981—. Guest lectr. NYU, 1975, 76; chmn. Congl. Radio-TV Galleries, Washington, 1975; guest lectr. Am. U., 1967; v.p. Nat. Press Bldg. Corp., 1974, Nat. Press Club, 1974; coverage participant ABC Peabody award, 2002. Recipient award of merit ARC, 1960, 61; Emmy award, 1978; Emmy nomination, 1979; N.Y.C. Firefighters award, 1979; Am. Bankers Assn. award, 1981. Mem. Radio and TV Corrs. Assn. (pres. 1975), White House Corrs. Assn., Fla. State U. Alumni Assn. (founding v.p. Washington chpt. 1974-75), ARC Lifeguard Alumni Assn. Episcopalian. Office: ABC Washington Bur 1717 Desales St NW Washington DC 20036-4407 E-mail: bill.greenwood@abc.com.

GREER, ALAN GRAHAM, lawyer; b. El Dorado, Ark., May 31, 1939; s. Arthur W. and Marie (Ross) G.; m. Patricia A. Seitz, Aug. 14, 1981. BS, U.S. Naval Acad., 1961; JD, U. Fla., 1969. Ptnr. Richmnan, Greer Weil Brumbaugh, Miami, Fla., 1969—. Chmn. emeritus WLRN Pub. Radio and TV Sta.; bd. dirs. Camillus Ho. Past chmn. Dade County Coun. Arts and Scis.; past mem. Fla. State Task Force on Water Issues, Gov.'s Bus. Adv. Coun. on Edn.; co-chmn. site selection com. Dem. Nat. Com., 1992, also trustee. With USN, 1961-67. Fellow Internat. Soc. Barristers, Am. Coll. Trial Lawyers; mem. ABA (standing com. on professionalism), Fla. Bar Assn. (cert., past chmn. internat. law com.). Home: 224 Ridgewood Rd Miami FL 33133-6614 Office: Richman Greer Weil Brumbaugh Miami Ctr 10th Fl 201 S Biscayne Blvd Miami FL 33131-4332 E-mail: agreen@richmangreer.com.

GREER, ALLEN CURTIS, II, lawyer, investment management executive; b. New Rochelle, N.Y., Dec. 6, 1951; s. Allen Wilkinson and Nancy (Carroll) G.; children: Katharine Burrage, Constance Carroll, Genevieve Forbes. AB, Harvard U., 1972, JD, 1975. Assoc. Cadwalader, Wickersham & Taft, N.Y.C., 1975-79, Palmer & Dodge, Boston, 1979-82; ptnr. Gaston & Snow, Boston and N.Y.C., 1982-91, Rogers & Wells, 1991-97, Cadwalader, Wickersham & Taft, N.Y.C., 1997-99, of counsel, 1999—; with Westbrook Real Estate Counsel, 1999—. Bd. dirs. various pvt. cos. Mem.: Urban Land Inst., Nat. Assn. Real Estate Investment Trusts. Office: Westbrook Ptnrs One Beacon St Ste 3400 Boston MA 02108 E-mail: cgreer@westbrookpartners.com.

GREER, CARL CRAWFORD, petroleum company executive; b. Pitts., June 12, 1940; s. Joseph Moss and Gene (Crawford) G.; m. Jerrine Ehlers, June 16, 1962 (div.); children: Caryn, Michael, Janet; m. Patricia Taylor, Feb. 4, 1989. BS, Lehigh U., 1962; PhD, Columbia U., 1966; PsyD, Ill. Sch. Profl. Psychology, Chgo., 1993. Lic. clin. psychologist and Jungian analyst. Assoc. in bus. Columbia U., 1964-66, asst. prof. banking and finance, 1966-67; retail mktg. mgr. Martin Oil Service Inc., Alsip, Ill., 1967-68, exec. v.p., 1968, pres., dir., 1968-76, chmn. bd., pres., 1976-85; pres., dir. Martin Mktg. Corp. GP Martin Oil Mktg. Ltd., 1982, MEMCO Mgmt. Corp. GP Martin Exploration Mgmt. Co., 1985. Bd. dirs. Fin. Assocs., Inc. Mem. Beta Theta Pi, Tau Beta Pi, Beta Gamma Sigma, Omicron Delta Kappa. Presbyterian.

GREER, CAROLE KILBY, reading specialist; b. Anawalt, W.Va., Jan. 11, 1950; d. Mark W. Kilby and Helen S. (Shepherd) Byrd; m. Jackie D. Greer Sr., July 3, 1965; children: Jackie D. Jr., Sara, Tara. BA in Edn., Emory & Henry Coll., 1979; MEd, U. Va., 1990. Tchrs. aide Head Start, Marion, Va.; tchr. Sugar Grove (Va.) Sch., 1979-2000; county reading specialist Smuth County Sch. Sys., Marion, Va., 2000—. Presenter in field. Vol. Falling Water Bapt. Ch., Marion, 1980—; sec. Sugar Grove PTO, 1979-80. Mem. Va. Reading Assn., S.W. Va. Reading Coun., Internat. Reading Assn. Home: 445 Wassona Dr Marion VA 24354-4425 Office: Smyth County Sch System Ste 300 121 Bagley Cir Marion VA 24354 E-mail: carolegreer@scsb.mail.org

GREER, CHARLES EUGENE, company executive, lawyer; b. Columbus, Ohio, Mar. 28, 1945; s. Earl E. Greer and Margaret I. Cavanass; 1 child, Erin Elizabeth. BS, Ind. U., 1972, JD, 1976. Bar: Ind. 1976. Pres. Willoughby Industries, Inc., Indpls., 1976-91, pres., CEO, 1991-93; ptnr. Ice Miller Donadio & Ryan, 1976-91; pres. ECM Corp., Indpls., 1993—, Loggins, Inc., Indpls., 1995—, bus. turnaround specialist, 1995—. Served to sgt. USAF, 1965-68, Vietnam. Mem. Ind. Bar Assn., Order of Coif, Phi Eta Sigma, Beta Gamma Sigma. Office: 5581 Sunset Ln Indianapolis IN 46228-1468

GREER, DAVID S. university dean, physician, educator; b. Bklyn., Oct. 12, 1925; s. Jacob and Mary (Zaslawsky) Greer; m. Marion Clarich, June 25, 1950; children: Jeffrey, Linda. BS, U. Notre Dame, 1948; MD, U. Chgo., 1953; MA (hon.), Brown U., 1975; LHD (hon.), Southeastern Mass. U., 1981. Diplomate Am. Bd. Internal Medicine. Intern Yale-New Haven Med. Center, 1953—54; resident in medicine U. Chgo. Clinics, 1954—57; instr. endocrinology and medicine U. Chgo., 1957; practice medicine specializing in internal medicine Fall River, Mass., 1957—74; chief staff dept. medicine Fall River Gen. Hosp., 1959—62; med. dir. Earle E. Hussey Hosp., Fall River, 1962—75; chief staff dept. medicine Truesdale Clinic and Truesdale Hosp., Fall River, 1971—74, pres. med. staff, 1968—70; sr. clin. instr. medicine Tufts U. Coll. Medicine, 1969—71, asst. clin. prof., 1971—78; clin. asso. prof. community health Brown U., 1973—75, dir. family practice residency program, 1975—78, prof. community health, 1975—93, prof. emeritus, 1993—, assoc. dean medicine, 1974—81, dean medicine, 1981—92, dean emeritus, 1992—, chmn. sect. community health, 1978—81. Mem. Gov.'s Task Force on Quality of Care, Medicaid Program, Commonwealth of Mass., 1969—70; del. White House Conf. Aging, 1971, 81; pres. Ind. Living Authority, State of R.I., 1975—81; mem. exec. com. Cancer Control Bd. R.I., 1975—80; mem. R.I. Gov.'s Task Force for Inst. of Mental Health, 1976—81; bd. dirs. Health Planning Coun., Inc., Providence, 1976—78; chmn. com. on aging Jewish Fedn. R.I., 1978—80; chmn. Gov.'s Commn. on Provision of Comprehensive Mental Health Svcs. in R.I., 1980—81; trustee Southeastern Mass. U., 1970—81, chmn., 1973—74, Providence Mayor's Sr. Citizens Task Force, 1975; bd. dirs. Assn. Home Health Agys. R.I., 1975—80; founding dir. Internat. Physicians for Prevention of Nuc. War, Inc., 1980—85; vis. prof. dept. medicine Georgetown U., 1992—93; scholar-in-residence Assn. Am. Med. Colls., 1992—93. Contbr. articles to profl. jours. Named Prof. of the Yr., Brown U., 1992; recipient Outstanding Svc. award, Mass. Easter Seal Soc., 1970, Outstanding Citizens award, Jewish War Vets. Aux., 1973, Disting. Svc. award, U. Chgo. Med. Alumni Assn., Cutting Found. medal, Andover Newton Theol. Sem., 1976; fellow in health, Kellogg Found. Internat., 1986—89, vis. fellow, Green Coll. Oxford U., 1985. Master: ACP; mem.: R.I. Med. Soc., Internat. Soc. Rehab. Medicine, Am. Congree Rehab. Medicine, Gerontol. Soc., Inst. Medicine. Jewish. Office: Brown U Box G Providence RI 02912 E-mail: Greer@brown.edu.

GREER, GEORGE RUSHTON, psychiatrist; b. Port Arthur, Tex., Apr. 13, 1950; s. Rushton Calhoun and Mary Louise Greer; m. Requa Tolbert, May 24, 1981; 1 child, Autry Greer Tolbert. BA, Vassar Coll., 1972; MD, U. Tex., 1976. Intern and resident in psychiatry San Mateo County Mental Health Svcs., 1976-79; pvt. practice San Francisco, 1979-82, Santa Fe, N.Mex., 1982—; clin. dir. mental health svcs. N.Mex. Corrections Dept., Santa Fe, 1992-98; med. dir. Heffter Rsch. Inst., Santa Fe, 1998—. Co-editor: Jour. Psychoactive Drugs, 1998. Fellow Am. Psychiat. Assn. (disting.); mem. Psychiat. Med. Assn. N.Mex. (pres. 1996-97, legis. rep. 1994-95, 98—). Office: 453 Cerrillos Rd Ste E Santa Fe NM 87501

GREER, GERMAINE, author; b. Melbourne, Australia, Jan. 29, 1939; d. Eric Reginald and Margaret May Mary (Lafrank) G. BA with honors in English, French Lit., U. Melbourne, 1959; MA with honors in English, U. Sydney, Australia, 1961; PhD (Commonwealth scholar), Newnham Coll. of Cambridge U., Eng., 1967; Doctorate (hon.), U. Griffith, 1996, U. York, Toronto, 1999, Manchester Inst. Tech., 2000. Sr. tutor U. Sydney, 1963-64; lectr. English U. Warwick, Eng., 1967-72; prof. modern letters U. Tulsa, 1980-83; dir. Tulsa Ctr. for Study of Woman's Lit.; prof. English and comparative studies U. Warwick, 1998—. Vis. prof. grad. faculty modern letters U. Tulsa, fall 1979; founder-dir. Tulsa Centre for the Study of Women's Lit.; founder, editor Tulsa Studies in Women's Lit., 1981; dir. Stump Cross Books, 1988—; spl. lectr. and unofcl. fellow Newnham Coll., Cambridge, 1989-98; lectr. in N.Am. Am. Program Bur., 1973-78. Author: The Female Eunuch, 1969, The Obstacle Race: The Fortunes of Women Painters and their Work, 1979, Sex and Destiny: The Politics of Human Fertility, 1984, Shakespeare, 1986, The Madwoman's Underclothes, 1986, Daddy, We Hardly Knew You, 1989 (J.R. Ackerly Prize, Premio Internazionale Mondello), The Change: Women, Aging and the Menopause, 1991, Slip-Shod Sibyls: Recognition, Rejection and the Woman Poet, 1995, The Surviving Works of Anne Wharton, 1997; editor: (with Susan Hastings, Jeslyn Medoff, Melinda Sansone) Kissing the Rod: An Anthology of Seventeenth Century Women's Verse, 1988, The Uncollected Verse of Aphra Behn, 1989, The Change: Women, Aging and the Menopause, 1991, Slip-Shod Sibyls: Recognition, Rejection and the Woman Poet, 1995, The Whole Woman, 1999, The Whole Woman, 1999; selected journalism published as The Madwoman's Underclothes, 1986, columnist Sunday Times, London, 1971-73, broadcaster/journalist/reviewer various publs. 1972-79. Jr. Govt. scholar, 1952, Diocesan scholar, 1956, Sr. Govt. scholar, 1956, Commonwealth scholar, 1964, Teacher's Coll. Studentship, 1956, Hon. Doctorate Univ. of Griffith, 1996.

GREER, GORDON BRUCE, retired lawyer, writer; b. Butler, Pa, Feb. 17, 1932; s. Samuel Walker and Winifred (Fletcher) G.; m. Nancy Linda Hannaford, June 14, 1959; children: Gordon Bruce, Alison Clark. BA, Harvard U., 1953, JD cum laude, 1959. Bar: Wis. 1959, Mass. 1961. Assoc. Foley, Sammond & Lardner, Milw., 1959-61; assoc. Bingham Dana LLP, Boston, 1961-67, ptnr., 1967-97, of counsel, 1997—2002; ret., 2002. Lectr. Boston U. Sch. Law, 1998-2002; bd. dir. Strong Mut. Funds., Menomonee Falls, Wis. Editor Harvard Law Rev. Vos. 71, 72; author: World in Conflict, 2003. Maj. USAFR (ret.) Mem. Mass. Bar Assn., Boston Bar Assn., Brae Burn Country Club, Harvard Club (Boston). Republican. Home: 45 Fieldmont Rd Belmont MA 02478-2606

GREER, K. GORDON, banker; b. Tulsa, Oct. 28, 1936; s. H.K. and Afton (Goodman) G.; m. Nancy Lang, Nov. 22, 1958; children— Keith G., Scott A. BS in Banking and Fin., Okla. State U., 1958; postgrad. Grad. Sch. Banking, U.

Wis.-Madison, 1964-67. Pres. Liberty Nat. Bank, Oklahoma City, 1958-84; CEO The First Nat. Bank and Trust Co., Tulsa, 1984—89, pres., 1989—96; vice chmn. BancFirst Corp., Tulsa. With Air Force N.G., 1958-64 Named to Hall of Fame, Bus. Adminstrn. Sch. Okla. State U., 1984 Mem. Am. Bankers Assn., Okla. Bankers Assn. (pres. 1983-84), Assn. Res. City Bankers Clubs: So. Hills Country, Tulsa (Tulsa). Republican. Methodist. Avocation: golf.

GREER, MACK VARNEDOE, retired physician; b. Valdosta, Ga., July 29, 1927; s. Lloyd Barton an dJulie Winn (Varnedoe) G.; m. Betty Dame English, Dec. 27, 1951; children: Betty June, Mack Varnedoe. AB, Emory U., 1951; MD, Med. Coll. Ga., 1960. Diplomate Am. Bd. Family Practice. Adjustor Crawford & Co., ins. adjusters, Atlanta, 1951—52; math and sci. tchr., football coach Clinch County (Ga.) and Waycross (Ga.) h.s., 1952—55; rotating intern Bapt. Meml. Hosp., Jacksonville, Fla., 1960—61; gen. practice medicine and surgery, Homerville, Ga., 1961—72; mem. staff South Ga. Me.d Ctr., 1972—95; chief staff South Ga. Med. Ctr., 1980; coll. physician, assoc. prof. biology Valdosta State U., 1972—95, emeritus prof., from 1995. Former bd. dirs. Valdosta Girls Club. With USMC, WWII, 1944-45, Korian War, 1950-51, ret., capt. M.C. USNR, 1944-87. Fellow Am. Acad. Family Practice; mem. AMA, Ga. Med. Assn., South Ga. Med. Soc., Valdosta Touchdown Club, Valdosta Country Club, Pi Kappa Alpha, Alpha Kappa Kappa. Presbyterian. Home: Valdosta, Ga. Died Sept. 6, 2002.

GREER, MELVIN, medical educator; b. N.Y.C., Oct. 14, 1929; s. Aaron and Ceil (Cohen) Jefkel; m. Arline Ebert, Dec. 16, 1951; children: Jonathan, Richard, Alison, David. BA magna cum laude, NYU, 1950, MD, 1954. Intern, resident Bellevue Hosp., N.Y.C., 1954-56; fellow N.Y. Neurol. Inst., Columbia, 1958-61; prof., chmn. dept. neurology U. Fla. Coll. Medicine, Gainesville, 1963-2000. Cons. NIH, 1971—, Fla. Div. Corrections, 1971— ; lectr., cons. Navy Dept.; prof. dept. neurol. dept. psychiatry, dept. pediatrics, U. Fla. Coll. Medicine; endowed professorship neurology U. Fla. Coll. Medicine, Gainesville, 1991—. Author: Mass Spectrometry of Biologically Important Aromatic Acids, 1969, Differential Diagnosis of Neurological Diseases, 1977; also articles.; Editorial bd.: Neurology, Geriatics, 1968— . Served to lt. comdr. USNR, 1956-58. Recipient Medallion award Columbia U., 1968, Hippocratic award U. Fla., 1970, Outstanding Clin. Tchr. award, 1975, 79; NIH grantee, 1962-71 Fellow Am. Acad. Neurology (councillor, sec.-treas. 1977-81, pres.-elect 1983-85, pres. 1985-87), Am. Acad. Pediatrics; mem. Am. Neurol. Assn. (councillor), Soc. Pediatric Research, Am. Pediatric Soc., Phi Beta Kappa, Alpha Omega Alpha. Home: 2058 NW 14th Ave Gainesville FL 32605-5245

GREER, RAYMOND WHITE, lawyer; b. Port Arthur, Tex., July 20, 1954; s. Mervyn Hardy Greer and Eva Nadine (White) Swain; m. Pamela V. Brown; children: Emily Ann, Sarah Kelly, Jonathan Collin. BA magna cum laude, Sam Houston State, 1977; JD, U. Houston, 1981. Assoc. Hoover, Cox & Shearer, Houston, 1980-83, Hinton & Morris, Houston, 1983-85; pvt. practice Houston, 1985-86; prin. Morris & Greer, P.C., Houston, 1986-90, Raymond W. Greer & Assocs., P.C., Houston, 1990-98, Rigg & Greer, Houston, 1998—. Lectr. in field; mem. dist. 4 grievance com. State Bar Tex. Mem. adv. com. Enterprising Girls Scouts Beyond Bars, San Jacinto coun., 1996-98. Recipient Outstanding Alumnus award, Dept. English, Sam Houston U., 1986, Disting. Alumni, Tex. Omicron chpt., Alpha Chi, 1996. Mem.: ABA, Ft. Bend County Bar Assn., Houston Bar Assn., State Bar Tex., Sam Houston State U. Alumni Assn. (combined charter and membership com. 1995—96, 1st v.p. 1996—97, pres. 1997—98, 2d v.p., chmn. membership com.), Rotary Club Houston (dir. 1999—2001, at large dir. 1998—99, chair Fresh Start com. 1997—98, asst. chair Fresh Start com. 1996—97). Avocations: golf, reading. Office: Rigg & Greer 13333 Southwest Fwy Ste 100 Sugar Land TX 77478-3545

GREER, ROBERT BRUCE, III, retired orthopedic surgeon, educator; b. Butler, Pa., 1934; BA, Haverford Coll., 1956; MD, Harvard U., 1960. Diplomate Am. Bd. Orthopaedic Surgery (bd. dirs. 1985-94, pres. 1990-91). Intern Mich. Med. Ctr., 1960-61, resident in surgery, 1961-62; resident in orthopaedic surgery Pitts. Med. Ctr., 1964-67, asst. prof. orthopedic surgery, 1967-71; orthopaedist MS Hershey Med. Ctr., Pa.; prof., chief orthopaedic surgery Pa. State U., 1971-91; ret. Med. dir. Howmedica, Inc., 1997-99. Capt. USAR, 1962-64. Mem. ACS, Am. Acad. Orthopaedic Surgeons, Am. Orthopaedic Assn., Ea. Orthopaedic Assn., Alpha Omega Alpha. Home: 166 Lake Meade Dr East Berlin PA 17316-9388

GREER, ROBERT E. insurance executive, retired; b. Louisville, July 24, 1937; s. William and Marguerite (Fleischaker) G.; m. Helen Dorothy Litton, July 1, 1976; children: Ashley, Alexis. BA, Cornell U., 1959; MBA, Harvard U., 1963. Mktg. research specialist Merrill Lynch, Inc. Co., N.Y.C., 1965-68; v.p. planning Hayden Stone Inc., N.Y.C., 1968-70, Reynolds Securities, Inc., N.Y.C., 1970-75; v.p. Chase Manhattan Bank, N.Y.C., 1975-80; v.p. mktg. research and planning Am. Stock Exchange, N.Y.C., 1980-83; v.p. fin. MBIA Ins. Corp., Armonk, N.Y., 1983-99; ret., 1999. Mem. exec. com. SEC Conf. on Small Bus. Capital Formation, 1982. Chmn. White Plains Dem. City Com., 1987-90; bd. dirs. Westchester County Assn., 1992-99, Westchester County chpt. ARC, 1992-96, Westchester Arts Coun., 1993-2001, Westchester Family Svcs., 2003—, Westchester County chpt. Habitat for Humanity, 1999—; mem. coun. Purchase Coll. Coun. SUNY, 1993-98; councilman City of White Plains, 1991—; trustee Purchase Coll. Found., 1999-2003; mem. White Plains Hist. Soc.; pres. White Plains Common Coun., 1996-98. With U.S. Armsdy, 1959-60. Mem. Govt. Finance Officers Assn., Urban Land Inst., Rotary. Avocation: collecting classical music recordings. Home: 20 Cushman Rd White Plains NY 10606-3706 E-mail: regreer@optonline.net.

GREER, SUZANNE MICHELLE, music educator; b. Duluth, Minn., May 14, 1968; d. Robert Leonard Moore and Beatrice Mae Sandum; m. David Lee Greer, May 20, 2000. MusB in Piano Performance, St. Olaf Coll., Northfield, Minn., 1990; MusM in Piano Performance, U. Minn., 1994. Cert. music tchr. Music Teachers Nat. Assn., 2001, motorcycle safety instr. Motorcycle Safety Found., 1999. Music dir. Trinity Episc. Ch., Anoka, Minn., 1997—98; piano instr. SG Studio, Minnetonka, Minn., 2002—; depot outreach artist-in-residence Depot Cmty. Outreach Program, Duluth, Minn., 1990—91; motorcycle safety instr. Mpls., 1999—; rider's edge new rider course instr. St. Paul Harley Davidson, 2001—; music instr. North Hennepin C.C., Brooklyn Park, Minn., 1994—2002, Anoka-Ramsey C.C., Coon Rapids, Minn., 2001—02; piano instr. Son-Sheim Music Sch., Anoka, Minn., 1994—2002; piano accompanist Robbinsdale All-District Choir, Robbinsdale, Minn., 2000—02. Liaison for bd. of dirs. Magnum Chorum (St Olaf Alumni Choir), St. Paul, 1998—2001; honors concert vol. coord. Minn. Music Tchrs. Assn., Mpls., 2002—. Scholar Music scholar, St. Olaf Coll., 1986, U. of Minn., 1993, Shar Products scholar, Suzuki Assn. of the Ams., 2002. Mem.: Suzuki Assn. for the Ams. (Shar Products Co. Scholarship for Tchr. Tng. 2002), Mpls. Music Tchrs. Forum (asst. recital com. chair 2003, My student won 2nd Pl. in Sr. Honors Contest 2001), Suzuki Piano Tchrs. Guild, Music Tchrs. Nat. Assn., West Suburban Music Tchrs. Assn., Minn. Music Tchrs. Assn. (honors concert vol. coord. 2002). D-Liberal. Presbyterian. Avocations: motorcycling, travel, weightlifting.

GREEVEN, RAINER, lawyer; b. Berlin, Dec. 6, 1936; s. Wolf and Marianne Kolck G.; m. Regina Jouvin, June 13, 1964; children— Andrea, Cristina. B.A., Cornell U., 1959; LL.B., Columbia U., 1962. Bar: N.Y. 1964, U.S. Dist. Ct. (so. dist.) N.Y. 1964. Assoc., Lord, Day & Lord, N.Y.C., 1963-67; assoc. Burke & Burke, N.Y.C., 1967-70, ptnr., 1971-77; ptnr. Morris & McVeigh, N.Y.C., 1977-87, Greeven & Ercklentz, N.Y.C., 1987—; dir. Continental Can Co., N.Y.C., Smith Barney World Funds, Smith Barney Travelers Funds; pres. Stuart (Fla.) Land Co., 1985-89. Founder, bd. dirs. South Fork Land Found., 1974. Mem. ABA, N.Y. State Bar Assn., Assn. Bar of City of N.Y., Internat. Bar Assn. Clubs: Knickerbocker (N.Y.C.); Meadow (Southampton, N.Y.). Home: 200 E 71st St New York NY 10021-5137 Office: Greeven & Ercklentz 630 5th Ave Ste 1905 New York NY 10111-0100

GREEVER, JANET GROFF, history educator; b. Philadelphia, Sept. 12, 1921; m. William St. Clair Greever, Aug. 24, 1951; 1 child. BA, Bryn Mawr Coll., 1942, MA, 1945, Harvard U., 1951, PhD, 1954. Resident head grad. houses Radcliffe Coll., Cambridge, Mass., 1947-48; resident head undergrad. hall Bryn Mawr (Pa.) Coll., 1949-51, instr. history, 1949-50; asst. prof. history Wash. State U., Pullman, 1962-63, U. Idaho, Moscow, 1965-66; ind. rschr., lectr. history Moscow, Idaho, 1954—. Interim lectr. history Whitman Coll., Walla Walla, Wash., 1978; Idaho regional admissions cons. and interviewer Bryn Mawr COll., 1955-81. Author: Jose Ballivian y El Oriente Boliviano, 1987. Bd. dirs. U. Idaho Libr. Assocs., Moscow, 1979-81, pres. 1980-81. Pa. State scholar, 1938-42, History fellow Bryn Mawr (Pa.) Coll., 1944-45, Margaret M. Justin fellow AAUW, Washington, 1948-49; grantee Lucius N. Littauer Found., N.Y.C., 1948-49. Mem. Am. Hist. Assn. (life), Conf. on Latin. Am. History (life), Latin Am. Studies Assn., Soc. for Am. Archaeology (life), Archaeol. Inst. Am. (life), Phi Alpha Theta. Avocations: travel, photography. Home: 315 S Hayes St Moscow ID 83843-3419

GREEVER, MARGARET QUARLES, retired mathematics educator; b. Wilkensburg, Pa., Feb. 7, 1931; d. Lawrence Reginald and Ella Mae (LeSueur) Quarles; m. John Greever, Aug. 29, 1953; children: Catherine Patricia, Richard George, Cynthia Diane. Cert. costume design, Richmond Profl. Inst., 1952; student, U. Va., 1953-56; BA in Math., Calif. State U., L.A., 1963; MA in Math., Claremont Grad. Sch., 1968. Cert. tchr. specializing in Jr. Coll. math., Calif. Tchr. math. Chaffey Unified H.S. Dist., Alta Loma, Calif., 1963-64, L.A. Unified Sch. Dist., 1964-65, Chino (Calif.) Unified Sch. Dist., 1965-81; from asst. prof. to prof. Chaffey Coll., Rancho Cucamonga, 1981-96, phys. sci. divsn. chmn. Alta Loma, 1985-92, dean, phys., life, health sci., 1992-96. Mem. AAUW (pres. local chpt. 1998-2000), Orcas Island Garden Club (treas. 1997-2000, pres.-elect 2000, pres. 2001), Orcas Island Yacht Club, Pi Lambda Theta. Avocations: quilting, cooking, sewing, gardening.

GREF, LYNN G. mathematician; BA in Math., U. Calif., Riverside, 1963, MA in Math., 1964, PhD in Math., 1966. Asst. prof. math. U. Mo., 1966—67; assoc. dir. Aerospace Corp., 1967—72; chief engr. R&D Assocs., 1972—89; program mgr./co-mgr. def. and civil programs office Jet Propulsion Lab., Pasadena, Calif., 1989—. Mem.Army Svc. Bd.; mem. naval rev. bd. NAS, 1994; quick depolyment evaluation panel mem. Ballistic Missile Def. Program Office, 1978; mem. M-X def. concept study panel Ballistic Missile Def. Systems Command, 1977. Office: Jet Propulsion Lab 4800 Oak Grove Dr Pasadena CA 91109

GREFE, ROLLAND EUGENE, lawyer; b. Ida County, Iowa, June 27, 1920; s. Alfred William and Zoma Corrine (Lasher) G.; m. Mary Arlene Cruikshank, June 12, 1943; 1 son, Roger Frederick. BA, Morningside Coll., 1941; JD, State U. Iowa, 1946. Bar: Iowa 1946. Assoc. Schaetzle, Williams & Stewart, Des Moines, 1946-48, Schaetzle, Swift, Austin & Stewart, Des Moines, 1948-52; ptnr. Schaetzle, Austin & Grefe (and related firms), Des Moines, 1952-60, Austin, Grefe & Sidney, Des Moines, 1960-71; sr. ptnr. Grefe & Sidney, Des Moines, 1971-95; mem. Grefe & Sidney P.L.C., 1995—. Dir. Freeman Decorating Co., 1969—, Cowles Syndicate, Inc., 1982-86; mem. bd. mgrs. Lawyers Com. Network, L.L.C., 1997-2000, chair, 1998-2000. Bd. dirs. Des Moines Area C.C., 1966-76, pres., 1967-76; bd. dirs. Westminster Presbyn. Ch. Found., 1975-89, Iowa State Bar Found., 1979-91; trustee Des Moines Water Works, 1984-99, pres., 1987, 91, 96. Lt. USNR, 1942-45. Fellow Am. Bar Found., Am. Coll. Trust and Estate Counsel; mem. ABA (ho. of dels. 1982-96, Iowa state del. 1992-93, bd. govs. 1993-96, standing com. on tech. and info. systems 1998-2001, sr. lawyers divsn. chair internet and tech. com. 2000-02), Assn. Endowment Found. Coll. (mem. pension plan adminstrn. com. 1994-2000), Polk County Bar Assn. (pres. 1971-72), Iowa State Bar Assn. (bd. govs. 1972-76, pres. 1978-79, chmn. com. on long-range planning 1979-81, Award of Merit 1982), Des Moines Estate Planners, Lincoln Inne. Clubs: Sertoma (Des Moines), Des Moines Embassy (Des Moines), Wakonda (Des Moines). Republican. Presbyterian. Home: 3524 Grand Ave Apt 803 Des Moines IA 50312-4344 Office: PO Box 10434 2222 Grand Ave Des Moines IA 50312-5306 E-mail: Rgrefe@grefesidney.com.

GREFRATH, PETER ALAN, marketing communications executive; b. Ridgewood, N.J., May 4, 1955; s. Warren Paul and Dorothy Lena (von Bieberstein) G.; m. Noeline Mary Dennis; children: Elizabeth Carmel, Victoria Noelle. BS in Journalism, U. Md., 1977; MBA in Mgmt., Fairleigh Dickinson U., 1991. Editor Met. Life, N.Y.C., 1977-80; editor, comm. specialist Sperry Corp., Lake Success, N.Y., 1980-81; mgr. internal comm. Alexander & Alexander Svcs., Inc., N.Y.C., 1981-89; mgr. mtkg. and client comm. Continental Asset Mgmt., N.Y.C., 1989-95; asst. v.p. Trust Co. of the West, N.Y.C., 1995—. Councilman Borough of Westwood, N.J., 1995, 97—, coun. pres. 2001—, mem. Planning Bd., Borough of Westwood, 1994, 96, Heritage Soc., Borough of Westwood, 1992; pres. Westwood Rep. Orgn., 1997; mem., sec. local assessment com., Borough of Westwood, 1997—; pres. Internat. Assn. Bus. Communicators, 1990-91. Republican. Episcopalian. Avocations: golf, skiing, baseball, soccer, gardening. Home: 17 Fifth Ave Westwood NJ 07675-2005 Office: Trust Co of West 200 Park Ave Ste 2200 New York NY 10166-0005 E-mail: peter.grefrath@tcw.com.

GREGA, ANDREW MICHAEL, music educator; b. Sharon, Pa., Nov. 26, 1971; s. William and Andrea Grega. MusB, Bowling Green State U., 1990—94; MA in music edn., The Ohio State U., 1998—2000. Cert. tchg. Dept. of Ohio, 1994. Dir. of choral activities St. Mary's City Schools, Ohio, 1995—99; grad. tchg. asst. Ohio State U., Columbus, 1999—2000; vocal music dir. Brookpark Mid. Sch., South-Western City Schools, Grove City, Ohio, 2000—03, Grandview Hts. High/Mid. Schs., Columbus, 2003—. Adult choir dir. Grace Luth. Ch., Elmore, Ohio, 1993—95; sr. choir dir. St. John Luth. Ch., Celina, Ohio, 1996—99; summer day camp counselor/dir./lifeguard Eastwood Family YMCA, Niles, Ohio, 1991—95. Actor: (plays) Fiddler On The Roof, The Sound of Music, The Music Man, Lost in Yonkers; dir.: You're A Good Man, Charlie Brown, Oklahoma!; singer: Lima Symphony Chorus, BGSU Men's Chorus, BGSU Collegiate Chorale, Ohio State U. Men's Glee Club, Ohio State U. Chorale, Columbus Symphony Chorus, 2002—. Recipient Golden Key Nat. Honor Soc., Bowling Green State U., 1994, Phi Eta Sigma Freshman Hon., 1991; Grad. Tchg. Assistantship, The Ohio State U., 1999—2000. Mem.: Music Educators Nat. Conf., Ohio Music Edn. Assn. (contest adjudicator), Am. Choral Directors Assn., BGSU Men's Chorus Alumni Soc., Phi Mu Alpha Sinfonia (music dir. 1993—94). Avocations: physical fitness, theater, outdoor recreation, dogs. Office: Grandview Hts HS 1587 W Third Ave Columbus OH 43212 Personal E-mail: agzeke@aol.com. Business E-mail: agrega@grandviewschools.org., agzeke@columbus.rr.com.

GREGAN, EDMUND ROBERT, landscape architect; b. New Haven, Feb. 4, 1936; s. Edmund Arthur and Elizabeth (Kochiss) G.; m. Janet Lamson Shaw, Aug. 22, 1959; children: Edmund Robert, Darianne Lee, Christyn Elizabeth. BS in Landscape Architecture, R.I. Sch. Design, 1960. Lic. landscape architect, Conn. Landscape architect and site planner Morton S. Fine & Assocs., Hartford, Conn., 1960-62; landscape architect New Haven Redevel. Agy., 1962-66, chief landscape architect, 1966-78; landscape architect, cons., lectr. E. Robert Gregan Landscape Architect, Northford, Conn., 1965—; chief landscape architect New Haven City Plan Dept., 1978-91. Instr. landscape architecture Guilford/Madison (Conn.) Adult Edn. Programs, 1979-88; tchr., critic Yale, R.I. Sch. Design, U. Conn. Conway Sch. Landscape Design, So. Conn. State U.; tchr. environ. design Yale Sch. of Forestry and Environtl. Studies Elem. Schs. New Haven, 1992; tchr. Federated Garden Clubs Conn. Sch. Landscape Design, 1979—; lectr. various orgns. and clubs. Contbr. numerous profl. jours. Bd. dirs. North Branford Land Conservation Trust, 1968-72, v.p., 1973—; mem. North Branford Conservation Commn., 1969-73, chmn., 1971-72, assoc. mem., 1973-92; cons. North Branford Ctr. Improvement Com., 1991-95; mem. North Branford-Northford Town Design Dists. Adv. Com., 1995—; bd. dirs. New Haven Urban Resources Initiative, 1991-96; mem. steering com. Long Wharf Nature Preserve, 1995-2000; landscape arch., vice chair spl. events 1995 Spl. Olympics World Games. Recipient Cert. of Achievement award Federated Garden Clubs. Conn., 1981, Bronze medal Federated Garden Clubs Conn., 1991, Cert. of Merit for Excellence in Study of Landscape Architecture, RISD, 1960, Outstanding Urban Forestry Profl. award Urban Forest Coun., 2001, numerous profl. design awards. Fellow Am. Soc. Landscape Architects; mem. Conn. Soc. Landscape Architects (bd. dir. 1981-86, hist. and landscape preservation com. 1987—, George A. Yarwood Cert. Svc. award 1987), Totoket Hist. Soc. (mem. design cons. 1972—), Garden Club New Haven (hon. mem.), Federated Garden Clubs of Conn., Inc. (hon. mem. landscape design critics coun. 1993). Episcopalian. Avocations: design, gardening, photography, travel. Home and Office: 7 Stair Brook Way Northford CT 06472-1495

GREGAN, JOHN PATRICK, finance executive, small business owner; b. Sigourney, Iowa, Nov. 24, 1947; s. Raymond Stephen and Ellen Mary (O'Brien) G.; m. Rhonda Mason Weissberg, Nov. 19, 1977; children: Brien Geoffrey, Audrey Jane. BA in Acctg., St. Ambrose Coll., Davenport, Iowa, 1970. Profl. lic. enrolled agt. Internal revenue agt. IRS, Davenport, Iowa, 1970-71; computer audit specialist OIO (office of internal ops.), Washington, 1971-79; tax acct. SMATAX Corp., Waldorf, Md., 1979—. Md. del. to Internat. Soc. Pub. Accts. Conv., 1987, 92. Diplomate, Rome, 1973; bd. dirs. The Home Inc., Alexandria, Va., 1992-96. Mem. Nat. Soc. Pub. Accts., Md. Soc. Pub. Accts., Nat. Assn. Enrolled Agts., Md. Soc. Enrolled Agts., Nat. Soc. Tax Profls. Democrat. Roman Catholic. Home: 13210 Breezy Ct Waldorf MD 20601-2000 Office: TS SMATAX 11865 Federal Sq Ste 106 Waldorf MD 20602-3226 E-mail: gr8full1040@yahoo.com., smatax@att.net.com.

GREGANTI, MAC ANDREW, physician, medical educator; b. Cleveland, Miss., Apr. 13, 1947; s. Mack Americo and Grace Margaret (Barbati) G.; m. Susan Taylor, Aug. 8, 1971; children: Paul Andrew, Mack Taylor, Mary Catherine. BS summa cum laude, Millsaps Coll., 1969; MD summa cum laude, U. Miss., 1972. Diplomate Am. Bd. Internal Medicine, Am. Bd. Geriat. medicine. Intern U. Rochester, N.Y., 1972-73, resident, 1973-75; instr. dept. medicine U. Miss. Sch. Medicine, Jackson, 1975-76, asst. prof., 1976-77, U. N.C. Sch. Medicine, Chapel Hill, 1977-83, assoc. prof., 1983-90, prof., 1990—, chief div. gen. medicine, 1986-91, assoc. chair for clin. affairs, 1991-99, acting chmn., 1999-2000, vice-chmn., 2000—. Dir. med./pediatric residency U. N.C. Dept. Medicine, Chapel Hill, 1980-86, dir. medicine residency, 1981-86. Contbr. articles on med. edn. and patient care to profl. jours. Fellow ACP; mem. Am. Geriatrics Soc., Alpha Oemga Alpha. Roman Catholic. Avocations: computers, tennis, golf. Office: Univ NC Chapel Hill Dept of Medicine 3029 Old Clinic Bldg Cb 7005 Chapel Hill NC 27599-7005

GREGERSEN, EDGAR ALSTRUP, anthropologist, educator, linguist, writer, researcher; b. New York, NY, Apr. 24, 1937; s. Carl and Solveig (Lamberg) Gregersen. BA, Queens Coll., NYC, NY, 1957; PhD, Yale U, New Haven, Conn, 1962. Instr. Columbia U, NYC, 1963—68, lectr., 1963—68; lang. coord. Nigerian Peace Corps, NYC, 1963—64, tchr. for E Africa, NYC, 1963—64; assoc. prof. Queens Coll., CUNY, NYC, 1968—74, Grad. Sch., CUNY, NYC, 1969—74; prof. Queens Coll., CUNY, NYC, 1974—, Grad. Sch., CUNY, NYC, 1974—. Supr., cultural tour of Italy(arch. sect.) Italian-Am Outreach Program, NYC, 1983. Author: Prefix and Pronoun in Bantu, 1967, Lang. in Africa, 1977, Sexual Practices (World of Human Sexuality), 1982, 1994, 1996. Recipient Phi Beta Kappa, Queens Coll./ NY, 1956, Sigma XI, Yale U/ New Haven, Conn, 1961; grantee Fulbright Hays Travel, NDEA, 1964. Fellow: Am. Anthrop. Assoc., Royal Anthrop. Inst., Explorers Club. Democrat. Agnostic. Avocations: spelling reform, Egyptology, photography, history. Home: 302 W 12th St Apt 16F New York NY 10014-6035 Office: Queens College Dept of Anthropology 65-30 Kissena Blvd Flushing NY 11367-1597

GREGERSEN, MAX A. structural, earthquake and civil engineer; b. Blackfoot, Idaho, Apr. 6, 1951; s. Garth Clifford and Ella Lavere (Adamson) G.; m. Fontaine Merritt, Dec. 6, 1997; children: Dusty Rae, Molly Malinda, Francesca, Claire, Jonathan. BSCE, U. Utah, 1976. Registered profl. engr. Ala., Alaska, Ark., Calif., Del., Fla., Ga., Idaho, Ind., Ill., Kans., La., Maine, Mich., Minn., Miss., Mo., Mont., Nev., N.J., N.Y., N.C., N.D., Ohio, Okla., Pa., S.C., Tenn., Tex., Utah, Vt., Wash., Wis., Wyo., Alta. Can., P.R.; cert. structural engr. Civil, structural engr. Kellogg-Rust Engring., Salt Lake City, 1976-83; mgr. civil-structural engring. dept. Ford, Bacon & Davis, Inc., Salt Lake City, 1983-95; prin. civil-structural engr. Centry Constructors and Engrs., Salt Lake City, 1995—99; pres. Gregersen Structural Engring., Inc., Midway, Utah, 1999—. Corres. mem. Fed. Emergency Mgmt. Agy. Nat. Earthquake Hazards Reduction Program; seismic provisions tech. subcoms. for steel and concrete structures Bldg. Seismic Safety Coun., Washington, 1994, seismic provisions update com. for steel structures, 1992—; vol. mem. applied tech. coun. Fed. Emergency Mgmt. Agy.-sponsored ATC-33 Project devel. guidelines for seismic rehab. existing bldgs. concrete team, 1993—; curriculum adv. bd., lectr. dept. civil engring. U. Utah, 1993—; adv. com. Utah Seismic Safety Commn. Engring. and Arch., 1995—. Mem. ASCE (structural engring. inst. seismic rehab. standards com. 1997—), Am. Concrete Inst. (com. 369 Seismic repair and rehab. 1992—), Nat. Inst. Bldg. Scis., Earthquake Engring. Rsch. Inst., Structural Engrs. Assn. Utah, Internat. Conf. Bldg. Ofcls., Assn. Profl. Engrs., Geologists, and Geophysicists Alta. Achievements include seismic evaluation and/or retrofit of existing heavy indsl. facilities, including: thermal catalytic cracking, olefin, gasoline stripping, depropanizing, solvent recovery, RDC deasphalting, waste heat boilers, synthetic crude, butane isomerization, frozen earth propane storage, solid fuel rocket motor prodn., copper smelting, silver and gold refining, hazardous waste incineration, machine shop, power house, change house, fire station, railroad switchhouse, mill bldg., rolling mill, open hearth and blast furnace, smoke stacks, coke oven, hazardous material tank storage and LNG petroleum tank storage facilities; seismic restraint of piping, and of mechanical, electrical and process equipment; engring. designs and/or constrn. of major petroleum refining or sulfur recovery units in the U.S., Spain and Aruba, hazardous waste incineration facilities in the U.S. and Can., indsl. wastewater treatment facilities in the U.S. and Mex.,gold, phosphates handling facilities in Morocco, Venezuela, and Brazil, chem. plants, mining, milling, smelting, coal processing, and material handling, power plant, slipformed concrete coal storage silos, solid fuel rocket motor production, roadway, railroad, dam, mcpl. waste composting, and geosynthetic-lined waste containment facilities.

GREGERSEN, R(OALD) GEORGE, newspaper publishing executive; b. Copenhagen, Mar. 14, 1935; came to U.S., 1948; s. Richard Vilhelm and Eva (Giertsen) G.; m. Gayle Froerer Richards, May 1, 1964 (div. 1978); m. Penney Losse, Dec. 21, 1982; children: Mary Anne Georgia, John Christian. Student, U. Utah, 1953-55. Pres., CEO Mortgage Investment Corp., Salt Lake City, 1955-68; pres., CEO Gregersen & Co., Salt Lake City, 1968-74; pub., CEO The Enterprise (weekly), Salt Lake City, 1974—. Editl. writer The Enterprise, 1974—. Bd. dirs. Utal Mil. & Vets. Affairs com., Salt Lake City, 1982-92. Named Utah Mil. Citizen of Yr., 1986; recipient Assn. U.S. Army Exceptional Svc. award, 1990. Mem. Alta Club (bd. dirs. 1993-96), Rotary. Republican. Episcopalian. Avocation: flyfishing. Home: 1427 Circle Way Salt Lake City UT 84103-4433 Office: Enterprise Newspaper Group Inc 136 S Main St Ste 721 Salt Lake City UT 84101-1676

GREGG, BILLY RAY, seed industry executive, consultant; b. Taylorsville, Miss., Aug. 31, 1930; s. Hinds and Lillie Mae (Moore) G.; m. Mary Frances Barber, Aug. 12, 1950 (div. Jan. 1987); children: Kathryn, Patricia, Lisa; m. Orawan Chonlavorn, Dec. 20, 1988; 1 child, Nathan Paul. AA, Perkinston (Miss.) Jr. Coll., 1950; BS, Miss. State U., 1954, MS, 1956, PhD, 1968; postgrad., Wash. State U., 1957-63. Asst. prof. Wash. State U., Pullman, 1956-63; mgr. Ala. Crop Improvement Assn., Auburn, Ala., 1964-66; seed technologist Miss. State U., 1966-68; chief party/processing specialist seed improvement project U.S. AID, New Delhi, India, 1968-72, chief party and seed specialist seed project Brasilia, Brazil, 1972-74, chief, seed industry devel. specialist Bangkok, 1977-87, seed industry devel. specialist Cairo, 1987-93; chief party and seed industry specialist IDB and GOB Agiplan Project, Brasilia, 1974-76; seed industry specialist Internat. Plant Breeders, Maringa, Parana, Brazil, 1976, Interam. Agrl. Sci. Inst., Brasilia, 1976-77; seed industry devel. specialist internat. programs Miss. State U., 1993—. Cons./advisor on seed tech. matters, mgmt., quality control and industry devel. nat. govts., pvt. cos., World Bank, Interam. Devel. Bank, FAO, GTZ, U.S. AID in more than 80 countries, 1960-95. Contbr. over 500 articles to profl. jours.; author 2 books. With U.S. Army, 1950-52; ETO. Indian Soc. Seed Technologists fellow, 1987. Mem. Kiwanis Internat. (dir., Kiwanian of the Yr. 1968), Agrl. Sci. Soc. Thailand (hon.), Wash. State Crop Improvement Assn. (hon. life), Phi Kappa Phi, Sigma Xi, Phi Theta Kappa. Buddhist. Avocations: vegetable and flower gardening, writing, travel. Home: PO Box 1756 Starkville MS 39760-1756 E-mail: topgregg@bully.net.

GREGG, CHARLES THORNTON, research company executive; b. Billings, Mont., July 27, 1927; s. Charles Thornton and Gertrude (Hurst) G.; m. Elizabeth Whitaker, Dec. 20, 1947; children: Paul, Diane, Brian, Elaine. BS in Physics, Oreg. State U., 1952, MS in Organic Chemistry, 1955, PhD in Biochemistry, 1959. Postdoctoral fellow Nat. Cancer Inst., Johns Hopkins Sch. Med., Balt., 1959-63; mem. staff Los Alamos (N.Mex.) Nat. Lab., 1963-85; sr. scientist Mesa Diagnostics, Los Alamos, 1985-86; v.p. rsch. Los Alamos Diagnostics, 1986-90; pres. Innovative Surg. Tech. Inc., 1991—. Pres. Bethco, Inc., 1972—; vis. prof. The Free U., Berlin, 1973-74; cons. internat. tech. div. Los Alamos Nat. Lab., 1985-90. Author: Plague, 1978, The Virus of Love, 1983, Tarawa,

1985; patentee bacterial identification apparatus, safe surg. knife. Bd. dirs. Friends of Mesa Pub. Libr., Los Alamos, 1981-83, County Libr. Los Alamos, 1983-85, Los Alamos Arts Coun., 1985-87, bd. dir., Lukens Med. Corp., 1996-97. Served in U.S. Navy, 1944-46. Fellow AAAS; mem. Am. Soc. Biochemistry and Molecular Biology, Am. Soc. Microbiology, Sigma Xi, Sigma Pi Sigma, Phi Lambda Upsilon. Democrat. Unitarian Universalist. Avocation: hiking. Office: 190 Central Park Sq Los Alamos NM 87544-4001 E-mail: cgregg3@yahoo.com., president@1stmedmart.com.

GREGG, DAVID, III, investment banker; b. N.Y.C., Jan. 29, 1933; s. David Gregg and Virginia (Wyckoff) Macgregor; m. May Foster Bowers, Dec. 21, 1963 (div. Apr. 1984); children: Justine Simms Barkstrom, David; m. Sarah Choate Massengale, Dec. 8, 1984. Assoc. Eastman Dillon Union Securities & Co., N.Y.C., 1959-67, ptnr., 1967-69; v.p. Blyth & Co., Inc., N.Y.C., 1969-72; 1st v.p. Blyth, Eastman, Dillon & Co., N.Y.C., 1972-73; exec. v.p. Overseas Pvt. Investment Corp., Washington, 1973-77; mng. dir. Pierce Internat., Ltd., Washington, 1978-85, Pierce Investment Banking Corp., 1985-97, Pierce Fin. Corp., Arlington, Va., 1986-2000, sr. advisor, 2000—03. Chmn. bd. dirs. Gator Broadcasting Corp., Del., 1986—; trustee Calvert Tax Free Res. Fund, 1978-83; dir. No. Ireland and Border Counties Trade and Investment Coun., 1994-98; dir. Monument Funds, 2000-02. Served with U.S. Army, 1955-57. Mem. Onteora Club (Tannersville, N.Y.) (dir. 1969-72), Chesapeake Bay Yacht Club (Easton, Md.), Amateur Ski Club N.Y. Republican. Episcopalian.

GREGG, ELLA MAE, writer; b. Appalachia, Va., Sept. 29, 1949; d. James Andrew Weatherly and Jewel Audrey Ramey; div.; children: Jeanie Barnett, Marcella Grooms, Jimmie Blazer. Offset pressman, Morritown, 1983; beautician, Knoxville Sch. Beauty, 1985; ins. Liberty Nat., Knoxville Sch. Ins., 1990. Tax cons. Exact Tax, Newport, Tenn.; owner, operator Hair Unltd., Tootie Fruitie's Beauty Shop, Newport. Mem. Mystery Writers Am., Women Guild Am., Police Writers Am. Avocations: walking, dancing, reading. Home: PO Box 1214 Newport TN 37822-1214 Office: 543 Freeman Ave Newport TN 37821-3840

GREGG, GARY L., II, political science educator; b. Coal Center, Pa., Oct. 2, 1967; s. Gary Lee and Carol Lee Gregg; m. Krysten Gregg, Aug. 17, 1991; children: Jacob, Emma, Landon, Nolan. BA, Davis and Elkins Coll., 1990; MA, Miami U., Oxford, Ohio, 1991, PhD, 1994. Asst. prof. Clarion (Pa.) U., 1994-96; nat. dir. Intercollegiate Studies Inst., Inc., Wilmington, Del., 1997-99; Mitch McConnell Chair in Leadership, prof. polit. sci. U. Louisville, 2000—. Dir., McConnell Ctr. Polit. Leadership, U. Louisville, 2000—. Author: The Presidential Republic; editor: Vital Remnants—America's Founding, 1999, Patriot Sage—George Washington, 1999, (monograph) The Senate—Great Forum of Constitutional Liberty, 2000, Securing Democracy-Electoral Coll., 2003. Mem.: Phila. Soc., Ky. Cols. Methodist. Avocations: golf, gardening, baseball, reading, woodwork. Office: U Louisville Ford Hall Louisville KY 40292 E-mail: GGregg@louisville.edu.

GREGG, GUY R. state legislator; State assemblyman dist. 24 State of N.J., 1995—. Home: 143 Drakestown Rd Hackettstown NJ 07840-5651*

GREGG, HUGH, former cabinet manufacturing company executive, former governor New Hampshire; b. Nashua, N.H., Nov. 22, 1917; s. Harry A. and Margaret R. (Richardson) G.; m. Catherine M. Warner, July 24, 1940; children: Cyrus Warner, Judd Alan. Grad., Phillips Exeter Acad., 1935; AB, Yale U., 1939; LLB, Harvard U., 1942; LLD, U. N.H., 1953; MA, Dartmouth Coll., 1953; DCL, New England Coll., 1954. Bar: N.H. 1942, Mass 1948. Mem. Sullivan & Gregg, Nashua; former pres., treas. Gregg & Son, Inc., Nashua; gov. of N.H., 1953-55. Chmn. bd. dirs., treas. Gregg Cabinets Ltd., Chambly, Que., Can.; former owner Greggs Greenhouse Restaurant, Sarasota, Fla.; clk., former co-pub. N.H. Profiles; pres. Resources of N.H., Inc., Nashua. Author: The Candidates: See How They Run, 1990, A Tall State Revisited, 1993, Birth of the Republican Party, 1995, Why NH?, 2003. Mem. Nat. Exec. Res.; alderman-at-large, City of Nashua, 1948-50, mayor, 1950; bd. dirs. New England Coun., 1952-55, pres., 1955-57; Rep. nat. committeeman from N.H., 1988; law commr. N.H. Ballot, 1992—; founder N.H. Polit. Libr., 1997—. Spl. agt. CIC, U.S. Army, 1942-46, 50-52. Mem.: VFW. Home: 17 Gregg Rd Nashua NH 03062-1002 E-mail: hgresources@charter.net.

GREGG, JAMES R. optometrist, educator; b. Napoleon, Ohio, Oct. 26, 1914; s. Edgar Macmillan Gregg, Minnie Lauerman Gregg; m. Bernice Rose Klopf; children: Janell Rose Gregg Bassett, Ronald Edgar. BSBA, Ohio State U., 1937, BS Optometry, 1942; D Optometry, L.A. Coll. Optometry, 1948, D (hon.) Ocular Science, 1955, DHL (hon.), 1965. Lic. optometrist 1944. Assoc. prof. L.A. Coll. Optometry, 1947—58; optometrist pvt. practice, Inglewood, 1947—73; prof. L.A. Coll. Optometry, 1958—73, So. Calif. Coll. Optometry, Fullerton, 1973—84, interim dean, 1975—76, grants adminstr., 1976—84, prof. emeritus, 1984—2002; freelance writer Anaheim, Calif., 1947—. Cons. U.S. Dept. of Health, Edn. and Welfare, Washington, 1967—69; bd. trustees AOA Members Retirement Plan, St. Louis, 1971—90. Author: The Story of Optometry, 1965 (AOA Distinguished Journalism award, 1970), The Sportman's Eye, 1971; editor: The Business of Optometric Practice, 1981; contbr. articles to profl. jours. Scoutmaster Boy Scouts Am. Troop 292, Inglewood, Calif., 1962—65; pres. Am. Field Svcs., 1968—69. Staff sgt. U.S. Army, 1943—46. Named Disting. Grad., Ohio State U., 1961. Mem.: Calif. Optometric Assn. (pres. 1958—59, Optometrist of Yr. 1956), Friends of Canyon Hills Libr. (pres. 1989—90), Rotary (bd. trustees 1984—86, Rotarian of Yr. 1985). Avocations: photography, writing, travel, hiking, camping. Home: 412 S Rolling Hills Pl Anaheim CA 92807

GREGG, JAY MASON, geology educator; b. Pitts., Jan. 24, 1951; s. Jay Buell and Patricia Louise (Mason) G.; m. Elizabeth Michelle Prudot, Sept. 3, 1977; children: Patricia Michelle, Nicholas Mason, Jay William. BS in Geology and Biology, Bowling Green State U., 1974; MS in Geology, Okla. State U., 1976; PhD in Geology, Mich. State U., 1982. Assoc. geologist Sun Exploration and Prodn. Co., Midland, Tex., 1976-78; sr. rsch. geologist St. Joe Minerals Corp., Viburnum, Mo., Tucson, 1982-87; prin. scientist Westinghouse Hanford Co., Richland, Wash., 1987-88; asst. prof. geology U. Mo., Rolla, 1988—91, assoc. prof. geology, 1991—95, prof., 1995—2000, Gulf Oil Found. Prof., 2000—. Co-editor SEPM Spl. Publ. on Basin-Wide Diagenetic Patterns; mem. editl. bd. Soc. of Econ. Geologists 75th Anniversary Volume. Fulbright scholar U. Coll., Dublin, 1995-96. Mem. AAAS, Geol. Soc. Am., Soc. for Sedimentary Geology. Democrat. United Methodist. Achievements include investigating, with others, the sources and flow-paths of hydrothermal mineralizing fluids in southern Missouri and the Irish Midlands using distribution of trace and minor elements, cathodoluminescence petrography, and fluid inclusions; co-development of classification system for dolomite rock textures. Home: 1321 Woodlawn Dr Rolla MO 65401-2591 Office: U Mo 125 Mcnutt Hall Rolla MO 65401

GREGG, JOHN MALCOLM HALL, pharmaceutical executive; b. Cambridge, Mass., Oct. 27, 1962; s. James Malcolm Hall and Dianne Gloria G.; m. Leisha Faye Koval Gregg, Aug. 28, 1993; children: Anna Kay, Ian James Ellis. BA in Biology, U. Chgo., 1987; MBA in Mktg. and Internat. Bus., NYU, 1995. Sr. med. sales rep. Mead Johnson Pharms., N.Y.C., 1987-93; sr. mkt. rsch. analyst Bristol-Myers Squibb Co., Princeton, N.J., 1993-95, assoc. mgr. sales analysis, 1994-95; mgr. market rsch. Ortho Biotech/Ortho McNeil Pharms., Raritan, N.J., 1995-97; assoc. dir. splty. market rsch. Novartis Pharms., East Hanover, N.J., 1997-98; dir. global new products, market analytics Pfizer, Inc., N.Y.C., 1998—. Rsch. technologist U. Chgo. Dept. Radiation Oncology, Chgo., 1985-87, U. Chgo. Ben May Cancer Lab., Chgo., 1984-85; rsch. asst. U. Chgo. Dept. Biophysics, Chgo., 1982-84; coll. promotions rep. Anheuser-Busch Corp., Chgo., 1982-84. Mem. ACS, AAAS, N.Y. Acad. Scis., Internat. Soc. for Hematotherapy and Graft Engring., Am. Soc. Microbiology, Pharm. Mktg. Rsch. Group. Presbyterian. Avocations: fly fishing, golf. E-mail address. Home: 657 Rosedale Rd Princeton NJ 08540-2217 E-mail: greggj@pfizer.com.

GREGG, JOHN PENNYPACKER, lawyer; b. Phila., May 25, 1947; s. William Pemberton and Sarah E. (High) G. AB, Trinity Coll., 1969; JD, Villanova U., 1974. Bar: Pa. 1974, U.S. Dist. Ct. (ea. dist.) Pa. 1974. Tchr., dir. student activities The Pennington (N.J.) Sch., 1969-71; atty. Pub. Defenders Office, Norristown, Pa., 1974—, High, Swartz, Roberts & Seidel, Norristown, 1975—. Bd. dirs. Rittenhouse Book Distbr. Inc., King of Prussia, Pa. Bd. dirs. Phila. Toboggan Co., Lansdale, 1987-91, Lower Merion Shared Housing Corp., Ardmore, Pa., 1991-95, Lower Merion Affordable Housing, Narberth, Pa., 1995—, The Episcopal Acad., Merion, Pa., 1986-89; ann. giving com. Inglis House, Phila., 1991-92. Recipient Legion of Honor Chapel of the Four Chaplains, Phila., 1980, Harry L. Green Svc. award, 1990, Disting. Svc. award Episcopal Acad., 1990. Mem. Pa. Bar Assn., Montgomery Bar Assn. (com. chmn. 1991-94). Home: 635 Walnut Ln Haverford PA 19041-1225 Office: High Swartz Roberts & Seidel 40 E Airy St Norristown PA 19401-4803

GREGG, JOHN RICHARD, lawyer; b. Sandborn, Ind., Sept. 6, 1954; s. Donald Richard and Beverly June (Blackwood) G.; m. Sherry L. Biddinger, Nov. 18, 1989; children: John Blackwood, Hunter W. AS, Vincennes U., 1974; AB, Ind. U., 1976, JD, 1984; MPA, Ind. State U., 1978. Real estate agt. Peabody Coal, Jasonville, Ind., 1978-79; govt. affairs agt. Amax Coal, Evansville, Indpls., Ind., 1979-85; ptnr. Gregg & Brock, Vincennes, Ind., 1985—2002; mem. Ind. Gen. Assembly, 1986—2002, house majority leader, 1990-94, minority leader, 1994-96, spkr., 1996—2002; ptnr. Sommer, Barnard, Ackerson, Attys., 2002—. Adj. prof. Vincennes (Ind.) U., 1985—. Active United Meth. Ch.; del. Nat. Dem. Conv., 1992, 96, 2000. Mem. Wabash Valley Human Svcs. (bd. dirs. 1982-85), Knox County Bar Assn. (pres. 1993), Columbia Club, Indpls. Press Club, Torpedo Club, Knights of Pythias, Masons (33 deg., past master 1979), Sigma Pi. Democrat. Home: PO Box 301 Sandborn IN 47578-0301

GREGG, JON MANN, lawyer; b. Louisville, Oct. 22, 1943; s. James Willard and Margaret Josephine (Mann) G.; m. Jeanette Ruth Brandner, June 18, 1966 (div. Oct. 1980); children: Heather Suzanne, Douglas Robert; m. Carol Ruth Slonneger, July 9, 1983; children: Catherine Marie, Emma Celeste. BS in Acctg., U. Ill., 1965; LLB, Harvard U., 1968. Bar: Ill. 1968. Assoc. Sidley & Austin, Chgo., 1968-74, ptnr., 1974—. Mem. ABA, Chgo. Bar Assn. Avocations: flying, aerobatics, tennis, sailing. Home: 344 W Wisconsin St Unit D Chicago IL 60614-5452 Office: Sidley Austin Brown & Wood 10 S Dearborn Bank One Plz Chicago IL 60603-2000 Business E-Mail: jgregg@sidley.com.

GREGG, JUDD, senator, former governor; b. Nashua, N.H., Feb. 14, 1947; m. Kathleen MacLellan, 1973; children: Molly, Sarah, Joshua. AB, Columbia U., 1969; JD, Boston U., 1972, LL.M., 1975. Bar: N.H. 1972. Ptnr. Sullivan, Gregg and Horton, Nashua, N.H.; mem. 97th-100th Congresses from 2d N.H. dist., Washington, 1981-89; governor of N.H., Concord, 1989-93; U.S. Senator from N.H., 1993—. Mem. Budget/Appropriations Com.; chmn. Appropriations Subcom. on Commerce, Justice, State, Judiciary; chmn. Labor and Human Resources Subcom. on Children & Families; mem. N.H. Gov.'s Exec. Coun., 1978-80. Pres. Crotched Mountain Rehab. Found. Mem. ABA, N.H. BAr Assn., Nashua Bar Assn. Republican. Office: US Senate 393 Senate Russell Bldg Washington DC 20510-0001*

GREGG, KATHY KAY, school system administrator; b. Washington, N.C., Aug. 26, 1956; d. Merwin Jack and Mary Elizabeth Gregg. BS, East Carolina U., 1978; MA, Appalachian State U., 1980; MEd, U. South Fla., 1993; PhD, Union Inst., Cin., 1998. Cert. educator Fla. Dept. Edn. Guidance counselor Waycross (Ga.) H.S., 1981—82; family life educator Family Svc. Ctrs., Clearwater, Fla., 1982—84; guildance counselor Pinellas County Schs., Largo, Fla., 1984—92, full svc. sch. coord., 1992—96, sch. adminstr., 1996—. Prof. Eckerd Coll., St. Petersburg, Fla., 1994—. Grantee Challenge Ropes Course, Jr. League St. Petersburg, 1997. Mem.: Assn. Experiential Edn. Avocations: reading, writing, sports, nature photography. Office: Northeast Cmty Sch 1717 54th Ave N Saint Petersburg FL 33714

GREGG, MARIE BYRD, retired farmer; b. Mount Olive, NC, Jan. 12, 1930; d. Arnold Wesley and Martha (Reaves) Byrd; m. Robert Allen Gregg, (deceased) July 11, 1953; children: Martha Susan, Kathryn Elizabeth, Kenneth Allen. BA in Elem. Edn., Furman U., 1951. Tchr. 3rd grade Greenville City Sch., SC, 1951-53; med. social worker Ctrl. Carolina Rehab. Hosp., Greensboro, NC, 1959-61; window display designer Kerr Rexall Drugs, Durham, NC, 1960's; shop owner Something Else Antiques, Lima, Ohio, 1979-81; farm owner Mt. Olive, 1978-92. Democrat. Methodist. Avocations: antique collecting, traveling, reading, interior decorating. Home and Office: 212 Baucom Park Dr Greer SC 29650-2972

GREGG, MICHAEL B. health science association administrator, epidemiologist; b. Paris, Jan. 6, 1930; married; three children. BA, Stanford U., 1952; MD, Case Western Res. U., 1956. Diplomate Am. Bd. Med. Examiners, Am. Bd. Preventive Medicine. Intern in internal medicine Presbyn. Hosp., N.Y.C., 1956-57, jr. asst. resident in internal medicine, 1957-58, sr. asst. resident in internal medicine, 1958-59; sr. asst. surgeon USPHS, NIH, Rocky Mountain Lab., 1959-61, surgeon, 1962; rsch. assoc. divsn. infectious diseases U. Md. Sch. Medicine, 1962-63; rsch. assoc. Inst. Internat. Medicine U. Md., 1963-64, asst. prof., 1964-66; acting assoc. dir. Pakistan Med. Rsch. Ctr., Lahore, 1964, dir. dept. malariology, 1964, dir. dept. serology and immunology, 1964-65; chief epidemic intelligence svc., epidemiology program Ctr. for Disease Control, 1966-68; dir. viral diseases divsn. Bur. Epidemiology, Ctrs. Disease Control, 1968-76, dep. dir., 1970-81; dep. dir. epidemiology program office Ctrs. for Disease Control, 1981-88, dir. epidemiology program office, 1988-89; pvt. practice specializing in epidemiology and disease control, 1989—. Editor Ctrs. for Disease Control Morbidity and Mortality Weekly Report, 1967-88; cons. on poliomyelitis WHO, Geneva, 1969; cons. to govt. of Indonesia for WHO, 1969, 70, 72, 74, 78; internat. cons. to various countries for WHO, 1969-81; mem. com. on Viral Hepatitis divsn. Med. Scis., NRC, Washington, 1970-74; mem. Ctrs. for Disease Control Study Sect. Office Rsch. Grants, 1970-72; mem. Data Registry Com. Nat. Cystic Fibrosis Found., Atlanta, 1972-78; mem. U.S. Influenza Del. to the USSR, 1973. Fellow Am. Coll. Epidemiology; mem. AAAS, Am. Pub. Health Assn., Am. Epidemiol. Soc., Alpha Omega Alpha. Home and Office: 855 Stony Hill Rd Guilford VT 05301-8266

GREGG, RICHARD, lawyer; b. Cananea, Mex., May 24, 1946; came to U.S., 1949; s. Enrique Francisco and Carolina (Rivas) G.; m. Jean Ann Pharris, June 2, 1973; 1 child, Jessica Raquel. BA, Calif. State U., 1972; JD, U. Calif., Davis, 1977. Bar: Calif. 1977, U.S. Dist. Ct. (ea. dist.) Calif. 1977, U.S. Dist. Ct. (no. dist.) Calif. 1984. Adminstrv. analyst City of Redondo Beach, Calif., 1972-74; ct. interpreter Yolo County Cts., Calif., 1975-79; legal asst. Calif. Dept. Motor Vehicles, Sacramento, 1976-77; ct. probate investigator Yolo County, 1978-83, ct. commr., 1983; ptnr. Lauricella & Gregg, Woodland, Calif., 1978-83; assoc. Boccado Law Firm, San Jose, Calif., 1983-89, Schneider & Wallerstein, San Jose, Calif., 1989-90, The Alexander Law Firm, San Jose, Calif., 1990-93, Zazueta & Gregg, San Jose, Calif., 1993-95, The Boccardo Law Firm, San Jose, Calif., 1995—. Editor Yolo County Bar Newsletter, 1981-83, Santa Clara County La Raza Lawyers Newsletter, 1984. Chmn. Safe Harbor Crisis House, Davis, Calif., 1982. 1st lt. U.S. Army, 1966-69, Vietnam. Decorated Air medal. Mem. Calif. State Bar Assn., Calif. Trial Lawyers Assn., Santa Clara County Bar Assn., Santa Clara County La Raza Lawyers Assn. (pres. 1986), Yolo County Bar Assn. (pres. 1983), La Raza Lawyers Assn. (pres. Santa Clara County chpt. 1986, TV moderator 1982), Toastmasters (pres. Sacramento 1982, pres. Woodland 1981, Dist. Toastmaster of Yr. 1982). Democrat. Office: Boccardo Law Firm 111 W Saint John St Fl 11 San Jose CA 95113-1113 E-mail: rgreggesq@msn.com.

GREGG, RODMAN WALTER, motion picture and television producer, publisher; b. Wilmington, Del., Sept. 1, 1953; s. Rodman I. and Elizabeth W. Gregg. BS in Plant Sci., U. Del., 1975. Asst. mgr. So. States Coop., Richmond, Va., 1977-79; tchr. New Castle County Sch. Dist., Wilmington, 1979-80; ind. prodr. L.A., 1981-90; prodr., ptnr. O'Hara/Gregg Films, Beverly Hills, Calif., 1990-94; pres. Mount/Kramer T.V., L.A., 1997-98, The Mount Co., Hollywood, Calif., 1998-2001; exec. RKO Pictures, 2001—02; cons., prodr. Idiom Films, 2002—03; prodr. RGO Pictures, 2003—. Pub. Packard House Books, Beverly Hills, 1984—; cons. Hollywood Broadcasting.com, L.A., 1999—2000; exec. sr. v.p. TV RKO Pictures, 2001; ind. prodr. and cons., 2002—03. Editor: (book series) Who's Who in the Motion Picture Industry, 1981—; writer (T.V. movie) The Prisoner of Zenda, 1996, (feature film) Manhattan Cowboys. With USMC, 1970-73, Vietnam. Producing fellow Am. Film Inst., Hollywood, 1984-86. Mem. Prodrs. Guild Am. Democrat. Avocations: writing, automobile restoration. Office: PO Box 2187 Beverly Hills CA 90213-2187 E-mail: filmbiz200@aol.com.

GREGGS, ELANORA, social worker; b. Barnwell County, S.C., Nov. 10, 1933; d. Daniel and Georgia (Cobb) Young; children: John, Christopher, Paulette, Doris. BA, Coll. of New Rochelle, 1985; MSW, Yeshiva U., 1987. Para-profl. Bd. Edn., Bklyn., 1965—67; salesperson Tira Exclusive, Laurelton, NY, 1982—85, Mary Kay Cosmetics, Stanley Home Products; human svcs. supr. Cath. Charities, Bklyn., 1986—87, social work supr. Jamaica, NY, 1987—95, Jamaica Support Sys., 1995. Tchr. Maranatha Bible Inst., 2001—. Author: Broken Pieces, 1998. Alumni Coll. New Rochelle, NY, 1985—, Yeshiva U., N.Y.C., 1987—; pub. rels. Lake Arbor Found., Mitchellville, Md., 2000—; vol. in nursing homes, 1996—; active Christian Women of Faith, Mitchellville, Md., 2001—; acting min. Evangel Cathedral, 1995—. Avocations: reading, writing, walking, swimming, gardening.

GREGGS, ELIZABETH MAY BUSHNELL (MRS. RAYMOND JOHN GREGGS), retired librarian; b. Delta, Colo., Nov. 7, 1925; d. Joseph Perkins and Ruby May (Stanford) Bushnell; m. Raymond John Greggs, Aug. 16, 1952 (dec. 1994); children: David M., Geoffrey B., Timothy C., Daniel R. BA, U. Denver, 1948. Children's librarian Grand Junction (Colo.) Pub. Library, 1944-46, Chelan County Library, 1948, Wenatchee (Wash.) Pub. Library, 1948-52, Seattle Pub. Library, 1952-53, Renton (Wash.) Pub. Library, 1957-61, dir., 1962, br. supr. and children's services supr., 1963-67; area children's supr. King County Library, Seattle, 1968-78, asst. coordinator children's services, 1978-86; head librarian Valley View Library of King County Library System, Seattle, 1986-90. Cons., organizer Tutor Ctr. Library, Seattle South Community Coll., 1969-72; mem. Puget Sound (Wash.) Council for Reviewing Children's Media, 1974—, chmn., 1974-76; cons. to children's TV programs. Editor: Cayas Newsletter, 1971-74; cons. to Children's Catalog, Children's Index to Poetry. Chmn. dist. advancement com. Kloshee dist. Boy Scouts Am., 1975-78; mem. Bond Issue Citizens Group to build new Renton Libr., 1958, 59; mem. exec. bd. Family Edn. and Counseling Ctr. on Deafness, 1991-94; mem. children's lit. tour People to People, South Africa, 1996. Recipient Hon. Service to Youth award Cedar River dist. Boy Scouts Am., 1971, Award of Merit Kloshee dist., 1977, winner King County Block Grant, 1990. Mem. ALA (Newbery-Caldecott medal com. 1978-79, com. chmn. 1983-84; membership com. 1978-80, Boy Scouts com. children's svcs. div. 1973-78, chmn. 1976-78, exec. bd. dirs. Assn. for Libr. Svc. to Children 1979-81, mem. coun. 1985-92, chmn. nominating com. 1986-87, councillor 1989-92, exec. bd. 1989-92, exec. com. 1989-92, coun. orientation com. 1987-89), Wash. Libr. Assn. (exec. bd. children's and young adult svcs. div. 1970-78, chmn. membership com. 1983-90, publs. com. 1988-92, emeritus 1991, mem. elections com.), King County Right to Read Coun. (co-chmn. 1973-77), Pierce-King County Reading Coun., Wash. State Literacy Coun. (exec. bd. 1971-77), Wash. Libr. Media Assn. (jr. high levels com. 1980-84), Pacific N.W. Libr. Assn. (young readers' choice com. 1981-83, chmn. div. 1983-85, exec. bd. 1983-85). Methodist. Home: 11448 Rainier Ave S Seattle WA 98178-3940

GREGOIRE, CHRISTINE O. state attorney general; b. Auburn, Wash. m. Michael Gregoire; 2 children. BA, U. Wash.; JD cum laude, Gonzaga U., 1977. Clerk, typist Wash. State Adult Probation/ Parole Office, Seattle, 1969; caseworker Wash. Dept. Social and Health Scis., Everett, 1974; asst. atty. gen. State of Wash., Spokane, 1977—81, sr. asst. atty. gen., 1981—82, dep. atty. gen. Olympia, 1982—88; dir. Wash. State Dept. Ecology, 1988—92; atty. gen. State of Wash., 1992—. Chair States/B.C. Oil Spill Task Force, 1989—92, Puget Sound Water Quality Authority, 1990—92, Nat. Com. State Environ. Dirs., 1991—92. Bd. dirs. Wash. State Dept. Ecology, 1988—92. Named Woman of Yr., Am. Legion Aux., 1999; named one of 25 Most Influential Working Mothers, Working Mother mag., 2000; recipient Conservationist of Yr. award, Trout Unlimited/N.W. Steelhead & Salmon Coun., 1994, Gov.'s Child Abuse Prevention award, 1996, Myra Bradwell award, 1997, Wyman award, 1997—98, Bd. of Gov.'s award for professionalism, WSBA, 1997, Kick Butt award, The Tobacco Free Coalition of Pierce County, 1997, Wash. State Hosp. Assn. award, 1997, Citizen Activist award, Gleitsman Found., 1998, Woman of Achievement award, Assn. for Women in Comm. Matrix Table, 1999, Pub. Justice award, WSTLA, 1999, Excellence in Pub. Health award, Wash. State Assn. Local Pub. Health Ofcls., 1999, Women in Govt. award, Good Housekeeping, 1999, Spl. Recognition award, Wash. State Nurses Assn., 2000. Mem.: Nat. Assn. Attys. Gen. (consumer protection and environment com., energy com., children and the law subcom.). Democrat. Office: Attorney Generals Office 1125 Washington St SE PO Box 40100 Olympia WA 98504-6200*

GREGOIRE, EUGENE HAROLD, music educator; b. Kankakee, Ill., Feb. 1, 1957; s. Harold Eugene and Phyllis Ann Gregoire; m. Holly Jean Palmateer, Mar. 27, 1959; children: Brittany, Jared. MusB in Edn., Ill. State U., 1979; M in Music Edn., Vandercook Sch. Music, Chgo., 1986. Dir. of bands Wilmington H.S., Ill., 1979—85, Herscher H.S., Ill., 1985—90, Hononegah H.S., Rockton, Ill., 1990—. Fine arts dept. head Hononegah H.S., 1999—2000, 2002. Dir. band (performance) Peach Bowl, 2000, Outback Bowl, 2003. Recipient Excellence In Edn. award, Ecolab, 1999—2001. Mem.: NEA, Ill. Edn. Assn., Hononegah Edn. Assn., Internat. Assn. of Jazz Educators, Ill. Music Educators Assn., Tri-M Music Nat. Honor Soc. Lutheran. Avocation: music arranging, golf, fishing. Home: 109 Fernridge Dr Rockton IL 61072 Office: Hononegah HS 307 Salem Rockton IL 61072 Office Fax: 815-624-5029. Personal E-mail: g_gregoire@hotmail.com.

GREGOR, CLUNIE BRYAN, geology educator; b. Edinburgh, Scotland, Mar. 5, 1929; came to U.S., 1968; s. David Clunie Gregor and Barbara Mary Moller-Beilby; m. Suzanne Assir, Apr. 24, 1955 (div. Apr. 1969); 1 child, Andrew James; m. Anna Bramanti, Apr. 15, 1969 (dec. Oct. 1993); children: Thomas James, Matthew James. BA, Cambridge (Eng.) U., 1951, MA, 1954; DSc, U. Utrecht, The Netherlands, 1967. Instr. Am. U. Beirut, 1958-64; rsch. asst. Delft (The Netherlands) Inst. Tech., 1964-65, dir. Crystallographic Lab., 1965-67; vis. prof. Case Western Res. U., Cleve., 1968-69; prof. West Ga. Coll., Carrollton, 1969-72, Wright State U., Dayton, Ohio, 1972—. Chmn. USA work group on geochem. cycles, 1972-88, vice chmn. panel on geochem. cycles NAS, 1988-90. Author: (monograph) Geochemical Behaviour of Sodium, 1967; editor: Chemical Cycles in the Evolution of the Earth, 1988, The Evolving Earth, 1997. Grantee NSF, 1977-82, Sicily, 1978-80. Fellow Geol. Soc. (London); mem. Geol. Soc. Am., Am. Geophys. Union, Geochem. Soc. (sec. 1983-89). Home: 136 W North College St Yellow Springs OH 45387-1563 Office: Wright State U Dept Geol Scis Dayton OH 45435

GREGOR, DOROTHY DEBORAH, retired librarian; b. Dobbs Ferry, N.Y., Aug. 15, 1939; d. Richard Garrett Heckman and Marion Allen (Richmond) Stewart; m. A. James Gregor, June 22, 1963 (div. 1974). BA, Occidental Coll., 1961; MA, U. Hawaii, 1963; MLS, U. Tex., 1968; cert. in Library Mgmt., U. Calif., Berkeley, 1976. Reference libr. U. Calif., San Francisco, 1968-69; dept. libr. Pub. Health Libr. U. Calif., Berkeley, 1969-71, tech. services libr., 1973-76; reference libr. Hamilton Libr., Honolulu, 1971-72; head serials dept. U. Calif., Berkeley, 1976-80, assoc. univ. libr. tech. svcs. dept., 1980-84, univ. libr., 1992-94; chief Shared Cataloging div. Libr. of Congress, Washington, 1984-85; univ. libr. U. Calif.-San Diego, La Jolla, 1985-92, OCLC asst. to pres. for acad. and rsch. libr. rels., 1995—98; docent Asian Art Mus., San Francisco, 1997—, ret. Instr. sch. libr. and info. studies U. Calif., Berkeley, 1975, 76, 83; cons. Nat. Libr. of Medicine, Bethesda, Md., 1985, Ohio Bd. Regents, Columbus, 1987; trustee Online Computer Libr. Ctr., 1988-96; dir. Nat. Coordinating Com. on Japanese Libr. Resources, 1995-98; docent Asian Art Mus., San Francisco, 1997-. Mem. ALA, Libr. Info. Tech. Assn., Program Com. Ctr. for Rsch. Librs. (bd. chair 1992-93, Hugh Atkinson award 1994). E-mail: dgregor@mcn.org.

GREGOR, EDUARD, laser physicist, consultant; b. Dnepropetrovsk, Ukraine, Jan. 9, 1936; came to U.S., 1955; s. Waldemar and Concordia (Teschke) G.; m. Marie L. Carlin, June 29, 1968; 1 child, Eduard Joseph. BS in Physics, Calif. State U., 1964, MS in Physics, 1966. Instr. Calif. State U., L.A., 1963-66; optical physicist TRW Instruments, El Segundo, Calif., 1966-68; laser physicist Union Carbide (Korad), Santa Monica, Calif., 1968-72; prodn. mgr. holography Quantrad Corp., El Segundo, Calif., 1972-75, ops. mgr., 1975-79; sr. project physicist Hughes Aircraft Co., El Segundo, 1979-82, dept. mgr., 1982-91, project mgr., 1992-93, sci., engr., 1993-95; pres. E. Gregor Assoc., Pacific Palisades, Calif., 1995—. Contbr. over 20 tech. articles on laser tech., coherent optics and holography to profl. jours. Sgt. U.S. Army, 1959-61. Recipient IR 100 award Indsl. Rsch. Mag., 1975. Mem. Optical Soc. Am., Soc. Photo-optical Instrumentation Engrs. Achievements include 8 patents for Mobile Laser Holocamera, Two Cavety Laser, Varible Lens and Birefringence Compensator,

Phase Conjugate Laser with a Temporal Square Pulse, Laser Reflective Cavety, Raman Converter with Variable Wavelength Distribution, Laser Head having a Conductively cooled Flashlamp, Compact Diode Pumped Solid State Laser. Home and Office: 820 Las Lomas Ave Pacific Palisades CA 90272-2428 E-mail: gregor820@earthlink.net.

GREGOR, MARLENE PIERCE, primary education educator, elementary science consultant; b. Oak Park, Ill., Apr. 22, 1932; d. Kenneth Bryant and Dorothy Rose Pierce; m. G. Ray Timmons, Aug. 1, 1953 (div. 1972); children: Gregg R., Todd P., Wendy S. Timmons McGuire; m. Harold L. Gregor, 1987. BS in Elem. Edn., U. Ill., 1953; MS in Elem. Edn., Ill. State U., 1974, postgrad., 1975-91. Tchr. 2d grade Wethersfield Community Unit Schs., Kewanee, Ill., 1953-54; primary tchr. Fairbury (Ill.) Cropsey Schs., 1965-84, Prairie-Cen. Community Unit #8 Schs., Fairbury, 1984-91; ret. Prairie-Ctr. Community Unit # 8 Schs., Fairbury, 1991. Item writer Stanford Achievement Test Psychol. Corp., San Antonio, 1989, sci. assessment Ill. State Bd. Edn., Springfield, 1987-88, Ill. student achievement test Metritech Corp., 2000-01; grant reader Ctr. Sci. Literacy, Springfield, 1991-93. Author: Bark Hunters, 2000, (with others) Horizons Plus Science Stories-Grade 2, 1992, Toys That Teach Science, 1993, Celebrating Science, 1990, Award Winning Nutrition Education Lessons and Units, 1994; mem. sci. tchrs. writing team Ill. State U., 1992; contbr. articles and stories to various publs. Bd. dirs. Friends of the Arts Ill. State U., Normal, 1980-86, 92-98, v.p., 1994-96; mem. Bloomington Mayoral Downtown Commn., 1993-98, sec., 1994-98; mem. adv. bd. Children's Mus., 1993-95; mem. steering com. Downtown Heritage Festival, Bloomington, 1995, 96; mem. steering com. Ill. State U. Fell Arboretum, 1994-2001, bd. dirs. and chair sch. outreach com., 1995-2001; mem. Leadership McLean County Class of 1996; mem. fundraising cabinet Fell Arboretum, Working Forum for Vision of Downtown, 1997-98; bd. dirs., chair visual arts com. Downtown Bloomington Assn., 1998-2000, mem. downtown aesthetics com., 1999—; bd. dirs. Sr. Profls., Ill. State U., 2001—; mem. Uniquely Bloomington Downtown Commn., sec., 1999—, art chair Sesquicentennial 2000 Festival, 1999-2000; bd. dirs. Ctrl. Ill. Neurosci. Found., 2000—; pub. art chair Corn-On-The-Curb, 2000, 01; bd. dirs. Ill. Symphony Guild, 2002—. Named Outstanding Tchr. Sci. NSF-Ill. State U., 1985, Honors Sci. Tchr. Ill. State U., 1985, 86, 87; Chpt. II Mini grantee Edn. Svc. Ctr. #13, 1985-90; recipient Creative Nutrition award Nutrition and Edn. Tng. Ctr., 1989, Women of Distinction award YWCA, 1999, Jean Anderson Downtown Improvement award, 2000. Mem. NEA, Nat. Sci. Tchrs. Assn. (presenter conv. 1985, 87), Coun. for Em. Sci. Internat., Ill. Edn. Assn. (Tchr. Excellence award 1989), Ill. Ctr. Sci. Literacy (adv. mem. 1991-93), Ill. Sci. Tchrs. Assn. (sec. 1989-93, Presdl. Excellence Sci. Tchg. award 1991, State Finalist), Delta Kappa Gamma (v.p. chpt. 1990-92). Presbyterian. Avocations: art, watercolor, travel, physical fitness, golf. Home: 107 W Market St Bloomington IL 61701-3917

GREGOR, TIBOR PHILIP, retired management consultant; b. Levoca, Czechoslovakia, Apr. 25, 1919; arrived in Can., 1951; s. Philip and Emma (Aufricht) Gregor; m. Helen Frances Lorenz, Sept. 15, 1942 (dec. 1989); children: Jan Michael, Charlotte Anne; m. Valma Costa, Dec. 17, 1994. Student, U. London, 1938—40. Gen. sales mgr. Eastern Steel Products Ltd., Toronto, Canada, 1952-57; pres., gen. mgr. Roneo Co. Ltd., Toronto, 1957-63, Roneo, Inc., Phila.; pres. Mcpl. Sand & Gravel Co., Kingston, Canada, 1964-71; exec. dir. Can. Soft Drink Assn., Toronto, 1972-86; pres. T.P. Gregor Assocs., Toronto, 1986—98, ret., 1998. Mem. Ont. Comml. Registration Appeals Tribunal, 1987—93. Vice chmn. Toronto Centennial Com., 1964—67; pres. Met. Toronto Assn. Mentally Retarded, 1961—64; past pres. Can. Assn. Mentally Retarded, 1969—71; founder, chmn. Friends Royal Can. Acad. Arts, 1985—89; chmn. Can. Fund Czech and Slovak Univs. Col. Czechoslovak Armoured Brigade, ret. Decorated Medal of Merit 1st class France; recipient commendation, City of Toronto, Centennial medal, Royal Can. Acad., Freedom award, City of Winnipeg. Mem.: Am. Soc. Assn. Execs., Can. Soc. Assn. Execs., Royal Can. Legion, Royal Can. Mil. Inst., Rotary (past gov. Rotary Dist. 7070, Toronto-Eglinton), Rotary Internat. (bd. dirs., past trustee, v.p. Rotary Found. Can.), Toronto Lawn Tennis Club. Mem. United Ch. Home and Office: 218 Glen Rd Toronto ON Canada M4W 2X3

GREGORIAN, RAFFI, diplomat; b. Redwood City, CA, Jan. 15, 1964; s. Vartan Gregorian, Clare Russell Gregorian; m. Bernadette Mary Dawson. PhD, Johns Hopkins School of Advanced International Studies, Washington, D.C., 1991—98; MA, King's College, University of London, London, 1988—89; BA (Hons), University of Pennsylvania, Philadelphia, PA, 1982—86. Historian U.S. Army Ctr. for Mil. History, Washington, 1986—88; policy analyst Ctr. for Arms Control and Tech. Assessment, EOS Technologies, McLean, Va., 1990—92; sr. analyst Sci. Applications Internat. Corp., McLean, Va., 1992—98; sr. adviser Dept. of Def. Interagency Task Force for Mil. Stblzn. in the Balkans, Washington, 1998—98; sr. advisor and chief of staff Office of the Spec. Adviser to the Pres. and Sec. of State for Kosovo and Dayton Implementation, Dept. of State, Washington, 1999—2001; acting office dir. Office of Kosovo Implementation Dep. of State, Washington, 2001—01; dir. for Bosnia policy Office of South Ctrl. Europe Dept. of State, Washington, 2001—. Author: (Book) The British Army, the Gurkhas, and Cold War Strategy in the Far East, 1947-54, 2002. Commd. officer USNR, 1993—. Mem.: Army-Navy Club, Society for Military History, Royal United Services Institute, International Institute for Strategic Studies. Home: 507 Queen Street Alexandria VA 22314 Office: Department of State 2201 C Street NW Washington DC 20520 Business E-Mail: gregorianr@state.gov.

GREGORIAN, VARTAN, foundation administrator; b. Tabriz, Iran, Apr. 8, 1934; came to U.S., 1956; s. Samuel B. and Shushanik G. (Mirzaian) G.; m. Clare Russell, Mar. 25, 1960; children: Vahe, Raffi, Dareh. Grad., Coll. Armenian, 1955; BA, Stanford U., 1958, PhD, 1964; hon. degree, Boston U., 1983, Brown U., 1984, Jewish Theol. Seminary, 1984, SUNY, 1985, Johns Hopkins U., 1987, NYU, 1987, U. Pa., 1988, Dartmouth Coll., 1989, Rutgers U., 1989, CUNY, 1990, Tufts U., 1994. From instr. to assoc. prof. history San Francisco State Coll., 1962—68; assoc. prof. UCLA, 1968; from assoc. prof. to prof. U. Tex., 1968—72, dir. spl. programs, 1970—72; Tarzian prof. Armenian and Caucasian history U. Pa., Phila., 1972—80; dean U. Pa. (Faculty Arts and Scis.), 1974—78, provost, 1978—80; pres. N.Y. Pub. Libr., 1981—89; prof. New Sch. Social Rsch., N.Y.C., 1984—89; prof. History and Near Eastern studies NYU, 1984—89; pres., prof. History Brown U., Providence, 1989—97; pres. Carnegie Corp., N.Y.C., 1997—. Author: The Emergence of Modern Afghanistan, 1880-1946, 1969. Bd. dirs. Aaron Diamond Found., 1990-97, Brookings Instns., 1994-97, Inst. for Internat. Edn., 1989-95, Internat. League of Human Rights, 1984-97, Inst. for Advanced Study, 1987—, J. Paul Getty Trust, 1988—, Aga Khan U., 1995—, Human Rights Watch, 1996—; chmn. bd. visitors Grad. Sch. and Univ. Ctr., CUNY, 1984-90; bd. trustees Mus. Modern Art, 1994—. Decorated Officier de l'Ordre des Arts et Lettres (France), Grand Oficial Ordem Infante D. Henrique Portuguese Govt., 1995; recipient Danforth E.H. Harbison Teaching award 1969, Cactus Teaching award 1971, award of distinction Phi Lambda Theta and Phi Delta Kappa, 1980, Silver Cultural medal Italian Ministry Fgn. Affairs, 1977, Gold medal of honor City and Province of Vienna, Austria, 1976, 1st Disting. Humanist award Pa. Humanities Coun., 1983, Nat. Fellowship award Fellowship Commn., Phila., 1984, Gold medal Nat. Inst. Social Scis., 1985, Disting. Svc. to the Arts award Third St. Music Sch. Settlement, 1997, Disting. Svc. to Pub. Edn. award N.Y. Acad. Pub. Edn., 1998, Friends of the Arts award Town Hall, 1998; fellow Social Sci. Rsch. Coun., 1960, Ford Found. Fgn. Area Tng., 1960-62, Am. Coun. Learned Socs.-Social Sci. Rsch. Coun., 1965, John Simon Guggenheim Found., 1971-72, Social Sci. Rsch. Coun., 1971-72, Am. Coun. Edn., 1973. Fellow Acad. Arts Scis., Am. Philos. Soc.; mem. Am. Antiquarian Soc., Am. Hist. Assn. (program chmn. 1972), Am. Philos. Soc. (grantee 1965, 66), Internat. Fedn. Libr. Assns. (co-chmn. program com. 1985), Assn. Advancement Slavic Studies (program chmn. Western Slavic Conf. 1967), Mid-East Studies Assn., Coun. Fgn. Rels., Grolier Club, Round Table, Century Club, Econ. Club, Phi Beta Kappa. Office: Carnegie Corp Office of the Pres 437 Madison Ave Fl 27 New York NY 10022-7001*

GREGORIE, CORAZON ARZALEM, operations supervisor; b. Bethesda, Md., Aug. 6, 1947; d. Faustino and Rosalina Arzalem. AA in Bus. Adminstrn., Palm Beach Coll., 1967; postgrad., Fla. Atlantic U., 1967; BA in Bus. Adminstrn., U. Fla., 1969. Mgmt. trainee Burdines Dept. Store, West Palm Beach, Fla., 1969; adminstrv. asst. divsn. econs. Nat. Food Processors Assn., Washington, 1970-71, statis. analyst divsn. econs. and stats., 1972-77, acting dir. divsn. econs. and stats., 1978; asst. editor Airfare Pub. Co., Washington, 1979-81; product specialist Arbitron Co., Beltsville, Md., 1982-83, tng. supr. Laurel, Md., 1984-87, night shift ops. supr. Columbia, Md., 1988—95, survey supr., 1996—. Collective mem., bd. dirs. Glut Food, Mt. Rainier, Md., 1973-78. Force vol. Nat. Park Svc., Washington, 1973-76; coord. College Park Food Coop., Md., 1970-72. Mem. Lotus Ltd. (bd. dirs. 1974—, treas., parts and tech. chmn., membership dir., corr. sec.). Avocations: photography, sports cars. Office: Arbitron Co 9705 Patuxent Woods Dr Columbia MD 21046-1572

GREGORY, ANN YOUNG, editor, publisher; b. Apr. 28, 1935; d. David Marion and Pauline (Adams) Young; m. Allen Gregory, Jan. 29, 1957; children: David Young, Mary Peyton. BA with high distinction with departmental honors, U. Ky., 1956. Sec. Ky. Edit. TV Guide, Louisville, summer 1956; traffic mgr. Sta. WVLK, Lexington, 1956-61; part-time tchr. adult basic edn. Wise County (Va.) Sch. Bd., St. Paul, 1966-72; adminstrv. asst. Appalachian Field Svcs., Children's TV Workshop, St. Paul, 1971-74; editor, co-pub. Clinch Valley Times, 1974—. Pres. Clinch Valley Pub. Co., Inc., St. Paul, 1974—; mem. mktg. com. Mountain Empire TechPrep Consortium, 1993—. Editor, text writer: The Flood of '77 in the St. Paul Area, 1977; weekly newspaper columnist: Of Shoes...and Ships...and Sealing Wax, 1974—. V.p. St. Paul PTA, 1970-73; trustee Lonesome Pine Regional Libr. Bd., 1972-80, chmn., 1978-80; chmn. com. to establish br. libr. in St. Paul, opened 1975; mem. adv. bd. Pro-Art, Wise County chpt. Va. Mus. Fine Arts, 1979-86; co-leader Brownie troop Girl Scouts U.S.A., 1971-76, bd. dirs. Appalachian coun., 1983-95, 1st v.p., 1985-91; mem. adv. bd. Wise County YMCA, 1977-80; mem. Wise County Bd. Edn., 1975—, vice-chmn., 1981-95, 99, chmn., 2000-01; pres. So. Region Sch. Bds. Assn., 1987-88; mem. Va. Edn. Block Grants Adv. Com., 1981-86, Region I State Literacy Coun., 1989-91; mem. Local Vocat. Adv. Coun., 1980—, chmn., 1981—; mem. statewide planning coun. Va. Dept. Edn.; mem. Va. Coun. on Vocat. Edn., 1987-95, chmn., 1989-91; mem. exec. com. Va. H.S. League, 1984-88 (Lifetime Achievement award, 2001); past pres. Wise County Humane Soc., Inc.; bd. dirs. Va. Sch. Bds. Assn., 1979-89, pres., 1985-86; bd. dirs. Va. Literacy Found., 1987-89, Appalachian Ednl. Lab., 1995-2001, bd. chmn., 2000, Quarter Century Club, Va. Sch. Bd. Assn., 2002; sec., treas. S.W. Va. Pub. Edn. Found. Bd., 1993—; mem. Mountain Empire C.C. Found. Bd., 1994—; mem. adv. com. Va. State Supt. Pub. Instrn., 1993-96; mem. devel. and comty. rels. com., mem. music adv. com. Clinch Valley Coll.; mem. adv. bd. Wise Appalachian Regional Hosp., 1995-98; mem. Wise County Info. Tech. Task Force, 1998—; bd. dirs., sec. St. Paul Tomorrow Steering Com., 1998-2000; mem. adv. com. WISE-FM, U. Va. Coll., Wise. Named Outstanding Clubwoman of Yr., St. Paul Jr. Women's Club, 1964, 66, Outstanding Citizen, S.W. Va. dist. Va. Fedn. Women's Clubs, 1968, Woman of Yr. Wise County/Norton Dem. Women's Club, 1986, Citizen of Yr., Wise County C. of C., 1990; recipient Rufus Beamer award Va. Poly. Inst., 1989, William P Kanto Meml. award for contbns. to edn. Clinch Valley Coll., Mountain Empire C.C. and Wise County and Norton Pub. Schs., 1990, Literacy award S.W. Reading Coun., 1994, Lifetime Achievement award Va. H.S. League, 2001; Ky. Broadcasters Assn. scholar, 1956 Mem. Va. Press Assn. (1st pl. award for editl. writing 1976), Nat. Press Women, Va. Press Women, Nat. Newspaper Assn., Women in Comms., Nat. Sch. Bds. Assn. (pub. rels. com., nominating com. 1987), Mortar Bd., Delta Kappa Gamma (hon. mem. Alpha Psi chpt.), Phi Beta Kappa, Alpha Delta Pi, Chi Delta Phi, Alpha Epsilon Rho, Alpha Lambda Delta, Theta Sigma Phi. Democrat. Methodist. Home: PO Box 303 Saint Paul VA 24283-0303 Office: PO Box 817 Saint Paul VA 24283-0817 E-mail: agregory@naxs.com.

GREGORY, BETTINA LOUISE, journalist; b. N.Y.C., June 4, 1946; d. George Alexander and V. Elizabeth Friedman; m. John P. Flannery, II, 1981; 1 child, Diana Elizabeth. Student, Smith Coll., 1964-65; diploma in acting, Webber-Douglas Sch. Dramatic Art, London, 1968; BA in Psychology, Pierce Coll., Athens, Greece, 1972; PsyD, George Washington U., 2002; LittD (hon.), Susquehanna U., 1988, St. Thomas Aquinas U., 1992; LLD (hon.), Wilmington Coll., 1989; D in Journalism (hon.), U. Findlay, 1990; LittD (hon.), Bethany Coll., 2000. Reporter Sta. WVBR-FM, Ithaca, N.Y., 1972-73, Sta. WCIC-TV, Ithaca, 1972; reporter, anchorwoman Sta. WGBB, Freeport, N.Y., 1973, Sta. WCBS, N.Y.; freelance reporter, writer AP, N.Y.C., 1973-74; freelance reporter N.Y. Times, 1973-74; with ABC News, 1974—, corr., 1977-79, White House corr., 1979—, sr. gen. assignment corr., 1980—, host The American Family, Goodlife TV Network, 1974—; ret., 2000. Elected rep. for corr.'s ABC News Women's Adv. Bd.; adj. prof. Robert H. Smith Sch. Bus.; adj. prof. exec. masters in bus. adminstrn. U. Md.; host Goodlife TV show "American Family." Reporter TV spl. Flaws in the Shield, 1989 (1st pl. Headliner award), A&E's Biography of Hillary Rodham Clinton, 1994 (Best Documentary ACE award 1994), Murder Trial O.J. Simpson (Edward R. Murrow award Best News Series 1996), Hannibal Lecter: the Honey in the Lion's Mouth, Am.Journal Psychotherapy, 2002. Recipient 1st Place award Nat. Feature News, Odyssey Inst., N.Y., 1978, Clarion award Women in Communications, Inc., 1979, hon. mention Nat. Commn. on Working Women, 1979, Media award for Am. Agenda segment on homeless World Hunger Found., 1990, Cable Ace Best Documentary award, 1995, Edward R. Murrow award for coverage of O.J. Simpson Murder trial, 1996; named one of top 10 investigative reporters, TV Guide, 1983. Mem. Radio TV Corrs. Assn., White House Corrs. Assn. Clubs: Newswomen's N.Y. (recipient Front Page award 1976); Nat. Press; Washington Press. Office: ABC News Washington Bur 1717 Desales St NW Washington DC 20036-4407 E-mail: bettinagre@aol.com.

GREGORY, CALVIN, insurance service executive; b. Bronx, N.Y., Jan. 11, 1942; s. Jacob and Ruth (Cherchian) G.; m. Rachel Anna Carver, Feb. 14, 1970 (div. Apr. 1977); children— Debby Lynn, Trixy Sue; m. 2d, Carla Deane Deaver, June 30, 1979. AA, L.A. City Coll., 1962; BA, Calif. State U.-L.A., 1964; MDiv, Fuller Theol. Sem., 1968; MRS, Southwestern Sem., Ft. Worth, 1969; PhD in Religion, Universal Life Ch., Modesto, Calif., 1982; DDiv (hon.), Otay Mesa Coll., 1982. Notary pub., real estate lic., casualty lic., Calif.; ordained to ministry Am. Baptist Conv., 1970. Youth minister First Bapt. Ch., Delano, Calif., 1964-65, 69-70; youth dir. St. Luke's United Meth. Ch., Highland Park, Calif., 1969-70; tchr. polit. sci. Maranatha High Sch., Rosemead, Calif., 1969-70; aux. chaplain U.S. Air Force 750th Radar Squadron, Edwards AFB, Calif., 1970-72; pastor First Bapt. Ch., Boron, Calif., 1971-72; ins. agt. Prudential Ins. Co., Ventura, Calif., 1972-73, sales mgr., 1973-74, casualty ins. agt. Allstate Ins. Co., Thousand Oaks, Calif., 1974-75; pres. Ins. Agy. Placement Svs., Thousand Oaks, 1975— ; head youth minister Emanuel Presbyn. Ch., L.A., 1973-74; owner, investor real estate, U.S., Wales, Eng., Can., Australia. Counselor YMCA, Hollywood, Calif., 1964, Soul Clinic-Universal Life Ch., Inc., Modesto, Calif., 1982. Mem. Apt. Assn. L.A., Life Underwriter Tng. Coun., Forensic Club (L.A.), X32 Club (Ventura, Calif.), Kiwanis (club spkr. 1971). Republican. Office: Ins Agy Placement Svc PO Box 4407 Thousand Oaks CA 91359-1407

GREGORY, CLAIRE DISTELHORST, television producer; b. Chgo., Mar. 6, 1926; d. Robert Henry and Genevieve (McCall) Distelhorst; children: Charles, Martha. Student, Cornell Coll., 1943-46; AB, Ind. U., 1947, MS, 1954. Tchr. pub. schs., Bismarck and Rossville, Ill., 1947-50, Helmsburg, Ind., 1950-51; grad. asst. Audio Visual Ctr. of Ind. U., 1953-55; dir. women's, children's/social svc. programs radio/TV, 1956-59; lectr., 1956-59; exec. dir. Cmty. Svc. Coun., Inc., Bloomington, Ind., 1971-75; asst. supr. instructional TV program devel. Ind. U. Radio and TV Svc., 1975-81, dir. spl. projects, 1982-92; chmn. Bloomington Telecomms. Coun., 1975-80. Writer, prodr: Russian Revolution and Arts, Parts I and II, 1976, Intro. to Immediate Access, 1977-80, Teleconference on Mass Transp., 1976, Transp. Briefing, 1977, videotapes on profl. devel. Internat. Devel. Inst., 1975-80, 16 videotapes on computer instrn., 1978-80, Getting There, 1980, Living Africa, 1979-82, Programming for Microcomputers, 1982, Negotiation, 1984, Ind. Collection, 1987, Joshua's Battle: The Story of Lyles Station, 1988, Charting New Courses teleconferences, 1988; prodr., videodisc instructional Clarity; prodr., dir., editor videotape SOUTH SHORE LINE: A Good Investment, 1990; prodr., editor Autism: Learning to Live, 1990 (Excellence award Autism Soc. Am. 1991), Autism: Stubborn Love, 1991 (Excellence award Autism Soc. Am. 1992), Autism: Being Friends, 1991; TV advisor Mostly Moliere Troupe, 1981-89; lay reader A Moment of Silence prodn., 1996. Mem. United Way of Monroe County, 1982. Recipient Communication Industry Silver award Assn. Visual Communicators, 1989. Mem. Blue Ridge Assn. (treas. 1978-81), Univ. Club, Theta Sigma Phi, Psi Iota Xi.

GREGORY, COLEMAN GEORGE, lawyer; b. Toronto, Ont., Can., Jan. 16, 1960; arrived in U.S., 1965; s. Thomas and Joan Gregory; m. Esther Louise-Toby Brodsky, June 19, 1983; children: Joseph, Aden, Benjamin. BA, U. Calif., Berkeley, 1982; JD, Harvard U., 1986. Bar: N.Y. 1987, Paris 1992. Assoc. Shearman & Sterling, N.Y.C and Paris, 1986-92; v.p., legal counsel BHF Bank AG, N.Y.C., 1992-99; sr. v.p., gen. counsel PB Capital Corp. (formerly BHF (USA) Capital Corp.), N.Y.C., 1999—. Mem. ABA, Bar of N.Y.C., Harvard Law Sch. Alumni Assn. Office: PB Capital Corp 590 Madison Ave New York NY 10022-2524 E-mail: cgregory@pb-us.com.

GREGORY, DEIRDRE DIANNE, secondary educator; b. Fairview Park, Ohio, Feb. 12, 1958; d. Richard Whiting and Ruth Elizabeth (Moody) Mason; m. Thomas Bradford Gregory, July 15, 1995. BS, Ashland U., 1981; MS, Ohio State U., 1986; MEd, Ashland U., 1989, U. Dayton, 1993. Cert. tchr., Ohio; cert. vocat. family and consumer sci. sch. guidance counselorand supr. Tchr. home econs. Mansfield (Ohio) City Schs., 1981-93, GRADS coord., 1993-99, guidance counselor, 1999—. Mem. adv. bd. Mansfield (Ohio) City Schs. Parents as Tchrs., 1993—, Pioneer Career and Tech. Ctr. GRADS Adv. Bd., Shelby, Ohio, 1993—; chair Children Family Health Svcs. Consortium, Mansfield, 1996-98. Named one of Tw Thousand Notable Am. Women, 1993, Outstanding Young Woman, 1987-88, 88-89, 97-98. Mem. AAUW (pres. 1997-99), Mansfield Sch. Employee Assn. (pres. 1994-95), Am. Assn. Family and Consumer Sci., Order of Eastern Star, Kappa Omicron Phi, Phi Delta Kappa (pres. 1994-96, historian 1996-98). Republican. Presbyterian. Avocations: reading, singing, music, cross stitch, walking. Home: 411 Overlook Rd Mansfield OH 44907-1533 Office: Mansfield Sr H S 145 W Park Blvd Mansfield OH 44906-2621 E-mail: DGregory@mansfield.k12.oh.us.

GREGORY, DICK, comedian, civil rights activist; b. St. Louis, Oct. 12, 1932; m. Lillian Smith, 1959; children: Michele, Lynne, Paula, Pamela, Stephanie, Gregory, Christian, Ayanna, Miss, Yohance. Student, So. Ill. U., 1951-53, 55-56. Lectr. univs. throughout U.S.; nutritionist world-heavyweight boxing champion Riddick Bowe, 1992. Entertainer, Esquire Club, Chgo., opened night club, Apex, Robbins, Ill., master ceremonies, Roberts Show Club, Chgo., 1959-60, night club appearances, Akron, Milw., Chgo., 1960, San Francisco, Hollywood, numerous other cities, 1961—, comedy act, Playboy Club, Chgo., 1961; TV guest appearances Jack Paar show, others; record albums Dick Gregory: The Light Side-Dark Side; others; Author: The Back of the Bus, 1962, Nigger, 1964, What's Happening, 1965, The Shadow That Scares Me, Write Me In, No More Lies, 1971, Dick Gregory's Political Primer, 1971, Dick Gregory's Natural Diet for Folks Who Eat, Cookin' With Mother Nature, 1973, Dick Gregory's Bible Tales, with Commentary, 1974, Up From Nigger, 1976, (with Mark Lane) Code Name Zorro: The Murder of Martin Luther King, Jr, 1977, Murder in Memphis, 1993, Callus on My Soul, 2002. Peace and Freedom Party presdl. candidate, 1968. Served with AUS, 1953-55. Winner Mo. mile championship, 1951, 52; named Outstanding Athlete So. Ill. U., 1953; recipient Ebony-Topaz Heritage and Freedom award, 1978 Achievements include creating Dick Gregory's Bahamian Diet Drink, 1984. Office: Dick Gregory Hlth Enterprises PO Box 3270 Plymouth MA 02361-3270

GREGORY, GEORGE ANN, writer, Native American educator; b. Ft. Smith, Ark., Aug. 17, 1945; d. George Eugene Miller and Maxine (Manuel) Eggensperger; children: Matthew Gregory, James Smiley. BA, U. Ark., 1969; MA, U. N.Mex., 1987, PhD, 1993. Ordained min., 1977. Instr. Oglala Lakota Coll., Kyle, S.D., 1989-90; lectr. No. Ariz. U., Flagstaff, 1990-92; dir. Ho Anumpoli!, Albuquerque, 1995—. Lit. cons. Pueblo of Santa Ana, 1999; cons., evaluator Indian Edn. Albuquerque, 1988-96; cons. emergency med. svcs. acad. U. N.Mex., 1994-95; cons. Okla. Native Am. Langs. Devel. Inst., 1990; adj. faculty U. N.Mex., 1993-98, Coll. Santa Fe, 2002—; faculty Azaliah U., 2001—. Author: (short story) People Before Columbus, 1993, (poetry) Neon Pow Wow, 1993, (juvenile) Mr. Finnegan and the Bear, 1990 (Honorable Mention), Grammar Works for Better Writing, 2000, A Basic Grammar Dictionary for Anyone, 2000, American English Punctuation for Anyone, 2000, American English Composition for Anyone, 2001, Holocaust of Native America, 2002; editl. staff S.W. Jour. of Linguistics, 2003—; sr. editlr MTG Pub., 2000-02; editor: Nizhoni mag., 1985; guest poet Writer's Alive, Corrales, N.Mex., 1995, 96. Ednl. task force Commn. on Indian Affairs, 1994-99; mem. Multicultural Task Force, Albuquerque, 1995; mem. ops. com. Women Studies U. N.Mex., 1994-95; mem. pres.'s ad hoc com. Native Am. Student Concerns U. N.Mex., 1986-87, Dept. Justice Seed com.; treas. Albuquerque Indian Ctr., 1999. Emma Mae Olson scholar Native Am. Coll. Edn. U. N.Mex., 1986; named Top Ten Native Am. Scholars Cornell U., Ithaca, N.Y., 1993. Mem. S.W. Linguistics Assn., Native Writer's Circle of Ams., Soc. Study Indigenous Langs., Nat. Strength and Conditioning Assn. Scientology. Avocations: aztec dancing, costuming, painting. Home: PO Box 40184 Albuquerque NM 87196-0184 Office: Ho Anumpoli! 1700 A Coal Ave SE Albuquerque NM 87106 E-mail: hoanumpoli@yahoo.com.

GREGORY, GEORGE G. retired lawyer; b. Whittier, Calif., Dec. 21, 1932; BA, Harvard U., 1954, LLB, 1957. Bar: Calif. 1957, U.S. Supreme Ct. 1962. Assoc. Gibson, Dunn & Crutcher, L.A., 1957-65, ptnr., 1966-69; v.p., sec. Cordura Corp. (formerly Computing & Software), L.A., 1969-74; ptnr. Collins, Gregory & Rutter, L.A., 1974-77, Hughes, Hubbard & Reed, L.A., 1977-83; exec. v.p. H.F. Ahmanson & Co., L.A., 1983-97; ret., 1997. Mem. State Bar Calif., Phi Beta Kappa.

GREGORY, JAMES ALEXANDER, editor, writer; b. Marshall, Mich., Apr. 11, 1930; s. Alexander and Chrissoula (Shoupilla) Gregory; life ptnr. Christopher Adams; children: Jim Davidson, Daniel G. B of English with honors, U. Mich., 1951, MA in English, 1952. Publicist Columbia Pictures, N.Y.C., 1956; press book editor-in-chief RKO Radio Pictures, N.Y.C., 1956-57; editor-in-chief Movieland and TV Time, N.Y.C., 1958-61; West Coast editor, writer Silver Screen, Screenland, Movieland, TV Time, L.A., 1960s; staff reporter Nat. Enquirer, 1974-76, freelance writer, 1976-80; editor Landscape and Irrigation, Van Nuys, Calif.; sr. editor Arbor Age, 1984-91, ret., 1992. Author: The Lucille Ball Story, 1974; co-author: The Wallaces of Alabama with George Wallace, Jr., 1975; author, editor: The Elvis Presley Story, 1960; author: David David David, 1972, The Soul of the Jackson 5, 1973, Donny!, 1973. Lt. (j.g.) USNR, 1953-55. Democrat. Avocation: art and autograph collector.

GREGORY, JEAN WINFREY, ecologist, educator; b. Richmond, Va., Feb. 13, 1947; d. Thomas Edloe and Kathryn (McFarlane) Winfrey; m. Ronald Alfred Gregory, Dec. 13, 1973. BS in Biology, Mary Washington Coll., 1969; MS in Biology, Va. Commonwealth U., 1975, postgrad., 1982-90; MA in Environ. Sci., U. Va., 1983. Cert. fisheries sci. Lab. specialist A Cardiovascular Divsn. Med. Coll. Va., Richmond, 1969-70; pollution specialist State Water Control Bd. (now Dept. Environ. Quality), Richmond, 1970-77, pollution control specialist B, 1977-81, ecologist, 1981-85, ecology programs supr., 1985-88, environ. program mgr., 1988-2000, environ. mgr. II, 2000—. Adj. faculty Va. Commonwealth U., Richmond, 1978-93. Contbr. articles to profl. jours. Named One of Outstanding Young Women of Am., 1974; EPA fellow, Va., 1974-76. Mem. Am. Soc. Limnology and Oceanography, N.Am. Lake Mgmt. Soc., N.Am. Benthological Soc., Sisters in Crime, Assn. Trad. Hooking Artists. Democrat. Methodist. Avocations: herb gardening, walking, rug hooking, dalmation rescue. Office: Office Water Quality Programs PO Box 10009 Richmond VA 23240-0009 E-mail: jwgregory@deq.state.va.us.

GREGORY, JEANNETTE T. publisher, writer; b. Newport News, Va., Sept. 25, 1954; d. Charlie James and Maggie Harris Tyson; m. Eric Gregory, Jan. 17, 1973; children: Derrick, Deitre, Alicia. AA, Rutledge Coll., Charlotte, NC, 1980. Mem. Bell South Advt. and Pub., Charlotte, NC, 1980—95; freelance motivational spkr. Charlotte, 1998—, life skill trainer and facilitator Transformation Ctr., Charlotte, 2000—; pres. Chosen Word Pub., Charlotte, 2000—. Author: (books) The Corridor of My Heart, 2000, Who Am I, 2002; contbr. columns in newspapers. Mentor Youth Network, Charlotte, NC, 2003. Recipient Editors Choice award, 1997. Avocations: writing, music, grandchildren. Office: Chosen Word Publishing Ste 307 1101 Tyvola Charlotte NC 28217

GREGORY, JOHN FORREST, information technology consultant; b. Springfield, Mass., Apr. 3, 1950; s. Howard Burdett and Mary Augustine (Reilly) G. BS of Fgn. Svc., Georgetown U., 1972; MSLS, Simmons Coll., 1974. Libr. Libr. of Congress, Washington, 1974-78, Sino-Soviet Inst., George Washington U., Washington, 1978-80, The Heritage Found., Washington,

1981-96; market rsch. and analysis staff U.S. Postal Svcs. Hdqrs., Washington, 1997—, market rsch. specialist, 1998—2003, sr. libr., 2003—. Cons. 1997-98. Author: Climber's Guide to Carderock, 1980, Rocksport! Tools Training and Technique for Climbers, 1989. Democrat. Roman Catholic. Home: 4114 Davis Pl NW Apt 105 Washington DC 20007-3948 Office: US Postal Svc HQ Rm 11800 475 L'Enfant Plz SW Washington DC 20260-1550 E-mail: gregoryj@mindspring.com., john.f.gregory@usps.gov.

GREGORY, KARL DWIGHT, economist, educator, consultant; b. Detroit, Mar. 26, 1931; s. Bertram and Sybil G.; m. Tenicia Ann Banks, June 7, 1959; children: Karin Diane, Sheila Therese, Kurt David. BA, Wayne State U., 1952, MA, 1957; PhD, U. Mich., 1962. Fiscal economist Office of Mgmt. and Budget, Washington, 1961-64; prof. Wayne State U., Detroit, 1960-61, 64-68, Oakland U., Rochester, Mich., 1968-96, disting. prof. emeritus, 1996—, ret. Chmn. bd., CEO Greater Detroit Bidco, Inc., 1990-96; mem. coun. econ. advisors Gov. Engler of Mich., 1992-96; cons. UN Devel. Program, Beijing, People's Republic of China, 1991; chief organizer, dir. First Ind. Nat. Bank Detroit, 1968-81, interim pres., 1980-81; vis. prof. SUNY, Buffalo, 1975; vis. scholar, mem. exec. staff U.S. Congl. Budget Office, Washington, 1975-76; chmn. bd., chief exec. officer Accord, Inc., Detroit, 1969-71. Author (with others) State of Black Michigan, 1984-87, 91; contbr. articles to pubns. Trustee Episcopal Diocese of Mich., Detroit, 1981-83, 84-87, 90-92; mem. Gov.'s Entrepreneurial Commn., Lansing, Mich., 1984-88, Regional Devel. Initiative S.E. Mich. Coun. Govts., 1990-91, Gov.'s Task Force on Tourism, Lansing, 1986-89; bd. dirs., United Way S.E. Mich., Mich. Ctr. High Tech., 1991-95, Detroit Alliance for Fair Banking, 1992-2002, Adult Well-Being Svcs., 1999—; mem. Detroit Workforce Devel. Bd., 2002—. 1st lt. U.S. Army, 1953-56. Recipient rsch. award Detroit chpt. NAACP, 1987, entrepreneurial awards Small Bus. Adminstrn., 1989, Mich. Dept. Commerce, 1992. Mem. Nat. Econ. Assn., Booker T. Washington Bus. Assn. Avocations: reading, music, photography, computers, travel. Home: 18495 Adrian St Southfield MI 48075-1803 E-mail: gregory_karl@hotmail.com.

GREGORY, LEWIS DEAN, trust company executive; b. Wichita, Kans., May 13, 1953; s. Harry Samuel III and Virginia Dorothy (Womer) G.; m. Laura Lorraine Davis, March 4, 1978; children: Paul Lewis, Erin Elizabeth. BA in Communications, U. Kans., Lawrence, 1975; MS in Journalism, U. Kans., 1976; JD, Washburn U., 1983. Bar: Kans. 1984, U.S. Dist. Ct. Kans. 1984. Cons. Delta Upsilon Frat., Inc., Indpls., 1973-76, mktg. rep. IBM, Kansas City, Mo., 1976-80; assoc. Frazey, Wix & Vetter, Wichita, 1983-84; trust mktg. mgr. Bank IV Wichita, 1984-86; v.p., trust officer, sales mgr. BancOklahoma Trust Co., Tulsa, 1986-88, Boatmen's Trust Co., Kansas City, 1988-97; sr. v.p., dist. trust mgr. Merrill Lynch Trust Co., 1997—. Dir. Am. Heart Assn., Wichita, Kans., 1985-86; pres. YMCA Men's Club, Tulsa, 1987-88; del. Rep. Party, Tulsa, 1988; trustee Leukemia Soc., 1992-96. Mem. ABA, Kans. Bar Assn., Johnson County Bar Assn., Kansas City Met. Bar Assn., Estate Planning Soc. (bd. dirs. 1996-98), Kiwanis, Kans. Univ. Alumni Assn. (pres. Greater Kansas City chpt. 1994-96, nat. bd. dirs. 1997-2002), Delta Upsilon (Indpls. dir. 1987-90, dir. Kans. chpt. 1977-90). Republican. Methodist. Avocation: running. Home: 12205 Aberdeen Rd Leawood KS 66209-1208 E-mail: lewis_gregory@ml.com.

GREGORY, MARGARET ELLEN, lawyer; b. Nebraska City, Nebr., Feb. 26, 1953; d. Edward Fugitt and Marjorie Ann (Elam) Askew; children: Megan, Mark, Scott, Robert. BA in Journalism, Iowa State U., 1974; JD, Coll. William Mary, 1977. Bar: Va. 1977, Colo. 1979. Lawyer U.S. Army, Ft. Carson, Colo., 1977-80, District Atty., Colorado Springs, Colo., 1980-83; pvt. practice Colorado Springs, Colo., 1983-2000; sr. atty. Office of Guardian-ad litem, El Paso County, 2000—. Editor League Peaks magazine, 1992-93. Chmn. Commn. Children Families (city and county chpts.), Colorado Springs, 1997-98; bd. dirs. Junior League, Colorado Springs, 1991-93, 98-2000, pres.-elect, 98-99, pres., 1999-2000. Capt. U.S. Army, 1977-80. Republican. Avocations: reading, volunteer work, travel. Office: 102 S Weber Colorado Springs CO 80903-3885 Fax: 719-635-7597. E-mail: mgregory@guardianadlitemelpaso.org.

GREGORY, MARY SHARON, educator; b. Washington, June 24, 1947; d. John Lynn and Dolores Katherine Sullivan; m. Brent E. Gregory, Aug. 16, 1969; children: Kathleen, Jean, Anne. BA, U.Ill., 1969; MA, Chgo. State U., 1973. Tchr. English Homewood/Flossmoor (Ill.) Jr. High Sch., 1969-72, U. Chgo. Lab. Schs., 1972-75, Dominican High Sch., Whitefish Bay, Wis., 1978-90, Homestead High Sch., Mequon, Wis., 1990—. Recipient Sen. Herb Kohl Tchr. award, 1990, Mequon-Thiensville Outstanding Educator of Yr. award, 1999. Mem. Nat. Coun. Tchrs. English, Wis. Coun. Tchrs. English, Milw. Alliance English Tchrs. (planning com. 1987—). Avocations: reading, travel. E-mail: msgregory@mtsd.k12.wi.us.

GREGORY, MAUGHN ROLLINS, education educator; b. Provo, Utah, Apr. 12, 1962; s. McKay and Joan Rollins; life ptnr. Troy D. Duty; 1 child, Nicole. PhD, U. Iberoamericana, Mexico City. Bar: Utah 1988. Dir. Philosophy for Children Inst. Montclair (N.J.) State U., 2001—, assoc. prof., 1997—. Dir. THISTLE critical thinking urban outreach, Newark, 1998—. Author: A Crash Course in Logic, 1999; contbr. articles to profl. jours.; guest editor: Inquiry: Critical Thinking Across the Disciplines, 2000. Mem. Gay Lesbian Straight Educators Network, Montclair, NJ, 2000—. Recipient Excellence in Tchg. award, Montclair State U. Student Govt., 1998, 1999; grantee, Victoria Found., Inc., 1998, 1999, 2000, 2001, USAI Devel. grantee, U.S. State Dept., 1999—2002. Mem.: Philosophy of Edn. Soc. Office: Montclair State U IAPC - 14 Normal Ave Montclair NJ 07043 Business E-Mail: gregorym@mail.montclair.edu.

GREGORY, MEL HYATT, JR., retired insurance company executive; b. Frankfort, Ky., Mar. 28, 1936; s. Mel Hyatt and Audrey (Fraley) G.; m. Joyce Klein, Sept. 9, 1955; children: Susan Gregory Lawson, Scott, Lisbeth Gregory Olesky. BS, Stetson U., 1958. Mgr., agt. Equitable Life Ins. Co., Louisville, 1959-66, agy., mgr. Dayton, Ohio, 1966-70, Atlanta, 1970-73, v.p. Cin., 1974-77, sr. v.p. N.Y.C., 1978-85, pres. so. ops. Atlanta, 1985-90, exec. v.p. N.Y.C., 1990-93; ret., 1993. Bd. dirs. Stetson U. Sch. Bus. Capt. U.S Army, 1958-62. Mem. Gen. Agts. and Mgrs. (pres. 1966-74), Canoe Brook Country Club, Cherokee Country Club. Republican. Home: 4570 Jett Rd NW Atlanta GA 30327-4562

GREGORY, MYRA MAY, religious organization administrator, educator; b. N.Y.C., Sept. 21, 1912; d. Thomas and Anna (Collins) G. Diploma, Maxwell Tchrs. Tng. Sch., Bklyn., 1933; BS in Edn., Bklyn. Coll., 1940, MA in History, 1952. Cert. music tchr. Tchr. N.Y.C. Bd. Edn., Bklyn., 1943-75; social worker Berean Bapt. Ch., Bklyn., 1932-48, supr., 1932-94, fin. sec. Sunday sch., 1935-94. Bd. dirs. Berean-Vacation Bible Sch., Bklyn., 1935-86; tchr. Protestant Coun., N.Y.C., 1940-81; bd. dirs. Recreation Bedford-Stuyvesant Area Project Inc., Bklyn.; dir. seminar Christian Teaching, Bklyn., 1974-86, 1990—. Bd. mgrs. Bklyn. Sun. Sch. Union, 1974—; bd. dirs. Bklyn. Divsn. Coun. of Chs. 1935—, pres., 1984-86, bd. dirs. Bklyn. Sunday Sch. Union, 1974—. Named Tchr. of Yr. Cmty. Sch. Bd. Dist. 14 N.Y.C. Bd. Edn., Bklyn., 1973, Outstanding Tchr., Stuyvesand divsn., Bklyn. Sunday Sch. Union, 1977, Educator/Leader Berean Bapt. Ch., 1977; recipient Ecumenism citation Borough Pres.'s Office, Bklyn., 1985, Religious Educator citation Bklyn. Ch. Women United, Inc., 1993, Cmty. Svc. awrd Mayors Office, N.Y.C., 1993, Ecumenical Svc./Educator Honors Office the Coun. City of N.Y., 1994, Lifetime Achievement award Bklyn. Coll., 1995, Outstanding Svc. award Coun. Chs. the City of N.Y., 1995, Leadership/Educator Citation Borough Pres. Office, Bklyn., 1999, Educator/Svc. Citation Berean Baptist Ch., 2000. Mem. ASCD, Am. String Tchrs. Assn., Am. Viola Soc., Assn. Childhood Edn. Internat., Orgn. Am. Historians, Ctr. Study of Presidency, Music Tchrs. Nat. Assn., Nat. Orch. Assn., Schomburg Ctr. Rsch. Black Culture. Democrat. Avocations: string ensemble, drama, writing. *When one reverently and humbly acknowledges that each individual is created by God to be his "temple", then life becomes a journey exemplifying the ideals and commands of His Son. Love's banner is seen regardless of challenging self-sacrifice.*

GREGORY, NELSON BRUCE, retired motel owner, retired naval officer; b. Syracuse, N.Y., Aug. 4, 1933; s. Nelson Bruce and Josephine (Sully) G.; m. Bonnie K. Bannowsky, May 2, 1961 (div. 1970); children: Elizabeth Jo, Jennifer Kay; m. Patricia Ann Greenhalgh, Oct. 15, 1977 (div. 1994); children: Peter Ward, Annette Frances, Michael John, Geoffrey Charles. BS, N.Y. Maritime Coll., 1955; postgrad., USN Pilot Tng., Pensacola, Fla., 1955-57; grad., NATO Weapons Sch., Oberammergau, Fed. Republic of Germany, 1966; diploma, Joint Warfare Sch., Salisbury, Eng., 1967, USN Counter Insurgency, Little Creek, Va., 1968, USAF Space Ops., Montgomery, Ala., 1969. Commd. ens. USN, 1955, advanced through grades to lt. comdr., 1964, operational pilot airborne Early Warning Squadron 2, 1957-60, flight instr. Airborne Early Warning Tng. Unit, 1960-63, command pilot Air Devel. Squadron 6 McMurdo Sound, Antarctica, 1963-64; airspace control officer NATO, Naples, Italy, 1964-68; chief pilot Naval Support Activity, Danang, Vietnam, 1968-69; space intelligence analyst NORAD, Colorado Springs, Colo., 1969-71; operational pilot Electronic Warfare Squadron 33 USN, Norfolk, Va., 1971-74, ops. officer Nat. Parachute Test Range El Centro, Calif., 1974-75, ret., 1975; owner, gen. mgr. Bonneville Motel, Idaho Falls, Idaho, 1975-99; ret., 1999. Bd. dirs. Am. Travel Inns, 1976-78. Newspaper contbr. Decorated Combat Air medals (3) USN; recipient Vietnamese Gallantry Cross Republic of Vietnam, 1969; Gregory Ridge in Antarctica named for him, 1964. Mem. VFW, Ret. Officers Assn. (life), Am. Legion, Heritage Found., Elks. Republican. Presbyterian. Avocations: yachting, camping, travel. Home: 474 Whittier St # 18 Idaho Falls ID 83401-2632

GREGORY, PHILIP J. pharmacist, editor; b. Fort Madison, Iowa, Sept. 6, 1970; s. Gregory. PharmD, U. of the Pacific, Stockton, Calif., 1999. Assoc. editor, dir. of natural medicines Therapeutic Rsch. Ctr., Stockton, 2001—02, assoc. editor, editl. dir., 2002—. Author: (reference book and database) Natural Medicines Comprehensive Database; editor: (monthly newsletter) Pharmacist's Letter & Prescriber's Letter; author: (book chpt.) Medication Misadventures; contbr. articles to profl. jours. Pres. No. Calif. Coll. of Clin. Pharmacy, Stockton, 2002—03. Specialist U.S. Army, 1991—93. Mem.: Am. Soc. of Health-Sys. Pharmacists, Am. Coll. of Clin. Pharmacy, Am. Pharm. Assn. Conservative. Home: 675 S Regent St Stockton CA 95204 Office: Therapeutic Rsch Ctr 3120 W March Ln Stockton CA 95219 Personal E-mail: pgregory@pletter.com.

GREGORY, ROGER LEE, federal judge; b. Phila., July 17, 1953; s. George Lee and Fannie Mae (Washington) G.; m. Carla Eugenia Lewis, Sept. 6, 1980; children: Adriene Leigh, Rachel Leigh. BA, Va. State U., 1975; JD, U. Mich., 1978. Bar: Mich. 1978, Va. 1980, U.S. Ct. Appeals (6th cir.) 1978, U.S. Ct. Appeals (4th cir.) 1980. Assoc. atty. Butzel, Long, Gust, Klein & Van Zile, Detroit, 1978-80, Hunton & Williams, Richmond, Va., 1980-82, ptnr. Wilder & Gregory, Richmond, 1982—2001; judge U.S. Ct. Appeals (4th cir.), Richmond, 2001—. Bd. visitors Va. Commonwealth U., Richmond, 1985—. Bd. dirs. Indsl. Devel. Authority, Richmond, 1984—, Richmond chpt. YMCA, 1989—. Me. Cen. Va. Legal Aid Soc. (exec. com.), Old Dominion Bar Assn. (pres.), Richmond Bar Assn. (bd. dirs.), Metro C. of C. (bd. dirs. 1989—), Alpha Kappa Mu, Alpha Mu Gamma. Baptist. Office: US Ct Appeals 4th Cir 1000 E Main St Rm 212 Richmond VA 23219*

GREGORY, SARA SUSAN, musician, lyricist, poet; b. DeQueen, Ark., June 24, 1952; d. Eugene Cluran Gregory and Maxine Louise Fulton; m. Steven Eugene Thomas, Nov. 18, 1977 (div. Dec. 1, 1995). Student, U. Okla., 1971, Southeastern Okla. State U., 1972—75, U. Denver, 1974, Oklahoma City U., 1981, San Francisco State U., 1996; master classes in trumpet with Maurice Andree, Nat. Trumpet Symposium. Auditor, payroll, ins. agt. Okla. Employment Svc., Oklahoma City, 1975—80; acct. Steven E. Thomas, CPA, Oklahoma City, 1980—82; musician, record prodr. World Evangelism Svcs., Oklahoma City, 1983—94; owner North Beach Rec., San Francisco, 1990—94, Times Two Records and Pub., Oklahoma City and San Francisco, 1986—94; audio/video engr. Bill Graham Presents, San Francisco, 1996; event staff San Francisco Performing Arts Found., 1996—98; publicist Daniel Castro Blues Band, 1996—98; prodr. Kimpton Prodns. Live from the Starlight Room TV show, 1998; hostess Little City & Tavolino Restaurants, 1998; enumerator U.S. Dept. Commerce-Census 2000, 2000; archivist Bill Graham Presents, San Francisco, 1996, George Tsongas, 2002; writer, 1986—2002; mng. editor San Francisco Oracle. Judge No. Calif. Songwriters Assn., San Francisco, 1997. Prodr.: (rec.) Sheer Joy, 1983; prodr., engr., writer, musician: rec. Steve & Sara, 1986, prodr., engr., writer, performer, distbr.: Frontlines, 1988; prodr., engr., writer, performer, distbr. : Songs of the Street, 1992; prodr., engr., writer, performer, distbr.: Streetsinger, 1992, Christmas by the Sea, 1992; author: Collected Lyrics and Poetry, 1999; mem. prodn. crew Black and White Ball, 1996, Bay Area Music Awards, 1996—98, mem. 150th prodn. crew Ann. Calif., 1999, audio and recording engr. Caffe Trieste Concerts & Recording, North Beach, San Francisco, 2003—. Mem. Common Cause, Telegraph Hill Dwellers Assn., San Francisco, 1994—; mem. comm. com. Pioneer Park Project at Coit Tower, San Francisco, 1996—2001, 400 Trees Project Telegraph Hill Dwellers and Friends of the Urban Forest, San Francisco, 1996—98; audio engr. Telegraph Hill Dwellers; mem. jazz band S.E. Okla. State U., 1972—75; concert band trumpet soloist Madrigal Singers and Opera Workshop; poll worker presdl. election San Francisco, 2000. Named to, Okla. All Dist. Band, 1965, Okla. All-State Band, 1969, 1970; recipient John Philip Sousa award, Broken Bow H.S., 1970, pvt. endowment, Elizabeth Styll Smith, 1983—94. Mem.: LWV, NARAS (staff 1997), Dixieland Combo-5E Okla. Dist. Tchrs., Okla. Music Educator's Conv., Band Masters Conv., Dist. 3 Dem. Club. Democrat. Roman Catholic. Avocations: cooking, sewing, ceramics. Home: PO Box 330522 San Francisco CA 94133 E-mail: sarasgregory@yahoo.com.

GREGORY, THOMAS BRADFORD, mathematics educator; b. Traverse City, Mich., Dec. 13, 1944; s. Philip Henry and Rhoda Winslow (Hathaway) G.; m. Deirdre Dianne Mason, July 15, 1995. *Father, Philip Henry Gregory, received a BS from Bowdoin College in 1926, a Bachelor of Sacred Theology from Yale Divinity School in 1935, and an MA from Oberlin College in 1937. A registered pharmacist, he became a minister, serving Baptist, Congregational and Presbyterian churches in Vermont, Massachusetts, Michigan and Ohio. Mother, Rhoda Winslow Hathaway, a member of the Massachusetts Society of Mayflower Descendants, studied at Massachusetts School of Art. Wife Deirdre Dianne Mason received a BSEd from Ashland College in 1981 and an MEd in 1989. She received an MS from Ohio State University in 1986 and an MEd from the University of Dayton in 1993. She is the former president, Mansfield School Employees Association and is currently guidance counselor, Mansfield City Schools.* BA, Oberlin (Ohio) Coll., 1967; MA, Yale U., 1969, M of Philosophy, 1975, PhD, 1977. Lectr. Ohio State U., Mansfield, 1977-78, asst. prof. math., 1978-84, assoc. prof. math., 1984—, pres. faculty, 2001—02. Reviewer: Math. Revs., 1984—; contbr. articles to profl. jours. Active Mansfield (Ohio) Symphony Chorus, 1977—, Presbytery Youth Ministries Com., New Philadelphia, Ohio, 1980-87, Ohio State U. Community Singers, Mansfield, 1985—; mem. Presbytery Biblical Authority task force, 1994-95; bd. dirs. Lay Acad. Religion, Wooster (Ohio) Coll., 1997—; commd. lay min. Presbytery of Muskingum Valley, New Philadelphia, Ohio, 1998—. Comdr. USNR, 1969-96. Fellow NSF, Washington, 1967; hon. fellow U. Wis., Madison, 1987-88, 92. Fellow Phi Beta Kappa; mem. Am. Math. Soc. (translator 1974-82), Ohio Coun. Tchrs. Math., Am. Soc. Naval Engrs., Res. Officers Assn., Naval Res. Assn., Navy League, Sigma Xi. Avocations: classical piano, singing. Home: 411 Overlook Rd Mansfield OH 44907-1533 Office: Ohio State U 1680 University Dr # O-15 Mansfield OH 44906-1547 E-mail: tgregory@math.ohio-state.edu.

GREGORY, WILTON D. bishop; b. Chgo., Dec. 7, 1947; s. Wilton and Ethel Duncan G.. Student, Niles Coll., Loyola U., Chgo., St. Mary of Lake Sem., Mundelein, Ill., Pontifical Liturgical Inst., Sant'Anselmo, Rome, D in Sacred Liturgy, 1980. Ordained priest Roman Cath. Ch., 1973, ordained bishop Roman Cath. Ch., 1983. Aux. bishop, Chgo., 1983—93; Bishop of Belleville, 1994—. Spkr. in field. Author (in field). Avocations: travel, music, racquetball, golf. Address: Chancery Office 222 S 3rd St Belleville IL 62220-1916*

GREGSON, MERRY CHRIS (MERRY SMITH), artist; b. Kansas City, Mo., Sept. 9, 1956; d. Leroy Zeddy Smith Jr. and Virginia Ann Fitzhugh; m. Ted C. Gregson, July 8, 2002. Art diploma, Internat. Correspondence Sch., 1994. Dog groomer, Sanford, N.C., 1980-85; cab driver Am. Yellow Cab, Sanford, 1998-2000. Exhibns. Ted's Mus., Sanford, N.C.; contbr. poetry to lit. publs. Historian Ted's Mus., Sanford, 2000—. Democrat. Avocations: bird watching, fishing, metal detecting, bicycling, walking.

GREGUS, LINDA ANNA, government official; b. Hartford, Conn., Mar. 24, 1956; d. Steven and Sylvia Christine (Ramunno) G. AB, Bowdoin Coll., 1978; MA in Law and Diplomacy, Tufts U., 1985. Vol. VISTA, Phoenix, 1978-79; research asst. Econ. Research Assocs., Boston, 1979; ops adminstr. CRT Inc., Hartford, Conn., 1980-82; program officer U.S. Dept. of State, Washington, 1986-90; intelligence officer CIA, Washington, 1990—. Recipient Milo Peck Scholarship Town of Windsor, Conn., 1984. Home: 1904 Wilson Ln Mc Lean VA 22102-1943

GREIF, GEOFFREY LEONARD, social work educator; b. Balt., Apr. 13, 1949; s. Leonard L. and Ann (Burgunder) G.; m. Maureen Lefton, Dec. 28, 1975; children: Jennifer, Alissa. BA, Ohio Wesleyan U., 1971; MSW, U. Pa., 1974; DSW, Columbia U., 1983. Lic. clin. social worker, Md. Social worker Camden (N.J.) Sch. System, 1974-76; psychiat. social worker Drenk Guidance Ctr., Burlington, N.J., 1976-79; tchr. Widener U., Chester, Pa., 1981-84; from asst. prof. to prof. U. Md., Balt., 1984—, assoc. dean, 1996—. Cons., supr. Cmty. Counseling Ctr., Cockeysville, Md., 1985-90; cons. drug program Sinai Hosp., Balt., 1990-96. Author: Single Fathers, 1985, (with others) Mothers Without Custody, 1988, The Daddy Track and the Single Father, 1990, When Parents Kidnap, 1993, Group Work with At-Risk Populations, 1997, Out of Touch: When Parents and Children Lose Contact After Divorce, 1997, Beating the Odds: Raising Academically Successful African-American Males, 1998, Overcoming the Odds: Raising Academically Successful African-American Young Women, 2002; contbr. over 90 articles and book chpts. Bd. dirs. Parents Anonymous, Balt., 1985-92, Park Sch., Balt., 1987-2000, Albert Schweitzer Fellows, Balt., 1999—; chair Gov.'s Commn. on Sexual Orientation Discrimination, 2000-01. Young scholar Sch. Social Wk., 1989. Office: U Md Sch Social Work 525 W Redwood St Baltimore MD 21201-1705 E-mail: ggreif@ssw.umaryland.edu.

GREIF, JOSEPH, lawyer; b. N.Y.C., June 25, 1943; s. Jacob J. and Dorothy (Harrison) G.; m. Aline Bohm, Jan. 1, 1966; children: Jeffrey, Julie. BBA, U. Pitts., 1964; JD, NYU, 1967. Bar: N.Y. 1967, D.C. 1968, U.S. Tax Ct. 1986; CPA, Md., D.C. Instr. No. Va. C.C., Annandale, 1967-68; mgmt. cons. Computer Sci. Corp., Silver Spring, Md., 1967-70; tax mgr. Arthur Andersen & Co., Washington, 1970-75; sr. assoc. Ginsberg, Feldman & Bress, Washington, 1975-77; ptnr. Touche Ross & Co., Washington, 1977-84, McGuffie, Greif, Whitney & Handal, Washington, 1984-90; of counsel McNeily, Rosenfeld & Rubenstein, Washington, 1991-98, Neimark & Nadel, Ft. Lauderdale, Fla., 1998—, Washington, 1998—. Lectr. George Washington U. Grad. Sch. Bus., Washington, 1993-95. Co-author, editor: Managing Membership Societies, 1979; contbr. articles on taxation, comml. leasing, computer systems contracting, exec. compensation, exec. contracts to profl. jours. Bd. dirs. Nat. Assn. for Mental Health, Washington, 1973-75, Combined Health Appeal, Washington, 1980-81, Assn. Devel. Coun., Washington, 1987-89; task force mem. White House Task Force on Charitable Giving, Washington, 1979-80. Mem. AICPA (chmn. fed. tax divsn. task force on exempt orgns. 1983-86), ABA, D.C. Bar Assn., Am. Soc. Assn. Execs. (mem. govt. affairs and long range planning coms., Outstanding Svc. award, tech. sect. coun. 1996—), D.C. Inst. CPAs, Greater Washington Soc. Assn. Execs. (tech. task force 1994—), Computer Law Assn. Avocations: boating, squash. Office: Greif Legal Econs Svcs 1717 K St NW Ste 600 Washington DC 20036 Fax: 202-204-2235.

GREIF, RALPH, mechanical engineer, educator; b. N.Y.C., Nov. 28, 1935; s. Harry and Anne (Reiter) G.; m. Judith Harriet Falk, June 29, 1958; children: Eve H. Karasik, William M., Daniel M. MusB in Edn., NYU, 1956; MS, UCLA, 1958; MA, PhD, Harvard U., 1962. Staff mem. Hughes R&D Labs., L.A., 1956-58; engr. Raytheon Mfg. Co., Bedford, Mass., 1958; post-doctoral fellow Harvard U., Cambridge, 1963; prof. U. Calif., Berkeley, 1963—. Vis. scholar Imperial Coll. of Sci. and Tech., London, 1969-70; vis. prof. Israel Inst. Technology, Haifa, 1977; cons. in field, 1965—; mem. adv. com. State Doctorate Thesis, France, 1983, exec. com. 15th Internat. Symposium on Shock Waves and Shock Tubes, 1985, scientific adv. com. 2d Internat. Symposium on Transport Phenomena in Turbulent Flows, Japan, 1985—. Mem. editl. bd. Jour. Materials Processing and Mfg. Sci., 1992—; hon. editl. adv. bd. Internat. Jour. Heat and Mass Transfer, 1995—, Internat. Commn. in Heat and Mass Transfer, 1995—; mem. adv. bd. Jour. Chem. Vapor Deposition, 1992—; mem. editl. adv. bd. Heat Transfer Rsch., 1997—. Recipient Best Paper award Am. Nuc. Soc., 1994; Charles Storer Storrow fellow Harvard U., 1961-62, John Simon Guggenheim Meml. Found. fellow, 1969-70, Lady Davis fellow Israel Inst. Tech., 1977, rsch. fellow Japan Soc. Promotion of Sci., 1995. Fellow ASME (heat transfer div., chmn. tech. com. on aircraft and astronautical heat tranfer 1970-73, computer technology com. 1975-79, chmn. honors and awards com. 1981-82, editor Jour. Heat Transfer, 1983—, vice chmn. Symposium on Automotive Engine Tech. 1985—, exec. com. 1990-95, chmn. 1993-94, Heat Transfer Meml. award 1985, Dedicated Svc. award 1996). Avocations: hiking, reading, music. Office: U Calif Berkeley Dept Mech Engring 6107 Etcheverry Hall Berkeley CA 94720-1740 Fax: 510-642-6163. E-mail: greif@me.berkeley.edu.

GREIF, ROBERT, mechanical engineering educator; b. N.Y.C., Jan. 17, 1938; s. Harry and Anne (Reiter) G.; m. Joyce Ambrose; children: Jessica, Andrew. BSME, NYU, 1958; SM, Harvard U., 1959, PhD, 1963. Registered profl. engr., Mass. Staff scientist Missile Systems div., Avco Corp., Wilmington, Mass., 1963-65, sr. staff scientist, 1965-67; asst. prof. mech. engring. Tufts U., Medford, Mass., 1967-70, assoc. prof., 1970-78, prof., 1978—, chmn. dept. mech. engring., 1981-89. Cons. Stone & Webster, Boston, 1971-78, U.S. Dept. Transp., Cambridge, Mass., 1977—; vis. scholar Harvard U., Cambridge, 1981; vis. research fellow U. Sussex, Eng., 1974; sr. rsch. assoc. NASA Langley Rsch. Ctr., 1988. Fellow AIAA (assoc.), ASME; mem. AAUP. Office: Tufts U Dept Mech Engring 200 College Ave Anderson Hall Medford MA 02155

GREIFELD, ROBERT A. corporate financial executive; BA Eng., Iona Coll., 1979; MBA, NYU, Stern Sch. of Bus., 1986. Pres. and chief op. officer Automated Securities Clearance, Inc., 1991—99; serves Bd. of Knight Securities, 1993; ECN Automated Securities Clearance, Inc., 1998; v.p. Sunguard Data Sys. Inc. and group CEO, Sunguard Brokerage Sys., 1999—2000; sr. v.p. Sunguard Data Sys., Inc., 2000—02; pres. and chief exec. The Nasdaq Stock Market, Inc., New York, NY, 2003—. In the role of Pres. and chief Op. Officer of Automated Securitites Clearance, he led a team that successfully made BRASS the industry std. trade order mgmt. sys. for NASDAQ stocks. He also spearheaded the founding of BRUT, the trading consortium whose mem. included Knight Trading, Morgan Stanley, Goldman Sachs and Merrill Lynch. Office: The Nasdaq Stock Market, Inc 1500 Broadway New York NY 10036*

GREIG, BRIAN STROTHER, lawyer; b. Austin, Tex., Apr. 10, 1950; s. Ben Wayne Greig and Virginia Ann (Strother) Higgins; m. Jane Ann Sentilles, June 17, 1972; children: Travis Darden, Grace Hanna. BA, Washington and Lee U., 1972; JD, U. Tex., 1975. Bar: Tex. 1975, U.S. Dist. Ct. (ea. dist.) Tex. 1976, U.S. Ct. Appeals (5th cir.) 1976, U.S. Dist. Ct. (so. dist.) Tex. 1977, U.S. Dist. Ct. (we. dist.) Tex. 1980, U.S. Supreme Ct. 1980, U.S. DIst. Ct. (no. dist.) Tex. 1984, U.S. Ct. Appeals (11th cir.) 1984. Law clk. to chief judge U.S. Dist. Ct., Beaumont, Tex., 1975-76; sr. ptnr. Fulbright & Jaworski L.L.P., Austin, 1976—. Mem. Austin Tomorrow On-Going Goals Assembly Com., 1981; pres. Austin Mgmt. Lawyers Forum, 1987, 93. Editor-in-chief Tex. Assn. Bus. Employment Law Handbook; mem. editl. bd. Tex. Labor Letter, 1994-2001. Pres. Austin Lawyers and Accts. for Arts, 1981; trustee Laguna Gloria Art Mus., Austin, 1983-91, pres., 1989-90, chmn., 1990-91; bd. dirs. Zachary Scott Theater Ctr., Austin, 1981; mem. devel. bd. Inst. Texan Cultures, 1991-98; trustee Westminster Manor Health Facilities Corp. of Travis County, Tex., 1991-96, sec., 1995-96; trustee St. Stephen's Episcopal Sch., 1995-2001; pres. Austin Mus. Art, 1991-92, trustee, 1991-93; bd. dirs. The Capital of Tex. Pub. Telecomms. Coun., Inc. (KLRU-TV), 2001—. Fellow Tex. Bar Found. (life), Am. Coll. Labor and Employment Lawyers (charter); mem. ABA, FBA, Am. Arbitration Assn. (employment adv. coun. 1995—), Tex. Bar Assn., Travis County Bar Assn., Tex. Commn. on Human Rights (chmn.'s task force), Tex. Assn. Bus. (bd. dirs. 2000—), Tarry House Club, Headliners Club (trustee 1998—), Austin Assembly. Methodist. Avocations: hunting, fishing. Office: Fulbright & Jaworski LLP 600 Congress Ave Ste 2400 Austin TX 78701-3271 E-mail: bgreig@fulbright.com.

GREIG, WILLIAM TABER, II, publishing company executive; b. Mpls., Apr. 16, 1924; s. William Taber and Margaret Naomi (Buckbee) G.; m. Doris Jane Walters, June 23, 1951; children: Kathryn Ann Greig Rowland, William Taber, III, Gary Stanley, Doris Jane. B.Arch., U. Minn., 1945. Jr. exec. Bur. Engraving, Mpls., 1946-48; partner, mgr. Praise Book Publns., Mound, Minn.,

1948-50; v.p., exec. v.p., gen. mgr. Gospel Light Publs., 1950-76, pres., owner, 1976—, chmn., 1983—. Bd. dirs. Lighthouse Ptnrs. Bookstores; founder, chmn., Gospel Light Worldwide, 2000-; founder, chmn. bd. Credo Pub., St. Petersburg, Russia. Ruling elder Presbyn. Ch. (U.S.A.); co-founder Minn. Sunday Sch. Assn., 1953; bd. dirs., chmn. Joy of Living Bible Studies, 1978—; trustee Concerts of Prayer Internat., 1988—; chmn John Perkins Found., 1990—. Served to lt. (j.g.) USNR, 1943-46. Mem. Evang. Christian Pubs. Assn. (co-founder 1974, bd. dirs., pres. 1981-83) Clubs: Tower. Republican. Home: 347 Lupine Way Ventura CA 93001-2201 Office: Gospel Light Publs 1957 Eastman Ave Ventura CA 93003

GREIL, ARTHUR LAWRENCE, sociology educator; b. Balt., Apr. 24, 1949; s. Ralph Steele and Adele Zelda (Wolpert) G.; m. Barbara Jean Eckstein, Aug. 11, 1974; children: Robert Isaac, Madeline Esther. Instr. sociology, Alfred (N.Y.) U., from 1977, asst. prof., assoc. prof., prof., Alfred (N.Y.) U. Instr. Alfred (N.Y.) U., 1977-79, asst. prof., 1979-83, assoc. prof., 1983-89, prof., 1989—. Bd. dirs., data cons. Ferre Inst., Utica, N.Y., 1983-96. Author: Georges Sorel and the Sociology of Virtue, 1981, Not Yet Pregnant: Infertile Couples in Contemporary America, 1991; editor: Between Sacred and Secular: Research and Theory on Quasi-Religion, 1994; also articles. Advisor Hillel, Alfred U., 1979—; chmn. Alfred Planning Bd., 1995—. Mem. Am. Sociol. Assn., Soc. for Sci. Study Religion (program chmn. 1989—, treas. 1996-2000, exec. officer 2000—), Soc. for Study Social Problems (divsn. chmn. 1985-86), Sociologists for Women in Society. Democrat. Jewish. Avocation: gardening. Office: Alfred U 1 Saxon Dr Alfred NY 14802-1232

GREILSHEIMER, JAMES GANS, lawyer; b. N.Y.C., Oct. 14, 1937; s. Jerome J. and Lillian (Gans) G.; m. Louise B. Steiner, Aug. 11, 1974; children: Lauren, Julie, Michael, Jeremy. AB cum laude, Princeton U., 1959; LLB, Harvard U., 1962. Bar: N.Y. 1963, D.C. 1969. Asst. U.S. atty. So. Dist. N.Y., 1963-68; litigating asst. corp. counsel City of N.Y., 1974-77, 1st asst. corp. counsel, 1978-80; ptnr. Blank Rome LLP and predecessor firms, N.Y.C., 1993—. Mediator mediation program U.S. Dist. Ct. (so. dist.) N.Y., 1993—. Mem., sec. N.Y.C. Charter Rev. Commn., 1982-83; pres. N.Y. chpt. Am. Jewish Com., 1981-84; v.p. Jewish Cmty. Rels. Coun. N.Y., 1981-85, bd. dirs., 1995-2001; bd. dirs. Com. on Decent Unbiased Campaign Tactics, 1983-93, Non-profit Coordinating Com., N.Y., 1985—, Vol. Cons. Group, Inc., 1986—; v.p., bd. dirs. Fund for Pub. Schs., Inc., 1986-91, pres., 1992-2002; mem. Citizens Budget Commn., Inc., 1991-93. Mem.: Assn. Bar of City of N.Y. (mcpl. affairs com. 1979—81, govt. ethics com. 1990—98, com. on condemnation and tax certiorari 1993—95, 2001—), N.Y. County Lawyers Assn. (bd. dirs. 1981—87, chmn. fed. cts. com. 1977—80, spl. com. on condemnation 1990—), N.Y. State Bar Assn. (spl. com. on cts. and cmty. 1975—81). Office: Blank Rome LLP 405 Lexington Ave New York NY 10174-0002 E-mail: jgreilsheimer@blankrome.com.

GREILSHEIMER, WILLIAM HENRY, lawyer; b. N.Y.C., Sept. 28, 1941; s. Jerome Jacob and Lillian (Gans) G.; m. Carol Leslie Horwitz, Sept. 6, 1970; children: Jeffrey Mark, Deborah Lynn. AB, Dartmouth Coll., 1963; JD, Yale U., 1966. Bar: N.Y. 1967, U.S. Ct. Appeals (2d cir.) 1968, U.S. Dist. Ct. (so. and ea. dists.) N.Y. 1968, U.S. Dist. Ct. Conn. 1997, U.S. Supreme Ct. 1970. Ptnr. Delson & Gordon, N.Y.C., 1967-73, Burns, Summit, Rovins & Feldeslman, N.Y.C., 1973-81, Ferber, Greilsheimer, Chan & Essner, N.Y.C., 1981-96, counsel, 1997-98. Lectr., co-author continuing legal edn. program, 1987. Trustee Stephen Wise Free Synagogue, N.Y.C., 1987-90. Mem. ABA, Assn. of Bar of City of N.Y. (com. on lectures and continuing edn. 1991-93, com. on corp. law 1993-95), N.Y. County Lawyers Assn. (corp. law com., securities and exchanges com.). Democrat. Jewish. Avocations: jogging, tennis, cross-country skiing. Home: 91 Central Park W New York NY 10023-4600 Office: 420 Lexington Ave New York NY 10170-0002 E-mail: whg@greils.com.

GREINER, JACK VOLKER, ophthalmologist, physician, surgeon, scientist; b. Fountain Hill, Pa., Aug. 25, 1949; s. Harry Sandt and Vera Lilian G.; m. Cynthia Ann Mis, May 17, 1980; children: Ashley Lauren, Logan Nicholas Jack, Jordan Dean Jack. AA, Valley Forge Mil. Coll., 1969; BA, U. Vt., 1971; MS in Anatomy, Purdue U., 1974; PhD, U. Toledo, 1975; OD, New England Coll. Optometry, 1978; DO, Midwestern U., 1982. Diplomate Am. Bd. Surgery in Ophthalmology. Rsch. fellow in ophthalmology Howe Lab. of Ophthalmology Harvard Med. Sch. and Mass. Eye and Ear Infirmary, Boston, 1974—76; rsch. fellow in ophthalmology Harvard Med. Sch., Boston, 1975—78, instr. ophthalmology, 1988—90, clin. instr., 1991—; rsch. fellow in cornea and external diseases of eye Schepens Eye Rsch. Inst., Retina Found., 1976—78, clin. assoc. scientist, 1991—; rsch. assoc. in ophthalmology U. Ill. Eye and Ear Infirmary, Chgo., 1979—81, rsch. asst. prof. ophthalmology, 1981-83; med. intern Cook County Hosp., Chgo., 1982—83; resident in ophthalmology Georgetown U. Med. Ctr., 1983—86; clin. assoc. prof. U. New Eng. Coll. Osteo. Medicine, 1999—; asst. clin. prof. dept. ophthalmology Tufts U. Sch. Medicine, Boston, 2000—. Adj. asst. scientist Eye Rsch. Inst., Retina Found., Boston, 1978; adj. asst. prof. ophthalmic pathology Midwestern U., 1978-82, asst. prof. dept. pathology, 1982-83, assoc. prof., 1983-87; co-dir. Eye Rsch. Lab., Chgo. Osteo. Hosp., 1980-87; clin. fellow in ophthalmology Harvard Med. Sch./Mass. Eye and Ear Infirmary, 1986-88; med. staff Beth Israel Deaconess Hosp., Boston, Winchester Hosp., Lawrence Meml. Hosp., Medford, Melrose-Wakefield Hosp., Spaulding Rehab. Hosp., Boston; founder, staff mem. Laser Eye Ctr. Boston, 1996—; founder, bd. dirs. Ocular Rsch. Boston, Inc., 1990—. Contbr. chpts. to books, over 140 articles to profl. jours.; patentee in ophthalmology and dermatology. Capt. C.E. USAR, 1971-78. Fight For Sight grantee, 1980-82, Nat. Soc. to Prevent Blindness grantee, 1981-82, NIH Nat. Eye Inst. grantee, 1982-85, 92-97. Fellow Am. Acad. Osteo. Surgeons (pres. 1995-96), Am. Acad. Optometry, Am. Acad. Ophthalmology (Achievement award 2001), Am. Acad. Specialists in Surgery (pres. 2002—, sec. 2001-02, Surgeon of Yr. 2003); mem. AMA (Physicians Recognition award 1985-87, 89-91, 94-97, 99), Nat. Acad. Practice (Disting. Practitioner), Mass. Soc. Eye Physicians and Surgeons, Am. Assn. Osteo. Specialists, Nat. Acads. Practice (editl. bd. Jour. Nat. Acad. Practice Forum), Am. Assn. Physician Specialists, Nat. Soc. Prevent Blindness (bd. dirs. Prevent Blindness Mass.), Contact Lens Assn. Ophthalmologists, Assn. Rsch. in Vision and Ophthalmology, Mass. Med. Soc., Sigma Xi, Phi Kappa Phi, Sigma Sigma Phi. Office: Harvard Med Sch 20 Staniford St Boston MA 02114-2508 E-mail: greiner@vision.eri.harvard.edu.

GREINER, KENNETH DONALD, JR., nursing home company executive; b. Cushing, Okla., Aug. 19, 1938; s. Kenneth Donald Greiner and Billie Alene (Williams) Greiner/Kannady; m. Leitner Louise Jarrell, Sept. 2, 1961; children: Katherine Louise Pierce, Kenneth Donald III, Jennifer Lee, Cheryl Sue. BS in Econs., Okla. State U., 1960; MBA, Harvard U., 1962; BS in Health Care Adminstrn., Okla. Bapt. U., 1977. Adminstrv. asst. Doric Corp., Oklahoma City, 1962-64; asst. to treas. Skelly Oil Co., Tulsa, 1964-66; loan officer AID, Lahore, Karachi, Pakistan, 1966-69; ptnr. Resource Analysis and Mgmt. Group, Oklahoma City, 1969-74; v.p., dir. Texal Internat. Co., Oklahoma City, 1974-76; chmn. Grace Living Ctrs. (formerly Amity Care Corp.), Oklahoma City, 1976—2002. Asst. trustee in bankruptcy Four Seasons Nursing Ctrs. Am., 1972—73; bd. dirs., mem. exec. com. Will Rogers Bank, 1983—94; br. adv. dir. Oklahoma City Nations Bank, 1994—97; trustee in bankruptcy Gulf South Corp., 1974, Cleanerator Corp., 1974, Preferred Commodity Options Corp., 1974—75. Treas., bd. dirs. Neighborhood Svcs. Orgn., Oklahoma City Met. Area, 1978—83; chmn. bd. New World Sch., Oklahoma City, 1973—74; mem. Putnam City Sch. Bd., 1988—93, pres., 1992—93; dir. Cowboy Golf, Inc., 1992—; trustee Hillcrest Hosp., Oklahoma City, 1989—93; dir. Emergency Med. Svcs. Authority, Oklahoma City, Tulsa, 1998—2001; mem. bd. govs. Okla. State U. Found., 1994—, trustee, 1998—; chmn. Cath. Social Ministries, Archdiocese of Oklahoma City, 1977—86. Mem.: Nat. Assn. Bds. Examiners Nursing Home Adminstrs. (pres. 1994—96), Okla. State Bd. Nursing Homes (bd. dirs. 1988—92), Nursing Home Assn. Okla. (exec. bd. 1988—2003, v.p. 1990—92), Okla. State U. CBA Assocs. (pres. 1993—94), Equestrian Order Holy Seplechre, Ski Island Lake Inc. (pres. 1984—87), Quail Creek Golf and Country Club (v.p., dir. 1998—2001), Harvard Bus. Sch. Alumni Club (pres. Oklahoma City 1970—71), Oklahoma City Dinner Club, Bus. Boosters Club (pres. 1985), Phi Delta Theta Alumni (pres. Oklahoma City 1969—71). Republican. Roman Catholic. Office: Nursing Home Properties 4350 Will Rogers Pky Ste 350 Oklahoma City OK 73108 Home: 6280 Estate Nazareth St Thomas VI 00802

GREINER, MARY LOUISE, lawyer, psychotherapist; b. St. Louis, Aug. 18, 1949; d. Theodore H. and Dorothy E. (Walters) G.; m. S. Charles Baber. BA, Hamline U., 1971; JD, U. Minn., 1974; MSSW, U. Tex., 1994. Bar: Minn. 1974, U.S. Dist. Ct. Minn. 1974, Hawaii 1976, U.S. Dist. Ct. Hawaii 1976, Tex. 1989. Staff atty. Fed. Res. Bank, Mpls., 1974-75; instr. L.A. Community Coll. Extension, Okinawa, Japan, 1975-76; assoc. Stubenberg Law Firm, Honolulu, 1976-77; spl. counsel State of Hawaii, Honolulu, 1977; counsel Control Data Corp., Mpls., 1978-87; pres. Greiner & Assoc., Bloomington, Minn., 1987-88; assoc. gen. counsel Electronic Data Systems Corp., Plano, Tex., 1989-92; clin. social worker, mediator Pastoral Counseling & Edn. Ctr., Dallas, 1994—. Mem. Internat. Inst. Bioenergetic Analysis, State Bar Tex., Tex. Lawyers Concerned for Lawyers (bd. dirs.). Unitarian Universalist. Avocations: travel, reading, needlepoint. Office: Pastoral Counseling and Edn Ctr 4525 Lemmon Ave Ste 200 Dallas TX 75219-2100 E-mail: mgreiner@flash.net.

GREINER, ROBERT PHILIP, lawyer, real estate broker; b. Herkimer, N.Y., July 3, 1930; s. Max Henry and Margaret Mary (O'Hara) G. BA, U. Rochester, 1951; MBA, Syracuse U., 1957; LLB, UCLA, 1964. Bar: Calif. 1965. CPA, Calif.; lic. real estate broker, Calif. Pvt. practice acct., CPA, 1962-64; lawyer L.A. Pub. Defenders Office, 1965-87; pvt. practice lawyer and real estate broker Calif., 1987—. Pres. Guide Dog Boosters, Los Alamitos, Calif., 1984. Staff sgt. USAF, 1951-55. Mem.: World Affairs Coun. Sonoma County. Home and Office: 730 Natalie Dr Windsor CA 95492-8870

GREINER, SANDRA, state legislator; b. Washington, Iowa, Oct. 26, 1945; m. Terrence Greiner. Student, Stephens Coll. Mem. Iowa Ho. Reps., 1992-2000, Iowa State Senate, 2001—, vice chair bus. and labor rels. com., mem. agr. com., ways and means com., small bus., econ. devel. and tourism com. Mem. Agr. Coun. Am. (former exec. com. mem.), Am. Feed Industry Assn., Corn and Soybean Growers, Pork Prodrs., Am. Agri-Women (past pres.), Agrl. Women's Leadership Network, Animal Industry Task Force, Daus. Am. Agr. (bd. dirs.), Keokuk County, Wapello County and Mahaska County Rep. Women, Washington County Rep. Women, Washington County Rep. Ctrl. Com., Keota Unltd. Republican. Home: 1005 Hwy 92 Keota IA 52248 E-mail: sandra_greiner@legis.state.ia.us.

GREINER, STEPHEN W. lawyer; b. N.Y.C., Dec. 14, 1944; BA, Syracuse U., 1965; JD, NYU, 1968. Bar: N.Y. 1969. Mem. Willkie Farr & Gallagher, N.Y.C. Mem. Assn. Bar City N.Y., Order of Coif. Office: Willkie Farr & Gallagher 787 7th Ave New York NY 10019-6018 E-mail: sgreiner@willkie.com.

GREINER, WILLIAM ROBERT, university administrator, educator, lawyer; b. Meriden, Conn., June 9, 1934; s. William Robert and Dolores (Quinn) G.; m. Carol A. Morrissey, Aug. 24, 1957; children: Kevin Thomas, Terrence Alan, Daniel Robert, Susan Lynn. BA, Wesleyan U., Conn., 1956; MA in Econs., Yale U., 1959, JD, 1960, LLM, 1966. Bar: Conn. 1961, N.Y. 1973. Asst. prof. Sch. Bus., U. Wash., 1960—64, assoc. prof., 1964—67, Sch. Law, SUNY, Buffalo, 1967—69, prof., 1969—, assoc. provost, 1970—74, assoc. dean, 1975—80; assoc. v.p. acad. affairs SUNY, Buffalo, 1980—83, interim v.p. acad. affairs, 1983—84, provost, 1984—91, pres., 1991—. Cons. in field. Author: (with Harold J. Berman) Nature and Functions of Law, 1966, 72, 80, 96; contbr. articles to profl. jours. Home: 889 Lebrun Rd Amherst NY 14226-4224 Office: U at Buffalo 506 Capen Hall Buffalo NY 14260-1600

GREINKE, EVERETT DONALD, corporate executive, international programs consultant; b. Elmhurst, Ill., Oct. 31, 1929; s. Herman and Marie Barbara (Kline) G.; m. Clara Joan Plasil, Sept. 29, 1951; children: Donald James, David Carl, Mark Andrew. BS with honors, No. Ill. U., 1951, MS with honors, 1956; postgrad., U. Wis., 1956, George Washington U., 1957. Project officer Bur. Aeronautics USN, Washington, 1956-60, asst. br. head Bur. Aeronautics, 1960-61, tech. advisor Automatic Data Processing Office Chief Naval Ops., 1961-65, asst. dir. command/control Office Chief Naval Ops., 1965-67; sr. staff specialist reconnaissance Office Dir. Def. Research and Engring., Washington, 1967-73, sr. staff specialist tactical command, control and intelligence, 1973-76, asst. dir. combat support, 1976-77, dir. combat support, 1977-80, dir. NATO/Europe affairs, 1980-82; acting dep. undersec. internat. programs and tech. Office UnderSec. Def. Research & Engring., Washington, 1982; scientific advisor to Supreme Comdr. NATO/Supreme Hdqrs. Allied Powers Europe, Casteau, Belgium, 1982-86; dep. undersec. internat. programs and tech. Office Undersec. Def. (Acquisition), Washington, 1986-88; internat. programs cons., 1988-90; v.p. corp. devel. Internat. Partnerships Group (Interpar), 1990-93; v.p. Internat. Planning and Analysis Ctr., 1993-96, Global Mktg. Devel. Solutions, 1996—. Lectr. on armaments cooperation various orgns., 1977—; mem. Army Sci. Bd., 2002—; cons. Def. Sci. Bd., 1988—, U.S. Industry on Internat. Coop. and High Tech. Programs, 1988—. Contbr. articles to profl. jours. Pres. Chapel Sq. Sch. PTA, Annandale, Va., 1966-67, v.p. 1965; pres. W.T. Woodson High Sch. PTA, 1972-73; pres. Hope Luth. Ch. Coun., Annandale, 1970-71, mem. ch. coun., 1987-89, mem. bd. elders, 1974-82, mem. planning com., 1986-87, chmn. bldg. com., 1987-92, trustee, 1993—; com. chmn. Boy Scouts Am., Annandale, 1966-68, chmn. Explorer Post, Annandale, 1972-73, scoutmaster, 1968-78; Santa Claus for local civic orgns., Annandale, 1961-94. Comdr. USNR, 1951-55. Decorated Def. D.S.M. (3), Def. Meritorious Service Medal; Comdr.'s Cross (Austria); recipient Def. Outstanding Pub. Service award, Service plaque W.T. Woodson High Sch. PTA, 1973, Service award Boy Scouts Am., 1975, Disting. Alumni award No. Ill. U., 1987. Mem. Nat. Def. Indsl. Assn. Lutheran. Avocations: gardening, fishing. Home: 8315 Toll House Rd Annandale VA 22003-4630

GREISING, DAVID WALTER, columnist; b. Chgo., Jan. 22, 1960; s. Robert Alan and Lynore Menze Greising; m. Cynthia Hedges Greising, Nov. 21, 1985; children: Wesley William, Margaret Lynore, Claire Rue. BA, DePauw U., 1982. Reporter City News Bur. Chgo., 1982—83, Chgo. Sun-Times, 1983—87, columnist, 1987—89; corr. Bus. Week, Chgo., 1989—94, Atlanta bur. chief, 1994—98; bus. columnist Chgo. Tribune, 1998—. Author (with Laurie Morse): Brokers, Bagmen & Moles: Fraud and Corruption in the Chicago Futures Markets, 1990; author: I'd Like the World to Buy a Coke: The Life and Leadership of Roberto Goizueta, 1997; author: (with Cynthia Hedges Greising) Toys Everywhere!, 1994. Pres. DePauw U. Alumni Bd., Greencastle, Ind., 1999—2001; trustee DePauw U., Greencastle, 1999—. Recipient Best Bus. Writing-Ill. award, UP Internat., 1985, Peter Lisagor award for best column, Chgo. Headline Club, 1998, 2000, Jefferson fellowship, East-West Ctr., Honolulu, 2001. Avocations: bicycling, gardening. Office: Chgo Tribune 435 N Michigan Ave Chicago IL 60611

GREIST, MARY COFFEY, dermatologist; b. Ft. Wayne, Ind., Jan. 31, 1947; d. George Alma and Irene Katherine (Zollinger) Coffey; m. Timothy William Greist, June 10, 1972; children: Heather Maria, Thomas Coffey, Timothy Michael. BA, Valparaiso (Ind.) U., 1969; MD, Ind. U., 1973. Intern in family medicine Duke U., Durham, N.C., 1973-74, resident in dermatology, 1974-77; asst. prof. dermatology sch. medicine Ind. U., Indpls., 1977-82, clin. asst. prof. dermatology sch. medicine, 1982—; pvt. practice Indpls., 1982—. Dermatology cons. Eli Lilly and Co., Indpls., 1977-86, Elizabeth Arden and Co., Indpls., 1978-86, Medicare-Blue Cross/Blue Shield, Indpls., 1989—. Mem. Ind. State Dermatological Soc. (sec. 1985, v.p. 1986, pres. 1987-88). Democrat. Avocation: gardening. Office: Greist & Ozols Dermatology 6820 Parkdale Pl Ste 211 Indianapolis IN 46254-6600 E-mail: mgreist@aol.com.

GREITZER, EDWARD MARC, aeronautical engineering educator, consultant; b. N.Y.C., May 8, 1941; s. Arthur O. and Harriet G.; m. Helen Moulton, Nov. 24, 1966; children: Mary Lee, Jennifer Elizabeth. BA, Harvard U., 1962, MS, 1964, PhD, 1970. Asst. project engr. Pratt & Whitney divsn. United Techs., East Hartford, Conn., 1969-76; indsl. fellow commoner Churchill Coll., Cambridge U., Eng., 1975-76; asst. prof. MIT, Cambridge, 1977-79, assoc. prof., 1979-84, prof., dir. Gas Turbine Lab., 1984-96, H.N. Slater prof. aero. and astronautics, 1988—, assoc. head dept., 1996—2002; sr. rsch. engr. United Techs. Rsch. Ctr., East Hartford, 1976-77, dir. aeromech., chem. & fluid sys., 1996-98. Royal Soc. guest fellow, SERC vis. fellow, overseas fellow Churchill Coll., Cambridge U., 1983-84; vis. fellow Japan Soc. for Promotion of Sci., 1987, Peterhouse, Cambridge U., 1990-91; mem. aeronautics adv. com. NASA, 1990-94; mem. sci. adv. bd. USAF, 1992-96. Contbr. articles to profl. jours., handbooks. Recipient T. Bernard Hall prize Instn. Mech. Engrs., London, 1978, Exceptional Civilian Svc. award USAF, 1996. Fellow AIAA (Air Breathing Propulsion Best Paper award 1987), Nat. Acad. Engring., ASME (gas turbine award 1977, 79, 96, Freeman scholar in fluids engring. 1980, bd. dirs. Internat. Gas Turbine Inst. 1993-98, chmn. 1996-97, chmn. turbomachinery com. 1989-91, chmn. gas turbine scholar selection com. 1989-93, turbomachinery com., Best Paper award 1991, 92, 95, Aircraft Engine Tech. award 1995, Controls and Diagnostics com. Best Paper award 1998). Avocations: jogging, photography, rock climbing. Home: 77 Woodridge Rd Wayland MA 01778-3611 Office: MIT Dept Aeronautics & Astronautics Bldg 31-264 Cambridge MA 02139 E-mail: greitzer@mit.edu.

GREJDA, GAIL FULTON, dean; b. Clarion, Pa., Aug. 31, 1937; d. Ralph Jay and Virginia Agnew Fulton; m. Edward Stanley Grejda, Aug. 31, 1958; children: Richard Edward, Steven Douglas. BS, Clarion U., 1966, MEd, 1968; PhD in Instrnl. Sys. Design, Pa. State U., 1988. Cert. level 2 in elem. edn. and spl. edn., Pa. Tchr. Brookville (Pa.) Area Sch. Dist., 1966-69, Clarion (Pa.) Area Sch. Dist., 1969-87, dir. gifted programs, 1977-82; tchr. Beijing Internat. Embassy Sch., 1980-81; computer instr. Sch. of Am. Embassy, Bridgetown, Barbados, 1987-88; asst. prof. Clarion U., 1988-93, assoc. prof., 1993-97, prof., 1997-98, dean Coll. Edn. and Human Svcs., 1998—. Author: (book chpt.) Guidelines for Interpreting Educational Research, 1994; contbr. articles to profl. jours. Grantee U.S. Dept. Edn., 1999, Bell Atlantic Found., 1998, NSF, 1999-2003, 2003—. Mem. Am. Assn. Colls. for Tchr. Edn., Assn. Tchr. Educators (commn. on utilizing tech. for ednl. reform 1988—), Tchr. Edn. Coun. State Colls. and Univs., Assn. for Ednl. Comms. and Tech., Pa. Assn. Coll. Tchr. Educators (bd. dirs. 1988—), Phi Delta Kappa (v.p. 1982—), Pi Lambda Theta. Avocations: travel, reading, golf. Office: Clarion U 101 Stevens Hall Clarion PA 16214 E-mail: grejda@mail.clarion.edu.

GRELL, LEWIS ADAM, retired association executive; b. New Castle, Pa., June 15, 1932; s. Adam Lewis and Mildred Mae (Barris) G.; m. Pamela L., June 9, 1961; children: Lewis Jr., Holly, Lynn, Jon. BS in Elem. Edn., Slippery Rock Coll., 1953; MEd, U. Pitts., 1957, EdD, 1963. Tchr. New Castle (Pa.) Sch. Dist., 1953, 55-59, prin., 1959-63; prin., dir. summer sch. Oak Park (Ill.) Elem. Sch. Dist., 1963-66; asst. supt. Am. Sch. Internat. Sch. of Hague, The Netherlands, 1966-68; supt. Eden (N.Y.) Cen. Schs., 1968-72, Am. Sch. of Hague, 1972-81, Hamburg (N.Y.) Cen. Sch. Dist., 1981-89; exec. dir. Assn. Advancement Internat. Edn., New Wilmington, Pa., 1989—, exec. dir. emeritus, 2001; ret., 2001. Chmn. Mid. States Accrediting Com., Frankfurt, Germany, 1987, European Coun. Internat. Schs., London, 1978-80; cons. Am. Sch. Brasilia, Brazil, 1987, Internat. Sch., Helsinki, 1985-88, Caracas Internat. Sch., Venezuela, 1986-88. Contbr. articles to profl. jours. Chmn. Western N.Y. Fin. and Legis. Com., Lancaster, 1983-85. With USN, 1953-55. Named to Assn. Advancement Internat. Edn. Hall of Fame, 1992. Avocations: showing American Saddlebred horses, playing softball, refereeing basketball games.

GREMBOWSKI, DAVID EMIL, educator, researcher; b. San Diego, May 26, 1951; s. Emil Dem and Delphine Joyce (Kurowski) G.; m. Mary West, June 22, 1974; children: Megan, Leda. BA, Wash. State U., Pullman, 1973, MA, 1975; PhD, U. Wash., Seattle, 1982. Rsch. analyst Stanford Rsch. Inst., Menlo Park, Calif., 1974-76; systems designer flexible intergovtl. grant project City of Tacoma, 1979-80; from rsch. instr. to prof. U. Wash., Seattle, 1981—. Prin. investigator of health svc. rsch. grants; instr. health program evaluation and health care system. Author: The Practice of Health Program Evaluation, 2001; contbr. articles to profl. jour. Mem. APHA, Internat. Assn. Dental Rsch. (officer in behavioral sci. and health svc. rsch. group 1988-94), Am. Assn. Dental Rsch., AcademyHealth, Am. Evaluation Assn., Phi Beta Kappa. Avocations: golf, travel, reading, painting. Office: U Wash Dept Health Svc Box 357660 Seattle WA 98195-0001

GREMILLION, ROBERT, publishing executive; b. New Orleans; Student, Loyola U., New Orleans. Station mgr. WGNO-TV Tribune, New Orleans, 1985-90; v.p., gen. mgr. CLTV News and Tribune Regional Programming, 1990-97; ceo, publ. Sun-Sentinel, Ft. Lauderdale, Fla., 1997—; gen. mgr. WBZL-TV, 2002—. Bd. dir. The Cardiology Coun. Broward. Office: Sun-Sentinel 200 E Las Olas Blvd Ste 1000 Fort Lauderdale FL 33301-2293*

GREMSE, DAVID ALBERT, pediatrician, educator; b. Montgomery, Ala., Oct. 14, 1956; s. Albert Rudolph and Jean (Faust) Gremse; m. Diane Blackwell, June 13, 1981; children: Jennifer, Albert, Christopher. BChE summa cum laude, Ga. Inst. Tech., 1970; MD, U. S. Ala., 1983. Lic. Ala., Ohio, diplomate Am. Bd. Pediat. and Pediat. Gastroenterology, Nat. Bd. Med. Examiners. Dir. Pediat. Gastroenterology and Nutrition divsn. U. South Ala., Mobile, 1990—. Asst. prof., assoc. prof. Pediat. U. South Ala., Mobile, 1990—99, asst. prof. Pharmacology, 1997—99, prof. pediat., 1999—, assoc. prof. Pharmacology, 1999—. Contbr. . Recipient Eagle Scout award, Boy Scouts Am., 1970; fellow, NIH, 1988—90; grantee, Cystic Fibrosis Found., 1994—95, 1996—97, TAP Holdings, Inc., 1998—99, 1998, Cell Pathways, Inc., 1999—2000, AstraZeneca, Inc., 1999—2000, Glaxo Wellcome, 1999—2000, 2000—01, Omnicare Clin. Rsch., Inc., 2001, 2002, Glaxo Wellcome, 2001—03, TAP Holdings, Inc., 2002, Wyeth Ayerst, 2002, GlaxoSmithKline, 2002—04. Fellow: Am. Coll. Gastroenterology (credentials com. 2001—, Pediat. Gastroenterology com. 2001); mem.: AMA (Physician's Recognition award 1997—2000), Soc. Pediat. Rsch. (reviewer Gastroenterology Abstract 2003), So. Soc. Pediat. Rsch. (moderator Gastroenterology session ann. meeting 1994, moderator Clin. Pharmacology ann. meeting 1997), Crohn's and Colitis Found. Am., Med. Soc. Mobile (Bd. Censors 1995—97), Mobile Pediat. Soc. (pres. 1994—95), Am. Bd. Pediat. (assoc.), So. Med. Assn., Med. Assn. State of Ala., N.Am. Soc. Pediat. Gastroenterology and Nutrition, Am. Gastroent. Assn., Am. Acad. Pediat. (chmn. Acad. Issues com. Ala. chpt. 1997—, Com. mem. Gastroenterology and Nutrition Edn. sect. 2001—, Nutrition com. 2001—, exec. bd. dist. VII rep. Ala. chpt. 2001—), Alpha Omega Alpha, Tau Beta Pi, Phi Kappa Phi, Phi Eta Sigma. Home: 803 Regents Dr E Mobile AL 36609 Office: Univ South Ala Divsn Pediat Gastroenterology 1504 Springhill Ave #5321 Mobile AL 36604

GRENALD, RAYMOND, architectural lighting designer; b. Louisville, Feb. 10, 1928; s. Samuel Solomon and Bertha (Borgenicht) Greenwald; m. Arlene Rubin, Nov. 21, 1961 (div. Nov. 1985); children: Seth Jonathan, Bethany Leigh; m. Elizabeth Pfaelzer Kapnek, Dec. 10, 1989. Student, U. Cin., 1945-46; BS in Engring., Wash. State U., 1951, BArch, 1954; postgrad., U. Wash., 1952-53. Registered architect, Pa., Md., Calif., Nat. Coun. Archtl. Registration Bds. Liaison engr. Boeing Airplane Co., Seattle, 1952-53; staff architect Thalheimer & Weitz, Architects, Phila., 1955-56, Nolen & Swinbourne, Architects, Phila., 1957-59; pvt. practice Phila., 1959-61; architect Vincent Kling, Architect, Phila., 1962-63, Wolfgang Rapp, Architect, Phila., 1963-64; asst. city architect Phila., 1964-66; archtl. lighting designer, assoc. Sylvan Shemitz & Assocs., New Haven, 1966-68; archtl. lighting cons. Phila., 1969—; chmn. Grenald Waldron Assocs., Narberth, Pa., 1968—. Instr. U. Pa., 1974-75, Drexel U., 1972-74, Temple U., 1964-67, U. Cin., 1977-80, UCLA, 1982-86, U. Conn., 1967; adj. assoc. prof. U. So. Calif., 1984-86; vis. lectr. Harvard U., Yale U., Moore Coll. Art, 1973-76. Designer archtl. lighting Carlsbad Cavern Nat. Park, 1976, Pennsylvania Avenue Devel. Corp., Washington, 1976-96, Boat House Row, Phila., 1978, Monumental Fed. Core, Washington, 1987—, motion picture Gremlins 2, Franklin Ct., Independence Mall Nat. Park, N.Mex. State Capitol, Puerto Cuervo, Sardinia, Hilton Hawaiian Village, Honolulu, Conn. Gen. Life Ins. Hdqrs., U.S. Supreme Ct., The Mall and Federal Triangle, Washington, West Wing White House, Washington, Balt. Bus. Dist., Phila. Bus. Dist., Akmerkaz Istanbul Beijing Fin. Ctr., China, Cempaka Mas, Jakarta, Inha Hosp., Inchon, Korea, Eastgate, Harare, Zimbabwe, U. Pa. Lighting Master Plan and Implementation, Naval Acad. Chapel, Annapolis, Md. With USAF, 1946-47; 2d lt. U.S. Army, 1950-51. Recipient Presdl. Design Award of Excellence, Nat. Endowment Arts and AIA, 1984, 88, Waterbury citation IIDA, 1996, Award of Excellence, GE, 1997, Eight Schuykill River Bridges, Memlyon Park Pretoria South Africa Dreamand (Resort, Mixed Use) Cairo, Egypt, Cocoa Walk, Bogata, Columbia; Fels fellow U. Pa., 1966. Fellow AIA, Internat. Assn. Lighting Designers (v.p. 1971-72, pres. 1973-74), Illuminating Engring. Soc. N.Am. (com. chmn. Nat. Mus. Lighting 1985-92, bd. dirs. EPRI Lighting Rsch. Orgn., Goddard trophy 1963, 97, Guth award of excellence 1984), Waterbury citation of excellence, 1996. Avocations: skiing, writing, traveling, photography. Office: Grenald Waldron Assoc PO Box 525 260 Haverford Ave Narberth PA 19072-2343

GRENANDER, ULF, mathematics educator; b. Våstervik, Sweden, July 23, 1923; came to U.S., 1966; s. Sven and Maria (Persson) G.; m. Emma-Stina Hallquist, Dec. 22, 1946; children: Sven, Angela, Charlotte. Fil. Dr., U. Stockholm, Sweden, 1950; DSc (hon.), U. Chgo. Prof. U. Stockholm, 1958-66, Brown U., Providence, R.I., 1966—. Author: General Pattern Theory, 1993. Fellow Inst. Math. Stats., Am. Acad. Arts and Scis.; mem. Royal Swedish Acad. Sci., Royal Statis. Soc. (hon.), Nat. Acad. Sci. E-mail: ulf-grenander@cox.net.

GRENDLER, PAUL FREDERICK, history educator; b. Armstrong, Iowa, May 24, 1936; s. August Paul and Josephine Lucy (Girres) G.; m. Marcella T. McCann, June 16, 1962; children: Peter, Jean. BA, Oberlin Coll., 1959; MA, U. Wis., 1961, PhD, 1964. Lectr. history U. Pitts., 1963-64, U. Toronto, Ont., Can., 1964-65, asst. prof., 1965-69, assoc. prof., 1969-73, prof., 1973-98; prof. emeritus, 1998; postdoctoral fellow Inst. for Research in Humanities, U. Wis., 1967-68. Author: Critics of the Italian World, 1530-1560, 1969, The Roman Inquisition and the Venetian Press, 1540-1605, 1977 (Marraro prize 1978), rev. Italian transl., 1983, Culture and Censorship in Late Renaissance Italy and France, 1981, Schooling in Renaissance Italy, 1989 (Marraro prize 1989), paperback, 1991, 1995, Italian transl., 1991, Books and Schools in the Italian Renaissance, 1995, The Universities of the Italian Renaissance, 2002 (Marraro prize 2002); editor: An Italian Renaissance Reader, 1987, 2d edit., 1992, Roman and German Humanism 1450-1550, 1993, Renaissance Quarterly, 2000-03; editor-in-chief: Ency. of Renaissance, 6 vols., 1999, 2d printing, 2000 (Dartmouth medal 2000, Roland H. Bainton prize 2000); mem. editl. bd., exec. com.: Collected Works of Erasmus, from 1976; contbr. articles to profl. jours. Fulbright fellow Italy, 1962-63; Can. Council fellow, 1970-71; Am. Council Learned Socs. fellow, 1971-72; I Tatti fellow Harvard U. Ctr. for Italian Renassance Studies, Florence, Italy, 1970-72; sr. fellow Soc. for Humanities Cornell U., 1973-74; Guggenheim Meml. fellow, 1978-79; Social Scis. and Humanities Research Council Can. fellow, 1979-80, 85-86; Woodrow Wilson Internat. Ctr. for Scholars fellow, 1982-83; Nat. Humanities Ctr. fellow, 1988-90; grantee NEH, 1989-92; Connaught fellowship, 1998. Mem. Renaissance Soc. Am. (v.p. 1991-92, pres. 1992-94), Am. Hist. Assn., Am. Cath. Hist. Assn. (pres. 1984), Am. Philos. Soc., Soc. Italian Hist. Studies (sr. scholar citation 1998; v.p. 2001-03, pres. 2003—). Address: 110 Fern Ln Chapel Hill NC 27514-4206 E-mail: pgrendler@cs.com.

GRENELL, JAMES HENRY, retired manufacturing company executive; b. Mpls., Feb. 19, 1924; s. Harrison Morton and Harriet Elizabeth (Kuch) G.; m. Naomi Betty Callerstrom, Sept. 15, 1945; children: Bonita (Mrs. Michael Wolfe), Suzanne Naomi, Andrea Bergine. BBA, U. Minn., 1947; postgrad. Advanced Mgmt. Program, Harvard U., 1974. With Honeywell Inc., Mpls., 1951-86, accountant, 1951-56, div. controller, 1956-68, group controller, 1968-71, asst. corp. controller, 1971-74, v.p., controller, 1974-82, v.p., staff exec., 1982-86. Instr. Mgmt. Inst. U. Wis.-Madison, 1960-69, Inst. Tech. U. Minn., Mpls., 1963-65; asso. dir. Mgmt. Center U. St. Thomas, 1959-69 Contbr. articles to profl. jours. Bd. dirs. Mpls. Soc. for Blind, 1963-71, pres., 1970-71; bd. dirs. U. Minn. Coll. Bus. Alumni Bd., 1975-82; mem. Acctg. Adv. Coun. U. Minn., 1977-83. Served to 1st lt. 1943-46, ETO. Decorated 4 Battle Stars, U.S. Army. Mem. Fin. Execs. Inst., Alpha Kappa Psi, Harvard Club of Ariz., Ariz. Club. Republican. Home: 10056 E Calle De Cielo Scottsdale AZ 85258-5652 also: 1201 Skyview Flagstaff AZ 86004-8718

GRENESTEDT, JOACHIM LENNART, educator; b. Uppsala, Sweden, Apr. 23, 1964; s. Edvard Lennart Natanael and Marie-Louise Signe Öyvindsdotter Grenestedt; m. Chiharu Tokura; children: Ken, Scott. MSc in Engring. Physics, Royal Inst. Tech., Stockholm, 1987, PhD, 1992, Docent, 1996. Rsch. fellow Brown Boveri & Cie Rsch. Ctr., Switzerland, 1987, Asea Brown Boveri Corp. Rsch., Baden, Switzerland, 1989-90; rsch. assoc. Kyoto (Japan) U., 1987-89; vis. rschr. Japan Nat. Aerospace Lab., Tokyo, 1990-91; rsch. assoc. dept lightweight structures Royal Inst. Tech., 1991-92, sr. rsch. engr. dept. aeronautics, 1992-98; CEO Ancos, 1991—; assoc. prof. Lehigh U., Bethlehem, Pa., 2000—. Vis. scholar divsn. engring. and applied scis. Harvard U., 1996; part-time rschr. Mid Sweden U., Östersund, 1998-2000; Class 1961 prof. Lehigh U., 2001—. Patentee peel-stopper for composite ships; contbr. numerous articles to profl. jours. Cpl. Royal Swedish Army, 1985-86. Recipient award Royal Swedish Acad. Scis., Tech. Dr. Marcus Wallenberg award, Saab-Scania award. Mem.: ASME, Soc. for Sandwich Constrn., NY Acad. Scis., Materials Rsch. Soc., Internat. Soc. Structural and Multidisciplinary Optimization, Sigma Xi. Avocations: flying, hang gliding, scuba diving, sailing. Office: Lehigh U Mech Engring & Mechs 553 Packard Lab 19 Memorial Dr W Bethlehem PA 18015 E-mail: jog5@lehigh.edu.

GRENEVICKI, LANCE FRANCIS, surgeon; b. Plainfield, N.J., May 21, 1967; s. Lawrence Francis and Joann Frances (Bengivenga) G.; m. Amy Lavonne Bridgers, Apr. 13, 1996. BS, Va. Poly. Inst. and State U., 1989; DDS, Med. Coll. Va., 1993; MD, U. Mo., Kansas City, 1997. Diplomate Am. Bd. Oral and Maxillofacial Surgery. Intern Truman Med. Ctr., Kansas City, Mo., resident, 1993-99; attending med. staff, chmn. med. records com. Holmes Regional Med. Ctr., Melbourne, Fla.; mem. med. staff, chmn. med. records com. Palm Bay (Fla.) Cmty. Hosp.; courtesy asst. prof. surgery U. Fla. Bd. dirs. Isaac Walton League of Am., Christiansburg, Va., 1988-89. Named Surg. Resident of Yr., Isaac Walton League Am., 1997; recipient Victim's Advocate award, State Atty.'s Office, 2002. Fellow Am. Assn. Oral and Maxillofacial Surgeons, Am. Coll. Oral and Maxillofacial Surgeons, Am. Acad. Cosmetic Surgery; mem. AMA, ADA, Fla. Soc. Oral and Maxillofacial Surgeons (trustee 2001-2004), Fla. Med. Assn., Fla. Dental Assn., Cen. Dist. Dental Soc., So. Med. Assn., Fla. Soc. Oral and Maxillofacial Surgeons (trustee 2001-, Young Eagle award 2001), Brevard County Dental Assn., Brevard County Med. Assn., Alpha Omega Alpha, Psi Omega, Pi Kappa Alpha. Roman Catholic. Avocations: trap and skeet shooting, hunting, fishing. Home: 3323 Burkeland Pl Melbourne FL 32934-2901 Office: Inst of Facial Surgery 1093 S Wickham Rd West Melbourne FL 32904-1652 Fax: 321-722-3303. E-mail: lgrenevicki@yahoo.com.

GRENIER, EDWARD JOSEPH, JR., lawyer; b. N.Y.C., Nov. 26, 1933; s. Edward Joseph and Jane Veronica (Farrell) G.; m. Patricia J. Cederle, June 22, 1957; children; Victoria-Anne, Edward Joseph III, Peter C. BA summa cum laude, Manhattan Coll., N.Y.C., 1954; LLB magna cum laude, Harvard U., 1959. Bar: D.C. 1959, N.Y. 1983, U.S. Ct. Appeals (D.C. cir.) 1959, U.S. Ct. Mil. Appeals 1960, U.S. Ct. Appeals (3d cir.) 1966, U.S. Supreme Ct. 1966, U.S. Ct. Appeals (9th cir.) 1973, U.S. Ct. Appeals (10th cir.) 1977, U.S. Ct. Appeals (5th cir., 11th cir.) 1982. Law clk. U.S. Ct. Appeals (D.C. cir.), 1959-60; assoc. Covington & Burling, Wahsington, 1960-68; ptnr. Sutherland, Asbill & Brennan, Wahsington, 1968—. Speaker in field of energy related issues to profl. orgns. Contbr. articles in field to legal jours. Chmn. bd. trustees, mem. exec. com. Connelly Sch. Holy Child, Potomac, Md., 1976-85, trustee, 1976-88; bd. dirs. D.C. Recording for the Blind, Washington, 1977-89. 1st lt. USAF, 1954-56. Fellow: Am. Bar Found.; mem.: ABA (chmn. sec. adminstrv. law 1986—87, sec., del. Ho. of Dels. 1991—97), Am. Inns of Ct. (master of bench Prettyman-Leventhal Inn of Ct. 1988—2000, pres. 1991—92, counselor 1997—98), Energy Bar Assn. (bd. dirs. 1986—89, 1995—2001, v.p. 1995—96, pres.-elect 1996—97, pres. 1997—98, del. Ho. of Dels. 1999—2001), D.C. Bar Assn., Fed. Bar Assn., Congl. Country Club, Met. Club. Office: Sutherland Asbill & Brennan LLP 1275 Pennsylvania Ave NW Washington DC 20004-2415 E-mail: edward.grenier@sablaw.com.

GRENIER, LAURA MARGIOTTA, medical/surgical nurse; b. L'Aquila, Italy, Jan. 18, 1963; arrived in U.S., 1964; d. Guido and Linda (Tedeschi) Margiotta; m. Arthur Jacob Grenier, III, May 3, 1986; children: Danielle Monique, Anthony James, Zachary Jon. Nursing degree, U. Conn., 1986; ADN, Greater Hartford C.C., 1998. Lic. arrhythmia interpretation, cert. health unit coord. Cardiology nurse Hartford (Conn.) Hosp., 1986—. Contbr. poetry to anthologies; author: (poetry) Beyond the Garden Gate, 2003, Convoluted Dream, 2003 (Pres.'s award, Hon. Mention, 2003). Mem. Hilstead Mus., Farmington, Conn., 2001—. Recipient Editor's Choice awards for poetry, 1997, 1998, 2001, Pres.'s award Literacy Excellence for poem "Convoluted" Dream, Illiad Press, 2003, hon. mention for poem "Convoluted" Dream, Summer Competition Illiad Press, 2002. Mem.: Brain Injury Assn. Conn., Am. Brain Tumor Soc., Acad. Am. Poets. Roman Catholic. Avocations: writing poetry, playing piano, going to the beach, travel, tennis.

GRENIG, JAY EDWARD, law educator; b. Salt Lake City, Apr. 18, 1943; s. Robert Edward and Betty (Gifford) G.; m. Sharon Flanigan, Dec. 22, 1967; children: Robert Jay, Alejandro Edward, Christian Michael. Student, U. Ariz., 1961-63; BA, Willamette U., Salem, Oreg., 1966; postgrad., Ariz. State U., 1968-69; JD, U. Calif.-Hastings Coll. Law, 1971. Bar: Calif. 1972, U.S. Dist. Ct. (no. dist.) Calif. 1973, U.S. Ct. Appeals (9th cir.) 1974, U.S. Ct. Claims 1974, Wis. 1980. Asst. dean Coll. of Law Willamette U., Salem, 1971-72; assoc. firm Johnson & Stanton, San Francisco, 1972-73; sole practice San Mateo, Calif., 1973-77; assoc. prof., dir. Employment Law Inst., Pepperdine U. Sch. Law, Malibu, Calif., 1977-79; prof. law Marquette U. Sch. Law, Milw., 1980—. Lectr. U. So. Calif. Grad. Sch. Pub. Adminstrn., L.A., 1978; reporter civil justice reform act adv. group U.S. Dist. Ct. (ea. dist.) Wis., 1991-97; pres., bd. dirs. Ctr. Pub. Representation, 1993-97; mem. Wis. Judicial Council, 2002—; reporter U.S. Dist. Ct. (ea. dist) Wis., 1991—. Author: (with others) Private Sector Labor Law, 1980, West's Federal Jury Practice and Instructions, 5th edit., 2001, West's California Education Code Forms, 1992, California Government Codes Forms with Practice Commentaries, 1998, Labor Arbitration Advocacy, 1989, West's Federal Forms, 1992, Wisconsin Civil Procedure, 1994, Wisconsin Civil Discovery, 1996, Alternative Dispute, 1997; editor Calif. Sch. Law Digest, 1973-84, Wisconsin Civil Discovery, 1996, West's Alternative Dispute Resolution, 1997, Illinois Civil Discover, 2000, West's Federal Jury Practice and Instructions (5th edit.), 2000; contbr. articles to legal publs. Bd. trustees Univ. Lake Sch., 1992-95. With U.S. Army, 1966-68. Mem.: Nat. Acad. Arbitrators (bd. govs.), State Bar Assn. Wis., Assn. Am. Law Schs. (chmn. labor and employment law sect. 1991—92), Am. Law Inst., Thurston Soc., Order of Coif. Home: 122 Birch Rd Delafield WI 53018-1305 Office: Marquette U Law Sch 1103 W Wisconsin Ave Milwaukee WI 53233-2313 E-mail: jgrenig@earthlink.net.

GRENITZ, ROBERT, retired obstetrician-gynecologist; b. Bklyn., May 3, 1935; MD, Albert Einstein Coll. Medicine, 1961. Cert. ob.-gyn. Intern Fitkin Meml. Hosp., Neptune, N.J., 1961-62; resident Bronx (N.Y.) Mcpl. Hosp.-Einstein, N.Y.C., 1962-66; asst. clin. prof. U. Miami Sch. Medicine, 1970-83; retired, 1994. Fellow Am. Coll. Ob-gyn., Am. Fertility Soc., Ft. Lauderdale Ob-gyn. Soc.; mem. AMA, Fla. Med. Assn., Broward County Med. Assn.

GRENQUIST, PETER CARL, consultant; b. East Orange, N.J., Feb. 15, 1931; s. Ernst Alexander and Carmela (Anastasia) G.; m. Barbara Ross Krone, Dec. 20, 1967; children: Carl Robert (dec.), Louisa Beatrice. BA, Dartmouth Coll., 1953; MA, Columbia U., 1957, PhD, 1963. Vice pres. Am. Assembly, Columbia U., 1957-62; dir. Spectrum Books, Prentice-Hall, Inc., 1962-70; v.p. coll. divsn. Prentice-Hall, Inc., 1970-72, pres. Trade Book divsn., 1972-80; CEO Arco Pub., Inc. (subs.), 1981-85; gen. mgr. gen. books divsn. McGraw-Hill Book Co., 1986-89; exec. dir. Assn. Am. Univ. Presses, Inc., N.Y.C., 1990-97; sr. assoc. Moseley Assocs. Inc., 1997—. Served to lt. (j.g.) USNR, 1953-56. Woodrow Wilson fellow, 1956-57 Mem. Devon Yacht Club, Phi Beta Kappa. Office: Moseley Assocs Inc 1202 Lexington Ave # 356 New York NY 10028 E-mail: grenquist@aol.com.

GREPPIN, JOHN AIRD COUTTS, philologist, editor, educator; b. Rochester, N.Y., Apr. 2, 1937; s. Ernest Haquette and Edna Barbara (Kill) G.; m. Mary Elizabeth Cleland Hannan, Sept. 30, 1961; children: Sarah Cleland Coutts, Carl Hannan Haquette. AB in Greek, U. Rochester, N.Y., 1961; MA in Classics, U. Wash., 1966; PhD in Indo-European Studies, UCLA, 1972; postdoctoral student, Yerevan State U., USSR, 1974-75. Tchr. Greek, Latin Stowe (Vt.) Prep. Sch., 1961-62; tchr. Woodstock (Vt.) Country Sch., 1962-65, admissions dir., 1968-69; interim asst. prof. U. Fla., Gainesville, 1971-72; tchr. Isidore Newman Sch., New Orleans, 1972-74; from asst. to assoc. to prof. linguistics Cleve. State U., 1975—, dir. program in linguistics, 1979-83, 99—. Vis. prof. linguistics Philipps U., Marburg, Germany, 1993. Author: Initial Vowel and Aspiration in Classical Armenian, 1973, Classical Armenian Nominal Suffixes, 1975, Classical and Middle Armenian Bird Names: A Taxonomic and Mythological Study, 1978, An Etymological Dictionary of the Indo-European Components of Classical Armenian, 1984, Bark Galianosi: The Greek Armenian Dictionary to Galen, 1985, A Handbook of Armenian Dialectology, 1986, An Arabic-Armenian Pharmaceutical Dictionary, 1997, The Diffusion of Greco-Roman Medicine into the Middle East and the Caucasus, 1999; editor: Proc. of 1st Internat. Conf. on Armenian Linguistics, Phila., 1979, (with others) Interrogativity: A Colloquium of the Grammar, Typology and Pragmatics of Questions in Seven Diverse Languages, 1984, When Worlds Collide: The Indo-Europeans and the Pre-Indo-Europeans: The Bellagio Papers, 1990, Studies in Classical Armenian Literature, 1994, Studies in Honor of Jaan Puhvel, Part One: Ancient Languages and Philology, 1997, Part Two: Mythology and Religion, 1997; founding editor Ann. Armenian Linguistics, 1980-2002, Armenian and Anatolian Studies, 1979—, Proc. 4th Internat. Conf. on Armenian Linguistics, 1992, Classical Armenian Literature: Studies in Early Armenian Authors; mng. editor Raft, A Jour. of Armenian Poetry and Criticism, 1987-2000; editor Jour. Soc. Armenian Studies, 2002—; contbr. over 200 articles to Am., European and Soviet jours., over 260 revs. to London Times Lit. Supplement, N.Y. Times Book Rev., others. Recipient Silver medal Congregazione Mekhitarista, Venice, Italy, 1979, Medal of David the Invincible award Armenian Philos. Acad., 2003; fellow Am. Coun. Learned Socs., 1965, NEH, 1978-79, NIH, 1984, Internat. Rsch. and Exchs. Bd., 1974-75, grantee, 1979-81, 84-87, 89, 92, 94, 98; grantee AGBU Manoogian Fund, 1977, 79-2001, Gulbenkian Found., 1982, 85, 96, Rockefeller Found., 1987, Am. Coun. Learned Socs., 1987. Mem. Assn. Internat. des Études Arméniennes, Soc. for Study of the Caucasus, Am. Philol. Soc., Linguistic Soc. Am., Soc. for Armenian Studies (mem. exec. bd. 1982-86, 2002—, sec. 1983-85), Am. Oriental Soc., Soc. Caucasologia Europaea. Avocations: pianist, chamber music assns., bird watching. Home: 3349 Fairmount Blvd Cleveland OH 44118-4262 Office: Cleve State U Dept Linguistics Cleveland OH 44115 Office Fax: 216-687-6943. E-mail: j.greppin@csuohio.edu.

GRESHAM, JACK WARREN, poet; b. Des Moines, Jan. 10, 1936; s. George Edwin and Nancy Marie (Smith) G.; m. Clara Vargas, Dec. 4, 1987; children: Shawn Leanne Kirby, John Kennedy Gresham. BA in Psychology, Bucknell U., 1957, MA in English Lit., 1960. Various staff positions CIA, Washington, 1961-86. Contbr. poetry to lit. publs. Soloist Marion Civic Chorale, Ocala, Fla., 1998-2002. Grad. scholarship Bucknell U., 1959-60; recipient poetry awards. Mem. Omicron Delta Kappa, Psi Chi, Phi Sigma Tau, Phi Gamma Delta. Democrat. Avocations: performing vocal music, collecting classical music, tennis. Home: 5385 SW 83rd Pl Ocala FL 34476

GRESHAM, JAMES THOMAS, foundation executive; b. Griffin, Ga., Dec. 6, 1937; m. Marcine Miller, June 12, 1960; children: Deborah G. Lynn, Elizabeth G.Harlin, James T. Gresham, Jr. BS in Textiles, Ga. Tech, 1960. With Callaway Found., Inc., La Grange, Ga., 1969—, now pres., gen. mgr., and treas.; pres., treas. Charitable Svcs. Co. Bd. trustees Ga. Tech Rsch. Corp., Ga. Heart Clin., Inc.; past pres., bd. trustees Ga. Tech Found., Inc.; pres., bd. trustees Med. Park Found., Inc.; pres., bd. trustees Enoch Callaway Cancer Clin. Past pres. LaGrange Rotary Club; former campaign chmn. United Way; deacon First Bapt. Church, LaGrange; mem. Highland Country Club. Mem. Sigma Chi; hon. mem. Tau Beta Pi, Phi Kappa Phi. Office: Callaway Found Inc PO Box 790 Lagrange GA 30241-0014

GRESHAM, ZANE OLIVER, lawyer; b. Mobile, Ala., Dec. 16, 1948; S. Charles Brandon and Lillian Ann (Oliver) G.; m. Marian Gan, Mar. 3, 1988. BA cum laude, Johns Hopkins U., 1970; JD magna cum laude, Northwestern U., 1973. Bar: Calif. 1973. Assoc. Morrison & Foerster, San Francisco, 1973-79, ptnr., 1980—, co-chair land use and environ. law group, 1987-97, co-chair airports and aviation law group, 1996—; chair Latin Am. Group, 1998—. Dir., v.p. (Latin Am.) Internat. Private Water Assn., 1999—; dir. Fromm Inst., 2000—. Cons. editor: Environ. Compliance and Litigation Strategy. Pres. San Francisco Forward, 1980-85; bd. dirs. Regional Inst. Bay Area, Richmond, Calif., 1989-95, Regional Parks Found., Oakland, Calif., 1992—, pres., 1995; spl. counsel Grace Cathedral, San Francisco, 1991—; dir., exec. v.p. Pan Am. Soc. Calif., 1995-97, pres. 1998—; vice chmn. Nat. Youth Sci. Found., 1997—. Mem. State Bar Calif., Urban Land Inst., Lambda Alpha. Avocations: opera, sketching. Office: Morrison & Foerster 425 Market St Ste 3100 San Francisco CA 94105-2482 E-mail: zgresham@mofo.com.

GRESS, EDWARD J(ULES), educator, consultant; b. Jerusalem, Jan. 11, 1940; came to U.S., 1966; s. Jules Charles and Mary (Alonzo) G.; m. Katie Lorenzo, Sept. 30, 1962; children: Albert, Richard, Alexander. BBA, Am. U. Beirut, 1961, MBA, 1964; PhD, U. Ariz., 1970. Instr. acctg. Am. U. Beirut, 1961-66; lectr. acctg. U. Ariz., Tucson, 1967-70; assoc. prof. acctg. U. Saskatchewan, Saskatoon, Can., 1970-72; vis. assoc. prof. Am. U. Cairo, 1973-74; assoc. prof. N.E. La. U., Monroe, 1972-76; prof. Canisius Coll., Buffalo, 1976-78, 81—; prof., dir. TAG Bus. Ctr., Buffalo, 1988—. Recipient Faculty award Haskins and Sells Found., 1968, George Washington Honor medal Freedoms Found., Valley Forge, 1986, 87, Outstanding Acct. of Yr. award, 1992, Disting. Prof. award, Canisius Coll., 1995; named Outstanding Prof. in MBA program at Canisius Coll., 1983, 86, Hon. Citizen, City of Tucson, 1969. Mem. Fin. Execs. Inst. (chmn. acad. rels. com.), Arab Soc. Cert. Accts., Am. Acctg. Assn., Am. Mgmt. Assn., Arab Mgmt. Soc. (founding mem., trustee, chmn. edn. com.). Republican. Roman Catholic. Avocations: cross country skiing, bicycling, swimming. Office: Canisius Coll 2001 Main St Buffalo NY 14208-1035

GRESSAK, ANTHONY RAYMOND, JR., sales executive; b. Honolulu, Jan. 22, 1947; s. Anthony Raymond and Anne Tavares (Ferreira) G.; m. Catherine Streb, Apr. 11, 1981; children: Danielle Kirsten, Anthony Raymond III, Christina Michelle. AA, Utah State U., 1967; postgrad., U.S. Army Inf. Officers Candidate Sch., 1968. Restaurant mgr. Ala Moana Hotel, Honolulu, 1970-72; gen. mgr. Fred Harvey, Inc., Ontario, Calif., 1972-73; regional mgr. So. Calif., 1972-73, regional mgr. tollway ops., 1973; divisional mgr. Normandy Lane, 1973; resident mgr. Royal Inns of Am., San Diego, 1974; food and beverage dir. Asso. Inns & Restaurant Co. of Am. (Aircoa), Big Sky, Mont., 1974-75; condominium mgr. Big Sky, 1975; asst. gen. mgr. Naples (Fla.) Bath and Tennis Club, 1975-76; food and beverage dir. Nat. Parks, Grand Canyon, Ariz., 1976-77; gen. mgr. Grand Canyon Nat. Park Lodges, 1977-79; divisional v.p. food services The Broadway, Carter Hawley Hale, Inc., Los Angeles, 1979-82; exec. v.p. Silco Corp., Los Angeles, 1982-84; mktg. mgr. Interstate Restaurant Supply, 1984-85; dir. mktg. and merchandising S.E. Rykoff & Co., Los Angeles, 1986-91; nat. accounts sales mgr. healthcare and hospitality Rykoff-Sexton, Inc., L.A., 1991-93; v.p. distbr. sales The Cheesecake Factory Bakery Inc., Calabasas Hills, Calif., 1993—. Maitre de table Chaine des Rotisseurs-Los Angeleno; mem. edn. culinary steering com. Los Angeles Trade Tech. Coll. With U.S. Army, 1967-70. Decorated Silver Star, Bronze Star, Purple Heart; South Vietnamese Cross of Gallantry. Mem. Nat. Restaurant Assn. (assoc.), Internat. Foodservice Mfrs. Assn., Internat. Order DeMolay (life, chevalier), Smithsonian Assocs., Am. Culinary Fedn. (assoc., Presdl. Medallion award 1991), Calif. Restaurant Assn. (assoc.), Les Toques Blanches Internat. Roman Catholic. Home: 20301 Minnehaha St Chatsworth CA 91311-2540 Office: The Cheesecake Factory 26950 Agoura Rd Agoura Hills CA 91301-5335 E-mail: tgressak@thecheesecakefactory.com. *Common sense isn't so common. Self discipline and respect for yourself will achieve success. Strive for perfection and you will attain it. Never give up. You never get a second chance to make a first impression.*

GRESSEL, GARY LEE, computer scientist; b. Columbus, Ind., Oct. 6, 1968; s. Daryl Lee and Jeanie Ramona (Willis) G.; m. Jeanne Williams Reynolds, June 1, 1996. BS in Computer Sci., Ball State U., 1991, MS in Info. and Communication Scis., 1992; cert. bus. contingency planner, Disaster Recovery Inst. Internat. Cons. Cummins Engine Co., Columbus, 1991-92, Kamdon Interactive, Muncie, Ind., 1991-92; rsch. fellow Ctr. for Info. and Comm. Scis., Muncie, 1991-92; supr. AT&T, Kansas City, Mo., 1992-96, tech. staff, 1996-98, supr., 2001—; corp. info. officer Bus. Ptnrs., Inc., Overland Park, Kans., 1997—. Cons. H&R Block, 1999—2000, Maxim Group, 1998—2001. Volleyball coach Holy Cross Luth. Sch., Gladstone, Mo., 1993—94; web master St. Paul's United Ch., Lenexa, Kans., 2000—; bd. dirs. East Columbus United Meth. Ch., 1984—85, Ctrl. Comm. Credit Union, Kansas City, 1993—, chmn. bd. dirs., 1995—. Mem. Electronic Frontier Found., Kansas City Pub. TV, Good Sam's Club. Methodist. Avocations: volleyball, model trains, golf, video production. Home: 16528 W 80th Ter Lenexa KS 66219-2814

GRESSMAN, EUGENE, lawyer; b. Lansing, Mich., Apr. 18, 1917; s. William Albert and Bess Beulah (Nagle) G.; m. Nan Alice Kirby, Aug. 6, 1944; children: William, Margot and Nancy (twins), Eric. AB, U. Mich., 1938, JD with distinction, 1940; LLD, Seton Hall U., 1994. Bar: Mich. 1940, D.C. 1948, Md. 1959, U.S. Supreme Ct. 1945. Atty. SEC, Washington, 1940-43; law clk. to Justice Frank Murphy, U.S. Supreme Ct., 1943-48; ptnr. firm Van Arkel, Kaiser, Gressman, Rosenberg & Driesen, Washington, 1948-77, of counsel, 1977-81, Bredhoff & Kaiser, Washington, 1981-84, Brand & Frulla, Washington, 1984—. Spl. counsel U.S. Ho. of Reps., 1976-84; William Rand Kenan Jr. prof. law U. N.C., Chapel Hill, 1977-87, prof. emeritus, 1987—; disting. vis. prof. Fordham U. Law Sch., 1982-83, 1987-88; Disting. vis. prof. Seton Hall U. Law Sch., 1987-94; vis. prof. law Ohio State U., 1967, Mich. Law Sch., 1969, George Washington U., 1971-77, Ind. U., 1976, Cath. U. Am., 1977; judge Appeals Tax Ct. Montgomery County, Md., 1959-62; chmn. rules com. U.S. Ct. Appeals for 4th Cir., 1984-89. Author: (with Robert L. Stern and others) Supreme Court Practice, 1950, 8th edit., 2002; (with Charles A. Wright and others) Federal Practice and Procedure: Jurisdiction, vol. 16, 1977; (with David Crump and David Day) Cases and Materials on Constitutional Law, 1989, 4th edit., 2002; contbr. articles to profl. jours. Fellow Am. Acad. Appellate Lawyers (hon.); mem. ABA, Fed. Bar Assn., D.C. Bar, Am. Law Inst., Am. Judicature Soc., Order of the Coif, Order of Barristers, Phi Beta Kappa, Delta Theta Pi (lifetime achievement award). Home: 325 Glendale Dr Chapel Hill NC 27514-5915 Office: U NC Sch Law Chapel Hill NC 27599-3380 E-mail: egressma@email.unc.edu.

GRETES, FRANCES CONSTANCE, information specialist; b. Norfolk, Va., Dec. 5, 1948; d. Ernest Peter G.; B.A. in Fine Arts, Coll. William and Mary, 1970; M.Librarianship, Emory U., 1973. Archtl. librarian John Portman & Assoc., Atlanta, 1973-76; adminstrv. librarian U.S. Army Libraries, Grafenwoehr, W. Ger., 1976-79; army librarian Pentagon, Washington, 1980; mktg. coordinator, info. dir. Skidmore, Owings & Merrill, N.Y.C., 1980-93; pres. Gretes Rsch. Svcs. Info. Broker, 1993—; dir. info. svcs. Rafael Viñoly Architects, 2002—. Recipient cert. of achievement U.S. Dept. Army, 1979. Mem. Spl. Libraries Assn., Art Libraries Soc. N.Am.,Assn. Ind. Info. Profls. Greek Orthodox. Author: Directory of International Periodicals and Newsletters on the Built Environment; contbr. articles to profl. jours.

GRETHER, DAVID MACLAY, economics educator; b. Phila., Oct. 21, 1938; s. Ewald T. and Carrie Virginia (Maclay) G.; m. Susan Edith Clayton, Mar. 24, 1961; children: Megan Elizabeth, John Clayton. BS, U. Calif., Berkeley, 1960; PhD, Stanford U., 1969. Research staff economist Cowles Found., Yale U., 1966-70; lectr. econs. Yale U., 1966-68, asst. prof., 1968-70; assoc. prof. econs. Calif. Inst. Tech., Pasadena, 1970-75, prof. econs., 1975—, exec. officer for social scis., 1978-82, chmn. Humanities and Social Scis. div., 1982-92. Author: (with M. Nerlove and J.L. Carvalho) Analysis of Economic Time Series: A Synthesis, 1979; contbr. articles to profl. jours. Mem. Econometric Soc., Am. Statis. Assn., Am. Econ. Assn. Home: 2116 N Craig Ave Altadena CA 91001-3519 Office: Calif Inst Tech Divsn Humanities Socia Pasadena CA 91125-0001

GRETICK, ANTHONY LOUIS, lawyer, judge; b. Chgo., June 26, 1936; s. Anton L. and Martha M. (Leinar) G.; m. Caroline Hogue, Dec. 30, 1955; children: Kirsten, David. AB, Northwestern U., 1958, JD, 1964. Bar: Ill. 1964, Ohio 1965, U.S. Supreme Ct. 1971. Assoc. Gebhard, Hogue, Dwyer & Wilson, 1964-67, ptnr., 1967-71; exec. asst. Atty. Gen. Ohio, 1971-72, also chief trial divsn. of spl. litigation sect., 1971-72; ptnr. Hogue, Dwyer, Gretick, Bish & Lowe, Bryan, Ohio, 1972-82, Gretick, Bish, Lowe & Roth, Bryan, Ohio, 1982—94. Pros. atty., Williams County, Ohio, 1977—94; judge gen. divsn. Ct. Common Pleas, Williams County, 1995—. Served with USNR, 1958-75. Fellow Ohio Bar Found.; mem. Ohio Pros. Attys. Assn. (dir. 1978-94, pres. 1982). Home: 115 Deerfield Cir Bryan OH 43506-9368 Office: 1 Courthouse Sq Bryan OH 43506-1751 Business E-mail: tgretick@msn.coun.

GRETSER, GEORGE WESTFALL, publisher; b. Frankfurt, Germany, Mar. 16, 1947; arrived in U.S., 1948; s. George Rushmore and Edythe (Westfall) G.; m. Linda J. Goff, Jan. 25, 1969; 1 child, Jennifer L. BJ, U. Tex., 1969; MBA, Keller Grad. Sch. Mgmt., Chgo., 1982. Advt. dir. Comms. Pub Corp., Denver, 1970-76; pub. Profl. Remodeling mag. Harcourt Brace Jovanovich Publs.,

Chgo., 1976-82; with Restaurants & Instns. mag. Cahners Pub. Co., Des Plaines, Ill., 1982-86; COO, pub. Brighton Sq. Pub., Austin, Tex., 1986-87; pub. East/West Network, N.Y.C., 1987-88; pres. ACPI pub. div. ClubCorp, pub. Pvt. Clubs mag. Assoc. Club Publs., Inc., Dallas, 1988-96; mag. mgr. L.A. Times Mag., 1996; advt. dir. Chgo. Mag., 1996-99, assoc. pub., 1999-2000, D Mag., 2000—01; pub. Ft. Worth Tex. Mag., 2001—02, Ft. Worth Bus. Press, 2002—03, Oxford Am. Mag., 2003—. Avocations: running, marathons, cycling, diving, golf, tennis.

GRETZ, KARL FREDERICK, training consultant, writer; b. Phila., June 27, 1947; s. William and Janis Gretz; m. Ingegärd Strömberg, Nov. 25, 1975; children: Michael, Anna, Maria, Sara. BA in History and Polit. Sci., Tufts U., 1973, MEd in Counseling and Guidance, 1974; PhD in Ednl. Psychology, Brigham Young U., 1978. Asst. adj. prof. CUNY, Staten Island, 1981-82; pvt. practice marriage and family therapist Staten Island, 1978-83; staff psychologist Staten Island Hosp., 1979-83; fin. cons. Merrill Lynch & Co., Manhattan, 1983-85, sr. tng. cons. Princeton, N.J., 1985-88; pres. Gretz & Assocs., Bensalem, Pa., 1988—; mng. dir. Drozdeck & Gretz Assocs. (formerly Tng. Groups Internat.), Bensalem, 1990-2000. Co-author: (with Steven. R. Drozdeck) Consultative Selling Techniques for Financial Professionals, 1990, The Effective Manager: Being the Best in Financial Sales Management, 1991, Empowering Innovative People: How Managers Challenge, Channel and Control the Truly Creative and Talented, 1992, The Broker's Edge: How to Sell Securities in Any Market, 1995, Professional Selling: A Consultative Approach, 1996, Managing Your Business for Success: A Guide for the Financial Consultant, 1997; contbr. articles to profl. jours. Capt. Spl. Forces U.S. Army, 1966-69, Viet Nam. Mem. Lds Ch. Office: 4431 Remo Crescent Rd Bensalem PA 19020-2931

GRETZINGER, RALPH EDWIN, III, management consultant; b. Louisville, Sept. 7, 1948; s. Ralph Edwin Jr. and Martha Irene (Jennings) G.; m. Jewel Jean Rocker, Mar. 21, 1970; children: Ralph Edwin IV, Sarah Elizabeth. BS in Applied Math., Ga. Inst. Tech., 1970; MBA, U. Utah, 1974. Group mgr. Prudential Ins. Co., Cin., 1974-76; owner, regional office mgr. Hewitt Assocs., Lincolnshire, Ill., 1976-78, Dayton, Ohio, 1978-81, Dallas, 1981—. Trustee Child Care Partnership of Dallas, 1985-90. Served with U.S. Army, 1971-74. Mem. S.W. Pension Conf., Ga. Tech. Club of North Tex. (pres. 1986-88), Beta Gamma Sigma. Roman Catholic. Avocation: golf. Office: Hewitt Assocs 2201 W Royal Ln Ste 100 Irving TX 75063-3205 E-mail: regretzi@hewitt.com.

GRETZKY, WAYNE DOUGLAS, retired hockey player, businessman; b. Brantford, Ont., Can., Jan. 26, 1961; s. Walter and Phyllis Gretzky; m. Janet Jones, July 16, 1988; children: Paulina, Ty Robert, Trevor Douglas. Center Peterborough Petes, Jr. Ont. Hockey Assn., 1977—78, Sault Ste. Marie Greyhounds, 1977—78, Indpls. Racers, World Hockey Assn., 1978, Edmonton Oilers NHL, Edmonton, Canada, 1988, L.A. Kings, NHL, 1988—96, St. Louis Blues, NHL, 1996, N.Y. Rangers, NHL, 1996—99, ret., 1999; investor Los Arcos Sports LLC/Phoenix Coyotes, 1999—. Player NHL All-Star Game, 1980—86, 1988—94; mem. Stanley Cup Championship Team, 1984, 85, 87, 88. Named Rookie of Yr., World Hockey Assn., 1978—79, Sportsman of Yr., Sports Illustrated, 1982, Sporting News NHL Player of Yr., 1980—81, 1986—87, Sporting News Man of Yr., 1981, Can. Athlete of Yr., 1985, Dodge Performer of Yr., 1984—85, 1986—87; recipient Art Ross Meml. Trophy, NHL, 1981—87, 1989—90, 1990—91, 1993—94, Conn Smythe Trophy, 1985, 1988, William Hanley Trophy, 1977—78, Lemms Family award, 1977—78, Hart Meml. Trophy, 1974—80, Lady Byng Meml. Trophy, 1979—80, 1990—91, 1991—92, 1993—94, Lester B. Pearson award, 1982, 1984—85, 1986—87, Emery Edge award, 1983—84, 1984—85, 1986—87, Lester Patrick Trophy, 1993—94. Achievements include the record holder for points, goals, assists, overtime assists and others. Office: c/o Phoenix Coyotes Cellular One Ice Den 9375 E Bell Rd Scottsdale AZ 85260-0101

GREVE, GUY ROBERT, lawyer; b. Bay City, Mich., Oct. 25, 1947; m. Nancy Lisbeth Mueller, Sept. 21, 1991; 1 child, Tyler James. BA, U. Mich., 1970; postgrad., U. Kent, Canterbury, Eng., 1974; JD, Detroit Coll., 1975. Bar: Mich. 1975, U.S. Dist. Ct. (ea. dist.) Mich. 1975. Ptnr. Patterson & Greve, Bay City, 1975-78; asst. atty. City of Bay City, 1975-76, atty., 1976-78; pvt. practice Bay City, 1978—. One-man shows include; co-chair Day in Life of Bay Country Photo Project, 2000. Bd. dirs. Am. Cancer Soc., 1975—2001, pres., 1982—83, Muse-Hopper Mobile Mus., Mich., 1980—82; co-chair Delta Coll. Scholarship Fundraiser, 2001; mem. steering com. Friends State Theater, 2001—; bd. dirs. Bay Arts Coun., 1999—, Women's Crisis Ctr., Bay City, 1977—79. Named Disting. Alumnus, Handy HS, 1985; recipient Disting. Svc. award, Bay City Jaycees, 1981. Mem.: ATLA, ABA, Mich. Trial Lawyers Assn., Bay County Bar Assn. (Liberty Bell chmn. 1994—98, bd. dirs. 1994—2000, pres. 1998—99), Mich. Bar Assn. (rep. assembly 1999—2001), Bay Area C. of C., Studio 23 (hon.), Saginaw Bay Yacht Club, U. Mich. Alumni Club (Bay City chpt. pres. 1994—97), Elks Club (lodge # 88), Optimists (pres. Bay City 1979—80, lt. gov. Mich. 1985—86, chmn. new club bldg. 1986—87, chmn. club svcs. 1989—90, founder, chair travel series 1993—, asst. gov. Mich. 1996—97, internat. conv. com. 1997). Home: 2300 Nurmi Dr Bay City MI 48708-6872 Office: PO Box 851 919 Washington Ave Bay City MI 48707 E-mail: ggreve@juno.com.

GREVE, JOHN HENRY, veterinary parasitologist, educator; b. Pitts., Aug. 11, 1934; s. John Welch and Edna Viola (Thuenen) G.; m. Sally Jeanette Doane, June 21, 1956; children— John Haven, Suzanne Carol, Pamela Jean BS, Mich. State U., East Lansing, 1956, D.V.M., 1958, MS, 1959; PhD, Purdue U., West Lafayette, Ind., 1963. Assoc. instr. Mich. State U., East Lansing, 1958-59; instr. Purdue U., West Lafayette, 1959-63; asst. prof. Iowa State U., Ames, 1963-64, assoc. prof., 1964-68, prof. dept. vet. pathology, 1968-99, interim chair dept. vet. pathology, 1992-95, counselor acad. and student affairs, 1991-92. Cons. to Dean on alumni affairs, Coll. Vet. Medicine; cons. parasitologist various zoos Mem. editl. bd. Lab. Animal Sci., 1971-83, Vet. Rsch. Comm., 1977-84, Vet. Parasitology, 1984-98; contbr. articles to sci. jours., chpts. to books. Dist. chmn. Broken Arrow Dist., Boy Scouts Am., Ames, Iowa, 1975-77 Named Disting. Tchr. Norden Labs., 1965, 99, Outstanding Tchr. Amoco Oil, Iowa State U., 1972, Faculty Mem. of Yr., Coll. Vet. Medicine, 1999; recipient Faculty Citation Iowa State U. Alumni Assn., 1978. Mem. AVMA (mem. editl. bd. jour. 1975-98, Excellence in Teaching award student chpt. 1990), Iowa Vet. Med. Assn., Am. Soc. Parasitologists, Midwestern Conf. Parasitologists (sec.-treas. 1967-75, presiding officer 1975-76), Am. Assn. Vet. Parasitologists (pres. 1968-70), Helminthological Soc. Washington, World Assn. for Advancement Vet. Parasitology, Am. Assn. Vet. Med. Colls., Izaak Walton League (bd. dirs. Iowa 1968-70), Honor Soc. Cardinal Key, Gamma Sigma Delta, Phi Eta Sigma, Phi Kappa Phi, Phi Zeta. Lodges: Kiwanis (Town and Country-Ames pres 1967, Nebr.-Iowa lt. gov. 1972-73). Republican. Avocations: philately, camping, gardening. Office: Iowa State U Coll Vet Med Found Ames IA 50011-1250 E-mail: sdgreve@isunet.net.

GREVE, SALLY DOANE, English educator; b. Detroit, June 2, 1934; d. Haven Frazelle and Keitha Maxine (Littler) Doane; m. John Henry Greve, June 21, 1956; children: John Haven, Suzanne Carol, Pamela Jean. BA, Mich. State U., 1956; MA in Tchg. English as Second Lang., Iowa State U., 1989. Adj. instr. ESL off-campus Des Moines Area C.C., Ankeny, Iowa, 1975-97, ESL cons., 1975-97, ret. Vol. tutor trainer Iowa Refugee Svc. Ctr., Des Moines, 1979-82; chmn. bldg. com. Episcopal Parish Ames, Iowa, 1972-74, supt. ch. sch., jr. warden, 1963-64, newsletter editor, 1991-2002, mem. choir, 1991—; sec., membership chair Ames Town and Gown Chamber Music Assn., 1999-2000, v.p., 2000-01, pres., 2001-02; bd. dirs. Story County Conservation Ptnrs., 1998-. Mem. TESOL, Mid-Am. TESOL (bd. dirs. 1985-91, pres. 1989-90), Missouri Valley Adult Edn. Assn., Iowa Assn. for Lifelong Learning, AVMA Aux., Internat. Hon. for Leadership in Univ. Apt. Cmtys. (hon.), Omega Tau Sigma (hon.). Avocation: church activities.

GREVILLE, FLORENCE NUSIM, secondary school educator, mathematician; b. Lynn, Mass., Nov. 19, 1913; d. Melach Joseph Nusim and Lillian Montrose; m. Thomas N.G. Greville (dec. Feb. 18, 1998). AB, Cornell U., 1935; MA, Columbia U., 1947. Sub. tchr Wis. Pub. Schs., Madison, 1975—80; tchr. math. Madison Area Tech. Coll., 1980—81; lectr. math. Piedmont C.C., Charlottesville, Va., 1982—84; sub. tchr. Charlottesville Pub. Schs., 1987—99. Instr. in math Oswego State Coll., 1947—48; tchr. Am. sch., Rio de Janeiro, 1953—54; program dir. AAUW, Monona, Wis., 1966—68, Charlottesville, Va., 2001—02. Author: (book) Computer Oriented Basic Math. 1970, Breafeast Gems, 2002. Fellow: AAAS; mem.: Math. Assn. Am. Avocation: playing classical piano. Home: 505 Pebble Hill Ct Charlottesville VA 22903-7873

GREW, PRISCILLA CROSWELL, university official, geology educator; b. Glens Falls, NY, Oct. 26, 1940; d. James Croswell and Evangeline Pearl (Beougher) Perkins; m. Edward Sturgis Grew, June 14, 1975. BA magna cum laude, Bryn Mawr Coll., 1962; PhD, U. Calif., Berkeley, 1967. Instr. dept. geology Boston Coll., 1967-68, asst. prof., 1968-72; asst. rsch. geologist UCLA, 1972-77, adj. asst. prof. environ. sci. and engring., 1975-76; dir. Calif. Dept. Conservation, 1977-81; commr. Calif. Pub. Utilities Commn., San Francisco, 1981-86; dir. Minn. Geol. Survey, St. Paul, 1986-93; prof. dept. geology U. Minn., Mpls., 1986-93; vice chancellor for rsch. U. Nebr., Lincoln, 1993-99, prof. dept. geoscis., 1993—, prof. conservation/survey divsn. Inst. Agr., 1993—; coord. Native Am. Graves Protection and Repatriation Act, 1998—. Dir. U. Nebr. State Mus., 2003—; vis. asst. prof. geology U. Calif., Davis, 1973-74; chmn. Calif. State Mining and Geology Bd., Sacramento, 1976-77; exec. sec., editor Lake Powell Rsch. Project, 1971-77; cons., vis. staff Los Alamos (N.Mex.) Nat. Lab., 1972-77; com. on minority participation in earth sci. and mineral engring. Dept. Interior, 1972-75; chmn. Calif. Geothermal Resource Task Force, 1977, Calif. Geothermal Resources Bd., 1977-81; earthquake studies adv. panel US Geol. Survey, 1979-83, adv. com., 1982-86; adv. coun. Gas Rsch. Inst., 1982-86, rsch. coord. coun., 1987-98, vice-chmn., 1994-96, chmn., 1996-98, sci. and tech. coun., 1998-2001; bd. on global change rsch. NAS, 1995-99, subcom. on earthquake rsch., 1985-88, bd. on earth scis. and resources, 1986-91, bd. on mineral and energy resources, 1982-88, Minn. Minerals Coord. Com., 1986-93, US nat. com. for internat. union of geological scis. (IUGS), 1985-93, US nat. com. for the internat. union of geodesy and geophysics 2001—, chmn., 2003—; mem. US Nat. Com. on Diversitas, 2000—; adv. bd. Stanford U. Sch. Earth Scis., 1989—, Sec. of Energy Adv. Bd., 1995-97; com. on equal opportunities in sci. and tech. NSF, 1985-86, adv. com. on earth scis., 1987-91, adv. com. on sci. and tech. ctrs. devel., 1987-91, adv. com. on sci. and tech. ctrs., 1996, adv. com. on geoscis., 1994-97; mem. State-Fed. Tech. Partnership Task Force, 1995-99, Fed. Coun. for Continental Sci. Drilling, 1992-98, Gt. Plains Partnership Coun., 1995-99; trustee Am. Geol. Inst. Found., 1988— (Ian Campbell medlist 1999). Contbr. articles to profl. jours. Bd. dirs. Abendmusik:Lincoln, 1995-97; trustee 1st Plymouth Congl. Ch., Lincoln, 1997-2000. Fellow NSF, 1962-66. Fellow AAAS (chmn. electorate nominating com. sect. E 1980-84, mem.-at-large 1987-91, chmn.-elect 1994, chmn. 1995, coun. del. 1997-98), Geol. Soc. Am. (nominations com. 1974, chmn. com. on geology and pub. policy 1981-84, audit com. 1988-90, chair 1990, com. on coms. 1986-87, 91-92, chmn. com. on coms. 1995, chair Day medal com. 1990, councilor 1987-91), Mineral. Soc. Am. (mem. Roebling medal com. 1999—), Geol. Assn. Can.; mem. Am. Geophys. Union (chmn. com. pub. affairs 1984-89), Soc. Mayflower Descs., Nat. Parks and Conservation Assn. (trustee 1982-86), Nat. Assn. Regulatory Utility Commrs. (com. on gas 1982-86, exec. com. 1984-86, com. on energy conservation 1983-84), Interstate Oil and Gas Compact Commn. (mem. Petroleum Profls. Task Force, 2001—), Cosmos Club, Country Club of Lincoln. Congregationalist. Office: U Nebr State Mus 307 Morrill Hall Lincoln NE 68588-0338 Office Fax: 402-472-8899.

GREW, RAYMOND EDWARD, mechanical engineer; b. Metamora, Ohio, Jan. 11, 1923; s. Edward F. and Coletta (Minck) G.; children: Elizabeth, Mary, Janet, John. BS in Mech. Engring., U. Mich., 1948. Registered profl. engr., Calif. Prin. engr. Hoffmann La Roche, Nutley, NJ, 1957-83. Navigator USAF. Mem. ASHRAE, Am. Assn. Energy Engrs. (specialist in rsch. lab. facilities), Am. Soc. Profl. Engrs., English Speaking Union, Pilgrims of U.S., Caterpiller Club. Achievements include patent for chromatographic device. Home: 28124 Hamden Ln Escondido CA 92026-6648

GREW, ROBERT RALPH, lawyer; b. Metamora, Ohio, Mar. 25, 1931; m. Anne Gano Bailey, Aug. 2, 1958. AB in Letters and Law, U. Mich., 1953, JD, 1955. Bar: Mich. 1955, N.Y. 1958. Assoc. Carter, Ledyard & Milburn, N.Y.C., 1957-68, ptnr., 1968-98, of counsel NYC, 1999—2002; ret., 2003. Lectr. legal problems in banking and in venture capital investments Practising Law Inst. Mem. Pilgrims of U.S., English Speaking Union (nat. v.p. 1989-93), Union Club, Lansdowne Club (London). Republican. Office: Carter Ledyard & Milburn 2 Wall St New York NY 10005-2001 also: 1401 Eye I St NW Washington DC 20005 E-mail: grew@clm.com.

GREWAL, PARWINDER S. biologist, educator; b. Dharour, Punjab, India, May 26, 1961; came to U.S., 1991; s. Joginder S. and Amarjit K. (Sekhon) G.; m. Sukhbir K. Battu, Feb. 22, 1987; children: Parbir, Sharanbir. BS with honors, Punjab Agrl. U., Ludhiana, India, 1981, MS in Nematology, 1983; PhD in Zoology, U. London, 1990; DIC Nematology, Imperial Coll., London, 1990. Scientist Indian Coun. Agrl. Rsch., Solan, 1984-87; higher sci. officer Horticulture Rsch. Internat., Littlehampton, Eng., 1987-91; postdoctoral rsch. assoc. Rutgers U., New Brunswick, N.J., 1991-93; mgr. nematode rsch. Biosys, Inc., Palo Alto, Calif., 1993-95, rsch. leader Columbia, Md., 1995-97; asst. prof. Ohio State U., Wooster, 1997—2002, assoc. prof., 2002—. Contbr. chpts. to books, over 100 articles to profl. jours. Recipient Team award for Environ. Achievement, Her Majesty the Queen, 1993, Young Scientist of Yr. award U.K. Mushroom Growers Assn., 1991, Lindbergh award 1999, Disting. Jr. Faculty award Ohio Agr. Rsch. and Devel. Ctr., 2002, Syngenta Crop Protection award 2002, Award of Excellance in Intergrated Pest Mgmt., 2003. Mem. AAAS, Soc. Nematologists, European Soc. Nematologists, Entomol. Soc. Am., Assn. Applied Biologists, Afro-Asian Soc. Nematologists (exec. bd. 1990—, editorial bd. 1990—). Avocations: running, travel, gardening. Office: Dept Entomology Ohio State U 1680 Madison Ave Wooster OH 44691-4114

GREWE, JOHN MITCHELL, orthodontist, educator; b. Eau Claire, Wis., Feb. 6, 1938; BS, U. Minn., 1960, DDS, 1962, MSD in Oral Pathology, 1964, PhD in Anatomy, 1966, Cert. in Orthodontics, 1967. Pvt. practice dentistry, Eau Claire, then Mpls., 1962-66; mem. dental staff U. Minn., 1967, VA Hosp. and Univ. Hosp., Iowa City, Iowa, 1968-69; practice orthodontics Univ. Md., 1969-77; pvt. practice orthodontics Towson, Md., 1977—. Asst. prof., chmn. pediatric dental div. U. Minn., 1966-67, U. Iowa, Iowa City, 1967-69, asst. prof. Coll. Dentistry and Coll. Medicine; assoc. prof. Coll. Dental Surgery, U. Md., Balt., 1969-75, prof., chmn. dept. orthodontics, 1969-78, part-time clin. prof., 1978-85; consulting orthodontist Johns Hopkins Hosp., Mercy Hosp.; cons. NIH, 1974, 76—, WHO, 1974-77, others. Contbr. articles to profl. jours.; assoc. editor Md. State Dental Jour., 1985-98. Fellow Internat. Coll. Dentists, Am. Coll. Dentists (chmn. Md. sect.); mem. Am. Assn. Dentistry Educators, ADA, Internat. Assn. Dental Rsch., Am. Assn. Orthodontics (coun. orthodontics edn. 1995—), Mid-Atlantic Soc. Orthodontists (past pres.), Md. Soc. Dentistry for Children (past pres.), Md. Soc. Orthodontics (past pres.), Fedn. Dentaire Internat. E-mail: grewgarc@bcpl.net.

GREWE, MARJORIE JANE, protective services official; b. Baltimore County, Md., Nov. 10, 1931; d. Wilbur Guy and Mary Alice (Stover) Gregory; m. Harold Henry, Oct. 31, 1954 (dec.); children: Dorothy Lee Gorkey, Eva-Maria Marjorie Shaeffer. Student, Essex County Coll., 1979 80, U. Md. Dep. sheriff Baltimore County Sheriff's Dept., Towson, Md., 1966-87; profl. interviewer U.S. Dept. Commerce, Phila., 1959-65; compiling stats., map making various orgns., Phila., 1959; profl. interviewer med. studies Johns Hopkins U., Balt., 1959; matron Balt. City Jail, 1957-58; demonstrator Tupperware, Balt., 1951-58; dep. area coord. civil def. City of Balt., 1956-59; ret., 1987. Freelance interviewer, 1959—65. Gossip columnist: local newspapers, 1959—65. Mem. Md. Sheriff's Youth Ranch; activist Am. with Disabilities, EPA, Animal Rights; mem. Adv. for Wildlife; sec. Dem. Clubs, Baltimore County, 1959—66; mem. polit. action com., 1965. Mem.: Baltimore County Sheriff's Dept., Nat. Sheriffs Assn. (state dir. 1986—87), Md. State Sheriffs Assn. (life; sec.), Fraternal Order Police (life), Moose Aux. Presbyterian. Avocations: doll collecting, travel, gardening, cooking, genealogy. Home: Baldwin Hills Estates Der Palast at 115 Baldwin Ln Staunton VA 24401-8950

GREWELL, JOHANNE H. FAIRS, librarian, consultant; b. Pittsfield, Mass., June 30, 1938; d. John H. and Eleanor (Brooks) Fairs; m. Donald Robert Grewell, Aug. 5, 1961 (div. Feb. 1970); 1 child, Dawn Rebecca. BS in Edn., Ea. Ill. U., Charleston, 1960; MS in LS, U. Ill., 1965. Cert. in h.s. teaching, instructional materials, Ill. Tchr. English, 10th grade Mattoon (Ill.) H.S., 1960-64; tchr. lang. arts, 8th grade Ctrl. Jr. H.S., Mattoon, 1964-66; 1st asst. cataloger Ea. Ill. U., 1966-71; media specialist Armstrong Jr. H.S., Jacksonville, Ill., 1971-77; libr. media specialist Peoria (Ill.) HS, 1977—2000; sch. libr. devel. cons. Alliance Libr. Sys., Pekin, Ill., 2000—. Instr. media/libr. svcs. Ill. Ctrl. Coll., East Peoria, 1978-95; subcom. on sys. Ill. State Libr. Adv. Coun., Springfield, 1994-97; cons. Libr. Book Selection Svc., Bloomington, Ill., 1992-2000, Alliance Libr. Sys. Adv. Coun., 1995-2000. Costume chmn. for numerous plays in cmty. theaters. Mem. ALA, Am. Assn. Sch. Librs., Ill. Sch. Libr. Media Assn. (bd. dirs., past pres.), PEO, Delta Kappa Gamma. Office: Alliance Libr Sys 845 Brenkman Dr Pekin IL 61554

GREY, BRAD, producer, agent; Mgr., prodr. Brillstein-Grey Entertainment, Beverly Hills, Calif., now chmn., CEO. Prodr.: (films) The Burning, 1981, (del.): Opportunity Knocks, 1990; exec. prodr.: (films) The Celluloid Closet, Cat and Mouse, 1995, Happy Gilmore, The Cable Guy, Bulletproof, 1996, The Replacement Killers, Dirty Work, 1998; (TV films) Don't Try This at Home!, 1990; (TV series) The Larry Sanders Show, 1992, Mr. Show, The Naked Truth, 1995, The Steve Harvey Show, 1996, Just Shoot Me!, Alright Already, C-16: FBI, 1997. Office: Brillstein Grey Entertainment 9150 Wilshire Blvd Ste 350 Beverly Hills CA 90212-3453

GREY, DEBORAH CLELAND, Canadian government official; b. Vancouver, B.C., Can., July 1, 1952; d. Mansell Caverhill Grey and Lilian Joyce (Russell) Levy; m. Lewis Larson, Aug. 7, 1993. Student, Burrard Inlet Bible Inst., 1973; student in Sociology and English, Trinity Western Coll., Langley, British Columbia, 1978; BA, U. Alta., Edmonton, Can., 1978, B of Edn. after degree, 1979. Tchr. Frog Lake (Alta.) Indian Res., 1979-80; tchr. jr. and sr. H.S. Dewberry (Alta.) Sch., 1980-89; M.P. Ho. of Commons, Ottawa, Ont., Can., 1989—. First mem. Reform Party Ho. Commons; Caucus chmn. Reform Party, 1993-2000, apptd. dep. parliamentary leader, 1995-2000, apptd. leader ofcl. opposition, 2000; dep. critic Human Resources Devel., 1998; caucus chair PC-DR Coalition Caucus, 2001; critic Aboriginal Affairs, 2001. Recipient Can. 125 medal, 1993, Alumni award of distinction Trinity Western U., 1996. Reform. Avocations: kayaking, gospel singing, motorcycles, drama, hiking. Office: House of Commons Parliament Bldgs Ottawa ON Canada K1A 0A6

GREY, FRANCIS JOSEPH, accountant, accounting company executive, educator; b. Yeadon, Pa., Nov. 30, 1931; s. William and Delia (Mullin) G.; m. Marlene M. Ward, June 24, 1961; children: Francis Joseph Jr., Melissa Ann. BS in Econs., Villanova U., 1958. CPA. Tax profl. Coopers & Lybrand, Phila., 1958-64, tax ptnr. in charge, 1964-72, mng. ptnr. tax, 1972—. Mem. devel. com. Villanova (Pa.) U., 1972—; bd. dirs. Del. County Hosp., Upper Darby, Pa.; adj. prof. Villanova Law Sch. Author: Tax Planning for Real Estate, 1978, 88, Pa. Taxation of Corporations, 1980; contbr. articles to profl. jours. Adv. com. Wharton Sch. Tax Conf., Phila., 1970-88, Internat. Bus. Forum, Phila., 1980-88. Sgt. U.S. Army, 1952-53, Korea. Mem. AICPAs, Pa. Inst. CPAs (v.p. 1988), Internat. Fiscal Assn. (treas. 1975), Phila. C. of C. (bd. dirs. 1975—), Phila. Country Club (bd. dirs. 1980-84), Union League of Phila., Locust Club, Beta Gamma Sigma. Republican. Roman Catholic. Avocations: golf, tennis, sports.

GREY, JERRY, science educator; b. N.Y.C., N.Y.C., Oct. 25, 1926; s. Abraham Lewis and Lillian Grey; m. Florence Maier, Feb. 21, 1969; children: Leslie, Jacquelyn(dec.). B of Mech. Engring., Cornell U., 1947, MS, 1949; PhD, Calif. Inst. Tech., 1952. Instr. Cornell U., Ithaca, NY, 1947—49; engine devel. engr. Fairchild Engines, Farmingdale, NY, 1949—50; mem. tech. staff Bell Labs., N.Y.C., 1947; hypersonic aerodynamicist Guggenheim Aero. Lab., Pasadena, Calif., 1950—51; sr. engr. Marquardt Aircraft Co., Van Nuys, Calif., 1950—51; prof. Princeton (N.J.) U., 1951—; adminstr. tech. activities and pub. policy, dir. sci. and tech. policy Am. Inst. Aeronautics and Astronautics, N.Y.C., 1971—, dir. sci. and tech. policy Reston, Va., 1987—. Pub., editor-at-large Aerospace Am., Reston, 1984—; adj. prof. environ. sci. L.I. U., Southampton, NY, 1978—83; v.p. publs. Am. Inst. Aeronautics and Astronautics, N.Y.C., 1966—71; vice-chmn. space power com. Internat. Astron. Fedn., Paris, 1986—90; v.p. tech. activities Internat. Acad. Astronautics, Paris, 1978—84; pres. Internat. Astronautical Fedn., Paris, 1984—86; mem. sci. adv. coun. NASA Inst. for Advanced Concepts, Atlanta, 1988—; chmn. solar adv. and other panels Office of Tech. Assessment, Washington, 1973—83; dep. sec. gen. UNISPACE-82, United Nations, N.Y.C., 1981—82; dir. Applied Solar Energy Corp., Industry, Calif., 1985—93; vice-chmn. comml. space transp. adv. com. FAA, Washington, 1985—87; chmn. coord. com. on energy Am. Assn. Engring. Socs., N.Y.C., 1976—78; mem. sci. adv. bd. Discover Mag., N.Y.C., 1980—84, George C. Marshall Inst., Washington, 1986—; mem., sec. energy adv. bd. U.S. Dept. Energy, Washington, 1989—92. Author: (book) Race for Electric Power, 1972, Facts of Flight, 1973, Enterprise, 1978, Aeronautics in China, 1981, Beachheads in Space, 1983. Seaman 2d class USN, 1943—46. Recipient Gen.-Interest Mag. award, Aviation/Space Writers Assn., 1985, E.E. Emme Publs. award, Am. Astron. Soc., 1986. Fellow: Am. Inst. Aeronautics and Astronautics; mem.: Cosmos Club, Key Biscayne Yacht Club. Achievements include patents for Calorimetric Probe. Avocations: tennis, swimming, theater. Home: Ste 22-A 881 Ocean Dr Key Biscayne FL 33149

GREY, ROBERT DEAN, academic administrator, biology educator; b. Liberal, Kans., Sept. 5, 1939; s. McHenry Wesley and Kathryn (Brown) G.; m. Alice Kathleen Archer, June 11, 1961; children: Erin Kathleen, Joel Michael. BA, Phillips U., 1961; PhD, Washington U., 1966. Asst. prof. Washington U., St. Louis, 1966-67; from asst. prof. to full prof. zoology U. Calif., Davis, 1967—, chmn. dept., 1979-83, dean biol. scis., 1985—, interim exec. vice chancellor, 1993-95, provost, exec. vice chancellor, 1995—2001, sr. advisor to chancellor, 2001—. Author: (with others) A Laboratory Text for Developmental Biology, 1980; contbr. articles to profl. jours. Recipient Disting. Tchg. awrd Acad. Senate U. Calif., Davis, 1977, Magnar Ronning award for tchg. Associated Students U. Calif., Davis, 1978, Disting. Alumnus award Phillips U., 1991. Mem. Am. Soc. Cell Biology, Soc. Developmental Biology, Phi Sigma. Avocations: music, hiking, gardening.

GREY, RUTHANN E. communications specialist, management consultant; b. Buffalo, N.Y., May 13, 1945; d. Wilson Campbell and Rosalie (Briggs) Evege; m. Daine A. Grey, Aug. 25, 1990; children: Daine, Jr., Keenan, Nichole. BS, SUNY, Buffalo, 1966, MS, 1970, PhD, 1980; postgrad., Harvard U., 1988. Tchr. Bennett H.S., Buffalo, 1966-69; prof. Erie C.C., Buffalo, 1970-73; adminstr. No. Va. C.C., Annandale, 1975-76, Wayne State U., Detroit, 1978-80; dir. pub. affairs Burroughs Corp., Detroit, 1981-86; exec. asst. to chmn. bd. dirs. The Equitable, N.Y.C., 1986-89; mgr. pub. affairs N.Y. Times, N.Y.C., 1989-90; mgr. divsn. corp. rels. Pub. Svc. Corp. Colo., Denver, 1990-93; v.p. comm. and pub. affairs Hoechst Celanese, Bridgewater, NJ, 1993—; v.p. global media and external rels. Hoechst Marion Roussel, Bridgewater, NJ, 1996—; comm. chief Ednl. Testing Svc., Princeton, NJ; with The Caunos Group, Watchung, NJ, 1998—. Cons. A+ For Kids, Newark, 1989-90, Rockefeller Found., N.Y.C., 1989-90. Bd. dirs. Citizens Scholarship Found., Minn., 1990-94. Mem. Pub. Rels. Seminar, Arthur Page Soc., The Wisemen, Pub. Rels. Rsch. Found. Avocations: gardening, walking. Home: 28 Stonegte Dr Watchung NJ 07069-5471 Office: The Caunos Group 28 Stonegte Dr Watchung NJ 07069 E-mail: regrey@optonline.net.

GREYSER, LINDA LORRAINE, education educator; b. Lynn, Mass., Oct. 8, 1942; d. Paul and Minnie E. (Sogoloff) Segel; m. Stephen A. Greyser, June 30, 1968; 1 child, Naomi Judith. BA, Lake Erie Coll., 1964; MA, Middlebury Coll., 1965; EdM, Harvard U., 1990, EdD, 1994. Tchr. Beverly (Mass.) Pub. Schs., 1965-67, Wayland (Mass.) Pub. Schs., 1967-73; cons. Edn. Coop., Wellesley, Mass., 1991-94; assoc. dir. programs in profl. edn. Grad. Sch. Edn. Harvard U., Cambridge, Mass., 1994—. Mem. Comm. for Common Core of Learning, Mass. Dept. Edn., 1993-94. Mem. sch. bd. Wayland Pub. Schs., 1981-90; mem. learning svcs. com. Pub. Broadcasting Svc., 1994-97. Democrat. Office: Harvard U Grad Sch Edn PPE 14 Gutman Ctr Cambridge MA 02138 Home: Apt A121 330 Beacon St Boston MA 02116-1179

GREYSON, CHARLES BRUCE, psychiatrist; b. Bklyn., Oct. 25, 1946; s. William Lawrence and Augusta Celia (DeBare) G.; m. Jane Alice Chapman, Mar. 23, 1968; children: Devon Lara, Eric Chapman. AB, Cornell U., 1968; MD, SUNY, Syracuse, 1973. Diplomate Nat. Bd. Med. Examiners, Am. Bd. Psychiatry and Neurology. Psychiat. resident U. Va., Charlottesville, 1973-76, asst. prof. psychiatry, 1976-78, U. Mich., Ann Arbor, 1978-84; assoc. prof. psychiatry U. Conn., Farmington, 1984-93, prof. psychiatry, 1993-95, U. Va., Charlottesville, 1995—, Bonner-Lowry prof. personality studies, 1998—2002,

Carlson prof. psychiatry, 2002—. Editor: The Near-Death Experience, 1984; editor Jour. Near-Death Studies, 1982—; contbr. sci. articles to profl. jours. Recipient William C. Menninger award Central Neuropsychiat. Assn., 1976, Fellow Am. Assn. Social Psychiatry, Am. Psychiat. Assn.; mem. Am. Assn. Suicidology, Parapsychol. Assn., Internat. Assn. for Near-Death Studies (pres. 1982-83, dir. rsch. 1981—). Home: 2700 Gray Fox Spur Charlottesville VA 22901-8867 Office: U Va Health Sys Divsn Personality Studies PO Box 800152 Charlottesville VA 22908-0152 E-mail: cbg4d@virginia.edu.

GREYSON, CLIFFORD RUSSELL, internist; b. N.Y.C., 1958; AB, Harvard Coll., 1980; MSEE, Stanford U., 1985, MD, 1987. Cert. internal medicine and cardiovascular diseases, critical care medicine. Resident in internal medicine Stanford U. Hosp., 1987-90, fellow in critical care, 1990-91; fellow in cardiovasc. disease U. Calif., San Francisco, 1991-95, faculty cardiology divsn., 1995-99, U. Colo. Health Scis. Ctr., Denver, 1999—. Co-dir. med. intensive care unit San Francisco VA Med. Ctr., 1998-99. Elected to city coun. Town of Woodside, Calif., 1995. Recipient Clinician Scientist award Am. Heart Assn., 1995-96, Clin. Investigator Devel. award NIH, 1996-01 Fellow Am. Coll. Cardiology; mem. ACP. Office: Denver VA Med Ctr Cardiology 111B 1055 Clermont St Denver CO 80220-3808

GRGIN, JOSEPH MICHAEL, environmental engineer; b. Bklyn., Sept. 21, 1946; s. Rudy and Mildred (Fatovich) G. BS in Engring., CCNY, 1969, MS in Engring., 1971; MS in Mgmt., Poly. Inst. N.Y., 1980. Registered profl. engr., N.Y., R.I., N.J., Mass. Engr. Syska & Hennessy Inc., N.Y.C., 1969-70; sr. engr. Parsons Brinckerhoff, Inc., N.Y.C., 1970-84; divsn. engr. N.Y.C. Transit Authority, Bklyn., 1984-86; prin. assoc. Clinton Bogert Assocs., Englewood Cliffs, N.J., 1986-96; assoc. Greeley and Hansen, N.Y.C., 1996—. Contbr. articles to profl. jours. Mem. ASCE, Am. Water Works Assn., Am. Mgmt. Assn., Water Environment Fedn. Home: 3 Litchult Ln Mahwah NJ 07430-1587

GRIBBEN, ALAN, English language educator, research consultant; b. Parsons, Kans., Nov. 21, 1941; s. J.S. and Ruth E. (North) G.; m. Irene Wong, Feb. 14, 1974; children: Walter Blake, Valerie Janet. BA in English, U. Kans., 1964; MA, U. Oreg., 1966; PhD, U. Calif., Berkeley, 1974. Rsrch. editor Mark Twain Papers, Bancroft Libr. U. Calif., Berkeley, 1967-74, instr. dept. English, 1972-73; asst. prof. dept. English, U. Tex., Austin, 1974-80, assoc. prof., 1980-88, prof., 1988-91, chmn. grad. studies dept. English, 1984-88; head dept. English and philosophy Auburn U. Montgomery, Ala., 1991—; disting. rsch. prof. Auburn U., 1998, pres. Heads Coun., 2002—. Mem. State Graduation Requirements Task Force, 1995-96; spl. cons. Mark Twain Libr. Assn., 1981; co-chair nat. conf. The State of Mark Twain Studies, 1993, nat. conf. Cotton: The Fiber, The Land, The People, 1994. Author: Am. Literary Scholarship: An Annual, 1995—, Mark Twain's Library: A Reconstruction, 1980; editor: Mark Twain's Rubaiyat, 1983; co-editor: Overland with Mark Twain: James B. Pond's Photographs and Jour. of the North American Lecture Tour of 1895, 1992; mem. editl. bd. Studies in Am. Fiction, 1988-97, U. Miss. Studies in English, 1986-96, Studies in Am. Humor, 1982—, Western Am. Lit., 1991-98, Am. Literary Realism, 2003—; nat. panel juror NEH, 1990-94; assoc. editor Libws. and Culture, 1980-91; contbr. articles to profl. jours. Recipient President's Assocs. Tchg. Excellence award U. Tex., 1983, Henry Nash Smith fellow Ctr. for Mark Twain Studies, Elmira Coll., 1997, Jervis Langdon Jr. fellow Ctr. for Mark Twain Studies, Elmira Coll., 1990. Mem. South Atlantic MLA, Mark Twain Cir. of Am. (hon. life, pres. 1987-89), Am. Lit. Assn. (exec. bd. 1989-96), Am. Humor Studies Assn., Western Am. Lit. Assn., Phi Kappa Phi. Avocations: bicycling, tennis, record and cd collecting (bands of 1930s and 1940s), rare book collecting, gardening. Home: 308 Arrowhead Dr Montgomery AL 36117-4108 Office: Auburn U Montgomery Dept English and Philosophy PO Box 244023 Montgomery AL 36124-4023 E-mail: agribben@mail.aum.edu. *Libraries constitute the heart of higher education and the essence of civilization itself, whether in modern-day San Francisco or ancient Alexandria. To befriend a library collection, then, is to contribute tangibly to general human knowledge, intellectual freedom, and aspirations for humanity.*

GRIBBEN, MONICA ANNE, social scientist, researcher; b. Honolulu, June 9, 1963; d. Jean B. Rositol; m. Hugh J. Gribben III, Aug. 26, 1989; children: Jennifer, Jake. BA, Yale U., 1985; MA, George Mason U., 1989, PhD, 1999. Tchr. Charles County Pub. Schs., La Plata, Md., 1985-86; tech. editor Nat. Systems Mgmt., Arlington, Va., 1986-87; rschr. Human Resources Rsch. Orgn., Alexandria, Va., 1987—. Brownie troop leader Girl Scouts, Laurel, Md., 2000-02; v.p. Bond Mill Elem. PTA, 2002-03, pres., 2003—. Recipient cert. of appreciation Office of Sec. of Def., 1993, Lola Zook award, 2000. Mem. APA (student travel award 1993), Am. Psychology Soc., Internat. Mil. Testing Assn.

GRIBBLE, CHARLES EDWARD, editor, Slavic languages educator; b. Lansing, Mich., Nov. 10, 1936; s. Charles P. and Elizabeth K. Gribble. BA, U. Mich., 1957; AM, Harvard U., 1958, PhD, 1967; postgrad., Moscow State U., 1960-61. Instr., asst. prof. Russian Brandeis U., Waltham, Mass., 1961-68; asst. prof. Slavic langs. Ind. U., Bloomington, 1968-75; assoc. prof. Slavic langs. Ohio State U., Columbus, 1975-89, prof. Slavic lang., 1989—, chairperson of dept., 1990-96. Pres., editor Slavica Pub., Inc., Columbus, 1966-97; vis. assoc. prof. Slavic lang. U. Va., 1977. Author: Russian Root List, 1973, A Short Dictionary of 18th Century Russian, 1976; editor-in-chief Folia Slavica, 1977-88; editor: Studies Presented to Professor Roman Jakobson by His Students, 1968, Medieval Slavic Texts, vol. 1, 1973; contbr. articles to scholarly jour. Woodrow Wilson fellow, 1957-58, Am. Coun. Learned Soc. fellow, 1972; Internat. Rsch. and Exch. Bd. grantee, 1960-61, 72, 80, Fulbright grantee, 1987. Mem. MLA, Am. Assn. Advancement Slavic Studies, Am. Assn. Tchr. Slavic and Ea. European Lang. (Disting. Contbn. to the Profession award 1992), Linguistic Soc. Am., Linguistic Soc. Europe, Bulgarian Studies Assn. (pres. 2002-03), Phi Beta Kappa. Office: Ohio State U Slavic Lang Dept 1841 Millikin Rd Rm 232 Columbus OH 43210-1215

GRIBBLE, MARY LOUISE, freelance/self-employed poet, writer; b. Atlanta, Nov. 10, 1928; d. Milton Allan and Martha Shippen Snyder; m. Stewart Webster Purdy (div. Apr. 11, 1969); children: Allan Stewart Purdy, Von Schrader Purdy; m. Donald Max Gribble, Feb. 14, 1970. BA in English, Draughan's Coll., San Antonio, 1951. Lic. real estate broker Calif. Asst. mgr. Travis Bldg. Beretta Enterprises, San Antonio, 1951—55; sec./bookkeeper/reservations Rennert Travel Svc., San Antonio, 1951—55; pvt. sec. of chief engr., CEO Grinnell of the Pacific, L.A., 1955—56; transcriber typist adult and juvenile hall L.A. Cts., 1960—64; acctg. sec. for project acctg. C.F. Braun Engring. Co., Alhambra, Calif.; mgr./bookkeeper Archtl. Woodworking Co., L.A.; sales rep. Waade Realty Co., Arcadia, Calif., 1972—75; broker/rep. United Farm Real Estate & self-employed, Pasadena, Calif., 1978—85; poet/writer San Marino, Calif., 1985—. Real estate cons., comml. and resdl. appraiser Republic Fed. Savs. and Loan Assn., Altadena, Calif., 1975—80. Writer for Amnesty Internat., 1986—2002; writer/supporter/peace marcher So. Calif. Ecumenical Coun. Interfaith Taskforce on Ctrl. Am., L.A., 1980—90; mem./writer/patron Reverse The Arms Race, anti-nuc. causes, Pasadena /San Marino, Calif., 1982—; petitioner for Ross Perot's presidency United We Stand, 1991—92. Named finalist, Writer's Digest Internat. Writing Competition, 1993—2002. Mem.: Nat. Soc. of Colonial Dames of Am. (chmn., vice-chmn., sec., treas., membership chmn. 1984—97, Nat. Roll of Honor 1987). Episcopalian. Avocations: researching U.S. policies, reading, human rights.

GRIBBON, DANIEL MCNAMARA, lawyer; b. Youngstown, Ohio, Jan. 27, 1917; s. James Edward and Loretta (Hogan) G.; m. Jane Retzler, Sept. 13, 1941; children: Diana Jane Gribbon Motz, Deborah Ann Gribbon Alt. AB, Case Western Res. U., 1938; JD, Harvard U., 1941. Bar: N.Y. 1942, D.C. 1946, U.S. Supreme Ct. 1950. Clk. Judge Learned Hand, N.Y.C., 1941-42; assoc. Covington & Burling, Washington, 1946-50, ptnr., 1950—. Chmn. adv. com. on procedures U.S. Ct. Appeals (D.C. cir.), 1983-88 Served with USNR, 1942-46. Fellow Am. Bar Found.; mem. Am. Coll. Trial Lawyers, D.C. Bar Assn. (chmn. bd. profl. responsibility 1976-79). Clubs: Met. (Washington) (pres. 1981-82); Chevy Chase (Md.). Roman Catholic. Office: Covington & Burling 1201 Pennsylvania Ave NW Washington DC 20004-2401 Fax: 202-778-5310. E-mail: dgribbon@cov.com.

GRIBSCHAW, VICTORIA MARIE, social sciences educator, department chairman; b. Pitts., Aug. 18, 1942; d. James S. and Elizabeth M. Gribschaw. BA, Seton Hill U., 1970; MS, W.Va. U., 1974; PhD, Ohio State U., 1985. Cert. Family and Consumer Scis. Upper elementary sci. and math tchr. Pitts. Cath. Schs., 1960—72; grad. tchg. asst. W.Va. U., Divsn. of Family Resources, Coll. of Human Resources and Edn., Morgantown, 1972—74; instr. home econs. Seton Hill Coll., Greensburg, Pa., 1974—78; rschr. Ohio Agrl. R&D Ctr. Ohio State U., Columbus, 1982—83; grad. rsch. assoc. Ohio Agrl. R&D Ctr. and Dept. of Home Mgmt. and Housing Ohio State U., Columbus, 1983—84; asst. prof. home econs. Seton Hill Coll., Greensburg, Pa., 1978—88, assoc. prof. home econs., dir. family studies, 1988—91, assoc. prof. home econs. with tenure, dir. family studies, 1991—93, assoc. prof. human ecology with tenure, dir. family studies, 1993—95, assoc. prof. family and consumer scis. with tenure, chair family and consumer scis. dept., dir. family studies, 1995—97, assoc. prof. of family and consumer scis. with tenure, chair divsn. mgmt., family and consumer scis., 1997—2002, chair divsn. social scis., 2002—. Editor: (proceedings) 1994 Conf. Proceedings Eastern Family Econs. and Resource Mgmt. Assn., 1994; contbr. articles to profl. jours. Mem. commn. on global mission and internationality Sisters of Charity of Seton Hill, Greensburg, 2000—01; mem. investment adv. bd. Sisters of Charity, Greensburg, 1999—2001; mem. fin. adv. bd. Sisters of Charity of Seton Hill, Greensburg, 1992—99; v.p. bd. dirs. Pregnant Adolescent Childcare Tng., Greensburg, 2001—; sec. bd. trustees Mercy Jeannette Hosp. (formerly Jeannette Dist. Meml. Hosp.), 1998—2001; trustee Mercy Jeannette Hosp., 1986—2003, chair med. and clin. affairs com., 2001—, mem. fin. com. bd. trustees, 1990—2003; treas. bd. dirs. JDMH HealthNet, Jeannette, 1996—2001; mem. Pregnant Adolescent Childcare Tng., Greensburg, 1988—2001; v.p. bd. dirs. Pregnant Adolescent Childcare Tng. Program, Greensburg, 2001; sec. Pregnant Adolescent Childcare Tng., Greensburg, 1999—2001, 1989—94; active Ctrl. Westmoreland Unemployment Steeering Com., Greensburg, 1988—90. Mem.: Am. Assn. Family Consumer Sci., Am. Assn. of Housing Educators, Nat. Coun. on Family Rels., Am. Coun. on Consumer Interests, Eastern Family Econs. and Resource Mgmt. Assn., Pa. Assn. of Family and Consumer Scis. (pres.-elect 2002—03, Western area v.p. 1998—2001, pres. 2003—), Alpha Sigma Lambda (pres. 2003—), Kappa Omicron Nu (leadership acad. scholarship 2000). Democrat. Roman Catholic. Office: Seton Hill Univ Seton Hill Box 307 Greensburg PA 15601-1599

GRICE, ROBERT E., JR., music educator, composer; b. Dothan, Ala., Sept. 27, 1964; s. Robert E. and Linda Hughes Grice. B in Music Edn., Troy State U., 1987, MS, 1996. Dir. Troy (Ala.) State Wesley Singers, 1983—87, band dir. Geneva (Ala.) City Schs., 1987—97, Enterprise (Ala.) City Schs., 1997—; mem. adj. faculty Enterprise State Jr. Coll., 1999—. Co-dir. Enterprise Indoor Percussion, 1997—2002; dir. Chamber Ensemble, Enterprise, 2002—. Composer: (symphonic music) Red Eclipse, 2000, Pinnacle, 2002, Myths and Legends, 2002. Recipient Golden Apple Tchr. award, WDHN-TV, Dothan, 2002. Mem.: Music Educators Nat. Conf., Phi Mu Alpha (pres. 1985—2002), Kappa Delta Pi. Methodist. Home: 464 Sandy Oak Enterprise AL 36330 Office: Daughin Jr HS 425 Dauphin St Enterprise AL 36330 E-mail: rgrice2607@aol.com.

GRIDLEY, MARK CHARLES, psychologist; b. Detroit, Jan. 5, 1947; s. Frederick William and Helen Lucille (Jones) G. BS, Mich. State U., 1969; MS, Case Western Reserve U., 1970, PhD, 1977. Psychometrist, research asst. Case Western Reserve Univ. Hosp., 1971-73; saxophonist/flutist free-lance Cleve., 1969—; cons., psychologist Cleve. Bd. Edn., 1977-81; vis. asst. prof. John Carroll U., Univ. Hgts., Ohio, 1981-84; prof. psychology Heidelberg Coll., Tiffin, Ohio, 1987—. Author: Jazz Styles: History and Analysis, 1978, 85, 88, 91, 94, 97, 2000, 03, Concise Guide to Jazz, 1992, 98, 2001, 03; contbr. articles to profl. jours.; contbr. to Encyclopedia of Britain, Encyclopedia of the Midwest, Grove Dictionaries of Music. Recepient Best Flutist award Notre Dame Collegiate Jazz Festival, 1968, Disting. Achievement award Ednl. Press Assn. Am., 1987 Mem. Internat. Assn. Jazz Educators, Col. Music Soc., Soc. Am. Music, Northeast Ohio Jazz Soc. Home: 47 Maple St Tiffin OH 44883-2719

GRIEB, KENNETH JOSEPH, historian, educator; b. Buffalo, N.Y. s. Joseph J. and Ida F. Grieb. BA, SUNY, Buffalo, 1960, MA, 1962; PhD, Ind. U., 1966. Lectr. Ind. U., South Bend, 1965-66; from asst. prof. to prof. U. Wis., Oshkosh, 1966—, coord. Latin Am. studies, 1968-77, coord. internat. studies, 1977—, John McNaughton Rosebush Univ. prof., 1983—; SNC Corp. univ. prof. of internat. rels., 1994—. Bd. dirs. Midwest Model UN, 1991-94. Mem. bd. editors: The Ams., 1966-93, The Historian, 1981—; author: The United States and Huerta, 1969, The Latin American Policy of Warren G. Harding, 1976, 77, Guatemalan Caudillo: The Regime of Jorge Ubico, Guatemala--1931-1944, 1979, Central America in the Nineteenth and Twentieth Centuries: An Annotated Bibliography, 1988; co-author: Essays on Miguel Angel Asturias, 1973; editor in chief: Research Guide to Central America and the Caribbean, 1985; co-editor: Latin American Government Leaders. Doherty Found. fellow, 1964-65; grantee U. Wis., 1966, 67-68, 71-72, 72-73, 74-75, 77, 80, 85; recipient Meritorious Svc. award Helicopter Assn. Internat., 1995, Tribute to Excellence award LWV of Wis., 1997, Tchg. Excellence award U. Wis. Sys. Bd. Regents, 1998, award for excellence Oshkosh C. of C., 1999. Mem. Am. Hist. Assn., Conf. on Latin Am. History (chair Caribe-CentroAm. studies com. 1978-80, 85-87), L.Am. Studies Assn., Midwest Assn. for L.Am. Studies (pres. 1972-73), Orgn. Am. Historians, North Cen. Coun. Latin Americanists (pres. 1967-68), Soc. for Historians of Am. Fgn. Rels., Internat. Studies Assn., UN Assn. USA, Phi Alpha Theta, Sigma Iota Rho (nat. coun. 1968—). Home: 1505 Porter Ave Oshkosh WI 54902-4249 Office: U Wis Internat Studies Program Oshkosh WI 54901

GRIECO, MICHAEL HENRY, allergy and infectious diseases physician; b. N.Y.C., Aug. 10, 1932; s. Henry and Angelina G. m. Dorothy; children: Michael, Angela, Susan. BA, NYU, 1954; MD, SUNY, Bklyn., 1957; JD, Fordham U., 1979. Diplomate Am. Bd. Legal Medicine, Am. Bd. Diagnostic Lab. Immunology, Am. Bd. internal Medicine; bd. cert. in allergy and clin. immunology, infectious diseases, pulmonary diseases, rheumatology, geriatric medicine, clin. tropical medicine and travelers' health. Intern in medicine St. Luke's Med. Ctr., N.Y.C., 1957-58, resident in medicine, 1960-61, resident in cardiology, 1961-62; resident in allergy The Roosevelt Hosp., N.Y.C., 1962-63; resident chest svc. Bellevue Hosp., N.Y.C., 1963-64; asst. attending physician The Roosevelt Hosp., 1964—, St. Luke's Hosp. Ctr., 1965-69, assoc. attending physician, 1969, assoc. dir. medicine, 1970, attending physician, 1973; prof. emeritus of clin. medicine Columbia U. Coll. of Physicians and Surgeons. Resident infectious disease svc. Cornell Med. Divsn., Bellevue Hosp., 1963-64; asst. outpatient dept. St. Luke's Hosp. Ctr., 1964-65, dir. allergy lab., 1965, dir. allergy and infectious disease sect., 1968; asst. in medicine Vanderbilt Clinic Presbyn. Hosp., N.Y.C., 1964; dir. Robert A. Cooke Inst. Allergy and Divsn. Allergy, The Roosevelt Hosp., 1973; attending, chief divsn. allergy, clin. immunology and infectious diseases, St. Luke's/Roosevelt Hosp. Ctr., 1980, dir. AIDS Ctr., 1987-97, dir. dept. medicine, 1993-97; v.p. med. affairs Christ Hosp., Jersey City, 1998—. Fellow ACP, Am. Coll. Legal Medicine, Infectious Diseases Soc. Am.; mem. ABA, Am. Assn. Immunologists, Am. Soc. Microbiology (com. chmn. 1984-87), Clin. Immunology Soc., N.Y. Allergy Soc. (pres. 1971-72, sec. 1968-70), N.Y. County Med. Soc. (v.p. 1989, sec. 1985-88, mem. health com. 1968-73, mem. CME com. 1978-79), N.Y. State Bar Assn. (mem. spl. com. on AIDS and the law 1988-89), Phi Beta Kappa, Alpha Omega Alpha. Home: 9 Mayflower Dr Tenafly NJ 07670-3129 E-mail: michael.grieco@verizon.net.

GRIEFEN, JOHN ADAMS, artist, educator; b. Worcester, Mass., Nov. 24, 1942; s. Robert John and Faith (Adams) G.; 1 child, Katherine Abigail Jacqueline. Student, Chgo. Art Inst., 1964-65, Bennington Coll., 1965-66; BA, Williams Coll., 1966; postgrad., Hunter Coll., 1966-68. Instr. Bennington Coll., 1968-69, Great Neck Adult Edn., N.Y., 1971-76. One-man shows Kornblee Gallery, 1969, 70, 73, Deitcher O'Reilly Gallery, N.Y.C., shows, William Edward O'Reilly Inc., N.Y.C., Martha Jackson Gallery, N.Y.C., Frank Watters Gallery, Sydney, Australia, 1979, Salander O'Reilly Galleries, N.Y.C., 1981, 82, 84, 85, 91, 93, 99, Harcus-Hrakow Gallery, Boston, Phyllis Kind Galley, Chgo., B.R. Kornblatt Gallery, Balt., Diane Brown Gallery, Washington, 1978, Sunne Savage Gallery, Boston, 1979, Williams Coll. Mus. Art, Williamstown, Mass., 1980, Martin Gerard Gallery, Edmonton, Alta., Can., 1981, Gallery Moos Ltd., Toronto and Calgary, 1981, Edmonton Art Gallery, 1984, Hirondelle Gallery, N.Y.C., 1986, Salander O'Reilly Galleries, L.A., 1991, Edmonton Art Gallery, Alberta, Can., 1993, Swift Current Art Gallery, Sask., 1993, S.C. Schultz Gallery, N.J., 1994; exhibited group shows Indpls. Mus. Art, Phoenix Mus., Sydney Mus., Whitney Mus. Purdue U., N.Y. Mus. Modern Art, Santa Barbara Mus., Boston Mus. Fine Arts; represented in pub. collections Larry Aldrich Mus. Contemporary Art, Allen Art Mus., Arthur A. Anderson Co., Bank of Ill., Calgary (Can.), Boston Mus. Fine Arts, Bklyn. Mus., Carnegie Inst. Mus. Art, Chase Manhattan Bank, Continental Resources Inc., Hines Indsl., Boston, N.Y.C., Washington, Dallas, Hirshhorn Mus. and Sculpture Garden, Washington, Met. Mus. Art, Michner Collections-U. Tex., Musnson-William-Proctor Art Inst., Mus. Modern Art, Newark Mus. Fine Arts, Reader's Digest Assn. Inc., Rose Art Mus., Brandeis U., Rothmans Art Gallery, St. Lawrence U., Sydney Mus., Australia, Whitney Mus., Williams Coll. Art Mus., Worcester Mus. Art, Mass., Met. Mus. Art, N.Y.C., Vassar Coll. Mus. Art, Poughkeepsie, N.Y., Lowcart Gallery, Miami. Recipient Esther Forbes award Bancroft Sch., Worcester, Mass., 1996. Home: 275 Park Ave Apt 6R Brooklyn NY 11205 Office: care Salander O'Reilly Galleries 20 E 79th St New York NY 10021-0106 *For the love of art and the kindness of strangers.*

GRIEGER, DONALD L. artist; b. Niles, Mich., Jan. 2, 1934; s. Clarence William and Alta Jenny Grieger; m. Mary Louise Grieger, Sept. 26, 1957; children: Dara Lynnette, Kimberly Karyl. BS in Engring., U. Mich., 1957; MS in Engring., Air Force Inst. Tech., 1966. Owner, operator Grieger Gallery, Rocky Neck Art Colony, Gloucester, Mass., 1986—91. Exhibitions include Salmagundi Club, N.Y., Mary Bryan Meml. Gallery, Jeffersonville, Vt., Represented in permanent collections. Fellow: Am. Artists Profl. League; mem.: Fine Arts League, North Shore Arts Assn., Internat. Soc. Marine Painters, Rochester Art Club, Salmagundi Club. Home: 5024 Terry Hills Dr Batavia NY 14020

GRIEM, HANS RUDOLF, physicist, educator; b. Kiel, Schleswig-Holstein, Germany, Oct. 7, 1928; came to U.S., 1954; s. Rudolf H. and Paula D. (Schwarz) Griem; m. Irmgard H. Hoehling, May 11, 1957; children: Jens, Torsten, Rowena, Bridget. Abitur, Max-Planck Sch. Kiel, 1949; PhD, U. Kiel, 1954; PhD (hon.), Ruhr U., Bochum, Fed. Republic Germany, 1990. Rsch. asst. U. Md., College Park, 1954-55, asst. prof., 1957-61, assoc. prof., 1961-63, prof., 1963-94; prof. emeritus, sr. rsch. scientist, 1994—; Wissenschaftlicher asst. U. Kiel, 1955-57; dir. Lab. for Plasma Rsch. U. Md., 1980-87. Cons. Naval Rsch. Lab., Washington, 1957-96, Lawrence Livermore (Calif.) Nat. Lab., 1979—. Author: Plasma Spectroscopy, 1964, Spectral Line Broadening by Plasmas, 1974, Principles of Plasma Spectroscopy, 1997; editor: Methods of Experimental Physics, Vol. 9A, 1970; contbr. articles to sci. jours., chpts. to books. NSF sr. postdoctoral fellow, 1963; Guggenheim Found. fellow, 1968; European Space Rsch. Orgn. fellow, 1971; recipient Humboldt prize, 1978, William F. Meggers award Optical Soc. Am., 1987. Fellow Am. Phys. Soc. (councilor 1983-87, J.C. Maxwell prize 1991). Achievements include devel. of quantitative spectroscopic methods for high temperature plasma diagnostics. Office: Univ of Md Inst Rsch in Electronics and Applied Physics College Park MD 20742-3511 E-mail: griem@glue.umd.edu.

GRIEM, JOHN MICHAEL, management consultant; b. San Francisco, Apr. 29, 1945; s. John Drysen and Gwendolyn (Pyeatt) G.; m. Peggy Clarke, Sept. 16, 1967; children: John Michael Jr., Marjorie Lynne. ScBE magna cum laude with high honors, Brown U., 1965, ScME, 1966; MBA, U. Chgo., 1968. Sr. economist USPHS, 1968-70; assoc. to v.p., dir. Cresap, McCormick and Paget, Chgo., 1970-81; mng. ptnr. subs. Cresap, McCormick and Paget do Brasil Servicos Ltda., 1978-81; v.p. A.T. Kearney, Chgo., 1981-95; pres. Kearney, Health Svcs. Cons., Chgo., 1981-87; pres., CEO, Griem & Co., Lake Bluff, Ill., 1995—. Bd. govs. Am. Soc. Sao Paulo, Brazil, 1979-81, John G. Shedd Aquarium, Chgo., 1992-98. Fellow NDEA, 1965-66, Ford Found., 1965, 67-68. Mem. Inst. Mgmt. Cons. (cert.; bd. dirs. 1998—, pres. 2000-01), MidAm.-Arab C. of C. (bd. dirs. 1989-91) Chgo. Coun. Fgn. Rels., Exmoor Country Club, Brown U. Club, Sigma Xi, Tau Beta Pi, Beta Gamma Sigma. Home and Office: 120 Indian Rd Lake Bluff IL 60044-2714 E-mail: griemco@ix.netcom.com.

GRIER, DOROTHY ANN PRIDGEN, secondary education specialist; b. Pitts, Jan. 14, 1936; d. Jay Lawrence and Myra (Morgan) Pridgen; m. Robert Warren Grier, Mar. 27, 1959; children: Cassandra Ann, Robert Warren Jr. BS, U. Pitts., 1959, MEd, 1981, PhD, 1989. Tchr. Pitts. Pub. Sch., 1960-63, 72-75, reading specialist, 1975-84, program specialist, 1984-85, supervisory instrl. specialist, 1985—. State evaluator Dept. Edn. State of Pa., Harrisburg, 1988—; mem. tech. com. strategic plan Pitts. Pub. Schs., 1995—; invited speaker 4th No. Am. Conf. on Adolescent/Adult Literacy, Washington, 1996; presenter in field, Internat. Reading Assoc. Adol. Lit. Comm.,"Adolescent Promising Practices", 2000; Nat. Mid. Sh. Urban Conf., Pitts., Pa., " Lit. Plus", 2001; Internat. Read. Assoc. Inst., Sa Francesco, Calif., "Lit. Improvement for Adolescents takes Collaboration at all Levels", 2002; Internat. Reading Assoc. Adolescent Lit. Comm., 2002. Mem. Strategic Planning Com. for Sewickley (Pa.) Acad., 1988-91; trustee Pine Richland Sch. Dist. Opportunities, Inc., 1994—. Mem. Internat. Reading Assn. (exec. com. Pitts.-Three Rivers coun. 1990-93, invited spkr. adolescent literacy commn. 2000, 2001-, 2002), Internat. Assn. Secondary Reading Interest Group (pres.-elect 1992, pres. 1994-96, com. media awards for broadcast and print 1998, 99—), Secondary Reading Interest Group (chmn. 1990-94, v.p. Pa. Keystone State coun. 1991—), Pitts. Women's Missionary Circle, Harty Bible Sch. Alumni Assn. (pres. 1992—), No. Allegheny County C. of C. (tchr. excellence award selection com. 1996, Pa. framework for reading, writing and talking across the curriculum com. 2000-), Nat. Mid. Sch. Urban Conf. (invited spkr. 2001). Avocations: walking, knitting, reading, golf.

GRIER, GEORGE EDWARD, music educator, musician; b. Seattle, Wash., Aug. 8, 1934; s. George Edward Grier and Phyllis Grace (Pruvey) Kaltenbach; m. Nancy Ruth Lumberg, Aug. 28, 1956; children: Kris Edward, Diane Elizabeth, Eric Karl, Michael Ray. MusB, Eastern Wash. Univ., Cheney, Wash., 1956, BE, 1957, ME, 1963. Educator music Bridgeport Pub. Sch., Bridgeport, Wash., 1956—58, Davenport Pub. Sch., Davenport, Wash., 1958—63; educator Port Angeles Pub. Sch., Port Angeles, Wash., 1963—89, Peninsula Coll., Port Angeles, Wash., 1974—2000. Condr. asst. Port Angeles Symphony, Port Angeles, Wash., 1985—2003; condr. Port Angeles Light Opera Assn., Port Angeles, Wash., 2000, Port Angeles, 03. Recipient Outstanding Music Educator, Washington Music Assn., 1988. Democrat. Office: Social Sci/Humanities Divsn Penisula Coll 1502 E Lauridsen Blvd Port Angeles WA 98362-6698

GRIER, JAMES EDWARD, hotel company executive, lawyer; b. Ottumwa, Iowa, Sept. 7, 1935; s. Edward J. and Corinne (Bailey) G.; m. Virginia Clinker, July 4, 1959; children: Michael, Susan, James, John, Thomas. BSc, U. Iowa, 1956, JD, 1959. Bar: Iowa 1959, Mo. 1959. Mng. ptnr. Hillix, Brewer, Hoffhaus & Grier, Kansas City, Mo., 1964-77, Grier & Swartzman, Kansas City, 1977-89; pres. Doubletree Hotels Corp., Phoenix, 1989-94; chmn. Sonoran Hotel Capital, Inc., Phoenix, 1994-96; mng. ptnr. Copa Investments, 1996—, Gainey Hotel Co., 1996—. Bd. dirs. Iowa Law Sch. Found., Iowa City, St. Joseph Healthcare Ariz., Phoenix, Homeward Bound, Phoenix. Home: 3500 E Lincoln Dr Phoenix AZ 85018-1010 Office: Copa Investments 7300 E Gainey Suites Dr Ste 169 Scottsdale AZ 85258-2061 E-mail: jegrier@mindspring.com.

GRIER, JEAN HEILMAN, lawyer; b. Rapid City, S.D., Jan. 27, 1947; d. Henry and Edna (Baum) Heilman; m. David Alan Grier, Mar. 20, 1986. BA in Polit. Sci., S.D. State U., 1969; JD, U. Minn., 1972; LLM, U. Wash., 1987. Bar: Minn., 1973, D.C., 1988. Asst. atty. gen. Minn. State Gov., St. Paul, 1972-83; sr. counsel trade agreements Dept. Commerce, Washington, 1987—2002; sr. procurement negotiator Office of U.S. Trade Representative, 2002—. Adj. asst. prof. George Washington U., Washington, 1994-98. Mem. editl. bd. Pub. Procurement Law Rev.; contbr. articles to profl. jours. Fellow Fulbright Assn. 1985-86. Mem. Asia Soc., Washington Fgn. Law Soc., Japan-Am. Soc. Office: Dept Commerce 14th and Constitution Washington DC 20016 E-mail: jgrier@ustr.gov.

GRIER, LEAMON FOREST, social services administrator; b. Augusta, Ga., Sept. 17, 1935; s. Gilbert Grier and Cleo Grier Norris; m. Marion Samuel Smith, Apr., 1960 (div. 1968); children: Frank O., Donald Smith, Susan Grier Bowman; m. Shirley Burroughs Graddy, June 19, 1992; children: Cheryl Cofer, Pamela N. Gordon. BA in Phys. Edn., Morris Brown Coll., 1959; postgrad., Rutgers U., 1964; MA in Community Psychology, U. D.C., 1979. Urban dir., dept. dir. CSRA EOA, Augusta, Ga., 1967-70; tng. officer Leadership Inst. for Community Devel., Washington, 1970-74; coll. coord. Moton Mission Edn. Opportunity Ctr., Washington, 1974-76; coord. rsch. devel. and planning psychologist Youth Pride, Inc., Washington, 1978-81; cons. Howard U. Sch

Edn., Washington, 1981-84; tng. provider NIH, Washington, 1985—; interim exec. dir. Bethlehem Community Ctr., Inc., Augusta, Ga., 1992-93, exec. dir., 1993—. Part-time prof. Voorhees Coll. Denmark, S.C., 1993—, cons. pres., 1974—; pres. Leamon F. Grier and Assocs., Washington, 1981-93; field reseacher U.S. Office Edn., Washington, 1992—; program developer Laney Walker BTC, Augusta, 1991-92; evaluator Shorter Coll. Title III Program, Little Rock, 1980-86; payment adminstr. Rent Rollback Tenants Movements, Washington, 1979-96; cons. mgmt. and manpower Fauquier County (Va.) Cmty. Action Agy., 1979-85. Author: Theory of Endowment Development, 1977, Roles and Responsibilities of Project Managers, 1981, Recruitment and Admissions, 1981. Active Good Hope Bapt. Ch.; vol. Ward I Dems. Coord. Com., 1980-83, First New Horizon Bapt. Ch., Clinton, Md.; bd. dirs. Dorchester House Tenants Assn., 1979-97; mem. Two Hundred Dollars A Year Club. With U.S. Army, 1960-62. Mem. Morris Brown Coll. Alumni Assn. (named to Hall of Fame 1981), John M. Tutt Quarterback Club, Kappa Alpha Psi (life, Man of Yr. 1997), Two Hundred Dollars A Year Club. Home: 2326 Shadowood Dr Augusta GA 30906-2936

GRIER, PHILLIP MICHAEL, lawyer, former association executive; b. Quitman, Ga., Aug. 31, 1941; s. Phillip Moore and Helen Dale Parrish (Cottingham) Grier. BA, Furman U., 1963; JD, U. S.C., 1969. Bar: S.C. 1969, U.S. Dist. Ct. S.C. 1969, U.S. Ct. Appeals (4th cir.) 1972, U.S. Supreme Ct. 1978, U.S. Ct. Appeals (fed. cir.) 1985. Assoc. Haynsworth, Perry, Bryant, Marion & Johnstone, Greenville, SC, 1969—70; asst. to pres. U. S.C., Columbia, 1969, staff counsel, 1970—74, gen. counsel, 1974—79; exec. dir., CEO Nat. Assn. Coll. and Univ. Attys., Washington, 1979—96; cons. Fulbright & Jaworski, Washington, 1996—2000. Bd. dirs. Am. Coun. Edn., 1992—94; mem. adv. bd. Ctr. for Constl. Studies, U. Notre Dame and Mercer U., 1981—92; mem. secretariat of nat. higher edn. orgns. Nat. Ctr. for Higher Edn., Washington, 1979—96. Author (with Joseph P. O'Neill): Financing in a Period of Retrenchment: A Primer for Small Private Colleges, 1984; editor: The Corporate Counsellors Deskbook (Non-Profit Organizations Supplement), 1983; editor, contbg. author: Legal Deskbook for Administrators of Independent Colleges and Universities, 1982, 1983, 1984; editor: Coll. Law Digest, 1980—96; mem. editl. adv. com.: West Pub. zco., 1980—96, editl. bd.: Jour. Coll. and Univ. Law, 1979—96. With U.S. Army, 1963—66, with USAR, 1966—74. Mem.: Ancient and Honorable Artillery Co., Mil. Order Fgn. Wars, St. Nicholas Soc. of N.Y., Soc. Colonial Wars, Order of St. John, Cosmos Club (legal affairs com. 1986—90, com. reciprocity 1988—90, house com. 1990—95, chmn. 1992—95), City Tavern Club (bd. govs. 1992—2000, sec. 1994, v.p. 1996—99).

GRIES, MICHAEL F. industrial maintenance industry executive; BS in Acctg. and Fin., Northeastern U. Ptnr., dir. restructuring and reorgn. Ernst & Young LLP; founder Conway, Del Genio, Gries, and Co.; chmn., chief restructuring officer Encompass Svcs. Corp., 2002—. Mem.: Assn. Insolvency Accts., NJ StateSoc. CPA, AICPA. Office: 3 Greenway Plaza Ste 2000 Houston TX 77046 Address: Olympic Tower 645 Fifth Ave New York NY 10022*

GRIESA, THOMAS POOLE, federal judge; b. Kansas City, Mo., Oct. 11, 1930; s. Charles Henry and Stella Lusk (Bedell) G.; m. Christine Pollard Meyer, Jan. 5, 1963. AB cum laude, Harvard U., 1952; LL.B., Stanford U., 1958. Bar: Wash. 1958, N.Y. 1961. Atty. Justice Dept., 1958-60; with firm Symmers, Fish & Warner, N.Y.C., 1960-61, Davis Polk & Wardwell, N.Y.C., 1961-72, partner, 1970-72; judge U.S. Dist. Ct. So. Dist. N.Y., 1972—, chief judge, 1993-2000. Mem.: Stanford Law Rev., 1956 58. Bd. visitors Stanford Law Sch., 1982 84; bd. dir. Greater N.Y. Coun. Boy Scouts of Am. Served to lt. (j.g.) USCGR, 1952-54. Mem. Bar Assn. City N.Y., Union Club N.Y.C. Christian Scientist. Office: US Dist Ct US Courthouse 500 Pearl St New York NY 10007-1316

GRIESAR, WILLIAM HOWARD, lawyer; b. NYC, Dec. 2, 1932; s. Otto Jonas and Ruby (Ozer) G.; m. Agnes Joan Mastrangelo, June 8, 1962; children: William, Katherine, Peter; m. Jane Mayo Roos, June 12, 1999. BA, U. Va., 1955, LLB, 1958. Assoc. Rogers, Hoge & Hills, N.Y.C., 1959-65, ptnr., 1965-83; v.p., gen. counsel Rockefeller U., NYC, 1983—2001. Home: 40 Clinton Ave Dobbs Ferry NY 10522-2202

GRIESBAUER, MICHELE ELAINE, newspaper official; b. Balt., July 29, 1964; d. Stanley Raymond and Leni Elfreide (Bischoff) Siminski; m. Melvin B. Griesbauer, Sept. 8, 1984 (div. June 1988). AS, SUNY, Albany, 1988; AA, Dundalk C.C., Balt., 1995; BS in Mass Comm., Towson U., 2000. Photoengraver Balt. Sun, 1988-96, classified advt. rep., 1996—. Contbr. articles to various mags. and poetry to various publs. With USN, 1983-88. Mem. Am. Legion, Nat. Honor Soc., Golden Key, Moose. Roman Catholic. Avocations: reading, arts and crafts, photography, music journalist and critic.

GRIESCHE, ROBERT PRICE, hospital purchasing executive; b. Berkeley, Calif., July 21, 1953; s. Robert Bowen and Lillian (Price) G.; m. Susan Dawn Albers, June 8, 1985 (div. Apr. 1989); 1 child, Sara Christine. AA, Coll. of the Canyons, Valencia, Calif., 1984. Warehouse supr. John Muir Hosp., Walnut Creek, Calif., 1973-82; purchasing mgr. Henry Mayo Newhall Hosp., Valencia, 1982-85; materials mgr. Foothill Presbyn. Hosp., Glendora, Calif., 1985-87; materials mgmt. dir. Huntington Meml. Hosp., Pasadena, Calif., 1987-96; sys. dir. purchasing So. Calif. Healthcare Sys., Pasadena, 1996—2002; materials mgmt. dir. Univ. Med. Ctr. of So. Nev., Las Vegas, 2002—. Chmn. Huntington Employee Campaign, 1990-92. V.p. Coll. of Canyons Found., Valencia, 1985-90. Named to Outstanding Young Men of Am., 1988. Mem. Am. Soc. Healthcare Materials Mgmt., Calif. Cen. Svc. Assn. (charter). Republican. Presbyterian. Avocations: swimming, gardening, photography. Home: 9621 Kinlock Ct Las Vegas NV 89117 Office: Univ Med Ctr 1800 W Charleston Blvd Las Vegas NV 89102

GRIESE, BRIAN, football player; b. Miami, Fla., Mar. 18, 1975; BS in political sci., Univ. Mich. Quarter back Denver Broncos, 1998—; winner Super Bowl 33. Office: Denver Broncos Football Club 13655 Broncos Pky Englewood CO 80112

GRIESÉ, JOHN WILLIAM, III, astronomer, educator, mental health advocate; b. Norwalk, Conn., Sept. 27, 1955; s. John William Jr. and Celia (Bolté) G. Student, Franklin and Marshall Coll., 1974-77, U. Bridgeport, 1977-78; diploma, Morse Sch. Bus., 1986; student, U. Conn., 1991-95, Trinity Coll., 1995-97, Wesleyan U., 1995-96; BS with honors, Charter Oak State Coll., 2003. Observer Stamford (Conn.) Obs., 1973, asst. dir., 1978—; observer Van Vleck Obs., Middletown, Conn., 1986, asst. astrometry program, 1992-99; user Perkin-Elmer PDS, Yale U., New Haven, 1992-99, rsch. asst., 1993-99; rsch. asst. astrometry-photometry group Wesleyan U., Middletown, 1997—2001; asst. editor Hartford Lit. mag. U. Conn., 1991-95; founder Morse Tutoring Svc., 1985. Tutor Math. Ctr., Trinity Coll., 1995-96; lectr. Stamford Mus., 1985-2001; presenter and lectr. in field, 1996—; adj. instr. Middlesex Cmty. Tech. Coll., Conn., 1996-99; course asst. Wesleyan U., 1998-2001, instr. adult edn., 1998—; alt. consumer rep. Nat. Alliance for Mentally Ill-CT (NAMI-CT), 1998-99, spkrs. bur., 2000—. Contbr. articles to Jour. Am. Assn. Variable Star Obs., Deep Sky Mag., The Astronomical Jour.; observations of variable stars pub. on circulars of Cen. Bur. for Astron. Telegrams, Internat. Astron. Union, Smithsonian Astrophys. Obs. Mem. consumer support coun. Conn. Alliance for Mentally Ill., Hartford, 1997-98; mem. Friends of the Ctr. for the History of Physics. Named one of Outstanding Young Man of Am., 1987. Mem.: Friends of the Ctr. for the History of Physics, Astron. Soc. Coonabarabran (NSW, Australia), Riverside Astron. Soc., Westport Astron. Soc., Astron. League (long range planning com. 1992—94), Astron. Soc. Greater Hartford (pres. 1992—93), Fairfield County Astron. Soc. (treas. 1985—88, pres. 1988—94, v.p. 1994—96, acting treas. 1996—99, pres. 1996—99, v.p. 1999—2002, v.p., treas. 2002—), L.A. Astron. Soc., We. Observatorium (bd. dirs. 1994—2000), Internat. Dark Sky Assn., Mt. Wilson Obs. Assn., Astron. Soc. Pacific, Hungarian Astron. Assn., Royal Astron. Soc. Can., Am. Astron. Soc., Am. Assn. Variable Star Observers (coun. 1985—90, liaison and rep. to mems. in Hungary, contbr. Variable Star Atlas, edits. I and II, preliminary charts com., supernova search com., telescopes com., Observer award 1994), Nat. Alliance Mentally Ill-Conn., Mental Health Assn. Conn. (facilitator self-help support groups and adv. com. 1998—), We. Amateur Astronomers (pub. info. coord. 1989—90, v.p., acting pres. 1992, v.p. 1992—94, Caroline Herschel Astronomy project award 1988), Phi Beta Lambda (pres. local chpt. 1985), Golden Key.

GRIESEMER, ALLAN DAVID, retired museum director; b. Mayville, Wis., Aug. 13, 1935; s. Raymond John and Leone Emma (Fischer) G.; m. Nancy Jean Sternberg, June 6, 1959; children: David, Paul, Steven. AB, Augustana Coll., 1959; MS, U. Wis., 1963; PhD, U. Nebr., 1970. With intern program Newark Mus., 1961—62; curator earth sci. & planetarium Dayton Mus. Natural History, 1962—65; curator; coordinator ednl. services U. Nebr., Lincoln State Museum, 1965-77, assoc. prof., assoc. dir., 1977-79, acting dir., 1980-81, assoc. dir. and coordinator, 1981-82, interim dir., 1982-84; dir. San Bernardino County Mus., Calif., 1984-97, dir. emeritus, 1997—; mem. faculty dept. geology U. Nebr., Lincoln, 1968-80; lectr. geology U. Nebr., Lincoln State Mus., 1968-80; CEO, dir., curator Mousley Mus. Natural History, San Bernardino County Mus., Yucaipa, Calif., 1984-97; ret., 1997. Adj. prof. Calif. State U., San Bernardino, 1986. Contbr. articles to sci. jours., mus. publs., 1965— . Bd. dirs. San Bernardino County Mus. Assn.; Redland Music Assn. Prospect Park; Fortnightly Club; Inland Harvest; Redlands Hist. Mus.; Redlands Cmty. Hosp. Found.; mem. adv. bd. Redlands Cmty. Hosp.; bd. dirs. Friends of Calico, 1999—2003. Recipient Hon. award Sigma Gamma Epsilon, 1958 Mem. Paleontol. Soc., Nebr. Mus. Conf. (pres. 1976 79), Nebr. Geol. Soc., Nebr. Acad. Scis., Mountain Plains Conf., Mountain Plains Mus. Assn. (pres. 1979), Am. Assn. Museums (v.p. 1983), Rotary. Lutheran. Home: 306 La Colina Dr Redlands CA 92374-8247

GRIESER, JEANNE K. writer; b. Newton, Kans., June 23, 1960; d. Richard L. and Lorita M. Regier; m. Edward J. Grieser, May 2, 1981; children: Adam E., Micah J., Zachary J. BS in Elem. Edn., Bethel Coll., 1983. Author: (novels) The Greatest Of These Is Love, Adventures With The Anabaptists, Hands On Nature, Worship Bulletins; contbr. articles to mags. Personal E-mail: scribble@southwind.net.

GRIEVE, PIERSON MACDONALD, retired chemicals executive; b. Flint, Mich., Dec. 5, 1927; s. P.M. and Margaret (Leamy) G.; m. Florence R. Brogan, July 29, 1950; children: Margaret, Scott, Bruce. BSBA, Northwestern U., 1950; postgrad., U. Minn., 1955-56. Staff engr. Caterpillar Tractor Co., Peoria, Ill., 1950-52; mgmt. cons. A.T. Kearney & Co., Chgo., 1952-55; pres. Rap-in-Wax, Mpls., 1955-62; exec. AP Parts Corp., Toledo, 1962-67; pres., CEO Questor Corp., Toledo, 1967-82; CEO Ecolab Inc., St. Paul, 1983-96; ret., 1996. Bd. dirs. St. Paul Cos. Inc., Bank of Naples, Mesaba Aviation; ptnr. Paladium Equity Ptnrs. LLC. Adv. coun. J.L. Kellogg Grad. Sch. Mgmt., Northwestern U.; bd. dirs. Guthrie Theatre; bd. trustees St. Thomas U. With USNR, 1945-46. Mem. Chevaliers du Tastevin, Mpls. Club, Royal Poincisun Club (Naples), Beta Gamma Sigma (dirs. table). Roman Catholic.

GRIEVES, FOREST LESLIE, political science educator; b. Beatty, Nev., Sept. 19, 1938; s. William Arthur and Alice Louise (Parman) G.; m. Irmgard Katharina Spengler, Mar. 31, 1963; children: Kevin Michael, Emily Katharina. BA in Polit. Sci., Stanford U., 1960; MA in Polit. Sci., U. Nev., 1964; PhD in Govt., U. Ariz., 1967. Tchg. assoc. U. Ariz., Tucson, 1964-67; asst. prof. Western Ill. U., Macomb, 1967-69; asst. prof. polit. sci. U. Mont., Missoula, 1969-72, assoc. prof., 1972-76, prof., 1976—, dept. chmn., 1990—91, 1997—2001. Guest prof. U. Saarlandes, Saarbrücken, Germany, 1978-79, 81; scholar-diplomat U.S. Dept. State, Washington, 1980; participant Friedrich Ebert Found. Seminar, Saarbrücken, 1982, Konrad Adenauer Found.-U.S. Dept. State Seminar, Bosen, Germany, 1982; Fulbright sr. lectr., Germany, 1978-79. Author: Supranationalism and International Adjudication, 1969, Conflict and Order, 1977; editor: Transnationalism in World Politics and Business, 1979; contbr. over 100 articles to profl. jours. and encys. 1st lt. U.S. Army, 1960-62. Rsch. grantee NEH, 1973, German Acad. Exch. Svc., 1978, 87; rsch. fellow Alexander von Humboldt Found., Germany, 1979, 81; Fulbright-Hays sr. scholar, Germany, 1984, 98. Mem. German Studies Assn. Office: U Mont Dept Polit Sci Missoula MT 59812-5832 E-mail: forest.grieves@umontana.edu.

GRIEVES, ROBERT BELANGER, engineering educator; b. Evanston, Ill., Oct. 15, 1935; s. Roy and Marie (Belanger) G.; m. Sandra Lee Artman, Dec. 10, 1966; children: Christopher Robert, Jaime Robert. BA in Russian, Northwestern U., 1956, MS in Chem. Engring, 1959, PhD in Chem. Engring, 1961. Asst. prof. civil engring. Northwestern U., Evanston, 1961-64; from asst. prof. to assoc. prof. civil and environ. engring. Ill. Inst. Tech., Chgo., 1964-67; prof., chmn. chem. engring. dept. U. Ky., Lexington, 1967-79, dir. Ky. Water Resources Rsch. Inst., 1973-82, assoc. dean adminstrn., grad. programs and rsch. Coll. Engring., 1976-82; dean Coll. Engring., prof. civil engring. U. Tex.-El Paso, 1982-89, prof. civil engring., instr. Slavic langs., 1989-94. Cons. to industry in air and water pollution control; spl. employee, mem. effluent stds. and water quality info. adv. com. U.S. EPA, Washington, 1975—79; mem. commn. on environ. health US Armed Forces Epidemiol. Bd. Office Surgeon Gen., Washington, 1962—79. Author articles on phys.-chem. separations, indsl. waste treatment. Mem. Phi Beta Kappa, Tau Beta Pi. Home: 705 Cresta Mira Dr El Paso TX 79912-2622

GRIFA, ROBERT JAMES, music educator; b. Waterloo, N.Y., Sept. 21, 1956; s. Mary Grifa; m. Bonnie Michelle Riehle, July 15, 1978; 1 child, Christopher. MusB, SUNY, 1978; MusM in in Conducting, VanderCook Coll. of Music, 1985. Cert. Music Educator Music Educators Nat. Conf., 1992. Band dir. Savannah-Chatham (Ga.) County Pub. Schools, 1978—83, Springville-Griffith (N.Y.) Inst. Pub. Schools, 1983—85, Jamestown (N.Y.) Pub. Schs., 1985—97, Chesapeake (Va.) Pub. Schs., Chesapeake, Va. Percussionist Savannah (Ga.) Symphony Orch., 1978—83, Va. Wind Symphony, Norfolk, Va., 1998—; percussion instr. Armstrong State Coll., Savannah, Ga., 1979—83. Musician: (albums) Music of Claude T. Smith, vol. 3; contbr. articles to profl. jours. Named Most Outstanding Instrumental Music Tchr. in Chautauqua County, Fredonia Chamber Players, 1996. Mem.: VicFirth, Inc., Scholastic Edn. Program, Va. Band and Orch. Directors Assn., Percussive Arts Soc., Va. Music Educators Assn., Music Educators Nat. Conf., Phi Mu Alpha Sinfonia. Avocations: computers, golf, tennis, reading, movies. Home: 458 Supplejack Ct Chesapeake VA 23320

GRIFF, HARRY, lawyer; b. Worcester, Mass., May 27, 1952; s. Joseph J. and Dorothy J. (Goldsmith) Griff; m. Joan G. Garovoy, May 27, 1973; children: Joshua, Jordana. BA with high distinction, U. Mich., 1973, JD with distinction, 1977. Bar: Mich. 1977, Colo. 1982. Legal counsel Social Security Adminstrn., HHS, Balt., 1978—79; trial atty. U.S. Dept. Justice, Washington, 1979—81; assoc. Dufford, Waldeck, Ruland, Wise & Milburn, Grand Junction, Colo., 1981—83; atty. Harmon & Griff, P.C., Grand Junction, Colo., 1983—86; ptnr. Foster, Larson, Laiche & Griff, Grand Junction, Colo., 1986—99, Griff, Larson, Laiche & Volkmann, Grand Junction, Colo., 1999—2001, Griff, Larson & Laiche, Grand Junction, Colo., 2001—. Legal counsel Grand Junction br., NAACP, Colo., 1983—84, Walker Field, Colo. Pub. Airport Authority, Grand Junction, 1984—97; bd. dirs. Paradise Hills Homeowners Assn., Grand Junction, Colo., 1984—87, Ptnrs., Inc., 1988—94, KPRN Pub. Radio Sta., 1989—91. Bd. dirs. Grand Junction Jewish Cmty. Ctr., 1984—89, Colo. Lawyers Trust Acct. Found., 1986—92, Mus. Western Colo., 1997—2001, Vol. Ctrl., 1996—99, Downtown Devel. Authority, 2002—, Avalon Theatre, 2002—, Friends of Kulture and Entertainment for the Grand Valley, 2003—; vol. KAFM Cmty. Radio, 1996—. Mem.: ABA, Mesa County Bar Assn. (bd. dirs. legal aid program 1984—89), Colo. Bar Assn., Assn. Trial Lawyers Am. Democrat. Home: 2636 Chestnut Dr Grand Junction CO 81506-8390 Office: Griff Larson & Laiche 422 White Ave Fl 3 Grand Junction CO 81501-2555 Business E-Mail: harry@gllvlaw.com.

GRIFFEL, L. MICHAEL, music educator, researcher; b. N.Y.C., Nov. 12, 1942, s. Joseph and Klara Griffel; m. Margaret Ross, Sept. 15, 1968; 1 child, David S. BA, Yale U., 1963; MS, Juilliard Sch. Music, N.Y.C., 1966; MA, Columbia U., 1968, PhD, 1975. Adj. lectr. music CUNY, 1970—85, prof. music, 1985—, asst. dean arts and scis., 1999—2000, assoc. dean arts and scis., 2000—02, acting assoc. provost, 2002—. Grad. faculty Mannes Coll. Music, N.Y.C., 1980—99, Juilliard Sch., N.Y.C., 1997—; artist-tchr. Merrywood Music Sch., Lenox, Mass., 1965—67; editor-in-chief Current Musicology, N.Y.C., 1970—72. Contbr. chapters to books, articles to profl. jours. Mem.: Am. Musicol. Soc. (coun. 1969—71), Am. Schubert Inst. (bd. advisors 1995—), Am. Beethoven Soc. (v.p. N.Y. chpt. 1995—). Achievements include research in Schubert's working methods as a symphonist. Home: 3135 Johnson Ave Apt 9E Bronx NY 10463 Office: Hunter Coll 695 Park Ave New York NY 10021 E-mail: lgriffel@hunter.cuny.edu.

GRIFFEN, AGNES MARTHE, library administrator; b. Ft. Dauphin, Madagascar, Aug. 25, 1935; d. Frederick Stang and Alvilde Margrethe (Torvik) Hallanger; m. Thomas Michael Griffen (div. Nov. 1969); children: Shaun Helen Griffen D'Antoni, Christopher Patrick, Adam Andrew; m. John H.P. Hall, Aug. 26, 1980. BA cum laude in English, Pacific Luth. U., 1957; MLS, U. Wash., 1965; Urban Exec. cert., MIT, 1976; postgrad., Harvard U., 1993. Cert. librarian, Wash., Md., Ariz. Area children's libr. King County Libr. Sys., Seattle, 1965-68, coord. instl. librs., 1968-71, dep. libr. for staff and program devel., 1971-74; dep. libr. dir. Tucson Pub. Libr., 1974-80; dir. Montgomery County Dept. Pub. Librs., Rockville, Md., 1980-96; libr. dir. Tucson-Pima Pub. Libr., 1997—. Lectr. Grad. Libr. Sch., U. Ariz., Tucson, 1976-77, 79; vis. lectr. Sch. Librarianship, U. Wash., Seattle, 1983. Contbr. articles to library periodicals and profl. jours. Active Md. Humanities Coun., Balt., 1986-92, Ariz. Humanities Coun., Phoenix, 1977-80; charter mem. Exec. Women's Coun. of So. Ariz., Tucson, 1979-80; mem. coun. Nat. Capital Area Pub. Access Network, 1992-94, pres. bd., 1993-94, Ariz. Statewide Libr. Devel. Commn., 2000-02' mem. adv. coun. to Ariz. State Libr., 1998--. Recipient Helping Hand award Md. Assn. of the Deaf, 1985, Cert. Recognition Montgomery County Hispanic Employees Assn., 1985; Henry scholar U. Washington Sch. Librarianship, 1965. Mem. ALA (exec. bd. 1989 93, divsn. pres. pub. libr. assn. bd. 1981 82, councilor-at-large 1972-76, 86-93, chmn. com. on program evaluation and support 1987-88, legis. com. 1998-2002), Ariz. State Libr. Assn. (legis. com. 1997--), Md. Libr. Assn. Democrat. Home: 1951 N El Moraga Dr Tucson AZ 85745-9070 E-mail: agriffe1@ci.tucson.az.us.

GRIFFEN, CLYDE CHESTERMAN, retired history educator; b. Sioux City, Iowa, July 29, 1929; s. Clyde Rumbaugh and Rosanna Susan (Chesterman) G.; m. Sarah Goldsborough Donoho, Feb. 14, 1959; children: John Winslow, Sarah Bolling, Robert Henry. BA, State U. Iowa, 1952; MA, Columbia U., 1953, PhD, 1960. Lectr. Columbia U., N.Y.C., 1954-57; instr. history Vassar Coll, Poughkeepsie, N.Y., 1957-61, asst. prof., 1961-67, assoc. prof., 1967-75, Lucy Maynard Salmon prof. Am. history, 1975-92, chmn. dept. history, 1982-85, dir. Am. culture program, 1977-79. Author: (with Sally Griffen) Natives and Newcomers: The Ordering of Opportunity in Mid-Nineteenth-Century Poughkeepsie, 1978; editor: New Perspectives on Poughkeepsie's Past, 1988; co-editor: Meanings for Manhood: Constructions of Masculinity in Victorian America, 1990; co-author: Full Steam Ahead in Poughkeepsie: The Story of Coeducation at Vassar, 1966-1974, 2000. NSF grantee, 1973-74; Nat. Humanities Inst. fellow, 1976-77; Fulbright rsch. scholar N.Z., 1984. Mem. Social Sci. History Assn. (editorial bd. 1976-89). Home: 9 MacCracken Ln Poughkeepsie NY 12604-0001

GRIFFEN, WARD O., JR., surgeon, educator, medical board executive; b. New Orleans, July 21, 1928; s. Ward O. and Dorothea (Rosenberg) G.; m. Margaret Mary Taylor, Dec. 27, 1952; children— Peter, Mary Ellen, Steven, Colleen, Timothy, Margaret Mary, Leah. AB, Princeton U., 1948; MD, Cornell U., 1953; PhD, U. Minn., 1963. Diplomate Am. Bd. Surgery, Am. Bd. Thoracic Surgery. Asst. prof. dept. surgery U. Minn, Mpls., 1962-65; assoc. prof. U. Ky. Coll. Medicine, Lexington, 1965-67, prof., chmn. dept. surgery, 1967-84; exec. dir., sec.-treas. Am. Bd. Surgery, Phila., 1984-94; prof. surgery U. Ky. Coll. Medicine, Lexington, 1994—. Contbr. articles to profl. jours. Served to comdr. USNR, 1955-67 John R. Markle Found. scholar, 1962-67 Fellow ACS (bd. govs. 1972-78, 2d v.p. 1995-96); mem. Am. Surg. Assn. (2d v.p. 1989), So. Surg. Assn. (1st v.p. 1995-96, pres. 1997-98), Assn. Acad. Surgery (pres. 1971), Ctrl. Surg. Assn. (sec. 1980-82, pres. 1984), Soc. Surgery Alimentary Tract (v.p. 1984-85), Halsted Soc. (sec. 1983-85, pres. 1986). Republican. Roman Catholic. Avocations: cooking, gardening, fishing. E-mail: popswog@coslink.net.

GRIFFENHAGEN, GEORGE BERNARD, trade association executive; b. Portland, Oreg., June 9, 1924; s. Richard Bernard and Clara (Schoenian) G.; m. Joan Helen Houston, June 21, 1946; children: Gary Bernard, Gordon Wesley, Barbara Clare. BS in Pharmacy, U. So. Calif., 1949, MS, 1950; student, Fresno State Coll., 1946, U. London, 1948. Dir. research Nion Corp., Hollywood, Calif., 1950-52; curator div. med. scis. Smithsonian Instn., Washington, 1952-59; sec. sect. history of pharmacy Am. Pharm. Assn., Washington, 1952-59, pres. local chpt., 1958-59, assoc. exec. dir., 1959-89, hon. pres., 1990-91; trustee Am. Pharm. Assn. Found., Washington, 1989-94; editor Jour. Am. Pharm. Assn., Washington, 1960-76; sec.-gen. 4th Pan Am. Congress Pharmacy and Biochemistry, Washington, 1957; sec. organizing com. 31st Internat. Congress Pharm. Scis., Washington, 1971; sec.-gen. Internat. Congress History of Pharmacy, Washington, 1983, Japan-U.S. Congress of Pharm. Scis., Honolulu, 1987; v.p. Pan Am. Pharm. and Biochem. Fedn., 1963-82, 85-91, Pharmacy World Congress, Washington, 1991. U.S. del. Internat. Pharm. Fedn. Gen. Assemblies, London, 1955, Brussels, 1958, Copenhagen, 1960, Vienna, 1962, Amsterdam, 1964, Hamburg, 1968, Geneva, 1970, Lisbon, 1972, Rome, 1974, Warsaw, 1976, Cannes, 1978; U.S. del. FIP Coun., Bucharest, 1969, Dublin, 1975, Montreal, 1985, Helsinki, 1986, Amsterdam, 1987, Sydney, 1988, Munich, 1989, Istanbul, 1990, Lyon, 1992, Tokyo, 1993, Lisbon, 1994, Jerusalem, 1996, Vancouver, 1997, The Hague, 1998, Barcelona, 1999, Vienna, 2000; congress coord., The Hague, 1977; U.S. del. Pan Am. Fedn. Pharmacy Congress, Mexico City, 1963, Buenos Aires, 1966, Caracas, 1969, Panama, 1972, Guatemala City, 1985, Santo Domingo, 1988, Buenos Aires, 1994, San Jose, Costa Rica, 1997, Rio de Janeiro, 2000; U.S. del. Internat. Congress History of Pharmacy, Budapest, Hungary, 1981, Fedn. Asian Pharm. Assns. Congress, Seoul, Korea, 1982; mem. Nat. Action Com. on Drug Edn., Office of Edn., 1970-71, Va. Gov.'s Coun. on Narcotic and Drug Abuse Control, 1970-72. Editor: Scalpel and Tongs, 1972-73; Contbr. articles to profl. jours. Mem. Fairfax County (Va.) Rep. Com., 1962-97; adminstrv. asst. to chmn. Va. State Rep. Com., 1969-71; life mem. Rep. Nat. Com., 1979—; founding pres. Nat. Coordinating Coun. on Drug Edn., 1968-69. Served with C.E. AUS, World War II, ETO. Recipient Pfizer Merit award U.S. CD Coun., 1964, U. So. Calif. Alumnus award, 1969; Hugo H. Schaefer award Am. Pharm. Assn., 1984; Disting. Svc. award Pharmacy Guild of Australia, 1988, Internat. Pharmacy Jour. Editor's prize, 1989, 95, Remington Honor medal Am. Pharm. Assn., 1991; named to Nat. Philatelic Writers Hall of Fame, 1990. Mem. Am. Inst. History of Pharmacy (pres. 1960-61, Edward Kremers award 1969, sec. 1991—), Friends of Hist. Pharmacy (pres. 1957-58), Pharm. Wholesalers Assn. (Distinguished Service award 1971), Am. Topical Assn. (1st v.p. 1972-75, pres. 1976-79, pres. med. subjects unit 1969-72, Distinguished Topical Philatelist award 1970, Myrtle Watt Med. Philately Topicalist award 1980, editor Topical Time 1992—), Am. Philatelic Congress (Jere Hess Barr award 1969), Am. Philatelic Soc. (sec.-treas. Writers Unit 1982— ; U.S. commr. to Internat. Exhbn. Thematic Philately, Basel, Switzerland 1983, Luff award 2003), Am. Revenue Assn. (named to Sterling Meml. Roll of Disting. Fiscalists 1979), Council Philatelic Orgns. (treas. 1983-91), Internat. Pharm. Fedn. (hon.), Philatelic Lit. Assn., Académie Internationale d'Histoire de la Pharmacie (treas. 1971-81, 1989-97), Pharm. Soc. Gt. Britain (hon.), Sigma Xi, Rho Chi, Phi Kappa Psi. Home: 2501 Drexel St Vienna VA 22180-6906 Office: Am Pharm Assn 2215 Constitution Ave NW Washington DC 20037-2907 E-mail: ggriffenhagen@aphanet.org.

GRIFFETH, LANDIS KING, nuclear medicine physician; b. Greenville, S.C., Aug. 3, 1956; s. Jesse Ellis and Mary Alice (King) G.; m. Terri Blount, Aug. 6, 1978. BA Chemistry & Zoology summa cum laude, Duke U., 1977, PhD in Pharmacology, 1983, MD, 1984. Diplomate Am. Bd. Nuclear Medicine. Postdoctoral rsch. fellow Duke U. Sch. Pharmacology, Durham, N.C., 1983-84; resident in diagnostic radiology Mallinckrodt Inst. of Radiology, Washington U., St. Louis, 1984-86, resident in nuclear medicine, 1986-87, chief resident in nuclear medicine, 1987-88, asst. prof. radiology, 1988-93; dir. nuclear medicine Baylor U. Med. Ctr., Dallas, 1993—; med. dir. North Tex. Clin. P.E.T. Inst., Dallas, 1998—. Dir. nuclear medicine and P.E.T., Am. Radiology Assn., Dallas, 1993—, nat. med. dir., P.E.T., U.S. Oncology, 2000—. Assoc. editor Radiology Jour., 1993-2000; cons. to editor Radiology, 2000-02; contbr. numerous articles to profl. jours; reviewer med. jours. Mem. Univ. Park United Meth. Ch.; bd. dirs. Cavalier Health Found. Mem. Am. Coll. Radiology (nuc. medicine accreditation com.), Am. Coll. Nuclear Physicians, Soc. Nuclear Medicine, Acad. Molecular Imaging (nat. patient adv. com.), Inst. for Clin. P.E.T., Radiol. Soc. N.Am., Am. Soc. for Law Enforcement Tng., Tex. Med. Assn., Tex. Radiol. Soc., Dallas County Med. Soc., Phi Lambda Upsilon, Alpha Omega Alpha. United Methodist. Avocations: target shooting, reading, dogs, travel. Office: Baylor U Med Ctr 3500 Gaston Ave Dallas TX 75246-2096 E-mail: LK.Griffeth@BaylorHealth.edu.

GRIFFEY, KAREN ROSE, special education educator; b. Phila., May 15, 1955; d. Arnold and Jacqueline (Wasserman) Salaman; m. Kenneth Paul Griffey, June 18, 1988; 1 child, Jessica; stepchildren: Kristina, Joseph. BS in Elem. Edn., W. Chester U., Pa., 1977; cert. Paralegal Studies, Nat. Ctr. Paralegal Tng., Atlanta, 1986; M in Edn., U. Ga., 1994. Adult habilitation program Jewish Vocat. Svc., Phila., 1977-79; instr. Phila. Sch. Sys., 1979-81; tchr. 3rd grade Fla. Sch. Sys., Fort Myers, 1981-86; paralegal Atlanta, 1986-89; tchr. Interrelated Sharp Middle Sch., Covington, Ga., 1989-91; tchr. Spl. Kindergarten Rorterdale and Fairview Elem., Covington, Ga., 1991-96; spl. edn. tchr. Hickory Flat Elem. Sch., 1997-99; interrelated resource tchr., spl. ed. chair Meml. Middle Sch., 1999—. Tchr., liaison, bd. mem., PAC rep., bldg. rep. Tchrs. Assn. Lee County, Fort Myers, Fla., 1981-86. Tchr. liaison Senators and Reps. in Fla. Legis., Tallahassee, 1981-86; PAC bd., 1981-86; exec. bd. mem. Leadership Team. of Tchrs. Assn. Lee County, Ft. Myers, Fla., 1981-86; Bargaining Team mdm. Tchrs. Assn. Lee County, Ft. Myers, Fla., 1981-86. Recipient Svc. award for working with handicapped, Phila. Sch. Sys., 1973; Phila scholarship Phils Sch. Sys., Mayor's Sch., Phila., 1973; NEA Svc. award in Edn., NEA, Ft. Myers, Fla., 1980. Mem. Coun. for Exceptional Children, Nat. Mus. of Women in the Arts, B'Nai B'rith, Spl. Olympics, Nat. Multiple Sclerosis Soc., Kappa Delta Pi. Democrat. Jewish. Avocations: reading, sewing, classical and jazz music, writing, arts and crafts. Home: 2580 Highland Dr Conyers GA 30013-1908 Office: Meml Middle Sch 3205 Underwood Rd SE Conyers GA 30013-2309

GRIFFEY, KEN, JR., (GEORGE KENNETH GRIFFEY JR.), professional baseball player; b. Donora, Pa., Nov. 21, 1969; Grad., H.S., Cin. Outfielder Seattle Mariners, 1987—99, Cin. Reds, 2000—. Named Most Valuable Player, All-Star Game, 1992; named to All-Star Team, 1990—95, Am. League Silver Slugger team, Sporting News, 1991, 1993—94, 1996, All-Star team, 1991, 1993—94; recipient Gold Glove award, 1990—96. Office: Cincinnati Reds 100 Cinergy Fld Cincinnati OH 45202-3543

GRIFFEY, LINDA BOYD, lawyer; b. Keokuk, Iowa, Aug. 6, 1949; d. Marshall Coulter and Geraldine Vivian (White) Boyd; m. John Jay Griffey, June 24, 1972. BS in Pharmacy, U. Iowa, 1972; JD, Duke U., 1980. Bar: Calif. 1980; lic. pharmacist, Iowa, N.C. Pharmacist Davenport (Iowa) Osteo. Hosp., 1972-75, Wagner Pharmacy, Clinton, Iowa, 1975-77, Durham (N.C.) County Gen. Hosp., 1977-80; assoc. O'Melveny & Myers, L.A., 1980-88, ptnr., 1988—. Spkr., writer in field of employee benefits and exec. compensation; former pres. L.A. chpt. Western Pension and Benefits Conf., 1998-99. Active L.A. Philharm. Bus. & Profl. Assn.; bd. dirs. Hillsides Home for Children, Pasadena Playhouse. Mem. ABA (employee benefits com. tax sect.), Am. Law Inst., L.A. County Bar Assn. (former chair employee benefits com. 1994-95), L.A. Duke Bar Assn. (pres. 1987-90, 91-92), Rotary (L.A. chpt. bd. dirs. 1995-97). Avocations: golf, reading, swimming. Office: O'Melveny & Myers 400 S Hope St Los Angeles CA 90071-2899 E-mail: lgriffey@omm.com.

GRIFFIE, GAYLE G. retired principal; b. York Springs, Pa., Mar. 27, 1941; d. Lawrence and Elsie Gulden; m. Harold Leon Griffie, Aug. 8, 1964. BSEd, Shippensburg State Coll., 1962, MEd, 1966; Prin.'s Cert., We. Md. Coll., 1979. Tchr. Spring Grove (Pa.) Area Sch. Dist., 1962-63; tchr. grade four to tchr. grade five Upper Adams Sch. Dist., Biglerville, Pa., 1963-82, prin. grades K-6, 1983-98. Adv. coun. mem. Adams County Children and Youth Svc., Gettysburg, Pa., 1979-82. Artist-in-edn. grantee Pa. Coun. for the Arts, 1987-88. Mem.: Susquehanna Iris Soc., Am. Iris Soc., Biglerville Hist. and Preservation Soc. (mem. com.), Adams County Water Garden Club, Delta Kappa Gamma (Beta Kappa chpt. first v.p. 2000—02, pres. 2002—).

GRIFFIN, ADELE, writer; b. Phila., Pa., July 29, 1970; d. Robert Earnest Watson and Priscillsa Goodwyn Sands; m. Erich Paul Mauff, Aug. 16, 1997. BS, U Pa., 1993. Writer Hyperion Books, 1996—, Putnam/G.P. Putnam's Sons, N.Y.C., 2000—. Author: Split Just Right, 1997 (Parents Choice Award), Sons of Liberty, 1997 (Nat. Book Award Finalist, Am. Lib. Assn. Best Book), The Other Shepards, 1998 (Pub. Weekly Bes Book of the Yr., Am. Lib. Assn. Best Book, Sch. Lib. Jour. Best Book of the Yr.), Dive, 1999, Amandine, 2001 (Pub. Weekly Bes Book of the Yr.), Hannah Divided, 2002 (Am. Lib. Assn. Best Book), Overnight, 2003, Witch Twins, Witch Twins at Camp Bliss, Witch Twins and Melody Malady, Witch Twins and the Ghost of Glenn Bly, books have been translated into Spanish, German, and Italian. Mem.: Soc. of Children's Book Writers adn Illustrators, N.Y. Pub. Lib., Southern Poverty Law Ctr. Democrat. Avocations: yoga, oil painting. Home: 163 East 71st St New York NY 10021

GRIFFIN, ALAN NASH, psychologist; b. Dallas, Oct. 23, 1943; s. Jack Forrest and Mary Helen (Nash) G. BA, U. North Tex., 1965, MA, 1966; PhD, U. Fla., 1971. Lic. psychologist, Tex.; cert. group psychotherapist; cert. cons. in clin. hypnosis. Psychologist Hillsborough County MHMR Ctr., Tampa, Fla., 1972-73; asst. prof. U. North Tex., Denton, 1973-74; pvt. practice Dallas, 1973-88, Austin, Tex., 1988—. Cons. Tex. Rehab. Commn., 1974-93, U.S. Dept. Labor, 1987-88, Plano, Tex. Sch. System, 1974-81, Mesquite Tex. Sch. System, 1974-75, Dallas Soc. for Crippled Children, 1974-75; asst. prof. psychology U. North Tex., 1973-74; adj. prof. So. Meth. U., 1975-77, U. South Fla., 1972-73; staff psychologist Dallas Child Guidance Clinic, 1969, Beverly Hills Hosp., 1967-69, Rusk, Tex. State Hosp., 1966-67. Editor (video series) Psychology Century Series, 1992; contbr. articles to profl. jours. Pres. Frontier Toastmasters, 1990; state del. Dem. Party, 1982-86, precinct chair 1968-69; pres., bd. dirs. Suicide Prevention Ctr., Dallas, 1978. Mem. Assn. of Psychol. Type (life), Am. Psychol. Assn., Am. Group Psychotherapy Assn. (clin. mem.), Am. Soc. of Clin. Hypnosis (clin. mem.), Am. Assn. of Marriage and Family Therapists (clin. mem.), Am. Assn. of Sex Educators, Conselors and Therapists (life). Avocations: traveling, sailing, concerts, reading, writing. Home: 2704 Oakhaven Dr Austin TX 78704-3832 Office: 1600 W 38th St Ste 428 Austin TX 78731-6409 E-mail: dralangriffin@austin.rr.com.

GRIFFIN, BETTY JO, elementary school educator; b. Monroe, La., Jan. 12, 1947; d. Julia Odell (Foster) Calhoun; divorced; 1 child, James Odell Griffin, Jr. BA, So. U., 1969; MA, San Francisco State U., 1975; PhD, LaSalle U., 2000. Cert. elem. tchr., Calif. Tchr. lang. arts Oakland (Calif.) Unified Sch. Dist., 1970-73, Garfield Elem. Sch., 1973-77, 1977-96; splty. prep. libr. and lang. arts tchr. Webster Acad., 1996—. Trustee Allen Temple Bapt. Ch., Oakland, Calif., 1987—; lit. tutor Delta Sigma Theta, Oakland, 1990—; chairperson African Am. Chain Read In, 1995—. Recipient Libr. Protection Fund award State Dept. Edn., 1997, Leadership award Dem. Nat. Com., 1997. Mem. NAACP, NEA, Oakland Edn. Assn. (bd. dirs.), Calif. Tchrs. Assn. (coun. of edn. 1996), Nat. Alliance Black Sch. Educators, Delta Sigma Theta, Phi Delta Kappa. Democrat. Avocations: reading, helping others, public speaking. Home: 2559 Oliver Ave Oakland CA 94605-4820 E-mail: BettyJGri@aol.com.

GRIFFIN, BETTY LOU, not-for-profit developer, educator; d. Julius Craven and Rachel Idell Best; m. Jack Wayne Griffin, May 28, 1960; children: Cheryle Louann, Melanie Lynn Young, Penelope. BS in Elem. Edn. magna cum laude, Campbell U., 1967; ME in Adult and Cmty. Coll. Edn., N.C. State U., 1974; ME in Adminstrn. and Supervision, Fayetteville State U., 1995. Tchr. Sampson County Schs., Clinton, NC, 1965-67, Clinton City Schs., 1967-87; founder, exec. dir. U Care Inc., Sampson County Domestic Violence Program, Clinton, 1996—; CEO, bd. dirs., exec. dir. On Track Youth Svcs., Clinton, 2000—02. Evening bus. math. instr. Sampson CC, 1973—75, instr., 1975—77; notary pub. State of N.C., 1995—. Author: (poems) Poetry Collection, 1997, Rhyme in Time, 1999. Founder, dir. Sampson County Women's Assembly, 1994, 1996, 1998; legis. chmn., monitor chmn. Youth Adv. Coun., Sampson, 1994—98; founder, pres., exec. dir. Sampson County Coun. Women, 1995—. Named N.C. Dem. Women Poet Laureate, 1997, Sampson County Disting. Woman of the Yr., Sampson County Coun. Women, 1998; recipient Carpathian award, N.C. Equity, 1996. Mem.: DAR, N.C. Dem. Women (mem. exec. bd. 1995—99, 1st poet laureate 1997—), Sampson County Dem. Women (v.p. 1993, 2d v.p. 1996—97, 2000—03, pres. 1994—95, 1998—99), Order of Eastern Star, Delta Kappa Gamma. Democrat. Methodist. Avocations: reading, creative writing, arts and crafts, hunting, fishing. Home and Office: 2535 Rosebory Hwy Clinton NC 28328

GRIFFIN, BRODERICK DEVOND, science educator, political consultant; b. Montgomery, Ala., Nov. 26, 1976; s. Marche Lanetta Griffin. AS, BS, Troy State U., Montgomery, Ala., 2000; BS, Ala. A&M U., 2000. Tchr. Montgomery Pub. Sch., Ala., 1999—2001. Mem. adv. bd. Troy State U., Montgomery, Ala., 2000—. Chmn. Montgomery County Young Dems., Ala., 2001; bd. dirs. So. Christian Leadership, Montgomery, Ala., 2001. Mem.: Ala. Young Dems. (rep. 1999—2001), Montgomery Dem. Club, Kappa Alpha Psi. Democrat. Baptist. Avocations: tennis, golf. Home: 3366 Rosa L Parks Ave Montgomery AL 36105

GRIFFIN, CAMPBELL ARTHUR, JR., retired lawyer; b. Joplin, Mo., July 17, 1929; s. Campbell Arthur and Clara M. (Smith) G.; m. Margaret Ann Adams, Oct. 19, 1958; children: Campbell A., Laura Ann. BA, U. Mo., 1951, MA in Acctg., 1952; JD, U. Tex., 1957. Bar: Tex. 1957. Assoc. Vinson & Elkins, LLP, Houston, 1957-67, ptnr., 1968-92, mgmt. com., 1981-90, mng. ptnr. Dallas, 1986-89. Adj. prof. adminstrv. sci. Jones Grad. Sch. Adminstrn., Rice U., 1992-94. Mem. ofcl. bd. Bethany Christian Ch., Houston, 1962-69, chmn. bd. elders, 1968; bd. dirs. Houston Pops Orch., 1982-87, Cornell Co. Inc. (NYSE), 1996-2000; councilman City of Hunters Creek Village, Tex., 1993-95; pres. Windcliff Property Owners Assn., Estes Park, Colo., 1995-96; bd. dirs. Cornell Cos., Inc. (NYSE), 1996-2000; active St. Martin's Epsicopal Ch., Houston. Mem. Houston Bar Assn., State Bar Tex. (bus. law sect. chmn. 1974-75), Tex. Bus Law Found. (chmn. 1988-89, dir. 1988-2000), Houston Racquet Club (dir. 1992-94).

GRIFFIN, CARLETON HADLOCK, accountant, educator; b. Richmond Heights, Mo., Oct. 30, 1928; s. Merle Leroy and Bernice Hilder Edwards (Nelson) G.; m. Mary Lou Goodrich, Dec. 26, 1953; children: Julia, Anne. BBA, U. Mich., 1950, JD, MBA, U. Mich., 1953. Mem. audit and tax staff Touche Ross & Co., Detroit, 1955-59, adminstrv. partner Denver, 1959-71, nat. tax dir. N.Y.C., 1971-72, nat. dir. ops. and adminstrn., 1972-74, chmn. bd., 1974-82, sr. ptnr., 1982-85, regional ptnr., 1983-85; prof. acctg. U. Mich., 1985-95. Dir. Paton Acctg. Ctr., U. Mich., 1997-2001. Contbr. articles to profl. jours. Sr. warden St. Paul's Episcopal Ch., Darien, Conn., 1979-81; trustee Siena Heights Coll., Adrian, Mich., 1988-2000. Served with Fin. Corps AUS, 1953-55. Mem. AICPA, Colo. Soc. CPAs (pres. 1970-71), N.Y. Soc. CPAs, Mich. Soc. CPAs. Republican.

GRIFFIN, CAROLYN LEIGH, English educator, genealogist; b. Ypsilanti, Mich, Nov. 2, 1945; d. William Beckwith Fuqua and Hazel Marie (Gray) Lucado; m. Earnest Ellsworth Griffin, June 17, 1967; 1 child, Michael Allen. BA, Eastern Mich. U., 1967, MA, 1972. Cert. tchr. English and history, Mich. Substitute English tchr. Ypsilanti, Lincoln, Willow Run, Ypsilanti, Mich., 1967-68; English tchr. Ypsilanti HS, 1968—. Spkr. in field Mich. Reading Assn., 1988—, Mich. Coun. Tchr. English, 1990—. Author: (genealogy/family history) Lucadou, Lookadoo, Luckado, and Lucado Family History, 1986, Lucadou, Lookadoo, Luckado, and Lucado Family History, supplements, 1987, 1991, Lucadou, Lookadoo, Luckado, and Lucado Family History, 4th supplement, 2001. Recipient 1st and 2d Pl. awards for The Palladian creative arts mag. for Ypsilanti HS, Am. Scholastic Press, 1993—2002. Mem. Mich. Coun. Tchr. English, Nat. Coun. of Tchr. of English, Geneal. Soc. Washtenaw County (edn. dir., spkr.), Assoc. of Profl. Geneologists. Baptist. Avocation: genealogy. Home: 1200 S Harris Rd Ypsilanti MI 48198-6513 Office: Ypsilanti HS 2095 Packard Rd Ypsilanti MI 48197-1833

GRIFFIN, CHRISTOPHER OAKLEY, healthcare professional, humanities educator, entrepreneur; b. Memphis, Apr. 27, 1970; s. Charles Ray Griffin and Gladys Lee (Oakley) Slappey. BA in English, Miss. Coll., 1992; MA in English, Baylor U., 1996; M in Humanities, U. Dallas, 1998. Tchg. asst. dept. English, Baylor U., Waco, Tex., 1993-95; hosp. worker Baylor Med. Ctr. at Irving, Tex., 1996-98; co-founder, dir. project devel. ReCare, Inc., Austin, Tex., 1999-2001; prin. C.O. Griffin Consulting, 2001—; assoc. curator of edn., univ. programs Blanton Mus. Art, 2002; co-founder, COO Talon Tech., 2002—. Adj. faculty Brookhaven Coll., Dallas, 1998. Author: poetry, criticism, philosophy. Scholar Presdl. scholar, Miss. Coll., Clinton, 1988—92. Avocation: guitar.

GRIFFIN, CLAYTON HOUSTOUN, retired power company engineer, lecturer; b. Atlanta, June 14, 1925; s. George Clayton and Eugenia (Johnston) G.; m. Gloria Giegel Handley; 1 child, Clayton Houstoun; m. Lela Lounsbery Griffin, June 6, 1953; children: Lela Griffin Lofgren, George Duncan Bryan, Phillips Lounsbery B.E.E., Ga. Inst. Tech., 1945, MS in E.E., 1950. Registered profl. engr., Ga. Tester Ga. Power Co., Atlanta, 1949-51, test engr., 1953-58, protection engr., 1958-63, chief protection engr., 1963-79, mgr. system protection and control, 1979-89. Contbr. tech. papers to profl. publs. Trustee Ga. Tech Nat. Alumni Assn., Atlanta, 1977-80. Served to lt. comdr. USNR, 1943-47, 51-53 Named Engr. of Yr., Ga. Power Engring. Soc., Atlanta, 1966, Ga. Soc. Profl. Engrs., Atlanta, 1984; named to Sch. of Engring. Hall of Fame, Ga. Inst. Tech., 2002. Fellow IEEE (chmn. Atlanta chpt. 1974, chmn. stds. com. on dispersed generation 1982-89, chmn. power sys. relaying com. 1987-89, Disting. Svc. award power sys. relaying com. 1990, Charles Proteus Steinmetz Major Contbns. to Devel. Elec. Engring. Stds. award 1994). Clubs: Cherokee Town and Country (Atlanta). Republican. Episcopalian. Avocations: stamp collecting, golfing. Home: 221 The South Chace NE Atlanta GA 30328-4262 E-mail: chg25@mindspring.com.

GRIFFIN, DEBORAH S. lawyer; b. N.Y., Oct. 31, 1953; d. William Daniel and Cora Shelton; m. James Robert Griffin, Mar. 1, 1982 (div. Mar. 1985); children: Jamal C. Wright, Jonathan James Griffin. BA, U. Pa., 1976; JD, U. Mo., 1988. Atty. Supreme Ct. Pa., 1988—. Recipeint Shirley Chisholm award for leadership, Nat. Political Congress Black Women, Phila. chapt., 1999. Mem. Nat. Assn. Criminal Defense Attys., Phila. Bar Assn. Avocations: tennis, singing, gourmet cooking. Office: 1315 Walnut St Ste 1105 Philadelphia PA 19107-4711 E-mail: eyedefendu@aol.com.

GRIFFIN, DONALD R(EDFIELD), zoology educator; b. Southampton, N.Y., Aug. 3, 1915; s. Henry Farrand and Mary Whitney (Redfield) G.; m. Ruth M. Castle, Sept. 6, 1941 (div. Aug. 1965); children: Nancy Griffin Jackson, Janet Griffin Abbott, Margaret, John H.; m. Jocelyn Crane, Dec. 16, 1965 (dec. Dec. 1998). BS, Harvard U., 1938, MA, 1940, PhD, 1942. Jr. fellow Harvard U., Cambridge, Mass., 1940-41, 46, rsch. assoc., 1942-45, prof., 1953-65, assoc. Mus. of Comparative Zoology, 1989—; asst. prof. Cornell U., Ithaca, N.Y., 1946-47, assoc. prof., 1947-52, prof., 1952-53, Rockefeller U., N.Y.C., 1965-86, prof. emeritus, 1986—, trustee, 1973-76. Vis. lectr. Princeton U., N.J., 1987-89; pres. Harry Frank Guggenheim Found., N.Y., 1979-83. Author: Listening in the Dark, 1958 (Nat. Acad. Scis. Elliot medal 1961), Echoes of Bats and Men, 1959, Animal Structure and Function, 1962, Bird Migration, 1964 (Phi Beta Kappa prize 1966), The Question of Animal Awareness, 1976, Animal Thinking, 1984, Animal Minds, 1992, rev. edit. 2001. Mem. Am. Ornithologists Union, Am. Soc. Zoologists, Am. Physiol. Soc., Ecol. Soc. Am., Am. Acad. Arts and Scis., Nat. Acad. Scis., Am. Philos. Soc., Animal Behavior Soc., Phi Beta Kappa, Sigma Xi. Office: Harvard U Concord Field Sta Old Causeway Rd Bedford MA 01730

GRIFFIN, DONALD SCOTT, physician assistant; b. Dothan, Ala., Mar. 7, 1962; s. James Donald Griffin and Betty Kay Colvin; 1 child, Danielle. BS Prelaw, U. Tenn., 1989; BS Physician Asst., Med. U. S.C., 1998. Cert. physician asst. Nat. Commn. of Physician Assts. Physician asst. Southeastern Med. Practice, Lumberton, NC, 1998—2002, Digestive Diseases Ctr., Panama City Beach, Fla., 2002—. Sr. intern Hon. Jim Sasser U.S. Senate, 1989. Author: (instrnl. manual) Basic Marksmanship of the M16A2, 2002. Home: PO Box 57 1415 Jasmine Ln Holly Hill SC 29059 Office: 204 E 19th St Panama City FL 32406 Home Fax: 803-496-5840. Personal E-mail: dsgriffn@aol.com.

GRIFFIN, DONALD SPRAY, mechanical engineer, consultant; BME, Cornell U., 1952; MS in Engring. Mechanics, Stanford U., 1953, PhD in Engring. Mechanics, 1959. From sr. engr. to mgr. structural mechanics Bettis Atomic Lab. Westinghouse, Pitts., 1959-72, with advance energy systems divsn., 1974-91; ind. cons. Pitts., 1972-74, 91—. Ad hoc visitor Accreditation Bd. Engring. and Tech., 1977-85. Assoc. editor Jour. Applied Mechanics, 1973-80; former mem. editl. bd. Internat. Jour. Computers and Structures, Jour. Structural Mechanics Software; contbr. articles, papers to profl. jours. Officer Civil Engring. Corps, USN, 1953-56. Recipient Literature award PVP, 1987. Fellow ASME (life, divsn. applied mechanics, chmn. divsn. pressure vessels and piping, publs. com., mem. com. computer tech., com. computing in applied mechanics, op. bd. materials and structures, subcom. boiler and pressure vessel code, com. solar energy standards codes, policy bds. comm. and rsch., Pressure Vessel and Piping award 1992), Nat. Rsch. Coun. (computational math. com.), Welding Rsch. Coun. (pressure vessel rsch. com.). Achievements include research in design methods, design criteria and software for structural analysis and computer operations for design of advanced energy systems. Home: 208 Oakcrest Ln Pittsburgh PA 15236-4208

GRIFFIN, ELEANOR, magazine editor; Exec. editor So. Living, Birmingham, 1993—. Office: Southern Living 2100 Lakeshore Dr Birmingham AL 35209-6721

GRIFFIN, GARY ARTHUR, technological products executive; b. Yonkers, N.Y., Nov. 23, 1937; s. William Edmund and Madeline G.; m. Jacqueline Cahill, June 21, 1958; children: Lynn, Elizabeth, Margaret. Student, Manhattan Coll., 1956-57, Westchester C.C., 1957-62; diploma, LaSalle Extension U., 1968. Engring. cons. IBM Corp., Yorktown, N.Y., 1960-61, Perkin Elmer Corp., Norwalk, Conn., 1961-63; product devel. mgr. Technicon Corp., Tarrytown, N.Y., 1963-69; chmn., pres. Dynacon Rsch. Corp., Rockland, N.Y., 1969-72; with Nat. Patent Devel. Corp., New Brunswick, N.J., 1973-82; corp. group v.p. new techs., 1977-82; pres. Hydromed Scis. div. NDP Dental Sys., Inc., NDP Epic Sys., Inc., 1978-82; pres., dir. Amalgamated Fin. Svcs., Inc., 1979-82; v.p., dir. NDP Productos Médicos, S.A., 1979-82; pres., dir. Applied Genetics, Inc., 1981-82; dir. FCS Industries, Inc., Flemington, NJ, 1982-98; sr. v.p. N.J., 1982-87; treas., 1984-87; chmn., COO, pres. Circuitech Inc., Eatontown, N.J., 1982-85; dir., 1985-87; chmn., pres., treas. Executrex Internat., Inc., New Brunswick, NJ, 1985—2002; chmn., CEO Renaissance Resource Group Ltd., New Brunswick, 2002—. Patentee in field. With USNR, 1954-62. Mem. IEEE, Am. Prodn. and Inventory Control Soc., Am. Mgmt. Assn., Am. Assn. Advancement Med. Instrumentation, Am. Entrepreneurs Assn., Internat. Entrepreneurs Assn., Turnaround Mgmt. Assn., Smithsonian Assocs., N.Y. Vet. Police Assn. Republican. Roman Catholic. Office: Executrex 100 Jersey Ave Bldg D New Brunswick NJ 08901-3200 E-mail: ggriffin@ren-consultants.net.

GRIFFIN, GLORIA JEAN, retired elementary school educator; b. Emmett, Idaho, Sept. 10, 1946; d. Archie and Marguerite (Johnson) G. AA, Boise (Idaho) Jr. Coll., 1966; BA, Boise Coll., 1968; MA in Elem. Curriculum, Boise State U., 1975. Cert. advanced elem. tchr., Idaho. Tchr. music, tutor, Boise, Idaho; sec. Edward A. Johnson, atty., Boise, Idaho; tchr. Head Start, Boise, Idaho; elem. tchr. Meridian Sch. Dist., Idaho, 1968—2002, ret., 2002. Developer multimodality individualized spelling program; co-developer program for adapting curriculum to student's individual differences. Author: The Culture and Customs of the Argentine People As Applied to a Sixth Grade Social Studies Unit. Sec. PTA. Named Tchr. of Yr., Meridian Sch. Dist., 1981. Mem. Actor's Guild, Alpha Delta Kappa (rec. sec.).

GRIFFIN, HARMON TERRELL, lawyer; b. Waycross, Ga., Sept. 6, 1942; s. Sion Pleasant and Margaret (Royal) G.; m. Jean Higgins, June 6, 1964; children: Gregory, Michael, Christopher. BA, Mercer U., Macon, Ga., 1966, JD, 1968. Bar: Fla. 1968, U.S. Dist. Ct. (mid. dist.) Fla. 1969, U.S. Ct. Appeals 1969. U.S. Supreme Ct. 1973; bd. cert. civil trial lawyer. Assoc. Maguire, Voorhis & Wells, Orlando, Fla., 1968-70, Troutman Griffin & Parrish, Winter Park, Fla., 1970-74; ptnr. Griffin & Linder P.A., Orlando, 1974—. Chmn. Orange County Rep. Party, Orlando, 1974-76; gen. counsel Rep. Party of Fla., Tallahassee, 1984-89. With U.S. Army, 1960-63. Office: Griffin & Linder PA 28 E Washington St Orlando FL 32801 E-mail: tgriffin@griflaw.com.

GRIFFIN, JAMES ANTHONY, bishop; b. Fairview Park, Ohio, June 13, 1934; s. Thomas Anthony and Margaret Mary (Hanousek) Griffin. BA, Borromeo Coll., 1956; JCL magna cum laude, Pontifical Lateran U., Rome, 1963; JD summa cum laude, Cleve. State U., 1972; DHL (hon.), Ohio Dominican Coll., 1994. Priest Roman Cath. Ch., 1960. Bishop Roman Cath. Ch., 1979; assoc. pastor St. Jerome Ch., Cleve., 1960—61; sec.-notary Cleve. Diocesan Tribunal, 1963—65; asst. chancellor Diocese of Cleve., 1965—68, vice chancellor, 1968—73, chancellor, 1973—78, vicar gen., 1978—79; pastor St. William Ch., Euclid, Ohio, 1978—79; aux. bishop Diocese of Cleve., vicar of western region Lorain, Ohio, 1979—83; bishop Diocese of Columbus, Ohio, 1983—. Mem clergy rels. bd. Diocese Cleve., 1972—75, mem clergy retirement bd., 1973—78, mem clergy pers. bd., 1979—83. Author (with A. J. Quinn): (book) Thoughts for Our Times, 1969, Thoughts for Sowing, 1970; author: (with others) Ashes from the Cathedral, 1974, Sackcloth and Ashes, 1976, The Priestly Heart, 1983, Reflections on the Law of Love, 1991, Summary of the New Catholic Catechism, 1994, A Lenten Walk, 1998. Chmn. bd. govs. N. Am. Coll., Rome, 1984—88; co-chair Columbus Cmty. Rels. Comn., 1992—95; mem Am's Promise, Columbus, 1997—2001, Columbus Coalition Domestic Violence, 2001—; mem. adv. coun. Cmty. Shelter Bd., 2001—; mem. adv. team Cmtys. in Sch., 2002—; chmn. Mayor's Coun Youth, 1986—90; trustee St Mary Sem, 1976—78; bd. dirs., mem pension comt Cath Cemeteries Assn., 1978—83; vice-chancellor Pontifical Col. Josephinum, 1983—; treas. Cath. Relief Svc. Bd., 1988—91, pres., 1991—96; bd. dirs. Holy Family Cancer Home, 1973—78, Meals on Wheels, Euclid, 1978—79, Franklin County United Way, 1984—90. Decorated Knight of the Holy Sepulchre; recipient Human Rights award, Anti-Defamation League B'nai B'rith, 1987, Gov's award, State of Ohio, 1994, Jessing award, Pontifical Coll., 1993, Don Bosco medal, 1997, NG Minuteman award, 1999, Cmty. Svc. award, Columbus Urban League, 1999, Bronze Pelican award, Cath. Boy Scouts, 2002, Charity Newsies award, 2002. Mem.: Columbus Bar Assn. (chmn. jud. advt. com. 1987—91, Liberty Bell award 1989), Am. Canon Law. Soc. Roman Catholic.

GRIFFIN, JAMES JOSEPH, physics educator; b. Phila., Oct. 20, 1930; s. James Joseph and Nellie (Nunan) G.; m. Mary Dolores Cornely, July 9, 1955; children: Kevin, Michael, Sean, Terence, Sheilagh. BS, Villanova U., 1952; MS, Princeton U., 1955, PhD, 1956. Fulbright scholar Niels Bohr Inst., Copenhagen, 1955-56; theoretical physicist Los Alamos (N.Mex.) Sci. Lab., 1956-65; vis. lectr. U. Wis., Madison, 1965-66; asst. prof. physics U. Md., College Park, 1966-68, assoc. prof., 1968-73, prof., 1973—, sr. investigator theoretical nuclear physics group, 1968—, rsch. prof. Inst. Phys. Scis. and Tech., 1981-82. A. von Humboldt U.S. sr. scientist Hahn-Meitner Inst., Berlin, 1975-76, U. Giessen, Germany, 1975-76; cons., vis. scientist Oak Ridge (Tenn.) Nat. Lab. and Lawrence Berkeley (Calif.) Lab., Brookhaven (N.Y.) Nat. Lab., Los Alamos (N.Mex.) Nat. Lab.; vis. scientist Inst. Atomic Energy, Beijing, Weizman Inst., Rehovot, Israel, gesellschaft f. Schwerionen Forschung, Darmstadt, Germany Sci. Nucleaire, Grenoble, France, Centre Nat. de Recherche Scientifique, Orsay, France, Centre d'Etudes Nucleaire, Saclay, France, Centre d'Etude Nucleaire, Bordeaux, France, also others; disting. vis. lectr. U. Toronto, 1978; disting. guest lectr., China, 1980. Translator: Group Theory and Its Applications to Quantum Mechanics (E.P. Wigner), 1959; contbr. over 100 articles to sci. jours. Nat. sci. fellow Birmingham (Eng.) U., 1959-60, Guggenheim fellow U. Calif., Berkeley, 1972-73. Fellow Am. Phys. Soc. (internat. travel grantee 1992). Avocations: running, sailing, skiing. Office: Univ of Maryland Dept Of Physics Astron College Park MD 20742-0001

GRIFFIN, JEAN (ALVA JEAN GRIFFIN), entertainer; b. Detroit, June 1, 1931; d. Henry Bethel White and Ruth Madelyn (Gowen) Durham; m. Francis Jay Griffin, July 8, 1958 (dec.); stepchildren: Patra, Rodney; 1 adopted child, Donald; children: Rhonda Jean, Sherree Lee. Student, Anderson Coll., 1952-53; DD (hon.), Ministry of Salvation, Chula Vista, Calif., 1990, Ministry of Salvation, 1990. Ordained minister, 1990. Supr. Woolworth's, Detroit, 1945-46; operator, supr. Atlantic Bell Tel. Co., Detroit, 1947-51, Anderson, Ind., 1952-56; sec. to div. mgr. Food Basket-Lucky Stores, San Diego, 1957-58; owner, mgr. Jay's Country Boy Markets, Riverside, Calif., 1962-87; entertainer, prodr., dir., singer Mae West & Co., 1980—. Past owner The Final Touch, Colorado Springs; owner Omega Communique Co., 1997—; tchr. art Grant Sch., Riverside, 1964-65; tchr., adviser Mental Retarded Sch., Riverside, 1976-77; instr. Touch for Health Found., Pasadena, Calif., 1975-79; cons., hypnotist, nutritionist, Riverside, 1976-79; mem., tchr. Psi field parapsychology. Writer children's stories and short stories. Mem. Rep. Presdl. Task Force, 1983. Recipient svc. award Rep. Presdl. Task Force, 1986. Mem. Parapsychology Assn. Riverside (pres. 1981-82). Mem. Ch. of Religious Science New Thought. Avocations: arts and crafts, photography, hiking, horseback riding, travel. Home: 201 W Chapel Rd Sedona AZ 86336-7031

GRIFFIN, JEAN LATZ, political strategist, writer; b. Joliet, Ill., Mar. 6, 1943; d. Carl Joseph and Helene Monica (Bradshaw) Latz; m. Dennis Joseph Griffin, Sept. 16, 1967; children: Joseph, Timothy, Peter. BS in Chemistry, Coll. St. Francis, Joliet, 1965; MS in Journalism, U. Wis., 1967. Clin. investigation coord. Baxter Labs., 1967-68; reporter Joliet Herald News, 1968-70, Raleigh

(N.C.) Times, 1974-75, Suburban Trib, Hinsdale, Ill., 1976-78, regional edn. reporter, 1978-82; gen. assignment reporter Chgo. Tribune, 1982-84, edn. writer, 1984-88, pub. health writer, 1988-94, govt., politics, and pub. policy reporter, 1994-97, econ. devel. reporter, 1997; strategist The Strategy Group, Chgo., 1998—; owner CyberINK, 1998—; adj. journalism instr. Roosevelt U., Chicago, 2001—. Bd. dirs. Residents for Emergency Shelter, Chgo., 1978-82, Genesis House, Chgo., 1995-98, vol. cook, 1994-98; devel. com. mem. Hope Now, Inc., 1998-2000; membership chair Arlington Hts. C. of C., 2001-2002; vol. Taoist Tai Chi instr., 2001—, pres. Taoist Chi Soc., Ill., 2003—. Recipient Writing award Am. Dental Assn., 1969, Alumna Profl. Achievement award Coll. St. Francis, Joliet, 1985, First Prize in ednl. writing Edn. Writers Am., 1986, Grand prize, 1988, Benjamin Fine award Nat. Assn. Secondary Sch. Prins., 1988, Edward Scott Beck award for reporting Chgo. Tribune, 1988, Peter Lisagor award for pub. svc. Soc. Profl. Journalists, Chgo. chpt., 1988, Mark of Excellence Chgo. Assn. Black Journalists, 1992, Cushing award for Journalistic Excellence, Chgo. Dental Soc., 1992, Human First award Horizon Cmty. Svcs., Chgo., 1993, Robert F. Kennedy Grand Prize in Journalism, 1994, Editl. Excellence award Ill. Merchandising Coun., 1994; finalist Pulitzer Prize, 1994. Mem. Women's Leadership Coun., Taoist Tai Chi Soc. USA-Ill., Arlington Heights C. of C. Office: CyberINK 621 N Belmont Ave Arlington Heights IL 60004 E-mail: jlgrif@earthlink.net. *Keep climbing mountains. Invent challenges if you have to. Love all life--amoeba to stars. Dive into the flow of the universe. And wash your dishes when you're done.*

GRIFFIN, JEFF, federal agency administrator, mayor; m. Marna Griffin; 2 children. Prin., owner Griffin Transport Svcs.; mayor City of Reno, Nev., 1995—2002; dir. region IX FEMA, 2002—. Co-chair USCM Spl. Task Force; bd. mem. U.S. Conf. Mayors; chmn. Pub. Safety Com.; co-chmn. Task Force on Gaming in Am.; mem. Aviation Security Task Force; mem. crime prevention policy com. Nat. League Cities. Named Pub. Ofcl. of Yr., 2001. Office: City Reno 490 S Center St Reno NV 89501-2105*

GRIFFIN, JERRY J. chaplain; b. Wauseon, Ohio, Feb. 13, 1938; s. Peter Clair Griffin and Sadie Irene (Stratton) Behnke; m. Jean Ann Sutherland, June 25, 1961 (div. Dec. 15, 1988); children: Anne Marie Kapral, John William; m. Ruth Emma Shook, Dec. 30, 1988; stepchildren: Michael J. Kapral Jr., MaryLynn Kapral Ahart, Mark D. Kapral. BA, Hiram Coll., 1961; MDiv, Drake U., 1965; ThM, Tex. Christian U., 1966. Cert. chaplain, Assn. Profl. Chaplains, Inc. Staff chaplain Iowa Meth. Hosp., Des Moines, 1966-68; pastor First Christian Ch., Coon Rapids, Iowa, 1968-70; chaplain Bethel Deaconess Hosp. & Home for Aged, Newton, Kans., 1970-79; chaplain, counselor Dorothy Love Retirement Cmty., Sidney, Ohio, 1979-83; chaplain Corning (N.Y) Hosp. & Founders Pavilion, 1983-93; sys. dir. spiritual svcs. Lee Meml. Health Sys., Ft. Myers, 1993—. Pres. bd. dirs. Midwest Area Alcohol Edn. & Tng. Program, Chgo., 1972-75. Bd. edn. Hesston (Kans.) Pub. Schs., 1978-79; bd. dirs. Fla. Bioethics Network, 1994-98, 99—. Mem. Assn. Profl. Chaplains, Inc. (pres. 1989-91), Samaritan Counseling Ctr. Southwest Fla. (bd. dirs. 1996-98). Avocations: reading, gardening. Home: 9100 Lady Bug Ct Fort Myers FL 33919-8342 Office: Lee Meml Health Sys PO Drawer 2218 Fort Myers FL 33902-2218 E-mail: Jerry.Griffin@leememorial.org.

GRIFFIN, JIM, secondary school educator; b. Leavenworth, Kans., Mar. 20, 1945; s. Jack Cailey and Jean (Barnes) Griffin; m. Karen Gayle McCluskey, Aug. 28, 1966; children: Shannon Griffin Jahn, John David, Cailey Jean. BA in History, Tex. Tech. U., 1968; MA in History, U. North Tex., 1979. Tchr., coach Richardson (Tex.) Ind. Sch. Dist., 1968—81; pers. mgr. Prophecy Corp., Carrollton, Tex., 1981—85; employment mgr. Sunbelt Sav., Dallas, 1985—86; tchr., coach Carrollton-Farmers Branch Ind. Sch. Dist., Carrollton, 1986—90, Coppell (Tex.) Ind. Sch. Dist., 1990—2000, tchr., dept. chair, 2000—. Tennis, baseball coach Richardson Ind. Sch. Dist., 1968—73; boys soccer coach Carrollton-Farmers Branch Ind. Sch. Dist., 1986—90; boys soccer coach, cross country coach Coppell Ind. Sch. Dist., 1990—2000. Mem.: Nat. Soccer Coaches Assn. Am. (Boys Soccer Coach of Yr., southwest region 1999), Tex. Assn. Soccer Coaches (Boys Soccer Coach of Yr. 1999, 2000), Orgn. Am. Historians. Avocations: reading, writing. Office: Coppell High Sch 185 W Parkway Coppell TX 75019

GRIFFIN, JO ANN THOMAS, retired financial planner, tax specialist; b. Dallas, July 20, 1933; d. John Baxton and Joan Marion (Ament) Thomas; m. John Barrett Brown, June 29, 1963 (div. 1972); children: John Barrett Jr., Daniel Thomas; m. Thomas Reese Griffin, Jan. 25, 1976; stepchildren: Gregory Crawford, Kevin Bradley. BA, U. Miss., 1955; BS magna cum laude, Lamar U., 1964; MEd, U. Del., 1972. Cert. fin. planner; enrolled agt. U.S. Treas. Dept. Site mgr. Motivational Ctr., Inc., Wilmington, Del., 1976-78; asst. dir. Indochinese social svcs. Assoc. Cath. Charities, New Orleans, 1978-79; dir. continuing edn. St. Mary's Dominican Coll., New Orleans, 1979-80; with fin. mgmt. U.S. Dept. Agr., New Orleans, 1981; tax auditor IRS, New Orleans, Phila., Del., 1981-86, revenue agt. Wilmington, Del., 1987-92; tax specialist Horty & Horty, CPA's, Wilmington, 1986-87; quality control H&R Block, Wilmington, 1992-94; counselor Svc. Corps Ret. Execs., Wilmington, 1992—96; dir. Wilmington River-City Com., 1997-2000. Docent Winterthur, New Orleans Mus. Art, Wilmington and New Orleans, 1966—85; sustaining mem., advisor Jr. League, Wilmington, 1989—92, 1998—2000, mem. cmty. adv. bd., 1998—2000; regent Vieux Carre chpt. DAR, New Orleans, 1984; bd. dirs. Neighborhood Watch, New Orleans, 1983—85, Waterfront Coalition, Inc., 1998—2000; sec., mem. exec. bd. Henrietta Johnson Med. Ctr., 1998—2001; treas., exec. bd. Civil War Round Table Wilmington, Inc., 1999—2002; bd. dirs. Common Cause Del., 2000—, Del. Medicare and Medicaid Fraud Project, 2000—; CASA vol. Family Ct., State of Del., 2000—01; pres. Wilmington chpt. Nat. Assn. Retired Federal Employees, 2001—03; lay reader, mem. outreach com. Episc. Ch. Diocese of Del., Wilmington, 1971—2000. Recipient Grad. Scholarship award AAUW, 1971, Sustained Superior Performance award IRS, New Orleans, 1984, Spl. Achievement award IRS, Wilmington, 1988, 89, Customer Svc. awards, 1989, 90. Mem. Am. Soc. Women Accts. (sec. 1986-89), Del. Valley Soc. Cert. Fin. Planners, Wilmington Tax Group, Estate Planning Coun. Del., Wilmington Women in Bus., Rotary, Blue and Gold Club, Mortar Bd., Phi Kappa Phi, Delta Delta Delta. Democrat. Episcopalian. Home: 900 N Broom St Unit 16 Wilmington DE 19806-4546

GRIFFIN, JOHN FRANCIS, cardiologist; b. Springfield, Mass., Nov. 18, 1926; s. Francis Joseph and Ethel Mary (Mould) G.; m. Janice Blanche Palmer, Sept. 22, 1951; children: Mary, John, Robert, Michael, Stephen. BS, St. Michael's Coll., Winooski, Vt., 1948; MD, Georgetown U., 1951. Diplomate in internal medicine and in cardiology Am. Bd. Internal Medicine. Intern N.C. Bapt. Hosp., Winston-Salem, N.C., 1951-52; resident in medicine Boston City Hosp., 1952-54; resident Georgetown U. Hosp., Washington, 1954-55; fellow in cardiology Nat. Heart Inst., Georgetown U. Hosp., Washington, 1955-56; internist Baystate Med. Ctr., Mercy Hosp., Springfield, Mass.; sr. clin. instr. medicine Tufts U., Boston. Mem. AMA, AHA, Am. Coll. Physicians, Am. Coll. Cardiology. Home and Office: 92 Deepwoods Dr Longmeadow MA 01106-2135

GRIFFIN, JOHN HENRY, medical researcher; b. Seattle, June 26, 1943; s. John Henry and Lillian Louise (O'Connell) G.; m. Antonia Lastreto, 1965 (div. 1984); children: John, Deanna, Paul. BS, U. Santa Clara, 1965; PhD, U. Calif., Davis, 1969. Tchg. asst. U. Calif., 1967-69; guest worker NIH, 1971-73; with staff Svc. Biochimie Ctr. Etudes Nucleaires, Saclay, France, 1973-74; asst. dept. immunopathology Scripps Clinic Rsch. Found., La Jolla, Calif., 1974-75, assoc. depts. immunopathology, molecular immunology, 1975-80; prof. dept. molecular exptl. medicine Scripps Rsch. Inst., La Jolla, 1994—. Peer rev. com. NIH, 1979—. Contbr. articles to profl. jours. Treas. San Diego Assn. Gifte Children, 1978-81; active Pub. Sch. Cluster Com., University City, S.D., 1984-85; mem. adv. com. High Sch. Cmty., University City, 1979-82, 86-88. Recipient Rsch. Career Devel. award NIH, 1976-81, fellow, 1966-69, 72-73, NIH Merit award, 1994—; RCA physics scholar 1961-64; Harvard Med. Sch. fellow, 1969-71, Helen Hay Whitney Found. fellow, 1969-72. Mem. Internat. Soc. Thrombosis Hemostasis, Am. Soc. Clin. Investigators, Am. Soc. Hematology, Am. Chem. Soc., Am. Soc. Biochem. Molecular Biologists, Am. Assn. Pathologists, Am. Heart Assn., Sigma Xi, Alpha Sigma Nu, Phi Kappa Phi. E-mail: griffin@scripps.edu.

GRIFFIN, KEITH BROADWELL, economics educator; b. Colon, Republic of Panama, Nov. 6, 1938; came to U.S., 1988; s. Marcus Samuel Griffin and Elaine Ann (Broadwell) Fabick; m. Dixie Beth, Apr. 2, 1956; children: Janice, Kimberley. BA, Williams Coll., 1960, DLitt (hon.), 1980; PhB, Oxford U., Eng., 1962, PhD, 1965. Fellow and tutor in econs. Magdalen Coll. Oxford (Eng.) U., 1965-76, fellow Magdalen Coll., 1977-79, pres., 1979-88, hon. fellow, 1988; acting warden, dir. Queen Elizabeth House, Inst. Commonwealth Studies, 1973, 77-78, warden, dir., 1978-79; prof. U. Calif., Riverside, 1988—, chmn. dept. econs., 1988-93, Presdl. prof., 1988-90, Disting. prof., 1997—. Vis. prof. Inst. Econs. and Planning U. Chile, 1962-63, 64-65; chmn. bd. UN Rsch. Inst. for Social Devel., 1988-95, sr. cons., 1971-72; mem. UN com. for devel. planning, 1987-94; mem. coun. UN Univ., 1986-92, chmn. fin. and budget com., 1988-90; mem. Marshall Aid Commemoration Commn., 1984-88; mem. World Commn. on culture and Devel., 1994-95; chief ILO Employment Adv. Mission to Ethiopia, 1982; econ. advisor Govt. of Bolivia, 1989-91; pres. Devel. Studies Assn., U.K., 1978-80; chief rural and urban employment policies br. ILO, 1975-76; cons. ILO on rurual devel. in Ecuador, 1974; sr. adviser OECD Devel. Centre, Paris, 1986-91; adviser to Inter-Am. Com. for Alliance for Progress on copper expansion programme in Chile, 1968, to FAO/ICO, IBRD World Coffee Study in Guatemala, El Salvador and Colombia, 1967; rsch. advisor Pakistan Inst. Devel. Econs., Karachi, 1965, 70; expert on agrl. planning to Govt. of Algeria, acting chief FAO Mission, Algiers, 1963-64; cons. IBRD on land reform in Morocco, 1973; head UN Devel. Program Poverty Alleviation Mission to Mongolia, 1994; head ILO Social Policy Review Mission to Uzbekis, 1995; cons. on econ. reform in Vietnam, UNDP, 1997; head ILO Employment and Social Protection Mission to Kazakstan, 1997; head UNDP mission to Mongolia, 2001, Armenia, 2002. Author: Underdevelopment in Spanish America, 1969, 2d edit., 1971, Spanish edit., 1972, The Green Revolution: An Economic Analysis, 1972, The Political Economy of Agrarian Change, 1974, 2d edit., 1979, Spanish edit., 1982, Hindi edit., 1983, Land Concentration and Rural Poverty, 1976, 2d edit., 1981, Spanish edit., 1983, International Inequality and National Poverty, 1978, Spanish edit., 1984, World Hunger and the World Economy, 1987, Alternative Strategies for Economic Development, 1989, 2d edit., 1999, Chinese edit., 1992, Studies in Globalization and Economic Transitions, 1996, Studies in Development Strategy and Systemic Transformation, 2000; co-author: Comercio Internacional y Politicas de Desarrollo Economico, 1967, Planning Development, 1970, Spanish edit., 1975, The Transition to Egalitarian Development, 1981, Globalization and the Developing World, 1992, Implementing a Human Development Strategy, 1994; editor: Financing Development in Latin America, 1971, Institutional Reform and Economic Development in the Chinese Countryside, 1984, The Economy of Ethiopia, 1992, Poverty and the Transition to a Market Economy in Mongolia, 1995, Social Policy and Economic Transformation in Uzbekistan, 1996, Economic Reform in Vietnam, 1998, Poverty Reduction in Mongolia, 2003; co-editor: Ensayos Sobre Planificacion, 1967, Growth and Inequality in Pakistan, 1972, The Economic Development of Bangladesh, 1974, Human Development and the International Development Strategy for the 1990s, 1990, The Distribution of Income in China, 1993, also numerous articles. Vis. fellow Oxford Ctr. Islamic Studies, 1998. Fellow AAAS; mem. Am. Econ. Assn. Avocation: travel. Office: Univ Calif Dept Econs Riverside CA 92521-0001

GRIFFIN, KELLY ANN, public relations executive, consultant; b. Buffalo, May 20, 1964; d. Michael Gerald and Patricia Frances (Lippert) G.; m. Thomas Richard Kleinberger, Oct. 11, 1992. B in Polit. Sci., SUNY, Geneseo, 1986; postgrad., CUNY, Bklyn., 1994—. Legis. asst. to N.Y. State Assembly Spkrs. Stanley Fink and Mel Miller, Buffalo, 1986-87; acct. exec. Griffin Media Group, N.Y.C., 1987-88, acct. supr., v.p., 1988-90, pres., CEO, 1990-94; pub. rels. cons. N.Y.C., 1994—. Assoc. dir. N.Y. State Funeral Dirs. Assn., N.Y.C., 1992-94, Met. Funeral Dirs. Assn., N.Y.C., 1992-94, County Execs. of Am., N.Y.C. and Washington, 1993-2000; dep. exec. dir. County Execs. Am., 2000—; instr. remedial reading Cornell U. Sch. Industry/Lab. Rels., Buffalo, 1987; v.p. Fairfield Owners Cooperative, Riverdale, 1996-2000. Editor N.Y. State AFL-CIO Unity, 1988-90, County Execs. News, 1993—, N.Y. State Funeral Dirs. Assn./Met. Funeral Dirs. Assn. News, 1992-94, Amalgamated Transit Union News, 1988-90. Cons. Interfaith Assembly on Homelessness, N.Y.C., 1994-97, Voter Assistance Commn., N.Y.C., 1990-92; participant, cons. Erie County Dem. Party, Buffalo, 1985-87; mem. assocs. steering com. Children's Health Fund, N.Y.C., 1991-97; bd. dirs. Kingsbridge Hts. Cmty. Ctr., Bronx, 1999-2000, sec., 2000-01, chair, 2001—; mem. Parents' Assn., Frances Schervier Home and Hosp. Childcare Ctr., Bronx, 1997-2000, Support Our Schs. Com., Bronx, 1999-2000; class parent Prospect Hill Sch. PTA, Pelham Manor, 2001-03, rec. sec., 2003—; mem. fundraising com. Transition Learning Ctr., New Rochelle, NY. Recipient Acad. award DAR, 1978. Mem. Pub. Rels. Soc. N.Y.C., The Manor Club (Pelham Manor, N.Y.). Roman Catholic. Avocations: reading, swimming, bike riding, running. Home: 1061 Hunter Ave Pelham NY 10803-3409 Office: Griffin Media Group 3rd fl 1010 Massachusetts Ave NW Washington DC 20001-5402 E-mail: kgrif@optonline.net.

GRIFFIN, LARRY PAUL, obstetrician-gynecologist, educator; b. Louisville, June 19, 1947; s. Elmer Paul and Emma Angella (Woehler) G.; m. Cara Anne Ciliberti; children: Eric Paul, Craig Alan, Anthony Ciliberti, Francesca Ciliberti. BA, U. Louisville, 1969, MD, 1973. Diplomate Am. Bd. Ob-gyn. (examiner 1991-96), Nat. Bd. Med. Examiners. Clk. Great Atlantic & Pacific Tea Co., Louisville, 1965-67; lab. asst. Celanese Coatings Co., Louisville, 1967-68; lab. tech. GE, Louisville, 1968-69; resident in ob-gyn. Louisville Gen. Hosp., 1973-76; fellow maternal/fetal medicine U. Louisville, 1976-77; ob-gyn., ptnr. Louisville Ob-Gyn. Assocs., 1977-90; asst. clin. prof. ob-gyn. U. Louisville, 1977-92, 99—; pvt. practice ob-gyn. 1970-90, 99—. Assoc. prof. Ind. U., 1989-94; dir. ob-gyn. residency program St. Vincent Hosp., 1989-93; v.p. program svcs. and fellowship divsn. ACOG, Washington, 1993-99; bd. dirs., chmn. Louisville mng. bd. PIE Mut. Ins. Co., 1989-96; dir. Ctr. for Med. Edn. and Health Policy Rsch., 1992-93. Mem. editl. bd. Jour. Gynecol. and Obstet. and Neonatal Nursing, 1982-86; contbr. articles to profl. jours. Bd. dirs. Ohio Valley chpt. March of Dimes, Louisville, 1979-89; task force mem. Jefferson County Drug Abuse Program, Louisville, 1986-89; chmn. Emergency Med. Svcs. Evaluation Task Force, 1986-87, State of Ky. Family Planning Task Force, 1988-92; mem. State of Ky. Health Svcs. Adv. Coun., 1988-92. Capt., MC, USNR, 1983 . Samuel McMurtry fellow U. Louisville Dept. Ob-Gyn., 1976; recipient William O. Johnson award Ob-Gyn. Soc., 1975. Fellow Am. Coll. Ob-Gyn. (chmn. Ky. sect., 1986-89, sec. dist. V 1989-93, dir. program svcs. 1993-99); mem. Ky. Med. Assn. (trustee 1987-89), Jefferson County Med. Soc. (pres. 1986-87, chmn. bd. 1987-88), Louisville Ob-Gyn Soc. (chmn. 1986-87), Jefferson Club, Hurstbourne Club, Historic Georgetown Club, Army Navy Club, Capitol Hill Club, Rotary. Republican. Office: 4130 Dutchmans Ln Ste 400 Louisville KY 40207-4711 E-mail: larrygriffin@home.com.

GRIFFIN, LAURA MAE, retired educator; b. Woodland, Calif., Aug. 14, 1925; d. George Everette Ramsey and Bertha (Storz) Ramsey Lowe; m. Roy J. Griffin, Nov. 19, 1944; children: Robert Eugene, Dennis Charles, Kathleen Ann. AA in Social Sci., Sacramento City Coll., 1969; BA in Geography, Calif. State U., Sacramento, 1972. Cert. elem. and secondary tchr., Calif.; Master Gardener. Sec. Alameda Naval Air, Alameda, Calif., 1944-45, Cal-Western Life Ins., Sacramento, 1945-47, Pacific Sch. Dist., Sacramento, 1956-57; substitute tchr. Sacramento Unified Sch. Dist., 1974-75; tchr. Mt. Diablo Unified Sch. Dist., Concord, Calif., 1976-91; ret., 1991. Dir. Heather Farm Garden Ctr., Walnut Creek, Calif., 1985-86, edn. chmn., 1986-87, pres., 1987-88, fin. sec., 1993-94; sec. investment group AAUW, Walnut Creek, 1978-79. Guardian Jobs Daus.-Bethel 325, Walnut Creek, 1978-79; leader Girl Scouts Am., Sacramento, 1971-72; den mother Boy Scouts Am., Sacramento, 1957-60; publicity chmn. membership Northgate Music Boosters, Walnut Creek, 1976-77. Recipient Bert A. Bertolero Gardening award, 1996. Mem. Calif. Garden Clubs (life), Heather Farm Garden Club (pres. 1987-88, Outstanding Svc. award 1995), Walnut Creek Garden Club (pres. 1983-84, civic project chmn. 1994-95, 95-96); Order Ea. Star. Republican. Avocations: reading, travel, bowling, golf, music, gardening.

GRIFFIN, LEAH G. art specialist; b. Nebraska City, Nebr., May 24, 1942; d. Leigh Addison and Ferne Gwendolyn (Ferguson) Sharp; m. Kenyon Neal Griffin, Mar. 2, 1962; children: Karol René, Shari Lené. Student, U. Nebr., 1960-61, U. Kans., 1964; BA, U. Wyo., 1981. Cert. in art K-12, elem. edn. K-6, Wyo. Teaching asst. Albany County Sch. Dist. 1, Laramie, Wyo., 1971-80, art specialist, 1981—2001. Instr. U. Wyo., 1993-94; panelist Wyo. Coun. on the Arts, 1985-92. Exhibited lithographs, etchings, woodcuts and silkscreen art in various shows, 1981—. Leader, camp dir. Camp Fire Girls, Laramie, 1971-84. Recipient Gov.'s Art award Wyo. Coun. on Arts, 1991; USIS acad. specialist grantee, United Arab Emirates, 1990; Fulbright Meml. fellowship, Japan, 1998. Mem. NEA, Nat. Art Edn. Assn., Colo. Art Edn. Assn., Albany County Edn. Assn. (Tchr. of Yr. 1985-86), PTA (life; v.p., pres.), Clowns of Am. Democrat. Episcopalian. Avocations: horseback riding, clowning, skiing, rollerblading, art. Home: 1808 Beaufort St Laramie WY 82072-1940

GRIFFIN, LINDA FRENCH, artist, activist, consultant; b. Cleve., Sept. 25, 1953; d. Park and Donna (Unger) French; m. Eugene Wilson Griffin III, June 15, 1974; children: Joshua Park, Margaret Ellen. BA magna cum laude, Hiram (Ohio) Coll., 1975. Ordained to priesthood Cmty. of Christ, 1988. Freelance artist, Durham, N.C., 1974-81, Elkin, 1981—. Author, illustrator: Building Kirtland Temple, 1985; artist, contbr.: Daily Bread, 1988-92; artist concept graphic works Peace Poster Project, 1990-99; artist, author graphic works and text Sabbath Prayer for Peace, 1994; contbg. artist/writer Herald Pub. House, Independence, Mo., 1988—; contbg. artist Brilliant Star Mag., Baha'i Nat. Ctr., Wilmette, Ill., 1990-95; commd. artist State Libr., N.C. Dept. Cultural Resources, Raleigh, 1991, 94. Grassroots organizer Priority: Peace, Elkin, 1983-90; bldg. project cons. Elkin City Schs., 1990-92; dist. rep. Outreach Internat., Independence, 1988-92; mem. Elkin Cmty. Chorus, 1983—, sec., 1990-91; bd. dirs. Foothills Art Coun., 1984-86; mem. Surry Cmty. Coll. Chorus, 1998—. Recipient 3d place Morrison Meml. Art Show, Elkin, 1989. Mem. Friends of Elkin Pub. Libr. (pres. 1990-92, 97), Elkin PTA (pres. 1991-92), Hiram Coll. Alumni Assn., Phi Beta Kappa (Mu chpt.), Phi Alpha Theta,(Gamma Delta Chpt.) Democrat. Avocations: choral singing, hiking, illuminated manuscript study.

GRIFFIN, LINDA LOUISE, English language and speech educator; b. Yale, Mich., Dec. 23, 1942; d. Benjamin and Ruth (Steenbergh) Hinton; m. James Griffin, Nov. 23, 1980. BA, U. Mich., 1965, MA, 1967; postgrad., Bowling Green (Ohio) State U., 1975, U. N.C., 1985; PhD, U. South Fla., 1996. Tchr. English and speech Sandusky (Mich.) H.S.; instr. Jackson (Mich.) C.C., Terra Tech. Coll., Fremont, Ohio, Edison C.C., Naples, Fla. Frequent speaker and presenter, including harp lecture programs; mem. NEH Shakespeare Seminar, 1985; keynote speaker Collier County Tchrs. Assn. Conf., 1987. Recipient Edison C.C. Excellence in Teaching award and endowed chair in comms.; Fulbright award winner No. Ireland. Mem. MLA, South Atlantic MLA, S.E. Medieval Assn., Medieval Inst., S.C. Renaissance Assn., Nat. Coun. Tchrs. English, Folger Shakespeare Libr., So. State Comm. Assn., Fla. Comm. Assn. (pres. 1989-90), Phi Kappa Phi. Home: 2292 Piccadilly Circus Naples FL 34112-3659 Office: 7007 Lely Cultural Pkwy Naples FL 34113-8976

GRIFFIN, MARVIN ANTHONY, industrial engineer, educator; b. Pine Apple, Ala., Mar. 28, 1923; s. Randolph Simpson and Linnie (Barrett) G.; m. Jane Pearle A. L'Herisson, Sept. 4, 1949 (dec. Dec. 1992); children: Margaret Lynn, John Marvin, Barbara Lee, Elizabeth Ann. BS, Auburn U., 1949; MS Engring, U. Ala., 1952; D.Eng., Johns Hopkins, 1960. Registered profl. engr., Ala. Chief ops. analysis Anniston Ordnance Depot, Ala., 1949-51; sr. mfg. engr. Western Electric Co., Winston-Salem, N.C., 1952-55, chief engring. Cumberland Mfg. Co., Chattanooga, 1955-57; instr. Johns Hopkins, 1957-60; chief indsl. engr. Matson Navigation Co., San Francisco, 1960-61, v.p. corporate devel., 1977-78, group v.p., 1978-79; prof. indsl. engring. U. Ala., 1961-76, chmn. dept., 1965-71, chmn. dept. computer sci. and ops. research, 1971-76, dir. computer sci., 1969-76, prof. indsl. engring. and computer sci., 1980—, prof. emeritus indsl. engring., 1987—, chmn. dept., 1983—. Mem. maritime transp research bd., maritime info. com. Nat. Acad. Sci., 1976— ; mgmt. cons. to industry, govt.; labor arbitrator Fed. Mediation and Conciliation Service, Am. Arbitration Assn.; cons. indsl. engring., ops. rsch., arbitration, mediation svcs., 1987-92. Contbr. articles to profl. jours. Served to comdr. USNR, 1943-47, PTO. Sr. postdoctoral fellow Johns Hopkins U., 1969 Mem. Operations Research Soc. Am., Am. Inst. Indsl. Engrs. (dir. 1954-55, chpt. pres. 1959-60), Am. Soc. Engring. Edn., Inst. Mgmt. Sci., Assn. Computing Machinery, Johns Hopkins Soc. Scholars. Home: 2013 Fox Ridge Rd Tuscaloosa AL 35406-3056

GRIFFIN, MARY FRANCES, retired library media consultant; b. Cross Hill, S.C., Aug. 24, 1925; d. James and Rosa Lee (Carter) G. BA, Benedict Coll., 1947; postgrad., S.C. State Coll., 1948-51, Atlanta U., 1953, Va. State Coll., 1961; MLS, Ind. U., 1957. Tchr., libr. Johnston (S.C.) Tng. Sch., Edgefield County Sch. Dist., 1947-51; libr. Lee County Sch. Dist., Dennis High, Bishopville, S.C., 1951-52, Greenville County (S.C.) Sch. Dist., 1952-66; libr. cons. S.C. Dept. Edn., Columbia, 1966-87. Vis. tchr. U. S.C., 1977. Bd. dirs. Greater Columbia Lit. Coun.; mem. Richland County unit Assault on Illiteracy. Recipient Cert. of Living the Legacy award Nat. Coun. Negro Women, 1980. Mem. ALA, Assn. Ednl. Comms. and Tech., S.C. Assn. Curriculum Devel., AAUW (pres. Columbia br. 1978-80), Southeastern Libr. Assn. (sec. 1979-80), S.C. Libr. Assn. (sec. 1979), S.C. Assn. Sch. Librarians, Nat. Assn. State Ednl. and Media Pers. Baptist. Home: PO Box 1652 Columbia SC 29202-1652 also: 1100 Skyland Dr Columbia SC 29210-8127

GRIFFIN, MERV EDWARD, former entertainer, television producer, entrepreneur; b. San Mateo, Calif., July 6, 1925; s. Mervyn Edward and Rita (Robinson) G.; m. Julann Elizabeth Wright, May 18, 1958 (div. June 1976); 1 son, Anthony Patrick. Student, San Mateo Coll., 1942-44; L.H.D., Emerson Coll., 1981. Owner Teleview Racing Patrol Inc., Miami, Fla., Video Racing Patrol Inc., Seattle, Beverly Hilton Hotel, Beverly Hills, Calif., The Scottsdale (Ariz.) Hilton, Wickenburg (Ariz.) Inn; chmn. bd. Griffin Group, Inc., Beverly Hills, Givenchy Hotel and Spa, Palm Springs, Calif., Blue Moon Hotel, So. Beach, Miami Beach, Fla.; owner Merv Griffin Entertainment, Beverly Hills, 1996—, Cleran's Manor Ho., Galway, Ireland. Performer Merv Griffin Show radio sta. KFRC, San Francisco, 1945-48, vocalist Freddy Martin's Orch., 1948-52; contract player, star So This is Love, Warner Bros., 1953-55; TV master ceremonies, 1958—, Merv Griffin Show, NBC-TV, 1962-63, Westinghouse Broadcasting Co., 1965-69, CBS-TV, 1969-72, syndication, 1972-86; currently exec. producing: Wheel of Fortune, Jeopardy. Mem.: Bohemian (San Francisco). Office: The Griffin Group 9860 Wilshire Blvd Beverly Hills CA 90210-3115 also: 780 3rd Ave Rm 1801 New York NY 10017-2024

GRIFFIN, MICHAEL SCOTT, communications educator, writer; b. Minneapolis, Minn., Feb. 9, 1953; s. Delmar Joseph and Joan Darlene Griffin; m. Martha Hollowell Nicoloff, Dec. 29, 2001; m. Dona Beth Schwartz, Aug. 20, 1978 (div. Oct. 13, 1998); children: Owen Michael Nicoloff, Daniel Joseph, Eric William, Lara Joan. BA in History, Carleton Coll., Northfield, Minn., 1975; MA in Comms., U. Pa., 1978; PhD in Comms., U. of Pa., 1986. Documentary filmmaker, Phila., 1977—80; CBS fellow, tchg. assoc. Annenberg Sch. for Comm., U. of Pa, Phila., 1980—82; lectr. mass comm. and film studies Sch. of Journalism and Mass Comms., U. of Minn., Mpls., 1982—90, asst. prof. of journalism and mass comm., 1990—98; Annenberg fellow, vis. lectr. Annenberg Sch. for Comm., U. of Pa, Phila., 1995—96; acting chair of comm. and media studies Macalester Coll., St. Paul, 2003—. Bd. dirs. Cursor, Inc., Mpls.; rsch. cons. St. Paul Pub. Access TV, St. Paul, 1988—90; vis. prof. comms. and Am. studies U. Amsterdam, Netherlands, 1994—95; vis. prof. journalism and mass comm. U. St. Thomas, St. Paul, 1998—99; vis. prof. media studies Macalester Coll., St. Paul, 1999—. Dir.: (documentary film) Handscapes (Spl. Selection, Paul Robeson Internat. Film Festival, 1978); editor: (book) International Media Monitoring, (comm. rsch. jour.) COMMUNICATION: Special double issue on Visual Communication. Neighborhood assn. leader St. Anthony Pk. Neighborhood Assn., St. Paul, 1986—97; writer, organizer Amnesty Internat., MoveOn, Ind. Media, Internat. Media Monitoring, and Cursor.org, 1986—2003; party del., com. chair Dem. Party, St. Paul, 1975—2002. Recipient U. Rsch. Grant-in-Aid, U. Minn., 1992—93, Pres.'s Disting. Tchr. and Mentor award, 1994, Faculty Exch. award, U. Amsterdam, 1994—95; CBS fellow, U. Pa., 1980—82, Annenberg Scholars Program fellow, Annenberg Sch. Comm., U. Pa, 1995—96. Mem.: Internat. Comm. Assn. (chair visual comm. interest group 2003—). Dfl. Avocations: music, movies, travel, reading, history, photography. Home: 859 Ivy Ave W Saint Paul MN 55117 Office: Macalester Coll 1600 Grand Ave Saint Paul MN 55105 E-mail: griffin@macalester.edu.

GRIFFIN, O. DANIEL, JR., reporter, writer, photographer, audio engineer, videographer; b. Portsmouth, Va., Oct. 26, 1960; s. Otto Daniel Sr. and Mary Lee (Gee) G. Student, Norfolk State U., 1980-83; BS in Fin., BA in Mass Media, Hampton U., 1986; BS in English, Old Dominion U., 1986; MFA in Film, Syracuse U., 1988. Lic. FCC. Audio & video engr. Afram Fest, Norfolk, Va., 1980—, Ujoma Fest, Portsmouth, Va., 1980—, Hampton Jazz Fest,

Hampton, Va., 1980—; telecomm. engr. officer USAFNG, 1980—; audio engr. Sta. WOWI-FM, Norfolk, Va., 1984—, Star Prodn., Norfolk, Va., 1988—; promotion, pub. rels. rep. McDonalds's, Portsmouth, Va., 1987; writer, reporter Citizens Press Am., Portsmouth, 1985—; asst. sport reporter Sta. WAVY-TV, Portsmouth, 1985—, Sta. WTKR-TV, Norfolk, 1987-93, Sta. WVEC-TV, Norfolk, 1991-92; owner Griffin's Photography, Audio & Video Post-Prodn. Inc., Portsmouth, 1987—, Step Above Post Prodn. Co.; writer, reporter Journal & Guide, Norfolk, 1988; mentor/computer programmer, writer, engr. Popular Hall Elem., 1992—; audio/video/light engr. cons. Treetop Co., Portsmouth, Va., 1993—; photographer Glamour Shots, Chesapeake, Va., 1996—, The New Jour. and Guide, Norfolk, 1995—. Cameraman Manor High Band, Portsmouth, 1985-88; audio engr. Hal Jackson's Talent Teens, Norfolk, 1984—; photographer Pre-Teen Pageant, Portsmouth, 1987; producer, dir. Va. Beach Joint Cable Ctr., 1990—, Quiet Storm Soundtrack, Sta. WOWI-FM, Norfolk, 1984; owner, producer, dir., writer Step Above Post Prodn. Co., Portmouth, Va., 1990—; asst. sport reporter Sta. WVEC-TV, Norfolk, 1991—; producer, dir. Va. Beach Joint Cable Ctr., 1990-91. Actor play Momma Don't, audio engr./mem. stage crew In Times Like These; audio & video engr. Play Just Us, 1997—, Summer in Suffolk, 1997—; contbr. articles popular mags., 1986—. Named one of Outstanding Young Men Am., 1988. Mem. Black Filmmaker Assn., Nat. Rec. Soc. Arts and Sci., Hampton Roads Black Media Profl. Assn., Citizens Press of Hampton Roads, Norfolk State U. Alumni Band, Hampton U. Alumni Band, Yearbook Club, Newspaper Club. Baptist. Avocations: reading, music, plays, bowling, running, modeling. Home: 1425 Horne Ave Portsmouth VA 23701-3126 Office: Sta WVEC-TV 613 Woodis Ave Norfolk VA 23510-1017

GRIFFIN, PATTI ELAINE, medical educator, consultant; d. Edgar Heerwald and Eva Irene Smith; m. Dennis W. Griffin; children: Lisa, Pat, Tim. BA, Stephens U., 1979; MA, U. Minn., 1984; MBA, S.W. Mo. State U., 1986; PhD in Healthservices and Social Change, Walden U., 1987. V.p. St. John's Regional Med. Ctr., Joplin, Mo., 1973—84, Franciscan Health Sys., Dayton, Ohio, 1987—93; cons. edn. specialist Johnson & Johnson, Cin., 1994—98; prof. Coll. Bus. Harding U., Searcy AR, 1998—99; prof. Coll. Bus. Lipscomb U., Nashville, 1999—2000, asst. provost, 2002—. Missionary Latin Am. Missions, Valdosta, Ga., 1987—99, Health Talents, Internat., Birmingham, Ala., 2000—02. Contbr. articles. Fellow: Am. Coll. Healthcare Exec. Mem. Ch. Of Christ. Avocations: singing, running, golf. Home: 101 Gillespie Dr Apt 8105 Franklin TN 37067 Office: Lipscomb Univ 3901 Granny White Pk Nashville TN 37204

GRIFFIN, PAULINE M. publishing executive; b. Bklyn., July 5, 1947; d. Timothy Joseph Griffin and Mary Christine Murphy. Author: Star Commandos, 1986, Star Commandos: Colony in Peril, 1987, Star Commandos: Mission Underground, 1988, Star Commandos: Death Planet, 1989, Star Commandos: Mind Slaver, 1990, Star Commandos: Return to War, 1990, Star Commandos: Fire Planet, 1990, Star Commandos: Jungle Assault, 1991, Seakeep/Storms of Victory, 1991, Star Commandos: Call to Arms, 1991, Falcon Hope/Flight of Vengeance, 1992, Redline the Stars, 1993, Firehand, 1994, Watchdogs of Space, 2002, (short stories) Covenant, 1986, Oath'Bound, 1987, Trouble, 1989, Knowledge, 1990, In Bastet's Service, 1991, Lizard, 1995, The Neighbor, 1996, Tenth-Life Cat, 1999, Partners, 1994. Mem.: Cat Writers' Assn. (Muse Medallion award 2000, 1994), Sci. Fiction and Fantasy Writers Am. Inc., Lewis and Clark Trail Heritage Found. (Portage Rte. chpt.). Roman Catholic. Avocations: cats, tropical fish, reading, music.

GRIFFIN, RICHARD J. federal agency administrator; b. Chgo., Oct. 9, 1949; m. Mary Jean Lang; three children. B in Econs., Xavier U., 1971; grad., Nat. War Coll., 1983; MBA, Marymount U., 1984. Agt. U.S. Secret Svc., Chgo., 1971, agt. in charge L.A., dep. asst. dir. Office of Investigations, asst. dir. protective ops., dep. dir.; inspector gen. Dept. Vets. Affairs, Washington, 1997—. Office: Dept Vets Affairs 810 Vermont Ave NW Washington DC 20420-0001

GRIFFIN, ROBERT F. military career officer; b. Ft. Pierce, Fla., Dec. 21, 1944; m. Ann Griffin; children: Carolyn, Laura, Thomas; children from previous marriage: James, Daniel, Robert Jr. Grad., U.S. Mil. Acad., 1967; MD, Emory U., 1974; grad., U.S. Army War Coll. Diplomate Am. Bd. Surgery. Commd. officer U.S. Army Infantry, advanced through grades to brig. gen.; intern and resident Letterman Army Med. Ctr., San Francisco; chief gen. surgery U.S. Army, Ft. Sill, Okla., brigade surgeon 193d Inf. Brigade Panama Canal Zone, divsn. surgeon 8th Inf. Divsn. (Mechanized), comdr. 3d Med. Bn., 3d Inf. Divsn. (Mechanized) Wuerzburg, Germany, chief dept. surgery, dep. comdr. 34th Gen. Hosp. Augsburg, Germany, comdr. USA Med. Dept. Activity and 98th Gen. Hosp. Nuernberg, Germany, corps surgeon VII (US) Corps Stuttgart, Germany, Saudi Arabia, dep. comdr. 332d Med. Brigade, comdr. USA Med. Dept. Activity, 45th Surgeon U.S. Mil. Acad.; command surgeon U.S. Army Forces Command; dep. comdr. Health Care Ops., chief Med. Corps Affairs U.S. Army Med. Command; commdg. gen. Dwight David Eisenhower Army Med. Ctr. S.E. Regional Med. Command. Decorated Silver Star, Legion of Merit with three oak leaf clusters, Bronze Star with oak leaf cluster, Purple Heart, Meritorious Svc. medal with four oak leaf clusters, Air medal, Army Commendation medal. Fellow ACS. Office: Dwight D Eisenhower Army Med Ctr SE Region Med Command DOD/TRICARE Region 3 Fort Gordon GA 30905

GRIFFIN, ROBERT H. career officer; b. Atlanta, Oct. 4, 1947; BS in Mech. Engring., MS in Geotech. Engring., Auburn U.; MBA, Long Island U.; grad., U.S. Army War Coll., Army Command/Gen. Staff Coll. Registered profl. engr., Va. Commd. 2d lt. U.S. Army, advanced through grades to brig. gen.; served in Dharan, Saudi Arabia; chief of staff Hdqrs., U.S. Army C.E., Washington, to 1996; comdr. and divsn. engr. U.S. Army C.E. Northwestern Divsn., Portland, Oreg., 1996-99, U.S. Army Great Lakes/Ohio River Divsn., Cincinnati, Ohio, 1999-. Decorated Legion of Merit with oak lead cluster, Bronze Star medal, others. Office: US Army Corps Engrs Great Lakes Ohio River Div PO Box 1159 Cincinnati OH 45201-1159 E-mail: robert.h.griffin.bg@usace.army.mil.

GRIFFIN, ROBERT PAUL, former United States senator, state supreme court justice; b. Detroit, Nov. 6, 1923; s. J.A. and Beulah M. G.; m. Marjorie J. Anderson, 1947; children— Paul Robert, Richard Allen, James Anderson, Martha Jill. AB, BS, Central Mich. U., 1947, LLD, 1963; JD, U. Mich., 1950, LLD, 1973; LL.D., Eastern Mich. U., 1969, Albion Coll., 1970, Western Mich. U., 1971, Grand Valley State Coll., 1971, Detroit Coll. Bus., 1972, Detroit Coll. Law, 1973; L.H.D., Hillsdale (Mich.) Coll., 1970; J.C.D., Rollins Coll., 1970; Ed.D., No. Mich. U., 1970; D. Pub. Service, Detroit Inst. Tech., 1971. Bar: Mich. 1950. Pvt. practice, Traverse City, Mich., 1950-56; mem. 85th-89th congresses from 9th Dist. Mich., Washington, 1957-66; mem. U.S. Senate from Mich., Washington, 1966-79; counsel Miller, Canfield, Paddock & Stone, Traverse City, 1979-86; assoc. justice Mich. Supreme Ct., Lansing, 1987-95. Trustee Gerald R. Ford Found. Served with inf. AUS, World War II, ETO. Named 1 of 10 Outstanding Young Men of Nation U.S. Jaycees, 1959 Mem. ABA, Mich. Bar Assn., D.C. Bar Assn., Kiwanis.

GRIFFIN, ROBERT THOMAS, automotive company executive; b. Somerville, Mass., July 3, 1917; s. Michael and Cecelia (Rourke) G.; m. Mary Ellen Mulcahy, Sept. 10, 1960; children: Mary Catherine, Christiane Marie, Justine Dufresne, Joseph Michael. BS, Boston Coll., 1939; MA in Pub. Adminstrn, Boston U., 1954; postgrad., Harvard U. Grad. Sch. Pub. Adminstrn., 1954-55. Regional mgr. War Assets Adminstrn., 1946-49; with GSA, Washington, 1950-56, 58-80, spl. asst. to adminstr., 1961-62, asst. adminstr., 1962-70, asst. commr. property mgmt., 1970-73; spl. asst. to adminstr. for coordination John F. Kennedy Library, 1973-77, acting adminstr., 1977—; dep. adminstr. GSA, 1977-78; sr. advisor Pres.'s Spl. Trade Rep., White House, 1977-78; sr. advisor to Personal Rep. of Pres. to Middle East Negotiations, White House, 1978-80. Staff exec. to pres. Chrysler Corp., 1980— ; dir. Van Pool Services, Inc.; mem. Pres.'s Inflation Task Force, 1978-79; conferee White House Conf. Natural Beauty, 1964, Pres.'s Fed. Agy. Task Force on Cost Reduction, 1965; adminstrv. cons. Govt. of Iran, 1956-58; mem. Pres.'s Com. Minority Enterprise. Bd. dirs. Hamlet Citizens Assn., Chevy Chase, Md., 1981—, John F. Kennedy Libr., 1991— (dir. emeritus). Served with USCGR, 1943-46. Mem. Am. Soc. Pub. Adminstrn., DAV Clubs: Washington Athletic, Columbia Country. Office: 1100 Connecticut Ave NW Washington DC 20036-4101

GRIFFIN, SHEILA MB, strategic marketing excutive; b. June 17, 1951; d. George Michael and Frances Josephine (Sheehan) Spielman; m. Woodson Jack Griffin, Dec. 30, 1972; children: Woodson Jack II, Kelly Sheehan. BS, U. Ill., 1975, MBA, 1979. Personal banking rep. Am. Express Banking, Boeblingen, Germany, 1973-74; market rsch. analyst Market Facts, Chgo., 1975-77; mgr. strategic rsch. Motorola, Inc., Schaumburg, Ill., 1977-83, mgr. mktg. resource, 1985-88, mgr. spl. projects corp. strategy office, 1988-89, dir. corp. advt. worldwide, 1989-93, dir. bus. assessment corp. strategy office, 1993-94, dir. multimedia strategy office, 1994-96, dir. global applied market rsch., 1996-98, v.p., dir. strategic mktg. office, 1999—2001; pres. Griffin Holdings, Inc., 2001—. Gen. mgr. mktg. rsch. and info. Ameritech Mobile Comm., Inc., Schaumburg, 1983-85. Founding trustee, chmn. Ill. Math. and Sci. Acad., 1985—; Lincoln Series for Excellence in the Pub. Sector fellow, 2002.. Mem. U. Ill. Chgo. MBA Alumni Assn. (founder, pres. 1984-86), U. Ill. Alumni Assn. (bd. dirs. 1984-86), Disting. Alumni 1985, Constituent Leadership award 1989). Home: 3017 Glen Eagles Ct Saint Charles IL 60174-8832 Office: Griffin Holdings Inc PO Box 3702 Saint Charles IL 60174

GRIFFIN, STANLEY RAY, machinist; b. Little Rock, Apr. 22, 1940; s. Stanley Earl and Era Mae (Overton) G.; m. Vicki Diane Harris, Aug. 3, 1958 (div. Apr. 1992); children: Kit Wade, Scott Allen, Diana Lee, Donna Sue; m. Thelma Alice Roberts, Sept. 4, 1993. Tech. asst. Tex. A&M Experiment Sta., Angleton, Tex., 1959-61; utility, chemist asst. Dow Chem. Co., Freeport, Tex., 1961-75; mgr. city parks City of Angleton, 1975-76; water dept. asst. South Tex. Farms, Rosharon, 1976-77; foreman body shop Scott Chevrolet, Oldsmobile, Angleton, 1977-78; material handler Collins Instrument Co., Angleton, 1978—. Author: (poetry book) Today I Saw the Sunrise, 2001, Because of You. Mem. Acad. Am. Poets. Avocations: writing poetry, poetry recitals and public readings. Home: 1053 CR 452 Sweeny TX 77480

GRIFFIN, SYLVIA GAIL, reading specialist; b. Portland, Oreg., Dec. 13, 1935; d. Archie and Marguerite (Johnson) G. AA, Boise Jr. Coll., 1955; BS, Brigham Young U., 1957, MEd, 1967. Cert. advanced teaching, Idaho. Classroom tchr. Boise Pub. Sch., Idaho, 1957-59, 61-66, 67-69, reading specialist, 1969-90, 91-95, 98-2001, inclusion specialist, 1995-98, early childhood specialist, 1990-91. Tchr. evening Spanish classes for adults, 1987-88; lectr. in field; mem. cons. pool US Office Juvenile Justice and Delinquency Prevention, 1991—. Author: Procedures Used by First Grade Teachers for Teaching Experience Readiness for Reading Comprehension; The Short Story of Vowels; A Note Worthy Way to Teach Reading; The Little Black Schoolhouse; Hellside Elementary School; Reading, Righting, and Revenge, Memorandum: Murder. Advisor in developing a program for dyslexics Scottish Rite Masons of Idaho, Boise. Mem.: NEA, Actor's Guild, Idaho Edn. Assn. (pub. rels. dir. 1970—72), Boise Edn. Assn. (pub. rels. dir. 1969—72, bd. dirs. ednl. polit. involvement com. 1983—89), Alpha Delta Kappa. Avocations: music, creative writing. Home: 9948 W Sleepy Hollow Ln Boise ID 83714-3665

GRIFFIN, TERESA BEVERLY, physician; b. Burke County, N.C., Mar. 7, 1951; d. Ivey Lawrence Jr. and Carolyn Doris (Ramsey) G. BS, East Carolina U., 1973; MA, U. No. Colo., 1974; PhD, U. Tenn., Knoxville, 1982; MD, Case Western Res. U., 1993. Diplomate Am. Bd. Family Practice. Tchr. phys. edn. Duffield (Va.) Elem. Sch., 1974-78; tchg. asst. dept. health edn. U. Tenn., Knoxville, 1980-82; asst. prof. health edn. Cleve. State U., 1982-88; intern Fairview Hosp., Cleve., 1993-94, resident in family practice, 1994-96; family physician Pigeon Forge (Tenn.) Family Medicine, 1996-98, MedCtrl., Cleve., 1999, Kaiser Permanente, Cleve., 2000—02, Sterling Med., 2003—. Cons. Am. Cancer Soc., Cleve., 1985-86, Am. Heart Assn., Cleve., 1985-86. Contbr. numerous articles to profl. jours. Advisor BEST program Am. Cancer Soc., Cleve., 1995-96. Mem. AMA, Am. Assn. Family Practice, Ohio Assn. Family Practice. Avocations: travel, skiing, scuba, historic house preservation. Home: 6921 Ottawa Rd Cleveland OH 44105-3713 E-mail: stardance6@pol.net.

GRIFFIN, THOMAS MCLEAN, retired lawyer; b. Lake Placid, N.Y., Sept. 12, 1922; s. Nathaniel Edward and Anne (McLean) G.; m. Hope Wiswall, July 16, 1949; children: Richard Wiswall, Anne McLean, Thomas McLean, David Coggin AB, Harvard Coll., 1943; LLB, Harvard U., 1949. Bar: Mass. 1950, U.S. Supreme Ct. 1976. Atty. State Mutual Life Assurance Co. Am., Worcester, Mass., 1949-58; assoc. counsel Old Colony Trust Co., Boston, 1958-67; sec., bd. dirs. 1st Nat. Bank Boston, 1967-87, gen. counsel, 1971-87, ret., 1987; gen. counsel Bank of Boston Corp., 1973-87, sec. bd. dirs., 1970-87, ret., 1987. Trustee Marlboro (Vt.) Coll., 1986-95, House of Seven Gables Settlement Assn., Salem, Mass., 1987-95, Salem Athenaeum, 1995-2001, Harmony Grove Cemetery, Salem; hon. chmn. Nathaniel Bowdithc Inst., 2003. Cmdr. USN, 1943-60, USNR, 1970—. Mem. Ea. Yacht Club, Whiting Club. Democrat. Avocation: bridge, sailing, sketching.. Home: 14 Beckford St Salem MA 01970-3206

GRIFFIN, WALTON W. performing company executive; b. Oakland, Tenn. With Dobbs Houses; with Memphis divsn. TMP Worldwide; gen. mgr. Ballet Memphis, 1995—. Ch. organist and choirmaster. Office: Ballet Memphis PO Box 3675 Cordova TN 38088-3675

GRIFFIN, WILLIAM MELL, III, lawyer; b. Tallahassee, Feb. 1, 1957; s. William Mell Jr. and June Winona (Cooper) G.; m. Kathryn Elizabeth Lawson, Dec. 11, 1993; children: William Mell IV, George Lawson, James Porter. BA, U. Va., 1979; JD, So. Meth. U., 1982. Bar: Ark. 1982, U.S. Dist. Ct. (ea. and we. dists.) Ark. 1982, U.S. Ct. Appeals (8th cir.) 1983. Assoc. Friday, Eldredge & Clark, Little Rock, 1982-87, ptnr., 1987—. Mem. ABA (torts and ins. practice sect.), Am. Bd. Trial Advocates (advocate), Ark. Bar Assn., Pulaski County Bar Assn., William R. Overton Inn of Ct., Ark. Def. Counsel, Def. Rsch. Inst., Fedn. Ins. and Corp. Counsel, Leadership Greater Little Rock, Phi Delta Phi. Avocations: running, hunting. Home: 420 Midland St Little Rock AR 72205-4177 Office: Friday Eldredge & Clark 2000 1st Commercial Bldg Little Rock AR 72201

GRIFFIN-BROWN, DIANNA LYNN, entrepreneur, educator; b. Moline, Ill., Oct. 9, 1957; d. Robert Edward and Bonita Pearl (Myers) Kirklin; m. Scott Martin Griffin, Dec. 1, 1982 (div. May 1995); 1 child, Robert Edward Griffin; m. William Brown Jr., 1978 (div. 1982); 1 child, Heidi Lynn Brown. Student, Black Hawk Coll., 1977, student, 1996. Shipper, truck driver, mail expediter Desaulniers Printing Co., Moline, Ill., 1975—89; propr. Angelic Fashions, Moline, Ill., 1989—94; dir., propr. Angelic Pageants, Mystical Starr Pageants, Moline, Ill., 1988—; propr. Golden Birthday Co., 1995—. Inventor numerous bridal and party goods. Author: The Complete Guide to Children in Pageants, 1995, 2002; creator: (party goods line) Golden Birthday, 1995, Star Birthday, 1995. Tchr. Literacy is for Everyone, Moline, Ill., 2001, 2002; tchr. poise and charm Y and Cmty. Pk. Bd., Moline, Ill., 2002; electoral judge Voter Registration, Moline, Ill., 1998. Democrat. Avocations: dancing, sewing, crafts, writing, reading. Office: Angelic Enterprises 2800 81/2 Ave Rock Island IL 61201

GRIFFIN-BURRILL, KATHLEEN R. F. See BURRILL, KATHLEEN R. F.

GRIFFING, GEORGE THOMAS, medical educator, endocrinologist; b. Lawrence, Kans., Apr. 3, 1950; s. George W. and Roberta J. (Brown) G.; m. Bonnie Anne Brennen, June 14, 1985; children: Nathaniel, Samuel, Emily. Student, U. Utah, 1971; MD, Wayne State U., 1975. From instr. medicine to asst. prof. medicine Boston U. Med. Sch., 1980-87, mem. dept. physiology, assoc. prof. medicine, 1987-92; prof. medicine U. Mo., Columbia, 1992-99, St. Louis U., 1999—. Asst. vis. physician Boston City Hosp., 1981-92; dir. Cosmo Internat. Diabetes Ctr./U. Mo., Columbia, 1992-99; dir. divsn. endocrinology/metabolism Sch. Medicine, U. Mo., Columbia, 1992-99, dir. divsn. gen. internal medicine St. Louis U., 1999-2001, dir. divsn. endocrinology, diabetes and metabolism, 2001—; vis. scientist dept. biochemistry Tufts U. Health Sci. Ctr., Boston, 1986-92; mem. Problem Based Learning Task Force, Columbia, 1995-99; chmn. admissions com. Sch. Medicine, U. Mo., 1994-99; chmn. activities com. Mo. regional chpt. Am. Coll. Medicine, 1994—. Author: (jours.) Jour. Clin. Endocrine, New Eng. Jour. Medicine. Mem. Cosmopolitan Internat., Columbia, 1992. Named New Investigator, NIH, 1983-86, Phi Zeta hon. lectr. U. Mo. Vet. Sch., 1994. Fellow Coun. for High Blood Pressure, ACP (dir. sub-splty. update regional meeting 1994—); mem. Am. Fedn. Clin. Rsch., Endocrine Soc. Achievements include investigation of new drug application for intranasal insulin. Home: 4 Cedar Crst Saint Louis MO 63132-4205 Office: St Louis U Fdt-12S 1402 S Grand Blvd-Univ Saint Louis MO 63104

GRIFFIN-THOMPSON, MELANIE, accounting firm executive; b. Corpus Christi, Tex., Oct. 25, 1949; d. Roy Albert and Ola Emma (Hunt) G.; m. Robert Thompson; children: Maurice Dale Griffin, Donald Dwight Griffin, Merideth Thompson Ferguson, Laura Thompson. BBA summa cum laude, Corpus Christi State U., 1977; MBA, Tex. A&M U., 1994. CPA Tex.; CVA, diplomate Assn. Forensic Examiners. Sec.-treas. Roy Hunt, Inc., Corpus Christi, 1970-78, dir., 1970-82; v.p. White, Sluyter & Co., Corpus Christi, 1978-80; pres. Whittington & Griffin, Corpus Christi, 1980-82, also dir.; sec.-treas., dir. Sand Express, Inc., Corpus Christi, 1982-84; v.p. Fields, Nemec & Co., P.C., Corpus Christi, 1984-97; ptnr. Corpus Christi, 1975-82; prin. Melanie Hunt Griffin & Assocs., CPAs, Corpus Christi, 1982-84; v.p. Fields, Nemec & Co., P.C., Corpus Christi, 1984-97; ptnr. Arthur Andersen, LLP, San Antonio, 1997-2000; cons. New Braunfels, Tex., 2000—02; prof. Tex. Luth. U., 2002—; prin. Melanie G. Thompson CPA, PC, 2002—. Mem. edn. and tng. task force White House Conf. Small Bus., 1993; adj. prof. Tex. A&M U., Corpus Christi; mem. Tex. State Bd. Pub. Accountancy, 2001—. Contbr. articles to profl. jours. Devel. chair Am. Heart Assn., chmn. bd. 1989-90, Leadership Corpus Christi Alumni, 1982—; mem. adv. coun. Tex. A&M U., Corpus Christi, NASBA Ethics Com. Recipient Women in Careers award YWCA, 1989. Mem.: AICPA (personal fin. planning dir. small bus. taxation com. 1990—93, mem. coun. 1997—), Exec. Women Internat. (chmn. philanthropy com. 1986—87), Tex. State CPAs Ednl. Found. (trustee 1990—93), Tex. Soc. CPAs (bd. dirs. 1987—, v.p. 1988—89, 1993—94, treas. 1995—96, pres. 1997—98, pres. Corpus Christi chpt. 1987—88, chmn. devel. new legis. leaders 1990—93, vice chair CPAs Helping Schs. 1994—95, Outstanding Svc. award 1990—91, Presdl. citation 1996—97, Outstanding Svc. award Corpus Christi chpt 1990—93, hon. fellow award 1998), Corpus Christi State U. Alumni Assn. (bd. dirs. 1987—90), New Braunfels Rotary. Home: 268 Eden Ranch Dr New Braunfels TX 78133-5410 E-mail: mgthompson97@hotmail.com.

GRIFFITH, ALAN RICHARD, banker; b. Mineola, N.Y., Dec. 17, 1941; s. Charles Ernest and Amalia (Guenther) G.; m. Elizabeth Ferguson, Nov. 28, 1964; children: Timothy, Elizabeth. BA, Lafayette Coll., Easton, Pa., 1964; MBA, CUNY, 1971. Asst. credit officer The Bank of N.Y., N.Y.C., 1968-72, asst. v.p., 1972-74, v.p., 1974-82, sr. v.p., 1982-85, exec. v.p., 1985-88, sr. exec. v.p., 1988-90, pres., 1990-94, vice chmn., 1994—. Trustee Amyothrophic Lateral Sclerosis Assn., Sherman Oaks, Calif., Chesapeake Bay Found., Annapolis, Md.; chmn. bd. trustees Lafayette Col. Mem. Univ. Club, (N.Y.C.). Office: The Bank of NY One Wall St New York NY 10286

GRIFFITH, ARNOLD KOONS, computer consultant; b. Providence, R.I., July 1, 1942; s. John Ramsbottom and Barbara Koons G.; m. Patricia Martino, July 10, 1971. BA, Swarthmore (Pa.) Coll., 1964; PhD, MIT, 1970. Divsn. mgr. Info. Internat., Inc., Culver City, Calif., 1971-82; owner A/P Systems, Santa Monica, Calif., 1982—. Contbr. articles to profl. jours. Mem. IEEE, Assn. for Computing Machinery, Jonathan Club, Phi Beta Kappa. Avocations: tennis, music, photography. Home: 802 Washington Ave Santa Monica CA 90403 E-mail: griffitha@acm.org.

GRIFFITH, B(EZALEEL) HEROLD, physician, educator, plastic surgeon; b. N.Y.C., Aug. 24, 1925; s. Bezaleel Davies and Henrietta (Herold) G.; m. Jeanne B. Lethbridge, 1948; children: Susan, Tristan. BA, Johns Hopkins U., 1992; MD, Yale U., 1948. Diplomate: Am. Bd. Plastic Surgery (dir. 1976-82, chmn. 1981-82). Asst. in anatomy Yale U., New Haven, 1947—48, asst. in surgery, 1948—49; intern Grace New Haven Cmty. Hosp.-Yale U., 1948-49; resident in surgery VA Hosp., Newington, Conn., 1949-50; asst. resident in surgery 2d (Cornell) Surg. Divsn., Bellevue Hosp., N.Y.C., 1952-53; instr. surgery Cornell U., 1956; resident in plastic surgery VA Hosp., Bronx, 1953-55; resident (sr. registrar) in plastic surgery U. Glasgow, Scotland, 1955; chief resident in plastic surgery N.Y. Hosp. Cornell Med. Ctr., N.Y.C., 1956; rsch. fellow in plastic surgery Cornell U. Med. Coll., 1956-57; pvt. practice specializing in plastic surgery Chgo., 1957-96; attending plastic surgeon Northwestern Meml., Children's Meml., VA Lakeside hosps., Rehab. Inst. Chgo.; instr. surgery Northwestern U., 1957-59, assoc. in surgery, 1959-62, asst. prof. surgery, 1962-67, assoc. prof., 1967-71, prof., 1971-96, prof. emeritus, 1996, chief divsn. plastic surgery, 1970-91; chief plastic surgery Shriners Hosp. for Crippled Children, Chgo., 1994-96; retired. Assoc. editor: Plastic and Reconstructive Surgery, 1972-78; contbr. articles to profl. jours. Lt. M.C., USNR, 1950-52. Fellow ACS, Am. Assn. Plastic Surgeons, Chgo. Surg. Soc., Royal Soc. Medicine; mem. AAAS, AMA, Am. Soc. Plastic and Reconstructive Surgeons (sec. 1972-74), Brit. Assn. Plastic Surgeons, Plastic Surgery Rsch. Coun. (chmn. 1969), Am. Cleft Palate Assn., N.Y. Acad. Scis., Ill., Chgo. Med. Socs., Midwestern Assn. Plastic Surgeons, Soc. Head and Neck Surgeons, Ill., Chgo. Hist. Socs., Civil War Round Table, Evanston Hist. Soc. (trustee 1974-78), Sigma Xi (pres. Northwestern U. 1986-87, 94-95). Clubs: Yale (Chgo.). Lodges: Masons. Achievements include research in transplantation, skin tumors, cleft palate, paraplegia.

GRIFFITH, CLARK DEXTER, risk management professional; b. Suffern, N.Y., Dec. 21, 1965; s. William Fredrick Jr. and Lillian Griffith. BA in Econs. and Japanese, San Diego State U., 1991; M Internat. Affairs and Fin., cert. East Asia Study, Columbia U., 2000. Realtor Elegado Realty & Prudential Calif. Realty, San Diego, 1988-92; coord. import housing projects Sotetsu Real Estate Co., Ltd., Yokohama, Japan, 1991-97; regional mgr. Intradex Corp., Pearl River, N.Y., 1995-2000; project mgr. pvt. client group Merrill Lynch Internat., 1999; with risk mgmt. GE Capital, 2000—. Customer svc. rep. Wells Fargo Bank, San Diego, 1988-90; cons. Kirin Breweries, Inc., Yokohama, 1989, Nichiei Co., Ltd., Yokohama, 1990, Perillo-Griffith Travel Svc., Pearl River, N.Y., 1976-86; lectr. Am. Assn. State Colls. and Univs. Japan Studies Inst. Nat. Summer Inst., 1998, 2000. Contbr. articles to profl. jours. Mem. Am. C. of C. in Japan (vice chmn. trade expansion com. 1992-97, chmn. import housing sub-com. 1995-97), Japan Studies Assn. (founder, pres. 1989-91). Avocations: scuba diving, golfing, jet skiing, snow skiing, reading, motorcycling. Home: 5050 Hacienda Drive Dublin CA 94568 Office: GE Capital 2840 Broadway 130 New York NY 10025-7816 E-mail: cg266@columbia.edu.

GRIFFITH, DANIEL ALVA, geography educator; b. Pitts., Nov. 15, 1948; s. Donald Sanford and Mary Jane (McClain) G.; m. Diane Elaine Swartz, Jan. 3, 1970; children: Darren Lee, Michele Renee. BS, Indiana U. of Pa., 1970, MA, 1972; MS, Pa. State U., 1985; PhD, U. Toronto, Ont., Can., 1978. Instr. Ryerson Polytech. U., Toronto, 1975-78; from asst. prof. to full prof. SUNY, Buffalo, 1978-88; prof. geography Syracuse (N.Y.) U., 1988—, dir. stats. program 1991-92, 93-95, chair, 1995-97; adj. prof. Coll. Environ. Sci. and Forestry 1992—. Vis. EPA/EMAP rsch. affiliate stats. dept. Oreg. State U., Corvallis 1990, 91, 92, 93; vis. rsch. prof. Erasmus U., Rotterdam, 1992, U. Rome, 1995 dep. dir. N.Y. State program in geographic info. and analysis Syracuse U. 1989-90; ASI dir. NATO Sci. Affairs, Brussels, 1979-80, 81-82, 85, cons. Peru Minister Edn., 2000-01; Leverhulme vis. prof. Cambridge U., 2004. Author Spatial Autocorrelation, 1987, Advanced Spatial Statistics, 1988, Statistical Analysis for Geographers, 1991, Spatial Regression Analysis on the PC, 1993 Multivariate Statistical Analysis for Geographers, 1997, A Casebook for Spatial Statistical Data Analysis, 1999; editor books; contbr. articles to profl. jours. NSF grantee, 1981, 83-84, 85, 88-90, 92-93, 95-97, 99, 2002—; Fulbright fellow 1992-93, rsch. fellow ASA/USDA-NASS, 1999, Guggenheim fellow, 2001-02 recipient Award Pa. Geog. Soc., 1999. Fellow N.Y. Acad. Scis.; mem. Am. Statis. Assn., Regional Sci. Assn. (pres. 1996-97), Assn. Am. Geographers (chair 1987-88, Nystrom Dissertation award 1980, Pub. Domain Computer Software award 1994, 97), Sigma Xi (Syracuse chpt. pres. 1999-2000) Democrat. Methodist. Avocation: traveling. Home: 5270 Wethersfield Rd Jamesville NY 13078-9727 Office: Syracuse U Geography Dept Syracuse NY 13244-1020

GRIFFITH, DAVID A, marketing educator, consultant; Research includes process standardization in intra and inter cultural relationships. Recipient Dennis Ching Excellence in Tchg. award, 2001.

GRIFFITH, DEWEY MAURICE, mechanical engineer, investor; b. Conway, S.C., Feb. 13, 1938; s. Edwin Dewey and Addie Lee (Pittman) G.; m. Margaret Louise Taylor, Aug. 18, 1963 (div.); 1 child, Jeffrey Scott. BSME, N.C. State Coll. Agr. & Engr., 1959. Mfg. engr. Westinghouse Electric Corp., Richmond,

Ky., 1960-63, design adminstrv. engr. Bloomfield, N.J., 1963-70; project mech. engr. PPG Industries, Shelby, N.C., 1970-71, GE, Lexington, Ky., 1971-72, E.D. Griffith Renaissance, Greenville, N.C., 1972-74, Catalytic Inc., Charlotte, N.C., 1974-75; profl. engr. D.M. Griffith Design and Rsch., Charlotte, N.C., 1975-79; The Delta Error-Sq. investor The Master E. with Accent Entity, Charlotte, N.C., 1979—. Inventor flashing miniature lamp. Mem. Math. Assn. Am. Republican. Methodist. Avocations: art, design, finance, geometry, mathematics. Home: Stonehaven Subdivision 5959 Kirkpatrick Rd Charlotte NC 28211-4200 E mail: desadept@earthlink.net.

GRIFFITH, DONALD KENDALL, lawyer; b. Aurora, Ill., Feb. 4, 1933; s. Walter George and Mary Elizabeth G.; m. Susan Smykal, Aug. 4, 1962; children: Kay, Kendall. Grad. in history with honors, Culver Mil. Acad., 1951; BA, U. Ill., 1955, JD, 1958. Bar: Ill. 1958, U.S. Supreme Ct. 1973. Assoc. Hinshaw & Culbertson, Chgo., 1959-65, ptnr., 1965-98, of counsel, 1999—. Spl. asst. atty. gen. Ill., 1970-72; lectr. Ill. Inst. Continuing Legal Edn., 1970-90. Mem. editl. bd. Ill. Civil Practice After Trial, 1970; co-editor The Brief, 1975-83; contbg. author Civil Practice After Trial, 1984, 89; contbr. articles to profl. jours. Trustee Lawrence Hall Youth Svcs., 1967-2000, v.p. for program, 1969-74; bd. dirs. Child Care Assn. Ill., 1970-73; bd. edn. Lake Forest HS, 1983-84; chmn. appellate adv. com. ABA, 1983-84. 2d lt. USAF, 1956. Fellow Am. Acad. Appellate Lawyers; mem. ABA (chmn. appellate advocacy com., tort and ins. practice sect. 1983-84), Ill. Bar Assn., Appellate Lawyers Assn. Ill. (pres. 1973-74), Univ. Club Chgo., Knollwood Club, Alpha Chi Rho (chpt. pres.), Phi Delta Phi. Office: Hinshaw & Culbertson 222 N LaSalle St Ste 300 Chicago IL 60601-1081 E-mail: kgriffithd@aol.com.

GRIFFITH, EDWARD, lawyer; b. Wilkes-Barre, Pa., Feb. 9, 1948; s. Edward Meredith Griffith and Jane (Randall) Griffith Jones; m. Linda Christine Scribner, Aug. 9, 1969 (div. July 1982); children: Trevor Scribner, Stewart Randall; m. Katherine Greybill, Oct. 24, 1987. BA, Lehigh U., 1970; JD, Dickinson Sch. Law, 1973. Bar: Pa. 1973, U.S. Dist. Ct. (ea. dist.) Pa. 1973, U.S. Ct. Appeal (3rd cir.) 1973, U.S. Supreme Ct. 1978. Ptnr. Duane, Morris LLP, Phila., 1973—. Cons. Pa. State Bd. Law Examiners, Phila, 1974-77. Master John E. Stively Inn of Ct.; mem. ABA, Pa. Bar Assn., Chester County Bar Assn. Republican. Presbyterian. Avocations: hunting, fishing, gardening. Office: Duane Morris LLP Station Square Three Ste 105 Paoli PA 19301 E-mail: griffith@duanemorris.com.

GRIFFITH, ELWIN JABEZ, lawyer, university administrator; b. Barbados, W.I., Mar. 2, 1938; came to U.S., 1956, naturalized, 1963; s. Vincent and Ermie G.; m. Norma Joyce Rollins, June 9, 1962; 1 child, Traci. BA, L.I. U., 1960; JD, Bklyn. Law Sch., 1963; LLM, NYU, 1964. Bar: N.Y. 1963. Asst. counsel Chase Manhattan Bank, N.Y.C., 1964-68, 68-71; asst. prof. law Cleveland Marshall Law Sch., Cleve. State U., 1968; asst. counsel Tchrs. Ins. and Annuity Assn., N.Y.C., 1971-72; asst. dean Drake U. Law Sch., 1972-73; assoc. prof. U. Cin., 1973-76, prof., 1976-78, assoc. dean, 1974-78; dean DePaul U. Law Sch., 1978-85; prof. Fla. State U. Coll. Law, Tallahassee, 1986—. Legal counsel Bedford-Stuyvesant Jaycees, 1968-71; vis. prof. colls.; vis. prof. Black Exch. program Nat. Urban League, 1970-75 Contbr. articles to law revs. Mem. ABA, N.Y. State Bar Assn. Office: Fla State U Coll Law Tallahassee FL 32306

GRIFFITH, EMLYN IRVING, lawyer; b. Utica, N.Y., May 13, 1923; s. William A. and Maud A. (Charles) G.; m. Mary L. Kilpatrick, Aug. 13, 1946; children: William L., James R. AB, Colgate U., 1942; JD, Cornell U., 1950; 10 hon. doctorates. Bar: N.Y. 1950, U.S. Supreme Ct. 1954. Pvt. practice law, Lockport, NY, 1950—52, Rome, 1952—. Bd. dirs. various corps. and founds.; chmn. N.Y. Photonics Devel. Corp., 2001—. Contbr. articles to profl. jours. in U.S. and U.K. Mem. N.Y. State Bd. Regents, 1973-96, Gov.'s Com. on Librs., 1976-80; co-chmn. State Conf. Professions, 1974-77, 85-90; mem. U.S. Forum Edn. Orgn. Leaders, 1978-80, Intergovtl. Adv. Coun. on Edn., 1982-86; del. to China-U.S. Joint Session on Trade and Law, Beijing, 1987, Soviet-Am. Conf. on Comparative Edn., Moscow, 1988, N.Y. State-USSR Lawyers Conf., Moscow, 1990; pres. Nat. Assn. State Bds. Edn., 1979-80, Nat. Assn. State Bds. Edn. Found., 1997-99; pres. Nat. Welsh-Am. Found., 1981-83; v.p. Hon. Soc. Cymmrodorion, London, 1988—; trustee, bd. pensions United Presbyn. Ch., 1966-72, Aerospace Edn. Found., 1979-96, Erie Canal Mus., 1996-2003, Cazenovia Coll., 1996—. Maj. USAAC, 1942-46. Recipient Disting. Svc. to Am. Edn. award Nat. Assn. State Bds. Edn., 1995, Conspicuous Svc. award State of N.Y., 1992, Exceptional Svc. citation Air Force Assn., 1980; Doolittle fellow Aerospace Edn. Found., 1988, Welsh Heritage award Nat. Welsh Am. Found., 1997. Fellow Am. Bar Found. (life), N.Y. Bar Found. (life, recipient Root-Stimson award for pub. svc. 1986, bd. dirs. 1989—); mem. ABA (com. pub. edn. 1974—), N.Y. State Bar assn. (ho. dels. 1974-76, co-chmn. com. atty. professionalism, 1989-92, mem. bd. editors Bar Jour. 1986-97), Oneida County Bar Assn. (pres. 1974-75), State Conf. County Bar Officers (chmn. 1974-76), Osgoode Soc. Can., Selden Soc., Eng., Phi Gamma Delta Internat. (pres. bd. trustees 1982-86, pres. edn. found. 1992-94). Office: 225 N Washington St Rome NY 13440-5742

GRIFFITH, G. LARRY, lawyer; b. Keokuk, Iowa, Mar. 6, 1937; s. Charles Floyd and Lillian Mae (McClinton) G.; children: Randall Dale, Kristin Lin, Barry Wynn. BA, DePauw U., 1959; JD, U. Iowa, 1962. Bar: Iowa 1962, Minn. 1963. Ptnr. Dorsey & Whitney, Mpls., 1962-2000, chair real estate dept., 1991-95, of counsel, 2001—. Instr. modern real estate transactions U. Minn., Mpls., 1970-71; bd. dirs. Brock-White Co. Comment editor U. Iowa Law Rev., 1961-62. Scout master Boy Scouts Am., Mpls., 1965-69; bd. dirs. Jr. Achievement, 1991—. Rector scholar De Pauw U., 1955-59 Mem. ABA, Minn. Bar Assn., Hennepin County Bar Assn., U.S. Ski Assn. (alpine competition com. cen. div. 1981-87, chmn. region I 1984-86), Mpls. Athletic Club, Burnsville Athletic Club (bd. dirs., legal advisor 1980-92), Phi Alpha Delta. Avocations: skiing, tennis, hunting, scuba diving, golf. Home: 8308 40th Ave N New Hope MN 55427 Office: Dorsey & Whitney LLP Ste 1500 50 S 6th St Minneapolis MN 55402-1553 E-mail: griffith.larry@dorseylaw.com.

GRIFFITH, GARY ERNEST, public affairs executive; b. Ft. Worth, Mar. 14, 1948; s. Ernest Clay and Doris Blanche (Jones) G.; m. Jacqueline Teresa McGaha, Mar. 12, 1970; children: Victoria, Amanda. BA, U. Tex., 1970. Fin. dir. Clements for Gov., Dallas, 1978; alumni assn. dir. SMU, Dallas, 1979-80; comm. dir., ptnr. Trammell Crow Co., Dallas, 1981-86; pres. Tex. Analyst Inc., 1987; v.p. pub. affairs and human resources Epic Healthcare Group, Dallas, 1988-94; pres. Jefferson Ptnrs., Dallas, 1994—. Mem. Dallas City Coun., 2003—; active Commn. on Jud. Conduct, Austin, Tex., 1988-91; bd. dirs. Child Care, Dallas, 1983-89, Tex. Optometry Bd., Austin, 1982-87, Dallas Ballet, 1987-88, Dallas Summer Musicals, 1996—; active Dallas Pk. Bd. Mem. N.Am. Interfraternity Conf., Rotary (found. pres.), Sigma Phi Epsilon (nat. pres.), Project Am. (nat. pres.). Home: 6930 Lakewood Blvd Dallas TX 75214-3556

GRIFFITH, H(OWARD) MORGAN, lawyer; b. Phila., Mar. 15, 1958; s. A. Hundley and Charlotte Virginia (Burford) G. BA, Emory and Henry Coll., 1980; JD, Washington and Lee U., 1983. Bar: Va. 1983, U.S. Dist. Ct. Va. 1985. Assoc. Lutins & Shapiro, Roanoke, Va., 1983-84; pvt. practice Salem, Va., 1984-87; ptnr. Griffith & Varney, Salem, 1987-89; pvt. practice Salem, 1989—; house majority leader, 2000—. Del. Va. Gen. Assembly, 1994—; dir. Salem Bank & Trust; bd. vis. Emory and Henry Coll. Vice-chmn. Salem Rep. Com., 1984-86, chmn., 1986-88, 91-93; bd. dirs. Legal Aid Soc. of Roanoke Valley, 1991-92; advisor, sponsor Legal Explorers Post Boy Scouts of Am., Salem, 1988-89; chmn. Catawba dist. Blue Ridge Mountains coun., Boy Scouts Am., 1984-86, vice chmn., 1987-88, dist. chmn., 1988-91, v.p. rels. and membership, 1991-93; com. mem. Stonegate Swim Club, Salem, 1984-88, bd. dirs., 1991—; mem. state bd. dirs. Easter Seals Va. Recipient Dist. Award of Merit, Boy Scouts Am., 1990-91, Silver Beaver award, 1994. Mem. Va. State Bar Assn., Roanoke County-Salem Bar Assn. (pres. 1995-96), Lions (bd. dirs. 1988-90). Episcopalian. Avocations: swimming, ornithology, ichthyology. Office: 113 E Main St Salem VA 24153-3804

GRIFFITH, JAMES D. retired lawyer; b. Evanston, Ill., Aug. 28, 1929; s. Wendell Crabtree and Mary Griffith; m. Elizabeth Meyer, Sept. 21, 1957 (div. July 1987); children: Ian Hunt, Alison Gail Griffith; m. Phyllis A. Zaruba Oct. 22, 1994. BA, DePauw U., 1951; MA in Modern European History, U. Ill., 1952; JD, Northwestern U., Chgo., 1953. Bar: Ill. 1953, Mich. 1973, Ind. 1980. Assoc. Campbell, Clithero & Fischer, Chgo., 1956-63; ptnr. Graham, Stevenson & Griffith, Chgo., 1963-67; prin. Pauker & Griffith, Ltd., Chgo., 1969-79; pvt. practice, Chgo., 1967-69, 80-95; ret., 1995. Magistrate Village of Glenview, Ill., 1961-65. Contbr. articles to profl. jours. Founder, pres. Com. on Lake Michigan Pollution, Wilmette, Ill., 1967-69, Fifty Percent, Chgo., 1991—; active Chgo. Crime Commn., 1967-72; mem. exec. com. New Trier Dem. Orgn.; pres. Lake Michigan Fedn., Chgo., 1973-74, 92-94; pres. Glenview Civic Party, 1981; dir. Family Svc. Ctr., Wilmette, 1997-2000; trustee Village of Wilmette, 2003-. With U.S. Army, 1954-56. Mem. Chgo. Coun. on Fgn. Rels., Sheridan Shore Yacht Club (Wilmette, commodore 1970), Wilmette Harbor Rotary (sec. 2002-03). Avocations: sailing, tennis, hiking, canoeing, bridge. Home: 1210 Glendenning Rd Wilmette IL 60091-1547

GRIFFITH, JAMES WILLIAM, systems engineer, consultant; b. Waco, Tex., Apr. 11, 1922; s. Paul Isaac and Willie Elizabeth (Rawlin) G.; m. Dorothy Louise Cannon., Oct. 17, 1949; children: Pamela D. (Mrs. John Fletcher Freeman), James William. Student, Tex. Tech U., 1940-41, U. Utah, 1943-44; BS, So. Meth. U., 1949, MS, 1956. Dir. engring. grad. div. So. Meth. U., 1960-67, chmn. dept. indsl. engring., 1965-67, prof., chmn. dept. systems engring., 1967-69; ptnr. K-G Assocs., 1970-80; prin. James W. Griffith Inc., Dallas, 1980—. U.S. expert in daylighting Commn. Internat. Eclairage, 1957—; cons. to govt. agys. including HUD, HEW, NAS; tech. cons. Nat. Fenestration Coun., 1984-87, LBL Windows and Daylighting, 1980-85; tech. cons. profl. devel. program AIA, 1982-86, instr., 1982-86, now cons.; mem. AIA Found. Contbr. articles to profl. jours. Served with USAAF, 1942-46. Named to Engrs. of Distinction Engrs. Joint Council, 1970 Fellow Illuminating Engrs. Soc. (nat. pres.); mem. ASHRAE, NSPE, Illuminating Engring. Rsch. Inst., Bldg. Environment and Thermal Envelope Coun., Nat. Fenestration Rating Coun., Bldg. Rsch. Inst. (bd. dirs. 1965-67, 73-75), Tex. Soc. Profl. Engrs., Soc. Mayflower Descs., Sigma Tau, Eta Kappa Nu. Achievements include a patent on the method of and assembly for measuring equivalent sphere illumination. Home and Office: 751 Sunset Hill Dr Rockwall TX 75087-3236 E-mail: billgsr@juno.com.

GRIFFITH, JOHN VINCENT, academic official; b. Oneida, N.Y., Dec. 24, 1947; s. William F. and Dorothy (Roberts) G.; m. Nancy E. Snell, Jan. 25, 1969; children: Matthew, Christopher. BA cum laude, Dickinson Coll., 1969; MDiv magna cum laude, Harvard U., 1972; PhD, Syracuse U., 1980. Dean admissions Davidson Coll., N.C., 1979-85, v.p. inst. advancement, 1985-89; pres. Lyon Coll., Batesville, Ark., 1989-97, Presbyn. Coll., Clinton, S.C., 1998—. Mem. Omicron Delta Kappa, Sigma Alpha Epsilon, Phi Mu Alpha Sinfonia. Office: Presbyn Coll Office of Pres PO Box 975 Clinton SC 29325-0975 E-mail: griffith@presby.edu.

GRIFFITH, JOHN RANDALL, health services administrator, educator; b. Balt., Mar. 22, 1934; s. Richard Robinson and Eleanor (Bond) G.; m. Helen Klenner, Sept. 17, 1955; children: Julia, Alison, Richard. BS Indsl. Engring., The Johns Hopkins U., 1955; MBA Hospital Adminstrn., U. Chgo., 1957. From asst. prof. to prof. U. Mich. Sch. Pub. Health Dept. Health Mgmt. Policy, Ann Arbor, 1960—, interim dept. chair, 1987-88, dept. chair, 1988-91, Andrew Pattullo Collegiate prof. Hosp. Adminstrn., 1982—; dir. program, chmn. dept. Bur. Hosp. Adminstrn., Ann Arbor, Mich., 1970-82. Examiner Baldridge Nat. Quality Award, 1997—98. Author: Quantitative Techniques for Hospital Planning and Control, 1972, Measuring Hospital Performance, 1978, The Well Managed Community Hospital, 1987 (award, 1988), Moral Challenges of Health Care Management, The Well-Managed Health Care Organization, 1995 (award, 1999, 2000), The Well-Managed Health Care Organization, 5th edit., 2002, Designing 21st Century Healthcare: Leadership in Hospitals and Health Systems, 1998; author: (with others) Thinking Forward: Six Strategies for Highly Successful Organizations, 2003. Bd. dirs., pres., Assn. Univ. Programs Health Adminstrn., 1974-75, Pattullo lectr., 1999; bd. dirs. Accredation Commn., 1977-83. Recipient Filerman Prize for Ednl. Leadership, Assn. Univ. Programs in Health Adminstrn., 2002. Fellow Am. Coll. Health Care Execs. (gold medal 1992, James A. Hamilton award), Tau Beta Pi, Omicron Delta Kappa. Home: 333 Rock Creek Ct Ann Arbor MI 48104-1857 Office: U Mich SPH II 109 Observatory St Ann Arbor MI 48109-2029

GRIFFITH, KATHERINE SCOTT, librarian; b. Atlanta, Jan. 16, 1942; d. Robert Sherrill and Emily Howell (Reynolds) G.; m. Henry Armand Terjen, Sept. 4, 1970 (div. Nov. 1979); 1 child, Henry Foster Terjen (dec.); m. Michael Christopher Healy, May 20, 1995. AB, Sweet Briar Coll., 1964; Masters, Emory U., 1968. Editor South Today, So. Regional Coun., Atlanta, 1969-72; editor Phoenix, Bklyn., 1972-73; dir. comm. N.Y. C. of C. and Industry, N.Y.C., 1978-79; dir. pub. liaison N.Y.C. Dept. Ports and Terminals, 1979-80; sr. pub. affairs officer Citicorp/Citibank, N.Y.C., 1981-83; asst. v.p., pub. rels. mgr. Citicorp Diners Club Media Svcs., N.Y.C., 1983-84; asst. v.p., pub. rels. dir. Citicorp Pub., N.Y.C., 1985-86, asst. v.p. corp. comms., 1986-87; v.p. First Atlanta Corp., Atlanta, 1984; sr. mgr. Can. Imperial Bank of Commerce, N.Y.C., 1987-88, v.p. USA corp. comm., 1989-95; dir. mktg. and comm. Can. Imperial Bank Commerce Wood Gundy divsn. of Can. Imperial Bank Commerce, N.Y.C., 1995-97; v.p., dir. corp. comm. Signet Banking Corp., Richmond, Va., 1997; comm. cons. Greenwich, Conn., 1998-99; pub. rels. supr. The Ferguson Libr., Stamford, Conn., 1999-2000; dir. comms. and external rels. N.Y. Regional Assn. Grantmakers, 2000—02, dir. comms. and govt. rels., 2002—03; libr. Bedford Free Libr., 2003—. Pres. 150 Joralemon Street Corp., Bklyn., 1987-89. Pres. 78th Precinct Cmty. Coun., Bklyn., 1977-78; mem. com. Cmty. Bd. 6, Bklyn., 1978-80; mem. coun. So. Regional Coun., Atlanta, 1984-98; bd. dirs. Atlanta Chamber Players, 1984; mem. Friends of Ferguson Libr., 2000—. Mem. Fin. Women's Assn. N.Y. (bd. dirs. 1995-96), Jr. League, Success by Six (mktg. com. 1999-2002), Beta Phi Mu. Democrat. Episcopalian. Home and Office: 596 Glenbrook Rd # 9 Stamford CT 06906 E-mail: ksgriff@optonline.net.

GRIFFITH, LAWRENCE STACEY CAMERON, cardiologist, educator; b. Washington, Sept. 16, 1937; s. Ernest Stacey and Margaret Dyckman (Davenport) G.; m. Anne Gorman Young, June 20, 1959; children: Lawrence, John, Melinda, Gordon. BA, Haverford Coll., 1959; MD with honors, U. Rochester, 1963. Diplomate Am. Bd. Internal Medicine, Am. Bd. Cardiovascular Disease. Intern in medicine and surgery Strong Meml. Hosp., Rochester, N.Y., 1963-64, asst. resident in surgery, 1964-65, asst. and assoc. resident in medicine, 1967-69; rsch. fellow in cardiology Johns Hopkins U., Balt., 1969-71, asst. prof. medicine Sch. Medicine, 1971-76, asst. prof. radiology, 1974-80, assoc. prof. medicine, 1976-88, prof. medicine, 1988—; med. dir. Johns Hopkins Medicine Internat., 1999—. Cons. VA Coop. Study Surgery for Coronary Artery Disease, Program on Surg. Control of Hyperlipidemias, U. Minn. Contbr. numerous articles to profl. jours. Bd. dirs. Julia Dychman Andrus Meml., Inc., Yonkers, N.Y., 1971—, chmn., 1976—; bd. dirs. John E. Andrus Meml. Home for Aged, Hastings-on-Hudson, N.Y., 1974-97; bd. dirs. Surdna Found., N.Y.C., 1976—, v.p., 1988-94; chmn. adv. bd. Balt. Pastoral Counseling Svc., 1971-80. With USPHS, 1965-67. Fellow ACP, Coun. Clin. Cardiology of Am. Heart Assn., Am. Coll. Cardiology; mem. Alpha Omega Alpha. Democrat. Methodist. Home: 802 W Saint Georges Rd Baltimore MD 21210-1409 Office: Johns Hopkins Hosp Carnegie 530 600 N Wolfe St Baltimore MD 21287-0005

GRIFFITH, LONZO, JR., technology specialist, educator, farmer; b. Lynnville, Ky., Nov. 20, 1948; s. Elisha Lonzo and Dorthy Lorene G.; m. Diane Louise Tucker, Dec. 21, 1969. BS, Murray State U., 1971, MS, 1980; postgrad., U. Mo., Rolla, 1984-85. Cert. sci., chemistry, physics, math., computer sci. tchr., Fla., sci., math., computer sci. tchr., Ky.' cert. project WILD facilitator, 2000. Assembler, machinist Midland Ross Corp., Paris, Tenn., 1977-80; tchr. Palmersville (Tenn.) H.S., 1980-81; instr. U. Tenn., Martin, 1981-84; tchr. Pahokee (Fla.) H.S., 1985-86, Clewiston (Fla.) H.S., 1986-96, technology specialist, tchr., 1996—. Mem. tech. com. Henry County Bd. Edn., LaBelle, Fla., 1996—; local tech. rep. Fla. Internet Resource Network, Tallahassee, 1996—; cert. facilitor Fla. Wildlife and Game Commn., 2000—. Recipient First Place Ky. award Nat. Corn Growers Assn., 1999, Second Place U.S. award, 1999. Mem. NEA, Henry County Edn. Assn., Fla. Assn. for Computers in Edn., Fla. Tchg. Profession. Democrat. Baptist. Avocations: fishing, carpentry, stamp collecting. Home: 711 Bowden Rd Clewiston FL 33440-5004 Office: Clewiston HS 1501 S Francisco St Clewiston FL 33440-5016 E-mail: mayfield@strato.net.

GRIFFITH, MADLYNNE VEIL, college administrator; b. Johnstown, Pa., Jan. 2, 1951; d. J. Donald and Mary Jane (Veil) G.; 1 child, Philip Bryce. BA, St. Mary's Coll., 1973; MBA, U. Notre Dame, 1975; DEd, Pa. State U., 1996. Cost and budget analyst U. Mich., Ann Arbor, 1980-81; acct. U. N.C., Wilmington, 1981, Johnstown Med. Devel. Corp., 1982-83; controller Mt. Aloysius Coll., Cresson, Pa., 1983-2000; v.p. Cambria County Area C.C., Johnstown, Pa., 2000-2001; CEO E-Education, Inc., Johnstown, Pa. Republican. Roman Catholic. Avocation: swimming.

GRIFFITH, MARTHA, controller; b. Brockton, Mass., Sept. 9, 1945; d. Ishmael Hayes and Jettie L. (Dudley) Davis; m. Jack C. Griffith, May 29, 1965 (dec. June 1984); Michael S., David M.; m. Dan H. Fries, Nov. 5, 1994. Student, U. Ark., 1962-64; BA, Ball State U., 1967. Prin. Griffith Acctg. Co., Indpls., 1968-70; probate adminstr. Johnson & Weaver, Indpls., 1970-74; personnel adminstr. Hercules Inc., Houston, 1974-76; adminstr. Lapin Totz & Mayer, Houston, 1976-80; bus. mgr. Pasadena (Tex.) Citizen, 1980-84; contr. Houston Community Newspapers, 1984-88, DCI Pub., Alexandria, Va., 1989-90, Telescan Inc., Houston, 1990-93, Advolink, Inc., 1993-99, Suncoast Post-Tension, Inc., Houston, 1999—. Commr. Houston council Boy Scouts Am., 1983. Recipient Dist. Merit awards Boy Scouts Am., Houston, 1983. Mem. Internat. Newspaper Fin. Execs. (com. mem. 1986-89), Collier Jackson Users Group (moderator 1986-89), Nat. Assn. Female Execs. Democrat. Baptist. Avocations: dancing, boating, traveling. Address: 14300 Ella Blvd #213 Houston TX 77014

GRIFFITH, MELVIN EUGENE, entomologist, public health official; b. Lawrence, Kans., Mar. 24, 1912; s. George Thomas and Estella (Shaw) G.; m. Pauline Sophia Bogart, June 23, 1941. AB, U. Kans., 1934, AM, 1935, PhD, 1938; postgrad., U. Mich., summers 1937-40. Instr. zoology N.D. Agrl. Coll., Fargo, 1938—39, asst. prof., 1939—41, assoc. prof., 1941—42; commd. officer USPHS, 1943—71; malaria control entomologist State Dept. Health, Oklahoma City, 1943—46, communicable disease ctr. entomologist, 1946—51; chief malaria adviser ICA, Bangkok, 1951—60; assoc. dir. Malaria Eradication Tng. Ctr., Kingston, Jamaica, 1960; regional malaria advisor SE Asia, AID, New Delhi, 1960—62, Near East and South Asia, AID, 1962—64; dep. chief malaria eradication br. AID, Washington, 1964—67, chief, 1967—71; ret. as capt., 1971. Assoc. prof. zoology scis. U. Okla., Norman, 1946-52, prof. 1952-56; cons. Office of Health, AID, Washington, 1971-75. Contbr. articles and monographs on entomology, malaria control and pub. health. Recipient citation for disting. svc. U. Kans., 1962. Mem. APHA, Am. Soc. Tropical Medicine and Hygiene, Am. Soc. Limnology and Oceanography, Entomol. Soc. Am., Explorers Club, N.Y. Acad. Scis., Siam Soc., Phi Beta Kappa, Sigma Xi. Address: PO Box 3550 Williamsburg VA 23187-3550 E-mail: melvinegriffith@cs.com.

GRIFFITH, NICOLA, writer; b. Leeds, Yorkshire, Eng., Sept. 30, 1960; life ptnr. Kelly Eskridge. Formerly ins. clk., waitress, singer, songwriter, tchr. self defense. Author: Ammonite, 1993 (Ga. and Atlanta Lit. prizes, Lambda Lit. award 1993, Tiptree Meml. award 1994), Slow River, 1995 (Lambda award, Nebula award), The Blue Place, 1999, Stay, 2002; co-editor: (short fiction series) Bending the Landscape. Office: care Shawna McCarthy Scovil Chichak Galen 381 Park Ave S Ste 1020 New York NY 10016*

GRIFFITH, OSBIE HAYES, chemistry educator; b. Torrance, Calif., Sept. 14, 1938; s. Osbie and Mary Belle (Neathery) G.; m. Karen Hedberg; 2 sons BA, U. Calif.-Riverside, Riverside, 1960; PhD, Calif. Inst. Tech., 1964; postgrad., Stanford U., 1965. NAS-NRC postdoctoral Stanford U., Eugene, 1965; asst. prof. chemistry U. Oreg., Eugene, 1966-69, assoc. prof., 1969-72; prof. chem. Inst. Molecular Biology, 1972—. Co-editor: Lipid-Protein Interactions, 1982; mem. edtl. bd. Biophysical Jour., 1974-78, Chemistry & Physics of Lipids, 1974-95, Microscopy and Microanalysis, 1995-2002; contbr. articles to profl. jours. Scholar Camille and Henry Dreyfus Found., 1970; Career Devel. award Nat. Cancer Inst., 1972-76; fellow Sloan Found., 1967-69, Guggenheim Found., 1972-76; Faculty Achievement award for Teaching Excellence, Burlington No. Found., 1987, Dean's Devel. award, 1991, Creativity Extension NSF, 1992. Mem. Am. Chem. Soc., Biophys. Soc., Microscopy Soc. Am. Home: 2550 Charnelton St Eugene OR 97405-3216 Office: U Oreg Inst Molecular Biology Eugene OR 97403 E-mail: hayes@molbio.uoregon.edu.

GRIFFITH, OWEN WENDELL, biochemistry educator; b. Oakland, Calif., June 19, 1946; s. Charles H. and Gladys C. (Farrar) G. BA, U. Calif., Berkeley, 1968; PhD, Rockefeller U., 1975. Asst. prof. Cornell U. Med. Coll., N.Y.C., 1978-81, assoc. prof., 1981-87, prof., 1987-92; prof., chmn. biochemistry Med. Coll. of Wis., Milw., 1992-2001, prof. biochemistry, 2001—; sci. founder, bd. dirs. ArgiNOx, Inc., Milw., 2000—. Mem., chmn. med. biochemistry study sect. NIH, Bethesda, Md., 1988-92. Contbr. more than 160 articles to profl. jours. Grantee NIH. Mem. Am. Chem. Soc., Am. Soc. Biochemistry and Molecular Biology, Am. Soc. Pharmacology and Exptl. Therapeutics. Achievements include more than 40 patents and patent applications in biomedical research. Office: Med Coll Wis Dept Biochemistry 8701 W Watertown Plank Rd Milwaukee WI 53226-3548 E-mail: griffith@mcw.edu.

GRIFFITH, PATRICIA KING, journalist; b. San Francisco, Jan. 20, 1934; d. Earl Beardsley and Frankie Mae (Kelly) King; m. Winthrop Gold Griffith, Oct. 4, 1958 (div. Jan. 1986); children: Kevin Winthrop, Christina Suzanne. BA, Stanford U., 1955. Copy asst., reporter Washington Post, 1956-57, 60-64; reporter San Francisco Examiner, 1957-59; Washington bureau chief Monterey Herald and Toledo Blade, Washington, 1979-81; investigative reporter Monterey (Calif.) Peninsula Herald, 1973-79, city editor, 1981-83, mng. editor, 1983-88; Washington bureau chief, White House corr. Toledo Blade and Pitts. Post-Gazette, Washington, 1988-99. Bd. dirs. Lyceum of Monterey Peninsula, 1977-79, All Sts. Episcopal Day Sch., Carmel, Calif., 1977-79, Monterey Coll. Law, 1978-79; sr. warden St. Dunstan's Episcopal Ch., Carmel Valley, Calif., 1983-84. Recipient Silver Gavel award ABA, 1978. Mem. Stanford Alumni Assn., Nat. Press Club, Gridiron Club, Stanford Club Washington, Stanford Cap and Gown Soc. Home: 103 Dockside Ln Belfast ME 04915

GRIFFITH, PATRICIA BARNES, music educator, pianist; b. Winston-Salem, N.C., June 7, 1950; d. Frank Tillman and Sarah H. (Hines) Barnes; m. Benjamin Griffith, Sept. 5, 1981; children: Treva Ann, Carrie Ellen. MusB, Salem Coll., Winston-Salem, N.C., 1972; MusM, Peabody Inst., Balt., 1974, Mus D in music arts, 1985. Prof. of music Ky. State U., Frankfort, 1977—. Organist Hope Luth. Ch., Frankfort, 1978—88. Author piano music. Grantee faculty rsch., Ky. State U., 2002. Mem.: Ky. State Tchrs. Assn. (bd. mem. 1994—, foundn. chmn. 1994—). Democrat. Mem. Soc. Of Friends. Avocations: cooking, gardening. Office: Ky State Univ E Main St Frankfort KY 40601

GRIFFITH, PETER, mechanical engineering educator, researcher; b. London, Sept. 23, 1927; came to U.S., 1930; s. Sanford and Katherine (Bennett) G.; m. Sylvia Biorn-Hansen, June 10, 1954 (dec. Sept. 1981); children: Sonja, Katherine; m. Kathleen Mayo, July 23, 1983. MSME, U. Mich., 1952; DSc, MIT, 1956. Rsch. asst. MIT, Cambridge, 1952, instr. mech. engring., 1954-56, asst. prof., 1956-59, assoc. prof., 1959-63, prof., 1963—. Cons. on heat transfer and two-phase flow, 1956—. Cpl. USAF, 1946-47. Fellow ASME. Home: 107 Louise Rd Belmont MA 02478-3968 Office: MIT 77 Massachusetts Ave Cambridge MA 02139-4307

GRIFFITH, PHILIP ARTHUR, elementary school educator; b. N.Y.C., Nov. 13, 1934; s. Jesse Lloyd and Anna (McGovern) G.; m. Nancy Sullivan, June 18, 1960; children: Philip, Margaret. BA, Hunter Coll., 1960; MS, CUNY, 1963. Cert. edn. Tchr. 6th grade N.Y.C. Pub. Schs., 1960-64; tchr. Central Islip (N.Y.) Pub. Schs., 1964—. Instr. Dowling Coll., Oakdale, N.Y., 1970-75; supr. N.Y.C. (N.Y.) Bureau of Cmty. Edn., 1970-80. Author: The History of Infant Jesus Parish; contbr. articles to profl. publs. Hockey coach Cath. Youth Orgn., Central Islip, 1976-82, St. Anthony's H.S., 1986-87; baseball coach Police Athletic League, Central Islip, 1976-86; del. L.I. Fedn. Labor, Mineola, N.Y., 1976-90; N.Y. state del. N.Y. State AFL-CIO, Albany, 1976-95, N.Y. Com. Health and Safety, N.Y.C., 1988-95; N.Y. State Tenure Hearing Panelist, Albany, 1978-99; mem. parents coun. Boston Coll., Chestnut Hill, Mass., 1990-92. Cpl. U.S. Army, 1954-56. Recipient N.Y. State PTA Jenkins award Charles Mulligan Sch. PTA, Central Islip, 1978, Leadership award United Way, L.I., 1978, Pride in the Union award Am. Fedn. Tchrs., 1990, 92, Influential Tchr. award MIT, Cambridge, 1980. Mem. Am. Fedn. Tchrs., Ctrl. Islip Tchrs. Assn. (pres. 1976-95), N.Y. State United Tchrs. (del. 1970-95), N.Y. State Tchrs. Retirement Sys. (del. 1974-95), U.S. Golf Assn., Port Jefferson Country Club, Port Jefferson Hist. Soc. (editor The Echoes of Port), Port Jefferson Civic Assn. (editor Jeffersonian), Nat. Geographic Soc., L.I. Pres. Coun. (dist. dir.), Indsl. Rels. Rsch. Assn., Chmn. Infrant Jesus R.C. Ch. History Comm.,Smithsonian

Inst., Am. Legion. Democrat. Roman Catholic. Avocations: golf, folk art, irish history, theatre, travel. Home: 14 Cove Ln Port Jefferson NY 11777-1103 Office: Central Islip Tchrs Assn Central Islip NY 11722

GRIFFITH, ROBERT CHARLES, allergist, educator, planter; b. Shreveport, La., Jan. 9, 1939; s. Charles Parsons and Madelon (Jenkins) G.; m. Loretta Dean Secrist, July 15, 1969; children: Charles Randall, Cameron Stuart, Ann Marie. BS, Centenary Coll., 1961; MD, La. State U., 1965. Intern, Confederate Meml. Med. Ctr., Shreveport, 1965-66, resident in internal medicine, 1966-68; fellow in allergy and chest disease, instr. U. Va. Med. Sch. Hosp., Charlottesville, 1968-70; practice medicine specializing in allergies, Alexandria, La., 1970-72, The Allergy Clinic, Shreveport, 1972; pres. Griffith Allergy Clinic, Shreveport, 1973—; faculty internal medicine La. State U., 1972—; owner, planter Riverpoint Plantation, Caddo Parish, La. and Miller and Lafayette Counties, Ark. Bd. dirs. Caddo-Bossier Assn. Retarded Citizens, 1977-84, Access (fomerly Child Devel. Ctr.), Shreveport, 1979-85; mem. (life) NRA, med. adv. com., spl. edn. adv. com. Caddo Parish Sch. Bd., 1977-89; mem. commission on missions and social concerns First Methodist Ch., 1981-84, mem. adminstrv. bd., 1981-84; mem. med. panel for transfer Caddo Parish Sch. Bd., 1974-94; mem. adopt a flag program Confederate Meml. Mus. New Orleans; co-chair Loyola Fund Drive, 1994-95. Served to maj. M.C., U.S. Army, 1965-71. Recipient Physician of the Yr. award Shreveport-Bossier Med. Assts., 1984. Fellow Am. Coll. Asthma, Allergy and Immunology, Am. Coll. Chest Physicians (assoc.), Am. Thoracic Soc.; mem. AMA, SAR (chpt. surgeon 1994—), Am. Acad. Allergy, Asthma and Immunology, Am. Legion, Jamestowne Soc., So. Med. Assn., La. Med. Soc., Shreveport Med. Soc. (allergy sposkesman 1984—), La. Allergy Soc. (charter; past pres.), U. Va. Med. Alumni Assn. (life), Pace Soc. Am., La. State U. Med. Alumni Assn., Confederate Soc. Am., Heritage Preservation Assn., League of the South (charter, sustainer), League of the South La. (bd. dirs.), Legion South, Am. Legion (Viet Nam), Mil. Order Stars and Bars, Order of So. Cross, Shreveport C. of C., Kappa Alpha, Methodist. Lodges: Masons (32 degree). Clubs: Shreveport Country, Petroleum of Shreveport, Shreveport, Ambs., Cotillion, Royal, Plantation, Shriners (El Kahruba Temple), Jesters, Les Bon Temps., Demoiselle Club. Home: 7112 E Ridge Dr Shreveport LA 71106-4749 also: Riverpoint Plantation Ida LA 71044

GRIFFITH, RUTH MARIE, religious studies educator; b. Chattanooga, May 7, 1967; d. Charles Russell, Jr. and Nannelle Stevenson Griffith; m. Leigh Eric Schmidt, Dec. 29, 1995; children: Zachary Griffith Schmidt, Ella Marie Schmidt. AB, U. Va., 1989; PhD, Harvard U., 1995. Lectr. and assoc. dir. Ctr. for Study of Religion Princeton (NJ) U., 1998—2001; assoc. prof. religion Princeton (N.J.) U., 2003—; rsch. assoc., vis. lectr. Harvard Div. Sch., Cambridge, Mass., 2002—03. Mellon fellow in the humanities Northwestern U., Evanston, Ill., 1996—98. Author: (scholarly book) God's Daughters: Evangelical Women and the Power of Submission, Born Again Bodies: Flesh and Spirit in American Christianity; contbr. articles, revs., essays to profl. publs. Fellow, The Whiting Found. and Harvard U., 1994—95, Material History of Am. Religion project, Lilly Endowment, 1996—2001, Women and Twentieth-Century Protestantism project, Pew Charitable Trusts, 1996—98, 1999—2001; grantee Women and Religion in the African Diaspora project, Ford Found., 2001—. Mem.: Orgn. of Am. Historians, Am. Studies Assn., Am. Soc. of Ch. History (coun. mem. 2000—03), Am. Hist. Assn., Am. Acad. of Religion. Office: Princeton U 1879 Hall Princeton NJ 08544 Home: 26 Linden Ln Princeton NJ 08540 E-mail: griffith@princeton.edu.

GRIFFITH, SIMA LYNN, investment banker, consultant; b. N.Y.C., Sept. 7, 1960; d. Morris Benjamin and Mary (Buberoglü) Nahum; m. Clark Calvin Griffith, Sept. 13, 1987. BA in English, Amherst Coll., 1982. Account exec. D.F. King & Co., Inc., N.Y.C., 1982-84, asst. v.p., 1984-86, v.p., 1986-88, Wells & Miller, Mpls., 1988; with Griffith, Levi Capital, Inc, Mpls., 1988-96; prin. Aethlon, Capital LLC, Mpls., 1996—. Co-chmn. PRSA, IR seminars, 1987; bd. adv. Pacer, Inc. Bd. govs. Children's Theater Co. Mem.: Pub. Rels. Soc. Am. (bod. govs., investor rels. sec. 1987—89), Assn. Bus. Communicators (bd. govs. 1987—88). Office: Aethlon Capital LLC 4920 IDS Ctr 80 S 8th St Minneapolis MN 55402-2100

GRIFFITH, STEVEN FRANKLIN, SR., lawyer, real estate title insurance agent and investor; b. New Orleans, July 14, 1948; s. Hugh Franklin and Rose Marie (Teutone) G.; m. Mary Elizabeth McMillan Frank, Dec. 9, 1972; children: Steven Franklin Jr., Jason Franklin. BBA, Loyola U., New Orleans, 1970, JD, 1972. Bar: La. 1972, U.S. Dist. Ct. (ea. dist.) La. 1975, U.S. Ct. Appeals (5th cir.) 1975, U.S. Supreme Ct. 1976. With Law Offices of Senator George T. Oubre, Norco, La., 1971-75; sole practice Destrehan, La., 1975—. Pres. 29th Jud. Dist. Bar Assn., 1999-2002. Fellow: La. State Bar Found.; mem.: ATLA, ABA, St. Charles Parish Bar Assn. (pres. 1999—2002), Fed. Bar Assn., New Orleans Trial Lawyers Assn., La. Trial Lawyers Assn., La. State Bar Assn. (ho. of dels. 1987—). Democrat.

GRIFFITH, TRACY COX, counselor, nurse; b. Des Moines, Feb. 8, 1965; d. William Arthur and Nancy Lea Cox; m. Rick Dean Griffith, June 7, 1985; children: Taylor Nicole (dec.), Rachel Nicole, Rebecca Renee. BSN, Mankato State U., 1988; MA in Counseling and Psychol. Svcs., St. Mary's Coll., Winona, Minn., 1994. RN, Tex.; lic. profl. counselor, Tex. Nurse/case mgr. Mayo Found., Rochester, Minn., 1988-93; utilization rev. nurse Mental Health Resource Ctr., Jacksonville, Fla., 1992-93; clin. coord. TEAM Chem. Dependency Treatment, Ponte Vedra Beach, Fla., 1994; adj. prof. U. North Fla., Jacksonville, 1994; psychotherapist Brenda Gross and Assocs., Jacksonville, 1994; counselor, assessment specialist Tex. Panhandle Mental Health Mental Retardation, 1995—2000, Amarillo (Tex.) Behavioral Cons., 1997-99; dir. substance abuse svcs. network Tex. Panhandle Mental Health Mental Retardation, Amarillo, 1998-2000; support group facilitator Harrington Cancer Ctr., 2002—. RN, 2002—. Vol. safe and drug free schs. and cmtys. adv. com. Amarillo Ind. Schs., 1999—; vol. Teen Pregnancy Prevention Coalition, Amarillo, 1998-99, Tex. Panhandle Prevention Coalition, 1999-2000. Mem. Internat. Bd. Examiners of Play Therapists (cert. play therapist, child psychotherapist). Avocations: volunteer work, children's ministry, music.

GRIFFITH, WILLIAM ALEXANDER, former mining company executive; b. Sioux Falls, S.D., Mar. 28, 1922; s. James William and Adeline Mae (Reid) G.; m. Gratia Frances Hannan, Jan. 27, 1949; children— Georgeanne Reid, James William, Wade Andrew. BS in Metall. Engring., S.D. Sch. Mines and Tech., 1947; MS in Metallurgy, M.I.T., 1950; Mineral Dressing Engr. (hon.), Mont. Coll. Mineral Sci. and Tech., 1971; D in Bus. Adminstrn. (hon.), S.D. Sch. Mines & Tech., 1986; D in Sci. (hon.), U. Idaho, 1990. With N.J. Zinc Co., 1949-57, chief milling and maintenance Bertha minerals divsn., 1956-57; metallurgist Rare Metals Corp. Am., Tuba City, Ariz., 1957-58; dir. rsch. Phelps Dodge Corp., Morenci, Ariz., 1958-68; with Hecla Mining Co., Coeur d'Alene, Idaho, 1968-87, exec. v.p., 1978, pres., chief exec. officer, 1979-86, chmn., chief exec. officer, 1986-87; pres. Granduc Mines Ltd., 1987-88; chmn. Inland N.W. Bancorp., Inc., 1989-96. Bd. dirs. The Coeur d'Alenes Co. With USNR, 1943-46. Mem. AIME (Gaudin award 1977, Richards award 1981, Disting. mem. 1977, Hon. 1987), NAE, Am. Mining Congress (past dir.), Idaho Mining Assn. (past pres.), Idaho Assn. Commerce and Industry (past bd. dirs.), Western Regional Coun. (chmn. 1986-87), Nat. Strategic Materials and Minerals Adv. Com. to Sec. Interior, Silver Inst. (past pres., past chmn.), Nat. Acad. of Engring., Sigma Tau, Theta Tau. Lodges: Rotary. Republican. Home: 630 S 14th St Coeur D Alene ID 83814-3820

GRIFFITH-BARBARA, MARTHA JAYNE, music educator; b. Ft. Smith, Ark., Aug. 12, 1968; d. Bob D. and Mary Jane Griffith; m. Donovan Scott Barbara, Dec. 20, 2002. MusB in Edn., U. Ctrl. Ark., 1990, MusM, 1993; PhD in Music Edn., U. Okla., 2003. Music dir. Norfork (Ark.) Pub. Sch., 1990—91; grad. asst. U. Ctrl. Ark., Conway, 1991—92; band dir. Lonoke (Ark.) Pub. Schs., 1993—94; beginning band coord. Pleasant Grove Ind. Sch. Dist., Texarkana, Tex., 1995—97; grad. tchg. asst. U. Okla., Norman, 1997—2000, vis. asst. prof., 2000—01. Dir. New Horizons Band, Norman, 2000—01. Pres. Columns Homeowner Assn., Norman, 2002—03. Mem.: Music Educators Nat. Conf. (life), Grad. Music Student Assn. (life; sec./treas. 1997—99), Pi Kappa Lambda (life), Sigma Alpha Iota (life; v.p., historian 1988—90). Home: 1303 Rebecca Ln Norman OK 73072 Personal E-mail: wheester@yahoo.com.

GRIFFITHS, BARBARA LORRAINE, psychologist, marriage-family therapist, writer; b. Glendale, Calif., July 15, 1927; d. David William and Mabel Augusta (Gaarder) G.; m. Dale Elmo Rumbaugh, Mar. 28, 1948; 1 child, David Wynn. AA in Journalism, Valley C.C., 1958; BA in Psychology, U. Calif. Riverside, 1972; MS in Rehab. Counseling, Calif. State U., 1976; PhD in Clin. Psychology, Calif. Grad. Inst., 1984. Cert. Diplomate Am. Psychotherapy Assn., 1998, cert. addiction specialist, Marriage and Family Therapist 1979. Alcoholism counselor Kaiser Permanente, L.A., 1976-82; pvt. practice Hollywood, L.A., 1979-89, Glendale, Burbank, Calif., 1989-97, L.A., 1997—. Mem. State of Calif. Med. Diversion Eval. Com., 1998—; screener 6th and 7th Prism awards Entertainment Industry Coun. Film, 2001—02; sci. expert reviewer 6th annual Prism Awards Entertainment Industry Coun., 2002—03; reviewer 6th and 7th Ann. PRISM awards Entertainment Industry Coun. Film, 2002; clinical psychologist Calif. Youth Authority, 2002—. Editor (child abuse newsletter): Directions, 1976—86; contbr. Mem. Glendale Rotary, 1990-95, Verdugo BPW, 1988-91; Nat. Ski Patrolwoman #122, 1952-56. Recipient Editor's Choice award for poetry, 1997. Mem. APA (assoc.), L.A. County Psychol. Assn. Avocations: script writing, tennis, skiing, swimming and water sports, reading. Home and Office: 3002 Hyperion Ave Los Angeles CA 90027-2564 Fax: 323-660-7911. E-mail: griffiths7@aol.com.

GRIFFITHS, DAVID, physicist, educator; b. Washington, Dec. 5, 1942; s. Gordon and W. Mary Griffiths; m. Terry Marshall, Dec. 20, 1970; children: Jennifer Beth, Timothy Seth. BA, Harvard U., 1964, MA, 1966, PhD, 1970. Postdoctoral fellow U. Utah, Salt Lake City, 1970-72, U. Mass., Amherst, 1972-74; asst. prof. physics Mt. Holyoke Coll., South Hadley, Mass., 1974-77, Trinity Coll., Hartford, Conn., 1977-78; prof. physics Reed Coll., Portland, Oreg., 1978—. Book rev. editor Am. Jour. Physics, 1996—. Author: Introduction to Electrodynamics, 1981, 2d edit., 1989, 3d edit., 1999, Introduction to Elementary Particles, 1987, Introduction to Quantum Mechanics, 1995; mem. editl. bd. Phys. Rev E, 1998—. Mem. Am. Phys. Soc., Am. Assn. Physics Tchrs. (Millikan award 1997). Office: Reed Coll Dept Physics Portland OR 97202 E-mail: griffith@reed.edu.

GRIFFITHS, DAVID NEAL, utility executive; b. Oxford, Ind., Sept. 11, 1935; s. David Scifres and Lorene Francis Griffiths; m. Alice Anne Goodpasture, Aug. 9, 1959 (div. 1972); children— Beth Anne, David Douglas; m. Barbette Suzanne Custoch, June 7, 1976; children— Michael, Megan BS in Indsl. Econs., Purdue U., 1957. Various positions Delco Remy div. Gen. Motors Corp., Anderson, Ind., 1957-69; dep. commr. revenue State of Ind., Indpls., 1969-71, adminstrv. asst. to gov., 1971-72; exec. dir. Environ. Quality Control, Inc., Indpls., 1972-75; project mgr. EDP Corp., Sarasota, Fla., 1975-76, v.p. adminstrn., 1977-78; asst. to pres. Citizens Gas and Coke Utility, Indpls., 1978-80, v.p. pub. affairs, 1980-82, sr. v.p. adminstrn., 1982-92, exec. v.p., 1995-98, exec. v.p., COO, 1998—, pres., CEO, 1999—. Mem. ind. Energy Devel. Bd., Indpls., 1980-92, Midwest Govs.' Energy Task Force, 1972-75; chmn. Fed. Home Loan Bank of Indpls., 1990-93; trustee Mfrs. Alliance; bd. dirs. Ind. Farmers Mut. Ins. Co., Am. Gas Assn., Meth. Med. Group. Author: Implementing Quality with a Customer Focus, Management in a Quality Environment. Pres. Indsl. Mgmt. Club, Anderson and Madison County, Inc., 1961; Cen. Coun. Indsl. Mgmt. Clubs 1966; bd. dirs., chmn. Environ. Quality Conrol, Inc., Indpls., 1983-98, Life/Ledership Devel., Inc.; bd.dirs. Greater Indpls. Progress Com., Goodwill Industries Found., Life/Leadership Devel., Inc., Indy Partnership. Recipient Exchange Industrialist with USSR award YMCA, 1963; named Sagamore of Wabash, Gov. of Ind., 1971, 75. Mem. Govtl. Affairs Soc. Ind. (past pres.), Ind. Gas Assn. (bd. dirs.), Greater Indpls. C. of C. (bd. dirs., vice chair), Columbia Club (Indpls.). Republican. Methodist. Avocations: golf, swimming. Home: 8158 Brent Ave Indianapolis IN 46240-2725 Office: Citizens Gas & Coke Utility 2020 N Meridian St Indianapolis IN 46202-1393

GRIFFITHS, GARETH, humanities educator, department chairman, theater critic, writer; b. Merthyr Tydfil, Wales, Mar. 15, 1943; arrived in U.S., 2002; s. John Henry and Annie Winifred Griffiths; m. Carolyn Margaret Aurisch; 3 children. BA, U. Wales, Cardiff, 1964, PhD, 1967. Lectr. U. Ea. Anglia, England, 1967—72; vis. prof. U. Mo., Kans. City, 1972—73; lectr. Macquarie U., Sydney, Australia, 1973—77, sr. lectr., 1977, assoc. prof., 1976—88; prof. U. Western Australia, Perth, Australia, 1989—2002, U. at Albany, NY, 2002—. French nat. disting. prof. U. Bourgogne, Dijon, France, 1995; Wineberg disting. prof. Guelph U., Ont., Canada, 1995. Author: (books) A Double Exile: African and West Indian Writing, 1978, The Empire Writes Back, 1989, Key Concepts in Post-Colonial Studies, 1998, African Lit. in Eng., 2002, editor. Mem.: Commonwealth Lit. and Letters (assoc.), Australian Drama Studies Assn. (pres. 1986—89). Office: University at Albany 1400 Washington Ave Albany NY 12222

GRIFFITHS, JOHN LIEBIG, retired foreign service officer, marketing consultant; b. L.A., Nov. 10, 1929; s. John Francis Griffiths and Jane Elizabeth Liebig; m. Graciela Baccara, June 24, 1966 (div. Sept. 1998); children: John, Alessandra, Glenn; m. Marguerite Trechter Giddings, Jan. 29, 1999. BA, UCLA, 1954; grad., U. So. Calif., 1958, Armed Forces Staff Coll., Norfolk, Va., 1969. Rsch. assoc. Navy Dept., 1958—60; various positions in fgn. svc. USIA/State Dept., Washington and Latin Am., 1960-88; internat. programs advisor U. So. Calif., L.A., 1994-97. Internat. mktg. cons., 1998—. Mem. Sister Cities Found., Ptnrs. of the Ams., Latin Am. and Washington, 1970-88. Lt. USNR, 1954-58. Decorated Order of Morazán, Govt. of Honduras for Humanitarian Svc., 1975, Hon. Col. State of La., Meritorious HOnor awards, U.S. Dept. State, USIA. Mem. Am. Fgn. Svc. Assn., Rotary Internat., Am. C. of C., Sigma Chi. Republican. Presbyterian. Avocations: linguistics, educational counseling, international exchange programs. Home: 251 S Medio Dr Los Angeles CA 90049-3911

GRIFFITHS, PHILLIP A. mathematician, academic administrator; b. Raleigh, N.C., Oct. 18, 1938; s. Phillip and Jeanette (Field) G.; m. Ann Lane Crittenden, 1958-67; children: Jan Kirsten, David; m. Marian Folsom Jones, 1968; children: Sarah, Rebecca. BS, Wake Forest U., 1959; PhD, Princeton U., 1962; D (hon.), Angers U., France, 1979; DSc (hon.), Wake Forest U., 1973, U. Peking, China, 1983; DSc (hon.), U. Oslo, 2002. Mem. staff U. Calif., Berkeley, 1964-67; prof. math. Princeton (N.J.) U., 1968-72; prof. Harvard U., Cambridge, Mass., 1972-83, Dwight Parker Robinson prof. math., 1983; provost, James B. Duke prof. math. Duke U., Durham, N.C., 1983-91; dir. Inst. for Advanced Study, Princeton, N.J., 1991—; sr. advisor Mellon Fedn., 2001—. Bd. dirs. Oppenheimer Funds, GSI Lumonics; vis. prof. Princeton U., 1967-68, mem. Inst. Advanced Study, 1968-70; chmn. bd. on math. scis. NRC, 1986-91, chmn. commn. on phys. scis., math. and applications, 1992, chmn. com. on sci., engring. and pub. policy, 1992-99; mem. Nat. Sci. Bd., 1991-96; sec. Internat. Math. Union, 1999—; chair Sci. Insts. Group, 1999—; sr. adv., Mellon Fedn., 2001—, coun. on Foreign Relations, 2002—. Editor Jour. Differential Geometry, 1980-90, Compositio Mathematica, 1980-92, Duke Math. Jour., 1983—, Selecta Mathematica, 1994—, Annals of Math., 1997—, Advances in Function Theory, 2002, Annals of Math. Studies, 2001. Bd. dirs. Rsch. Triangle Inst., 1983-91; trustee Woodward Acad., N.C. Sch. Sci. and Math. Decorated Nat. Order of Sci. Merit (Brazil); recipient LeRoy P. Steel prize Am. Math. Soc., 1971, Dannie Heineman Preis, Acad. Scis. Gottingen, 1979, Ordem Nat. Mérito Cientifico, Ministry of Sci. and Tech., Brazil, 2002; Miller fellow U. Calif. Berkeley, 1962-64, 1975-76, Guggenheim fellow, 1980-82. Fellow: Accademia Lincei (assoc.; fgn.), Third World Acad. Scis. (assoc.; fgn.); mem.: NAS (disting. sr. pres. fellow internat. rels. 2002—), Coun. on Fgn. Rels., Am. Acad. Arts and Scis., Am. Philos. Soc., N.Y. Yacht Club. Office: Inst Advanced Study Office of Dir Einstein Dr Princeton NJ 08540 Home: 67 River Rd Stockton NJ 08559

GRIFFITHS, RACHEL, actress; b. Melbourne, Australia, 1968; BEd in Drama and Dance, Victoria Coll. Actor: (films) Muriel's Wedding, 1994 (Best Supporting Actress Australian Film Critics award, Best Supporting Actress Australian Film Inst. award, 1995), Jude, 1996, To Have and To Hold, 1997, My Best Friend's Wedding, 1997, Hilary and Jackie, 1998 (nominee Best Supporting Actress Oscar, 1999), My Son, the Fanatic, 1998, Among Giants, 1998, Amy, 1998, Me Myself I, 1999, Blow, 2001, The Rookie, 2002, The Hard Word, 2002; (TV series) Secrets, 1993, Jimeoin, 1994, Six Feet Under, 2001— (Best Suppporting Actress Golden Globe award, 2001). Office: c/o SAG 5757 Wilshire Blvd Los Angeles CA 90036-3635

GRIFFITHS, ROBERT PENNELL, banker; b. Chgo., May 6, 1949; s. George Findley and Marion E. (Winterrowd) G.; m. Susan Hillman, Jan. 31, 1976 (div. 2002). BA, Amherst Coll., 1972; MS in Mgmt., Northwestern U., 1974. From comml. banking officer to v.p. No. Trust Co., Chgo., 1978—85; sr. v.p. comml. lending UnibancTrust Co., Chgo., 1985-88; pres., CEO Old Kent Bank of Naperville, Ill., 1988—90; sr. v.p. Old Kent Bank, Chgo., 1991—92; pres., CEO Uptown Nat. Bank Chgo., 1993—2001; mng. dir. Pvt. Bank and Trust Co., Chgo., 2002—. Mem. Univ. Club (Chgo.), Onwentsia Club. Office: Pvt Bank and Trust Co 517 Green Bay Rd Wilmette IL 60091 Home: 2726 Aspen Ct Glenview IL 60025

GRIFFITHS, SYLVIA PRESTON, physician, educator; b. London, Dec. 25, 1924; d. Wheeler Bate and Dorothy (Hartley) Preston; m. Raymond B. Griffiths; 1 dau., Wendy Elizabeth. BA, Hunter Coll., 1944; MD, Yale U., 1948. Intern Grace-New Haven Community Hosp., 1948-49, resident, 1949-52; fellow in pediatric cardiology Yale U., 1952-54; asst. to prof. clin. pediatrics Columbia U., N.Y.C., 1955, prof. clin. pediatrics, 1977-90, prof. emeritus, 1990—. Recipient career scientist award Health Research Council, City of N.Y., 1963-69 Mem. N.Y. Heart Assn. (dir. 1977-83), Am. Acad. Pediatrics, Am. Pediatric Soc., Am. Heart Assn., Am. Coll. Cardiology, Babies Hosp. Alumni Assn. (pres. 1991-92). Office: Columbia Presbyterian Med Ctr 622 W 168th St New York NY 10032-3720

GRIFFY, THOMAS ALAN, physics educator; b. Oklahoma City, Dec. 16, 1936; s. Judson H. and Dicie (Johnston) G.; m. Peggy Lynn Walker, June 6, 1958; children— David, Alan, Marjorie BA, Rice U., 1959, MA, 1960, PhD, 1961. Asst. prof. physics Duke U., Durham, N.C., 1961-62; research assoc. High Energy Physics Lab., Stanford U., Calif., 1962-65; assoc. prof. physics U. Tex., Austin, 1965-68, prof., 1968—, chmn. dept., 1974-84, assoc. dean grad. sch., 1970-73, 96-00. Contbr. articles to profl. jours. Fellow Am. Phys. Soc. Methodist. Office: U Tex Dept Physics Austin TX 78712

GRIGG, WILLIAM HUMPHREY, utility executive; b. Shelby, N.C., Nov. 5, 1932; s. Claud and Margy (Humphrey) G.; m. Margaret Anne Ford, Aug. 11, 1956; children: Anne Ford, John Humphrey, Mary Lynne. AB, Duke U., 1954, LL.B., 1958. Bar: N.C. 1958. Gen. practice, Charlotte, 1958-63; with Duke Power Co., 1963-97, v.p. finance, 1970-71, v.p., gen. counsel, 1971-75, sr. v.p. legal and finance, 1975-82, exec. v.p., 1982-90, vice chmn., 1990-94, chmn., pres., CEO, 1994-97, also dir., 1997; chmn. emeritus Duke Energy Corp., Charlotte, 1997—. Bd. dirs. NationsFunds, Inc., Aegis Ins. Svcs., Shaw Group, Inc. Editor-in-chief Duke Law Jour, 1957-58; contbr. articles to profl. jours. Bd. dirs. Found. for the Carolinas. Capt. USMC, 1954—56. Mem. AMA, N.C. Bar Assn., Charlotte Country Club. Methodist. Office: Duke Power Co 422 S Church St Charlotte NC 28242-0001

GRIGGER, JANE ELIZABETH, earth science educator, photographer; b. Phila., June 7, 1947; d. John Casimer and Rozanne Marie (Peters) G. BS in Geology, Bucknell U., 1969; EdM in Earth Sci. Edn., Temple U., 1971. Tchr. secondary sci. Bensalem Twp. Sch. Dist., Cornwells Heights, Pa., 1970-72, Princeton Regional Schs. (N.J.), 1972-75; tchr. middle sch. earth sci. and phys. sci. Princeton Day Sch., 1975—. Tchr. ptnrs. in edn. geology program Princeton U., 1985, photographer jours. Troop advisor S.E. Pa. coun. Girls Scouts U.S.A., 1969—; photographer Girl Scout Internat. Event, 1975, 76. Mem. Phila. Geol. Soc., Field Conf. Pa. Geologists, N.J. Sci. Tchrs. Assn., Roster Women Geoscis., N.J. Earth Scis. Tchrs. Assn., Nat. Assn. Geology Tchrs., Nat. Sci. Tchrs. Assn., Bucknell Alumni Club. Episcopalian. Home: 64-13 Ravens Crest Plainsboro NJ 08536 Office: Princeton Day Sch PO Box 75 Princeton NJ 08542-0075 E-mail: jane_grigger@pds.org.

GRIGGS, GARY BRUCE, science administrator, oceanographer, geologist, educator; b. Pasadena, Calif., Sept. 25, 1943; s. Dean Brayton and Barbara Jayne (Farmer) G.; m. Venetia Gina Bradfield, Jan. 11, 1980; children: Joel, Amy, Shannon, Callie, Cody. BA in Geology, U. Calif., Santa Barbara, 1965; PhD in Oceanography, Oreg. State U., 1968. Registered geologist, Calif.; cert. engr. geologist, Calif. Rsch. asst., NSF grad. fellow in oceanography Oreg. State U., 1965-68; from asst. prof. to prof. earth scis. U. Calif., Santa Cruz, 1969—; Fulbright fellow Inst. for Ocean & Fishing Rsch., Athens, Greece, 1974-75; oceanographer Joint U.S.A.-N.Z. Rsch. Program, 1980-81; chair earth scis. U. Calif., Santa Cruz, 1981-84, assoc. dean natural scis., 1992-95; dir. Inst. of Marine Scis., 1991—2002. Vis. prof. Semester at Sea program U. Pitts., 1984-96; guest lectr. World Explorer Cruises, 1987; chair marine coun. U. Calif., 1999-02; bd. govs. Consortium for Oceanographic Rsch. and Edn., 1995—. Author: (with others) Geologic Hazards, Resources and Environmental Planning, 1983, Living with the California Coast, 1985, Coastal Protection Structures, 1986, California's Coastal Hazards, 1992; mem. editl. bd. Jour. of Coastal Rsch., Geology; contbr. numerous articles to profl. jours. Mem. Am. Geophys. Union, Am. Geol. Inst., Coastal Found. Achievements include research in coastal processes; coastal erosion and protection; coastal engineering and hazards; sediment yield, transport and dispersal; geologic hazards and land use. Office: U Calif Inst Marine Scis Santa Cruz CA 95064 E-mail: griggs@emerald.ucsc.edu.

GRIGGS, JOHN ROBERT, financial and consumer credit services executive; b. Franklin, N.J., Oct. 19, 1949; s. Frank E. and Verna L. (Geddes) G.; m. Sally Shutt, June 15, 1974; children: Brian, Dan, Carole. BS in Acctg., U. Tulsa, 1971, MBA, 1973. Cert. fin. and ops. prin. Nat. Assn. Securities Dealers, consumer credit exec. Fin. analyst Citicorp Person to Person, St. Louis, 1974, dir. fin. planning and analysis and various positions, 1975-78, chief of staff, 1978-79, sr. area mgr. Seattle, 1979; area v.p. Citicorp Acceptance Co., Seattle, 1979-82, v.p., chief fin. officer, treas. St. Louis, 1982-85, v.p. ops. Atlanta, 1985-86; v.p., gen. mgr. Household Fin. Svcs., Chgo., 1986-91, sr. v.p., 1991-93; exec. v.p., CFO, treas., dir. Hamilton Investments, subs. Household Internat., Chgo., 1993-94; v.p. Household Internat., Prospect Heights, Ill., 1994-96; sr. v.p. nat. ops. mgr. Banc One Credit Corp., Columbus, Ohio, 1996-97; exec. v.p., COO First Merchant's Acceptance Corp., Deerfield, Ill., 1997, mgmt. cons., 1997-98; divsn. pres. First Plus Fin., Dallas, 1998-99. Exec. v.p. ops. Centex Home Equity Corp., Dallas, 1999-2001; dir. loan servicing Capital One Auto Fin., Dallas, 2001-; chmn., bd. dirs. Consumer Credit Counseling Svc. Greater Chgo. (cert. consumer credit exec.). Coach Little League baseball, St. Louis, Atlanta, Chgo.; advisor Cub Scouts, Atlanta; trustee, treas. Homeowner's Assn., St. Louis; mem., bd. dirs., treas. Barrington (Ill.) Youth Baseball. Mem. Am. Fin. Svcs. Assn. (bd. dirs., exec. com.), Nat. Second Mortgage Assn. (bd. dirs., exec. com.), Internat. Credit Assn., Nat. Automotive Fin. Assn. (bd. dirs.), Alpha Phi Omega, Omicron Delta Kappa, Beta Gamma Sigma. Avocations: softball, racquetball.

GRIGGS, LEONARD LEROY, JR., airport executive; b. Norfolk, Va., Oct. 13, 1931; s. Leonard LeRoy and Mary (Blair) G.; m. Denise Ziegler, Mar. 18, 1977; children: Margaret Rosalyn, Virginia Lorraine Williams, Julia Blair Havey, Deborah Branham Taylor. BS, U.S. Mil. Acad., 1954; MS in Aero. Engring., Air Force Inst. Tech., 1960; MS in Internat. Affairs, George Washington U., 1967; disting. grad., Naval War Coll., 1967, Army War Coll., 1971. Registered profl. engr., Mo. Commd. 2d lt. U.S. Army, 1954; advanced through grades to col. USAF, 1970; served in Vietnam; ret., 1977; dir. Lambert St. Louis Internat. Airport, 1977-87; v.p. Ross & Baruzzini, Inc., 1987-89, Bangert Bros. Constrn. Co., St. Louis and Denver, 1989—; asst. adminstr. for airports FAA, Washington, 1990-93; airport dir. St. Louis Internat. Airport, 1993—. Adj. prof. St. Louis U.; apptd. to Nat. Civil Aviation Rev. Commn., 1997. Bd. dirs. USO, St. Louis/Lambert, Airports Coun. Internat., 1997-98. Decorated Silver Star, D.F.C. with 4 oak leaf clusters, Bronze Star, Meritorious Service medal, Air medal with 22 oak leaf clusters, Purple Heart, Air Force Commendation medal with 2 oak leaf clusters, Army Commendation medal; Medal of Honor; Medal of Gallantry (Vietnam); recipient Aviation Engring. Safety award FAA, 1979 Mem. Airport Operators Coun. Internat., Am. Assn. Airport Execs., Profl. Engring. Soc. St. Louis, Order of Dadelians, St. Louis Air Force Assn., Engr. Club, Mo. Athletic Club, Army Navy Club, Univ. Club., Order DeMolay. Home: 4400 Lindell Blvd Apt 17M Saint Louis MO 63108-2427 Office: Lambert-St Louis Intl Airport PO Box 10212 Lambert Airport MO 63145-0212

GRIGGS, NINA M. realtor; b. NYC, Sept. 21, 1932; d. John Malcolm Miller and Kathryn Ruth Wilenzick; m. Charles Guy Moseley, Aug. 28, 1954 (dec. Feb. 1970); children: Charles Edward Keeble Moseley, Kathryn Drew Moseley Kristofik; m. Bancroft Gerardi Davis, Dec. 31, 1971 (dec. Dec. 1980); m.

Richard Curtis Miles, Feb. 5, 1983 (dec. Sept. 1987); m. Northam Lee Griggs, Feb. 13, 1993 (dec. Mar. 2002). BA, Vassar Coll., 1954; MA, U. Va., 1956; postgrad., Columbia U. Exec. assoc., part-time rsch. assoc., 1961-63; founder, pres. Adventures Abroad, Ltd., 1964-71; also asst. to dir. profl. exams. divn. Psychol. Corp., N.Y.C., 1968-71; program officer Internat. Inst. Ednl. Planning/UNESCO, Paris, 1971-72; program adminstr. French and German lang. tchg. asst. prog. Inst. Internat. Edn., N.Y.C., 1973-85; dir. women's program Internat. Exec. Svc. Corps, 1988-91; real estate associate New England Land Co, Greenwich. Founder, dir. Women's Talent Corps, 1965-67; mem. N.Y. Jr. League; dir. Masters Nursery and Children's Ctr., 1962-81. Author: U.S. Citizenship Today, 1963; editor: (with Kertis, O'Driscoll) English Language and Orientation Programs in the United States, 1978, 80; contbr. articles to profl. jours. Trustee, chmn. nominating com. Dobbs Sch., 1968-71. Mem. Hyannisport Club, N.Y. Jr. League, Harvard Club of N.Y., Regency Club, Delta Delta Delta. Episcopalian. Home: 9 Country Rd Westport CT 06880 2524 Office: New England Land Co 783 North St Greenwich CT 06831 3105 Fax: 203-222-7497.

GRIGGS, ROBERT CHARLES, physician; b. Wilmington, Del., Jan. 8, 1939; s. Albert Bertin and Virginia (Robertson) G.; m. Rosalyne Hoggard, June 16, 1964; children— Jennifer, Heather. AB, U. Del., 1960; MD, U. Pa., 1964. Intern Case Western Reserve U., Cleve., 1964-65, resident, 1965-66, Nat. Inst. Neurol. Disease and Blindness, Bethesda, Md., 1966-68; resident in medicine, neurology U. Rochester, N.Y., 1968-71, prof. neurology, medicine, pathology, pediatrics, co-dir. neuromuscular disease ctr., 1972—, chmn. dept. neurology, 1986; practice medicine specializing in neurology Rochester, 1971—; hon. cons. Univ. Coll. Hosp., London, 1981-82. Author: Evaluation and Treatment of Myopathies; editor in chief Neurology, 1997—. Served to lt. comdr. USPHS, 1966-68. ACP Rsch. and Teaching grantee, 1971-74. Office: Strong Meml Hosp Dept Neurology 601 Elmwood Ave Dept Rochester NY 14642-0002

GRIGGS, STEPHEN LAYNG, management consultant; b. Morristown, NJ, 1947; s. Paul and Frances G.; m. Margaret Anne Hastings, 1970; children: Jocelyn Hastings, Diana Hastings. BSME, Villanova (Pa.) U., 1969; MS, MIT, 1971; MBA, Harvard U., 1974. Mem. tech. staff Bell Telephone Labs., Holmdel, N.J., 1969-72; div. mgr. Norlin Industries, Carlisle, Pa., 1974-77, contr., chief fin. officer, 1977-79; sr. assoc. Booz Allen & Hamilton, N.Y.C., 1979-82; v.p. ops., chief fin. officer Phys. Acoustics Corp., Princeton, N.J., 1982-83; sr. ptrn. KSM Group Inc., Short Hills, N.J., 1983-88; pres. The Tewksbury Group Inc., Oldwick, N.J., 1988—. Mem. IEEE, Am. Inst. Ultrasound Medicine, Am. Assn. Clin. Chemists, Soc. Competitive Intelligence Profls., Parenteral Drug Assn., Med. Mktg. Assn., Am. Soc. Materials, Soc. for Advancement of Materials and Process Engring., Am. Soc. for Microbiology, Am. Soc. Echocardiography, Hunterdon County Hist. Soc., Geneal. Soc. N.J., Nat. Geneal. Soc., New Eng. Hist. Geneal. Soc., Controlled Release Soc., Sigma Xi, Tau Beta Pi, Pi Tau Sigma. Republican. Episcopalian. Avocations: trout fishing, architecture. Office: Tewksbury Group Inc PO Box 48 Oldwick NJ 08858-0048

GRIGSBY, BYRON LEE, dean; b. Newburgh, NY, Sept. 24, 1968; s. Leslie Earle and Tina Marie Grigsby; m. Carolyn Elaine Coulson, Oct. 13, 1996; 1 child, Eliza Marie. BA, Moravian Coll., 1990; MA, Wake Forest U., 1992; PhD, Loyola U., Chgo., 2000. Adj. faculty mem. Olive-Harvey Coll., Chgo., 1995—97; writing specialist, tchr. Ea. Conn. State U., Willimantic, 1997—98, instr. writing, lit., western soc., 1998—2000; asst. prof., dir. writing ctr. Centenary Coll., Hackettstown, NJ, 2000—03, dean grad. and profl. programs, 2003—. Presenter in field; grad. asst. Wake Forest U., 1990—92. Author: Pestilence in Medieval and Early Modern English Literature, 2003, Misconceptions of the Middle Ages, 2003; contbr. articles to profl. jours. Mem. festival com. Warren County C. of C., 2001—; literacy tutor, dir. Willimantic Pub. Libr., Ea. Conn. State U., 1999; trustee, pub. theology coord. Waterloo (NY) United Meth. Ch., 2002—. Grantee, Ea. Conn. State U., 1998—99, Centenary Coll., 0022. Mem.: MLA, Coll. Composition and Comm., Nat. Coun. Tchrs. English, Delaware Valley Medieval Assn., N.E. MLA, Medica: Soc. for Study of Healing in Mid. Ages (pres. 1999—). Methodist. Office: Centenary Coll 400 Jefferson St Hackettstown NJ 07840

GRIGSBY, HENRY JEFFERSON, editor; b. Denver, Dec. 29, 1930; s. Henry Jefferson and Thelma Pearl (Nispel) G.; m. Joan Shirley Rinker, Sept. 6, 1953 (div. 1973); children: Kevin, Lisa, Lincoln. BA, U. Colo., 1954. Reporter Sterling (Colo.) Jour.-Advocate, 1954-55; reporter, Sunday editor Lewiston (Idaho) Morning Tribune, 1955-57; reporter Denver bur. UPI, 1958-59, mgr., 1961-66, bur. mgr., 1959-61, S.W. div. news editor Dallas bur., 1966-69, mgr. San Francisco bur., 1969-72, night mng. editor, 1972-74, mng. editor for news, 1974-75; assoc. editor Forbes mag., N.Y.C., 1976-77, sr. editor, 1977-81, exec. editor, 1981-86; sr. editor Fin. World mag., N.Y.C., 1988-90. Pres. Dallas chpt. Nat. Soc. Autistic Children, 1967-69. Served with USAF, 1950-52. Mem. N.Y. Fin. Writers Assn., Sigma Delta Chi, Phi Delta Theta. Home: 160 W 16th St Apt 1E New York NY 10011-6267

GRIGSBY, WILLIAM P. surgeon; b. Pulaski, Va., Apr. 13, 1932; MD, Med. Coll. Va., 1956. Diplomate Am. Bd. Surgery. Intern Queens Hosp., Honolulu, 1956-57; resident Chesapeake-Ohio R.R. Hosp., Clifton Forge, Va., 1960-61, Peter Bent Brigham Hosp., Boston, 1962-67; mem. staff Holston Valley Hosp., Kingsport, Tenn. Fellow ACS; mem. AMA. Office: 5712 Chestnut Hills Dr Kingsport TN 37664

GRIJALVA, RAUL, congressman; b. Tucson, Feb. 19, 1948; m. Ramona F. Grijalva; children: Adelita, Raquel, Marisa. BA, U. Ariz. Dir. El Pueblo Neighborhood Ctr.; asst. dean Hispanic student affairs U. Ariz.; mem. Pima County Bd. Suprs., 1989—2003; congressman 7th Dist. Ariz. U.S. Ho. Reps., 2003—. Democrat. Office: 1440 Longworth House Office Bldg Washington DC 20515-0307*

GRIJNS, LAINE, investment company executive; Chmn. bd. Internat. Nederlanden, N.Y.C.; CEO Patricof & Co. Capital Corp, N.Y.C.; sr. adv. BNY Capital Mkts., Inc., N.Y.C., 1998—2002.

GRILES, J. STEVEN, federal agency administrator; b. Clover, Va., Dec. 13, 1947; s. Frazior Lee and Elsie (Neal) G.; m. Mary L. Disque, Mar. 26, 1978; children— Matthew Disque, Maegan Elizabeth; children by previous marriage— Kimberly Neal, Timothy Neal BA, Univ. Richmond, 1970. Exec. asst. Va. Dept. Conservation, Richmond, Va., 1968-81; dep. dir. Office Surface Mining U.S. Dept. Interior, Washington, 1981-83, dep. asst. sec. land and minerals, 1983-85, asst. sec. of the interior for land and minerals mgmt., 1985-89; sr. v.p. environ. and pub. affairs The United Co., Bristol, Va., 1989—; dep. secy. U.S. Dept. Interior, Washington, 2001—. Served with Va. USNG, 1970-78 Republican. Office: US Dept Interior Off Secy 1849 C St NW Washington DC 20240

GRILL, LAWRENCE J. lawyer, accountant, corporate/banking executive; b. Chgo., Nov. 5, 1936; s. Samuel S. and Evelyn (Wollack) G.; m. Joan V. Krimston, Dec. 16, 1961; children: Steven Eric, Elizabeth Anne. BS with honors, U. Ill., 1958; postgrad., U. Chgo., 1959-60; LL.B., Northwestern U., 1963. CPA Ill.; bar: Ill. 1963, Calif. 1965. Audit and tax mgr. Arthur Anderson & Co., Chgo., 1958-60; with firm Aaron, Aaron, Schimberg & Hess, Chgo., 1963-64, Gendel, Raskoff, Shapiro & Quittner, Los Angeles, 1964-66; sec., gen. counsel Traid Corp., Los Angeles, 1966-69; v.p., sec., gen. counsel Kaufman & Broad, Inc., Los Angeles, 1969-78; pres. Kaufman & Broad Asset Mgmt., dir. subs.; v.p., sec., gen. counsel AM Internat., Inc., Century City, 1979-82, dir. subs.; sr. v.p., group ops. officer, dir. subs. Wickes Cos., Inc., Santa Monica, 1982-85; acting chief exec. officer, chief operating officer, mem. exec. com. Barco of Calif., Gardena, 1985-86; pres. Lawrence J. Grill & Assocs., L.A., Calif., 1985-94; pres., CEO Pan Am. Bank and United Pan Am. Fin. Corp., San Mateo, Calif., 1994-2000, also bd. dirs., 1994—. Chmn., pres., CEO Universal Savs. Bank, Orange, Calif., 1988-90; cons. bd. dirs. World Trade Bank, N.A., 1992, Marathon Nat. Bank, 1992-93; spl. advisor to Fed. Home Loan Bank Bd. San Francisco, Fed. Deposit Ins. Co. for Distressed Savs. Instns., 1986-88; arbitrator Am. Arbitration Assn. Served with AUS, 1958-59. Home: 48437 Vista Palomino La Quinta CA 92253 Office: 1300 S El Camino Real San Mateo CA 94402-2963 E-mail: Larg36@yahoo.com.

GRILL, RICHARD LOUIS, music educator; b. Chgo., Oct. 9, 1943; s. Emil Joseph and Rose Jean (Retel) Grill; m. Mary Bernadette Moran, Dec. 30, 1967; 1 child, Rick. MusB, DePaul U., Chgo., 1965; MusM, Cleve. Inst Music, 1970. Lic. Tchr. Ind. Dir. of music St. Paul Ch., Chgo., 1962—64, St. Denis Ch., Chgo., 1964—66, Our Lady of Angels Ch., Cleve., 1966—72, St. Mary Ch., Muncie, Ind., 1972—. Condr. Dubois Seven Last Words Our Lady Angels Ch., Cleve., 1966—72, condr. Beethoven Mass in C, 1972; mem. music commn. Diocese Cleve., 1969—72; mem. of music commn. Diocese Lafayette-in-Indiana, 1980—90; organ cons. St. John Evangelist Ch., Hartford City, Ind., 1987—88; advisor Muncie Symphony Children's Concerts, 1994—; mem. del. to Hungary, Poland, Czech Republic People to People, Seattle, 1998. Contbr.: articles on liturgy Explanation of the Catholic Mass, Voice of St. Mary, 2000—. Mem.: Am. Guild of Organists (treas., dean 1986—90, Colleague 1984). Roman Catholic. Avocations: harpsichord building, photography, travel. Home: 3000 W Applewood Ct Muncie IN 47304-7503 Office: St Mary Church 2300 W Jackson St Muncie IN 47303 Personal E-mail: ducks3000@earthlink.net.

GRILLAKIS, MANOUSSOS, mathematician, educator; b. Canea, Greece, Nov. 8, 1958; arrived in U.S., 1982; s. George and Maria Grillakis; m. Kristi-Anna Dobrovolski, Jan. 8, 1989; children: Antigone, Clio. Diploma in chem. engring., Nat. Tech. U. Athens, 1981; M in Applied Math., Brown U., 1983, PhD in Applied Math., 1986. Instr. Courant Inst. NYU, 1986—87; visitor Inst. Advanced Studies, Princeton, NJ, 1988; prof. U. Md., College Park, 1989—91, 1992—; assoc. prof. U. Mich., Ann Arbor, 1991—92. Named Sloan fellow, 1991—92; recipient Presdl. Young Investigators award, NSF, 1990—95. Mem.: MAA, SIAM. Office: U Md Dept Math College Park MD 20742 Business E-Mail: mng@math.umd.edu.

GRILLER, DAVID, economics and technology consultant; b. London, May 29, 1948; came to Can., 1977; s. Lewis and Renee (Kellinger) G.; m. Alexis Myers, Aug. 22, 1971; children: Hannah, Mark, Nadia. BS, U. Coll. London, 1969, PhD, 1972. Salters Co. fellow, London, 1973; postdoctoral fellow NRC of Can., Ottawa, 1973-75, head organic chemistry, 1977-91; mgmt. cons. Deloitte, Haskins and Sells, London, 1975-77; sr. ptnr. Secor Inc., Ottawa, Ont., Can.; 1991—. Author over 180 sci. papers and books. Recipient CNC-Iupac award Internat. Union Pure and Applied Chemists, 1984, Rutherford medal Royal Soc. Can., 1986, Organic Reaction Mechanisms award Royal Soc. of Chemistry, 1986. Fellow Royal Soc. Can., Can. Inst. Chemistry (Merck Sharp and Dohme award 1985). Avocations: squash, skiing. Home: 2026 Delmar Ct Ottawa ON Canada K1H 5R6 Office: Groupe Secor 38 McArthur Ave Ste 200 Ottawa ON Canada K1L 6R2 E-mail: dgriller@secor.ca.

GRILLER, GORDON MOORE, court administrator; b. Sioux City, Iowa, Feb. 3, 1944; s. Joseph Edward and Arlene (Searles) G. m. Helen Mary Friederichs, aug. 20, 1966; children: Heather, Chad. BA in Political Sci., U. Minn., 1966, MA in Pub. Affairs, 1969. Mgnt. analyst Hennepin County Adminstr., Mpls., 1968-72, asst. court adminstr. Hennepin County Municipal Ct., Mpls., 1972-77, ct. adminstr., 1977-78; judicial dist. adminstr. 2nd Dist. Ct. Minn., St. Paul, 1978 87; ct. adminstr. Superior Ct. Ariz., Phoenix, 1987—2002, Trial Cts. in Maricopa County Ariz., Phoenix, 2002—. Bd. dirs. Nat. Ctr. State Cts., 1997—, Nat. Conf. Metro Cts., 1999—. Vice-chmn. Bloomington Sch. Bd., Minn., 1981-87. Sgt. USAAF, 1968-74 Res. Recipient Warren E. Burger award Inst. Ct. Mgnt.,1988, Leadership Fellows award Bush Leadership Program, 1974. Mem. Nat. Assn. Trial Ct. Adminstrs.(pres. 1983-84), Ariz. Ct. Assn., Nat. Assn Ct. Mgmt. (award of merit), Am. Judicature Soc., (bd. dirs. 1997—). Lutheran. Avocations: running, kyaking, racquetball, scuba diving. Home: 8507 E San Jacinto Dr Scottsdale AZ 85258-2576 Office: Superior Ct Ariz 201 W Jefferson St Fl 4 Phoenix AZ 85003-2205

GRILLO, ISAAC ADETAYO, surgery educator, consultant; b. Lagos City, Nigeria, Jan. 15, 1931; s. Jeremiah Aina and Rachel Oni (Aluko) G.; m. Elizabeth Arinade Adejunmobi, July 18, 1957; children: Adewale, Adedayo, Adebola, Aderonke, Adeola, Adebusola, Adedamola, Adegboyega, Adedunmoye, Adebukola, Adeboye, Adejoke. BS cum laude, BA in Edn./Psychology, McPherson (Kans.) Coll., 1955, DSc (honoris causa), 1987; MD, U. Kans., 1960. Diplomate Am. Bd. Gen. Surgery, Am. Bd. Thoracic Surgery. Intern Menorah Med. Ctr., Kans. City, Mo., 1960-61; resident in gen. surgery Homer G. Phillips Hosp., St. Louis, 1961-65; resident in cardiothoracic surgery Olive View Hosp., Calif., 1965-66, Highland-Alameda County Hosp., Oakland, Calif., 1966-67; physician II Fairmont Hosp., San Leandro, Calif., 1967-68; from lectr. to prof. U. Ibadan, Nigeria, 1968-89; cons. to chief cons. U. Coll. Hosp. Ibadan, 1968-89; head dept. surgery U. Ibadan and U. Coll. Hosp. Ibadan, 1985-88; chief cons., head of surgery King Fahad Ctrl. Hosp., Gizan, Saudi Arabia, 1988-90; sr. cons. cardiothoracic surgery Assir Ctrl. Hosp., Abha, Saudi Arabia, 1990-99; prof. cardiothoracic surgery Coll. of Medicine, King Saud U., Abha, 1991-98, King Khalid U., Abha, 1998-99; physician and surgeon Salinas Valley State Prison, Calif. Dept. Correction, Soledad, 2000—. Cons. surgeon, (1971-88) acting med. supt (1971) Ogbomosho (Nigeria) Bapt. Hosp. Contbr. articles to profl. jour. Active choir McPherson Coll. Chapel and Ch. of the Brethren, McPherson, 1952-55, Ch. of the Brethren, Kansas City, Kans., 1956-60; active choir, violinist Orita Mefa Bapt. Ch., Ibadan, 1968—, New Haven Bapt. Ch., Ibadan, 1990—. Lt. col. Nigerian Army MC, 1969. Chemistry and Fgn. Students scholar McPherson Coll., 1952-55, Japanese Overseas Cooperation Agy. scholar Japanese Govt., 1971; Fulbright-Hayes fellow in cardiothoracic surgery U.S. Govt., 1977. Fellow ACS, Am. Coll. Angiology, Internat. Coll. Surgeons, Coll. Chest Physicians, West African Coll. Surgeons, Nigeria Med. Coun. Surgery. Avocations: playing music, writing poetry. Office: PO Box 4095 UI Post Office Ibadan Nigeria also: PO Box 367 Soledad CA 93960-0367 E-mail: isaacgrillo@aol.com.

GRILLO, ROBERT S. private investigator, protective services official; b. Johnstown, Pa., Mar. 28, 1923; s. George Angelo Grillo and Louise Marie Prevoreschi; m. Aurora M. Grillo; children: Robert G., Michael J., George V. Address: 5125 Cabrilla Ct New Port Richey FL 34652-3095

GRILLY, EDWARD ROGERS, physicist; b. Cleve., Dec. 30, 1917; s. Charles B. and Julia (Varady) G.; m. Mary Witholter, Dec. 14, 1942 (dec. 1971); children: David, Janice; m. Juliamarie Andreen Langham, Feb. 1, 1973. BA, Ohio State U., 1940, PhD, 1944. Rsch. scientist Carbide & Carbon Chemicals Corp., Oak Ridge, Tenn., 1944-45; asst. prof. Chemistry U. N.H., Durham, 1946-47; mem. staff U. Calif. Nat. Lab., Los Alamos, N.Mex., 1947-80, cons., 1980—. Contbr. articles to books and profl. jours. Mem. N.Mex. House of Reps., Santa Fe, 1967-70, Los Alamos County Coun., Los Alamos, 1976-78. Mem. Am. Physical Soc., Kiwanis Club, Los Alamos Golf Club (pres. 1974-75). Republican. Avocation: golf. Home: 705 43rd St Los Alamos NM 87544-1807 *The key to my life is discovery. It always amazes me how learning can be so fascinating. Of course, the ultimate is discovery in my own vocation-physics-whether it is of my own doing or learning of a colleague's work. But, I also found that intense involvement in community work can lead to surprising results.*

GRILLY, GERALD E. publishing executive; Publ. Anchorage Daily News, 1978-93; CEO Denver Post, 1993-98, publ., 1998—2001; exec. v.p. and COO Media News Group, Denver, 2001—. Office: 1560 Broadway Ste 2100 Denver CO 80202-6000 E-mail: ggrilly@medianewsgroup.com.

GRIM, BRIAN KEITH, music educator; b. Pottstown, Pa., Aug. 3, 1963; s. James Stanley and Joan Lynn Grim; m. Erin Jane McConihay, July 26, 1986; 1 child, Adam. MusB in Edn., Capital U., 1985; MA in Edn., U. of Findlay, 2000. Cert. tchr. Ohio Dept. of Edn., 1985. Dir. of bands Perry Local Schs., Lima, Ohio, 1985—86, Delphos (Ohio) St Johns, 1986—89, Waynesfield-Goshen (Ohio) Schs., 1989—94; band dir. Kenton (Ohio) City Schs., 1994—2002, Bath Local Schs., Lima, Ohio, 2002—. Lectr. in music Ohio No. U., Ada, Ohio, 1995—. Mem.: Ohio Music Edn. Assn. Republican. Avocations: travel, business, golf. Home: 4801 Township Road 25 Ada OH 45810 Office: Bath Local Schools 2850 Bible Road Lima OH 45801 Personal E-mail: b-grim@onu.edu.

GRIM, ELLEN TOWNSEND, artist, retired art educator; b. Boone County, Ind., Nov. 1, 1921; d. Horace Wright and Sibyl Conklin (Lindley) Townsend; m. Robert Little Grim, Apr. 5, 1952; children: Nancy Ellen Grim Garcia, Howard Robert. Student, Our Lady of the Lake U., 1939-41, U. Tex., 1941-42; BA in Art, U. Wash., 1946; MA in Art, UCLA, 1950; postgrad., Otis Art Inst., L.A., 1970-71. Cert. secondary tchr., Calif. Art tchr., chairperson secondary Calif. and L.A. Unified Sch. Dist., 1947—82; retired, 1982; artist, 1975—. Guest speaker on art TV and cable, L.A., 1993. One-woman shows include Ventura County Mus. Art, 1982, Riverside Mcpl. Mus., 1984, Craft and Folk Art Mus., L.A., 1986, S.W. Mus., L.A., 1987, Calif. Heritage Mus., 1991, Brand Art Ctr., Glendale, 1996, Wurdermann Gallery, L.A., 1997, others; exhibited in more than 100 group shows. 1st lt. USMC, 1943-45. Recipient Purchase prize Gardena Fine Arts Collection, 1982, Watercolor West award San Diego Watercolor Soc. Internat., 1983, N.Mex. Watercolor Soc. award, 1989, 1st pl. award Fine Arts Fedn., 1987, 1st pl. award Art Educators L.A., 1988, 89, 1st pl. award Collage Artists Am., 1995, 2002, Brand Art Ctr. Watercolor West award, 1999, Painting award Valley Inst. of Visual Art, San Fernando Valley, 1999, 2001, Long Beach Arts painting award, 1999, 2000. Mem.: Alliance of Women Vets., Women Marines Assn., Collage Artists Am. (1st Place award 1995, 2002), Pasadena Soc. Artists (Painting award 1986, 1988, 1990, 1992, 1993, 1999, 2001, 2002), L.A. Art Assn. (bd. dirs. 1993—95), Women Painters West (membership chair, mem.-at-large 1983—89, Painting award 1985, 1986, 1989, 1992, 1993, 1995, 1999, Best of Show award 2000, Painting award 2000, 2001), Nat. Watercolor Soc. (historian 1989—90, Painting award 1984, 1999, 2000), Women in Mil Svc. for Am., Pi Lambda Theta, Alpha Phi. Avocations: Native American and Latin American culture, travel, Southwestern history.

GRIM, PATRICIA ANN, retired banker; b. Everett, Pa., Sept. 7, 1940; d. Harry Grant and Nellie Elizabeth (Koontz) Foor; m. James Woodrow Grim, Feb. 21, 1970. Student, Am. Inst. Banking, Rolling Meadows, Ill., Bank Adminstrn. Inst., The Bus. Women's Tng. Inst., Penn State Univ. Sec. William H. Snyder, Atty. at Law, Bedford, Pa., 1958-60; sec., loan teller First Nat. Bank of Everett, Pa., 1960-70; teller Orrstown (Pa.) Bank, 1970-81, asst. cashier, asst. sec., 1981-82, v.p., asst. sec., 1982-94; officer, mgr. Mellon Bank, Shippensburg, Pa., 1994-2000; ret., 2000. Recipient Family Tng. Hour Leader of Yr. award Ch. of God State of Pa., Layman of Yr. award, 1979; nat. nominee Layperson of Yr., 1984. Mem. Ch. of God.

GRIM, PATRICK NEAL, philosopher, logician, educator; b. Pasadena, Calif., Oct. 29, 1950; s. Elgas Shull Grim and Dorathy Mae O'Neal; m. L. Theresa Watkins. AB in Philosophy and Anthropology, U. Calif., Santa Cruz, 1971; BPhil, U. St. Andrews, 1975; PhD, Boston U., 1976. Mellon faculty fellow Wash. U., St. Louis, Mo., 1977-78; from asst. prof. to prof. SUNY, Stony Brook, 1978-94, prof., 1994—2001, disting. tchg. prof., 2001—. Author: The Incomplete Universe, 1991, The Philosophical Computer, 1998; editor: The Philosopher's Annual, Vols. 1-25, 1979-2003, Philosophy of Science and the Occult, 1982, 91; contbr. articles to profl. jours. Fulbright fellow, St. Andrews, Scotland, 1971-72, Mellon Faculty fellow Washington U., St. Louis, 1977-78. Fellow Acad. of Tchr./Scholars; mem. Internat. Assn. Philosophy of Law, Am. Philosophical Assn., Cognitive Sci. Soc. Avocations: art, music. Home: Toad Hall 99 Swezey St Patchogue NY 11772 Office: Dept of Philosophy Suny At Stony Brk Stony Brook NY 11794-3750 E-mail: pgrim@notes.cc.sunysb.edu.

GRIM, SAMUEL ORAM, chemistry educator; b. Landisburg, Pa., Mar. 11, 1935; s. Oram Michael and Esther Blanche (Gable) G.; m. Faith H. Rojahn, June 8, 1957 (div. 1982); children: Stephen W., Amy R., Lucy G.; m. Caren L. Klarman, Mar. 11, 1983 (div. 1993); 1 child, Christina K.; m. Rebecca A. Allen, Aug. 11, 2001. BS, Franklin and Marshall Coll., 1956; PhD, MIT, 1960. Faculty U. Md., College Park, 1960—, prof. chemistry, 1968—, chmn. inorganic chemistry divsn., 1970-77, 80-86, 1995—96, assoc. chmn., chemistry dept., 1996-98. Program officer in inorganic chemistry NSF, 1988-90. Contbr. articles to profl. jours. Union Carbide Co. scholar, 1954-56; NSF fellow, 1958-60; summer teaching fellow, 1960; research fellow Imperial Coll., London, 1961-62; Sir John Cass's Found. sr. research fellow City of London Poly., 1979-80 Fellow AAAS, Am. Inst. Chemists, Royal Soc. Chemistry (London); mem. Am. Chem. Soc., N.Y. Acad. Scis., Internat. Union Pure and Applied Chemistry, Internat. Coun. Main Group Chemistry, Chem. Soc. Washington, Phi Beta Kappa, Sigma Xi (Sci. Achievement award 1983), Phi Lambda Upsilon, Alpha Chi Sigma. Clubs: Terrapin (College Park). Republican. Home: 14219 Greenview Dr Laurel MD 20708-3215 Office: U Md Dept Chemistry College Park MD 20742-2021

GRIMALDI, JAMES THOMAS, investment fund executive; b. Elizabeth, N.J., Dec. 8, 1928; s. Anthony and Helen (Bernatt) G.; m. Norma Miriello, June 17, 1951; children: Patricia Ann, Pamela Gay, Donna Lynne. BS in Econs., U. Pa., 1951; MBA, Columbia U., 1955. CLU, 1964. Br. acct. Watson-Flagg Engring. Co., Paterson, N.J., 1953-56; from agt. to sr. asst. dist. mgr. Met. Life Ins. Co., Paterson, Ridgewood, N.J., 1956-61; reg. agy. dir., asst. v.p. Am. Amicable Life Ins. Co., Ft. Lauderdale, Fla., 1961-66; v.p. mktg. Inland Life Ins. Co., Chgo., 1966-69; exec. v.p. Peoples Home Life Ins. Co. Ind., 1969-71, Fed. Life & Casualty Co., Battle Creek, 1970-71; pres., chief exec. officer, also dir. Peoples Home Life Ins. Co. of Ind., 1971-74; pres., CEO, bd. dirs. Fed. Life & Casualty Co., 1971-74, Keystone Co., Boston, 1974-76, Cornerstone Fin. Svcs., Inc., Boston, 1974-76; exec. v.p. sales Keystone Custodian Funds, Inc., Boston, 1974-76; engaged in pvt. investments, 1976—. Mem. faculty De Paul U., Chgo., 1969. 1st lt. USAF, 1951-53. Recipient Spl. Tribute as Outstanding Citizen, State of Mich., 1974. Mem. Sales Mktg. Execs. Internat., Am. Soc. CLU, Nat. Assn. Life Underwriters, Am. Mktg. Assn., Assn. Individual Investors, Life Assn. Mich. (pres. 1973, exec. com.), Nat. Assn. Security Dealers, Acad. Polit. Sci., U. Pa. Alumni Assn., Columbia U. Alumni Assn. Home: 4904 Sentinel Post Rd Charlotte NC 28226-7445

GRIMALDI, NICHOLAS LAWRENCE, fundraising executive; s. Dominick Lawrence and Marian Theresa (Colucci) G. Student, Manhattan Coll., Fordham U. Exec. assoc. Nat. Assn. Regional Ballet, N.Y.C., 1979-87; exec. dir. Nikolais/Louis Found. for Dance, Inc., N.Y.C., 1987-89; dir. devel. Hartley House, N.Y.C., 1989-93, Fountain House, Inc., N.Y.C., 1993—. Cons. mgmt. and fund raising; mem. steering com./pastoral coun. Ch. of St. Francis Xavier, N.Y.C., 1993-97. Mem.: Assn. Fundraising Profls., Phi Sigma Tau, Phi Kappa Phi, Alpha Sigma Nu. Office: Fountain House Inc 425 W 47th St New York NY 10036-2397

GRIMALDI, VINCE, artist; b. NYC, July 21, 1929; s. Vincenzo and Sebastiana Grimaldi. Student, Art Students League, N.Y.C., 1947-50, New Sch. Social Rsch., 1952-55. One-man shows include Falmouth (Mass.) Art Guild, 1968, Michael's Gallery, N.Y.C., 1976, Soho Photo Gallery, 1977, Cin. Art Acad., 1984, Claire Dunphy Studio, N.Y.C., 1986, 1989, Ednl. Alliance, 1989, 1992, Monaco Studio, Providence, 1995, Café La France, 1996, Providence Art Club, 1998, Central Congregational Ch., 1998, Bodi Gallery, Newport, R.I., 2001, Peck Gallery, Providence, 2001, Centercity Gallery, 2002, Wells Coll., Aurora, N.Y., 2002, exhibited in group shows at March Gallery, N.Y.C., 1954, East Hampton Gallery, 1967, Taniger Gallery, 1955, Ball State Coll., Muncie, Ind., 1963—64, Scorpio Gallery, Rome, 1965, Feiner Gallery, N.Y.C., 1967, Cape Cod Assn., Hyannis, Mass., 1967, Falmouth Art Guild, 1967, Soho Photo Gallery, N.Y.C., 1975—76, Floating Found. Photography, 1982, Donnell Libr., 1985, Kenkeleba Gallery, 1985, Castle Gallery, New Rochelle, N.Y. State Mus., N.Y.C., 1986, New Rochelle N.Y. Mus., 1986, Ctrl. Pk. Gallery, N.Y.C., 1986, Silvermine Gallery, Conn., 1987, Window Box Gallery, N.Y.C., 1987, 1989, Ch. Ctr., 1988, Claire Dunphy Studio, 1988, AMMO Gallery, Bklyn., 1989, Vasarely Mus., Budapest, Hungary, 1991, Forum Gallery Jamestown Coll., N.Y., 1992, Madrid, 1993, Sarajevo, Bosnia, 1993, Glasgow (Scotland) Gallery, 1994, West Broadway Gallery, N.Y.C., 1994, Sarah Doyle Gallery, Providence, 1995, 1997, 2001, Providence Art Club, 1996—97, Centercity Gallery, Providence, 1999—2000, R.I. State House, 2000, Spring Bull Gallery, Newport, R.I., 2001, Bodi Gallery, Newport, 2001, Attleboro (Mass.) Mus., 2003, Station 29 Gallery, Newport, RI, 2003, Represented in permanent collections Hambidge Ctr. Arts, Tate Gallery, London, Bklyn. Mus. Art, N.Y.C., Butler Inst. Am. Art, Met. Mus. Art, UCLA, N.Y. Pub. Libr., Newark Pub. Libr., Mus. Modern Art, N.Y.C., Louis Held Collections, Wells Coll., Aurora, U. Mass., pvt. collections, 2,000 Years in Rome, 1967, Celebrating the Statue of Libery, 1986, slide talks, Galapagos Islands, 1993 , With U.S. Army, 1951-53, Korea. Avocations: swimming, beach combing, travel, slide talks. Home: 280 Washington St (509) Providence RI 02903-3605 E-mail: grimvin@sacbeemail.com.

GRIMBALL, CAROLINE GORDON, retail sales professional; b. Columbia, S.C., Dec. 21, 1946; d. John and Caroline Grimball. B.A. in Polit. Sci., Converse Coll., 1968; postgrad., S.C. Law Sch., 1968-69. Asst. buyer, buyer Rich's, Inc., Atlanta, 1971-78, spl. events fashion coordinator, Columbia, S.C.,

1978-83; gen. mdse. mgr. Rackes, Inc., Columbia, 1983-84, Parasol Boutique, Columbia, 1984-86; retail cons. Retail Mdsg. Service Automation, Columbia, 1986-88; sales rep. Palmetto Promotions, 1989-93; retail mdse. supr. Riverbanks Zoo & Garden, 1993-94; retail mgr., buyer Riverbanks Zoo & Garden, 1994-2000; retail mngr., Aramark Entertainment, 2000-. Pres. Columbia Action Coun., 1990-92; bd. dirs. Palmetto Leadership Coun., 1991-92, Palmetto State Orch. Assn., Columbia, 1979-89, Women's Symphony Assn., Columbia, 1985; com. chmn. Columbia Action Coun., 1984-85, exec. com., 1989-92; Piedmont Found. S.C., Columbia Classical Ballet. Named one of Outstanding Young Women Am., 1979, 80; recipient Community Service award Rich's, Inc., 1981. Mem. Nat. So. Colonial Dames Am., Columbia Jr. League. Democrat. Episcopalian. Club: Columbia Drama. Avocations: bridge, reading, needlepoint, tennis. Home: 109 Walden Ct Columbia SC 29204-4043

GRIMBERG, ADDA, pediatrician; MD, Cornell U., 1989—93. General Pediatrics Am. Bd. of Pediat., 1996, Pediatric Endocrinology Am. Bd. of Pediat., 1999. Asst. prof., pediat. U. of Pa., Sch. of Medicine, 2000—; attending, ped. endocrinology Children's Hosp. of Phila., 1999—. Recipient Student Award in Clin. Nutrition, The Regional Ctr. for Nutrition Edn., The NY Acad. of Medicine, 1991, Clin. Scholar award, Lawson Wilkins Pediatric Endocrine Soc., 2000—02; Merrill Presdl. scholar, Cornell U., 1989, Rsch. fellowship, Lawson Wilkins Pediatric Endocrine Soc., 1998—99, NIDDK rsch. grant, NIH/NIDDK, 2002—. Mem.: Joseph Stokes Rsch. Inst., U. of Pa. Cancer Ctr., The Endocrine Soc., Lawson Wilkins Pediatric Endocrine Soc., Phila. Endocrine Soc. (bd. mem. 2002—). Achievements include research in relationships between p53 and IGF pathways; (clinical) growth in children. Office: Children's Hosp of Phila Abramson rm 802; 3615 Civic Center Blvd Philadelphia PA 19104-4318 Office Fax: 215-590-1605. E-mail: grimberg@email.chop.edu.

GRIMES, CRAIG ALAN, electrical engineering educator; b. Ann Arbor, Mich., Nov. 6, 1956; s. Dale Mills and Janet LaVonne (Moore) G.; m. Elizabeth Carol Dickey, 1998; children: Keltin Maxwell, Kyra Megan. BS in Physics, BSEE, Pa. State U., 1984; MS, U. Tex., 1985, PhD, 1990. Engr. Applied Rsch. Labs., Austin, Tex., 1981-83; pres. Crale, Inc., Austin, 1985-90; rsch. scientist Lockeed Rsch. Labs., Palo Alto, Calif., 1990-92; dir. advanced materials lab. Southwall Techs., Palo Alto, Calif., 1992-94; asst. prof. dept. elec. engring. U. Ky., Lexington, 1994-98, assoc. prof., 1998-2000, Frank J. Derbyshire prof., 2000-01, dir. Ctr. for Micro-Magnetic and Electronic Devices, 2000-01; assoc. prof. dept. elec. engring. Pa. State U. and Materials Rsch. Inst., 2001—; pres. Sentechbiomed Corp., 1999—. Rsch. asst. U. Tex., Austin, 1985-88, teaching asst., 1987-90; cons. Eastman Kodak, San Diego, 1989, Storage Tech., Boulder, Colo., 1989, Read-Rite, Fremont, Calif., 1994, AT&T Bell Labs., Murray Hill, N.J., 1995; mem. Clark County Rural Electric Coop.; founder, pres. Sentech Biomed Corp., 1999—. Co-author: Essays on the Formal Aspects of E&M Theory, 1992, Advanced Electromagnetism: Foundation, Theory and Applications, 1995, The Electromagnetic Origin of Quantum Theory and Light, 2002; editor-in-chief: Sensor Letters, 2003—; contbr. articles to profl. jours. Active Nature Conservancy, 1988-95, Austin Triathletes, 1987-90. Mem.: IEEE, AAAS, Bluegrass Masters. Achievements include 6 patents, 8 pending in field; development and manufacture of permeameters, magnetic measurement tools for high frequency permeability measurements; development of size independent antennae. Home: 615 Windmill Rd Boalsburg PA 16827 Office: PSU 217 Materials Rsch Lab University Park PA 16802-4801 E-mail: cgrimes@engr.psu.edu.

GRIMES, DALE MILLS, physics and electrical engineering educator; b. Marshall County, Iowa, Sept. 7, 1926; s. LeRoy and Helen (Mills) G.; m. Janet LaVonne Moore, Mar. 22, 1947; children: Prudence Rae, Craig Alan. BS in Physics, Math. and Chemistry, Iowa State U., 1950, MS in Physics and Math, 1951; PhD in Elec. Engring, U. Mich., Ann Arbor, 1956. From rsch. assoc. to assoc. prof. elec. engring. U. Mich., 1951-61, prof. elec. engring., 1961-76; chief scientist Conductron Corp., Ann Arbor, 1960-63; prof. elec. engring., chmn. dept. U. Tex., El Paso, 1976-79; prof. elec. and computer engring. Pa. State U., 1979-91, prof. emeritus, 1992—, chmn. dept., 1979-86. Adj. prof. physics U. Ky., 1996—2000; cons. Environ. Rsch. Inst. Mich., U.S. Dept. Transp., GM Corp., 1968—91; vis. prof. elec. and computer engring. U. Tex.-Austin, 1985—86; chief scientist Crale, Inc., 1985—95. Author: Electromagnetism and Quantum Theory, 1969, Automotive Electronics, 1974, Advanced Electromagnetics: Foundations, Theory, Applications, 1995, Electromagnetic Origin of Quantum Theory and Light, 2002, also articles on automotive radar, biconical antennas, quantum theory, electromagnetic radiation; patentee in field. Served with USNR, 1943-46. Fellow AAAS; mem. IEEE, Am. Phys. Soc., Lexington Acad. Sr. Profls. Home: 1325 Megan Dr State College PA 16803

GRIMES, DAVID LYNN, communications company executive; b. Oklahoma City, June 9, 1947; s. Glenn Ross and Kathleen Sue G.; m. Sandra Kay Belt, Mar. 6, 1970; children: David Edwin, Emily Kathleen. BBA in Mktg., Cen. State U., Edmond, Okla., 1979; grad. internat. sr. mgrs. program, Harvard U. Grad. Sch. Bus., 1988. With Southwestern Bell Telephone, 1970-83, rates and tariff, 1975-77, industry mgr., 1977-79, dist. mgr. sales ops. St. Louis, 1979-80, mktg. mgr. Kansas City, Mo., 1980-82, Houston, 1982-83; div. mgr. Am. Bell, Houston, 1983-84; br. mgr. nat. accts. AT&T, Houston, 1984-85, v.p. sales Dallas, 1986-98; chief operating officer Sharetech, Parsippny, N.J., 1985-86; pres., COO Sykes Enterprises, 1998-2000, pres., CEO, 2000; sr. v.p. Tropic Networks, 2001—. Mem. Nat. Bd. of Visitors Tex. Christian U., 1990-96; mem. adv. coun. Sch. Nat. Sci., U. Tex., Austin, 1988-93; bd. dirs. Tex. Bus. Hall of Fame Found., Dallas, 1988-93. Mem. Dallas C. of C. (mem. exec. com. econ. devel. 1991-93), Harvard Bus. Club Dallas, Univ. Club (Dallas), Avila Country Club, Pinnacle Country Club, Tampa C. of C. (bd. dirs. 2000-01). Republican. Methodist. Avocations: golf, tennis, fishing, hunting. Home: 5510 Merrimac Ave Dallas TX 75206

GRIMES, GARY A. music educator; b. Belvidere, Ill., Mar. 15, 1954; s. Roy A. and Alice M. Grimes. BMus, Ill. State U., Normal, 1977, MMus, 1979; DMus, U. Ill., Urbana, 1996. Instr. Lincoln Coll., Normal, Ill., 1984—; owner, instr. Ctr. Performing Arts, Bloomington, Ill., 1984—; instr. Ill. Wesleyan U., Bloomington, 1986—2001, U. Ill., Urbana, 2002—. Pres. Ill. Fedn. of Music Clubs, 1988—93; mem. exec. bd. Nat. Fedn. of Music Clubs, Indpls., 1993—96. Dir. Singing Y'ers (boy choir YMCA), Bloomington, Ill., 2002—. Avocations: dogs, cooking.

GRIMES, HEILAN YVETTE, publishing executive; b. Hamilton, Ohio, Sept. 16, 1949; d. J and Claudette (Hinkle) G. Grad., New Eng. Sch. Photography, 1987. Founder, pres. Dot & Line Graphics, 1975—, Color Computer Weekly, 1982—, Hollow Earth Pub., 1983—. Author: Norse Mythology, 1984, Legend of Niebelungenlied, 1984, Using QuarkXPress 3.3, 1994, Beginning Internet, 1994, Filemaker Pro Developer's Guide, 1997; founder Byte Mag., 1974, Macpower Mag., 1993. Recipient various photographic awards and grants. Democrat. Avocations: magic, juggling, hiking, traveling. Office: PO Box 51480 Boston MA 02205-1480 E-mail: yvettegr@hotmail.com.

GRIMES, HOWARD RAY, management consultant; b. Manilla, Iowa, July 24, 1918; s. Ray Herb and Sarah Alice (Saunders) G.; m. Nancy Palmer, Nov. 17, 1993; children from previous marriage: Patricia, Susan, Nancy, Sarah, Laura. Student, U. Wis., 1939; BA, Grinnell Coll., 1940. With Aetna Life & Casualty Co., 1940-82, field supr., regional mgr., 1950-74, regional dir., v.p. field, 1974-82; mgmt. cons., 1983-95; chmn. Benefit Svcs. Inc., 1968-93. Bd. dirs. Waterville Co. Inc. Served with USAAF, 1942-45. Sports-Illustrated Silver Anniversary All-Am. Mem. Down Town Club (Boston), Weston Golf Club (Mass.), Bald Peak Colony Club (N.H.), The Moorings Club (Fla.). Home: PO Box 513 10 W Branch Rd Waterville Valley NH 03215-0513 also: 1180 Reef Rd Vero Beach FL 32963-2971 E-mail: hrgrimes8@aol.com.

GRIMES, JAMES CAHILL, retired publishing executive, advertising executive; b. Oklahoma City, July 20, 1918; s. James Arthur Grimes and Kathryn Shanahan; m. Roma Ellison, Oct. 18, 1958; children: Joseph Edward, Jill. BA in Journalism, U. Okla., 1940. With J.C. Grimes & Assocs., Oklahoma City, 1946-49, 75-98; fundraiser Girl Scouts U.S.A., Kansas City, Mo., 1963-70; ptnr. Grimes-Valentine, Arlington, Tex., 1972-75; co-publ., S.W. Travel & Recreation Quarterly, Ariz., 1983-97. Publ. Cochise County Mag., 1988-96, Nogales/Santa Cruz County Mag., 1990-96, Okla. Home Builder Mag., 1946-49; co-publ. Ariz...Discover It! mag., 1992-94; founding pres. Old West Country, N.M., 1984-88. Officer-in-charge Beachhead News, 1944-45; publ. League of Young Dem. Newspaper, Oklahoma City, 1946-49; pres. O'Odham Tash (Indian Days), 1996-97; chmn. Mining Days, Silver City, N. Mex., 1985; chmn. Winter Art Festival, Sierra Vista, Ariz., 1990; dist. commr. Boy Scouts Am., Phoenix, 1982-86 (silver beaver award 1985), commr. Boy Scouts Am., Tucson, 1998- (disting. commisioner, 2003), Maj. U.S. Army, 1942-46. Decorated Bronze Star; named Tourism Citizen of Yr. C. of C., Silver City, N.M., 1985, Sierra Vista, 94. Mem. Rotary Internat., Masons, Tex. Rabbit Breeders Assn., N. Mex. Rabbit Breeders Assn. (pres.), Ariz. Rabbit Breeders Assn., Sigma Delta Chi, Delta Upsilon Fraternity (gen. sec. 1949-56). Republican. Mem. Lds Ch. Home and Office: 3245 S Wilmot Rd Apt 3109 Tucson AZ 85730-2286

GRIMES, JAMES GORDON, geologist; b. Kenosha, Wis., Mar. 18, 1951; s. James Gordon Bennett Jr. and Alyce Louise (Gannaway) G. BS in Earth Sci., U. Wis., Parkside, 1974; MS in Geology, Mich. Tech. U., 1977. Registered profl. geologist, Tenn. Geologist nat. uranium resource evaluation project Union Carbide Corp. Nuclear Div., Oak Ridge, 1977-84; geol. cons. UCC-ND Mercury Task Force, Oak Ridge, 1983; geologist Lockheed Martin Energy Systems Inc., Oak Ridge, 1984-99. Tech. mgr. Y-12 plant Meterol. Info. Support System, 1987-96, ind. cons., Kenosha, 1999—. Mem. AAAS, Am. Statis. Assn., Am. Meteorol. Soc., Am. Mgmt. Assn., Am. Water Resources Assn., Nat. Weather Assn., Geol. Soc. Am., Am. Nuc. Soc., Air and Waste Mgmt. Assn., Internat. Assn. Math. Geology. E-mail: xjg@worldnet.att.net.

GRIMES, JULIA PATRICE, physician, researcher; b. Milw., Sept. 22, 1966; d. Patrick Gerald and Maureen Anne Grimes; m. Joseph Scala, May 28, 1995; children: Anthony, Daniel. BA, Rutgers Coll., New Brunswick, N.J., 1988; DO, UMDNJ- Sch. of Osteopathic Medicine, Stratford, N.J., 1994; MPH, UMDNJ-Sch. of Pub. Health, Stratford, N.J., 2002. Cert. Am. Bd. of Internal medicine. Clin. asst. prof. of medicine UMDNJ-Robert Wood Johnson Med. Sch., New Brunswick, NJ, 2002. Contbr. articles to profl. jour. Fellow: ACP; mem.: Am. Womens Med. Assn., La Leche League. Avocations: bicycling. Office: UMDNJ Robert Wood Johnson Med Sch New Brunswick NJ 08903

GRIMES, KATHERINE ELIZABETH, child psychiatrist, researcher; b. Durham, N.C., July 29, 1950; d. Alan Pendleton and Margaret (Whitehurst) Grimes; m. David Wedgewood Green, May 5, 1979; children: Sarah Elizabeth Green, Daniel Grimes Green. Student, Oberlin Coll., 1968—69; BA, Mich. State U., 1974, MD, 1978; MPH, Harvard U., 2001. Instr. Mich. State U., East Lansing, 1978—79; resident in adult psychiatry Menninger Sch. Psychiatry, Topeka, 1979—81; resident in child psychiatry Harvard Med. Sch., Boston, 1981—83, fellow, 1981—83, instr., 1984—2001, asst. prof., 2001—. Dir. child & adolescent mental health Harvard Pilgrim Health Care, Brookline, Mass., 1989—96, dir. abuse & trauma intervention program, 1990—99; dir. Mass. mental health svcs. program youth Neighborhood Health Plan, Boston, 1997—, assoc. med. dir. mental health, 2001—. Contbr. Who Model Policy Report. Founder abuse and trauma intervention program Best Practice, 1998; founder child mental health model program Am. Prospect, 2001; founder Model Program Mass. Child Mental Health Sys. Care, 2001; mem. Lexington Youth Summer Theater, Mass., 1992—. Mem.: Mass. Med. Soc., New Eng. Coun. Child & Adolescent Psychiatry, Am. Acad. Child & Adolescent Psychiatry, Am. Psychiat. Assn. Avocations: gardening, running, musical theater.

GRIMES, MARGARET WHITEHURST, artist, educator; b. New Bern, N.C., June 5, 1943; d. Alan Pendleton and Margaret (Whitehurst) G. BA, Gov. State U., 1975, MA, 1976; postgrad., Notre Dame U., 1977; MFA, U. Pa., 1980. Instr. drawing and design Thornton C.C., Chgo., 1974-79; prof. painting and drawing Western Conn. State U., Danbury, 1980—, asst. chair, 1991-92, coord., master fine arts program, 2000—. Guest lectr./critic Vt. Coll. of Norwich U., Montepelier, 1995-96, Vt. Studio Ctr., Johnson, 1995, Tanglewood Inst., Lenox, Mass., 1997, S.V.A. Conf. on Liberal Arts and the Edn. of Artists, 1997, Ctrl. Conn. State U., New Britain, 1997, Weir Farm Nat. Hist. Site, Wilton, Conn., 1998, Gunn Mus., Washington, 2000; vis. artist Am. U., Corciano, Italy, 2001-03, Hendrix Coll., Conway, Ark., 2002, Chautauqua (N.Y.) Inst., 2003. Co-editor New Art Assn. Newsletter, 1971; one woman shows include Green Mountain Gallery, N.Y., 1979, (biennial) Blue Mountain Gallery, N.Y., 1980-2003, Fischbach Gallery, N.Y., 1986, Moravian Coll., Bethlehem, Pa., 1990, Western Conn. State U., 1990, 98, Ctrl. Conn. State U., 1997, Washington Art Assn., 1990, 2000, Weir Farm Nat. Trust, Wilton, Conn., 2003, 100 Pearl Gallery, Hartford, Conn., 2003, NAS, Washington, 2003; three-person show Provincetown Group Gallery, Mass., 1987; exhibited in group shows at Internat. Women's Art Festival, Walker Art Inst., 1976, Woodmere Mus., Phila., 1977, Provincetown Art Mus., Mass., 1978, Reading Mus., Pa., 1983, Queens Mus., N.Y., 1983, Rahr-West Mus., Manitowac, Wis., 1983, Columbus (Ohio) Mus. of Art, 1987, Katherina Rich Perlow Gallery, 1987, 88, 89, 76th Am. ann. show Newport (R.I.) Mus., 1988, Erector Sq. Gallery, New Haven, Conn., 1994, Kline Gallery, 1994, Creiger-Dane Gallery, Boston, 1995, Park Ave. Atrium, N.Y.C., 1995, Wilmington (Del.) Ctr. for Contemporary Art, 1996, Conn. State U. biennial, 1987-99, Blue Mountain Gallery, 1980-2001, Bachelier-Cardonsky Gallery, Kent, Conn., 1996, 97, 98, Philbrook Museum, Tulsa, Okla., Ringling Museum of Art, Sarasota, Fla., Davenport Museum, Iowa, 1999-2000, NAS, 2001-02; represented in permanent collections at Pitts. Plate Glass Co., Conn. Ins. Group, N.Am. Christian Sci. Ch. Ctr., Boston, U.S. Tobacco Co., Bellevue Hosp., N.Y., NAS, Washington, Nat. Acad. Sci. Recipient Disting. Lectureship award Henry Barnard Found., 1990; rsch. grantee in painting Conn. State U., 1985; named Univ. Prof. Conn. State U., 1992. Mem. AAUP (grantee 1986, 90, 91, 93, 95, 99, 2003), Coll. Art Assn. Home: 27 Wykeham Rd Washington CT 06793-1308

GRIMES, MICHAEL DAVID, podiatrist; b. Berkeley, Calif., Jan. 29, 1973; s. Charlie Alfred and Ruth Elaine Grimes; stepfather, Roger Lloyd Sharpe. BS, U. Calif., Berkeley, 1994; D of Podiatric Medicine, Calif. Coll. Podiatric Medicine, San Francisco, 1998. Resident in podiatry Houston Podiatry Found., 1998-99, surg. resident in podiatry, 2000—. Pvt. practice, 1999—. Named one of Outstanding Young Men in Am., 1998. Mem. AAMS, Am. Podiatric Med. Assn., Am. Chem. Soc., Tex. Podiatric Med. Assn. Avocations: running, biking, swimming, hiking, fishing.

GRIMES, PAMELA RAE, retired elementary school educator; b. Cumberland, Md., Dec. 30, 1943; d. Robert Elmer and Mary Evelyn (Hill) McFarland; m. George Edward Grimes, Feb. 9, 1962; children: George Edward Jr., Robert Eric, Jonathon William, David James, Richard Allen. AA, American River Coll., 1965; BA, MA, Calif. State U., Sacramento, 1975, adminstrv. credential, 1999; cert. in computer literacy, Sacramento Unified Sch. Dist., 1981. Cert. elem. tchr., Calif.; cert. adminstrv. credential. Tchr. aide O.W. Erlewine Elem. Sch., Sacramento, 1965-67, elem. gate tchr., 1969-71; tchr. aide Cohen Elem. Sch., Sacramento, 1967-69; libr., tchr. 1st through 6th grades Golden Empire Elem. Sch., Sacramento, 1979-89; tchr. Hubert Bancroft Elem. Sch., Sacramento, 1989-95; staff tng. specialist Literacy Curriculum & Instrn. Dept., 1995-97; reading coach Sacramento Unified Sch. Dist., 1998—2002; ret., 2002. Mentor tchr. Sacramento City Unified Sch. Dist., 1985-95; fellow, mem. Calif. History/Social Sci. course of study, 1991; mem. libr./lit. course of study, 1975, mem. CORE lit. com., 1979, mem. lang. arts assessment com., 1990—, mem. CLAS adv. com., 1993-94, mem. literacy task force, 1995-97, mem. adv. com. on assessment testing, 1995, co-chairperson 20-1 class size reduction program, mem. Young Authors program, mem. curriculum alignment project; literacy leader, facilitator CSIN, 1995—; No. Calif. coord. Ottawa U., 1991—; mem. lang. arts/literacy/ ELD Task Force, 1996-97. Ednl. cons. Children's Mus. Com., 1985—, Sacramento History Ctr., 1985. Fellow Calif. Lit. Project, 1989, Area III Writing Project, 1988, Calif. Social Studies Inst., 1990. Fellow Calif. Geog. Inst., East Asian Humanities Inst.; mem. NEA, ASCD, SARA, CRA, IRA, Nat. Coun. Tchrs. English, Geography Inst. (mem. social studies project. sch. com. 1991), Calif. Alliance Elem. Edn., Calif. English Tchrs. Assn., Calif. Tchrs. Assn. Democrat. Methodist. Avocations: reading, writing, gardening, grandchildren. Home: 9005 Harvest Way Sacramento CA 95826-2203

GRIMES, RICHARD ALLEN, economics educator; b. Toledo, Ohio, Apr. 24, 1929; s. Robert Howell and Mary Mildred Grimes; m. Helen Ann Schaeffer, Aug. 25, 1951; children: Gregory Allen, Julianne, Frank Edwin, Mary Ann. BS major in Chemistry, U. Ga., 1951; MS in Mgmt., Ga. Inst. Tech., 1959; postgrad., Ga. State U., 1979. Commd. lt. U.S. Army, 1951, advanced through grades to lt. col., ret. 1971; asst. prof. econs. Clayton State Univ., Morrow, Ga., 1971-74; assoc. prof. econs. Ga. Perimeter Coll., Decatur, 1974-97. Adj. prof. Jacksonville State U., 1959—63, Va. Commonwealth U., 1964—67, Ga. Mil. Coll., 1979—91, Ctrl. Tex. Coll., 1997—2001, Gordon Coll., 1998—; ednl. cons.; real estate broker, instr. Author: (book) Economics and Finance Study Guide, 2000; reviewer: Economics, 1979—99. Organizing dir. Cmty. Bank, 2001—; umpire Atlanta Area Football Ofcsl. Assn., treas., 1971—95; evaluator Ga. H.S. Football Ofcls., 1996—; active Spl. Olympics, Atlanta, 1971—; founding pres. Rex Civic Assn., 1973; sec.-treas. Villages Homeowners Assn., 1994—95; tax cons., instr. AARP, 2001—. Decorated Soldier's medal for valor Vietnam; named Rotarian of the Yr., 1976, Football Ofcl. of the Yr., Atlanta area, 1980; recipient Eagle Scout award, 1944. Mem.: AAUP (pres. Ga. Perimeter Coll.chpt. 1987—97), VFW (life), Mil. Officers Assn. Am., Nat. Soc. Pub. Acctgs., Ga. Assn. Acctg. Profls. (past pres.), Ga. Assn. Econs. and Fin. (past pres.), Am. Acctg. Assn., So. Econ. Assn., U. Ga. Varsity Letterman, South Atlanta U. Ga. Alumni Club, So. Metro. Ga. Tech. Alumni Club (sec., scholarship chmn.), Am. Legion, Delta Pi Epsilon. Presbyterian. Avocations: football, golf, camping, swimming. Home: Eagles Landing 118 Carron Ln Stockbridge GA 30281-6302 E-mail: r_grimes@bellsouth.net.

GRIMES, RICHARD MICHAEL, public health educator; b. Detroit, Nov. 20, 1940; s. James Bernard and Ruth Hall Grimes; m. Deanna C. Evans, Jan. 26, 1963; children: Mary Jeanine Van Baalen, Maureen Ann Croft, Patrick Joseph, Kevin Anthony. BBA, U. of Mich., 1962, MBA, 1963; PHD, U. of Mo., 1972. Grad. rsch. asst. U. of Mich., Ann Arbor, 1962—65; mng. dir. Cmty. Systems Found., Ann Arbor, Mich., 1964—68; rsch. assoc. U. of Mo., Columbia, 1968—72; asst. prof. U. of Tex. Health Sci. Ctr., Houston, 1972—76, assoc. prof., 1976—. Pres. bd. dirs. Montrose Clinic, Houston, 1987—93; mem. spl. sci. rev. panels Nat. Inst. of Allergy and Infectious Diseases, Bethesda, Md., 1994—2002. Author: (book) AIDS and HIV Infection, 65 sci. articles, 19 book chpts. Chmn. of bd. AIDS Ministry of Houston/Galveston Diocese, Houston, 1988—93. Recipient Hon. membership, Romanian Acad. of Med. Scis., 1996. Mem.: U.S.- Mex. Border Health Assn., Am. Acad. of Scis., APHA. Office: The Univ of Tex Health Sci Ctr PO Box 20186 Houston TX 77225-0186

GRIMES, RICHARD STUART, editor, writer; b. Wheeling, W.Va., June 28, 1939; s. Harold George and Sarah G.; m. Katheryn Perrine Johnson, Nov. 7, 1964; children: Sara Jane, Richard Harold, Stephen Ross. Grad., W.Va. U., 1961. Reporter Charleston (W.Va.) Daily Mail, 1964-2000, polit. editor, 1985-2000, also regular columnist. Master of ceremonies TV show Underfire, Pub. TV, 1989-99. Author: Old Money, New Politics, 1984; syndicated columnist in some 20 newspapers. Chmn. of bd. Meth. Ch., 1990. Sgt. U.S. Army, 1961-64. Mem. Southridge Lions Club (pres. 1994-98). Republican. Avocations: woodworking, furniture building, music. Home: 679 Gordon Dr Charleston WV 25314-1751

GRIMES, RUSSELL NEWELL, chemistry educator, inorganic chemist; b. Meridian, Miss., Dec. 10, 1935; s. Newell Cleveland and Marion Esther (Zehner) G.; m. Nancy Farrow Hall, Sept. 21, 1962; children— Susan, David BS in Chemistry, Lafayette Coll., 1957; PhD in Chemistry, U. Minn., 1962; postdoctoral, Harvard U., 1962, U. Calif., Riverside, 1962-63. Asst. prof. chemistry U. Va., Charlottesville, 1963-68, assoc. prof. chemistry, 1968-73, prof. chemistry, 1973—2003, chmn. dept. chemistry, 1981-84, prof. emeritus, 2003—. Guest prof. U. Canterbury, N.Z., 1974-75, U. Heidelberg, Fed. Republic of Germany, 1986, 1997-98. Author: Carboranes, 1970; editor: Metal Interactions with Boron Clusters, 1982, Inorganic Syntheses Vol. 29, 1992; contbr. over 240 articles to profl. jours. Grantee Office Naval Rsch., 1965-83, Army Rsch. Office, 1983—, NSF, 1976—; Fulbright sr. rsch. scholar, New Zealand, 1974-75; recipient Alexander von Humboldt Sr. Rsch. prize, 1996. Fellow AAAS; mem. Am. Chem. Soc. (sec.-treas. inorganic divsn. 1981-84, grantee 1965—), Corp. Inorganic Syntheses, Sigma Xi (President's and Visitors' rsch. prize 1981, 85, 96). Office: U Va Dept Chemistry Mccormick Rd Charlottesville VA 22904-0001 E-mail: rng@virginia.edu.

GRIMES, RUTH ELAINE, city planner; b. Palo Alto, Calif., Mar. 4, 1949; d. Herbert George and Irene (Williams) Baker; m. Charles A. Grimes, July 19, 1969 (div. 1981); 1 child, Michael; m. Roger L. Sharpe, Mar. 20, 1984; 1 child, Teresa. AB summa cum laude, U. Calif., Berkeley, 1970, M in City Planning, 1972. Rsch. and evaluation coord. Ctr. Ind. Living, Berkeley, 1972-74; planner City of Berkeley, 1974-76, sr. planner, 1983—, analyst, 1976-83. Bd. dirs. Vets. Asssistance Ctr., Berkeley, pres., 1978-93; bd. dirs. Berkeley Design Advocates, treas., 1987-94. Author: Berkeley Downtown Plan, 1988; contbr. numerous articles to profl. jours. and other publs. Bd. dirs. Berkeley-Sakai Sister City Assn., 1994—, pres., 1995-97, Ctr. Ind. Living. Honored by Calif. State Assembly Resolution, 1988; Edwin Frank Kraft scholar, 1966. Mem. Am. Inst. Cert. Planners, Am. Planning Assn., Mensa, Lake Merrit Joggers and Striders (sec. 1986-89, pres. 1991-93), Lions Internat. (bd. dirs. Berkeley club 1992-94, 2000-02, v.p. 1997-98, pres. 1998-99, chair membership com. 1999-2000), U. Calif. Coll. Environ. Design Alumni Assn. (bd. dirs. 1992-98, treas. 1994-96, disting. alumnus com. 1997—). Avocation: long distance running. Home: 1330 Bonita Ave Berkeley CA 94709-1925 Office: City of Berkeley 2118 Milvia St 3rd Fl Berkeley CA 94704 E-mail: rgrimes@ci.berkeley.ca.us.

GRIMES, STEPHEN HENRY, retired state supreme court justice; b. Peoria, Ill., Nov. 17, 1927; s. Henry Holbrook and June (Kellar) G.; m. Mary Fay Fulghum, Dec. 29, 1951; children: Gay Diane, Mary June, Sue Anne, Sheri Lynn. Student, Fla. So. Coll., 1946-47; BS in Bus. Adminstrn. with honors, U. Fla., 1951, LLB with honors, 1954; LLD (hon.), Stetson U., 1980. Bar: Fla. 1954, U.S. Dist. Ct. (no. and so. dists.) 1954, U.S. Ct. Appeals (5th cir.) 1965, U.S. Supreme Ct. 1972. Since practiced in, Bartow, Fla.; ptnr. Holland and Knight and predecessor firm, Tallahassee, 1954-73, 98—; judge Ct. Appeal 2d Dist. Fla., Lakeland, Fla., 1973-87, chief judge, 1978-80; chmn. Conf. Fla. Dist. Cts. Appeal, 1978-80; justice Fla. Supreme Ct., Tallahassee, 1987-97, chief justice, 1994-96; chair Article V Task Force, 1994-96, Supreme Ct. Workload Study Commn., 2000-2001. Mem. Fla. Jud. Qualification Commn., 1982-86, vice chmn., 1985-86; chmn. Fla. Jud. Coun., 1989-94. Contbr. articles U. Fla. Law Rev., 1951, 54. Bd. dirs. Bartow Meml. Hosp., 1958-61, Bartow Library, 1968-78; trustee Polk Community Coll., Winter Haven, Fla., 1967-70, chmn., 1969-70; bd. govs. Polk Pub. Mus., 1976-97; bd. dirs., chmn. Elder Care. Lt. (j.g.) USN, 1951-53. Fellow Am. Coll. Trial Lawyers; mem. ABA, Fla. Bar Assn. (bd. govs. jr. bar 1956-58, bd. dirs. trial lawyers sect. 1967-69, sec. 1969, vice chmn. appellate rules com. 1976-77, vice chmn. tort litigation rev. commn. 1985-86), 10th Cir. Bar Assn. (pres. 1966), Am. Judicature Soc., Bartow C. of C. (pres. 1964), Rotary (dist. gov. 1960-61). Episcopalian (sr. warden 1964-65, 77). Office: Holland & Knight LLP 315 S Calhoun St Tallahassee FL 32301-1856 E-mail: sgrimes@hklaw.com.

GRIMES, SUZANNE, publishing executive; With TV Guide, 1990—94, nat. advt. dir., 1994—95, sr. v.p., pub., 1995—97; pub. Women's Sports & Fitness, 1997—2000, Allure, 2000—01; pub., v.p. Glamour Mag., 2001—. Office: Glamour Mag Conde Nast Bldg 4 Times Sq New York NY 10036-6522

GRIMES, TRESMAINE JUDITH RUBAIN, psychology educator; b. N.Y.C., Aug. 3, 1959; d. Judith May (McIntosh) Rubain; m. Clarence Grimes, Jr., Dec. 22, 1984; children: Elena Joanna, Elijah Jeremy. BA, Yale U., 1980; MA, New Sch. for Social Rsch., 1982; MPhil, PhD, Columbia U., 1990. Advanced tchg. fellow Jewish Bd. Family and Childrens Svcs., N.Y.C., 1980-82; tchg./rsch. asst. Columbia U. Tchrs. Coll., N.Y.C., 1983—84; rschr., historian Youth Action Program, N.Y.C., 1984-86; psychologist Hale House for Infants, N.Y.C., 1986-89; asst. rschr. Bank St. Coll., N.Y.C., 1988; addiction program adminstr. Harlem Hosp. Ctr., N.Y.C., 1989-91; asst. prof. psychology S.C. State U., Orangeburg, 1991-96, assoc. prof., 1996—2000, chmn. dept. psychology, 1998—2000, chmn. psychology & sociology, 1998-2000; asst. prof. psychology Iona Coll., 2001—02, assoc. prof., 2002—. Adj. prof. psychology Tchrs. Coll., Columbia U., N.Y.C., 1990-91; adj. prof. Iona Coll., New Rochelle, N.Y., 2000-01. Named one of Outstanding Young Women of Am., 1981. Mem.: APA, Soc. for Tchg. of Psychology, Assn. Black Psychologists, Ea. Psychol. Assn., Psi Chi, Kappa Delta Pi, Delta Sigma Theta. Democrat. Avocations: singing, drama. Office: Iona Coll 715 North Ave New Rochelle NY 10801 E-mail: newgrimes@yahoo.com.

GRIMLEY, JEFFREY MICHAEL, dentist; b. Alton, Ill., Feb. 3, 1957; s. John Richard and Joyce Imogene (Mallin) G.; m. Julie Ellen Gardner, Aug. 2, 1980; children: Joel Michael, Christopher Mark, Benjamin Jeffrey. BS, U. Iowa,

1979, DDS, 1983; cert., Miami Valley Hosp, Dayton, Ohio, 1984. Gen. practice dentistry, Naperville, Ill., 1984—. Mem. ADA, Acad. Gen. Dentistry, Ill. Dental Soc., Chgo. Dental Soc. Methodist. Avocations: sports, photography. Office: 14 S Main St Naperville IL 60540-5365

GRIMLEY, ROBERT THOMAS, chemistry educator; b. North Attleboro, Mass., Jan. 3, 1930; s. John Thomas and Ivy (Frost) G.; m. Margaret Rockwood, June 21, 1952; children: Mark, Maureen, Kevin, Terrence, Peter. BS, U. Mass., 1951; PhD, U. Wis., 1958. Rsch. chemist Corning (N.Y.) Glass, Inc., 1957-59; fellow U. Chgo., 1959-61; prof. chemistry Purdue U., West Lafayette, Ind., 1961-94, prof. emeritus, 1995—. Vis. prof. Calif. Inst. Tech., Pasadena, 1992—96; vis. scholar Dartmouth Coll., 2001—. 1st lt. USAF, 1951—53. Mem. Am. Chem. Soc. (chmn. Purdue U. sect.), Am. Phys. Soc., Sigma Xi, Alpha Chi Sigma. Home: PO Box 550 Grantham NH 03753-0550

GRIMM, BEN EMMET, former library director and consultant; b. Jersey City, Sept. 27, 1924; s. Benjamin Harrison and Eunice Blanche (Whitenack) G.; m. Jean Kay Bohrer, Aug. 19, 1950 (div. 1982); children: Jeffrey, Kevin, Mark, Wendy; m. Lucy Ann Taylor, Jan. 21, 1989. BA, Washington and Lee U., 1949; MS, Columbia U., 1950. Librarian youth services Detroit Public Library, 1950-52; sr. librarian Fair Lawn (N.J.) Public Library, 1952-54; reference and reading librarian Montclair (N.J.) Public Library, 1955-56, asst. dir., 1956-61; dir. Belleville (N.J.) Public Library, 1961-72, Jersey City Public Library, 1973-85; prin. Grimm/McPherson Assocs., Montclair, N.J., 1988-92; ind. libr. cons., 1992-93. Chmn. Hudson County Audio-Visual Aids Commn., 1975-85; cons. libr. bldgs., svcs. and adminstrn., 1966-93; cons., mem. state aid constrn. adv. bd. N.J. State Libr., 1985-88, chmn. adv. coun. Libr. Svcs. and Constrn. Act, 1979-83. Mng. editor Libr. Trustee Newsletter, 1978-80. Bd. dirs. Orange County (Va.) Hist. Soc., 1994-96, pres., 1995; bd. dirs. Orange County Libr. Found., 1995-98, v.p., 1997-98; bd. dirs. Rapidan Found., 1999—; bd. dirs. The Arts Ctr. in Orange, 2002—. With USAAF, 1942-45. Decorated D.F.C., Air medal with oak leaf clusters. Mem. N.J. Libr. Assn. (pres. 1968-69). Home and Office: PO Box 145 Rapidan VA 22733-0145 E-mail: bgrimm@ns.gemlink.com.

GRIMM, CLAYFORD THOMAS, architectural engineer, consultant; b. Buchannon, W.Va., July 31, 1924; s. Clayford Thomas and Genevieve Fallon Grimm; m. Elide Lucy Medone, Dec. 27, 1946; 1 child, Rose Marie. BArchE, Cath. U. Am., 1949. Sr. lectr. archtl. engring. U. Tex., Austin, 1969-91; pres. Clayford T. Grimm, P.E., Inc. Cons. archtl. engrs., Austin. Contbr. more than 185 articles to profl. jours. Pres. Sierra Club, Austin, 1970—71. With U.S. Army, 1943—46. Fellow ASTM (Walter C. Voss award 1994), ASCE (life); mem. The Masonry Soc. (hon., Pres. award 1995), Constrn. Specifications Inst. (spl. award edn.), Brit. Masonry Soc. (hon.). Republican. Roman Catholic. Home: 1904 Wooten Dr Austin TX 78757-7702

GRIMM, DONALD LEE, executive; b. Uniontown, Pa., Feb. 19, 1954; s. James Richard and Edna Arlene (Savage) G.; m. Linda Diane Ferris, Oct. 6, 1979; children: Patrick Ryan, Jason Thomas. Student, Clarion (Pa.) State Coll., Washington, Pa. Sales Budd Baer Buick/Pontiac Inc., Washington, Pa., 1976-78; svc. mgr., asst. mgr. Uniroyal, Pleasant Hills, Pa., 1978, store mgr. Kendalville, Ind., 1978-79, Am. Automotive, Morgantown, W.Va., 1979-80; owner, CEO Car Care Ctr., Washington, Pa., 1981—. Bd. dir. Nat. Duncan Miller Glass Soc. Deacon, elder Presbyn. Ch.; bd. dirs. Automotive Svc. Assn. Pa. Fed. Credit Union, 1999—; v.p. Trinity Boys Soccer Boosters, 1999. Mem. NRA, Elks, Dormont Mt. Lebanon Sportsmens Assn., Jaycees (bd. dirs. 1984-85). Republican. Avocations: boating, target shooting, historical research. Office: Car Care Ctr 887 Henderson Ave Washington PA 15301-1361 E-mail: grimmy.mail@worldnet.att.net.

GRIMM, JAMES R. (RONALD GRIMM), multi-industry executive; b. Monroe, Mich., Nov. 5, 1935; s. Carl S. and Annie B. (Platt) G.; m. Carol Ann Forman, Aug. 24, 1957; children: James R., Phillip H. BS in Bus. Adminstrn, Ariz. State U., 1958. Dir. internal audit Motorola, Inc., Phoenix, 1961-68; bus. and fin. mgr. Europe Motorola Semicondr. Co., Geneva, 1968-70; dir. internat. fin. Fairchild Camera & Instrument Co., Mountain View, Calif., 1970-71; v.p. internat. fin. Computer Scis. Corp., Los Angeles, 1971-74; sr. v.p., chief fin. exec. Pertec Computer Corp., Los Angeles, 1974-80; exec. v.p. fin. and adminstrn. MAPCO, Inc., Tulsa, 1980-84; v.p., chief fin. officer Greyhound Corp., Phoenix, 1984-88; pres. Internat. Bus. Cons., Phoenix, 1988—; sr. v.p., CFO Gulf States Steel Ala., Gadsden, 1998-2000. Bd. dirs. Petro Star Inc., Fairbanks, Alaska, Infinite Tech. Corp., Dallas. Contbr. articles to Inst. Internal Auditors publs., 1964-68. Inducted into Ariz. State U. Hall of Fame, 1982 Mem. Inst. Internal Auditors (founder and 1st pres. Phoenix chpt. 1963), Fin. Exec. Inst., Gadsden Country Club. Home: 527 Mistletoe Holw Gadsden AL 35901-5739 E-mail: gjim4a1@aol.com.

GRIMM, JOHN LLOYD, business executive, marketing strategist; b. N.Y.C., Oct. 21, 1945; s. Judson Lloyd and Nanette Grimm; m. Stephanie L. Cassagne, Dec. 23, 1969; children: Samantha, Jonathan. BBA, Tulane U., 1967, MBA, 1969. Asst. prof. Dillard U., New Orleans, 1969-82; pres. Multi-Quest Internat. Inc., New Orleans, 1966—, Analytical Studies Inc., New Orleans, 1966—, Sybersurveys Inc., New Orleans, 1966—. Author: Interviewer's Handbook & Training Manual, 1970. Chmn. rsch. com. United Way, New Orleans, 1988-89, 94—, mem. mktg. com., 1986-88; mem. mktg. com. YMCA, New Orleans, 1985-98; mem. pub. rels. com. Goodwill Industries, New Orleans, 1986-89. Named Prof. of the Yr., Dillard U., 1981. Mem. Am. Mktg. Assn. (pres. New Orleans chpt. 1985-87, 94-95, treas. 1984-85, sec. 1983-84), Market Rsch. Assn. Avocation: stamp collecting. Office: Multi-Quest Internat Inc 708 Rosa Ave Metairie LA 70005-2145

GRIMM, LARRY LEON, psychologist; b. Goshen, Ind., Aug. 16, 1950; s. Warren Arden and Elizabeth Ann (Rassi) G.; m. Ann Mae Nelson, July 16, 1977; 1 child, Kirsten Ann. BS in Elem. Edn., No. Ariz. U., 1975, MA in Early Childhood Edn., 1977, EdD in Ednl. Psychology, 1983. Lic. psychologist; cert. sch. psychologist, elem. tchr., Ariz. Nat. Tchr. elem. sch. Page (Ariz.) Unified Sch. Dist., 1975-76; tchr. elem. sch. Litchfield Sch. Dist., Litchfield Park, Ariz., 1976-80; sch. psychologist intern Peoria (Ariz.) Unified Dist., 1981-82; adj. faculty Grand Canyon Coll., Phoenix, 1982; sch. psychologist Child Study Svcs., Prescott (Ariz.) Unified Sch. Dist., 1982-87; postdoctoral fellow in pediat. psychology Child Devel. Ctr., Georgetown U. Med. Ctr., Washington, 1988-89; pvt. practice pediat. psychologist, 1989—. Adj. assoc. prof. No. Ariz. U., Flagstaff, 1984—; cons. in field; presenter at convs. Contbr. articles to profl. jours. Chmn. project devel. com. Infant & Toddler Network, 1989-92; mem. family resource ctr. adv. bd. Yavapai Regional Med. Ctr., 1990—. Mem. Am. Psychol. Assn. (publs. com. div. 16), Nat. Assn. Sch. Psychologists (Ariz. del. fiscal com. 1987-88, Capitol Network 1988-89), Soc. Pediat. Psychologists, Ariz. Psychol. Assn., Ariz. Assn. Sch. Psychologists (bd. dirs. No. Ariz. chpt., regional dir. 1983-84, pres. 1986-87, newsletter editor 1986-87, Pres.'s award 1985, 88, 89), Granite Mt. Psychol. Soc. (pres. 1998-99).

GRIMM, LOUIS JOHN, mathematician, educator; b. St. Louis, Nov. 30, 1933; s. Louis and Florence Agnes (Hammond) G.; m. Barbara Ann Mitko, May 6, 1967; children: Thomas, Mary. BS, St. Louis U., 1954; MS, Ga. Inst. Tech., 1960; PhD, U. Minn., 1965. Chemist USPHS, Savannah, Ga., 1958-61; asst. prof. U. Utah, Salt Lake City, 1965-69; assoc. prof. U. Mo., Rolla, 1969-74, prof., 1974—, chmn. dept. math. and stats., 1981-87, dir. Inst. Applied Math., 1983-87. Vis. asst. prof. U. Minn., Mpls., 1966; vis. prof. U. Nebr., Lincoln, 1978-79, U. So. Calif., L.A., 1987-88; exch. scientist Polish Acad. Scis., Warsaw, Poland, 1981. Contbr. articles to profl. jours. With Med. Svc. Corps, AUS, 1956-58. Jefferson Smurfit fellow Univ. Coll. Dublin (Ireland), 1984; NSF rsch. grantee. Mem. AAUP, Soc. for Indsl. and Applied Math., Polish Math. Soc., Gesellschaft für angewandte Mathematik und Mechanik, Math. Assn. Am. (disting. tchg. award, 2001), Sigma Xi. Office: U Mo Dept Math & Stats Rolla MO 65409-0001

GRIMM, MARY M. development professional; d. George Francis and Ethel Corrine Madigan; m. Edgar C. Grimm, 1964; children: Michael Madigan, Kelly Ann. BA cum laude, U. Md., 1963. Cert. fund raising exec. Asst. dir. adminstrn. Health Examinetics, White Plains, 1981; dir. Young People's Theatre, Scarsdale, NY, 1982; contbns. asst. Gen. Foods Corp., White Plains, N.Y., 1983-86; adminstrv. specialist, editor Maxwell House Coffee Co., Jacksonville, Fla., 1986-93; exec. dir. Duval Pub. Edn. Found., Jacksonville, 1993-97; dir. devel. Woodrow Wilson House, Washington, 1998—2000; assoc. dir. devel. Ind. Sector, Washington, 2000—. Mem.: Assn. Fundraising Profls. (bd. dirs.), Leadership Jacksonville, Jacksonville Women's Network, Jr. League Washington. Office: Ind Sector Ste 200 1200 Eighteenth St Washington DC 20036

GRIMM, REINHOLD, humanities educator; b. Nuremberg, Germany, May 21, 1931; s. Eugen and Anna (Käser) G.; m. Anneliese E. Schmidt, Sept. 25, 1954; 1 dau., Ruth Sabine. Student, U. Erlangen, Germany, 1951-56, PhD, 1956; student, U. Colo., 1952-53; Dr. honoris causa, Georgetown U., 1988. Faculty German lit. U. Erlangen, 1957-61, U. Frankfurt, Germany, 1961-67; vis. prof. Columbia, also N.Y.U., spring 1967, U. Va., fall 1978; Alexander Hohlfeld prof. German U. Wis., 1967-80, Vilas prof. comparative lit. and German, 1980-90; Presdl. prof. German and comparative lit. U. Calif., Riverside, 1990-92, prof., 1992-97, disting. prof., 1997—, prof. emeritus, 2003—. Mem. Inst. for Research in Humanities, U. Wis., spring 1981. Author: numerous books including Nach dem Naturalismus: Essays zur modernen Dramatik, 1978, Von der Armut und vom Regen: Rilkes Antwort auf die soziale Frage, 1981, Love, Lust and Rebellion: New Approaches to Georg Büchner, 1985, Echo and Disguise: Studies in German and Comparative Literature, 1989, Versuche zur europäischen Literatur, 1994, Felix Pollak as Self-Translator, 2002; translator: Hans Magnus Enzensberger, Lighter than Air: Moral Poems, 2000, (with I. Hunt) German Twentieth Century Poetry, 2001, others; editor: numerous books, jours. including Monatshefte, 1979-90, German Quar., 1991-94, Deutsche Romantheorien, 2d edit., 1974, Deutsche Dramentheorien, 3d edit., 1981; co-editor: numerous books, yearbooks including Basis, 1970-80, Brecht Yearbook, 1971-81; contbr. articles to profl. jours. Recipient Förderungspreis der Stadt Nürnberg, 1964; Guggenheim fellow, 1969-70; Hilldale award, 1988, Elisabeth Fraser deBussy Prose prize, 2002. Mem. Am. Assn. Tchrs. German (hon., pres. 1974-75), PEN. Home: 6315 Glen Aire Ave Riverside CA 92506-5304 Office: Dept Comparative Lit and Fgn Langs U Calif Riverside Riverside CA 92521

GRIMMET, ALEX J. clergyman, school administrator, elementary and secondary education educator; b. July 17, 1928; s. Alex A. and Edna Mae (Boyd) Grimmet; m. Lois Jean Grimmet, June 24, 1949; children: Larry Bruce, Raven Alexis. AB, Ky. Christian Coll., 1949; MEd, U. Cin., 1964; postgrad. in math., Washburn U., 1967, U. Cin., 1968—69, Georgetown U., 1968. Ordained to ministry Ch. of Christ, 48. Elem. tchr. Highland County schs., Hillsboro, Ohio, 1957—62; tchr. math. Warren County, Morrow, Ohio, 1964—67, Lebanon H.S., Ohio, 1967—85, head dept., 1969—84; student min. Olympia Christian Ch., Owensville, Ky.; min. Choatville Christian Ch., Frankfort, Ky., 1949—51, Evang. Mountains Ky. and W.Va., Pike County, Ky., Mingo County, W.Va., 1951—52, Jefferson and Capella Chs. of Christ near Winston Salem, NC, 1952—57, Danville Ch. of Christ, Hillsboro, Ohio, 1957—62, Loveland (Ohio) Ch. of Christ, 1962—66, Lerado Ch. of Christ, 1966—. Adminstr. Christian Schs. of Greater Cin., 1991—96; chmn. math. curriculum revision com. Lebanon City Schs., 1969—70, 1982—85, chmn. competency based edn. program for math., 1982—85, with IRS, 1986—89, sub. tchr. Cin. Hills Ch. Sch., 1996—. Vol. math. instr. GED program Loveland Lit. Program, 1986—, Adult Literacy Program, 1996; sub. tchr. Cin. Hills Christian Acad., Loveland; precinct exec. Dems. Hamilton County, Loveland, 1980—. Mem.: NEA, Lebanon Tchrs. Assn. (mem. liaison com.), Ohio Coun. Tchrs. Math. (dist. dir. 1981—84, v.p. 1984—87, conv. program chmn. 1986), Ohio Edn. Assn., Kiwanis (sec. local chpt., sec.-treas. 8th Ohio divsn.). Home: 848 Kenmar Dr Loveland OH 45140-2819 *My life has been centered around helping my fellow man. I believe in the Bible as the inspired Word of God and accept it without change and compromise. I believe in and try to follow Matthew 6:33, "Seek you first the Kingdom of God and His Righteousness and all these things shall be added unto you." If we put Him and His church first in our lives I believe the necessities of life will be provided by our loving heavenly Father.*

GRIMMETTE, MARK, Olympic athlete; b. Ann Arbor, Mich., Jan. 23, 1971; Mem. U.S. Olympic Luge Men's Doubles Team, 1989. Named U.S. Nat. Champion in Doubles, 1996, winner 6 World Cup medals, World Cup champion, 1998, Bell Atlantic Nat. champion Silver medal, 1998; recipient Bronze medal Luge Men's Doubles, Nagano Olympics, Japan, 1998, Bronze medal, Lillehammer Olympics, 1996, All-Japan Championships, Nagano, World Championship, 2000, Silver medal, Luge Challenge Cup, 2000. Office: US Luge Assn 35 Church St Lake Placid NY 12946-1805

GRIMMOND, C. SUSAN B. atmospheric scientist, educator; b. Dunedin, New Zealand, Feb. 16, 1959; arrived in U.S., 1988; d. Nicola M. Grimmond; life ptnr. C. J. Souch. BSc with honors, U. Otago, Dunedin, New Zealand, 1980; MSc, U. B.C., Vancouver, B.C., Can., 1983, PhD, 1988. Asst. prof. Ind. U., Bloomington, 1989—95, assoc. prof., 1995—2001, prof., 2001—. Contbr. articles to profl. jours. Mem.: Internat. Assn. Urban Climate (pres.-elect 2002), Am. Meteorol. Soc. (chair bd. urban environment 1999—2002). Office: Ind Univ 701 E Kirkwood Ave Bloomington IN 47405 Office Fax: 812-855-1661. Business E-Mail: grimmon@indiana.edu.

GRIMSHAW, DAVID NORMAN, physician, educator; b. Brazil, Ind., Nov. 1, 1960; s. Norman Charles and Mary Ellen (Shepler) G.; m. Elizabeth Jones, June 6, 1981; children: Benjamin Charles, Ashley Elizabeth, Kelsey Irene. BS, Butler U., 1982; DO, Mich. State U., 1986. Diplomate Am. Bd. Osteo. Family Practice, Am. Bd. Ostepathic Manipulative Medicine; bd. cert. in cranial osteopathy, 2002. Intern Lansing (Mich.) Gen. Hosp., 1986—87; fellow in osteo. manipulative medicine Mich. State U. Coll. Osteo. Medicine, 1987—88; pvt. practice family physician Okemos, Mich., 1988-91; family physician USPHS, Plmetto, Ga., 1991-93; emergency rm. physician Coastal Emergency Svcs., Atlanta, 1993-95; osteopathic manipulative medicine speciliast Drs. Hosp., Massillon, Ohio, 1995-96, D. T. Watson Rehab. Hosp., Pitts., 1996-97; asst. prof. Mich. State U. Hosp., E. Lansing, 1997—; owner Ctr. for Integrated Medicine, Okemos, Mich., 2002—. Prin. investigator Mich. State U., E. Lansing, 1997—. Mem. Am. Osteopathic Assn., Am. Acad. Osteopathy, Cranial Acad., Am. Holistic Med. Assn., N.Am. Spine Soc., Am. Back Soc., Mich. Osteopathic Assn. Democrat. Mem. United Ch. of Christ. Avocations: camping, hiking, jazz musician, yoga. Home: 5853 Carlton St Haslett MI 48840-8857 Office: Ctr for Integrated Medicine 4655 Dobie Rd Ste 270 Okemos MI 48864 E-mail: grimshaw@msu.edu.

GRIMSHAW, LYNN ALAN, lawyer; b. Portsmouth, Ohio, Sept. 14, 1949; s. Vaughn Edwin and Margaret (Jordan) G.; m. Beverly Gay Moore, Oct. 21, 1978; children: Jordan, Stuart. BS in Indsl. Mgmt., Purdue U., 1971; JD, U. Cin., 1975. Bar: Ohio 1978. Atty. Gerlach & Grimshaw, Portsmouth, 1975-76; pros. atty. Scioto County, Portsmouth, 1977—. Mem. Gov.'s Organized Crime Cons. Com., Ohio, 1984. Chmn. Scioto County Dem. Party, 1980-81. Mem. Ohio Pros. Atty. Assn. (pres. 1985), Nat. Dist. Atty.'s Assn. (bd. dirs. 1987), Scioto County Bar Assn. (pres. 1997), Kiwanis. Democrat. Methodist. Office: Scioto County Courthouse 6th and Courts Sts Portsmouth OH 45662

GRIMSHAW, THOMAS TOLLIN, lawyer; b. Mpls., Oct. 31, 1932; s. U.L. and Judith (Austrid) G.; children: Scott, Lynn, Steve, Lisa, Shane. Student, Hamline U., 1951; BA, U. Minn., 1953; JD, Northwestern U., 1956. Bar: Ill., Colo. 1956. Assoc. Calkins, Rodden & Kramer, Denver, 1956-62; pvt. practice Denver, 1963-64; ptnr. Calkins, Kramer, Grimshaw & Harring, Denver, 1965-84, of counsel, 1984-94; ptnr. Grimshaw & Harring, 1994—. Bd. dirs. Colo. Housing Fin. Authority, Denver, 1987-98; mem. Nat. Conf. Commrs. on Uniform State Laws, 1987—, Colo. Coun. on Econ. Edn., 1987-2000; bd. dirs. Sturm Financial Group Inc., Exempla, Inc., LMC Found., Inc., Cmty. Found., Exempla Healthcare, The Edn. Found. State rep. Colo. Gen. Assembly, Denver, 1967-70; mem., chmn. Colo. Housing Bd., Denver, 1970-74; bd. dirs., chmn. State Bd. for Comm. Colls. and Occupl. Edn., Denver, 1979-86; bd. dirs. Cen. Bapt. Theol. Sem., Kansas City, Kans., 1978-88, 94—. Mem. Denver Bar Assn. (chmn. pub. relations com. 1969-70), Colo. Bar Assn. (bd. govs. 1969-70, chmn. pub. relations com. 1970-71, sr. v.p. 1971-72, chmn. legis. com. 1972-77), ABA, Denver Athletic Club (past bd. dirs.), Jacques DeMolay, Colo. Consistory. Republican. Baptist. Office: Grimshaw & Harring 1700 Lincoln St Ste 3800 Denver CO 80203-4538 E-mail: tomg@grimshawharring.com.

GRIMSLEY, BESSIE BELLE GATES, retired special education educator; b. Iola, Kans., Feb. 22, 1938; d. Dwight Leonard and Ruth Bebee (Colwell) Gates; m. Dale Dee Grimsley, Feb. 14, 1959; 1 child, Lendi Lea Grimsley Bland. BS in Edn., Emporia State U., 1962, MS in Edn., 1970. Music tchr., Hamilton, Kans., 1957-58; music tchr. Belle Plaine, Kans., 1958-59; 3rd grade tchr. Johnson, Kans., 1959-61; mid. sch. tchr. Kendall, Kans., 1961-63-68; kindergarten tchr. Alma, Kans., 1968-69; music, reading, phys. edn., math. tchr. Council Grove, Kans., 1969-94; Title I reading and math tchr., 1994-2000. Polit. chmn. USD #417 Tchr.'s Orgn., Council Grove, 1992-94, pres., 1987-89, uniserve rep., 1987-93, sec., 1997-2000; adv. prof. Emporia State U., 2003. Vice chmn. Lyon County Dem. com., 1988-94; mem. planning bd. Americus, Kans. zoning commn., 1985-97; mem. Americus Fall Festival com., parade chmn., 1992-94, 97; pres. WKDC, 1997-98; chmn. Americus Days, 1997-2000. Mem. Americus C. of C. (pres. 1993-95, 97-99), Emporia Antique Auto Club (sec.-treas. 1993-94, pres. 2001-2003), 4-H Alumni, VFW Aux., Am. Legion Aux., Woman's Kans. Day Club (2d v.p. 1994, state pres. 1997-98), Delta Kappa Gamma (pres. 2000-2002). Presbyterian. Avocations: tennis, tap dancing, running, softball, bowling. Home: PO Box 147 Americus KS 66835-0147

GRIMWADE, RICHARD LLEWELLYN, lawyer; b. Chgo., Apr. 26, 1945; s. Eric Illingworth and Pauline J. (Crandall) G.; m. Alexandra M. Galbraith, Feb. 22, 1981; children: Eric Montgomery, Sara Elizabeth. BA, Lawrence U., 1967; JD cum laude, U. Wis., 1971. Bar: Wis. 1971, N.Y. 1971, Ill. 1978, Calif. 1981, U.S. Dist. Ct. (so. and ea. dists.) N.Y., 1971, U.S. Dist. Ct. (no. dist.) Wis., 1971, U.S. Dist. Ct. (no. dist.) Ill., 1978, U.S. Dist. Ct. (ctrl. dist.) Calif., 1981, U.S. Ct. Appeals (2d cir.) 1971, U.S. Ct. Appeals (7th cir.) 1978, U.S. Ct. Appeals (9th cir.) 1981. Atty. Davis Polk, N.Y.C., 1971—76; ptnr. Barton Klugman, L.A., 1983-93; pvt. practice L.A., 1993—. Mem. U. Wis. Law Rev., 1969-71. Bd. mgrs. Ketchum Downtown YMCA, L.A., 1991-97; trustee Reform L.A. Pub. Schs. (LEARN), 1993-97. Recipient 3 Am. Jurisprudence awards for evidence, legis., and acctg. and law Bancroft-Whitney, 1970. Mem.: State Bar Calif., Toastmasters (Best Performer award 1996, Best Table Topics award 1997, Best Spkr. award 1997), Order of Coif. Avocations: gardening, poetry, running, public speaking, history. Home: 22372 Dardenne St Calabasas CA 91302

GRINALDS, JOHN SOUTHY, military officer, academic administrator; b. Balt., Jan. 5, 1938; Grad., West Point, 1959; B in Geography, M in Geography, Oxford (Eng.) U.; MBA with distinction, Harvard U. Commd. 2d lt. USMC, 1959, advanced through grades to maj. gen.; commdg. gen. Marine Corps Recruit Depot, San Diego, 1989—91; headmaster Woodberry Forest Sch., Woodberry Forest, Va., 1991—97; pres. The Citadel, Charleston, SC, 1997—. Decorated Silver Star; recipient Legion d'Honneur, French Pres., Francois Mitterand. Office: The Citadel 171 Moultrie St Charleston SC 29409

GRINBERG, RAUL, internist; b. Buenos Aires, Aug. 15, 1922; came to U.S., 1958; s. David Grinberg and Ana Tabachicoff; m. Raquel Funes, Feb. 12, 1945 (div. 1962); children: George Anibal, Ricardo Adrian, Diego Xavier. Bachelor's degree, Mariano Moreno, Buenos Aires, 1939; MD, Buenos Aires Med. Sch., 1946. Rsch. assoc. Columbia U., N.Y.C., 1958-62; sr. internist Roswell Pk. Meml. Inst., Buffalo, 1963-64; clin. instr. SUNY, Binghamton, N.Y., 1970-74; pvt. practice Binghamton, 1970—. Vis. prof. Cornell U., Ithaca, N.Y., 1964-66; mem. adv. bd. oncology N.Y. State Med. Soc., Lake Success, 1970-96. Author: (books) Computers and Obesity, 1989, Sexual Education for Doctors, 1998. Mem. Roberson Art Mus., Binghamton, 1964-99, H. Johnson Art Mus., Ithaca, 1980-99, Philharmonic Orch., Binghamton, 1964-99; Met. Mus., N.Y.C., 1997-99. Recipient Bronze award Am. Cancer Soc., 1997. Fellow ACP; mem. Endocrine Soc., Am. Assn. for Cancer Rsch, Am. Coll. Forensic Examiners, Inc. Avocations: painting, writing, collecting antiques. Home and Office: Apt 3A Bldg 4 201 Evergreen St Vestal NY 13850

GRINDAL, MARY ANN, former sales professional; b. Michigan City, Ind., Sept. 9, 1942; d. James Paxton and Helen Evelyn (Koivisto) Gleason; m. Bruce Theodore Grindal, June 12, 1965 (div. Sept. 1974); 1 child, Matthew Bruce. BSBA, Ind. U., 1965. Sec. African studies program Ind. U., Bloomington, 1965-66; rsch. aide Ghana, West Africa, 1966-68; exec. sec. divsn. biol. scis. Ind. U., Bloomington, 1968-69; office asst. Dean of Students office Middlebury (Vt.) Coll., 1969-70; exec. sec. Remo, Inc., North Hollywood, Calif., 1974-76; sec., asst. to product mgrs. in cosmetic and skin care Redken Labs., Canoga Park, Calif., 1976-79; various sec. and exec. sec. positions L.A., 1979-81, 85-89; exec. sec. Sargent Industries, Burbank, Calif., 1981-85; sales asst. Chyron Graphics, Burbank, Calif., 1989-97; adminstrv. sec. divsn. instructional svcs. Burbank Unified Sch. Dist., 1998—. Author of poems and essays. Mem. U.S. Navy Meml. Found. Mem. DAR (chpt. registrar 1988-91, chpt. regent 1991-94, chpt. chmn. pub. rels. and pub. 1994-2001, chpt. chaplain 1994-2001, mem. spkrs. staff 1995-2001, state chmn. Am. Heritage 1994-96, state chmn. Calif. DAR scholarship com. 1996-98), Daus. of Union Vets. of Civil War, 1861-65, Inc., Ladies of the Grand Army of the Republic, Nat. Soc. Dames of the Ct. of Honor (state chaplain 1997-2001). Episcopalian. Avocations: travel, writing, genealogy.

GRINDLAY, JONATHAN ELLIS, astrophysics educator; b. Richmond, Va., Nov. 9, 1944; s. John Happer and Elizabeth (Ellis) G.; m. Sandra Kay Smyrski, Oct. 10, 1970; children: Graham Charles, Kathryn Jane. AB, Dartmouth Coll., 1966; MA, Harvard U., 1969, PhD, 1971. Jr. fellow Harvard U., Cambridge, Mass., 1971-74, asst. prof., 1976-81, prof. astronomy, 1981—2001, Paine prof. astronomy, 2001—, chmn. dept. astronomy, 1985—90, 2001—03; astrophysicist Smithsonian Obs., 1974—76. Cons. MIT Lincoln Lab., Bedford, Mass., 1982—; mem. vis. com. astronomy U. Chgo., 1983, Astrophys. Lab. Saclay, France, 1988—, NASA/Goddard Space Flight Ctr., 1995—96; mem. vis. com. dept. physics Columbia U., 1998; chmn. NASA/Goddard Space Flight Ctr., 1997; mem. vis. com. Naval Rsch. Lab., 1998; mem. vis. com. dept. astronomy and space physics Rice U., 1999; mem. users com. Cerro Tololo Interam. Obs., La Serena, Chile, 1981—84; mem. Aspen Ctr. for Physics, Colo., 1991—2001, trustee, 1989—90; chmn. high energy astrophysics mgmt. ops. group NASA, 1986—88; mem. users com. Compton Gamma Ray Obs., 1992—94; chair users com. NASA High Energy Astrophysics Sci. Archive Ctr., 2000—02; mem. space sci. bd. NAS, 1986—89; mem. com. astronomy and astrophysics NRC, 1992—98, mem. com. on internat. programs, 1996—98, mem. high energy astronomy forum space panel, 1998—99; mem. Space Telescope Inst. Coun., 1993—96, 1989—90, Space Telescope Ind. Sci. Rev. Com., 1996—97; chmn. binary panel Space Telescope Cycle 7 Time Allocation Commn.; chmn. space sci. working group AAU, 1990—92; mem. sci. orgn. com. for numerous internat. mtgs. Contbr. articles to profl. jours. and books. Recipient Bart J. Bok prize dept. astronomy Harvard U., 1976; NSF and NASA rsch. grantee, 1978—; Guggenheim fellow, 1991-93, Sloan fellow, 1981-84. Fellow: AAAS, Am. Astron. Soc. (high energy divsn. nat. sec.-treas. 1982—84, councilor 1989—90, nat. v.p. 1994—97, nat. vice chair 2000—01, nat. chair 2002—), Am. Phys. Soc. (nat. chair divsn. astrophysics 1998—99); mem.: Internat. Astron. Union (pres. commn. 6 1991—94, organizing com. 1997—). Home: 195 Lincoln Rd Lincoln MA 01773-4102 Office: Harvard Coll Obs 60 Garden St Cambridge MA 02138-1516 E-mail: josh@cfa.harvard.edu.

GRINDLEY, BRUCE ALAN, real estate agency executive; b. Woking, England, Mar. 1, 1948; s. Ernest and Ivy (Mummery) G.; children: Andrée, Paul. Brokerage clk. Leslie & Godwin, Lloyds Brokers, London, 1965-67; from enquiry clk. to br. mgr. Abbey Life, London, Croydon, Crawley, England, 1967-86; dir. Sunway Properties, Tenerife, Spain, 1986-94, Tenerife Property Shop, 1994—. Recipient Winner Best Internat. Estate Agt. Gold award 1996-97, Best Internat. Residential Estate Agent, 1997-98, Best Spanish Estate Agent Gold award, 1998-99, 99-2000, 2000-01, 2001-02, 2002-03, Best Property Website award, 2000, 2002-03, Safe Home award, 2000, Best Property Advt., 2001-03, Best Internat. Estate Agt., 2002-03. Fellow Life Ins. Assn.; mem. Internat. Real Estate Inst., Nat. Assn. Estate Agts., Liga Internat. de Prpresentacion y Agencia Comml., Coll. Ofcl. Agts. Comml. Office: Tenerife Property Shop SL 117 Puerto Colon Playa de las Americas Adeje Tenerife Spain E-mail: info@tenerifepropertyshop.com.

GRINDSTAFF, MARK JOSEPH, historian; b. Colorado Springs, Colo., Aug. 7, 1974; s. James Dwight and Connie Ann Grindstaff; m. Rebecca Elizabeth Urech, Oct. 9, 1999. BA in History and Philosophy, Berry Coll., Rome, Ga., 1997; MA in History and Pub. History, Mid. Tenn. State U., 2002; postgrad., Ga. State U., 2002—. Grad. rsch. asst. Ctr. for Hist. Preservation, Murfreesboro, Tenn., 1998—2000; historian, transp. planner Ga. Dept. of Transp., Atlanta,

2000—. Ind. cons. in the field of hist. preservation. Mem.: Am. Hist. Assn., Nat. Coun. on Pub. History, Orgn. of Am. Historians, Phi Alpha Theta. Avocations: writing, travel, music. Personal E-mail: gstaff@mindspring.com.

GRINE, FLORENCE MAY, secondary education educator; b. Sycamore, Ohio, Apr. 21, 1927; d. Murray J. and Ethel (Kingseed) G. BS, Bowling Green State U., 1949, MEd, 1966. Cert. tchr., Ohio. Bus. tchr. McCutchenville (Ohio) Sch., 1949-51, Fostoria (Ohio) High Sch., 1951-60, Tiffin (Ohio)-Columbian High Sch., 1960-90. Mem. NEA, AAUW, Nat. Bus. Edn. Assn., Ohio Edn. Assn., N.W. Ohio Edn. Assn., Ohio Vocat. Assn., Ohio Bus. Tchrs. Assn., Tiffin Edn. Assn. (pres. 1965-66), Tiffin Bus. and Profl. Women (pres. 1955, 63, Woman of Yr. award 1987), Delta Kappa Gamma (chpt. pres. 1970-72, state pres. 1989-91). Republican. Presbyterian. Avocations: travel, gardening.

GRINER, PAUL FRANCIS, physician; b. Phila., Jan. 1, 1933; s. John and Josepha (Snyder) G.; m. Miriam Millard; children: Laura, Paul Jr. BA, Harvard U., 1954; MD with honors, U. Rochester, 1959. Diplomate Am. Bd. Internal Medicine, Nat. Bd. Med. Examiners. Intern in medicine Mass. Gen. Hosp., Boston, 1959-60, asst. resident, 1960-61, sr. resident, 1963-64; chief resident in medicine Strong Meml. Hosp., Rochester, N.Y., 1964-65; fellow in pathology U. Rochester Sch. Medicine & Dentistry, 1956-57, instr. medicine, fellow in hematology, 1964-65, clin. instr., 1965-66, clin. sr. instr., 1966-67, asst. prof. medicine, 1967-69, assoc. prof., 1969-73, Samuel E. Durand prof. medicine, 1973-95, head. gen. medicine unit, 1976-84, acting chmn. dept. medicine, 1977-79, chmn. dept. health svcs., 1985-94; gen. dir. Strong Meml. Hosp., 1984-95; v.p. Assn. Am. Med. Colls., Washington, 1995-2000. Dir. med. edn. Rochester Gen. Hosp., 1965—67, cons., 1969—95, Genesee Hosp., 1969—95, Highland Hosp., 1969—95; chmn. bd. dirs. Acad. Med. Ctr. Consortium, 1991—92; emeritus prof. medicine U. Rochester Sch. Medicine and Dentistry; sr. fellow Inst. for Healthcare Improvement, 2002—. Contbr. numerous articles to profl. jours., chpts. to books. Mem. N.Y. Gov.'s Health Care Adv. Bd., 1990-94, Mayoral Commn. on Health and Hosps. Corp. of City of N.Y., 1991-92. Capt. USAF, 1961-63. Decorated Air Force Commendation medal; recipient Duran Stephens prize, U. Rochester, 1959. Master: ACP (mem. health and pub. policy com. 1981—84, 1987—88, chmn. 1988—90, chmn. bd. regents 1991—92, chmn. clin. efficacy assessment subcom. 1986—88, pres. 1993—94); mem.: Inst. Medicine Nat. Acad. Scis. (com. quality rev. and assurance in Medicare 1987—90, mem. bd. healthcare svcs. 1987—2000, mem. com. on future primary care 1994—95), Soc. Med. Adminstrs., So. Gen. Internal Medicine Soc., Assn. Am. Physicians, Am. Clin. and Climatol. Assn., AAAS, Alpha Omega Alpha. Avocations: skiing, golf, surf fishing, travel.

GRINNELL, ALAN DALE, neurobiologist, educator, researcher; b. Mpls., Nov. 11, 1936; s. John Erle and Swanhild Constance (Friswold) G.; m. Verity Rich, Sept. 30, 1962 (div. 1975); m. Feelie Lee, Dec. 23, 1996. BA, Harvard U., 1958, PhD, 1962. Jr. fellow Harvard U., 1959-62; research assoc. biophysics dept. Univ. Coll. London, 1962-64; asst. research zoologist UCLA, 1964-65, from asst. prof. to prof. dept. biology, 1965-78, prof. physiology, 1972—; dir. Jerry Lewis Neuromuscular Research Ctr. UCLA Sch. Medicine, 1978—2003; head Ahmanson Lab. Cellular Neurobiology UCLA Brain Research Inst, 1977—; dir. tng. grant in cellular neurobiology UCLA, 1968—, rsch. assoc. Fowler Mus. Cultural History, 1990—, chmn. dept. physiol. sci., 1997—2001. Author: Calcium and Ion Channel Modulation, 1988, Physiology of Excitable Cells, 1983, Regulation of Muscle Contraction, 1981, Introduction to Nervous Systems, 1977, others; contbr. editorial revs. to profl. jours., pub. houses, fed. granting agys. Guggenheim fellow, 1986; recipient Sr. Scientist award Alexander von Humboldt Stiftung, 1975, 79, Jacob Javits award NIH, 1986. Mem. AAAS (mem.-at-large neurosci. steering group 1998-2002), Muscular Dystrophy Assn. (mem. med. adv. com. L.A. chpt. 1980-92), Soc. for Neurosci. (councilor 1982-86), Am. Physiol. Soc. (mem. neurophysiol. steering com. 1981-84), Soc. Fellow, Phi Beta Kappa, Sigma Xi, others. Avocations: music, anthropology, archaeology, travel. Home: 510 E Rustic Rd Santa Monica CA 90402-1116 Office: UCLA Sch Medicine Dept Physiology Los Angeles CA 90095-0001 E-mail: adg@ucla.edu.

GRINNELL, HELEN DUNN, musicologist, arts administrator; b. N.Y.C., Nov. 22, 1936; d. Kempton and Susan Barret (Gill) Dunn; m. Alexander Grinnell; children: Taylor, James Bodman. Ed., New Eng. Conservatory, 1957-60; BMus in Music Theory, San Francisco Conservatory, 1968; MA in Musicology, Am. U., 1982. Dir. Opera and Symphony Previews, San Francisco, 1966-67; arts coord. Del. State Arts Coun., 1977-78; mgr. Performing Arts Libr. Am. U., 1981-84; pres. Music Info. Specialists, 1984—; cons. Met. Mus. Art, 1996—. Cons. China Inst. in Am., 1999, Carnegie Hall, 2000—; vis. com. mus. instruments Mus. Fine Arts, Boston, 2002—, bd. dirs. Author: Chinese Musical Iconography: A History of Musical Instruments Depicted in Chinese Art, 1987; program annotator Dumbarton Concert Series, Smithsonian Instn., Kennedy Ctr., Stagebill; editor: Am. Women Composers' Forum, 1986—88; contbr. Orientation, Music in Art, 1995—. Mem. steering com. Friends of Music Smithsonian Instn., 1978—88; bd. dirs. Nat. Symphony Orch., Washington, 1979—82, Nat. Orchestral Assn., 1993—95, East-West Music Exch. Assn., 2000—. Sping Opera San Francisco, 1967—71, Jr. League of San Francisco, 1967—71, Wilmington Music Sch., 1973—78, Washington Performing Arts Soc., 1980—90, Bergemusic Ltd., N.Y.C., 1992—94, Shelter Island Hist. Soc., 1993—95, New Eng. Conservatory Alumni Coun., 1994—; bd. overseers New Eng. Conservatory, 1985—90; bd. dirs. Cape Cod Chamber Music Festival, 2000—; chair acad. policy com., trustee San Francisco Conservatory of Music, 1967—71; chair archtl. rev. bd. Village of Dering Harbor, NY, 1991—95. Mem. Am. Musical Instruments Soc., Am. Musicol. Soc., Soc. Ethnomusicology, Cosmopolitan Club.

GRINNELL, JOSEPH FOX, lawyer; b. July 4, 1923; s. Robert L. and Mary King G.; m. Marjorie Volwiler, Aug. 24, 1946; children: Stephen F., Christine K. Burcham, James W. BA, Yale U., 1945; JD, Northwestern U., 1949. Bar: Ill. 1949, U.S. Dist. Ct. (no. dist.) Ill. 1949, Minn. 1954. Assoc. Winston-Strawn, Chgo., 1949-54; sr. v.p. law Investors Diversified Svcs., Mpls., 1954-83; of counsel Pepin Dayton Herman Graham & Getts, Mpls., 1983-87. Bd. dirs. Guthrie Theater, Mpls., 1970-71, Minn. Orch. Assn., Mpls., 1976-78; bd. dirs., chmn. Minn. Pollution Control Agy., Mpls., 1973-81. Served to lt. (j.g.) USN, 1942-46, PTO. Democrat. Presbyterian. Home: 8155 Parkview Ln Bloomington MN 55438

GRINOLS, EARL LEROY, III, economist, educator; b. Bemidji, Minn., May 2, 1951; s. Earl Leroy and Betty Annette (Wolfe) G.; m. Anne Dudley Bradstreet, Feb. 2, 1978; children: Kimberly Anne, Lindsay Elizabeth, Daniel Stephen. BS in Econs., BA in Math. summa cum laude, U. Minn., 1973; PhD in Econs., MIT, 1977. Asst. prof. econs. Cornell U., Ithaca, N.Y., 1977-84; assoc. prof. U. Ill., Champaign, 1984-87, prof., 1988—; sr. economist Coun. of Econ. Advisers, Washington, 1987-88; vis. prof. U. Chgo., 1991. Cons. Dept. Labor, Washington, 1985-86. Author: Uncertainty and the Theory of International Trade, 1987, Microeconomics, 1994. Grad. fellow NSF, 1973-76. Mem. Am. Econ. Assn., Econometric Soc., Assn. Christian Economists, Royal Econ. Soc., Phi Beta Kappa. Home: 1104 Galen Dr Champaign IL 61821-6913 Office: U Ill 1206 S 6th St Champaign IL 61820-6978

GRINSHPUN, SERGEY A. science educator, science administrator; b. Odessa, Ukraine, Jan. 13, 1960; arrived in U.S., 1991; s. Alexander E. Grinshpun and Lidia M. Grinchpoun; m. Victoria S. Appatova, Aug. 5, 1983; children: Sasha, Leah. MS Physics, Odessa U., 1982, PhD Thermophysics (Aerosol Sci.), 1987. Jr. rsch. fellow Odessa U., 1982—87, rsch. scientist, 1987—89, sr. rschr., 1989—91; vis. faculty mem. U. Cin., 1991—93, rsch. assoc. prof. environ. health, 1993—97, assoc. prof., 1997—2003, prof., 2003—, dir. Ctr. for Health Related Aerosol Studies, 2000—. Lectr. in field; spkr. in field; vis. prof. Inst. Nuclear Safety and Protection, Saclay-Paris, France, 2001. Ad hoc reviewer (jours.) Aerosol Sci. and Tech., 1989—, Am. Indsl. Hygiene Assn. Jour., 1994—, editl. bd. dirs., 2000—, ad hoc reviewer Environ. Rsch., 1997, Atmospheric Environ., 1992—93, 2000, Jour. Aerosol Sci., 1990—, Jour. Exposure Analysis and Environ. Epidemiology, 1998, Jour. Air and Waste Mgmt. Assn., 1998, Meteorology and Hydrology, 1987, 1990—92, Physics of Aerodispersed Sys., 1983—91; contbr. 90 articles to profl. jours., 70 chpts. to books. Recipient Nat. Young Scientist award, USSR, 1982, Internat. Smoluchowski award, European Aerosol Assembly, 1996, Best Practice award, U.S. Dept HUD, 2000. Mem.: Pan-Am. Aerobiology Assn., Internat. Assn. Aerobiology, European Assn. Aerosol Rsch., Am. Soc. Microbiology, Am. Indsl. Hygiene Assn. (Outstanding Aerosol Paper award 1997, John M. White award 1997, 1998, cert. excellence Best Poster award 1999, David L. Swift Meml. award for Outstanding Aerosol Paper 2001), Am. Conf. Govtl. Indsl. Hygienists, Am. Assn. Aerosol Rsch., Air & Waste Mgmt. Assn. Achievements include 300 publications and 3 patents. Home: 4433 Classic Dr Cincinnati OH 45241 Office: U Cin Dept Environ Health 3223 Eden Ave POB 670056 Cincinnati OH 45267-0056 Business E-Mail: sergey.grinshpun@uc.edu.

GRINSTEAD, PAUL LEE, materials company official; b. Chilhowie, Va., May 3, 1951; s. Fred Love Grinstead and Anna (Lee) Eller; m. Barbara Ann Sturgill, Aug. 5, 1972; children: Paul Jeremy, Justin Ross. AS, Va. Highlands C.C., 1994; BS, U. Va., 1996; cert. in Bible, Belle Meadows Bible Coll., Va., 1998. Prodn. coord. Brunswick Corp., Marion, Va., 1976-81, material specialist, 1982-86, program specialist II, 1987-96; estimator Marion Composites, TPG, 1996-97, program coord. II, 1998—2002; program coord. II armament and tech. products Marion ops. Gen. Dynamics, 2002—. Mem. gov.'s adv. com. Commonwealth of Va., Richmond, 1998—; apptd. by gov. to Tobacco Indemnification and Cmty. Revitalization Commn., Gov.'s Outreach Network; bd. trustees S.W. Va. Higher Edn. Ctr. Dir. children's ch. and youth Bapt. chs., Smyth and Tazewell Counties, Va., 1976—; chmn. 5th Legis. and 39th Senatorial dists. Smyth County Rep. Com., 1994—; vice chmn. Smyth County Planning Commn., 1994-2001, chmn., 2001; mem. Smyth County Sch. Sys. Sch. Bd., 1998—. Mem. Masons (worshipful master 1988-89). Avocations: hunting, fishing, camping, hiking. Home: 323 Greystone Rd Marion VA 24354-6501 E-mail: pgrinstead@smyth.net.

GRINSTEIN, GERALD, transportation executive; b. 1932; married. BA, Yale U., 1954; LL.B., Harvard U., 1957. Bar: (D.C.), (Wash.). Counsel to merchant marine and transp. subcoms., chief counsel U.S. Senate Commerce Com., Washington, D.C., 1958-67; adminstrv. asst. U.S. Senator Warren G. Magnuson, Washington, D.C., 1967-69; ptnr. Preston Thorgrimson Ellis & Holman, 1969-83; chmn. bd. Western Air Lines Inc., Los Angeles, 1983-84, pres., COO, 1984-85, CEO, 1985-86, chmn., CEO, 1986-87; vice chmn. Burlington Northern Inc., Ft. Worth, 1987-88; pres., CEO Burlington Northern, Inc., Ft. Worth, 1989-90, chmn., CEO, 1990-95; pres., CEO, Burlington No. R.R. Co., 1989-90; chmn., CEO Burlington Northern R.R. Co., 1990-95; chmn. Delta Air Lines, Inc., 1997-99, also bd. dirs.; chmn. Agilent Techs., 1999—2002. Bd. dirs. Paccar, Inc., Vans Inc., Delta Air Lines, Brinks Co. Office: 1000 2nd Ave Ste 3700 Seattle WA 98104-1053

GRIPE, ALAN GORDON, minister; b. Indpls., Sept. 8, 1920; s. Otto Herman and Bertha (Anderson) G.; m. Elizabeth Howell, Sept. 29, 1951 (div. 1972); children: Stephen, David. BA, Lake Forest (Ill.) Coll., 1942; BD, Princeton Theol. Sem., 1946; STM, Union Theol. Sem., N.Y.C., 1953. Ordained to ministry, Presbyn. Ch. (U.S.A.), 1946. Asst. prof. Silliman U., Dumaguete City, Philippines, 1946-50; chaplain Davidson Coll., NC, 1951-52; asst. chaplain U.S. Mil. Acad., West Point, 1952-55; pastor First Presbyn. Ch., Westfield, NY, 1955-65; exec. coord. Personnel Svcs., United Presbyn. Ch. USA, 1965-88; interim pastor Genesee Valley Presbytery, Rochester, NY, 1991-99, acting exec. presbyter, 2001—02, ret., 2002. Author: The Interim Pastor's Manual, 2d edit., 1997. Treas. John Milton Soc. for Blind, N.Y.C., 1988-90. Mem. Assn. of Presbyn. Interim Ministry Specialists (coun. mem. 1987-90). Home: 95 Penarrow Rd Rochester NY 14618-1721

GRIPPI, SALVATORE WILLIAM, artist; b. Buffalo, Sept. 30, 1921; s. Leonardo and Josephine (Orlando) G.; m. Rosalind Ratzenberg, Apr. 14, 1945. Student, Mus. Modern Art, N.Y.C., 1944-45, Art Students' League, 1945-48, Atelier 17, 1951-53; student (Fulbright grantee), Istituto Statale d'Arte, Florence, Italy, 1953-55. Instr. Atelier 17, summer 1953, Cooper Union Art Sch., 1956-59, Sch. Visual Arts, N.Y.C., 1961-62; asso. prof. art Claremont Grad. Sch., 1962-68, Pomona Coll., 1962-68; prof., founder art dept. Ithaca Coll., 1968—. Invited participant Ford Found. Conf. Visual Artists, 1961 One-man shows include, N.Y. U., N.Y.C., 1958, Zabriskie Gallery, N.Y.C., 1956, 59, Krasner Gallery, N.Y.C., 1962, 64, 79, 81, Feingarten Galleries, 1967, 70, Everson, Mus., Syracuse, N.Y., 1978, Handwerker Gallery, Ithaca Coll., 1978, group shows include, Met. Mus. Art, N.Y.C., 1952, Schneider Gallery, Rome, 1954, Galleria La Fontanella, Rome, 1955, Whitney Mus. and Smithsonian Inst. Traveling show, 1958-59, Corcoran Gallery Art, Washington, 1959, 63, Whitney Mus., N.Y.C., 1960, Mus. Modern Art, N.Y.C., 1962, 1994-95, Hunter Coll. Leubsdorf Gallery, N.Y.C., 1995; represented in permanent collections, Whitney Mus., Met. Mus. Art, N.Y. Pub. Library, N.Y.C., Joseph Hirshorn Collection, Washington, Milw.-Downer Coll., Ithaca Coll., St. Lawrence U., Everson Mus. Served with USNR, 1942-45. Mem. Art Students' League (life, treas. 1961-62, bd. control 1961-64), Coll. Art Assn. Home: 9 Orchard Hill Rd Ithaca NY 14850 Office: Ithaca Coll Art Dept Ithaca NY 14850

GRISCHKE, ALAN EDWARD, lawyer; b. Milw., Mar. 2, 1945; s. Rupert Edward and Velma Pearl (Springer) G.; m. Christine A. Bremer, July 4, 1981 (div.). BS, U. Wis., Stevens Point, 1968; postgrad., U. Miami, Fla., 1969; JD, Loyola U., Chgo., 1971. Bar: Ill. 1971, Wis. 1982, U.S. Dist. Ct. (no. dist.) Ill. 1971, U.S. Dist. Ct. (we. and ea. dist.) Wis. 1982, U.S. Ct. Appeals (7th cir.) 1979, U.S. Supreme Ct. 1979; cert. civil trial specialist. Asst. atty. gen. Ill. Atty. Gens. Office, Chgo., 1971-73; regional counsel Ill. Dept. Mental Health, Chgo., 1973-75, gen. counsel, 1975-80; ptnr. Grischke & Assocs., Ltd., Chgo., 1980-82; assoc. Trembath, Hess, Miller & Seidl, Wausau, Wis., 1982; ptnr. Mallery Law Offices SC, Wausau, Wis., 1983-85; pvt. practice Wausau, Wis., 1985-89; pres. Grischhke & Bremer LLSC, Wausau, Wis., 1989—2003, Grischke, Molinaro & Laughlin, LLSC, Wausau, 2003—. Adj. prof. John Marshall Law Sch., Chgo., 1975-81; faculty U. Ill., Abraham Lincoln Sch. Medicine, Chgo., 1976-80, Loyola U., Stritch Sch. Medicine, Chgo., 1980-82; chmn. Midwest Consortium Mental Health Attys., 1975-76, Nat. Assn. State Mental Health Attys., 1976-80; bd. dirs. Dept. Natural Resources, Wis., 2003—. Mem. ABA (sustaining), Am. Trial Lawyers Assn., Wis. State Bar Assn. (bd. profl. responsibility dist. 16 1990-98), Marathon County Bar Assn., Wis. Acad. Trial Lawyers (sustaining, bd. dirs. 1986-88). Home: 608 Excel Dr Wausau WI 54401-2165 Office: PO Box 847 1400 Merrill Ave Wausau WI 54402-0847 E-mail: aeg@alangrischke.com.

GRISCHKOWSKY, DANIEL RICHARD, research scientist, educator; b. St. Helens, Oreg., Apr. 17, 1940; s. Oscar Edward and Christine Hazel (Olsen) G.; m. Frieda Rosa Bachmann; children: Timothy and Stephanie (twins), Daniela BS, Oreg. State U., 1962; AM in Physics, Columbia U., 1965, PhD in Physics, 1968. Postdoctoral studies Columbia U., N.Y.C., 1968-69; mem. rsch. staff IBM Watson Rsch. Ctr., Yorktown Heights, N.Y., 1969-77; sci. advisor to dir. rsch. div. IBM, Yorktown Heights, 1978; mgr. atomic physics with lasers group IBM Watson Rsch. Ctr., Yorktown Heights, 1979-83, mgr. ultra-fast sci. with lasers group, 1983-93; Regents prof., Bellmon chair optoelectronics Sch. Elec. and Computer Engring. Okla. State U., Stillwater, 1993—. Chmn. Internat. Coun. on Quantum Electronics, 1989-93, Am. Phys. Soc./Optical Soc. Am./IEEE Joint Coun. on Quantum Electronics, 1989-93. Contbr. articles to profl. jours.; patentee in field. Recipient Boris Pregel award N.Y. Acad. of Sci., 1985. Fellow IEEE, Am. Phys. Soc. (chmn. laser sci. topical group 1993-94), Optical Soc. Am. (R.W. Wood prize 1989, William F. Meggers award 2003). Office: Okla State U Sch Elec Computer Engring Stillwater OK 74078-0001

GRISE, MARK ANDREW, cardiologist; b. Haverhill, Mass., June 16, 1966; s. Gerard Emile and Corinne DeLuca Grise; m. Kimberlee Michele Reed, Aug. 2, 1997. BS in engring., Tufts U.; MD, U. Mass. EIT Tufts U., 1987; MD U. Mass., 1992, Diplomate in Internal Medicine Am. Bd. of Internal Medicine, 1995, Diplomate in Critical Care Am. Bd. of Internal Medicine, 1997, Diplomate in Cardiovascular Disease Am. Bd. of Internal Medicine, 2001. Physician UCLA, Los Angeles, 1997—98; physician/interventional cardiologist Scripps Clinic, La Jolla, Calif., 2001—. Contbr. articles. Mem.: Am. Coll. of Cardiology. Home: 466 Avenida Primavera Del Mar CA 92014 Office: Scripps Clinic 10666 North Torrey Pines Rd La Jolla CA 92037 Home Fax: 858-554-6883; Office Fax: 858-554-6883. Personal E-mail: markgrisemd@yahoo.com. E-mail: markgrisemd@yahoo.com.

GRISHAM, ANDREW FLETCHER, aerospace engineer, consultant; b. Nashville, Feb. 23, 1937; s. Albert Harding and Gladys Katella (Harmon) G.; m. Marilyn Jean Crerar, Sept. 2, 1967; children: David Andrew Fletcher Grisham, Mary Kathryn Grisham Wright, Elizabeth Ann Grisham Volz. BSCE, Vanderbilt U., 1958; MSCE, U. Calif., Berkeley, 1960, postgrad., 1958-60. Civil engring. tchg. asst. U. Calif., Berkeley, 1958-59; sr. structural engr. Boeing Co., Seattle, New Orleans, 1958-73, sr. specialist engr. Renton, Everett, Wash., 1973-82; prin. engr. Boeing Space Group/Marine Sys., Kent, Renton, Wash., 1982-89; sr. prin. engr. Boeing Mil. Airplane Group, Seattle, 1989-94; cons. Boeing Comml. Airplane Group, Seattle, 1989-94, Boeing Def. and Space Group Rsch., Seattle, 1994-96. Cons. The Raisbeck Group, Rockwell Internat., Seattle, 1977, Superior Design Co., Bellevue, Wash., 1994-96, The Boeing Co., Bellevue, 1994-96; instr. finite element methods Boeing grad. engr. tng., Kent, Wash., 1979; chmn. cross-corp. maj. structural analysis sys., Boeing Co., Phila., Wichita, Kans., Renton, Wash., Kent, Wash., Everett, Wash., Seattle, 1988-91. Author: (Boeing mainframe sys. handbooks and software) Interfaced Structural Analysis System, 1965-87, (Boeing workstation sys. handbooks and software) Multidisciplinary Design, Analysis and Optimization System, 1987-96; author papers. Chmn. worship and music com. Trinity Methodist Ch., Seattle, 1969-75, mem. Rep. precinct com., Seattle, 1978-86, ch. organist, Seattle, 1954-73. U. Calif. grantee NSF, 1959-60; A.J. Dyer scholar Vanderbilt U., 1954-58, scholar U. Calif., 1958-60. Mem. Seattle Prof. Engring. Employees Assn., Queen City Yacht Club, Holiday Ramblers, Tau Beta Pi. Republican. Nazarene. Achievements include devel. of Boeing finite element pre- and post-processors for modeling, optimization and commonality analysis for joint (Marine, Navy, Air Force) strike fighter; developed methods for nonlinear geometric analysis of Apollo Saturn booster tank penetrations, and for analysis, including post buckling in aerospace structural finite element models for multiple load conditions using pre-strains. Home and Office: 8713 Golden Gardens Dr NW Seattle WA 98117-3942

GRISHAM, GEORGE ROBERT, mathematics educator; b. Wheeler, Miss., Nov. 30, 1930; s. George B. and Maggie (Oakley) G.; m. Garnette S. Swinney, May 28, 1955; children: Deborah K. Grisham O'Neal, Jennifer L. Grisham Rochford. BS, Miss. State U., 1952, MEd, 1956. Cert math. tchr., K-14 gen. supervision, Ill.; cert. math. tchr., Tex. Tchr. Streator (Ill.) Twp. High Sch., 1956-68; prof. math. Ill. Cen. Coll., East Peoria, Ill., 1968-86, chmn. dept., 1981-86; tchr. N.E. Ind. Sch. Dist., San Antonio, 1986-87; asst. prof. Bradley U., Peoria, Ill., 1987-92; ret., 1992. Author algebra study guides; editor The Math Connexion, 1972-75. Bd. dirs. Am. Field Svc., Morton, Ill., 1972. With USN, 1952-54, Korea, comdr. USNR, ret. Named Tchr. of Yr., Peoria Savs. and Loan Assn., 1972. Mem. ACLU, Math. Assn. Am., Nat. Coun. Tchrs. Math. (conv. chmn. Peoria 1980), Ill. Coun. Tchrs. Math. (pres. 1976, co-chmn. conv. 1989), Interfaith Alliance, Ill. Math. Assn. C.C.'s (life, pres. 1981), Mil. Officers Assn. (life), Moose, Elks. Democrat. Unitarian Universalist. Avocations: reading, gardening, ballroom dancing, genealogy. Home: 22 Maple Ridge Dr Morton IL 61550-1152 E-mail: gg@insightbb.com.

GRISHAM, JEANNIE, artist; b. Opportunity, Wash., June 26, 1942; d. Lyle Gordon and Lela Georgia (Miller) Jacklin; m. John Paul Grisham, July 4, 1965; children: Jill Jacklin Grisham Ross, Jennifer Jean Grisham Marks, John Paul Jr. Attended, Wash. State U., 1960-62; grad., Burnley Sch. Profl. Art (now Seattle Art Inst.), 1962-64; postgrad., Lyme (Conn.) Acad. Fine Art, 1981-82; studied with, Gerald Brommer, Jerry Caron, Brent Heighton, Katherine Chang Liu, Marilyn Hughy Phillis, Barbara Nechis, Carol Orr, Lou Taylor, Alex Powers, Irving Shapiro, Frank Webb. Exhibits include U.S. Naval Acad., Annapolis, Md., 1974, San Diego Watercolor Soc., 1982-83, San Diego Art Inst., 1982-83, Western Fedn. Watercolor Soc., 1982-83, Deerpath Art Festival, Lake Forest, Ill., 1985-88, Deerpath Art Gallery, Lake Forest, 1985-88, David Adler Show, Libertyville, Ill., 1987-88, Curtis Gallery, Libertyville, 1987-88, Eastside Assn. Fine Art, Kirkland, Wash., 1989, 90, Ea. Wash. Watercolor Soc., Richland, 1989, Mercer Island (Wash.) Art Festival, 1989, Frye Art Mus., Wash., 1990, 91, 93, Bainbridge Arts and Crafts Solo Show, 1989, 91, 93, 94, N.W. Watercolor Soc., 1991, 92, 94, 95, 96, 97, Women Painters Wash., 1993-99, Midwest Watercolor Soc., 1992, 93, 97, 98, NWWS Waterworks, 1992, 94-99, Nat. Watercolor Soc., 1996, 97, Nat. Acad. 1998, Millennium Images Ireland and America, Ireland, 1999, many others; works included in various publs. Recipient A. & C. Obrig award NAt. Acad. Mem. Am. Watercolor Soc. (assoc.), Midwest Watercolor Soc. (signature mem.), Nat. Watercolor Soc. (signature mem.), N.W. Watercolor Soc. (pres. emeritus, signature mem.), Women Painters Wash., Watercolor West Juried Assn. Home: 10044 Edgecombe Pl NE Bainbridge Island WA 98110-4333

GRISHAM, JOE WHEELER, pathologist, educator; b. Smith County, Tenn., Dec. 5, 1931; s. William Wince and Grace (Allen) G.; m. Jean Evelyn Malone, July 2, 1955. BA, Vanderbilt U., 1953, MD, 1957. Intern Washington U.-Barnes Hosp., St. Louis, 1957-58, resident in pathology, 1958-60; mem. faculty Washington U., Med. Sch., 1960-73; prof. pathology and anatomy Washington U. Med. Sch., 1969-73; assoc. pathologist Barnes Hosp., 1969-73; vis. instr. Makerere Med. Coll., Kampala, Uganda, 1961; prof. pathology, chmn. dept. U. N.C. Med. Sch., Chapel Hill, 1973-99, Kenan prof., 1992—; also pathologist-in-chief U. N.C. Hosp., 1973-99; mem. pathology study sect. A NIH, 1969-73, chmn., 1970-73, chmn. pathology study sect. B, 1979-83; Norma Berryhill disting. lectr. U. N.C., 1998—. Bd. sci. counsellors Nat. Inst. Environ. Health Scis., 1974-78; mem. sci. advisory panel Chem. Industry Inst. Toxicology, 1977-88, chmn., 1980-88; adv. bd. Given Inst. Pathobiology, 1983-87; Berryhill lectr. U. N.C., 1998; Leon Goldberg Meml. lectr. Chem. Industry Inst. Tech., 1989; Paul Brindley lectr. U. Tex. Med. Br., 1993; Norma Berryhill Disting. lectr. U. N.C., 1998; Claude P. Brown Meml. lectr. Assn. Clin. Scientists, 2001. Contbr. articles to med. jours. Served to lt. comdr. USNR, 1961-63. Fogarty scholar NCI/NIH, 2000—; John and Mary R. Markle scholar Acad. Medicine, 1964-69; fellow Life Ins. Med. Rsch. Fund, 1959-61, Nat. Cancer Inst., 1958-59; Brindley prof. U. Tex. Med. Br., 1993; named Disting. Med. Alumnus Vanderbilt U., 1994; named to Order of Long Leaf Pine, State of N.C., 1996. Mem. Am. Assn. Pathologists (pres. 1984-85), Am. Assn. Cancer Research, Fedn. Am. Soc. Exptl. Biology (pres., chmn. bd. 1984-85), Am. Assn. Study Liver Diseases, Am. Soc. Cell Biology, Univ. Assn. Rsch. and Edn. in Pathology (v.p. 1985-86), Tissue Culture Assn., Internat. Acad. Pathology, Cell Kinetics Soc., AMA, AAAS. Home: 1703 Curtis Rd Chapel Hill NC 27514-7614 Office: Univ NC Med Sch Dept Pathology Cb # 7525 Chapel Hill NC 27599-0001

GRISHAM, JOHN, writer; b. Jonesboro, Ark., Feb. 8, 1955; m. Renee Jones; children: Ty, Shea. BS, Miss. State U., 1977; JD, U. Miss., 1981. Bar: Miss. 1981. Practiced law, Southaven, Miss., 1981-91; mem. Miss. Ho. Reps., 1984-90. Author: A Time to Kill, 1988, The Firm, 1991, The Pelican Brief, 1992, The Client, 1993, The Chamber, 1994, The Rainmaker, 1995, The Runaway Jury, 1996, The Partner, 1997, The Street Lawyer, 1998, The Testament, 1999, The Brethren, 2000, A Painted House, 2001, Skipping Christmas, 2001, The Summons, 2002, The King of Torts, 2003, Bleachers, 2003, (screenplay) The Gingerbread Man, 1998. Office: Doubleday Pub 1540 Broadway New York NY 10036-4039*

GRISHAM, LARRY RICHARD, physicist, consultant; b. Henderson, Tex., Feb. 2, 1949; s. James Marion and Eva Fay (Powell) G.; m. Jacqueline Lea Criswell, June 24, 1972; children: Austin Nathanial, Rachel Nicole, Hilary Jane. BS in Physics, U. Tex., 1971; PhD in Physics, Oxford (Eng.) U., 1974. Postdoctoral fellow Princeton (N.J.) U., Plasma Physics Lab., 1974-75, staff rsch. physicist, 1975-82, rsch. physicist, 1982-89, prin. rsch. physicist, 1989—, head beam physics, 1988—. Cons. Northrop Corp., L.A., 1985, Phys. Dynamics, La Jolla, Calif., 1986-88, Teledyne Brown Engring., Huntsville, Ala., 1989—; mem. and chmn. various rev. panels U.S. Army Strategic Def. Command, 1986—. Contbr. numerous articles to profl. jours. Mem. N.J. Rhodes Scholar Selection Com., Morristown, 1986—. Recipient Tex. Exes Centennial Honored Alumnus award U. Tex., Austin, 1985, Wolfson Grad. award, 1972, Kaul Found. prize for excellence in plasma physics and tech. devel., 2001; winner Westinghouse Sci. Talent Search, Washington, 1967; Rhodes scholar, 1971; Woodrow Wilson fellow, 1971, invited rsch. fellow Japan Atomic Energy Rsch. Inst., 1996. Methodist. Achievements include research in energy confinement properties of tokamak plasmas as a fuction of major and minor radius; physics and technology of high power neutral beam systems physics of excited nuclear states. Home: 2 Dennick Ct Princeton NJ 08540-2202 Office: Princeton Univ Plasma Physics Lab PO Box 451 Princeton NJ 08543-0451

GRISHAM, RICHARD BOND, lawyer, retired oilfield service company executive; b. Dallas, Feb. 18, 1945; s. Nellson Norman and Patricia Jean (Ritchie) G.; children: Jeffrey Claassen, Rebeccah Claassen, Blair. BA in Math., Centenary Coll., 1967; JD, So. Meth. U., 1972. Bar: Tex. 1972. V.p. legal Halliburton Energy Svcs., Houston, 1993-2000; ret., 2000. Mem. State Bar Tex. E-mail: meowbark@houston.rr.com.

GRISHMAN, LEE HOWARD, college program administrator; b. L.A., Dec. 16, 1946; s. Milton and Sadie Edith (Kisner) G.; children: Melissa Leigh, Julia Anne, Andrea Joy. BA, Brigham Young U., 1973; MA in Religion, Yale U., 1975; AM in Higher Edn., Columbia U., 1977, EdD in History of Am. Edn., 1983. Instr., religion and edn. U. Utah, 1978-79, Columbia U.; dir. admission and acad. svcs. Sch. Bus. and Econs., Calif. State U., L.A., 1984-88; dir. counseling and matriculation Chaffey Coll., Rancho Cucamonga, Calif., 1988-90; asst. vice chancellor for student devel. Pima County C.C. Dist., Tucson, 1991-93; coord. transfer edn. and articulation Antelope Valley Coll., 1995-2001, dean student devel., 2001—. Adj. sr. lectr., dept. policy, planning and adminstrn. U. So. Calif. Contbr. articles to profl. jours. Capt. USNR. Fellow Yale U., 1974, Union Theol. Sem., Columbia U., 1976-78. Mem. ASTD, Phi Delta Kappa. Home: 26615 Purple Martin Ct Santa Clarita CA 91351-5542 E-mail: lgrishman@AVC.edu.

GRISKEY, RICHARD GEORGE, chemical engineering educator; b. Pitts., Jan. 9, 1931; s. George and Emma (Maskell) G.; m. Pauline Anne Becker, June 11, 1955; children: Paula Louise, David Richard. BChemE, Carnegie-Mellon U., 1951, MChemE, 1955, PhD, 1958. Registered profl. engr., Wis. Sr. engr. E. I. duPont Co., Seaford, Del., 1958-60; asst. prof. U. Cin., 1960-62; assoc. prof. Va. Poly. Inst., 1962-64, prof., 1964-66; prof., head chem. engring. dept. U. Denver, 1966-68; dir. rsch. and found. rsch. prof. Newark Coll. Engring., 1968-71; prof. chem. engring., dean U. Wis., Milw., 1971-82; prof. chem. engring., dean engring. U. Ala., Huntsville, 1982-85; v.p., provost Stevens Inst. Tech., 1985-86, exec. v.p., provost, 1986-88, The Institute prof. chemistry and chem. engring., 1988—. Vis. scientist Polish Acad. Sci.-NAS, 1971; OAS vis. prof. Multi Nat. Food Project, Brazil, 1973; vis. prof. Monash U., Australia, 1974, Algerian Inst. Petroleum, 1975-76; cons. in field. Editor, Marcel Dekker Inc., 1974— ; referee, reviewer: Canadian Jour. Chem. Engring., Am. Inst. Chem. Engrs. Jour., Jour. Polymer Sci., Jour. Fluid Mechanics, Jour. Heat Transfer; author: Chemical Engineering for Chemists, 1997; author: Polymer Process Engineering, 1995, Chemical Engineers Portable Handbook, 2000, Transport Phenomena and Unit Operations, 2001; contbr. articles to profl. jours. With AUS, 1951-53. Fellow ASME, Am. Inst. Chemists, Am. Inst. Chem. Engrs.; mem. Soc. Rheology, Am. Soc. Engring. Edn., Am. Assn. Higher Edn., Plastics Inst. Am. (bd. dirs. 1986—), Soc. Plastics Engrs., Am. Chem. Soc. (congl. counselor, Exceptional Achievement award 1991), Tau Beta Pi, Sigma Xi, Triangle, Scabbard and Blade. Office: Stevens Inst Tech Dept Chem & Chem Engring Hoboken NJ 07030

GRISMORE, ROGER, physics educator, researcher; b. Ann Arbor, Mich., July 12, 1924; s. Grover Cleveland and May Aileen (White) G.; m. Marilynn Ann McNinch, Sept. 15, 1950; 1 child, Carol Ann. BS, U. Mich., 1947, MS, 1948, PhD, 1957; BS in Computer Sci., Coleman Coll., 1979. From asst. to assoc. physicist Argonne (Ill.) Nat. Lab., 1956-62; assoc. prof. physics Lehigh U., Bethlehem, Pa., 1962-67; specialist in physics Scripps Inst. Oceanography, La Jolla, Calif., 1967-71, 75-78; prof. physics Ind. State U., Terre Haute, 1971-74; from mem. staff to sr. scientist JAYCOR, San Diego, 1979-84; lectr. Calif. Poly. State U., San Luis Obispo, 1984-92, rsch. prof., 1992—, lunar sample investigator, 1994—. Contbr. numerous articles to profl. jours. Served as ensign USNR, 1945-46, PTO. Mem. Am. Phys. Soc., Am. Geophys. Union, N.Y. Acad. Scis., Sigma Xi. Achievements include co-discovery of the radioisotope silver-108m in the general marine environment, and development of the technique of radiosilver dating. Home: 535 Cameo Way Arroyo Grande CA 93420-5574 Office: Calif Poly State U Dept Physics San Luis Obispo CA 93407

GRISSO, ROBERT DWIGHT, JR., engineering educator; b. Radford, Va., Feb. 24, 1956; s. Robert Dwight and Mary Lee (Huff) G.; m. Teresa Faith Gill, Dec. 16, 1978; children: Steven Elliott, Lauren Christine. BS, Va. Poly. Inst. & State U., 1979, MS, 1981; PhD, Auburn (Ala.) U., 1985. Registered profl. engr., Nebr. Rsch. assoc. Va. Poly. Inst. and State U., Blacksburg, 1980-81, Auburn U., 1981-85; asst. prof. engring. U. Nebr., Lincoln, 1985-90, assoc. prof. engring., 1990-96, prof., 1996—2001, Va. Tech., 2001—. Cons. engr. Tenn. Valley Irrigation, Oneonta, Ala., 1987-95. Contbr. articles to profl. jours. State del. Nebr. Rep. Party, 1989-90. Recipient Ext. award merit Gamma Sigma Delta, 1994, Disting. Svc. award Nebr. Coop. Ext. Assn., 1996, Faculty Svc. award, 1997; named Outstanding Young Specialist, Nebr. Coop. Extension Assn., 1989, Team Rsch. award U. Nebr., 1991. Mem. Am. Soc. Agrl. Engrs. (Blue Ribbon award for excellence 1988-91, 97, 2002, Nolan Mitchell Young Ext. Worker award 1994), Soc. Automotive Engrs., Nebr. Coop. Extension Assn. (disting. svc. award 1989, 96), Sigma Xi, Alpha Epsilon, Epsilon Sigma Phi. Republican. Avocations: computers, woodworking, running. Office: Va Tech Biol Systems Engring 211 Seitz Hall Blacksburg VA 24061-0303

GRISSOM, GARTH CLYDE, lawyer, director; b. Syracuse, Kans., Jan. 24, 1930; s. Clyde and Bernice Minnie (Eddy) G.; m. Elena Joyce Kerst, Aug. 17, 1958; children: Colin, Grady, Cole, Kent. BS, Kans. State U., 1951; LL.B., Harvard U., 1957. Bar: Colo. 1957, U.S. Dist. Ct. (fed. dist.) Colo., 1957, U.S. Ct. Appeals (10th crct.) 1957, U.S. Supreme Ct. 1989. Ptnr., mem., counsel Sherman & Howard, L.L.C., Denver, 1963—. Sec., counsel, trustee Mile High United Way, Denver, 1985-88; trustee Kans. State U. Found., Manhattan, 1962-89; mem. Colo. Gov.'s Commn. on Life and the Law, 1990-99, chmn., 1996-99. Mem. ABA, Colo. Bar Assn., Denver Bar Assn. (pres. 1985-86, award of merit 1994), Rotary (sec. Denver 1983-84, bd. dirs. 1983-86, pres. 1989-90), Pi Kappa Alpha (pres. 1968-70). Home: 1777 Larimer St Apt 1610 Denver CO 80202-1548 Office: Sherman & Howard LLC 633 17th St Ste 3000 Denver CO 80202-3665

GRIST, JOHN, retired government official, engineering consultant; b. Nov. 17, 1928; (parents Am. citizens); s. John Rivers and Raphaela Matilda (Santiesteban) Grist; m. Ana Dolores D'Almonte, Nov. 22, 1961; children: Anna Cecilia, John Alexander, Paul Steven. Aircraft indsl. engring. cons. Parr Engring., Atlanta, 1958; food mfg. indsl. engring. cons. USDA, Washington, 1958—60; postal mechanization indsl. engr. U.S. Post Office Dept., Washington, 1962—64; hosp. indsl. engr. cons. VA, Washington, 1962—64; bldgs. mgmt. indsl. engr. cons. GSA, Washington, 1964—65; parks mgmt. sr. mgmt. analysis cons. Nat. Park Svc., Washington, 1965—71; sr. indsl. engring. cons. U.S. Postal Svc., N.Y.C., 1971—74, sr. indsl. cons. Western Mass. Springfield, 1974—89; internat. bilingual export-import tech. cons., 1958. Pres. Parents' Coun., Lexington Sch. for Deaf, Queens, NY, 1972—74; mem. fund raising com. Clarke Sch. for Deaf, Northampton, Mass., 1975—76. With USAF, 1951—55. Mem.: Ga. Tech. Nat. Alumni Assn. Roman Catholic. Home: 15102 SW 104 St #809 Miami FL 33196

GRISWELL, J. BARRY, insurance company executive; b. Ga. Bachelor's, Berry Coll., 1971; master's, Stetson U., 1972. Pres., CEO MetLife Mktg. Corp. (subs. MetLife Ins. Co.); agy. v.p. The Prin. Fin. Group, Des Moines, 1986-91, sr. v.p. individual ins. dept., 1991-96, exec. v.p., 1996-98, pres., 1998—, pres., CEO, 1999—. Past chair LIMRA Internat.; past chair bd. trustees Life Underwriting Tng. Coun.; trustee Ctrl. Coll., Pella, Iowa, dir. bus. com. for arts. Office: The Prin Fin Group 711 High St Des Moines IA 50392-0002

GRISWOLD, FRANK TRACY, III, bishop; b. Bryn Mawr, Pa., Sept. 18, 1937; s. Frank Tracy Jr. and Louisa Johnson (Whitney) G.; m. Phoebe Wetzel, Nov. 27, 1965; 2 children. AB, Harvard Coll., 1959; student, Gen. Theol. Sem., 1959—60; BA, Oxford U., 1962, MA, 1966. Ordained deacon Episc. Ch., 1962, ordained priest Episc. Ch., 1963. Bishop coadjutor Diocese of Chgo., 1985—87, bishop, 1987—97; presiding bishop Episcopal Ch. in USA, N.Y.C., 1998—. Former dep. to Gen. Conv.; former chmn. Pa. Liturgical Commn. Former chair Standing Liturgical Commn., Episcopal Ch. U.S.; former co-chair Anglican-Roman Cath. Dialogue U.S.; co-chair Anglican-Roman Cath. Internat. Episcopalian. Office: Episcopal Ch Ctr 815 2d Ave New York NY 10017

GRISWOLD, JONATHAN DEWITT, pediatric anesthesiologist, pharmacology educator; b. Bridgeport, Conn., Feb. 6, 1956; BS in Molecular Biochemistry, MS in Molecular Biochemistry, Yale U., 1978; MD, Columbia U., 1982. Intern Evanston (Ill.) Hosp., 1982-83; resident in anesthesiology Mass. Gen. Hosp., Boston, 1984-86, fellow in pediatric anesthesiology, 1986-87; asst. prof. anesthesiology Tufts U., Boston, 1987—, lectr. pharmacology, 1991-94, asst. prof. pharmacology, 1994—, acting dir. sect. pediatric anesthesia, 1998-2000, dir. pediatric fellowship program, 2001—, dir. sect. pediatric anesthesia, 2001—. Bd. dirs. Mass. Anesthesia Coun. Edn., Boston, v.p., 1991-92, pres., 1992-94. Fellow Am. Acad. Pediatrics (sect. on anesthesiology, 1987-); mem. Am. Soc. Anesthesiologist, Mass. Soc. Anesthesiologist. Office: New Eng Med Ctr Dept Anesthesiology 750 Washington St Boston MA 02111-1526

GRISWOLD, KIM, physician, researcher; b. Hartford, Conn., Sept. 25, 1950; d. Brendan and Adelaide Griswold. BA in Drama/English, Bard Coll., 1972; AS, RN, SUNY, Syracuse, 1977; MPH, Yale U., 1984; MD, SUNY, Buffalo, 1994. Diplomate Am. Bd. Family Practice, Neurol./surg. nurse Mass. Gen. Hosp., Boston, 1977—82; adminstr., rsch. assoc. Dept. Pediat. SUNY, Buffalo, 1985—88, rsch. edn. specialist, 1988—90, asst. prof. family medicine and psychiatry, 1998—. Active refugee outreach, NY, 1988—2003. Mem.: Am. Acad. Family Physicians. Avocation: canine therapy programs. Office: Dept Family Medicine 462 Grider St Buffalo NY 14215

GRISWOLD, PAUL MICHAEL, clinical psychologist, consultant; b. Milw., Sept. 26, 1945; s. Willard Matthew and Evelyn (Haerle) G.; m. AnnMari Gerardine La Valle, Aug. 2, 1969; children: Matthew Paul, Jennifer Jean. BA, Marquette U., 1967, MS, 1969; PhD, Kent State U., 1972. Sr. staff psychologist Wis. Div. Corrections, Milw., 1972-83; pvt. practice clin. and cons. psychology Menomonee Falls, Wis., 1973—. Lectr. Mount Mary Coll., Milw., 1973-78; faculty Wis. Sch. of Profl. Psychology, Milw., 1981—; cons. Ethan Allen Sch. Wis. Div. Corrections, Wales, Wis., 1984—. Contbr. articles to profl. jours. Mem. Am. Psychol. Assn., Wis. Psychol. Assn., Milw. Area Psychol. Assn. Avocations: old cars, sailing, ice boating. Home: 1366 County Hwy 164 Hubertus WI 53033-9426 Office: Clin Psychology Assocs W156 N8327 Pilgrim Rd Menomonee Falls WI 53051-3776

GRISWOLD, SARA Y. language educator; arrived in U.S., 1988; m. George Griswold; children: Carlos, George. BA in Edn., Nat. U. Trujillo, 1977; Cert. D'aptitude Dans L'enseignement Du Français langue etrangere, U. Grenoble, France, 1981; MA in Edn., U. Kans., 1986; doctoral student language edn., U. Georgia. ESL tchr. Santa Rosa H.S., Trujillo, 1977—79; ESL instr. Cath. U., Trujillo, 1979; French tchr. Alliance Française, Trujillo, 1979—84; ESL tchr. Inst. Cultural Peruano-Americano, Trujillo, 1979—88, acad. coord., 1988; part-time ESL instr. Prince George's C.C., Largo, Md., 1989; part-time Spanish instr. Augusta (Ga.) State U., 1989—90, temporary full time Spanish instr., 1992—93, full time Spanish instr., 1993—99, full time Spanish asst. prof., 1999—. Recipient Study award, French Govt., 1980—81, Delta Kappa Gamma, 1984—86; scholar, Fulbright, 1984—86, U. Kans., 1984—86. Mem.: Peru-TESOL, Fgn. Lang. Assn. for Internat. Rapport, Am. Assn. Tchrs. Spanish and Portuguese, Cultural Hispanic Assn. of the Ctrl. Savannah River Area, Augusta, Ga. 1992, Alpha Mu Gamma (advisor/sponsor Iota Phi chpt. 1992). Avocations: travel, collecting post cards, reading. Office: Augusta State Univ 2500 Walton Way Augusta GA 30904

GRITSCH, RUTH CHRISTINE LISA, editor; b. Duisburg, Germany, July 18, 1931; came to the U.S., 1941; d. Carl and Maria Augusta (von Schuman-Janssen) Sandman; m. Eric Walter Gritsch, June 4, 1955 (div. 1993); children: Deborah, Erika. BA, NYU, 1953. Assoc. Inst. for Internat. Edn., N.Y.C., 1953-55; sec. Zeigler Bros., Inc., Gardners, Pa., 1993—2003. Translator: (books) Liberty, Equality, Sisterhood, 1978, Hildrich Zwingli, 1983, I Am a Palestinian Christian, 1995, Violence, 1996; co-translator: Luther's Works, Vols. 39, 41, 1966, 67; editor: Roly, 1988; translator, editor: Justification of the Ungodly, 1968; editor, co-translator: Thomas Müntzer, A Tragedy of Errors, 1989. Active So. Poverty Law Ctr., Adams Co. Arts Coun. Mem.: LWV (bd. dirs., v.p. 1969—90, 1999—2001), Internat. Platform Assn. Democrat. Lutheran. Avocations: reading, collecting art. Home: 1 West St Gettysburg PA 17325-2130

GRITTNER, JAMES RUSSELL, artist, educator, department chair; b. Westboro, Wis., July 21, 1934; s. Frank George Grittner and Rilla Sofia Vought; m. Patricia Gayle McKnight; children: Leah Palomo, Rachel Bruzek. BS in Art, U. Wis., Superior, 1958; MS in Ceramics, U. Wis., Madison, 1961; MFA, Rochester Inst. Tech., N.Y., 1966. Co-creator, sales rep. Paoli (Wis.) Clay Co., 1960-61; asst. and acting dir. Rochester (Minn.) Art Ctr., 1961—2002; mem. art faculty U. Wis., Superior, 1963—, chmn. dept. art., 1989—. Creator Lake Superior Nat. Craft Exhbn. Duluth Art Inst., Minn., 1971; guest artist Lakehead U., Thunder Bay, Ont., Can., 1977, Notre Dame U., South Bend, Ind., 1979, Art Sch. Chgo. Art Inst., 1981; guest tchr. N. Adelaide Sch. Art, Australia, 1984-85. Represented in permanent collection Everson Mus., Syracuse, N.Y., Bemidgi State U., Minn. Dem. co-chmn. Don Anderson for gov. campaign, Wis., 1968. Avocations: golf, white water canoeing, downhill skiing. Home: 2325 Hughitt Ave Superior WI 54880 Office: U Wis Art Dept Belknap & Catlin Box 2000 Superior WI 54880 E-mail: jgrittne@facstaff.uwsuper.edu.

GRITTON, EUGENE CHARLES, nuclear engineer, director; b. Santa Monica, Calif., Jan. 13, 1941; s. Everett Mason and Matilda (Benne) Gritton; m. Gwendolyn O. Gritton; children: Dennis Mason, Kathleen Wanda. BS, UCLA, 1963, MS, 1965, PhD, 1966. Research engr., def. systems analyst RAND, Santa Monica, Calif., 1966-73, project leader advanced undersea tech. program, 1973-76, program dir. marine tech., 1974-76, program dir. applied sci. and tech., 1976-94, head dept. phys. scis., 1975-77, head engring. and applied scis. dept., 1977-86, RAND resident scholar for tech., 1990-93, dep. v.p. Nat. Security Rsch. Divsn., 1986-93, dep. v.p. Rsch. Ops. Group, 1986-90, dir. Acquisition and Tech. Policy Ctr., 1994—; acting dir. Nat. Security Rsch. Divsn., 1997-98. Vis. lectr. dept. mech. engring. U. So. Calif., L.A., 1967-72; vis. lectr. dept. energy and kinetics UCLA, 1971, 73; mem. Def. Sci. Bd. Study, 1996, 98. Recipient Engring. Alumnus of Yr. award UCLA Sch. Engring. and Applied Sci., 1985-86; AEC fellow, 1963, NSF Coop. Grad. fellow, 1964-66. Mem. Am. Nuclear Soc. (mem. exec. com. aerospace and hydrospace div. 1974-75), AIAA Home: 3616 The Strand # C Manhattan Beach CA 90266-3276 Office: Rand PO Box 2138 1700 Main St Santa Monica CA 90407-2138 E-mail: gene_gritton@rand.org.

GRITTS, GERALD LEE, home health nurse, AIDS care nurse, AIDS educator; b. Tulsa, Okla., May 14, 1956; s. Arlie Lee and Kathleen Joyce (Thomas) G. A in Nursing Sci., Greenville (S.C.) Tech. Coll., 1993. RN, Colo. With Preferred Mobile Nurses, Greeley, Colo., 1993-94; grad. RN Fair Acres Manor, Greeley, Colo., 1993-94, Quality Home Healthcare Svcs., Greeley, Colo., 1994—99, dir. nursing, 1996-99; subacute care coord. Fair Acres Manor, 1999-2000, staff devel., nursing assessment coord., 2000-01; hospice nurse for homecare and inpatient unit Hospice and Palliative Care No. Colo., 2000—. Advisor/cons. HIV services Quality Infusion Services, 1994—99; adj. instr. nursing U. No. Colo., 1996—; adj. instr. death, dying, grief Colo. State U., 1993 —. Author: (pamphlets) Losing a Loved One to AIDS, 1994, When Your Partner Has AIDS, 1994; author, co-editor, co-producer: (videos) Tears, Smiles and Remembrances, 1993, Healthcare and AIDS: The PWA, Family, and Medical Professionals, 1996. Co-founder, advisor, media chairperson AIDS Pub. Edn. League, Ft. Collins, Colo., 1991 96; cons. HIV vols.; cons. student HIV svcs. Colo. State U., Ft. Collins, 1993—; vol. HIV patients No. Colo. AIDS Project, Ft. Collins, 1993—, bd. dirs., 1995-2002, sec., 1997—; vol. Parents, Friends of Lesbians and Gays, Denver, 1986—, Friends of the Names Project Quilt, 1994—. Recipient AIDS Health Educator award Straight, But Not Narrow Group, Ft. Collins, 1994, Profls. for AIDS Edn. award AIDS Pub. Edn. League, Ft. Collins, 1994, award of merit Wednesday Noon Moms Group for AIDS Care of Children, Adolescents and Adults, 1995. Mem. Assn. Nurses in AIDS Care, No. Colo. Aids Project (bd. dirs. 1995-2002, mem. speakers bur. 1994—), Grief and Loss Task Force of Weld County. Avocations: outdoors, travel, reading, music. Office: Hospice of No Colo 2726 W 11th St Rd Greeley CO 80634

GRIZANTI, ANTHONY J. lawyer; b. Cin., Jan. 27, 1949; s. Anthony Joseph and Mary Emma (Schroeder) G.; m. Judith L. Grizanti, July 26, 1969; children: Virginia A. Madonna, Christina E., Anthony J. III, Michael F. BA, Canisius Coll., 1971; MBA, SUNY, Buffalo, 1980; JD, Syracuse U., 1984. Bar: N.Y. 1985, Pa. 1990, U.S. Dist. Ct. (no. dist.) N.Y. 1986, U.S. Ct. Claims 1985, U.S. Supreme Ct. 1991. V.p. Grizanti Music Co., Inc., Niagara Falls, N.Y., 1972—; atty. advisor U.S. Tax Ct., Washington, 1984-85; ptnr. Scolaro, Shulman, Cohen, Lawler & Burstein, P.C., Syracuse, N.Y., 1985—. Dir. Syracuse Symphony Orch., 1993-98. Mem. Estate Planning Coun. Ctrl. N.Y. (pres. 1996-97), Performing Arts Medicine Assn. (pres. 1994-97). Office: Scolaro Shulman Cohen Lawler & Burstein PC 90 Presidential Plz Ste 500 Syracuse NY 13202-2200

GRIZZARD, GEORGE, actor; b. Roanoke Rapids, N.C., Apr. 1, 1928; s. George Cooper and Mary Winifred (Albritton) G. BA, U. N.C., 1949. Appeared at Arena Stage, Washington, 1950, 52-54; Broadway appearances include The Desperate Hours, 1955, The Happiest Millionaire, 1956-57, The Disenchanted, 1958-59 (nominee Tony award), Face of a Hero, 1960, Big Fish, Little Fish, 1961 (nominee Tony award), Mary, Mary, 1962, Who's Afraid of Virginia Woolf?, 1962, The Glass Menagerie, 1965, You Know I Can't Hear You When the Water's Running, 1967, Sweet Potato, 1968, The Gingham Dog, 1969, Inquest, 1970, The Country Girl, 1972, The Creation of the World and Other Business, 1972, Crown Matrimonial, 1973, The Royal Family, 1975, California Suite, 1976, Man and Superman, 1978, A Delicate Balance, 1996 (Best Leading Actor Tony award 1996), Judgement At Nuremberg, 2001; also appeared with Assn. of Producing Artists, N.Y.C., 1961-62, Tyrone Guthrie Theatre, Mpls., 1963-65, Show Boat, Toronto, 1995, London, 1998; film appearances include From the Terrace, 1960, Advise and Consent, 1961, Warning Shot, 1967, Happy Birthday, Wanda June, 1971, Comes a Horseman, 1978, Firepower, 1979, Seems Like Old Times, 1980, Wrong is Right, 1981, Bachelor Party, 1983, The Wonder Boys, 2000, Small Time Crooks, 2000; TV appearances include Twilight Zone, The Adams Chronicles (nominated Emmy award), 1976, The Oldest Living Graduate (recipient Emmy award 1980), Caroline?, 1988, Simple Justice, 1993, Breaking the Silence, 1993, Queen, 1993, Scarlett, 1994, Suspicion of Innocence, 1997. Mem. Kappa Alpha. Office: PO Box 2275 New Preston Marble Dale CT 06777-0275

GRIZZARD-BARHAM, BARBARA LEE, artist; b. Roanoke, Va., Apr. 4, 1935; d. Alton Lee and Mable (Jewell) Grizzard; m. Charles Thomas Barham, Sr., June 25, 1955; children: Charles Thomas, Christopher. BS, Va. Commonwealth U., 1971, postgrad. Educator Colonial Heights (Va.) Sch. Sys., 1971—88; represented by Agora Gallery, N.Y.C., 1999—2001, Amsterdam Whitney Gallery, NYC, 2003. One-woman shows include Wakefield (Va.) Ctr. for Arts, 1993, 1994, Petersburg (Va.) Area Art League, 1993, 1995, 2000, Rappahannock Westminster-Canterberry Gallery, Va., 1995, Assn. for Visual Artists Gallery, Chattanooga, Tenn., 1999, Rappahanock Westminster Canterberry Gallery, Va., 1999, Williamsburg Regional Libr./Gallery/Theater Complex, 1999, exhibited in group shows at Richmond (Va.) Jewish Cmty. Ctr., 1991, 1993, Rappahannoc Art League Show, Va., 1995, Assoc. Artists Winston-Salem, N.C., 1991, 1992, 1996, Hoyt Inst. Fine Arts, Pa., 1998, Fredericksburg (Va.) Creative Ctr. Art, 1999, Richmond Shockoe Creative Ctr. Art, 1999, Richmond Women's Caucus for Art, 1999—2000, Shockoe Bottom (Va.) Art Ctr., 1999—2000, Agora Gallery, 1999, 2000, N.Y.C., 2001, 2002, Amsterdam Whitney Gallery, 2003, Limner Gallery, 2001. Recipient awards for art. Mem. Petersburg Area Art League, Shockoe Bottom Art League, 1708 Art Gallery, Va. Mus. Art, Whitney Mus. Art, Mus. Modern Art. Republican. Episcopal. Avocations: investing, amateur genealogist, breeding Am. Cocker Spaniels champions, piano, Civil War tours. Home: 701 Forestview Dr Colonial Heights VA 23834-1116

GRIZZLE, TREVOR LLOYD, religious studies educator, minister; b. Hanover, Jamaica, Dec. 22, 1947; arrived in Eng., 1962,arrived in USA, 1973; s. Stanford Augustus and Ida Grizzle; m. Maureen Elaine Clarke, Oct. 18, 1997; children: André Mark, Reneé Leann; m. Beryl Beverly Bean, July 24, 1974 (dec. July 31, 1994). PhD, Southwestern Bapt., Ft. Worth, Tex., 1984, MDiv, 1978; BA, Lee Univ., Cleve., TN, 1975. Cert. commissioned New Testament Ch. of God as a missionary to Ghana, W. Africa, 1968. Prof. of New Testament and Greek Oral Roberts Univ. Grad. Sch. of Theology and Missions, Tulsa, Okla., 1982—; missionary tchr. Ch. of God, Ghana, 1968—72. Rev. Grizzle blends the best insights of practical ministry and scholarly endeavor in communicating the word of God. An ordained minister in the Ch. of God, he has over thirty years experience in the ch. and classroom. Over the years, God has placed upon him a burden for the spiritual well-being of ministers and families. This has led to enriching Ministerial/leadership and Marriage seminars, which he conducts with great results on both the national and international levels. Fundraiser Am. Heart Assoc., Tulsa, Okla., 1996—, Am. Cancer Assoc., Tulsa, Okla., 1996—. Recipient Outstanding Faculty of the Yr., Oral Roberts Univ., 1991, 1998. Mem.: Soc. for Pentecostal Studies, Evangelical Theological Soc., Curriculum Comm., Oral Roberts Univ., PhD Comm., Oral Roberts Univ., 21st Century, Acad. Comm., Oral Roberts Univ. Ch. Of God. Dr. Grizzle is the founder and pastor of Hope Internat. Ministries in Tulsa, Okla., and a popular speaker at conventions and conferences nationally and internationally. Home: 7606 So Quebec Ave Tulsa OK 74136-8101 Office: Oral Roberts Univ 7777 South Lewis Ave Tulsa OK 74171

GRMEK, DOROTHY ANTONIA, accountant; b. Cleve., July 7, 1930; d. Louis and Antonia (Korosec) Lipanye; m. Charles Stelmach, June 13, 1953 (div. May 1977); children: Monica Doran Meade, Dwayne Alan Stelmach, Dale Richard Stelmach; m. William Edward Grmek, Aug. 18, 1978. BBA in Acctg., Fenn Coll., 1953. Chief acct. Pyromatics, Inc., Willoughby, Ohio, 1975-87; acct., exec. sec. Auctor Assocs., Inc., Cleveland Heights, 1972-96; ptnr., tax cons. Diversified Bus. Svc., Avon, Ohio, 1980—; contr., human rels. specialist Telefast Industries, Inc., Berea, Ohio, 1988-94; treas., buyer River Toy Box, Inc., Rocky River, 1990-2001. Mem.: Slovene Nat. Benefit Soc. (ins. agt. 1982—, charter mem., fin. sec. lodge 781 1982—, Cleve. Fedn. Lodges rec. sec. 1968—72, fin. sec. 1972—82). Home: 1925 Pembrooke Ln Avon OH 44011-1659

GROAH, LINDA KAY, nursing administrator, educator; b. Cedar Rapids, Iowa, Oct. 5, 1942; d. Joseph David and Irma Josephine (Zitek) Rozek; m. Patrick Andrew Groah, Mar. 20, 1975; 1 child, Kimberly; stepchildren: Nadine, Maureen, Patrick, Marcus. Diploma, St. Luke's Sch. Nursing, Cedar Rapids, 1963; student, San Francisco City Coll., 1976-77; BA, St. Mary's Coll., Moraga, Calif., 1978; BSN, Calif. State U., 1986; MSN, U. Calif., 1989. Staff nurse to head nurse U. Iowa, 1963-67; clin. supr., dir. oper. and recovery rm. Michael Reese Hosp., Chgo., 1967-73; dir. oper. rms. Med. Ctr. Ctrl. Ga., Macon, 1973-74; dir. oper. and recovery rms. U. Calif. Hosps. and Clinics, San Francisco, 1974-90, asst. dir. hosps. and clinics, 1982-86; v.p. patient care svcs., dir. hosp. ops. Kaiser Found. Hosp., San Francisco, 1990—. Asst. clin. prof. U. Calif. Sch. Nursing, San Francisco, 1975—; cons. to oper. room suprs., to div. ednl. resources and programs Assn. Am. Med. Colls., 1976—; condr. seminars. Author: Perioperative Nursing Practice, 1983, 3d edit., 1996; contbr. articles to project jours. and textbooks; author, prodr. audio-visual presentations; author computer software. Mem. San Francisco C. of C. Fellow Am. Acad. Nursing; mem. ANA (vice chmn. oper. rm. conf. group 1974-76), Assn. Oper. Rm. Nurses (com. on nominations 1979-84, treas. 1985-87, 93-95, bd. dirs. 1991-93, pres.-elect 1995-96, pres. 1996-97, found. bd. trustees 1995-97, pres. found. 1992-95, Excellence award in Preoperative Nursing 1989), Nat. League for Nurses, Ctr. for Study Dem. Instns., San Francisco C. of C. Home: 5 Mateo Dr Belvedere Tiburon CA 94920-1071 Office: 3020 Bridgeway Ste 399 Sausalito CA 94965-2839 E-mail: lindag1005@aol.com.

GROAT, CHARLES GEORGE, geologist, science administrator; b. Westfield, N.Y., Mar. 25, 1940; married, 1963; 2 children. AB, U. Rochester, 1962; MS, U. Mass., 1967; PhD in Geology, U. Tex., 1970. Rsch. geologist Bur. Econ. Geology, U. Tex., Austin, 1968-71, assoc. dir., 1971-75, assoc. prof. dept. geol. sci., 1971-76, acting dir. Bur. Econ. Geology, 1975-76; assoc. prof. geol. sci., chmn. U. Tex., El Paso, 1976-78; dir. La. Geol. Survey, 1978-90; exec. dir. Am. Geol. Inst., 1990-92; dir. La. State U. Ctr. Coastal Energy & Environ. Rsch. Lab., Baton Rouge, 1992-95, U. Tex. Ctr. for Environ. Resource Mgmt., El Paso, 1995-98; assoc. v.p. rsch. U. Tex., El Paso, 1998. Mem. Geol. Soc. Am., Am. Assn. Petrol Geologists, Am. Geophys. Union, Am. Assn. for Higher Edn. Achievements include research in geology of energy resources, environmental aspects of resource extraction, geomorphology of coastal and arid areas, water resources, science education. Office: US Geol Survey 12201 Sunrise Valley Dr Reston VA 20192-0002

GROAT, LINDA NOEL, architectural educator; b. Stamford, Conn., Aug. 18, 1946; d. Everett Linwood and Vivian (Smith) G.; m. Lawrence K. Stern, Apr. 29, 1979; 1 child, Laura Linwood. BA, Conn. Coll., 1968; MA in Teaching, Yale U., 1969; MFA, Calif. Inst. Arts, 1972; MS, U. Surrey, 1979, PhD, 1985. Designer Charles Moore Assocs., New Haven, 1969-70, McCue Boone Tomsick Architects, San Francisco, 1974-77; cons. Kaplan, McLaughlin, Diaz Architects, San Francisco, 1979-80; asst. prof. U. Wis., Milw., 1980-86, assoc. prof., 1986-87; assoc. dean Coll. Arch. and Urban Planning U. Mich., Ann Arbor, 1987-92, assoc. prof., 1987-99, prof., 1999—, prof. architecture and women's studies, 2001—. Faculty assoc. Ctr. for Rsch. on Learning and Tchg., 1996-97. Co-author (with David Wang): Architectural Research Methods, 2002; editor: Giving Places Meaning, 1995—; mem. editl. bd. Jour. Archtl. Edn., 1989—95, Jour. Environ. Psychology, 1990—, Jour. Archtl. and Planning Rsch., 1990—. Mem. Archtl. Theory Rev., 1998—, Nat. Mus. Women in the Arts, Washington, 1987—2001. Recipient Environ. Graphics award Print Casebooks, 1979, Sarah Goddard Power award, 1998; design rsch. grantee Nat. Endowment for the Arts, 1982, 92, Graham Found. for Advanced Studies in Fine Arts, 1991. Mem. AIA (assoc.), Internat. Assn. for Study People and Their Phys. Surroundings, Assn. Collegiate Sch. Architecture (east ctrl. region dir. 1992-95), Environ. Design Rsch. Assn. Avocations: swimming, horseback riding, gardening. Office: U Mich Coll Architecture & Urban Planning 2000 Bonisteel Dr Ann Arbor MI 48109-2069

GROB, GEORGE FREDERICK, health, social services association administrator; M in Math., Georgetown U., 1969. Comptroller Office of Asst. Sec. Def.; ops. rsch. analyst Office of Asst. Sec. Navy for Fin. Mgmt.; dir. planning and policy coordination Office of Asst. Sec. Planning and Evaluation, USHHS, 1976-88; chair evaluation and inspection round table PCIE, Washington, 1994—2002; dep. insp. gen. for evaluation and inspections USHHS, Washington, 1988—2002, dep. insp. gen. mgmt. and policy, 2002—. Chair evaluation and inspections round table Pres.'s Coun. on Integrity and Efficiency, 1994—2002. Mem. Am. Evaluation Assn. (co-chair Evaluation Mgrs. and Supr. Group). Home: 38386 Millstone Dr Purcellville VA 20132-3739 Office: USHHS 330 Independence Ave SW Washington DC 20201-0001 E-mail: georgegrob@compuserve.com.

GROB, GERALD N. historian, educator; b. N.Y.C., Apr. 25, 1931; s. Sidney and Sylvia G. Grob; m. Lila Kronick, Dec. 25, 1954; children: Bradford S., Evan D., Seth A. BS, CCNY, 1951; MA, Columbia U., 1952; PhD, Northwestern U., 1958; D.Litt. (hon.), Clark University, 2002. From instr. history to prof. Clark U., Worcester, Mass., 1957—69; Henry E. Sigerist prof. of the history of medicine Rutgers U., New Brunswick, NJ, 1969—, chmn. dept., 1969—71, 1973—74, 1981—84. Mem. fellowship adv. com. NEH, 1975—76; chmn. study sect. history of medicine NIH, 1975—77, 1987—89, 1993—98. Author: books including Ed Jarvis and the Mecical World of 19th Century America, 1978, Workers and Utopia, 1961, The State and the Mentally Ill, 1966, Mental Institutions in America, 1973, Mental Ilness and American Society, 1875-1940, 1983, The Inner World of American Psychiatry, 1890-1940, 1985, From Asylum to Community, 1991, The Mad Among Us, 1994, The Deadly Truth: A History of Disease in America, 2002; contbr. articles. Elected to inst. medicine NAS. With U.S. Army, 1955—57. Fellow, NEH, 1972—73, 1989—90, Am. Coun. Learned Socs., 1976—77, Guggenheim fellow, 1980—81, Davis Ctr., Princeton U., 1985—86; grantee, NIH, 1960—65, 1967—81, 1984—92. Mem.: Orgn. Am. Historians, Am. Antiquarian Soc., Am. Assn. History of Medicine (coun. mem. 1978—81, v.p. 1994—96, pres. 1996—98, William H. Welch medal 1986). Jewish. Home: 821 Starview Way Bridgewater NJ 08807-1824 Office: Rutgers U Inst Health Care Policy 30 College Ave New Brunswick NJ 08901-1293 E-mail: ggrob@rci.rutgers.edu. *My philosophy of history is essentially a tragic one; a study of the past, if undertaken in as honest and objective a manner as is humanly possible, should render us less certain about our omniscience and ability to control the future.*

GROBE, CHARLES STEPHEN, lawyer, accountant; b. Columbus, Ohio, May 5, 1935; s. Harry A. and Bertha S. (Swartz) G.; m. Ila Silverman, Aug. 30, 1964; children— Eileen, Kenneth. BS, U. Calif. at Los Angeles, 1957; JD, Stanford, 1961. Bar: Calif. 1962; CPA, Calif. Tax accountant, Beverly Hills, Calif., 1961-63; tax atty. Los Angeles, 1963—. Author: Guide to Investing Pension and Profit-Sharing Trust Funds, 1973, Guardianship, Conservatorship and Trusts on Behalf of Persons Who Are Mentally Retarded— An Assessment of Current Applicable Laws in the State of California, 1974, Using an Individual Retirement Savings Plan and the Related Rollover Provisions of the Pension Reform Act of 1974, 1975, Guide to Setting Up a Group Term Life Insurance Program Under IRC Section 79, 1976, Practical Estate Planning, 1988, Planning for Incapacity, 1989, Planning to Reduce the Generation Skipping Tax, 1989, Estate Planning Considerations for Community Property Interests, 1990, Legal and Tax Problems of Joint Tenancy as a Form of Ownership, 1990, The Tax Economics of Using the Generating Skipping Tax Exemptions, 1992, The Tax Economics of Gifting Property, 1992, Saving Estate Taxes with Life Insurance and a Life Insurance Trust, 1992, Family Wealth Transfer Planning, The Tax Economics of a Qualified Personal Residence Trust, also articles. Capt. AUS, 1957-64. Mem. ABA, State Bar Calif., L.A. County Bar Assn., Beverly Hills Bar Assn., Calif. Soc. CPAs. Home: 11349 Homedale St Los Angeles CA 90049 Office: 12110 Wilshire Blvd Los Angeles CA 90025-1104

GROBERG, JAMES JAY, information sciences company executive; b. Bklyn., May 29, 1928; s. David and Anna (Gross) G.; m. Marcia J. Black, June 25, 1950 (div. June 1986); children: Neil H., Richard L., Eric L.; m. Carol Ann De Barros, Sept. 4, 1986. BS in Econs., U. Pa., 1951. Asst. v.p. Economy Fin. Corp., Indpls., 1959-62; v.p. Rosenthal & Rosenthal, Inc., N.Y.C., 1962-68, Brandon Applied Systems, Inc., N.Y.C., 1970-71; fin. v.p. Telco Mktg. Svcs., Inc., Chgo., 1971-73; exec. v.p. Volt Info. Scis., Inc., N.Y.C., 1973-81, sr. v.p., CFO, 1985—, bd. dirs.; chmn., CEO Multivest, Inc., Ft. Lauderdale, Fla., 1981-82, Mego Corp., N.Y.C., 1982-85, also bd. dirs. Chmn. bd. dirs. Am. Community Pubs. Inc., 1989-91; bd. dirs. Autologic Info. Internat., Inc. Capt. USAFR, 1950-66. Mem. Fin. Execs. Inst. Office: Volt Info Scis Inc 560 Lexington Ave New York NY 10022-6828 E-mail: jgroberg@volt.com.

GROBLEBE, JIMMY LEE, graphics designer; b. Denver, Colo., Oct. 9, 1952; s. John Troy Groblebe,Sr. and Jeneatte Mary Ashland, Louis Leroy Ashland (Stepfather) and Lucy Groblebe(Stepmother); children: Amy Bono, Jason, Jimmy Groblebe,Jr., Jessica, Ashely Miller. CEO Bent and Twisted Enterprizes,Inc., Aurora, Colo., 1999—, designer, 1999—. Composer (graphic artist, songwriter): With your shield or on it/The Best Is Yet To Come., 1998; CD covers and life size paintings, My fish tank, acrylic on stretched canvas 192"x50", 1999, Grandfather Spirit, 1999, Blue Macaws, 1999, Brown-eyed Clown, 1999, Tuts FM, 2000, The Best is Yet to Come, 2002; composer: musical compositions CD on MP3, (musical composition MP3) Bring on the Clowns, 2002. Spec 4 U.S. Army, 1985—88. Mem.: DAV (life). Republican. Avocation: finish life's work publishing music i have writen.. Home: 1247 S Troy St Aurora CO 80012-4419 Office: Bent Twisted Enterprizes Inc 1247 S Troy St Aurora CO 80012-4419 Business E-Mail: jimmyleeg@excite.com.

GROBMAN, ARNOLD BRAMS, retired biology educator and academic administrator; b. Newark, Apr. 28, 1918; s. Samuel H. and Sophia (Brams) G.; m. Hulda Gross, Feb. 20, 1944; children: Marc Ross, Beth Burruss. BS, U. Mich., 1939; MS, U. Rochester, 1941, PhD, 1943. Instr. zoology U. Rochester, 1943-44; research asso. Manhattan project, 1944-46; from asst. prof. to asso. prof. biology U. Fla., 1946-59; research participant Oak Ridge Inst. Nuclear Studies, summer 1950, research specialist, med. center study, 1951-52; dir. Fla. State Mus., 1952-59; dir. biol. scis. curriculum study U. Colo., 1959-65, dean Coll. Arts and Scis.; prof. zoology Rutgers U., New Brunswick, N.J., 1965-72, dean Rutgers Coll., 1966-72; vice chancellor for acad. affairs, prof. biol. scis. U. Ill., Chgo., 1973-74, spl. asst. to pres., 1974-75; chancellor U. Mo.-St. Louis, 1975-85, chancellor emeritus, 1985—, prof. biology, 1975—, research prof., 1986—; adj. curator Fla. Mus. Natural History, 1982—. Vis. lectr. Utah State U., U. Ind./Purdue U., U. So. Ill., Nat. Taiwan Normal U., U. Campinas, Brazil, U. New Delhi, India, U. No. Sumatra, Indonesia, U. Sind, Pakistan, Chulalongkorn U., Bangkok, Thailand, U. Singapore, Sophia U., Japan, Internat. Christian U., Japan, Chiang Mia U., Thailand; cons. to govt., industry, founds. and ednl. instns., 1954— ; Mem. div. biology and agr. NRC-Nat. Acad. Scis., 1954-58, com. adult edn., 1956-58; sec. U.S. nat. com. Internat. Union Biol. Scis., 1966-69; Chmn. Ednl. Opportunity Center of Met. St. Louis, 1976-78; mem. advisory team sci. soc., Thailand, 1971; fgn. observer Treaty Plebiscite, Gov. Panama, 1977-78; mem. Commn. on Adult Learner Author: (with others) Island Life: A Study of the Land Vertebrates of Eastern Lake Michigan, 1948, Our Atomic Heritage, 1951, Genetics Effects of Chronic X-irradiation Exposure in Mice, 1960; author: BSCS Biology Implementation in the Schools, 1964, The Changing Classroom, 1969, Urban State Universities, 1988; editor: Social Implications of Biological Education, 1970; also articles to profl. jours., encys. and newspapers. Bd. dirs. in St. Louis United Way, Laumeier Sculpture Park, Narcotics Service Council, Regional Commerce and Growth Assn., St. Louis Higher Edn. Ctr., St. Louis Pub. Libr.; v.p. St. Louis Conf. on Edn., 1980-82; adv. bd. Indian River County Pub. Libr., 1997-2003. Recipient Fred H. Stoye prize Am. Soc. Ichthyologists and Herpetologists, 1941; A Cressy Morrison prize N.Y. Acad. Scis., 1943; Macalaster award Nat. Assn. Biology Tchrs., 1966; award of merit Urban League, 1984; Commanders Cross, Order of Merit, Fed. Republic Ger., 1985. Mem. Acad. Zoology in India (exec. com. 1967-69), Am. Assn. Higher Edn., AAAS (council 1961-65), Am. Assn. Museums (mus. tng. com. 1960-63), Am. Assn. State Colls. and Univs. (urban affairs com. 1977-85), Am. Ednl. Research Assn., Am. Inst. Biol. Scis. (exec. com. 1958-61, Disting. Service award 1984), Am. Soc. Ichthyologists and Herpetologists (bd. govs. 1952—, pres. 1964), Am. Soc. Naturalists, Am. Soc. Zoologists, Assn. Am. Med. Colls., Assn. Southeastern Biologists, Assn. Supervision and Curriculum Devel., Assn. Tropical Biology, Asian Assn. Biol. Edn., Biol. Scis. Curriculum Study (chmn. steering com. 1965-69), Biol. Soc. China, Biol. Soc. Washington, Council on Fgn. Relations, NEA, Edn. Programs Improvement Corp. (trustee 1970-74), Colo.-Wyo. Acad. Sci., AAUP, Explorers Club, Fla. Acad. Sci., Fla. Found. Future Scientists (chmn. 1957-59), Herpetologists League, Mo. Council Pub. Higher Edn. (exec. com. 1977-82, v.p. 1978, pres. 1979), Mo. Bot. Garden, Nat. Council Accreditation Tchr. Edn. (chmn. 1970-71), Genetics Soc., Herpetologists League, Philippine Assn. Sci. Tchrs., Nat. Assn. Biology Tchrs. (pres. 1966, editorial bd. 1974-77, dir. 1978-80), Nat. Assn. Research Sci. Teaching, Nat. Assn. State Univs. and Land Grant Colls. (exec. com. 1979-80, council on acad. affairs 1974-76, chmn. div. urban affairs 1978-79), Nat. Sci. Tchrs. Assn., Nature Conservancy, Newcomen Soc., N.J. Acad. Scis., Orgn. Tropical Studies, Sci. Soc. Thailand, Soc. Study Amphibians and Reptiles, Soc. Study Evolution, Soc. Systematic Zoology, Soc. Vertebrate Paleontology, Southeastern Museums Conf. (pres. 1955-57), Phi Beta Kappa, Sigma Xi, Phi Kappa Phi, Phi Sigma, Alpha Sigma Lambda, Alpha Epsilon Delta. Home: 855 Live Oak Ln Vero Beach FL 32963-2926 E-mail: agrobman@aol.com.

GROBMAN, GARY M. writer; b. Phila., Nov. 11, 1952; s. Leon and Freda M. Grobman; m. Linda M. May, July 22, 1990; 1 child, Adam Gabriel. BS, Drexel U., 1975; MPA, Harvard U., 1982; PhD, Pa. State U., Middletown, 2002. Legislative asst. U.S. Rep. Robert W. Edgar, Washington, 1975—79; legislative affairs analyst Smith & Howard Assocs., Washington, 1979—80; exec. dir. Pa. Jewish Coalition, Harrisburg, 1983—96; v.p. for spl. projects White Hat Comm., Harrisburg, Pa. Author: (book) The Nonprofit Handbook, The Nonprofit Organization's Guide to E-Commerce, Improving Quality and Performance in Your Nonprofit Organization, The Nonprofit Internet Handbook, The Holocaust: A Guide for Teachers; composer: (music) Russian Dance for Klezmer Band and Orchestra. Founder and chair Nonprofit Advocacy Network, Harrisburg, 1987—96; chair Pa. Human Svcs. Coalition, Harrisburg, 1995—96; v.p. The Greater Harrisburg Concert Band, 1998—2003. Named Runner of the Yr., Harrisburg Area Rd. Runners Club, 1988, Profl. of the Yr., Coun. of Jewish Federation's Govt. Affairs Network, 1993. Mem.: ARNOVA, Am. Assn. for Pub. Adminstrn., Pa. Assn. Nonprofit Orgns. (assoc. Cert. of Appreciation 1996). Jewish. Home: 3009 N Second St Harrisburg PA 17110 Office: White Hat Communications PO Box 5390 Harrisburg PA 17110 Home Fax: 717-238-2090; Office Fax: 717-238-2090. Personal E-mail: gary.grobman@paonline.com. E-mail: gary.grobman@paonline.com.

GROBMAN, HULDA GROSS (MRS. ARNOLD B. GROBMAN), retired health sciences educator; b. Phila., Aug. 2, 1920; d. Joseph and Dora (Abrahams) Gross; m. Arnold B. Grobman, Feb. 20, 1944; children— Marc Ross, Beth Alison Burruss. AB, U. Pa., 1940; MPA, U. Mich., 1941; EdD, U. Fla., 1958. Rsch. asso. Western Interstate Commn. on Higher Edn., Boulder, Colo., 1959-60; staff cons. Biol. Scis. Curriculum Study, Boulder, 1960-65, Joint Council on Econ. Edn., N.Y., 1965-66; prof. edn. N.Y. U., 1966-72, Bklyn. Coll., City U. N.Y., 1972-73; sr. rsch. assoc. ADA, Chgo., 1973-74; dir. edn./career mobility, area health edn. system, prof. med. edn. U. Ill. Med. Center, 1973-75; prof. health scis. edn. St. Louis U. Med. Ctr., 1975-88; prof. emeritus St. Louis U. Med. Center, 1988—. Cons. Sci. Edn. Center, U. Sao Paulo, Brazil; vis. prof. Asian Assn. Biol. Edn., Hebrew U. Jerusalem Inst. on Test Writing, 1972; cons. Fundacao Carlos Chagos, Sao Paulo, Brazil. Author: Developmental Curriculum Projects, 1970, Evaluation Activities of curriculum Projects, 1968, also articles; cons. editor Jour. Ednl. Rsch., 1973-80, Am. Ednl. Rsch. Jour.; mng. editor Serin Press. Bd. dirs. LWV Fla., 1950-55; candidate for City Commn., Gainesville, Fla., 1955; mem. Bd. State Dept. Children and Families, Dist. 15, 1997-2000. Recipient A-Individual Achievement award 3d Army Res. Command, 1956. Fellow AAAS (council 1967-73); mem. Asian Assn. Biology Edn. (charter hon. mem.), Am. Ednl. Research Assn. (sec. div. I 1979-81). Home: 4817 SW 34th St Ste 3 Gainesville FL 32608

GROCE, JAMES FREELAN, financial planning specialist; b. Lubbock, Tex., Nov. 24, 1948; s. Wayne Dee and Betty Jo (Rice) G.; m. Patricia Kay Rogers; 1 child, Jason Eric. BS cum laude, Tex. Tech U., 1971. Registered profl. engr., Tex. Petroleum engr. Texaco, Inc., Sweetwater, Tex., 1971-74, drilling and prodn. engr. Wichita Falls, Tex., 1974-77, asst. dist. engr. Midland, Tex., 1977-78; sr. prodn. engr. Bass Enterprises Prodn., Midland, 1978-81; petroleum engr. Murphy H. Baxter Co., Midland, 1981-82, Henry Engring., Midland, 1982-87, Fasken Oil and Ranch Interests, Midland, 1987, mgr. engring./ops., 1987-95; 2d v.p. investments, fin. planning specialist Salomon Smith Barney, Midland, 1996—. Scoutmaster Boy Scouts Am., Midland, 1980-83, merit badge counselor, 1987; mem. Community Bible Study, Midland, 1987-93. Mem. Soc. Petroleum Engr. (local sect. chmn. 1987, 25 Yr. Mem.), Soc. Petroleum Evaluation Engr. (local sect. chmn. 1996), Mensa, Tex. Tech. Ex-Student Assn., Century Club, Tau Beta Pi, Rotary Club of Midland. Presbyterian. Avocations: individual investments, real estate, gardening. Home: 2117 Bradford Ct Midland TX 79705-1726 E-mail: james.f.groce@smithbarney.com.

GROCE, STEVEN FRED, lawyer; b. Springfield, Mo., Aug. 6, 1956; s. Robert V. and Celeste Groce. BA in Psychology, S.W. Mo. State U., 1980; JD, U. Mo., Kansas City, 1984. Bar: Mo. 1984, U.S. Dist. Ct. (we. dist.) Mo. 1984, U.S. Supreme Ct., 1990. Ptnr. Groce & DeArmon, P.C., Springfield, 1984—. Mem. U.S. Supreme Ct. Bar, Mo. Bar Assn., Tex. Bar Assn., Internat. Bar Assn., Nat. Assn. Criminal Def. Lawyers (life). Office: Ste B-100 1200 E Woodhurst Dr Springfield MO 65804-4261

GROCOTT, HILARY PETER, adult education educator; b. Regina, Saskatchewan, Canada, Mar. 5, 1966; s. Hubert Clifford and Dorothy Margaret Grocott; m. Shivaun Noel Berg, Dec. 30, 1964; children: Bronwen Berg, Jane Rhiannon. MD, U. of Sask., 1984—90. FRCPC Royal Coll. of Physicians and Surgeons of Can., 1995. Assoc. prof. of anesthesiology Duke U., 1997—. Office: Duke University Medical Center Box 3094 Durham NC 27710 Office Fax: 919-681-8994. E-mail: h.grocott@duke.edu.

GRODD, LESLIE ERIC, lawyer; b. N.Y.C., Feb. 18, 1946; s. Abe and Celia G.; m. Judith Cota, June 18, 1967; children: Elissa, Katharine, Matthew. BA, U. Vt., 1966; JD, St. John's U., 1969; MBA, NYU, 1971. Bar: N.Y. 1969, Conn. 1974, D.C. 1982, U.S. Dist. Ct. Conn. 1975, U.S. Tax Ct. 1980, U.S. Supreme Ct. 1975. With tax dept. Coopers & Lybrand, N.Y.C., 1969-74; prin. Blazzard, Grodd & Hasenauer, PC, Westport, Conn., 1974—. Mem. ABA (chair closely held bus. com., tax sect. 1998-99, vice chair 2000-2001, chair 2001—), AICPA, Conn. Soc. CPAs (chmn. fed. tax com. 1988-89), Conn. Bar Assn. (chmn. tax sect. 1991-94), N.Y. Bar Assn., D.C. Bar Assn. Jewish. Office: Blazzard Grodd & Hasenauer PC 943 Post Rd E PO Box 5108 Westport CT 06880-5399 E-mail: lgrodd@aol.com., leslie.grodd@bghpc.com.

GRODEN, GERALD, psychologist; b. Cambridge, Mass., Apr. 11, 1931; s. Eugene and Ruth (Patten) G.; m. June Handwerger, Mar. 28, 1975; 1 son, John. AB, U. Vt., 1957, MA, 1960; PhD, Purdue U., 1963. Instr., then asst. prof. dept. neurology Ind. U. Med. Sch., Indpls., 1963-66, assoc. faculty mem. dept. pscyhology, 1964-66, U. R.I. ext., Providence, 1966—, clin. assoc. prof. Kingston, 1969—. Instr. dept. pediatrics Brown U., Providence, 1969, vis. assoc. prof. psychology; vis. adj. assoc. prof., 1999—, dir. psychology dept. R.I. Hosp. Child Devel. Center, Providence, 1966-78; dir. Groden Ctr., Providence, 1976—; dir. Behavioral Assocs., Providence, 1980-88; cons. R.I. Child Policy Coalition, 1995—; cons. in field. Contbr. articles to profl. jours. Bd. dirs. Sophia Little Home, R.I. Protective and Advocacy Sys., Providence; mem. R.I. Gov.'s Adv. Commn. on Mental Retardation, R.I. Gov.'s Adv. Commn. on Children and Youth, R.I. Senate Adv. Commn. on Early Intervention. Served with USNR, 1952-54. State of R.I. grantee, 1972. Mem. APA, R.I. Psychol. Assn. (dir.), Assn. for Advancement of Behavior Therapy, Assn. for Behavioral Analysis, Sigma Xi. Home: 99 Fosdyke St Providence RI 02906-3537 Office: 86 Mount Hope Ave Providence RI 02906-1648 E-mail: ggroden@grodencenter.org.

GRODEN, MICHAEL LEWIS, English literature educator; b. Buffalo, May 30, 1947; s. Sheldon Robert and Maxine (Helper) G.; m. Molly Peacock, 1992. BA, Dartmouth Coll., 1969; MA, Princeton U., 1972, PhD, 1975. Vis. asst. prof. English U. Western Ont., London, Can., 1975-77, asst. prof. English, 1977—78, assoc. prof., 1978—83, prof., 1983—. Author: Ulysses in Progress, 1977, James Joyce's Manuscripts: An Index, 1980; gen. editor: James Joyce Archive, 63 vols., 1977-79; co-editor: Johns Hopkins Guide to Literary Theory and Criticism, 1994; contbr. articles to profl. jours. Fellow John Simon Guggenheim Meml. Found., 1979-80, Social Scis. and Humanities Rsch. Coun. of Can., 1983-84, 91-94, 95-98. Mem.: MLA, Assn. for Computers and Humanities, Soc. for Textual Scholarship, Assn. Can. Coll. and Univ. Tchrs. English, Internat. James Joyce Found. Office: Univ Western Ontario Dept English London ON Canada N6A 3K7 E-mail: mgroden@uwo.ca.

GRODMAN, RICHARD STEPHEN, internist, cardiologist; b. S.I., N.Y., July 2, 1947; BS in Biology, C.C.N.Y., 1969; MD, SUNY-Downstate Med. Ctr., 1973. Diplomate Am. Bd. Internal Medicine with subspecialty in cardiovascular disease. Intern King's County-SUNY Med. Ctr., Bklyn., 1973-74, resident in medicine, 1974-76, resident in critical care medicine, 1976-77; fellow in cardiovascular disease Brown U.-R.I. Hosp., Providence, 1977-79; pvt. practice S.I.; attending physician St. Vincent's Med. Ctr.-Richmond, S.I., 1979—, dir. cardiology, 1981—; assoc. prof. medicine N.Y. Med. Coll., 1985—. Fellow ACP, Am. Coll. Cardiology, N.Y. Cardiology Soc., CCP. Office: St Vincent's Med Ctr Richmond 355 Bard Ave Staten Island NY 10310-1664 E-mail: rgrodman@svcmcny.org.

GRODNER, GEOFFREY MITCHELL, lawyer; b. Houston, Aug. 22, 1950; s. Murray and Leah (Cohen) G.; m. Lorelei Meeker, Dec. 22, 1974; 1 child, Andrew Meeker. B.A., Ind. U., 1972, J.D. cum laude, 1975. Bar: Ind. 1975, U.S. Dist. Ct. (so. dist.) Ind. 1975, U.S. Ct. Appeals (7th cir.) 1978. Assoc., Rogers Wilder & McDonald, Bloomington, Ind., 1975; counsel Subcom. on Constl. Amendments, U.S. Senate, Washington, 1975-76; ptnr. Rogers McDonald & Grodner, Bloomington, 1977-81, Grodner & Fore, Bloomington, 1981-85; sole practice, Bloomington, 1985— ; pres., dir. Westside Mgmt., Inc., Bloomington, 1983— ; ptnr. gen. Devel. Group, Bloomington, 1983— ; dir. Bloomington Datsun, Inc., Chmn., bd. dirs. Bloomington Pub. Transp. Corp., 1982— ; mem. Bloomington Ind. Bd. Pub. Works, 1972-75; pres., bd. dirs. Girl's Club, Bloomington, 1978-82. Mem. Monroe County Bar Assn., Ind. Bar Assn. Democrat. Home: 705 S Meadowbrook Dr Bloomington IN 47401-4230

GRODSKY, GEROLD MORTON, biochemistry educator; b. St. Louis, Jan. 18, 1927; s. Louis and Goldie B.; m. Kayla Deane Wolfe, Dec. 6, 1952; children: Andrea, Jamie. BS, U. Ill., 1946, MS, 1947; PhD, U. Calif., Berkeley, 1954; postgrad., Cambridge (Eng.) U., 1954-55. Prof. biochemistry U. Calif. Med. Sch., 1961-92, prof. emeritus (active status), 1992—. Vis. prof. U. Geneva, 1968—69, U. Paris VII, 1989; Somogyi Meml. lectr., 72; Helen Martin lectr., 76; Herman Rosenthal lectr., 86; cons. various pharm. houses; cons. to UCSF Diabetes Ctr., 1993—. Mem. editl. bd. Diabetes, 1965-73, 86-90, Am. Jour. Physiology, 1977-94, Diabetologia, 1990-92, Endocrinology, 1992-96; founding adv. editor: Diabetes Tech. and Therapy, 1998—, Diabetes New World (China); contbr. chpts. to books; contbr. over 200 articles on diabetes and storage, secretion of insulin to profl. jours. Mem. med. adv. bd. Juvenile Diabetes Found., 1974-77, 80-85; program dir. NIH Diabetic Animal Program, 1978-82, chmn. diabetes rsch. adv. bd. to Sec. Health, 1982-87. Lt. (s.g.) USNR, 1944-54. Recipient David Rumbough Internat. award Juvenile Diabetes Found., 1984, Williams-Levine award, 1990, NIH Merit award, 1987, Juvenile Diabetes Found. endowed Grodsky award for basic rsch. in diabetes, 1994—; named as one of 1000 most cited world scientists. Mem.: Am. Diabetes Assn. (rsch. bd. 1974—77, chmn. rsch. policy com. 1977, bd. dirs. Calif. chpt. 1989—91, nat. grant rev. com. 1992—96), Endocrine Soc., European Diabetes Assn., Am. Fedn. Clin. Rsch., Soc. Exptl. Biology, Am. Soc. Biol. Chemists, Internat. Diabetes Found., Meadowood Club, Harborpoint Club, Calif. Tennis Club. Home: 3969 Washington St San Francisco CA 94118-1613 Office: U Calif Sch Medicine Diabetes Ctr PO Box 0540 San Francisco CA 94143-0001

GRODSKY, JAMIE ANNE, law educator; b. San Francisco; d. Gerold Morton and Kayla Deane (Wolfe) G. BA in Human Biology/Natural Scis. and History with distinction, Stanford U., 1977; MA in Econ. Geography, U. Calif., Berkeley, 1986; JD, Stanford Law Sch., 1992. Ednl. dir. Oceanic Soc., San Francisco, 1979-81; rsch. asst. Woods Hole (Mass.) Oceanographic Inst., 1983; analyst Office Tech. Assessment U.S. Congress, Washington, 1984-89; counsel Com. Natural Resources, U.S. Ho. of Reps., Washington, 1993—95; counsel to Com. on Judiciary U.S. Senate, Washington, 1995-97; jud. clk. with chief judge U.S. Ct. Appeals (9th cir.), 1997-98; sr. advisor to the gen. counsel U.S. EPA, Washington, 1999—2001; assoc. prof. law U. Minn. Law Sch., Mpls., 2001—. Articles editor Stanford Law Rev.; contbr. articles to profl. jours. Trustee Desert Rsch. Inst. Found. Mem.: D.C. Bar Assn., Calif. Bar Assn., Supreme Ct. Bar Assn.

GRODY, DONALD, actor, judge, lawyer, arbitrator; b. N.Y.C., Dec. 18, 1927; s. Charles E. and Jeannette (Kessler) G.; m. Judith Anderson Weston, Oct. 21, 1989; children by previous marriage: Dion, Gordon, James, Jeremy. Student, Royal Acad. Dramatic Art, 1949-50; BA cum laude, Hunter Coll., 1951; LLB, N.Y. Law Sch., 1959. Bar: N.Y. State bar 1959. Profl. actor, singer, 1950-58; atty. U.S. Dept. Labor, Washington, 1959-60; labor union atty. N.Y.C., 1960-65; atty.-advisor Nat. Labor Relations Bd., Washington, 1965-67; asst. gen. counsel Retail Clerks Internat. Assn., Washington, 1967-69; gen. counsel dist. 65 Distributive Workers Am., N.Y.C., 1970-73; exec. sec. Actors Equity Assn., N.Y.C., 1973-80; asst. exec. dir. NFL Players Assn., Washington, 1980-81, arbitrator, mediator, 1984-93; sole practice law N.Y.C., 1981-89; supervising adminstrv. law judge N.Y.C. Parking Violations Bur., 1989-93. Mem. theatre adv. panel Nat. Endowment for the Arts; mem. exec. bd., dept. profl. employees AFL-CIO.; Chmn. Equity-League Pension and Welfare Trust Funds, 1973-80 Appeared: (pre-Broadway tour) Yiddle with a Fiddle, 1994-95, Little Shop of Horrors, Tenn. Repertory Theatre, 1995, Sweeney Todd, Pitts. Pub. Playhouse, 1995-96, Let's Do It, Long Wharf Theatre, 1996, Jekyll & Hyde, Broadway, N.Y.C., 1997-98, Gypsy, Paper Mill Playhouse, 1998, Golf With Alan Shepard, Buffalo Studio Arena Theatre, 1998, Guys and Dolls, Dallas Theater Ctr., 2000, Parade (nat. tour), 2000, (returned to theatre) Nat. Co. Guys & Dolls, 1993-94 (nat. tour 2000), (TV show) Law & Order, 1999. Served with AUS, 1945-47. Mem. AFTRA, SAG, Actors Equity Assn., Dramatists Guild.

GRODY, MARK STEPHEN, public relations executive; b. Milw., Jan. 1, 1938; s. Ray and Betty (Rothstein) G.; m. Karen Goldstein, Mar. 6, 1965 (div. 1972); 1 child, Laura; m. Susan Tellem, Mar. 25, 1979 (div. 1989); 1 child, Daniel; m. Jackie Black, June, 2, 2002. BS, U. Wis., 1960. Pub. rels. exec. GM, Detroit, 1961-74; v.p. pub. affairs Nat. Alliance of Businessmen, Washington, 1973-74; v.p. Carl Terzian & Assocs., L.A., 1974-75; chmn. Mark Grody Assocs. and Grody Tellem Comm., Inc. (now The Rowland Co.), L.A., 1975-90; pres. Mark Grody Assocs., L.A., 1990-93; exec. v.p., gen. mgr. Ogilvy Pub. Rels., L.A., 1993-96; pres. Mark Grody Assocs., L.A., 1996—. Ptnr. Mktg. Golf Resources, L.A., 1996-99, thegolfspot.com, 1998; founder corporategolf-.com, L.A., 1999—. Co-author: Corporate Golf: How to Play the Game for Business Success, 1996. Capt. U.S. Army, 1960. Mem. Internat. Network Golf (bd. dirs.), Pub. Rels. Soc. Am., The Lakes Country Club. Avocations: golf, bridge. E-mail: mgrody@aol.com.

GRODY, WAYNE WILLIAM, physician; b. Syracuse, N.Y., Feb. 25, 1952; s. Robert Jerome and Florence Beatrice (Kashdan) G.; m. Gaylen Ducker, July 8, 1990. BA, Johns Hopkins U., 1974; MD, Baylor Coll. Medicine, 1977, PhD, 1981. Diplomate Am. Bd. Pathology, Am. Bd. Med. Genetics; lic. physician,

Calif. Intern/resident UCLA Sch. Medicine, 1982-85, postdoctoral fellow, 1985-86, asst. prof., 1987-93, dir. DNA Diagnostic Lab., 1987—, assoc. prof., 1993-97; prof. depts. pathology and lab. medicine, pediatrics, human genetics, 1997—. Panelist Calif. Children's Svcs., 1987—, U.S. FDA, Washington, 1989—; mem. DNA tech. com. Pacific Southwest Regional Genetics Network, Berkeley, Calif.,NIH Task Force on Genetic Testing, others, 1987—; med., tech. cons. and writer Warner Bros., NBC, Tri-Star, CBS, Twentieth Century Fox, Universal, others, 1987—; chair, molecular genetics com. Coll. Am. Pathologists, Am. Coll. Med. Genetics, Assn. Molecular Pathology, others. Contbg. editor, film critic: MD Mag., 1981-91; assoc. editor Diagnostic Molecular Pathology, 1993—; contbr. articles to profl. jours., books, websites. Recipient best paper award L.A. Soc. Pathology, 1984, Joseph Kleiner Meml. award Am. Soc. Med. Technologists, 1990; Basil O'Connor scholar March of Dimes Birth Defects Found., 1989, Nakamura Lectureship Scripps Clinic, 1996, Moss Lectureship LSU, 1998, Stop Cancer Fdn. Rsch. Award, 1998, Am.'s Top Doctors, 2001-. Mem. AAAS, AMA, Am. Soc. Clin. Pathology (DNA workshop dir. 1988—), Am. Soc. Human Genetics, Coll. Med. Geneticist Am. (bd. dirs. 2001), Soc. Inherited Metabolic Disorders, Soc. Pediat. Rsch. Democrat. Jewish. Achievements include application of molecular biology to clinical diagnosis and genetic screening, molecular genetics research and AIDS and cancer research. Office: UCLA Sch Medicine Divsns Med Genetics and Molecular Pathology Los Angeles CA 90095-1732 E-mail: wgrody@mednet.ucla.edu.

GRODZICKER, TERRI I. research scientist, educator, academic administrator; b. N.Y.C., N.Y., Nov. 18, 1942; d. Harry Grodzicker and Anna Blanche Lowen. BA, Wellesley Coll., 1963; MS, Columbia U., 1965, PhD, 1969. Postdoctoral fellow Harvard Med. Sch., Boston, 1969—72; staff investigator Cold Spring Harbor (N.Y.) Lab., 1973—74, sr. staff investigator, 1974—79, sr. scientist, 1979—2000, prof., 2000—, asst. dir. for acad. affairs, 1986—. Cons. Cancer Rsch. Fund, N.Y.C., 1984—; adj. assoc. prof. Med. Sch., SUNY, Stony Brook, NY, 1981—. Editor: Genes and Development, 1989—. Mem.: Am. Soc. for Cell Biology, Am. Soc. Microbiology, Sigma Xi. Office: Cold Spring Harbor Lab 1 Bungtown Rd Cold Spring Harbor NY 11724

GROEBLI, WERNER FRITZ, professional ice skater, realtor; b. Basel, Switzerland, Apr. 21, 1915; s. Fritz and Gertrud (Landerer) G.; m. Yvonne Baumgartner, Dec. 30, 1954. Student architecture, Swiss Fed. Inst. Tech., 1934-35. Lic. realtor, Calif. Chmn. pub. relations com. Profl. Skaters Guild Am., 1972—. Performed in ice shows, Patria, Brighton, Eng., 1937; command performance in, Marina, London, 1937, Symphony on Ice, Royal Opera House, 1937; mem. Ice Follies, 1939-81, partner (with Hans Mauch) in comedy team Frick & Frack, 1939-53; solo act as Mr. Frick (assisted by comedy team), 1955-81; numerous TV appearances including Snoopy on Ice, 1973, Snoopy's Musical on Ice, 1978, Sportsworld, NBC-TV, 1978, Donnie and Marie Osmond Show, 1978, Mike Douglas Show, 1978, Dinah Shore Show, 1978; films include Silver Skates, 1942, Lady Let's Dance, 1943, Jinxed, 1981; interviewed by Barbara Walters NBC Today, 1974; appeared in Christmas Classics on Ice at Blue Jay Ice Castle, 1991. Served with Swiss Army, 1934-37. Named Swiss jr. skating champion, 1934; named to Madison Sq. Garden Hall of Fame for 10,000 performances in Ice Follies, 1967, U.S. Figure Skating Assn. World Hall of Fame, 1984; recipient Hall of Fame Ann. award Ice Skating Inst. Am.; used skates exhibited at Smithsonian Inst. Lasted 15,000 performances in Ice Follies; originator of "Frick" cantilever spread-eagle skating movement; comedic choreography consultant. Address: 77 Wildbachstr 8008 Zurich Switzerland

GROENHEIM, HENRI ARNOLD, psychologist, consultant; b. Bklyn., Oct. 18, 1927; s. Herman and Suzanna May (Bierman) G.; m. Gail Thacker, June 29, 1957; children: Lisa Gail, Gary Thomas. BA in Psychology, Pa. State U., 1950; MA in Counseling, George Washington U., 1954; PhD in Counselor Edn., Fla. State U., 1968. Lic. psychologist Md. State Bd. Examiners of Psychologists. Sch. counselor Brookville (Pa.) Jr.-Sr. H.S., 1950-51; dean of boys Derry Twp. Jr.-Sr. H.S., Hershey, Pa., 1951-52; sch. counselor Frederick (Md.) H.S., 1952-54; counselor Nurnberg Am. H.S., Germany, 1954-55; sch. counselor Kenwood Sr. H.S., Balt., 1955-61; sch. counselor, guidance dept. chair Overlea Sr. H.S., Balt., 1961-66; coll. counselor Catonsville C.C., Balt., 1968-69; assoc. prof. Johns Hopkins U., Balt., 1970-74; assoc. prof. psychology Towson State U., Balt., 1969-94. Cons. psycholog. testing Divsn. Rehab. Svcs., Balt., 1973—, Disability Determination Svcs., Balt., 1973—, Kennedy Inst., Balt., 1985-86, Balt. City Pub. Schs., 1990-98; sr. counseling profl. mentor dept. counseling George Washington U., 1996—; med. staff allied health profl. Harford Meml. Hosp., Harford County, Md. Contbr. articles to profl. jours.; moderator TV program, 1987. Bd. dirs. Cmty. Counseling & Resource Ctr., Cockeysville, Md., 1985-90; com. mem. State Democratic Election Com., Balt., 1994. Recipient Sparks medal for outstanding scholarship Pa. State U., 1948. Fellow Md. Psychol. Assn. (ins. com.); mem. APA, Balt. Psychol. Assn., Johns Hopkins Club, Downtown Towson Rotary Club. Avocations: swimming, travel, golf. Home and Office: 526 St Francis Rd Baltimore MD 21286-1325

GROENIER, JAMES SCOTT, civil engineer; b. Madison, Wis., Jan. 17, 1963; s. James Edward and Darlene Gelaine (Frye) G.; m. Mary Elizabeth Ruhland Groenier, May 17, 1986 (div. Jan. 26, 1988). BS in Civil Engring., U. Wis., Madison, 1986; MS in Civil Engring., Mont. State U., Bozeman, 1995. Registered profl. engr. Wis. Civil engr. Ill. Dept. Transp., Dixon, 1987-88; staff engr. Ayres & Assocs., Eau Claire, Wis., 1988-90; rsch., tchg. asst. Mont. State U., Bozeman, 1990-92; civil engr. USDA Forest Svc., Petersburg, Alaska, 1992-95, Vernal, Utah, 1995-2000; east zone structural engr. USDA Forest Svc., Region 9, Milw., 2000—. Contbr. technical papers in field. Baseball Coach, 1993-95, soccer coach Petersburg Youth Soccer, 1992, 95, Eau Claire Youth Soccer, 1989, 90. Mem. ASCE. Avocations: hunting, fishing, sports, outdoor activities. E-mail: jgroenier@fs.fed.us.

GROENING, MATTHEW, writer, cartoonist; b. Portland, Oreg., Feb. 15, 1954; s. Homer Philip and Margaret Ruth (Wiggum) G.; m. Deborah Lee Caplan; 2 children. BA, Evergreen State Coll., 1977. Cartoonist Life in Hell weekly comic strip (syndicated by Acme Features Syndicate), Sheridan, Oreg., 1980—; pres. Matt Groening Prodns., Inc., L.A., 1988—, Bongo Entertainment, Inc., L.A., 1993—. Creator, prodr. The Simpsons, 1989—; cartoonist for tv cartoon Futurama, 1999. Named New Pub. of Yr. Diamond Distbn. Gem awards, 1993.

GROETSCH, CHARLES WILLIAM, mathematics educator; b. New Orleans, Feb. 15, 1945; s. Gilbert G. and Lillian (Dooley); m. Sandra Carver, Sept. 3, 1966; children: Kurt, Heidi. BS, La. State U., 1966, MS, 1968, PhD, 1971. Rsch. assoc. USAF Flight Dynamics Lab., 1978; exch. scientist East German Acad. Sci., 1979; asst. prof. U. Cin., 1971-76, assoc. prof., 1976-81, prof., 1981—, head dept. math., 1985—90; dean McMicken Coll. Arts and Scis., 2000—01. Vis. prof. U. Manchester, Eng., 1980, U. Kaiserlautern, Fed. Republic of Germany, 1983, Australian Nat. U., 1986, U. Queensland, 1996; cons. NRC, NSF, Mgmt. Decision Devel. Corp.; vis. asst. prof. U. R.I., 1974-75. Author 8 books, 91 rsch. papers. Grantee Air Force Office Sci. Rsch., Sci. Rsch. Coun. Gt. Britain, NSF, NATO. Mem. Am. Math. Soc., Math. Assn. Am. (George Polya award 1994), Soc. Ind. Applications Math. Home: 5320 Eagleswatch Ct Cincinnati OH 45230-1380 Office: U Cin Math 025 Cincinnati OH 45221-0001

GROETZINGER, JON, JR., lawyer, consumer products executive; b. N.Y.C., Feb. 12, 1949; s. Jon M. and Elinor Groetzinger; m. Carol Marie O'Connor, Jan. 24, 1981; 3 children. AB magna cum laude, Middlebury Coll., 1971; JD in Internat. Legal Affairs, Cornell U., 1974. Bar: N.H. 1974, N.Y. 1980, Mass. 1980, Fla. 1982, Md. 1985, Ohio 1991, U.S. Supreme Ct. 1980. Assoc. McLane, Graf, Greene, Raulerson and Middleton, P.A., Manchester, N.H., 1974-76; atty. John A. Gray Law Offices, Boston, 1978-81; pvt. practice N.H., Boston, 1977-81; chief internat. counsel Martin Marietta Corp., Bethesda, Md., 1981-88; pres., exec. v.p. Martin Marietta Overseas Corp., Bethesda, 1984-88; sr. v.p., gen. counsel, corp. sec. Am. Greetings Corp., Cleve., 1988—. Chmn. internat. adv. bd. Case Western Res. U. Law Sch., 1995—, disting. adj. prof., 1992—. Trustee Middlebury (Vt.) Coll., 1974—76, mem. bd. overseers, 1977—; bd. dirs. Cleve. Coun. on World Affairs, 1992—98, 2000—, vice chmn., 2002—, chmn. strategic planning com., 2000—02, mem. exec. com., 2000—03, trustee, 1992—96, 1998—, Can.-U.S. Law Inst.; mem. exec. com. The Conf. Bds. Coun. Chief Legal Officers, 1996—, membership chmn., 1997—98, program chair, 1999—2000, coun. chmn., 2000—02; chmn., pres. Greater Cleve. Gen. Counsel Assn., 2001—; bd. dirs. Lake Erie Coll., 2002—. Mem. ABA, N.H. Bar Assn., Fla. Bar Assn., Ohio Bar Assn., Cleve. Bar Assn., Md. Bar Assn., Am. Soc. Corp. Secs. (sec. Ohio chpt. 1995—, v.p. 1996-97, pres. 1997-98, adv. com. 1998—), Soc. of Benchers, Phi Beta Kappa. Office: Am Greetings Corp 1 American Rd Cleveland OH 44144-2301 E-mail: jgroetzi@yahoo.com.

GROFF, JOANN, organization administrator; b. Ft. Leonardwood, Mo., Oct. 10, 1956; d. Barry T. Groff and Ann (Ferry) Ragsdale. Student, Georgetown U., 1974-76; BS in Bus. Adminstrn., Babson Coll., Wellesley, Mass., 1978. Office mgr. Morgan Smith for Congress, Northglenn, Colo., 1978; fair and rodeo asst. Adams County Commrs., Brighton, Colo., 1979; mktg. devel. officer Columbine Title Co., Lakewood, Colo., 1979-80; express agt., loan officer Wells Fargo Credit Corp., Englewood, Colo., 1981-84; pub. banking rep. Cen. Bank of Denver, 1985-89; mem. Colo. Ho. of Reps., Denver, 1983-89, chmn. audit com., 1989; fin. com.; dir. Leadership Giving Mile High United Way, 1991-92; pres. Colo. Retail Coun., 1992—. Past pres. Westminster Cmty. Artist Series; mem. bd. Pub. Svc. Credit Union, Colo. State Dem. Com., 1980-93, Colo. State Exec. Com., 1988-93, del. Nat. Conv., 1980, 84, alt. del., 1976; bd. dirs. Westminster (Colo.) Cmty. Artist Series, Marycrest H.S.; apptd. mem. Colo. State Bd. Equalization, 1994—, Colo. Transp. Com., 1999—. Roman Catholic. Office: Colo Retail Coun 451 E 58th Ave Denver CO 80216-8412 E-mail: jag@coloradoretail.org.

GROFF, TRACEY ANNE, social worker; b. Lancaster, Pa., Dec. 20, 1965; d. James David and Peggy Louise (Ulrich) G. BSW, Elizabethtown Coll., 1988; MSW, Temple U., 1995. Lic. social worker. Sales assoc. Watt & Shand Dept. Store, Lancaster, Pa., 1983-90; social worker Masonic Homes, Elizabethtown, Pa., 1989—. Mem. NASW, Alpha Delta Mu. Democrat. Roman Catholic. Home: 862 Fountain Ave Lancaster PA 17601-4533

GROGAN, MICHAEL KEVIN, lawyer, negotiator; b. Chgo., Sept. 26, 1951; s. William P. and Margaret (Campbell) Grogan; m. Nancy Ann Wilson, July 24, 1974; children: Margaret Lindsay, Kathryn Eileen, Michael Patrick. BS, MacMurray Coll., 1972; JD, Mercer U., 1976. Bar: Fla. 1972, Ga. 1976, U.S. Ct. Appeals (5th cir.) 1976, U.S. Ct. Appeals (11th cir.) 1982, cert.: The Fla. Bar (labor and employment and city, county and local govt. law). Ptnr. Coffman, Coleman, Andrews & Grogan P.A. and predecessors, Jacksonville, Fla., 1976—. Mem. labor law chpt. Specialized Legal Rsch. Little, Brown & Co., 1987—. Chmn. Fla. Pub. Employment Labor Rels. Forum, 1985—. Recipient Marsicano award for local govt. work, 1999; scholar Ill. State, 1969—72. Mem.: ABA, Acad. Fla. Mgmt. Attys., Ga. Bar Assn., Fla. Bar Assn., Tournament Players Club, River Club. Roman Catholic. Office: Coffman Coleman Andrews & Grogan PA PO Box 40089 Jacksonville FL 32203-0089 E-mail: mgrogan@claglaborlaw.com.

GROGAN, PAUL J. retired engineering educator; b. Adrian, Minn., Nov. 20, 1918; s. William Edward and Amelia (Steinbach) Grogan; m. Dorothy Wells, Sept. 7, 1946; children: William, Jane, Katherine, Mary, JoAnne, Tom. BSME, Purdue U., 1943; student in diesel engring., Pa. State U., 1943; student in naval architecture, U. Mich., 1944—45; MSME, U. Wis., 1949. Cert. profl. engr., Wis. Asst. prof. U. Notre Dame, Ind., 1950—51; dir. OSTS, Dept. Commerce, Washington, 1966—68; from instr. to asst. prof. U. Wis., Madison, 1947—50, from asst. prof. to prof., 1951—66, prof., 1968—85, prof. emeritus, 1985—. Power cons. City of Marshfield, Wis., 1952—56; loss analysis Madison Gas and Electric, 1972—85. Editor: (two volume set) History of Tech.: Tech. in Western Civilization 1961-1965; contbr. articles to profl. jours.; illustrator:. Mem. various state and county coms. Lt. USN, 1943—46, PTO. Recipient various awards. Mem.: Am. Soc. Engring. Edn. (life), Nat. Soc. Power Engrs. (life), Am. Legion, Triangle Fraternity. Avocations: crossword puzzles, mathematics, science, word games, puzzles. Home: 18 Southwick Cir Madison WI 53717 E-mail: pjgrogan@facstaff.wisc.edu.

GROGAN, ROBERT HARRIS, lawyer; b. Feb. 25, 1933; s. Robert Michael and Nora Howarth (Johnson) G.; m. Delia Ann Grossi, Dec. 23, 1967 (div. 1982); m. Lynn D. Habian, June 20, 1987. AB, Harvard U., 1955; LLB, U. Va., 1961. Bar: Va. 1961, N.Y. 1962, Ill. 1977, Fla. 1986; cert. cir. ct. mediator, Fla. Assoc. Milbank, Tweed, Hadley & McCloy, N.Y.C., 1961-66; counsel Anaconda Co., N.Y.C., 1966-68; assoc. Shearman & Sterling, N.Y.C., 1968-75; v.p., gen. counsel staff Citibank, N.Y.C., 1975-76; ptnr. Mayer, Brown & Platt, Chgo., 1976-81; of counsel Olwine, Connelly, Chase, O'Donnell & Weyher, N.Y.C., 1981-87; sr. v.p., dep. sr. counsel S.E. Bank, N.A., Miami, Fla., 1987-91; sr. v.p., gen. counsel Republic Nat. Bank of Miami, 1992-96; ind. bank, bus. and legal cons., 1996-2001; program adminstr. Broward County (Fla.) Legal Aid Svc., 2001—. Vice chmn. exec. adv. coun. Andreas Bus. Sch. Barry U., Miami Shores, Fla., 1995-97; lectr. in field. Contbg. author: The Local Economic Development Corporation, 1970. Sec., bd. dirs. 3d Equity Owners Corp., coop. housing corp., 1975-77, pres., bd. dirs., 1982-86. With Signal Corps, U.S. Army, 1956-58. Mem. Fla. Bar, N.Y. Bar, Va. State Bar Assn., Ill. State Bar Assn., Am. Arbitration Assn. (comml. panel neutral arbitrators 1997-2001), Harvard Club (N.Y.C.), Harvard Faculty Club (Cambridge, Mass.). Home: 1441 Brandywine Dr Apt 900G West Palm Beach FL 33480-0666 Fax: 561-848-5922. E-mail: rgrogan@legalaid.org.

GROGAN, STANLEY JOSEPH, educational and security consultant; b. N.Y.C., Jan. 14, 1925; s. Stanley Joseph and Marie (Di Giorgio) G.; m. Mary Margaret Skroch, Sept. 20, 1954; 1 child, Mary Maureen. AA, Am. U., 1949, BS, 1950, MA, 1955; grad., Fed. Emergency Mgmt. Agy. Staff Coll., 1970; degree, Indsl. Coll. Armed Forces Air War Coll., 1972; MS, Calif. State Coll., Hayward, 1973; EdD, Nat. Christian U., 1974. Cert. Protection Profl. Personal asst., recruitment asst. CIA, Washington, 1954-56; disting. grad. acad. instr., allied officer course Air Command and Staff Coll., Maxwell AFB, Ala., 1962; asst. prof. air sci. U. Calif., Berkeley, 1963-64, Chabot Coll., 1964-70, Oakland Unified Sch. Dist., 1962-83, Hayward Unified Sch. Dist., 1965-68; instr. ednl. methods, edn. rsch. methods instrn. Nat. Christian U., 1975—, Nat. U. Grad. Studies, Belize, 1975—. Pres. SJG Enterprises, Inc., cons., 1963—; cons. pub. rels., 1963—; bd. dirs. We T.I.P., Inc., 1974. Contbr. articles to profl. jours. and newspapers. Asst. dir. Nat. Ednl. Film Festival, 1971. With AUS, 1945; lt. col. USAFR, 1948-76; col. Calif. State Mil. Res. Decorated Air medal with oak leaf cluster, Korean Svc. medal with four battle stars, Cold War medal; named to Hon. Order Ky. Cols., Commonwealth of Ky., 1970; recipient Air Force Commendation medal (2), UN Svc. medal, citation, Korea, RCVP Korean Vets. Assn. medal, 1994. Fellow: Internat. Inst. Security and Safety Mgmt. (vice chmn., mem. bd. dirs. 2001—, Vet. of Millennium award 2000); mem.: DAV (life), VFW (life), NRA (life), Nat. Def. Exec. Res./FEMA, Am. Soc. Indsl. Security, Res. Officers Assn. (life), Air Force Assn. (life), Night Fighter Assn. (nat. publicity chmn. 1967), Assn. Nat. Def. and Emergency Resources (bd. dirs. 1995—98), Am. Def. Preparedness Assn. (life), Marines Meml. Home: 2585 Moraga Dr Pinole CA 94564-1236

GROGAN, TIMOTHY JAMES, business executive, golf professional; b. Hillsboro, Oreg., Aug. 5, 1940; s. James John and Joan Louise (Harper) G.; m. Jean Louise Egbert, Aug. 3, 1963 (div. June 1984); children: Susan, Erin; m. Kathryn Stetson, Aug. 9, 1985; children: Stephanie, Katherine. BS, U.S. Mil. Acad., 1963; MA in English, Columbia U., 1971; postgrad., U.S. Army War Coll., 1980-81, Royal Coll. Def. Studies, London, 1986. Commd. 2d lt. U.S. Army, 1963, advanced through grades to gen., 1987; asst. div. comdr. 8th Inf. Div. U.S. Army, Europe, 1987-88; chief of staff Hdqrs. U.S. V Corps, Frankfurt, Germany, 1988-89; asst. dep. chief staff for concepts and doctrine Hdqrs. Training and Doctrine Commd., Ft. Monroe, Va., 1989-93; ret., 1993; exec. Perot Sys. Corp., Dallas, 1993-98; golf tchg. profl. Hank Haney Golf Sch., 2000—; COO, Custom Homes Group, LLC. Decorated DSC, Silver Star, Legion of Merit, Purple Heart. Republican. Roman Catholic. Avocations: golf, basketball, skiing, scuba, guitar. Home: 3501 Lakebluff Way Plano TX 75093-7522

GROGG, TERRIE LYNN, factory assembler; b. Ft. Wayne, Ind., Feb. 27, 1956; d. Robert Emor and Margaret Berneice Foreman; m. Randy Ray Grogg (div. 1985); 1 child, Justin Robert. Cert. advanced model and finishing, Charmaine Finishing, Ft. Wayne, 1973; student, Ind. U., Ft. Wayne, 1979; cert. solder elec. contractor, ITT Industries, Ft. Wayne, 1989; student, Ivy Tech. State Coll., Ft. Wayne, 1997—2001. Instr. English riding Lomond Farms, Ossian, Ind., 1972; factory worker Tony's Pizza Co., Salina, Kans., 1974-76; clk. N.Am. Vanlines, Ft. Wayne, 1976-79; factory worker Ft. Wayne Wire & Die, 1979-80; clk. Temp. Agys., Ft. Wayne, 1981-84; policy change clk. Mut. Security Ins., Ft. Wayne, 1984-87; die maker AJAX Industries, Ft. Wayne, 1987-88; inspector Ind. Coatings Corp., Ft. Wayne, 1989—2001; assembler ITT Industries, Ft. Wayne, 1989—, asst. co. mgr. ElectroAire dept. Flickinger, Ind., 2001—03, assembler Ft. Wayne, 2003. Mem. adv. bd. edn. ITT Industries, 1995. Contbg. poet The World of Poetry, 1990, The Sound of Poetry, 1994; self-pub. book Our Lives, 1999, In This World, 2001. Recipient Golden Poets award Nat. Libr. Poetry, Owings Mills., Md., 1990, 91, 92, Editors Choice award, 1994, named to Internat. Poetry Hall of Fame, 1996. Mem. Ind. Poets (Mack chpt.), N.E. Ind. Poets (sec. 2001), Am. Health and Fitness (life), Paradigm Soc. Religious Scientist. Avocations: writing, drums, art, camping. Home: PO Box 8001 Fort Wayne IN 46898-8001

GROH, JENNIFER CALFA, law librarian; b. Patchogue, N.Y., Mar. 28, 1970; d. Anthony Bernard and Mary (Fogerty) C.; m. William Matthew Groh, May 10, 1997. BA in Social Sci., St. Joseph's Coll., 1992; MA in Internat. Edn., NYU, 1993; MSLS, Pratt Inst., Bklyn., 1996. Reference page Patchogue (N.Y.)-Medford Libr., 1986-93; from libr. asst. to sr. libr. Morgan & Finnegan, N.Y.C., 1994—. NYU grad. scholar, 1992, Law Libr. Assn. scholar, N.Y. 1995, Am. Assn. Law Librs. scholar, 1996. Mem. ALA, Spl. Librs. Assn., Law Libr. Assn. Greater N.Y. Home: 21 Mohawk Dr North Babylon NY 11703-3303 Office: Morgan & Finnegan 345 Park Ave New York NY 10154-0053

GROHE, LINDA SQUIRES, dean; b. San Francisco, Aug. 1, 1944; d. Alan Francis Squires and Edna May Rafael; m. William Grohe. BA in Speech-Comm., San Jose State U., 1966, MA in Speech-Comm., 1969. Cert. life cert. c.c. supr. Calif., life cert. std. tchg. credential in speech and social scis. Instr. Humboldt (Calif.) State U., 1968-69, City Coll. San Francisco, 1969-75, pub. rels. officer, 1975-79, acting asst. dean of instrn., 1979-82, dean of instrn., 1982-92, contract edn. coord., 1992-96, dean John Adams campus Sch. Health and Phys. Edn., 1997—. Bd. dirs. Stonestown YMCA, San Francisco, Hotel & Restaurant Scholarship Found., San Francisco, 1987—99; mem. program com. Pvt. Industry Coun.; mem. San Francisco Citizens Com. for Cmty. Devel. Mem.: NAACP, Am. Assn. Women in Cmty. and Jr. Colls. (mem. Bay Area chpt., pres. Bay Area chpt. 1981—82), Assn. Calif. C.C. Adminstrs. Avocation: golf, reading, swimming. Office: City Coll San Francisco 1860 Hayes St San Francisco CA 94117-1220 E-mail: lgrohe@ccsf.cc.ca.us.

GROHSKOPF, BERNICE, writer; b. Troy, N.Y. m. Herbert Grohskopf (div.); 1 child, Margaret Ellen. MA, Columbia U., 1954. Writer-in-residence Sweet Briar (Va.) Coll., 1980—82; rsch. assoc. Work and Correspondence of William James, Charlottesville, Va., 1984—95; freelance writer. Author: The Treasure of Sutton Hoo, 1970, 1973, 2000. Mem.: PEN, Nat. Book Critics Cir., Authors Guild. Home: Apt 11 116 Turtle Creek Rd Charlottesville VA 22901-6760

GROISS, FRED GEORGE, lawyer; b. Glen Cove, N.Y., Mar. 12, 1936; s. Frederick F.W. and Dorothy C. (Roberts) G.; m. Jacqueline C. Grosse; children— Frederick C., Katherine E., Jennifer L. AB, Cornell U., 1958, LL.B., 1961. Bar: N.Y. 1961, Wis. 1963, U.S. Dist. Ct. (ea. dist.) Wis., 1963, U.S. Ct. Appeals (7th cir.) 1965. Assoc. Sage, Gray, Todd & Sims, N.Y.C., 1961-63; assoc. Porter, Quale, Porter & Zirbel, Milw., 1963-65, Brady, Tyrrell, Cotter & Cutler, Milw., 1965-70; ptnr. Quarles & Brady, Milw., 1970-2000; ret. Lectr. various labor law confs. Mem. Gov.'s Commn. on Civil Service Reform, Madison, Wis., 1977-78 Mem.: Wis. Bar Assn. (bd. dirs. labor law sect. 1975—77), Greencroft ACAC Club. Republican. Avocation: sports. Home: 2460 Dunmore Rd Charlottesville VA 22901-9447 E-mail: fgg@cstone.net.

GROLLER, RICHARD J. music educator, musician; b. Allentown, Pa., Jan. 9, 1951; s. Elwood and Angela Groller. MusB in Edn., Phila. Music Acad, 1975; MusM, Temple U., 1995. Cert. principal Temple U. Music tchr. Harrison-Morton M.S., Allentown, 1985—87; band dir. Raub M.S., Allentown, 1987—2002, Trexler M.S., Allentown, 2002—. Percussionist Allentown Symphony, 1970—. Mem.: Percussive Arts Soc., Allentown Musicians Assn. (exec. bd. 2000—). Office: Trexler Middle School 851 N 15th St Allentown PA 18104

GROLLI, FRANK THOMAS, retired pharmacist; b. Bklyn., July 25, 1933; s. Frank and Theresa D. G.; mem. Maria T. Cerbone, Mar. 30, 1974. BS in Pharmacy, Bklyn. Coll. Pharmacy, 1956. Registered pharmacist Ferro's Pharmacy, Bklyn., 1959-61; mgr., owner Associated Drugs, N.Y.C., 1961-66; mgr., pharmacist Frank's Pharmacy, Staten Island, 1966-76; asst. mgr., pharmacist Savon SuperX, Staten Island, 1976-84, asst. mgr., pharmacy supr., 1984-88, pharmacy coord., 1988-94; northeast region pharmacy coord. H.S.I., Rutherford, N.J., 1994; pharmacy supr. Revco D.S., Carteret, N.J., 1994-95, ret., 1995. Col. Med. Svc. Corps, 1961-86. Decorated Nat. Def. Svc. medal. Army Reserve Comp. Achievement medal, Meritorous Svc. medal. Mem. APHA, Pharm. Soc. of N.Y., N.Y.C. Pharm. Soc., Italian Pharm. Soc., Reserve Officers Assn., Assn. of Mil. Surgeons. Avocations: gardening, stamp collecting, fishing, home repairs.

GROLLMAN, JULIUS HARRY, JR., cardiovascular and interventional radiologist; b. L.A., Nov. 26, 1934; s. Julius Harry and Alice Carolyn (Greenlee) G.; m. Alexa Jule Silverman, May 20, 1959; children: Carolyn, David, Elizabeth. BA, Occidental Coll., 1956; MD, UCLA, 1960. Diplomate in radiology and vascular and interventional radiology Am. Bd. Radiology. Intern L.A. VA Hosp., 1960-61; resident in radiology UCLA Med. Ctr., 1961-64; chief cardiovascular radiology Walter Reed Gen. Hosp., 1965-67; chief cardiovascular radiology Ctr. Health Svcs. UCLA, 1967-78; chief cardiovascular and interventional radiology Little Company of Mary Hosp., Torrance, Calif., 1978—; clin. prof. radiol. sci. UCLA, 1978—. Contbr. over 150 articles to profl. jours., 9 chpts. to med. books. Fellow Soc. for Cardiac Angiography and Interventions (trustee 1992-95), Am. Coll. Radiology, Coun. Cardiovascular Radiology, Am. Heart Assn., Soc. Cardiovascular and Interventional Radiology; mem. AMA, Am. Roentgen Ray Soc., Radiol. Soc. N.Am., Western Angiographic and Interventional Soc. (pres. 1976-77), N.Am. Soc. for Cardiac Imaging (pres. 1991-92). Republican. Presbyterian. Office: Little Company of Mary Hosp Dept Radiology 4101 Torrance Blvd Dept Torrance CA 90503-4664 also: RPM 100 Oceangate Ste 1000 Long Beach CA 90802-4347 E-mail: jgrollma@ucla.edu.

GROLLMAN, SIGMUND SIDNEY, physiology educator; b. Stevensville, Md., Feb. 12, 1923; s. Ellis Phillip and Rachel Naomi (Krystal) G. BS, U. Md., 1947, MS, 1949, PhD, 1952. Cert. biochem. physiology. Teaching asst. U. Md. Zoology Dept., College Park, 1947-49, instr., 1949-51, asst. prof., 1952-55, assoc. prof., 1955-58, prof., 1958-84, chair div. physiology, 1966-73, dir. grad. studies, 1973-83, prof. emeritus, 1984; pres. Sigmund Grollman Ltd., Balt., 1970—. Author: (textbook) The Human Body--Its Structure and Function, 1964, 4th rev. edit., 1984, (manual) Anatomy and Physiology, 1960-84, Experimental Mammilian Physiology, 1971-83; contbr. articles to profl. jours. Sgt. U.S. Army, 1940-43, ETO. Fellow Am. Coll. Sports Medicine; mem. Soc. Exptl. Biology and Medicine, N.Y. Acad. Sci., Sigma Xi. Home: 4001 N Charles St Baltimore MD 21218-1749

GROMADA, THADDEUS V. historian, academic administrator; b. Passaic, N.J., July 30, 1929; s. John W. and Aniela (Pudzisz) Gromada; m. Theresa M. Michalski, Aug. 25, 1951; children: Joseph, John, Ann. BS magna cum laude, Seton Hall U., 1951; MA, Fordham U., 1953, PhD, 1966. From asst. prof. history to prof. European history N.J. City U., 1959-92; v.p., exec. dir. Polish Inst. Arts and Scis., N.Y.C., 1991—. Chmn. Gov.'s Commn. Ea. European History, Trenton, NJ, 1985—89; cons. ethnic heritage Dept. Edn., Washington; cons. NEA, 1975—. Author, editor: book Essays on Poland's Foreign Policy 1918 1939, 1969; co-editor: Polonia Amerykanska, 1988; editor: Jadwiga of Anjou & Rise of East Central Europe, 1991; founder, co-editor: Tatra Eagle, 1947—. Mem. awards com. Korczak lit. prize, 1980—85; co-organizer Conf. Germany, Poland & Europe, 1992; organizer Conf. Jagiellonian U.and Polish Acad. Arts and Scis., Cracow, Poland, 2000; vice chmn., trustee Kosciusko Found., N.Y.C., 1981—; mem. dialog com. Nat. Polish Am.-Jewish Am. Coun., Washington, 2001—. Sgt. U.S. Army, 1953—55. Decorated Officer's Cross of Merit Pres. Poland, Comdrs. Cross, L'Ordre du Merite Culturel Poland's Min. of Culture and Arts; recipient Haiman medal, Polish Am. Hist. Assn., 1985. Mem.: Polish Am. Hist. Assn. (pres. 1995—96), Am. Hist. Assn., Am. Assn. Advancement Slavic Studies. Roman Catholic. Avocations: classical music,

violin, polish highlander folklore, hiking. Home: 2722 Old Oak Walk Johns Island SC 29455-6213 Office: Polish Inst Arts & Scis 208 E 30th St New York NY 10016-8202 E-mail: tgromada@mindspring.com.

GROMEN, RICHARD JOHN, historian, educator; b. Cleve., Dec. 3, 1930; s. John Rudolph and Rena Marie (Calcagni) G.; m. Joyce Margaret Pawlak, Jan. 27, 1951; children: Margot Lynn, Doreen Rae, Richard John. *Wife Joyce, BA 1983, MA 1985 Edinboro, taught dance and communication for Allegheny College and Penn State Erie. Daughter Margot, BSED 1976, MED 1981 Edinboro, has co-authored several conference presentations on science teaching and is president of Richmond Area Speleological Society. Daughter Doreen, BS 1977 Indiana University of Pennsylvania, MED 1984 Cleveland State, is a principal at Cloverleaf High School, Lodi, Ohio. Son Richard, BA 1983 Wittenberg, JD 1986 Akron, is practicing law in the Lancaster/Harrisburg Pennsylvania area.* BA, Adelbert Coll., 1953; MA, Western Res. U., 1961; PhD, 1969. Salesman Beck Shoe Store, Parma, Ohio, 1946-48; cowboy Minor Cattle Ranch, Hyannis, Nebr., 1949; with classified advt. dept. Cleve. News, 1949-50; office mgr. Parma Cut Stone, 1950-60; part-time bookkeeper Cleve., 1960-64; acct., bookkeeper Broadview Savs. and Loan, Cleve., 1960-64; tchr., summer sch. dir. Brunswick (Ohio) High Sch., 1960-64; mem. faculty Edinboro U. of Pa., 1964-98, prof., dean faculty arts and scis. Author: British Historians and Their View of the British Policy of Appeasement, 1931-39, 1969; contrb. to Hist. Abstracts, 1972-98. Treas. Edinboro Found.; bd. dirs. Edinboro State Coll. United Cerebral Palsy Joint Coun.; past pres. Ams. for Competitive Enterprise System; pres. Tri-Boro Little League, 1979-89. Tuition scholar, 1949-55 Mem. NEA (life), AAUP, Am. Hist. Assn., N.Am. Conf. Brit. Studies, Phi Alpha Theta. Lutheran. *The standards one sets should be for oneself and not for others. Nor should one express a view on a controversial issue until one can understand why someone as sincere and honest as oneself can hold the opposite view.*

GROMOSIAK, PAUL, historian, consultant, writer, science and math educator; b. Niagara Falls, N.Y., Aug. 21, 1942; s. John and Anna (Rimanosky) G. BS in Chemistry, Niagara U., 1964. Chemist Eastman Kodak, Rochester, N.Y., 1965, Durez Plastics div. Occidental, North Tonawanda, N.Y., 1966-68; tchr. Niagara Falls Bd. Edn., 1969-89; author Western N.Y. Wares, Inc., Buffalo, 1990—. Guest lectr. Ctr. of Renewal, Stella Niagara, N.Y., 1991—. Author: Soaring Gulls and Bowing Trees, 1990, Answers to the 100 Most Common Questions About Niagara Falls, 1990, Zany Niagara, 1992, Sensing the Wonders of Niagara, 1994, Water Over the Falls, 1996, Daring Niagara, 1998, Nature's Niagara, 2000, Owahonton, Maid of the Mist, 2002, Goat Island, Niagara's Scenic Retreat, 2003. Vol. historian Schoellkopf Geol. Mus., Niagara Falls, 1984-90. Mem. Old Fort Niagara Assn. (life). Avocations: public speaking, gardening, hiking. Home: 5819 Grauer Rd Niagara Falls NY 14305-1455

GROMULTS, JOSEPH MICHAEL, JR., internist; b. Ansonia, Conn., Nov. 8, 1932; s. Joseph Michael and Mary Margaret (Marcelynas) G.; m. Paula Ruth Beeler Casella, July 6, 1967; 1 stepchild, Stephen. BA in History, Yale U., 1954; MD, NYU, 1958. Diplomate Am. Bd. Internal Medicine. Intern in medicine Bellevue Hosp., N.Y.C., 1958—59, resident in medicine, 1959—61; rsch. fellow NYU Sch. Medicine, N.Y. Heart Assn., 1961—62; pvt. practice Stamford, Conn., 1965—. Attending physician St. Joseph Hosp., Stamford, 1966-98, merged with Stamford Hosp., 1965-2002; clin. instr. medicine N.Y. Med. Coll., Valhalla, N.Y., 1970-97; clin. instr. medicine Columbia Med. Sch., 1997-2002. Capt. USAF, 1962-65. Mem. AMA, ACP, Conn. Med. Soc. (del. 1980-2000), Am. Legion. Republican. Roman Catholic. Avocations: gardening, handyman, music appreciation, travel. Home: 268 Golden Bear Dr Pawleys Island SC 29585-7351

GRONER, ISAAC NATHAN, lawyer; b. Buffalo, Oct. 22, 1919; s. Louis and Lena (Blinkoff) Groner; m. Estelle Kaye Groner, Sept. 14, 1941; children: Phyllis Gross, Robert, Lois. BA econ. and gen. studies with distinction, Cornell U., 1939; MA, NYU, 1942; LLB cum laude, Yale U., 1948. Bar: NY 1948, US Supreme Ct. 1953, DC 1954, US Ct. Appeals (DC cir.) 1954, Md. 1955. Law clk. Chief Justice Fred M. Vinson US Supreme Ct., Washington, 1948—50; chief counsel Wage Stblzn. Bd., Washington, 1951—53; pvt. practice Washington, 1953—64, 1990—2000; ptnr. Cole & Groner, P.C., Washington, 1964—90. Contbr. articles. Tech. sgt. U.S. Army, 1943—46. Mem.: Order of Coif, ABA (co-chmn. com. on law govt. employee rels. sect. labor rels. law 1962—64), Phi Kappa Phi, Phi Beta Kappa. Home: 3304 Wake Dr Kensington MD 20895-3217

GRONER, JONATHAN JACOB, periodical editor, freelance writer, lawyer; b. Trenton, N.J., Dec. 8, 1950; s. Oscar and Mildred (Shapiro) G.; m. Arlene Pianko, Aug. 17, 1975; children: Samuel, Daniel, Sarah. BA, Columbia Coll., N.Y.C., 1972; JD, Columbia U., 1975. Bar: D.C. 1975. Lawyer U.S. Dept. Justice, Washington, 1975-78, FTC, Washington, 1978-86; assoc. editor Legal Times, Washington, 1986-93, exec. editor D.C. Counsel Connect, 1994-95, sr. editor, 1995-97, mng. editor, 1997-99; editor Legaltimes.com, 1999-2000; editor-at-large Legal Times, 2000—. Adj. prof. dept. govt. Am. U., Washington, 1993-95; freelance book reviewer ABA Jour., Washington Post, Washington Times, Jewish Week, Moment, Balt. Jewish Times, The Forward, Salon.com. Author: Hilary's Trial: The Elizabeth Morgan Case, 1991. Bd. dirs. Hebrew Acad. Greater Washington, Silver Spring, Md., 1993-96, mem. bd. edn., 1999—. Avocation: tennis. Home: 807 Kersey Rd Silver Spring MD 20902-3003 Office: Legal Times 1730 M St NW Washington DC 20036-4505 E-mail: jgroner@legaltimes.com.

GRONLUND, ROBERT B. art collector, fund raising consultant; b. Duluth, Minn., May 2, 1926; s. Bernard S. and Lena J. (Manske) G.; m. Dorothy M. Dahlstrom, June 2, 1951; children: Gaye, Robin, Gregg, Jamie. BA, Wartburg Coll., Waverly, Iowa, 1949; MDiv, Wartburg Sem., Dubuque, 1953; LittD, Thiel Coll., Greenville, Pa., 1973. Ordained Luth. Ch., 1953. Pastor Newport Harbor Luth. Ch., Newport Beach, Calif., 1953-56; exec. dir. Inter Ch. Fellowship, L.A., 1956-59; asst. to pres. Calif. Luth. U., Thousand Oaks, Calif., 1959-62; exec. dir. Am. Luth. Ch. Found., Mpls., 1962-63; v.p. devel. Capital U., Columbus, Ohio, 1963-69, U. Tampa, Fla., 1969-76; founding ptnr. Gronlund Sayther Brunkow, West Palm Beach, Fla., 1976—; pres. Fla. campus Northwood U., West Palm Beach, 1981-83. Mem. works of art com. Norton Mus., West Palm Beach, 1993-96; chair PBCC Art Gallery, Palm Beach Gardens, Fla., 1995-96; chair Tampa Bay Art Ctr., Tampa, 1973-74; chair Vision for Mission Com., Evang. Luth. Ch. Am., Chgo., 1995-99. Exhibited collection at Norton Mus., Pensacola Mus., Tampa Mus., Wartburg Coll., Lighthouse Gallery, Tequesta, Fla., Ctr. for Arts, Vero Beach, Fla., others. Chair Fla. Repertory Theater, West Palm Beach, 1990—92; founding pres. Planned Giving Coun., West Palm Beach, 1982—84; sr. warden Bethesda By Sea Episcopal Ch., 1995; founding chair S.E. Diocese Episcopal Found., 1999—2002. Cpl. U.S. Army, 1943—46, ETO. Mem.: Men Bethesda (chmn. 2002—). Republican. Episcopalian. Avocations: golf, travel, grandchildren. Home: 2320 Saratoga Bay Dr West Palm Beach FL 33409-7222 E-mail: bobgronlund@gsbfr.com.

GROOM, DIANE V. not-for-profit developer; b. Providence, Aug. 16, 1954; d. Daniel Marland, Jr. and Shirley Anne Swailes; m. Larry Willis Martin Grooms, Oct. 13, 1984; 1 child, Robert Marland Grooms. BA, San Jose State U., 1982; MBA, U. Redlands, 1992. Cert. fund-raising exec. Nat. Soc. Fund-Raising Execs. Sect. editor Salinas Calif., 1978—83; ptnr., owner PR Plus, Salinas, 1983—87; devel. assoc. Antelope Valley Hosp., Lancaster, Calif., 1987—92; regional v.p. United Way Greater L.A., 1992—. Bd. mem. Mental Health Assn. Adv. Bd., Lancaster, Calif., 2001—03. Mem. bond oversight com. Lancaster Sch. Dist., Calif., 2000—03; past pres. Rotary Internat., Lancaster, 2002. Office: United Way 42442 10th St West A Lancaster CA 93534

GROOM, ROBERT CRAIG, perfusionist; b. Sewickley, Pa.A, Jan. 1, 1956; s. John Wilson and Ann Marie Groom; m. Holly Marple Groom, June 17, 1978; children: Zachary, Sarah, Jesse, Hannah, Jacob. BSc, Geneva Coll., 1977; attended, Tex. Heart Inst. Sch. of Perfusion Tech., 1981, Dartmouth Med. Sch. Ctr. for the Evaluative Clin. Sci., 2002—. Cert. Clinical Perfusionist Am. Bd. Cardiovascular Perfusionists, 1981. Asst. chief perfusionist The Va. Heart Ctr., Falls Church, Va., 1987—95; chief perfusionist Maine Med. Ctr., Portland, Maine, 1996—. Clinical instr. Northeastern U, Boston, 1996—, SUNY, Syracuse, NY, 2001—, Quinnipac U., Hamden, Conn., 2000—; course dir. Soc. Cardiovascular Anesthesia, Richmond, Va., 2000—; bd. dir. Maine Med. Ctr. IRB, Portland; adv. bd. Perfusion Rsch. Edn. Found., 1997—2001. Contbr. chapters to books, articles to profl. jours.; mem. editl. adv. bd. : Jour. Extracorporeal Tech., 1999—; mem. editl. adv. bd. Perfusion, 1996—. Bd. dir. Calvary Ch. of the Nazarene, Annandale, 1985—92, Cmty. of Hope Ch., Washington, 1993—96, treas., 1994—96, Calvary Ch. of the Nazarene, Annandale, 1985—92. Mem.: Am. Acad. of Cardiovascular Perfusion (sec. 1989—96, pres. 2000—01). Office: Maine Medical Center 22 Bramhall Street Portland ME 04102 Business E-Mail: groomr@mmc.org.

GROOMS, HENRY RANDALL, civil engineer; b. Cleve., Feb. 10, 1944; s. Leonard Day and Lois (Pickell) G.; m. Tonie Marie Joseph; children: Catherine, Zayne, Nina, Ivan, Ian, Athesis, Shaneya, Yaphet, Rahsan, Dax, Jevay, Xava. BSCE, Howard U., 1965; MSCE, Carnegie-Mellon U., 1967, PhD, 1969. Hwy. engr. D.C. Hwy. Dept., Washington, 1965; structural engr. Peter F. Loftus Corp., Pitts., 1966; structural engr., engring. mgr. Rockwell Internat. (now Boeing), Downey, Calif., 1969—. Contbr. articles to profl. jours. Scoutmaster Boy Scouts Am., Granada Hills, Calif., 1982-87; basketball coach Valley Conf., Granada Hills, 1984—; coach Am. Youth Soccer Orgn., Granada Hills, 1985-90, 94—; tutor Watts Friendship Sports League, 1989—; co-founder Project Reach Scholarship Found., 1993. Recipient Alumni Merit award Carnegie-Mellon U., 1985; named Honoree Black History Project Western Res. Hist. Soc., 1989. Fellow Inst. Advancement Engring. (Outstanding Engring. Vol. award, 1999), African Sci. Inst.; mem. ASCE, Tau Beta Pi, Sigma Xi. Office: Boeing Mail Code H013-C326 5301 Bolsa Ave Huntington Beach CA 92647-2099 E-mail: henry.r.grooms@boeing.com.

GROOS, ARTHUR BERNHARD, JR., German literature and music educator; b. Fullerton, Calif., Feb. 5, 1943; s. Arthur Bernhard and Nancy Elizabeth (Stowe) G.; m. Bonnie Cleo Buettner, May 16, 1979; children: Peter, Jan. AB magna cum laude, Princeton U., 1964; MA, Cornell U., Ithaca, N.Y., 1966; PhD, Cornell U., 1970; postgrad., Freie Universitat Berlin, 1966-67. Asst. prof. UCLA, 1969-73; asst. prof. German lit. Cornell U., 1973-76, assoc. prof., 1976-82, prof., 1982—, dir. medieval studies, 1974-86, chmn. dept. German studies, 1986-91, 96-99. Chmn. German dept. adv. coun. Princeton U., N.J., 1981-85; vis. prof. U. Paderborn, W.Ger., 1982, Freie U. Berlin, 2001-02; bd. dirs. Centro Studi Giacomo Puccini (Lucca). Author: Puccini: La Boheme, 1986, Romancing the Grail, 1995; co-author: Medieval Christian Literary Imagery, 1988; editor: Dichtkunst und Lebenkunst, 1981, Magister Regis, 1986, Reading Opera, 1988, Cambridge Opera Jour., 1988-98, Studi pucciniani, 1998—, Perceval/Parzival, 2002; gen. editor: Cambridge Opera Monographs. Fulbright fellow Berlin, 1966, Fulbright sr. fellow Munich, 1979, Guggenheim fellow Munich, 1979; recipient ASCAP-Deems Taylor prize, 1993, Humboldt Rsch. prize 1999. Mem. MLA, Internat. Arthurian Soc., Medieval Acad. Am., Wolfram v. Eschenbach Gesellschaft, Internat. Courtly Lit. Soc., Am. Musicol. Soc., Phi Beta Kappa. Home: 492 Valley Rd Brooktondale NY 14817-9701 Office: Cornell U Dept German Studies 185 Goldwin Smith Hall Ithaca NY 14853-3201

GROPMAN, SAUL I. music educator; b. L.A., Mar. 12, 1955; s. Paul Aron and Helen Gropman; m. Anne Katharina Moller-Racke, May 26, 1995; children: Dorothe, Louis, Hannah. MusB, Manhattan Sch. Music, 1978, MusM, 1980; studied with Andres Segovia, 1980—81. Lectr. in music Calif. State U., Sacramento, 1983—85, San Francisco State U., 1986—, artistic dir., Morrison Artists Series, 1989—. Adv. bd. Sonoma Valley Mus. Art, 1999—; judge Irving H. Klein Internat. String Competition, San Francisco, 1992, San Francisco, 94. Recording artist Soundings: Music for Classical Guitar, 1984. Office: San Francisco State U Sch Music and Dance 1600 Holloway Ave San Francisco CA 94132 E-mail: sgropman@sfsu.edu.

GROPP, LOUIS OLIVER, editor-in-chief; b. LaPorte, Ind., June 6, 1935; s. Hosea Howard and Carol Gladys (Pagel) G.; m. Jane Margaret Goodwin, Aug. 15, 1965; children: Amy Alison Forbes, Lauren Elizabeth Lowry. BA in Communication Arts, Mich. State U., 1957. Design editor Home Furnishings Daily, Chgo. and N.Y.C., 1960-67; v.p. Milo Baughman Design, Wellesley, Mass., 1967; exec. editor House & Garden Guides, Conde Nast Co., N.Y.C., 1968-72, editor-in-chief, 1973—80, House and Garden mag., N.Y.C., 1981-88; v.p. design and creative svcs., consumer products div. Westpoint-Pepperell, N.Y.C., 1988-89; editor in chief Elle Decor, Hachette Pub. co., N.Y.C., 1990-91; editor-in-chief House Beautiful, Hearst Mags. Div., N.Y.C., 1991-2000. Author: Solar Houses, 1978. Chmn. bd. deacons Riverside Ch., N.Y.C., 1973-75; pres. bd. Christianity and Crisis, 1988-90; bd. dirs. Am. Soc. Mag. Editors, 1990-94, N.Y. Theol. Sem., 1999—, N.Y. Sch. Interior Design, N.Y.C., 2001—, Long House Res., Easthampton, N.Y., 2001—. Home: 140 Riverside Dr Apt 6G New York NY 10024-2605 also: 44 Old Depot Rd Quogue NY 11959 E-mail: lougropp@earthlink.com.

GROPPER, ALLAN LOUIS, bankruptcy judge; BA, Yale U., 1965; JD, Harvard U., 1969. Bar: N.Y. 1969, U.S. Dist. Ct. (so. and ea. dists.) N.Y. 1971, U.S. Ct. Appeals (2d cir.) 1971, U.S. Supreme Ct. 1974. Atty. Civil Appeals Bur., Legal Aid Soc., N.Y.C., 1969-71; assoc. White & Case, N.Y.C., 1972-77, ptnr., 1978-2000; bankruptcy judge U.S. Bankruptcy Ct., N.Y.C., 2000—. Adj. prof. Fordham Law Sch., 2003—. Bd. dirs. Browning Sch., 1990—, pres., 1997-2000; bd. dirs. Legal Aid Soc., 1990-2000, v.p., 1996-2000; bd. dirs. N.Y. Lawyers for Pub. Interest, 1990-2000. Mem. ABA, Assn. of Bar of City of N.Y. (v.p. 1995-96, mem. exec. com. 1991-96, chmn. 1994-95), N.Y. State Bar Assn. Office: US Bankruptcy Ct Alexander Hamilton Custom House 1 Bowling Green New York NY 10004

GROPPER, DANIEL MICHAEL, college assistant dean, business educator; b. Takoma Park, Md., June 3, 1959; s. Bernard Adolph and Roberta Gropper; m. Sareen Stepnick, July 31, 1982; children: Michelle Lauren, Michael James. BA, U. Md., 1981; MS, Fla. State U., 1985, PhD, 1989. Planning/rsch. economist Fla. Pub. Svc. Com., Tallahassee, 1984; economist Econ. Rsch. Svc. (ERS) Inc., Tallahassee, 1985-88; from instr. to asst. prof. Auburn (Ala.) U., 1988-94, assoc. prof., 1994—, dir. MBA programs, 1995-99, asst. dean, exec. dir. MBA program, 1999—. Cons. Conn. Atty. Gen., Hartford, 1995-96, Sabel & Sabel, LLP, Montgomery, Ala., 1995-96, Ala. Power Co., Birmingham, 1990. Contbr. articles to profl. jours. Recipient Outstanding Prof. award Auburn Panhellenic Coun., 1995; Fed. Home Loan Bank grantee, 1989-90; Richard Weaver fellow Intercoll. Studies, Wilmington, Del., 1985-86. Mem. Assn. Grad. Bus. Dirs. (sec., v.p. 1995-97), Am. Econ. Assn., So. Fin. Assn., Phi Kappa Phi, Beta Gamma Sigma, Mensa. Republican. Avocations: golf, fishing. Office: Auburn U Coll Bus 415 W Magnolia Ste 503 Auburn AL 36849

GROSBARD, ULU, director; b. Antwerp, Belgium, Jan. 9, 1929; came to U.S., 1948; s. Morris and Rose (Tennenbaum) G.; m. Rose Gregorio, Feb. 25, 1965 BA, U. Chgo., 1950, MA, 1952; postgrad., Yale U. Sch. Drama, 1952-53. Dir. plays The Days and Nights of Beebeem, 1962, The Subject Was Roses, 1964 (Tony nomination 1965), A View from the Bridge, 1965 (Obie award 1965), The Investigation, 1966, The Price, 1968, American Buffalo, 1977 (Tony nominations), The Woods, 1980, The Floating Light Bulb, 1981, Weekends Like Other People, 1982, The Wake of Jamie Foster, 1982, The Tenth Man, 1989, Family Week, 2000; (films) The Subject Was Roses, 1968, Who is Harvey Kellerman, 1971, Straight Time, 1978, True Confessions, 1981, Falling in Love, 1984, Georgia, 1994, The Deep End of the Ocean, 1999. Served with U.S. Army, 1953-55 Mem. Dirs. Guild Am., Soc. Dirs. and Choreographers Jewish.

GROSCH, LAURA DUDLEY, artist, teacher, consultant; b. Worcester, Mass., Apr. 1, 1945; d. Daniel Swartwood and Edith Dudley (Taft) G. BA in Art History, Wellesley Coll., 1967; BFA in Painting, U. Pa., 1968. Solo exhbns. include Mint Mus. Art, Charlotte, N.C., 1974, Jerald Melberg Gallery, Charlotte, 1984, 87, Greenville (N.C.) Mus. Art, 1987, Greenville County Mus. Art, 1987, Christa Faut Gallery, Davidson, N.C., 1990, 93, 96, Rock Sch. Arts Found., Valdese, N.C., 2000, Millennium exhbn., Valdese, 2000, others; group exhbns. include Impressions Gallery, Boston, 1973, Rose Mus. Glenbow-Alberta Gallery, Can., 1974, New Orleans Mus. Art, 1975, Bklyn. Mus., 1976, Visual Arts Ctr. Alaska, 1978, Print Club, Phila., 1980, Palazzo Venezia, Rome, 1984, Syracuse U., N.Y., 1987, Wellesley (Mass.)Coll., 1997, Mint Mus., Charlotte, N.C., 2002, Christa Faut Gallery, Cornelius, N.C., 2003; represented in pub. collections Boston Pub. Libr., Brit. Mus., London, Bklyn. Mus., Fla. State U., Manhattan Coll., Mus. Fine Arts, Boston, N.Y. Pub. Libr., Ringling Mus., Sarasota, Fla., Smithsonian Inst., Washington, UCLA, Newark Pub. Libr., Minn. Inst. Arts, Honolulu Acad. Arts, Dayton (Ohio) Art Inst., Carnegie Mellon U., Pitts., Free Libr. Phila., Victoria and Albert Mus., London, many others. Office: PO Box 10 497 S Main St Davidson NC 28036-8006

GRÖSCHEL, DIETER HANS MAX, physician, educator; b. Würzburg, Germany, May 13, 1931; came to U.S., 1963, naturalized, 1969; s. Friedrich Wilhelm and Anne (Burger) G.; m. A. Margarete Pustelny, June 9, 1958; chldren: Anne, Henrike. Med Grad., U. Würzburg, Erlangen, Cologne, 1957; MD, U. Cologne, 1958. Intern U. Cologne, 1957-59, resident, 1959-60, assoc. instr. Inst. Hygiene, 1960-63; assoc. Wistar Inst., Phila., 1963-65; assoc. prof. microbiology Temple U., 1965-68; dir. microbiology and infectious diseases Baystate Med. Ctr., Springfield, Mass., 1968-71; prof. pathology U. Tex./M.D. Anderson Hosp. and Tumor Inst., Houston, 1971-79; assoc. prof. medicine and pathology U. Tex. Med. Sch., Houston, 1973-79; mem. staff Hermann Hosp., Houston, 1973-79; prof. pathology and medicine U. Va. Med. Ctr., Charlottesville, 1979-96, prof. emeritus, 1996—. Served with Deutscher Volkssturm, 1945. Fulbright scholar U. Colo., 1954-55. Fellow Am. Acad. Microbiology, Infectious Diseases Soc. Am.; mem. Am. Soc. Microbiology, Fedn. Am. Scientists. Home: 150 Terrell Rd E Charlottesville VA 22901-2165 E-mail: dhg@virginia.edu.

GROSCOST, JEFF, former state legislator, small business owner; b. Tooele, Utah, Apr. 29, 1961; m. Dana Groscost; 5 children. Student, Ariz. State U., Mesa C.C., Brigham Young U. Mem. Ariz. Ho. of Reps., 1993—2001, past chmn. ways and means com., past mem. appropriations com., past mem. block grants com., past mem. joint legis. budget com., past mem. joint legis. tax com., past majority whip, past chmn. apropriations sub-com. gen. gov., past chmn. states rights and mandates com., former spkr. house. Gem broker; mem. adv. bd. Gov.'s Motion Picture and TV. Bd. dirs. S.W. Shakespeare Fest., bd. mem., vol. youth coach Mesa Family YMCA, East Valley, Mesa So. Little League; bd. dirs. Mesa United Way; exec. bd. mem. Grand Canyon Coun. of the Boy Scouts Am, Mem. State Bd. Chartered Schs., Constl. Def. Coun. Mem. Lds Ch.

GROSE, ANDREW PETER, foundation executive; b. Washington, July 16, 1940; s. Peter Andrew and Mildred (Holston) G.; m. Jacqueline Stamm, Aug. 17, 1963; children: Peter Andrew II, Tracey Christine. BS with high honors, U. Md., 1962, MA, 1964. Mem. legis. staff Fla. Ho. of Reps., Tallahassee, 1972-74; rsch. dir. Nev. Legislature, Carson City, 1974-83; chief of staff Office of Gov. Nev., Carson City, 1983-84, dir. econ. devel., 1984-90; dir. Western region Coun. of State Govt., San Francisco, 1990-95; pres. Westrends, 1990-95; CEO Pub. Policy Inst. Calif., 1995—. Mem. exec. com. Nat. Conf. State Legislatures, Denver, 1982-83; bd. dirs. Am. Lung Assn., San Francisco and San Mateo Counties. Author: Florida Model City Charter, 1974, The West Comes of Age: Hard Times, Hard Choices, The West on a Slippery Slope, High Growth, Low Pay; mem. editl. bd. Nev. Rev. of Bus. and Econs., Reno, 1976-90. Bd. dirs. African Am. Shakespeare Co., 2002—. Capt. USAF, 1964-70, to brig. gen., Res. Mem. Air Force Assn., Res. Officers Assn., Nat. Assn. State Devel. Agys. (1st v.p.), Western Govt. Rsch. Assn. (pres. 1993-95), Kiwanis (pres. 1981-82, bd. dirs. 1994-97, treas. 1997-2000, pres. 2001-2002). Democrat. Home: 405 Hazelwood Ave San Francisco CA 94127-2129 Office: Public Policy Inst Calif 500 Washington St Ste 800 San Francisco CA 94111-2934 E-mail: grose@ppic.org.

GROSE, CHARLES FREDERICK, pediatrician, infectious disease specialist; b. Faribault, Minn., Apr. 15, 1942; s. Frederick G. and Marie A. (Swelland) G. BA, Beloit Coll., 1963; MD, U. Chgo., 1967. Bd. cert. in pediatric infectious disease. Resident Albert Einstein Coll. Medicine, Bronx, N.Y., 1967-68, fellow, 1970—75, U. Calif., San Francisco, 1975-76; asst. prof. Health Sci. Ctr. U. Tex., San Antonio, 1976-84; prof. pediatrics U. Iowa Hosp., Iowa City, 1985—. Cons. NIH, Bethesda, Md., 1988—. Editor Pediat. Infectious Disease Jour., 2003—; mem. editl. bd. Virology Jour.; contbr. articles to profl. and sci. jours. Capt. U.S. Army Med. Corps., Vietnam, 1968-70. Grantee NIH, 1978—. Fellow Infectious Disease Soc. Am., Pediatric Infectious Disease Soc., Am. Acad. Pediatrics, Am. Soc. Virology. Achievements include research on diagnosis and treatment of chickenpox and shingles, and on the etiologic agent which is varicella virus. Office: U Iowa Hosp Pediatrics 200 Hawkins Dr Iowa City IA 52242-1009 E-mail: charles-grose@uiowa.edu.

GROSE, WILLIAM RUSH, publishing executive; b. Charleston, W.Va., Jan. 29, 1939; s. William Ellis and Mary W. (Morrison) G. Grad., Haverford Coll., 1961. With Prentice-Hall, Inc., Englewood Cliffs, N.J., 1962-70, Warner Communications, Inc., N.Y.C., 1970-72; editor-in-chief Dell Pub. Co., Inc., N.Y.C., 1972-79; v.p., pub. Jove Publs., Inc., N.Y.C., 1979-81; v.p., editorial dir. Berkeley/Jove Pub. Group, 1981-82; v.p., editor-in-chief New Am. Library Inc., 1982-83; exec. v.p., editorial dir. Pocket Books, 1983—. Mem.: Knickerbocker; Groucho (London). Democrat. Episcopalian. Home: 929 Park Ave New York NY 10028-0211 also: 128 Blackville Rd Washington CT 06794-1209 Office: Simon and Schuster Ste 383 1230 Avenue Of The Americas Fl Conc1 New York NY 10020-1586

GROSECLOSE, EVERETT HARRISON, retired editor; b. Childress, Tex., June 25, 1938; s. Everett Jackson and Eula Margaret (Snider) G.; m. Edna Kathryn Hunter, Dec. 24, 1962 (div. 1986); children: Kirsten Lee, Megan Margaret; m. Susan Kahne Greer, Dec. 22, 1990. BA in Journalism, Tex. Tech. U., Lubbock, 1961. Reporter Wall St. Jour., Dallas and N.Y.C., 1965-70; asst. mng. editor Cleve., 1970-76; dir. pub. affairs Dow Jones & Co., N.Y.C., 1976-80; mng. editor Dow Jones News Services, N.Y.C., 1980-88; exec. editor Dow Jones Profl. Investor Report, N.Y.C., 1988-92; dir. product devel. Dow Jones Info. Services, N.Y.C., 1988-92; dir. internat. mktg., news and database svcs. Telerate, Inc. subs. Dow Jones, N.Y.C., 1992-94; mng. editor Dow Jones Emerging Markets Report, N.Y.C., 1994-97, Servicio Dow Jones Americas, N.Y.C., 1996-97; founder Internet Pub. Group, Inc. (formerly VertiNews.com, Inc.), 1999—. Served with AUS, 1961-64. Decorated Army Commendation medal. Unitarian Universalist. Home: 57 Goodnight Trl E Santa Fe NM 87506-7925 E-mail: egroseclose@starband.net.

GROSECLOSE, WANDA WESTMAN, retired elementary school educator; b. Clarks, Nebr., Oct. 5, 1933; m. B. Clark Groseclose; children: D. Kim, Byron C. Jr., Eric P., A. Glenn. B degree, Brigham Young U., 1976; M in Tchg., St. Mary's Coll., Moraga, Calif., 1981. Cert. tchr., Calif. 5th grade tchr. Brentwood (Calif.) Union Sch. Dist., 1977-97; ret. Art tchr., mentor tchr. Contra Costa County Program of Excellence. Author: American Music in Time, 1992, In the Shadow of Our Ancestors, 2003, The Lees of Southwest Virginia, 2003. Human rels. bd. dirs. City of Livermore, 1968—70. Republican. Mem. Lds Ch. Avocations: oil painting, sewing, gardening, genealogy. Home: 83 Payne Ave Brentwood CA 94513-4701 E-mail: grosclose@ecis.com.

GROSENHEIDER, DELNO JOHN, lawyer; b. Litchfield, Ill., Feb. 10, 1935; s. Junas Louis Henry and Esther O'Neil (Knabel) G.; m. Margaret Noel Adams, Aug. 30, 1959; children— John Stephen, Michael Del. Student So. Ill. U., 1953-54; B.A., U. Tex., 1961, LL.B., 1964. Bar: Tex. 1963, U.S. Dist. Ct. (we. dist.) Tex., 1966, U.S. Ct. Appeals (5th cir.) 1985, U.S. Supreme Ct., 1986. Atty. Tex. Securities Bd., Austin, 1964-66, House, Mercer, House & Brock, Austin, 1966-77; ptnr. Wilson, Grosenheider & Burns, Austin, 1977—. Judge, City of Rollingwood, Tex., 1968; city atty. City of Rollingwood, 1969; mem. Bd. of Adjustment, City of Rollingwood, 1975-84. Mem. State Bar of Tex., Travis County Bar Assn., Tex. Assn. Def. Counsel, Def. Rsch. Inst., Internat. Assn. Ins. Counselors, Met. Club. Republican. Episcopalian. Home: 3005 Stratford Dr Austin TX 78746-4650 Office: 400 W 15th St Ste 1100 Austin TX 78701-1674

GROSFELD, JAY LAZAR, surgeon, educator; b. N.Y.C., May 30, 1935; m. Margie Faulkner; children: Lisa, Denise, Janice, Jeffrey, Mark. AB cum laude, NYU, 1957, MD, 1961. Diplomate Am. Bd. Surgery (spl. qualification Pediatric Surgery). Intern in gen. surgery dept. surgery Bellevue and Univ Hosps. NYU, N.Y.C., 1961—62; resident in gen. surgery Bellevue and Univ. Hosps. NYU, N.Y.C., 1962—66; resident in pediatric surgery Ohio State U. Coll. Medicine, Children's Hosp., 1968—70; instr. surgery Ohio State U. Coll. Medicine, 1968—70; clin. instr. surgery NYU Sch. Medicine, N.Y.C., 1965—66, asst. prof. surgery and pediatrics, 1970—72; prof., dir. pediatric surgery Ind. U. Sch. Medicine, Indpls., 1972—. Lafayette F. Page prof., 1981—, chmn. Dept. Surgery, 1985—; surgeon-in-chief James Whitcomb Riley Hosp. Children. Author: Common Problems in Pediatric Surgery, 1991, Central Surgical

Association: The First 50 Years, 1991, Progress in Pediatric Trauma, 1992, Essentials of Pediatric Surgery, 1995, Pediatric Surgery, 5th edit., 1998, The Surgery of Childhood Tumors, 1999; contbr. ; editor-in-chief : Jour. Pediat. Surgery; editor: Seminars in Pediat. Surgery. Capt. M.C. U.S. Army, 1966—68. Recipient Commendation medal, recipient numerous fellowships, grants, teaching awards. Fellow: ACS (bd. govs. 1985—91), Royal Coll. Physicians and Surgeons Glasgow, Am. Acad. Pediats. (exec. com. surg. sect. 1989—95, chmn. surg. sect. 1994—95, sec. surg. sect., Ladd medal 2002—), Royal Coll. Surgeons of Eng. (hon.); mem.: AMA, Halsted Soc. (v.p. 1995—96, pres. 1996—97), Accreditation Coun. Grad. Med. Edn. (vice chair surg. residency rev. com. 2000—01), Am. Bd. Med. Specialities, World Fedn. Assns. Pediat. Surgeons (pres. 1998—2001, v.p.), Am. Bd. Surgery (bd. dirs. 1989—97, vice chair 1995, chmn. 1996—97, chmn.-elect), Am. Pediatric Surg. Assn. Found. (chmn. bd. dirs.), Internat. Soc. Surgery (sec., treas. Internat. Soc. Surgery Found. 2001—), Western Surg. Assn. (pres. 1997—98), Soc. Surg. Oncology, Brit. Assn. Pediat. Surgeons (exec. coun. 1990—93, Denis Browne Gold medal 1998), Ctrl. Surg. Assn. (sec. 1987—, pres.-elect 1988, pres. 1990), Soc. Surgery Alimentary Tract, Am. Trauma Soc., Ind. State Med. Assn., Marion County Med. Soc., Soc. Univ. Surgeons, Am. Surg. Assn., Am. Pediat. Surg. Assn. (pres. 1994—95, bd. govs., pres.-elect), N.Y. Cancer Soc., Assn. Acad. Surgery, Pediat. Surgery Biology Club, Alpha Omega Alpha, Phi Beta Kappa. Office: J W Riley Childrens Hosp 702 Barnhill Dr Rm 2500 Indianapolis IN 46202-5128 also: Ind U Med Ctr Dept Surgery 545 Barnhill Dr Dept Surgery Indianapolis IN 46202-5112 Office Fax: 317-274-5777. E-mail: jgrosfel@iupui.edu.

GROSHNER, MARIA STAR, nuclear engineer; b. Las Vegas, Nev., Aug. 31, 1961; d. Robert Leroy and Stepheny (Higby) Groshner; m. Robert Clay Singleterry, Jr., May 18, 1984. BS in Nuc. Engring., U. Ariz., 1984. Engr. in tng., Idaho. Reactor operator EG&G Idaho, Inc., Idaho Falls, 1985-89, engr., 1989-90, sr. engr., 1990-91; export control reviewer EG&G Idaho Inc., Idaho Falls, 1990-91; engr. III Westinghouse Idaho Nuc. Co., Idaho Falls, 1991-92, sr. engr. I, 1992-94; prin. engr., safety analyst Lockheed Martin Idaho Techs. Co., Idaho Falls, 1994-96, staff engr., 1996-97; prin. mem. Quantum Solutions LLC, 1995-96; sr. engr. BWX Techs., Inc., Lynchburg, Va., 1999—. Sci-by-mail mentor, 1998—2000. Mem. Citizen Energy Alert Network Nuc. Energy Inst., Washington, 1987—96; mem. Planned Parenthood, 1992—96. Mem.: Soc. Women Engrs. (chpt. sect. rep. 1990—91, treas. 1993—96, v.p. southeastern Idaho chpt. 1989, coord. young women's conf. 1990), Am. Nuc. Soc. (media rels. chmn. Idaho chpt. 1990, comm. 2001), Toastmasters Internat. (chpt. pres. 1990, chpt. pres. Lynchburg unit 2000, adminstrv. v.p. Jack C. High unit 1989, v.p. pub. rels. 1995, Competent Toastmaster, Able Toastmaster), U.S. Golf Assn. Avocations: aviation, golf, camping, handcrafts, communications. Home: 407 Chadwick Drive Lynchburg VA 24502- Office: BWX Techs Inc PO Box 785 Lynchburg VA 24505-0785

GROSHOLZ, EMILY ROLFE, philosophy educator, poet; b. Phila., Oct. 17, 1950; d. Edwin DeHaven and Frances Skerrett Grosholz; m. Robert Roy Edwards, Jan. 2, 1987; children: Benjamin, Robert, William, Mary-Frances. BA, U. Chgo., 1972; PhD in Philosophy, Yale U., 1978. Fellow Nat. Humanities Ctr., Research Triangle Park, N.C., 1985-86; sr. rsch. fellow Inst. History & Philosophy of Sci. & Tech. U. Toronto, Can., 1988-89; assoc. Ctr. for Philosophy of Sci. U. Pitts., 1992—. Adj. assoc. prof. dept. philosophy U. Pa., Phila., 1992; prof. philosophy Pa. State U., University Park, 1993—, affiliate African and African-Am. studies, 1997—, fellow Inst. for the Arts and Humanities, 1995—; mem. poets' prize com. Nicholas Rsch. Mus., N.Y.C., 1993—. Author: Cartesian Method and the Problem of Reduction, 1991, Eden, 1992, The Abacus of Years, 2002; co-author: Leibniz's Science of the Rational, 1998; adv. editor: The Hudson Rev., 1984—, mem. editl. bd.: Jour. History of Ideas, 1998—, Studia Leibnitiana, 2001—. Fellow Nat. Humanities Ctr., 1985-86, Guggenheim Found., 1988-89, Am. Coun. Learned Socs., 1997; Transatlantic Cooperation Rsch. grantee Alexander von Humboldt Found., 1994-97. Mem. Am. Philos. Assn., Leibniz Soc. N.Am., Leibniz Assn., Clare Hall U. Cambridge (life), Philosophy Sci. Assn. Democrat. Episcopalian. Home: 116 Kennedy St State College PA 16801-7805 Office: Pa State Univ Dept Philosophy 240 Sparks Bldg University Park PA 16802 E-mail: erg2@psu.edu.

GROSKOPF, AUBREY BUD, motion picture television executive, lawyer; b. Milw. s. George Norman and Rose (Becker) G.; 1 child, James E. BS, U. Wis., 1952, LLB, 1956. Bar: Wis. 1957. Dir. bus. affairs CBS-TV Network, N.Y.C., 1958-73; exec. v.p. Four Star Internat., L.A., 1973-76; pres. Republic Pictures Corp., L.A., 1976-87; ind. motion picture and TV prodr., 1987—. Prodr. motion picture Boys of Paul Street, 1969 (Best Fgn. Film award 1969); writer, prodr., dir. TV spl. and video A Norman Rockwell Christmas, 1994; creator Tales of Edgar Allan Poe, 1998. 1st lt. U.S. Army, 1952-54, Korea. Decorated Bronze Star. Mem. NATAS, Acad. Motion Picture Arts and Scis. E-mail: aubrey@roskopf.webtv.

GROSLAND, EMERY LAYTON, banker; b. Holden, Alta., Can., July 19, 1929; s. Arne and Lillie Olivetta (Jacobson) G.; m. Margaret Grace Woodward, Sept. 3, 1952; 1 child, Roberta Jayne Student pub. schs., Holden; student Amos Tuck Sch. Exec Program, Dartmouth Coll., 1980. With The Royal Bank of Can., 1949—, sr. v.p., 1983—, ret., 1987. Cons. in field. Mem.: N. Halton Golf and Country. Avocation: golf.

GROSMAN, ALAN M. lawyer; b. Mar. 13, 1935; s. Charles M. and Grace (Fishman) G.; m. Bette Bloomenthal, Dec. 27, 1967; children, Ellen, Carol. BA, Wesleyan U., 1956; MA, Yale U., 1957; JD, N.Y. Law Sch., 1965. Bar: N.J. 1965, U.S. Dist. Ct. N.J. 1965, U.S. Supreme Ct. 1969. Ptnr. Grosman & Grosman and predecessors, Millburn, N.J., 1965—; asst. prosecutor Essex County, N.J., 1968-69; prosecutor Millburn, 1981—. Mem. family practice com. NJ Supreme Ct., 1984—88, mem. dispute resolution task force, 1987—88, mem. com. on women in the cts., 1991—93; chmn. NJ Trade Coun., 1975—77, dir., 1978—; adj. prof. family law Rutgers U. Sch. Law, 2002—; lectr. in field. Author: New Jersey Family Law, 1999, with supplement, 2003; reporter: New Haven Jour., 1959—60, Newark Evening News, 1961—62; contbr. articles to profl. jours. Mem. ABA (chmn. alimony, maintenance and support com. family law sect. 1983-87, editor ABA Family Law Quar. 1993—), N.J. State Bar Assn. (exec. editor N.J. Family Lawyer 1980-91, mem. exec. com. family law sect. 1980—, chmn. sect. 1987-88, appellate practice com. 1995—), Am. Acad. Matrimonial Lawyers (pres. N.J. chpt. 1983-85, nat. bd. govs. 1984-88, editor Jour. AAML 1980-90), Essex County Bar Assn. (chmn. family law com. 1970-72), N.Y. Law Sch. Alumni Assn. (bd. dirs. 1988-98), Millburn-Short Hills Rep. Club, Inc. (counsel 1988—), Phi Beta Kappa. Address: 75 Main St Ste 205 Millburn NJ 07041-1322

GROS-PIETRO, GIAN MARIA, economics educator; b. Turin, Italy, Feb. 4, 1942; Degree in econs., U. Turin. Tchr. prodn. econs. Sch. Indsl. Adminstrn. U. Turin, 1965-72, prof. indsl. econs., 1974—, full prof. indsl. policy and econs., 1994—. Rschr. CERIS-Istituto di Ricerca sull'Impresa e lo Sviluppo, Nat. Rsch. Coun., 1965-72, dir., 1977-95; coord. plan for instrumental mechs. Ministry of Industry, Italy, 1977-80; econ. cons. Italian Union Machine Tool Constructors, 1983; mng. dir. Fincimu, 1983-85; rep. Ministry Public Investment; mem. various sci. couns.; v.p. sci. com. Nomisma; chmn., CEO IRI, 1997-99; chmn. ENI, 1999-2002, Autostrade, 2002—. Author numerous texts in field. Bd. dirs. U. Turin, 1985—96. Mem. Soc. Italiana degli Economisti. Office: 4 Piano Corso Unione Sovietica 218 bis I-10134 Turin Italy

GROSS, ALAN ELLIS, psychologist, educator, researcher, mediator, consultant; b. Detroit, Mar. 5, 1936; s. Carl J. and Mamie Ellis Gross; m. Sarah Miller Davies, Dec. 30, 1990; children: Molly Bianca, Matthew Terry, Elise Adrianna Quagliata, Justin Michael Quagliata. BS, Purdue U., 1959; MBA, Stanford U., 1962, PhD, 1967. Prof. psychology various univs. including U. Mo., U. Wis., U. Calif. Irvine and Ohio State U., 1966—77; dir. Office of Social and Ethical Responsibility, APA, Washington, 1977—78; prof., chair dept. psychology U. Md., College Park, 1978—86; pres. Best Price Enterprises, Inc., N.Y.C., 1979—; disaster vol. and mediation coord. Safe Horizon, N.Y.C., 2001—. Vis. scholar U. Calif., L.A., 1984—86; broadcaster and talk show host WVOX, New Rochelle, NY, 1988—; vol. mediator Safe Horizon, Cmty. Mediation Svcs., N.Y.C., 1996—. Contbr. chapters to books, articles to profl. jours. With U.S. Army, 1955—57. Grantee, NIH, 1969—73. Fellow: APA, Am. Psychol. Soc. Home: 341 West 29th St New York NY 10001

GROSS, ALAN GERALD, rhetoric educator; b. N.Y.C., June 2, 1936; s. Jacob and Celia Gross; m. Myra Eder, May 1970 (div. 1978); children: Jessica Gross Griffith, Sarah, Joshua; m. Suzanne Lee Shumate, Sept. 10, 1978. BA, NYU, 1956; PhD, Princeton U., 1958. Asst. prof. English, Wayne State U., Detroit, 1962-66; prof. comm. Macomb County C.C., Warren, Mich., 1966-76; prof. English, Purdue U.-Calumet, Hammond, Ind., 1976-91, dean gen. studies, 1976-80; prof. rhetoric U. Minn.-Twin Cities, St. Paul, 1991—. Vis. scholar Inst. for Advanced Study, Hebrew U., 1995; vis. prof. Brit. Assn., 1998; vis. fellow Internat. Rsch. Ctr. Soc. Sci., 1999-2000. Author: Rhetoric of Science, 1996, Communicating Science, 2002, Chaim Perelman, 2002; editor: Rhetorical Hermeneutics, 1996, Rereading Aristotle's 'Rhetoric', 2000. With U.S. Army, 1958-59. Fellow Ctr. for Philosophy Sci., U. Minn., 1996, U. Pitts., 1997. Avocation: classical music. Home: 2482 N Sheldon Roseville MN 55113 Fax: 651-638-9021. E-mail: grossalang@aol.com.

GROSS, ALLEN JEFFREY, lawyer; b. Wheeling, W.Va., May 2, 1948; s. Arthur and Bertyl (Kahn) G.; m. Carolyn McGuire, May 2, 1982; children: Alexander, Lindsay. BS, Ohio State U., 1970; JD, Georgetown U., 1974. Bar: Pa. 1974, U.S. Dist. Ct. (ctrl. and we. dists.) Pa., Calif. 1989, U.S. Dist. Ct. (no., so. and ctrl. dists.) Calif. 1989, U.S. Ct. Appeals (3d and 6th cirs.). Ptnr. Morgan, Lewis & Bockius, Phila., 1974-89, Orrick, Harrington & Sutcliffe, L.A., 1989-93; now with Mitchell, Silberberg & Knupp, L.A. Mem. Corp. Counsel Inst. adv. bd. Georgetown U. Law Ctr. Author: Survey of Wrongful Discharge Cases in the United States, 1979, Employee Dismissal Laws, Forms, Procedures, 1986, 2d edit. 1992. Fellow Coll. Labor and Employment Lawyers Inc.; mem. ABA (chair trial advocacy supcom. 1989-93, employee rights and responsibilities com. 1991—, co-chair Nat. Advocacy Inst. 1992), Calif. Bar Assn., Pa. Bar Assn. (mgmt. chair Employee Rights Responsibilities com., Sect. Insts. Spl. Programs sub-com.), L.A. County Bar Assn. Office: Mitchell Silberberg & Knupp 11377 W Olympic Blvd Los Angeles CA 90064-1625

GROSS, AMY, publishing executive; Features editor and spl. projects editor Vogue, 1978—88; founding editor Mirabella, 1988—93, editor-in-chief, 1996—97; editl. dir. Elle, N.Y.C., 1993—96; editor-in-chief O, The Oprah Mag., 2000—. Office: O The Oprah Mag 224 W 57th St New York NY 10019-6708*

GROSS, ARIELA JULIE, law educator; b. San Francisco, Sept. 22, 1965; d. David Jonathan and Shulamith Pia Gross; m. Jon Edward Goldman, Sept. 2, 1990; children: Raphaela, Sophia. BA, Harvard U., 1987; JD, Stanford U., 1994, PhD, 1996. Bar: Calif. 1995. Acting asst. prof. law Stanford (Calif.) Law Sch., 1996; asst. prof. law U. So. Calif. Law Sch., LA, 1996—98, assoc. prof. law, 1998—2001, prof. law and history, 2001—. Steering com. Ctr. for Law, History & Culture, LA, 1999—; juror Frederick Douglass Book prize Gilder Lehrman Ctr., 2002—03. Author: Double Character: Slavery & Mastery in the Antebellum Southern Courtroom, 2000 (Phi Kappa Phi award, 2001); contbr. articles to profl. jours. Grantee Fgn. Lang. Area Studies scholar, US Dept. Edn., 1993, Littleton-Griswold grant, Am. Hist. Assn., 1995, Zumberge Rsch. Innovation grant, U. S.C., 1997—98, Guggenheim fellow, 2003—, Huntington fellow, NEH, 2003—, Burkhardt fellow, Am. Coun. Learned Socs., 2003—. Mem.: Law and Soc. Assn. (Willard Hurst prize com. 1999—), Am. Soc. Legal History (exec. com., bd. dirs., program chair 2001—). Office: Univ SC Law Sch Los Angeles CA 90089 Business E-mail: agross@law.usc.edu.

GROSS, BEATRICE SCHAAP, education educator, consultant, writer; b. N.Y.C., Jan. 23, 1935; married; 2 children. BA in Am. Studies, Syracuse U., 1956; MS in Edn., Bank Street Coll. Edn., N.Y.C., 1958. Cert. pre-sch. and elem. tchr. Adj. faculty NYU, N.Y.C., 1968-81, New Sch. Social Rsch., N.Y.C., 1983-87; vis. prof. Vassar Coll., 1985; assoc. prof. humanities SUNY, Old Westbury, 1972-76; cons. to govt., industry and founds., 1976—. Participant univ. seminars Columbia U.; adj. prof. Queens Coll., 1993-95; author tchg. materials McGraw Hill, Sci. Rsch. Assocs. Program adv. Beacon Coll., 1978-82; assoc. dir. Writers in the Pub. Interest, 1981-96; assoc. project dir. Ind. Scholars Project, 1982-96; adj. assoc. prof. La Guardia C.C., 1992—, CUNY, Queens, 1994-95; exec. com. Womanspace, Great Neck, N.J. Author: Radical School Reform, 1970, Will It Grow in a Classroom?, 1974, The Children's Rights Movement, 1977, The New Old, 1978, Teaching Under Pressure, 1979, Towards Improved Compensatory Education, 1982, Independent Scholarship: Promise, Problems and Prospects, 1983, The Great School Debate: Which Way for American Education, 1985; syndicated columnist: The Family Viewpoint, 1979-82; co-editor: Ind. Scholarship newsletter; contbr. articles to profl. jours.; exhibited in juried art show Nassau County Mus. Fine Arts, 2002. Recipient Disting. Achievement award Ednl. Press Assn. Am., 1974, winner Peacock Showcase award Nassau Office Cultural Devel., 1999, Hon. Mention Artist Network of Great Neck Small Works Show, 2001; Faculty Exch. scholar SUNY, 1975; selected for competitor show Nassau County Mus. Art Juried Art Exhbn., 2002. Mem. Am. Soc. Journalists and Authors, Manhasset Art Assn. (bd. dirs. 1999—), Artists Network Great Neck (bd. dirs. 1994), Great Neck Artist Assn. (bd. dirs. 2000—). Home: 17 Myrtle Dr Great Neck NY 11021-1807

GROSS, BRYON WILLIAM, lawyer; b. Rochester, N.Y., Jan. 28, 1964; s. William E. Gross and Diana L. Peets; children: Adam M., Matthew W., Sarah H. BA, St. Lawrence U., 1986; JD, We. New Eng. Coll., 1990. Pvt. practice, Springfield, Mass., 1993-98; assoc. Gallo & Iacovangelo, Rochester, N.Y., 1998—. Vol. VITA, 1989-98. Mem. N.Y. State Bar Assn., A.B. Best Rated, Monroe County Bar Assn. (guardian and ct. evaluations com. 1998). Office: Gallo and Iacovangelo 39 State St Rochester NY 14614

GROSS, CAROL ANN, lawyer; b. St. Louis, Mo., May 25, 1951; m. William H. Gross. B in journalism, U. Mo., 1973; JD cum laude, Seton Hall U. Sch. Law, 1985. Bar N.J., 1985, Pa., 1985, N.Y., 1995, U.S. Dist. Ct., 1985. Law clerk N.J. office atty. gen., Trenton, 1983-85; assoc. Lowenstein, Sandler, Kohl, Fischer & Boylan, Roseland, N.J., 1985-90, Jones, Day, Reavis & Pogue, N.Y., 1990-96; ptnr. pvt. practice, Somerville, N.J., 1996—. Co-Author: (book) N.J. Environmental Law Handbook, 1989; contbr. Environmental Reporter's Handbook, 1988; co-editor (newsletter) Enviro-Notes, 1989-90; contbr. author: Legal Guide to Working with Environmental Consultants. Recipient Responsible Journalism award, N.J. Press Assn., 1982, Interpretive Writing award, N.J. Press Assn., 1980, Journalistic Excellence Under Deadline Pressure award, Soc. Profl. Journalists, 1979, Good Citizen award, Gannett Co., Inc., 1979, Merit award, Union Co. Civil Defense/Disaster Control, 1978. Mem. ABA, N.J. Bar Assn., Pa. Bar Assn. Avocations: gardening, guitar, cooking. Office: 79 Davenport St Somerville NJ 08876-1921

GROSS, CATHERINE MARY (KATE GROSS), writer, educator; b. Seattle, Jan. 21, 1931; d. Daniel Bergin Hutchings and Eleanor Paris (Miller) Bold. Student, Northwestern U., Evanston, Ill., 1958; BA, U. Wash., 1962, postgrad, 1984, cert. fiction grad., 1996. Cert. vocat. tchr. Copywriter Pacific Nat. Advt., Seattle, 1963; prodn. coord. Sta KRON-TV, San Francisco, 1963-65, acting program mgr., 1965; chief copywriter, TV and radio producer Teawell-Shoemaker Advt., San Diego, 1966-68; asst. pub. rels. dir. San Diego Zoo, 1968-70; pub. relations dir. Univ. Village, Seattle, 1975-77; pub. rels. dir. Seattle/King County Bd. Realtors, 1978; adj. instr. bus. Seattle Pacific U., 1980-89; instr. ASUW Exptl. Coll., 1980—; instr. humanities Heritage Inst. Antioch U., 1991—; instr. humanities Bellevue C.C., 1992-96; instr. U. Wash. Exptl. Coll., 1985—. Instr. Wonder Sch. Art, 1998; instr. writing by formula Women's Ctr. of U. Wash.; cons. in field. Author: Advertising for a Small Business, 1984, Fund Raising Magic, 1984, Conversations With Writers, 1993, Sunshine the Magician's Rabbit, 1996 (juvenile fiction award Wash. Press Assn. 1996, 2d place best book Rocky Mountain Outdoor Writers 1996, creative nonfiction award Klondike Centennial Anthology 1997); author, pub. Mary, The Mouse and the Coal Mine, 1999; editor: Hiking and Bushwalking in Papua, New Guinea, 1987; tech. editor oceanography and medicine U. Wash., 1974-75; contbr. short stories to Compass and Sea Classics, 1982. Vol. sponsor Big Sisters of Puget Sound, Seattle, 1978-87, Seattle Parks; vol. coordinator World Affairs Council, Seattle, 1986; bd. dirs. Seattle Aquarium, 1985-87. Recipient Non-Fiction Book award Pacific Northwest Writers' Conf., 1979, Juvenile Story award Pacific Northwest Writers' Conf., 1984, Short Story award Fictioneers, 1993, Juv. Fiction award Washington Press Assn., 1997, Writers Digest award for Secrets of the Whispering Waters, 2002. Mem. AAUW (internat. rep. 1988), Seattle Freelance Writers Assn., Wash. Press Assn., Wash. Ornithol. Soc., Rocky Mountain Outdoor Writers, Mountaineers, Issaquah Alps Trails Club, Audubon Soc. Republican. Avocation: hiking. Office: Kate Finegan Books Box 381 117 E Louisa St Seattle WA 98102-3203

GROSS, CHARLES GORDON, psychology educator, neuroscientist; b. NYC, Feb. 29, 1936; s. Frank and Sara (Gordon) G.; m. Gaby Ellen Peierls, Sept. 23, 1961 (div. Mar. 1985); children: Melanie, Monica (dec.), Derek, Rowena; m. Greta Berman, May 1, 1988. BA, Harvard U., 1957; PhD, Cambridge U., Eng., 1961. From postdoctoral fellow to asst. prof. psychology MIT, 1961-65; vis. lectr., asst. prof., then lectr. Harvard U., 1963-70; prof. psychology Princeton U., 1970—. Vis. prof. U. Calif., Berkeley, 1970-71, MIT, 1975-76, Beijing U., 1986; vis. scientist Tokyo Met. Inst. Neurosci., 1988-89, Nencki Inst. Exptl. Biology, Warsaw, Poland, 1961; Fulbright lectr. Inst. Biophysics, Fed. U. Rio de Janeiro, 1986; U.S. Nat. Program vis. scientist Shanghai Inst. Physiology, 1987; vis. fellow Magdalen Coll., Oxford U., 1990, vis. scholar Wolfson Coll., 1995, McDonnell-Pew vis. fellow Med. Rsch. Coun. Ctr. in Brain and Behaviour, 1995, chair, Psychology Section (J), Am. Assoc. for the Advancement of Science. Author books and papers on brain, visual function and history of science. Grantee NIH, NSF, Spencer Found., Sloan Found., McDonald-Pew Found., Office Naval Rsch. Fellow APA, AAAS, Soc. Exptl. Psychologists, Brazilian Acad. Sci.(fgn.), Nat. Acad. Sci., am. Acad. Arts and Sci. Home: 45 Woodside Ln Princeton NJ 08540-5417 Office: Princeton Univ Green Hall Princeton NJ 08544

GROSS, CHARLES ROBERT, bank executive, state senator; b. St. Charles, Mo., Aug. 20, 1958; s. Jack Robert and Margaret Ellen (Stumberg) G., m. Leslie Ann Goralczyk, May 27, 1984; children: Megan Marie, Madelynn Ann. BS in Pub. Adminstrn., U. Mo., 1981, MPA, 1982. Pers. mgr. Army and Air Force Exch. Svc., various cities, 1983-89; pers., safety dir. Ever-Green Lawns Corp., St. Charles, 1989-92; state rep. Mo. Legislature, Jefferson City, 1993—; real estate appraiser, 1994—2001; v.p. UMB Bank, 2001—. Pres. St. Charles County Young Reps., 1990-92; active Youth in Need, Bridgeway Counseling. Mem. St. Charles DARE, Kiwanis, Pacaderms, Alpha Kappa Psi (life). Lutheran. Avocations: golf, scuba diving, ice hockey. Home: 3019 Westborough Ct Saint Charles MO 63301-4550 E-mail: chuckgross58@hotmail.com.

GROSS, CYNTHIA SUE, petrochemicals manufacturing executive; b. Palmyra, Mo., Aug. 14, 1959; d. Floyd Raymond and Carolyn Elizabeth (Howell) Mette; m. Edward Lee Gross, June 8, 1985; 1 child, Ray E.; stepchildren: Troy A., Christina M. BS in Metall. Engring., U. Mo., Rolla, 1980. Metallurgist Bryon Jackson Pump, Tulsa, Okla., 1981-82; metall. engr. Conoco, Inc., Ponca City, Okla., 1982-84, Vista Chem., Houston, 1984-89; staff maintenance engr. Hoechst Celanese, Clear Lake, Tex., 1989-92; instr. of welding metallurgy San Jacinto Coll., 1992; sect. leader maintenance engring. Hoechst Celanese, Bishop, Tex., 1992-93, sect. leader maintenance, 1993-95; prodn. supt. for polyester Hoechst Celanese, Trevira, Spartanburg, S.C., 1995-97; process hazards prevention leader Celanese, Clear Lake, 1997-98, methanol and maintenance mgr., 1999-2000, tech. and maintenance mgr., 2000—01, corp. reliability and maintenance dir., 2001—. Spkr. symposium Nat. Petroleum Refiners Assn., San Antonio, 1993, San Antonio, 2000, San Antonio, 02; instr. welding metallurgy San Jacinto Coll., Houston, 1992. Mem. quality mgmt. com. Houston Bus. Roundtable, 1990-92, chmn. Quality Day '91. Mem. NPRA (com. mem. 2001), Alpha Chi Sigma. Avocations: youth baseball, piano. Office: Celanese Clear Lake Plant 9502 Bayport Blvd Pasadena TX 77507-1402

GROSS, DAVID LEE, geologist; b. Springfield, Ill., Nov. 20, 1943; s. Carl David and Shirley Marie (Northcutt) G.; m. Claudia Cole, June 11, 1966; children: Oliver David, Alexander Lee AB, Knox Coll., 1965; MS, U. Ill., 1967, PhD, 1969. Registered profl. geologist, Ill., Calif. Asst. geologist Ill. State Geol. Survey, Champaign, 1969-73, assoc. geologist, 1973-80, geologist, 1980—, coord. environ. geology, 1979-84, head environ. studies, 1984-89, asst. chief, 1991-99, sr. geologist emeritus, 1999—. Exec. dir. Gov.'s Sci. Adv. Com., Chgo., 1989-91; bd. dirs. First State Bank, Beardstown, Ill., chmn. 2001—. Contbr. numerous articles to profl. jours. Bd. govs. Channing-Murray Found., 1973-76, pres., 1976; trustee Unitarian Universalist Ch., Urbana, 1977-80, 99—, chmn., 1977-79, 99-2001; bd. dirs. Vol. Action Ctr., 1981-85, chmn., 1984-85; bd. dirs. United Way Champaign County, 1984-89, exec. com., 1984-85, chmn. United Way Campaign, U. Ill., 1986; bd. dirs. Vol. Cu., 1994-97; mem. Gov.'s Sci. Adv. Com., 1989-97; vol. summer camp counselor for teenage youth, 1984-03; bd. dirs. Ill. Prairie chpt. ARC, 1997—. NDEA fellow, 1969 Fellow Geol. Soc. Am., AAAS; mem. Internat. Union Quaternary Rsch., Am. Quaternary Assn., Internat. Assn. Gt. Lakes Rsch., Am. Inst. Profl. Geologists (pres. Ill.-Ind. sect. 1980), Ill. State Acad. Sci., Rotary (pres. Urbana, Ill. chpt. 1986-87), Columbia (Chgo.) Yacht Club, Sigma Xi. Home: 3 Flora Ct Champaign IL 61821-3216 Office: Ill State Geol Survey 615 E Peabody Dr Champaign IL 61820-6918 *Strive for reasonable balance among family, volunteer and professional responsibilities. All are essential for a healthy life.*

GROSS, DONALYN ANN, counselor; b. Springfield, Mass., July 5, 1950; d. Harold Arnold and Estelle (Eisenstock) Gross. BS in Human Svcs./Social Work, U. Chattanooga, 1973; MEd in Counseling, Springfield Coll., 1979; PhD in Counseling/Thanatology, Columbia Pacific U., 1981. LCSW; cert. music practitioner/harpist. Thanatologist Conn. Dept. Corrections, 1991—95; activity dir. Genesis Eldercare, Heritage Woods Assisted Living Ctr., Agawam, Mass., 1997—98; social worker, dir. Good Endings Program SunBridge Care and Rehab. for East Longmeadow, 1998—. Adj. prof. Springfield Coll., Bay Path Coll., 1999; vol. coord. VNA and Home Care of Manchester, Conn.; workshop presenter Jewish Geriatric Svcs., 2000—01; dir. Good Endings program Heritage Hall West, Agawam, Mass., 2002—. Author: Dying in Prison - Counseling the Terminal Inmate, 1991, Voices of the Dying - Reflections of the Living, 1995, Good Endings - Caring for the Dying Resident - The Training Manual, 1999, Earth Angels - One Year of Vigil, 2000; contbr. articles to profl. publs.; musician: (CD) Remembering Music for Memorial Services. Harpist for dying; presenter, cons., spkr. on death and dying. Jewish. Avocations: professional musician, spinning wool. Home: 189 Porter Lake Dr Springfield MA 01106

GROSS, DOROTHY-ELLEN, library director, dean; b. Buffalo, June 13, 1949; d. William Paul and Elizabeth Grace (Hough) Gross. BA, Westminster Coll., 1971; MLS, Benedictine U., 1975; MDiv, McCormick Theol. Sem., 1975. Jr. cataloger McCormick Theol. Sem., Chgo., 1972-75; head tech. svcs. Barat Coll., Lake Forest, Ill., 1975-79, head libr., 1980-82; dir. coll. libr. North Park Coll. and Theol. Sem., Chgo., 1982-87, dir. coll. and sem. librs., 1987-96, assoc. dean, 1990-96, prof., 1991—. Cons. acad. librs.; spkr. various profl. meetings and confs. Author (with Karsten): From Real Life to Reel Life, 1993; editor: LIBRAS Handbook and Directory, 1982—96; co-editor: North Park Faculty Publs. and Creative Works, 1992; contbr. chpt. in book, articles, book reviews to profl. jours. Dir. rsch. United Way, Chgo., 1996—99; bd. dirs. Eldredge Libr., 2000—. Recipient Melvin R. George award, 1996. Mem.: LIBRAS (pres. 1983—85), ALA, Pvt. Acad. Librs. Ill. (pres. 1981—83, 1994—95, newsletter editor, contbr.), Assn. Coll. and Rsch. Librs. Presbyterian. E-mail: dgross@northpark.edu.

GROSS, EDWARD, sociologist, educator; b. Nagy Genez, Romania; s. Samuel and Dora (Levi) G.; m. Florence Rebecca Goldman, Feb. 18, 1943; children—David P., Deborah L. Teagardin. BA, U. B.C., Can., 1942; MA, U. Toronto, Ont., Can., 1945; PhD, U. Chgo., 1949; JD, U. Wash., 1991. Prof. Wash. State U., Pullman, Wash., 1947-51, 53-60; prof. U. Wash., Seattle, 1951-53, 65-89, prof. emeritus, 1990—; prof. sociology U. Minn., Mpls., 1960-65. Vis. prof. Australian Nat. U., Canberra, 1971, U. Queensland, U. New South Wales, Griffith U., Australia, 1977; invited lectr. Cen. China Poly. Inst., 1987; lectr. arts and sci. honor program U. Wash., 1998—. Author: Work and Society, 1958, Univ. Goals and Academic Power, 1968, Changes in Univ. Orgn., 1964-71, The End of a Golden Age: Higher Ed. in a Steady State, 1981, Orgn. in Soc., 1985, Embarrassment in Everyday Life, 1994; contbg. author: Handbook of Sociology and Encyclopedia of Sociology, 2d edit.; former assoc. editor Social Problems, Symbolic Interaction, Can. Jour. Sociology; contbr. numerous articles to profl. jour. Trustee Temple Beth Am, Seattle, 1993-97. Fulbright scholar Australia, 1977, 87. Mem.: Am. Sociol. Assn. (emeritus), Pacific Sociol. Assn. (pres. 1971, coun. 1983—85). Office: U Wash Dept Sociology Seattle WA 98195-0001 E-mail: egross@u.washington.edu.

GROSS, FELIKS, writer; b. Cracow, Poland, June 17, 1906; came to U.S., 1941; s. Adolf and Augusta (Alexander) G.; m. Priva Baidaff, July 25, 1937; 1 child, Eva Helena Gross Friedman. LLM, Jagiellonian U., 1930; LLD, Jagiellanian U., 1931. Bar: Poland 1937. Sec., gen. Cen. Ea. European Planning Bd., 1941-45; editor New Europe and World Reconstrn. jour., N.Y.C., 1942-45; prof. sociology and anthropology grad. ctr. Bklyn. Coll., N.Y.C., 1946-77, prof. emeritus, 1977—, resident prof. CUNY grad. ctr., 1988—. Vis. prof. NYU, 1945-68; vis. prof., dir. Inst. Internat. Affairs, U. Wyo., Laramie, summers 1945-52; vis. prof. Woodrow Wilson Sch. Fgn. Affairs, U. Va., Charlottesville, 1951, 54-56, U. Vt., Burlington, 1957; sr. Fulbright sr. lectr. U. Rome, 1957-58, 64-65, 74; lectr. other European, Am. univs.; mem. rsch. coun. Fgn. Policy Rsch. Inst., Phila., 1966—; vis. prof. Columbia U., N.Y.C., 1973; lectr. U. Florence, 1977, Italian Fgn. Office, Rome; cons. Nat. Com. on Causes and Prevention of Violence, 1968. Pres., Taraknath Das Found., N.Y., 1965; hon. pres. CUNY Acad. Humanities and Scis., 1985; co-founder, bd. dirs. Non-Profit Coordinating Com. N.Y., 1984-86. Author: Nomadism, 1936; Polish Worker, 1945; Foreign Policy Analysis, 1954; Seizure of Political Power, 1957; Valori Sociali e Struttura, 1967; World Politics and Tension Areas, 1967; Violence in Politics, 1973; Il Paese, Values and Social Change in an Italian Village, 1974; The Revolutionary Party, 1974; Ethnics in the Borderland, 1979; Ideologies, Goals and Values, 1986; Working Class and Culture (in Polish), 1986, Toleration and Pluralism (in Polish), 1992, European Federation & Confederations, Origin and Visions (in Polish), 1994, The Civic and the Tribal State, 1998, Citizenship and Ethnicity, 1999, The Civic and Tribal State, 1998, others; contbr. numerous articles to profl. jours. Decorated Golden Cross of Phoenix (Greece); Order Polonia Restituta (Poland); Carnegie scholar, Paris, 1931, Pub. Affairs Found. NYU, 1962-63; recipient Ethnic New Yorker award N.Y.C., 1987, Alfred Jurzykowski Price award for scholarship contbn., Polish Nat. Archives award, 1995, award Polish Ministry Culture and Art, 1995, N.Y.C. commendation for serving the Polish-Am. Cmty., 1998; ILO/League of Nations scholar, Geneva, 1930, Carnegie Scholarship, 1931; grantee Sloan Found., 1963, City U. Rsch. Found., 1971-74, NSF, 1972, Rockefeller Found., 1974; Fulbright grantee, 1956-57, 64-65, 74. Fellow Polish Inst Arts and Scis. (pres. F-7 1988-99); mem. Internat. League Rights of Man (dir. 1960-88), Am. Sociol. Assn., Acad. Polit. Sci., N.Y. Acad. Scis., Polish Acad. Scis. (fgn.), Polish Sociology Soc. (hon.), Sigma Xi. Home: 310 W 85th St New York NY 10024-3819 Office: CUNY Acad for Human and Science 365 Fifth Ave New York NY 10016-4309

GROSS, GARY NEIL, allergist, physician; b. Fort Lewis, Wash., July 25, 1944; s. Norman Harold and Dorothy Naomi (Bercie) G.; m. Elaina Wee, Mar. 23, 1974; children: Risa, Lara. BA, U. Tex., 1967; MD, Southwestern Med. Sch., Dallas, 1969; MBA, Southern Methodist U., Dallas, 1987. Diplomate Am. Bd. Internal Medicine, Am. Bd. Allergy and Clin. Immunology. Intern U. Utah Med. Ctr. Hosp., Salt Lake City, 1969-70, resident, 1970-71; fellow Nat. Jewish Hosp., Denver, 1971-74; founding physician Dallas Allergy and Asthma Ctr., Tex., 1979—; med. dir. Pharm. Rsch. and Cons., Dallas, 1992—; clin. prof. internal medicine Southwestern Med. Sch., Dallas, 1994—. Contbr to profl. jours. Bd. dirs. Am. Jewish Com., Dallas, 1990-94, Am. Lung Assn., 1978-88, Temple Emanuel Brotherhood, 1978-80. Fellow Am. Coll. Physicians, Am. Acad. Allergy Immunology (chmn. seminars com., 1987-88, chmn. pub. edn. com., 1989-90); mem. Fedn. Regional State Local Allergy Socs. (gov. reg. 5, 1992—, chmn. 1993-94), Joint Coun. Allergy Clin. Immunology (sec. bd. dirs. 1992-96, exec. v.p. 1998—). Jewish. Avocations: cycling, skiing, photography. Office: 5499 Glen Lakes Dr Ste 100 Dallas TX 75231-4383 E-mail: ggross144@yahoo.com.

GROSS, GEOFFREY FRIES, systems engineer; b. Cin., Apr. 26, 1950; s. Merrill Jay and Ann Fries Gross; m. Diantha Louise Perry, May 9, 1970 (dec. July 1998); 1 child, Abraham Hart; m. Wendy Robin Levine, Aug. 12, 2000. BA in Math. cum laude, SUNY, Buffalo, 1973, MEd in Math. Instrn., 1976. Acting chmn. math. dept., instr. U. New Eng., Biddeford, Maine, 1979-80; tchr. math. Laconia (N.H.) H.S., 1980-81; programmer Franklin, N.H., 1982; project leader Mellen Co., Webster, N.H., 1983-87; sys. engr. Analysis and Computer Sys. Inc., Burlington, Mass., 1987-90; sys. arch., project mgr. Sys. Resources Corp., Burlington, 1990-95; sr. prin. sys. arch. Raytheon, St. Petersburg, Fla., 1996—. Mem. Sch. Budget Com., Milford, N.H., 1990-91; pres. Congregation Betenu, Amherst, N.H., 1991-97; trustee Congregation B'nai Israel, St. Petersburg, 2002—; bd. dirs. Sun Island Assn., South Pasadena, Fla., 2002-03; cons. Mus. Fine Arts, Boston, 1995. Mem. N.Y. Acad. Scis., Phi Beta Kappa (Omicron chpt.). Jewish. Avocations: american art, presidential campaign materials, chess. Office: Raytheon 1501 72nd St N Saint Petersburg FL 33710 Fax: 727-302-4851. E-mail: grossg@tampabay.rr.com.

GROSS, HANNS, history educator; b. Stockerau, Austria, June 20, 1928; came to U.S., 1961; s. Arthur and Gabriele (Schneider) G.; m. Bonnie Jean Rotter, July 20, 1991. BA with honors, U. London, 1950; AM, U. Chgo., 1963, PhD, 1966. Tchr. Emmanuel Grammar Sch., Swansea, Wales, 1950-61; tutor Bible Coll. Wales, Swansea, 1950-61; asst. prof. So. Ill. U., Carbondale, 1966-67; asst. prof., assoc. prof. history Loyola U., Chgo., 1967-78, prof., 1978-99, emeritus, 1999—. Author: Empire and Sovereignty, 1973, Rome in the Age of Enlightenment, 1990. Elder Moody Ch. Mem.: Deutsche Gesellschaft fuer Erforschung des 18. Jahrhundert, Soc. Italian Hist. Studies, Conf. on Faith and History, Am. Soc. for 18th Century Studies, Am. Soc. for Legal History, Am. Hist. Assn. Avocations: travel, walking, conversation. Office: Loyola U Dept History 6525 N Sheridan Rd Chicago IL 60626-5344

GROSS, HARRIET P. MARCUS, religious studies and writing educator; b. Pitts., July 15, 1934; d. Joseph William and Rose (Roth) Pincus; children: Sol Benjamin, Devra Lynn. AB magna cum laude, U. Pitts., 1954; cert. in religious tchg., Spertus Coll. of Judaica, Chgo., 1962; MA, U. Tex., Dallas, 1990, postgrad., 1998—. Assoc. editor Jewish Criterion of Pitts., 1955-56; publs. writer B'nai B'rith Vocat. Svc., 1956-57; group leader Jewish Cmty. Ctrs. Met. Chgo., 1958-63; columnist Star Publs., Chicago Heights, Ill., 1964-80; pub. info. specialist Operation ABLE, Chgo., 1980-81; dir. religious sch. Temple Emanu-El, Dallas, 1983-86; freelance writer, 1986—; columnist Dallas Jewish Life Monthly, 1992-96, Dallas Jewish Week, 2000—. Lectr. U. Tex., DAllas, 1994-98; tchr. writing Homewood-Flossmoor (Ill.) Park Dist., Brookhaven Jr. Coll., Dallas; advisor journalism program Prairie State Coll., Chicago Heights, 1978-80; mem. adv. bd. The Creative Woman Quar. Publ., Gov.'s State U., Governors Park, Ill., The Mercury U. Tex., Dallas. Bd. dirs., sec. Family Svc. and Mental Health Ctr. of South Cook County, Ill., 1965-71; active Park Forest (Ill.) Commn. on Human Rels., 1969-80, chmn., 1974-76; bd. dirs. Ill. Theatre Ctr., 1977-80, Jewish Family Svc. of Dallas, 1982-95, Dallas Jewish Hist. Soc., 1995—; mem. Dallas Jewish Edn. Com., 1992-95. Recipient Humanitarian Achievements award Fellowship for Action, 1974, Honor award Anti-Defamation League of B'nai B'rith, 1978, Cmty. Svc. award Dr. Charles E. Gavin Found., 1978, 1st Ann. Leadership award Jewish Family Svc., 1990, Katie award Dallas Press Club, 1995; inducted into Park Forest (Ill.) Hall of Fame, 2000, Tex. Press Women State Writing award, 2003. Mem. Nat. Fedn. Press Women, Tex. Press Women, Ill. Woman's Press Assn. (named Woman of Yr. 1978), Intertel (pres. Gateway Forum of Dallas 1984-85), Nat. Assn. Temple Educators, Mensa, Soc. Profl. Journalists, Dallas Press Club, Nat. Soc. of Newspaper Columnists, Am. Jewish Press Assn., Phi Sigma Sigma. Jewish. Achievements include development of 1st community newspaper action line column, 1966. Office: 8560 Park Ln Apt 23 Dallas TX 75231-6312 E-mail: hgross@utdallas.edu.

GROSS, JAMES DEHNERT, pathologist; b. Harvey, Ill., Nov. 15, 1929; s. Max A. and Marion (Dehnert) G.; m. Marilyn Agnes Robertson, Jan. 9, 1960; children: Kathleen Ann, Terrence Michael, Brian Andrew, Kevin Matthew. BS in Biology, U. Chattanooga, 1951; MD, Vanderbilt U., 1955. Diplomate Am. Bd. Pathology, Am. Bd. Med. Mgmt. Rotating intern U.S. Naval Hosp., St. Albans, N.Y., 1955-56; resident in anatomic and clin. pathology Nat. Naval Med. Ctr., Bethesda, Md., 1956-59; dir. labs. U.S. Naval Hosp., Memphis, 1959-62, St. Mary's Hosp., Streator, Ill., 1962-93, pres. med. staff, 1972-73. Instr. pathology and microbiology U. Tenn. Med. Sch., 1960-62; bd. dirs. La Salle County bd. Am. Cancer Soc., 1966-68 Mem. parish council St. Anthony's Roman Catholic Ch., Streator, 1969-72. Served to lt. comdr. M.C., USNR, 1955-68 Fellow Am. Soc. Clin. Pathologists, Coll. Am. Pathologists, Assn. Clin. Scientists (founder); mem. AMA, Ill. Med. Soc., Sigma Chi, Alpha Kappa Kappa Lodges: K.C., Rotary (past bd. dirs.). Republican. Home and Office: 374 MacEwen Dr Osprey FL 34229-9233 E-mail: marigro@comcast.net.

GROSS, JAMES HOWARD, lawyer; b. Springfield, Ohio, Sept. 21, 1941; s. Cyril James and Virginia (Stieg) G.; m. Gail Sue Helmick, July 13, 1968; children: Karin G. Cramer, David James. BA, Ohio State U., 1963; LLB, Harvard U., 1966. Bar: Ohio 1966, D.C. 1975. Assoc. Vorys, Sater, Seymour and Pease, Columbus, Ohio, 1966-75, resident ptnr. Washington, 1975-77; ptnr. Vorys, Sater, Seymour and Pease LLP, Columbus, 1975—. White House fellow, spl. asst. to sec. HUD, Washington, 1972-73; city atty. City of Bexley, Ohio, 1985—. Mem. Franklin County Rep. Cen. Com., 1973-75, Bexley City Coun., 1981-85. Lt. comdr. USNR, 1968-74. Mem. ABA, Ohio Bar Assn. (corp. law com.), Columbus Bar Assn. (securities law com.), D.C. Bar Assn. Lutheran. Home: 5 Sessions Dr Bexley OH 43209-1440 Office: Vorys Sater Seymour and Pease LLP 52 E Gay St # 1008 Columbus OH 43215-3161

GROSS, JEFFREY, software engineer; b. Chgo., Feb. 23, 1963; s. Mickey and Evelyn (Udwin) G. BSEE, Ill. Inst. Tech., Chgo., 1985. Software engr. Gen. Dynamics, San Diego, 1986-91; sci. programmer Biosym Technologies, San Diego, 1991-94; sr. software engr. Qualcomm, San Diego, 1994-99; ind. software engring. cons. San Diego, 1999—; prin. software cons. SynergyWare, Inc., 1999—. Ill. State scholar; recipient Gen. Dynamics Excel award. Mem. Assn. Computing Machinery, Mensa. Home: 10878 Cloverhurst Way San Diego CA 92130-4800

GROSS, JONATHAN LIGHT, computer scientist, mathematician, educator; b. Phila., June 11, 1941; s. Nathan K. and Henrietta E. (Light) G.; m. Susan Fay Kodner, Aug. 29, 1976; children: Aaron, Jessica, Joshua, Rena Lea, Alisa Sharon BS, M.I.T., 1964; MA, Dartmouth Coll., 1966, PhD, 1968. Instr. math. Princeton (N.J.) U., 1968-69; asst. prof. math. stats. Columbia U., N.Y.C., 1969-72, assoc. prof., 1973-78, prof. computer sci., math. and stats., 1978—, vice-chmn. dept. computer sci., 1982-89; dir. edn. Ctr. for Advanced Tech., 1989-93. Cons. Russell Sage Found., Inst. Def. Analyses., AT&T Bell Labs., Alfred P. Sloan Found., IBM, Oak Ridge Nat. Lab.; vis. scientist Carnegie-Mellon U., Pitts., 1984-85. Co-author: Fundamental Programming Concepts, 1972, FORTRAN 77 Programming, 1978, Introduction to Computer Programming, 1979, Pascal Programming, 1982, Measuring Culture, 1985, PASCAL, 1991 FORTRAN 77 Fundamentals and Style, 1985, Topological Graph Theory, 1987, WATFIV-S Fundamental Style, 1986, Graph Theory and Its Applications, 1999; editor: Handbook of Discrete and Combinatorial Mathematics, 2000; adv. editor: Columbia U. Press, Jour. Graph Theory, Computers and Electronics, CRC Press; contbr. articles to profl. jours. IBM postdoctoral fellow, 1972-73; Sloan fellow in math., 1973-75; rsch. grantee NSF, Office of Naval Rsch., Exxon Found., ARCO Found., Mellon Found., Russell Sage Found., N.Y. State Sci. and Tech. Found., Citicorp. Mem. Am. Math. Soc., Assn. Computing Machinery, Soc. Indsl. and Applied Math. (sec. discrete math. 1994-96), Jewish Ctr. of Princeton (v.p. 1997-99, pres. 2000—). Jewish. Home: 3 Stuart Ln W Princeton Junction NJ 08550-1844 Office: Columbia U Dept Computer Sci New York NY 10027 *The essence of acquiring an education is internalizing an acute awareness of the distinctions among feeling, conjecturing, doing, and actually knowing.*

GROSS, JOSEPH H. lawyer, educator; b. Tel Aviv, Feb. 28, 1934; s. Woolf and Mali (Timberg) G.; m. Zvia Armon, July 21, 1959; children: Raz, Aeyal, Vardit. LLB, Tel Aviv U., 1955, LLM, 1958; PhD, U. London, 1962. Bar: Israel 1959, N.Y. 1989. Legal advisor Discount Bank Investment Co., Tel Aviv, 1963-76; prof. law Tel Aviv U., assoc. dean Law Sch., 1973-78; chmn. law firm Gross, Kleinhandler, Hodak, Halevy, Greenberg & Co., Tel Aviv, 1979—. Vis. scholar Harvard U. Law Sch., Boston, 1977; chmn. com. on mergers Govt. of Israel, 1975—77, com. to reform co. law, 1985—94, chmn. adv. bd. govt. cos., 1986—91; chmn. Israel Bar Pub. House; bd. dirs. Ta'agidim Ltd., Sano Ltd., Ramot Ltd., Saniv Ltd., Carmel Bank Holding Ltd.; chmn. Bloostein-Genosar Ltd.; ct. appeals on mergers and monopolies, 1995—2000; pub. com. on taxing nonprofit orgns. Israel Income Tax Authority, 1989—90. Author: Israel's Company Law, 1970, Company Promoters, 1972, Securities Law, 1973, Directors in Government Companies, 1977, Tax Planning of Investments, 1984, Corporation Tax, 3 edits., 1987, V.A.T., 1987, Directors and Officers of Corporations, 1989, Director's Manual, 9th edit., 1999; editor: The Director in Practice, 2d edit., 1997, The New Companies Law, 1999, 2d edit., 2000, The New Tax Law, 3th edit., 2003. Maj. Israeli Army, 1954-57. Mem.: Israel Bar Assn. Home: 10 Berkovitz St 64238 Tel-Aviv Israel Office: 1 Azrieli Ctr 67021 Tel Aviv Israel E-mail: joseph@gkh-law.com.

GROSS, KAREN CHARAL, lawyer; b. N.Y.C., Nov. 25, 1940; d. Harry B. and Adele (Hook) Charal; m. Meyer A. Gross, Aug. 16, 1964; children: Dana Leslie, Jennifer P., Pamela A. AB, Barnard Coll., 1962; JD, NYU, 1965. Bar: N.Y. 1965. Atty. Wolder & Gross, N.Y.C., 1965-78, Wolder, Gross & Yavner, N.Y.C., 1978-86; sr. v.p. legal and bus. affairs GoodTimes Entertainment LLC, N.Y.C., 1986—. Editor NYU Law Rev., 1963-65. Parent liaison Ramaz Sch., N.Y.C., 1980-86; del. Dem. County Com., N.Y.C., 1988—; legal mentor to students Barnard Coll., N.Y.C. John Norton Pomeroy scholar NYU, 1963-65. Mem. INTA, Copyright Soc. USA., INTA Avocation: travel. Office: GoodTimes Entertainment LLC 16 E 40th St New York NY 10016-0104

GROSS, KATHLEEN ALBRIGHT, interventional radiology nurse, educator, writer; b. Mechanicsburg, Pa., June 10, 1951; d. Clyde Nelson and Louise Albright; m. Richard Joseph Gross, Oct. 15, 1972; children: David, Jonathan. Diploma, Harrisburg Hosp. Sch. Nursing, 1972; BS summa cum laude, Pa. State U., Harrisburg, 1977; BSN summa cum laude, Coll. Notre Dame Md., 1982; MSN, U. Phoenix, 2001. Cert. med.-surg. nurse, radiology nurse, ACLS, PALS. Staff nurse ICU M.S. Hershey (Pa.) Med. Ctr., 1972-74; rsch. asst. in dermatology Johns Hopkins Bayview Med. Ctr. (formerly Balt. City Hosps.), 1977; rsch. asst. dept. health svcs. rsch. Johns Hopkins Sch. Hygiene and Pub. Health, Balt., 1978; staff nurse crit. care unit, ICU, med.-surg. Upjohn Healthcare, Balt., 1978-81; camp nurse Friends Sch., Balt., 1985; office nurse Balt., 1982-94; instr. Greater Balt. Med. Ctr. Sch. Radiologic Tech., Balt., 1991—; staff nurse interventional radiology Greater Balt. Med. Ctr., 1988—; staff nurse Patient First, 1994—. Cons. Edumed, 1996—. Instr. BCLS, Am. Heart Assn., Balt., 1983—, vol. fundraiser, 1985, 87, 88, author, 1999; vol. Gilman Sch., Balt., 1981—; vol. naturalist Irvine Natural Sci. Ctr., Stevenson, Md., 1987-91; vol. fundraiser Leukemia Soc. Am., Balt., 1989; aux. membership chairperson Balt. City Hosps., 1976, 77. Mem. Am. Radiol. Nurses Assn. (sec. 1997-2000, pres.-elect 2001-02, pres. 2002-03, bd. dirs. 2003—, mem. exec. com. 1994-96, ANA-nursing orgn. liaison forum, sec. 1997—), Am. Coll. Radiology Patient Safety Task Force, Md. Radiol. Nurses Assn. (v.p. 1991-92, pres. 1993-94, bd. dirs. 1995-96, rep. to 1st Nursing Summit 1991, sec. 1997-98), Soc. for Vascular Nursing, Balt. Interventional Radiol. Technologists Assn., Delta Tau Kappa, Sigma Theta Tau. Avocations: gardening, reading. Home: 1243 Berans Rd Owings Mills MD 21117-1641 Office: Greater Balt Med Ctr Interventional Radiology 6701 N Charles St Baltimore MD 21204-6808

GROSS, LARRY PAUL, communications educator; b. Washington, Nov. 22, 1942; s. Bertram Myron and Nora (Faine) G. BA, Brandeis U., 1964; PhD, Columbia U., 1968; MA (hon.), U. Pa., 1973. Asst. prof. U. Pa., Phila., 1968-73, assoc. prof., 1973-82, prof., 1982—, Sol Worth prof., 1998—, assoc. dean for grad. studies, 1989-93, chair faculty senate, 2000-01, dep. dean, 2001—03; prof., dir. Sch. Comm., U. So. Calif., 2003—. Author: Contested Closets: The Politics and Ethics of Outing, 1993; editor: Communications Technology and Social Policy, 1973, Between Men-Between Women book series, 1991—, Studying Visual Communication, 1981, Image Ethics, 1988, Studies in Visual Communications, 1977-85, On the Margins of Art Worlds, 1995, The Columbia Reader on Lesbians and Gay Men in Media, Society and Politics, 1999, Up From Invisibility: Lesbians, Gay Men and the Media in America, 2001; assoc. editor Internat. Ency. Comm., 1989; contbr. articles to profl. jours. Chair Phila. Lesbian and Gay Task Force, 1981-2000; mem. Pa. Humanities Coun., 1985-90. Guggenheim fellow, 1998-99. Fellow Am. Anthrop. Assn. (co-chmn. rsch. group on homosexuality 1981-84); mem. Internat. Comm. Assn. (chair task force on diversity 1992—, lesbian and gay studies interest group 1993-96), Nat. Comm. Assn., Phi Beta Kappa, Sigma Xi. Home: 2334 Clark Ave Venice CA 90291 Office: U So Calif Annenberg Sch Los Angeles CA 90089 E-mail: lgross@asc.upenn.edu.

GROSS, LAURA ANN, marketing and communications professional, acupuncturist, herbalist; b. Kew Gardens, N.Y., July 11, 1948; d. Melvin Fredericks and Harriette (Levy) G. BA, Boston U., 1970; MA, Columbia U., 1974; MS, Pacific Coll. Oriental Medicine, 1996. Staff writer Am. Banker, N.Y.C., 1974-82, assoc. editor, 1982-88; dir. fin. svcs., instns., communications Am. Express Travel/Related Svcs. Co., N.Y.C., 1988-89; dir. sales promotion and pub. rels. Am. Express Travelers Cheque Group/Am. Express Travel Svcs., N.Y.C., 1989-92; dir. strategic bus. comm. Am. Express Travel Related Svcs., N.Y.C., 1992-93; pres. Strategic Comm. Cons., N.Y.C., 1993-2000; founder Alternative Ctr. for Natural Healing, 1997—; exec. v.p. mktg. Letsgotrade, Inc., 2000-01; sr. v.p. mktg./ebusiness Muriel Siebert & Co., Inc., 2001—. Spkr. fin. svcs. and Chinese medicine. Author, editor consumer surveys and articles. Recipient editorial awards Pannell Kerr Forster, 1984, N.E. Bus. Press Editors, 1986, N.Y. Bus. Press. Editors, 1987, first Boston U. Coll. of Liberal Arts Young Alumni award, 1985. Avocations: fiction writing, travel, snorkeling.

GROSS, LEROY, sugar company executive; b. N.Y.C., Aug. 11, 1926; s. Morris and Sarah (Leichter) G.; m. Betty Koch, Aug. 28, 1949; children: Michael Stephen, Kenneth Richard, Emily Jayne Gross Eider. BS in Acctg., NYU, 1948; postgrad., Fordham U., 1951-53; MBA in Acctg., NYU, 1955. With SuCrest Corp., N.Y.C., 1948-77, internal audit mgr., 1962-65, corp. acctg. mgr., 1965-69, contr., 1969-75, asst. sec., 1971-77; v.p. N.Y.C., 1975-77; v.p., contr. Revere Sugar Corp., 1977-86. Lectr. NYU, 1968-71; cons. in field. With USAAF, 1946-47. Mem. Inst. Internal Auditors, Nat. Assn. Accountants, Fin. Execs. Inst. Home and Office: 118 Winder Rd Yorktown VA 23693-3222

GROSS, LESLIE PAMELA, sales executive, consultant; b. N.Y., Aug. 23, 1952; d. Gerald Jay and Pearl (Meltzer) G.; m. Ned T. Ashby (div. Mar. 1997); 1 child, James Warren Taylor Ashby. AB, Cornell U., 1976. Ins. agt. Equitable Life, San Francisco, 1976-79; sales assoc. Digital Equipment Corp., San Francisco, 1979-81, from sales rep. to sales exec. Santa Clara, Calif., 1981-87, corp. acct. mgr. San Francisco, 1987-92; area mgr. WordPerfect Corp., Orem, Utah, 1992-94; sr. account mgr. Novell, Inc., Santa Clara, Calif., 1994-97; sr. client rep. IBM, Menlo Park, Calif., 1997—2001, client exec., 2001—. Missionary, LDS Ch., Boston, 1973-75; jr. Sunday sch. tchr., Menlo Park, Calif., 1993-95, 1996-98, 2002—; pres. Women's Relief Soc., Stanford, Calif., 1986, counselor, Palo Alto, Calif., 1987-88, counselor, stake pres., Menlo Park, 1991-92, edn. com. 1999-2001; sec. Channing Pl. Homeowners Assn., Palo Alto, 1987-88, 90-91, pres., 1988-90. Avocations: travel, cinema, fitness. E-mail: lpgross@us.ibm.com.

GROSS, LILLIAN, psychiatrist, educator; b. N.Y.C., Aug. 18, 1932; m. Harold Ratner, Feb. 4, 1961; children: Sanford Miles, Marcia Ellen. BA, Barnard Coll., 1953; postgrad., U. Lausanne, Switzerland, 1954-56; MD, Duke U., 1959. Diplomate Bd. Pediatrics, Am. Bd. Psychiatry and Neurology, Am. Bd. Child Psychiatry. Intern Kings County Hosp., Bklyn., 1959-60, resident, 1967-70, psychiatrist devel. evaluation clinic, 1970-72; resident Jewish Hosp., Bklyn., 1960-62; physician in charge pediatric psychiat. clinic Greenpoint (N.Y.) Hosp., 1964-67; pvt. practice pvt. practice, Great Neck, N.Y., 1970—. Clin. instr. psychiatry Downstate Med. Ctr., Bklyn., 1970-74, clin. asst. prof., 1974-99; lectr. in psychiatry Columbia U., 1974-99; psychiat. cons. N.Y.C. Bd. Edn., 1972-75, Queens Children's Hosp., 1975-96; mem. med. bd. Saras Ctr., Great Neck, N.Y., 1977—. Child psychiatry fellow Kings County Hosp., 1969-70, pediatric psychiatry fellow, 1962-63. Fellow Am. Acad. Pediatrics, Am. Acad. Child Psychiatry, N.Y. Soc. Clin. Hypnosis (pres.); mem. AMA, Nassau Pediatric Socs., Soc. Adolscent Psychiatry, N.Y. Coun. Child Psychiatry, Am. Med. Women's Assn. (Nassau, pres. 1985-86, 95-96), N.Y. Med. Socs., Internat. Soc. Study of Multiple Personality and Dissociation (founder, pres. L.I. component study group), Greater Long Island Psychiat. Soc. Home and Office: 55 Blue Bird Dr Great Neck NY 11023-1001 E-mail: drlillian@aol.com.

GROSS, MARILYN AGNES, artist, business owner, speech audiologist; b. Rolla, Mo., Jan. 23, 1937; d. John Andrew and Florence Margaret (White) Robertson; m. James Dehnert Gross, Jan. 9, 1960; children: Kathleen Ann, Terrence Michael, Brian Andrew, Kevin Matthew. Student, U. Mo., 1955; BS, St. Louis U., 1958; Cert., Washington Sch. Art, 1978. Audiologist Bur. Maternal and Child Health U.S. Dept. Pub. Health, Washington, 1959; pvt. practice speech therapist Millington, Tenn., 1959—60; owner, dir. Marilyn's Studio, Creative Systems for Creative People, Streator, Ill., 1983—93, Osprey, Fla., 1993—; bus. mgr. Pathology Services, Streator, 1984—93; art represented by Toby Falk N.Y.C., 1988—90. Exhbn. coord. Arts Week Community Project, Streator, 1982; visual arts rep. Ill. Pub. Sch. System on Improvement of Fine Arts Curriculum, 1986; speaker numerous civic orgns. and clubs; participant numerous art seminars and confs. Exhbns. include: Ill. Valley Art League (award) 1975, 76, Town and Country, Ottawa, Ill. (award), 1975, 76, 77, (award) 78, (2 awards) 79, (award) 81, Streator Centennial, 1976, North Light mag. Competition, Westport, Conn., 1977, Internat. Soc. Artists Competition, N.Y.C., 1978, Ann. Town and Country State Art Show, Peru, Ill., (3 awards) 1979, (4 awards) 80, (award) 81, 82, Urbana, Ill., 1979, 80 (State award), Pekin, 1980, Ill. Valley Art League Silver Ann. Show, 1980, Ducks Unlimited Contest, 1980, Link Gallery, Oglesby, Ill., 1981, Streator Arts Happening, 1982, Ill. Watercolor Exhbn., Glenview (traveling exhbn. award), 1983, Springfield, 1985, Ill. Art League Lakeview Mus., 1984, Springfield (Ill.) Art Assn., 1985, Gallery 100 Premier Exhbn., Chgo., 1985, Limelight Club, Chgo., 1986, Galesburg Civic Art Ctr., 1987, N. Coast Coll. Soc., 1988 (2 awards), Hiram (Ohio) Coll., 1988, Adirondack Nat. Exhbn. of Am. Watercolors, Old Forge, N.Y., 1988, Riverlands '88 Exhbn., Hopkinsville, Ky., 1988, Ft. Wayne (Ind.) Mus. Art, 1988, 89, Alice and Arthur Baer Competitive Exhbn., Chgo., 1988 (award), 48th Nat. Competition, Fine Arts Mus. of South, Watercolor Soc. Ala., Mobile, 1989, Soc. Experimental Artists Nat. Juried Exhibit, U. North TX, 1994, Western Colo. Watercolor Exhibition, Nat. Juried Exhibition, Grand Junction CO (Juror's Award), 1997, Watercolor USA, Nat. Juried Exhibition Springfield Mus. Art, MO, 1998, Am. Watercolor Soc. Exhbn., Salmagundi Club, N.Y.C., 1998, Internat. Soc. Exptl. Artists, Internat. Juried Exhibit, U. North Tex., Ft. Worth, Tex., 1998 (award), Ariz. Aqueous, 1999, Nat. Juried Exhbn., Tubac (Ariz.) Ctr. for the Arts, 1999, 8th Annual Internatl. Soc. of Experimental Artists Exhibition, Huntsville Mus. of Art, 1999, 19th Annual Faber Birren Natl. Color Exhibition, Univ. of Conn., Stamford, CT, 1999, Intuitive Art, Rosemary Ct. Galleries, Sarasota, 2000, No. Trust Exhbn., Longboat Key, Fla., 2000, Internat. Soc. Exptl. Artists Exhbn., Dennos Mus., Traverse City, Mich., 2001, 6th Ann. Nat. USA Acrylic Painters' Assn. Exhbn., Segretto Contemporary Art Gallery, Santa Fe, 2002, Watermedia, 2003, Houston, 2003, Challenge of the Champions, 2003; one-woman shows include: Engle Ln. Gallery, Streator, 1980, 81, 82, 84, 85, Illini Union Gallery, Urbana, 1982, Dai-Ichi Kangyo, Ltd., Chgo., 1983, Atrium Gallery We. Ill. U., Macomb, 1983, John G. Blank Ctr. for Arts, Michigan City, Ind., 1984, 1st Nat. Bank of Morton (Ill.) Gallery, 1985, Birchwood Farms Estate, Harbor Springs, Mich., 1988, L'Attitude Gallery, Sarasota, Fla., 2003; gallery shows include Copley Soc., Boston, 1983-86, Lakeview Mus. Gallery, Peoria, Ill., 1983-88, Springfield Art Assn. Gallery, 1983—, The Prism Gallery, Evanston, Ill, 1987-88, Ft. Wayne Mus. Art Gallery, 1988, Artisan's Gallery, Petoskey, Mich., 1988-90, Hodgell Gallery, Sarasota, Fla., 1995-2002, L'Attitude Gallery, Sarasota, 2002-03, Boston, 2002—; represented in numerous corp. and pvt. collections; painting selected for books: Best of Watercolor, 1995, Creative Watercolor, 1996, Abstracts in Watercolor, 1996, Creative Inspiration, 1997, Painting Color, Best of Watercolor Series, 1997, Watercolor Mag., Spring 2001, The Collected Best of Watercolor, 2002, Splash 7: A Celebration of Light, 2002; Watercolor Magic Mag., Spring, 2002; Painting Composition, Best of Watercolor Series, 1997; author: Gift of Love, 1975 (Peter Herring Poetry award), The President's Book, 1971, Studio Log: Making it Happen-Creative Systems for Creative People, 1988. Mem. St. Anthony's Parents Club, 1966-82; rep. White House conf. on library and info. services, 1978. Recipient photography award CICCA Interclub Comp., 1981, 82, (3 awards) 83, 2 photography awards Pictorialists Comp., 1982, painting award Binney & Smith Corp., 1982, photography award Fuji Photo Comp., 1983, profl. award Ill. Art League, 1984; named Artist of Month Springfield (Ill.) Art Assn. Gallery, 1983; represented in numerous biographies and revs. in newspapers and books. Mem. Am. Med. Soc. Aux., Assn. Clin. Scientists Aux., Am. Soc. Clin. Pathologists Aux., Coll. Am. Pathologists Aux., LaSalle County Med. Soc. Aux., Am. Speech and Hearing Assn. (cert.), Internat. Soc. Artists (charter), Associated Photographers Internat., Am. Watercolor Assn. (assoc.), Nat. Watercolor Assn. (assoc.), Midwest Watercolor Assoc., Nat. Collage Soc. (signature mem.), Watercolor Soc., Ill. Art League, Ky. Watercolor Soc., Ala. Watercolor Soc., Nat. Acrylic Painters Assn. (signature mem.), Internat. Soc. Exptl. Artists (signature mem.), Knickerbocker

Artists N.Y., Soc. Painters in Casein and Acrylics, Chgo. Artists Coalition, Pictoralists Club, Delta Sigma Epsilon, Sigma Alpha Eta, Delta Zeta (State Day award 1958). Republican. Roman Catholic. Home: 374 MacEwen Dr Osprey FL 34229-9233

GROSS, MICHAEL ROBERT, writer, editor; b. N.Y.C., July 16, 1952; s. Milton and Estelle (Murov) G.; m. Barbara Hodes, June 21, 1986. BA, Vassar Coll., Poughkeepsie, N.Y., 1974. Music columnist Andy Warhol's Interview, N.Y.C., 1973-74; editor-in-chief Rock Mag., N.Y.C., 1976-78, Fire Island News, N.Y.C., 1978; contbg. editor, columnist Manhattan, Inc., N.Y.C., 1984-85; reporter, columnist N.Y. Times, N.Y.C., 1985-88; contbg. editor N.Y. Mag., N.Y.C., 1988-94; commentator CBS This Morning, N.Y.C., 1992-93; sr. writer Esquire Mag., N.Y.C., 1994-95; contbg. editor Tatler mag., London, 1994-99; writer at large GQ Mag., N.Y.C., 1996-00; contbg. editor N.Y. Mag., N.Y.C., 1997-00, Travel and Leisure mag., N.Y.C., 1997—; sr. editor George Mag., N.Y.C., 2000; contbg. writer Talk mag., N.Y.C., 2001—02; columnist Daily News, N.Y.C., 2002—03; contbg. writer Radar mag., 2003—. Author: Robert Plant, 1975, Bob Dylan, 1978, Model: The Ugly Business of Beautiful Women, 1995, My Generation: Fifty Years of Sex, Drugs, Rock, Revolution, Glamour, Greed, Valor, Faith and Silicon Chips, 2000, The More Things Change: Why the Baby Boom Won't Fade Away, 2001, Genuine Authentic: The Real Life of Ralph Lauren, 2003; co-author: The Rock Yearbook, 1980, Temple Kent, 1982, Shattered Mask, 1983, Precious Objects, 1984; contbr. articles to profl. jours. Mem. Am. Soc. Journalists and Authors, Authors Guild. Office: Trident Media Group 41 Madison Ave New York NY 10010

GROSS, PATRICK WALTER, business executive, management consultant; b. Ithaca, N.Y., May 15, 1944; s. Eric T. B. and Catharine B. (Rohrer) G.; m. Sheila Eve Proby, Apr. 12, 1969; children: Geoffrey Philipp, Stephanie Lovell. Student, Cornell U., 1962 63; B in Engring. Sci., Rensselaer Poly. Inst., 1965; MSE in Applied Math., U. Mich., 1966; MBA, Stanford U., 1968. Cons. info. mgmt. operation Gen. Electric Co., Schnectady, 1965-67; sr. staff mem. Office Sec. Def., Washington, 1968-69, spl. asst., 1969-70; founder, prin. exec. officer, chmn. exec. com. Am. Mgmt. Systems, Inc., Arlington, Va., 1970—, also bd. dirs. Also bd. dirs.; chmn. bd. dirs. Medlantic Enterprises, Inc., 1988-94, Baker and Taylor Holdings, Inc., 1994—, dir., 1992—, Medlantic Healthcare Group, Capital One Fin. Corp., Net 2000 Comm., Landmark Sys. Corp., Powersim Corp., Computer Network Tech. Corp., Net 2000 Comm.; adv. coun. Stanford Grad. Sch. of Bus., 1999—, Ctr. for Strategic and Internat. Statis., 1998—. Trustee Washington Hosp. Ctr., 1977-87, Georgetown Med. Ctr., 2000—, Sidwell Friends Sch., 1980-88, 92—, Wolf Trap Found. Performing Arts, 1997—, Com. for Econ. Devel., Georgetown U. Hosp., 2000—, Aspen Inst., 2001—; mem. exec. com., treas. Youth for Understanding, 1984-90, 93—, vice chmn., 1996—, Youth for Understanding Found., Germany, 1989—; mem. Econ. Policy Coun. UNA-USA, mem. Coun. on Competitiveness, Fed. City Coun., Washington, 1992—; bd. dirs. Wolf Trap Fund. for the Performing Arts, 1997—; mem. adv. bd. Ctr. Strategic Internat. Studies; adv. coun. Stanford Grad. Sch. Bus.; adv. bd. Stanford Inst. for Econ. Policy Rsch. Mem. Fgn. Policy Assn. (bd. govs., bd. dirs., mem. exec. com. 1977-86, 87—), World Affairs Coun. Washington (bd. dirs., founding vice chmn. 1980-91, chmn. 1991—), Coun. Excellence in Govt. (bd. dirs. 1996—, v. chmn. 1999—), Jamestown Found. (bd. dirs. 1997—), Aspen Inst. (bd. dirs. 2001—), Coun. Fgn. Rels., Washington Inst. Fgn. Affairs, Internat. Inst. Strategic Studies (London), World Econ. Forum (Geneva), Econ. Club Washington, Nat. Economists Club, Aspen Inst. Soc. Fellows, Pilgrims of U.S., Smithsonian Luncheon Group, Met. Club Washington, Chevy Chase Club, Univ. Club N.Y.C., Useless Bay Country Club (Wash.), Sigma Xi, Tau Beta Pi. Home: 7401 Glenbrook Rd Bethesda MD 20814-1327 Office: Am Mgmt Sys Inc 4050 Legato Rd Fairfax VA 22033-4087 E-mail: pat_gross@ams.com.

GROSS, PAUL ALLAN, health service executive; b. Va., VA, Oct. 1, 1937; s. Albert and Cynthia (Saxe) G.; m. Gail Byrd, Nov. 19, 1966; children: Lorri, Garry, Randy. Student, U. Richmond, 1956-59; BA, U. Ga., 1961; M.H.A., Va. Commonwealth U., 1964; cert. in hosp. adminstrn., U. Miami, Jackson Meml. Hosp. Adminstrv. resident in hosp. adminstrn. Tampa Gen. Hosp., Fla., 1964; adminstrv. asst. Dallas County Hosp. Dist., 1964-66, asst. adminstr., 1966-69, sr. asst. adminstr., 1969-70, assoc. adminstr., 1971-72; clin. assoc. prof. hosp. med. care U. Tex. Southwestern Med. Sch., 1964-72, Sch. Allied Health Scis., Dallas, 1964 72; exec. dir. Humana Inc. Suburban Hosp., Louisville, 1972-76; v.p. Fla. region Humana Inc., Miami, 1976-81; sr. v.p. Pacific Region Humana Inc., Newport Beach, Calif., 1981-84, exec. v.p., pres. hosp. div., 1984-92; ret. Humana Inc., 1992; prof., health adminstr. Va. Commonwealth U./Med. Coll. Va., 1992-95, prof. emeritus, 1996—. Nat. cons. emeritus Surgeon Gen. USAF, 1987—; vice chmn. bd. trustees MedEcon, Inc., Louisville, 1993-96, also bd. dirs.; bd. dirs. St. Anthony Pub. Co., Washington, 1993-96; advisor KBL Healthcare Inc., Comprehensive Med. Mgmt., Inc., N.Y.C. 1993-96. Contbr. articles to profl. jours. Mem. health adv. com. Senator Paul Carpenter, Cypress, Calif., 1983; mem., chmn. U.S. Selective Svc. System Local Bd. 154, Newport Beach, 1983, Bd. 13, Louisville, 1982-2002; bd. assocs. U. Richmond, Va., 1990-96; bd. dirs. St. Francis High Sch., Louisville, 1989-92, Louisville Zool. Found. Bd., 1989-96, chmn. investment com., 1992; mem. adv. bd. Sch. Nursing, 1992-96, Spalding U., 1997; chmn. devel. bd. Jefferson County Community Coll., Kentuckiana Edn. and Work Force Com.bd. dirs U.S. Selective Svc. Bd., 1981-2002, dir.emeritus 2001—; preceptor Fellowship Program-Education with Industry, USAF, 1986-92; bd. dirs. Spaulding U., 1996-97, bd, dirs.Med. Coll. Va. Found. (chmn. audit and applications com. 1993-2000; pres. bd. dirs. Pelican Cove Two Condo Assn. With USNR, 1955—63. Named Outstanding Adminstr., Ctrl Region Humana, 1975, 1976; recipient Humana Club award, Ctrl. Region, Louisville, 1974—76, Presdl. medallion, Va. Commonwealth U., 1995. Fellow Am. Coll. Health Care Execs. (ethics com., chmn. inv. droped sect. 1993—); mem. Tex. Hosp. Assn., Hosp. Coun. So. Calif. (chmn. multi-instnl. corp. liaison com. 1983—), United Hosp. Assn. Calif., Fedn. Am. Healthcare Sys. & Am. Hosp. Assn. (hon. life). Mailing: 1730 Peninsula Dr Tavares FL 32778 Fax: 352-742-0483.

GROSS, PETER ALAN, epidemiologist, researcher; b. Newark, Nov. 18, 1938; s. Meyer P. and Nathalie (Bass) Denburg) G.; m. Regina Teri Gittlin, May 30, 1964; children: Deborah Karen, Michael Philip, Daniel Brian. BA cum laude, Amherst Coll., 1960; MD, Yale U., 1964. Diplomate Am. Bd. Internal Medicine. Intern Yale-New Haven Hosp., 1964-65, jr. resident, 1965-66; sr. resident Peter Bent Brigham Hosp., Boston, 1968-69; research and edn. assoc. Va Hosp., West Haven, Conn., 1971-73, acting chief infectious disease sect., 1972-73; chief infectious disease sect. VA Hosp., West Haven, Conn., 1973-74, Hackensack (N.J.) U. Med. Ctr., 1974—, chmn. dept. medicine, 1980—, chmn. med. bd., 1986; prof. medicine N.J. Med. Sch., Newark, 1981—, vice chmn. dept. medicine, 1994—. Assoc. clin. prof. medicine Columbia U. Coll. Physicians and Surgeons, N.Y.C., 1971—81, asst. clin. prof., 1974—77; asst. prof. medicine Yale U. Sch. Medicine, New Haven, 1971—74; ad hoc reviewer rsch. grants NIH, Nat. Inst. Allergy and Infectious Diseases; investigator Ctr. for Biologic Evaluation and Rsch. FDA, 1974—95; chmn. drug safety and risk mgmt. adv. com. Ctr. for Drug Evaluation and Rsch. FDA, 2002; mem. clin. indicators task force Joint Commn. on Accreditation of Healthcare Orgns., 1987—89, chmn. pneumonia clin. adv. panel, 1999—2001; project dir. Phase I and Phase II Pursuing Perfection! Raising the Bar for Health Care Performance Robert Wood Johnson Found. and Inst. for Healthcare Improvement; mem. Sentinel Event Alert Adv. Group; mem. expert panels on cmty.-acquired pneumonia, HCQIP surg. dir. prevention HCQIP Ctrs. for Medicare and Medicaid Svc., 1998—2002; co-chmn. N.J. Quality Improvement Adv. Com. Author: Gram Strain Recognition, 1975, 2d edit., 1980, Managing Your Health, 1991; past assoc. editor: Clinical Performance and Quality Health Care; mem. editorial bd. Jour. Clin. Microbiology, 1980—, Infection Control, 1980-90, mem. editl. bd. Managed Care, 1998—; editl. adv. bd. Joint Commn. Jour. Quality Improvement. Served to lt. comdr. USPHS, CDC, 1966-68. NIH fellow Yale U., 1969-71. Fellow Infectious Diseases Soc. Am. (clin. affairs com., past chair practice guidelines com., councillor 2000-02); mem. ACP (task force on adult immunization), Am. Acad. Microbiology, Am. Soc. Virology, Am. Soc. Microbiology, Soc. Healthcare Epidemiologists Am. (councillor 1986-88, v.p. 1992, pres.-elect 1993, pres. 1994, past pres. 1995), Assn. Profs. Medicine. Office: Hackensack U Med Ctr Dept Internal Medicine Hackensack NJ 07601

GROSS, RICHARD EDMUND, education educator; b. Chgo., May 25, 1920; s. Edmund Nicholas and Florence (Gallistel) G.; m. Jane Clare Hartl, May 25, 1943; children: Kathryn Ann, Elaine Clare, Edmund Ralph, John Richard. BS, U. Wis., 1942, MS, 1946; EdD, Stanford U., 1951. Jr. personnel officer FSA, Milw., 1942-43; tchr. Central High Sch., Madison, Wis., 1943-48; instr. Menlo Sch. and Coll., Menlo Park, Calif., 1948-51; asso. prof. Fla. State U., 1951-55; mem. faculty Sch. Edn., Stanford U., 1955—, prof., 1965—87, chmn. curriculum and tchr. edn., 1977-90. Chief cons. central com. social studies Calif. Dept. Edn., 1958-60; Fulbright lectr. tchr. edn. U. Wales, Swansea, 1961-62; guest prof. Am. Inst., U. Frankfurt, Germany, 1968-69; ednl. adviser World Bank Pilot Center project U. Santiago, Spain, 1973; vis. prof. Monash U., Melbourne, Australia, 1976; curriculum cons. to schs., 1952— ; guest lectr. Taiwan Tchrs. Inst., Taipei, 1990, Seoul Nat. U., Republic of Korea, 1995; Bicentennial lectr. U. Alaska, Anchorage, 1987; adv. bd. Edn. Policy Com., 1958-68; chmn. nat. advisory bd. E.R.I.C. Social Sci. Center, U. Colo., 1969-71; dir. social studies, adviser Addison-Wesley Publs., 1970-83; bd. dirs. Calif. Inst. Internat. Studies, Inst. Devel. Human Resources; co-dir. nat. citizenship edn. study, 1985-93. Author: How to Handle Controversial Issues, 1952, The Problems Approach and the Social Studies, 1955, The Sociology of the School, 1957, The United States Congress, 1957, Educating Citizens for Democracy, 1958, The Heritage of American Education, 1962, British Secondary Education, 1965, Civics in Action, 1966, Man's World: A Physical Geography, 1966, The History of Education: A Timeline, 1967, Teaching the Social Studies, 1969, Profile of America, 1971, Quest for Liberty, 1971, Teaching Social Studies Skills, 1973, The Human Experience, 1974, Social Studies for Our Times, 1978, American Citizenship: How We Govern, 1979, Learning to Live in Society, 1980, What Should We Be Teaching in the Social Studies, 1983, Ciencias Sociales, 1983, What Chinese Children Have Learned About the United States, 1990, Social Science Perspectives on Citizenship, 1990, Designing Effective Instruction for Secondary Social Studies, 1998, 3d edit., 2003; editor: Phi Delta Kappa Bi-centennial Fast-Backs, 1976, Calif. Social Sci. Rev., 1962—68; contbr. articles to encys., profl. jours.; creator Scholastic World-Affairs Multitext Publs., 1963, K. and E. overhead viewer transparencies for U.S. History, 1964. Mem. ASCD, AAUP, NEA, Nat. Coun. Social Studies (pres. 1967, Career Rsch. award 1990), Nat. Soc. Study Edn., Am. Acad. Polit. and Social Sci., History of Edn. Soc., World Assn. Civic Edn. (exec. com.), Phi Alpha Theta, Kappa Delta Tau, Phi Delta Kappa (Hilda Taba hon. award, 1988). Home: 26304 Esperanza Dr Los Altos CA 94022-2653 Office: Stanford Univ Cubberley Hall Stanford CA 94305

GROSS, ROBERT ALAN, history educator; b. New Haven, Feb. 17, 1945; s. Samuel and Roslyn (Chadys) G.; m. Ann Leslie Goldman, May 22, 1966; children: Matthew Benjamin, Stephen Alexander, Eleanor Elizabeth. BA, U. Pa., 1966; MA (Woodrow Wilson nat. fellow), Columbia U., 1968, PhD, 1976; MA (hon.), Amherst Coll., 1986. Gen. sec. U.S. Student Press Assn., Washington, 1966-67; asst. editor Newsweek, N.Y.C., 1968-70; NIMH trainee in social history Columbia U., 1970-72; adj. asst. prof. Worcester Poly. Inst., 1973-76; asst. prof. history and Am. studies Amherst Coll., 1976-80, assoc. prof., 1980-86, prof., 1986-88; prof. Am. studies and history, dir. Am. studies Coll. of William and Mary, 1988-98, Forrest D. Murden prof. Am. studies, 1992—2003; James L. and Shirley A. Draper chair of early Am. hist. U. Conn., 2003—. Prof. Am. studies U. Sussex, Brighton, England, 1981-83; vis. prof., dir. studies Ecoles des Hautes Etudes en Sciences Sociales, Paris, 1985; vis. assoc. prof. Brandeis U., 1985; core scholar New England and the Constitution, 1986-88, Am. Studies specialist U.S. Info. Agy., 1991-92; dir. NEH Summer Inst., 1993; Fulbright chair of Am. studies Odense (Denmark) U., 1998-99, Fulbright sr. specialist (Brazil), 2003; book rev. editor William and Mary quar., 1999—2002. Author: The Minutemen and Their World, 1976 (Nat. Hist. Soc. Book award, Bancroft prize), Books and Libraries in Thoreau's Concord, 1988, In Debt to Shays: The Bicentennial of an Agrarian Rebellion, 1993; mem. editorial bd. Jour. Am. History, 1995-98. Bd. dirs. Rose Brook Sch., 2003—. Guggenheim fellow, 1979-80, Charles Warren fellow Harvard U., 1979-80, Amherst Coll. Trustees faculty fellow, 1979-80, Bibliog. Soc. Am. fellow, 1984, Kate and Hall Peterson fellow Am. Antiquarian Soc., 1984, Howard Found. fellow, 1988-89, Old Sturbridge Village Rsch. fellow, 1991, NEH fellow, 1994; residency Rockefeller Found.'s Study and Conf. Ctr., Bellagio, Italy, 1994. Fellow Soc. Am. Historians; mem. Am. Hist. Assn., Orgn. Am. Historians, Am. Studies Assn. (Mary C. Turpie award 2001, Am. Antiquarian Soc. (chair program in the history of the book in Am. culture 1993-98, coun. 1999-2002, Mellon Disting. scholar in residence 2002-03), Colonial Soc. Mass., Mass. Hist. Soc., New Eng. History Tchrs. Assn. (Kidger award 1987), Phi Beta Kappa. Democrat. Jewish. Home: 235 Grant Hill Rd Tolland CT 06084-4907 Office: U Conn 241 Glenbrook Rd Unit 2103 Storrs Mansfield CT 06269-8795 E-mail: robert.gross@uconn.edu., robert5725@cox.net.

GROSS, RONALD MARTIN, forest products executive; BA, Ohio State U., 1955; MBA, Harvard U., 1960. With Battelle Meml. Inst., Columbus, Ohio, 1957-58, Champion Internat., 1960-68, Can. Cellulose Co. Ltd., Vancouver, B.C., 1968-78, pres., CEO, dir., 1973-78; pres., COO ITT Rayonier, Inc., Stamford, Conn., 1978-81, pres., CEO, 1981-84, chmn., pres., CEO, 1984-96; chmn., CEO, 1996-98; chmn. emeritus, 1999—. Bd. dirs. Rayonier Inc., Pittston Co., Corn Products Internat. Office: 6 Landmark Sq Ste 400 Stamford CT 06901-2704

GROSS, ROSALIE-ETHELYN, secretary; b. N.Y.C., Feb. 24, 1914; d. Jacob Samuel Jr. and Julia Ethelyn Lavall; m. Charles Ray Gross, Sept. 20, 1942 (dec. July 1980); 1 child, Eunice Elaine. Grad., Washington Irving H.S., N.Y.C., 1932. Sec. Doles Sr. Citizens, Mt. Vernon, N.Y., 1987-95, Cmty. Sch. Initiative, Mt. Vernon, 1996-99. Sec. newsletter for srs., Mt. Vernon, 1987-95. Recipient 12 awards United Way, 1995—. Mem.: Nat. Coun. Negro Women (corr. sect. 1995—, Westchester sect. recording sec. 1987—95, 7 achievement awards 1992—98). Avocations: art, theater, museums, ice skating shows, soap operas.

GROSS, RUTH TAUBENHAUS, former pediatrician; b. Bryan, Tex., June 24, 1920; d. Jacob and Esther (Hirshenson) Taubenhaus; m. Reuben H. Gross, Jr., Aug. 22, 1942 (div. June 1952); 1 child, Gary E. BA Barnard Coll., 1941, MD Columbia U., 1944. Intern Charity Hosp., New Orleans, 1944; resident in pediat. Tulane U., New Orleans, 1945, Columbia U., N.Y.C., 1946—47; instr. Radcliffe Infirmary, Oxford, England, 1949—50; instr. pediat. Stanford (Calif.) U., 1950—53, asst. prof., 1953—56, assoc. prof., 1956—60, prof., 1973—92, prof. emerita, 1992, acting exec. pediat., 1957—59, assoc. dean student affairs, 1973—75, dir. divsn. gen. and ambulatory pediat., 1975—85, dir. Stanford-Children's Ambulatory Care Ctr., 1980—85. Nat. study dir. Infant Health and Devel. Program, 1983—92; assoc. prof. pediat., co-dir. divsn. human genetics Albert Einstein Coll. Medicine, Yeshiva U., N.Y.C., 1960—64, prof. pediat., 1964—66; clin. prof. pediat. U. Calif. Med. Ctr., San Francisco, 1966—73; dir. dept. pediat. Mt. Zion Hosp. and Med. Ctr., San Francisco, 1966—73. Contbr. articles to profl. jours. Fellow Commonwealth human genetics, Instituto de Genetica, Pavia, Italy, 1959—60. Mem.: Soc. Rsch. in Child Devel., Ambulatory Pediatric Assn., Am. Acad. Pediat., Soc. Pediatric Rsch., Am. Pediatric Soc., Am. Fedn. Clin. Rsch., Inst. Medicine NAS, Sigma Xi, Alpha Omega Alpha, Phi Beta Kappa. E-mail: rpgross@nas.edu.

GROSS, SAMSON RICHARD, geneticist, biochemist, educator; b. N.Y.C., July 27, 1926; s. Isidor and Ethel (Mermelstein) G.; m. Helen Hudi Steinmetz, Sept. 16, 1952; children: Deborah Ann, Michael Robert, Eva Elizabeth. BA, NYU, 1949; A.M., Columbia, 1951, PhD (USPHS fellow), 1953. Asst. prof. genetics Stanford U., 1956-57; asst. prof. genetics Rockefeller U., N.Y.C., 1957-60; assoc. prof. dept. microbiology and immunology Duke, Durham, N.C., 1960-65, prof. genetics and biochemistry, 1965-91, prof. emeritus genetics and biochemistry, 1991—, dir. div. genetics dept. biochemistry, 1965-77, dir. univ. program in genetics, 1967-77. Bd. dirs. Cold Spring Harbor Lab. Quantitative Biology, N.Y., 1967-72 USPHS Spl. fellow Weizmann Inst., 1969-70; Josiah Macy Found. fellow Hebrew U., 1977-78; John Simon Guggenheim fellow Hebrew U., 1985-86. Mem. Genetic Soc. Am., AAAS, Am. Soc. Microbiology, Am. Soc. Biol. Chemists, Phi Beta Kappa. Home: PO Box 498 Little Switzerland NC 28749-0498 also: 2411 Prince St Durham NC 27707

GROSS, SHARON RUTH, forensic psychologist, researcher; b. L.A., Mar. 21, 1940; d. Louis and Sylvia Marion (Freedman) Lackman; m. Zoltan Gross, Mar. 1969 (div.); 1 child, Andrew Ryan; m. Ira Chroman, June 1994. BA, UCLA, 1983; MA, U. So. Calif., L.A., 1985, PhD, 1991. Diplomate Am. Bd. Psychol. Spltys. Tech. Rytron, Van Nuys, Calif., 1958-60; computress on tetrahedral satellite Space Tech. Labs., Redondo Beach, Calif., 1960-62; owner Wayfarer Yacht Corp., Costa Mesa, Calif., 1962-64; electronics draftsperson, designer stroke-writer characters Tasker Industries, Van Nuys, 1964-65; pvt. practice cons. Sherman Oaks, Calif., 1965-75, 77-80; printed circuit bd. designer Systron-Donner, Van Nuys, Calif., 1975-76; design checker, tech. writer Vector Gen., Woodland Hills, Calif., 1976-77; undergrad. adv. U. So. Calif., L.A., 1987-89, rsch. asst. prof., rsch. assoc. social psychology, 1991—. Owner Attitude Rsch. Litigation and Orgn. Cons.; prof. Pierce Coll., Woodland Hills, Calif., 2000—. Contbr. articles to profl. jours., chpts. to books. Recipient Haynes Found. Dissertation fellowship U. So. Calif., 1990. Fellow Am. Coll. Forensic Examiners, mem. APA, AAAS, Computer Graphics Pioneers, Am. Psychol. Soc., Western Psychol. Assn. Democrat. Jewish. Office: 4570 Van Nuys Blvd #357 Sherman Oaks CA 91403 E-mail: sharonrgross@cs.com.

GROSS, STANLEY CARL, marketing consultant; b. Bklyn., Apr. 3, 1938; s. Sidney and Estelle Gross; m. Anita Jackson, Oct. 3, 1971; 1 child, Amanda Rae. BA, Bklyn. Coll., 1959; MBA, St. John's U., 1966; PhD in Mktg. and Orgn. Devel., Union Exptl. Colls. and Univs., 1978. Sales rep. Avery Products Co., N.Y.C., 1959-62; v.p. sales Ranger Rsch., Inc., N.Y.C., 1962-68; v.p. mktg. Brian Lloyd Co. Inc., N.Y.C., 1969-71; pres. Stan Gross Assocs. Inc., Haverford, Pa., 1971—. Pvt. practice mktg. Marketing Maps; instr. Phila. Community Coll., 1973, Manor Jr. Coll., 1974; asst. prof. mktg. Rider Coll., 1975-81; keynote speaker Mature Mktg. Inst., N.Y.C. Author: Reconstituting Advertising Effectiveness, 1979, Market Directed Corporate Effectiveness, 1983, Marketing Maps, 1986, The Inner Mind of the Mature Market, 1989, Marketing Strategy is Best Achieved Through Inner Mind Marketing Maps, 1994, Advertising Learning: To Add a 92 Percent Assurance that the Marketer's new Planned Band Advertisement and Campaign Will Be Successful or Not, 1995, The Five Feelings That Determine the Prescriptions Physicians Write, 2000, Focusing the Creative Advertising Development Process, 2001, Getting on the Same Page as the Target Market, 2002; contbr. articles to profl. jours. With USAR, 1960-65. Recipient Pub. Svc. award Delaware County (Pa.), 1978, Faculty Adv. award Mktg. Club, Rider Coll., 1976. Mem. Am. Mktg. Assn. (awards 1979, 80), Assn. for Consumer Rsch. Republican. Jewish. Home and Office: 518 Waldron Park Dr Haverford PA 19041-1928 E-mail: stangross@aol.com.

GROSS, STEPHEN MARK, pharmacist, academic dean; b. Bklyn., July 31, 1938; s. Arthur S. and Hazel F. (Marks) Gross; m. Susan S. Farber, Nov. 5, 1961; 1 child, Julie S. BS, Columbia U., 1960, MA, 1969, EdD, 1975. Registered pharmacist N.Y., 1961. Pharmacist/mgr. C.O. Bigelow Chemists Inc., N.Y.C., 1960-65, Bigelow-Americana Chemists Inc., N.Y.C., 1963-65; asst. to dean Coll. Pharm. Scis., Columbia U., 1965-68, asst. dean, 1968-71, assoc. dean, 1971-72, acting dean, 1972-74, dean, 1974-76; dean grad. studies Arnold & Marie Schwartz Coll. Pharmacy and Health Scis. L.I. U., 1976-79; dean Sch. Bus. and Pub. Adminstrn., Bklyn. Ctr. L.I. U., 1983-84; dean grad. studies and research Conolly Coll. L.I.U., 1979-83, dean Faculties Pharmacy and Health Professions, 1984-88; dean Schwartz Coll. Pharmacy L.I. U., 1985—, dean Sch. of Health Professions, 1990—. Mem. health care quality improvement steering com. Island Profl. Rev. Orgn., 1995—2000; mem. NY State Bd. Pharmacy, 1991—2002, chmn., 1997—98, extended mem., 1991—. Contbr. Bd. dirs. Israel Humanitarian Found. Recipient numerous grants instnl. improvement. Mem.: Am. Soc. Health-Sys. Pharmacists, Nat. Cmty. Pharmacists Assn., Pharm. Soc. State N.Y., Am. Assn. Colls. Pharmacy (chmn. sect. continuing edn. 1979—80), Am. Pharm. Assn., Soc. Am. Magicians (v.p. N.Y. Assembly 1981—83, pres. 1983—84). Home: 43 Knott Dr Glen Cove NY 11542-4116 Office: LI U 1 University Plz Brooklyn NY 11201-5301 E-mail: sgross@liu.edu.

GROSS, STEPHEN RANDOLPH, accountant; b. Newark, Oct. 8, 1947; s. Edward Thomas and Frances (Randolph) G.; m. Barbara Louise Schutz, June 14, 1969 (div. Jan. 1981); children: David Randolph, Matthew Jeffrey; m. Tami Marie Haddad, Dec. 30, 1999. AB, Duke U., 1970. CPA Ga.; cert. CFE, fraud examiner, CVA, valuation analyst Ga. From staff acct. to ptnr. Lester Witte & Co., Atlanta, 1970—74, ptnr. Chgo., 1974—79, nat. dir. tng., 1978—79, exec. com.; founder HLB Gross Collins, Atlanta, 1979—. Trustee nds; bd. dirs. ebank.atlanta, Anderson Calhoun, Ltd., Healthfield, Inc.; treas. Henry Aaron Ent., Inc., Milw.; v.p. Coventry Holding Group, Inc., Decatur, Ga.; sec. Carint of NA, Milan; mng. dir. Next Tech. Golf, LLC. Bd. dirs. Henry Grady Found.; active Atlanta Symphony Orch., 1975—, High Mus. Art, Atlanta, 1985—, Ga. Pub. Policy Found., 1991—. Mem. AICPA, Ga. Soc. CPAs, Nat. Assn. Cert. Valuation Analysis, Assn. Cert. Fraud Examiners, Inst. Bus. Appraisers, Cherokee Town amd Country Club, Chaine des Rotisseurs (Paris), Reynolds Plantation Club. Home: 175 River North Dr NW Atlanta GA 30328-1111 Office: HLB Gross Collins PC 2625 Cumberland Pkwy SE Ste 400 Atlanta GA 30339-3993 E-mail: sgross@grosscollins.com.

GROSS, STEVEN ROSS, lawyer; b. N.Y.C., June 15, 1946; s. Alexander and Lola (Mandelbaum) Gross; m. Georgette Francine Kleinhaus, Dec. 14, 1968; children: Amy, Jillian. BA, Columbia U., 1968, MA, 1969; LLB, Cambridge U., 1971; JD, Yale U., 1973. Bar: U.S. dist. Ct. (ea. and so. dists.) N.Y. 1974. Assoc. Debevoise & Plimpton, N.Y.C., 1973-80, ptnr., 1981—. Co-author: Collier Business Workout Guide; contbr. Mem.: ABA, Assn. of Bar of City of N.Y. Jewish. Home: 145 E 74th St New York NY 10021-3225 Office: Debevoise & Plimpton 919 3rd Ave 42nd Fl New York NY 10022-3094 E-mail: srgross@debevoise.com.

GROSS, THEODORE LAWRENCE, university administrator, author; b. Bklyn., Dec. 4, 1930; s. David and Anna (Weisbrod) G.; m. Selma Bell, Aug. 27, 1955 (dec. 1991); children: Donna, Jonathan; m. Joellen Gross, 2001. BA, U. Maine, 1952; MA, Columbia U., 1957, PhD, 1960. Prof. English CCNY, 1958-78, chmn. dept., 1970-72, assoc. dean and dean humanities, 1972-78, v.p. instl. advancement, 1976-77; provost Capitol Campus, Pa. State U., Middletown, 1979-83; dean Sch. Letters and Sci. SUNY Coll., Purchase, 1983-88; chmn. SUNY-Purchase Westchester Sch. Partnership, 1984-88; pres. Roosevelt U., Chgo., 1988—2002, chancellor, 2002—03. Vis. prof., Fulbright scholar, Nancy, France, 1964-65, 68-69, Dept. State lectr., Nigeria, Israel, Japan, Austria. Author: Albion W. Tourgée, 1964, Thomas Nelson Page, 1967, Hawthorne, Melville, Crane: A Critical Bibliography, 1971, The Heroic Ideal in American Literature, 1971, Academic Turmoil: The Reality and Promise of Open Education, 1980, Partners in Education: How Colleges Can Work with Schools to Improve Teaching and Learning, 1988, Roosevelt University: From Vision to Reality, 2002; also essays, revs.; editor: Fiction, 1967, Dark Symphony: Negro Literature in America, 1968, Representative Men, 1969, A Nation of Nations, 1971, The Literature of American Jews, 1973; gen. editor: Studies in Language and Literature, 1974, America in Literature, 1978. With AUS, 1952-54. Grantee, Rockefeller Found., 1976-77, Am. Coun. Learned Socs. Mem. MLA, PEN, Nat. Coun. Tchrs. of English (chmn. lit. com.), Century Assn., Univ. Club, Chgo. Club. Home: 1100 N Lake Shore Dr Chicago IL 60611-1070 E-mail: tgross@roosevelt.edu.

GROSS, THOMAS LESTER, obstetrician-gynecologist, researcher; b. Decatur, Ill., Aug. 17, 1945; s. Gilbert Wayne and Anna (Graham) G.; m. Judy Beth Osburn, Dec. 30, 1967; children: Elizabeth, Matthew, Joshua. BA in Chemistry, Bluffton (Ohio) Coll., 1967; MD, U. Ill., 1971. Diplomate Am. Bd. Ob-Gyn., subsplty. maternal/fetal medicine. Intern, resident Akron (Ohio) Gen. Med. Ctr., 1973-77; fellow maternal/fetal medicine Case Western Res. U., Cleve., 1977-79; asst. to dir perinatal clin. rsch. ctr. Cleve. Met. Gen. Hosp., 1982-85; acting dir. Perinatal Clin. Rsch. Ctr., 1985-86; asst. prof. ob-gyn. Case Western Res. U., Cleve., 1977-85, assoc. prof., 1985-86; assoc. prof. ob-gyn. U. Ill. Coll. Medicine, Peoria, 1986—, chmn. dept., 1986-97; dir. perinatology St. Francis Med. Ctr., Peoria, 1987—. Instr. Internat. Symposium Fetal Evaluation, Lima, Peru, 1983. Contbr. numerous articles to sci. jours. Mem. Physicians for Social Responsibility, Am. Coll. Obstetricians and Gynecologists (1st prize rsch. 1984), Ctrl. Assn. Obstetricians and Gynecologists (Cmty. Hosp. Rsch. award 1981, Ann. prize award for rsch. 1982), Soc. Perinatal Obstetricians, Soc. Gynecologic Investigation, Perinatal Rsch. Soc., Peoria Ob-Gyn. Soc. Office: Maternal Fetal Diagnostic Ctr 4911 Executive Dr Peoria IL 61614

GROSS, WILLIAM ALLEN, mechanical engineer; b. L.A., Nov. 17, 1924; s. William Allen and Margaret Florence (Hill) G.; m. Shirley Mae Jackson, Aug. 10, 1948 (dec. 1968); children: Constance, Ellen, Mark, David; m. Sharon Carol Philbrick, Aug. 22, 1970. BS, USCG Acad., New London, Conn., 1945; MS, U. Calif., Berkeley, 1949, PhD, 1951. Registered profl. engr., N.Mex. Lectr. to asst. prof. U. Calif., Berkeley, 1949—52; asst. prof. Iowa State U., Ames, 1952—55; mem. tech. staff Bell Telephone Labs., Murray Hill, NJ, 1955—56; mem. rsch.

staff, mgr. applied mechanics dept. IBM, San Jose, 1956—61; v.p. adv. tech. div., dir. rsch. AMPEX, Redwood City, Calif., 1961-72; vis. lectr. U. Calif., Berkeley, 1973—74; dean engring. U. N.Mex., Albuquerque, 1974—80, prof. mech. engring., elec. and computer engring., 1974—93, prof., dean emeritus, 1993—; dir. new techs. Tejas Power Corp., 1993—97. Vis. prof. Poly. U. Bucharest, 1991,93; dir. Lovelace Inhalation Toxicology Rsch. Inst., Albuquerque, 1976-97, U. N.Mex. Tech. Innovative Prog., 1978-87; dir. Renewable Energy Program, Vols. in Tech. Assistance, 1980-81; mem. bd. advisors Lovelace Respiratory Rsch. Inst., 1997—; cons. in field. Editor, author: Fluid Film Lubrication, 1961; author: Gas Film Lubrication, 1962; editor/author: Fluid Film Lubrication, 1982; patentee in field; contbr. articles to profl. jours. Bd. dirs. Am. Friends Svc. Com., 1970-72, Lovelace Respiratory Rsch. Inst., 1997—, Inhalation Toxicology Rsch. Inst., 1974-97, Futures for Children, Albuquerque, 1982-88, Trinity Forum, 1989-92. Recipient Chief Manuelito award, Navajo Tribe, 1982, Lifetime Achievement award N.Mex. Solar Energy Assn.; named N.Mex. Engr. of Yr., 1991, Disting. Alumnus U. Calif. Berkeley Coll. Engring., 1995, Disting. Alumnus, USCG Acad., 1997. Fellow AAAS, ASME (life; Centennial award 1978), IEEE (Third Millennium award); mem. Nat. Acad. Engrs., Nat. Soc. Profl. Engrs. N.Mex. Soc. Profl. Engrs. Democrat. Mem. Soc. Of Friends. Home: 1401 Las Lomas Rd NE Albuquerque NM 87106-4529 Office: U NMex Dept Mech Engring Albuquerque NM 87131-0001 E-mail: wgross@unm.edu.

GROSS, WILLIAM H. financial analyst, investment company executive; b. Middletown, Ohio, Apr. 13, 1944; children: Jeff, Jennifer. BA in Psychology, Duke U., 1966; MBA in Fin., UCLA, 1971. Chartered Fin. Analyst. Investment analyst Pacific Mut. Life Ins. Co., Newport Beach, Calif., 1971-73, sr. analyst, 1973-76, asst. v.p., Fixed Income Securities, 1976-78, 2d v.p., Fixed Income Securities, 1978-80, v.p. Fixed Income Securities, 1980-82; from mng. dir. to chief investment officer Pacific Investment Mgmt. Co. subs. Pacific Mut. Life Ins. Co., Newport Beach, Calif., 1982—. Regular panelist Wall Street Week with Louis Rukeyser TV program. Mem. L.A. Soc. Fin. Analysts. Office: 840 Newport Center Dr Newport Beach CA 92660-6310

GROSSBARD-SHECHTMAN, AMYRA, economist, educator, researcher; b. Antwerp, Belgium, Oct. 23, 1948; d. Chaim and Anna (Propper) Grossbard; m. Amos Shechtman, June 15, 1978; children— Michelle Anna, Zev Mordechai, Haim Joshua. B.A., Hebrew U., Jerusalem, 1971; M.A., U. Chgo., 1975, Ph.D., 1978. Fellow Ctr. for Advanced Study in Behavioral Scis., Stanford, Calif., 1980-81; assoc. prof. econs. San Diego State U., 1981-87 ; lectr.; acting dir. Lipinsky Inst. Judaic Studies. Bar Ilan Univ., Israel, 1983-84. Contbr. articles to profl. jours. Mem. Am. Econ. Assn., Soc. for Advancement Behavioral Econs. (adv. bd.), Population Assn. Am. Jewish. Office: San Diego State Univ, Dept Econs, San Diego CA 92182

GROSSBERG, DAVID ALAN, lawyer; b. Evanston, Ill., Oct. 13, 1950; s. Edmund J. and Alice (Kaven) G.; m. Robyn DeKoven, Apr. 11, 1981; children: Jonathan, Samuel. AB, U. Calif., Berkeley, 1972; JD, U. Chgo., 1975. Bar: Ill. 1976; U.S. Dist. Ct. (no. dist.) Ill. 1976; U.S. Ct. Appeals (7th cir.) 1977; U.S. Supreme Ct. 1982. Law clk. to Hon. Lewis R. Morgan U.S. Ct. Appeals (5th cir.), New Orleans, 1975-76; assoc. D'Ancona & Pflaum, Chgo., 1976-81, ptnr., 1982-93, Sachnoff & Weaver, Ltd., Chgo., 1993-98, Schiff, Hardin & Waite, Chgo., 1998—. Pres. midwest region Am. Jewish Congress, Chgo., 1987-91, nat. v.p.; chmn. domestic concerns Jewish community rels. coun. Jewish United Fund of Met. Chgo., 1989-91; bd. dirs. Med. Rsch. Inst. coun. Michael Reese Hosp., Chgo., 1988-91, Pub. Interest Law Initiative, Chgo., 1987-90; pres. North Shore Congregation Israel, 1995-97; mem. bd. edn. New Trier Twp. H.S. Dist. 203, 1999-2003. Office: Schiff Hardin & Waite 6600 Sears Tower 233 S Wacker Dr Chicago IL 60606-6473 E-mail: dgrossberg@schiffhardin.com.

GROSSBERG, DAVID BURTON, cardiologist; b. Bronx, N.Y., Oct. 28, 1956; s. Jules Harold and Florence (Greenbaum) G.; m. Karen Leslie Sonin, Apr. 17, 1988; children: Samuel Benjamin, Hannah Rachel. BA, SUNY, Binghamton, 1977; MD, SUNY, Syracuse, 1981. Diplomate Am. Bd. Internal Medicine, Am. Bd. Cardiology. Resident in internal medicine Overlook Hosp., Coll. Physicians and Surgeons, Columbia U., Summit, N.J., 1981-84; asst. clin. prof. medicine George Washington U., Washington; adj. asst. prof. medicine Baylor U. Sch. Medicine; staff physician St. Mary's Hosp., East Orange, N.J., 1982; internist Sumter County Pub. Health, Wildwood, Fla., 1984-86; cardiology fellow Albany (N.Y.) Med. Ctr. Hosp., 1986-88; cardiologist Md. Cardiology Assoc., Silver Spring, 1988-91; pvt. practice Silver Spring, Rockville, Md., 1991-97; ptnr. Assocs. in Cardiology, Silver Spring, Md., 1997—. Mem., dir. Cen. Fla. Ambulance Svcs., Sumterville, 1984-85; active attending staff Washington Adventist Hosp., Holy Cross Hosp., Laurel Hosp., Montgomery Gen. Hosp., Washington Hosp. Ctr.; co-investigator gusto trial-thrombolytic therapy post myocardial infarction; chmn. dept. cardiology Laurel Hosp., 1999—. Recipient Elsbeth Kroeber Meml. award N.Y. Biology Tchrs. Assn., 1973, Regents scholar, 1973. Fellow Am. Coll. Cardiology, Am. Coll. Chest Physicians; mem. Physicians for Social Responsibility, Md. Med. Soc. (alt. del. 1992-95, del. 1995—), Sierra Club (vol. physician Wilderness Project 1982), Audubon Soc., Montgomery County Med. Soc. Avocations: Karate, hiking, philately, numismatics. Office: 2415 Musgrove Rd Ste 307 Silver Spring MD 20904-5223

GROSSBERG, GEORGE THOMAS, psychiatrist, educator; b. Hungary, Aug. 20, 1948; came to the U.S., 1957; s. Henry and Barbara (Rothman) G.; m. Darla Jean Brown, June 13, 1976; children: Jonathan, Anna-Leah, Aviva, Aliza Rebecca, Jeremy. BA, Yeshiva U., 1971; MD, St. Louis U., 1975. Diplomate Am. Bd. Psychiatry and Neurology. Chief resident in psychiatry St. Louis U., 1978-79, instr., 1979-81, asst. prof., 1982-86, assoc. prof., 1986-90, prof., 1990-98, Samuel W. Fordyce prof. and chmn. dept. psychiatry, 1995-98, Samuel w. Fordyce prof., dir. divsn. geriat. psychiatry, 1998—. Cons. on aging U.S. VA Hosps. Assn., Washington, 1990—. Contbr. articles to profl. jours. Adv. bd. St. Louis Alzheimers Assn., 1983—. Recipient Pub. Svc. award, St. Louis Alzheimers Assn., 1989, Donovan-Sheer award, St. Louis Mental Health Assn., 1999, Fleischman-Hilliard award, Jewish Ctr. for Aged, 2000, Physician of Year award, Mo. Adult Daycare Assn., 2001. Mem. Am. Assn. Geriat. Psychiatry (pres. 1989-90), Am. Psychiat. Assn. (cons. on aging 1990—, Falk fellow 1977-79), Am. Geriat. Soc., Gerontol. Soc. Am., Internat. Psychogeriat. Assn. (treas. 1997—, pres. 2003-05). Avocations: collectibles, art, skiing. Office: Saint Louis U Med Ctr 1221 S Grand Blvd Saint Louis MO 63104-1016 E-mail: grossbgt@slu.edu.

GROSSBERG, MARC ELIAS, lawyer; b. Houston, Dec. 26, 1940; s. Sylvester and Leah (Hochman) G.; m. Eva M. Wolski, Jan. 3, 1981; 1 child, Nicole; children from previous marriage: Lee Ann Krishnan, Toni Oreck. BS in Polit. Sci., U. Houston, 1961; JD with honors, U. Tex., 1965. Bar: Tex. 1965, Calif. 1966, Fla. 1980, U.S. Supreme Ct. 1980; bd. cert. fed. income taxation, Tex. Acct. Brochstein Toomim & Co CPAs (now Deloitte Touche), Houston, 1961-62; law clk. hon. Walter Ely U.S. Ct. Appeals (9th cir.), L.A., 1965-66; assoc. Fulbright & Jaworski, Houston, 1966-71; ptnr. Schlanger Mills Mayer & Grossberg, LLP, Houston, 1974-99, Thompson & Knight LLP, Houston, 1999—. Pres. Imprint, Inc., 2000—02, chmn. bd. dirs., 2002—. Articles editor: Tex. Law Rev. Advanceman, speech writer 1968 Hubert Humphry Presdl. Campaign; pres. Tex. Bill of Rights Found., Houston, 1971-72, Jewish Family Svc., Houston, 1986-87, U. Tex. Law Rev. Assn.; commr. Housing Authority City of Houston, 1974-78. Mem. ABA (tax sect. and litig. sects.), Order of Coif. Democrat. Jewish. Avocations: family, writing, reading, exercise. Office: Thompson & Knight LLP Ste 3300 333 Clay St Houston TX 77002 E-mail: marc.grossberg@tklaw.com.

GROSSBERG, MICHAEL LEE, theater critic, writer; b. Houston, Sept. 7, 1952; s. Fred Samuel and Esther R. (Rosenstein) G. BA, U. Tex., 1979, BS in Journalism, 1983. Film, theater critic, reporter Victor Valley Daily News, Victorville, Calif., 1983-85; film, theater critic Columbus (Ohio) Dispatch, 1985-87, theater critic, 1987—. Co-founder Free Press Assn., Mencken awards for outstanding journalism, dir., 1981-94. Contbr. Otis Guernsey/Burns Mantle Theater Yearbook: Best Plays, 1993-02; regional report columnist Backstage, 1997—. Mem. Outer Critics Cir., Am. Theatre Critics Assn. (chmn. awards new plays com. 1993-99, exec. com. 1996-2002, vice chmn. 2001-02), Libertarian Futurist Soc. (chmn. Prometheus award judges com. 1997—, pres. bd. 1999-2002). Avocations: reading, traveling, meditation, public speaking. Home: 3164 Plymouth Pl Columbus OH 43213-4236 Office: Columbus Dispatch 34 S 3rd St Columbus OH 43215-4241 E-mail: mikegrossb@aol.com., mgrossberg@dispatch.com.

GROSSBLATT, NORMAN, science editor; b. Newark, Feb. 13, 1935; s. Philip and Dorothy G.; m. Marilyn Jean Nusbaum, May 31, 1958; children: Philip W., Benjamin D. BA, Haverford Coll., 1956. Cert. ELS(D). Rsch. analyst Documentation Inc., Washington, 1956-58; tech. editor Allis-Chalmers Mfg. Co., Washington, 1958-63; sr. editor NAS, Washington, 1963—. Mem. Bd. Editors in Life Scis. (founding mem., pres. 1991-99), Am. Med. Writers Assn. (fellowship, pres. award), Coun. Sci. Editors, European Assn. of Sci. Editors. Unitarian Universalist. Home: 6711 Georgia St Chevy Chase MD 20815-4139 Office: Nat Acad Scis 500 5th St NW Washington DC 20001 Fax: 413-581-3640. E-mail: normang@bellatlantic.net.

GROSSENBURG, JOHN ANTHONY, minister; b. Gregory, S.D., June 26, 1970; s. John Michael and Patricia Elaine Grossenburg. BA, Creighton U., 1993; MDiv, Pontifical Coll. Josephinum, 1999. Ordained pastor Diocese of Rapid City, S.D., 1999. Assoc. pastor Blessed Sacrament Cath. Ch., Rapid City, 1999—99; adminstr. Sacred Heart Parish, Philip, SD, 1999—2000; pastor Sacred Heart Cath. Ch., Philip, 2000—. Bd. dirs. Western S.D. Cath. Found., Rapid City; pres. Philip Ministerial Assn., 2002—. Republican. Roman Catholic. Avocations: reading, computers, classical music, skiing, gardening. Office: Sacred Heart Cath Ch PO Box 309 Philip SD 57567 E-mail: sacred@gwtc.net.

GROSSER, BERNARD IRVING, psychiatry educator; b. Boston, Apr. 19, 1929; s. John and Katherine (Russman) G.; children: Steven, Mark, Minda; m. Karen Grosser. BA, U. Mass., 1950; MS, U. Mich., 1953; MD, Case-Western Res. U., 1959. Diplomate Am. Bd. Psychiatry and Neurology. Intern U. Utah, 1959-60, resident in psychiatry, 1960-65; asst. prof. psychiatry U. Utah Sch. Medicine, Salt Lake City, 1967-71, assoc. prof., 1971-75, prof., 1975—, chmn. dept., 1978—. Mem. pre-clin. and clin. psychopharm. rev. com. NIMH, Washington, 1974-79, 80-84, mem. sci. adv. bd., 1984-88; mem. merit rev. bd. VA, Washington, 1988-91; sr. sci. advisor Alcohol, Drug Abuse and Mental Health Adminstrn., Washington, 1987-88; ad hoc mem. Mental Health Clin. Rsch. Ctr. rev. com. NIMH, 1997, ad hoc mem. mental health clin. contracts rev. com., 1998, ad hoc mem. spl. emphasis panel, 2000, 2002, 2003. Contbr. chpts. to books, articles to profl. jours. Capt. USAF, 1965-67. Grantee NIMH, 1959-84, FDA, 1985-88; recipient Exemplary psychiatrist award Nat. Alliance for Mentally Ill, 1997. Fellow Am. Psychiat. Assn. (disting. life); mem. Internat. Soc. Psychoneuroendocrinology (treas. 1974-88), Utah Psychiat. Assn. (pres. 1995-96), Psychiat. Rsch. Soc. (pres. 1986-87), Am. Coll. Neuropsychopharmacology, Soc. Neurosci., N.Y. Acad. Scis., Collegium Internat. Neuropsychopharmacologicum, Am. Assn. Psychiatry Dept. Chairmen (coun. 1997—. Republican. Jewish. Home: 511 Perrys Hollow Rd Salt Lake City UT 84103-4245 Office: U Utah Sch Medicine Dept Psychiatry 50 N Medical Dr Salt Lake City UT 84132-0001 Business E-Mail: bernard.grosser@hsc.utah.edu.

GROSSER, T.J. administrator, developer, fundraiser; b. Milw., Oct. 17, 1938; s. Owen Henry and Ethel Clare (Hathazy) G.; m. Mary Janet McClanahan, Apr. 3, 1976; children: Paul Howard, Julie Anne, Philip Owen, Peter John, Elizabeth Michelle. BA, U. Wis., 1958, MA, 1962, EdD, 1971; DD (hon.), Union Theol. Sem., Richmond,Va., 1972. Min. edn. Cross Luth. Ch., Milw., 1957-62; assoc. Christ Luth. Ch., Oshkosh, Wis., 1962-65; preacher/tchr. Trinity Luth. Ch., Santa Barbara, Calif., 1966-71; pres. Amigos de las Ams., Houston, 1972-79, Vols. in Internat. Svc. & Awareness, L.A., 1980-84; v.p. Pacific Clinics, Pasadena, Calif., 1985-87; pres., chief exec. officer Children's Aid Internat., San Diego, 1987-97; pres., CEO Angelcare, 1998—. Bd. dirs. Am. Devel. Found., Washington, 1981-95; bd. dirs., pres. End Hunger Network, L.A., 1983-87; bd. dirs., v.p. Ind. Charities of Am., San Francisco, pres., 1988—; bd. dirs. Children's Charities Am.; advisor numerous internat. and religious agys. Contbr. 200 artices to profl. jours. Advisor African Refugee Ctr., L.A., 1989—; worker priest Hope Luth. Ch., Hollywood, Calif., 1983—. Named Educator of Yr. Am. Luth. Ch., Mpls., 1966, exec. of Yr. Coun. Internat. Vol. Orgn., Geneva, 1975, 76; recipient Papal medal Pope John Paul II, Rome, 1979. Mem. Fund Raising Execs., Rotary (Paul Harris fellow) 1987). Democrat. Avocations: reading, speaking, travel, promoting internat. adoptions. Home: 6457 Elmhurst Dr San Diego CA 92120-3959 Office: Anglecare PO Box 600370 San Diego CA 92160-0370 E-mail: tjgrosser@angelcare.org.

GROSSET, JESSICA ARIANE, computer analyst; b. Paris, Aug. 31, 1952; came to U.S., 1970; d. Raymond Louis and Barbara Ann (Byrne) G.; m. Bruce Edward Kaskubar, May 23, 1986. AA, Berkshire Community Coll., Pittsfield, Mass., 1972; BS, SUNY, Potsdam, 1979; postgrad., Ariz. State U., 1980, U. Minn., 1980-81. Computer programmer Kay-Bee Toy and Hobby Shops, Lee, Mass., 1974-78; computer analyst Mayo Clinic, Rochester, Minn., 1981—. Voting staff Mayo Clinic, Rochester, 1996. Mem. Nat. Assn. Female Execs. Avocations: reading, sailing, travel, horseback riding, skiing. Office: Mayo Clinic 200 1st St SW Rochester MN 55905-0002

GROSSETT, DEBORAH LOU, psychologist, consultant; b. Alma, Mich., Feb. 16, 1957; d. Charles M. and Margaret A. (Roethlisberger) G. BS, Alma Coll., 1979; MA, Western Mich. U., 1981, PhD, 1984. Lic. psychologist, Tex.; cert. in diagnostic evaluation, Tex.; bd. cert. behavior analyst, Tex. Grad. rsch. and teaching asst. Western Mich. U., Kalamazoo, 1979-84; asst. group home supr., cmty. outreach Residential Opportunities, Kalamazoo, 1982-84; psychologist Richmond (Tex.) State Sch., 1984-87, Shapiro Devel. Ctr., Kankakee, Ill., 1987-88; clin. coord. Monroe Devel. Ctr., Rochester, N.Y., 1988; chief psychologist Denton (Tex.) State Sch., 1989-90; dir. psychol./behavioral svcs. Ctr. for the Retarded, Houston, 1990—2002; psychologist Mental Health and Mental Retardation Authoruty Harris County, Houston, 2002—. Behavioral cons. Ctr. for Developmentally Disabled Adults, Kalamazoo, 1984, Goodman-Wade Enterprises, Houston, 1987; instr. psychology Houston Community Coll., 1985-86, U. Houston-Clear Lake, 1987, 92, 95—. Contbr. chpt. to book, articles to profl. jours. Western Mich. U. fellow, 1984. Mem. Am. Psychol. Assn., Am. Assn. on Mental Retardation, Assn. for Behavior Analysis (chair Outreach Bd. 1989-91), Tex. Assn. for Behavior Analysis (bd. dirs. 1989-91, program chair 1996, pres. 1997). Democrat. Presbyterian. Avocations: golf, camping, gardening. Home: 9750 Ravensworth Dr Houston TX 77031-3130 Office: MHMRA Harris County 5901 Long Dr Houston TX 77087 E-mail: deb_grossett1@email.com.

GROSSHANS, MERILYN LA VONNE, librarian, consultant; b. Plaza, N.D., July 16, 1939; d. John Rudolph and Lillian (Erickson) Willey Peterson; m. Dennis Grosshans, Apr. 20, 1970 (div. Sept. 1983). BA, Northwestern Coll., Mpls., 1961; postgrad. Valley City State Coll., 1962; MLS, U. N.D., 1969. Tchr. Engish, Stanley (N.D.) High Sch., 1963-65, Williston (N.D.) High, 1965-67; children's librarian L.A. Pub. Libr., 1969-70; libr. Vermillion (S.D.) High, 1970-72, Las Vegas HS, Clark County Sch. Dist., 1973-96, ret., 1996. Author: (Nev. sect.) Exploring the Mountain States Through Literature, 1994; contbr. articles to profl. jours. Vol. Nev. State Prison, Jean and Indian Springs. Elected to bd. Assembly on Adolescent Lit., 1990-92; mem. Gov.'s Conf. on Librs. Com., 1989-90; del. Gov.'s Conf. on Librs., 1990. Recipient Exceptional Tchr. award Clark County Bd. Sch. Trustees and PTA, 1983. Mem. ALA (com. best of the best books for young adults 1988, young adult svc. div. 1983, humor genre list com. 1990, chair fantasy genre com. 1992-93, chair Wilson Publ. award, 1993-94), Nev. Libr. Assn. (intellectual freedom chair 1990-92, membership chair 1984-85, chair so. dist. 1991, spkr. 1994, Librarian of Yr. 1996), Nev. Assn. Sch. Librs. (pres. 1983, Spl. Achievement award 1988), Am. Assn. Sch. Librs. (com. 1984-86, Bill Backer Meml. scholar 1989), Clark County Sch. Library Assn. (pres. 1976-77, program chair reading conf., 1987-97), Mountain Plains Libr. Assn. (pres. children's and sch. div. 1987-88), Alpha Delta Kappa (sec. 1986, treas. 1986-87). Democrat. Home: 7060 Picaroon Ln Las Vegas NV 89145-0166

GROSSI, RALPH EDWARD, agricultural conservation organization executive, farmer, rancher; b. San Rafael, Calif., Feb. 16, 1949; s. James Joseph and Rose Marie (Halter) G.; m. Judy Arlene Lamb, Sept. 9, 1972; children: Amy, Erin, Kathryn. BS, Calif. Poly. State U., San Luis Obispo, 1971. Mng. ptnr. Marindale Dairy, Novato, Calif., 1971-87, Marindale Ranch, Novato, 1987—; pres. Am. Farmland Trust, Washington, 1985—, also bd. dirs. Founder, chmn. Marin Agrl. Land Trust, Marin County, Calif., 1980-82; pres. Marin County Farm Bur., 1979-81; water adv. com. Calif. Agrl., 1979-81, U.S. Implementation Bd. of N.Am. Waterfowl Mgmt. Plan, Washington, 1988-94; chmn. Smart Growth Am., 2001--. Adv. com. Calif. Poly. State U. Sch. Agr., 1988—; bd. dirs. Wildlife Habitat Enhancement, Washington, 1989-94; v.p. Alpha Gamma Rho Found., Kansas City, Mo., 1991-94; active Yale Forest Forum, 1998-, U. Calif. Pres.'s Commn. on Agr. and Natural Resources, 2000-. Named Man of Yr., Progressive Farmer Mag., 2002; recipient Feinstone Environ. award, Sol Feinstone Awards Com., 1985. Mem. Soil and Water Conservation Soc., Calif. Farm Bur. Fedn. (Outstanding Young Farmer and Rancher award 1976). Presbyterian. Avocations: golf, hunting, fishing. Office: Am Farmland Trust 1200 18th St NW Ste 800 Washington DC 20036-2524

GROSSMAN, ALLEN NEIL, lawyer; b. Bklyn., May 14, 1946; s. William Lester and Shirley Miriam (Jacobson) G.; m. Pamela Jean Pearson, June 8, 1969; children: Steven Mueller, Elizabeth Jane. AB, Princeton U., 1968; JD, Harvard U., 1971. Bar: Pa. 1971, N.J. 1973. Assoc. Dechert Price & Rhoads, Phila., 1971-73, Smith Stratton Wise & Heher, Princeton, N.J., 1973-75, ptnr., 1975-81; dir. bus. devel. Dow Jones Info. Svcs. Group, Princeton, 1981-91, exec. dir. bus. ops. and devel., 1991-92; exec. dir. prodn. mktg. and devel. Dow Jones Bus. Info. Svcs. Group, Princeton, 1992-93, exec. dir. corp. products, 1993-94, exec. dir. content and distbn., 1994-96, Dow Jones Interactive Pub., Princeton, 1997-99; v.p., dir. strategic relationships Factiva, a Dow Jones and Reuters Co., Princeton, 1999—2001; mgmt. cons., 2002; of counsel Mason, Griffin & Pierson, P.C., Princeton, NJ, 2002—. Dir. Princeton Area United Way, 1978-79; mem. Princeton Regional Bd. Edn., 1980-84, 86-91, Coun. of Princeton U. Cmty., 1990-92; coach Princeton Youth Soccer Assn., 1984-91. Democrat. Jewish. Avocations: running, photography, cycling. Home: 101 Poor Farm Rd Princeton NJ 08540 E-mail: skip@mgplaw.com.

GROSSMAN, ANN, professional tennis player; b. Columbus, Ohio, Oct. 13, 1970; Grad., Am. Sch., Chgo., 1989. Profl. tennis player; advanced to 2d round French Open, 1998. MVP U.S. Jr. Wightman Cup team, 1987; rep. U.S. on Maureen Connolly Brinker team and Nat. team, 1988, Ohio H.S. AAA State and Regl. champion, 1985; co-ranked No. 1 in U.S. 18 singles in 1987, winner Nat. Singles Title, 1987 Office: USTA 70 W Red Oak Ln White Plains NY 10604-3602

GROSSMAN, CISSY, curator, art historian, art exhibit designer, appraiser; b. N.Y.C., 1932; BA, Lehman Coll., N.Y., 1972; MA in Art History, Hunter Coll., N.Y., 1979; PhD in Art History, CUNY, 1998. Asst. curator judaica The Jewish Mus., N.Y., 1972-79; lectr. art history Rutgers U., New Brunswick, N.J., 1978-86; lectr. George Washington U., Washington, D.C., 1979; curator Cen. Synagogue, N.Y., 1986-98; appraiser of Judaica N.Y., 1992—. Sr. rschr. Mus. of Jewish Heritage, N.Y.C., 1992—; exhbn. designer, Judaica connoisseur, appraiser, curator Michael and Judy Steinhardt Collection. Author: (book) A Temple Treasury, 1989, A Jewish Family's Book of Days, 1989; curator, author catalog The Collector's Room: Selections From the Michael and Judy Steinhardt Collection, 1993; art exhbn. designer Fragments of Greatness, Walters Art Gallery, N.Y.C., Americana from The Jewish Mus., N.Y.C. Bd. dirs. Grad. Ctr. for Jewish Art, Jerusalem, Textile Conservation Workshop, South Salem, N.Y. Mem. Am. Assn. Mus. (curator's com.), Appraiser's Assn. of Am. E-mail: cissyg@earthlink.net.

GROSSMAN, DAN STEVEN, lawyer; b. N.Y.C., Apr. 6, 1953; s. George M. and Jeanne L. (Stickle) G.; m. Patrice Irene Michaelson, June 27, 1976; children: Deborah, Andrea. BA, SUNY, Albany, 1975; JD, Albany Law Sch., 1978; LLM, Georgetown Law Ctr., 1980. Bar: D.C. 1978, N.Y. 1979. Law clk. to judge U.S. Tax Ct., Washington, 1978-80; assoc. Webster and Sheffield, N.Y.C., 1980-84, Finley Kumble Wagner, N.Y.C., 1984-87, Willkie Farr and Gallagher, N.Y.C., 1987-90, ptnr., 1991—. Mem. ABA (tax sect.), N.Y. State Bar Assn. (tax sect.), Assn. of Bar of City of N.Y., D.C. Bar Assn. Office: Willkie Farr and Gallagher 787 7th Ave New York NY 10019-6018

GROSSMAN, DEBRA A. lawyer, real estate manager, radio talk show host; b. Cleve., July 29, 1951; d. Morris M. and Idelle R. (Bialosky) G. BA, Syracuse U., 1973; JD, Suffolk U., 1976. Bar: Mass. 1977, U.S. Dist. Ct. Mass. 1977. Sole practice, Lexington, Mass., 1977-79; ptnr. Kurland & Grossman, P.C., Lowell, Mass., 1979-94; property mgr. KD Mgmt. Co., Lowell, 1983—94, Chelmsford, Mass., 1994—; talk show host "Legal Briefs" WCCM Radio, Lawrence, Mass., 1989-97. Lectr. Greater Lowell Alzheimers Assn., 1987; vice chair Lowell Hist. Bd., 1995—97, chair, 1997—2001; mem. corp. adv. bd. Suitability, Inc., 2001—; Bd. dirs. Downtown Lowell Bus. Assn., 1987. Mem. ATLA, Mass. Assn. Women Lawyers (asst. treas. 1981-82, bd. dirs. 1979-81), Mass. Bar Assn. (law practice mgmt. sect. coun. 2003—), Mass. Acad. Trial Lawyers, Greater Lowell Bar Assn. (bd. dirs. 1993-96, Lawyer for the Day program dir. 1990-92), Syracuse U. Alumni Club, Greater Boston Club, Mass. Family and Probate Am. Inn Ct. Office: Kurland & Grossman PC 139 Billerica Rd Chelmsford MA 01824-3619 E-mail: dgrossman@nrmail.com.

GROSSMAN, ELMER ROY, pediatrician; b. LA, Jan. 30, 1929; s. Harry and Reta (Frankel) G.; m. Rosalind Nagin, June 24, 1951 (div. 1976); children— Deena, Marianna; m. Pamela Canfield Antoncich, July 29, 1976; stepchildren: Camilla Sutter, Michael A. Antoncich. AB, U. Calif.-Berkeley, 1949; MD, U. Calif. Sch. Medicine, San Francisco, 1953. Intern Orange County Gen. Hosp., Orange, Calif., 1953-54; resident U. Calif. Hosps., San Francisco, 1957-59; practice medicine specializing in pediatrics Berkeley Pediatric Med. Group, Calif, 1959-92. Assoc. clin. prof. health and med. scis. U. Calif., Berkeley, 1978-80; clin. prof. pediat. emeritus U. Calif. Sch. Medicine, San Francisco; chmn. dept. pediat. Alta Bates Hosp., Berkeley, 1972-74, chmn. infant care ethics com., 1984-90. Author: Everyday Pediatrics, 1993, Everyday Pediatrics for Parents, 1996; columnist The Everyday Pediatrician; contbr. articles to profl. jours. Mem. Berkeley Schs. Master Plan Com., 1966—68, Berkeley Schs. Child Care Com., 1968—70, Berkeley Cmty. Environ. Adv. Commn., 2000—02, Berkeley Cmty. Health Commn., 2002; pres. Temple Beth El, Berkeley, 1970—72. Served to capt USAF, 1954—56. Fellow Am. Acad. Pediatrics; mem. Alameda-Contra Costa Med. Assn., Physicians for Social Responsibility, Physicians for a Nat. Health Program. Democrat. Jewish. Avocations: wine making, gardening. Home and Office: 899 Euclid Ave Berkeley CA 94708-1305 E-mail: elmergrossman@attbi.com.

GROSSMAN, GEORGE STEFAN, library director, law eductor; b. Poltar, Czechoslovakia, May 31, 1938; m. Suzi Herczeg, 1960; 1 child, Zoltan BA, U. Chgo., 1960; LL.B., Stanford U., 1966; MA in Library Sci., Brigham Young U., 1971. Bar: Calif. 1966, Minn. 1974. Tech. processes law librarian U. Pa., 1966-68; assoc. prof. law, law librarian U. Utah, 1968-70, prof., law librarian, 1970-73; prof., dir. law library U. Minn., 1973-79, Northwestern U., Chgo., 1979-93; prof., dir. law libr. U. Calif., Davis, 1993—. Cons. to univs. Author: Legal Research: Historical Foundations of the Electronic Age, 1994, The Spirit of American Law, 1999; contbr. articles to legal jours. Mem. Indian rights com. ACLU, 1973-92, pres. Utah affiliate, 1972-73, bd. dirs. Ill. affiliate, 1982-87. Mem. Am. Assn. Law Libraries, Internat. Assn. Law Libraries. Office: U Calif Sch Law Libr King Hall 400 Mrak Dr Davis CA 95616 Fax: 530-752-8766.

GROSSMAN, HERBERT BARTON, urologist, researcher; b. Tampa, Fla., June 25, 1945; s. Benjamin and Pauline (Mattis) G.; m. Amy C. Becker, Aug. 24, 1969; children: Beth, Sara, Rebecca. BA, La Salle Coll., Phila., 1966; MD, Temple U., 1970. Diplomate Am. Bd. Urology. Surg. intern U. Mich. Med. Ctr., Ann Arbor, 1970-71; surg. resident St. Joseph Mercy Hosp., Ann Arbor, 1973-74; urology resident U. Mich. Med. Ctr., Ann Arbor, 1974-77; instr. U. Mich. Med. Sch., Ann Arbor, 1977-78; rsch. and clin. fellow Meml. Sloan-Kettering Cancer Ctr., N.Y.C., 1978-80; asst. prof. U. Mich. Med. Sch., Ann Arbor, 1980-85, assoc. prof., 1985-90, prof., 1990-94; dir., urologic oncology U. Mich. Cancer Ctr., Ann Arbor, 1986-94; prof. U. Tex. M.D. Anderson Cancer Ctr., Houston, 1994—, dep. chair Dept. Urology, 1998—. Cons. Taubman Med. Libr., 1985-94, The Med. Letter, 1991, Jour. Vascular Surgery, 1991; reviewer VA Merit Rev. Bd. for Surgery, 1986, NIH Pathology B Ad Hoc (SI) Study Sect., 1988, NIDDK Ad Hoc Rev. Groups 12 and 13, 1992; spl. reviewer NIH Exptl. Therapeutics Study Sect., 1986, reviewer spl. study sect., 1995, reviewer cancer ctr. support grant, 1996; reviewer NGI Rev. Group/subcom. 4, 1997; external reviewer Alberta Cancer Bd., 1998; mem. surg. quality control and edn. com. SW. Oncology Group, 1980-90, GU com., 1980—, organ site chmn. for local bladder cancer, 1991-2000; surg. oncology adv. com. dept. surgery U.

Mich. Med. Ctr., Ann Arbor, 1981-82, dept. surgery computer sys. adv. com., 1983-88, cancer ctr. clin. rsch. com., 1987-94, laser safety com., 1987-94, med. sch. admissions com., 1988-94, patient care com., 1989-90, hosps. quality mgmt. com., 1990-94, rsch. coord. sect. urology, 1991, fin. adv. com., adv. promotion com. for primary rsch. staff dept. surgery, 1993-94; med. practice subcom. U. Tex. M.D. Anderson Cancer Ctr., Houston, 1994—, grad. med. edn. com., 1994—, surveillance com., 1994-95, dir. clin. rsch., 1994—, dep. chmn. dept. urology 1998—; prostate cancer adv. com. Mich. Dept. Pub. Health, 1993-94, clin. rsch. com. mem. 1994-2000, chmn. 1997-2000, dir. bladder cancer multidisciplinary rsch. program, 1999—; mem. scientific adv. bd. Anthra Pharms., Inc., 1994—, Fujirebio Diagnostics Inc., 2003-; reviewer Med. Rsch. Coun., U.K., 1999, Dutch Cancer Soc., 1999, NCI Spl. Emphasis Panel, 1999, 2000; molecular biology review panel, FAMRI, 2001, 2002; ad hoc reviewer U.S. Army Med. Rsch. and Materiel Command, 1999; with clin. study sect. revue grants program M.D. Anderson Cancer Ctr., 2002-, vice chmn. 2002-03, chmn. 2003-04. Mem. editl. bd. Oncology Reports, 1998—, Jour. Urology, 1999-2004; sect. editor Urologic Oncology, 2000—; contbr. 180 articles to profl. jours.; authored 24 book chpts. Capt. USAF, 1971-73. Recipient 2d prize Ferdinand C. Valentine Urology Essay Contest, 1980, also numerous rsch. grants; named to W.A. "Tex" and Deborah Moncrief, Jr. Disting. Chair in Urology, 1994; Ferdinand C. Valentine fellow N.Y. Acad. Medicine, 1979-80, clin. fellow Am. Cancer Soc., 1979-80. Office: U T MD Anderson Cancer Ctr 1515 Holcombe Blvd # 110 Houston TX 77030-4009

GROSSMAN, HERSCHEL I. economics educator; b. Phila., Mar. 6, 1939; BA with highest honors, U. Va., 1960; BPhil, U. Oxford, Eng., 1962; PhD, Johns Hopkins U., 1965. Asst. prof. econs. Brown U., Providence, R.I., 1964-69, assoc. prof. econs., 1969-73, prof. econs., 1973—, Merton P. Stoltz prof. social scis., 1980—, chmn. dept. econs., 1982-85, 86-91. Rsch. assoc. Nat. Bur. Econ. Rsch., 1979—; faculty rep. NCAA, 1985 90; vis. scholar Russell Sage Found., 2000-01. Author: Money, Employment and Inflation, 1976, Chinese translation, 1981, Japanese translation, 1982, Italian translation, 1982; mem. editl. bd. European Jour. Polit. Economy, 2000—, Econ. of Governance, 1997—, Jour. Monetary Econs., 1977-83, rev. editor, 1984-91; bd. editors Am. Econ. Rev., 1980-83; contbr. numerous articles to profl. jours. John Simon Guggenheim Meml. Found. fellow, 1979-80; grantee NSF, 1969, 72, 76, 78, 82, 84, U.S. Dept. Labor, 1974, 80, Social Sci. Rsch. Coun., 1982: IRIS scholar, 1991. Office: Brown U Dept Econs Box B Providence RI 02912-9079 E-mail: Herschel_Grossman@Brown.edu.

GROSSMAN, IRVING GROSS, retired geologist; b. N.Y.C., Mar. 4, 1917; s. Harry and Charlotte (Gross) G.; m. Rose Opas, Aug. 28, 1944 (div. July 1953); 1 child, Barbara Louise; m. Ann Safran, Aug. 12, 1956; children: Joshua Seth, Gilbert Elias. AB, Bklyn. Coll., 1944; MA, Columbia U., 1947. Instr. geology U. N.D., Grand Forks, 1946-49; asst. state geol. North Dakota, 1948; groundwater geologist U.S. Geol. Survey, Reston, Va., 1949-86; geology editor, rsch. scientist N.J. Geol. Survey, Trenton, 1986-95, ret., 1995. Cons. N.J. Geol. Survey, 1999—; prof. environ. geology Beijing U. Sci. & Tech., 1987, lectr. earth sci. Bucks County C.C., Newtown, Pa., 1993; vis. lectr. Am. U., Washington, 1980-81; lectr. geology U. Conn., Willimantic, 1968. Contbr. articles to profl. jours. Pres. Natural History Soc. P.R., San Juan, 1960-62. Recipient Geostrider award U.S. Geol. Survey, 1982. Fellow Geol. Soc. Am.; mem. AAAS, Am. Geophys. Union, Soc. Econ. Geologists, Assn. Geoscientists for Internat. Devel., Geol. Assn. N.J., Sigma Xi. Jewish. Avocations: sketching, genealogy, classical music, swimming, biking. Home and Office: 224 S Flint Ct Yardley PA 19067-5716

GROSSMAN, JACK, advertising agency executive; b. N.Y.C., Mar. 22, 1925; s. Benjamin Robert and Sarah Dora (Bender) G.; m. Esther Arline Goldman, Nov. 23, 1949; children— Barbara Ruth, Neil David. B.Sc., NYU, 1950, MBA, 1952. With Biow Co., Inc., N.Y.C., 1952-56, mgr. sales research, 1954-56; with William Esty Co., Inc., N.Y.C., 1956-87, mgr. research dept., then v.p. research, 1964-73, sr. v.p., dir. research, 1973-87; pres. MBN Research Assocs., N.Y.C., 1987—. Adj. asso. prof. mktg. Pace U., 1962-74, adj. prof., 1988; adj. prof. mktg. Parsons Sch. Design, 1988; lectr. Baruch Coll., CUNY, 1990. Bd. dirs. L.I. Cons. Center, 1979— . Served with AUS, 1943-47. Decorated Bronze Star with oak leaf cluster, Purple Heart. Jewish. Home: 1365 York Ave New York NY 10021-4035 Office: MBN Rsch Assocs 1365 York Ave New York NY 10021-4035

GROSSMAN, JAMES A. public relations executive; b. Altoona, Penn., Feb. 24, 1942; s. Irwin Isaac and Ruthe (Hytowitz) Grossman; m. Sarah A. Reyes, July 29, 1968; children: Liliana Michelle, Luis Manuel. BA summa cum laude, U. Pitts., 1964; MS cum laude, Columbia U., Grad.Sch. Journalism, 1968. Reporter Pitts. Press, 1967, Charlotte Observer, NC, 1968, San Juan Star, PR, 1969; copy editor Wall St. Jour., N.Y., 1969—70; asst. editor Consumer Reports, Mt. Vernon, NY, 1970—76; asst. dir. pub. rels. Muscular Dystrophy Assn., N.Y., 1976—77; exec. asst. N.Y. State Assembly, Albany, 1977—82; exec. v.p. Rubenstein Assoc., Inc., N.Y., 1982—. 1st lt. U.S. Army, 1964—66, Korea. Mem.: Phi Beta Kappa. Democrat. Jewish. Achievements include Public Rels. clients include David Merrick, Marv Albert, Michael Bolton, Pamela Harriman, Madame Dewi Sukarno, F. Lee Bailey, George Steinbrenner. Avocation: photography. Home: 525 W 238th St Bronx NY 10463 Office: Rubenstein Assoc 1345 Ave of Americas New York NY 10105

GROSSMAN, JANICE, former magazine publishing company executive; b. Montreal, Que., Can., Nov. 3, 1949; m. Daniel Rubinstein, July 11, 1978; 1 child, Lauren Alexandra. MA, NYU, 1970; BA, New Sch. Social Research, 1971. Advt. sr. exec. recruiter Merrill, Lynch, Pierce, Fenner & Smith Inc., N.Y.C., 1976-78; advt. sales rep. Ms. mag., N.Y.C., 1978-80; N.Y. advt. mgr. Ms. Mag., N.Y.C., 1980-82, advt. dir., 1982-84, New Woman Mag., N.Y.C., 1984-86, assoc. pub., 1986-88, became pub., 1989, In Fashion Mag., N.Y.C., 1988, N.Y. Mag., 1991; pub. Seventeen mag., N.Y.C., 1992-96; v.p., group pub. PRIMEDIA Mags., N.Y.C., 1992-96; pres. Advt. & Mktg., N.Y.C., 1996—2000; exec. v.p. Primedia Consumer mags., N.Y.C., 1997—2000. Mem. Am. Mag. Conf. Com. Mem. adv. bd. Strang-Cornell Breast Ctr. Mem. Fragrance Found., Fashion Group, Advt. Women N.Y., Cosmetic Exec. Women, Advt. Club N.Y.

GROSSMAN, JEROME BARNETT, retired service firm executive; b. Kansas City, Kans., Sept. 9, 1919; m. Marian Navran, Sept. 19, 1945; children: Jean Zeldin, Janet Zwillenberg. AB, U. Mich., 1941. Exec. v.p., gen. mgr. Helzberg's Diamond Shop Inc., 1941-66; dir. mktg. H & R Block, Inc., Kansas City, Mo., 1966-69, asst. to pres., 1969-71, exec. v.p., chief oper. officer, 1971-88, sr. exec. v.p., chief oper., 1988-89, vice chmn. of the bd., 1989-92, vice chmn. emeritus, 1992—. Bd. dirs. Spherion Corp. Served to maj. USAF, 1941 45. Office: H & R Block Inc 4400 Main St Kansas City MO 64111-1812

GROSSMAN, JEROME KENT, lawyer, accountant; b. St. Louis, Apr. 15, 1953; s. Marvin and Myra Lee (Barnholtz) G.; m. Debbie Ada Kogan, Aug. 7, 1977; children: Hannah Felicia, Marni Celeste. AB cum laude, Georgetown U., 1974, JD, 1977. Bar: Mo. 1977, D.C. 1978, U.S. Ct. Claims 1979, U.S. Tax Ct. 1979, Del. 1980, U.S. Dist. Ct. Del. 1982; CPA, Mo. Acct., controller U.S. Dept. State, Washington, 1974-77; acct. Arthur Andersen & Co., St. Louis, 1977-79; mem. firm Bayard, Handelman and Murdoch, P.A., Wilmington, Del., 1979-88; ptnr. Young Conaway Stargatt & Taylor LLP, Wilmington, 1988—. Co-author: ALI-ABA Course of Study on the Reform Act of 1984, 86. V.p. Jewish Cmty. Ctr., Wilmington, 1986—88, 1989—90, treas., 1989—90; trustee Milton & Hattie Kutz Found., 2001—, Harry Cohen Found., 2002—; bd. dirs. Congregation Beth Shalom, Wilmington, 1985—, pres., 1990—92; treas. Jewish Fedn. Del., 1989—90; pres. Del. Gratz Hebrew H.S., 1997—2000, trustee, 1995—, Jewish. Com. of Del. Endowment Fund., 1988—95; co-chmn. Del. State Com. State of Israel Bonds, 1992—95, chmn., 1995—2000; bd. dirs., trustee Del. Symphony Assn., 1998—, vice chmn., 1999—2001. Fellow: Am. Coll. Tax Counsel; mem.: AICPA (mem. coun. 2000—01), ABA (chmn. inventories subcom. 1982—86, vice chmn. 1986—88, chmn. 1988—90, tax sect., com. on tax acctg.), Del. Soc. CPAs (chmn. tax com. 1980—85, coun. 1985—87, ethics com. 1989—92, coun. 1993—2002, pres. 2000—01), Del. Tax Inst. (planning com. 1985—86, 1994—), Del. Bar Assn. (chair sect. of taxation 1996—97), Alpha Sigma Nu. Democrat. Avocations: choir, opera, bridge. Home: 803 Westover Rd Wilmington DE 19807-2978 Office: Young Conaway Stargatt & Taylor LLP PO Box 391 Wilmington DE 19899-0391 E-mail: jgrossman@ycst.com.

GROSSMAN, JERROLD B. pharmaceutical executive; b. N.Y.C., Oct. 23, 1947; BA, Fairleigh Dickinson U., 1969, MBA, 1973; D of Profl. Studies in Bus. Mgmt., Pace U., 1989. Gen. mgr. Nomis Svc. Stores, Bklyn., 1969-72; fin. analyst Irving Trust Co., N.Y.C., 1972-74; sr. adminstr. Greater N.Y. blood program ARC, N.Y.C., 1974-79; dir. mktg., sales and biologic resources N.Y. Blood Ctr., 1979-85; v.p., dir. mktg. N.Am. Immuno-U.S., Inc., N.Y.C., 1985-90; pres. Genesis Bio-Pharm., Inc., Hackensack, NJ, 1990—. Bd. dirs. Govan, Inc., Pascack Cmty. Bank, Westwood, NJ; cons. Can. Red Cross, 1996. Author: Overview of Plasma Derivatives, 1984 (ency. sect.) Impact of Technology on the Plasma Derivative Industry, 1989, Blood and Plasma Industry, 1992-94. Bd. dirs., 1st vice chmn. Cmty. Blood Ctr., Paramus, NJ, 2000—; sec., bd. dirs. N.J. Soc. Blood Bank Profls., 2000—01; mem. Blood Bank Task Force N.J.; mem. fin. com. Congressman Robert Torricelli, 1995—96; bd. dirs. Temple Sinai Bergen County. Sgt. N.Y. Nat. Guard, 1969—75. Mem. Am. Assn. Blood Banks.

GROSSMAN, JOEL B(ARRY), political science educator; b. N.Y.C., June 19, 1936; s. Joseph and Selma G.; m. Mary Hengstenberg, Aug. 23, 1964; children: Alison, Joanna, Daniel. BA, Queens Coll., 1957; MA, U. Iowa, 1960, PhD, 1963. Faculty dept. polit. sci. U. Wis., Madison, 1963-96, prof., 1971-96, chmn. dept., 1975-78; prof. Johns Hopkins U., 1996—. Fellow in law and polit. sci. Harvard Law Sch., Cambridge, Mass., 1965-66; Fulbright lectr. U. Strathclyde, Glasgow, 1968-69; vis. prof. law U. Stockholm, 1973, John Hopkins U., 1995-96. Editor: Law and Soc. Review, 1978-82; author: Lawyers and Judges, 1965, Frontiers of Judicial Research, 1969, Law and Change in Modern America, 1971, Constitutional Law and Judicial Policy Making, 1972, 80, 88; contbr. articles to profl. jours. Chmn. Wis. Jud. Commn. 1985-87. Served with USAR, 1960-66. Mem. Wis. Civil Liberties Union (vice chmn. 1970-72), Am. Polit. Sci. Assn., Midwest Polit. Sci. Assn. (v.p. 1988-90), So. Polit. Sci. Assn., Law and Soc. Assn. Democrat. Home: 6606 Walnutwood Cir Baltimore MD 21212-1213 E-mail: jbgrossm@jhu.edu.

GROSSMAN, JOYCE RENEE, pediatrician, internist; b. Bklyn., Nov. 15, 1951; d. Norman and Sydell (Rashbaum) Katz; m. Arthur Robert Grossman (div.); 1 child, Justin. BS, Bklyn. Col., 1973; MS, Cornell Med. Col., 1980; MD, Downstate Med. Col., 1986. Adj. prof. Downstate Med. Ctr., Bklyn., 1994—; attending physician N.Y. Hosp. Network, Bklyn., 1996-97, Beth Israel Med. Ctr., Bklyn., 1997; assoc. med. dir. Cigna of N.Y., N.Y.C., 1998—. Author: (with others) Pediatric Aspects of Tuberculosis & Clinical Handbook, 1995. Fellow Am. Acad. Pediatrics, Am. Acad. Physicians. Achievements include patents in field of gene therapy, antibiotics and chemotherapeutic agents.

GROSSMAN, KATE NADIA, journalist; b. Chgo., Dec. 8, 1969; d. Robert Mayer and Frances Rosenbacher Grossman; m. Peter Fidler, Aug. 29, 1999. BA, Cornell U., 1992; M in Pub. Policy, MS in Journalism, Columbia U., 1997. Prodn. asst. ABC News 20/20, Washington, 1993-94; tchr. Chgo. Pub. Schs., 1994-95; reporter Providence Jour., 1997-99, AP, Chgo., 1999-2000, Chgo. Sun-Times, 2000 . Big sister Big Bros./Big Sisters Met. Chgo., 1999. Recipient 2 first pl. awards R.I. Press Assn., 1997, 1st and 2nd pl. awards R.I. Press Assn., 1998, Journalism award Am. Planning Assn., 2002, award Nat. Edn. Writers Assn., 2002. Mem. Assn. for Women Journalists, Soc. for Profl. Journalists (award 2002). Avocations: biking, jogging, hiking, camping, reading. Office: Chgo Sun Times 401 N Wabash Chicago IL 60611

GROSSMAN, LAWRENCE MORTON, nuclear engineering educator; b. N.Y.C., Aug. 2, 1922; married; 1 child. B.Chem. Engring., City Coll. N.Y., 1942, M.Sc. (Standard Oil Co. Calif. fellow), 1944; PhD in Engring. Sci., U. Calif. at Berkeley, 1948. Chem. engr. E.I. du Pont de Nemours & Co., Niagara Falls, N.Y., 1942-43; instr. mech. engring. U. Calif., Berkeley, 1944-46, lectr., 1946-48, asst. prof., 1948-54, assoc. prof. mech. engring., 1954-59, prof., 1959—, chmn. dept. nuclear engring., 1969-74. Fulbright lectr. U. Delft, 1952-53; NSF sr. research fellow Saclay Nuclear Research Center, France, 1961-62; NATO sr. fellow, 1974 Recipient Berkeley Citation, 1991. Mem. A.A.A.S., Am. Nuclear Soc. Office: U Calif Etcheverry Hl Berkeley CA 94720-0001 E-mail: grossman@nuc.berkeley.edu.

GROSSMAN, LISA ROBBIN, clinical psychologist, lawyer; b. Jan. 22, 1952; d. Samuel R. and Sarah (Kruger) G. BA with highest distinction & honors, Northwestern U., 1974, JD cum laude, 1979, PhD, 1982. Bar: Ill. 1981; registered psychologist, Ill. Jud. intern U.S. Supreme Ct., Washington, 1975; pre-doctoral psychology intern Michael Reese Hosp. and Med. Ctr., Chgo., 1979-80; therapist Homes for Children, Chgo., 1980-83; psychologist Psychiat. Inst. Cir. Ct. Cook County, Chgo., 1981-87; pvt. practice Chgo., 1984—. Invited participant workshop HHS, Rockville, Md., 1981. Contbr. articles to profl. jours. Mem.: APA (com. on legal issues 1992—95, state leadership organizing com. 1996—98, com. on profl. practice and stds. 1996—99, chair 1998, mem. exec. com. caucus of state and provincial reps. 2000—02, coun. reps. 2000—, bd. profl. affairs 2001—03, chair 2003, exec. com. women's caucus), ABA, Soc. Personality Assessment, Chgo. Bar Assn., Ill. State Bar Assn., Chgo. Assn. for Psychoanalytic Psychologists (parliamentarian 1982), Ill. Psychol. Assn. (pres. 1995—96), Alpha Lambda Delta (pres. forensic forum 2003), Shi-Ai, Phi Beta Kappa, Mortar Bd. Office: 500 N Michigan Ave Ste 1520 Chicago IL 60611-3758 E-mail: LRGrossman@aol.com.

GROSSMAN, MARC, federal agency administrator; b. L.A., Sept. 23, 1951; s. Melvin and Estelle Grossman; m. Mildred Patterson, May 29, 1982; 1 child, Anne. BA, U. Calif., Santa Barbara, 1973; MSc in Internat. Rels., London Sch. Econs./Polit. Sci., 1974. Polit. officer U.S. Embassy, Islamabad, Pakistan, 1977-79; staff asst. Bur. Near Eastern and South Asian Affairs U.S. Dept. State, 1979-80; dep. spl. adviser to Pres. Carter The White House, Washington, 1980; chief profl. staff State Dept. Transition Team, 1980; country officer for Jordan Dept. of State, 1981-83; polit. officer U.S. Mission to NATO, 1983; dep. dir. pvt. office of sec. gen. NATO, 1984-86; exec. asst. to dep. sec. Dept. State, 1986-89; dep. chief U.S. Mission in Turkey, 1989-92; exec. sec., spl. asst. to sec. Dept. of State, Washington, 1993-94, U.S. amb. to Turkey Ankara, 1995-97, asst. sec. for Europe and Can. affairs Washington, 1997-98, asst. sec. European affairs, 1998-2000, dir. gen. Fgn. Svc., 2000-01, under sec. of state for polit. affairs, 2001—. Mem. Am. Friends of the London Sch. of Econs., Army and Navy Club (Washington). Avocations: reading, travel, sports.

GROSSMAN, MARY MARGARET, elementary education educator; b. East Cleveland, Ohio, Sept. 26, 1946; d. Frank Anthony and Margaret Mary (Buda) G. Student, Kent State Univ., 1965-67; BS in Elem. Edn. cum laude, Cleveland State Univ., 1971; postgrad, Lake Erie Coll., 1974-77, John Carroll Univ., 1978, 81, 82, 83, 85, Cleveland State Univ., 1985. Cert. elem. sch. tchr. grades 1 to 8, Ohio; cert. data processing, Ohio. Tchr. Cleve. Catholic Diocese, Cleve., Ohio, 1971-72, Willoughby-Eastlake Sch. Dist., Willoughby, Ohio, 1972—. Participant Nat. Econ. Edn. Conf., Richmond, Va., 1995. Eucharistic min. St. Christine's Ch., Euclid, 1988—, mem. parish pastoral coun., 1995-00. Recipient Samuel H. Elliott Econ. Leadership award, 1986-87, Consumer Educator award N.E. Ohio Region, 1986, 1st pl. award for excellence in tchg. Tchrs. in Am. Enterprise, 1984-85, 89-90; Martha Holden Jennings scholar, 1984-85. Mem. NEA, Ohio Edn. Assn. (human rels. award 1986-87, cert. merit 1987-88), N.E. Ohio Edn. Assn. (Positive Tchr. Image award 1988). Roman Catholic. Avocations: racquetball, softball, walking, tennis, bicycling. Home: 944 E 225th St Cleveland OH 44123-3308 Office: McKinley Elem Sch 1200 Lost Nation Rd Willoughby OH 44094-7324

GROSSMAN, MICHAEL, economics educator; b. Bklyn., July 12, 1942; s. Mortimer and Doris (Orent) G.; m. Ilene Joy Gordon, Sept. 11, 1966; children: Sandra Diane, Barri Lynn. BA, Trinity Coll., Hartford, Conn., 1964; Ph.D, Columbia U., 1970. Asst. prof. Ctr. Health Adminstrn. Studies, Grad. Sch. Bus., U. Chgo., 1969-71; research assoc., co-program dir. health econs. research Nat. Bur. Econ. Research, N.Y.C., 1972—; prof. econs. CUNY Grad. Sch., 1974, disting. prof. econs, 1988. Cons. in field. Author: The Demand for Health: A Theoretical and Empirical Investigation, 1972; contbr. articles to profl. jours. Member Social Sciences, Nursing, Epidemiology, and Methods Study Section, Center for Scientific Review, National Institutes of Health, Washington, 2000—01. Ford Found. fellow Columbia U. Mem. Am. Econ. Assn., Population Assn. Am., Am. Pub. Health Assn., Health Econs. Research Assn., Phi Beta Kappa, Pi Gamma Mu Independent. Jewish. Avocations: tennis, skiing, boating. Home: 115 E 9th St Apt 14C New York NY 10003 Office: Nat Bur Econ Rsch 365 5th Ave 5th Flr New York NY 10016-4309 Office Fax: 212-817-1597. E-mail: mgrossman@gc.cuny.edu.

GROSSMAN, MORLEY KEITH, music educator; b. Columbia, SC, Mar. 17, 1945; s. David L. and Sylvia Sarah Grossman; m. Nancie A. Hack, Aug. 28, 1969; 1 child, Lili Miriam Blanche. Student, Calif. Inst. Arts, 1963—64, Calif. State U., Fullerton, 1964—66; BA, Calif. State U., Long Beach, 1967; D in Musical Arts (with hons.), Ind. U., 1978. Faculty prep. divsn. Peabody Inst., Balt., 1971—72; instr. piano Ind. U., Bloomington, 1972—78; assoc. prof. piano U. Tex.-Pan Am., Edinburg, Tex., 1978—. Fellow tchg. fellow, Cleve. Inst. Music, 1967—71. Republican. Jewish. Avocations: travel, videography, judaica. Home: 2417 River Oaks Lane Edinburg TX 78539 Office: University of Texas-Pan American W University Drive Edinburg TX 78539 Home Fax: 956-380-1379. Personal E-mail: drmorleyg@aol.com. E-mail: drmorleyg@aol.com.

GROSSMAN, MURRAY, neurologist; b. Montreal, Que., Can., Jan. 5, 1952; arrived in U.S., 1986; s. Samuel and Roslyn Grossman; m. Francine Nelson, Apr. 15, 1977; children: Joshua, Scott. BA, Union Coll., 1972; EdM, EdD, Boston U., 1972-77; MD, McGill U., 1985. Diplomate Am. Bd. Neurology. Postdoctoral fellow MIT, Cambridge, Mass., 1979; resident in neurology U. Pa., Phila., 1986-89, neurologist, 1989—. Scholar Union Coll., 1972, McGill U., 1985. Mem. Acad. Aphasia (chmn. 1998—), Am. Acad. Neurology, Soc. Neurosci., Cognitive Neurosci. Soc., Am. Soc. for Clin. Investigation. Office: U Pa Dept Neurology 3400 Spruce St Philadelphia PA 19104-4206 E-mail: mgrossma@mail.med.upenn.edu.

GROSSMAN, PAMELA LYNN, education educator; d. Moses and Verle Anne Grossman; m. David Ezra Kahn; children: Ben Grossman-Kahn, Rebecca Grossman-Kahn, Sarah Grossman-Kahn. BA, Yale U., 1975; MA, U. of Calif., Berkeley, 1981; PhD, Stanford U., 1988. Boeing prof. of tchr. edn. U. of Wash., Seattle, 1996—2000; prof. English Edn. Stanford (Calif.) U., 2000—. Author: The Making of a Teacher: Teacher Knowledge and Teacher Education, 1990 (CEE Richard A. Meade Award for Disting. Rsch. in English Edn., 1991). Fellow Dissertation, The Spencer Found., Postdoctoral. Mem.: Am. Edn. Rsch. Assn. (v.p. divsn. K 2002—). Office: Stanford U Sch of Edn 485 Lasuen Mall Stanford CA 94305

GROSSMAN, ROBERT ALLEN, transportation executive; b. Port Jervis, N.Y., July 24, 1941; s. George and Helen (Garson) G.; m. Joan Ward, June 15, 1962 (div.); children: Jeffrey, Wendy; m. Gloria Schwartz, Nov. 22, 1987. Student, Cornell U., 1959-60, U. Pa., 1960-62. Fin. divsn. North Shore Packing Co., Inc., North Bellmore, N.Y., 1962-64; mgr. refin. and legal dept. Coburn Corp. Am., Rockville Centre, N.Y., 1964-67; stockbroker Weis, Volson & Cannon, Inc., N.Y.C., 1967-69, Nadel & Co., N.Y.C., 1969-70; v.p. Emons Industries, Inc., York, Pa., 1971—79, chmn. bd., CEO, 1979—2002; chmn., CEO Emons Transp. Group, 1986—2002; exec. v.p. Genesee & Wyoming Inc., Greenwich, Conn., 2002—. Mem. legis. policy com. Am. Assn. Shortline and Regional R.R. Assn., 1998—. Bd. dirs. Better York, Inc., 1996—. Mem. Am. Assn. Short Line and Regional Railroads (dir. 1998—). York Area C. of C. (dir. 1978-83), Pa. Rail Freight (adv. com. 1993-2002), Me. Rail Task Force, Keystone State Railroad Assn. (pres. 1996-99, exec. com. 1996-2002), Nat. Indsl. Transp. League. Office: Genesee & Wyoming Inc 204 North George St Ste 230 York PA 17401

GROSSMAN, ROBERT GEORGE, physician, educator; b. N.Y.C., Jan. 24, 1933; s. Ferenc and Vivian (Isenberg) G.; m. Ellin Friedman, June 26, 1955; children— Amy, Kate, Ruth. BA, Swarthmore Coll., 1953; MD, Columbia U., 1957. Diplomate Am. Bd. Neurosurgery. Intern Strong Meml. Hosp., Rochester, N.Y., 1957-58; resident Presbyn. Hosp., Columbia U., N.Y.C., 1960-63; acad. practice medicine, specializing in neurol. surgery Houston, 1973—; instr., assoc. prof. neurol. surgery U. Tex. SW Med. Sch., 1963-68; assoc. prof., prof. neurol. surgery Albert Einstein Coll. Medicine, 1969-73; prof., chmn. div. neurol. surgery U. Tex. Med. Br., Galveston, 1973-80; prof., chmn. dept. neurol. surgery Baylor Coll. Medicine, 1980—; assoc. dean clin. affairs Baylor Coll. Medicne, 2002—; chief neurosurg. service Meth. Hosp., Houston, 1980—. Chmn. neurology B study sect. USPHS, NIH, 1972-74; mem. bd. sci. counsellors Nat. Inst. Neurol. Diseases and Stroke, NIH, 1989-93; mem. nat. adv. coun. Nat. Inst. Neurol. Diseases and Stroke, NIH, 1993-96. Author: (with W. D. Willis) Medical Neurobiology, 3d edit, 1981; chmn. editorial bd. Jour. Neurosurgery, 1987. Served with AUS, 1958-60. Mem. Am. Assn. Neurol. Surgeons, ACS, Soc. Univ. Surgeons, Am. Bd. Neurol. Surgery (chmn. bd. 1989-90), Am. Acad. Neurol. Surgery (v.p.), Soc. Neurol. Surgeons (pres. 1995). Home: 2002 Sunset Blvd Houston TX 77005-1651 Office: Tex Med Ctr Scurlock Tower 6560 Fannin St Ste 944 Houston TX 77030-2706 E-mail: grossman@bcm.tmc.edu.

GROSSMAN, ROBERT JAMES, retired architect; b. Spokane, Wash., Feb. 3, 1936; s. George Christian and Corinne (Shelton) G.; m. Charleigh Rozelle, Aug. 7, 1956; children: Kevin James, Heidi Rozelle. B Archtl. Engring. with highest honors, Wash. State U., 1959. Lic. architect, Wash. Architect Heylman-Trogdon, Spokane, 1962-64, Trogdon-Smith, Architects, Spokane, 1964-72; prin. architect Trogdon-Smith-Grossman, TSG Architects, Spokane, 1973-83; mng. prin. N.W. Archtl. Co. (A Joint Venture), Spokane, 1979-83; pres., prin. N.W. Archtl. Co., P.S., Seattle, 1983-85, 98-99, mng. prin., 1986-99; ret., 1999. Coord. architect for site planning and devel. Expo'74 World's Fair, Spokane, 1971-74; mem. adv. coun. Sch. Architecture Wash. State U., Pullman, 1986-93, mem. adv. bd. Coll. Engring. and Architecture, 1991-99, 2001—; bd. dirs. Evergreen Bancorp. Inc. Prin. works include 40 sch. projects throughout Wash.; Wash. State U. Alumni Ctr., Pullman; instnl. and comml. projects. Bd. dirs., pres. Salvation Army-Booth Care Ctr., Spokane, 1972-85; bd. dirs. Med. Svc. Corp., Spokane, 1984-86; mem. state adv. bd. Lien Law Reform, 1990; founding pres. Downtown Exch. Club of Seattle Found., 1990—; mem. adv. bd. for master planning Children's Hosp., Seattle, 1991-94; chair Wash. State Archs. and Engrs. Legis. Coun., 1994-97, 1st lt. C.E., U.S. Army, 1960-62. Recipient Disting. Svc. award Govt. State of Wash. and State Commn. for Expo '74, 1974. Mem. AIA (pres. Spokane chpt. 1976), Wash. State Coun. Architects (bd. dirs. 1975-78), Wash. State U. Alumni Assn. (Alumni Achievement award 1990), Exch. Club (bd. dirs. 1988-91). Avocations: travel, music.

GROSSMAN, ROBERT LOUIS, lawyer; b. Cleve., Dec. 20, 1954; s. Sidney and Lillian Belle (Davis) G.; m. Rochelle Carol Shear, Nov. 7, 1987; children: Zachary, Jonathan, David, Andrew. BA with honors, Ohio State U., 1975, JD with Honors, 1978, MA with honors, 1979. Bar: Ohio 1978, U.S. Ct. Appeals (5th cir.) 1979, Fla. 1982. Law clk. U.S. Dist. Ct. (so. dist.) Ohio, Columbus, 1977-78; sr. atty. U.S. Govt. EEOC, Houston, 1979-82; shareholder Greenberg, Traurig, P.A., Miami, 1982—. Editor: Florida Corporate Practice, 2d edit., 1991. Chmn. South Dade Jewish Leadership Coun., 1997-99; bd. dir. Greater Miami Jewish Fedn. South Dade, Miami, 1987—, campaign chmn., 1995-97, chmn., 1997-99; bd. dir. Greater Miami Jewish Fedn., 1995—, exec. com., 1997-99, Alper Jewish Comm. Ctr., 1997-2000, exec. com., 1998-2000; bd. dir. Children's Bereavement Ctr., 2000—, Orgn. Leadership Advancement Miami, 2001-; chmn. Exec. Inst. OLAM, 2001-; bd. dir., Beacon coun., 2000—; chmn. Exec. Inst. for Orgn. for Leadership Advancement in Miami, 2001-03; chmn. Fedn. Agy., Day Sch. and Synagogue Campaign, 2003—; bd. dir. Temple Beth Am., 2003—. Donald Becker Meml. scholar Ohio State U., 1975, 76, fellow, 1978; Robert Russell fellow Greater Miami Jewish Fedn., 1998; recipient Stanley C. Myers Young Leadership award Greater Miami Jewish Fedn., 1999, Put Something Back Cmty. award, 2003. Mem. ABA (corp. securities sect.), Fla. Bar Assn., Dade County Bar Assn., Order of Coif. Avocations: sports, reading, travel. Office: Greenberg Traurig 1221 Brickell Ave Miami FL 33131-3224

GROSSMAN, SANFORD JAY, economics educator; b. Bklyn., July 21, 1953; s. Sloane and Florence G.; m. Naava. BA in Econs. with honors, U. Chgo., 1973, MA in Econs., 1974, PhD in Econs., 1975. Asst. prof. econs. Stanford U., Calif., 1975-77; economist Bd. Govs. Fed. Res., 1977-78; assoc. prof. econs. U. Pa., Phila., 1978-79, prof. econs., 1979-81, U. Chgo., 1981-85; John L. Weinberg prof. econs. Princeton U., N.J., 1985-89; Steinberg trustee prof. fin. U. Pa., Phila., 1989—2000; dir. Wharton Ctr. Quantitative Fin., 1994—2001, Quantitative Fin. Strategies, Inc., Stamford, Conn., 2001—. Pub. dir., bd. dirs.

Chgo. Bd. Trade, 1992-96. Mem. editl. bd. Finance India, 1994—; mem. adv. bd. Math. Finance, 1994—; contbr. articles to profl. jours. Recipient Irving Fisher grad. monograph award, award for best article, Graham and Dodd Scroll, Fin. Analyst Jour., 1988, Roger F. Murray 1st Prize award, Q Group, 1988, Math. Fin. Best Paper award, 1993, Profl. Achievement citation, U. Chgo., 2002, 2004, Mathematical Fin. Best Paper award, 1993; fellow, Lilly Found., Guggenheim Meml., Sloan Found., Am. Econometric Soc., 1980, Lilly Found. Fellow AAAS, Econometric Soc., Am. Fin. Assn. (v.p. 1992, pres.-elect 1993, pres. 1994, bd. dirs., fellow 2000); mem. Am. Econ. Assn. (John Bates Clark medal 1987). Office: Quantitative Fin Strategiges Inc Four Stamford Plz 107 Elm St Ste 500B Stamford CT 06902 Office Fax: 203-602-7746. Business E-Mail: qfs@qfsfunds.com.

GROSSMAN, STANLEY LAWRENCE, surgeon; b. Bklyn., Aug. 14, 1929; MD, SUNY, Bklyn., 1954; MPH, N.Y. Med. Coll., 1986. Diplomate Am. Bd. Surgery. Intern Maimonides Hosp., Bklyn., 1954-55, resident in surgery, 1955-59; with St. Lukes Hosp., Newburgh, N.Y., Cornwall Hosp., N.Y. Fellow ACS, N.Y. Acad. Medicine; mem. AMA, Med. Soc. State N.Y. Office: 460 Gidney Ave Newburgh NY 12550-3117 E-mail: slgrossman@compuserve.com.

GROSSMAN, STUART ALAN, oncologist, medical educator; b. Athens, Ohio, Feb. 12, 1947; s. Morton Charles and Sylvia Grossman; m. Linda Sullivan, Dec. 30, 1972; children: Julia, Elizabeth, Susan. BA, Harvard Coll., 1969; MD, U. Rochester, N.Y., 1973. Diplomate Am. Bd. Internal Medicine, Am. Bd. Med. Oncology. Resident internal medicine Strong Meml. Hosp., Rochester, 1973-76; physician Nat. Health Svc. Corps, Greenwood, Wis., 1976-78; fellow med. oncology Johns Hopkins Hosp., Balt., 1979-81; faculty med. oncology Johns Hopkins Oncology Ctr., Balt., 1981—, dir. neuro-oncology, 1981—; prof. oncology medicine and neurosurgery Johns Hopkins Sch. Medicine, Balt., 1998—. Patentee in field. Lt. comdr. USPHS, 1976-78. Mem.: Soc. Neuro-oncology (pres. 1999—2001). Office: Johns Hopkins Hosp Cancer Rsch Bldg Rm G93 1650 Orleans St Baltimore MD 21231-1000 E-mail: grossman@jhmi.edu.

GROSSMAN, THEODORE MARTIN, lawyer; b. N.Y.C., Dec. 31, 1949; s. Albert and Sylvia Pia (Greenstein) G.; m. Linda Gail Steinbook, Dec. 3, 1976; children: Andrew Scott, Michael Steven. AB, Cornell U., 1971, JD, 1974. Bar: N.Y. 1975, U.S. Ct. Appeals (D.C. cir.) 1981, U.S. Ct. Appeals (2nd cir.) 1982, U.S. Ct. Appeals (5th cir.) 1984, U.S. Dist. Ct. (no. dist.) Ohio 1986, Ohio 1987, U.S. Dist. Ct. (so. dist.) N.Y. 1988, U.S. Dist. Ct. (ea. dist.) N.Y. 1988, U.S. Ct. Appeals (6th cir.) 1988. Assoc. Debevoise, Plimpton, Lyons & Gates, N.Y.C., 1974-77, Rosenman Colin Freund Lewis & Cohen, N.Y.C., 1977-80; trial and appellate counsel fed. programs br. of civil div. U.S. Dept. Justice, Washington, 1980-84; assoc. Jones Day, Cleve., 1984-86, ptnr., 1987—. Editor Cornell U. Law Rev., 1974. Trustee Cleve. Ctr. for Contemporary Art, 1992-96, treas., 1992-94. Fellow: Am. Coll. Trial Lawyers; mem.: ABA. Home: 2979 Broxton Rd Cleveland OH 44120-1819 Office: Jones Day 901 Lakeside Ave E Cleveland OH 44114-1190 E-mail: tgrossman@jonesday.com.

GROSSMAN, VICTOR G. lawyer; b. N.Y.C., Nov. 21, 1951; s. Jacob and Frances (Gaezer) Grossman; m. Jamie Williams, Apr. 8, 1984; children: Robert William, Sarah Frances. BA in Am. Studies with honors, Brandeis U., 1973; JD, Hofstra U., 1978. Bar: NY 1979, US Dist Ct (so and ea dists) NY 1980, US Supreme Ct 1984. Pvt. practice, White Plains, N.Y., 1979-82; atty. Aurnou Kurzman Midler & Friedman, White Plains, 1982-87; pvt. practice Carmel, N.Y., 1987—. Mem zoning bd appeals Town of Southeast, Brewster, NY, 1989—91, dep supr, 1994—96; legislator Putnam County Legis, Carmel, 1990—92. Home: 40 Seven Oaks Ln Brewster NY 10509-1610 Office: Nine Fair St Carmel NY 10512-1213

GROSSMAN, WILLIAM, medical researcher, educator; b. N.Y.C., 1940; MD, Yale U., 1965. Intern Peter Bent Brigham Hosp., Boston, 1965-66, resident in medicine, 1968-69, rsch. fellow in cardiology, 1969-71; dir. cardiac catheterization labs. N.C. Meml. Hosp., Chapel Hill, 1971-75, Peter Bent Brigham Hosp., Boston, 1975-81; chief cardiovasc. divsn. Beth Israel Hosp., Boston, 1981-94; tchg. fellow in medicine Harvard U., Boston, 1968-71, assoc. prof., 1975-81, prof., 1981-84, Herman Dana prof. medicine, 1984-94; exec. dir. cardiovasc. rsch. Merck & Co., West Point, Pa., 1994-95, v.p., 1996-97; prof. medicine U. Calif., San Francisco, 1997—, chief cardiology, 1997—. Served as sr. asst. surgeon USPHS, 1966-68. Fellow Am. Coll. Cardiology, Am. Heart Assn., Assn. Am. Physicians, Am. Physiol. Soc., Am. Soc. Clin. Investigation. Office: UCSF Med Ctr Dept Cardiology Box 0124 San Francisco CA 94143-0124

GROSSMANN, IGNACIO EMILIO, chemical engineering educator; b. Mexico City, Nov. 12, 1949; s. Donat and Marie-Louise (Epper) G.; m. Ignacio E. Blanca Espinal, Nov. 26, 1977; children: Claudia, Andrew, Thomas. BSc ChemE, U. Iberoamericana, 1974; MSc ChemE, hon. diploma, Imperial Coll., 1975, PhD ChemE, 1977; DTech (hon.), Abo Akademi, 2002. Research and devel. engr. Inst. Mexicano del Petroleo, Mexico City, 1978; asst. prof. chem. engring. Carnegie Mellon U., Pitts., 1979-83, assoc. prof., 1983-86, prof., 1986-90, Rudolph R. and Florence Dean prof. chem. engring., 1990—, head dept. chem. engring., 1994—. Robert W. Vaughan lectr. Calif. Inst. Tech., Pasadena, 1986; Mary Upson vis. prof. engring. Cornell U., Ithaca, N.Y., 1986-87; acad. trustee Computer Aids for Chem. Engring. Edn. (CACHE), Austin, Tex., 1983-2000; mem. governing bd. Coun. for Chem. Rsch. Assoc. editor: AIChE Jour., 2000—, mem. editl. bd.: Computers and Chem. Engring. Jour., 1987—, Jour. Global Optimization, 1991—, Optimization and Engring.; contbr. articles to profl. jours. Recipient Presdl. Young Investigator award NSF, Washington, 1984, Tech. Achievement award HEENAC, 2000. Fellow: Inst. Operation Rsch. and Mgmt. Svc.; mem.: AIChE (chmn.computing and sys. tech. divsn. 1992, Computing in Chem. Engring. award 1994, William H. Walker award 1997), Mex. Acad. Engring., Nat. Acad. Engring., Am. Chem. Soc., Sigma Xi. Roman Catholic. Avocation: classical music. Home: 6385 Douglas St Pittsburgh PA 15217-1821 Office: Carnegie Mellon Univ Dept of Chem Engring Pittsburgh PA 15213

GROSSMANN, RONALD STANYER, lawyer; b. Chgo., Nov. 9, 1944; s. Andrew Eugene and Gladys M. Grossmann; m. Jo Ellen Hanson, May 11, 1968; children: Kenneth Frederick, Emilie Beth. BA, Northwestern U., 1966; JD, U. Mich., 1969. Bar: Oreg., 1969. Law clk. Oreg. Supreme Ct., Salem, 1969-70; assoc. Stoel Rives LLP, Portland, Oreg., 1970-76, ptnr., 1976—. Mem.: Am. Coll. Employee Benefits Counsel, Oreg. Bar Assn., ABA. Office: Stoel Rives LLP 900 SW 5th Ave Ste 2600 Portland OR 97204-1268 E-mail: rsgrossmann@stoel.com.

GROSSO, STACIA STROUSS, foundation administrator; b. Sweickley, Pa., May 27, 1966; d. Richard Lowell and Sara Anna Strouss; m. Frank Anthony Grosso, Oct. 28, 1997; children: Katherine Angelina, Alyssa Felice. BA, Dickinson Coll., 1988; MBA, George Washington U., 1994. Profl. svcs. rep. Pa. Bly Shield, Camp Hill, 1989—90; bus. dir. Fairfax Radiological Cons., Va., 1990—95; asst. v.p. Nat. Com. Quality Assurance, Washington, 1995—2000; CEO Nat. Coalition Cancer Survivorship, 2000—02, chief devel. officer, 2002—03. Democrat. Roman Catholic. Office: NCCS 1010 Wayne Ave Ste 770 Silver Spring MD 20910 E-mail: sgrosso@canceradvocacy.org.

GROSU, DANIEL, computer scientist; s. Constantin and Gherghina G.; m. Sanda Guseila, Aug. 22, 1992; 1 child, Ioana. MS, U. Tex., San Antonio, 2002. Lectr. Transylvania U., Brasov, Romania, 1994—99; rsch. asst. U. Tex., San Antonio, 1999—. Contbr. articles. Rsch. Assistantship scholar, NASA, 2000-2002, PhD fellow, U. Tex., 2000. Mem.: IEEE Computer Soc., SIAM, AMS, ACM, IEEE. Achievements include research in distributed systems. Office: University of Texas/Computer Science 6900 N Loop 1604 West San Antonio TX 78249

GROSVENOR, GILBERT MELVILLE, journalist, educator, business executive; b. Washington, May 5, 1931; s. Melville Bell and Helen (Rowland) Grosvenor; m. Donna C. Kerkam, June 16, 1961 (div.); children: Gilbert Hovey II, Alexandra Rowland; m. Wiley Jarman, June 1, 1979; 1 child, Graham Dabney. BA, Yale U., 1954; D in Pub. Svc. (hon.), George Washington U., 1983; LHD (hon.) (hon.), U. Colo., 1983, Curry Coll., 1984; LLD (hon.) (hon.), Coll. of Wooster, Ohio, 1983; LHD (hon.) (hon.), Coll. William and Mary, 1987, Miami U., Oxford, Ohio, 1988, Syracuse U., 1989, R.I. Coll., 1991, Old Dominion U., 1993, Longwood Coll., Worcester, Mass., 1997, Ind. Univ., 1998, Univ. S.C., 1998, Pa. State Univ., 1999. With Nat. Geog. Soc., 1954—, trustee, 1966—, v.p., 1966—80, assoc. editor, 1967—70, editor, 1970—80, pres., 1980—96, chmn. bd. dirs., 1987—. Bd. dirs. Chevy Chase Bank, FSB, Marriott Internat., Inc., Saul Ctrs., Inc., Ethyl Corp.; former fellow Yale Corp. Bd. visitors Duke U. Nicholas Sch. Environment; former bd. visitors Coll. William and Mary; ann. corp. mem. Children's Hosp.; former mem. Pres.'s Commn. on Environ. Quality; mem. Washington Cathedral Bldg. Com.; trustee Nat. Wildflower Rsch. Ctr., Fed. City Coun., B.F. Saul Real Estate Trust, Saul Ctrs., Inc., Wildlife Conservation Soc.; past vice chmn. Pres.'s Commn. Ams. Outdoors; chmn. emeritus, found. bd. Alexander Graham Bell Assn. for Deaf; bd. dirs. Conservation Fund, Environmentors Project, Dian Fossey Gorilla Fund Internat. Recipient Editor of Yr. award, Nat. Press Photographers Assn., 1975, Disting. Achievement award, U. So. Calif. Sch. Journalism and Alumni Assn., 1977, Pres. medal, George Washington U., 1993, Golden Plate award, Am. Acad. Achievement, 1996. Mem.: Assn. Am. Geographers, Chevy Chase (Md.) Club, Cosmos Club, Alibi Club, Alfalfa Club, Newcomen Soc., Explorers Club (citation of merit 1997). Office: Nat Geog Soc 1145 17th St NW Washington DC 20036-4701

GROSZ, BARBARA JEAN, computer science educator; b. Phila., July 21, 1948; d. Joseph Eugene and Judith Phyllis (Zander) Gross. AB in Math., Cornell U., 1969; MA in Computer Sci., U. Calif., Berkeley, 1971, PhD in Computer Sci., 1977. Rsch. mathematician Artificial Intelligence Ctr., SRI Internat., Stanford, Calif., 1973-77, computer scientist, 1981-82, sr. computer scientist, 1981-82, program dir. nat. lang. and representation, 1982-83, sr. staff scientist, 1983-86; co-founder, mem. exec. com., prin. researcher Ctr. for Study of Lang. and Info. Stanford U. and SRI Internat., 1983-86; with divsn. engring. and applied scis. Harvard U., Cambridge, Mass., 1986—, interim assoc. dean for affirmative action, 1993-94, Higgins prof. natural scis., 2001—, dean of sci. Radcliffe Inst. Advanced Study, 2001—. Vis. faculty dept. computer sci. Stanford U., fall 1982, cons. assoc. prof. computer sci. and linguistics, 1984-85, computer sci., 1985-87; vis. scholar dept. computer and info. sci. U. Pa., Jan.-June 1982; conf. chair Internat. Joint Conf. on Artificial Intelligence (IJCAI-91), chair bd. trustees IJCAI Inc., 1989-91, mem. bd. trustees 1987-97 program com. 1982; Harold Perlman vis. prof. faculty sci. Hebrew U., Jerusalem, 1992; invited spkr. numerous nat. and internat. profl. assns., confs., symposia; reviewer program proposals NSF; participant adv. meetings for rsch. and funding various govtl. agys. Author: (with others) Elements of Discourse Understanding, 1982, Understanding Spoken Language, 1982, Foundations of Cognitive Science, 1988, Intentions in Communications, 1988; editor: (with Sparck Jones, Webber) Readings in Natural Language Processing, 1986; assoc. editor: Ann. Rev. Computer Sci., 1982-1985; editl. bd.: Artificial Intelligence Jour., 1982—, Am. Jour. Computational Linguistics, 1981-83; contbr. articles and papers to profl. jours., workshops and conf. procs. Recipient Disting. Alumna award in computer sci. and engring., U. Calif., Berkeley, 1997, Donald E. Walker Disting. Svc. award, IJCAI, 2001. Fellow AAAS, Am. Assn. Artificial Intelligence (exec. coun. 1981-84, 86-89, pres.-elect 1991-93, pres. 1993-95, past pres. 1995-97, disting. svc. award, 1999); mem. NRC (computer sci. & telecom. bd. 1994-98), Assn. Computational Linguistics (exec. com. 1986-88), Assn. Computing Machinery (vice chair 1979-81, chair 1981-83, mem. SIGART), Am. Philos. Soc. Avocations: hiking, wildflower photography, snorkeling. Address: 33 Oxford St Rm 249 Cambridge MA 02138-2901

GROSZ, MORTON ERIC, lawyer; b. N.Y.C., Feb. 1, 1944; s. Armand A. and Gisele (Zucker) G.; m. Judith Harriet Armour, June 15, 1969; children: David, Jeffrey. BS in Econs., U. Pa., 1965; LLB, Boston U., 1968; LLM in Internat. Law, NYU, 1969. Bar: N.Y. 1968. Assoc. Barrett Smith Schapiro Simon & Armstrong, N.Y.C., 1969-76; ptnr. Barrett, Smith Schapiro Simon & Armstrong, N.Y.C., 1976-88, Chadbourne & Parke, N.Y.C., 1988—. Mem. Assn. of Bar of City of N.Y. (corp. law com. 1975-77, 89-92). Office: Chadbourne & Parke 30 Rockefeller Plz Fl 31 New York NY 10112-0129

GROTE, DICK (RICHARD CHARLES GROTE), management consultant, educator, author, radio commentator; b. N.Y.C., Dec. 14, 1941; s. Charles Henry and Muriel (Steele) G.; m. Jacqueline Center, May 11, 1991. BA, Colgate U., 1959; M Liberal Arts, So. Meth. U., 1992. Pers. mgr. GE, Schenectady, 1964-67; mgr. mgmt. devel. United Air Lines, Chgo., 1967-72; mgr. tng. and devel. Frito-Lay, Inc., Dallas, 1972-77; pres. Performance Systems Corp., Dallas, 1977-87; prin. Grote Cons. Corp., Dallas, 1987—. Adj. prof. U. Dallas Grad. Sch. Mgmt., 1977—; commentator NPR, 1993—; reviewer Inst. Mus. Svcs., 1974-77. Author: Positive Discipline, 1985, Discipline Without Punishment, 1995, The Complete Guide to Performance Appraisal, 1996, The Performance Appraisal Q&A Book, 2002; host (film series) Respect and Responsibility; contbr. articles to profl. jours. Trustee, pres. Schaumburg (Ill.) Pub. Libr., 1969-72; bd. dirs. Shakespeare Festival Dallas, 1981-84, Dallas Opera, 1981-88; chmn. So. Meth. U. Conservatory Soc., 1988—; bd. councillors U. Dallas, 1989—. Recipient Torch award ASTD, 1979, Disting. Svc. award Malaysian Soc. for Tng. and Devel., 1984, Bapindo award Govt. of Indonesia, 1984. Republican. Office: Grote Consulting Corp 15303 Dallas Pkwy Ste 645 Addison TX 75001-6725 E-mail: dickgrote@groteconsulting.com.

GROTEN, BARNET, energy company executive; b. Bklyn., Oct. 25, 1933; s. Irving and Pearl G.; m. Iris Diane Brand, Aug. 1955; children: Eric Allen, Kurt David, Jessica Amy. BS, Bklyn. Coll., 1954; PhD, Purdue U., 1961. Joined Exxon Co., various locations, 1961; dir. rsch. and bus. devel. Tex. Eastern Corp., Houston, 1977-87; exec. v.p. Tex. Eastern Devel., Inc., 1980-87; sec. Gulf Univs. Research Consortium, 1980-81; chmn. bd. Gulf Univs. Rsch. Consortium, 1982-83; exec. dir. Energy Ctr. U. Okla., Norman, 1987-91; v.p. Energy Internat., Inc., Bellevue, Wash., 1991-99; pres., CEO Grait Techs., LLC, Bellevue, 1999—, Power Genix Systems, Inc., Bellevue, 2001—03. Contbr. articles to profl. jours. Mem. Gov.'s Energy Adv. Coun.; chmn. Natural Gas Vehicle Task Force. Office: Grait Techs LLC 13706 NE 36th Pl Bellevue WA 98005-1413 E-mail: barnet@wolfenet.com.

GROTENHUIS, MARSHALL, retired nuclear engineer; b. Oostburg, Wis., Oct. 17, 1918; s. William and Isabel Grotenhuis; m. Marilynn Johnson; children: Susan Kidd, Alan, Judith, Brian. BS in Sci. and Math., Milw. State Tchrs. Coll., 1941; MS in Physics and Math., Marquette U., Milw., 1948. Tchr. Wakefield H.S., Mich., 1941—42; instr. physics Marquette U., Milw., 1947—48; with Argonne Nat. Lab., Downers Grove, Ill., 1949—71, dir. Office of Indsl. Coop., 1965—67, supt. ctrl. shops dept., 1967—70, sr. mgmt. engr., 1970—71; environ. project mgr. U.S. Nuclear Regulatory Commn., Rockville, Md., 1971—75, operating reactor project mgr., 1976—88. Mem. IAEA Shielding Panel, 1964; vis. lectr. nuclear engring. dept. U. Wis.; lectr. in field; chmn. Ill. State Tech. Svc. Bd. Commr. Boy Scouts Am., 1959—; mem. Gaithersburg Hist. Assn., 1980—. Sgt. USAAF, 1942—46. Recipient Silver Beaver award, Boy Scouts Am., 1971. Mem.: PTA (life), Am. Nuclear Soc. (bd. dir., editor Nuclear Structural Engring., editl. adv. com. Nuclear Tech., Disting. Svc. award, Meritorious Svc. award, Spl. Achievement award), Sigma Xi, Sigma Pi Sigma, Delta Chi Sigma. Home: 415 Russell Ave Apt 505 Gaithersburg MD 20877

GROTH, ALEXANDER JACOB, political science educator; b. Warsaw, Mar. 7, 1932; came to U.S., 1947; s. Jacob and Maria (Hazenfuss) Goldwasser; m. Marilyn Ann Wineburg, Dec. 15, 1961; children: Stevin James, Warren Adrian. BA magna cum laude, CCNY, 1954; MA, Columbia U., 1955, PhD, 1960. Instr. polit. sci. Trinity Coll., Hartford, Conn., 1957-58, CUNY, 1960-61; asst. prof. Harpur Coll., Binghamton, N.Y., 1961-62, U. Calif., Davis, 1962-71, prof., 1971—. Cons. Ency. Am., Danbury, Conn., 1965—. Author: Comparative Politics, 1971, Major Ideologies, 1971, 2d rev. edit., 1983, People's Poland, 1972, Progress and Chaos, 1984, Lincoln: Authoritarian Savior, 1995, Democracies Against Hitler, 1999; co-author: Contemporary Politics: Europe, 1976, Comparative Resource allocation, 1984, Public Policy Across Nations, 1985; editor: Revolution and Political Change, 1996; contbr. numerous articles to encys., scholarly jours. Recipient Ward medal dept. govt. CCNY, 1954, T. R. Dye award, 2000; grantee Am. Co. Learned Socs. and Social Sci. Research Council, 1965-66. Mem. Western Polit. Sci. Assn., Policy Studies Assn., Far West Slavic Assn., Phi Beta Kappa. Republican. Avocations: baseball, baseball history, research and writing. Business e-mail: ajgroth@u cdavis.edu. Personal e-mail: marilynag@aol.com. Home: 1848 Rushmore Ln Davis CA 95616-6654 Office: U Calif Dept Polit Sci Davis CA 95616

GROTON, JAMES PURNELL, lawyer; b. Newport News, Va., Oct. 29, 1927; s. Lafayette Watson and Mary (Skidmore) G.; m. Lora Frances Webster, June 13, 1953 (dec. March 3, 1999); children: James Purnell, Hunter W., Molly Groton Urban, Lora Groton Rust. AB cum laude, Princeton U., 1949; LLB, U. Va., 1954. Bar: D.C. 1954, Ga. 1955, U.S. Supreme Ct. 1964. Assoc. Sutherland, Asbill & Brennan, Atlanta, 1954-61, ptnr., 1961-2001; lectr. to profl. socs. on alternative dispute resolution and constrn. Editor articles Va. Law Rev., 1953-54; contbr. to profl. jours. Bd. dirs. Atlanta Council for Internat. Visitors, 1968-75; bd. dirs., treas. N.W. Ga. council Girl Scouts U.S., 1973-79; trustee South Kent Sch., Conn., 1973-77, Nat. Assn. Women in Constrn. Edn. Found., 1993-98; chmn. Constrn. Industry Dispute Avoidance and Resolution Task Force, 1991-94. Capt. USMC, 1946-48, 50-52. Recipient medal Excellence, Engineering News-Record, 1993. Fellow Am. Coll. Constrn. Lawyers (pres. 2000-2001), Coll. of Comml. Arbitrators, Chartered Inst. of Arbitrators; mem. Nat. Acad. of Construction, State Bar Ga., Atlanta Bar Assn. (chmn. construction sect., 1992-93), AIA (hon., Bronze medal 1984), Am. Arbitration Assn. (nat. panel constrn. arbitrators 1970—, bd. dirs. 1990-2002, nat. constrn. dispute resolution com., 1992—, Whitney North Seymour medal 1983), Nat. Sch. Bds. Assn. Council of Sch. Attys., Nat. Assn. Coll. and Univ. Attys., Ga. Council Sch. Bd. Attys. (exec. com. 1971-78), Ctr. for Pub. Resources (Alternative Dispute Resolution awards 1988, 1994), Princeton Alumni Assn. Ga. (v.p. 1964-77), Phi Delta Phi. Democrat. Episcopalian. Clubs: Peachtree, Piedmont Driving, Old War Horse Lawyers. Home: 7 Park Ln NE Atlanta GA 30309 Office: 2300 First Union Plaza 999 Peachtree St NE Atlanta GA 30309-3996

GROTTA, SANDRA BROWN, interior designer; m. Louis William Grotta; m. Louis William Grotta. Pres. S.G. Interiors, New Vernon, NJ, 1964—. Mem.: Am. Soc. Interior Designers. E-mail: sandy@sginteriors.com.

GROTTANELLI, PAMALA N. nursing administrator, educator; b. Corinth, Miss. d. William Robert and Estelle (Carter) Stewart; m. Richard Grottanelli. ASN, Miss. Univ. Women, 1975, BSN, 1980; MSN, U. Ala., Birmingham, 1983. RN Miss. Asst. dir. staff devel. Golden Triangle Regional Med. Ctr., Columbus, Miss., 1980-81, staff/charge nurse ICU, 1981-82; nursing instr. Auburn U., Montgomery, Ala., 1983-84, La. State U., New Orleans, 1984-85; staff nurse ICU East Jefferson Gen. Hosp., Metairie, La., 1984-85; nursing instr. Itawamba CC, Fulton, Miss., 1985-86, 90-92; varied hourly critical care nurse U. Colo. Health Scis. Ctr., Denver, 1986-87; mgr. nursing systems U. Community Hosp., Tampa, Fla., 1987-89; critical care float Northside Hosp., Atlanta, 1989-90, N.E. Miss. CC, Corinth, 1992-95; nurse educator Valparaiso U., 1995; dir. profl. divsn. Horizon Career Coll., 1995-96; dir. Hope Hospice House, 1998—. Malpractice cons. to various law firms, 1978—; dir. nursing and curriculum devel. GREC, 1996—98; spkr. Miss. Student Nurses Assn., Biloxi, 1991. Affiliate faculty Am. Heart Assn., Miss., 1982—86. Alumnae scholar, Alcorn County MSCW Alumnae, 1973. Mem.: ANA, AACN, Emergency Nurses Assn., Nat. League Nursing, Sigma Theta Tau. Avocations: genealogy, cooking. Home: 7499 Barrancas Ave Bokeelia FL 33922-3808

GROTTEROD, KNUT, retired paper company executive; b. Sarpsborg, Norway, Feb. 12, 1922; emigrated to Can., 1945, naturalized, 1954; s. Klaus and Maria Magdalena (Thoresen) G.; m. Isabel Edwina MacMaster, Feb. 25, 1950; children: Ingrid, Christopher, Karen. Grad., Tech. Coll., Horten, Norway, 1945; BME, McGill U., Can., 1949, postgrad, 1951; DSc (hon.), U. Maine, 1987; Exec. in Residence (hon.), U. New Brunswick, 1989. With Consol. Bathurst Ltd., Que., 1951-70; v.p. prodn., gen. mgr. N.S. Forest Industries, Port Hawkesbury, 1970-73; v.p. mfg. Fraser Cos. Ltd., Edmundston, N.B., Can., 1973-75, sr. v.p. ops., 1975-80; exec. v.p. Fraser Inc., Edmundston, 1980-85, pres., chief operating officer, 1985-87, chmn., chief exec. officer. Chmn. bd. Atlantic Waferboard, Chatam, N.B., 1985-87, Island Paper Mills, Vancouver, B.C., 1985-87, Alta. Newsprint Co. Ltd., Whitecourt, 1988-90, Rsch. and Productivcity Coun., Fredericton, N.B., 1986—. Incutech Brunswick, 1988-94, Potato Devel. and Mktg. Coun., Fredericton, 1989-90. Bd. dirs. Canadian-Scandinavian Found., Montreal, 1974-75, v.p., 1975-77, pres., 1978-94; mem. bd. govs. U. New Brunswick. With Norwegian Underground Army, 1941-45. Mem. N.B. Forest Products Assn. (dir. 1983-88, pres. 1985-88), Can. Pulp and Paper Assn., Corp. Profl. Engrs. N.B., Rotary Internat. (dist. gov. 1996-97). Home: 67 Castleton Ct Fredericton NB Canada E3B 6H3 Office: Rsch & Productivity Coun 921 College Hill Rd Fredericton NB Canada E3B 6Z9

GROTTO, DOUGLAS THOMAS MATTHEW, music educator; b. S.I., N.Y., Jan. 3, 1964; s. John Peter and Shirley (Fiorello) G. BS in Music Edn., Concordia Coll., Bronxville, N.Y., 1989. Cert. tchr. music, N.Y., N.J. Composer songs. Home: 364 Church Rd Brick NJ 08723

GROTZINGER, LAUREL ANN, librarian, educator; b. Truman, Minn., Apr. 15, 1935; d. Edward F. and Marian Gertrude (Greeley) G. BA, Carleton Coll., 1957; MS, U. Ill., 1958, PhD, 1964. Instr., asst. libr. Ill. State U., 1958-62; asst. prof. Western Mich. U., Kalamazoo, 1964-66, assoc. prof., 1966-68, prof., 1968—, asst. dir. Sch. Librarianship, 1965-72, chief rsch. officer, 1979-86, interim dir. Sch. Libr. and Info. Sci., 1982-86, dean grad. coll., 1979-92, prof. univ. libr., 1993—. Author: The Power and the Dignity, 1966; mem. editl. bd. Jour. Edn. for Librarianship, 1973-77, Dictionary Am. Libr. Biography, 1975-77, Mich. Academician, 1990—; contbr. articles to profl. jours., books. Trustee Kalamazoo Pub. Libr., 1991-93, v.p., 1991-92, pres., 1992-93; pres. Kalamazoo Bach Festival, 1996-97, bd. dirs. 1992-98, exec. com. 1996-98. Mem. ALA (sec.-treas. Libr. History Round Table 1973-74, vice chmn., chmn-elect 1983-84, chmn. 1984-85, mem.-at-large 1991-93), Spl. Librs. Assn., Assn. Libr. Info. Sci. Edn., Mich. acad. Sci., Arts and Letters (mem.-at-large, exec. com. 1980-86, pres. 1983-85, exec. com. 1990-94, pres. 1991-93, vice chmn. libr./info. scis. 1996-97, chair 1997-98), Internat. Assn. Torch Clubs (v.p. Kalamazoo chpt. 1992-93, pres. 1993-94, exec. com. 1989-95), Soc. Collegiate Journalists, Phi Beta Kappa (pres. S.W. Mich. chpt. 1977-78, sec. 1994-97, pres. 1997-99), Beta Phi Mu, Alpha Beta Alpha, Delta Kappa Gamma (pres. Alpha Psi chpt. 1988-92), Phi Kappa Phi. Home: 2729 Mockingbird Dr Kalamazoo MI 49008-1626 E-mail: grotzinger@wmich.edu.

GROULX, AIMÉ RENÉ, artist, photographer; b. Goffstown, N.H., Oct. 12, 1942; s. René Robert and Cecile Jeanie Groulx; m. Adele Elizabeth Freedman (div.); m. Ly Thi Le, Oct. 9, 1999. Diploma in photography, Manchester Inst. Arts & Scis., 1992. Exhbn. technician Wadsworth Antheneum, Hartford, Conn., 1968-69; artist-in-residence Elliot U. Ctr. U. N.C., Greensboro, 1972. Exhbns. include Morehead Planetarium, U. N.C., Chapel Hill, 1973, Washington and Lee U., Lexington, Va., 1974, Lisbon Pub. Libr., Wadworth Athneum, Huntington Gallery, 1968-69, Greensboro Pub. Libr., 1975, Robert Frost House, Franconia, N.H., 1977, others. Mem. U.S. Naval Inst. Avocations: conceptual biology, medical science, natural science. Home: PO Box 1385 Manchester NH 03105 Office: Inter Net Work Gallery PO Box 1385 Manchester NH 03105

GROVAS, CARLOS, orthopedic surgeon; b. San Juan, P.R., Feb. 17, 1942; s. Carlos Grovas and Teresa Badrena; m. Aracelis Grovas, Sept. 10, 1999; children: Carlos, Rafael, Jorge, Abnelis, Yamilis. Degree in medicine, San Juan, 1967; BS Georgetown U., 1963. Cert. Qualified Am. Bd. Orthopaedic Surgeons, Am. Bd. Ind. Med. Examiners, Am. Acad. Disability Evaluating Physicians, lic. physician N.Y., P.R., Ohio. Resident Orthop. U. Hosp. San Juan, 1968—72; fellow in reconstructive surgery Harvard Med. Sch., Boston, 1971; chief surgery Pavia, Hato Rey, PR, 1998—, head orthopaedic surgery dept., 1978—. Cons. in field; instr. orthopaedics U. P.R. Sch. Medicine; faculty pres. Hato Rey Cmty. Hosp., San Juan, 1981, 1993—94, 1996—98. Capt. med. corps P.R. N.G., 1967—73. Fellow: Am. Bd. Orthopaedic Surgeons, Am. Acad. Disability Evaluating Physicians, Interam. Coll. Surgeons; mem.: AMA, Am. Coll. Sport Medicine, P.R. Med. Assn. (founding mem. sport medicine sect., pres. ethics com. orthopaedic sect.), Assn. Medica de P.R. Avocation: tennis. Office: Midtown Plz Ste B-12 421 Munoz Rivera Ave San Juan PR 00918

GROVDAHL, STEVEN NOEL, court commissioner; b. Tacoma, Wash., Feb. 21, 1948; s. Harvey M. and Eleanor A. Grovdahl; m. Judy K. Scharbach, Apr. 17, 1971; children: Echo L., Raina, Tiffany. BA in Econs., Wash. State U., 1970; JD, Gonzaga U., 1975. Bar: Wash. 1975. Pvt. practice, Spokane, Wash.,

1975—91; atty. Taft, Mackin, Grovdahl, Henault & Hancock, Spokane, 1991—98; ct. commr. Spokane County Superior Ct., Spokane, 1998—. Instr. Spokane C.C., Spokane, 1992—99; trustee Spokane County Bar Assn., Spokane, 1996—98; mem. family law & juvenile commn. Wash. Bd. Judicial Adminstrn., Wash., 1998—. Chmn. Northland Credit Union, Spokane, 1994, bd. dirs., 1989—99. Mem.: Spokane County Bar Assn. (hon. mention pro bono atty. 1994), Wash. Bar Assn., Eagles, Kiwanis Club (pres. 1980—2001). Roman Catholic. Avocations: computer, reading, golf. Office: Spokane Superior Ct W 1116 Broadway Spokane WA 99210

GROVE, ANDREW S. electronics company executive; b. Budapest, Hungary, 1936; married; 2 children. BS, CCNY, 1960, DSc (hon.), 1985; PhD, U. Calif., Berkeley, 1963; DEng (hon.), Worcester Poly. Inst., 1989; LLD (hon.), Harvard U., 2000. With Fairchild Camera and Instrument Co., 1963—67; pres., COO Intel Corp., Santa Clara, Calif., 1967—87, pres., 1979—, CEO, 1987—98, chmn. bd., 1998—; also bd. dirs. Lectr. Stanford Grad. Sch. of Bus. Author: Physics and Technology of Semiconductor Devices, 1967, High Output Management, 1983, One on One with Andy Grove, 1987, Only the Paranoid Survive, 1996, Swimming Across, 2001. Named Exec. of Yr., U. Ariz., 1993, Citizen of Yr., World Forum Silicon Valley, 1993, Statesman of Yr., Harvard Bus. Sch., 1996, Tech. Leader of Yr., Industry Week, 1997, Man of Yr. Time mag., 1997, CEO of Yr., CEO mag., 1997; recipient Am. Inst. Chemists medal, 1960, Merit cert., Franklin Inst., 1975, Townsend Harris medal, CCNY, 1980, Enterprise award, Profl. Advt. Assn., 1987, George Washington award, Am. Hungarian Found., 1990, Achievement medal, Am. Electronics Assn., 1993, Heinz Family Found. award, 1995, John von Neumann medal, Am. Hungarian Assn., 1995, Steinman medal, CCNY, 1995, Internat. Achievement award, World Trade Club, 1997, Cinema Digital Technols. award, Internat. Film Festival, 1997, Cinema Digital Tech. award, Cannes Film Festival, 1997, IEEE Medal of Honor, 2000, Disting. Exec. of the Yr., Acad. of Mgmt., 1998, Lifetime Achievement award, Strategic Mgmt. Soc., 2001. Fellow: IEEE (Achievement award 1969, J.J. Ebers award 1974, Engring. Leadership Recognition award 1987, Computer Entrepreneur award 1997), Nat. Acad. Engring. (award 1979), Am. Acad. Arts and Scis. Office: Intel Corp PO Box 58119 2200 Mission College Blvd Santa Clara CA 95054-1549

GROVE, BRANDON HAMBRIGHT, JR., diplomat; b. Chgo., Apr. 8, 1929; s. Brandon Hambright and Helen Julia (Gasparska) G.; m. Marie Cheremeteff, 1959 (div. 1983); children: John C., Catherine C.G. Jones, Paul C., Mark C. ; m. Mariana Alfaro Moran, 1988; 1 step child, Michele Parsons Shotts. AB, Bard Coll., 1950; M.P.A., Princeton U., 1952. Joined U.S. Fgn. Svc., 1959; vice consul Abidjan, Ivory Coast, also Upper Volta, Niger, and Dahomey, 1959-61; staff asst. to undersec. state, 1961-62; spl. asst. to dep. undersec. state for adminstrn., 1962-63; spl. asst. to Am. ambassador, 1963-65; U.S. liaison officer to city govt. Berlin, 1965-69; dir. Office Panamanian Affairs, State Dept., 1969-71; mem. Sr. Seminar in Fgn. Policy, 1971-72; dep. dir. State Dept. policy planning staff, Washington; also staff dir. Under Secretaries Com. of NSC, 1972-74; chargé d' affaires, then dep. chief of mission Am. Embassy to German Dem. Republic, Berlin, 1974-76; fgn. svc. sr. insp. Dept. State, 1976-78; dep. asst. sec. state for Inter-Am. affairs, 1978-80; consul gen., 1980-83; Capstone fellow Nat. Def. U., Fort McNair, Washington, 1984; ambassador to Zaire, Kinshasa, 1984-87; coord. State Dept. Budget Rev., Washington, 1987 88; dir. Fgn. Service Inst., Washington, 1988-92; diplomat-in-residence Georgetown U., Washington, 1992-93; sr. advisor State Dept. Policy Planning Staff, Washington, 1993-94; retired U.S. Fgn. Svc., 1994. Asst. instr. Princeton U., 1953; sr. cons. APCO Assocs., Inc., Washington, 1996-2000, Sol M. Linowitz prof. internat. affairs, Hamilton Coll. Editorial bd. chmn. Fgn. Svc. Jour., 1992-94. Served to lt. USNR, 1954-57. Recipient Pres.'s Meritorious Service award, 1985, 90, 92, John Dewey medal for disting. pub. svc. Bard Coll., 1990. Mem. Am. Acad. Diplomacy (bd. dirs.), Am. Fgn. Svc. Assn. (achievement award 2000), Washington Inst. Fgn. Affairs, Coun. on Fgn. Rels., Georgetown U. Inst. for Study of Diplomacy (bd. dirs.), Assn. for Diplomatic Studies and Tng. (bd. dirs.), Atlantic Coun. of U.S., Diplomatic and Consular Officers Ret., Met. Club of Washington. Home: 2029 Connecticut Ave NW Washington DC 20008-6141

GROVE, DAVID LAVAN, lawyer; b. Johnstown, Pa., Nov. 4, 1937; s. William Morgan and Edith Elizabeth (Boyd) G.; m. Barbara Pearson Fogg, Aug. 26, 1961; children: Jonathan Morgan, Amy Pearson. BA in Polit. Sci. with honors, Dickinson Coll., 1959; LLB, Yale U., 1962. Bar: Pa. 1965, U.S. Dist. Ct. (ea. dist.) Pa. 1966, U.S. Ct. Appeals (3d cir.) 1972, U.S. Supreme Ct. 1976, U.S. Ct. Internat. Trade 1977, U.S. Dist. Ct. (mid. dist.) Pa. 1990. Vol. U.S. Peace Corps, Nigeria, West Africa, 1962-64, atty-advisor Washington, 1967-69; assoc. Montgomery, McCracken, Walker & Rhoads, LLP, Phila., 1964-67, 69-72; ptnr. Montgomery, McCracken, Walker & Rhoads, Phila., 1972—. Asst. lectr. law faculty U. Lagos, Nigeria, 1962-64, Office of Peace Corps Gen. Counsel, Washington, 1967-69; advisor on fed. law and regulations Peace Corps ofcls.; U.S. del. to Coun. Internat. Secretariat for Vol. Svc., Washington, 1968, Geneva, 1969. Bd. sch. dirs. Wallingford (Pa.)-Swarthmore Sch. Dist., 1975-87, bd. pres., 1977-79, 82-84; mem. Wallingford-Swarthmore Sch. Authority, 1988-99, pres., 1995-99; bd. dirs. Recs. for Blind and Dyslexic, Phila., 1994—. Fellow: Am. Coll. Trial Lawyers; mem.: ABA, Phila. Bar Assn., Rolling Green Golf Club (Springfield, Pa.), Theta Chi, Omicron Delta Kappa, Pi Gamma Mu, Delta Phi Alpha. Democrat. Mem. Soc. Of Friends. Avocations: tennis, golf, snorkeling, scuba diving. Home: 80 Yale Ave Swarthmore PA 19081-1607 Office: Montgomery McCracken Et Al 123 S Broad St 24th Fl Philadelphia PA 19109 Office Fax: 215-731-3821. E-mail: dgrove@mmwr.com., dlgrove@att.net.

GROVE, DAVID LAWRENCE, economist, director; b. Boston, Apr. 25, 1918; s. Lawrence Roger and Emily (Becker) G.; m. Lois Pawlowski, May 13, 1942; 1 child, Carolyn Anne. Grad., Boston Latin Sch., 1935; AB magna cum laude, Harvard U., 1940, MA, MPA, Harvard U., 1942, PhD, 1952. Economist Fed. Res. Bd., 1944-52; adviser monetary and banking problems Paraguay, 1944, 51, 1947, 57, 58, 1945, 46, 56, 62, 65, 1948, 49, 1950, 1964; chief economist Bank Am., San Francisco, 1952-58, v.p., head internat. relations, 1961-62, v.p., head bond investment dept., 1962-63, v.p., 1959-63; v.p., econ. advisor Fed. Res. Bank San Francisco, 1963-64; v.p., economist Blyth & Co., N.Y., 1965-66; chief economist IBM, 1966-69, v.p., chief economist, 1969-78; pres. David L. Grove Ltd., 1978-85, Grove-Andersen Farms, Armonk, N.Y., 1985—. Sr. econ. adviser Marine Midland Bank, 1978-83; past lectr. Am. U., Ctr. Latin Am. Monetary Studies, Mex.; bd. dirs. ING Mutual Funds; mem. Time Mag. Bd. Economists, 1969-80, N.Y. State Coun. Econ. Advisers, 1973-74, several govt. adv. coms.; trustee Com. Econ. Devel., N.Y. Med. Coll., 1972-75; governing body Internat. Labor Office, Geneva, 1980-84. Author articles in field.; mem. editorial bd. Fin. Analysts Jour. Served with OSS, 1942-44. Decorated officer Order of Merit, Ecuador). Mem. Am. Econ. Assn., C. of C. of U.S. (bd. dirs. 1967-78), U.S. Coun. Internat. Bus. (pres. 1978-84), Am. Orchid Soc. (v.p. 1990-94), Phi Beta Kappa. Episcopalian. Home and Office: 5 The Knls Armonk NY 10504-1022

GROVE, DENISE WHITLOCK, accounting and financial professional; b. Marietta, Ga., July 5, 1959; d. J. Winston and Martha Josephine (Phillips) Whitlock. BSBA, Auburn U., 1981. CPA, Ga. Audit profl. KPMG, Dallas, 1982-85, with exec. office N.Y., 1985-86, audit mgr. Atlanta, 1986-87; fin. analyst Columbian Chem. Co. div. Phelps Dodge Corp., Atlanta, 1987-90; asst. v.p. acctg. policy Bank of Am. (formerly C&S/Sovran Corp.), Atlanta, 1990-91, v.p. acctg. policy, 1991-92; controller CryoLife, Inc., Marietta, 1992-94; sr. analyst N.W. Airlines, Inc., Atlanta, 1994-96, mgr. fin. projects, 1996-97; fin. mgr. Hewlett-Packard Co., Atlanta, 1997-98; CFO DBS Mfg., Inc., Atlanta, 1998; founder, owner Denise Whitlock Grove, CPA, Bus. and Fin. Cons., Peachtree City, Ga., 1998—. CFO Support, Inc., Atlanta, 1998—. Vol. CFO Cochran Mill Nature Ctr., 2000—. Treas., chmn. fundraising Atlanta Symphony Assn., 1987-89; bd. dirs., treas. Morningside Terrace Condominium Assn., Atlanta, 1987-90. Recipient Vol. of Yr. award, CFO Cochran Mill Nature Ctr., 2001. Mem.: AICPA (editl. advisor 1990—97), Ga. Soc. CPAs (continuing profl. edn. com. 1990—99, bd. dirs. 1994—, v.p. Atlanta chpt. 1997—98, pres. 1998—99, chmn. CPAs in industry, govt. and edn. com. 2000—02, coun. 1994—, leadership team industry sect.), Auburn U. Alumni Assn., U.S. Tennis Assn., Atlanta Lawn Tennis Club, Delta Gamma. Avocations: tennis, reading. Office: CFO Support Inc 1507 River Green Dr Atlanta GA 30327 E-mail: d.Whitlock@get.net.

GROVE, JEFFREY SCOTT, family practice physician; b. Paxton, Ill., Sept. 21, 1964; s. Ronald Edwin and Delores Ann (Martensen) G.; m. Karen Beth Hanlon, June 17, 1989; 1 child, Garrett Jeffrey. BS in Biology, Fla. So. Coll., 1986; DO, Southeastern Coll. Osteo Med., North Miami Beach, Fla., 1990. Diplomate Am. Bd. Quality Assurance and Utilization Rev. Physicians; bd. cert. family practice and in geriatrics. Intern Suncoast Hosp., Largo, Fla., 1990-91, resident in family practice, 1991-93; pvt. practice SunCoast Family Med. Assocs., Largo, 1993—. Med. dir. Barrington Properties, Largo, 1994-97, Oak Manor Nursing Ctr., Largo, 1993-2000, Drew Village Nursing Ctr., Clearwater, Fla., 1996-99, Highland Pines Nursing Ctr., 1999-2000; rep.-at-large exec. com. Suncoast Hosp., 1995-2000, chief adminstrv. resident, 1992-93, family practice tchg. staff, geriatrics program dir., 1993-96, faculty devel. com., 1994—, legal compliance comm., 1998—; mem. quality assurance/utilization rev. com., 1993—, med. dir. of quality assurance/utilization rev. dept., 1995—; bd. dirs. Suncoast Cmty. Care PHO, Largo, 1994-98, med. dir., 1998; clin. asst. prof. family medicine Nova Southeastern U. Coll. Osteo. Medicine, North Miami Beach, 1994-2000, clin. assoc. prof., 2000—; clin. instr. Kirksville Coll. Osteo. Medicine, 1993—; trustee SunCoast Hosp. Found., 1996-2002, SunCoast Hosp., 1998—; regional med. dir. Tampa Bay for Elder Health. Vice chmn. bd. trustees SCH Found., 1997-98, chmn., 1998-99; trustee St. Paul's Sch., 2003—. Named to Outstanding Young Men of Am.; recipient Disting. Trustee award SCH Found., 2000. Mem.: Pinellas County Osteo. Med. Soc. (bd. govs. 1995—, treas. 1996—99, pres. 2000—03, Physician of Yr. 2002—03), Am. Coll. Osteo. Family Physicians (chair membership com. 1997—99, trustee 1997—, treas. 1999—2000, v.p. 2000—01, pres. 2001—02, Physician of Yr. 2003—04), Fla. Osteo. Med. Assn. (trustee 2001—), Am. Osteo. Assn., Nova Southeastern U. Coll. Osteo. Medicine Alumni Assn. (v.p. 2000—01, pres. 2002—03, Disting. Alumni award 2001), Scouting Res., Nat. Eagle Scout Assn. (life). Republican. Methodist. Avocations: golf, stamp collecting, travel, snow skiing. Home: 301 Osceola Rd Clearwater FL 33756-1453 Office: SunCoast Family Med Assocs 12020 Seminole Blvd Largo FL 33778

GROVE, MYRNA JEAN, elementary education educator; b. Bryan, Ohio, Oct. 24, 1949; d. Kedric Durward and N. Florence (Stombaugh) G. Student, Bowling Green State U., 1970-71; BA in Edn., Manchester Coll., 1971; postgrad., U. No. Colo., 1974-76, Purdue U., 1977, St. Francis Coll., Ft. Wayne, Ind., 1986, Coll. Mount St. Joseph, Ohio, 1986; MLS, Kent State U., 1999. Cert. elem. tchr., Ohio, 1971, permanent cert., 1999. Tchr. elem. sch. Bryan City Schs., 1972—. Author: Asbestos Cancer: One Man's Experience, 1995, Legacy of One-Room Schools, 1999; editor newspaper column Education Today, 1975-82, newsletter N.W. Ohio Emphasis, 1981-83 (award 1981). Dir., violinist Bryan String Ensemble, 1981—; organist Trinity Episc. Ch., Bryan, 1979-89; active Lancaster Mennonite Hist. Soc., Hans Herr Found.; trustee Bryan Area Cultural Assn., 1984-89; bd. dirs. Williams County Cmty. Concerts; sec. Black Swamp Arts Coun., 2001—. Jennings scholar Martha Holden Jennings Found., Bowling Green State U., 1982-83. Mem. ALA, NEA (Ohio del., state contact 1986-87), Am. Booksellers Assn. (assoc. mem.), Ohio Edn. Assn. (presenter 1984, del. global issues 1986, sec. N.W. Ohio Tchrs. Uniserv. 1975-78), Bus. and Profl. Women Ohio (individual devel. com. 1986-90, speaking skills cert. 1987), Ohio Libr. Coun., Ohioana Libr. Assn., N.W. Ohio Manchester Coll. Alumni Assn. (past pres.), Bryan Edn. Assn. (exec. com., pres. 1985-86), Williams County Geneal. Soc., Williams County Hist. Assn., P. Buckley Moss Soc., Trees of Life (v.p. 1994-2001, region moss docent), Alpha Delta Kappa (pres. 1996-98). Alpha Mu. Avocations: collecting dolls, playing piano, organ and violin, reading, travel.

GROVE, NANCY CAROL, academic administrator; b. Johnstown, Pa. d. Henry and Marie (Boerstler) Frambach; m. William M. Grove; children: Eric William, Carol Ann. BS in Nursing, U. Pitts., 1968, MEd, 1972, PhD, 1988; MS in Nursing, Duquesne U., 1980. Staff nurse Conemaugh Valley Meml. Hosp., Johnstown, 1963-66, head nurse, 1967, 70, nursing care supr., 1968-71, instr., course dir. Sch. Nursing, 1971-79, dir. Sch. Nursing, 1979-91; assoc. prof. RN-BSN program, dir. Sch. Nursing U. Pitts., Johnstown, 1990—. Instr. refresher course Votech. Sch., Johnstown, 1973-76; adj. assoc. prof. U. Pitts., 1979-91; site visitor Nat. League for Nursing, N.Y.C.; chair Cambria/Somerset Coun. for Health Profls., Inc., Johnstown, 1984-89, Cambria/Somerset Mgmt. Com., 1994-96. Recipient Tribute to Women award for excellence in edn. YWCA, 1988, Sch. Nursing Dean's Disting. Tchg. award, 2001. Mem. Soroptimist Internat. (pres. 1994-96), Sigma Theta Tau. Lutheran. Avocations: calligraphy, art. Home: 810 Linden Ave Johnstown PA 15902-2856 Office: U Pitts 141 Biddle Hall Johnstown PA 15904 E-mail: ngrove@pitt.edu.

GROVE, RICHARD CHARLES, retired power tool company executive; b. Bethlehem, Pa., Aug. 13, 1940; s. Dale Addison and Mary Elizabeth (Ripple) G.; m. Cynthia Ann Dimmick, Dec. 7, 1963; 1 child, Jeffrey. BEE, Cornell U., 1962; MBA, U. Pitts., 1967. Mgmt. cons. Touche Ross & Co., Detroit, 1967-72; mgr. bus. planning Amstar Corp., N.Y.C., 1972-75, treas. Spreckels Sugar div. San Francisco, 1975-82, treas. N.Y.C., 1983-84, v.p., controller Stamford, Conn., 1985-88, v.p., chief fin. officer, 1988-89; sr. v.p. Esstar Inc., New Haven, 1989, exec. v.p., dir., 1995; exec. v.p. Milw. Electric Tool Corp., 1990-91, pres., chief exec. officer, 1991-2000. Bd. dirs. Carolinas Concert Assn., Charlotte Repertory Theatre. Served to 1st lt. U.S. Army, 1964—66. Mem.: The Point Lake and Golf Club. Republican. Avocations: golf, reading, travel. E-mail: richardgrove@adelphia.net.

GROVE, TIMOTHY LYNN, geology educator; b. York, Pa., July 15, 1949; s. Arthur Leib and Ruby Janette (Finger) G.; m. Madeline Scadden, June 15, 1971; m. Ann Marie Reilly, June 19, 1979; children: Matthew Brian, Michael Thomas. BA, U. Colo., 1971; AM, Harvard U., 1975, PhD, 1976. Rsch. asst. SUNY, Stony Brook, 1975-79; from asst. prof. to assoc. prof. dept. earth, atmospheric and planet sci. MIT, Cambridge, Mass., 1979-91, prof. dept. earth, atmospheric and planet sci., 1991—. Vis. prof. divsn. geology and sci. Caltech, Pasadena, Calif., 1979. Editor Contbns. to Mineralogy and Petrology, 1985—. Fellow: Am. Geophys. Union (Bowen award 1993), Mineral Soc. Am.; mem.: Geochem. Soc., Geol. Soc. Am. Home: 87 Menotomy Rd Arlington MA 02476-6111 Office: MIT Earth Atmospheric & Planet Sci 77 Massachusetts Ave # 541220 Cambridge MA 02139-4307

GROVE, WILLIAM JOHNSON, physician, surgery educator; b. Ottawa, Ill., Mar. 23, 1920; s. Joseph Roy and Florence (Johnson) G.; m. Betty Pedigo, Mar. 23, 1944; children: William Johnson, Pamela J. Holly Lynn. BS, U. Ill., 1941, MD, 1943, MS in Surgery, 1949. Intern U. Ill. Research and Ednl. Hosps., 1944, asst. resident surgery, 1949-50, chief resident surgery, 1951-52; asst. resident surgery Hines VA Hosp., 1950-51; mem. faculty U. Ill. Coll. Medicine, 1951—; prof. surgery, 1964-81, prof. emeritus, 1981—, dean, 1968-70, exec. dean, 1970-76; vice chancellor for acad. affairs U. Ill. Coll. Medicine (U. Ill. Med. Center), 1976-80, vice chancellor emeritus, 1981—; acting dir. U. Ill. Coll. Medicine (Center for Study of Patient Care), 1980-81. Attending surgeon U. Ill. Hosp.; cons. W.K. Kellogg Found., 1981-86; prof. med. edn. U. Ill., Chgo., 1981-86. Author numerous articles in field. Served to capt. AUS, 1944-46. Fellow ACS; mem. Assn. Am. Med. Colls., Central, Chgo. Surg. Socs., Soc. Univ. Surgeons, Warren H. Cole Soc., Soc. Clin. Surgery, Am. Surg. Assn., Sigma Xi, Alpha Omega Alpha, Phi Delta Epsilon. Home: 2221 Viewpoint Dr Naples FL 34110-7949

GROVER, DORYS C. English educator; d. H. Mildred Bowman and John W. Crow. BA, Oreg. State U., 1951; postgrad., U. Hawaii, 1962; PhD, Wash. State U., 1969. Editor The Pendleton (Oreg.) Record, 1959-69; news mgr. KUMA Radio, Pendleton, 1959-64; news writer KCRL-TV, Reno, Nev., 1970-71; asst. instr. English Wash. State U., Pullman, 1964-69; prof. English Drake U., Des Moines, 1971-72, Tex. A&M U., Commerce, 1972-93, emerita prof., 1993—. Author: A Solitary Voice: Collection of Critical Essays, 1973, John Graves, 1990, The Valley of the Tutuilla, and Other Lines, 1997; editl. bd. Am. Lit. Manuscripts, 1977; contbr. essays, poetry, short stories to profl. publs.; contbr.: Pioneer Trails. Mem. MLA, Western Am. Lit. Assn., Soc. for Study of Midwestern Lit., Sherwood Anderson Soc., Melville Soc., James Branch Cabell Soc. (v.p., editor Kalki 1980-93), Western Lit. Assn. (editl. bd. Yeats-Eliot Rev. 1980—), Tex. Am. Studies Assn. (pres. 1990). Home: Visa Village Electra Ct #122 3300 Carpenter Rd SE Lacey WA 98503 Office: A & M U Commerce 71330 Tutuilla Rd Pendleton OR 97801 E-mail: dg888@ucinet.com.

GROVER, JAMES ROBB, chemist, editor; b. Klamath Falls, Oreg., Sept. 16, 1928; s. James Richard and Marjorie Alida (van Groos) G.; m. Barbara Jean Ton, Apr. 14, 1957; children: Jonathan Robb, Patricia Jean. BS summa cum laude, valedictorian, U. Wash., Seattle, 1952; PhD, U. Calif., Berkeley, 1958. Rsch. assoc. Brookhaven Nat. Lab., Upton, N.Y., 1957-59, assoc. chemist, 1959-63, chemist, 1963-67, chemist with tenure, 1967-77, sr. chemist, 1978-93, rsch. collaborator, 1993—. Cons. Lawrence Livermore (Calif.) Nat. Lab., 1962; assoc. editor Ann. Rev. of Nuclear Sci., Ann. Revs., Inc., Palo Alto, Calif., 1967-77; vis. prof. Inst. for Molecular Sci., Okazaki, Japan, 1986-87; vis. scientist Max-Planck Inst. für Strömungsforschung, Göttingen, Fed. Republic Germany, 1975-76. Contbr. numerous articles to profl. jours. With USN, 1946-48. Mem. Am. Chem. Soc. (chmn. nuclear chemistry and tech. 1989), Am. Phys. Soc., Triple Nine Soc., Sigma Xi, Phi Beta Kappa, Phi Lambda Upsilon, Zeta Mu Tau, Pi Mu Epsilon. Libertarian. Presbyterian. Achievements include naming of the nuclear yrast levels and discovery of their importance in nuclear reactions; invention of use of short-lived radioactivity in molecular beams; first to successfully use radioactivity for detection in chemically reactive scattering experiments; invention of threshold photoionization method for measuring the dissociation energies of neutral weak complexes in molecular beams. Home and Office: 1536 Pinecrest Ter Ashland OR 97520-3427 E-mail: jrobbgrover@cs.com.

GROVER, MARK DONALD, computer scientist; b. Augusta, Maine, July 12, 1955; s. Donald William and Aletha D. (Wells) G. BA, U. Fla., 1976; MS, Northwestern U., 1978, PhD, 1982. Cert. EMT, CPR instr. Instr. Northwestern U., Evanston, Ill., 1978-81; mem. tech. staff TRW Def. Sys., Redondo Beach, Calif., Fairfax, Va., 1981-85; sr. computer scientist Advanced Decision Sys., Arlington, Va., 1985-89; prin. software engr. Oberon Software Inc., Cambridge, Mass., 1990-94; software design engr. DeLorme Mapping, Yarmouth, Maine, 1995—. Program chmn. Nat. Symbolics User Group Conf., Washington, 1986; mem. computer sci. dept. adv. bd. U. So. Maine; presenter to confs. in field. Contbr. articles to sci. jours. Mem. mcpl. comprehensive plan com. Town of Gray; vol. Town of Gray, Citizen Corps.; trustee First Congl. Ch., Gray, Maine. Mem. NRA (endowment life), Phi Beta Kappa, Tau Beta Pi. Avocations: travel, rare books, drama, marksmanship, history. Office: DeLorme Mapping PO Box 298 Yarmouth ME 04096-0298 E-mail: mgrover@delorme.com.

GROVER, NORMAN LAMOTTE, theologian, philosopher; b. Topeka, Feb. 9, 1928; s. LaMotte and Virginia Grace (Alspach) G.; m. Anne Stottler, June 24, 1950; children: Jennifer Jean, Peter Neal, Rebecca Louise Grover Verna, Sandra Christine Grover. B. Mech. Engring., Rensselaer Poly. Inst., 1948; B.D., Yale, 1951, S.T.M., 1952, PhD, 1957. Mem. faculty, chaplain Hollins (Va.) Coll., 1954-57, asst. prof. religion, 1956-57; ordained to ministry Presbyn. Ch., 1952; head dept. philosophy and religion Va. Poly. Inst. and State U., 1957-75, prof. philosophy and religion, 1961-83, prof. religion, 1983-91, prof. emeritus, 1991—. Adj. prof. Ctr. for Study Sci. in Soc., 1983-86; mem. supervising com. So. leadership tng. project Fund for Republic, 1955-56; assoc. Danforth Found., 1958—, sr. assoc., 1962—, chmn. Va., N.C. and S.C. conf., 1962; psychotherapeutic counsellor Blacksburg Community Counselling Center, 1962-65 Bd. dirs. YMCA at Va. Tech. (Gold Triangle award 1962), bd. dirs. United Campus Ministries of Blacksburg, 1986-95; mem. Amnesty Internat., Blacksburg Master Chorale and Va. Tech. Concert Choir Concert Tour in Berlin, Poland, Czech Republic, Salzburg, 1992, Germany, Austria, Czech Republic, 1995, England, Scotland, 2003; concert under Robert Shaw, 1998; study trip to Costa Rica, Nicaragua, El Salvador and Guatemala Presbyn. Ch. U.S.A. Presbytery of Peaks Partnership with CEDEPCA, 1989, 91; mem. Habitat for Humanity, New River Valley chpt., Montgomery County Race Rels. Work Group, Ecumenical Alliance of New River Valley; mem. local convening com. Interfaith Social Concerns Network, 1999—. Mem. AAUP (pres. Va. Poly. Inst. and State U. chpt. 1961-62, 81-82, sec.-treas. chpt. 1959-60, 77-80, v.p. chpt. 1960-61, 80-81, 92-94), NAACP (exec. bd. Montgomery, Floyd, Radford chpt., 1999--), ACLU, Amnesty Internat., Va. Philos. Assn. (pres. 1969), So. Soc. Philosophy and Psychology, Am. Acad. Religion (chmn. S.E. region theology/philosophy religion sect. 1983-85, mem. citizen amb. team to Ukraine and Russia 1993, China 1994), Coalition for Justice in Ctrl. Am. (bd. dirs., v.p. 1990-94), Bread for the World, Sierra Club, Smithsonian Assocs., Wilderness Soc., Am. Assn. Ret. Persons, People to People Internat. (Am. People amb. del. to India, Nepal and Tibet 1996, China 2000). Home: Warm Hearth Village 1622 Hawthorne Ridge Blacksburg VA 24060-6143 E-mail: ngrover@vt.edu.

GROVER, ROBERT LAVERN, retired auto worker; b. Mpls., May 21, 1938; s. La Vern Wilber and Opal Elizabeth (Thompson) G.; m. Carolyn Sue Donavant, Oct. 6, 1962; children: Denise Marie, David Scott, Kevin Robert, Richard Thomas. Grad., Graphic Arts Tech. Sch., Mpls., 1963, Am. Computer Sch., Kansas City, Mo., 1971. Printer Raytown (Mo.) News, 1963, Phoenix Box & Label, Kansas City, Mo., 1963-65, Gustion Bacon, Kansas City, Mo., 1965; utility relief man Claycomo (Mo.) plant Ford Motor Co., 1965-97. Author: Compendium of Microfilm and Census in Missouri and Kansas, 1980, Missouri Genealogical Periodical Index A County Guide 1960-1982, 1983, others. Served with USN, 1957-61. Mem. MOSSAR SAR (registrar 1992-94, v.p. 1995-97, exec. v.p., 1998, pres., 1999, nat. trustee 2000-01, comdr. color guard 1995, 97—, pres., treas., sec., historian, sgt.-at-arms and v.p. Harry S Truman chpt. 1989-93, Mo. Color Guardsman of Yr. 1996, 98, Vietnam War Svc. medal 1993, Bronze Good Citizenship medal 1993, 96, Cert. of Disting. Svc. 1993, 97, 98, Meritorious medal 1994, 2002, 2003, Liberty medal 1994, 98, 2002, 2003, Centennial medal, Nat. Gold medal Color Guardsman of Yr. 1999, Patriot medal, Disting. medal, 2002, Silver Good Citizenship medal, 2003, SAR South Ctrl. Dist. Color Guard Vice Comdr., 2002, Comdg. Gen., 2003), Jackson County Genealogy Soc. (v.p. 1979-81, 98—, pres. 1999-2000), Heart of Am. Geneal. Soc. (publ. coord. 1975-79), Mo. State Geneal. Soc. (founder, charter mem. 1979), Sons of Union Vets., Soc. War 1812 in State of Minn., Nat. Soc. Sons and Daus. of the Pilgrims, SAR. Avocations: genealogy, muskie fishing, blues music. Home: 3929 S Milton Dr Independence MO 64055-4043 also: RR 2 Box 2706 Wheatland MO 65779-9809

GROVER, ROSALIND REDFERN, oil and gas company executive; b. Midland, Tex., Sept. 5, 1941; d. John Joseph and Rosalind (Kapps) Redfern;m. Arden Roy Grover, Apr. 10, 1982; 1 child, Rosson. BA in Edn. magna cum laude, U. Ariz., 1966, MA in History, 1982; postgrad. in law, So. Methodist U., Dallas. Libr. Gahr H.S., Cerritos, Calif., 1969; pres. The Redfern Found., Midland, 1982—; ptnr. Redfern & Grover, Midland, 1986—; pres. Redfern Enterprises Inc., Midland, 1989—. Chmn. bd. dirs. Flag-Redfern Oil Co., Midland. Sec. park and recreation commn. City of Midland, 1969-71, del. Objectives for Convocation, 1980; mem., past pres. women's aux. Midland Cmty. Theatre, 1970; chmn. challenge grant bldg. fund, 1980, chmn. Tex. Yucca Hist. Landmark Renovation Project, 1983, trustee, 1983-88; chmn. publicity com. Midland Jr. League, Midland, Inc., 1972, chmn. edn. com., 1976, corr. sec., 1978; 1st v.p. Midland Symphony Assn., 1975; chmn. Midland Charity Horse Show, 1975-76; mem. Midland Am. Revolution Bicentennial Commn., 1976; trustee Mus. S.W., 1977-80, pres. bd. dirs., 1979-80; co-chmn. Gov. Clements Fin. Com., Midland, 1978; mem. dist. com. State Bd. Law Examiners, Hockaday Sch. Bd. Visitors, 2001—; trustee Midland Meml. Hosp., 1978-80, Permian Basin Petroleum Mus., Libr. and Hall of Fame, 1989-98. Recipient HamHock award Midland Cmty. Theatre, 1978. Mem. Ind. Petroleum Assn. Am., Tex. Ind. Producers and Royalty Owners Assn., Petroleum Club, Racquet Club (Midland), Horseshoe Bay (Tex.) Country Club, Phi Kappa Phi, Pi Lambda Theta. Republican. Office: PO Box 2127 Midland TX 79702-2127 E-mail: rozgrover@aol.com.

GROVER, SCOTT W, surgeon; b. Rexburg, Idaho, May 21, 1964; s. Dean R. and Lois M. Grover; m. Sandy M. Grover, May 2, 1986; children: Coltin, Carissa, Michael, Daniel, Ciara. AA, Ricks Coll., 1987; BS, Idaho State U., 1991; DO, Des Moines U., 1995. Diplomate Am. Bd. Med. Examiners; cert. BLS, ACLS, ATLS. Intern Des Moines Gen. Hosp., 1995-96; resident in surgery Des Peres Hosp., St. Louis, 1996-00; emergency physician St. Louis, 1996-00. Contbr. articles to profl. jours. Sunday sch. instr., young men advisor, 1991-94; varsity scout master Boy Scouts Am., 1992-94; ch. quorum sec., 1998-2000, quorum counselor to quorum pres., 1997-98, chair com., 1996-97, chair cub scout com., 1999-00, new scout leader, 2001-03. Named Eagle Scout Boy Scouts Am., 1981. Mem.: AMA, Utah Med. Assn., Idaho Med. Assn., Mo. Assn. Osteo. Physicians and Surgeons, Am. Osteo. Assn., Am. Coll. Osteo. Surgeons.

Avocations: family, woodworking, outdoor recreation. Home: 2042 N 550 E North Logan UT 84341-8829 Office: Cache Valley Surg Cos 550 E 1400 N Ste D Logan UT 84341 E-mail: surgn@aol.com.

GROVES, JOHN TAYLOR, III, chemist, educator; b. New Rochelle, N.Y., Mar. 27, 1943; s. John Taylor and Frances (Gaylor) G.; m. Karen Joan Morrison, Apr. 15, 1967; children: Jay, Kevin. BS, M.I.T., 1965; PhD, Columbia U., 1969. Asst. prof. U. Mich., Ann Arbor, 1969-76, assoc. prof., 1976-79, prof. organic chemistry, 1979-85; prof. organic and inorganic chemistry Princeton (N.J.) U., 1985—, chmn. dept. chemistry, 1988-93, Hugh Stott Taylor prof. chemistry, 1991—. Morris S. Kharasch Vis. Prof. U. Chgo., 1993; cons. in field; dir. Mich. Center for Catalytic and Surface Scis., Ann Arbor, 1981-85 Bd. editors: Bioorganic Chemistry, 1984—, Bioorganic and Medicinal Chemistry, 1994—, Bioorganic and Medicinal Chemistry Letters, 1994—; mem. editl. bd.: Reaction Kinetics and Catalysis Letters, 1989—, Jour. of Biol. Inorganic Chemistry, 1995—; contbr. articles to profl. jours.; mem. adv. bd. Inorganic Chemistry, 1995-97. Recipient Phi Lambda Upsilon award for outstanding teaching and leadership, 1978, NSF Extension award, 1990-92. Fellow AAAS, Am. Acad. Arts and Scis.; mem. Am. Chem. Soc. (Arthur C. Cope Scholar award 1991, Alfred Bader award in bio-organic and bioinorganic chemistry 1996), N.Y. Acad. Sci., Sigma Xi. Office: Princeton U Dept Chemistry 203 Hoyt Lab Princeton NJ 08544-0001

GROVES, MICHAEL, banker; b. London, Jan. 2, 1936; came to U.S., 1969; s. Percy Reginald and Lily Sarah (Bentley) G.; m. Monica Rosario, June 8, 1963; children: Christopher, Carolyn, Jonathan. Grad., Inst. Chartered Accts., London, 1958; licentiate and tchg. cert., Royal Acad. Music, 1959; grad., Sch. Bank Adminstrn., U. Madison, Wis., 1976. Chief acct. Malaysian Estate Agys. Group Ltd., Kuala Lumpur, Malaysia, 1959-61; chief acct. Flour Mills Nigeria, Ltd., Lagos, 1961-62; asst. fin. mgr. Fábrica de Tejidos La Union Ltda, Lima, Peru, 1963-69; asst. to comptr. internat. Firstar, Milw., 1969-70, asst. auditor, 1970-72; loan rev. officer First Wis. Corp., 1972-79; sr. v.p. AmSouth Bancorp., Birmingham, 1979-82; v.p., mgr. credit rev. Merc. Bancorp, St. Louis, 1982-84; sr. v.p. internat. banking, sr. v.p. risk mgmt. Merc. Trust Co., St. Louis, 1985-87, chief credit policy officer, 1988-90; dir. risk mgmt. Integra Fin. Corp., Pitts., 1990-96. Mem. faculty Sch. Bank Adminstrn., U. Madison, 1979-92. Author: Loan Review: A Guide, 1978, 2d edit., 1987, Management of Problem Loans, 1989, mus. compositions, arrangements. Mus. dir., com. mem. Selangor Philharm. Soc., Kuala Lumpur, 1959-61, Brit. Coun. Activities, Lima, 1963-69. Fellow Inst. Chartered Accts. Eng. and Wales; mem. Robert Morris Assocs. (mem. faculty loan rev. seminars 1977-80, chmn. 1978-79), Bank Adminstrn. Inst. (faculty, audit course 1970-74 Sch. for Bank Adminstrn. 1977-90).

GROVES, MICHAEL G. dean; DVM, Tex. A&M U., 1964; MPH in Epidemiology, Tulane U., 1966; PhD in Microbiology, Cath. U. Am., 1975. Comdr. rsch. lab. U.S. Army Vet. Corps, Malaysia, 1964—90; dir. Army/Navy consol. infectious disease program U.S. Army Vet. Corps., dep. dir. Walter Reed Army Inst. Rsch.; ret. U.S. Army; mem. faculty, head dept. epidemiology and comty. health La. State U. Vet. Medicine, 1990, dir. La. Vet. Med. Diagnostic Lab.; dean La. State U. Sch. Vet. Medicine, Baton Rouge, 2000—. Mem., past chair Nat. Bd. Exams. Com. for vet. licensing; mem. Joint FDA and USDA Nat. Adv. Com. on Microbiol. Criteria for Foods. Mem.: Am. Assn. Food Hygiene Vets. (bd. dirs.), Am. Coll. Vet. Microbiologists (diplomate), Am. Coll. Vet. Preventive Medicine (diplomate, charter diplomate epidemiology specialty, past pres., exams. com., bd. counselors). Office: La State U Sch Vet Medicine Baton Rouge LA 70803-8404

GROVES, RAY JOHN, accountant; b. Cleve., Sept. 7, 1935; m. Anne Keating, Aug. 18, 1962; children: David, Philip, Matthew. BS summa cum laude, Ohio State U., 1957. CPA, Conn., N.Y., Ohio. With Ernst & Whinney, Cleve. and N.Y.C., 1957-94, ptnr., 1966-71, nat. ptnr., 1971-77, chmn., chief exec. officer, 1977-89; co-CEO, Ernst & Young, N.Y.C., 1989-91, chmn., CEO, 1991-94; chmn. Legg Mason Merchant Banking, Inc., 1995—2001; pres., COO Marsh, Inc., 2001—02, chmn., CEO, 2003—. Bd. govs. Am. Stock Exch., 1987-93; bd. dirs. Inc., Boston Sci. Corp., Gillette, Marsh & McLennan Cos., Inc., EDS. Bd. overseers Wharton Sch. U. Pa., 1986-95; vice chmn. bd. trustees Ursuline Coll., Cleve., 1970-86; mng. dir., treas. Met. Opera Assn., 1988—; trustee Pub. Policy Inst. N.Y. State, 1988—, Bus. Coun UN, 1993-99; dir. Ohio State U. Found., 1994—, chmn., 1999-2001. Mem. AICPA (chmn. bd. dirs. 1984-85), Nat. Assn. Securities Dealers (bd. govs. 1981-84), Union Club, Pepper Pike Club, Links Club, Met. Club, Blind Brook Club. Republican. Home: 1566 Ponus Rdg New Canaan CT 06840-3430 also: 15 W 53rd St Apt 20A New York NY 10019-5401 Office: Marsh Inc 1166 Ave of Americas 44th Flr New York NY 10036-2774

GROVES, RICHARD THOMAS, III, conductor, minister; b. Dallas, Tex., Sept. 19, 1974; s. Richard Thomas Groves, Jr. and Daena Marie Groves; m. Tamara Downey, Mar. 8, 1997; 1 child, Taylor Renee. MusB, Howard Payne U., 1997. Property & Casualty Ind., 2002. Music min. Southside Bapt. Ch., Brownwood, Tex., 1996—98; asst. band dir. Early Ind. Sch. Dist., Early, Tex., 1997—98; youth and music pastor Bosqueville Bapt. Ch., Waco, Tex., 1998—2000, Living Hope Christian Fellowship, Waco, Tex., 2000—01; band dir. St. Peter's Luth. Sch., Columbus, Ind., 2001—; support staff/renter's specialist Scott Wilson State Farm Ins., Columbus, Ind., 2001—; youth pastor Lakeside Fellowship Ch., Columbus, Ind., 2001—; asst. band dir. Bosqueville I.S.D., Waco, Tex., 2000—01. Asst. team leader/worship leader Super Summer - So. Bapt. of Ind., Ind., 2002—; support staff/renter's specialist Scott Wilson State Farm Ins., Columbus, 2001—; youth pastor Lakeside Fellowship Ch., Columbus, 2001—; asst. band dir. Bosqueville Ind. Sch. dist., Waco, 2000—01. Actor: (musical) Music Man, Guys and Dolls, Seven Brides for Seven Brothers, Kiss Me Kate. Mem. Columbus Area Youth Minister's Alliance, Columbus, Ind., 2001—02; leader Young Life, Columbus, Ind., 2002; mem. Waco Area Youth Ministers Orgn., Waco, Tex., 1998—2001. Mem.: Music Educators Nat. Conv., Kappa Kappa Psi (alumni sec., sec., v.p./membership edn. officer 1994—97). Conservative. Avocations: music, sports, movies, technology. Home: 1130 Saylor Apt 1A Columbus IN 47201 Office: St Peter's Lutheran School 719 5th St Columbus IN 47201 Personal E-mail: indianayouthguy@hotmail.com.

GROVES, SHERIDON HALE, orthopedic surgeon; b. Denver, Mar. 5, 1947; s. Harry Edward Groves and Dolores Ruth (Hale) Finley; m. Deborah Rita Threadgill, Mar. 29, 1970 (div. Apr. 1980); children: Jason, Tiffany; m. Nanely Marie Lamont, July 1, 1980 (div. Dec. 1987); 1 child, Dolores; m. Elaine Robbins, Feb. 7, 1991. BS, U.S. Mil. Acad., 1969; MD, U. Va., Charlottesville, 1976. Commd. 2nd lt. U.S. Army, 1969, advanced through grades to maj., 1979, ret., 1992, surg. intern, 1976-77, resident in orthop. surgery, 1977-80, staff orthop. surgeon Killeen, Tex., 1980-83, ret., 1992; staff emergency physician various emergency depts. State of Tex., 1983-84, 87; emergency dept. dir. Victoria (Tex.) Regional Med. Ctr., 1984-86; med. dir. First Walk-In Clinic Victoria, 1986-87; tchr. U. Tex. Med. Br., Galveston, 1986-90; emergency dept. dir. Gulf Coast Med. Ctr., 1988-89; with Amerimed Corp., 1990-92, Primedex Corp., 1992-93; clinic med. dir, staff orthop. surgeon Pain Relief Network, 1993-99; ret., 1999—. Lectr. Spkrs. Bur., Victoria, 1984-86, Cato Inst., Ludwig Von Mises Inst. Host radio talk show, 1996-97; contbr. articles to profl. jours. Mem. Victoria Interagy. Coun. Sexual Abuse, 1984-86; treas. bd. dirs. Youth Home Victoria, 1986-90; vol. Bible tchg. Calif. Penal Sys. Recipient Physician's Recognition award, AMA, 1980, 83, 86, 89, 92, 95. Fellow Am. Acad. Neurologic and Orthop. Surgeons; mem. Soc. Mil., Orthop. Surgeons, Am. Coll. Emergency Physicians, Tex. Med. Found., Assn. Grads. of U.S. Mil. Acad. (life), Am. Assn. Disability Evaluation Physicians, Coalition of Med. Providers, Am. Coll. Sports Medicine, Am. Running and Fitness Assn. (cert. of recognition 1987), Internat. Coll. Surgeons (pres., vice regent), Internat. Martial Arts Assn., Hurricane Sports Club of Houston, Smithsonian Assocs., So. Calif. Striders Track Club. Avocation: martial arts.

GROVES, STEPHEN PETERSON, SR., lawyer; b. Charleston, SC, June 4, 1956; s. George Francis Jr. and Helen (Peterson) G.; m. Amy B. Rothschild; children: Danel, Joshua, Stephen Jr., Sumter. BA, Coll. Charleston, 1979; JD, U. S.C., 1986. Bar: S.C. 1986, U.S. Dist. Ct. S.C. 1987, U.S. Ct. Appeals (4th cir.) 1987, U.S. Supreme Ct. 1990, U.S. Ct. Appeals (7th, 11th, Fed. cirs.) 1991, U.S. Ct. Appeals (5th, 6th and 9th cirs.) 1993, U.S. Ct. Appeals (10th cir.) 1996. Asst. to city planner Charleston Dept. Planning and Urban Devel., 1976-77; asst. to legal coordinator Neighborhood Legal Asst. Program, Charleston, 1978; police officer, detective Charleston County Police Dept., 1980-83; law clk. to dean U. S.C. Law Sch., 1983-86; assoc. Young, Clement, Rivers & Tisdale, Charleston, 1986-91, ptnr., 1991—2003; spl. coun. Nexsen, Pruet, Jacobs, Pollard & Robinson, LLC, 2003—. Contbg. editor S.C. Civil Procedure, 1985, Domestic Relations in South Carolina, 1986, ABA Tips Property Insurance Law Subcommittee-Annotations Standard, Fire and Extended Coverage, 1994, Coverage Litigation Insurance, 1998, others. Mem. ATLA, ABA (co-editor ABA-YLD Arson Reporter 1988-90, ABA TIPS Comml. Torts Newsletter 1991—, chair ABA TIPS bus. torts com. 1997—, vice chair ABA TIPS appellate adv. com. 1994—, vice chair ABA TIPS civil procedure and evidence com. 1994—), Internat. Bar Assn., S.C. Bar (ethics adv. com. 1995—, profl. responsibility com. 1995—), Charleston County Bar Assn., Am. Judicature Soc., S.C. Def. Trial Lawyers Assn. (amicus curaie brief com. 1990—), Libel Def. Resource Ctr. (contbg. editor 50-state ann. survey), Def. Rsch. Inst., Christian Legal Soc., Sigma Nu, Pi Sigma Alpha, Omicron Delta Kappa. Republican. Roman Catholic. Avocations: sports, coaching. Office: Nexsen Pruet Jacobs Pollard & Robinson LLC Box 486 205 King St Ste 400 Charleston SC 29401 E-mail: sgroves@npjp.com.

GROW, ROBERT THEODORE, economist, association executive; b. Newton, Mass., Aug. 14, 1948; s. William and Lempi (Kangas) G.; m. Anita L. Capps, Nov. 20, 1982; 1 child, Margaret Celia. BS magna cum laude, U. Mass., 1970, MS, 1973. Regional economist Southeastern Va. Planning Dist. Commn., Norfolk, 1973-80; dir. met. coord. Met. Washington (D.C.) Coun. Govts., 1980-85; exec. dir. Washington/Balt. Regional Assn., Washington, 1985-94; dir. transportation The Greater Washington Bd. Trade, 1994—. Chmn. met. com. Capital Area chpt. Am. Planning Assn., Washington, 1988-89. Appeared on Comedy Central's Daily Show, 1999. Mem. design selection panel Woodrow Wilson Bridge, 1999; alternate citizens adv. com. Met. Washington Transp. Planning Bd., 2001. Fellow Am. Ctr. for Internat. Leadership; mem. Am. Soc. Assn. Execs., Va. Econs. Devel. Assn., Md. Indsl. Devel. Assn., Phi Kappa Phi. Avocations: sailing, skiing, golf. E-mail: bobgrow@bot.org.

GROWICK, PHILIP, advertising executive; b. New York, Dec. 28, 1944; s. Morris and Rose G.; m. Maiju; children: Matthew, Kevin. BA, Hunter Coll., 1966. Pres. Philip Growick Assocs., N.Y.C., 1975-91; mng. dir. Jerry Fields Assocs., Inc., 1994—; v.p. bd. dirs. Skyview on the Hudson, 1992—. Author: Hail to the Chief, 1964. Editor: Nudeniks, 1964. Avocations: history studies, political history, scuba, ancient Rome.

GROW-MAIENZA, JANICE, education educator; d. Cecil Herbert Grow and Ruby McMillan; children: Michael Antony Maienza, John Andrew Maienza, Charles David Maienza. PhD, U. Chgo., 1981. Chmn. dept. of edn. Sinte Gleska Coll., Rosebud Sioux Reservation, SD, 1982—84; asst. prof. St. Mary's Coll., Notre Dame, Ind., 1984—86; prof. Truman State U., Kirksville, Mo., 1988—; exch. prof. Pusan (Republic of Korea) Nat. U., 1995—96. Cons. Indonesian Dept. of Edn. and Culture, Jakarta, Java, 1986—88. Contbr. articles to profl. jours. Recipient Eisenhower Profl. Devel. awards, Mo. Coordinating Bd. of Higher Edn., 2001—02, Curriculum Devel. award for Native Am. lit. in the curriculum, Eli Lilley Found., 1986; fellow, NEH, 1983, 1984; grantee, NSF, 2000. Mem.: Nat. Coun. Tchrs. of Math., Am. Ednl. Rsch. Assn. Achievements include research in anlysis of mathematics instruction in Korean classrooms and analysis of Korean primary mathematics textbooks. Home: RR 3 59 White Oak Ln Kirksville MO 63501 Office: Truman State U 100 East Normal Kirksville MO 63501 Personal E-mail: jgrow@truman.edu. E-mail: jgrow@truman.edu.

GRUB, PHILLIP DONALD, business educator; b. Medical Lake, Wash., Aug. 8, 1931; s. Carl Dryer and Barbara Rosalie (Johnson) G. BA in Econs. and Bus. Edn. with honors, Eastern Wash. State U., 1953; MBA (Scottish Rite Found. fellow), George Washington U., 1960, DBA (Am. Security and Trust scholar), 1964; DBus (hon.), U. Internat. Bus. and Econs., Beijing, 1986. Pres. Phillip D. Grub, Inc., Spokane, Wash., 1953-54; pvt. practice, 1956-62; co-owner, co-mgr. 7G Ranch, Medical Lake, 1962-70; assoc. prof., dir. programs in internat. bus. George Washington U., Washington, 1964-70, chmn. dept. bus. adminstrn., 1968-70, prof. bus. adminstrn., 1971-73, Aryamehr prof. multinat. mgmt., 1974-94, Aryamehr prof. emeritus, 1994—, spl. asst. to pres., 1974-80; chmn. Phillip Grub and Assocs., 1994—; disting. internat. exec. in residence Ea. Washington U., Cheney, 1997—. Cons. Summa Group, Jakarta, Indonesia, 1991-92; mgmt. cons. to industry and govts.; sr. ptnr. C & P Properties, Medical Lake, Wash., 1988—, Pacific Costal Investments, Medical Lake, Wash., 2001—; mem. Md.-D.C. Export Expansion Coun., 1968-89; vis. prof. internat. bus. adminstrn., acting dir. Ohio World Trade Edn. Ctr., Cleve. State U., 1972-73; dir., chmn. exec. com. Diplomat Nat. Bank, 1978-80; mem. bd. adv. Donaldson, Luftkin & Jenrette, 1980-83; bd. dirs. U.S.-Japan Culture Ctr.; dir. Washington World Trade Inst., 1983-91, pres., 1983-86; dir. U.S. Vietnam Ednl. Found., 1990—; sr. advisor Shanghi Ctr. Internat. Studies, 1987—. Author: A Guide to Personnel Development, 1966, A Handbook for Term Papers, Theses and Dissertations, 1967, American-East European Trade: Controversy, Progress, Prospects, 1968; (with Norma M. Loeser) Executive Leadership: The Art of Successfully Managing Resources, 1969, Management U.S.A., 1968; (with Mika S. Kaskimies) International Marketing in Perspective, 1971; (with Ashok Kapoor) The Multinational Enterprise in Transition, 1972, 3d edit., 1986; (with Ghadar and Khambata) Asia Dimensions of International Business, 1982, Foreign Investment Analysis: Cases and Country Studies, 1986, Global Business Management in the 1990's, 1990, Foreign Direct Investment in China, 1991, The Re-Emerging Securities Market in China, 1992, Vietnam, The New Investment Frontier in Southeast Asia, 1992, (with Dara Khambata) The Multinational Enterprise: Strategies for Global Competitiveness, 1993, Global Business Strategies for the Year 2000, 1995; contbr. articles to profl. jours. Bd. dirs. U.S. Forestry, 1987-90; sr. advisor Shanghai Ctr. Internat. Studies, 1987—. With U.S. Army, 1954-56. Named a Univ. Prof. in Peoples Republic of China, 1986. Mem. Acad. Internat. Bus. (pres. 1975-77), Acad. Mgmt., Am. Mgmt. Assn., U.S.-Japan Culture Soc. (bd. dirs., exec. sec.), Fellows Acad. Internat. Bus., Masons, Alpha Kappa Psi, Beta Gamma Sigma. Home: 4810 S Saint Andrews Ln Spokane WA 99223-4304 Office: C & P Properties PO Box 220 Medical Lake WA 99022-0220 E-mail: phillipg54@aol.com.

GRUBB, DAVID H. construction company executive; b. Jan. 22, 1936; married BSCE, Princeton U.; MSCE, Stanford U. With Swinerton and Walberg Co., San Francisco, 1964—, then exec. v.p. Structural divsn., exec. v.p. ops., pres., also bd. dirs.; pres. Swinerton Inc., 1993-96, CEO and chmn. bd. Chmn. bd. Swinerton Builders. Office: Swinerton Incorp 260 Townsend St San Francisco CA 94107-1790

GRUBB, DONALD HARTMAN, paper industry company executive; b. West Chester, Pa., Oct. 22, 1924; s. Donald C. and Bessie (Hanthorne) G.; m. Jean Louise Flounders, Sept. 7, 1946; children: Donna Jean (Mrs. Robert Kanich), Deborah Anne (Mrs. James R. Jackson), Donald Philip. BA, U. Pa., 1949; MA, Am. U., 1954; postgrad., NYU, 1963-64. With U.S. Treasury Dept., Washington, 1949-57, recruitment officer, 1951-53, dir. personnel, 1953-57; mgr. personnel Westvaco Corp., N.Y.C., 1957-59, regional adminstrv. mgr. Hoboken, N.J., 1959-61, mgr. sales, 1961-64; asst. to v.p. Huyck Corp., Stamford, Conn., 1964, v.p. adminstrn. and mktg., 1969-70, exec. v.p., 1970-73, pres., dir., chief exec. officer, 1973-81; chmn. BTR Paper Group, 1981-82; pres. Gedon Enterprises, 1982—; v.p., gen. mgr. Formex Co. of Can., Kentville, N.S., 1965-67; also dir.; v.p., gen. mgr. Huyck Formex Co. of U.S., Greeneville, Tenn., 1967-69. Mgr. Grubb Assocs., LLC dba Fasteners Supply of Goldsboro; retired dir. various cos. in U.S. and U.K. Bd. dirs. Blanchard-Fraser Meml. Hosp., Kentville, N.S., Can., 1966-67, Wake County Hosp. System, Raleigh, 1983-87, N.C. State U. Pulp and Paper Found.; mem. N.C. State U. Sch. Engring. Foun., N.C. State U. Sch. Humanities Found. Served with AUS, 1943-46. Decorated Bronze Star AUS. Mem. Raleigh C. of C. (dir. 1976-78), Phi Beta Kappa. Presbyterian. Office: 6713 Foxfire Pl Raleigh NC 27615-7011 E-mail: dongrubb@earthlink.net.

GRUBB, ROBERT L., JR., neurosurgeon; b. Charlotte, N.C., May 9, 1940; MD, U. N.C., 1965. Intern Barnes Hosp., St. Louis, 1965-66, resident in gen. surgery, 1966-67, resident in neurosurgery, 1969-73; fellow NIH, Bethesda, Md., 1968-69; mem. staff Barnes-Jewish Hosp., St. Louis, St. Louis Children's Hosp.; prof. neurosurgery Washington U., St. Louis. Fellow ACS; mem. Am. Acad. Neurol. Surgery, AANS, CNS, SNS. Office: Washington U Sch Medicine 660 S Euclid Ave Box 8057 Saint Louis MO 63110-1010 E-mail: grubbr@nsurg.wustl.edu.

GRUBB, ROBERT LYNN, computer system designer; b. Knoxville, Tenn., Nov. 23, 1937; s. Willian Henry and DeLores Alfisi (Pierucci) Hollinshead; m. Donna Jean Chicado, May 28, 1973; children: Barbara, Robert Lynn, Paul, Werner, Luke, Jubal. BS, Ctrl. State Coll., Edmond, Okla., 1972. Air traffic contr. FAA, Ft. Worth, 1955-62; engr. Philco-Ford Corp., Oklahoma City, 1962-65; svc. co. exec. lear-Siegler, Inc., Oklahoma City, 1965-67; computer specialist USN, Corpus Christi, Tex., 1967-71, U.S. Army, Petersburg, Va., 1971-77, U.S. CSC, Washington, 1977-79, U.S. Justice Dept., San Antonio, 1979-89, Def. Mapping Agy., Acad. Health Scis., 1989-93; CEO Tex. Office Systems Co., Inc., Wetmore, 1980-92; pres., CEO Dot Com Websites, Inc., 1998—. Cons. Corpus Christi Pub. Sch. Bd. Author: Conversion and Implementation of CS3 Computer System, 1973, Economic Analysis of Automated System-TOPS, 1977—; contbr. articles and stories on Western history to various periodicals. Committeeman Boy Scouts Am., 1963-64; bd. dirs., athletic coach Southside Youth League, 1970. With USNR, 1945-46, PTO. Mem. Western Writers Am. Home and Office: 122 E Terra Alta Dr San Antonio TX 78209-2766

GRUBB, WENDY STANDLEY, school counselor; b. Emmett, Idaho, May 30, 1952; d. Irl T. and Margaret T. (Smith) Standley; m. Robert J. Grubb, July 13, 1974; children: Michael, Catherine. BA, Boise State U., 1974; MS, Loyola U., 1981. Cert. nat. counselor, lic. profl. counselor La. Payroll clk. Le Pavillion Hotel, New Orleans, 1974; food & beverage controller Pontchartrain Hotel, New Orleans, 1975; educator Carrollton Presbyn. Sch., New Orleans, 1975-81; counselor St. Mary's Dominican H.S., New Orleans, 1981—, adv. coll. Mem. Am. Counseling Assn., La. Counseling Assn., Caledonian Soc. New Orelans (past pres.), Chi Sigma Iota (charter mem. Alpha Zeta chpt. pres. 1993-94). Avocations: scottish country dancing, sewing, needlework, family. Office: St Marys Dominican High Sch 7701 Walmsley Ave New Orleans LA 70125-3429

GRUBB, WILLIAM, musician, music educator; b. Greencastle, Ind., Mar. 30, 1951; s. Cassel William Grubb and Bernice Anne Flanagan; m. Laurie Carney Grubb, Oct. 17, 1976. MusB, The Juilliard Sch., 1975, MusM, 1976, D of Musical Arts, 1981. Dir. chamber music Aspen (Colo.) Music Festival, 1976—; cellist Aspen Soloists, N.Y.C., 1976—90; prof. music Bklyn. Coll., 1985—90, Butler U., Indpls., 1991—, U. Cin., 1997—. Trustee Aspen Music Festival, 1997—2002. Recipient award, Concert Artists Guild, 1975. Office: Butler U Indianapolis IN

GRUBB, WILLIAM FRANCIS XAVIER, consumer software executive, marketing executive; b. N.Y.C., Aug. 11, 1944; s. William Martin and Eileen F. (Donnelly) G.; m. Eileen B. O'Leary, Apr. 4, 1964; children: Catherine E., William M., Kerri A., Christopher M. BA in Econs., Fordham U., 1966; MBA in Mktg. and Fin., Seton Hall U., 1972. bd. dirs. several privately-held cos. Mktg. and sales exec. Black & Decker, Towson, Md., 1968-79; v.p. mktg. Atari, Sunnyvale, Calif., 1979-81; chmn., pres. New West Mktg., Mountain View, Calif., 1981; pres., chief exec. officer, chmn. Imagic, Los Gatos, Calif., 1981-84; exec. v.p. Dataspeed, 1984-85; pres. Axlon Inc., 1985-86; exec. v.p., gen. mgr. Worlds of Wonder, Inc., Freemont, Calif., 1986-87; pres., chief exec. The Complete PC, San Jose, Calif., 1987-93; CEO, ICTV Inc., Los Gatos, Calif., 1994-96; CEO Millenia Software Inc., Saratoga, Calif., 1996—; pres. Toolz Ltd., Palo Alto, Calif., 1998-99; CEO Grubb Enterprises LLC, Pawleys Island, SC, 1999—. Bd. regents Holy Names Coll. Home: 57 Britt Ct Alameda CA 94502-7778 Office: Grubb Enterprises LLC 93 Rookery Trl Pawleys Island SC 29585-5266 E-mail: wfxgrubb@aol.com.

GRUBBS, ARLENE BUSSE, social worker, consultant; b. Pitts., May 29, 1937; d. Robert Ramsey and Rosemarie (Foley) Busse; m. Alfred Kimes Grubbs, Jan. 30, 1960; children: James Ramsey, Tracy Ann, Robert Kimes, Kathryn Ruth. BA, Allegheny Coll., 1959; MSW, U. Pitts., 1961. Cert. Acad. Cert. Social Workers; lic. social worker, Pa. Coord. Vis. Nurse Assn., Pitts., 1976-86; employee assistance counselor Mercy Hosp., Pitts., 1988-95, West Penn Hosp., Pitts., 1990-95. Adj. faculty Community Coll. Allegheny County, Pitts., 1984—; trainer-cons. in field, Pitts., 1986—. Author: (with others) Older Adult Ministry, 1987, Volunteer Recognition Skit Kit, 1992. Bd. dirs. Zoar Home, Pitts., 1985-90, pres., 1987-89; bd. dirs. North Hills Affordable Housing, Pitts., 1989-2000, pres., bd. mem., 1989-95; chair nom. com., Girl Scouts Southwe. Pa., 1999-2001. Named YWCA Woman of the Yr. for Cmty. Svc. Award, 1995, Rotary Club of McCandles Paul Harris Fellow, Outstanding Visionary 2002. Mem. NASW, Pa. Assn. for Volunteerism (bd. dirs., pres. 1988-89), Vol. Adminstrs. Southwestern Pa. (bd. dirs., pres. 1984-86), Assn. for Vol. Adminstrn., Phi Beta Kappa. Home: 21 Briar Cliff Rd Pittsburgh PA 15202-1305 Office: 21 Briar Cliff Rd Pittsburgh PA 15202-1305

GRUBBS, CONWAY E. marine company executive; b. Tribbey, Okla., Mar. 26, 1918; s. Harvey Kendrick and Ida Irene (Wright) G.; m. Clyde Laverne Mason, Aug. 23, 1941; children: Jimmy Conway, Barri Lynn. Student, Northeastern Okla. A&M Coll., 1937-38. Mgr. ops., mgr. mktg., gen. mgr, v.p., dir. Caribbean, Ctrl. and So. Am. Chgo. Bridge & Iron Co., Oakbrook, Ill., 1955-69, asst. mgr. marine ops., dir. underwater welding rsch., 1969-76, mgr. worldwide underwater constrn. Prairieville, La., 1976-79; pres., owner D&W Underwater Welding Svc., Inc., Baton Rouge, 1979-84; dir. underwater welding R & D Global Divers and Contractors, Inc., Lafayette, La., 1984—. Cons. U.S. Nat. Rsch. Coun., U.S. Dept. Interior; chmn. exec. com. Joint Industry Underwater Welding Devel. Program. Contbr. articles to profl. jours. With USAAF, 1941-44. Recipient award in recognition of significant achievements in comml. diving, Assn. Diving Contractors Internat. Mem. Am. Welding Soc. (chmn. coms., tech. rep., Meritorious Award for Outstanding Achievements in the Sci. of Welding 1987), Internat. Inst. Welding (chmn., del.). Achievements include patents for Method of Underwater Welding Using Pressurized Welding Electrode Transfer Capsule and Dry Welding Electrode Insitu Storage, Viewing Scope for Turbid Environment and Use in Underwater Welding, and Method of Underwater Welding Using Viewing Scope; major advancements in underwater 'wet' welding. Office: Global Divers & Contractors PO Box 10840 New Iberia LA 70562-0840 Address: 7414 Prairie Dr Greenwell Springs LA 70739-3055

GRUBBS, DONALD RAY, educational director, educator, welder; b. Houston, Tex, Oct. 22, 1947; s. J. W. and Imo Gene (Williams) G.; Glenda Carol Nowell, Nov. 27, 1967; 1 child, Sean Lynn. EdB, Lamar U., 1974, AAS, 1983. Welder Bethlehem Steel, Beaumont, Tex., 1968-73; pipefitter, welder Pipefitters Local 195, Beaumont, 1973-86; regents instr. Lamar U., Beaumont, 1973-87, placement dir. tech. arts, 1986-87; chief instr. Am. Welding Soc., Miami, Fla., 1987—, dir. qualification and cert., 1988-92; welding quality mgr. Base Line Data Inc., Portland, Tex., 1993-95; dir. edn. Am. Welding Soc., Miami, Fla., 1992—; v.p. Guardian NDT, Corpus Christi, Tex., 1995—; edn. dir. Base Line Data, Portland, Tex., 1996-98; sr. insp. Longview Inspection, Tex., 1998—. Cons. in field. Scoutmaster Boy Scouts Am., Beaumont, 1978-86. Served with USMC, 1968-70, Vietnam. Mem. Am. Welding Soc. (chmn. 1983-84, dir. edn. Miami chpt. 1992—), Tex. Jr. Coll. Tchrs. Assn. (chmn. 1980-83), Placement Assn. Tex., Lamar Ex-Students Assn. Democrat. Mem. Christian Ch. (Disciples Of Christ). Avocation: outdoor sports. Home: PMB 498 1137 E 42nd St Odessa TX 79762 Office: Longview Inspection 12410 W Hwy 80E Odessa TX 79765

GRUBBS, DONALD SHAW, JR., retired actuary; b. Bellvue, Pa., Dec. 15, 1929; s. Donald Shaw and Zora Fay (Craven) G.; m. Margaret Helen Crooke, Dec. 27, 1969; children: David, Deborah, Daniel, Dawson, Dwight, Douglas. AB, Tex. A&M U., 1951; postgrad., L.A. State Coll., 1953-54, Fresno State Coll., 1954-55, Boston U., 1955-57, Princeton Theol. Sem., 1959-60, Westminster Theol. Sem., 1960-61; JD, Georgetown U., 1979. Bar: D.C. 1979. Actuarial asst. New Eng. Mut. Life Ins. Co., Boston, 1955-58, Warner Watson, Inc., Boston, 1958-59; cons. actuary John B. St. John, Penllyn, Pa., 1959-65, Grubbs & Co., Phila., 1965-72; v.p. actuary Nat. Health and Welfare Retirement Assn., N.Y.C., 1972-74; dir. actuarial div. IRS, Washington, 1974-76; cons. actuary Buck Cons., Inc., Washington, 1976-86; pres. Grubbs and Co., Inc., Silver Spring, Md., 1986-95, retired, 1995—. Chmn. Joint Bd. for Enrollment Actuaries, Washington, 1975-76. Author: (with G.E. Johnson) The Variable Annuity, 1967; (with D.M. McGill) Fundamentals of Private Pensions, 6th edit., 1989. V.p. NAACP, Ambler, Pa., 1961-62; chmn. Warminster (Pa.) Child Day Care Assn., 1962-64. 1st lt. U.S. Army, 1951-53, Korea. Decorated Bronze Star with V U.S. Army, 1953; recipient Employee Benefits Outstanding Achievement award Pension World, 1986. Fellow Soc. of Actuaries (sec. 1983-84),

Conf. Consulting Actuaries; mem. ABA, Middle Atlantic Actuarial Club (pres. 1981-82), UN Assn. (v.p. nat. capital area divsn. 1996-98, 2000-02). Democrat. Unitarian Universalist. Home: 10216 Royal Rd Silver Spring MD 20903-1613 E-mail: dongrubbs@aol.com.

GRUBBS, ELVEN JUDSON, retired newspaper publisher; b. Taylor County, Fla., Dec. 26, 1930; s. Judson Omer and Nancy Lourainie (Lundy) G.; m. Loretta Caruthers, June 4, 1950; 1 son, Russell Elven. Student public schs., Ocala, Fla. With Ocala Star-Banner, 1947-77, advt. dir., 1964-77, gen. mgr., 1968-77; v.p., publisher The Ledger, Lakeland, Fla., 1977-82; pub. Sarasota (Fla.) Herald-Tribune, 1982-91, ret., 1991. Former trustee John and Mable Ringling Mus. Art, Sarasota. Republican. Baptist. Home: PO Box 962 Steinhatchee FL 32359-0962

GRUBBS, JUDITH EVANS, classical studies educator; b. Atlanta, Nov. 30, 1956; d. Trevor and Ellen Enid (Lovell) Evans; m. Charles Thompson Grubbs, Aug. 18, 1979; 1 child, Charlotte. BA with highest honors, Emory U., 1978; postgrad., Am. Sch. Classical Studies, Athens, Greece, 1978-79; PhD in Classics, Stanford U., 1987. Lectr. Intercollegiate Ctr. Classical Studies, Rome, 1984-85; tchg. fellow classics Stanford (Calif.) U., 1983-84, 85-87; asst. prof. Sweet Briar (Va.) Coll., 1987-93, dir. honors program, 1995-96, assoc. prof. classical studies, 1993-2000, prof. classical studies, 2000—. Author: Law and Family in Late Antiquity: The Emperor Constantine's Marriage Legislation, 1995, Women and the Law in the Roman Empire: A Sourcebook on Marriage, Divorce and Widowhood, 2002; contbr. articles and book revs. to profl. jours. Recipient ITT internat. fellowship, Greece, 1978-79, grad. fellowship Stanford U., 1979-83, Mednick grant Va. Found. Ind. Colls., 1988, Jessie Ball Dupont fellowship Nat. Humanities Ctrs., N.C., 1993-94, fellowship for coll. tchrs. NEH, 1997-98. Mem. Am. Philol. Assn., Assn. Ancient Historians, Classical Assn. Mid. West and South, Classical Assn. Va., Women's Classical Caucus, N.Am. Patristics Soc. Episcopalian. Office: Sweet Briar Coll Dept Classical Studies Sweet Briar VA 24595 E-mail: evansgrubbs@sbc.edu.

GRUBBS, ROBERT HOWARD, chemistry educator; b. Calvert City, Ky., Feb. 27, 1942; s. Henry Howard and Faye (Atwood) G.; m. Helen Matilda O'Kane; children— Robert B., Brendan H., Kathleen M. BS, U. Fla., 1963, MS, 1965; PhD, Columbia U., 1968. NIH postdoctoral fellow Stanford U., Calif., 1968-69; asst. prof. Mich. State U., East Lansing, 1969-73, assoc. prof., 1973-78; prof. chemistry Calif. Inst. Tech., Pasadena, 1978—, Victor and Elizabeth Atkins prof., 1989. Contbr. articles to profl. publs.; patentee in field. Fellow Sloan Found., 1974-76, Alexander von Humboldt Found., 1975; Dreyfus Found. scholar, 1975-78. Mem. AAAS, NAS, Am. Chem. Soc. (Organic Chemistry award 1989, Polymer Chemistry award 1995, Benjamin Franklin medal in chemistry 2000, Herman F. Mark polymer chemistry award 2000, Herbert C. Brown award for creative rsch. in synthetic methods 2001, Arthur C. Cope award, 2002, Richard C. Tolman medal 2003). Democrat. Achievements include research in homogeneous or heterogeneous catalysis. Home: 1700 Spruce St South Pasadena CA 91030-4721 Office: Calif Inst Tech Dept Chemistry 164 30 Pasadena CA 91125-0001

GRUBE, ELIZABETH, investment company executive; b. Indpls., 1917; d. Emery Warner and Jessie (Foster) Hanes; m. William F. Grube, Mar. 15, 1937; children: Carol Buck, F. William. Student, Consol. Bus. Coll., 1936, Ind. U.-Purdue U., Indpls., 1984. Pres. Prospect Investment Co. Bd. dirs. Indpls. Water Co., IWC Resources Corp., Indpls. Bd. dirs. Jameson Camp for Children, Indpls., 1981—, Greenwood Village South, Indpls., 1982—; mem. Rep. Senatorial Inner Circle, Washington, 1984. Methodist. Avocation: traveling. Home: 285 Celtic Cir Greenwood IN 46143-2458

GRUBE, KARL BERTRAM, judge; b. Elmhurst, Ill., Jan. 13, 1946; s. Karl Ludwig and Gerturde (Bertram) G.; m. Mary B. Harr, May 4, 1974 (div. Aug. 1991); m. Julia Ross, Dec. 28, 1998. BSBA, Elmhurst Coll., 1967; JD, Stetson U., 1970; M in Judicial Studies, U. Nev., 1992. Asst. pub. defender State of Fla., Clearwater, 1970-73, county ct. judge St. Petersburg, 1977—; pvt. practice Seminole, Fla., 1973-76; city atty. City of Redington Beach, Fla., 1975-76. Asst. dean Fla. Jud. Coll., Tallahassee, 1984-85; faculty mem., course coord., mem. faculty coun. Nat. Jud. Coll., chair faculty coun., 2000—; mem. Nat. Hwy. Traffic Safety Jud. Tng. Implementation Bd. Contbr. articles to profl. jours. Dir. Pinellas Comprehensive Addiction Svcs., Clearwater, 1982-88. Jud. fellow U.S. Dept. Transp., 1998, Nat. Hwy. Traffic Safety Adminstn., 1999. Mem. ABA (conf. chmn. divsn. jud. adminstrn. 1992, del. to jud. divsn. coun. 1997—, Dedicated Svc. award 1991), Fla. Bar Assn. (civil rule com.), Colo. Bar Assn., Fla. Conf. County Ct. Judges (pers. com. 1984-85), Rolls Royce Owner's Club (editor 1982-84). Lutheran. Avocations: collecting fountain pens, collecting antique watches, auto restoration. Office: Pinellas County Ct 501 1st Ave N Ste A212 Saint Petersburg FL 33701-3732

GRUBER, FREDRIC FRANCIS, financial planning and investment research executive; b. Pekin, Ill., July 16, 1931; s. Louis Simon and Lillian Frances (Klein) G.; m. Dolores Rae Hanson, Aug. 15, 1960; children: Darrell Grant, Eric Tyson. BS in Acctg., Bradley U., 1956; postgrad., Northwestern U. CPA; CFP, Fla. Audit mgr. Arthur Young & Co., Chgo., 1956-63; controller Associated Coca-Cola Bottling Co., Inc., Daytona Beach, Fla., 1963-66, asst. treas., 1964-66, treas., 1966-83, v.p., 1976-83; exec. v.p. Rich-United Corp., 1983-84; pres. Aquaculture Food Farms Inc., 1984-85; fin. cons., 1985-86; exec.v.p. G.A. Repple Fin. Group, Inc., Maitland, Fla., 1986-87; registered rep. Mut. Svc. Corp., 1987-93; CFP Investment Mgmt. and Rsch., Inc., 1993-96; assoc. G.A. Repple & Co., 1996—. Reg. repr. NASD. Served with USCG, 1950-53. Mem. AICPA, Fin. Execs. Internat., Fla. Inst. CPAs, Inst. CFP (registry practitioners), Nat. Coun. Cert. Estate Planners, Fin. Planning Assn.

GRUBER, GEORGE MICHAEL, accountant, financial systems consultant; b. Euclid, Ohio, Sept. 9, 1951; s. George and Cecilia Marie (Cantwell) G.; m. Alice Armas Peralta, June 22, 1985; 1 child, Christian Alexander. BS in Acctg. and Fin., San Francisco State U., 1983, MBA in Fin., 1991. Letterpress printer Custom Printing Assocs., San Francisco, 1973-78; voucher examiner U.S. Dept. Labor, San Francisco, 1980-81; teamster United Courier, Inc., San Francisco, 1979-81; bookkeeper, tile setter Curry Tile, Albany, Calif., 1982; sr. staff acct., fin. analyst Marriott Corp. divsn. Farrells Restaurants Inc., San Francisco, 1983-85; asst. contr. Bay Area Seating Svc., Oakland, Calif., 1985-87; mgr. acctg. and fin. divsn. Grand Met. Plc (Pillsbury) The Häagen Dazs Co. Inc., Hayward, Calif., 1987-90; corp. contr. Andronico's Park & Shop Inc., Albany, Calif., 1991; divsn. contr. Core-Mark Internat., Hayward, 1991-93; founder, owner Gruber Fin. Sys. Svcs. (GFS), 1993—; mid-Pacific regional fin. acctg. contr. DFS, L.P., Tamuning, Guam, 1993-95; CFO, treas. Tool&Garden.com, 1999-2000; v.p. fin. Golden State Internat., Inc., Oakland, Calif., 2000—01. Guest lectr. fin. San Francisco State U., 1990-91; CFO, sr. v.p. Indoor Air Quality Inc. Coach Willie Mays Youth Baseball, San Francisco; umpire San Fransciso Youth Baseball League, No. Calif. Little League, San Francisco; coach Pony League Baseball Team; mem. No. Calif. Umpire Assn. Mem. Inst. Mgmt. Accts. (v.p. edn. 1991-92, pres. 1992-93, cert. of appreciation 1992-93), Assn. for Fin. Profls., Nat. Soc. Pub. Accts., VFW, Am. Legion. Avocations: cycling, archery, pistol, martial arts (tang soo do). Home and Office: Gruber Fin Svcs Co 432 Congo St San Francisco CA 94131-3111 Home Fax: 415-680-2540. E-mail: GGruber@PacBell.net.

GRUBER, IRA DEMPSEY, historian, educator; b. Phila., Jan. 6, 1934; married; 3 children. AB, Duke U., 1955, AM, 1959, PhD, 1961. Instr. history Duke U., 1961-62; fellow Inst. Early Am. History and Culture, 1962-65; asst. prof. Occidental Coll., 1965-66; from asst. prof. to assoc. prof., 1966-74; prof. Rice U., Houston, from 1974, now Harris Masterson prof. history, chmn. dept. history, 1983-87. Master Hanszen Coll., Rice U., 1968-73; John F. Morrison prof. U.S. Army Command and Gen. Staff Coll., 1979-80; vis. prof. mil. history U.S. Mil. Acad., 1984-85, 92-93; mem. hist. adv. com. USAF, 1987-91, Dept. Army, 1992-95; trustee Soc. for Mil. History, 1987-95. Author: Lord Howe and Lord George Germain, 1965, The American Revolution as a Conspiracy: The British View, 1969, The Howe Brothers and the American Revolution, 1972, The Education of Sir Henry Clinton, 1990; co-author: Classical Traditions in Early America, 1976, Reconsiderations on the Revolutionary War, 1978, Limits of Loyalty, 1980, Arms and Independence, 1984, Against All Enemies, 1986, America's First Battles, 1986, Warfare in the Western World, 1996; editor: John Peebles American War, 1998; mem. editl. bd. Jour. of Mil. History, 1995—, chair editl. bd., 1999—. Office: Rice Univ Dept History 6100 Main St Houston TX 77005-1892 E-mail: gruber@rice.edu.

GRUBER, JACK, virologist, cancer research program administrator, medical researcher; b. Bklyn., Apr. 18, 1931; s. Harry and Rose (Kramer) Gruber; m. Patricia Ann Mason, June 28, 1964; 1 child, Harry Mason. BS, CUNY, Bklyn., 1954; PhD, U. Ky., 1963. Rsch. asst., lab. instr. dept. microbiology U. Ky., Lexington, 1955-61; rsch. bacteriologist U.S. Army Biol. Labs., Ft. Detrick, Frederick, Md., 1962-63; bacterial immunology microbiologist Med. Scis. Lab., Ft. Detrick, 1963-67, viral immunology microbiologist, 1967-70; microbiologist, rsch. program adminstr. viral biology br. Nat. Cancer Inst., NIH, 1970-72, chief office of program resources and logistics, viral oncology program, 1972-78, asst. chief biol. carcinogenesis br., divsn. cancer etiology, 1978-80, dep. chief biol. carcinogenesis br., divsn. cancer biology, 1980—84, chief, 1984—2003, chief cancer etiology br., divsn. cancer biology, 2003—. Editor (with others): Primates and Human Cancer, 1979; contbr. articles to profl. jours. Achievements include research in and publications on rheumatic fever and group A streptococci; on highly pathogenic bacteria; on development of various arbovirus vaccines; on the role of biological agents, especially viruses, in the etiology of human cancer. Office: National Cancer Institute NIH Exec Plz N # 5012 Bethesda MD 20892-0001 E-mail: jg65y@nih.gov.

GRUBER, JOHN BALSBAUGH, physics educator, university administrator; b. Hershey, Pa., Feb. 10, 1935; s. Irvin John and Erla R. (Balsbaugh) G.; m. Judith Anne Higer, June 20, 1961; children: David Powell, Karen Leigh, Mark Balsbaugh. BS, Haverford (Pa.) Coll., 1957; PhD, U. Calif. at Berkeley, 1961. NATO postdoctoral fellow Inst. Tech. Physics, Tech. U. Darmstadt, Germany, 1961-62, gastdozent, 1961-62; asst. prof. physics UCLA, 1962-66; assoc. prof. physics Wash. State U., Pullman, 1966-71, prof. chem. physics, 1971-75; asst. dean Wash. State U. (Grad. Sch.), 1968-70, assoc. dean, 1970-72; prof. physics, dean Coll. Sci. and Math., N.D. State U., Fargo, 1975-80; prof. physics and chemistry, v.p. for acad. affairs Portland (Oreg.) State U., 1980-84; prof. physics San Jose State U., 1984—, acad. v.p., 1984-86, v.p. devel., 1986, dir. Inst. for Modern Optics, 1992—, chmn. dept. physics, 2001—. Vis. prof. Joint Ctr. Grad. Study, Richland, Wash., 1964, 65, 66, Ames Lab., Dept. of Energy, Iowa State U., 1976-80; Disting. vis. prof. U.S. Navy Naval Weapons Ctr., China Lake, Calif., 1984-93, Stanford U., 1993—; invited lectr., U.S., Can., Europe, 1966—; cons. in laser physics and spectroscopy Aerospace Corp., El Segundo, Calif., 1962-65, Douglas Aircraft and McDonnell Douglas Astronautics Co., Santa Monica, Calif., 1963-69, N.Am. Aviation, Space and Info. Systems, Downey, Calif., 1964-66, Battelle-Northwest, Richland, Wash., 1964-69, Los Alamos (N.Mex.) Sci. Lab., 1969-71, 73-74; mem. task force lunar exploration sci. Apollo, NASA, 1964-69, 71-73; cons. Army Rsch. Lab., Adelphi Ctr., U.S. Army, 1991—, IBM, 1985-90, GTE, 1986-89, Lasergenics, 1986—, Night Vision Lab. U.S. Army, Ft. Belvoir, 1993—, Deltron, 1990-91, Rey Tech Corp., 1998-2002, Laser Sci. and Tech., 1999—, Bicron Corp., 2000—, Spectragen Corp., 2000, SAIC, 2002--, Battelle, 1994—; mem. Rare Earth Rsch. Conf. Com., 1976-83, exec. com., 1977-83, sec. bd. dirs., 1979-84, gen. conf. chmn. XIV Internat. Rare Earth Rsch. Conf., 1979, Novel Laser Sources and Materials, 1992; exec. sec. Internat. Frank H. Spedding Award, 1979, 83, Willig award, 1986, Internat. Spencer prize for outstanding contbrn. to sci., 1987, Pres.'s Scholar, 1994-95, Outstanding Achievement awards U.S. Dept. Def., 1995, 96, 98, 01, 02, Nom. U.S. Asst. Sec. Def. (Spl. Ops.), 1986-87; chmn. U.S. Navy/ASEE Postdoctoral Selection Bd., 1988-2002, U.S. Nat. Inst. Sci. and Tech. Postdoctoral Selection Bd., 1989-91; mem. rev. panel U.S. Navy/ASEE Grad. Fellowship Program, 1990—; chmn., mem. NASA/ASEE program rev. bd., 1994-98; chmn. Internat. Conf. on Novel Laser Sources and Applications, San Jose, Calif., 1993, chmn. Battelle U.S. Dept. Def. Scholarship Program, 1994-2001; mem. Battelle Sci. Bd. for selection of grad. scholarship fellows, 1998-99; vis. scholar Stanford U., 1993—. Contbr. articles to profl. jours., chpts. to books; holder numerous patents in laser sci. and tech. Trustee Symphony Bd. Fargo-Moorhead Symphony Orch., 1978-80; mem. N.D. State Bd. PTA; chmn. Univ., Coll. and Pub. Sch. Rels. Bd., 1979-80; active Boy Scouts Am.; trustee Pullman Pub. Libr., 1973-75, N.D. Symphony Orchs. Assn., 1978-80; mem. planning commn. City of Pullman, 1972-75; bd. dirs. Westminster Found., 1982-84. Recipient Outstanding Merit and Performance award San Jose State U., 1990, San Jose State Pres.'s Scholar award, 1994-95, Dist. Tchr./scholar award, 1996, 97, 99, Disting. Performance award in the field of lasers and electro-optics U. Chgo., 1995, Citation for Svc. and Achievement Dept. of Def., 1996, Award for Rsch. into night vision devices U.S. Army, 1997, Outstanding World Leadership in Sci. award Acad. Scis., Poland, 1998; grantee AEC-ERDA, 1963-75, NSF, 1966-72, 76-78, 92—, U.S. Army Rsch. Office, Durham, 1979-80, Am. Chem. Soc. Petroleum Rsch. Funds, 1979-80, Dept. Energy, 1979-84, Dept. Def., 1984—, Office Naval Rsch., 1987—, Office Naval Tech., 1988-93, Dept. Def., DARPA, 1998—; fellow NASA Ames Lab., 1993-95; vis. scholar Stanford U., 1993—. Fellow Am. Soc. Engring. Edn. (disting.), Am. Phys. Soc. (chmn. nat. mtg. sessions), Am. Acad. Spectral Scis.; mem. AAAS, IEEE (sec. lasers and electro-optics 1995-96), NSF (reviewer and panel mem. divsn. material sci. 1994—), N.Y. Acad. Scis., N.D. Acad. Sci., Oreg. Acad. Sci., Acad. Scis. of Ukraine, Nat. Acad. Scis. (com. on lasers and electro-optics), Coun. Colls. Arts and Scis., Optical Soc. No. Calif. (v.p. 1992, pres. 1993), Lasers and Electro-optics Soc. (mem. program com. nat. meeting 1995), Internat. Soc. Optical Engring. (bd. dirs. 1993), Phi Beta Kappa, Sigma Xi, Phi Kappa Phi, Sigma Pi Sigma, Phi Sigma Iota. Office: San Jose State U Dept Physics San Jose CA 95192-0106 E-mail: jbgruber@email.sjsu.edu.

GRUBER, JOHN EDWARD, editor, railroad historian, photographer; b. Chgo., May 18, 1936; s. Edward David and Leah Elizabeth (Diehl) G.; m. Bonnie Jean Barstow, May 12, 1962; children: Richard J., Timothy J. BA in Journalism, U. Wis., 1959, postgrad., 1981-84. Editor, writer U. Wis., Madison, 1960-95; editor Vintage Rails, Waukesha, Wis., 1995-99. Author: Focus on Rails, 1989, (pamphlet) Madison's Pioneer Buildings, 1987; co-author: Caboose, 2001, (posters) Travel by Train, 2002, Railway Photography, 2003; acting editor Rail News, 1999; also articles; contbr. photographs to Trains mag., 1960—; contbg. editor: Classic Trains, 2000—. Dir. Historic Madison, Inc., 1981-89. Recipient Nat. Award in R.R. History for photography Rwy. and Locomotive Hist. Soc., 1994, James J. Hill rsch. grantee Hill Reference Libr., 1986. Mem. Mid-Continent Railway Hist. Soc. (bd. dirs. 1984-87, 88-97, pres. 1988-89, sec. 1990-95, v.p. 1995-97, editor Mid-Continent Railway Gazette 1982-99), Ctr. for R.R. Photography and Art (pres. 1997—). Home: 1430 Drake St Madison WI 53711-2211

GRUBERG, CY, educational administrator; b. Kingston, N.Y., Aug. 23, 1928; s. Joseph and Sara J. (Jacobson) G. BS, Rider U.; MA, Syracuse U., 1949; postgrad. guidance and counseling, Columbia U.; postgrad., NYU, Hofstra U., Adelphi U., U. Maine, U. Vt.; PhD, Columbia Pacific U., 1980. Tchr., guidance counselor Wellington C. Mepham High Sch., Bellmore, N.Y., 1949-60; guidance counselor, dean and dir. guidance Lynbrook (L.I.) High Sch., 1960-66; asst. prof. State U. N.Y. at New Paltz, 1966-67; dir. pupil pers. svcs. and guidance Hastings-on-Hudson (N.Y.) Pub. Schs., 1967-85; dir. coll. counseling Univ. Sch. Nova Southeastern U., Ft. Lauderdale, Fla., 1985-2000, pvt. ind. cons., 2000—. Group leader summer resident camps, 1950— ; mem. faculty Inst. Beau Soliel, Villars, Switzerland, 1955; tour dir. summer tours, U.S., Europe, Russia, Israel, Mexico, Can., 1961— ; instr. adult edn. Mepham High Sch., 1950-55; mem. faculty Roosevelt Sch., summers 1949-50; admissions interviewer Columbia U., 1985; faculty of Focus at Tufts U., Medford, Mass., summer 1990-91. Cons. N.C.C.J.; Active local drives Nat. Cerebral Palsy Assn., Am. Cancer Soc., Muscular Dystrophy Found., Cystic Fibrosis Found. (bd. dirs. Mid-Hudson Valley Region, N.Y.), Leukemia Soc. Am., also, Community Scholarship drives; exec. bd. Nassau County Boys and Girls Week Com.; adv. com. Hastings Youth Employment Svc.; adv. coun. Graham Home; chmn. Hastings Student Project Com.; Mem. Hastings Safety Commn.; bd. dirs. Echo Hills Mental Hill Clinic, Dobbs Ferry, N.Y.; vol. Cleve. Clinic Hosp., Weston, Fla. Served to 1st lt. AUS, World War II. Recipient Nat. citation Parents' mag., 1960-65; scholar workshop human rels. U. Maine, 1958; recipient William O. Hamilton award Key club N.Y. State, 1964, 72; June 3, 1981 proclaimed Cy Gruberg Day, Westchester County, N.Y. Execs.; named to Sr. Hall of Fame, Broward County, Fla, 2000. Mem. VFW, N.Y. State Tchrs. Assn., N.Y. State Pers. and Guidance Assn., Am. Guidance and Pers. Assn., Westchester-Putnam-Rockland Pers. and Guidance Assn., NEA, So. Assn. Coll. Admissions Counselling, Am. Ednl. Rsch. Assn., Nat. Assn. for Coll. Admissions Counseling, Am. Legion, Jewish War Vets., Phi Delta Kappa, Zeta Beta Tau. Clubs: B'nai B'rith, Kiwanis. E-mail: DocCy24@aol.com. *Counseling is not advice-giving pep talks or lectures— this may be the most important thing we can say about it. Counseling is an art that takes much training, understanding, and practice. Counseling is an interaction between two people to produce change. In schools it is a process of relationship and interaction between an adult and an adolescent through which the youngster may achieve goals personal to himself. The concern is always a personal one and frequently private to the pupil concerned. Progress comes through the thinking that the individual-with-the-problem does for himself rather than through solutions suggested by the counselor. The counselor's function is to make this kind of thinking possible rather than to do it himself.*

GRUBERG, MARTIN, political science educator; b. N.Y.C., Jan. 28, 1935; s. Benjamin and Mollie (Stolnitz) G.; m. Rosaline Kurfirst, Mar. 25, 1967 (dec. 1980); m. Humaira Sayeed, Aug. 15, 1983. BA, CCNY, 1955; PhD, Columbia U., 1963. Agt.-adjudicator Passport Agy., Dept. State, N.Y.C, 1960-61; tchr. social studies Pelham (N.Y.) High Sch., 1961-62; instr. polit. sci. CUNY-Hunter Coll., 1961-62; tchr. social studies James Monroe and Seward Park High Schs., N.Y.C., 1962-63; asst. prof. polit. sci. U. Wis., Oshkosh, 1963-66, assoc. prof., 1966-69, prof., chmn. dept., 1969-72, dir. pre-law program, 1966-69, 83—, coord. criminal justice program, 1983-87. Author: Women in American Politics, 1968, A Case Study in U.S. Urban Leadership: The Incumbency of Milwaukee Mayor Henry Maier, 1996, A History of Winnebago County Government, 1998, Introduction to Law, 2003; newspaper column: Women: Our Largest Minority, The Paper for Ctrl. Wiso., 1970-71, Spotlight on Women for Oshkosh Northwestern, 1971-73; Broadcast 16 weeks Civil Rights Revolution, Wis. State FM Network, 1974; editor: Wis. Polit. Scientist, 1986-91; contbr. articles to encys., profl. jours. Pres. Oshkosh Human Rights Coun., 1966-68; v.p. Winnebago chpt. NOW, 1970-71, sec. Oshkosh chpt., 1980-81, pres., 1981-83; pres. Women's Caucus of Midwest Polit. Scientists, 1980-81; pres. Fox Valley ACLU, 1985—. Recipient Am. Legion Aux. Americanism award, 1949, Buckvar award, 1955, Steigman award, 1955; N.Y. State scholar, 1952; Columbia grantee, 1961, 62, Wis. Regents' rsch. grantee, 1964-70, 73-75. Mem. AAUP (state sec. 1975-81, pres.-elect 1981-82, 91-92, pres. 1982-83, 92-93), Am. Polit. Sci. Assn., Midwest Polit. Sci. Assn., Wis. Polit. Sci. Assn. (pres. 1974-75), Law and Soc. Assn., Acad. Criminal Justice Scis., Candlelight Club, Optimists. Home: 2121 Oregon St Oshkosh WI 54902-7058 Office: U Wis Clow Hall Oshkosh WI 54901 E-mail: gruberg@uwosh.edu.

GRUBIN, SHARON E. lawyer; b. Newark, Feb. 9, 1949; d. Harold and Blanche (Dultz) G. AB with honors, Smith Coll., 1970; JD with honors in Legal Writing and Analysis, Boston U., 1973. Bar: N.Y. 1974, U.S. Dist. Ct. (so. and ea. dists.) N.Y. 1974, U.S. Ct. Appeals (2nd cir.) 1974. Litigator White & Case, N.Y.C., 1973-84; judge U.S. Dist. Ct. (so. dist.) N.Y., N.Y.C., 1984-2000; gen. counsel Metroplitan Opera, N.Y.C., 2000—. Chair 2d Cir. Task Force on Gender, Racial and Ethnic Fairness in the Cts.; lectr. NYU Sch. Law, Yale Law Sch., Bklyn. Law Sch., N.Y. Law Sch.; dir., sec., exec. com. Lawyers' Com. on Violence, Inc. Author: (with others) Advocacy-The Art of Pleading a Cause, 1985, Removal, Federal Civil Practice, 1989, and supplement, 1993; spkr. seminars in field. Mem. ABA (chair spl. projects com. 1996-97, nat. conf. fed. trial judges, jud. adminstrn. divsn.), Nat. Assn. Women Judges (chair fed. gender bias com., publicity and pub. affairs com., newsletter com.), Fed. Bar Coun. (trustee, exec. com., chair nominating com. 1994, v.p. 1990-94, award com. 1988-94, com. on 2d cir. cts. 1982-96, long-range planning com. 1992-96), N.Y. State Bar Assn. (exec. com., nominations com., fed. cts. task force, comml. and fed. litig. sect.), N.Y. State Assn. Women Judges (bd. dirs.), Assn. of Bar of City of N.Y. (long-range planning com., chair nominating com. 1995—, chair spl. com. on legal history 1994-96, chair spl. com. on Orison S. Marden Meml. lectrs., chair 1994-96, exec. com. 1990-94, spl. com. on gender bias in fed. cts. 1991-94, coun. on jud. adminstrn. 1986-90, prof. and jud. ethics com. 1986-89, nominating com. 1984-85, 95-96, com. on jud. 1982-83, chair young lawyers com. 1979-81, com. on entertainment law, 2001-), Am. Judicature Soc. (editl. com. 1994-97). Office: Metropolitan Opera Lincoln Ctr New York NY 10023

GRUBMAN, ALLEN J. lawyer; b. Bklyn., Dec. 30, 1942; BBA, CCNY, 1965; JD, Bklyn. Law Sch., 1967. Bar: N.Y. 1968. Ptnr. Grubman Indursky Schindler & Godlstein P.C., N.Y.C. Office: Grubman Indursky Schindler & Goldstein 152 W 57th St New York NY 10019-3310*

GRUBMAN, WALLACE KARL, chemical company executive; b. N.Y.C., Sept. 12, 1928; s. Samuel and Mildred G.;/ m. Ruth R. Winer, July 29, 1950; children: James (dec.), Steven L., Eric P. BSChemE, Columbia U., 1950; MS, NYU, 1954. With Nat. Starch and Chem. Corp., 1950-93, corp. v.p., gen. mgr. adhesive div., 1972-77, group v.p., 1977-78, pres., chief operating officer, dir., 1978-83, pres., chief exec. officer, 1983-84, chmn., chief exec. officer, 1984-85; group head chems. Unilever PLC and Unilever NV, 1986-91, also bd. dirs., 1986-91; pres. Ridge Assocs. Mgmt. Cons. Bd. dirs. Jorin Ltd., U.K. Fellow London Inst. Dirs., Instn. Chem. Engrs. London; mem. Soc. Chem. Industry, Am. Inst. Chem. Engrs., Princeton Club, Sky Club (N.Y.C.), Mid-Ocean (Bermuda) Club, Wentworth Golf (Eng.) Club, Chmns. Club (London). Office: PO Box 977 Ascot Berkshire SL5 ORD England

GRUCCI, FELIX J., JR., former congressman; Former pres Grucci Fireworks, NY; congressman NY First Dist., 2000—02. Republican. Office: 1505 Longworth House Office bldg Washington DC 20515 also: 1 Grucci Ln Brookhaven NY 11719

GRUCHACZ, CRAIG M. financial executive; b. Glen Ridge, N.J., Nov. 13, 1954; s. Thaddeus Adam and Edith (Wilby) G.; m. Rita Maria Maltino, May 25, 1980; children: Christina Maria, Gabrielle Lyn. BS in BA, Montclair (N.J.) State Coll., 1978; MBA in Fin., Seton Hall U., 1983. With Inspiration Copper Consol. Co., Morristown, N.J., 1978-79, Westinghouse Elec. Co., Bloomfield, N.J., 1979-83, Philips Lighting Co., Bloomfield, 1983-84, corp. cost mgr., 1984-86; group contr. Philips Electronics, N.Y.C., 1986-90; v.p., CFO Philips Electronic Instruments, Mahwah, N.J., 1990-92; sr. v.p., CFO Philips Credit Corp., N.Y.C., 1992-95; v.p., CFO Philips Lighting Co., Somerset, N.J., 1995—. Chmn. SAP steering com. Republican. Roman Catholic. Avocations: politics, financial markets, gardening, children. Home: 7 Vale Rd Whippany NJ 07981-2317 Office: Philips Lighting Co 200 Franklin Square Dr Somerset NJ 08873-4186 E-mail: craig.gruchacz@philips.com.

GRUCHACZ, ROBERT S. real estate executive; b. Bloomfield, N.J., May 15, 1929; s. Stanley A. and Mae (Zalenski) G.; m. LaVerne T. Stein, Mar. 2, 1957; children— Robert S., Thomas A., Christopher J. BS, Seton Hall U., 1950; MBA, NYU, 1971; student, Advanced Mgmt. Program, Harvard U., 1973. C.P.A., N.J. With Arthur Young & Co., C.P.A.'s, 1955-58, Sterling Drug Inc., N.Y.C., 1958-65; controller Nabisco Inc., 1965-72, asst. to pres., 1973-74, 76—, v.p., 1979-84; broker Dunes Mktg. Group and Sea Pines Realty, 1985-2001; exec. v.p. Aurora Products, 1974-76. Served as 1st lt. USAF, 1952-54. Mem. Am. Inst. CPAs. Home: 11 Timber Marsh Ln Hilton Head Island SC 29926-2790 Office: 6 Queens Folly Rd Hilton Head Island SC 29928-5110

GRUCHOT, LINDA, secondary school educator; Master's degree, St. Xavier U., 1997. Tchr. Cmty. H.S Dist. 218, Oak Lawn, Ill., 1992—. Mem.: NFCA, ICTM, NCTM, Phi Delta Kappa, Kappa Delta Pi.

GRUDA, BENJAMIN JOSEPH, pharmacist; b. New Brunswick, N.J., Mar. 22, 1947; s. Benjamin Joseph and Sophie Dolores (Michalowski) G.; m. Rita Lorraine Krzyzkowska, Oct. 17, 1970; children: Benjamin Joseph, Bryan Michael. BS in Pharmacy, St. John's U., Jamaica, N.Y., 1970; postgrad., St. Lawrence U., Canton, N.Y., 1984, U. R.I., 1991. Registered pharmacist, N.Y., N.J., Vt., Pa. Pharmacy intern Easton Pharmacy, New Brunswick, 1970-71; staff pharmacist Hawley's Drugs, Moravia, N.Y., 1971-72, Fay's Drugs, Syracuse, N.Y., 1972, pharmacy mgr. Potsdam, N.Y., 1972-85, regional pharmacy supr. Liverpool, N.Y., 1985-90, pharmacy mgr. Potsdam, 1991-97; chief pharmacist, dept. head Riverview Correctional Facility, Ogdensburg, N.Y., 1990-91; pharmacy mgr. Eckerd Drug, Potsdam, 1997—. Mem. adv. com. Glaxo SmithKline, Phila., 1997, 2003; mem. Pharmacy Technician Cert. Coun., Washington, 1997-2000, chmn., 1999; mem. adv. group System-Based Prescription Errors in the Outpatient Setting, Chgo., 1996; mem. editl. adv. bd. Jour. Am. Pharm. Assn., 1999-2002. Contbr. articles to profl. jours. Mem. Am. Pharm. Assn./Acad. Pharmacy Practice and Mgmt. (acad. officer 1989-97, pres. 1996-97); fellow Am. Pharm. Assn., Pharmacists Soc. State N.Y.(bd. dirs.

2000—, pres.-elect 2003, Spl. Recognition award 1997), Pharmacists Soc. No. N.Y. (pres. 1988-95), KC, Racquette River Toastmasters, Delta Sigma Theta Avocations: amateur radio, writing, outdoor sports, travel. Home: 80 Root Rd Potsdam NY 13676-3444 Office: Eckerd Drug 201 Market St Ste H Potsdam NY 13676-1200 E-mail: bgruda@northnet.org.

GRUDEN, JON, professional football coach; b. Sandusky, Ohio, Aug. 17, 1963; Student, U. Dayton. Asst. coach U. Tenn., 1986-87, U. Southeast Mo., 1988-89, San Francisco 49ers, 1990, U. Pitts., 1991, Green Bay Packers, 1992-94; offensive coord. Phila. Eagles, 1994-97; head coach Oakland Raiders, 1998—2002, Tampa Bay Buccaneers, 2002—. Office: Tampa Bay Buccaneers One Buccaneer Pl Tampa FL 33607

GRUDER, YARON E. foundation administrator; Dir. gen. The Wolf Found., Herzlia, Israel. Office: The Wolf Found PO Box 398 Herzlia BET46103 Israel also: 39 Hamaapilim St 46103 Herzlia Pitauach Israel

GRUE, ANN) LEE MEITZEN, poet, consultant; d. LeRoy Robert Meitzen and Catherine Bernice McCullar; m. Ronald David Grue, Oct. 28, 1963 (div. Sept. 5, 2000); children: Celeste Holiday Delafosse, Ian Bowditch, Teal Murdoch. BA in English, U. New Orleans, 1963; MFA in Fiction, Warren Wilson Coll., Asheville, North Carolina, 1982. Cert. cosmetologist La. Dir. New Orleans Poetry Forum, 1972—90; editor New Laurel Rev.; vis. writer Tulane U., New Orleans, 1993—98. Author: In the Sweet Balance of the Flesh, 1990, French Quarter Poems, 1994, Goodbye, Silver, Silver Cloud; editor: World Port, 1984, New Laurel Rev., 1982—. Recipient Syndicated Fiction award, PEN, 1984, Poetry and Short Story award, Deep South Writer Assn., 1994; fellow Residency, Va. Ctr. Creative Arts, 1986, 1988, 1991, Ledig Ho., 1998; grantee, NEA, 1984—85. Fellow: Newcomb Ctr. Resarch on Women (hon.; vis. scholar 2003—). Independent. Avocations: swimming, travel, yoga, jazz history. Home and Office: New Laurel Review 828 Lesseps Street New Orleans LA 70117 Personal E-mail: leeleegrue@aol.com. E-mail: leeleegrue@aol.com.

GRUE, THOMAS ANDREW, lawyer; b. Plattsburgh, N.Y., Sept. 21, 1959; s. Ellsworth Charles and Emily Ruth (Noseworthy) G., m. Karen Sue Couch, Apr. 19, 1986; children: Robert Thomas, Rachel Mae. BA, Cornell U., 1981; JD, SUNY, Buffalo, 1984. Bar: N.Y. 1984, U.S. Army Ct. Military Review, U.S. Dist. Ct. (no. dist.) N.Y. 1996, U.S. Supreme Ct. 1998. Assoc. Couch, White, Brenner, Howard & Fiegenbaum, Albany, N.Y., 1988-90; ptnr. Poissant, Nichols & Grue, P.C., Malone, N.Y., 1990—. Instr. Bus. Law, Kans. State U., Manhattan, 1985-86. Sr. editor Buffalo Law Review, 1982-83. Capt. U.S. Army, 1984-88. Mem. Franklin County Bar Assn., N.Y. State Bar Assn., N.Y.C. Civil and Criminal Bar Assn. Home: 21 Morton St Malone NY 12953-1614 Office: Poissant Nichols & Grue PC 367 W Main St Malone NY 12953-1813

GRUEBELE, MARTIN, chemistry, physics, and biophysics educator; b. Stuttgart, Federal Republic of Germany, Jan. 10, 1964; came to U.S., 1980; s. Helmut and Edith Victoria (Berner) G.; m. Nancy Makri, July 10, 1992; 2 children. BS in Chemistry, U. Calif., Berkeley, 1984, PhD in Chemistry, 1988. Rsch. fellow Calif. Inst. Tech., Pasadena, 1989-92; asst. prof. dept. chemistry U. Ill., Urbana, 1992-98, assoc. prof., 1998-99, prof. chemistry and biophysics, 1999—2000, prof. chemistry, physics, and biophysics, 2000—01, Alumni Scholar prof. chemistry, prof. physics, biophysics and computational biology, 2002—. Sr. editor Jour. Phys. Chemistry; mem. editl. bd. Jour. Chem. Physics., Chem. Phys. Lett., Ann. Rev. Phys. Chem., Chem. Physics. Recipient New Faculty award Dreyfus Found., 1992, Nat. Young Investigator award NSF, 1994, Coblentz award, 2000; fellow IBM, 1986-87, Dow Chem. Co., 1987-88, David and Lucile Packard Found., 1994, Sloan fellow, 1997; Cottrell scholar, 1995, Camille and Henry Dreyfus scholar, 1998, Alfred P. Sloan fellow, 1998; Univ. scholar U. Ill., 1998. Fellow Am. Phys. Soc.; mem. Am. Chem. Soc., Biophys. Soc., Sigma Xi. Achievements include research of theoretical and experimental studies of novel transient molecular species, studies in laser-control of chemical reactions and molecular vibrational relaxation, as well as fast time-resolved protein folding dynamics. Office: U Ill Dept Chemistry Box 5-6 600 S Mathews Ave Urbana IL 61801-3602

GRUEN, DAVID HENRY, financial executive, consultant; b. Buffalo, Aug. 12, 1929; s. Edward Charles and Florence (Knoche) G.; m. Joan Willard, Jan. 3, 1976; children by previous marriage: David E., Stephen P., Cathryn E., Edward Charles II, William A. BA, Cornell U., 1951, MBA, 1954. C.P.A., N.Y. Sr. accountant Arthur Andersen & Co., N.Y.C., 1954-59; asst. treas. Marine Midland Banks, Inc., 1959-60, asst. v.p., 1960-63, v.p., treas., 1963-69; sr. v.p. Marine Midland Bank-Western, 1969-74; sr. v.p., treas. Marine Midland Banks, Inc., Buffalo, 1974-80; sr. v.p., gen. auditor, 1980-85; cons. Gruen Assocs., Buffalo, 1986—; v.p., chief fin. officer Niagara Envelope Group Inc., Buffalo, N.Y., 1986-89. Served from 2d lt. to 1st lt. USAF, 1951-53. Mem. Am. Inst. C.P.A.s, Tax Execs. Inst., N.Y. Soc. C.P.A.s, Fin. Execs. Inst. Home: 34 Middlesex Rd Buffalo NY 14216-3616

GRUEN, GERALD ELMER, psychologist, educator; b. Granite City, Ill., July 19, 1937; s. Elmer George and Velma Pearl G.; m. Karol Jane Selvidge, Mar. 20, 1960; children— Tami Jane, Christy Lynn. BA, So. Ill. U., 1959; MA, U. Ill., 1963, PhD, 1964. Postdoctoral fellow Heinz Werner Inst. of Developmental Psychology, Clark U. and Worcester (Mass.) State Hosp., 1964-66; asst. prof. dept. psychol. scis. Purdue U., West Lafayette, Ind., 1966-69, assoc. prof., 1969-74, prof., 1974—, head dept. psychol. scis., 1987-97. Author: (with T. Wachs) Early Experience and Human Development; contbr. chpt. to The Structuring of Experience, 1977; contbr. articles to profl. jours. Deacon Calvary Baptist Ch., West Lafayette. Recipient USPHS rsch. awards, 1968-71, Nat. Rsch. Svc. award NIMH, 1976-80, Research award Nat. Insts. Child Health and Human Devel., 1981—; recipient Ind. Psychol. Assn. Gordon Barrows award for disting. career contbns., 2000. Fellow APA, Am. Psychol. Soc. (charter mem.); mem. Midwestern Psychol. Assn., Soc. for Rsch. in Child Devel., Sigma Xi. Home: 3738 Westlake Ct West Lafayette IN 47906 Office: Purdue U Psychology Dept West Lafayette IN 47907 E-mail: gruen@psych.purdue.edu.

GRUEN, JANE SWAN, retired educator, lecturer; b. Chester, Pa., Nov. 10, 1925; d. Roscoe Frederick and Elizabeth (Cochran) Ballard; m. Alfred Swan, June 1947 (dec. June 1970); child: Alexis; m. Robert Gruen, May 17, 1979. BA, Swarthmore Coll., 1947; MA, U. Penn., 1949, PhD, 1955. Mem. faculty Agnes Irwin Sch., Wynnewood, Pa., 1969-70, Moore Coll. Art, Phila., 1970-75; prof. Russian history West Chester (Pa.) U., 1975-97. Bd. dirs. Delaware Valley Historians; lectr. in Russian history, French history, world civilization. Author: Biography of Patriarch Tikhon, 1964, The Lost Children: A Russian Odyssey, 1989. Jane B. Swan Scholarship named in her honor, 1982; Bennett Fellow Univ. Pa., 1949, Disting. Tchg. Fellow with Chair in History, Commonwealth Pa., 1980-83. Mem.: Phi Delta Theta, Alpha Lambda Delta. Home: 523 Old Buck Ln Haverford PA 19041

GRUEN, MARGARET, actress; b. N.Y.C., July 24, 1949; d. Arno G. and Judith (Goldstein) Milenbach. Student, Yale Sch. Drama. Actress. Writer, performer (theatre) Tanya Talks: The Last Jew, 1997, The Young Sophisticate, 1994, What A Wonderful World, 1990, Dracula, 1970; one-woman show: Grenfell's Eccentric Characters; appeared in theatre, TV, and radio prodns., including Uncle Vanya, Garcia Lorca's New York; mem. comedy team The Chamansky Sisters. Mem. Am. Fedn. Television & Radio Artists, Actors Equity Assn., Screen Actors Guild.

GRUEN, MICHAEL STEPHAN, lawyer; b. L.A., Mar. 25, 1942; s. Victor and Elsie Caroline (Krummeck) G.; m. Susanna Lloyd, July 18, 1964; m. Vanessa Elisabeth Ahlfors, Jan. 3, 1976; children: Madeleine Gruen, Alexis Cutchins, Viveca Gruen; stepchildren: Stefan Keneas, Sebastian Keneas. BA cum laude, Harvard U., 1963; LLB, UCLA, 1966. Bar: Calif. 1966, N.Y. 1967, U.S. Ct. Appeals (2d cir.) 1976, U.S. Supreme Ct. 1975, U.S. Dist. Ct. (so. and ea. dists.) N.Y. 1986. Assoc. Paul, Weiss, Rifkind, Wharton & Garrison, N.Y.C., 1966-69, Gilinsky, Stillman & Mishkin, N.Y.C., 1969-70, Wolf, Popper, Ross, Wolf & Jones, N.Y.C., 1970-74; gen. counsel Bio-Med. Scis., Inc., Fairfield, N.J., 1974-75; pvt. practice N.Y.C., 1975-80; mem. Gruen & Muskin, N.Y.C., 1980, Gruen, Muskin & Thau, N.Y.C., 1981-88, Gruen, Gilliatt & Livingston, N.Y.C., 1989-90, Gruen & Livingston, N.Y.C., 1990-97, Gruen & Farrelly LLP, N.Y.C., 1998—2001; counsel Vandenberg & Feliu, LLP, 2002—. Contbr. articles to legal and gen. publs. Chmn. Historic Dists. Coun., 1974—79; dir. Learning Through an Expanded Arts Program, 2001—; mem. bd. advisors Prep divsn. Bklyn. Coll. Ctr. for Performing Arts, 1980—83; mem. law com. Mcpl. Art Soc., 1987—; pres. Riverside Dems., N.Y.C., 1971—72; bd. dirs. Columbia Land Conservancy, 1986—2002, pres., 1988—91; bd. dirs. N.Y. Landmarks Conservancy, 1972—94, mem. adv. coun., 1994—97; dir. Abingdon Theatre Co. N.Y., 2001—; bd. dirs. Boys' Athletic League, 1966—82. Mem. ABA (litig. sect.), N.Y. State Bar Assn., Assn. of Bar of City of N.Y. Office: Ste 1502 110 E 42nd St New York NY 10017-8521 E-mail: mgruen@vanfeliu.com.

GRUENBECK, LAURIE, librarian; b. Sebewaing, Mich., Mar. 4, 1936; d. Ernest R. and Gertrude M. (Dierks) G. BA, Valparaiso (Ind.) U., 1961; MS in Libr. Sci., Our Lady of the Lake U., 1971. Deaconess Zion Luth Ch., Oklahoma City, 1961-62, Caracas, Venezuela, 1962-64; 3rd and 4th grade tchr. Zion Luth. Sch., Hemlock, Mich., 1964; 4th grade tchr. Saginaw Pub. Schs., 1965-67; substitute, cataloger San Antonio Pub. Libr., 1967-72, cataloger, 1972-77, br. mgr., 1977—98; ret., 1998. Adminstr. of adult edn. classes Bazan Br. Libr., San Antonio, 1983-96. Mem. ALA, Internat. Reading Assn., Tex. Libr. Assn., Hymn Soc. U.S. and Can. Democrat. Roman Catholic. Avocations: collecting christmas carol (religious) books and records, mexican cookbooks. Home: 3103 Saunders Ave San Antonio TX 78207-4050

GRUENBERG, GLADYS WALLEMAN, economics educator, arbitrator; b. Milw., June 22, 1920; d. John Matthew and Olive Anna (Glassner) Walleman; m. Harold Gruenberg, Dec. 27, 1946; children: Sandra Louise Gruenberg Davis, Dorothy Laura, Daniel Richard. AB, Marquette U., Milw., 1940; AM, St. Louis U., 1949, PhD, 1952. Life sr. profl. human resources. Field examiner NLRB, St. Louis, 1944-46; rsch. dir. Retail, Wholesale and Dept. Store Union, St. Louis, 1946-47; grad. instr. St. Louis U., 1949-52, asst. prof., 1952-55, assoc. prof., 1969-77, prof. econs. and indsl. rels., 1977-83; prof. emeritus, 1983—. Mem. labor and employment arbitration panel Am. Arbitration Assn., N.Y.C., 1970—; mem. arbitration panel Fed. Mediation and Conciliation Svc., Washington, 1972—, Nat. Med. Bd., 1974—, State PERBS, Iowa, Ill. and Kans., 1974—. Co-author: International Payoffs, 1977, Ethical Perspectives on Business and Society, 1977, Fifty Years in the World of Work: A History of the National Academy of Arbitrators, 1997; author: Biography of Father Leo C. Brown S.J., 1981, Career Planning Manual for HRM/Personnel, 1980, editor Annual Proc. Nat. Acad. of Arbitrators, 1987-95. Pub. mem. Spl. Com. on Labor Rels. in Pub. Employment, 1977, Gov. Coun. on Campaign Reform, 1978, Ad Hoc Com. on Nursing Homes in Mo., 1979; mem. Gov.'s Com. on Mgmt. and Productivity, 1994. Mem. Nat. Acad. Arbitrators (bd. govs. 1987-90, v.p. 1996-98), Assn. for Social Econs. (exec. bd. 1981-83), Indsl. Rels. Rsch. Assn. (exec. bd. 1977-80), Soc. Human Resource Mgmt. (life), Midwest Econ. Assn. (1st v.p. 1975-76), Phi Beta Kappa (hon.), Omicron Delta Epsilon, Beta Gamma Sigma. Office: St Louis U 3674 Lindell Blvd Saint Louis MO 63108-3302

GRUENBERGER, PETER, lawyer; b. Czechoslovakia, May 19, 1937; came to U.S., 1941; s. Leslie and Olga (Zollman) G.; m. Carin Lamm; children: Karen, Richard, Lauren. AB, Columbia U., 1958, LLB, 1961. Bar: N.Y. 1962, U.S. Dist. Ct. (so., ea. and no. dists.) N.Y. 1962, U.S. Ct. Appeals (1st and 2d cirs.) 1963, U.S. Supreme Ct. 1964. Assoc. Hughes, Hubbard & Reed, N.Y.C., 1962-69; ptnr. Weil, Gotshal & Manges, N.Y.C., 1970—, mng. ptnr. Tex. office Houston, 1988-90. Contbr. articles on litigation to profl. jours. Served as 1st lt. U.S. Army, 1961-62. Harlan Fiske Stone scholar, 1959-61. Mem. ABA (chmn. various coms. 1973-75, 79-86, spl. com. on class actions and discovery 1977-86, governing council 1975-78, litigation sect.), Assn. of Bar of City of N.Y. (grievance com. 1975-77). Office: Weil Gotshal & Manges 767 5th Ave Fl Concl New York NY 10153-0119

GRUENFELD, KEVIN E. marketing professional, researcher; b. Jackson, N.J., Apr. 22, 1973; s. Norman G. and Judy F. (Barbash) G. BA in Psychology, Coll. of N.J., 1995; MA in Clin. Psychology, No. Ill. U., 1997. Computer lab mgr. Coll. of N.J., Trenton, 1993-95; intern/asst. counselor SERV/Mercer, Trenton, 1994; therapist Psychol. Svcs. Ctr./No. Ill. U., DeKalb, 1995-97; tchg. asst. psychology dept. No. Ill. U., 1995-96, rsch. assoc. Anxiety Disorders Rsch. Lab., 1996-97; project dir. Nat. Youth Leadership Coun./Nat. Svc. Learning Conf., 1997-98; opers. mgr. Nat. Analysts, Inc., Phila., 1998—2003. Contbr. Ency. of AIDS, 1998. Mem. Bugles Across Am., Logan Square Town Watch, Phila., 2001—, others; pres., co-founder, Philly Runners running club. Mem.: APA, Am. Psychol. Soc., Psi Chi. Avocations: performing and composing music, fitness, photography, cooking, theatre.

GRUENWALD, GEORGE HENRY HENRY, new products development management consultant, writer; b. Chgo, Ill, Apr. 23, 1922; s. Arthur Frank and Helen (Duke) G.; m. Corrine Rae Linn, Aug. 16, 1947; children: Helen Marie Gruenwald Orlando, Paul Arthur. BS in Journalism, Northwestern U., 1947; student, Evanston Acad. Fine Arts, 1937-38, Chgo. Acad. Fine Arts, 1938-39, Grinnell Coll., 1940-41. Asst. to pres. UARCO, Inc., Chgo., 1947-49; creative dir., mgr. mdse. Willys-Overland Motors Inc., Toledo, 1949-51; new products, brand and advt. mgr. Toni Co./Gillette, Chgo., 1951-53; v.p., creative dir., account supr. E.H. Weiss Agy., Chgo., 1953-55; exec. v.p., mgmt. supr. North Advt., Chgo., 1955-71; pres., treas., dir. Pilot Products, Chgo., 1963-71; pres., dir. Advance Brands, Inc., Chgo., 1963-71; owner Venture Group, 1971—; exec. v.p., dir. Campbell Mithun Inc., Chgo., 1971-72, pres., dir., 1972-79, chmn., dir., 1979-81, CEO, dir., 1981-83, chief creative officer, dir., 1983-84; vice-chmn., dir. Ted Bates Worldwide, NYC, 1979-80, mgmt. cons. new product devel., 1984—; exec. v.p., dir. Campbell Mithun Inc., Mpls. Author: New Product Development-What Really Works, 1985, 2d edit., New Product Development-Responding to Market Demand, 1992, How to Create Profitable New Products, 1997, (workbook) New Product Development Checklists: From Mission to Market, 1991, (videos) New Products Seven Steps to Success, 1988, New Product Development, 1989; editor-in-chief Oldsmobile Rocket Cir. mag., 1955-65, Hudson Family mag., 1953-56; feature writer Mktg. News, 1988—; contbr. articles to profl. jour. Trustee Chgo. Pub. TV Assn., 1969-73, Mpls. Soc. Fine Arts, 1975-83, Linus Pauling Inst. Sci. and Medicine, Palo Alto, 1984-92, 95-96; advisor Linus Pauling Inst., Oreg. State U., Corvallis, 1996—; chmn., v.p., chmn. class reps. Northwestern U. Alumni Fund Coun., Chgo., 1965-68; trustee, chmn., chmn. exec. com. Twin Cities Pub. TV Corp., 1971-84; trustee Minn. Pub. Radio Inc., 1973-77, vice chmn., 1974-75; bd. dirs., mem. exec. com. PBS, Alexandria, Va., 1978-86, 88-94, mem. comm. adv. com., 1993-95, vice chmn. task force on funding, 1991-92; chmn. task force on tech. applications, lay rep., 1971—; del. Am.'s Pub. TV Stas., Washington, 1971—; bd. dirs. St. Paul Chamber Orch., 1982-84, San Diego Chamber Orch., 1986-88; mem. adv. bd. San Diego State U. Pub. Broadcasting Comty., 1986—, pub. rels. specialist, editor. With USAAF, 1943-45, MTO. Recipient Hermes award Chgo. Federated Advt. Clubs, 1963, Ednl. TV awards, 1969, 71, 86, Best of the Best award San Diego Book Awards, 1997; charter mem. Medill Sch. Journalism Hall of Achievement, 1997. Mem. Am. Mktg. Assn., Am. Assn. Advt. Agys. (mgmt. com. 1976-84), Nat. Soc. Profl. Journalists, Am. Inst. Wine and Food (bd. dir. 1985-92). Office: PO Box 1696 Rancho Santa Fe CA 92067-1696 *To learn. To teach. To make a difference.*

GRUENWALD, GEZA, plastics consultant; b. Budapest, Hungary, Sept. 13, 1919; s. Julius and Martha (Ebner) G.; m. Marianne Pabst, Mar. 9, 1949; 1 child, Claudia. DEng, Tech. U., Berlin, 1943. Registered profl. engr., Pa. Chemist, tech. svc. Farbwerke Hoechst, Frankfurt-am-Main, Germany, 1950-57; devel. chemist Gen. Electric, Pittsfield, Mass., 1957-60, material sci., mgr. Erie, Pa., 1960-80; plastics cons. Erie, 1980—. Author: (textbook) Thermoforming, A Plastics Processing Guide, 1987, 2d edit., 1998, Plastics, How Structure Determines Properties, 1993; contbr. articles to profl. jours.; patentee in field. Mem. Am. Chem. Soc., Soc. Plastics Engrs., German Chem. Soc. Home and Office: 36 W 34th St Erie PA 16508-2812 E-mail: ggruenwald9@cs.com.

GRUENWALD, JAMES HOWARD, association executive, consultant; b. Cin., Aug. 30, 1949; s. Howard Francis and Geraldine Emma (Mueller) G. BS, Xavier U., 1971. Cert. profl. in recreation and leisure svc., Ill. Rep. pub. rels. Cath. Youth Orgn., Cin., 1969-72; sales rep. Spade Trucking Co., Cin., 1972-73; field rep. Ohio Dept. Transport, Columbus, 1973-76; editl., sales rep. Cin. Suburban Newspaper, 1977-79; nat. exec. dir. Say Soccer USA, Cin., 1979-93; co-founder, exec. dir. U.S. Indoor Soccer Orgn., 1985-93, 1985-90; bd. dirs. Buckeye Men's Baseball, Cin., 1982-90, chmn., 1982-86, 89-90; dir. Amateur Athletic Union, Indpls., 1983-85; nat. membership coord. Am. Youth Soccer Orgn., L.A., 1993-2001. Cert. trainer Am. Coaches Effectiveness Program, Champaign, Ill., 1983-92. Editor Touchline jour., 1980-92, Parents Guide to Soccer, 1985-92. Adv. bd. Church Parish, Cin., 1974-76. Recipient cmty. svc. award State of Mich., 1986. Mem. Nat. Coun. Youth Sports Dirs., Nat. Recreation and Parks Assn., Mich. Recreation and Parks Assn. (cmty. svc. award 1986), Soc. for Non Profits. Avocations: hiking, reading, writing, teaching, conducting workshops. Home and Office: Apt 4 4886 Holiday Dr Fairfield OH 45014-2862 E-mail: jimmygee@aol.com.

GRUENWALD, MARK EDWARD, mathematics educator; b. Swift Current, Sask., Can., Aug. 29, 1959; came to U.S., 1968; s. Edward George and Florence Virginia (Hecht) G.; m. Margaret Lee Davis, June 26, 1982; children: David, Benjamin, Matthew. BA, Concordia Coll., River Forest, Ill., 1981; MS, No. Ill. U., 1985, PhD, 1989. Computer programmer Concordia Coll. Computer Network, 1981-83; part-time instr. Concordia Coll., 1982-83; grad. asst., part-time instr. No. Ill. U., DeKalb, 1983-89; asst. prof. math. U. Evansville, Ind., 1989-95, assoc. prof. math., 1995—2003, prof. math., 2003—, chair math. dept., 1998—. Co-author: College Algebra, 1995, College Algebra and Trigonometry, 1997; contbr. articles to profl. jours. Dissertation fellow No. Ill. U., 1987; ARTS grantee U. Evansville, 1990, 91. Mem. Math. Assn. Am., S.W. Ind. Coun. Tchrs. Math. (bd. dirs. 1990-92, pres. 1993-94). Lutheran. Office: U Evansville 1800 Lincoln Ave Evansville IN 47722

GRUENWALD, RENEE, special education educator; b. Bklyn., Oct. 8, 1948; d. Isidor and Monia (Kaczanowska) Oshinsky; m. Laurence David Gruenwald, June 22, 1969; children: Kate, Sara. BA, Brandeis U., 1969; MA, Kean Coll., 1983. Cert. elem., spl. edn., learning disabilities tchr., cons. supervision and adminstrn. Tchr. Marlboro (Mass.) Pub. Schs., 1969-71, Colegio Anglo-Mexicano, Guadalajara, Mex., 1971-73, So. Orange/Maplewood (N.J.) Pub. Schs., 1981—. Mem. N.J. Edn. Assn. (negotiations cons. 1993-97), South Orange-Maplewood Edn. Assn. (v.p. 1984-86, pres. 1986-88, negotiations chair 1991-94, grievance chair 1994-96, grievance com. 1999—), N.J. Assn. Learning Cons., Kappa Delta Pi. Home: 364 Redmond Rd South Orange NJ 07079-1505 Office: South Orange Middle Sch 70 N Ridgewood Rd South Orange NJ 07079-1518 E-mail: rgru@infioline.net.

GRUHL, ANDREA MORRIS, librarian; b. Ponca City, Okla., Dec. 9, 1939; d. Luther Oscar and Hazel Evangeline (Anderson) Morris; m. Werner Mann Gruhl, July 10, 1965; children: Sonja Krista, Diana Krista. BA, Wesleyan Coll., 1961; MLS, U. Md., 1968; postgrad., Johns Hopkins U., 1970-71, U. Md., 1968, 71-73, Oxford U., 1996. Tchr. Broward County, Fla., U.S. Dept. Def. Montgomery County, Md., 1961-66; libr. Prince Georges County (Md.) Pub. Libr., 1966-68, 81-83, U. Md., College Park, 1970-72; art. history rschr. Joseph Alsop, Washington, 1972-74; libr. Howard County Pub. Libr., Columbia, Md., 1969-70, 74-79; European exch. staff Libr. of Congress, Washington, 1982-86; cataloger fed. documents GPO, Washington, 1986-93, supervisory libr., 1993—2001. Women's program adv. com., processing dept. rep. Libr. of Congress, 1983-86, mem. ofcl. Libr. of Congress delegation to Internat. Fedn. Libr. Assn. ann. conf., Munich, 1983, Chgo., 1985; state del. White House Conf. on Librs., 1978, 90. Indexer, editor: Learning Vacations, 3d edit., 1980; editor: Federal Librarian, 1994-99; LCPA Index to Libr. of Congress Info. Bull., 1984. Trustee Howard County (Md.) C.C., 1989-95, Howard County Pub. Libr., Columbia, Md., 1979-87; publ. chmn. LWV Howard County, 1974, bd. dirs., 1996-97, sec., 2002--; bd. dirs. LWV Nat. Capitol Area, 2002—; chair Homeland Security Com., citizens rep. Howard County, exec. bd. Balt. Regional Planning Coun. Libr. com., 1976-79; Friends of Libr., Howard County, pres., 1976; vol. Nat. Gallery Art Libr., Washington, 1978-80. Mem. ALA (councilor 1997-2001, co-chair coun. caucus 2000-01, fed. libr. round table 1988—, v.p. 1997-98, pres. 1998-99, editor 1994-99, govt. documents roundtable 1986—), Libr. Adminstrn. and Mgmt. Assn. (planning and evaluation libr. svcs. 1996-97), D.C. Libr. Assn. (co-chair mgmt. interest group 1996-97, v.p./pres.-elect 2001-02, pres. 2002-03), Assn. Coll. and Rsch. Librs., Internat. Fedn. Libr. Assns. and Instns. (sect. on cataloging, internat. std. bibliographic description/cartographic materials working group 1999-2001), UN Assn. (Nat. Capitol area chpt., membership com., Md . telephone chair 1992-94), Art Librs. Soc. N.Am. (coord. mems.' publ. exhbn. 1980-82), Libr. Congress Profl. Assn. (coord. ann. staff art shows 1982-83, chair libr. sci. interest group 1985-87), Libr. Congress Am. Fedn. State County and Mcpl. Employees Union (program chair 1984-86), Md. Libr. Assn. (pres. trustee divsn. 1982-83), Md. Assn. C.C. Trustees (sec. 1991-92, bd. dirs. 1992-93), Md. Assn. C.C. (bd. dirs. 1992-95), Oxford Univ. Soc., Fed. and Armed Forces Librs. Round Table (chmn. constn. and bylaws com. 2001—, disting. Svc. award 2001), Beta Phi Mu. Democrat. Lutheran. Home: 5990 Jacobs Ladder Columbia MD 21045-3817

GRUHL, JAMES, energy scientist, artist; b. Milw., Apr. 9, 1945; s. Alfred and Helen (Vanderveer) G.; m. Nancy Lee Huston, July 4, 1974; children: Amanda Natalie, Steven Christopher. BS, MS, MIT, 1968, PhD, 1973. Lectr. MIT, 1969-83; rsch. scientist MIT Energy Lab., Cambridge, 1973-83, program mgr., 1978-83, rsch. affiliate, 1984; sci. adv. bd. U.S. EPA, 1986-93; energy cons. U.S. Congress, rsch. insts., internat. energy industries, 1973—. Ednl. counselor MIT, 1978—. Recipient Silver Beaver award Boy Scouts Am., 1986, numerous art awards, 1990—; NSF grantee. Mem. IEEE, AAAS, Math. Programming Soc., MIT Alumni Assn. (officer 1978—), Tau Beta Pi, Eta Kappa Nu. Achievements include research on uncertainties and validity of analytic models, validity of government and industry energy policy models, and climate change models. Office: Gruhl Assocs PO Box 36524 Tucson AZ 85740-6524

GRUHN, ROBERT STEPHEN, retired parole officer; b. N.Y.C., Dec. 9, 1938; s. Jerome and Beatrice (Fuchs) G.; m. Shirley Darlene Brayfield, Sept. 14, 1984. BS, NYU, 1961; MA in Criminology, Sam Houston State U., 1975; AB in Legal Studies, Drury Coll., 1987. Cert. criminal investigator, gang crime specialist, State of Ill. Collection mgr. Sears, Roebuck & Co., Albuquerque, 1961-64; adjuster Gen. Adjustment Bur., Albuquerque, 1964-65; indsl. engr. LTV Aerospace Corp., Dallas, 1965-66; agy. sec. Am. Nat. Ins., Dallas, 1966-72; parole officer Tex. Bd. Parole, Dallas and Houston, 1974-80, Mo. Bd. Parole, Springfield, 1980-99; investigator Greene County (Mo.) Prosecuting Atty. Office, 1999—. With Springfield Police Dept. Tng. Acad. Facility, 1984-90; presenter Gang Awareness Program, S.W. Mo., 1992-99, Mo. State Hwy. Patrol Tng. Acad., 1997-99. Author Collision Course, 1984. Bd. dirs. Wayback Halfway House, Dallas, 1977-80; chmn. Gang Task Force, Springfield, 1996-97, So. Mo. Fugitive Task Force, Springfield, 1992-93; bd. dirs. youth svcs. Mo. Dept. Corrections, 1993—; sr. v.p. One Missing Link, Children Non-Profit Orgn., 1994—, active P.E.A.C.E. Project, Springfield, 1994-95; mem. Missing Persons Task Force, 2000—, Utility Theft Divsn. Task Force, 2000—. Recipient commendation cert. N.Y. Police Dept., 1961, Cert. of Achievement in Extremism and Terrorism, Mo. Dept. Corrections, 1986, Cert. of Achievement in Satanism and the Occult, Mo. Dept. Corrections, 1989, Cert. of Achievement in Dangerous Gangs, 1989, Cert. Achievement, Mid States Organized Crime Info. Ctr., 1990, Cert. of Appreciation, U.S. Treasury Dept., 1992. Mem. Am. Mgmt. Assn. (internat. v.p. 1971-74), Soc. for Advt. Mgmt. (sec. 1968-71, pres. 1971-72), Soc. for Advancement of Mgmt. (Profl. Achievement award 1972), Mo. Corrections Assn., Midwest Gang Investigations Assn., Mu Gamma Tau. Avocation: writing. Home: 6226 N State Hwy 2 Willard MO 65781-9720 Office: 1010 N Boonville Ave Springfield MO 65802-3804

GRULIOW, AGNES FORREST, artist, educator; b. Davenport, Iowa, July 5, 1912; d. James Lindsay and Agnes (Johnston) F.; m. Leo Gruliow, Sept. 25, 1945; children: Frank Forrest, Rebecca Agnes Lindsay. BA, Antioch Coll., Yellow Springs, Ohio, 1938; student, Art Students League, N.Y.C., 1963-66. Resident dir. Am. Peoples Sch., N.Y.C., 1937-41; asst. nat. sec. Nat. Fedn. Settlements, N.Y.C., 1941-43; assoc. pers. dir.,asst. prof. Antioch Coll. Extramural Sch., Yellow Springs, 1943-45; index designer-editor Current Digest of Soviet Press, Washington and N.Y.C., 1949-53; freelance editor N.Y.C., 1954-57; tchr. art City & Country Sch., N.Y.C., 1966-68; hostess Am. Friends Svc. Com. Internat. Seminar, Oestgeest, The Netherlands, 1960, Poughkeepsie, N.Y., 1961; sr. vis. fellow Woodrow Wilson Found., 1977-80; proprietor art studio N.Y.C., 1961-69, Worthington, Ohio, 1970-72; art therapy asst. Harding Hosp., Worthington, 1970-72. One-woman show at Antioch Coll., 1967; group shows Herndon Gallery, Yellow Springs, Ohio, 2000, Northwood Art Space, Columbus, Ohio, 2003. Pres. Columbia U. Greenhouse Nursery Sch., N.Y.C., 1954-59; bd. mem. Open Door Day Care Ctr., N.Y.C., 1954-59; mem. founding and adv. bd. East Harlem Tutoring Program, N.Y.C., 1965-73; mem. bd. Columbus Area Internat. Program, 1970-72, 79-87, sec., 1981, pres., 1982-85, chair adv. bd., 1983-87; del. Nat. Bd. Coun. Internat. Programs, Cleve.,

1981-83; mem. bd. Cmty. Svc., Inc., Yellow Springs, 1981-99. Mem. AAUW, Columbus Meml. Soc., Columbus Mus. Art, South Ctrl. Ohio Preservation Soc., UNA, UNICEF, World Federalist Assn. Ctrl. Ohio (membership sect. 1987-94), Crichton Club (Columbus), Order Eastern Star. Home: 163 E Lane Ave Columbus OH 43201-1212

GRULIOW, REBECCA AGNES LINDSAY, editor, translator, artist; b. N.Y.C., Jan. 28, 1956; d. Leo and Agnes (Forrest) G.; m. Michael Barnhart, Jan. 1977 (div. 1982). BA in Russian studies and lit. with honors, Bryn Mawr Coll., 1979; BFA in glass and ceramics with honors, Temple U., 1989; MS, Drexel U., 2002. Prodn. editor J.B. Lippincott Co., Phila., 1980-83; project editor Saunders Coll. Pub., Phila., 1983, 1987-88; prodn. editor Extracorporeal, Inc., 1983-84, W.B. Saunders Co., Phila., 1984-85; free-lance, 1985—. Devel. editor Mosby, Phila., 1996, Phila., 1997—, sr. devel. editor, 1999—2001, Elsevier Sci., 2001—03, mng. editor, 2003—. One-person shows include The Hunterdon Art Ctr., Clinton, N.J., 1991, The Clay Studio, Phila, 1995, Abington Art Ctr. Gallery Store, Jenkintown, Pa., 1997; exhibited at group shows at Temple Gallery, 1987, Franklin Plaza, 1987, The Armory, 1987, del Mano Gallery, 1988, Gallery 479, 1990, The Clay Studio, 1990, 1995-2002, Luckenbach Mill Gallery, 1990, Hunterdon Art Ctr., 1991, Noyes Mus., 1991, Nat. Mus. Ceramic Art, 1991, Paley Design Ctr., 1992, Long Beach Island Found Arts & Scis., 1992, 93, 98, Gallery Am. Craft at Wheaton Village, 1994-97, Abington Art Ctr., 1996, Bryn Mawr Coll. Alumni Exhbn., 1998; co-translator: Lysenko and the Tragedy of Soviet Science, 1994; contbr. articles to profl. jours. Mem. Am. Craft Coun., Clay Studio. Office: 625 Walnut St Philadelphia PA 19106-3323

GRUMAN, ROBERT RICHARD, energy management consultant; b. Calgary, Alta., Can., Mar. 21, 1967; came to U.S., 1976; s. William Paul and Pauline Adams Gruman; m. Olga Vladimirovna Bordanova, Jan. 27, 1996, 1 child, Aleksander Robert. BS summa cum laude, Ariz. State U., 1989. Fin. analyst Conoco, Inc., Casper, Wyo., 1989, staff supr. Lafayette, La., 1990-91, fin. analyst, 1991-93, sr. fin. analyst Moscow, 1993, material and logistics supr., 1993-95, sr. staff fin. analyst, 1995-96, region fin. analyst Lafayette, La., 1996; dir. mgmt. cons. PricewaterhouseCoopers LLP, Houston, 1996—2002; assoc. ptnr. IBM Bus. Cons., Houston, 2002—. Contbr. papers to profl. jours. Bd. advisors Ariz. State U. Coll. Bus. Dept Fin. Mem. Beta Gamma Sigma, Phi Kappa Phi, Alpha Lambda Delta. Republican. Roman Catholic. Avocations: golf, reading, exercise, running, traveling. Home: 8610 Malardcrest Dr Humble TX 77346-8114 E-mail: bob.gruman@us.ibm.com.

GRUMMAN, CORNELIA, newswriter; B in Pub. Policy, Duke U.; M in Pub. Policy, Harvard U. Stringer Washington post News and Observer, Beijing, 1989; met., state, govt. and Internet reporter Chgo. Tribune, mem. editl. bd., 2000—. Recipient Casey medal for meritorious journalism, Studs Terkel award for coverage of disadvantaged communities, Herman Kogan award for editls. on death penalty, Peter Lisagor award for commentary, Pulitzer prize for editl. writing, 2003. Office: Chgo Tribune 777 W Chicago Ave Chicago IL 60610

GRUMMER-STRAWN, LAURENCE M. public health service officer, researcher; b. Albuquerque, May 2, 1964; s. Mary Rose and Charles J. Grummer; m. Sara J. Strawn, July 25, 1987; children: Jessica R., Zachary K. BS, Tex. Christian U., 1982—86; MPA, Princeton U., 1987—89, MA, PhD, Princeton U., 1989—91. Epidemic intelligence officer Centers for Disease Control, 1991—93, epidemiologist, 1993—96; adj. prof. Emory U., 1996—; br. chief Centers for Disease Control, 1996—. Comdr. Pub. Health Svc., Atlanta, 1991—; tech. advisor Salvadoran Demographic Assoc., San Salvador, 1992—; tech. resource group UNICEF Multiple Indicator Cluster Surveys, 1994—2000; mem. U.S. Breastfeeding Com., Washington, 1998—; steering com. WHO Growth Reference Study, Geneva, 1998—. CDC Growth Charts for U. S., 2000; contbr. over 50 scientific pubs. in peer review jours., chapters to books. Cantor Holy Cross Cath. Ch., Doraville, Ga., 1991—. Mem.: Internat. Soc. for Rsch. on Human Milk and Lactation, Population Assn. of Am., APHA. Roman Catholic. Avocations: marathon runner, singing, acting in musical theater, swimming, camping, hiking. Office: Centers for Disease Control & Prevention 4770 Buford Hwy MS K25 Atlanta GA 30341

GRUNBAUM, ADOLF, philosophy educator, author; b. Cologne, Germany, May 15, 1923; came to U.S., 1938, naturalized, 1944; s. Benjamin and Hannah (Freiwillig) G.; m. Thelma Braverman, June 26, 1949; 1 child, Barbara Susan. BA, Wesleyan U., Middletown, Conn., 1943; MS in Physics, Yale U., 1948, Ph.D in Philosophy, 1951; Dr. Honoris Causa, U. Konstanz. Mem. faculty Lehigh U., 1950-60, prof. philosophy, 1955-56, Selfridge prof. philosophy, 1956-60; vis. rsch. prof. Minn. Ctr. Philosophy of Sci., 1956, 59; Andrew Mellon prof. philosophy of science U. Pitts., 1960—, rsch. prof. psychiatry, 1979—, dir. Ctr. Philosophy of Sci., 1960-78; now chmn. U. Pitts. (Ctr. Philosophy of Sci.). Chmn. sect. philosophy of phys. scis. Internat. Congress for Logic and Philosophy of Sci., Jerusalem, Israel, 1964, Bucharest, Rumania, 1971, Salzburg, Austria, 1983; physicist div. war research Columbia U., World War II; Werner Heisenberg lectr. Bavarian Acad. Scis., 1985; Gifford lectr., Scotland, 1985; vis. Mellon prof. Calif. Inst. Tech., 1990; Leibniz lectr. U. Hannover, Germany, 2003. Author: Philosophical Problems of Space and Time, 1963, 2d edit., 1973, Russian edit., 1969, Modern Science and Zeno's Paradoxes, 2d edit, 1968, Geometry and Chronometry in Philosophical Perspective, 1968, The Foundations of Psychoanalysis: A Philosophical Critique, 1984, German, Italian, French, Hungarian, Japanese edits., 1988, Psicoanalisi: Obiezioni E Risposte, 1988, Validation in the Clinical Theory of Psychoanalysis, 1993, La Psychanalyse à L'Épreuve, 1993; also numerous articles; mem. editorial bd.: Ency. Philosophy, 1961—; bd. editors Philosophy Sci., 1959—, Am. Philos. Quar., Psychoanalysis and Contemporary Thought, Studies in History and Philosophy of Science, The Philosopher's Index; co-editor Pitts. Series in Philosophy and History of Sci.; assoc. editor Behavioral and Brain Scis. Served with M.I.S. U.S. Army, 1944-46. Recipient J. Walker Tomb prize Princeton U., 1958, honor citation Wesleyan U., 1959, U.S. sr. scientist award Alexander von Humboldt Found., 1985, Fregene Prize in Sci., Italian Parliament, 1989, Wilbur Lucius Cross medal Yale U., 1990. Fellow AAAS (v.p. sect. L 1963); mem. Acad. Internat. de Philosophie des Scis., Am. Philos. Assn. (pres. Ea. divsn. 1982-83), Philosophy of Sci. Assn. (pres. 1965-70), Am. Acad. Arts and Scis., Acad. Humanism (laureate 1985), Phi Beta Kappa, Sigma Xi. Achievements include being subject of numerous books. Home: 7141 Roycrest Pl Pittsburgh PA 15208-2737 Office: U Pitts 2510 Cathedral Of Learning Pittsburgh PA 15260-2510 Fax: (412) 648-1068.

GRUNBERG, ROBERT LEON WILLY, nephrologist, educator; b. Bucharest, Romania, July 23, 1940; came to U.S., 1972, naturalized, 1977; s. William A. and Isabelle L. (Rosen) G.; m. Donna M. Fishman, Oct. 19, 1975; children: Wendie I., Andrea B. MD, U. Orleans-Tours, France, 1969. Diplomate Am. Bd. Internal Medicine, Am. Bd. Nephrology; cert. hypertension specialist in clin. hypertension. Intern, then resident in cardiology Vichy (France) Hosp., 1968-72; resident in internal medicine Albert Einstein Med. Ctr., Phila., 1972-74; fellow in nephrology-hypertension Hahnemann Univ. Hosp., Phila., 1974-76, sr. clin. instr. then asst. clin. prof. div. nephrology, 1976; pvt. practice medicine specializing in nephrology Allentown, Pa., 1976—. Attending physician St. Luke's Hosp., Bethlehem, Pa., Lehigh Valley Ctr. (now Lehigh Valley Hosp.), Allentown; attending charge divsn. nephrology Easton (Pa.) Hosp.; courtesy staff Hahnemann Univ. Hosp.; dir. Renal Dialysis Ctr. at Easton (Pa.) Hosp., 1989; chief dialysis Warren Hosp., Phillipsburg, N.J., 1999. Fellow ACP; mem. AMA (Physician's Recognition award 1975, 79, 82, 85, 88, 89-92, 92-95, 95-98, 2001), Pa. Med. Soc., Am. Soc. Nephrology, Am. Soc. Artificial Internal Organs, Internat. Soc. Hypertension, Am. Soc. for Parenteral and Enteral Nutrition, Internat. Soc. for Artificial Organs, Internat. Soc. Nephrology, Assn. for Advancement of Med. Instrumentation, Internat. Soc. for Peritoneal Dialysis, Nat. Kidney Found., N.Y. Acad. Scis. Office: 50 S 18th St Easton PA 18042-3912 also: 401 N 17th St Allentown PA 18104-5034

GRUNBERG, SLAWOMIR, film and television producer and director, director of photography; b. Lublin, Poland, Apr. 6, 1951; came to the U.S., 1981; s. Karol Nathan and Danuta Czosnowska (Ostrowska) G.; m. Wanda Turek, Aug. 15, 1976; children: Karolina, Sarah, Joanna. MA, SGGW, Warsaw, 1974; cert. film and TV dir., Polish Film Sch., Lodz, 1981. Vis. scholar MIT, Boston, 1982; asst. prof. U. Cin., 1982-84, Govs. State U., Chgo., 1984-85; vis. prof. Webster U., St. Louis, 1985-86; asst. prof. Ithaca (N.Y.) Coll., 1986-90; TV and film prodr., cameraman, editor Log In Prodns., Spencer, NY, 1987—. Prodr., dir.: School Prayer: A Community At War, 1998 (selected by PBS Broadcast 1999, Emmy award 2000), From Chechnya To Chernobyl, 1996, Chelyabinsk: The Most Contaminated Spot, 1994, Fenceline: A Company Town Divided, 2002 (selected by PBS Broadcast 2002); co-prodr.: Messenger to Poland, 1989; second unit prodr.: Shtetl, 1997 (Grand Prix award, Cinema du Reel Festival 1996, Silver Baton for Excellence in Radio/TV Journalism duPont-Columbia U. 1997); co-dir. photography: Legacy, 2001 (Acad. award nomination); contbg. dir. photography, editor (PBS series) Frontline, NOVA, AIDS Quarterly, The American Experience, The People's Century; Guggenheim fellow in documentary film making, 1997; NYU Found. for Arts fellow, 2002. Prodn. grantee Ind. TV Svc., 1997, Soros Documentary Fund, 1996; recipient Silver Apple award, Grand Prix Best in Prague, 1998, Golden Cine award, Grand Prix award Internat. Environ. Film Fest, 1996, Best Journalistic award Okomedia Film Festival, 1995. Mem. Assn. Ind. Video and Filmmakers, Internat. Documentary Assn. Avocation: nature. Office: Log In Prodns 4 La Rue Rd Spencer NY 14883-9657

GRUNBLATT, HILDA RUTH, translator, editor; b. Bklyn., Mar. 20, 1922; d. Samuel and Anna (Robson) Waterman; m. Jacques Grunblatt, Nov. 27, 1947 (dec. Jan. 1989); children: Ellen Miriam, Jesse Elliott, Mark Henry. BA, Bklyn. Coll., 1943. Tchr. N.Y.C. Bd. of Edn., Bklyn., 1946-49; med. asst., bookkeeper Offices of Dr. Jacques Grunblatt, North Creek, N.Y., 1949-75; freelance co-translator and editor North Creek, 1981—. Bd. dirs. Johnsburg Pride, North Creek, N.Y., 1993-98; trustee Johnsburg Pub. Libr., 1995-98. Editor: Seven Hells, 1990; editor: (co-translator) The Shattered Dream, 1989; author: numerous poems; feature editor: Temple Beth El Sisterhood Sun, 1997—. Organizer, vol. Town of Johnsburg (N.Y.) Headstart, 1962-73; vol. Literacy Vols. Am., Glens Falls, 1990-1995; bd. dirs. Warren County Planned Parenthood, Glens Falls, 1966-75, Adirondack Ctr. for the Arts, Blue Mountain Lake, N.Y., 1966-75, Warren County Homemaker Svc., Glens Falls, 1967-75; bd. dirs. Glens Falls Warren County Com. on Children and Pub. Welfare, 1960-75, Warren County Mental Health Assn., 1964-70; del. from Temple Sisterhood to bd. dirs. Temple Beth El, 1999-2000, mem. Hadassah, 1955—. Recipient Golden Poet award World of Poetry, 1985, 87, Editor's Choice award The Nat. Libr. of Poetry, 1994. Mem.: Physicians for Social Responsibility, Union of Concerned Scientists, The Ocean Conservancy, So. Poverty Law Ctr., Internat. Physicians for Prevention of Nuclear War, Environ. Def., Natural Resources Def. Coun., Amnesty Internat. Jewish. Avocation: music. Home: 39 Longview Dr # 205 Queensbury NY 12804-5894

GRUNDER, FRED IRWIN, industrial hygienist, consultant; b. Detroit, Aug. 17, 1940; s. Fritz and Mary Kathrine (Irwin) G.; m. Barbara Ann Ward, May 7, 1966; children: John Frederick, Robert William. BS in Engr. Physics, U. Mich., 1963, MS in Physics, 1967. Diplomte Am. Bd. Indsl. Hygiene; cert. indsl. hygienist. Rsch. assoc. U. Mich., Ann Arbor, 1960-69; chemist G.D. Clayton & Assocs., Southfield, Mich., 1969-72; lab. dir. Bethlehem (Pa.) Steel Corp., 1972-85; dir. indsl. hygiene Am. Med. Labs., Fairfax, Va., 1985-92; mgr. lab. accreditation programs Am. Indsl. Hygiene Assn., Fairfax, 1992—2002; indsl. hygiene cons., 2002—. Sect. editor: Methods for Biological Monitoring, 1988. Scoutmaster Boy Scouts Am., Bethlehem, 1972-84; pres. U. Mich. Club, Lehigh Valley, 1980-84; mem. toxic planning and oversight panel Chesapeake Rsch. Consortium, Solomons Island, Md., 1990-91, site assessor AIHA Lab., 1992; bd. dirs., vice-chair Nat. Coop. Lab. Accreditation, 1997 98, pres., 1998-2000, past pres., 2000-01; bd. dirs. Saw Habitat for Humanity. Fellow Am. Indsl. Hygiene Assn. (President's award 2001); mem. ASTM, Am. Chem. Soc., Am. Acad. Indsl. Hygiene. Democrat. Methodist. Avocations: reading, stamp and coin collecting, gardening. E-mail: fgrunder@mindspring.com.

GRUNDFAST, KENNETH MARTIN, otolaryngologist; b. Bklyn., Mar. 12, 1944; s. Theodore Harvey and Anne Gertrude (Goldberg) G.; m. Ruthanne Blatt Grundfast, May 26, 1974; children: Rena Brett, Dara Beth. BA, Johns Hopkins U., 1965; MD, SUNY, Syracuse, 1969. Clin. instr. dept. of community medicine Georgetown U. Sch. of Medicine, Washington, 1972-74, prof. depts. otolaryngology and pediat., 1996-99, interim chmn. dept. otolryngology; resident otolaryngology Boston U. Hosp., 1974-77; fellow in pediatric otolaryngology Childrens Hosp. of Pitts., 1977-78, staff otolaryngologist, 1978-79, asst. prof. of otolaryngology, 1978-79; prof. dept. otolaryngology, 1980-96; chmn. dept. otolaryngology Children's Nat. Med. Ctr., Washington, 1980-94, vice-chmn., 1994-96; prof., chmn. dept. otolaryngology Sch. Medicine Boston U., 1999—. Lectr. in field. Author: (with others) Ear Infections in Your Child, 1987, Pediatric Otology/Neurotology, 1997; contbr. articles to profl. jours. Lt. comdr. USPHS, 1971-73. Recipient Sylvan Stool Achievement award Sentac, 2000. Fellow ACS, Am. Acad. Pediat., mem. AMA (Humanitarian award 1973), Soc. for Ear, Nose and Throat Advancement in Children (bd. dirs. 1985, v.p. 1988, pres. 1989), Am. Bronchoesophagologic Soc.,Soc. of U. Otolaryngologists, Am. Neurotology Soc., Trilogical Soc. (hon. mention clin. rsch. thesis), Am. Soc. Pediatric Otolaryngology (pres. 1993-94), Am. Acad. Otolaryngology (v.p. 1994-96, Presdl. Citation award 1996). Avocations: swimming, bicycling. Office: Dept Otolaryngology One Boston Med Ctr Pl Boston MA 02118-2393

GRUNDHOFER, JERRY A. bank executive; BA, Loyola Marymount U., 1967. With Union Bank, 1967-81; pres. Alliance Bank, 1981-83; sr. v.p. So. Calif. corp. banking, sr. v.p. So. Calif. retail banking ops. Wells Fargo Bank, 1983-85, exec. v.p. 440 br. statewidef retail banking sys., 1985-87; vice chmn. Security Pacific Nat. Bank, 1987-90, pres., CEO, 1990-93, Star Banc Corp., Cin., 1993—, also chmn. bd. dirs.; pres., CEO Star Bank, N.A., 1993—, also bd. dirs.; CEO Firstar Corp., Milw., U.S. Bancorp (formerly Firstar Corp.), Minneapolis, 2001—. Bd. dirs. Arete Assocs., Cin. Equity Fund, L.L.C., Hennegan Co., Visa Internat., Visa U.S.A., Inc., mem. exec. com. Trustee Children's Hosp. Med. Ctr., Health Found. Greater Cin., Cin. Symphony Orch., United Appeal/Cmty. Chest, United Way, U. Cin. Found., Xavier U.; co-chair Fine Arts Fund Campaign, 1995, chmn., 1996; co-chmn. Urban Capital Campaign, 1995, 96; chmn. corp. exec. com. 13th ann. tribute dinner Jewish Inst. Rel. Hebrew Union Coll., 1995; chmn. ann. dinner Nat. Conf. Christians and Jews, 1997; bd. dirs. Nat. Underground Railroad Freedom Ctr. Honoree 15th ann. tribute dinner Jewish Inst. Rel. Hebrew Union Coll., 1997. Mem. Am. Bankers Assn. (bd. dirs.), Internat. Fin. Conf. (bd. dirs.), Bankers Roundtable (bd. dirs.), Greater Cin. C. of C. (bd. dirs.), Over-the-Rhine C. of C. (bd. dirs.), Birnan Woods, Cin. Country Club, Comml. Club (mem. exec. com.), Double Eagle Golf Club, Queen City Club. Office: US Bancorp US Bank Pl 601 2nd Ave S Minneapolis MN 55402

GRUNDHOFER, JOHN F. banking executive; b. L.A., 1939; Student, Loyola U., 1960, U. So. Calif., 1964. Formerly with Wells Fargo & Co., San Francisco, also vice chmn.; now chmn., pres., CEO U.S. Bancorp (formerly First Bank System, Inc.), Mpls., 1990—2001, chmn., 2001—, also dir. Office: US Bancorp 601 2nd Ave S Minneapolis MN 55402-4303

GRUNDIG, JOHN PATRICK, director; s. Nina Spiller and John George Grundig; m. Shawna DeAnn Miller, Mar. 6, 1993; children: John Patrick Jr., Anna Elizabeth, Sarah Renee'. BS in Health, U. of North Fla., 1993; MBA, Jacksonville U., 1998. Rsch. asst. U. of Fla., Dept. Cmty. Health and Family Medicine, Jacksonville, 1993—96; dir. instl. rsch. Jacksonville U., Jacksonville, 1996—2001, dir. enrollment ops., 2001—02, dir. admissions, 2002—. Author: (rsrch. article) Jour. of the Nat. Med. Assn. Mem.: Assn. for Internat. Educators, Nat. Assn. for Coll. Admission Counseling, Am. Assn. of Collegiate, Registrars and Admissions Officers. Office: Jacksonville U 2800 University Blvd N Jacksonville FL 32211-3394 Office Fax: 904-256-7012. E-mail: jgrundi@ju.edu.

GRUNDLEHNER, CONRAD ERNEST, information company executive, economic consultant; b. N.Y.C., Mar. 12, 1942; s. Ernest and Elise Louise (Eicks) G.; m. Marietta Ferebee Guidon, Feb. 19, 1977; children: Marietta Ferebee Karen, Guidon Steven. BS, MIT, 1964; MA, U. Pa., 1968. V.p. Simumatics, Inc., Haddonfield, N.J., 1969-72; mgr. Hay Assocs., Phila., 1973-79, Strategic Planning Assocs., Washington, 1980-82; chief economist Donoghue Orgn. Inc., Holliston, Mass., 1982-84; pres. Conrad Grundlehner Inc., McLean, Va., 1984—. Bd. dirs. Conrad Grundlehner Inc., McLean, 1984—, bd. dirs., cons. economist W.E. Donoghue & Co., Inc., Holliston, Mass., 1986—. Editor: Donoghue's Mutual Funds Alamanac, 1984-86, contbg. editor: Donoghue's Mutual Funds Alamanac, 1987. 1st lt. U.S. Army, 1971. Mem. MIT Enterprise Forum, Am. Econ. Assn., Nat. Assn. Bus. Econs., MIT Club Washington. Republican. Episcopalian. Avocation: photography. E-mail: ablution@aol.com.

GRUNDY, KENNETH WILLIAM, political science educator; b. Phila., Aug. 6, 1936; s. William and Alma (Hahn) G.; m. Martha Jonet Paxson, June 25, 1960; children: William MacIntyre, Thomas Paxson, Anne Edmunds. BA with honors, Ursinus Coll., 1958; MA, Pa. State U., 1961, PhD, 1963. Asst. prof. polit. sci. San Fernando Valley State Coll., Northridge, Calif., 1963-66; assoc. prof. Case Western Res. U., Cleve., 1966-74, prof., 1974-88, Marcus A. Hanna prof., 1988—, chmn. dept. polit. sci., 1974-76, dir. Ctr. for Policy Studies, 1998-2000. Vis. sr. lectr. Makerere U. Coll., Kampala, Uganda, 1967-68; vis. scholar Inst. Social Studies, The Hague, The Netherlands, 1972-73, U. Pretoria, 1998; vis. Fulbright prof. U. Zambia, Lusaka, 1977, Nat. U. Ireland, Galway, 1979-80; vis. adj. prof. Cleve. State U., 1992—; editl. adv. bd. Ctr. Internat. Race Rels., 1968—. Author: Conflicting Images of the Military in Africa, 1968, Guerrilla Struggle in Africa, 1971, Confrontation and Accommodation in Southern Africa, 1973, (with Weinstein) The Ideologies of Violence, 1974, We're Against Apartheid, But, 1974, Defense Legislation and Communal Politics, 1978, (with V. McHale and B. Hughes) Evaluating Transnational Programs in Government and Business, 1980, Soldiers Without Politics, 1983, The Militarization of South African Politics, 1986, rev. edit., 1988, South Africa: Domestic Crisis and Global Challenge, 1991, The Politics of the National Arts Festival, 1993; also articles; book rev. editor Internat. Jour. Comparative Sociology, 1973-83; assoc. editor Jour. African Policy Studies, 1991—; contbg. editor Current History, 1982—; mem. editl. adv. bd. African Affairs, 1983-93; mem. editl. bd. Jour. Third World Studies, 1988—, South African Jour. Internat. Affairs, 1993-98. Fellow NDEA, 1959-62, Rhodes U., Grahamstown, South Africa, 1989-90, Ctr. Internat. Race Rels., 1969-70; 1st Bradlow fellow South African Inst. Internat. Rels., 1982; grantee Rockefeller Found., 1967-68, Social Sci. Rsch. Coun., 1972, 79-80, Earhart Found, 1979. Mem. African Studies Assn. (mem. exec. coun.), Inter-Univ. Seminar on Armed Forces and Soc., Internat. Studies Assn. Home: 2602 Exeter Rd Cleveland OH 44118-4246 Office: Case Western Res U Dept Polit Sci Cleveland OH 44106

GRUNDY, RICHARD DAVID, engineer; b. San Mateo, Calif., Mar. 17, 1937; s. John Richard and Violette Grundy; m. Claudia Copeland, 1977 (div. 1992); m. Jamei C. Haswell, 1997. BSEE, Stanford (Calif.) U., 1958; MS, U. Calif., 1963, postgrad., 1964, George Washington U., 1965-67, Harvard U., 1980. Exec. sec. Nat. Fuels and Energy Policy Study U.S. Senate, Washington, 1971-76, mem. sr. profl. staff Com. on Environment and Pub. Works, 1967-76, mem. sr. profl. staff Com. on Energy and Natural Resources, 1977-94; pres. Alexandria (Va.) Energy Assoc., Inc., 1995—. Bd. mem., North Coast Region Regional Water Quality Control Bd., EPA, State of Calif., 2001—; chmn. protocol com. 2d Internat. Clear Air Congress, Internat. Union Air Prevention Assns., 1970; steering com. Aspen Inst. Energy Forum, 1985-91; observer White Ho. Conf. on Global Climate Change, Washington, 1990, 93-94, UN Negotiations on Climate Change, Geneva, 1993, 94; participant UN Conf. on Clean Coal Tech. in Devel. Countries, Beijing, 1991. Author: (with others) Air Pollution and Industry, 1972; co-editor: Consumer Health and Product Hazards, 1974; contbr. numerous articles to profl. jours. Mem. adminstrv. bd. Foundry United Meth. Ch., Washington, 1960-62, 66-70, mem. coun. of mins., 1967-70, chmn. membership commn., 1968-70; mem. nat. planning com. Nat. Youth Govs. Conf., YMCA and Readers Digest Found., Washington, 1975-80; mem. Air Pollution Control Assn., 1967-82; pres. Nat. Capitol Orchid Soc., Washington, 1989-90; exec. dir. Ea. Orchid Congress, 1997-2000. Comdr. USPHS, 1959-67. Recipient Disting. Svc. award U.S. Senate, 1981. Fellow AAAS; mem. IEEE, NSPE, Assn. of Energy Engrs., D.C. Soc. Profl. Engrs. (Young Engr. of the Yr. 1970), Am. Orchid Soc. (conservation com.), U.S. Energy Assn. Methodist. Home and Office: 950 Wikiup Dr Santa Rosa CA 95403-1305 E-mail: richardgrundy@att.net.

GRUNE, STEVEN, publishing executive; Acct./bus. mgr. McCalls; sales positions Parents Mag., adv. dir., 1994—97, Redbook, 1997, assoc. pub., 1998; pub. Midwest Living, 1999—2000, Country Living, 2000, Country Living Gardener, 2000; v.p. Country Living, 2002—, Country Living Gardener, 2002—. Office: Country Living 224 West 57th St New York NY 10019

GRUNEBAUM, ERNEST MICHAEL, investment banker; b. London, Dec. 26, 1934; came to U.S., 1941; naturalized, 1947; s. Erich Otto and Gabrielle (Neumann) G.; m. Marjorie Bleetstein, Aug. 20, 1957; children: Edward, Lauren, David. BA, Dartmouth Coll., 1956; MA, Brown U., 1958. With N.Y. Hanseatic Corp., investment bankers, N.Y.C., 1956-74, pres., 1973-74; gen. ptnr., mgr. Hanseatic divsn. Stuart Bros., N.Y.C., 1974-81; exec. v.p., mgr. Hanseatic divsn. The Securities Groups, N.Y.C., 1981-85; sr. exec. v.p. Yamaichi Internat. (Am.) Inc., N.Y.C., 1985-87; mng. dir. Hanseatic Hirschland Ptnrs. Inc, Katonah, NY, 1987—. Mem. exec. com. Self-Help Cmty. Svcs. Inc.; hon. pres., mem. exec. bd. Greater N.Y. Coun. of Reform Synagogues; trustee, mem. exec. com. Union of Am. Hebrew Congregations, 1989—; mem. exec. com. Am. Fedn. Jews from Ctrl. Europe, 1992; dir. United Help, Inc., 1996—. Mem. Money Marketeers (bd. govs., pres.). Jewish (pres., trustee temple). Home: 31 Austin Hill Rd Pound Ridge NY 10576-1811 Office: 282 Katonah Ave # 250 Katonah NY 10536

GRUNEICH, JEFFREY ALAN, biotechnology executive; b. Berkeley, Calif., July 27, 1973; s. John A Gruneich and Angie A Holdaway. BS in Chemistry and Math., U. Calif., Berkeley, 1996, MA in Chemistry, 1997; PhD, U. Pa., 2002. Chief bus. officer Infoceutics, Inc., Phila., 2001—; subject matter expert IBM, Phila., 2003—. Chief strategy officer eTechtransfer.com, Phila., 1999—2000. Musician: (performance) Dear Mandy (Conan O'Brien, Best Coll. Band, 1995). Co-pres. U. Pa Biotech Club, Phila., 1999—2000. Recipient Magna cum laude, So. Meth. U., 1996; fellow Grad. Student fellowship, Chemistry, NSF, 1996-2001. Mem.: Am. Soc. of Gene Therapy, Am. Assn. of Pharm. Scientists (assoc.), World Future Soc. (assoc.), Am. Assn. for the Advancement of Sci. (assoc.), Am. Chem. Soc. (assoc.), Phi Beta Kappa. Achievements include patents pending for synthesis and use of reagents for improved DNA lipofection and/or slow release prodrug and drug therapies. Avocations: skiing, weightlifting, travel, guitar, trumpet. Home: 1035 Spruce St Apt 302 Philadelphia PA 19107

GRUNER, GEORGE RICHARD, retired secondary education educator; b. Springfield, Mo., Apr. 6, 1940; s. George Fredrick and Elsie Rachel (Souders) G.; m. Grayce Anne Hartman, Mar. 29, 1957 (div. June 1977); children: Mark Randall, Stephen Eric; m. Rita Marie Torres, May 31, 1982; children: Gregory Lee, Dawn Marie. BA in History, Lincoln U. of Mo., 1961; tchg. credentials, U. Puget Sound, 1965; MS in Edn., Calif. State U., Fullerton, 1972; postgrad., U.S. Army War Coll., Carlisle, Pa., 1986. Cert. tchr. Calif. History tchr. Huntington Beach (Calif.) High Sch., 1965-69; tchr., coord. for gifted/talented edn. Edison High Sch., Huntington Beach, 1969-81, English tchr., 1983-90, chmn. English dept., 1991-98, chmn. site restructuring com., 1992-97, cross-curricular integration mentor, 1993-95; commandant Calif. Mil. Acad., Sacramento, Calif., 1986-90; dep. dir. Nat. Interagy. Counterdrug Inst., San Luis Obispo, Calif., 1991; lectr., student tchr. supr. Calif. Poly. State U., San Luis Obispo, 2001—. Acad. bd. dirs. Calif. Mil. Acad., Sacramento, 1986-91; mem., nat. rep. State Mil. Acad. Adv. Coun., Region VII, Calif., Nev., Utah, Ariz., Hawaii, 1986-90; cons. Calif. Army Nat. Guard, L.A., 1992—; mem. Orange County Vital Link Assessment Com., 1993-98; adminstrv. coord. Ctr. for Internat. Bus. and Comm. Studies, 1994-99. Contbr. articles to regional and nat. jours., author pubs. in field. Exec. bd. PTA Edison High Sch., 1971-75; adult leader, cubmaster Boy Scouts Am., Huntington Beach, 1967-74; mem. Huntington Beach Dist. Tech. Coun., 1994-95, Action Planning Com., 1993-95; steering com. CIBACS Found., 1995-99; dir. Ret. and Sr. Vols. Program, San Luis Obispo County, 2001—; exec. dir. Lifespan Found. for Human Svcs., 2003; bd. dirs. Camp Roberts Mil. Mus.; commr. at large San Luis Obispo County Commn. on Aging, 2003—; adv. coun. Ctrl. Coast Commn. Sr. Citizens. Col. U.S. Army, 1962-92. Decorated Legion of Merit, Order of Calif., 1992; grantee AST Rsch. Corp., 1993, Calif. Dept. Edn., 1994-98; recipient Hon. Svc. award Calif. Congress of Parents, Tchrs. and Students, 1995. Mem. AARP (cmty. presence team), Dist. Educators Assn. (faculty rep.), Calif. Tchrs. Assn., NEA, Nat. Coun. Tchrs. English, Nat. Guard Assn. U.S. and Calif., Am. Legion, Mil. Officers Assn. Am. (sec. Ctrl. Coast chpt.), So. Calif. RSVP Dirs. Assn., Calif. Ret. Tchrs. Assn. (exec. bd. divsn. 86), Lions Club, Audubon Soc., Nature Conservancy. Avocations: hiking, camping, nature study. Home: 1535 Via Arroyo Paso Robles CA 93446 E-mail: rgruner@tcsn.net.

GRUNES, DAVID LEON, research soil scientist, educator, editor; b. Paterson, N.J., June 29, 1921; s. Jacob and Gussie (Griggs) G.; m. Willa Freeman Grunes, June 26, 1949; children— Lee Alan, Mitchell Ray, Rima Louise BS, Rutgers U., 1944; PhD, U. Calif., 1951. With USDA, 1950-96, tech. assistance expert to Internat. Atomic Energy Agy., UN, 1963-64, rsch. soil scientist, 1964-96; assoc. prof. crop and soil scis. Cornell U., Ithaca, 1967-76, prof., 1976-97; collaborator USDA, Ithaca, 1996—. Cons. editor soils, agr. McGraw-Hill Ency., Sci. and Tech., 1965-88. Contbr. chpts. to books, articles to profl. jours. Served with U.S. Army, 1944-45 Recipient Rsch. award USDA, 1959, 82, 89, 92, Am. Soc. Agronomy (Northeastern chpt.), 1988. Fellow AAAS, Am. Inst. Chemists, Am. Soc. Agronomy, Soil Sci. Soc. Am.; mem. Internat. Soc. Soil Sci., Council for Agrl. Sci. and Tech., Sigma Xi Home: 307 Salem Dr Ithaca NY 14850-1915 Office: US Plant Soil and Nutrition Lab Tower Rd Ithaca NY 14853-2901 E-mail: dlg3@cornell.edu.

GRUNIG, JAMES ELMER, communications educator, researcher, public relations consultant; b. Storm Lake, Iowa, Apr. 18, 1942; s. Roy Albert and Gladys Erma (Harjes) G.; m. Juretta Ann Weisgerber, Sept. 11, 1965 (dec. May, 1984); children: Andrew, John, Neil; m. Larissa Ann Johnson, May 11, 1985; 1 stepchild, Lara Schneider. BS, Iowa State U., 1964; MS, U. Wis., 1966, PhD, 1968. Asst. prof. Land Tenure Ctr. U. Wis., Madison, 1968-69; asst. prof. communications Coll. Journalism, U. Md., College Park, 1969-72, assoc. prof., 1972-78, prof., 1978-99, prof. dept. comm., 1999—. Pub. rels. cons. numerous orgns. Author: Decline of the Global Village, 1976, Managing Public Relations, 1984, Excellence in Public Relations and Communication Management, 1992, Public Relations Techniques, 1993, Manager's Guide to Excellence in Public Relations and Communication Management, 1995, Excellent Public Relations and Effective Organizations, 2002; co-editor Pub. Rels. Rsch. Ann., 1989-91, Jour. Pub. Rels. Rsch., 1992-94; contbr. articles to profl. jours. Scoutmaster Boy Scouts Am., Hyattsville, Md., 1985-90; tchr. Rockville (Md.) United Ch., 1980-92. Recipient Pathfinder award for rsch., Inst. for Pub. Rels. Rsch. and Edn., N.Y., 1984, James W. Schwartz award, Greenlee Sch. Journalism and Comm., Iowa State U., 2002; grantee, Internat. Assn. Bus. Communicators Found., 1986—95. Mem. Assn. for Edn. in Journalism and Mass Comm. (Paul J. Deutschmann award 2000), Internat. Comm. Assn., Pub. Rels. Soc. Am. (Outstanding Educator award 1989, Jackson, Jackson and Wagner award for behavioral sci. rsch. 1992), Internat. Assn. Bus. Communicators, Nat. Comm. Assn., Internat. Pub. Rels. Assn., Cosmos Club (Washington). Democrat. Avocation: sport. Home: 41 Brinkwood Rd Brookeville MD 20833-2300 Office: U Md Dept Comm 2130 Skinner Bldg College Park MD 20742-7635 E-mail: jgrunig@umd.edu.

GRUNNET, MARGARET LOUISE, pathology educator; b. Mpls., Feb. 20, 1936; d. Leslie Nels and Grace Harriet (Thomson) Grunnet; m. Irving Noel Einhorn, Mar. 10, 1972; stepchildren: Jeffrey Allan, Franne Ruth, Eric Carl, Stanley Glenn. BA summa cum laude, U. Minn., Mpls., 1958; MD, U. Minn., 1962; MS, Ohio State U., 1969. Resident in psychiatry U. Pa. Sch. Medicine, Phila., 1963-64; resident anatomic pathology Presbyn.-U. Pa. Med. Ctr., Phila., 1965-66; fellow neuropathology Phila. Gen. Hosp., 1967, Ohio State U. Hosp., Columbus, 1968-69; instr. Ohio State U., 1969; asst. prof. U. Utah Sch. Medicine, Salt Lake City, 1970-76, assoc. prof., 1976-80; assoc. prof. pathology U. Conn. Sch. Medicine, Farmington, 1980-90, prof., 1990—. Contbr. articles to profl. jours. Mem. Am. Med. Women's Assn., Internat. Soc. Neuropathology, Conn. Soc. Pathologists, World Muscle Soc., Am. Assn. Neuropathologists, Phi Beta Kappa, Alpha Omega Alpha. Mem. Ch. of Christ. Avocations: reading, music, travel. Home: 1550 Asylum Ave West Hartford CT 06117-2805 Office: U Conn Health Ctr Dept Pathology Farmington CT 06032

GRUNOW, RICHARD F. music educator; b. Mineral Point, Wis., Nov. 22, 1945; s. Frederick Henry and Ruby Lucille Grunow. BS in Secondary Edn., U. Wis.-Platteville, 1967; M in Music Edn., U. Mich., 1974, PhD in Music Edn., 1980. Instrumental music tchr. Beloit (Wis.) Pub. Schs., 1967—74; lectr. in music edn. U. Mich., Ann Arbor, 1977—78; prof. music edn. Eastman Sch. of Music, Rochester, NY, 1979—. Co-author: (method book) MLR Instrumental and Choral Score Reading Programs, 1979—84, Creativity in Improvisation, 1997—98, Jump Right In: The Instrumental Series, 1987—2002. Recipient Disting. Alumnus award, U. Wis., 1994. Mem.: Early Childhood Music and Movement Assn., Orgn. of Am. Kodaly Educators, Gordon Inst. for Music Learning, Music Educators Nat. Conf. Home: 3 Tobey Woods Pittsford NY 14534 Office: Eastman Sch of Music 26 Gibbs St Rochester NY 14604

GRUNSFELD, ERNEST ALTON, III, architect; b. Chgo., June 5, 1929; s. Ernest Alton Jr. and Mary Jane (Loeb) G.; m. Sally Riblett, July 10, 1954 (dec. 1999); children: Marcia Grunsfeld Henner, John Mace. Student, Inst. Design, Chgo., 1945, Art Inst. Chgo., 1946; BArch, MIT, 1952. Registered architect, Ill., Conn., Ind., Mich., N.C., Ohio, Mo., Wis. Ptnr. Yerkes & Grunsfeld, Chgo., 1956-65; owner Grunsfeld & Assocs., Architects, Chgo., 1965-75, sr. ptnr., 1975-84, owner, 1984—2001; prin. Grunsfeld Shafer Architects, LLC, 2001—. Corp. mem. Woodlawn Hosp., Chgo., 1968-70; mem. Highland Park (Ill.) Planning Commn., 1969-75; pres. Grunsfeld Meml. Fund, Chgo., 1970—. Contbr. articles to profl. jours. Bd. dirs. Urban Gateways, Chgo., 1968-89, mem. adv. bd., 1989—; life mem. Field Mus. Natural History, Chgo., 1970—, Chgo. Symphony Orch. Assn., 1975—, governing mem., 1995—; mem. exec. com. Coun. for Arts MIT, Cambridge, 1977-89, bd. dirs., 1977—; hon. life mem. Chgo. Hort. Soc., 1995—, governing mem., 2001—; benefactor, hon. governing mem. Art Inst. Chgo., 1980—. Recipient 1st Honor award Burlington Mills, 1968. Fellow AIA (corp. mem. Chgo. chpt., Honor award 1962, citation of merit 1969); mem. Tavern Club, Lake Shore Country Club, Arts Club of Chgo. Office: Grunsfeld Schafer Architects LLC 211 E Ontario St Chicago IL 60611-3219

GRÜNWALD, HANS WOLFGANG, internist, hematologist, oncologist; b. Stuttgart, Germany, July 24, 1935; came to U.S., 1968; s. Walter I. and Lotte (Strauss) G.; m. Doris Heine, Jan. 4, 1969; children: Michael, Judy, David. Medico-Cirujano, U. Chile, Santiago, 1960. Diplomate Am. Bd. Internal Medicine, Am. Bd. Hematology, Am. Bd. Med. Oncology. Intern, resident in internal medicine Mount Sinai Hosp., Chgo., 1960-63; fellow clin. hematology Tufts/N.E. Med. Ctr., Boston, 1963-65; asst. prof. pathophysiology U. Chile Sch. Medicine, Valparaiso, 1965-68; coord. dept. medicine Sisters of Charity Hosp., Buffalo, 1968-72; staff hematologist Queens Hosp. Ctr., N.Y.C., 1972-75, assoc. dir. hematology, 1975-78, chief divsn. hematology, 1978-92, chief divsn. hematology-oncology, 1992—. Asst. prof. medicine SUNY, Buffalo, 1968-72; asst. assoc. prof. medicine SUNY, Stony Brook, 1972-86; assoc. prof. medicine Albert Einstein Coll. medicine, Bronx, N.Y., 1986-93, Mt. Sinai Sch. Medicine, N.Y.C., 1993—. Co-author: (book chpt.) Chemicals and Leukemia, 1982, 88, 94; author: (book chpt.) Treatment of Adult Leukemia, 1994. Fellow Am. Coll. Physicians; mem. N.Y. Soc. Study of Blood (exec. comm. membership com. 1991-92, v.p. 1995-96, pres. 1996-97), Am. Soc. Hematology, Am. Soc. Clin. Oncology, Internat. Soc. Hematology, N.Y. Acad. Scis., Am. Cancer Soc. (chmn. med. affairs Queens divsn. 1995—). Democrat. Jewish. Avocations: sailing, skiing, photography, classical music. Office: Queens Hosp Ctr 82-68 164th St Jamaica NY 11432-1140 E-mail: hans.grunwald@mssm.edu.

GRUNWALD, HENRY ANATOLE, ambassador, editor, writer; b. Vienna, Dec. 3, 1922; arrived in U.S., 1940, naturalized, 1948; s. Alfred and Mila (Loewenstein) G.; m. Beverly Suser, Jan. 7, 1953 (dec. 1981); children: Peter, Madeleine, Lisa; m. Louise Melhado, May 1, 1987. AB, NYU, 1944, LHD, 1975; LLD, Iona Coll., 1981; LHD, Bennett Coll., 1983; LittD (hon.), Webster U., Vienna, 1989. Editorial staff Time mag., 1945-87, sr. editor, 1951-61, fgn. editor, 1961-66, asst. mng. editor, 1966-68, mng. editor, 1968-77; corp. editor Time Inc., 1977-79, editor-in-chief, 1979-87; amb. to Austria, 1988-90. Author: Salinger, a Critical and Personal Portrait, 1962, Churchill, The Life Triumphant, 1965, One Man's America, 1997, Twilight, 1999; contbr. to Time, Life, New Yorker, Fgn. Affairs and Wall St. Jour. Trustee Am. Austrian Found.; mem. adv. bd. Nat. Press Inst. Russia, World Press Freedom Com.; bd. dirs. Lighthouse Internat., Internat. Rescue Com., Met. Opera Guild, Am. Friends of the Salzburg Easter Festival; mem. bd. overseers faculty arts and scis. NYU. Named sr. fellow Salzburg Seminar. Fellow Royal Soc. Arts; mem. ASCAP, Am. Coun. on Germa, Coun. Am. Ambassadors, Coun. Fgn. Rels., Met. Opera Assn., Internat. Press Inst., Century Assn., Knickerbocker Club, Phi Beta Kappa. Office: 654 Madison Ave New York NY 10021-8404

GRUPE, ROBERT CHARLES, corporate training consultant; b. Alice, Tex., Sept. 3, 1948; m. Dorothy E. Cleveland, Nov. 22, 1975; children: Amber, Robert, Elisabeth, Jonathan. BA, MBA, Calif. Coast U., 1977, PhD, 1992. Announcer Stein Broadcasting Co., Sweetwater, Tex., 1966-68; news announcer Ea. Okla. TV Co., Ada, 1969-72; announcer Anadarko (Okla.) Broadcasting Co., 1972-74; news dir. Cleveland County Broadcasting Co., Norman, Okla., 1974-75; instr. Elkins Inst., Oklahoma City, 1975-77; mng. editor Okla. World Media, Oklahoma City, 1977-78; pres., owner Quality Prodns. Inc., Oklahoma City, 1978—. Job skills cons. Okla. Pvt. Industry Coun., Oklahoma City, 1989; vol. trainer U.S. Olympic Festival, Oklahoma City, 1989; mem. Total Quality Mgmt. Faculty Okla. State U., 1990-95; TV prodr./host Cox Cable Pub. Programming, Oklahoma City, 1990-96; syndicated radio commentator, 1993-99; talk show host WKY Radio, Oklahoma City, 1999-2000, ind. networking specialist, 2000—; TV host Pathways to Success Produced for Oklahoma City Ednl. TV Consortium, 2001—. Author: The Miracle of Speech, 1981, The Change, 1993, Creating The Future, 1994, Creating Your Future in Network Marketing, 2002; contbr. articles to profl. jours. Vol. media devel. Vol. Action Com. Oklahoma City, 1991. Mem. ASTD (v.p. 1992), Internat. Assn. Bus. Communicators (v.p. 1996-97), Neuro Linguistic Programming Assocs. (v.p. 1991-92). Avocation: historical research. Office: Quality Prodns Inc 4230 NW 36th St Oklahoma City OK 73112-2910 E-mail: dgrupe@drgrupe.com.

GRUPPE, CHARLES CAMILLE, artist; b. N.Y.C., July 1, 1928; s. Paulo Mezdag and Camille Louise (Plasschaert) G.; divorced. BFA, Columbia U., 1954, MFA, 1955. Free-lance artist, U.S.A., Europe, 1960—. Numerous one-man shows, group shows in Boothbay Harbor, Maine, Stamford, Conn., Key West, Fla., Palm Beach, Fla., and Barcelona, Spain; represented in over 5,000 pvt. collections; workshops include Jupiter, Fla., Marathon, Fla., Greenwich, Conn., Oyster Bay, L.I., Hilton Head, S.C., 1991, Greece- 1999, France-2000, Portugal-2001, Spain-2002. With USAAF, 1946-47, PTO. Fulbright Found. fellow, 1957; Columbia U. fellow, 1958; Huntington Hartford Found. fellow, 1959. Mem. Nantucket Art Assn., North Shore Art Assn., Salmagundi Art Assn., Hudson Valley Art Assn., Silvermine Guild. Avocations: stamp collecting, travel. Home and Office: PO Box 6126 Jensen Beach FL 34947

GRUSH, OWEN CHARLES, psychiatry educator; b. Beverly, Mass., Jan. 7, 1940; s. Maurice and Martha (Weisholz) G.; m. Susan Ann Naman, Apr. 5, 1970 (div. Aug. 1990); children: Eric Nathan, Emily Beth; m. Ellen Margaret Wenz, Jan. 18, 1992; stepchildren: Ivy, Jonathan Benjamin. BA, Columbia U., 1960; MD, U. Rochester, 1964. Diplomate Am. Bd. Pediats., Am. Bd. Pediat. Hematology, Am. Bd. Psychiatry and Neurology. Intern in pediats. Children's Hosp., Boston, 1964-65, resident in pediats., 1965-66, sr. resident in pediats. Cin., 1966-67; fellow in pediat. hematology-oncology Children's Rsch. Found., Cin., 1967-69; asst. prof. pediats. Emory U., Atlanta, 1969-72, assoc. prof. pediats., chief hematologist, oncologist, 1972-74; assoc. prof. Med. U. S.C., Charleston, 1974-90, resident in psychiatry, 1991-94, clin. asst. prof. psychiatry, 1994-98; fellow in med. ethics Inst. Med. Humanities, Galveston, Tex., 1985-86; attending psychiatrist Inst. Psychiatry, Charleston, 1994-98, clin. assoc. prof. psychiatry, 1998—2003, clin. prof. psychiatry, 2003—; attending psychiatrist VA Hosp., Charleston, 1995—. Clin. investigator Pdiat. Oncology Group, St. Louis, Mo., 1974-90. Contbr. articles to profl. jours., chpts. to books. Pres. Synagogue Emanu-El, Charleston, S.C., 1988-90; mem. med. missions team St. Philip's Episcopal Ch., Charleston, 1989-95; med. advisor Camp Happy Days for Children With Cancer, Charleston, 1982-91; mem. Jewish Fedn. Bd., Charleston, 1987-91; bd. dirs. Grief and Loss Ctr. of s.C., 1997—. Fellow Am. Acad. Pediats., Am. Psychiat. Assn., Hypnosis Soc. S.C.; mem. Chamber Music Soc. Charleston, Grief and Loss Ctr. S.C. Jewish. Avocations: gardening, theology, ethics. Office: 1064 Gardner Rd Ste 101 Charleston SC 29407-5711

GRUSHOW, SANDY, broadcast executive; BA in Communication, UCLA, 1983. Former v.p. creative advtg. 20th Century Fox Film Corp.; sr. v.p. advtg. and promotion Fox Broadcasting Co., 1988—90, exec. v.p. programming and scheduling, 1990—91; exec. v.p. Fox Entertainment Group, 1991—92, pres., 1992—95, Tele-TV Media, 1995—97, Twentieth Century Fox TV, LA, 1997—; chmn. Fox Entertainment Group. Office: Fox Entertainment Group PO Box 900 Beverly Hills CA 90213-0900

GRUSIN, RICHARD ARTHUR, literature educator, writer; b. Chicago, Ill., Sept. 29, 1953; s. Edward Maxwell and Marcia Jean Grusin; m. Ann Eleanor Gregory, July 28, 1973; children: Sarah Lynne, Samuel Gregory. BA in English with honors, U. Ill., 1976; PhD, U. Calif., Berkeley, 1983. Asst. prof. English Coll. of William and Mary, Williamsburg, Va., 1983—86, Ga. Inst. Tech., Atlanta, 1986—91, assoc. prof., sch. of lit., comm., and culture, 1991—96, assoc. prof. and chair, sch. of lit., comm., and culture, 1996—99; fellow, Robert Penn Warren Ctr. Humanities Vanderbilt U., Nashville, 1999—2000; prof., sch. of lit., comm., and culture Ga. Inst. Tech., Atlanta, 2000—01; prof. and chair of English Wayne State U., Detroit, 2001—. Author: Transcendentalist Hermeneutics: Instl. Authority and the Higher Criticism of the Bible, 1991, Remediation: Understanding New Media, 1999 (Lewis Mumford award in media ecology, 2001), Culture, Tech., and the Creation of America's Nat. Parks, 2003. Office: Wayne State U 51 W Warren Detroit MI 48202 Office Fax: 313-577-8618. E-mail: r.grusin@wayne.edu.

GRUSKY, ROBERT R. investor; b. N.Y.C., Aug. 19, 1957; s. Burton and Barbara (Rudoy) G.; m. Hope Holmes Eiseman, Feb. 25, 1989; children: Robert R. Jr., Katherine Elizabeth, Alexandra Rose. BA in History cum laude, Union Coll., 1979; MBA with distinction, Harvard U., 1985. Banking assoc. to banking officer to 2nd v.p. U.S. Banking Dept. Continental Ill. Nat. Bank and Trust Co., Chgo., 1979-83; assoc. to v.p. investment banking divsn. Goldman Sachs & Co., N.Y.C., 1985-93, v.p., prin. investment, 1993-97; asst. to the sec. of def. for spl. projects The Pentagon, Washington, 1990-91; sr. advisor Hon. Ronald S. Lauder, N.Y.C., 1997-2000; pres. RSL Investments Corp., N.Y.C., 1998-2000; mem. New Mountain Capital, N.Y.C., 2000—. Mng. mem., gen. ptnr. Hope Capital Ptnrs., 2000—. Trustee Hackley Sch., Tarrytown, N.Y., 1992—. White House fellow, 1990-91. Mem. Harvard Club N.Y.C., Manursing Island Club. Presbyterian. Office: 712 5th Ave Fl 23D New York NY 10019-4108

GRUSON, MICHAEL, lawyer; b. Berlin, Sept. 17, 1936; came to U.S., 1962; s. Rudolf and Barbara Gruson; m. Hiroko Tsubota, July 11, 1964; children; Rudolf, Andreas, Sebastian, Matthias, Florian, Konrad. LLB, U. Mainz, Fed. Republic of Germany, 1962; M in Comparative Law, Columbia U., 1963, LLB, 1965; Dr. iur, Freie Univ., Berlin, 1966. Bar: N.Y. 1969, U.S. Ct. Appeals (2d cir.) 1969, U.S. Dist. Ct. (so. dist.) N.Y. 1971, U.S. Supreme Ct. 1977. Assoc. Shearman & Sterling, N.Y.C., 1966-73, ptnr., 1973—2000, of counsel, 2000—. Bd. dirs. Mizuho Corp. Bank. Author: Die Bedurfniskompetenz, 1967; co-author: Sovereing Lending: Managing Legal Risk, 1984, Legal Opinions in International Transactions, 4th edit., 2003, Regulation of Foreign Banks, 2 vols., 4th edit., 2003, Acquisition of Shares in a Foreign Country, 1993; contbr. articles to profl. jours. Mem. Am. Law Inst., Internat. Bar Assn. (past vice chmn. com. banking law, past chmn. subcom. on legal opinions, hon. treas. Am. br.), N.Y. State Bar Assn. (com. internat. banking, securities and fin. transaction, internat. law and practice sect.), Internat. Law Assn. (com. on internat. monetary law, hon. treas. Am. br.). Home: 108 E Hook Cross Rd Hopewell Junction NY 12533 Office: Shearman & Sterling 599 Lexington Ave Fl C2 New York NY 10022-6069

GRUTMAN, JEWEL HUMPHREY, lawyer, writer; b. N.Y.C., Mar. 13, 1931; d. Robert and Gladys Humphrey; m. Robert W. Bjork, June 26, 1954 (div. Apr. 22, 1975); 1 child, Bruce Bjork; m. Roy Grutman, Oct. 30, 1975 (wid. 1994); m. Fredrick Yonkman, July 4, 1998. BA magna cum laude, Mt. Holyoke Coll., 1952; LLB, Columbia U., 1955. Bar: N.Y., U.S. Dist. Ct. (So. Dist.) N.Y. 1971, U.S. Dist. Ct. (ea. dist.) N.Y. 1974, U.S. Dist. Ct. Conn. 1984, U.S. Supreme Ct. 1984. Atty. Debevoise & Plimpton, N.Y.C., 1954-60; ptnr. Eaton Van Winkle, N.Y.C., 1976-79, Grutman Greene & Humphrey, N.Y.C., 1979—. Co-author: (with CD-ROM) The Ledgerbook of Thomas Blue Eagle, 1994 (Christopher award 1995, Internat. Reading Assn. award), The Sketchbook of Thomas Blue Eagle, 2001, (CD-ROM) The Journey of Thomas Blue Eagle, 1995 (Best Project award Intermedia, Asia, 1995, Creative NGe ANN Disting. award 1995, EMMA award best visual content 1996); asst. prodr., editor (ednl. film on art) Where Time is a River (1st prize Women's Film Festival); contbr. photograph illustrations: The Reforming Power of the Scriptures, 1996; developer series of designs based on Native Am. art; contbr. articles to mags. and newspapers. Dir. Inwood Ho., N.Y.C., 1970-80; past mem. various coms. Mt. Holyoke Coll.; mem. com. sr. advisors N.Y. Commn. for Internat. Bus. and UN, 1997; past chmn. com. to establish Barbara Black Fellowship at Columbia U. Law Sch.; past pres. 85th St. Playground Assn., N.Y.C.; active supporter The Children's Storefront, Harlem, N.Y.C., N.Y. Jr. League. Mem. Assn. Bar City N.Y., The Stanwich Club (Greenwich, Conn.). Avocations: opera, golf, tennis, poetry. E-mail: bijou203@optonline.net.

GRUVER, WILLIAM ROLFE, investment banker; b. Denver, May 31, 1944; s. John and Marion Jean (Plummer) G. AB with distinction, Dartmouth Coll., 1966; MBA, Columbia U., 1968. Ptnr. Goldman, Sachs & Co., N.Y.C., 1972-99; ret., 1999. Disting. exec. in residence, prof. Bucknell U., 1993—; dir. eSocrates, Allentown, Pa., 2002—; mem. investment com. Geisinger Found., Danville, Pa., 2002—; mem. adv. bd. Hirtle, Callaghan & Co., West Conshocken, Pa., 1996—, Cornell U. Park Leadership Fellows, Ithaca, N.Y., 2002—. Vol. Big Bros., Morristown, NJ, 1981—84; mayor Eagles Mere Borough, 1994—; trustee Eagles Mere (Pa.) Cmty. Ch., 1993—; chmn. bd. trustees Woodbridge (N.J.) Devel. Ctr., 1982—87; trustee Berea Coll., 1995—, Eagles Mere Found., 1998—2003; mem. advisor bd. The Lymphoma Found., N.Y.C., 1985—; founder, faculty advisor Bucknell Harvest, 1997—; arbitrator NASD, 1993—. Lt. USN, 1968—72. Mem. Am. Legion. Home: PO Box 359 Eagles Mere PA 17731-0359 E-mail: gruver@bucknell.edu.

GRUY, HENRY JONES, engineering company executive, petroleum engineer; b. Victoria, Tex., June 10, 1915; s. Heinrich and Bessie (Jones) G.; m. Evelyn Hudson, Nov. 15, 1941 (dec. Feb. 1977); children: Robert Henry, Janet Gruy Winter, William Alan; m. Erma Bell Jopling, Jan. 7, 1978 (dec. Oct. 1980). BS, Tex. A&M U., 1937, Profl. Engr. degree, 1956. Registered profl. engr., Tex. Field engr. Standard Oil Co., Midland, Tex., 1937-38; exploitation engr. Shell Oil Co., Ark., La., Tex., 1938-42, dist. engr., 1942-45; engr., geologist DeGolyer & MacNaughton, Dallas, 1945-50; chmn. H.J. Gruy and Co., Houston, 1950—. Author: (with others) Petroleum Exploration and Economics, Vol. 19, 1981; contbr. articles to profl. jours. Recipient Alumni Hon. award Coll. Engring., Tex. A&M U., 1986, Disting. Alumnus award Tex. A&M U., 1990. Fellow Inst. Petroleum (U.K.), Australasian Inst. Mining & Metallurgy, mem. Soc. Petroleum Engrs. (hon., pres. 1968-69, DeGolyer award 1983), AIME (hon., v.p. 1969-70), Soc. Petroleum Evaluation Engrs. (life, pres. 1963-64), Am. Assn. Petroleum Geologists (cert., del.), Nat. Acad. Engrs., Petroleum Engrs. Club Ft. Worth (pres. 1953), Petroleum Engrs. Club Dallas (pres. 1950)

GRUZINSKA, ALEKSANDRA, language educator; BA, SUNY, Buffalo, 1964, MA, 1966; PhD, Pa. State U., 1973. Instr. French Sweet Briar Coll., Va., 1971-73; asst. prof. French Ariz. State U., 1973—. Co-translator (with Murray D. Sirkis) of Antoine Pecquet's Diverse Thoughts on Man (from the French Pensées diverses sur l'homme 1738), 1999; editor, contbr.: Essays on E.M. Cioran Rasinari 1911-Paris 1995, 1999; contbr. articles to profl. jours. Fulbright scholar, Paris, 1968-69. Mem. Phi Beta Kappa. Home: 1929 W Javelina Ave Mesa AZ 85202-5724 Office: Dept Langs & Lits Ariz State U PO Box 870202 Tempe AZ 85287-0202 E-mail: gruzinska@asu.edu.

GRYC, STEPHEN MICHAEL, composer, music educator; b. St. Paul, June 26, 1949; s. George and Jean (Funk) G.; m. Judith Drake King, May 7, 1977; 1 child, William Edward. MusB, U. Mich., 1971, MusM, 1978, D of Musical Arts, 1983. Prof. music composition U. Hartford, Conn., 1980—. Composer: Wind Machine for Organ and Orch., 1978 (ASCAP grant to Young Composers 1979), 3 Fantasies for Orch., 1983 (Rudolph Nissim prize 1986), Dance Concerto for Clarinet & Orch., 1989 (Conn. Commn. on Arts grant 1988), Fantasy Variations for Oboe and String Quartet, 1992 (New Music Del. prize 1996). Official town composer Town of Farmington, Conn., 1995. MacDowell Colony fellow, Peterborough, N.H., 1985, 88; recipient citation of merit Gen. Assembly State of Conn., 1995, Ucross (Wyo.) Found. residency, 1996; Meet the Composer grantee, 1997. Mem. ASCAP, Am. Composers Forum, Am. Music Ctr., Soc. Composers, Inc., Conn. Composers, Inc., Pi Kappa Lambda. Avocations: geyser study and observation, regional U.S. cuisine. Home: 19 Tanglewood Rd Farmington CT 06032-1162 Office: U Hartford The Hartt Sch 200 Bloomfield Ave West Hartford CT 06117-1545 E-mail: stevegryc@aol.com.

GRYKA, GEORGE EDWIN, chemical company executive; b. Belmont, Mich., Nov. 22, 1932; s. George John and Helen Elizabeth (Powlowski) G.; m. Madeline E. Barko, Sept. 28, 1957; 1 child, Cynthia Mary (dec.). BSChemE, U. Mich., 1954, MS, 1955. With Monsanto Co., St. Louis, 1955-68, planning mgr., 1966-68; corp. planning analyst GAF Corp., N.Y.C., 1969; with Stauffer Chem. Co., Westport, Conn., 1970-84; pres. Mt. Pleasant Chem. Co., Westport, 1978-81, divsn. gen. mgr., 1981-84; prin. Phoenix Internat. Enterprises, Southport, Conn., 1984—. Bd. dirs. TODD Credfeld Inc., Roanwell Corp., PIPco, Inc. Mem. Planning Forum (past pres. N.Y. chpt., past nat. v.p.), Soc. Chem. Industry, Am. Coun. Sci. and Health Comml. Devel. Assn., Southport Racquet Club. Home: 893 Sasco Rd Southport CT 06490 Office: PO Box 656 Southport CT 06890-0656 E-mail: ggryka@compuserve.com.

GRYSON, JOSEPH ANTHONY, orthodontist; b. Rahway, N.J., Feb. 11, 1932; s. Elmer Joseph Anthony and Joyce Asher (Toms) G.; m. Patricia Ann Huddleston, Nov. 22, 1961; children— Karen Ann, David Joseph. B.Chem. Engring., Cornell U., 1954; D.D.S., U. Calif., San Francisco, 1964. Diplomate: Am. Bd. Orthodontics. Engr. div. refinery tech. service Standard Oil of Calif., Richmond, 1954, 58-60; individual practice dentistry specializing in orthodontics San Rafael, Calif., 1964-96; clin. instr. orthodontics U. Calif., San Francisco, 1965-87, assoc. clin. prof. orthodontics, 1987-99, clin. prof. orthodontics, 1999—. Referee Am. Jour. Orthodontics and Dentofacial Orthopedics. Contbr. articles to profl. jours. Treas., pres., dir. Hmeowners Assn., San Rafael, 1970-74. Served as carrier pilot USN, 1954-58. Mem. ADA, Pacific Coast Soc. Orthodontists (dir. 1980-85, pres. 1985-86, award of merit 1992), Am. Assn. Orthodontists (ho. of dels. 1982-87, 94-95, spkr. ho. of dels. 1988-91, James E. Brophy Disting. Svc. award 1996), Calif. Dental Assn. (Disting. Svc. award 1994), E.H. Angle Soc. (sec. No. Calif. component 1992-96). Home: 1060 Lea Dr San Rafael CA 94903-3726 E-mail: jagryson@comcast.net.

GRZANKA, LEONARD GERALD, writer, consultant; b. Ludlow, Mass., Dec. 11, 1947; s. Stanley Simon and Claire Genevive Grzanka; m. Christine Duncan Pearson, May 15, 1997 (div. Dec., 2000). BA, U. Mass., 1972; MA, Harvard U., 1974. Asst. prof. Gakushiun U., Tokyo, 1975-78; pub. rels. specialist Pacific Gas and Electric Co., San Francisco, 1978-80; sales promotion writer Tymshare Transaction Svcs., Fremont, Calif., 1980-81; account exec. The Strayton Co., Santa Clara, Calif., 1981-82; mng. editor Portable Computer Mag., San Francisco, 1982-84; prin. Grzanka Assocs., San Francisco, 1984-86; San Francisco bur. chief Digital News, 1986-91; battery program cons. Bevilacqua Knight Inc., Oakland, Calif., 1991-97; freelance writer, cons., 1997—. Staff asst. Electric Power Rsch. Inst./U.S. Advanced Battery Consortium, Palo Alto, Calif., 1991-96; lectr. Golden Gate U., San Francisco, 1985-87; instr. Diablo Valley Coll., Pleasant Hill, Calif., 2002—. Author: Neither Heaven Nor Hell, 1978; translator, editor: (art catalog) Masterworks of Japanese Crafts, 1977; translator: (book chpt.) Manajo: The Chinese Preface to the Kokinwakashu, 1984 (Literary Transl. award 1984), Spanish translation, 1994. Sgt. USAF, 1965—69. Fellow, Danforth Found., 1974. Mem. Harvard Club of San Francisco (bd. dirs. 1984-88, Cert. Appreciation 1986, 88), Phi Beta Kappa, Phi Kappa Phi. Avocations: writing, fishing. Home: 2909 Madison St Alameda CA 94501-5426

GRZEBIENIAK, JOHN FRANCIS, psychologist; b. New Castle, Pa., Jan. 9, 1949; s. John and Helen (Mielcuszny) G.; married; children: Anna Helen, Sarah Mary, Andrew John. BA, Youngstown (Ohio) State U., 1970, MS in Edn., 1974; PhD, U. Pitts., 1982. Lic. psychologist, Ohio, Pa.; cert. chem. dependency counselor. Substance abuse counselor, mental health counselor Columbiana County Mental Health Counseling Ctr., 1974-82, intern in psychology, 1982-84; cons. psychologist Diagnostic and Evaluation Clinic, Youngstown, 1985—; dir. diagnostic assessment Columbiana County Mental Health Ctr., 1984-95, sr. psychologist, 1995—, dir. diagnostic svcs., 1997—. Cons. psychologist Beaver (Pa.) Valley Psychol. Svcs., 1988-90; adj. prof. dept. psychology Kent (Ohio) State U., 1989—; mem. consulting staff Salem (Ohio) Cmty. Hosp., 1996-99;

bd. dirs. Forensic Psychiat. Ctr. Northeastern Ohio, Inc., Youngstown; presenter numerous seminars. Contbr. articles to Salem (Ohio) News, profl. publs. Fellow: Pa. Psychol. Assn.; mem.: APA. Roman Catholic. Avocations: woodworking, gardening, fishing, sausage making. Office: Psychological Svcs 128 Leeper Dr New Castle PA 16102-2716 E-mail: jgrzeb@prodigy.net.

GRZESIK, JAN ALEXANDER, electronics engineer, mathematician; b. Rybnik, Upper Silesia, Poland, Aug. 7, 1939; arrived in U.S., 1952; s. Aleksander Franciszek Grzesik and Anna Makowska; m. Ewa Wiktoria Michalak, July 24, 1965 (div. Dec. 1970); m. Renata Ewa Wisniewska, Jan. 4, 1971; children: Renata Katarzyna, John Michael. BA in Physics summa cum laude, UCLA, 1960, PhD in Nuc. Engring., 1977; MA in Physics, Harvard U., 1961. Physicist U. Calif. Lawrence Livermore Lab., 1963; tchg. fellow dept. physics Harvard U., Cambridge, Mass., 1963—64; sr. staff antennas TRW Space and Electronics, Redondo Beach, Calif., 1968—; physicist RAND Corp., Santa Monica, Calif., 1973—75; rsch. engr. Sch. Engring. Applied Sci. UCLA, 1975—76. Contbr. articles to profl. jours. Fellow, Woodrow Wilson Found., 1960—61, NSF, 1961—62. Mem.: Math. Assn. Am., IEEE Antennas and Propogation Soc. Avocation: music. Home: 5517 Babcock Ave Valley Village CA 91607-1530 Office: Northrop Grumman Space Tech Onc Space Pk R11/2856AA Redondo Beach CA 90278

GRZYMALA-BUSSE, JERZY WITOLD, engineering educator; b. Warsaw, Apr. 3, 1942; s. Witold Lech and Estera Maria Grzymala-Busse; m. Dobrosława Melania Thomas, Feb. 11, 1967; children: Anna Maria, Witold Jakub, Jan Pawel. MSEE, Tech. U., Poznan, 1964, PhD, 1969; MS in Math., Wroclaw U., 1967; Habilitation in Engring., Tech. U., Warsaw, 1972. Asst. prof. Tech. U. Poznan, Poland, 1970-73, assoc. prof., 1973-80; prof. U. Kans., Lawrence, 1980—. Contbr. over 150 articles to profl. publs. Mem.: AAAI, NRC, Assn. Computing Machinery, Internat. Rough Set Soc., Upsilon Pi Epsilon. Avocation: running. Home: 4713 Wimbledon Dr Lawrence KS 66047-9301 Office: U Kans 415 Snow Hall Lawrence KS 66045-7523 Fax: 785-864-3226. E-mail: jerzy@ku.edu.

GSCHNEIDNER, KARL ALBERT, JR., metallurgist, educator, editor, consultant; b. Detroit, Nov. 16, 1930; s. Karl and Eugenie (Zehetmair) Gschneidner; m. Melba E. Pickenpaugh, Nov. 4, 1957; children: Thomas, David, Edward, Kathryn. BS, U. Detroit, 1952; PhD, Iowa State U., 1957. Mem. staff Los Alamos Sci. Lab., 1957-62, sec. chief, 1961-62; vis. asst. prof. U. Ill., Urbana, 1962-63; assoc. prof. materials sci. and engring. Iowa State U., Ames, 1963-67, prof., 1967-79, Disting. prof., 1979—, metallurgist, 1963-67, sr. metallurgist, 1967—, dir. Rare-earth Info. Ctr., 1966-96; vis. prof. U. Calif.-San Diego, La Jolla, 1979-80; cons. Los Alamos Nat. Lab., 1981-86, Teltech, 1987-2000. Author: Rare Earth Alloys, 1961, Scandium, 1975, others; editor: (33 vol. book) Handbook on the Physics and Chemistry of Rare Earths, 1978-2003, Industrial Applications of Rare Earth Elements, 1981; contbr. numerous chpts. in books and articles to profl. publs. Recipient William Hume-Rothery award AIME, Warrendale, Pa., 1978, Burlington No. award for Excellence in Rsch., Iowa State U., 1989, Significant Implication for Energy Related Techs. in Metallurgy and Ceramics award Dept. Energy, 1997; co-recipient Outstanding Sci. Accomplishment in Metallurgy and Ceramics award Dept. Energy, Washington, 1982, Frank H. Spedding award Rare Earth Rsch. Confs., 1991, Russell B. Scott Meml. award Cryogenic Engr. Conf., 1995, David R. Boyland Eminent Faculty award in Rsch. Coll. Engring., Iowa State U., 1997; named Sci. Alumnus of 2000, U. Detroit-Mercy. Fellow Minerals, Metals and Materials Soc., Am. Soc. for Materials Internat., Am. Phys. Soc.; mem. AAAS, Am. Chem. Soc., Am. Crystallographic Assn., Materials Rsch. Soc., Iowa Acad. Sci., Materials Rsch. Soc. India (hon.), Cryogenic Soc. Am., Japan Inst. Metals (hon.). Roman Catholic. Office: Iowa State U Ames Lab Ames IA 50011-3020 E-mail: cagey@ameslab.gov.

GSCHWIND, DONALD, management and engineering consultant; b. Youngstown, Ohio, July 3, 1933; s. Mark Leon and Esther Lillian (Wauschek) G.; s. Eleanor Ann Tyken, May 27, 1961; children: Sandra J., Kurt L. BSME, Case Western Res. U., 1955; MS in Auto Engring., Chrysler Inst. Engring., 1957; MBA, Mich. State U., 1975. With Chrysler Corp., Detroit, 1955-58, mgr. steering and suspension engring., 1968-72, mgr. product engring., 1972-74, mgr. quality control, 1974-76, dir. chassis engring., 1976-80, v.p. product planning, 1980-84, v.p. program mgmt., 1984-88; dir., master automotive engring. Lawrence Tech. U., 1994-96. Served to capt. USAF, 1957—59. Mem. Soc. Auto Engrs., Tau Beta Pi

GSCHWINDT DE GYOR, PETER GEORGE, SR., economist; b. Budapest, Hungary, Jan. 1, 1945; came to U.S., 1975; s. George and Marie Henrietta (Haggenmacher) G.; m. Michele Herman, Oct. 14, 1972; children: Henrik, Marie. MA in Econs., Brussels U., Belgium, 1967. Grad. trainee Samuel Montagu and Co., London, 1967-69; dep. mgr. Europe Chase Manhattan Bank, London, 1970; credit officer Banque de Commerce (Chase), Antwerp and Brussels, 1971-75; ops. officer IMF, Washington, 1975-80, economist, 1980-90, with govt. fin., balance of payments, 1990—2002; ret., 2002. Dir. Hosp. Relief Fund for Caribbean, Chevy Chase, Md., 1982—. Decorated knight Magistralis Grace Sovereign Mil. Order Malta, Rome, 1975. Roman Catholic. Avocation: golf. Home: 5710 Grosvenor Ln Bethesda MD 20814-1834 Personal E-mail: pgdegyor@aol.com.

GU, BAOHUA, soil scientist, chemist; b. Changshu, Jiangsu, China, Nov. 22, 1958; came to U.S., 1986; s. Dexing and Liushi G.; married, Aug. 1984; children: Alice P., Jessie P. BS, Nanjing (China) Agrl. U., 1982; MS, U. B.C., Vancouver, Can., 1986; PhD, U. Calif., Berkeley, 1991. Postdoct. fellow Oak Ridge (Tenn.) Nat. Lab., 1992-93, rsch. scientist, 1993—. Inventor resin regeneration. Grantee, U.S. PTO, 2002—. Office: 1 Bethel Valley Rd Oak Ridge TN 37830-8050

GU, HENRY HONGSHENG, pharmacist, researcher; s. Yuanqing Gu and Xiuwen Cao; m. Linda Yihong Yihong Ding, Mar. 20, 1993; children: Rachel Shinran, Sophie Yiran. MS, Ohio U., 1996; BS, Shanghai Jiao Tong U., 1987. Rsch. scientist Bristol-Myers Squibb Co., Princeton, NJ, 1997—; rsch. chemist Sanle GE, Nanjing, China, 1987—93. Patent advisor Bristol-Myers Squibb Co., Princeton, NJ, 2002—. Mem 80-20. Scholar Nanyang Scholarship, Shanghai Jiao Tong U., 1987, Scholarship, Ohio U., 1993—96, U. of Pa, 1996. Mem.: Am. Chem. Soc. Achievements include patents for Us 6, 399, 773; Us 5, 990, 109; patents pending for Wo 0026197; Wo 0181340; research in Jour. of Bioorganic & Medicinal Chemistry; Jour. of Medicinal Chemistry; Organic Letters; Tetrhedron Letters; Synlett; discovery of new drug discovery. Office: Bristol-Myers Squibb Co Po Box 4000 Princeton NJ 08543-4000

GU, JENG YUL, radiologist; b. Kyung Nam Do, Republic of Korea, 1936; came to U.S., 1965; MD, Coll. Medicine, Seoul, 1962. Diplomate Am. Coll. Radiology. Intern Bon Secours Hosp., Grosse Point, Mich., 1965-66; resident radiology Detroit Gen. Hosp., 1966-69; resident pathology Victoria Hosp., London, 1969-70; resident radiology Toronto Gen. Hosp., 1970-71; pvt. practice Sayre, Pa., 1971—. Instr. SUNY Upstate Med. Ctr. Mem. Radiol. Soc. N.Am. Office: Guthrie Clinic Guthrie Sq Sayre PA 18840-1606

GU, JIANMIN, mechanical engineer, researcher; b. Shanghai, Sept. 6, 1970; arrived in U.S., 1995; parents Shunfa Gu and Lingjiu Zhang. BS, Shanghai Jiao Tong U., 1992, MS, 1995; PhD, U. Mich., 2000. Lab. and rsch. asst. Nat. Lab. Ocean Engring. Shanghai Jiao Tong U., 1991-92, rsch. investigator/asst. Structural Mech. Lab., 1992-95; rsch. asst. thermotractive thin film rsch. group Mich. State U., East Lansing, 1995—96; rsch. asst. Computational Mech. Lab. U. Mich., Ann Arbor, 1995—2000, instr. dept. mech. engring. and applied mech., 1999; devel. and test engr. core analysis tools Mech. Dynamics, Inc., Ann Arbor, Mich., 1997-99; rsch. engr. rsch. and vehicle tech. Ford Motor Co., Dearborn, Mich., 2000—. Summer rsch. engr. Tech. and Equipment Rsch. Inst. Shengil Oil Field Complex, Shandong, China, 1992; cons., reviewer jours. in field. Contbr. articles to profl. jours. Recipient 3d prize, Shanghai Sci. and Tech. Assn., 1993, Best Paper award, Nat. Conf. Offshore Engring., 1994, Disting. Achievement award, U. Mich. Coll. Engring., 1998, Vehicle NVH Recognition award, Ford Motor Co., 2002, 2003; Nat. Congress Computational Mech. scholar, 1999, Horace H. Rackham Travel grantee, 1999, Computational Dynamics fellow, Mech. Dynamics, Inc., 1999. Mem.: AIAA, ASME, Internat. Assn. Computational Mechanics (Finalist award Robert J. Melosh medal 1999), Soc. Automotive Engrs., U.S. Assn. Computational Mechanics (Computational Mechanics scholar 1999), Chinese Soc. Naval Arch. and Marine Engrs. (Fellowship award 1991), Am. Acad. Mechanics, Sigma Xi. Avocations: travel, reading, music. Office: Ford Motor Co Product Devel Ctr 1D-M32 20901 Oakwood Blvd Dearborn MI 48124 Fax: 313-322-0312. E-mail: jgu2@ford.com.

GU, KEQIN, mechanical engineering educator; b. Lanxi, China, Nov. 23, 1957; came to U.S., 1985; s. Lijian Gu and Jieping Jiang; m. Xinxin Zhu, Apr. 20, 1985; children: Siyao, Patrick. BS, Zhejiang U., 1982, MS, 1985; PhD, Ga. Tech. Inst., 1988. Instr. Zhejiang U., China, 1985; rsch. asst. Ga. Tech. Inst., Atlanta, 1985-88; rsch. assoc. Oakland U., Rochester, Mich., 1989-90; from asst. prof. to prof. So. Ill. U., Edwardsville, 1990—, grad. program dir., 1998—2002, acting chair, 2003—. Faculty advisor Siue Me Club, Edwardsville, 1990-91; co-organizer NSF-CNRS Workshop on Advances in Time-delay Systems, 2003; program com. mem. Conf. on Decision and Control, 2001-03. Contbr. articles to profl. jours.; assoc. editor IEEE Transactions on Automatic Control, 2000-02; program editor IFAC Workshop on Time-delay Systems, 2001. Mem. IEEE, ASME, Am. Soc. Engring. Edn., Control Sys. Soc. (conf. assoc. editor 1995-99). Achievements include research in time-delay systems, robust control theory, robotics, nonlinear dynamics. Office: So Ill U Dept ME/IE Edwardsville IL 62026

GU, YANPING, neuroscientist, researcher; b. Xuzhou, Jiangsu, China, Jan. 22, 1956; d. Xiangtong Gu and Huifang Su; m. Xiaofu Wang, Jan. 22, 1985; children: Jane Wang, Jonathan Wang. MD, Nanjing Med. Coll., China, 1978, MS, 1984. Tchg. asst. Nanjing Med. Coll., 1979—81, instr., 1985—88; vis. scientist U. of Tex. Med. Br., Galveston, 1989—96, asst. prof., 1997—. Contbr. articles to profl. jours. Recipient Sci. and Advantage Tech. award, Jiangsu Province Health Bur., 1987, Nat. Youth Excellent Physiology Thesis award, Chinese Physiology Soc., 1988. Mem.: Soc. for Neurosci. Achievements include discovery of new in vitro priming procedure that generates a nearly pure population of neurons from fetal human neural stem cells transplanted into adult rat central nervous system. Avocations: reading, gardening. Office: U Tex Med Br 301 University Blvd Galveston TX 77555 Office Fax: 409-762-9382. Personal E-mail: yagu@utmb.edu. E-mail: yagu@utmb.edu.

GUADAGNO, MARY ANN NOECKER, social scientist, consultant; b. Springville, N.Y., Sept. 21, 1952; d. Francis Casimer and Josephine Lucille (Fricano) Noecker; m. Robert George Guadagno, Aug. 29, 1970 (div. Mar. 1981). BS in Edn. cum laude, SUNY, Buffalo, 1974; MS, Ohio State U., 1977, PhD, 1978. Grad. teaching assoc. Ohio State U., Columbus, 1974-77, grad. rsch. assoc., 1977-78; asst. prof. U. Minn., St. Paul, 1978-83; cons. Nationwide Ins. Co., Columbus, 1982-83, rsch. assoc. Corp. Rsch., 1983-86, product devel. assoc., Office of Mktg., 1986-89; adjunct prof. Coll. Bus. & Pub. Adminstrn. Franklin U., Columbus, Ohio, 1985-89; lectr. Coll. Bus. Adminstrn. and Econ. Ohio Dominican Coll., Columbus, 1986-89; scientist family econ. rsch. group USDA, Washington, 1989-93; survey statistician Nat. Ctr. for Health Stats., HHS, Washington, 1993—. Chair Women's Coun., DHHS, Hyattsville, Md., 1993-96; mem. women in sci., 1991-93; health scientist adminstr. Nat Inst. Health, Nat. Inst. Aging DDHS, Washington. Author: Family Inventory of Money Management, 1982, Family Inventory, 1982; contbr. articles to profl. jours., 1978—. Com. mem. United Way, Mkt. Rsch. Info. Exchange, Columbus, Ohio. Recipient Spl. Recognition award Ohio House Reps., 1987, Cert. Grad. award Columbus Area Leadership Program, 1987, Cert. Appreciation award Am. Mktg. Assn., 1987, Cert. Merit award U.S. Dept. Agr., 1991. Mem. Columbus Area Leadership Program, Ohio State U. Coll. Human Ecology Alumni. Republican. Roman Catholic. Avocations: horseback riding, classical music, eastern philosophy, gardening. Home: 4853 Cordell Ave Apt 921 Bethesda MD 20814-3024 Office: Nat Inst Health Ctr for Sci Rev 6701 Rockledge Dr Bethesda MD 20817 E-mail: guadagma@csr.nih.gov.

GUADAGNOLI, MICHAEL JOHN, music educator; b. Walsenberg, Colo., Sept. 22, 1974; s. Albert W. and Mary Ann Guadagnoli. BA, Adams State Coll., Alomosa, CO, 1997; MA, Adams State Coll., Alamosa, CO, 2001. Band dir. Windsor (Colo.) HS, 1997—98, Monte Vista (Colo.) Mid. Sch., 1998—2003. Mem.: San Luis Valley Music Educators Assn. (pres. 1998—2001), Colo. Band Masters Assn., Colo. Music Educators Assn. (rep. 1993—2002, treas. 2003), Elks Club (esquire / chaplin 1997—2002, lctr. knight, loyal knight 1998—2003), Phi Beta Mu. Roman Catholic. Office: Monte Vista Mid Sch 3720 Sherman St Monte Vista CO 81144 Office Fax: 719-852-6199.

GUAJARDO, ELISA, counselor, educator; b. Roswell, N. Mex., Nov. 13, 1932; d. Alejo Najar and Hortensia (Jiminez) Garcia; m. David Roberto Guajardo, Oct. 15, 1950; 1 child, Elsie Edith. BS, Our Lady of the Lake U., 1962, MEd, 1971; MA, Chapman U., 1977. Cert. tchr., adminstr., counselor, Calif. Elem. tchr. San Antonio (Tex.) Sch. Dist., 1962-63; tchr. social sci. Newport Mesa Sch. Dist., Costa Mesa, Calif., 1963-67, Orange (Calif.) Unified Sch. Dist., 1967-70, project dir., 1970-71, tchr. English, 1972-73, counselor, 1973—. Pres. Bilingual, Bicultural Parent Adv. Bd., Orange, Calif., 1971-72; reader bilingual projects Calif. State Dept. Edn., Orange, 1971-72; vis. lectr. We. Wash. Univ., Bellingham, 1972-73; mem. curriuculum and placement couns., Orange Unified Sch. Dist., 1973-78, 95-96. Author: (Able)Adaptations of Bilingual/Bicultural Edn, Fed. Project Proposal. Mem. NEA, AAUW, Calif. Tchrs. Assn., Orange Unified Edn. Assn, Hon., Alpha Chi, Our Lady of Lake U., Tex. chpt. Democrat. Mem. Assemblies of God Church. Avocations: choir and solo singing, piano, marimba, organ. Home: 335 E Jackson Ave Orange CA 92867-5743 Office: Canyon HS 220 S Imperial Hwy Anaheim CA 92807-3945 E-mail: davielisa2@juno.com.

GUAJARDO TOUCHÉ, RICARDO, bank executive; BS in Mech. and Elec. Engring., ITESM; MBA, U. Calif., Berkeley; MSEE, U. Wis. With VISA, VAMSA; CEO Grupo Financiero BBVA Bancomer, S.A. de C.V., Mexico, chmn. Bd. dirs. Mex. Stock Exch., FEMSA, VAMSA, ITESM, TMM, Grupo Industry Alfa, El Puerto de Liverpool, Grupo Aeropuertario del Sureste. Mem.: Mex. Bankers Assn. (pres. 1993). Office: Grupo Financiero BBVA Banomer SA de CV Montes Urales 424 11000 Col Lomas de Chapultepec Mexico

GUALTIERI, JOSEPH PETER, museum director; b. Royalton, Ill., Dec. 25, 1916; s. Simone and Teresa (Toracca) G.; m. Marie E. MacDonald, Nov. 21, 1939; children: Ricardo Simone, Renee Marie; m. Angeline Lanzetta, Sept. 19, 1987. Diploma, Art Inst. Chgo., 1939; postgrad. study in, Italy, 1969-70, Mex., 1939-40. Tchr. art Hull House, Chgo., 1942, Lyman Allyn Mus., New London, Conn., 1945-46, Eastern Conn. State U., Willimantic, Conn., summers 1950-52, Hillyer Coll., Hartford, Conn., 1957-58, Norwich (Conn.) Art Sch., 1943-79; tchr. Norwich Free Acad.; dir. Slater Meml. Mus., Norwich, 1962—2000. One-man exhbns. include Chgo. Art Inst., 1941, Contemporary Art Gallery, N.Y.C., 1951, Nexus Gallery, Boston, 1965, Parnassus Gallery, Chgo., 1941-42, Cummings Art Ctr., New London, Conn., 1979, retrospective exhbn. Slater Mus., 1992. Bd. dirs. Otis Library, Norwich, 1975-81; mem. Norwich Charter Revision Com. Recipient 1st prize Chgo. Art Inst., 1941, Logan medal, 1941; purchase prize Pa. Acad. Fine Arts, 1948, 51; prize Eastern States Exposition Conn. Artists, 1951 Mem. Conn. Acad. Fine Arts, United Italian Soc. (chmn.). Democrat. Roman Catholic. Home: 179 Liberty St Pawcatuck CT 06379-1335

GUAN, SHANGBO G. physician; b. Aug. 15, 1951; MD, Guangzhou (China) Med. Coll., 1983; PhD, Tulane U., 1992. Instr. Guangzhou Med. Sch., 1983 88, asst. prof., 1988-90; rsch. scientist Tulane Med. Sch., New Orleans, 1992-96; intern, resident Morehouse Sch. Medicine, Atlanta, 1996-99; physician Prompt Med. Care, Atlanta, 1999-2000; pvt. practice physician Atlanta, 2000—. Contbr. articles to profl. jours.

GUAN, ZHUANG-DAN DANIEL, mathematician, educator; arrived in U.S., 1987; s. Yusen Guan and Xinfan Zhuang; m. Zhiqiang Susan Zhu; children: Grace Esther, John Nathanael. PhD, U. Calif., Berkeley, 1993; degree, Amoy U., Xiamen, China, 1982. Asst. prof. Princeton (N.J.) U., 1993—2000, U. Calif., Riverside, 2000—. Asst. rschr. Inst. Math. Academia Sinica, Beijing, 1986—87. Partitcipant Christian chs., Riverside, Calif., 2000—. Grantee, NSF, 1993—2003. Achievements include research in classification of compact complex homogeneous spaces.

GUARE, JOHN, playwright, educator; b. N.Y.C., Feb. 5, 1938; s. John Edward and Helen Clare (Grady) Guare; m. Adele Chatfield-Taylor, 1981. AB, Georgetown U., 1961; MFA, Yale U., 1963; PhD (Hon.), Georgetown U., 1991. Seminar in writing fellow Saybrook Coll., Yale U., New Haven, 1977—78; adj. prof., 1978—81; fellow Juilliard Sch., 1993—94; lectr. NYU, CCNY; vis. artist Harvard U., 1990—91. Author: (plays) Universe, 1949, Thirties' Girl, 1959, The Toadstool Boy, 1960, The Golden Cherub, 1962, Did You Write My Name in the Snow, 1962, To Wally Pantoni, We Leave a Credenza, 1964, The Loveliest Afternoon of the Year, Something I'll Tell You Tuesday, 1966, Muzeek, 1967 (Obie award, 1968), Cop-out, 1968 (N.Y. Drama Critics' award, 1969), A Play by Brecht, Home Fires, Kissing Sweet, 1969, The House of Blue Leaves, 1971 (N.Y. Drama Critics' Circle award, 1971, Outer Critics' Circle award, 1971, Obie award, 1971, Tony award, 1986), (musical) Two Gentlemen of Verona, 1971 (N.Y. Drama Critics' Circle award, 1972, 2 Tony awards, 1972, 2 Drama Desk awards, 1972), A Day for Surprises, 1971, Un Pape a New York, 1972, Marco Polo Sings a Solo, Optimism, or the Adventures of Candide, 1973, Rich and Famous, 1974, Landscape of the Body, 1977 (Joseph Jefferson award, 1977), Take a Dream, 1978, Bosoms and Neglect, 1979, In Fireworks Lie Secret Codes, 1981, Lydie Breeze, Gardenia, 1982, Hey, Stay a While, Women and Water, 1984, Gluttony, The Talking Dog, 1985, Moon Over Miami, 1989, Six Degrees of Separation, 1990 (N.Y. Drama Critics' Circle award, 1991), London, 1993 (Olivier Best Play award, 1993), Four Baboons Adoring the Sun, 1992 (Tony award nomination Best Play, 1992), Moon Under Miami, 1995, The General of Hot Desire, 1997; co-adapter, lyricist: plays Two Gentlemen of Verona, 1971; author: (screenplays) Taking Off, 1970, Atlantic City, 1981 (Academy award nomination Best Original Screenplay, 1981, N.Y. Film Critics' award, 1981, L.A. Film Critics' award, 1981, Nat. Soc. Film Critics' award, 1981, Venice Film Festival Grand prize, 1981), Six Degrees of Separation, 1993, Chuck Close: Life and Work 1988-1995, War Against the Kitchen Sink, 1996; playwright-in-residence N.Y. Shakespeare Festival, 1976—77; co-editor: Lincoln Ctr. Rev. Named Lit. Lion, N.Y. Pub. Libr., 1986; recipient Award of Merit, Am. Acad. Arts and Letters, 1981; Rockefeller grantee. Mem.: Am. Acad. Arts and Letters, Dramatist Guild Council. Address: Kay Collyer & Boose LLP 1 Dag Hammarskjold Plz New York NY 10017-2201

GUARENTE, LENNY, medical geneticist, educator; b. Chelsea, Mass., June 6, 1952; s. Leonard and Norma Guarente; m. Barbara Weiffenbach, Sept. 6, 1981 (div. 1985); 1 child, Jeffrey. BS, MIT, 1974; PhD, Harvard U., 1978. Prof. MIT, Cambridge, 1981—. Founder, dir. Elixir Pharm., Cambridge, 2000—. Author: Ageless Quest, 2003; contbr. Mem.: Am. Acad. Microbiology. Achievements include patents in field; discovery of gene that regulates aging.

GUARINI, FRANK JOSEPH, lawyer, real estate developer; b. Jersey City, N.J., Aug. 20, 1924; s. Frank J. G., Sr. and Caroline Loretta Critelli. BA, Dartmouth Coll., 1946; JD, NYU, 1950, LLM, 1955; LHD (hon.), St. Peter's Coll., 1994; DLitt (hon.), N.J. City U., 1993. Bar: N.J. 1951, D.C. 1994, N.Y. 1995. Sr. ptnr. Guarini & Guarini, Jersey City, N.J., 1951—; senator State of N.J., Trenton, 1966-73; mem. Ho. of Reps., Washington, 1979-93; U.S. rep. UN Gen. Assembly, 1995—96. Bd. dirs. John Cabot U., Rome, 1994—; founder Guarini Ctr. for Govtl. Affairs St. Peter's Coll., Jersey City, N.J., 1994—, bd. dirs. Washington Ctr. for Interns, 1993-96, The New Cmty. Found., Newark, 1993-94; pres., chmn. Nat. Italian Am. Found., 1999—; rep. U.S. UN, N.Y.C., 1997-98; alumni trustee Hague (The Netherlands) Acad. Internat. Law, 1956-60. Fellow ABA; mem. Am. Trial Lawyers Assn. (nat. bd. govs. 1975-78), N.J. State Bar Assn. (mem. gen. coun. 1960-63), N.Y. Athletic Club. Democrat. Roman Catholic. Avocations: skiing, tennis, archeology, travel. Office: Guarini & Guarini 30 Montgomery St Ste 15 Jersey City NJ 07302-3821 Fax: 201-938-1503. E-mail: gsdinc@msn.com.

GUARINO, ANTHONY MICHAEL, pharmacologist, educator, consultant, counselor; b. Framingham, Mass., Dec. 11, 1934; s. Alfred V. and Nellie L. (Beatrice) G.; m. Aida Iris Gerena, Nov. 9, 1957; children: Theresa, Elizabeth, Barbara, Cathy, Tom, Gregory, Paula, Phil, Richard, Paul. BS in Chemistry, Boston Coll., 1956; MS in Chemistry, U. R.I., 1963, PhD in Pharmacology and Toxicology, 1966; MA in Counseling, Liberty U., 1993. Lic. profl. counselor. Lt. comdr. USPHS, 1966, advanced through grades to capt., 1979; staff fellow pharmacology-toxicology rsch. assoc. program Nat. Heart Inst., NIH, Bethesda, Md., 1966-68; rsch. pharmacologist NCI Nat. Cancer Inst., NIH, Bethesda, Md., 1968-73, chief lab. toxicology, 1973-80; regulatory pharmacologist Ctr. for Drugs and Biologics-FDA, Md., 1980-84; lab. dir. fishery rsch. br. FDA, Dauphin Island, Ala., 1984-93. Adj. prof. U. South Ala. Coll. Medicine, Mobile, 1984—, U. South Ala. Coll. Allied Health Professions, Mobile, 1996—; marriage and family counselor Cath. Social Svcs., Mobile, 1993—; vice chmn. com. on animals as monitors in environ. hazards NAS. Contbg. author: Handbook of Experimental Pharmacology—Concepts in Biochemical Pharmacology, 1971, Handbook of Experimental Pharmacology, Antineoplastic and Immunosuppressive Agents, 1974, Methods in Cancer Research, 1979, Pesticides and Xenobiotics Metabolism in Aquatic Organisms, 1979, Pesticides and Xenobiotics Metabolism in Aquatic Organisms, 1979, Cisplatin—Current Status and New Developments, 1980, Modern Pharmacology, 1982; contbr. 106 articles to profl. jours. Mem. Am. Soc. Pharmacology and Exptl. Therapeutics, Soc. Toxicology, Am. Chem. Soc., Am. Assn. Christian Counselors. Roman Catholic. Home: 968 Westbury Dr Mobile AL 36609-3332 Office: U So Ala Coll Medicine Dept Pharmacology Msb 3130 Mobile AL 36688-0001 E-mail: amguarino@cssmobile.org.

GUARNIERI, GIULIA, literature educator; d. Giancarlo Guarnieri and Lucilla Seghi. Laurea in Fgn. Languages, U. of Bologna, Italy, 1987—93; PhD in Romance Languages and Lit., U. of Wash., 1994—2002. Cert. tchr. Italy, 2000. Tchg. assoc. U. of Wash., Seattle, Wash., 2000—02; asst. prof. Monmouth U., Long Br., NJ, 2002—. Dir. of italian honor soc. Monmouth U., 2003—, advisor for the italian minor, 2002—; book reviewer for the italian textbook Prego McGraw Hill, N.Y.C. Author (elem. italian) lang. tapes and cd's; contbr. jour. article in italian quarterly, book article, jour. article. Fellow Ege Fellowship, U. of Bologna, 1991-1992; scholar Edn. abroad, U. of Wash., 1998, Fritz scholarship, 1998. Mem.: MLA (corr.). Office: Monmouth U 400 Cedar Ave West Long Branch NJ 07764

GUARNO, PETER GARY, consumer products company executive; b. White Plains, N.Y., July 25, 1952; s. Peter Vincent and Betty Omejean (Baker) G. BS, Elizabeth Seton Coll., 1976. V.p., CFO, auctioneer White Plains Auction Rms., 1976-80; pres., CFO, auctioneer Westchester County Auctions, Larchmont, N.Y., 1981-88; pres., CFO 7-11 Corp, Larchmont, 1988-92, Schmieg & Kotzian Custom Furniture, Mamaroneck, N.Y., 1990-96; CEO, CFO Judgement Review Group, White Plains, 1996—. CEO, CFO Antique Advt. Network, White Plains, 1996—. E-mail: pgman725@aol.com.

GUASTAFERRO, ANGELO, science administrator, consultant; b. Hoboken, NJ, June 4, 1932; s. Carlo and Rafaela Nancy (Gioffi) G.; m. Eleanor Lago, Sept. 12, 1954; children: Carl, Mark, John Brian. BS in Mech. Engring, N.J. Inst. Tech., 1954, MBA, Fla. State U., 1963; A.M.P., Harvard U., 1984. With NASA, 1963-85, dep. mgr. Viking project, 1974-76; dir. planetary programs NASA Hdqs., Washington, 1979-81; dep. dir. Ames Research Center, Moffett Field, Calif., 1981-85; v.p., program dir. Lockheed Missiles & Space Co., 1985-96, exec. dir., 1994-96; CEO, CFO, chmn. bd. N View Corp., Newport News, Va., 1996; pres., CEO View Corp., Newport News, Va., 1996—98; exec. cons. Ag Cons., Williamsburg, Va., 1998—. Bd. trustees Internat. Space U., 1993-96; bd. dirs. View Corp., 1995-2002; sci. adv. com. NJIT. Chair bd. dirs. Hampton Rds. Tech. Coun. Served with USAF, 1955-58. Recipient Langley Spl. Achievement award NASA, 1974, 77, 78, Outstanding Leadership medal, 1977, Superior Performance award, 1980, Exceptional Service medal, 1981, Presdl. Meritorious rank, 1982; Disting. Alumnus NJIT, 1997. Fellow AIAA (Space Systems medal 1982), Am. Astronautics Soc.; mem. Mars First Landing Soc. (pres. 1978-79), Internat. Astronautics Fedn. (bd. dirs.), Tau Beta Pi (eminent engr. 1989). Roman Catholic. Office: Ag Cons 124 Peter Lyall Williamsburg VA 23185-8902

GUAY, DAVID ADALBERT, biology educator; b. Lewiston, Maine, June 14, 1973; s. Raymond R. and Diane Lauziere G. BS in Biology, Bates Coll., 1995; MS in Marine Biology, U. Calif., San Diego, 1997. Cert. EMT. Instr. dept. biology Bowdoin Coll., Brunswick, Maine, 1997—, field dir. Coastal Studies Ctr., Orr's Island, Maine, 1998; EMT Orr's and Bailey Islands Rescue/Cundy's Harbor Rescue, Harpswell, Maine, 1999—. Ednl. cons. in

marine biology, 2000-02; mem. steering com. New Meadows River Watershed Project, 1999-2001. Chmn. Harpswell Conservation Commn., 1998-2001; bd. dirs. Orr's and Bailey Island Fire Dept., 2000-2002. Fellowship Beinecke Bros. Meml. Found., 1994-97, Calif. Regent's fellowship U. Calif., 1995-97. Mem. Soc. for the Study of Evolution, Nat. Marine Educators Assn., Gulf of Maine Marine Educators Assn. (sec. bd. dirs. 2003—), New Eng. Estuarine Rsch. Soc., Phi Beta Kappa, Gamma of Maine, Sigma Xi. Democrat. Roman Catholic. Avocations: writing, natural history, science education, sports, cooking. Office: Bowdoin Coll Dept Biology 6500 College Station Brunswick ME 04011-8465 Fax: 207-725-3405. E-mail: dguay@bowdoin.edu.

GUAY, GORDON HAY, federal agency administrator, marketing educator, consultant; b. Hong Kong, Aug. 1, 1948; came to U.S., 1956; s. Daniel Bock and Ping Gin (Ong) G. AA, Sacramento City Coll., 1974; BS, Calif. State U., Sacramento, 1976, MBA, 1977; postgrad., U. of the Pacific, 1978; PhD, U. So. Calif., 1981. Mgmt. assoc. U.S. Postal Svc., Sacramento, 1980-82, br. mgr., 1982-83, fin. mgr., 1983-84, mgr. quality control, 1984-86, mgr. tech. sales and svcs. divsn., 1986-91, dir. mktg. and comm., 1991-95, postmaster, 1996—. Prof. bus. adminstrn., mktg. and mgmt. Calif. State U., Sacramento, 1981-85; prof. mktg. Nat. U., San Diego, 1984—; pres. Gordon Guay and Assocs., Sacramento, 1979—; cons. Mgmt. Cons. Assocs., Sacramento, 1977-79. Author: Marketing: Issues and Perspectives, 1983; also articles to profl. jours. With U.S. Army, 1968-70. Recipient Patriotic Svc. award U.S. Treasury Dept., San Francisco, 1985. Fellow Acad. Mktg. Sci.; mem. NEA, AAUP, Am. Mgmt. Assn., Am. Mktg. Assn. (Outstanding Mktg. Educator award 1989), Am. Soc. Pub. Adminstrn., Soc. Advancement Mgmt. (Outstanding Mem. 1976), Assn. MBA Execs. Democrat. Avocations: teaching, golf, tennis, fishing, camping.

GUBBINS, KEITH EDMUND, chemical engineering educator; b. Southampton, Eng., Jan. 27, 1937; came to U.S., 1962; m. Pauline Margaret Payne, June 28, 1960; children: Nick, Vanessa. B.Sc. in Chemistry, Queen Mary Coll., U. London, 1958; Diploma in Chem. Engring., King's Coll., U. London, 1959, PhD in Chem. Engring., 1962. Vis. lectr. U. London, Eng., 1960-62; postdoctoral fellow U. Fla., Gainesville, 1962-64, asst. prof., 1964-68, assoc. prof., 1968-72, prof., 1972-76; T.R. Briggs prof. engring. Cornell U., Ithaca, N.Y., 1976-98, dir. Sch. Engring., 1983-90; W.H. Clark Disting. Univ. prof. N.C. State U., Raleigh, 1998—. Vis. cons. theoretical physics divsn., U.K. Atomic Energy Authority, Harwell, U.K., 1971; vis. prof. physics dept. U. Guelph, 1971-73, 76, U. Kent, Canterbury, Eng., 1975; vis. prof. chemistry U. Oxford, 1979-80, 86-87; vis. prof. chem. engring., U. Calif., Berkeley, 1982, Australian Nat. U., Canberra, 1993, Imperial Coll., London, 1970-71, 94, 2002, U. Paris-Sud, 2001-02; McCabe lectr. N.C. State U., 1986, Lindsay lectr. Tex. A&M, 1989, Dodge lectr. Yale U., 1990, Katz lectr. U. Mich., 1991, Wohl lectr. U. Del., 1991, Merck lectr. Rutgers U., 1992, Olaf Hougen vis. prof. chem. engring., U. Wis., 1993, Chiba U., Japan, 1999, U. Paris-Sud, 2001-2002; Miles lectr. U. Pitts., 1995, Merck lectr. U. P.R., 1995, Robb lectr. Pa. State U., 1997, Fair lectr., U. Okla., 1997, Leland lectr. Rice U., 2001; vis. fellow Fulbright Sr. scholar Australian Nat. U., 1993-94; T.W. Leland lectr. Rice U., 2001; cons. Mobil Oil, 1979, 80, Exxon Engring., 1980-81, Union Carbide Corp., 1981, Process Simulation Internat., 1982, Nat. Bur. Stds., 1983, BP Rsch., U.K., 1985, 89, Exxon Rsch. and Engring. Co., Clinton, N.J., 1985-95, Unilever Rsch., Port Sunlight, U.K., 1985, Linde divsn. Union Carbide Corp., 1988, Mobil Rsch., Princeton, 1991, Exxon Chem. Co., 1991, BHP, Melbourne, Australia, 1993, Johnson Matthey, 1994, Chevron Rsch., 1995, Westvaco, 2000, Gaz de France, 2001, Dow Chem., 2002; mem. NAS com. to study formation of Nat. Resource Ctr. for Computing in Chemistry, 1976-77, NRC Assessment Bd. to rev. NIST programs, 1988-91. Mem. editl. bd. Molecular Physics, 1978-87, 95—, Jour. of Chem. Physics, 1995-98, Molecular Simulation, 1986—, assoc. editor, 1990—; assoc. editor Am. Inst. Chem. Engrs. Jour., 1988-91; editor: Topics in Chem. Engring., Oxford U. Press, 1991—; del. Oxford U. Press, 1991—. Recipient best paper ann. award Can. Soc. Chem. Engring., 1973; nemed Eppley Found. fellow Imperial Coll. London, 1970-71, Guggenheim fellow, 1986-87, sr. vis. fellow (SERC award) U. Oxford, 1986-87, vis. fellow (SERC award) Imperial Coll., London, 1994. Mem. NAE, AAAS, Am. Chem. Soc., Am. Inst. Chem. Engrs. (program com. 1974-81, Alpha Chi Sigma award 1986, William H. Walker award 2000), Am. Inst. Physics, Chem. Soc. (London). E-mail: keg@ncsu.edu., kgubbins@aol.com.

GUBER, PETER, executive producer; b. Boston, Mass., Mar. 1, 1942; m. Linda Gellis. BA, Syracuse U.; SSP, JD, LLM, U. Florence, Italy; postgrad., NYU. Bar: N.Y., Calif., D.C. Exec. asst. Columbia Pictures, studio chief, co-chmn., 1989-94; prin. Peter Guber's Filmworks; co-prin., chmn. bd. Casablanca Record and Filmworks (merger Peter Guber's Filmworks and Casablanca Records), 1976-80; prin. Polygram Pictures, 1980-83, Guber-Peters, 1983-88; co-chmn., mng. dir. Guber-Peters-Barris Entertainment Co, 1988-89, chmn., 1989; chmn., chief exec. officer Sony Pictures Entertainment, 1989-94; chmn., CEO Mandalay, incl. Mandalay Pictures, Mandalay Television, Mandalay Sports Entertainment, Mandalay Media Arts, Mandalay E-Media. Vis. prof., chmn. producer's dept. UCLA Sch. Theatre Arts. Author: Inside the Deep, Above the Title, (with Peter Bart) Shoot Out: Surviving Game and (Mis)Fortune in Hollywood, 2002; prodr.: (films) The Deep, 1977; (with Jon Peters) Vision Quest, 1985, Batman, 1989, Tango & Cash, 1989; (with Peters and Neil Canton) The Witches of Eastwick, 1987, Caddyshack II, 1988; (television) Stand By Your Man, 1981, Brotherhood of Justice, 1986, Bay Coven, 1987, Nightmare at Bitter Creek, 1988, Finish Line, 1989; exec. prodr.: Midnight Express, 1978; (with Peters) An American Werewolf in London, 1981, Six Weeks, 1982, Missing, 1982 (Academy award nomination for best picture 1982), Flashdance, 1983, D.C. Cab, 1983, Head Office, 1985, The Legend of Billie Jean, 1985, The Color Purple, 1985 (Academy award nomination for best picture 1985), Youngblood, 1986, Gorillas in the Mist, 1988, Rain Man, 1988 (Academy award for best picture 1988), Missing Link, 1989, The Bonfire of the Vanities, 1990, This Boy's Life, 1993, With Honors, 1994; (with Peters, George Folsey, Jr., and John Landis) Clue, 1985; (with Peters, Mark Damon, John Hyde, and Sydney Kimmel) The Clan of the Cave Bear, 1986; (with Peters, Kathleen Kennedy, Frank Marshall, and Steven Speilberg) Innerspace, 1987; (with Peters and Roger Birnbaum) Who's That Girl?, 1987, (with Peters, Benjamin Melniker, and Michael E. Uslan) Batman Returns, 1992, Galapagos: The Enchanted Voyage, 1999, Alex and Emma, 2003; (television) The Toughest Man in the World, 1984; (with Peters) Television and the Presidency, 1983 (Emmy award nomination 1984), Rude Awakening, 1998; asst. prodr.: High Spirits, 1988. Named Producer of Yr., NATO, 1979; Albert Gallatin fellow NYU. Office: Mandalay Entertainment Astaire Bldg 10202 W Washington Blvd Culver City CA 90232-3119*

GUBERMAN, JAYSETH, financial analyst; b. Bridgeport, Conn., Apr. 4, 1960; s. Maurice and Sylviaselma Guberman; m. Ronda Faith Fabian, May 24, 1990; 1 child, Lily Imanuela. BA, Sacred Heart U., Fairfield, Conn., 1981; MA, NYU, 1985. Tchr. 7th Grade Congregation B'nai Torah, Trumbull, Conn., 1986—89; claims analyst Peerless Ins. Co., Hartford, 1997—. Contbr. articles to profl. jours. Recipient Two Star Internat. Website award, Fedn. Internat. de Philatelie, 2000, Bronze award, Midaphil Nat. Philatelic Website awards, 1999, 2000. Mem.: Soc. Israel Philatelists, Am. Philatelic Soc. Avocations: philately, Chinese, Islamic & classical numismatics, travel, historical research, reading. Home: PO Box 270357 West Hartford CT 06127-0357 Personal E-mail: IT2IK3@yahoo.com.

GUBERMAN, SIDNEY, painter, writer; b. Greenville, S.C., Aug. 24, 1936; s. Morris and Louise (Cook) G.; m. Jennifer Glidden, June 5, 1965 (div. 1977); children: Maxwell, Angus; m. Rebecca Wilson, July 31, 1977; children: Elizabeth Tindall, Dore Hopkins Brooks. BA, Princeton U., 1958; MArch, U. Pa., 1967. Asst. prof. Ecole Polytechnique, Lausanne, Switzerland, 1973-75. Vis. artist U. S.C., Columbia, 1991-92, Atlanta Coll. Art, 1989, 91; vis. lectr. Princeton (N.J.) U., 1981; artist invité Federale de Lausanne Ecole des Beaux-Arts, Switzerland, 1971-73; chmn. bd. dirs. New Visions Gallery, Atlanta, 1987-93; bd. dirs. Atlanta Arts Festival, 1986-88. Solo exhbns. include Henri Gallery, Washington, 1970, 73, 75, Galerie R-B, Fribourg, Switzerland, 1975, 79, Image South Gallery, Atlanta, 1976, Harcus/Krakow/Rosen/Sonnabend, Boston, 1976, Fraser's Stable Gallery, Washington, 1978, Heath Gallery, Atlanta, 1979, Leah Levy Gallery, San Francisco, 1979, Diane Brown Gallery, Washington, 1980, Galerie Jonas, Cortaillod, Switzerland, 1980, Barbara Fiedler Gallery, Washington, 1981, Fay Gold Gallery, Atlanta, 1981, 82, 83, 85, Gertrude Herbert Gallery, Augusta, Ga., 1985, Gibbes Art Mus., Charleston, S.C., 1988, Galerie von der Milwe, Aachen, Germany, 1990, Hodges-Taylor, Charlotte, N.C., 1990, Louisa McIntosh Gallery, Atlanta, 1991, Susan Conway Carroll Gallery, Washington, 1991, "New Paintings" Weslyn Coll Gallery, Macon, Ga., 1999; group exhbns. include Prix de peinture, Vevey, Switzerland, 1974, City Gallery Contemporary Art, Raleigh, N.C., 1987, SECCA, Winston-Salem, N.C., 1988, Birmingham (Ala.) Mus. Art, 1988-89; permanent collections include The High Mus., Atlanta, The Hunter Mus., Chattanooga, Tenn., The Nat. Mus. Am. Art, Washington, Princeton (N.J.) U. Mus., Colo. Springs Fine Arts Ctr.; author: Frank Stella: An Illustrated Biography, 1995; curator Frank Stella-Imaginary Landscapes exhbn. The Gibbes Mus., 2001, Charleston, S.C., William Christenberry: Hale County on My Mind, various museums. Individual Artist's grantee NEA, 1980; Guggenheim fellow, 1988-89. Mem. The Ivy Club. Democrat. Avocations: films, tennis, opera. Home: 131 Montgomery Ferry Dr NE Atlanta GA 30309-2712 Office: 1174 Zonolite Pl NE # C Atlanta GA 30306-2002 E-mail: st.gubie@mindspring.com.

GUBERNATIS, MARY LORETTO, filmmaker, agent, writer; b. Glasgow, Scotland, Apr. 27, 1949; arrived in U.S., 1958; d. Robert Shadbolt and Anne McDonagh; m. Louis E. Gubernatis, June 7, 1969; children: Angela, Bridgette, Christine, Debbie, Joseph, Kevin. BA in English, U. Md., Balt., 1968. Pres., agt. McDonagh Davis Assocs., Balt., 1987—, McDonagh David Newberg & Quante, Balt., 1990—92; owner, mgr. Closet Classics, Balt., 1994—96; owner Abracadabra West, Balt., 1996—2003, Hanbury Cross Pub., Balt., 2000—, Zendo Enterprises, Balt., 2000—. Agt. distbr. Ind. Feature Project, N.Y.C., 1989—; program dir. Women in Film & Video, Balt., 1988—; prodr. through Mayor DuBurns office, organizer Welcome Whoopie to Balt., 1988. Author: (books) The Burning of the Bag and What It Begot, 1986, Observation of an Idiosyncratic, 1999, (35 screenplays, including) Every Woman Bleeds, 1991, (screenplays) The Trashman Cometh, Grand Doggy; prodr.: Stagefright; prodr., dir. Loneliest Journey (Telly award); appeared on : Top of the Morning talk show. Sec. Meals on Wheels, Dundalk, Md., 1971—74; active Bea Gaddy Found., Balt., 1995—; prodr. Top of the Morning Promotion and Art in Balt., Balt., 2002—; founder, creator Children's Corner website for charity; founder, min. Order of Angelical Reformation, 1999—. Mem.: Silicon Alley Entrepreneur Club. Democrat. Avocation: writing children's stories. Home and Office: McDonagh Davis Assocs 203 S Castle St Baltimore MD 21231 E-mail: mcdonaghdavis@msn.com.

GUBITS, DAVID BARRY, lawyer; b. New Brighton, Pa., July 12, 1941; s. Harry William and Florence Leonore (Weiner) G.; m. Ruth Miriam Farkas, Apr. 11, 1965; children: Jonathan, Daniel. AB, Brown U., 1963; JD, NYU, 1966. Bar: N.Y. 1967, U.S. Dist. Ct. (no. dist.) N.Y. 1967, U.S. Ct. Appeals (2nd cir.) 1969, U.S. Dist. Ct. (so. and ea. dists.) N.Y. 1977, U.S. Supreme Ct. 1978. Assoc. Appellate Div. 3rd Dept., Albany, N.Y., 1966-68, Gerald N. Jacobowitz, Walden, N.Y., 1967-72; ptnr. Jacobowitz & Gubits, LLP., Walden, 1973—. Dep. atty. Village of Washingtonville (N.Y.), 1973—, Village of Highland Falls (N.Y.), 1976—, Village of Maybrook (N.Y.), 1983—; mem. adv. coun. Stewart Airport Land Authority, New Windsor, N.Y., 1972-81; pres. UJA/Fedn. Rockland County, 1991-92, exec. bd., 1988—. Mem.: ABA (fed. grants com. 1979—84, banking law com. 2000—), Orange County Bar Assn. (chmn. continuing legal edn. com. 1979—80), NY State Bar Assn. (land use control com. 1979—81, real estate devel. com. 1982—84, real estate fin. com. 2000—, atty. opinion letters com. 2000—), Maverick Concerts (pres. 2002—), John Burroughs Soc., Mohonk Preserve (land protection com. 2001—). Avocations: wilderness canoeing, history. Home: PO Box 162 Stone Ridge NY 12484 Office: Jacobowitz & Gubits LLP 158 Orange Ave PO Box 367 Walden NY 12586-0367 E-mail: dbg@jacobowitz.com.

GUBLER, DUANE J. research scientist, administrator; b. Santa Clara, Utah, June 4, 1939; s. June and Thelma (Whipple) G.; m. Bobbie J. Carroll, Mar. 1, 1958; children: Justin Chase, Stuart Jefferson. BS, Utah State U., 1963; MS, U. Hawaii, 1965; ScD, Johns Hopkins U., 1969; AS, So. Utah State U., 1962, DSc (hon.), 1988. Asst. prof. pathobiology Sch. Hygiene Johns Hopkins U., Balt. and Calcutta, 1969-71; assoc. prof. tropical medicine Sch. Medicine U. Hawaii, Honolulu, 1971-75; head virology dept. Naval Med. Rsch. Unit Number 2, Jakarta, Indonesia, 1975-78; assoc. prof. entomology and microbiology U. Ill., Urbana, 1978-79; rsch. microbiologist divsn. vector-borne viral diseases Ctrs. for Disease Control and Prevention, Fort Collins, Colo., 1980-81, dir. San Juan (P.R.) Labs., 1981-89, dir. divsn. vector-borne infectious diseases, 1989—. Cons. NRC, 1972, South Pacific Commn., 1972-76, WHO, Geneva, 1974—, AID, Washington, 1977—, Pan Am. Health Orgn., 1981—, Internat. Devel. Rsch. Ctr., Ottawa, Can., 1977—, Rockefeller Found., N.Y.C., 1987—, numerous nat. ministries of health, 1972—; Bailey K. Ashford meml. lectr. U. P.R. Sch. Medicine, 1999; chmn. bd. coun. Pediat. Dengue Vaccine Initiative, 2002; mem. scientific adv. bd. Novartis Inst. Tropical Diseases, 2003—. Contbr. numerous articles to profl. jours. Lt. USN, 1975-77; capt. USPHS. Recipient Commendation medal, 1984, Outstanding Svc. medal, 1988, Meritorious Svc. medal, 1991, Outstanding Unit citation, 1995, 98, 2000, Outstanding Alumni award for sci. and rsch. Johns Hopkins U. Sch. Pub. Health, 1997, Chuck Alexander Operational award La. Mosquito Control Assn., 1998, Disting. Svc. award Dept. HHS, 2001, Charles Shepard award in Sci., Ctr. for Disease Control, 2001; selected as one of 90 Illustrious Alumni in celebration of U. Hawaii's 90th year, 1997, Woodward Lectr. award USN Preventive Medicine Unit, 2000. Mem. AAAS, Am. Soc. Tropical Medicine (Charles Franklin Craig lectr. 1988, pres.-elect 1998, pres. 2000), Am. Soc. Parasitologists, Am. Mosquito Control Assn., Entomol. Soc. Am. (highlights in med. entomology lecture 1979, 95), Soc. Vector Ecologists, Infectious Disease Soc. Am., Rotary (Rotarian of Yr. San Juan chpt. 1986, Meritorious Svc. award Rotary Found., Evanston, Ill. 1990, Svc. Above Self award Fort Collins Club 1999, Internat. Svc. Above Self award 2000). Home: 717 Dartmouth Trl Fort Collins CO 80525-1522 Office: USPHS Ctrs Disease Control & Prevention PO Box 2087 Fort Collins CO 80522-2087 E-mail: dgubler@cdc.gov.

GUBRIUM, JABER F. sociology educator; b. Hull, Que., Can., July 17, 1943; arrived in U.S., 1950; children: Aline, Erika. MA, Mich. State U., 1966; PhD, Wayne State U., 1970. Prof. Marquette U., Milw., 1970—87, U. Fla., Gainesville, 1987—2002, U. Mo., Columbia, 2002—. Author: Living and Dying at Murray Manor, 1975, Oldtimers and Alzheimer's, 1985, Speaking of Life, 1990. Recipient Disting. Mentor award, Gerontol. Soc. Am., 1991, Disting. Career Contbn. award, 2000, Disting. Scholar award, Am. Sociol. Assn., 1996. Office: Dept Sociology U Mo 312 Middlebush Hall Columbia MO 65211-6100

GUBSER, PETER ANTON, political scientist, writer, educator; b. Tulsa, May 9, 1941; s. Eugene Herbert and Mary (Douglass) G.; m. Annie Yeni-Komshian, Aug. 15, 1969; children: Sasha Mary-Helen, Christi Valerie. BA, Yale U., 1964; MA, Am. U. Beirut, 1966; PhD, Oxford (Eng.) U., 1970. Rsch. fellow U. Manchester, Eng., 1970-72; assoc. rsch. scientist Am. Insts. for Rsch., Washington, 1972-74; asst. rep. Ford Found., Beirut, 1974-77; pres. Am. Near East Refugee Aid, Washington, 1977—. Bd. dirs. Internat. Svc. Agys., Washington, Am. Coun. Vol. Internat. Action, Internat. Coll., Beirut, Nat. Coun. on U.S.-Arab Rels., Washington, Found. for Mid. East Peace, Washington, Global Devel. Forum, Amman, Jordan; adj. prof. Georgetown U., Washington, 1990—; lectr. various govt. and non-govt. instns., 1977—. Author: Politics and Change at Karak, Jordan, 1973, Jordan: Crossroads of Middle East Events, 1983, Historical Dictionary of Hashemite Kingdom of Jordan, 1991. Mem. Somerset (Md.) Town Coun., 1994—. Mem.: Washington Inst. Fgn. Affairs, Middle East Studies Assn., Middle East Inst., Am. Polit. Sci. Assn., Cosmos Club, Order of the Hosp. of St. John of Jerusalem. Democrat. Mem. Christian Ch. Avocations: hiking, reading, travel. Office: Am Near East Refugee Aid 1522 K St NW Ste 202 Washington DC 20005-1202 E-mail: peter@anera.org., gubser@mindspring.com.

GUBTA, INDRAJIT, trade association administrator; Pres. World Fedn. of Trade Unions, Prague, Czech Republic. Died Feb. 2001.

GUCALP, RASIM AHMET, oncologist; b. Erzurum, Turkey, Jan. 31, 1951; MD, Haceteppe U., Ankara, Turkey, 1975. Intern Downstate Med. Ctr., Bklyn., 1982-83, resident, 1983-84; fellow Albert Einstein Cancer Ctr.-Montefiore Med. Ctr., Bronx, N.Y., 1984-86, rsch. fellow, 1986-91; attending physician VA Med. Ctr., Amarillo, Tex., 1991-92; asst. prof Tex. Tech U. Sch. Medicine, Amarillo, 1991-92; attending physician Montefiore Med. Ctr., 1992—; asst. prof. medicine Albert Einstein Coll. Medicine, Bronx, 1992-93, assoc. prof. medicine, 1993—. Fellow Am. Coll. Physician; mem. Am. Soc. Clin. Oncology. Office: Montefiore Med Ctr 111 E 210th St Bronx NY 10467-2401 E-mail: rgucalp@montefiore.org.

GUCCIONE, ROBERT CHARLES JOSEP, publisher; b. Bklyn., Dec. 17, 1930; s. Anthony and Nina G.; children: Tonia, Bob, Jr., Nina, Tony, Nick; m. Kathy Keeton, Jan. 17, 1988. Mng. editor London Daily American. Pub. Forum mag., Variations mag., Viva mag. Omni mag., Four Wheeler mag., Saturday Review, Longevity mag.; chmn. Gen. Media Internat. Inc., 1988—. Artist, 1948-55, 92—; several gallery exhibits and museum shows, 1992-93; formerly cartoonist and greeting card designer; producer film Caligula, 1979; exec. producer TV shows Omni: The New Frontier, Omni: Visions of Tomorrow; pub. Omni, Longevity, Compute, Four Wheeler, Variations, Penthouse Letters, Saturdy Rev., Hot Talk, Girls of Penthouse, Open Wheel, Superstock and Drag, Stock Car Racing, Forum; contbr. articles to profl. jours. Avocations: collecting art, mostly impressionist, some old masters.

GUCKENHEIMER, DANIEL PAUL, financial advisor; b. Tel Aviv, Oct. 10, 1943; came to U.S., 1947, naturalized, 1957. s. Ernest and Eva Guckenheimer; m. Helen Sandra Fox, Dec. 21, 1969; children: Debra Ellen, Julie Susan. BBA in Fin., U. Houston, 1970; cert. hosp. adminstrn., Trinity U., San Antonio, 1973. Asst. adminstr. Harris County Hosp. Dist., Houston, 1970-76; pres. Mid Am. Investments, Kansas City, Kans., 1976; exec. dir. Allen County Hosp., Iola, Kans., 1977-78; comml. loan officer Traders Bank, Kansas City, Mo., 1979; v.p., mgr. Traders Ward Pkwy. Bank, 1980; v.p., mgr. installment loans Traders Bank, 1981, v.p., comml. loan officer, 1982; sr. v.p., mgr. comml. loans United Mo. Bank South, 1982-91; sr. v.p., mgr. lending United Mo. Bank, N.A., 1991-93; pres. Guckenheimer Fin. Svcs., 1993—. Bd. dirs. Robert Morris Assocs., 1988-92, Food Distbn., Inc., 1983-88, Crime Stoppers Greater Kansas City, 1989—; clinic adminstr. 190th USAF Clinic, 1977-84. With USAF, 1962-66, maj. Res. ret. Mem. N.G. Assn., Olympic Soc., Internat. Platform Assn., Assn. Mil. Surgeons U.S., Mil. Order World Wars, B'nai Brith (v.p. 1982-83, pres. 1984-85, treas. 1986-95). Home: 8439 W 113th St Overland Park KS 66210-2437

GUCKER, DOUGLAS, agronomist, consultant; s. Richard and LaVerne Gucker; m. Jane Gleason, July 5, 1975. BS in Biology, Va. Poly. Inst. and State U., 1973, BS in Agronomy, 1975; MS in Agronomy, U. Ill., 1995. Cert. crop advisor Am. Soc. Agronomy/ Ill., 1993. Tech. svc. rep. Chemagro Divsn., Bayer, Sun Prairie, Wis., 1975—75; farmer Gucker Farms Inc., Cisco, Ill., 1976—. Instr. U. Ill. Ext., Monticello, 1992—; tech. adviser Upper Sangamon River Watershed Com., Decatur, Ill., 1994—; sec.-treas. Heartland Ill. Resource Conservation and Devel., Decatur, 2002—. Chmn. dept. youth devel. Episcopal Diocese Springfield, Ill., 1995—99; pres. Piatt County Farm Bur. Found., Monticello, 2002. With USAR, 1974—86. Mem.: Soil and Water Conservation Soc. (state bd. dir. 1998—2000), Am. Soc. Agronomy. Independent. Episcopalian. Avocations: gardening, travel, youth work. Office: Univ Ill Ext - Piatt 210 S Market St Monticello IL 61856 Office Fax: 217-762-2703. E-mail: dgucker@uiuc.edu.

GUCKERT, NORA JANE GASKILL, medical and surgical nurse, hospice nurse, holistic consultant; b. Pitts., June 17, 1945; d. James E. and Nora L. (McAllister) Gaskill; m. Ray H. Guckert, Aug. 1, 1964 (div. May 2001); children: Brian K. Sr., Bruce M., Brenda L. Jansen. LPN, C.C. Allegheny County, Pitts., 1976, AS in Nursing, 1982; BS, Clayton Coll. Holistic Med., 1998, MS, 1999, PhD, 2001. Staff nurse St. Margaret's Meml. Hosp., Aspinwall, Pa., 1976-86; vis. nurse Personal Touch Home Care, Pitts., 1986-87, Norfolk, Va., 1995-98; staff nurse Kimberly Quality Home Care/Portsmouth (Va.) Naval Hosp., 1988-90; pvt. practice, 1988—; liason Sentara Home Health, 1992—92; dir. nursing Med. Staff Svcs., Inc., Virginia Beach, Va., 1997-98; cons. Holistic Health of Tidewater, Inc., Va., 1995-99; dir. nursing edn. Virginia Beach, Newport News and Richmond campsuses Med. Careers Inst., 2000—; cons. Holistic Health of Virginia Beach Cons. Svc., 1997—; hospice dir. Personal Tech Home Care, Va., 1997—99; home health nurse Tender Loving Care/Staff Builders Inc., 2000—02, Comfort Care Home Health, 2003—. Dir. 1st holistic conf. by profls., Virginia Beach, 1997. Author materials on nutritional needs. Vol. Chesapeake Indigent Care Clinic. Home: 3280 Winterberry Ln Virginia Beach VA 23456-5910 E-mail: nonniejphd@earthlink.net., nguckert@comfortcarehomehealthstaff.com.

GUDE, ALBERT VALDEMAR, retired anesthesiologist; b. Atlanta, Oct. 15, 1922; s. Albert Valdemar and Helen (O'Brien) G.; m. Donna Rae Currier, Dec. 22, 1945; children: Anne, Helen, Margaret, Donna, Doris. BA, Emory U., 1943; MD, Johns Hopkins U., 1946. Diplomate Am. Bd. Anesthesiology. Intern Union Meml. Hosp., Balt., 1946-47; resident in anesthesia Lawson VA Hosp. Emory U., Atlanta, 1949-51; pvt. practice anesthesiology Atlanta, 1951-87; chief anesthesiologist Piedmont Hosp., Atlanta, 1976-83; ret. Pres. med. staff Piedmont Hosp., Atlanta, 1968. Mem. AMA, Med. Assn. Ga., Med. Assn. Atlanta, Am. Soc. Anesthesiologists, Rotary Club (charter sec. Jasper, Ga.). Republican. Roman Catholic. Home: 2769 Peachtree Rd NE Apt 9 Atlanta GA 30305-2946

GUDE, GILBERT, former state and federal legislator, nurseryman, writer; b. Washington, Mar. 9, 1923; s. Adolph Elbert and Inez Elinor (Gilbert) G.; m. Jane Wheeler Callaghan, June 19, 1948; children: Sharon, Gilbert Jr., Gregory, Daniel, Adrienne. BS, Cornell U., 1948; MA, George Washington U., 1958; DSc (hon.), Georgetown U., 1977. Del. Md. Gen. Assembly, Annapolis, 1953-58, senator, 1962-66; mem. U.S. Congress from Md. dist., 1967-76; dir. Congl. rsch. svc. Library of Congress, Washington, 1977-86; ind. cons. Bethesda, Md., 1987—. Mem., past chmn. consultative com. Ctr. Parliamentary Documentation Inter-Parliamentary Union, Geneva, 1984-89; mem. exec. com. Environ. and Energy Study Inst., Washington, 1986-89, 1999—; exec. dir. Potomac River Basin Consortium, Bethesda. Author: Where the Potomac Begins, 1984, Small Town Destiny, 1989; contbr. articles on rsch. and info. systems in support of legis. bodies to various publs. Trustee Montgomery County Hist. Soc., Rockville, Md., Md. Hist. Trust, 1992—; bd. dirs. Pks. and History Assn., 1999—. With U.S. Army, 1943-46, PTO. Mem. Nat. Acad. Pub. Adminstrn., Chevy Chase Club, Capitol Hill Club. Republican. Roman Catholic. Home and Office: 5411 Duvall Dr Bethesda MD 20816-1871 E-mail: gjgude@aol.com.

GUDE, NANCY CARLSON, lawyer; b. Kane, Pa., Aug. 5, 1948; d. Edward Walter and Theo Alberta (Herzog) Carlson. BA in History, Pa. State U., 1969; MS in Computer Sci., U. Central Fla., 1981; JD, Thomas M. Cooley Law Sch., 2001. Bar: Fla. 2001. Programmer Group Hospitalization, Inc., Washington, 1969-70; programmer analyst Space Age Computer Sys., Washington, 1970-73, Ky. Fried Chicken, Louisville, 1973-75; sys. analyst Sentinel Comm. Co., Orlando, Fla., 1975-77, programming supr., 1977-78, sys. and programming mgr., 1978-80, asst. dir. data processing, 1980, mgr. staff devel., 1981-82; mgmt. info. svcs. mgr. Sun-Sentinel Co., Ft. Lauderdale, Fla., 1982-83, v.p., dir. info. sys., 1983-94, sys. cons., 1994-98; assoc. atty. Walton Lantaff Schroeder & Carson, Ft. Lauderdale, 2002—. Adj. instr. U. Ctrl. Fla., Orlando, 1981—82. Participant Leadership Broward X; chair LBX Artserve Intervention Group. Recipient Thomas M. Cooley Leadership Achievement award, 2001. Mem.: Pa. State U. (Ft. Lauderdale chpt., treas. 1990—92, v.p. 1992—93, pres. 1993—95). Presbyterian. Home: 1101 River Reach Dr Apt 216 Fort Lauderdale FL 33315-1177

GUDEA, DARLENE, publishing company executive; Group pub. Call Ctr./CRM group Advanstar Tech. Comms., Santa Ana, Calif., 2000—. Office: Advanstar Comms 201 Sandpointe Ave Ste 600 Santa Ana CA 92707-8700 Fax: 714-513-8640.

GUDEMA, NORMAN H. civil engineer; b. Bronx, N.Y., Nov. 7, 1936; s. Daniel and Theresa Gudema; m. Roberta Zacker; children: Michelle, Daniel, Jonathan. BCE, CUNY, 1959; MBA, Fairleigh Dickinson U., 1969. Cert. prof. engr., N.J., N.J., Pa., Ill., Ariz. Project engr. Exxon Rsch. & Engring., Florham Park, N.J., 1966-68, Witco Chem., Oakland, N.J., 1968-70; project mgr. Warner Lambert, Morris Plains, N.J., 1970-81, Lehrer-Mcgovern, N.Y.C., 1985; dir. engring. Cosmair, inc., Clark, N.J., 1985-88, Revlon, Inc., N.Y.C., 1988-89, 81-85; site mgr. Liberty Sci. Ctr., Jersey City, N.J., 1989-93; project mgr.

Hoffman LaRoche, Nutley, NJ, 1994—97, Foster Wheeler, 1997—2001. 1st lt. U.S. Army, 1959. Mem. ASCE, Chi Epsilon. Democrat. Jewish. Home: 27 Coddington Ter Livingston NJ 07039-3633 Office: Hoffmann LaRoche 340 Kingsland St Nutley NJ 07110-1150

GUDEMAN, STEPHEN FREDERICK, anthropology educator; b. Chgo, Ill, June 29, 1939; s. Edward and Frances (Alschuler) G.; m. Roxane Harvey, Sept. 20, 1965; children: Rebecca, Elise, Keren AB, Harvard U., 1961, MBA, 1965; MA, Cambridge U., Eng., 1963, PhD, 1970. Asst. prof. anthropology U. Minn.-Mpls., Minn., 1969-74, assoc. prof. anthropology, 1974-78, prof. anthropology, 1978—, chmn. dept., 1984-89, 96-97, 98-2001; mem. Inst. Advanced Study, Princeton, NJ, 1978-79; fellow Ctr. for Advanced Study, Palo Alto, Calif., 1995-96, Swedish Collegium for Advanced Study in the Social Sci., 2002—03. Sr. fellowship NEH, 1983-84; mem. selection com. Marshall Scholarships, 1983-86; Benedict Disting. vis. prof. Carleton Coll., 1981; Hardy Chair lecture Hartwick Coll., 1985 Author: Relationships, Residence and the Individual, 1976, Demise of a Rural Economy, 1978, Econ. As Culture, 1986, Conversations in Colombia, 1990; The Anthrop. of Econ., 2001; editor Cambridge Studies in Anthropology, 1989-96; contbr. numerous articles to profl. jour. Marshall scholar, 1961-63. Fellow Am. Anthropol. Assn. (bd. dir. 1987-91), Am. Ethnological Soc. (pres. 1989-91, bd. dir. 1987-91, assoc. editor 1981-84), Royal Anthropol. Inst. (sec., chmn. N.Am. com. 1983-88, Curl Bequest Essay prize 1971), Soc. Econ. Anthropology Avocations: tennis, jogging, music. Home: 1650 Dupont Ave S Minneapolis MN 55403-1101

GUDENBERG, HARRY RICHARD, arbitrator, mediator; b. Frankfurt, Germany, May 20, 1933; m. Sharon Rickey; children— Lori, Bruce. BS, N.Y. U., 1960, MBA, 1964; JD, Seton Hall U., 1970. Bar: N.J. bar 1970, U.S. Supreme Ct 1973. With ITT, N.Y.C., 1970-88, v.p., dir. indsl. and employee relations, employment and labor law, 1978-88; cons. on benefits, compensation and employment law William M. Mercer Inc., N.Y.C., 1988-93. Arbitrator, mediator fact finder, dispute resolution, employment and labor law, panel mem. Am. Arbitration Assn., Fed. Mediation and Conciliation Svc., N.J. State Bd. Mediation, N.J. Pub. Employment Rels. Commn., 1994—, also various pvt. panels. Served with U.S. Army, 1953-55. Mem. ABA, Nat. Acad. Arbitrators, N.J. Bar Assn., Indsl. Res. Rsch. Assn.

GUDERIAN, RONALD HOWARD, pathologist; b. Morden, Man., Can., Jan. 31, 1942; s. Harry Fred and Edna Elizabeth (Hildabrand) G.; m. Eleanor Joy Corey, Dec. 27, 1966; children: Jeffrey, Joy, Janell. BSc, Seattle Pacific U., 1967, DSc (hon.), 1990; PhD, U. Wash., 1970; MT, U. Calif., San Francisco, 1972; MD, Cath. U., Cuenca, Ecuador, 1978. Dir. clin. lab. Hosp. Vozandes, Quito, Ecuador, 1975-80, dir. dept. clin. investigation, 1980-97, dir. primary health care program, 1980-97; dir. nat. control program onchocerciasis Ministry of Health, Quito, 1990-96; assoc. prof. medicine Cath. U., Cuenca, 1986—; adj. prof. medicine U. Miami, Fla., 1995—. Mem. expert com. on parasitic diseases WHO, Geneva, 1985-99, cons. on onchocerciasis, 1981-95; cons. for malaria U.S. AID, Quito, 1984-85; internat. cons. on tropical medicine Cath. U., 1995—. Author: Oncocerosis en el Ecuador, 1996; patentee use of electric shock with venemous snake bites; contbr. over 150 articles to profl. jours. Pres. Healing Fund, Seattle, 1990-92. Named Alumnus of Yr. Seattle Pacific U., 1987, Hon. Citizen of Ecuador, 1995. Fellow Royal Soc. Tropical Medicine and Hygiene; mem. World Fedn. Parasitologists, Am. Soc. Tropical Medicine, Ecuadorian Acad. Medicine, Lions. Avocations: hiking, camping, fishing, gardening. Office: Northwest Med Teams Internat 6955 SW Sandburg St Portland OR 97223-8081

GUDERJAN, THOMAS HAROLD, archaeologist, educator; b. Toluca, Ill., July 27, 1954; s. Harold August and Marie Guderjan. BA, So. Ill. U., 1976; MA, So. Meth. U., 1983, PhD, 1988. Dir. exhibits Inst. Texan Cultures, U. Tex., San Antonio, 1983-86, sr. rsch. assoc., 1986-91; pres. Maya Rsch. Program, Ft. Worth, 1990—; asst. prof. archaeology St. Mary's U., San Antonio, 1992-2000; asst. prof. Tex. Christian U., Ft. Worth, 2000—. Adj. asst. prof. San Francisco State U., 1998—; co-dir. Ambergris Caya Archaeol. Project, 1986—88; dir. Blue Creek Archaeol. Project, 1992—2001, Ichpartun Archaeol. Project, 2003—; lectr. in field. Author or co-author books, book chpts., also articles in field. Mem. Mayor's Japan coun. City of San Antonio, 1987; advisor Youth Odyssey, Corpus Christi, Tex., 1986—; sponsor U.S. study for several Ctrl. Am. students. Fulbright fellow, Belize, 1990. Fellow Explorers Club; mem. Alamo Pre-Columbian Soc. (bd. dirs. 1988-2002). Democrat. Avocations: scuba diving, hiking, exploring. Office: Maya Rsch Program 2800 S University Dr Fort Worth TX 76129-0001 E-mail: guderjan@tcu.edu.

GUDMUNDSON, BARBARA ROHRKE, ecologist; b. Chgo. d. Lloyd Ernest and Helen (Bullard) Rohrke; m. Valtyr Emil Gudmundson, June 14, 1951 (dec. Dec. 1982); children: Holly Mekkín Leighton, Martha Rannveig. BA, U. Tenn., 1950; MA, Minn. State U., 1965; PhD, Iowa State U., 1969. Microbiologist Hektoen Inst. & Ill. Ctr. Hosp., Chgo., 1950-52; immunologist Jackson Meml. Lab., Bar Harbor, Maine, 1952-54; dist. ecologist Corps of Engrs., St. Paul, 1971-72; sr. ecologist North Star Rsch. Inst., Mpls., 1972-76; staff engr. Met. Waste Control Commn., St. Paul, 1976-77; pres., prin. ecologist Ecosystem Rsch. Svc./Upper Midwest, Mpls., 1978-99. Pvt. practice as cons. ecologist, Des Moines and Mpls., 1968-70; mem. Citizens League Task Force on the Mississippi Riverfront, 1973-74; mem. adv. com. Mpls. Lakes Water Quality, Mpls., 1974-75; river ecologist Mississippi River Canoe Expdn., Coll. of the Atlantic, Bar Harbor, 1979. Author: V. Emil Gudmundson: Icelandic Canadian Unitarian, A Personal Biography, 1991; editor-in-chief The Icelandic Unitarian Connection, 1984; contbr. articles to profl. jours. Mem. from 61st dist. Dem.-Farmer-Labor Ctr. Com., Minn., 1978-80; mgr. Minnehaha Creek Watershed Dist., 1979-83, sec., 1982-83; mem. Capital Long-Range Improvements Com., Mpls., 1981; mem. steering com. Nokomis East Neighborhood Assn., 1995-97, bd. dirs. 1997-2003. Recipient Leadership award Izaak Walton League, 1982; River Basin Ecology grantee Iowa Acad. Scis., Cedar Falls, 1976, Mississippi River Ecology grantee Freshwater Biol. Rsch. Found., Navarre, Minn., 1979; Fulbright Sr. Rsch. grantee USA/Iceland Fulbright Commns., Washington, Reykjavik, 1986, 92. Mem. NOW (Minn. state bd. 1989-96, Anita Hill Courage and Justice award Twin Cities chpt. 1994, Minn.-NOW's Charlotte Striebel Long Distance Runner award 1998), Ecol. Soc. Am. (pres. Minn. chpt. 1971-75), Geol. Soc. Minn. (pres. 1981), Phycological Soc. Am., Internat. Assn. Diatom Rsch., Icelandic Am. Assn. Minn., Hekla Icelandic Club (pres. 1977), Fulbright Assn., Minn. Interfaith Campaign Climate Change, 2001—, Sigma Xi, Phi Kappa Phi, Sigma Delta Epsilon-Grad. Women in Sci. (nat. mem. com. 1990-93, chmn. 1991-93). Unitarian Universalist. Achievements include discovery of diatom genus Biddulphia in the state of Iowa; establishment of Diatom Herbarium of Iceland. Home: 5505 28th Ave S Minneapolis MN 55417-1957

GUDMUNDSSON, FINNBOGI, library administrator; b. Reykjavik, Iceland, Jan. 8, 1924; s. Gudmundur Finnbogason and Laufey Vilhjalmsdottir; m. Kristjana P. Helgadottir, Oct. 1, 1955 (dec.); 1 child, Helga Laufey. Cand. mag., U. Iceland, 1949, Dr. phil., 1961. Assoc. prof. U. Man., Winnipeg, Can., 1951-56; lectr. Icelandic Univs., Oslo and Bergen, 1957-58; tchr. Icelandic Reykjavik Gymnasium, 1958-64; docent U. Iceland, Reykjavik, 1962-64; dir. Nat. Library of Iceland, Reykjavik, 1964-94. Author: Sveinbjörn Egilsson's Translations of Homer, 1960, Stephan G. Stephansson in Retrospect: Seven Essays, 1982, The Humour of Snorri Sturluson, 1991; contbr. articles to profl. jours.; editor: Orkneyinga saga, 1965; Selected Letters Written to Stephan G. Stephansson I-III, 1971-75, Arbok Landsbokasafns, 1964-93, Andvari, 1968-82; Poets' Letters to Gudmundur Finnbogason, 1987. Mem. Icelandic Studies Soc. (chmn. 1962-64), Icelandic Research Librarians (chmn. 1966-73), Icelandic Patriotic Soc. (pres. 1967-82), Nordinfo (bd. dirs. 1976-79), Icelandic Nat. League (hon.), Icelandic Libr. Assn. (hon.), Rotary (sec. 1983-84). Lutheran.

GUEDRY, JAMES WALTER, lawyer, retired paper corporation executive; b. Morgan City, La., Jan. 7, 1941; s. J. Walter and P. Marie (McNulty) G. AB magna cum laude, Georgetown U., 1962; postgrad., U. Brussels, 1962-63; LL.B., U. Va., 1966. Bar: N.Y. 1967. Assoc. Lord, Day & Lord, N.Y.C., 1966-76; v.p., corp. sec./assoc. gen. counsel Internat. Paper Co., N.Y.C., 1976-2000; retired, 2000. Mem. Assn. Bar City N.Y. Home: 79 Charles St New York NY 10014-2638

GUELLER, SAMUEL, civil and environmental engineer; b. Casares, Argentina, Feb. 9, 1935; came to U.S., 1985; s. Abraham and Paulina (Bilik) G.; m. Berta Fanny Awruch, Feb. 12, 1981; children: Daniel Horacio, Eduardo Javier. MSc, U. Cin., 1987, PhD, 1991. Registered profl. engr., Argentina. Asst. prof. Northeast U., Resistencia, Argentina, 1968-81; sr. engr. Ministry Pub. Works, Corrientes, Argentina, 1970-82, Elscint Ltd., Sao Paulo, Brazil, 1982-85, Farlow, Inc., Indpls., 1989-90, Rumpke, Inc., Cin., 1990-92, Inter-Am. Devel. Bank, Washington, 1992-95, URS Greiner Cons., Virginia Beach, Va., 1995-98, Dekalb County, Decatur, Ga., 1998—. Founding mem. Congress Big Hydroelectric Works, Buenos Aires, 1970—. Author: Frontiers of Physics, 1987, Supergravity, 1995; author tech. reports and sci. rsch. papers. Recipient Internat. Cooperation award Delft (The Netherlands) U., 1971-72, Technion U., Haifa, Israel, 1973-74, U. Graz, Austria, 1976. Fellow ASCE; mem. Am. Water Works Assn., Water Environ. Fedn., Inter-Am. Soc. Sanitary Engrs., Sigma Xi. Achievements include research in engineering and physics math models. Home: 3400 Garson Dr # 4302 Atlanta GA 30324 Office: Dekalb County 4327 Memorial Dr Decatur GA 30032-1233 E-mail: gueller@aol.com.

GUENTHER, CHARLES JOHN, librarian, writer; b. St. Louis, Apr. 29, 1920; s. Charles Richard and Hulda Clara (Schuessler) G.; m. Esther G. Klund, Apr. 11, 1942; children: Charles John, Cecile Anne, Christine Marie. AA, Harris Tchrs. Coll., 1940; postgrad., St. Louis U., 1952-54; BA, Webster Coll., 1973, MA, 1974; LHD (hon.), So. Ill. U., Edwardsville, 1979. Editl. asst. St. Louis Star-Times, 1938; with Social Security Commn. Mo., Dept. Labor, U.S. Employment Service, War Dept., C.E., St. Louis, 1941-43; head archives unit USAAF Aero Chart Svc., St. Louis, 1943-45, head rsch. unit, 1945-47; asst. chief, chief of library, translator, historian, geographer, supervisory cartographer, librarian USAF Aero Chart and Info. Center (name changed to DMA Aerospace Center), St. Louis, 1947-57, chief tech. libr., 1957-75. Civilian library specialist Project Crossroads, USAF, 1946; instr. creative writing Peoples Art Center, St. Louis, 1953-56; lectr., poetry workshop leader various U.S. writers confs. Author: Modern Italian Poets, 1961, Paul Valery in English, 1970, (poems) Phrase.Paraphrase, 1970, Voices in the Dark, 1974, Moving the Seasons, 1994; translator: (with others) Selected Poems in Alain Bosquet, 1963, Selected Translations, 1986; contbr. to Anthology of Spanish Poetry, 1961, Modern European Poetry, 1966, New Directions, 1968-80, Roots and Wings, 1976; contbr. articles to profl. jours.; book reviewer: St. Louis Post-Dispatch, 1953—, Globe-Democrat, 1972-82. Decorated commendatore Ordine al Merito della Repubblica Italiana; recipient Shell Co. Found. grant for book Phrase/Paraphrase, 1970, Witter Bynner grant, 1979; recipient Lit. award Mo. Libr. Assn., 1974, Mo. Writers Guild award, 1987, 94, 96, Mo. and St. Louis Arts awards, 2001. Mem. Poetry Soc. Am. (Midwest regional v.p., James Joyce award 1974), St. Louis Writers Guild (v.p. 1958, pres. 1959, 76-77), St. Louis Poetry Center (chmn. bd. chancellors 1965-72, pres. 1974-76), Mo. Writers Guild (v.p. 1971-73, pres. 1973-74), Spl. Libraries Assn. (pres. Greater St. Louis chpt. 1969-70), Rose Soc. Greater St. Louis; corr. mem. Academie d'Alsace (diplome d'honneur 1957); hon. mem. Les Violetti Picards et Normands, Paris, Academia de Ciencias Humanisticas y Relaciones, Mexico, Academie Chablaisienne, Thonon-les-Bains, France, Biblioteca Partenopea, Naples, asso. mem. Internat. Am. Inst. Home: 9877 Allendale Dr Saint Louis MO 63123-6450 *A poet's relation to his time is complex and mutable. A poet's temperament, attitudes, and sense of the function of poetry are all changeable and conflict with each other throughout his life. In a world which tends to be imitative, regimented, and standardized, each poet is his own definition of poet, his own conscience, his own value.*

GUENTHER, GEORGE CARPENTER, travel company executive, retired; b. Reading, Pa., Aug. 27, 1931; s. John H. and Eleanor (Carpenter) G.; m. Kathleen Lance Coyle, Oct. 20, 1962; children: George Carpenter, Todd C., John E., Gregory C. AB in Psychology, Amherst Coll., 1952. Pres. John H. Guenther Hosiery Co., Reading, 1955-67; dep. sec. Pa. Dept. Labor and Industry, 1967-69; dir. Bur. Labor Standards, Dept. Labor, 1969-71, asst. sec. labor for occupational safety and health, 1971-73; sr. v.p. Ins. Co. N. Am., Phila., 1973-75; v.p. Talmage Tours, Inc., Phila., 1975-77, pres., 1977-96; ret., 1996. Bd. dirs., exec. com. Phila. Convention and Visitors Bureau, 1979-96. Served with USNR, 1952-55. Mem. Nat. Tour Assn. (bd. dirs., exec. com. 1982-90, pres. 1990). Home: 44 Overlook Cir Berwyn PA 19312-2531 E-mail: g.c.guenther@worldnet.att.net.

GUENTHER, GORDON P. mechanical engineer; b. La Cross, Wis., July 11, 1934; BS, U. Mich., 1968; MA, La. Tech. U., 1978, MBA, 1983. Registered profl. engr., La. Instr. navigation 2 Bomb Wing, Barksdale AFB, La., 1974-75; chief design engr. 2 Civil Engring. Squadron, Barksdale AFB, La., 1975-76; project engr. Riley Beard, Inc., Shreveport, 1976-77; sr. product engr. WKM Wellhead Sys., Shreveport, 1977-83; chief energy mgmt. sys. 2 Civil Engring. Squadron, 1983-86; chief engr. 1 Electronic Combat Range Group, Barksdale AFB, 1986-95; chief contracts 2 Civil Engring. Squadron, 1995-99. Adj. instr. Embry-Riddle Aero. U., Barksdale AFB, 1998—. Mem. ASME (chmn. 1998-99), So. Am. Mil. Engrs. (pres. 1976-77). Home: 1081 Harmon Loop Homer LA 71040-5821

GUENTHER, JACK DONALD, banker; b. Little Rock, Jan. 21, 1929; s. Gottlob and Josephine Margaret (Presley) G.; m. Margaret Adah Beltz, June 11, 1956; children— Elizabeth, Katherine, John BA, Yale U., 1950; postgrad., King's Coll., Cambridge U., Eng., 1952-53; MA, Harvard U., 1957, PhD, 1959. Various staff positions IMF, Washington, 1960-79; sr. v.p., sr. advisor internat. ops. Citibank, N.Y.C., 1979-95; cons. MBIA, N.Y.C., 1995-98. Served as sgt. U.S. Army, 1953-55 Home: 4231 42d St Washington DC 20016

GUENTHER, KENNETH ALLEN, business association executive, economist; b. Rochester, N.Y. s. Walter K. and Erna (Ahrenz) G.; m. Lilly Hoesli, Jan. 11, 1964; 1 child, Christine R. BA cum laude, U. Rochester, 1957; postgrad., Johns Hopkins U. Sch. Advanced Internat. Studies, 1957-58, Rangoon Hopkins Ctr., Burma, 1958-59, Yale U., 1959-60. Internat. economist Dept. Commerce, Washington, 1960—65; fgn. svc. officer Dept. State, Washington, 1965, 68-69, Santiago, Chile, 1966-68; spl. asst. to Senator Jacob Javits U.S. Senate, Washington, 1969-73; exec. dir. Inter-Am. Devel. Bank, Washington, 1973-74; asst. spl. trade rep. White House, Washington, 1974-75; asst. to bd. govs. Fed. Res System, 1975-79; assoc. dir. Ind. Cmty. Bankers of Am., Washington, 1980-82, exec. dir., 1982-85, exec. v.p., dir., 1985-2001, pres., CEO, 2001—. Bd. dirs. Ind. Cmty. Bankers Am., Cmty. Banking Network Inc., Ind. Cmty. Bankers Securities Corp. Inc., Ind. Cmty. Bankers Bancard Inc., Ind. Cmty. Bankers Fin. Svcs. Inc. Contbr. articles on banking to profl. jours. Mem. adv. com. on The Golden Dollar, U.S. Mint, 1999-2000; bd. dirs. Homeownership Alliance, 2001--, chmn., 2003--; bd. dirs. Washington campus, 2002--; mem. Bush-Cheney Transition Adv. Com. for U.S. Treasury; mem. Fin. Svcs. Sector Coord. Coun. for Critical Infrastructure Protection and Homeland Security, 2002. With U.S. Army, 1961-66. Recipient spl. achievement award Fed. Res. System, 1977, presdl. pen for work on Monetary Control Act, 1980, electronic funds transfer achievement award U.S. Treasury, 1995. Mem. Bretton Woods Com., Russian Am. Bankers Forum (bd. overseers 1993), Small Bus. Adminstrn. (nat. adv. coun. 1994-2000), Social Compact (bd. dirs. 1994-99), Exchequer Club, Diplomatic and Counsellor Officers Ret., Kenwood Country Club. Home: 4513 Dalton Rd Bethesda MD 20815-3732 E-mail: ken_guenther@icba.org.

GUENTHER, PAUL BERNARD, volunteer; b. N.Y.C., May 1, 1940; s. Bernard and Elsie G.; m. Diane Erceg, July 31, 1965; children— Matthew, Elizabeth, Christopher BS in Econs., Fordham U., 1962; MBA in Fin., Columbia U., 1964. Credit analyst Mfrs. Hanover Trust, N.Y.C., 1964-66; various positions Paine Webber Inc., N.Y.C., 1966-80, exec. asst. to chief exec. officer, 1981, sr. v.p., dir. adminstrn. div., 1981-82, exec. v.p., dir. adminstrv. div., 1982-84, exec. v.p., chief adminstrv. officer, 1984-87, exec. v.p., adminstrn., ops., systems and consumer markets, 1987-88, pres., 1988-95; cons., 1995; retired, 1995. Bd. dirs. Vox Media, Consol. Freightways, Gabelli Asset Mgmt.; mem. adv. com. Walden Capital Ptnrs. L.P. Trustee, chmn. Fordham U.; mem. bd. overseers grad. sch. bus. Columbia U.; chmn. N.Y. Philharm., Frost Valley YMCA; trustee Gov.'s Com. on Scholastic Achievement, Mary Flagler Cary Charitable Trust, Lincoln Ctr. for Performing Arts, Lenox Hill Hosp. Mem. Inst. Chartered Fin. Analysts. Democrat. Lutheran. Office: Walden Ptnrs 21st Fl 708 3rd Ave Fl New York NY 10017-4201

GUENTHER, WILLIAM H. management consultant; b. Rome, Mar. 11, 1950; (parents Am. citizens); s. J. Jordan and May Monstield (Ferry) Guenther; m. Deirdre Goobyloew Guenther, Nov. 6, 1982; children: Caroline, Charles. BA cum laude, Harvard Coll., 1972; JD, NYU, 1975. Bar: N.Y. 1975. Pres., founder Mass. Insight Corp., Boston, 1989—, Mass. Insight Edn. Rsch. Inst., Boston, 1997—. Office: Mass Insight Corp 18 Trenat St Boston MA 02108

GUENTNER, GAIL MARIE, software engineer; b. Milw., Apr. 17, 1961; d. Theodore Edward and June Dolores (Carlson) G. BS in Computer Sci., U. Wis., Milw., 1985. Software engr. Norland Corp., Ft. Atkinson, Wis., 1986-87; software support engr. Heurikon Corp., Madison, Wis., 1987-89, tech. support mgr., 1989-90, software engr., 1990-93; software support mgr. NeuroConcepts, Inc., Madison, 1993; software engr. cons. Insight Ind., Platteville, Wis., 1993—94; sys. analyst Telephone and Data Sys., Madison, Wis., 1994—96; sr. software engr. GE Spacenet-Tridom, Marietta, Ga., 1996—97; sys. integrator Lockheed Martin, Marietta, 1997—. Mem. IEEE, Computer Soc. of IEEE, Soc. Women Engrs., Assn. Computing Machinery, World Wildlife Fund. Avocations: downhill skiing, camping, hiking, volleyball, photography. Office: Lockheed Martin EIS 86 S Cobb Dr Marietta GA 30063

GUENTNER, JAMES FRANCIS, JR., art educator, artist; b. Glenshaw, Pa., Feb. 23, 1949; s. James Francis Guentner and Elizabeth McCloskey; m. Linda Louise Kauffman Guentner; 1 stepchild, Ronald Kauffman; m. Cheryl Guentner (div. Apr. 28, 1973); 1 child, Rachel. A, Allegheny C.C., Pa., 1969; BA, Carlow Coll., Pa. Art tchr. Shaler Sch. Dist., Glenshaw, Pa., 1999—; painting instr. North Hills Art Ctr., Pa., 1986—94; truck driver GAGE Co., Pa., 1979—99, Local 249 Union Hall, Pa., 1976—79; med. equipment installer Robert A. Fulton Co., Pa., 1973—76; substitute art tchr. Shaler Sch. Dist., Glenshaw, Pa., 1972—73. Exhibitions include Borelli-Edwards Gallery, Carnegie Mus. Art. Avocations: guitar, magic, bodybuilding. Home: 220 Lucille St Glenshaw PA 15116

GUEQUIERRE, JOHN PHILLIP, manufacturing company executive; b. Milw., Sept. 10, 1946; s. Gerald Herbert and Louise Ann (Fenske) G.; m. Mary Rowlands Speer, Aug. 17, 1968; children: William Edward, Robert John, Elizabeth Louise. BA, U. Wis., 1968; MBA, U. Chgo., 1972. Systems analyst Inland Steel Co., East Chgo., Ind., 1968-72; analyst inventory INRYCO, Milw., 1972-73, supr. material planning, 1973-74, mgr. contract adminstrn., 1974-76; mgr. fin. Inland Steel Devel. Corp., Washington, 1976-78; mgr. fin. analysis Inland Steel Urban Devel. Corp., Chgo., 1978-80; v.p. adminstrn. Scholz Homes Inc., Tol., 1980-83; sr. v.p. adminstrn., dir. Schult Homes Corp., Middlebury, Ind., 1983-92, sr. v.p. ops., dir., 1992-95, pres. manufactured housing group, 1995-99; sr. v.p. mfg. Oakwood Homes, Middlebury, 1999-2000; pres., CEO Pleasant St. Homes, LLC, 2000—. Chmn. budget subcom. United Way, Elkhart, Ind., 1983-89, bd. dirs. 1989-2000, treas., 1990-92, chmn. 1992; adult leader 4H, Elkhart County, 1983—; bd. dirs. Elkhart Chamber Found., 1993-98; bd. dirs. Ind. Assn. United Ways, 1993-2000, vice chmn., 1995-97, chmn., 1997. Mem.: Beta Gamma Sigma, Phi Kappa Phi, Phi Beta Kappa. Republican. Presbyterian. Office: Pleasant St Homes LLC 51700 Lovejoy Dr Middlebury IN 46540

GUÉRARD, GENEVIÈVE, dancer; Student, École Pierre Laporte. Apprentice Les Grands Ballets Canadiens de Montréal, 1993—96, soloist, 1996—99, prin. dancer, 1999—. Dancer (ballets) The Nutcracker, Agon, Le Corsaire, Thème et variations, 1999, Carmen, Jardi Tancat. Office: Les Grands Ballets Canadiens de Montréal 4816 rue Rivard Montreal QC Canada H2J 2N6

GUERIN, BILL, professional hockey player; b. Wilbraham, Mass., Nov. 9, 1970; With New Jersey Devils, 1991—98, Edmonton Oilers, 1998—2001, Boston Bruins, 2001—02, Dallas Stars, 2002—. Played on World Cup Championship team, 1996, Team USA Olympic team, 1998. Office: Southwest Sports Group 1000 Ballpark Way Ste 400 Arlington TX 76011

GUERIN, DEAN PATRICK, executive; b. St. Paul, Feb. 21, 1922; s. Joseph Henry and Della (Booth) G.; m. Jo Alice Maryman, Sept. 3, 1959; children: Dean William, Stephen Patrick, Mark Joseph. BSBA, Boston U., 1949. With Sperry Gyroscope Co., N.Y.C., 1940-42; registered rep. Chas. A. Day & Son, Boston, 1946-49, Dallas Rupe & Son, 1949-51; from exec. v.p. to chmn. bd. dirs. Eppler, Guerin & Turner, Inc., Dallas, 1951-89; CEO, chmn. bd. dirs. Gen. Aluminum Corp., 1990—94; ind. dir. cos., 1994—. Bd. dirs. Components Corp.; chmn. Archaea Solutions, Inc. Past trustee Marine Mil. Acad. With USMCR, 1942-46, PTO. Mem. Dallas Country Club, Dallas Petroleum Club. Republican. Episcopalian. Home: 9016 Broken Arrow Ln Dallas TX 75209-2406

GUERIN, DIDIER, magazine executive; b. Neuilly/Seine, France, Aug. 2, 1950; came to U.S. 1973; s. Jacques Guerin and Jeanine (Vaesken) Florange; m. Margaret Moray, Dec. 31, 1982; 1 son, Didier Guy Jr. BA in Pub. Law, BA in Comm., U. Paris, 1973; MA in Journalism, Mich. State U., 1975. Editor Soc. Gen. de Presse, Paris, 1976-79; asst. pub. Look mag., N.Y.C., 1979-81; mng. dir. Hachette Comm. Ltd., London, 1982-93; exec. v.p., dir. Hachette Publs., Inc., N.Y.C., 1983-86, Publs. Filipacchi, N.Y.C., 1983-86; pub. ELLE Mag., 1984-85; pres., CEO, dir. Hachette Publs., Inc., N.Y.C., 1987-91; pres., CEO Publs. Filipacchi, N.Y.C., 1987-91, Interdeco Inc., N.Y.C., 1989-91, Hachette-Filipacchi Asia-Pacific, Sydney, 1991-95, Conde Nast Asia-Pacific, Sydney, 1995-2000, Media Convergence Asia-Pacific, Sydney, 2000—. Chmn. The Conde Nast Publs. Pty. Ltd. (VOGUE Australia), Sydney, 1995-2000, The Conde Nast Publs. Pte. Ltd. (VOGUE Singapore), Singapore, 1995-97, The Conde Nast China (VOGUE, GQ Taiwan), Taipei, 1996-2000, Nikkei-Conde Nast (VOGUE Nippon), Tokyo, 1997-2000, Interculture Comm. Ltd., Taipei, 1996-2000; chmn. bd. Toyo Fashion Kaihatsu, Tokyo, 1984-92, Hachette-Consol. Press. (ELLE Australia), Sydney, 1990-95, Hachette Filipacchi Australia, Sydney, 1990-95, Hachette-Interculture, (ELLE Taiwan), Taipei, 1992-95, Hachette Mags. Ltd., Hong Kong, 1993-95, ELLE Mag. Ltd. (ELLE Hong Kong), 1993-95, Hachette Filipacchi-Post, Bangkok (ELLE Thailand), 1994-95, Hachette Filipacchi Japan Ltd., Tokyo (Elle Japan); fgn. trade advisor French Govt., 1988—. Office: Media Convergence Asia-Pacific Knox Manor 17 Knox St Double Bay Sydney NSW 2028 Australia E-mail: didier@mediaconv.com.

GUERIN, JOHN WILLIAM, artist; b. Houghton, Mich., Aug. 29, 1920; s. Omer Francis and Mildred Montague (Miller) G.; m. Anne Walden Dewey, Dec. 28, 1948 (dec. 1979); m. Martha McAshan, Apr. 10, 1982. Student, Am. Acad. Art, Chgo., Art Students League, N.Y.C., Escuela de Bellas Artes, San Miguel, Mexico. Prof. art U. Tex., 1953-80, prof. emeritus, 1980—. Artist in residence, Skowhegan (Maine) Sch. Painting and Sculpture, 1960; one-man shows, Kraushaar Galleries, N.Y.C., 1960, 63, 68, Ft. Worth Art Center, 1956, 64, 65, Marion Kooglar McNay Art Inst., San Antonio, 1961, 65, Centennial Mus., Corpus Christi, Tex., 1963, Carlin Galleries, Ft. Worth, 1962, 64, 67, 70, 77, 81, 87, Nat. Acad. Design, N.Y.C., 1987; one-man retrospective show, Nave Mus., Victoria, Tex., 1982, group exhbns. include, Met. Mus. Art, Whitney Mus. Art, Art Inst. Chgo., Corcoran Mus. Art, Carnegie Inst.; represented in permanent collections, Chrysler Mus., Provincetown, Mass., Joslyn Mus., Omaha, New Britain (Conn.) Mus., Houston Mus., Dallas Mus., U. Notre Dame Art Gallery, Colorado Springs (Colo.) Fine Art Center., Archives Am. Art, Smithsonian Instn., Washington. Served with USAAF, 1942-45. Grantee Am. Acad Arts, Nat. Inst. Arts & Letters, 1960, Ford Found., 1978; recipient Henry Ward Ranger Fund Purchase prize NAD, 1958; Research Inst. grant U. Tex., 1960, 66 Mem. Art Students League N.Y.C. (life), Nat. Acad. Design (academician). Episcopalian. Home and Office: 3400 Stoneridge Rd Austin TX 78746-7716

GUERNSEY, LOUIS HAROLD, retired oral and maxillofacial surgeon, educator; b. Port Chester, N.Y., Sept. 22, 1923; s. Harold Allen and Odette Marcelle (Caillat) G.; m. Isabelle Margaret Napoli, Mar. 15, 1946; children: John Allen, Nancy Jean, Paula, Louis Harold. BS, N.Y. U., 1959; D.D.S., U. Pa., 1947, M.Sc. in Dentistry, 1956. Diplomate Am. Bd. Oral and Maxillofacial Surgery. Gen. practice dentistry, Gooding, Idaho, 1947-52; commd. 1st lt. Dental Corps U.S. Army, 1953, advanced through grades to col., 1967; service in W. Ger.; ret., 1974; prof. oral surgery, chmn. dept. oral and maxillofacial surgery U. Pa. Sch. Dental Medicine, 1974-80, prof. oral and maxillofacial surgery, from 1980, dir. postgrad. oral surgery programs, 1974-86; dir. oral surgery U. Pa. Hosp., 1974-90, prof., chief oral surgery, 1980-86, prof. emeritus

oral and maxillofacial surgery, 1986—; prof. emeritus, attending oral maxillofacial surgery Hosp. U. of Pa., 1986-90; ret., 1990. Mem. staff U. Pa. Med. Ctr. Editor: Reconstructive Implant Surgery/Implant Prosthodontics Dental Clinics of North America, 2 edits., 1986; contbr. articles profl. jours. Decorated Legion of Merit; recipient Harold Krogh Oral Cancer award Washington chpt. Am. Cancer Soc., 1974 Fellow Internat. Coll. Dentists, Am. Coll. Dentists, Am. Dental Soc. Anesthesiology; mem. ADA, Am. Soc. Oral and Maxillofacial Surgeons, Brit. Assn. Oral Surgeons, Internat. Assn. Oral Surgeons, Am. Assn. Hosp. Dentists, Pa. Soc. Oral and Maxillofacial Surgeons. Republican. Roman Catholic. Home: 14 Highfield Ln Wayne PA 19087-2760

GUERRA, ARMANDO J. corporate professional; b. St. Clara, Las Villas, Cuba, Nov. 3, 1951; arrived in U.S., 1961; s. Armando and Ofelia (Bolanos) G.; m. Maria Cata, Sept. 7, 1974; children: Adrianne, Corinne, Eric. BS in Pharmacy, U. Fla., 1974. Staff pharmacist Eckerd Drugs, Miami, 1975-77; pres. Sedano's Pharmacy & Discount, Miami, 1977—; also CEO 14 brs. Sedano's Pharmacies, Miami. Dir. U.S. Century Bank; vice chmn., Century Ptnrs. Ltd.; bd. dirs., v.p. Sedano's Supermarkets, Inc., Miami. Bd. dirs. South Fla. Cmty. Blood Bank, Everglades Nat. Park Trust; mem. Met. Dade County Econ. Devel. Program Com. Recipient City of Hialeah Proclamation, Mayor, City of Hialeah, 1982, 86, The Merck award U. Fla., Gainesville, 1975, Dade County Proclamation, Dade County Mayor, Miami, 1986. Mem. Nat. Assn. Retail Druggists, Am. Pharm. Assn., Fla. Pharmacy Assn., Dade County Pharm. Assn., Century 100 Club (U. Fla.). Republican. Roman Catholic. Avocations: automobile driving clubs, tennis, racquetball.

GUERRA, GONZALO ENRIQUE, economist; b. Chinandega, Nicaragua, June 6, 1972; arrived in U.S.A., 1986; s. Rene Guerra and Nidia (De Jesus) Navarro. BA in Polit. Sci., U. Calif., Riverside, 1995; MA in Applied Econ., MPP, U. Mich., 1998. Team leader Target, Pontana, Calif., 1992—95, tng.team leader Livonia, Mich., 1995—96; program evaluator Mexicantown Cmty. Devel. Corp., Detroit, 1997; internat. policy analyst Ford Motor Co., Dearborn, Mich., 1996—99; sr. economist Potomac Mgmt. Group, Inc., Washington, 1999—2001, program mgr., 2001—. Bd. mem. U.S.-Mex. C. of C., Detroit, 1998—2000; women in action conf. com. Soc. Hispanic Profl. Engrs., Dearborn, 1998—2000. Recipient award, Hispanic Youth Found., 1998. Mem.: Nat. Economists Club. Office: Potomac Management Group 610 King St Ste 200 Alexandria VA 22314 E-mail: nguerra@umich.edu.

GUERRA, MARY LOUISE, human resources executive; b. El Paso, Tex., Mar. 28, 1946; d. Luis and Mary Ruth Alvidrez; m. Victor Guerra, Apr. 15, 1965; children: Paul, Cristina. BSN, U. Tex., 1971. RN, 1968. Adminstrv. dir. Dallas County Mental Health, 1979-85; dir. human resources Prudential, Newark, 1985-97; sr. v.p. human resources CIT, Livingston, N.J., 1997—. Mem. Alto Lakes Country Club, Kokopelli Country Club. Office: CIT 650 CIT Dr Livingston NJ 07039

GUERRANT, DAVID EDWARD, retired food company executive; b. Elizaville, Ky., Sept. 27, 1919; s. William Upton and Claire (Jordan) G.; m. Charlotte L. Lander, Feb. 6, 1942; children: Stephen, Jeffrey. BS, Kans. State U., 1941. With Potts-Turnbull Agy., Kansas City, Mo., 1941-48; creative dir. Campbell-Ewald Co., Chgo., 1948-51; with John W. Shaw Advt., Inc., Chgo., 1951-61, pres., 1959-61, MacFarland, Aveyard & Co., Chgo., 1961-64; pres., v.p. mktg. Libby, McNeill & Libby, Chgo., 1964-68, pres., CEO, 1968-73, chmn. bd., 1971-77; chmn., pres., CEO Nestlé Co., Inc., White Plains, N.Y., 1973-81, Nestlé Enterprises Inc. (holding co. for Nestlé Co. Inc., Libby, McNeill & Libby and Stouffers Inc.), 1977-83; ret., 1983. Mem.: Island Country (Marco Island, Fla.). Presbyterian. Home: 591 Hammock Ct Marco Island FL 34145-5848

GUERRANT, MARY THORINGTON, music educator; b. Taft, Tex., May 7, 1925; d. William Lord Thorington and Mary Guerrant Burnett; m. William Barnett Jr., Sept. 3, 1946; 1 child, William B. Guerrant III. BA in English, Austin Coll., 1946; MusM in Piano, Tex. Tech. U., 1971, PhD in Fine Arts, 1976. Piano instr. Austin Coll., Sherman, Tex., 1957-58; assoc. prof. piano and composition Tunghai (Taiwan) U., 1976-77, vis. prof., 1984-86; vis. scholar (piano) Hong Kong Bapt. Coll., 1986-88. Adjudicator Nat. Guild of Piano Tchrs., Sherman and Lubbock, Tex., 1966-84, Lubbock Music Tchrs. Assn. Solo piano recitals include First United Meth. Ch., Albuquerque, 1995, U. N.Mex., 1992, Hong Kong Bapt. Coll., 1988, St. John's Cathedral, Hong Kong, 1988, and others; composer (chamber opera) The Shepherds, 1976, (ensemble) Pecos Ruins, 1974; contbr. articles to profl. publs. Vol. Cmty. Concerts, Sherman, 1954-66, Albuquerque Literacy Program, 1988-90, Meals on Wheels, Albuquerque, 1989; bd. dirs. Friends of Music, Albuquerque, 1991, 92. Heard fellowship in English Austin Coll., 1945-46, Disting. Alumni award, 1979. Mem. Music Tchrs. Nat. Assn. (cert. master tchr.), Profl. Music Tchrs. of N.Mex., Albuquerque Music Tchrs. Assn., Alpha Chi, Pi Kappa Lambda. Avocations: traveling, camping, hiking, foreign language study, tennis. Home: 14217 Turner Ct NE Albuquerque NM 87123-1836

GUERRERA, VITTORIO, priest; b. Waterbury, Conn., Dec. 15, 1963; BA in Psychology and Sociology, Quinnipiac U., 1985; MDiv, Christ the King Sem., 1990; STL, Pontifical Gregorian U., Rome, 1999. Ordained priest Roman Cath. Ch., 1991. Parochial vicar Sacred Heart Ch., Suffield, Conn., 1991-93, St. Pius X Ch., Wolcott, Conn., 1993-98; chaplain K. of C. Coun. 3961, Wolcott, 1993—98; dir. formation of diaconate Archdiocese of Hartford, 1999—2003; columnist The Cath. Transcript, 1996-97; parochial vicar St. Ann Ch., Avon, Conn., 1999—2003; attache, permanent observer Mission of the Holy See to the UN, 2003—. Author: Medjugorje-A Closer Look, 1995, Let the Children Come To Me: Homilies for Children, 1996, The Shroud of Turin: A Case for Authenticity, 2001. Avocations: reading, writing.

GUERRERO, LILIA, school nurse; b. McAllen, Tex., Aug. 5, 1953; d. Manuel C. and Olivia (Garza) G. BSN, Tex. Woman's U., 1975; MS, Calif. Coll. Health Scis., 1999. RN, Tex.; nat. cert. sch. nurse. Emergency rm. supr. McAllen (Tex.) Med. Ctr., 1975-80; staff nurse Mission (Tex.) Hosp., 1980-85; nurse Mission Cen. Ind. Sch. Dist., 1980—. Tchr., insvc. trainer Am. Cancer Soc., 1991—92; mem. planning com. Region One ESC Wellness Conf.; spkr. Tex. All Well Conf., Tex. Sch. Health Assn. State Conf., 2002, 21st Cent. Lifeline Programs Conf., 2002. Editor (newsletter): Mission Pediat. Ctr., 1990—92; featured in Asthma Manual by Chgo. Health Corps, U. Ill., Coll. Nursing. Past dist. pub. edn. chmn. Am. Cancer Soc.; mem. Super Saturday Asthma Day Planning Com., 1990, planning com. Epilepsy Conf., 1991; co-facilitator Asthma Summer Day Camp, 1997—, Mission Hosp. Asthma Support Group, 1999—, Camp Energy, 2001-03; chmn. adv. bd. Mission CISD Wellness, 1994-95. Recipient Achievement award Am. Cancer Soc. Mem. Nat. Assn. Sch. Nurses, Tex. Assn. Sch. Nurses (pres. region 1, bd. dirs. ann. conv. 1991, regional pres. 1989-91).

GUERRERO, VLADIMIR, professional baseball player; b. Nizao Bani, Dominican Rep., Feb. 9, 1976; Outfielder Montreal Expos, 1996—. Achievements include being a holder of Expo franchise records including most extra base hits, 1996, RBIs by a right fielder, 1996, total bases, others. Office: Montreal Expos PO Box 500 Station M Montreal QC Canada H1V 3P2 also: Montreal Expos Olympic Stadium 4549 Ave Pierre de Coubertin H1V3N7 Montreal PQ Canada

GUERRETTE, RICHARD HECTOR, priest, psychotherapist, management consultant, writer; b. Bristol, Conn., June 26, 1930; s. Hector and Leona (Marcel) G. BA, St. Mary's Sem. and U., 1955; MA, U. Notre Dame, 1971; STM, Yale U., 1971; PhD, U. Conn., 1981. Ordained priest Roman Cath. Ch., 1959; diplomate Am. Acad. Forensic Counseling; cert. family therapist. Lectr., rschr. Ecumenical Continuing Edn. Ctr. at Yale, New Haven, 1972-73; adj. prof. Goddard Coll., Plainfield, Vt., 1980-81, Vt. Coll. Norwich U., Montpelier, Vt., 1981-83, 90—; rsch. fellow Yale U. Div. Sch., New Haven, 1971, 84-87; lectr., researcher U. Conn., West Hartford, 1984-89; dir., cons. EquiPax Retreat Ctr. Human and Ethical Resources, Newport, Vt., 1988—; dir., curator EquiPax Art Gallery, Newport, 1989—; dir., psychotherapist EquiPax Counseling Svcs., Newport, 1988—. Resource cons. Vt. Dept. Edn., Montpelier, 1988—; cons. Internat. Career Mgmt. Specialists, Toronto, Ont., Lewiston, N.Y., 1995—; invited lectr. at internat. confs. Author: A New Identity for the Priest: Toward an Ecumenical Ministry, 1971, The Emmanuel Servant Community: Study of Social Movement Organization, 1981, (with others) Ethics and Economic Affairs, 1994; contbr. articles on family therapy, psychotherapy, sociotherapy, and corp. and mgmt. ethics to profl. publs., articles on theology and liturgy to religious publs.; book reviewer Jour. Bus. Ethics, 1988. Named for Disting. Svc. in Counseling and Devel., The Nat. Disting. Svc. Registry, 1989-90. Mem. Am. Counseling Assn., Internat. Assn. Marriage and Family Counselors, Nat. Acad. Cert. Family Therapists (cert.), Nat. Career Devel. Assn., Nat. Employment Counseling Assn., Assn. Religion and Intellectual Life, Soc. Advancement Socio-Econs. Avocations: skiing, sailing, canoeing, antiques, opera. Office: EquiPax Retreat Ctr Human/Ethical Resources 96 School St Newport VT 05855-5040

GUERRI, WILLIAM GRANT, lawyer; b. Higbee, Mo., Mar. 30, 1921; s. Grant and Pearl (Zambelli) G.; m. Millicent K. Branding; children: Paula Ann Guerri Baker, Glenda Kay, William Grant. AB, Central Meth. Coll., 1943; LLB, Columbia, 1946. Bar: NY 1946, Mo. 1947. Ptnr. Thompson Coburn LLP, St. Louis, 1956—. Mem. bd. editors: Columbia Law Rev, 1945-46. Hon. mem. bd. dirs. St. Louis Heart Assn., chmn., 1972-73; bd. dirs. United Way Greater St. Louis, 1976-94; curator Ctrl. Meth. Coll., 1981-97. Fellow The Fellows of Am. Bar; mem. ABA, Mo. Bar Assn. (trustee 1984-92), Bar Assn. Met. St. Louis, Assn. of Bar of City of N.Y., Am. Law Inst., Am. Judicature Soc., Noonday Club, Round Table Club, Phi Delta Phi. Home: Apt 308 14300 Conway Meadows Ct E Chesterfield MO 63017-9612 Office: Thompson Coburn LLP Ste 3000 1 US Bank Plz Saint Louis MO 63101-1643 E-mail: wguerri@thompsoncoburn.com.

GUERRIERO, CAROL MARIE, librarian; b. Sept. 10, 1963; BA in Radio/TV/Film, Wayne State U., 1985, MLS, 1988. Libr. Livonia (Mich.) Pub. Librs., 1991—. Office: Livonia Pub Libr 32777 Five Mile Rd Livonia MI 48154-3045

GUERRIERO, DAVID JOHN, physician; b. Chgo., Oct. 2, 1963; s. E. John and Theresa (Cea) G.; m. Ranell Katea Guerriero; children: Alexandra Nichole, Grantly. BA, Taylor U., 1985; BS, DC, Palmer U., 1990; MS, Lynn U., 2000. Diplomate Am. Acad. Pain Mgmt., Am. Acad. Biomech. Trauma. Adj. prof. anatomy Valencia C.C., Orlando, Fla., 1991-93; chiropractor Fla. Chiropractic Medicine, Inc., Orlando, 1991—. Adj. prof. pathophysiology and anatomy Fla. Hosp. Coll. Health Scis., bd. dirs. Fla. Chiropractic Medicine Inc. Contbr. articles to profl. jours. Fellow Am. Back Soc.; mem. Am. Chiropractic Assn., Fla. Chiropractic Assn., Nat. Assn. Chiropractic Medicine, Nat. Bd. Forensic Chiropractic, Am. Acad. Biomed. Trauma, Aircraft Owners and Pilots Assn., Exptl. Aircraft Assn., Profl. Assn. Diving Instrs. Office: 5104 N Orange Blossom Trl Ste 208 Orlando FL 32810

GUERS, CHRISTIAN ALAIN, information systems specialist; b. Santiago, Chile, Mar. 21, 1964; s. Henri Louis and Lucie Rose (Galaz) G. Ingeniero en Informatica, U. Tecnica Federico Santa María, Valparaiso, Chile, 1987. Cert. engr. info. sys. Sys. cons. Dipac-Manta, Quito, Ecuador, 1988; sys. analyst Banco de Chile, Santiago, 1988-90; sys. engr. Bancosorno, Santiago, 1990-93; info. sys. mgr. Nike, Santiago, 1993-99; regional tech. mgr. Nike Inc., Beaverton, Oreg., 1999—. Founder, dir. Intersoft jour., 1984. Mem. IEEE-Computer Sci., Assn. Computing Machinery. Avocations: sports, short story writing. Office: Nike Inc 1 SW Bowerman Dr Beaverton OR 97005-0979

GUERTIN, ROBERT POWELL, physics educator, university dean; b. Trenton, N.J., July 5, 1939; s. Alfred N. and Rhoda (Thomas) G.; m. Margaret Eipper, Aug. 13, 1966 (div. 1999); children: Lynn Frances, Laura Thomas. BS, Trinity Coll., 1961; MA, Wesleyan U., 1963; PhD, U. Rochester, 1969. Asst. prof. physics Tufts U., Medford, Mass., 1968-75, assoc. prof., 1975-83, prof., 1983—, dean Grad. Sch. Arts and Scis., 1985-96, dean Grad. Sch. Rsch. and Profl. Edn., 1994-96. Bd. govs. Univ. Press New England, Hanover, N.H., 1985-96, chmn., 1986-87, 93-94; vis. scientist Nat. High Magnetic Field Lab., Fla., 1996—. Editor books on crystalline electric fields and anomalous rare earth magnetic effects, 1980, 83, 90, 94; contbr. articles to profl. jours. Mem. Lucretia Crocker adv. council Commonwealth Mass., 1986—; bd. dirs. N.E. Assn. Grad. Schs. NSF and NIH rsch. award, 1972-90. Mem. Am. Phys. Soc. (mem. various coms. 1968—). Unitarian Universalist. Avocations: piano, swimming. Home: 478 Beacon St Apt 3 Boston MA 02115-1021

GUESON, EMERITA TORRES, obstetrician, gynecologist; b. Angeles City, The Philippines, Jan. 4, 1942; came to U.S., 1964; d. Lina (Torres) Gueson. AA, U. Sto. Tomas, Manila, Philippines, 1958, MD, 1963. Resident in ob-gyn. Phila. Gen. Hosp., 1966-71; attending physician Nazareth Hosp., Phila., 1973—, Holy Redeemer Hosp., Meadowbrook, Pa., 1983—. Bd. dirs. Physicians Who Care; lectr. healthcare issues to consumer groups, Phila. Author: Doctors Under Fire, 1989, Scales of Justice: Exploring the Wilderness of Health Care and Society's Moral Conscience, 1992, Do HMO's Cut Costs...and Lives, 1997, Survival Guide for HMO Patients, 1997; pub. ThereseVision Publs.; also med. writer, screenplay writer, line dir., prodr. Hon. co-chair physicians adv. bd. Republican Nat. Com. Fellow ACOG, ACP; mem. AMA, Pa. Med. Soc., Philadelphia County Med. Soc., Pro-Life Ob.-Gynecologists (charter). Avocations: writing, painting, refinishing furniture. Office: 3336 Aldine St Philadelphia PA 19136-3802 E-mail: therese44@aol.com.

GUESS, AUNDREA KAY, accounting educator; b. Seth, W.Va., Feb. 7, 1953; d. Hobert and Inez Elizabeth (Howell) Adams; children: Renae, Rhonda. BBA, Baylor U., Waco, Tex., 1988; MBA, Auburn U., 1989; PhD, U. North Tex., 1993. CPA, Ala., Fla. Co-owner Stevenson (Ala.) All-Mart, 1967-94; grad. rsch. asst. Auburn (Ala.) U., 1988-89; teaching fellow U. North Tex., Denton, 1989-90, lectr., 1990-93; prof., dir. acctg. program Samford U., Birmingham, Ala., 1993—97, dir. new masters of acctg. degree program; prof. U. Tex., 1997—; dir. acctg. MBA profram St. Edwards U., Austin, Tex., 1998—. Cons. Kay Guess Cons., Birmingham, 1993—, activity based costing Coca-Cola; presenter Southwestern Bus. Adminstrn. Conf., 1994; discussant, 1995 track chair for acctg. and fin. Southwestern Case Rsch., pres. 2003—; owner Kay's Designer Dresses, Stevenson; prof. St. Edwards U., 2003; bd. dir. N.Am. Case Rsch. Assn. Contbr. pubs. to various jours. Recipient Fin. Execs. Inst. award, 1987, 89; Rsch. grantee Samford U.Heloise Brown Canter scholar Am. Women's Soc. CPA and Am. Soc. Women Accts., 1992. Mem. AICPA, Am. Acctg. Assn., Am. Soc. Women CPAs (South Birmingham chpt., Laurel scholar 1992, scholar 1989), Fla. Inst. CPAs, Inst. Mgmt. Accts. (bd. dirs. 1994—, dir. tech. meetings 1994—), Acad. Acctg. Historians, Inst. Internal Auditing, Phi Theta Kappa, Alpha Kappa Psi, Beta Alpah Psi (treas. Auburn chpt. 1989), Phi Kappa Phi, Beta Gamma Sigma. Baptist. Avocations: sewing, cake decorating, running. Home: 651 Martin Rd Dripping Springs TX 78620-3506

GUESS, DAVID LYNN, education educator; b. Austin, Tex., May 18, 1958; s. James Lynn and Virginia Townsend Guess; m. Rebecca Diane Sherrod, June 16, 1984; children: Braden James, Natalie Erin. MusB, U. of Mary Hardin-Baylor, 1983; MusM, U. of Okla., 1993. Min. of music & youth First Bapt. Ch., Eagle Lake, Tex., 1979—81; asst. dir. of admissions U. of Mary Hardin-Baylor, Belton, Tex., 1983—86; admissions counselor U. of Tex. at San Antonio, 1986—90; min. of music Alameda Bapt. Ch., Norman, Okla., 1990—94; choral dir. Waco H.S., Tex., 1994—97; dir. of choral activities U. of Mary Hardin-Baylor, 1997—. Dir. Tex. Bapt. All-State Youth Choir, 1999, 2003. Dir.: various region choir concerts. Mem.: Chorus Am., Tex. Music Educators Assn., Tex. Choral Directors Assn., Am. Choral Directors Assn., Phi Kappa Phi. Avocations: golf, woodworking. Home: 12002 Woodfall Circle Waco TX 76712 Office: University of Mary Hardin-Baylor UMHB Box 8012 900 Coll St Belton TX 76513

GUESS, JAMES DAVID, lawyer; b. Lampasas, Tex., Jan. 21, 1941; s. David Ira and Lila Blanch (Reagan) G.; m. Susan Lawyer, Dec. 19, 1981; children: Corey, Stephanie, Casey, Chris. BS in Edn., Southwestern U., 1963; JD, St. Mary's U., 1968. Bar: Tex. 1968, U.S. Dist. Ct. (we. dist.) Tex. 1974, U.S. Ct. Appeals (5th cir.) 1974, U.S. Dist. Ct. (so. dist.) Tex. 1978, U.S. Dist. Ct. (no. dist.) Tex. 1982. Assoc. Groce Locke & Hebdon, San Antonio, 1968-74, ptnr., 1975-86; shareholder Groce Locke & Hebdon P.C., San Antonio, 1986-96, Jenkens & Gilchrist, San Antonio, 1996-99, Law Offices of James D. Guess, San Antonio, 1999—. Sustaining mem. Products Liability Adv. Coun.; mem. Am. Bd. Trial Advs. With USN, 1961—67, Vietnam. Mem.: Internat. Assn. Def. Counsel, Def. Rsch. Inst. (bd. dirs. 1998—2001), Tex. Assn. Def. Counsel (past pres.). Avocations: sports, golf, hunting. Home: 13318 Southwalk St San Antonio TX 78232-4843 E-mail: jamesdguess@sbcglobal.net.

GUEST, ABBI TAYLOR, lawyer, judge, educator; b. Plainview, N.Y., Oct. 28, 1966; d. Leonard and Kelli Taylor; m. John Bradford, June 6, 1998; 1 child, Maryann Nicole. BA, New Coll., Sarasota, Fla., 1988; JD, Mercer U., Macon, Ga., 1991. Bar: Ga. 1991, Fla. 1991, U.S. Ct. Appeals (11th cir.) 1991, U.S. Dist. Ct. (no. dist.) Ga. Atty. Fain Mayor & Wiley, Atlanta, 1991-92, Office of Dekalb County Pub. Defender, Decatur, Ga., 1992-95; magistrate judge Dekalb County, Decatur, 1997—; atty. Peters Roberts Borsuk & Guest, Decatur, 1995-2001; adj. prof. law Ga. State U., Atlanta, 1998—. Mem. Ga. Assn. Criminal Def. Lawyers (area v.p. 1996—, chmn. membership com. 1997—), Nat. Assn. Criminal Def. Lawyers, Dekalb Bar Assn. (chmn. Law Day 1995), Ga. Trial Practice and Litigation. Office: Law Firm of Abbi Taylor Guest 500 Commerce Plz 755 Commerce Dr Decatur GA 30030 E-mail: abbiguest@criminal-defense.net.

GUEST, BARBARA, author, poet; b. Wilmington, NC, Sept. 6, 1920; d. James Harvey and Anna (Hetzel) Pinson; m. Lord Stephen Haden-Guest, 1948 (div. 1954); 1 child, Hon. Hadley; m. Trumbull Higgins, 1954 (dec.); 1 child, Jonathan van Lennep. AB, U. Calif., Berkeley, 1943. Editorial assoc. Art News, 1951-59. Author: (plays) The Ladies Choice, 1953, The Office, 1961, Port, 1965, (with Kevin Killian) Often, 2000; (poems) The Location of Things, 1960, Poems, 1963, The Blue Stairs, 1968, Moscow Mansions, 1973; (with Sheila Isham) I Ching: Poems and Lithographs, 1969, The Countess from Minneapolis, 1976, The Türler Losses, 1980, Biography, 1981, Quilts, 1981, Fair Realism, 1989; (with June Felter) Musicality, 1989; (with Richard Tuttle) The Altos, 1991, Defensive Rapture, 1993, Selected Poems, 1995, Stripped Tales, 1995; (novel) Seeking Air, 1978 (reprint 1997), (biography) Herself Defined, 2002, The Poet H.D. and Her World, 1984, (poems) Quill Solitary Apparition, 1996, Rocks on a Platter: Notes on Literature, 1999, If So, Tell me, 1999, The Confetti Trees: Motion Picture Stories, 1999, (with Laurie Reid) Symbiosis, 2000, Miniatures and Other Poems, 2002, (essay) Forces of Imagination: Writing on Writing, 2003, Dürer in the Window, 2003. Recipient Longview award Longview Found., 1960, Laurence Lipton prize in lit., 1990, San Francisco State U. award for poetry, 1994, Fund for Poetry award, 1995, The America award, 1996, Pen West Josephine Miles award, 1996, Robert Frost medal Poetry Soc. Am., 1999; Yaddo fellow, 1958; Nat. Endowment for the Arts grantee, 1978. Address: 1301 Milvia St Berkeley CA 94709-1934 E-mail: barbgues@aol.com.

GUEST, FLOYD EMORY, JR., lawyer; b. Oglethorpe, Ga., May 5, 1929; s. Floyd Emory and Eula Belle (Jones) G.; m. Mary E. Vick, Oct. 12, 1955 (div. 1959); 1 child, Victoria Elizabeth; m. Martha J. Roy, Oct. 12, 1963; children: Alyson Jane, Emory Roy. AB in Bus. Adminstrn., Duke U., 1952; JD, U. Tex., 1962; MS in Fin. Svcs., Am. Coll., 1980. Bar: Tex. 1962. V.p., controller Cosmopolitan Life, Houston, 1952-59; trust officer Bank of Southwest, 1962-67, Capital Nat. Bank, 1967-69; chmn. Profl. Businessmen Assn. Retirement Plans Co., Houston, 1969—. Pres. Southgate Civic Assn., Houston, 1967, 68. Served to capt. USAFR, 1952-67. Mem. SAR, Tex. Bar Assn., Houston Bar Assn., Houston Estate Planning Coun. Delta Theta Phi Law Frat. (pres. Houston alumni 1964). Lodges: Downtown Optimist (pres. 1982-83), Masons, K.T. Republican. Home: 5826 Doliver Dr Houston TX 77057-2470 Office: PBA Retirement Plans Co 5005 Mitchelldale St Ste 192 Houston TX 77092-7242 E-mail: floydguest@hotmail.com.

GUEST, LINDA SAND, education educator; b. Ft. Morgan, Colo., Sept. 9, 1945; d. Robert E. and Leona Mae (Prettyman) Sand; m. Richard E. Guest, June 5, 1966; children: Elise M., Gregory D. BA, Colo. State U., 1967, MEd, 1983; EdD, Harvard U., 1990. Ednl. cons. Nat. Office for Rural Edn., Ft. Collins, Colo.; tchr. Denver Pub. Schs., East Maine Sch. Dist. 63, Niles, Ill., Poudre R-1 Sch. Dist., Ft. Collins, 1979-91; asst. prof. curriculum and instrn. U. Denver Sch. Edn., 1991-94; project coord. Rocky Mountain Tchr. Edn. Collaborative, Greeley, Colo., 1994-98; dir. curriculum Am. Honda Eagle Rock Sch. and Profl. Devel. Ctr., Estes Park, Colo., 1998—. Adj. faculty mem. Sch. Edn. Colo. State U., 1997—. Mem. ASCD, Am. Ednl. Rsch. Assn., Phi Delta Kappa. Office: Eagle Rock Sch PO Box 1770 Estes Park CO 80517-1770

GUEST, RITA CARSON, interior designer; b. Atlanta, Aug. 17, 1950; d. Walter Harold and Doris Rebecca Carson; m. John Franklin Guest Jr., Jan. 20, 1979. B of Visual Arts, Ga. State U., 1973. Registered interior designer Ga., Fla., D.C., Ala. Pres., dir. design Carson Guest, Inc., Atlanta, 1984—. Lectr. in field. Bd. dirs. Atlanta Nat. Mus., 2002—. Recipient 5 1st place awards Gwinnett Home Show and Interior Design Expo, 1991. Fellow: ASID (Ga. chpt. dir. 1984, treas. 1985—86, nominating com. 1987, chmn. interprofl. devel. com. 1988—90, pres.-elect 1991—92, pres. 1992—93, nat. office coun. of pres.'s steering com. 1993—94, nat. dir. for region 14 1995—96, legis. adv. coun. 1997—98, mem. fellows coun. 1997—99, nat. bd. dirs. 2000—02, Comml. Design Project award 1983, Ga. chpt. Presdl. citation 1984, Residential Design award 1987, Ga. chpt. 1st place Office Design award 1987, Comml. Offices 1st place Project award 1989, Profl. Office Design award 1989, 1st place Libr. Design/1st place Comml. Offices award 1991, Pres. citation 1991, Designer of Yr. 1992, 2 Comml. Project awards 1992, 1st place Nat. Project award 1993, 1st place Instnl. Design award 1994, 1st place Healthcare Project award 1995, Ga. chpt. Silver Contract Design award 2000, Bronze Contract Design award 2001, Gold Instl. award 2002, Gold Comml. award 2003); mem.: Ga. Alliance Interior Design Profls. (pres. 1991—92, bd. advisors), Atlanta C. of C., Midtown Bus. Alliance. Presbyterian. Avocation: painting. Office: Carson Guest Inc 1720 Peachtree St NW Ste 1001 Atlanta GA 30309-2459 E-mail: ritaguest@carsonguest.com.

GUEST, ROBERT HENRY, state legislator, management educator; b. East Orange, N.J., May 3, 1916; s. James Henry and Charlotte (Newbould) G.; m. Kate Hay, Dec. 18, 1942; children: David Hartley, Gregory Alan, John Hay, Peter Staples. AB cum laude, Amherst Coll., 1939, LHD, 1974; MA, Columbia U., 1941, PhD, 1960; MA (hon.), Dartmouth Coll., 1963. Dir. indsl. relations Limerick Yarn Mills, Me., 1941-42; sr. field examiner NLRB, 1946-47; mem. field research staff Labor and Mgmt. Center Yale, 1948-52; assoc. dir. research tech. project, 1952-60; ptnr. Charles R. Walker Assocs. (mgmt. cons.), New Haven, 1952-61; prof. organizational behavior Amos Tuck Sch. Dartmouth, 1960-81; mng. dir. Health Mgmt. Assocs. (mgmt. cons.), 1975. Mediator Conn. Labor-Mgmt. Com. Econ. Devel., 1960; mem. N.H. Gov's. Mental Health Com., 1964, N.H. Aeros. Commn., 1968; mem. mgmt. adv. panel NASA, 1969; disting. lectr. U. Leeds, U.K. 1959, U. Strathclyde, U.K. 1969, U. Canterbury, New Zealand, 1981, U. Sapporo, Japan, 1982. Author: (with C. R. Walker) The Man on the Assembly Line, 1952, (with C. R. Walker and A. N. Turner) The Foreman on the Assembly Line, 1957, Organizational Change: The Effect of Successful Leadership, 1962, Hospital Policy: Process and Action; contbg. editor: Changing Forces In American Society, 1964, Organizational Research in Health Institutions, 1973, IL Mutamento Della Organizzazione Aziendale, 1976, (with Paul Hersey and Kenneth H. Blanchard) Organizational Change Through Effective Leadership, 1977, rev. edit., 1986, Innovative Work Practices, 1981, Robotics: The Human Dimension, 1984, Work Teams and Team Building, 1986, As Good Luck Would Have it: An Autobiography on the Light Side, 1987. Exec. com. N.H. Dem. Party; ofcl. U.S. Winter Olympics, Lake Placid, N.Y., 1980; rep. N.H. State Legislature, 1988-2000; prime sponsor First Physician-Assisted Suicide Legis. in USA, 1991. With USNR, 1942-45. Reicpient Book of Yr. award Nat. Orgn. Devel. Coun., 1963, Article of Yr. awards Can. Assn. Mgmt., 1967, Am. Coll. Hosp. Adminstrs., 1974, Disting. Svc. medal Amherst Coll., 1986; marshal Brit. Open Golf Championship, 1990. Mem. Alpha Delta Phi. Clubs: Royal and Ancient Golf (St Andrews, Scotland). Home: 8 Barrett Rd Hanover NH 03755-2421

GUEST, SUZANNE MARY, adult education educator, artist; b. Monroe, Mich., Sept. 24, 1935; d. Hubert George Guest and Lola Viola Anne Pfeffer. BA, Marygrove Coll., 1957; MFA, U. Notre Dame, 1969. Chmn. art dept. Marian H.S., Birmingham, Mich., 1960—66, St. Mary H.S., Akron, Ohio, 1966—68, Am. Sch., London, 1971—91; adult educator Wordens World of Art, Pompano, Fla., 1994—, Ft. Lauderdale (Fla.) H.S., 1994—, First Presbyn. Ch., Pompano, 1999—; mem. sisterhood Immaculate Heart of Mary, Detroit, 1957—69. Freelance artist Alan Kent Design Group, London, 1970; presenter workshops in field; calligraphy sabbatical Oreg. Sch. Arts and Crafts, Portland,

1988—89. Author: Calligraphy for Those Who Are Young at Heart, 1988; contbr. ; exhibitions include various schs., restaurants, art stores, chs. Recipient Outstanding Svc. in Secondary Edn. award, European Coun. Internat. Schs., London, 1977—90, Calligraphy award, Soc. Scribes and Illuminators, London, 1991. Mem.: So. Fla. Watercolor Soc., Mus. for Women in Arts, Humane Soc. Democrat. Roman Catholic. Avocations: music, meditation, watercolor. Home: 3051 NE 48th St Apt 104 Fort Lauderdale FL 33308-4903

GUETHLEIN, WILLIAM O. lawyer; b. Cin., May 4, 1927; s. William O. and Catherine (Sandmann) G.; m. Bette Mivelaz, Aug. 4, 1961 (dec. 1974). LLD, U. Louisville, 1950. Bar: Ky. 1950, U.S. Dist. Ct. Ky. 1954, U.S. Ct. Appeals (6th cir.) 1954. Assoc. Boehl Stopher and Graves, Louisville, 1950-60, sr. ptnr., 1960—. Lt. USAR, 1952-60. Fellow Am. Acad. Trial Lawyers; mem. ABA, Jefferson County Bar Assn., Ky. Bar Assn., Am. Assn. Hosp. Attys. Avocation: tennis. Office: Phillips Parker Orberson and Moore PLC 716 W Main St Ste 300 Louisville KY 40202-2634

GUETTEL, HENRY ARTHUR, retired arts executive; b. Kansas City, Mo., Jan. 8, 1928; s. Arthur Abraham and Sylva (Hershfield) G.; 1 dau. by previous marriage, Laurie C. (dec.); m. Mary Rodgers, Oct. 14, 1961; children: Matthew Rodgers (dec.), Adam Arthur, Alexander Burton. Student, Wharton Sch. of U. Pa., 1944-47, U. Kansas City, 1947-48. Stage mgr. on Broadway and TV, also stock cos., 1949-60; gen. mgr. Royal Ballet, Can., 1953-54; producer nat. touring cos. The Best Man, Sound of Music, Camelot, Oliver; then also gen. mgr. Music Theatre of Lincoln Center; touring cos. The Merry Widow, Kismet, Carousel, Annie Get Your Gun, Show Boat, 1964-67; mng. dir., then v.p. Am. Nat. Opera Co., 1967-68; prodn. supr. exploratory music theatre prodns., forum Vivian Beaumont Theater and theatre concerts Philharmonic Hall, N.Y. State Theatre, 1966-69; assoc. Kaplan Veidt, Ltd., 1970-72; v.p., prodn. assoc. Cinema 5, Ltd., 1972-78; v.p. creative affairs Columbia Pictures, 1978-80; sr. v.p. East Coast Prodn. Twentieth Century-Fox, 1980-82; exec. dir. Theatre Devel. Fund, 1982-92. Mem. theatrical adv. panel N.Y. State Coun. of Arts, 1965-70; cons. theatre to SUNY, 1969-70; bd. dirs. Chelsea Theatre Ctr., N.Y.C., 1966-72, Performing Arts Repertory Theatre, N.Y.C., 1971-82, Theatre Devel. Fund, 1980-93, AFS Internat., 1987-89, Alliance for Arts, The Actor's Fund of Am., 1980—, Lit. Vols. N.Y.C., 1995-97, The New 42nd St., 1995—, Young Concert Artists, 1998—. Mem. Century Assn., Quogue Field Club, Quogue Beach Club. Address: 211 Central Park W New York NY 10024-6020

GUETZKOW, DANIEL, technology company entrepreneur; b. Ann Arbor, Mich., May 19, 1949; s. Harold S. and Lauris G. Student, Columbia U., 1967-70; BSBA in Accountancy, Thomas Edison State Coll., 1989; MS in Bus. and Mgmt., Acctg. Systems, U. Md., 1991. CPA, D.C., MD; cert. mgmt. acct. Prodn. mgr. plastics inj. molding Rehrig-Pacific, Inc., L.A., 1975-78; plastics blow molding maintenance mgr. Setco, Inc., Culver City, Calif., 1978-79; plastic/plywood plant mgr. Veneer Tech., Inc., L.A., 1979; co-founder, chief fin. officer, chief ops. officer, exec. v.p. Networld, Inc., Riverdale, Md., 1981-91, also dir.; pres. Roadside Table Ahead, Ltd., Del., 1990—2000, RTA Techs., Ltd., 1990-92; founder, CFO, exec. v.p. Global Coherence Inc., 1990-95; dir., treas. The Compassion Ctr., Inc., 1996—. Author: (book) Indemnification of Officers and Directors, 1988, (software) Telemarketing Database Mgr., 1984 86, Systems Accounting Control, 1985, Electronic Mail Switcher, 1982, 84, Compute Marginal IRS Tax Rate Using Linear Programming Sensitivity Analysis, 1989, Working Capital Liquidity Mgmt. Simulation, 1990, Use of Information Theory to Determine When to Post-Audit Capital Budgeting Decisions, 1991, Leading/Lagging Paradigm for Classifying Performance Indicators for Total Quality Management, 1991, Plan, Plant, Product Busn Re-Engr Software, 1994; contbr. articles to profl. jours. Mem. AICPA, D.C. Inst. CPAs (chief fin. officers and mgmt. cons. svcs. com.), Ops. Rsch. Soc. Am., Inst. Mgmt. Accts., Md. Assn. CPAs, Nat. Assn. Corp. Dirs. Home and Office: Compassion Ctr Inc PO Box 888 Riverdale MD 20738-0888 E-mail: daniel@guetzkow.org.

GUEVARRA, MANUEL ROBINSON, artist, retired military officer; b. San Roque, Cavite, The Philippines, June 17, 1931; s. Jose Andico and Frances (Robinson) G.; m. Carol Ann Bennett, June 15, 1963; children: Mark Bennett, Christian Benjamin. AA, Valencia Coll., 1979. Actor Cor-Qui Films Inc., Manila, 1950-51; enlisted USN, 1953, advanced through grades to chief petty officer, ret., 1976; procurement specialist Naval Tng. Ctr., Orlando, Fla., 1977-79; supr. dist. ops. USPS, Orlando and Lake Mary, Fla., 1979-97; sculptor Crealde Sch. of Arts, Winter Park, Fla., 1997—. Prin. works include The General, 1997, bronze life-size bust of Gen. MacArthur (donated to Pacific War Meml., Phillippines), 2002; Winston Churchill, 1997, George Patton, 1997; works exhibited at Art-Works Gallery and Studio, Oviedo, Fla. Assoc. mem. Orlando Mus. of Art, mem. Crealde Sch. of Art; com. mem. St. Stephen's Ch., Winter Springs, Fla., 1989-90; counselor Boy Scouts Am., Winter Park, 1976-78. Recipient Hon. Mention award, Williams and Jenkins Gallery, 2002. Mem. Fleet Res. Assn., Nat. Assn. Postal Suprs., Fil-Am. Club of Ctrl. Fla. (auditor, v.p. 1976-78). Democrat. Roman Catholic. Avocations: sculpture, stamp collecting, coin collecting, gardening, carpentry.

GUFFEY, BARBARA BRADEN, elementary education educator; b. Pitts., Pa., Aug. 10, 1948; d. James Arthur and Dorothy (Barrett) Braden; 1 child, William Butler Guffey III. BA in Elem. Edn., Westminster Coll., New Wilmington, Pa., 1970; MEd in Elem. Edn., Slippery Rock State Coll., 1973; postgrad., U. Pitts., Duquesne U., Westminster Coll. Cert. tchr., elem. and secondary history and govt. edn, elem. prin. Tchr. Shaler Area Sch. Dist., Glenshaw, Pa., 1970—, lang. arts area specialist, 1988—91, 1992—93, grad. level chmn., 1991—92, curriculum support math./sci., 1994—, mem. instrnl. support team, 1995—. Mem. Shaler Area Stretegic Planning Core Team, 1992—; mem. A.S.S.E.T. Leadership Team, 1995—; condr. seminars and workshops in field. Pres. alumni coun. Westminster Coll., 1996—97, v.p., 1995—96, chmn. homecoming all-alumni luncheon, 1991—93, chmn. homecoming, 1995—96, trustee, 1999—, mem. sesquicentennial com., 2002, mem. enrollment mgmt., ednl. policy and student affairs com. institut. advancement, vice chmn. instl. advancement com., 2003—; chairperson Westminster Fund; active Burchfield Elem. Sch. PTA; chmn. publicity Shaler Area Choir Parents Assn., 1996—2000; vice chmn. Dist. Adv.; mem. Child Care Adv. Bd.; elder, chair Christian edn. com. Glenshaw Presbyn. Ch., 1995—2001, mem. Presbyn. Women. Mem.: NEA, Shaler Area Edn. Assn. (mem. at large, negotiator, former rec. sec., v.p., bldg. rep., editor newsletter), Pa. Edn. Assn., Nat. Geneal. Soc. (local arrangements chair Pitts. conf. 2003), Armstrong County Hist. and Mus. Soc., Ind. County Geneal. and Hist. Soc., Western Pa. Geneal. Soc. (bd. dirs. 1992—, chair 25th Anniversary 1999, pres. 1999—2000, publicity 2000—03, pres. 2002—03), Perry Historians, Juniata County Hist. Soc., First Families of Western Pa. (charter mem.), Westminster Coll. Women's Club Pitts. (pres. 1975—76, treas. 1994—99, pres. 2001—03, v.p., sec., chair ways and means), Kappa Delta Pi. Office: Burchfield Elem Sch 1500 Burchfield Rd Allison Park PA 15101-4099

GUGEL, CRAIG THOMAS, advertising and strategic research executive; b. Detroit, Jan. 18, 1954; s. Paul Walter and Patricia Angela (Sullivan) G. BA, U. Windsor, Ont., Can., 1976. Asst. br. mgr. Mich. Nat. Bank, Livonia, 1975—77; analyst media rsch. Kenyon & Eckhardt, Inc., Birmingham, Mich. and N.Y.C., 1977—81, supr. media rsch. N.Y.C., 1981—82; v.p., asst. dir. media rsch. McCann-Erickson, Inc., N.Y.C., 1982—84; v.p., dir. media rsch. Foote, Cone & Belding, Inc., N.Y.C., 1984—86; sr. v.p., corp. dir. media resources Bozell, Jacobs, Kenyon & Eckhardt, Inc., N.Y.C., 1986—88; sr. v.p., dir. media research Bates Worldwide, Inc., N.Y.C., 1988—91, sr. v.p., exec. dir. media rsch. and tech., 1991—94, sr. v.p., exec. dir. interactive media and rsch., 1994—95, exec. v.p. new media and interactive rsch., 1995—97, exec. v.p., dir. media resources and rsch., 1997; pres., CEO Manhattan-Pacific Multimedia Inc., N.Y.C., 1997—; chief rsch. svcs. officer Organic, Inc., N.Y.C., 1997—98; exec. v.p., dir. strategic insights Optimedia Internat., N.Y.C., 2001—. Mem.: Advt. Rsch. Found. (bd. dirs. 1995—2001, chmn. interactive media com., co-chmn. digital media measurement coun.). Avocations: reading, theatre, computers.

GUGEL, M. SUE, artist; b. Van Wert, Ohio, Nov. 22, 1938; d. Merlin Harvey Smith and Margaret Ann Louise Miller; m. Lorenz Walter Gugel, Dec. 28, 1959 (dec. 1980); children: Scott, Craig, Kristina. Studied with David Humphreys Miller, 1957; student, U. N.Mex., 1965-67, U. Alaska, 1967-71. Tchr. art therapy ARC, El Paso; art tchr. Shiva Paint Co., El Paso, 1972 74, Officers Club, El Paso, Fairbanks, Alaska, 1975-80, Umpqua C.C., 1975—; art tchr. spl. arts, disabilities Umpqua Valley Arts Ctr. Group shows include Rickerts Gallery, Newport, Oreg., Fischer Galleries, Washington, D.C. One person shows include, Tolly's Art and Antiques, Oakland, Oreg., Art Mill Gallery, Roseburg, Oreg., Umpqua Valley Art Ctr., Roseburg, Bend (Oreg) City Hall, 2003; represented in permanent collections including Bapt. State Conv. Bldg., Anchorage, Pioneer Hall of Fame, Burrough Pub. Libr., Fairbanks, Alaska, Roseburg Forest Products, Trent Colleges, Wash., Oreg., Starfire Lumber, Marsha Leaptrout Collection, Ford Found., others. Charter mem. Nat. Mus. Women in the Arts. Mem. Fairbanks Art Assn. (pres., award), Umpqua Valley Arts Assn. (pres., award), Nat. Soc. Lit. and the Arts, Willamette We. Artists Assn. Republican. Avocations: music, politics. Home: PO Box 367 Dillard OR 97432-0367 E-mail: lindaf@teleport.com.

GUGGENHEIM, FREDERICK GIBSON, psychiatry educator; b. Chgo., July 8, 1935; s. Melvin Elias and Marjorie Stone (Gibson) G.; m. Bethany Reed (div. Apr. 1976); m. Olivia Bishop Rogers, Nov. 23, 1984; children: Jennifer, Hannah, Russell Alderson, Rhoades Alderson. BA, Yale U., 1957; MD, Columbia U., 1961 Resident in medicine Bellevue Hosp., N.Y.C., 1961-63, Columbia Presbyn. Med. Ctr., N.Y.C., 1963-64; clin. assoc. NIMH, Bethesda, Md., 1964-66; resident in psychiatry Strong Meml. Hosp., Rochester, N.Y., 1966-69; asst. prof. Harvard Med. Sch., Boston, 1970-79; from asst. in psychiatry to assoc. psychiatrist Mass. Gen. Hosp., Boston, 1969-79; assoc. prof. Southwestern Med. Sch. in Tex., Dallas, 1979-85; Marie Wilson Howells prof. and chair dept. psychiatry U. Ark. for Med. Scis., Little Rock, 1985-2000, prof., 2001—02; chief psychiat. cons. svc. Univ. Hosp., Little Rock, 2001—02; staff psychiatrist East Bay Mental Health Ctr., Providence, 2002—. Mem. nat. adv. com. clin. scholars program Robert Wood Johnson Found., Princeton, N.J., 1988-94; mem. com. on career devel. awards VA, Washington, 1990-95; mem. nat. adv. coun. Substance Abuse and Mental Health Svcs. Adminstrn., 1993-96; chief of staff U. Hosp., 1992-94, sec. med. bd., 1998-2000. Recipient Allison travel fellowship Yale U., 1956, 57, Saybrook Fellows prize, 1957, Nancy CA Roeske cert. of recognition for excellence in med. student edn., 2002. Fellow Am. Psychiat. Assn., Am. Coll. Psychiatrists, Acad. Psychosomatic Medicine; mem. So. Assn. Rsch. in Psychiatry (pres. 1991-92), Am. Assn. Chairmen of Depts. Psychiatry (pres. 1995-96), Ark. Psychiat. Soc. (pres. 1988-89), Assn. Acad. Psychiatry (pres. 1992-93), Cosmos Club of Wash., Alpha Omega Alpha (faculty). Home: 690 Angell St Providence RI 02906-5552 Office: Adams Farley Counseling Ctr 610 Wampanoag Trail East Providence RI 02915

GUGGENHEIM, MARTIN FRANKLIN, law educator, lawyer; b. N.Y.C., May 29, 1946; s. Werner and Fanny (Monatt) G.; m. Denise Silverman, May 29, 1969; children: Jamie, Courtney, Lesley. BA, SUNY, Buffalo, 1968; JD, NYU, 1971. Bar: N.Y. 1972, U.S. Dist. Ct. (so. dist. and ea. dist.) N.Y. 1973, U.S. Ct. Appeals (2d cir.) 1974, U.S. Ct. Appeals (3d cir.) 1979, U.S. Ct. Appeals (6th cir.) 1977, U.S. Supreme Ct. 1976. Staff atty. Legal Aid Soc., N.Y.C., 1971-72, dir. spl. litig. unit, juvenile rights divsn., 1972-73; clin. instr. NYU Sch. Law, N.Y.C., 1973-75; staff atty. juvnile rights project ACLU, N.Y.C., 1975-79, acting dir., 1976-77; asst. prof. clin. law NYU, N.Y.C., 1975-77, assoc. prof. clin. law, 1977-79, prof. clin. law, 1980—; of counsel Mayerson & Stutman LLP, N.Y.C., 2001—. Exec. dir. Washington Sq. Legal Svcs., Inc., N.Y.C., 1986-2000; pres. Nat. Coalition for Child Protection Reform, 2000—, pres., founding dir. Family Def. Law Project, Inc., N.Y.C., 1992-2000; advisor program for children Edna McConnell Clark Found., 1993-2001; dir. clin. and advocacy programs NYU, 1989-2002; founding dir. Ctr. for Family Representation, N.Y.C., 2002--; cons. juvenile justice stds. project ABA/Inst. Jud. Adminstrn., 1979-81; acting dir. Clin. Advocacy Programs, Sch. of Law NYU, 1988-89. Author: (with Alan Sussman) The Rights of Parents, 1980, Abuse and Neglect Volume, 1982, The Rights of Young People, 2d edit., 1985, (with Anthony G. Amsterdam and Randy Hertz) Trial Manual for Defense Attorneys in Juvenile Court, 1991, (with Alexandra Lowe and Diane Curtis) The Rights of Families, 1996. Dir. William J. Brennan Ctr., NYU, 1995-2000; mem. adv. bd. N.Y.C. Adminstrn. Children, 1997—; pres. Nat. Coalition for Child Protection Reform, 2000—. Arthur Garfield Hays Civil Liberties fellow, 1970-71, Criminal Law Edn. and Rsch. fellow, 1969-70; Kathryn A. McDonald award Assn. of the Bar of the City of N.Y., 2000. Mem. ABA, Am. Assn. Law Schs., Assn. of Bar of City of N.Y. Office: NYU Sch Law 161 Ave of the Americas New York NY 10013 E-mail: martin.guggenheim@nyu.edu.

GUGGENHEIMER, HEINRICH WALTER, mathematician, educator; b. Nurnberg, Germany, July 21, 1924; arrived in U.S., 1959; s. Siegfried and Marguerite Erna (Bloch) G.; m. Eva Auguste Horovicz, June 6, 1947; children: S. Michael, Esther H., Tobias I.S., Hanna Y. Diploma in math., Swiss Fed. Inst. Tech., Zurich, 1947, DSc in Math., 1950. Lectr. Hebrew U., Jerusalem, 1954-56; prof. Bar Ilan (Israel) U., 1956-59; assoc. prof. Wash. State U., Pullman, 1959-60, U. Minn., Mpls., 1960-62, prof., 1962-67, Poly U. (formerly Poly. Inst. Bklyn.), 1967-89; prof. emeritus Poly. U. N.Y. (formerly Poly. Inst. Bklyn.), 1989—. Author: Differential Geometry, 2d edit., 1977, Plane Geometry and Its Groups, 1967, Mathematics for Engineering and Science, 1976, Applicable Geometry, 1977, BASIC mathematical Programs for Engineers and Scientists, 1987, (with Eva H. Guggenheimer) Jewish Family Names and Their Origins: An Etymological Dictionary, 1992, German edit., 1996, The Scholar's Haggadah, 1995, Seder Olam: A Translation and Commentary, 1998 (bilingual edit.), The Jerusalem Talmud, part I, vol. 1, vol. 2 (bilingual edit.), 2000, vol. 3, 2001, vol. 4, 2002, vol. 5, 2003; contbr. articles to profl. jours. With Swiss Army, 1944-54. Mem. Swiss Math. Soc. (life), Math. Assn. Am., Soc. Indsl. Applied Math. Home: PO Box 401 West Hempstead NY 11552-0401

GUGGENHEIMER, TOBIAS IMMANUEL SIMON, architect; b. Basel, Switzerland, Jan. 30, 1953; s. Heinrich Walter and Eva Augusta (Horowicz) G.; m. Lisa Ann Shapiro, June 27, 1976 (div. 1999); children: Anna Bella, Leanora Margaret. BA in Lit., SUNY, Binghamton, 1975; MArch, U. Colo., 1985. Registered architect, N.Y., N.J. Pres. Tobias Guggenheimer Arch., P.C., Dobbs Ferry, N.Y., 1991—. Educator Pratt Inst. Sch. of Architecture, Bklyn., 1987-99; asst. prof., dir. interior design program Marymount Coll., Tarrytown, N.Y., 1999-03; lectr. in field. Author: A Taliesin Legacy: The Architecture of Frank Lloyd Wright's Apprentices, 1995; contbg. editor: Jour. of Taliesin Fellows, 1996-97; architect: (restorations) Frank Lloyd Wright's Serlin Residence, 1996-97; (projects) Mittman Residence, Spearfish, S.D., 2000; (renovations) Yannuzzi Residence, Tuxedo Park, N.Y., 1997-99, Malek Residence, 1999, Shore Residence, 1999, Howe Bldg., 2000-02, Holtz-Lamb Residence, 2000, Frank-Mermelstein Residence, 2002, Hunter Residence, 2002, Hanlon Residence, 2002; curator: A Taliesin Legacy: The Independent Work of Frank lloyd Wright's Apprentices, Pratt Inst. Gallery, 1993, Architectural Competitions in America, 2000. Cons. Village Tuxedo Park, 1999, Frank Lloyd Wright's Reisley Residence, 1999. Mem. AIA, Nat. Coun. Archtl. Registration Bds. Home: 215 W 95th St New York NY 10025- Office: Tobias Guggenheimer Arch PC 145 Palisade St Dobbs Ferry NY 10522-1617 E-mail: tobiasarch@aol.com.

GUGGENHIME, RICHARD JOHNSON, lawyer; b. San Francisco, Mar. 6, 1940; s. Richard E. and Charlotte G.; m. Emlen Hall, June 5, 1965 (div.); children: Andrew, Lisa, Molly; m. Judith Perry Swift, Oct. 3, 1992. AB in Polit. Sci. with distinction, Stanford U., 1961; JD, Harvard U., 1964. Bar: Calif. 1965, U.S. Dist. Ct. (no. dist.) Calif. 1965, U.S. Ct. Appeals (9th cir.) 1965. Assoc. Heller, Ehrman, White & McAuliffe, 1965-71; ptnr. Heller, Ehrman, White & McAuliffe, 1972—. Spl. asst. to U.S. Senator Hugh Scott, 1964; bd. dirs. Comml. Bank of San Francisco, 1980-81, Global Savs. Bank, San Francisco, 1984-86, North Am. Trust Co., 1996-99. Mem. San Francisco Bd. Permit Appeals, 1978—86; bd. dirs. Marine World Africa USA, 1980—86; mem. San Francisco Fire Commn., 1986—88, Recreation and Parks Commn., 1989—92; chmn. bd. trustees San Francisco Univ. H.S., 1987—90; trustee St. Ignatius Prep. Sch., 1987—96. Mem.: Am. Coll. Probate Counsel, Mayacama Golf Club, Olympic Club (bd. dirs. 1999—2002, pres. 2002), Thunderbird Country Club (Rancho Mirage, Calif.), Chevaliers du Tastevin (San Francisco), Wine and Food Soc., Bohemian Club. Home: 2621 Larkin St San Francisco CA 94109-1512 Office: Heller Ehrman White & McAuliffe 333 Bush St San Francisco CA 94104-2878

GUGINO, CARL FRANK, orthodontist, educator; b. Buffalo, Nov. 7, 1928; s. Anthony Samuel and EmoiJane (Ursitti) G.; divorced; children: Megan Eileen Schapp, Carla Neill, Carl Anthony; m. Linda Barrett, Nov. 19, 1995. DDS, SUNY, Buffalo, 1956. Gen. practice dentistry, Buffalo, 1955-59; tng. in orthodontics SUNY, 1964; pvt. practice orthodontics Buffalo, 1961—, Sarasota, Fla.; pres. Aperio Svcs., 2001—. World lectr. on orthodontics, 1964—; vis. prof. Howard U., Washington, 1983—; hon. pres., hon. chmn., advisor to ZeroBase Bioprogressive Therapy Groups, Italy, France, Japan; former mem. bd. dirs. and rsch. dir. Found. for Orthodontic Rsch. Lt. comdr. USN, 1953-55. Named hon. citizen, Paris and Monte Carlo; recipient honors Assoc. Orthodontic Jour. Europe. Fellow Am. Coll. Dentists, Internat. Coll. Dentists; mem. ADA, Am. Assn. Orthodontists, Northeastern Soc. Orthodontists, Erie County Dental Soc., 8th Dist. Dental Soc., Soc. Francaise Orthopedic Dento-Faciale, Bioprogressive Study Club Japan (chmn.), Ricketts Club France (hon. pres.). Avocations: skiing, walking, homeopathic studies, travel, golf.

GUGLIELMINO, LUCY MARGARET MADSEN, education educator, researcher, consultant; b. Charleston, S.C., Feb. 20, 1944; d. Robert Allen and Margaret Webb (Rodgers) Madsen; m. Paul Joseph Guglielmino, July 31, 1965; children: Joseph Allen, Margaret Rose. BA in English magna cum laude, Furman U., 1965; MEd in English and Edn., Savannah Grad. Ctr., 1973; EdD in Adult Edn., U. Ga., 1977. Tchr. English various pub. schs., Mass., 1965-72; vis. asst. prof. adult and cmty. edn. Fla. Atlantic U., Boca Raton, 1978-87, asst. prof., 1987-88, assoc. prof., 1988-90, prof., 1991—, chmn. dept. ednl. leadership, 1991-94, dir. Melby Cmty. Edn. Ctr., 1994—2000. Cons. AT&T, Motorola, Westvaco, S.E. banks, 1979—; bd. dirs. South Fla. Ctr. for Ednl. Leaders. Author: Adult ESL Instruction: A Sourcebook, 1991, Community Education and Florida's Future: Proceedings of the Commissioner's Summit, 1997; co-author: Administering Programs for Adults, 1997; author: (adult form) Self-Directed Leaning Readiness Scale, 1978, 3 other forms and translations into 17 other langs., 1979—94, Learning Preference Assessment (self-scoring format for business), 1991; editor: Florida GED Teachers' Handbook, 1999, 2001, Florida GED Teachers' Lesson Bank, 2001; co-editor: Internat. Jour. Self-Directed Learning, 2003—; contbr. over 90 articles to profl. jours., chapters to books. Mem. Fla. Literacy Coalition, 1990—. Recipient Tchr. of Yr. award Coll. Edn., Fla. Atlantic U., 1990, Outstanding Achievement award 1991, Presdl. Merit award, 1993, Profl. Excellence award, 1998, Malcolm Knowles Meml. award for outstanding lifelong contbn. to rsch. in self directed learning, 2002; named to Fla. Adult and Cmty. Edn. Hall of Fame, Fla. Adminstrs. Adult and Cmty. Edn., 1992; numerous grants, 1979—. Mem. AAUW, Nat. Cmty. Edn. Assn., Am. Assn. for Adult and Continuing Edn., Commn. Profs. Adult Edn. (chmn. self directed learning task force 1987-88, 90-91), Fla. Adult Edn. Assn. (bd. dirs. 1989-90), Phi Kappa Phi, Phi Delta Kappa. Episcopalian. Avocations: reading, swimming, biking, flower arranging, gardening. Home: 7339 Reserve Creek Dr Port Saint Lucie FL 34986 Office: Fla Atlantic U CO 113 500 NW California Blvd Port Saint Lucie FL 34986 E-mail: lguglie@fau.edu.

GUGLIELMINO, PAUL JOSEPH, educator; b. Bklyn., May 19, 1942; s. Carl and Rose (Loreto) G.; m. Lucy Margaret, July 31, 1965; children: Joseph Allen, Margaret Rose. BA, The Citadel, 1964; MA, U. Ga., 1970, EdD, 1978. Capt. transfer pt. U.S. Army, Ft. Devens, Mass., 1964-66; dir. ctr. for mgmt. Fla. Atlantic U., Boca Raton, Fla., 1978-81, adj. prof. mgmt., 1981-86, exec. dir., asst. prof., 1986-94, assoc. prof. mgmt., 1994—. Patentee in field. Mem. Boca Forum, Boca Raton, 1989-90. Mem. Acad. Mgmt., Assn. Citadel Men., Acad. Internat. Bus. Episcopalian. Home: 7339 Reserve Creek Dr Port Saint Lucie FL 34986

GUHA, SUJATA, education educator; b. Calcutta, West Bengal, India, Dec. 13, 1969; d. Ashoke Kumar and Minu Guha. BS, U. of Dubuque, Iowa, 1994, MS, Purdue U., Ind., 1997, PhD, 2000. Grad. instr. chemistry Purdue U., West Lafayette, Ind., 1994—2000; asst. prof. chemistry Rocky Mountain Coll., Billings, Mont., 2000—. Author: (book chapter) Stratospheric Bromine Chemistry: Insights from Computational Studies. Presdl. Scholarship, U. of Dubuque, 1991—94. Mem.: Am. Chem. Soc., Am. Assn. for the Advancement of Sci., N.Y. Acad. of Scis., The Math. Soc. of Am., Mont. Sci. and Tech. Consortium, NASA-Montana Spage Grant Consortium, Phi Lambda Upsilon, Alpha Chi (bd. dirs. 1992—94). Achievements include research in Atmospheric chemistry of novel transient species in the gas phase. Home: 2460 Village Ln #310B Billings MT 59102 Office: Rocky Mountain Coll 1511 Poly Dr Billings MT 59102 Office Fax: 406-259-9751. Personal E-mail: sujata_guha@yahoo.com. E-mail: guhas@rocky.edu.

GUHAROY, ROY, pharmacy director, medical educator; b. Calcutta, India, June 20, 1959; s. B M and Gita Guharoy; m. Sue Guharoy, May 3, 1983; 1 child, Victor. D of Pharmacy, U. Minn., 1982; MBA, Claremont Grad. Sch., 1992. Clin. pharmacist Porterville (Calif.) State Hosp., 1982-83, John F. Kennedy Meml. Hosp., Indio, Calif., 1983-86, dir. pharmacy svcs., clin. coord., 1986-98; dir. pharmacy svcs. Canyon Springs Hosp., Cathedral City, Calif., 1988-90, U. Hosp., Syracuse, N.Y., 1998—; assoc. prof. Union U., Albany Coll. of Pharmacy, 1998—; assoc. prof. Sch. of Nursing SUNY Health Sci. Ctr., Syracuse, 1998—, assoc. prof. Sch. Medicine, vice chmn. clin. pharmacology, 1998—. Asst. prof. U. So. Calif. Sch. Pharmacy, 1991-98; profl. rels. com. Am. Coll. of Clin. Pharmacy. Contbr. over 100 articles to profl. publs. Fellow Am. Soc. of Hosp. Pharmacists; mem. N.Y. Soc. of Health System Pharmacists (editl. bd.). Office: Univ Hosp 750 E Adams St Syracuse NY 13210-1834

GUHR, DANIEL JOHANNES, management consultant; b. Kirch-Brombach, Germany, Oct. 22, 1967; s. Ekkehard E.F. and Sigrid G. Guhr; m. Erin Nicole Dunlop, 2001. BA Equivalent, U. Bonn, Germany, 1991; MA, Brandeis U., 1995; MSc, Oxford U., England, 1995, PhD, 1999. Intern The Libr. of the German Parliament, Bonn, Germany, 1990, Embassy of the U.S., Bonn, Germany, 1990—91; mgmt. cons. The Boston Cons. Group, Munich, 1997—99, San Francisco, 1999—2000; dir. bus. devel. SAP Markets, Inc., Palo Alto, Calif., 2000—01; mng. ptnr. Illuminate Consulting Group, 2002—. Author: (novels) Access to Higher Education in Germany and California, 2002; editor DAAD North American Studies Yearbook 1991/92, 1992. Scholar, Friedrich-Naumann-Found., 1990, Brandeis U., 1992; fellowship for doctoral studies at Oxford U., Econ. and Social Rsch. Coun., Eng., 1994, scholarship and stipend for studies at Harvard U., German Acad. Exch. Svc., 1991, Travel grantee, Heinz-Schwarzkopf-Found., 1990. Mem.: Comparative and Internat. Edn. Soc., Max-Planck-Soc., The Acad. Polit. Sci., Turnerschaft Germania (Bonn, Germany) (life), Oxford U. Alumni Assn., U. Bonn Alumni Assn., U. Calif. Berkeley Alumni Assn., Brandeis U. Alumni Assn., German Acad. Exch. Svc. Alumni Assn., U. Harvard Alumni Assn., The Churchill Club, The Commonwealth Club of Calif. Home: 2109 Ellen Ave San Jose CA 95125 E-mail: guhr@illuminateconsultinggroup.com.

GUI, JAMES EDMUND, architect; b. Wooster, Ohio, Aug. 13, 1928; s. Harry Ludwig and Mabel Josephine (Olson) Gui; m. Anne Louise Outram, Oct. 15, 1955; children: Linda Anne, Jeffrey Allen. BArch, Ohio State U., 1954. Assoc. firm Charles F. McKirahan & Assocs., Archs., Ft. Lauderdale, Fla., 1958—63; chief specifications Archs. Collaborative, Cambridge, Mass., 1963—67; propr. James E. Gui, Archtl. and Specifications Cons., Belmont, Mass., 1967—. Prin. works include Archs. Collaborative, Benjamin Thompson & Assocs., Cambridge Seven Assocs., Archtl. Resources Cambridge, Inc., Harvard, MIT, Juilliard Sch. Music, Lincoln Ctr., NYC, U.S. Pavillion Expo 67, Montreal, New Eng. Aquarium, Children's Hosp. Med. Ctr., Harvard U. Law Sch. Complex, Harvard Gutman Libr., Harvard Obs., Kirkland Coll., Berkshire CC, Tufts U. Dental Health Ctr., Independence Nat. Hist. Pk. Visitors Ctr., Navy Pier, Chgo., Wilmington Jewish Cmty. Ctr., Faneuil Hall Marketplace, Boston, Harborplace, Balt., Seaport Market, NYC, Pier 17, Bayside Marketplace, Miami, Century City Market, LA, Harvard Kennedy Sch. Govt., Cambridge, Ordway Music Theater, Mpls., Union Sta. Restoration, Washington. Mem.: Constrn. Specifications Inst. Address: 50 Starfish Dr Unit 307 Hilton Head Island SC 29928-6901 E-mail: jandagui@aol.com.

GUIBBORY, ACHSAH, English educator, writer; b. Norwalk, Conn., June 30, 1945; d. Moses and Bathyah (Rasmussen) Guibbory; m. Anthony D. Kaufman, June 11, 1972; 1 child, Gabriel Benjamin. BA, Ind. U., 1966; MA, UCLA, 1967, PhD, 1970. Asst. prof. U. Ill., Urbana, 1970-76, assoc. prof., 1976-89, prof. English, 1989—. Vis. prof. Barnard Coll., 2003. Author: The Map of Time, 1986, Ceremony and Community from Herbert to Milton, 1998; editor Jour. English and Germanic Philology, 1976-95, mng. editor, 1995-01. Recipient U. Ill. Campus Undergrad. Tchg. award, 1979, Luckman Tchg. award, U. Ill., 1995, Prokasky Tchg. award, 1995; grantee Ctr. for Advanced Study, U. Ill., 2001—02;, NEH fellow, 2001—02, Ctr. Advanced Study fellow, U. Ill., 2002. Mem.: MLA (exec. com. 17th Century English Lit. divsn. 1999—2003), John Donne Soc. (Disting. Publ. award 1992, 1994), Milton Soc. Am. (exec. com. 1991—93, v.p. 2000, pres. 2001). Office: U Ill Dept English 608 S Wright St Urbana IL 61801-3630 E-mail: aguibbor@uiuc.edu.

GUIBERTEAU, MILTON J. radiologist; b. Aug. 11, 1945; BA, Rice U., Houston, 1967; MD, Baylor U., 1971. Resident in radiology Harvard U. Hosps., Boston, 1972-76; prof. radiology U. Tex. Med. Sch., Houston, 1985—; chmn. dept. radiology St. Joseph Hosp., Houston, 1989—; diagnostic/nuclear radiologist/physician Christus/St. John Hosp., Houston, 1980—. Pres. SJR Assocs. Author: Essentials of Nuclear Medicine Imaging, 1983, 4th edit., 2000, Cardiovascular Nuclear Medicine, 1995. Chmn. bd. dirs. Tex. Radioactive Waste Commn., 1991-99; mem. human use com. Internat. Commn. on Radiation Protection, 1996—; bd. chancellors Am. Coll. Radiology. Mem.: Tex. Radiol. Soc. Home: 3465 W Alabama St Houston TX 77027-6028 Office: St Joseph Hosp Dept Radiology PO Box 27705 Houston TX 77227-7705 E-mail: mjgmd@aol.com.

GUICE, STEPHEN WAYNE, lawyer; b. Woodbury, N.J., Feb. 18, 1958; s. Marvin Ray and Shirley Guice. BS, Wagner Coll., 1980; JD, Rutgers U., 1984. Bar: N.J. 1984, Pa. 1984, U.S. Ct. Appeals (3d cir.) 1984, U.S. Supreme Ct. 1989. Law clk. Gloucester County Superior Ct., Woodbury, N.J., 1984-85; assoc. Horn, Goldburg, Gorny, Daniels, Atlantic City, 1985-86, Friedman, Bafundo & Porter, Cherry Hill, N.J., 1986-92; pvt. practice, Barrington, N.J., 1992—. Avocations: volleyball, skiing. Office: 413 Clements Bridge Rd Barrington NJ 08007-1809

GUIDA, PAT, information broker, literature chemist; b. Highland Park, Mich. d. Wilfred Bernard and Patricia Mary (Kelly) Graham; m. Edward Silvio Guida, Aug. 29, 1965; chidren: Niels Bohr, Eric Bohr. Student, Regis Coll., 1946-48, Rutgers U., 1952-55; BS cum laude, Fairleigh Dickinson U., 1961. Asst. librarian Warner-Lambert Research Inst., Morris Plains, N.J., 1961-64; librarian Reaction Motors Div. Thiokol, Denville, N.J., 1964-69; mgr., info. ctr. Foster D. Snell Div., Booz Allen & Hamilton Inc., Florham Park, N.J., 1969-80; pres. Pat Guida Assocs., Fairfield, N.J. Mem. Sci. Adv. Bd. EPA, Washington, 1978-82, Library Com. Chemists Club, N.Y.C., 1983-89. Editor: Chemical Digest, 1971-74. Pres. PTA, Sparta, N.J., 1959-60. Avocations: theatre, west highland white terriers, music, travel. Home and Office: 5 Cedar Tree Ln Sparta NJ 07871-2306 E-mail: vjrs@sys.uea.ac.uk .

GUIDA, TONI M. lawyer; b. Bklyn., Nov. 10, 1961; d. Peter and Susan G.; m. Jeffrey P. Rogan, Apr 1, 1989; children: Madeline Elsie, Peter Dylan Jeffrey. BA with honors, Binghamton U., 1984; JD with honors, Syracuse U., 1987. Bar: N.Y. 1987, U.S. Dist. Ct. (ea. and so. dists.) N.Y. 1989. Jud. clk. appellate divsn. 3rd dept. N.Y. Supreme Ct., Albany, 1987-88; litig. atty. Kelley, Drye & Warren, N.Y.C., 1988-93; sr. spl. counsel divsn. enforcement N.Y. Stock Exch., N.Y.C., 1993-94; founding ptnr. Rogan, Guida & Orenstein, White Plains, N.Y., 1996—. Alumni admissions rep. Binghamton U., 1996—. Notes and Comments editor Syracuse Jour. Internat. Law & Commerce, 1985-86. Vol. White Plains Sch. Dist., 1997—; mem. The Women's Guild, White Plains, 1997—. Mem. N.Y. Met. Club. Harper Coll./Binghamton U., Syracuse Met. Alumni Assn. Avocations: writing instructional books and articles, reading. Office: Rogan Guida & Orenstein 235 Mamaroneck Ave White Plains NY 10605-1315

GUIDICE, REBECCA MONETTE, strategic management educator; d. Phillip Joseph and Iris Eileen Guidice; m. David G. Wolf, Aug. 10, 1996 (div. May 1, 2000); 1 child, Logan Dante Wolf. BSBA, Whitworth Coll., 1991; MBA, Ea. Wash. U., 1994; PhD, Wash. State U., 2001. Assoc. dir. ops. Internat. Amb. Programs, Spokane, 1985—94; prof. Wash. State U., Pullman, 1991, instr., rsch. asst., 1991—94; prof. U. Miss., Oxford, 1991—. Mem.: S.W. Acad. Mgmt., So. Mgmt. Assn., Acad. Mgmt. Office: U Miss PO Box 1848 University MS 38677

GUIDO, MICHAEL ANTHONY, evangelist; b. Lorain, Ohio, Jan. 30, 1915; s. Mike and Julia (DePalma) G.; m. Audrey Forehand, Nov. 25, 1943. Student, Moody Bible Inst., Chgo., 1933-35. Ordained to ministry So. Bapt. Conv., 1939. Min. youth and music 1st Presbyn. Ch., Sebring, Fla., 1936-38, 1st Bapt. Ch., Lake Charles, La., 1939; evangelist Moody Bible Inst., 1940-50; founder, pres., speaker Guido Evangelistic Assn., Metter, Ga., 1950—. Writer, speaker daily telecast A Seed from the Sower, 1972—, daily broadcaster The Sower, A Seed from the Sower, Seeds from the Sower, Your Favorite Ten, 1957—. Author: (autobiography) Seeds from the Sower, 1990, rev. edit., 1998, Treasury of Illustrations, 1999; editor Sowing and Reaping mag., 1957—; daily newspaper columnist Seeds from the Sower, 1957—. Named Alumnus of Yr., Moody Bible Inst., 1982, Citizen of Yr., Kiwanis Club, Metter, 1982. Baptist. Interstate bridge named in honor of Michael A. Guido, 1998. Home: PO Box 508 Metter GA 30439-0508 Office: 600 N Lewis St Metter GA 30439-1428 *Life to me is loving God and serving Him by finding a need and supplying it, and searching for a lost soul and bringing that one home to God.*

GUIGON, JOHN V. corporate lawyer; V.p. Schering-Plough Corp., Madison, NJ, gen. counsel. Office: Schering-Plough Corp 1 Giralda Farms Madison NJ 07940-1010

GUIHER, JAMES MORFORD, JR., publisher, writer; b. Clarksburg, W.Va., Feb. 21, 1927; s. James Morford and Ruth Holt (Souders) G.; m. Elizabeth Ewing Hart, Aug. 20, 1954; children: Catharine Brownfield, Deborah Hart. BA, Princeton U., 1951; postgrad., Harvard U., 1951-52, Boston Mus. Sch. Fine Arts, 1953-54. Editor coll. textbooks Prentice-Hall, Inc., Englewood Cliffs, N.J., 1954-66, exec. editor Ednl. Book div., 1966-68, editor-in-chief, 1968-74, v.p., gen. mgr., 1974-76; publishing cons. Author: (play) Aphrodite, 1999. Served with AUS, 1945-47. Home: 4 E 88th St New York NY 10128-0509

GUILAK, FARSHID, biomedical engineering researcher, educator; b. Tehran, Iran, Sept. 17, 1964; arrived in U.S., 1970; s. Hooshang and Nahid (Toufigh) G. BS, Rensselaer Poly. Inst., 1985, MS in Biomed. Engring., 1987; MPhil, Columbia U., 1990, PhD in Mech. Engring., 1991. Computer programmer U. Houston, 1982; rsch. asst. Rensselaer Poly. Inst., Troy, N.Y., 1983, grad. rsch. asst., 1985-86; computer programmer Houston Mus. Natural Sci., 1983-84; rsch. fellow Columbia U., N.Y.C., 1986-91; asst. prof. orthopaedic surgery and mech. engring. SUNY, Stony Brook, 1991-94; asst. prof. orthop. surgery, biomed. and mech. engring. Duke U., Durham, NC, 1994—2000, assoc. prof. orthop. surgery, 2001—. Reviewer Jour. Biomechanics, 1991—, editor-in-chief, 2002—; reviewer NSF, Washington, 1991—, NIH, Washington, 1998, Jour. Biomech. Engring., 1992—, Jour. Orthopedic Rsch., 1993—, Bone, 1993—; co-editor Cell Mechanics and Cellular Engring., Functional Tissue Engring.; contbr. articles to profl. jours., chpts. to books. Nat. Merit scholar, 1982; Frank E. Stinchfield fellow, 1990; recipient Young Investigator's award World Congress on Med. Physics, 1991, George W. Thorn award Whitaker Found., Kappa Delta award, 1998. Mem. ASME (Best Paper award 1990), Orthopaedic Rsch. Soc. (Young Investigators award 1991, New Investigator Recognition award 1994). Achievements include development in cell mechanics and cellular engineering using microscopy and finite element modeling; rsch. in use of stem cells derived from subcutaneous fat to regenerate cartilage and bone. Office: Orthopaedic Rsch Labs Duke U Med Ctr PO Box 3093 Durham NC 27715-3093 Business E-Mail: guilak@duke.edu.

GUILD, ALDEN, retired lawyer; b. Boston, July 3, 1929; s. Howard Redwood and Frances Allen (Warren) G.; m. Ruth Ineta Creighton, Sept. 14, 1957; 1 child, Heather Louise. BA, Dartmouth Coll., 1952; JD, U. Chgo., 1957; LLD (hon.), Norwich/Vt. Coll., 1977. Bar: Vt. 1958, U.S. Dist. Ct. Vt. 1958. With law dept. Nat. Life Ins. Co., Montpelier, Vt., 1957-90, asst. v.p., counsel, corp. sec., 1974-83, v.p., gen. counsel, 1983-89, sr. v.p., gen. counsel, 1989-90; ret. McKee, Giuliani & Cleveland, Montpelier, of counsel, 1990-97. Author: Stock-Purchase Agreements, 1960, Professional-Partnership Purchase Agreements, 1961, Business-Partnership Purchase Agreements, 1962; contbr. articles to legal jours. Trustee Norwich U., 1972-96, Vt. Coll., 1967-72, Kimball U. Acad., 1972-74, Wood Art Gallery, 1961-72; mem. Dartmouth Coll. Alumni Council, 1975-78. Served with USAF, 1950-53, Korea. Recipient Disting. Service award Montpelier Jr. C. of C., 1962 Mem. Vt. Bar Assn., Assn. Life Ins. Counsel, Am. Coun. Life Ins., VFW, Am. Legion, Order of Colf, Lake Mansfield Trout Club (Stowe, Vt.), Masons, Elks, Phi Beta Kappa, Theta Chi. Republican. Home: 63 Murray Rd Montpelier VT 05602-8514

GUILD, CLARK JOSEPH, JR., lawyer; b. Yerington, Nev., May 14, 1921; s. Clark Joseph and Virginia Ellen (Carroll) G.; m. Elizabeth Ann Ashley, July 20, 1945 (div. 1977); children: Clark J. III, Jeffrey S., Daniel E. (dec.), Jann Cademartori. BA, U. Nev., 1943; JD, Georgetown U., 1948. Bar: Nev. 1948, D.C. 1948, U.S. Dist. Ct. (no. dist.) Nev. 1948, U.S. Ct. Appeals (D.C. cir.) 1948, U.S. Supreme Ct. 1959, U.S. Ct. Appeals (9th cir.) 1984. Ptnr. Guild, Hagen & Clark, Ltd., Reno, Nev., 1953-88, Guild, Russell, Gallgher & Fuller Ltd., Reno (formerly Guild, Hagen & Clark Ltd.), 1988—. Pres. YMCA, Reno, 1954, 64; regent U. Nev. System, 1972. Capt. inf. U.S. Army, 1942-46. Recipient Disting. Nevadan award U. Nev., 1989. Fellow Am. Coll. Trial Lawyers; mem. ABA, State Bar Nev., Clark County Bar Assn., Washoe County Bar Assn. (pres. 1959-60), Masons, Elks. Democrat. Episcopalian. Office: Guild Russell Gallagher & Fuller Ltd 100 W Liberty St Reno NV 89501-1962

GUILD, NELSON PRESCOTT, retired state education official; b. Keene, N.H., Nov. 20, 1928; s. Louis F. and Hope (Mason) Guild; m. Margaret Adele Graf, June 24, 1950; children: Douglas, Matthew(dec.), BA, U. N.H., 1953; MA, Pa. State U., 1955, PhD, 1958. Asst. prof. govt. Hamilton Coll., Clinton, N.Y., 1958-64, assoc. prof., 1964-66; dean Frostburg (Md.) State Coll., 1966-69, pres., 1969-85; interim exec. dir. bd. trustees Md. State Univs. and Colls., 1985-87. Author: (with Kenneth T. Palmer) Introduction to Politics: Essays and Readings, 1968. Served with USAF, 1946-49.

GUILD, RICHARD SAMUEL, trade association management company executive; b. Boston, Nov. 5, 1925; s. Walter Rayford and Anna (Hollander) G.; m. Susan Jane Coughlin, July 3, 1965; children: Laura Ann, Linda Jean. BS, Boston U., 1949. Cert. assn. exec. With Guild Assocs., Inc., Boston, 1949—, mng. dir., 1960-65, pres., 1965—. Owner Copypro, 1975-92; treas. Resource Matching System, Inc., 1982-83; exec. sec. New Eng. Marine Trade Assn., 1963, Liquified Petroleum Gas Assn. New Eng., 1972-1985; mng. dir. Shoe Pattern Mfrs. Assn., 1951-94, Mass. Automatic Merchandising Coun., 1964-99, Tel. Answering Assn. New Eng., 1983-99; exec. v.p. Am. Boat Builders and Repairers Assn., 1979-90; treas. Wet Ground MICA Assn., 1983-87. With USNR, 1944-45. Mem. Multiple Assn. Mgmt. Inst. (past pres.), Am. Soc. Assn. Execs. (past bd. dirs.), N.Am. Paddlesports Assn. (exec. v.p. 1987-90), Boston Soc. Assn. Execs. (past pres.), Def. Orientation Conf. Assn., Soc. Mgmt. of Profl. Computing (exec. sec. 1985-94), New Eng. Honda Automobile Dealers Assn. (exec. sec. 1985-95), Acura Dealers of N.E. (exec. sec. 1989-93, 96—). Home: 5 Glengarry Rd Winchester MA 01890-2511 Office: 389 Main St Malden MA 02148-5017

GUILERMO, FIGUEROA, conductor; Studied under Pablo Casals; studied under Oscar Shumsky, Felix Galimir, Juilliard Sch; tng., Conservatory of Music, P.R. Music dir., prin. guest conductor PR Symphony Orch., 2001—. Guest conductor Iceland Symphony, N.J. Symphony, N.Mex. Symphony, Orquestra Sinfonica do Teatro Municipal, Ballet Memphis, Cayuga Chmaber Orch., N.Y.C. Ballet, El Salvador Symphony, Rio de Janeiro. Conductor Colo. Symphony, Kansas City Symphony, Iceland Symphony, Four Seasons, (collaborated) with Janos Starker, Vladimir Feltsman, Glenn Dicterow, Horacio Guttierrez, Paul Neubauer, concertmaster N.Y.C. Ballet Orch., 1992, soloist (violin concerts) Brahms, Berg, Glass, Barber, Mikhail Baryshnikov, Deutsche Grammophon, Reverie, Bourgeois Getilhomme, Violin Concerto, Duo Fantasy, Synchronisms No.9; musician: Scherzo-Tarantelle, Liebesleid, Concertino for violin and chamber orch., premiere of John Adams' violin concert, premiere of two sonatas for violin and piano written by German Caceres, perfomed with Houston de Camera Latin Am. Festival, Music in the Vineyard Chamber music festival, Pro Arts Chamber Music Soc. Recipient Victor Herbert prize, Julliard Sch., 1st prize, Washington Internat. Competition, 1979. Mem.: Orpheus Chamber Orch. (concertmaster, soloist U.S., Europe, Asia). Office: PR Symphony Orch PO Box 41227 Minillas Sta San Juan PR 00940-1221

GUILES, RONALD DAVIS, biochemist, educator; b. San Mateo, Calif., Nov. 23, 1951; s. Richard Charles and Doris May Guiles. PhD, U. of Calif., 1988. Post-doctoral rsch. assoc. U. of Calif. San Francisco, San Francisco, 1988—91; asst. prof. U. of Md., Baltimore, Md., 1991—96, assoc. prof., 1996—, U. of Md. Biotechnology Inst., 1996—2003. Mem.: Am. Chem. Soc. Office: Univ Md 20 North Pine Street Baltimore MD 21201 Office Fax: 410-706-0346. Personal E-mail: rguiles@rx.umaryland.edu. E-mail: rguiles@rx.umaryland.edu.

GUILFORD, ANDREW JOHN, lawyer; b. Santa Monica, Calif., Nov. 28, 1950; s. Howard Owens and Elsie Jennette (Hargreaves) G.; m. Loreen Mary Gogain, Dec. 22, 1973; children: Colleen Catherine, Amanda Joy. AB summa cum laude, UCLA, 1972, JD, 1975. Bar: Calif. 1975, U.S. Dist. Ct. (ctrl. dist.) Calif. 1976, U.S. Ct. Appeals (9th cir.) 1976, U.S. Supreme Ct. 1979, U.S. Dist. Ct. (so. dist.) Calif. 1981, U.S. Dist. Ct. (no. and ea. dists.) Calif. 1990. Assoc. Sheppard, Mullin, Richter & Hampton, L.A. and Orange County, Calif., 1975-82, ptnr. Orange County, 1983—. Lectr. The Rutter Group, Encino, Calif., 1983—, Continuing Edn. of the Bar, Berkeley, 1978—, Hastings Ctr. for Advocacy, San Francisco, 1988; judge pro tem, arbitrator Calif. Superior Ct., 1983—; mem. commn. future legal profession and state bar; mem. adv. task force on multi-juristictional practice, task force on self-represented litigants. Author UCLA Law Review, 1975. Mem. Amicus Publico, Santa Ana, Calif., 1986; bd. dirs. Constl. Rights Found., 1990, Pub. Law Ctr. Orange County, 1990—, Baroque Music Festival, 1992-96, NCCJ, 1995-99, UCLA Law Alumni Assn., 1992-95; subdeacon, warden, del. Episcopal Ch. Recipient resolution of commendation Calif. State Senate and Assembly, Outstanding Svc. award Poverty Law Ctr., 1991, Bernard E. Witkin Amicus Curiae award Calif. Jud. Coun., Jurisprudence award Anti-Defamation League, J. Reuben Clark award, cert. of recognition U.S. Congress, others; co-recipient President's Pro Bono award State Bar; Regents scholar U. Calif., Berkeley, 1968-72; named one of Calif.'s 100 Most Influential Attys., The Daily Jour., Bus. Litig. Trial Lawyer of Yr., Orange County Trial Lawyers Assn. Fellow Am. Coll. Trial Lawyers; mem. ABA, FBA (bd. dirs. 2001—), Assn. Bus. Trial Lawyers (founding officer Orange County chpt., pres. 2000-2001), Am. Arbitration Assn. (arbitrator large complex case program 1993-95), Calif. Bar Assn. (pres. 1999-2000, bd. govs. 1996-2000), Orange County Bar Assn. (bd. dirs. 1985-87, officer 1988-90, pres. 1991, chmn. bus. litigation sect. 1983, state bar conv. 1986, 87, law-motion com. 1982, standing com. trial ct. delay reduction 1987-93), 9th Cir. Jud. Conf. (rep. 1990-93, 99—), Phi Beta Kappa (sec.-treas. 1978-80, v.p. 1980-84), Pi Gamma Mu, Sigma Pi. Republican. Avocations: theater, photography, sports, gardening, poetry. Office: Sheppard Mullin Richter & Hampton 650 Town Center Dr Fl 4 Costa Mesa CA 92626-1993 Home: 31852 Camino del Cielo Trabuco Canyon CA 92679-3400 E-mail: aguilford@sheppardmullin.com.

GUILFOYLE, ROBERT THOMAS, retired lawyer; b. Chgo., Mar. 23, 1936; s. Joseph Leo and Nellie (Powers) Guilfoyle; m. Jacqueline Gardner, May 21, 1964 (dec.). BS, U. San Francisco, 1958; JD, DePaul U., 1964. Bar: Ill. 1964. Atty. Allstate Ins. Co., Chgo., 1964—95; ret., 1995. With USN, 1958—60. Mem.: Ill. Bar Assn., Chgo. Bar Assn. Roman Catholic. Home: 524 N 5th Ave Des Plaines IL 60016-1125 Office: 200 N La Salle St Chicago IL 60601-1014 Personal E-mail: robertguilfoyle@aol.com.

GUILIANO, FRANCIS JAMES, office products manufacturing company executive; b. Feb. 1, 1932; s. James V. and Mary C. Guiliano; m. Mary Beth Eberly, Jan. 9, 1957; children: Barbara Jean, James Francis, Janet Marie, John Alden. BBA in Fin., U. Mass., 1959; MBA, U. Pa., 1978. Salesman Continental Can Co., 1959-63; sales mgr. State of Mich., 1964-65; plant gen. mgr. Internat. Paper Co., Greensburg, Pa., 1966-67, gen. mktg. mgr. container divsn., 1967-69, world-wide gen. mktg. mgr., 1969-72, v.p., gen. mgr. Folding Carton divsn. N.Y.C., 1972-76; exec. v.p. Simkins Industries, New Haven, 1977; chmn., CEO, pres. Ampad Corp., Holyoke, Mass., 1979-90; owner, CEO Rite-Now Container Corp., East Longmeadow, Mass., 1990—. CEO 4M Corp., 1987—; dir. Shawmut First Bank & Trust; CEO and pres. PCL Industries, 1990-93. Bd. dirs. United Way, 1981-82; chmn. bus. adv. coun., mem. exec. com. U. Mass. Sch. Bus., 1980-82; bd. govs. Holyoke Libr. Served with USN, 1951-55. Mem. Am. Mgmt. Assn., Ind. Box Makers Assn., Paper Converters Assn., Nat. Office Products Assn., Wholesale Stationers Assn., Colony Club (Springfield, Mass.), Longmeadow Country Club. E-mail: ritenow@capecod.net.

GUILL, MARGARET FRANK, pediatrics educator, medical researcher; b. Atlanta, Jan. 18, 1948; d. Vernon Rhinehart and Margaret N. (Tichenor) Frank; m. Marshall Anderson Guill III, July 6, 1974; children: Daniel Marshall, Laura Elizabeth. BA, Agnes Scott Coll., 1969; MD, Med. Coll. Ga., 1972. Diplomate Am. Bd. Pediatrics, Am. Bd. Pediatrics subbd. pulmonology, Am. Bd. Allergy and Immunology, Nat. Bd. Med. Examiners. Resident in pediatrics Kaiser Found. Hosp., San Francisco, 1976-78, fellow in allergy, 1978-79; staff physician Waipahu (Hawaii) Clinic, 1973-76; intern in internal medicine Med. Coll. Ga., Augusta, 1973, resident in pediatrics, 1974, fellow in allergy and immunology, 1979-80, from asst. prof. to prof. pediatrics, 1981—, also chief sect. pediatric pulmonology and dir. Asthma Ctr., dir. Cystic Fibrosis Ctr., 1990—, vice chair dept. pediat., 2000—, Dorothy A. Hahn chair pediats., 2001—. Pres. Physician Practice Group, 2001—04; pres. staff Childrens Med. Ctr. Hosp., 2000—01; spkr. in field. Host Healthwatch weekly program WJBF-TV, 1982-83; contbr. articles to profl. jours. Active Reid Meml. Presbyn. Ch.; vol. tchr. Episcopal Day Sch., 1982-85; career day participant Acad. Richmond County, 1982, 83; med. advisor Augusta Area Allergy and Asthma Support Group, 1984-86; adv. bd. East Cen. br. Am. Lung Assn. Ga., 1985—, program of work com., 1987—, bd. dirs., 1987—, program coordinating com., 1990-91, exec. bd., 1989-91; med. staff Camp Breathe Easy, 1985—, med. dir., 1996-98. Recipient Mosby Book award, 1973; grantee rsch. grantee, BRSG, 1981—86, Del Labs., 1982, Merrell-Dow, 1983—84, Elan Pharms., 1986, Am. Lung Assn. Ga., 1986—87, Hollister-Stier, 1986, Fisons Corp., 1989, 1991—93, 1995, Med. Coll. Ga., 1989, Am. Heart Assn., 1991, Genentech, 1991—, Miles, 1992, Clintrials, 1990—95, PathoGenesis, 1995—99, Smith-Kline Beecham, 1996, Kaleida Health, 2002, Chiron, 2002. Fellow Am. Acad. Pediat., Am. Coll. Chest Physicians, Am. Acad. Allergy, Asthma and Immunology, Am. Coll. Allergy, Asthma and Immunology, Am. Assn. Cert. Allergists; mem. Med. Assn. Ga., Richmond County Med. Soc., Allergy and Immunology Soc. Ga., S.E. Allergy Assn. (Hal Davison award 1985), Am. Assn. Clin. Immunologists and Allergists, Ga. Thoracic Soc. (Med. Profl. of Yr. 1998), Am. Thoracic Soc., Assn. for Care Asthma, Alpha Omega Alpha. Home: 2247 Pickens Rd Augusta GA 30904-4462 Office: Med Coll Ga Dept Pediatrics Augusta GA 30912 E-mail: mguill@mail.mcg.edu.

GUILLAMA-ALVAREZ, NOEL JESUS, merchant banker, healthcare executive; b. Havana, Cuba, Nov. 30, 1959; came to U.S., 1966; s. Jesus Mario Guillama and Rosa Maria Alvarez Guillama; 1 child, Jahziel Mikhail Guillama; m. Susan E. Darby, Dec. 13, 2002; 1 stepson, Patrick James Jacobs. Student, Palm Beach C.C., Lake Worth, Fla., 1978-80; BS in Constrn. Mgmt., Allstate Coll., Tampa, Fla., 1983; postgrad., MIT, 1997-99. Cert. bldg. contractor, Fla.; lic. real estate broker, mortgage broker, gen. ins. agt. Dir. programing Teleprompter Corp., West Palm Beach, Fla., 1976-79; pres., CEO JMG Holdings Inc, Palm Beach, Fla., 1980-90; v.p. ops. Quality Care Networks, Boca Raton, Fla., 1990-95; v.p. devel. Medpartners, Inc., Birmingham, 1995; pres., CEO Met. Health Networks, Boca Raton, 1995-2000; chmn., mng. ptnr. Millenium Capital Ptnrs., Boca Raton, 1997—; chmn. The Quantum Group, Inc., Wellington, Fla., 1991—; chmn., CEO Tektonica, Inc., Tequesta, Fla., 2001—; chmn. TargitInteractive, Portsmouth. Vice-chair Palm Beach County Adv. Bd., West Palm Beach, 1990-92; co-founder, vice-chair Lake Worth Cmty. Devel. Corp., 1990-92; co-founder Project Lake Worth, 1989-92; dir. Fl. Internat. U. Found., Miami, 2001. Writer weekly column Palm Beach Latino Newspaper, 1991-92. Bd. dirs. Fla. Internat. U. Found., Miami, 2002—. Recipient award Leukemia Soc. Am., 1979, Chin de Plata award Todo Mag., Miami, Fla., 1978. Mem. Am. Fin. Assn., Am. Coll. Healthcare Execs. (assoc.), Med. Group Practice Assn. Avocations: scuba diving, tennis, golf, fishing. Office: 12230 Forest Hill Blvd Ste 157 Wellington FL 33414 E-mail: noel@guillama.com.

GUILLAUME, GERMAINE CORNELISSEN, chronobiologist, researcher; b. Schaerbech, Belgium, Nov. 22, 1949; came to U.S., 1975; d. Alphonse and Helene (Minne) Cornelissen; m. Francis Guillaume, Nov. 22, 1975. BS in Physics, U. Libre de Bruxelles, Brussels, Belgium, 1969, MED, MS, U. Libre de Bruxelles, Brussels, Belgium, 1971, PhD in Physics, 1976. Tchr. Lycee Emile Max, 1971-73; fellow U. Libre de Bruxelles, Brussels, 1974-76; internat. vis. Chronobiology Lab. U. Minn., Mpls., 1975, vis. rsch. fellow, 1976-79, rsch. fellow, 1979-82, rsch. assoc., 1982-92, sr. rsch. assoc., dir. biometry, 1992-93, 94—, co-dir. chronobiology labs., 1999—. Referee GERB, Chronobiologia, Circulation, Chronobiology Internat., Clin. Sci., Hypertension, Internat. Jour. for Chronobiology, Jour. Nutrition, Life Scis., Nature, Psychol. Reports: Perceptual and Motor Skills, CRC Press, Italian Jour. Gastroenterology, Neuroendocrinology, Am. Jour. Ob-Gyn.; bd. dirs. Underlab Project, Pioneer Frontier Explorations and Rsch. Srl, Ancona, Italy. Guest editor Psychophysiology; mem. editl. bd. Il Policlinico, 1991-96, Chronobiologia, 1989-91, co-editor, 1991-94; contbr. more than 350 articles to profl. jours. including Am. Jour. Cardiology, Am. Jour. Perinatology, Annales Geophysicae, Annals of the N.Y. Acad. Scis., Clin. Cardiology, Clin. Chemistry, Clin. Drug Investigation, Jour. Clin. Endocrinology, Jour. Interdisciplinary Cycle Rsch., JAMA, New Trends in Exptl. and Clin. Psychiatry, Peptides, Psychol. Reports, The Statistician, among others. Mem. Internat. Soc. for Chronobiology, Internat. Soc. for Rsch. on Civilization Diseases and the Environment (sec. N.Am. chpt. 1987—), Sigma Xi. Avocations: hiking, reading, cooking. Home: 511 Ryan Ave W Saint Paul MN 55113-6605 Office: U Minn Chronobiology Lab Mayo Mail Code 8609 Minneapolis MN 55455-0351 E-mail: corne001@umn.edu.

GUILLAUME, RAYMOND KENDRICK, banker; b. June 19, 1943; s. William Raymond and Marguerite (Lyons) G.; m. Ann Greenwell, June 26, 1965; children— Lee Kendrick, Jill Lyons Kissel. BS, Western Ky. U., 1965. Asst. cashier Liberty Nat. Bank, Louisville, 1968, asst. v.p., 1969-70, v.p., 1970-72, sr. v.p., 1973-78, exec. v.p., 1978-92, pres., 1993-95, also bd. dirs.; vice chmn., CEO Bank of Louisville, 1995—2002; pres. Ky. and Louisville metro region Br. Banking & Trust, 2002—. Chmn., bd. dirs. ARC, Louisville, 1985; treas., bd. dirs. Met. United Way, Louisville, 1984-92, 93—, St. Anthony's Hosp., Louisville, 1985; trustee Christ Ch. United Meth., Louisville, 1984; chmn. Leadership Louisville, 1992-95; chmn. bd. dirs. Metro United Way, Western Ky. Univ. Found., Ky. Ctr. for the Arts Endowment Fund; bd. dirs. Norton Healthcare, The Healing Pl., The Housing Partnership. Mem. Western Ky. U. Nat. Alumni Assn. (pres. 1985), Ky. Bar Assn. (bd. dirs.), Pendennis Club, Louisville Boat Club, Jefferson Club, Kentuckians of N.Y. Home: 415 Rolling Ln Louisville KY 40207-1807 Office: Br Banking & Trust PO Box 1101 Louisville KY 40201-1101

GUILLEMETTE, MARK EDGAR, textile technologist; b. Fall River, Mass., Sept. 13, 1956; m. Elaine Marie Sylvain, Oct. 5, 1996. BS, U. Mass., Dartmouth, 1978; MS, Inst. Textile Tech., Charlottesville, Va., 1980. Tech. svc. mgr. Globe Mfg. Co., Fall River, Mass., 1980-2001, Radicispandex, F, 2001—. Recipient Harry Riemer Vets. award No. Textile Vets. Assn., 1978. Mem. Am. Chem. Soc. (sr.), Am. Assn. Textile Chemists and Colorists (sr.; pub. spkr.). Avocation: golf. Office: Radicispandex 125 Hartwell St Fall River MA 02721-

GUILLEMIN, ROGER C. L. physiologist; b. Dijon, France, Jan. 11, 1924; arrived in came to US, 1953, naturalized, 1963; BA, U. Dijon, 1941, B.Sc., 1942; MD, Faculty of Medicine, Lyons, France, 1949; PhD, U. Montreal, 1953; PhD (hon.), U. Rochester, 1976, U. Chgo., 1977, Baylor Coll. Medicine, 1978, U. Ulm, Germany, 1978, U. Dijon, France, 1978, Free U. Brussels, 1979, U. Montreal, 1979, U. Man., Can, 1984, U. Turin, Italy, 1985, Kyung Hee U., Korea, 1986, U. Paris, Paris, 1986, U. Barcelona, Spain, 1988, U. Madrid, 1988, McGill U., Montreal, Can., 1988, U. Claude Bernard, Lyon, France, 1989, Laval U., Quebec, Can., 1996, Sherbrooke U., Quebec, 1997, U. Franche-Comté, France, 1999. Intern, resident univs. hosps., Dijon, 1949-51; asso. dir., asst. prof. Inst. Exptl. Medicine and Surgery, U. Montreal, 1951-53; asso. dir. dept. exptl. endocrinology Coll. de France, Paris, 1960-63; asst. prof. physiology Baylor Coll. Medicine, 1953-57, assoc. prof., 1957-63, prof., dir. labs. neuroendocrinology, 1963-70; resident fellow, chmn. labs. neuroendocrinology Salk Inst., La Jolla, Calif., 1970-89, adj. rsch. prof., 1989-94; Disting. Scientist Whittier Inst., 1989-97, med. and sci. dir., 1993-94; adj. prof. medicine U. Calif., San Diego, 1995-97; disting. prof. Salk Inst., La Jolla, Calif., 1997—. Bd. dir. ICN Pharms. Decorated chevalier Legion d'Honneur France, officer; recipient Gairdner Internat. award, 1974, award, Lasker Found., 1975, Dickson prize in medicine, 1976, Passano award sci., 1976, Schmitt medal neurosci., 1977, Barren Gold medal, 1979, Dale medal, Soc. for Endocrinology, UK, 1980, Ellen Browning Scripps Soc. medal, Scripps Meml. Hosps. Found., 1988, Disting. Scientist award, Nat. Diabetes Rsch. Coalition. Fellow: AAAS; mem.: NAS, Western Soc. Clin. Rsch., Internat. Soc. Neurosci. (charter), Acad. Royale de Medecine de Belgique, Acad. Sci., Academie Internat. Medicine, French Acad. Scis., Am. Acad. Arts & Scis., Soc. Neuro-scis., Internat. Soc. Rsch. Biology Reprodn., Internat. Brain Rsch. Orgn., Soc. Exptl. Biology and Medicine, Endocrine Soc. (pres. 1986), Assn. Am. Physicians, Am. Physiol.

Soc., Can. Soc. Endocrinal Metabolism (hon.), Swedish Soc. Med. Sci. (hon.), Am. Peptide Soc. (hon.), Club of Rome. Office: The Salk Inst 10010 N Torrey Pines Rd La Jolla CA 92037-1099 Address: The Salk Inst PO Box 85800 San Diego CA 92186-5800*

GUILLERY, RAINER WALTER, anatomy educator; b. Greifswald, Germany, Aug. 28, 1929; came to U.S., 1964; s. Hermann and Eva (Hackel) G.; m. Margot Cunningham Pepper, Dec. 21, 1954, (div. 2000); children: Peter, Edward, Philip, Jane. B.Sc. in Anatomy, U. Coll., London, Eng., 1951, PhD, 1954. Asst. lectr. Univ. Coll., London, Eng., 1953-57, lectr., 1957-63, reader, 1963-64, assoc. prof. U. Wis. at Madison, 1964-68, prof. anatomy, 1968-77; prof. dept. pharm. and physiol. Scis. U. Chgo., 1977-84; Dr. Lee's prof. anatomy Oxford U., Eng., 1984-96; vis. prof. anatomy U. Wis., Madison, 1996—2002, emeritus prof. anatomy, 2002—. Author: (with M.S. Sherman) Exploring the Thalamus, 2001; mem. editl. bd. Jour. Comparative Neurology, 1971-2002, Jour. Neurocytology, 1972-76, Jour. Neurophysiology, 1975-81, Neurosci, 1979—, Jour. Neurosci, 1980-90; editor-in-chief European Jour. Neurosci., 1987-92, mem. editl. bd., 1987—. Fellow U. Coll. London, 1987. Fellow Royal Soc.; mem. Soc. Neurosci., Anatomical Soc. G.B., Ireland (pres 1994-96). Achievements include rsch. on central nervous system, synapses, degeneration, devel. visual pathways. Office: U Wis Dept Anatomy Sch Medicine 1300 University Ave Madison WI 53706-1510 E-mail: rguiller@wisc.edu.

GUILLIOUMA, LARRY JAY, JR., performing arts administrator, music educator; b. Massillon, Ohio, Apr. 23, 1950; s. Larry Jay and Molly (Galob) G. BS, U. North Ala., 1972, MA, 1975; postgrad., U. Miss., 1976-78. Cert. tchr., Tex. Band dir. Phil Campbell (Ala.) H. S., 1972-76; grad. asst. U. Miss. Band, Oxford, 1976-78; asst. dir. Victoria (Tex.) H. S., 1978-81; dir. bands Harlingen (Tex.) H. S., 1981-87, McAllen (Tex.) Pub. Schs., 1991—. Musician Huntsville (Ala.) Symphony Orchestra, 1970-76, Victoria (Tex.) Symphony Orchestra, 1978-81. Named Outstanding Dir. Alamo Tournament of Bands, San Antonio, 1985, Best in Class, World of Music Festival, Dallas, 1986; named to Nata. Band Dirs. Hall of Fame, Daytona Beach, Fla.; Harlingen High Sch. Big Red Cardinal Band marched in Pasadena Tournament of Roses Parade, 1987. Mem. Nat. Band Assn., Tex. Music Educators Assn. (bd. dirs, region vice chmn., region band chmn.), Tex. Band Masters Assn., Phi Beta Mu Avocations: bicycling, travel, computers, telecommunications. Home: Apt 1215 7150 Smiling Wood Ln Houston TX 77086-3142

GUILLORY, ANN VERRETT, psychologist, educator; b. New Orleans, Dec. 10, 1948; d. Wilbert A. and Augusta Bell Verrett; m. Samuel Guillory (div.); children: Elizabeth, Christine. BS, Loyola U. of the South, New Orleans, 1970; MEd in Guidance and Counseling, Loyola U. of the South, 1972; MEd in Gerontology, Columbia U., N.Y.C., 1981; EdD in Applied Human Devel., Columbia U., 1983. Cert. student svcs. and sci. tchr. La., N.J. Dir. Ednl. Opportunity Fund Felician Coll., Lodi, NJ, assoc. prof. psychology. Bd. trustees Care Plus, N.J., Paramus, 1994—, Care Plus Found., Paramus, 2001—, Westside Daycare Ctr., Englewood, NJ, 2001—. Mem.: Am. coll. Personnel Assn., Assoc. Gerontology in Higher Edn. Roman Catholic. Avocations: gardening, needlepoint. Office: Felician College 262 S Main St Lodi NJ 07644

GUILLORY, J. KEITH, pharmacist, educator; b. Bunkie, La., Feb. 4, 1935; s. Edgar and Alma Decuir Guillory. PhD, U. Wis., 1961. Asst. prof. Wash. State U., Pullman, 1961—64; prof. U. of Iowa, Iowa City, 1964—98. Bd. dirs. Elder Svcs., Iowa City, 2000—02. Recipient rsch. achievement award, Am. Assn. Pharm. Scientists, 1997. Mem.: Am. Assn. Pharm. Scientists. Office: U Iowa College of Pharmacy Iowa City IA 52242 Business E-Mail: guillory@uiowa.edu.

GUILLORY, JOHN FERREL, journalism educator; b. Lutcher, La., Mar. 5, 1947; s. Daniel Peter and Dorothy (Deroche) G.; m. Kathleen Ann Augusta, May 18, 1968; children: Kristen Guillory Skordinski, Lesley Guillory Wade, Justin. BA, Loyola U., New Orleans, 1969; MS in Journalism, Columbia U., 1970. Reporter The States Item, New Orleans, 1970-72; columnist, Washington correspondent, editorial page editor The News and Observer, Raleigh, N.C., 1972-96; writer-in-residence, sr. fellow MDC, Inc., Chapel Hill, NC, 1995—; dir. program on so. politics, media and pub. life U. N.C., Chapel Hill, 1997—; Batten prof. pub. policy Davidson Coll., 2000. Co-author: The Carolinas--Yesterday, Today, Tomorrow, 1999, (Reports to Region) State of the South, 1996, 98, 2000, 02; co-editor: Southern Politics, Southern Cultures, 1997; moderator (Pub. TV Panel) Evening with Five Living Govs., 1994. Bd. dirs. Agape Pl. Homeless Shelter, 1980-86, N.C. Inst. Polit. Leadership, Wilmington, 1995—; bd. visitors Loyola Dept. Comm., New Orleans, 1996—; mem. adv. bd. Statelme.org, 2001—; vice chmn. adv. bd. Cath. Campus Min., Raleigh, N.C., 2002-. Recipient Faith Active award N.C. Coun. of Chs., Raleigh, 1990. Home: 4628 Gramercy Ct Raleigh NC 27609-5579 Office: U NC PO Box 3365 Chapel Hill NC 27599-3365 E-mail: guillory@unc.edu.

GUILLOT, CYRIL ETIENNE, international organization administrator; b. Paris, Sept. 24, 1962; s. Jacques Rene and Jacqueline (Lageat) G. Cert., U. de Belgrano, Buenos Aires, 1984, U. de Los Andes, Bogota, Colombia, 1984; BA, Johns Hopkins U., 1984, MA, 1985. Field implementation officer UN Capital Devel. Fund, N'Djamena, Chad, 1987-89; assoc., sr. project mgmt. officer UN Office for Project Svcs., N.Y.C., 1989-93; country officer UN Capital Devel. Fund, N.Y.C., 1993-96, program specialist, 1997—2001, dep. dir. local governance unit, 2002—. Study grantee Orgn. of Am. States, 1984. Mem. Fgn. Policy Assn. Avocation: travel. Office: UN Capital Devel Fund 1 UN Plz # Dc2-2623 New York NY 10017-3515 Home: 16 Springdale Rd New Rochelle NY 10804-4317 E-mail: cyril.guillot@undp.org.

GUILLOT, PATRICK CARL, lawyer, judge; b. Dallas, Apr. 12, 1945; s. L.E. and Helen Ruth (Gallagher) G.; m. Rebecca Nichols, Jan 20, 1945; children—Christian, Claire, Drouard. B.A., U. Tex., 1967, J.D., 1969. Bar: Tex. 1969, U.S. Dist. Ct. (no. dist.) Tex. 1969, U.S. Ct. Appeals (5th cir.) 1973. Assoc. Bailey & Williams, Dallas, 1969-73; mem. Collie, McSpedden & Roberts, Dallas, 1969-79; judge 254th Dist. Ct., Dallas, 1979-81; judge Ct. Appeals, Dallas, 1981-86; mem. Godwin & Carlton 1986-93; mem. True, Rohde & Sewell, 1993—. mem. Nat. Conf. Commrs. on Uniform State Laws, 1982— . Fellow Tex. Bar Found. Republican. Roman Catholic. Office: Ste 250 2929 Carlisle St Dallas TX 75204-4069

GUILMET, GEORGE MICHAEL, cultural anthropologist, educator; b. Seattle, Feb. 8, 1947; s. Michael D. and Avis M. (Degerness) G.; m. Glenda J. Black, May 24, 1980; children: Michelle R., Douglas J. BS in Metallurg. Engring., U. Wash., Seattle, 1969, MA in Anthropology, 1973; PhD in Anthropology, UCLA, 1976. Lectr. anthropology Calif. State U., Bakersfield, 1976-77, program dir. urban anthropology internship program, 1977-78; asst. prof. comparative sociology U. Puget Sound, Tacoma, 1977-82, assoc. prof., 1982-88, prof., 1988—2002, prof. emeritus, 1992—. Reader dept. anthropology UCLA, 1974-75; rsch. cons. dept. psychiatry UCLA, 1975-76; rsch. assoc. Nat. Ctr. Am. Indian Alaska Native Mental Health Rsch., U. Colo., 1986—; disting. vis. prof. anthropology San Diego State U., 1991; grant reviewer NIMH, Bethesda, 1991, 92; spkr. in field. Author, co-author: (chpts.) Research in Philosophy and Technology, vol. 8, 1985, Technology and Responsibility: Philosophy and Technology, vol. 3, 1987, Behavioral Health Issues among American Indians and Alaska Natives: Explorations on the Frontiers of the Biobehavioral Sciences, 1988, Native America in the Twentieth Century: An Encyclopedia, 1994, (rsch. monograph) The People Who Give More, 1989; contbr. articles to profl. jours.; keyboardist, vocals Brave New World; singles released include It's Tomorrow, 1967. Evaluation cons. Chief Leschi Sch., Puyallup Tribe Indians, Tacoma, 1989, 96—, vol. musician Puyallup Tribe Indians, Tacoma, 1996, 97, cultural needs assessment cons., 1996-97, juvenile justice program cons., 1997-98. Kaiser Aluminum Chem. Corp. scholar, 1968-69; grantee Carnegie Found., 1974, U. Puget Sound, 1977-79, 83-84, 86, 88, 89, 91, 93, 2001. Fellow Am. Anthrop. Assn. (bd. dirs. coun. anthropology edn. 1983-85, anthropology and environ. sect.); mem. Soc. Philosophy Tech., Fedn. Small Anthropology Programs, Pacific N.W. Historians Guild. Home and Office: 652 Old Blyn Hwy Sequim WA 98382-9695 E-mail: guilmet@ups.edu.

GUILMET, GLENDA JEAN, artist; b. Tacoma, Wash., Mar. 28, 1957; d. Cody Calvin Black and Maria Isabel Rivera; m. George Michael Guilmet, May 24, 1980; children: Michelle Rene, Douglas James. Student, Clover Park Vocat. Tech. Inst., 1982-83; BA in Bus. Adminstrn., U. Puget Sound, 1981, BA in Art, 1989. Freelance photographer, Tacoma and Blyn, 1976—; women's sports photographer U. Puget Sound, Tacoma, 1977-78, asst. photographer, 1978-79; visual artist Tacoma and Blyn, 1982—; photographic cons. Puyallup Tribe of Indians, Tacoma, 1984; on-call photographer Puyallup Tribal Health Authority, Tacoma, 1984-86. Instr. sculpture Tacoma Arts Commn., 1989; guest lectr. U. Puget Sound, 1990, 94; grants juror Artist Trust, Seattle, 1990; video festival juror Tacoma Mcpl. TV, 1990; photography competition juror Washington State PTA Reflections Com., 1995; art dir., Tacenda and Willo Trees Press, Marshfield, Mo., 1993. Contbr. photographs to various publs.; one-woman shows include, Stage Door Gallery, Tacoma Little Theatre, 1993, Seattle U. Women's Ctr., 1994, Inst. de Cultura Puertorriquena, Jayuya, Carolina and Caguana, P.R., 1994, 1995, Galleria on Broadway, Tacoma, 1996, 1998, Sacred Cir. Gallery of Am. Indian Art, Seattle, 1996, 1997, 1999, exhibited in group shows, Nat. Mus. of Women in the Arts, Washington, U. Puget Sound, Tacoma, 1989, Windhorse Gallery, Seattle, 1990, Chase Gallery, Spokane City Hall, 1990, Hanforth Gallery, Tacoma, 1990, 1991, Wash. State Capital Mus., Olympia, 1990, Foyer of the Okean Theater, Vladivostok, Russia, 1992, First Night Gallery, Tacoma, 1992, 1996, 1997, Sacred Cir. Gallery of Am. Indian Art, 1993, 1996, Cunningham Gallery U. Wash., 1993, Western Gallery, Western Wash. U., Bellingham, 1993, Seattle Art Mus., 1993, Bibliotheque Nat. de France, 1994, Street Level Photography Gallery, Glasgow, Scotland, 1995, Tacoma Art Mus., 1995, Park Ave. Armory, N.Y.C., 1995, Westfalische Mus. fur Naturkunde, Munster, Germany, 1995, 1996, Iverness (Scotland) Mus., 1997, Ione Gallery Highland Folk Mus., Kingussie, Scotland, 1997, U. Ariz. Mus. Art, 1997, Coos Art Mus., Coos Bay, Oreg., 1998, Pratt Fine Arts Ctr., Seattle, 2000, Wash. State Conv. and Trade Ctr., Seattle, 2000, Represented in permanent collections, Steilacoom (Wash.) Tribal Mus., Bibliotheque Nat. de France, U. Puget Sound, Chief Leschi Schs., Puyallup Tribe of Indians, also pvt. and corp. collections; art dir. Tacenda, Marshfield, Mo., 2003. Recipient 1st Place Photography award, Crosscurrents Art Contest, 1988, Hedgebrook Invitational Residency, Hedgebrook Found., Langley, Wash., 2000. Mem. Artist Trust, En Foco, Atlatl, Women's Caucus for Art, Nat. Mus. Women in the Arts. Home and Studio: 652 Old Blyn Highway Sequim WA 98382-9695 E-mail: glendaguilmet@yahoo.com.

GUILMETTE, JONATHAN, Olympic athlete; b. Montreal, Que., Can., Aug. 18, 1978; Profl. speed skater, Canada. Named Can. champion, 1999, 2001; recipient Silver medal 500m, World Championships, 2001, Gold medal 5000m men's relay, 2002 Olympic Games. Avocations: computers, video games, movies, reading. Office: Speed Skating Can 2781 Lancaster Rd Ste 402 Ottawa ON K1B 1A7 Canada

GUIN, DON LESTER, insurance company executive; b. Shreveport, La., Nov. 5, 1940; s. Lester and Ethelyn (Dumas) G.; m. Mary Ann Guin, Feb. 3, 1979. BBA in Ins., U. Ga., 1962; BS in Law, Kensington U., Glendale, Calif., 1987, JD, 1989. Bar: Calif. 1990, U.S. Ct. Appeals (5th and 9th cirs.) 1990, U.S. Dist. Ct. (no. dist.) Calif. 1990, U.S. Ct. Appeals (fed. cir.) 1991, U.S. Dist. Ct. (ea. dist.) Tex. 1991, U.S. Ct. Internat. Trade 1991, U.S. Ct. Fed. Claims 1992, U.S. Supreme Ct. 1994. Adjuster, supr. Lindsey & Newsom, Beaumont, Tex., 1963-71, mgr. Port Arthur, Tex., 1968-71, asst. to pres. Tyler, Tex., 1971-74, v.p. ops., 1977-84, sr. v.p., 1984—; sr. v.p. adminstrn. and legal Lindsey Morden, 1990— ; sr. v.p., corp. sec. Lindsey Morden Claims Svc. Inc., Lindsey Morden Claims Mgmt., 1992-93, sr. v.p., treas. U.S. Ops., 1993—, sr. v.p., corp. treas., chief legal officer, 1995 —; sr. v.p., corp. treas. and sec. Vale Nat. Training Ctrs, Inc., 1993—; exec. v.p., corp. treas, corp. sec., chief legal officer, 1995—; exec. v.p. Cunningham Lindsey U.S., Inc., 2000—, Vale Nat. Tng. Ctr., 2001—. Bd. dirs. Lindsey Morden Claims Svc., Inc., Lindsey Morden Claims Mgmt., Inc., exec. com., mgmt. com., compensation com., incentive com., Vale Nat. Tng. Ctrs., Lindsey & Newsom Inc.; trustee Lindsey and Newsom Benefit Trusts, 1990-91, plan adminstr. Lindsey Morden Profit Sharing Retirement Trust, 1994, Lindsey & Newsom Retirement Funds, 1990—; sr. v.p., corp. sec., CLO Lindsey Morden Group, Inc., 1996—; mem. adv. bd. Kemper Ins. Group; sr. v.p., corp. sec. Lindsey & Newsom, Vale Nat; bd. dirs. Tyler Mus. Art, chmn. pers. policy com., chair fin. com., 1999; exec. v.p. Cunningham Lindsey, U.S., Inc., 2000. Author: Analysis of Garage Liability, 1972, Dishonesty Claims Handling, 1973, Casualty Reporting Manual, 1975, Sexual Harassment in the Workplace, 1986, (audio cassette) Beating the Bears of Bad Faith, 1991, (video cassette) Bad Faith and Preventing Errors and Omissions Claims, 1987. Trustee Lindsey Morden Benefit Trusts, Lindsey Morden Retirement Trusts, 1992—; dir. assoc. U. Tex Health Ctr., 1995; budget allocation panelist United Way Tyler/Smith County, Tex., 1995; bd. dirs. Tyler Mus. of Art, 1996. Mem. ABA (internat. law sect., corp. law sect.), Can. Bar Assn., Nat. Assn. Def. Counsel, Nat. Assn. Ind. Ins. Adjusters (data processing com. 1976, legis. com. 1990), Bar Assn. D.C., Bar Assn. U.S. Fed. Cir., Defense Inst. Trial Lawyers Assn. (ins. law com.), State Bar Calif. (internat. law sect., tort sect., litigation sect., labor and employment law sect.), Nat. Employee Benefit Found., Def. Rsch. Inst., Alameda County Bar Assn., Inter-Pacific Bar Assn., Italian-Am. Bar Assn., Bar Assn. 5th Fed. Cir., Optimist Club, Kiwanis Club, Sabre Club, Lawyers Club San Francisco, Ins. Soc. U. Ga. (charter mem.), Circle K-Kiwanis. Home: 17389 Hidden Valley Ln Flint TX 75762-9611 Office: Lindsey Morden Claims Svcs Inc 211 Brookside Dr Tyler TX 75711

GUIN, JUNIUS FOY, JR., federal judge; b. Russellville, Ala., Feb. 2, 1924; s. Junius Foy and Ruby (Pace) G.; m. Dorace Jean Caldwell, July 18, 1945; children: Janet Elizabeth Smith, Judith Ann Mullican, Junius Foy III, David Jonathan. Student, Ga. Inst. Tech., 1940-41; AB magna cum laude, U. Ala., JD with honors, 1947; LLD, Magic Valley Christian Coll., 1963. Bar: Ala. 1948. Pvt. practice law, Russellville; sr. ptnr. Guin, Guin, Bouldin & Porch, 1948-73; fed. dist. judge U.S. Dist. Ct. (no. dist.) Ala., Birmingham, from 1973, now sr. judge; commr. Ala. Bar, 1965-73, 2d v.p., 1969-70. Pres. Abstract Trust Co., Inc., 1958-73; sec. Iuka TV Cable Co., Inc., Haleyville TV Cable Co., Inc., 1963-73; former dir., gen. counsel First Nat. Bank of Russellville, Franklin Fed. Savs. & Loan Assn. of Russellville.; Lectr. Cumberland-Samford Sch. Law, 1974—, U. Ala. Sch. Law, 1977— Chmn. Russellville City Planning Com., 1954-57; 1st chmn. Jud. Commn. Ala., 1972-73; mem. Ala. Supreme Ct. Adv. Com. (rules civil procedure), 1971-73; mem. adv. com. on standards of conduct U.S. Jud. Conf., 1980-87, mem. com. on Fed.-State Jurisdiction, 1982-88, mem. ad hoc com. on cameras in the courtroom, 1982-83; Rep. county chmn., 1954-58, 71-72, Rep. state fin. chmn., 1972-73; candidate for U.S. Senator from, Ala., 1954; Ala. Lawyers' Finance chmn. Com. to Re-elect Pres., 1972; former trustee Ala. Christian Coll., Faulkner U., Magic Valley Christian Coll., Childhaven Children's Home; elder Ch. of Christ. Served to 1st lt., inf. AUS, 1943-46. Named Russellville Citizen of Year, 1973; recipient Dean's award U. Ala. Law Sch., 1977 Mem. ABA (mem. spl. com. on resdl. real estate transactions 917-73), Am. Radio Relay League, Ala. Bar Assn. (com. chmn. 1965-73, Award of Merit 1973), Jefferson County Bar Assn., Fed. Bar Assn., Am. Law Inst., Ala. Law Inst. (dir. 1969-73, 76—), Am. Judicature Soc., Farrah Law Soc., Farrah Order Jurisprudence (now Order of Coif), Phi Beta Kappa, Omicron Delta Kappa, Delta Chi. Office: US Dist Ct 619 US Courthouse 1729 5th Ave N Birmingham AL 35203-2000

GUINIER, LANI, law educator; BA cum laude, Harvard U., 1971; JD, Yale U., 1974; MA (hon.), U. Pa., 1992; LLD (hon.), Northeastern U., 1994, Swarthmore Coll., 1996, Smith Coll., 1999, U. D.C., 2001; D in Civil Law (hon.), Hunter Coll., 1994, Spelman Coll., 1998; LHD (hon.), U. R.I., 1999. Bar: Mich. 1975, U.S. Supreme Ct. 1979, D.C. 1980, U.S. Ct. Appeals (5th, 6th, 8th and 11th cirs.). Law clk. hon. Damon J. Keith U.S. Ct. Appeals (6th cir.), 1974—76; juvenile ct. referee Wayne County Juvenile Ct., 1976—77; spl. asst. civil rights divsn. U.S. Dept. Justice, 1977—81; asst. counsel NAACP Legal Def. and Ednl. Fund, Inc., 1981—88; assoc. prof. U. Pa. Law Sch., 1988—92, prof. law, 1992—98, Harvard Law Sch., 1998—2001, Bennett Boskey prof., 2001—. Adj. prof. NYU Sch. Law, 1985—89; of counsel NAACP Legal Def. Fund, Inc., 1988—91; trustee Phila. Cmty. Legal Svcs., 1989—90, Open Soc. Inst., 1996—; mem. adv. bd. com. on acad. freedom and tenure Assn. Am. Law Schs., 1992—93; mem. small grants adv. com. So. Regional Coun., 1992—95; founder, pres. Commonplace, Inc., 1994—99; vis. prof. Harvard Law Sch., 1996; mem. Penn Nat. Commn. on Soc., Cmty. and Culture, 1996—98; mem. vis. com. for diversity Brown U., 2000; presenter in field. Author: The Tyranny of the Majority: Fundamental Fairness in Representative Democracy, 1994, Lift Every Voice: Turning a Civil Rights Setback into a New Vision of Social Justice, 1998; co-author (with Michelle Fine and Jane Balin): Becoming Gentlemen: Women, Law Schools and Institutional Change, 1997; co-author: (with Susan Sturm) Who's Qualified: A New Democracy Forum on Creating Equal Opportunity in School and Jobs, 2001; co-author: (with Gerald Torres) The Miner's Canary: Enlisting Race, Resisting Power, Transforming Democracy, 2002; contbr. articles to profl. jours. Mem.: Am. Law Inst. Office: Harvard Law Sch 1525 Massachusetts Ave Cambridge MA 02138-2903

GUINN, JANET MARTIN, psychologist, consultant; b. Rapid City, S.D., Aug. 16, 1942; d. Verne Oliver and Carolyn Yetta (Clark) Martin; m. David Lee Guinn, Oct. 27, 1962 (div. June 1988); children: Cynthia Gail, Kevin Scott, Garrett Lee. BS in Psychology, U. Alaska, 1980, MS in Counseling Psychology, 1983; PhD in Clin. Psychology, Calif. Sch. Profl. Psychology, 1988. Lic. psychologist, Alaska, Nev. Pvt. practice, Anchorage, 1988-93, Carson City and Reno, Nev., 1993—; clinician Behavior Medicine Cons., 1983-84; pvt. practice clinician, 1983-84; supr. Southcentral Counseling Ctr., Anchorage, 1984-85; cons. City/Borough of Juneau, Alaska, 1988; psychologist youth treatment program Alaska Psychiat. Inst., Anchorage, 1989-90; psychologist Nev. Mental Health Inst., Sparks, 1994-97. Cons. in field; cons. Alaska Small Bus. Coalition, Anchorage, 1990-92; reviewer Blors Corp. Contbr. articles to profl. jours. Active in politics. Mem. APA, Am. Coll. Forensic Examiners, Nev. Psychol. Assn., Internat. Neuropsychol. Soc., Rotary, Psi Chi. Republican. Avocations: skiing, gourmet cooking, dancing.

GUINN, KATHLEEN ANNE, human resources specialist; b. Phila., June 18, 1947; d. Robert Walter Jr. and Gladys (Murray) McGowan; m. Stephen Lee Guinn, July 18, 1969; 1 child, Shanan Lee. BS in Psychology, Va. Commonwealth U., 1969; MA in Indsl. Rels., St. Francis Coll., 1975. Supr. affirmative EEO, 1971-75; exec. dir. Cannery Industry Trust Fund, Oakland, Calif., 1976-81; regional cons. Devel. Dimensions Internat., Pitts., 1981-83, program devel. mgr., 1983-85, sr. cons., cons. svcs. group, 1985-88, mgr. maximizing performance product line, 1988-90; cons. Hay Group, Pitts., 1990-93; sr. cons., regional dir. human resources planning & devel. Human Resources Planning and Devel. cons. svcs., Pitts., 1993-94; sr. cons. William M. Mercer, Inc., Pitts., 1994-95, prin., 1995-98; nat. practice leader performance & devel. consulting, 1997-98; pres. Human Capital Ptnrs., Inc., 1998—, also bd. dirs. Adj. faculty St. Francis U., Pitts., 1999—; presenter in field. Contbr. articles to profl. publs. Mem. ASTD (Excellence award 1991), Human Resource Planning Soc. (v.p. programs 1993-94), Pitts. Human Resources Assn. (bd. dirs. 2002), Exec. Women's Coun. Greater Pitts. (pres. 1988), Soc. for Human Resource Mgmt. Avocations: travel, reading. Office: Human Capital Ptnrs Inc 83 Fair Oaks Dr Pittsburgh PA 15238-1936

GUINN, KENNY C. governor; b. Garland, Ark., Aug. 24, 1936; married BA, MA, Calif. State U., Fresno; EdD, Utah State U. Supt. Clark County Sch. Dist.; v.p. adminstrn. Nev. Savs. and Loan Assn. (PriMerit Bank), 1978-80, pres., chief operating officer, 1980-85, chief exec. officer, 1985-92, now chmn. bd.; pres. Southwest Gas Corp., 1987-88, chmn., chief exec. officer, 1988-93; chmn. bd. S.W. Gas Corp.; gov. State of Nev., Carson City, 1999—; interim pres. U. Nev., Las Vegas, 1994. Republican. Office: Governors Office 101 N Carson St Carson City NV 89701*

GUINN, STANLEY WILLIS, lawyer; b. Detroit, June 9, 1953; s. Willis Hampton and Virginia Mae (Pierson) G.; m. Patricia Shirley Newgord, June 13, 1981; children: Terri Lanae, Scott Stanley. BBA with high distinction, U. Mich., 1979, MBA with distinction, 1981; MS in Taxation with distinction, Walsh Coll., 1987; JD cum laude, U. Mich., 1992. CPA Mich., cert. mgmt. acct., Mich.; bar: Calif., U.S. Dist. Ct. (so. dist.) Calif., U.S. Tax Ct. Tax mgr. Coopers & Lybrand, Detroit, 1981-87; tax cons. Upjohn Co., Kalamazoo, 1987-89; litigation atty. Brobeck, Phleger & Harrison, 1992-94, Coughlan, Semmer & Lipman, San Diego, 1994-95; consumer fin. atty. Bank Am. NT & SA, San Francisco, 1995-98, GreenPoint Credit, LLC, San Diego, 1998—. Served with USN, 1974-77. Mem.: ABA, AICPA, Conf. on Consumer Fin. Law, Inst. Cert. Mgmt. Accts., Atty.-CPA, Inc., San Diego County Bar, Calif. State Bar Assn., Delta Mu Delta, Beta Alpha Psi, Beta Gamma Sigma, Phi Kappa Phi. Republican. Mem. Christian Ch. Avocations: tennis, racquetball, hiking. Home: 3125 Crystal Ct Escondido CA 92025-7763 Office: GreenPoint Credit 10089 Willow Creek Rd San Diego CA 92131-1603 E-mail: stan.guinn@greenpoint.com.

GUINNESS, KENELM L. civil engineer; b. London, Dec. 13, 1928; came to U.S., 1948; s. K. Lee and Josephine (Strangman) G.; m. Jane Nevin, June 3, 1961; children: Kenelm, Sean. BSc, MIT, 1953. Sr. engr. World Bank (Internat. Bank for Reconstrn. and Devel.), Washington, 1954-75; ind. engring. cons., 1975—90. Lt. Royal Horse Guards, Brit. Army, 1946-48. Mem. ASCE, ICID. Home: 10799 Rich Neck Rd Claiborne MD 21624

GUINOUARD, DONALD EDGAR, psychologist; b. Bozeman, Mont., Mar. 31, 1929; s. Edgar Arthur and Venabell (Ford) G.; m. Irene M. Egeler, Mar. 30, 1951; children: Grant M., Philip A., Donna I. BS, Mont. State U., Bozeman, 1954; MS, Mont. State U., 1955; EdD, Wash. State U., Pullman, 1960; postdoctoral, Stanford U., 1965; grad., Indsl. Coll. of the Armed Forces, 1964, Air War Coll., 1976. Lic. psychologist, Ariz., counselor, Wash., Mont.; cert. secondary tchr. and sch. adminstr., Wash., Mont.; diplomate Am. Psychotherapy Assn., Am. Bd. Forensic Counselors, Am. Bd. Psychol. Specialities. Advanced through grades to col. USAFR, 1946-84, ret., 1984; dir. counseling Consol. Sch. Dist., Pullman, Wash., 1955-60; assoc. prof. Mont. State U., Bozeman, 1960-66; field selection officer Peace Corps, U.S., S.Am., 1962-68; prof. counseling, counseling psychologist Ariz. State U., Tempe, 1966-90; prof. emeritus, 1990; co-owner Forensic Cons. Assocs., Tempe, 1970—; pvt. practice, 1990—. Admissions liaison officer USAF Acad., Colo. Springs, 1967-84; assessment officer Fundamental Edn. Ctr. for the Devel. of the Latin American Community, Patzcuaro, Mex., 1963-64; expert witness on vocat. and psychol. disability for fed. and state cts. Contbr. articles to profl. jours. Mem. Ariz. Psychol. Assn., Am. Assn. Counseling & Devel., Reserve Officers Assn., Am. Psychotherapy Assn., Am. Coll. Forensic Examiners. Democrat. Methodist. Avocations: photography, woodworking, camping, fishing, silversmithing. Home and Office: 112 E Cairo Dr Tempe AZ 85282-3606 E-mail: donaldg516@aol.com.

GUINSBURG, PHILIP FRIED, alcohol and substance abuse counselor; b. N.Y.C., Sept. 13, 1946; s. Theodore and Elena (Fried) G.; m. Debrah Josias Guinsburg, June 15, 1968; children: Mark, Michael. BA, Columbia Coll., 1968; MA, U. N.D., 1970, PhD, 1973. Diplomate Am. Bd. Med. Psychotherapy; lic. alcohol and drug abuse counselor. Clin. dir. Nashville Drug Treatment Ctr., Dede Wallace Ctr., 1973-78; pvt. practice Nashville, 1974—. Asst. clin. prof. psychiatry Vanderbilt U., Nashville, 1987-93; cons. Crisis Intervention Ctr., 1974-99; pres. Dreammakers, Inc., Nashville, 1989-91; cons. Campus For Human Devel. Co-author: Making Love Safe, 2003. Baseball coach Brentwood (Tenn.) Civitan Little League, 1982-92. Mem. Am. Counseling Assn., Am. Group Psychotherapy Assn., Am. Acad. Psychotherapists (pres.-elect), Assn. for Spiritual, Ethical and Religious Values in Counseling, Nat. Assn. Alcoholism and Drug Abuse Counselors, Tenn. Assn. Alcohol and Drug Abuse Counselors (pres., Tenn. Profl. of Yr. 2002, Lifetime Achievement award 2003). Jewish. Avocations: gardening, sports, gourmet foods. Home: 8121 Maryland Ln Brentwood TN 37027-7341 Office: 2313 21st Ave S Nashville TN 37212-4908 E-mail: PFG1946@aol.com.

GUION, ROBERT MORGAN, psychologist, educator; b. Indpls., Sept. 14, 1924; s. Leroy Herbert and Carolyn (Morgan) Guion; m. Mary Emily Firestone, June 8, 1947; children: David Michael, Diana Lynn, Keith Douglas, Pamela Sue, Judith Elaine. BA, State U. Iowa, 1948; MS, Purdue U., 1950, PhD, 1952. Vocat. counselor Purdue U., 1948-51, research fellow, 1951-52; mem. faculty Bowling Green (Ohio) State U., 1952—, prof. psychology, 1964—, univ. prof., 1983-85, univ. prof. emeritus, 1985—, chmn. dept., 1966-71. Vis. prof. U. Calif., Berkeley, 1963—64, U. N.Mex., 1965; tech. adviser Dept. Pers. Svcs., State of Hawaii, 1970; vis. rsch. psychologist Ednl. Testing Svc., 1971—72; cons. in field. Author: (book) Personnel Testing, 1965, Assessment, Measurement and Prediction for Personnel Decisions, 1998; editor: Jour. Applied Psychology, 1983—88. With AUS, 1943—46. Recipient Stephen E. Bemis award, Internat. Pers. Mgmt. Assn., 2000. Mem.: APA (pres. divsn. 14 1972—73, pres. divsn. 5 1982—83, James McKeen Cattell award divsn. 14 1965, 1981, Disting. Sci. Contbn. award divsn. 14 1987, Disting. Svc. award

divsn. 14 1993, Lifetime Contbn. award divsn. 5 1997), Am. Psychol. Soc. (James McKeen Cattell award 2000). Methodist. Home: 632 Haskins Rd Bowling Green OH 43402-1615 E-mail: rmguion@wcnet.org.

GUIRGUIS, RAOUF ALBERT, health science executive; b. Cairo, Aug. 25, 1953; came to U.S., 1983; s. Albert Amin Guirguis and Georgette Dahabi; m. Dana Lynn Lebo, Aug. 26, 1982 (div. June 1988); 1 child, Sandra Gene; m. Loretta Elisabeth Moschetti, July 14, 1989; 2 children. MD, U. Alexandria, Arab Republic of Egypt, 1980, MS, 1983, Georgetown U., 1987, PhD, 1988. Intern Alexandria U. Sch. Medicine, 1979-80, navy fellow, 1980-83; rsch. assoc. Lombardi Cancer Ctr., Washington, 1983-84; pathology fellow Nat. Cancer Inst., NIH, Bethesda, Md., 1984—89; chmn. bd. Antibody Resources Inc., Gaithersburg, Md., 1989-93; pres., CEO Cancer Diagnostics Inc., Rockville, Md., 1989-94; chmn. bd. Fingerprint Diagnostics Inc., Rockville, Md., 1989—94; chmn., pres. La Mina, Inc., Wilmington, Del., 1992—2002; chmn. Comprehensive Cancer Care Ctrs. LLP, 1994—, Cancer Diagnostics Holding Co., Fairfax, Va., 1995—; co-founder, chmn., CEO Point of Care Techs. Inc., Fairfax, Va., 1996-97; pres., CEO Point of Care Techs., Inc., Fairfax, Va., 1999—2002, MonoGen, Inc., Fairfax, Va., 1996—99. Cons. Nephrology Cancer Ctr., Mansura, Arab Rep. of Egypt, 1988-94; adj. prof. dept. physiology and biophysics Georgetown U. Med. Sch., Washington, 1988-93. Contbr. articles to profl. jours. Assoc. Smithsonian, Washington, 1990; mem. Kennedy Ctr., Washington, 1990, Georgetown Club, Washington, 1989; mem. Balt. Coun. on Fgn. Affairs; bd. dirs. U.S. Israel Biotech. Coun. Georgetown U. scholar, 1985-88, Saudi Minister of Health scholar, 1986-88; Nat. Coun. of Churches Rsch. grantee, 1986, Hoffmann-LaRoche Innovation Rsch. grantee, 1986. Mem. AMA (chief exec. divsn.), AAAS, IEEE, Am. Math. Assn., Am. Assn. for Clin. Chemistry, Am. Soc. for Microbiology, Am. Chem. Soc., Am. Mgmt. Assn., NY Acad. Sci., Soc. for Computer Simulation, Sigma Xi (presdl. roundtable). Republican. Coptic Orthodox. Achievements include patents and trademarks for CDI Shuttle System, a cancer screening and laboratory testing device, a method for CytoShuttle a monolayer cytology device, a method for LC-Shuttle a chromatography device for multiple marker panels, for Assay-Shuttle a bead based immuno-assay, a Cell Chamber for chemotaxis assay, a Modular Multiple Fluid Sample Preparation Assembly, a Blood Withdrawing Apparatus and a Antigen Testing Method, a Enviromental Sample Collection and Testing Device, a Blood Testing and Fingerprint Identification Method; patents pending for Preparation and Isolation of Intact Pseudopodia Fragments, a Urine Testing Apparatus with Urinary Sediment Device, a Intact and Isolated Pseudopodia Fragments/A Model SYstem for Cell Migration, a Possible Role for Membrane Fusion in Tumor Cell Invasion and Metastasis, and a New Method and Device for the Early Detection of Cancer Using Body Fluids (mainly urine). Office: Point of Care Techs Inc Ste 800 1901 N Fort Myer Dr Arlington VA 22209

GUISE, DAVID EARL, architect, educator; b. N.Y.C., Dec. 29, 1931; s. Jack I. and Frances (Haberman) G.; m. Gretchen Grunenfelder, Nov. 21, 1962; children: Gabrielle Ann, John George, Jacqueline Alexis, Ursula Claire. BArch with honors, U. Pa., 1957. Job capt. Kahn & Jacobs, Architects, N.Y.C., 1957-60; designer draftsman E.J. Robin, Architect, N.Y.C., 1961; architect David Guise, Architect, N.Y.C., 1962—; asst. prof. Sch. Architecture, CCNY, 1966-70, assoc. prof., 1970-76, prof., 1976-91; prof. emeritus CCNY, 1991—. Adj. prof. Columbia U., 1983-85, CCNY, 1993—; vis. prof. U. Pa., 1990. Author: Design and Technology in Architecture, 1985, rev. edit., 1991; contbr. articles to profl. jours., Ency. Britannica yearbook; architect numerous comml. and residential bldgs. Mem. nat. panel Am. Arbitration Assn., 1967—; sec. Irvington Planning Bd., N.Y., 1974-88. Mem. Bldg. Rsch. Inst. Home: PO Box 132 Georgetown ME 04548-0132 Office: 250 W 57th St New York NY 10107

GUITRY, LORAINE DUNN, community health nurse; b. Bryan, Tex., Apr. 12, 1930; BS Elem. Edn., Paul Quinn Coll., 1954. Registered nurse U. Tex. Med. Br., Galveston, 1958—67, U.S. Pub. Health Svc., Galveston, 1967—. Home: 701 Chadley Ct Bryan TX 77803

GUITTAR, LEE JOHN, retired newspaper executive; b. St. Louis, May 4, 1931; s. LeRoy and Edna Mae (Johnston) G.; m. Elizabeth Madden Shedrick, Aug. 23, 1980; children: David Lee, Stephen Joseph, Mitchell John, Jeanne Marie Kessler, Richard Laughran; step-children: Elisabeth F. Brew, Kathryn S. Shedrick, Daniel C. Shedrick. AB, Columbia U., 1953; postgrad., U. Mass., 1962; MA, Columbia U., 1993. With Gen. Electric Co., 1955-65, mgr. community and govt. relations programs, 1963-65; mgr. employee and pub. relations Tidewater Oil Co., N.Y.C., 1965-66; from personnel dir. to circulation dir. Miami (Fla.) Herald, 1967-71; v.p., bus. mgr. Detroit Free Press, 1972-74, v.p., gen. mgr., 1974-75, pres., dir., 1975-77; pub. Dallas Times Herald, 1977-80; Publisher The Denver Post, 1980-83; chmn. Denver Post, 1983; pres. U.S.A. Today, 1984-86; v.p. group exec. newspapers The Hearst Corp., N.Y.C., 1986-98; editor, pub. San Francisco Examiner, 1995-98, ret., 1998. Lt. (j.g.) USNR, 1953-55, Korea. Mem. Farm Neck Golf Club (Martha's Vineyard, Mass.), Edgartown Yacht Club, Phi Beta Kappa. Republican. Roman Catholic.

GUIVENS, NORMAN ROY, JR., mathematician, engineer; b. Brockton, Mass., May 8, 1957; s. Norman Roy and Lula Elizabeth (Wager) G. SB in Math., SM in Meteorology, MIT, 1979; MTS in Pastoral Ministry, St. Meinrad Sch. Theology, 1992. Teaching asst. MIT Dept. Ocean Engring., Cambridge, Mass., 1979; cons. to Lincoln Lab. Mass. Tech. Lab., West Newton, 1984; sr. engr. SPARTA, Inc., Lexington, Mass., 1984—. Contbr. over 15 articles to profl. jours. Lt. USN, 1979-84. Mem. IEEE (chpt. chmn. 1990-93), U.S. Naval Inst. Roman Catholic. Achievements include devel. of first successful simulation of coherent laser radars, comprehensive model for optical detection system, defense laser/target signatures (DELTAS) code, application of genetic algorithms to design of unconventional imaging systems, modular software architecture for control of robots and peripheral equipment, devel. of scene description language compiler for 3-D solid models, devel. of adaptive topographic model with automatic resolution matching capability. Office: SPARTA Inc 900 Middlesex Tpke Bldg 8 Billerica MA 01821-3929 E-mail: norm_guivens@sparta.com.

GUJRAL, JASPAL SINGH, physician, internist; b. Meerut, India, June 9, 1953; s. Jaswant Singh and Prem Kaur (Bindra) G.; m. Ravinder Kaur Duggal, Jan. 30, 1983; children: Amandeep Singh, Harpreet Singh. BSc, U. Delhi, India, 1972; M.B.BS, Maulana Azad Med. Coll., New Delhi, 1976. Sr. house officer Manor Hosp., Walsall, Birmingham, Eng., 1988-89, Sheppey Gen. Hosp., Gillingham, Kent, Eng., 1989-90; registrar U. Wales & Assoc. Hosp., Cardiff, 1990-92; clin. rsch. fellow Leicester U., 1992-94; resident SUNY, Buffalo, 1994-97; attending physician Univ. Hosp., Augusta, Ga., 1997-99; asst. prof. medicine Med. Coll. Ga., Augusta, 1999—. Med. officer/physician Ctrl. Hosp., Almarj, Libya, 1984-88. Capt. Indian Army Med. Corps, 1977-82. Fellow ACP-ASIM; mem. Royal Coll. Physicians U.K. Home: 3657 Camelback Ln Martinez GA 30907-9423 Office: Med Coll of Ga Dept Internal Medicine Augusta GA 30912 E-mail: jgujral@mail.mcg.edu.

GULAN, BONNIE MARION, writer, researcher; b. Kenosha, Wis., Feb. 27, 1922; d. Matthew and Elizabeth Ummy Thomas; m. Edward J. Gulan, Nov. 26, 1949; children: John, Michael, Kathryn. Beauty cons. Globe Dept., Kenosha, Wis., 1950—54; inventor & pitch artist Beauty Blush Cosmetic Line, Waukegan, Ill., 1954—56; creator & founder Felture's Inc., Brookfield, Ill., 1956—59; gen. mgr. & designer Eichling's Flowers Inc., Skokie, Ill., 1960—64; founder, dir. An-Oix-Is In-home Youth Ministry, Winnetka, Ill., 1965—75; founder & ceo The Christmas Tree Story Ho. Mus., Multiple Locations, Ill., 1970—90; author & rschr. Milwaukee, Wis., 1990—98; author Saukville, Wis., 1998—. Founder, pres. World-Wide Women's Inventor's Orgn., Libertyville, Ill., 1961—65; creator, lectr. Miracle Thinking Lecture Series, Mundelein, Ill., 1965—69; spkr. in field. Author: (book) Family Miracles, 1981, Stories From The Christmas Tree Story House, 1981, The Great Bible Dig, 2001, The House of the Seven Cats - An Adventure, 2001, Lost Adventures-House of the 7 Cats, 2001, 7 Cats Promised Land Adventure, 2001, Over the Fence Non-Sense Tales, 2001, Lamp Of Hope, 2001, Back Yard Critter Tales, 2001, A Collection Of Mrs. Claus' Christmas Stories, 2001, The Master Toy Maker, 2001, Adventures Down Nursery Rhyme Lane, 2001, A Collection Of Nodding Off Stories, 2001, Christmas In Our Town, 2002, The Great Journey in Pursuit of Jesus' Way, Truth & Life, 2002; composer: (albums) Sounds of The Christmas Tree Story House, 1975. Founder, pres. & lectr. T.H.E Anti-Drug Youth Program, Winnetka, 1971—75. Home: 1053 South Main Street Saukville WI 53080 Personal E-mail: bmgulan@aol.com.

GULATI, GENE L. hematologist, educator, consultant; m. Usha Usha Sood, Jan. 18, 1979; children: Nishi, Vineet. PhD, St. John's U., New York, 1973. Specialist in Hematology Am. Soc. for Clin. Pathology, Bd. of Registry, 1976, Clinical Laboratory Director, Hematology Dept. of Health, NY City/State, 1978, Diplomate in Laboratory Management Am. Soc. for Clin. Pathology, Bd. of Registry, 1991, Diplomate in Clinical and Applied Thrombosis, Hemostasis and Vascular Medicine Internat. Bd. of Clin. and Applied Thrombosis, Hemostasis and, 1995. Tech. specialist/rsch. assoc. Brookhaven Nat. Lab., Upton, NY, 1967—73; sect. chief hematology lab. Muhlenberg Regional Med. Ctr., Plainfield, NJ, 1973—89; clin. prof. pathology Jefferson Med. Coll., Phila., 1989—. Assoc. dir. hematology lab. Thomas Jefferson U. Hosp., Phila., 1989—; presenter numerous workshops. Contbr. articles to profl. jours. Fellow: Internat. Acad. Clin. and Applied Thrombosis and Hemostasis; mem.: Clin. Lab. Mgmt. Assn., Am. Soc. for Clin. Pathology, Am. Soc. of Hematology. Office: Thomas Jefferson Univ Hosp 307 Pav Bldg 125 S 11th St Philadelphia PA 19107

GULATI, RANJAY, finance educator; arrived in U.S., 1983; s. Satya Paul and Sushma Gulati; m. Anuradha Dayal-Gulati; 1 child, Varoun. BA in Econs. with honors, St. Stephen's Coll., Delhi, 1983; BS in Computer Sci. summa cum laude, Wash. State U., 1985; MS, MIT, 1987; PhD, Harvard U., 1993. Asst. prof. mgmt. and orgns. Northwestern U., Kellogg Sch. Mgmt., Evanston, 1993—96, assoc. prof. mgmt. and orgns., 1996—2001, prof. mgmt. and orgns., 2001—, Michael L. NemmersDisting. prof. strategy and orgns., 2001—, rsch. dir. Ctr. for Rsch. on Tech., Innovation and E-Commerce, 2000—02. Presenter in field. Co-author: Tech Venture: New Rules on Value and Profit from Silicon Valley, 2001, Kellogg on Technology and Innovation, 2002; co-editor: Kellogg TechVenture, 2000, mem. editl. bd.: Acad. Mgmt. Rev., 1996—99, Adminstrv. Sci. Quarterly, 1996—, Orgn. Sci., 1996—, mem. editl. bd.: Strategic Mgmt. Jour., 2000, Strategic Orgns., 2002—; contbr. articles to profl. jours. Fellow, Consortium on Competitiveness and Cooperation, Sloan Found., 1991—92; Harvard MacArthur fellow, MacArthur Found., 1992—93. Mem.: Macro-Orgnl. Behavior Soc., Acad. Mgmt. (program chair bus. policy and strategy divsn. 1999—, mem. exec. com. bus. policy and strategy divsn. 1997—), Beta Gamma Sigma, Phi Kappa Phi. Avocations: writing, skiing. Home: 2238 Iroquois Rd Wilmette IL 60091 Office: Northwestern Univ 2001 Sheridan Rd Evanston IL 60208

GULATI, SUNIL, sports administrator; b. Allahabad, India, 1959; m. Marcela Gulati; 1 child, Emilio. BA magna cum laude, Bucknell U.; MA, MPhil in Econs., Columbia U. Asst. prof. econs. Columbia U., 1986-90; with World Bank, 1991; mng. dir. Kraft Soccer Properties, 1993—. Mng. dir. nat. teams, chmn. internat. games com., nat. teams com., U.S. Cup 1992 and 1993 U.S. Soccer Fedn., 1987-94; exec. v.p., chief internat. officer, mem. mgmt. com. World Cup USA, 1994; bd. dirs. 1999 Women's World Cup, U.S. Soccer, U.S. Soccer Found. Mem. Phi Beta Kappa. Office: 725 5th Ave Ste 1700 New York NY 10022-2519

GULATI, TERESA ANTOINETTE, nursing educator; b. Marikuppam, Mysore, India, Aug. 9, 1932; came to U.S., 1959; d. Vincent and Mabel (Talent) Davids; m. Suresh T. Gulati, Aug. 19, 1961; children: Raj, Prem, Sonya. RN, cert. midwife, J.J. Sch. Nursing, Bombay, India, 1952; BSN, Alfred U., 1980; MS in Edn., Elmira Coll., 1984. Staff nurse J.J. Group of Hosps., Bombay, 1952-59; staff nurse operating rm. St. Luke's Hosp., N.Y.C., 1959-60, Michael Reese Hosp., Chgo., 1960-62, Community Hosp., Boulder, Colo., 1962-64, Boulder (Colo.) Meml. Hosp., 1964-67, Corning (N.Y.) Hosp., 1967, Arnot Ogden Meml. Hosp., Elmira, N.Y., 1967-79, nursing instr. peri operative nursing, 1979—. Faculty workload com. Arnot Ogden Sch. Nursing, Elmira, 1983—, quality assurance com., 1985—, procedures com., 1988-91. RN Family Health Ctr., Elmira, 1972—. Mem. Assn. Oper. Rm. Nurses, Am. Field Svc. (historian 1985-90), Internat. Club Finger Lakes, Elmira Rotary Club (coord. group study exchange 1990-92), Delta Kappa Gamma. Democrat. Roman Catholic. Home: 49 Saddleridge Dr Elmira NY 14903-7976

GULBRANDSEN, NATALIE WEBBER, religious association administrator; b. Beverly, Mass., July 7, 1919; d. Arthur Hammond and Kathryn Mary (Doherty) Webber; m. Melvin H. Gulbrandsen, June 19, 1943 (dec. Feb. 23, 1991); children: Karen Ann Bean, Linda Jean Goldsmith, Eric Christian, Ellen Dale Williams, Kristin Jane Morgan. BA, Bates Coll., 1942, LLD (hon.), 1996; LHD (hon.), Meadville/Lombard Theol. Sch., Chgo., 1991. Social worker Bur. Child Welfare, Bangor, Maine. Leader Girl Scouts USA, Auburn, Mass., 1941—42, 1942—43, exec. dir., 1943—45, leader, 1952—65, leadership trainer, 1946—63, bd. dirs. Welleseley, Mass., 1950—63, pres., 1960—63; mem. Wellesley town meeting, 1967—71; trustee Unitarian Universalist Women's Fedn., 1971—81, pres., 1977—81, mem. commn. on appraisal, 1981—85; moderator Unitarian Universalist Assn., U.S. and Can., Boston, 1985—93; bd. dirs. Unitarian Universalist Ch. of the Larger Fellowship, 1992—98, chairperson bd. dirs., 1996—98, ch. search com., 1998—99, chair ministerial rels. com., 1999—2001; bd. dirs. Unitarian Universalist Women's Heritage Soc., 1994—2002, ch. bd., 2001—02; chair denominational affairs Unitarian Universalist Soc. Wellesley Hills, 2002—; bd. dirs. Am. Field Svc., 1964—70; mem. permanent sch. accomodations com. Welleseley, 1970—76; mem. Wellesley Youth Commn., 1968—70; trustee Wellesley Human Rels. Svc., 1964—76, pres., 1973—76; bd. dirs. Newton Wellesley Weston Needham Area Mental Health Assn., 1975—78; co-chairperson METCO Program of Wellesley, 1965—69. Recipient Wellesley Ctr. Cmty. award, 1981, Unitarian Universalist Disting. Svc. award, 2002. Mem. AAUW, Boston Bates Alumnae Assn. (pres. 1966-69), Internat. Assn. Religious Freedom (mem. coun. 1981-90, v.p. 1990-93, pres. 1993-96, co-pres. U.S. chpt. 1997—, Clara Barton birthplace com. 1997-01). Unitarian Universalist. Home: 2251 Commonwealth Ave Auburndale MA 02466-1817 Office: Internat Assn for Religious Freedom 2 Market St Oxford 0X1 3EF England

GULBRANDSEN, PATRICIA HUGHES, physician; b. May 9, 1940; d. Patrick Boland and Anne Hughes; m. Jon Alf Gulbrandsen, Mar. 6, 1972 (dec. Oct. 1984). BA, Cornell U., 1962; MD, U. Pa., 1967; MPH, Johns Hopkins U., 1980. Cert. Am. Bd. Disability Analysts; diplomate Am. Bd. Phys. Medicine and Rehab., Am. Bd. Occupl. Medicine. Rotating intern Chgo. Wesley Meml. Hosp., 1967-68; resident in neurology Pa. Hosp., Phila., 1968-69, Georgetown U. Hosp., Washington, 1972-74; fellow in gynecologic endocrinology Chelsea Hosp. for Women, London, 1969-71; resident in phys. medicine and rehab. Good Samaritan Hosp., Phoenix, 1974-76; commd. maj. U.S. Army, 1979, advanced through grades to lt. col., 1982; with Walter Reed Army Med. Ctr., Washington, 1979-81; occup. medicine officer U.S. Army/Army Environ. Hygiene Agy., Aberdeen Proving Ground, Md., 1981-83; resigned U.S. Army, 1983; med. dir. USN/Naval Surface Warfare Ctr., White Oak, Md., 1984-89, NASA Hdqs., Washington, 1990-93; acting chief med. officer Hdqs. FBI, Washington, 1995; med. officer Orgn. Am. States, Washington, 1999—2001; occupl. health phys., cons. Def. Intelligence Agy., Bolling AFB, Washington, 2001—. Occuptl. medicine Profl. Occuptl. Health Svcs., 1997-98; staff physiatrist, head consultation svc. New Eng. Med. Ctr. Hosps., Boston, 1977-78; instr. neurology and phys. medicine and rehab. Tufts U. Sch. Medicine, Boston, 1977-78; med. cons. Fairfax County (Va.) Health Dept., 1990, Hummer and Assocs., Cleve., 1990-93, Allied Med. Cons., Inc., Washington, 1994-95, AspenMed Svcs., Inc., 1995-96, 2001--, Occu Save, Inc., Lanham, Md., 1996, staff privileges Drs. Cmty. Hosp., Lanham, Md., 1996-98, Hummer Whole Health Mgmt., 1998-99. Mem. Am. Coll. Preventive Medicine, Am. Coll. Occupl and Environ. Medicine, Montgomery County Med. Soc., Med. and Chirurg. Faculty Md. Republican. Avocations: phys. fitness, noetic scis., computer applications. Fax: 301-585-6519. E-mail: laska20910@yahoo.com.

GULCHER, ROBERT HARRY, aircraft company executive; b. Columbus, Ohio, Aug. 26, 1925; s. Alban H. and Beatrice (Plohr) G.; m. Barbara Witherspoon, June, 1949 (div.); 1 child, Robert; m. Anne Cummings, Dec. 14, 1959 (dec.); children: Jeffrey, Donald; m. Suzanne K. Kane, Apr. 12,1969; children: Andrew, Kristin. BS, U.S. Marine Acad., 1945; B.E.E., Ohio State U., 1950. Third asst. engr. Am. Petroleum Transp. Co., N.Y.C., 1945-46; engr. Capital Elevator & Mfg. Co., Columbus, Ohio, 1949-51, Columbus div. N. Am. Aviation, 1951-53, various mgmt. engring. positions, 1953-66; chief engr. Columbus div. Rockwell Internat., 1966-79, v.p. rsch. and engring. N.Am. aircraft ops., 1979-85, v.p. advanced programs N.Am. aircraft ops., 1985-87, v.p., program mgr. nat. aerospace plane, 1987-90, v.p. hypersonic programs, 1990-91; retired, 1991; aerospace cons., 1992—. Trustee Little Co. of Mary Hosp. Found., 1992—, chmn. bd. trustees, 1996-97; trustee coun. LCMH Hosp., 1997—. Fellow AIAA, IEEE (sr. mem.); mem. Rotary Internat. Republican. Lutheran. E-mail: rgulcher@aol.com.

GULDA, EDWARD JAMES, business acquisitions executive; b. Detroit, Oct. 28, 1945; s. Alfred and Lucy Irene (Ball) G.; m. Nancy Mary Greenlee, Nov. 28, 1964; children: Kimberly Sue Marsh, Nicholas Edward. BS in Aerospace Engring., U. Mich., 1968, MBA, 1979. Systems engr. LTV Aerospace Corp., Sterling Heights, Mich., 1966-72; mgr. systems engring. Ford Motor Co., Dearborn, Mich., 1972-78; mgr., prodn. plan. Rockwell Internat. Corp., Dearborn, Mich., 1978-79, dir. prod. plan. Troy, Mich., 1979-80, dir. mkt. electronics, 1980-81, gen. mgr. auto electronics, 1981-84, v.p. rsch. and engring., 1984-85; pres. ITT Teves Am., Troy, 1985-87; group v.p. engring. ITT Auto, Inc., Troy, 1987-88; pres., chief exec. officer Dayton Walther (Varity) Corp., Dayton, Ohio, 1988-89; pres. Varity Brake Group Kelsey-Hayes Brake Group N.Am., Romulus, Mich., 1989-94; pres. Kelsey-Hayes Co., Romulus, Mich., 1994-95, chief exec. Livonia, Mich., 1995; chmn. and CEO Peregrine Inc., Southfield, Mich., 1996-98; pres. Kinnick Group LLC, 1998—. Mem. MENSA, Birmingham Country Club, Golf Club Fiddler's Creek, Tarpon Bay Club. Avocations: hunting, golf. Office: 2706 Horseshoe Dr S Naples FL 34104 E-mail: ed@ejgulda.com.

GULDEN, SIMON, lawyer, investment/real estate development executive, business and legal consultant; b. Montreal, Que., Can., Jan. 7, 1938; s. David and Zelda (Long) G.; m. Ellen Lee Barbour, June 12, 1977. BA, McGill U., Montreal, 1959; cert., U. Rennes, 1961; LL.L., U. Montreal, 1962; cert., Wharton Sch., 1979; ADR cert., York U., Toronto, 1999. P. Adminstrn. Inst. Chartered Secs. and Adminstrs., 1982; Bar: Que. Ptnr. Genser, Philips, Friedman & Gulden, Montreal, 1963-68; sec., legal counsel Pl. Bonaventure, Inc., 1969-72; legal counsel real estate Steinberg Inc., Montreal, 1972-74; solicitor, prime atty. Bell Can., Montreal, 1975-76; v.p., gen. counsel, sec., dir. Nabisco Ltd, Toronto, 1975-98; pres., dir. Interlude Capital Corp., Unionville, Ont., Can., 1997—; dir. legal affairs Stream Intelligent Networks Corp., 2000-2001; v.p. corp. and legal affairs Canderel Stoneridge Equity Group, 2001—02. Mem.: ABA, Bar of Que., Inst. Chartered Secs. and Adminstrs. (cert.), Osgoode Law Soc., Lord Reading Law Soc. Que., Can. Bar Assn. Home and Office: 23 Danbury Ct Unionville ON Canada L3R 7S1 E-mail: simongulden@rogers.com.

GULFO, ADELE MADELYN, pharmaceutical marketing executive; b. East Orange, N.J., Dec. 3, 1962; d. Felix Thomas and Adelaide (Balletti) Vitello; m. Joseph Vincent Gulfo, June 21, 1987. BS in Biology and Chemistry, Seton Hall U., 1984; MBA, Fairleigh Dickinson U., 1993. Analytical chemist Fisher Sci. Co., Fair Lawn, N.J., 1986-88, sr. rsch. chemist, 1988-90; mgr. sales and mktg. Spectra Tech. Co., Stamford, Conn., 1990-91; sr. med. writer Parke-Davis divsn. Warner Lambert, Morris Plains, Conn., 1991-94, internat. mktg. mgr., 1994-95, sr. dir. mktg., 1995-2000, Astra Zeneca v.p. cardiovascular therapy area, 2000—. Spkr. in field. Contbr. chpt. to book, articles to newspapers and profl. jours. Recipient Best Rx Product Launch award Fin. Times, 1999; named among Top 100 Marketers, Advt. Age, 1999. Mem. Healthcare Bus. Women's Assn. (Rising Star 1999), Healthcare MKtg. Coun., Am. Heart Assn. (pharm. round table). Roman Catholic. Avocations: fitness, golf, tennis. Home: 406 Gulph Ridge Dr King Of Prussia PA 19406-3211 Office: Warner Lambert 201 Tabor Rd Morris Plains NJ 07950-2693 E-mail: Adele.Gulfo@AstraZeneca.com.

GULGOWSKI, PAUL WILLIAM, German language, social science, and history educator; b. Oberhausen, Germany, July 4, 1940; s. Paul and Katharina (van Look) G.; m. Heide Anna Maria Hegenscheidt, July 6, 1989; children: Audrey-Annette, Paul William. BSc, U. Tex., El Paso, 1970; MA, Marquette U., 1992; PhD, U. Bremen, Germany, 1981. Cert. tchr., social sci., German and history. Commd. 2d lt. U.S. Army, 1970, advanced through grades to maj., 1981; gen. staff officer, comdr. combat and support forces U.S. Army, worldwide, 1970-80; polit. advisor, forces comdr. U.S. Army, Germany, 1980-82; prof. German U.S. Mil. Acad., West Point, N.Y., 1982-85; personal rep. of NATO Land Forces comdr., Heidelberg, Germany, 1985-87; ret. U.S. Army, 1987; lectr. German and fgn. lang. study methodology U. Wis., Whitewater, 1993—. Author: U.S. Military Government in Germany, 1983, Flucht aus Ostpreussen, 1986, Die unglaubliche Story des Peter V., 2001; author articles. Chief historian USCG Aux., Washington, 1992-94; comdr. northwestern USCG 9th, 1994—; v.p. Wis. Profl. Edn. & Info. Coun., 1997-99, pres., 2000—. Decorated D.S.M. with four oak leaf clusters; comdr.'s cross German Order of Merit. Mem. Phi Kappa Phi. Roman Catholic. Avocations: classical music, literature, skiing, boating, travel. Home: PO Box 180347 Delafield WI 53018-0347 E-mail: phgulgow@milwpc.com.

GULICK, DONNA MARIE, accountant; b. N.Y.C., Jan. 25, 1956; d. H.R. and M.G. Gulick. MBA, Fairleigh Dickinson U., 1981, MS, 1986. Programmer Wash. State U., Pullman, 1983; acctg. analyst IBM, Tarrytown, N.Y., 1983-89, program mgr., 1989-91, program mgr. long-term disability plan Purchase, N.Y., 1991-92, staff acctg. analyst labor charges Tarrytown, N.Y., 1992-94, project mgr. Somers, NY, 1994—97; staff acct. Somers, N.Y., 1997—2002. Mem. Assn. MBA Execs., ACM, Inst. of IEEE, Nat. Assn. Unknown Players, Delta Mu Delta. Roman Catholic. Avocations: flying, skiing. Home: 395 State Route 28 Bridgewater NJ 08807-2471 Office: IBM Rt 100 Somers NY 10589

GULICK, WALTER BROOKS, philosopher, educator; b. Boston, Aug. 10, 1938; s. Luther Hervey and Helen Sutton Gulick; m. Barbara Ann Jacobus, July 12, 1940; children: John Lawrence, Edward Brooks. BA, Pomona Coll., 1960; MA, Columbia U., 1966; PhD, Claremont U., 1974. Tchr. Tarsus (Turkey) Am. Coll., 1960—63; group ins. adminstr. Tchrs. Ins. and Annuity Assn., N.Y.C., 1965—68; vis. instr. Oreg. State U., Corvallis, 1971—74; instr. prof. Mont. State U., Billings, 1974—, interim acad. vice chancellor, 1994—96. Bd. mem. N.Am. Soc. for Social Philosophy, 1983—90; book rev. editor Tradition and Discovery, St. Joseph, 1990—; pres., gen. coord. Polanyi Soc., St. Joseph, Mo., 1999—. Mem. editl. bd.: Polanyiana, 1992—; contbr. articles to profl. jours. Bd. mem. Justice and Witness Ministries, United Ch. Christ, Cleve., 1999; mem., pres. Billings Symphony and Chorale, 1995—2001; mem. Mont. Com. for the Humanities, Missoula, 1979—83. Recipient Disting. Work in the Humanities award, Mont. Com. for the Humanities, 1993; grantee, NEH, 1977, 1983, 1987; Fulbright scholar, Fulbright Commn., Hungary, 1993, Fulbright Commn., Moldova, 2001. Mem.: Inst. on Religion in an Age of Sci., Polanyi Soc. (pres. 1999), Am. Acad. Religion. Office: Montana State Univ 1500 University Dr Billings MT 59101

GULICK, WALTER LAWRENCE, psychologist, former college president; b. Summit, N.J., July 4, 1927; s. Walter Lawrence and Carol (Dewey) G.; m. Winifred Bourn Frazee, Oct. 18, 1952; children— Hans, Tod, Kristina. AB, Hamilton Coll., Clinton, N.Y., 1952; MA (Theta Delta Chi fellow), U. Del., 1955; MA (hon.), Dartmouth, 1968; PhD (psychology scholar 1955-57), Princeton U., 1957; LHD (hon.), St. Lawrence U., 1989. Mem. faculty U. Del., 1957-65, prof. psychology, 1963-65, chmn. dept., 1964-65; prof. psychology Dartmouth, Hanover, N.H., 1965-74, chmn. dept., 1970-73, 74-75, Distinguished Class of 1925 prof., 1973-75; dean of coll. Hamilton Coll., 1975-79, prof. psychology, 1975-81, William R. Kenan prof., 1979-81; pres. St. Lawrence U., 1981-87, Gulick Assocs., 1987—. Vis. prof. U. Vt., summer 1977; resident scholar U. Del., 1988-02; cons. Presbyn. Hosp., Phila., 1961-63; editl. cons. Oxford U. Press, 1963—, McGraw-Hill Pub. Co., 1966-67, Harper & Row, 1971-73, Cambridge U. Press, 1979—; dir. Key Bank, N.A., 1981-87, NGM Ins. Co., 1981-86. Author: Hearing: Physiology and Psychophysics, 1971, Human Stereopsis: Psychophysical Analysis, 1976, Hearing: Physiological Acoustics, Neural Coding and Psychoacoustics, 1989; contbr. to Encyclopedia of Human Behavior, 1994; contbr. articles to profl. jours. Mem. Hanover Sch. Bd., 1972-75, Dresden Bd. Sch. Dirs., 1972-75; Mem. grad. council Princeton U., 1972-75; mem. adv. council Nat. Inst. for Humanities, 1975— ; mem. teaching evaluation project HEW. Served with AUS, 1946-48. Recipient nat. svc. award 1955, 81; Dale prize music Hamilton Coll., 1952, alumni achievement medal Hamilton Coll., 1995. Mem. N.Y. Acad. Scis., Ea. Psychol. Assn., Psychonomic Soc., Phi Beta Kappa, Omicron Delta Kappa, Sigma Xi (pres. Dartmouth chpt. 1967-68, Gold Medal Lifetime Achievement award

1995), Psi Chi (pres. U. Del. chpt. 1954-55). Achievements include rsch. vision and hearing. Home: 347 Greenbriar Ln West Grove PA 19390 Office: Gulick Assocs Inc PO Box 1036 Newark DE 19715-1036

GULINO, DENNY, communications executive; Bur. chief Market Internat. News, Washington, 1994—. Office: Market Internat News 552 National Press Building Washington DC 20045-1501

GULKIN, HARRY, arts administrator, film producer; b. Montreal, Que., Can., Nov. 14, 1927; s. Peter Oliver and Raya (Shinderman) G. Portrait photographer, 1942-44; mcht. seaman, trade union organizer, 1944-49; labour journalist, critic, trade union organizer, 1950-56; market researcher, cons., 1956-71; ind. film producer, 1971—; exec. and artistic dir. Saidye Bronfman Ctr., 1983-87; dir. projects Soc. Developpement Entreprises Culturelles, 1987—; producer BAYO, 1985. Challenger Nat. Film Bd., Can., 1979; adv. coun. film dept. Concordia U. Producer: Penny and Ann (2d prize Film Festival Internat. Congress Rehab. Centres 1976, award Amtec Media Festival 1977), 1974 (Red Ribbon Am. Film Festival 1977), Lies My Father Told Me (Hollywood Fgn. Critics award as best fgn. film 1975, Canadian Film award 1976, Grand prize V.I. Internat. Festival 1975, Christopher awards 1975, Assn. Can. TV and Radio Artists award 1976, Can. Motion Picture Distbrs. Assn. award 1976), Jacob Two Meets The Hooded Fang, 1976 (Gold medallion spl. jury award Miami Internat. Film Festival 1978, Spl. Jury award 8th Internat. Children's Film Festival, Los Angeles 1979), Two Solitudes, 1977; editor: The Marketer Jour., 1966. Mem. Motion Picture Inst. Can. (pres. 1977), Can. Film Inst. (past pres., chmn.), Assn. Que. Film Producers, Cinematheque Québecoise (v.p. 1995-2000), Am. Mktg. Assn. (past chpt. pres.), Acad. Can. Cinema, Quebec Soc. for Promotion of English Lang. Lit. (mem. adv. coun.). Home: 111 St Joseph Blvd W Montreal QC Canada H2T 2P7 Office: Bur 800 215 Rue St JAcques Montreal QC Canada H2Y 1M6

GULKO, EDWARD, health care executive, consultant; b. Paterson, N.J., Nov. 22, 1950; s. Benjamin and Anita (Yankelevsky) G.; m. Judith Ilene Lee, May 29, 1977. BS in Indsl. Engring., N.J. Inst. Tech., 1972; MBA, Temple U., 1974. Cert. healthcare exec., med. practice exec.; lic. nursing home adminstr. Health program analyst Morrisania Hosp., Bronx, N.Y., 1974-75; assoc. dir. Mission Health Ctr., San Francisco, 1976; supervising sys. analyst Health and Hosp. Corp., N.Y.C., 1977-78; dep. exec. dir. Greenpoint Hosp., Bklyn., 1978-82; assoc. exec. dir. Woodhull Med. Ctr., Bklyn., 1982-84; adminstr. Montclair (N.J.) Med. Group, 1984-87; asst. adminstr. Summit (N.J.) Med. Group, N.J., 1987-91; adminstr. Wooster (Ohio) Clinic, Inc., 1991-96; COO Grove Hill Med. Ctr., New Britain, Conn., 1996-99; exec. dir. Old Bridge (N.J.)-Sayreville Med. Group, 1999—2002, Digestive Healthcare Ctr. and Ctrl. Jersey Ambulatory Surgery Ctr., Hillsborough, NJ, 2002—. Trustee Society Hill Townhouse Assn., 1986-90, v.p., 1987-88, pres., 1988-89; bd. dirs. Residential Support Svcs., 1993-96, v.p. 1993-96. Lt. cmdr. Med. Svcs. Corp. USNR, 1982—. Fellow: Am. Coll. Med. Practive Execs.; mem.: N.J. Med. Group Mgmt. Assn. (exec. bd. 2000—, treas. 2002—), Am. Acad. Med. Adminstrs. (N.J. state dir. 2000—), Naval Res. Assn. (dist. v.p. 1987—91), Med. Group Mgmt. Assn. (nat. comm. com. 1993—95, jour. editl. bd. 2000—), Assn. Mil. Surgeons U.S. (exec. com. N.J. chpt. 1985—87, pres. 1988—89), Am. Coll. Healthcare Execs. Democrat. Home: 230 Seton Hall Dr Freehold NJ 07728-8878 Office: Digestive Healthcare Ctr 511 Courtyard Dr Hillsborough NJ 08844 E-mail: edgulko@aol.com.

GULKO, PAUL MICHAEL, insurance executive; b. Boston, Feb. 19, 1944; s. Jacob and Helen (Bornstein) G.; m. Judith Silbert, Sept. 20, 1970 (div. Mar. 1983); children: Harlan David, Brett Robert; m. Donna Gold, Oct. 6, 1991 (dec. June 1993); m. Myra Feldman, Aug. 11, 2002. BA, Northeastern U., 1966; JD, Suffolk U. Law Sch., 1970. Bar: Mass. 1971, U.S. Dist. Ct. Mass. 1971, U.S. Supreme Ct. 1978. Counsel Mass. Divsn. Ins., Boston, 1971-75; mgr., exec. sec. Mass. Insurers Insolvency Fund, R.I. Insurers Insolvency Fund, Conn., N.H., Wash. D.C., Vt., Maine, Va. Ins. Guaranty Assn., Boston, 1975; pres. Guaranty Fund Mgmt. Svcs., Boston, 1981—. Bd. dirs. Temple Israel, Swampscott, Mass., 1975-78, Jewish Rehab. Ctr. North Shore, Swampscott, 1976-80; pres. North Shore Hebrew Sch., 1987-91. Mem. ABA (past chmn. pub. regulation ins. law com., pub. regulation ins. law com.), Nat. Assn. Ins. Commrs. (rehabilitators and liquidators task force, past chmn. industry adv. com.), Nat. Conf. Ins. Guaranty Funds (task force mem. ops. com., vice chmn. bd. dirs. 1990-91, chmn. 1991-922, bd. dirs. 1990—, exec. com. 1990—). Democrat.

GULL, HAZEL JOY (CONNIE GULL), retired nursing administrator; b. Rumford, Maine, Sept. 15, 1944; d. Robert Crisp and Ellen (Hall) Constantine; m. Theodore R. Gull, July 1, 1967; children: Michael Stephen, Matthew Christopher. Diploma, New Eng. Deaconess Hosp., Boston, 1967; BSN, U. Ariz., 1975; M in Policy Scis., U. Md., Baltimore County, 1998. RN NY, Ariz., Tex., Md., cert. peri anesthesia nurse. Evening supr. Tompkins County Hosp., Ithaca, N.Y., 1967-70; charge nurse St. Joseph's Hosp., Tucson, 1973-75; staff nurse Clear Lake Hosp., Webster, Tex., 1975-77; nurse mgr. post anesthesia care unit Howard County Gen. Hosp., Columbia, Md., 1977-91, peri-operative info. mgr., 1991—2003; ret., 2003. Author: (with others) The Nursing Clinics of North America, 1987. Parish nurse Christ United Meth. Ch., Columbia, 2000—. Mem. ASPAN, Phi Kappa Phi. Home: 9275 Brush Run Columbia MD 21045-5302

GULL, PAULA MAE, adult nurse practitioner; b. L.A., Mar. 7, 1955; d. Gerald Henry and Artemis (Cubillas) Balzer; m. Randell Jay Gull, July 10, 1976. AA, Cypress (Calif.) Coll., 1976; AS with high honors, Rancho Santiago Coll., Santa Ana, Calif., 1985; BSN with high honors, Calif. State U., Fullerton, 1993; MSN, Calif. State U., Long Beach, 1996. Cert. med. surg. nurse, nephrology nurse, nurse practitioner, clin. transplant coord. Staff RN U. Calif. Irvine Med. Ctr., Orange, Calif., 1986-87, asst. nurse mgr., 1987-88, nurse mgr., 1988; med.-surg. nurse N000, 1990—; renal transplant nurse practitioner, coord. U. Calif.-Irvine Med. Ctr., Orange, 1992—, St. Joseph Hosp., Orange, 1997—. Mem.: Calif. Coalition Nurse Practitioners, N.Am. Transplant coord. Orgn., Am. Nephrology Nurses Assn. Mem. Lds Ch. Home: 24974 Enchanted Way Moreno Valley CA 92557-6410 E-mail: p.gull@worldnet.att.net.

GULLACE, MARLENE FRANCES, information engineer, systems analyst, consultant; b. Ft. Belvoir, Va., Jan. 12, 1952; d. Amerigo Francis and Martha Arlene Guy; m. Gerald Lynn Tolley, June 26, 1970 (div. Nov. 1974); 1 child, Gerald Lynn Tolley Jr.; m. Salvatore Gullace, Nov. 19, 1976 (div. Apr. 1991). AA in Pre-Law, Cochise Coll., 1979; BA in Polit. Sci., U. Ariz., 1982; AA in Computer Sci., Bus., Chaparral Coll., 1985. Realtor, entrepreneur, inventor, Sierra Vista, Ariz., 1977-84; ADP instr. Chaparral Coll., Tucson, 1985; model Barbizon, Tucson, 1986-87; clk. HUD/FHA, Tucson, 1987-88; computer programmer DOD Inspector Gen., Arlington, 1988-89; programmer analyst U.S. Army Corps of Engrs., USAF, Washington, 1989-91, Calibre Systems Inc., Falls Church, Va., 1991; cons., systems analyst/programmer EDP, Vienna, Va., 1991-93; info. engr. Ogden/Anteon Corp., Vienna, 1993-96, Orkand Corp., 1996, SRA Internat., Inc., 1997-00, SRA Internat., 2000—01, SAIC, 2002—. Patented toy, registered trademark. Realtor assoc. Cochise County Bd. Realtors, 1977-84. Mem. IEEE, Fed. Women's Program at SBA (sec. 1976). Methodist. Avocations: art, design, crafts, sewing. Home: 7829 Piccadilly Dr Warrenton VA 20186-8623

GULLAND, EUGENE D. lawyer; b. Endicott, N.Y., Aug. 27, 1947; s. George Raymond and Virginia (Fisher) G.; m. Kristin Spearing, Aug. 29, 1970; children: Michael Spearing, Molly Spearing, Samuel Spearing. AB, Princeton U., 1969; JD, Yale U., 1972. Bar: D.C., Va., U.S. Supreme Ct., U.S. Ct. Appeals (1st, 2d, 3d, 4th, 6th, 7th, 9th, D.C., Fed. cirs.), U.S. Dist. Ct. D.C., (ea. dist.) Va., Md., Ariz., Ind. Assoc. Covington & Burling, Washington, 1973-80, ptnr., 1980—. Practitioner before London Ct. Internat. Arbitration, Internat. C. of C., Am. Arbitration Assn., also other arbitral tribunals; mem. faculty Nat. Inst. for Trial Advocacy, Am. Judicature Soc. Trustee Loudoun Day Sch., Leesburg, Va., 1986-98; vestryman, treas. Our Redeemer Ch., 1987-97; mem. alumni schs. com. Princeton U. Capt. U.S. Army, 1972-73. Woodrow Wilson scholar Princeton U., Princeton U. scholar. Mem. Nat. Assn. Coll. and Univ. Attys., Phi Beta Kappa. Am. Judicature Soc., Henlopen Acres Beach Club Home: Little River Farm Aldie VA 20105 Office: Covington & Burling 1201 Pennsylvania Ave NW Washington DC 20004-2401 E-mail: egulland@cov.com.

GULLEDGE, IRENE O. retired music educator; b. Santa Rosa, Fla., June 28, 1913; d. Ira Peter Olds and Edna Emma Oakley; children: Imogene, Marshall, Ronnie, Ocie, Gaylord. Grad. H.S., Foley, Ala. Ch. pianist Christian Missionary Alliance, Elberta, Ala., 1927—30; ch. pianist and organist Meth. Ch., Rosinton, Ala., 1930—79, ch. organist Loxley, Ala., 1979—. Tchr. grades 3 and 4 Rosinton Elem., 1941—44. Author poetry. Active Helping Hand Club, Robertsdale, Ala., 2001—02, Rep. Nat. Com. Methodist. Avocation: composing gospel songs.

GULLEDGE, SANDRA SMITH, publishing executive, film producer; b. Great Lakes, Ill., July 6, 1949; d. Dennis Murrey and Olga (Grosheff) Smith. BS, Northwestern U., 1971; MA, Annenberg Sch Comm., U. So. Calif., 1986. Columnist Camarillo Daily News, Calif., 1971-76; editor Fillmore Herald, Calif., 1976-78; pub. info. officer Oxnard Union High Sch. Dist., Calif., 1980-82, Ventura County Cmty. Coll. Dist., 1982-83; pub. rels. dir. Murphy Orgn., Oxnard, Calif., 1983-84; editor Forum and Solutions GTE, Irving, Tex., 1988-89; mktg. spec. USAA Alliance Svc., San Antonio, 1995-99; pres. Crimson Horse Entertainment & Publ.Co., LLC, 2000—. E-mail: guidepublishing@usa.net.

GULLEN, CHRISTOPHER ROY, lawyer; b. Detroit, Feb. 17, 1950; s. George Edgar and Mary Ruth Gullen; m. Sheila Rae Collins, Aug. 25, 1973; children: Brian Christopher, Katelyn Elizabeth. BA, U. Mich., 1972; JD, Ohio Northern U., 1975. Bar: Mich. 1975, U.S. Dist. Ct. (ea. dist.) Mich. 1975, U.S. Ct. Appeals (6th cir.) 1978. Law clk. Mich. Ct. Appeals, Lansing, 1975-77; ptnr. Gullen & Fitzsimmons, Rochester, Mich., 1977-82, Sarvis, Gullen & Herrmann, Birmingham, Mich., 1982-86; pub. liability atty. Kmart Corp., Troy, Mich., 1986-90, pub. liability counsel, 1990-99, dir. risk mgmt. and pub. liability, 2000—02. Mediator Oakland County Cir. Ct., 1986—. Author: Rules and Regulations of the Science Court, 1980. Mem. ABA, Mich. Bar Assn. Office: James E Logan & Assocs Ltd 7011 Orchard Lake Rd West Bloomfield MI 48322 E-mail: cgullen@jeloganltd.com.

GULLER, IRVING BERNARD, forensic, clinical psychologist, consultant; b. N.Y.C., July 27, 1932; s. Hyman and Mildred (Rothman) G.; m. Adele Horowitz, Apr. 5, 1955; children: Robert, Matthew. BA, CCNY, 1954, MS, 1956; PhD, NYU, 1962. Diplomate clin. psychology Am. Bd. Profl. Psychology (fellow), Am. Coll. Forensic Examiners. Dir. psychol. tng. and rsch. Maine Dept. Mental Health and Corrections, Augusta, 1962-63; asst. prof. psychology, coll. psychologist Franklin and Marshall Coll., 1963-67; assoc. prof. psychology John Jay Coll., N.Y.C., 1967-71, prof. psychology, 1971-92, prof. emeritus, 1992—; doctoral faculty criminal justice CUNY, 1981—92, prof. emeritus, 1992—. Founder, dir. Inst. Forensic Psychology, 1971—. attending psychologist, cons. St. Joseph's Hosp., Paterson, N.J., 1970-99; cons. to police depts. and criminal justice agys. in forensic psychology; family therapist in pvt. practice, Oakland, N.J., 1962—; founding assoc. N. Jersey Mental Health Assocs., Oakland. Author: Clinical Psychology Training Guide and Handbook, 1963, The Clinical Psychologist in Institutional Settings, 1976, A Brief Introduction to Protective Techniques, 1982, Stop Panic, 2001; contbr. articles to profl. jours. Served with AUS, 1954-56. Recipient Founder's Day award NYU, 1963. Mem. Am., Ea., N.J. Psychol. Assns., Am. Coll. Forensic Examiners. Office: 5 Fir Ct Ste 4 Oakland NJ 07436-1821 E-mail: copdoc@aol.com.

GULLET, LEON ESTLE, retired cartographer; b. St. Clair, Mo., June 15, 1930; s. Estle Reece and Gertie Ethel (Maupin) G.; m. Willodean House, June 27, 1959 (dec. Nov. 1983). AA, Jeff City Jr. Coll., 1950; BS, S.W. Mo. State U., 1953. Cartographic aid Aero. Chart & Info. Ctr., St. Louis, 1955-57, cartographer, 1957-78; sr. cartographer Def. Mapping Aerospace Ctr., St. Louis, 1978-85, ret., 1985. Coord., writer for converting plant manual to oper. instrns., 1975. Author: Life's Greatest Decision, 1996, After Life's Greatest Decision, 1997, My Travelog 1936-2001, 2001; composer hymns: author one-act plays; editor ch. history First Bapt. Ch., St. Clair, Mo., 1922-92; writer Franklin County Bapt. Camp History, 1947-93; author, editor, rschr.: Brief History of the Gullet Family, 1998, Brief History of the Maupin Family, 1999, Brief History of the Franklin County Baptist Association, 2000; contbr. articles to profl. jours. Music dir. First Bapt. Ch., St. Clair, 1967-76, 83-85, chmn. constn. and by-laws com., 1995-97, chmn. ch. history com., 1993-97; chmn. ops. manual compilation com. Franklin County Bapt. Assn., 1994. With U.S. Army, 1953-55. Decorated Nat. Def. Svc. medal, Army of Occupation medal. Democrat. Avocations: hunting, fishing, livestock farming, travel. Home: 615 E Gravois Ave Saint Clair MO 63077-1609

GULLEY, JAMES CLARENCE, JR., television producer, marketing specialist, internet consultant; b. Detroit, Apr. 2, 1948; s. James Clarence Sr. and Mildred Lee (Griffin) G.; m. Anita Oliver; m. Jeanola Jackson; m. Phyllis Antoinette Hill, May 25, 1991; children: Marc, Darnell, James, Melanie, Delano. Pres. Big G Prodns., Detroit, 1972-94; v.p. ATAC Internat., Detroit, 1994-95, P.J. Internat., Detroit, 1995; pres. Gulley Group, Detroit, 1995—. Co-pub. King Kong Souvenir Book, 1976 (Movie Industry Champ award 1978); co-prodr. (music video) The Real Side TV Show, 1973-74; co-founder The Promoter, The Entertainment Resource Guide, 2002. Mem. bd. United Citizens of Detroit, 1990.; bd. dirs. 15th Congrl. Dist. Dems., Detroit; Dem. precinct del., Detroit; mem. Barton-Mcfarlane Neighborhood Assn., Detroit. With USMC, 1966-69, Vietnam. Recipient Wayne County (Mich.) cert. of appreciation, 1994, Assn. Govt. Accts. cert. achievement, 1984, Black United Fund of Mich. cert. appreciation, 1990. Mem. Detroit Million Man March Orgn., Adults Asserting Themselves, Internat. Masons. Democrat. Home: 10367 Beechdale St Detroit MI 48204-2564 E-mail: gulleygroup@aol.com.

GULLEY, JOAN LONG, banker; b. Balt., Sept. 10, 1947; d. Thomas F. and Florence (Waldron) Long; m. Philip Gordon Gulley, aug. 2, 1969; 1 child, Colin Jason. BA, U. Rochester, 1969; postgrad., Harvard U., 1985. Analyst U.S. Dept. Commerce, Washington, 1969-70, Fed. Res. Bd., Washington, 1970-74; sr. analyst 5, Washington, 1979-81; asst. v.p. Fed. Res. Bank Boston, 1975-79, v.p., 1981-83; sr. v.p. 5, 1983-86; exec. v.p. The Mass. Co., Boston, 1986-94, pres., CEO, 1994, also bd. dirs.; chmn., CEO PNC Bank New Eng., 1995-97; sr. v.p., mgr. strategic planning PNC Bank Corp., 1997-98, exec. v.p., dep. mgr. consumer bank, 1998—, dep. mgr. regional cmty. bank, 1999—2000; CEO PNC Bus. Banking, 2000—02, PNC Advisors, 2002—. Chmn. PNC Bank, New Eng., 1997-99. Mem. Boston Econ. Club, Allegheny Country Club, Nantucket Golf Club, Duquesne Club, Phi Beta Kappa. Office: PNC Bank Corp 1 PNC Plz 249 5th Ave Pittsburgh PA 15222-2709

GULLEY, WILBUR PAUL, JR., retired savings and loan association executive; b. Little Rock, Aug. 8, 1923; s. Wilbur Paul and JaJa Douglas (Ashburn) Gulley; m. Mary Elizabeth Bragg Hunt, Mar. 13, 1971; children from previous marriage: Wilbur Paul III, William H., James Ransom, Michael Pierce. AB in Bus. Adminstrn., Duke U., 1947. With Gulley Ins. Agy., Little Rock, 1947, ptnr., mng. officer, 1947-58; with Savers Fed. Savs. & Loan Assn., Little Rock, 1947-89, sec., 1948-52, v.p., 1952-58, pres., 1959-83, chmn. bd. dirs., 1983—89, also bd. dirs.; ret., 1989. Bd. dirs. Little Rock br. Fed. Res. Bank St. Louis, 1983—87. Gen. campaign chmn. United Fund, Pulaski County, Ark., 1963—64; v.p. Little Rock Boys Club, 1970—71, pres., 1971—72; commr. Metrocenter Improvement Dist., 1977—81, chmn., 1981; bd. stewards 1st United Meth. Ch. Little Rock, 1960—90, fin. chmn., 1989; trustee Savs. & Loan Found., 1977—81, Hendrix Coll., Conway, 1980—92, Roselawn Meml. Pk., 1975—, v.p. bd. trustees, 1994—; pres. BBB, Ark., 1962; trustee George W. Donaghey Found., 1958—2001, pres., 1969—72, 1981—83, 1995—96; trustee Ark. State U., 1968—73, sec.-treas., 1971—72, chmn., 1972—73. With USNR, 1943—46. Mem.: Ark. Savs. and Loan League, Pulaski County Savs. and Loan League, U.S. League Savs. Instns., Fin. Instns. Retirement Fund, Southwestern Savs. and Loans Conf., Little Rock C. of C., Little Rock Country Club, Phi Beta Kappa, Beta Omega Sigma, Sigma Alpha Epsilon. Home: 3500 Cedar Hill Rd Unit 3 Little Rock AR 72202-1914 Office: PO Box 3573 Little Rock AR 72203-3573

GULLICKSON, GLENN, JR., physician, educator; b. Mpls., July 9, 1919; s. Glenn and Grace (Stellwagen) G.; m. Glenna A. Swore, May 18, 1957; children: Mary, Glenn III. BA, U. Minn., 1942, MD, 1945, PhD, 1961. Diplomate: Am. Bd. Phys. Medicine and Rehab. Intern Gallinger Municipal Hosp., Washington, 1944-45; faculty U. Minn. Med. Sch., Mpls., 1946—, assoc. prof. phys. medicine and rehab., 1961-66, prof. phys. medicine and rehab., 1966-86, prof. emeritus, 1986—, acting head dept., 1974-75, interim head, 1982-85, asst. dir. Rehab. Center, 1954-61, dir. Rehab. Center, 1961-86. Exec. dir. Am. Congress Phys. Medicine and Rehab., 1960-66; mem. exam. com. phys. therapists Minn. Bd. Med. Examiners, 1961-71, pres., 1968-71; mem. med. adv. com. Minn. Soc. for Crippled Children and Adults, 1967-72; fellow stroke council Am. Heart Assn., mem. exec. com., 1971-74; mem. neurol. scis. research tng. com. Nat. Inst. Neurol. Diseases and Blindness, 1965-69; exec. com. Joint Com. Stroke Facilities, 1969-78. Served to lt. (s.g.), M.C. USNR, 1945-46, 53-54. Mem. AMA (prin. rep. interspìty. com. 1968-72, mem. residency review com. phys. medicine, rehab. 1971-79), AAUP, Minn. Med. Soc., Hennepin County Med. Soc., Minn. Med. Found., Am. Acad. Phys. Medicine and Rehab. (gov., v.p. 1968-69, pres. 1970-71), Am. Bd. Phys. Medicine and Rehab. (chmn. 1976-81, asst. to exec. dir. 1987-90), Am. Congress Rehab. Medicine (v.p. 1978-84, pres. 1984-85), Assn. Acad. Physiatrists, Sigma Xi. Home: # 225 9550 Collegeview Rd Bloomington MN 55437-2175 Office: Health Scis Ctr Univ Minn Minneapolis MN 55455

GULLIFORD, ANDREW JELLIS, historian, photographer; b. St. Paul, Nov. 2, 1953; s. David Oliver and Mildred Christine (Jellis) G.; m. Stephanie Bruce Moran, Aug. 13, 1977; children: Tristan David, Duncan Jewett. BA, Colo. Coll., 1975, MA in Teaching, 1976; PhD, Bowling Green State U., 1986. Tchr. 4th grade Silt (Colo.) Elem. Sch., 1976-83; historian, folklorist Am. House, Inc., Lima, Ohio, 1986-87; mus. dir. Western N.Mex. U., Silver City, 1987-90; asst. prof., dir. pub. history/hist. preservation program Mid. Tenn. State U., Murfreesboro, 1990-2001; prof. S.W. studies and history, dir. Ctr. of S.W. Studies, Ft. Lewis Coll., Durango, Colo., 2001—. Instr. Colo. Mountain Coll., Rifle, 1977-83; grant writer Colo. Endowment Humanities, Boulder, 1977-78; project dir. Country Sch. Legacy, 1980-83, As Far As the Eye Can See, 1975-76, The Years Ahead, 1977-79; writer, photographer El Paso County (Colo.) Hist. sites, 1975-76. Author: America's Country Schools, 1984, 1991, Boomtown Blues: Colorado Oil Shale 1885-1985, 1989, Sacred Objects and Sacred Places: Preserving Tribal Traditions, 2000. Mem. Nat. Register Rev. Bd.; bd. dirs. Nat. Coun. on Pub. History. Recipient Nat. Vol. award U.S. Forest Svc.; grantee Can. Embassy, Victoria, B.C., 1987, NEH, 1982, Colo. Endowment for the Humanities, 1975, 77; fellow Smithsonian Instn., 1986. Mem. Am. Culture Assn. (bd. govs.), Western History Assn., Am. Studies Assn., Colo. Hist. Soc., Mt. Plains Mus. Assn. Democrat. Avocations: hiking, photography, writing. Office: Ctr of SW Studies Ft Lewis Coll Durango CO 81301

GULLIFORD, JAMES B. government agency administrator; b. ST. Paul; m. Yvonne Gulliford; children: Keri, Jason. BS in Forestry Mgmt., Iowa State U., 1973, MS in Forestry Econs. and Mktg., 1975. Asst. dir. ops. coal extraction utilization rsch. ctr. So. Ill. U., 1979—81; dir. Iowa Dept. Soil Conservation, 1982—86; dir. divsn. soil conservation Iowa Dept. Agr. Land Stewardship, 1986—2001; regional adminstr. region 7 US EPA, Kansas City, Kans., 2001—. Mem.: Iowa Environ. Coun., Nat. Assn. Conservation Dists., Soil Water Conservation Soc. (pres. 1993—94), Nat. Assn. State Conservation Agys. (pres. 1989), Iowa Assn. Soil Water Conservation Dist. Commrs. (hon.), Gamma Sigma Delta (Alumni Merit award 1990), Xi Sigma Pi (pres. 1974—75). Office: US EPA Region 7 Office External programs 901 N 5th St Kansas City KS 66101

GULLIVER, JOHN STEPHEN, civil engineering educator, consultant; b. Torrence, Calif., Sept. 9, 1950; s. Robert David and Jane Elizabeth (Loeffler) G.; m. Karen Lyum, Nov. 27, 1972; children: Djuna, Teigan, Hallon. BSChemE, U. Calif., Santa Barbara, 1974; MSCE, U. Minn., 1977, PhD in Civil Engring., 1980. Registered profl. engr., Minn. Rsch. assoc. U. Minn., Mpls., 1980-81, asst. prof. civil engring., 1981-87, assoc. prof., 1987-96, prof., 1996—, acting head civil engring., 1997-98, head, 1998—. Editor: Handbook of Hydropower Engineering, 1990, Air-Water Mass Transfer: Selected Papers From the Second Symposium on Gas Transfer at Water Surfaces, 1991; tech. editor Hydro Rev., 1987-2001, Hydro Rev. Worldwide, 1993-2001; contbr. 87 publs. to sci. and engring. jours. Mem ASCE (Rickey medal 1990, 2003), Internat. Assn. for Hydraulic Rsch. (editor Proc. 27th Congress, Vol. D), Internat. Assn. Water, Am. Soc. Engring. Edn., Assn. Environ. Engring. and Sci. Profs., Am. Pub. Works Assn., Minn. Surveyors and Engrs. Soc., N.Am. Lake Mgmt. Soc. Home: 942 Forest Dale Rd Saint Paul MN 55112-2517 Office: U Minn Civil Engring Dept Minneapolis MN 55455

GULLO, STEPHEN PERNICE, psychologist, corporate executive; b. N.Y.C. s. Anthony V. and Rose (Pernice) G. PhD Columbia U. Pres., chmn. bd. Inst. Health and Weight Scis., N.Y.C., 1980—; co-dir. Family Bereavement Project Columbia U. Med. Sch., N.Y.C. Asst. clin. prof. Columbia-Presbyn. Med. Ctr., 1980-96; chair Nat. Obesity and Weight Control Edn. Inst., Am. Inst. for Life-Threatening Illness, Columbia U., 1996-98; chair profl. adv. bd. Am. Inst. for Life Threatening Illness, Columbia-Presbyn. Med. Ctr., 1996-2000; mem. com. grants and profl. edn. N.Y.C. region Am. Cancer Soc., 1980-99; mem. sci. adv. com. Inst. Cancer Rsch.; co-chmn. Internat. Conf. Child and Death, Columbia-Presbyn. Med. Ctr., N.Y.C., 1979; co-chair Nat. Obesity Symposium, Am. Inst. for Life Threatening Illness, Columbia U. Med. Ctr., 1994; expert witness City Coun. N.Y. Author: (with J. Schowalter et al) When People Die, 1978, The Child and Death, 1983, Education in Thanatology, 1984, Loveshock: How to Survive a Broken Heart and Love Again, 1988, Thin Tastes Better, 1995, (with T. Van Italie, A. Simopoulos and W. Futterweit) Obesity, 1995; cons. editor Jour. Thanatology, 1974-80, Archives Found. Thanatology, 1974—; chmn. editl. bd. Thanatology Abstract Series, 1974-76; cons. editor Advances in Thanatology, 1980-97; assoc. editor Loss, Grief & Care, 1990, Illness, Crises and Loss; contbg. editor: SELF, 1994-2002; contbr. articles and chpts. to med. textbooks. Vice chair ann. dinner Boys' Town of Jerusalem, 1981, assoc. chmn. ann. dinner Girls' Town Jerusalem, 1984; co-chmn. fundraising com. Found. Thanatology, 1982—; life hon. mem. Foss Found. Recipient gran croce al merito Accademia Italiana per lo Sviluppo Economico e Souale, Rome, 1985, Schoenberg award Am. Inst. for Life Threatening Illness, 1990; Knight Order St. John of Jerusalem, 1986; Patterson Found. fellow, 1972-73; NIH Rsch. grantee, 1973-75. Mem. N.Y. Acad. Scis., Found. Thanatology (exec. bd., profl. adv. bd.), Columbia U. Coll. Physicians and Surgeons, Rolls Royce Owners Found.. Home: 420 E 80th St Penthouse New York NY 10021-1052 Office: 16 E 65th St New York NY 10021-7030

GULLY, RUSSELL GEORGE, lawyer; b. San Angelo, Tex., Feb. 18, 1955; s. Frank Arthur and Dolores Ann (Dierschke) G.; m. Patricia Prost, Aug. 4, 1984; children: Monica, Tessa, Rachel. BA in Math., U. Tex., 1976, MA in Math., 1978, JD, 1984. Bar: Tex. 1984. Computer software instr. Tex. Instruments, Austin, 1978-81; atty. Thompson & Knight L.L.P., Dallas, 1984—. State advocate KC, 1996-98. Mem. ABA, S.W. Benefits Assn., Dallas Benefits Soc., Tex. Bar Assn., Dallas Bar Assn. Avocations: audiobooks, gardening. Office: Thompson & Knight LLP 1700 Pacific Ave Ste 3300 Dallas TX 75201-4693 E-mail: russell.gully@tklaw.com.

GULOTTA, STEPHEN J. cardiologist; b. Bklyn., Mar. 5, 1933; s. Vito and Dora Gulotta; m. Lee Scaringella Gulotta, June 27, 1954; 1 child, Stephen Gulotta Jr.;children: Ronald, Eric. BS in Chemistry, Bklyn. Coll., 1954; MD, SUNY, Bklyn., 1958. Diplomate Am. Bd. Internal Medicine with subspeciality in cardiovascular diseases. Med. intern Montefiore Hosp., Bronx, NY, 1958—59, resident in medicine, 1959—61; fellow in cardiology N.Y. Hosp. Cornell Med. Ctr., N.Y.C., 1961—62; chief cardiology North Shore Univ. Hosp., Manhasset, NY, 1967—79; dir. catheterization labs. St. Francis Hosp., Roslyn, NY, 1979—2000. Mem. editl. bd. Circulation, Jour. Am. Coll. Cardiology, 1962—; contbr. over 50 articles to profl. jours. Pres. Nassau Heart Assn., 1978—80, Am. Heart Assn., N.Y. Affiliate, 1981—83; bd. dirs. Commn. on Human Rights, Mt. Vernon, NY, 1964—70. Recipient Disting. Svc. award, Am. Heart Assn., 2000. Fellow: Am. heart Assn. Coun. of Clin. Cardiology, Am. Coll. Chest Physicians, Soc. Coronary Angiography and Interventions, Am. Coll. Cardiology, Am. Coll. Physicians. Avocations: skiing, collecting 20th Century American painters. Office: St Francis Hosp 100 Port Washington Blvd Roslyn NY 11576

GULTEKIN, EBRU KADRIYE, pediatrician; b. Balt., Nov. 13, 1964; d. Muharrem and Fazilet (Ozsoylu) G. BA, U. Louisville, 1986, MD, 1990. Intern, resident Kosair Children's Hosp., Louisville, 1990-93; fellow pediat. endocrinology Children's Hosp. Med. Ct., Cin., 1993-95; pediatrician pvt. practice, Louisville, 1995-98, Ft. Thomas, Ky., 1998—. Mem. AMA, Am. Med. Women's Assn., Ky. Med. Assn., Ky. Pediatric Soc., Jefferson County Med.

Soc., Louisville Pediatric Soc. Moslem. Avocations: chess, reading, crossword puzzles. Office: 602 S Fort Thomas Ave Fort Thomas KY 41075-2208 Fax: 859-572-3021. E-mail: ekgmd@msn.com., lokum64@hotmail.com.

GULYA, AINA JULIANNA, neurotologist, surgeon, educator; b. Syracuse, N.Y., Feb. 3, 1953; d. Aladar and Sylvia E. Gulya; m. William R. Wilson, May 21, 1983. AB cum laude, Yale Coll., 1974; MD with distinction in rsch., U. Rochester, 1978. Diplomate Am. Bd. Otolaryngology. Intern, jr. resident in gen. surgery Beth Israel Hosp., Boston, 1978-80; resident in otolaryngology Mass. Eye and Ear Infirmary, Boston, 1980-83; fellow in otology/neurotology Bapt. Hosp. Ear Found., Nashville, 1983-84; asst. prof. surgery George Washington U., Washington, 1984-87, assoc. prof. surgery, 1987-90; assoc. prof. otolaryngology and head and neck surgery Georgetown U., Washington, 1990-94, prof., 1994-96; chief clin. trials br. Nat. Inst. on Deafness and other Comm. Disorders, Bethesda, Md., 1996-2000, chief clin. trials epidemiology biostatistics sect., 2000—; clin. prof. surgery, otolaryngology, head and neck surgery George Washington U., 1998—. Assoc. examiner Am. Bd. Otolaryngology, 1993-97, bd. dirs., 1997-2002, oral exam. leader for otology, 2000-02, chair neurotology sub-specialty cert. com., 2000-02. Co-author: Anatomy of the Temporal Bone With Surgical Implications, 1986, 95; assoc. editor Am. Jour. Otology, 1989-99. Bd. dirs. Deafness Rsch. Found., 1994—2001. Recipient Libr. award, Rochester Acad. Medicine, 1975, presdl. citation, Am. Otol., Rhinol. and Laryngol. Soc., 1999. Mem.: Am. Acad. Otolaryngology, Head and Neck Surgery (bd. dirs. 1995—97, Honor award 1991, Disting. Svc. award 2001), Am. Neurotology Soc. (coord. for continuing med. edn. 1990—95), Am. Otological Soc. (coun. 1993—, editor-libr. 1995—2000, trustee rsch. fund 1993—2001, pres.-elect 1999—2000, pres. 2000—01). Avocation: water skiing. Office: EPS 400D-7 6120 Executive Blvd Rockville MD 20852-4909

GUMA, MICHAEL JOSEPH, music educator, band director, musician; b. New Orleans, Jan. 31, 1949; s. Alphonse John and Dorothy Thomson Guma; m. Cheryl Ann Ott, Feb. 13, 1971; children: Lora Shea, Michelle Theriot children: Virginia. BA in Music Therapy, Loyola U. of the South, New Orleans, 1970. Cert. tchr. La. Band dir. Isidore Newman Sch., New Orleans, 1972—79, 1991—, Our Savior Luth. Sch., New Orleans, 1979—85, Jefferson Parish Pub. Schs., Kenner, La., 1980—91. Freelance musician Am. Fedn. of Musicians, New Orleans, 1966—. Musician: (recording) The Milneburg Joys New Orleans Jazz, 1984, Rene Netto & The Sounds Of New Orleans Shades of New Orleans, 1991, Original Dixieland Jazz Band 80 Years of Jazz, 1997. Civic assn. bd. mem. Driftwood Pk. Civic Assn., Kenner, 1986—88; wage committe mem. Am. Fedn. of Musicians Local 174-496, New Orleans, 1980—84. Recipient Father/Son Achievement award for Contributions to Music Edn., New Orleans Music Colloquium, 2001. Mem.: La. Music Educators Assn. (honor band chmn. 1991—95), Music Educators Nat. Conf. Roman Catholic. Avocations: fishing, snorkeling, travel. Home: 1413 Feronia St Metairie LA 70005 Office: Isidore Newman Sch 1903 Jefferson Ave New Orleans LA 70118

GUMBEL, BRYANT CHARLES, broadcaster; b. New Orleans, Sept. 29, 1948; s. Richard Dunbar and Rhea Alice (LeCesne) Gumbel; m. June Carlyn Baranco, Dec. 1, 1973; children: Bradley Christopher, Jillian Beth. BA, Bates Coll., 1970. Writer Black Sports mag., N.Y.C., 1971; editor Black Sports mag, N.Y.C., 1972; sportscaster KNBC-TV, Burbank, Calif., 1972—76, sports dir., 1976—81; sports host NBC Sports, N.Y.C., 1975—82; co-host Today Show NBC, N.Y.C., 1982—97; host, Real Sports with Bryant Gumbel Home Box Office, 1995—; host The Early Show CBS, N.Y.C., 1997—2002. Recipient Emmy award, 1976, 1977, Golden Mike award, L.A. Press Club, 1978, 1979, Edward R. Murrow award, Overseas Press Club, 1988. Mem.: AFTRA. Office: Home Box Office Inc 100 Ave of the Americas New York NY 10036*

GUMBINER, ANTHONY JOSEPH, investment banker, lawyer; b. Bradford, Eng., Jan. 2, 1945; s. Samuel and Marie (Sweeney) Gumbiner; m. Heather Howie, 1971; 1 child, Charles Maxwell; m. Mylene Monsillon, Feb. 17, 1981; 1 child, Celine Marie. Student Coll. of Law, Brighton Coll., 1962, U. Guildford, Eng., 1965. Sole practice, London, 1965—77; with Hallwood Group Cos. BV, Amsterdam, 1977—; joint mng. dir. Interallianz Hallwood BV, Zurich, Switzerland, 1977—; mng. dir. Hallwood Fin. Corp., 1980—. Chmn., mng. dir. Anglo Met. Holdings Ltd., London, 1979—; chmn., CEO Atlantic Met. Corp., Cherry Hill, NJ, 1983; chmn. First Pa. Mortgage Trust, 1978—; vice chmn., dir. UMET Properties Corp., 1979—; chmn., CEO, pres. Instl. Investors Corp., N.Y.C., 1983—; dir. Saxon Oil Co.; chmn. bd. Stanwick Internat. Corp. NV and predecessors. Mem.: Law Soc. Eng., Lodge Of Light. Jewish. Office: The Hallwood Group Inc 3710 Rawlins Ave Ste 1500 Dallas TX 75219-4236

GUMBINER, KENNETH JAY, lawyer; b. Chgo., Sept. 2, 1946; s. Bernard and Sylvia (Oguss) G.; m. Christy Habecost, June 11, 1972; children: Rebecca, Benjamin, Sara. BS in Indsl. Engring., Purdue U., 1968; JD, U. Ill., 1971. Bar: Ill. 1971, Mass. 1981, N.C. 1985, U.S. Supreme Ct. 1985; cert. mediator, N.C. Assoc. Neuman, Williams, Anderson & Olson, Chgo., 1971-72; asst. atty. gen. environ. divsn. Ill. Atty. Gen.'s Office, Chgo., 1972-74; ptnr. Pedersen & Houpt, Chgo., 1974-81; v.p., gen. counsel Riley Stoker Corp., Worcester, Mass., 1981-84; ptnr. Patton Boggs, LLP, Greensboro, N.C., 1984-2000, Tuggle, Duggins & Meschan, Greensboro, 1999—. Author: Construction Law Digest, 1986-99, Construction Industry Forms, 1988, Alternative Dispute Resolution, A Litigators Guide, 2001. Mem.: ABA (litig., dispute resolution and constrn. sects.), Mass. Bar Assn., Ill. Bar Assn., N.C. Dispute Resolution Commn., N.C. Bar Assn. (past chmn. dispute resolution sect.). Office: Tuggle Duggins & Meschan 228 W Market St Greensboro NC 27401-2536 E-mail: kgumbiner@tuggleduggins.com.

GUMBINNER, PAUL S. advertising and executive recruitment agency executive; b. N.Y.C., Aug. 30, 1942; s. Paul G. Gumbinner and Ruth (Gumpert) Coben; m. Nancy Levin (div. 1978); children: Elizabeth Susan, Jeffrey Michael; m. Amye Hope Price, Sept. 12, 1982. BS, Temple U., 1964. Asst. account exec. Richard K. Manoff, N.Y.C., 1964-66; account exec. DKG, Inc., N.Y.C., 1966-68; v.p. Kenyon & Eckhardt, N.Y.C., 1969-73; sr. v.p. McCaffrey & McCall, N.Y.C., 1974-77; pres. Anesh, Viseltear, Gumbinner, N.Y.C., 1977-82, The Gumbinner Co., Inc., N.Y.C., 1982—. Contbr. articles to Ad Week, Advt. Age. Pres. Friends Emelin Theatre, Mamaroneck, N.Y., 1976-78; v.p. Larchmont (N.Y.) Pub. Libr., 1975-77; chmn. bd. dirs. Urban Glass, Bklyn., chmn., 2000—; bd. dirs. Art Alliance for Contemporary Glass; pres. Southgate Owners Assn., 2000—. Recipient Effie award Am. Mktg. Assn., 1985. Mem. Ad Club N.Y. (guest lectr.). pres. Southgate Owens Assn., 2000-. Democrat. Avocations: photography, glass collecting. Office: The Gumbinner Co Inc 509 Madison Ave Ste 708 New York NY 10022-5501

GUMM, MARGARET R. lawyer; b. East Orange, N.J., June 25, 1940; d. John R. Gumm and Margaret M. (Clay) Wahl. B.A., William Smith Coll., 1962; J.D., NYU, 1969. Bar: NY 1970. Asst. to pub. relations officer Exec. Council Episc. Ch., N.Y.C., 1963-70; assoc. Ponzan & Goldblum, Queens, N.Y., 1970-73, Norman S. Reich, 1973-78; atty. Human Resources Adminstrn. Office of Legal Affairs, City of N.Y., 1978-83, assoc. atty., 1983— ; counsel Episc. Women's Caucus, 1971-73, mem. Exec. Council, Episc. Diocese of N.Y., 1972-75. Mem. Canons Com., Episc. Diocese of N.Y., 1971-76; sr. warden St. Clement's Episc. Ch., N.Y.C., 1982—, mem. vestry, 1973— . Mem. Hobart and William Smith Club. of N.Y. (bd. govs. 1978-84), Phi Beta Kappa, Phi Sigma Iota. Office: Human Resources Adminstrn Office of Legal Affairs 220 Church St Fl 6 New York NY 10013-2904

GUMMEL, HERMANN KARL, retired physicist, laboratory administrator; b. Hannover, Germany, July 6, 1923; came to U.S., 1953; s. Johannes and Charlotte (Elgeti) G.; m. Erika Ilse Reich, Aug. 31, 1952; children— Monica Ruth, Margaret Grace MS, Syracuse U., 1952, PhD, 1957; diploma in Physics, Philipps U., Marburg-Lahn, 1952. Mem. tech. staff Bell Telephone Labs, Murray Hill, N.J., 1957-62, supr., 1962-67, dept. head, 1967-82, asst. dir., 1982-84; dir. AT&T Bell Labs, Murray Hill, N.J., 1984-86, ret., cons. Contbr. articles to profl. jours.; patentee in field Recipient Phil Kaufman award Electronic Design Automation Co., 1994. Fellow IEEE (David Sarnoff award 1983, Guillemin-Cauer prize paper award Circuits and Systems Soc. 1977, Tech. Achievement award Circuit and Systems Soc. 1990, Golden Jubilee medal 2000, Third Millennium medal 2000); mem. Am. Phys. Soc., Nat. Acad. Engring., Sigma Xi Presbyterian.

GUMMERE, JOHN, insurance company executive, director; b. Mt. Holly, N.J., Feb. 12, 1928; s. John Westcott and Ruth (Clark) G.; m. Eleanor Frances Greene, Oct. 9, 1954; children: Cynthia Clark, John Greene. BA, Yale U., 1948. With Phoenix Mut. Life Ins. Co., Hartford, Conn., 1949—92, sec. charge underwriting dept., 1961—64, v.p., 1965—72, sr. v.p., 1972—78, exec. v.p., 1978—81, dir., pres., COO, 1981—83, pres., CEO, 1983—87, chmn. bd., CEO, 1987—92, Phoenix Home Life Mut. Ins. Co., Hartford, 1992—94. Mem. exec. com. Med. Info. Bur., 1972-77, chmn., 1977; past bd. dirs. Hartford Grad. Ctr., Old State House, Am. Coun. Life Ins. and Health Ins. Assn. Am. Fellow Soc. Actuaries; mem. Greater Hartford C. of C. (past chmn., bd. dirs.), Sigma Xi.

GUMMERE, WALTER COOPER, educator, consultant; b. Columbus, Ohio, Apr. 24, 1917; s. Walter Cooper and Glenn (Becker) G.; m. Virginia Lee Jeffries, Jan. 10, 1942; children: Virginia Glenn Gummere Stewart, Deborah Gummere Lilgendahl (dec.), Rebecca Jane Gummere Pivetta. AB, Brown U., 1940; MBA, U. Louisville, 1953. Chief indsl. engr. Colgate Palmolive Co., 1947-53; gen. supt., dir. Rich's Inc., Atlanta, 1953-57; personnel adminstr. Montgomery Ward & Co., Chgo., 1957-60; v.p., gen. mgr. Plasti-Line Inc., Knoxville, Tenn., 1960-62; mgmt. cons., 1962-63; with Tappan Co., 1963-73, exec. v.p., 1966-72, pres., chief exec. officer, 1972-73; also dir.; chmn., chief exec. officer The Vendo Co., 1974-78; pres. Square Pegs Assocs., Inc., 1978—. Exec.-in-residence U. Central Fla., 1982-83, Centre Coll. Ky., winter 1983, Am. Coll., London, spring and summer 1984; Goodyear exec. prof. Sch. Bus., U. Akron, 1984-85; vis. prof. Clemson U., 1986, Lander Coll., 1987, Am. Coll., London, 1988, Centre Coll. Ky., 1990, U. Louisville, 1990—. Served to capt. AUS, 1942-46. Mem. Newcomen Soc., Acad. Mgmt., Delta Upsilon, Phi Beta Kappa, Delta Sigma Pi, Sigma Iota Epsilon, Omicron Delta Kappa Republican. Presbyterian. Home and Office: 202 Meadowvista Ln Sun City Center FL 33573-5562

GUMPEL, LISELOTTE, retired language educator; b. Berlin; d. Karl and Gretchen (Philipps) G. BA summa cum laude, State U. of San Francisco, 1964; MA, Stanford (Calif.) U., 1966, PhD, 1971. Asst. prof. U. Minn., Morris, 1968-72, assoc. prof., 1972-80, full prof. in German, 1980—98, ret., 1998, prof. German lang. and lit. emerita, 1999—. Lectr. in field. Author: Concrete Poetry from East and West Germany: The Language of Exemplarism and Experimentalism, 1976, Metaphor Reexamined: A non-Aristotelian Perspective, 1985; contbr. MLA, 2000, Poetry for Today and Tomorrow, Goethe-Inst. Inter Nationes, 2002; contbr. poetry and articles to profl. jours. Nat. Endowment fellow, 1972, Helen Cam fellow Girton Coll., Cambridge, Eng., 1977. Mem. MLA (life), Am. Assn. Tchrs. German, Soc. for Internat. Germanistics, Internat. Union of Germanic Lang. and Lit., Older Women's League. Democrat. Jewish. Avocations: reading, visiting museums, libraries, theatres, concerts, writing.

GUMPERT, GUNTHER, artist; b. Krefeld, Germany, Apr. 17, 1919; came to U.S., 1967, naturalized, 1971; s. Karl and Erna (Cordes) G.; m. Anita Von Kahler, Nov. 28, 1967. Grad., Human. Gymnasium, Krefeld, 1937, Sch. Fine Arts, 1938, Sch. Fine Arts, Wuppertal, 1939. Numerous one-man shows in, Europe and U.S. including: Zurich, 1955, Winterthur, 1959, Paris, 1960, Vienna, 1961, Rome, 1962, N.Y.C., 1963, 96, 98, Chgo., 1963, 64, London, 1963, Pforzheim, 1964, Seattle, 1965, 68, 70, 73, 76, Denver, 1972, Washington, 1966, 68, 69, 72, 75, 79, 82, 85, 87, 88, 90, 93, Cleve., 1971, Santo Domingo, 1978, group shows include, Suermondt Mus., Aachen, Ger., 1948, Kaiser-Wilhelm Mus., Krefeld, 1949, 50, 51, Internat. Exhibit Abstract Art, Pistoia, Italy, 1961, Salon Realites Nouvelles, Paris, 1959, 60, 61, Salon De Mai, Paris, 1962, Gruppe Z, Wuppertal, 1960, Internat. Exhbn. Contemporary Art, London, 1964, European Acad. Fine Art, Trier, 2000, Die Grosse Abstraktion, Wichtrach/Bern, 2002; represented in permanent collections, Met. Mus. Art, N.Y.C., Victoria and Albert Mus., London, Albertina, Vienna, The Phillips Collection, Washington, Kaiser-Wilhelm Mus., Krefeld, Museo Nacional de Bellas Artes, Santiago, Chile, Sch. Design, Providence, R.I., Princeton U. Art Mus., Mus. Fine Arts, Dallas, Denver Art Mus., Finch Coll. Mus., N.Y.C., Wesleyan U., Middletown Conn., Ohio U. Mus. Am. Art, Athens, Roosevelt House, New Delhi, India, Museo de Arte Moderno, Santo Domingo, George Washington U., Washington, and others; TV film Gumpert At Work, 1963. Address: 3752 Mckinley St NW Washington DC 20015-2510

GUMPERT, GUSTAV, public relations executive; b. Phila., Nov. 28, 1922; s. Hibbard Gustav and Lillian (Heebner) G.; A.B., Lehigh U., 1944. Reporter, Allentown (Pa.) Morning Call, 1945-46; asso. editor Musical Digest, N.Y.C., 1946-49; health edn. dir. Dept. Public Health, Phila., 1950-52, health info. officer, 1952-60; writing unit head pub. rels. dept. SmithKline Beecham, Phila., 1962-63, mgr. writing, editorial svcs., 1965-66, mgr. planning, editorial svcs., 1966-73, dir. spl. projects, 1973-78, dir. creative sers., 1978-89; ret., 1989. Contbr. articles to profl. jours. Pres. bd. Planned Parenthood Assn. Phila., 1960-62; bd. dirs. Found. for Study Cycles, 1959-60. Mem. Phi Beta Kappa.

GUMPERT, LYNN, gallery director; Student, Sorbonne, Paris, 1971-72; cert. completion first year, Ecole du Louvre, Paris, 1971-72; BA in History of Art with honors, U. Calif., Berkeley, 1974; MA in History of Art, U. Mich., 1977. Curatorial asst. The Jewish Mus., N.Y.C., 1978-80; curator The New Mus. Contemporary Art, N.Y.C., 1980-84, sr. curator, 1984-88; adj. curator Mus. Contemporary Art, L.A., 1988-89, We. States Arts Fedn., Santa Fe, 1988-89; coord. Eighth Biennale of Sydney Art Gallery N.S.W., Sydney, Australia, 1989-90; guest curator, adminstrv. dir. Amway (Japan) Ltd. and Setagaya Art Mus., Tokyo, 1989-91, Nat. Mus. Art, Osaka, Japan, 1989-91; cons. curator Gallery at Takashimaya, Inc., N.Y.C., 1992-95; guest curator, U.S. coord. ARC/Musée d'Art Moderne de la Ville de Paris, 1994-95; guest curator Grey Art Gallery, N.Y.C., 1996-97, dir., 1997—; interim dirl mus. studies program NYU, 1999-2000. Lectr. in field; juror in field; panelist in field; ind. curator/cons., 1988-97; mem. adv. com. Asia Soc. Galleries. Exhbns. include Grey Art Gallery, The New Mus. Contemporary Art, 1980, 81, 82, 84, 86, 89, Pitts. Ctr. Arts, 1983, Mus. Contemporary Art, Chgo., 1988, Galerie Ghislaine Hussenot, Paris, 1992, The Gallery at Takashimaya, N.Y.C., 1994, 95, numerous others; author: Christian Boltanski, 1993, reprint, 1996; editor: The Art of the Everyday: The Quotidian in Postwar French Culture, 1997. Decorated chevalier Order Arts and Letters (France); Univ. fellow U. Mich., 1975. Mem. Internat. Assn. Art Critics, ArtTable (N.Y.). Office: Grey Art Gallery NYU 100 Washington Sq E New York NY 10003-6688 Fax: 212-995-4024. E-mail: greygallery@nyu.edu.

GUMPERTZ, WERNER HERBERT, structural engineering company executive; b. Berlin, Dec. 26, 1917; s. Richard and Olga H. (Prenzlau) G.; m. Elizabeth Mildred Lewit, Nov. 25, 1949; children: Richard H., Ruth O. Gumpertz Moses. BCE, Swiss Fed. Inst. Tech., 1939; SBCE, MIT, 1948, SM in Bldg. Engring. and Constrn., 1950, advanced profl. degree in bldg. engring. and constrn., 1954. Registered profl. engr., Mass., Pa., Calif., Colo., Okla., Md., Kans., Tex., Ga., La. Constrn. supr., expeditor, draftsman Homes & Gardens Inc., N.Y.C., 1940; engring. draftsman, surveyor Lockwood Kessler & Bartlett, Bklyn., 1940-41; office engr., estimator, constrn. supr. M. Shapiro & Sons Constrn. Co., N.Y.C. and Newport News, Va., 1941-43; engring. asst. to head Kaiser Co. Inc. Shipyard, Vancouver, Wash., 1943; structural engr. U.S. Army C.E., ETO, 1946-47; office and field engr. United Engrs. & Constructors Inc., Phila. and Devon, Conn., 1948-49; prof. civil engring. MIT, Cambridge, Mass., 1949-57; sr. prin. Simpson Gumpertz & Heger Inc., Arlington, Mass., 1956—. Part-time instr. structural engring. Bridgeport Engring. Inst., 1948-49, U. Mass. Extension, 1953-62; cons. bldg. constrn. and material tech., bldg. systems and assemblies of materials; lectr. Harvard Grad. Sch. Design, 1985, 87. Contbr. articles to profl. jours. Mem. Adv. Com. on Pub. Bldg. Constrn., City of Newton, Mass., 1956-68; guidance lectr. Cambridge Pub. Sch. System, 1955-57. Served to cpl. U.S. Army, 1943-46, ETO. Fellow ASCE (nat. com. on stds., sec.-treas., joint com. on profl. conduct Mass. sect.), ASTM (chmn. com. D-8 on roofing, waterproofing and bituminous materials 1981-85, real estate com. 1988-95, Award of Merit 1986, Walter C. Voss award to Engr. for Outstanding Contbn. to Advancement of Bldg. Tech. 1987); mem. Am. Concrete Inst. (com. on residential concrete slabs, cellular concrete com.), U.S. Metric Assn. (cert. advanced metrication specialist), Am. Soc. Engring. Edn. (chmn. archtl. engring. divsn.), Am. Arbitration Assn. (nat. panel arbitrators), Nat. Fire Protection Assn., Midwest Roofing Contractors Assn. (assoc.), Nat. Roofing Contractors Assn. (assoc.), Sigma Xi. Office: Simpson Gumpertz & Heger Inc 41 Seyon St Waltham MA 02453-8335 E-mail: whgumpertz@sgh.com.

GUMPRECHT, BLAKE, geographer; b. Wilmington, Del., Dec. 30, 1959; s. William H and Jan Bannan Gumprecht; m. Josephine Lenardi, Jan. 28, 1989; 1 child, Ezekiel Hackberry. BS in journalism, U. of Kans., 1977—83; MLS, La. State U., 1990; MA in geography, Calif. State U., 1990—95; PhD in geography, U. of Okla., 1995—2000. Asst. prof. of geography U. of SC., Columbia, SC, 2001—; lectr. U. of Okla., Norman, Okla., 2000—01. Contbr. articles to journals including (Muriel H. Wright award, Okla. Hist. Soc., 1997); author: (book) The Los Angeles River: Its Life, Death, and Possible Rebirth (J.B. Jackson Prize, Assn. of Am. Geographers, 1999, Donald Flueger Local History award, Hist. Soc. of So. Calif., 2002), (article) Historical Geography (Andrew Hill Clark award, Assn. of Am. Geographers, 2000), Great Plains Quarterly (Frederick C. Luebke award, Ctr. for Gt. Plains Studies, 1998), Southern California Quarterly (Doyce B. Nunis Jr. award, Hist. Soc. of So. Calif., 1998). Grant, Graham Found. for Advanced Studies in the Fine Arts, 2000. Mem.: Assn. of Am. Geographers (program dir., cultural geography splty. group 2001—03). Independent. Office: University of New Hampshire Dept of Geography James Hall, 66 College Rd Durham NH 03824-3589 Office Fax: 603-862-2649. E-mail: gumprech@unh.edu.

GUMPRECHT, JANE CAROLINE DOERING, retired physician; b. Lewistown, Mont., Feb. 6, 1922; d. Gotthilf Johann Doering and Martha Elizabeth Strauss; m. Donald Max Gumprecht, Sept. 1944; children: Donald George, Ruth Ellen Carlson, Thomas Frank, Ernest Charles. BS, Mont. State U., 1942; BM, MD, U. Minn., 1946. Diplomate Am. Bd. Medicine. Pvt. practice, Three Forks, Mont., 1948—49, Coeur d' Alene, Idaho, 1951—87; ret., 1987. Sec., bd. dirs. Kootenai Meml. Hosp., Coeur d'Alene; inspirational spkr. Author: Holistic Health: A Medical and Biblical Critique of New Age Deception, 1986, New Age Health Care: Holy or Holistic? 2d edit., 1988, Abusing Memory: The Healing Theology of Agne Sanford, 1997. Com. for the handicapped City of Coeur d' Alene, 1961—62; cand. for Idaho legislature Rep. Party, Boise, Idaho, 1960, state com. woman, 1962—64; founding mem. Coeur d' Alene Bible Ch., Coeur d' Alene; sec. Kootenai County Med. Soc., Coeur d' Alene, 1957—58, pres., 1959—60. With USPHS, 1949—51. Named Idaho Mother of the Yr., Am. Mothers, Inc., 1981. Mem.: PEO, Alpha Omicron Pi, Phi Sigma, Phi Kappa Phi. Republican. Avocations: golf, travel, gardening. Home: 317 Military Dr Coeur D Alene ID 83814

GUNASEKERA, THILAK WIJENAYAKA, mathematician, educator; b. Colombo, Sri Lanka, Jan. 14, 1939; came to U.S., 1989; s. James and Sisiliya Stella (Wijesinghe) G.; m. Padmini Senaratna, June 8, 1964; children: Prasad, Pradeep, Prabath, Kumudini, Geethani, Indira, Prasanna. BS in Math. with honors, U. Ceylon, Peradeniya, Sri Lanka, 1962; MEd in Math. Edn., Wayne State U., 1992, PhD in Ednl. Evaluation and Rsch., 1997. Tchr. math. Ananda Coll., Colombo, 1962-81, Sokoto (Nigeria) Tchrs. Coll., 1981-89, Highland Park (Mich.) Schs., 1990-92; worksite edn. specialist UAW/Ford Rouge Acad., Dearborn, Mich., 1992-99; faculty math. Wayne County C.C., Detroit, 1993—, Devenport U., Warren, 1993—; mem. math. faculty Henry Ford C.C., Dearborn, 1998—; tchr. Trombly Alternative H.S., Detroit, 1999—. Tchr. Trombly Alternative H.S., 1999. Wilmer Menge Meml. scholar for leadership in math. edn. Wayne State U., 1993. Mem. Nat. Coun. Tchrs. Math., Mich. Coun. Tchrs. Math. Avocations: tennis, film, photography. Office: Trombly Alternative High Sch 1095 Hubbard St Detroit MI 48214- E-mail: gunthila@dpsnet.detpub.k12.mi.us., pgunaseker@aol.com.

GUNBERG, EDWIN WOODROW, JR., counseling psychologist, consultant, researcher; b. Sioux Falls, S.D., Nov. 13, 1950; s. Edwin Woodrow and Eileen Marie Elizabeth (Youngdahl) G.; m. Elizabeth Ann Robbins, June 5, 1976; children: Edwin Christian, Emily Elizabeth. BA, Gustavus Adolphus Coll., St. Peter, Minn., 1972; MA, George Mason U., 1975; postgrad., Va. Poly. Inst. and State U., 1975-79; PhD, U. N.D., 1981. Diplomate Am. Bd. Forensic Examiners, Am. Bd. Forensic Medicine, Am. Bd. Psychol. Specialties. Asst. prof. counseling U. N.D., Grand Forks, 1981-82; prin. PSYCON, Round Hill, Va., 1982—; pres. MARS Assessment Tech., Inc., Sterling, 1990-2001; v.p. United Bus. Svcs., 1996-98. Cons. HumRRO Internat., Inc., Alexandria, Va., 1985-91. Bd. dirs. Loudon Symphony Assn., 1994—, pres., 1996—99; mem. Round Hill Econ. Devel. Com., 2003—; mem. Rep. Senatorial Inner Cir., 1989; mem. Loudon County Rep. Com., 1992—97. Mem. Am. Assn. for Marriage and Family Therapy (clin.), Am. Psychol. Soc., Aircraft Owner and Pilot Assn., Exptl. Aircraft Assn., Mooney Aircrft Pilots Assn. Lutheran. Avocation: aviation. Address: PO Box 636 Round Hill VA 20142

GUNCZLER, PETER, pediatric endocrinologist; b. Caracas, Venezuela, June 13, 1948; s. Enrique and Aranka (Gross) G.; m. Jeannette Pariente, Mar. 28, 1974; children: Sam, David, Patricia. BSc, Moral y Luces, Caracas, 1965; MD, U.C.V., Caracas, 1972. Diplomate Am. Bd. Pediat. Intern in pediat. Hosp. de Niños, Caracas, 1972-74, attending physician, 1979-87; resident in pediat. NYU-Bellevue Hosp., 1974-76; fellow in pediat. endocrinology Cornell-N.Y. Hosp., 1976-79; dir. pediat. endocrinology Centro Medico, Caracas, 1979-89, Hosp. Clinicas Caracas, 1989—. Dir. Avepane, Caracas, 1981-95, ASEREME med. jour.'s assn., 1987-89. Chief editor Venezuelan Jour. Pediat., 1987-92. Recipient Eli Lilly award Endocrine Soc., Caracas, 1991, Pediat. Nat. award Pediat. Soc., Puerto La Cruz, 1994, Maracaibo, 1995. Mem. Venezuelan Pediat. Soc. (bd. dirs. 1984-89), Venezuelan Pediat. Assn. (bd. dirs. 1990—). Office: Hosp Clinicas Caracas Ave Panteon San Bernardino Caracas Venezuela E-mail: petergunczler@hotmail.com

GUND, AGNES, art museum administrator; Pres. Mus. of Modern Art, N.Y.C., 1991—. Office: care Museum Modern Art 11 W 53rd St New York NY 10019-5401

GUND, GORDON, venture capitalist, professional sports team executive; b. Cleve., Oct. 15, 1939; s. George and Jessica (Roesler) G.; m. Llura Liggett; children: Grant Ambler, Gordon Zachary. BA, Harvard U., 1961; DPubSvc (hon.), U. Maryland, 1980; DHL, Whittier Coll., 1993; LLD (hon.), U. Vt., 1994; PhD (hon.), Goteburg U., Sweden, 1997. Pres., chmn., CEO Gund Investment Corp., Princeton, N.J.; prin. owner Cleve. Cavaliers, NBA, 1983—. Mem. bd. govs. NBA; bd. dirs. Kellogg Co., Corning Inc. Mem. U.S. Olympic Com.; co-founder The Found. Fighting Blindness, 1971; mem. Nat. Adv. Eye Coun., 1980—84. Office: Gund Investment Corp PO Box 449 14 Nassau St Princeton NJ 08542-4523 also: Cleveland Cavaliers Gund Arena One Center Ct Cleveland OH 44115

GUNDERSEN, LARRY EDWARD, academic administrator; b. Detroit, Mich., June 3, 1940; s. Marius Christian and Katherine Belle Gundersen; m. Penny Faye Harrell, May 19, 1989; m. Laura Anita Ribble, Feb. 2, 1963 (div. May 12, 1989); children: Katherine Marie Dundas, Erik Anders, Christina Beth, Bjorn Lauritz. BS in Chemistry, Bowling Green State Univ., 1962; MS in Chemistry, U. of Ill., 1964; PhD in Biochemistry, U. Iowa, 1968. Cert. Regulatory Affairs Certified Regulatory Affairs Profl. Soc., 2001. Postdoctoral fellow Scripps Clinic & Rsch. Found., San Diego, 1968—71; dir., regulatory affairs programs San Diego State U., San Diego, 1999—; assoc. dir., regulatory affairs Mead Johnson and Co., Evansville, Ind., 1971—76; dir., divsn. of sci. info. and regulatory affairs Pennwalt Pharm. Divsn., Rochester, NY, 1976—83; dir., tech. and regulatory affairs Bausch & Lomb, Rochester, NY, 1985—84; dir., clin. rsch. and regulatory Nelson Rsch., Irvine, Calif., 1985—87; exec. dir., regulatory affairs Beecham Laboratories, Bristol, Tenn., 1987—89; group dir., u.s. regulatory affairs SmithKline Beecham, Philadelphia, Pa., 1989—92; v.p., worldwide regulatory & quality (& clin.) Genta, Inc., San Diego, 1992—97; regulatory affairs cons. Carlsbad, Calif., 1997—99. Recipient Spl. Recognition Award: Increasing Understanding of Regulatory Affairs, Regulatory Affairs Professionals Soc., 2001. Mem.: Drug Info. Assn., Regulatory Affairs Profls. Soc. (Spl. Recognition Award: Increasing Understanding of Regulatory Affairs 2001). Independent. Avocations: lapidary, genealogy. Office: San Diego State Univ 5500 Campanile Dr San Diego CA 92182-4610

GUNDERSEN, MARY LISA KRANITZKY, finance company executive; b. Schenectady, N.Y., July 20, 1955; d. Charles William Kranitzky and Shirley Ann (Thomas) Ballou. BS in Fin., U. Ala., 1982. Fin. specialist GE Co., Birmingham, Ala., 1981-83, supv. acctg. adminstrn. Atlanta, 1984-85, corp. auditor Schenectady, 1985-87; mgr. fin. analysis and auditing GE Constrn. Svcs., Burkville, Ala., 1988-90; mgr. fin. Manheim Auctions Inc., Atlanta, 1990-92; program fin. mgr. Latin Am. Sales Gen. Elec. Indsl. and Power Systems, Schenectady, 1992-94; dir. fin. GE Capital/PT Astra Sedaya Fin.,

Jakarta, Indonesia, 1995-97, GE Capital Asia Pacific, Hong Kong, 1997-99; comml. mgr. finance GE Energy Parts, Atlanta, 2000—. Bd. dirs. Birmingham Opera Theater, 1980—. Recipient Acad. Excellence medal Fin. Execs. Inst., 1982. Mem. Beta Gamma Sigma, Phi Kappa Phi, Omicron Delta Epsilon. Episcopalian. Avocations: music, water skiing, reading, travel. Home: 2920 Perrington Ct Marietta GA 30066-8717 Office: GE Energy Parts 4200 Wildwood Pkwy Atlanta GA 30339-8402 E-mail: lisa.gundersen@ps.ge.com.

GUNDERSEN, WAYNE CAMPBELL, management consultant, oil and gas consultant; b. Elgin, Ill., May 27, 1936; s. LeRoy Arthur and Jean Ellen (Campbell) G.; m. Gail Andrews, Mar. 21, 1959; children: Thomas Dexter, Lori Ann, Kathy Lee. BS, U. Nebr., 1959, MS, 1961. Advisor fgn. ops. Standard Oil of Calif., San Francisco, 1974-76; asst. to v.p. Chevron Overseas Petroleum, San Francisco, 1976-80; dir. oil and gas Kaiser Aluminum & Chem. Corp., Oakland, Calif., 1980-81; v.p., gen. mgr. Kaiser Energy, Inc., Oakland, 1983-85, pres., 1985-87; v.p. Kaiser Aluminum and Chem. Corp., Oakland, 1983-87; pres. Kaiser Aluminum Exploration Co., Oakland, Kaiser Exploration and Mining Co., Oakland, 1985-87; cons. in oil and gas., 1987—. Chmn. bd., chief exec. officer The Petroleum Synergy Group, Inc., 1988—; mem. geology adv. bd. U. Nebr., Lincoln, 1984-87. Co-authored articles in field. Pres. Parents Club Foothill Sch., Walnut Creek, Calif., 1978—79. Named Man-of-Yr., New Orleans Jaycees, 1973; Sinclair fellow, 1960-61. Mem.: Am. Assn. Petroleum Geologists. Republican. Methodist. Office: The Petroleum Synergy Group Inc PO Box 34300 Reno NV 89533 E-mail: renooilman@aol.com.

GUNDERSHEIMER, WERNER LEONARD, library director; b. Frankfurt, Hesse, Germany, Apr. 7, 1937; s. Herman Samuel and Frieda (Siegel) G.; m. Karen Rosenwald, Oct. 16, 1939; children: Joshua, Benjamin. BA, Amherst Coll., 1959, DHL (hon.), 1984; MA, Harvard U., 1960, PhD, 1963; MA (hon.), U. Pa., 1971; DHL (hon.), Williams Coll., 1989, Muhlenberg Coll., 1991, Davidson Coll., 1998, Washington Coll., 2003. Asst. prof. history U. Wis., Madison, 1963-64; jr. fellow Harvard U., Cambridge, Mass., 1962-66; asst. prof. U. Pa., Phila., 1966-68, assoc. prof., 1968-72, prof., 1972-85, chmn. history dept., 1976-78; dir. Folger Shakespeare Library, Washington, 1984—2002, dir. emeritus, 2002—; vis. prof. history Williams Coll., 2003. Trustee Rosenbach Mus. and Library, Phila., 1969-89, The Medici Found., Princeton, N.J., 1984-2000, Brit. Inst. of the U.S., Washington, 1985-90; vis. prof. Tel Aviv (Israel) U., 1982; adj. prof. history Amherst (Mass.) Coll., 1986-02. Author: Life and Works of Louis LeRoy, 1966, Ferrara: The Style of a Renaissance Despotism, 1973, Art and Life of the Court of Ercole I d'Este, 1972; editor: The Italian Renaissance, 1965; contbr. articles to profl. jours. Trustee Shakespeare Theatre at the Folger, Washington, 1985-92, PEN/Faulkner Found., 1990-95; v.p. Nat. Humanities Alliance, 1992-95, pres., 1996-00; cons. NEH, 1982—. Fellow Inst. for Advanced Study, 1970-71, Guggenheim fellow, 1974-75, I Tatti fellow Harvard Ctr. for Renaissance Study, 1974-75. Mem. Am. Philos. Soc., Am. Hist. Assn., Ind. Rsch. Libr. Assn. (pres. 1994-97), Renaissance Soc. Am., Med. Acad. Am., Century Assn., Grolier Club, Phi Beta Kappa (senator 1994-2000). Democrat. Jewish. E-mail: wgundersheimer@folger.edu.

GUNDERSON, BRENT MERRILL, lawyer; b. Vernal, Utah, Apr. 16, 1960; s. Merrill Ray and Betty Velate (Norton) G.; m. Julie Phillips, Oct. 28, 1983; children: Adam Brent, Jeremy Phillip, Matthew Norton, Hannah, Rachel, Mariah, Kayla, Jacob Elden. BA, Brigham Young U., 1984; JD, Columbia U., 1987. Bar: Ariz. 1987, U.S. Dist. Ct. Ariz. 1987, U.S. Tax Ct. 1994. Ptnr. Brown & Bain, Phoenix, 1987—96; pvt. practice Gunderson Denton & Profitt, P.C., Mesa, Ariz., 1996—. Pres. Ariz. Mgmt. Soc., Phoenix, 1996-97. Asst. dist. commr. Boy Scouts Am., Mesa, Ariz., 1994-97, scoutmaster troop 611, Mesa, 1991-94, troop 761, Mesa, 1999-2002, mem. varsity scout com., 2002--, chair, 1997-98; precinct capt. Mesa Rep. Precincts 47 & 17, 1988-94; cubmaster pack 761, Boy Scouts Am., 1998-99; mem. Ariz. Cmty. Found. Breakfast Series com., 2001—; mem. profl. advisors. com. Leave a Legacy, Ariz. Recipient Mesa Dist. award of Merit, 1997, Scoutmaster award of Merit Boy Scouts Am., 1992, named to Scout Leader Hall of Fame, 1993, Scouting Family Hall of Fame, 1999. Mem. Am. Immigration Lawyers Assn. (v.p. Ariz. chpt. 1992-93, Maricopa County Bar Found. (bd. dirs. 1991-95), East Valley Estate Planning Coun. (bd. dirs. 1997-2001, pres. 1999-2000), Am. Immigration Lawyers Assn., Ariz. Mgmt. Soc. (bd. dirs. 1997—). Mem. Lds Ch. Avocations: backpacking, fishing, China. Office: Gunderson Denton & Profitt PC 123 N Centennial Way Ste 150 Mesa AZ 85201-6747

GUNDERSON, CLARK ALAN, orthopedic surgeon; b. Watertown, S.D., Aug. 27, 1948; s. Harvey Alfred and Eugenie (Tulson) G.; m. Robbie Gunderson; children: Ashley, Camille Student, U. Minn., 1966-69; BS, U. S.D., 1971; MD, Baylor Coll. of Medicine, 1973. Diplomate Am. Bd. of Orthopaedic Surgery, 1979. Intern in gen. surgery Charity Hosp., New Orleans, 1973-74, resident in orthopedic surgery, 1974-78; chief of surgery Lake Charles (La.) Meml. Hosp., 1980-83, 90-91, sec., treas. med. staff, 1983-87, pres. med. staff, 1992-93, also trustee, 90-94, chief of surgery, 1998-99; clin. assoc. prof. La. State U. Sch. of Medicine, New Orleans, 1987-90. Bd. dirs. Arthritic Found. La., 1987. Mem. AMA, ACS, Am. Acad. Orthopaedic Surgeons (bd. councilors 2002, com. on state com. 2002), La. Orthopaedic Assn. (pres. 1995-96), Calcasieu Parish Med. Soc., La. State Med. Soc., N.Am. Spine Assn., Mid Am. Orthopaedic Assn., La. Orthopaedic ASsn. (exec. com. 1993—), Lake Charles Country Club (pres. 1987-89), Clin. Orthopedic Rsch. Soc., Sigma Chi. Avocation: golf. Office: 2615 Enterprise Blvd Lake Charles LA 70601-7675

GUNDERSON, CLEON HENRY, management consultant corporation executive; b. Great Falls, Mont., June 5, 1932; s. Leon H. and Mona (Emmett) G.; m. Virginia Ellen Hudson, Aug. 26, 1972; children: Craig H., Robert S., Laura E. BS, Inst. Tech., Dayton, Ohio, 1971, Mont. State U., 1957; MAPA, U. Okla., 1975. Communications engr. Mountain States Tel & Tel, Helena, Mont., 1953-54; aerospace engr. Boeing Co., Seattle, 1957-58; commd. 2nd lt. USAF, 1958, advanced to col., 1974, ret., 1976; pres. Precision Prodn. & Engring., Walla Walla, Wash., 1976-79, Western Skies Energy Systems, Spokane, Wash., 1979-88, Computer Central, Olympia, Wash., 1988-90, C.H. Gunderson & Assocs., Littlerock, Wash., 1990—. Mem. Am. Inst. Elec. Engrs., Seattle, 1957-60, Am. Inst. Indsl. Engrs., Spokane, 1982-85. Inventor heatexchange solar panels, comml. solar panels. Past pres. Tumwater Lions Club. Decorated Silver Stars, Disting. Flying Crosses, Purple Heart, Air medals. Mem. Soc. Mfg. Engrs. (sr. mem.), Soc. Mil. Engrs., Nat. Assn. Small Businesses, Toastmasters Internat., Walla Walla C. of C.; Canto Blanco Gun Club (Madrid, v.p. 1973-75, Scott Air Force Base Gun Club (v.p. 1975-76), Spokane Gun Club, Evergreen Gun Club (Littlerock). Republican. Avocations: hunting, fishing, competitive shooting. Home: 7136 Holmes Island Rd SE Olympia WA 98503-3436 Office: 7136 Holmes Island Rd SE Lacey WA 98503-3436 E-mail: lvgunder@juno.com.

GUNDERSON, GERALD AXEL, economics educator, administrator; b. Seattle, May 24, 1940; s. Marian A. and Ethel Ann (Hamon) G.; m. Margaret Jean Overway, Sept. 10, 1965; children: David Eric, Laura Lynn. BA in Econs., U. Wash., 1962, MA in Econs., 1965, PhD in Econs., 1967. Asst. prof. econs. U. Mass., Amherst, 1967-74; vis. assoc. prof. econs. Mt. Holyoke Coll., South Hadley, Mass., 1974-75; spl. lectr. econs. N.C. State U., Raleigh, 1975 78; prof. econs. Trinity Coll., Hartford, Conn., 1978-82, Shelby Cullom Davis prof. Am. bus. and econ. enterprise, 1982—, dir. S.C. Davis Endowment, 1982—. Bd. dirs. exec. com. Yankee Inst. for Pub. Policy Studies; acad. adv. com. Inst. on Research on Econs. of Taxation. Author: A New Economic History of America, 1976, The Wealth Creators: An Entrepenurial History of the United States, 1989; contbg. author: Explorations in Econs. History, 1973—, Jour. Econ. History, 1974, Social Sci. History, 1977, Wall Street Jour.; editor Jour. Pvt. Enterprise. Grantee Freedom Found. at Valley Forge, 1980 Mem. Assn. Pvt. Enterprise Edn. (pres. 1984-85), Econ. History Assn. Home: 6 Andrew Dr Weatogue CT 06089-9725 Office: Trinity Coll 300 Summit St Hartford CT 06106-3100

GUNDERSON, JUDITH KEEFER, golf association executive; b. Charleroi, Pa., May 25, 1939; d. John R. and Irene G. (Gaskill) Keefer; m. Jerry L. Gunderson, mar. 19, 1971; children: Jamie L., Jeff S.; stepchildren: Todd G. (dec.), Marc W. Student pub. schs., Uniontown, Pa. Bookkeeper Fayette Nat. Bank, 1957-59, gen. leader bookkeeper, 1960-63; head bookkeeper 1st Nat. Bank, Broward, Fla., 1963-64; bookkeeper Ruthenberg Homes, Inc., 1966-69; bookkeeper, asst. sec.-treas. Peninsular Properties, Inc. subs. Investors Diversified, Mpls., 1969-72; conptr., pres. Am. Golf Fla., Inc. (doing bus. as Golf and Tennis World), Deerfield Beach, Fla., 1972-89, stockholder, 1972-92; sales assoc. Realty Brokers Internat., Inc., 1990; sec.-treas. Internat. Golf, Inc., 1974-89, stockholder, 1974-99; dir. Mary Kay Cosmetics, 1993-97; wellness cons. Nikken, Inc., 1997—; wellness cons., advisor USA+; assoc. Premier Travel Internat., 2002—.

GUNDERSON, MARGARET STEEBLE, music educator; b. Boston, Aug. 5, 1944; d. Murray Ellzey and Janet Hale (Dormon) Steeble; m. Hans Magelssen Gunderson, Dec. 27, 1969; 1 child, Sharon Marie. B in Music Edn., Wheaton Coll., 1966; MusM in Voice, U. Ill., 1968. Grad. asst. U. Ill., Urbana, 1967-68; instr. in voice Bemidji (Minn.) State U., 1968-71, U. Grand Forks, N.D., 1971-74, No. Ariz. U., Flagstaff, 1975-93, sr. lectr. in voice, 1993—. Instr. in voice and piano Preparatory Sch. Music, Flagstaff, 1983—; pianist/organist various chs., 1968—; singer various chs., 1968-71, Luth. Ch., Grand Forks, 1971-74; singer and pianist 3 Luth. chs., Flagstaff, 1974—. Mem. Nat. Assn. Tchrs. Singing (treas. No. Ctrl. chpt. 1994-98), Music Tchrs. Nat. Assn. Republican. Lutheran. Avocations: hiking, historical trips, reading, listening, walking. Home: 3455 N 4th St Flagstaff AZ 86004-1763 Office: No Ariz Univ Coll Fine Arts PO Box 6040 Flagstaff AZ 86011-0001

GUNDERSON, MICHAEL ARTHUR, lawyer; b. Flint, Mich., Nov. 3, 1952; s. Robert Edward and Phyllis Elaine (Cronin) G.; m. Patricia Beatrice Holstein, Jan. 4, 1980; children: Eric Brendan, Ryan Dane. BA, U. Mich., 1974; postgrad. Gonzaga U. Law Sch., 1974; JD, Detroit Coll. Law, 1978. Bar: Mich. 1978, U.S. Dist. Ct. (ea. dist.) Mich. 1978, U.S. Dist. Ct. (we. dist.) Mich. 1980. Mem. firm Harvey, Kruse & Westen, P.C., Detroit, 1978-79, Fitgerald, Hodgman, Kazul, Rutledge, Cawthrone & King, P.C., Detroit, 1979-85; ptnr. Rutledge, Manion, Rabaut, Terry & Thomas, P.C., Detroit, 1986—; rep. assembly State Bar Mich., 1987—. Notes and comment editor Detroit Coll. Law Rev., 1976-77. Mem. ABA, Catholic Lawyers Soc. Detroit (pres. 1984-86, bd. dirs. 1981—), Mich. Bar Assn., Detroit Bar Assn., Oakland County Bar Assn., Def. Research Inst., Am. Arbitration Assn. (arbitrator), Mich. Def. Trial Counsel, Incorp. Soc. Irish Am. Lawyers (bd. dirs. 1987—), Assn. Def. Trial Counsel, Wayne County Mediator Tribunal (mediator), Delta Theta Phi. Republican. Roman Catholic. Home: 659 Rivard Blvd Grosse Pointe MI 48230-1253 Office: Rutledge Manion Rabaut Terry & Thomas PC 2300 Buhl Bldg Detroit MI 48226

GUNDERSON, SCOTT LEE, state legislator; b. Oct. 24, 1956; m. Lisa Gunderson, Oct. 17, 1981; children: Joshua, Hannah, Rebecca. Grad. H.S., Waterford, Wis. Former supr. Town of Waterford, Wis.; assemblyman Wis. State Dist. 83. Owner Gundy's Sport. Mem. Racine County Fair Bd., Wis. State Fair Park Bd. Mem. Wind Lake C. of C. (past pres.), Waterford Lions, Wings Over Wis. Address: State Capitol Rm 7W PO Box 8952 Madison WI 53708 E-mail: rep.gunderson@legis.state.wi.us.

GUNDERSON, TED LEE, security consultant; b. Colorado Springs, Colo., Nov. 7, 1928; BBA, U. Nebr. Sales rep. George A. Hormel Co., Austin, Minn., 1950-51; spl. agt. in charge U.S. Dept. Justice FBI, Los Angeles, Dallas, Memphis, Phila., 1951-79; internat. security cons. Ted L. Gunderson & Assocs., Santa Monica, Calif., 1979—; chmn. bd. dirs. HEB Inc., pubs. of Am. Free Press, Washington. Cons. Calif. Narcotic Authority; lectr., cons. on terrorism, cults and related topics. Author: How to Locate Anyone Anywhere, 1989, Be Smart, Be Safe, 1994; appeared on numerous nat. and local TV and radio talk shows; prodr. TV documentary on Satanism. Mem. Bel Air U.S. Navy League, Internat. Assn. Chiefs of Police, Internat. Footprinters Assn., Philanthropic Found. (Los Angeles chpt.), Royal Soc. Encouragement of Arts, Mfrs. and Commerce, Sigma Alpha Epsilon. Avocations: golf, racquetball.

GUNDLACH, HEINZ LUDWIG, investment banker, lawyer; b. Dusseldorf, Germany, July 6, 1937; came to U.S., 1969, naturalized, 1980; s. Heinrich Otto and Ilse (Schuster) G.; m. Cornelia T. Gundlach; children: Andrew, Annabelle, Julia Olivia. ML, LLD, U. Heidelberg, 1962. V.p. Thyssen A.G. Dusseldorf, 1964-68; v.p., partner Loeb, Rhoades & Co., N.Y.C., 1969-75; vice-chmn., CEO Fed-Mart Corp., San Diego, 1975-81; vice chmn., chief exec. officer successor cos. Sunbelt Investment Holdings, Inc., 1981-88; chmn. successor cos. Trucolor Foto Inc., 1981-88, Clearfoto, Inc., 1981-88; mng. dir. Dean Witter Reynolds, Inc., N.Y.C. and London, 1988-91; prin., chmn. Cardinal Capital Corp., Palm Beach, Fla., 1991—. Served with W. Ger. Army, 1958-59. Mem. St. James's Club (London). Republican. Office: Cardinal Capital Corp 217 Peruvian Ave Palm Beach FL 33480-4688

GUNDY, JEFFREY GENE, English educator; b. Bloomington, Ill., Aug. 7, 1952; s. Roger Eugene and Arlene (Ringenberg) G.; m. Marlyce Martens, Oct. 27, 1973; children: Nathan, Ben, Joel. BA, Goshen Coll., 1975; MA, Ind. U., 1978, PhD, 1983. Instr. Hesston (Kans.) Coll., 1980-84; prof. English, Bluffton (Ohio) Coll., 1984—. C. Henry Smith peace lectr. C. Henry Smith Trust, 1989, 99. Author: Inquiries: Poems, 1992, Flatlands: Poems, 1995, A Community of Memory: My Days with George and Clara, 1996, Rhapsody with Dark Matter, 2000, Scattering Point: The World in a Mennonite Eye, 2003. Creative writing fellow Ohio Arts Coun., 1988, 91, 96, 99, 2002. Mem. MLA, Nat. Coun. Tchrs. English. Mennonite. Avocations: guitar, soccer. Office: Bluffton Coll English Dept Bluffton OH 45817 E-mail: gundyj@bluffton.edu.

GUNDY, RICHARD L. freelance/self-employed writer; b. San Pedro, Calif., Jan. 25, 1956; s. William Clarence and Irma Rachut Gundy; m. Terri Lynn Waters, July 29, 1989. Student, Harbor Jr. Coll., Wilmington, Calif., 1974—77. Tchr.'s aide San Pedro H.S., 1974; asst. mgr. J.J. Newberry Co., San Pedro, 1977—80; chief engr. Ch. of Scientology, L.A., 1980—99. Author: (poem) The Ghost of McBee in True Reflections, 2001 (Editors Choice award, 2001). Adv. bd. chmn. Ch. of Scientology, L.A., 1985—97, mem. adv. bd., 1997—98. Mem.: Handyman Club of Am. Scientologist. Avocations: writing, cooking, gardening, walking.

GUNDY-REED, FRANCES DARNELL, marketing executive; b. Muskegon, Mich., Aug. 19, 1947; d. Joseph Leo and Olaverne (Mathis) Merle; m. Russell Norman Gundy, Sept. 18, 1965 (div. 1985); 1 child, Raymond Joseph; m. Robert A. Reed, Aug. 26, 1995 (dec. 1997). AS, Aquinas Coll., 1988, BA, 1991; MLS, Wayne State U., 1993. Mktg. dir. Pine and Dunes coun. Girl Scouts Mich., Muskegon, Mich., 1999—. Active Mich. Strategic Planning Com., Muskegon Cmty. Health Project. Mem.: AAUW, ALA (specialized svcs. coordination com.), Muskegon Heights Alliance of Bus. and Edn. (pres.), Mich. Libr. Assn., Intellectual Freedom Roundtable, Am. Bus. Clubs (former dist. gov.), East Muskegon Heights Neighborhood Assn. (treas.). Home: 145 S Green Creek Rd Muskegon MI 49445-2272 E-mail: darnellgundy_reed@yahoo.com.

GUNEWARDENE, ROSHANI MALA, lawyer; b. London, July 30, 1961; d. Swarna L. Gunewardene. BA, Sweet Briar Coll., 1985; JD, U. Conn., 1988; LLM, Columbia U., 1990. Bar: Fla. 1988, U.S. Ct. Appeals (llth cir.) 1988, U.S. Dist. Ct. (mid. and so. dists.) Fla. 1989, U.S. Supreme Ct. 1992. Cert. legal intern Office of Pub. Defender, West Palm Beach, Fla., summer 1987; assoc. Blackwell & Walker, PA, Miami, Fla., 1988-89, George T. Ramani, PA, Coral Gables, Fla., 1990-91, 92-93, Melton & Assocs., PA, Orlando, Fla., 1992; on-call assoc. Leon B. Cheek, III, Esquire, Fern Park, Fla., 1995-98; pvt. practice Altamonte Springs, Fla., 1993—. Mem. arbitrator panel U.S. Dist. Ct. for Mid. Dist. Fla., 1996—; cons., assoc. Orange County Bar Assn., Orlando, 1998-99, 2000-02. Contbr. articles to law jours. Mem. Human Rels. Bd., Orlando, Fla., 1993-99, vice chmn., 1995-97, chmn., 1997-98; mem. Seminole County Sheriff's Civilian Rev. Bd., Sanford, Fla., 1998-01; adv. charter rev. com. City of Altamante Springs, 2000-01; vol. pub. interest law grant chpt. U. Conn. Sch. Law, 1986-87; vol. Ryan's Nursing Home, Amherst, Va., 1983-84; vol. worker braille transl. project Blind Coun., Colombo, Sri Lanka, 1976-78. Scholar Sweet Briar Coll., 1984-85. Mem.: Better Bus. Bureaus Inc. (arbitrator 2000—), Fla. Bar (student edn. and admissions to the bar com. 1993—94, profl. ethics com. 1996—99, 2002—), Am. Immigration Lawyers Assn., Nat. Assn. Securities Dealers (arbitrator 1997—2002). Avocations: stamp collecting, music, movies. Office: San Sebastian Sq PO Box 162032 Altamonte Springs FL 32716-2032 E-mail: roshanigunewardene@hotmail.com.

GUNHUS, GAYLORD T. military career officer; b. Enderlin, N.D., May 22, 1940; m. Ann Broten; children: Kevin, Michael, Holly. BS, Seattle Pacific U., 1962; MDiv, Luth. Brethren Sem., 1967; ThM, Princeton Theol. Sem., 1976; grad., Armed Forces Staff Coll., 1980, Army War Coll., 1989. Ordained clergyman Luth. Ch., Ch. Luth. Brethren of Am. Synod, 1967. Army chaplain U.S. Army, 1967, advanced through grades to maj. gen., asst. brigade chaplain Arty. Officer Candidate Sch., 1967-68, bn. chaplain 520th Transp. Bn. Phu Loi, Vietnam, 1968-69, asst. ctr. chaplain U.S. Army Pers. Ctr. Ft. Lewis, Wash., 1969-72, group chaplain 164th Aviation Group Can Tho, Vietnam, 1972-73, cmty. chaplain Stanley R. Mikkelson Safeguard Complex Nekoma, N.D., 1973-75, asst. cmty. chaplain Heidelberg, Germany, 1976-79, chief Concepts and Studies Divsn., chief Concepts Divsn. Ft. Benjamin Harrison, Ind., 1980-85, divsn. chaplain 9th Inf. Divsn. Ft. Lewis, Wash., 1985-87, I Corps and Installation chaplain, 1987-88, USAREUR chaplain, 1989-92, TRADOC chaplain, 1992-94, dep. chief of chaplains Washington, 1994-99, chief of chaplains Arlington, Va., 1999—. Decorated Legion of Merit with oak leaf cluster, Bronze Star medal with oak leaf cluster, Meritorious Svc. medal with two oak leaf clusters, Air medal, Army Commendation medal with oak leaf cluster. Office: US Army Chief of Chaplains 2511 Jefferson Davis Hwy Arlington VA 22202-3923

GUNN, ALAN, law educator; b. Syracuse, N.Y., Apr. 8, 1940; s. Albert Dale and Helen Sherwood (Whitnall) G.; m. Bertha Ann Buchwald, 1975; 1 child, William BS, Rensselaer Poly. Inst., 1961; JD, Cornell U., 1970. Bar: D.C. 1970. Assoc. Hogan & Hartson, Washington, 1970-72; asst. prof. law Washington U., St. Louis, 1972-75, assoc. prof., 1975-76; assoc. prof. law Cornell U., Ithaca, N.Y., 1977-79, prof., 1979-84, J. duPratt White prof., 1984-89; prof. law U. Notre Dame, Ind., 1989-96, John N. Matthews prof., 1996—. Apptd. spl. advocate St. Joseph County Probate Ct., 2001—. Author: Partnership Income Taxation, 1991, 3d edit., 1999; (with Larry D. Ward) Cases, Text and Problems on Federal Income Taxation, 5th edit., 2002; (with Vincent R. Johnson) Studies in American Tort Law, 1994, 2d edit., 1999. Methodist. Office: U Notre Dame Law Sch Notre Dame IN 46556

GUNN, ALBERT EDWARD, JR., internist, educator, lawyer, administrator; b. Port Washington, N.Y., Oct. 31, 1933; s. Albert Edward and Esther Frances (Williams) G.; m. Joan Marie Jacoby, May 18, 1968; children: Albert Edward III, Emily Williams Gunn Hebert, Andrew Robert, Clare Margaret Gunn Berchelmann, Catherine Ann, Philip David. *Albert E. Gunn Sr. was born on September 16, 1891, in Port Washington, New York, and died there on October 14, 1952. His father, Edward Mott Gunn, was married to Sarah Olivia (Nelson) G. He was valedictorian at the Port Washington High School in 1910. He received an LL.B. from the Brooklyn Law School of St. Lawrence University in 1912, and was admitted to the New York Bar in 1914. He had a law practice in New York City until 1919, and then relocated to Port Washington with the firm Gunn and Gunn, and then Gunn, Neier and Gunn until 1952. He was the president of the Port Washington Chamber of Commerce in 1932. He was a Regimental Sergeant Major with the Judge Advocate Generals Department from 1918-19. He married Esther Frances (Williams) G., daughter of Edward Williams and Ellen (Bevan) W. on April 27, 1924. She was born on October 22, 1898 in New York, and died April 30, 1969 in Stuart Florida.* BS, Fordham Coll., 1955, LLD, 1958; MB BCh BAO, Nat. U. Ireland, Galway, 1967. Bar: NY 1958, U.S. Ct. Mil. Appeals 1959, D.C. 1972, U.S. Supreme Ct. 1972, U.S. Ct. Appeals (D.C. cir.) 1972; diplomate Am. Bd Internal Medicine, lic. physician Pa., NY, Fla., Va., Ga., Tex., Eng., Wales. Owner, agt. Albert E. Gunn Ins. Agy., Port Washington, 1953-65; intern Montefiore Hosp., N.Y.C., 1967-68; resident in medicine Roosevelt Hosp., N.Y.C., 1968-70; USPHS trainee in neurology U. Rochester, NY, 1970-72; asst. dir. govtl. rels. AMA, Washington, 1972-74; med. dir. Geriat. Svcs. Suffolk County, Hauppauge, NY, 1974-75, Rehab. Ctr., U. Tex./M.D. Anderson Cancer Ctr., 1975-88, chief rehab. sect., 1988-93, chief geriat. sect., 1993-2000, dep. chmn. dept. internal med. spltys., 1998-2000; prof. mgmt. and policy scis. U. Tex. Houston Sch. Pub. Health, 2001—. Asst. prof. medicine U. Tex. Med. Sch., Houston, 1976-80, assoc. prof., 1980-2000, prof., 2000—, also assoc. dean for admissions; med. dir. Region IV, Tex. Med. Found., 1986-93; del.-at-large White House conf. on Handicapped Individuals, 1977; pres. Mus. Med. Sci., 1990; cons. CDC, Legal Svcs. Corp., Nat. Libr. Medicine. Co-author: Rehabilitation of the Cancer Patient, 1976, AIDS in Africa, 1988; editor, contbg. author: Cancer Rehabilitation, 1984; mem. editl. bd. Cancer Bull., 1977-90, Gerontology and Geriatrics Edn., 1984-2003, Linacre Quar.; contbr. articles to profl. jours. Mem. nat. adv. health coun. HEW, 1974-75; mem. adv. com. Nat. Inst. Law Enforcement and Criminal Justice, Law Enforcement Assistance Adminstrn., U.S. Dept. Justice, 1974-76; mem. bd. regents Nat. Libr. Medicine, NIH, 1983-87, chmn., 1986-87, chmn. lit. selection tech. adv. com., 1988-91; bd. dirs. Right to Life Advs., 1977-78, Tex. Med. Ctr. Libr., 1990. With USAF Strategic Air Command, 1958-61, capt. Res., 1961-75. Fellow ACP; mem. Tex. Med. Assn. (trustee ins. trust, chmn. bd. trustees 1997-2000), Harris County Med. Soc. (exec. bd. 1986-90, v.p. 1998), Royal Coll. Physicians London (licentiate), Royal Coll. Surgeons Eng., Houston Acad. Medicine (bd. dirs. 1986-90, pres. 1990), Houston Bar Assn., D.C. Bar, Cath. Med. Assn. (regional bd. dirs. 1992—, Thomas Linacre award 1997), Sons of Union Vets. of Civil War, Am. Legion, KC, Army and Navy Club, Cosmos Club, Petroleum Club (Houston), Giraud (San Antonio). Roman Catholic. Home: 2329 Watts Rd Houston TX 77030-1139 Office: U Tex MD Anderson Cancer Ctr 1515 Holcombe Blvd Box 515 Houston TX 77030-4009

GUNN, ALEXANDER N., II, surgeon; b. Evanston, Ill., 1936; s. Alexander Hunter Gunn III and Mary Clark Stanley Magee; divorced. BA, Yale U., 1958; MD, Northwestern U., 1962. Diplomate Am. Bd. Surgery. Intern Cook County Hosp., Chgo., 1962-63; resident Marquette Affil Residency, Milw., 1965-69, Boston Children's Hosp., 1969-70; hon. staff Addison Gilbert Hosp, Gloucester, Mass.; chief med. officer Medic Ambulance Svc., Vallejo, Calif.; field staff surveyor Commn. on Cancer/ACS, Folsom, Calif. Exec. com Sacramento Ballet Co., bd. dirs. Mem. ACS, Am. Coll. Physician Execs., Essex Surg. Soc., Mass. Med. Soc. Office: 560 Couch St Vallejo CA 94590- E-mail: gunn.alex.scott@aya.yale.edu.

GUNN, BERT DENNIS, social worker; b. New Rochelle, N.Y., Sept. 14, 1946; s. David Bolton and Ruth (Davega) Gunn. BS, U. Conn., 1968, MSW, 1970. Lic. clin. social worker, Conn. Social worker United Workers, Norwich, Conn., 1970-74, Conn. Coll., New London, 1974-80; clin. social worker Chaplin, Conn., 1980—. Pub. (newsletter) Another Life, 1990—; editor, pub.: Nahui Mitl, The Journey of the Four Arrows. Bd. dirs. United Svcs., Dayville, Conn., 1989-94; pres. Kalpulli Chaplin, 1990—; coord. Ea. tributary Peace and Dignity Journeys (Mass. to Mexico City Relay Run), 1992; U.S. coord. Tekpan Tonantzin Pyramid of Peace, Mex., 1999—, Zihuakoatl Internat. Confedn. Kalpultin, 2000—. Mem. NASW. Home: 18 Bedlam Rd Chaplin CT 06235-3325 Office: Kalpulli Chaplin 18 Bedlam Rd Chaplin CT 06235-3325 E-mail: bertgunn33@earthlink.net.

GUNN, CAROLYN JEAN, retired elementary school educator; b. Albuquerque, Dec. 8, 1939; d. Eugene Maurice and Ruby Parsons Jontz; m. Gordon McKay, III Gunn, Apr. 12, 1996; 1 child, Dean Carter Hines. BA in Edn., U. N.Mex., 1961; MA in Edn., U. N.Mex, 1968. Cert. tchr. N.Mex. Educator Albuquerque Pub. Schools; ret., 1992. V.p. Academic Advisers Corp., Albuquerque, 1999—2002. Author: Second Grade Learning Methods. Fellow: Pi Beta Phi (assoc.; alumni v.p., treas. 1962—2002, numerous awards 1962—2002). Democrat. Presbyterian. Home: 3413 Harwood Court NE Albuquerque NM 87110-2115 Office: Acad Advisers Corp 3413 Harwood Court NE Albuquerque NM 87110-2115 Home Fax: 505-881-6131; Office Fax: 505-881-6131. Personal E-mail: jeanniegunn@msn.com. E-mail: jeanniegunn@msn.com.

GUNN, CLARE ALWARD, travel consultant, writer, retired educator; b. Grandville, Mich., Oct. 28, 1916; s. Fred Melvin and Lila Barton (Alward) G.; married; children: Thomas, Bruce, Richard, William. BS, Mich. State U., 1940, MS in Land and Water Conservation, 1952; PhD in Landscape Architecture, U. Mich., 1965. Prof. dept. tourism-recreation devel. Mich. State U., East Lansing, 1945-66; vis. prof. tourism Sch. Travel Industry Mgmt. U. Hawaii, 1966-67; prof. tourism-recreation devel. Tex. A&M U., College Station, 1967-74, prof. dept. recreation, park and tourism scis., 1975-85, prof. emeritus, 1985—. Prof. resources recreation Oreg. State U., summer 1974; prof. Sch. Landscape Arthitecture, U. Guelph, Ont., Can., 1974-75; vis. prof. Clemson U., 1989; cons. state tourism plans N.Y., 1986, Okla., 1987, Wash., 1988, Del., 1990, Ill., 1993; cons. analysis tourism potential Whiteman Park, Perth, Australia, 1989; cons. South African Tourism Bd., 1988, natural resource potential for Tourism in Del., 1991; mem. task force Moorea & Tourism, French Polynesia, 1990, tourism

potential Finger Lakes Region, N.Y., 1989-91, resort devel. plan Chun-Cheon Lake Area, Korea, 1991; tourism plan Newfoundland, Labrador, Can., 1994; prepared Agenda Item 13 World Tourism Conf., The Philippines, 1980, major destination zone study for Can., 1982. Author: A Concept for the Design of a Tourism-Recreation Region, 1965, An Annotated Bibliography of Resource Use of the Texas Gulf Coast, 1969, Vacationscape: Designing Tourist Regions, 3d edit., 1997, Chinese edit., 1998, Tourism Planning, 3d edit., 1994, 4th edit., 2002, others; contbr. articles to profl. jours. Mem. George Bush Libr. Com., College Station, 1994; chair adv. com. CVB of Bryan, College Station, 1992-93; mem. sch. bd. Okemos (Mich.) Dist., 1958-64. Recipient Tex. Gov. award, 1984, Disting. Alumni award Landscape Architecture Program, Mich. State U., 1999; named mem. emeritus Internat. Acad. for Study of Tourism, 2001. Fellow Am. Soc. Landscape Architects (Spl. award 1973); mem. Travel and Tourism Rsch. Assn. (bd. dirs., Lifetime Achievement award 2001), Rotary Internat. (chmn. dist. group study exch. com. 1992-93, chair dist. exch. com. 1992-94, Role of Fame award 1990), Gamma Sigma Delta, Epsilon Sigma Phi, Beta Gamma Sigma, Phi Kappa Phi, Sigma Lambda Alpha (Disting. Mem. award 1991). Republican. Methodist. Avocations: photography, travel, sketching. Home: 1602 Glade St College Station TX 77840-4365

GUNN, ELIZABETH MARKS, educator; b. Richmond, Va., Aug. 21, 1946; d. Richard Harrison Jr. and Carrie Lee Chewning Marks; stepfather, Albert Kash; stepmother, Blanche Kash Clark; m. Richard McDowell Gunn, Aug. 3, 1968 (div. June 1989): m. Don Eldon Kash, July 27, 1995; 1 child, Andrew McDowell Gunn; stepchildren: Kelli Mulloy, Jeffrey Kash. BA, Mary Baldwin Coll., 1968; MLS, U. Okla., 1975, MPA, 1981, PhD, 1986. Social worker State of Del., Dover, 1969-71, State of Iowa, Des Moines, 1972-74; mem. faculty U. Okla., Norman, 1975-94; sr. analyst Office Tech. Assessment, Washington, 1993-95; sr. analyst, office of sci. and tech. policy Exec. Office of the Pres., Washington, 1995-96; vis. asst. prof. George Mason U., Fairfax, Va., 1996-98, assoc. prof., 1998—. Mem. editl. bd. Internat. Jour. Global Environ. Issues, London, 2000—. Morris K. Udall fellow Office Tech. Assessment, 1993-94. Mem. AAAS (Sci. and Engring. Congl. fellow 1993-94), AWIS. Home: 3428 Stoneybrae Dr Falls Church VA 22044-1227 Office: George Mason U MSN5D3 4400 University Drive Fairfax VA 22030-4444 Fax: (703) 993-1439. E-mail: egunn@gmu.edu.

GUNN, GILES BUCKINGHAM, language educator, religious studies educator, global and international studies educator; b. Evanston, Ill., Jan. 9, 1938; s. Buckingham Willcox and Janet (Fargo) G.; m. Janet Mears Varner, Dec. 29, 1969 (div. July 1983); 1 child, Adam Buckingham; m. Deborah Rose Sills, July 9, 1983; 1 child, Abigail Rose. BA, Amherst Coll., 1959; student, Episc. Theol. Sch., Cambridge, Mass., 1959-60; MA, U. Chgo., 1963, PhD, 1967. Prof. religion and lit. U. Chgo., 1966-74; prof. religion and Am. studies U. N.C., Chapel Hill, 1974-85; prof. English and Religion U. Fla., 1984-85; prof. English U. Calif., Santa Barbara, 1985—, chmn. English dept., 1993-97, prof. global and internat. studies, 1998—, chmn. global studies, 2001—. Vis. asst. prof. religion Stanford U., Palo Alto, Calif., 1973; Benedict Disting. vis. prof. religion Carleton Coll., Northfield, Minn., 1977; William R. Kenan Disting. vis. prof. humanities Coll. William and Mary, Williamsburg, Va., 1983-84; Humanities Disting. vis. prof. U. Colo., 1989; Eric Yoegelin Disting. prof. Am. Studies, U. Munich, 1994-95; dir. NEH summer sems. for coll. and univ. tchrs., 1979, 81, 85, 94, for sch. tchrs., 1987, 88, 89, 91; cons. Libr. of Am. Author: F.O. Matthiessen, The Critical Achievement, 1975, The Interpretation of Otherness: Literature, Religion and the American Imagination, 1979, The Culture of Criticism and The Criticism of Culture, 1987, Thinking Across the American Grain: Ideology, Intellect, and the New Pragmatism, 1992, Beyond Solidarity: Pragmatism and Difference in a Globalised World, 2001; editor: Literature and Religion, 1971, Henry James, Senior: A Selection of His Writings, 1974, New World Metaphysics: Readings on the Religious Meaning of the American Experience, 1981, The Bible and American Arts and Letters, 1983, Church, State, and American Culture, 1984, Early American Writing, 1994, William James, Pragmatism and Other Writings, 2000; co-editor: Redrawing the Boundaries: The Transformation of English and American Literary Studies, 1992; contbr. numerous articles to profl. jours. Bd. dirs. Fund for Santa Barbara. Edward John Noble Leadership grantee, 1959-63; Amherst-Doshisha fellow, Kyoto, Japan, 1960-61, Kent fellow, Danforth Found., 1963-65, Guggenheim fellow, 1978-79, Nat. Endowment for Humanities fellow, 1990, U. Calif. Pres.'s Rsch. fellow, 1990; Phi Beta Kappa vis. scholar, 2000-01. Mem. MLA, Am. Acad. Religion (dir. research and pubs. 1974-77), Am. Studies Assn., Soc. Religion, Arts and Contemporary Culture, Soc. Am. Phil., Nat. Critics Book Circle. Democrat. Avocations: walking, motorcycling, traveling. Office: U Calif Dept English Santa Barbara CA 93106 Home: 5488 Rincon Beach Park Dr Ventura CA 93001-9749

GUNN, GORDON MCKAY, III, retired investment banker, retired entrepreneur; b. El Paso, Tex., Jan. 25, 1939; s. Gordon McKay, Jr. and Barbara Ann Gunn; m. Carolyn Jean Hines, Apr. 12, 1996; children: Gordon McKay, IV, Walter Martin, Tyler Christopher, Carson Porter, Jason Martin, Kimberly Marisa. MBA(hon.), Pace Coll., 1973. Exec. v.p. IBM Corp., Armonk, NY, 1966—73; founder TicketMaster Corp., Phoenix, 1975—80; pres. Acad. Advisers Corp., Albuquerque, 1992—. Buena Comida Corp., Albuquerque, 1994—98. V.p. Verdugo Hills coun. Boy Scouts Am., Glendale; dir. Glendale Kiwanis, Glendale, Calif., 1981—91. Master: Toastmasters Internat. (State Winner 1975, 1976). Republican. Presbyterian. Avocations: physical fitness, tennis, automobile restoration, flying. Home: 3413 Harwood Court NE Albuquerque NM 87110-2115 Office: Academic Advisers Corp 3413 Harwood Court NE Albuquerque NM 87110-2115 Home Fax: 595-881-6131; Office Fax: 505-881-6131. Personal E-mail: gmgunn3rd@msn.com. E-mail: gmgunn3rd@msn.com.

GUNN, JAMES E. English language educator; b. Kansas City, Mo., July 12, 1923; s. J. Wayne and Elsie M. (Hutchison) G.; m. Jane Frances Anderson, Feb. 6, 1947; children: Christopher Wayne, Kevin Robert. BS, U. Kans., 1947, MA, 1951. Editor Western Printing and Litho, Racine, Wis., 1951-52; asst. dir. Civil Def., Kansas City, Mo., 1953; instr. U. Kans., Lawrence, 1955, mng. editor Alumni Assn., 1956-58, adminstrv. asst. to the chancellor for univ. rels., 1958-70, lectr. English, 1970-74, prof., 1974-93, emeritus prof., 1993—. Cons. Easton Press, Norwalk, Conn., 1985-98; lectr. in field. Author: over 25 books including Station in Space, 1958, The Immortals, 1962, The End of Dreams, 1975, Alternate Worlds: The Illustrated History of Science Fiction (World Sci. Fiction Conv. Spl. award, 1976, Pilgrim award Sci. Fiction Rsch. Assn., 1976), The Listeners, 1972, The Dreamers, 1980, Isaac Asimov: The Foundations of Science Fiction, 1982 (Hugo award World Sci. Fiction Conv., 1983), The Science of Science-Fiction Writing, 2000, The Millennium Blues, 2001, Human Voices, 2002, numerous plays, screenplays, radio scripts; editor: The Road to Science Fictions, 6 vols., 1977—2002, 8 other books; contbr. 99 stories to mags.; contbr. articles. Dir. Ctr. for Study Sci. Fiction, Lawrence, 1984—. Lt. (j.g.) USN, 1943-46, PTO. Recipient Eaton award Eaton Conf., 1992, Hugo award, 1983; Mellon fellow U. Kans., 1981, 84. Mem. Author's Guild, Sci. Fiction and Fantasy Writers Am. (pres. 1971-72), Sci. Fiction Rsch. Assn. (pres. 1981-82, Pilgrim award 1976)., Avocations: golf, bridge. Home: 2215 Orchard Ln Lawrence KS 66049-2707 Office: U Kans English Dept Lawrence KS 66045-0001

GUNN, JANET PENELOPE, engineer; b. Worcester, U.K., Jan. 10, 1954; d. J.B. and Freda Elizabeth (Pilcher) G.; m. Timothy Michael Horn, May 11, 1996. BA in Math., Hampshire Coll., 1975; postgrad., U. N.C., 1975-79. Various positions IBM Research, Yorktown Heights, N.Y., 1972-77; tech. Bell Labs, Holmdel, N.J., 1978; tech. staff, sr. tech staff Network Analysis Corp. (became Contel/GTE), Fairfax, Va., 1979-91; tech. dir. NMI, Fairfax, 1991-93, Price Waterhouse Coopers, Vienna, Va., 1993—2001, Nyquetek Inc., 2001—02, CSC, Chantilly, Va., 2002—. Mem. Commonwealth Dresage and Combined Tng. Assn. (treas. 1988—, bd. dirs.). Avocations: horses, motorcycles.

GUNN, JOAN MARIE, health care administrator; b. Binghamton, N.Y., Jan. 29, 1943; d. Andrew and Ruth Antoinette (Butler) Jacoby; m. Albert E. Gunn, Jr., May 18, 1968; children: Albert E. III, Emily W. Hebert, Andrew R., Clare M. Berchelmann, Catherine A.B., Philip D. Diploma, Binghamton State Hosp., 1966; BS summa cum laude, Tex. Women's U., 1983; MSN, U. Tex., Houston, 1989. RN, N.Y., Tex., Va., Gt. Britain. Staff nurse Columbia/Presbyn. Med. Ctr., N.Y.C., 1966-67; head nurse, ICU Montefiore Hosp. and Med. Ctr., N.Y.C., 1967-68; staff nurse Nat. Orthopedic and Rehab. Hosp., Arlington, Va., 1972-73, Woman's Hosp. of Tex., Houston, 1976-80; staff nurse geriatrics St. Anthony's Ctr., Houston, 1985-86; charge nurse gero psychiatry Bellaire Gen. Hosp., Houston, 1986; from head nurse gero psychiat. unit to dir. patient svcs. Harris County Psychiat. Ctr. U. Tex., Houston, 1986—2001, dir. patient svs. Harris County Psychiat. Ctr., 2001—. Mem. NRA, Nat. Soc. Colonial Dames of the XVII Century, Daus. of Union Vets. of Civil War, Sigma Theta Tau. Roman Catholic. Avocation: reading history. Home: 2329 Watts St Houston TX 77030-1139 Office: U Tex Harris County Psychiat Ctr 2800 S Macgregor Way Houston TX 77021-1032

GUNN, JOSEPH RIDGEWAY, III, consulting economist; b. Ross, Calif., Nov. 28, 1928; s. Joseph Ridgeway, Jr. and Melvine Henrietta (Longley) G.; BS in Bus. Adminstrn., U. Calif., Berkeley, 1954, MA in Econs., 1958; spl. studies Oxford (Eng.) U., 1967; m. Marie Elsie Thurlow, June 16, 1951; children: Dana Carolyn Gunn Winslow, Anita Jayne Gunn Shirley, Janice Marie Gunn Smeallie. Econ. analyst Standard Oil Co., Calif., 1954-61; econ. adv. Ministry Commerce, Govt. Afghanistan, Kabul, 1961-67; cons. economist, 1967—95; sr. v.p. Nathan Assocs., Inc., Arlington, Va., 1986—1995, chmn. bd. dirs. 2001-, Mem. Am. Econ. Assn., Asia Soc., Cosmos Club. Democrat. Episcopalian. Author articles, reports. Home: 10917 Picasso Ln Potomac MD 20854-1711 Office: Nathan Assocs Inc 2101 Wilson Blvd Arlington VA 22201-3062

GUNN, LARRY CHARLES, physician; b. Amarillo, Tex., Jan. 3, 1939; Student, Purdue U., 1956-58, U. Ill., 1958-59, MD, 1963. Intern U. Ill. Hosp., 1963-64, resident, 1964-68; with Hinsdale (Ill.) Hosp., asst. dir. breast care ctr.; with Good Samaritan Hosp., Downers Grove, Ill. Asst. prof. surgery U. Ill. Mem. AMA, Am. Coll. Surgeons, Alpha Omega Alpha. Home: 34 Briarwood S Oak Brook IL 60523-8703 Office: 908 N Elm St Hinsdale IL 60521-3635

GUNN, LEE FREDRIC, career officer; Grad., UCLA, 1965. Commd. ensign USN, 1965, advanced through ranks to vice-adm.; various assignments to comdr. Amphibious Group Three and Combined Naval Forces; inspector gen. Dept. of the Navy. Decorated Disting. Svc. medal, Def. Superior Svc. medal, Legions of Merit (6 times), Meritorious Svc. medal (2 times), Navy Commendation medal with Combat V, Navy Achievement medal, others.

GUNN, MARY ELIZABETH, retired English language educator; b. Great Bend, Kans., July 21, 1914; d. Ernest E. and Elisabeth (Wesley) Eppstein; m. Charles Leonard Gunn, Sept. 13, 1936 (dec. Apr. 1985); 1 child, Charles Douglas. AB, Ft. Hays State U., 1935, BS in Edn., 1936, MA, 1967. Tchr. English Unified Sch. Dist. 428, Great Bend, 1963-80, Barton County C.C., Great Bend, 1977-84, tchr. adult edn., 1985-87, tchr. ESL, 1988-94; ret., 1994. Conf. Am. Studies fellow De Pauw U., 1969; recipient Nat. Cmty. Svc. award DAR, 1996. Mem. AAUW (Outstanding Mem. 1991), NEA, Bus. and Profl. Women (Woman of Yr. 1974), Kans. Adult Edn. Assn. (Master Adult Educator 1986), Kans. Assn. Tchrs. English, PEO, Delta Kappa Gamma, Alpha Sigma Alpha. Democrat. Mem. United Ch. of Christ. Avocations: travel, driving, needlepoint, crossword puzzles, reading. Home: 3009 16th St Great Bend KS 67530-3705

GUNN, MICHAEL PETER, lawyer; b. St. Louis, Oct. 18, 1944; s. Donald and Loretto Agnes (Hennelly) G.; m. Carolyn Ormsby Ritter, Nov. 27, 1969; children: Mark Thomas, Christopher Michael, John Ritter, Elizabeth Jane. JD, St. Louis U., 1968. Bar: Mo. 1968, U.S. Dist. Ct. (ea and we. dists.) Mo. 1968, U.S. Tax Ct. 1972. Assoc. Gunn & Gunn, St. Louis, 1968-81; ptnr. Gunn & Lane, St. Louis, 1981-86; pvt. practice Ballwin, Mo., 1986—. Rep. ea. dist. Mo. Ct. Appeals. Sgt. U.S. Army, 1969-75. Mem. ABA (ho. of dels. 1988—), St. Louis Bar Assn., The Mo. Bar (bd. govs. 1990-2001, exec. com. 1993-94, pres.-elect 1998-99, pres. 1999-2000), Lawyers Assn. St. Louis (pres. 1981-82), St. Louis Bar Found. (pres. 1988-89), Bar Assn. Met. St. Louis (pres. 1987-88), Nat. Conf. Bar Founds. (trustee 1990-95, pres. 1993-94). Roman Catholic. Home: 2232 Centeroyal Dr Saint Louis MO 63131-1910 Office: The Gunn Law Firm PC Ste 240 1714 Deer Tracks Trail Saint Louis MO 63131

GUNN, MOREY WALKER, JR., secondary education educator, choir director, organist; b. Orangeburg, S.C., June 23, 1939; s. Morey Walker Sr. and Marjorie (Dusek) G.; m. Sheila Dianne Taylor, Nov. 26, 1994; 1 child, Andrew Walker. BA in Music, Furman U., 1961, MA, 1967. Cert. specialist music edn. tchr., S.C. Band dir. Holly Hill (S.C.) H.S., 1961-65, Orangeburg H.S., 1965-71, Greer (S.C.) H.S., 1971-73, Ft. Johnson H.S., Charleston, SC, 1973-77, Berkeley County Schs., Goose Creek, SC, 1978-92; organist St. Andrews United Meth. Ch., 1992—. Mem. Nat. Rep. Senatorial Com. 1978-97; deacon 1st Presbyn, Ch., 1965-71; elder James Island Presbyn. Ch., 1974-76, 78-80, choir dir., organist, 1965-94; organist St. Andrews United Meth. Ch., Orangeburg, S.C., 1994—; bd. dirs. excellence in tchg. award com. Charleston County Youth Symphony, 1975; bd. dirs. Charles Towne Landing Band Festival Com., 1988-89; class agt. Furman U., 2003—. Mem. Am. Guild Organists, Sertoma Club (bd. dirs. 1989-90), Kiwanis Club (bd. dirs. 1997-2001, sec. 1998-99, pres. 1999-2000, Disting. sec. 1998-99, Disting. pres. 1999-2000, Disting. Kiwanian award 1998-2000), Hibernian Soc., Elks, Phi Mu Alpha (hon. life). Avocations: dancing, reading, dining out, family outings, collecting seascape prints. Home: 2 Waters Edge Ct Charleston SC 29414-7327

GUNN, THOM(SON) (THOMSON WILLIAM GUNN), poet, retired English educator; b. Gravesend, Eng., Aug. 29, 1929; came to U.S., 1954; s. Herbert Smith and Ann Charlotte (Thomson) G. BA, Trinity Coll., Cambridge (Eng.) U., 1953. Tchr. English, sr. lectr. U. Calif., Berkeley, 1958-66, 73-99; ret., 1999. Author: Fighting Terms, 1954, The Sense of Movement, 1957, My Sad Captains, 1961, Touch, 1967, Moly, 1971, Jack Straw's Castle and Other Poems, 1976, Selected Poems, 1979, The Passages of Joy, 1982, The Occasions of Poetry, 1982, expanded edit., 1985, The Man with Night Sweats, 1992, Shelf Life, 1993, Collected Poems, 1993, Boss Cupid, 2000. Recipient Robert Kirsch award L.A. Times, 1988, Shelley Meml. award Poetry Soc. Am., 1990, Forward 1st prize, 1992, Bay Area Book Reviewers award for poetry, 1973, 93, PEN USA West Poetry award, 1973, 93, Lenore Marshall Poetry prize, 1993, Medal of Merit for poetry Am. Acad. Arts and Letters, 1998, David Cohen prize for lit., 2003; Lila Wallace Reader's Digest grantee, 1991; MacArthur fellow, 1993. Address: 1216 Cole St San Francisco CA 94117-4322

GUNNELS, LEE O. retired finance and management educator, manufacturing/research company director, inventor; b. Huntington Park, Calif., Sept. 11, 1933; s. LeRoy O. and Marrion W. Gunnels; m. Laura Gunnels, Nov. 7, 1958; children: Cornelia, Amelia, Sarah. BA in Math./Physics, U. Hawaii, 1960; MBA, Xavier U., Cin., 1970, PhD in Edn., 1983. Nuc. physicist Battelle Meml. Inst., Columbus, Ohio; ret. assoc. prof. fin. and mgmt. Muskingum Tech. Coll., Zanesville, Ohio, past chmn. faculty senate; inventor, developer Gunnels Rsch. LLC. Contbr. articles to various publs. Home: 1849 Drugan Ct SW Reynoldsburg OH 43068-8181 also: Stoney Meadow Farms Adamsville OH 43802

GUNNER, MURRAY, religious organization administrator; b. NYC, Mar. 26, 1918; s. Abraham and Sadie (Schnee) G.; m. Pearl O. Katz, June 12, 1949; children: Marilyn Ruth, Janet Marie. BS, CCNY, 1938; MSW, Columbia U., 1946; cert., Hebrew U., 1971. Cert. social worker. Social worker, acting supr. N.Y.C. Dept. Welfare and Camp LaGuardia, 1940-45; adminstrv. asst. Coun. House, St. Louis, 1946-50; program dir. Jewish Community Ctr., Hartford, Conn., 1950-54, exec. dir. Newburgh, N.Y., 1954-62, Bklyn., 1962-66, Yonkers, N.Y., 1966-83; cons. Jewish Community Ctr., Jewish Fedn., 1983-89; exec. dir. Jewish Coun. of Yonkers, 1989—. Cons. Hudson River Mus., Elizabeth Seton Coll., 1989-89; co-chmn. commn. of synagogue rels. United Jewish Appeal Fedn., N.Y.C., 1980-81, co-chmn. Jewish Community Ctrs., 1981-82; co-chair adult edn. com. Greystone Jewish Ctr., Yonkers, 1980-82, bd. dirs., 1978-80. Contbr. author to various books. Active Charter Revision Commn., Yonkers, 1979, Mayor's Holocaust Commn. Yonkers, 1979, Mayor's Com. on Jewish Affairs, Yonkers, 1990—, Yonkers Crime Commn., 1975, Yonkers Mental Health Coun., 1978—83, Mayor's Cmty. Rels. Com., Yonkers, 1992—, task force City/County Youth Violence; exec. com. Edn. 2000, Yonkers, 1992; cmty. planning coun. Substance Abuse Prevention Com., 1997—; shared decision making commn. Gorton H.S., 1997; exec. com. Yonkers Mayor's Cmty. Rels. Commn., 1997; edn. com. Yonkers City Coun., 1998—; chair Yonkers Flag Day Commn., 1998; mem. Yonkers Family and Cmty. project Columbia U., 1998, N.Y. State Assemblyman Adv. Com., 1997; active Yonker Mayor's Health Commn., 1998—2002; older adults com. Yonkers Mayor Health Commn., 1999; active Older Adult Task Force, Substance Abuse Task Force; apptd. mem. partnership com. Yonkers Bd. Edn., 1999; apptd. bd. dirs. Yonkers Libr. Found., 2001; apptd. by Benedict Found. Elder-Friendly Com., City of Yonkers, 2001; apptd. sec. adv. com. Westchester Jewish Chronicle; apptd. Yonkers Libr. Found. Commn., 2001; adv. com. to senator N.Y. State Senate, 1997—; active Mentoring Com. for Youth at Risk, 1993, Mayor's Commn. on AIDS, 1997—; bd. dirs. Greystone Jewish Ctr., 2000—, Yonkers United Way, 1981—83, Cmty. Planning Agy., Yonkers, 1992—. Recipient Israel Cummings award Commn. on Synagogue Rels. Fedn., 1963, cert. of merit, 1992, Am. Com. on Italian Migration, 1992, cert. of recognition for outstanding svc. and contbns. Charles Gorton H.S., Yonkers, 1995, Yonkers Martin Luther King Commn. award, 1995, Cmty. Svc. award Mayor of City of Yonkers, 1995, Multi-Cultural Edn. award Yonkers Pub. Schs., 1998, honors for outstanding leadership Westchester County Exec. Dirs., 2001, Outstanding Leadership award S.W. Yonkers Planning Assn., 2001, Outstanding Profl. award Westchester County Execs. of U. A Fedn., Humanitarian award, C. of C., 2002, Griffon award Untrmeyer Performing Arts Coun., 2002; honored for cmty. svc. Jewish Coun. Yonkers Bd. Dirs., City of Yonkers, County of Westchester, U.S. Congress, Rockland County YM-YWHA, 1998; Murray Gunner Day named in his honor City of Yonkers, 1983, County of Westchester, 1983; named guest of honor Westchester chpt. Am. Heart Assn., 1997. Mem.: NASW (Gold Care mem., Disting. Svc. award Westchester chpt. 2001, Lifetime Achievement award N.Y. State chpt. 2001), Rotary (chair pub. rels. com. 1988, chair cmty. svcs., bd. dirs. 1993—94, Paul Harris fellow 1994). Home: 10 Gateway Rd Yonkers NY 10703-1200 Office: Jewish Coun of Yonkers 584 N Broadway Yonkers NY 10701-1731 *The struggle for survival we face each day, can be exhilerating or threatening. The manner, in which we handle each challenge, is dependent on the degree of our faith in God, coupled with the strength of belief in ourselves.*

GUNNESS, ROBERT CHARLES, retired chemical engineer; b. Fargo, N.D., July 28, 1911; s. Christian I. and Elizabeth (Rice) G.; m. Beverly Osterberger, June 18, 1936; children: Robert Charles, Donald Austin, Beverly Anne. BS, U. Mass., Amherst, 1932; MS, MIT, 1934, D.Sc., 1936. Asst. prof. chem. engring. MIT, 1936-38; research dept. Standard Oil Co. Ind., 1938-47, mgr. research, 1947-51, asst. gen. mgr. mfg., gen. mgr. supply and transp., 1952-56, exec. v.p., 1956-65, pres., 1965-74, vice chmn., 1974-75, dir., 1953-75. Vice chmn. research and devel. bd. Dept. Def., 1951 Trustee U. Chgo., Rush-Presbyn.-St. Lukes Hosp., life mem. Mass. Inst. Tech. Corp.; past chmn. Nat. Merit Scholarship Corp.; past pres., trustee John Crerar Library. Fellow Am. Inst. Chem. Engrs. (council 1951); mem. Nat. Acad. Engring., Am. Chem. Soc., Am. Acad. Arts and Scis., Sigma Xi, Phi Kappa Phi, Kappa Sigma. Home: 852 Morningside Dr Fullerton CA 92835-3546

GUNNING, FRANCIS PATRICK, lawyer, insurance association executive; b. Scranton, Pa., Dec. 10, 1923; s. Frank Peter and Mary Loretta (Kelly) G.; m. Nancy C. Hill, Aug. 10, 1951; 1 son, Brian F. Student, City Coll. N.Y., 1941-43; LLB, St. John's U., 1950. Bar: N.Y. 1950. Legal editor Prentice Hall Pub. Co., N.Y.C., 1950-51; legal specialist Tchrs. Ins. & Annuity Assn. Am., Coll. Retirement Equities Fund, N.Y.C., 1951-53, asst. counsel, 1953-57, assoc. counsel, 1957-60, counsel, 1960-65, asst. gen. counsel, 1965-67, assoc. gen. counsel, 1967, v.p., assoc. gen. counsel, 1967-73, sr. v.p., gen. counsel, 1973-74, exec. v.p., gen. counsel, 1974-88, ret., 1988. Trustee, mem. exec. and audit coms. Mortgage Growth Investors (now MGI Properties). Contbr. articles on mortgage financing to profl. jours. With USAAF, 1943-46. Mem. ABA, N.Y. State Bar Assn., Am. Land Title Assn., Am. Law Inst., Assn. of Bar of City of N.Y., Assn. Life Ins. Counsel, Nat. Assn. Coll. Univ. Attys., Am. Coll. Real Estate Lawyers. Republican. Roman Catholic. Home and Office: 32 Kewanee Rd New Rochelle NY 10804-1324

GUNNING, ROBERT CLIFFORD, mathematician, educator; b. Longmont, Colo., Nov. 27, 1931; s. Clifford Henry and Inez (Wilhelm) G.; m. Wanda S. Holtzinger, July 9, 1966. AB, U. Colo., 1952; MA, Princeton U., 1953, PhD, 1955. NSF fellow U. Chgo., 1955-56; mem. faculty Princeton U., 1956—, prof. math., 1966—, chmn. dept., 1976-79, dean of faculty, 1989-95. Vis. prof. U. São Paulo, Brazil, 1957, U. Munich, 1967, ULCA, 1972, Oxford (Eng.) U., spring 1968, fall, 1980, 88, 95; Sloan fellow, 1958-61; asst. dir. studies, math. St. Catharines Coll., Cambridge (Eng.) U., 1959-60; mem. editl. bd. Princeton (N.J.) U. Press, 1969-73. Author: Lectures on Modular Forms, 1962, (with H. Rossi) Analytic Functions of Several Complex Variables, 1965, Lectures on Riemann Surfaces, Vol. I, 1966, Vol. II, 1967, Vol. III, 1972, Complex Analytic Varieties, Vol. I, 1970, Vol. II, 1974, Generalized Theta Functions, 1976, Uniformization of Complex Manifolds, 1978, Introduction to Holomorphic Functions of Several Variables, 3 vols., 1990; editor: Problems in Analysis, 1970, Theta Functions, 1989, Collected Papers of Salomon Bochner, 4 vols., 1991; contbr. articles to profl. jours. Fellow AAAS; mem. Am. Math. Soc., Princeton Club (N.Y.C.), Nassau Club (Princeton), Phi Beta Kappa, Sigma Xi. Episcopalian. Office: Fine Hall Washington Rd Princeton NJ 08544-1000

GUNNING, TOM, art educator; PhD in Cinema Studies, NYU. Prof. dept. art history U. Chgo. Author: (book) D.W. Griffith and the Origins of American Narrative Film: The Early Years, 1991; contbr. Guggenheim fellow, 1998. Office: Dept Art History U Chgo 5540 S Greenwood Ave Chicago IL 60637-1506 Fax: 773-702-5901. E-mail: tgunning@midway.uchicago.edu.

GUNSALUS, CAROLYN KRISTINA, law educator, consultant; b. Urbana, Ill., Oct. 1, 1957; d. I.C. and Carolyn Foust Gunsalus; m. Michael Walker, July 21, 1979; children: Kearney T., Anna Shea. AB with distinction, U. Ill., 1978, JD magna cum laude, 1984. Bar: Ill. 1984. Specialist in automated edn. Plato Lab, Uiuc U. Ill., Urbana, 1974—84, assoc. vice chancellor rsch., 1989—94, assoc. provost, 1994—2002, spl. counsel, adj. prof., 2002—. Cons. computer sci. and tech. bd. NRC, Washington, 1988-90. Contbr. articles to profl. jours. Active Urbana Planning Commn., 1983-91; bd. dirs. Planned Parenthood Assn. Champaign County, 1987-91, bd. dirs., East Cen. Ill., 1991-93; active Urbana Dist. #116 Bd. Edn., 1991—, pres., 1994-97. Recipient Lifetime award meritorious svc., PTA, Urbana, Champaign, Ill.; Kellogg Nat. Leadership fellow, Kellogg Found., 1984. Mem. ABA (patent, trademark and copyright law sect.), Ill. Bar Assn., Nat. Assn. State Univs. and Land Grant Colls. (higher edn. tech. com. 1986—, tax com. 1988—), Nat. Coun. Univ. Rsrch. Adminstrs., Soc. Univ. Patent Adminstrs., Licensing Execs. Soc., AAAS (com. on sci. freedom and responsibility 1991-97, chair 1993-97). Office: U Ill Coll Law 504 E Pennsylvania Ave Champaign IL 61820-5711 E-mail: gunsalus@uiuc.edu.

GUNSEL, SELDA, chemical engineer, researcher; b. Istanbul, Turkey, Nov. 10, 1958; d. Nejat and Hikmet (Suntekin) G.; m. Donald Lee Pferdehirt, June 6, 1987; children: Melisa, Lara. BSc in Chem. Engring., Istanbul Tech. U., 1981; MSc in Chem. Engring., Pa. State U., 1983, PhD in Chem. Engring., 1986. Advanced rsch. engr. Pennzoil Prods. Co., The Woodlands, Tex., 1986-90, sr. rsch. engr., 1990-94, rsch. assoc., 1994-97, sr. rsch. assoc., 1997-98, dir. tech. devel., 1999-2000, v.p. tech. devel., 2000—02; bus. team mgr. automotive lubricants Shell Global Solutions (U.S.) Inc., Houston, 2002—. Editor: Current Research in Tribology in North Am., 1993; mem. editl. rev. bd. CRC Handbook Lubrication and Tribology, Vol. III; mem. editl. bd., Jour. of Lubrication Sci.; Assoc. editor, Lubrication Engrg. Jour., contbr. articles to profl. jours. Fellow Soc. Tribologists Lubrication Engr. (exec. com. 2000-); mem. Am. Chem. Soc., Am. Soc. Heating, Refrigeration, Air Conditioning Engrs., Soc. Automotive Engrs. (Excellence in Oral Presentation 1996, chmn. lubricant rsch. award bd. 1997-99), Soc. Tribologists and Lubrication Engrs. (Captain Alfred E. Hunt award 1998, bd. dirs. 1996—, instr. edn. courses 1990, 97, 99), Sigma Xi, Phi Lambda Upsilon. Achievements include patents for non-aqueous lamellar liquid crystalline lubricants, liquid crystal-surfactant technology; contributions in the field of lubrication science and tribology; leadership in the advancement of knowledge and application of science and lubrication and tribology; research in areas of thermal/oxidative stability of lubricants, friction/wear mechanisms in boundary and elastohydrodynamic lubrication, vapor-phase lubricants, liquid crystal lubricants, refrigeration lubricants. Office: Shell Global Solutions (US) Inc Westhollow Tech Ctr 3333 Hwy 6 S Houston TX 77082

GUNTER, BRADLEY HUNT, capital management executive; b. Norfolk, Va., Dec. 8, 1940; s. J.A. and Virginia (Whalen) G.; m. Susan Mason Hart, Dec. 27, 1962 (div. 1977); children: Bradley Hunt, Valerie Mason; m. Anne A. Macon, Nov. 7, 1985 (dec. 1994); 1 child, Bradford Macon Gunter; m. Meredith Laura Strohm, Dec. 16, 1994. BA, U. Richmond, 1962; MA, U. Va., 1963, PhD, 1969.

Instr. Washington and Lee U., Lexington, Va., 1967-69; asst. prof. Boston Coll., 1969-71; editor Econ. Rev. Fed. Res. Bank, Richmond, Va., 1971—80; pres. Bartleby's Inc., Richmond, 1980-85; dir. found. rels. U. Va., Charlottesville, 1985-86; investment broker Scott and String fellow, Richmond, 1987-89; mng. dir. Scott & Stringfellow Capital Mgmt., Richmond, 1989-97, pres., CEO, 1997—2000; pres. Investment Mgmt. of Va., LLC, Richmond, 2000—03, Charlottesville, Va., 2000—03. Cons. NEH, Washington, 1975-80. Author: Studies in The Waste Land, 1971, Guide to T.S. Eliot, 1970, Checklist of T.S. Eliot, 1969; contbr. articles to profl. jours. Vestryman St. Paul's Ch., Richmond, 1975-78; chmn. fund drive United Way, Richmond, 1980; mem. arts and scis. alumni coun. U. Va., mem. Emeritus Soc., Coll. Found., Annual Giving Adv. Bd.; pres., bd. dirs. New Va. Review; bd. dirs. Va. Ctr. for the Book, U. Va. Cancer Ctr., St. Christopher's Sch. Found., Richmond, 1981-85, Richmond Ballet, Big Bros. Richmond Inc., Va. Found. for Humanities and Pub. Policy, Scott and Stringfelow Ednl. Found., Elk Hill Farm; trustee St. Paul's Endowment Fund, Inc., United Way Greater Richmond; pres. Arts Coun. Richmond, Hist. Richmond Found., Poe Found., Va. Ctr. for the Book; bd. dirs., chmn. U. Va. Cancer Ctr., U. Va. Health Scis. Coun., U. Va. Libr. Bd.; mem. regional bd. Sorensen Inst. for Polit. Leadership; mem. U. Va. Ann. Giving Adv. Bd. Mem. Richmond Assn. Bus. Economists, Assn. for Investment Mgmt. and Rsch., U. Va. Alumni Assn. (chpt. pres. Richmond 1981), Va. Soc. Mayflower Descs. (bd. dirs.), Country Club Va., Colonnade Club, Focus Club, Univ. Club, Farmington Country Club, Phi Beta Kappa, Omicron Delta Kappa. Episcopalian. Avocations: tennis, walking. Office: Investment Mgmt of Va 310 4th St NE Charlottesville VA 22902-5266 E-mail: bradhg@adelphia.net.

GUNTER, CHRISTIE D. geneticist; PhD, Emory U., Atlanta, 1998. Postdoctoral fellow dept. genetics Case Western Res. U., Cleve., 1998-2001; assoc. editor Nature Mag., 2002—. Editl. fellow Human Molecular Genetics jour., 2000-2001. Recipient Pres.'s award U. Ga., 1992, Nat. Rsch. Svc. award NIH, 2000. Mem. Am. Soc. Human Genetics, Coun. of Sci. Editors, Sigma Xi. Office: 968 Nat Press Bldg 529 14th St NW Washington DC 20045 E-mail: girlscientist@yahoo.com.

GUNTER, EMILY DIANE, communications executive, marketing professional, real estate developer, author, educator; b. Atlantic City, N.J., Apr. 5, 1948; d. Fay Gaffney and Verlee (Wright) G.; children: Saliha, Kadir, Amin, Shedia. BA in Math. Stats., Am. U., 1970, postgrad., 1971, San Diego C.C., 1986. Cert. Qualtec Total Quality mgmt. trainer. Traffic engr. C&P Bell, Washington, 1970-71; market analyst Market Towers Inc., Atlantic City, N.J., 1978-79; outside plant engr. N.J. Bell, Atlantic City, 1979-81; market analyst Empcor Group, Atlantic City, 1981-83; outside plant engr. Pacific Bell, San Diego, 1983-91, account exec., 1991-93; v.p. Black Am. of Achievement, Inc., San Diego, 1994-95; founder Women's Wholistic Enpowerment Ctr., 1996-97; pres. Gunter Devel. Enterprises, 1987—. Lectr. women and minorities in engrng. and math. Princeton (N.J.) U., 1979-81, Atlantic C.C., Atlantic City, 1979-81; customer coord. Pacific Bell-Telsam, San Diego, 1983-85; prof. math. Grossmont Coll., 1992-94, instr. super learning skills seminar, 1992—; motivational spkr. Author: Superlearning 2000: The New Technologies of Self-Empowerment, 1993, Supermath 2000: How to Learn Math Without Fear, 1993, Achieve Goals 2000: A Personal Handbook for the Lifelong Learner, 1995, Living, Learning & Healing Through the Right Use of Your Mind, 1996, SL2000 Learning Made Easy-Everybody Can Learn, 1997, A Rite of Passage to Spiritual Enlightenment-Living with Compassion, 2000, Whole Women-Whole World, 2003. Bd. dirs. Lead, San Diego, Atlantic City Transp. Authority, 1981-82, San Diego Urban Math. Collaborative; trustee Reuben H. Fleet Sci. Found., 1989, San Diego Sci. Found., 1989-97, 1990 class Lead-Leadership Edn. Awareness Devel., San Diego; mem. steering com. United Negro Coll. Fund, San Diego; mem. Atlantic City Urban Area Transp. Commn., 1982-83; mem. Am. Humanics Bd. U. San Deigo, 1991-91; pres. bd. World Beat Cultural Ctr., Balboa Park, Calif., 1992-93; internat. exec. dir. Rites of Passage Youth Empowerment Programs of Am., 1997—; youth advocate, chmn., founder and CEO Rites of Passage Youth Empowerment Found., 1998; chmn. and CEO Heart of Africa Holding Corp., 1998—. Mem. African Am. Womens Conf., Women on Tour (exec. bd. 1992—), Coalition Women's Groups (bd. dirs. 1996-97), Sigma Gamma Rho (hon. mem., rites of passage coord. 1996—). Democrat. Avocations: chess, painting, water aerobics, walking, piano. Home: PO Box 72372 Durham NC 27722-2372 also: Gunter Devel Enterprises PO Box 72372 Durham NC 27722-2372 Fax: 919-403-8885. E-mail: edgunter@ritesofpassageonline.org.

GUNTER, JOSEPH CLIFFORD, III, lawyer; b. Ft. Worth, Apr. 26, 1943; s. Joseph Cliford Jr. and Helen (Wright) G.; children: Joseph Clifford IV, Grant Norwood. BA, U. Tex., 1965, JD, 1967. Bar: Tex. 1967. Assoc. McDonald Sanders Ginsberg New Kirk Gibson & Webb, Ft. Worth, 1967-68; ptnr. Bracewell & Patterson, Houston, 1968—. Adv. Am. Bd. Trial Advocates. Lt. USNR, 1967-73. Fellow Am. Coll. Trial Lawyers, Tex. Bar Found., Houston Bar Found.; mem. ABA, State Bar Tex., State Bar Colo. Episcopalian. Avocations: golf, tennis. skiing, sailing. Office: Bracewell & Patterson 711 Louisiana St Ste 2900 Houston TX 77002-2781 E-mail: clifford.gunter@bracepatt.com.

GUNTER, MICHAEL DONWELL, lawyer; b. Gastonia, N.C., Mar. 26, 1947; s. Daniel Cornelius and DeNorma Joyce (Smith) G.; m. Barbara Jo Benson, June 19, 1970; children: Kimberly Elizabeth, Daniel Cornelius III. BA in History with honors, Wake Forest U., 1969; JD with honors, U. N.C., 1972; MBA with honors, U. Pa., 1973. Bar: N.C. 1972, U.S. Dist. Ct. (mid. dist.) N.C. 1974, U.S. Tax Ct. 1975, U.S. Supreme Ct. 1979, U.S. Claims Ct. 1982, U.S. Ct. Appeals (D.C. cir.) 1985, U.S. Ct. Appeals (4th cir.) 1992. Ptnr. Womble Carlyle Sandridge & Rice PLLC, Winston-Salem, N.C., 1974—; chmn. employee benefits practice group. Bd. dirs. G & J Enterprises Inc., Gastonia, Indsl. Belting Inc., Gastonia. Contbr. articles to profl. jours. Coach youth basketball Winston-Salem YMCA, 1981-90; advisor Winston-Salem United Way Christmas Cheer Toy Shop, 1975; fundraiser Deacon Club Wake Forest U., also mem. exec. com., strategic planning com., athletic coun., 1987—, v.p., pres., 1990-92; bd. dirs. Goodwill Industries, Winston-Salem, 1987—, chmn. bd., sec., chmn. fin. com.; bd. dirs. Centenary Meth. Ch., 1980; mem. cmty. problem solving com. United Way, 1988-99; mem. Leadership Winston-Salem, former mem. Alumni Coun. Wake Forest U., Cert. Com. NCAA, long range planning com. athletic dept. William E. Newcombe scholar U. Pa., 1972-73; selected One of Best Employee Benefits and Corp. Lawyers in Am., Nat. Law Jour. Fellow Am. Coll. Employee Benefits Counsel (charter); mem. ABA, So. Pension Conf., N.C. Bar Assn. (former chmn. tax sect., mem. continuing legal edn. com., sports and entertainment law com.), Forsyth County Bar Assn., Forsyth County Employee Benefit Coun., Winston-Salem Estate Planning Coun. (past bd. dirs.), Profit Sharing Coun. Am., ESOP Assn., Profit Sharing Coun., Assn. of Pvt. Pension and Welfare, Forsyth Country Club (former pres., bd. dirs.) Order of Coif, Rotary (former bd. dirs. Reynolda club). Democrat. Avocations: golf, fishing. Home: 128 Ballyhoo Dr Lewisville NC 27023-9633 Office: Womble Carlyle Sandridge & Rice PLLC One West Fourth St Winston Salem NC 27101 E-mail: mgunter@wcsr.com.

GUNTER, NORMA, artistic director; Dance tchr., 1953-82; artistic dir. Parkersburg (W.Va.) Civic Ballet Co., 1982—, Mid Ohio Valley Ballet Co., Parkersburg. Office: Mid Ohio Valley Ballet Co PO Box 4204 Parkersburg WV 26104-4204

GUNTER, RUSSELL ALLEN, lawyer; b. Amarillo, Tex., Feb. 21, 1950; s. J.B. and Shirley Ann (Russell) G.; children: Kim, Sarah, Laura, Rachel, Lindsay. BS in Polit. Sci., So. Ark U., 1972; JD, Tex. Tech U., 1975. Bar: Ark., 1975, Tex, 1975, U.S. Dist. Ct. (ea. and we dists.) Ark. 1975, U.S. Supreme Ct. (8th cir.) 1975, U.S. Dist. Ct. (no. dist.) Tex. 1976, U.S. Ct. Appeals (5th cir.), 1980, U.S. Supreme Ct. 1986. Assoc. Gaines N. Houston, Little Rock, 1975-79, Wallace, Dover & Dixon, P.A., Little Rock, 1979-90, McGlinchey Stafford Lang P.L.L.C., Little Rock, 1990-97; Cross, Gunter, Witherspoon & Galchus P.C., Little Rock, 1997—. Mem. ABA (com. on practice and procedure before NLRB labor sect.), Soc. for Human Resource Mgmt. (cert. sr. profl. in human resources), Ark. Bar Assn., Tex. Bar Assn. Office: 500 E Markham St Ste 200 Little Rock AR 72201-1747

GUNTER, WILLIAM DAWSON, JR., (BILL GUNTER), insurance company executive, consultant; b. Jacksonville, Fla., July 16, 1934; s. William Dawson Gunter and Tillie S. Gunter; children— Bart, Joel, Rachel, Rebecca. BSA. with high honors, U. Fla., 1956. Tchr. pub. schs., Live Oak and Orlando, Fla., 1956, 58; ins. agt., agy. mgr. Central Fla., 1959-72; mem. Fla. State Senate, 1966-72, U.S. Congress from 5th Fla. dist., 1973-74; treas., ins. commr. State of Fla., Tallahassee, 1976-88; CEO, chmn. Rogers, Gunter, Vaughn Ins., Inc., Tallahassee, 1997—; chief exec. officer Bill Gunter & Assocs. (govt. cons.), Tallahassee, 1989—. Sr. v.p. Southland Equity Corp., Orlando, Fla.; pres. Southland Capital Investors, Inc., Orlando, 1975-76. Deacon Baptist Ch.; bd. dirs. Central Fla. Fair Assn. Served with U.S. Army, 1956-58. Recipient good govt. award Fla. State Jaycees, 1972 Mem. U. Fla. Nat. Alumni Assn. (pres. 1985-86), Orlando Area C. of C. (past dir.). Clubs: Jaycees, Kiwanis, Masons. Democrat. Office: 1117 Thomasville Rd Tallahassee FL 32303-6223 E-mail: wgunter@ragainsurance.com.

GUNTER, WILLIAM DAYLE, JR., physicist, consultant; b. Mitchell, S.D., Jan. 10, 1932; s. William Dayle and Lamerta Berniece (Hockensmith) G.; m. Shirley Marie Teshera, Oct. 24, 1955; children: Maria Jo, Robert Paul. BS in Physics with distinction, Stanford U., 1957, MS, 1959. Physicist Ames Rsch. Ctr. NASA, Moffett Field, Calif., 1960-81, asst. br. chief electronic optical engrng., 1981-85; pvt. practice cons. Photon Applications, San Jose, Calif., 1985-98, Modesto, Calif., 1998-2000; ret. Patentee in field; contbr. articles to profl. jours. With U.S. Army, 1953-55. Recipient Westinghouse Sci. Talent Search award, 1950; Stanford U. scholar, 1950. Mem. IEEE (sr.), Am. Phys. Soc., Optical Soc. Am., Nat. Space Soc., NASA Alumni League.

GUNTERN, GOTTLIEB, foundation executive, physician; b. Ritzingen, Valais, Switzerland, Apr. 26, 1939; s. Quirinus and Angelina (Schmid) G.; m. Greta Gallati, Aug. 28, 1971. MD, U. Basel, Switzerland, 1969. Med. asst. U. Bern, Switzerland, 1970-71, Hosp. Sandoz, Lausanne, Switzerland, 1975-76; fellow in mental health U. Lausanne, clinic chief, 1973-75; rsch. in systems sci. and therapy Children's Hosp., Phila., 1976-78; founder, med. dir. of pilot project Psychiatry Ctr., Brig, Switzerland, 1978-89; founder, dir. Internat. Found. for Creativity and Leadership, Martigny, Switzerland, 1979—. Founder, chmn. Internat. Zermatt (Switzerland) Symposium on Creative Leadership, 1990—; rschr. in creativity and leadership. Author: Social Change, Stress and Mental Health in the Pearl of the Alps, 1979, Therápodos - la via del terapeuta, 1989, Im Zeichen des Schmetterlings, 1992, 7 goldene Regeln der Kreativitätsförderung, 1994, Maskentanz der Mediokratie, 2000, La médiocratie démasqueé, 2001, Les 7 règles d'or de la Créativité, 2001, Götter, Helden und Schamanen, 2001, Himbeer-Hulda, 2002, Mit den Schwingen des Adlers, 2003. Recipient Priz Duboux for extraordinary accomplishments in psychiatry and philosophy U. Lausanne, 1975, Rünzi award for achievements honoring the canton of Valais, 1997. Fellow Collegium Internat. Medicae Psychosomaticae, World Econ. Forum; mem. Internat. Soc. for Systems Sci., Internat. Systems Inst. (rsch. bd.), Swiss Psychiat. Soc., Jane Goodall Inst. Avocations: song writing, novel writing, mountain climbing, skiing, golf. Office: Internat Found for Creativity and Leadership Furkastrasse 3 3900 Brig Switzerland

GUNTHER, LEON, physicist, educator; b. Bklyn., Aug. 22, 1939; s. Joseph and Esther Gunther; m. Harriet S. Gamrin, Oct. 10, 1962; children: David Michael, Benjamin Gene, Rachel Leah; m. Johanna Ellen Cotter, Nov. 11, 1979; 1 stepchild, Erika Rae Brown; 1 child, Avi Yosef. BS, CCNY, 1960; PhD, MIT, 1964. Asst. prof. Tufts U., Medford, Mass., 1965-72, assoc. prof., 1972-78, prof., 1978—. Cons. in field; vis. prof. Technion, Tel-Aviv U., Louis Néel Lab. of Magnetism, Grenoble, France. Co-editor Proceedings of NATO Workshop in Quantum Tunneling of Magnetization, 1995; contbr. over 100 articles to profl. jours. Prin. 2d violinist Newton Symphony Orch., Mass., 1974-83; founder, dir. Mak'hay lah chorus Temple Emunah, Lexington, Mass. NATO Postdoctoral fellow NSF, 1965-66, Research grantee. Mem. AAUP, Am. Phys. Soc. Office: Tufts Univ Dept Of Physics Medford MA 02155

GUNTHER, MARGOT WEBSTER, interior design; b. Mpls. d. Gustav A. and Henrietia (Webster) G. BA, Brown U., 1956, R.I. Sch. Design, 1956; postgrad., Columbia U. Sch. Architecture. Asst. designer Casa Linda, Wilmette, Ill., 1956; designer Sarra, Inc., Chgo., 1956-58, Whitaker Guernsey, Chgo., 1958-59, B. Altman, N.Y.C., 1959-61; designer owner Gunther-Watson, N.Y.C., 1961—; owner Antique House, Nantucket, Mass. Mem. Am. Soc. Interior Designers, Internat. Furnishings and Design Assn. Democrat. Roman Catholic. Avocation: restoring old houses. Home: 107 E 63rd St New York NY 10021-7331 Office: Gunther-Watson 107 E 63rd St New York NY 10021-7331

GUNTHER, WILLIAM DAVID, university administrator, economics educator; b. Balt., Oct. 11, 1940; s. Geneva (Gee) G.; m. Irene Leveja Reineks, Jan. 8, 1966; children: William B., Kristine A., Jennifer R. BS, Kent State U., 1962, MA, 1965; PhD, U. Ky., 1969. Asst. prof. econs. U. Ala., Tuscaloosa, 1968-72, assoc. prof. econs., 1972-76, prof. econs., 1976—, assoc. dean for rsch., 1988-98; dean sch. bus. U. So. Miss., Hattiesburg, 1998—. Contbr. articles to profl. jours. Fulbright scholar Fulbright Commn., 1972, Faculty fellow USAF, 1979. Mem. Assn. Coll. Honor Socs. (exec. coun. 1983—), Nat. Assn. Bus. Economists, Am. Econs. Assn., So. Regional Sci. Assn. Avocations: boating, coin collecting, paper money collecting. Office: U So Miss PO Box 5021 Hattiesburg MS 39406-1000 E-mail: william.gunther@usm.edu.

GUNTHEROTH, WARREN GADEN, pediatrician, educator; b. Hominy, Okla., July 27, 1927; s. Harry William and Callie (Cornett) G.; m. Ethel Haglund, July 3, 1954; children: Kurt, Karl, Sten. MD, Harvard U., 1952. Diplomate: Am. Bd. Pediatrics, Am. Bd. Pediatric Cardiology, Nat. Bd. Med. Examiners. Intern Peter Bent Brigham Hosp., Boston, 1952-53; fellow in cardiology Children's Hosp., Boston, 1953-55, resident in pediatrics, 1955-56; rsch. fellow physiology and biophysics U. Wash. Med. Sch., Seattle, 1957-58, mem. faculty, 1958—, prof. pediatrics, 1969—, head divsn. pediatric cardiology, 1964-91. Author: Pediatric Electrocardiography, 1965, How to Read Pediatric ECGs, 1981, 3d edit., 1992, Crib Death (Sudden Infant Death Syndrome), 1982, 3d edit., 1995, Climbing With Sasha, a Washington Husky, 1995; also numerous articles; mem. editl. bd. Am. Heart Jour., 1977-80, Circulation, 1980-83, Am. Jour. Noninvasive Cardiology, 1985-94, Jour. Am. Coll. Cardiology, 1988-94, Am. Jour. Cardiology, Jour. Noninvasive Cardiology, 1996-00; sect. editor Practice of Pediatrics, 1979-87. Served with USPHS, 1950-51. Spl. research fellow NIH, 1967. Mem. Soc. Pediatric Rsch., Biomed. Engrng. Soc. (charter), Am. Heart Assn. (chmn. N.W. regional med. rsch. adv. com. 1978-80), Cardiovascular System Dynamics Soc. (charter), Am. Coll. Cardiology. Democrat. Home: 13201 42nd Ave NE Seattle WA 98125-4626 Office: U Wash Med Sch Dept Pediatrics PO Box 356320 Seattle WA 98195-6320 E-mail: wgg@u.washington.edu. *My career includes medical practice, teaching and research; my hobby is mountain climbing. Both work and hobby benefit from courage. Encouraging students to ask difficult— and even embarrassing— questions, reaching a timely diagnosis, starting treatment in a dangerously ill patient, and raising challenging questions in research that may provoke anger or scorn; all require courage. Silent convictions are not enough.*

GUNTY, CHRISTOPHER JAMES, newspaper editor; b. Hometown, Ill., Oct. 13, 1959; s. Harold Paul and Therese Agnes Gunty; div.; children: William, Amy, Timothy. BA, Loyola U., Chgo., 1981. Circulation mgr. The Chgo. Catholic, 1981-83, assoc. mnging. editor, 1983, mng. editor, 1983-85; editor, mng. editor The Catholic Sun, Phoenix, 1985-96; assoc. pub. The Cath. Sun, Phoenix, 1996—. Author: He Came to Touch Us, 1987; co-author videotape script The Pope in Arizona, 1987; contbg. author: (anthologies) Freedom of Journalist, 1990, Mission and Future of the Catholic Press, 1998; contbr. articles to spl. Catholic news svcs. as well as papers where employed. Mem. Fiesta Bowl Com., Phoenix, 1987-92; bd. dirs. Catholic Journalism Scholarship Fund, 1990—, pres., 1995-96, 99-2001. Named Honoree Summer U. Internat. Cath. Union of the Press, Switzerland, 1988. Mem. Cath. Press Assn. (bd. dirs. 1988-99, sec. 1990-92, v.p. 1994-96, pres. 1996-98, St. Francis de Sales award 2000), Assoc. Ch. Press, Ariz. Newspapers Assn., Soc. Profl. Journalists. Roman Catholic. Avocations: bicycling, sci. fiction. Office: The Catholic Sun 400 E Monroe St Phoenix AZ 85004-2336

GUNZENHAUSER, GERARD RALPH, JR., management consultant, investor; b. Mt. Vernon, N.Y., Sept. 26, 1936; s. Gerard Ralph and Helen Elizabeth (Carey) G.; m. Alfa Marjorie Vendetti, Sept. 17, 1960; children: Cathy Susan, Michael Gerard, Christopher John, Eric David. BBA, Iona Coll., 1965; postgrad., NYU Sch. Bus. Adminstrn., 1967-68. Asst. mgr. fin. analysis Gen. Foods Corp., White Plains, N.Y., 1962-68; dir. fin. planning and analysis RJR Foods, Inc., Winston-Salem, N.C., 1968-76; area fin. dir. R.J. Reynolds Tobacco Internat., Winston-Salem, 1976-79; comptroller R.J. Reynolds Tobacco. Co., Winston-Salem, 1979-81; v.p., comptroller R.J. Reynolds Tobacco Co., Winston-Salem, 1981-83, v.p. fin., chief fin. officer, 1983-84; sr. v.p., chief fin. officer Del Monte Corp., San Francisco, 1984-85; sr. v.p. fin., controller RJR Nabisco, Inc., Winston-Salem, 1986-87; sr. v.p. fin. R.J. Reynolds Tobacco Co., Winston-Salem, 1987-88, exec. v.p., chief fin. officer, 1988-91, also exec. com., bd. dirs.; pres., chief exec. officer GRG Assocs., Inc., Winston-Salem, 1991—. Mem. local adv. bd. Branch Banking & Trust Co., 1987-99; mem. Consumer Credit Counseling Svc., 1983-84, 87-90; mem. Reynolds Carolina Credit Union Bd., 1973-83. Trustee Winston-Salem Arts Coun., 1987-94; bd. dirs. Winston-Salem Piedmont Triad Symphony, 1986—, Piedmont Opera Theatre, 1989—, Tanglewood Pk. Found., 1991-98; mem. N.C. Gov.'s Bus. Coun. on Arts and Humanities, 1987-91; chmn. fund appeal Bishop McGuinness High Sch., Winston-Salem, 1982-83, mem. bd. edn., 1987-90, chmn. bd., 1988-90; chmn. St. Leo's Parish Coun., Winston-Salem, 1974-77; exec. v.p. Winston-Salem Nat. Little League, 1981-84; chmn. sch. budget task force C. of C., 1976; mem. bd. advisors Catholic Conf. Ctr., 1990-93; exec. com., bd. trustees Forsyth County Park Authority, 1992-99; bd. dirs., vice chmn. Found. Roman Cath. Diocese of Charlottee. Named to Hon. Order Ky. Cols., 1983 Mem. Fin. Execs. Inst. Roman Catholic. Home: 2814 Galsworthy Dr Winston Salem NC 27106-5107 Office: GRG Assocs Inc 101 S Stratford Rd Ste 201 Winston Salem NC 27104-4224

GUNZENHAUSER, MICHAEL GERARD, mathematician, educator; b. White Plains, N.Y., Feb. 26, 1965; s. Gerard Ralph Gunzenhauser Jr. and Alfa (Vendetti) Gunzenhauser; m. Deborah Ann Desjardins, May 1, 1999. AB, U. N.C., 1987; MEd, U. Vt., 1992; PhD, U. N.C., 1999. Residential counselor N.C. Sch. Sci. and Math., Durham, 1987—90; coord. pre-coll. programs Duke U., Durham, 1992—94; asst. prof. Okla. State U., Stillwater, 1999—. Rschr. Arts Edn. Partnership, Washington, 2002—03, Kenan Inst. for Arts, Winston-Salem, NC, 1995—2000. Bd. dirs. DaVinci Inst., Oklahoma City. Recipient Mary Catherine Ellwein award, Am. Ednl. Rsch. Assn., 2001. Mem.: Philosophy Edn. Soc., Am. Ednl. Studies Assn., Am. Ednl. Rsch. Assn. (Mary Catherine Ellwein award 2001). Roman Catholic. Avocations: music, gardening, cooking. Office: Okla State Univ 204 Willard Hall Stillwater OK 74078

GUNZENHAUSER, STEPHEN CHARLES, conductor; b. N.Y.C., Apr. 8, 1942; s. M(ax) Kurt and Ruth (Sorsky) G.; m. Rochelle E. Davis, June 14, 1970; children— Marisa, Amy. MusB, Oberlin Coll., 1963; diploma, Salzburg (Austria) Mozarteum, 1962; MusM, New Eng. Conservatory Music, 1965; artist diploma, Hochschule, Cologne, Fed. Republic Germany, 1968; LittD (hon.), Widener U., 1987. Guest condr. Rhenish Chamber Orch., Cologne, 1967-69, City of Gelsenkirchen Orch., 1972, Nat. Orch. Costa Rica, 1975, Del. Pro Musica, 1974-75, Lancaster (Pa.) Symphony, 1979, Radio Orch. Ireland, Dublin, 1979, 82, Hessian State Broadcasting Network Orch., 1969, RIAS Orch. of Berlin, 1969, Knoxville (Tenn.) Symphony, 1982, Duluth-Superior (Wis.) Wymphony, 1982, Ala. Symphony, 1983, Spokane Symphony, 1983, Laredo (Tex.) Symphony, 1983, Slovak Philharm., 1988, 90, Silesia Philharm., Poland, 1988, Seoul Philharm., Republic of Korea, 1988, Innsbruck Symphony, Austria, 1989, Hagen Symphony, Germany, 1990; resident condr. Costa Verde and Sintra Festival, Portugal, 1984, Va. Symphony, 1984, Sacramento Symphony, 1985, Symphony N.S., 1986, Peoria Symphony, 1987, Okla. Symphony, 1987, 96, Charlotte Symphony, 1987, Israel Chamber Orch., 1993, Berlin Symphony Orch., 1995, 96, 97, 99, 2000, Colo. Music Festival, 1996, 99, Munich Symphony, 1996, Nat. Kibbutz (Israel) Chamber Orch., 1996, Hagen (Germany) Philharm., 1996, 98; asst. condr. Monte Carlo Nat. Orch., 1968-69, Am. Symphony Orch., N.Y.C., 1969-70, Nat. Orch. Argentina, 2001, music dir. Bklyn. Ctr. Chamber Orch., 1970-72, Kennett (Pa.) Symphony Orch., 1974-78, Wilmington (Del.) Chamber Orch., 1976-79, Del. Symphony, 1978-2002; exec. Lancaster Symphony, 1978—, music dir., 1981; artistic dir. Wilmington Music Sch., 1974-82, artistic advisor, 1982-87, clarinettist, rec. artist; recs. with HNH Internat., 1985-92, also for Pro Arte, Israel, Elan and Albany Records Trustee Nat. Guild Community Schs. Arts, 1977-83. Recipient 1st prize Santiago (Spain) Competition, 1967, medal of distinction U. Del., 1990, Collector's Choice prize Classic CD mag.; apptd. Cultural Amb., State of Del., 1990; Fulbright grantee, 1965-68. Mem. Musicians Union, Condrs. Guild, Am. Symphony Orch. League Home: 901 Shallcross Ave Wilmington DE 19806-3232 Office: Del Symphony Orch PO Box 1870 Wilmington DE 19899-1870 *As musician, I can neither build nor repair the tangible aspects of life. My hope is to minister successfully to the spirit.*

GUO, DAQING, medical researcher; b. Jiangsu, China; MD, Nanjing Med. U., Jiangsu, China, 1987. Rsch. fellow New Eng. Med. Ctr., Boston, 1998—2002. Named Baxter Asia Young Investigator, 1998.

GUO, DONG-SHENG, physicist; PhD in Physics, Ill. Inst. Tech., Chgo., 1984. Rsch. assoc. U. Notre Dame, South Bend, Ind., 1984-86, U. Oreg., Eugene, 1986-90, U. Windsor, Ont., Can., 1990-92; summer physicist Lawrence Livermore Nat. Lab., Livermore, Calif., 1993—; assoc. prof. physics Southern U., Baton Rouge, 1992—. Contbr. articles to profl. jours. Rsch. grantee U.S. Dept. Energy, 1994-96, NASA, 1996—, NSF, 1997—. Mem. Am. Phys. Soc. Achievements include development of a systematic nonperturbative quantum electrodynamics theory; interpretation of Kapitza-Dirac effect in intense laser fields discovered by P.H. Bucksbaum et al and predictions of ponderomotive momentum, spin-other-orbit effect of photon modes. Office: Southern Univ and A&M Coll Dept Physics Baton Rouge LA 70813-0001 E-mail: dsguo@grant.phys.subr.edu.

GUO, JAMES CHWEN-YUAN, civil engineer, educator; b. Taipei, Taiwan, Mar. 8, 1952; arrived in U.S., 1978; m. Lucy Lai Hsu, Dec. 25, 1977; 1 child, Wei S. PhD, U. Ill., 1982. Prof. dept. civil engrng. U. Colo., Denver, 1982—. Author: (book) Street Hydraulic, 1996, Channel Design, 1997; contbr. Recipient Svc. award, U. Colo.-Denver, 1999, Rsch. award, 2000, Outstanding award, Colo. Engrng. Coun., 1996. Mem.: ASCE. Achievements include development of 12 computer models in the area of flood predictions. Office: Univ of Colorado at Denver Dept Civil Engrng 1200 Larimer St Denver CO 80217

GUO, MEIWEN, structural engineer; b. Fugu, Shaanxi, China, Dec. 4, 1954; s. Houyang Guo and Gaizhi Hao; m. Yun Wang, Feb. 10, 1983; 1 child, Chuan. BCE, Xian Inst. Hwy. Engrng., China, 1982; MCE, Chungqing Archtl. Engrng. Inst., 1987; PhDCE, U. Ky., 1995. Registered profl. engr., Minn., Ky., ND. Structural engr. HMB, Frankfort, Ky., 1996—97, Parsons Transp. Group, Salt Lake City, 1997—98; lead structural engr. and profl. assoc. Parsons Brinckerhoff Inc., Mpls., 1998—. Contbr. articles to profl. jours. Recipient award for contbn. to composite rsch., Composite Inst., Cin., 1996. Mem.: ASCE, Minn. Concrete Coun. Achievements include development of new finite element models in predicting behavior of stiffened laminated plates; engaged in bridge design. Avocation: fishing. Office: Parsons Brinckerhoff 510 First Ave N #550 Minneapolis MN 55403 Office Fax: 612-371-4410.

GUO, MINTONG, pharmaceutical scientist; arrived in U.S., 1997; s. Daqun Guo and Lunyin Wu. PhD, U. of Md., 2002. Rsch. scientist Peking U. Med. Ctr., Beijing, 1994—97; rsch. asst. U. of Md., Balt., 1998—2002; sr. scientist Geneva Pharm. A Novartis Co., Dayton, NJ, 2002—. Author: (book) Chinese Nutraceutical Supplements, 1993. Recipient Outstanding Student fellowship, Peking U. Med. Ctr., 1987—90. Mem.: Controlled Release Soc. (assoc.), Am. Chem. Soc. (assoc.), Am. Assn. of Pharm. Scientists (assoc.), Rho Chi Soc. (life). Achievements include patents for Formulation Composition For Sumatriptan; research in Synthesis of Boc-Asn-OCH2-Polystyrene Ester; patents pending for Micropellets with Taste Masking Property; Pharmaceutical Formulation For Urinary Tract Infection; Colonic Drug Delivery System; research in SMCC's Potential Application in High Dose Nutraceutical Hardgelatin Capsule Formulation; Potential Application of SMCC In Hard Gelatin Capsule Formulation Pharmaceutical Development and Technology; A Hybrid Intelligent System For Formulation Of BCS Class II Drugs In Hard Gelatin Capsules, Proceedings of the International Conference on Neural Information Processing; first to A Prototype Intelligent Hybrid System For Hard Gelatin Capsule Formulation Development Pharmaceutical Technology; research in Evaluation of the Plug Formation Process of Silicified Microcrystalline Cellulose International Journal of Pharmaceutics. Office: Geneva Pharm A Novartis Co 2400 Rte 130 N Dayton NJ 08810 Home Fax: 609-275-8731; Office Fax: 732-274-8989. Personal E-mail: mguo001@yahoo.com. E-mail: mintong.guo@gx.novartis.com.

GUO, PING, cancer researcher; PhD in Pharmaceutics, West China U. of Med. Sci., Chengdu, Sichuan, 1996. Assoc. dir. Ctr. of Analysis and Test Coll. of Pharmacy, West China Univ. of Med. Sci., Chengdu, 1986—93, assoc. prof., 1996—98; postdoctoral assoc. Coll. of Pharmacy, U. of Minn., Mpls., 1998—99; rsch. assoc. Fox Chase Cancer Ctr., Phila., 1999—. Author: (acdemic book) Targeted Drug Delivery System; contbr. Recipient Second Pl. award, Innovation Ctr. for Life Sci., China Nat. Sci. Com., 1995, Exellent Rsch. Article award, Editl. Bd. of Chinese Pharm. Jour. Mem.: Am. Asssociation of Pharm. Scientists, Am. Assn. for Cancer Rsch. Achievements include research in Successfully reduced the toxicity of Amphotericin B, a highly toxic but most effective agent in treatment of serious systemic fungal infections by a drug delivery system; successfully developed many innovative assays for measuring anticancer agents in tumor tissues. Office: Fox Chase Cancer Ctr 7701 Burholme Ave W232 Philadelphia PA 19111 E-mail: p_guo@fccc.edu.

GUO, QIZHONG, engineering educator, researcher, consultant; b. Guangdong, China, Oct. 8, 1962; came to U.S., 1984; m. Xiaolan Wang; children: Lillian, Joshua. B of Engring., Tianjin (China) U., 1982; MS, U. Minn., 1987, PhD, 1991. Registered profl. engr., Minn. Rsch./tchg. asst. U. Minn., Mpls., 1985-91, rsch. assoc., 1991-92; R & D engr. Lemna Corp., St. Paul, 1992; asst. prof. Rutgers U., Piscataway, N.J., 1992-98, assoc. prof., 1998—. Tech. adv. steering com. Barnegat Bay Nat. Estuary Program, Trenton, N.J., 1996—; tech. adv. com. Whippany Watershed Project, Trenton, 1996—. Contbr. articles to profl. jours. Mem. ASCE, Am. Waterworks Assn., Am. Geophysical Union, Am. Water Resources Assn. (U. Minn. student chpt. pres. 1990-91), Water Environ. Fedn. Achievements include research in solutions to hydraulic problems in deep tunnel project for Greater Chicago; revealing environmental problems that may occur as a result of processing hazardous waste derived fuel in cement kilns; developing a new method for quantifying freshwater input and flushing time in estuaries. Office: Rutgers Univ 623 Bowser Rd Piscataway NJ 08854-8014 E-mail: qguo@rci.rutgers.edu.

GUO, RUYAN, engineering educator, researcher; b. Beijing; arrived in U.S., 1985, naturalized; BSEE, Xi'an Jiaoting U., China, 1982; MSEE, Xi'an Jiaotong U., China, 1984; PhD in Solid State Sci., Pa. State U., 1990. Assoc. lectr. elec. engring. dept. Xi'an Jiaotong U., 1984—85; faculty rsch. assoc. Materials Rsch. Lab. Pa. State U., University Park, 1991—94, faculty rsch. assoc., asst. prof. materials, 1995—96, sr. rsch. assoc., assoc. prof. materials, assoc. prof. elec. engring., 1996—99, assoc. prof. elec. engring. and materials rsch., dept. elec. engring. and Materials Rsch. Inst., 1999—. Presenter in field. Editor on bd.: jour. Phase Transitions, 2001—, Jour. of Korean Ceramic Soc., 2002—; contbr. tech. papers to refereed jours., conf. procs., book chpts. Mem.: AAAS, IEEE (sr. Cert. Recognition and Appreciation for Organizing the 9th IEEE Internat. Symposium on Application of Ferroelectrics 1994), IEEE Computer Soc., Lasers and Electro-optics Soc., SPIE Internat. Soc. for Optical Engring., Am. Soc. for Engring. Edn., Ultrasonic, Ferroelectric and Frequency Control Soc., Materials Rsch. Soc., Am. Ceramic Soc. (Cert. of Excellence in Svc. Orgn. of Electronics Divsn. Meeting 2000 2001). Achievements include research in science and technology of electronic and optoelectronic materials and devices; ferrous oxides; low loss and tunable microwave materials; optical fiber communications and tunable wireless optical interactions. Office: Pa State U Dept Elec Engring 187 Materials Rsch Lab University Park PA 16802

GUO, SHENG MING, retired history educator; b. Zhengjiang, Jiangsu, China, Dec. 25, 1915; came to U.S., 1989, naturalized, 1996; s. Dun Xue Guo and Xiao Chun Wu; m. Hong Yi Wang, Jan. 24, 1945; children: Victor Kuo, John Kuo, Meide Guo. BA in History, Nat. Ctrl. U., Chongching, China, 1938; MA, Ctrl. Inst. Polit. Sci., Chongching, 1941; postgrad., Tulane U., 1949. Vice consul Chinese Consulate, New Orleans, 1945-47, acting consul, 1948-50; prof. history Kuangsi (China) U., 1951-53, Hunan (China) U., 1953-56, East China Normal U., Shanghai, 1957-89. Advisor Chinese Assn. Medieval History, Beijing, 1976—, Shanghai Assn. Social Sci., 1983—; U.S. State Dept. vis. prof., Georgetown U., Harvard U., U. Chgo., Stanford U., also others, 1983. Author: A Survey of Western Historiography, 1983 (State prize 1985), An Outline of World Civilization, 1989 (State prize 1991); editor-in-chief: Dictionary of World History, 1986; editor History of Foreign Countries in Ency. Sinica, 1987. Presbyterian. Avocation: gardening.

GUO, XIAOFENG, physicist; b. Fuzhou, China, Jan. 15, 1967; came to U.S., 1990; m. Jianwei Qiu, June 20, 1996. BS, Beijing U., 1988; PhD, Iowa State U., 1996. Postdoctoral rsch. scientist Columbia U., N.Y.C., 1996-98; postdoctoral rsch. fellow U. Ky., Lexington, 1998—. Contbr. articles to profl. jours. Mem. Am. Phys. Soc., Assn. Women in Sci.

GUO, YANPING, physicist; m. Shouxiang Hu; 1 child, Han Hu. BS, Huazhong U., Wuhan, China, 1982; MS in Physics, Cath. U. Am., 1990, PhD in Physics, 1992. Prin. profl. staff Johns Hopkins U. Applied Physics Lab., Laurel, Md., 1994—. Mission design lead NASA new horizons pluto-kuiper belt mission Johns Hopkins U., mission design lead NASA solar probe mission, sci. sequence planning lead NASA Near earth asteroid rendezvous mission, prin. investigator autonomous interplanetary navigational project, prin. investigator diffusion tomography project. Co-patentee imaging objects in a dissipative medium by nearfield electromagnetic holography. Recipient Group Achievement award for NEAR Mission, NASA, 1998. Mem.: Am. Astron. Soc. Office: Johns Hopkins Univ Applied Physics Lab 11100 Johns Hopkins Rd Laurel MD 20723-6099

GUO, ZENGKUI, research scientist; b. Pingyao, Shanxi Province, China, Sept. 17, 1951; arrived in U.S., 1986; s. KaiQi H. Guo and AiYing K. Zhang; m. Lendia L. Zhou, Oct. 22, 1963; children: Winston, Yugene. PhD, U. of Mo., 1990. Physiology lectr. Shanxi Coll. of Vet. Scis., Taigu, 1976—80; rsch. fellow Chinese Acad. of Agrl. Scis., Beijing, 1983—86; postdoctoral rsch. fellow Cedars-Sinai/Harbor UCLA Med Ctr, L.A., 1990—91; rsch. assoc. U. of Chgo., 1991—92; sr. rsch. assoc. U. of Cin., 1993—95; NIH grant trainee Mayo Found., Rochester, Minn., 1995—98, rsch. assoc., 1998—2002, assoc. cons., 2002—. Co-author: (textbook) Animal Anatomy and Physiology. Recipient Pilot and Feasibility Project award, Minn. Obesity Ctr., 1999—2000; grantee, NIH NIDDK, 2001—06. Mem.: North Am. Soc. for the Study of Obesity, Nat. Inst. of Nutritional Scis. Achievements include research in established procedures for studying skeletal muscle metabolism using stable isotopes; histological establishment of adipocyte distribution in skeletal muscle and the techniques for its removal; development of model for the oxidation of blood and intramuscular fatty acids by skeletal muscle; establishment of in vivo techniques for stress-free investigation of metabolism in rodents. Home: 4616 Manor Park Dr NW Rochester MN 55901 Office: Mayo Found 5-194 Joseph Rochester MN 55905 Office Fax: 507-255-4828. E-mail: guo.zengkui@mayo.edu.

GUO, ZIBIN, medical anthropologist; b. Nanjing, China, Jan. 18, 1961; came to U.S., 1986; s. Wenxue Guo and Yueqing Wu. BA, Nanjing U., 1982; MA, U. Conn., 1988, PhD, 1994; postgrad., Harvard U., 1995-97. Dir. clin. studies New Eng. Sch. Acupuncture, Watertown, Mass., 1995; lectr. Harvard Med. Sch., Boston, 1997-98; asst. prof. dept. sociology and anthropology U. Tenn., Chattanooga, 1998—. Cons. N.Y. Task Force on Immigrant/Health, N.Y.C., 1993-94, U. Conn. Med. Ctr., Farmington, 1995, Women's Rsch. Ctr., Wellesley (Mass.) Coll., 1998-2000; mem. adv. com. Inst. Cmty. Rsch., Hartford, Conn., 2000—. Author: Ginseng and Aspirin, 2000; contbr. chpts. to books. Grantee Nat. Ctr. for Health Stats., 1992-93; fellow Nat. inst. Aging., 1995-97, summer, 1996, U. Tenn., summer 1999. Mem. Am. Anthropol. Assn., Soc. for Applied Anthropology, U.S. Judo Assn. (life). Avocations: tai chi, martial arts. Office: U Tenn 615 McCallie Ave Chattanooga TN 37403 E-mail: Zibin-Guo@utc.edu.

GUP, BENTON EUGENE, banking educator; b. Reading, Pa., Mar. 5, 1936; married; children: Lincoln, Andrew, Jeremy. BA, U. Cin., 1961, MBA, 1963, PhD, 1966. Economist Fed. Res. Bank of Cleve., 1967-70; prof. fin. U. of Tulsa, 1970-82, prof., chair banking, 1970-82; vis. prof., chair banking U. Va., Charlottesville, 1980-81; prof., chair banking U. Ala., Tuscaloosa, 1983—. Author: Guide to Strategic Planning, 1980, Financial Intermediaries, 2d editl, 1980, Principles of Financial Management, 1983, 2d edit., 1987, Management of Financial Institutions, 1984, The Basics of Investing, 5th edit., 1992, (with Charles Meiburg) Cases in Bank Management, 1986, Personal Investing: A Complete Handbook, 1987, Commercial Bank Management, 1989, Bank Mergers: Current Issues and Perspectives, 1989, Bank Fraud: Exposing the Hidden Threat to Financial Institutions, 1990, (with Robert Brooks) Interest Rate Risk Management, 1993, Targeting Fraud: Uncovering and Detering Fraud in Financial Institutions, 1995 (with Donald Fraser and James Kolari) Commercial Banking: The Management of Risk, 1995, The Bank Director's Handbook, 1996, Bank Failures in the Major Trading Countries of the World, 1998, International Banking Crises, 1999, The New Financial Architecture, 2000, Megamergers in a Global Economy, 2002, The Future of Banking, 2003, Investing OnLine, 2003. Served with USAF, 1954—58. Mem. Fin. Mgmt. Assn. (chmn. site selection 1975-85), Midwest Fin. Assn. (pres. 1982-83), Am. Fin. Assn., Fin. Execs. Inst., Acad. Fin. Svcs. (v.p., dir. 1988-91). Home: 1124 Forest Oaks Ln Tuscaloosa AL 35406-2673 Office: U Ala Dept Fin PO Box 870224 Tuscaloosa AL 35487-0154

GUPCHUP, GIREESH VIJAY, pharmacist, educator; b. Bombay, Dec. 28, 1965; arrived in U.S., 1988; s. Vijay Narhar and Vijaya Gupchup; m. Chatura Chitale-Gupchup, Dec. 27, 1994; 1 child, Samay. BS in Pharmacy, U. Bombay, 1988; MS, U. Toledo, 1990, MS, 1993; PhD, Purdue U., 1996. Lic. pharmacist Maharashtra State Pharmacy Coun., India. Purdue-Merck fellow in pharm. economics, grad. asst. Purdue U., West Lafayette, Ind., 1993—96; chmn. pharmacy adminstrn. grad. program U. N.Mex, Albuquerque, 1996—2000, asst. prof. pharmacy, 1996—2002, assoc. prof. pharmacy, 2002—; dir. N.Mex Medicaid Retrospective Drug Utilization Rev. Program, Albuquerque, 2000—. Pharmacoeconomics cons. N.Mex Medicaid Drug Utilization Rev. Program, Albuquerque, 1996—2000. Mem. editl. adv. bd.: Jour. Am. Pharm. Assn.; author: (21 journal articles) Several Pharmacy-related journals of repute. Recipient Alumni Achiever's award, KMK Coll. of Pharmacy, U. Bombay, 2000; grantee, various state, fed. and industry sources, 1996—2002. Mem.: N.Mex Pharm. Assn. (2d v.p. 2002—), Internat. Soc. Pharmacoeconomics and Outcomes Rsch., Am. Pharm. Assn., Kappa Psi, Phi Kappa Phi, Rho Chi. Achievements include development of two instruments to measure health-related quality of life among Native American asthma and diabetes patients. Avocations: golf, swimming. Office: U NMex 2502 Marble NE Albuquerque NM 87131

GUPTA, AARON DAS, mechanical engineer; b. India, Nov. 20, 1943; came to U.S., 1969, naturalized, 1974; s. Krishna Das and Amita Das G.; B.S., Indian Inst. Tech., 1963; M.S. (DRB Research fellow 1965-67), Nova Scotia Tech. Coll., 1967; Ph.D., Va. Poly. Inst., 1975; m. Runu Biswas, Mar. 9, 1972; children— Elora Das and Debraj Das (twins). Design engr. Whittaker, Gardener, Calif., 1969-70; project engr. Kingsport (Tenn.) Press, 1973-75; stress analyst Sundstrand Aviation, Rockford, Ill., 1975-76; sr. mech. research engr. U.S. Army Ballistic Research Lab., Aberdeen Proving Ground, Md., 1976— . Registered profl. engr., Ill., Va. Mem. ASME, N.Y. Acad. Scis., Am. Acad. Scis., Sigma Xi, Phi Kappa Phi, Pi Tau Sigma. Hindu. Contbr. articles in field to profl. jours. Home: 104 John St Perryville MD 21903-2630 Office: US Army Rsch Lab B309 Tbd Apg Rm 226 Aberdeen Proving Ground MD 21005 E-mail: adsgpt@cs.com.

GUPTA, ANJU, risk management consultant; b. Bangalore, India, Sept. 14, 1971; d. Darshan Singh and Neera Gupta; m. Parag Gupta. PhD, Stanford U., California, USA, 1997. Postdoctoral rsch. scholar Stanford U., Palo Alto, Calif., 1997—98; sr. engr. Risk Mgmt. Solutions Inc., Newark, Calif., 1998—2000, product mgr., weather risk, 2000—01, dir. product devel., 2001—. Cons. Wharton team on NSF project, Palo Alto, 1996; mem. Curee, L.A., 1998; mem. com. earthquake risk financing and transfer Earthquake Engring. Rsch. Inst., Oakland, Calif., 1999. Contbr. articles to profl. jours. Vol. for adult literacy, Mountain View, Calif., 1998; vol. for childhood literacy New Delhi, 1995—97. Mem.: Earthquake Engring. Rsch. Inst. Achievements include development of financial risk model for Central America; a standardized national earthquake loss estimation software tool, Hazards US (HAZUS); participation in project dealing with urban search and rescue requirements for responding to catastrophic disasters in the U.S; project to assess annualized losses from earthquakes in the U.S; project to validate and calibrate the HAZUS methodology. Home: 25800 Industrial Blvd # K191 Hayward CA 94545 Office: Risk Mgmt Solutions Inc 7015 Gateway Blvd Newark CA 94560 Office Fax: 510-505-2501. Personal E-mail: anjurisk@yahoo.com. E-mail: anju.gupta@rms.com.

GUPTA, ASHMIT, otolaryngologist, researcher; b. Ahmedabad, India, Sept. 16, 1971; s. Devkumar and Krishna Gupta. BA, U. of Pa, Philadelphia, PA, 1989—93; MD, George Wash. U., Washington, D.C., 1993—97, M.P.H., 1997. Spl. vol. rsch. fellow NIH, Bethesda, Md., 1995—98; rsch. fellow George Wash. U., Washington, 1997—98, resident physician, 1998—. Author: (poster) Early Arytenoid Adduction for Vagal Paralysis after Skull Base Surgery, 1999 (Most outstanding poster presentation award, 1999); contbr. book, articles to profl. jours. Co-chair of agenda com. Nat. Student Campaign against Hunger and Homelessness, Philadelphia, Pa., 1990—93; health care worker Zaccheus Free Clinic, Washington, 1995—96. Recipient Pub. Health Scholarship, George Wash. U., 1995. Mem.: ACS, Am. Acad. of Otolaryngic Allergy, Am. Acad. of Facial Plastic and Reconstructive Surgery, Am. Acad. of Otolaryngology-Head and Neck Surgery (Otolaryngology Resident award 2001, 2002). Conservative-R. Hindu. Avocations: history, jazz, music, travel, golf. Office: George Washington Univ Med Ctr 2150 Pennsylvania Ave NW #6-301 Washington DC 20037 Personal E-mail: agupta@mfa.gwu.edu.

GUPTA, ASHWANI KUMAR, mechanical engineering educator; b. Punjab, India, Oct. 23, 1948; s. Ram Nath and Vidya G. BSc, Panjab U., India, 1966; MSc, Southampton U., U.K., 1970; PhD, Sheffield (Eng.) U., 1973, DSc, 1986. Chartered engr., fuel technologist, U.K. Rsch. engr. Internat. Combustion Co., Derby, Eng., 1967-71; rsch. asst. Sheffield U., 1971-73, rsch. fellow, ind. rsch. worker, 1973-76; mem. rsch. staff MIT, Cambridge, 1977-82; prof. dept. mech. engring. U. Md., College Park, 1983—. Mem. sci. adv. bd. State of Md., 1985—. Author: Swirl Flows, 1984, Flowfield Modeling and Diagnostics, 1985; editor 8 books in Energy and Engineering Science series, 1980—; founding co-editor: Environmental and Energetics series, 1990—; author over 250 tech. papers. Fellow AIAA (chmn. propellants and combustion tech. com. 1988-90, chmn. terrestrial energy systems tech. com. 1991-2000, dep. dir. energy 2000—, Energy Sys. award 1990, Propellant and Combustion award 1999), Inst. Energy U.K., ASME (chmn. Fuels and Combustion Tech. divsn. 1998-2000, mem. computers and info. in engring. divsn. 2002-03, George Westinghouse Gold medal 1998, James Harry Potter Godl Medal 2003); mem. Soc. Automotive Engrs., Combustion Inst., Am. Soc. Engring. Edn. Avocations: flying, swimming, squash, photography. Office: U Md Dept Mech Engring College Park MD 20742-0001 E-mail: akgupta@eng.umd.edu.

GUPTA, GIAN CHAND, environmental scientist; b. Delhi, India, Oct. 10, 1939; s. Bhagat Ram and Shanti Gupta; m. Hirdesh Bindu, Apr. 18, 1972; children: Tarra, Suneal. BS, Panjab (India) U., 1959; MS, Vikaram U., Bhopal, India, 1962; PhD, Roorkee (India) U., 1966. Cert. profl. soil scientist. Postdoctoral rsch. fellow U. Miss., 1968-69; assoc. prof. Rust Coll., Holly Springs, Miss., 1969-70; dir. environ. health M.E. Comprehensive Health Ctr., Fayette, Miss., 1970-72; dir. environ. health edn. J.H. Comprehensive Health Ctr., Utica, Miss., 1972-77; asst. prof. U. Md., Princess Anne, 1977-83, assoc. prof., 1983-90, prof., 1990—. Contbr. articles to profl. jours. Mem. Am. Soc. Agronomy, Am. Chem. Soc., Nat. Environ. Health Assn. Office: U Md Eastern Shore Dept Environ Sci Princess Anne MD 21853

GUPTA, KRISHAN LAL, physician, medical educator; b. Bhiwani, India, May 21, 1946; s. Sat Narain and Chameli (Devi) G.; m. Veena Gupta, Dec. 2, 1972; children: Shalini, Sheila. MD, Med. Coll., Rohtak, India, 1970. Tng. in, India and Eng., from 1970; assoc. prof. medicine N.Y. Med. Coll., Valhalla, 1985-91, prof. clin. medicine, divsn. geriatric medicine, 1991-96, prof. medicine, 1996—, dir. divsn. geriatric medicine, 1994—; attending physician Franklin Delano Roosevelt Vets. Hosp., Montrose, N.Y., 1985-97, Univ. Hosp. at Westchester County Med. Ctr., Valhalla, 1985—, St. Agnes Hosp., White Plains, N.Y., 1995—; dir. geriatric fellowship program Westchester County Med. Ctr., 1994—; dir. med. svcs. Ruth Taylor Geriatric and Rehab. Inst., Hawthorne, N.Y., 1993-96. Author: 100 Short Cases for the MRCP, 1983, 2d edit., 1994, German transl., 1987, High Blood Cholesterol: Causes, Prevention and Treatment, numerous others; contbr. numerous articles to profl. jours. Fellow ACP, Royal Coll. Physicians Edinburgh, Gerontol. Soc. Am., N.Y. Acad. Medicine; mem. Am. Geriatrics Soc. E-mail: sgup178@aol.com.

GUPTA, KRISHNA CHANDRA, mechanical engineering educator; b. 1948; m. Karuna Gupta; 1 child, Anupama B.Tech. with distinction, Indian Inst. Tech., 1969; MS in M.E., Case Inst. Tech., 1971; PhD in M.E., Stanford U., 1974. Grad. asst. Case Inst. Tech., Cleve., 1969-71; research asst. Stanford U., Calif., 1971-74; from asst. prof. mech. engring. to assoc. dean U. Ill., Chgo., 1974—2002, assoc. dean, 2002—. Mem. editorial adv. bd. Jour. Applied Mechanisms and Robotics; assoc. editor Mechanism and Machine Theory; contbr. articles to profl. jours. Recipient award of merit Procter & Gamble Co., 1978, South Pointing Chariot award, 1989, AM&R G.N. Sandor award, 1997; grantee in field. Fellow ASME (assoc. editor Jour. Mech. Design 1981-82, mem. editorial adv. bd. Applied Mechanics Rev. 1985-93, chmn. mechanisms com. 1989-90, gen chmn. 1990 design tech. conf., chmn. 1990 mechanisms conf., mem. design divsn. exec. com. 2001—, editor newsletter divsn. design engring., best paper computers in engring. conf. 1991, Henry Hess award 1979, Design Divsn. Mechanisms and Robotics award 2002). Avocations: investments, speed reading. Office: Univ Ill College of Engring m/c 159 851 S Morgan St Chicago IL 60607-7043 Fax: 312-413-3365. E-mail: kcgupta@uic.edu.

GUPTA, MADAN LAL, cardiologist; b. New Delhi, Dec. 25, 1938; came to U.S., 1969; MD, Rajasthan U., Jaipur, India, 1961. Diplomate Am. Bd. Internal Medicine, Am. Bd. Cardiovasc. Disease. Resident internal medicine Flushing Hosp., N.Y.C., 1969-70, Brooklyn VA Hosp., N.Y.C., 1971-72; resident cardiology Grasslands Hosp., Valhalla, N.Y., 1970-71; fellow cardiology Maimonides Med. Ctr., N.Y.C., 1972-73; staff St. Marys Hosp., Galesburg, Ill., 1973—, Galesburg Clinic, 1973—. Fellow ACP, Am. Coll. Cardiology. Office: Galesburg Clinic 3315 N Seminary St Galesburg IL 61401-1224

GUPTA, MADHU SUDAN, electrical engineering educator; b. Lucknow, India, June 13, 1945; came to U.S., 1966; s. Manohar Lal and Premvati Gupta; m. Vijaya Lakshmi Tayal, July 9, 1970; children: Jay Mohan, Vineet Mohan; m. Manorama Vyas, May 29, 1985. BS, Lucknow U., India, 1963; MS, Allahabad U., India, 1966, Fla. State U., 1967; MA, U. Mich., 1968, PhD, 1972. Registered profl. engr., Ont. Asst. prof. elec. engring. Queen's U., Kingston, Ont., Can., 1972-73, MIT, Cambridge, 1973-78, assoc. prof. elec. engring., 1978-79, U. Ill., Chgo., 1979-84, prof. elec. engring., 1984-87, dir. grad. studies, 1980-83; vis. prof. elec. and computer engring. U. Calif., Santa Barbara, 1985-86; sr. staff engr. Hughes Aircraft Co., 1987-95; prof. elec. engring., chmn. dept. elec. engring. Fla. State U., Tallahassee, 1995-2000; prof. elec. engring., RF comm. sys. industry chair San Diego State U., 2000—; dir. Comm. Sys. and Signal Processing Inst., 2000—; adj. prof. elec. engring. U. Calif., San Diego, 2002—. Cons. Lincoln Lab. MIT, Lexington, 1976-79, Hughes Research Labs., Malibu, Calif., 1986-87. Editor: Electrical Noise, 1977, Teaching Engineering, 1987, Noise in Circuits and Systems, 1988, IEEE Microwave Mag., 2003—; contbr. articles to profl. jours.; editor in chief IEEE Microwave & Guided Wave Letters, 1998-2000. Lilly fellow, 1974-75. Fellow IEEE; mem. IEEE Microwave Soc. (vice chmn. 1984-85, chmn. 1986-87). Achievements include patents in field. Office: San Diego State U Dept Elec Engring 5500 Campanile Dr San Diego CA 92182-1309 E-mail: m.gupta@ieee.org. *A person's level of maturity is measured by what he wants from other members of the society: something for nothing, equal return for everything, or nothing except the opportunity to put something back in the kitty.*

GUPTA, PAUL R. lawyer; b. Cambridge, Eng., Mar. 7, 1950; came to U.S., 1953; naturalized, 1963. s. Suraj Narayan Gupta and Letty J.R. Paine; m. Mary Lee Gupta, Sept. 30, 1978; children: Adam, Margaret. BA, Yale U., 1971; JD, Harvard U., 1974. Bar: Mass., N.Y. Assoc. Simpson, Thacher & Bartlett, N.Y.C., 1974-79, Cravath, Swaine & Moore, N.Y.C., 1980-83; ptnr. Sherin and Lodgen, Boston, 1983-91, Nutter, McClennen & Fish, Boston, 1991-94, Sullivan & Worcester, LLP, Boston, 1995—. Dir. technology law group Sullivan & Worcester, LLP. Corres. European Intellectual Property Review; bd. editors Multimedia Strategist; contbr. articles to profl. jours.; editl. adv. bd. Elec. Banking Law and Commerce Report; mem. editl. bd. Am. Lawyer Y2K Counselor. Mem. ABA (co-chair year 2000 subcom., internat. property litigation com.), Boston Bar Assn. (chair ct. tech. com. 1994—), Boston Patent Law Assn. (co-chair anti-trust com. 1994—), Assn. of the Bar of the City of N.Y. (mem. computer law com. 1994—), Phi Beta Kappa. Office: Leboeuf Lamb Greene & MacRae LLP 125 W 55th St New York NY 10019 Office Fax: 617-439-0341. Business E-Mail: em.pgupta@llgm.com.

GUPTA, RAJAT KUMAR, lawyer, accountant; b. New Delhi, Apr. 22, 1960; arrived in U.S., 1970; s. Ravindra Kumar and Rama G. BBA, Rutgers Coll., New Brunswick, N.J., 1978-82; JD, Rutgers U., Newark, 1985-88. Bar: N.J. and Pa. 1989, U.S. Tax Ct. 1992; lic. CPA; lic. title ins. prodr. N.J. Dept. Banking and Ins. Staff acct. Borrelli & Assocs., Highland Park, NJ, 1983-84, S. Kirschenbaum & Co., CPA, East Brunswick, N.J., 1984-85; tax assoc. Coopers & Lybrand, Princeton, N.J., 1988-89; pvt. practice atty. New Brunswick, 1989-98; sr. assoc. Spevack & Cannan, P.A., Iselin, NJ, 1998—2000; fin. specialist N.J. Supreme Ct. - Office Atty. Ethics, Trenton, 2000—03; gen. counsel Premier Abstract and Title Agy., Inc., Cranbury, NJ, 2003—. Mentor Rutgers Law Sch., Seton Hall Law Sch., Asian and Pacific Law Students Assn. Prodn. editor Rutgers Computer & Technology Law Jour., 1987-88, Cannonball-One Lap of America, 1988; contbr. articles to profl. jours. Arbitrator Better Bus. Bur., Newark, 1986—87; vol. atty. Rutgers U. Off Campus Housing Ctr., 1996—2000; mem. com. on character N.J. Supreme Ct., 1997—2000. Mem.: AICPA, ABA, Accts. for Pub. Interest, Mercer County Bar Assn., Asian and Pacific Lawyers Assn. Hindu. Avocations: tennis, travel, photography, art. Office: 1006 Eastpark Blvd Cranbury NJ 08512

GUPTA, RAJENDRA PRASAD, physician; b. Marhura, India, May 19, 1948; naturalized, 1981; s. Ramji Das and Somvati Devi Gupta; m. Vinod K. Gupta, Dec. 14, 1974; children: Vanita, Vikram, Vishal. BSc, Agra U., Mathura, 1964; B Medicine B Surgery, Rajisthan U., Udiapur, India, 1969, MD, 1973; MBA, U. South Fla., 1999. Diplomate Am. Bd. Internal Medicine, Am. Bd. Gastroenterology, Am. Bd. Utilization and Quality Review Physicians. Rotating intern R.N.T. Med. Coll., Udaipur, Ind., 1969-70, resident in internal medicine, 1970-71, casualty med. officer in internal medicine, 1972; med. officer Seema Nursing Home, Udaipur, 1972, cons. physician, 1972-73; resident tng. in internal medicine Nat. Health Svc. Hosps., 1973-75; resident in internal medicine category "C" St. Francis Med. Ctr., Trenton, N.J., 1975-77; fellow in gastroenterology U. Medicine and Dentistry of N.J., Newark, 1977-79; pvt. practice in gastroenterology and internal medicine Trenton, 1979—; practice medicine Hopewell Valley Med. Group PA, Trenton, N.J. Tchr. Ravindra Nath Tagore Med. Coll.; clin. instr. U. Medicine and Dentistry of N.J., 1977-79, Robert Wood Johnson Med. Sch., Piscataway, NJ, 1992-95; clin. sr. instr. Hahneman Med. Coll., Phila., 1981-92; asst. prof. Robert Wood Johnson Med. Sch., Piscataway, 1995—; affiliated Capital Health Sys., Trenton, Robert Wood Johnson at Hamilton Hosp., N.J.; chmn. audit com. Mercer Med. Ctr., Trenton, 1982-83, chmn. utilization rev., 1983-88, mem. constitution and bylaws, 1984-88, mem. med. records com., 1983-85, exec. com., 1985-88, chmn. risk mgmt. com., 1987—, chief gastroenterology sect., 1993-95, chmn. com. sect. chiefs, 1995-97, chmn. physician/hosp. orgn. com., 1993-94, mem. steering com., 1994-95, mem. computer com., 1993, co-chmn. joint conf. com., 1995—, mem. strategic planning com., 1995-96, chmn. dept. medicine, 1995-97, mem. search com., med. dir., 1995, pres. med. staff, 1995-96, mem. fin. com., 1995-97; assoc. med. dir. Ctrl. N.J. Mercer, Middlesex Preferred Orgn., Prucare, 1985-86; pres. Healthpath Mercer County, Aetna Health Plan Ind. Practice Assocs., Mt. Laurel, N.J., 1992-93, 93-94; chmn. med. adv. bd. Morris Hall Home for Aged, Lawrenceville, N.J., 1987-90; treas. Physician's Healthcare Plan of N.J., Lawrenceville, 1993-95, sec., 1995-96, v.p., 1996-97, mem. fin. com., 1993-97; cons. gastroenterology Bd. Med. Examiners, Trenton, 1990—. Active Am. Cancer Soc. Mercer County chpt., 1990-92; bd. trustees Chapin Sch., Princeton, NJ, 1993-94; mem. Healthcare Adv. Group for Christie Whitman, 1993; chmn. Capital Health Sys. Found., Trenton, NJ, 2003—. Fellow ACP, Internat. Coll. Physicians, Am. Coll. Gastroenterology, Coll. Utilization Rev. Physicians; mem. AMA (category I award cert. 1979—, Physician Outreach award Presentation 1997, 99), Am. Soc. Gastrointestinal Endoscopy, Acad. Medicine N.J., Med. Soc. N.J. (mem. bd. trustees 1996—, mem. legis. com. 1992-94, mem. internat. med. grad. com. 1992-93, mem. pres. coun. 1992-93, vice-chmn. internat medicine grad. com. 1993-94, chmn. reference com. B house of dels. 1993, chmn. house of dels. 1994, vice-chmn. coun. on legis. 1994-95, del. organized med. staff sect. 1995—, mem. exec. com. coun. on legis. 1996—, cons. coun. legis. 1996—), N.J. Gastrointestinal

Soc., Mercer County Med. Soc. (v.p. 1990-91, chmn. numerous coms., pres. 1992-93), Capital Health Found. Republican. Hindu. Avocations: tennis, swimming, skiing. Office: Hopewell Valley Med Group PA 1871 Pennington Rd Trenton NJ 08618-1208

GUPTA, RAJESH, engineer, consultant; b. New Delhi, June 10, 1962; s. K.L. and Urmilla Varshney; m. Jaishree Gupta, Mar. 7, 1993; children: Sameer, Salil. BSc in Elec. Engring., Aligarh U., India, 1980—85. Asst engr. Hindustan Aeronautics Ltd., Lucknow, India; sr. systems analyst Emirates Airlines Group, Dubai, United Arab Emirates, 1989—94; cons. Compaq Can. Inc., Toronto, Canada, 1995—99; prin. cons., pres. E3i Technologies Inc., Mississauga, Canada, 2000—. Mem.: Metro. Profl. and Exec. Registry (hon.). Home: 3724 Crabtree Crescent Mississauga ON Canada L4T 1S6

GUPTA, RAJIV LOCHAN, chemical company executive; b. Muzzafarnagar, India, Dec. 23, 1945; s. Phool Prakash and Rukmini (Sahai) G.; m. Kamla Varshney, Jan. 24, 1968; children: Amita, Vanita. B of Tech. in Engring. with honors, Indian Inst. Tech., Bombay, 1967; MS in Ops. Rsch., Cornell U., 1969; MBA in Fin., Drexel U., 1971. Mgmt. sci. analyst Scott Paper Co., Phila., 1969-71; treasury mgr. Rohm & Haas Co., Phila., 1971-74, asst. to chief exec. officer, 1974-76, fin. planning mgr., 1976-79, fin. dir. East Croydon, Eng., 1979-81, planning dir. London, 1981-83, dir. gen. adj. Paris, 1983-84; dir. gen. Duolite Internat. SA, Paris, 1984-87; bus. dir. plastics Rohm & Haas Co., London, 1987-89, global bus. dir., 1989-93, v.p. Pacific Region Phila., 1993-96; chmn. comm. electronic materials bus. group Rohm & Haas Co., Phila., 1996-98, vice-chmn., 1999, chmn., CEO, 1999—. Bd. dirs. Agere Sys., Vanguard Group, Technitool. Sec. Indian Children Orgn., Phila., 1970-71. Hindu. Avocations: bridge, tennis, golf, travel, reading. Office: Rohm and Haas Co Independence Mall W Philadelphia PA 19105

GUPTA, RAKESH KUMAR, internist; b. India, July 31, 1953; MD, All India Inst. Med. Scis., 1976. Diplomate Am. Bd. Internal Medicine. Intern Jewish Hosp. - Med. Ctr., Bklyn., 1977-78; resident in internal medicine Chgo. Med. Sch., North Chicago, 1978-80; fellow in cardiology Wayne State U. Sch. Medicine, Detroit, 1980-82; internist VA Med. Ctr., Wilmington, Del.; instr. medicine Jefferson Med. Coll. Fellow Am. Coll. Cardiology. Office: VA Med Ctr 1601 Kirkwood Hwy Wilmington DE 19805-4917

GUPTA, SANJEEV, physician, researcher; b. Jaipur, Rajasthan, India, Apr. 23, 1954; came to U.S., 1985; s. Krishan Dayal and Kusum Lata Gupta; m. Neena Mangalick, Jan. 26, 1984; children: Sanchit, Sonika. MB, BS, Sardar Patel Med. Coll., Bikaner, India, 1977; MD, Postgrad. Inst. Med. Edn. & Rsch., Chandigarh, India, 1980. Diplomate Am. Bd. Internal Medicine. Intern Sardar Patel Med. Coll., 1976-77; resident, resident tchg. fellow Postgrad. Inst. Med. Edn. and Rsch., 1977-80, sr. resident in medicine, 1980-81; fellow in gastroenterology Hammersmith Hosp., London, 1981-85; fellow in hepatology U. So. Calif., L.A., 1985-87; sr. fellow in hepatology Albert Einstein Coll. of Medicine, Bronx, N.Y., 1987-89, asst. prof. medicine, 1989-94, assoc. prof. medicine, 1994-98, prof. medicine, 1998—. Sci. cons. Am. Liver Found., N.J., 1995—. Mem. editl. bd. Hepatology, 1994—, Am. Jour. Physiology, 1997-2000; contbr. over 200 articles to profl. jours. Recipient Gold medal Pfizer Inc., India, 1980, Clin. Investigator award NIH, 1989, numerous grants NIH, 1987—, Irma T. Hirschl award Hirschl/Weil Caulier Trust, 1995. Fellow Am. Coll. Physicians, Royal Coll. Physicians London; mem. Am. Gastroenterol. Assn., Am. Assn. for Studies of Liver Diseases, Brit. Soc. Gastroenterology, Assn. Physicians of India, Am. Fedn. for Clin. Rsch. Avocations: travel, reading, classical music, tennis, swimming. Office: A Einstein Coll Medicine 1300 Morris Park Ave Bronx NY 10461-1926

GUPTA, SANJEEV KUMAR, pharmaceutical executive, director; b. Asansol, India, Nov. 14, 1962; arrived in U.S.A., 1985; s. Birendra Prasad and Raj Kumari Gupta; m. Kavita Gupta, July 6, 1988; children: Tanya, Tushar. BS in Pharmacy, Birla Inst. Tech., India, 1985; MS in Indsl. Pharmacy, St. John's U., 1987, PhD in Pharm. Scis., 1992. Registered pharmacist N.Y. Post doctoral rsch. fellow Wyeth Labs., Peral River, NY, 1992—93; from formulation scientist to dir. R&D Barr Labs., Inc., Pomona, NY, 1993—2002, dir. R&D, 2002—. Mem.: Am. Assn. Pharm. Scientists, Rho Chi. Avocations: art, music, reading, tennis, teaching. Home: 650 McKinley Ave Washington Twps NJ 07676 Office: Barr Labs Inc 2 Quaker Rd Pomona NY 10970

GUPTA, SRABANA, economist, researcher; b. Calcutta, West Bengal, India, Feb. 3, 1964; arrived in U.S., 1988, permanent resident; d. Mithil Ranjan and Bharati Gupta; m. Farshad Araghi. PhD in Econs., U. Fla., Gainesville, 1994—94. Adj. instr. Santa Fe C.C., Gainesville, Fla., 1993; instr. U. of Fla., Gainesville, 1993—94; asst. prof. econs. Fla. Atlantic U., Fort Lauderdale, 1994—2002, Pa. State U., Erie, Pa., 2002—. Contbr. articles to profl. jours. and to World Bank. Recipient Nat. Merit Scholarship, West Bengal Secondary Bd., 1981; grantee Rsch. Grant, Fla. Atlantic U., 1998. Mem.: Internat. Atlantic Econ. Assn., Am. Econ. Assn., Rand Corp., Phi Kappa Phi. Avocations: art, literature, music, travel. Office: Pa State U Station Rd Erie PA 16563

GUPTA, SUDHIR, immunologist, educator; b. Bijnor, India, Apr. 14, 1944; came to U.S., 1971; s. Tej S. and Jagdishwari Gupta; m. Abha, Jan. 28, 1980; children: Ankmalika Abha, Saurabh Sudhir. MD, King George's Med. Coll., Lucknow, India, 1966, PhD, 1970. Diplomate Am. Bd. Allergy and Immunology, Am. Bd. Diagnostic Lab. Immunology, Clin. Immunology Bd., Royal Coll. Physicians and Surgeons Can. Intern King George's Med. Coll., Lucknow, 1966, resident in medicine, 1967-70; teaching faculty fellow dept. medicine Tufts U. Med. Sch., Boston, 1971-72; vis. fellow in medicine Columbia U., N.Y.C., 1972-74; rsch. fellow Sloan-Kettering Inst. Cancer Rsch., N.Y.C., 1974-76, asst. prof., 1976-78, assoc. prof., 1978-82; instr. Cornell U., N.Y.C., 1976-77, asst. prof., 1977-79, assoc. prof., 1979-82; prof. medicine U. Calif., Irvine, 1982—, prof. microbiology and molecular genetics, 1984—, prof. pathology, 1986—, prof. neurology, 1988—, vice chair Dept. Medicine, 1994—2002. Mem. adv. panel FDA, Washington, 1989—; sci. advisor Inst. Immunopathology, Kohn, Germany, 1990—; mem. allergy-immunology subcom. NIH, Bethesda, Md., 1985-89; vis. prof. Hematologic Rsch. Found., Roslyn, N.Y., 1992. Editor-in-chief Jour. Clin. Immunology, 1980—; editor: Immunology of Clinical and Experimental Diabetes, 1984, Mechanisms of Lymphocyte Activities and Immune Regulation I-VII, 1985-98, New Concepts in Immunodeficiency Diseases, 1993, Multidrug Resistance in Cancer, 1996, Immunology of HIV Infections, 1996. Pres. Nargis Dutt Meml. Found., So. Calif., 1990; vice-chair AIDS Task Force, Orange County (Calif.) Med. Assn., 1987-95; mem. Indo-Am. Republican Club, Orange County, 1991—. Recipient Arthur Manzel Rsch. award R.A. Cooke Inst., N.Y.C., 1976, Outstanding Achievement award in med. scis. Nat. Fedn. Asian Indians in N.Am., 1986, Lifetime Achievement award Jeffrey Modell Found., N.Y.C., 1990, Disting. Scientists award Assn. Scientists Indian Origin in Am., 1994, Disting. Physician award Indian Med. Assn. Master ACP; fellow Royal Coll. Physicians and Surgeons Can., Am. Soc. Medicine (London); mem. Am. Assn. Immunologists. Achievements include description of the presence of K+ channels in human T cells, their role in T cell function and assn. with exptl. autoimmune diseases, reversal of multidrug resistance of cancer cells by cyclosporin A both in vitro and in vivo, described a new human intracisternal retrovirus associated with CD4+ cell deficiency without HIV infection; increased apoptosis in T cells in human aging. Office: U Calif Dept Medicine C240 Med Sci I Irvine CA 92697-0001 Fax: 949-824-4362. E-mail: sgupta@uci.edu.

GUPTA, SURAJ NARAYAN, physicist, educator; b. Haryana, India, Dec. 1, 1924; came to U.S., 1953, naturalized, 1963; s. Lakshmi N. and Devi (Goyal) G.; m. Letty J.R. Paine, July 14, 1948; children: Paul, Ranee. MS, St. Stephen's Coll., India, 1946; PhD, U. Cambridge, Eng., 1951. Imperial Chem. Industries fellow U. Manchester, Eng., 1951-53; vis. prof. physics Purdue U., 1953-56; prof. physics Wayne State U., Detroit, 1956-61, disting. prof. physics, 1961-99, disting. prof. emeritus physics, 1999—. Researcher on high energy physics, nuclear physics, relativity and gravitation. Author: Quantum Electrodynamics, 1977. Fellow Am. Phys. Soc., Nat. Acad. Scis. of India. Achievements include quantum theory with negative probability and quantization of the electromagnetic field; flat-space interpretation of Einstein's theory of gravitation and quantization of the gravitational field; regularization and renormalization of elementary particle interactions; development of the theory of bound states in quantum electrodynamics and quantum chromodynamics; mass matrix formulation of quark mixing and CP violation in weak interactions; investigation of phenomena at supercollider energies. Home: 30001 Hickory Ln Franklin MI 48025-1566 Office: Wayne State U Dept Physics Detroit MI 48202

GUPTA, SURENDRA KUMAR, chemical firm executive; b. Delhi, India, Apr. 5, 1938; came to U.S., 1963, naturalized, 1971; s. Bishan Chand and Devki G.; m. Karen Patricia Clarke, Oct. 12, 1968; children—Jay, Amanda. BSc with honors, Delhi U., 1959, MSc, 1961; MTech, Indian Inst. Tech., Bombay, 1963; Ph.D., Wayne State U., 1968. Rsch. assoc. Western Mich. U., Kalamazoo, 1968-73; indsl. postdoctoral fellow Starks Assocs., Buffalo, 1973-74; group leader New Eng. Nuc. Co., Boston, 1974-80, Pathfinder Labs., St. Louis, 1981-83; chmn. bd., chemist Am. Radiolabeled Chem., Inc., St. Louis, 1983—. Contbr. numerous articles to internat. sci. jours. Mem. Am. Chem. Soc. (chmn. pub. relations com. 1970-73). Hindu. Avocations: table tennis; stamp collecting; traveling. Home: 22 Muirfield Ln Saint Louis MO 63141-7380 Office: Am Radiolabeled Chems Inc 101 ARC Dr Saint Louis MO 63146-3506

GUPTA, TEJ P. physician; b. Jodhpur, Raj, India, Aug. 18, 1954; came to U.S., 1983; s. Badri P. and Kamla Gupta; m. Anuradha Jain, June 15, 1983; children: Richa, Samir. Grad., U. Rajasthan, Jaipur, India, 1971; MD, S.M.S. Med. Coll., Jaipur, 1977. Diplomate in Internal medicine and gastroenterology Am. Bd. Internal Medicine. Resident S.M.S. Hosp., Jaipur, 1977-80; sr. house officer in medicine Barnsley Gen. Hosp., Yorkshire, Eng., 1981-83; resident in internal medicine Wayne State U. Sch. Medicine, Detroit, 1983-86, fellow in gastroenterology, 1986-88, instr. medicine, 1988-89; asst. prof. medicine Tex. Tech U. Sch. Medicine, El Paso, 1989-91; pvt. practice gastroenterology, El Paso, 1991—. Contbr. articles to med. jours. Grantee FDA, 1988-89, G.D. Searle & Co., 1990. Fellow ACP, Am. Coll. Gastroenterology. Office: 1733 Curie Dr Ste 200 El Paso TX 79902-2909

GUPTA, VIJAY KUMAR, chemistry educator; b. Ambala Cantt, Haryana, India, Apr. 27, 1941; m. Surjit Mohini Aggarwal, Sept. 5, 1968; children: Sonia, Angela, Ashish. BS in Chemistry with honors, Panjab U., Chandigarh, India, 1961, MS in Chemistry with honors, 1962, PhD in Chemistry, 1969. Asst. prof. chemistry Punjab Engring. Coll., Chandigarh, India, 1962-64, 67-68; postdoctoral rsch. assoc. Wright State U., Dayton, Ohio, 1968-69; rsch. chemist Lawrence Livermore Nat. Lab., Livermore, Calif., summer 1980; adj. faculty mem. Lebanon Correctional Inst., Ohio, fall 1977, 78, summer 1982; fellow Wright Patterson AFB, Dayton, summer 1981, with aero-propulsion lab., 1981-83, with materials lab., 1984, fellow materials lab., 1985, summers 1987, 88, 91, vis. scientist materials lab., 1985-87; adj. faculty mem. Wright State U., 1985; adj. faculty in chemistry Wilberforce U., Ohio, spring/summer 1981, 82, 83, 84, 1983-84, fall 1986-87; prof., chmn. chemistry, researcher Cen. State U., Wilberforce, Ohio, 1969-98, prof. emeritus, 1998—. Cons. E.G.&G. Mound Labs., summer, 1989, 90, 92, 93; researcher in environ. pollution, lubricant devel. and characterization, devel. of radioluminescent light sources, thermodynamics, electrochemistry, chem. kinetics, trace metals analysis, energy conversion and storage, for IBM Corp., Pitts. Plate Glass Fiber Glass Tech. Ctr., NASA, Johnson Johnson Controls Inc., Lawrence Livermore Nat. Lab., Wright Patterson AFB, Universal Energy Systems Inc., AF Office of Sci. Research, San Jose State U., United Tech. Systems Inc., SCEEE, Systran Corp., E.G.&G. Mound Techs., Inc., U. Dayton Rsch. Inst. Contbr. numerous articles to profl. jours. Recipient Appreciation award Ctrl. State U., 1975-76, Talmadge McKinney award, 1986, Excellence in Rsch. award, 1995, Outstanding Svc. to Cmty. award India Club of Greater Dayton, 1985, Clarence E. Bowman award for Comm. Svcs., 1991, others; Nat. Urban League fellow, IBM Corp. fellow, summer 1973, Pittsburgh Plate Glass Fiberglass Tech. Ctr., summer 1976, Johnson Johnson Control Inc. fellow, 1979, NSF summer fellow, 1979; USAF grantee, 1982-83, NASA grantee, 1976-79, U.S. Army grantee, 1994-98, USN grantee, 1995-96. Mem.: Divine Love Mission, Am. Chem. Soc. (chmn. Dayton sect. 1988, Outstanding Sect. award 1988), India Club (Dayton). Democrat. Hindu. Home: 2810 Dennis Ct Beavercreek OH 45434-6522

GUPTA, VISHAL K, pharmaceutical scientist; b. India; s. Jagdish and Pratima Gupta; m. Stuti Sinha, Sept. 11, 2001. B in pharmacy, Amravati U., 1992; PharmM, Banaras Hindu U., 1994; PhD, U. of Ga., 2000. Rsch. assoc. Ranbaxy Labs, Gurgaon, India, 1994—95; vis. scientist Rohm GmbH, Darmstadt, Germany, 1999; rsch. investigator Pharmacia Corp., Skokie, Ill., 2000—. Sec.-treas. Am. Assn. of Pharm. Scientists - Pharm. Technologies Sect., Arlington, Va., 2003—. Recipient IDMA-GP Nair Best Grad. award, Indian Drug Manufacturer's Assn., 1993, Tchg. Asst. Mentor award, U. of Ga., 1999; Grad. assistantship, 1997—2000. Mem.: Am. Assn. of Pharm. Scientists, Phi Beta Delta, Rho-Chi. Achievements include patents for development of Novel oral site-specific drug delivery system; patents pending for new technology for production of compressed tablets. Office: Pharmacia 4901 Searle Pkwy Bldg P120 Skokie IL 60077 Office Fax: 847-982-4900. E-mail: vishalgupta100@hotmail.com.

GURALNICK, SIDNEY AARON, civil engineering educator; b. Phila., Apr. 25, 1929; s. Philip and Kenia (Dudnik) G.; m. Eleanor Alban, Mar. 10, 1951; children: Sara Dian, Jeremy. BSc, Drexel Inst. Tech., Phila., 1952; MS, Cornell U., 1955, PhD, 1958. Registered profl. engr., Pa.; lic. structural engr., Ill. Instr., then asst. prof. Cornell U., 1952-58, mgr. structural research lab., 1956-58; mem. faculty Ill. Inst. Tech., Chgo., 1958—, prof. civil engring., 1967—, disting. prof. engring., 1982—, dir. structural engring. labs., 1968-71, dean Grad. Sch., 1971-75, exec. v.p., provost, 1975-82, trustee, 1976-82, dir. Advanced Bldg. Materials and Sys. Ctr., 1987—. Devel. engr. Portland Cement Assn., Skokie, Ill., 1959-61; participant internat. confs.; cons. to govt. and industry. Author numerous papers in field. Trustee Inst. Gas Tech., 1976-81, Rsch. Inst. of Ill. Inst. Tech., 1976-82; commr.-at-large North Ctrl. Assn. Schs. and Colls., 1985-89, cons., evaluator, 1989-93. With C.E., U.S. Army, 1950-51. McGraw fellow, 1952-53; Faculty Rsch. fellow Ill. Inst. Tech., 1960; European travel grantee, 1961 Fellow: ASCE (Collingwood prize 1961, Lifetime Achievement award Ill. sect. 1997, Civil Engr. of Yr. award Ill. sect. 1998); mem.: Ill. Univs. Transp. Rsch. Consortium (adminstrv. com. 1983—93), Transp. Rsch. Bd., Structural Engrs. Assn. Ill. (bd. dirs., pres.-elect 1989—90, pres. 1990—91, John F. Parmer award 1993), Soc. Exptl. Mechanics, Am. Concrete Inst., Chi Epsilon, Tau Beta Pi, Phi Kappa Phi, Sigma Xi. Office: Ill Inst Tech 3300 S Federal St Chicago IL 60616-3793 E-mail: guralnick@iit.edu.

GURAM, GURPAL SINGH, mathematician, educator; b. Ludhiana, India, Aug. 12, 1946; s. Arjan Singh and Bhagwant (Kaur) G.; m. Mohinder Kaur Guram, Aug. 17, 1975; children: Gurpreet, Jaspreet. BSc, Panjab (India) U., 1965; MSc, U. Roorkee, India, 1968; MS, U. Windsor, Can., 1971; PhD, U. Windsor, 1974. Assoc. prof. math. N.Y. Inst. Tech., Old Westbury, 1982—. Home: 106 Bagatelle Rd Dix Hills NY 11746

GURASH, JOHN THOMAS, insurance company executive; b. Oakland, Calif., Nov. 25, 1910; s. Nicholas and Katherine Restovic Gurash; 1 child, John N. Student Loyola Univ. Sch. Law, 1934. With Pacific Employers Ins. Co., 1944—53; pres., organizer Meritplan Ins. Co., 1953—59; exec. vpres. Pacific Employers Ins. Co., 1959—60, pres., 1960—68, chmn. bd., 1968—76; vpres. Ins. Co. N. Am., 1966—70; exec. vpres. INA Corp., 1968—69, dir., 1968—69, chmn., 1969—74, pres., 1969—74, CEO, 1969—74, chmn., 1974—75, CEO, 1974—75, chmn. bd., 1975, chmn. exec. comt., 1975—79; chmn. bd. Certain-Teed Corp. and Saint Gobain Corp., 1978—92, chmn. emeritus, 1992—; chmn. Horace Mann Educators Corp., Springfield, Ill., 1989—96, chmn. emeritus, 1996—; dir. St. Gobain Corp., chmn. bd. dirs., 1991—92; trustee emeritus Occidental Col., Los Angeles; former trustee Orthopaedic Hosp., Los Angeles; dir. Weingart Found., bd. dirs. bd. dirs. Weingart Found. Office: 1000 Wilshire Blvd Ste 610 Los Angeles CA 90017-2463 E-mail: jtgurash@aol.com.

GUREVICH, GRIGORY, visual artist, educator, mime; b. St. Petersburg, Russia, Dec. 26, 1937; came to U.S., 1976; s. Abram Grigoryevich Gurevich and Klara Mihailovna (Olshvang) Fleitman; m. Mongita Zalmanovna Freedman, Aug. 8, 1958 (div. Feb. 1967); 1 child, Jelena Gurevich Scherbina; m. Erika Wittmann, Jan. 17, 1987; d. Sept. 6, 2001. 1 child, Alexander. Diploma, Acad. Fine & Indsl. Art, St. Petersburg, 1966. Interior designer Lenprojekt, St. Petersburg, Lenzneeap, 1961-63, 63-65; founder Grigur's Pantomime Theater, St. Petersburg, 1966-69; founder mime sch. St. Petersburg, 1969-75; founder Grigur's Pantomime Theater, N.Y.C., 1977; tchr. visual arts Bergen Sch., Jersey City, 1980-82; instr. sculpture Newark Sch. Fine and Indsl. Art, 1982-96; prof. St. Johns U., Jamaica, N.Y., 1994-97. Conductor workshops on sculpture U.S., Italy, Denmark; founder Art Workshops Festival, Arts on the Hudson, Jersey City. Exhibited in solo and group exhbns. U.S., Russia, France, Denmark, Germany; bronze sculpture tableau Commuters for Newark Penn Sta., 1985, bronze bust Kazuo Hashimoto, 1996; represented in numerous pvt. collections, Russia, U.S. and Europe, Hermitage Mus., N.Y. Pub. Libr., Libr. Newark Mus., Montclair Mus., Libr. St. Bonaventure U., Yad Vashem Mus., Israel; pub. poetry Reflections, 1992; author: Book of Numbers 1-10, 10-1, 1993 (collection Bklyn. Mus. 1994); inventor process of wood firing, 1963, manifolding book, 1995. Founder Arts on the Hudson Sch., Jersey City, N.J., 1998. Recipient Grumbacher award, Marian Reitman award, others. Mem. N.Y. Artists Equity Assn., Am. Artists Profl. League (1st Place Nat. award 1993, 98), Hudson Artists (Artist of Yr. 1995, other awards), Screen Actors Guild. Home: 282 Barrow St Jersey City NJ 07302-3502 E-mail: grigur@netzero.net.

GURFEIN, PETER J. lawyer; b. N.Y.C., Sept. 13, 1948; m. Pamela Hedin, June 23, 1976; children: Diana, William, Eva. BA, NYU, 1969; JD, George Washington U., 1973. Bar: N.Y. 1976, U.S. Supreme Ct. 1976, US. Dist. Ct. (so. and ea. dists.) N.Y. 1976, U.S. Ct. Appeals (2d cir.) 1979, Internat. Ct. Trade 1979, U.S. Ct. Appeals (9th cir.) 1986, Calif. 1986, U.S. Dist. Ct. (no., ea., so. and cen. dists.) Calif. 1987, D.C. 1993. Project dir. Commn. on Correctional Facilities and Scs. ABA, Washington, 1973-75; asst. dist. atty., spl. narcotics prosecutor Dist. Atty.'s Office N.Y. County, N.Y.C., 1976-81; assoc. Zalkin, Rodin & Goodman, N.Y.C., 1981-83, Moses & Singer, N.Y.C., 1983-86; ptnr. Morrison & Foerster, San Francisco, 1986-92, Sonnenschein, Nath & Rosenthal, L.A. and San Francisco, 1993-2000, Akin, Gump, Strauss, Hauer & Feld, LLP, L.A., 2001—. Editor-in-chief The Calif. Bankruptcy Jour., 1995-2000; contbr. articles to handbooks and profl. jours. Mem. Bar Assn. San Francisco (chmn. bankruptcy and comml. law sect. 1993), L.A. County Bar Assn.; dir. L.A. Bankruptcy Forum, 1995—. Office: Akin Gump Strauss Hauer & Feld LLP Ste 2400 2029 Century Park E Los Angeles CA 90067 E-mail: pgurfein@akingump.com.

GURFEIN, RICHARD ALAN, lawyer; b. N.Y.C., Nov. 4, 1946; s. Jack and Ruth (Kronowitz) G.; m. Erica P. Temchin, Oct. 20, 1978; children: Jared L., Amanda, Jessica M., Sarah R. BE, NYU, 1967; JD, Bklyn. Law Sch., 1971. Bar: N.Y. 1972, U.S. Dist. Ct. (so. and ea. dists.) N.Y. 1973, U.S. Supreme Ct. 1976, U.S. Ct. Appeals (2d cir.) 1990. Assoc. Mark B. Wiesen, PC, N.Y.C., 1972-78; ptnr. Wiesen & Gurfein, N.Y.C., 1978-82, Wiesen, Gurfein & Jenkins, N.Y.C., 1982-2001; pres. Trial1.com, Inc., 1997—; prin. Richard A. Gurfein & Assocs., PLLC, 2001—02; founder and ptnr. Gurfein Douglas LLP, 2002—. Moderator, lectr. Nassau Acad. Law, 1984—, N.Y. State Trial Lawyers Inst., 1985—, treas., 1989-91, pres. 1995-96. Recipient Crown of Good Name award Inst. Jewish Humanities, 1996. Mem. Assn. Trial Lawyers Am., N.Y. State Trial Lawyers Assn. (lectr. continuing legal edn. 1985—, bd. dirs. 1986—, chmn. com. on coms. 1987-88, exec. com. 1987—, dep. treas. 1988-89, treas. 1989-91, sec. 1991-92, v.p. 1992-94, pres. elect 1994-95, pres. 1995-96, past pres. 1996—), N.Y. County Lawyers Assn., Nassau County Bar Assn. (chmn. com. on med. jurisprudence 1983-86), Million Dollar Advocates Forum, N.Y. State Bar Assn., Bklyn. Bar Assn. Avocations: astronomy, amateur radio, photography, golf, computing. Office: Gurfein Douglas LLP 11 Park Pl Rm 1100 New York NY 10007-2889 E-mail: rgurfein@trial1.com.

GURIAN, BENNETT SHEPPE, psychiatrist; b. New Haven, Conn., May 21, 1932; s. Harry and Pauline (Caplan) G.; m. Elaine Gurian; children: Aaron, Josef, Eve; m. Tanya T. Terry, May 22, 1983; children: Amy, Andrew. AB, Brandeis U., 1954; MS, Brown U., 1956; MD, Boston U., 1965. Diplomate Am. Bd. Psychiatry and Neurology with added qualifications in geriatric psychiatry. Ind. rschr. Mass. Gen. Hosp., Boston, 1956-61; dir. geriatrics Mass. Mental Health Ctr., Boston, 1969-92; sr. cons. geriatric psychiatry Deaconess Hosp., Boston, 1992-95; N.E. regional dir. UPBEAT Dept. Vet.'s Affairs, Brockton/West Roxbury, Mass., 1995-97; psychiatrist Beth Israel Deaconess Med. Ctr., Boston, 1997—; medical dir. Jewish Family and Children's Svcs., Newton, Mass., 2000—. Editor: Jour. Geriatric Psychiatry, 1995—; contbr. articles to profl. jours. Founder For Fathering project Med. Found., Boston, 1995—; bd. dirs. SPRY Found., Washington, 1990-2000, Boston Soc. for Gerontol. Psychiatry, 1995-2001; v.p. Physicians for Social Responsibility, 1961-70. Recipient Significant Achievement award Am. Psychiat. Assn., 1990, resolution and recognition Mass. Ho. Reps., 1989. Fellow Am. Geriatrics Soc., Gerontol. Soc. Am. Avocation: watercolorist. Home: 328 Mason Ter Brookline MA 02446-2779

GURIAN, MAL, telecommunications executive; b. N.Y.C., Nov. 17, 1926; s. George Joseph and Rose (Graff) G., m. Gloria Dickler; children: Randy Harlan, Nancy Ellen Newman. Ptnr. Mal Gurian Assocs., N.Y.C., 1946-77; v.p. Radio Telephone Corp., N.Y.C., 1960-83; sr. v.p. Aerotron, Inc., Raleigh, N.C., 1965-81; v.p. Oki Advanced Comm., Hackensack, N.J., 1981-84; pres. Oki Telecom, Fairlawn, N.J., 1984-88, Cartell, Inc., Romulus, Mich., 1988, Cellcom Cellular Corp., Fairfield, N.J., 1989-91; CEO Universal Cellular, Inc., Anaheim, Calif., 1992; chmn., CEO Global Link Comm., Inc., Irvine, Calif., 1993—; pres., CEO Authentix Network, Inc., Tucson, 1995-98, 99—, chmn., 1998-2001; pres., CEO SimplySay, LLC, Tucson, 2001—02, Mal Gurian Assocs., Bradenton, Fla., 2002—; advisor I-Control, Campbell, Calif., 2002—03. Pres. Ea. Profl. Photographers Assn., N.Y.C., 1951-53; exec. advisor TRW Wireless Commn., Sunnyvale, Calif., 1994; advisor Sims Comms., Inc., Delray Beach, Fla., 1994-98; arbitrator Am. Arbitration Assn., 1994—; bd. dirs. N.E. Digital Networks, 1998-99, Rangestar Internat., San Jose, Calif., 1999-2001, bd. electronic comm., 1996-98. Life mem. Old Tappan (N.J.) First Aid Corp., 1966—. Cpl. USMC, 1943-46. Decorated Air medal; named to Wireless Hall of Fame, 2003; recipient Alexander S. Popov Hon. medal, St. Petersburg Electrotech. U., Russia, 1995. Fellow Radio Club Am. (life mem., v.p. 1976-92, exec. v.p. 1993, pres. 1994, pres. emeritus 1995—, Spl. Svcs. award 1986, Sarnoff citation 1988, Fred Link award 1989, inducted into Wireless Hall of Fame, 2003); mem. Am. Assn. Pub. Safety Comm. Officers, Nat. Assn. Bus. and Ednl. Radio (bd. dirs. 1977-84, Chmn.'s award 1986, named to Wireless Hall of Fame 2003). *Advances in technology is rapidly moving on. Mankind must strive to utilize our developments in a positive vein and promote compatibility amongst each other.*

GURION, HENRY BARUCH, lawyer; b. Duluth, Minn., Mar. 30, 1950; s. Maximilian and Gina (Spinner) Gurion; m. Joanne Francesca Bohman, Aug. 21, 1971; children: Lisa, David, Daniel, Charles. BA, U. Ill., 1972; JD, Loyola U. Chgo., 1975. Assoc. Law Offices of Thomas J. Keevers, Chgo., 1975—79, Garretson & Santora, Chgo., 1979—81, Purcell & Wardrope Chartered, Chgo., 1981—85, Henry B. Gurion and Assocs., 1985—88; mng. atty. midwest region AIG Inc., 1988—91; v.p., gen. counsel MJMC, Hazel Crest, Ill., 1991—. Mem.: Ill. Bar Assn. Office: MJMC 3111 167th St Hazel Crest IL 60429 1025 E-mail. Hgurion@MJMC.com.

GURLEY, CURTIS RAYMOND, lawyer; b. Joplin, Mo., Apr. 5, 1959; s. Carl R. and Glenda (Cummins) G.; m. Rebecca Lynn Miller; 2 children: Jackson M. and Davis C. AB, U. Mo., 1986, JD, 1989. Bar: N.Mex. 1989, U.S. Ct. Appeals (10th cir.) 1989, Mo. 1990, U.S. Dist. Ct. N.Mex. 1991, Colo. 1998. Ptnr. Hynes, Hale & Gurley, Farmington, N.Mex. Mem. NACDL, San Juan County Bar (pres. 1993), N.Mex. Trial Lawyers Assn. (bd. dirs. 1993-97), N.Mex. Criminal Def. Attys. Assn., Elks. Republican. Presbyterian. Office: Gurley Law Firm PO Box 1982 Farmington NM 87499 E-mail: curtisgurley@gurleylawfirm.com.

GURLEY, FRANKLIN LOUIS, lawyer, military historian; b. Syracuse, N.Y., Nov. 26, 1925; Swiss national, 1994 (dual nationality); s. George Bernard and Catherine Veronica (Moran) G.; m. Elizabeth Anne Ryan, June 17, 1950. AB, Harvard U., 1949, JD, 1952. Bar: Mass. 1952, N.Y. 1956, Ill. 1956, Mich. 1956, D.C. 1956. Fgn. service staff officer Dept. State, Washington and Germany, 1953-55; atty. N.Y. Central R.R. Co., 1955-56; asst. dist. atty. New York County, 1956-57; atty. firm Dewey, Ballantine, Bushby, Palmer & Wood, N.Y.C., 1957-63; gen. counsel, sec. IBM Europe Corp., Paris; also mng. atty. IBM Corp., Armonk, N.Y., 1963-68; sr. v.p., gen. counsel Nestle S.A., Vevey, Switzerland, 1968-83, spl. legal adv., 1984-85; internat. legal cons., 1985—. Author: 399th in Action in World War II, 1946, Into the Mountains Dark, 2000, (play) King Philip's War, 1952; chief editor Beachhead News (Germany), 1945-46; contbr. articles to profl. and mil. jours. Pres. Tappan Landing Assn. Tarrytown N.Y. 1958-60. Served with inf. AUS, 1944-46, ETO. Decorated Bronze Star, Combat Inf. Badge; 7th Army mile run champion, 1945; set West

Point and Heptagonal 1000-yard records in track, 1948. Mem. SAR (sec., bd. mgrs. N.Y. chpt. 1957-63, founding mem. Swiss chpt. 1970), 100th Inf. Divsn. Assn. (historian 1984—). Home and Office: 1626 Romanens Fribourg Switzerland

GURNACK, DEAN HILTON, artist; b. East Orange, N.J., Apr. 1, 1945; s. Walter A. and Virginia (Hilton) G.; m. Elizabeth Anne Lehman, June 7, 1980. AB, Colgate U., 1967; MBA, Columbia U., 1970; AA, Am. Acad. Art, Chgo., 1981. Exhibited in group shows at Covenant Club, Chgo., 1980, Libertyville (Ill.) Arts Ctr., 1981-85, Salmagundi Club, N.Y.C., 1985, Bennett Galleries, Knoxville, Tenn., 1991, 92, 94, 96, Nashville, 1993, Bryant Galleries, Birmingham, Ala., 1992, Indpls. Mus. Art Regional Juried Exhbn., Columbus, Ind., 1998 (award of merit), Nat. Oil and Acrylic Painters' Soc. Juried Exhbn., Osage Beach, Mo., 1998, Hoosier Salon Juried Exhbn., Indpls., 1998, 99; represented in permanent collections Knoxville Mus. Art, 1st Knoxville Bank, Suntrust Bank, Knoxville, Hyatt Rescorp., Chgo., others. 2d lt. U.S. Army N.G., 1967-68. Union League Club of Chgo. scholar, 1978, 79, 80. Avocations: flying, computers. Home: 22436 Norfolk Ct Novi MI 48374 E-mail: gurnack@gurnack.com.

GURNEY, ALBERT RAMSDELL, playwright, novelist, educator; b. Buffalo, Nov. 1, 1930; s. Albert Ramsdell and Marion (Spaulding) Gurney; m. Mary Forman Goodyear, June 8, 1957; children: George, Amy, Evelyn, Benjamin. BA, Williams Coll., 1952, DDL (hon.), 1984; MFA, Yale U., 1958; LLD (hon.), Buffalo State U., 1992. Mem. faculty MIT, 1960-96, prof. lit., 1970-96. Contbr., ; author: (plays) The Golden Fleece, 1969, Public Affairs, 1970, Scenes from American Life, 1971, Children, 1974, Richary Cory, 1976, The Middle Ages, 1977, The Wayside Motor Inn, 1977, The Golden Age, 1980, The Dining Room, 1981, What I Did Last Summer, 1982, The Perfect Party, 1985, Another Antigone, 1985, Sweet Sue, 1986, The Cocktail Hour, 1988, Love Letters, 1988, The Snow Ball, 1991, The Old Boy, 1991, The Fourth Wall, 1992, Later Life, 1993, A Cheever Evening, 1994, Sylvia, 1994, Overtime, 1995, Let's Do It!, 1996, The Guest Lecturer, 1998, Labor Day, 1998, Far East, 1999, Ancestral Voices, 1999, Human Events, 2000, Buffalo Gal, 2001, The Fourth Wall (revised), 2002, O Jerusalem, 2003, Big Bill, 2003, (teleplays) O Youth and Beauty, 1979, The Hit List, 1988, Love Letters, 1999, (novels) The Gospel According to Joe, 1974, Entertaining Strangers, 1977, The Snow Ball, 1984, (one-act opera) Strawberry Fields, 1999. With USNR, 1952—55. Recipient award, N.Y. Drama Desk, 1971, Rockefeller Playwrights, 1977, Playwriting award, Nat. Endowment Arts, 1981—82, Award of Merit, Am. Acad. and Inst. Arts and Letters, 1987, Lucille Lortel award for Body of Work, 1994, William Inge award, 2000. Mem.: Dramatists Guild, Writers Guild, Authors League Am. Home: 40 Wellers Bridge Rd Roxbury CT 06783-1616 E-mail: a.r.gurney@worldnet.att.net.

GURNEY, DANIEL SEXTON, race car manufacturing company executive, racing team executive; b. L.I., Apr. 13, 1931; s. John R. and Roma (Sexton) G.; m. Evi B., July 7, 1969; children: Justin B., Alexander R.; children by previous marriage: John, Lyndee, Danny, Jimmy. Grad., Menlo Jr. Coll., 1951. Profl. race car driver, 1955-70; pres., owner Dan Gurney's All Am. Racers, Inc. (doing bus. as); Dan Gurney Eagle Racing Cars, U.S.A., Santa Ana, Calif., 1964-65; mgr. Eagle Racing Team (Indpls. 500 winners 1968, 73, 75, U.S. Auto Club Nat. Championship winners 1968, 74), Formula A Championship winners 1968, 69); TV sports commentator. Mem. Automobile Competition Com. for U.S.A.; car owner, builder Fed Ex Championship Series, Santa Ana, Calif. Served with U.S. Army, 1952-54, Korea. Recipient numerous racing awards including GTO driving championship Internat. Motor Sports Assn. (driver Chris Cord), 1987, GTO Mfrs.' championship Interrnat. Motor Sports Assn. (mfr. Toyota), 1987, Norelco Cup championship (driver Willy T. Ribbs), 1987, IMSA Camel GTP championship, 1992, 93, IMSA mfrs. championship for Toyota, 1992, 93. Mem. Screen Actors Guild, AFTRA, U.S. Auto Club, Sports Car Club Am., U.S. C. of C., Championship Auto Racing Teams, Inc., Soc. Automotive Engrs., Fedn. Internationale de L'Automobile, Internat. Motor Sports Assn. Clubs: Balboa Bay, Eagle.

GURNEY, MARY KATHLEEN, pharmacist; b. Chgo., Mar. 8, 1964; d. John Lewis and Sylvia Yvonne (Lopatka) G. BS in Pharmacy, Drake U., 1987; MS in Social and Adminstrv. Pharmacy, U. Wis., 1999. From pharmacist to pharmacy mgr. Osco Drug/Albertson's, Beloit, Wis., 1987—. Vol. Children's Mus. Indpls., Ind., 1990-93. Mem. Am. Pharm. Assn. (del. 1994, 95, 99, postgrad. officer Acad. Pharm. Rsch. and Sci.-Econ., Social and Adminstrv. Sci. sect. 1999-2001), Ind. Pharmacists Assn. (chmn. pub. affairs 1993-95, Marion Merrell Dow Disting. Young Pharmacist award for Ind. 1993), Pharm. Soc. Wisc., Pi Beta Phi (bd. dirs. 1999-2001), Phi Lamdba Sigma. Avocations: ballroom dancing, walking, bicycling. Home: 6610 Offshore Dr Madison WI 53705-4236

GURNIS, MICHAEL CHRISTOPHER, geological sciences educator; b. Boston, Oct. 22, 1959; s. George Albert and Barbara (Dempsey) G. BS, U. Ariz., 1982; PhD, Australian Nat. U., Canberra, 1987. Rsch. fellow in geophysics Calif. Inst. Tech., Pasadena, 1986-88, assoc. prof. geophysics, 1994-96; asst. prof. geol. scis. U. Mich., Ann Arbor, 1988-93, assoc. prof., 1993—; asst. dir. Seismological Lab. Calif. Inst. Tech., Pasadena, 1995—, prof. geophysics, 1996—. Recipient Presdl. Young Investigator award NSF, 1989, fellowship David and Lucile Packard Found., 1991. Fellow Am. Geophys. Union (Macelwance medal 1993), Geol. Soc. Am. (sr., Donath medal 1993). Achievements include research in the linkage of sedimentary rocks deposited in the interiors of continents to geodynamic processes within the earth; global dynamics, mantle convection, plate tectonics, sea level changes, evolution of mantle and crust; computational and visual fluid mechanics. Office: Calif Inst Tech Seismol Lab-252-21 Pasadena CA 91125-0001

GURNOW, MICHAEL ERWIN, literature and film educator, art educator; s. Michael Erwin and Delia S. Gurnow; m. Heather K. Gurnow. MA in English, S.E. Mo. State U., 2001. Adj. faculty, English Dept. Shawnee Cmty. Coll., 2003—, S.E. Mo. State Univ., 2001—. Author: (author of various short stories/drama) The Killing Joke and Other Stories/Apartment of Atreus.

GURR, JIM R. statistician; b. Warner Robins, Ga., Oct. 24, 1964; s. Rufus Baker and Jannette Carroll Gurr; m. Stephanie Dawn Pycus, Jan. 10, 1995; children: Hayden T., Jillian A. BS, Ill. State U., 1998, MS, 2000. Commd. 2d lt. US Army, 1987; adj. faculty Ill. State U., Normal, 1998—2000; rsch. statistician Nielsen Media Rsch., Dunedin, Fla., 2000—. Adj. faculty math. St. Petersburg Coll., Tarpon Springs, Fla., 2000—02. Active PTA, Palm Harbor, Fla., 2001—02. Mem.: WAPOR, AAPOR, Am. Statis. Assn. Republican. Home: 875 Delaware Ave Palm Harbor FL 34683 Office: Nielsen Media Rsch 375 Patricia Ave Dunedin FL 34698

GURR, TED ROBERT, political science educator, author; b. Spokane, Wash., Feb. 21, 1936; s. Robert Lucas and Anne (Cook) G.; m. Erika Brigitte Klie, Feb. 20, 1960 (dec. May 1980); children: Lisa Anne, Andrea Mariel; m. Barbara Harff, Jan. 14, 1981. BA, Reed Coll., 1957; postgrad., Princeton U., 1957-58; PhD, NYU, 1965, Sofia U., 2002. From asst. editor to assoc. editor Am. Behavioral Scientist, 1961-64; asst. to dir. NYU Office Research Services, N.Y.C., 1962-64; research assoc. Princeton (N.J.) U., 1965-67, asst. prof., 1967-69, assoc. dir. workshop in comparative politics, 1966-69; assoc. prof. polit. sci. Northwestern U., Evanston, Ill., 1969-72, prof., 1972-74, Payson S. Wild prof. polit sci., 1974-84, chmn. dept., 1977-80; prof. polit. sci., dir. Ctr. for Comparative Politics U. Colo., Boulder, 1985-89; prof. govt. and politics U. Md., College Park, 1989—, disting. univ. prof., 1995—. Co-dir. hist. and comparative task force Nat. Commn. Causes and Prevention of Violence, 1968-69; vis. fellow Inst. Criminology Cambridge (Eng.) U., 1976; dir. Minorities at Risk project Ctr. Internat. Devel. and Conflict Mgmt. U. Md., College Park, 1987-2002; fellow U.S. Inst. Peace, Washington, 1988-89, PIOOM fellow Leiden U., 1993, sr. cons. Task Force on State Failure, U.S. Govt., 1994—; Olof Palme vis. prof. Uppsala U., 1996-97. Author: (with A. de Grazia) American Welfare, 1961; Why Men Rebel (Woodrow Wilson Found. award 1970), 1970, Politimetrics, 1972; (with C. Ruttenberg) Cross National Studies of Civil Violence, 1969; (with H.D. Graham) Violence in America: Historical and Comparative Perspectives, 1969, rev. edit., 1979; (with H. Eckstein) Patterns of Authority, 1975; Rogues, Rebels, Reformers, 1976; (with P. Grabosky and R.C. Hula) The Politics of Urban Crime and Conflict, 1977; Handbook of Political Conflict: Theory and Research, 1980; (with D.S. King) The State and the City, 1987; Violence in America, Vol. 1: History of Crime, Vol. 2: Protest, Rebellion, Reform, 20th ann. edit., 1989; (with J.A. Goldstone and F. Moshiri) Revolutions of the Late Twentieth Century, 1991, Minorities at Risk: A Global View of Ethnopolitical Conflict, 1993; (with B. Harff) Ethnic Conflict in World Politics, 1994; (with J.L. Davies) Preventive Measures: Building Risk Assessment and Crisis Early Warning Systems, 1998, Peoples Versus States: Minorities at Risk in the New Century, 2000; (with R. Alker and K. Rupesinghe) Journeys Through Conflict: Narratives and Lessons, 2002; (with M.G. Marshall) Peace and Conflict, 2003; mem. editl. bd. World Politics, 1970-73, Comparative Polit. Studies, 1968-99, Nationalism and Ethnic Politics, 1994—; co-editor Sage Professional Papers in Comparative Politics, 1969-73; editor: Comparative Political Studies, 1979-80. Fellow Wilson Nat., 1957, Ford Found., 1970, Guggenheim, 1972-73, German Marshall Fund., 1976, Fulbright, Australia, 1981. Mem. Am. Polit. Sci. Assn. (coun. 1989-91, Lifetime Achievement award 1991), Peace Sci. Soc., Internat. Studies Assn. (chmn. profl. rights and responsibilities com. 1985-88, chmn. govtl. rels. com. 1989-91, pres. 1994-95), Phi Beta Kappa. Home: 3551 Narragansett Ave Annapolis MD 21403-4937

GURRIA TREVINO, JOSÉ ANGEL, former Mexican government official; b. Mexico, May 8, 1950; BA in Econs., Nat. Autonomous U., 1972; MA in Pub. Fin., Leeds U., Eng.; studentInternat. Rels., U. So. Calif.; student Fin., Harvard U. Analyst Fed. Electricity Commn., Mexico, 1968-71; pvt. sec. to Sec. Gen. Fed. Dist. dept. Govt. of Mexico, Mexico City, 1971-74, pvt. sec. to dir. gen. pub. fin. dept.; permanent rep. Internat. Coffee Orgn., London, 1976-78; adv. pub. debt. Secretariat of Treasury, Mexico, 1978, dir. pub. debt., 1979; dir. gen. pub. credit, negotiator pub. fgn. debt Govt. of Mexico, Mexico City, 1983-88, undersec. internat. fin., negotiator free trade treaty, 1989-93; dir. gen. Nat. Bank for Fgn. Trade, Mexico, 1993-94; sec. fgn. affairs Govt. of Mexico, Mexico City, 1995—98, sec. fin. and pub. credit, 1998—2000. Mem. Com. Internat. Affairs, Modernization and Ideology. Institutional Revolutionary Party. Office: Partido Revolucionario Inst Insurgentes Norte No 9 Edif 2 Col Buenavista Deleg Cuauhtemoc 06359 Mexico City Mexico

GURSKY, ANDREAS, artist; b. Leipzig, Germany, Jan. 15, 1955; Student, Folkwangschule, Essen, 1978—81, Kunstakademie, Dusseldorf, 1981—87; studied with Bernd Becher, 1985. One-man shows include Flughafen Dusseldorf, 1987, Galerie Johnen and Schottle, Cologne, 1988, 1991, 303 Gallery, N.Y.C., 1989, 1991, 1995, Mus. Haus Lange, Krefeld, 1989, P.S. 1 The Clocktower, N.Y., 1989, Ctr. Genevois de Gravure Contemporaine, Geneva, 1989, Kunstlerhaus, Stuttgart, 1991, Galerie Rudiger Schottle, Paris, 1991, Munich, 1991, Hypobank, N.Y., 1992, Galeria Lia Rumma, Naples, 1992, Victoria Miro Gallery, London, 1992, Kunsthalle, Zurich, 1992, Monika Spruth Galerie, Cologne, 1993, Deichtorhallen, Hamburg, 1994, De Appel Found., Amsterdam, 1994, Le Case D'Arte, Mailand, 1994, Portikus, Frankfurt, 1995, Tate Gallery, Liverpool, Eng., 1995, Galerie Mai 36, Zurich, 1995, Rooseum Ctr. Contemporary Art, Malmo, 1995, Galerie Ghislaine Hassenot, Paris, 1996, Matthew Marks Gallery, N.Y., 1997, Milw. Art Mus., 1998, others, exhibited in group shows at Kunstlerwerkstatt Lothringer Str., Munich, 1985, Galerie Rudiger Schottle, 1986, 1988, Galerie Wittenbrink, 1987, Galerie Mosel and Tschechow, 1988, Galleria Lia Rumma, Naples, 1989, Nat. Mus. Modern Art, Tokyo, 1990, Castello di Rivoli, 1991, Musee d'art Moderne de la Ville de Paris, 1992, Hayward Gallery, London, 1992, Mus. Folkwang, 1993, Galerie des Archives, Paris, 1994, Matthew Marks Gallery, N.Y.C., 1995, Berlinische Galerie, 1997, The Photographer's Gallery, London, 1998, numerous others. Office: care Matthew Marks Gallery 523 W 24th St New York NY 10011-1104

GURSOY, DOGAN, hospitality and tourism educator, researcher; b. Tokat, Turkey, Mar. 10, 1969; arrived in U.S., 1994; s. Ismail and Fatma Gursoy. PhD, Va. Tech, 2001. Cert. hospitality educator Am. Hotel and Lodging Assn. Instr. Va. Tech., Blacksburg, 1999—2001; asst. prof. Wash. State U., Sch. of Hospitality Bus. Mgmt., Pullman, Wash., 2001—. Advisor Sigma Iota, Pullman, 2001—02; presenter in field. Contbr. articles to profl. jours. (Best Paper award, 2000, Haworth Hospitality Press award for best conf. paper, 2000). Recipient grad. fellowship, U. of New Haven Grad. Sch., 1995—96; fellow, Coll. Bus., Wash. State U., 2002—03; grantee, Taiwan NSF, 2002, Sch. of Hospitality Bus. Mgmt., 2001—02; scholar, Turkish Govt., 1994—2001; Internat. Bus. fellow, Wash. State U., 2003—. Mem.: Travel and Tourism Rsch. Assn., Coun. on Hotel, Restaurant and Instl. Edn., Internat. Soc. of Quality of Life Studies. Office: Wash State U Sch Hospitality Bus Mgmt 479 Todd Hall PO Box 644742 Pullman WA 99164 Office Fax: 509-335-3857. Personal E-mail: dgursoy@wsu.edu. E-mail: dgursoy@wsu.edu.

GURSPAN, MITCHELL SCOTT, technology architect, author; b. New York, NY, Jan. 12, 1962; s. Wallace Gurspan, Liliane Gurspan; m. Susan J Weiss; 1 child, Marcy Corinne. BS in Physics and Math., CUNY, 1984. Lic. mortgage broker Fla. President Digitech Software Systems, New York, NY, 1985—87; Systems Analyst Standard and Poor's Trading Systems, New York, NY, 1987—89, ILX Systems, New York, NY, 1989—91; Senior Systems Analyst Garban Inc., New York, NY, 1991—95; Principal Technology Specialist Sybase, Rockaway, NJ, 1995—2001. Author: (book) Upgrading and Migrating to Sybase SQL Server11, 1996. Event committee member Crohn's and Colitis Association, New York, NY, 1994—2001. Mem.: IEEE. Avocation: Third degree black belt instructor, Tai chi chuan instructor, author, tennis. E-mail: mgurspan@optonline.net.

GURSPAN, SUSAN JUDITH, English as Second Language educator, consultant; b. New York, NY, Dec. 6, 1964; d. Samuel Abraham and Alice Weiss; m. Mitchell Scott Gurspan; 1 child, Marcy Corinne. BA in Arts/Applied Linguistics and Edn. summa cum laude, Queens Coll., Flushing, NY, 1981—86, MS in Edn. summa cum laude, 1988; Hebrew Lang. and Judaic Studies, Orot Coll., Petach Tikvah, Israel, 1982—83. Cert. English as second lang. tchr./common branches N.Y.C. Bd. of Edn., 1986, Real Estate Agt. NJ Bd. of Realtors, 2001. Adj. lectr., intensive english lang. immersion program English Lang. Inst., Queens Coll., Flushing, NY, 1986—88; tchr. of English as a second lang. Pub. Sch. 9, New York, NY, 1988—99; model teacher/staff developer/teacher-trainer Dist. 3 Office of Multilingual/Multicultural Edn., New York, NY, 1990—99; presenter/trainer NYC Bd. of Edn., New York, NY, 1990—99, Staff Devel. Resources, Torrance, Calif., 1998—2001. Curriculum developer/editor Libros: Encouraging Cultural Literacy, Long Beach, NY, —; real estate agt. Century 21/JJ Laufer, Highland Park, NJ, 2001—. Author: (corporate training business course) The "SPEED" Approach to Effective Business-English Skills in the Corporate Environment, 2001, (Tchr's Guide for Tchrs. of ESL students) "Accelerating the Progress of ESL Students", 2001. Recipient Elaine Goran Newman award in TESOL Achievement, Queens Coll., 1989, Jonas E. Salk scholarship, 1990. Mem.: TESOL, ASTD, NJ. Assn. of Realtors. Avocations: skiing, tennis, travel. Personal E-mail: sgurspan@optonline.net.

GURTIN, MORTON EDWARD, mathematics educator; b. Jersey City, Mar. 7, 1934; children: Amy Lynn, William Robert. B.M.E., Rensselaer Poly. Inst., 1955; PhD, Brown U., 1961; PhD in Civil Engring. (hon.), U. Rome, 1994. Structures engr. Douglas Aircraft Co., 1955-56, Gen. Electric Co., 1956-59; research asso. Brown U., 1961-62, asst. prof., 1962-64, assoc. prof., 1964-66; prof. math. Carnegie Mellon U., 1966—; alumni prof. math., 1992—. Sr. Fulbright-Hays fellow, Guggenheim fellow U. Pisa, Italy, 1974; lectr., Europe, South Am., Japan, Can; cons. to industry. Author: (with B.D. Coleman, I Herrera, and C. Truesdell) Wave Propagation in Dissipative Media, 1965, An Introduction to Continuum Mechanics, 1981, Thermomechanics of Evolving Phase Boundaries, 1993, Configurational Forces as Basic Concepts of Continuum Physics, 2000; assoc. editor Archive for Rational Mechanics and Analysis, Jour. Elasticity; contbr. articles to profl. jours., including Handbuch der Physik. Recipient Disting. Grad. Sch. Alumnus award Brown U., 1995, Agostinelli prize Acad. dei Lincei, Rome, 2001. Mem. Soc. Natural Philosophy, Sigma Xi. Office: Dept Math Carnegie-Mellon U Pittsburgh PA 15213

GURULÉ, JIMMY, legal educator, federal agency administrator; b. Salt Lake City, June 14, 1951; BA, U. Utah, 1974, JD, 1980. Bar: Utah 1980. Spl. asst. U.S. Atty.'s Office, Washington, 1981, U.S. Atty.'s Office So. Dist., Miami, Fla., 1982; trial atty. criminal div. U.S. Dept. Justice, Washington, 1980-82, asst. atty. gen., 1990-93, asst. U.S. atty. L.A., 1985-89; prof. law sch. U. Notre Dame, South Bend, Ind., 1989-90, 93; Under Secy Enforcement Dept Treasury, Washington, 2001—. Recipient Atty. Gen.'s Disting. Svc. award, 1990, Drug Enforcement Adminstrn. award, 1991, Hispanic Leaders award SER Jobs for Progress, Inc., 1991. Mem. ABA, Utah State Bar, Hispanic Nat. Bar Assn. (pres. 1988-89, Lifetime Achievement award 1991). Republican. Office: Dept Treasury Under Sec for Enforcement 1500 Pennsylvania Ave NW Washington DC 20220

GURUSWAMY, DHARMITHRAN, urban planner; b. Colombo, Sri Lanka, Oct. 2, 1972; came to U.S., 1978; s. Lakshman D. and Vinodini (Chanmugam) G. BA, U. Md., 1994; M of City Planning, Ga. Inst. Tech., 1997, MS, 1998. Rsch. asst. Internat. Inst. Energy Conservation, Washington, 1994, 95; grad. rsch. asst. Ga. Inst. Tech., Atlanta, 1994-95, 95-97; assoc. Apogee Rsch., Bethesda, Md., 1997-98, Hagler Bailly Svcs., Arlington, Va., 1998-99; cons. Inter-Am. Devel. Bank, Washington, 1999—2001; mgr. comml. partnerships Amtrak, Washington, 2002—03, planning and policy officer, 2002—. Contbr. or co-contbr. articles to profl. publs. Mem. student-at-large bd. Md. Media Inc., College Park, 1993-94; newsletter editor Action Com. for Transit, Silver Spring, Md., 1997-98. Mem. Am. Planning Assn., Transp. Rsch. Bd. (mem. com. on nonmotorized transport 1997—, newsletter editor), Inst. Transp. Engrs. (assoc.), Urban Land Inst. (assoc.), Assn. Collegiate and Schs. of Planning (ind.), Am. Inst. Cert. Planners. Democrat. Methodist. Office: Amtrak 60 Massachusetts Ave NE Washington DC 20002- E-mail: dguruswamy@hotmail.com.

GURVAL, ROBERT ALAN, education educator; b. Kingston, Pa., Aug. 2, 1958; s. John James and Lenore Louise Oram Gurval. BA, Brown U., 1980; MA, U. of Calif. at Santa Barbara, 1982; PhD, U. of Calif. at Berkeley, 1988. Lectr. UCLA, Dept. of Classics, 1988—89; asst. prof. U. of Oreg., Dept. of Classics, 1989—90, UCLA, Dept. of Classics, 1990—96, assoc. prof., 1996—, chmn., 2000—. Author: (book) Actium and Augustus, 1995. Docent Gamble Ho., Pasadena, 1991—. Recipient Rome Prize fellow, Am. Acad. Rome, 1997. Mem.: Vergilian Soc. (life), Am. Classical League (life), Am. Numismatic Soc. (life), Am. Philol. Assn. (life). Avocations: architecture, films, tennis. Home: 8527 Nash Dr Los Angeles CA 90046 Office: UCLA, Dept of Classics 405 Hilgard Ave/DODD 100 Los Angeles CA 90095 Office Fax: 310-206-1903. Business E-Mail: gurval@humnet.ucla.edu.

GURVICH, VICTOR ALEXANDER, physicist, engineer; b. Moscow, Dec. 24, 1951; s. Alexander and Galina (Shtykanova) G.; m. Irina Makarova, Apr. 29, 1988; children: Marina, Yury. MSME, Moscow Inst. Electronics, 1974; PhD in Med. Engring. Inst. of Med. Devices, Moscow, 1986. Engr. Russian Rsch. Inst. for Light Engring., Moscow, 1974-77; chief lab. x-ray image intensifiers Mosroentgen, Inc., Moscow, 1977-92; gen. mgr. Alvim R&D Ltd. at Shaare Zedec Med. Ctr., Jerusalem, 1993-98, Alvim R&D Ltd., Toronto, 1998—; SQA specialist MDS Sciex, Canada, 2000—02; med. physicist Windsor Regional Cancer Ctr., 2003—. Head project Min. Industry and Trade, Jerusalem, 1995—98; scientific sec. Mosroentgen, Inc., Moscow, 1982—92. Contbr. articles to profl. jours. Inventor State Com. on Discoveries and Inventions Affairs, 1986; silver medalist Exhbn. of Econ. Achievement, USSR, 1985; recipient diploma Internat. Tech. Exhbns. in Plovdiv, Bulgaria, 1985, and Leipzig, Germany, 1987. Mem. Am. Assn. Physicists in Medicine, Russian Assn. Physicists in Medicine, N.Y. Acad. Scis., Israeli Assn. New Entrepreneurs. Achievements include patents for. Avocations: tourism, guitar, poetry. Office: 2361 Rossini Blvd Windsor ON Canada N8W 4P7 E-mail: victor.gurvich@sciex.com.

GURWITCH, ARNOLD ANDREW, communications executive; b. Hamburg, Germany, Jan. 29, 1925; came to U.S., 1946; s. Max and Bertha Ida (Schereschevsky) G.; m. Barbara Anne Guthrie, July 21, 1961; children: Laurence Andrew, Sara Anne. Student, U. Basle, Switzerland, 1943-46; LLB, Bklyn. Law Sch., 1955. Bar: N.Y. Resident atty. Leeds Music Corp., N.Y.C., 1956-60; ptnr. Rosen, Seton and Sarbin, N.Y.C., 1960-64; internat. rep. ASCAP, N.Y.C., 1964-74, head fgn. dept., 1974-78, fgn. mgr., 1978-89, dir. internat. rels., 1989-94, cons. internat. rels., 1995-96. Editor: Guide to Jazz, 1956. V.p., bd. dirs. Statesmen of Jazz, Ltd. Mem. N.Y. State Bar Assn., Copyright Soc. U.S.A. Democrat. Unitarian Universalist.

GURWITZ-HALL, BARBARA ANN, artist; b. Ayer, Mass., July 7, 1942; d. Jack and Rose (Baritz) Gurwitz; m. James M. Marshall III, Mar. 12, 1966 (div. 1973); m. William D. Hall, May 3, 1991; 1 child, Amanda Posner. Student, Boston U., 1960-61, Katherine Gibbs Sch., Boston, 1961-62. Represented by Wilde-Meyer Gallery, Scottsdale and Tucson, Ariz., Martin and Roll Gallery, Durango, Colo., Courtyard Gallery, New Buffalo, Mich., Joanne Coia Gallery, Delray, Fla. Artist-in-residence Desert House of Prayer, Tucson, 1989—91. One-woman shows include Henry Hicks Gallery, N.Y.C., 1971, Karin Newby Gallery, Ariz., 1989—99, CCGV Artist of Month, 1997, Martin and Roll Gallery, Durango, 1998, exhibitions include Data Mus., Einhod, Israel, 1987, one-woman shows include others, exhibitions include juried show Santa Cruz Valley Art Assn., 1989—2000 (Best of Show award, 1989, award for excellence, 1992, Hon. Mention, 1990), exhibitions include SCV/aa 25 Anniversary Invitational, 1997, Scharf Gallery, Santa Fe, N.Mex., 1998, NLAPW/GV Juried Exhibit, 1997 (2d prize, 1997, hon. mention, 1998, 2d prize, 1999), exhibitions include juried exhibit U. Tampa, 1998 (award of Honor, 1998), exhibitions include Tucson Mus. of Art, 1998—2000, 2002, Craig Gall. Annual Christmas, 2003, Los Cabaleros Mus., Wickerburg, Ariz., 2001, Wilde-Meyer, Tucson, 2002, Tohono Chul Mus., 2002, Ponies del Pueblo, 2002—03, Pima County Project, 2003, Thono Chul Mus., 2003—, Phippen Mus., 2002—03, many others, Represented in permanent collections Nat. Mus. Women in The Arts, Washington, Tucson Mus. Art, Goldman Sachs and Co., N.Y.C., Diocese of Tucson, Data Mus., Israel, Haiku Mus., Japan, Nat. Haiku Archive, Calif., Tubac Elem. Sch., Phippeu Mus., Prescott, Ariz., Sheriton Corp., Represented in permanent collections, one-woman shows include Heary Hicks Gallery, NYC, 1971. Mem. Tubac Village Coun., 1979-86; bd. dirs. Pimeria Alta Hist. Soc., Nogales, Ariz., 1982-84; creator Children's Art Walk, Tubac Sch. Sys. and Village Coun., 1980; set designer, choreographer DeAnza Ann. Pageant, Tubac Ctr. Arts, 1982-97; bd. dirs. Cath. Found., 2003—. Mem. Nat. League Am. PEN Women (pres. pro tem Sonora Desert br. 1999-2000, pres. 2000-2002), Tucson Mus. Art, Nat. Mus. of Women in Arts Washington. Avocations: golf, theater, singing, travel.

GUSAIN, LAKHAN, ancient language educator, researcher; b. Hanumangarh, India, Nov. 3, 1966; s. Sultangir and Santo Devi Gusain; m. Shalinee Gusain, July 1, 2000; 1 child, Aadesh. BSc, U. of Rajasthan, Jaipur, India, 1987; MA, U. of Ajmer, 1989, Jawaharlal Nehru U., New Delhi, 1992, MPhil, 1994, PhD, 2000. Lectr. U. of Mich., 2001—. Dir. Ctr. for Rajasthani Studies, Purabsar, India, 2001—. Author: (book) Bagri Grammar, 2000, Shekhawati Grammar, 2001, Mewati Grammar, 2003. Recipient UNESCO cert., Basque country, 1998; grantee Merit scholarship, JNU, New Delhi, 1990—92, UGC fellowship, UGC, India, 1998—2000. Mem.: Rajasthani Acad., Linguistic Soc. of Am., Assn. for Asian Studies. Hindu. Avocation: Rajasthani lang., linguistics, lit. and culture. Home: 1972 Traver Rd Ann Arbor MI 48105 Office: U of Mich 3511 Frieze Bldg Ann Arbor MI 48109-1285

GUSCIORA, REED, assemblyman; b. Passaic, N.J., Mar. 27, 1960; BA, Cath. U. of Am., 1982; JD, Seton Hall U. Sch. of Law, 1988. Staff asst. Rep. Mike Synar, 1983—85; atty. Labor and Employment Law, 1988—, Stark & Stark, Princeton, NJ, 1990—92; assemblyman N.J. Gen. Assembly Dist. 4, 1996—. Campaign mgr. N.J. Dem. Congl. Candidate Betty Holland, 1988; field coord. Barbara Boggs Sigmund N.J. Gubernatorial Campaign, 1989; candidate Mercer County Freeholder, 1994; mem. Govs. Adv. Bd. on AIDS, 1997—; asst. minority leader, 1998—2001. Mem. Mercer County HIV Consortium, 1998—, N.J. Beach Erosion Commn., 1996—; chair Environ. & Solid Waste; vice chair Transp. Mem.: United Progress Inc. (bd. mem. 1998—), Trenton Magnet Theatre (bd. mem. 1998—). Democrat. Roman Catholic. Office: 226 W State St Trenton NJ 08608 E-mail: AsmGusciora@nileg.org., reednj15@aol.com.*

GUSEH, JAMES SAWALLA, public administration educator; b. Zenalomai, Liberia, Dec. 5, 1951; s. Abraham Massawalla and Sonie Kennedy; m. Thelma Amy Broderick, Mar. 3, 1984; children: Sawalla J., Sonie K., Nahsan S. BA in Econs., Brandeis U., 1976; MS in Econs., U. Oreg., 1977; JD, MPA in Pub. Adminstrn., Syracuse U., 1980; PhD in Polit. Economy, U. Tex.-Dallas, Richardson, 1991. Counsellor-at-law, Republic of Liberia. Legal advisor, economist Ministry of Fin. Republic of Liberia, Monrovia, 1980-83, asst. atty. gen. Ministry of Justice, 1983-87; asst. prof. SUNY, Fredonia, 1991-92; asst. prof., dir. Shaw U., Raleigh, N.C., 1992-97; assoc. prof. pub. adminstrn. N.C.

Ctrl. U., Durham, 1997-2000, asst. interim dir. pub. adminstrn. program, 1999—, assoc. prof., 2000—. Rsch. fellow U. Tex., Dallas, 1990-91; cons. in field. Mem. editl. bd. African Social Sci. Rev., 1998—; contbr. articles to profl. jours. Mem. legis. com. Kannapolis (N.C.) C. of C., 1996-97; proposal reviewer Gov.'s Commn. on Nat. and Com. Svc., Raleigh, 1999—. Wien Internat. scholar, 1973-76. Mem. ASPA, Policy Studies Orgn., Liberian Studies Assn. (bd. dirs.), Conf. Minority Pub. Adminstrs., Assn. Third World Studies. Avocations: soccer, basketball, swimming, writing. Office: NC Ctrl U Dept Pub Admins rn Durham NC 27707 E-mail: guseh@juno.com.

GUSEV, YEUGENIY MIKHAILOVICH, research scientist; b. Moscow, Nov. 1, 1947; s. Mikhail Mikhailovich and Taisiya Timofeevna (Mordashova) G.; m. Elena Nikolaevna Moskvina, Nov. 19, 1977 (div. Aug. 1990); children: Mikhail, Yeugeniy; m. Klara Vasilievna Plyuscheva, Nov. 15, 1992. MSc, Moscow Phys. Engring. Inst., 1972; PhD, Russian Acad. Agrl. Sci., St. Petersburg, 1979; D in Biol. Sci., Moscow State U., 1993. Cert. engring.-physicist, hydrologist, agrl. physicist. Engr. Sci. Product Co. Red Star, Moscow, 1972-74; postgrad. staff Water Problems Inst., Russian Acad. Sci., Moscow, 1974-77, jr. rschr., 1978-81, sr. rschr., 1981-89, head lab., 1989—. Mem. sci. coun. Water Problems Inst., Russian Acad. Sci., 1979—; educator Ecol. Lyceum N232, Moscow, 1992-93; cons. Inst. Agrl. Modernization, Shijiazhuang, China, 1996. Author: Formation of Soil Water Regime and Resources for the Winter-Spring Period, 1993; mem. editl. bd. Jour. Hydrol. and Hydromechanics, 1997—; contbr. articles to profl. jours. Grantee U.S. Dept. State, Washington, 1993, Internat. Sci. Found., N.Y.C., 1993, Govt. Russia, Moscow, 1994, 97, Russian Found. Basic Rsch., Moscow, 1995, 98, 2002, Russian Found. Basic Rsch. and Internat. Sci. Found., 1995, Fulbright Found. Scholar Program, 2000-01. Mem. N.Y. Acad. Sci. Avocations: mini-soccer, tennis, drawing. Home: Apt 45 Marshala Nedelina St 4 121596 Moscow Russia Office: Water Problems Inst RAS Gubkina St 3 117971 Moscow Russia E-mail: gusev@iwapr.msk.su., sowa@online.ru.

GUSEWELLE, ANNE ELIZABETH, lawyer; b. Kansas City, Jan. 7, 1969; d. Charles Wesley and Katie Jane Gusewelle. BA, Vassar Coll., 1991; JD, U. Kans., 1996. Bar: Mo. 1996, Kans. 1997. Atty., law clk. hon. Joseph E. Stevens, Jr. U.S. Dist. Ct. (we. dist.) Mo., Kansas City, 1996-98; assoc. Shughart Thomson & Kilroy, Kansas City, 1998—. Mem. ABA, Kans. Bar Assn., Kansas City Met. Bar Assn. Democrat. Avocations: travel, skiing, painting, wine tasting, fishing. Office: Shughart Thomson & Kilroy 120 W 12th St Ste 1500 Kansas City MO 64105-1929 E-mail: agusewelle@kc.stklaw.com.

GUSEWELLE, CHARLES WESLEY, journalist, writer, documentary maker; b. Kansas City, Kans., July 22, 1933; s. Hugh L. and Dorothy (Middleton) G.; m. Katie Jane Ingels, Apr. 17, 1966; children— Anne Elizabeth, Jennifer Sue. BA in English, Westminster Coll., 1955; LHD (hon.), Park Coll., 1990. Reporter Kansas City (Mo.) Star, 1955-66, editorial writer of fgn. affairs, 1966-76, fgn. editor, 1976-79, asso. editor, columnist, 1979—. Author: A Paris Notebook, 1985, An Africa Notebook, 1986, Quick as Shadows Passing, 1988, Far from Any Coast, 1989, A Great Current Running, 1994, Another Autumn, 1996, The Rufus Chronicle, 1998, A Buick in the Kitchen, 2000, On the Way to Other Country, 2001; contbr. short stories to Brit., Am. lit. quars.; writer, narrator, host: A Great Current Running, This Place Called Home (Regional Emmy 1998), Water and Fire: A Story of the Ozarks. 1st lt. AUS, 1956-58. Recipient Aga Khan prize for fiction, 1977, Thorpe Menn Lit. award, 1989; inducted Writers Hall of Fame, 2000. Home: 1245 Stratford Rd Kansas City MO 64113-1325 Office: 1729 Grand Ave Kansas City MO 64108-1413

GUSHEE, RICHARD BORDLEY, lawyer; b. Detroit, Aug. 25, 1926; s. Edward Tisdale and Norine Amelia (Bordley) G.; m. Marilyn Lucy Flynn, June 9, 1951; children: Jacqueline Lowe (dec. 1977), Peter Hale. BA, Williams Coll., 1947; JD, U. Mich., 1950. Bar: Mich. 1951, U.S. Supreme Ct. 1961. Assoc. Miller, Canfield, Paddock and Stone, Detroit, 1950-58, ptnr., 1959-93, of counsel, 1994—. Chmn. Tri-county Hearing Panel #18 of Atty. Discipline Bd. Former trustee United Community Svcs.; former chancellor Episc. Diocese Mich. With USAF, 1945. Mem. ABA. Office: Miller Canfield Paddock & Stone 150 W Jefferson Ave Ste 2500 Detroit MI 48226-4416 E-mail: gushee@millercanfield.com.

GUSHÉE-MOLKENTHIN, ALLISON, financial advisor; b. Hartford, Conn., Apr. 6, 1962; d. Stephen Hale and Anne (Taylor) Gushée; m. Steven M. Molkenthin. BA in Mech. Engring. & Comparative Lit., Brown U., 1984; MBA, Insead, Fountainebleau, France, 1987. Assoc. Bankers Trust Co., N.Y.C., Paris, Milan, London, 1984-89; pres., COO UI-USA, Inc., N.Y.C., 1989-98; sr. advisor Bentley Assocs., LP, 1998—. Fulbright scholar U. Mohammed V, Rabat, Morocco, 1985. Mem. NAFE, Princeton Brown Club. Episcopalian. Avocations: french, italian, spanish, german and arabic languages. Home: 195 Hollow Tree Ridge Rd Darien CT 06820 E-mail: gusheemolkenthin@BentleyLp.com.

GUSHIN, STEPHEN RALPH, psychiatrist; b. Elizabeth, N.J., July 17, 1932; AB, Princeton U., 1954; MD, NYU, 1958. Diplomate Am. Bd. Psychiatry and Neurology. Intern USPHS Hosp. S.I., N.Y., 1958-59; resident in psychiatry VA Hosp., Bronx, N.Y., 1961-62; attending psychiatrist Gracie Sq. Hosp., N.Y.C., 1964-70; resident in psychiatry Bellevue Hosp. Ctr., N.Y.C., 1962-64, clin. asst. attending neuropsychiatrist, 1964-66, asst. attending neuropsychiatrist, 1965-74, assoc. attending psychiatrist, 1974-93, Univ. Hosp., N.Y.C., 1964—; from tchg. asst. to clin. assoc. prof. psychiatry NYU Med. Ctr., 1964-76, clin. assoc. prof., 1976—. Unit chief psychiat. med. unit Bellevue Hosp. Ctr., 1964-66, unit chief maximally disturbed ward, 1966-69, dir. psychiat. walk-in clinic, 1969-78, dir. psychiat. admitted-med. unit, dir. psychiat. intake/emergency svcs., 1979-80; dirADEPT Day Hosp., 1981-91; unit chief dual diagnosis unit Bergen Pines Hosp., Paramus, 1991-94, chief rehab. unit, 1994-97; ready res. USPHS, Fed. Bur. Prisons, Butner, N.C., 1990; locum tenens various med. facilities, 1989—; lectr. profl. seminars and symposia, 1974, 77, 80. Sr. asst. surgeon USPHS, 1959-61. Mem. Am. Psychiat. Assn., N.Y. State Med. Soc., New York County Med. Soc. Office: 344 E 84th St New York NY 10028-4405 E-mail: srg.32@juno.com.

GUSKI, RICHARD HENRY, software engineer; s. Edmund and Majorie Guski; m. Cheryl Ann Bradley; children: Tad, Honora, Matthew. BS, N.Y. Inst. Tech., 1971. Cert. info. sys. security profl. Computer programmer Mountain Bell Tel. Co., Denver, 1971—81; sr. tech. staff mem. IBM Corp., Poughkeepsie, NY, 1981—. Contbr. articles to profl. jours. Specialist 4th class U.S. Army, 1966—68, Ft Hood, TX and Vietnam. Achievements include patents for computer software. Avocation: amateur radio. Office: IBM Corp 2455 South Rd Poughkeepsie NY 12601 Personal E-mail: guski@attglobal.net. Business E-Mail: guski@us.ibm.com.

GUSKIN, ALAN E. university president; b. Bklyn., Mar. 22, 1937; s. David N. and Frances (Midler) G.; m. Lois La Shell, 1990; children from previous marriage: Sharon, Andrea. BA with honors, Bklyn. Coll., 1958; PhD, U. Mich., 1968; LHD (hon.), Saybrook Inst., 1989, Antioch U., 1997. Instr., Peace Corps. vol. Chulalongkorn U., Thailand, 1961-64; dir. of selection VISTA, 1964-65; asst. dir. Ctr. for Research on the Utilization of Scientific Knowledge, Inst. for Social Research, 1968-69; lectr. dept. of psychology and residential coll. U. Mich., 1968-71, dir. ednl. change team, Sch. of Edn., 1969-71, assoc. prof. edn., 1971; provost Clark U., Worcester, Mass., 1971-73, acting pres., 1973-74, prof. sociology and edn., 1973-75; chancellor, prof. edn. U. Wis.-Parkside, Kenosha, 1975-85; pres., prof. Antioch Coll. and Antioch U., Yellow Springs, Ohio, 1985-94; chancellor, Disting. univ. prof. Antioch U., 1994-97, disting. prof., 1997—. Author: (with Samuel Guskin) A Social Psychology of Education, 1970; editor New Directions on Teaching and Learning, The Administrator's Role in Effective Teaching, 1981; contbr. numerous articles and reports to profl. jours. Chmn. bd. Coun. on Adult and Experiential Learning, 1993-95. Mem. Am. Assn. Higher Edn.

GUSKOV, SERGEY, security firm executive; b. Moscow, Aug. 31, 1973; BS in Engring. and Econs. with honors, Moscow Aviation Inst., 1995; MBA, U. Pa., 2000. Sr. auditor KPMG, Moscow, 1995—98, Leeds, England, 1998; assoc., mgmt. consulting A.T. Kearney, New York, NY, 2000—01; mgr. bus. analysis Brink's Inc., Darien, Conn., 2001—. Investment banking summer assoc. CIBC World Markets, N.Y.C., 1999. Co-author: (study book) Securities, 1998. Co-founder, v.p. Russian Digital Alliance, Washington, 2001—03. Home: 150 E 37th St Apt 2C New York NY 10016

GUSKY, DIANE ELIZABETH, state agency administrator, planner; b. Orange, N.J., Mar. 4, 1948; d. Marvin Leonard and Mary Elizabeth (Frayne) Gusky; m. John Bertram Broster, May 21, 1983. B of Univ. Studies, U. N.Mex., 1981, M Cmty. and Regional Planning, 1984. Cert. cmty. planner. Cmty. planner Planning divsn. City of Albuquerque, 1983-84; aviation planner Aeronautics office Tenn. Dept. Transp., 1985-88; chief planner Greater Nashville Regional Coun., 1988-90; sr. planner Buchart-Horn, Inc., Nashville, 1990-92, Espey, Huston & Assocs., Inc., Nashville, 1992-97; dep. dir. Aeronautics divsn. Tenn. Dept. Transp., Nashville, 1997-2000, asst. dir. Office Strategic Planning, 2000—. Mem. Title VI adv. bd. Tenn. Dept. Transp., 1998—, vice chmn., 2001—. Co-author: Land Use Compatibility and Airports, A Guide for Effective Land Use Planning. Recreational therapist Assn. for Retarded Children, N.J. and N.Mex., 1974-77; mem. Metro Greenways Citizens Adv. Com., Nashville, 1993—, chair planning and devel. com., 2000—; mem. Nat. Women's Polit. Caucus. Recipient So. Regional Adminstr.'s Top Flight award FAA, Atlanta, 1998; named to Outstanding Young Women of Am., 1983. Mem.: Am. Inst. Cert. Planners, Rebuild Tenn. Coalition (chmn. 1997—98). Office: Tenn Dept Transp Office Strategic Planning 505 Deaderick St Ste 300 Nashville TN 37243 E-mail: Diane.Gusky@state.tn.us.

GUSMAN, ROBERT CARL, lawyer; b. NYC, Nov. 17, 1931; s. Samuel and Esther (Zuckerman) G.; m. Harriet Wish, Aug. 21, 1955; children: Amy, Jennifer, Julie. BA, NYU, 1953; JD, Cornell U., 1956. Bar: N.Y. 1957, D.C. 1960, Calif. 1962. Asst. counsel Office Gen. Counsel, Dept. of Navy, Washington, 1956-58; spl. legal advisor fleet ballistic missile program USN, Washington, 1958-60; asst. gen. counsel Aerojet-Gen. Corp., El Monte, Calif., 1960-70, Lockheed Corp., Calabasas, Calif., 1970-87, asst. sec., 1987-95, v.p., asst. gen. counsel, 1992-95. Editl. cons. fed. contract reports Bur. Nat. Affairs, Washington, 1970-84, adv. bd., 1984-95; spl. legal advisor Commn. on Govt. Procurement, Washington, 1970; instr. law Loyola U., L.A., 1971-72; chmn. indemnification project group Aerospace Industries Assn., Washington, 1984-86, chmn. legal com., 1986-88. Contbr. articles to profl. jours. Mem. ABA (chmn. pub. contract law subcoms.), Fed. Bar Assn. (conf. chmn. 1985-88), Am. Arbitration Assn. (arbitrator 1964—).

GUSOFF, PATRICIA KEARNEY, retired elementary education educator; b. Phila., Jan. 25, 1951; d. William Anthony and Helen Frances (Budnik) Kearney; m. Ronald Gusoff, June 22, 1975; children: Wayne Kenneth, Howard Brandon. BS in Edn., Temple U., 1973, MEd, 1977, EdD, 1988. Cert. elem. tchr., supr., adminstr., Pa., N.J. Elem. sch. tchr. Sch. Dist. Phila., 1973—2001, elem. sci. tchr., 1989-90, basic skills tchr., 1990-96, tchr. remedial work primary grades, 1990-96; asst. facilitator, tutor William McKinley Elem. Sch., Phila., 1992-96; ret., 2001. Coord. sch. recycling Phila. Pride, 1990-96. Mem. ASCD (assoc.), Pa. ASCD, Phila. Fedn. Tchrs. Home: 1119 Hedgerow Ln Philadelphia PA 19115-4808

GUSSIN, ROBERT ZALMON, retired healthcare company executive; b. Pitts., Jan. 5, 1938; s. Carl and Yetta G. BS in Pharmacy, Duquesne U., 1959, MS in Pharmacology, 1961; PhD in Pharmacology, U. Mich., 1965. Rsch. fellow dept. pharmacology SUNY, 1965-67; rsch. pharmacologist Lederle Labs., N.Y.C., 1967-69, group leader dept. cardiovascular renal pharmacology, 1969-73, dir. cardiovascular renal disease therapy sect., 1973-74; exec. dir. rsch. McNeil Labs., Ft. Washington, Pa., 1974-78, v.p. rsch. div., 1978, v.p. R & D, 1978-79; v.p. sci. affairs McNeil Pharm., Pa., 1979-86; corp. v.p., sci. and tech. Johnson & Johnson, New Brunswick, N.J., 1986-2000. Author: Introduction to Cardiovascular Pharmacology, 1976; mem. editorial bd. New Drug Evaluations, Drug Devel. Pharmaco Therapy; contbr. in field. Mem. Am. Soc. Clin. Pharmacology and Therapeutics, Am. Soc. Nephrology, Am. Soc. Pharmacology and Exptl. Therapeutics, Am. Fedn. Clin. Research, AAAS, N.Y. Acad. Scis., Am. Heart Assn. Office: Johnson & Johnson 410 George St New Brunswick NJ 08901-2021 E-mail: rgussin@corus.jnj.com.

GUST, DAVID R. military career officer; b. Platte City, Mo., Oct. 20, 1942; m. Peggy A. Gimbel; children: Scott, Thomas. BEE, U. Denver, 1974; M in Sys. Mgmt., U. So. Calif., 1976; grad., Command and Gen. Staff Coll., Naval War Coll. Drafted U.S. Army, 1966, commd. 2d lt. Signal Corps, 1967, advanced through grades to maj. gen., various positions, European tel. sys. and AUTOVON officer 5th Signal Command, 1974-77, bn. CE officer 1st Bn., 40th Field Arty., with 74th Signal Co., 3rd Bn., 3rd Arty., 194th Brigade, project officer Def. Comm. Sys. Comm. Sys., sys. project leader Directorate for Sys. Mgmt., Comm., product mgr. PEO Fire Support, acting project mgr. PEO Intelligence and Electronic Warfare; fielding officer Program Exec. Office, Comm. Sys.; project mgr. Mobile Subscriber Equipment PEO Comm. Sys.; program exec. officer for comm. sys., 1992-95; program exec. officer for Intelligence & Electronic Warfare, 1995-99; dep. chief staff rsch. devel. and acquisition U.S. Army Material Command, Alexandria, Va., 1999—. Decorated Bronze Star medal, Purple Heart, Legion of Merit, Meritorious Svc. medal with two oak leaf clusters, Army Commendation medal with two oak leaf clusters, Good Conduct medal, Vietnam Svc. medal with four campaign stars. Office: DCS RD&A US Army Materiel Command 5001 Eisenhower Ave Alexandria VA 22333-0001

GUSTAFSON, ALBERT KATSUAKI, lawyer, engineer; b. Tokyo, Dec. 5, 1949; arrived in U.S., 1951; s. William A. and Akiko (Osada) Gustafson; m. Helen Melissa Laird, July 31, 1971 (div. 1975); m. Karen Jane Ekblad, Dec. 31, 1978 (div. 1987). BA with distinction, Stanford U., 1972; JD, U. Wash., 1980. Bar: Wash. 1981, U.S. Dist. Ct. (we. dist.) Wash. 1981, U.S. Ct. Appeals (9th cir.) 1984, NY 1993. Acoustics analyst Boeing Co., Seattle, 1973—74, material buyer, 1974; legal editor Book Pub. Co., Seattle, 1975—76; rsch. analyst Batelle Inst., Seattle, 1975—76; legal intern Office of U.S. Atty., Seattle, 1976; engr. U.P.R.R., 1977—85; corp. counsel Dorden, Inc., Centralia, Wash., 1984—87, Ansette Fin. Corp., Inc., Seattle, 1987—89, Precision Forms, Inc., 1988, Endo and Mamba, 1989—93; of counsel Barkats and Assocs., 1991—98; prin. Albert K. Gustafson, P.S., Seattle, 1981—93; pres. Shomei Corp., 1990—95, Shomei, Kokusai, Kabushki, Kaisha, 1991—95; v.p. Sierra Capital Mgmt., Inc., 1992—93; prof. internat. bus. law Sch. Internat. Studies Nichibei Kaiwa Gakuen, Tokyo, 1989—90, Nippon Tel. & Tel., 1989—90. Bd. dirs. Daiki, Inc.; v.p. ops. BND Sea and Airlines Corp., 1997—98; dir., counsel Zinza K.K., 1998—, pres., rep. dir., 2002—; rep. dir. Multipro K.K., 1998—2002. Mem. nat. bd. editors Prentice-Hall Rigos CPA Review, 1991—93. Sec. local 117-E United Transp. Union, 1984, local vice-chmn., 1984; Dem. precinct chmn., 1984. Named Kraft scholar, 1968, Calif. State scholar, 1968—72. Mem.: ABA, Japan Am. Soc., Roppongi Bar Assn., Seattle-King County Bar Assn., Inter-Pacific Bar Assn., Asian Bar Assn., Internat. Bar Assn., Imperial Club, Century Ct. Club, City Club, College Club, Rotary, Order of DeMolay (master councilor 1968), Shriners, Masons. Presbyterian. Address: #404 Asahi Iidabashi Mansion 1-9-6 Iidabashi Chiyoda-ku Tokyo 102-0072 Japan also: 75 Shoe Ln London England EC4 BQ also: 3917 Interlake Ave N Seattle WA 98103 also: 5 Krasnoznamenny By-str 690000 Vladivostok Russia also: PO Box 12 600 Main St Cobleskill NY 12043 also: 67 Wall St 22nd Fl New York NY 10005 Business E-Mail: ananda@gol.com.

GUSTAFSON, ANNE-LISE DIRKS, lawyer, foreign consul; b. Vejle, Denmark, Aug. 14, 1934; came to U.S., 1955; d. Hans and Edith Margerita Dirks; m. William L. Gustafson, June 23, 1958. BA cum laude, U. Miami, 1963, JD, 1971, LLM, 1973. Vice consul Nation of Denmark, Miami, Fla., 1973-76; consul, 1976 ; assoc. atty. Aronovitz & Weksler, Miami, 1976-83; pvt. practice Miami, 1983—. Knighted by Queen of Denmark, 1976, 96. Mem. Fla. Bar Assn., Consular Corps Miami, Alpha Lambda Delta, Delta Phi Alpha, Kappa Delta Pi. Republican. Lutheran. Home and Office: 2655 S Le Jeune Rd Ph 1D Coral Gables FL 33134-5827 Fax: 305-448-4151, 305-448-9707.

GUSTAFSON, CRAIG THOMAS, theatrical director, playwright, graphic artist; b. Oak Park, Ill., Aug. 26, 1958; s. Eric O. and Mary Louise (Howlett) G.; m. Marjorie L. Weitzenfeld, July 11, 1998. Student, Second City, Chgo., 1978; AA, Coll. DuPage, 1979. Board operator Wells Fargo Alarm, Elmhurst, Ill., 1978-81; ops. employee Coll. DuPage, Glen Ellyn, 1981—. Prodr., dir. Ad Hoc Theatre Co., Lisle, Ill., 1986-89; dir., writer The Summer Place, Naperville, Ill., 1989-96, Village Theatre Guild, Glen Ellyn; dir., composer, graphic artist Wheaton (Ill.) Drama, Inc., 1990—; artistic dir. Top Banana, Oakbrook Terrace, Ill., 1997-99; v.p., dir., composer, graphic artist First St. Playhouse, Batavia, Ill., 2002-; actor, dir., prodr., composer, choreographer, others, Village Players, Oak Park, Ill., 1995, West Suburban Players, Villa Park, Ill., 1996-98, Music On Stage, Palatine, Ill., 2001, Village Theatre of Palatine, 2002. Actor: The Foreigner, The House of Blue Leaves, Chicago, Bobby Gould in Hell, Rumors, Waiting for Godot, The Fantasticks, Twelfth Night; dir.: Assassins, Luv, Lucky Stiff, Lend Me a Tenor, The Odd Couple, Tartuffe, A Funny Thing Happened on the Way to the Forum, Nunsense, Mingle, Among the Demons; writer, performer (with Joy Kenyon) Tongues and Animal Crackers, Vic Theatre, Chgo., 1992. Named Funniest Person in Chgo., Chgo. Sun-Times, 1981, Best Cmty. Prodn. for "The Nerd," Acad. Theatre Artists and Friends, Chgo., 1996. Mem. Sons of the Desert (vice-shiek 1994-95). Democrat. Avocations: studying history of comedy, irritating conservatives.

GUSTAFSON, DEBORAH LEE, educational administrator, educator; b. Boston, Dec. 17, 1948; d. Edward Michael and Patricia Frances (Curtin) Lee, m. Robert Edward Gustafson, Oct. 1, 1977; children: Lauren Elizabeth, Jared Lee. BS in Edn., Wagner Coll., 1970, MEd, 1973; cert. advanced grad. studies, Bridgewater State Coll., 1993. Tchr. Trinity Luth. Sch., Staten Island, N.Y., 1970-74, Town of Wareham, Mass., 1974—, elem. curriculum developer, 1983—, dir. acad. Olympics program, 1999-2000, core acad. lead tchr., 2000—. Chmn. com. to write statement of mission and goals Wareham Pub. Schs., 1987—89. Mem. Wareham 250th Anniversary Commn., 1987-89, Constn. Bicentennial Commn. Wareham, 1986-88; chmn. 250th Anniversary Sch. Planning Commn., Wareham, 1988-89; pres. Wareham Hist. Soc., 1989-95; tour guide Fearing Tavern Mus., Wareham, 1988—; reader Talking Infor Ctr. for the Visually Impaired, 1988—; aquatic fitness instr., 2000—. Horace Mann grantee State of Mass., 1988-89. Mem. Mass. Tchrs. Assn. (regional rep., 1995—), Plymouth County Tchrs. Assn. (honor 1985, citation 1988), Plymouth County Edn. Assn. (bd. dirs. 1989-95, 2000—, profl. recognition com. 1990-92, chmn. profl. devel. com. 2001—), Wareham Edn. Assn. (sec. 1978-83, pres. 1983-89, chmn. profl. rights and responsibilities com. 1990-2000, pres. 2000—), People to People Student Amb. Program (tchr. leader 1995-99), Delta Kappa Gamma. Roman Catholic. Avocations: needlework, travel. Office: Minot Forest Sch Minot Ave Wareham MA 02571

GUSTAFSON, ERIC WILLIAM, real estate investor, wildlife habitat conservationist; b. Monterrey, Mex., Feb. 12, 1945; s. Bertel and Elenor (Ceder) G.; m. Mina Villarreal, June 16, 1973; children: Eric Alain, Karini, Elyn Michelle. BS, Duke U., 1966; MBA cum laude, Monterrey Inst. Tech., 1970; PhD, U. Mass., 1975. Founder, dir. ITESM, 1971-73, Univ. Tchg. Excellence Ctr. and LASCA Computer Degree, Monterrey, 1973-74; from strategic planning mgr. to internat. v.p. Cuauhtemoc Brewing Co., Monterrey, 1975-80; internat. dir. Femsa/Visa Group, Monterrey, 1980-82; C.E.O. & nat. v.p. Ducks Unltd. of Mex. Wildlife Conservation Orgn., 1982-97; ptnr. Metroalianza SA, 1998—. Assoc. World Bus. Coun. Sustainable Devel., Switzerland, 1991—, pres. U.S.-Mex. C. of C., NE Mexico, 1996—; founder, ptnr. Craidero Estrella, S.A., 1999; cons. U. Nuevo Leon, 1975-76, Clemente Jacques Food Corp.; Mex. rep. Can./U.S./Mex. Trilateral Wildlife Com., 1997, rep. of Mex. at UNCED World Summit Brazil, 1992, rep. of Mex. on N.Am. Waterfowl Mgmt. Plan, 1995—. Author: Organization and Development of Teaching Improvement Center, 1975, Eco-efficiency and Sustainable Development, 1992, The White Winged Dove in Ne Mexico, 2000, Laguna Flamingos, 2001, Soto La Marina, 2002 editor: Mexico: Monterrey and You, 1984. Pres. bd. dirs. Am. Sch. Found., Monterrey, 1988-90; nat. bd. dirs. Mex. Nat. Coun. Parks and Res., 1996; Mex. rep. N.Am. Waterfowl Mgmt. Plan, 1995—; pres. Conservation Mex., 1999-2004. Recipient Excellence in Environment Spain-Mex. award, 1995; N.Am. Wetlands Conservation Act grantee, 1999-2002; Ford Found. scholar, Nat. Coun. Sci. & Tech. Mex. scholar. Mem. Valle Alto Golf Club, Casino de Monterrey, U.S.-Mex. C. of C. (pres. 1996—), Phi Kappa Psi, Union ch., ASFM Devel. (chmn.); bd. mem. USMCOC Biational, 2002, Avocations: hiking, hunting, tennis, horseback riding, golf. Office: Arbol 182 Santa Engracia Garza Garcia Nuevo Leon 66267 Mexico Fax: (52) 818-356-5010. E-mail: karini@usa.net., drericgustafson@hotmail.com.

GUSTAFSON, JOHN ALFRED, biology educator; b. Boston, Mar. 31, 1925; s. Walter Alfred and Lilly Christine (Anderson) Gustafson; m. Nancy Gay Johnson, June 30, 1951; children: Walter A., Laura E., Paul E.(dec.), Daniel D., Martha E., J. Olaf. AB, Dartmouth, 1948; PhD, Cornell U., 1954. Asst. prof. biology State U. N.Y. Coll., Brockport, 1954-55, asst. prof. biology Cortland, 1955-57, asso. prof. biology, 1957-63, prof. biology, 1963-81, chmn. dept. biol. scis., 1965-77; project dir. NSF Grant for Outdoor Sci. Edn., 1980-82. Participant NSF Inst., 1962; pres. Alliance for Environ. Edn., 1974; mem. Temporary State Commn. on Youth Edn. in Conservation, N.Y., 1969-73; owner, pub. Slingerland-Comstock Co., 1976-91. Author: (with B.A. Hall) Laboratory Studies in Botany, 1960; Editor: Nature Study, Jour. Environ. Edn. and Interpretation, 1965-79, Alliance Exchange, 1975-76. Chmn. Town of Homer (N.Y.) Zoning Bd., 1959-69, Town of Homer Planning Bd., 1969-75; chmn. Homer Plan Rev. Com., 2001-02, vice chmn. Eastern Susquehanna Water Resources Bd., 1969-76; pres. Highvista Nature Center, Inc., 1973-92; mem. Labrador Hollow Unique Area Adv. Coun., 1978—; chmn. Cortland County Environ. Mgmt. Council, 1980-82, Cortland County Anderson-Lucey campaign, 1980; mem. bd. edn. Homer Cen. Sch. Dist., 1982-88; treas. Pocono Environ. Edn. Ctr., 1988-91, Lime Hollow Nature Ctr., 1992—; Cortland County rep. to open space com. N.Y. State, Region 7, 1996—; bd. dirs. Iroquois Assn., Am. Baptist Chs., 1986-89, 97—, moderator, 1987; pres. Cortland County Council of Chs., 1986-89; adminstr. 1st Bapt. Ch., Homer, N.Y., 1990-94, treas., 1995-99, bd. elders, 2001-02, bd. deacons, 2002-03; mem. steering com. N.Y. State Grazing Lands Conservation Initiative, 1997—. Served with USMCR, 1943-46, 51-53. Recipient Taft Campus award No. Ill. U., 1989, Griffith-Balcom Leadership award Am. Bapt. Chs., 1998. Fellow AAAS (coun. 1968-73); mem. Am. Nature Study Soc. (pres. 1962-63, treas. 1964-75, 79-97, Disting. Svc. award 1969, John Gustafson award for exemplary svc., 1995), Nature Conservancy (dir., treas., chmn. ctrl. N.Y. chpt., chmn. N.Y. State bd. dirs. 1983-87, vice chmn., ctrl/western N.Y. chpt. 1994-96, Oak Leaf award 1984), Phi Delta Kappa. Republican. Baptist. Home: 5881 Cold Brook Rd Homer NY 13077-9709 *As I think back over my life, I am impressed by the evidence that God, through my commitment to him, has given guidance and direction at those times when crucial decisions were made. So often what seemed at the time to be a relatively insignificant decision turned out to have been a key turning point. It is God's Spirit within me, and his love and concern, that gives meaning to what I do.*

GUSTAFSON, KARIN ELISABETH, foundation executive; b. Engelmannsreuth, Germany, Nov. 9, 1943; came to U.S., 1953; d. Erwin and Auguste (Limmer) Hofmann; m. Nels R. gustafson, Dec. 31, 1971. Grad., Brown's Bus. Coll., Springfield, Ill., 1963. Sec. Office of Gov., State of Ill., Springfield, 1963-64; adminstv. asst. Ill. Dept. Agr., Springfield, 1964-69; office mgr. Hahn & Assocs., Springfield, 1969-76; dep. dir. Ill. Dept. Motor Vehicles, Springfield, 1977-80; treas. City of Springfield, 1980-84; exec. dir. Women's Resource Ctr., Sarasota, Fla., 1985-90; prs. YMCA Found., Sarasota, 1990—. Former participant polit. campaigns Otto Kerner, Alan J. Dixon, Richard Durbin, Paul Simon and others, Ill., 1962—84. Named One of 200 Most Influential People, Sarasota Herald-Tribune, 1993, 100 Most Influential, Sarasota Mag., 2001. Mem.: Nat. Soc. Profl. Fund Raising Execs. (pres. S.W. Fla. chpt. 1977—, cert.), Sarasota Univ. Club (pres. 1995). Democrat. Lutheran. Avocation: collecting royal commemoratives and art. Office: YMCA Found One S School Sarasota FL 34237-8133

GUSTAFSON, LEWIS ALLAN, retired geologist; b. Lansing, Mich., Dec. 12, 1931; s. Palmer Leonard and Erma Beryl (Washburn) Gustafson; m. Mary Joanne Porter, Oct. 1, 1955; children: Lori, Steven, Leslie. BS in Geology, Mich. State U., 1955, MS in Geology, 1960; postgrad., U. Minn., 1974. Cert. engring. geologist, Wash., Oreg. . Staff geologist Walla Walla dist. U.S. Army Corps Engrs., 1963-68, staff geologist Omaha dist., 1968-74, resident geologist RIRIE Dam Idaho Falls, 1974-75, chief, geology sect. Portland dist., 1975-81, divsn. geologist North Pacific divsn., 1981-88, chief geologist Hdqtrs. Washington, 1988-92. Cons. in field. Lt. U.S. Army, 1956. Mem.: U.S. Soc. Dams, Assn. Engring. Geologists, Soc. Am. Mil. Engrs. Avocations: hunting, shooting, fishing, hiking, history. Home: 1275 NE Paula Dr Bend OR 97701-6058

GUSTAFSON, MARDEL EMMA, secondary school educator, writer; b. Waukesha, Wis., June 10, 1922; d. Otto Robert and Emma Bertha (Steffan) Hoppe; m. Wayne Carroll Gustafson, Nov. 1, 1950; children: Faith, Keith, Richard, Wayne, John, Beverly. BE, U. Wis., Madson, 1946. Sec. Waukesha Motor Co., 1944—45, Wis. Gen. Hosp., Madison, 1945—46; tchr. Hannibal HS, Wis., 1946—49, St. John Pub. Sch., ND, 1949—50. Author: What Is Happening To Our Children?, 1993, Why A Role Mother?, 2001, All My Love, 2001. Mem.: Wis. Alumni Assn., TOPS Club (sec. 1978—). Lutheran. Avocations: sewing, knitting, crocheting, gardening, walking. Home: W289 S2915 Hwy Dt Waukesha WI 53188

GUSTAFSON, RANDALL LEE, city manager; b. Sidney, Nebr., Nov. 11, 1947; s. Robert John and Hilda Lydia (Sims) G.; m. Cynthia Ann Taylor, Oct. 18, 1974. Student, U. Kans., 1965-68, Rockhurst Coll., 1968-70; BS in Pub. Adminstrn., Upper Iowa U., 1992; MS in Pub. Adminstrn., PhD in Pub. Adminstrn., Hamilton U., 1998. City mgr. City of Bonner Springs, Kans., 1970-77; bus. owner Lambquarters, Dix, Nebr., 1977-83; city mgr. City of Aurora, Mo., 1983-85, City of Sterling, Colo., 1985—2002; city mgr. City of Hays, Kans., 2002—. Bd. dirs. Logan Area Devel. Co., Sterling. Bd. dirs. Fire and Police Pension Assn. Colo., Denver, 1987-95, 13th Jud. Dist. Cmty. Corrections, Brush, Colo., 1988-90; mem. Colo. Mcpl. League Policy Com., Denver, 1987-89. Recipient Disting. Svc. award Jaycees, 1976. Mem.: Govs. Fin. Assn., Kans. Assn. City Mgmt., Am. Soc. for Pub. Adminstrn.., Colo. Assn. City Mgmt., Internat. City Mgmt. Assn. (credentialed mgr., Mark E. Keane award for Excellence 1999), Mensa, Elks, Rotary. Republican. Lutheran. Office: 1507 Main PO Box 490 Hays KS 67601

GUSTAFSON, RICHARD ALRICK, university president; b. Peekskill, N.Y., May 15, 1941; s. Richard Alrick Sr. and Faye Alice (Jones) G.; m. Joanne Marie Walters, Sept. 5, 1964; children: Richard III., Peter. AB in Biology and Chemistry, Boston U., 1963, MEd in Sci. Edn., 1964; PhD in Statistics and Measurement, U. Conn., 1970; attended, Harvard Inst. Ednl. Mgmt., 1982; MEd in TESOL, Notre Dame Coll., 1997. Tchr. sci. Newtown (Conn.) Pub. Sch., 1964-65; tchr. chemistry Greenwich (Conn.) Pub. Schs., 1965-68; rsch. specialist Ctr. for Planning and Evaluation, San Jose, Calif., 1970-71; dir. mgmt. svcs. New Eng. Resource Ctr. for Occupl. Edn., Newton, 1971-73; asst. dean career studies Keene (N.H.) State Coll., 1973-78, assoc. dean acad. affairs, 1978-81, v.p. acad. affairs, 1981-87; pres. So. N.H. U. (formerly N.H. Coll.), Manchester, 1987—2003, pres. emeritus, 2003—. Bd. dirs. Optima Health, 1997-98. Contbr. articles to profl. jours. Bd. dirs. Keene Family YMCA, 1975-80, 1st No. Bank, Keene, 1984-86, Cheshire Med. Ctr., Keene, 1986-88, Federated Arts Bd., 1989-92, Leadership Manchester Bd., 1989-91, Manchester United Way Bd., 1990-97, chmn., 1993, Hillcrest Terr. Bd., 1991-93, Elliot Hosp., 1999—; vice chair N.H. Tuition Savings Plan Commn., 1997—; mem. ops. com. Forum for Higher Edn. in N.H., 2000-2003; bd. dirs. N.H. Symphony Orch., 2003—, AAA No. New Eng., 2000—. Recipient Granite State award, 2000; Augustus Howe Buck scholar Boston U., 1960-62; Fulbright sr. rsch. fellow, Thailand, 1999. Mem. Am. Vocat. Assn. (Svc. award 1980), Nat. Assn. Ind. Colls. and Univs. (bd. dirs. 1991-94), N.H. Coll. and U. Coun. (bd. dirs. 1987-2003, chmn. 1995-97), N.H. Postsecondary Edn. Commn. (chmn. 1994-96, bd. dirs. 1987—), Greater Manchester C. of C. (bd. dirs. 1990-97, chmn. 1996), Rotary (bd. dirs. Keene 1985-87). Episcopalian. Avocations: skiing, tennis. E-mail: r.gustafson@snhu.edu.

GUSTAFSON, SANDRA LYNNE, retired secondary school educator; b. Phila., Mar. 8, 1948; d. William Henry Gustafson and Ruth Blossom (Berger) Watson. BS in Edn., Temple U., 1969. Tchr. Lincoln H.S., Phila., 1969—78, Germantown H.S., Phila., 1978—85, Lincoln H.S., Phila., 1985—88, Germantown-Lankenau Motivation H.S., Phila., 1988—98, dean of discipline, 1994—96; tchr. Germantown H.S., Phila., 1998—99, Saul H.S., Phila., 1999—2003; ret., 2003. Asst. to vice prin. Lincoln H.S., Phila., 1970-78; sponsor Nat. Honor Soc., Phila., 1989-92, 93-96, Peer Counselors and Peer Tutors, Phila., 1989-98, records mgr., testing coord. Germantown-Lankenau Motivation H.S., 1997-98; chaperone on choir's trip to Europe, Lincoln H.S., 1973, coord. Freshman Orientation Program, Phila., 1993-98. Sponsor Big Brother/Big Sister Program, 1994-98. Mem. MLA, Phila. Fedn. Tchrs. (del. to state conv. 1973, del. to nat. conv. 1973, 74), Phila. Area Spanish Educators, Sigma Delta Pi, Kappa Delta Epsilon. Democrat. Jewish. Avocations: theater, music, ballet, opera, reading. Personal E-mail: slgandcats@aol.com.

GUSTAFSON, THOMAS, administrator; b. Mar. 31, 1947; married; 3 children. BA magna cum laude, Williams Coll., 1969; PhD in Econs., Yale U., 1982. Rsch. asst. Boston Cons. Group, 1970-71; acting dir. divsn. policy rsch. Office of Income Security Policy, U.S. Dept. Health and Human Svcs., 1983-84, economist, 1976-85; dir. divsn. Medicaid and long term care Office Legis. and Policy, Health Care Financing Adminstrn., Washington, 1985-88, dir. office policy analysis, 1988-90, dep. dir., 1990-96; dep. dir. Office Rsch. & Demonstration Health Care Financing Adminstrn., Balt., 1996-97, dep. dir. Office Strategic Planning, 1997-98, dir. Hosp. and Ambulatory Policy Group, Ctrs. Medicare and Medicaid, 1998—2003; dep. dir. Ctr. for Medicare Mgmt., Balt., 2003—. Presenter in field. Contbr. articles to profl. jours. Office: Ctr Medicaid Mgmt 7500 Security Blvd # 40126 Baltimore MD 21244-1849

GUSTAFSON, WILLIAM GENE, oil industry executive; b. El Reno, Okla., Sept. 16, 1930; s. Oliver B. and Madelyn (Morrison) Gustafson; children: Patricia Ownbey, Cindi Inman, William G. II. Student, U. Okla., 1948—50. Cert. risk mgmt. oil and gas Wharton Sch., U. Pa., 1982. Gen. agt., supt. agys. Penn Mut. Life Ins. Co., Omaha, 1958—60, Phila., 1960—62, Oklahoma City, 1962—78; pres., chmn. bd., CEO Petra Resources, Inc., Oklahoma City, 1980—. Chmn. bd. Petra-Graphic Labs., Inc., Oklahoma City, 1981—, Whitetail Oilfield Equipment, Inc., Edmond, Okla., 1983—. Served with U.S. Army, 1950—53, Korea. Decorated Purple Heart, Combat Infantryman's Badge. Republican. Roman Cath. Office: Petra Resources Inc 420 W Main St Ste 1000 Oklahoma City OK 73102-4401

GUSTAFSON, WINTHROP ADOLPH, aeronautical and astronautical engineering educator; b. Moline, Ill., Oct. 14, 1928; s. Gustav A. and Katherine (Wenger) G.; m. Sarah Elizabeth Garner, Aug. 3, 1957; children: Charles Lee, Stanley Scott, John Winthrop, Richard Neil. BS, U. Ill., 1950, MS, 1954, PhD, 1956. Research scientist Lockheed Missiles & Space Co., Palo Alto, Calif., 1956-60; asso. prof. Sch. Aeros. and Astronautics, Purdue U., Lafayette, Ind., 1960-66, prof., 1966-98, assoc. head sch., 1980-98, acting head sch., 1984-85, 93, prof. emeritus, 1998—. Vis. prof. U. Calif. at San Diego, 1968; research engr. Allison div. Gen. Motors Co., Indpls., summer 1962; mem. tech. staff Bell Telephone Labs., Whippany, N.J., summer 1966, NASA-Dryden Flight Research Center, summer 1976; cons. Goodyear Aerospace Corp., Akron, Ohio, 1964, Los Alamos Sci. Lab., 1977, U.S. Army, 1986-87. Contbr. articles to profl. jours. Served to 1st lt. USAF, 1951-53. Mem. AIAA. Home: 209 Lindberg Ave West Lafayette IN 47906-2109 Office: Purdue U Sch Aeros & Astronautics Lafayette IN 47907

GUSTAFSSON, LARS ERIK EINAR, writer, educator; b. Västerås, Sweden, May 17, 1936; came to U.S., 1983; s. Einar H. and Lotten Margaretha (Carlson) G.; m. D. Alexandra Chasnoff, 1982 (div. 2002); children: Benjamin, Karen. PhD, Uppsala (Sweden) U., 1978. Editor-in-chief Bonners Pub. House, Stockholm, 1961-72; rsch. fellow Ctr. Advanced Studies, Bielefeld, Germany, 1980-81; Aby Warburg rsch. prof. Warburg Found. U. Hamburg, Germany, 1997-98. Bd. dirs. Svenska Dagbladet Found.; bd. regents Uppsala (Sweden) U., 1994-97; adj. prof. U. Tex., Austin, 1983—; Jamail Disting. prof., 1998—. Author numerous novels and poetry collections. John Simon Guggenheim Meml. fellow of poetry, 1993. Mem. Acad. of Arts (Berlin), Acad. Scis. and Lit. (Mainz, Germany), Royal Swedish Acad. Engring. (Stockholm), Bavarian Acad. Fine Arts (Munich). Avocation: painting. Office: U Tex Austin Dept Philosophy Austin TX 78712 E-mail: lars.gustafsson@mail.utexas.edu.

GUSTAVSON, MARK STEVEN, lawyer; b. Berkeley, Calif., Jan. 3, 1951; s. Dean Leonard and Barbara (Knight) G.; m. Janet Daly, Jan. 24, 1974; children: Eric Karl, Stephen Earl, Jennifer Ann. BA in Philosophy magna cum laude with hons., U. Utah, 1973, JD, 1976. Bar: Utah 1976. Gen. counsel The Gustavson Group, Inc., Salt Lake City, 1976-91; pvt. practice Salt Lake City, 1976-82; sr. ptnr. Gustavson & Williams Attys., 1983-85, Gustavson, Hall & Williams, Salt Lake City, 1985-86, Gustavson, Schultz, Hall & Williams, Salt Lake City, 1986-93; corp. counsel, sec. Christensen Boyles Corp., Salt Lake City, 1993-96; pvt. practice Gustavson Law Assoc., 1999—. Pres. Concours Automotive Restoration, Inc., 1981—, Championship Pub., LLC, 1998—, Custon Styling Studio, LLC, 2001—; adj. prof. philosophy Utah C.C., 1991; mem. devel. com. Tanner Humanities Ctr., U. Utah. Columnist Scale Auto Enthusiast, Car Modeler, Model Car Jour., Model Cars, IPMS Jour., The Builder; contbr. articles to profl. jours. Founder Nat. Model Car Builders' Mus, GSL Internat. Model Car Championship. Faculty scholar, U. Utah, 1972-73. Mem. Utah Bar Assn., Salt Lake County Bar Assn., Sunstone Found., Owl and Key. Libertarian. Mem. Lds Ch. Avocations: model automotive building, gardening, restoring old cars.

GUSTIN, MARK DOUGLAS, hospital executive; b. Bklyn. BS in Acctg., N.Y. Inst. Tech., 1969, MBA in Bus. Mgmt., 1973; M Profl. Studies, L.I. U., 1975; residency diploma in hosp. adminstrn., Kings County Hosp. Ctr., 1979; health care fin. mgmt. cert., Molloy Coll., 1993, elder care studies cert., 1994. Cert. behavioral health care executive; diplomate in healthcare adminstrn. Acct. Fass, Tuchler & Muster, N.Y.C., 1969-74; asst. adminstr. Manhattan Kidney Ctr., Nat. Nephrology Found., Inc., N.Y.C., 1974-76; adminstr. Carter Cmty. Health Ctr., Jamaica, N.Y., 1976-77; resident in hosp. adminstrn. Kings County Hosp. Ctr., N.Y.C. Health and Hosps. Corp., Bklyn., 1978-79, evening dir. (asst. dir.), 1979-80, assoc. dir., 1980-92, sr. assoc. dir., 1992—. Mem. surrogate decision making program N.Y. State Commn. on Quality of Care for the Mentally Disabled, 1993—. Fellow Am. Acad. Med. Adminstrs. (bd. dirs. N.Y. State 1989—, pres. N.Y. Met. chpt. 1990—, State Dir. of Yr. award 1994), Am. Coll. Healthcare Execs., Assn. Behavioral Healthcare Mgmt. (bd. dirs. N.Y. chpt. 1993—, dep. gov. region II 1993-96, gov. 1997—, treas. 1998—), Royal Soc. Health; mem. Healthcare Execs. Club (treas. 1996-98) Home: 32 Jasmine Ln Valley Stream NY 11581-2412 Office: Kings County Hosp Ctr 451 Clarkson Ave Brooklyn NY 11203-2097

GUSTUS, STACEY A. legal secretary; b. Lakewood, Colo., Sept. 10, 1961; d. Norman Gaylord and Sandra S. (Melton) Holder; m. Wayne A. Gustus, Jr., June 14, 1980; children: Gregory K., Cynthia Jo. Student, U. North Colo., 1979-80. Cert. paralegal. County ct. tech. Adams County Dist. Atty., Brighton, Colo., 1980-83; legal sec. Peter L. Mattisson, Esq., Westminster, Colo., 1983-85, Hall & Evans, Denver, 1985-90; paralegal Machol & Machol, Denver, 1990-91; legal sec., mktg. liaison McKenna Long & Aldridge, LLP, Denver, 1991—. Mem. Nat. Contract Mgmt. Assn. (Denver chpt., sec., registrar 1994—, treas. and newsletter editor 1994-99). Avocations: sewing, crafts, bowling, fishing. Office: McKenna Long & Aldridge LLP 1875 Lawrence St Ste 200 Denver CO 80202 E-mail: sgustus@mckennalong.com.

GUTEKUNST, RICHARD RALPH, microbiology educator; b. Allentown, Pa., Jan. 20, 1926; s. George D. and Jennie L. (Alsop) G.; m. Anna Frances Fetterman, Dec. 27, 1946; children: Mary Jane Ellickson, Richard M., Jo Anne Loughery. BS, Phila. Coll. Pharmacy and Sci., 1951; MS, Cornell U., 1957, PhD, 1958. Commd. ensign USN, advanced through grades to comdr., 1968; mem. faculty Hahnemann Med. Coll. and Hosp., Phila., 1968-80, prof. microbiology and immunology, 1974-80; dir. Clin. Micro Lab., 1968-75; dean Coll. Allied Health Professions, 1975-80, Coll. Health Related Professions; prof. dept. med. tech. and microbiology U. Fla., Gainesville, 1980-95; dean emeritus, 1995—.,.p. Lower Gwynedd (Pa.) Twp. Commrs., 1972-80; mem. coun. St. Peter's Luth. Ch., North Wales, Pa., 1972-77, pres., 1974-77; No. Ctrl. Fla. Regional Planning Coun., 1987-92; bd. dirs. Citizens' Crime Commn., Alachua County, 1984-88, vice-chmn., 1986-87; bd. dirs. United Way Alachua County, 1984-90, 98—, pres., 1988; bd. dirs. ARC of Alachua County, 1989-93; pres. Fla. Alliance of 100, Healthcare Manpower, 1988-90; mem. adv. bd. AIDS Inst., UF; mem. com. on pub. health FMA, 1986-95, mem. com. on allied health, 1991-94, mem. task force on nursing shortage, 1990-95; bd. dirs. DAYTOP Fla., 1996-98, chmn. 1998; bd. dirs. Phoenix Ho. of Fla., 1999—, chmn. 1999—. Recipient Lindback award, 1975; Faculty Achievement award Coll. Allied Health Professions; Faculty Achievement award Hahnemann Med. Coll. and Hosp., Phila., 1980 Fellow Am. Acad. Microbiology, Am. Soc. for Allied Health Professions (pres.-elect 1981-82, pres. 1982-83); mem. Assn. Practitioners Infection Control, Am. Soc. Microbiology, N.Y. Acad. Scis., Masons. Republican. Lutheran. Home: 3942 NW 25th Cir Gainesville FL 32606-7435 Office: U Health Sci Ctr PO Box 100014 Gainesville FL 32610-0014 E-mail: RGutekun@vpha.ufl.edu., RRGutekunst@aol.com.

GUTENTAG, PATRICIA RICHMAND, social worker, family counselor, occupational therapist; b. Newark, Apr. 10, 1954; d. Joseph and Joan (Miller) Leflein; m. Herbert Norman Gutentag; children: Steven, Jesse. BS in Occupational Therapy, Tufts U., 1976; MSW, Boston Coll., 1979. Lic. family and marriage counselor, lic. clin. social worker, N.J.; diplomate Am. Bd. Examiners in Clin. Social Work; registered occupational therapist, N.J. Social worker Jewish Family Svc., Salem, Mass., 1979-82; pvt. practice family and marriage counselor Westfield and Red Bank, N.J., 1982—. Cons. high stress, Westfield and Red Bank, 1982—. Fellow N.J. Soc. for Clin. Social Work; mem. NASW, Am. Occupational Therapists Assn., Registered Occupational Therapists Assn., Soc. for Advancement Family Therapy in N.J., Am. Anorexia-Bulimia Assn., Am. Assn. Marriage and Family Therapy. Avocation: reading. Office: 200 Maple Ave Red Bank NJ 07701-1732

GUTER, JAMES L. music educator; b. Newark, Jan. 2, 1939; s. Noah J. and Jean Guter; m. Janis D. Chamberlin, Nov. 30, 1985; m. Joyce Bauer, June 24, 1960 (div.); children: Ellen Howard, Mark. MusB Edn., Montclair State U., 1964, M Music Edn., 1968. Cert. K-12 music tchr. Music tchr. Madison (NJ) Jr./Sr. H.S., 1964—68; dir. of bands John F. Kennedy Meml. H.S., Iselin, NJ, 1968—73, Franklin Twp. H.S., Somerset, NJ; music coord. k-12/dir. of bands Gloucester (Mass.) Pub. Schools, 1975—82; chmn., music dept./dir. of bands Clovis West H.S., Fresno, Calif., 1982—84; exec. dir. of bowl games of am. Heritage Festivals, Salt Lake City, 1984—88; pres. and owner Events Am., Inc., Groton, Mass., 1988—92; chmn., music and performing arts dept., k-12/dir. of bands Acton-Boxborough Regional Sch. Districts, Acton, Mass., 1988—93; dist. coord. of fine arts and gifted and talented programs K-12 Consol. Sch. Sys. of New Britain, New Britain, Conn., 1993—95; music dept. chmn. Lincoln-Way Cmty. H.S., New Lenox, Ill., 1995—97; fine arts dept. chair, dir. of bands Cmty. H.S. Dist., West Chicago, Ill., 1997—. V.p. Fox Valley Music Festival, Ill., 1999—2000, pres., Ill., 2000—01; bd. of dirs. New Britain (Conn.) Symphony, 1993—95; edn. bd. mem. New Britain Mus. of Am. Art, 1993—95; founder and past pres. New Eng. Scholastic Band Assn., Mass., 1976—82; founder/dir. Ctrl. Jersey Wind Ensemble, Iselin, NJ, 1968—75; dir. of bands Paris All Star Marching Band, 2001—02; founder/dir. West Chicago-C.O.D. Cmty. Concert Band, 2000—. Contbr. articles to profl. publs. With USN, 1957—60. Recipient Disting. Svc. Award, NJ Jr. C. of C., 1970, First Starward, Am. Bandmasters Found., 1974, Outstanding Svc. to Music Edn. award, Conneticut Music Educators, 1995. Mem.: NEA (Citation of Excellence for outstanding contbns. to band and band music 2000), Nat. Art Edn. Assn., Internat. Assn. of Jazz Educators, Nat. Band Assn., Ill. Music Educators Assn. (Outstanding Svc. to Music Edn. award 1999), Music Educators Nat. Conf., Phi Mu Alpha Sinfonia (historian and v.p. 1962—64). Avocation: travel. Home Fax: 630-876-6379; Office Fax: 630-876-6379. Personal E-mail: jguter@d94.org. E-mail: jguter@d94.org.

GUTERMUTH, SCOTT ALAN, accountant, pharmaceutical company executive; b. South Bend, Ind., Nov. 24, 1953; s. Richard H. and Barbara Ann (Bracey) G. BS in Bus., Ind. U., 1976. CPA, Ind. With Coopers & Lybrand, Indpls., 1976-83, supervising auditor, 1980-83, audit mgr., 1983; v.p., contr. Society Nat. Group, Indpls., 1983-89; v.p., CFO Am. Svc. Life Ins. Co., 1989-90; CFO Quad Pharms., Inc., 1990-96; CFO, treas. Lilly Ranbaxy Pharms. LLC, 1996—. Instr., nat. update analyst Becker CPA Rev. Course, 1980—. Advisor Jr. Achievement; mem. Marion County Rep. Com., 1978—, Rep. Nat. Com., 1972—. Fellow Life Mgmt. Inst.; mem. AICPA, Nat. Assn. Accts., Ins. Acctg. and Statis. Assn., Ind. Assn. CPAs (ins. com. 1984—), Life Mgmt. Inst. (assoc.). Methodist. Home: 3132 Sandpiper South Dr Indianapolis IN 46268-3229 Office: 8910 Purdue Rd Ste 230 Indianapolis IN 46268-1177

GUTFELD, NORMAN E. lawyer; b. Pitts., Dec. 8, 1911; s. Adolph and Fannie (Haupt) G.; m. Evelyn Kirtz, Aug. 9, 1938 (dec. Jan. 1989); children: Nancy Gutfeld Brown, Howard, Charles, Joan Gutfeld Miller, Rose Gutfeld Edwards, Steven. BA, Case-Western Res. U., 1933, LL.B., 1935. Bar: Ohio 1935. Individual practice law, Cleve., 1935-43; atty. U.S. Regional War Labor Bd., Cleve., 1944; assoc. firm Benesch, Friedlander & Morris, Cleve., 1944-53; treas. Builders Structural Steel Corp., Cleve., 1953-59; partner Garber, Gutfeld & Jaffe, Cleve., 1959-73, Simon, Haiman, Gutfeld, Friedman and Jacobs, Cleve., 1973-80; of counsel Hertz Kates Friedman & Kammer, Cleve., 1981-93; pvt. practice Cleve., 1993-95; retired, 1995. Mem. Cleveland Heights-University Heights Bd. Edn., 1956-63, pres., 1958-59; treas. Bur. Jewish Edn. Cleve., 1974-79; trustee Cleve. Jewish Community Fedn., 1976-77. Mem. Bar Assn. Greater Cleve., Ohio State Bar Assn., Citizen's League Cleve. Clubs: Cleve. City. Home: 3151 Mayfield Rd Cleveland Heights OH 44118

GUTFINGER, DAN ELI, cardiologist, surgeon; b. New Haven, June 17, 1964; s. Chaim and Tamak Gutfinger; m. Shari Gutfinger, Mar. 27, 1998; 1 child, Bradley. BS, U. Calif., Irvine, 1983, MS, 1986, PhD, 1990, MD, 1996. Engring. specialist Ford/Loral Aerospace, Newport Beach, Calif., 1984—91; dir. artificial heart program U. Calif., Irvine, 1991—92; gen. surgery resident Allegheny Gen. Hosp., Pitts., 1996—2001; cardiothoracic surgery fellow U. Ariz., Tucson, 2001—. Editor: Mechanical Cardiac Assist, 1993. E-mail: gutfinger@yahoo.com.

GUTH, ALAN HARVEY, physicist, educator; b. New Brunswick, N.J., Feb. 27, 1947; s. Hyman and Elaine (Cheiten) G.; m. Susan Tisch, Mar. 28, 1971; children: Lawrence David, Jennifer Lynn. SB and SM, MIT, 1969, PhD in Physics, 1972. Instr. Princeton U., 1971-74; research assoc. Columbia U., N.Y.C., 1974-77, Cornell U., Ithaca, N.Y., 1977-79, Stanford Linear Accelerator Ctr., Calif., 1979-80; assoc. prof. Physics MIT, Cambridge, 1980-86, prof., 1986-89, Jerrold Zacharias prof. physics, 1989-91, Victor F. Weisskopf prof. physics, 1992—. Physicist Harvard-Smithsonian Ctr. for Astrophysics, 1984-89, vis. scientist, 1990-91. Alfred P. Sloan fellow, 1981; on Sci. Digest's list of America's 100 Brightest Scientists Under 40, 1984; on Esquire Mag.'s list of Men and Women Under 40 Who Are Changing the Nation, 1985; on Newsweek's list of 25 Top Am. Innovators, 1989. Fellow AAAS, Am. Phys. Soc. (mem. exec. com. astrophysics div. 1986-88, vice chmn. astrophysics div. 1988-89, chmn. div. 1989-90, recipient Lilienfeld Prize 1992), Benjamin Franklin medal for Physics, Franklin Inst., 2001; Am. Acad. Arts and Scis.; mem. NAS, Am. Astron. Soc. Achievements include being originator of inflationary model of early universe. Office: MIT Ctr Theor Physics 6209 77 Massachusetts Ave Cambridge MA 02139-4307

GUTH, CARYL JOY, retired anesthesiologist; b. Peoria, Ill., 1935; m. John Faistad, 1968 (dec. 2001). AA, Mars Hill Coll., 1955; BS, Wake Forest U., 1957, MD, 1962. Diplomate Am. Bd. Anesthesiology. Intern U. Kans. Med. Ctr., Kansas City, 1962-63; resident in anesthesiology U. Pa. Hosp., Phila., 1963-65; fellow in anesthesiology Queen Victoria Hosp., Sussex, Eng., 1966; former chmn. dept anesthesiology Mills-Peninsula Hosps., San Mateo, Calif., ret.; instr. U. Nijmegan, Netherlands, 1966; ind. Nikken wellness cons., 1996—; spl. interest-complementary medicine, 1998—; wellness cons. Bd. dirs. Mills-Peninsula Health Sys., Mills Hosp.; mem. bd. sci. and policy advisors Am. Coun. Sci. and Health, 2000—. Mem. AMA, Am. Soc. Anesthesiology (del. 1976-2000, chair com. on comms. 1987-90, chair com. profl. diversity 1995-97, ann. meeting program organizer 1983-84, 87-88, 94, 97), Calif. Med. Assn. (chair com. splty. socs. 1983-84), Calif. Soc. Anesthesiology (past pres., editor bull. 1976-79, asst. treas. 1979-81, pres.-elect 1981-82, pres. 1982-83), San Mateo County Med. Assn. (bd. dirs. 1984-86, chair med. staff affairs com. 1985-86), Wake Forest U. Med. Alumni Assn. (bd. dirs. 1999—, sec. 2003—, establisher, fundraiser endowed chair integrative medicine 2002). Home: 512 Bermuda Village Dr Advance NC 27006 E-mail: wellconsultant@5pillars.com.

GUTH, SHERMAN LEON (S. LEE GUTH), psychologist, educator; b. N.Y.C. s. Arthur and Caroline (Laub) G.; children from previous marriage: Melissa, Victoria; m. Ling Zhao; 1 child, Lillian. BS, Purdue U., 1959; MA, U. Ill., 1961, PhD, 1963. Lectr. dept. psychology Ind. U., Bloomington, 1962-63, instr., 1963-64, asst. prof., 1964-67, assoc. prof., 1967-70, prof., 1970—; dir. research and grad. devel. Sch. Optometry, 1980-88, chmn. dept. visual scis., 1982-85. Vis. assoc. prof. psychology Mich. State U., 1968-69; NIH spl. research fellow in psychology U. Calif., Berkeley, 1971-72; NSF program dir. for sensory physiology and perception, 1977-78 NIH research grantee, 1964-70, NSF research grantee, 1963-86. Fellow Optical Soc. Am. Achievements include being the creator of the ATD model for visual adaption and color perception. Office: Ind U Dept Psychology Bloomington IN 47405

GUTHART, LEO A. electronics executive; b. N.Y.C., Sept. 26, 1937; s. Harry and Lillian (Singer) G.; m. Laura Carrol, June 16, 1960; children:: Rebecca, Margaret. AB, Harvard U., 1958, MBA, 1960, D in Bus. Adminstrn., 1966. Rsch. assoc. Bus. Sch Harvard U., Boston, 1960-62; with Pittway Corp., 1963—, vice chmn., 1988—; exec. v.p. Ademco divsn., Syosset, N.Y., 1963-71, pres., 1971-99; chmn., CEO Pittway Security Group, Syosset, 1999—; exec. v.p. Home and Bldg. Control, Honeywell Internat.; mng. ptnr. Topspin Ptnrs., LP, Roslyn Heights, N.Y., 2000—. Chmn. bd. trustees Hofstra U., Hempstead, N.Y., 1993-96; bd. dirs. Aptargroup, Acorn Fund, Symbol Technologies, L.I. Venture Fund; chmn. Cylink Corp., Sunnyvale, Calif., 1996—; chmn. Alarm Industry Rsch. and Edn. Found., 1997—. Contbr. articles to profl. jours. Fellow Ford Found., 1961; named Baker scholar, Harvard U., 1960. Mem. Harvard Club, Racquet Club, Beta Gamma Sigma (hon.). Avocation: tennis. Office: 3 Expressway Plz Roslyn Heights NY 11577-2045

GUTHEIL, IRENE A. social work educator, researcher; b. St. Louis, June 17, 1944; m. John Gordon Gutheil, June 9, 1968 (dec.); children: David Arthur, Robert Douglas. BA, Brandeis U., 1966; MS, Columbia U., 1968, D Social Welfare, 1988. Lic. social worker, N.Y. Psychiat. social worker Karen Horney Clinic, N.Y.C., 1968-69; social work cons. New Rochelle (N.Y.) Nursing Home, 1973-76, 77-83, Westledge Extended Care Facility, Peekskill, N.Y., 1973-84; social worker Geriatric Assocs., Montefiore Med. Ctr., Bronx, NY, 1986; from adj. instr. to prof. Fordham U. Grad. Sch. Social Svc., N.Y.C., 1982—2001, Henry C. Ravazzin prof. of gerontology, 2001—; dir. Ravazzin Ctr. Social Work Rsch. in Aging Fordham U., N.Y.C., 1995—. Adj. instr. Mercy Coll., Dobbs Ferry, NY, 1981—83; mem. human svcs. adv. bd, Actors Fund Am., N. Y.C., 1982—92; mem. rssch. adv. bd. Found. for Long Term Care, Albany, NY, 1997—; mem. adv. bd. Health Advocates for Older People, N.Y.C., 1998—; bd. dirs. Aging in Am. Cmty. Svcs., Bronx, 1998—; mem. disaster svcs. adv. com. ARC Greater NY, N.Y.C., 2001—02. Contbg. author: (with R. Chernesky) Adult Psychopathology: A Social Work Perspective, 1999; editor: Work with Older People: Challenges and Opportunities, 1994; contbr. articles to profl. jours., including Jour. Gerontol. Social Work, Social Work, Ednl.Gerontology. Grantee Fordham U., 1991, Grotta Found., 1999, Fan Fox and Leslie R. Samuels Found., 1999, The Philanthropic Group, 2000, John A. Hartford Found., 2002, Helen Andrus Benedict Found., 2002, Fan Fox & Leslie R. Samuels Found., 2002. Fellow Gerontol. Soc. Am. (postdoctoral fellow 1989); mem. NASW, Coun. on Social Work Edn., Am. Soc. on Aging, Assn. for Gerontology in Social Work Edn., State Soc. on Aging N.Y. (exec. bd. 1992-94, 98-99). Office: Fordham U Grad Sch Social Svc Neperan Rd Tarrytown NY 10591 E-mail: gutheil@fordham.edu.

GUTHEIM, ALLEN HERMAN, economist; b. Washington, June 2, 1945; s. August George and Mary (Walsh) G.; m. Susan Haynam, July 19, 1969; children: Daniel August, Katherine Estelle. BS, Case Inst. Tech., 1967; MA, Case Western Res. U., 1977. Staff analyst Ernst & Ernst, Cleve., 1967-71; stockbroker Paine, Webber, Jackson & Curtis, Cleve., 1971-72; sales rep. Al Schulte & Assocs., Cleve., 1972; economist Wharton Econometric Forecasting Assocs., Phila., 1978-83; sr. economist First Nat. Bank of Boston, 1983-85, Data Resources, Inc./McGraw-Hill, 1985—2001, regional account mgr., 1990-91, sr. assoc., 1991—2001; prin. Global Insight, Inc., 2001—. Instr. Case Western Res. U., 1974-77; mem. bus. rsch. adv. coun. Bur. Labor Stats., 1985-87. Contbr. articles to profl. jours. Home: 47 Cedar Creek Rd Sudbury MA 01776-1004 Office: 24 Hartwell Ave Lexington MA 02421-3103 E-mail: allen.gutheim@globalinsight.com.

GUTHEINZ, JOSEPH RICHARD, JR., lawyer, former politician, investigative consultant, retired army officer and NASA official, educator, author; b. Camp Lejune, N.C., Aug. 13, 1955; s. Joseph R. Sr. and Rita C. (O'Leary) G.; m. Lori Ann Bentley, Jan. 16, 1976; children: Joseph, Christopher, Michael, Jim, Bill, Dave. AS, AA, Monterey Peninsula Coll., Calif., 1975; BA, Calif. State U., Sacramento, 1978, MA, 1979; postgrad., U. Calif., Davis, 1979-80; grad. U.S. Army Mil. Intelligence Officer Basic Course, U.S. Army Tactical Intelligence Sch., 1980; grad., U.S. Army Flight Sch., 1984; MS in Sys. Mgmt.,

U. So. Calif., 1985; JD, S. Tex. Coll. Law, 1996; grad. Criminal Investigators Basic Course (hon.), Fed. Law Enforcement Tng. Ctrs., 1988; grad. (disting.), Fed. Law Enforcement Tng. Ctrs. Office Inspector Gen., 1989. Bar: Tex. Supreme Ct. 1997, U.S. Dist. Ct. (so. dist.) Tex. 1997, U.S. Vets. Ct. Appeals 1998, U.S. Armed Forces Ct. Appeals 1998, U.S. Ct. Appeals (5th, 10th, 11th and fed. cirs.) 1998, U.S. Tax Ct. 1998, U.S. Supreme Ct. 2001; lic. FAA comml. pilot, cert. fraud examiner, tchr. credentials in aeronautics, mil. sci., bus. and indsl. mgmt., pub. svcs. and adminstrn., sociology and police sci. Calif. Officer U.S. Army, Kitzigen, Fed. Rep. Germany, 1980-82, capt., mil. intelligence officer Stuttgart, Fed. Rep. Germany, 1982-84, capt., aviator Ft. Polk, La., 1984-86; spl. agt. civil aviation security FAA, Oklahoma City, 1986-87; spl. agt. U.S. Dept. Transp., Denver, 1987-90; sr. spl. agt., acting sr. resident agent in charge Office Insp. Gen. NASA, Houston, 1990-2000; pvt. practice atty. Houston, 1996—; mentor, instr. organized crime U. Phoenix, 2002—. Police sci. instr. Ctrl. Tex. Coll., Nelligan, 1983; case agt. FAA Air Traffic Control Acad. Cheating Scandal, 1987, New Denver Airport Investigation, 1988—2000; case agt. in pilot match investigation FBI/FAA Pilot Match Investigation, 1989—90; case agt. in charge of investigating space shuttle temperature transducers Grounded Shuttle Fleet, 1991; task force leader Nine Agy. Fed. Omniplan, 1992—96; task force leader leaseback scheme investigation Lockheed Engring. Sci. Corp., 1999—2000; guest spkr. Internat. Bus. Forum, 1995, Assn. Govt. Accts., 1996, NASA OIG Auditor Conf., 2000; chief NASA OIG investigator Russian Mir Space Stas. fire and collision, 1997; task force leader Bid and Proposal Investigation Rockwell Space and Ops. Co., 1996—2000; criminal def. atty., expert witness, 1997—; chief investigator and arresting agt. Jerry Whittridge the astronaut and CIA assassin impersonator, 1998, Op. Lunar Eclipse, 1998—2000; investigator Civilian Astronaut Corps., 1999—2002; task force leader Fed. Agy. Investigation Rockwell Internat./Boeing N.Am. and U.S. Alliance, 2000; task force leader Fed. Agy. Investigation, Lockheed Martin; extensively quoted on Columbia disaster, 2003. Author: The Moon Rock Con, Stealing the Dream, Is it Legal to Privately Own Space Shuttle Tiles. Pres. Calif. State U. United Students for Life, 1976—79; chairperson Calif. Rally for Life, 1980; atty./activist against San Jacinto C.C. spl. election to annex parts of Clear Lake Texas; proponent Calif. Pro-Life Initiative, 1977; organizer Morton Downey Dem. Presdl. Campaign, 1979; bd. dirs. Sea Isle Property Owners, 2001—02; briefed Pres. Yeltsin's econ. advisors, 1995. Decorated U.S. Army Meritorious Svc. medal, Army Commendation medal; recipient letter of commendation FBI Dir. Louis Frech, 1995, Tex. Spl. Commendation U.S. Atty. Office So. Dist., 1996, NASA Exceptional Svc. medal, 2000, Pres.'s Coun. for Integrity and Efficiency Career Achievement award, 2000, Cert. of Appreciation U.S. Atty. (so. dist.) Tex., 2003, Cert. of Commendation Univ. Phoenix, 2003; named Hon. Lt. Gov. Okla., 1987; Merit scholar South Tex. Coll. Law. Mem.: Haris County Lawyers assn., Nat. Rep. Lawyers Assn., Tex. Criminal Def. Lawyers Assn., Tex. Bar Assn., Cert. Fraud Examiners. Republican. Roman Catholic. Avocations: reading, teaching, public speaking, political activism, helping the poor. Office: 205 Woodcombe Houston TX 77062 E-mail: jguteinz@sbcglobal.net.

GUTHERY, JOHN M. lawyer; b. Broken Bow, Nebr., Nov. 22, 1946; s. John M. and Kay G.; m. Diane Messineo, May 26, 1972; 1 child, Lisa. BS, U. Nebr., 1969, JD, 1972. Bar: Nebr. 1972. Pres. Perry, Guthery, Haase & Gessford, P.C., L.L.O., Lincoln, Nebr., 1972—. Bd. govs. Nebr. Wesleyan U. Mem. ATLA, ABA (mem. litigation section), Nebr. Bank Attys. Assn. (past pres., 1985-86), Nebr. Assn. Trial Attys., Nebr. State Bar Assn. (pres. 1998-99, mem. Nebr.State Bar Found. mem ho. dels. 1979-83, 87-95, exec. coun. 1988-94 pres. elect. 1997-98, chair Nebr. bankruptcy sect.), Lincoln Bar Assn. (bd. trustees, 1985-88, pres. 1990-91), mem. Bd of Gov., Wesleyan Univ., Nebr. Office: Perry Guthery Haase & Gessford PC LLO 233 S 13th St Ste 1400 Lincoln NE 68508-2003 E-mail: jguthery@perrylawfirm.com.

GUTHIKONDA, MURALI, neurosurgeon; s. Sreeramulu and Jayamma Guthikonda; m. Winifred M Yavorsky, May 1, 1976; children: Shaila, Shyam. MD, Guntur Med. Coll., India, 1973. Practicing neurosurgeon Murali Guthikonda, PC, Youngstown, Ohio, 1980—92; assoc. prof. Dept of Neurol. Surgery, Detroit, 1992—2002. Interim chmn./program dir. Dept of Neurol. Surgery/ Wayne State U., Detroit. Lt. col USAR, 1989—98, Ft. Lewis, Tacoma. Mem.: Am. Assn. of Neurol. Surgeons. Office: Dept of Neurological Surgery 4160 John R Ste 930 Detroit MI 48201 Personal E-mail: mguthikonda@hotmail.com. E-mail: mguthikonda@neurosurgery.wayne.edu.

GUTHKE, KARL SIEGFRIED, foreign language educator; b. Lingen, Germany, Feb. 17, 1933; came to U.S., 1956, naturalized, 1973; s. Karl Hermann and Helene (Beekman) G.; m. Dagmar von Nostitz, Apr. 24, 1965; 1 child, Carl Rickfel, MA, U. Tex., 1953; PhD, U. Göttingen, Germany, 1956; MA (hon.), Harvard U., 1968. Faculty U. Calif., Berkeley, 1956-65; prof. German lit. U. Calif. at Berkeley, 1962-65, U. Toronto, Ont., Can., 1965-68, Harvard U., 1968-78, Kuno Francke prof. German art and culture, 1978—. Vis. prof. U. Colo., 1963, U. Mass., 1967; vis. fellow Sidney Sussex Coll., Cambridge U., Nat. Rsch. Ctr., Wolfenbüttel, Inst. for Adv. Studies, U. Edinburgh, Humanities Rsch. Ctr., Australian Nat. U., Canberra. Author: Englische Vorromantik und deutscher Sturm und Drang, 1958, (with Hans M. Wolff) Das Leid im Werke Gerhart Hauptmanns, 1958, Geschichte und Poetik der deutschen Tragikomödie, 1961, Gerhart Hauptmann: Weltbild im Werk, 1961, rev. edit., 1980, Haller und die Literatur, 1962, Der Stand der Lessing-Forschung: Ein Bericht über die Literatur, 1932-1962, 1965, Modern Tragicomedy: An Investigation into the Nature of the Genre, 1966, Wege zur Literatur: Studien zur deutschen Dichtungs-und Geistesgeschichte, 1967, Hallers Literaturkritik, 1970, Die Mythologie der entgötterten Welt: Ein literarisches Thema von der Aufklärung bis zur Gegenwart, 1971, Das deutsche bürgerliche Trauerspiel, 1972, 5th rev. edit., 1994, G.E. Lessing, 3d edit., 1979, Literarisches Leben im 18. Jahrhundert in Deutschland und in der Schweiz, 1975, Das Abenteuer der Literatur, 1981, Haller im Halblicht, 1981, Der Mythos der Neuzeit, 1983, Erkundungen, 1983, Das Geheimnis um B. Traven entdeckt, 1984, B. Traven: Biographie eines Rätsels, 1987, The Last Frontier: Imagining Other Worlds, 1990, Letzte Worte, 1990, B. Traven: The Life Behind the Legends, 1991, Last Words, 1992, Trails in No-Man's Land, 1993, Die Entdeckung des Ich, 1993, Schillers Dramen, 1994, Ist der Tod eine Frau, 1997, The Gender of Death, 1999, Der Blick in die Fremde, 2000, Goethes Weimar und die grosse Öffnung in die weite Welt, 2001, Epitaph Culture in the West, 2003, Lessings Horizonte, 2003, also others; transl.: Die moderne Tragikomodie: Theorie und Gestalt, 1968; editor: Haller, Die Alpen, 1987; co-editor: (Hanser) Gotthold Ephraim Lessing, Werke, 1970-72, Joh. H. Füssli, Sämtliche Gedichte, 1973, B. Traven: Briefe aus Mexiko, 1992, Lessing Yearbook, Colloquia Germanica, Twentieth Century Literature, German Quar. Honored in History and Literature: Essays in Honor of Karl S. Guthke, 2000. Fellow Humanities Rsch. Ctr., Canberra Australia, Inst. Advanced Studies, Edinburgh, Scotland, Rsch. Ctr., Wolfenbuttel; mem. Lessing Soc. (past pres.), Inst. Germanic Studies (London corr. fellow). Office: Harvard U Dept German Cambridge MA 02138

GUTHMAN, JACK, lawyer; b. Cologne, Germany, Apr. 19, 1938; came to U.S., 1939, naturalized, 1945; s. Albert and Selma (Cahn) G.; m. Sandra Polk, Nov. 26, 1967. BA, Northwestern U., 1960; LL.B., Yale U., 1963. Bar: Ill. bar 1963. Law clk. to dist. judge U.S. Dist. Ct. No. Ill., 1963-65; since practiced in Chgo.; ptnr. Sidley & Austin, 1970-94, Shefsky & Froelich Ltd., Chgo., 1995—. Mem. City Chgo. Zoning Bd. Appeals, 1970-75, chmn., 1975-87. Democrat. Jewish. Office: Shefsky & Froelich Ltd 444 N Michigan Ave Ste 2500B Chicago IL 60611-3998

GUTHRIDGE, BILL, university basketball coach; b. Parsons, Kans., July 27, 1937; m. Leesie Guthridge; children: Jamie, Stuart, Megan. BS in Math., Kans. State U., MEd, 1963. Coach Scott City (Kans.) H.S; asst. football coach Kans. State U.; freshman basketball coach, co-asst. varsity coach U. N.C., Chapel Hill, from 1973, asst. coach, 1968-97, head coach, 1998—. Coach Puerto Rican AAU Summer Leagues; coach Puerto Rican Olympic Team, 1968. Named Coach of Yr., Puerto Rican AAU, Nat. Coach of Yr., Nat. Assn. Basketball Coaches, Sporting News, CBS/Chevrolet, Columbus Touchdown Club, Atlantic Coast Conf., 1998; recipient Naismith award Atlanta Tipoff Club. Office: U NC Office Basketball PO Box 2126 Chapel Hill NC 27515-2126

GUTHRIE, CATHERINE S. (CATHERINE S. NICHOLSON-GUTHRIE), research scientist; b. Jackson, Miss. d. James Benjamin and Catherine Cornelia Nicholson; m. George Drake Guthrie, Aug. 5, 1961; 1 child, George Drake Jr. BS, Auburn U., 1957; MS, Fla. State U., 1960; PhD, Ind. U., 1972. Instr. Fla. State U., Tallahassee, 1960, Boston State Coll., 1963-64; rsch. asst. Calif. Inst. Tech., Pasadena, 1960-62, MIT, Cambridge, 1964-65; trainee NIH, 1967-71; vis. asst. prof. U. Evansville, Ind., 1972-73; profl. staff mem. com. sci. and tech. U.S. Ho. of Reps., Washington, 1981; instr., then adj. rsch. scientist Ind. U. Sch. Medicine, 1974-92, ind. rsch. scientist Area GABA/Ovarian Cancer, 1992—. Cons. Mead Johnson Co., Evansville, Ind., 1976, Com. on Environment and Pub. Wks., U.S. Senate, Washington, 1981. Contbr. articles to profl. jours. State bd. dirs. Citizens Energy Coalition, Indpls., 1975-76; bd. dirs. Child Find Orgn., Evansville, 1985-86. Mass Media Sci. fellow AAAS, 1979, Sarah Berliner fellow AAUW, 1978-79. Avocation: bird watching. Home: 4 Tres Hermanas Santa Fe NM 87508 E-mail: gguthrie@usi.edu.

GUTHRIE, DIANA FERN, nursing educator; b. N.Y.C., May 7, 1934; d. Floyd George and A. May (Moler) Worthington; m. Richard Alan Guthrie, Aug. 18, 1957; children: Laura, Joyce, Tammy. AA, Graceland Coll., 1953; RN, Independence (Mo.) Sanitarium, 1956; BS in Nursing, U. Mo., 1957, MS in Pub. Health, 1969; EdS, Wichita State U., 1982; PhD, Walden U., 1985. Cert. diabetes educator, bd. cert. advanced diabetes mgmt.; RN Mo., Kans., cert. holistic nursing, RN advanced practitioner; lic. profl. counselor Kans., cert. stress mgmt. edn., clin. hypnosis, healing touch, lic. marriage and family therapist. Instr. red cross U.S. Naval Sta., Sangley Point, Philippines, 1961-63; acting head nurse newborn nursery U. Mo., Columbia, 1963-64, birth defect nurse dept. pediat., 1964-65, nursing dir. clin. research ctr., 1965-67, research asst., 1967-73; diabetes nurse specialist Sch. Medicine U. Kans., Wichita, 1973—, asst. then assoc. prof. Sch. Medicine, 1974-85, prof. dept. pediat. and psychiatry Sch. Medicine, 1985-99, prof. emeritus, 2000; prof. dept. nursing Kans. U. Med. Ctr., Wichita, 1985-99, ret., 1999. Nurse cons. diabetes Mo. Regional Med. Program, Columbia, 1970-73; nat. advisor Human Diabetes Ctr. for Excellence, Lexington, Ky., 1982-90, Phoenix, 1983-92, Charlottesville, Ky., 1990-95; adj. prof. Sch. Nursing Wichita State U., 1985—. Author: Nursing Management of Diabetes, 1977, Nursing Management of Diabetes, 5th edit., 2002, The Diabetes Source Book, 1990, 2003, Alternative and Complementary Diabetes Case, 2000; contbr. articles to profl. jours. Mem. health adv. bd. Mid-Am. All Indian Ctr., Wichita, 1978-80; bd. dirs. Wichita Urban Indian Health Clinic, 1980-82; bd. trustees Graceland Univ., Lamoni, Iowa, 1996-2001, bd. dirs. emeritus, 2002—. Fellow: Am. Acad. Nursing; mem.: APHA, ANA, Am. Assn. Med. Psychotherapists (profl. adv. bd. 1985—), Am. Assn. Diabetes Educators (Kans. area Disting. Svc. award 1999), Am. Diabetes Assn. (Kans. area prof. edn. and youth com. 1988—, affiliate bd. dirs. 1979—83, pres. Kans. affiliate 1980—81, 1990—91, Outstanding Educator award 1979, Regional Outstanding Svc. award 1984), Sigma Theta Tau (Exemplary Recognition award Epsilon Gamma chpt. 1996). Democrat. Mem. Cmty. Of Christ Ch. Avocations: harp, piano, oil painting, crafts, reading. Office: 200 S Hillside Wichita KS 67211-2127 E-mail: dguthrie@kumc.edu.

GUTHRIE, EDGAR KING, artist; b. Chenoa, Ill., May 12, 1917; s. David McMurtrie and Emily Henrietta (Streid) G.; m. Eva Ross Harvey, Dec. 8, 1945 (dec. Jan. 1978); children: Melody Bliss Johnson, Mark King Guthrie. BEd, Ill. State U., 1939; MA, Am. U., 1958, graduate, Command and General Staff Coll., Ft. Leavenworth, Kan., 1967. Artist W.L. Stensgaard Co., Chgo., 1939-40, The Diamond Store, Phoenix, 1941-42; presentation artist CIA, Washington, 1955-72; instr. Columbia Tech. Inst., Arlington, Va., 1966-72; owner, later ptnr. Guthrie Art & Sign Co., Winchester, Va., 1976—; instr. U. Hawaii, Lihue, 1980-81; cartoonist The Kauai Times, Lihue, 1981-90; owner Alo-o-oha-ha-ha Caricatures, Lihue, Honolulu, 1980—. Cons., artist Shenandoah Apple Blossom Festival, Winchester, 1975-78; cartoonist Internat. Salon of Caricature, Montreal, Can., 1976-77; co-chmn. Kauai Soc. of Artists Art Show, Lihue, 1981. One man shows include 50 Yrs. of Painting-A Retrospective, Lihue, 1984; inventor Artists' Kit; Filmic Artist: (documentary film) The River Nile, 1960 (NBC Emmy Award). Bd. dirs. Civil Def., Virginia Hills, 1954; publicity com. Frederick County Taxpayers Assn., Winchester, 1973, Exch. Club, Winchester, 1977. Lt. col. U.S. Army, 1942-54. Decorated Purple Heart, Bronze Star with oak leaf cluster; recipient Spl. Merit award Boy Scouts Am. Aloha Coun., Lihue, 1982. Mem. Mus. of Cartoon Art, U.S. Naval Combat Artist, Daniel Morgan Mus. (contbr. 1976), Nat. Soc. Mural Painters (contbr. 1976), Allied Artists of Am. (contbr. 1977), Pastel Soc. Am. (contbr. 1977-78), Am. Watercolor Soc. (contbr. 1982—), Greek Expeditionary Forces (hon.). Mem. Ch. LDS. Avocations: animation, cinematography, hiking, swimming, genealogy. Home and Office: 2444 Hihiwai St Apt 703 Honolulu HI 96826-5104 E-mail: eg@edguthrie.com. *Have short term and long term righteous goals. Be able to take risks in those things that most interest you, and gain wisdom from those risks that are least effectual. Instead of merely abandoning a project, try to give it more quality.*

GUTHRIE, FRANK ALBERT, chemistry educator; b. Madison, Ind., Feb. 16, 1927; s. Ned and Gladys (Glick) G.; m. Marcella Glee Farrar, June 12, 1955; children: Mark Alan, Bruce Bradford, Kent Andrew, Lee Farrar. AB, Hanover Coll., 1950; MS, Purdue U., 1952; PhD, Ind. U., 1962. Mem. faculty Rose-Hulman Inst. Tech., Terre Haute, Ind., 1952—, assoc. prof., 1962-67, prof. chemistry, 1967-94, prof. emeritus, 1994—, chmn. dept., 1969-72, chief health professions adviser, 1975-94. Kettering vis. lectr. U. Ill., Urbana, 1961-62; vis. prof. chemistry U.S. Mil. Acad., West Point, N.Y., 1987-88, 93-94, admissions coord., 1989—; vis. prof. chemistry Butler U., spring 2000. Mem. exec. bd. Wabash Valley coun. Boy Scouts Am., 1971-87, scoutmaster, 1979-82, adv. bd., 1988—, v.p. for scouting, 1976; selection chmn. Leadership Terre Haute, 1978-80. Served with AUS, 1945-46. Recipient Vigil Honor Order of Arrow, Wabash Valley coun. Boy Scouts Am., 1975, Wood badge, 1976, Dist. award of merit, 1976, Silver Beaver award, 1980. Fellow Ind. Acad. Sci. (pres. 1970, chmn. acad. found. trustees 1986—); mem. Am. Chem. Soc. (sec. 1973-77, editor directory 1965-77, chmn. divsn. analytical chemistry 1979-80, chmn. 1958, counselor Wabash Valley sect. 1980—, local sect. activities com. 1982-86, nominations and elections com. 1988-94, sec. 1992-94, coun. policy com. 1995, constn. and bylaws com. 1996-2002, membership affairs com., 2003—, steering com. for Joint Ctrl.-Gt. Lakes Regional Meetings, Indpls., 1978, 91, vis. assoc. com. profl. tng. 1984—, chmn. analytical chemistry exam inst. std. exam. 1994, membership affairs com., 2003—), Coblentz Soc., Midwest Univs. Analytical Chemistry Conf., Hanover Coll. Alumni Assn. (pres. 1974, Alumni Achievement award 1977), Masons (32 deg.), Sigma Xi (treas. Wabash Valley chpt. 1994-98), Phi Lambda Upsilon, Phi Gamma Delta, Alpha Chi Sigma (E.E. Dunlap scholarship selection com. 1986—, chmn. 1990—, dir. expansion 1995-99, profl. rep. 1997-2000). Presbyterian. Home: 120 Berkley Dr Terre Haute IN 47803-1708 Office: Rose Hulman Inst Tech 5500 Wabash Ave Terre Haute IN 47803-3999 E-mail: frank.guthrie@rose-hulman.edu., fguthrie@chilitech.com.

GUTHRIE, GLENDA EVANS, academic counselor, development specialist; b. De Funiak Springs, Fla., Aug. 10, 1945; d. Owen Clement and Vera Mae (Adams) Evans; m. Theron Asbury Guthrie Jr., June 10, 1967; children: Michael Patrick, Jennifer Leigh. BS in Elem. Edn., Samford U., 1967; MA in Elem. Edn., U. Ala., 1983, EdS in Ednl. Leadership, U. Fla., 1990. Tchr. grades 8-9 Warrington Jr. High, Pensacola, Fla., 1967; tchr. grades 4-5 Birmingham (Ala.) City Schs., 1967-69; tchr. grade 5 Faith Christian Sch., Bessemer, Ala., 1969-70; tchr. grade 4 Fairfield Highlands Christian Sch., Birmingham, 1973-74, First Bapt. Sch., Pleasant Grove, Ala., 1974-83; tchr. grade 5 Ctrl. Park Christian Sch., Birmingham, 1983-84, elem. dir., 1984-86; tchr. grades 5-6 Duval County Sch., Jacksonville, Fla., 1986-90; ednl. cons. Jostens Learning Corp., Phoenix, 1990-92, sr. ednl. cons., 1993-95; profl. devel. specialist CompassLearning, 1995—; acad. counselor U. Phoenix-Nashville Campus, 2003. Co-founder Success Unlimited Learning Ctr., Birmingham, 1985-86; judge Sci. Fair, Jacksonville, 1988-90; seminar/workshop leader; mem. elem. textbook com. Duval County Schs., 1988-89. Active Brentwood Bapt. Ch. Named Tchr. of Yr. Livingston Sch., Jacksonville, 1989, Ednl. Cons. of Yr., 1991-92. Mem. ASCD, Internat. Reading Assn., Nat. Coun. Tchrs. Math., Kappa Delta Pi. Republican. Baptist. Avocation: reading. Home and Office: 159 Carphilly Cir Franklin TN 37069

GUTHRIE, HUGH DELMAR, chemical engineer; b. Murdo, S.D., May 11, 1919; s. John Arlington and Farol Venus (Smith) G.; m. Elizabeth Anne Harris, Mar. 4, 1950; children: Katherine Farol, Gretchen, Mary Melissa, Elizabeth Lenore, Emily Jo. BSChemE with highest distinction, State U. Iowa, 1943. Jr. engr., engr., group leader Shell Devel. Co., San Francisco, 1943-52; technologist, sr. technologist, asst. dept. mgr. Shell Oil Co., Wood River, Ill., 1952-56, staff engr., group leader N.Y.C., 1956-60, dept. mgr. Wood River, 1960-62, asst. mgr. to mgr. mktg. N.Y.C., 1962-70, from dept. mgr. to sr. staff Houston, 1970-76; div. dir. ERDA, Dept. Energy, Washington, 1976-78; dir. Energy Ctr., Stanford Rsch. Inst., Menlo Park, Calif., 1978-80; v.p. licensing, mgr. tech. assessment Occidental Rsch. Corp., Irvine, Calif., 1980-83; v.p. licensing, mgr. rsch. planning Cities Svc., Tulsa, 1983-86; dir. extraction divsn. Morgantown (W.Va.) Energy Tech. Ctr. Dept. Energy, 1987-92, gen. engr. products tech. mgmt., mgr. gas products, 1992-97, sr. mgmt., tech. advisor, 1997-99, Dept. Energy Strategic Ctr for Natural Gas, Morgantown, WVa., 1999—. Cons. Hugh D. Guthrie & Assocs., Tulsa, 1986-87; mem. adv. bd. U. Iowa, U. Calif., Berkeley, Tulsa U., U. Tex., U. Pitts., W.Va. U. Former sr. warden Episcopal chs., Conn., Ill., Tex., W.Va. Fellow AIChE (pres. 1969, chair Assembly of Fellows 1990-92, chair mgmt. divsn. 1991, chair membership campaign found. 1992-98, Founder's award 1974, F.J. Van Antwerpen award 1986, Robert L. Jacks Meml. award 1992); mem. AAAS, Am. Chem. Soc., Soc. Petroleum Engrs., N.Y. Acad. Scis., Sigma Xi, Tau Beta Pi, Phi Lambda Upsilon, Omicron Delta Kappa. Republican. Achievements include patents on distillation equipment. Home: 901 Stewart Pl Morgantown WV 26505-3688 Office: Dept Energy Morgantown Energy Fed Ctr 3610 Collins Ferry Rd Morgantown WV 26505-2353 E-mail: hguthr@netl.doe.gov.

GUTHRIE, JAMES ERNEST, accounting educator; b. Melbourne, Victoria, Australia, June 25, 1952; s. James and Gwen (Barton) G.; children: Fiona, Jamie, Laura Hill-Guthrie. B.Bus. (acctg.), Royal Melbourne Inst. Tech., 1976; Grad. Diploma in Acctg., Deakin U., 1980; M.Bus., Curtin U., 1983; PhD, U. N.S.W., 1995. Faculty Royal Melbourne Inst. Tech., 1976, Deakin U., 1977-84; sr. lectr. acctg. and auditing U. N.S.W., Sydney, 1984-94; prof. mgmt., dep. dir. grad. sch. mgmt. Macquarie U., Sydney, 1995—. Cons. Pub. Accounts Com., Canberra, Indsl. Rels. Commn., N.S.W., N.S.W. EPA, Orgn. for Econ. Coop. and Devel.; dir. Sector Rsch. Pty. Ltd.; assoc. dir. Centre for Social and Environ. Acctg. Rsch., Dundee U., Scotland. Co-editor: The Public Sector, Contemporary Readings in Accounting and Auditing, 1990; editor: Australian Public Sector Pathways to Change in the 1990's; joint editor Acctg., Auditing and Accountability Jour.; joint founding editor Social Acctg. Monitor Newsletter. Recipient Royal Melbourne Inst. Tech. Centenary medallion for contbn. to cmty., 1987, Best Editors prize MCB Univ. Press, 1993, 95 Fellow Australian Soc. CPA; mem. Inst. Chartered Accts. Australia, Australian Evaluation Soc., Royal Inst. Pub. Inst. Australia, Accountability Interest Group, Acctg. Assn. Australia and New Zealand. Avocations: music, reading, cooking, push bike racing. Home: PO Box 401 Paddington NSW 2021 Australia Office: Macquarie U Grad Sch Mgmt Sydney NSW 2109 Australia

GUTHRIE, JAMES UHL, retired surgeon; b. Logansport, Ind., Nov. 27, 1926; MD, Ind. U., 1950. Diplomate Am. Bd. Surgery. Resident in surgery Ind. U. Hosps, 1951-53, 55, St. Elizabeth's Hosp., Lafayette, Ind., 1956; surgeon Peru, Ind., 1956—. Surgeon Duke's Meml. Hosp., Peru. Mem. AMA, Soc. Am. Gastrointestinal Endoscopic Surgeons, Ind. State Med. Assn., Miami County Med. Assn., Alpha Omega Alpha.

GUTHRIE, JANET, professional race car driver; b. Iowa City, Mar. 7, 1938; d. William Lain and Jean Ruth Guthrie. BS in Physics, U. Mich., 1960. Comml. pilot and flight instr., 1958-61; research and devel. engr. Republic Aviation Corp., Farmingdale, N.Y., 1960-67; publs. engr. Sperry Systems, Sperry Corp., Great Neck, N.Y., 1968-73; racing driver Sports Car Club Am. and Internat. Motor Sports Assn., 1963-86; profl. racing driver U.S. Auto Club and Nat. Assn. for Stock Car Racing, 1976-80; pres. Janet Guthrie Racing Enterprises Inc., 1978—. Highway safety cons. Met. Ins. Co., 1980-87. Named to Women's Sports Hall of Fame, 1980; recipient Curtis Turner award, Nat. Assn. for Stock Car Racing-Charlotte World 600, 1976, First in class award, Sebring 12-hour, 1967. Mem. Madison Ave. Sports Car Driving and Chowder Soc., Women's Sports Found., Les Dames d'Aspen, Internat. Wine and Food Soc., Nat. Spkrs. Assn. Achievements include being the first woman to qualify for and race in Daytona 500, 1977, Top Rookie; first woman to qualify for and race in Indpls. 500, 1977, finished 9th, 1978; North Atlantic Road Racing Champion, 1973.

GUTHRIE, JUDITH K. federal judge; b. Chgo., July 13, 1948; d. David Curtis and Kathleen McAfee G.; m. John H. Hannah, Jr., May 9, 1992. Student, Ariz. State U., 1966-68; BA, St. Mary's U., 1971; JD cum laude, U. Houston, 1980. Bar: Tex. 1981, U.S. Dist. Ct. (ea. dist.) Tex. 1982, U.S. Ct. Appeals (5th cir.) 1982, U.S. Dist. Ct. (no. dist.) Tex. 1983, U.S. Dist. Ct. (we. dist.) Tex. 1984. Editor Am. Coun. Edn., Washington, 1972-73; exec. asst. Tex. Ho. Reps., Austin, 1973-75; lobbyist Bracewell & Patterson, Austin, 1975-80, assoc. Houston, 1980-81; briefing atty. Tex. Ct. Appeals, Tyler, 1981-82; ptnr. Hannah & Guthrie, Tyler, Tex., 1982-86; magistrate judge U.S. Dist. Ct. (ea. dist.) Tex., Tyler, 1986—. Instr. legal asst. program, Tyler Jr. Coll., 1986-87; apptd. Tex. Judicial Coun., 1991-97, gender bias task force, 1991-92; lectr. in field. Contbr. articles to profl. jours. Adv. bd. Main St. Project; legal asst. adv. bd. Tyler Jr. Coll., 1986—, chmn. adv. bd., 1996—; mem. Citizens Commn. Tex. Jud. Sys., 1992—93; bd. dirs. Habitat for Humanity, 2003—; former Dem. chmn. Smith County; former bd. dirs. Found. Women's Resources, Leadership Am., Leadership Tex. Mem.: ABA ((Fed. trial judges legis. com. 1991-93)), Smith County Bar Assn. ((chmn. law libr. com. 1985-2001)), State Bar Tex. (various coms., including dist. 2A grievance com. 1990—, chmn. 1995—96), 5th Cir. Bar Assn., Fed. magistrate Judges Assn., Am. Judges Assn. Office: US District Court 300 Federal Bldg & US Ct House 211 W Ferguson St Tyler TX 75702-7212

GUTHRIE, LAWRENCE SIMPSON, II, law librarian, journalist; b. Thomas, Okla., Dec. 2, 1953; s. Lawrence Simpson and Helen Marie (Janning) G. BS, Georgetown U., 1976, Anna Freud Ctr., London, 1979; MA, U. Okla., 1980; MS in Libr. Sci., Cath. U. Am., 1988. Asst. prof. psychology Tulsa Cmty. Coll., 1982—86; grad. libr. nursing/biology Cath. U. Am., Washington, 1986-89; law libr. interlibr. loan George Washington U. Law Libr., Washington, 1989-95, Covington & Burling, Washington, 1995—. Author: Sports Libraries, 1995, Medieval Library Taxonomies, 2003; contbr. articles to profl. jours. including History of Cataloging, 2003; start-up cons., D.C. corr. Urban Tulsa newspaper, 1990-93; founder Today's Events col. Tulsa World Newspaper, 1978-79; columnist Copyright Corner, Information Outlook, 1997—. Bd. dirs. Cath. U. Sch. Libr. and Info. Sci. Alumni Assn., Washington, 1990-92; moderator White House Conf. on Librs., Washington, 1991; donated Okla. flag to John F. Kennedy Ctr. Hall of States, Washington, 1988. Recipient commendation as educator of all levels Okla. Gov. & Legislature, 1989. Mem. Am. Assn. Law Librs., Spl. Librs. Assn. (copyright com. 1992-95, govt. rels. com. 1995—, chmn. 1996—, chmn. legal divsn. 1999-2000, Liverpool del. 2002), Nat. Press Club. Democrat. Roman Catholic. Avocations: ice skating, baseball, walking. Home: 2450 Virginia Ave NW Apt E317 Washington DC 20037-2654 Office: Covington & Burling 1201 Pennsylvania Ave NW Washington DC 20004-2401

GUTHRIE, M. PHILIP, corporate financial executive; b. Vicksburg, Miss., Mar. 26, 1945; s. Marion P. Jr. and Aileen (Perry) G.; m. Beverly Alice Blackmon, June 2, 1966; children: Philip Todd, Edward Tait, Stuart Trent. BS, La. Tech U., 1967; MBA, U. Mich., 1968. CPA, La., Tex. Sr. cons. Price Waterhouse & Co., Houston, 1968-72; v.p. fin. and mfg. Vicra div. Baxter Labs., Dallas, 1972-78; v.p. fin., CFO, treas. S.W. Airlines Co., Dallas, 1978-81; exec. v.p., CFO, Braniff Internat., Dallas, 1981-84; pres. Diamond Mgmt. Group, Dallas, 1984-89; mng. dir. Mason Best Co., Dallas, 1989—; chmn., CEO, Am. Eagle Group, Inc., Dallas, 1992—96; CEO Aircraft Interior Resources Group Inc., 1998—. Bd. dirs. Mainstream Data, Inc., Salt Lake City, Safeguard Bus. Sys., Ft. Washington, Pa., Internat. Autotech, Dallas, Westmark Sys., Inc., Austin, Tex., Sunrise Pubs., Inc., Bloomington, Ind., Bristol Group (Buenos Aires), Alpargatas (Buenos Aires). Assoc. bd. dirs. So. Meth. U. Grad. Sch. Bus., Dallas, 1985—. Mem. AICPA, Fin. Execs. Inst., Nat. Assn. Casualty and Surety Execs., Soc. Internat. Bus. Fellows, Tex. Soc. CPA's, Coun. of Ins. Co. Execs., Phi Kappa Phi, Omicron Delta Kappa, Beta Gamma Sigma, Delta Sigma Pi, Beta Alpha Psi. Office: Galleria Tower 2 13455 Noel Rd Ste 1000 Dallas TX 75240 E-mail: pguthrie@airresource.com.

GUTHRIE, MICHAEL STEELE, magnetic circuit design engineer; b. Murray, Ky., Nov. 22, 1954; s. Steele G. and Lunelle (Holmes) G. BS in Physics, Murray State U., 1976. Engr. quality control & mfg. Allegheny Ludlum, Princeton, Ky., 1977-79; engr. applications & design Hitachi Magnetics Corp., Edmore, Mich., 1979-86; engr. applications & design Delco Remy div. GM, Anderson, Ind., 1986-91; regional mgr. applications engring. Carbone of Am., Farmville, Va., 1991-96, Stackpole Magnetic Systems, Kane, Pa.,

1991-98; mgr. application & design engring. Crumax Magnetics Inc., Elizabethtown, Ky., 1998-99, Morganite Crumax, Inc., Elizabethtown, Ky., 1999—2002; physicist Multicraft Auto/Consumer divsn. Morgan Crucible, Ltd., Brandon, Miss., 2002—. Co-author: Rapidly Solidified Alloys, 1993. Mem. IEEE, Magnetics Soc., Am. Phys. Soc., Clan Guthrie, Ky. Cols. Home: 2014 Ashley Ave Brandon MS 39047 Office: Multicraft 148 Michel St Brandon MS 39042-3044 E-mail: mike.guthrie@morganplc.com.

GUTHRIE, PHILLIP PATRICK, division production manager; b. Balt, Md, Aug. 19, 1962; s. Dion Francis and Sandra Ann (Fiscaro) G. Bachelor's degree, U. Md., 1984; diploma, Dale Carnegie Mgmt., 1990. Restricted radiotelephone operator permit. Exec. prodr. Sta. WBFF-TV/Fox 45, Balt., 1985-92; sr. prodr., program mgr. Cable 17, Balt., 1992-95; pub. affairs prodr. Sta. WMAR-TV/News channel 2, Balt., 1995; divsn. prodn. mgr. Comcast Prod., Balt., 1995—. Intern. Sta. WJLA/TV, Washington, 1984; writer Warner Bros. Writing for TV Program, Balt., 1991-93. Writer, prodr., editor, performer: (radio drama) Nothing but Time, 1984 (Grand Prize Audio Entertainment 1984); writer: (screenplay) Prisoner of the Heart, 2000. Nominated Emmy award, 1997, 2001, Cable Ace award, 1998; recipient 5 Telly awards, 1998, 3 Telly awards, 1999, 2 Telly awards, 2000, Telly award, 2001, 02; Cable Advt. Bur. award, 2000, Cable Advt. Bur. award and Best of Show, 2002. Mem. NATAS, Internat. TV Assn. (3d pl. award for orgnl. news 1992, 2d pl. award for orgnl. news 1994, Silver award for pub. svc. announcements 1997), Am. Film Inst., Advt. Assn. Batl. (2 Best in Balt. Addy awards 1999). Avocations: acting, painting, traveling. Home: 8113 Glen Arbor Dr Rosedale MD 21237 Office: Comcast Prodns 10946 Golden West Dr ste 190A Hunt Valley MO 21031 E-mail: sitcom@comcast.net.

GUTHRIE, RANDOLPH HOBSON, JR., plastic surgeon, consultant; b. N.Y.C., Dec. 8, 1934; s. Randolph Hobson and Mabel Edith (Welton) G.; m. Beatrice Mills Holden, Mar. 20, 1965; children; Randolph Hobson III, Michael Phipps, Philip Holden. AB, Princeton U., 1957; MD, Harvard U., 1961. Intern N.Y. Hosp., N.Y.C., 1961-62, resident, 1962-63, 69-71, chief resident, 1971; resident St. Luke's Hosp., N.Y.C., 1963-66, chief resident, 1966—, chief plastic & reconstructive surgery svc. Meml. Sloan-Kettering Cancer Ctr., N.Y.C., 1971-77; chief dept. plastic and reconstructive surgery N.Y. Downtown Hosp., N.Y.C., 1979-2000; asst. prof. Cornell U. Med. Coll., 1971-74, assoc. prof., 1974-89, prof., 1989—. Asst. attending surgeon, N.Y. Hosp., 1971-74, assoc. attending surgeon, 1974-89, attending surgeon, 1989—; attending surgeon Sloan-Kettering Cancer Ctr., 1977-93, cons., 1994—. Author: The Truth About Breast Implants, 1994; co-author: Reconstruction and Esthetic Mammoplasty, 1989; contbr. articles to profl. jours., books. Pres. East River Med. Found., N.Y.C., 1970-80, Acacia Found., N.Y.C., 1980-94; alumni dir. St. Paul's Sch., Concord, N.H., 1979-83, form agt., 1983-87, term trustee, 1985-89, life trustee, 1989-94; trustee Episcopal Sch., N.Y.C., 1976-84; bd. dirs. Am.-Italian Found. Cancer Rsch., N.Y.C., 1985-94; bd. dirs., treas. Save Venice, Inc., 1985-89, pres., 1989-97, chmn., 1997—; trustee N.Y. Downtown Hosp., 1985-92, Isabella Stewart Gardner Mus., Boston, 1998-2000. Maj. M.C. AUS, 1966-69. Decorated Cavaliere nell 'Ordine Al Merito della Repubblica Italiana; rsch. fellow Sloan Kettering Cancer Ctr., 1971-77. Mem. ACS, Plastic Surgery Rsch. Coun., Am. Geriatrics Soc., Am. Soc. Plastic and Reconstructive Surgeons, Pan Am. Med. Soc., N.Y. Soc. Plastic and Reconstructive Surgery, N.Y. Med. Soc., Med. Soc. County N.Y., Herbert Conway Soc., Doubles Club, Century Club, Knickerbocker Club (N.Y.C.). Home and Office: 15 E 74th St New York NY 10021-2604 E-mail: RHGNYC@aol.com.

GUTHRIE, RICHARD ALAN, physician; b. Pleasant Hill, Ill., Nov. 13, 1935; s. Merle Pruitt and Cleona Marie (Weaver) G.; m. Diana Fern Worthington, Aug. 18, 1957; children: Laura, Joyce, Tamara. AA, Graceland Coll., 1955; MD, U. Mo., 1960. Diplomate Am. Bd. Pediatrics, Am. Bd. Pediatric Endocrinology; cert. Nat. Bd. for Diabetes Educators. Intern U.S. Naval Hosp., Camp Pendleton, Calif., 1960-61, dir. dependent svcs. Sangley Point, The Philippines, 1961-63; asst. instr., resident in pediatrics U. Mo., 1963-65, NIH fellow in endocrinology and metabolism, 1965-68, asst. prof., dir. newborn svcs., 1968-71, assoc. prof. pediat., 1971-73; prof., chmn. dept. pediatrics U. Kans. Med. Sch., Wichita, 1973-82; exec. dir. Kans. Regional Diabetes Ctr., Wichita, 1982-84; pres. Mid-Am. Diabetes Assocs., Wichita, 1984—. Dir. Robert L. Jackson Diabetes Treatment, Edn. and Rsch. Ctr., 1985—. Author: Nursing Management in Diabetes Mellitus, 1976, 5th edit., 2003, 4th edit., 1997, 5th edit., 2002, The Child with Diabetes, 1970, Physiologic Management of Diabetes in Children, 1986, Diabetes Source Book, 1990, 5th edit., 2003; mem. editl. bd. Practical Diabetology, 1982-92, Diabetes Self-Management, 1984-97, Diabetes Educator, 1985-89; assoc. editor Diabetes Spectrum, 2000—; contbr. articles to profl. jours. Mem. health ministries bd. Reorganized Ch. Jesus Christ Latter-day Saints; mem. adv. bd. Kans. Action for Children, 1978—, Kans. State Diabetes, 1988-93, 95—. With USN, 1960-63. Recipient grants NIH, 1968—, Outstanding Faculty award Wichita State U., 1976, 2000, Disting. alumnus award Graceland Coll., 1984, Humanitarian award Wesley Med. Found., 1997, award for outstanding cmty. svc. Am. Diabetes Assn., 2001; Dr. McIver Furman Disting. lectureship in health scis. Del Mar Coll., Corpus Christi, Tex., 1986. Fellow Am. Acad. Pediatrics, Am. Coll. Endocrinology; mem. AMA, Am. Diabetes Assn. (bd. dirs. 1972-77, Outstanding Contbn. to Camping award 1992, Outstanding African award 2003, Outstanding Physician Clinician award 2003), Kans. Diabetes Assn. (pres. 1974, chmn. bd. 1974-77, 85-87), Kans. State Med. Soc., Sedgewick County Med. Soc., Am. Pediat. Soc., Soc. Pediat. Rsch., Wichita Pediat. Soc. (bd. dirs. 1988, pres. 1990-92), Lawson Wilkins Pediat. Endocrinology Soc., Midwest Soc. Pediat. Rsch., Internat. Soc. for Pediat. and Adolescent Diabetes (edn. com. 1995—), Am. Assn. Diabetes Educators (bd. dirs. 1994-97), Am. Assn. Clin. Endocrinology 1992—), Sigma Xi, Alpha Omega Alpha. Home: 14210 SW 60th St Andover KS 67002-8237 Office: Mid-Am Diabetes Assocs 200 S Hillside St Wichita KS 67211-2127 E-mail: rag33@hotmail.com.

GUTHRIE, ROBERT VAL, retired psychologist and educator; b. Chgo., Feb. 14, 1930; s. Paul Lawrence and Lerlene Yvette (Cartwright) G.; m. Elodia S. Guthrie, Sept. 15, 1952; children: Robert S., Paul L., Michael V., Ricardo A., Sheila E., Mario A. BS, Fla. A&M U., 1955; MA, U. Ky., 1960; PhD, U.S. Internat. U., 1970. Tchr. San Diego City Schs., 1960-63; instr. psychology San Diego Mesa Coll., 1963-68, chmn. dept., 1968-70; assoc. prof. U. Pitts., 1971-73; sr. research psychologist Nat. Inst. Edn., Washington, 1973-74; asso. dir. orgnl. effectiveness and psychol. scis. Office Naval Research, Arlington, Va., 1975; supervising research psychologist Naval Pers., R & D Center, San Diego, 1975-82; pvt. practice psychology, San Diego, 1982-90; prof. psychology So. Ill. U., Carbondale, 1991-95; ret., 1995. Adj. assoc. prof. George Washington U., Washington, 1975; lectr. Georgetown U., 1975; adj. assoc. prof. U. Pitts., 1977, adj. prof. San Diego State U., 1989. Author: Psychology in the World Today, 1968, 2d edit., 1971, Encounter, 1970, Black Perspectives, 1970, Man and Society, 1972, Psychology and Psychologists, 1975, Even the Rat Was White, 1976. Served with USAF, 1950-59, Korea. Mem. AAAS, Am., Western, Calif. psychol. assns., Fedn. Am. Scientists, Am. Acad. Polit. and Social Scis., Kappa Alpha Psi. Achievements include research on social psychology, organizational and personnel psychology variables in small groups.

GUTHRIE, WALLACE NESSLER, JR., naval officer; b. N.Y.C., Feb. 22, 1939; s. Wallace Nessler and Rena Otis (Robertson) G.; m. Virginia Dale Sargeant, June 7, 1961; children: Wallace Edward, Gail Elizabeth, Virginia Lynn. BS, U.S. Naval Acad., Annapolis, Md., 1961; MS, Rollins Coll., 1972, EdS, 1981. Commd. ensign USN, 1961, advanced through ranks to rear adm., 1987; edn. specialist Naval Tng. Systems Ctr., Orlando, Fla., 1967-89; dep. dir. Naval Res., Washington, 1989-92; dir. tng., supt. schs. Am. Forces Info. Svc., 1993-97. Past head Naval Acad. Candidate Selection Com., 9th Congl. Dist., Fla. Sr. officer adv. panel Joint Mil. Intelligence Coll.; bd. dirs., trustee Navy Mut. Aid Assn. Mem. Naval Res. Assn. (life), Res. Officers Assn. (life), Surface Navy Assn. (life), Naval Submarine League. Republican. Avocations: camping, boating, fishing, hiking. E-mail: wallaceg5@aol.com.

GUTHRIE, WILLIAM ANTHONY, minister; b. Bartica, Essequibo, Guyana, May 11, 1949; came to U.S., 1980; s. Charles and Lachmin (Bridjlall) G.; m. Elizabeth Ann Feidtkou, June 24, 1977; children: Tony, Pat, Carol. BA (hon.), U. West Indies, Barbados, 1972, Licentiate in Theology, 1974; Diploma in Theology, Codrington Coll., Barbados, 1974; D Ministry, Va. Theol. Sem., 1986. Ordained to ministry Episcopal Ch. as deacon, 1973, as priest, 1974. Asst. to dean St. George's Cathedral, Georgetown, Guyana, 1974-77; rector St. Patrick's Ch., Canje, Guyana, 1977-79; priest-in-charge Berbice River Missions, Berbice, Guyana, 1977-79; vicar Trinity Episcopal Ch., Charlottesville, Va., 1980-88; dean of region XV Diocese of Va., Charlottesville, 1985-88; rector St. Cyprian's Episcopal Ch., San Francisco, 1989-90, Christ Episcopal Ch., East Orange, N.J., 1992—. Mem. Diocesan Commn. on Race Rels., Richmond, Va., 1982-87, Commn. on Evangelism, Diocese of Calif., 1989-90. Mem. bd. mgmt. Trinity Child Care Ctr., Charlottesville, 1980-88, sec. 4-H Club, Bartica, 1960-62; elected clergy del. nat. conv., Diocese of Va., 1987. Named one of Outstanding Young Men Am., 1985; recipient fellowship Va. Theol. Sem., 1987, Bp. Allin Fellowship, Geneva. Mem. NAACP, Nat. Orgn. Episcopalians for Life, East Orange Clergy Assn. (sec. 1995—), Black Clergy Caucus in Diocese of Newark (sec. 1995-98). Avocations: reading, swimming, travel. Home: 8 Rosemont Ct West Orange NJ 07052-2212 *Perhaps, the only thing worse than evil itself is to sit back and do nothing in the face of evil.*

GUTHY, GEORGE EDWARD, retired information systems executive; b. N.Y.C., Nov. 11, 1936; s. Adam William and Edna Louise (Sanders) G.; m. Adelaide Musto, May 12, 1973. BS in Physics and Chemistry, C.C.N.Y., N.Y.C., 1957; MS in Applied Math., Adelphi U., 1966; LLB, LaSalle U., 1970; MBA in Finance, Iona Coll., 1973. Cert. data processing Inst. Cert. Computer Profls. Mathematician Boeing, Seattle, 1957-58, Airborne Instrument Lab., L.I., 1958-66; cons. Manned Spacecraft Ctr., ITT, Bankers Trust, 1966-77; mgr. planning European Am. Bank, N.Y.C., 1977-80; dir. sys. Commodity Exchange, Inc., N.Y.C., 1980-86; v.p. syss. and tech. Citicorp, N.Y.C., 1986-91; dir. advanced tech. Charles River Computers, N.Y.C., 1992-94; dir. advanced info. svcs. Reserve Mgmt. Corp., N.Y.C., 1994-97; ret., 1997. Cons. in field. Author: Strategic Planning and Corporate Forecasting, 1972. Mem. Mensa Internat. Avocations: flying, scuba diving, Karate. Home: 97-13 72 Dr Forest Hills NY 11375

GUTIERREZ, CARL T. C. former governor; b. Agana Heights, Guam, Oct. 15, 1941; s. Tomas Taitano Gutierrez and Rita Benavente Cruz; m. Geraldine Chance Torres, 1963; children: Carla Stahl, Tommy, Hannah. Mem. Senate Guam, beginning 1972, spkr., chmn. of ways and means com., chmn. HUD; vice chmn. rules com., tourism comm, transp. com.; gov. Guam, Agana, 1994—2003. Democrat. Roman Catholic. Mailing: PO Box 404 Hagatna GU 96932-0404*

GUTIERREZ, CARLOS M. grocery manufacturing company executive; Student, Monterrey Inst. Tech., Queretaro, Mex. Sales rep., various sales and mktg. positions Kellogg de Mex., Mexico City, 1975-82, gen. mgr., 1984-89; pres., CEO, Kellogg Can., 1989-90; supr. L.Am. mktg. svcs. Kellogg Co., Battle Creek, Mich., 1982-83, mgr. internat. mktg. svcs., 1983-84, corp. v.p. product devel., 1990, v.p., 1990-93, exec. v.p., 1994-96, exec. v.p. bus. devel., 1996-98, pres., COO, 1998-99, pres., CEO, 1999—, also bd. dirs. Exec. v.p. sales and mktg. Kellogg USA, Battle Creek, 1990—93, exec. v.p., 1993—94, gen. mgr. cereal divsn., 1993—94; pres. Kellogg Asia-Pacific, 1994—96. Mem.: Grocery Mfrs. Am. (bd. dirs.). Office: 1 Kellogg Sq Battle Creek MI 49017-3534

GUTIERREZ, EDITH G. freelance/self-employed music educator, composer, lyricist; b. Houston, Tex., Nov. 29, 1914; d. John Monroe Gribbin and Maria Paulina Viglini; m. Patricio Gutierrez, June 10, 1955 (dec.); m. John Bernardo Oliveros II (dec. Sept. 15, 1985); children: Pauline, John Bernardo. Cert. tchr. piano Am. Coll. of Musicians. Jobbing musician Houston Profl. Musicians Orgn., Houston, 1930—; pvt. piano instr. Houston, 1930—. Lyracist, composer of children's plays. Author (author-composer): (plays) Rumplestiltskin, 1991, Magic of the Woods, 1992, Pocahontas, 1993, Boogie Woogie Aesop, 1994. Mem.: Houston Music Tchrs. Assn. (bd. dir. 1950—, charter mem.). Avocations: hosting foreign students, pets. Home and Studio: 2202 Colquitt St Houston TX 77098 E-mail: egg@webtv.net.

GUTIERREZ, FRANKLIN ABEL, Spanish language-Latin America literature educator; b. Santiago, Dominican Republic, Jan. 25, 1951; came to U.S., 1978; s. Santos and Gloria M. (Gutierrez) C.; m. Amarilis Rivera Lantigua, Nov. 27, 1987; children: Ariel, Melissa. BA in Edn. and Lit., Autonoma U. Santo Domingo, 1975; MA in Hispanic Lit., CUNY, 1990, PhD in L.Am. Lit., 1997. Instr. Spanish lang. and L.Am. lit. York Coll., CUNY, Jamaica, 1989-95, asst. prof., 1995-2000, assoc. prof., 2000—, coord. Spanish program, 1997—. Author: (poems) Canto a mi pueblo sufrido, 1973, Hojas de octubre, 1982, (anthology Deominican poets) Niveles del iman, 1983, (poems) Inriri, 1984, Helen, 1988, Reflexiones acerca de la literatura latinoamericana, 1986, Aproximaciones a la narrativa de Juan Bosch; author: (with Daisy Cocco De Filippis) Historias de Washington Heights y otros rincones del mundo, 1994; author: Seis Historias Casi Falsas, 1993, Antologia Historica de la Poesia dominicana del siglo XX, 1995, Enriquillo: Radiografia de un heroe galvaniano, 1999, Evas Terrenales, 2000, palabras de ida y Vuelta, 2002, Literatura dominicana en los Estados Unidos, 2001, 33 historiadores dominicanos, 2002. Recipient nat. essay prize Dominican Republic Bd. Edn., 1999. Mem. MLA, Assn. Dominican Studies, Dominican Assn. Lit. Criticism, Dominican Studies Inst. (bd. dirs.). Avocation: tennis. Office: CUNY Fgn Langs Dept Jamaica NY 11451 E-mail: alcance66@yahoo.com.

GUTIERREZ, GERALD ANDREW, theatrical director; b. N.Y.C., Feb. 3, 1955; s. Andrew and Obdulia A. (Concheiro) G.; m. Wendy J. Wasserstein, Dec. 3, 1983 (div. Dec. 1986); children: Ginger Joy, Phyllis Kate, Edna Elizabeth. BS in Theater Arts, Juilliard Sch., 1972; postgrad., Yale U., 2000—01. Resident dir. St. Nicholas Theater, Chgo., 1977-80, Playwrights Horizons, N.Y.C., 1980-84; assoc., artistic dir. Lincoln Ctr. Thea., N.Y.C., 1993—. Co-author Sunset at Camp O'Henry, 1984; co-author play for TV Latenite, 1985; author film script A Bag of Shells, 1980; dir. A Delicate Balance, 1996 (Tony award 1996). Recipient Award for best direction of a musical Conn. Drama Critics, 1991, L.A. Drama Critics Circle award Best Direction of a Musical, 1992; nominated Tony award for Abe Lincoln in Illinois, 1994; recipient Tony award for The Heiress, 1995. Democrat. Episcopalian. Avocation: gourmet chef.

GUTIERREZ, GUILLERMO, human services administrator, medical educator; b. Palma Soriano, Cuba, Jan. 10, 1946; came to U.S., 1961; s. Armando Gutierrez and Edelmira Cabezas; m. Ellin Lee Groh, Dec. 21, 1968 (div. Oct. 1981); m. Marian Elizabeth Wulf, June 18, 1983; children: James, LeAnna, Alexandra, Susan. B in Engring., CUNY, 1968; MME, U. Dayton, 1970; MD, Case Western Res. U., 1977, PhD in Engring., 1978. Diplomate Am. Bd. Internal Medicine, Am. Bd. Pulmonary Diseases and Critical Care Medicine. Devel. engr. GM Corp., Dayton, Ohio, 1968-71; sr. scientist GM Tech. Ctr., Detroit, 1977-78; med. resident U. Mich., Ann Arbor, 1978-81, pulmonary fellow, 1981-83; prof. medicine Med. Sch. U. Tex., Houston, 1983—2001, prof. health informatics, 1998—2001; pres. VistaLink Med. Comm., Inc., Houston, 1996—2001. Prof. medicine George Washington U., Washington, 2001—. Author: Tissue Oxygen Utilization, 1991; editor-in-chief Jour. Critical Care, 1994—. Named Outstanding Young Engr. of the Yr. Engring. Soc. Detroit, 1979; recipient Am. Lung Career Investigator award Am. Lung Assn., 1990. Fellow Royal Soc. Medicine; mem. Argentinian Critical Care Soc. (hon.), Venezuelan Critical Care Soc. (hon.), Green Coll. Soc., Tex. Thoracic Soc. (treas.). Avocations: skiing, travel, music. Office: Dept Medicine 2150 Pennsylvania Ave NW Washington DC 20037 Home: 6791 Father John Ct Mc Lean VA 22101 Fax: 703-893-0944.

GUTIERREZ, LINO, diplomat; b. Havana, Cuba, Mar. 26, 1951; s. Lino Gabriel and Maria C. (Fernandez) G.; m. Miriam A. Messina, Nov. 12, 1979; children: Alicia, Diana, Susana. Student, U. Miami, 1968-69; BA, U. Ala., 1972, MA, 1976. Tchr. social studies Urban League, Miami, 1973-75; Nicaragua desk officer ARA U.S. Dept. State, Washington, 1981-83, Portugal desk officer EUR, 1985-87; consular officer Am. Embassy, Santo Domingo, PR, 1977-79, polit. officer Lisbon, Portugal, 1979-81, polit. sect. chief Port-au-Prince, Haiti, 1983-85, polit./internal chief Paris, 1987-90, dep. chief of mission Nassau, The Bahamas, 1990-93; mem. Sr. Seminar Dept. Seminar, 1993-94; dir. policy planning Bur. Inter-Am. Affairs Dept. State, Washington, 1994-96, U.S. amb. to Nicaragua, 1996-99, prin. dep. asst. sec. Bur. Western Hemisphere Affairs, 1999—2002; internat. affairs advisor Nat. War Coll., 2002—03; U.S. amb. to Argentina U.S. Dept. State, Washington, 2003—. William P. Bloom scholar U. Ala., Tuscaloosa, 1972. Avocations: tennis, fishing, boating, reading, chess. Office: American Embassy Unit 4334 APO AA 34034 Buenos Aires Argentina*

GUTIERREZ, LUIS V. congressman, elementary education educator; b. Chgo., Dec. 10, 1953; BA magna cum laude in English, Northeastern Ill. U., 1975. Social worker Ill. Dept. Children and Family Svcs.; adminstrv. asst. Mayor's Subcom. on Infrastructure, 1984-85; alderman for 26th ward Chgo. City Coun., 1986-93, pres. pro tempore, 1992; mem. U.S. Congress from 4th Ill. Dist., 1993—; mem. banking and fin. svcs. com., vet. affair com. Chmn. Housing, Land Acquisition and Disposition com., 1989-93. Democrat. Office: US Ho of Reps 2367 Rayburn House Off Bldg Washington DC 20515-0001*

GUTIÉRREZ, MARY CARMEN, artist; b. Villarro Bledo, La Mancha, Spain, Sept. 13, 1946; came to U.S., 1965; d. Francisco Gutiérrez and Asuncion Maroto; children: Ann Frances, Carol Stephanie. BA in Spanish, Visual Arts, Ctrl. U. Langs., Madrid, 1962. Tchr. arts and crafts Annunciation Pvt. Sch., Cleve., 1971-75; mgr., nat. sales dir. Murfoley Internat. Creations Inc., Manhattan, N.Y., 1975-79; graphic design dir. Lloyderson Internat., Ltd., Lancaster, Pa., 1979-95; ind. artist/designer, muralist San Remo, Fla., 1995—; owner One King St. Gallery, St. Augustine, Fla., 1998, Salon Art Boutique, St. Augustine, 1999; ofcl. translator City of St. Augustine, 1998. One-woman exhbns. include King St. Gallery, St. Augustine, Fla., Franklin and Marshall Coll. Square/Dioh's, Lancaster, Pa. State Coll. Ctr., Lancaster, Homestead Village Ctr., Lancaster, House of Lloyderson, Manhattan, N.Y., Lancaster County Art Assn., Byers/Basciano Phys. Therapy and Rehab. Ctr., Lancaster, Twin Brook Winery, Gap, Pa., Art Walk Week-End, Lancaster, Willow Valley Manor, Lancaster; group exhbsn. include Weber House Gallery, Springfield, Ill., Rosseti's, St. Augustine, St. Augustine Art Ctr., Galerie 110, Harrisburg, Pa., Lebanon (Pa.) Campus C.C., Pa. Acad. Music, Lancaster, Art Assn. Harrisburg, Mus. Art, Lancaster, Lancaster Dispensing Co., Heritage Ctr. at Penn Square, Lancaster, Artworks at Donecker's, Ephrata, Pa., Art Sundays, Lancaster, Lancaster Mus. Art, Art Walk, Lancaster, Arts Celebration Downtown Pub. Libr., Cleve., Barefoot in the Park, Cleve., Three Rivers Festival, Pitts.; designed and coordinated mural for Downtown Lancaster; designer, painter 3 murals for City Festival, 1999, flags and banners, 2000, permanent collection, Lancaster (Pa.) General Hosp.; illustrator numerous books, 1998-2001. Bd. dirs. Lancaster County Art Assn., Red Rose Ctr. for Arts, Spanish Profls. Am., Countdown New Yr. Celebration, Lancaster, Lancaster Mus. Art, Art Assn. Harrisburg, Nat. Mus. Women in Arts, Washington; bd. advisors Spain-U.S. C. of C., N.Y.C.; mem. St. Augustine Art Assn., Fla.; advisor Bd. of St. Augustine Textile Art Guild; coach/chmn. Art Walk, instr. All Around the World, Heritage Ctr., Lancaster; day camp dir. Summer Youth Ctr., Ohio; apptd. hon. vice-consul Jacksonville and St. Augustine representing Spain, 2002; advisor, assessor sister cities Aviles, Spain and Island of Menorca, Spain, 1999-2002. Recipient Michael Angel award, 1993. Mem. Lancaster County Art Assn., Lancaster Mus. Art, Art Assn. Harrisburg, Springfield Art League, Lloyderson Internat. Gallery, N.Y., Nat. Mus. Women in Arts, Catharine Lorillard Wolfe Art Club, St. Augustine Art Assn., Textile Art Guild; Historic Preservation and Heritage Tourism, 1999-02, St. Augustine Historical Soc., 1999-02.

GUTIERREZ, RAMON A. history educator; s. Arthur and Nellie (Alderete) G. BA, U. N. Mex., 1973; MA, U. Wis., 1976, PhD, 1980. Lectr. in history U. Wis., Madison, 1980; prof. history Pomona Coll., Claremont, Calif., 1980-82; from asst. to full prof. U. Calif. San Diego, La Jolla, 1982--. Mem. exec. bd. Am. Studies Assn., Bloomington, Ind., 1998—2001; mem. bd. govs. U. Calif.-Humanities Rsch. Ins., Irvine, Calif., 2000—; mem. bd. Calif. Coun. Humanities, Calif., 2001—03. Author: When Jesus Came the Corn Mothers Went Away, 1991, Contested Eden, 1998; contbr. articles to profl. jours. Fellow Fulbright Found., 1973, Danforth Found., 1974-80, MacArthur Found., 1983-88; mem. adv. bd. Nat. PArk Svc., Wash., 1995-99; mem. Latino adv. bd. Smithsonian, Wash., 1995-2003. Mem. Am. Hist. Assn. (Bolton prize 1992), Latin Am. Studies Assn., We. History Assn., Chicano Studies Assn., Nat. Endowment Humanities (mem. nat. coun. 1994-2001). Avocations: photography, ceramics, hiking. Office: U Calif San Diego Ethnic Studies 9500 Gilman La Jolla CA 92093-0522

GUTIERREZ, SIDNEY M. federal agency administrator; b. Albuquerque, June 27, 1957; BS in Aero. Engring., USAF Acad., 1973; MA in Mgmt., Webster U., 1977. Commd. 2d lt. USAF, advanced through grades to col., test pilot, ret.; dir. satellite ctr. Sandia Nat. Labs., Albuquerque; space shuttle pilot and comdr. NASA, mem. aerospace safety adv. panel, 2000—03. Chmn. Goodwil Industries of N.Mex., N.Mex. Bd. regents N.Mex. Inst. Mining and Tech. Office: Sandia Nat Labs PO Box 5800 Albuquerque NM 87185 E-mail: smgutie@sandi.gov.

GUTIERREZ, YEZID, retired pathologist; b. Santa-Rosa, Caldas, Colombia, Oct. 3, 1936; came to U.S., 1962; naturalized, 1970; m. T. Janovy, 1965; children: Anita, Nicole, David. MD, Univ. de Caldas, Colombia, 1962; MPH, TM, Tulane U., 1963, MS, 1964; PhD, U. Okla., 1971. Asst. in parasitology dept. preventive medicine Sch. of Medicine, Manizales, Colombia, 1959-62, asst. prof. parasitology, 1962-67, chmn. parasitology divsn, 1965-67; instr. med. parasitology U. Okla. Med. Sch., 1968-71; resident Inst. Pathology Case Western Res. U., Cleve., 1972-75; asst. prof. dept. pathology U. Cin. Med. Coll., 1975-77; med. staff Cin. Gen. Hosp., 1976-77; from asst. prof. to assoc. prof., dir. autopsy svc. Case Western Res. U. Inst. Pathology, Cleve., 1977-96; ret. Case Western Res. U., Cleve., 1996. Vis. prof. Med. Sch., Saigon, South Vietnam, 1969, U. Nebr. Med. Ctr., 1987-93, Bapt. Meml. Hosp. and U. Tenn. Med. Sch., 1988, M.D. Anderson Tumor Inst. U Tex., 1988; adj. staff Cleve. Clinic Found., 1989—; with dept. medicine Cin. Coll. Medicine, 1976-77; microbiology testing com. Am. Bd. Pathology, 1989-94; speaker in field. Author: Diagnostic Pathology of Parasitic Infections with Clinical Correlations, 1990; co-author: Diagnostic Pathology of Infectious Diseases, 1993, 2d edit. rev., 2000; contbg. author chpts. in 10 books; contbr. articles to profl. jours.; mem. editl. bd. Human Pathology, 1989—; referee nine other publs. U.S. AID fellow, Tulane U., 1962-64; U.S. Pub. Health fellow U. Okla., 1967-72. Mem. Am. Soc. Parasitology, Am. Soc. Tropical Medicine and Hygiene, Internat. Acad. Pathology, Am. Soc. Clin. Pathologists, Cleve. Soc. Pathologists (CME coord. 1979-86, gov. 1982-84, v.p. 1984-85, pres. 1985-86), Ohio State Soc. Pathologists, Latin Am. Found. Pathology, Binford-Dammin Soc. Infectious Diseases Pathologists, Sigma Xi. Home: 14280 Sweetbriar Ln Novelty OH 44072-9787

GUTIERREZ-JONES, CARL SCOTT, English educator; b. Cheverly, Md., Feb. 22, 1960; s. Jose and Joyce (Coleman) G.; m. Leslie Sampson Jones, Aug. 18, 1989; children: Marina, Natalia. BA, Stanford U., 1982; PhD, Cornell U., 1991. Asst. prof. english U. Calif., Santa Barbara, 1990-95, assoc. prof., 1995-2001, full prof., 2001—. Chair English dept., U. Calif. Santa Barbara, July 2000—. Author: (books) Rethinking the Borderlands: Between Chicano Culture and Legal Discourse, 1995, Critical Race Narratives: A Study of Race, Rhetoric and Injury, 2001; editl. bd. (jour.) Aztlan: A Journal of Chicano Studies, 1998—. Mem. leadership coun., So. Poverty Law Ctr., Montgomery, Ala., 1990—, Amnesty Internat., Santa Barbara, 1990—, Nat. Coun. of La Raza, N.Y., 1992—; vol. Head Start, 1990-92. Recipient post-doctoral fellowship, Ford Found., 1993-94, Humanities Faculty fellowship, U. Calif. Regents, 1997-98, Harold J. Plous award, U. Calif. Santa Barbara, 1993, Rockefeller Found. award, 2000—; grantee Calif. State Legislature, 1992—. Mem. Modern Language Assn., Am. Studies Assn., U. Calif. Santa Barbara faculty Assn. (pres. 1999-2001). Democrat. Avocation: rock climbing. Office: U Calif Santa Barbara English Dept 2702 South Hall Santa Barbara CA 93106 Fax: 805-893-4622. E-mail: carlgj@english.ucsb.edu.

GUTIN, MYRA GAIL, communications educator; b. Paterson, N.J., Aug. 13, 1948; d. Stanley and Lillian (Edelstein) Greenberg; m. David Gutin, Sept. 5, 1971; children: Laura, Sarah, Andrew. BA, Emerson Coll., 1970, MA, 1971; PhD, U. Mich., 1983. Asst. prof. comm. Cumberland County Coll., Vineland, N.J., 1972-80, Rider U., Lawrenceville, N.J., 1981-88, prof., 1989—. Adj. instr. Essex County Coll., Newark, 1971-72, Nassau C.C., Garden City, N.Y., 1972, Trenton (N.J.) State Coll., 1981-84; adj. asst. prof. Rider U., 1981-85; lectr. in field. Author: The President's Partner The First Lady in the 20th Century, 1989; contbr. articles to profl. jours. Officer Emerson Coll. Nat. Alumni Bd., 1994—2002, pres., 1998—2000; bd. dirs. Harry B. Kellman Acad., 1999—2002, vice chair bd. dirs., 1998—2000, chair bd. dirs., 2000—02; bd. dirs. Jewish Cmty. Relations Coun., 2003—. Recipient Alumni Achievement award, Emerson Coll., Boston, 1991. Mem. Ctr. for Study of the Presidency, Nat. Comm. Assn., Ea. Comm. Assn. Avocations: travel, theatre. Home: 119 Greenvale Ct Cherry Hill NJ 08034-1701

GUTKNECHT, GILBERT WILLIAM, JR., congressman, former state legislator, auctioneer; b. Cedar Falls, Iowa, Mar. 20, 1951; s. Gilbert William Sr. and Joan (Kerns) G.; m. Mary Catherine Keefe, June 3, 1972; children: Margaret, Paul, Emily. BA, U. No. Iowa, 1973. Sales rep. J. S. Latta, Cedar Falls, 1973-78, Valley Sch. Supplies, Appleton, Wis., 1978-81; auctioneer Rochester, Minn., 1978-95; state legis. State of Minn., Rochester, 1982-95; mem. U.S. Congress from 1st Minn. dist., 1995—, mem. sci. com., budget com., agriculture com., 1997—. Republican. Avocations: fishing, boating, baseball. Office: US House Reps 425 Cannon House Office Bldg Washington DC 20515-2301 also: Midway Office Plaza 1530 Greenview Dr SW Ste 108 Rochester MN 55902-1080*

GUTMAN, HARRY LARGMAN, lawyer, educator; b. Phila., Feb. 23, 1942; s. I. Cyrus and Mildred B. (Largman) Gutman; m. Anne G. Aronsky, Aug. 28, 1971; children: Jonathan, Elizabeth. AB cum laude, Princeton U., 1963; BA, U. Coll., Oxford, Eng., 1965; LLB cum laude, Harvard U., 1965; MA (hon.), U. Pa., 1984. Bar: Mass. 1968, U.S. Tax Ct. 1969, Pa. 1989, DC 1996. Assoc. Hill & Barlow, Boston, 1968-75, ptnr., 1975-77; clin. assoc. Law Sch. Harvard U., Cambridge, Mass., 1971-77; instr. Boston Coll., 1974-77; atty.-advisor Office Tax Legis. Counsel U.S. Dept. Treasury, 1977-78, dep. tax law legis. counsel, 1978-80; assoc. prof. law U. Va., Charlottesville, 1980-84; prof. Law Sch. U. Pa., 1984-89; ptnr. Drinker Biddle & Reath, Phila., 1989-91; chief staff joint com. taxation U.S. Congress, 1991-93; ptnr. King & Spalding, Washington, 1994-99, KPMG LLP, Washington, 1999—. Cons. Office Tax Policy U.S. Dept. Treasury, 1980, Am. Law Inst., 1980—84; reporter Generation-Skipping Tax Project Arden Ho. III Conf.; vis. prof. Law Sch. U. Va., 1985—89, Ill. Inst. Tech., 1986. Author: (book) Transactions Between Partners and Partnerships, 1973, Minimizing Estate Taxes: The Effects of Inter Vivos Giving, 1975; author: (with F. Sander) Tax Aspects of Divorce and Separation, 1985; author: (with D. Lubick) Treaury's New Views on Carryover Basis, 1979, Effective Federal Tax Rates on Transfers of Wealth, 1979; author: (with others) Federal Wealth Transfer Taxes after ERTA, 1983, Reforming Federal Wealth Transfer Taxes after ERTA, 1983, A Commnet on the ABA Tax Section Task Force Report on Transfer Tax Restructuring, 1988, Where Does Congress Go From Here? Base Timing and Measurement Issues in the Transfer Tax, 1989. Trustee Washington Opera. Fellow: Am. Coll. Tax Counsel (trustee); mem.: Am. Tax Policy Inst. (trustee). Office: KPMG LLP 2001 M St NW Washington DC 20036-3310 E-mail: hgutman@kpmg.com.

GUTMAN, LUCY TONI, school social worker, educator, counselor; b. Phila., July 13, 1936; d. Milton R. and Clarissa (Silverman) G.; divorced; children: James, Laurie. BA, Wellesley Coll., 1958; MSW, Bryn Mawr Coll., 1963; MA in History, U. Ariz., 1978; MEd, Northwestern State U., 1991, MA in English, 1992; postgrad., U. So. Miss., 1992—. Cert. sch. social work specialist, Nat. Bd. Cert. Counselor; diplomate in clin. social work; cert. secondary tchr., La.; cert. counselor, La.; cert. Acad. Cert. Social Workers, La. Bd. Cert. Social Workers. Social worker Phila. Gen. Hosp., 1963-65; sr. social worker Irving Schwartz Inst. Children and Youth, 1965-66; sr. psychiat. social worker Child Study Ctr. Phila., 1966-68; chief social worker Framingham (Mass.) Ct. Clinic Juvenile Offenders, 1968-72; dir. clinic, supr. social work Tucson East Cmty. Mental Health Ctr., 1972-74; coord. spl. adoptions program Cath. Social Svcs. So. Ariz., Tucson, 1974-75; social worker Met. Ministry, 1983; supr. social work Leesville (La.) Mental Health Clinic, 1984; sch. social worker Vernon Parish Sch. Bd., Leesville, 1984—. Cons. Nashua (N.H.) Cmty. Coun., 1969-72; adj. instr. English, sociology, Am. and European history Northwestern State U., Ft. Polk, La., 1984—; part-time counselor River North Psychol. Svcs., Leesville, 1989-92; presenter La. Sch. Social Workers Conf., 1986, 87, Ann. Conf. NASW, 1987, 88, La. Spl. Edn. Conf., 1988, La. Conf. Tchrs. English, 1991, 94, So. Assn. Women Historians, 1994, Mid-Am. Conf. History, 1997, Conf. Contemporary So. Women's Lit., 1997, La. Hist. Assn. Conf., 1998. Contbr. articles to profl. jours. Nat. Soc. Colonial Dames scholar, 1978-79; fellow Pa. State, 1961-62, NIMH, 1962-63. Mem. NASW (diplomate), La. Hist. Assn., So. Hist. Assn., So. Assn. Women Historians, Gamma Beta Phi, Phi Alpha Theta, Phi Kappa Phi. Home: 2004 Allison St Leesville LA 71446-5104

GUTMAN, RICHARD, electrical engineer; b. July 8, 1948; m. Monica Gutman; children: Sandra Mae, Kimberly Jane. BSEE magna cum laude, Polytechnic Inst. N.Y., 1974, MSEE, 1976; MBA (Weidler scholar), Ohio State U., 1985. Registered profl. engr., N.Y., Ohio. Tech. asst. Am. Elec. Power, N.Y.C., 1968-74, engr., 1974-80, asst. mgr. Columbus, Ohio, 1980-85, mgr., 1985-93, prin. engr., 1993—. Contbr. articles to profl. jours. Recipient Innovators award Elec. Power Rsch. Inst., 1996. Mem. IEEE (sr.), N.Y. Acad. Scis., Phi Kappa Phi, Beta Gamma Sigma, Tau Beta Pi. Avocations: travel, reading, cycling. Home: 1407 Beechlake Dr Columbus OH 43235

GUTMAN, RICHARD EDWARD, lawyer; b. New Haven, Apr. 9, 1944; s. Samuel and Marjorie (Leo) G.; m. Jill Leslie Senft, June 8, 1969 (dec.); 1 child, Paul Senft; m. Rosann Seasonwein, Dec. 10, 1987. AB, Harvard U., 1965; JD, Columbia U., 1968. Bar: N.Y. 1969, U.S. Ct. Appeals (2d cir.) 1969, U.S. Dist. Ct. (so. and ea. dists.) N.Y. 1975, U.S. Supreme Ct. 1982, Tex. 1991. Counsel Exxon Corp., N.Y.C., 1978-90, Dallas, 1990-91, asst. gen. counsel, 1992-99, Exxon Mobil Corp., Dallas, 1999—. Pres. 570 Park Ave Apts., Inc., N.Y.C., 1984-89, past bd. dirs. Fellow Am. Bar Found. (life); mem. ABA (fed. regulation securities com., vice-chmn. 1995-98), Am. Law Inst., N.Y. State Bar Assn. (exec. com. 1983-86, 93—, securities regulation com. 1980—, chmn. 1993-97, chmn. bus. law sect. 2001-02), Assn. of Bar of City of N.Y. (securities regulation com. 1980-81, 83-86), Dallas Bar Assn., Coll. of the State Bar of Tex., N.A.M. (corp. fin. and mgmt. com.), Harvard Club (N.Y.C., admissions com. 1983-86, chmn. 1985-86, nominating com. 1986-87, bd. dirs. 1988-91, v.p. 1990-91), Harvard Club (Dallas bd. dirs. 1998-2001).

GUTMAN, RICHARD MARTIN, lawyer; b. Chgo., Mar. 12, 1946; s. Raymond Tobias and Frieda (Garber) G.; m. Linda Ellen Fisher, June 14, 1987; children: Miriam, Eve. BA cum laude, Harvard U., 1967; JD, U. Chgo., 1973. Bar: Oreg. 1973, Ill. 1974, U.S. Dist. Ct. (no. dist.) Ill. 1974, U.S. Ct. Appeals (7th cir.) 1977, Pa. 1990, U.S. Dist. Ct. (mid. dist.) Pa. 1991, U.S. Supreme Ct. 1991, U.S. Ct. Appeals (3d cir.) 1993, N.J. 1996, U.S. Dist. Ct. N.J. 1996. Vol. Peace Corps, 1967-69; staff atty. ACLU Police Project, Chgo., 1973-74; pvt. practice, Chgo., 1975-90, Carlisle, Pa., 1990-95, Montclair, N.J., 1995—; dir. Polit. Surveillance Litigation Project, Chgo., 1975-90; investigator, writer Ralph Nader Congress project, Washington, 1972. Author: (with others) The Environment Committees, 1975; contbr. articles to prof. jours. Recipient 5th Anniversary award Alliance to End Repression, Chgo., 1975, Legal Eagle award Ind. Voters Ill.-Ind. Precinct Orgn., Chgo., 1981, Award of Distinction, 1st Unitarian Ch., Chgo., 1982, 1st Amendment award Citizens Alert, chgo., 1997. Mem. ACLU (pres. South Cen. Pa. chpt. 1992-95). Office: 55 Warfield St Montclair NJ 07043-1116

GUTMAN, ROBERT WILLIAM, retired educator; b. N.Y.C., Sept. 11, 1925; s. Theodore and Elsie G. BA, NYU, 1945, MA, 1948. Instr. New Sch. for Social Research, 1955-57; founder, lectr. Bayreuth Festival Master Classes, 1959-61; lectr. design history art and design div. Fashion Inst. Tech., SUNY, N.Y.C., 1957-66, asst. prof., 1966-71, assoc. prof., 1971-76, prof., 1971-88, dean div. art and design, 1974-79, dean grad. studies, 1979-88, ret., 1988. Vis. prof. Bard Coll., 1991; lectr. PBS Telecast of Bayreuth Festival, 1983. Author: Richard Wagner, The Man, His Mind, and His Music, 1968, German transl., 1970, Italian transl., 1983, Mozart, A Cultural Biograpghy, 1999; editor: Volsunga Saga (transl. by William Morris), 1961. Bd. dirs. Am. Friends of Internat. Found. Mozarteum, 1991—, The Collegiate Chorale, 1990—. Biography juror Nat. Book Awards, 1973; Guggenheim fellow, 1979 Mem.: Nat. Arts (N.Y.C.), Princeton (N.Y.C.), Lotos (N.Y.C.). Home: 37 W 12th St New York NY 10011-8502

GUTMAN, ROY WILLIAM, reporter; b. N.Y.C., Mar. 5, 1944; s. Ira H. and Linda (Snyder) Gutman; m. Elizabeth Jane Dribben, May 17, 1979; 1 child, Caroline. BA, Haverford Coll., 1966; MS, London Sch. Econs., 1968; DLitt (hon.), Haverford Coll., 1995. Reporter UPI, Frankfurt, Germany, 1968—70; corr. Reuters News Agy., Bonn, Germany, 1971—72, bur. chief Belgrade, Yugoslavia, 1973—75, Dept. State corr. Washington, 1976—80, Capitol Hill bur. chief, 1981; nat. security reporter Newsday, Washington, 1982—89, European bur. chief Bonn, 1990—94, fgn. affairs reporter Washington, 1994—2000; corr. Newsweek, Washington, 2001—. Jennings Randolph sr. fellow U.S. Inst. Peace, 2002—03; adj. prof. Medill Sch. Journalism, 2003. Author: (book) Banana Diplomacy, 1988 (named one of best 200 books of 1988, N.Y. Times, Best Am. Book of the Yr., Times Lit. Supplement, London, 1988), A Witness to Genocide, 1993; co-editor: Crimes of War, 1999; contbr. Named one of best fgn. affairs reporters in Washington, The Washingtonian, 1989; recipient Human Rights in Media award, Internat. League for Human Rights, 1992, Pulitzer Prize for internat. reporting, 1993, George Polk Fgn. Reporting award, 1993, Selden Ring Investigative Reporting award, U. So. Calif., 1993, Nat. Headliner Outstanding News Reporting award, 1993, Heywood Brown award, Newspaper Guild, 1993, Excellence in Series/Investigation award, Deadline Club, 1993, Hal Boyle award, Overseas Press Club, 1993, Exemplary Cmty. Svc. Alumni award, Haverford Coll., 1994. Mem.: Inst. Current World Affairs. Jewish. Avocations: gardening, photography. Home: 13132 Curved Iron Rd Herndon VA 20171-2930 Office: Newsweek 1750 Pennsylvania Ave NW Washington DC 20006 E-mail: RoyGut@Newsweek.com. *Facts matter. And collecting them requires a readiness to get your fingernails dirty.*

GUTMAN, STEVEN IFOR, pathologist; b. New Orleans, Dec. 8, 1948; s. Emil and Charlotte Gutman; m. Ruth Ronnie Solomon; children: Tracy Emily, Hilary Laura. BS in Zoology, Ohio State U., 1970; MD, Cornell U., 1974; MBA, SUNY, Buffalo, 1990. Diplomate Am. Bd. Pathology. Chief pathologist Buffalo VA Med. Ctr., 1985—92; med. officer divsn. clin. lab. devices FDA, Rockville, Md., 1992—93, dir. divsn. clin. lab. devices, 1993—2002, dir. office of in vitro diagnostic device evaluation and safety, 2002—. Mem. U.S. tech. adv. group for ISO/TC 212 NCCLS, Villanova, Pa., 1995—; FDA rep. task force on genetic testing NIH-DOE, Bethesda, Md., 1995—97; mem. clin. lab. improvement amendment com. Ctr. for Disease Control, Atlanta, 1992—. Recipient John E. Foley award for outstanding fed. profl., Fed. PA of Western NY, 1984, Group Honors award for compliance injunction activity, HHS, 2000. Fellow: Am. Soc. Clin. Pathologists (corr.), Coll. Am. Pathologists (corr.); mem.: Fed. Physicians Assn. (corr.), Am. Assn. Clin. Chemistry (corr.). Office: Office of In Vitro Diagnostics CDRH FDA HFZ 440 2098 Gaither Rd Rockville MD 20950 Office Fax: 301-594-3084. E-mail: sig@cdrh.fda.gov.

GUTMANN, AMY, political science and philosophy educator, academic administrator; b. Bklyn., Nov. 19, 1949; 1 child, Abigail. BA, Radcliffe Coll.-Harvard U., 1971; MS in Polit. Sci., London Sch. Econ., 1972; PhD in Polit. Sci., Harvard U., 1976. Dir. grad. studies dept. politics Princeton (N.J.) U., 1986-88, dir. polit. philosphy program, 1987-89, dir. ethics and pub. affairs program, 1990-95, founding dir. Ctr. Human Values, 1990-95, 97-99, dean faculty, 1995-97, Laurance S. Rockefeller U. prof., 1990—. Tanner lectr., Stanford U., 1994-95; provost, Princeton U., 2001—. Author: Liberal Equality, 1980, Democratic Education, 1987, 2nd edit., 1999; co-author: (with Dennis Thompson) Democracy & Disagreement, 1996, (with Anthony Appiah) Color Conscious, 1996 (award N.Am. Soc. Social Philosophy), Identity in Democracy, 2003; editor: Democracy and the Welfare State, 1988, Multiculturalism, 1992, Freedom of Association, 1998, (with Dennis Thompson) Ethics and Politics, 3d edit., 1997. Bd. trustees Princeton U. Press, 1996—, Ctr. for Advanced Study in the Behavioral Scis., U. Calif., Stanford, 1998—; mem adv. coun. Kennedy Sch. Govt.-Harvard U., 1996—. Recipient award AAAS, 1997, Ralph J. Bunche award Am. Polit. Sci. Assn., 1997. Mem. Assn. Practical and Profl. Ethics (bd. dirs.), Am. Soc. Political and Legal Philosophy (pres. 2000—). Office: Princeton U Three Nassau Hall Princeton NJ 08544-0001

GUTMANN, DAVID LEO, psychology educator; b. N.Y.C., Sept. 17, 1925; s. Isaac and Masha (Agronsky) G.; m. Joanna Redfield, Aug. 18, 1951; children: Stephanie, Ethan. MA, U. Chgo., 1956, PhD, 1958. Lectr. psychology Harvard U., Cambridge, Mass., 1960-62; prof. U. Mich., Ann Arbor, 1962-76, Northwestern U., Chgo., 1976-97, prof. emeritus, 1998—, chief of psychology, 1976-81, dir. older adult program, 1978-95. Vis. emeritus prof. Hebrew U., Jerusalem, 1997. Author: Reclaimed Powers: Toward a New Psychology of Men and Women in Later Life, 1987, Reclaimed Powers: Men and Women in Later Life, 1994, The Human Elder in Nature, Culture, and Society, 1997; co-author: (with Bardwick, Douvan and Horner) Feminine Personality and Conflict, 1979. With U.S. Mcht. Marine, 1943-46. Recipient Career Devel. award NIMH, 1964-74. Fellow Gerontol. Soc. Am.; mem. Am. Vets. of Israel, Nat. Assn. Scholars. Jewish. E-mail: d-gutmann@northwestern.edu., dgutmann@aol.com.

GUTMANN, JOSEPH, art history educator; b. Wuerzburg, Unterfranken, Germany, Aug. 17, 1923; came to U.S., 1936; s. Henry and Selma (Eisemann) G.; m. Marilyn Tuckman, Oct. 8, 1953; children: David H., Sharon D. BS, Temple U., 1949; MA, NYU, 1952; PhD, Hebrew Union Coll., 1960, DD, 1984, DHL, 1999. Ordained Rabbi. Assoc. prof. art history Hebrew Union Coll., Cin., 1960-69; adj. prof. art. Univ. of Cin., 1961-68; vis. prof. art. Antioch Coll., Yellow Springs, Ohio, 1964; prof. art history Wayne State U., Detroit, 1969-89, prof. art history emeritus, 1989—. Vis. prof. art history U. Mich., Ann Arbor, 1985, Spertus Coll. Judaica, Chgo., 1989; vis. prof. religious studies U. Windsor, Ont., Can., 1990-92, U. Ctrl. Fla., Orlando, 1998-2001, cons. Spertus Mus. Chgo., Skirball Cultural Ctr., L.A., The Jewish Mus., N.Y., Yeshiva U. Mus., N.Y.; adv. bd. Internat. Survey of Jewish Monuments of CAA-SAH. Author: Juedische Zeremonialkunst, 1963, Jewish Ceremonial Art, 1964, 2d edit. 1968, Images of the Jewish Past, 1965, (with S.F. Chyet) Moses Jacob Ezekiel: Memoirs from the Baths of Diocletian, 1975, Ephraim Moses Lilien's Jerusalem, 1976, Hebrew Manuscript Painting, 1978, (with V. Mann) Danzig 1939: Treasures of a Destroyed Community, 1982, The Jewish Sanctuary, 1983, The Jewish Life Cycle, 1987, Sacred Images: Studies in Jewish Art from Antiquity to the Middle Ages, 1989; editor Beauty in Holiness: Studies in Jewish Customs and Ceremonial Art, 1970, No Graven Images: Studies in Art and the Hebrew Bible, 1971, Die Darmstaedter Pessach-Haggadah, 1972, The Dura-Europos Synagogue: A Re-Evaluation, 1973, rev. 2d edit., 1992, The Synagogue: Studies in Origins, Archaeology and Architecture, 1975, The Temple of Solomon: Archaeological Fact and Medieval Tradition in Christian, Islamic and Jewish Art, 1976, The Image and the Word: Confrontations in Judaism, Christianity and Islam, 1977, Ancient Synagogues: The State of Research, 1981; author (monthly column) Gutmann on Art Nat. Jewish Post and Opinion, For Every Thing a Season: Proceedings of the Symposium on Jewish Ritual Art, 2002. Chmn. Community Forum Midrasha, Birmingham, Mich., 1986-88. Served as cpl. USAF, 1943-46. Recipient Faculty Recognition award Wayne State U., 1980; Gershenson Disting. Faculty fellow, 1986-88, Henry Morgenthau fellow Hebrew Union Coll., 1957-58, Meml. Found. Jewish Culture grantee 1959, 72; Am. Council of Learned Socs. grantee, N.Y., 1983, Am. Philos. Soc. grantee, Phila., 1965. Mem. Cen. Conf. Am. Rabbis, Coll. Art Assn. Jewish. Avocations: reading, painting. Home: 13151 Winchester Ave Huntington Woods MI 48070-1726

GUTMANN, REINHART BRUNO, clergyman, social worker; b. Munich, May 1, 1916; came to U.S., 1942, naturalized, 1946; s. Franz and Berta G.; m. Vivian Carol Brunke, Oct. 7, 1944 (dec. Jan. 2003); children: Robin Peter Edward, Martin Francis. Student, History Honours Sch., Manchester U., Eng., 1936-38; MA in Social Scis, St. Andrews U., Scotland, 1939; postgrad., Coll. of Resurrection, Eng., 1939-41, Coll. Preachers, Washington, 1948, 52, U. Wis., summer, 1951, St. Augustine's Coll., Eng., 1964. Ordained deacon Ch. of Eng., 1941, ordained priest, 1942; curate St. Michael's Parish, Golders Green, London, 1941-42; rector St. Mark's Parish, Green Island, N.Y., 1944-45, St. Andrew's Parish, Milw., 1952-54; chaplain and mem. faculty Hoosac (N.Y.) Sch., 1943-45; founder, exec. dir. Neighborhood House and Episcopal City Mission, Milw., 1945-60; exec. dir. Friendship House, Washington, 1960-62; cons. Indian Social welfare Exec. Council of Episcopal Ch., N.Y.C., 1962-64; exec. sec. div. community services Exec. Council of Episcopal Ch., 1964-68, exec. for social welfare and field services, 1968-71; part-time priest-in-charge St. Thomas of Alexandria, Pittstown, N.J., 1968-75; hon. asst. priest St. Martin's Ch., Pawtucket, R.I., 1980. Priest-in-charge St. Peter's Mission, North Lake, Wis., 1958-60; mgr. spl. projects Human Resources Adminstrn., NYC, 1971-72, spl. asst. to asst. adminstr., 1972-73, dir. mgmt. office cmty. svcs., 1973, spl. asst. to dep. adminstr. social svcs., 1973-75; nat. exec. dir. Foster Parents Plan, Inc., Warwick, R.I., 1975-82; pres. Cedar Brook Cons., Inc., 1982-86, ret., 1987. Organizer Gordonstoun Am. Found., 1983; chmn. dept. Christian social relations Province of Midwest, Episcopal Ch., 1954-60; chmn. social edn. and action Nat. Fedn. Settlements, 1960-62; hon. canon All Saints Cathedral, Milw., 1971; founder Silver Spring Neighborhood Ctr., Milw., 1958; founder Northcott Neighborhood House, Milw., 1959. Mem. Acad. Cert. Social Workers, Nat. Assn. Social Workers. Democrat. *Personal success is not measured by wealth or public recognition. It is the knowledge that one has done everything possible to help people achieve dignity, security, and fulfillment; and in so doing has transmitted a sense of personal caring for the needs of others.*

GUTNIK, ZHANNA, physician, gastroenterology consultant; b. Novomoskovsk, Ukraine, Apr. 30, 1966; came to U.S., 1991; d. Valerey and Yelizaveta Keybol; m. Igor Gutnik, Apr. 20, 1986; children: Liliya, Annette. MD, Ivano-Frankovsk Med. Inst., Ukraine, 1989. Diplomate Am. Bd. Internal Medicine, Am. Bd. Gastroenterology. Resident in internal medicine Brooklyn Hosp. Ctr., N.Y.C., 1994-97, fellow in gastroenterology, 1997-2000. Mem. Am. Gastroenterol. Assn., Am. Soc. for Gastrointestinal Endoscopy. Home: 2873 Valerie Ct Merrick NY 11566

GUTOW, BERNARD SIDNEY, packaging manufacturing company executive; b. Chgo., Nov. 11, 1939; s. Max and Betty (Warshawsky) G.; m. Carol Lerch, June 5, 1960; children: Jeffrey, Bryon. BS in Engring., U. Ill., 1961, MS in Engring., 1962; MBA, U. Santa Clara, 1965; JD, Golden Gate U., 1997, LLM, 1998. Registered profl. engr., Ill. Sr. engr. Lockheed Missiles, Sunnyvale, Calif., 1962-65; project engr. U.S. Steel Co., Chgo., 1965-67; engr., prin. A.T. Kearney Co., Chgo., 1967-78; dir. Shaklee, San Francisco, 1978-79; v.p. H.S. Crocker, San Bruno, Calif., 1979-85; v.p., gen. mgr. First Data Resources subs. Am. Express Corp., Tustin, Calif., 1985-88; gen. ptnr. Mgmt. Resource Ptnrs., Redwood Shores, Calif., 1988-96; pres., CEO Bayline Ptnrs./Bayline Paper Supply, Union City, Calif., 1991—. Pres. CEO Bayline Ptnrs., Bayline Paper Supply, Union City, Calif., 1991—. Editor: Plant Engineering Management, 1974; contbr. articles to profl. jours. Pres. Morton Grove Park Dist., Ill. 1973-78; mem. Morton Grove Youth Commn., 1973-78. Recipient Plaque, Morton Grove Park Dist., 1978, cert. Soc. Mfg. Engrs., Chgo., 1975, Bronze award Internat. Film and TV Festival N.Y., N.Y.C., 1984, 1st place internat. law writing competition award N.Y. State Bar Assn., 1998. Mem. ASME (chpt. chmn. 1972-73). Home: 3263 La Mesa Dr San Carlos CA 94070-4244 E-mail: bgutow@gguol.ggu.edu.

GUTOWICZ, MATTHEW FRANCIS, JR., radiologist; b. Camden, N.J., Feb. 23, 1945; s. Matthew F. and A. Patricia (Walczak) G.; m. Alice Mary Bell, June 27, 1977; 1 child, Melissa. BA, Temple U., 1968; DO, Phila. Coll. Osteo. Medicine, 1972. Diplomate Am. Bd. Radiology, Am. Bd. Nuclear Medicine. Intern Mercy Hosp., Denver, 1972-73; resident in diagnostic radiology Hosp. of U. Pa., Phila., 1973-76, fellow in nuclear medicine, 1976-77; chief dept. radiology and nuclear medicine Fisher Titus Med. Ctr., Norwalk, Ohio, 1977—; pres. Firelands Radiology, Inc., Norwalk, 1977—. Ptnr. Pacifica in the Desert Restaurant, Palm Desert, Calif. Republican. Roman Catholic. Avocations: photography, tennis, scuba diving. Home: 23 Patrician Dr Norwalk OH 44857-2463 Personal E-mail: matthewg@neo.rr.com..

GUTREUTER, JILL STALLINGS, financial consultant, financial planner; b. Chgo., Mar. 25, 1937; d. C.G. and Ann (Subject) Stallings; m. Robert L. Gutreuter, June 5, 1971; 1 child, Julia E. BA, U. Ill., 1967; postgrad., Chgo.-Kent, 1968-69, Coll. Fin. Planning, Denver, 1994. Staff dir. ABA, Chgo., 1969-71; trust officer Peoples Trust/Summit Bank, Ft. Wayne, Ind., 1980-87; fin. cons. Merrill Lynch, Ft. Wayne, Ind., 1987—2003; 2d v.p. investments Smith Barney, Ft. Wayne, Ind., 2003—. Fin. planning tchr., continuing edn. divsn. Ind. U.-Purdue U., Ft. Wayne, 1990—2000. Bd. dirs., mem. fin. com. YWCA, Ft. Wayne, 1997—2003; pres. Art League, Ft. Wayne Mus. Art, 1992—93; trustee Episcopal Diocese of North Ind. Found., South Bend, 1995—2000; Bd. dirs. Girl Scouts of the Limberlost, No. Ind., 1997—2000. Recipient Women of Achievement award YWCA, Ft. Wayne, 1994. Mem.: Inst. CFPs, Altrusa Internat. (pres. Ft. Wayne chpt. 1992—94), DAR, Rotary Internat. Episcopalian. Avocations: swimming, walking, painting, knitting. Home: 2312 Forest Park Blvd Fort Wayne IN 46805-3619 Office: Smith Barney One Summit Sq 20th Fl Fort Wayne IN 46869-3429

GUTSCH, WILLIAM ANTHONY, JR., astronomer; b. Newark, Jan. 14, 1946; s. William Anthony and Mary (Ellenback) G. BS, St. Peter's Coll., 1967; MS, U. Va., 1973, PhD, 1978; LHD, St. Peter's Coll., 1995. Staff astronomer Rochester Museum and Sci. Ctr., N.Y., 1973-82; chmn. Am. Mus.-Hayden Planetarium, N.Y.C., 1982-95; ind. cons., writer, prodr. for sci. ctrs., pubs. and TV, Computer & Multi-Media, 1995—. Cons., lectr. in field; news columnist Rochester Times-Union, 1980-84; sci. reporter Sta.-WOKR-TV, Rochester, N.Y., 1976-82; sci. corr. Sta.-WABC-TV, N.Y.C., 1982-84, sci. editor., 1984-88; on-air meteorologist, spl. sci. corr. ABC Network, 1986-93; sci. columnist Gannett, 1980-90; cons. U. Santiago, Chile, 1982; sci. corr. USA Network, 1993—. Author: The Search for Extraterrestrial Life, 1991, 1001 Things Everyone Should Know About the Universe, 1998, (with Isaac Asimov) The Exploding Suns, 1996; author other books, also newspaper articles, TV news and planetarium scripts; writer, contbg. editor New Book of Knowledge, 1992—; writer Discovery Channel, 1994-95. Recipient award of svc. U. Santiago, 1982, City of Buenos Aires, 1983, City of San Juan, 1991, City of Jaharta, Indonesia, 1991; Emmy nominee, 1987. Mem. Am. Astron. Soc., Am. Meteorol. Soc., Am. Assn. Physics Tchrs., Internat. Planetarium Soc. (pres. 1992-94, past pres. 1994-96). E-mail: BillGutsch@cs.com.

GUTSCHE, CARL DAVID, chemistry educator; b. LaGrange, Ill., Mar. 21, 1921; s. Frank Carl and Vera (Mutchler) G.; m. Alice Eugenia Carr, June 4, 1944; children: Clara Jean, Betha Lynn, Christopher Glenn. BA, Oberlin Coll., 1943; PhD, U. Wis., 1947. With Office Sci. Devel., USDA, 1943-44; instr. chemistry Washington U., St. Louis, 1947-48, asst. prof., 1948-51, assoc. prof., 1951-59, prof., 1959-89, prof. emeritus, 1989—, chmn. dept., 1970-76; Robert A. Welch prof. chemistry Tex. Christian U., Ft. Worth, 1989—2002; vis. scholar U. Ariz., Tucson, 2002—. Cons. in field; mem. adv. bd. Petroleum Rsch. Fund., 1971—74; chmn. medicinal chemistry study sect. NIH, 1978—81. Author: The Chemistry of Carbonyl Compounds, 1967, Carbocyclic Ring Expansion Reactions, 1968, Fundamentals of Organic Chemistry, 1975, Calixarenes, 1989, Calixarenes Revisiited, 1998; mem. adv. bd.: Jour. Organic Chemistry, 1979-83; mem. editorial bd.: Organic Preparations and Procedures Internat., 1968—, Jour. Inclusion Phenomena, 1993-2000; contbr. articles to profl. jours. Bd. dirs. St. Louis Conservatory and Schs. for Arts, 1978—82, Ft. Worth Chamber Music Soc., 1999—2002. Recipient Alumni award Washington U., 1977; Guggenheim fellow, 1981. Fellow AAAS; mem. Am. Chem. Soc. (chmn. St. Louis sect. 1959, mem. pub. com. 1974-77, com. on coms. 1977-80, com. on profl. tng. 1980-89, cons. to com. 1990-98, councilor and dir., St. Louis sect. award 1971, Midwest award 1988, Doherty award 1998, Izatt-Christensen award 2002), Chem. Soc. (London), AAUP, Phi Beta Kappa (mem. qualifications com. 1992—), Sigma Xi. Home: 7607 S Galileo Ln Tucson AZ 85747 Office: U Ariz Dept Chemistry Tucson AZ 85721-0041 E-mail: d.gutsche@tcu.edu.

GUTSCHE, HENRY WILLIAM, retired scientist, writer; b. Frankfurt, Germany, June 21, 1922; s. Wilhelm Hans and Frieda Gutsche; m. Brigitte Giescla Gutsche, July 18, 1957; children: Susan, Martin, Carol, Michael; m. Maria Gutsche (div.); 1 child, Heimar. Asst. prof. U., Erlaugeu, Germany, 1954—54; scientist Siemens, Erlaugeu, Germany, 1954—57, Merck Co., Danville, Pa., 1957—64; sr. scientist Monsanto, Saint Louis, Mo., 1964—85; writer, from 1985. Recipient Semi condr., Semry, 1979. Achievements include patents for Semi Conductor Materials. Home: Saint Louis, Mo. Died June 24, 2002.

GUTSHALL, THOMAS L. clinical diagnostics company executive; b. Huntingdon, Pa., Feb. 24, 1938; s. Joseph Boyd and Katherine Pauline (Wear) G.; m. Jane Kipp Taylor, Aug. 22, 1959; children: Jennifer, Douglas, Jodi. BS ChemE, U. Del., 1960. Process engr. Union Carbide Corp., S. Charleston, W.Va., 1960-61, 63-69; mfg. supt. Mallinckrodt, Inc., St. Louis, 1969-72, plant mgr. Raleigh, N.C., 1972-75, v.p., gen. mgr. St. Louis, 1975-81; group v.p. Syntex Corp., Palo Alto, Calif., 1981-83, sr. v.p., 1985-86, exec. v.p., 1987—94; pres. Syva Co., Palo Alto, Calif., 1983-85; pres., Coo CV Therapeutics, Palo Alto, Calif., 1994—96; chmn., CEO Cepheid, Sunnyvale, Calif., 1996—. Chmn. City Team Ministries, San. Jose, Calif., 1984—. Served to 1st lt., U.S. Army 1961-62. Mem. Inst. Chem. Engrs., Tau Beta Pi. Republican. Presby[illegible] Home: 24968 Okeefe Ln Los Altos CA 94022-4612 Office: Ce[illegible] Caribbean Dr Sunnyvale CA 94089-1189

GUTSTEIN, CAROL FEINHANDLER, realtor; b. Chgo., Aug. 31, 1941; d. Emanuel Joshua and Rose (Paster) Feinhandler; m. Solomon Gutstein, Sept. 3, 1961; children: Jonathan, David, Daniel, Joshua. BS in Edn., Loyola U., 1962; MA in Spl. Edn., DePaul U., 1969. Cert. comml. investment mem.; grad. residential real estate; cert. comml. real estate. Spl. cons. Mayor's Office of Sr. Citizens and Handicapped, Chgo., 1977-79; realtor C-21 Shoreline, Evanston, Ill., 1982-84, Matanky, Chgo., 1985, Hallmark & Johnston, Chgo., 1986-95, L.H. Properties, Ltd., Lincolnwood, Ill., 1996—. Cons. Nursing Homes, Chgo., 1978—80. Compiler, editor Community Resources for the Disabled Person in the Chicago Metropolitan Area, 1978. Active campaigner Paul Simon for Senate campaign, 1984-85, 89-90; mgr., dir. Aldermanic campaigns, Chgo., 1975, 79, 95; del. 11th Congrl. Dist. Dem. Nat. Conv., 1980; mem. Dist. 1 Chgo. Sch. Coun., 1989-91. Fellowship Northwestern U., 1962. Mem. WCR (bd. dirs. 1997-98), CCIM (bd. dirs. 1997-2003), Camp Ramah (bd. dirs. 1985-2004), Hadassah (corr. sec. 1998, bd. dirs. 1999-2004). Democrat. Jewish. Fax: (312)649-1598. E-mail: carolfg1@aol.com.

GUTTENBERG, ALBERT ZISKIND, planning educator; b. Chelsea, Mass., Nov. 6, 1921; s. Harry and Edith (Bernstein) G.; m. Mariella Mascardi, June 29, 1964. AB in Social Rels., Harvard U., 1948; postgrad. in sociology, U. Chgo., 1949-51; postgrad. in city planning, U. Pa., 1958-59. Planning asst. Planning Bd., City of Portland, Maine, 1954-56; planning analyst Planning Commn., City of Phila., 1956-60; chief gen. plans and programming sect. Comprehensive Planning div., 1960-61; sr. planner Nat. Capital Downtown Com., Washington, 1962-63; assoc. prof. urban planning U. Ill., 1964-69, prof. urban and regional planning, 1969-89; chair in urban and regional renewal Dept. Geodesy, Delft U. Tech., The Netherlands, 1977-78. Cons. in field. Author: (with others) Explorations Into Urban Structure, 1964, New Directions in Land use Classification, 1965, (with others) Human Ecology, 1975, The Language of Planning, 1993; editor Planning and Public Policy, 1974-89; contbr. articles on land use planning to profl. pubs. Served with U.S. Army, 1942-46. Guggenheim fellow, 1970-71; Brookings Inst. guest scholar, 1970-71; Gelderman Fund grantee Delft U. Tech., 1977; German Marshall Fund Travel grantee, Holland, 1979; recipient Fulbright Travel award Italy, 1986. Mem. Am. Planning Assn., Am. Inst. Cert. Planners (coll. fellows), Soc. Am. City and Regional Planning History, Fulbright Alumni Assn. Home: 711 Hamilton Dr Champaign IL 61820-6811 Office: 111 Temple Hoyne Buell Hall 611 E Lorado Taft Dr Champaign IL 61820-6921 E-mail: a-gutten@uiuc.edu.

GUTTENPLAN, HAROLD ESAU, retired food company executive; b. Flushing, N.Y., Oct. 12, 1924; s. Adolph and Mollie (Penner) G.; m. Jeanette Harris, Apr. 17, 1948; children— Bruce David, Mark Stuart. BA, Queens Coll., 1948; MBA, NYU, 1951. Statistician printing ink div. Sun Chem. Corp., 1948-49; cost accountant, chief accountant, asst. treas. DCA Food Industries, Inc., N.Y.C., 1949-66, treas., 1966-96, asst. sec., 1972-73, sec., dir., 1973-96; ret., 1996. Bd. dirs. Nisshin-DCA. Co-chmn. Queens Coll. 50th Alumni Day Reception, 1998; cub Scout leader Nassau County Thunderbird coun. Boy Scouts Am., 1955-63. With USAAF, 1943-45, PTO. Recipient Anti-Defamation League citation award, 1968. Mem. Daus. of Jacob Relatives Assn. (pres. 1976-77), Alpha Phi Omega (pres. 1947-48), B'nai B'rith (pres. Sagamore lodge 1963-64), Am. Assn. Ret. Persons (asst. state coord. Driver Safety Program 1998). Home: 69 Joyce Ln Woodbury NY 11797-2124

GUTTENPLAN, JOSEPH B. biochemist, educator; b. N.Y.C., May 16, 1943; s. Henry L. and Elizabeth (Phillips) G.; m. Hilde Krohn, Sept. 20, 1971; children: Nils, Alys. BS, Bklyn. Coll., 1965; MS, PhD, Brandeis U., 1970; MPH, Columbia U., 1992. Postdoctoral fellow Max Planck Inst., Goettingen, Germany, 1969-71, U. Calif., Berkeley, 1971-73; rsch. asst. prof. Mt. Sinai Sch. Medicine, N.Y.C., 1973-74; from asst. prof. to assoc. prof. biochemistry NYU Dental Ctr., N.Y.C., 1974-87, prof. biochemistry, 1987, coord. biochemistry/microbiology, 1991—, dir. rsch., 1993—; assoc. prof. environ. medicine NYU Med. Ctr., 1983—, prof., 1998—. Cons. Mt. Sinai Med. Ctr., 1980-84; pvt. cons. toxicology. Co-author: Biochemistry, 1995; mem. editl. bd. Mutation Rsch., 1997—; Nutrition and Cancer, 2002. contbr. chpt. to book, articles to profl. jours. Mem. NCI site visit team U. Cinn. Med. Sch., Eppley Inst., mem. study sect. to rev. superfund grants. Grantee NIH, 1976, 79, 83, 87, 94, 98, 99, 2000, 2001, 2002, Am. Inst. Cancer Rsch., 1996, Air Force, 1996, Smokeless Tobacco Rsch. Coun., 1998. Fellow Am. Inst. Chemists; mem. Am. Assn. Cancer Rsch., Environ. Mutagen Soc., Am. Soc. Biol. Chemists, Soc. Toxicology, Internat. Assn. Dental Rsch., Am. Assn. Dental Rsch. Home: 110 E Brookside Dr Larchmont NY 10538-1736

GUTTENTAG, JACK MARK, economist, educator; b. Bklyn., Dec. 9, 1923; s. Sidney W. and Fannie (Coon) Guttentag; m. Doris Wallach, June 5, 1955; children: William, Adam. BS, Purdue U., 1948; PhD, Columbia, 1958. Market analyst FHA, 1952- 54; economist Fed. Res. Bank N.Y., 1954-62; prof. finance Wharton Sch., U. Pa., 1962—96, prof. emeritus, 1996—, chair banking, 1969—96. Cons. in field, 1962—; mem. sr. rsch. staff Nat. Bur. Econ. Rsch., 1965—71; chmn. GHR Sys., Inc., 1989—. Author: (book) Lender of Last Resort in an International Context, Disaster Myopia in International Banking; contbr. articles to profl. jours.; mng. editor: Jour. Fin., 1974—76, Housing Fin. Rev., 1984—89, syndicated columnist on home mortgages:. With inf. U.S. Army, 1943—46, ETO. Mem.: Am. Fin. Assn. (bd. dirs. 1968—70, 1978—80). Home: PO Box 574 Valley Forge PA 19481-0574 Personal E-mail: jguttentag@mtgprofessor.com.

GUTTENTAG, JOSEPH HARRIS, lawyer, educator; b. Boston, Feb. 8, 1929; s. Samuel Alexander and Sara (Hurwitz) G.; m. Merna Fay Cohn, June 18, 1961; children: Steven, Adam, Alice AB, U. Mich., 1950; LLB, Harvard U., 1953. Bar: DC 1953, Mich. 1954. Internat. tax counsel US Treasury, Washington, 1967-68; ptnr. Surrey & Morse, Washington, 1965-67, 68-79, Arnold & Porter, Washington, 1979-94, 1991-94; dep. asst. sec. internat. tax affairs US Treasury, Washington, 1994-99, sr. advisor Office of Tax Policy, 1999-2000. Adj. prof. Howard Law Sch., Washington, 1964-67; professorial lectr. George Washington U. Sch. Law, 1968-75 Chmn. com. fiscal affairs Orgn. Econ. Coop. and Devel., Paris; mem. adv. commn. Elec. Commerce, 1999-2000; trustee Levine Sch. Music. Capt. USAF, 1954-57. Mem. DC Bar Assn., Am. Soc. Internat. Law. Democrat. Jewish.

GUTTERIDGE, THOMAS G. academic administrator, consultant and labor arbitrator; b. Flint, Mich., Oct. 31, 1942; s. George Ernest and Mary Ruth (Stewart) G.; m. Judith Kay Grubbs Gutteridge, Aug. 28, 1965; children: Theresa, Debbie, Cindy. BS in Industrial Engring., Gen. Motors Inst., 1965; MS in Ind. Admin., Purdue U., 1966, PhD, 1971. Teaching asst. Purdue U., Lafayette, Ind., 1967-70; asst., assoc. prof. SUNY, Buffalo, 1970—83; dean, full prof. So. Ill. U., Carbondale, 1983—92; dean, disting. prof. U. Conn., Storrs, 1992—2002, emeritus dean, disting. prof., 2002—03; dean, prof. mgmt. Coll. Bus. Adminstrn. U. Toledo, 2003—. Safety engr. Buick Motors, Flint, Mich., 1964-65; corp. recruiter Industrial Nucleonics, Columbus, Ohio, 1966-67; labor arbitrator Am. Arbitration Assn., Fed. Mediation and Conciliation Svc., 1972—; mem. Conn. State Bd. Labor Rels., 1995-98. Co-author: Organizational Career Development: Benchmarks for Building a World-Class Workforce, Organizational Career Development: State of the Practice; contbr. numerous articles to profl. jours. Recipient Career Devel. awards Am. Soc. for Tng. and Devel., 1983. Mem. Acad. of Mgmt. Human Resource Planning Soc., Golden Key Honor Soc., Beta Gamma Sigma. Democrat. Avocation: sports. Home: 523 Foret Lane Holland OH 43528 Office: U Toledo Coll Bus Adminstrn Mail Stop # 103 2801 W Bancroft St Toledo OH 43606

GUTTERMAN, ALAN J. lawyer; b. Bklyn., Nov. 21, 1942; s. Hyman and Madeline (Wolfe) G.; m. Emily Scharer, June 23, 1966; children: David, Andrew, Glenn, Jamie. BA with honors, U. Rochester, 1964; JD, Rutgers U., 1967. Bar: N.J. 1967, U.S. Ct. Claims 1970, U.S. Ct. Appeals (3rd cir.) N.J. 1967, U.S. Supreme Ct. 1977. Law clk. U.S. Ct. Appeals 3rd Cir., 1967-68; assoc. Sills, Beck, Cummis, Radin & Tischman, Newark, 1968-71; sole practice Union, N.J., 1972-75; ptnr. Gutterman,Markowitz & Klinger, LLP and predecessor firms, Westfield, NJ, 1975—. Editor: Rutgers Law Rev., 1966-67; contbr. N.J. Law Jour. Councilman, Westfield, N.J., 1979-83. Mem.: Union County Bar Assn., N.J. State Bar Assn. Republican. Jewish. Office: Gutterman Markowitz & Klinger LLP PO Box 2850 240 E Grove St Westfield NJ 07091-2850 E-mail: ajgesq@verizon.net.

GUTTERSEN, MICHAEL, ranching and investments professional; b. San Francisco, Mar. 26, 1939; s. William L. and Grace Tooee (Smith) Vogler; m. Penny Leonora Quinn, Aug. 29, 1959; children: Michael William, Arthur Roy, Shawn Patrick. Student, U. Col., 1957-58. Foreman Crow Creek Ranch, Ault, Colo., 1960-61; owner/mgr. Flying G Ranch, Briggsdale, Colo., 1961-86; pres. Two E Ranches Inc., Greeley, Colo., 1969-86, PX Ranch, Elko, Nev., 1969-71, Indian Creek Ranch, Encampment, Wyo., 1970-83, Lake Farms Co., Eaton, Colo., 1969-86; gen. ptnr. Guttersen & Co./Guttersen Ranch, Kersey, Colo., 1986—. Mgr. ins. agy. Am. Nat. Ins. Co., Greeley, 1962-70; owner FGF Ins. Brokers, Inc., Greeley, 1962-70. Bd. dirs. United Way, Weld County, Colo., 1979-81, Greeley Philharmonic Orch., 1991-94, Nat. Cowboy Hall of Fame, Oklahoma City, 1994—. With U.S. Army, 1958-60. Mem. Nat. Cattlemens Assn., Colo. Cattlemens Assn., Colo. Cattle Feeders Assn., Tex. and S.W. Cattle Raisers Assn., Weld County Livestock Assn., Greeley Country Club. Republican. Roman Catholic. Avocations: fishing, hunting in africa. Home: Woods Lake Farm 13696 RD 74 Eaton CO 80615 Office: Guttersen and Co PO Box 528 Kersey CO 80644-0528

GUTTING, GABRIELLE L. literature educator, researcher; d. Walter H. and Ruth E. Gutting; m. Helge E. Dreher, Sept. 16, 1959. PhD in Am. Lit. and English magna cum laude, U. Trier. Instr., Am. lit. and English. Rsch. and consulting, so. culture and lit. Fla. Atlantic U., Boca Raton, 2000—. Author: (book, critical study) Yoknapatawpha (on William Faulkner), (exhibition catalog) William Faulkner, (photo exhibition with texts) William Faulkner's Mississippi; prodr.: (video documentaries) Various Video productions on the European Union, the European Council, and European Institutions; contbr. articles and essays to jour. Mem.: SAMLA, MLA, Ctr. Study So. Culture, William Faulkner Soc., Soc. Study So. Lit. Office: Florida Atlantic Univ 777 Glades Rd Boca Raton FL 33431 E-mail: ggutting@fau.edu.

GUTTMACHER, SALLY JEANNE, education educator; d. Alan Frank and Leanore Florence Guttmacher; 1 child, Benjamin Alan Guttmacher Holtzman. PhD, MPhil, Columbia U., 1975. Prof. NYU, 1990—. Bd. mem. Pub. Health Assn. of N.Y.C., 1972. Grantee Rsch., NIH, 1998—2000. Mem.: Pub. Health Assn. of N.Y.C. (pres. 1996—99). Achievements include research in Cmty. based health promotion and disease prevention interventions and evaluations. Home: 15 Claremont Ave (#83) New York NY 10027 Office: New York Univ Pub Health Rm 515 726 Broadway New York NY 10003 Personal E-mail: sg2@nyu.edu. E-mail: sg2@nyu.edu.

GUTTMAN, ARNOLD R. chemist, educator; b. Chgo., Oct. 22, 1947; s. Joseph Reese and Sally (Meyers) G.; m. Cheryl L. Krader, Aug. 20, 1978; children: Lawrence, Mark. BA, DePaul U., 1970; BS in Chemistry, Northeastern Ill. U., 1982; MEd, Nat. Louis U., 1990. Chemist G.D. Searle & Co., Skokie, Ill., 1980-83, Abbott Labs., North Chicago, Ill., 1983-84; phys. sci. tchr. Hardey Prep Sch., Chgo., 1988-91; chemistry tchr. Waukegan (Ill.) H.S., 1991—. Tchr. rsch. assoc. Argonne (Ill.) Nat. Labs., 1995; tchr. materials rsch. ctr. Northwestern U., Evanston, Ill., 1999, 2000, 2001, participant, 2003. Contbr. articles to profl. jours. Recipient Excellence in tchg. Sci. award Ill. Jr. Acad. Sci., 1989; Am. Soc. Biochemistry and Molecular Biology fellow The Chgo. Med. Sch., 1996. Mem. Am. Chem. Soc. (chpt. h.s. com., 2001 h.s. chemistry exam. com.), Ill. Chemistry Tchrs. Assn., Ill. Sci. Tchrs. Assn. Avocations: tennis, chess, walking. Home: 701 Indian Hill Rd Deerfield IL 60015-4048

GUTTMAN, EGON, law educator; b. Neuruppin, Germany, Jan. 27, 1927; came to U.S., 1958, naturalized, 1968; s. Isaac and Blima (Liss) G.; m. Inge Weinberg, June 12, 1966; children: Geoffrey David, Leonard Jay. Student, U. Cambridge, 1945-48; LLB, U. London, London, England, 1950, LLM, 1952; post grad., Northwestern U. Sch. Law, 1958-59. Barrister: Eng. 1952. Sole practice, England, 1952-53; faculty Univ. Coll. and U. Khartoum, 1953-58; legal advisor to chief justice, 1953-58; founder, editor Sudan Law Jour. & Reports, Sudan, 1956-57; researcher, lectr. Rutgers U. Sch. Law, Newark, 1959-60; asst. prof. U. Alta., Edmonton, Canada, 1960-62; prof. Howard U. Law Sch., Washington, 1962-68, vis. adj. prof., 1968-96; adj. prof. law Washington Coll. Law, Am. U., Wash., 1964-68, Levitt Meml. Trust scholar-prof., 1968—; dir. JD-MBA joint degree program, 1990-2000; lectr. Practicing Law Inst., 1964—. Adj. prof. law Georgetown U. Law Ctr., 1972-74, Johns Hopkins U., Balt., 1973-81; vis. prof. Faculty of Law, U. Cambridge, Wolfson Coll., Eng., 1984, U. Haifa, Israel, 2000; atty.-fellow SEC, 1976-79; cons. to various U.S. agys. and spl. commns.; U.S. rep. to UNCITRAL working groups; mem. various ALI-ABA working groups on the revision of the uniform comml. code; mem. Sec. of State's Adv. Com. on Pvt. Internat. Law; arbitrator NY Stock Exch. and NASD, 1997—. Author: Crime, Cause and Treatment, 1956; author: (with A. Smith) Cases and Materials on Domestic Rels., 1962; author: Modern Securities Transfers, 3d edit., 2002; author: (with R.G. Vaughn) Cases and Materials on Policy and the Legal Environment, 1973, rev., 1978, 3d edit., 1980; author: Problems and Materials on Sales Under the Uniform Comm. Code and the Convention on Internat. Sale of Goods, Comm. Transactions, vol. 2, 1990; author: (with L.F. Del Duca and A.M. Squilante) Problems and Materials on Secured Transactions Under the Uniform Comm. Code, Comm. Transactions, vol. 1, 1992; author:, 1997, Problems and Materials on Negotiable Instruments Under the Uniform Comm. Code and the UN Conv. on Internat. Bills of Exch. and Internat. Promissory Notes, Comm. Transactions, vol. 3, 1993, supplement, 1995; author: (with R.B. Lubic) Secured Transactions-A Simplified Guide, 1996; author: Securities Laws in the United States-A Primer for Fgn. Lawyers, 1996—99; author: (with L.F. Del Duca, F.H. Miller, P. Winship, W.H. Henning) Secured Transactions Under the Uniform Comm. Code and Internat. Commerce, 2002; contbr. numerous articles, revs., briefs to profl. lit. Howard U. rep. Fund for Edn. in World Order, 1966-68; trustee Silver Spring Jewish Ctr., Md., 1976-79; mem. exec. com. Sha'are Tzedek Hosp., Washington, 1971-72, 97—. Leverhulme scholar, 1948-51; U. London studentship, 1951-52; Ford Found. grad. fellow, 1958-59, NYU summer workshop fellow, 1960, 61, 64; Levitt Meml. Trust scholar-professor 1982—; recipient Outstanding Svc. award Student Bar Assn., Am. U., 1970, Law Rev. Outstanding Svc. award, 1981, Washington Coll. of Law Outstanding Contbn. to Acad. Program Devel. award, 1981. Mem. Am. Law Inst., ABA, Fed. Bar Assn. Assn. Trial Lawyers Am., Brit. Inst. Internat. and Comparative Law, Soc. Pub. Tchrs. Law (Eng.), Hon. Soc. Middle Temple, Hardwick Soc. of Inns of Ct., Sudan Philos. Soc., Assn. Can. Law Tchrs., Am. Soc. Internat. Law, Can. Assn. Comparative Law, B'nai Brith, Argo Lodge, Phi Alpha Delta (John Sherman Myers award 1972). Home: 14801 Pennfield Cir Silver Spring MD 20906-1580 Office: Am U Washington Coll Law 4801 Massachusetts Ave NW Washington DC 20016-8196 Fax: (202) 274-4130. E-mail: guttman@wcl.american.edu.

GUTTMAN, HELENE NATHAN, biomedical research consultant, transpersonal counselor, regression therapist; b. N.Y.C., July 21, 1930; d. Arthur and Mollie (Bergovoy) Nathan. BA, Bklyn. Coll., 1951; AM, Harvard U., 1956; MA, Columbia U., 1958; PhD, Rutgers U., 1960. Registered and cert. profl. past-life regression therapist; bd. cert. nutrition specialist; bd. cert. and registered hypnotherapist; registered and cert. transpersonal counselor; certified and registered neurolinguistic therapist. Rsch. technician Pub. Health Rsch. Inst., N.Y.C., 1951-52; control bacteriologist Burroughs-Wellcome, Inc., Tuckahoe, N.Y., 1952-53; vol. researcher Haskins Labs., N.Y.C., 1952-53, rsch. asst., 1953-56, rsch. assoc., 1956-60, staff microbiologist, 1960-64; lectr. dept. biology Queens Coll., N.Y.C., 1956-57; rsch. collaborator Brookhaven Nat. Labs., Upton, L.I., N.Y., 1958; guest investigator Botanisches Institut der Technisches Hochschule, Darmstadt, Germany, 1960; rsch. assoc. dept. biol. scis. Goucher Coll., Towson, Md., 1960-62; vis. asst. rsch. prof. dept. medicine Med. Coll. Va. Richmond, 1960-62; asst. prof., then assoc. prof. dept. biology NYU, 1962-67; from assoc. prof. to prof. dept. biol. scis. U. Ill.-Chgo., 1967-75, prof., 1969-75; prof. dept. microbiology U. Ill. Med. Sch., 1969-75; assoc. dir. for rsch. Urban Systems Lab. U. Ill., 1975; expert Office of Dir. Nat. Heart, Lung and Blood Inst., NIH, Bethesda, Md., 1975-77, coordinator rsch. resources Office Program Planning and Evaluation, 1977-79; dep. dir. Sci. Adv. Bd., Office of Adminstr., EPA, 1979-80; program coordinator, post-harvest tech., food safety and human nutrition, sci. and edn. adminstrn. USDA, 1980-83, assoc. dir. Beltsville Human Nutrition Rsch. Ctr., Agrl. Rsch. Svc., 1983-89; pres. HNG Assocs., 1983—; nat. animal care coord. Nat. Program Staff Agr. Rsch. Svc./USDA, Beltsville, Md., 1989-95. Bd. advisors The Monroe Inst., 1993—. Sr. author: Experiments in Cellular Biodynamics, 1972; co-editor (procs.) First Joint USA-USSR Joint Symposium on Blood Transfusion, Moscow, 1976, DHEW Publ. No. (NIH) 78-1246, 1978; editorial bd. Jour. Protozoology, 1972-75, Jour. Am. Med. Women's Assn., 1978-81, Methods in Cell Science, 1994—; sr. editor: Science and Animals: Addressing Contemporary Issues, 1989; editor: Guidelines for Well-being of Rodents in Research, 1990, Rodents and Rabbits: Current Research Issues, 1994; (with others) Rodents and Rabbits: Addressing Current Issues, 1994; contbr. articles profl. jours. Mem. edn. com. Ill. Commn. on Status Women, 1974-75; cons. EPA, sci. adv. bd., 1974-79; bd. dirs. Du Page County Comprehensive Health Care Agy., 1974-75. Andelot fellow Harvard U., 1956, Rutgers scholar Rutgers U., 1960; recipient Thomas Jefferson Murray prize Theobald Smith Soc., 1959; spl. award for work in Germany Deutscher Forschungs Gemeinschaft, 1960; Fellow Dazian Found., 1956; research grantee. Fellow: AAAS, N.Y. Acad. Scis., Am. Acad. Microbiology, Am. Inst. Chemists (chmn. com.); mem.: Am. Assn. Pastoral Counselors, Univ. and Coll. Women Ill. (past v.p.), Fed. Orgn. Profl. Women (past chmn. task force, past pres.), Assn. Women in Sci., Soc. Protozoology (past mem. exec. com., past com. chmn.), Am. Soc. Clin. Nutrition, Am. Soc. Cell Biology (past com. chmn.), Am. Soc. Microbiologists, Neuroscis. Soc., Am. Soc. Biol. Chemistry and Molecular Biology, Tissue Culture Assn. (com. chmn. Nat. Capital Area br. 1988—90), Soc. Sci. Exploration, Soc. for In Vitro Biology (chmn. constn. and bylaws com. 1994—2002, Disting. Svc. award 1995, 1999), Assn. for Transpersonal Psychology (profl. mem.), Soc. Am. Bacteriologists (pres.'s fellow), Internat. Assn. Regression Therapies (life profl.), Am. Running and Fitness Assn. (bd. dirs., mem. editl. bd., mem. bd. advisors 1993—95), Sigma Xi, Sigma Delta Epsilon (past coord. regional ctrs.). Home and Office: 5607 Mclean Dr Bethesda MD 20814-1021 E-mail: hguttman@soundbalance.net. *Personal philosophy: If it's worth having, it's worth fighting for.*

GUTWIRTH, MARCEL MARC, French literature educator; b. Antwerp, Belgium, Apr. 11, 1923; s. Jacob Nahum and Frieda (Willner) G.; m. Madelyn Katz, June 20, 1948; children: Eve, Sarah, Nathanael. Student, NYU, 1941-42; AB, Columbia, 1947, MA, 1948, PhD, 1950. Mem. faculty Haverford (Pa.) Coll., 1948-87, William R. Kenan, Jr. prof. French lit., 1977-82, John Whitehead prof., 1983-87; Disting. Prof. Grad. Ctr. CUNY, 1987-94, exec. officer PhD program in French, 1987-93. Vis. prof. Johns Hopkins U., 1967, Queens Coll., 1968, Bryn Mawr Coll., 1969, 76; Andrew Mellon vis. prof. humanities Tulane U., 1980; lectr. Folger Inst., 1985. Author: Molière ou l'Invention Comique, 1966, Jean Racine: Un Itinéraire Poétique, 1970, Stendhal, 1971, Michel de Montaigne ou le Pari d'Exemplarité, 1977, Un Merveilleux sans Eclat: La Fontaine ou la Poésie Exilée, 1987, Laughing Matter, 1993. Bd. dirs. Childbirth Edn. Assn. Greater Phila., 1961-64. With AUS, 1943-46, ETO. Fulbright postdoctoral fellow Paris, 1953-54, Am. Coun. Learned Socs. fellow, 1964-65, Guggenheim fellow, 1971-72, 85, Nat. Humanities Ctr. fellow, 1985-86. Mem. ACLU, MLA (mem. editl. bd. publs. 1973-76), Am. Assn. Tchrs. of French. Jewish. Home: 640 Valley View Rd Ardmore PA 19003-1029

GUY, ARTHUR WILLIAM, electrical engineering educator, researcher; b. Helena, Mont., Dec. 10, 1928; s. Arthur Jack and Evelyn (Hebb) G.; m. Vivian Ruth Walker, June 12, 1952; children: William, Sandra, Fred, Arla. BSEE, U. Wash., 1955, MSEE, 1957, PhDEE, 1966. Rsch. asst. elec. engring. dept. U. Wash., Seattle, 1956-57; rsch. engr. Boeing Airplane Co., Seattle, 1957-63; cons. engr. rehab. medicine U. Wash., Seattle, 1963-65, rsch. engr. elec. engring. dept., 1964-66, prof. elec. engring. dept., rehab. medicine, 1966-83, prof., dir. bioelectromagnetics rsch. lab. Ctr. for Bioengineering, 1983-91, prof. emeritus, 1991—. Cons. Bioelectromagnetics Cons., Seattle, 1991-2000; mem. telecomms. facilities adv. com. Seattle City Coun., 1991-92; mem. Sci. Adv. Group on Wireless Tech., 1993-95; active Wireless Tech. Rsch., L.L.C., 1993-97. Contbr. articles to profl. jours. Mem. Electromagnetic Field Task Force State Dept. Health, Olympia, Wash., 1991-92. Sgt. USAF, 1947-52. Recipient Achievement award Westinghouse Co., 1954, spl. award for the decade internat. Power Inst. for Med. and Biol. Rsch., 1980. Fellow AAAS, IEEE (life, vice chair SCC 28 stds. bd. 1989-94, mem. COMAR 1974-89, 92-98, chair COMAR 1987-89); mem. Nat. Coun. on Radiation Protection and Measurements (hon.), Bioelectromagnetic Soc. (charter mem., pres. 1984, d'Arsenval award 1987). Methodist. Home and Office: 18122 60th Pl NE Kenmore WA 98028-8901

GUY, DAVID MCCUTCHEON, literature educator; b. Pitts., Aug. 19, 1948; s. William Barker Guy and Mary Jane McCutcheon; m. Elizabeth Heard, June 20, 1970 (div. Aug. 1991); 1 child, William Barker; m. Alma G. Blount, Jan. 10, 1994. AB, Duke U., 1970, MAT, 1977. Tchr. English Forsyth Country Day Sch., Winston-Salem, NC, 1970—76; tchr. creative writing U. NC, Chapel Hill, 1970—91, Duke U., Durham, NC, 1999, writing instr., 2001—02. Author: (novels) Second Brother, 1985, Autobiography of My Body, 1991, Red Thread of Passion, 1998. Home: 2117 Wilson St Durham NC 27705 E-mail: davidguy@mindspring.com.

GUY, ELEANOR BRYENTON, writer; b. Pitts., Sept. 6, 1930; d. Lloyd Charles and Verda Eleanor (Hooper) Bryenton; m. Daniel Sowers Guy, Dec. 22, 1962; children: Stanley, Sharon. BA, Ohio Wesleyan U., 1953. Program dir. Lakewood Br. Cleve. Met. YWCA, Lakewood, Ohio, 1953-56, ctr. dir., 1956-57; residence dir., mem. faculty St. Luke's Hosp. Sch. Nursing, Shaker Heights, Ohio, 1957-59; pers. asst., counselor Acacia Mutual Life Ins. Co., Washington, 1959-62; admissions counselor Ohio No. U., Ada, 1963-64; freelance writer, photographer Kenton (Ohio) Times, 1984-88, Ada Herald, 1988-96; coord. external affairs, editor the Writ, Pettit Coll. of Law, Ohio No. U., 1995-96. Sec. bd. trustees, chmn. pub. rels. com. Ada Pub. Libr., 1982—86; mem. pub. rels. com., bd. dirs. Hardin County Alcohol and Drug Abuse Ctr., Kenton, 1989—92; chmn. publicity Town and Gown Planning Com., Ada, 1988; tchr., mem. co-chair edn. com., mem. missions com., mem., sec. adminstrv. coun., mem. centennial com., publicist local ch., 1985—, lay dist. del. to West Ohio Ann. conf., 1998—; dist. spiritual growth coord. Ch. United Meth. Women, 2000—03. Mem. AAUW (pres. local br. 1978-80), Ohio No. U. Women (parliamentarian, pub. rels. chair Christmas Arts Festival 1990-96), P.E.O. (v.p. 1994-96, sec. 1998-99), Twice Ten Art Club (pres. 1984-85, 90-91, 97-98, sec. 1988-89, 99-01, mem. v.p. 2003—). Methodist. Avocations: photography, travel, music.

GUY, JAMES MATHEUS, lawyer, realtor; b. Wichita, Kans., Aug. 26, 1945; s. Jesse Milton and Roberta Aldine (Housholder) G.; m. Cindy K. Sundell, Dec. 31, 1978. BA, U. Kans., 1967; JD, Washburn Coll., 1970. Bar: Kans. 1970, U.S. Dist. Ct. Kans. 1970. Assoc., Coombs & Brick, Wichita, Kans., 1970-71; atty. Fed. Land. Bank, Wichita, 1971-76, sr. atty., 1976-78, prin. atty., 1978-84, asst. gen. counsel litigation, 1985-86; realtor, gen. counsel and owner Century 21 Consol. Realty, Inc., Wichita, 1986—. Founding mem. Kans. Preservation Alliance, Topeka, 1979—; pres. Midtown Citizens Assn., Wichita, 1984-85, mem MCA Exec. Bd., 1984-87; bd. dirs., exec. com. Hist. Wichita-Sedgwick County, Inc., 1974—; mem. Wichita Hist. Landmarks Preservation Com., 1981—; bd. dirs., pres. Victorian Soc. in Am., Kans. chpt., Wichita, 1974-84, Skinner Lee Victorian House Mus., Wichita, 1976-84; mem., chmn. Wichita Hist. Landmarks Preservation Council, 1981—. Washburn U. law scholar, 1967, law research fellow, 1968-70. Mem. Wichita Area Corp. Counsels (sec. 1982-83), Washburn Law Sch. Assn., Kans. U. Alumni Assn. Lodges: Mason, Shriners. Home: 1043 Jefferson St Wichita KS 67203-3575 Office: Century 21 Consolidated Realty Inc 1999 Amidon St Ste 105 Wichita KS 67203-2122

GUY, JOHN MARTIN, lawyer; b. Detroit, July 16, 1929; s. Alvin W. and Ann G. (Martin) G.; B.S., Butler U., 1958; J.D., Ind. U., 1961; children— Janice Lynn, Robert John. Bar: Ind. 1962. Practice law, Monticello, 1962— ; atty. firm Guy, Christopher, Loy, 1962— ; mem. Ind. Ho. of Reps., 1971-74, house majority leader, 1973-74; mem. Ind. Senate, 1977-84, majority leader, 1979-80; Pros. atty. 39th Jud. Circuit, 1963-67. Pres. White County Mental Health Assn., 1965-68. Trustee Monticello-Union Twp. Library Bd., pres., 1970-71. Served with USAF, 1951-55. Named Outstanding Republican Freshman Ind. Ho. of Reps., 1971, Ind. Senate, 1977. Mem. Ind., Monticello Bar Assns., Monticello C. of C. (pres. 1975-76), Am. Legion, Masons, Shriners, Moose. Office: 115 W Broadway PO Box 925 Monticello IN 47960-0925

GUY, L(EONA) RUTH, medical educator; b. Kemp, Tex., Mar. 17, 1913; d. Henry Luther and Minnie Elizabeth (Murphy) G. AB, Baylor U., 1934, MS, 1949; PhD, Stanford (Calif.) U., 1953. Rsch. fellow NOOO Stanford U., 1951-53, teaching asst., 1951; with Southwestern Med. Sch. U. Tex., Dallas, 1953—77; prof. U. Tex. Southwestern Med. Sch., Dallas, 1977-82, prof emeritus, 1982—. Assoc. dir. Parkland Meml. Hosp. Blood Bank, Dallas

1953-78; cons. VA Hosp., Dallas, 1960-80, Temple, 1964-80; vis. prof. to Far East, China Med. Bd. of N.Y., N.Y.C., 1969-70. Author: (with others) Modern Blood Banking and Transfusion Practices, 1982; editor: Technical Manual, 1966; contbr. numerous articles to profl. jours. Bd. dirs. Dallas Repertory Theater, Dallas, 1983-89. Named Disting. Alumnus Baylor U., 1994; inducted into Tex. Women's Hall of Fame, Gov.'s Commn. for Women, 1989. Fellow Am. Soc. Clin. Pathologists (hon., assoc., Disting. Svc. award 1989); mem. Bus. and Profl. Women's Club Dallas (pres. 1970-71), Baylor Women's Coun. (Woman of Distinction award 1988), Baylor Heritage Club (pres. Dallas chpt. 1991-92), Zonta (pres. Dallas chpt. 1961-62, Spirit of Zonta award 1994). Baptist. Avocation: painter. Home: 5455 La Sierra Dr Dallas TX 75231-4146

GUY, MARC DUANE, assistant city manager; b. Hays, Kans., July 8, 1956; s. Duane Francis and Donna Lynette Guy; m. Sue Rae Helweg, Mar. 30, 1985; children: Alexa Rae, Aric Duane. BA, U. Tex., Austin, 1978; M in Urban Planning, Tex. A&M U., 1981. City planner City of Grapevine, 1981-83; sr. planner City of Grand Prairie, Tex., 1983-85, City of Carrollton, 1985-88, planning dir., 1988-93, asst. city. mgr., 1993—. Mem. profl. com. Coll. Arch., Tex. A&M U., College Station, 1992-94, mem. profl. adv. com. dept. urban planning, 1992-94. Mem. Am. Planning Assn. (membership chair 1991-93, treas. 1987-91), City Planners Assn. Tex., Urban Land Inst. (assoc.). Office: 1945 E Jackson Rd Carrollton TX 75006-1737 E-mail: mguy@cityofcarrollton.com.

GUY, MARY ELLEN JOHNSTON, political science educator; b. Carlinville, Ill., Dec. 2, 1947; d. Charles Oren and Marilyn Elinor (Denby) Johnston; divorced. BA cum laude, Jacksonville U., 1969; M of Rehab. Counseling, U. Fla., 1970; MA in Psychology, U. S.C., 1976, PhD in Polit. Sci., 1981. Rehab. counselor Ga. Dept. Human Resources, Augusta, 1970-73; psychologist S.C. State Hosp., Columbia, 1973-80, quality assurance coord., 1980-82; Collins prof. public admin. Fla. State U., 1997—; prof. polit. sci. and pub. affairs U. Ala., Birmingham, 1982-97. Adv. bd. Cooper Green Hosp., Birmingham. Editor: Women and Men of the States, 1992; author: Ethical Decision Making, 1990, From Organizational Decline, 1989, Professionals in Organizations, 1985. Mem. Am. Soc. Pub. Adminstrn. (Disting. Rsch. award 1992, Outstanding Paper award 1992, coun. mem. 1987-90, pres. 1997-98), So. Polit. Sci. Assn. (pres. 2001-2002), Am. Polit. Sci. Assn., Women's Caucus in Polit. Sci./South (pres. 1990-92). Unitarian Universalist. Avocations: golf, breeding and showing purebred dogs. Office: Fla State U Askew Sch Pub Adminstrn & Policy Tallahassee FL 32306-2250

GUY, MATTHEW JOEL, gastroenterologist, educator; b. Aug. 23, 1945; s. Rubin and Gertrude (Feinberg) Guy; m. Barbara Mae Sachartof, Oct. 21, 1979; children: Reuven Maxwell, Judah Philip, Alan Louis, David Charles, Goldie Hannah-Cheryl. Diplomate Am. Bd. Internal Medicine. Intern Maimonides Hosp., Bklyn., 1970-71, resident, 1971-72, St. Luke's Hosp., N.Y.C., 1972-73, Columbia-Presbyn. Med. Ctr., N.Y.C., 1973-74; pvt. practice Bklyn. and Belle Harbor, NY, 1974—. Mem. staff Beth Israel Kings Hwy. Hosp., Bklyn., 1974—, dir. gastro-intestinal endoscopy, 1976—; mem. staff Maimonides Hosp., Bklyn., Peninsula Hosp., Rockaway, N.Y., 1997—, Brook Plz. Surgictr., Bklyn., 2001--; asst. prof. medicine SUNY Downstate Med Ctr., Bklyn Trustee, mem. bd. edn. Yeshiva of Flatbush. Fellow Am. Coll. Gastroenterology, Am. Soc. Gastrointestinal Endoscopy; mem. ACP, AMA, Kings County Med. Soc., Phi Beta Kappa, Sigma Xi. also: 3043 Ocean Ave Brooklyn NY 11235 Office: 119-15 Rockaway Beach Blvd Rockaway Park NY 11694 E-mail: harborhealthcare@aol.com.

GUY, MATTHEW WAYNE, education educator, writer; b. Charleston, SC, May 4, 1969; m. Kristina Alexis Zoch, May 27, 2000. BA, U. of Miami, 1987—92; MA, Clemson U., 1992—95; PhD, La. State U., 1995 -2003. Instr. in english Trident Tech. Coll., Charleston, SC, 1994—95, La. State U., 1995 -2001, Baton Rouge C.C., Baton Rouge, 2001—. Fellow, Internat. Sch. for Theory in the Humanities, 1998. Mem.: North Am. Soc. for the Study of Romanticism, MLA. Home: 527 East Blvd Baton Rouge LA 70802 Personal E-mail: mguy@lsu.edu.

GUY, MILDRED DOROTHY, retired secondary school educator; b. Brunswick, Ga. d. John and Mamie Paul (Smith) Floyd; m. Charles H. Guy, Aug. 18, 1956 (div. 1979); 1 child, Rhonda Lynn. BA in Social Sci., Savannah State Coll., 1949; MA in Am. History, Atlanta U., 1952; postgrad., U. So. Calif., U. Colo. Tchr. social studies L.S. Ingraham H.S., Sparta, Ga.; tchr. English and social studies North Jr. H.S., Colorado Springs, 1958-84, ret., 1984; cooperating tchr. Tchr. Edn. Program, Col. Coll., 1968-72. Fund raiser for Citizens for Theatre Auditorium, Colorado Springs, 1979; bd. dirs. Urban League, 1971-75; del. to County and State Dem. Conv., 1972, 76, 80, 84, 92, 96; mem. Pike's Peak C.C. Coun., 1976-83; mem. Colo. Springs Opera Coun. of 500, 1984-88; mem. nominating com. Wagon Wheel coun. Girl Scouts U.S.A., 1985-87; active Fine Arts Ctr., Pikes Peak Hospice, mem. St. John's Bapt. Ch., former sanctuary choir mem.; mem. Svcs. of Charity (local and nat.); life mem. Friends of Colorado Springs Pioneers Mus. Recipient Viking award North Jr. H.S., 1973, Woman of Distinction award Girl Scouts Wagon Wheel Coun., 1989, 94; Outstanding Black Woman of Colorado Springs award, 1975; named Pacesetter, Atlanta U., 1980-81, Outstanding Black Educator of Yr., Black Educators of Dist. II, Colorado Springs, 1984, Outstanding Ednl. Svc. award Colo. Dept. and State Bd. Edn., 1983, Dedicated Svc. award Pikes Peak C.C., 1983, Outstanding Cmty. Leadership award Alpha Phi Alpha, 1985, Action award Colo. Black Woman for Polit. Action, 1985, Sphinx award, 1986; named in recognition sect. Salute to Women, Colorado Springs Gazette Telegraph, 1986; Wall of Fame honoree Nat. Women's Hall of Fame, 1997. Mem.: AAUW, NEA, NAACP (life), LWV (Colo. chpt.), Women's Ednl. Soc. Colo. Coll. (bd. mgrs. 1992—98), Afro-Am. Life and History, Colo. Social Studies Assn., Women's Found. Colo., Negro Hist. Assn. Colorado Springs, Assn. for the Study of Afro Am. Life and History, Inc. (life), Colo. Springs Pioneers Mus. (life), Golden Heritage (life), Alpha Kappa Alpha (pres. Iota Beta Omega chpt. 1984—85, Chpt. Pres. award 1985), Alpha Delta Kappa. Home: 3132 Constitution Ave Colorado Springs CO 80909-2177

GUY, RALPH B., JR., federal judge; b. Detroit, Mich., Aug. 30, 1929; s. Ralph B. and Shirley (Skladd) G.. AB, U. Mich., 1951, JD, 1953. Bar: Mich. 1953. Sole practice, Dearborn, Mich., 1954—55; asst. corp. counsel City of Dearborn, 1955—58, corp. counsel, 1958—69; chief asst. U.S. Atty.'s Office (ea. dist.), Detroit and Mich., 1968—70, U.S. Atty., 1970—76; judge U.S. Dist. Ct. (ea. dist.) Mich., Ann Arbor, 1976—85, U.S. Ct. Appeals (6th cir.), Ann Arbor, 1985—94, sr. judge, 1994—. Treas. Detroit-Wayne County Bldg. Authority, 1966—73; chmn. sch. study com. Dearborn Bd. Edn., 1973; mem. Fed. Exec. Bd., 1970—, bd. dirs., 1971—73. Recipient Civic Achievement award, Dearborn Rotary, 1971, Distinguished Alumni award, U. Mich., 1972. Mem.: FBA (pres. 1974—75), ABA (state chmn. sect. local govt. 1965—70), Out-County Suprs. Assn. (pres. 1965), Mich. Municipal League, Mich. Assn. Municipal Attys. (pres. 1962—64), Nat. Inst. Municipal Law Officers (chmn. Mich. chpt. 1964—69), Am. Judicature Soc., Dearborn Bar Assn. (pres. 1959—60), Detroit Bar Assn., State Bar Mich. (commr. 1975—), U. Mich. Alumni Club (local pres. Dearborn 1961—62), Rotary (local pres. 1973—74), Lambda Chi Alpha, Phi Alpha Delta. Office: US Ct Appeals PO Box 7910 200 E Liberty St Rm 226 Ann Arbor MI 48107 also: Potter Stewart US Courthouse 100 E 5th St Cincinnati OH 45202-3988

GUY, RICHARD P. retired state supreme court justice; b. Coeur d'Alene, Idaho, Oct. 24, 1932; s. Richard H. and Charlotte M. Guy; m. Marilyn K. Guy, Nov. 16, 1963; children: Victoria, Heidi, Emily. JD, Gonzaga U., 1959. Bar: Wash. 1959, Hawaii 1988. Former judge Wash. Superior Ct., Spokane, from 1977; chief justice Wash. Supreme Ct., Olympia, 1998—2001; mediator, arbitrator Judicial Arbitration and Mediation Svc., 2001—. Capt. USAS. Recipient Herbert Harley Award, Am. Judicature Soc., Outstanding Judge Award, Wash. St. Bar Assn., Supreme Ct. Medal, Canada. Mem. Wash. State Bar, Spokane County Bar Assn. Roman Catholic. Office: Wash Supreme Ct Temple Justice PO Box 40929 Olympia WA 98504-0929 also: JAMS Seattle 600 University St Ste 1910 Seattle WA 98101

GUY, WILLIAM ACHILLES, JR., (ROD GUY JR.), urban planner, economic development consultant; b. Monroe, La., Dec. 19, 1953; s. William Achilles Sr. and Lula (Newberry) G.; m. Shannon Lewis; children: William A. IV, Susannah Grace. BA in Polit. Sci., N.E. La. U., 1976, MA in History, 1982; M in Urban Regional Planning, U. New Orleans, 1991; postgrad., U. Ctrl. Ark., 1992-94. Varsity football coach River Oaks Sch., Monroe, La., 1980; cons. Office Sys., Shreveport, La., 1982-83; sales rep. Burroughs Corp. (Unisys), Monroe, La., 1983-86; computer trainer State Farm Ins., Monroe, La., 1987-89; cons. N.E. La. Econs. Devel. Alliance, Monroe, La., 1991-95; exec. dir. Poverty Point Cmty. Devel. Corp., Monroe, La., 1996-98; pres. Urban Planning & Econ. Devel., Monroe, La., 1990—. Cons., founder N.E. La. Scenic By Ways, Monroe, Piney Hills Town, Ctrl. La., North Ctrl. La. Econ. Devel. Alliance. Contbr. articles to profl. publs. 1st lt. U.S. Army, 1977-84. Recipient Enterprise Cmty. award Dept. Agr., Cert. Appreciation, State of La., 1994. Mem. Am. Planning Assn., Sewanee Alumni Assn., N.E. U. Alumni Assn., Masons, Rotary, Am. Legion, Am. Vet. Episcopalian. Avocation: tennis. Office: Urban Planning & Econ Devel 1106 Hilton St Monroe LA 71201-4320

GUYBERSON, RANDY ALAN, writer; b. South Bend, Ind., Mar. 9, 1950; s. William J. Guyberson, Sr. and Lucille M. Guyberson. Diploma, Inst. Children Lit., West Redding, Conn., 1999; home study course, McColl's Cooking Sch., South Bend, Ind., 1980. Chef several restaurants, South Bend; owner, painter, paper hanger Guyberson's Painting Co., South Bend; owner, oper. Granny's Spot Restaurant, Wyatt, Ind.; owner, oper. launderette Denever County; writer. Avocations: cooking, designing, writing, dogs. Home: 219 E Dayton St South Bend IN

GUYER, CHARLES GRAYSON, II, psychologist; b. High Point, NC, May 22, 1949; s. Charles Grayson Sr. and Mildred Louise (Wrokman) G.; m. E.R. Ward, June 24, 1986; children: Charles Grayson III, Jarvis Griffith. BA, Appalachian State U., 1972, MA, 1974; EdD, Coll. William & Mary, 1978. Bd. cert. in counseling psychology and family psychology Am. Bd. Profl. Psychology. Resident No. Wyo. Mental Health, Buffalo, 1978-80; pvt. practice High Point, N.C., 1980-83, Greensboro, NC, 1988—98; chief sch. psychologist Perquimans County Schs., Hertford, NC, 1998—2002; pvt. practice Jacksonville, NC, 2002—. Pres. Am. Bd. Family Psychology, 1992-94, bd. dirs., 1991-96, 2000--, Am. Bd. Counseling Psychology, 1991-93. Contbr. articles to profl. jours., chpts. to books. Lt. USN, 1983—88. Recipient Irving I. Sector award, Am. Soc. Clin. Hypnosis, 1997. Fellow APA, Am. Soc. Clin. Hypnosis (chair ethics com. 1993-97), Acad. Family Psychology (pres. 1995-96), Am. Acad. Counseling Psychology (bd. dirs. 1991-93, pres. 1993-95), Soc. Clin. Exptl. Hypnosis; mem. Am. Group Psychotherapy Assn., Nat. Assn. Sch. Psychologists, Va. Acad. Clin. Psychologists, Va. Psychol. Assn., NC Soc. Clin. Hypnosis, NC Psychol. Assn., Guilford County Psychol. Assn. (treas. 1997-98). Methodist. Avocations: running, reading. Home: 371 Great Hope Church Rd Hertford NC 27944 Office: Ste 204 1703 Country Club Rd Jacksonville NC 28546 E-mail: drguyer@hotmail.com.

GUYETTE, JAMES M. airline executive; b. 1945; married; 5 children. BS Bus. Adminstrn., Econs., St. Mary's Coll., Moraga, Calif., 1967. With United Air Lines Inc., Chgo., 1967—, various mgmt. positions, 1967-79, v.p. personnel, sr. v.p., 1979-85, exec. v.p. ops., 1985—, v.p. mktg. planning., 1992. Bd. Regents St. Mary's Coll., U. Ill. Bus. Adv. coun.; devel. coun. Alexian Bros. Med. Ctr., Elk Grove Village, Ill.; various leadership positions United Way Crusade Mercy; bd. dirs. United Way, PrivateBancorp. Office: United Air Lines Inc PO Box 66100 AMF Ohare IL 60666-0100

GUYMON, GARY LEROY, civil engineering educator, consultant; b. Farmington, N.Mex., Nov. 5, 1935; s. Leland W. and Grace E. (Cumming) G.; m. Lucinda A. Kemmis, June 11, 1988; children by previous marriage: Gary Jr., Richard, Marisa, Michael. BS, U. Calif., Davis, 1966, MS, 1967, PhD, 1970. Asst. civil engr. Calif. Dept. Water Resources, L.A., 1955-66; asst. rsch. engr. U. Calif., Davis, 1969-71; assoc. prof. U. Alaska, Fairbanks, 1971-74; prof. U. Calif., Irvine, 1974-94, chmn. dept. civil engring., 1984-88, prof. emeritus, 1994—. Mem. coordinating bd. U. Calif. Water Resources Ctr., Berkeley, 1985-89; del. Univs. Coun. on Water Resources, Carbondale, Ill., 1980-94. Author: Unsaturate Zone Hydrology, 1994; contbr. numerous articles to profl. jours.; assoc. editor Advances in Water Resources, Southampton, U.K., 1981-89. Fellow ASCE; mem. Am. Geophys. Union, U.S. Com. on Large Dams, Phi Beta Kappa, Tau Beta Pi, Chi Epsilon. Independent. Avocations: woodworking, physical fitness. E-mail: gguymon@att.net.

GUYNES, DEMI See MOORE, DEMI

GUYNN, ROBERT WILLIAM, psychiatrist, educator; b. Streator, Ill., Oct. 27, 1942; s. William Digby and Helen Louise (Dancey) G. BA, Mich. State U., 1963; MD, Johns Hopkins U., 1967. Diplomate Am. Bd. Psychiatry and Neurology. Clin. fellow Nat. Inst. of Mental Health, Washington, 1970-73; asst. prof. Dept. of Psychiatry and Behaviorial Scis. U. Tex., Houston, 1973-76, assoc. prof., 1976-83, vice-chmn., prof. psychiatry, 1983-87, interim chmn., 1987-89, chmn., 1989—. Dir. U. Tex. Mental Scis. Inst., Houston, 1987—; exec. dir. Harris County Psychiat. Ctr., 1988—; sr. examiner Am. Bd. Psychiatry and Neurology, 1997—. Contbr. articles to profl. jours. and book chpts.; mem. editl. bd. Internat. Rev. Psychiatry, 1988-93, editor-in-chief, 1989-93. Bd. dirs. Vols. of Am., Houston, 1982-88, Harris County Mental Health Assn., Houston, 1992-97. Full surgeon USPHS, 1970-73. Fellow Am. Psychiat. Assn., Am. Coll. Psychiatrists; mem. Am. Soc. Biol. Chemistry, Tex. Rsch. Soc. on Alcoholism (pres. 1985-87), Tex. Soc. of Am. Assn. Psychiat. Adminstrs. (treas. 1990-91, pres. 1992-93), Biochem. Soc., Rsch. Soc. on Alcoholism, Houston Psychiat. Soc. (v.p. 1989-90, pres. 1991-92), Harris County Med. Soc. (bd. ethics 1989-92), Tex. Dept. Mental Health and Mental Retardation (med. adv. com. 1997—, chair 1999—). Avocation: printmaking. Office: U Tex Health Sci Ctr PO Box 20708 Houston TX 77225-0708

GUYTON, SAMUEL PERCY, retired lawyer; b. Jackson, Miss., Mar. 20, 1937; s. Earl Ellington and Eulalia (Reynolds) G.; m. Jean Preston, Oct. 11, 1959; children: Tamara Reynolds, William Preston, David Sage. BA, Miss. State U., 1959; LLB, U. Va., 1965. Bar: Colo. 1965, U.S. Dist. Ct. Colo. 1965, U.S. Tax Ct. 1977, U.S. Ct. Appeals (10th cir.) 1965, U.S. Ct. Appeals (5th cir.) 1981. Ptnr. Holland & Hart, Denver, 1965-92, ret., 1992. Mem. faculty Am. Law Inst. ABA, 1976-88, bd. dirs. Royal St. Corp., Royal St. Utah Inc., Deer Valley Ski Resort. Co-author: Cattle Owners Tax Manual, 1984, Supplement to Federal Taxation of Agriculture, 1983, Colorado Estate Planning Desk Book, 1984, 90; author: (chpt.) Success Briefs For Lawyers, 2000; contbr. articles to profl. jours., mags.; bd. advs. Agrl. Law Jour., 1978-82; mem. editl. bd. Jour. Agrl. Tax and Law, 1983-92. Sec., trustee Colo. Hist. Found., 1971-92, pres., 1983-87; trustee Music Assn. Aspen and Aspen Music Festival, 1980-88; precinct com. chmn. Dem. Party, 1968-70; mem. Gov.'s Mansion preservation com., 1989-92; bd. advisors Coll. Arts and Scis., Miss. State U., 1996-98; mem. com. govt. and legal affairs Hampshire Coll., 1996-2000; chmn. com. on legis. Woodmen of the World, 1972-2000. Fellow Am. Coll. Tax Counsel (bd. regents 1985-92, chmn., pres. 1989-91), Am. Tax Policy Inst. (trustee 1989-92, v.p. 1989-92); mem. ABA (sect. taxation 1967-92, chmn. sect.'s com. on agr. 1980-82), Colo. Bar Assn. (tax coun. 1983-86, sec. 1983, chmn. 1985-86), Colo. Bar Found. (life), Greater Denver Tax CslS. Assn. (chmn. 1978), Law Club Denver, Little River Lectures Assn. (bd. dirs., v.p. 1985-96, pres. 1996-2000), Am. Alpine Club (life), Colo. Mountain Club (life, planned giving com.), Eleanore Mullen Weckbaugh Found. (trustee 1983-95), William P. Guyton Found. (co-trustee), Humphreys Found. (sec., treas., v.p., trustee), Colo. Trail Found. (trustee 1987-99), Colo. Mountain Club Found. (dir., v.p.), Colo. Hist. Soc. (bd. dirs., chmn. nominating com. 1997-2001, co-chair dirs. coun.), Holland & Hart Found. (bd. dirs., pres.). Mem. Unity Ch. Home and Office: 12345 W 19th Pl Lakewood CO 80215-2516 *To live fully and consciously in the present is both challenge and reward.*

GUYTON, WILLIAM LEHMAN, JR., retired surgeon; b. Balt., Sept. 22, 1914; MD, U. Md., 1938. Diplomate Am. Bd. Surgery. Intern Church Home-Hosp., Balt., 1938-39, resident in surgery, 1939-42; hosp. staff Church Hosp., Balt. Fellow ACS, Internat. Coll. Surgeons.

GUZAK, KAREN JEAN WAHLSTROM, artist; b. Cambridge, Mass., May 21, 1939; d. Ernest E. and Kathryn E. (Kemp) Wahlstrom; m. Steven V. Guzak, Aug. 29, 1959 (div. 1983); children: Gretchen, Christopher, Lauren. BS, U. Colo., 1961; BFA, Cornish Sch. Allied Arts, Seattle, 1976. Pres. Karen Guzak Inc., Seattle, 1982—. One-woman shows include Foster White Gallery, Seattle, 1981, 1984, 1987, 1989, 1991, 1994, 1996, 1998, 2000, Davidson Galleries, 1981, 1984, 1987, Tom Luttrell Gallery, San Francisco, 1981, Harris Gallery, Houston, 1982, Laura Russo Gallery, Portland, Oreg., 1987, 1989, 1991, 1996, Musee Hyacinth Rigaud, Perpignan, France, 1988, exhibited in group shows at Bklyn. Mus., 1981, Brentwood Gallery, St. Louis, 1982, Seattle Art Mus., 1983, San Francisco Mus., 1983, Portland Art Mus., 1985, Davidson Gallery, 1992, Stifel Fine Arts Ctr., Wheeling, W.Va., 1993, Bellevue Art Mus., Wash., 1988, 1990, 1995—96, DeCordova Mus., 1991, Purdue U., 1995, U. Brighton, Eng., 1997, Bronx Mus., 1987, Portland Art Mus., 1997, Ctr. on Contemporary Art, 2000, Tacoma Art Mus., 2002, Represented in permanent collections Portland Art Mus., Jundt Mus. Gonzaga U., Bklyn. Mus., NYC Libr., Pratt Inst., City of Seattle, King County Wash., pub. commns. include South Seattle C.C., So. Oreg. State Coll., King County Coun. Chambers, Overlake Ctr. for Sound Transit, Redmond, Wash. Bd. commrs. King County Arts Commn., Seattle, 1981—86, commr., 1984—85; arts adv. com. METRO Arts Program, Seattle, 1985—91; contemporary coun. Seattle Art Mus., 1990—96; pres., developer Sunny Arms Coop., Seattle, 1988—90; co-developer, pres. Union Arts Coop., Seattle, 1992—93; hist. design rev. bd. City of Snohomish, 2000—03; bd. dirs. Ctr. Contemporary Art, 1987—88; pres. bd. dirs. Artist Trust, Seattle, 1996—99. Boettcher scholar Univ. Colo., 1957-61; recipient Housing Designs that Work award Seattle Design Commn., 1991, Home of Yr. award Seattle Times and AIA, 1994. Democrat. Avocation: yoga. Home and Office: Karen Guzak Inc 230 Avenue B Snohomish WA 98290-2841

GUZDA, HENRY PETER, industrial relations specialist; b. Stamford, Conn., Jan. 9, 1950; s. Henry and Marion (Wujcik) G. BA in History, Alliance Coll., 1971; MA in History, Edinboro U., 1974; postgrad., Cath. U., 1986—. Historian U.S. Dept. Labor, Washington, 1976-84, indsl. rels. specialist, 1984—. Hist. advisor U.S. Dept. Labor Libr.; dir. internat. visitor program Office of Am. Workplace, Washington, 1989—; cons. Readers Digest, Pleasantville, NY, 1993, Gale Rsch., Detroit. Contbr. articles to profl. jours. Block capt. Neighborhood Watch, Foxwood Cmty. Assn., Burke, Va., 1986-92; chief steward Office of Am. Workplace, Am. Fedn. Govt. Employees, Washington, 1993-94. Mem. Indsl. Rels. Rsch. Assn. (exec. bd. D.C. chpt. 1989-94, pres. 1992-93, award 1993). Democrat. Achievements include research in tracing origins and development of new forms of work organization/labor-mgmt. coop., research in covering origins of equal employment opportunity programs in Dept. of Labor. Home: 5654 Sutherland Ct Burke VA 22015-1850 Office: Office Asst Sec for Policy Dept Labor 200 Constitution Ave NW Washington DC 20210-0001

GUZIK, ESTELLE MARION, professional society administrator; b. Bklyn., Sept. 12, 1939; d. David and Helen G. BA in Polit. Sci., Bklyn. Coll., 1961; MS in Urban Planning, Hunter Coll., 1967. Dir. Fed. Regional Coun., N.Y.C., 1971-80; dir. Fair Housing and Equal Opportunity N.Y. area office HUD, N.Y.C., 1980-83; dir. compliance divsn. U.S. Dept. Housing and Urban Devel., N.Y.C., 1983-95; pres. Jewish Genealog. Soc. Inc., N.Y.C., 1997—. Mem. genealogy task force Ctr. for Jewish History, N.Y.C., 1996—; coord. computerized index-web Kings County Naturalization Index, 2001. Editor: Genealogical Resources in New York, 2003. Mem. Phi Beta Kappa.

GUZMAN, BELINDA F. elementary school educator; b. Guadalajara, Jalisco, Mexico, Jan. 8, 1965; arrived in U.S., 1970; d. Ralph Loran and Modesta DeBelle; m. Alfonso Guzmán, Aug. 10, 1990; children: Alfonso, Daniela. B in Indisciplinary Studies, U. Tex. Pan Am., 1995, MEd, 2001. Cert. educator Tex., 1995. Legal sec. Law Office of Vernon Hill Jr., McAllen, Tex., 1982—93; educator Pharr, San Juan, Alamo Ind. Sch. Dist., Pharr, Tex., 1993—. Mem.: Mission Jr. Svc. League, Kappa Delta Pi (historian 2001—). Roman Catholic. Avocations: reading, dancing. Office: North San Juan Elem Sch 2900 N Raul Longoria San Juan TX 78589

GUZMAN, JOSE JAVIER, aeronautical engineer; b. Bayamon, Pr, Oct. 27, 1970; s. Jose Dolores Guzman and Nydia Margarita Rivera; m. Natalia Ramirez, May 12, 2001. BSEngr. in Aero/Astronautical Engring., Purdue U., West Lafayette, Ind., 1993, MS in Aero/Astronautical Engring., 1995, PhD in Aero/Astronautical Engring., 2001. Mission analyst a.i. solutions, Inc., Lanham, Md., 2001—. Contbr. articles. Recipient Indsl. Roundtable Leadership Award, Purdue U., 1991, Triana Project Group Achievement award, NASA Goddard Space Flight Ctr., 2002; award, Nat. Hispanic Scholarship Fund, 1991, scholar, McDonnell Douglas Found., 1992, Grad. Student Rschrs. Program fellowship, NASA Goddard Space Flight Ctr., 1996-1999. Mem.: AIAA (assoc.; evolution of flight chair 2002—03), Planetary Soc., Am. Astronautical Soc. (assoc.).

GUZMAN, MARIE ELVIRA, school guidance counselor; b. Quito, Ecuador, July 19, 1937; Came to U.S., 1968; d. Jose Amable Rubio and Sarah Maldonado; m. Antonio Guzman, Dec. 26, 1958; children: Miriam, Renato, Freddy, Scott. BA, 1975; MEd, Montclair State U., 1982. Cert. tchr., guidance counselor, N.J.; cert. Spanish, elem., bilingual, ESL, student pers. svcs. guidance counselor. Tchr. Pub. Pilot Sch., Quito, 1958-68, Paterson (N.J.) Pub. Schs., 1975-83, Paterson Adult Sch., Paterson, 1978—; guidance counselor Paterson (N.J.) Pub. Schs., 1983—. Mem. ASCD, N.J. Counselors Assn. Roman Catholic. Avocation: reading. Home: 4212 No Dancer Way Orlando FL 32826-4293

GUZMAN-ARENAS, ADOLFO, computer science researcher, electronics engineer; b. Ixtaltepec, Oaxaca, Mex., July 22, 1943; s. Bartolo (dec.) and Piedad (Arenas) G.; m. Carina Favela (dec.); children: Mara, Flora, Victor; m. Carime Vargas, 1998; children: Alfa, Adolfo. BS in Telecommunications and Electronics, Nat. Poly. Inst., Mex., 1965; MS in Electrical Engring., MIT, 1967, PhD in Computer Sci., 1969. Registered profl. engr., Mex. Asst. prof. elec. engring. dept. MIT, Cambridge, Mass., 1969-70; research fellow dept. machine intelligence U. Edinburgh, Scotland, 1970; prof. elec. engring. dept. Centro de Investigacion y Estudios Avanzados, Nat. Poly. Inst., Mexico City, 1970-73; dir. Nat. Computer Ctr., Mexico City, 1971—72, IBM Latin Am. Sci. Ctr., Mexico, 1973—76; prof. computer sci. dept. Nat. U. Mex., Mexico City, 1975-83; chmn. computer sci. dept. Centro de Investigacion y Estudios Avanzados Nat. Poly. Inst., Mexico City, 1983-86; sr. mem. tech. staff Microelectronics and Computer Co., Austin, Tex., 1986-88; chief scientist Internat. Software Systems, Inc., Austin, Tex., 1989, v.p. engring., 1990—92; dir. and founder Ctr. for Computing Rsch. Nat. Poly. Inst., Mexico City, 1997—2002. Cons. Mexican Ministry Telecommunications and Transp., 1972, State Govt. Oaxaca (Mex.), 1983-84; mem. editorial bd. Computerworld, Mexico City, 1983—. Assoc. editor, founding mem. Jour. Computer Vision, Graphics and Image Processing, Pattern Recognition Jours., Pattern Recognition Letters Jour., Netherlands, editor-in-chief Jour. Computacion y Sistemas, 1997-2002; assoc. editor CIENCIA mag. Mex. Acad. Sci., 2000—; contbr. numerous articles on computer sci., elec. engring., image understanding, artificial intelligence, parallel processing, and geographical data bases to profl. publs., also contbr. to books. Named Nat. Scientist, Fed. Govt. Mex., 1984, 2000—; recipient BanaMex Nat. prize for outstanding work on remote sensing, Mexico City, 1977, Medina prize for outstanding work in computer sci., Morelia, Mex., 1980, Nat. prize in Scis. and Arts, Fed. Govt., Mex., 1996. Fellow. Assn. for Computing Machinery (mem. pubs. bd. 2002—); mem.: IEEE (sr.), NY Acad. Scis., Mex. Acad. Scis., Nat. Acad. Engring. Mex. (founder,). Home: Fresnillo 6 Mexico City 10610 Mexico Office: Nat Poly Inst Ctr Investigacion Av Juan de Dios Batiz/Othon de Mendizaba Col Zacatenco Mexico City 07738 Mexico E-mail: a.guzman@acm.org., aguzman@ieee.org.

GUZY, CAROL, photojournalist; b. Bethleham, PA, Mar. 7, 1956; ADN, Northampton County Area C.C., Pa.; AAS in Photography, Art Inst. Ft. Lauderdale. Staff photographer The Miami Herald, 1980-88, The Washington Post, 1988—. Recipient Best Portfolio award Atlanta Seminar Photojournalism, 1982, 85, 90, Robert F. Kennedy award, 1984, Excellence citation Overseas Press Club, 1986, Pulitzer Prize in spot news photography, 1986, 95, Leica Excellence medal, 1994; named Newspaper Photographer of Yr. Nat. Press Photographer Assn., 1989, 92, Photographer of Yr. White House News Photographers Assn., 1991, 93, 94, 96, Pulitzer Prize in feature photography, 2000. Office: The Washington Post 1150 15th St NW Washington DC 20071-0002

GUZZO, GLENN, former newspaper editor; V.p. news Knight Ridder Inc., 1989-93; editor The Philadelphia Inquirer, Ft. Worth Star-Telegram; mng. editor Akron Beacon Jour., 1993-99; editor Denver Post, 1999—2002.

GWADOSKY, DAN A. secretary of state; b. Fairfield, Maine, Feb. 16, 1954; m. Cheryl Norton; children: Joshua, Jessica. BS in Mgmt., LHD (hon.), Thomas Coll. Mem. Maine Ho. of Reps., Augusta, 1978-96, asst. majority floor leader, house majority leader, 1988-94; spkr. Maine Ho. Reps., 1994-96; sec. of state State of Maine, Augusta, 1997—. Adminstr. Atrium Hotels Corp., 1985—. Mem. adv. bd. Kennebec Valley Vocat. Tech. Coll., State YMCA; bd. trustees Thomas Coll.; bd. dirs. State Leaders Found.; mem. exec. com. Coun. of State Govts.; co-chair Fairfield Cmty. Fest; co-chair bldg. com. Lawrence Pub. Libr.; active Lawrence HS Alumni Assn., Booster Club; coach boys and girls baseball, soccer, and basketball teams. Democrat. Home: 12 Mckenzie Ave Fairfield ME 04937-3341 Office: Nash Bldg 148 State House Sta Augusta ME 04333-0148 E-mail: sos.office@state.me.us.*

GWALLA-OGISI, NOMSA, education educator, consultant; b. Greytown, South Africa, Feb. 21, 1952; arrived in U.S., 1972; d. Johannes Peter and Clarice Thoko Gwalla; 1 child, Sbusiso Jube Ogisi. BA, Univ. Zululand, Empangeri, South Africa, 1973; MSED, So. Ill. Univ., Ewardsville, Ill., 1975, PhD, 1980. Divsn chair devel. of spl. edn. Univ. Zululand, South Africa, chair and sch. guidance dept.; asst. prof. Mo. Valley Coll., Marshall, Mo., Ind. State Univ., Terre Haute, Ind., 1987—88; assoc. prof. Univ. Wis., Whitewater, Wis., 1988—. Contbr. articles to numerous profl. jour., scientific papers to numerous confs. and profl. jour., chapters to books. Fund raiser YMCA, 1979. Mem.: Internat. for Spl. Edn., Coun. for Exceptional Children Internat., Coun. for Children with Behavior Disorders, Phi Delta Kappa. Avocations: tennis, racquetball, flower arranging, gardening. Home: 1298 W Ct St PO Box 551 Whitewater WI 53190 Office: Spl Edn Dept Univ Wis 800 W Main St Whitewater WI 53190

GWALTNEY, CORBIN, editor, publishing executive; b. Balt., Apr. 16, 1922; s. Howell Corbin and Margaret (Bell) G.; m. Doris Jean Kell, July 13, 1946 (dec.); children: Margaret Kell, Jean Corbin, Thomas Stewart; m. Jean Caryl Wyckoff, June 20, 1973 (dec.). BA, Johns Hopkins U., 1943; LHD (hon.), L.I. U., 1970; DHL (hon.), Johns Hopkins U., 1998. Instr., English Johns Hopkins U., 1946; with indsl. relations dept. Western Electric Co. and Locke div. Gen. Electric Co., 1946-49; editor Johns Hopkins Mag., 1949-59; editor, exec. dir., chmn. Editorial Projects for Edn., Inc., Balt. and Washington, 1959-78; exec. editor Chronicle Higher Edn., Washington, 1966-2000, chmn., 2000—; exec. editor Chronicle of Philanthropy, 1988—, chmn., 2000—. Served with AUS, 1943-45. Recipient Robert Sibley award Am. Alumni Council, 1951, 56, 59, Disting. Service to Higher Edn. awards Columbia U. Alumni Fedn., 1964, Disting. Service to Higher Edn. awards Am. Coll. Public Relations Assn., 1971; George Polk award for edn. reporting, 1979 Home: 5104 Brookview Dr Bethesda MD 20816-1602 also: 4755 Bayfields Rd Harwood MD 20776-9576 Office: Chronicle Higher Edn 1255 23rd St NW Ste 700 Washington DC 20037-1146 E-mail: corbin@chronicle.com.

GWALTNEY, THOMAS MARION, education educator, writer; b. Sikeston, Mo., Sept. 17, 1935; s. Thomas Marion and Niva (Kem) G.; m. Dolores Doreen Barrow, Dec. 23, 1962; children: Anne Elise, Karen Lee Gwaltney Holder, Kristen Diane. BS, S.E. Mo. State U., 1957; MS, So. Ill. U., 1959, PhD, 1963; BA, Ea. Mich. U., 1979; postgrad., U. Mich., Harvard U. Cert. elem. and secondary tchr. Mich., humanities profl. Mich. Tchr. Wyatt (Mo.) Elem. Sch., 1955-56; jr. high tchr. Scott County Sch. Dist., Sikeston, 1957-58, elem. supr. Benton, 1958-60; vis. lectr. So. Ill. U., Carbondale, 1960-63; asst. prof. edn. No. Mich. U., Marquette, 1963-64; prof. Ea. Mich. U., Ypsilanti, 1964—, assoc. dean grad. sch., 1989-90, honors advisor, 1984—, cons., 1986—, coord. grad. advising, 1992—, coord. social founds. program, 1995-96, 2002—03. Ednl. cons. Computing and Ednl. System, Dallas, 1969-70, World Coll., 1986, cons., 1987-89; vis. prof. U. Autónoma Met., Mexico City, 1990—, sr. Fulbright lectr., rschr., 1990-91; vis. prof. sch. langs. and sch. sociology U. Autónoma de Querètaro, Mex., 1994; mem. Fulbright Selection Com., U.S. Embassy, Mex. City, 1990-91; rschr., tchr. edn. U.S., Russia, 1991-93; vice chair Collegium for Advanced Studies, 1992-93, chair, 1993-95, bd. dirs., 1995—; vis. prof. Escuela de Idiomas U. Autónoma de Querètaro, Mex., 1993; cons. Field-Intensive Tchr. Tng. Bilingual Program, 1988—; cons. rschr. and supr. bilingual edn. spl. transition project Ea. Mich. U., Farmington Pub. Schs., U.S. Dept. Edn., 1993-94; invited lectr. (in Spanish) Fundación Gran Mariscal Ayachucho, Venezuela, 1994; vis. prof. Escuela de Idiomas and Escuela Sociology, 1994; mem. Fulbright Commn. on the Environ., 2001—; presenter in field Author: EDUSIM: Educational Simulation, 1972, Teaching Cultural Foundations, Handbook for Freshman, 1979; editor: Orientation Course, 1984, Teacher and Educational Foundations; book reviewer Houghton Mifflin Co., 1994-95; contbg. poet: Amidst the Splendor, 1996; contbr. articles to profl. jours. Active desegregation bd. Ypsilanti Pub. Schs., 1975-76, campaign organizer, 1983-84; cons. Latin-Am. Initiative, 1989-90. Recipient Disting. Faculty award Ea. Mich. U., 1984-87, award Collegium for Advanced Studies, 1986—, Excellence in Higher Edn. Tchg. award State of Mich., 1990, Alumni Assn. Excellence in Teaching award Ea. Mich. U., 1993, Excellence award Mich. Assn. Governing Bds., 1996, alumni merit award Southeast Mo. State U., 1999. Mem.: AAUW, Mich. Directories of Humanities Profls., Soc. Profl. of Edn., Mich. Assn. Bilingual. Edn. Advocates, Mich. Assn. Bilingual Edn., Mich. Assn. Staff Devel. and Sch. Improvement (exec. bd. 1992—), Coun. Grad. Schs., Spanish and Portuguese, Am. Edn. Studies Assn., Am. Assn. Tchrs., Southea. Mich. Fulbright Assn. (bd. dirs. 1993—2000, treas. 1999—, mem. Fulbright commn. of environ. 2001—, Tech. award Renaissance Group 2000—), Fulbright Assn. on the Environment, Fulbright Assn., Mich. One Rm. Sch. Assn. (exec. bd. 1993—, 2002—, trustee), Hist. Soc. Mich., Mich. Ethnic Heritage Found., Detroit Inst. Arts (founder's soc. 1982—), Internat. Assn. Poets (disting.), Kappa Delta Pi (Mich. area rep. 1990—, internat. com. 1992—, Latin Am. rep. 1992—, co-founder 1st Latin Am. chpt. in Mex. 1994, Queré taro Quo Mex. chpt. 1994, installing officer 1994, internat. constn. and bylaws com. 1994—, lectr. internat. convocation 1995, Honor Key 1992, Outstanding Counselor award 1998—2000), Phi Kappa Phi, Phi Delta Kappa. Baptist. Avocations: photography, writing, bicycling, walking, reading. Home: 6154 Eagle Trace Dr Ypsilanti MI 48197-6223 Office: Ea Mich U Dept Tchr Edn 313 W Porter Bldg Ypsilanti MI 48197-2210 E-mail: Thomas.Gwaltney@emich.edu.

GWARTNEY, PATRICIA ANNE, sociology educator; b. Glendale, Calif., Mar. 30, 1951; d. Robert Alan and Marilyn Arline (Sanborn) G.; m. Stanley Morshead Gibbs, July 31, 1971 (div. Feb. 1994); children: Loren, Spencer; m. George Gordon Goldthwaite Jr., Apr. 29, 1995; children: Emily Eleanor, Lisa Margaret, Adam Michael. AB, U. Calif., Berkeley, 1973; MA, U. Mich., 1979, PhD, 1981. Asst. prof. U. Oreg., Eugene, 1981-88, assoc. prof., 1988-96, prof. sociology, 1996—, affiliate Ctr. for Study of Women in Soc., 1984—, founding dir. Oreg. Survey Rsch. Lab., 1992—. Contbr. articles to profl. publs.; editl. bd. Jour. Marriage and the Family, 1995-97. Cons. Task Force on Gender Fairness Oreg. Supreme Ct., 1996-98. Fulbright fellow U. Auckland, New Zealand, 1986. Mem. AAAS, AAUP, Am. Sociol. Assn., Pacific Sociol. Assn. (coun.), Population Assn. Am., Am. Assn. Pub. Opinion Rsch. Democrat. Congregationalist. Home: 2875 Spring Blvd Eugene OR 97403-2510 Office: U Oreg Dept Sociology Eugene OR 97403-1291 E-mail: pattygg@oregon.uoregon.edu.

GWATHMEY, CHARLES, architect; b. Charlotte, N.C., June 19, 1938; s. Robert and Rosalie Dean (Hook) G.; m. Bette-Ann Damson, Dec. 15, 1974. Student, U. Pa., 1956-59; M.Arch., Yale U., 1962. Partner firm Gwathmey-Siegel and Assocs. Architects, N.Y.C., 1971—. Vis. prof. archtl. design Pratt Inst., Yale U., Princeton U., Harvard U., Columbia U., Cooper Union, UCLA. Pres. bd. trustees Inst. Architecture and Urban Studies, N.Y.C., 1978. Recipient Arnold Brunner prize AAAL, 1970; William Wirt Winchester traveling fellow, 1962-63; Fulbright grantee France, 1962-63; recipient AIA Nat. Honor awards for Straus residence, Purchase, N.Y., 1969, Whig Hall, Princeton U., 1976, Dormitory, Dining and Student Union SUNY, Purchase 1976, Taft Residence, Cin., 1984, Westover Sch., Middlebury, Conn., 1988, AIA N.Y. awards for Sch. Agr. Cornell U., 1991, Guggenheim Mus., N.Y.C., 1995, Yale Arts award for outstanding achievement, 1985, Lifetime Achievement medal in visual arts Guild Hall Acad., 1988, Lifetime Achievement award N.Y. State Assn. Archs., 1990. Fellow AIA (firm award 1982, Medal of honor 1983); mem. Am. Acad. Arts and Letters. Office: Gwathmey Siegel & Assoc Arch 475 10th Ave 3d Fl New York NY 10018-1198 E-mail: c.gwathmey@gwathmeysiegel.com.

GWATHMEY, JOE NEIL, JR., broadcasting executive; b. Brownwood, Tex., Jan. 4, 1941; s. Joe Neil and Grace Christine (Henry) G.; m. Linda Sue Sams, Aug. 22, 1965; children: Sara Lynn, David Alan. BA, Howard Payne Coll., 1963; postgrad., U. Denver, 1963-64, George Washington U., 1964-65. Sta. mgr. Sta. KUT-FM, Austin, 1965-71; various mgmt. positions Nat. Pub. Radio, Washington, 1971-83, v.p., 1983-88; pres. Tex. Pub. Radio, San Antonio, 1988—. Review panel chair United Way Bexar County, San Antonio, 1994-97; adv. coun. mem. Coll. Fine Arts Univ. Tex., Austin, 1990-93; trustee Tex. Student Publs., Austin, 1995-98, World Affairs Coun., San Antonio, 1999—; bd. adv. N.Y. Festivals, 1986—. Recipient Edward R. Murrow award Corp. Pub. Broadcasting, 1988. Mem. Rotary. Democrat. Protestant. Avocations: singing, acting, public speaking, reading. Home: 2926 Meadow Cir San Antonio TX 78231-1720 Office: Tex Pub Radio 8401 Datapoint Dr Ste 800 San Antonio TX 78229-5903

GWAZDAUSKAS, FRANCIS CHARLES, animal science educator, dairy scientist; b. Waterbury, Conn., July 25, 1943; s. Francis Julian (dec.) and Agnes Eva Gwazdauskas; m. Judy Keller, Mar. 20, 1971; children: Jennifer, James (dec.), John, Peter. BS in Animal Sci., U. Conn., 1966; MS in Dairy Sci., U. Fla., 1972, PhD in Animal Sci., 1974. Asst. prof. dairy sci. Va. Polytechnic Inst. and State U., Blacksburg, 1974-80, assoc. prof. dairy sci., 1980-86, prof. dairy sci., 1986—. Cons. PPL (Pharm. Proteins Ltd.), Blacksburg, 1992-97. Contbr. articles to profl. jours. Treas. Blacksburg High Athletic Boosters, 1990—. Sgt. U.S. Army, 1967-68, Vietnam. Recipient award for rsch. excellence Va. Poly. Inst. and State U. Alumni Assn., 1995, David R. and Magaret Lincicome endowed professorship, 1996, Pharmacia/Upjohn Physiology Rsch. award Am. Dairy Sci. Assn., 1996, Gamma Sigma Delta Rsch. award, 1998. Avocation: golf. Office: Va Polytechnic Inst State U Dept Dairy Sci Blacksburg VA 24061-0315 E-mail: guaz@vt.edu.

GWIAZDA, STANLEY JOHN, retired university dean; b. Phila., Feb. 14, 1922; s. Nicholas and Pauline (Stanczak) G.; m. Regina R. Grzeskowiak, Nov. 26, 1944; 1 dau., Marianne C. BS in Mech. Engring., Drexel Inst. Tech., 1944, MS, 1952. Mem. faculty Drexel U., 1946-87, assoc. prof. mech. engring., 1952-87, dean evening coll., 1963-87, assoc. prof. emeritus mech. engring., dean emeritus evening coll., 1987—97; ret., 1997. Bd. dirs. Phila. Govt. Tng. Inst.; mem. pres.'s coun. Holy Family Coll., 1984-89, acad. affairs com., 1989-2002. Author: (with J. H. Billings) Advanced Machine Design, 1958. Lt. (j.g.) USNR, 1944-46, PTO; lt. comdr. Res. ret. Stanley Gwiazda Professorship named in his honor Drexel U., recipient Vol. Svc. award Holy Family Coll., 1994. Mem. Assn. Univ. Evening Colls. (chmn. com. on faculty devel. 1971-72), Am. Soc. Engring. Edn., Assn. Continuing Higher Edn. (dir. 1976-79, chmn. ethics com. 1979-83, pres. 1985-86, chmn. adv. com. 1986-87, Educator of Yr. award Region IV 1991), Res. Officers Assn. (pres. N.J. dept. 1973-74), Naval Res. Assn., Ret. Officers Assn., Cross Keys, Pi Tau Sigma, Alpha Sigma Lambda (assoc. dir. adult edn. found. 1984-90, bd. dirs. 1990-2002, Alpha Sigma Lambda Leadership award in Adult Edn. 1986). Roman Catholic. Home: 2001 Wayne Ave Haddon Heights NJ 08035-1036

GWIN, JAMES ELLSWORTH, librarian; b. Chattanooga, Mar. 1, 1947; s. Madison Taylor and Juanita Elizabeth (Wallace) G.; m. Sheena Margaret Mackenzie, Oct. 5, 1985; children; Colleen Mackenzie, Elizabeth Maureen. AB, U. Tenn., 1969; M Library, Emory U., 1970; MPA, Va. Commonwealth U., 1984. Instr., cataloger U. Chattanooga, 1970; asst. prof., asst. head U. Tenn., Chattanooga, 1972-75; head bibliographic svc. U. Richmond, Va., 1975-85, acting univ. librarian, 1985-86, acting dir. LRC, 1986, dir. tech. svc., 1987-99, acting univ. libr., 1990-91, 96-98, dir. libr. collections/spl. collections and rare books, 2000—. Adj. prof. Cath. U. Am., 1994—. Editor Terminal Talk, 1980-81. Dir. Cen. Va. Union List of Serials Project, 1990—. 1st lt. U.S. Army, 1971-72. Lyndhurst Found. grantee, Chattanooga, 1974-75. Mem. ALA, Am. Soc. Pub. Adminstrn., Assn. Coll./Rsch. Libraries (chmn. Va. chpt. 1986), Va. Libr. Assn. (2d v.p. 1992-93), Phi Kappa Phi, Pi Alpha Alpha. Democrat. Episcopalian. Home: 1506 Palmyra Ave Richmond VA 23227-4422 Office: U Richmond Boatwright Meml Libr Richmond VA 23173 E-mail: jgwin@richmond.edu.

GWIN, JOHN MICHAEL, emeritus educator, consultant; b. Montgomery, Ala., June 21, 1949; s. Emmett Brindley Jr. and Irma Rebecca (Watkins) G.; m. Pamela Jane Blair, Sept. 7, 1970 (dec. Dec. 1998); children: Colin Blair, Connor Brindley. BBA, Auburn U., 1971; MBA, U. Ga., 1973; PhD, U. N.C., 1979. Fiscal officer U. Ga., Athens, 1971-73; ops. mgr. Bedsole & Gwin Inc., Fairhope, Ala., 1973-75; instr. Faulkner Coll., Bay Minette, Ala., 1975-76; rsch. asst. U. N.C., Chapel Hill, 1976-78, vis. lectr., 1978-79; asst. prof. Ind. U., Bloomington, 1979-81, U. Va., Charlottesville, 1981-83, assoc. prof., 1983-2000, mktg. area coord., 1990-93, dir. Ctr. for Entrepreneurial Studies, 1992-96, prof. emeritus, 2000—; mng. dir. QuixCinch, Inc. Fulbright prof. Trinity Coll., Dublin, Ireland, 1986-87;, vis. prof., 1993; exec. educator numerous U.S. firms, 1981—; cons. numerous internat. and U.S. firms, 1983—; invited lectr. Sorbonne, U. Paris, Alsace Inst., Strasbourg, France, 1987. Inventor LaMaze Timer and audio text. Sesquicentennial Research Assoc., U. Va., 1986-87, 93-94; named Outstanding Young Man Am., U.S. Jr. C. of C., 1976. Mem. Am. Counseling Assn., Am. Psychol. Assn., Am. Mktg. Assn. (conf. coord. Cen. Va. chpt. 1986), Am. Personal Contsct Assn., Am. Soc. Bus. & Behavioral Studies, So. Mktg. Assn., Acad. Mktg. Sci. Episcopalian. Avocations: fiction writing, golf, sailing, blue-water fishing. Home: 8 Rolling Oaks Dr Fairhope AL 36532-3060 E-mail: jgwin621@aol.com., jmg4z@virginia.edu.

GWINN, MARY ANN, newspaper reporter; b. Forrest City, Ark., Dec. 29, 1951; d. Lawrence Baird and Frances Evelyn (Jones) Gwinn; m. Richard A. King, June 3, 1973 (div. Jan. 1981); m. Stephen E. Dunnington, June 10, 1990. BA in Psychology, Hendrix Coll., 1973; MEd in Spl. Edn., Ga. State U., 1975; MA in Journalism, U. Mo., 1979. Tchrs. aide DeKalb County Schs., Decatur, Ga., 1973—74, tchr., 1975—78; reporter Columbia (Mo.) Daily Tribune, 1979—83, Seattle Times, 1983—, internat. trade and workplace reporter, 1992—96, asst. city editor, 1996—98, book editor, 1998—. Instr. ext. divsn. U. Wash., Seattle, 1990; instr. journalism Seattle U., 1994. Recipient Edn. Reporting award, Charles Stewart Mott Found., 1980, Enterprising reporting award, C.B. Blethen Family, 1989, Pulitzer Prize for Nat. Reporting, 1990. Mem.: Newspaper Guild. Avocations: writing, gardening, reading, camping. Office: Seattle Times PO Box 70 Seattle WA 98111-0070

GWINN, MARY DOLORES, business developer, organizational theorist, philosopher, writer, speaker; b. Oakland, Calif., Sept. 16, 1946; d. Epifanio and Carolina (Lopez) Cruz; m. James Monroe Gwinn, Oct. 23, 1965; 1 child, Larry Allen. Student, Monterey Peninsula Jr. Coll., 1965. Retail store mgr. Consumer's Distbg. divsn. May Co., Hayward, Calif., 1973-78; mktg. rep. Dale Carnegie Courses, San Jose, Calif., 1978-79; founder, pres. Strategic Integrations, Ariz.'s Innovative Bus. Devel. Ctr., Scottsdale, 1985—, Gwinn Genius Inst., Scottsdale, 1998—. Speaker St. John's Coll. U. Cambridge, England, 1992, INC. Mag., U.S.A., 1996, Clemson Univ., 1996, Antelope Valley Coll., Lancaster, Calif., 1998; founder, pres. Internat. Inst. for Conceptual Edn., Scottsdale, 1993—; chairperson Keble Coll., Oxford (Eng.) U., 1997; spkr. Willard Internat. Hotel, Washington, 2000. Founder new fields of study Genestics and NeuroBus.; profiled the Thought Process of Genius; conceived Whole Brain Business Theory, 1985; author: Genius Leadership Secrets from the Past for the 21st Century, 1995; writer bus. column Gwinn on Bus., IMAGE Networker, Pa., 1996; contbr. articles to profl. jours. Chairperson Keble Coll., Oxford (Eng.) U. Republican. Avocations: reading, imagination games, playing with grandchildren. Home and Office: 5836 E Angela Dr Scottsdale AZ 85254-6410

GWINN, ROBERT P. publishing executive; b. Anderson, Ind., June 30, 1907; s. Marshall and Margaret (Cather) G.; m. Nancy Flanders, Jan. 20, 1942 (dec. 1989); 1 child, Richard Herbert. PhB, U. Chgo., 1929. With Sunbeam Corp., Chgo., 1936-51, gen. sales mgr. elec. appliance div., 1951-52, v.p., dir., 1952-55, pres., chief exec. officer, 1955-71, chmn. bd., chief exec. officer, 1971-82, also bd. dirs.; chmn. bd., chief exec. officer Ency. Britannica, Inc., Chgo., 1973-93, chmn. emeritus, 1993—. Chmn. bd., CEO Titan Oil Co., Riverside; bd. dirs. Continental Assurance Co., Continental Casualty Co., CNA/Fin. Corp., Inst. for Philos. Rsch., Alberto-Culver Corp. Trustee Chgo. Zool. Soc., U. Chgo.; mem. Citizens Adv. Com., Chgo.; bd. fellows Harvard Med. Sch., James Madison Coun., Libr. of Congress. Mem. Soc. Chgo., Internat. Food and Wine Soc. Chgo., Mid. Am. Club, Elec. Mfrs. Club (hon.), Comml. Club Chgo., Casino Club, Execs. Club, Bird Key Yacht Club, Riverside Golf Club, U. Chgo. Club, Alpha Sigma Phi.

GWYNN, ANTHONY KEITH (TONY GWYNN), former professional baseball player; b. L.A., May 9, 1960; m. Alicia Gwynn; children: Anthony, Anisha Nicole. Student, San Diego State U. Player minor league teams, Walla Walla and Amarillo, Hawaii, 1981—82; outfielder San Diego Padres, 1982—2001. Named MVP, N.W. League, 1981; named to All-Star Team, 1984—87, Silver Slugger Team, Sporting News Nat. League, 1984, All-Star Team, 1984; recipient Batting Title award, Nat. League, 1984, 1987, 1988, 1989, 1995, Gold Glove award, 1986—87, 1989—91, All-Star Team, 1989—96, Silver Slugger Team, Sporting News Nat. League, 1986—87, 1989—91, All-Star Team, 1986—87, 1986—87, 1989, 1994. Office: San Diego Padres Qualcomm Stadium PO Box 2000 San Diego CA 92112-2000

GWYTHER, ROBERT EDWIN, physician, consultant; b. Evansville, Ind., Aug. 15, 1944; s. Robert Edwin and Ruth Marguerite Gwyther; m. Lisa Pepper, June 25, 1967; children: Marni Gwyther Holder, Ryan Reiff. BA, Adelbert Coll., Western Res. U., 1962—66; MBA, Case Western Res. U., 1966—68; MD, Med. Coll. of Ohio, 1975—78. Diplomate Am. Bd. of Family Practice, 1978, Cert. Am. Soc. of Addiction Medicine, 1994. Prof, UNC Sch. of Medicine, Dept. of Family Medicine, Chapel Hill, NC, 1994—; dir. of med. student programs UNC Dept. of Family Medicine, Chapel Hill, NC, 1996—. Pres. NC Acad. of Family Physicians, Raleigh, NC, 2001—02. Lt. (jr. grade) U.S. Coast Guard, 1968—72, U.S. Coast Guard Acad. New London Conn. Recipient Alpha Omega Alpha, UNC Chpt., 2002, Beta Gamma Sigma, Case Western Res. Chpt., 1968. Mem.: Assn. for Med. Edn. and Rsch. in Substance Abuse, NC Soc. of Addiction Medicine (secretary-treasurer 1994—95), Am. Soc. of Addiction Medicine, NC Acad. of Family Physicians (pres. 2001—02), Am. Acad. of Family Physicians.

GYAMFI, PHYLLIS, research scientist, researcher; b. Wurzburg, Germany, Apr. 20, 1968; d. Anthony and Mary Gyamfi; m. McGregor Ottley. BA, U. Miami, 1990; MA, Columbia University, 1995, PhD, 2001. Grad. rsch. fellow Ctr. Children and Families, N.Y., NY, 1995—2001; rsch. scientist ORC Macro, Atlanta, 2001—. Intern grad. rsch. Ednl. Testing Svc., Princeton, NJ, 1998. Recipient Outstanding Rsch. award, Soc. Social Work Rsch., 2000, 1st place winner grad. rsch. paper competition, APA, 1999, Dissertation Fellowship award, Woodrow Wilson Nat. Fellowship Found., 2001; fellow pre-doctoral fellow, Ednl. Testing Svc., 1998. Mem.: Soc. Rsch. in Child Devel. Office: ORC Macro 3 Corporate Sq NE Ste 370 Atlanta GA 30329 E-mail: phyllis.gyamfi@orcmacro.com.

GYEKENYESI, ANDREW, mechanical engineer; DEng, Cleve. State U., 1997. Resident rsch. scientist OAI/NASA Glenn Rsch. Ctr., Cleve., 1993—, tech. lead nondestructive evaluation. Organizer, chair internat. sci. confs. Contbr. articles to profl. jours.; editor: Proceedings of SPIE: NDE and Health Monitoring of Aerospace Materials and Composites, 2003, Proceedings of SPIE: Nondestructive Evaluation and Health Monitoring of Aerospace Materials and Civil Infrastructures, 2002. Mem.: ASME, Am. Soc. Nondestructive Testing.

GYEKENYESI, JOHN PAUL, mechanical engineer; b. Nagykanizsa, Hungary, May 16, 1938; came to U.S., 1951; s. George Laszlo and Katherine (Korcsmar) G.; m. Erika Eva Sari, June 17, 1961; children: John, Thomas, Andrew. BSME, Case Inst. Tech., 1961, MSME, 1966; PhD in Mechanics, Mich. State U., 1972. Registered profl. engr., Ohio. Test engr. Ohio Crankshaft Co., Cleve., 1961-62; design engr. NASA-Lewis Rsch. Ctr., Cleve., 1962-72, rsch. engr., 1972-82, sr. scientist structures, 1982-85, rsch. mgr. structures, 1985-99, NASA-Glenn Rsch. Ctr., Cleve., 1999—. Cons. in structures Sari Corp., Cleve., 1978-90. Contbr. over 70 articles to profl. jours., chpts. to books. Pres. Ohio Soccer Assn., Cleve., 1992—. Recipient Yr.'s Best Paper in Structures award NASA, 1986, 91, Software of Yr. award NASA, 1994, Excellence in Tech. Transfer award Consortium of Fed. Labs., 1994, R&D 100 award, 1995, Excellence in Engring. award NASA, 1996, Turning Goals into Reality award NASA, 2000. Mem. ASME (ceramics com. 1990—, Best Paper in Ceramics award 1987, 97, EDI Tech. Innovation award 1998), ASTM (ceramics com. 1985—), Am. Ceramic Soc. (structural ceramics 1987—), ASM Internat. Roman Catholic. Achievements include development of computational techniques by applying the method-of-lines in analytical fracture mechanics to obtain new solutions to 3-D crack problems; first to devel. gen. purpose ceramic component life prediction software (CARES); rsch. in failure mechanisms in ceramic matrix composites. Office: NASA Glenn Rsch Ctr 21000 Brookpark Rd Cleveland OH 44135-3191 E-mail: John.P.Gyekenyesi@grc.nasa.gov.

GYEMANT, ROBERT ERNEST, diversified financial services company executive, merchant; b. Managua, Nicaragua, Jan. 17, 1944; arrived in U.S., 1949, naturalized, 1954; s. Emery Gyemanat and Magda (Von Rechnitz) Gyemant; m. Sally Bartch Libhart, Oct. 17, 1992; children: Emily Bartch, Amanda Nancy, Katherine Libhart;children from previous marriage: Robert Ernest Jr., Anne Elizabeth. AB magna cum laude, UCLA, 1965; JD, U. Calif., Berkeley, 1968. CPA Calif.; bar: Calif. 1969, NY 1981. Tax acct. Ernst & Ernst, CPAs, Oakland, Calif., 1966—68; assoc. atty. Orrick, Herrington, Rowley & Sutcliffe, San Francisco, 1968—69; ptnr. law firm Skornia, Rosenblum & Gyemant, San Francisco, 1969—74, law offices Robert Ernest Gyemant profl. corp., San Francisco, 1975; exec. v.p. fin. Topps & Trowsers, San Francisco, 1977—79; cons., pvt. investor, 1979; with ComDial Corp., San Francisco; co-founder Com Vu Corp., N.Y.C., 1979—83, San Francisco, 1993—97; prin. Knapp, Petersen & Clarke, P.C., Glendale, Calif., 1997—99, Hill, Farrer & Burrill, LLP, L.A., 1999—2000; mng. dir. Trinity River Capital Ventures, LLC; pres. Trioindustries Holdings, LLC. Instr. U. Calif., Berkeley, 1968. Editor: Calif. Law Rev., 1967—68; author: publs. in field. Hon. vice consul Republic of Costa Rica, 1981—; trustee French-Am. Bilingual Sch., San Francisco, 1978—82; mem., prin. Calif. Council Criminal Justice Jud. Process Task Force, 1971—73; mem. Calif. State Rep. Ctrl. Com. Mem.: AICPA, ABA, Calif. Trial Lawyers Assn., Assn. Def. Counsel, Calif. CPA Soc. (mem. accounting prins. com. 1969), State Bar Calif. (cert. specialist criminal law 1988—93, com. on unauthorized practice law 1974—76, spl. com. on juvenile justice 1974, commr. San Francisco County juvenile justice comm. 1976—), San Francisco Bar Assn. (co-chmn. sect. on juvenile justice 1971), San Francisco Downtown Assn., Racquet and Tennis Club, N.Y. Athletic Club (N.Y.C.), Brook Haven Country Club. Office: 8411 Preston Rd #850 Dallas TX 75225 E-mail: rgyemant@TRCVentures.com.

GYENES, GABOR, physician, educator; b. Budapest, Dec. 14, 1959; s. George and Marianne (Ferenczi) G.; m. Erika Müllner, July 13, 1991; children: Balázs, Dóra. MD, Semmelweis U. Med. Sch., Budapest, Hungary, 1984; postgrad., Karolinska Inst., Stockholm, 1994-97. Asst. prof. 3rd Dept Med. Semmelweis Med. U., 1984-98; clin. fellow adult cardiology U. Toronto, Ont., Can., 1998-2001; asst. prof. divsn. cardiology U. Alta., Edmonton, Can., 2001—. Author: Pharmindex Kompendium, 1995, Hypertension: Data and Facts, 1997, Handbook of Coronary Angiography and Angioplasty, 2001; editor: Cardiology, 2000, Melania Pub. Ltd., Budapest. Sgt. Hungarian Army, 1985-86. Recipient Eminent Young Scientist award Internat. Rsch. Promotion Coun., 2000. Mem. Hungarian Soc. of Cardiology, Hungarian Soc. Internal Medicine, Can. Cardiovascular Soc. Avocations: rock and classical music, tennis, soccer. Office: U Alta Walter Mackenzie Health Ctr 2C2 Edmonton AB Canada T6G 2B7 E-mail: gyenesgabor@hotmail.com., ggyenes@CHA.AB.CA.

GYLES, MARY FRANCIS, retired history educator; b. Blackville, S.C., Dec. 24, 1918; d. Ronald Corbin and Valeria (Gyles) G. BA, U.N.C., Greensboro, 1939; MA, U. N.C., Chapel Hill, 1945, PhD, 1949. Asst. prof. Memphis State U., 1949-57; asst. prof. ancient and medieval history Bklyn. Coll., CUNY, 1957-63, assoc. prof., 1963-65, prof., 1965-79, prof. emerita, 1979—, chmn. dept. history, 1963-70; part-time instr. U. S.C., Aiken, 1981-91. Author: (essays in ancient history) Laudatores Temporis Acti, 1964, (with Caldwell) The Ancient World, 1966, Public Gardens of South Carolina 1999-2000, 2001. Chmn. Garden Club S.C., Columbia, 1989—, bd. dirs., chmn. hist. trails 1998-99, chmn. hort. 1997-99, chmn. botanic gardens 1999—, columnist, writer S.C. Gardener, 1995—; master flower show judge Nat. Garden Clubs, St. Louis, 1985—. Recipient Pres.'s citation Garden Club S.C., 1997, also Dir.'s award, Helen S. Hull plaque Nat. Garden Club, Inc., 2003, Literary Horticulture

Interest award, Nat. Garden Club, 2003. Mem. Judges Club S.C. (2d v.p. 1999—, ednl. displayer), DIA Study Club (pres. 2002-03), Phi Beta Kappa, Phi Alpha Theta. Democrat. Episcopalian. Avocations: reading, writing, gardening, travel.

GYLL, JOHN SÖREN, company executive; b. Skorped, Västernorrland, Sweden, Dec. 26, 1940; s. Josef and Gertrud G.; m. Lilly Margareta Hellman, 1974; 3 children. Higher cert. exam. and univ. degrees. Mktg. mgr., v.p. Rank-Xerox AB, 1963-77; pres. Uddeholm-Sweden, 1977-79, exec. v.p., 1979-81; pres., CEO Uddelholm-Sweden, 1981-84; CEO Procordia AB, Stockholm, 1984-92, AB Volvo, Göteborg, Sweden, 1992-97. Bd. dirs. SCA AB, Skanska AB, SKF AB. Mem.: Confedn. of Swedish Enterprise (chmn.), Royal Swedish Acad. Engring. Scis. Avocations: hunting, golf, skiing. Office: H&B Advisors AB Riddargatan 23 SE-11457 Stockholm Sweden

GYLSETH, DORIS HANSON (DORIS LILLIAN GYLSETH), retired librarian; b. Helena, Mont., May 26, 1934; d. Richard E. and Lillie (Paula) Hanson; m. Arlie Albeck, Dec. 26, 1955 (div. Apr. 1964); m. Hermann M. Gylseth, Apr. 29, 1983 (dec. Aug. 1985). BS in Edn., Western Mont. Coll. Edn., 1958; MLS, U. Wash., 1961. Tchr. Helena Sch. Dist., 1955-56, Dillon (Mont.) Elem. Sch., 1957-59, Eltopia (Wash.) Unified Sch. Dist., 1959-60; sch. libr. Shoreline Sch. Dist., Seattle, 1960-64, Dept. of Def., Chateauroux, France, Hanau, Fed. Republic Germany, Tachikawa, Japan, 1964-68, Long Beach (Calif.) Unified Sch. Dist., 1968-70; br. libr. Long Beach Pub. Libr., 1970-74, coord. children's svcs., 1974-85; libr. Long Beach (Calif.) Unified Sch. Dist., 1986-94; realtor Century 21, All Pacific, 1994-96. Bd. dirs. Children's Svcs. divsn. Calif. Libr. Assn., 1985, Literary Guild of Orange County, 1993—; co-chmn. Long Beach Authors Festival, 1978-86; mem. planning coun. Third Pacific Rim Conf. on Children's Lit., UCLA, 1986. Mem.: So. Calif. Coun. on Lit. for Children and Young People (bd. dirs. 1974—88, pres. 1982—84), Men of Mystery, Lit. Guild of Orange County, Friends of Long Beach Pub. Libr. (bd. dirs. 1988—), Helen Fuller Cultural Carousel (bd. dirs. 1985—), Over-the-Hill Gang, Zonta (pres. 1978—80). Avocations: cats, traveling. Home: 5131 Kingscross Rd Westminster CA 92683-4832

GYOHTEN, TOYOO, economist; b. Yokohama, Japan, 1931; married; 2 children. BA in Econs., U. Tokyo, 1955; postgrad., Princeton U., U.S.A., 1956-58. With Ministry Fin., Tokyo, 1955-89, Japan Desk, Internat. Monetary Fund, Washington, 1964-66; spl. asst. to pres. Asian Devel. Bank, Manila, Philippines, 1966-69; dir. gen. Internat. Fin. Bur., Ministry of Fin., Tokyo, 1984-86; vice min. fin. for internat. affairs Ministry of Fin., Tokyo, 1986-89; with The Bank of Tokyo, Ltd. (merged with Mitsubishi Bank Ltd.), Tokyo, 1991—; chmn. bd. dirs. The Bank of Tokyo, Ltd., Tokyo, 1992-96; sr. advisor The Bank of Tokyo-Mitsubishi, Ltd., 1996—; spl. advisor to Prime Minister of Japan, 1998. Pres. Inst. for Internat. Monetary Affairs, 1995—; chmn. working party III OECD, Paris, 1988-90; vis. prof. Harvard U., 1990, Princeton U., 1990-91, U. St. Gallen, Switzerland, 1991; trustee Princeton in Asia, N.J.; mem. adv. panel East African Devel. Bank, Uganda, Asia Pacific Adv. Comm., N.Y. Stock Exch.; mem. exec. com. Trilateral Comm., N.Y., Paris, Tokyo; mem. internat. coun. The Asia Soc., N.Y., Group of Thirty, Washington. Co-author: (with Paul Volcker) Changing Fortunes, 1992. Office: Inst Internat Monetary Aff 1-3-2 Nihombashi-Hongokucho Chuo Tokyo 103-0021 Japan

GYORFI, JULIUS STEVEN, electrical engineer, researcher; BSEE, U. Toledo, 1993; MSEE, Northwestern U., 1996, PhD in Elec. Engring., 1998. Lic. profl. engr., Ill. Dept. Profl. Regulation. Sr. engr. Motorola, Inc., Libertyville, Ill., 1998—2000; staff engr. Motorola Labs, Schaumburg, Ill., 2000—02; sr. staff engr. Motorola Labs., Schaumburg, Ill. Contbr. articles to profl. jours. Recipient Nat. Coll. Engring. award, U.S. Achievement Acad., 1993; fellow Walter P. Murphy fellow, Northwestern U., 1993; scholar AEE scholar, Assn. Energy Engrs., 1991, Jesse W. and Leona Probst scholar, U. Toledo, 1991, Norma Richards scholar, 1991, AEE scholar, Assn. Energy Engrs., 1992, Norma Richards scholar, U. Toledo, 1992. Mem.: NSPE, IEEE, Ill. Soc. Profl. Engrs., Phi Kappa Phi, Phi Eta Sigma, Pi Mu Epsilon, Eta Kappa Nu, Tau Beta Pi. Office: Motorola Labs 1301 East Algonquin Rd Schaumburg IL 60196 Business E-Mail: Julius.Gyorfi@Motorola.com.

GYORGYEY, CLARA M. educator, writer; b. Budapest, Hungary, May 23, 1933; came to the U.S., 1957; d. Laszlo Takacs and Sarolta Mendel; m. Ferenc A. Gyorgyey, Feb. 20, 1960; children: Katalin, Maria. BA, U. Budapest, 1954; MA, Acad. Fgn. Langs., Budapest, 1956; MAT, Yale U., 1959. Master tchr. No. Haven H.S. for Yale Tchrs. Program, New Haven, 1960-89; assoc. dir. program for humanities in medicine Yale Med. Sch., New Haven, 1989—; lectr., instr. Yale U. Sch. Medicine, New Haven, 1989—. Author: Catsplay, 1976, Ferenc Molnar, 1980, With Arrogant Humility, 1987, Mirrors to the Cage, 1993; editor PEN's Quarterly Newsletter, 1982—, World Lit. Today Recipient Trans. award Nat. Endowment for Arts, 1986, Ady award Hungary PEN Club, 1992, Cross of the Order of Merit, Hungarian Govt., 1993; named Tchr. of Yr., State Conn., 1969; Rockefeller scholar, 1958-59, Fulbright scholar, 1989-90. Fellow Yale's Jonathan Edward Coll.; mem. Internat. PEN Club/Writers in Exile Ctr. (pres.), Writers' Union Hungary, Authors League/Dramatist Guild, Conn. Acad. Arts and Scis., Conn. Critics' Cir., elected mem. Hungarian Acad. Arts and Scis. Roman Catholic. Home: 42 Derby Ave Orange CT 06477 Fax: 203-397-5439. E-mail: gyorgyey@aol.com.

GYSBERS, NORMAN CHARLES, education educator; b. Waupun, Wis., Sept. 29, 1932; s. George S. and Mabel (Landaal) Gysbers; m. Mary Lou Ziegler, June 23, 1954 (dec. July 1997); children: David, Debra, Daniel; m. Barbara K. Townsend, May 12, 2001. AB, Hope Coll., 1954; MA, U. Mich., 1959, PhD, 1963. Tchr. Elem. and Jr. High Sch., Muskegon Heights, Mich., 1954-56; lectr. edn. U. Mich., 1962-63; prof. counseling psychology U. Mo., Columbia, 1963—. Cons. U.S. Office Edn.; mem. nat. adv. coms. ERIC Clearinghouses in Career Edn. and Counseling and Personnel Services; research and devel. com. for CEEB, Am. Insts. for Research Project on Career Decision Making, Comprehensive Career Edn. Model, TV Career Awareness Project KCET-TV, Los Angeles; dir. 10 nat. research projects and state projects in career devel.-guidance; Francqui prof. Universite Libre de Bruxelles. Editor: Vocat. Guidance Quar. 1962-70; (with L. Sunny Hansen) spl. issue Personnel and Guidance Jour., May 1975, Jour. Career Devel., 1979—, (with E. Moore and W. Miller) Developing Careers in the Elementary School, 1973, (with E. Moore and H. Drier) Career Guidance: Practices and Perspectives, 1973; author: (with E. Moore) Improving Guidance Programs, 1981, Designing Careers, 1984, (with E. Moore) Career Counseling, 1987, (with P. Henderson) Developing and Managing Your School Guidance Program, 1988, 3d edit., 2000, (with C. McDaniels) Counseling for Career Development, 1992, (with P. Henderson) Guidance Programs that Work, 1997, (with M. Heppner and J. Johnston) Career Counseling, 1998, 2d edit., 2003, (with P. Henderson) Leading and Managing Your School Guidance Program Staff, 1998, (with P. Henderson) Implementing Comprehensive School Guidance Programs, 2002; contbr. articles to profl. jours. and chpts. to textbooks. Elder Presbyn. Ch. Served with arty. U.S. Army, 1956-58. Recipient Am. Spirit award USAF, 1987. Mem.: ACA (pres. 1977—78, disting. profl. svc. award 1983), Internat. Assn. Ednl. and Vocat. Guidance, Mo. Guidance Assn. (outstanding svc. award 1978), Am. Vocat. Assn. (v.p. 1979—82, merit award guidance divsn. 1978), Am. Sch. Counselor Assn. (post-secondary sch. counselor of yr. 2001), Assn. for Counselor Edn. and Supervision, Nat. Career Devel. Assn. (pres. 1972—73, nat. merit award 1981, Eminent Career award 1989). Home: 4 Bingham Rd Columbia MO 65203 Office: U Mo 201 G Student Success Ctr Columbia MO 65211-6060 E-mail: gysbersn@missouri.edu.

GYURAS, BRIAN JOSEPH, music educator; b. Oregon, Ohio, Oct. 15, 1968; s. John Louis and Barbara Ann Gyuras. EdB with hons., U. of Toledo, 1992; MusM, Bowling Green (Ohio) State U., 1998. Cert. tchr. Ohio, 1998. Dir. of bands Clay HS Oreg. City Schs., Oregon, Ohio, 1999—; asst. dir. of bands Napoleon (Ohio) Area Schs., 1995—99; dir. of bands Edgerton (Ohio) Local Schs., 1994—95; grad. asst. Bowling Green (Ohio) State U. Scholar, Bowling Green State U., 1992—94. Mem.: Nat. Band Assn., Ohio Music Educators Assn. (licentiate), Kappa Kappa Psi (pres. 1990—92). Roman Catholic. Avocations: biking, travel, music.

GYURO, PAULA CANDICE, financial planner; b. Phillipsburg, N.J., May 23, 1947; d. Alfred Eugene Gyuro and Pauline Johanna (Tinnes) Caldwell. BA, Ohio Wesleyan U., 1969; MBA, Xavier U., 1984. Cert. fin. planner. Events coord. The Nestle Co., Marysville, Ohio, 1969-73; sr. technologist R&D The Kroger Co., Cin., 1973-88; personal fin. advisor Am. Express Fin. Advisors Inc., Cin., 1989—. Mem. Fin. Planning Assn., Greater Cin. chpt. Fin. Planning Assn. Office: Am Express Fin Advisors Inc 225 Pictoria Dr Ste 110 Cincinnati OH 45246-1614

HA, CHANG SIK, polymer science educator; b. Pusan, Korea, Jan. 30, 1956; s. Won Do and Bong Soon (Eh) H.; m. Sun Ja Han, Jan. 13, 1983; children: Ji Won, Ji Hyun, Jae Hun. BS, Pusan Nat. U., 1978; MS, Korea Adv. Inst. Sci. & Tech., Seoul, 1980, PhD, 1987. Engr. Lucky Chem. Co. Ltd., Pusan, 1982; from instr. to asst. prof. Pusan Nat. U., 1982-89, faculty advisor univ. English newspaper, 1987, assoc. prof., 1989-94, chmn. dept., 1992-94, prof., 1994—, assoc. dean of planning, 2000-01. Vis. scholar U. Cin., 1988-89, Stanford U., 1997-98; mem. editl. adv. bd. Materials Sci. Found. (Trans Tech. Publs. Switzerland). Author: Polymer Chemistry, 1990, Polymer Processing, 1991, Polymer Engineering, I, 1995, II, 1997; editor: Polymer: Structure and Properties, 1988; mem. editl. bd. Material Sci. Found., 1998—, assoc. editor Macromolecular Rsch.; contbr. numerous articles to sci. jours. on polymer blends and composites or electroluminescent devices. Mem. Am. Chem. Soc., Am. Phys. Soc., N.Y. Acad. Scis., Polymer Soc. Korea (Polymer Science award 1995), Soc. Polymer Sci. Japan, Korean Inst. Rubber Industries (Best Paper of Yr. award 1989). Avocations: classical music, climbing. Office: Pusan Nat U Dept Polymer Sci & Engring Pusan 609-735 Republic of Korea Fax: 82-51-514-4331. E-mail: csha@pnu.edu.

HA, CHONG WAN, information technology executive; b. Chin-ju, Kyung-Nam, South Korea, Oct. 25, 1938; came to U.S., 1963; s. Kyung-sik and Kyung-Nam (Park) H.; m. Karen Hye-Ja Han, Aug. 19, 1968; children: Jean Frances, Julie Ann. BA in Econs., UCLA, 1970; MA in Mgmt., Claremont (Calif.) U., 1985. Sr. systems analyst Atlantic Richfield Co., Los Angeles, 1972-78; asst. v.p. 1st Interstate Services Co., Los Angeles, 1978-85; v.p. Ticor Title Ins. Co., Los Angeles, 1985-91; assoc. dir. MCA/Universal Studios, 1991; dir. State of Calif. Stephen P. Teale Data Ctr., Sacramento, 1991-97; v.p. LCS, Inc., Sacramento, 1997-99; pres., chief tech. officer Ha Technologies, Burbank, Calif., 1999-2000; v.p. enterprise tech. svcs. 21st Century Ins. Group, Woodland Hills, Calif., 2000—. Exec. com. Calif. Forum on Info. Tech.; adv. bd. Govt. Tech. Conf., 1994. Res. police officer Monterey Park (Calif.) Police Dept., 1981-82; bd. dirs. Asian Pacific Alumni Assn., UCLA, 1988, Asian Pacific Am. Legal Found., L.A., 1988, Korean Youth Ctr., Korean Am. Music Acad.; mem. alumni coun. Claremont Grad. Sch., 1993. Recipient Peter Drucker Ctr. Alumni award, 1994, Calif. State Atty. Gen. award, 1994, Carnegie Mellon U. and AMS Achievement award in mng. info. tech., 1995. Mem. Soc. of Info. Mgmt., Leadership Edn. for Asian Pacifics, UCLA Chancellers Circle. Avocations: golf, classical music, reading. Home: 7801 Via Foggia Burbank CA 91504-1208 E-mail: chongha@aol.com.

HA, CHUL S, radiation oncologist; b. Nov. 2, 1959; m. Jung Hyun Lee. BA, Rice U., 1982; MD, Havard U., 1987. Diplomate Nat. Bd. of Med. Examiners, 1988, Am. Bd. of Radiology, 1993. Assoc. prof. U. Tex. M.D. Anderson Cancer Ctr., Houston, 1998—, assoc. med. dir. Radiation Oncology Ctr., 2001—02, med. dir. Radiation Oncology Med. Ctr., 2002—. Co-dir. Gamma Knife Radiosurgery Unit, Hermann Hosp., Houston, 1993—94; assoc. dir. Multidisciplinary Lymphoma Ctr., U. Tex. M.D. Anderson Cancer Ctr., Houston, 2000—; svc. chief Lymphoma Svc., Radiation Oncology, U. Tex. M.D. Anderson Cancer Ctr., Houston, 2001—. Recipient Daniel Ripley scholarship, Rice U., 1979-1980, Travel award, Am. Soc. for Therapeutic Radiology and Oncology, 1997, Max Roy scholarship, Rice U., 1980-1981, 1981-1982, Raymond Pearson scholarship, 1980-1981, 1981-1982, Honor scholarship, Korean Govt., 1982-1983; Karin Grunebaum Cancer Rsch. Found. fellowship, Harvard Med. Sch., 1985-1986, Am. Cancer Soc. Clin. Oncology fellowship, 1990-1991. Mem.: Radiol. Soc. N.Am., Am. Soc. Hematology, Am. Radium Soc., Am. Soc. Clin. Oncology, Harris County Med. Soc., Am. Soc. for Therapeutic Radiology and Oncology, Gilbert H. Fletcher Soc., Harvard U. Club (Houston), Phi Lambda Upsilon, Phi Beta Kappa. Office: Univ Tex MD Anderson Cancer Center 1515 Holcombe Blvd Box 97 Houston TX 77030 Office Fax: 713-503-2331. E-mail: chulha@mdanderson.org.

HA, QUAN MANH, adult education educator; b. Da Lat, Vietnam, July 17, 1979; arrived in U.S., 2001; s. Huy Ha and Hai Thi Dinh. BA in English, U. Da Lat, 2000; MEd in English, Troy State U., 2003. Instr. English U. Da Lat, Vietnam, 2000—01; instr. English as 2d lang. Troy State U., Ala., 2002—. Mem.: Sigma Tau Delta, Phi Kappa Phi. Home: 29 Cho Chi Lang P9 Lam Dong Da Lat Vietnam E-mail: manhquan2001@yahoo.com.

HA, YONGGANG, optical engineer; b. Nanjing, Jiiangxi, China, Oct. 30, 1974; s. Genzhu Ha and Fengsheng Yang; m. Shuxin Li, July 26, 2000; 1 child, Lucy. PhD, Beijing Inst. Tech., 2000. Cert. optical designer, OSA. Postdoc CREOL, Orlando, Fla., 2000—01, assoc. dir. optical design, 2001—. Contbr. articles to profl. jours. Mem.: Sci. Rsch. Soc., Internat. Soc. Optical Engring. Achievements include patents for Compact Lenses for Head Mount Displays. Office: Univ Ctrl Fla 4000 Central Florida Blvd Orlando FL 32816-2700 E-mail: ha@odalab.ucf.edu.

HAACK, JOHN SCOTT, special education educator, historian; b. Mankato, Minn., Oct. 4, 1945; s. Paul Frank (Stepfather) and Juanita (Fuller) Haack, Burnett Scott Clatterbaugh; m. Debra Sue Sellin, June 9, 1972 (div. Sept. 1992); children: Thomas Jeffer, John Paul. BS, Mankato State Coll., 1967; MA, St. Cloud State U., 1992, postgrad., 2002—. ESL tchr. U.S. Peace Corps, Ilagan, Isabella, Philippines, 1967—68, Virac, Catduanes, Philippines, 1968—69; social studies, English tchr. Spring Valley (Wis.) Schs., 1969—70; social studies tchr. Buffalo (Minn.) Jr./Sr. H.S., 1970—90; spl. edn. tchr. Ramsey Internat. Fine Arts Ctr., Mpls., 1998—2000, Edison Ptnrs. in Pride and Learning, Mpls., 2000—01, Armstrong H.S., Plymouth, Minn., 2001—02, North Br. Campus Pub. Schs., 2002—03. Pub., editor Voice of Catanduanes newspaper, historical corr. Mankato Free Press. Pres. Wright County Hist. Soc., Buffalo, 1990; state bd. dir., pres. MADD-Minn., 1980—; active MADD-Wright County, 1980—; city councilman Maple Lake (Minn.) City Coun., 1976—79. Avocation: collecting coins, stamps, books, antiques and military items. Home: 118 First St E Maple Lake MN 55358 Address: 3864 150th St NW Clearwater MN 55320

HAACK, RICHARD WILSON, retired police officer; b. Chgo., July 7, 1935; s. Arthur Frank and Mildred Ann (Meyer) H.; m. Ruth Marie Tietz, May 27, 1972; children: Laura Marie, Karl Richard. Grad., Sheriff's Police Acad., Cook County (Ill.), 1967; AS, Triton Coll., 1973; cert., Chgo. Police Acad., 1974; BA, Lewis U., 1975; MA, Northeastern Ill. U., 1979; BS in Bus. Adminstrn., Elmhurst Coll., 1982. Shipping clk. Am. Furniture Mart, Chgo., 1955-60; quality control insp. Nat. Can Co., Chgo., 1961-67; police officer Northlake (Ill.) Police Dept., 1967-92, watch comdr. patrol divsn., 1978-85, dept. chief of police, 1986-87, in-svc. tng. coord., 1991-92, retired, 1992. Realtor Internat. Realty World-Norton & Assocs., 1984-87. Author Ency. Am. Judiciary; contbr. articles to profl. publs. Mem. Bill Bruce fundraising com. Aid Assn. Luths., Christ Evang. Luth. Ch., Northlake, 1981-82, mem. Gala Varsity Show, 1982, chmn. evang. bd., 1981-85, ch. rep. Internat. Luth. Laymen's League, 1984—, pub. rels. dir., usher, 1873-85; choir Apostles Luth Ch., 1985-87; membership chmn. Redeemer Luth. Ch. Men's Club, 1995-99; dir., emcee German-Am. Police Assn., 1980-2001, emcee Oktoberfest, 1980-99, chmn. entertainment, 1984-2001, assoc. membership chmn., 2001—; coach Northlake Little League baseball team, 1985; trustee Northlake Police Pension Fund, 1997—; active March of Dimes-Mothers March, 1997-99; chmn. program com. Immanuel Ch., 2002—. Served with USMC, 1952-55, Korea, with res. 1955-60. Recipient John Edgar Hoover Meml. Gold medal, 1987, numerous letters of commendation, competitive shooting awards. Mem. NRA, Internat. Assn. Chiefs of Police, Ill. Police Assn. (life), Fraternal Order Police (life, sec.-treas. Perri-Nagle Meml. Lodge 18 1977-85), St. Jude Police League, Nat. Police Officers Assn., Internat. Police Assn. (life), German/Am. Police Assn. (life, bd. dirs), Combined Counties Police Assn., Internat. Juvenile Officers Assn., Ill. Juvenille Officers Assn., Ill. Police Assn. (life), Emerald Soc. Ill. Irish/Am. Police Assn., Northeastern Ill. U. Alumni Assn. (bd. dirs. 1980-86), Am. Polit. Sci. Assn., Schwaben Verein, N.W. Real Estate Bd., Leyden Real Estate Bd. (inner circle 1984-87), Sharkhunters, Internat. Platform Assn., Realtors Polit. Action Com. Ill. (inner circle 1984-87), Am. Legion, Ret. and Disabled Police of Am., Kaire Ind. Distbr., Die Hard Cub Fans, Moose Lodge, Korean War Vets.-Navy League. Republican. Home: 244 E Palmer Ave Northlake IL 60164-1735 Office: 55 E North Ave Northlake IL 60164-2518 E-mail: haackpack@aol.com.

HAACKE, HANS CHRISTOPH CARL, artist, educator; b. Cologne, Germany, Aug. 12, 1936; s. Carl and Antonie Haacke; m. Linda Snyder, 1965; 2 sons. MFA, State Acad., Kassel, 1960; DFA (hon.), Oberlin Coll., 1991; D (hon.), Bauhaus U., Weimar, Germany, 1998. Asst. prof. Cooper Union for Advancement of Sci. and Art, N.Y.C., 1971-75, assoc. prof., 1975-79, prof., 1979—2002, prof. emeritus, 2002—. Guest prof. Hochschule für Bildende Künste, Hamburg, 1973, 94, Gesamthochschule, Essen, 1979. One-man shows include Galerie Schmela, Düsseldorf, 1965, Howard Wise Gallery, N.Y.C., 1966, 68, 69, Galerie Paul Maenz, Cologne, 1971, 74, 81, Museum Haus Lange, Krefeld, 1972, John Weber Gallery, N.Y.C., 1973, 75, 77, 79, 81, 83, 85, 88, 90, 92, 94, Kunstverein, Frankfurt, 1976, Galerie Durand-Dessert, Paris, 1977, 78, Mus. of Modern Art, Oxford, 1978, Stedelijk Van Abbemuseum, Eindhoven, 1979, Renaissance Soc., Chgo., 1979, Galerie France Morin, Montreal, Que., Can., 1983, Tate Gallery, London, 1984, Neue Gesellschaft für Bildende Kunst, Berlin, 1984, Kunsthalle, Berne,, 1985, Le Consortium, Dijon, France, 1986, The New Mus. Contemporary Art, N.Y.C., 1986, Victoria Miro Gallery, London, 1987, Centre Georges Pompidou, Paris, 1989, Biennale Venice, Italy, 1993, Fundació Antoni Tàpies, Barcelona, 1995, Mus. Boijmans Van Beuningen, Rotterdam, 1996, German Parliament Bldg., Berlin, 2000, Portikus, Frankfurt, 2000, Serpentine Gallery, London, 2001, Generali Found., Vienna, 2001; group exhbns. Stedelijk Mus., Amsterdam, 1962, 65, 82, Mus. Modern Art, N.Y.C., 1968, 70, 88,99, Tokyo Biennale, 1970, Jewish Mus., N.Y.C., 1970, 94, Documenta Kassel, 1972, 82, 87, 97, Biennale Venice, 1976, 78, Mus. van Hedendaagse Kunst, Ghent, Belgium, 1980, Hirshhorn Mus., Washington, 1984, Palais des Beaux-Arts, Brussels, 1984, Sydney (Australia) Biennale, 1984, 90, Sao Paulo (Brazil) Biennale, 1985, Nationalgalerie, Berlin, 1984, Centre Georges Pompidou, 1987, 89, 90, 92, 96, 2000, Musée d'Art Moderne de la Ville de Paris, 1981, 89, L.A. Cty. Mus., 1987, 2001, Whitney Mus., NY, 1989, 1999, 2000, State Russian Mus., St. Petersburg, 1990, Irish Mus. Modern Art, Dublin, 1992, Musée d'art contemporain, Montreal, 1992, 2003, Bundeskunsthalle, Bonn, Germany, 1992, Kunsthalle Basel, Basel, Switzerland, 1994, Mus. Contemporary Art, L.A., 1995, Mus. Contemporary Art, Tokyo, 1995; Stage set: Ernst Jünger, Volksbühne, Berlin, 1994, Skulptur Projekte Münster, Germany, 1997, Deutschlandbilder, Gropius-Bau, Berlin, 1997, 2003, Berlin-Moskow/Moskow-Berlin Johannesburg Biennale, 1997, Mus. Hamburger Bahnhof, Berlin, 1999, Mus. Contemporary Art, Barcelona, 2000, Tate Modern London, 2000, Nat. Portrait Gallery, London, 2000, Hayward Gallery, London, 2000, Haus der Kunst, Munich, 2000, Zentrum für Kunst und Medientechnologie, Karlsruhe, Germany, 2002, Musée d'art contemporain, Bordeaux, France, 2002; author: (with Edward F. Fry) Werkmonographie, 1972, (with others) Framing and Being Framed, 1975, Nach allen Regeln der Kunst, 1984, (with others) Unfinished Business, 1987, Artfairismes, 1989, (with others) Bodenlos, 1993, Mia san mia, 2001, (with Pierre Bourdicu) Libre-Echange, 1994, Obra Social, 1995; AnsichtsSachen/ViewingMatters, 1999, contbr. articles to profl. jours. Recipient Golden Lion Venice Biennale. Office: The Cooper Union Cooper Square New York NY 10003

HAAG, CAROL ANN GUNDERSON, marketing professional, consultant; b. Mpls. d. Glenn Alvin and Genevieve Esther (Knudson) Gunderson; m. Lawrence S. Haag, Aug. 30, 1969; 1 child, Maren Anne. BJ, U. Mo., 1969; postgrad., Roosevelt U., Chgo., 1975—. Pub. rels. writer, advt. copywriter Am. Hosp. Supply Corp., Evanston, Ill., 1969-70; asst. dir. pub. rels. Rush-Presbyn. St. Luke's Med. Ctr., Chgo., 1970-71; asst. mgr. pub. and employee comm. Quaker Oats Co., Chgo., 1971-72, mgr. editl. comm., 1972-74, mgr. employee comm. programs, 1974-77; dir. pub. rels. Shaklee Corp., San Francisco, 1978-82; pres. CH & Assocs., San Francisco, 1982-84; dir corp. comm. BRAE Corp., San Francisco, 1984; dir. mktg. St. Francis Meml. Hosp., San Francisco, 1985-89, dir. mktg. and planning svcs., 1989-91; ptnr. Haag & Rohan, San Francisco, San Diego, 1991—; pres. Sci. Symposiums Internat., Moraga, 1998—. Examiner Calif. Coun. for Quality and Svc., 1997, 98, sr. examiner, 1999; cons. in field. Bd. dirs. Calif. League Handicapped; mem. adv. bd. San Francisco Spl. Olympics; mem. pub. relations com. San Francisco Recreation and Parks Dept., San Francisco Vol. Bur. Recipient 1st place cert. Printing Industry Am., 1972, 74, 1st place spl. comm. award Internat. Assn. Bus. Communicators, 1974, 1st place citation Chgo. Assn. Bus. Communicators, 1974, gold award Healthcare Mktg. Reports, 1989, 90. Mem. NATAS, Indsl. Com. Coun., Pub. Rels. Soc. Am., San Francisco C. of C. (grad. leadership program 1991, bd. dirs. leadership coun.). Home and Office: 133 Fernwood Dr Moraga CA 94556-2315 E-mail: haagassoc1@aol.com.

HAAG, EVERETT KEITH, architect; b. Cuyahoga Falls, Ohio, Jan. 27, 1928; s. Arnold and Lois (Martz) H.; m. Eleanor Jean Baker, Nov. 1, 1961; children—Kurt, Paula, Pamela. BS in Architecture, Kent State U., 1951; B.Arch., Western Res. U., 1953. Founder, prin. firm Keith Haag & Assocs. (architects), Cuyahoga Falls, 1955-72; founder, pres. Keith Haag Assos. Inc. (architecture-engring.-planning), Cuyahoga Falls, 1972-81; archtl. and planning cons. Cuyahoga Falls, 1981—. Instr. Kent State U., 1952-54 Pres. Tri-County Planning Commn., 1960-61; chmn. Urban Renewal Review Commn., Cuyahoga Falls, 1971—. Regional Planning Group, Northampton Twp., 1970— ; mem. Akron Regional Devel. Bd.; bd. dirs. Goodwill Industries, chmn. strategic planning com., 1988—, Akron, Stan Hywet Hall Found., Inc. (pres. 1991-92); chmn. Historic Bldgs. Com., 1988—; mem. alumni bd. Kent State U., 1970-72, co-developer Polymer Housing system, 1989. Recipient 46 archtl. design awards. Fellow AIA (past pres. Akron chpt., nat. com. on office practice); mem. Architects Soc. Ohio (exec. com., sec. 1975-76, v.p. 1977-78, pres. 1979, Gold medal 1986), Northampton C. of C. (pres. 1972), Summit County Hist. Soc. (dir. 1974—) Clubs: President's (Kent State U.), Hilltoppers (Akron U.). Home: 1007 W Steels Corners Rd Cuyahoga Falls OH 44223-3111 Office: PO Box 1147 Cuyahoga Falls OH 44223-0147

HAAG, JOEL EDWARD, architect; b. Wayne, Nebr., June 30, 1962; s. Robert James and Shirley Ann (Kruty) Haag; m. Kathleen M. Kerwood, Oct. 20, 2001. BS, N.E. Mo. State U., 1984; BArch, U. Kans., 1986. Registered architect, Mo. Architect Hollis & Miller Group, Prairie Village, Kans., 1986-90; arch. Tognascioli, Gross, Kautz Architects, Inc., Kans. City, Mo., 1991-92; engr., structural design draftsman Borton Inc., Hutchinson, Kans., 1992-93; registered architect Mann & Co., Hutchinson, Kans., 1993—. Co-chmn. Archtl. Explorer Post, Kans. City, Mo., 1989-92. Mem. Hutchinson Chamber Chorale; chmn. Hutchinson Landmarks Commn., 1995—2001; bd. mem. computer drafting adv. coun. Hutchinson C.C., 1998—; vice chmn. Hutchinson Housing Commn., 1999—2001; treas. Kans. Kids, Inc., 2000—; chmn. Hutchinson Housing Authority, 2000—; S.W. Dist. rep. Hutchinson City Coun., Hutchinson, 2001—03; trustee Redeemer Luth. Ch., Lawrence, Kans., 1987—88; mem. choir Bethany Luth. Ch., Overland Park, Kans., 1989—92; bd. dir., treas. Kans. Kios, Inc. Mem. Reno Choral Soc., Kans. Mennonite Men's Chorale. Home: 407 E 1st Ave Hutchinson KS 67501-7148 Office: Mann & Co 335 N Washington St Ste 110 Hutchinson KS 67501-4862 E-mail: joel@mannandcompany.com.

HAAG, WALTER M(ONROE), JR., philatelist; b. Williamsport, Pa., Apr. 25, 1940; s. Walter Monroe and Julia Maria (Halabura) H.; m. Joanne Marie Spudis, May 22 1971; 1 child, Steven Joseph. BSI.E., Pa. State U., 1962, MS in Indsl. Engring., 1968; M.P.H., U. Mich., 1971. Indsl. engr. Sylvania, Montoursville, Pa., 1962-64, supr. quality control, 1965-66; commd. lt. (j.g.) U.S. Pub. Health Services, 1966; advanced through grades to capt., 1977; mgmt. analyst NIH, Bethesda, Md., 1966-69; global community health career fellow USPHS, Washington, 1969-71; tech. officer WHO, Geneva, 1972-73; br. chief resource mgmt. Nat. Inst. Occupational Safety and Health, Rockville, Md., 1973-74, dep. dir. planning, 1974-76, dir. phys. scis. and engring. Cin., 1976-87; cons. Assn. Media-Based Continuing Edn. for Engrs., Atlanta, 1979, assoc. dir. div. tng. and manpower devel., 1987-95, indsl. engr., 1995-96; philatelist Loveland, Ohio, 1997—. Adminstr. research for instruments, fibrous aerosol monitor Indsl. Research 100 award, 1972 Speaker Am. Lung Assn., Las Vegas, Nev., 1979; speaker Air Pollution Control League, Cin., 1982, 87; mem. indsl. and profl. adv. council Pa. State Coll. Engring. Recipient Commendation medal USPHS, Rockville, 1976, Citation award USPHS, Cin., 1986, Unit Commendation medal USPHS, 1988, 92, Meritorius Svc. medal USPHS, 1992; named Supr. of Yr., Federally Employed Women, Cin., 1980. Mem. Inst. Indsl. Engrs. (sr. treas.

chpt. 1964-65, v.p. chpt. 1966), Am. Mgmt. Assn., Am. Soc. for Tng. and Devel., Am. Conf. Govtl. Indsl. Hygienists (bd. dirs. 1986-89), Air Pollution Control League Greater Cin. (trustee 1982—). Republican. Roman Catholic.

HAAGA, JOHN GREGORY, demographer; b. Washington, D.C., Sept. 7, 1953; s. Paul Galarneaux and Virginia (Coughlan) Haaga; m. Elin Mair Lewis; children: Owen, Bethan, Daniel. MA with 1st class honors, Oxford (Eng.) U., 1974; MA, Johns Hopkins U., 1978; PhD, Rand Grad. Sch., Santa Monica, Calif., 1983. Dep. dir. Cornell Nutritional Surveillance, Ithaca, NY, 1982—85; rsch. assoc., economist Rand Corp., Washington, 1985—90; project dir. Internat. Ctr. Diarrheal Disease Rsch., Dhaka, Bangladesh, 1990—94; dir. com. on population NAS, Washington, 1994—97; dir. Measure Project Population Reference Bur., Washington, 1997—99, dir. domestic programs, 1997—; dir. Ctr. Pub. Info. on Population Rsch., Washington, 2002—. Adv. com. Rockefeller Found., N.Y.C., 1995—2000; cons. Helen Keller Internat., World Bank, 1985—95. Election judge Montgomery County, Md., 2002, adv. bd. on substance abuse prevention, 1986—88. Mem.: Internat. Union Scientific Study of Population, Assn. Population Ctrs. (pres. 2003—), Population Assn. Am. (sec.-treas. 1997—2000). Democrat. Roman Catholic. Avocations: running, gardening, British political history. Office: Population Ref Bur 1875 Connecticut Ave NW Washington DC 20009 E-mail: jhaaga@prb.org.

HAAGE, ROBERT MITCHELL, retired history educator, organization leader; b. Garden City, Kans., Mar. 10, 1924; s. William Russell and Mayme Levice (Mitchell) H.; m. Lila Marie Baker, Sept. 7, 1947; children: Lori Deane, Lisa Anne, Melanie Sue. BA, Southwestern Coll., 1947; MDiv, Garrett Bibl. Inst., 1952. Cert. tchr., Kans., Calif. Min. Meth. Ch., Copeland, Kans., 1947-48, Meth. Chs., Ingleside, Spring Grove, Ill., 1948-50; asst. min. First Meth. Ch., Emporia, Kans., 1952-53; tchr. core curriculum Marshall Intermediate Sch., Wichita, Kans., 1953-56; tchr. U.S. history Bellflower (Calif.) High Sch., 1956-57; tchr. math. Chaffey Joint Union High Sch. Dist., Ontario, Calif., 1957-59, tchr. U.S. history and econs., 1959-85. 1st faculty pres. Montclair High Sch., 1959-60; founding pres. Inland Empire Counties Coun. for Social Studies, San Bernardino, Calif., 1961-62; dean student activities Western CUNA Mgmt. Sch., Pomona Coll., Claremont, Calif., 1980-84; treas. Tchrs. Adv. Group/Tchrs. Farm and Ranch Co-op, 1984-93. Conservation editor Desomount Dustings Newsletter, 1990-92, gen. editor, 1993—. Founding officer Chaffey Dist. Employees Fed. Credit Union, Ontario, 1964-69; chair, bd. dirs. Chaffey Fed. Credit Union, Ontario, 1979-87, dir., 1969—; officer, bd. govs. Mt. Baldy chpt. Calif. Credit Union League, Pomona, 1977-86; bd. dirs., treas. Upper Westwood Homeowners Assn., Pomona, 1982-84, 91-92; conservation chair Desomount Environ. Orgn.; mem. Nat. Wildlife Fedn. Recipient We Honor Ours award Calif. Tchrs. Assn., 1985, Outstanding Svc. award Associated Chaffey Tchrs., 1985. Mem. Univ. Club Claremont (sec.-v.p.-pres. 1986-92, editor newsletters 1986-90, bd. dirs. 1993-96, chair fin. com. 1993-97, co-chair planning com., Sept. chair program com. 1999—, Leadership award 1992), Toastmasters Club 12 (pres. 1964-65, Best Evaluator award 1982, 83, 85), Sierra Club, Fedn. of Western Outdoor Clubs (v.p. So. Calif. chpt. 1990—, gen. v.p. 1994-95, treas. 1995-98, mem. Sequoia strategy com. 1998—, chair Sequoia strategy com. 1999—), Claremont Sr. Computer Club, Phi Delta Kappa (pres. 1977-78, Disting. Svc. award 1978), Kappa Delta Pi (hon. soc. in edn. 1953—). Democrat. Avocations: woodworking, reading, camping, hiking, photography. Home: 9541 Tudor Ave Montclair CA 91763-2219 E-mail: rhaage@juno.com.

HAAK, HAROLD HOWARD, university president; b. Madison, Wis., June 1, 1935; s. Harold J. and Laura (Kittleson) H.; m. Betty L. Steiner, June 25, 1955; children— Alison Marie, Janet Christine. BA, U. Wis., 1957, MA, 1958; PhD, Princeton U., 1963. From asst. prof. to assoc. prof. polit. sci., pub. adminstrn. and urban studies San Diego State Coll., 1962-69, dean coll. profl. studies, prof. pub. adminstrn. and urban studies, 1969-71; acad. v.p. Calif. State U., Fresno, 1971-73, pres., 1980-91, pres. emeritus, 1991—, trustee prof., 1991-2000, trustee, prof., vice chancellor acad. affairs, 1992-93; v.p. U. Colo., Denver, 1973, chancellor, 1974-80; pres. Fresno Pacific U., 2000—02. Trustee William Saroyan Found., 1981-91; mem. NCAA Pres. Commn., 1987-91; bd. dirs. Fresno Econ. Devel. Corp., 1981-91, Cmty. Hosps. Ctrl. Calif., 1989-92, Pacific Luth. Theol. Sem., 1998-2002; bd. visitors Air Univ.; mem. Army adv. panel on ROTC affairs, 1988-92; vice-chair Calif. Commn. on Agr. and Higher Edn., 1993-96; pres., trustee Ctrl. Calif. br. Leukemia and Lymphoma Soc., 2002—; pres., bd. dirs. Armenian Agribus. Edn. Fund, 2002—. Recipient U. Colo. medal, 1980. Mem.: Phi Kappa Phi, Phi Beta Kappa.

HAALAND, GORDON ARTHUR, psychologist, university president; b. Bklyn., Apr. 19, 1940; s. Ole E. and Ellen R. (Hansen) H.; m. Carol E. Anderson, Jan. 19, 1963; children: Lynn, Paul. AB, Wheaton (Ill.) Coll., 1962; PhD, SUNY, Buffalo, 1966. Instr. SUNY, Buffalo, summer, 1965; asst. to assoc. prof. psychology U. N.H., Durham, 1965-74, prof., 1974-83, chmn. dept. psychology, 1970-74, v.p. for acad. affairs Coll. Arts and Scis., 1979-83, interim pres. of univ., 1983-84, pres., 1984-90; dean Coll. Arts and Scis., prof. psychology U. Maine, Orono, 1975-79; pres. Gettysburg (Pa.) Coll., 1990—. Vis. prof. U. Bergen, Norway, 1972-73; mem. New Eng. Land-Grant Univs., chmn. 1985-86; v.p. N.H. Coll. and Univ. Coun., 1985-87; bd. dirs. New Eng. Bd. Higher Edn., 1986—, chmn., 1988-90; bd. dirs. Eisenhower World Affairs Inst.; chmn. N.H. Postsecondary Edn. Commn., 1986-88; dir. Maine Coun. Econ. Edn., 1975-79; evaluator NSF CAUSE Project, U. Maine, 1980-83; bd. dirs. First N.H. Banks, Inc., 1987—, mem. First NH Investment Svcs., 1987—; corporator Bangor (Maine) Savs. Bank, 1975-79. Contbr. articles, papers to profl. publs. and confs. procs. Incorporator N.H. Charitable Fund, 1985-88, Trust for N.H. Lands, 1986—; bd. dirs. Ctr. for N.H.'s Future, 1980—, N.H. Coun. World Affairs, 1986-89; mem. Gov.'s Commn. on N.H. in 21st Century, 1989—; trustee Theater-by-the-Sea, Portsmouth, N.H., 1980-83, N.H. Higher Edn. Assistance Found., 1986—; co-dir. series pub. workshops Dickey-Lincoln and Passamaquoddy Hydroelectric Projects; chair Coun. Higher Edn. Accreditation, dir., 1997-2002. Norwegian Rsch. Coun. fellow, 1972-73; grantee NSF, NIMH, HEW, 1966-75. Mem. AAAS, AAUP, NCAA (pres. commn. 1996-2000), Council of Colls. of Arts and Scis. (bd. dirs. 1977-79), Nat. Assn. State Univs. and Land-Grant Colls. (commn. on arts and scis. 1978-81, chair exec. com. council on acad. affairs 1983, internat. affairs com. 1985-87, exec. com. 1986—, chair commn. edn. for teaching professions 1987-88), Nat. Assn., Ind. Colls. and Univs. (bd. dirs. 1993—), Am. Psychol. Assn. (div. 8 and 26, coun. of reps. N.H., Vt., Maine and R.I. 1968-71, com. on structure and function of coun. 1968-71), Eastern Psychol. Assn., N.H. Psychol. Assn. (program dir. 1971), Eisenhower World Affairs Inst. (bd. dirs. 1991—), Soc. Exptl. Social Psychology, Phi Kappa Phi, Sigma Xi. Office: Gettysburg Coll Office of Pres Gettysburg PA 17325-1486

HAAR, ANA MARIA FERNANDEZ, advertising and public relations executive; b. Oriente Province, Cuba, Mar. 25, 1951; came to U.S., 1960; naturalized, 1970; d. Gilberto and Esmeralda Emiliana (Diaz) Fernández. Grad., Miami Dade C.C., 1971; student, Barry Coll., 1972-78. Adminstrv. asst. through asst. v.p. nat. accounts Flagship Bank, Miami Beach, Fla., 1971-77; v.p. comml. lending Jefferson Nat. Bank, Miami Beach, Fla., 1977-78; chmn., CEO, IAC Group, Inc., Miami, Fla., 1978—. Instr. Women in Mgmt. program Miami Dade C.C., 1980-81; hostess Sta. WPBT Program Viva; exec. com. World Trade Ctr., Miami; mem. Dade County Commn. on Status of Women, 1979-82; chmn. Econ. Devel. Task Force of Commn. on Status of Women, 1979-82; bd. dirs., chmn. Human Capital Group, New Am. Alliance; bd. dirs. Cuban Am. Nat. Found.; mem. adv. com. John S. and James L. Knight Found. Bd. dirs., vice-chmn. CAMACOL-Latin C. of C.; chmn. World Trade Ctr.; Miami dir. SCORE; mem. Exec. Assn. Greater Miami; vice chair New America Alliance; bd. dirs. Cuban Am. Nat. Found.. Recipient Gran Orden Martiana of Cuban Lyceum for excellence in community svc., 1976, Up and Comers award South Fla. Bus. Jour., 1988, Red Cross Spectrum award, 2000; named one of 100 Most Infulential Hispanics, Hispanic Bus. Mag., So. Fla. Leading Women Business Owners, 1990, Entrepeneur of the Yr. Inc. Mag. (natl. finalist), 1992. Mem. Advt. Fedn. Greater Miami, Greater Miami Advt. Fedn. (bd. dirs.) Asociación de Publicitarios Latino-Americanos (v.p.), Japan Soc. (bd. dirs.), Miami Beach C. of C. (hon. life, trustee), Greater Miami C. of C., Hispanic Heritage Festival Com., Cuban Women's Club (past pres.), Assn. Hispanic Advt. Agys. (pres. 1998-99), New Am. Alliance. Office: IAC Advt Group 2725 SW 3rd Ave Miami FL 33129-2335 E-mail: iac@iacadgroup.com.

HAAR, CHARLES MONROE, lawyer, educator; b. Dec. 3, 1920; came to U.S., 1921; s. Benjamin and Dora (Eisner) H.; children: Jeremy, Susan Eve, Jonathan. AB, N.Y.U., 1940; LLB, Harvard, 1948; MA, U. Wis., 1941; LLD, Lake Erie U., 1968, Hebrew Coll., 1988. Bar: N.Y. 1949, U.S. Dist. Ct. (so. dist.) N.Y. 1950, U.S. Supreme Ct. 1968, Mass. 1978. Practice law, N.Y.C., 1949-52; asst. prof. law Harvard, 1952-54; prof., 1954-66, 69—, Louis D. Brandeis prof. law, 1972—; disting. prof. U. Miami Law Sch., 1998—. Chmn. Joint Ctr. for Urban Studies, Mass. Inst. Tech. and Harvard, 1969—, chmn. land policy roundtable Lincoln Inst. Land Policy; dir. Charles River Assocs.l asst. sec. met. devel. Dept. Housing and Urban Devel., Washington, 1966-69. Author: Land Planning Law in a Free Society, Feeral Credit and Private Housing, 1960, Law and Land, 1964, Golden Age of American Law, 1966, The End of Innocence, 1972, Housing the Poor in Suburbia, 1973, Suburban Problems, 1973, Property and Law, 1977, 2d edit., 1985, Of Judges, Politics and Flounders: Perspectives on the Cleaning Up of Boston Harbor, 1985; (with others) The Wrong Side of the Tracks, 1986, Fairness and Justice, 1987, Land-Use Planning: A Casebook in the Use, Misuse and Re-use of Urban Land, 4th edit., 1989, Landmark Justice, 1989, Zoning and the American Dream, 1989; editor: Beacon Classics of the Law, Suburbs Under Siege, 1992; contbr. articles to profl. jours. Chief reporter Am. Land Inst. project model code land devel. 1964-66; mem. Cambridge Redevel. Authority, Met. Area Planning Coun., Mass. Gov.'s Com. on Resource Mgmt., 1974, Fin. Adv. Bd., 1978—, Uniform Commn. State Laws, 1979—, Jerusalem Com., 1970—; chmn. Pres.'s Task Force Preservation Natural Beauty, Task Force on Model Cities, on Suburban Problems; chmn. com. on met. governance RFF, 1970-72; cons. WHite House AID, HHFA, U.S. Senate state and city agys.; mem. U.S. del. to UN Conf. on Habitat, 1976; pres. Regional and Urban Planning Implementation, Onc., bd. dirs. Zelda Zinn Found.; trustee Mass. Gen. Hosp., 1979—. Lt. (j.g.) USNR, 1942-46. Fellow Urban Land Inst.; mem. Am. Acad. Arts and Scis., Am. Inst. Planners, Brit. Town Planning Inst., Am. Bar Assn., Am. Law Inst., Phi Beta Kappa. Office: Harvard Law Sch Griswold 300 Cambridge MA 02138

HAAR, FRANKLIN DUANE, musician, writer; b. Marysville, Kans., Dec. 12, 1935; s. Maxmilian Herman and Thelma Grace (Umphries) Haar. Freelance musician, Austin, Tex., 1955—; freelance calligrapher, 1968—. Contbr. ; photographer U. Tex. Chemistry Dept., 1977—86. Vol. V.I.S.T.A., 1965—68. With USAF, 1952. Mem.: Capital City Scribes. Avocations: literature, music. E-mail: franklharr@aol.com.

HAAR, ROBERT THEODORE, lawyer; b. St. Louis, Apr. 11, 1950; s. Robert Edwin and Mary Ann (Rose) H.; m. Cathleen Annette Sanford, Jan. 21, 1981; children: Alexandra, Matthew, Mark. BS in Elec. Engring., Stanford U., 1972; BPh in Econs., Oxford (Eng.) U., 1974; JD, Yale U., 1977. Law clk. to Hon. Harold Leventhal U.S. Ct. Appeals (D.C. cir.), Washington, 1977-78; law clk. to Justice William H. Rehnquist U.S. Supreme Ct., Washington, 1978-79; atty.-advisor Office of Legal Counsel, U.S. Dept. Justice, Washington, 1979-80; asst. U.S. atty. U.S. Atty.'s Office, St. Louis, 1980-85; ptnr. Kohn, Shands, Elbert, Gianoulakis & Giljum LLP, St. Louis, 1986-97, Haar & Woods, LLP, St. Louis, 1997—. Chair civil justice reform act adv. group U.S. Dist. Ct. (ea. dist.) Mo., 1995-97. Police commr. St. Louis Met. Police Dept., 1994-98. Rhodes scholar, 1972. Home: 3635 Flora Pl Saint Louis MO 63110-3703 Office: Haar & Woods LLP 1010 Market St Ste 1620 Saint Louis MO 63101-2000 E-mail: roberthaar@haar-woods.com.

HAARMEYER, DAVID ALAN, computer programmer/analyst, educator; b. Buffalo, Oct. 30, 1958; s. Robert Charles and Irene (Gorniak) H.; m. Valerie Jean Frank, May 14, 1983. BS in Mgmt., SUNY, Buffalo, 1980, MBA, 1986. Cert. computer profl. Software cons. DVH Software Devel., Kenmore, N.Y., 1986—; computer instr. Kenmore-Tonawanda (N.Y.) Sch. Dist., 1990-92; sys. analyst M&T Bank, Buffalo, 2002—. Treas. Alliance Men's Fellowship, Kenmore Alliance Ch., 1990—. Mem.: Western N.Y. Soc. Info. Processors. Republican. Avocations: tennis, white water rafting. Home: 74 Irving Ter Buffalo NY 14223-2740 Office: M&T Bank One M&T Center Buffalo NY 14223

HAAS, BRADLEY DEAN, pharmacy director, clinical pharmacist, consultant; b. Albion, Nebr., Nov. 24, 1957; s. Ernest Duane Jr. and Joy Lou (Fusselman) H. Student, Kearney State Coll., 1976-78; PharmD with distinction, U. Nebr. Coll. Pharmacy, Omaha, 1981. Registered pharmacist, Nebr., Colo.; cert. hosp. pharmacy residency, basic life support instr. and provider, advanced cardiac life support instr. and provider. Resident hosp. pharmacy U. Nebr. Med. Ctr., Omaha, 1981-82; intensive care clin. pharmacist Mercy Med. Ctr., Denver, 1982-85; home care pharmacist Am. Abbey Homecare, Englewood, Colo., 1985; pharmacy dir. Charter Hosp. of Aurora, Colo., 1989-90; clin pharmacy coord. Porter Meml. Hosp., Denver, 1987-92; asst. dir. clin. pharmacy svcs. Luth. Med. Ctr., Wheat Ridge, Colo., 1992-94; dir. pharmacy Integrated Pharmacy Solutions, Inc./Pru Care Pharmacies, Denver, 1994-96; sr. med. info. scientist AstraZeneca L.P. (formerly Astra Merck), 1996—. Cons. Porter Meml. Hosp. Chronic Pain Treatment Ctr., 1987-89, Charter Hosp., 1989-90; adj. asst. prof. pharmacy U. Colo., 1983-96; mem. leadership adv. coun. sch. pharmacy U. Colo., 1987-89; mem. State Colo./ Medicare D.U.R. Com., 1992-96. Author, co-author in field. Vol. Colo. Hosp. Pharmacists Week, Poison Prevention Week, KUSA-TV Health Fair; active Colo. Trust. Named Disting. Young Pharmacist of the Year Marion Labs., Colo., 1987, one of Outstanding Young Men of Am., 1987; recipient Acad. Scholarship U. Nebr. Med. Ctr, 1978-81, Excellence in Pharmacy Practice award U. Colo. Sch. Pharmacy, 1988; Marjorie Merwin Simmons Meml. scholar U. Nebr. Found. Fund., 1980; scholar VFW, 1978-81. Mem. Am. Soc. Health-Sys. Pharmacists (state chpt. grants program selection com. 1989, nominations com. 1990-91, ho. of dels. 1987, 90-92), Acad. Managed Care Pharmacy, Colo. Managed Care Pharmacy Dirs., Colo. Soc. Health-Sys. Pharmacists (presdl. officer 1987-89, chmn. numerous couns. and coms., Hosp. Pharmacy Practitioner Excellence award 1988, 89), LoDo Sertoma Club (charter mem., sec. 1999-2000, v.p. sponsorship 2000-2001, v.p. programs 2001-2002, v.p. membership 2002—). Avocations: snow/water skiing, bicycling, photography, golf, community service activities. Office: AstraZeneca LP 10115 Granite Hill Dr Parker CO 80134-9515 E-mail: bradley.haas@astrazeneca.com.

HAAS, CAROLYN BUHAI, elementary education educator, publisher, writer, consultant; b. Chgo., Jan. 1, 1926; d. Michael and Tillie (Weiss) Buhai; m. Robert Green Haas, June 29, 1947 (dec. June 30, 1984); children: Andrew Robert, Mari Beth, Thomas Michael, Betsy Ann, Karen Sue. BEd, Smith Coll., Northampton, Mass., 1947; postgrad., Nat. Coll. Edn., Evanston, Ill., 1956-59, Art Inst. Chgo., 1958-59. Tchr. Francis W. Parker Sch., Chgo., 1947-49; tchr. art Glencoe (Ill.) Pub. Schs., 1967-68, substitute tchr., 1964-72. Co-founder PAR Leadership Tng. Found., Northfield, Ill., 1969-81; pres., editor CBH Pub., Inc., Northfield, 1979-92; cons., writer, adv. bd. The Learning Line; cons. presch. sci. program Mus. Sci. and Industry, Chgo.; adv. bd. My Own Mag.; cons. in field. Author: (with Ann Cole and Betty Weinberger) I Saw a Purple Cow, 1972, A Pumpkin In A Pear Tree, 1974, Children Are Children Are Children, 1976, Backyard Vacation, 1978, Purple Cow to the Rescue, 1982, Recipes for Fun and Learning, 1982, Recetas Para Divertirse, 1997; (with A.C. Friedman) My Own Fun, 1990, The Big Book for Recipes for Fun, 1979, Look at Me: Activities for Babies and Toddlers, 1985; co-editor: Know Your Town/East Hampton League Women Voters of the Hamptons, 1993; contbr. articles to profl. jours. Pres. West Sch. PTA, Glencoe, Jr. Bd. Scholarship and Guidance, Chgo.; bd. dirs. Family Counseling Svc. of Glencoe, Glencoe Human Rels. Com.; pres., sec, bd. dirs. Glencoe Pub. Libr.; pres. Friends of Glencoe Pub. Libr.; co-founder Glencoe Patriotic Days Com.; co-chair Frank Lloyd Wright Bridge Com., Glencoe; pres., bd. dirs. Chgo. League Smith Coll.; mem. women's bd. Northwestern U.; bd. dirs. Chgo. chpt. Am. Jewish Com.; mem. women's com. Chgo. Symphony Orch. Clubs; bd. dirs. Art Resources in Tchg.; vol. Parish Art Mus., The Retreat. Mem. AAUW, LWV (bd. dirs.), Internat. Reading Assn., Soc. Children's Bookwriters, Children's Reading Roundtable, Nat. Assn. Edn. Young Children, Assn. Childhood Edn. Internat., NEA, Artists Alliance of East Hampton (bd. dirs.), Ladies Village Improvement Soc. (bd. dirs.). Democrat. Jewish. Avocations: art, reading, sports, travel. E-mail: cbhpub@aol.com.

HAAS, CHARLIE, screenwriter; b. Bklyn., Oct. 22, 1952; s. Philip and Eunice (Dillon) H.; m. Barbara K. Moran, Dec. 21, 1981. BA, U. Calif., Santa Cruz, 1984. Editorial dir. Warner Bros. Records, Burbank, Calif., 1974-76; contbg. editor New West Mag., Beverly Hills, Calif., 1976-80; freelance writer L.A., 1976-80, Oakland, Calif., 1980—. Co-author: (movies) Over the Edge, 1979, Tex, 1982, Gremlins 2, 1990, Matinee, 1993, Runaway Daughters, 1994; contbr. articles to mags. Mem. Friends of Oakland Parks & Recreation, Friends of Oakland Pub. Libr. Avocations: fountain pens, mountain bikes.

HAAS, EDWARD LEE, business executive, consultant; b. Camden, N.J., Nov. 9, 1935; s. Edward David and Mildred Haas; m. Maryann Lind, Dec. 27, 1958; children: John Eric, Gretchen Haas Theodore. BA, LaSalle U., 1958. Cryptanalyst Nat. Security Agy., Ft. Meade, Md., 1958—59; mgr. systems devel. RCA Corp., Cherry Hill, NJ, 1966-71; mgr. computer tech. svcs. Gencorp, Akron, Ohio, 1971-74; sr. mgr. computer applications R & D Ernst & Young LLP, Cleve., 1974-75, dir. nat. systems group, 1976-77, chief info. officer, nat. dir. software products, 1977-80, nat. ptnr., 1978-82, cons. ptnr. Phila., N.Y.C., L.A., 1983-95; ind. mgmt. cons. L.A., N.Y.C., 1996—. 1st lt. arty. U.S. Army, 1958-59. Mem.: Tournament Players Club, Union League of Phila., Plantation Country Club. Republican. Roman Catholic.

HAAS, EDWARD NORBERT, financial consultant, writer; b. New Orleans, Apr. 13, 1936; s. Arnold Aloysius Haas and Palma Josephine Neely; 1 adopted child, Kenneth Quigley. Lic. comml. pilot FAA, 1977. Sec.-treas. Honey Island Timber Co., Inc., Pearl River, La., 1976—2000, pres., 2000—. Dir. Honey Island Timber Co., Inc., Pearl River, 1976—. Author: Introspective Cosmology II, 2000, The Nature & Origins Of Murder Worship, 2001, In The Beginning Was The Internet, 2001, The Love Song Tree, A Fairy Tale Portrait Of God, 1999, The Story Of Drawden The Pig, 1999, Letters Against Murder Worship, 2000, Letters And Thoughts On Homosexuality, 2000, Pieces Of Moral And Dogmatic Theology, 2000, Two Letters For 1993, 2000, A Letter From A Father To His Son In 1994, 2001, Miscellaneous Letters, 2001, On Philosophy, 1 Long & 4 Short, 2001. With USAF, 1955—60. Roman Catholic. Avocation: bicycling. Home and Office: 39193 Haas Rd - Haaswood Pearl River LA 70452 Personal E-mail: htoknow@yahoo.com.

HAAS, EILEEN MARIE, homecare advocate; b. Pitts., Feb. 27, 1948; d. Michael Joseph and Bridget Agnes (Connolly) McNulty; m. Jerry Albert Haas, July 19, 1975; 1 child, Melissa. Student, York Coll. of Pa., 1975-78, Messiah Coll., Grantsville, Pa., 1978-80. Clk. Exch. Bur. Pitts., 1966-67; debt. collector Nat. Account Sys., Pitts., 1967-71; preadoptive advocate Hershey, Pa., 1983-84, Phila., 1984-85; homecare advocate Dillsburg, Pa., 1985-88, Deer Lodge, Mont., 1988-92, Gibsonia, Pa., 1992—. Interpreter svcs. St. Victors Ch., Bairdsford, Pa., 1992—; presenter Harrisburg (Pa.) Area C.C., 1985, Pa. Soc. Respiratory Therapy, Ctrl. Pa. chpt., 1985; co-presenter Coun. Exceptional Children, Salt Lake City, 1997; rschr. in pulmonary rehab. With USN, 1971-74. Mem. DAV, Am. Soc. Deaf Children, Coun. Exceptional Children, Assn. Severe Handicaps, Profl. Networking for Excellence in Svc. to Deaf and Hard of Hearing. Republican. Roman Catholic. Avocations: deaf education research, dysphagia research, writing, needlepoint, knitting. Home: 90 Kaufman Rd Gibsonia PA 15044-7950

HAAS, ELEANOR A. (MRS. PETER RALPH HAAS), business advisor; b. Jersey City; d. Nicholas Mark and Eleanor (Cochran) Alter de Csanytelek; m. Peter Ralph Haas. BA, Smith Coll. Account exec. Ruder & Finn, Inc., N.Y.C., 1966-68; founder, pres. The Haas Group, Inc., N.Y.C., 1968-86, MarketQuest, N.Y.C., 1986-98; v.p., dir. HMG Planning The Howard Marlboro Group, N.Y.C., 1988-91; managing dir. E-Technologies Assocs., LLC, N.Y.C., 1998-99; founder, editor CyberScout, N.Y.C., 1996—2000; mng. dir. The Calyx Group, N.Y.C., 2000—. Adj. assoc. prof. dept. journalism NYU, 1980-83, lectr. Sch. Continuing Edn. NYU, 1981-83. Mem. MIT Enterprise Forum of N.Y.; mem. adv. bd. Women's Leadership Exch., Oddcast Inc. Mem. Am. Mktg. Assn., Columbia Bus. Sch. Club N.Y., N.Y. New Media Assn., Fin. Women's Assn., N.Y. Software Industry Assn. Office: The Calyx Group 59 E 54th St Rm 73 New York NY 10022-4211 E-mail: eleanor@thecalyxgroup.com.

HAAS, FREDERICK CARL, retired paper and chemical company executive; b. Buffalo, Feb. 16, 1936; s. Karl A. and Marie S. (Shilling) H.; m. Dorothy A. Wittlief, Aug. 31, 1957; children— Kenneth Karl, Lawrence Frederick, Sandra Dorothy. BS in Chem. Engring, Purdue U., 1957; MS in Nuclear Engring, Rensselaer Poly. Inst., Troy, N.Y., 1959, PhD in Chem. Engring, 1960; grad., Advanced Mgmt. Program, Harvard U., 1978. Registered profl. engr., N.Y. Research engr. Cornell Aero. Lab., 1960-63; with Westvaco Corp., 1963-98, corp. research dir., then v.p., 1978-81, sr. v.p. ops., 1982—. Asst. prof. Potomac State Coll., 1966; mem. curriculum com., research com. U. Maine; chmn. research adv. com. Inst. Paper Chemistry; mem. president's key exec. com. Rensselaer Poly. Inst. Author papers in field. Bd. dirs. Syracuse Pulp and Paper Found. AEC fellow, 1957, Tappi fellow, 1994; recipient Disting. Engring. Alumnus award Purdue U., 1993, Outstanding Chem. Engring. award, 1993. Mem. Am. Mgmt. Assn. (research and devel. council), Am. Inst. Chem. Engrs., Am. Chem. Soc., TAPPI, Nat. Soc. Profl. Engrs., Indsl. Research Inst., Dirs. Indsl. Research, Can. Pulp and Paper Assn., Tri-State Shetland Sheep Dog Club, Sigma Xi. Methodist.

HAAS, GEORGE AARON, lawyer; b. N.Y.C., July 6, 1919; s. Herman Joseph and Violet (Cowen) H.; m. Miriam Durkin, Aug. 1942; children— Thomas Leonard, Karen Ann (Mrs. Michael Davenport), James G.D. AB, Princeton U., 1940; LL.B., Yale U., 1947. Bar: Ga. 1947. Since practiced in, Atlanta; partner Haas, Bridges & Kane (and predecessor firms), 1947—. Sec., dir. Lucerne Corp., East Freeway Corp., Crescent View Corp., Mountain View Corp., Lake Placid Corp. Mem. hosp. and health div. Atlanta Community Council, 1962-68; mem. tech. assistance com., del. White House Conf. on Children and Youth, 1970; state trustee from Ga. Nat. Easter Seal Soc. for Crippled Children and Adults, 1959-65, mem. exec. com., 1961-65, v.p., 1963-65, 1st v.p., 1965-66, mem. ho. of dels., 1965-73, pres. 1971-73; bd. dirs. 1965-73, chmn. formula rev. bd., mem. relations and standards rev. com., 1967-69, pres., 1969-71; trustee Ga. Easter Seal Soc. for Crippled Children and Adults, 1955-65, 78—, sec., 1957-58, pres., 1959-61, chmn. ho. of dels., 1967-69; Bd. dirs. Fulton-DeKalb chpt. Nat. Found.; mem. med. adv. bd. Ga. chpt. Am. Phys. Therapy Assn. Served to capt. F.A. AUS, World War II. Mem. ABA, Ga. Bar Assn., Atlanta Bar Assn. Clubs: Standard (Atlanta) (past sec., dir.). Lodges: Kiwanis. Home: 2575 Peachtree Rd NE Atlanta GA 30305-3694 Office: 2964 Peachtree Rd NW Atlanta GA 30305-2153

HAAS, HOWARD GREEN, retired bedding manufacturing company executive; b. Chgo., Apr. 14, 1924; s. Adolph and Marie (Green) H.; m. Carolyn Werbner, June 4, 1949; children: Jody, Jonathan. Student, U. Chgo., 1942; BBA, U. Mich., 1948. Promotion dir. Esquire, Inc., Chgo., 1949-50; advt. mgr. Mitchell Mfg. Co., Chgo., 1950-52, v.p. advt., 1952-56, v.p. sales, 1956-58; sales mgr. Sealy, Inc., Chgo., 1959-60, v.p. marketing, 1960-65, exec. v.p., 1965-67, pres., treas., 1967-86, 87. Bd. dirs. Brogden Tool & Die Co., Aurora Custom Machinery, Inc.; chmn. Howard Haas Assocs.; vis. prof. strategic mgmt. U. Chgo. Grad. Sch. Bus., 1989—. Author: The Leader Within, 1993. Past mem. nominating com. Glencoe Sch. Bd.; mem. print and drawing com. Art Inst. Chgo.; past chmn. parent's com. Washington U., St. Louis; past bd. dirs. Jewish Children's Bur.; mem. vis. com. Oriental Inst., U. Chgo., Meet the Composer. 1st lt. USAAF, 1943-45, ETO. Decorated Air medal with 3 oak leaf clusters; recipient Brotherhood award NCCJ, 1970, Human Relations award Am. Jewish Com., 1977 Mem. Nat. Assn. Bedding Mfrs. (past vice chmn., trustee), Birchwood Tennis Club (Highland Pk., Ill.), Masons. Jewish. Office: Howard Haas Assocs 208 S La Salle St Ste 1275 Chicago IL 60604-1101 E-mail: hghhaas@aol.com.

HAAS, JAMES WAYNE, accountant; b. Merrill, Wis., Sept. 27, 1944; s. Frank Joseph and Verna Antoinette (Beilke) H.; m. Patrice Marie Will, June 2, 1973 (div. Sept. 1997); children: Christopher Jon, Scott James. A in Acctg., N. Cen. Tech. Coll., 1968. Lic. ins. agt., Minn., Wis.; cert. tax profl. Contr., asst. treas. House of Merrill, Inc., Merrill, 1968-72; controller Semling Menke Co., Inc., Merrill, 1968-72; treas., dir. North Star Comms., Ltd., Gleason, Wis., 1971-72; pres., dir. Profl. Acctg. Systems, Inc., La Crosse, Wis., 1975-88; pres. Haas Enterprises, Inc., 1971-82; pres., treas. Adventure Capital, Ltd., 1971—; treas., prodn. mgr., dir. Modu-Line Windows, Wausau, Wis., 1977—78. Treas. Sys. Mgmt., Inc., St. Paul, 1983—84, Gateway Acctg. Svcs., Inc., Ft. Myers, Fla., 1982—83; v.p., treas., ops. mgr. Acctg. Bookkeeping Co., Inc., Wauwatosa, Wis., 1975—76; v.p. Marathon Mining & Mfg. Corp., Wausau, Wis., 1976, pres., 1977—78; mng. ptnr. Haas Properties, Mosinee, Wis., 1979—83; owner Midwest Investments, Winona, Minn., 1980—; pres., dir. Acctg. Bookkeeping

Cons., Ltd., 1987—88; owner Jim Haas Assocs., 1988—; pres. Jim Haas Assocs., LLC, Winona, 1999—; chmn., sec., dir. Consol. Bus. Svcs., Inc., La Crosse, Wis., 1992—; treas. Am. Bending Supply, Inc., Galesville, Wis., 1992—94; owner Tri-State Markers, La Crosse, 1995—; chmn., sec., treas., dir. Ferrous, Inc., Winona, 1996—, Mid-Am. Heat Treat, Inc., Winona, 1998—, Mid Am. Core and Mold, Inc., Winona, 2000—; sec. Goodview Clin., Ltd., 1998—; treas. M2 Comms., Ltd., Reno, 1998—; pres. The Watch Dog Group, Ltd., Shakopee, Minn., 2001—; chmn. The Aichalden Group, Ltd., La Crosse, Wis., 2002—. Mem. Adminstrv. Mgmt. Soc., Inst. Internat. Auditors, Nat. Notary Assn., Inst. Record Mgrs. and Adminstrs., Am. Soc. Notaries, Nat. Assn. Accts., Am. Inst. Profl. Numismatists (charter mem.), Am. Acctg. Assn., Nat. Soc. Pub. Accts., Nat. Soc. Tax Profls., Nat. Assn. Life Underwriters, Internat. Cmty. Corrections Assn., Am. Assn. Altruistic CPAs and Fin. Planners, Am. Soc. Tax Profls., Am. Soc. Metallurgists, Inst. Mgmt. Cons., Soc. of Cath. Order of Foresters, KC, Kiwanis (New Club Bldg. award), Optimists, Winona Lions. Office: 1005 W 5th St # D Winona MN 55987-5126 Home: 1339 Lauderdale Pl Onalaska WI 54650-3277 Office: 312 W Main St Arcadia WI 54612

HAAS, JERE DOUGLAS, nutritional sciences educator, researcher; b. Lancaster, Pa., Sept. 15, 1945; s. Jacob Charles and Dorothy Louise (Graeter) H.; m. Sharon Faye Pitt, June 22, 1968; children: Jeremy Michael, Jonathan Andrew. AB, Franklin and Marshall Coll., 1967; MA, Pa. State U., 1970, PhD, 1973. Trainee in human biology USPHS, Peru, 1971-73; asst. prof. anthropology U. Mass., Amherst, 1973-75; asst. prof. nutrition Cornell U., Ithaca, N.Y., 1975-80, assoc. prof., 1980-87, prof., 1987—; Nancy Schlegel Meinig prof. maternal and child nutrition; dir. human biology program, dir. divsn. nutritional scis. Cornell U., Ithaca, N.Y. Hon. rsch. fellow anatomy dept. U. Aberdeen, Scotland, 1982; vis. prof. Food Rsch. Inst., Stanford (Calif.) U., 1988-89; mem. com. on nutrition during pregnancy and lactation Inst. Medicine, NAS, 1988-90; advisor panel on nutrition WHO, 1991—; chair subcom. on maternal anthropometry, 1991-94; tech. adv. group on food and nutrition Pan Am. Health Orgn., 1996—; dir. divsn. nutrition and health Nat. inst. Pub. Health, Cuernavaca, Mex., 1998. Mem. editl. bd. Human Biology, 1984-88, Annals Human Biology, 1985—, Am. Jour. Human Biology, 1990-2002; contbr. more than 200 articles to profl. jours., chpts. to books. Rsch. grantee NSF, Bolivia, Peru, 1975-96, NIH, N.Y., Kans., Guatemala, 1978-94, 1998-2003, USDA, 1996-2003, Micronutrient Initiative, Philippines, 2001—. Fellow AAAS, Human Biology Assn. (exec. com. 1981-85); mem. Am. Assn. Phys. Anthropologists (v.p. 1992-94, pres. 1995-97), Am. Soc. Nutritional Scis., Soc. Internat. Nutrition Rsch. (exec. coun. 2000—), Am. Soc. Clin. Nutrition, Assn. Nutrition Depts. and Programs (treas. 1998—, chair 2003). Office: Cornell U #127 Savage Hall Ithaca NY 14853-6301

HAAS, JOHN C. architect; b. Columbus, Ohio, Nov. 3, 1934; s. John Clyde and Margaret (Merideth) H.; m. Jean Ann Scigliano, June 12, 1958 (dec. Apr. 1986); m. Joyce Conklin, May 9, 1987; children: Jeffrey, Joel, John. BArch, Pa. State U., 1958. Registered architect Pa., Ohio, N.J., N.Y., Del., W.Va., Md., Va., Mass., Fla., N.C. Archtl. draftsman Arthur E. Tennyson, Pitts., 1959-62; archtl. designer Diehl and Stein Architects, Princeton, NJ, 1962—63; staff architect Hankin and Hyres, Trenton, NJ, 1963—67; architect Mahony and Zvosec, Princeton, NJ, 1967-71; dir. archtl. planning dept. Gen. Housing Industries, State College, Pa., 1971-72; pres., CEO John C. Haas Assocs., Inc., State College, Pa., 1972—. Sec., treas. Pa. Archs. Licensure Bd., 1998—2002, v.p., 2002—; adv. bd. dir. PNC Bank of Ctrl. Pa. Prin. works include Nittany Apt. Housing, The Meadows Clinic, Fraser St. Parking Garage, BCH Office Bldg., Geisinger Med. Clinic, The Bryce Jordan Convocation Ctr., Pa. State U. (all State Coll.), Beaver Stadium Expansion, Pa. State U. Active Centre County United Way Campaign Cabinet, 1994, 95, 96; county chmn. United Way Campaign, 1997; mem. bd. dirs. Chamber of Bus. and Ind. of Centre County, 1996—, Centre County United Way, 1998—. Capt. U.S. Army, 1958-59. Mem. AIA (pres. mid. Pa. chpt. 1986-87), Nat. Coun. Archtl. Registration Bds., Pa. Soc. Architects (pres. 1993), State College Area C. of C. (pres. 1990-91, bd. dirs. 1984-92), Rotary (pres. 1988-89, bd. dirs.). Republican. Presbyterian. Home: 14 High Meadow Ln State College PA 16803-1853 Office: John C Haas Assocs Inc Architects Engrs Planners 1301 N Atherton St State College PA 16803-2932 E-mail: JHaas@HaasAEP.com.

HAAS, JOSEPH ALAN, court administrator, lawyer; b. Riverside, Calif., June 30, 1950; s. Garland August and Pauline (Anderson) H.; m. Barbara Roberts, May 27, 1978; children: Natalie C., Christina R. BA in Econs., U. Wash., 1972, MA in Econs., 1974; JD, Seattle U., 1983. Bar: Wash. 1984, U.S. Dist. Ct. (we. dist.) Wash. 1984, Md. 1986, U.S. Ct. Appeals (4th cir.) 1986. Regional coord. Adminstrv. Office U.S. Cts., Washington, 1975-80; chief dep. clk. U.S. Dist. Ct. for Western Wash., Seattle, 1981-84; clk. U.S. Dist. Ct. Md., Balt., 1984-96, U.S. Dist. Ct. for S.D., Sioux Falls, 1996—. Mem. Nat. Assn. for Ct. Mgmt., Fed. Ct. Clks. Assn. (pres. 1987-88, pres. elect 2000-01, pres. 2001-03), Wash. State Bar Assn. Office: US Dist Ct 400 S Phillips Ave Rm 128 Sioux Falls SD 57104-6851

HAAS, JOSEPH MARSHALL, petroleum consultant; b. Alexandria, La., June 21, 1927; s. Samuel and Lulu Susan (Haupt) H.; m. Mary Louise Nance, June 4, 1949 (dec. Jan. 1950); 1 child, Samuel Douglas; m. Marion Barker, Apr. 9, 1954; children: Joseph Marshall, Suzanne M., Thomas B., Katherine L. B of Mech. Engring., Ga. Inst. Tech., 1949. With Gen. Am. Oil Co., Dallas, 1949-78, asst. v.p. prodn. and engring., 1957-60, v.p. engring., 1960-78; petroleum cons. Haas Engring., 1978—. Pres., bd. dirs. Conejo Investments Inc., 1994—. With USNR, 1945-46. Mem. Am. Inst. Mining and Metall. Engrs., Masons (32 degree, Shriner), Dallas Petroleum Club, Tau Beta Pi, Sigma Chi, Pi Tau Sigma. Methodist. Home: 1119 Challenger St Austin TX 78734-3801 Office: 1123 Challenger St Austin TX 78734-3801

HAAS, JULIAN L. researcher, educator; b. Antonino, Kans., Sept. 27, 1938; s. Alfred A. and Thecla C. Haas. BA, St. Fidelis Coll., Herman, PA, 1961; MA, Capuchin Coll., Washington, DC, 1965; STL, Gregorian U., Rome, Italy, 1985; STD, Seraphicum Franciscan U., Rome, Italy, 1994. Prof. St. Fidelis H.S., Herman, Pa., 1966—71; dir. youth ctr. Thomas More Prep, Hays, Kans., 1971—77, dir. admissions, 1971—77; pastor St. Joseph's Parish, Hays, Kans., 1977—83; assoc. and pastor Annunciation Ch., Denver, 1985—89; rsch. staff Capuchin Hist. Inst., Rome, 1989—94; rschr., writer and lectr. Capuchin Friars, Saint Louis, Mo., 1994—2002, Colorado Springs, 2002—. Assoc. dean Diocese Salina, Hays, Kans., 1980—83; v.p. Salina Diocesan Priests' Senate, Salina, Kans., 1982—83. Chaplain KC, Hays, Kans., 1978—83; active Hays, Kans., 1979—83; bd. mem. Marian H.S., Hays, Kans., 1977—83. Recipient Fourth Degree, KC, 1982. Roman Catholic. Home: 15 W View PL Colorado Springs CO 80903 Personal E-mail: haas1938@yahoo.com.

HAAS, LESTER CARL, retired architect; b. Shreveport, La., Apr. 9, 1913; s. Jacob and Hanna (Kahn) H.; m. Niki Kal, Nov. 1, 1942; children: Dale Frances, Catherine Kal (Mrs. Fred Donald Youngswick). BA, Johns Hopkins U., 1933; BArch, U. Pa., 1936; postgrad., Ecole Des Beaux-Arts, N.Y.C., 1936-37; diplome, Ecole Des Beaux-Arts, Fontainebleau, France, 1939; vis. student in residence, Am. Acad., Rome, Italy, 1940. Archtl. apprentice W. Pope Barney, Phila., 1936-39; architect Robert & Co., 1940-41; prin. Lester C. Haas, Architect, Shreveport, 1946-65; ptnr. Haas, Massey & Assocs. (architects), Shreveport, 1966-88; mng. partner TAG-The Archtl. Group, 1978-85; prin. Lester C. Haas, FAIA(E), CCS-Architect, 1989-98, ret., 1998. Co-author: weekly column Ark-La-Texture, 1967-71. Principal works include, Pioneer Bank and Trust Co., Shreveport main office and 9 br. banks, 1948-78, KTBS offices, radio and TV studios, Shreveport, 1948-76, Caddo Sch. Exceptional Children, Shreveport, 1956, also addition, 1977, La Sands Western Hills Motel, Bossier City, La., 1957, St. Pius X Sch., convent and sanctuary alterations, North Shreveport, 1962, Barksdale Officer Club, Barksdale AFB, La. Alteration and Addition, 1965, Northwestern State U. at Shreveport, 1966, Restoration and Renovation of the Strand Theatre, Shreveport, 1978-85, C-Barc Adult Workshop, Shreveport, 1970, additions, 1979, Adminstrv. Center, Caddo Parish Sch. Bd., Shreveport, 1971, Master Plan and Adminstrn. Bldg., Delgado Coll., New Orleans, 1979-81, Shreveport Chamber Pla., 1983, Caddo Parish Communications Dist. Number 1, Emergency Communication Ctr. E-911, 1988. Chmn. rev. com. N.W. La. Areawide Health Planning Council, 1973-75, pres., 1975-76; pres. Travelers Aid, 1951, Children's Service Bur., 1952, Courtyard Players Civic Theatre, 1954, ARC, 1963-65, NCCJ, 1965-69; nat. bd., 1970-73, St. Vincent Acad. Parents Club, 1966-67, Lyric Ball, 1967, Caddo Found. for Exceptional Children, 1972-74; v.p. Caddo-Bossier Assn. Retarded Citizens, 1957, United Fund, 1963-67, Caddo Found. Exceptional Children, 1967-72; adv. bd. Congregation Daughters of Cross, 1965-69; community adv. com. Jr. League, 1973-76, all Shreveport; mem. Shreveport Bldg. Bd., 1979-83; pres. Mental Health Assn. Caddo-Bossier, 1981-82; founding mem. Caddo-Bossier Assn. Retarded Citizens Found., 1997. Lt. USNR, 1942-45. Decorated Navy Commendation ribbon; recipient Merit award 2d Internat. Lighting Exposition, 1947; Ann. Brotherhood citation Shreveport chpt. NCCJ, 1974; John Stewardson Travelling scholar in architecture, 1939-40; honoree Martin Luther King Health Ctr. Christian Svc. Inst., 1991; recipient 5 CSI Regional Specification awards. Fellow AIA (pres. N.La. chpt. 1955, exec. com. Gulf States regional council 1956, pres. Shreveport chpt. 1984); mem. Constrn. Specifications Inst. (cert. constrn. specifier 1979, pres. Shreveport chpt. 1970-71, Nat. Jury Fellows 1974-76), La. Architects Assn. (rep. to Gov.'s Com. to Rewrite Fire Marshal's Act 1973, bd. dirs. 1984), Shreveport Jr. C. of C. (past v.p.), Shreveport C. of C. (bd. dirs., officer), Am. Legion, D.A.V., Tau Sigma Delta. Jewish (pres. congregation 1967, 68). Club: Greater Shreveport Racquet. Home: 1031 Dudley Dr Shreveport LA 71104-4732

HAAS, LU ANN, counselor; b. Waterloo, Iowa, Oct. 16, 1956; d. Leonard Edward and Naomi Lee (Binley) H.; divorced; children: Shauna Lee Haas, Nicholas William Smith. AAS, Ctrl. Tex. Coll., 1986; BA magna cum laude, Mt. mercy Coll., 1992; MA, U. Iowa, 1993. Cert. rehab. counselor; cert. lay spkr. Meth. Ch. Ind. truck driver, 1982-83; night supr. Four Oaks-John Mcdonald Residential Treatment, Monticello, Iowa, 1991-92; security officer RA-CO Security Co., 1993-94; substance abuse counselor Area Substance Abuse Coun., Anamosa, Iowa, 1993-94; counseling psychologist Dept. Vets Affairs, Cin., 1994-96, Dallas, 1996-97; mentor host program Fairfield Elem. Sch., Copperas Cove, Tex., 1994-97; ret., 1997. Spkr. in field; cons. in field. Unit sec. United Meth. Women. Sgt. U.S. Army, 1975-81, 83-87. Leonard A. Miller scholar, 1993. Mem. ACA, Nat. Rehab. Assn., Am. Rehab. Counseling Assn., Nat. Rehab. Counseling Assn. (sec./treas. 1997, 98, bd. dirs. 1995, 96, membership chmn. 1995-97), Tex. Rehab. Counseling Assn., Disabled Am. Vets. (life), U. Iowa Alumni Assn., Kappa Gamma Pi (liaison Mt. Mercy Coll.), Am. Legion, Vietnam Vets. Am. (assoc. Miami Valley (Ohio) chpt.). Democrat. Methodist. Avocations: crocheting, reading, writing. Home: 1404 Janet Ln Copperas Cove TX 76522-1228

HAAS, NEIL B. psychiatrist; b. Detroit, Feb. 27, 1941; s. Abraham Haas and Florence Nita Pearlman; m. Rowena Marie Haas, June 10, 1965; 1 child, Jeremy Channing. Student, U. Mich., 1958-61, MD, 1965; M in Social Psychiatry, UCLA, 1973. Psychiat. resident UCLA, 1968-71; pvt. practice L.A., 1971—. Chief chem. dependency Sepulved VA Med. Ctr., North Hills, Calif., 1994-2000; asst. clin. prof. psychiatry UCLA, 1974—. Active L.A. County Narcotics and Dangerous Drugs Commn., 1985—. Mem. Am. Acad. Addiction Psychiatry, Am. Soc. Addictive Medicine, Am. Psychiat. Assn., So. Calif. Psychiat. Soc. (ethics com.). Office: Ste 211 1800 Fairburn Los Angeles CA 90025-4968 E-mail: nhaas@ucla.edu.

HAAS, PAUL RAYMOND, petroleum company executive; b. Kingston, N.Y., Mar. 10, 1915; s. Frederick J. and Amanda (Lange) H.; m. Mary F. Diedrick, Aug. 30, 1936; children: Rheta Marie, Raymond Paul, Rene Marie. AB, Rider Coll., 1934, LL.D., 1976. C.P.A., Tex. Acct. Arthur Andersen & Co. (C.P.A.s), N.Y.C. and Houston, 1934-41; with La Gloria Oil & Gas Co., Corpus Christi, Tex., 1941-59, v.p., treas., dir., 1947-59; adminstrv. v.p. Tex. Eastern Transmission Corp., Houston, 1958-59; pres., chmn. bd. Prado Oil & Gas Co., 1959-66, Wiltex Corp., 1950-65, Garland Co., 1956-65, Citronelle Oil & Gas Co., 1967-69, Corpus Christi Oil and Gas Co., 1968-90, Corpus Christi Leaseholds Inc., 1990—, Corpus Christi Exploration Co., 1976-90; ltd. partner Salomon Bros., 1973-81. Ind. oil and gas operator, 1959—. Trustee Corpus Christi Ind. Sch. Dist., 1951-58, pres., 1956-58; mem. Tex. Bd. Edn., 1962-72, vice chmn., 1970-72; mem. Gov.'s Com. Edn., 1966-69; Trustee Paul and Mary Haas Found., 1954—, Robert T. Wilson Found., 1954-72, Rider Coll., 1959-67, Moody Found., 1966-73, Found. Center, 1970-75, Council on Founds., 1970-76, Commn. on Philanthropy and Pub. Needs, 1973-75, Univ. Cancer Found. M.D. Anderson Hosp. and Tumor Inst., 1975— . Presbyn. (elder). Home: 4500 Ocean Dr Apt 9A Corpus Christi TX 78412-2572 Office: Corpus Christi Holding Co PO Box 779 Corpus Christi TX 78403-0779

HAAS, PETER M. political science educator; b. Oakland, Calif., Jan. 23, 1955; s. Ernst B. and Hildegarde Haas; m. Julie Zuckman, Apr. 28, 1986; 1 child, David. BA (hons.), Univ. Mich., 1977; PhD, Mass. Inst. Tech., 1986. Teaching fellow Harvard Univ., 1984, 85; marine policy rsch. fellow Marine Policy Ctr. Woods Hole Oceanographic Inst., 1986-87; asst. prof. political sci. dept. Univ. Mass., Amherst, 1986-92; project dir. Ctr. for Internat. Affairs Harvard Univ., 1990-92; assoc. prof. political sci. dept. Univ. Mass., 1992-98, prof. political sci. dept., 1998—. Vis. asst. prof. Yale Univ. Political Sci. dept. 1986; editl. bd. Jour. of European Public Policy, 1999—, Global Environmental Politics, 1999—, Policy Studies Jour., 2003—; adj. rsch. fellow Ctr. for Sci. and International Affairs Harvard Univ., 1990—; vis. prof. Oxford U., 2002, The Watson Inst., Brown U., Providence, 2002-03; presenter at numerous confs. Author: Knowledge, Power and International Policy Coordination, 1997, Institutions for the Earth: Sources of Effective International Environmental Protection, 1993, Saving the Mediterranean: The Politics of International Environmental Cooperation, 1990, The International Environment in the Global Economy, 2003, Emerging Forces in Environmental Governance, 2003; contbr. numerous articles to profl. jours.; and book chpts. Recipient rsch. fellowship German Marshall Fund, 1992, Peace and World Security Studies Program, Hampshire Coll., 1989, 99, Nat. Sci. Found. 1990, 92, Rockefeller Brothers Fund Project grant, 1991 and others. Office: Univ Mass political sci dept 216 Thompson Hall Amherst MA 01003 E-mail: Haas@polsci.umass.edu.

HAAS, RAYMOND P. lawyer; b. Corpus Christi, Tex., Dec. 9, 1942; BA cum laude, Yale U., 1964, LLB, 1967. Bar: Calif. 1967. Law clk. to Hon. Roger J. Traynor Supreme Ct. of Calif., 1967-68; atty. Howard, Rice, Nemerovski, Canady, Falk & Rabkin, San Francisco. Trustee San Francisco U. High Sch., 1973-78, 85-88, chmn., 1973-76, treas., 1986-88; trustee Pacific Presbyn. Med. Ctr., 1979-91, vice chmn. 1986-91. Mem. ABA (forum com. on franchising, antitrust law sect., bus. law sect., internat. law sect., patent, copyright and trademarks sect., sci. and tech. sect.), State Bar Calif., Bar Assn. San Francisco (computer law sect.), Licensing Execs. Soc., Computer Law Assn., Order of Coif. Office: Howard Rice Nemerovski Canady Falk & Rabkin 3 Embarcadero Ctr Ste 7 San Francisco CA 94111-4074

HAAS, RICHARD, lawyer; b. Glens Falls, N.Y., Sept. 1, 1924; s. Marc and Henrietta (Vogelsanger) H.; m. Dorothy J. Walz, Aug. 2, 1946; children: Eric, Marco, Gregory. AB, UCLA, 1951; LLB, U. Calif., Berkeley, 1950. Bar: Calif. 1951, U.S. Dist. Ct. (no., cen., ea. and so. dists.) Calif. 1951, U.S. Supreme Ct. 1970. Ptnr. Brobeck, Phleger & Harrison, San Francisco, 1959-79; mem. Lasky, Haas & Cohler, San Francisco, 1979-94. Served to lt. USNR, 1941-46. Fellow Am. Bar Found., Am. Coll. Trial Lawyers; mem. Order of Coif. Clubs: Claremont Country (Oakland, Calif.); Berkeley Tennis. Republican. Home: 2901 Forest Ave Berkeley CA 94705-1310 Office: Lasky Haas & Cohler 505 Sansome St Fl 12 San Francisco CA 94111-3106 E-mail: mugford389@aol.com.

HAAS, ROBERT DOUGLAS, apparel manufacturing company executive; b. San Francisco, Apr. 3, 1942; s. Walter A. Haas Jr. and Evelyn (Danzig) Haas; m. Colleen Gershon, Jan. 27, 1974; 1 child, Elise Kimberly. BA, U. Calif., Berkeley, 1964; MBA, Harvard U., 1968. With Peace Corps, Ivory Coast, 1964-66; fellow White House, Washington, 1968-69; assoc. McKinsey & Co., 1969-72; with Levi Strauss & Co., San Francisco, 1973—, sr. v.p. corp. planning and policy, 1978-80, pres. new bus. group, 1980, pres. operating groups, 1980-81, exec. v.p., COO, 1981-84, pres., CEO, 1984-89, CEO, chmn. bd., 1989-99, chmn. bd. dirs., 2000. Pres. Levi Strauss Found.; mem. Global leadership team. Hon. dir. San Francisco AIDS Found.; trustee Ford Found.; bd. dirs. Bay Area Coun.; past bd. dirs. Am. Apparel Assn. Fellow White House fellow, 1968—69. Mem.: Meyer Friedman Inst. (bd. dirs.), Calif. Bus. Roundtable, Trilateral Commn., Coun. Fgn. Rels., Conf. Bd., Bay Area Coun., Brookings Inst. (trustee), Phi Beta Kappa. Office: Levi Strauss & Co 1155 Battery St San Francisco CA 94111-1256

HAAS, ROBERT JOHN, aerospace engineer; b. Dayton, Ohio, Apr. 14, 1930; s. Robert J. Haas and Harriett (Longstreth) Bevan; m. Florence A. Eldred, June 6, 1952 (div. June 1984); adopted children: Jeffrey (dec.), Lisa Haas Cappuccio; m. Gayle F. Byrne, Dec. 14, 1984; stepchildren: Patrick Barton, Marissa Barton; children: Amber Haas, Robert J. Haas III. Student, U.S. Mil. Acad., 1948-51; BS in Petroleum Engring., U. Tulsa, 1954. Petroleum engr. Skelly Oil Co., Tulsa, 1953-54; propulsion engr., supr. Marquardt, Van Nuys, Calif., 1957-64, mgr. rocket programs, 1964-69, dir. test and facilities, 1969-72, gen. mgr. environ. systems, 1972-75; plant gen. mgr. Williams Internat., Ogden, Utah, 1975-79, sr. v.p. engring. Walled Lake, Mich., 1979-86, sr. v.p. product planning and mktg., 1986-90; sr. advisor, cons. Las Vegas, Nev., 1990—; CEO Haas Enterprises, Consulting Firm, Las Vegas, 1992—. Cons. Marquardt, Van Nuys, 1961-75; bd. dirs. Verile Corp. Author: Approach to Aerospace Plane Propulsion, 1960. Lectr. and advisor Weber State Coll., U. Utah and various high schs. and clubs., 1975-79; pres. Marquardt Mgmt. Club, 1971. 1st lt. USAF, 1954-56. Mem. AIAA, Navy League (lifetime). Republican. Roman Catholic. Achievements include contribution to devel. and prodn. of world's smallest turbofan for cruise missiles; discoveries in the field of integrated propulsion modules for missiles, economical methods of testing ramjets, turbines and rocket engines. Home and Office: Haas Enterprize PO Box 33126 Las Vegas NV 89133-3126

HAAS, ROBERT LANCE, surgeon, consultant; b. N.Y.C., Oct. 7, 1933; s. Kalman and Ruth Haas; m. Lois Feldman, Apr. 14, 1957; children: Kara, Robyn, Bradley, Felice. BS in Biology, Ohio State U., 1953; DDS, Columbia U., 1957, MPH, 1973. Diplomate Am. Bd. Oral & Maxillofacial Surgery. Intern in maxillofacial surgery Harlem Hosp., N.Y.C., 1958; resident in maxillofacial surgery Grasslands Hosp., Valhalla, N.Y., 1960; pvt. practice; assoc. attending maxillofacial surgeon N.Y. Med. Coll.-Grassland Hosp., Valhalla, Bronx (N.Y.)-Lebanon Med. Ctr., Fordham-Misericordia Med. Ctr., The Bronx; attending maxillofacial surgeon Royal Hosp., The Bronx; attending surgeon, chief maxillofacial surgery & dentistry Newark Beth Israel Med. Ctr., dir. out-patient dept. Contbr. articles to profl. jours. Adminstrv. judge City of Tampa; co-chmn. New Tampa Emergency Prepared Com.. Fellow Am. Coll. Oral and Maxillofacial Surgeons, Am. Acad. Cosmetic Surgeons, Internat. Soc. Oral and Maxillofacial Surgeons, Am. Dental Soc. Anesthesiology, Internat. Assn. Study Pain, Am. Pain Soc.; mem. APHA, state and local affiliates of ADA, Internat. Assn. Maxillofacial Surgery, Hillsborough County Hosp. Authority, Am. Assn. Oral and Maxillofacial Surgeons, Nat. Ctr. Health Edn. (charter assoc.), N.Y. Acad. Scis., Alpha Omega. Home: 17627 Nathans Dr Tampa FL 33647-2273

HAAS, SIR RUSSELL (DUKE OF ELBASAN), federal agency administrator; b. Casper, Wyo., June 18, 1940; s. Darrell Harland Haas and Sue Ellen (Reynolds) Ferguson. M of Engring., Scranton, PA, 1976; Engring. degree, UCLA, 1977; Doctor Religous Humanities, Pheonix, AZ; Doctor Divinity, Modesto, CA. Engr. Lockheed, Palmdale, Calif., 1963-95; dir., CEO R.L. Haas Corp.; postmaster gen. The Principality of St. Michel de Clermont. Mem. Space Shuttle Orbiter Structural Test Team. Author, Editor: The Teaching of the Magi, 2000. Charter mem. Presdl. Task Force, 1993—2001. With U.S. Army, 1963—69. Mem. N.Y. Acad. Scis. (life), Archaeological Conservancy of the U.S. (life), Elbasan Coll. Arms (chiar harold). Balenl. Home: 36633 N 94th St E Littlerock CA 93543 Office: PO Box 397 Littlerock CA 93543

HAAS, SHEILA SPERBER, writer, consultant; b. Richmond, Va., July 27, 1942; d. Gustave Howard and Mae (Toobert) Sperber; m. François Haas, June 2, 1974; children: Alex Oliver, Ariane Esther. BA, NYU, 1964; PhD, CUNY, 1980. Freelance writer, 1990—; mng. editor, writer Complementary Medicine for the Physician newsletter WellMet Publs., N.Y.C., 1996—2000; mng. editor Dermatology Focus newsletter Dermatology Found., Evanston, Ill., 1990—. Co-author: The Essential Asthma Book, 1987, The Chronic Bronchitis and Emphysema Handbook, 2000. Pres. Washington Sq. Pk. Coun., N.Y.C., 1983—95; bd. mem. Washington Sq. Assn., N.Y.C., 1978—90. Recipient Cmty. Svc. award, Village Reform Dem. Club, 1988. Mem.: AAAS. Avocations: photography, gardening, French culture.

HAAS, WILLIAM PAUL, humanities educator, former college president; b. Newark, May 31, 1927; s. Joseph J. and Elizabeth (Ryan) H. AB, Providence Coll., 1948; STL, Pontifical Inst., Washington, 1954; PhD, U. Fribourg, Switzerland, 1962; DBA (hon.), Bryant Coll., Providence, 1966; LLD, U. R.I., 1967, Brown U., 1969; DD, Conn. Wesleyan U., 1969; DHL, R.I. Coll., 1970, Salve Regina Coll., 1971. Ordained priest Roman Cath. Ch., 1953, laicized, 1973; prof. theology and philosophy Emmanuel Coll., Boston, 1954-60; prof. philosophy Providence Coll., 1962-63, 71-72, pres., 1965-71; asso. prof. U. Notre Dame, 1963-65; on leave as post-doctoral research asso. Boston U., 1972-73; vice chancellor for acad. affairs Mass. State Coll. System, 1973-79; pres. North Adams State Coll., Mass., 1979-83; prof. humanities Bryant Coll., Smithfield, R.I., 1983-96. Inaugurated spl. program religious studies Purdue U., 1963-65; vis. prof. contemporary theology Wabash Coll., Crawfordsville, Ind., 1964-65; vis. distinguished prof. U. R.I., 1971-72; Mem. R.I. Council Arts, 1967-70, R.I. Adv. Council State Tech. Services Act, 1965, 1967-71; mem. commn. learning Assn. Am. Colls., 1966-69; adv. council extension and continuing edn. Dept. Health, Edn. and Welfare, 1966-70; mem. commn. humanities in schs. Nat. Found. on Arts and the Humanities, 1967-71; chmn. R.I. Higher Edn. Council, 1969-71 Author: The Conception of Law and the Unity of Peirce's Philosophy, 1964, The Contemporary Arts, 1965; Contbr. articles to profl. jours. Bd. dirs. R.I. Philharmonic Orch., 1965-68, R.I. Found. Repertory Theatre, 1966-71, R.I. Urban Coalition, 1969-71, Packard Manse (center ecumenical studies), Boston, 1965-67; trustee John F. Kennedy Meml. Fund R.I., 1966-71, New Eng. Colls. Fund, 1970-71, Rocky Hill Sch., 1971-73, Bryant Coll., 1971-79; bd. dirs. United Fund R.I., 1967-71, Howard Found., Brown U., 1969-73; chmn. R.I. com. Rhodes Scholarship Trust, 1969, mem., 1970; bd. dirs. Humanities Forum of R.I., 1989—; mem. R.I. Com. for the Humanities, 1991-98. Mem. Am. Soc. Aesthetics, Nat. Cath. Edn. Assn. (exec. com. coll. and univ. dept. 1970-73) Home: 2 Vanderbilt Ave Newport RI 02840-4342

HAASE, ASHLEY THOMSON, microbiology educator, researcher; b. Chgo., Dec. 8, 1939; s. Milton Conrad and Mary Elizabeth Minter (Thomson) H.; m. Ann DeLong, 1962; children: Elizabeth, Stephanie, Harris. BA, Lawrence Coll., 1961; MD, Columbia U., 1965. Intern Johns Hopkins Hosp., Balt., 1965-67; clin. assoc. Nat. Inst. Allergy and Infectious Disease, Bethesda, Md., 1967-70; vis. scientist Nat. Inst. Med. Rsch., London, 1970-71; chief infectious disease sect. VA Med. Ctr., San Francisco, 1971-84, med. investigator, 1978-83; prof. microbiology U. Minn., Mpls., 1984-99, head dept., 1984—, Regents' prof., 1999—. Mem. fellowship screening com. Am. Cancer Soc., San Francisco, 1978-81; mem. UNESCO Internat. Cell Rsch. Orgn., India, 1978; mem. nat. adv. coun. Nat. Inst. Allergy and Infectious Diseases, 1986-91, mem. task force on microbiology and infectious diseases, 1991, Method to Extend Rsch. in Time investigator, 1989—, chair AIDS rsch. adv. com., 1993-96, chmn. vaccine subcom.; Javits neurosci. investigator Nat. Inst. Neurol. and Communicative Disorders and Stroke, 1988-95; chmn. panel on AIDS, U.S.-Japan Coop. Med. Sci. Program, 1988-95; mem. OAR AIDS Rsch. Evaluation Working Group, 1995-96; mem. adv. com. for career awards in biomed. scis. Burroughs-Wellcome Fund, 1995-2000; trustee Lawrence U., 1997-2000; adv. coun. NIH Office AIDS Rsch., 2002-. Editor: Microbial Pathogenesis, 1988-94; contbr. articles on AIDS pathogenesis and other topics in neurovirology to profl. jours. Recipient Lucia R. Briggs Disting. Achievement award Lawrence Coll., 1990. Mem. Am. Soc. Microbiology, Assn. Am. Physicians, Am. Soc. Clin. Investigation, Am. Soc. Virology, Assn. Med. Schs. Microbiology Chmn., Infectious Diseases Soc. Am., Nat. Multiple Sclerosis Soc. (adv. com. 1978-84), Am. Assn. Immunologists, Phi Beta Kappa, Alpha Omega Alpha. Democrat. Home: 14 Buffalo Rd Saint Paul MN 55127-2136 Office: U Minn Dept Microbiology 420 Delaware St SE Minneapolis MN 55455-0374 E-mail: haase001@umn.edu.

HAASE, DIXIE CAROL, retired manufacturing worker, writer; b. Granby, Mo., July 26, 1934; d. Fred Alton McDaniel and Helen Maurine Capps; m. Loren Alva Haase, Oct. 5, 1952; children: Kathleen, Leslie, Beverly and Barbara (twins). Grad., Granby (Mo.) H.S., 1952. Seamstress Granby Mfg. co., 1952, 53-70; with Miller Mfg. Co., La-Z Boy, Neosho, Mo., 1971-97. Freelance writer Newton County News, Granby, 1986—, Neosho Post, 1998—; author: Granby—Oldest Mining Town, Vol. I, 1982, Vol. II, 1986, Searching Shoal Creek, 1993, also 2 cemetery books, 10 books on mines and miners. City

Historian Granby City Coun., 1993. Mem. Granby Hist. Soc., Neosho Hist. Soc., Genealogy Soc. (vol. over 10,000 hrs. in rsch.). Republican. Avocations: research, photography, church, family. Home: 1298 S Main St Granby MO 64844-8128

HAASE, DONALD PAUL, German language, literature and culture educator; b. Cin., Mar. 20, 1950; m. Harry Paul and Evelyn Blanche Haase; m. Connie Lee Kordenbrock, Mar. 18, 1972; children: Emily Marie, Rebecca Anne, Sarah Elizabeth. BA, U. Cin., 1972, MA, 1973; PhD, U. N.C., 1979. Vis. asst. prof. Miami U., Oxford, Ohio, 1979-81; asst. prof. German, Wayne State U., Detroit, 1981-85, assoc. prof., 1985—, chmn. dept., 1989—, dir. jr. yr. in Germany programs, 1993-95. Mem. editorial bd. Wayne State U. Press, Detroit, 1989—. Editor: Reception of Grimms' Fairy Tales, 1993, English Fairy Tales and More English Fairy Tales, 2002; contbg. author: Deutsches Literatur-Lexikon, 1986; mng. editor Carolina Quar., 1974-75; editor Marvels and Tales: Jour. Fairy-Tale Studies, 1997—; mem. editl. bd. The Child and the City Series, 2000—; contbg. editor Oxford Companion to Fairy Tales, 2000; contbr. articles to profl. jours. Bd. dirs. St. Cyril Sch., Taylor, Mich., 1982; mem. strategic planning com. Livonia (Mich.) Pub. Schs., 1992. Recipient Probus award for acad. achievement Probus Club, Detroit, 1987, Pres.'s award for excellence in tchg. Wayne State U., 1985; grantee German Acad. Exch. Svc., 1976, 90, NEH, 1985, 87, 88, 90, 94. Mem. MLA (regional del. 1989-91), Brueder Grimm-Gesellschaft, Am. Assn. Tchrs. German, Am. Folklore Soc, Internat. Soc. for Folk Narrative Rsch., Phi Beta Kappa. Office: Wayne State U 443 Manoogian Hall Detroit MI 48202

HAASE, GERALD MARTIN, pediatric surgeon; b. Shanghai, Jan. 29, 1947; s. Warner A. and Jean E. Haase; children: Sean Hale, Ryan Eric, Jessica Ann; m. Peggy Newman. BA, Johns Hopkins U., 1968; postgrad., Wayne State U. Med. Sch., 1968-70; MD, Tufts U., 1972. Diplomate Am. Bd. Surgery, Pediatric Surgery, Critical Care. Resident in surgery U. Colo., Denver, 1972-74, 75-77; resident in pediat. surgery Children's Hosp., Boston, 1974-75, fellow pediat. surgery Columbus, Ohio, 1977-79; practice medicine Denver Pediat. Surgeons, 1979—99; profl. LLC, 1999—. Chmn. dept. pediatric surgery Children's Hosp., Denver, 1980—91; cons. pediat. surgeon Fitzsimons Army Med. Ctr., Aurora, Colo., 1982—96; clin. asst. prof. surgery U. Colo. Health Sci. Ctr., Denver, 1979—84, assoc. prof., 1985—91, prof., 1992—; chmn. surg. steering com. Children's Cancer Group, 1987—92, group V chmn., 1992—2001; chmn. bd. sci. counselors Cancer Treatment Rsch. Found., 1994—2002, Bd. dirs. Am. Cancer Soc., 1991—96. Mem. AMA, ACS, Denver Med. Soc., Colo. Med. Soc., Am. Acad. Pediatrics, Am. Pediat. Surg. Assn. (chmn. cancer com. 1995-98), Soc. Surg. Oncology, Internat. Soc. Pediat. Oncology, Nat. Childhood Cancer Found. (med. and sci. adv. bd. 1995-2000), Internat. Soc. Pediat. Surg. Oncology (charter mem. exec. coun.), Extracorpeal Life Support Orgn. (charter mem.), Am. Soc. Clin. Oncology, Pacific Assn. Pediat. Surgery, N.Y. Acad. Sci., Children's Oncology Group (charter mem.), Internat. Consortium Cure Childhood Cancer China (vice chmn.), Sigma Phi Epsilon, Delta Phi Alpha. Office: Professional LLC 1056 E 19th Ave # B190 Denver CO 80218-1007 E-mail: haase.gerald@tchden.org.

HAASLER, GEORGE BRUCE, cardiothoracic surgeon; b. Hamburg, Germany, Aug. 14, 1952; came to U.S., 1959; m. Barbara Haasler; children: Erik, Christopher, Brian, Benjamin, Molly. BA in Math., SUNY, Buffalo, 1973; MD, Columbia U., 1977. Diplomate Am. Bd. Surgery, Thoracic Surgery, Laser Surgery. Intern gen. surgery Columbia U., N.Y.C., 1977-82, resident thoracic and cardiac surgery, 1982-85; asst. prof. cardiothoracic surgery Med. Coll. Wis., Milw., 1985-91, assoc. prof. cardiothoracic surgery, 1991—. Chief cardiothoracic surgery sect. Zablocki Vets. Hosp., Milw., 1986-92; mem. thoracic surgery subcom. Radiation Therapy Oncology Group, Phila., 1988-96; mem. exam. cons. com. Am. Bd. Thoracic Surgery, Evanston, Ill., 1996-97. Contbr. chpts. in med. textbooks and articles to profl. jours. Fellow ACS; mem. Internal Soc. for Heart and Lung Transplantation, Gen. Thoracic Surg. Club, Soc. Thoracic Surgeons, Tri-State Thoracic Soc. (gen. chmn.), Wis. Thoracic Soc., Pi Mu Epsilon. Avocations: classical musician, mathematics. Office: Dept Cardiothoracic Surgery 9200 W Wisconsin Ave Milwaukee WI 53226-3522

HAASS, RICHARD NATHAN, federal agency administrator, educator; b. Bklyn., July 28, 1951; s. Irving B. and Marcella Haass BA, Oberlin (Ohio) Coll., 1973; M in Philosophy, Oxford U., Eng., 1975, PhD, 1982. Legis. asst. U.S. Sen. Claiborne Pell, Washington, 1975; research assoc. Internat. Inst. for Strategic Studies, London, 1977-79; spl. asst. to undersec. def. U.S. Dept. Def., Washington, 1979-80; dir. office regional security affairs U.S. Dept. State, Washington, 1981-82, dep. for policy bur. European and Can. affairs, 1982-85, spl. Cyprus coordinator, 1983-85; lectr. pub. policy John F. Kennedy Sch. govt. Harvard U., Cambridge, Mass., 1985-89; spl. asst. to pres. Nat. Security Affairs, 1989-93; sr. dir. near east and south Asia Nat. Security Coun., 1989-93; sr. assoc. Carnegie Endowment for Internat. Peace, Washington, 1993-94; dir. nat. security programs, sr. fellow Coun. on Fgn. Rels., Washington, 1994-96; v.p., dir. fgn. policy programs Brookings Instn., 1996—2000; dir. policy planning Dept. State, 2001—. Author: Congressional Power: Implications for American Security Policy, 1979, Beyond the INF Treaty: Arms, Arms Control and the Atlantic Alliance, 1988, Conflicts Unending: The United States and Regional Disputes, 1990, The Power to Persuade, 1994, Intervention: The Use of American Military Force in The Post-Cold War World, 1994, The Reluctant Sheriff: The United State after the Cold War, 1997, The Bureaucratic Entrepreneur, 1999; editor: Superpower Arms Control: Setting the Record Straight, 1987, Economic Sanctions and American Diplomacy, 1998, Transatlantic Tensions, 1999, Honey and Vinegar: Incentives, Sanctions, and Foreign Policy, 2000. Recipient Superior Honor award Dept. State, 1982, Presdl. Citizens medal, 1991; Rhodes scholar Oxford U., 1973. Mem. Internat. Inst. for Strategic Studies, Coun. on Fgn. Rels., Trilateral Commn. Office: Dept of State 2200 C Street NW Washington DC 20520

HAAYEN, RICHARD JAN, university official, insurance company executive; b. Bklyn., June 30, 1924; s. Cornelius Marius and Cornelia Florence (Muskus) H.; m. Marilyn Jean Messner, Aug. 30, 1946; children— Richard Jan, Peter Wyckoff, James Carell. BS, Ohio State U., 1948; D in Pub. Svc. (hon.), Nat. Coll. Edn., Evanston, Ill. With Allstate Ins. Co., 1950—, v.p. underwriting, 1969-75, exec. v.p., 1975-80, pres., 1980-86, chmn., chief exec. officer, 1986-89; exec.-in-residence So. Meth. U., Dallas, 1989—. Bd. dirs. Guaranty Fed. Savs. Bank, Dallas, R.L.I. Ins. Co., Peoria, Ill. Bd. dirs. Dallas World Salute, Communities-in-Schs., Dallas, Dallas Opera. Mem. Nat. Assn. Ind. Insurers, Am. Arbitration Assn. (arbitrator), Phi Delta Theta. Republican. Home: 9 Glenshire Ct Dallas TX 75225-2040 Office: 7557 Rambler Rd Ste 1424 Dallas TX 75231-2390

HABACHY, SUZAN SALWA SABA, development economist, non profit administrator; b. Cairo, July 15, 1933; came to the U.S., 1952; d. Saba and Gameela (Gindy) H. BA, Bryn Mawr (Pa.) Coll., 1954; MA, Harvard U., Cambridge, Mass., 1956. Teaching fellow Ohio U., Athens, 1957-58; economist Mobil Oil Co., N.Y.C., 1959-64; reporter, editor Petroleum Intelligence Weekly, N.Y.C., 1964-65, McGraw Hill News Bur., London, England, 1965-68; program officer UN, N.Y.C., 1969-75, section chief, 1975-88; focal point for women UN Office of Pers., N.Y.C., 1988-93; exec. dir. The Trickle Up Program, N.Y.C., 1994-2001. Avocations: theatre, travel, reading. Home: 1056 5th Ave New York NY 10028-0112

HABAL, MUTAZ BILLAH, plastic surgeon; b. Damascus, Syria, Apr. 27, 1938; s. Monier and Rabia (Rick) H.; m. Randa Habal, June 22, 1964; children: Rula, Bassam. MD, Am. U. Beirut, 1964; cert. and fellow, Coll. of Surgeons, Toronto, Can., 1972. Intern, resident U. Pa., Phila., 1964-65; resident, chief SUNY, Syracuse, 1965-69; resident Peter Bent & Children, Harvard U., Boston, 1969-71; fellow Harvard U., Boston, 1971-72; asst. prof. U. Ind., Indpls., 1972-74; assoc. prof. U. Fla., Gainesville, 1974-78; prof. and chmn. U. South Fla., Tampa, 1978-80, rsch. prof. and chmn., 1980—. Clin. prof. U. Fla., Tampa, 1980—. Contbr. articles to profl. jours. Col. USAR, 1984—. Fellow ACS, Royal Coll. Surgeons, Internat. Coll. Surgeons, Am. Acad. Pediatric Surgeons, Country Med. Soc. (pres. 1995—). Republican. Moslem. Home: 6358 Maclaurin Dr Tampa FL 33647-1164 Office: Tampa Bay Craniofacial Ctr 801 W Martin Luther King Blvd Tampa FL 33603-3301

HABECK, JAMES ROY, lawyer; b. Berlin, Wis., Aug. 11, 1954; s. Roy J. and Phyllis J. (Hazelwood) H.; m. Penny Ann Gillman. BS, U. Wis., Stevens Point, 1976; JD, Marquette U., 1979. Bar. Wis. 1979, U.S. Dist. Ct. (ea. and we. dists.) Wis. 1979, U.S. Supreme Ct. 1990. Atty. Rutgers Law Office, Sheboygan Falls, Wis., 1979-80; pvt. practice Shawano, Wis., 1980—2002; judge Shawano County Courthouse, Shawano, Wis., 2002—. Family ct. commr. Shawano, Menominee County, 1983-2002; corp. counsel Shawano County, 1984-87, 90, 93; legal counsel Wis. Towns Assn., Shawano, 1987-2002. Pres. Big Brothers/Big Sisters, Shawano, 1984-88; v.p. Rep. Ctrl. Com., Shawano County, 1993-99, chmn. 1999-2002; atty. St. James Lutheran Ch., Shawano, 1983-2001. Named Friend of 4-H Shawano County 4-H, 1990. Mem.: Wis. Family Ct. Commrs. Assn. (sec.-treas, pres. 1992—96, bd. dirs. 1998—2002), Shawano County Bar Assn. (sec-treas, pres. 1987—93), Wild Turkey Fedn., White Tails Unltd., Shawano Area C. of C. (bd. dirs. 2000—03), Rotary (bd. dirs. 2001—), Shawano County Agrl. Soc. Lutheran. Avocations: scoring high sch. basketball games.

HABECKER, EUGENE BRUBAKER, religious association executive; b. Hershey, Pa., June 17, 1946; s. Walter Eugene and Frances (Miller) H.; m. Marylou Napolitano, July 27, 1968; children: David, Matthew, Marybeth. AB, Taylor U., 1968; MA, Ball State U., 1969; JD, Temple U., 1974; PhD, U. Mich., 1981. Bar: Pa. 1974. Asst. dean Ea. Univ., St. Davids, Pa., 1970-74; dean students, asst. prof. polit. sci. George Fox U., Newberg, Oreg., 1974-78; exec. v.p. Huntington (Ind.) Coll., 1979-81, pres., 1981-91; pres, CEO Am. Bible Soc., N.Y.C., 1991—. Evaluation cons. North Ctrl. Assn., Chgo., 1982-91; dir. Christian Colls. and Univs., Washington, 1982-88; bd. dirs. Christianity Today Internat., United Bible Socs. internat. exec. com., 1992-2001, LeTourneau U. Author: Affirmative Action in Independent College, 1977, The Other Side of Leadership, 1987, Leading With a Follower's Heart, 1990, Rediscovering the Soul of Leadership, 1996; contbr. articles to profl. jours. Recipient Christian Mgmt. award Christian Mgmt. Assn., 1989. Mem. Nat. Assn. Intercollegiate Athletes (coun. of pres.' 1985-90), Nat. Assn. Evangs. (bd. dirs. 1985-90), Am. Mgmt. Assn., Christian Mgmt. Assn. Republican. Presbyterian. Office: Am Bible Soc 1865 Broadway New York NY 10023-7503

HABECKER, SANDRA K. retired nurse; b. Columbia, Pa., Apr. 5, 1937; d. Ralph Marvin and Emma Hubley (Eshleman) Kilheffer; m. Charles N. Habecker, Oct. 4, 1958; children: Jean, Marianne, Lisa, Susan. AS, RN, Lancaster (Pa.) Gen. Hosp., 1958. Pediatriac nurse Montgomeryville (Pa.) Pediatrics, 1975-90; sch. nurse Calvary Bapt. Sch., Lansdale, Pa., 1988-99; ret., 1999. Republican. Baptist. Avocations: gardening, reading, cooking, playing bassoon. Home: 361 Oakland Ave Lansdale PA 19446-3223

HABEDANK, GARY L. brokerage house executive; b. Glendive, Mont., Feb. 17, 1944; s. Otto T. and Arleen T. (Miller) H.; m. Kathryn Ann Czyhold, June 18, 1967; children: Silke, Anne. BBA, Pacific Lutheran U., 1966; postgrad., U. Mont., 1966-67. CFP, 1980. Sr. v.p., fin. cons. Smith Barney Inc., Tacoma, 1968—. Adv. coun. John Nuveen & Co., Chgo., 1986—; adv. bd. Planned Giving & Fin. Bd. of Visitors. Trustee Tacoma Art Mus., 1984-90; trustee, pres. Tacoma Philharm., Inc., 1977-83; sec. Annie Wright Sch., 1985-91; mem. Christ Episc. Ch. (vestry, fin. chmn. 1987-91) Recipient Community Svc. award Jr. League of Tacoma, 1990, Disting. Alumnus Centennial award, Pacific Lutheran U., 1990. Mem. Tacoma Club, Tacoma Elks, Boy Scouts Am. Republican. Episcopalian. Avocations: community service, writing, classical music, reading, gardening. Home: 3 N Rosemount Way Tacoma WA 98406-7117 Office: Tacoma Fin Ctr 1145 Broadway Ste 1400 Tacoma WA 98402-3587 E-mail: Dakota003@aol.com., gary.habedank@rssmb.com.

HABEEB, HABEEBA HUSSAIN, library director; b. Male, Republic of Maldives, Sept. 9, 1930; d. Hussain Habeeb and Shahima Shamsuddin; m. Abdulla Zubair, May 18, 1923; children: Ibrahim, Shafeea, Shahida. Grad. High Sch. Urdu Medium, Osmania, Hyderabad, India, 1948; grad. High Sch. English Medium, Holy Family Convent, Colombo, Sri Lanka, 1952. Cert. librarian. Asst. prin. Govt. Service, Male, Maldives, 1956-62; sec. Prime Minister's Office, Male, 1962-67, Foreign Affairs, Male, 1968-70, Transp. Dept. Govt. Service, Male, 1974-78, Aid Dept. Ministry of Justice Govt. Service, Male, 1974-75; librarian Nat. Library, Male, 1978-86, deputy dir., 1986-90; dir., 1990-95; dir. gen., 1995—. Author: Mohammed Thakurufaan The Great, 1990; co-author: Innovation in Primary School Construction, 1986; translator: How to Write Short Stories, 1984, other lit. works from Urdu to Dhivehi and English to Dhivehi; editor Jour., Niru Libr. newsletter, Children's Club mag. including Faithoova mag.; contbr. articles to cultural publs. Recipient Pres.'s award Gold Pen, Presdl. award for 25 yrs. govt. svc., Presdl. Encouragement award transl. Mem. Nat. Ctr. for Linguistic and Hist. Rsch. (adv. mem.). Home: Mandoovilla 8 Bodufulah Str Male Machchangolhi 20-03 Maldives Office: Nat Libr 59 Majeedi Magu Galolhu Male 20-24 Maldives

HABEGER, STEVEN RICHARD, science administrator; b. Vallejo, Calif., July 25, 1945; s. Richard John and Georgette (Dyce) H.; m. Cathleen Anne Henigan, June 21, 1969; children: Scott, Kelly. BSME, Va. Tech., 1968. Engr. Naval Surface Warfare Ctr., Dahlgren, Va., 1968-86; tech. dir. Naval Sea Sys. Command Detachment, Wallops Island, Va., 1986-89; exec. dir. Surface Combat Sys. Ctr., Wallops Island, 1989—; v.p. P'zazzz, Pocomoke, Md., 1994—. Chmn. bd. dirs. Samaritan Shelter, Pocomoke, 1986-89; chmn. fin. coun. Parish, Pocomoke, 1994-99; bd. dirs. Reachout, Inc. Mem. Am. Field Svc. (pres. Pocomoke chpt.), JC Internat. (senator), Va. Jaycees (life), Knights of Columbus (charter), Benevolent & Protective Order of Elks. Roman Catholic. Office: Surface Combat Sys Ctr Bldg R-30 Wallops Island VA 23337-5000 E-mail: shabege@scsc.wal.nswc.navy.mil., VTHawk@comcast.net.

HABEGGER, CYNTHIA A. medical/surgical nurse; b. Van Wert County, Ohio, Dec. 14, 1953; d. Palmer Paul and Donna Jean (Hertel) Johnson; m. Alan Duane Habegger, Oct. 13, 1979; children: Duane Alan, Rebekkah Ann. ADN, Purdue U., Ft. Wayne, 1985, AD in Supervision, 1991; BSN, Luth. Coll. Health Profls., Ft. Wayne, 1994. RN, Ind.; lic. supr. Staff nurse Swiss Village, Berne, Ind., 1985-87; staff nurse med.-surg. unit Caylor Nickel Clinic, Bluffton, Ind., 1987-88; DON geriatric Decatur (Ind.) Community Care, 1988; charge nurse Cooper Community Care Corp., Bluffton, 1988; psychiat. staff nurse and charge nurse Caylor Nickel Clinic, Bluffton, 1988-92; ADON Meadowvale Nursing Home, Bluffton, 1992-93; intermittent RN Vis. Nurse Svc. and Hospice, Fort Wayne, Ind., 1993-94; instr. nursing Ivy Tech State Coll., 1994-95; DON, ExtendaCare Bluffton (Ind.), 1995-96; pvt. duty nurse, 1996-99; staff nurse Swiss Village, Berne, Ind., 1999—. Home: 1132 W 400 S Berne IN 46711

HABER, DIANE LOIS, psychotherapist, clinical specialist; b. Bklyn., Oct. 4, 1937; d. Philip and Ida (Kleinfield) H.; m. Paul Friedman, Sept. 27, 1959 (div. Feb. 1978); children: Philip Friedman, Andrew Friedman, Melanie Friedman; m. Robert Bruce, Mar. 29, 1992. Diploma, Mt. Sinai Hosp. Sch. Nursing, N.Y.C., 1959; BA, Marymount Manhattan Coll., 1976; MS, Yeshiva U., 1981. RN, N.Y.; cert. clin. specialist psychiat./mental health nursing cert. in gerontology, behavioral psychotherapy, hypnosis, EMDR. Clin. supr. psychiat. St. Barnabas Hosp., Bronx, N.Y., 1982-84; psychiat. nurse clinician Frances Schervier Home and Hosp., Riverdale, N.Y., 1984-88; staff devel. coord. Holliswood (N.Y.) Hosp., 1988-93; psychotherapist in pvt. practice Great Neck, N.Y., 1991—; primary psychotherapist Coney Island Hosp., Bklyn., 1993-96; psychiat. clinician Frances Schervier Home Care, Riverdale, N.Y., 1997-99. Tchr. Bd. Edn., Queens, N.Y., 1985-88; cons. nursing homes N.Y.C. Dept. Health, 1985-87; workshop presenter. Mem. N.Y. Soc. Ericksonian Psychotherapy and Hypnosis (bd. dirs., chmn. 1991-95), Network of N.Y. Clin. specialists (rec. sec., bd. dirs.), Am. Soc. Clin. Hypnosis (cons.). Democrat. Jewish. Avocations: music, dancing, hiking, travel, theater. Home: 58-46 246 Crescent Douglaston NY 11362 Office: 15 Canterbury Rd Apt A4 Great Neck NY 11021-2615 E-mail: dhaber@villagenet.com.

HABER, IRA JOEL, artist, art educator; b. N.Y.C., Feb. 24, 1947; s. Oscar and Rosalind (Tilzer) H. Student public schs. Instr. art SUNY, Stony Brook, 1981—, U. Calif.-San Diego, 1982, 84, Ohio State U. (Columbus), 1984. One-man shows include Fischbach Gallery, N.Y.C., 1971, 72, 74, Kent (Ohio) State U., 1977, Pam Adler Gallery, N.Y.C., 1978, 80, 82, Rutgers U., 1980, SUNY, Stony Brook, 1981, Phila. Art Alliance, 1984, J.N. Herlin Inc., N.Y.C., 1984, 86, 55 Mercer St. Gallery, N.Y.C., 1991; group shows include Mus. Modern Art, N.Y.C., 1970, Whitney Mus., N.Y.C., 1971, 73, Public Sch. One, L.I., N.Y., 1976, Albright-Knox Gallery, Buffalo, 1979, Ohio State U., 1984; represented in permanent collections NYU, Guggenheim Mus., N.Y.C., Hirshhorn Mus., Washington, Allen Meml. Art Mus., Oberlin (Ohio) Coll., Albright-Knox Gallery, Buffalo. NEA fellow, 1974, 77, 84; grantee Creative Artists Public Service, 1974, 77, Ariana Found., 1982, Pollock-Krasner Found., 1986-87, 2001. Address: 311 85th St Brooklyn NY 11209

HABER, JOEL ABBA, lawyer; b. N.Y.C., Sept. 17, 1943; BS, U. Buffalo, 1964; JD, U. Wis., 1967. Bar: Wis. 1967, Ill. 1968, U.S. Supreme Ct. 1973. Trial atty. SEC, Washington and Chgo., 1967-70; assoc. Schiff, Hardin & Waite, Chgo., 1970-71; ptnr. Chatz, Sugarman, Abrams & Haber, Chgo., 1972-82, Fagel, Haber & Maragos, Chgo., 1982-90, Fagel & Haber, Chgo., 1991—. Spl. counsel to Ill. Dept. Ins., 1983—. Mem. ABA, Wis. Bar Assn., Chgo. Bar Assn., U. Wis. Law Alumni Assn. (pres. 1987-89).

HABER, LEO M. writer, editor-in-chief; b. N.Y.C., May 28, 1927; s. Aaron Haber and Anna Sales Haber; m. Sylvia Bittkower Haber, June 16, 1951; children: Howard Eli, Edward Marc. BA, CCNY, 1947; MA, Columbia U., 1948; diploma, Herzliah Hebrew Tchrs. Inst., 1948. Tchrs. secondary sch. license in English and Hebrew N.Y. State Dept. Edn., suprs. secondary sch. license N.Y. State Dept. Edn. Tchr. Hebrew H.S. Bd. Hebrew Edn., Essex County, NJ, 1948—50; tchr. English and Hebrew Pub. H.S., Bklyn., 1950—52; tchr. English, Hebrew and Latin Lawrence H.S., Cedarhurst, NY, 1952—89, chmn. dept. fgn. lang., 1965—89; cons. editor Midstream Mag., N.Y.C., 1990—2001, editor-in-chief, 2001—. Adj. lectr. Hebrew Baruch Coll., N.Y.C., 1950—64; adj. asst. prof. English CCNY, N.Y.C., 1964—76; adj. prof. Hebrew Hebrew Union Coll., N.Y.C., 1994—2000; working mem. Regents Examination Com., N.Y. State, NY, 1960—, Coll. Bds. Achievement Examination Com., NJ, 1980. Author: (novels) The Red Heifer, 2001, poetry, articles and short stories. Recipient awards in fiction, Negative Capability, Literal Latté, Serpentine, Red Rock Rev., Pif Mag., Explorations '99, award in poetry, Embers, Poetpourri, Quick Brown Fox Lit. Jour., Icarus, Gramercy Pictures, El Dorado Writers' Guild, Rome Art and Cmty. Ctr., Pawtucket (R.I.) Arts Coun., Poetry Soc. Dallas. Jewish. Home: 2569 W 2nd St #1F Brooklyn NY 11223 Office: Midstream Mag 21st Fl 633 Third Ave New York NY 10017

HABER, LYNN BECKER, English language educator; b. River Vale, N.J., Oct. 20, 1961; d. Murray Leonard and Anita (Goodman) Becker; m. Samuel Myles Haber, Nov. 6, 1994; children: Gary, Craig. BA in Psychology, Muhlenberg Coll., 1983; MA in Teaching, Montclair State U., 1987; PhD in English Edn., NYU, 1987. Cert. elem. tchr., English tchr., N.J. Tchr. English Cedar Grove (N.J.) H.S., 1987-89; writing instr. Middlesex County Coll., Edison, N.J., 1989; instr. English Union County Coll., Cranford, N.J., 1990; teaching fellow NYU, N.Y.C., 1990-92, adj. asst. prof., 1995—; asst. prof. English So. Conn. State U., New Haven, 1995-99. Rep. NYU Grad. Student Orgn., N.Y.C., 1991-92. Mem. Nat. Coun. Tchrs. English, Kappa Delta Pi. Avocations: reading, travel, jogging, Scrabble.

HABER, RALPH NORMAN, psychology consultant, researcher, educator; b. Lansing, Mich., May 15, 1932; s. William and Fannie (Gallas) H.; m. Ruth Lea Boss, 1961 (div. 1974); children— Sabrina Beth, Rebecca Ann; m. Lyn R. Roland, 1974. BA, U. Mich., 1953; MA, Wesleyan U., Middletown, Conn., 1954; PhD, Stanford U., 1957; Postdoctoral fellow, Med. Research Council, Applied Psychology Unit, Cambridge, Eng., 1970-71. Rsch. assoc. Inst. for Comm. Rsch., Stanford, 1957-58; instr. psychology San Francisco State Coll., Calif., 1957-58; asst. prof. psychology Yale, 1958-64; assoc. prof. psychology U. Rochester, N.Y., 1964-67, prof. psychology, 1967-70, prof. psychology and visual sci., 1970-79, chmn. dept. psychology, 1967-70, mem. faculty senate, 1968-70, sec., mem. steering com., 1969-70; prof. psychology U. Ill., Chgo., 1979-91, rsch. prof., 1991-94, rsch. prof. emeritus, 1994—; ptnr. Human Factors Cons., Swall Meadows, Calif., 1988—; rsch. assoc. psychology U. Calif., Santa Cruz, 1995. Adj. prof. U. Calif., Riverside, 1997-99; vis. prof. Air Force Human Resources Lab., Williams AFB, Ariz., 1981-83; ptnr. Human Factors Cons., Highland Park, Ill.; vis. scientist Med. Rsch. Coun. Applied Psychology Unit, Cambridge, Eng., 1970-71; chmn., divisional maj. III Yale, 1959-64; vis. asst. prof. New Sch. for Social Research, 1963; research cons. VA, 1967-71; adv. editor for exptl. psychology Holt, Rinehart & Winston Book Pubs., 1969-77. Author: (with Hershenson) The Psychology of Visual Perception, 1973, 2d edit., 1980, (with Fried) An Introduction to Psychology, 1975, (with others) Discovering Psychology, 1977; editor: Current Research on Motivation, 1966, Contemporary Theory and Research on Visual Perception, 1968, Information Processing Approaches to Visual Perception, 1969; Contbr. articles to profl. jours. Committeeman 18th Ward, Brighton (N.Y.) Democratic Com., 1967-70; founding mem., trustee Coll. Admission Prep. Program, Rochester, 1968-70; commr. Wheeler Crest Fire Prevention Dist., Swall Meadows, Calif., 1995-2000; founder, 1st pres., bd. dirs. Eastern Sierra Conservancy, 2000-2002. Recipient Outstanding Achievement award U. Mich., 1977; Behavioral Sci. fellow Ford Found., 1953-54; grantee NSF, NIH, Nat. Inst. Edn., Air Force Office Sci. Research, Dept. Army Fellow APA, AAAS, Am. Psychol. Soc.; mem. Psychonomics Soc., Brit. Psychol. Assn., Optical Soc. Am., Human Factors and Ergonomics Soc., Am. Contract Bridge League (dir. Bishop unit 517 1996—), Sigma Xi, Pi Lambda Phi.

HABER, STEPHEN K. lawyer; b. Phila., Jan. 3, 1945; s. Benjamin F. and Dorothy L. (Kurtz) H.; A.B. cum laude, U. Pa., 1964; J.D., Yale U., 1968; m. Dorine Myriam Caddous, Nov. 4, 1982. Admitted to Pa. bar, 1968; with Sheriff Securities Corp., N.Y.C., 1968—, pres., dir., 1979— . Pres., Am. Friends of Haifa Maritime Mus., Inc. Mem. Pa. Bar Assn., N.Y. Bar Assn., N.Y. Stock Exchange. Jewish. Clubs: Explorers, Yale (N.Y.C.). Home: 5 E 22d St Penthouse C New York NY 10010 Office: 630 5th Ave Ste 2415 New York NY 10111-0100

HABERL, VALERIE ELIZABETH, physical education educator, company executive; b. N.Y.C., July 6, 1947; d. William Anthony and Rose Mary (Hoholecek) H. BS, So. Conn. State U., 1969, postgrad., 1979. Cert. elem. tchr., Conn. Tchr. phys. edn. West Haven (Conn.) Bd. Edn., 1969—. Pres. Creative Studio, 1992—; inventory control specialist, 1997-2001. Mem. Conn. Assn. Health, Phys. Edn., Recreation and Dance. Republican. Roman Catholic.

HABERLY, DAVID TRISTRAM, language educator; b. Tucson, Dec. 11, 1942; s. Loyd and Virginia Dean Haberly; m. Susan Smith, July 25, 1985; children: Duncan Charles, Anne Sills, Jacqueline Isabella Young, Caroline Anne Sion. AB, Harvard Coll., Cambridge, Mass., 1963; AM, Harvard U., 1964, PhD, 1966. Asst. prof. of Portuguese Harvard U., Cambridge, Mass., 1966—73; assoc. prof. of Portuguese U. of Va., Charlottesville, 1973—84, dept. chair, 1973—78, prof. of Portuguese, 1984—. Author: (academic book) Three Sad Races: Racial Identity and National Consciousness in Brazilian Literature; editor (author): (academic reference book) Cambridge History of Latin American Literature, vol. 3; editor: (edition of novel in translation) Quincas Borba, by Joaquim Maria Machado de Assis. Dir. Ptnrs. of the Ams., Virginia-Santa Catarina, Richmond, Va., 1978—90. Grantee Sesquicentennial Rsch. grantee, U. of Va., 1979, 1985, 1999. Mem.: Am. Portuguese Studies Assn. (treas., dir. 1997—2001). Office: University of Virginia Wilson Hall 115 Charlottesville VA 22904

HABERMAN, CHARLES MORRIS, mechanical engineer, educator; b. Bakersfield, Calif., Dec. 10, 1927; s. Carl Morris and Rose Marie (Braun) H. BS, UCLA, 1951; MS in Mech. Engring., U. So. Calif., 1954, MS in Aeronautical Engring., 1960. Lead, sr. and group engr. Northrop Aircraft, Hawthorne, Calif., 1951-59, cons., 1959-61; asst. prof. to prof. mech. engring. Calif. State U., L.A., 1959-91. Cons. Royal McBee Corp., 1960-61. Author: Engineering Systems Analysis, 1965, Use of Computers for Engineering Applications, 1966, Vibration Analysis, 1968, Basic Aerodynamics, 1971. Served with AUS, 1946-47. Mem. Am. Soc. Engring. Edn. Democrat. Roman Catholic.

HABERMAN, F. WILLIAM, lawyer; b. Princeton, N.J., Apr. 20, 1940; s. Frederick William and Louise (Power) H.; m. Carmen Marie Duffy, June 15, 1963; children: Frederick, Sarah. BA, U. Wis., 1962; LLB, Harvard Law Sch., 1965. Bar: Wis. 1965, Fla. 1993, U.S. Dist. Ct. (ea. dist.) Wis. 1966, U.S. Dist. Ct. (we. dist.) Wis. 1967. Ptnr. Michael, Best & Friedrich, Milw., 1965—. Mem. adv. bd. Johnson Bank, 1994-97. Co-author: Marital Property Law in Wisconsin, 1986. Trustee Pub. Policy Forum, Milw., 1998—; bd. dirs. Ctrl. YMCA, Milw., 1988-93, Richard and Ethel Herzfeld Found., Milw., 1985—, Wis. affiliate Am. Heart Assn., 1993-97; mem. Greater Milw. Com., 2000—; mem.

adv. bd. Milw. Fair Housing Coun., 1989-90; mem. deferred giving adv. bd. Milw. Sch. Engring., 1989-93; bd. dirs. Milw. Children's Hosp. Found., 1994-98, Milw. Repertory Theater, 1997-2002. Fellow Am. Coll. Trust & Estate Counsel; mem. ABA, Wis. Bar Assn., Phi Beta Kappa. Home: 2727 E Shorewood Blvd Milwaukee WI 53211-2459 Office: Michael Best & Friedrich 100 E Wisconsin Ave Ste 3300 Milwaukee WI 53202-4108

HABERMAN, LOUISE SHELLY, consulting company executive; b. N.Y.C. d. Harry Martin and Rebecca (Binstock) H.; m. Gordon Joel Schochet. BA, Cornell U., 1971; PhD, Princeton (N.J.) U., 1984. Mem. faculty numerous colls. and univs., 1975-84; researcher pub. policy U.S. Dept. Commerce, 1976; prin. investigator pub. policy study State of N.J., Trenton, 1979-80; pvt. practice cons. Highland Park, N.J., 1984-86; head regional bank svcs. Multinational Strategies, Inc., N.Y.C., 1986-90; pres. Haberman Assocs., Inc., Edison, N.J., 1990—. Author: (monograph) Regional Banks: International Strategies for the Future, 1987; editor: (with Paul Sacks) Ann. Rev. of Nations, 1988; contbr. articles to profl. jours. Issues advisor selected polit. candidates and civil liberties causes. Avocations: gardening, painting. Office: Haberman Assocs Inc 315 N 8th Ave Edison NJ 08817-2914

HABERMAN, SHELBY JOEL, statistician, educator; b. Cin., May 4, 1947; s. Jack Leon and Miriam Leah (Langberg) H.; m. Elinor Penny Levine, Feb. 18, 1979 (dec. 1996); children: Shoshanah, Chasiah, Sarah, Milcah, Boaz, Devorah. AB, Princeton U., 1968; PhD, U. Chgo., 1970. Asst. prof. to prof. U. Chgo., 1970-82; prof. Hebrew U., Jerusalem, 1982-84; prof. stats. Northwestern U., Evanston, Ill., 1984—2002, chmn. dept., 1986-88; dir. Ctr. for Statis. Theory and Practice, Ednl. Testing Svc., Princeton, NJ, 2002—. Author: Analysis of Frequency Data, 1974, Analysis of Qualitative Data, Vol. I, 1978, Vol. II, 1979, Advanced Statistics, Vol. I, 1996; contbr. articles to profl. jours. Guggenheim fellow, 1977-78. Fellow AAAS, Inst. Math. Stats., Am. Statis. Assn. Home: 414 S 4th St Highland Park NJ 08904- Office: Ednl Testing Svc Rosedale Rd 08541 Princeton NJ 08541-0001 E-mail: SHaberman@ets.org.

HABERMANN, HELEN MARGARET, plant physiologist, educator; b. Bklyn., Sept. 13, 1927; AB, SUNY, Albany, 1949; MS, U. Conn., 1951; PhD, U. Minn., 1956. Asst. botanist U. Conn., Storrs, 1949-51; asst. U. Minn., Mpls., 1951-53, asst. plant physiologist, 1953-55, head residence counselor, 1955-56; rsch. assoc. U. Chgo., 1956-57; rsch. fellow Hopkins Marine Sta. Stanford (Calif.) U., 1957-58; from asst. prof. to prof. biol. scis. Goucher Coll., Towson, 1958—82, chmn. dept. biology, 1963-66, 68, 78-79, Lilian Welsh prof. biol. scis., 1982-92; prof. emeritus, 1992—. Co-author Biology: A Full Spectrum, 1973, Mainstreams of Biology, 1977. NIH spl. rsch. fellow Rsch. Inst. Advanced Study, Balt., 1966-67. Fellow AAAS; mem. Phytochem. Soc. N.Am. (sec. 1987-93), Am. Soc. Plant Physiologists, Am. Soc. Hort. Sci., Soc. Devel. Biology, Am. Soc. Photobiology, Am. Inst. Biol. Scis., Scandinavian Soc. Plant Physiology, Internat. Soc. Plant Molecular Biology, Japanese Soc. Plant Physiology, Soc. Exptl. Biology and Medicine, Am. Camellia Soc., Pioneer Camellia Soc. (pres. 1994-95, sec. 2000-01), Am. Hort. Soc., Sigma Xi. Office: Goucher Coll Dept Biol Scis 1021 Dulaney Valley Rd Baltimore MD 21204-2753 E-mail: hhabermann@wans.net.

HABERMANN, JAMES HERBERT, retired pathologist; b. Cassville, Wis., June 18, 1926; s. Matthew Herbert and Clara Cordelia (Reilly) H.; m. Helen Audrey Howe, June 14, 1952; children: Thomas, Patrick, Michael, Jane, Mary Ann. MD, Marquette U., Milw., 1952. Diplomate in anat. and clin. pathology Am. Bd. Pathology. Family practice physician, Mt. Calvary, Wis., 1953-60; resident in pathology Denver Gen. Hosp., 1960-64; dir. labs. Mercy Hosp. and Luth. Hosp. (merged into Trinity Hosp.), Ft. Dodge, Iowa, 1964-77; staff pathologist Freeman Hosp., Joplin, Mo., 1977-80, St. John's Med. Ctr., Joplin, 1980-91. Pres. bd. dirs. Trinity Regional Hosp., Ft. Dodge, 1973-77; chief of staff St. John's Med. Ctr., Joplin, 1984-85. 1st lt. U.S. Army, 1944-47, Germany. Fellow Am. Soc. Clin. Pathologists, Coll. Am. Pathologists. Roman Catholic. Avocation: woodworking. Home: 2111 E 36th St Joplin MO 64804-4232 E-mail: JHHabermann@webtv.net.

HABERMEHL, LAWRENCE LEROY, philosophy educator; b. Joplin, Mo., June 13, 1937; s. Roland William and Ruth Esther (Kelly) H.; m. Kathryn J. Barnes, June 8, 1958 (div. 1974); children: Elizabeth Anne, R. William, Edward Hale; m. Sue Ellen Lovejoy, Sept. 16, 1989 (div. 1996). AB, Phillips U., 1959; BD, Union Theol. Sem., 1961; PhD, Boston U., 1967. House mgr. Boston Seaman's Friend Soc., 1963-65; teaching fellow Boston U., 1965-66; asst. prof. philosophy Am. Internat. Coll., Springfield, Mass., 1966-73, assoc. prof., 1973—. Author: The Counterfeit Wisdom of Shallow Minds. A Critique of Some Leading Offenders of the 1980s, 1994; author/editor: Morality in the Modern World, 1976. Mem. AAUP, Am. Philos. Assn., Metaphys. Soc. Am., Common Cause, Amnesty Internat., Assn. Informal Logic and Critical Thinking. Unitarian-Universalist. Home: 1235 Enfield St Enfield CT 06082 Office: Am Internat Coll Dept Philosophy Springfield MA 01109 E-mail: LawLH@aol.com.

HABERSTROH, RICHARD DAVID, insurance agent; b. St. Louis, Mar. 21, 1943; s. Richard J. and Helen M. (Jones) H.; m. Patricia Steinlage, Aug. 22, 1964; children: Michelle, Stacy, Richard David. BS, S.E. Mo. State U., Cape Girardeau, 1965; MSFS, Am. Coll., Bryn Mawr, Pa., 2000. CLU. Ins. agt. Constitution Life, Chgo., 1963-70; gen. agt. Monarch Life, Springfield, Mass., 1971-78; pres. Richard D. Haberstroh, CLU, Inc., St. Louis, 1978—. Bd. mem. Jefferson Bank, St. Louis, Family Physician Health Svc. Corp. of Ind., Ind. Acad. Family Physicians; cons. Purdue U. Ins. Mktg. Inst., West Lafayette, Ind., 1992, Investeel. Contbr. articles to profl. jours. Bd. mem., chmn. United Cerebral Palsy, 1982. Named Ins. and Fin. Adv. of the Yr., Mo. Assn. of Ins. and Fin. Adv., 2003. Mem. St. Louis Assn. Life Underwriters (bd. mem. 1992), St. Louis Soc. CLUs (bd. dirs.), Gateway Chpt. Nat. Speakers (pres. 1987), King's Men (bd. mem. 1978—), Million Dollar Round Table (life). Republican. Roman Catholic. Avocations: golf, hunting, fishing, reading, public speaking. Office: Richard D Haberstroh CLU Ste 2 1023 Executive Pky Dr Saint Louis MO 63141-6323

HABGOOD, ANTHONY JOHN, corporate executive; b. Woodbastwick, Eng., Nov. 8, 1946; s. John Michael and Diana Margaret (Dalby) H.; m. Nancy Ray Atkinson, June 29, 1974; children: Elizabeth Ann, John Alan, George Michael. BA in Econs., Gonville and Caius Coll., Cambridge U., 1968; MA, Cambridge U., 1971; MS in Indsl. Adminstrn., Carnegie-Mellon U., Pitts., 1970. From staff to v.p., dir. Boston Cons. Group Inc., 1970-86, exec. com., 1983-86; dir. Tootal, PLC, London, 1986-91, CEO, 1991; dir. Geest, PLC, London, 1988-93; CEO Bunzl, PLC, London, 1991-96, chmn., 1996—; dir. Powergen, PLC, London, 1993-2001, Schroder Ventures Internat. Investment Trust, PLC, London, 1995—, Nat. Westminster Bank, PLC, London, 1998-2000. W.L. Mellon fellow, 1968-70 Mem.: Royal Norfolk and Suffolk Yacht. Mem. Ch. Of Eng. Office: 110 Park St London W1K 6NX England

HABIAN, BRUCE GEORGE, lawyer; b. Nov. 23, 1947; s. George and Doris Marie (Cipollina) H.. AB, Boston Coll., 1969; JD, Villanova U., 1972. Bar: N.Y. 1973, N.J. 1974, U.S. Dist. Ct. (so. and ea. dists.) N.Y. 1975, U.S. Ct. Appeals (2nd cir.) 1975, U.S. Supreme Ct. 1976. Asst. corp. counsel Office Corp. Counsel, N.Y.C., 1972—73; assoc. Martin, Clearwater & Bell, N.Y.C., 1973—79, ptnr., 1979—, sr. ptnr., 1983—. Lectr. Law Jour. Seminars Press; cons. N.Y. State Commr. Health, N.Y.C., NY, 1983. Mem.: ABA (litigation sect.), Internat. Assn. Def. Coun., Def. Rsch. Coun., Assn. Bar City N.Y., University (N.Y.C.). Republican. Roman Catholic. Home: 993 Park Ave Apt 1B New York NY 10028-0809 Office: Martin Clearwater and Bell 220 E 42nd St New York NY 10017-5806

HABIB, IBRAHIM WAHBY, computer networks engineer, educator, consultant; b. Cairo, Aug. 16, 1959; arrived in U.S., 1988; s. Wahby Mohamed Habib and Salwa Kamel Essawy. BSEE, Ain Shams U., Cairo, 1981; MSEE, Poly. U. N.Y., 1984; PhD in Elec. Engring., CUNY, 1991. Cons., N.J., N.Y., 1998—; assoc. prof. CUNY, 1998. Part-time tech. cons. AT&T, 1997—2000, Telecordia, 2000—01; spkr. at several Am. and European univs. Guest editor IEEE JSAC, IEEE Comms. Mag., John Wiley Jour. on Wireless Networks; contbr. over 70 articles to profl. pubs. Mem. IEEE (sr., reviewer 1991—, editor 1993-97, mem. tech. program com. numerous internat. confs.). Achievements include patents pending Adaptive Allocation of Resources in Communication Networks. Office: CUNY Elec Engring Dept 137 St and Convent Ave New York NY 10031 Fax: 212-650-7110. E-mail: ibrahimhabib@hotmail.com.

HABIB, THOMAS MARK, musician, educator; b. Augusta, Ga., May 14, 1963; s. Roshdy and Elizabeth Gertrude Habib; m. Barbara Annette Bentley, June 19, 1988; 1 child, Daniel Bentley. MusB in Guitar Performance, U. South Ala., 1988; MusM in Guitar Performance, U. So. Miss., 1994. Spl. courses instr. U. South Ala., Mobile, 1994—97; guitar instr. U. Mobile, 1998—. CDs include Thomas Mark Habib-Classical Guitarist, Thomas Mark Habib-Classic Guitar. Active Guitar Found. Am., 2002—. Recipient 1st place, MTNA Competition, 1990, Pine Belt Guitar Competition, 2002. Republican. Avocations: hiking, mountain biking, golf, swimming. Office: Univ Mobile PO Box 13220 Mobile AL 36663

HABICH, ELIZABETH CHAMBERLAIN, librarian; b. Boston, Mar. 23, 1955; d. Eugene Randolph and Helen Howard Chamberlain; m. Michael Paul Habich, Sept. 10, 1977. BA in English, Wellesley Coll., 1977; MS in Libr. and Info. Sci., Simmons Coll., 1980, MBA, Northeastern U., 1990. Libr. asst., page Hingham Pub. Libr., 1971-78; circulation asst. MIT, Cambridge, 1978-80; reference libr. Saugus (Mass.) Pub. Libr., 1980-82; head res. svcs. Northeastern U. Libr., Boston, 1982-87, bldg. projects officer, 1986-91, adminstrv. svcs. officer, 1991—. Cons. in field. Author: Moving Library Collections: A Management Handbook, 1998; contbr. chpts. to books. Trustee North Reading (Mass.) Pub. Libr., 1992—; chair Libr. Orgn. and Mgmt. Sect. Fiscal and Bus. Officers Discussion Group, 2000-2002, mem., 2002—. Mem. ALA, Assn. Coll. Rsch. Libr., Libr. Adminstrn. Mgmt. Assn. (bldg. equipment sect. 1987—, vice-chair, chair-elect 1993-94, chair 1994-95, past chair 1995-96), program com. 1996-2000, fin. com. 2000—, chair nominating com. 1997-98, Beta Phi Mu, Beta Gamma Sigma. Avocations: quilting, gardening, music. E-mail: e.habich@neu.edu.

HABICHT, CHRISTIAN HERBERT, history educator; b. Dortmund, Germany, Feb. 23, 1926; came to U.S., 1972; s. Hermann Christian and Emile Julie (Diefenbach) H.; m. Freia Renate Wilkowski, Aug. 15, 1952; children: Susanne, Christoph, Nikolaus. Dr.Phil., U. Hamburg, 1952, Habil, 1957. Asst. to assoc. prof. U. Hamburg, 1952-61; prof. ancient history U. Marburg/Lahn, 1961-65; prof. U. Heidelberg, 1965-73, dean, 1966-67; prof. Inst. Advanced Study, Princeton, N.J., 1973-98; vis. prof. Princeton U., 1973-80. Author books; contbr. articles to profl. jours. Mem. British Acad., Am. Philos. Soc., Acad. Heidelberg, Acad. Athens, German Archeol. Inst., Austrian Archeol. Inst., Am. Inst. Archeology, Assn. Ancient Historians (Reuchlin-Price award 1991, Moe-Price award 1996, Criticos-Price award 1998). Office: Inst Advanced Study Sch Hist Studies Princeton NJ 08540 E-mail: habicht@ias.edu.

HABICHT, FRANK HENRY, retired industrial executive; b. Chgo., Sept. 4, 1920; s. Geroge Jr. and Gertrude A. (Tronc) H.; m. Jeanne Ellen Patrick, Mar. 9, 1943; children: Pamela, Patricia, Frank Henry II. BSME, Purdue U., 1942; postgrad., Cornell U., 1942, Am. U., 1944. From sales engr. to pres. Marshall & Huschart Machinery Co., Chgo., 1946-70; vice chmn. Cone-Blanchard Machine Co., Windsor, Vt. and Aldridge, Eng., 1971-74; chmn. bd., pres. United Tech. Corp., Chgo., 1970-81; pres. Steego Tech. Corp., West Palm Beach, 1981 86; chmn., pres. Corp. Assocs., Inc., 1986-97. Tech. cons. U.S. Dept. Def., Washington, 1963-64; pres. UNISIG Corp., 1980-86, King & Gavaris Cons. Engrs. Inc., 1980 84; U.S. projects mgr. Boehringer GmbH, Germany, 1989-95; 1997; lectr. in field; bd. dirs. Am. SIP Corp., Botemp Corp., Switzerland. Author: Modern Machine Tools, 1964; contbr. articles to profl. jours. Mem. def. indsl. plant equipment com. Dept. Def. Lt. comdr.USN, 1942-45. Mem. ASME, Am. Machine Tool Distbrs. Assn. (dir., past pres.), Fabricating Mfrs. Assn. (dir., past pres.), Assn. of RAF Warbirds, Conf. Bd. (exec. coun.), Order Knights St. John of Jerusalem, Oakbrook Polo Club, Palm Beach Club, Beach Club, Palm Beach Yacht Club, Governor's Club, Soc 4 Arts (Palm Beach, Navy League (bd. dirs.), Masons. Episcopalian. Avocations: hunting, fishing, tennis. Office: Corp Assocs Inc PO Box 746 Palm Beach FL 33480-0746

HABICHT, JEAN PIERRE, healthcare educator, nutritionist; b. Geneva, Dec. 15, 1934; arrived in US, 1962; s. Max H. and Elizabeth (Peterson) Herzog; m. Pat Hinxman, Jan. 3, 1959 (div. Oct. 1990); children: Heidi, Christopher, Oliver; m. Gretel H. Pelto, June 13, 1997. MD, U. Zurich, 1962, MD, 1964; MPH, Harvard U., 1968; PhD, MIT, 1969. Cert. in clin. nutrition Am. Bd. Nutrition. Biochem. rsch. asst. Merck, Sharpe, andDohme, Rahway, NJ, 1958-59; pediat. intern Children's Hosp. Med. Ctr., Boston, 1965-66; med. officer WHO, Guatemala, 1969-74; prof. maternal and child health U. San Carlos, Guatemala, 1972-74; spl. asst. Nat. Ctr. Health Stats., Washington, 1974-77; James Jamison prof. nutritional epidemiology Cornell U., Ithaca, NY, 1977—. Cons. pub. health issues nat. and internat. govt., profl. agy., 1975—; mem. expert com. nutrition WHO, Geneva, 1975—, mem. com. epidemiology and disease prevention, 1986—89, chmn., expert com. phys. status, 1991—93; me.. epidemiology and disease control study sect. NIH, Washington, 1980—83; mem. joint nutrition monitoring and evaluation com. HHS-USDA, 1982—86; mem. adv. group coordinating subcom. nutrition U.N., 1983—89, chmn., 1986—87; mem. food and nutrition bd. NAS, Washington, 1994—96, mem-.com. internat. nutrition, 1994—97, mem. com. uses dietary reference intakes Inst. Medicine, 1997—2000; chmn. expert com. optimal duration exclusive breastfeeding, 2001; mem. tech. adv. com. Child and Adolescent Health and Devel., 2001—. Contbr. articles to profl. jour., chapters to books. Fellow: Soc. Internat. Nutrition Rsch. (pres. 2002—), Am. Soc. Nutritional Scis. (Atwater Meml. lectr. 1998, Kellogg prize 1994, Conrad A. Elvehjem award 1999), Am. Coll. Epidemiology; mem.: APHA, Internat. Soc. Rsch. Human Milk and Lactation (exec. com. 1995—96), Internat. Epidemiol. Assn., Soc. Epidemiologic Rsch., Am. Soc. Clin. Nutrition, Delta Omega, Gamma Sigma Delta, Sigma Xi. Office: Cornell Univ Div Nutritional Sci Savage Hall Ithaca NY 14853

HABICH WOLF, LYNN CHARLOTTE, education educator, department chairman, educational consultant; b. Madison, Wis., June 28, 1944; d. Frank Lucas and Charlotte Clara Habich; m. Russell Murray Wolf, June 15, 1968; 1 child, Nicole Jenee Wolf. BS, U. N.C., Greensboro, 1962—66; MS, Radford U., 1978—80; EdD, Nova Southeastern U., 1989—93. Cert. adminstrn. and supervision State Va., 1966, spl. edn. State Va., 1966, K - 12 educator State N.C, - Fla. and Va., 1966, reading specialist State Va., 1986. Spl. edn. tchr. Henry County Schools, Va., 1966—94, asst. prin. high sch., 1995—96, elem. prin., 1997—2000; asst. prof., chairperson edn. dept. Averett U., Danville, Va., 2000—. Cons. and spkr. aha! Process, Inc., Highlands, Tex., 2002—. Bd. mem. Internat. Dyslexia Assn., Richmond, Va., 1993—99, 2003—. Recipient Learning Disabilities Tchr. Yr. State Va., Va. Coun. Learning Disabilities, 1988 - 1989, Exemplary Program Award Va., 1993. Home: 730 Lady Mary Rd Ridgeway VA 24148 Office: Averett U 420 W Main St Danville VA 24541 Office Fax: 434-791-5020.

HABING, BRETT WILLIAM, music educator; b. Indpls., June 2, 1972; s. John William and Nancy Jean Habing; m. Deborah Sue Mongold, July 16, 1994; 1 child, Aidan James. MusB, Bob Jones U., 1994, MEd, 1997. Mem. voice and conducting faculty, chmn. music edn. dept. Northland Bapt. Bible Coll., Dunbar, Wis., 1997—, rec. prodr., 2002—. Choral clinician. Composer: various gen. and sacred choral and vocal works. Singer Dickinson Area Cmty. Chorus, Iron Mountain, Mich., 1999—2002; deacon Grace Bapt. Ch., Iron Mountain, 2002. Mem.: Nat. Assn. for Music Edn., Am. Choral Directors Assn. Baptist. Home: 1608 River St Niagara WI 54151 Office: Northland Bapt Bible Coll W10085 Pike Plains Rd Dunbar WI 54119 Office Fax: 715-324-6133. E-mail: bhabing@nbbc.edu.

HABKIRK, SUE ANN, education educator, consultant; b. Flint, Mich., July 1, 1957; d. Kenneth Albert and Dora Jean (Haley) Habkirk; m. Vincent Guerriero Jr., May 5, 1990; 1 child, Kent Vincent Guerriero. BS, U. Ariz., 1979, MEd, 1981, PhD, 1987, postgrad. Cert. secondary tchr., cmty. coll. educator Ariz. Lectr. in health edn. U. Ariz., Tucson, 1981-85, grad. asst. in student svcs., 1985-87, curriculum specialist, substance abuse prevention edn., 1987-91; health and phys. edn. resource tchr., sch. outreach coord. Tucson Unified Sch. Dist., 1997—; sch. health specialist Ariz. Dept. of Edn., 1992-97. Contbr. Mem.: AAHPERD, Ariz. Sch. Health Assn., Ariz. Alliance for Health, Phys. Edn., Recreation and Dance, Am. Sch. Health Assn.

HABOUB, WAEL JOUMAA, political scientist, educator; b. Jabalia, Gaza Strip, Palestine, Sept. 6, 1974; s. Joumaa Mohammed and Etedal Haboub. BA cum laude, Northeastern Ill. U., 1997, MA, 2000. Polit. sci. vis. lectr. Northeastern Ill. U., Chgo., 2001—. Pres. Politics Club-Northeastern Ill. U., Chgo., 1997—98. Mem.: Pi Sigma Alpha. Home: 1909 N Kimball Ave Chicago IL 60647-3725 Office: Northeastern Ill Univ 5500 N St Louis Ave Chicago IL 60625-4699 Personal E-mail: haboub@ameritech.net. E-mail: w-haboub@neiu.edu.

HABRE, SAMER S, mathematician, educator; b. Beirut, Beirut, Lebanon, Dec. 24, 1962; s. Said and Layla Hobeika Habre; m. Paula Abboud, Apr. 30, 1995; children: Nadeem, Sari. Ph.D., Syracuse U., New York, NY, 1986—91. Assoc. prof. of math. Lebanese Am. U., Beirut, Lebanon, 1991—, asst. prof. of math., 1992—98; vis. asst. prof. of math. Cornell U., Ithaca, NY, 1998—99, SUNY, Geneseo, NY, 1991—92. Author: (academic paper) Writing in a Reformed Differential Equations Course; reviewer (review of a book) Differential Equations and Linear Algebra; author: (academic paper) The ODE Curriculum: Traditional vs. Non-Traditional, The Case of One Student., Visualization Enhanced by Technology in the Learning of Multivariable Calculus, The Convergence of an Euler Approximation of an Initial Value Problem Is Not Always Obvious, Visualization in Multivariable Calculus The Case of 3D-Surfaces, Exploring Student's Strategies to Solve Ordinary Differential Equations in a Reformed Setting, Innovative Methods in the Teaching of Calculus - A Case Study, [00b7]The Fredholm Alternative for Second Order Linear Elliptic Systems with VMO Coefficients., Homotopic Classification of Euler-Lagrange Systems. Mem. of the adv. bd. Sci Quest Mag., Beirut, Lebanon, 1992—97; sec. Internat. Conf. on Tech. in Math. Edn. (Lebanese Am. U.), Beirut, Lebanon, 2000; chmn. Internat. Conf. on Trends in Math. Edn. (Lebanese Am. U.), Beirut, Lebanon, 2003. Recipient Fulbright, Am. Govt., 1999-2000. Mem.: Math. Assn. of Am. Avocations: travel, music, reading. Office: Lebanese American University Mme Curie Beirut Beirut Chouran 1102-2801 Lebanon E-mail: shabre@lau.edu.lb.

HABUSH, ROBERT LEE, lawyer; b. Milw., Mar. 22, 1936; s. Jesse James and Beatrice (Liebenberg) Habush; m. Miriam Lee Friedman, Aug. 25, 1957; children: Sherri Ellen, William Scott, Jodi Lynn. BBA, U. Wis., 1959, JD, 1961. Bar: Wis. 1961, U.S. Dist. Ct. (ea. and we. dists.) Wis. 1961, U.S. Ct. Appeals (7th cir.) 1965, U.S. Supreme Ct. 1986. Pres. Habush, Habush & Rottier, S.C., Milw., 1961—. Lectr. U. Wis. Law Sch., Marquette U. Law Sch., State Bar Wis., others. Author: (book) Cross Examination of Non Medical Experts, 1981; contbr. articles to profl. jours. Capt. U.S. Army, 1959—75. Recipient Evan P. Helfaer Donor award, Nat. Assn. Fundraising Execs., 2000. Mem.: ABA, ATLA (bd. govs. 1983—86, pres. 1986—87, Harry Philo award 1999, Leonard Ring Champion of Justice award 2002, Robert L. Habush ATLA Endowment re-named in his honor), Trial Lawyers Pub. Justice, Inner Cir. Advs., Wis. Acad. Trial Lawyers (pres. 1968—69, named Robert L. Habush Trial Lawyer of the Yr. award in his honor 2000), Wis. Bar Assn., Am. Soc. Writers Legal Subjects, Am. Bd. Trial Advs., Nat. Bd. Trial Advs., Nat. Coll. Advocacy, Internat. Soc. Barristers, Internat. Acad. Trial Lawyers (bd. dirs. 1983—87, 1991—92), Roscoe Pound Found. Office: Habush Habush & Rottier 777 E Wisconsin Ave Ste 2300 Milwaukee WI 53202-5381

HACCOUN, DAVID, electrical engineering educator; b. Bizerte, Tunisia, July 4, 1937; arrived in Can. 1957; s. Charles and Emma (Melloul) H.; m. Lyson Tobaly, Dec. 26, 1971; children— Nathalie, Laurent. B.Sc. Engring. Physics, U. Montreal, 1965; SM, MIT, 1966; PhD, McGill U., 1974. Registered profl. engr., Que. Communications engr. City of Montreal, Que., Can., 1965; research asst. MIT, Cambridge, 1965-66; prof. Ecole Polytech. U., Montreal, Que., Can., 1966—; vis. research prof. Concordia U., Montreal, Que., Can., 1984-85. Project leader Can. Inst. for Telecom. Rsch. under Nat. Ctrs. Excellence of Govt. Can., 1990-2003; vis. rsch. fellow Advanced Study Inst., U. BC, Vancouver, 1992; vis. rschr. INRIA, Paris, 1992, 1998-99; co-founder, pres. Can. Soc. Into. Theory, 1986-87; vis. rsch. prof. Higher Sch. Tech., Montreal, 1999, U. Victoria, B.C., Can., 1999; mem. exec. com. Telecom. Engring. Mgmt. Inst. Can., 1997—; cons. in field. Co-author: Digital Communications by Satellite, 1981, translated in Japanese, 1984, in Chinese, 1989, The Communications Handbook, 1997, 2001, The Encyclopedia of Telecommunications, 2002; contbr. articles to profl. jours. Mem. exec. com. Can. Jewish Congress, 1996—; bd. dirs. Comm. Rsch. Ctr., Ottawa, 1999—. Commonwealth fellow London, 1965; Grass fellow MIT, 1966, MIT scholar, 1965-66; Hydro-Que. fellow, Montreal, 1969-72. Fellow IEEE (life), 1993; mem. AAAS, 1997, Order of Engrs. of Que., 1968-, NY Acad. Scis., Sigma Xi. Avocations: photography, swimming, skiing. Office: Ecole Polytechnique PO Box 6079 Sta Centre Ville Montreal QC Canada H3C 3A7 E-mail: david.haccoun@polymtl.ca.

HACHEY, THOMAS EUGENE, British and Irish history educator, consultant; b. Lewiston, Maine, June 8, 1938; s. Leo Joseph and Margaret Mary (Johnson) H.; m. Jane Beverly Whitman, June 9, 1962. BA, St. Francis Coll., 1960; MA, Niagara U., 1961; PhD, St. John's U., 1965. Asst. prof. history Marquette U., Milw., 1964-69, assoc. prof., 1969-77, prof., 1977—, chmn. dept. history, 1979-93, dean Coll. Arts and Scis., 1993-2000; exec. dir. Irish programs, endowed chair dept. history Boston Coll., 2000—. Vis. prof. history Sch. Irish Studies, Dublin, 1977-78; cons. investments in Ireland Frost & Sullivan, N.Y.C., 1978-82; pres. Am. Conf. Irish Studies, 1983-85; dir. Bradley Inst. for Democracy and Pub. Values, 1988-99. Author: Problem of Partition: Peril to World Peace, 1972, Britain and Irish Separatism, 1977; co-author: The Irish Experience, 1988, expanded edit., 1996, Perspectives of Irish Nationalism, 1988; editor: Voices of Revolution, 1972, Confidential Despatches, 1975; contbr. over 100 articles and revs. to Brit., Irish and Am. jours. and newspapers. Danforth assoc., 1979-85. Fellow Anglo-Am. Assocs. Roman Catholic. Home: 20 Deerpath Rd Dedham MA 02026 Office: Boston Coll Connolly House 300 Hammond St Chestnut Hill MA 02467-3930

HACHTEN, WILLIAM ANDREWS, journalism educator, author; b. Wichita, Kans., Nov. 30, 1924; s. George Charles and Emma Elizabeth (Andrews) H.; m. Harva Kaaren Sprager, Apr. 5, 1952; children: Elizabeth, Marianne. BA, Stanford U., 1947; MS, UCLA, 1952; PhD, U. Minn., 1961. Profl. football player N.Y. Giants, 1947; reporter Santa Paula (Calif.) Chronicle, 1948-49, Long Beach (Calif.) Press-Telegram, 1952 54, Santa Monica (Calif.) Outlook, 1954; copy editor L.A. Examiner, 1955-56; prof. Sch. Journalism and Mass Communication U. Wis., Madison, 1959-89, asst. dir., 1973-75, dir., 1975-80. Fulbright lectr. U. Ghana, 1972-73. Author: The Supreme Court on Freedom of the Press, 1968, Muffled Drums: The News Media in Africa, 1971, Mass Communications in Africa: An Annotated Bibliography, 1971, World News Prism, 1981, 92, 96, 99, 2002, The Press and Apartheid, 1984, Growth of Media, 1993, The Troubles of Journalism, 1998, 2001; assoc. editor Journalism Quar., 1972-75. Served with USMCR, 1943-46. Recipient Sigma Delta Chi award for rsch. in journalism, 1968, Fulbright-Hays Rsch. award for Africa, 1968. Mem. Assn. Edn. Journalism, Internat. Press Inst., Internat. Assn. Mass Communication Rsch. Unitarian Universalist. Home: 90 Oak Creek Trl Madison WI 53717-1510

HACK, ELIZABETH, artist; b. Frankfurt, Germany, Feb. 27, 1954; d. Sidney Hack and Eleanor Barbara (Bermak) H. BFA, U. Miami, Coral Gables, Fla., 1976; M Media Arts, U. S.C., 1979. Art instr., Berkeley, Calif., 1991-97; art instr. W. Contra Costa (Calif.) Adult Sch., 1994-96. Lectr., workshops Nat. League Am. Pen Women, El Cerrito Cmty. Ctr., Albany Sr. Ctr., 1992—Featured artist Commonwealth Club gallery, San Francisco, 1994; solo exhbns. Newall Assocs., 1997, Henry Hardy Gallery, Univ. Club, San Francisco, 1992, Gallery 57, Fullerton, Calif., 1992, AMEX, San Rafael, Informative Edge, San Francisco, 1991, Conv. Plz. Bldg., San Francisco, 1990, Heller Gallery, U. Calif. Berkeley, Sumitomo Bank, San Francisco, ASUC Studio, U. Calif. Berkeley, 1988, Musical Offering, Berkeley, Coldwell Banker, Kensington home, French Hotel Berkeley, 1987, Coffee Cantata, San Francisco, 1985; group exhbns. include Gloria Delson Fine Art, L.A., 1995, 96, Cameo Art Gallery, Columbia, S.C., 1992, 94, Ashkenazy Galleries, L.A., 1991; group shows include: Art in Embassy Program, U.S. State Dept., 2003, Hayward Arts Coun., Nat. League of Am. Pen Women Exhibit, Hayward, Calif., 1999, Cruising the Triton, Santa Clara, Calif., 1999, Palos Verdes Cultural Ctr., 1997, Orlando Gallery, Sherman Oaks, Calif., 1997, Triton Mus. of Art, Benefit Auction, Santa Clara, Calif., 1997, Richmond Art Ctr., Holiday Acution, Calif., 1997, Newall Assocs., Santa Monica, Calif., 1997, Soolip Gallery, West Hollywood, Calif., 1997, Hayward Arts Coun., 1998, Nat. League Am. Pen

Women, Hayward, 1998, Triton Mus. Art, Santa Clara, 1997, 98, 3 Com Corp., Santa Clara, Calif., 1998, Network Assoc., Menlo Park, Calif., 1998, Triton Mus. Art, Santa Clara, Calif., 1998, Mad River Post Nancy Sadler Fine Arts, Calif., 1998, Triton Mus., 2000, 01, Lindsay Dirkx Brown Art Gallery, San Ramon, Calif., 2000, 2001, 2002, 2003, Alameda Bd. Suprs. Gallery, Oakland, Calif., 2002. Curator multiple abstractions W. Contra Costa Adult Sch., 1995, 4th ann. Gift of Life Ctr. for Visual Arts, Oakland, 1996—, AIDS auction, 1994; mem. Hayward Art Coun., 1999. Recipient Critic's Choice award San Francisco Bay Guardian, 1990, award of distinction Berkeley Art Ctr., 1989, Golden Web award Internat. Assn. Webmasters and Designers, 2001. Mem. Nat. League Am. Pen Women (sec. 1994-96, v.p. 1996-98, pres. Diablo-Alameda chpt. 1998-2000, membership chair 2002, 2d v.p. 2002-04). Avocations: skiing, hiking, music. Home and Office: PO Box 8057 Berkeley CA 94707-8057 E-mail: studio@elizabethhack.com.

HACK, GARY ARTHUR, dean; b. Abernethy, Sask., Can., Apr. 8, 1942; came to U.S., 1964; s. Arthur and Marie (Banerd) H.; m. Lynda Lloy Lewis, Sept. 5, 1964 (dec.); children: Andrew Arthur, Carolyn Sarah; m. Lynne Beyer Sagalyn, Jan. 1, 2002. BArch, U. Manitoba, 1964; MArch, U. Ill., 1966, M in Urban Planning, 1967; PhD, MIT, 1976. Project mgr. Gruen Assocs., N.Y.C., 1967-69; asst. prof. MIT, Cambridge, 1970-75; gen. mgr. Can. Mortgage and Housing Corp., Ottawa, Ont., 1975-79; prof. MIT, Cambridge, 1979-96; prin. Carr Lynch Hack & Sandell, Cambridge, 1986-94; dean, Paley prof. U. Pa., Phila., 1996—. Co-author: Site Planning, 3d edit., 1984, Global City Regions, 2000; chief planner West Side Waterfront, N.Y.C., 1986-91, Prudential Ctr. Redevel., Boston, 1988-91. Chair Phila. City Planning Commn., 2000—. Recipient 1st award Progressive Architecture, 1975. Fellow Urban Land Inst.; mem. Am. Inst. Cert. Planners. Avocations: travel, architectural photography, collecting yi cheng teapots. Office: U Pa 101 Meyerson Hall/6311 Philadelphia PA 19104 E-mail: hackga@aol.com.

HACK, RANDOLPH C. advocate, educator, counselor; b. N.Y.C., Feb. 14, 1947; s. Sidney and Eleanor (Bermak) Hack. BA, U. Hawaii, Honolulu, 1980. Per diem tchr. Hawaii Dept. Edn., Honolulu, 1984—92; dir. consumer adv. United Self-Help, Honolulu, 1989—95; program dir. United Self Help, Honolulu, 1992—95, exec. dir., 1995—99; consumer advisor Adult Mental Health Divsn., Honolulu, 1999—2003, dir. consumer affairs, 2003—. Counselor Armed Svcs. YMCA, Schofield Barracks, Hawaii, 1987—93, participant White Ho. Conf. Mental Health, Washington, 1999; bd. dirs. Statewide Ind. Living Coun. Vice chmn. State Coun. Mental Health, 1995—99; mem. Diamond Head Svc. Area Bd. Mental Health & Substance Abuse, Honolulu, 1989—92; precinct chmn. Dem. Com. Hawaii, Honolulu, 2000; bd. dirs. Mental Health Assn. Hawaii, 1984—86, Waikiki Health Ctr., 1999—, Mental Health Kokua, 1990—. Recipient Cmty. Svc. award, Mental Health Assn., 1991, Senator Daniel K. Inouye award, Hawaii Psychol. Assn., 1998. Mem.: Nat. Alliance Mentally Ill (state rep., nat. consumer coun. 1998—, bd. dirs. Hawaii 1997—, bd. dirs. Oahu 1997—). Avocation: swimming. Home: 1117 12th Ave Apt 8 Honolulu HI 96816-3747 Office: Adult Mental Health Divsn 1250 Punchbowl St Honolulu HI 96813 E-mail: rchack@mail.health.state.hi.us.

HACKAM, REUBEN, electrical engineering educator; b. Baghdad, Iraq, Feb. 18, 1936; arrived in Can., 1978; s. Yechiel and Rachel (Cohen) H.; m. Estelle Malkinson, June 7, 1964; children: Judy, David, Abby, Dan. BSc, Israel Inst. Tech., Haifa, 1960; PhD, U. Liverpool, Eng., 1964, DEng, 1988. Sr. engr. GE, Stafford, Eng., 1964-69; lectr. elec. engring. U. Sheffield, Eng., 1969-73, sr. lectr., 1973-74, reader, 1974-78; prof. U. Windsor, 1978—2001, prof. emeritus, 2001—, chmn. dept., 1981-82, 84-86. Vis. staff dept. math. Staffordshire Poly., Stafford, 1964-69, Sheffield Poly, 1970-78, Hong Kong Poly. U., 1990-91; cons. Brit. Rail, Derby, Eng., 1975-78, English Electric Co., Stafford, 1975-77, Windsor Star, 1981-91, Corp. City of Windsor, 1983-92, Green Shield Prepaid Svcs., Inc., 1982—, County of Essex Libr., 1986—, Can. Salt Co., 1988—, Windsor Real Estate Bd., 1996—; vis. prof. Kumamoto U., Japan, 1998-99. Contbr. articles to profl. jours. Cons. Windsor Bd. Edn., 1988, Essex Bd. Edn., Windsor, 1989-94. Fellow: IEEE (bd. dirs. conf. on elec. insulation and dielectric phenomena 1985—91, gaseous dielectrics tech. com. 1985—, mem. tech. program com.IEEE-CEIDP 1986—97, mem. editl. bd. IEEE Insulation Mag. 1990—98, asst. editor Digest IEEE Transactions on Dielectrics and Elec. Insulat 1990—99, mem. permanent sci. com. int. synomps. on discharges and elec. insulat 1991—2001, sec. 1992—93, fellows award com. 1993—96, vice chmn. conf. on elec. insulation and dielectric phenomena 1994—95, chmn. 1996—97, various working groups 1997—, mem. editl. bd. IEEE Insulation Mag. 1999—2001, assoc. editor 1999—2001, editor-in-chief 2002—, program com. publicity and pub. chmn., Third Millennium medal 2000, Eric O. Forster Disting. award 2000, Innuishi Meml. lecture award 1998); mem.: IEEE Dielectrics and Elec. Insulation Soc. (nominating and adv. coms. 1988—91, pub. com. 1988—96, chmn. publ. com. 1990—91, edn. com. 1990—95, asst. treas. 1991, treas. 1993—94, v.p. adminstrn. 1995—96, pres. 1997—98, mem. IEEE meetings and svcs. com. 1997—98, chair 1999—2000, treas. 1999—2001, pub. com. 1999—2001). Jewish. Office: U Windsor 401 Sunset Ave Windsor ON Canada N9B 3P4 E-mail: hackam@u.windsor.ca.

HACKBIRTH, DAVID WILLIAM, aluminum company executive; b. Butler, Ind., Jan. 25, 1935; s. Ernest William and Bessie Mae (Snyder) H.; m. Anna Katherine Shaffer, July 19, 1959; children: Cynthia Kay, David William. Student, Defiance Coll., 1953; BS, Ind. U., 1959; JD, Wayne State U., 1963, postgrad., 1965; MBA, U. Detroit, 1965. Bar: Mich. bar 1963. Auditor Ernst & Ernst, Indpls., 1958-59; fin. and budget analyst Ford Motor Co., Dearborn, Mich., 1959-62; legal adminstr. Chrysler Corp., Detroit, 1962-63, tax atty., 1963-66, Glidden Co., Cleve., 1966-67; asst. to treas. Alcan Aluminum Corp., Cleve., 1967-70, asst. to group v.p. ops., 1970-73; pres., dir. Aluminio de Colombia S.A., 1973-76; v.p. Alcan Bldg. Products div. Alcan Aluminum Corp., Warren, Ohio, 1976-78, pres., 1978-83, Alcan Sheet and Plate div., 1983-86, Alcan Bldg Products div., 1986-89, Alcan Extrusions USA div., 1989-90; pres., dir. Alcan Aluminum Corp., 1990-95, Bus. Concepts, Inc., 1995—. Bd. dirs. Luxfer USA Ltd., Alcan-Toyo-Am., Inc., Lanxide Corp., Liberty Mutual Ins. Co. Bd. dirs. ARC, NCCJ. Served with U.S. Army, 1954-56. Mem. ABA, Am. Arbitration Assn., Mich. Bar Assn., Cleve. Growth Assn. (dir.), Akron Regional Devel. Bd., Pine Lake Trout Club, Country Club of Hudson, Union Club, Cotillion Soc. Cleve., Scottish Rite, Beta Alpha Psi, Delta Theta Phi. Home: 290 Bicknell Dr Hudson OH 44236-2922 Office: 920 Key Bldg 159 S Main St Akron OH 44308-1317

HACKEL, ADAM WILLIAM, music educator; s. William Michael and Geraldine Ann Hackel. BFA, Tulane U., 1994; MA in Edn1. Leadership, Kean U., 2000; EdD, Rowan U., 2002; postgrad., Combined Arms and Services Staff Sch., 2002—. Cert. Music tchr. 1996, Chem. Def. Tng. 1995, Combat Life saver 1996, Supr. K-12 2001, Prin. 2001, Chem. Def. Tng. 2001, Army Instr. 1999, Army Course Mgr. 2000. Band dir. Montgomery Twp. Sch. Dist., Skillman, NJ, 2002—; commdg. officer 3 BN 391st Rgt. 7th Brigade, 98th Divsn., FT Dix, NJ, 2002—; jazz band dir. Montgomery Twp. Sch. Dist., Skillman, NJ, 2002—; dep. comdt., U.S. Army Chem. Sch. region a 4th Bn. Chem., 98th Divsn., FT Dix, NJ, 1999—2002; broadcase mgr. U.S. Army, 2003—. Musician: (music education work book) Master Teacher collaborative, 2000 (NJ. Symphony Orch. Master Tchr. Award, 2000). Capt. U.S. Army, 1994. Decorated Nat. Def. Svc. Medal U.S. Army Chem. Sch.; recipient Dunnaway Medal, Valley Forge Mil. Acad., 1990, Wayne Rotary Club Medal for selfless svc., 1989, Master Music Tchr. Collaborative, N.J. Symphony Orch., 2000, Aerospace Edn. Disting. Svc. Award, CAP, 2000, Disting. Svc. Award, Tulane Police Dept., 1994, David Price Trainer Award, Valley Forge Mil. Acad., 1990, Dunnaway medal, 1998. Master: Music Honor Soc. (life; faculty advisor 1995); mem.: Music Educators Nat. Conf. (assoc.), Kappa Delta Pi (assoc.). Avocations: music composition, camping, theater, singing, hiking. Office: Montgomery Township School System Burnt Hill Rd Skillman NJ 08558 Personal E-mail: tiamat9408@earthlink.net.

HACKEL, EMANUEL, science educator; b. Bklyn., June 17, 1925; s. Henry N. and Esther (Herbstman) H.; m. Elisabeth Mackie, June 24, 1950 (dec. Apr. 1978); children: Lisa M., Meredith Anne, Janet M.; m. Rachel A. Fisher, Oct. 18, 1981; stepchildren: Daniel E., Tabitha A., and Jessica K. Harrison. Student, N.Y. U., 1941-42; BS, U. Mich., 1948, MS, 1949; PhD, Mich. State U., 1953. Fisheries biologist Mich. Dept. Conservation, 1949; mem. faculty Mich. State U., East Lansing, 1949—, prof. natural sci., 1962-74, chmn. dept. natural sci., 1963-74, prof. medicine, 1974-95, prof. emeritus, 1995—, prof. zoology, 1974-95, prof. emeritus, 1995—. Asst. dean coll. 1958-63; rsch. fellow Galton Lab., U. Coll., London, 1970-71, 77-78; vis. investigator blood group rsch. unit Lister Inst., London, 1956-57; cons. Mpls. War Meml. Blood Bank, 1983-95. Author: Guide to Laboratory Studies in Biological Science, 1951, Studies in Natural Science, 1953, Natural Science, 1955, Vols. 1, 2, 3, 1952-63. Editor: The Search for Explanation-Studies in Natural Science, Vols. 1, 2, 3, 1967-68, Laboratory Manual for Natural Science, Vol. 1, 2, 3, 1967-68, Human Genetics, 1974, Theoretical Aspects of HLA, 1982, Bone Marrow Transplantation, 1983, HLA Techniques for Blood Bankers, 1984, Human Genetics 1984: A Look at the Last Ten Years and the Next Ten, Transfusion Management of Some Common Heritable Blood Disorders, 1992, Advances in Transplantation, 1993, HLA Typing Section, Clinical Laboratory Medicine, 1994, Human Genetics '94: A Revolution in Full Swing, 1994; contbr. articles on genetics, human blood group immunology and chem. nature of blood group antigens, human biochem. genetics, tissue typing, human histocompatibility antigens to sci. jours. Served to lt. (j.g.) USNR, 1943-47; now lt. comdr. USNR Ret. Recipient Cooley Meml. award Am. Assn. Blood Banks, 1969, Elliott Meml. award Am. Assn. Blood Banks, 1987, alumni disting. faculty award Coll. Natural Sci. Mich. State U., 1995. Mem. Assn. Gen. and Liberal Studies (sec.-treas. 1962-65), AAUP, AAAS, Genetics Soc. Am., Am. Soc. Human Genetics, Am. Assn. Blood Banks (dir. 1983-84, chmn. sci. sect. 1983-84), Mich. Assn. Blood Banks (v.p. 1970, pres. 1975-77), Am. Inst. Biol. Sci., Biometric Soc., Transplantation Soc. Mich. (dir. 1975-84), Am. Assn. for Clin. Histocompatability Testing, N.Y. Acad. Scis., Sigma Xi, Phi Kappa Phi. Home: 244 Oakland Dr East Lansing MI 48823-4747

HACKEL-SIMS, STELLA BLOOMBERG, lawyer, former government official; b. Burlington, Vt., Dec. 27, 1926; d. Hyman and Esther (Pocher) Bloomberg; m. Donald Herman Hackel, Aug. 14, 1949; children: Susan Jane, Cynthia Anne; m. Arthur Sims, Aug. 28, 1980. Student, U. Vt., 1943-45; JD cum laude, Boston U., 1948. Bar: Vt. 1948, Mass. 1948, D.C. 1979, Va. 1982. Individual practice law, Burlington, 1948-49, Rutland, Vt., 1949-59, 73—; city prosecutor City of Rutland, 1957-63; commr. Vt. Dept. Employment Security, 1963-73; treas. State of Vt., 1975-77; dir. U.S. Mint, Dept. Treasury, Washington, 1977-81. Chmn. Vt. Municipal Bond Bank, 1975-77 Mem. Vt. Adv. Com. on Mental Retardation, Interdept. Council on Aging, Commn. on Status Women, Human Resource Inter-Agency Com., Emergency Resource Priorities Bd., Info. Planning Council, Legis. Council Equal Opportunity Com., Vt. Indsl. Devel. Authority, Vt. Housing Fin. Agy., Vt. Claims Commn., Vt. Tchrs. Retirement Fund. Bd., Vt. Home Mortgage Guaranty Bd.; chmn. Vt. State Employees Retirement Fund; ex-officio mem. Nat. Manpower Adv. Com., 1971-72, Fed. Adv. Council on Unemployment Ins., 1971-72; Pres. Rutland Girl Scouts Leaders Assn., 1949-50, Rutland League Women Voters, 1951-52, Rutland Council Jewish Women, 1955-56; chmn. womens div. Rutland Community Chest Dr., 1952, Rutland County-Vt. Assn. for Blind, 1953-56; pres. Rutland County Democratic Women's Assn., 1956-63; treas. Rutland City Dem. Com., 1957-63; former rep. office women's activities Dem. Nat. Com., Regional Council I., Women's CD Councils; mem. Vt. bd. Girl Scouts U.S.A.; chmn. Arlington County Tenant-Landlord Commn., Va., 1986— . Mem.: LWV, AAUW (pres. Rutland County br. 1961—62), Interstate Conf. Employment Security Agys. (v.p. region I 1966—68, legis. com. 1969, sr. v.p. 1970—71, pres. 1971—72), Am. Soc. Pub. Adminstrn., Vt. Coun. Social Agys., Bus. and Profl. Women's Club, Rutland County Bar Assn. (pres. 1973), Vt. Bar Assn., Emblem (dir. 1960-63), Woodmont Country; Internat. (Washington), Moorings Country Club (Naples, Fla.), Emblem Club (dir. 1960—63), Delta Phi Epsilon.

HACKENBERG, BARBARA JEAN COLLAR, retired advertising and public relations executive; b. Venango County, Pa., Apr. 15, 1927; d. Guy Lamont and Marion Leona (Kingsley) Collar; m. George Richardson, June 13, 1953; children: Kurt Edward, Kim Ellen, Caroline Kingsley. BA, Grove City (Pa.) Coll., 1948; ML, U. Pitts., 1949. Advt. dir. The Halle Bros. Co., Erie, Pa., 1950-52, advt. and sales promotion dir. Pa. divsn., 1952-54; exec. dir. Wyomissing (Pa.) Inst. Fine Arts, 1970-74; dir. and cmty. liason Freedman Gallery, Albright Coll., Reading, Pa., 1976-78; selling supr. Pomeroy's Children's Dept., Wyomissing, Pa., 1981-83; pub. rels. account exec. Wentworth Assocs., Lancaster, Pa., 1983-84; exec. dir. World Affairs Coun., Reading, 1987—97; ret. The WRITE Place, Reading, 1997, owner, 1979—. V.p. Harrisburg (Pa.) Foreign Policy Assn., 1964-67; various fund-raising activities, 1954-70; pub. relations chmn. Erie World Affairs Ctr., 1957-60; mem. mil. affairs com. Berks County chpt. ARC, 1998—; apptd. to Parks and Recreation Bd., Twp. of Cumru, 1998—; mem. Internat. Com. YMCA, Berks County, Pa., 1999—. Mem. Women in Communications, Inc. (pub. relations chmn. ctrl. Pa. chpt., 1984-87, sec. ctrl. Pa. chpt., 1986-87). Avocations: writing, theater, art, concerts, bicycling. Home and Office: 1334 Welsh Rd Reading PA 19607-9334

HACKER, ANDREW, political science educator; b. N.Y.C., Aug. 30, 1929; s. Louis Morton and Lilian (Lewis) H.; 1 child, Ann. AB, Amherst Coll., 1951; MA, Oxford (Eng.) U., 1953; PhD, Princeton U., 1955. Instr. govt. Cornell U., Ithaca, N.Y., 1955-56, asst. prof., 1956-60, asso. prof., 1960-66, prof., 1966-71; prof. polit. sci. Queens Coll., CUNY, 1971—. Cons. Conf. Bd., Brookings Instn., Rockefeller Bros. Fund, NBC, Ency. Brit. Author: Political Theory: Philosophy, Ideology, Science, 1960, Congressional Districting, 1963, The Study of Politics, 1973, The Corporation Take-Over, 1964, The End of the American Era, 1970, The New Yorkers, 1975, Free Enterprise in America, 1977, U.S.: A Statistical Portrait of the American People, 1983, Two Nations: Black and White, Separate, Hostile, Unequal, 1992, updated edit., 2003, Money: Who Has How Much and Why, 1997, 2d edit., 1998, Mismatch: The Growing Gulf Between Women and Men, 2003. Mem. Phi Beta Kappa. Home: 20 W 64th St Apt 16K New York NY 10023-7180 Office: CUNY Queens Coll Dept Polit Sci Flushing NY 11367

HACKER, BARTON CLYDE, historian, writer; b. Chgo., July 17, 1935; s. Carl and Ida (Genstel) Hacker; m. Sally Lynn Swank, June 10, 1966; 1 child, Richard Mark. BA in Liberal Arts, U. Chgo., 1955, BA in History, 1960, MA in History, 1962, PhD in History, 1968. Lectr.U. Chgo., 1965—66; sr. historian Manned Spacecraft Ctr., Houston, 1965—69; asst. prof. Iowa State U., Ames, 1970—75; rsch. assoc. MIT, Cambridge, Mass., 1975—77; radiation dosimetry historian REECo, Las Vegas, Nev., 1978—86; vis. asst. prof. Oreg. State U., Corvallis, 1986—91; lab. historian Lawrence Livermore Nat. Lab., Livermore, Calif., 1992—98; curator Armed Forces history Smithsonian Mus. Am. History, Washington, 1998—. Cons. in field; chmn. program com.ICOHTEC, 2002—03. Author: (short story) Go and Catch a Falling Star, 1960 (Mennn prize, 1960), (essay) The Idea of Rendevous, 1971 (Goddard prize, 1972), Radiation Safety, the AEC and Nuclear Weapons Testing, 1992 (Madison prize, 1993), The Dragon's Tail, Elements of Controlversy (Leopold prize, 1996), World Military History Bibliography, 2003; co-author: Project Gemini Technology, 1969, On the Shoulders of Titans, 1978; co-editor: West Point in the Making of America, 2002; editor: Annotated Index to Technology and Culture, 1991 (Usher prize, 1993); co-editor: The Martians, Hungarian Emigré Scientists, 1997; contbr. Co-founder, sec. Houston br. NOW, 1968; precinct chmn. Dem. Party, Cambridge, Iowa, 1972. With U.S. Army, 1956—59. Mem.: U.S. Commn. on Mil. History, Soc. for Mil. History, History of Sci. Soc., Columbia History of Sci. Group (chmn. program com. 1997—99, pres. 1998—2000), Mil. Tech. Interest Group (founder, chmn. 1985—), World Hist. Assn., Soc. for History of Tech. (chmn. editl. com. 1993—94, chmn. Dexter prize com. 1998—99, chmn. Robinson prize com. 1981—82, mem. adv. coun. 1983—88, Leonardo da Vinci medal 2003), Orgn. Am. Historians (life), Am. Hist. Assn. (life). Home: 150 12th St NE Washington DC 20002-6471 Office: Smithsonian Instn NMAH-4013 Washington DC 20560-0620 E-mail: hackerb@si.edu.

HACKER, MICHELLE WENDY, auditor, researcher, finance educator; b. Chgo., Feb. 19, 1955; d. George Edward and Katharine Rosino Hacker. BS, Fla. Met. U., Tampa, Fla., MBA, 1995; DBA, U. of Sarasota (Fla.), 2001. Mgr. SuperAm., Mpls., 1985—92; machinist Sargent-Lelich Sci., Chgo., 1975—85; tax auditor Dept. of Revenue, Tampa, Fla., 1995—; adj. prof. internat. bus Fla. Met. U., Tampa, Fla., 2001—. Composer: (symphonies) #1 The Egotistical, 1998, #2 The Esoteric, 2000, #3 The Quintessens, Complete book of Preludes Piano Opus 30, Complete Book of Nocturnes Piano Opus 41. Counselor AA, Tampa, Fla. Mem.: LWV, NOW. E-mail: michelledoc2003@yahoo.com.

HACKER, THOMAS OWEN, architect; b. Dayton, Ohio, Nov. 4, 1941; s. Homer Owen and Lydia (McLean) H.; m. Margaret (Brooks) Stewart, Mar. 21, 1965; children: Jacob, Sarah, Alice. BA, U. Pa., 1964, MArch, 1967. Registered arch., Oreg.; registered Nat. Coun. Archtl. Registration Bds. Intern architect Office of Louis I. Kahn, Phila., 1964-70; mem. faculty architecture U. Pa., Phila., 1967-69, U. Oreg., Eugene, 1970-84; design prin. Thomas Hacker and Assocs. Architects P.C., Portland, Oreg., 1983—. Vis. profl. architecture, U. Oreg., 1985—. Prin. works include Biomed. Info. Comm. Ctr., Oreg. Health Scis. U., Sch. Nursing, Oreg. Health Scis. U., Portland Art Mus., High Desert Mus., Bend, Oreg.; designer crystal vase for Steuben Inc., Spokane Pub. Libr., Yellowstone Art Mus., Billings, Mont., Lewis & Clark Coll. Signature Project, Multnomah County Librs., Columbia Gorge Interpretive Ctr., Portland State U. Urban Ctr., Whitman Coll. Penrose Meml. Libr., Portland 1st Unitarian Ch., Bend Pub. Libr. Office: 34 NW 1st Ave Ste 406 Portland OR 97209-4017 Home: 2762 SW Montgomery Dr Portland OR 97201-1693

HACKERMAN, NORMAN, chemist, academic administrator; b. Balt., Mar. 2, 1912; s. Jacob and Anne (Raffel) Hackerman; m. Gene Allison Coulbourn, Aug. 25, 1940; children: Patricia Gale, Stephen Miles, Sally Griffith, Katherine Elizabeth. AB, Johns Hopkins U., 1932, PhD, 1935. Asst. prof. Loyola Coll., Balt., 1935—39; rsch. chemist Colloid Corp., 1936—40; asst. chemist USCG, S.I., 1939—41; prof. Va. Poly. Inst., Blacksburg, 1941—43; rsch. chemist Kellex Corp., 1944—45; asst. prof. chemistry U. Tex., 1945—46, assoc. prof., 1946—50, prof., 1950—70, chmn. dept. chemistry, 1952—61, dir. corrosion rsch. lab., 1948—61, dean rsch. and sponsored programs, 1960—61, v.p., provost, 1961—63, vice chancellor acad. affairs, 1963—67, pres., 1967—70, prof. emeritus chemistry, 1985—; prof. chemistry Rice U., Houston, 1970—85, Disting. prof. emeritus, 1985—, pres., 1970—85, pres. emeritus, 1985—. Chmn. Gordon Corrosion Rsch. Conf., 1950; cons. in corrosion, 1946—; chmn. Inter Soc. Corrosion Com., 1956—58, Gordon Rsch. Conf. on Surface Chemistry, 1959; mem. nat. sci. bd. NSF, 1968—80; chmn., 1974—80; mem. Def. Sci. Bd., 1978—85; chmn. sci. adv. bd. Welch Found., 1982—; chmn. bd. energy studies NAS/NRC Commn. Natural Resources, 1974—77; mem. Energy Rsch. Adv. Bd., 1980—82, Tex. Gov.'s Task Force on Higher Edn., 1981—82; trustee MITRE Corp., 1980—85. Editor Jour. Electrochem. Soc., 1969—89, editl. bd., adv. edn. bd. Corrosion Sci., 1965—70, editl. bd. Catalysis Revs., 1968—73. Recipient Whitney award, Nat. Assn. Corrosion Engrs., 1956, Joseph J. Mattiello Meml. lectr., Fedn. Socs. Paint Tech., 1964, Gold medal, Am. Inst. Chemists, Mirabeau B. Lamar award, Assn. Tex. Colls. and Univs., 1981, Disting. Alumnus award, Johns Hopkins U., 1982, Alumni Gold medal for disting. svc. to Rice U., 1984, Vannevar Bush award, NSF, 1993, Nat. medal of Sci., 1993. Fellow: AAAS (Phillip Hauge Abelson prize 1987), N.Y. Acad. Scis., Am. Acad. Arts and Scis.; mem.: NAS, Am. Philos. Soc., Argonne Univs. Assn. (chmn. bd. trustees 1969—73), Nat. Corrosion Engrs. (bd. dirs. 1952—55, chmn. com. edn. Corrosion Rsch. Coun. 1957—60), Faraday Soc., Electrochem. Soc. (pres. 1957—58, Palladium medal 1965, Edward Goodrich Acheson award 1984), Am. Chem. Soc. (bd. editors 1955—62, exec. com. colloid divsn. 1955—58, chmn. chemistry and pub. affairs com. 1982—88, S.W. Regional award 1965, Charles Lathrop Parsons award 1987), Sigma Xi, Phi Kappa Phi, Alpha Chi Sigma, Phi Lambda Upsilon. Home: 3 Woodstone Sq Austin TX 78703 Office: The Robert A Welch Found 5555 San Felipe St Ste 1900 Houston TX 77056-2732

HACKERMAN, WILLARD, construction services executive; BS, Johns Hopkins U, Baltimore. CEO, pres. Whiting-Turner Contracting, Balt. Office: Whiting-Turner Contracting 300 E Joppa Rd Baltimore MD 21286*

HACKETT, CAROL ANN HEDDEN, physician; b. Valdese, N.C., Dec. 18, 1939; d. Thomas Barnett and Zada Loray (Pope) Hedden; m. John Peter Hackett, July 27, 1968; children: John Hedden, Elizabeth Bentley, Susanne Rochet. BA, Duke U., 1961; MD, U. N.C., 1966. Intern Georgetown U. Hosp., Washington, 1966-67, resident, 1967-69; clinic physician DePaul Hosp., Norfolk, Va., 1969-71; chief spl. health svcs. Arlington County Dept. Human Resources, Arlington, Va., 1971-72; gen. med. officer USPHS Hosp., Balt., 1974-75; pvt. practice family medicine Seattle, 1975—. Mem. staff, chmn. dept. family practice Overlake Hosp. Med. Ctr., 1985-86; clin. asst. prof. Sch. Medicine U. Wash. Bd. dirs. Mercer Island (Wash.) Presch. Assn., 1977-78; coord. 13th and 20th Ann. Inter-profl. Women's Dinner, 1978, 86; trustee Northwest Chamber Orch., 1984-85. Fellow Am. Acad. Family Practice; mem. King County Acad. Family Practice (trustee 1993-96, pres.-elect 1997-98, pres. 1998-99), King County Med. Soc. (chmn. com. TV violence), Wash. Acad. Family Practice, Wash. State Med. Soc., DAR, Bellevue C. of C., N.W. Women Physicians (v.p. 1978), Seattle Symphony League, Eastside Women Physicians (founder, pres.), Seattle Yacht Club, Sigma Kappa. Episcopalian. Home: PO Box 3098 Bellevue WA 98009-3098 Office: 1414 116th Ave NE Bellevue WA 98004-3801 Fax: 425 462 5313.

HACKETT, EARL RANDOLPH, neurologist; b. Moulmein, Burma, Feb. 16, 1932; s. Paul Richmond and Martha Jane (Lewis) H.; m. Shirley Jane Kanehl, May 25, 1953; children: Nancy, Raymond, Susan, Lynn, Laurie, Richard, Alicia. BS, Drury Coll., Springfield, Mo., 1953; MD, Western Res. U., 1957. Diplomate Am. Bd. Psychiatry and Neurology, Am. Bd. Electrodiagnostic Medicine. Intern, then resident in neurology Charity Hosp., New Orleans, 1957-62; resident in internal medicine VA Hosp., New Orleans, 1958-59; mem. faculty La. State U. Med. Sch., New Orleans, 1962—, prof. neurology, 1973-88, head dept., 1977-88; clin. prof. neurology U. Mo., Columbia, 1988—. Mem. med. adv. bd. Myasthenia Gravis Found. Fellow Am. Acad. Neurology; mem. Am. Assn. Electrodiagnostic Medicine, Soc. Clin. Neurologists, Mo. Med. Assn., Greene County Med. Soc., AOA. Methodist. Home: 2517 S Brentwood Blvd Springfield MO 65804-3201 Office: 1965 S Fremont Ave Ste 2800 Springfield MO 65804-2258

HACKETT, JOHN BYRON, advertising agency executive, lawyer; b. N.Y.C., Dec. 28, 1933; s. John Joseph and Cecelia Elizabeth (Meehan) H.; m. Patricia P. Briordy, May 23, 1964 (div. 1980); children: Kimberly, John; m. Kathryn Meyer, Mar. 28, 1982. BBA, Iona Coll., 1956; JD, St. Johns U., 1960. Bar: N.Y. 1961. Sales adminstr. NBC, N.Y.C., 1962-65; with J. Walter Thompson Co., N.Y.C., 1965-85, v.p. legal dept., 1971-76, sr. v.p. adminstrn., 1976-80, sr. v.p., gen. mgr. entertainment div., 1980-83, sr. v.p., dir. spot broadcasting U.S.A., 1983-85; pvt. legal practice, 1985—. Home and Office: 1 Toms Point Ln Apt 10B Port Washington NY 11050-2120

HACKETT, JOHN THOMAS, retired economist; b. Fort Wayne, Ind., Oct. 10, 1932; s. Harry H. and Ruth (Greer) H.; m. Ann E. Thompson, July 24, 1954; children: Jane, David, Sarah, Peter. BS, Ind. U., 1954, MBA, 1958; PhD, Ohio State U., 1961. Instr. Ohio State U., 1958-61; asst. v.p., economist Fed. Res. Bank, Cleve., 1961-64; dir. planning Cummins Engine Co., Columbus, Ind., 1964-66, v.p. finance, 1966-71, exec. v.p., 1971-88, also dir.; v.p. fin. and adminstrn. Ind. U., Bloomington, 1988-91; mng. gen. ptnr. CID Equity Ptnrs., L.P., Indpls., 1991—2002, ret., 2002. Bd. dirs. Irwin Fin. Corp., Ind. Corp. for Bus. Modernizationand Tech.; chmn. bd. dirs. Wabash Nat. Corp. 1st lt. AUS, 1954-56. Mem. Ind. Acad., Beta Gamma Sigma. Home: PO Box 2337 Columbus IN 47202-2337

HACKETT, KEVIN JAMES, insect pathologist; b. Phila., Apr. 24, 1947; s. James Patrick and Betty Corrine (Hulsey) H.; m. Kathleen Ruth Schmitt, Mar. 22, 1969; children: Ryan Hale, Aislinn Elizabeth. BS, Rutgers U., 1969, MS, 1971; PhD, U. Calif., Berkeley, 1980. Ea. coord. John Muir Inst. Environ. Studies, Washington, 1979-83; rsch. entomologist insect biocontrol lab. USDA Agrl. Rsch. Svc., Beltsville, Md., 1983—, nat. program leader for biocontrol, invasive species, bees and pollination, and insect genomics, 1998—. Author: The Mycoplasmas, 1990 (novel) Sen, Secluded, 2001; contbr. articles to jour. Sci. Founder, coord. Dept. of Peace and Conflict Studies (formerly Ind. Peace Studies), U. Calif., Berkeley, 1972-74. Mem. AAAS, Internat. Orgn. Mycoplasmology (team leader spiroplasma working team 1990-96, Derrick Edward award 1988), Soc. Invertebrate Pathology, Am. Soc. Microbiology, Entomology Soc. Am. Unitarian Universalist. Achievements include development of insect cell spiroplasma coculture, hypothesis for spiroplasma evolution. Office: USDA/ARS/Nat Program Staff 5601 Sunnyside Ave Bldg 4 Beltsville MD 20705-5000

HACKETT, KEVIN R. lawyer; b. Atlantic City, N.J., Apr. 16, 1949; BA summa cum laude, Boston Coll., 1971; JD, Harvard U., 1974. Bar: N.Y. 1975. Ptnr. Shearman & Sterling, N.Y.C. Fellow Am. Coll. Real Estate Lawyers; mem. ABA, N.Y. State Bar Assn., Assn. Bar City of N.Y., Phi Beta Kappa. Office: 599 Lexington Ave Fl 1448 New York NY 10022-6030

HACKETT, MIMS, JR., state legislator; b. Sept. 28, 1941; BS in Biology, Paul Quinn Coll., 1963; MS in Adminstrn. and Supervision, Seton Hall U., 1976. Mayor City of Orange Twp., NJ, 1996—; assemblyman N.J. Gen. Assembly, 2002—. Vice chair, state govt. com. N.J. Gen. Assembly, mem. appropriations com. Democrat. Office: 15 Village Plz Ste 1B South Orange NJ 07079 E-mail: AsmHackett@njleg.org.

HACKETT, PATRICIA JO, academic administrator, dean; b. Rushville, Ill., Feb. 23, 1954; d. James Ralph and Pauline Bernice Perry; m. Keith Thomas Hackett, July 17, 1976; children: Katie Rae, James Thomas. BA, Tarkio Coll., Mo., 1976; MS, U. of Memphis, 1986. Placement dir. Baker U., Baldwin City, Kans., 1978—80; freshman dean Oklahoma City U., 1988—89, dir. of student acad. support, 1992—97; dir. of retention St. Gregory's U., Shawnee, Okla., dean of students, 1998—. Home: 1937 NW 18th St Oklahoma City OK 73106 Office: St Gregory's U 1900 W MacArthur Dr Shawnee OK 74804 Office Fax: 405-878-5372. Personal E-mail: hackett7@aol.com. E-mail: pjhackett@sgc.edu.

HACKETT, ROBERT JOHN, lawyer; b. N.Y.C., Feb. 6, 1943; s. John P. and Marie S. (Starace) Hackett; m. Anita Carlile, Apr. 19, 1969; children: Robert John Hackett Jr., John Peter, Kathryn Marie. AB, Rutgers U., 1964; JD, Duke U., 1967. Bar: N.Y. 1967, Ariz. 1972. Assoc. Milbank, Tweed, Hadley, McCloy, N.Y.C., 1967—71; ptnr. Evans, Kitchel & Jenckes, Phoenix, 1971—89; dir. Fennemore Craig, Phoenix, 1989—, course dir. seminar on mergers and acquisitions, 1996, 1999. Mem. editl. bd. Duke Law Jour., 1966—67. Former bd. dirs. Xavier Coll. Prep., mem. steering com. for Fine Arts Ctr. capital campaign. Mem.: ABA (com. on fed. securities regulation), Maricopa County Bar Assn., State Bar Ariz. (past chmn. securities regulation sect.), Assn. Corp. Growth (past bd. dirs., past pres. Ariz. chpt.), Phoenix Duke U. Law Alumni Club (past pres.), Pi Sigma Alpha. Republican. Roman Catholic. E-mail: rhackett@fclaw.com.

HACKETT, ROGER FLEMING, history educator; b. Kobe, Japan, Oct. 23, 1922; s. Harold Wallace and Anna Luena (Powell) H.; m. Caroline Betty Gray, Aug. 24, 1946; children: Anne Marilyn, David Gray, Brian Vance. BA, Carleton Coll., 1947; MA, Harvard U., 1949, PhD, 1955. Prof. history Northwestern U., Evanston, Ill., 1953-61; prof. history U. Mich., Ann Arbor, 1961-93, prof. emeritus, 1993—, chmn. dept., 1975-77; dir. Center for Japanese Studies, 1968-71, 78, 79. Cons. Office of Edn., HEW; mem. sub-com., joint com. Social Sci. Research Council. Author: Yamagata Aritomo in the Rise of Modern Japan 1838-1922, 1971; Editor: Jour. Asian Studies, 1959-62; contbr. articles and chpts to profl. jours. and books. Served with USMC, 1942-46. Social Sci. Research Council fellow; Japan Found. fellow; Fulbright-Hays fellow; fellow St. Antony's Coll. Oxford U. Mem. Japan Soc., Assn. for Asian Studies (exec. com., bd. dirs. 1966-69), Internat. House of Japan, Phi Beta Kappa. Clubs: Racquet (Ann Arbor). Home: 2122 Dorset Rd Ann Arbor MI 48104-2604 Office: U Mich Dept History Ann Arbor MI 48109 E-mail: fhackett@umich.edu.

HACKETT, ROGER JAMES, editor; b. N.Y.C., July 8, 1941; s. James Roger and Ruth (Paro) H. BA, Fordham U., 1963; grad. student, NYU, 1963-64. Instr. Latin and English Manhattan Coll. High Sch., Riverdale, N.Y., 1964-68; dir. sports info. Fordham U., N.Y.C., 1966-73; assoc. editor Bill Commn., N.Y.C., 1973-80; editor Columbia U., N.Y.C., 1980-98, exec. asst., assoc. v.p. pub. affairs, 1998-2000, comm. coord., 2000—02. Recipient Best in Nation award Cosida, 1971. Democrat.

HACKETT, WESLEY PHELPS, JR., lawyer; b. Detroit, Jan. 3, 1939; s. Wesley P. and Helen (Decker) H.; children: Kelly D. Hackett Pell, Robin C. BA, Mich. State U., 1960; JD, Wayne State U., 1968. Bar: Mich. 1968, U.S. Dist. Ct. (we. dist.) Mich. 1971, U.S. Ct. Appeals (6th cir.) 1972, U.S. Dist. Ct. (ea. dist.) Mich. 1972, U.S. Supreme Ct. 1972, U.S. Ct. Mil. Appeals 1991. Law clk. Mich. Supreme Ct., Lansing, 1968-70; ptnr. Brown & Hackett, Lansing, 1971-73; pvt. practice Lansing, 1973-84; ptnr. Starr, Bissell & Hackett, Lansing, 1984-87; pvt. practice East Lansing, Mich., 1987-98, Saranac, Mich., 1998—. Adj. prof. Thomas M. Cooley Law Sch., Lansing, 1973—; instr. Lansing C.C., 1981-99. Author: Evidence: A Trial Manual for Michigan Lawyers, 1981, Hackett's Evidence: Michigan and Federal, 2d edit., 1995, Michigan Lawyers Manual Part L, 1994, revised, 2002; co-author: Hiring Legal Staff, 1990. Mem. City of East Lansing Planning Commn., 1969-72; mem. Village of Saranac Planning Commn., 2000—; bd. dirs. St. Vincent Home for Children, Lansing, 1974-82. 1st lt. USAF, 1961-65. Fellow Coll. Law Practice Mgmt.; mem. ABA (sec. gen. practice sect. 1990-91, vice-chair 1991-92, chair 1993-94, standing com. on lawyer referral and info. svcs. 1997-2000, sole practitioner of yr. 1994, founders award 1997), State Bar Mich. (chair legal econs. sect. 1990-91).

HACKL, ALPHONS J. publisher; b. Warman, Can. s. John J. and Anna (Moser) H.; m. Muriel J. Forster, Feb. 2, 1946; 1 son, John Raymond. Grad., Handelsschule, Salzburg, Austria, 1934; student, Nat. U., 1937-38, Corcoran Sch. Art, 1938-40, U. Chgo., 1941; BA, Sussex Coll. Tech., 1945; postgrad., Internat. Summer Sch., St. Peter Coll., Oxford U., 1976; JD, LaSalle U., 1991. Apprentice Funder & Mueller, printers, Salzburg, 1934-36; advt. copywriter, art dir., account exec. advt. agy. and dept. store Washington, 1936-40; founder, chmn. emeritus Colortone Press, Washington, 1946—; founder Acropolis Books, Ltd., Washington, 1959—; lectr., instr. George Washington U., 1974-78. Past mem. adv. coun. SBA; mem. adv. bd. publ. specialist program George Washington U.; adv. bd. Washington Tech. Inst.; adj. prof. LaSalle U., 1992; counselor Svc. Corps Ret. Execs. (S.C.O.R.E.), chmn. chpt. Manasota #116. Contbr. articles to profl. publs.; patentee programmed instruction device. Chmn. Met. Sch. Printing, 1972-74. Capt. AUS, 1941-45. Decorated Bronze Star.; recipient George Washington Honor medal Freedoms Found., Award of Excellence Image Industry Coun. Internat. Fellow Corcoran Art Gallery; mem. Pub. Rels. Soc. Am., Assn. Am. Pubs., Nat. Press Club, Svc. Corp Ret. Execs. (chmn. chpt. # 116), Sarasota Yacht Club, Lotos Club (N.Y.C.), U.S. Power Squadron Club. Episcopalian. Home: 415 Wood Duck Dr Sarasota FL 34236-1823 E-mail: ahackl3@yahoo.com. *Always do more than is expected of you, and keep your promises.*

HACKL, DONALD JOHN, architect; b. Chgo., May 11, 1934; s. John Frank and Frieda Marie Hackl; m. Bernadine Marie Becker, Sept. 29, 1962; children: Jeffrey Scott, Craig Michael, Cristina Lynn. BArch., U. Ill., 1957, MS in Architecture, 1958. With Loebl Schlossman & Hackl Architects, Chgo., 1963—, assoc., 1967-74, exec. v.p., dir., 1974, pres., dir., 1975—. Prof. architecture Internat. Acad. Architecture, Sofia, Bulgaria; mem. Nat. Coun. Archtl. Registration Bds., 1980—; bd. dirs. Chgo. Bldg. Congress, 1983-94, v.p., 1985-94; design juries include: Reynolds Metals, Western Mont. Regional Design, Am. Inst. Steel Constrn., Precast Concrete Inst., Okla. Soc. Architects, UIA/UNESCO (4); chmn. Ariz. Soc. Architects, Midwest Design Conf., 1983; design critic dept. arch. U. Ill., 1975-76, 81; vis. critic sch. architecture U. Notre Dame, 1977, 78, 80, 82; adj. prof. Kent Coll. Law, Ill. Inst. Tech., 1983—; adj. faculty Shenzhen (China) U., 1998-; cons. Pub. Svcs. Adminstrn., Washington, 1974-76; cons. urban planning, Changchun, China. Prin. works include Water Tower Place, Chgo., 1976, King Faisel Specialist Hosp. and Rsch. Ctr., Riyadh, Saudi Arabia, 1978, Household Internat. Hdqrs., Prospect Heights, Ill., 1978, Shriners Hosp. for Children, Chgo., 1979, Square D Co. Hdqrs., Palatine, Ill., 1979, West Suburban Hosp., Oak Park, Ill., 1981, Allstate Pla. West, Northbrook, Ill., 1990, Sears Roebuck & Co. stores of future concept, 1985-89, Ford City Shopping Ctr. Redevel., Chgo., 1989, Commerce Clearing House, Riverwoods, Ill., 1986, Physicians' Pavilion Greater Balt. Med. Ctr., 1987, Two Prudential Plaza, Chgo., 1990, City Place with Omni Hotel, Chgo., 1990, 350 N. LaSalle, Chgo., 1990, Infinitec, Assistive Tech. Application Ctr. for United Cerebral Palsy Assn., Chgo., 1992, Shenzhen AVIC Plaza Bldg., Shenzhen, China, 1993, Ill. State U. Biol. and Chemistry Scis. Lab. Bldg., Normal, 1995, Old Orchard Shopping Ctr. Redevel., Skokie, Ill., 1994, Sun Comml. City, Changchun, China, 1993, Shekou Harbor Bldg., Shenzhen, 1995, East Shanghai Film and TV Ctr., 1995, Luo-Hu Comml. Ctr., Shenzhen, 1994, Shenzhen Internat. Exch. Plz., 1996, Jin Hui Plz., Shanghai, 1996, Shenzhen Cultural Ctr., 1997, Changchun Sun Housing Estates, China, 1999, Hdqrs. for Almacenes Paris LTDA, Santiago, Chile, 1999, Cook County Hosp. Replacement Facility, 2002, Grand Pier Ctr., Chgo., 1998, Computer/Engring. Bldg. U. Ill., 1999—, Bank of Mauritius, Port Louis, 1999. Mem. Met. Am. Cancer Crusade, 1973; life trustee West Suburban Hosp., 1983—, mem. exec. com., 1986-87; vice chmn. North Ctrl. Coll., 1990—; mem. Pres.'s Coun. U. Ill. Found.; mem. curricula adv. com. Dept. Architecture, U. Ill.; bd. dirs. World Trade Ctr., Chgo., 1995—. Fellow AIA (treas. Chgo. chpt. 1977-78, exec. com. 1978-81, v.p. 1981, pres. 1981, bd. dirs. Chgo. AIA Found. 1981-83, nat. v.p. 1985, 1st v.p. 1986, nat. pres. 1987, chmn. design com. 1985, exec. com. 1985-87, bd. dirs. 1981-87, documents com. 1974-79, chmn. 1980, exec. com. AIA Svc. Corp. 1983-84, chmn. internat. com. 1987-91), Royal Archtl. Inst. Can. (hon.), Colegios Architectos Mexicanos (hon.), Internat. Acad. Architecture (hon.); mem. Union Internat. Archs. (bd. dirs., del. 1987—, 1st v.p. 1990-93, coun. 1993-96, v.p. region III 1996-99, treas. 2000—), Union Bulgarian Archs. (hon.), Soc. Cuban Archs., Japan Inst. Archs. (hon.), Colegio Arquitectos Cochabamba (Bolivia), Colegios Arquitectos Espana (hon.), Instituto do Arquitectos do Brazil (hon.), Art Inst. Chgo., Tavern Clubs, Carlton Club, Econ. Club, Lake Zurich Club. Office: Loebl Schlossman and Hackl Inc 233 N Michigan Ave ste 3000 Chicago IL 60601-5708

HACKLER, RUTH ANN, retired educator; b. Rogers, Ark., Feb. 2, 1924; d. Ezekiel Burton and Effie Lena (Paschal) Ruddick; m. Eugene T. Hackler, Dec. 27, 1946; children: Amy E., Susan Hackler Fetsch, Nancy Hackler Beaver. BA, Washburn U., 1946. Cert. secondary tchr., Kans. Asst. registrar Washburn U., Topeka, 1947-49; tchr. bus. Washburn Rural High Sch., Topeka, 1949-50, Olathe (Kans.) High Sch., 1950-52; mem. bd. edn. Olathe Pub. Schs., 1969-91; state rep. Kans. Ho. of Reps., Topeka, 1991-92; part-time legal sec. Hackler Law Firm, Olathe, 1949-90; ret. Mem. Gov.'s Edn. Cabinet, 1983-84; apptd. to Kansas. Interagy. Coord. Coun. on Early Childhood Devel. Svcs. Mem. Olathe Pub. Sch. Bd., 1969-91, pres., v.p.; mem. youth adv. bd. Johnson County Cmty. Corrections; former dir., mem. found. bd. Johnson County C.C.; mem. rsch. adv. com. League Kansas Municipalities, 1988—; treas., mem. ch. coun. St. Mark's Luth. Ch., Olathe; bd. dirs. Cedar House, Inc., 1969—; bd. dirs. Met. Kansas City United Cmty. Svcs., Inc.; organizer Olathe Children Initiatives, 1992; bd. dirs., sec. Olathe Pub. Libr.; mem. adv. coun. Olathe and Metro Parents as Tchrs.; bd. mem. Kans. Assn. Sch. Bds., 1978-85, pres., 1984; treas. St. Mark's Luth. Ch., 1993-94, pres., 1995-97. Recipient Lifetime Achievement award Johnson County Parks and Recreation, 1990, Friend of Edn. award Phi Delta Kappa. Mem. Met. Coun. on Child Care, Nat. Sch. Bds. Assn. (del. fed. rels. network, alternate nat. assembly del. 1982, del. 1983, 84, 85, Disting. Svc. award 1984), Kans. Assn. of Sch. Bds. (bd. dirs. 1977-82, chmn. sex edn./human sexuality/AIDS statewide com., chair state conf. on human sexuality/AIDS edn. 1988, past chmn. edn. PAC, pres. 1984), Olathe C. of C. (legis. com.), Chrysantas (past pres.), Delta Kappa Gamma. Democrat. Lutheran. Home: 685 W Cedar St Olathe KS 66061-4001

HACKLEY, DAVID KENNETH, lawyer; b. Chgo., Mar. 31, 1940; s. Kenneth Lewis and Helen (Sievers) H.; m. Janey D., June 2, 1962 (div. 1970); children: Gretchen Ann, David Edward; m. Sara E. Hayward, Mar. 5, 1985 (div. 1990). BA, Miami U., Oxford, Ohio, 1960; MA, U. Wyo., 1961; postgrad., U. Minn., 1961-62, JD, 1965. Bar: Minn. 1965. Law clk. Hennepin County Dist. Ct., Mpls., 1965-66; pvt. practice Mpls., 1966-83, 85—. Author: New Panama Canal Company and American Isthmian Diplomacy; 1894-1904, 1961. Chmn. Mpls. Bd. Housing Appeals, 1968-83. Mem. Minn. State Bar Assn., Hennepin County Bar Assn. (ethics com. 1982-87, fee arbitration com. 1977-88, chmn. 1986-87), Toastmasters. Office: 3400 W 66th St # 325407 Minneapolis MN 55435-2111

HACKMAN, GENE (EUGENE ALDEN HACKMAN), actor; b. San Bernardino, Calif., Jan. 30, 1930; s. Eugene Ezra H.; m. Faye Maltese, 1956 (div. 1985); m. Betsy Arakawa; children: Christopher, Elizabeth, Leslie. Appeared in stage prodns. The Natural Look, Death and the Maiden, others; film roles include Lilith, 1964, Hawaii, 1966, Bonnie and Clyde, 1967, First to Fight,1967, The Split, 1968, Riot, 1969, The Gypsy Moths, 1969, Downhill Racer, 1969,I Never Sang for My Father, 1969, Marooned, 1970, Doctor's Wives, 1971, The French Connection 1971 (Acad. Best Actor award, Golden Globe award, Brit. Acad. award, N.Y. Film Critics award), Cisco Pike, 1971, Scarecrow, 1973 (Cannes Film Festival award), The Poseidon Adventure, 1972 (Brit. Acad. award), The Conversation, 1974, Zandy's Bride, 1974, The French Connection II, 1975, Bite the Bullet, 1975, Night Moves, 1975, Lucky Lady, 1975, A Bridge Too Far, 1977, The Domino Principle, 1977, March or Die, 1977, Superman, 1978, All Night Long, 1980, Superman II, 1981, Eureka, 1983, Under Fire, 1983, Uncommon Valor, 1983, Target, 1985, Twice in a Lifetime, 1985, Power, 1986, Superman IV, 1987, No Way Out, 1987, Another Woman, 1988, Bat 21, 1988, Mississippi Burning, 1988 (Best Actor award Nat. Soc. Film Critics, Acad. Award nomination), Full Moon in Blue Water, 1988, The Package, 1989, Postcards From The Edge, 1989, Class Action, 1989, Loose Cannons, 1990, Narrow Margin, 1990, Company Business, 1991, Unforgiven, 1992 (Acad. Award Best Supporting Actor, Golden Globes, N.Y., L.A., Boston Film Critics, Nat. Soc.Film Critics awards), The Firm, 1993, Geronimo, 1993, Wyatt Earp, 1994, The Quick and the Dead, 1995, Crimson Tide, 1995, Get Shorty, 1995, Extreme Measures, 1996, The Chamber, 1996, The Birdcage, 1996, The Magic Hour, 1997, Absolute Power, 1997, Enemy of the State, 1998, Antz (voice), 1998, Twilight, 1998, Under Suspicion, 1999, The Replacements, 2000, The Mexican, 2001, Heartbreakers, 2001, Heist, 2001, The Royal Tenenbaums, 2001 (Golden Globe/Best Actor in a Comedy 2001, Chgo. Film Critics award for best actor 2002, Nat. Soc. Film Critics award 2002, AFI award 2002), Behind Enemy Lines, 2001; various TV and stage roles. Hon. chmn. Permanent Charities Com. of the Entertainment Industries. Named Star of Year, Nat. Assn. Theatre Owners, 1974 Office: care Fred Spector 9830 Wilshire Blvd Beverly Hills CA 90212-1804

HACKMAN, GWENDOLYN ANN, private duty nurse; b. Phila., Mar. 22, 1932; d. Stanley Heaney and Joy Hayes (Sands) H. Diploma, Phila. Gen. Hosp. Sch. Nursing, 1953; postgrad., La. State U., Tulane U. RNC, La.; cert. gerontol. nurse. Staff nurse pediatrics Phila. Gen. Hosp., 1953; staff nurse premature ctr. Charity Hosp., New Orleans, 1953-55, head nurse premature ctr., 1955; asst. instr. fundamentals of nursing, 1956-57; asst. instr. med. surg. nursing Touro Infirmary Sch. Nursing, 1957-60; rsch. assoc. maternal and child health sect. Tulane U., New Orleans, 1965-67; pvt. duty nurse New Orleans, 1955, 60-65, 67—. Mem. ANA, New Orleans Dist. Nurses Assn., Nat. Gerontol. Assn., La. State Nurses Assn. (profl. practice com. 1962-63, 2d vice chmn. pvt. duty sect. 1962-66, chmn. 1968-69, bd. dirs. 1966), New Orleans Dist. Nurses Assn. (chmn. pub. rels. com. 1962, chmn. pvt. duty sect. 1962-67, bd. dirs. 1962-67, One of Great 100 Nurses 1998), Phila. Gen. Hosp. Sch. Nursing Alumnae (life mem. 1999), DAR. Home: 1750 Saint Charles Ave Apt 427 New Orleans LA 70130 6746

HACKMAN, JOHN CLEMENT, neuropharmacology educator, neurophysiologist; b. Dayton, Ohio, May 16, 1947; s. Clem Frank and Martha Virginia (Schneble) H.; m. Susan Joan Pollard, June 3, 1968; children: Dawn, Jeffrey, Mark. BS, U. Miami, 1969, MS, 1976, PhD, 1979. Rsch. technologist VA Med. Ctr., Miami, Fla., 1975-78, rsch. physiologist, 1978—; rsch. asst. prof. Sch. Med. Neurology U. Miami, 1980-82, asst. prof., 1982-87, assoc. prof., 1988-95, prof., 1995—, asst. prof. Sch. Med. Pharmacology, 1991-96, assoc. prof., 1983-91, prof., 1996—. Chief proctor Nat. Bd. Med. Examiners, Phila., 1987-99. Contbr. chpts. to books, articles to profl. jours. Pres. Devonaire Villas Homeowners Assn., Miami, 1980-83; mem. boundary com. Dade County Pub. Schs., Miami, 1981-82; v.p. Devonaire PTA, Miami, 1981; treas. Devonaire Master Homeowners Assn., Miami, 1982-89; bd. dirs. S. Fla. Vet. Affairs Found. for Rsch. and Edn., 2001-02; com. chair Pack 811 Boy Scouts Am., 1991-93, cubmaster, 1993-94, asst. scoutmaster, Troop 599, Miami, 1994—, com. chmn., 1995-98. Decorated Army Commendation medal; Dept. Vets. Affairs grantee, 1994—. Mem. Soc. for Neurosci., Am. Physiol. Soc., Am. Soc. for Pharmacology and Exptl. Therapeutics, N.Y. Acad. Sci., Southeastern Pharm. Soc. Avocations: camping, fishing. Home: 13611 SW 109th St Miami FL 33186-3309 Office: U Miami Sch Medicine 1600 NW 10th Ave Miami FL 33136-1090

HACKMAN, MARVIN LAWRENCE, lawyer; b. Jasper, Ind., Jan. 29, 1934; s. Theodore Peter and Sarah Rose (Bellner) H.; m. Jane Marie Sermersheim, Aug. 23, 1958; children: Stephen J., Anne M., Michael A., Daniel T. AB summa cum laude, St. Joseph Coll., 1956; JD magna cum laude, Ind. U., 1959. Bar: Ind. 1959, U.S. Dist. Ct. (so. dist.) Ind. 1959, U.S. Ct. Appeals (7th cir.) 1960. Law clk. to chief judge U.S. Dist. Ct., Indpls., 1959-61; mem. Hackman Hulett & Cracraft LLP, Indpls., 1961—. Mem. ABA, Ind. State Bar Assn., Indpls. Bar Assn., Phi Delta Phi, Order of Coif. Home: 4021 Royal Pine Blvd Indianapolis IN 46250-2272

HACKNEY, CLINT PORTER, lawyer, lobbyist; b. Lufkin, Tex., Mar. 5, 1952; s. Don Vernon and Mary Lynne Hackney; m. Susan Adrain Longo, Aug. 9, 2002; m. Gail Brown, Nov. 30, 1974 (div. Nov. 30, 1990); children: John Clinton, Jennifer Gail, Laura Lynne, Caroline Victoria. BA polit. sci., Tex. A & M Univ., Coll. Sta., Tex, 1974; JD, Univ. Houston, Houston, 1977. Bar: Am. and Tex. Assoc. Bresenhan, Martin & Wingate, Houston, 1977—79; ptnr. Ford, Reiff & Burgess, Houston, 1979—81, Kennedy, Burleson & Hackney, Houston, 1981—89, Ford & Ferraro, Austin, Tex., 1990—96; prin. Clint Hackney & Co., Austin, Tex., 1996—. Dir. Cornerstone Savings, Houston, 1984—89; bd. chmn. Intergrated Recovery Corp., Austin, Tex., 1999—; adv. bd. mem. Texas A & M Dept. of polit. sci., Coll. Sta., Tex., 1998—. Commentator (radio program) The Texas Shootout, 1992—94. Adv. bd. mem. Am. Diabetes Assn., 1984—86; founder Forest Pines Civic Club, Houston, 1979; mem. dist. 184 Tex. Ho. of Reps., Austin, Tex., 1981—88. 2nd lt. paratrooper U.S. Army, 1974—75, Ft. Gordon. Recipient Disting. Student award, Tex. A & M Univ., 1974, Comparative Study award, Oxford Univ., Eng., 1976, Legis. Excellence award, Assn. of Cmty. Action Agencies, 1987. Fellow: Tex. Bar Found.; mem.: The Austin Soc., Austin Club. Achievements include Author of current Tex election laws code, co-author og legis. creating Tex. dept. of Commerce, instrn. supr. at Unniv. of Houstoon Trail Advocacy program. Avocations: golf, baseball, travel, crossword puzzles, kids. Home: 3316 Lookout Ln Austin TX 78746 Office: Clint Hackney & Co 816 Coongress Ave Ste 1125 Austin TX 78701

HACKNEY, HUGH EDWARD, lawyer; b. McGregor, Tex., July 17, 1944; BA, So. Meth. U., 1966, JD, 1969. Bar: Tex. 1970. Mem. Fulbright & Jaworski, LLP, Dallas, 1970-97; lawyer Locke Purnell Rain Harrell, Dallas, 1998-99, Locke Liddell & Sapp LLP, Dallas, 1999—. Fellow: Coll. of Labor and Employment Lawyers; mem. ABA, London Ct. Internat. Arbitration, Chartered Inst. Arbitrators (London), State Bar Tex., Dallas Bar Assn., Houston Bar Assn., Phi Alpha Delta, Soc. Internat. Bus. Fellows, Internat. Bar Assn. Office: Locke Liddell and Sapp LLP 2200 Ross Ave Dallas TX 75201-6776

HACKNEY, JACK DEAN, physician; b. Marion, Ill., Oct. 11, 1924; s. William F. and Betty (Monical) H.; m. Dorothy Anne Stublefield, Sept. 8, 1946; children: Richard W., Robert J. Student, So. Ill. Univ., 1941-43, Yale U., 1943; MD, St. Louis U. Sch. Medicine, 1948. Diplomate Am. Bd. Internal Medicine, Acad. Toxicol. Scis. Resident in internal medicine VA Hosp., St. Louis, 1949-51, White Meml. Hosp., L.A., 1953-54; rsch. assoc. Loma Linda U., L.A., 1954-57, asst. to assoc. prof., 1957-69; prof. medicine U. So. Calif., L.A., 1969-94, prof. emeritus, 1994—; dir. pulmonary lab. Rancho Los Amigos Med. Ctr., Downey, Calif., 1969-92, chief environ. health, 1970-94, emeritus, 1994—. Mem. EPA Sci. Adv. Bd., Washington, 1984-86; cons., 1986-92. Editor/author: Inhalation Toxicology of Air Pollution, 1993; contbg. author: Bronchial Asthma: Mechanics and Therapeutics, 1985, 93; contbr. articles to profl. jours. Mem. air quality adv. com. Dept. Health Svcs., State of Calif., 1974-91, med. adv. panel South Coast Air Quality Mgmt. Dist., 1985-92. 1st lt. AMC, 1951-53, Korea. Recipient Calif. medal Am. Lung Assn. Calif., 1992. Fellow Am. Coll. Chest Physicians, Am. Coll. Toxicology; mem. Am. Physiol. Soc., Am. Thoracic Soc., Alpha Omega Alpha, Sigma Xi. Achievements include development of indirect method for measuring respiratory ventilation; extraction of gases from blood for Gas Chromatographic analysis; control of exposure facilities and methods to study human inhalation toxicology and use of these facilities to demonstrate ozone toxicity, adaptation to ozone, and determine exposure responses to many inhaled gas and particle pollutants. Home: 5181 Duenas Laguna Hills CA 92653-1878 Office: Environmental Health Svc RLAMC 7601 Imperial Hwy # 51 Downey CA 90242-3456

HACKNEY, JAMES ACRA, III, industrial engineer, consultant, retired manufacturing company executive; b. Washington, N.C., Sept. 27, 1939; s. James Acra Jr. and Margaret Dunston (Hodges) H.; m. Constance Garrenton, June 5, 1961; children: Kenneth Ross, Jane H. Kemsley. BSME, N.C. State U., 1961, BS in Indsl. Engring, 1962. Registered profl. engr., N.C. With Hackney Industries, Inc., Washington, N.C., 1961-95, chief engr., 1961-63, asst. gen. mgr., 1963-65, exec. v.p., gen. mgr., 1965-70, pres., chief exec. officer, 1970-90; chmn. bd. dirs. Hackney & Sons, Inc., Washington, NC, 1990-95, mng. dir. The Hackney Group, Washington, NC, 1995—. Bd. dirs. Sprint Mid-Atlantic Telecom, Wake Forest, N.C., 1987-97, Bank of Am., North Coast region, N.C., chmn., 1995—. Chmn. Blackbeard dist. Boy Scouts Am., 1970-74, pres. East Carolina coun., 1976-77, mem. nat. exec. bd., 1987—, pres. S.E. region, 1987-89; chmn. bd. trustees Beaufort County Hosp., 1975-77; trustee N.C. State U., Raleigh, 1979-87, chmn. bd. trustees, 1985-87; mem. Interam. Scout Com., World Orgn. of Scout Movement, 1984-88; lay Eucharistic min. Zion Episcopal Ch., Washington, NC, 2002--; gen. campaign chmn. Beaufort County United Way, 1998-2000. Recipient Disting. Service award Washington Jaycees, 1970; Silver Beaver award Boy Scouts Am., 1975, Silver Antelope award, 1982, Disting. Eagle Scout award, 1980, Silver Buffalo award, 1992; Youth of the Ams. award World Orgn. Scout Movement, 1990, John Southam Journalism award Sail Am., 1997; named N.C. Small Businessman of Yr., SBA, 1971, Young Engr. of Yr., NSPE, 1971. Fellow NSPE; mem. Inst. Indsl. Engrs. (chpt. pres. 1967-68), Profl. Engrs. N.C. (pres. Ea. Carolina chpt. 1971-72, state sec. 2000-01, state treas. 2001-02, pres.-elect 2002-03, pres. 2003—, Outstanding Young Engr. 1970-71), N.C. Engring. Found. (bd. dirs. 1977—, N.C. Citizens for Bus. and Industry (bd. dirs. 1979-86), Washington C. of C. (pres. 1972-74, Outstanding Cmty. Svc. award 2000), N.C. State U. Alumni Assn. (bd. dirs. 1976-80, Outstanding Young Alumnus 1975, Disting. Engring. Alumnus 1984, Watauga Medal 1997), Rotary (pres. 1978-79), Pamlico Plantation Yacht Club (commodore 1993). Home and Office: PO Box 1987 117 Riverview Dr Washington NC 27889-9763

HACKNEY, ROBERT WARD, plant pathologist, nematologist, parasitologist, molecular geneticist, commercial arbitrator; b. Louisville, Dec. 11, 1942; s. Paul Arnold and Ovine (Whallen) H.; m. Cheryl Lynn Hill, June 28, 1969 (div. Dec. 1995); 1 child, Candice Colleen; m. Jacqueline Monica Eisenreich, Dec. 27, 1995; 1 child, Sarah Ashley. BA, Northwestern U., 1965; MS, Murray State U., 1969; PhD, Kans. State U., 1973. Postgrad. rsch. nematologist U. Calif., Riverside, 1973-75; plant nematologist Calif. Dept. Food and Agr., Sacramento, 1975-85, sr. plant nematologist, supr., 1985-89, sr. plant nematologist, 1989—. Comml. arbitrator Am. Arbitration Assn., 1980—; chmn. Calif. Nematode Diagnosis Adv. Commn., Sacramento, 1981—. Assoc. editor Jour. Nematology, Annals of Applied Nematology, 2000; contbr. articles to profl. jours. Hon. dep. Sheriff, Sacramento, 1992-93. Served with USMC, 1966. NSF grantee, 1974. Mem. Soc. Nematologists, Internat. Coun. Study of Viruses and Virus Diseases of the Grape, Delta Tau Delta, Sigma Xi. Democrat. Baptist. Office: Calif Dept Food & Agriculture Plant Pest Diagnostic Ct 3294 Meadowview Rd Sacramento CA 95832-1437

HACKNEY, SHELDON, former federal agency administrator, history educator; b. 1933; Pres. Univ. of Penn., Philadelphia, Penn., 1981-93; chmn. NEH, Washington, 1993-97; prof. history U. Pa., Phila., 1997—. Author: The Politics of Presidential Appointment: A Memoir of the Culture War, 2002. Office: U Pa Dept History 208 CH/6379 3451 Walnut St Philadelphia PA 19104

HACKNEY, VIRGINIA HOWITZ, lawyer; b. Phila., Jan. 11, 1945; d. Charles Rawlings and Edith Wrenn (Pope) Howitz; m. Barry Albert Hackney, Feb. 15, 1969; children: Ashby Rawlings, Roby Howison, Trevor Pope. BA in Econs., Hollins Coll., 1967; JD, U. Richmond, 1970. Bar: Va. 1970. Assoc. Hunton & Williams, Richmond, Va., 1970-77, ptnr., 1977—. Pres. Am. Acad. Hosp. Attys. Chgo., 1992-93. Mem. agy. evaluation com. United Way of Greater Richmond, 1981-86; sustainer Jr. League of Richmond; mem. Am. Health Lawyers Assn. (pres. 1992-93, bd. dirs. 1988-94). Named Outstanding Woman in field of law, YWCA, Richmond, 1981. Mem. ABA (bus. law sect. 1984—, forum com. on health law 1982—), Va. State Bar (long range planning com. 1985-90, chmn. standing com. lawyer discipline 1986-90, exec. com. 1988-90, Bar Coun. mem. 1984-90). Avocations: book tapes, reading, boating, jogging/walking. Office: Hunton & Williams Riverfront Plz East Tower 951 E Byrd St Richmond VA 23219-4074

HACKWOOD, SUSAN, electrical and computer engineering educator; b. Liverpool, Eng., May 23, 1955; came to U.S., 1980; d. Alan and Margaret Hackwood. BS with honors, DeMonfort U., Eng., 1976; PhD in Solid State Ionics, DeMonfort U., Eng., 1979; PhD (hon.), Worcester Poly. Inst., 1993; DSc (hon.), DeMonfort U., 1993. Rsch. fellow DeMonfort U., Leicester, Eng., 1976-79; postdoctoral rsch. fellow AT&T Bell Labs., Homdel, N.J., 1980-81, mem. tech. staff, 1981-83, supr. robotics tech., 1983-84, dept. head robotics tech., 1984-85; prof. elec. and computer engring. U. Calif., Santa Barbara, 1985-89, dir. Ctr. Robotic Systems in Microelectronics, 1985-89, dean Bourns Coll. Engring. Riverside, 1990-95; exec. dir. Calif. Coun. on Scis. and Tech., Riverside, 1995—. Editor Jour. Robotic Systems, 1983, Recent Advances in Robotics, 1985; contbr. over 100 articles to tech. jours.; 7 patents in field. Fellow AAAS, IEEE (sr.). Office: 5262 King St Riverside CA 92506-1623

HADA, JERRIANNE, librarian; b. Alva, Okla., Dec. 19, 1944; d. David Leroy and Thelma Joyce (Rader) H. BA, Northwestern Okla. State U., 1966; MLS, Emporia State U., 1971; postgrad., Okla. State U., 1976, Kans. State U., 1985. Cert. secondary sch. libr. media specialist, Kans. Libr. jr. and sr. high sch. Unified Sch. Dist. 274, Oakley, Kans., 1966-68; libr. sr. high sch. Unified Sch. Dist. 443, Dodge City, Kans., 1968-72, Stuttgart (Germany) Am. High Sch., 1972-74, Cleveland (Okla.) Ind. Sch. Dist. 6, 1974-80, Unified Sch. Dist. 254, Medicine Lodge, Kans., 1980-81; libr. jr. and sr. high sch. Unified Sch. Dist. 397, Lost Springs, Kans., 1981-84; libr. sr. high sch. Unified Sch. Dist. 331, Kingman, Kans., 1984—. Mem. Friends of the Libr., Kingman, 1990. Grantee NDEA, 1967. Mem. NEA, ALA, AASL, Kans. Edn. Assn., Kans. Assn. Sch. Librs., Kappa Delta Pi, Delta Kappa Gamma. Methodist. Avocations: genealogy, travel, embroidery. Home: 540 W A Ave Kingman KS 67068-1205 Office: Unified Sch Dist 331 Kingman High Sch 260 W Kansas Ave Kingman KS 67068-1028

HADALLER, DAVID LAWRENCE, dean; b. Chelsea, Mass., Oct. 21, 1954; s. David Lawrence I and Ruth M.; m. Mirela Mustaca, Mar. 19, 1990; children, David Lawrence III, Nicholas Edward. BA, Gonzaga U., 1976; MA, St. Louis U., 1979, Columbia U., 1999; PhD, Washington State U., 1993. English instr. St. Louis U., 1976-79, Washington State U., Pullman, 1980-83, 85-86; asst. prof. Mayville (N.D.) State U., 1983-84, 86-87; Fulbright prof. Iasi, Romania, 1987-88; English dept. faculty Clovis (N.Mex.) Coll., 1989-92; rschr. N.Y.C., 1993-95; coord. spl. projects Hostos C.C., CUNY, N.Y.C., 1996-98, asst. dean, 1998—2001; assoc. dean of curriculum Dutchess Cmty. Coll., Pougkeepsie, 2001—. Tech., mktg. writer Topaz, Inc., San Diego, 1984-85. Author: Gynicide: Women in the Novels of William Styron, 1996. Mem. Fulbright Assn., Kappa Delta Pi, Alpha Sigma Nu, Phi Theta Kappa (hon.). Office: Dutchess Comm College 53 Pendell Rd Poughkeepsie NY 12601-1595

HADAS, ELIZABETH CHAMBERLAYNE, editor; b. Washington, May 12, 1946; d. Moses and Elizabeth (Chamberlayne) H.; m. Jeremy W. Heist, Jan. 25, 1970 (div. 1976); m. Peter Eller, Mar. 21, 1984 (div. 1998). AB, Radcliffe Coll., 1967; postgrad., Rutgers U., 1967-68; MA, Washington U., St. Louis, 1971. Editor U. N.Mex. Press, Albuquerque, 1971-85, dir., 1985-2000, spl. acquisitions editor, 2000—. Bd. dirs. N.M. Endowment for the Humanities, 2001—. Mem. Assn. Am. Univ. Presses (pres. 1992-93). Democrat. Home: 2900 10th St NW Albuquerque NM 87107-1111 Office: U New Mexico Press 1720 Lomas Blvd NE Albuquerque NM 87106-3807 E-mail: ehadas@unm.edu.

HADAS, JULIA ANN, social services administrator; b. Rome, Ga., May 23, 1947; d. Robert Franklin and Myrtle Julia (Patrick) Richmond; m. John R. Hadas, Apr. 22, 1967 (div.); children: Kevin, Brian. BS magna cum laude, No. Mich. U., 1972, MA, 1977. Cert. social worker; lic. profl. counselor. Placement worker adult community Mich. Family Independence Agy., Marquette, 1976-80, supr. vol. svcs., 1980-86, supr. children svcs., 1986-93, dir. Marquette/Baraga Local Office, 1993—. Chair Parent Adv. Coun. Marquette Area Pub. Schs., 1984-85; pres. Upper Peninsula Children's Coalition, 1986-96; adv. bd. Student Vol. Orgn. No. Mich. U., 1984-85; sec., pers. com. Women's Ctr.; treas. Alger-Marquette Human Svcs. Coordinating Body, 1994-2000; mem. Lake Superior Cmty. Ptnrship., 1999-2001, Lake Superior Ptnrs. in Edn., 2000—, Med. Care Access Coalition, Inc.; mem. Domestic and Sexual Violence Coalition, 2001—; Alger-Marquette Human Svcs. Coord. Body, 1994—(chair 2002—). Named one of Outstanding Young Women in Am., 1982. Mem. Childbirth Edn. Assn. (pres. 1975-76), Mich. Assn. Vol. Adminstrs., Zonta (pres. Marquette chpt. 1982-83). Episcopalian. Avocations: reading, travel, interior decorating, skiing, gardening.

HADAS, RACHEL, poet, educator; b. N.Y.C., Nov. 8, 1948; d. Moses and Elizabeth (Chamberlayne) H.; m. Stavros Kondilis, Nov. 7, 1970 (div. 1978); m. George Edwards, July 22, 1978; 1 child, Jonathan. BA in Classics, Radcliffe Coll., 1969; MA, Johns Hopkins, 1977; PhD, Princeton U., 1982. From adj. to assoc. prof. Rutgers U., Newark, N.J., 1981-92, prof., 1992—, Bd. Govs. Prof., 2002—; adj. prof. Columbia U., N.Y.C., 1992-93. Vis. prof. Hellenic studies program Princeton U., spring 1995. Author: (poetry) Slow Transparency, 1983, A Son From Sleep, 1987, Pass It On, 1989, Living in Time, 1990, Mirrors of Astonishment, 1992, Other Worlds Than This, 1994, The Empty Bed, 1995, The Double Legacy, 1995, Halfway Down the Hall: New and Selected Poems, 1998, Indelible, 2001. Recipient award Am. Acad. Inst. Arts and Letters, 1990; Guggenheim fellow in poetry, 1988-89. Fellow Am. Acad. Arts and Scis.; mem. MLA, Poets, Essayists and Novelists, Nat. Book Critics Cir. Democrat. Avocation: reading. Home: 838 W End Ave Apt 3A New York NY 10025-5365 Office: Rutgers U Dept English Hill St Fl 5 Newark NJ 07102-2607

HADDA, JANET RUTH, Yiddish language educator, lay psychoanalyst; b. Bradford, Eng., Dec. 23, 1945; came to U.S., 1948; d. George Manfred and Annemarie (Kohn) H.; m. Allan Joshua Tobin, Mar. 22, 1981; stepchildren: David, Adam. BS in Edn., U. Vt., 1966; MA, Cornell U., 1969; PhD, Columbia U., 1975. Prof. Yiddish UCLA; rsch. psychoanalyst So. Calif. Psychoanalytic Inst., L.A., 1988—, tng. and supervising analyst, 1995—, Inst. Contemporary Psychoanalysis, 1993—. Author: Yankev Glatshteyn, 1980, Passionate Women, Passive Men: Suicide in Yiddish Literature, 1988, Isaac Bashevis Singer: A Life, 1997, with New Introduction, 2003; mem. editl. bd.: Prooftexts, Yivo Ann; contbr. articles. Mem. MLA, Assn. Jewish Studies, Am. Psychoanalytic Assn., Inst. Contemporary Psychoanalysis, So. Calif. Psychoanalytic Inst., Phi Beta Kappa. Office: UCLA Dept English 1335 Rolfe Hl Los Angeles CA 90095-0001

HADDAD, ABRAHAM HERZL, electrical engineering educator, researcher; b. Baghdad, Iraq, Jan. 16, 1938; came to U.S., 1963; s. Moshe M. and Masuda (Cohen) H.; m. Carolyn Ann Kushner, Sept. 9, 1966; children: Benjamin, Judith, Jonathan. BSEE, Technion-Israel Inst. Tech., Haifa, 1960, MSEE, 1963; MA in Elec. Engring., Princeton U., 1964, PhD in Elec. Engring., 1966. Asst. prof. elec. engring. U. Ill., Urbana, 1966-70, assoc prof., 1970-75, prof., 1975-81; sr. staff cons. Dynamics Research Corp., Wilmington, Mass., 1979; program dir. NSF, Washington, 1979-83; prof. Ga. Inst. Tech., Atlanta, 1983-88; Dever prof., chmn. elec. engring and computer sci. dept. Northwestern U., 1988-98, Dever prof. dept. elec. and computer engring., 1996—, interim chair dept., 2001—02, dir. master info. and tech., 1998—. Dir. Computer Integrated Mfg. Sys. Program, 1987—88; adv. U.S. Army Missle Command, Huntsville, Ala., 1969—79; vis. assoc. prof. Tel Aviv U., Israel, 1972—73; cons. Lockheed-Ga. Co., 1984—88; gen chmn. Am. Control Conf., 1993; sec. Am. Automatic Control Coun., 1990—2003; chmn. policy com. Internat. Fedn. Automatic Control, 1996—2002, chmn. awards com., 2002—. Editor: Non-linear Systems, 1975; assoc. editor Control Engring. Practice, 1999—. Fellow AAAS, IEEE (editor Trans. on Automatic Control 1983-89, Centennial medal 1984, mem. awards bd. 1997-99, third millenium medal 2000); mem. Control Systems Soc. of IEEE (gen. chair 1984 Conf. on Decision and Control, Disting. mem. award 1985, v.p. fin. affairs 1989-90, pres.-elect 1991, pres. 1992, assoc. editor at large Trans. Automatic Control 1998-2003, chair Axelby award com. 2002-03). Jewish. Office: Northwestern U Dept ECE Evanston IL 60208-3118

HADDAD, CAROLINE N. mathematics educator, researcher; d. Nabeeh and Georgette Haddad. D in Math., Rensselaer Poly. Inst., Troy, N.Y., 1993. Vis. asst. prof. Middlebury Coll., Vt., 1993—95; assoc. prof. SUNY, Geneseo, 1995—. Spkr., presenter in field. Contbr. articles to profl. jours. Mem.: Math. Assn. Of Am. (assoc. editor), Golden Key Honor Soc. Office: SUNY 1 College Cir Geneseo NY 14423 Office Fax: 585-245-5128. E-mail: haddad@geneseo.edu.

HADDAD, EDWARD RAOUF, civil engineer, consultant; b. Mosul, Iraq, July 1, 1926; came to U.S., 1990. s. Raouf Sulaiman Haddad and Fadhila (Sulaiman) Shaya; m. Balquis Yousef Rassam, July 19, 1961; children: Reem, Raid. BSc, U. Baghdad, Iraq, 1949; postgrad., Colo. State U., 1966-67; PhD (hon.), 1995. Project engr., cons. Min. Pub. Works, Baghdad, 1949-63; arbitrator Engring. Soc. & Ct., Kuwait City, Kuwait, 1963-90; tech. advisor Royal Family, Kuwait, 1987-90; cons. pvt. practice Haddad Engring., Albuquerque, 1990-95; owner, pres. Overseas Contacts-Internat. Bus. and Consulting, Albuquerque, 1995—. Organizer reps abroad, Kuwait, 1990. Pres. Parents Assn., U. N.Mex., 1995. Recipient Hon. medal Pope Paul VI of Rome, 1973, Men of Achievement award Internat. Biog. Ctr., 1994. Mem. ASCE, NSPE, ABA (assoc.), Am. Arbitration Assn. (mem. adv. bd.), Sierra Cath. Internat. (trustee), Lions (bd. dirs. 1992), Inventors Club (bd. dirs. 1992), KC (chancellor 1992). Address: 1425 Monte Largo Dr NE Albuquerque NM 87112-6378 E-mail: edward.haddad@yahoo.com.

HADDAD, EMILY ANNE, literature educator; d. Robert Mitchell and Helen Rogerson Haddad; m. John William Erikson, Aug. 26, 1990; children: Philip David Erikson, Robert George Erikson, Theodore Haddad Erikson. BA in Lit., Harvard-Radcliffe Coll., 1986; MA in Comparative Lit., Harvard U., 1992, PhD in Comparative Lit., 1997. Asst. prof. English U. S.D., Vermillion, 1997—2001, assoc. prof. English, 2001—. Author: Orientalist Poetics, 2002. Grantee, Fulbright Assn., Egypt, 1986—87. Mem.: Phi Beta Kappa. Office: Univ SD English Dept 414 E Clark St Vermillion SD 57069

HADDAD, ERNEST MUDARRI, lawyer; b. Boston, Oct. 30, 1938; s. Abraham and Elaine (Mudarri) H.; m. Kathleen L. Tracy; 1 child, Barton Edward; children from previous marriage: Scott Cochrane, Mark Mudarri. BA, Trinity Coll., Hartford, Conn., 1960; LLB, Boston U., 1964. Bar: Mass. 1964, U.S. Dist. Ct. Mass. 1966, U.S. Supreme Ct., 1981. Asst. dean sch. law Boston U., 1966-71; asst. sec., gen. counsel Commonwealth of Mass. Exec. Office Human Svcs., Boston, 1971-76; gen. counsel Blue Cross and Blue Shield Mass. Inc., Boston, 1976-80; sec., gen. counsel The Mass. Gen. Hosp., Boston, 1981—2002, Ptnrs. HealthCare Sys., Inc., Boston, 1995—2002; assoc. dean, prof. law Boston U. Sch. Law, 2002—. Bd. dirs. Internat. Inst. Boston, 2002—. Program chmn., mem. exec. com. Boston Study Group, 1979—; Bd. dirs. New Eng. Legal Found., 2001—. Recipient Trinity Coll. Alumni medal for Excellence, 1990. Mem. ABA, Am. Health Lawyers Assn., Boston Bar Assn. (mem. coun. 1998-2002, exec. com. 1999-2002, fin. com. 1999-2002, treas. 2001-02, mem. audit com. 2003—), Boston Bar Found. (trustee, 1998—), Boston U. Law Sch. Alumni Assn. (pres. 1998-99). Home: 144 Mount Vernon St Boston MA 02108-1128 Office: 765 Commonwealth Ave Boston MA 02215 E-mail: ehaddad@bu.edu.

HADDAD, FREDDIE DUKE, JR., hospital development administrator; b. Charleston, W.Va., Oct. 18, 1952; s. Freddie Duke Haddad Sr. and Betty Jane (Perry) Campbell; m. Cynthia Ann LaMaster, July 17, 1976; children: Freddie Duke III, Jamie Lynn, Shannon Lynn. BS, W.Va. U., 1974; MPA, Marshall U., 1976; EdD, W.Va. U., 1986. Grad. asst. W.Va. Grad. Coll., Charleston, 1974-75; assoc. dir. devel. U. Louisville, Ky., 1976—77; dir. alumni affairs Fla. Internat. U., Miami, 1977-79; dir. alumni/devel. U. Charleston, W.Va., 1979-81; pvt. practice bus. cons. Charleston, 1981-82; dir. alumni/devel. Butler U., Indpls., 1982-89; dir. devel. St. Vincent Hosp. Found., Indpls., 1989-98, v.p. devel., exec. dir., 1998—; exec. dir. St. Vincent Mercy Hosp. Found., Elwood, Ind., 1995-99. Adj. prof. Nova U., Ft. Lauderdale, Fla., 1978-79; cons. in field. Contbr. articles to profl. jours. Mem. parish coun. St. George Orthodox Ch., Indpls., 1990-93; mem. com. Hall of Fame awards com. ARC, Indpls., 1991—; sec., v.p. Lawrence Twp. Babe Ruth League, Indpls., 1991-93; bd. dirs. Lawrence Twp. Edn. Found., Indpls., 1994-98, pres., 1999. Recipient Disting. Alumnus award Marshall U. Grad. Coll., 2002, Hon. Sec. of State award State of Ind., 2002; named Ky. Col., Gov. Ky., Frankfort, 1976, Outstanding Young Men of Am., 1986, Outstanding West Virginian, Gov. W.Va., Charleston, 1994, Sagamore of Wabash, Gov. Ind., 1996. Mem.: Assn. Healthcare Philanthropy (Jour. award 1993), Assn. Fundraising Profls. (cert.fund raising exec., bd. mem. 1990—95, v.p., pres.-elect Ind. chpt. 1992—94, pres. 1995, nat. AFP edn. curriculum com. 1996, Red Cross Hall of Fame com. 1992—, Pres.'s award 1993), Ascension Health Nat. Coun. Philanthropy (1st v.p. 1998—99, pres. 1999—2000, bd. dirs. 2001—), W.Va. U. Alumni Assn. (mountaineer amb. 1991—). Avocations: reading, writing, race walking, golfing. Office: St Vincent Hosp Found 11595 N Meridian St Ste 800 Carmel IN 46032-6948 E-mail: fdhaddad@stvincent.org.

HADDAD, GABRIEL G. pediatrician, educator; b. Beirut, Mar. 20, 1947; arrived in U.S., 1974; s. George Gabriel and Ida (Bitar) Haddad; m. Karen Chmielski, June 14, 1975; children: Christopher, Diana, Justin. BS in Biology and Chemistry, Am. Univ. Beirut, 1969, MD, 1973. Diplomate Am. Bd. Pediat. Jr. resident pediat. Am. U. Beirut Med. Ctr., 1973—74; sr. resident pediat. U. Tex. Med. Ctr., Houston, 1974—75; fellow in pediat. pulmonary divsn. Columbia U., N.Y.C., 1975—78, asst. prof. pediat., 1978—84, assoc. prof. pediat., 1984—88, dir. sleep physiology lab. dept. pediat., 1980—88; dir. sect. and chief clin. svc. respiratory medicine Yale U. Sch. Medicine, New Haven, 1988—, assoc. prof. pediat., 1988—90, prof. pediat., 1990—, prof. cellular and molecular physiology, 1993—. Mem. NIHD study sect. NIH, Md., 1982; mem. editl. bd. Jour. Applied Physiology, 1983—85, assoc. editor, 1989—93; NIHLB site visitor NIH Program Project, Cleve., 1985; conf. chmn. NIHLB, 1987, NICHD, 1988; NIH subcom. chmn.; with dept. physiology and biophysics U. Iowa, 1986—87; with dept. genetics Yale U. Sch. Medicine, Boyer Ctr. for Molecular Medicine, 1996. Editor 2 books, contbr. over 173 articles and abstracts to profl. jours. and books. Recipient Edward Livingston Trudeau award, Am. Lung Assn., 1979—82, Pediat. Faculty Tchg. award, Yale U. Sch. Medicine, 1991, Excellence in Pediat. Rsch. award, Am. Acad. Pediat., 1992; fellow Parker B. Francis, 1976—79, Milton Singer, Columbia U. Coll. Physicians, 1977—78. Mem.: AAAS, Soc. for Neurosci., Am. Thoracic Soc. (respiratory neurobiology and sleep sect.), Am. Physiol. Soc., Soc. for Pediat. Rsch., Am. Heart Assn. (established investigator 1985—90), Alpha Omega Alpha. Office: PO Box 208234 New Haven CT 06520-8234 Fax: 203-785-6337. E-mail: gabriel.haddad@yale.edu.

HADDAD, HESKEL MARSHALL, ophthalmologist, educator; b. Baghdad, Iraq, Sept. 26, 1930; came to U.S., 1953, naturalized, 1962; s. Moshe M. and Masuda (Cohen) H.; m. Doris I. Fatzer, July 4, 1963; children: Ava Masuda, Andreas Moshe, Michael Albert. Student, Royal Coll. Medicine, Baghdad, 1945-50; MD, Hebrew U., Jerusalem, 1953. Diplomate Am. Bd. Pediatrics, Am. Bd. Ophthalmology; ordained rabbi, 1997. Intern Donolo Hosp., Jaffo-Tel Aviv, Israel, 1950-51; rotating intern Hadassah U. Hosp., Jerusalem, 1951-53; pediatric resident Children's Med. Center, Boston, 1953-56; fellow in pediatric endocrinology Johns Hopkins Hosp., Balt., 1956-58; fellow in clin. endocrine br. Nat. Inst. Arthritis and Metabolic Diseases, NIH, Bethesda, Md., 1958-59, pediatrician sect. clin. endocrinology, 1959-60; asst. prof. pediatrics sch. medicine Howard U., Washington, 1959-60; resident, asst. dept. ophthalmology sch. medicine Washington U., St. Louis, 1960-64; leave of absence, 1962-63; fellow pediatric ophthalmology Inst. Visual Sci., San Francisco, 1962; research fellow Hôpital des Quinze-Vingts, Laboratoire de Physiologie de Vision, Ecole des Hautes Etudes, Paris, 1962-63; ophthalmologist Hôpital Beni Messous, Algiers, Algeria, 1964; asst. attending ophthalmic surgeon, also asst. prof. ophthalmology Mt. Sinai Hosp. and Sch. Medicine, N.Y.C., 1964-67; dir. dept. ophthalmology Beth Israel Med. Center, N.Y.C.; also assoc. prof. ophthalmology Mt. Sinai Sch. Medicine, 1967-71; clin. prof. ophthalmology N.Y. Med. Coll., 1971—. Author: Endocrine Exophthalmos, 1973, Metabolic Eye Diseases, 1974, Metabolic-Peditric Eye Diseases, 1979, Metabolic Ophthalmology: Diagnostic Techniques Vols. I and II, 1985, Jews of Arab and Islamic Countries: History, Problems and Solutions, 1984, (autobiography) Flight from Babylon, 1986; editor-in-chief: Metabolic Ophthalmology, 1976-79, Metabolic and Ophthalmology, 1976-79, Metabolic and Pediatric Ophthalmology, 1979-82, Metabolic, Pediatric and Systemic Ophthalmology, 1982—; contbr. numerous articles and revs. to profl. jours.; holder 7 U.S. patents. Pres. Am. Com. for Rescue and Resettlement of Iraqui Jews, World Orgn. Jews from Arab Countries, Parents' Assn. of Sch. of Performing Arts, 1980-83. Fellow ACS, Am. Inst. Chemists; mem. Am. Endocrine Soc., Am. Fedn. Clin. Research, Assn. Research Ophthalmology and Vision, AMA, New York County Med. Soc., AAAS, Am. Acad. Ophthalmology, N.Y. Acad. Medicine, N.Y. Acad. Scis., N.Y. Soc. Clin. Ophthalmology, Soc. Eye Surgeons, Société Française d'Ophthalmologie, German Ophthal. Soc., Internat. Soc. Metabolic Eye Disease (founder, sec.-treas. 1973—), World Soc. on Systemic Ophthalmology (founder, sec.-treas. 1982, chmn.), N.Y. County Med. Soc. (chmn. com. fgn. med. grads. 1985-90, del. N.Y. State Med. Soc. 1985-86). Achievements include patents in field. Office: 1125 Park Ave New York NY 10128-1243 E-mail: optogdcorp@aol.com., optogdcorp@hotmail.com. *The Commandment of "loving one's neighbor" should read "Thou shalt love for thy neighbor as for thy self." Whereas we cannot always control the emotion of love, we are consciously able to stop doing unto others what we do not like for ourselves.*

HADDAD, JAMES HENRY, chemical engineering consultant; b. Willimantic, Conn., Jan. 30, 1923; s. William Addy and Nellie (Birbarie) H.; m. Isabel Serrano, Feb. 3, 1962; children: Frederick William, Francis Xavier. BS in Engring., Yale U., 1944. Chem. engr. Conn. Hard Rubber Co., New Haven, 1943-44; engr. rsch. dept. Mobil Rsch. Devel. Corp., Paulsboro, N.J., 1944-52, engr. engring. dept. N.Y.C., 1952-70, sr. engring. cons. Princeton, N.J., 1971-89; ind. cons. worldwide Catalytic Processing/Solids Sys., Princeton Junction, N.J., 1989—. Contbr. articles to profl. publs.; patentee in field, petroleum refining and shale retorting sys. Mem. budget com., trustee Princeton Area Communities United Way, 1977-90. Mem. Am. Chem. Soc., Am. Inst. Chem. Engrs., Alpha Chi Sigma. Avocation: swimming. Home and Office: 120 Tunicflower Ln Princeton Junction NJ 08550-1645

HADDAD, JAMIL RAOUF, physician; b. Mosul, Iraq, Aug. 18, 1923; came to U.S., 1952, naturalized, 1965; s. Raouf Sulaiman and Fadhila (Shaya) Haddad; m. Mary Lou Scorsone, Aug. 1, 1959 (dec. 2001); children: Ralph J.(dec.), John L., James M. M.B., Ch.B., Iraqi Royal Coll. Medicine, Baghdad, Iraq, 1946. Med. officer Khanaqin (Iraq) Hosp., 1946-52; asst. resident pathology Crawford W. Long Meml. Hosp., Atlanta, 1953-54; resident Bellevue Hosp., N.Y.C., 1954-56; practice medicine specializing in pathology N.Y.C., 1963—, Passaic, N.J., 1981—; chmn. dept. anatomic and clin. pathology St. Clare's Hosp. and Health Center, N.Y.C., 1971-81; dir. pathology and clin. lab. Gen. Hosp. Ctr. at Passaic, 1981—. Assoc. Sloan-Kettering Inst. for Cancer Rsch., N.Y.C., 1960—66; asst. prof. pathology NYU Coll. Medicine, 1959—65, asst. clin. prof. pathology, 1965—67, assoc. clin. prof. pathology, 1967—70, clin. prof. pathology, 1970—85; asst. prof. exptl. cell biology Mt. Sinai Grad Sch. Biol. Scis., N.Y.C., 1966—70, lectr., 1971—83, adj. asst. prof., 1983—88. Mem. Coll. Am. Pathologists, Am. Soc. Clin. Pathologists, AMA, N.Y. Pathol. Soc., N.Y. State, New York County med. socs. Home: 420 E 23rd St Apt MC New York NY 10010-5043 Office: 350 Boulevard Passaic NJ 07055-2840

HADDAD, LOUIS NICHOLAS, paralegal; b. Beggs, Okla., Sept. 3, 1923; s. Abraham and Tammam (Lelo) H.; m. Jacqueline Marie Pratali, Sept. 22, 1945 (div. 1952); children: Carole, Shirley, Charles; m. Martha Maria Laengst, Dec. 31, 1954; children: Sheila, Stephanie. Co-owner Haddad Bros. Wholesalers, Lancaster, Calif., 1955-57; regional v.p. Nulite Corp., No. Calif., 1957-60; owner, mgr. Shamrock Motors, Seaside, Calif., 1960-68, Gateway Liquors, Seaside, 1968-70, Wagontown Auto Sales, Seaside, 1971-73, Camptown West Motor Homes, Seaside, 1973-79; co-owner, mgr. Monterey (Calif.) Bay Tribune, 1983-89. Councilman City of Seaside, 1964-66, 78-80, mayor, 1966-72; charter bd. dirs. Monterey Peninsula Boys Club; bd. dirs. Alliance on Aging, Assn. Monterey Bay Area Govts., Monterey Peninsula Water Mgmt. Dist., 1993-97; chmn. Laguna Grande Agy., Seaside County Sanitation Dist., Monterey Overall Econ. Devel. Com.; chmn. adv. com. Project Aquarius; mem. Seaside Planning Comn.; vice chmn. So. Monterey Bay Water Pollution Control Agy.; chmn. tri-county bd. Calif. Coun. on Criminal Justice; former vice chmn. Monterey County Local Agys. Formation Com. Capt. U.S. Army, 1940-46, 50-55. Mem. VFW, NCO Assn. Am. (hon.), Am. Legion, Seaside C. of C. (bd. dirs.), K.C., Lions (past pres. Seaside chpt.), Rotary (past pres. Seaside chpt.). Republican. Roman Catholic. Home: 5 Deer Stalker Path Monterey CA 93940-6311 E-mail: haddad@redshift.com.

HADDAD, REEM MARIAM EDWARD, physician; b. Kuwait, Mar. 6, 1969; came to U.S., 1990; MD, U. N.Mex., 1994. Resident Duke U. med. Ctr., Durham, N.C., 1994-97; intern Lovelace Med. Ctr., Albuquerque, N.Mex., 1997. Mem. AMA, ACP, Alpha Omega Alpha, Phi Kappa Phi. Roman Catholic. Avocations: dancing, swimming, tennis, ballet. Office: Lovelace Med Ctr 5400 Gibson Blvd SE Albuquerque NM 87108-4763

HADDAWAY, JAMES DAVID, retired insurance company official; b. Louisville, July 25, 1933; s. Charles Montgomery Jr. and Viola (Sands) H.; m. Myrna Lou Harris, June 5, 1954 (dec. Sept. 1999); children: Peggy Ann, Robert Marshall, Susan Gayle; m. Janie Louise Young, Mar. 25, 2000. BS in Commerce, U. Louisville, 1960; MBA, Xavier U., 1973. Cert. adminstrv. mgr., purchasing mgr., sr. profl. human resources mgr. Ins. cons. Met. Life Ins., Louisville, 1955-59; supt. Byck Bros. & Co., Louisville, 1959-61; purchasing mgr. Liberty Nat. Bank, Louisville, 1961-63; v.p., mgr. gen. svcs. adminstrn. Citizens Fidelity Bank, Louisville, 1963-79; asst. v.p., mgr. human resources Ky. Farm Bur. Ins. Co., Louisville, 1979-95; ret., 1995. Founder, chmn. emeritus Kentuckiana Expn. Bus. and Industry, 1973-85. With 11th Airbourne Divsn., U.S. Army, 1953-55. Named Boss of Yr., Louisville chpt. nat. Secs. Assn., 1978, 79. Mem.: Nat. Assn. Purchasing Mgmt. (dir. nat. affairs 1970—71), Louisville Soc. Advancement Mgmt. (pres. 1993—94, dir. 1994—95, charter), Ky. C. of C. (chmn. banking and ins. health and welfare subcom. project 21 1988), Nat. Assn. Ind. Insurers (pers. com. 1987—95), Soc. Human Resource Mgmt. (chmn. conf. com. region 9 1984, dist. dir. for western Ky. 1984, v.p. region 9 1985—86, Ky. coun. chmn. 1986), Conf. Casualty Ins. Co. (chmn. nat. pers. conf. com. 1983), Louisville Soc. Human Resource Mgmt. (pres. 1983—84, chmn. reorgn. com. 1992, Profl. Excellence award 1993), Purchasing Mgmt. Assn. Louisville (pres. 1969—70), Adminstrv. Mgmt. Soc. (pres. Louisville 1975—76, bd. dirs. 1976—92, nat. dir. 1979—81, charter mem. Found.), Am. Assn. Individual Investors (life), Bass Anglers Sportsman Soc. (life), Land Yacht Port O'Call Club (co-chmn. computer club 1998, chmn. 1999), Wally Byam Caravan Club Internat. (pres. Ky. unit 1993, chmn. long range planning com. 1994, 2d v.p. region 5 1996—97, 1st v.p. region 5 1998—99, pres. region 5 2000—01, internat. 2d v.p. 2002—03, internat. 1st v.p. 2003—04), Good Sam Recreational Vehicle Club (life), Univ. Club Louisville (charter), Shriners, Masons, Am. Legion, Order Ky. Cols., Nat. Eagle Scout Assn. (life). Home: 974 Breckenridge Ln # 155 Louisville KY 40207-4619 E-mail: jdhaddaway@juno.com.

HADDEN, ARTHUR ROBY, lawyer; b. San Antonio, Feb. 13, 1929; s. Will Alexander and Kathleen (Westerman) H.; m. Marellyn Frances Denton, June 23, 1956; children: Neilson, Lynne, Wesley, Arthur. BBA, U. Tex., 1952, LLB, 1957. Bar: Tex. 1957, U.S. Dist. Ct. (ea. dist.) Tex. 1959, U.S. Ct. Appeals (5th cir.) 1961, U.S. Supreme Ct. 1970, U.S. Dist. Ct. (no. dist.) Tex. 1975. Lawyer Ramey, Brelsford, Hull and Flock, Tyler, Tex., 1957-70; U.S. atty. Ea. Dist. Tex., Tyler, 1970-77; lawyer, sole practice Law Offices Roby Hadden, Tyler, 1977-94; justice 12th Ct. Appeals, Tex., 1995-2000, 5th Ct. Appeals, Tex., 2001—. Mem. Fed. State Law Enforcement Commn. Tex., Austin, 1976-77. Mem. Human Subjects Investigation Commn. U. Tex. Hosp., Tyler, 1980-90, Mayor's Anti-Crime Task Force, Criminal Justice Div., Tyler, 1986-88. Capt. USAF, 1952-54. Fellow Tex. Bar Found.; mem. Smith County Bar Assn., Nat. Assn. Former U.S. Attys., Coll. of State Bar of Tex., Downtown Rotary Tyler, Rotary Internat. Republican. Avocations: jogging, mountaineering, snow skiing, tennis, swimming. Home and Office: 3335 Heines Dr Tyler TX 75701-9034

HADDEN, JOHN WINTHROP, immunopharmacology educator; b. Berkeley, Calif., Oct. 23, 1939; s. David Rodney Hadden; m. Elba Mas, July 31, 1964; children: John W. II, Paul J. BA, Yale U., 1961; MD, Columbia U., 1965. Asst. prof. pathology U. Minn., Mpls., 1972-73; assoc. prof. Cornell Grad. Sch., N.Y.C., 1973-82; assoc. mem., dir. lab. immunopharmacology Sloan-Kettering Meml. Cancer Inst., N.Y.C., 1973-82; prof. medicine, dir. div. immunopharmacology U. South Fla., Tampa, 1982-99; chmn. bd. dirs. ImmunoRx, N.Y.C., 1999—. Cons. in field.; vis. prof. U. South Fla. Med. Coll., Nat. Cancer Inst., Mex. Assoc. editor Internat. Jour. Immunopharmacology, 1978-86, editor, 1986-99; editor 12 textbooks; contbr. chpts. to books, more than 300 articles to profl. jours. Mem. Am. Assn. Immunologists, Am. Soc. Pharm. & Exptl. Therapy, Internat. Soc. Immunopharmacology (v.p. 1982-85, pres. 1985-88, publ. officer 1988-99, treas. 1999—), Tampa Yale Club (v.p. 1986-91). Achievements include patents for methods of imparting immunomodulating activity. Home: 428 Harbor Rd Cold Spring Harbor NY 11724-2108 Office: Immuno-Rx Inc 140 W 57th St Ste 9C New York NY 10019-3326 E-mail: jwhadden@optonline.net.

HADDEN, ROBERT LEE, librarian; b. Clarksville, Tenn., Sept. 4, 1951; s. William James and Margaret Shumate H.; cert. Europaisches Inst., Bonn, Germany, 1972; B.A., U. N.C., 1973; M.L.S., East Carolina U., 1977; B.S., SUNY, 1982. Salesman, School Bookhouse, Inc., Charlottesville, Va., 1973-76; restaurateur Die Hooghuis, Doel aan de Schelde, Belgium, 1974; library intern N.C. State Mus. Natural History, Raleigh, 1976-77; plant librarian Burroughs Wellcome Co., Greenville, N.C., 1977-81; med. librarian King Fahad Hosp., Al Baha, Saudi Arabia, 1981-83; med. library cons. King Khaled Eye Specialist Hosp., Riyadh, Saudi Arabia, 1982-83; indexer Pharm. Tech., Pharm. Tech. Pub. Co., Marina Del Rey, Calif., 1979-81; supervisory librarian USAG Camp Page, Chunchon, Korea and USAG Camp Long, Wonju, Korea, 1984-85; med. librarian USAF Regional Med. Ctr., Clark AFB, Philippines, 1985; engring. systems librarian U.S. Army Ballistic Research Lab., Aberdeen Proving Grounds, Md., 1985— . Mem. Spl. Libraries Assn., Med. Library Assn., Middle East Library Assn., Am. Soc. Indexers, N.C. Library Assn., U.S. Chess Fedn., N.C. Wildlife Fedn., Mensa (Gifted and Talented Children's Program Coordinator for Md., 1987—), Royal Asiatic Soc., N.C. On-Line Users Group. Episcopalian. Clubs: Unicorn Computer, N.C. Wildlife Fedn., Pitt County Wildlife. N.C. Vols. (4th regiment, Inf.). Home: 100 Hickory St Apt D103 Greenville NC 27858-1676

HADDEN, SALLY, historian, educator; b. Charlotte, N.C., Oct. 14, 1962; m. Robert Berkhofer, III, Sept. 3, 1994. BA, U. N.C., 1984; AM, Harvard U., 1985, JD, 1989, PhD, 1993. Bar: Mass. 1990. Asst. prof. history and law U. of Toledo, 1993—95; asst. prof. of history and aw Fla. State U., Tallahassee, 1995—2001, assoc. prof. of history and law, 2001—. Author: (book) Slave Patrols: Law and Violence in Virginia and the Carolinas. Recipient New Eng. Rsch. fellowship, NERFC, 2002. Mem.: Am. Hist. Assn., Am. Soc. for Legal History (life), So. Hist. Assn. (life), Phi Beta Kappa. Office: Fla State U History Dept 401 Bellamy Bldg Tallahassee FL 32306-2200 E-mail: shadden@mailer.fsu.edu.

HADDOCK, FRED(ERICK) T(HEODORE), JR., astronomer, educator; b. Independence, Mo., May 31, 1919; s. Fred Theodore Sr. and Helen (Sea) H.; m. Margaret Pratt, June 24, 1941 (div. Sept. 1976); children: Thomas Frederick, Richard Marshall; m. Deborah J. Fredericks, Dec. 7, 2003. SB, MIT, 1941; MS, U. Md., 1950; DSc (hon.), Rhodes Coll., 1965, Ripon Coll., 1966. Physicist U.S. Naval Rsch. Lab., Washington, 1941-56; assoc. prof. elec. engring. and astronomy U. Mich., Ann Arbor, 1956-59, prof. elec. engring., 1959-67, prof. astronomy, 1959-88, emeritus prof., 1988—. Lectr. radio astronomy Jodrell Bank U. Manchester, Eng., 1962; vis. assoc. radio astronomy Calif. Inst. Tech., 1966; vis. lectr. Raman Inst., Bangalore, India, 1978; sr. cons. Nat. Radio Astron. Obs., W.Va., 1960-61; founder, dir. U. Mich. Radio Astron. Obs., 1961-84. Author: (chpts. in books) Space Age Astronomy, 1962, Radio Astronomy of the Solar System, 1966; contbr. articles to prof. jours. and publs. Mem. Union Radio Sci. Internat., nat. chmn. commn. on radio astronomy, 1954-57; trustee Associated Univs., Inc., 1964-68; prin. investigator, five Orbiting Geophys. Observatories, 1960-74, and Interplanetary Probe 9, 1964-77; co-investigator on Voyager planetary probes, 1970-86, NASA, Washington; mem. astronomy adv. panel NSF, Washington, 1957-60, 63-66. With USN, 1944-45. Fellow IEEE (life), Am. Astron. Soc. (v.p. 1961-63); mem. Internat. Astron. Union (commn. on radio astronomy 1948—), NAS (adv. panel astronomy facilities 1962-64), AIA (hon. mem. Huron Valley chpt. 1980—), Sigma Xi (past pres. U. Mich. chpt. 1956). Achievements include design and development of first submarine periscope radar antenna, 1943-44; early discoveries in microwave astronomy, gaseous nebulae in 1953 and early space detection of kilometer waves from galaxy and the sun, 1962. Home: 3935 Holden Dr Ann Arbor MI 48103-9415 Office: U Mich Astronomy Dept Ann Arbor MI 48109 E-mail: fhaddock@umich.edu.

HADDOCK, HAROLD, JR., retired accounting firm executive; b. Newark, July 26, 1932; s. Harold and Lilian (Smith) H.; m. Constance M. Beltz, June 23, 1962 (div. 1986); children: Anita Jane, Carolyn Jeanne; m. Margot Mahoney, Dec. 31, 1986. AA, Union Coll., 1957; BS, Rutgers U., 1959. CPA, N.J., Fla., Mich., N.C. Sr. acct. Price Waterhouse, Newark, 1959-64; exec. asst. to treas. AP, N.Y.C., 1964-68; mgr. Price Waterhouse, N.Y.C., 1969-74, ptnr., 1974, nat. dir. fin., chief fin. officer N.Y.C. and Tampa, Fla., 1975-90, nat. dir. adminstrn., 1990-93. Pres. Scotch Plains-Fanwood (N.J.) YMCA, 1979—80, bd. dirs., trustee, 1975—84; pres., dir. The Westshore Alliance, Tampa, 1991—93; bd. dirs. The Eastman Cmty. Assn., 1997—2003, pres., 1998—2002; trustee Lebanon Coll., 2000—, chair, 2002—; mem. Bd. of Selectmen, Grantham, Minn., 2003—. Fellow AICPA, Fla. Inst. CPA, N.J. Soc. CPA; mem. Rockefeller Ctr. N.Y.C. (pres. 1979). Republican. Roman Catholic. Avocations: flying, golf, spectator sports.

HADDOCK, RAYMOND EARL, career officer; b. Oklahoma City, Sept. 26, 1936; s.Clyde William and Ida Belle (Lemmon) H.; m. Brunhilde Ernestine Becker, Oct. 21, 1960; children: Ralph William, Ronald Raymond, Karen Elizabeth Haddock Fralen. BS in Chemistry, W. Tex. State U., 1958; MS in Pub. Adminstrn., Shippensburg Coll., 1977; grad., U.S. Army War Coll., Carlisle Barracks, Pa., 1977. Commd. 2d lt. U.S. Army, advanced through grades to maj. Gen., bn. comdr. Pershing Missile Bn., 56th F.A., 1973-75, pers. staff officer (G-1) 8th Inf. Div., 1975-76, dir. internat. programs Tng. and Doctrin Command, 1977-80, comdr 9th Div. Arty. Fort Lewis, Wash., 1980-83, chief of staff Tng. Ctr. Fort Dix, N.J., 1983-84, comdg. gen. Pershing Missile Command 56th F.A., 1984-87; U.S. comdr. U.S. Command and U.S. Army, Berlin, 1988-90; comdg. gen. Security Assistance Command U.S. Army, Alexandria, Va., 1990-92; v.p. ITT Def. Internat., McLean, Va., 1993—, ret., 2003. Participator fall of Berlin wall, reunification of Germany and U.S.-Soviet nuclear forces treaty, 1987. Decorated D.S.M. with two oak leaf clusters; Fed. Order of Merit, Berlin Order of Merit (Fed. Republic Germany); Gold Nat. Def. medal (France). Avocations: sailing, fishing, jogging, hunting, genealogy. Home: 143 Northampton Blvd Stafford VA 22554

HADDOCK, ROBERT LYNN, information services entrepreneur, writer, inventor; b. Vallejo, Calif., May 12, 1945; s. Orville Walter and Lee Ellen (Alexander) H. BA, Union Coll., 1967; postgrad., NYU, 1977-81. Editor So. Pub. Assn., Nashville, 1969-74, controller, 1974-75; mktg. analyst Bus. Publs. div. Prentice-Hall, Englewood Cliffs, N.J., 1975-78, bus. mgr., 1978-81, Ziff-Davis Pub. Co., N.Y.C., 1981-82, dir. bus. devel., 1982-83; pres. Personal Access, Inc., N.Y.C., 1983-84; v.p., dir. product devel. Citicorp Global Report, N.Y.C., 1984-86, v.p., dir. mktg., 1986-88; v.p., dir. product devel. Citibank, N.A., N.Y.C., 1989-90; v.p., dir. product devel. and mktg. Enhanced Telephone Svcs., Inc., N.Y.C., 1990-91; pres. M-Power Corp., N.Y.C., 1991-98, Global Strategy Ptnrs., N.Y.C., 1998—2002, 2002—. Author: The Broken Web, 1973, How to Stop Smoking, 1974; inventor database accessing system, 1983, enhanced telephone, 1989, digital screen phone, 1993. Mem. IEEE, Am. Assn. Artificial Intelligence, Software and Info. Industry Assn., Mensa. Home: 105 W 13th St Apt 15F New York NY 10011-7848 E-mail: rhaddock@globalstrategypartners.com.

HADDOX, JEFFREY LYNN, vision scientist; b. Panama City, Fla., Sept. 28, 1953; s. Robert Arthur and Doris Lillian (Stubbs) H.; m. Marjorie Marie Castleberry, May 25, 1974; children: Jennifer Marie, Christina Lynn. BS, U. Ala., Huntsville, 1975; postgrad., Clemson (S.C.) U., 1975-77. Rsch. biologist Diabetes Rsch. and Tng. Ctr., Birmingham, Ala., 1977-78; electron microscopist, supr. sci. lab. Eye Found. Hosp./Ellen Gregg Ingalls Eye Rsch. Inst., Birmingham, 1978-82; spr. eye rsch., sr. scientist Eye Rsch. Labs., Brookwood Med. Ctr., Homewood, Ala., 1982-99; dir. eye rsch., sr. scientist Ala. Eye Bank, Birmingham, 1999-2000; exec. dir., sr. scientist Sight Savers of Ala., Birmingham, 2000—. Contbr. articles to profl. jours. Co-founder Sight Savers of Ala., 1996—; co-founder Children's Eye Care Network, 1996. Independent. Baptist. Achievements include design of a novel chemotactic assay for evaluating cell movement; research in the discovery and inhibition of inflammatory mediators, especially in eye trauma; work on synthetic complementary peptides and ophthalmologic uses thereof; patent in field. Home: 520 Meadow Ridge Cir Birmingham AL 35242-2979 Office: Sight Savers Ala 500 Robert Jemison Rd Birmingham AL 35209-3070 E-mail: jhaddox@sightsaversofalabama.org.

HADDY, FRANCIS JOHN, physician, educator; b. Walters, Minn., Sept. 6, 1922; s. Thomas J. and Frances (Shaheen) H.; m. Theresa Eileen Brey, Sept. 21, 1946; children: Richard, Carol, Alice. Student, Luther Coll., Decorah, Iowa, 1940-42; BS, U. Minn., 1943, M.B., 1946, MD, 1947, MS in Physiology, 1949, PhD in Physiology (Am. Heart Assn. fellow), 1953. Diplomate: Am. Bd. Internal Medicine. Intern Mpls. Gen. Hosp., 1946-47; fellow internal medicine Mayo Found., 1949-51; asst. prof. physiology and medicine Northwestern U. Med. Sch., 1953-61; clin. investigator VA Research Hosp., Chgo., 1957-59; prof. physiology, chmn. dept., asso. prof. medicine U. Okla. Med. Center, 1961-66; prof. physiology, chmn. dept. Mich. State U., East Lansing, 1966-76; prof. physiology Uniformed Services U., Bethesda, Md., 1976-98, chmn. dept. physiology, 1976-87. Mem. cardiovasc. study sect. NIH, 1963-69; tng. com. Nat. Heart and Lung Inst., NIH, 1970-73; mem. atherosclerosis and hypertension adv. com. Nat. Heart, Lung and Blood Inst., NIH, 1983-86; rsch. com. Am. Heart Assn., 1974-80; mem. life scis. adv. com. NASA, 1986-92, chmn., 1988-92, mem. aerospace med. adv. com.. 1988-93, mem. NASA-NIH adv. com., 1993-95; sr. scientist NASA/Johnson Space Ctr. S.C. med. scis. divsn., Houston, 1989-90; cons., peer rev. adminstr. for cardiopulmonary, integrative physiology, and clin. areas NASA, 1995,— cons. 2003—. Mem. editorial bd. Am. Jour. Physiology, 1963-69, 80-86, Jour. Applied Physiology, 1963-69, Procs. Soc. Exptl. Biology and Medicine, 1969-72, Circulation Rsch., 1975-81, Microvascular Rsch., 1978-81, Hypertension, 1978-81, Jour. Am. Coll. Nutrition, 1993-99. Recipient Med. Sci. Achievement award Am. Heart Assn., 1987, Scientist Emeritus awrd Soc. Exptl. Biology and Medicine, 1996-97, Disting. Alumnus award Mayo Found., 2003. Fellow Am. Coll. Nutrition (coord. hypertension and cardiovasc. diseases 1992-98, bd. dirs. 1993-97, publs. com. 1994-99, ann. award 1996); mem. Am. Physiol. Soc. (steering com. circulation group 1972-75, chmnm. com. on coms. 1974-77, mem. coun. 1976-79, pres. 1981, fin. com. 1983-89, chmn. fin. com. 1985-89, select com. on animal care 1988-91, chmn. long range planning com. 1990-93, hon. mem. com. 1993-95, chmn. 1995, Carl J. Wiggers award 1966), Am. Soc. Clin. Investigation, Fedn. Am. Socs. Exptl. Biology (bd. dirs. 1980-83, treas. 1990-92, rep. to Am. Assn. Accreditation Lab. Animal Care trustees 1993-96, exec. com. 1995-96), Internat. Union Physiol. Scis. (U.S. nat. com. 1976-79, 81-84), Nat. Hypertension Assn. (trustee 1979—, v.p. 2003—), NAS (basic biomed. scis. panel, com. on nat. needs for biomed. and behavioral rsch. pers. Inst. Medicine 1983-86), Assn. Chairmen Depts. Physiology (chmn. animal welfare com. 1986-87), Aerospace Med. Assn. (publ. com. 1994-95), Am. Soc. for Gravitational and Space Biology (awards com. 1994-99), Montgomery County Art Assn. (pres. 1997-98), Mayo Found. (Disting. Alumnus award, 2003). Achievements include left heart catherization, small vein and artery catherization, mechanisms of pulmonary edema, fluid flux across the capillary membrane, local regulation of blood flow, ionic action on blood vessels, and low renin hypertension. Home: 211 2nd St NW Apt 1607 Rochester MN 55901-2896 E-mail: fhaddy@hq.nasa.gov.

HADDY, RICHARD IAN, family physician, educator; b. Rochester, Minn., Jan. 8, 1950; s. Francis John and Theresa Eileen (Brey) H.; m. Cheryl Lynn Mitchell, June 11, 1976; children: Kari Valia, Jennifer Robin, Michael Francis, Sarah Elizabeth. BA, St. Olaf Coll., 1972; MD, Mich. State U., 1976. Diplomate Am. Bd. Family Practice. Resident U. Iowa Hosps. and Clinics, 1976-79; fellow in infectious diseases Mich. State U., Coll. Human Medicine, Saginaw, 1979-80; pvt. practice Mid-Mich. Family Medicine, Grand Ledge, 1980-81; residency faculty St. Joseph Hosp., Flint, Mich., 1981-83; asst. prof. dept. family practice and cmty. medicine U. Fla., Gainesville, 1983 86; dir. rsch., assoc. prof. dept. family practice Wright State U., Dayton, Ohio, 1986-93, prof. dept. family medicine, 1993-97; prof. dept. family/cmty. medicine, vice chair clin. affairs U. Louisville, Ky., 1997-99, vice-chair acad. affairs, 1999—. Contbr. articles to profl. jours. Recipient Reuben B. Widmer Alumni Rsch. award U. Iowa dept. Family Practice, 1992; John C. Gillen Rsch. scholar Wright State U. Sch. Medicine, 1995-97; grantee Hoechst-Rousel Pharms., Inc., 1984, U. Fla. Coll. Medicine, 1984-85, Dept. Health and Human Svc., 1986-87, 91, 94, 96, 2000, Lederle Labs., 1987, Am. Cancer Soc., 1987, Wright State U. Sch. Medicine, 1991-93, Am. Acad. Family Physicians Found., 1992, Am. Heart Assn., 1992. Fellow Am. Acad. Family Physicians; mem. AMA (Physician's Recognition award in continuing med. edn. 1988-91, 91-94, 94-97, 97-2000, 2000-2003), Soc. Tchrs. Family Medicine, N.Am. Primary Care Rsch. Group, Ky. Med. Assn., Ky. Acad. Family Physicians, Jefferson County Med. Soc., Phi Delta Epsilon. Avocations: swimming, model trains, coin collecting, wwii and civil war history. Home: 6900 Windham Pkwy Prospect KY 40059-7801 Office: U Louisville Dept Famioly and Cmty Svcs Med Center One Louisville KY 40202

HADEN, BENJAMIN, minister, retired publishing executive, broadcast executive; b. Fincastle, Va., Oct. 18, 1925; s. Benjamin and Anne Spiller Haden; m. Charlene Gay Edwards, July 22, 1950; 1 child, Dallas Haden Gibbons. BA in polit. sci., U. Tex., Austin, 1947; JD, Washington and Lee U., Lexington, Va., 1949; MDiv magna cum laude, Columbia Theol. Sem., Atlanta, 1963; DD (hon.), King Coll., Bristol, Tenn., 1968. Bar: DC 1953; ordained minister 1962. Owner and pres. Long Oil Co., Harrisonburg, Va., 1949—50; with CIA, Washington, 1950—51; news, advt., circulation Mansfield News Jour., Ohio, 1951—53; nat. advt. Jefferson City News Tribune, Mo., 1953—54; CEO Kingsport Times News, Tenn., 1954—60; interim pastor Riviera Presbyn. Ch., Miami, Fla., 1962; youth dir. North Ave. Presbyn. Ch., Atlanta, 1962—63; sr. pastor Key Biscayne Presbyn. Ch., Miami, 1963—67; spkr. Bible Study Hour, NBC radio, Phila., 1967—68; sr. pastor First Presbyn. Ch., Chattanooga, 1967—99; founder, spkr. Changed Lives TV/Radio Internat., Chattanooga, 1968—. Mem. Am. Newspaper Pubs. Assn., 1954—60, So. Newspaper Pubs. Assn., 1954—60; dir. The Bible For You, Atlanta, 1963—70; assoc. evangelist Billy Graham Crusade, Vancouver, Canada, 1965; Bible tchr. Leadership Inst., Atlanta, 1968, Monterey, Calif., 70; trustee King Coll., Bristol, Tenn., 1968—74; mem. Nat. Religious Broadcasters, 1968—2001; mem. originating bd. Debbie Fox Found., 1969; dir. Christianity Today, Chgo., 1975—2000, Electric Sys., Chattanooga, 1985—2000; spkr. first Conv. of Evangelists, Moscow, 1990; dir. Race Found., Cedar Rapids, Iowa, 1965—2002, Electric Motor Sales, Chattanooga, 1985—, Metal Sys., Inc., Chattanooga, 1994—. Author: (books) Kingsport - Modern Am. City, 1962, I See Their Faces, 1962; co-author: Why I am at Seminary, 1961; author: Rebel to Rebel, 1971, Pray!, 1974; contbr. articles to newspapers; interviewer (in print and broadcast media). Pres. Kingsport Rotary Club, 1959; mem. race rels. com. Mayor Jim Rose, Chattanooga, 1970; chmn. Salvation Army Bd., Kingsport, 1954; deacon First Presbyn, Ch., Kingsport, 1955, mem. pulpit com., 1956; mem. exec. com. Kingsport C. of C., 1956; pres. Community Chest, Kingsport, 1957; dir. Ridgefields Country Club, Kingsport, 1957. Recipient Merit in Program Prodn. award, Nat. Religious Broadcasters, 1987, Love of Chattanooga award, 1986, Nat. Heritage award, Chattanooga Sertoma Club, 1988. Mem.: Tenn. Bar Assn., Chattanooga Golf and Country Club, Mountain City Club, Rotary Club of Chattanooga, Kappa Sigma (pres. Washington and Lee chpt. 1948). Avocations: current events, hiking, writing. Office: Changed Lives Ste 200 1200 Mountain Creek Rd Chattanooga TN 37405

HADEN, BILLY HARPER, research biochemist; b. Jackson, Miss., Mar. 8, 1940; s. Billy Sunday and Fannie Lou (Ware) H.; m. Linda Lee Mims, Feb. 23, 1963; children: Billy, Stacey, Andrew. BS in Chemistry, Miss. State U., 1963; MS in Chemistry, U. Notre Dame, 1968, postgrad., 1968-71, Mich. State U., 1971-72. Researcher Ames Co. div. Miles Labs., Inc., Elkhart, Ind., 1963-68, assoc. research biochemist, 1968-72; applications and customer service chemist Analytical Systems Mktg. div. Bausch and Lomb, Rochester, N.Y., 1972-74; mgr. devel. applications Syva Co., Palo Alto, Calif., 1974-77; mgr. applications and clin. investigations Beckman Instruments, Inc., Brea, Calif., 1977-94; dir. tech. and regulatory Reagents Applications, San Diego, 1994-95; mgr. devel. Med. Analysis Systems, Camarillo, Calif., 1995-99; v.p. sci. and regulatory Precision Systems Inc, Natick, Mass., 1999—. Patentee in field; contbr. articles to profl. jours. Advisor Boy Scouts Am./Cub Scouts, Elkhart and Rochester, 1971-74;chief, asst. chief Y Indian Guides/Princesses, Elkhart and Rochester, 1970-82, com. mem., 1972-73; v.p. bd. dirs. Elkhart Civic Theater, 1969-72. Recipient Career Devel. award Syntex Corp., Palo Alto, 1975, Mgmt. Supervisory Devel. U. Calif., 1982, Excellence in Leadership award Beckman Instruments, Inc., Brea, Calif., 1985. Mem.: Am. Assn. Clin. Chemists (treas. N.E. sect.), Am. Chem. Soc. Avocations: outdoor activities, traveling, coin collecting. Office: Precision Systems Inc 16 Tech Cir Natick MA 01760-1038

HADEN, CHARLES HAROLD, II, federal judge; b. Morgantown, W.Va., Apr. 16, 1937; s. Charles H. and Beatrice L. (Costolo) H.; m. Priscilla Ann Miller, June 2, 1956; children: Charles H., Timothy M., Amy Sue. BS, W.Va. U., 1958, JD, 1961. Ptnr. Haden & Haden, Morgantown, W.Va., 1961-69; state tax commr. W.Va., 1969-72; justice Supreme Ct. Appeals W.Va., 1972-75, chief justice, 1975; judge U.S. Dist. Ct. No. and So. Dists. W.Va., Parkersburg, 1975-82; chief judge U.S. Dist. Ct. (so. dist.) W.Va., 1982—2002. Mem. W.Va. Ho. of Dels., 1963-64; asst. prof. Coll. Law, W.Va. U., 1967-68; mem. com. adminstrn. probation system Jud. Conf., 1979-86; mem. 4th Cir. Jud. Coun., 1986-91, 96-2000, U.S. Jud. Conf., 1997—2002, chair exec. com., 2000-02. Mem. Bd. Edn., Monongalia County, W.Va., 1967-68; bd. dirs. W.Va. U. Found., 1986—; past. mem. vis. coms. W.Va. U. Coll. Law & Sch. Medicine. Recipient Outstanding Alumnus award W.Va. U., 1986; named Outstanding Appellate Judge in W.Va., W.Va. Trial Lawyers Assn., 1975, Outstanding Trial Judge in W.Va., 1982, Justicia Officium, W. Va. U. Coll. of Law award Fellow Am. Bar Found., W.Va. State Bar Found.; mem. ABA, W.Va. Bar Assn., W.Va. State Bar Assn., Am. Judicature Soc., 4th Cir. Dist. Judges Assn. (pres. 1993-95), W.Va. U. Alumni Assn. (pres. 1982-83), W.Va. U. Order of Vandalia. Office: US Dist Ct PO Box 351 Charleston WV 25322-0351 E-mail: judge_haden@wvsd.uscourts.gov.

HADEN, CLOVIS ROLAND, university administrator, engineering educator; b. Houston, Apr. 10, 1940; s. Clovis Newton and Mary Aline (Baker) H.; m. Joyce Elaine Weathers, Aug. 8, 1956; children: Cathy, Kimberly, Clay. Student, Navarro Coll., 1958-59; BSEE, U. Tex.-Arlington, 1961; MSEE, Calif. Inst. Tech., 1962; PhD, U. Tex., 1965. Lic. profl. engr., Tex., Okla. Asst. prof. U. Okla., 1965-68; dir. Sch. Elec. Engring. and Computing Scis., 1972-78; asso. prof. Tex. A&M U., College Station, 1968-71, prof., 1971-72, dir. Inst. Solid State Electronics, 1969-72; dean Coll. Engring and Applied Scis. Ariz. State U., Tempe, 1978-87, 89-91, v.p. for acad. affairs, 1987-88, provost west campus Phoenix, 1988-89, mem., pres. Research Park bd. Tempe, 1983-91; bd. dirs. Ariz. Transp. Research Ctr., 1980-91; vice chancellor for acad. affairs La. State U., Baton Rouge, 1991-93; vice chancellor/dean engring., dir. engring. experiment sta. Tex. A&M U., 1993—2002. Mem. Ariz. Gov.'s Commn. on Sci. and Tech., 1980-82, chmn. transp. subcom., 1981-83, mem. adv. coun. for engring., 1979-91; mem. Ariz. Gov.'s High Tech. Coun., 1990-91; mem. Tex. Gov.'s Coun. Sci. & Tech., 1997-2002; chair strategic planning La. Edni. Quality Support Fund, 1991-93; mem. Nat. Engring. Dean's Exec. Bd., 1984-87, 95-2000; mem. adv. group Coun. on Competitiveness, 1994-95; chmn. bd. Ariz. R&D Co., 1983-90; mem. adv. bd. A.T. Kearney, 1986-90; mem. Tex. Bd. Profl. Engrs., 2002—. Exec. editor: Electric Power Systems Research jour, 1978—. Bd. mgrs. Tempe YMCA, 1982-84; mem. Ariz. Econ. Devel. Bd., 1982-85; bds. dirs. Harrington Arthritis Rsch. Ctr., 1983-87, Inter-tel, Inc., 1983-, Square D. Co., 1985-91, E Sys., 1994-95, WAVO Corp., 1990-99, Crosstex Energy, 2002—. Recipient George Washington Honor medal Freedoms Found., 1989, Disting. Alumnus award U. Tex., Arlington, 1995, Econ. Devel. award Phoenix area, 1985; Bur. Engring. rsch. fellow, 1964. Fellow IEEE (Oklahoma City Engr. of Yr. award 1977), Am. Soc. Engring. Edn. (chair pub. policy com. 1997-99, Marlowe award 1998); mem. NSPE, Ariz. Soc. Profl. Engrs. (Engr. of Yr. award 1983), Ariz. Assn. Indsl. Devel., Coun. Tex. Engring. Deans (chmn. 1995-98), Tex. Soc. Profl. Engrs. (bd. dirs. 1995-98), Soc. Mfg. Engrs., Sons of Republic of Tex., Golden Key, Sigma Xi, Phi Kappa Phi, Eta Kappa Nu, Tau Beta Pi. Republican. Mem. Ch. of Christ. E-mail: r-haden@tamu.edu.

HADFIELD, CHRIS A. astronaut; b. Sarnia, Aug. 29, 1959; s. Roger and Eleanor Hadfield; m. Helene Walter; 3 children. B of Mech. Engring., Royal Mil. Coll., Kingston, Ont., Can., 1982; MS in Aviation Systems, U. Tenn., 1992; DEng (hon.), Royal Mil. Coll., 1996; LLD (hon.), Trent U., 1999. Commd. 2d lt. Can. Air Force, 1978, advanced through grades to col.; with 425 Squadron; exch. officer Strike Test Directorate, Naval Air Sta., Patuxent River, Md.; astronaut NASA, Houston, 1992—, with Shuttle Ops. Devel., chief CAPCOM; chief astronaut Can. Space Agy.; dir. ops. NASA, Gagarin Cosmonaut Tng. Ctr., Star City, Russia. Decorated Meritorious Svc. Cross; named Test Pilot of Yr., USN, 1991; recipient Liethen-Tittle award, USAF Test Pilot Sch., 1988, Vanier award, 2001. Mem.: Can. Aeronautics and Space Inst., Soc. Exptl. Test Pilots, Order of Ont., Royal Mil. Coll. Club. Achievements include mission specialist STS-74 (1995), STS-100 (2001). Office: Astronaut Office/CB NASA Johnson Space Ctr Houston TX 77058

HADFIELD, MICHAEL JAMES, electrical engineer; b. Waukesha, Wis., Jan. 25, 1934; s. Raymond James and Viola Emma (Hardke) H.; m. Arlene Rita Echaust, June 11, 1955 (dec. 1996); children: Steven Michael, Linda Frances, Mary Arlene (dec. 1998), Dayna JoAnne; m. Judy Kay Hadfield; children: Franklin Dennis, David Lawrence Miller. BSEE, Marquette U., 1955; postgrad., U. Wis., 1960, U. South Fla., 1968-69. Commd. USMC, 1955, advanced through grades to capt., 1965, resigned; project engr. GM, Milw., 1958-60; guidance sys. engr. Honeywell, Inc., Clearwater, Fla., 1960-93, prin. staff engr., 1991-93, ret., 1993; mktg. mgr., program mgr. USAF, Holloman AFB, 1994-99, ret., 1999; cons., 1999—. Pres., chmn. Sta. WQXM-FM/FM Enterprises, Largo, Fla., 1968-69; v.p. Real Property Ctr., 1975-79; v.p. Luten Properties, Inc., 1979-93; broker-salesman Prudential Fla. Realty, Clearwater, 1993-94. Contbr. chpts. to books, 32 articles to tech. jours. Pres. Ch. Coun. Recipient: Gold Medal AFCEA and SAME. Fellow: AIAA (assoc.); mem.: IEEE (program and exhibits chmn., exec. com.), Inst. of Navigation (v.p.Eastern region, chmn. Inertial div.), Air Force Assn., Fla. Bd. Realtors, Nat. Bd. Realtors, Assoc. Proposal Mgmt. Profls., Scabbard and Blade, Tau Beta Pi, Pi Mu Epsilon, Eta Kappa Nu, Alpha Sigma Nu. Republican. Home and Office: PO Box 1189 Cloudcroft NM 88317-1189

HADGES, THOMAS RICHARD, media consultant, consultant; b. Brockton, Mass., Mar. 13, 1948; s. Samuel Charles and Ethel Toli (Prifti) H.; m. Beth Evelyn Rastad, Oct. 22, 1988. BA in Biology magna cum laude, Tufts U., 1969; student, Harvard Sch. Dental Med., 1969-71. Announcer Sta. WOKW, Brockton, 1965-67, Sta. WTBS-FM, MIT, Cambridge, 1966-68; announcer, program dir. Sta. WTUR, Medford, Mass., 1967-69; announcer Concert Network, Sta. WBCN-FM, Boston, 1968-78, program dir., 1977-78, Sta. WCOZ-FM, Blair Broadcasting, Boston, 1978-80, Sta. KLOS-FM, ABC, L.A., 1980-85; sr. programming advisor Pollack Media Group, Pacific Palisades, Calif., 1985-89, pres., 1989—, Pollack/Hadges Enterprises, Pacific Palisades, 1985-89. Named Program Dir. of Yr., L.A. Times, 1981. Mem. Phi Beta Kappa. Avocations: jogging, electronics. Office: Pollack Media Group 860 Via De La Paz Ste D2 Pacific Palisades CA 90272-3663

HADIDIAN, CALVIN Y. retired surgeon; b. Beirut, Apr. 26, 1924; s. Yenovk and Helen (Koundakjian) H.; m. Betty Ann Myers, May 15, 1960 (div. 1989); children: Gwynne Ann, Jocelyn Kate. BA, Am. U., Beirut, 1943, MD, 1947. Diplomate Am. Bd. Surgery, Am. Bd. Thoracic Surgery. Asst. thoracic surgery U. Md. Sch. Medicine, Baltimore, 1955-56; thoracic-vascular surgery pvt. practice, Cumberland, Md., 1957-85; clin. asst. prof. U. Pitt., Pa., 1995—. Contbr. articles to profl. jours. Mem. Soc. Thoracic Surgeons (founding). Independent. Avocations: tennis, singing, theater, writing. Home: 21 Monmouth Dr Cranberry Township PA 16066-5745 E-mail: calhad@stargate.net.

HADIPRIONO, FABIAN CHRISTY, engineering educator, researcher; b. Cirebon, Java, Indonesia, Oct. 6, 1947; came to U.S., 1976; s. Robertus Sudarjo and Wertriani (Yoyoh) H. BCE, MCE, Parahyangan U., 1973; MS, U. Calif., Berkeley, 1978, M of Engring., 1980, DEng, 1982. Registered profl. engr., Ohio. Project engr. various design and constrn. cos., SE Asia, 1965-75; project mgr. Phoenix Inc., Jakarta, Indonesia, 1974-75; engr., asst. bd. dirs. Mahkota Group, Indonesia, 1975-77; instr., teaching assoc. U. Calif., Berkeley, 1981-82; asst. prof. civil and constrn. engring. and mgmt. Ohio State U., Columbus, 1982-89, assoc. prof. civil engring., constrn. engring. and mgmt., 1989—, prof. civil and constrn. engring. and mgmt., 1995—. Tech. cons. various attys. at law for forensic engring. cases, 1984—; advisor to numerous constrn. cos. and univs. in Indonesia, 1984—; dir. Constrn. Lab. for Automation and System Simulation, Ohio State U., 1993—. Contbr. more than 200 articles to profl. jours.; presenter in field. Recipient Dale Carnegie Human Rels. award, 1976, Rsch. award Ohio State U. Coll. Engring., 1989, Lichtenstein Meml. award 1989; Ohio State U. grantee, 1985, 86, U.S. Army C.E. grantee, 1986, USAF fellow and grantee, 1986, Newhouse Found. fellow U. Calif., Berkeley, 1978, Harry H. Hilp fellow U. Calif., Berkeley, 1981, Robert B. Rothchild Jr. fellow U. Calif., Berkeley, 1982. Fellow ASCE; mem. NSPE, ASME, Internat. Assn. Bridge and Structural Engring., Am. Concrete Inst., Archtl. and Engring. Roman Catholic. Avocations: nature, cultural arts, classical music, tennis. Home and Office: Ohio State U 2070 Neil Ave Columbus OH 43210-1226

HADJIISKI, LUBOMIR MINTCHEV, computer scientist, researcher; b. Moscow, Aug. 16, 1966; arrived in US, 1996; s. Mincho Bankov and Zdravka Ananieva Hadjiiski; m. Veronika Ivanova Shopova, May 30, 1992; 1 child, Zornica. BS, Tech. U., Sofia, Bulgaria, 1990, MS, 1991; PhD, U. Kassel,

Germany, 1996. Vis. rschr. U. Reading, Eng., 1992-93, Kassel U., 1993; rsch. assoc. Clarkson U., Potsdam, N.Y., 1996-97; postdoctoral rsch. fellow U. Mich., Ann Arbor, 1997-99, rsch. investigator, 1999-2001, asst. rsch. scientist, 2001—. Contbr. articles, reviewer jours. in field. Grantee OCULUS Optikgerate GmbH, Germany, 1994-95, Heraeus Quarzglas GmbH, Germany, 1994-95, U.S. Army Med. Rsch. and Materiel Command, 1998—. Mem. IEEE Control Sys. Soc., IEEE Engring. in Medicine and Biology Soc., IEEE Neural Networks Soc., Internat. Soc. Optical Engring. Avocations: skiing, tennis, literature. Office: U Mich Hosp CGC B2103 1500 E Medical Ctr Dr Ann Arbor MI 48109-0904 Fax: (734) 647-8557. E-mail: lhadjisk@umich.edu.

HADLEY, JANE BYINGTON, psychotherapist; b. N.Y.C., Apr. 24, 1929; d. David and Ruth (Johnson) Millar; m. Arthur Twining Hadley, Feb. 24, 1979; children: Elisabeth Jane Wheeler, Caroline Anne Thies. BA, U. Va., 1951; MA, Columbia U., 1967; analytic tng., Met. Ctr. for Mental Health, 1970-73. Intern Queens Coll., 1969; pvt. practice psychotherapy N.Y.C., 1971—. Bd. mem. Am. Liver Found., Greater N.Y. Chpt. Mem. APA, Cosmopolitan Club, Century Assn. Democrat. Episcopalian.

HADLEY, JOHN LIVINGSTON, V, management executive, writer; b. Nashville, Apr. 8, 1928; s. John Livingston Hadley IV and Eugenia Margaret Johnston-Hadley; m. Mary Lou Burt, Aug. 26, 1950; children: Pamela Diane, John Livingston, Burt Alexander. Student, Peabody Coll., 1946—47; BS in Indsl. Mgmt., U. Tenn., 1951. Messenger Western Union, Pryor, Okla., 1943—45; projectionist Pryor Theater, 1944—45; supr., foreman E.I. DuPont Co., Seaford, Del., 1952—53, supr. tech. lab. Kinston, NC, 1953—60, shift supr. mfg. Old Hickory, Tenn., 1960—78, supr. power engring., 1978—88; dir. Miss Rodeo Am. Pageant, Tenn., 1985—91; pres., corp. agt. Miss Rodeo Tenn. Pageant Inc., 1991—; amb./del. Miss Rodeo Am. Pageant, Pueblo, Colo., 1985—2004. Amb./del. Miss Rodeo Am. Pageant, Pueblo, Colo., 1985—2002. Author: Trail Legacy, 1998, Alien Trail, 1999, Jonas One Horse Trail, 2000, The Two Horse Trail, 2001, Vicks Gold, 2002, Black Mountain Lair, 2003. Mem.: Nat. Rifle Assn. (patron), Gallatin Gun Club (past pres.). Republican. Avocations: reading, genealogy, hunting, rodeo, target shooting. Home and Office: Miss Rodeo Tenn Pageant Inc PO Box 53 Madison TN 37116

HADLEY, LAWRENCE HAMILTON, economics educator; b. Detroit, June 9, 1945; s. Wayne Nelson and Virginia Margret (Jominy) H.; m. Linda Beblo, June 20, 1970; children: Mark Jonathan, Eric Christopher, Alena Michelle. BA, Rutgers U., 1967; MA in Econs., U. Conn., 1969, PhD in Econs., 1975. Asst. prof. econs. Hartwick Coll., Oneonta, N.Y., 1971-75; vis. asst. prof. Am. U. Cairo, 1975-77; assoc. prof. U. Dayton, Ohio, 1977—. Participant seminars profl. orgns. including Grad. Sch. Bus., U. Chgo., 1975, NSF, 1980, 81; presenter various confs. and convs.; cons. econ. analysis; referee publs. including Growth and Change, Internat. Migration Rev., Jour. of Devel. Areas, Jour. Econs., Jour. Econs. and Bus., Jour. Forensic Econs.; proposal reviewer NSF; textbook reviewer Bus. Publs. Inc., Dryden Press. Contbr. articles to profl. jours. Mem. Am. Econ. Assn., Nat. Assn. Forensic Economists. Avocations: reading, physical fitness, watching baseball. Home: 321 Dellwood Ave Dayton OH 45419-3524

HADLEY, LEILA ELIOTT-BURTON (MRS. HENRY LUCE III), writer; b. N.Y.C., Sept. 22, 1925; d. Frank Vincent and Beatrice Boswell Eliott Burton; m. Arthur T. Hadley, II, Mar. 2, 1944 (div. Aug. 1946); 1 child, Arthur T. III; m. Yvor H. Smitter, Jan. 24, 1953 (div. Oct. 1969); children: Victoria C. Van D. Smitter Barlow, Matthew Smitter Eliott, Caroline Allison F.S. Nicholson; m. William C. Musham, May 1976 (div. July 1979); m. Henry Luce III, Jan. 1990. MD, St. Timothy's Sch., 1943. Author: Give Me the World, 1958, reprinted, 1999, How to Travel with Children in Europe, 1963, Manners for Children, 1967, Fielding's Guide to Traveling with Children in Europe, 1972, rev., 1974, 1984, Traveling with Children in the U.S.A., 1974, Tibet-20 Years After the Chinese Takeover, 1979; author: (with Theodore B. Van Itallie) The Best Spas: Where to Go for Weight Loss, Fitness Programs and Pure Pleasure in the U.S. and Around the World, 1988, rev., 1989; author: A Journey with Elsa Cloud, 1997, paperback edit. with afterword, 2003, Give Me the World, 1999; assoc. editor Diplomat mag., N.Y.C., 1964—65, Saturday Evening Post, 1965—67, contbg. editor ICON: World Monuments Mag., editl. cons. TWYCH, N.Y.C., 1985—87, book reviewer Palm Beach Life, Fla., 1967—72, consulting editor Tricyle, The Buddhist Rev., 1991—, garden columnist Fishers Island Gazette; contbr. articles to various newspapers, mags. Mem. bd. advisors Tricycle, the Buddhist Rev., 1991—; bd. dirs. Wings Trust, Inc., Tibet House, 1995, Fishers Island Conservancy, 1995, Donald & Shelley Rubin Cultural Trust, 2001, Bd. Heliki Found. Recipient Norman Vincent Peale award, 2002. Mem. Acad. Am. Poets, Soc. Woman Geographers (exec. council 1984—), Authors Guild, Nat. Writers Union, Nat. Press Club, PEN, Explorers Club, Central Park Conservancy, Ocean Conservancy (bd. dirs.), N.Y. Acad. Medicine (guest bd.), Nat. Arts Club, Lansdowne Club (Eng.). Home: 4 Sutton Pl New York NY 10022-3056 E-mail: leilahadleyluce1@aol.com.

HADLEY, MARLIN LEROY, direct sales financial consultant; b. Mankato, Kans., Jan. 5, 1931; s. Charles LeRoy and Lillian Fern (Dunn) H.; m. Clarissa Jane Payne, Sept. 17, 1949; children: Michael LeRoy, Steven Lee. BS, U. Denver, 1953; postgrad., Harvard U., 1966. Pres. Jewel Home Shopping Service div. Jewel Cos., Inc., Barrington, Ill., 1953-72; pres., chief exec. officer, dir. Beeline Fashions, Inc., Bensenville, Ill., 1972-82; chmn. bd. HAS Originals, Blairstown, NJ, 1984—; fin., bus. cons. Pres., dir. Beeline Real Estate Corp., Act II Jewelry, Inc., Home Galleries, Inc.; dir. Goulder Co., Inc., Climax Spltys., Inc. Mem.: Economics (Chgo.). Home and Office: 4298 W Lake Cir Littleton CO 80123

HADLEY, PAUL BURREST, JR., (TABBIT HADLEY), domestic engineer; b. Louisville, Apr. 26, 1955; s. Paul Burrest and Rose Mary (Ruckert) H. Grad. in Computer Ops. and Programming, No. Ky. Vocat. Sch., 1975. Floor mgr. reconciling dept. Cen. Trust Co., Cin., 1974-76; freelance photographer Ky., Ohio, Colo., 1975—; chef mgr. The Floradora, Telluride, Colo., 1978-96; domestic engr. Telluride Resort Accomodations, 1996—2001, The River Club, 2001. Pres. Tabbit Enterprises; freelance recipe writer, Telluride, 1978— Author poetry (Golden Poet award 1989, Silver Poet award 1990); actor: (plays) Of Mice and Men, The Exercise, Crawling Arnold, A Thousand Clowns, The Authentic Life of Billy The Kid, others. Actor The Plunge Players, Telluride; v.p. Telluride Coun. for Arts and Humanities, 1989. Mem. Plan Internat. USA, Christian Children's Fund. Avocations: mountain climbing, hiking, photography, travel. Home: PO Box 923 Telluride CO 81435-0923

HADLEY, PAUL ERVIN, international relations educator; b. South Ovid, Mich., July 17, 1914; s. Ervin C. and Viola M. (Barnes) H.; m. Virginia Faye Last, May 15, 1945; 1 dau., Deborah Faye. AB, Occidental Coll., Los Angeles, 1934; A.M., U. So. Calif., 1946, PhD in Comparative Lit, 1955; L.H.D., Nat. U., 1980. Tchr. El Monte (Calif.) Union High Sch., 1935-42; exec. sec. Centro Cultural Paraguayo Americano, Asunción, Paraguay, 1943-44; head Cultural Insts. unit U.S. Dept. State, Washington, 1945; instr. internat. relations U. So. Calif., Los Angeles, 1945-47, asst. prof., 1947-55, assoc. prof., 1955-64, prof., 1964-81, emeritus prof., 1981—, disting. emeritus prof., 1992. Dean summer session, 1960-73; dean Coll. of Continuing Edn., 1966-73, assoc. v.p. acad. adminstrn., 1973-77, interim acad. v.p., 1975-77, acad. v.p., 1977-81, dir. emeriti ctr., 1997-2001; exec. sec. Inst. World Affairs, 1948-73, chmn. Pacific Coast Council Latin Am. Studies, 1956-57; mem. Woodrow Wilson Fellowship selection com. Region XV, 1960-67; fgn. leader and specialist program Am. Council on Edn., 1960-62; mem. State Com. on Continuing Edn., 1966-76; mem. adv. com. Servicemembers Opportunity Colls., 1978-81; chmn. edn. sect. Town Hall of Calif., 1965-68, chmn. internat. relations sect., 1969-71; trustee Latin Am. Scholarship Program Am. Univs., 1972-74; trustee So. Calif. Presbyn. Homes(chmn. 1988-89). Pres. Assn. Retirement Orgns. in Higher Edn., 2001-03. Mem. Assn. Univ. Summer Sessions (pres. 1970-71), Inst. Internat. Edn. (adv. bd. West Coast region), Nat. U. Extension Assn. (chmn. region VI 1970-71, pres. 1976-77), Adult Educators Greater Los Angeles (chmn. 1970-71), Phi Beta Kappa, Pi Sigma Alpha, Sigma Alpha Epsilon, Phi Kappa Phi. Presbyn. (elder, stated clk. Presbytery 1983-87). Home: 1230 E Windsor Rd Apt 305 Glendale CA 91205-2642

HADLEY, RALPH VINCENT, III, lawyer; b. Jacksonville, Fla., Aug. 20, 1942; s. Ralph V. and Clare (Cason) H.; m. Carol Fox Hadley, Sept. 18, 1993; children: Graham Kimball, Christopher Bedell, Blair Vincent. BS, U. Fla., 1965, JD, 1968. Bar: Fla. 1968, Calif. 1972. Assoc. Kurz, Toole, Taylor & Moseley, Jacksonville, 1968-69; asst. atty. gen. State of Fla., Orlando, 1972-73; ptnr. Davids, Henson & Hadley, Winter Garden, Fla., 1973-80; sr. ptnr. Hadley & Asma, Winter Garden, 1980-89, Parker, Johnson, Owen, McGuire, Michaud, & Hadley, Orlando, 1989-91, Owen & Hadley, Orlando, 1991-94, Hadley, Gardner & Ornstein, P.A., Winter Park, Fla., 1994-95; Swann, Hadley & Alvarez, P.A., Winter Park, 1995-2000; with Swann & Hadley, 2000—. Vice chmn. bd. dirs. Tucker State Bank, Winter Garden, 1981-88; vice chmn. bd. dirs., sec. Tucker Holding Co., Jacksonville, 1984-88; bd. dirs. BankFIRST. Bd. dirs. Orange County Dem. Exec. Com., Orlando, 1974-81, Spouse Abuse, Inc., Orlando, 1975-81. Lt. comdr. USN, 1969-72, Vietnam. Recipient Navy Achievement medal, Award of Merit, Orange County Legal Aid Soc., 1987, Disting. Svc. award Judge J.C. Jake Stone Legal Aid Soc., 1989, Pres. Pro Bono Svc. award Fla. Bar, 1992. Mem. ABA, Fla. Bar Assn., Calif. Bar Assn., Orange County Bar Assn. (legis. chmn. 1979, 82), Am. Inn of Ct. (master), Winter Park C. of C. (bd. dirs. 1979-80), West Orange C. of C. (bd. dirs. 1979-82), Rotary. Presbyterian. Office: 1031 W Morse Blvd Winter Park FL 32789-3715 E-mail: ralphh@swannhadley.com.

HADLEY, ROBERT JAMES, lawyer; b. Wilmington, Ohio, Oct. 27, 1938; s. Robert Edwin and Ethel Edith (Slade) H.; m. Judith Ellen Gilbert, Aug. 11, 1962; children: Scott, Laura, Stephen. BA in History cum laude, Ohio State U., 1960; LLB, Harvard U., 1963. Bar: Ohio 1963. Assoc. Smith & Schnacke, Dayton, 1963-69, ptnr., 1970-89, Thompson Hine LLP, Dayton, 1989—. Pres. Man-to-Man Assocs., 1978-84, Dayton Habitat for Humanity, 1988; v.p. COPE Halfway House, Dayton, 1982-85; dir., sec. Friendship Village of Dayton, 1985—; bd. dirs. Cmty. Blood Ctr., Dayton, 1987—; loaned exec. United Way, 1980-82, cabinet 2001-02; mem. Kettering Civic Band, 1968—, v.p. Parish Resource Ctr., 1996-99, pres., 1999-2000; bd. dirs. South Cmty. YMCA, 1996-98, Greater Dayton Youth for Christ, 1980-86, Dayton Area Peace Accords Project; mem., treas. Ministry of Money bd., 1992—. Named Kettering Man of the Yr., 1986; Rotary Found. grantee, Israel, 1974. Mem. ABA, Ohio Bar Assn., Dayton Bar Assn., Dayton Racquet Club, Rotary (pres. Kettering 1986-87, dist. gov., group rep. Dist. 667 1989-90, dist. gov. 1993-94), Phi Beta Kappa. Republican. Methodist. Avocations: music, travel, sports. Home: 4848 Glenmina Dr Dayton OH 45440-2002 Office: Thompson Hine LLP PO Box 8801 2000 Courthouse Plz NE Dayton OH 45401-8801 E-mail: bob.hadley@thompsonhine.com.

HADLEY, STANTON THOMAS, international manufacturing and marketing company executive, lawyer; b. Beloit, Kans., July 3, 1936; s. Robert Campbell and Helen (Schroeder) H.; m. Charlotte June Holmes, June 9, 1962; children: Gayle Elizabeth, Robert Edward, Stanton Thomas, Steven Holmes. BS in Metall. Engring., Colo. Sch. Mines, 1958; LL.B., U. Colo., 1962. Bar: Colo. 1962, U.S. Dist. Ct. 1962, U.S. Patent Office 1963. Metallurgist ASARCO, Leadville, Colo., 1957; tng. engr. Allis-Chalmers Co., West Allis, Wis., 1958-61; adminstrv. engr. Ball Corp., Boulder, Colo., 1961-62, atty., 1962-65; patent counsel Scott Paper Co., Phila., 1965-71, USG Corp., Chgo., 1971-76, gen. mgr. metals div., 1976-79, group v.p. indsl. group, 1979-84, sr. v.p. adminstrn., sec., 1984, sec., 1984-87, sr. v.p. staff services, 1987-89; pres. Ansco Photo-Optical Products Corp., Chgo., 1989-93, Visador Co., Marion, Va., 1994-98. Bd. dirs. Masonite Corp., WJE Assocs. Inc., USG Found. Bd. dirs. Ill. Safety Council, North Suburban YMCA, Northbrook Symphony Orch.; former mem. founders' council Field Mus.; mem. Chgo. United, Chgo. Assn. Commerce and Industry. Served with U.S. Army, 1959. Mem. Am. Soc. Metals, Licensing Execs. Soc., Assn. Corp. Patent Counsel. Clubs: Union League, Sunset Ridge Country, Executives. Republican. Home: 555 Valley Way Northfield IL 60093-1067 Office: STH Cons 555 Valley Way Northfield IL 60093-1067

HADLEY, SUSAN MARIE, librarian; b. Buffalo, Nov. 25, 1952; d. Frank Joseph and Antionette (Gerace) Coniglio; m. Steven R. Hadley, Sept. 1, 1984. BA, SUNY, Buffalo, 1975; MLS, U. Mich., 1976; cert., U. Calif., Berkeley, 1986. Reference libr. Mont. Coll. Mineral Sci. and Tech., Butte, 1977-78; rsch. libr. Sandia Nat. Labs., Livemore, Calif., 1978-85; libr. cons. Townsend & Townsend, San Francisco, 1987-97, Howe-Lewis Internat., Palo Alto, Calif., 1988-90, Beyer Weaver Thomas, 1993—, TomlinsonZisko Morosoli Maser, 1998—2001, Silicon Valley Intellectual Property Group, 2000—. Mem. NOCALL. Avocation: travel. Home: 2385 Kilkare Rd Sunol CA 94586-9461

HADLEY, WILLIAM MELVIN, retired dean; b. San Antonio, June 4, 1942; s. Arthur Roosevelt and Audrey Merle (Barrett) H.; m. Dorothy J. Hadley, Jan. 21, 1967 (div. July 1989); children: Heather Marie, William Arthur; m. Jane F. Walsh, Oct. 13, 1990. BS in Pharmacy, Purdue U., West Lafayette, Ind., 1967, MS in Pharmacology, 1971, PhD in Toxicology, 1972. Teaching and grad. asst. Purdue U., West Lafayette, 1967-72; asst. prof. U. N.Mex., Albuquerque, 1972-76, assoc. prof., 1976-82, prof., 1982—2002, asst. dean Coll. Pharmacy, 1984-86, acting dean Coll. Pharmacy, 1985, dean Coll. Pharmacy, 1986—2002; prof. and dean emeritus Coll. Pharmacy, 2002—. Vis. scientist Lovelace Inhalation Toxicology Inst., Albuquerque, 1981, adj. scientist, 1991-2002, sr. scientist, 2002—; adv. bd. Waste Edn. Rsch. Consortium, Las Cruces, N.Mex., 1989—; dirs. adv. com. Nat. Ctr. for Eviron. Health, CDC, 2002—, mem. NIH Proposal Rev. Panels, Bethesda, Md., 1983-84; mem. Gov.'s PCB Expert Adv. Panel, Santa Fe, 1985-86; sci. adv. bd. Carlsbad Environ. Monitoring Ctr., 1992-97; sci. adv. com. S.W. Regional Spaceport, Las Cruces, 1992-94; cons. in field. Steering com. United Fund, U.N.Mex., 1987, key person, 1988-97. NIH grantee, 1974-80, 83-87. Mem. AAAS, Am. Pharm. Assn., Am. Assn. Colls. of Pharmacy, Soc. Toxicology (pres. Rocky Mt. chpt. 1990-91), Western Pharmacology Soc., Southwestern Assn. Toxicologists. Achievements include research in biotransformation of xenobiotics with emphasis on nasal tissue; effects of heavy metals on biotransformation with emphasis on cadmium; toxic effects of xenobiotics on the immune system. E-mail: wmhadley@aol.com.

HADLOW, WILLIAM, retired veterinarian, pathologist; Rsch. vet. in pathology NIAD; ret. vet. and pathologist. Editor (with Stalney Prusiner): Slow Transmissible Diseases of the Nervous System, 1979; contbr. articles to profl. publs. Hon. trustee Charles Louis Davis, DVM Found. Mem.: Inst. Medicine. Achievements include research in prions play a role in causing neurodegenerative diseases, including kuru. Office: Rocky Mountain Labs 903 S 4th St Hamilton MT 59840-2932

HADYK-WEPF, SONIA MARGARET, artist, real estate manager; b. May 30, 1931; d. Albert and Margaret (Rodriguez) Wepf; m. Walter Hadyk, Feb. 14, 1957 (div.June 1976); 1 child, W. Gordon Hadyk. BS in Art Edn., Pratt Inst., 1954. Tchr. art Midland Park (N.J.) Jr. H.S., 1954-55, Lyncourt (N.Y.) Pub. Sch., 1969-70; staff artist Norcross Greeting Cards, N.Y.C., 1955-56, Spencer Advt. Art, Union City, N.J., 1956-58, L.W. Peckham Advt., Syracuse, N.Y., 1958-59; freelance artist Syracuse, 1959-74; mgr. jewelry dept. Naum's, DeWitt, N.Y., 1974-75; owner Hadyk House of Gem Design, Syracuse, 1975—; mgr. Walter Hadyk Rental Homes, Syracuse, 1993—. Guest lectr. Carrier Women's Club, Syracuse, 1972, Nat. League Pen Women, Syracuse, 1972; juror Arts and Crafts Festival, Camillus (N.Y.) Hist. Soc., 1973. Designer, craftsman (cultured pearl necklace) Golden Claws, 1971, (bracelet) Bubbles, 1971, (ring) Elipses, 1983; designer, goldsmith numerous pieces including All Done With Mirrors, 1980 (Judges prize for Most Creative); designer, platinumsmith (earrings) Snowflake, 1982 (1st Runner-up). Recipient numerous awards Diamond Info. Ctr., N.Y.C., 1973, DeBeers Mines, N.Y.C., 1977, 1st prize award Jewelers' Circular Keystone, Radnor, Pa., 1979; finalist in color catalog of winning designs "Colored Gemstone Design award 2000,"; sponsored by Signity N.Y. Ltd., Stuller, Jewelers of Am., Nat. Jeweler Mag.; numerous others. Mem. Real Estate Investors Ctrl. N.Y., Gem and Mineral Soc. Syracuse Inc. Unitarian-universalist. Avocations: gem carving, gardening. Office: 102 Dewey Ave Fayetteville NY 13066-1607

HAEBERLE, ROSAMOND PAULINE, retired educator; b. Clearwater, Kans., Oct. 23, 1914; d. Albert Paul and Ella (Lough) H. BS in Music Edn., Kans. State U., 1936; MusM, Northwestern U., 1948; postgrad., Wayne State U., 1965-66. Profl. registered parliamentarian. Tchr. sch. dist., Plevna, Kans., 1936-37, Esbon, Kans., 1937-41, Frankfort, Kans., 1941-43, Garden City, Kans., 1943-44, music supr. Waterford Twp., Mich., 1944-47, tchr. Pontiac, Mich., 1947-80, ret., 1980. Pres. Pontiac Fedn. Tchrs., 1961-63. Bd. dirs. Pontiac Oakland Town Hall; adv. coun. Waterford Sr. Citizens, chmn., 1990-93; pres. Oakland County Pioneer and Hist. Soc., 1992-94. Recipient Tchrs. Day award Mich. State Fair, 1963. Mem. AAUW (pres. Pontiac br. 1970-72, founds. chair Pontiac br.), Mich. Fedn. Music Clubs (state pres. 1993-95, chmn. state bylaws and citations, chair parliamentarian 2001—, pres. Tuesday musicale of Pontiac 1984-86, pres. S.E. dist. 1986-90, chmn. Music for the Blind Northeastern region 2000), Mich. Fedn. Bus. and Profl. Womens Club (Woman of Achievement award dist. IX 1994), Mich. DARS (state parliamentarian 1985-2002), DAR (Gen. Richardson chpt., regent 1983-85, libr. and parliamentarian, Excellence in Cmty Svc. award 1995), Waterford-Clarkston Bus. and Profl. Womens Club (bylaws and parliamentarian), Pontiac Area Ret. Sch. Pers. (parliamentarian, pres. 1981-84), Mich. Assn. Retired Sch. Pers. (Disting. Svc. award 1994), Mich. Bus. and Profl. Women's Club (dir. dist. 10 1965-67), Mich. Fedn. Music Clubs (Honored Recognition award 2000, Citations award 2000), Pontiac Bus. and Profl. Women (pres. 1959-61, Woman of the Yr. award 1974), Pontiac Area Fedn. Women's Clubs (pres. 1976-78, 81-84), Mich. Registered Parliamentarians, Louise Saks Parliamentary Unit (pres. 1990-92), Bloomfield Rep. Women's Club (parliamentarian 1999-2003), Detroit Women's Club, Eastern Star, Mu Phi Epsilon, Beta Sigma Phi (life), Zeta Tau Alpha. Republican. Methodist. Avocations: travel, playing piano, reading, bell ringing, dance.

HAEBERLE, WILLIAM LEROY, corporate director, business educator, entrepreneur; b. Marion County, Ind., May 19, 1922; s. Louis Leroy and Marjorie Ellen (Jared) H.; m. Yvonne Carlton, June 17, 1947; children: Patricia, William C., David C. BS, Ind. U., 1943, MBA, 1947, DBA, 1952. Mem. faculty Ind. U., Bloomington, 1946—, prof. mgmt., 1963-85, prof. emeritus, 1985—. Sr. fellow Johnson Ctr. for Entrpreneurship and Innovation, Kelly Sch. Bus. Ind. U., 1989—; pres., dir. Nat. Entrepreneurship Found., 1982—; bd. dirs. Ind. Inst. for New Bus. Ventures, Inc., 1983-91, Nat. Assn. Corp. Dirs., 1983-84, Internat. Consortium Univ. Exec. Edn. Dirs., 1972-93; chmn. Command Corp., 1996—, vice chmn. Prime Tech. Inc., 1994-2002, Syndicate Sales Inc., 1994—, Norcote Internat. Inc., 1994—, Impact Forge Inc., 1995—; bd. dirs. Wildbirds Unltd. Inc., 1995—, St. Elmo Inc., 1996—, Command Equity Group, 1998—, Johnson Ventures, Inc.; bd. dirs., pres. Cambridge Aircraft Leasing Co. Inc., 1969—. Capt. U.S. Army, 1943-46; lt. col. USAFR, 1982, ret. Recipient Entrepreneur of Yr. award Ernst & Young, 1989, Entrepreneur of Yr., Inst. Hall of Fame. Mem. VFW, Air Force Assn., Res. Officers Assn. Sagamore of the Wabash, Am. Legion, Met. Club N.Y., Union League Club Chgo., Columbia Club Indpls., Sigma Alpha Epsilon.

HAEFELE, EDWIN THEODORE, political theorist, consultant; b. Burnt Prairie, Ill., Oct. 5, 1925; s. Monroe Edwin and Lola Amanda (Coles) H.; m. Ruth Anne Woods, Dec. 23, 1948; children: Ann Katherine, Douglas Monroe, John Joseph. Student, Mich. State U., 1943, Ill. Wesleyan U., 1946-48, U. Chgo., 1948-50. Staff asst. Pub. Adminstrn. Clearing House, Chgo., 1951-54; asst. dir. Transp. Center, Northwestern U., 1954-62; mem. sr. staff Brookings Instn., Washington, 1962-67; mem. sr. research staff Resources for Future, Inc., Washington, 1967-73; prof. polit. sci. U. Pa., Phila., 1973-82, prof. emeritus, 1982-84, 88—, prof., chmn. dept. polit. sci., 1985-88; exec. v.p. Consortium of Govtl. Counselors Inc., 1989-96. Author: Government Controls on Transport, 1965, Representative Government and Environmental Management, 1973; editor: Transport and National Goals, 1967, The Governance of Common Property Resources, 1974, What Constitutes the American Republic?, 1993. Served with AUS, 1943-46. Decorated Purple Heart, Presdl. Unit citation. Republican. Congregationalist. Home: 1215 Box Butte Ave Alliance NE 69301-2522

HAEGELE, JOHN ERNEST, business executive; b. Phila., July 11, 1941; s. Ernest F. and Cecilia (Wheeler) H.; m. Victoria J. Brasten, July 31, 1965; children: John, Scott, Lisa. BS Drexel U. in Acctg. and Fin., 1964. C.P.A., N.Y. Acct. Arthur Young & Co., N.Y.C., 1964-68, mgr., 1968-71; asst. controller Indian Head Inc., N.Y.C., 1971-76, v.p., controller, 1976-82; exec. v.p. dir. Interpool, Ltd., N.Y.C., 1982-85, chmn., chief exec. officer, 1987-88; sr. v.p. fin. TBG Group, N.Y.C., 1985-87, exec. v.p., 1988-92. Pres., COO TBG Group, Inc., N.Y.C., Monte Carlo, 1992-96; chmn. bd. dirs., CEO TBG Industries Inc., N.Y.C., 1997—, TriPoint Global Comm. Inc., 1998—. Mem. bus. sch. adv. bd. Drexel U. Served with U.S. Army, 1964-69. Mem. AICPA, N.Y. Soc. CPAs. Republican. Roman Catholic.

HAEGELE, PATRICIA, publishing executive; b. Wheeling, W.Va., Dec. 19, 1950; d. Thomas J. and Marcella (Kissell) Cook. Student, W. Liberty Coll., 1970-71, Brevard Community Bus. Coll., 1973-74, Rollins Coll., 1974-76. Retail advt. rep. Coca Today/Gannett Co., Cocoa, Fla., 1973-76, Tampa Tribune Co., Tampa, Fla., 1976-79; corp. advt. rep. Washington Post Co. Inc., Washington, 1979-82; corp. advt. mgr. USA Today/Gannett Co. Inc., N.Y.C., 1982-84, div. sales mgr., 1984-85, v.p., eastern sales mgr., 1985, v.p., advt. dir., 1985-86; pub. USA Weekend, N.Y.C., 1986-88; sr. v.p. advt. USA Today, N.Y.C., 1988—95; pub. Travel Holiday mag.; pres. gen. mgr. Newspaper Nat. Network, 1995—97; sr. v.p., pub. Good Houseeping, 1997—. Selected to YWCA's Acad. of Women Achievers, 1988; profiled On The Rise column Fortune mag., Aug., 1988. Mem. Am. Newspapers Pubs. Assn., Internat. Newspaper Advt. Mktg. Assn., Am. Mktg. Assn. Republican. Roman Catholic. Avocations: running, biking, body tng. Home: 510 E 80th St #6C New York NY 10021 Office: Good Housekeeping 959 Eighth Ave New York NY 10019

HAEGER, JOHN DENIS, academic administrator; Doctoral, Loyola U., Chgo.; M, Loyola U., Chgo.; BA, Loyola U., Chgo. Pres. Northern Ariz. U., 2001—, provost, academic student affairs divsn.; prof., history dept. Ctrl. Mich. U., chair, history dept., interim dean, coll. grad. studies, assoc. dean, coll. grad. studies, dean, coll. arts & sci., dir. student affairs; provost, v.p. Towson U. Contbr. articles. Office: No AZ U S San Fransisco St Flagstaff AZ 86011

HAEGI, MARCEL, physicist; b. Geneva, Oct. 29, 1931; arrived in Italy, 1962; s. Emile and Rosa (Voegeli) Haegi; m. Sybilla Kool, Apr. 14, 1961; children: Vlasta, Anita, Eric, Tamara. D in Phys. Scis., U. Geneva, 1968. Cert. thermonuclear physicist. Scientist U. Geneva, 1960—62, Euratom, Brussels, 1962—78, prin. scientist, 1978—. Cons. Inst. Parliamentary Studies, Rome, 1992—. Guest editor: Fusion Tech., 1994; contbr. articles to profl. jours. Pres. European Fedn. Rd. Crash Victims, Geneva, 1991—. Mem.: European Phys. Soc., Swiss Phys. Soc. Home: via del Piscaro No 4 I-00044 Frascati Italy E-mail: mhaegi@virgilio.it.

HAEMIG, MARY JANE, religious studies educator; b. Mpls., Aug. 21, 1954; d. Ernest Albert and Jean Louise Haemig. AB, U. Minn., 1977; MTheol. Studies, Harvard Div. Sch., 1981; JD, Harvard U., 1981, ThD, 1996. Bar: Ill. 1981. Atty., law dept. Continental Ill. Bank & Trust Co. of Chgo., 1982-89; asst. prof. religion Pacific Luth. U., 1994-99; assoc. prof. ch. history Luther Sem., 1999—. German Acad. Exch. fellow, 1981-82. Mem. ABA. Lutheran. Office: Luther Sem 2481 Como Ave Saint Paul MN 55108 E-mail: mhaemig@luthersem.edu.

HAENER, JUAN A. physicist; s. Georghe Haener and Elena Frederica Roth; children: Georgina Kammel, Carmen Calica, Cristian, Juan, Mila Fadely. PhD in Physics, Tech. U., Berlin, Germany, 1947. Engineering Tech. U., Berlin-Charlottenburg, 1942. Chief scientist Whittaker Corp., San Diego, 1962—72; pres. Haener Block Co. LLC, San Diego, 1975—. Mem.: NY Acad. of Sci. (life). Achievements include patents for Interlocking Mortarless Block System. Home: 8215 Harton Pl San Diego CA 92107 Office: Haener Block Company LLC 4102 Catalina Pl San Diego CA 92107 Home Fax: 619-224-6401; Office Fax: 619-224-6401. Personal E-mail: info@haenerblock.com. E-mail: info@haenerblock.com.

HAENICKE, DIETHER HANS, academic administrator emeritus, educator; b. Hagen, Germany, May 19, 1935; came to U.S., 1963, naturalized, 1972; s. Erwin Otto and Helene (Wildfang) H.; m. Carol Ann Colditz, Sept. 29, 1962; children: Jennifer Ruth, Kurt Robert. Student, U. Gottingen, 1955-56, U. Marburg, 1957-59; PhD magna cum laude in German Lit. and Philology, U. Munich, 1962; DHL (hon.), Cen. Mich. U., 1986; DHL, We. Mich. U., 1998. Asst. prof. Wayne State U., Detroit, 1963-68, assoc. prof., 1968-72, prof. German, 1972-78, resident dir. Jr. Year in Freiburg (Ger.), 1965-66, 69-70, dir. Jr. Year Abroad programs, 1970-75, chmn. dept. Romance and Germanic langs. and lits., 1971-72, assoc. dean Coll. Liberal Arts, 1972-75, provost, 1975-77, v.p., provost, 1977-78; dean Coll. Humanities Ohio State U., 1978-82, v.p. acad.

affairs, provost, 1982-85; pres. Western Mich. U., Kalamazoo, 1985-98. Asst. prof. Colby Coll. Summer Sch. of Langs., 1964-65; lectr. Internationale Ferienkurse, U. Freiburg, summers 1961, 66, 67 Author: (with Horst S. Daemmrich) The Challenge of German Literature, 1971, Untersuchungen zum Versepos des 20. Jahrhunderts, 1962; editor: Liebesgeschichte der schonen Magelone, 1969, Der blonde Eckbert und andere Novellen, 1969, Franz Sternbalds Wanderungen, 1970, Wednesdays with Diether, 2003, University Governance and Humanistic Scholarship (Festschrift), 2002; contbr. articles to acad. and lit. jours. Mem. Mich. State Atty. Discipline Bd. Fulbright scholar, 1963-65 Mem. MLA, AAUP, Am. Assn. Tchrs. of German, Mich. Acad. Arts and Scis., Mich. Coun. for Arts and Cultural Affairs, Phi Beta Kappa. Office: Western Mich U 3019 Waldo Library Kalamazoo MI 49008-3804 E-mail: diether.haenicke@wmich.edu.

HAENSLY, PATRICIA ANASTACIA, psychology educator; b. Kronenwetter, Wis., Dec. 4, 1928; d. Paul Frank and Valeria (Woyak) Banach; m. William E. Haensly, 1954; children: Paul, Robert, Thomas, James, John, David, Mary, Katherine. BS, Lawrence U., 1950; MS in Genetics, Iowa State U., 1953; PhD in Ednl. & Devel. Psychology, Tex. A&M U., 1982. Histo technique specialist dept. vet. pathology Iowa State U., Ames, 1958-63; asst. prof. dept. ednl. psychology Tex. A&M U., College Station, 1982-97; instr. Blinn Jr. Coll., College Station; prin. Investigator Project Mustard Seed, U.S.D.O.E. Javits Grant, 1993-96; assoc. dir. programs Inst. for Gifted and Talented Tex. A&M U., College Station, dir. summer presch. program Minds Alive, 1987-95. Mem. adj. faculty psychology Western Wash. U., Bellingham, 1996—. Contbg. editor Roeper Rev., 1996—; contbr. articles to profl. jours., chpts. to books; mem. editl. bd. Gifted Child Quar., 1996—, Gifted Child Today, 1997—; guest editor: (spl. issue) Gifted Teachers/Teachers of Gifted Learners, Parenting the Gifted. Alt. U.S. del. World Coun. Gifted and Talented Children, 1997-99, 2001-02, del., 1999-2001; del. People to People amb. program Pacific N.W. Initiative to the People's Rep. of China., 1998. Recipient Outstanding Woman award AAUW, 1980, Govt. Rsch. Javits grante, 1993-96, Hon. Mention Hollingworth award Intertel Found., 1993. Mem. Tex. Assn. for Gifted and Talented (1st v.p. 1988, 89, editor news mag. 1988, 89), Nat. Assn. Gifted Children (co-chmn. rsch. and evaluation com. 1985-87, John Curtis Gowan Rsch. award 1981, program chair Conceptual Found. divsn. 1997-99, chair 2000-01), World Coun. for Gifted and Talented Children, Inc., Soc. for Rsch. in Child Devel., Coun. for Exceptional Children, Assn. for Childhood Edn. Internat., Am. Creativity Assn. (charter), Am. Psychol. Soc., Phi Kappa Phi. Home: 3384 Northgate Rd Bellingham WA 98226-9263 E-mail: haensly@cc.wwu.edu.

HAERING, EDWIN RAYMOND, chemical engineering educator, consultant; b. Columbus, Ohio, Dec. 8, 1932; s. Edwin Jacob and Mary Mildred (Kunst) H.; m. Suzanne Rowe, June 9, 1956; children: Cynthia, David Arthur, Elizabeth. BChemE, MS, Ohio State U., 1956, PhD, 1966. Mem. faculty Ohio State U., Columbus, 1959-91, assoc. prof., 1973-82, prof. chem. engring., 1982-91, prof. emeritus, 1991—, vice chmn. dept., 1974-76, chmn. dept., 1977-78. Cons. in field, 1966—. Author: Laboratory Manual for Unit Operations Laboratory, 1980; also tech. articles to profl. jours. Disaster svcs. vol. ARC, 1997—. Lt. (j.g.) USNR, 1956—59. NROTC scholar, 1951-56, Dow Chem. Co. scholar, 1956; Keppers tchg. fellow, 1962. Mem. AIChE (treas. Cen. Ohio sect. 1974-79), Am. Chem. Soc., Port Clinton Power Squadron (exec. com. 2003—), Sigma Xi, Tau Beta Pi, Ohio State U. Faculty Club (pres. 1988-89), Mid. Bass Yacht Club, Lake Erie South Shore Hunter Sailing Assn. (treas. 1997-99). Avocations: golf, gardening, sailing. Home: 701 Stoutenberg Dr Lakeside Marblehead OH 43440-2049 Office: Ohio State Univ Dept Chem Engring 701 Stoutenberg Dr Lakeside Marblehead OH 43440-2049

HAERLE, PAUL RAYMOND, judge; b. Portland, Oreg., Jan. 10, 1932; s. George William and Grace (Soden) H.; m. Susan Ann Wagner, May 30, 1953 (div. Apr. 1973); children: Karen A. Haerle D'Or, David A.; m. Michele A. Monson, June 1, 1991. AB, Yale U., 1953; JD, U. Mich., 1956. Bar: Calif. 1956, U.S. Supreme Ct. 1962. Assoc. Thelen, Marrin, Johnson & Bridges, San Francisco, 1956-64, ptnr., 1965-67, 69-94, mng. ptnr., 1990-93; appointments sec. Office of Gov., State of Calif., Sacramento, 1967-69; assoc. justice Calif. Ct. Appeal (1st dist.), San Francisco, 1994—. Lawyer rep. 9th Cir. Jud. Conf., 1985-88. Editor-in-chief Mich. Law Rev., 1955-56 Presdl. elector, 1972; del. Rep. Nat. Conv., 1972; vice chmn. Calif. Rep. Com., 1973-75, chmn., 1975-77; mem. Rep. Nat. Com., 1975-77; trustee World Affairs Coun. No. Calif., 1997-2003; mem. adv. com. on internat. law U.S. Dept. State, 2002—. Fellow Am. Coll. Trial Lawyers; mem. Yale Club of San Francisco, Order of Coif. Avocations: tennis, travel, hiking. Office: Calif Ct Appeal 350 McAllister St San Francisco CA 94102-3600

HAESELER, CARL WILLIAM, pomology and viticulture educator; b. Northampton, Mass., Feb. 25, 1929; s. Rudolph Friedrich and Ruth Edna Haeseler; m. Martha Elizabeth Haeseler; children: Carolyn, Ruth, Stephen. PhD, Pa. State U., State College, Pennsylvania, 1950; MSci, Cornell U., Ithaca, New York, 1949; BSci, U. of Mass., Amherst, Massachusetts, 1947. Pomology ext. educator Pa. State U., State College, 1962—66, pomology and viticulture educator North East, 1966—78, pomology and vitian hure educator, 1978—94, prof. emeritus pomology and viticulture State College, 1994—. Chmn. Iroquois Sch. Dist. Bldg. Commn., Erie, Pa., 2002. Pvt. first class US Army, 1954—56. Mem.: Am. Soc. of Enology and Viticulture, Am. Soc. Hort. Sci., Am. Pomological Soc., Soc. of Sigma Xi. Avocations: wine making, woodworking, photography, watercolors. Home: 156 Lake Cliff Drive Erie PA 16511-1242 also: 1810 Woodstock Ln Sarasota FL 34243-3051

HAESSLE, JEAN-MARIE GEORGES, artist; b. Buhl/Haut/Rhin, France, Sept. 12, 1939; came to U.S., 1967; s. Georges and Marguerite H. Student, Ecole Nationale des Beaux Arts, Paris, France, 1965-67, École de la Grande Chaumiere, Paris, 1966-67. Painter, Paris, 1965-67, N.Y.C., 1967—. One man shows include Panoras Gallery, N.Y.C., 1968, West Broadway Gallery, N.Y.C., 1973, Atlantic Gallery, Washington, 1979, Nat. Acad. Sci., Washington, 1979, RR Gallery, N.Y.C., 1980, Gabrielle Bryers Gallery, N.Y.C., 1981, Kerr Gallery, N.Y.C., 1984-85, Little John Smith Gallery, N.Y.C., 1986, Lucien Durand Galerie, Paris, 1987-91; exhibited in groups shows U.S. and abroad including Salon de la Jeune Peinture, Musee d'Art Moderne, Paris, 1968, Palace of Fine Arts, Mexico City, 1972, Aldrich Mus. Contemporary Art, Ridgefield, Conn., 1978; represented in permanent collections U.S. and abroad including So. Ill. U., Edwardsville, Bank of N.Y., N.Y.C., Atlantic-Richfield, Los Angeles, Am. Express, Fla., IBM, Los Angeles, Exxon, Fla., Chase Manhattan Bank, Los Angeles, Citibank, Los Angeles, Oven Corning Fiberglass, Toledo; works reviewed in profl. and popular publs. Roman Catholic. Home: 106112 Spring St New York NY 10012

HAEUSER, MICHAEL JOHN, library administrator; b. LaCrosse, Wis., July 5, 1943; s. Loyal Eldon and Kamilla (Brenengen) H.; m. Linda Kay Johnsrud, Aug. 31, 1968 (div. 1981); 1 child, Britton; m. Irene Jeanette Morris, June 20, 1987. BS in History, U. Wis., 1970, MA in History, 1972, MLS, 1973, cert., 1986. Readers svcs. libr. Knox Coll., Galesburg, Ill., 1973-74, head readers svcs., 1974-76; head libr. Linfield Coll., McMinnville, Oreg., 1976-81; dir. learning resources, head libr. Gustavus Adolphus Coll., St. Peter, Minn., 1981-97, coll. archivist, 1997—. Co-instr. Mil. History WWII, 1979; presenter in field. Author: With Grace, Elegance and Flair: The First 25 Years of Library Associates, 2002; cons. to editor books for coll. librs., Choice mag.; contbr. articles to profl. jours. Chmn. Core Curriculum Rev. Task Force, Linfield Coll., 1977 7; mem. coll. libr. com. Nat. Commn. Preservation and Access, 1989, team Bibliographic Instrn., 1982—; bd. dirs. Minn. Humanities Commn., 1990-97. With U.S. Army, 1963-66. NEH fellow, 1978; grantee, 1980, 83; grantee: Japan Found., 1978, U.S. Office Edn., 1979, 80, Murdock Trust, 1979, Hearst Found., 1980, Collins Found., 1980, Nat. Archives and Records Svc., 1983, Presser Found., 1983; recipient John Cotton Dana Libr. pub. rels. award 1983, 94. Mem. ALA (selected vol. pres.' program Chgo. chpt. 1985, sec. coll. libr. sect. 1990, Outstanding Pub. Rels. 1983), Assn. Coll. And Rsch. Librs., Assn. Coll. and Resource Librs. (nat. adv. coun. libr. sect. 1985), Am. Hist. Assn., Minn. Libr. Assn. (pres. 1988-90), Minn. Assn. Libr. Friends (bd. dirs. 1990), Minn. Humanities Commn. (bd. dirs. 1991-97). Lutheran. Avocations: skiing, outdoor work, reading, traveling, association activities. Office: Gustavus Adolphus Coll Folke Bernadotte Meml Libr 800 W College Ave Saint Peter MN 56082-1485 E-mail: haeuser@gac.edu.

HAEUSSLER, CHARLES LOUIS, II, oil company executive; b. NYC, Feb. 1, 1938; s. Ernest Frederick and Frieda Wilhelmina (Erdmann) H.; m. Judith Lindsay Dymock, Mar. 20, 1964; children: Linda Jane, John Lindsay. BA, Dickinson Coll., Carlisle, Pa., 1960; M Govt. Adminstrn., U. Pa., Phila., 1962; cert. project mgmt., Harvard U., 1978; Grad. Econ. Devel. Inst., U. Okla., 1983. Planning dir. Lebanon (Pa.) County Planning Commn., 1962-68, fin. planner McDonnell Co., N.Y.C., 1968-69; planning cons. Kendree & Shepard, Phila., 1969-71; chief planner N.W. Pa. Planning Commn., Oil City, 1971-74; exec. dir. Fifth Planning Dist., Roanoke, Va., 1974-81; capital planning specialist Saudi Arabian Oil Co., Dhahran, Saudi Arabia, 1981-98; lectr. Tucker Internat., Boulder, Colo., 2000—. Mem. geog. adv. com. Va. Poly. Inst. and State U., Blacksburg, 1977-81; preparer land devel. plans, control packages, capital investment programs for govts. and corps. in N.Am., Mid. East; Mid. East Bus. Cons., Doylestown, Pa.; lectr. on Middle East bus. practices Tucker Internat. Sch., Boulder, Colo., 2000-. County chmn. Com. to Revise the State Constitution, Lebanon, Pa., 1966. Fels fellow U. Pa., Phila., 1960-62; recipient Disting. Svc. award U. Pa., Phila., 1967. Mem. Am. Inst. Cert. Planners, Am. Econ. Devel. Coun., Masons (32 degree), Kiwanis (treas. 1966). Republican. Presbyterian. Avocation: investments. Home: 145 Selner Ln # D Doylestown PA 18901-3821 E-mail: chas@quadnet.net.

HAFEMEISTER, DAVID WALTER, physicist; b. Chgo., July 1, 1934; s. Lester David and Alma Doris (Schmidt) H.; m. Gina Rohlander, June 10, 1961; children: Andrew, Jason, Heidi. MS in Physics, U. Ill., 1959, PhD in Physics, 1964. Asst. prof. physics Carnegie-Mellon U., Pitts., 1966-69; prof. physics Calif. Poly. State U., San Luis Obispo, 1969-2000; study dir. on arms control on beyond START NAS, Washington, 2000—02. Sci. advisor Sen. John Glenn U.S. Senate, Washington, 1975-77; spl. asst. to Under Sec. State Benson and Nye U.S. State Dept., Washington, 1977-79; vis. scientist U. Groningen, The Netherlands, 1971, 80, Program Sci. Tech. in Internat. Security, MIT, Cambridge, 1983-84, Ctr. for Bldg. Scis. Lawrence Berkeley (Calif.) Lab., 1985-86, Office Strategic Nuc. Policy U.S. Dept. State, 1987, Ctr. Internat. Security and Arms Control Stanford U., 1988; program on nuc. policy alternatives Princeton U., 1989; mem. profl. staff Senate Fgn. Rels. Com., 1990-92; staff Senate Gov. Affairs Com., 1992-93, Sch. Pub. Affairs, U. Md., 1996; Foster fellow Office of Strategic Negotiations, U.S. Arms Control and Disarmament Agy., 1997-98. Author: Physics of Societal Issues, 2003; co-author: Physics of Modern Architecture, 1983; co-editor: Energy Sources: Conservation and Renewables, 1985, Arms Verification, 1986, Nuclear Arms Technologies in the 1990s, 1988, Physics and Nuclear Arms Today, 1990, Global Warning: Physics and Facts, 1991, Biological Effects of Low-Frequency Electromagnetic Fields, 1998. Fellow Am. Phys. Soc. (chmn. forum on physics and soc. 1985-86, chair panel on pub. affairs 1996, Leo Szilard award for Physics in the Pub. Interest 1996); mem. AAAS (congl. fellow 1975-76, arms control fellow 1987), Fedn. Am. Scientists, Arms Control Assn., Am. Inst. Physics (co-editor books). Home: 553 Serrano Dr San Luis Obispo CA 93401 E-mail: dhafemei@calpoly.edu.

HAFER, BARBARA, state official; b. L.A., Aug. 1, 1943; BS, Duquesne U., Pitts., 1969; postgrad., U. Pitts., U. London. Auditor gen. State of Pa., Harrisburg, 1989-96, state treas., 1997—. Office: State of Pennsylvania Treasury Dept 129 Finance Building Harrisburg PA 17120-0018 E-mail: barbarahafer@patreasury.org.

HAFER, FREDERICK DOUGLASS, utility executive; b. West Reading, Pa., Mar. 12, 1941; s. Charles Frederick and Irene Naugle (Renninger) H.; m. Martha Louise Gartner, Apr. 6, 1963; children: Frederick, Craig, Keith. Student, Drexel Inst. Tech., 1959-62; LHD, Alvernia Coll., 1993. With Met. Edison Co., Reading, Pa., 1962-68; with Gen. Pub. Utilities Corp., N.Y.C., 1968-78, asst. treas., 1970, treas., 1970-78; v.p. rates GPU Service Corp., 1977-86; v.p. Met. Edison Co., Pa. Electric Co., 1982-86; pres. Met. Edison Co., 1986—; pres., CEO, chmn. bd. GPU Inc, 1994—, also bd. dirs. Bd. dirs. Met. Edison Co., Pa. Electric CO., GPU Service Corp., GPU Nuclear Corp., Utilities Mut. Ins. Co., Meridian Bancorp, Inc., Meridian Bank. Bd. dirs. Reading Hosp. and Med. Ctr., Leadership Pa., Leadership, Pa.; bd. dirs. Found. For Drug-Free Pa., Berks Festivals, Inc., Berks Bus.-Edn. Coalition, Kutztown U. Found. Mem.: Pa. Electric Assn. (exec. com.), Mfrs. Assn. Berks County (bd. dirs.), Berks County C. of C. (formerly bd. dirs.), Berkshire Country. Office: GPU Inc 300 Madison Ave PO Box 1911 Morristown NJ 07962-1911

HAFER, JOSEPH PAGE, lawyer; b. Harrisburg, Pa., June 28, 1941; s. George Horace and Betty (Page) H.; m. Margaret B. Cady; children: Bradford G., Susan P., David E. AB, Lafayette Coll., 1963; JD with distinction, U. Mich., 1966. Bar: Pa. 1966, U.S. Dist. Ct. (mid. dist.) Pa. 1966, U.S. Supreme Ct. 1969, U.S. Ct. Appeals (3d cir.) 1976. Assoc. Metzger, Hafer, Keefer, Thomas & Wood, Harrisburg, 1966-77; mng. ptnr. Thomas, Thomas & Hafer, Harrisburg, 1977—. Adj. prof. law Dickinson Law Sch., Carlisle, Pa. Pres. Cumberland Valley Sch. Bd., Mechanicsburg, Pa., 1976-85; pres. Hampden Twp. Rep. Assn., Camp Hill, Pa. Fellow Am. Coll. Trial Lawyers; mem. ABA, Pa. Bar Assn., Assn. Trial Lawyers Am., Pa. Trial Lawyers Assn., Dauphin County Bar Assn. (ct. rels. com.). Methodist. Home: 1530 Waterford Camp Hill PA 17011-9000 Office: Thomas Thomas & Hafer PO Box 999 Harrisburg PA 17108-0999 E-mail: jph@tthlaw.com.

HAFETS, RICHARD JAY, lawyer; b. N.Y.C., Apr. 23, 1951; s. Meyer Hafets and Marilyn (Glanzrock) Bell; m. Claire Margolis, June 18, 1972; children: Brooke, Amy. BS in Bus. summa cum laude, Am. U., Washington, 1973, JD magna cum laude, 1976. Bar: Md. 1976, U. S. Dist. Ct. Md. 1976, U.S. Ct. Appeals (4th cir.) 1976, U.S. Supreme Ct. 1981, D.C. 1997, U.S. Dist. Ct. (D.C.) 1997. Assoc. Piper & Marbury, Balt., 1976-84, ptnr., 1984—, chmn. labor and employment practice, 1990—, chmn. hiring and assoc. coms., 1988-91. Labor atty. Balt. Symphony Orch., 1986-93; bd. dirs., gen. counsel Am. Cancer Soc., Balt., 1983-89; bd. dirs. Md. Ballet, Balt., 1978-80. Mem. ABA, Md. Bar Assn., Balt. City Bar Assn., Order of Coif. Avocations: horses, skiing. Home: 7346 Narrow Wind Way Columbia MD 21046-1262 Office: Piper Marbury Rudnick & Wolfe 6225 Smith Ave Baltimore MD 21209-3600 E-mail: richard.hafets@piperrudnick.com.

HAFEY, JOSEPH MICHAEL, health association executive; b. Annapolis, Md., June 25, 1943; s. Edward Earl Joseph and Verna (Hedlund) H.; m. Mary Kay Miller, Dec. 30, 1978; children: Erin Catherine, Ryan Michael. BA, Whittier Coll., 1965; MPA, UCLA, 1967. Sr. asst. health officer HHS, Washington, 1967-69; dir. govt. relations Alliance for Regional Community Health, St. Louis, 1969-71; exec. dir. Contra Costa Comprehensive Health Assn., Richmond, Calif., 1971-74, Bay Area Comprehensive Health Planning Coun., San Francisco, 1974-76, Western Ctr. for Health Planning, San Francisco, 1976-86, Western Consortium for Pub. Health, Berkeley, 1980-95; pres., CEO Pub. Health Inst. (formerly Calif. Pub. Health Found.), 1985—. Chmn. Contra Costa Pub. Health Adv. Body, Martinez, Calif., 1987-93; founder Calif. Coalition for Future of Pub. Health, Sacramento, 1988—; co-founder Calif. Healthy Cities Program, Berkeley, 1987—. Chmn. United Way Com. for the Uninsured, San Francisco, 1985-93; bd. dirs. Eugene O'Neill Found., 1980-89. With USPHS, 1967-69. Recipient fellowship WHO, Geneva, 1987. Mem. Am. Pub. Health Assn. (governing coun. 1984-87), Am. Health Planning Assn. bd. dirs., chmn. annual meeting 1982). Avocations: jogging, tennis, skiing, collecting political campaign buttons. Home: 1749 Toyon Rd Lafayette CA 94549-2111 Office: Pub Health Inst 2001 Addison St Ste 200 Berkeley CA 94704-1103

HAFF, GUY GREGORY, exercise science educator, researcher; b. Montclair, N.J., Sept. 25, 1969; s. Guy Gordon and Sandra K. H. BS, East Stroudsburg U., 1993; MS, Appalachian State U., 1996; PhD, U. Kans., 1999. Cert. strength and conditioning specialist. Graduate asst. Appalachian State U., Boone, 1993-96, cardiac rehab. intern, 1994; personal trainer Milburne (N.J.) Short Hills Athletic Club, 1995; grad. tchg. asst. U. Kans., Lawrence, 1996-99; asst. prof. exercise physiology Appalachian State U., Boone, NC, 2000—02, neuromuscular lab. dir., 2000—02; asst. prof. Midwestern State U., Wichita Falls, Tex., 2002—, dir. human performance lab. Mem. com. USA Weightlifting, 1993-; mem. Human Performance Lab. com., Appalachian State U., 1999-2002. Reviewer Strength and Conditioning, 1999—. Mem. Nat. Strength and Conditioning Assn. (scholarship 1996, Young Investigation of the Yr. 2001), Am. Coll. Sports Medicine, U.S. Weight Lifting Assn. (athletic coach), European Coll. Sport Scis. Avocations: weightlifting, computers, reading, hiking, cycling. Home: 5007 Trinidad Dr Wichita Falls TX 76310 Office: Midwestern State U Ligon Hall 3410 Taft Blvd Rm 215 Wichita Falls TX 76308 E-mail: greg.haff@mwsu.edu.

HAFFNER, ALDEN NORMAN, university official; b. Bklyn., Oct. 3, 1928; s. Irving and Irene (Gutfleisch) H. AB, Bklyn. Coll., 1948; OD, Pa. Coll. Optometry, 1952; MPA, NYU, 1960, PhD, 1964; DOS (hon.), Mass. Coll. Optometry, 1960; ScD (hon.), Pa. Coll. Optometry, 1973. Exec. dir. Optometric Center of N.Y., N.Y.C., 1957—; acting chief adminstrv. officer State Coll. Optometry, SUNY, N.Y.C., 1970-71, dean, 1971-76, pres., 1976-78; assoc. chancellor for health scis. SUNY, Albany, 1978-82, vice chancellor for research, grad. studies and profl. programs, 1982-87, pres. coll. optometry, 1987—. Pub. svc. prof. health poligy Rockefeller Coll., SUNY-Albany, 1986; chmn. N.Y. State Com. on Health Personnel and Productivity, 1990—; cons. in field. Contbr. articles in field to profl. jours. Mem. adv. com. Commn. for Blind and Visually Handicapped, State Dept. Social Services, 1966-70; mem. bd. nat. study commn. on optometry Nat. Commn. on Accrediting, 1968-70; mem. health manpower planning com. Comprehensive Health Planning Agy., N.Y.C., 1969-73; project dir. Fed. Program of Identification, Counseling, Guidance and Recruitment of Minority Students in Profession of Optometry, 1968-74; mem. Mayor's Com. for Study of Aging, N.Y.C., 1958; chmn. bd. trustees Manhattan Health Plan, Inc., 1976-81. Served to 1st lt. M.C. U.S. Army, 1953-55. Recipient Albert Fitch Meml. award, 1962; Prof. Frederick A. Woll Meml. award, 1961; Distinguished Achievement award Alumni Assn., N.Y. U. Grad. Sch. Pub. Health Adminstrn., 1974 Fellow Am. Pub. Health Assn., AAAS, Am. Sch. Health Assn., Am., N.Y. Acad. Optometry; mem. N.Y. Acad. Scis., Group Health Assn. Am., Am. Pub. Welfare Assn., Am. Soc. Pub. Adminstrn., Nat. Rehab. Assn., Illuminating Engring. Soc., Am. Optometric Assn., N.Y. State Optometric Assn., Gerontol. Soc., Am. Assn. Univ. Adminstrs., Pub. Health Assn. City of N.Y. (dir. 1967—), Nat. Assn. Land Grant Colls. and State Univs. (com. health affairs 1981), Community Family Planning Coun., Am. Coun. on Edn., Assn. Cad. Health Ctrs., Hermann Biggs Soc., Beta Sigma Kappa (Gold Medal award 1974), Home: 201 E 36th St New York NY 10016-3668 Office: SUNY Coll Optometry 33 W 42nd St New York NY 10036-8003

HAFFNER, CHARLES CHRISTIAN, III, retired printing company executive; b. Chgo., May 27, 1928; s. Charles Christian and Clarissa (Donnelley) H.; m. Anne P. Clark, June 19, 1970. BA, Yale U., 1950. With R.R. Donnelley & Sons Co., Chgo., 1951—, treas., 1962-68, v.p. and treas., 1968-83, vice-chmn. and treas., 1983-84, vice-chmn., 1984-90, ret., 1990. Bd. dirs. DuKane Corp. Chmn. Morton Arboretum, 1975-2001, Newberry Libr., 1986-2000, Sprague Found., 1996-2000; trustee Art Inst. Chgo., Latin Sch., Chgo., 1974-84, Ill. Cancer Coun., 1984-92, Chgo. City Day Sch., Lincoln Pk. Zool. Soc., Brooks Sch., 1987-95, Newberry Libr.; life trustee Sprague Found.; bd. govs. Nature Conservancy, 1973-84, chmn. Ill. chpt., 1984-87, life trustee, 1987—; mem. Chgo. Plan Commn., 1986-91. 1st lt. USAF, 1952-54. Mem. Chgo. Club, Comml. Club, Commonwealth Club, Racquet Club, Caxton Club, Casino Club. Home: 1530 N State Pkwy Chicago IL 60610-1610 Office: 35 E Wacker Dr Ste 2650 Chicago IL 60601-2398

HAFFNER, JAMES W., JR., opera educator, director; b. Cleve., Oct. 31, 1970; s. James W., Sr. and Linda J. Haffner; life ptnr. Timothy H. Swaim, Dec. 29, 2001. MFA, Artist's diploma, U. of Cin., 1997; BA, Baldwin-Wallace Coll., Ohio, 1993. Dir. opera U. of the Pacific, Stockton, Calif., 1993—. Cons. Opera Am., Washington, 2003—; dir. Nat. Opera Assn., Canyon, Tex., 2003—. Dir.: (production) La Cenerentola (Kennedy Ctr., Am. Coll. Theatre Festival, 2001). Fellow, Goethe Institut, 1995; grantee, Fulbright, 1996—97. Mem.: Lincoln Ctr. Dirs. Lab. Office: U of the Pacific 3601 Pacific Ave Stockton CA 95211

HAFFNER, WILLIAM H.J. obstetrician, gynecologist; b. Jersey City, Mar. 31, 1939; s. William S. and Jean W. (Krueger) H.; m. Marlene E. Brings, Aug. 13, 1963; children: Stephanie E., Andrea J. AB, Wesleyan U., 1961; MD with distinction, George Washington U., 1965. Diplomate in surgery Am. Bd. Ob-Gyn., Nat. Bd. Med. Examiners. Surg. intern George Washington U. Hosp., Washington, 1965-66; resident in ob-gyn. Sloan-Columbia-Presbyn. Hosps., N.Y.C., 1966-71; head ob gyn. Gallup (N.Mex.) Indian Med. Ctr., 1971-81; staff Nat. Naval Med. Ctr., Bethesda, Md., 1981—; attending staff ob-gyn. Uniformed Svcs.-U. Health Scis., Bethesda, 1981—, resident program dir. ob-gyn., 1985-94, prof., 1992—, chmn., 1992—2003. Chief med. officer Office of Surgeon Gen. USPHS, 1990—94. Editor: Obstetric Neonatal and Gynecologic Care, 1993—. Fellow AMA, ACOG (Disting. Svc. award 2002), Am. Soc. Reproductive Medicine; mem. Assn. Profs. Gynecology and Obstetrics (coun. mem. 2000-2003, sec.-treas. 2003—), Coun. Univ. Chairs in Ob-Gyn., D.C. Gynecol. Soc., Alpha Omega Alpha. Office: Uniformed Svcs-U Health Sci Dept Ob-Gyn Bethesda MD 20814-4799 E-mail: whaffner@usuhs.mil.

HAFFORD, FAYE O'LEARY, writer; b. St. John Plantation, Maine, Apr. 27, 1925; d. Lee and Clara Mills O'Leary; m. Joseph Lee Hafford, Nov. 5, 1949 (dec. 1993); children: Michael Lee, Randi Lou. Student, Colby Coll., 1942—44; BS in Edn., U. Maine, 1965. Cert. elem. sch. tchr. Maine. Tchr. towns of Allagash, Limestone, Brunswick, Ft. Kent, Maine, 1951—76; ret. Author: 14 booklets on folklore of St. John Valleyl, 1986—. Contbr. curriculum guide Town of Brunswick; organizer, pres., vol. librarian Allagash Pub. Libr., 1998. Recipient County All Star award, Aroostook County, Presque Isle, Maine, 2000, Calendar award, Maine Ctr. for Women, 2000, Meritorious award, Nat. Coun. Geographic Edn., 1970, commendations for work on Allagash waterway, Gov. Maine, commendation, Maine Legis., Ken York award for work on Allagash Wilderness Waterway. Mem.: NEA, Aroostook Ret. Tchrs. Assn., Maine Ret. Tchrs. Assn., AARP. Republican. Congregationalist. Avocations: knitting, crocheting, fishing, camping, reading. Home: RFD # 1 Box 130 Allagash ME 04774 Office: Allagash Pub Libr 894 Allagash Rd Allagash ME 04774

HAFKENSCHIEL, JOSEPH HENRY, JR., cardiologist, educator; b. Youngstown, Ohio, Apr. 2, 1916; s. Joseph Henry and Anna Marie (Conroy) H.; m. Lucinda Buchanan Thomas, July 18, 1942 (dec. 1983); children: Joseph Henry III, Benjamin A. Thomas, Mark Conroy, John Proctor; m. Carol MacDonald Smith Rush, Jan. 25, 1985. AB, Swarthmore Coll., 1937; MD, Johns Hopkins U., 1941. Diplomate Am. Bd. Internal Medicine. Intern U. Pa. Hosp., Phila., 1941-42, resident, 1948-49, fellow in cardiology, 1949; instr. pharmacology U. Pa. Sch. Medicine, Phila., 1946-47, instr. medicine, 1949-51, assoc. medicine, 1951-66; cardiovasc. disease physician in pvt. practice Phila., 1949-65, Palo Alto, Calif., 1969-78; med. dir. West Coast Office Sandoz Pharm., San Francisco, 1965-67; staff physician Cowell Student Health Svcs. Stanford U., Calif., 1967-69, clin. instr. medicine, 1966-69, asst. to assoc. prof., 1969-84, emeritus clin. assoc. prof. medicine, 1984—. Staff physician Extended Care Svc. VA Med. Ctr., Palo Alto, 1978-84. Contbr. articles to profl. jours. Pres. Peninsula Meml. and Funeral Soc., Palo Alto, 1984. Maj. M.C., USAAF, 1942-46. Fellow ACP, Coll. Physicians Phila., Am. Heart Assn., Am. Physiol. Soc.; mem. Air Force Assn., Am. Irish Hist. Soc., San Francisco Golf Club, Merion Golf Club, Gulph Mills Golf Club, Ballybunion Golf (Ireland) Club, Am. Legion (post comdr. 1960-62), Sigma Xi. Republican. Roman Catholic. Avocations: world travel, golf, gardening, art history. Home: 870 Lesley Road Villanova PA 19085-1118 also: Box 191 11 Harborside Rd Northeast Harbor ME 04662-0191

HAFLING, MARILYN ELIZABETH, lawyer; b. Apr. 26, 1950; BA in Psychology, BS in Comm. Disorders, U. Minn., 1972; MS in Counseling Psychology, Nova U., 1984; JD, Stetson U., 1992. Bar: Fla. 1992. Clk. typist, tchr. asst., presch. dir., rsch. asst., 1966-73; speech pathologist Faribault (Minn.) State Hosp., 1973-75; program dir. REM Inc., Mpls., 1975-78; human svcs. counselor, supr. devel. svcs. State of Fla. Human Resource Svcs., 1979-89; atty. in pvt. practice Largo, Fla., 1992—. Mem. legal panel Pinellas ACLU, 1992—, bd. dirs., 1996-97; pres. bd. dirs. Resource Ctr. for Women, 1998—; mem. Women On the Way. Mem. NOW (pres. Pinellas chpt. 2002—), ABA, Fla. Bar Assn., Clearwater Bar Assn., Assn. Women Lawyers (pres. 1992). Office: 11740 Currie Ln Largo FL 33774-3843

HAFNER, JOSEPH A., JR., food company executive; b. San Bernadino, Calif., Oct. 9, 1944; s. Joseph Albert and Mary Florence (McGowan) H.; m. Merrill Hafner; children: John Michael, Daniel Stephen, Caroline Elizabeth. AB cum laude, Dartmouth Coll., 1966; MBA with high distinction, Amos Tuck Sch. Bus. Adminstrn., 1967. C.P.A. Intern Latin Am. Cornell U.-Ford Found., Lima,

Peru, 1967-69; sr. cons. Arthur Andersen & Co., Houston, 1969-71; controller C/A div. Riviana Internat., Inc., Guatemala City, Guatemala, 1972-73, treas., v.p. fin. Houston, 1973-77; v.p. Riviana Foods Inc., Houston, 1977-81, pres., chief operating officer, 1981-84, pres., chief exec. officer, 1984—, dir., 1985—. Recipient C.P.A. Gold medal Ark. State Bd. Pub. Accountancy, 1969 Mem. AICPA, Coun. on Fgn. Rels. Office: Riviana Foods Inc 2777 Allen Pky Houston TX 77019-2141

HAFNER, THOMAS MARK, lawyer; b. Evansville, Ind., Aug. 8, 1943; s. Theodore Paul and Josephine Margaret (Herpolsheimer) H.; m. Joy Ruth Roller, June 10, 1967; children: Mark, Sharon, Matthew, Michael, Martin. BA with distinction, Valparaiso U., 1965, JD, 1968. Bar: Ind. 1968, Tenn. 1980. Assoc. Nieter, Smith, Blume, Wyneken & Dixon, Ft. Wayne, Ind., 1968-70; atty. Magnavox Co., Ft. Wayne, Ind., 1970-73, group counsel, 1973-77; sr. counsel N.Am. Philips Corp., Ft. Wayne, Ind., 1977-80, Knoxville, Tenn., 1980-87, divsn. gen. counsel, 1988-89; v.p., gen. counsel Philips Consumer Electronics Co., Knoxville, Tenn., 1989-97, Atlanta, 1997-2000, Philips Consumer Electronics N.Am., Atlanta, 2000—. Dir. Cherokee Health Sys., Inc., 1995-97. Mem. Electronic Industries Assn. (chmn. govt. and consumer affairs coun. 1981-86, vice chmn. law com. 1986, chmn. 1987-88, bd. dirs. consumer electronics group 1991-94), Am. Corp. Counsel Assn. (bd. dirs. at large Tenn. chpt. 1986-88, 90-97).

HAFNER-EATON, CHRIS, health services researcher, medical educator, policy analyst; b. N.Y.C., Dec. 9, 1962; d. Peter Robert and Isabelle (Freda) Hafner; m. James Michael Eaton, Aug. 9, 1986; children: Kelsey James, Tristen Lee, Wesley Sean. BA, U. Calif., San Diego, 1986; MPH, UCLA, 1988, PhD Health Svcs. Rsch./Policy Analysis, 1992. Cert. health edn. specialist; internat. bd. cert. lactation cons. Cons. dental health policy UCLA Schl. Dentistry, 1989; grad. teaching asst. UCLA Sch. Pub. Health, 1987-92; health svcs. researcher UCLA, 1987-92; cons. health policy U.S. Dept. Health & Human Svcs., Washington, 1988—; analyst health policy The RAND/UCLA Ctr. Health Policy Study, Santa Monica & L.A., 1988-94; asst. prof. health care adminstrn. Oreg. State U. Dept. Pub. Health, Corvallis, 1992-95; pres. Health Improvement Svcs. Corp., 1994—; dir. rsch. rev. La Leche League Internat., 1996-99. Adj. faculty pub. health Linn-Benton Coll., 1993—, bd. dirs. Benton County Pub. Health Bd., Healthy Start Bd.; mem. Linn-Benton Breastfeeding Task Force, Samaritan Mother-Baby Dyad Team., Am. Public Hlth. Assn. (sect. Council Med. Care). Peer reviewer for NIH jours., others; contbr. articles to profl. jours. including JAMA, Midwifery Today, Jour. Ambulatory Care Mgmt.; other numerous lay publs. such as Mothering Mag.. Rsch. grantee numerous granting bodies, 1988—. Mem. AAUW, NOW, Internat. Lactation Cons. Assn., La Leche League Internat. (area profl. liaison for Oreg.), Am. Pub. Health Assn. (med. care sect. coun., women's caucus), Am. Assn. World Health, Oreg. Pub. Health Assn., Oreg. Health Care Assn., Assn. Health Svcs. Rsch., Soc. Pub. Health Edn., Physicians for Social Responsibility, UCLA Pub. Health Alumni Assn. (life), Pub. Health Honor Soc., Delta Omega. Home: 1807 NW Beca Ave Corvallis OR 97330-2636 E-mail: drmom@proaxis.com.

HAFT, GAIL KLEIN, pediatrician; b. N.Y.C., Mar. 5, 1938; d. Herbert and Pearl (Mittleman) Klein; m. Jacob I. Haft, Mar. 27, 1964; children: Bethanne, Ian. AB in Chemistry, Vassar Coll., 1959; MD, U. Rochester, 1963. Diplomate Nat. Bd. Med. Examiners, Am. Bd. Pediatrics. Intern Albert Einstein Coll. Medicine, N.Y.C., 1963-64, resident, 1964-65, Mt. Sinai Hosp., N.Y.C., 1967-68; pediatrician Dept. Health, Staten Island, N.Y., 1965-67, Head Start, Englewood, N.Y., 1969-71, Dept. Health, Hackensack, N.J., 1970-71; utilization rev. physician Hosp. Corp., N.Y.C., 1973-76; pediatrician Westchester County Health Dept., N.Y., 1974-76; sch. physician Bd. Edn., Yonkers, N.Y., 1974-76; bus. mgr. Heartronics, Newark, 1980-94; chief med. officer Bergen County Spl. Svcs., Paramus, N.J., 1984—; physician Tenafly (N.J.) Sch. Bd. Edn., 1990-94. Mem. Tenafly Bd. Edn., 1983-89, pres., 1986-88.

HAFTER, DARYL M. educator; b. Elizabeth, N.J. d. Harry and Theresa (Rothberg) Maslow; m. Monroe Z. Hafter, June 18, 1957; children: Matthew Ian, Naomi Eve. BA, Smith Coll., 1956; MA, Yale U., 1957, PhD, 1964. Lectr. U. Mich., Ann Arbor, 1967-68; asst. prof. Ea. Mich. U., Ypsilanti, 1969-73, assoc. prof., 1973-81, history prof., 1981—. Bd. dirs. women's studies Ea. Mich. U., 1982—84. Mem.: Soc. for History of Tech. (pres. 2001—03). Home: 1325 Brooklyn Ave Ann Arbor MI 48104-4414 Office: Ea Mich U Dept History & Philosophy Ypsilanti MI 48197

HAFTER, JEROME CHARLES, lawyer; b. Orlando, Fla., May 16, 1945; s. Jerome Sidney and Mary Margaret (Fugler) H.; m. Jo Cille Dawkins, July 18, 1976; 1 child, Jerome Bryan. BA summa cum laude, Rice U., 1967; BA with first class honours, Oxford U., Eng., 1969, MA, 1976; JD, Yale U., 1972. Bar: Miss. 1974, U.S. Ct. Appeals (5th cir.) 1974, U.S. Dist. Ct. (no. and so. dists.) Miss. 1974. Law clk. to presiding judge U.S. Ct. Appeals (5th cir.), Jackson, Miss., 1972-73; assoc. Lake, Tindall, Hunger & Thackston (now Lake Tindall LLP), Greenville, Miss., 1973-76, ptnr., 1976—2001, Phelps Dunbar LLP, Jackson, Miss., 2001—. Chmn. Miss. Bd. Bar Admissions, Jackson, 1979-2002; sec., treas. Hafter Realty Inc., Greenville, 1969-92, pres., 1992—; mem. gov.'s constn. commn., Jackson, 1985-87; sec., gen. counsel Delta and Pine Land Co., Scott, Miss., 1993— Author: Family History of Peter Quin, 1964, 2d. rev. edit., 1970. Pres. Downtown Improvement Assn. Greenville, 1980—, Common Cause/Miss., 1976-78; mem. Greenville City Election Commn., 1978—, Greenville Mcpl. Sch. Bd., 1988—, pres., 1995-96, 99-2000, 02-03; chmn. com. on tax Miss. Econ. Council, Jackson, 1985, 87, 96-98, pres., Greenville Area C. of C., 1992. Served to 1st lt., C.E., U.S. Army, 1972, maj., USAR, 1972-92, ret. Marshall scholar, 1967-69; Leadership Miss. Program fellow, 1976-77; Best Lawyers in Am., 2001-02, 2003-04 Fellow Miss. Bar Found.; mem. ABA (vice chmn. com. on issues affecting legal profession, young lawyers div., 1980-82, law sch. accreditation com. 1998-2002, mem. coun. sect. legal edn. and admissions to bar 2000—), Miss. Bar Assn. (bd. dirs. young lawyers divsn. 1976-79, pres. fellows young lawyers divsn., 2000-01, chmn. sect. corp. fin. bus. law 1989-90), Fed. Bar Assn. (v.p. no. Miss. 1977-78, 81-82), Nat. Conf. Bar Examiners (MBE com. 1986-88, trustee 1989-2000, chmn. 1998-99), Am. Judicature Soc., Am. Law Inst., Greenville C. of C. (bd. dirs. 1976-79, pres. 1992-93), Washington County Hist. Soc. (pres. Greenville chpt. 1981), Miss. Bankruptcy Conf. (chmn. com. on bankruptcy rules 1988), Phi Beta Kappa. Clubs: Greenville Golf and Country (v.p. 1977-79); Huntercombe Golf (Nuffield, Eng.), Annandale Golf (Madison, Miss.); Vincents (Oxford, Eng.). Lodges: Kiwanis (Greenville pres. 1978-79, lt. gov. 1982-83). Episcopalian. Home: 315 Wetherbee St Greenville MS 38701 Office: Phelps Dunbar LLP PO Box 23066 111 E Capitol Ste 600 Jackson MS 39201 E-mail: hafterj@phelps.com, hafter@tecinfo.net.

HAGA, ENOCH JOHN, computer educator, author; b. L.A., Apr. 25, 1931; s. Enoch and Esther Bonser (Higginson) H.; m. Elna Jo Wright, Aug. 22, 1957. AA, Grant Tech. Coll., 1950; AB, Sacramento State Coll., 1955, MA, 1958; PhD, Calif. Inst. Integral Studies, 1972. Tchr. bus. Calif. Med. Facility, Vacaville, 1956-60; asst. prof. bus. Stanislaus State Coll., Turlock, Calif., 1960-61; engring. writer, publs. engr. Hughes Aircraft Co., Fullerton, Calif., 1961-62, Lockheed Missiles & Space Co., Sunnyvale, Calif., 1962, Gen. Precision, Inc., Glendale, Calif., 1962-63; sr. adminstrv. analyst Holmes & Narver, Inc., L.A., 1963-64; tchr., chmn. dept. bus. and math. Pleasanton (Calif.) Unified Dist., 1964-92, coord. computer svcs., adminstrn., instrn., 1984-85. Vis. asst. prof. bus. Sacramento State Coll., 1967-69; instr. bus. and computer sci. Chabot Coll., Hayward, Calif., 1970-89; instr. bus. and philosophy Ohlone Coll., Fremont, Calif., 1972; prof., v.p., mem. bd. govs. Calif. Inst. Asian Studies, 1972-75; pres., prof. Pacific Inst. East-West Studies, San Francisco, 1975-76, also mem. bd. govs.; dir. Cert. Couns., Livermore, Calif., 1975-80; mem., chmn. negotiating team Amador Vly. Secondary Educators Assn., Pleasanton, 1976-77, pres. 1984-85. With USAF, 1949-52, with USNR, 1947-49, 53-57. Coordinating editor Total Systems, 1962; editor Automation Educator, 1965-67, Automated Educational Systems, 1967, Data Processing in Biomedicine and Medicine, 1973; contbg. editor Jour. Bus. Edn., 1961-69, Data Processing mag., 1967-70; author, compiler: Understanding Automation, 1965; author: Simplified Computer Arithmetic, Simplified Computer Logic, Simplified Computer Input, Simplified Computer Flowcharting, 1971-72, Before the Apple Drops, 15 Essays on Dinosaur Education, 2d edit., 1997, Exploring Prime Numbers on Your PC and the Internet, 2001, How to Prepare Your Genealogy for Publication on Your Home Computer, 2001, TAROsolution: A Complete Guide to Interpreting Tarot, 1994, The 2000-Year History of the Haga-Helgoy and Krick-Keller Families, Ancestors and Descendants, 1994; editor Data Processor, 1960-62, Automedica, 1970-76, FBE Bull., 1967-68. Mem. Internat. Assn. Computer Info. Sys. (exec. dir. 1970-74). Home: 983 Venus Way Livermore CA 94550-6345 E-mail: Enokh@aol.com.

HAGAN, ANN P. lawyer; b. Mexico, Mo., Oct. 6, 1955; d. Ray J. and Margaret B. H.; m. James M. DeLong, June 4, 1983; children: Shelley, Ross. BA, Rockhurst Coll., 1978; JD, U. Mo., Kansas City, 1981. Bar: Mo. 1981, Ill. 1982, U.S. Dist. Ct. (ea. and we. dists.) Mo., U.S. Ct. Appeals (8th cir.), U.S. Supreme Ct. Assoc. Brown & James, St. Louis, 1981-83; shareholder Seigfreid, Runge et al, Mexico, 1983-93; ptnr. Hagan, Hamlett, Maxwell, L.L.C., Mexico, 1993—. Vice-pres. Altrusa Internat., Mexico, 1984, pres., 1993-94; legal com. chair United Way, Mexico, 1990; pres. St. Brendan sch. bd.; bd. mem. Audrain County Health Care, Inc. Mem. ABA, Mo. Bar Assn., Mo. Def. Lawyers, Def. Rsch. Inst., Audrain County Bar Assn. Avocations: fishing, horses, music. Office: Hagan Hamlett Maxwell LLC 210 E Love St Mexico MO 65265-2880 E-mail: hhmlaw@sbcglobal.net.

HAGAN, DAVID, musician, educator; b. Frederick, Md., Feb. 18, 1943; s. Henry David Hagan and Bettina Adele Colliflower; m. Karin Storm Ulanowsky. MusB, Peabody Conservatory of Music, Balt., 1966, MusM, 1965. Piano instr. Peabody Conservatory Prep. Sch., Balt., 1964—66, Coll. Notre Dame of Md., Balt., 1966—68, Dickinson Coll., Carlisle, Pa., 1966—68; piano instr. New England Conservatory, Boston, 1968—78; instr. piano, duo-piano, chamber music New England Coservatory Preparatory and Continuing Edn., 1975—; piano instr. Conn. Coll., New London, Conn., 1985—90, Milton Acad., Milton, Mass., 1996—. Musician: (performances) N.Y. recital debut, 1968, London recital debut, 1974, (recitals) ea. U.S., Cen. Am., Germany, (recs.) Bruch: Concerto for Two Pianos and Orchestra, 1977, Bach-Reger: Brandenburg Concertos for piano duet, 1975, Bach-Reger: Orchestral Suites for piano duet, 1976, Mendelssohn-Moscheles: Duo Concertante, 1977, (world premiere performance) Bruch Concerto for Two Pianos and Orchestra, 1977, (music of George Crumb) Night Music II, 1979. Stoeckel fellow, Yale U., 1967. Avocations: photography, steam railways, model railways, cathedral architecture. Office: New England Conservatory 290 Huntington Ave Boston MA 02115 Personal E-mail: haganpiano@yahoo.com.

HAGAN, JOHN AUBREY, financial executive, retired; b. Pulaski, Tenn., Sept. 30, 1936; s. Edwin Jackson and Rebecca Maria (Smith) H.; m. Nicole Emilie Thiltges, Sept. 7, 1958; children— Mark, Alex, Micheline. AB, Harvard U., 1958, MBA, 1963. With R. J. Reynolds Tobacco Co. (name later changed to R. J. Reynolds Industries, then to RJR Nabisco), Winston-Salem, NC, 1963-85, asst. contr., 1970-75, contr., chief acctg. officer internal auditing and fin. info. sys., 1975-79, v.p., contr., 1979-85; CFO Embrex Inc., Research Triangle Park, NC, 1986-95, v.p. fin. and adminstrn., 1988-95, ret., 1995. Bd. dirs. United Way of Forsyth County, 1976-80, pres., 1979. Officer USN, 1958-61. Mem. Fin. Execs. Inst. (com. on corp. reporting 1979-85, pres. N.C. chpt. 1981-82), Common Cause, Greater Winston-Salem C. of C. (speakers bur. 1977-85), Am. Mgmt. Assn. (fin. coun. 1981-86). Home: 104 W Lochwood Dr Cary NC 27511-9744 Personal E-mail: njhagan@att.net.

HAGAN, JOHN CHARLES, III, ophthalmologist; b. Mexico, Mo., Oct. 7, 1943; s. John Charles Hagan II and Cleta L. (Book) Neely; m. Rebecca Jane Chapman, July 15, 1967; children: Carol Ann, Catherine Elizabeth. BA, U. Mo., 1965; MD, Loyola U., Chgo., 1969. Diplomate Am. Bd. Ophthalmology. Intern Med. Coll. Wis., Milw., 1969-70; resident in ophthalmology Emory U., Atlanta, 1972-75; practice medicine, Kansas City, Mo., 1975—. Cons. Am. Running and Phys. Fitness Assn., Washington, 1973—. Editor: Mo. Medicine: The Jour. of the Mo. State Med. Assn.; contbr. over 100 articles to med. jours. Capt. M.C., USAF, 1970-72. Fellow ACS; mem. AMA, Am. Soc. Cataract and Refractive Surgery, Mo. Soc. Eye Physicians and Surgeons (pres. 1998), Kansas City Soc. Ophthalmology. Office: Discover Vision Ctrs 9401 N Oak Trafficway Kansas City MO 64155

HAGAN, JOSEPH HENRY, higher education consultant; b. Providence, Mar. 2, 1935; s. Joseph Henry and Claire Veronica (Gorman) H.; m. Patrice O'Malley; 1 child, Kevin O'Malley. AB, Providence Coll.; EdM, Boston U.; D. Min., EdD, Grad. Theol. Found.; hon. degree (hon.), Salve Regina Coll., Mount St. Joseph Coll., Bryant Coll., Boston U., Providence Coll., Assumption Coll., Rivier Coll. Tchr. Providence Public Schs., 1958-61; legis. asst. U.S. Ho. of Reps., 1961-64; staff asst. Pres.'s Com. on Juvenile Delinquency, 1964-65; spl. asst. OEO, 1965-68; dir. planning, devel. and fed. relations Bryant Coll., Smithfield, R.I., 1968-70, v.p. for public affairs, 1970-73, lectr. public adminstrn., adj. prof. social scis.; asst. to chmn. Nat. Endowment for Humanities, Washington, 1973-78; pres., lectr. politics Assumption Coll., Worcester, Mass., 1978-98, pres. emeritus, 1998—; pres. Roger Williams U., Bristol, RI, 1999—2001. Chmn. bd. trustees John Cabot U., Rome; mem. Nat. Coun. on the Humanities, 1992-2000; pres., trustee Cardinal Tardini Charitable Trust; chmn. budget com. Little Compton, R.I., 1999-2001, mem. zoning bd., 2001—. Decorated Knight of Honor and Devotion in Obedience of Malta, Knight Grand Cross, St. Gregory the Great, comdr. Palmes Academiques (France), Knight Grand Cross of Justice of the Sacred Mil. Constantinian Order St. George, Knight comdr. Order of Saints Maurice & Lazarus, Knight Comdr. with star of the Holy Sepulchre, Comdr. of Order of Merit, Knights of Malta, Gentleman-in-Waiting to Pope John Paul II. Mem. Am. Antiquarian Soc., N.Am. Assn. Constantinian Order (pres.), Univ. Club (Providence), Sakonnet Golf Club, Circulo della Caccia (Rome), KC, Univ. Club (Washington). Roman Catholic.

HAGAN, JUDITH ANN, social worker; b. Chgo., May 7, 1943; d. Glenn Dean and Laura May Phillips; children: Stephen L. Curtis, Michael L. Curtis; m. George Leonard Hagan, Nov. 13, 1993. AA with highest distinction, Scottsdale (Ariz.) C.C., 1978; BS magna cum laude, Ariz. State U., 1979, MSW, 1985. Cert. ind. social worker, Ariz.; cert. in critical incident stress mgmt., FEMA. Bus. assoc. Am. Express, Phoenix, 1980-89; client svcs. rep. Pharm. Card System, Scottsdale, 1986-87; case mgr. Child Protective Svcs., State of Ariz., Phoenix, 1985; dir. social svcs. S.W. Adoptions, Scottsdale, 1989-92; employee assistance profl. Ariz. Dept. Transp., Phoenix, 1992-96; pvt. practice psychotherapy; program and projects specialist with procurement staff Ariz. Dept. Transp., Phoenix, 1996—2002; owner, operator Complete Counseling Svcs., Phoenix; mobil therapist Terros Behavioral Health Agy., Phoenix, 2002—03; counselor II Valle Del Sol, Inc., 2003—. Presenter programs on reconstituted families, relationships and mental health, drug abuse, stress mgmt.; freelance writer, editor. Writer, editor Ariz. Dept. Transp. Women's Resource Group Newsletter; editor pub. newsletter Procurement Update, 1997-2002; author, dir., pub. tng. film Panorama of County Services for Managers, 1984; author Ariz. Dept. Transp. Intellectual Properties Drug Abuse Program, 1993; column writer Moon Valley Tattler, 1999-2003. Vol. in cmty. devel. Battered Women's and Children's Shelter Maricopa County, Phoenix, 1979; activist Civil Rights, Sumter, S.C., 1962, Green Peace, L.A., 1971, NOW, 1980, Citizens against Cockfighting, 1998, Yr. of the Humane Child, 2000. With U.S. Women's Army Corps, 1973-74. Recipient seal Acad. Cert. Social Workers, Washington, 1996-97. Mem.: Women in Mil. Svc. for Am. (charter), Ariz. Counselors Assn. (policy com., editor newsletter 2003—), Phi Theta Kappa. Avocations: healthy gourmet cooking, yoga, public speaking. Address: 1209 S 1st Ave Phoenix AZ 85003

HAGAN, PETER ANTHONY, lawyer; b. Staten Island, N.Y., Nov. 30, 1947; s. Peter Anthony and Frances Theresa (Golumb) H.; m. Barbara Ann Sibulski, Apr. 29, 1973; children: Marygrace, Patrick, Michael, Elizabeth. AB, Fordham U., 1969; JD, St. John's U., 1972; MLS, Pratt Inst., 1978; LLM, NYU, 1983. Bar: N.Y. 1973, U.S. Dist. Ct. (ea. and so. dists.) N.Y., U.S. Ct. Appeals (2nd cir.) 1977, Pa. 1989. Sr. atty. Consol. Edison, N.Y.C., 1973—. Atty. Pax Christi, N.Y.C., 1983—. Author: Scout Leaders Legal Guidebook. Lt. JAGC USMC, 1969-73. Recipient Eagle Scout award Boy Scouts Am. Mem. Emerald Soc., Right to Life Party, Phi Beta Kappa. Roman Catholic. Avocations: running, weightlifting, scouting. Home: 134 Greeley Ave Staten Island NY 10306-3213 Office: Consol Edison 4 Irving Pl New York NY 10003-3502

HAGAR, JOANNE MARIE, physician assistant; b. Wellsboro, Pa., Mar. 30, 1961; d. Fordyce John and Theresa Mary Hagar. BSEd in Biology and Chemistry, Mansfield U., 1985; cert. physician assistant, Gannon U., 1991. Cert. Nat. Commn. Cert. Physician Assts., Inc. Family practice physician assistant 5th Ave. Med. Assocs., Inc., Coraopolis, Pa., 1991-93, Mars (Pa.) Med. Clinic, 1993-95; emergency room physician assistant Greene County Meml. Hosp., Waynesburg, Pa., 1995-97, Citizens Gen. Hosp., New Kensington, Pa., 1995-97; internal medicine physician assistant Surinder S. Bajwa & Daniel R. Casper, New Kensington, 1997-99; family practice physician asst. Office of Elizabeth-Ann Ruberg, Moon, Pa., 2000—. Mem. Am. Assn. Physician Assts., Pa. Soc. Physician Assts. (Region I rep. 2002—), Bus. and Profl. Women's Club (v.p. 1995-97). Democrat. Presbyterian. Avocations: skiing, running, working out. Home: 428 Scottsdale Dr Moon Township PA 15108

HAGAR, RICHARD JOSEPH, music educator, musician; b. Brockton, Mass., July 15, 1954; s. Preston Irving and Marie Mahoney Hagar; m. Charlene Ann Hagar, Aug. 2, 1986. B in Music and Music Edn., Hartt Coll. of Music, 1976. Cert. tchr. music K-12 Mass., Conn., N.Y. Tchr. string instruments, orch. and chorus dir. Delaware Acad., Delhi, NY, 1976—78; tchr. string instruments, orch. dir. Bedford (Mass.) Pub. Schs., 1978—88, Westborough (Mass.) Pub. Schs., 1988—. Named Mass. Orch. Dir. of Yr., 2000; recipient Lowell Mason award for outstanding contbns. to music edn., 1999. Mem.: Mass. Music Educators' Assn. (treas. Northea. Dist. 1982—86, all-state conf. exec. bd. 1993—98, 2002—, membership coord. Northea. Dist. 1980—93, all-state orch. mgr. 1998—2000), Westborough Tchrs. Assn., Mass. Tchrs. Assn., Am. String Teachers Assn. with Nat. Sch. Orch. Assn. (pres. Mass. chpt. 1982—86, exec. bd. Mass. chpt. 1990—), Music Educators' Nat. Conf. Home: 20 Greybert Ln Worcester MA 01602

HAGART-ALEXANDER, CLAUD, software engineer; b. Edinburgh, Scotland, Nov. 5, 1963; s. Claud and Hilda Etain Hagart-Alexander; m. Elaine Susan Park, June 24, 1994; 1 child, Claud Miles Park Alexander. BS in Engring. (hons.), U. of Glasgow, Scotland, U.K., 1985. Software engr. Hawker Siddeley Dynamics Engring., Welwyn Garden City, England, 1985—87, Dynamic Control Systems, Vancouver, Canada, 1987—88; control sys. software engr. Devron-Hercules, North Vancouver, Canada, 1987—92; control sys. dir. Measurex-Devron, North Vancouver, Canada, 1992—98; application controls dir. Honeywell, Cupertino, Calif., 1998—. Author: (several tech. papers) Pulp and Paper. Mem.: Pulp and Paper Tech. Assn. of Can. (assoc.). Achievements include patents for Paper stock shear and formation control; Wet end control for papermaking machine; Fast CD and MD control in a sheetmaking machine; Paper stock zeta potential measurement and control; Means of correcting a measurement of a property of a material with a sensor that is affected by a second property of that material. Home: 514 Jeter St Redwood City CA 94062 Personal E-mail: claudha@comcast.net.

HAGARTY, EILEEN MARY, pulmonary clinical nurse specialist; b. Chgo., June 17, 1950; d. Lawrence C. and Eleanore R. (Mark) Pauls; m. Jon R. Hagarty, June 23, 1979; children: Patrick Michael, Rita Kristine. BSN, DePaul U., Chgo., 1974; MS, No. Ill. U., 1975. RN, Ill.; cert. clin. specialist in med.-surg. nursing. Staff nurse Edward Hines Jr. VA Hosp., Hines, Ill., 1971-75, pulmonary clin. nurse specialist, 1975—. Chair membership com. of nursing assembly Chgo. Lung Assn., 1980-86; co-chairperson accreditation subcom. Great Lakes VA Health Care Sys.; nat. recognized lectr. in the field of pulmonary nursing, funded prin. investigator. Contbr. articles to profl. jours. Recipient Excellence in Nursing award Dept. VA, 1992. Mem. ANA (task force), Ill. Nurses Assn., Respiratory Nursing Soc. Avocations: boating, fishing, travel. Home: 7824 Mayfair Ln Darien IL 60561-4864 Office: Edward Hines Jr Hosp 118B Dept VA Hines IL 60141 E-mail: Eileen.Hagarty@med.va.gov.

HAGBERG, CHRIS ERIC, lawyer; b. Steubenville, Ohio, Dec. 19, 1949; s. Rudolf Eric and Sara (Smith) H.; m. Viola Louise Wilgus, Feb. 19, 1978. BS, Duke U., 1975; JD, U. Tulsa, 1978; postgrad., Nat. Law Ctr., George Washington U. Bar: Okla. 1978, Va. 1979, U.S. Ct. Appeals (4th cir.) Calif. 1986. Law clk. to presiding justice U.S. Dist. Ct. (no. dist.) Okla.; asst. counsel ADP Selection Office Dept. Navy, Navy Regional Contracting Ctr., Washington; counsel Naval Supply Ctr., Pearl Harbor, Hawaii; Pacific area counsel Naval Supply Sys. Command, Dept. Navy, Makakilo, Hawaii; assoc. counsel Navy Supply Sys. Command, Washington; atty. Pettit & Martin, L.A., 1985-87, Seyfarth, Shaw, Fairweather and Geraldson, Washington, 1988-91, U.S. Coast Guard HQ, Washington, 1992-93, USN, 1993-95; Dept. Navy OGC/NSWC Carderock, West Bethesda, Md., 1995—. Contbr. articles to legal jours. Lt. USN, 1970-74. Recipient David I. Milsten award, 1978, 7 Am. Jurisprudence awards, 1976-78, First prize Dept. Navy Legal Writing Contest, 1981. Mem. ABA, FBA, Nat. Contract Mgmt. Assn., Order of Coif. Presbyterian. Home: 9810 Meadow Valley Dr Vienna VA 22181-3215

HAGBERG, VIOLA WILGUS, lawyer; b. Salisbury, Md., July 3, 1952; d. William E. and Jean Shelton (Barlow) Wilgus; m. Chris Eric Hagberg, Feb. 19, 1978. BA, Furman U., Greenville, S.C., 1974; JD, U. S.C., 1978, U. Tulsa, 1978; DOD Army Logistics Sch. honor grad. basic mgmt. def. acquisition, def. small purchase, advanced fed. acquisition regulation, Fort Lee, Va., 1981-82. Bar: Okla. 1978, Va. 1979, U.S. Ct. Appeals (4th cir.) 1979. With Lawyers Com. for Civil Rights, Washington, 1979; pub. utility specialist Fed. Energy Regulatory Commn., Washington, 1979-80; contract specialist U.S. Army, C.E., Ft. Shafter, Hawaii, 1980-81; contract officer/supervisory contract specialist Tripler Army Med. Ctr., Hawaii 1981-83; supervisory procurement analyst and chief policy Procurement Div. USCG, Washington, 1983; contracts officer and chief Avionics Engring Contracting Br., 1984; procurement analyst office of sec. Dept. Transp., 1984-85; contracting officer Naval Regional Contracting Ctr., Long Beach, Calif., 1985-87; chief acquisition rev. and policy, Hdqrs. Def. Mapping Agy., Washington, 1987-92, dir. acquisitions, Fairfax, Va., 1992-93, dir. acquisition policy, 1994-96; dir. acquisition polity, tech., and legis. programs Nat. Mapping and Imagery Agy., 1996-97, Office of Gen. Counsel. Mem. ABA (law student div. liaison 1977-78), Nat. Contract Mgmt. Assn., Va. State Bar Assn., Okla. Bar Assn., Phi Alpha Delta, Kappa Delta Epsilon. Home: 9810 Meadow Valley Dr Vienna VA 22181-3215 Office: Nat Imagery and Mapping Agy Office Gen Counsel 4600 Sangamore (MS-D-10) Bethesda MD 20816

HAGE, GEORGE CAMPBELL, social studies educator, minister, and counselor; b. Huntington, W.Va., Nov. 12, 1944; s. Campbell Joseph and Martha (George) H.; m. Ellen Elaine Harner, July 1, 1972; 1 child, Shauna Kristin. BA, Marshall U., 1971; BRE, Washington Bible Coll., 1971; M in Edn., U. N.C., Greensboro, 1984, EdD, 1990. Lic. tchr., N.C.; lic. profl. counselor, N.C.; ordained to ministry Christian Ch. (Disciples of Christ), 1982. Religious educator, 1971—; tchr. adult and continuing edn. Forsyth Tech. C.C., Winston Salem, N.C., 1979-85; min. New Hope Christian Ch., Winston Salem, N.C., 1982-88; rsch. asst. Sch. Edn. U. N.C., Greensboro, 1986-89; social studies tchr. Guilford Tech. C.C., Greensboro, 1986-88, Carver High Sch., Winston Salem, 1988-89; min. South Pk. Christian Ch., Reidsville, N.C., 1988-89; social studies tchr. Forsyth Tech. C.C., Winston Salem, 1990—; social worker/therapist Children's Home, Inc., Winston Salem, 1989-92; assoc. min. Trinity Christian Ch., 1990—; social worker/therapist Elon Homes for Children, 1993; youth and family therapist Host Homes of Cath. Social Svcs., Winston Salem, 1992-98; program dir., therapist, chaplain Seven Homes: A Residential Youth Devel. Alternative, Inc., High Point, NC, 1999—. Author: The Seed Within You, 1976, A Symbolic Analysis of the Dimensions of Holiness in American Culture and Curriculum: Toward a Symbolic Synthesis of Wholeness, 1990; author poems (winner of George Herbert Meml. Poetry Competition 1982); composer booklet: Rhapsodia Fantsia: A Musical Design for an Autobiographical Theory of Curriculum, 1986. Recipient Editor's Choice award Nat. Libr. Poetry, 1996; named Poet of Yr. Internat. Soc. Poets, 1996. Fellow Nat. Coun. Social Studies (presdl. appointee adv. com. religion 1986-90), Winston-Salem Profl. Piano Tchrs. Assn.; mem. Internat. Soc. Poets (disting. mem.), Chi Alpha Omega. Avocations: writing poetry, writing music, pianist, organist, painting and drawing. Address: 1514 Berwick Rd Winston Salem NC 27103-4704 E-mail: drqchage@wmconnect.com.

HAGEDORN, DONALD JAMES, phytopathologist, educator, agricultural consultant; b. Moscow, Idaho, May 18, 1919; s. Frederick William and Elizabeth Viola (Scheyer) H.; m. Eloise Tierney, July 18, 1943; 1 child, James William BS, U. Idaho, 1941, DSc (hon.), 1979; MS, U. Wis., 1943, PhD, 1948. Prof. agronomy and plant pathology U. Wis., Madison, 1948-64, prof. plant pathology, 1964—. Courtesy prof. plant pathology Oreg. State U., Covallis, 1972-73; vis. scientist DSIR Lincoln Rsch. Ctr., Christchurch, N.Z., 1980-81; cons. Asgrow Seed Co., 1987-93; affiliate prof. plant pathology U. Idaho, 1991—. Contbr. chpts. to books, articles to profl. jours. With USAAF, 1943-46.

Recipient Campbell award AAAS, 1961, CIBA-Geigy award, 1974, Meritorious Svc. award Nat. Pea Improvement Assn., 1979, Bean Improvement Coop., 1979, Forty-Niners award, 1983, Citation for Outstanding Sci. Achievement, Wis. Acad. Letters, Arts and Scis., 1986; NSF sr. fellow, 1957; named Disting. Centennial Alumnus, U. Idaho, 1989; named to U. Idaho Alumni Hall of Fame, 1990. Fellow Am. Phytopath. Soc.; mem. Kiwanis, Sigma Xi, Gamma Sigma Delta, Alpha Zeta. Methodist. Home: 927 University Bay Dr Madison WI 53705-2248 Office: U Wis 583 Russell Labs 1630 Linden Dr Madison WI 53706-1520

HAGEDORN, LINDA SERRA, education educator, researcher; b. Chgo., Dec. 12, 1951; d. Genaro Victor Serra and Ruth Bass; m. Timothy William Hagedorn, June 5, 1981; children: Aaron, Serra. BA, Elmhurst Coll., 1973; MEd, Nat. Louis U., 1990; PhD, U. Ill., Chgo., 1995. Electronic exch. engr. GTE Automatic Electric, Northlake, Ill., 1973-77; electronics instr. Triton Coll., River Grove, Ill., 1977-85; tchr. Cmty. Consol. Sch. Dist. 15, Palatine, Ill., 1985-91; rsch. assoc. Nat. Ctr. for Tchg. Learning and Assessment, Chgo., 1991-94, postdoctoral fellow, 1994-96; assoc. prof. U. So. Calif., L.A., 1996—; assoc. dir. Ctr. for Higher Edn. Policy Analysis, 2001—; dir. transfer and retention project L.A. C.C. Dist., L.A., 2002—. Trustee Sias U., Zhengzhou, China, 1999—. Mem. editl. bd. Rev. Higher Edn., 1999—; contbr. articles to profl. jours. Grantee Assessment for Student Devel. Rsch. grant Am. Coll. Pers. Assn., 1996-97, Improving Instnl. Rsch. in Postsecondary Edn. Instns. Database Inst. scholar NCES, Washington, 1997, grantee U.S. Dept. Edn., 2000-03; recipient Mertes award for excellence in cmty. coll. rsch., Assn. Calif. C.C. Adminstrs., 1997, Promising Scholar award Assn. for Study Higher Edn., 2000, Socrates award for Tchg., 2000, Mem. Am. Ednl. Rsch. Assn. (bd. mem., exec. coun. 1998-2000, v.p. divsn. J -2004. Home: 23545 Estrella Pl Valencia CA 91355-2132 Office: Univ So Calif 3470 Trousdale Pkwy Los Angeles CA 90089-0017 Fax: 213-740-3889. E-mail: lsh@usc.edu.

HAGEE, JESKO MICHAEL, naval officer; b. Calif., 1973; BS in Sys. Engring., U.S. Naval Acad., Annapolis, 1995; MS in Elec. Engring. and Computer Sci., MIT, 1997. Commd. ensign USN, 1995, advanced through grades to lt., 1995, aux. officer, 1997-98, tng. officer, 1998-99, navigator, 1999-2000; instr. U.S. Naval Acad., Annapolis, Md., 2000—. Mem. Phi Kappa Phi, Sigma Xi, Tau Beta Pi.

HAGEE, MICHAEL W. commandant of the US Marine Corps; BS in Engring. with distinction, U.S. Naval Acad., 1968; MSEE, U.S. Naval Postgrad. Sch., 1969; MA in Nat. Security/Strategic Studies, Naval War Coll., 1987; Grad., Command and Staff Coll., 1982, U.S. Naval War Coll., 1987. Commd. 2d lt. USMC, 1968, advanced through grades to brig. gen., 1996—; command positions include 1st Btn., 8th Marines, 1988-90; commanding officer 11th Marine Expeditionary Unit, 1992-93; various to exec. asst. to asst. commandant USMC, 1993-94; dir. Character Devel. Divsn. U.S. Naval Acad., 1994-95; sr. mil. asst. to dep. sec. of def. Office of Sec. of Def., Washington, 1995-96; exec. asst. to dir. CIA, Washington, 1995-96; dep. dir. opers. Hdqtrs., U.S. European Command, Stuttgart, Germany, 1996-98; dir. strategic planning and policy U.S. Pacific Command, 1999—2000; commd. gen. I Marine Expeditionary Force, 2000—02; commd. US Marine Corps, Washington, 2003—. Decorated Def. Disting. Svc. medal, Legion of Merit with two gold stars, Bronze Star with Combat "V", Def. Meritorious Svc. medal with one gold star, Navy Achievement medal with one gold star, Combat Action Ribbon, Nat. Intelligence Disting. Svc. medal. Office: Commd USMC Petangon Washington DC 20350*

HAGEL, CHARLES, senator; b. North Platte, Nebr., Oct. 4, 1946; m. Lilibet Ziller; 2 children. Student, Brown Inst. Radio & TV, Minn., 1966; BA, U. Nebr., 1971. Dep. adminstr. VA, 1981-82; pres./CEO World USO, 1987-90; pres. McCarthy & Co., 1991-96; U.S. senator from Nebr., 1996—. Mem. internat. fin., fgn. rels. coms. U.S. Senate, chmn. senate global climate change observer group, mem. NATO observer group; mem. coms. banking, housing and urban affairs, 1997—, spl. com. on aging, 1997—; founder/dir. Vanguard Cellular Syss. Inc. Active Bellevue U., Red Cross, No Greater Love, World USO; chair Paralyzed Veterans of Am., 10 Anniversary Vietnam Vets. Meml. With U.S. Army, 1967-68. Mem. Am. Legion VFW, Omaha C. of C. (trustee). Republican. Office: 248 Russell Senate Office Bldg Washington DC 20510-0001*

HAGEL, JOHN, III, management consultant; b. Berlin, N.H., Sept. 14, 1950; s. John Jr. and Evelyn Gertrude (Parent) H. BA, Wesleyan U., 1972; PhB, Oxford U., 1974; MBA, JD, Harvard U., 1978. Bar: Mass. 1978. Cons. Boston Cons. Group, 1978-80; pres. Sequoia Group, Larkspur, Calif., 1980-82; v.p. Atari, Inc., Sunnyvale, Calif., 1982-83, sr. v.p., 1983-84; sr. engagement mgr. McKinsey and Co., N.Y.C., 1984-87, prin. San Francisco, 1987-2000; chief strategy officer 12 Entrepreneuring, Inc., San Francisco, 2000—02; pres. Bus. Performance Network, Burlingame, 2002—. Author: Alternative Energy Strategies, 1976, Assessing The Criminal, 1977, Net Gain: Expanding Markets Through Virtual Communities, 1997, Net Worth: Shaping Markets When Customers Make the Rules, 1999, Out of the Box: Strategies for Achieving Profits Today and Growth Tomorrow through Web Services, 2002; contbr. articles to profl. jours. Keasbey Found. fellow, 1972-74; Forum fellow World Econ. Forum, 1999-2003. Mem. ABA, Mass. Bar Assn. Episcopalian. E-mail: jh@johnhagel.com.

HAGEL, RAYMOND CHARLES, publishing company executive, educator; b. Jersey City, Sept. 5, 1916; s. Morris and Theresa (Feigenbaum) H.; m. Ruth Block, May 30, 1941; children: Keith W., Wendy A. BS cum laude, NYU, 1937. Promotion mgr. McGraw-Hill Pub. Co., 1937-38, 41-42, 45-46; with bus. dept. N.Y. World-Telegram, 1939-40; with Asso. Mag. Contbrs., Inc., 1947-48; pres. Smith, Hagel & Knudsen, Inc., N.Y.C., 1948-59, P.F. Collier & Son Corp., N.Y.C., 1959-60, chmn. bd., 1961-65; exec. v.p. Crowell-Collier Pub. Co. (name changed to Crowell Collier and Macmillan, Inc. 1965, Macmillan Inc., 1973), 1959-60, pres., 1960-76, chief exec. officer, 1963-80, chmn. bd., 1964-80, also bd. dirs. David L. Tandy exec.-in-resident, vis. prof. M.J. Neeley Sch. Bus., Tex. Christian U., 1980-81, mem. adv. bd. dept. journalism, 1981—; prof. mgmt. Barney Sch. Bus. and Public Adminstrn., U. Hartford, 1981-90, chmn. dept. mgmt., 1983-84; mem. Rockefeller Center adv. bd. Chem. Bank, N.Y.C.; mem. Council Internat. Exec. Service Corps.; disting. adj. prof. Coll. Bus. and Pub. Adminstrn., NYU, 1972-79, mem. dean's adv. council, 1973 Trustee, Coll. of New Rochelle, 1970-76, 77-80. Served with USNR, 1942-45. Recipient John T. Madden Meml. medal NYU, 1972; Disting. Service award in investment edn. Investment Edn. Inst. of Nat. Assocs. Investment Clubs, 1973; Madden asso., Gallatin asso. NYU Mem. Fgn. Policy Assn., Am. Assn. Higher Edn., Dirs. Table, Assn. Am. Pubs., Alpha Delta Sigma, Beta Gamma Sigma, Beta Alpha Psi, Econ. Club, Metro. Club, Pub.'s Lunch Club.

HAGEL, WILLIAM CARL, metallurgical consultant; b. Pitts., Apr. 5, 1927; s. William and Mabel Florence (Geary) H.; m. Mary Ellen Roosa; children: Lisa Christine, Karen Andrea, Juliana Margaret. B in Metall. Engring., Cornell U., 1951; MS, PhD in Metallurgy, Carnegie-Mellon U., 1954. Metallurgist GE Co. Rsch. Lab., Schenectady, N.Y., 1954-66; prof., chmn. metallurgy dept. U. Denver, Colo., 1966-70; mgr. materials devel. GE Aircraft Engines, Evendale, Ohio, 1970-72; mgr. advanced materials Kelsey-Hayes R & D, Ann Arbor, Mich., 1972-73; mgr. R&D Climax Molybdenum Co. Mich., Ann Arbor, 1973-84; pres. Arbormet Ltd., Ann Arbor, 1984—. Disting. vis. prof. Minas Inst. Tech., Minas Gerais, Brazil, 1969. Co-editor: The Superalloys, 1972, Superalloys II, 1987; contbr. articles to profl. jours.; patentee in field. Chair adv. bd. Northside Cmty. Ch., Ann Arbor, 1993-94. With USN, 1945-46. Fellow Am. Soc. for Metals, Am. Inst. for Chemists; mem. Am. Inst. Mining and Metall. Engrs., Am. Ceramic Soc., Electrochem. Soc., N.Y. Acad. Sci., Sigma Xi, Phi Kappa Phi. Avocations: archaeology, numismatics. Home: 929 Greenhills Dr Ann Arbor MI 48103-2721 E-mail: hagelite@umich.edu.

HAGELSTEIN, ROBERT PHILIP, publisher; b. N.Y.C., Dec. 15, 1942; s. H. Robert and E. Ann (Buhrow) H.; m. Ann G. Linguvic, Apr. 26, 1970; children: Christopher R., Jonathan W. BA in English Lit., L.I. U., 1964. Prodn. mgr. Johnson Reprint Corp., N.Y.C., 1965-68, editor-in-chief, 1968-70; v.p. Greenwood Press, Inc., Westport, Conn., 1970-73; pres. Greenwood Pub. Group, 1973-99; pub. and electronic pub. cons., 1999—. Bd. dirs. Aldwych Press, London. Contbr. articles to scholarly and profl. jours.; author Converticalc computer software program. Mem.: U.S. Power Squadron, South Norwalk Boat Club, North Palm Beach Yacht Club.

HAGEMAN, KATHERINE ELIZABETH, secondary school educator; b. Denver, Colo., Feb. 27, 1970; d. William Ross and Mary Elizabeth Hageman. BA in Social Sci., U. No. Colo.; postgrad., Metro State Coll., Denver. Lic. tchr. Colo. Tchr. Taylor's Rainbow Learning Ctr., Northglenn, Colo., 1989—94, Adams County Sch. Dist. 1, Thornton, Colo., 1994—95, Falcon Sch. Dist. 49, Colorado Springs, Colo., 1997—98, Adams County Sch. Dist. 50, Westminster, Colo., 1998—, dept. chair math., 1999—2002, curriculum devel. com. mem., 2000—01. Highland Hills instr. Adams County Sch. Dist. 50, Westminster, 1998. Actor: poetry to jours., anthologies. Mem. Colo. Share Holy Cross Cath. Ch., Thornton, 1995, religious tchr., 1992—94. Named to Internat. Poetry Hall of Fame, 1997. Mem.: NEA, Colo. Edn. Assn. Roman Catholic. Avocations: reading, cross stitch, poetry.

HAGEMAN, RICHARD PHILIP, JR., educational administrator; b. Derby, Conn., Dec. 21, 1941; s. Richard Philip and Elizabeth (Serafinowicz) H.; m. Patricia Steele; children: Margaret Anne, Sheila Marie. BS, Cen. Conn. State U., 1964; MS, U. Bridgeport, 1968, profl. diploma, 1972. Cert. counselor Nat. Bd. Cert. Counselors; cert. tchr., Conn. Tchr. Stony Brook Sch. Stratford (Conn.) Bd. Edn., 1964—69, elem. sch. guidance counselor, 1969—81, secondary sch. guidance counselor, 1981—83; asst. prin. Stratford Acad., 1983—90; prin. Whitney Sch., 1990—95, Ctr. Sch., 1995—99; ret., 1999; univ. supr. Sacred Heart U., Fairfield, Conn. Lectr. edn. Fairfield U. Grad. Sch. Edn., 1971-93; head counselor Stratford Continuing Edn. Program, 1983-91, program facilitator, 1999—; chief examiner Gen. Ednl. Devel., 1986-91; assessor, trainer Beginning Educator Support and Tng. program Conn. State Dept. of Edn.; mem. adv. bd. counselor edn. Fairfield (Conn.) U., 1970-74; co-chmn. Stratford Juvenile Deliquency Prevention Team, 1979-81; pres. Stratford Elem. Prin. Assn., 1991-92; chief reader Conn. Adminstrs. Test, 1999—. Mem. Youth Adv. Bd. Stratford, 1981-85, chairperson, 1984-85; radio announcer Sta. WMNR, Monroe, Conn., 1982—. Mem. ACA, ASCD, NEA (life), Stratford Edn. Assn. (pres. 1978-79), New Eng. Assn. Specialists Group Work (pres. 1982-83, v.p. 1999-2003), Phi Delta Kappa. Roman Catholic. Democrat. E-mail: hagemanrandp@msn.com.

HAGEMANN, DOLORES ANN, water company official; b. Parkston, S.D., June 5, 1935; d. Jacob George and Margaret Marie (Mayer) Schumacher; m. Norbert Bernard Hagemann, June 8, 1954; children: Douglas, Pamela, Susan. AS, Des Moines Community Coll., 1984. Cert. notary pub., Iowa. Sales rep. Stanley Home Products, Westfield, Mass., 1970-76; owner, mgr. Hagemann Gen. Store, Lidderdale, Iowa, 1974-77; motor rt. carrier Des Moines Register, 1977-82; accounts receivable clk. City Water Dept., Lidderdale, 1981—. Owner, designer Dolores' Silk Flower Shop, Lidderdale, 1986—; bd. dirs. Lidderdale Apts., Inc., sec., 1974-91. Author: (with other) The Official Carroll County Democrat Cookbook, 1984. Com. person Carroll County Dems., 1970-96, 98-2000, sec., 1985-86, 2d vice chair, 1989-90, 1st vice chair, 1990-92, chair, 1992-94, chmn. chairs and vice chairs assn. 5th Congl. Dist. Iowa, 1990-92, chmn. county affirmative action com., 1994-96; mem. affirmative action com. 5th Congl. Dist.; mem. Iowa Dem. Party Election Rev. Com., 1991-93; hospice mem. Community Hospice of Stewart Meml. Community Hosp., 1988-2001; counselor Carroll Help Line, 1982-87; mem. adv. bd. We. Iowa Transit, 1990-97; mem. Carroll County steering com. Child Support Pub. Awareness Project, 1992 ; mem. Iowa Sen. Harkins Older Iowa Com., 1986—; mem. nat. steering com. Clinton/Gore Campaign, 1996, Gore Presdl. Campaign, 1999-2000; capt. Carroll County Precinct Gore Presdl. Campaign, 1999-2000, 03; charter mem. Gephardt for Pres. Com., 2003; Nat. Dem. Conv. del., 2000; mem. leadership cir. Nat. Com. Preserve Social Security Medicare, 1997—, mem. leadership cir., 2000—. Mem. Am. Assn. Ret. Persons, Holy Family Parish Guild (chair person 1976), Des Moines Community Coll. Alumni, Stewart Meml. Community Hosp. Aux. Democrat. Roman Catholic. Avocations: reading, gardening, canning, traveling, sewing. Home: PO Box 68 Lidderdale IA 51452-0068

HAGEMIER, HERMAN FREDERICK, chemist; b. Linton, Ind., Oct. 23, 1908; s. Clarence Frederick and Estella (Davidson) H.; m. Georgia Emmiline Tracy, Jan. 28, 1939 (dec. 1966); children: Evelyn Louise, Frederick Louis; m. Loueva Elizabeth Stoner Helton, Nov. 4, 1971. BS in Botany and Chemistry, Butler U., 1953. Independent researcher, 1962-2000. Author: Magnetic Double Helix, 1992, Magnetic Double Helix II, 1996, Magnetic Double Helix III, 1998.

HAGEN, AGNES MARY, adult education educator, writer; b. Albany, N.Y., June 14, 1938; d. Terrence Francis and Julia Treanor Hagen. BA in English, Medaille Coll., Buffalo, 1968; MEd as Reading Specialist, U. Va., 1974. Cert. adult edn., elem. edn. and spl. edn. 1-6 Va., lic. postgrad. profl. Elem. tchr. SNJM, Albany, 1958—72; reading specialist Washington parochial schs., 1972—76; social worker St. Ambrose Housing Aid/Balt. Cath. Charities, 1976—83; adult edn. tchr. Susquehanna/Chesapeake Job Corps Ctr. U.S. Dept. Labor, Port Deposit, Md., 1983—86; adult edn. tchr. Va. Dept. Correctional Edn., Staunton, 1986—. Lectr. in field. Author: The Jack Sloan series, 2002 (Top Titles for Adult New Readers award, Pub. Libr. Assn., 2000), The Tony Jefferson series, 2001. Mem.: AARP (v.p. 2000—), Va. Assn. for Adult Continuing Edn., Va. Assn. Correctional Educators (bd. dirs. 1994—), Delta Kappa Gamma. Roman Catholic. Avocations: reading, travel, kyaking. Home: PO Box 1444 Staunton VA 24402 Office: Staunton Correctional Ctr 301 Greenville Ave Staunton VA 24401

HAGEN, BARBARA C. music educator; b. Beaumont, Tex., June 3, 1952; d. Bobbie Carlyle and Doris Mae (Lindberg) Mabry; m. Keith Thomas Hagen, Dec. 21, 1973; children: Holly Hagen Buche, Heidi Noel. BS in Music Theory, Lamar U., 1974. Piano accompianist First Bapt. Ch. Youth Choir, Beaumont, Tex., 1972—73; viola player Symphony of S.E. Tex., 1972—74; viola player, music arranger various ch. activities, 1972—98, San Antonio, 1972—98; viola player profl. string quartet for weddings, Beaumont, 1990—98; tchr. piano & strings Hagen's Happy Notes, 1972—. Recipient Nat. award Gladys Robinson, Nat. Fedn. Music Clubs, 1995. Mem.: Beaumont Music Tchrs. Assn. (pres. 1996—98), Kingwood/Humble Music Tchrs. Assn. (sec. 1999—), Delta Omicron, Delta Omega, Delta Delta Delta (music chmn. 1987—88). Avocations: composing music, piano, viola, drawing, reading. Home: 2331 Crimson Valley Ct Kingwood TX 77345-2101

HAGEN, DANIEL RUSSELL, physiologist, educator; b. Springfield, Ill., Sept. 29, 1952; s. Robert William and Russella Mae (Lane) H.; m. Rosemary Ellen Simonetta, Mar. 25, 1978; children: Matthew, Mark, Lane, Elise. BS, U. Ill., 1974, PhD, 1978. Rsch. assoc. Cornell U., Ithaca, N.Y., 1978; asst. prof. Pa. State U., University Park, 1978-84, assoc. prof., 1984-93, prof., 1993—. Vis. assoc. prof. U. Wis., Madison, 1988-89, interim dept. head, 1995-98. Mem. editl. bd. Jour. Animal Sci., 1983—86, 1993—96, Biology Reprodn., 1997—2000; contbr. numerous articles to profl. jours. Mem.: Soc. for Study Fertility, Soc. for Study Reprodn., Am. Soc. Animal Sci., Sigma Xi. Office: Pa State U 324 Henning Bldg University Park PA 16802-3503 E-mail: drh@psu.edu.

HAGEN, DAVID WARNER, judge; b. 1931; BBA, U. Wis., 1956; LLB, U. San Francisco, 1959. Bar: Washoe County 1981, Nev. 1992. With Berkley, Randall & Harvey, Berkeley, Calif., 1960-62; pvt. practice Loyalton, Calif., 1962-63; with Guild, Busey & Guild (later Guild, Hagen and Clark Ltd. and Guild & Hagen Ltd.), Reno, 1963-93; judge U.S. Dist. Ct. Nev., Reno, 1993—, chmn. 9th Cir. Art. III, Judge's Edn. Com., 1998—2000. Lectr U. Nev., 1968-72; acting dean Nev. Sch. of Law, 1981-83, adj. prof., 1981-87; mem. Nev. Bd. Bar Examiners, 1972-91, chmn., 1989-91; chmn. Nev. Continuing Legal Edn. Com., 1967-75; mem. Nev. Uniform Comml. Code Com. Sgt. USAF, 1949—52. Fellow Am. Coll. Trial Lawyers (state chmn. 1983-85); mem. Nev. Bar Assn., Calif. Bar Assn., Washoe County Bar Assn., Am. Bd. Trial Advocates (advocate), Nat. Maritime Hist. Soc., VFW, U.S. Sailing Assn. Office: US Dist Ct Fed Bldg & US Courthouse 400 S Virginia St Reno NV 89501-2193

HAGEN, DONALD FLOYD, university administrator, former military officer; b. Ambrose, N.D., Jan. 2, 1938; s. Alvin Hagen and Edith I. (Abell) Olsen; m. Karen Pizzino, May 11, 1973; children: Dana, Lisa Amanda. BA, Concordia Coll., Moorhead, Minn., 1959; BS in Medicine, U. N.D., 1961; MD, Northwestern U., Evanston, Ill., 1963. Diplomate Am. Bd. Surgery. Commd. ensign USN, 1964, advanced through grades to rear adm., 1989; internship L.A. County Gen. Hosp., 1963-64; residency gen. surgery Portmouth (Va.) Naval Hosp., 1970-73; staff surgeon Naval Aerospace Med. Ctr., Pensacola, Fla., 1973-75; chief surgery U.S. Naval Hosp., Yokosuka, Japan, 1973-79, dir. clin. svcs. Jacksonville, Fla., 1979-81, commdg. officer Camp Pendleton, Calif., 1984-86; dir. contingency planning div. Bur. Medicine and Surgery, Washington, 1981-82; dir. med. edn. and tng. Office of Surgeon Gen., Washington, 1982-84, dir. health care ops., 1986-88; dep. comdr. health care ops. Naval Med. Command, Washington, 1988; comdr. Nat. Naval Med. Ctr., Bethesda, Md., 1988-91; surgeon gen., vice admiral USN, 1991-95, retired, 1995; exec. vice chancellor U. Kans. Med. Ctr., Kansas City, 1995—. Mem. bd. regents Uniformed Svcs. U. Health Scis., Bethesda, 1988-90; asst. chief Navy Med. Corps., 1989-90. Decorated bronze star; recipient Fed. Exec. award of excellence Am. Hosp. Assn., 1989. Mem. AMA, Am. Coll. Physician Execs., Assn. Mil. Surgeons of the U.S. (Founder award 1984), Army-Navy Club (Washington). Republican. Avocations: piano playing, church choir. Office: U Kans Med Ctr 3901 Rainbow Blvd Kansas City KS 66160-0001

HAGEN, GLENN W. lawyer; BS in Chemistry, U. Ala., 1970; JD, Valparaiso U., 1973. Bar: Mich. 1973, U.S. Dist. Ct. (we. dist.) Mich. 1974, Colo. 1981, U.S. Dist. Ct. Colo. 1982. Ptnr. Peters, Seyburn & Hagen, Kalamazoo, 1973-76; dep. city atty. City of Battle Creek, Mich., 1976-79; staff and regulatory counsel CF&I Steel Corp., Pueblo, Colo., 1979-81; gen. counsel Commonwealth Investment Properties Corp., Littleton, Colo., 1981-82; assoc. Berkowitz & Brady, Denver, 1982-83, Zarlengo, Mott, Zarlengo & Winbourn, Denver, 1983-87; pvt. practice Glenn W. Hagen, P.C., Denver, 1987—. Lectr. law office mgmt., constrn. law, small and mid-size bus. issues, corp. entity and formation issues Colo. Bar Assn. and Nat. Bus. Inst. Referee property tax appeals Douglas and Jefferson Counties; del. Colo. Rep. Com., 1986, 1990—2002; chmn. 18th Jud. Dist., 1999—; small bus. cons. South Met. Denver C. of C., 1994—2000. Mem.: ABA (young lawyers exec. coun. 1978—81, chmn. small bus. enterprises 1986, regional dir. constabars 1992—94, nat. editors conf. 1995, mem. constrn. forum 1996—), Highlands Ranch C. of C. (founder, bd. dirs., chmn. elect, treas. 2000—), Colo. Lawyers for Arts, Am. Arbitration Assn., Douglas-Elbert County Bar Assn., Denver Bar Assn, Colo. Bar Assn. (chmn. long range planning com. 1983—86, gen. practice exec. coun. 1985, bus. law sect. 1986—91, mem. exec. bd. chmn. budget com. 1987—89, mem. svcs. com. 1987—89, alt. dispute resolutions com. 1990—94, chmn.small firm section 1991—96, law office mgmt. com. 1995—, constrn. law sect. 1996—, chmn. 2001—), Mich. Bar Assn. (young lawyers exec. coun. 1978—80). Office: Highlands Ranch Bus Pk Ste 108 8925 S Ridgeline Blvd Highlands Ranch CO 80129-2354 Fax: 303-683-3521. E-mail: hagenlaw4biz@earthlink.net.

HAGEN, JOHN WILLIAM, psychology educator; b. Mpls., May 11, 1940; s. Wayne Sigvart and Elfie Marie (Erickson) H.; adopted children— Darus Gene, Lonny John, Frederick F. BA, U. Minn., 1962; PhD, Stanford U., 1965. Asst. prof. psychology U. Mich., Ann Arbor, 1965-69, assoc. prof., 1969-73, prof., 1973—, chmn. developmental program, 1971-83, dir. Ctr. Human Growth and Devel., 1982-93. Mem. Mich. Gov.'s Spl. Commn. on Age of Majority, 1970-71; dir. Reading and Learning Skills Ctr., 1985—1996 ; exec. officer Soc. for Rsch. in Child Devel., 1989—; adv. coun. Mich. Dept. Edn., 1972-74; chmn. Univ. Com. on Internat. Year of Child, 1979-80; rsch. rev. com. Nat. Inst. Child Health and Human Devel., 1980—. Co-author: Perspectives on the Development of Memory and Cognition, 1977; cons. editor Merrill Palmer Quar, 1968-80, Child Devel, 1972—; contbr. articles to profl. jours. Bd. dirs. Guild House Campus Ministry, Ann Arbor, 1972-83; bd. dirs. Humane Soc. Huron Valley, 1991-2000; profl. adv. bd. Nat. Assn. Learning Disabilities, 2001-. Recipient Standard Oil Found. award, 1967; USPHS trainee, 1963-65; Woodrow Wilson fellow, 1962-63; James Neubacher Award, 1997. Fellow Am. Psychol. Assn., Internat. Acad. for Rsch. in Learning Disabilities (exec. com. 2001-), Am. Psychol. Soc.; mem. Am. Edn. Rsch. Assn., Midwestern Psychol. Assn., Soc. Research in Child Devel. (chmn. program com. 1981-83), Internat. Soc. Study of Behavioral Devel., Phi Beta Kappa. Clubs: Univ. (Ann Arbor), Alumni (Ann Arbor). Unitarian Universalist. Home: 3421 Burbank Dr Ann Arbor MI 48105-1518 Office: Soc Rsch in Child Devel 3131 S State St #302 Ann Arbor MI 48108

HAGEN, MICHAEL DALE, family physician educator; b. St. Louis, Nov. 11, 1949; s. Hubert Dale and Gwendel (Carden) Hagen; m. Barbara Carroll Keifer, Aug. 21, 1971; children: Laura Carrol, Sandra Ann. BS in Biology, Denison U., 1971; MD cum laude, U. Mo., Columbia, 1975. Cert. family practice bd. Pvt. practice Family Medicine Assocs., Aurora, Mo., 1978—81; asst. prof. dept. family practice U. Ky., Lexington, 1981—87, assoc. prof. dept. family practice, 1987—92, prof. dept. family practice, 1993—, interim chmn. dept. family practice, 1992—93, assoc. chmn. dept. family practice, 1993—97, project dir., computer-based assessment, 1996—; assoc. dir. assessment methods Am. Bd. Family Practice, 2003—. Fellow clin. decision making New Eng. Med. Ctr., Boston, 1987—89; at-large dir. Am. Bd. Family Practice, Lexington, 1991—96, pres., 1995—96; residency rev. com. family practice Accreditation Coun. for Grad. Med. Edn., Chgo., 1994—97. Author: Saunders Review Family Practice, 1992, 1997, 2002; contbr. articles. Mem.: AMA, Omicron Delta Kappa, Soc. for Med. Decision Making, Am. Acad. Family Physicians (clin. policies task force 1994—95), Phi Kappa Phi, Alpha Omega Alpha. Presbyterian. Avocations: amateur radio, gardening. Home: 2012 Blairmore Rd Lexington KY 40502-2435 Office: Assessment Techs Inc 2224 Young Dr Lexington KY 40505-4219 E-mail: hagenmd@prodigy.net., mhagen@assesstech.com.

HAGEN, NICHOLAS STEWARD, medical educator, consultant; b. Plentywood, Mont., Aug. 6, 1942; s. William Joseph and June Janette (Reuter) H.; m. Mary Louise Edvalson, July 26, 1969; children: Brian Geoffrey, Lisa Louise, Eric Christopher, Aaron Daniel, David Michael. BS in Chemistry, Ariz. State U., 1964; MBA in Internat. Bus., George Washington U., 1969; MD, U. Ariz., 1974. Lic. physician Ariz., Utah, Idaho.; diplomate Nat. Bd. Med. Examiners. Intern., resident Good Samaritan Hosp., Phoenix, 1974-75; pvt. practice Roy, Utah, 1975-77; dir. clin. rsch. Abbott Labs., North Chicago, Ill., 1977-84; v.p. med. affairs Rorer Group, Inc., Ft. Washington, Pa., 1984-88; clin. prof. Ariz. State U., Tempe, 1988-90. Pres. Southwestern Clin. Rsch., Tempe, 1987—, Travel Profl. Internat., Tempe, 1989-98; mem. Ariz. Bd. Med. Student Loans, 1998-2002. Author: Valproic Acid: A Review of Pharmacologic Properties and Clinical Use in Pharmacologic and Biochemical Properties of Drug Substances, 1979; contbr. articles to med. jours.; patentee in field. Bishop Ch. Jesus Christ of Latter-day Saints, Gurnee, Ill., 1981-84; various positions with local couns. Boy Scouts Am., 1988—; active Rep. campaigns, Mesa, Ariz., 1988—; 2d vice chmn. Maricopa County Rep. Assembly, 1997-99; dist. republican chmn., 1996-98; mem. governing bd. East Valley Inst. Tech., 1998-2003. Lt. comdr. USCG, 1965-69. Joan Mueller-Etter scholar Ariz. State U., 1960, Phelps-Dodge scholar Ariz. State U., 1961; NASA fellow Brigham Young U., 1964. Mem. Am. Coll. Sports Medicine, Eagle Forum, Nat. Right-to-Life Assn., Utah Hist. Soc., Nat. Geneal. Soc., Bucks County Geneal. Soc., Sons of Norway, Soc. Descendants Emigrants from Numedal, Hallingdal and Hedmark, Norway, Blue Key, Archons, Kappa Sigma (treas. Greater Phoenix alumni chpt. 1999—), Beta Beta Beta, Alpha Epsilon Delta, Phi Eta Sigma, Sophos. Republican. Mem. Lds Ch. Avocations: genealogy, swimming, philately, medieval history, art collecting. Office: 2251 N 32d St Lot 20 Mesa AZ 85213-2445

HAGEN, PAUL BEO, physician, medical scientist; b. Sydney, Australia, Feb. 15, 1920; emigrated to Can., 1959, naturalized, 1965; s. Conrad and Mary (McFadzean) von H.; m. Jean Himms, Sept. 29, 1956; children— Anna, Nina. M.B., BS, U. Sydney, 1945. Intern, resident New South Wales Dept. Health, Sydney, 1945-48; lectr. physiology U. Sydney, 1948-50; sr. lectr. physiology U. Queensland, 1950-52; research fellow Oxford U., 1952-54; asst. prof. pharmacology Yale U., 1954-56, Harvard U., 1956-59; head biochemistry dept. U. Man., 1959-64, Queens U., 1964-67; dir. NRC, Ottawa, Ont., 1967-68; dean grad. studies U. Ottawa, 1968-83, chmn. pharmacology dept., 1983-86. Mem. med. bd. Muscular Dystrophy Assn. Can., 1961-87, chmn., 1976-87, nat. pres., 1980-83; vice chmn. Med. Research Council, 1967; trustee Can. Inst. Particle Physics, 1971-79 Mem. Editorial bd. Biochem. Pharmacology, 1961-66, Jour. Pharmacology and Exptl. Therapeutics, 1960-64, Can. Jour. Biochemistry, 1963-67; contbr. to books and periodicals on physiol., biochem. and pharm. subjects. Chmn. Ont. Bd. Libr. Coordination, 1971-73; trustee Ottawa Gen. Hosp., 1984-94. Recipient Lederle Faculty award Yale U., 1956, Centennial medal Govt. of Can., 1967; Jubilee medal, 1977; C.J. Martin fellow Oxford U., 1952; J.H. Brown fellow Yale U., 1954; Fulbright fellow, 1954 Fellow Chem. Inst. Can. (v.p., pres. biochem. div. 1962-64); mem. Brit. Pharm. Soc., Am. Soc. Pharmacology. Home: 233 Todor Pl Ottawa ON Canada K1L 7Y1

HAGEN, THOMAS BAILEY, business owner, former state official, retired insurance company executive; b. Buffalo, Sept. 19, 1935; s. Walter B. and Isabella S. (Bailey) H.; m. Susan R. Hirt, May 31, 1958; children: Jonathan, Sarah. Student, Pa. State U., Erie, 1953-55; BS in Commerce, Ohio State U., 1957; DPubSvc (hon.), Edinboro U. Pa., 1996. With Erie (Pa.) Ins. Group, 1953-98, exec. v.p., 1976-82, pres., 1982-90, chmn., CEO, 1990-93, spl. asst. to chmn., 1993-95, also bd. dirs., 1979-98; sec. of commerce Commonwealth of Pa., 1995-96, sec. cmty. and econ. devel., 1996-97; chmn. bd. dirs. Custom Engring. Co., 1997—; chmn. Team Pa. Found., 1997-2001; chmn., bd. dirs. Venango Machine Co., 1999—, Lamjen, Inc., 2000—, Custom Group Industries, Ltd., 2000—. Bd. dirs. Pa. Housing Fin. Agy., Bliley Techs., Inc.; chmn. Pa. Indsl. Devel. Authority, 1995-97, Pa. Econ. Devel. Fin. Authority, 1995-97, Pa. Ben Franklin/IRC Partnership, 1995-97. Bd. dirs. Erie Philharmonic, 1962-75, pres., 1970-71; bd. dirs. Erie Coun. Navy League U.S., 1977-86; pres. Erie Tomorrow Corp., 1979-86; vice chmn., bd. dirs. Bayfront East Side Taskforce, Erie, 1978-96; bd. dirs. Erie Conf. on Community Devel., 1985-93, hon. dir., 1993-2003; bd. dirs. Pa. Chamber Bus. and Industry, Harrisburg, 1986-95, 99—, Pa. Econ. Devel. Partnership, 1987-94, Pa. for Effective Govt., 1987-95. Capt. USNR ret. Alumni fellow Pa. State U., 1988; recipient Ins. Mentor award U. Ala., 1976, Golden Baton award Erie Philharmonic, 1974, Disting. Pennsylvanian award Gannon U., 1987, Phila. C. of C., 1980, Outstanding Community Service award Multiple Sclerosis Soc., 1980, Alumni Citizenship award Ohio State U., 1981, Man of the Yr. award Erie and Chautauqua Mag., 1986, Preservationist of the Yr. award (now Otto Haas award) Pa. Hist. and Mus. Commn., 1987, Honor award Pa. Soc. Architects, 1993. Mem. Internat. Ins. Soc. (bd. dirs. 1978-92, hon. counselor award 1982), Ins. Fedn. Pa. (bd. dirs. 1970-91, chmn. 1984-86), Ins. Inst. Am. (inst. for property and liability underwriters, trustee 1987-93), Griffith Found. (v.p. 1985-92, trustee 1985-95, trustee emeritus 1995—), The Pa. Soc. (pres. 1995-97, bd. dirs. 1990—). Office: 100 State St Ste 440 Erie PA 16507-1456

HAGEN, UTA THYRA, actress; b. Göttingen, Germany, June 12, 1919; came to U.S., 1926; d. Oskar F. L. and Thyra A. (Leisner) H.; m. Herbert Berghof, Jan. 25, 1957 (dec. Nov. 1990); 1 child, Leticia. DFA (hon.), Smith Coll., 1978; LHD (hon.), De Paul U., 1981, Wooster Coll., 1982; DFA (hon.), U. Wis., Madison, 2000, Pa. State U., 2000. Tchr. acting Herbert Berghof Studio, N.Y.C., 1947—, now chmn. Appeared as Ophelia, Dennis, Mass., 1937, as Nina in Sea Gull, N.Y.C., 1938, Key Largo, 1939, Vicki, 1942, Othello, 1943-45, Masterbuilder, 1947, Faust, 1947, Angel Steet, 1948, Street Car Named Desire, 1948, 50, Country Girl, 1950, G.B. Shaw's Saint Joan, 1951-52, Tovarich, City Center, 1952, In Any Language, 1952, The Deep Blue Sea, 1953, The Magic and the Loss, 1954, The Island of Goats, 1955, A Month in the Country, 1956, Good Woman of Setzuan, 1957, Who's Afraid of Virginia Woolf, 1962-64 (Antoinete Perry award 1963), The Cherry Orchard, 1968, Charlotte, 1980; also univ. tour 1981-82, Mrs. Warren's Profession, Roundabout Theatre, N.Y.C., 1985—, You Never Can Tell, Circle in the Square, 1986—, Mrs. Klein, Lortel Theatre, 1995-96, on tour, 1996-97, Collected Stories, Lortel Theatre, 1998-99, Six Dance Lessons in Six Weeks, Geffen Theatre, 2001; (films) The Other, 1972, The Boys from Brazil, 1978, Reversal of Fortunes, 1990; TV appearances include A Month in the Country, 1956, Out of Dust, 1959; appeared in numerous TV spls. and guest star appearances including Lou Grant, 1982, A Doctor's Story, 1984, PBS Am. Playhouse prodn. The Sunset Gang, 1991, 02, 1999; author: Respect for Acting, 1973, Love for Cooking, 1976, Sources, a Memoire, 1983, A Challange for the Actor, 1991; appearances include numerous roles with the H.B. Playwrights Found., 1965-98. Chmn. bd. HB Playwrights Found., 1991—. Recipient Antoinette Perry award, 1951, 63, N.Y. Drama Critics award, 1951, 63, Donaldson award for best actress, 1951, London Critics award for best actress, 1963-64 season, Outer Cir. award, Mayor's Liberty medal, 1986, Drama Legend award 1986, John Houseman award for disting. svc., 1987, Campostella award for disting. svc., 1987, Living Legacy award Women's Internat. Ctr., 1994, Lucille Lortell Lifetime Achievement award, 1995, Lortell award, 1996, Drama League Lifetime Achievement award, 1996, Obie Lifetime Achievement award 1996, Jeffry award, chgo., 1997, Antoinette Perry Lifetime Achievement award, 1999; named to Theatre Hall of Fame, 1981. Mem. Am. Acad. of Arts and Scis. Office: Herbert Berghof Studio 120 Bank St New York NY 10014-2126

HAGENBECK, FRANKLIN LEE, military officer; b. Rabat, Morocco, Nov. 25, 1949; m. Judy Vaughn; children: Kelly, Leeann. BS, U.S. Mil. Acad., 1971; MS, Fla. State U., 1978; MBA, L.I. U., 1979. Advanced through grades to maj. gen., 2001; brigade comdr. 3rd Tng. Brigade, Ft. Leonard Wood, Mo., 1993—95; chief of staff 10th Mountain Divsn., Ft. Drum, 1995—97; dir., officer pers. mgmt. directorate U.S. Army, Washington, 1997—98; asst. divsn. comdr. ops. 101st Airborne Divsn., Ft. Campbell, Ky., 1998—99; dep. dir. global/multilateral issue/internat. American affs., J-5 Joint Staff, Washington, 1999—2000, dep. dir. ops., J33, 2000—01; commanding gen. 10th Mountain Divsn., Ft. Drum, NY, 2001—03; commdg. gen., coalition task force-mountain Operation Anaconda, Afghanistan, 2001—02. Decorated Legion of Merit with 3 oak leaf clusters, Bronze Star, numerous others. Mem.: Assn. of U.S. Army, Am. Legion.

HAGENBUCH, JOHN JACOB, investor, real estate company executive; b. Park Forest, Ill., May 31, 1951; s. David Brown and Jean Iline (Reeves) H.; m. Kimberly A. Steel, Aug. 20, 2000; children: Henry, Hunter, Hilary, Sydney, John. AB magna cum laude, Princeton U., 1974; MBA, Stanford U., 1978. Assoc. Salomon Bros., N.Y.C., 1978-80, v.p. San Francisco, 1980-85; gen. ptnr. Hellman & Friedman, 1985-93; chmn. M&H Realty Ptnrs., L.P., 1993—. Mem. Burlingame Country Club, Pacific-Union Club, Calif. Tennis Club, Villa Taverna Club, Bohemian Club, Valley Club. Office: M&H Realty Ptnrs 353 Sacramento St Fl 21 San Francisco CA 94111-3620

HAGENBUCH, RODNEY DALE, consulting principal, financial consultant; b. Saxville, Wis. s. Herbert Jenkin and Minnie Leona (Hayward) Hagenbuch; children: Kris, Beth, Patricia; m. LaVerne Julia Scoonover, Sept. 1, 1956. BS, Mich. State U., 1980. Cert. fin. mgr. Designer Olds div. Gen. Motors, Lansing, Mich., 1960-66; institutional account exec. Merrill Lynch, Lansing, 1966-75, institutional mgr., 1975-80, sales mgr. Columbus, Ohio, 1980-82, sr. resident v.p. Tacoma, 1982-93, L.A., 1993-98; ret., 1998; prin. Quantum Group, 1999—; portfolio analyst Affinity Investment Advisors, 2001. Prin. Securities Expert Witness Network, 1999, Quantum Leap Inst., 1999, Quantum Leap Securities, 2001; mem. adv. bd. U. Wash. Sch. Bus., Tacoma, 1998—2002; bd. dirs. Employers Group. Author (with Richard J. Capalbo): Investment Survival: How to Use Investment Research to Create Winning Portfolios, 2002. Mem. adv. bd. Charles Wright, 1989—93; mem. econ. devel. bd. City of Tacoma, 1986—93, chmn., 1987—88; pres. Downtown Tacoma Assn., 1986; chmn. Corp. Coun. for the Arts, 1986, L.A. United Way, 1993—2000; pres. Tacoma Symphony, 1988; chmn. human resource commn. Meridian Twp., 1972—74; mem. Meridian Planning Commn., Lansing, 1964—70, Meridian Police and Fire Commn., Lansing, 1964—70; pres. adv. bd. U. Wash., Tacoma, chmn., 1992; mem. State Wash. Arts Stblzn. Bd.; sec. bd. dirs. Tacoma Art Mus., 1992; legis. chmn. N.W. Securities Industry Assn.; campaign chmn. Pierce County United Way, 1991—92; non-resident dir. Tacoma Art Mus., 1994—, Tacoma Urban League, 1983—93; exec. com. fraternity of friends L.A. Music Ctr.; hon. mem. bd. govs. Streetlights L.A., 1998—; bd. dirs. L.A. Acad. Fin., 1993—98, L.A. United Cerebral Palsy, 1994—; bd. dirs., chmn. L.A. Red Cross; bd. dirs. Forward Wash., New L.A. Mktg. Plan, 1995—97; bd. dirs., mem. dist. 2 com. NASD, 1996—99; bd. govs. L.A. Children's Hosp. Rsch. Inst., 1994—99, mem. fin. com., 1999—; bd. govs. L.A. Town Hall, 1996, mem. fin. com., 1999—; bd. govs. L.A. Employers Group. Recipient Outstanding Citizen award Mcpl. League Pierce County, 1988; named Nat. Vol. of Yr., Urban League Western Divsn., 1987. Mem.: Tacoma C. of C. Avocations: running, skiing. Home: 16826 Monte Hermoso Dr Pacific Palisades CA 90272-1910 E-mail: rdhagen@earthlink.net.

HAGENDORF, STANLEY, lawyer, writer; b. Bklyn., Mar. 1, 1930; s. David and Fanny (Hammer) H.; m. Tilbeth Greene, Nov. 18, 1962; children: Lauren, Wayne, Richard. BS in Econs., U. Pa., 1953; JD cum laude, Harvard U., 1956; LLM in Taxation, NYU, 1961. Bar: N.Y. 1956, Fla. 1975. Assoc. Hellerstein, Rosier & Brudney, N.Y.C., 1957-59; pvt. practice N.Y.C., 1960-70; ptnr. Karow & Hagendorf, N.Y.C., 1970-75, Hagendorf & Schlesinger, N.Y.C., Coral Gables, Fla., 1975-84, Hagendorf, Deason & Frank, 1984-85; pvt. practice N.Y.C., 1985-2000, Hagendorf Law Firm, Las Vegas, Nev., 2000—. Assoc. prof. U. Miami Law Sch., Coral Gables, 1975-80; dir.-lectr. Hagendorf Tax Workshop, N.Y.C. Author: Tax Manual for Corporate Liquidations, Redemptions and Estate Planning Recapitalizations, 1978, Liquidations, Redemptions and Recapitalizations: Taxation and Planning, 1986, Tax Guide for Buying and Selling a Business; editor: Tax Hotline, 2001; contbr. articles to profl. jours. Emeritus fin. and estate planning adv. bd. Commerce Clearing House. With U.S. Army, 1948-51. Recipient Disting. Lectr. award Nat. Soc. Pub. Accts. Scholarship Found., 1980, Cert. Appreciation, N.Y. County Lawyers Assn., 1982. Mem. ABA, N.Y. State Bar Assn., Fla. Bar Assn. (cert. tax lawyer). Office: Hagendorf Law Firm 2000 S Jones Blvd Ste 240 Las Vegas NV 89146 E-mail: stanleyhagendorf@hagendorflaw.com.

HAGENDORN, WILLIAM H. lawyer; b. Bklyn., Sept. 1, 1925; s. William V. and Florence (Hull) H.; m. Patricia Yarvote, Apr. 6, 1974; children: Katherine Florence, Patricia Ann. AB, Princeton U., 1944; JD, Harvard U., 1949; LL.M., NYU, 1952. Bar: N.Y. 1949. Practiced in N.Y.C., 1949—; assoc. firm Debevoise, Plimpton & McLean, N.Y.C., 1953-61, Carter, Ledyard & Milburn, N.Y.C., 1961-65; gen. counsel Am. Express Co., 1965-72, Wells Fargo & Co., 1965-68, Equitable Securities, Morton & Co., N.Y.C., 1966-72; sr. atty. Shearman & Sterling, N.Y.C., 1973-91; ptnr. Burlingham Underwood, N.Y.C., 1991—2002; pvt. practice Bronxville, NY, 2002—. Adviser to com. uniform consumer credit code Nat. Conf. Uniform State Laws, 1966-68; adj. prof. Rutgers Law Sch., Newark, 1991, 93. Served with inf. AUS, 1944-46. Mem.: Assn. of Bar of City of N.Y., N.Y. State Bar Assn. (chmn. com. admiralty law 1990—93, exec. com. internat. law sect. 1990—, chmn. com. admiralty law 1998—2000), Univ. Club (N.Y.C.). Home and Office: 25 Parkview Ave Apt 3A Bronxville NY 10708-2936 E-mail: whagendorn@aol.com.

HAGENLOCKER, EDWARD E. retired automobile company executive; b. 1939; married. BS, MS, Ohio State U., 1962, PhD, 1964; MBA, Mich. State U., 1982. With Ford Motor Co., 1964-98, chief engr., 1973—77, gen. mgr., 1978—80, dir., v.p. ops., 1984-85, dir., pres., 1985-86, v.p., gen. mgr. truck ops., 1986-92, exec. v.p. N.Am. automative ops., 1992-94, pres. Ford automotive ops., 1994-96, vice chmn., 1996-98. Office: 39400 Woodward Ave Ste 165 Bloomfield Hills MI 48304-5151

HAGENS, WILLIAM JOSEPH, state official, public health educator; b. Bay City, Mich., June 3, 1942; s. Francis Bernard and Lillian May (O'Neill) H.; m. Noel Scantlebury, Apr. 15, 1967; children: Clara O'Neill, Nicholas Barlow. BA, Saginaw Valley Coll., 1969; MA, Wayne State U., 1971. VISTA vol. Pierce County Legal Assistance, Tacoma, 1971-73; sr. rsch. analyst Wash. Ho. of Reps., Olympia, 1974-99; dep. commr. Wash. State Office Ins. Commr., Olympia, 1999—2002; sr. health policy advisor Wash. State Dept. Social and Health Svcs., Olympia, 2002—. Instr. Pacific Luth. U., Tacoma, 1979-81; clin. prof. Sch. Pub. Health U. Wash., Seattle, 1984—, mem. vis. com. Sch. Nursing, 1993, mem. vis. com. Sch. Pub. Health, 2002; mem. health policy project George Washington U., Washington, 1985-91; bd. dirs. Area Health Edn. Ctr., Seattle, 1988-90; mem. Nat. Acad. State Health Policy, 1990—; mem. adv. com. Wash. State Ctr. Health Stats., 1988-94; mem. Nat. Conf. State Legislatures' Forum for Health Policy Leadership, 1991-2000; mem. vis. com. U. Wash. Sch. Pub. Health, 2003—; cons. health care sys. devel. Russian Republic of Sakha, 2002. Contbg. author: Analyzing Poverty Policy, 1975. Participant AIDS symposium Pasteur Inst., Paris, 1987; mem. North End Neighborhood Coun., Tacoma, 1998-2002; mem. pub. affairs com. Seattle Symphony, 1997-99. Recipient Pres. award Wash. State Pub. Health Assn., 1986, Ann. award Wash. State Pub. Health Assn., 1994, award Wash. Health Found., 2002; NIMH fellow, 1979, WHO internat. travel fellow, 1992. Mem. Am. Pub. Health Assn., Am. Polit. Sci. Assn., Policy Studies Orgn., English Speaking Union, World Affairs Coun., Pi Sigma Alpha. Avocations: opera, classical music, history, big band jazz, paintings and engravings. Home: 3214 N 27th St Tacoma WA 98407-6208 Office: Med Assistance Adminstrn Dept Social and Health Svcs PO Box 45500 Olympia WA 45500-5500 E-mail: gmahler@u.washington.edu.

HAGENSTEIN, WILLIAM DAVID, forester, consultant; b. Seattle, Mar. 8, 1915; s. Charles William and Janet (Finigan) H.; m. Ruth Helen Johnson, Sept. 2, 1940 (dec. 1979); m. Jean Kraemer Edson, June 16, 1980 (dec. 2000). BS in Forestry, U. Wash., 1938; MForestry, Duke, 1941. Registered profl. engr., Wash., Oreg. Field aid in entomology U.S. Dept. Agr., Hat Creek, Calif., 1938; logging supt. and engr. Eagle Logging Co., Sedro-Woolley, Wash., 1939; tech. foreman U.S. Forest Svc., North Bend, Wash., 1940; forester West Coast Lumbermen's Assn., Seattle and Portland, Oreg., 1941-43, 45-49; sr. forester FEA, South and Central Pacific Theaters of War and Costa Rica, 1943-45; mgr. Indsl. Forestry Assn., Portland, 1949-80, exec. v.p., 1956-80, hon. dir., 1980-87; pres. W.D. Hagenstein and Assocs., Inc., Portland, 1980—. H.R. MacMillan lectr. forestry U. B.C., 1952, 77; Benson Meml. lectr. U. Mo., 1966; S.J. Hall lectr. indsl. forestry U. Calif. at Berkeley, 1973; cons. forest engr. USN, Philippines, 1952, Coop. Housing Found., Belize, 1986; mem. U.S. Forest Products Trade Mission, Japan, 1968; del. VII World Forestry Congress, Argentina, 1972, VIII Congress, Indonesia, 1978; mem. U.S. Forestry Study Team, West Germany, 1974; mem. sec. Interior's Oreg. and Calif. Multiple Use Adv. Bd., 1975-76; trustee Wash. State Forestry Conf., 1948-92, Keep Oreg. Green Assn., 1957—, v.p., 1970-71, pres., 1972-73; adv. trustee Keep Wash. Green Assn., 1957-95; co-founder World Forestry Ctr., dir., 1965-89, v.p., 1965-79, hon. dir. for life, 1990. Author: (with Wackerman and Michell) Harvesting Timber Crops, 1966; Assoc. editor: Jour. Forestry, 1946-53; columnist Wood Rev., 1978-82; contbr. numerous articles to profl. jours. Trustee Oreg. Mus. Sci. and Industry, 1968-73. Served with USNR, 1933-37. Recipient Hon. Alumnus award U. Wash. Foresters Alumni Assn., 1965, Forest Mgmt. award Nat. Forest Products Assn., 1968, Western Forestry award Western Forestry and Conservation Assn., 1972, 79, Gifford Pinchot medal for 50 yrs. Outstanding Svc., Soc. Am. Foresters, 1987, Charles W. Ralston award Duke Sch. Forestry, 1988, Lifetime Achievement award Oreg. Soc. Am. Foresters, 1995; Honored as only surviving co-founder World Forestry Ctr., 2000. Fellow Soc. Am. Foresters (mem. coun. 1958-63, pres. 1966-69, Golden Membership award 1989); mem. Am. Forestry Assn. (life, hon. v.p. 1966-69, 74-92, William B. Greeley Forestry award 1990), Commonwealth Forestry Assn. (life), Internat. Soc. Tropical Foresters, Portland C. of C. (forestry com. 1949-79, chmn. 1960-62), Nat. Forest Products Assn. (forestry adv. com. 1949-80, chmn. 1972-74, 78-80), West Coast Lumbermen's Assn. (v.p. 1969-79), Forest History Soc. (bd. dirs. 2001—), David Douglas Soc. Western N. Am., Lang Syne Soc., Hoo Hoo Club, Xi Sigma Pi (outstanding alumnus Alpha chpt. 1973). Republican. Home: 3062 SW Fairmount Blvd Portland OR 97239-1439 Office: 921 SW Washington St Ste 803 Portland OR 97205-2826

HAGER, ANTHONY WOOD, mathematics educator; b. Marshfield, Wis., Dec. 16, 1939; s. Cyril Francis and Margaret Ruth (Wood) H.; 1 child, Amanda D. BS, Pa. State U., 1960, PhD, 1965. Rsch. scientist Leeds & Northrup Co., N. Wales, Pa., 1960-61; instr. U. Rochester, N.Y., 1965-67, asst. prof., 1967-68, Wesleyan U., Middletown, Conn., 1968-69, assoc. prof., 1969-75, prof., 1975—, chmn. dept. math., 1976-77, 88-90, 93, 95-96. Contbr. articles to profl. jours. NAS vis. rschr., Prague, 1973, 75; Italian N.C.R. vis. rschr. Padua, 1978; U. Fla. vis. rschr., Gainesville, 1995. Mem. Am. Math. Soc. Office: Wesleyan U Math Dept Middletown CT 06459-0001 E-mail: ahager@wesleyan.edu.

HAGER, EDWARD PAUL, development executive; b. Pottsville, Pa., Jan. 15, 1948; s. Edward Louis and Pauline Ann (Macalush) H.; m. Kathleen C. Roseman. BA magna cum laude, St. Charles Borromeo, Phila., 1970. Dist. exec. Hawk Mountain coun. Boy Scouts Am., Reading, Pa., 1971-78, sr. dist. exec. Hawk Mountain coun., 1978-80, devel. dir. Hawk Mountain coun., 1980-83, fin. dir. Nassau county coun. Roslyn, N.Y., 1983-85; dir. devel. Luth. Home, Topton, Pa., 1985-94, St. Vincent Archabbey, Latrobe, Pa., 1994-99; cons. Cmty. Counseling Svc. Co., Inc., 1999-2000; pres. LAS Found., Zelienople, Pa., 2000—. Campaign worker United Way So. Schuykill, Pottsville, Pa., 1977-79, United Way Berks County, Reading, 1982, 85-92; com. chmn. Hawk Mountain coun. Boy Scouts Am., 1986-89. Named one of Outstanding Young Men Am., 1977; recipient St. George award Nat. Cath. Com. on Scouting, 1978. Mem.: Assn. Fundraising Profls. (bd. dirs. northeastern Pa. chpt. 1986—94, v.p. 1988, pres. 1989, 1992), Luth. Brotherhood (br. v.p. 1991—93), Rotary (bd. dirs. West Reading Club 1980—83, Reading Club 1990—94, dist. Rotary Found. group study exch. 1991—94, Outstanding Fund Raising Exec. 1993). Roman Catholic. Avocations: aquatics, hiking, backpacking, furniture refinishing. Home: 1407 Clearview Dr Greensburg PA 15601-3703 E-mail: ehager@lassenior.com.

HAGER, ELIZABETH SEARS, state legislator, social services organization administrator; b. Washington, Oct. 31, 1944; d. Hess Thatcher and Elizabeth Grace (Harper) Sears; m. Dennis Sterling Hager, Sept. 3, 1966; children: Annie Elizabeth, Lucie Caroline. BA, Wellesley Coll., 1966; MPA, U. N.H., 1979. Prin. Philbrook Ctr., Concord, N.H., 1970-71; rep. N.H. Gen. Ct., Concord, 1973-76, 85-94, 1996—; del. N.H. Constitutional Conv., Concord, 1974, 84; campaign coord. Anderson for Pres. Rep. Primary, N.H., 1980; mem. Concord City Coun., 1982-90; mayor City of Concord, 1988-90; exec. dir. United Way of Merrimack County, Concord, 1996—. Bd. dirs. Jefferson Pilot Funds, Concord, Bank of NH. Pres. Greater Concord United Way, 1980-81; campaign chair United Way of Merrimack County, Concord, 1986. Republican. Episcopalian. Office: 46 N Main St Concord NH 03301-4913 Home: 5 Pleasant View Ave Concord NH 03301-2555

HAGER, JOHN HENRY, state official, former lieutenant governor; b. Durham, N.C., Aug. 28, 1936; m. Margaret Dickinson Chase, Feb. 27, 1971; children: John Virgil, Henry Chase. BSME, Purdue U., 1958; MBA, Harvard U., 1960; hon. degree, Averett Coll., 1999, Mary Washington Coll., 1999, U. No. Va., 1999. Various positions Am. Tobacco Co., 1961-94; lt. gov. and pres. State Senate State of Va., Richmond, 1998—2002, asst. to the gov. for Commonwealth preparedness, 2002—. Chmn. of Disability Commn.; co-chmn. com. on Edn1. Infrastructure; chmn. Faith Based Cmty. Svcs. Task Force; vice-chmn. Gov.'s Commn. on Transp. Policy; bd. dirs., vice-chair Aerospace State Assn.; trustee, v.p. Jamestown Yorktown Found.; chmn. Greater Richmond Conv. Ctr. Expansion; dir., pres. Sorensen Inst. Polit. Leadership; dir. Ctr. for Politics, U. R.I., Jamestown 2002; past dir. Partnership for Urban Va., past dir. Va. State C of C; trustee, exec. com., fin. com. Va. Mus. Fine Arts; 1st v.p., dir. Va. Pub. Safety Found., Inc.; past pres., trustee, exec. com. Children's Hosp.; Met. Richmond Conv. and Vis. Bur. (past chmn., dir., founding dir.); Va. Health Care Found. (past chmn., dir., exec. com.); 7th Dist. Rep. Party (past vice chmn. 3rd district, exec. com. mem. past precinct, ward and campaign chmn.); Rep. Party of Va. and del./alt. to 4 natl. convs. (past treas., past exec. com. mem., state central com. mem., numerous others); ruling elder 1st Presbyn. Ch., Richmond; mem. drug task force Va. State Crime Commn. 2nd lt. U.S. Army, 1960-61, capt. USAR. Named one of Outstanding Young Men of Am., 1976, Man of Yr., Tobacco Internat. Mag., 1990; recipient Alumni Citizenship award Purdue U., 1987, Svc. award Richmond Rep. Com., 1992, Disting. Alumni award Durham Acad., 1992, Good Govt. award Richmond First Club, 1996, Tourism Leadership award Met. Richmond Convention and Visitors Bur., 1997, Lettie Pate Whitehead Evans award Westminster Canterbury, 1997, Citizenship award Va. Coun. Indians, 1998. Mem. Am. Legion, Va. C. of C. (dir.), Nat. Assn. Lt. Govs. (mem. exec. com., So. sector chmn.), So. Growth Policies Bd., Adv. Bd. Tobacco History Corp., Jamestown, Richmond Rep. Party Com., Richmond German, Richmond Hundred (past pres., dir.), City of Richmond Electoral Bd. (past chmn.) Pub. Affairs Group (past chmn.), Forum Club (past pres.), Commonwealth Club (past dir.), Custis Fishing and Hunting Club (past dir.), Country Club Va. (past pres. and CEO, past dir.). Republican. Office: PO Box 1475 202 N 9th St Richmond VA 23218

HAGER, LOUISE ALGER, retired chaplain; b. Spokane, Wash., Dec. 15, 1923; d. Russel S. and Thelma Ella (Geib) Alger; m. Bernard Coe, Nov. 16, 1945 (dec. July 1965); children: Cynthia W., Marjorie L.; m. Onslow B. Hager, Jan. 16, 1970 (dec. Dec. 1983). BEd, Nat. Coll. Edn., 1946; M of Theol. Studies, St. Paul Sch. Theology, 1997. Kindergarten tchr. Edgewater Park Bd. Edn., Beverly, N.J., 1946-47, 59-83; pres. bd. mgrs. Cinnaminson (N.J.) Home, 1985-88; chaplain Rsch. Med. Ctr., Kansas City, Mo., 1986-88; assoc. chaplain John Knox Village, Lee's Summit, Mo., 1988-98; ret., 1998; vol. chaplain, psychogeriatric inpatient unit Sheppard Pratt Health Sys., 1999—; vol. chaplain Hollowell and Taylor Halls health care units Inpatient Nursing Svcs. at Broadmead Retirement Cmty., 1999—. Chaplain vol. Burlington County Hosp., Mt. Holly, N.J., 1987-88; lay minister. Recipient Disting. Alumni award, Nat. Louis U., 2002, Vol. Impact award for extrordinary svc., Sheppard Pratt Health Hosp., 2002. Mem. NEA, Lee's Summit Ministerial Soc., Coll. Chaplains, Am. Soc. on Aging, Mid-Am. Congress on Aging. Democrat. Mem. Soc. Of Friends. Avocations: reading, piano playing, singing, sewing, walking. Home: Broadmead 13801 York Rd Apt M1 Cockeysville MD 21030-1891

HAGER, LOWELL PAUL, biochemistry educator; b. Girard, Kans., Aug. 30, 1926; s. Paul William and Christine (Selle) H.; m. Frances Erea, Jan. 22, 1949; children: Paul, Steven, JoAnn. AB, Valparaiso U., 1947; MA, U. Kans., 1950; PhD, U. Ill., 1953. Postdoctoral fellow Mass. Gen. Hosp., Boston, 1953-55; asst. prof. biochemistry Harvard U., Cambridge, Mass., 1955-60; mem. faculty U. Ill., Urbana, 1960—, prof. biochemistry, 1965—, head biochem. div., 1967-89, dir. Biotech. Ctr., 1987—. Chmn. physiol. chemistry study sect. NIH, 1965—; vis. scientist Imperial Cancer Rsch. Fund, 1964; cons. NSF, 1976. Editor life scis. Archives Biochemistry and Biophysics, 1966—; assoc. editor Biochemistry, 1973—; mem. editorial bd. Jour. Biol. Chemistry, 1874—. With USAAF, 1945. Guggenheim fellow U. Oxford, Eng., 1959-60, Max Planck Inst. Zellchemie, 1959-60. Mem. NAS (elected), Am. Chem. Soc., Am. Soc. Biol. Chemists, Am. Soc. Microbiology (chmn. physiology divsn. 1967). Achievements include rsch. in enzyme mechanisms, intermediary metabolism, tumor virus. Home: 5 Fields East Champaign IL 61822 E-mail: l-hager@uiuc.edu.

HAGER, MICHAEL W. museum director; m. Denise Hager; children: Amy, Brian. BA in Biology, Grinnell Coll.; PhD in Geology, U. Wyo. Prof. geology Augustana Coll., 1973-78; dir. Mus. of the Rockies, 1978-89, Va. Mus. Natural History, 1989-91; exec. dir. San Diego Natural History Mus., 1991—. Mus. cons. Exec. prodr. (film) Baja California, 2000. Bd. dirs. Elem. Inst. Sci. and Harborside Sch.; head cultural com. Binational Com. Edn. and Culture, San Diego/Tijuana. Mem. Assn. Sci. Mus. Dirs. (pres.). Office: San Diego Natural History Mus PO Box 121390 San Diego CA 92112-1390 Fax: 619-232-0248. E-mail: mhager@sdnhm.org.

HAGER, PAULA MICHELE, critical care nurse; b. Palmerton, Pa., Sept. 29, 1957; d. Edward L. and Pauline A. (Macalush) H. Diploma, Hazleton (Pa.) State Gen. Hosp, 1978. CCRN; cert. BLS, ACLS, pediatric advanced life support. Staff nurse, med./surgical Coaldale (Pa.) State Gen. Hosp., 1978-86, staff nurse ICU/CCU, 1986-92, St. Luke's Miners Meml. Med. Ctr., 1992—. Instr. ACLS, CPR. Vol. Am. Heart Assn. Mem. AACN, Pa. Nurses Assn. E-mail: PMH57@webTV.net.

HAGER, ROBERT WORTH, retired aerospace company executive; b. Longview, Wash., June 20, 1928; s. Josiah Denver and Merle (Worth) H.; m. Margaret Goodnough, Aug. 25, 1950; children: Stephen M., Sandra Hager Dahl, Shane D. BS in Civil Engring, U. Wash., 1949, MS in Civil Engring, 1950; DSc (hon.), U. Ala., 1995. Rsch. fellow U. Wash., 1949-50; rsch. engr. U.S. Navy Civil Engring. Lab., Port Hueneme, Calif., 1950-53; mem. staff Sandia Corp., Albuquerque, 1953-55; with Boeing Co., Seattle, 1955-93, Minuteman program mgr., 1973-78, v.p., gen. mgr. ballistic missile and space div., 1978-80, v.p. engring., 1980-84, v.p. space sta. Huntsville, Ala., 1984-89, v.p., gen. mgr. Huntsville div. Boeing Aerospace and Electronics, 1989-91, v.p., gen. mgr. Missiles and Space Div. Boeing Def. and Space Group, 1991-93. Past chmn. bd. Univ. Space Rsch. Assn.; past chmn. Bus. Coun. Ala.; co-chmn. Lower Hood Canal Watershed Com.; bd. dirs. Hood Canal Salmon Enhancement Group; treas. Pacific N.W. Salmon Ctr., 2002—. Fellow AIAA, Am. Astron. Soc. Methodist. Home: 51 E Sunset Beach Dr Belfair WA 98528-9534

HAGER, SUSAN KULKA, public relations executive; b. Washington, Oct. 19, 1944; d. Joseph A. and Mary Margaret (Berry) Kulka; m. C. Eric Hager, Nov. 3, 1967; 1 child, Elizabeth Hager Finley. BA in Sociology, Brescia U., 1966. VISTA vol., vol. leader Office Econ. Opportunity, White Mountain, Alaska, 1966—67; VISA and Peace Corps recruiter, cons. Gale Assocs., Washington, 1968; program asst. Office Econ. Opportunity, Washington, 1969—70, program analyst, 1970—71; program dir. Nat. Ctr. for Voluntary Action, Washington, 1971—73; chair, CEO Hager Sharp, Inc., Washington, 1973—. Founder, first pres. Nat. Assn. Women Bus. Owners, Washington, 1974; chmn. U.S. Dept. Trustees Small Bus. Adv. Coun., Washington, 1980—82; pres. Nat. Small Bus. United, Washington, 1992; vis. prof., mentor Brescia U. Editor: (monthly column) Washington Bus. Jour., 1995—97. Bd. dirs. Greater Washington Bd. Trade, Washington, 1990—, Lab Sch. Washington, 1991—95, pres. bd. dirs., 1996—. Named Bus. Woman of the Yr., Nat. Assn. Women Bus. Owners, Washington, 1985, Small Bus. of the Yr., D.C. C. of C., Washington, 1995, Bus. Woman of the Yr., United Cerebral Palsy, Washington, 1998; named one of 25

Heroines and Heroes Whose Actions Over the Last Quarter Century Have Given Women in the Workplace a Better Shot, Working Women mag., 2001. Mem.: Leadership Washington (bd. mem. 1987—), Cosmos Club. Office: Hager Sharp Inc 1090 Vermont Ave NW Washington DC 20005

HAGERMAN, JOHN DAVID, lawyer; b. Houston, Aug. 1, 1941; s. David Angle and Noima L. (Clay) H.; m. Linda J. Lambright, June 25, 1975; children: Clayton Robert, Holly Elizabeth. BBA, So. Meth. U., 1963; JD, U. Tex., Austin, 1966. Bar: Tex. 1966, U.S. Ct. Appeals (5th cir.) 1967, U.S. Supreme Ct. 1969; cert. civil trial law, 1980-95; real estate broker Tex. Pres., owner Hagerman & Sereau, Inc., The Woodlands, Tex., 1966—. Condr. bank creditor rights seminars; mem. adv. bd. Klein Bank. Contbr. articles to profl. jours. Res. dep. sheriff Montgomery County, Tex.; former bd. dirs. Montgomery County Fair Assn., 1978—, Montgomery County Hosp. Dist. Found., Seven Coves Homeowners Assn. Mem. ABA, Tex. Bar Assn., Houston Bar Assn., Houston Outdoor Advtsg. Assn., Tex. Assn. Civil Trial Splsts., Tex. Assn. Bank Counsel, Comml. Real Estate Assn. Montgomery County, Houston Philosoph. Soc., Petroleum Club (Houston), Woodlands Country Club, Beta Theta Pi. Republican. Avocations: swimming, tennis, jogging, shooting. Office: Hagerman & Sereau Inc 24800 Interstate 45 Ste 100 The Woodlands TX 77386-1987

HAGERMAN, MICHAEL CHARLES, lawyer, arbitrator, mediator; b. Webster City, Iowa, Aug. 20, 1951; s. Charles Arnold and Jill Hamilton (Son de Regger) H.; m. Birgit A. Hagerman; children: Kelly, Douglas, Alexander, Christine, Jacqueline. BA with honors, U. Iowa, 1973; MBA, U. Utah, 1978; JD, Drake U., 1981; Grad., U.S. Army Command/Gen. Staff, Coll., Ft. Leavenworth, Kans., 1988. Bar: Iowa 1981, Mass. 1995. Clk. Iowa Resources, Legal Aid of Polk County, and State of Iowa, Des Moines, 1978-81; contract atty. Fisher Controls Internat., Inc., Marshalltown, Iowa, 1981-84; contracts mgr. Emerson & Cuming, Inc., Canton, Mass., 1984-85; contract atty. GTE Govt. Sys., Taunton, Mass., 1986-90, v.p., gen. counsel, sec. ISI Sys., Inc., Andover, Mass., 1990-94; legal counsel Swan Tech. Inc., Marlboro, Mass., 1994-95; pvt. practice Franklin, Mass., 1995—; counsel Fleet Boston Fin., 1998—. Contbr. articles to profl. jours. Capt. U.S. Army, 1973-78, Germany; lt. col. U.S. Army Res. ret. Mem. Sigma Chi (chpt. Balfour award 1973), Phi Alpha Delta (chpt. pres. 1980-81). Avocations: sailing, writing, travel. E-mail: mchagermanesq@msn.com.

HAGERTHEY, GWENDOLYN IRENE, retired music educator; b. Sheffield, Eng., Sept. 28, 1937; arrived in U.S., 1938; d. Colin Clifford and Dorothy Abbott Oldfield; m. George Robert Hagerthey, June 23, 1962; children: Wendy Lee Hagerthey Canfield, Scot Edward. BS in Music, Trenton State Coll., 1959. Tchr. music Northfield Pub. Schs., NJ, 1959—64, 1971—74, Enfield Pub. Schs., Conn., 1974—78, Mt. Olive Twp. Pub. Schs., Budd Lake, NJ, 1978—99; ret., 1999. Organist, choir dir. various chs. including Stanhope (N.J.) Meth. Ch., 1950—98; camp music dir. Willow Lake Day Camp, Lake Hopatcong, NJ, 1985—97. Vol. Shore Meml. Hosp., Somers Pt., NJ, 1999—, Meadowview Nursing Home, Northfield, 1999—; dir. Atlantic County Hist. Soc., Somers Pt., 1999—. Named Rookie of Yr., Shore Meml. Hosp., 2000; recipient Govs. award for Outstanding Tchg., 1991. Mem.: AAUW (1st v.p. 1959—61). Home: 26 E Meyran Ave Somers Point NJ 08244

HAGERTY, POLLY MARTIEL, financial analyst, construction executive; b. Joliet, Ill., Aug. 17, 1946; d. George Albert and Gene Alice (Roush) Jerabek; m. Theodore John Hagerty, Feb. 12, 1972. BS in Elem. Edn., Midland Luth. Coll., 1968; MEd in Early Childhood Edn., U. Ill., 1977; MBA in Fin., U. Tex., 1986. Elem. tchr. Madison Heights (Mich.) Sch. Dist., 1968-70, Taft Sch. Dist., Lockport, Ill., 1970-72; systems clerk U.S. Army, The Pentagon, Washington, 1972-74; psychology aide Psychology Clinic U. Ill., Urbana, 1974-75; elem. tchr. Champaign (Ill.) Sch. Dist., 1975-77; with recruitment Standard Oil of Ohio, Cleve., 1977-78; v.p. NCNB Texas-Houston, 1981-88, Citibank, Tucson, 1988-92; substitute tchr. Austin (Tex.) Ind. Sch. Dist., 1993-94; project adminstr. Taylor Woodrow Comtys./Steiner Ranch, Ltd., Austin, 1994—; co-owner Hagerty Constrn. Co., Austin, 1994—. Pres. Christus Victor Luth. Ch., League City, Tex., 1985-88, Luth. Ch. of the Foothills, Tucson, 1990-92; treas. Holy Cross Luth. Ch., Austin, 1996—2002. Recipient Golden Circle Sales and Svc. award, 1991. Mem. NAFE, AAUW, U. Ill. Alumni Club. Republican. Lutheran. Avocations: jazzercise, skiing, needlework, spectator sports, gourmet cooking. Office: 3405 Grimes Ranch Rd Austin TX 78732-2141 Home: 22101 W Summit Dr Spicewood TX 78669 E-mail: polly.hagerty@us.taylorwoodrow.com.

HAGG, REXFORD A. lawyer, former state legislatorr; b. Sioux Falls, S.D., May 10, 1957; m. Cindy Hagg; 1 child. Student, Nebr. U., S.D. State U. City atty. City of Box Elder, S.D., 1984—; mem. S.D. Ho. of Reps., 1988—98, vice chmn. judiciary com., mem. legis. procedure and taxation coms., speaker, 1997-98; atty. Whiting, Hagg & Hagg, Rapid City, S.D. Home: 1721 West Blvd Rapid City SD 57701-4555 Office: Whiting Hagg & Hagg 601 West Boulevard PO Box 8008 Rapid City SD 57709

HAGGARD, GERALDINE LANGFORD, primary school educator, adult education educator, consultant; b. Wellington, Tex., Dec. 12, 1929; d. Frank and Zelma Dell (Edmondson) Langford; children: Colby, Sarah, Mary. MEd, Tex. Women's U., 1973, EdD, 1980; Cert. in Reading Recovery, Ohio State U., 1989. Elem. sch. tchr. Denton County (Tex.) Schs., 1949-62, Plano (Tex.) Ind. Sch. Dist., 1963-69, reading tchr., reading dir., 1999-2001. Vis. prof. Tex. Woman's U. Editor and author lang. arts texts; contbr. articles to profl. jours.; author: Teaching and Assessing Comprehension Strategies, 2003. Sunday Sch. tchr. Prairie Creek Baptist Ch., Plano, 1994—; vol. facilitator Journey of Hope program for grief counseling. Named Hero Plano ISD centennial celebration, 1998. Mem. N.Am. Coun. Reading Recovery (bd. mem. 1995-99), Internat. Reading Assn., Tex. State Coun. Reading, Tex. Assn. Improvement of Reading, Coalition Reading English Suprs. Tex. (sec. 1994-97), Tex. Ret. Tchrs. Assn. (Plano chpt.), Alpha Delta Kappa, Delta Kappa Gamma, Phi Delta Kappa. Home: 2017 Meadowcreek Dr Plano TX 75074-4663

HAGGARD, JOAN CLAIRE, church musician, piano instructor, accompanist, adjudicator; b. Ann Arbor, Mich., July 7, 1932; d. Clifford Buell and Bertha (Woodhurst) Wightman; m. Harold Wallace Haggard, June 30, 1956; children: Alan C., Stephen T., John A., Marian E. BA, Carleton Coll., 1954; postgrad., Ecole des Beaux Arts, Fontainebleau, France, 1954, U. Mich., 1954-55; A., Am. Guild Organists, 1980. Cert. pvt. piano tchr. Organist, choir dir. St. Paul's Episc. Ch., Riverside, Ill., 1955-59; dir. of music St. Andrew's Episc. Ch., Livonia, Mich., 1960-72; organist Christ Episc. Ch., Dearborn, Mich., 1973-83; dir. of music St. Philip's Episc. Ch., Rochester, Mich., 1983-92; organist, music coord. 1st United Meth. Ch., Farmington, Mich., 1992-2000. Pvt. piano tchr., Livonia, 1960—; piano instr. Southfield (Mich.) Sr. Adult Ctr., 1992-99; accompanist Creative and Performing Arts High Sch., Livonia, 1987-90; accompanist many solo instrumental and vocal performances, 1959—; student performance on piano and voice adjudicator Nat. Fedn. Music, Mich. State Band and Orch. Assn. Editor Livonia Youth Symphony Soc. newsletter, 1972-77; contbr. articles to profl. jours. Pres. Livonia Youth Symphony Soc., 1973-76; program dir. Episcopal Diocese Mich. Jr. Choir Camp, 1981-84, 87-89; coord. daily worship Triennial Conv. Episcopal Ch., Detroit, 1988. Mem. Am. Guild Organists (dean Detroit chpt. 1976-79, gen. chmn. nat. conv. 1986, councillor Region V 1986-92), Nat. Guild Piano Tchrs. (judge piano auditions 1987—), Music Tchrs. Nat. Assn., Assn. Anglican Musicians, Hymn Soc. in the U.S. and Can., Assn. Diocesan Liturgy and Music Commns., Music Commn. Episcopal Diocese Mich. (chmn. 1980-81), Mich. Fedn. Music Clubs (pres. eastern dist. 1998-2000), Mich. Music Tchrs. Assn. (local assn. chmn. 1996—, student performance on piano and voice adjudicator), Piano Tchrs. Forum (Livonia area, pres. 1995-97), SAI Friend of Arts, PEO. Avocations: bird watching, nature, reading (especially murder mysteries). Home: 33974 Hampshire St Livonia MI 48154-2722

HAGGARD, WILLIAM ANDREW, lawyer; b. Miami, Feb. 20, 1942; s. Curtis Andrew and Marjorie (Tumlin) H.; m. Carole Ann Erali; children: Michael Andrew, Rebecca M. BA, Fla. State U., 1964; JD, Mercer U., 1967. Bar: Fla. 1967, U.S. Dist. Ct. (5th cir.) 1972, U.S. Supreme Ct. 1972, U.S. Ct. Appeals 1981. Clk. Fla. State Atty.'s Office, 1967; asst. state atty. Eleventh Jud. Cir., 1967-68; chief prosecutor, mil. judge, trial counsel USAF, 1968-71; assoc. Frates, Floyd, Pearson & Stewart, 1971-72; ptnr. Rentz, McClellan & Haggard, 1972-79, Rentz & Haggard, 1979-82; sr. ptnr. Haggard & Kirkland, 1982-89, Wm. Andrew Haggard & Assoc., 1989-93, Haggard & Stone, Coral Gables, Fla., 1993-95, Haggard Parks & Stone, P.A., 1995—, Haggard & Parks, P.A., 1999—2001, Haggard Parks Haggard & Bologna, P.A., 2001—. Instr. Fla. bar continuing legal edn., 1977-82; vis. lectr. U. Fla. Law Sch., 1977-82 Commr. Fla. Commn. on Ethics, 1990-91; mem. Mercer U. Alumni Bd.; bd. dirs. Fla. State U. Found.; chmn. Fla. State U. Coll. of Arts and Scis. Leadership Counsel; Gov. Bush appointee Fla. State Bd. Trustees. Fellow Internat. Acad. Trial Lawyers (state chair); mem. ATLA, ABA, Am. Bd. Trial Advocates, Dade County Bar Assn., Acad. Fla. Trial Lawyers (bd. dirs. 1995-96), Internat. Soc. Barristers, Million Dollars Advocates Club, Phi Delta Phi, Sigma Chi. Office: 330 Alhambra Cir Coral Gables FL 33134-5004 E-mail: mail@haggardparks.com.

HAGGARD, WILLIAM HENRY, meteorologist; b. Woodbridge, Conn., Nov. 20, 1920; s. Howard Wilcox and Josephine Cecelia (Foley) H.; m. Blanche Woolard, Mar. 21, 1944 (div. May 1967); children: William Henry Jr., Robert H.; m. Martina Wadewitz, Oct. 1, 1967. BS in Physics, Yale U., 1942; cert. in profl. meteorology, MIT, 1942; MS in Meteorology, U. Chgo., 1946; postgrad., Fla. State U., 1958-59. Instr. meteorology N.C. State U., Raleigh, 1946-47; rsch. meteorologist U.S. Weather Bur., 1947-48; forecaster USWB Nat. Airport, 1949-50; instr. U.S. AID, Washington, 1950-51; staff weather rsch. project U.S. Navy, Norfolk, Va., 1951-54; chief adv. svcs. br. U.S. Weather Bur., Washington, 1954-59, asst. chief Office of Plans, 1960-61; dep. dir. Nat. Weather Records Ctr., Asheville, N.C., 1961; dir. Nat. Climatic Ctr., Asheville, 1963-75; pres. Climatol. Cons. Corp., Asheville, 1976-97, v.p., 1998; cons., 1999—. Mem. weather com. U.S. Power Squadron, Raleigh, N.C., 1988-98. Contbr. articles to tech. jours., 1947-99. Bd. dirs. ARC, Asheville, 1965-70, United Way, Asheville, 1964-70. Capt. USN, 1942-45, with Res. 1951-54. Recipient Tech. Adminstr. award NOAA, Washington, 1970, Am. Meteor. Soc. award outstanding Contbrns. to Applid Meteorology, 2001. Fellow Am. Meteorol. Soc. (cert. cons. meteorologist, bd. dirs. pvt. sector meteorology sect. 1989-92, mem. cert. cons. meteorologist bd. 1983-88), Nat. Coun. Indsl. Meteorologists (pres. 1988-89, bd. dirs. 1987-90, 94-96, 99-2001, sec., treas. 1994-2002). Republican. Presbyterian. Avocations: sailing, photography. Office: William H Haggard CCM LLC 150 Shope Creek Rd Asheville NC 28805-9795 E-mail: cccavl@aol.com.

HAGGEN, DONALD E. food products executive; CEO Haggen Foods, Bellingham, Wash., co-chmn., 1996—. Office: Haggen's Inc PO Box 9704 Bellingham WA 98227-9704

HAGGERSON, NELSON LIONEL, JR., education educator; b. Silver City, N.Mex., June 11, 1927; s. Nelson L. and Gladys Lenore (Jackson) H.; m. B. Kate Baldwin, June 1, 1949 (dec. 2001); children: Patrick, Frederick, Teresa, Rebecca, Lionel, Mary; m. Catherine Ramsey, Dec. 1, 2001. BA, Vanderbilt U., 1949; MS, Western N.Mex. U., 1952; PhD, Claremont Grad. U., 1960. Cert. secondary tchr.; cert. adminstr. Dir. Exptl. Sch. Webster Coll., Webster Groves, Mo.; asst. prof. edn. Western N.Mex. U., Silver City; prin. Cobre High Sch., Bayard, N.Mex.; prof. emeritus edn. Ariz. State U., Tempe. Vis. prof. U. W.I., St. Augustine, Trinidad and Tobago, 1993-99, U. Pitts., 1982, 91, 92, R.I. Coll., 1991, Western N.Mex. U., 1988, 97, 98, 99, 2000, 01. Author: Secondary Education Today, 1967, To Dance With Joy, 1971, Naturalistic Research Paradigms: Theory and Practice, 1983, Informing Educational Policy and Practice Through Interpretive Inquiry, 1992, From Geronimo's Lookout, Growing Up and Living in the Southwest: An Autobiography, 1993, Oh Yes I Can!, A Biography of Arlena Seneca, 1994, A Celebration: The Life of Father Ramon Estivill, Renaissance Man of God, 1999, Expanding Curriculum Research and Understanding, 2000, Stories of the Academy: Learning From the Good Mother, 2002, The Mission of the Scholar: Research and Practice, A Tribute to Nelson Haggerson, 2002, also 12 book chpts.; guest editor: Education in Asia, Silver Ann Edit., World Coun. Curriculum and Instrn., Winter, 1995; contbr. over 50 articles to profl. jours. With USN, 1945-46. Fulbright fellow, 1986; recipient Award in Curriculum, MacDonald, 1986, Lifetime Achievement award Am. Biog. Inst.; named Outstanding Researcher, Coll. Edn., 1987, Outstanding Tchr., 1988; Rsch. grantee Deakin U., Victoria, Australia, 1988, The Mission of the Scholar, Research and Practice: A Tribute to Nelson Haggerson, 2002. Mem. AERA, ASCD, Profs. Curriculum, Soc. for Study of Curriculum History, World Coun. for Curriculum and Instrn. (program chmn. 1989), Order Internat. Fellowship, Phi Delta Kappa, Phi Kappa Phi, Kappa Delta Pi. Home: PO Box 24177 Tempe AZ 85285-4177 E-mail: haggerson@asu.edu.

HAGGERTY, JAMES JOSEPH, lawyer; b. Scranton, Pa., June 12, 1936, s. James J. Haggerty and Margaret W. Cummings; m. Cecelia Ellen Lynett; children: Jean Margaret McGrath, Mauri Elizabeth Collins, James Joseph Jr., Matthew Edward, Cecelia Ellen, Daniel Patrick, Kathleen Mary. BA in Econs., Holy Cross Coll., Worcester, Mass., 1957; JD, Georgetown U., 1960; LLD (hon.), U. Scranton, 1987; LHD (hon.), Villanova U., 1995. Bar: Pa. 1961, Ct. Common Pleas Lackawanna County 1961, U.S. Dist. Ct. (mid. dist.) Pa. 1961, U.S. Ct. Appeals (3d cir.) 1962, U.S. Ct. Claims 1985. Assoc. Farrell Butler Kearney & Parker, Scranton, 1961-62; law clk. to Hon. William J. Nealon U.S. Dist. Ct. (mid. dist.), Scranton, 1963-64; ptnr. Casey Haggerty and McDonnell, Scranton, 1965-70, Haggerty McDonnell O'Brien, Scranton, 1970-87; former sec. of commonwealth State of Pa., Harrisburg, 1987-89; gen. counsel to gov. Commonwealth of Pa., Harrisburg, 1989-93; ptnr. Haggerty, McDonnell & O'Brien, Scranton, 1993—. Apptd. by U.S. Dist. Ct. trustee in bankruptcy of Blue Coal Corp., 1976-86; mem. hearing com. 3.03 Disciplinary Bd. Pa. Supreme Ct.; permanent mem. Jud. Conf. U.S. 3d Jud. Cir.; mem. Fed. Jud. Screening Com., 1996-2001; chmn. bd. dirs. Shamrock Comm. Corp.; past bd. dirs. Specialty Plastics Products Inc.; past. bd. dirs., solicitor 1st Nat. Community Bank Dunmore. Trustee U. Scranton, 1979—86, chmn. bd., 1982—86, mem.Pres.'s Cir., mem. Pres.'s Club; chmn. Real Bob Casey Com., 1985—86; trustee Scranton Prep. Sch., 1995—2000, chmn. bd., 1999—2000; former bd. dirs. Lackawanna United Way, former chmn. profl. and geog. divsn.; bd. dirs. assocs. Scranton Area Found. With U.S. Army, with Pa. N.G. Mem. ABA, ATLA, Am. Bankers Assn., Pa. Bar Assn. (Spl. Achievement award 1988-89), Pa. Trial Lawyers Assn., Pa. Bankers Assn., Lackawanna Bar Assn. (past pres., bd. dirs.), Greater Scranton C. of C. (bd. dirs., former v.p.), Holy Cross Coll. Alumni Assn. N.E. Pa. (past pres., Outstanding Alumnus award 1982), Scranton Prep. Sch. Alumni Assn. (past mem. bd. govs., T. Donald Reinfret S.J. award Outstanding Alumnus of Yr. 1985), Friendly Sons of St. Patrick Lackawanna County (mem. exec. com., past pres.), Country Club Scranton (bd. dirs.). Roman Catholic. Office: Haggerty McDonnell & O'Brien 203 Franklin Ave Ste 1 Scranton PA 18503-1989 E-mail: hmolaw@epix.net.

HAGGERTY, JEAN MARIE, journalist; b. Suffern, N.Y., Jan. 18, 1975; d. Francis Michael Haggerty and Margaret Murphy; m. Clinton van der Spuy. BA Polit. Sci., SUNY, Oneonta, 1995; MA Internat. Journalism, City U., London, 1997. Rschr. house ops. N.Y. State Assembly, Albany, 1996; reporter-in-tng. Newsweek Internat., London, 1997; reporter, mng. editor Instnl. Investor Newsletters, N.Y.C., London, 1997—2000; reporter Internat. Fin. Rev., N.Y.C., 2000—. Contbr. articles to profl. jours. Recipient 1st Pl. award analytical newswriting newsletter journalism category, Nat. Press Club, 2000. Mem.: Soc. Profl. Journalists, Nat. Fedn. Press Women, N.Y. Fin. Writers Assn. Roman Catholic. Avocations: writing, photography, hiking, travel. Home: 31 Tower Ct 1A Canonbury St Islington London N12 US England Office: Thomson Fin Internat Fin Rev 33 Aldgate High St London EC3N England

HAGGERTY, ROBERT HENRY, lawyer; b. N.Y.C., Feb. 25, 1919; s. Daniel A. and Helen Marie (Henry) H.; m. Mary Rita O'Neil, Aug. 28, 1945 (dec. 1990); children: Robert Jr., Daniel J., Nancy D., Thomas H; m. Nadia Ismail, 1991. BBA, Manhattan Coll., 1940; LLB, Harvard U., 1953. Bar: N.Y. 1954, Fla. 1977. Assoc. Root, Ballantine, Harlan, Bushby & Palmer (now Dewey, Ballantine), N.Y.C., 1953—56, 1962—95, ptnr., 1965—; atty. Gen. Electric Co., N.Y.C. and Schenectady, N.Y., 1956-62. Bd. dirs. Ticor Title Guarantee Co., N.Y.C. Editor: PLI Real Estate Construction Current Problems, 1973; editor (vols. 8, 29, 58) PLI Real Estate Construction, 1969-72. Bd. dirs. Plandome (N.Y.) Property Assocs., 1965-76, pres., 1970-76; pres. Plandome Mills Property Owners, 1980-82; village justice of Plandome Manor, 1983-89, mayor, 1989-93. Served to maj. USMC, 1941-45, PTO. Decorated Silver Star, Purple Heart. Mem. Plandome Country Club, Grand Harbor Golf and Country Club. Roman Catholic. Address: Dewey Ballantine 1301 Avenue of the Americas New York NY 10019-6092 Home: 1870 Paseo del Lago Vero Beach FL 32967-7260

HAGGERTY, ROBERT JOHNS, physician, educator; b. Saranac Lake, N.Y., Oct. 20, 1925; s. Gordon Abbott and Nina (Johns) H.; m. Muriel Ethel Protzmann, Oct. 29, 1949; children: Robert, Janet, Richard, John. AB, Cornell U., 1946, MD, 1949; AM (hon.), Harvard U., 1975; DSc (hon.), Ind. U., 1990. Diplomate Am. Bd. Pediatrics. Intern Strong Meml. Hosp., Rochester, N.Y., 1949-51; from resident to chief resident pediatrics Children's Hosp. Med. Ctr., Boston, 1953-55; med. dir. family health care program Harvard Med. Sch., also asst. prof. pediatrics, 1953-64; prof. pediatrics, chmn. dept. U. Rochester Sch. Medicine, 1964-75; Roger I. Lee prof. health services, chmn. dept. health services Harvard Sch. Pub. Health, 1975-78; prof. pediatrics Harvard Med. Sch., Boston, 1975-78, clin. prof., 1978-80; pres. Wm. T. Grant Found., N.Y.C., 1980-92; clin. prof. pediatrics Cornell U. Med. Sch., N.Y.C., 1980-92; prof. pediatrics emeritus U. Rochester Sch. Medicine, 1992—; exec. dir. Internat. Pediatric Assoc., 1993-98. Dir. gen. pediatrics acad. devel. program Robert Wood Johnson Found., 1978-88; mem. health svcs. rsch. sect. USPHS, 1964-70, 82-84, chmn., 1968-70, 82-84; mem. N.Y. State Health Planning Adv. Coun., Carnegie Coun. on Children, 1972-77; chmn. panel health scis. rsch. com. on nat. needs for biomed. and behavioral rsch. per. NRC, 1975-78; mem. bd. U.S. Com. on UNICEF, 1981-87; mem. Gov.'s Coun. on Grad. Med. Edn., N.Y. State, 1989-93. Editor: (with M. Green) Ambulatory Pediatrics, 1968, 5th edit., 1999, (with J. Lucey) Pediatrics, 1973-80, Pediatrics in Rev., 1978—, Bull. N.Y. Acad. Medicine, 1992-99; assoc. editor New Eng. Jour. Medicine, 1959-64; contbr. articles to med. jours. Mem. vis. com. Grad. Sch. Edn., Harvard U., 1982-88; bd. dirs. Grantmakers in Health, 1985-89; bd. overseers, social scis. dept., Tufts U., 1990-94; bd. visitors U. Okla. Sch. Pub. Health, 1991-94. Capt. USAF, 1951-53. Recipient Martha M. Eliot award Am. Pub. Health Assn., 1976, Disting. Alumni award Cornell U. Med. Coll., 1987, 6 awards various pediatric socs., 1989, Primary Care Achievement award PEW Found. Health Professions Commn., 1994; Markle scholar in acad. medicine, Markle Found., N.Y.C., 1962-67, fellow Ctr. for Advanced Study Behavioral Scis., Stanford, Calif., 1974-75 Mem.: Alliance for Health Care for All (trustee 1991—94), Am. Health Fedn. (trustee 1989—92), NY Acad. Medicine (trustee, sec. 1989—92), Inst. of Medicine (coun. 1974—77, chmn. com. on prevention of mental illness 1992—93, chmn. steering com. nat. study quality assurance programs 1975—76, Gustave Lienhard award 1989), Soc. Pediat. Rsch. (v.p. 1970—71), Internat. Epidemiol. Assn., Assn. Am. Med. Colls., Ambulatory Pediat. Assn. (chmn. 1963—64, George Armstrong award 1969), Am. Pediat. Soc. (Joseph St. Geme award 1989, John Howland award 1998, E.H. Christopherson award for internat. child health 2001), Am. Acad. Pediats. (v.p., pres. 1983—85, Grulee award 1981, Dale Richmond award 1981, Aldrich award 1986, Job Smith award 1987, Abraham Jacobi award 1996, Lifetime Edn. award 2002), Am. Assn. Poison Control Cus. (pres. 1962—64), Assn. Med. Sch. Pediat. Dept. Chairmen (pres. 1969—70), Brit. Paediatric Soc. (hon.), Harvard Club N.Y.C., Alpha Omega Alpha, Phi Beta Kappa. E-mail: robert_haggerty@urmc.rochester.edu.

HAGGERTY, ROSANNE, entrepreneur; BA, Amherst Coll., 1982; postgrad., Columbia U. Coord. housing devel. Bklyn. Cath. Charities; founder, exec. dir. Common Ground, N.Y.C., 1990—. Bd. dirs. N.Y.C. Citizens Housing and Planning Coun., Ctr. Urban Cmty. Svcs., The Echorey Green Found., Fordham Preparatory Sch. Trustee Amherst Coll.; dir. Times Sq. Bus. Improvement Dist. MacArthur fellow, 2001. Office: Common Ground Cmty 505 8th Ave 15th Fl New York NY 10018

HAGGETT, ROSEMARY ROMANOWSKI, academic administrator; BA in Biology summa cum laude, U. Bridgeport, 1974; PhD in Physiology, U. Va., 1979. Postdoctoral fellow Northwestern U., Evanston, Ill., 1979-82, asst. prof. biology Loyola U. Chgo., 1982-87; asst. rsch. scientist zoology U. Md., College Park, 1987-88; from program dir. to divsn. dir. animals and nutrition USDA, 1988-94, dep. assoc. adminstr., 1988-94; dean Coll. Agr., Forestry and Consumer Scis. W.Va. U., Morgantown, 1994-99, assoc. provost acad. programs, 1999—. Office: WVa Office of Provost PO Box 6203 Morgantown WV 26506-6203 E-mail: rrhaggett@mail.wvu.edu.

HAGGLUND, CLARANCE EDWARD, lawyer, publishing company owner; b. Omaha, Feb. 17, 1927; s. Clarance Andrew and Esther May (Kelle) H.; m. Dorothy Souser, Mar. 27, 1953 (div. Aug. 1972); children: Laura, Bret, Katherine; m. Merle Patricia Hagglund, Oct. 28, 1972. BA, U. S.D., 1949; JD, William Mitchell Coll. Law, 1953. Bar: Minn. 1955, U.S. Ct. Appeals (8th cir.) 1974, U.S. Supreme Ct. 1963; diplomate Am. Bd. Profl. Liability Attys. Ptnr. Hagglund & Johnson and predecessor firms, Mpls., 1973—; mem. Hagglund, Weimer and Speidel, PA; publ., pres. Common Law Publishing Inc., Golden Valley, Minn., 1991—. Pres. Internat. Control Sys., Inc., Mpls., 1979—, Hill River Corp., Mpls., 1976—, gen. counsel Minn. Assn. Profl. Ins. Agts., Inc., Mpls., 1965-86; CFO, Pro-Trac, software for profl. liability ins. industry. Contbr. articles to profl. jours. Served to lt. comdr. USNR, 1945-46, 50-69. Fellow Internat. Soc. Barristers; mem. Lawyers Pilots Bar Assn., U.S. Maritime Law Assn. (proctor), Acad. Cert. Trial Lawyers Minn. (dean 1983-85), Nat. Bd. Trial Advocacy (cert. in civil trial law, bd. dirs.), Douglas Amdahl Inns of Ct. (pres.), Ill. Athletic Club (Chgo.), Edina Country Club (Minn.), Calhoun Beach Club (Mpls.). Roman Catholic. Avocation: flying. Home: 3168 Dean Ct Minneapolis MN 55416-4386 Office: Common Law Publishing Inc 3601 W 76th St #250 Minneapolis MN 55435-5149 E-mail: hagglund@pro-ns.net.

HAGIN, T. RICHARD, lawyer; b. Thomasville, Ga., Sept. 13, 1941; s. Wesley R. and Elizabeth (Skinner) H.; m. Deborah Hayes, June 19, 1981; children: Jennifer Bridges, Lori Mikula; children from previous marriage: John Wesley Hagin, Grace Elizabeth Hagin. AA, North Fla. C.C., Madison, 1961; student, Fla. State U., 1961-62; JD, Stetson U., 1964. Fla. 1964, Oreg. 1992, U.S. Dist. Ct. (mid. dist.) Fla. 1965, U.S. Ct. Appeals (5th cir.) 1965, U.S. Ct. Appeals (11th cir.) 1981, U.S. Ct. Mil. Appeals 1991, U.S. Supreme Ct. 1971. Atty. Law Offices of David A. Davis, Bushnell, Fla., 1964; ptnr. Davis and Hagin, Bushnell, 1965; atty. in pvt. practice Bushnell, 1966-67; ptnr. Hagin, Hughes, Rardon & Rodriguez, Bushnell, 1989-1996, Getzen and Hagin, Bushnell, 1967-71; pres. Getzen & Hagin, P.A., Bushnell, 1971—. Local counsel CSX R.R., Bushnell, 1967-87, gen. counsel Tax Collector of Sumter County, Bushnell, 1976-95; forfeiture atty. Sumter County Sheriff Dept., Bushnell, 1983-89; county atty. Sumter County, Fla., 1969-76; city atty. City of Webster, Fla., 1966-87, City of Coleman, Fla., 1969-73; gen. counsel Sumter County Indsl. Authority, Bushnell, 1979-89, Sumter County Hosp. Authority, Bushnell, 1969-85. Mem. City Coun., Bushnell, 1967-69; pros. atty. Sumter County, 1969-73; chmn. Withlacochee Regional Planning Coun., Ocala, Fla., 1973-75; chmn. 5th Jud. Cir. Grievance Com., 1973-76. Mem. ABA, Assn. Trial Lawyers Am., Fla. Bar, Oreg. Bar Assn., Acad. Fla. Trial Lawyers. Democrat. Office: Getzen and Hagin PO Box 248 Bushnell FL 33513-0019

HAGLUND, THOMAS ROY, research biologist, consultant, educator; b. Beloit, Wis., Jan. 19, 1950; s. Roy Wilhelm and Marguerite Jean (Anderson) H.; m. Doris Anne Mendenhall, Oct. 22, 1988; 1 child, Victoria Tamsin. BS in Earth Sci., U. Wash., 1972; postgrad., U. Ill., Chgo., 1972-74; PhD in Biology, UCLA, 1981. Lectr., biology Calif. State Univ., L.A., 1981-83; sci. chair Windward Sch., L.A., 1983—97, 2002—; rsch. biologist UCLA, L.A., 1985—98; dir. Windward Conservation Biology Inst., 1997—. Adj. prof. biology Calif. State Poly. U., Pomona, 1991—; cons. U.S. Army C.E., L.A., 1979-80, Calif. Dept. Fish and Game, 1986—, Met. Water Dist., L.A., 1991, 93, 94, Dept. Pub. Works, Los Angeles County, 1991, 94—, U.S. Fish Wildlife Svc., 1992—, Perrier Corps of Am., 1998—; chair So. Calif. Native Fishes Working Group, 1996—. Contbr. chpt. to Historial Biogeography of North American Fish, 1991, articles to Jour. Paleontology, Evolution, Paleobiology, Biochem. Systematics Ecology, Copeia. Grantee NSF, 1978, Calif. Dept. Fish and Game, 1986, 87, 90, 91, 92, 93, 94, 99, World Bank, 1999-2001. Mem. AAAS, Am. Soc. Ichthyology and Herpetology, Am. Fisheries Soc., Desert Fishes Coun., European Ichthyological Congress. Achievements include research in systematics and population genetics of minnows, suckers and sticklebacks, conservation genetics of endangered North American fish, recovery strategies for endangered fishes; biological impacts of sediment management associated with dams. also: Windward Sch 11350 Palms Blvd Los Angeles CA 90066-2104

HAGMAN, SALLY WINGCHONG, physical therapist; b. Hong Kong, Nov. 26, 1962; came to U.S., 1968; d. Bruce Chiu-Lap and Shau King (Lai) Chan. BS in Kinesiology, UCLA, 1984; MS in Phys. Therapy, U. So. Calif., 1986. Phys. therapist San Gabriel (Calif.) Valley Med. Ctr., 1986-88; outpatient phys. therapist, clin. instr. UCLA, 1988-91; orthopaedic therapist South Valley Phys. Therapy, Littleton, Colo., 1991-94, Operation Mobilization, Littleton, 1994—.

Rsch. asst. Chesapeake Biol. Labs., Balt., 1988—89; bd. dirs. Internat. Student Connection. Contbr. articles to profl. jours. Mem. Am. Phys. Therapy Assn., Nat. Athletic Trainers Assn. Republican. Avocations: traveling, cooking. Home: 2697 West Long Pl Littleton CO 80120

HAGMANN, LILLIAN SUE, violin instructor; b. Fontana, Calif., Mar. 10, 1931; d. Riley Royston and Winifred Lillian (Humphry) Green; m. Armand P. Oueilhe, Dec. 17, 1950 (div. 1971); children: Ellen Lynne Oueilhe Keene, Karen Sue Oueilhe Stanton, A. Louis Oueilhe (dec. 1971), Gregoire Pierce Oueilhe; m. Rolf Hagmann, May 19, 1971. AA, Chaffey Coll., 1951; Travel Counselor, Internat. Travel Tng., Chgo., 1974; student, Suzuki Violin Tchr. Tng. Inst., Guelph, Can., 1992, Suzuki Violin Tchr. Tng. Inst., Forest Grove, Oreg., 1993, 97, Occidental Coll., Eagle Rock, Calif., 1994, Suzuki Violin Tchr. Tng. Inst., Stevens Point, Wis., 1995, Suzuki Violin Tchr. Tng. Inst., Aspen, Colol., 1998, Suzuki Violin Tchr. Tng. Inst., Chgo., 2000. Pricer MacNall Bldg. Materials, Santa Barbara, Calif., 1964-67; office mgr. Laguna Blanca Sch. Devel. Program, Santa Barbara, 1968; pub. rels. asst. to mgr. Goleta (Calif.) Savs. and Loan, 1969-71; travel counselor Around The World Travel, Palatine, Ill., 1974-77; travel mgr./dir. pub. rels. Newport Area Travel, Newport Beach, Calif., 1977-80; travel counselor Cresenta Valley Travel, La Crescenta, Calif., 1981; violin instr. Arise Acad. Arts, Pomona, Calif., 1989-94, U. Redlands (Calif.) Cmty. Sch. Music, 1989—2003, Arts Encounter, Rowland Heights, Calif., 1996—97. Del. 1st Stringed Instrument Edn. Del., China, 1997. Mem. The Fandango Chamber Group. Violinist Santa Barbara Symphony, 1962-70, Riverside (Calif.) City Coll. Symphony, 1990-97; judge Search for Talent contest Riverside Exch. Clubs, 2000-02; active Adams Sch. PTA, Santa Barbara, 1967—; bd. dirs. Calif. Congress PTA; organizer, pres. Assn. for Neurologically Handicapped Children, 1970-71; choir Corona Cmty. Ch., 1995-97; mem. five piece ensemble Evang. Free Ch. of Corona; organizer violin concerts for children including MC Orange County Suzuki Festival, 2002-03. Democrat. Avocations: gardening, artist. Home: 1143 Via Santiago Corona CA 92882-3950 E-mail: mrbeethoven@prodigy.net.

HAGMEIER, CLARENCE HOWARD, retired anesthesiologist; b. Pitts., Dec. 23, 1914; s. Clarence Howard and Bertha May (Rogers) H.; m. Hilda Marie Bronder, Oct. 30, 1942 (dec. Feb. 10, 2000); children: Clarence, Roberta, Susan, David, Michael. BS with honors U. Pitts., 1943; MD, 1950. Diplomate Am. Bd. Anesthesiology; Oreg. State Bd. Med. Examiners. Intern Good Samaritan Hosp., Portland, Oreg., 1950-51; resident Oreg. Med. Sch. and Hosp., 1951-53; pvt. practice Portland, 1953-87; ret., 1987. Chmn. Mulrnomah County Rep. Com., 1980—82; pres. Portland Ronald McDonald House, 1991—93; mem. internat. adv. bd. Ronald McDonald House, 1993—95; mem. exec. com. Oreg. Presch. Immunization Consortium, 1992—2000; sr. role model OASIS, 1993, Vols. of Am. Allstar, 1996. With USN, World War II. Fellow Am. Coll. Anesthesiologists, Internat. Coll. Surgeons; mem. Oreg. Med. Assn. (pres. 1976-77), Multnomah County Med. Soc. (pres. 1974), Oreg. Health Sci. U. Sch. Medicine Alumni Assn. (mem. exec. coun.), Rotary (pres. Portland club 1979-80, dist. gov. 1983-84, nat. coord. PolioPlus, 1986-88, mem. exec. com. Nat. PolioPlus Immunization Task Force 1992-94, Found. citation for meritorious svc. 1991, Svc. Above Self award 1993, Found. Disting. Svc. award 1995, del. to Coun. on Legis. 1995, 98, PolioPlus Partners Com.), Theta Chi, Chi Rho Nu, Phi Rho Sigma. Republican. Avocation: gardening. Home: 4907 SW Canterbury Ln Portland OR 97219-3326

HAGN, GEORGE HUBERT, electrical engineer, researcher; b. Houston, Sept. 15, 1935; s. H. John and Lucile Emilie H.; m. Rose Marie Meier (dec. Apr. 1997); children: Cheryl Ann, David John. BSEE, Stanford U., 1959, MSEE, 1961. Registered elec. engr., Calif. Rsch. engr. Stanford Rsch. Inst. (name changed to SRI Internat. 1977), Menlo Park, Calif., 1959—69, sr. rsch. engr., 1969—73; asst. dir. SRI Washington Office, Arlington, Va., 1973—76, 1976—80; program dir. SRI Telecomm. Sci. Ctr., Arlington, 1980—84, asst. dir. Telecom. Scis. Ctr., 1984—86, asst. dir. Info. Sci. and Tech. Ctr., 1986—88, asst. dir. Info. and Telecom. Scis. Ctr., 1988—93, sr. staff advisor Info. and Telecom. Scis. Ctr., 1991—93, sr. staff advisor Info. Telecom. and Automation Divsn., 1993—96, sr. staff advisor signals tech. program, 1996—2000. U.S. industry mem., electromagnetic propagation panel NATO Adv. Group for Aerospace R & D, 1989-91. Assoc. editor Radio Sci., 1975-78. Adult leader Boy Scouts Am., Annandale, Va.; bd. dirs. Annandale Christian Community for Action, 1990-93; active Annandale United Meth. Ch. Fellow IEEE (life, spectrum mgmt. and electromagnetic compatibility, guest editor IEEE Transactions, EMC 1977, 81, spl. issues spectrum mgmt., mem. adminstrv. com. Antenna and Propagation Soc. 1993-96, sec. IEEE wave propagation stds. com. Antenna and Propagation Soc. 1989-2002, chair IEEE antenna stds. com. 1998-2002, assoc. editor stds. AP-S mag. Antenna and Propagation Soc. 1991—), Washington Acad. Scis. (life, bd. mgrs. 1994-97, v.p. adminstrn. 1996-97); mem. AAAS, Am. Geophys. Union, N.Y. Acad. Sci., Pa. Acad. Sci., Internat. Union Radio Sci. (chmn. U.S. URSI com. 8 on radio noise 1974-75, vice chmn. internat. URSI com. E 1975-78, U.S. com. E on electromagnetic noise and interference 1975-78, chmn. internat. URSI com. E on electromagnetic noise and interference 1978-81, vice chmn., treas. U.S. nat. com. 1978-81, mem. internat. URSI liaison com. with Internat. Telecom. Union's Internat. Radio Consultative Com. and Internat. Telegraph and Telephony Consultative com. 1981-90, chmn. 1984-90, mem. ITU radioncomm., sector study groups 1, 3, and 4). Home: 4208 Sleepy Hollow Rd Annandale VA 22003-2046 E-mail: ghagn@erols.com.

HAGOOD, LEWIS RUSSELL, lawyer; b. Persia, Tenn., July 13, 1930; s. Hobart Verlin and Stella Rose (Carter) Hagood; m. Mary Evelyn Morrisette, Mar. 15, 1952; children: Lewis Russell Jr., Mary Victoria, Paul Gregory. Student, Lincoln Meml. U., Harrogate, Tenn., 1947-49; BS, E. Tenn. State U., 1952; JD, U. Tenn., 1963. Bar: Tenn. 1964, U.S. Dist. Ct. (ea. dist.) Tenn. 1964, U.S. Dist. Ct. (ea. dist.) Ky. 1975, U.S. Tax Ct. 1984, U.S. Ct. Appeals (6th cir.) 1968, U.S. Supreme Ct., cert.: Ea. Dist. Tenn. (fed. mediator), approved mediator: Tenn. Supreme Ct. Ptnr. McLellan, Wright, Hagood, Attys., Kingsport, Tenn., 1964-65; assoc. Arnett & Draper, Attys., Knoxville, Tenn., 1965-67; ptnr. Arnett, Draper & Hagood, Knoxville, 1967—. Mem., pres. Tenn. Bd. Law Examiners, 1994—2002; spkr., lectr. in field. Editor-in-chief: Tenn. Law Rev., 1963—64; contbr. articles to profl. jours. Mem. E. Tenn. chpt. March of Dimes, 1981—84; bd. dirs. Knoxville Symphony, 1977—, Knoxville Teen Ctr., Inc., 1975—97. With U.S. Army, 1954—56. Fellow: Tenn. Bar Found.; mem.: ABA, Knoxville Bar Assn., Tenn. Bar Assn. (past chmn. labor law sect.). Republican. Presbyterian. Avocations: golf, fishing, antique autos. Office: Arnett Draper & Hagood Plz Towers Ste 2300 Knoxville TN 37929

HAGOOD, MURL FELTON, surgeon; b. Marietta, Ga., Oct. 18, 1941; s. Murl Miller and Mary Evelyn (Jones) H.; m. Martha Addie James, June 20, 1965; children: Gregory Felton, Robert Miller, Richard James. MD, Emory U., 1966. Diplomate Am. Bd. Surgery. Am. Bd. Colon & Rectal Surgery. Intern U. Va. Hosp., Charlottesville, 1966-67, surg. resident, 1967-68; med. officer Charleston Naval Hosp. U.S. Navy, 1968-70; resident gen. surgery Med. U. S.C., 1970-73; fellow colon & rectal surgery Ochsner Found. Hosp., New Orleans, 1973-74; pvt. practice-colon & rectal surgery Kennestone Hosp., Marietta, 1974—. Lt. cmdr. USNR, 1968-70. Mem. Cobb County Med. Soc. (pres. 1993-94), Kiwanis Club, Phi Beta Kappa, Alpha Omega Alpha. Methodist. Avocations: golf, boating. Home: 577 Keeler Woods Dr Marietta GA 30064 Office: Surg Assocs of Marietta 790 Church St NW Ste 570 Marietta GA 30060-8967 E-mail: mfhagood@bellsouth.net.

HAGOOD, RICHARD A. academic administrator, educator; Assoc. provost office of exec. v.p. and provost Washington State U.; pres. N.W. Nazarene U., 1993—. Spkr. in field. Mem. bd. dirs. Nampa Sch. Dist., Ch. Nazarene, mem. gen. bd.; chmn. bd. dirs. Mercy Med. Ctr. Office: NW Nazarene U 623 Holly St Nampa ID 83686

HAGOOD, SUSAN STEWART HAHN, clinical dietitian; b. Balt., May 31, 1953; d. Paul Gilbert and Phyllis Jeanette (Mann) Hahn; m. Thomas Richard Hagood, Jr., Nov. 25, 1978; 1 child, Margaret Foster. BS, Western Ky. U., 1975; MS, Ga. State U., 1992. Registered and lic. dietitian; cert. diabetes educator. Dietetic trainee U. Hosp., Jacksonville, Fla., 1975-76; clin. dietitian VA Med. Ctr., Lake City, Fla., 1976-80, in-service and staff devel. dietitian, 1980-85; clin. specialist Clayton Gen. Hosp., Riverdale, Ga., 1985-88; grad. teaching asst. Ga. State U., 1991; primary care and rsch. dietitian VA Med. Ctr., Atlanta, 1992—. Pres. Lake City Hist. Preservation Bd., Fla., 1982—83; chmn. youth adv. com. Columbia County 4-H, Lake City, 1981—84; vol. instr. Tech. Assistance Health Resource Group, 1982—84; co-chmn. Com. for Restoration Columbia County Hist. Mus., 1983—84; bd. dirs. Clayton County unit Am. Heart Assn., 1987—88; mem. Dekalb unit nutrition and cancer work group Am. Cancer Soc., 1993—96, past bd. dirs.; leader Decatur svc. unit Girl Scouts U.S.A., 1993—; mem. Winter Park Hist. Assn., Fla. Mem. Am. Dietetic Assn., Atlanta Dist. Dietetic Assn., Atlanta English Speaking Union, DAR, Colonial Dames Am., Colonial Dames XVII Century, Woodward Acad. Parents Club, Phi Upsilon Omicron, Alpha Xi Delta. Republican. Presbyterian. Avocations: rug making, traveling, hiking, camping. Home: PO Box 982 Decatur GA 30031-0982 Office: VA Medical Ctr 1670 Clairmont Rd Decatur GA 30033-4004

HAGOOD, THOMAS RICHARD, JR., minister, publisher; b. Charlotte, NC, Sept. 16, 1954; s. Thomas Richard and Donna Gwendolyn (Williams) H.; m. Susan Stewart Hahn, Nov. 25, 1978; 1 child, Margaret Foster. BA, Davidson Coll., 1976; MDiv, Columbia Theol. Sem., 1996. Ordained to Presbyn. Ch., 1997. Editor Columbia Publ., Inc., Decatur, Ga., 1976-88, publ., 1988—; min. Barnesville Presbyn. Ch., Ga., 1997-2000; sr. min. Columbia Presbyn. Ch., 2000—. Mem. small ch. com., 1997-00, com. preparation ministry Presbytery Greater Atlanta, 1998—, com. World Wide Mins., 1999-2000. Scoutmaster Boy Scouts of Am., Lake City, Fla., 1982-85; pres. Columbian Countians, Lake City, 1982-85; mem. Govt. Study Com., Columbia County, Fla., 1984; elder Presbyn. Ch., Atlanta. Recipient Silver Beaver award North Fla. coun. Boy Scouts Am., 1986. Mem. English Speaking Union, Lake City Rotary (bd. dirs. 1982-85), Woodward Acad. Parent Club. Avocations: backpacking, camping, reading, woodworking. Home: PO Box 982 Decatur GA 30031-0982

HAGOORT, THOMAS HENRY, lawyer; b. Paterson, N.J., May 30, 1932; s. Nicholas Hugh and Rae (Sytsma) H.; m. Lois Ann Bennett, Sept. 6, 1954; children: Nancy Hagoort Treuhold, Susan Audrey Bick. AB cum laude, Harvard U., 1954, LL.B. magna cum laude, 1957. Bar: N.Y. 1959. Assoc. firm Cleary, Gottlieb, Steen & Hamilton, N.Y.C., 1957-67, ptnr., 1968-90; gen. counsel Albany Internat. Corp., 1991—2002, Sr. V.P., 2002—. Note editor: Harvard Law Rev., 1956—57. Pres. Mountainside Hosp., Montclair, N.J., 1983-85, chmn. bd. trustees, 1985-88; pres. Internat. Baccalaureate of N.Am., N.Y.C., 1980-91, Montclair Bd. Edn. 1966-70; mem., Coun. of Found. Internat. Baccalaureate Orgn., Geneva, 1982-96, pres. and chair exec. com., 1990-96. Mem.: ABA, N.Y. State Bar Assn., Sea Pines Country Club, S.C. Yacht Club, Harvard Club of N.J. (pres. 1977—78). Democrat. Home: PO Box 3229 Hilton Head Island SC 29928-0229

HAGOPIAN, JACOB, federal judge; b. Providence; s. Bedros and Varvar (Leylegian) H.; m. Mary L. Pomoranski; children: Mark Jay, Dana Aquinas, Mary Lou, Jan Christian, Jon Gregory. AB, George Washington U., 1957; JD, Am. U., 1960; grad. thesis in internat. law, Judge Advocate Gen.'s Sch., 1964; postgrad., Indsl. Coll. Armed Forces, 1967. Bar: Va. 1961, R.I. 1964, U.S. Supreme Ct. 1964, U.S. Dist. Ct. R.I., U.S. Dist. Ct. (ea. dist.) Va., U.S. Ct. Appeals (D.C. cir.), U.S. Ct. Customs and Patent Appeals, U.S. Ct. Claims, U.S. Tax Ct. Enlisted U.S. Army, 1944, advanced through grades to 1st sgt. 11th Airborne Divsn., 2d lt. to 1st lt. 82d Airborne Divsn., parachutist, glider pathfinder, & jumpmaster qualified, 1948-50; capt. U.S. Army Security Agency, Washington, 1950-53, 56-60, with 501st Recon group, 1953, 1954-56; advanced through grades to col. U.S. Army, 1953-68; appellate judge U.S. Ct. Mil. Rev. (U.S. Army Ct. Criminal Appeals), Washington, 1968-70; ret. colonel U.S. Army, 1970; appellate judge U.S. Army Judiciary, Washington, 1968-70; dir. law ctr. Roger Williams Coll., Providence, 1970-71; U.S. magistrate judge U.S. Dist. Ct., Providence, 1971—. Legal advisor to intelligence cmty. Spl. Ops., Berlin, 1960—63; group supr. def. appellate divsn. USA Judiciary, Washington, 1964—66; dep. and chief criminal law divsn. OTJAG dept. of the army The Pentagon, Washington, 1966—68; mem. U.S. Army and U.S. Air Force Clemency and Parole Bd.; lectr. Fed. Jud. Ctr., Washington; adj. prof. Am. U., 1971—, Suffolk U. Law Sch.; vis. prof. Naval War Coll.; mem. hon. faculty fellow AV, 1997—, hon. program U. R.I.; mem. code com. Uniform Code of Mil. Justice, Sec. of Def., 2000—; U.S. magistrate judge Jud. Coun., 1st Cir. Ct. of Appeals; qualified parachutist, gliderist, jumpaster and pathfinder. Contbr. articles to profl. jours. Decorated Legion of Merit (2) with first oak leaf cluster; recipient Army Commendation medal with oak leaf cluster. Mem. ABA (former cons. sect. criminal justice, vice chmn. com. on adequate def. and incentives in mil., former sec.-reporter com. mil. law, Houston Justice Assist award 1987, mem. code com. uniform code mil. justice 2000—), Fed. Bar Assn. (past pres. R.I. chpt., mem. nat. coun., mem. nat. chmn. com. criminal law, chmn. U.S. magistrate judge's com.), Inst. Jud. Adminstrn., U.S. Naval War Coll. Found., Nat. Def. U. Found. Office: US Dist Ct Two Exchange Ter Providence RI 02903 Fax: 401-752-7006.

HAGSTEN, IB, animal scientist, livestock consultant; b. Assens, Denmark, May 18, 1943; arrived in U.S., 1971, naturalized, 1980; s. Kresten and Marie (Jakobsen) H.; m. Patricia Ellen Dettman, July 13, 1968; children: Ellen Marie, Scot (dec.), Lisa R. BS, Bygholm Landbrugskole, Horsens, Denmark, 1965; MS, Royal Danish Agr. U., Copenhagen, 1971, Purdue U., 1973, PhD, 1975. Cert. animal scientist; diplomate Am. Coll. Animal Nutrition. Farm laborer, foreman various livestock farms, Denmark, Eng., Germany, Can., 1958-65; tchg. asst. Royal Danish Agr. U., 1969-70; rsch. assoc. Nat. Danish Rsch. Found., Copenhagen, 1971; cons. nutritionist M.D. King Milling Co., Pittsfield, Ill., 1976-77; acting product mgr. Am. Hoechst Corp., Somerville, N.J., 1978, tech. specialist, 1977-83; profl. sales rep. Hoechst Roussel Agri-Vet. Co., Gladstone, Mo., 1983-89, tech. svc. specialist, 1989-90, sr. profl. svc. specialist, 1990-98; pres. Hagsten Enterprises, Internat., livestock cons. svc., Kansas City, Mo., 1999—. Cons. Shell Farm, Inc., Ørum, Denmark, 1970—71, Agri-Bus. Tng. and Devel., Inc., Roswell, Ga., 1979—95, Nat. Renderer's Assn., Hong Kong, 1989, USDA Trade Mission, Moldova, 1995, HRVet-Asia Workshop, Thailand, 1998, Hoechst Asia, Bangkok, 1998; cons. employee-tng. Ukraine and Moldova, 2000, Ukraine, Moldova and Kazakhstan, 2001, Moldova and Hungary, 2002; adj. prof. Rutgers U., New Brunswick, NJ, 1981—84, U. Mo., Columbia, 1990—97; vis. prof. Saratov State Agrarian U., Russia, 2001; pres. Personal Growth Alternatives, 1982—; cert. assessor environ. assistance program Nat. Pork Prodrs. Coun.; cert. agrl. cons., United States, 2001—, Canada, 2002—; cert. assessor environ. assistance program Environ. Mgmt. Svcs. LLC. Author: Energy Metabolism Evaluations, 1971; contbr. articles to profl. jours. and popular publs. Bd. dirs. MACOS handicapped support group, Macomb, Ill., 1976-77; co-chair Cmty. Hunger Walks (CROP), Western N.J., 1978-82; mem. family curriculum bd. Lopatcong Twp. Sch., Phillipsburg, N.J., 1982; vice moderator Pilgrim Presbyn. Ch., Phillipsburg, 1980-83, elder, 1979-83, Gashland Presbyn. Ch., Gladstone, 1990-93; regional exec. bd. mem. United Marriage Encounter, Mo., Kans., 1983-95; bd. dirs. Gashland Christian Presch., 1991-93, World-In-Need Internat., 2002- ; mem. Core of Advocates, Coll. Vet. Medicine Kans. State U.; bd. dirs. Heartland Presbyn. Pro-Life, 1993—, pres., 1999-2002; v.p. Trade Palms, a mission-funding corp., 2001—; bd. dirs. World In Need Internat., 2002-. Sgt. Danish King's Royal Guard, 1959-61. Mem.: Am. Registry Profl. Animal Scientists (chmn. ethics com. 1982—85, cert.), Nat. Feed Ingredient Assn., Am. Coll. Animal Nutrition (charter, diplomate), Am. Soc. Agrl. Cons. Internat. (charter), Am. Soc. Agrl. Cons. (bd. dirs. 1978—81, sec.-treas. 1990—2000, bd. dirs. 1992—94, chmn. ethics com. 1992—94, bd. dirs. 1995—97, v.p. 2000—01, pres. 2002—03, Disting. Svc. award 1980), Danish Soc. Animal Sci., Greater Kans. City Scandinavian Club (bd. dirs. 1992—96). Republican. Avocations: people, gardening, travel, reading. Home and Office: 7212 N Woodland Ave Kansas City MO 64118-2263 E-mail: hagsten@bww.com.

HAGSTROM, JACK WALTER CARL KLING, retired pathology educator; b. Rockford, Ill., Dec. 2, 1933; s. Walter Carl Paul Hagstrom and Loretta Christine (Kling) Pearson; life ptnr. Thomas J. Fleming. AB, Amherst Coll., 1955; MD, Cornell U., 1959. Instr. dept. pathology Cornell U. Med. Coll., N.Y.C., 1962-65, asst. prof., 1965-68; assoc. prof. Case We. Res. U., Cleve., 1968-70, Columbia U., N.Y.C., 1970-75, prof. pathology, 1975-91, prof. emeritus, 1991—. Attending pathologist Univ. Hosp., Cleve., 1968—70, Presbyn. Hosp., N.Y.C., 1981—91; dir. dept. pathology Harlem Hosp., N.Y.C., 1981—91; hon. curator modern poetry Amherst Coll. Libr., Amherst, Mass., 1981—. Author: Thom Gunn: A Bibliography, 1979, Dana Gioia: A Descriptive Bibliography with Critical Essays, 2002; contbr. Mem. corporator Holden Arboretum, Mentor, Ohio; chmn. Friends of Amherst Coll. Libr., 1973—90. Fellow: Am. Coll. Cardiology; mem.: Pvt. Librs. Assn., Acad. Am. Poets, Printing History Soc., Bibliograph. Soc. London, Bibliograph. Soc. U. Va., Bibliograph. Soc. Am., Kiambu Club, Northport Yacht Club, Durban Club, Jockey Club, Club Odd Vols., Grolier Club, Pratts Club, Travellers' Club, Garrick Club. Episcopalian. Home: PO Box 105 Seven Ponds Towd Rd Water Mill NY 11976

HAGSTROM, RICHARD MICHAEL, lawyer; b. Eau Claire, Wis., Feb. 19, 1951; s. Robert James and Edna Marie Hagstrom; m. Deirdre Abbey, Dec. 17, 1977; children: Lindsey Starr, Kevin Ford. BS, U. Minn., 1973; JD, U. Utah, 1976. Bar: Minn. 1976, Utah 1977, U.S. Ct. Appeals (8th cir.) 1981, U.S. Ct. Appeals (10th cir.) 1987, U.S. Ct. Appeals (6th cir.) 1995, U.S. Supreme Ct. 1987, U.S. Dist. Ct. Minn. 1976, U.S. Dist. Ct. Utah 1987, U.S. Dist. Ct. (ea. dist.) Wis. 1989, Ariz. 1994, U.S. Dist. Ct. (ea. dist.) Mich. 1994. Atty. Meagher, Geer, Mpls., 1976—77, Sydney Berde, P.A., St. Paul, 1978—81; shareholder Berde & Hagstrom, P.A., St. Paul, 1981—85; chief antitrust sect. Utah Atty. Gen. Office, Salt Lake City, 1985—88; assoc. Zelle, Hofmann, Voelbel, Mason & Gette LLP, Mpls., 1988—91, ptnr., 1992—. Pub. chmn. No. Suburban br. Luth. Brotherhood, St. Paul, 1993-96. Mem. ABA, Minn. Bar Assn., Utah State Bar Assn. Avocations: skiing, water skiing, scuba diving, jet skiing. Office: Zelle Hofmann Voelbel Mason & Grette LLP 33 S 6th St Ste 4400 Minneapolis MN 55402-3710

HAGUE, WILLIAM EDWARD, editor, author; b. Duquesne, Pa., Feb. 2, 1919; s. William Edward and Edith (Osburn) H.; m. Margaret Cleland Anderson, July 22, 1950 (div.). AB, Princeton U., 1940; postgrad., U. Pitts. Sch. Law, 1940-41. Assoc. editor Tide mag., 1947-49; promotion dir. Living for Young Homemakers mag., 1949-50, copy editor, 1951-54, mng. editor, 1954-61; editor Living's Guide to Home Planning mag., 1958-61; with Conde Nast Publs., N.Y.C.; sr. editor House & Garden, 1961; editor-in-chief House & Garden Guides, 1962-72; asst. account exec. Fitzgerald Advt. Agy., New Orleans, 1950-51. Author: How to Decorate With Color, 1964, What You Should Know About Furniture, 1965, Planning Your Vacation Home, 1968, Plan Your Baths for Beauty and Efficiency, 1969, Plan The Kitchen That Suits You, 1969, Making The Most of The One-Room Apartment, 1969, Your Vacation House, How To Plan It, 1972, Doubleday's Complete Basic Book of Home Decorating, 1976, Know Your America, California, 1978, Remodel, Don't Move, 1981, The New Complete Basic Book of Home Decorating, 1983; editor: Country Kitchens and Baths, 1987; contbg. editor: Reader's Digest's Household Hints, 1987. Lt. USNR, 1942—46. Recipient Dorothy Dawe award for disting. journalistic coverage in home furnishings field, 1969 Mem. Princeton Triangle Club. Home: 49 E 73rd St Apt 5F New York NY 10021-3560

HAHIN, CHRISTOPHER, metallurgical engineer, corrosion engineer; b. Buffalo, Dec. 26, 1945; s. Leo Paul and Nancy (Morabito) H.; children: Bonnie L., Terence J., Jonathan R. BS, Mich. State U., 1968; MS, U. Ky., 1974. Cert. profl. engr., Ill., Calif. Missile facilities engr. USAF, Strategic Air Command, Minot AFB, N.D., 1968-72; rsch. metallurgist U.S. Army Corps of Engrs. Constrn. Engr. Rsch. Lab., Champaign, Ill., 1974-81; prin. engr. Container Corp. Am., Carol Stream, Ill., 1981-84; chief metallurgist Avondale Ind., Danly Machine Divsn., Chgo., 1984-86; engr. structural materials and bridge investigations Bur. Materials and Phys. Rsch., Ill. Dept. Transp., Springfield, 1987—. Prin. assoc. Materials Protection Assn., Springfield, Ill., 1984—; panel mem. Transp. Rsch. Bd., Nat. Acad. of Scis., 1997—. Author: Book Science Baseball, 1983; contbr. Advanced Casting Technology Conf., Kalamazoo, 1986, ASM Metals Handbook vol. 13, 1987, 2003; patentee in field; contbr. over 120 articles to profl. and tech. jours. With USAF 1968-72. Fellow Ashland Oil U. Ky., 1971; decorated A.F.C.M. 1st Oak Leaf Cluster; recipient U.S. Army Spl. Act Svc., 1981; named Statewide Engr. of Yr., Ill. Dept. Transp., 2001. Mem. ASTM (mem. com. steel, stainless steel and related alloys), Am. Soc. for Metals, Nat. Corrosion Engrs. Assn., Am. Welding Soc. Independent. Office: Ill Dept Transp 126 E Ash St Springfield IL 62704-4766 E-mail: hahinc@nt.dot.state.il.us.

HAHM, DAVID EDGAR, classics educator; b. Milw., Sept. 30, 1938; s. Edgar David and Loraine Emily (Stebnitz) H.; m. Donna Lorraine Seifert, Aug. 8, 1964; children: Melanie Davida, Christopher David, Geoffrey Kenneth, Martha Maria. BA, Northwestern Coll., 1960; student, Wis. Luth. Sem., 1960-61; MA, U. Wis., 1962, PhD, 1966. Asst. prof. U. Mo., Columbia, 1966-69; asst. prof. classics Ohio State U., Columbus, 1969-72, assoc. prof., 1972-78, prof., 1978—, chmn., 1999—. Vis. fellow Corpus Christi Coll., Cambridge, Eng., 1990-91. Author: The Origins of Stoic Cosmology, 1977; contbr. articles to jours., chpts. to books. Trustee Dublin Hist. Soc., 1974-79, pres., 1974-76; active Archtl. Rev. Bd., Dublin, Ohio, 1976-83, chmn., 1980-82; mem. exec. bd. Worthington Hist. Soc., 1981-89, 93—; trustee Old Dublin Assn., 1996—, treas., 1997—. Fellow Ctr. Hellenic Studies; mem. AAUP, Am. Philol. Assn., Am. Philos. Assn., Classical Assn., Mid. West and South, History of Sci. Soc., Soc. Ancient Greek Philosophy. Lutheran. Office: Ohio State U Dept Greek and Latin 230 N Oval Mall Columbus OH 43210-1335 E-mail: hahm.1@osu.edu.

HAHN, BESSIE KING, library administrator, lecturer; b. Shanghai, People's Republic of China, May 14, 1939; came to U.S., 1959; d. Jen Fong and Wei (Lok) King; m. Roger Carl Hahn, 1962 (div. 1983); children: Angela Yee-mei, Michael King-yau, Belinda Shee-wei; m. David Ware Duhme, 1989. BA, Mt. Marty Coll., Yankton, S.D., 1961; MSL.S., Syracuse U., 1972. Librarian Carrier Corp., Syracuse, N.Y., 1972; life sci. bibliographer Syracuse U. Libraries, 1973-75, head sci. and tech., 1975-78; asst. dir. reader services Johns Hopkins U. Library, Balt., 1978-81; dir. libraries Brandeis U., Waltham, Mass., 1981-96, asst. provost for librs., univ. libr., 1996-2000, nat. women's com. libr., asst. provost, 2000—03, univ. libr. emerita, 2003—. Cons. Shanghai Jiao Tong U. Library, Shanghai, 1983—, hon. prof., 1984 Editor Jour. Ednl. Media and Library Scis., 1983-99; contbr. articles to profl. jours. Bd. govs. Abraham Lincoln Brigade Archives, 1989-99; commr. New England Assoc. Schs. and Colls., Inc., 1991-97; exec. dir. Newton Symphony Orch., 2003—. Recipient Golden Cup award Johns Hopkins U. Class of 1980, 1980. Mem. ALA, Chinese-Am. Librarians Assn. (pres. 1982-83). Home: 148 Sudbury Rd Weston MA 02493-1351 Office: Brandeis U Libr 415 South St Waltham MA 02453-2728 E-mail: bhahn@brandeis.edu.

HAHN, BEVRA HANNAHS, medical educator; b. Wheeling, W.Va., Dec. 9, 1939; d. Chester Hobart and Isa May (Quillen) Hannahs; m. Theodore J. Hahn, May 3, 1964; children: Alysanne Yvonne, April Dianne. BS, Ohio State U., 1960; MD, Johns Hopkins U., 1964. Diplomate Am. Bd. Internal Medicine, Am. Bd. Rheumatology. Intern Barnes Hosp., Washington U., St. Louis, 1964-65; resident in medicine Washington U., St. Louis, 1965-66, from instr. to assoc. prof. medicine, 1969-83; fellow in rheumatology Johns Hopkins U., Balt., 1966-69; prof. medicine, chief of rheumatology UCLA, 1983—. Chmn. Immunologic Scis. Study Sect. NIH, Washington, 1983-85; mem. Nat. Arthritis Adv. Bd., U.S. Dept. Health and Human Services, Washington, 1983-85. Contbr. articles to profl. jours. Mem. Am. Coll. Rheumatology (pres.1999), Am. Soc. Clin. Investigation, Am. Assn. Immunologists, Lupus Found. Am. (med. advisor 1980—), Arthritis Found., Phi Beta Kappa, Alpha Omega Alpha. Presbyterian. Avocations: tennis, swimming, music, reading. Office: UCLA Rheumatology 37-139 1000 Veteran Ave Los Angeles CA 90024-2704

HAHN, CATHY ANN CLIFFORD, sales executive; b. Celina, Ohio, June 6, 1947; d. William Eugene and Kathleen (McNally) Clifford; m. John Hahn (div.) BS, U. Dayton, 1969. Sales rep. J.T. Baker Instruments, Bridgeport, Conn., 1972-76, E.I. duPont de Nemours & Co., Dallas, 1976-81, new bus. developer Wilmington, Del., 1981-83, sr. tng. designer, 1983-84, sales tng. mgr., 1984-85, ter. mgr., trainer Dallas, 1985-94; v.p. Planet Cadillac Clothing Co., Plano, Tex., 1994-95; owner Metaluna Ltd. Co., Dallas, 1996—2000, Party Animals!, Plano, Tex., 1998—; realtor Coldwell Banker, Plano, 2000—. Vol. Am. Cancer Soc., Dallas, 1986—. Home and Office: 5217 Old Shepard Pl Plano TX 75093-5002 E-mail: realcathy@comcast.net.

HAHN, DAVID BENNETT, hospital administrator, marketing professional; b. Louisville, Ohio, June 5, 1945; s. Bennett E. and Betty J. (McGaughey) H.; m. Elizabeth Burdine, Oct. 4, 1975; children: Stephen, Sarah, Scott. BS in Agrl. Econs., Ohio State U., 1967; MBA, U. Toledo, 1977. Social worker, supr. Franklin County Welfare, Columbus, Ohio, 1968-71, pers. asst., 1971-73; pers. dir. Mansfield (Ohio) Gen. Hosp., 1973-76; adminstr. Kettering Hosp., Loudonville, Ohio, 1978-81; v.p. Marietta (Ohio) Hosp., 1981-92; CEO City Hosp., Bellaire, 1992-94, mktg. dir. med. integrated svcs., 1995—; pres. Advanced Practice Systems, 1996—2001; v.p. Tech Risk Mat. Group, 1998—2002. Coach

St. Clairsville H.S. Soccer. Mem. East Muskingham Civic Assn. Bd., 1982-92; bd. dirs., recreation coord. Marietta Soccer League; v.p. Mid Ohio Mktg. Assn., 1992; boys soccer coach St. Clairsville HS, 1999—; bd. dirs. Belmont County Salvation Army, 1992—. Fellow Am. Coll. Health Care Execs.; mem. Assn. MBA Execs., Am. Mktg. Assn. (local chpt. bd. dirs.), Ohio Hosp. Assn. Com., Ohio Hosp. Soc. for Planning and Mktg., Loudonville C. of C. (pres. bd. dirs. 1981), Bellaire C. of C. (bd. devel. com. 1992-93), Wheeling Soccer Assn. (coach), St. Clairsville Area Soccer Assn. (bd. pres.), Pioneer Alumni Ohio State U. (bd. dirs., pres.), Rotary (bd. dirs. Loudonville club 1978-81), Lions (1st v.p.), Masons. Mem. Calvary Presbyterian. Avocations: soccer, reading, gardening, running. Office: PO Box 575 Saint Clairsville OH 43950

HAHN, DAVID LOUIS, family practice physician, educator; b. Chgo., July 22, 1945; s. Erwin L. and Marion E. (Failing) H.; m. Carolyn A. Fruehling, Apr. 22, 1978; children: Andrew D., Christopher W. AB, Stanford U., 1967, MD, 1973; MS in Epidemiology & Preventive Medicine, U. Wis., 1997. Diplomate Am. Bd. Family Practice, Nat. Bd. Med. Examiners. Resident in family practice U. Iowa, 1977-79; family practitioner Dean Med. Ctr., Madison, Wis., 1981—; clin. prof. family medicine U. Wis. Med. Sch., Madison, 1997—. Med. dir. Dean Found. Health Rsch. and Edn., Madison, 1992—96; dir. rsch. project devel. Wis. Rsch. Network, 1996—2001; reviewer med. jours. and non-profit orgns. Contbr. numerous articles to profl. jours. Mem.: European Respiratory Soc., Am. Thoracic Soc., N.Am. Primary Care Rsch. Group, Am. Acad. Family Physicians (Advanced Rsch. Tng. grantee 2000—02). Avocation: prairie restoration. Office: Arcand Park Clin 3434 E Washington Ave Madison WI 53704-4155 E-mail: dlhahn@facstaff.wisc.edu.

HAHN, ELLIOTT JULIUS, lawyer; b. San Francisco, Dec. 9, 1949; s. Leo Wolf and Sherry Marion (Portnoy) H.; m. Toby Rose Mallen; children: Kara Rebecca, Brittany Atira Mallen, Michael Mallen, Adam Mallen. BA cum laude, U. Pa., 1971, JD, 1974; LLM, Columbia U., 1980. Bar: N.J. 1974, Calif. 1976, D.C. 1978, U.S. Dist. Ct. N.J. 1974, U.S. Dist. Ct. (cen. dist.) Calif. 1976, U.S. Supreme Ct. 1980. Assoc. von Maltitz, Derenberg, Kunin & Janssen, N.Y.C., 1974-75; law clk. L.A. County Superior Ct., 1975-76; atty. Atlantic Richfield Co., L.A., 1976-79; prof. Summer in Tokyo program Santa Clara Law Sch., 1981-83; assoc. prof. law Calif. Western Sch. Law, San Diego, 1980-85; atty. Morgan, Lewis & Bockius, L.A., 1985-87; assoc. Whitman & Ransom, L.A., 1987-88, ptnr., 1989-93, Sonnenschein Nath & Rosenthal, L.A., 1993-97, Hahn & Bolson, LLP, 1997—. Vis. scholar Nihon U., Tokyo, 1982; vis. lectr. Internat. Christian U., Tokyo, 1982; adj. prof. law Southwestern U. Sch. Law, 1986-93, Pepperdine U. law Sch., 1986-93, U. So. Calif. Law Sch., 1997-98; lectr. U. Calif., Davis, Law Sch. Orientation in U.S.A. Law Program, 1994-97. Author: Japanese Business Law and the Legal System, 1984; contbr. chpt. on Japan to The World Legal Ency.; internat. law editor Calif. Bus. Law Reporter. Vice-chmn. San Diego Internat. Affairs Bd., 1981-85; bd. dirs. San Diego-Yokohama Sister City Soc., 1983-85, L.A.-Nagoya Sister City Soc., 1986-1996; mem. master planning com. City of Rancho Palos Verdes, Calif., 1989-91; advisor, exec. com. Calif. Internat. Law Sect., 1990-91, 95, appointee exec. com., 1991-94, vice-chmn., 1992-93, chair, 1993-94; appointee, trustee Palos Verdes Libr. Dist., 1993-94; bd. dirs. Internat. Student Ctr. UCLA, 1996—, pres., 2000-01. Mem. ABA, State Bar Calif., LA County Bar Assn. (bd. dirs. internat. sect., exec. com. Internat. Legal Sec. 1987—, sec. 1995-96, 2d v.p. 1996-97, 1st v.p. 1997-98, chmn. 1998-99, appointee Pacific rim com. 1990-98, chmn. 1991-92, 95-98, trustee 1997-98), Assn. Asian Studies, U. Pa. Alumni Club (pres. San Diego chpt. 1982, pres. coun. Phila. 1983), Anti Defamation League, Japanese-Am. Soc. (book rev. editor Seattle 1983-85). Jewish. Office: Hahn & Bolson LLP 1000 Wilshire Blvd # 1600 Los Angeles CA 90017-2457 E-mail: ehahn@hahnbolsonllp.com.

HAHN, ERWIN LOUIS, physicist, educator; b. Sharon, Pa., June 9, 1921; s. Israel and Mary Hahn; m. Marian Ethel Failing, Apr. 8, 1944 (dec. Sept. 1978); children: David L., Deborah A., Katherine L.; m. Natalie Woodford Hodgson, Apr. 12, 1980. BS, Juniata Coll., 1943, D.Sc., 1966; MS, U. Ill., 1947, PhD, 1949; D.Sc., Purdue U., 1975, U. Stuttgart, Germany, 2001; DrRerNat, U. Stuttgart, 2001. Asst. Purdue U., 1943-44; research assoc. U. Ill., 1950; NRC fellow Stanford, 1950-51, instr., 1951-52; research physicist Watson IBM Lab., N.Y.C., 1952-55; assoc. Columbia U., 1952-55; faculty U. Calif., Berkeley, 1955—, prof. physics, 1961—, assoc. prof., then prof. Miller Inst. for Basic Rsch., 1958-59, 66-67, 85-86. Eastman vis. prof. Balliol Coll., Oxford, Eng., 1988-89; cons. Office Naval Rsch., Stanford, 1950-52, AEC, 1955—; spl. cons. USN, 1959; adv. panel mem. Nat. Bur. Stds., Radio Stds. div., 1961-64; mem. NAS/NRC com. on basic rsch.; advisor to U.S. Army Rsch. Office, 1967-69; faculty rsch. lectr. U. Calif., Berkeley, 1979. Author: (with T.P. Das) Nuclear Quadrupole Resonance Spectroscopy, 1958. Served with USNR, 1944-46. Fellow Guggenheim Found., 1961-62, 69-70, NSF, 1961-62; recipient prize Internat. Soc. Magnetic Resonance, 1971, Humboldt Found. award, 1977, 94, Alumni Achievement award Juniata Coll., 1986, citation U. Calif., Berkeley, 1991; co-winner prize in physics Wolf Found., 1984; named to Calif. Inventor Hall of Fame, 1984; vis. fellow Brasenose Coll., Oxford U., 1969-70, life hon. fellow, 1984—. Fellow AAAS, Internat. Soc. Electron Paramagnetic Resonance, Am. Phys. Soc. (past mem. exec. com. div. solid state physics, Oliver E. Buckley prize 1971), Soc. Magnetic Resonance in Medicine (hon.), The Inst. of Physics Great Britain; mem. NAS (co-recipient Comstock prize in electricity, magnetism and radiation 1993), Slovenian Acad. Scis. and Arts (fgn.), French Acad. Scis. (fgn. assoc.), Berkeley Fellows, Royal Soc. U.K. (fgn. mem.). Home: 69 Stevenson Ave Berkeley CA 94708-1732 Office: U Calif Dept Physics 367 Birge Berkeley CA 94720-0001

HAHN, FRANK HORACE, economics educator; b. Berlin, Apr. 26, 1925; s. Arnold and Maria (Katz) H.; m. Dorothy Salter, 1946. BSc in Econs., London, 1945, PhD, 1951; MA, Cambridge (Eng.) U., 1960; D in Social Scis. (hon.), Birmingham (Eng.) U., 1981; DLitt (hon.), U. East Anglia, Norwich, 1984; Doctor honoris causa, U. Strasbourg, 1984; DSc in Econs. (hon.), London, 1985; D (hon.), U. York, 1991; LittD (hon.), U. Leicester, 1993; PhD (hon.), U. Athens, 1993; doctor honoris causa, De L'Univ. Paris X, Nanterre, 1999. Lectr., reader math. econs. Birmingham U., 1948-60; lectr. econs. Cambridge U., 1960-66; prof. econs. London Sch. Econs., 1967-72, prof., 1972-92, prof. emeritus, 1992; prof. ordinario U. Siena, 1989—2000; hon. fellow London Sch. Econs., 1989; fellow Churchill Coll., Cambridge, 1960—; emeritus U. Siena, 2000—. Co-author (with Kenneth J. Arrow): General Competitive Analysis, 1971; author: The Share of Wages in the National Income, 1972, Money and Inflation, 1982, Equilibrium and Macroeconomics, 1984, Money, Growth and Stability, 1985; co-author (with Robert Solow): A Critical Essay on Modern Macroeconomic Theory, 1995; editor: The Economics of Missing Markets, Information, and Games, 1989; co-editor (with Ben Friedman): Handbook of Monetary Economics, 1990; co-editor: (with Fabio Petri) General Equilibrium: Problems and Prospects, 2003; mng. editor Rev. Econ. Studies, 1965—68, assoc. editor Jour. Econ. Theory, 1971—76. Recipient Palacky gold medal Czechoslovak Acad. Scis., 1991. Fellow Brit. Acad., Econometric Soc. (pres. 1968-69), NAS (fgn. assoc. 1988), Am. Acad. Arts and Scis. (hon.), Am. Econ. Assn. (hon.), Royal Econ. Soc. (pres. 1986-89), Brit. Assn. Advancement Sci. (pres. sect. F 1990).

HAHN, FREDERIC LOUIS, lawyer; b. Chgo., Apr. 28, 1941; s. Max and Margery Ruth (Goodman) H.; m. Susan Firestone, Mar. 26, 1967; 1 child, Frederic Firestone. AB with highest distinction, Cornell U., 1962, MBA with highest distinction, 1963; JD magna cum laude, Harvard U., 1966. Bar: Ill. 1966; CPA, Ill. Assoc. Hopkins & Sutter, Chgo., 1966-72, ptnr., 1973-94, Mayer, Brown & Platt (now Mayer, Brown, Rowe & Maw), Chgo., 1994—. Bd. dirs. Lyric Opera of Chgo., 1988—. Recipient Gold medal (CPA exam) State of Ill., 1963. Mem. Phi Beta Kappa. Home: 1377 Scott Ave Winnetka IL 60093-1444 Office: Mayer Brown Rowe & Maw 190 S La Salle St Ste 3100 Chicago IL 60603-3441 E-mail: fhahn@mayerbrownrowe.com.

HAHN, GEORGE LEROY, agricultural engineer, biometeorologist; b. Muncie, Kans., Nov. 12, 1934; s. Vernon Leslie and Marguerite Alberta (Breeden) H.; m. Clovice Elaine Christensen, Dec. 3, 1955; children— Valerie, Cecile, Steven, Melanie. BS, U. Mo., Columbia, 1957, PhD, 1971; MS, U. Calif., Davis, 1961. Agrl. engr., project leader and tech. advisor Agrl. Research Service, U.S. Dept. Agr., Columbia, Mo., 1957, Davis, Calif., 1958-61, Columbia, 1961-78, Clay Center, Nebr., 1978—. Contbr. articles to profl. jours. and books on impact of climatic and other environ. factors on livestock prodn., efficiency, and well-being, evaluation of methods of reducing impact and techniques for measuring dynamic responses and characterizing stress in meat animals. Recipient award Am. Soc. Agrl. Engrs.-Metal Bldgs. Mfrs. Assn., 1976 Fellow Am. Soc. Agrl. Engrs. (dir. prof. coun. 1991-93); mem. Am. Meteorol. Soc. (award for outstanding achievement in bioclimatology 1976), Internat. Soc. Biometeorology (treas. 1999—), Am. Soc. Animal Sci. Office: US Meat Animal Rsch Ctr PO Box 166 Clay Center NE 68933-0166 E-mail: hahn@email.marc.usda.gov.

HAHN, GEORGE THOMAS, materials engineering educator, researcher; b. Vienna, July 28, 1930; came to U.S., 1938; s. Rudolph and Stella (Honig) H.; m. Charlotte Minovitz, June 10, 1956; children: Claudia Abbott, Elizabeth. BSME, NYU, 1952; MS in Metall. Engring., Columbia U., 1956; ScD in Metall. Engring., MIT, 1959. Rsch. engr. Westinghouse Rsch. Labs., Pitts., 1952; cons. Mfg. Labs., Cambridge, Mass., 1956-60; rsch. assoc. metal sci. sect. Battelle Meml. Inst., Columbus, Ohio, 1960-66, mgr. metal sci. sect., 1966-79; prof. materials sci. and engring. Vanderbilt U., Nashville, 1979-98, prof. materials sci. and engring. emeritus, 1998—, chmn. dept. materials sci. and engring/, 1988-93; co-dir. Ctr. Materials Tribology, Nashville, 1987-96; pres. Mechanics & Materials Techs. Inc., Nashville, 1988—. Co-editor: Fracture, 1959, Fast Fracture and Crack Arrest, 1977, Crack Arrest Methods, 1980; contbr. numerous articles to profl. jours. Capt. USAF, 1953-57. Fellow Am. Soc. Metals (Campbell Meml. Lectr. 1981), Metall. Soc., Am. Soc. Lubrication Engrs. Avocation: painting. Office: Vanderbilt U Dept Mech Engring Box 1592 Sta B Nashville TN 37235 E-mail: hahngt@vuse.vanderbilt.edu.

HAHN, GORDON MARTIN, political scientist, writer; b. Frankfurt, Germany, Feb. 19, 1955; (parents Am. citizens); s. Gordon Martin and Carol Marie (Lombardy) Hahn; m. Marina Markovna Styogantseva, Dec. 30, 1993; 1 child, Gordon Martin III. BA in Polit. Sci., Boston Coll., 1986, MA in Polit. Sci., 1988; PhD in Polit. Sci., Boston U., 1995. Vis. asst. prof. The Am. Univ., Washington, 1995; rsch. fellow Hoover Inst. Stanford (Calif.) U., 1995—96; rsch. scholar Am. Coun. Tchrs. of Russian, Washington, 1996—97; archival rsch. coord. Hoover Instn. Stanford U., 1997—2000; vis. lectr. dept. polit. sci. Stanford U., 2001; vis. scholar Hoover Instn., Stanford U., 2000—; lectr. dept. polit. sci. San Jose State U., 2002—03; Fulbright tchg. and rsch. fellow St. Peterburg (Russia) State U., 2003—. Grad. rsch. scholar Inst. for Study of Conflict, Ideology and Policy, Boston, 1989—93; internat. rels. cons. Wm. Robinson & Assocs., Boston, 1989. Author: (book) Russia's Revolution from Above, 2001; contbr. articles to profl. jours. Recipient Rsch. scholarship, Hoover Instn., Stanford U., 1995—96, Title VIII Rsch. scholarship, Am. Coun. Tchrs. of Russian, 1996; grantee, Kennah Inst. for Advanced Russian Studies, 1994. Avocations: baseball, jazz. Office: Stanford Univ Hoover Instn Palo Alto CA 94305-6010

HAHN, HAROLD THOMAS, physical chemist, chemical engineer; b. N.Y.C., May 31, 1924; s. Gustave Hahn and Lillie Martha (Thomas) H.; m. Bennie Joyce Turney, Sept. 5, 1948; children: Anita Karen, Beverly Sharon, Carol Linda, Harold Thomas Jr. Student, Hofstra U., 1941-43; BSChemE, Columbia U., 1943-44; PhD in Chemistry, U. Tex., 1950-53. Chem. engr. Manhattan Dist. U.S. Army, Los Alamos, N.Mex., 1945-47; chem. engr. U. Calif., Los Alamos, 1947-50; sr. scientist Gen. Electric Co., Hanford, Wash., 1953-58; sect. chief, chem. research dept. Phillips Petroleum Co., Idaho Falls, Idaho, 1958-64; sr. staff scientist Lockheed Missiles & Space Co., Palo Alto, Calif., 1964-92; private cons., 1992—. Contbr. articles to profl. jours.; patentee in field. Pres. Edgemont Gardens PTA, Idaho Falls, 1963-64; commr. cub scout div. Stanford area council Boy Scouts Am., Palo Alto, 1973-76, also cubmaster pack 36, 1973-80, chmn. troops 36 and 37, 1975-77; mem. adminstrv. bd. Los Altos Meth. Ch. Served to col. U.S. Army, 1944-46, with res., 1946-84, col. res. ret. Humble Oil Co. fellow, 1952, Naval Bur. Ordnance fellow, 1953. Fellow Am. Inst. Chemists; mem. AIAA, Magnetics Soc. IEEE (elected sr. mem.), Calif. Acad. Scis., Internat. Platform Assn., Am. Chem. Soc., Sigma Xi, Phi Lambda Upsilon, Kappa Rho. Home and Office: 661 Teresi Ln Los Altos CA 94024-4162

HAHN, HELENE B. motion picture company executive; b. N.Y.C. BA, Hofstra U.; JD, Loyola U., Calif., 1975. Bar: Calif. 1975. V.p. bus. affairs Paramount Pictures Corp., L.A., sr. v.p. bus. affairs, 1983-84; sr. v.p. bus. and legal Walt Disney Studios, Burbank, Calif., 1984-87, exec. v.p., 1987-94; with Dreamworks, 1994—. Recipient Frontrunner award in bus. Sara Lee Corp., 1991, Big Sisters Achievement award, 1992, Clairol Mentor award, 1993, Women in Bus. Magnificent Seven award, 1994.

HAHN, JAMES KENNETH, mayor, lawyer; b. L.A., July 3, 1950; s. Kenneth and Ramona Hahn; m. Monica Ann Teson, May 19, 1984; children: Karina Natalie, Jackson Kenneth. BA in English magna cum laude, Pepperdine U., 1972, JD, 1975. Bar: Calif. 1975. Law clk. L.A. County Dist. Atty.'s Office; city pros. L.A. City Atty.'s Office, 1975-79; pvt. practice Marina del Rey, 1979-81; city contr. City of L.A., 1981-85, city atty., 1985—2001, mayor, 2001—. Office: City Hall 200 N Spring St Rm 303 Los Angeles CA 90012

HAHN, JAMES MAGLORIE, former librarian, farmer; b. Grey Eagle, Minn., June 2, 1936; s. Frank John and Mabel Leone H.; m. Ellen MacMonagle, Sept. 7, 1976; children by previous marriage: Michele Diane, Nichola Darcy, Jennifer Deirdre, Gillian Dana, Kristan Desiree. BA, U. Minn., 1960, MA, M.L.S., U. Minn., 1962. Dir. Libraries and Information Center, Minn. Dept. Corrections, 1961-63; chief librarian Royal Air Force, Lakenheath, Eng., 1963-68; asst. command librarian Hdqrs. U.S. Air Force Europe and Near East, Wiesbaden, Ger., 1968-69; staff librarian Hdqrs. 1st Air Force, Newburgh, N.Y., 1969; asst. chief for network devel. Library of Congress, Washington, 1970-75; chief library div. VA, Washington, 1975-79, dir. learning resources service, 1979-81, dir. continuing edn. resources services, 1981-89; treas. SABIL Inc., 1983-89; farmer Castleton, Va., 1988—. Assoc. prof. library sci. Cath. U. Am., Washington, 1977-89; adviser on libraries and patient edn. Am. Hosp. Assn., 1977-89; bd. regents Nat. Library Medicine, 1980-89; sec./treas. Solitude Farms Property Owners Assn., 1994—. Home: 6437 Campground Ln Castleton VA 22716-1703

HAHN, JOAN CHRISTENSEN, retired secondary education educator, travel agent; b. Kemmerer, Wyo., May 9, 1933; d. Roy and Bernice (Pringle) Wainwright; m. Milton Angus Christensen, Dec. 29, 1952 (div. Oct. 1 1971); children: Randall M., Carla J. Christensen Teasdale; m. Charles Henry Hahn, Nov. 15, 1972. BS, Brigham Young U., 1965. Profl. ballroom dancer, 1951-59; travel dir. E.T. World Travel, Salt Lake City, 1969—; tchr. drama Payson (Utah) H.S., 1965-71, Cottonwood H.S., Salt Lake City, 1971-95; owner Travel Passport, 1992—. Dir. performing European tours, Salt Lake City, 1969—76, Broadway theater tours, 1976—. Regional dir. dance LDS Ch., 1954—72; pres. Elder Quest, Utah divsn. Elderhostel, Utah Valley State Coll., 2002—; bd. dirs. Salem (Utah) City Days, 1965—75. Named Best Dir. H.S. Musicals, Green Sheet Newspapers, 1977, 82, 84, 91, Utah's Speech Educator of Yr., 1990, 91, to Nat. Hall of Fame, Ednl. Theatre Assn., 1991, Cottonwood H.S. Hall of Fame, 1995, Nat. Women's Hall of Fame, 1999, Ohio Thespians Hall of Fame, 2000, Outstanding Educator, Utah Ho. of Reps., 1995; recipient 1st place award Utah Drama Tournament, 1974, 77, 78, 89, 90, 91, 94, 95, Tchr. of Yr. award Cottonwood H.S., 1989-90, Limelight award, 1982, Exemplary Performance in Tchg. Theater Arts award Granite Sch. Dist., Salt Lake City, 1982; Joan C. Hahn Theatre named in her honor Cotonwood H.S., 1997. Mem. NEA, Internat. Thespian Soc. (internat. dir. 1982-84, trustee 1979-84), Utah Speech Arts Assn. (pres. 1976-78, 88-90), Utah Edn. Assn., Granite Edn. Assn., Profl. Travel Agts. Assn., Utah H.S. Activities Assn. (drama rep. 1972-76), AAUW (pres. 1972-74). Republican. Avocations: reading, travel, dancing. Home: PO Box 36 Salem UT 84653-0036 E-mail: joanhahn@juno.com.

HAHN, JOAN MARJORIE, public relations consultant, marketing consultant; b. N.Y.C., Dec. 17, 1937; d. Chester Arnold and Malvina Therese (Orwan) H.; m. Robert Harold Perilla, Dec. 20, 1959; children: Beth Perilla Esbin, Mindy, Wendy. BS in edn., Hofstra, 1959; MS in edn., Queens Coll., 1963. Tchr. UFSD # 3, Cedarhurst, N.Y., 1959-62, tchr. gifted children, 1962-64; acct. exec. Bob Perilla Assocs., Inc., N.Y.C., 1981-85, acct. supr., 1985-92; ptnr. Pub. Rels. Mktg., Inc., Roslyn, N.Y., 1993—. Pres. Nudge, Inc., 2000—, Nudge Inc., 2000—; creator, implementor nat. promotional image campaigns, including Dutch Cut Flowers, Tinkerbell Children's Toiletries, Am. Dream Enterprises; med. billing Nassau Cmty. Coll., 2003—. Contbg. author: Easy Wedding Planning Plus, 1996. Pres. cmty. svc. Nat. Coun. Jewish Women, Roslyn, 1974-78; bd. dirs. Bldg. Block Day Care Ctr., Roslyn, 1973 , Child Abuse Prevention Svc., 1991-93; pres. Roslyn High Parent Assn., 1978-80; creator, implementor pilot Roslyn After Sch. program, 1975; East Hills cand. village trustee, East Hills, N.Y., 1992. Mem.: L.I. Assn., Nat. Coun. Jewish Women (pres., Hannah G. Solomon award 1982, Woman of Yr. 1982), High Hopes Investment Club (pres. 2000—02). Avocations: travel, reading, decorating. Home: 30 Walnut Dr Roslyn NY 11576-2333 Office: Public Rels Mktg Inc PO Box 508 Glenwood Landing NY 11547-0508

HAHN, JOHN WILLIAM, retired insurance company executive; b. N.Y.C., July 12, 1940; s. Ferdinand J. and Evelyn H. H. (Hauser) H.; m. L. Dale Mazza, 1963; children: Nancy, John. BA, Queen's Coll, 1962; postgrad., Harvard U., 1973-74. With Atlantic Mut. Cos., N.Y.C., 1963—, v.p., adminstrv. svcs., 1963—, sr. v.p., adminstrv. svcs. Roanoke, Va., 1978-85, exec. v.p., adminstrn. Madison, N.J., 1985—. Exec. com., bd. dir. Ins. Value Added Network Svc., Conn., 1985-92; mem. std. com. Agy. Co. Orgn. for R&D; bd. dir. Sun Trust Bank, Roanoke, Va., 1983-, Luxury Market Coun., NYC, 2002—; spl. advisor Artbase, NYC, 2003—. With USMC, 1959—66. Mem. Marines Meml. Assn., AGENA Corp. (chmn. bd. dirs. 1993-95), Alliance for Productive Tech. (chmn. bd. dirs. 1997-98), Harvard Club (N.Y.C.), Roanoke (Va.) Country Club, Hidden Valley Country Club (Va.). Home: 85 Loving Cir Penhook VA 24137-5225

HAHN, LEWIS EDWIN, philosopher, retired educator; b. Swenson, Tex., Sept. 26, 1908; s. Edwin D. and Ione (Brewster) H.; m. Elizabeth Herring, June 30, 1932 (dec. 1991); children: Helen Elizabeth, Mary, Sharon; m. Mary Anne King, Sept. 1, 1992; children: Michael H. King, Mary Susan King. BA, MA, U. Tex., 1929; PhD, U. Calif., 1939. Tchg. fellow U. Calif., 1931-34; from instr. philosophy to assoc. prof. U. Mo., Columbia, 1936-49; prof. philosophy Washington U., St. Louis, 1949-63, chmn. dept., 1949-63; from assoc. dean to dean Washington U. Grad. Sch. Arts and Scis., St. Louis, 1953-63; rsch. prof. philosophy So. Ill. U., Carbondale, 1963-77, prof. emeritus, 1977—; editor emeritus So. Ill. U. Libr. of Living Philosophers, 2001—, vis. prof., editor, 1981-2001. Disting. vis. prof. Baylor U., 1977-80; Mem. U.S. Nat. Commn. UNESCO, 1965-67; vis. lectr. Princeton U., 1947. Author: A Contextualistic Theory of Perception, 1942, (with others) Value: A Cooperative Inquiry, 1949, Enhancing Cultural Interflow Between East & West, 1998, A Contextualist Worldview, 2001; co-author: Guide to the Works of John Dewey, 1970; editor: Library of Living Philosophers, 1981—; co-editor: The Philosophy of Gabriel Marcel, 1984, The Philosophy of W.V. Quine, 1986, expanded edit., 1998, The Philosophy of G.H. von Wright, 1989, Charles D. Tenney's Discovery of Discovery, 1991, The Philosophy of Seyyed Hossein Nasr, 2001; editor: The Philosophy of Charles Hartshorne, 1991, The Philosophy of A.J. Ayer, 1992, The Philosophy of Paul Ricoeur, 1995, The Philosophy of Paul Weiss, 1995, The Philosophy of Hans-Georg Gadamer, 1997, The Philosophy of Roderick M. Chisholm, 1997, The Philosophy of P.F. Strawson, 1998, The Philosophy of Donald Davidson, 1999, Perspectives on Habermas, 2000. Recipient Disting. Svc. award So. Ill. U., 1993. Fellow AAAS; mem. Am. Philos. Assn. (exec. bd. 1950-54, 70-73, chmn. com. placement, available pers. 1951-54, sec.-treas. West divsn. 1949-51, sec.-treas. 1960-66, com. on internat. coop. 1967-80, history com. 1993), AAUP, Am. Soc. Aesthetics, S.W. Philos. Soc. (pres. 1955), Mo. Philos. Assn. (pres. 1949-50), So. Soc. for Philosophy and Psychology (pres. 1958-59), Ill. Philosophy Conf. (pres. 1969-71), Soc. Advancement Am. Philosophy (Herbert W. Schneider award 1998), Phi Beta Kappa. Office: So Ill U Dept Philosophy Carbondale IL 62901-4505 Home: 5550 Harvest Hill Rd Dallas TX 75230-1684

HAHN, MARC B. dean, anesthesiologist; b. Providence, 1958; DO, U. Osteo. Medicine and Health Scis., Des Moines, 1984. Intern Walter Reed Army Med. Ctr., Washington, 1984-85, resident in anesthesiology, 1985-87; fellow in pain mgmt. Nat. Inst. Health, Bethesda, Md., 1987-88; prof. dept. anesthesiology Pa. State U. Coll. Medicine, Hershey, 1995—2001; dean Texas Coll. of Osteopathic Med., 2001—. Mem. AMA, Am. Osteo. Assn., Am. Pain Soc., Am. Soc. Anesthesiologists, Am. Acad. Pain Medicine, Internat. Assn. Study of Pain. Office: Tex Coll of Osteopathic Med 3500 Camp Bowie Blvd Fort Worth TX 76107-2699

HAHN, MARY DOWNING, writer; b. Washington, Dec. 9, 1937; d. Kenneth Ernest and Anna Elisabeth (Sherwood) Downing; m. William Edward Hahn, Oct. 7, 1961 (div. 1977); children: Katherine Sherwood, Margaret Elizabeth; m. Norman Pearce Jacob, Apr. 24, 1982. BA in Fine Arts and English, U. Md., 1960, MA in English, 1969. Asst. libr. children's sect. Prince George's County (Md.) Meml. Libr. System, 1975-91; instr. English U. Md., College Park, 1970-74; free-lance illustrator PBS/WETA, Arlington, Va., 1973-75. Author: The Sara Summer, 1979, The Time of the Witch, 1982, Daphne's Book, 1983 (William Allen White Children's Choice award 1985-86), The Jellyfish Season, 1985, Wait Till Helen Comes: A Ghost Story, 1980 (11 Children's Choice awards), Tallahassee Higgins, 1987, Following the Mystery Man, 1988, December Stillness, 1988 (Book award Child Study Assn. 1989, Calif. Young Readers' medal 1990-91), The Doll in the Garden, 1989 (Md. Children's Book award 1990-91, 7 Children's Choice awards), The Dead Man in Indian Creek, 1990 (4 Children's Choice awards), The Spanish Kidnapping Disaster, 1991, Stepping on the Cracks, 1991 (Scott O'Dell Hist. Fiction award 1992, ALA notable 1991, Joan G. Sugarman award, Hedda Seisler Mason award, Children's Choice awards), The Wind Blows Backward, 1993 (ALA Best Books for Young Adults), Time for Andrew, 1994 (7 Children's Choice awards), Look for Me by Moonlight, 1995 (Yalsa Quick Picks for Reluctant Readers), The Gentleman Outlaw and Me-Eli, 1996, Following My Own Footsteps, 1996, As Ever, Gordy, 1998, Anna All Year Round, 1999, Promises to the Dead, 2000, Anna on the Farm, 2001, Hear the Wind Blow, 2003. Recipient Scott O'Dell award for hist. fiction, 1992, author's award Md. Libr. Assn., 1997. Mem. Soc. Children's Book Writers, Washington Children's Book Guild. E-mail: mdh12937@aol.com.

HAHN, PAUL BERNARD, lawyer; b. Prague, Czechoslovakia, Aug. 13, 1947; came to U.S. 1949, naturalized, 1954; s. George and Edith (Blum) H.; m. Denise Szabo, Aug. 7, 1976; children: Aaron, Ross. BA, Queens Coll., 1969; MS, L.I.U., 1971; JD, Bklyn. Law Sch., 1976. Bar: N.Y. 1977, U.S. Dist. Ct. (ea., so. dists.) N.Y. 1977. Tchr. Bklyn. Pub. Schs., 1969-77; assoc. J.V. Salierno Law Firm, Middle Village, N.Y., 1977-78; dist. office counsel SBA, N.Y.C., 1978-82; sr. assoc. Goldman, Horowitz & Cherno, Mineola, N.Y., 1982-83; sr. atty. Heller Fin., Inc., N.Y.C., 1983—; spl. asst. U.S. Atty. U.S. Atty.'s Office, so. dist., N.Y.C., 1981-82. Contbr. articles to profl. jours. Mem. ABA, Assn. of Bar of City of N.Y., Assn. Comml. Fin. Attys. (sec., bd. dirs.). Office: Heller Financial Inc 101 Park Ave New York NY 10178-0002

HAHN, PETER MATHIAS, electrical engineer, consultant; b. Vienna, May 15, 1937; came to U.S., 1941; s. Ernest and Sabine (Hafner) H.; m. Susanne Elkins Zumbro, Sept. 16, 1962 (div. Nov. 1979); children: Karen Anne, Paul Frederick, Roger Joseph; m. Bonnie Wendy Silver, July 14, 1980. BEE, CCNY, 1958; MSEE, U. Pa., 1962, PhD, 1968. Sys. engr. RCA Corp., Moorestown, N.J., 1965-67, divsn. staff tech. advisor, 1979 84, engring. leader Camden, N.J., 1976-77; head engring. sect. Ford Aerospace and Comm. Corp., Willow Grove, Pa., 1967-76; chief engr. Sonic Scis., Inc., Warminster, Pa., 1977-79; mgr. comm. analysis and simulation Fed. and Electronic Sys. divsn. GE, King of Prussia, Pa., 1985-88; sr. staff engr., mgr. strategic sys. dept. GE, Bluebell, Pa., 1988-90; sci. assoc. Wiltec, Paris, 1991-93; v.p., gen. mgr. ARI Corp., Elverson, Pa., 1994-98, also bd. dirs.; cons. Sci-Tech Svcs., Inc., Phila., 1998—. Lectr. dept. electronic physics Lasalle Coll., Phila., 1968-79; adj. prof. elec. engring. Drexel U., Phila., 1980-85, 97-2001; adj. assoc. prof. U. Pa., 1984-95, 98—; univ. program evaluator Accreditation Bd. for Engring. and Tech., Washington, 1989-93. Contbr. numerous articles to profl. jours. and procs.; reviewer European Jour. Operational Rsch. and Mgmt. Sci., 1980-90; patentee directory search technique. 1st lt. U.S. Army, 1959. Mem. IEEE (chmn. tech. transfer com. 1988, sr. mem. Phila. sect. com. 1975-80, reviewer comm. transactions 1980-85, presenter various meetings 1966-80), Inst. Ops. Rsch. and Mgmt. Scis., Soc. Indsl. and Applied Math., Sigma Xi. Avocations: research on math. optimization techniques (quadratic assignment problem). Home and Office: 2127 Tryon St Philadelphia PA 19146-1228 E-mail: hahn@seas.upenn.edu.

HAHN, ROBERT ALAN, philosophy educator; b. N.Y.C., Aug. 25, 1952; s. Stanley Lawrence and Shirley Laura (Wishner) Hahn; m. Amy Lynn Knoblock; 1 child, Zoë Shirley. BA summa cum laude, Union Coll., 1973; MA in

Philosophy, MPhil, Yale U., 1975, PhD, 1976. Postdoctoral rsch. fellow U. Calif., Berkeley, 1976; lectr. philosophy Yale U., New Haven, 1977; asst. prof. philosophy U. Tex., Arlington, 1977—78; asst. prof. philosophy and history of ideas Brandeis U., Waltham, Mass., 1978—81; asst. prof. Harvard U., Cambridge, Mass., 1979—81; from asst. prof. philosophy to assoc. prof. philosophy So. Ill. U., Carbondale, 1982—, prof. philosophy, 2002—. Vis. prof. Am. Coll. Greece, 1980. Author: Kant's 'Newtonian Revolution' in Philosophy, 1988, Self-Identity and Moral Decisions, 1989, 2nd edit., 1991, Formal Deductive Logic, 1993, 7th edit., 2003, Conduct and Contraints: Testing the Limits of the 'Harm Principle', 1994, 6th edit., 2001, Anaximander and the Architects: The Contribution of Egyptian and Greek Architectural Technologies to the Origins of Greek Philosophy, 2001, Anaximander in Context: New Studies on the Origins of Greek Philosophy, 2003; contbr. articles to profl. jours. including Phronesis, Jour. History of Philosophy, Apeiron, Southwest Jour. Philosophy, Philos. Rsch. Archives, Jour. Chinese Philosophy. Fellow, Yale U., 1974—76; Regents scholar, N.Y. State, Archibald scholar, 1972—73. Mem.: Am. Philol. Assn., Ill. Philos. Soc., N. Am. Kant Soc., Soc. Ancient Greek Philosophy, Archeol. Inst. Am., Am. Philos. Assn., Nat. Classics Honor Soc. (hon.), Phi Beta Kappa. Avocation: semi-profl. tennis player. Office: So Ill U Dept Philosophy Carbondale IL 62901-4505 Business E-Mail: rhahn@jinx.umsl.edu.

HAHN, STANLEY ROBERT, JR., lawyer, financial executive; b. Louisville, Dec. 8, 1946; s. Stanley Robert and Dorothy Dodd (Moseley) H.; children from previous marriage: Laura, Valerie, Kathy; (div.); m. LaDonna Marie Dees, Nov. 9, 1996. BBA in Fin., MBA, Ga. State U.; LLM in Litigation, JD, Atlanta Law Sch. Bar: Ga. 1983, U.S. Dist. Ct. (no. dist.) Ga. 1983, U.S. Ct. Appeals (11th cir.) 1983, U.S. Ct. Apppeals (4th cir.) 1985, U.S. Supreme Ct. 1986. Mgr. credit White-Westinghouse Corp., Atlanta, 1975-77; mgr. fin. Am. Can Co., Greenwich, Conn., 1977—; pvt. practice Atlanta, 1983—. Bd. dirs. HDC Investments Inc., Atlanta, Interest Unltd. Inc., Atlanta. Mem.: ABA, Nat. Assn. Credit Mgmt., Assn. Trial Lawyers Am., Assn. MBA Execs. Baptist. Avocations: golf, tennis, chess, billiards. Office: Bldg E Ste 600 6185 S Buford Hwy Norcross GA 30071 Fax: 770-416-0195. E-mail: Robert@atlantalawyersonline.com.

HAHN, THERESA, epidemiologist, researcher; b. Kingston, N.Y., July 10, 1970; d. John W. Norton, Jr. and Margaret A. Norton; m. Anthony M. Mrozik, Jr., July 26, 2002; 1 child, Ava E. Mrozik. BS in Biochemistry, SUNY, Geneseo, 1992; MS in Epidemiology, SUNY, Buffalo, 1994, PhD in Epidemiology, 2000. Asst. mem. Roswell Park Cancer Inst., Buffalo, 2003—. Cons. Am. Soc. for Blood and Marrow Transplantation, Arlington Hts., Ill., 2000—. Contbr. Mem.: Am. Soc. for Blood and Marrow Transplantation, Am. Soc. Hematology. Avocations: painting, hiking. Office: Roswell Park Cancer Inst Elm and Carlton Sts Buffalo NY 14263

HAHN, THOMAS JOONGHI, accountant; b. Seoul, Korea, Apr. 12, 1955; came to U.S., 1979; s. Sang Jin and Seong Soon (Hong) H.; m. Linda Young Kim, May 26, 1984; children: Gina K., Michael J., Catherine S. BS, U. Md., 1982; MS, U. Va., 2002. CPA, CFP. Jr. acct. VerKenteren, Anerbach & Olson, CPAs, Silver Springs, Md., 1982-83; sr. acct. Chough, Oh & Co., CPAs, Silver Springs, 1983-85; ptnr. Lee & Hahn, CPAs, Falls Church, Va., 1985-87; prin. Thomas J. Hahn, CPA, Falls Church, 1987—. Bd. dirs. STG, Inc., Fairfax, Va. Host weekly radio talk show, 1996—. Recipient Svc. award Posung H. S. Alumni Assn. of Greater Washington Area, 1992. Mem. AICPA, Va. Soc. CPAs. Roman Catholic. Office: Thomas J Hahn CPA 7639 Leesburg Pike 1st Fl Falls Church VA 22043-2520

HAHN, YOON SUN, pediatric neurosurgeon, educator; b. Seoul, Republic of Korea, Sept. 23, 1937; came to U.S., 1970; s. D..C. and Kyung S. Hahn; m. Wonjae Cho, Sept. 25, 1965; children: Susie, David, Jimmy. BS, Yonsei U., Seoul, 1958; MD, Yonsei U., 1962. Diplomate Am. Bd. Pediat. Neurosurgery, Am. Bd. Neurol. Surgery, Korean Bd. Neurol. Surgery. Chief neurosurgery 101 Evacuation Hosp., Vungtao, Vietnam, 1968-69; fellow in neurosurgery, vis. asst. prof. U. Mich., Ann Arbor, 1970-71; spl. fellow neurosurgery and craniofacial surgery Hôpital Foch U. Paris, Suresnes, France, 1976; assoc. prof. neurosurgery Yonsei U. Med. Sch., Seoul, 1976; asst. prof. neurosurgery Children's Meml. Hosp., Chgo., 1979-88; prof., chief pediat. neurosurgery Loyola U. Med. Ctr., Chgo., 1988-95; dir. pediat. neurosurgery, surgeon-in-chief Hope Children's Hosp., Oak Lawn, Ill., 1995—; prof., chief divsn. pediat. neurosurgery U. Ill. Coll. Medicine, Chgo., 1996—. Contbr. chpts. to books; inventor in field. Major Korean Army, 1967-70. Recipient Silver medal Republic of Korea Army, Vietnam, 1969. George Joost award for outstanding tchg. Northwestern U. Med. Sch., 1999; named Best Neurosurgery Resident of Yr., Northwestern U. Children's Meml. Hosp., Chgo., 1975. Fellow ACS, Am. Acad. Pediat.; mem. Am. Assn. Neurol. Surgery, Am. Soc. Pediat. Neurosurgeons, Congress of Neurol. Surgery, Internat. Soc. Pediat. Neurosurgeons. Avocations: golf, skiing, reading. Office: U Ill Coll Medicine Pediat Neurosurgery 912 S Wood St Chicago IL 60612-7329 Fax: 312-996-9018.

HAHN, YUKAP, physics educator, researcher; b. Seoul, July 28, 1932; came to U.S., 1952; s. Chi Jin Hahn and Bock Hee Chung; m. Cora Byung Chai Chang, May 1956; children: Chisong, Chiwon, Chihoe. Student, George Pepperdine U., 1952—54; BS magna cum laude, U. So. Calif., 1956; MS, Yale U., 1958, PhD, 1962. Rsch. scientist NYU, N.Y.C., 196l-65, vis. prof., 1972-73; asst. prof. physics U. Conn., Storrs, 1965-67, assoc. prof., 1967-73, prof., 1973—2001, prof. emeritus, 2001—. Vis. prof. U. Calif., Berkeley, 197l-72, U. Toronto, 1972, U. London, 1979, Cath. U. Louvain (Belgium), 1985. Contbr. over 250 articles on theoretical physics to profl. rsch. pub. Dept. Energy grantee, 1977—. Fellow Am. Phys. Soc.; mem. Phi Beta Kappa, Sigma Xi, Phi Kappa Phi. Office: U Conn Dept Physics Storrs Mansfield CT 06269 Home: 5916 Old Greenway Dr Glen Allen VA 23059-7062

HAIDET, KEITH R. radiologist; b. Cleve., Jan. 17, 1957; s. Walter and Carmela Haidet; m. Kim K. Haidet, Aug. 18, 1984; 1 child, Jared. BS, Allegheny Coll., Meadville, Pa., 1979; MD, Pa. State U., 1983. Diplomate Am. Bd. Radiology, Nat. Bd. Med. Examiners. Intern Hahnemann U., Phila., 1983-84; resident Pa. State U., Hershey, 1984-88, chief resident in radiology, 1987-88; fellow Thomas Jefferson U., Phila., 1988-90; staff radiologist Quantum Radiology, Harrisburg, Pa., 1990—. Bd. dirs. Am. Cancer Soc., 1993-97. Named Homer Branch fellow, Thomas Jefferson U., 1989. Mem. Am. Coll. Radiology, Am. Inst. Ultrasound in Medicine, Soc. of Ultrasound in Radiology, Radiol. Soc. N.Am., Pa. Radiol. Soc., Pa. Med. Soc. Office: Quantum Radiology 3508 Trindle Rd Camp Hill PA 17011-4439

HAIDOSTIAN, ALICE BERBERIAN, concert pianist, civic volunteer and fundraiser; b. Highland Park, Mich., Sept. 21, 1925; d. Harry M. and Siroun Vartabedian Berberian; m. Berj H. Haidostian, Oct. 1, 1949; children: Cynthia Esther Haidostian Wilbanks, Christine Rebecca Haidostian Garry, Dicran Berj. MusB, U. Mich., 1946, MusM, 1949. Pvt. piano tchr., 1946-48; tchr. music Detroit Pub. Sch., 1953; dir. vocal trio The Haidostians, 1959—71; dir. youth choral group Cultural Soc. Armenians from Istanbul, 1965—72. Chmn. adv. coun. Armenian Studies Program, U. Mich., 1984-99. Initiator (Operas) Anoush, Mich. Opera Theatre, 1981—82, 2001—02, Transparent Anatomical Manikin exhibit, Detroit Sci. Ctr., 1976. Founder Centennial Celebration U. Mich. Sch. Music, Detroit, 1980; mem. Armenian Gen. Benevolent Union Alex Manoogian Sch., 1981—91, Detroit chpt. core group com., 1992—; chmn. Marie Manoogian group Armenian Gen. Benevolent Union Alex Manoogian Sch, 1993—; active Detroit Women's Symphony Orch, Mich. Opera; bd. trustees Mich. Opera Theatre, 1982—; active Oakway Symphony Orch.; mem. Save Orch. Hall women's divsn. Project HOPE, 1964—, pres. Save Orch. Hall women's divsn., 1995—96; pres. Detroit Armenian Women's Club, 1964—65, 1973—75; active women's chpt. Armenian Gen. Benevolent Union, Detroit, 1944—93; bd. dirs. Childhelp USA Greater Detroit Aux., 1998—; active Detroit Sci. Ctr., 1976—, bd. trustees, 1999—; organist, choir dir. Armenian Congl. Ch., Detroit, 1946—48; mem. Chancel Choir Westminster Ch. Detroit, 1965—80; bd. dirs. Detroit Symphony Orch. Opera, 1986—88. Recipient Spirit of Detroit award, 1980, Heart of Gold award United Found. City Detroit, 1981, Nat. Svc. citation U. Mich. Alumnae Coun., 1980, Disting. Alumni Svc. award U. Mich., 1981, Leadership plaque Detroit Symphony Orch., 1988, Magic Flute award Internat. Found. Mozarteum, Salzburg, Austria, 1989, Lifetime Achievement award Outstanding Woman Mich. Project HOPE, 1998, Cmty. Svc. award Wayne County Med. Soc. Alliance, 2000; named Armenian Mother of Yr., Internat. Inst. Detroit, 1981. Mem. Detroit Assn. Univ. Mich. Women (pres. 1969-71), Mich. Fedn. Music Clubs, Mich. State Med. Soc. Aux., Pro Mozart Soc. Greater Detroit (pres. 1982-02, pres. emeritus 2002-, Cert. Appreciation 2002), Pro Musica Detroit (sec. 1969-90, 1st v.p. 1990—), Tuesday Musicale Detroit (pres. 1970-72), Univ. Mich. Alumni Assn. (chmn. alumnae coun. 1977-79), Univ. Mich. Sch. Music Alumni Soc., Women's Assn. Detroit Symphony Orch. (pres. 1986-88, vol. coun. Detroit Symphony Orch.), U. Mich. Alumni Assn. (bd. dirs.), U. Mich. Emeritus Club (pres. 1997-98). Avocation: piano. Home: 6838 Valley Spring Dr Bloomfield Hills MI 48301-2845

HAIES, EVELYN S(OLOMON), fundraiser, educator, writer; b. Bkyln., Oct. 26, 1944; d. Samuel and Marion (Dickstein) Solomon; m. Jay W. Haies, May 30, 1966; children: Elissa Rachel Grunwald, Deborah Scop, Lila Shleifstein, Daniel, David. BA, Hunter Coll., 1964; MFA, Bklyn. Coll., 1989. Cert. jr. h.s. tchr. social studies, jr., sr. h.s. lang. arts & social studies. Tchr., N.Y.C., 1964—; finance profl. N.Y.C. Ins., 1986—; founder, pres. Rachel's Children Reclamation Found. Inc., N.Y.C., 1996—. Organizer Ann. Internat. Writing Contest, 1998—; program dir., initiator N.Y. Citywide Yartzheit Commemorations for Matriarch Rachel, 1999-2001; Bklyn. borough pres.; inaugerated Jewish Mother's Day Pres. Bnei Rachel. Author: Four Years of Glory, 1964, (poetry) Frozen Shadows, 1989, Parallel Parashas, 1995, The Eleventh Plague, Twins, 2002, The Twelfth Plagues: Generations, 2003; author lyrics We Are Rachel's Children, 1995, Hagolan & Od Josef Chai, 1996; contbr. articles to profl. jours. Bd. dirs. sisterhood Manhattan Beach Jewish Ctr., Bklyn., 1990—; nat. v.p. Women's Br., N.Y.C., 1994—, chair nat. conv., Washington, 1995. Recipient Women of Yr. award Prospect Park Yeshiva, Bklyn., 1975, Women United Redeption, Bkyln., 1996, 2000, Bonei Yerushalayim award JPP, N.Y.C., 2002, Nachshon Ben Aminadau award Beit Brot, 2002. Avocations: poetry readings, lecturing. Office: Rachels Children Reclamation Found PO Box 220 Valley Stream NY 11582-0220

HAIG, ANDREW JOHN, physical medicine and rehabilitation physician, writer; b. Milw., Mar. 22, 1958; s. Gerald Thomas and Margaret Haig; m. Brigit Jensen, June 15, 1985; children: Molly, William. BS, U. Wis., Milw., 1979; MD, Med. Coll. Wis., 1983. Diplomate Am. Bd. Phys. Medicine and Rehab., Am. Bd. Electrodiagnostic Medicine, Am. Bd. Pain Mgmt. Resident in phys. medicine and rehab. Northwestern U., Chgo., 1983-86, asst. prof. orthop. and rehab. U. Vt., Burlington, 1986-89; dir. Ctr. for Rehab. Svcs. Theda Clark Regional Med. Ctr., Neenah, Wis., 1989-96; assoc. prof. phys. medicine and rehab. and surgery U. Mich., Ann Arbor, 1996—. Dir. Interdepartmental Spine Program, U. Mich., Ann Arbor, 1996—2002, dir. WorkWise Occupl. Rehab. Program, 1997-99, co-dir. Mich. Rehab. Engring. Rsch. Ctr. for Ergonomics, 1998—; former clin. assoc. prof. Med. Coll. Wis., Milw.; co-dir., founder Novus Occupl. Health Program, Appleton, Wis., 1992-93; pres. Rehab. Team Assessment, LLC, 2001—. Author: This Weekend, 1992 (winner Am. Club Writing Contest 1992), The Locked-In Syndrome, 1998 (finalist creative med. writing Jour. Gen. Internal Medicine 1998), This Happens Only to My Patients, 1999 (finalist med. econs. writing contest 1999); mem. editl. bd. The Spine Jour. Founder Ind. Options Fund, Burlington, Vt., 1987-89. Fellow Am. Acad. Phys. Medicine and Rehab. (multiple com. positions, Richard and Hilda Rosenthal Found. award 1994), Am. Assn. Electrodiagnostic Medicine (chair multiple coms.), Internat. Soc. Study of Lumbar Spine, Archives of Phys. Medicine and Rehab. (editl. bd.), Assn. Acad. Physiatrists. Presbyterian. Avocations: swimming, diving, coaching water polo. Office: U Mich Spine Program 325 E Eisenhower Ann Arbor MI 48108 Fax: (734) 615-1770. E-mail: andyhaig@umich.edu.

HAIG, DAVID M. property and investment manager; b. New Rochelle, N.Y., May 20, 1951; s. Alexander Salusbury and Joan (Damon) H. Student, Marlboro Coll., 1974. Trustee Estate of S.M. Damon, Honolulu, 1982—, chmn., 1982—. Bd. dirs. BancWest Corp., First Hawaiian Bank, Honolulu. Bd. dirs. YMCA Honolulu, 1985—, chmn., 1999—; dir. Aloha United Way, 1990-94; trustee YMCA Retirement Fund, 1991-99, Hawaii Pacific U., 1988-94; nat. bd. mem. YMCA of U.S.A., 1990-94, bd. dirs. internat. com., 1989-93; chmn. Hawaii Food Bank, 1990-94, dir., 1982-94. Mem. Young Pres.'s Orgn., Oahu Country Club, Waialae Country Club, Rotary, 200 Club, Pacific Club, Honolulu Club. Address: David M Haig Trustee 999 Bishop St Ste 2800 Honolulu HI 96813-4432

HAIG, FRANK RAWLE, physics educator, clergyman; b. Phila., Sept. 11, 1928; s. Alexander M. and Regina A. (Murphy) H. AB, Woodstock Coll., Md., 1952, S.T.L., 1960; Ph.L., Bellarmine Coll., Plattsburgh, N.Y., 1953; PhD, Catholic U., 1959; LHD honoris causa, SUNY, 1987. Ordained priest Roman Cath. Ch. 1960. Joined S.J., 1946; postdoctoral fellow U. Rochester, N.Y., 1962-63; asst. prof. Wheeling Coll., W.Va., 1963-66, pres., 1966-72; asst. and assoc. prof. Loyola Coll., Balt., 1972-81; pres. Le Moyne Coll., Syracuse, N.Y., 1981-87; prof. physics Loyola Coll., Balt., 1987-2000, emeritus prof., 2000—. Editor Jour. Md. Assn. Higher Edn., 1979-81; contbr. articles on nuclear physics, bibl. theology and internat. politics to profl. publs. Pres., Wheeling C. of C., 1969-71; pres. Syracuse Opera Co., 1983-85, chmn. bd., 1985-87; gen. campaign chmn. United Way Onondaga County, Syracuse, 1985-86 Recipient Mayor's Achievement award Mayor of Syracuse, 1983; Harry J. Carman award Middle States Council for Social Studies, 1985; NSF fellow, 1962-63 Mem.: AAUP (v.p. Md. Conf. 1990—92, 1995, pres. 1995—98), Charles Carroll House of Annapolis (chmn. bd. 2001—), Washington Acad. Scis. (pres. 1993—94, treas. 1999—), Am. Phys. Soc., Am. Assn. Physics Tchrs. (pres. Chesapeake sect. 1976—77, 1990—92). Republican. Roman Catholic. Office: Loyola Coll Dept Physics 4501 N Charles St Baltimore MD 21210-2699

HAIG, MONICA ELAINE NACHAJSKI, special education educator; b. Bay Shore, N.Y., Nov. 17, 1963; d. Walter Andrew and Elaine Gilda (Guerringue) Nachajski; m. Michael Haig, June 24, 1989; children: Kathleen Mary, Michael Christopher, Christina Jean. BS in Edn., SUNY, Geneseo, 1985; MS in Edn. with high honors, L.I. U., 1989. Cert. permanent spl. and elem. edn. tchr., N.Y. Tchr. spl. edn. Convalescent Hosp. for Children, Rochester, N.Y., 1985, Patchogue-Medford Sch. Dist., Patchogue, N.Y., 1985. Edn. cons., mem. Suffolk County Exec.'s Conf. on Youth, Alcohol and hwy. Safety, Ronkonkoma, N.Y., 1990; presenter internet usage in elem. sci. classroom curriculum, CEC Conv. N.Y. State, 1999; participant seminars, workshops and confs.; presenter in field. Mem. Coun. for Exceptional Children. Avocations: reading, movement therapy. Office: Oregon Mid Sch Oregon Ave Medford NY 11763

HAIG, ROBERT LEIGHTON, lawyer; b. Plainfield, N.J., July 30, 1947; s. Richard Randall and Edith (Remington) Haig. AB, Yale U., 1967; JD, Harvard U., 1970. Bar: N.Y. 1971, U.S. Dist. Ct. (so. and ea. dists.) N.Y., U.S. Ct. Appeals (2d cir.). Assoc. Kelley Drye & Warren, N.Y.C., 1970-79, ptnr., 1980—. Mem. bd. advisors Law Dept. Mgmt. Advisor, 1995—. Co-author: Preparing for and Trying the Civil Lawsuit, 1987, 1991, 1994, 1997, 2000, Federal Civil Practice, 1989, 1993, 1997, 2000, Federal Litigation Guide, 1992, 1993, 1994, Corporate Counsel's Guide, 1996, 1997, Products Liability in New York, 1997, 2002; contbr. . Co-chair Comml. Cts. Task Force, 1995—; mem. legis. com. Com. for Modern Cts., N.Y.C., 1986—, bd. dirs., exec. com., 2001—; mem. Am. Law Inst., 1998—; mem. exec. coun. N.Y. State Conf. Bar Leaders, 1988—90, dept. disciplinary com. appellate divsn., 2003—, hearing panel chair, 1999—2001, policy com. mem., 2003—; mem. N.Y. State Jud. Salary Commn., 1997—, policy com., 2003—, Nat. Ctr. State Ct. Lawyers Com., 2002—. Recipient Excellence in CLE award, Assn. CLE Adminstrn., 1991. Fellow: N.Y. Bar Found. (life; v.p. 2002—03, pres. 2003—, bd. dirs.), Am. Bar Found. (life); mem.: ABA (del. 1991—, standing com. on jud. selection, tenure and compensation 1995—96, bus. cts. com. 1996—, chair subcom. on rels between inside and outside counsel 1997—, spl. advisor standing com. fed. judiciary 2002), N.Y. State Bar Assn. (lectr. 1985—, chmn. com. on fed. cts. 1986—88, chmn. comml. and fed. litig. sect. 1988—90, del. 1988—, exec. com. 1991—94, steering com. on commerce and industry 1997—, chair com. on multi-disciplinary practice and legal profession 1998—99, 1st Ann. award for Disting. Pub. Svc. Comml. and Fed. Litig. Sect. 1995), N.Y. County Lawyers Assn. (chmn. com. on supreme ct. 1984—86, lectr. 1984—, v.p. 1986—92, exec. com. 1986—95, chmn. fin. com. 1988—90, pres. 1992—94, pres. Found. 1992—94, dir.), Assn. of Bar of City of N.Y. (jud. com. 1985—88, chmn. 1989—92, coun. on jud. adminstrn. 1989—92, chmn. 1996—99). Office: Kelley Drye & Warren LLP 101 Park Ave Fl 30 New York NY 10178-0062 E-mail: rhaig@kelleydrye.com.

HAIG, SUSAN, ecologist, educator; BA, Northland Coll., 1979; post graduate, Univ. Wis.-Madison, 1981; PhD, Univ. N.D., 1987. Asst. prof. Clemson Univ., 1989—92; asst. unit leader S.C. Coop. Fish and Wildlife Rsch. Unit, 1989—94, acting unit leader, 1990—94; assoc. prof. Clemson Univ., 1992—94, Oreg. State Univ., 1994—2000, prof., 2000—; wildlife ecologist USGS Forest and Rangeland Ecosystem Sci. Ctr., 1994—. Contbr. scientific papers, articles to profl. jour., chapters to books; invited lectr. numerous Univs. Recipient Environ. Achievement award, Northland Coll., 2002, Outstanding Scientist award, USGS-FRESC, 2001; grantee Population Genetic Structure in Snowy Plovers, U.S. Fish and Wildlife Svc., 2003—, An Evaluation of the use of stable isotopes in defining geographic origin of vertebrates N. Am., 2002—, Devel. of a potential nesting habitat model for Snowy Plovers Oreg., 2003—, A genetic evaluation of hybridization between Spotted Owls and Barred Owls, 2001—03, many others; Friends of the Nat. Zoo Postdoctoral Fellowship, 1989, Smithsonian Inst. Molecular Genetics Fellowship, 1989, Smithsonian Inst. Postdoctoral Fellowship, 1987, Univ. N.D. Doctoral Fellowship, 1986. Fellow: Am. Ornithologists Union; mem.: Wilson Ornithological Soc., Wader Study Group, Soc. for the Study of Evolution, Soc. For Conservation Biology (life), Wis. Soc. for Ornithology (hon.), Cooper Ornithogical Soc., Assn. of Field Ornithologists, Sigma Xi Scientific Rsch. Soc. Office: USGS Forest and Rangeland Ecosystem Sci Ctr 3200 SW Jefferson Way Corvallis OR 97331

HAIGH, CHARLES, criminal justice educator; b. Paterson, N.J., Oct. 29, 1939; s. Wallace Glover and Myrtle (Lewis) H.; m. Patricia Brennan, Apr. 12, 1986; children: Michael C., Charles E. BS in Law Enforcement Adminstrn., U. New Haven, 1972, MPA, 1976; CAS in Ednl. Adminstrn./Supervision, Fairfield (Conn.) U., 1980; EdD in Ednl. Mgmt., U. Bridgeport, 1989. Dir. tng. Milford (Conn.) Police Dept., 1965-91; asst. prof., adj. prof. criminal justice/criminology program Ctrl. Conn. State U., New Britain, 1991—. Adj. prof. criminal justice program U. New Haven, West Haven, Conn., 1979—. Adv. bd. criminal justice program Housatonic C.C., Bridgeport, 1985-92; deacon First United Ch. of Christ, Congl., Milford, 1993—, chmn., 1995, cons./lectr. Milford, Conn. Police Acad., 1997—. With USN, 1957-60. Ctrl. Conn. State U. grant, 1994. Mem. Acad. Criminal Justice Scis., Northeastern Assn. Criminal Justice Scis. (Outstanding Svc. to Assn. award 1994), Elks (chmn. Most Valuable Student scholarship program 1990—), Masons (lodge historian 1998—). Democrat. Avocations: golf, biking, swimming. Home: 25 Art St Milford CT 06460-4318

HAIGH, PETER LESLIE, software company executive, consultant; b. London, Aug. 27, 1940; came to U.S., 1941; s. Leslie Baines and Winifred (Hutchins) H.; 1 child, Deborah Elizabeth. BSEE, Princeton U., 1963. Engr. Electronic Assocs., Inc., Long Branch, N.J., 1963-67, XLO Computer Systems, Englewood, N.J., 1967-70; sr. engr. Sweda Internat., Morristown, N.J., 1970-78; sr. cons. engr. NCR Corp., Dayton, Ohio, 1978-90; pres., founder High Performance Software, Inc., Dayton, 1990—; pres. HPS Mktg., Dayton, 1994—. Organizer confs.; developer of techniques and products for performance analysis of computer systems and networks. Editor: Winter Simulation Conf., 1988; contbr. articles to profl. jours. Bd. chmn. Head Start Program, Orange, N.J., 1974. 1st lt. U.S. Army, 1964-66. Recipient ROTC Disting. Mil. Grad. award, NCR Corp. R & D award for Meritorious Tech. Achievement, 1986. Mem. IEEE (computer soc., comm. soc.), Assn. Computing Machinery, Annual Simulation Symposium (exec. v.p. 1983-86, officer), Greater Dayton Assn. Computing Machinery (chmn. 1991-92), Project Mgmt. Inst. (cert.). Avocations: simulation modeling, skiing, outboard motorboat racing, country western dancing. Office: 227 Broadleaf Cir Miamisburg OH 45342-7609

HAIGH, ROBERT WILLIAM, business administration educator; b. Phila., Aug. 22, 1926; s. Harry E. and Mildred (Elliott) H.; m. Jane Stanton Sheble, June 19, 1948; children: Cynthia Jane, Anne Sheble, Robert William, Barbara Lynne. Student, Muhlenberg Coll., 1944-45; AB cum laude, Bucknell U., 1948; MBA with high distinction, Harvard U., 1950, DCS, 1953. Research and teaching faculty Harvard U. Grad Sch. Bus. Adminstrn., 1950-56, asst. prof., 1953-56; asst. to pres. Helmerich & Payne, Inc., Tulsa, 1956, controller and asst. to pres., 1956-57, fin. v.p., dir., 1957-61, White Eagle Internat. Oil Co., 1957-60; v.p. corp. planning and devel. Standard Oil Co. (Ohio), Cleve., 1963-66; pres. Sohio Chems. & Vistron Corp. Subs., 1966-67, Sohio Chemicals and Vistron Corp. Subs., 1966-67; group v.p., pres. edn. group, dir. Xerox Corp., Stamford, Conn., 1967-72; exec. v.p. Swedlow Corp., 1973-74, pres., chief exec. officer, dir., 1974; pres. Hillsboro Assocs., 1974-75; sr. v.p. Freeport Minerals Co., 1975-76; chmn. bd., chief exec. officer Photo Quest, Inc., Cognitrex, Inc., 1977-78; dir. Wharton Applied Rsch. Ctr., lectr. U. Pa., Phila., 1978-79; Disting. prof. bus. adminstrn. Darden Grad. Sch. Bus. U. Va. Tayloe Murphy Internat. Bus. Studies Ctr., 1979-95; prof. emeritus U. Va., 1995—. Author: (with John G. McLean) The Growth of Integrated Oil Companies, 1954, Leading Virginia Industries series: Textiles and Apparel, A Business Update, 1986, Wood and Paper Products, 1987, Investment Strategies and the Plant-Location Decision: Foreign Companies in the U.S., 1989, Global Markets for Pollution-Control Equipment: An Export Opportunity for Virginia Business, 1991, Medical Products Companies in Virginia: Export Status Report. Served with USNR, 1944-45. Mem. Phi Beta Kappa, Phi Lambda Theta. Home: 404 Ednam Dr Charlottesville VA 22903-4716

HAIGHT, CAROL BARBARA, lawyer; b. Buffalo, May 3, 1945; d. Robert H. Johnson and Betty R. (Walker) Hawkes; m. H. Granville Haight, May 28, 1978 (dec. Nov. 1983); m. Dennis M. Nagel PE, Oct. 19, 1996; children: David Michael, Kathleen Marie. BSW summa cum laude, BA in Psychology summa cum laude, Widener U., Chester, Pa., 1980; JD cum laude, Widener U., Wilmington, Del., 1984. Assoc. Pepper, Hamilton & Scheetz, Phila., 1985-88, Hodgson, Russ, Andrews, Woods & Goodyear, Buffalo, 1988-90; pvt. practice Boca Raton, Fla., 1990—; corp. counsel Eilink Corp, Fremont, Calif., 2000. Arbitrator Am. Arbitration Assn., mediator, 1989—, mediation instr.; founding dir. Mediation Ednl. Svc., Fla. Supreme Ct. Cert. mediator and arbitrator, 1999-; vol. spkr. and coun. Hospice. Contbr. articles to profl. jours. Mem. Pa. Bar, Fla. Bar, Phi Kappa Phi Hon. Soc., Phi Alpha Delta, Phi Gamma Mu. Republican. Episcopalian. Avocations: scuba diving, skiing, tennis, sailing, ballroom dancing, flying. Home: Braemar Isle Townhouse 9 4744 S Ocean Blvd Highland Beach FL 33487-5321 Fax: 561-368-1582. E-mail: cbhaight@yahoo.com.

HAIGHT, CATHY, artist; b. Washington, Jan. 22, 1948; d. William Harrison Haight and Pauline Ikel. Student, Northwestern U., 1966-68. English tchr. various schs., Colombia, South America, 1970-71, 73-77; coding supervisor Inst. Rsch. in Social Behavior, Oakland, Calif., 1978-80; field interviewer various nat. social sci. organizations, Albuquerque, 1983-91; from field mgr. to divsn. field mgr. Nat. Opinion Rsch. Ctr. U. Chgo., Albuquerque, 1991—98. Standards dir. N.Mex. Arts & Crafts Fair, Albuquerque, 1991; co-dir Amapola Gallery, Albuquerque, 1995. Exhbns. include Contemporary Crafts, Albuquerque, 1984, Thompson Gallery, U. N.Mex., 1985, Fuller Lodge Art Ctr. Gallery, Los Alamos, N.Mex., 1986, 89, 93, South Broadway Cultural Ctr., Albuquerque, 1988, Placitas (N.Mex.) Artists Series, 1993, Art of Albuquerque, 1994, 96, N.Mex. State Fair Profls. Artists, 1995-2002, Historic San Ysidro Ch. Gallery, N.Mex., 1996. Conservation chair N.Mex. Mtn. Club, Albuquerque, 1984. Mem.: Nat. Mus. of Women in the Arts. Avocations: travel, hiking, photography. Home: 1045 Red Oaks Loop NE Albuquerque NM 87122-1343

HAIGHT, CHARLES SHERMAN, JR., federal judge; b. N.Y.C., Sept. 23, 1930; s. Charles Sherman and Margaret (Edwards) H.; m. Mary Jane Peightal, June 30, 1953; children: Nina E., Susan P. BA, Yale U., 1952, LL.B., 1955. Bar: N.Y. State 1955. Trial atty., admiralty and shipping dept. Dept. Justice, Washington, 1955-57; assoc. firm Haight, Gardner, Poor & Havens, N.Y.C., 1957-68, ptnr., 1968-76; judge U.S. Dist. Ct. for So. Dist. N.Y., 1976—. Bd. dirs. Kennedy Child Study Ctr.; adv. trustee Am.-Scandinavian Found., chmn., 1970-76; bd. mgrs. Havens Fund. Mem. Maritime Law Assn., U.S., N.Y. State Bar Assn., Bar Assn. City N.Y., Fed. Bar Council. Episcopalian. Office: US Dist Ct US Courthouse 500 Pearl St New York NY 10007-1316

HAIGHT, DAVID B. religious organization administrator. s. Hector C. and Clara Tuttle Haight; m. Ruby Olson, three children. Attended Utah State U; Former Mayor, Palo Alto, Calif.; Asst. to the twelve 1970-76, Apostle, Quorum of the Twelve, 1976—. Mormon Ch., Salt Lake City; Comdr. Navy, WW2. Office: LDS Church 50 E North Temple Salt Lake City UT 84150-0002 also: Bonneville Internat Corp Broadcast House 55 E 3rd S Salt Lake City UT 84111-2201*

HAIGHT, DAVID HULEN, ophthalmologist; b. Highland Park, Ill., Mar. 30, 1954; s. Thomas Hulen and Virginia Ellen (Olsson) H. AB in Biochemistry magna cum laude, Brown U., 1976; MD, Johns Hopkins U., 1980. Diplomate Am. Bd. Ophthalmology. Resident ophthalmology Manhattan Eye, Ear and Throat Hosp., N.Y.C., 1981-84, fellow in cornea dept., 1984-85, resident instr., ophthalmology, 1985-87, residency coord., 1989-91, chief Contact Lens Clinic I, 1986—, chief coord. investigator, 1991—, with laser rsch. study, 1991—. Quality assurance com. Manhattan Eye, Ear and Throat Hosp., N.Y.C., 1987—, chmn. ophthalmology credentials com. 1993—; surgeon dir. Manhattan Eye, Ear and Throat Hosp., 1997—, dir. refractive surgery, 1997—; mem. adv. bd. N.Y. Eye Bank for Sight Restoration, N.Y.C., 1992—; sec. med. adv. bd. N.Y. Eye Bank for Sight Restoration, 1995-97; skills transfer adv. com. Am. Acad. Ophthalmology, San Francisco, 1992-96; lectr. ophthalmology Columbia U., N.Y.C., 1997—; clin. asst. prof. ophthalmology N.Y. Weill-Cornell Med. Coll., N.Y.C., NYU Sch. Medicine. Contbg. author: Corneal Surgery, 1986, 2nd edit., 1993, 3d edit., 1999, Color Atlas of Ophthalmology, 1999. Fellow Am. Acad. Ophthalmology (honor award 1993); mem. Med. Soc. of State of N.Y., N.Y. State Ophthalmologic Soc., Internat. Soc. Refractive Surgery, Contact Lens Assn. of Ophthalmologists, Am. Soc. Cataract and Refractive Surgery, Phi Beta Kappa, Sigma Xi (assoc.). Avocations: photography, golf, travel, aviation, birding. Office: 155 E 72nd St New York NY 10021-4371

HAIGHT, JAMES THERON, lawyer, corporate executive; b. Racine, Wis., Dec. 10, 1924; s. Walter Lyman and Geraldine (Foley) H.; m. Patricia Aloe, Apr. 26, 1952; children: Alberta, Barbara, Catherine, Dorothy, Elaine. Student, U. Nebr., 1943-44, U. Bordeaux, France, 1947; diplome d'Etudes, U. Paris, 1948; BA, U. Wis., 1950, LL.B., 1951. Bar: D.C. 1952, U.S. Supreme Ct. 1955, Calif. 1968. Atty. Covington & Burling, Washington, 1951-56, Goodyear Tire & Rubber Co., Goodyear Internat. Corp., Akron, Ohio, 1956-61; gen. counsel, sec. George J. Meyer Mfg. Co., Milw., 1961-66; sr. v.p., sec., chief corp. counsel Thrifty Corp., L.A., 1966-92, spl. counsel, 1992-96. Adv. bd. Edward Roybal Inst. Applied Gerontology, Calif. State U., LA. Fellow: Am. Bar Found. (life); mem.: ABA (chmn. internat. law sect. 1974—75), Am. Soc. Corp. Secs., Pasadena Bar Assn., Calif. Bar Assn., Order of Coif. Home and Office: 1390 Ridge Way Pasadena CA 91106-4514

HAIGHT, WARREN GAZZAM, investor; b. Seattle, Sept. 7, 1929; s. Gilbert Pierce and Ruth (Gazzam) H.; m. Suzanne H., Sept. 1, 1951; children— Paula Lea, Ian Pierce; m. Ottina Mehau, June 25, 1985 AB in Econs, Stanford U., 1951. Asst. Treas. Hawaiian Pineapple Co., Honolulu, 1955-64; v.p., treas. Oceanic Properties, Inc., Honolulu, 1964-67, pres., dir., 1967-85, chmn., 1983-85; pres. Hawaii, Castle & Cooke Inc., 1983-85, Warren G. Haight & Assocs., 1985—; chmn. Molokai Ranch, Ltd., 1996—2002, Pacific Is. Resources, LLC, 2000—03. Bd. dirs. Round Hill Enterprises, Inc., Las Positas Land Co., Inc., Baldwin Pacific Properties, Inc., Hawaii Project Mgmt., Inc., Transamerica Realty Advisors, Inc., Queen Emma Corp., Queens Devel. Corp., Dole Corp., Standard Fruit and Steamship Co., Inc., Bumble Bee Seafoods, Inc. Bd. dirs. Downtown Improvement Assn., Oahu Devel. Conf., Hawaii Island Econ. Devel. Bd., Econ. Devel. Corp. Honolulu, Intellect, Inc., Hawaii Resort Developers Conf., Homeless Solutions, Inc., Mutual Housing of Hawaii, Inc.; mem. Transit Coalition, Honolulu, Govs. Com. on Econ. Futures; pres., bd. dirs. Land Use Rsch. Found. of Hawaii, Pacific Found. for Cancer Rsch., Hawaii Nature Ctr.; mem. policy adv. bd. for elderly affairs State of Hawaii. Lt. USNR, 1951-55. Mem. Housing Coalition, Calif. Coastal Council. Clubs: Outrigger Canoe, Round Hill Country, Plaza, Pacific. Home: 319 Lala Pl Kailua HI 96734-3224 Office: 220 S King St Ste 1465 Honolulu HI 96813-4542 E-mail: haighthawaii@aol.com.

HAILE, ALLEN CLEVELAND, educator and administrator; b. Forbes Rd., Pa., Aug. 26, 1930; s. Wesley Matthew and Mary Olivia (Hall) H.; m. Barbara Honey, Dec. 30, 1975; children: Mark, Brice, Scott, Marybeth, Jonathan, Courtney. AB, U. Nebr., Omaha, 1959; MS, U. So. Calif., 1966, MPA, PhD, U. So. Calif., 1971. Commd. 2d lt. USAF, 1953, advanced through grades to lt. col., retired, 1973; v.p. urban affairs Pepperdine U., L.A., 1969-73; sr. rschr. Dept. Info. Scis. Rand Corp., Santa Monica, Calif., 1972-73; regional rep. Pacific Basin U.S. Sec. Commerce, L.A., 1977-81; dept. mgr. human resources devel. Bechtel Civil, Inc., Jubail City, 1981-85, mgr. bus. devel. for bldgs. and infrastructure ops., 1985-87, mgr. mktg., 1987-89, mgr. infrastructure devel. Pacific Rim countries, 1991—; dean Coll. of Bus. Calif. Poly State U., San Luis Obispo, 1993-94, dir. cmty. and govt. rels., 1994—. Adj. prof. Golden Gate Univ., 1992. V.p., bd. dirs. San Luis Obispo ARC, C. of C.; pres. Filipino Am C. of C., 1991; bd. dirs. United Way, San Luis Obispo, Econ. Forecast Project, San Luis Obispo, Larkin St. Youth Ctr., San Francisco Edn. Fund, Ct. Appointed Spl. Advocates for Children, Western Govtl. Rsch. Assn., pres. 1989; pres. San Francisco Social Svcs. Commn. 1989, San Francisco Planning and Urban Rsch. Assn., 1992. Decorated DFC and seven air medals. Mem. Am. Soc. Pub. Adminstrn. (bd. trustees found., chmn. constitution revision com. 1988, 89). Home: 1022 Islay St San Luis Obispo CA 93401-4026 Office: Calif Poly State U Cmty and Govt Rels San Luis Obispo CA 93407

HAILE, BENJAMIN CARROLL, JR., retired chemical engineer, retired mechanical engineer; b. Shanghai, Apr. 6, 1918; arrived in U.S., 1925; s. Benjamin Carroll and Ruth Temple (Shreve) Haile; m. Lola Pauline Lease, Dec. 28, 1957 (dec. Dec. 17, 2002); children: Thomas Benjamin, Ronald Frederick. BS, U. Calif., Berkeley, 1941; cert., Harvard-MIT, 1945; postgrad., U. So. Calif., 1950-51. Registered profl. chem. and mech. engr., Calif. Chem. engr. Std. Oil Calif. (Chevron), San Francisco, El Segundo, 1941-43, 46-48; sr. project chem. engr. C.F. Braun & Co., Alhambra, Calif., 1948-50, 54-56, 67-71, 72; contract chem. and mech. engr. Dow Chem., Stearns-Roger, Fluor et al, Tex., Colo., Ill., 1951-54, 56-57; sr. process engr. Aerojet-Gen. Corp., Sacramento, Covina, Calif., 1957-67; mech. engr. So. Calif. Edison Co., Rosemead, 1972-84; pvt. practice chem. engr. Fontana, Montclair, Calif., 1986, 88, 92; sr. mem. tech. staff Ralph M. Parsons Co., Pasadena, Calif., 1971, 88-91; ret., 1992. 2d lt. USAAF, 1943—46. Mem.: AIChE (mem. emeritus), NSPE (life; pres. Sacramento chpt. 1960—62), Toastmasters Internat. (chpt. v.p. 1979, Outstanding Toastmaster 1984), Psi Upsilon. Republican. Achievements include design of oil refineries, chemical plants, others with estimated cumulative inflation adjusted value of one billion dollars during lifetime; development of new fluid bed adsorption process for air separation; research in economic optimization studies of complete aerospace programs; static electricity protection study for Polaris propellant manufacturing facility; design of world's largest boring machines. Home: 159 N Country Club Rd Glendora CA 91741-3919

HAILE, GETATCHEW, retired archivist, educator; b. Shenkora, Shewa, Ethiopia, Apr. 19, 1931; came to U.S., 1976; s. Haile Woldeyes and Assegge-detch Wolde Yohannes; m. Misrak Emitu Amare, July 12, 1964; children: Rebecca, Sossina, Elizabeth, Dawit, Mariam-Sena, Yohannes. BD, Coptic Theol. Coll., Cairo, 1957; BA, Am. U. at Cairo, 1957; PhD, Tübingen (Fed. Republic Germany) U., 1962. Advisor Middle Eastern affairs Ethiopian Ministry Fgn. Affairs, Addis Ababa, 1962; prof. Ethiopian studies Addis Ababa U., 1962-73; mem. parliament State of Ethiopia, Addis Ababa, 1974-75; cataloguer Oriental manuscripts Hill Monastic Manuscript Libr. St. John's U., Collegeville, Minn., 1976-99, regents prof. medieval studies, 1988-99, retired, 1999. Co-editor Acta Ethiopica, 1974-89; mem. internat. adv. bd. Jour. Ethiopian Studies, 1991—, Ethiopian Jour. of Edn., 1992—; contbg. editor Northeast African Studies; mem. adv. bd. Analecta Bellandiana, 1993—, Aethiopica, Zeitschrift für Äthiopistische Studien, 1996—; mem. Ethiopian Register, 1994-2001; author monographs and contbr. articles to scholarly jours. Mem. Cen. Com. of World Coun. of Chs., Geneva, 1968-74; mem. adv. bd. Ethiopian Orthodox Ch., Addis Ababa, 1973-74. MacArthur fellow, 1988. Corr. fellow Brit. Acad. Home: 17903 County Road 9 Avon MN 56310-8624 Office: St John's U Hill Monastic Manuscpt Libr Collegeville MN 56321 E-mail: ghaile@csbsju.edu., ghaile@albanytel.com.

HAILE, H. G. German language and literature educator; b. Brownwood, Tex., July 31, 1931; s. Frank and Neil (Goodson) H.; m. Mary Elizabeth Huff, Sept. 1, 1952; children: Jonathan, Christian, Constance Haile Hunsaker. BA, U. Ark., 1952, MA, 1954; student, U. Cologne, Germany, 1955-56; PhD, U. Ill., 1957. Instr. U. Pa., 1956-57; asst. prof., then asso. prof. U. Houston, 1957-63; mem. faculty U. Ill., Urbana, 1963—, prof. German, 1965—, head dept., 1964-73; asso. mem. U. Ill. (Center for Advanced Study), 1969—. Vis. prof. U. Mich., U. Ga. Author: Das Faustbuch nach der Wolfenbuttler Handschrift, 1963, 95, The History of Doctor Johann Faustus, 1965, 1996, Artist in Chrysalis: A Biographical Study of Goethe in Italy, 1973, Invitation to Goethe's Faust, 1978, Luther: An Experiment in Biography, 1983, We Are All Sonsabitches Now, 2000; contbr. numerous articles to profl. and popular jours. Fulbright fellow, 1955; Fellow Am. Coun. Learned Socs., 1961 62. Office: U Ill 3072 Foreign Languages Urbana IL 61801 E-mail: harryhaile@aol.com. *A child of the Dust Bowl who became a foreign language teacher, I was skeptical about America. I have learned to accept skepticism as the American trait which protects us from correctness, collectivism and coercion.*

HAILE, LAWRENCE BARCLAY, lawyer; b. Atlanta, Feb. 19, 1938; children: Gretchen Vanderhoof, Eric McKenzie (dec.), Scott McAllister. BA in Econs, U. Tex., 1958, LLB, 1961. Bar: Tex. 1961, Calif. 1962. Law clk. to U.S. Judge Joseph M. Ingraham, Houston, 1961-62; pvt. practice San Francisco, 1962-67, LA, 1967—. Instr. UCLA Civil Trial Clinics, 1974, 76; lectr. law Calif. Continuing Edn. of Bar, 1973-74, 80-89; nat. panel arbitrators Am. Arbitration Assn., 1965—. Mem. editl. bd. Tex. Law Rev, 1960-61; contbr. articles profl. jours. Mem. State Bar Calif., Tex., U.S. Supreme Ct. Bar Assn., Internat. Assn. Property Ins. Counsel (founding mem., pres. 1980), Vintage Motorsports Coun. (past pres.), Phi Delta Phi, Delta Sigma Rho. Office: 425 E Ocean Blvd Unit 340 Long Beach CA 90802-4951 E-mail: lhaile1938@aol.com. *Gold is like brass/Except less crass.*

HAILEY, ARTHUR, author; b. Luton, Eng., Apr. 5, 1920; arrived in Can., 1947, naturalized, 1952, (also Brit. citizen); s. George and Elsie (Wright) H.; m. Sheila Dunlop, July 28, 1951; children: Roger, John, Mark (by previous marriage), Jane, Steven, Diane. Student elementary schs., Eng. Author: (with John Castle) Runway Zero-Eight, 1958, The Final Diagnosis, 1959, In High Places, 1962, Hotel, 1965, Airport, 1968, Wheels, 1971, The Moneychangers, 1975, Overload, 1979, Strong Medicine, 1984, The Evening News, 1990, Detective, 1997; author 12 internat. TV plays including No Deadly Medicine (Emmy nomination 1957); (TV series) Hotel; collected plays Close-up on Writing for Television, 1960; motion pictures include Zero Hour, 1956, Time Lock, 1957, The Young Doctors, 1961, Hotel, 1966, Airport, 1970, The Moneychangers, 1976, Wheels, 1978, Strong Medicine, 1986, Detective, 2003; (poem) A Last Request; first editor RAF aircrew tng. mag, Airclues. Air Ministry staff officer, London, 1945-47; pilot, flight lt. RAF, 1939-47; commd. RCAF Res. flight lt., 1951. Recipient Air Efficiency award RAF; subject TV program This Is Your Life, Eng., 1991. Mem. Writers Guild Am. (life), Authors League Am., Alliance of Canadian Cinema, Television and Radio Artists (hon. life), Writers Guild Can. (life). Home: Lyford Cay PO Box N-7776 Nassau The Bahamas Office: Nancy Stauffer Assocs PO Box 1203 Darien CT 06820-1203 E-mail: ahailey@coralwave.com.

HAILEY, HANS RONALD, lawyer; b. Boston, Feb. 9, 1950; s. William C. and renate (Weiss) H.; m. Rosalie A. Caprio, May 2, 1981 (div.); 1 child, Alexa Emily. BA, Boston U., 1973, JD, 1976. Bar: Mass. 1977, U.S. Dist. Ct. Mass. 1977, U.S. Ct. Appeals (1st cir.) 1978; cert. civil trial specialist, Nat. Bd. Trial Lawyers, U.S. Supreme Ct. Pvt. practice law, Boston. Mem Mass. Archtl. Barriers Bd., 1978-82. Author: So You Think You Have Better Thing To Do Than Stay Married, 1991; contbr. articles to profl. jours. Bd. dirs. Boston Ctr. for Ind. Living, 1979-88, Easter Seal Soc., 1988-93; mem. Mass. Archtl. Barriers Bd., 1978-82. Named One of ten Outstanding Young Leaders Boston Jaycees, 1981. Mem. Mass. bar Assn., Boston Bar Assn., Mass Trial lawyers Assn. (exec. coun.). Democrat. Roman Catholic. Home: 74 Highview St Westwood MA 02090-3019 Office: 225 Friend St Boston MA 02114 E-mail: hhailey@erols.com.

HAILS, ROBERT EMMET, aerospace consultant, business executive, former air force officer; b. Miami, Fla., Jan. 20, 1923; s. Daniel Troy and Jean (Burke) H.; m. Ethel Fitzgerald Gayle, Mar. 2, 1957; children: Robert Emmet Jr., Merrily Hails Joiner, Florence T. Hails Patton, Laura Hails Smith. BS in Aero. Engring., Auburn U., 1947; MS in Indsl. Engring., Columbia U., 1950; postgrad., C&CS Air U., 1955; postgrad. AMP, Harvard U. Sch. Bus., 1965. Enlisted USAAF, 1942, commd. 2d lt., 1944, advanced through grades to lt. gen., 1974, combat pilot Pacific Theater, 1944-45; assigned to SAC, 1947-48; inspector gen. Hdqrs. USAF, 1950-53; program devel. officer Marcel Dassault Mystere IV Jet Aircraft, French Air Force Am. embassy, Paris, 1953-55; air staff project officer F-104/F-105 aircraft HQ USAF, 1956-60; comdr. procurement dist. USAF, San Francisco, 1960-62; mil. asst. for weapons systems acquisition Office Sec. AF, 1962-66; system program dir. Joint USAF/USN A-7D Aircraft Engring., Devel., Test & Prodn., AF Systems Commd., 1966-68; dep. chief staff maintenance engring. Air Force Logistics Command, 1968-71; comdr. Def. Pers. Support Ctr. Def. Log. Agy., Phila., 1971-72; comdr. Air Logistics Ctr. USAF, Warner Robins AFB, Ga., 1972-74, vice comdr. Tactical Air Command Langley AFB, Va., 1974-75; dep. chief staff systems and logistics Hdqrs. USAF, Washington, 1975-77; ret. USAF, Washington, 1977; mgmt. cons. Atlanta, 1978-80; sr. v.p. internat. ops. LTV Corp., Dallas, 1980-84; pres. Hails Assoc. Inc., Macon, Ga., 1984—. Mem. sci. bd. Loral Corp., Yonkers, NY, 1992-96. Regional exec. Boy Scouts Am.; mem. Auburn U. Alumni Engring. Coun., 1982—; bd. advisors Wesleyan Coll., 1985-90; mem. Found. Bd., Macon State Coll., 1998-2001. Decorated DSM with 2 oak leaf clusters, legion of Merit with 2 oak leaf clusters, Air medal with 2 oak leaf clusters; Order of Nat. Security (Korea); recipient Engring. Achievement award Auburn U., 1998; inducted into State of Ala. Engring. Hall of Fame, 2001, State of Ga. Aviation Hall of Fame, 2001. Mem. AIAA, Air Force Assn., Daedalians, Auburn U. SPADES, Army-Navy Country Club (Arlington, Va.), Idle Hour Golf and Country Club, Omicron Delta Kappa, Sigma Alpha Epsion. Roman Catholic. Achievements include introduction of heads-up-display (HUD) in a US military aircraft. E-mail: bobehails@cox.net.

HAILSTON, EARL B. career officer; b. Utica, N.Y., May 27, 1947; m. Nancy Anne Carlson; children: Kelly Anne, Ashley Elizabeth. Enlisted USMC, 1967, commd. officer through Enlisted Commissioning Program, 1968, advanced through grades to lt. gen., 1999; various assignments include comdr. Marine Aircraft Group 31, 1992-94; comdg. gen. 3DFSS6, 1994-96; asst. dep. chief of staff Installations and Logistics, Hdqtrs. USMC, Washington, 1996; dir. for strategic planning and policy J-5, USCINCPAC, Camp H.M. Smith, Hawaii, 1997-99; comdg. gen. III MEF, 1999—2001, MARFORPAC, Hawaii, 2001—. Decorated Silver Star, Legion of Merit, Bronze Star, Def. Meritorious Svc. medal, Meritorious Svc. medal, Navy Commendation medal, Combat Action Ribbon, Def. Disting. Svc. medal. Office: Box 64134 Camp H M Smith HI 96861

HAILU, BROOK, media analyst, analyst; s. Hailu Beshah and Rosa Terefe; m. Tsehainesh K/Mariam Gebru, May 5, 1989; children: Hailu Brook, Tegist Brook, Natna Brook. B in polit. sci. and internat. rels., Addis Ababa U., 1976—80; M in polit. sci. and internat. rels., Leipzig U., 1985—87; PhD, Inst. For Media & Communication Sciences, 1991—97. Dir. in the european & am. directorate Ministry Of Fgn. Affairs, Addis Ababa, Ethiopia, 2000—01; dep. amb. Embassy Of Ethiopia, Washington D.C., 2001—. External rels. head Addis Ababa U., Ethiopia, 1998—2000, asst. prof., polit. sci. & internat. rels., 1997—2001. Founder & v.p. The Ethiopian Polit. Sci. Assn., Ethiopia, 1999—2001. Mem.: The Ethiopian Polit. Sci. Assn. (v.p. 1999—2001). Home: 13207 Stravinsky Terrace Silver Spring MD 20904 Office: Embassy of Ethiopia 3506 International Dr NW Washington DC 20008 Home Fax: 202-686-9573; Office Fax: 202-686-9573. E-mail: brookh@ethiopianembassy.org.

HAIMAN, FRANKLYN SAUL, author, communications educator; b. Cleve., June 23, 1921; s. Alfred Wilfred and Stella (Weiss) H.; m. Louise Goble, June 11, 1955; children— Mark David, Eric Saul. BA, Case Western Res. U., 1942; MA, Northwestern U., 1946, PhD, 1948. Mem. faculty Northwestern U., Evanston, Ill., 1948—, chmn. dept. communication studies, 1964-75, prof. communication studies, 1970-88, John Evans prof. communication studies, 1988-91, John Evans prof. emeritus, 1991—. Adj. prof. U. of San Francisco, 1992—. Author: Group Leadership and Democratic Action, 1951, Freedom of Speech: Issues and Cases, 1965, Freedom of Speech, 1976, Speech and Law in a Free Society, 1981, "Speech Acts" and the First Amendment, 1993, Freedom, Democracy, and Responsibility: The Selected Works of Franklyn S. Haiman, 2000, Religious Expression and the American Constitution, 2003; co-author: The Dynamics of Discussion, 1960, 2d edit., 1980; editor: (book series) To Protect These Rights, 1976-77; contbr. articles to profl. jours. Pres. ACLU of Ill., 1964-75, nat. bd. dirs., 1965-96, nat. corp. sec., 1976-82, nat. v.p., 1987-96, vice chair nat. adv. coun., 1996—. With USAAF, 1942-45. Mem. ACLU, Nat. Comm. Assn., Am. Psychol. Assn., AAUP, Phi Beta Kappa. Home: 5283 Broadway Ter Apt 4-b Oakland CA 94618-1491

HAIMAN, IRWIN SANFORD, lawyer; b. Cleve., Mar. 19, 1916; s. Alfred W. and Stella H. (Weiss) H.; m. Jeanne D. Jaffee, Mar. 8, 1942; children: Karen H. Schenkel, Susan L. BA, Western Res. U., 1937; LL.B., Cleve. Marshall Law Sch., 1941; JD, Cleve. State U., 1969. Bar: Ohio 1941, U.S. Ct. Appeals (6th cir.) 1961, U.S. Supreme Ct. 1961. Asst. to pres. Tremco Mfg. Co., Cleve., 1936-42; house counsel William Edwards Co., Cleve., 1947-48; pvt. practice Cleve., 1948-68; ptnr. firm Garber, Simon, Haiman, Gutfeld, Friedman & Jacobs, 1968-80; ptnr. McCarthy, Lebit, Crystal & Haiman, 1981—. Lectr. in speech Western Res. U., 1948-70; dir. Washington Fed. Savs. and Loan Assn.; asst. law dir., prosecutor City of Lyndhurst, Ohio, 1965-79, law dir., 1979-84. Trustee Montefiore Home, Cleve., 1974-88 (life trustee 1988—)—, East End Neighborhood House, 1962-68; councilman City of South Euclid, 1948-54, pres., 1952-54; pres. Young People's Congregation, Fairmount Temple, 1951-52; sec., trustee Surburban Temple, 1962-65, trustee, 1983—, pres., 1984-87; chmn. speakers div., bd. dirs. Cleve. chpt. ARC, 1959-62; chmn. speaker and film div. Cleve. United Appeal, 1961-62; chmn. speakers div. Jewish Welfare Fund Cleve., 1973-79. Served as 1st lt. AUS, 1943-47. Mem. Ohio, Cleve. bar assns., Assn. Trial Lawyers Am., Zeta Beta Tau. Clubs: Oakwood Country, Lake Forest Country (pres. 1971-72, 75-79). Home: 20201 N Park Blvd Cleveland OH 44118-5000

HAIMAN, ROBERT JAMES, newspaper editor, journalism educator, media consultant; b. Norwich, Conn., May 6, 1936; s. Albert and Letta (Cone) H.; m. Elizabeth Royce Greenlaw, Sept. 26, 1964 (div. Aug. 1996); 1 child, Robert Greenlaw. Student, U. Conn., 1953-55; BS, U. Fla., 1957. Reporter St. Petersburg (Fla.) Times, 1958-60, copy editor, 1962-63, nat. editor, 1964-66, mng. editor, 1966-76, exec. editor, 1976-83; pres., mng. dir. Poynter Inst. Media Studies, 1983-96, pres. emeritus, disting. editor in residence, 1997—. Bd. dirs. Times Pub. Co., St. Petersburg; trustee Fla. InterAm. Scholarship Found.; mem. minority mgmt. task force Inst. Journalism Edn. Mem. pres. round table Eckerd Coll.; trustee Poynter Inst. Media Studies, St. Petersburg; mem. Pulitzer Prize jury, 1977, 90, 91, 96, 97; internat. adv. bd. Inst. Advancement Journalism, Johannesburg, South Africa; mem. nat. adv. bd. Inst. for Journalists and Pub. Policy Gordon Pub. Policy Ctr. Brandeis U. Elder Presbyn. Ch.; trustee Bayfront City Found.; sr. fellow Freedom Forum, Washington, 1998—; mem. Pres.'s coun. U. Fla., U. South Fla., chmn. campus adv. bd., 1989—91; mem. adv. bd. U. Fla. Internat. Ctr.; mem. journalism adv. bd. Knight Found., Inst. Current World Affairs, Hanover, NH, Tampa Bay Com. Coun. on Fgn. Rels. Served with USMC, 1961. Named Disting. Alumnus, U. Fla., 1988. Mem. AP Mng. Editors Assn. (pres. 1982), Am. Soc. Newspaper Editors (dir. 1992-98), Internat. Press Inst. (Vienna), World Editors Forum (Paris), Interam. Press Assn., St. Petersburg Yacht Club, Dragon Club, Quarterback Club, Golden Triangle Club, Soc. Profl. Journalists. Democrat. Home: 5155 Isla Key Blvd S Apt 103 Saint Petersburg FL 33715-1687 Office: 801 3rd St S Saint Petersburg FL 33701-4920

HAIMES, TODD, artistic director; m. Alison Haimes, children: Hilary, Andrew. Grad., Yale Sch. of Mgmt., U. Pa. Artistic dir. Roundabout Theatre Co., N.Y.C., 1990—. Office: Roundabout Theatre Co 231 W 39th St Ste 1200 New York NY 10018-3109

HAIMES, YACOV YOSSEPH, systems and civil engineering educator, consultant; b. Baghdad, Iraq, June 18, 1936; came to U.S., 1965, naturalized, 1972; s. Yosseph and Rose (Elani) H.; m. Sonia E. Jamison, June 16, 1968; children: Yosef, Michelle. BS, Hebrew U., Jerusalem, 1964; MS, U. Calif., 1967, PhD with distinction, 1970. Jr. petroleum engr. Ministry of Devel., Jerusalem, 1962-65; asst. prof. engring. Case-Western Reserve U., Cleve., 1970-71, assoc. prof. systems engring., 1971-76, dir. grad. program water resources and systems engring., 1972-87, prof. systems engring. and civil engring., 1976-87, dir. Center for Large Scale Systems and Policy Analysis, 1980-84, chmn. systems engring. dept., 1983-86; Lawrence R. Quarles Prof. of Engring. and Applied Sci. U. Va., Charlottesville, 1987—; dir. Ctr. for Risk Mgmt. of Engring. Systems, U. Va., Charlottesville, 1987—. Pres. Environ. Systems Mgmt. Inc., Ohio, 1974—; mem. staff Office of Sci. and Tech. Policy, Exec. Office of President, 1977, Com. on Sci. and Tech., Ho. of Reps., 1978; cons. in field.; chmn. UNESCO Working Group on Water Resources Planning, 1980-87; mem. bd. on water sci. and tech. NRC, 1982-84; chmn. tech. adv. com. Internat. Ground Water Modeling Ctr. Holcomb Research Inst., 1985-88, mem. 1983-88; cons. Congl. Office of Tech. Assessment, 1977-89; cons. Sci. Adv. Bd. U.S. EPA, 1986-96, Oil and Gas Regulatory Commn. State of Ohio, 1986-87, chmn. regulatory com., 1986-87. Author: (with W.A. Hall and H.T. Freedman) Multiobjective Optimization in Water Resources Systems, 1975; Hierarchical Analyses of Water Resources Systems, 1977; (with V. Chankong) Multiobjective Decision Making: Theory and Methodology, 1983; (with J. Pet-Edwards, V. Chankong, H. Rosenkranz and F. Ennever) Risk Assessment and Decisionmaking Using Test Results: The Carcinogenicity Prediction and Battery Selection (CPBS) Approach, 1989; (with K. Tarvainen, T. Shima and J. Thadathil) Hierarchical Multiobjective Analysis of Large-Scale Systems, 1990; (with V. Chankong) Multiobjective Problems: Theory and Methods, 1996; Risk Modeling, Assessment, and Management, 1998; editor: Scientific, Technological and Institutional Aspects of Water Resource Policy, 1980; (with P. Laconte) Water Resources and Land Use Planning, 1982; Energy Auditing and Conservation, 1980; Risk/Benefit Analysis in Water Resources Planning and Management, 1981: Large Scale Systems, 1982; (with D. Allee) Multiobjective Analysis in Water Resources, 1984; (with V. Chankong) Decision Making with Multiple Objectives, 1985; (with J.H. Snyder) Groundwater Contamination, 1986; (with E.Z. Stakhiv) Risk-Based Decision Making in Water Resources, 1986; (with J. Kindler and E. Plate) The Process of Water Resources Planning: A Systems Approach, 1987; (with D. Baumann) Water Resources Planning and Management: The Role of the Social Sciences, 1988; (with E. Stakhiv) Risk Analysis and Management of Natural and Man-Made Hazards, 1989; (with J. Bear, F. Walters and G. Jousma) Modeling of Groundwater Contamination, 1989: (with E.Z. Stakhiv) Risk-Based Decision Making in Water Resources, 1990; (with E.Z. Stakhiv and D. Moser) Risk-Based Decision Making in Water Resources, 1992; (with E.Z. Stakhiv and D. Moser), Risk Based Decision Making in Water Resources VI, 1994, (with E.Z. Stakhiv and D. Moser), Risk Based Decision Making in Water Resources, VII, 1996, (with E.Z. Stakhiv and D. Moser) Risk Based Decision Making in Water Resources VIII, 1998, (with E.Z. Stakhiv and D. Moser) Risk Based Decision Making in Water Resources IX, 2001; assoc. editor IEEE Trans. on Systems, Man and Cybernetics, 1979-2001, Automatica, 1981-92, Large Scale Systems: Theory and Applications, 1981-88, Jour. Control, Theory and Advanced Tech., 1985-92, Info. and Decision Techs., 1988-91, Reliability Engring. and Systems Safety, 1990—, Risk Analysis Internat. Jour., 1991—. Mem. UNESCO IHP IV Panel Water Resources, 1991-97. Case Centennial Scholar Case Inst. Tech., Case Western Res. U., 1980. Fellow IEEE, AAAS, ASCE (com. on water resources systems 1975-80, outstanding rsch. paper award 1990), Am. Water Resources Assn. (pres. Ohio sect. 1974-75), Internat. Water Resources Assn., Soc. Risk Analysis, Internat. Coun. Engring. Sys., IEEE Systems, Man and Cybernetics Soc. (v.p. for tech. activities 1990-91, v.p. for publs. 1992-93, Norbert Weiner award 2001), Univs. Council on Water Resources (chmn. com. on environ. quality 1977-79, dir. 1979-85, v.p. 1983-84, pres. 1984-85, Pub. Svc. award 1991, Warren A. Hall medal 1997), Internat. Fedn. Automatic Control (chmn. working group on water resources 1973-87, vice-chmn. systems engring. com. 1987-90), Am. Automatic Control Council (vice-chmn. systems engring. com. 1976-79), Am. Geophys. Union (com. on water resources systems 1970-74, chmn. water resource environ. mgmt. com. 1980-82), Ops. Rsch. Soc. Am., Soc. for Risk Analysis (chmn. com. on confs. and workshops 1989 91, Disting. Achievement award 2000), Multiple Criteria Decision Making Soc. (exec. com. 1984-98), Sigma Xi (past pres. local chpt.), Tau Beta Pi. Home: 3160 Waverly Dr Charlottesville VA 22901-9576 Office: U Va Olsson Hall Rm 112 Dept Systems and Info Engring Charlottesville VA 22903

HAIMS, BRUCE DAVID, lawyer; b. N.Y.C., Nov. 25, 1940; s. Samuel Harold and Judith (Feller) H.; m. Judith Jackson; children: Carolyn, Daniel, Nolan. BS in Econs., U. Pa., 1962; LLB magna cum laude, Harvard U., 1965; LLM in Taxation, NYU, 1972. Bar: Conn. 1965, N.Y. 1967, U.S. Ct. Appeals (2d cir.) 1968, U.S. Tax Ct. 1972. Assoc. Debevoise & Plimpton, N.Y.C., 1967-72, ptnr., 1973—. Bd. dirs. Axe Houghton Found., Brookfield Craft Ctr. Capt. U.S. Army,

1965-67. Mem. N.Y. State Bar Assn., Assn. of Bar of City of N.Y., Internat. Fiscal Assn. Home: 470 W End Ave Apt 14A New York NY 10024-4933 Office: Debevoise & Plimpton 919 3rd Ave Fl 2 New York NY 10022-3904

HAIN, PATRICIA A. music educator; d. Alfred Charles and Myrtle Marie Walsh; m. Raymond Fisher, Apr. 3, 1975; children: Raymond, Marie-Amanda, Deborah, David. BA in History, Rosemont Coll., Pa., 1971; BA in Edn., U. Portland, Oreg., 1972. Cert. tchr. State of Oreg., 1972, State of Wash., 1994. Tchr. Mayfield Jr. Sch., Pasadena, Calif., 1968—70, Govt. of Guam, Agana, 1972—76; pvt. piano tchr., 1978—; ch. pianist St. Vincent de Paul Ch., Federal Way, Wash., 1981—92; tchr. Visitation Sch., Tacoma, 1991—92; ch. pianist St. Paul's Ch., Athens, Ala., 1993—99; sub. pianist, organist St. John The Beloved Ch., Wilmington, Del., 2002—. Composer: Religious Hymns; contbr. articles to profl. jours. Mem.: Nat. Fedn. of Music Clubs, Music Tchrs. Nat. Assn., Northern Del. Music Tchrs. Assn. (v.p. membership 2003—).

HAINE, THOMAS WILLIAM NICHOLAS, educator; b. Oxford, England, Feb. 23, 1967; s. Stephen Robert and Jennifer Susan Haine; m. Barbara Jean Souter, Sept. 13, 1997. BA in Physics & Theoretical Physics, U. Cambridge, England, 1988, MA; PhD in Phys. Oceanography, U. Southampton, England, 1993. Rsch. assoc. U. Eas Anglia, England, 1993-94; lectr. U. Oxford, England, 1996-99; asst. prof. Johns Hopkins U., Balt., 2000—01, assoc. prof., 2002—. Contbr. rsch. papers to profl. pubs. Rsch. grantee Natural environment Rsch. Coun., England, 1996, 97, 2000, NSF, 2000-02; rsch. scholar MIT, Cambridge, Mass., 1994-96; rsch. fellow Wolfson Coll, Oxford, 1996-99. Fellow Royal Meteorol. Soc.; mem. Am. Meteorol. Soc., Am. Geophys. Union. Office: Earth and Planetary Scis The Johns Hopkins U 301 Olin Hall Baltimore MD 21218

HAINE, WILLIAM R. state senator; b. Alton, Ill., Aug. 8, 1944; m. Anna Haine; children: Cecilia, Elizabeth, Mary, Margaret, Alice, Thomas, Joseph. BA, St. Louis Univ., 1967; JD, St. Louis Univ. Sch. of Law, 1973. State Senator US Senate, Dist. 56, 2002—; State's Atty. Madison County, 1988—2002; lawyer Alton & Wood, 1976—88. Bd. mem. Madison County, 1978; chair Metro-Fast Transit Bd. of Trustees, 1981—88; bd. mem. Madison County, 1982—88; chair Local Gov.; mem.. Dem. Ctrl. Comm., 1975—90; mem. Environ. & Energy, Judiciary, Lic. Activities. 1st Calvalry Div. USAR, 1967—69, Vietnam. Mem.: Ill. State Bar Assoc., Vet. of Fgn. Wars, St. Anthony Hosp. Health Ctr. Bd., Alton Cemetery Bd. of Trustees, Knights of Columbus, past comdr., Am. Legion. Democrat. Roman Catholic. Office: Capitol M120 Capitol Bldg Springfield IL 62706 Home: 307 Henry St #120 Alton IL 62002 Address: 1407 Liberty St Alton IL 62002*

HAINES, CATHY JEAN, middle school education educator; b. Philipsburg, Pa., Nov. 21, 1949; d. George Clark and Mary Frances (Taylor) Moore; 1 child, Franklin Cole Whitby. BS in Music Edn., U. Mary-Hardin Baylor, 1973; MA in Music Theory, U. Iowa, 1981, MA in Ednl. Adminstrn., 1990, postgrad., 1997. Cert. tchr. Tex., Ark., music tchr., secondary adminstr. Iowa, secondary adminstr. Ark. Tchg. asst. U. Iowa, Iowa City, 1976-77; tchr. Pulaski County Spl. Sch. Dist., Little Rock, 1979-83, Kennedy H.S., Pierce, Hiawatha and Nixon Elem. Schs., 1983-87; music tchr. Harding Mid. Sch., Cedar Rapids, 1983—. Lead orch. tchr. Interlochen (Mich.) Ctr. for Arts, 1993-96, Blue Lake Fine Arts Camp, 1999, Very Spl. Arts; mem. NCA evaulation team Anson Jr. H.S., Marshalltown, Iowa, 1990; mem. S.E. Iowa Symphony Orch., Waterloo-Cedar Falls Symphony Orch., Ottumwa Symphony Orch., Oskaloosa Symphony Orch., Dubuque Symphony Orch.; mem. summer chamber music workshops Raphael Trio, Adamant, Vt. Violinist Hancher Auditorium, Iowa City, Interlochen Ctr. for Arts, Blue Lake Fine Arts Camp; contbr. articles to profl. publs. Mem. NEA, ASCD, Nat. Sch. Orch. Assn. (nat. exec. bd. 1988-90, Disting. Svc. award), Iowans for Arts Edn. (state bd. dirs. 1988-90), Phi Delta Kappa (rec. sec. 1995-96). Office: Cedar Rapids Cmty Sch Dist Cedar Rapids IA 52246

HAINES, DANIEL WEBSTER, engineering consultant, educator; b. Nashville, Nov. 8, 1937; s. I. Snowden and Elsie (Davis) Haines; m. Brynne Levinson, Nov. 9, 1962; children: Gordon, Laurel. BS, Rutgers U., 1959; MS, Lehigh U., 1961; ScD in Engring., Columbia U., 1968. Registered prof. engr., N.Y., SC. Rsch. asst. Lehigh U., 1959—61; vol. Peace Corps, Ibadan, Nigeria, 1961—63; trainee NASA, 1964—66; prof. engring. U. SC, Columbia, 1969—77; product engring. mgr. Ciba-Geigy Corp., Ardsley, NY, 1977—81; prin. Midlantic Testing and Cons., White Plains, NY, 1982—87; prof. Manhattan Coll., Riverdale, NY, 1983—, chair mech. engring. dept., 1995—99. Vis. lectr. Yale U., 1975—76; vis. assoc. prof. Stevens Inst., Hoboken, NJ, 1975—76; cons. Institut National de la Recherche Agronomique, Nancy, France, 1999—. Editor (in chief): CAS Jour., 1989—95; mem. editl. adv. bd. CAS Jour., 1999—2002; contbr. articles to profl. jours. Fellow, Sloan Found., Princeton U., 1968—69; grantee, NSF, 1969—77. Mem.: ASME, ASCE, Catgut Acoustical Soc. (treas. 1982—90, trustee 1981—99). Home: 142 Greenridge Ave White Plains NY 10605-3109 E-mail: danhaines@juno.com.

HAINES, DENNIS G. military officer; BS in Bus. Adminstrn. and Mgmt., U. Wyo., 1968, MS in Bus. Adminstrn. and Mgmt., 1969; disting. grad., Squadron Officer Sch., 1972; grad., Air Command and Staff Coll., 1978. Commd. 2d lt. USAF, 1968, advanced through grades to maj. gen., 1997; maintenance control officer 19th Tactical Air Support Squadron, 314th Air Divsn., Osan Air Base, South Korea, 1972-73; chief, maintenance control divsn. comdr. 18th Equipment Maintenance Squadron, Kadena Air Base, Japan, 1980-83; dep. dir., dir. for maintenance engring. Hdqs. Pacific Air Forces, Hickam AFB, Hawaii, 1983-87; dep. comdr. for maintenance 37th Tactical Fighter Wing, Nellis AFB, Nev., 1988-90; chief fighter propulsion mgmt. divsn. San Antonio Air Logistics Ctr., Kelly AFB, Tex., 1990-91; dir. aircraft directorate Ogden Air Logistics Ctr., Hill AFB, Utah, 1991-93; dir. logistics Hdqs. Air Edn. and Tng. Command, Randolph AFB, Tex., 1993-95; dir. of supply Hdqs. USAF, Washington, 1995-96; dir. of logistics Hdqs. Air Force Materiel Command, Wright-Patterson AFB, Ohio, 1996-97, Hdqs. Air Combat Command, Langley AFB, Va., 1997-99, dir. combat weapon systems, 1999-2000, comdr. Warner Robins Air Logistics Ctr. Robins AFB, Ga., 2000—. Decorated Legion of Merit with oak leaf cluster, Meritorious Svc. medal with 4 oak leaf clusters. Office: WRALC / CC 215 Page Rd Ste 235 Robins Afb GA 31098-1662

HAINES, HERBERT H. sociology educator; b. Kansas City, Kans., July 6, 1952; s. Hadley H. and Blanche M. Haines; m. Cynthia G. Moy; children: Evan M., Colin M. PhD, U. Kans., 1982. Asst. prof. Western New Eng. Coll., Springfield, Mass., 1983—85; prof. SUNY, Cortland, NY, 1985—. Author: Against Capital Punishment: The Anti-Death Penalty Movement in America, 1972-1994, 1996, Black Radicals and the Civil Rights Mainstream, 1954-1970, 1988 (Outstanding Book Gustavus Myers Ctr. for Study of Human Rights in the U.S., 1989). Mem.: Midwest Sociol. Soc., Soc. for Study of Social Problems, Am. Sociol. Assn. Office: SUNY Cortland Cornish Hall Cortland NY 13045

HAINES, JOHN MEADE, poet, translator, writer; b. 1924; Homesteader in Alaska, 1947-69; poet-in-residence U. Alaska, Anchorage, 1972-73; vis. prof. English U. Wash., Seattle, 1974; vis. lectr. U. Mont., Missoula, 1974-75; Guggenheim fellowship, 1984-85; disting. vis. lectr. U. Calif., Santa Cruz, 1986; writer-in-residence Montalvo Ctr. for the Arts, 1987-88, Djerassi Found., 1988; vis. prof. Ohio U., Athens, 1989-90. Vis. writer George Washington U., 1991-92; Elliston fellow in poetry U. Cin., 1992; chmn. creative arts Austin Peay State U., Clarksville, Tenn., 1993—; vis. lectr. Ann. Summer Wordsworth Conf., Grasmere, Eng., 1996; writer-in-residence Bellagio Ctr., Italy, 2000; poet-in-residence Bucknell U., 2001. Translator: El Amor Ascendia, 1967; author: Winter News: Poems, 1966, Suite for the Pied Piper, 1967, The Legend of Paper Plates, 1970, The Mirror, 1971, The Stone Harp, 1971, Twenty Poems, 1971, Leaves and Ashes: Poems, 1974, In Five Years Time, 1976; The Sun on Your Shoulder, 1976, Cicada, 1977, In a Dusty Light, 1977, Living Off the Country: Essays on Poetry and Place, 1981, Of Traps and Snares, 1981, Other Days, 1982, News from the Glacier: Selected Poems 1982, Forest Without Leaves, 1984, Stories We Listened To, 1986, The Stars, The Snow, The Fire, 1989, Meditation On a Skull Carved in Crystal, 1989, New Poems, 1980-88, 1990 (Western States Art Fedn. award, Lenore Marshall/Nation award, Poets prize 1990), (poetry) Rain Country, 1990, The Owl in the Mask of the Dreamer, Collected Poems, 1993, A Guide to the Four-Chambered Heart, 1996, At the End of this Summer, 1948-54, 1997, (essay) Fables and Distances, New and Selected Essays, 1996, For the Century's End, Poems 1990-1999, 2001. Recipient Acad. award in Lit. Am. Acad. of Arts and Letters, 1995; 63d fellow Acad. Am. Poets, 1997; named Alaska Poet Laureate, 1969-73; Gugggenheim fellow, 1965-66, NEA fellow, 1967-68. Home: 717 Longstaff Missoula MT 59801-3605

HAINES, JOYBELLE, retired elementary school educator; b. Geronomo, Okla., Oct. 20, 1930; d. William Tommie and Ruby Dell Heffington; m. Meredith C. Haines, Aug. 22, 1953; children: Cynthia Elaine, Stephen Michael, Lisa Joy. Grad., Asbury Coll., Wilmore, Ky.; postgrad., Ball State Tchrs. Coll., Calif. State U. Missionary tchr., Seoul, Republic of Korea, 1954—56; tchr. Hartford City, Ind., 1956—65, Muncie, Ind., 1965—66, Stockton (Calif.) Unified Sch. Dist., 1966—2000; ret., 2001. Cons. new tchrs., tutor, Stockton, 1999—. Mem.: AAUW, Rep. Women's Club. Baptist. Home: 9530 Springfield Way Stockton CA 95212

HAINES, KATHLEEN ANN, physician, educator; b. N.Y.C., July 28, 1949; d. George Raymond and Gertrude Ann (Driscoll) H.; m. Emil Claus Gotschlich, May 24, 1975; 1 child, Emily Claire. BA, CUNY, 1971; MD, Albert Einstein Coll. Medicine, 1975. Diplomate Am. Bd. Pediatrics, Am. Bd. Allergy and Immunology. Intern, resident N.Y. Hosp./Cornell U., N.Y.C., 1975-77, fellow in allergy/immunology, 1977-80; instr. in pediatrics NYU Sch. of Medicine, N.Y.C., 1980-84, asst. prof. pediatrics, 1984-91, asst. prof. medicine, 1989-91, assoc. prof. clin. pediatrics and medicine, 1991—; dir. pediat. rheumatology Hosp. for Joint Diseases/NYU Med. Ctr., 1994—2002; dir. clin. immunology lab. Hosp. for Joint Diseases, 1995—2002; sect. chief pediat. immunology Hackensack U. Med. Ctr., 2002—. Mem. rsch. coun. N.Y. Heart Assn., 1988-90; program com. Am. Coll. Rheumatology, 2000-03, vis. prof., 2001. Contbr. articles to profl. jours., chpts. to books in field. Med. and Scientific Com. N.Y.C. chpt. Arthritis Found., 1993-99. Grantee N.Y. Arthritis Found., 1990, 96, NIH, 1993-98. Fellow Am. Acad. Allergy and Immunology, Am. Acad. Pediatrics; mem. Am. Fedn. Med. Rsch., Allergy, Asthma and Immunology Soc. of Greater N.Y. (sec. 1995-97, pres.-elect 1997-98, pres. 1998-99), Harvey Soc., Soc. Pediatric Rsch. Office: Hackensack U Med Ctr 30 Prospect Ave Hackensack NJ 07601

HAINES, KENNETH H. sports television broadcasting and marketing executive; b. Spokane, Sept. 5, 1942; s. Kenneth A. and Helen Elizabeth (Evans) H.; m. Stephanie Marie Phelps, Nov. 23, 1981; 1 child, Avery Jordan. *Father, Kenneth A. Haines, 30 years with United States Department of Agriculture, most recently Director of International Research, Washington, DC. Married 65 years to Helen Haines. Brother, Thomas R. Haines, 33 years employed by Washington State Department of Social and Health Services, currently as the Community Service Office Administrator, Seattle. Wife, Stephanie, BS Virginia Tech, MS Radford University. Faculty member in English, King's College, Charlotte, received the college "teaching excellence" CPCC award, 1992. Daughter, Avery, student at Providence Day School Charlotte, selected as member of the National Honor Society in 1999.* BA, Dakota Wesleyan U., 1964; MA, U. Wyo.; MS, Troy State U., 1970; CAGS, Va. Tech., 1976. News dir. KORN TV, Mitchell, S.D., 1962-64; sta. mgr. KUWR Radio, Laramie, Wyo., 1965-67; gen. mgr. KLME Radio, Laramie, 1967-68; instr. flight ops. U.S. Army, Ft. Rucker, Ala., 1968-70; from dir. radio, tv, film to dir. pub. affairs, univ. rels. Va. Tech., Blacksburg, 1970-81; from exec. v.p., COO to pres., CEO, Raycom Sports, Charlotte, NC, 1981—2002, pres., CEO, 2002—. Bd. dirs. Charlotte Sports Commn., ACC Properties; trustee Dakota Wesleyan U.; exec. dir. Continental Tire Bowl, 2002—. *Kenneth Haines negotiates Raycom contracts for all network coverage and sports properties, including ACC basketball. He developed innovative projects such as "Glasnost Bowl", "Blockbuster Bowl", "Emmy Awards for Sports", Continental Tire Bowl, LPGA golf tournaments, and live programming from Graceland. He authored studies of collegiate conferences initiating major restructuring of traditional college athletic alignments. In 1991, he negotiated a partnership with ABC-TV to produce all its college basketball games. A frequent speaker at sports marketing conferences, he travels extensively to college campuses and television studios, and frequently quoted by such publications as USA Today, Wall Street Journal, Broadcasting and Associated Press.* Bd. dirs. Sunshine Football Classic, 1989—, Charlotte Basketball Challenge, 1987—; tournament dir. LPGA Golf, 1989—; exec. dir. Continental Tire Bowl. Named Reporter of Yr., UPI, 1967, Opperman Disting. Lectr., Dakota Wesleyan U., 1998, Outstanding TV Sports Exec., All-Am. Football Found., 1999; recipient golden award Coun. Support Higher Edn., 1978. Mem. Am. Assn. Agr. Writers, Am. Coll. Pub. Rels. Assn. (exceptional achievement award 1974), Va. Press Assn., Coun. for Advancement and Support of Edn. (pres. univ. faculty club 1980-82), Nat. Acad. TV Arts and Scis. (judge), Charlotte C. of C. (bd. dirs.), Phi Kappa Delta, Pi Delta Epsilon, Omicron Delta Kappa. Avocations: sports, photography, television, travel, reading. Home: 1909 Carmel Rd Charlotte NC 28226-5021 Office: Raycom Sports 2815 Coliseum Centre Dr Ste 200 Charlotte NC 28217-1378

HAINES, LEE MARK, JR., religious denomination administrator; b. Marion, Ind., Dec. 9, 1927; s. Lee M. Sr. and Anna (Stevens); m. Maxine Louise Shockey, June 8, 1948 (dec. September 16, 2002); children: Mark Edward, Rhoda Lynn. B of Religion, Ind. Wesleyan U., 1950; MDiv, Christian Theol. Sem., Indpls., 1959; ThM, Christian Theol. Sem., 1973; D Ministry, Bethel Theol. Sem., St. Paul, 1981; DD (hon.), Ind. Wesleyan U., 1981; LittD (hon.), Houghton Coll., N.Y., 1981; DD (hon.), So. Wesleyan U., 1996. Ordained to ministry Wesleyan Ch., 1950. Pastor Peru (Ind.) Wesleyan Meth. Ch., 1948-51, Blue River Wesleyan Meth. Ch., Arlington, Ind., 1951-56, Jonesboro (Ind.) Wesleyan Meth. Ch., 1956-61; editor Adult Sunday Sch. Lessons Wesleyan Meth. Ch., Marion, Ind., 1961-63; pastor Eastlawn Wesleyan Ch., Indpls., 1963-70; assoc. prof. religion Ind. Wesleyan U., 1970-80; gen. sec. edn. and the ministry The Wesleyan Ch., Indpls., 1980-88, gen. supt., 1988-2000, gen. supt. emeritus, 2000—. Historian The Wesleyan Ch., 1976-88; vice-chair Wesleyan World Fellowship, 1996-00. Assoc. editor/writer: The Wesleyan Bible Commentary; co-author: An Outline History of the Wesleyan Church; co-editor: Conscience and Commitment: History of the Wesleyan Methodist Church; Days of Our Pilgrimage: History of the Pilgrim Holiness Church; contbg. author Reformers and Revivalists: The History of the Wesleyan Church. Mem. Evang. Theol. Soc., Wesleyan Theol. Soc. (editor 1978-81), Christian Holiness Partnership (treas. 1994-97). Mem. Wesleyan Ch. E-mail: lmhmlh@aol.com. *God is the divine lover of each human person, and seeks through Jesus Christ to bring about a loving relationship with each one. Our highest task is to help bring that to pass.*

HAINES, MICHAEL ROBERT, economist, educator; b. Chgo., Nov. 19, 1944; s. James Joshua and Ann Marie (Welch) H.; m. Patricia Caroline Foster, Aug. 19, 1967 (div. Dec. 1986); children: James, Margaret; m. Eileen Margaret Mulhare, Jan. 5, 1995. BA, Amherst Coll., 1967; MA, U. Pa., 1968, PhD, 1971. Asst. prof. econs. Cornell U., Ithaca, N.Y., 1972-79; rsch. assoc. prof. Sch. Pub. and Urban Policy, U. Pa., Ithaca, 1979-80; assoc. prof. econs. Wayne U., Detroit, 1980-86, prof. econ., 1986-90; Banfi Vintners Disting. prof. econs. Colgate U., Hamilton, N.Y., 1990—. Vis. lectr. econs. U. Pa., Phila., 1979; cons. NIH, Bethesda Md., 1980-84, 90-91, 93, 95-2000, The World Bank, Washington, 1983, Nat. Rsch. Coun., 1995; rsch. assoc. Nat. Bur. Econ. Rsch., 1987—; rsch. affiliate Population Studies Ctr., U. Mich., Ann Arbor, 1990—. Author: Economic-Demographic Interrelations in Developing Agricultural Regions, 1977, Fertility and Occupation, 1979, Fatal Years, 1991, A Population History of North America, 2000; contbr. articles to profl. jours. Grantee: NIH, 1974-77, 78-82, 89—. Mem. Internat. Union Sci. Study Population, Econ. History Assn. (bd. dirs. 1987-91), Social Sci. History Assn. (bd. dirs. 1983-85, treas. 1985-87, v.p. 1997-98, pres. 1998-99), Am. Econ. Assn., The Cliometrics Soc. (bd. editor 1988-94), Population Assn. Am. Roman Catholic. Avocations: numismatics, wine, book collecting. Office: Colgate Univ Dept Econs 13 Oak Dr Hamilton NY 13346-1338 E-mail: mhaines@mail.colgate.edu.

HAINES, RICHARD FOSTER, retired psychologist; b. Seattle, May 19, 1937; s. Donald Hutchinson and Claudia May (Bennett) H.; m. Carol Taylor, June 17, 1961; children: Cynthia Lynn, Laura Anne. Student, U. Wash., 1955-57; BA, Pacific Luth. Coll., Tacoma, 1960; MA, Mich. State U., 1962, PhD, 1964. Predoctoral rsch. fellow NIH, 1964; Nat. Acad. Sci. postdoctoral resident rsch. assoc. Ames Rsch. Ctr./NASA, Moffett Field, Calif., 1964-67, rsch. scientist, 1967-86, chief of space human factors office, 1987-88, rsch. scientist Rsch. Inst. Advanced Computer Sci., 1988-90; assoc. prof. dept. psychology San Jose State U., 1988-89; computer scientist RECOM Techs., Inc., Moffett Field, Calif., 1993-2000, Raytheon Corp., 2000—01; ret., 2001. Rsch. cons. to NASA Foothill Coll.; cons. Stanford U. Sch. medicine, 1966-67, TRW-Systems Group, 1969-70; mem. adv. com. on vision NRC; founding mem. advanced tech. applications com. Calif. Coun. AIA and NASA, 1975-80; mem. adv. bd. Space Scis. Ctr.-Foothill Coll., 1976-78; bd. advisors Fund for UFO Rsch., Washington; chmn. bd. Novosibirsk Christian Pub.-Calif., 1993—; chief scientist Nat. Aviation Reporting Ctr. on Anomalous Phenomena, 2001—. Author: UFO Phenomena and the Behavioral Scientist, 1979, Observing UFOs, 1980, Melbourne Episode: Case Study of a Missing Pilot, 1987, Advanced Aerial Devices Reported During the Korean War, 1990, Night Flying, 1992, Project Delta, 1994, Close Encounters of the Fifth Kind, 1999; mem. editl. and sci. bd. Jour. UFO Studies, Internat. UFO Reporter, Cuadernos de Ufologica; contbr. articles to profl. jours. Mem. Palo Alto (Calif.) Mayor's Com. on Youth Activities, 1967; chmn. adv. coun. Christian Cmty. Progress Corp., Menlo Park, Calif.; v.p., dir. Ctr. Counseling for Drug Abuse, Menlo Park; bd. dirs., chmn. sci. adv. team Threshold Found.; founding co-dir. Joint Am.-Soviet Aerial Anomaly Fedn., 1991—97. Named Alumnus of Yr., Pacific Luth. U., 1972 Fellow Aerospace Med. Assn. (assoc.); mem. Optical Soc. Am., Soc. for Sci. Exploration, Sigma Xi. Achievements include patents for device of advanced detection of glaucoma, optical projector of vision performance data for design engineers, visual simulator optical alignment device, grooming aid for use by astronauts in space. Home: 325 Langton Ave Los Altos CA 94022-1055

HAINES, RONALD H. retired bishop; b. New Castle, Del., Aug. 14, 1934; m. Mary Ferrell; six children. BS in Engring., U. Del., 1956; student; M. Div., S.T.M., Gen. Theol. Sem. Ordained deacon Episcopal Ch., 1966, ordained priest, 1967. Bus. career; asst. St. Paul's Ch., Bronx, N.Y., 1967-68; rector St. Francis Ch., Rutherfordton, N.C., until 1981; bishop's dep. Diocese of Western N.C., 1981-86; suffragan bishop Diocese of Washington, 1986-90, bishop, 1990-2000; ret., 2000. Episcopalian. Address: 316 Wickshire Cir Lititz PA 17543

HAINES, STEPHEN JOHN, neurological surgeon; b. Burlington, Vt., Sept. 4, 1949; s. Gerald Leon and Frances Mary (Whitcomb) H.; m. Jennifer Lea Plombon; children: Christopher, Jeremy. AB, Dartmouth Coll., 1971; MD, U. Vt., 1975. Diplomate Am. Bd. Neurol. Surgery; diplomate Nat. Bd. Med. Examiners. Intern U. Minn., Mpls., 1975-76; neurol. surgery resident U. Pitts., 1976-81; asst. prof. neurosurgery U. Minn., Mpls., 1982-87, assoc. prof. neurosurgery and otolaryngology, 1987-93, prof. neurosurgery and otolaryngology and pediatrics, 1993-97, head. div. pediatric neurosurgery, 1985-97; prof. neurosurgery, otolaryngology and pediatrics, chmn. dept. neurological surgery Med. U. S.C., Charleston, 1997—. Contbr. articles to profl. jours. Fellow ACS; mem. AMA, Am. Assn. Neurol. Surgeons (Van Wagenen fellow 1981), Congress Neurol. Surgeons (pres. 1996), Soc. Clin. Trials, Neurosurg. Soc. Am., Am. Acad. Neurol. Surgery, Soc. Neurol. Surgeons. Office: Med U SC Dept Neurol Surgery 96 Jonathan Lucas St Ste 428 Charleston SC 29425-8900 E-mail: hainesj@musc.edu.

HAINES, STUART TILMAN, pharmacist, educator; b. Hartford, Conn., Oct. 6, 1961; s. Ronald James Haines and Rayann Burnham Cummings. BS in Pharmacy, Mass. Coll. Pharmacy, 1985; PharmD, U. Tex., 1994. Bd. cert. pharmacotherapy specialist; cert. anticoagulation care provider; cert. diabetes educator. Pharmacy practice residency Brigham and Womens Hosp., Boston, 1985-86; pharmacy mgr. Freedom Drug, Inc., Peabody, Mass., 1986-87, dir. pharmacy Amesbury, Mass., 1987-91; ambulatory care pharmacy residency Audie Murphy Vets. Med. Ctr., San Antonio, 1993-94; asst. prof. U. Md., Balt., 1994-98, assoc. prof., 1998—; dir. anticoagulation svc. U. Md. Med. Sys., Balt., 1994—. Dir. cmty. pharmacy residency programs U. Md., Balt., 1994—2001; mem. adv. bd. nat. diabetes edn. program Ctrs. for Disease Control and NIH, 2000—. Contbr. articles to profl. jours. U. Tex. fellow, 1991-94. Fellow: Am. Coll. Clin. Pharmacy (chair ambulatory care PRN 2000—02, bd. regents 2002—), Am. Soc. Health-Sys. Pharmacists (anticoagulation traineeship preceptor 1995—); mem.: Am. Assn. Colls. Pharmacy, Am. Pharm. Assn., Am. Assn. Diabetes Educators (cert. diabetes educator), Am. Diabetes Assn. (editor Diabetes Forecast 1997—2000). Office: U Md Sch Pharmacy Rm 240H 100 Penn St Baltimore MD 21201-1082 E-mail: shaines@rx.umaryland.edu.

HAINES, THOMAS HENRY, biochemist, educator, biochemist, researcher; b. N.Y.C., Aug. 9, 1933; s. Charles and Elizabeth Cubbon Haines; m. Mary Manning Cleveland, Aug. 6, 1986; m. Adrian Sheila Rappaport, Nov. 26, 1960 (dec. May 5, 1985); 1 child, Avril Danica. BS, CUNY, 1957; PhD, Rutgers U., 1965; MS, CUNY, 1999. Rsch. biochemist Boyce Thompson Inst. for Plant Rsch., Yonkers, NY, 1959—62; asst./assoc. prof. chemistry City Coll. CUNY, N.Y.C., 1964—72; prof. chemistry and biochemistry doctoral program CUNY, N.Y.C., 1972—; acting dean, founder Sophie Davis Biomed. Program CUNY Med. Sch., N.Y.C., 1971—73, dir. biochemistry, 1973—. Vis. assoc. prof. U. Calif., Berkeley, 1970—71, vis. rsch. scientist, 1993—94; chair symposium on lipids Internat. Union Pure and Applied Biochemistry, Riga, Latvia, 1970; vis. scholar Nat. Ctr. for Sci. Rsch., Gif-sur-Yvette, France (incl. Monaco), 1970—71; vis. prof. U. Minn., Mpls., 1978—79, Beijing Med. Sch., 1986—87; vis. scientist Mitsubishi-Kasai Inst. for the Life Scis., Machida, Tokyo, Japan, 1986—87; mem., exec. com. Levich Inst. for Hydrodynamics, N.Y.C., 1991—2001; ad hoc mem. biochemistry and cell biology study sect. Nat. Inst. Alcoholism and Alcohol Abuse, Washington, 1992—95; cons. Liposome Tech. Inc., Menlo Park, Calif., 1993—95, Sequus, Inc., Menlo Park, 1995—2000. Co-founder Partnership for Responsible Drug Info., N.Y.C., 1993—2002, Voluntary Com. Lawyers, N.Y.C., 1994—2002. Grantee, NIH, 1972—78, NSF. Mem.: AAAS (life), Assn. Grad. and Med. Schs. Biochemistry Chairs, N.Y. Acad. Scis. (life; chair biophysics sect. 1991—94), City Coll. Sci. Alumni Assn. (pres. 1993—). Achievements include design of created model for why animals need cholesterol; research in Lipid Structure and Function. Avocations: gardening, politics, travel. Home: 14 West 68 St New York NY 10023 Office: City Univ New York 139 St at Convent Ave New York NY 10031 Home Fax: 212-721-9557. Personal E-mail: thaines@prdi.org. E-mail: thaines@sci.ccny.cuny.edu.

HAINES, THOMAS W. W. lawyer; b. Balt., Oct. 10, 1941; s. John Summer and Clara Elizabeth (Ward) H.; m. Vivienne Wilson, Jan. 3, 1981; children: Robert S., Elizabeth E., John M. BA, Cornell U., 1963; LLB, U. Md., 1967. Bar: Md. 1967, U.S. Dist. Ct. Md. 1968, U.S. Ct. Appeals (4th cir.) 1972, U.S. Tax Ct. 1973, U.S. Supreme Ct. 1975. Assoc. Semmes, Bowen & Semmes, Balt., 1968-75, ptnr., 1975-95, Venable, Baetjer & Howard, LLP, Balt., 1995—. Fellow Am. Coll. Trust and Estate (counsel); mem. ABA, Md. Bar Assn., Bar Assn. Balt. City, Gibson Island Club, Maryland Club. Office: Venable Baetjer & Howard LLP 1800 Mercantile Bank Trust 2 Hopkins Plz Ste 2100 Baltimore MD 21201-2982 E-mail: twhaines@venable.com.

HAINES, WALTER WELLS, retired economics educator; b. Stamford, Conn., Dec. 1, 1918; s. Thomas Kelly Peterson and Carrie Hooker (Williams) H.; m. Hazel Ellen Maxwell, Jan. 1, 1945 (div.); children: Jennifer Jean, Deborah Lee, Pamela Ann, Christopher Alan, Liseli Ellen, Timothy Maxwell; m. Mary Lou Peck, Nov. 30, 1991. *Mother is daughter of Mosely Hooker Williams, congregational minister and editor for the American Sunday School Union. She is descended from Thomas Hooker, non-conformist minister, who arrived in America in 1663 and founded Hartford, Connecticut, in 1636. Father is a descendent of Richard and Margaret Haines, Quakers from Banbury Monthly Meeting in England, who came to Burlington, New Jersey, in 1682. He is the inventor of the Domart sewing box. Wife Mary Lou Peck, EdD, Columbia University, 1983, is associate professor of nursing, Russell Sage College, and was instrumental in establishing the Nurse Practitioner program in the Graduate School there.* BA, U. Pa., 1940, MA, 1941, Harvard U., 1942, PhD (Lehman nat. fellow), 1943. Instr. econs. Kenyon Coll., 1946-47; mem. faculty NYU, 1947—, prof. econs., 1960-89, emeritus prof. of econs., 1989—, chmn. dept. Univ. Coll., 1956-68, dir. undergrad. studies, 1983-89; adminstr. Friends Hosp., Tiriki, Kenya, 1969-70. Fulbright prof. econs. U. Peshawar, Pakistan, 1962-63; Fulbright prof. environ. conservation Middle East Tech. U., Ankara, Turkey, 1973-74; lectr. Siena Coll., 1989-92. Author: Money, Prices and Policy, 1961, also articles. Lehman Nat. fellow Harvard U., 1941-43. Fellow Internat. Inst. for Social Econs.; mem. AAAS, World Future Soc., Internat. Assn. for Rsch. in Econ. Psychology, Fulbright Alumni Assn., Cultural Survival, Human Economy Ctr. (bd. dirs.), Am. Econ. Assn., Fellowship of Reconciliation, Fedn. Am. Scientists, Assn. for Social Econs., Soc. for Advancement of Socio-Econs., Internat. Soc. for Intercommunication New Ideas (Disting. fellow 1992, mem. consultative coun.), Internat. Soc. Ecol. Econs., Nat. Peace Inst. Found., Global

Edn. Associates, Amnesty Internat., World Federalists, Parliamentarians for Global Action, Economists Allied for Arms Reduction, Internat. Physicians for the Prevention of Nuclear War, Nature Conservancy, Nat. Wildlife Fedn. Wilderness Soc., Union of Concerned Scientists, Carter Ctr., Albert Einstein Inst., UN Assn. U.S., World Federalists, Habitat for Humanity, Natural Resources Def. Coun., Phi Beta Kappa. Mem. Religious Soc. of Friends. Home: 196 Vosburgh Rd Averill Park NY 12018-5710 E-mail: hainesww@earthlink.net., peckm@sage.edu. *The wellspring of my life is a belief that there is something of God in every person. From this universality of the divine spark emerge many principles of faith; the brotherhood of man, the importance of the golden rule, the primacy of love. These in turn call for social action to promote civil rights, nondiscrimination, peace, cooperation, democracy, world equality, the preservation of a quality environment, and conservation of resources for future generations. I have no illusion that this belief has brought me "success", but it has contributed much to the richness of life.*

HAINES, WILLIAM JOSEPH, pharmaceutical company executive; b. Crawfordsville, Ind., Sept. 26, 1919; s. Burt and Lala R. (Luster) Haines; m. Wilma M. Hester, June 6, 1993; 2 children, Paula Sue Haines Curtis-Burn, Eric J. AB summa cum laude, Wabash Coll., 1940, DSc (hon.), 1970; PhD, U. Ill., 1943; grad. exec. program in bus. adminstrn., Columbia Bus. Sch., 1965. Rsch. biochemist Upjohn Co., Kalamazoo, 1943-50, head dept. endocrinology rsch., 1950-54; tech. dir. Armour Labs., Kankakee, Ill., 1954-58; v.p. dir. rsch. Ortho Pharm. Corp., Raritan, N.J., 1958-65, exec. v.p., 1965-67; vice chmn. Johnson & Johnson Internat., 1967-69; dir., mem. exec. com. Johnson & Johnson, New Brunswick, N.J., 1969-79, v.p. corp. office sci. and tech., 1979 82; pres. Bucks-Tech Assocs., Inc. (cons. in mgmt., sci. and tech.), Doylestown, Pa., 1982—. Chmn. sci. adv. com. Alliance Internat. Health Care Trust, 1983-87; former dir. Quidel Corp., La Jolla, Calif.; invited lectr. Laurentian Hormone Conf., 1952, Gordon Rsch. Conf., 1952. Contbr. numerous sci. articles to profl. jours., including pioneer paper on human requirement for essential amino acids, 1942. One of initial investigators to identify essential amino acids for human nutrition; patentee biosynthesis of adrenal cortex hormones, paper chromatography and automatic partition column chromatography of steroids. Trustee Wabash Coll., 1972-93, trustee emeritus, 1993—; trustee Hood Coll., 1975-87, vice chmn. bd., 1982-87, trustee emeritus, 1989—; Joslin Diabetes Found. Inc., Boston, 1974-79; elder Thompson Meml. Presbyn. Ch., New Hope, Pa. Recipient William E. Upjohn prize and medal, 1952, Alumni Merit award Nat. Assn. Wabash Men, 1973. Fellow AAAS, Am. Inst. Chemists; mem. Am. Chem. Soc. (med. cheistry div.), N.Y. Acad. Scis., Endocrine Soc., Am. Soc. Biol. Chemists, Soc. Chem. Industry (former chmn. Am. sect.), Pharm. Mfrs. Assn. (former chmn. R&D sec.), Assn. Rsch. Dirs., Indsl. Rsch. Inst., (dir. emeritus), N.J. Acad. Scis., Soc. Exptl. Biology and Medicine, Pacific Coast Fertility Soc., Am. Fertility Soc., Internat. Soc. Rsch. in Biology Reproduction (charter), Am. Inst. Mgmt. (exec. council), Am. Mgmt. Assn., Am. Found. Pharm. Edn. (Century Club), Ind. Covered Bridge Soc., Sons of Ind. (N.Y.C. chpt.), Chemists Club (N.Y.C.), Masons, Elks, Kiwanis (emeritus), Lake Naomi Club, Phi Beta Kappa, Phi Lambda Upsilon, Phi Kappa Phi, Sigma Xi, Alpha Chi Sigma. Republican. Home: 5 Bedford Dr Doylestown PA 18901-9463 Office: Johnson & Johnson 1 Johnson And Johnson Plz New Brunswick NJ 08933-0002

HAINING, JEANE, psychologist; b. Camden, N.J., May 2, 1952; d. Lester Edward and Adina (Rahn) H. BA in Psychology, Calif. State U., 1975; MA in Sch. Psychology, Pepperdine U., 1979; MS in Recreation Therapy, Calif. State U., 1982; PhD in Psychology, Calif. Sch. Profl. Psychology, 1985. Lic. clin. psychologist 1987, lic. ednl. psychologist 1982. Crisis counselor Calif. State U., Northridge, 1973-74; recreation therapist fieldwork Camarillo (Calif.) State Hosp.-Adolescent/Children's Units, 1974; Intern recreation therapist UCLA Neuropsychiatric Inst., L.A., 1975-76; substitute tchr./recreation therapist New Horizons Sch. for Mentally Retarded, Sepulveda, Calif., 1976-79; sch. psychologist Rialto (Calif.) Unified Sch. Dist., 1979-82; clin. psychologist field work San Joaquin County Dept. Mental Health, Stockton, Calif., 1982-83; intern clinical psychologist Fuller Theol. Sem. Psychology Ctr., Pasadena, Calif., 1984-85; clin. psychologist U.S. Dept. Justice, Terminal Island, Calif., 1985-86; cmty. mental health psychologist L.A. County Dept. Mental Health, 1987-89; clin. psychologist Calif. Dept. Corrections, Parole Outpatient Clinic, L.A., 1990—, Mary Magdeline Project, Commerce, Calif., 1992-2000. Adv. bd. Camarillo (Calif.) State Hosp., 1994-97, vice-chmn. adv. bd., 1996-97, examiner Lic. Ednl. Psychologist Oral Examinations, Calif. Bd. Behavioral Sci. Examinations, Sacramento, 1985. Recipient award Outstanding Achievement Western Psychology Conf., Calif., 1974. Mem. APA, Forensic Mental Health Assn. (con. planning com. 1993). Democrat. Lutheran. Avocations: rock climbing, skiing, skating, tennis, piano.

HAINKEL, JOHN J., JR., state senator; BA, JD with honors, Tulane U. Mem. La. Ho. Reps., Baton Rouge, 1968-88, speaker of ho., 1980-84; mem. La. State Senate, Baton Rouge, 1988—, pres., 2002—, chmn. fin. com., mem. ins. com., judiciary A com., mem. labor and indsl. rels. com., revenue & fiscal affairs, vice-chmn. jt. legis. com. on budget. Republican. Office: PO Box 94183 Baton Rouge LA 70804-9183 also: La State Senate 6th Dist 704 Carondelet St New Orleans LA 70130-3706*

HAINLINE, BRIAN, neurologist; b. Detroit, Dec. 23, 1955; s. Forrest Arthur Jr. and Nora Marie (Schrot) H.; m. Pascale Clauzet, Dec. 22, 1979; children: Clotilde, Arthur, Juliette. BA, U. Notre Dame, 1978; MD, U. Chgo., 1982. Intern U. Chgo. Hosps. and Clinics, 1982-83; resident in neurology N.Y. Hosp., N.Y.C., 1983-86; attending neurologist North Shore U. Hosp., Manhasset, N.Y., 1986-91, program dir., acting co-chmn. dept. neurology, 1990-91; dir. sports and clin. neurology Hosp. for Joint Diseases, N.Y.C., 1991-97, vice chmn. dept. neurology, 1994-97, co-dir. The Pain Ctr., 1996-97; chief neurology and integrative pain medicine ProHealth Care Assocs., N.Y.C., 1997—. Instr. neurology Cornell U. Med. Coll., N.Y.C., 1986-87, asst. prof. neurology, 1987-91, NYU Sch. Medicine, 1991-95, clin. assoc. prof. of neurology, 1995—; med. rev. officer U.S. Tennis Assn., N.Y.C., 1991—; chief med. officer U.S. Open Tennis Championships, Flushing Meadows, N.Y., 1992—; mem. med. commn. Internat. Tennis Fedn., London, 1993—; mem. sports medicine com. U.S. Olympic Com., 1997—. Author: USTA Drug Education Handbook, 1992; co-author: Drugs and the Athlete, 1989; co-editor: Neurological Complications of Pregnancy, 1994, 2d edit., 2002; contbr. articles to profl. jours. and chpts. to books. Recipient Ednl. Merit award, Internat. Tennis Hall of Fame, 2001. Mem. Am. Acad. Neurology, Physicians for Social Responsibility, Am. Coll. Sports Medicine. Avocations: tennis, piano, writing. Home: 122 Grosvenor St Flushing NY 11363-1007 Office: ProHealth Care Assocs 2800 Marcus Ave New Hyde Park NY 11042-1052

HAINSWORTH, MELODY MAY, information professional, researcher; b. Vancouver, B.C., Can., May 13, 1946; m. Robert John Hainsworth, Jan. 6, 1968; children: Kaleeg William, Shane Alan. BA with honors, Simon Fraser U., Vancouver, 1968; MLS, Dalhousie U., Halifax, N.S., Can., 1976; PhD, Fla. State U., Tallahassee, 1992. Libr. Dept. Edn. of Tanzania, Mbeya, 1969-72, Dept. of Edn. of Zambia, Mwinilunga, 1972-74; law libr., deptl. libr. Dept. of Atty. Gen. of N.S., Halifax, 1975-77; regional libr. Provincial Ct. Librs. Dept. of Atty. Gen. of Alta., Calgary, 1977-80, So. Alta. Law Soc. libr., 1980-89; dir. librs. Keiser Coll., Tallahassee, 1992-93; v.p. info. resources and svcs. Internat. Coll., Naples, Fla., 1993—. Adj. instr. Sch. Libr. and Info. Studies, Fla. State U., Tallahassee, 1990-91; speaker in field; rschr. in law and info. sci.; co-founder Naples Free-Net, World Class Acad.; mem. faculty Practising Law Inst.; active Women's Polit. Caucus; co-founder Naples Free-Net; rschr. in law and info. sci. World Class Acad.; evaluator SACS/COC, 1999—; mem. external rev. panel ALA/COA, 1999—; spkr. Practising Law Inst. Author monographs; contbr. articles to profl. jours. Pres. Naples Free Net, 1993—; co-chair adv. com. com. on edn. and tech. Fla. State Bd. Ind. Colls. and Univs., 1993-2001; founding mem. Pub. Access to the Law of Fla., 1990—; mem. exec. bd. Calgary Legal Guidance, 1985-89, vice chmn., 1988-89, hon. life mem.; tech. grant com. Collier County Edn. Found., 1994-96, sec./webmaster World Class Collier; supt. search com., 1998; chair edn. com. East Naples Civic Assn., 1998; bd. dirs. Seacrest Country Day Sch., 1996-2002. Student Leader Bursaries Simon Fraser U. scholar, 1966-68; H.W. Wilson scholar Dalhousie U., 1974; recipient Woman of Distinction award AAUW, 1999. Mem. Spl. Librs. Assn (pres. 1994-95), Assn. Online Profls., Fla. State, Ct. and County Librs. Assn., Tallahassee Law Librs. Assn., Fla. Libr. Assn., Assn. Libr. and Info. Sci. Edn., Alta. Legal Archives Soc. (hon. life), Collier County Bar Assn., Women's Polit. Caucus (webmaster 1999—), Tempo Internat., bd. dirs. 2003—, Naples Press Club. Avocations: squash, hiking, travel. Office: Internat Coll 2655 Northbrooke Dr Naples FL 34119-5707

HAIR, GILBERT MARTIN, foundation administrator; b. Manila, Philippines, Mar. 16, 1941; came to U.S., 1945; s. Jack and Jane McMahon Hair; m. Joanne Walsh, June 1966 (div.); m. Susan Christian, Apr. 5, 1969 (div. 1979); 1 child, Nicole. BA, Am. U., 1966; postgrad., San Fernando Valley Coll. Law, 1973-74. Cert. travel counsel, cert. Cruise Line Internat. Assn., Calif. Landscape Contractors Assn. With CIA, 1963-66; sales rep. Pan Am. World Airways, N.Y.C., 1966-71; dir. mktg. Continental Airlines, L.A., Micronesia, 1972-79; sr. v.p. mktg. Air North Am., Pasadena, Calif., 1979-83; instr., program dir. Jostens, Inc., L.A., Ventura, Calif., 1982-87; stockbroker, investment banker Thousand Oaks, Calif., 1987-93; pres., exec. dir. The Ctr. for Internee Rights Inc., Newbury Park, Calif., 1990—92, Miami Beach, 1992—. Mem. Rep. Nat. Com., Washington, 1964—; pres. Conejo Valley (Calif.) Rep. Action Com., 1992—. With USMC, 1960—63. Mem.: Admiral Nimitz Found., Explorer's Club, Coalition Retired Mil. Vets. (life), Disabled Am. Vets. (life), Philippine Scouts Heritage Soc. (life), Am. Defenders of Bataan and Corregidor (life), Am. Ex POW Assn. (life), Marines' Meml. Club, Westlake Tennis and Swim Club, Royal Bangok Sports Club (life), Am. Legion (life). Roman Catholic. Avocations: golf, tennis, fishing, travel, politics, computers. Home: 6060 La Gorce Dr Miami Beach FL 33140 Office: CFIR Inc 6060 La Gorce Dr Miami Beach FL 33140 E-mail: expows@bigfoot.com.

HAIR, KITTIE ELLEN, secondary educator; b. Denver, June 12, 1948; d. William Edward and Jacqueline Jean (Holt) H. BA, Brigham Young U., 1971; MA in Social History, U. Nev., Las Vegas, 1987, cert. paralegal, 1995. cert. tchr., Nev. Health educator Peace Corps, Totota, Liberia, 1971-72; tchr. Clark County Sch. Dist., Las Vegas, Nev., 1972-77, 1979—, chair dept. social studies, 1993-95; missionary Ch. Jesus Christ Latter-Day Saints, Alta., Can., 1977-79. Assessor Nat. Bd. Profl. Tchg. Stds. Chairwoman Nev. H.S. Mock Trial Competition, 2003—. Recipient Outstanding Faculty award U. Nev./Southland Corp., Las Vegas, 1991; named Educator of Yr. Kiwanis Club, 1998-99. Mem.: Nev. HS Mock Trial Bd. (chairperson 2003), Phi Alpha Theta, Phi Kappa Phi. Democrat. Avocations: collecting western and native american art, gardening. Office: Advanced Technologies Acad 2501 Vegas Dr Las Vegas NV 89106-1643 E-mail: Khair@atech.org.

HAIR, MATTOX S. mediator, arbitrator, former judge, lawyer; b. Coral Gables, Fla., Jan. 18, 1938; s. Henry Horry and Frances Alberta (Strickland) H. BS, Fla. State U., 1960; JD, U. Fla., 1964. Bar: Fla. 1964. Ptnr. Marks, Gray, Conroy & Gibbs, Jacksonville, 1965-88; asst. atty. gen. Fla., 1964-65; mem. Fla. Ho. of Reps. from 22d Dist., 1972-74, Fla. Senate from 9th Dist., 1974-88; cir. judge Duval County Ct., Jacksonville, 1989-92; ptnr. Gabel & Hair, Jacksonville, 1992 97. Mediator, arbitrator, pvt. judge, 1992—. 2d lt. U.S. Army, 1963-64; capt. Fla. N.G., 1955-58, 61-67. Mem. ABA, Fla. Bar Assn., Jacksonville Bar Assn. (bd. govs. 1968-72), Chester Bedell Inn of Ct. (master of the bench), Rotary Club of Jacksonville, Phi Delta Phi. Baptist. Home: 505 Lancaster St #16A Jacksonville FL 32204-4143 Office: 225 Water St Ste 2100 Jacksonville FL 32202-5154

HAIR, ROBERT EUGENE, editor, writer, historian; b. Winamac, Ind., Apr. 11, 1921; s. Charles Franklin and Lucy Agnes (Zellers) H.; m. Marian Martha Emerson, Dec. 11, 1949; children: Donald Edward, Martha Anne. AB, DePauw U., Greencastle, Ind., 1942; postgrad., U. Mich., Ann Arbor, 1943-44, 53-56. Newspaper writer and editor; editor Mich. Dept. Health, Lansing, 1956-60; asst. editor Encyclopedia Britannica, Chgo., 1960-64; exec. editor Battelle Rsch. Outlook, Columbus, 1964-69; editor Cordis Corp., Miami, 1969-80. Author: (books) Sturgis, Michigan: Its Story to 1930, 1992, Sturgis, Michigan: 1930-1945, 1996, Sturgis and Its Industrial Growth, 1998, Klinger Lake...Its Origins and Growth, 2001; contbr. articles to profl. jours. Pres. Civic Auditorium Bd., Sturgis, 1994, St. Joseph County Hist. Soc., Centreville, Mich., 1995; v.p. Sturgis Hist. Soc., Mich., 1996, Centennial Celebration Com., Sturgis, 1996. Recipient Award of Merit Hist. Soc. of Mich., 1996, 2001. Mem. Am. Med. Writers Assn., Soc. Profl. Journalists, Masonic Blue Lodge, Sturgis Exch. Club (pres. 1951-52), Lambda Chi Alpha. Republican. Presbyterian. Avocations: preserving history, philately, music, photography, collecting antiques. Home: 428 Mortimer St Sturgis MI 49091-2228

HAIRE, JACK, magazine publisher; married; children: Billy, John. Grad., American U., D.C., 1974. With McGraw Hill, 1974-78; joined Time Inc., 1978; sales rep. Fortune mag., N.Y.C., 1978-80, mgr. New England sales office Boston, 1980-82, mgr. Chgo. sales office Chgo., 1982-84, dir. U.S. advt. sales, 1986-89, Time mag., 1989-91; v.p. advt. sales Entertainment Weekly mag., 1989-91; v.p. regional advt. sales Time Inc., Chgo., 1991-93; pub. Time mag., N.Y.C., 1993-2000; pres. Fortune Group, N.Y.C., 2000—01; exec. v. p. Time Inc, 2001—. Office: Time Time & Life Bldg Rockefeller Plz New York NY 10020-1393

HAIRSTON, HAROLD B. protective services official; m. Anne Hairston; children: Harold, Jr., Jennifer. Student, A&T U., N.C., Pa. State U., Abington; DHL (hon.), Holy Family Coll. With Phila. Fire Dept., 1964—, lt. Ladder Co. # 6, 1971-78, chief battalion, dep. fire marshal, 1981-86, dep. chief, chief divsn. fire prevention, 1986-92, commr., 1992—. Expert witness Mcpl. and Common Pleas Ct.; testifier Consumer Products Safety Commn., Washington. Bd. dirs. Delaware Valley Burn Found., Hero Scholarship Fund, Police Athletic League, Dad Vail Regatta, ARC S.E. Pa. Named Fire Ofcl. of Yr., Nat. Burglar and Fire Alarm Assn.; recipient Outstanding Achievement award, Conf. of Mayors, Excellence in Govt. award, Am. Soc. Pub. Adminstrn. Mem. Nat. Fire Protection Assn., Urban Fire Forum, Bldg. Ofcls. and Code Adminstrs., Internat. Assn. Black Profl. Firefighters, Internat. Assn. Fire Chiefs, Metro Fire Chiefs Assn. (Met. Fire Chief of Yr. 2003). Office: Fire Department Fire Administration Bldg 240 Spring Garden St Fl 2D Philadelphia PA 19123-2923

HAIRSTON, JAMES CHRISTOPHER, food service distribution executive; b. Dallas, Nov. 23, 1960; s. James Loy and Beverly Gail (Van Duzen) H.; m. Cheryl Alice Wilson, Mar. 3, 1984; children: Mary Alice, Emily Elizabeth, James Christopher Jr., William Michael. Student, St. Edward's U., Austin, Tex., 1979; BS in Psychology, So. Meth. U., 1983; postgrad., U. Tex., Tyler, 1984-85. Sales rep. Hairston Produce Co., Dallas, 1980-83; pres. Bullet Distbg. Co., Dallas, 1981-82; sales mgr. Southland Corp./Dist. Ctr., Tyler, 1984 86; pres. Airline Distbn. Svcs., Inc., Dallas, 1986-93, Contra Pak, Inc., Dallas, 1993—; owner Milk Buds Co., 1994—; exec. Lindley Food Svc., 2001—03, CP7 Foods, Inc., 2003—. Owner Hairston Produce Co., 1991-93; ptnr. HST Acquisition Group, 1996—; political cons. Radicalmail.com; contbr. KLIF Radio, 1994-2001, WBAP Radio, 2001-03. Contbr. numerous articles to trade jours. and newspapers. Mem. Rep. Nat. Com., 1984—; sponsor Dallas Can Acad., 1987—, Am. Heart Assn., 1987 ; cand. Highland Park Ind. Sch. Dist. Sch. Bd., 1993, 97; Rep. precinct chmn., 1997—; Rep. election judge, 1997—; mem. Gov. George Bush Election Com., 1998, Rich Perry for Gov. campaign, 2001, George W. Bush Re-election Campaign Com., 2002—; mem. bd. mgmt. Park Cities YMCA, 1999—, Rich Perry Re-electon Campaign, 2002-03, Bush Cheney '04, 2003--. Mem. Tex. Restaurant Assn., Dallas Jaycees, Masons, Shriners, Premier Club (Dallas). Roman Catholic. Avocations: golf, cycling, running, reading.

HAIRSTON, NELSON GEORGE, JR., ecologist, educator; b. Asheville, NC, Sept. 26, 1949; s. Nelson George and Martha Turner (Patton) H.; m. Deborah Susan (Whitaker)Hairston, Nov. 30, 1974; 1 child, Peter Whitaker Hairston. BS, U. Mich., 1971; PhD, U. Wash., 1977. Asst. prof. U. R.I., Kingston, 1977-81, assoc. prof., 1981-85, Cornell U., Ithaca, NY, 1985-87, prof., 1988—. Frank H.T. Rhodes prof. environ. sci., 1996—, chmn. dept. ecology and evolutionary biology, 2001—. Vis. disting. ecologist U. Mich. Biol. Sta., Pelston, 1984; vis. eminent ecologist Mich. State U. Biol. Sta., Hickory Corners, 1989; cons. Westinghouse Savannah River Co., 1990-95, NSF Program in Population Biology and Physiol. Ecology, 1985-87, Swedish Nat. Rsch Coun., 1991, 99, U. Stockholm, 1996, Max Planck Inst. for Limnology, 1997, U. Uppsala, 1998; Douglas Disting. lectr. Rocky Mountain Biol. Lab, Crested Butte, Colo., 1992. Mem. editl. bd. Limnology and Oceanography, 1986-89, 2003, Ecology/Ecol. Monographs, 1989-92, 94-96; contbr. more than 75 articles and papers to sci. jours. NSF grantee, 1980, 83, 86, 88-89, 89-90, 91-92, 92-93, 95, 97, 99, 2000; EPA grantee, 1997, 2001; Andrew Mellon Found. grantee, 1997,2003. Mem. Ecol. Soc. Am. (coun. reps. 1990-93, chair awards com. 1992-95, governing bd. 1996-99, 2001-2004), Internat. Assn. Theoretical and Applied Limnology (nat. rep. 1992-95, 2002—). Avocations: boating, skiing, reading. Home: 6125 Perry City Rd Trumansburg NY 14886-9011 Office: Cornell U Dept Ecology and Evolutionary Biology Ithaca NY 14853 E-mail: NGH1@cornell.edu.

HAISCH, BERNARD MICHAEL, astronomer, researcher; b. Stuttgart-Bad Canstatt, Federal Republic of Germany, Aug. 23, 1949; s. Friedrich Wilhelm and Gertrud Paula (Dammbacher) H.; m. Pamela S. Eakins, July 29, 1977 (div. 1986); children: Katherine Stuart, Christopher Taylor; m. Marsha A. Sims, Aug. 23, 1986. Student, St. Meinrad (Ind.) Coll., 1967-68; BS in Astrophysics, Ind. U., 1971; PhD in Astronomy, U. Wis., 1975. Rsch. assoc. Joint Inst. Lab. Astrophysics, U. Colo., 1975-77, 78-79; vis. scientist space rsch. lab. U. Utrecht, The Netherlands, 1977-78; rsch. scientist Lockheed Rsch. Lab., Palo Alto, Calif., 1979-83, staff scientist, 1983-99; dep. dir. Ctr. for EUV Astrophysics U. Calif., Berkeley, 1992-94; dir. Calif. Inst. Physics and Astrophysics, 1999—2002; chief sci. officer Many One Networks, 2002—. Guest investigator Internat. Ultraviolet Explorer, Einstein Obs., Exosat, ROSAT Obs., EUVE Obs., Astro-D (ASCA), X-Ray Timing Explorer, 1980—; vis. fellow Max Planck Inst. Extraterr. Physik, Garching, Germany, 1991-94. Editor-in-chief Jour. Sci. Exploration, 1988-99, Solar and Stellar Flares, 1989; sci. editor The Astrophys. Jour., 1993-2003; monograph The Many Faces of the Sun, 1999; mem. editl. bd. Solar Physics, 1992-95, Speculations in Sci. and Tech., 1995-99; contbr. articles to profl. jours. Fellow Royal Astron. Soc., AIAA (assoc.); mem. AAAS (patron), Internat. Astron. Union, Am. Astron. Soc., European Astron. Soc., Am. Assn. Physics Tchrs., Sigma Xi, Phi Beta Kappa, Phi Kappa Phi. Avocations: Tae Kwon Do, international folk dance, downhill skiing, songwriting. Office: ManyOne Networks 901 Mariner's Island Blvd Ste 325 San Mateo CA 94404 E-mail: haisch@calphysics.org.

HAITHCOCK, WILLIAM DANA, JR., physician; b. Bennettsville, S.C., Feb. 19, 1946; s. William Dana and Clarice Anna (Skaggs) H.; m. Nancy Lee, Feb. 10, 1973; children: Judson Legare, Walker Calloway, William Franklin. BS, Wofford Coll., 1968; MD, Med. U. S.C., 1973. Diplomate Am. Bd. Ob-Gyn. Intern William Beaumont Army Med. Ctr., El Paso, 1973-74, resident, 1974-77; practice medicine specializing in ob-gyn. Fayetteville (N.C.) Woman's Clinic, 1980—; med. dir. ob-gyn. svc. line Cape Fear Health System, 2002. Mem. staff Cape Fear Valley Med. Ctr., Highsmith-Rainey Meml. Hosp.; mem. Cumberland County Mental Health Bd., 1980-84 . Trustee Fayetteville Area Health Edn. Found., 1993-99, v.p., mem. exec. com., 1996-99; mem. Fayetteville Regional Airport Commn., 1994-96. Served to maj. U.S. Army, 1973-80. Decorated Army Commendation medal. Fellow Am. Coll. Ob-Gyn.; mem. So. Med. Assn., N.C. Med. Soc., N.C. Ob-Gyn. Soc., So. Clin. Congress Ob-Gyn., Palmetto Soc., Pi Kappa Alpha. Presbyterian.

HAITINK, BERNARD J. H. conductor; b. Amsterdam, Mar. 4, 1929. MusD (hon.), U. of Oxford, 1988, U. of Leeds, 1988. Condr., Netherlands Radio Philharmonic Orch., 1955-61; guest condr. Concertgebouw Orch., Amsterdam, then joint condr., 1956-64, prin. condr., music dir., 1964-88; chief conductor Concertgebouw, 1964-88; prin. condr. London Philharm. Orch., 1967-79; guest condr. Glyndebourne Festival Opera, 1972-77, music dir. Glyndebourne, 1978-88; music dir. Royal Opera House, Covent Garden, London, 1988-2002; pres. London Philharm. Orch., 1990—; music dir. European Union Youth Orch., 1994-1999; guest condr. Boston Symphony, 1995-; guest condr. Cleve. Philharm., Vienna Philharm., N.Y. Philharm.; chief condr. Dresden Staatskapelle, 2002-; guest condr. Chgo. Symphony, Bayerische Rundfunk Symphony, Munich, Berlin Philharm., Salzburg Festival, London Philharm., Glyndebourne. Recordings include Don Giovanni, Cosa fan Tutte, Figro, Der Rosenkavalier, The Magic Flute, Daphne, Tannhauser, The Ring, Peter Grimes, Fidelio; recorded with Philips, Decca and EMI. Decorated Order Oranje Nassau; chevalier Ordre des Arts et des Lettres; Hon. knight Brit. Empire, 1977; officer Order of Crown (Belgium); recipient Bruckner medal of honor Bruckner Soc., 1970, Gold medal Royal Philharm. Soc., 1991, Erasmus prize The Netherlands, 1991. Fellow Royal Coll. Music; mem. Royal Acad. Music (London) (hon.), Internat. Gustav Mahler Soc. (hon.; gold medal 1970). Office: Sächsische Staatsoper Dresden Orchesterdirektion Theaterplatz 2 Dresden D-01067 Germany*

HAIZLIP, HENRY HARDIN, JR., real estate consultant, former banker; b. Pine Bluff, Ark., Dec. 18, 1913; s. Henry Hardin and Rebecca (Porter) H.; m. Emily Williamson, Feb. 15, 1947; children: Henry Hardin III, Wilson, Jean Hunter, Selden. Student, Tulane U., 1932-33. With W.N. Ballou Cotton Co., Memphis, 1933-36; with First Nat. Bank Memphis, 1936-73, exec. v.p., 1968-70, chmn. exec. com., 1970-73; pres. First Memphis Realty Trust, 1970-73, chmn., 1973-76; pres. First Tenn. Corp., 1973-78; real estate cons. Haizlip/Lovitt, Memphis, 1979—. Dir. Mid South Title Co., Union Service Industries Inc.; vice chmn. First Tenn. Nat. Corp., until 1979; ret.; instr. in mortgage financing La. State U., Ohio State U. Pres. Memphis Cotton Carnival Assn., 1966, bd. dirs., 1967—; vice chmn. Shelby United Good Neighbors, 1967-68; mem. Chickasaw coun. Boy Scouts Am.; pres. Future Memphis, Inc., 1974-77; bd. dirs. Memphis and Shelby County unit Am. Cancer Soc., 1967-68; trustee Comty. Found. Greater Memphis, chmn., 1978; mem. pres.'s coun. Tulane U., New Orleans, Rhodes Coll., Memphis; vice-chmn. The Trezevant Manor Episcopal Home. Capt. AUS, 1941-46. Mem. Am. Bankers Assn., Downtown Assn. Memphis (chmn. bd.), Kappa Alpha. Clubs: Memphis Country; Menasha Hunting and Fishing (Turrell, Ark.); Memphis Hunt and Polo. Episcopalian. Home: 965 Audubon Dr Memphis TN 38117-4601 Office: 600 Perkins Memphis TN 38117

HAJE, PETER ROBERT, lawyer; b. N.Y.C., July 31, 1934; s. Arnold John and Edna Marie (Bossert) H.; m. Helen Heineman, Aug. 13, 1943; children: Michael James, Katherine Joy, Lily Elizabeth. BA, Cornell U., 1955; LLB, Harvard U., 1960. Bar: N.Y. 1961, U.S. Dist. Ct. (so. dist.) N.Y. 1965, U.S. Ct. Appeals (2d cir.) 1965, D.C. 1970, U.S. Ct. Appeals (D.C. cir.) 1981. Assoc. Paul, Weiss, Rifkind, Wharton & Garrison, N.Y.C., 1960-68, ptnr., 1969-90; exec. v.p., gen. counsel Time Warner Inc., N.Y.C., 1990-99, gen. counsel emeritus, 2000—; counselor AOL Time Warner, 2000—02; bus. and legal cons., 2000—. Office: 1285 Ave of the Americas Ste 3021 New York NY 10019

HAJEK, ANN ELIZABETH, insect pathologist; b. San Francisco, Apr. 27, 1952; d. Ernest Emil and Dorothy Fern (Moller) H.; m. James K. Liebherr, July 1, 1984; children: Lisa, Jonathan. MS, U. Calif., Berkeley, 1980, PhD, 1984. Rsch. affiliate, rsch. entomologist USDA Agrl. Rsch. Svc., Ithaca, N.Y., 1985-90; rsch. assoc., sr. rsch. assoc. Boyce Thompson Inst., Ithaca, N.Y., 1990-94; asst. prof. to assoc. prof. Cornell U., Ithaca, NY, 1994—. Vis. fellow Cornell U., Ithaca, 1984-94; assoc. editor, BioControl., 1997—; editl. bd., Jour. Invertebrate Pathology, 1998-99, Biol. Control, 2000—. Contbr. articles to profl. jours. Grantee USDA Competitive grants CSRS, 1987, 90, 93, 96, 2002; recipient Cert. of Merit USDA, ARS, Ithaca, N.Y., 1988. Mem. AAAS, Internat. Orgn. Biol. Control (exec. com. mem. at large 1998 2000), Soc. Invertebrate Pathology (sec., treas. microbial control divsn. 1989-93, chairperson divsn. 1995-97, soc. sec. 1998-2000), Entomol. Soc. Am. Democrat. Achievements include research in the epizootiology of an Asian fungal pathogen of gypsy moth in North America, and use of fungi to control Asian long-horned beetle. Office: Cornell U Dept Entomology Comstock Hall Ithaca NY 14853-0901

HAJEK, FRANCIS PAUL, lawyer; b. Hobart, Tasmania, Australia, Oct. 21, 1958; came to U.S., 1966; s. Frank Joseph and Kathleen Beatrice (Blake) H. BA, Yale U., 1980; JD, U. Richmond, 1984. Bar: Va. 1984, U.S. Dist. Ct. (ea. dist.) Va. 1984, U.S. Ct. Appeals (4th cir.) 1986. Law clk. to presiding magistrate U.S. Dist. Ct., Norfolk, Va., 1984-85; assoc. Seawell, Dalton, Hughes & Timms, Norfolk, 1985-87, Weinberg & Stein, Norfolk, 1987-89, I'Anson-Hoffman Am. Inn of Ct., 1991-97; ptnr. Wilson, Hajek & Shapiro, P.C., Virginia Beach, Va., 1989—. Legal counsel United Transp. Union, 1999—. Mem. ABA, ATLA, Am. Rail Labor Acad., Va. Bar Assn., Norfolk-Portsmouth Bar Assn. (chmn. exec. com. young lawyer's sect. 1990-91). Roman Catholic. Avocations: squash, tennis. Home: 1001 Caton Dr Virginia Beach VA 23454 Office: Hajek & Shapiro PO Box 5369 Virginia Beach VA 23471-0369 E-mail: fhajek@whslaw.com.

HAJEK, OTOMAR, mathematician, educator; b. Beograd, Serbia, Jugoslavia, Dec. 22, 1930; arrived in U.S., 1966, naturalized, 1974; s. Frantisek Josef and Ruzena (Houdekova) Hajek; m. Olga Barbara Nemcova, Feb. 12, 1955; 1 child,

Michael. Diploma in math., Caroline U., Prague, Czechoslovakia, 1953, candidate sci., 1963, RNDr, 1966. Asst. prof. Czech Inst. Tech., Prague, 1953-56, sr. asst. prof., 1956-60; sci. officer Research Inst. Computing Machinery, Prague, 1960-65; sr. sci. officer Caroline U., Prague, 1965-66; assoc. prof. Case Western Res. U., Cleve., 1966-69, prof. math., 1969—, prof. sys. engring., 1988-96, prof. emeritus, 1996—. Author: (book) Dynamical Systems in the Plane, 1968, Pursuit Games, 1975, Control Systems in the Plane, 1991; co-author: Local Semi-Dynamical Systems, 1969; co-editor: Global Differentiable Dynamics, 1970. Recipient von Humboldt award, 1975; Deutsche Forshungsgemeinschaft fellow, Bonn, 1979, 1990, Fulbright fellow, 1990. Mem.: Union Czech Math. and Physics, Fulbright Assn., von Humboldt Assn., Czechoslavak Soc. Arts and Scis., Am. Math. Soc. Lutheran. Home: 11330 Savannah Dr Fredericksburg VA 22407-9109 E-mail: oohajek@webtv.net.

HAJEK, ROBERT J., SR., lawyer, real estate broker, commodities broker, nursing home owner; b. May 17, 1943; s. James J. Sr. and Rita C. (Kalka) H.; m. Maris Ann Enright, June 19, 1965 (div. Oct. 1991); children: Maris Ann, Robert J., David, Mandie BA, Loras Coll., 1965; JD, U. Ill., 1968. Bar: Ill. 1968, U.S. Tax Ct. 1970, U.S. Dist. Ct. (no. dist.) Ill. 1971, U.S. Ct. Appeals (7th cir.) 1972, U.S. Supreme Ct. 1972; lic. real estate broker, Ill., Nat. Assn. Securities Dealers; registered U.S. Commodities Futures Trading Commn. Ptnr. Hajek & Hajek, Berwyn, Ill., 1968-76; pres., bd. chmn. Hajek, Hajek, Koykar & Heying, Ltd., Westchester, Ill., 1976-85; pres., CEO Land of Lincoln Real Estate, Ltd., Glendale Heights, Ill., 1985-89, also bd. dirs.; ptnr., owner Camelot Manor Nursing Home, Streator, Ill., 1978—, Ottawa (Ill.) Care Ctr., 1981—, Glenwood House Nursing Home, Streator, 1988—, Sullivan House Nursing Home, Ottawa, 1991—, Law Ctr. Bldg., Westchester, 1976-91. Exec. v.p., gen. counsel Ottawa Long Term Care, Inc.; owner Garfield Ridge Real Estate, Chgo, 1973-78, Centre Realty, Westchester, 1976-85; ptnr. Westbrook Commodities, Chgo., 1983; v.p., bd. mem., gen. counsel DeHart Gas and Oil Devel., Ltd., 1970-73; prin. Northeastern Okla. Oil and Gas Prodn. Venture, Tulsa, 1982—; exec. v.p., gen. counsel Garrett Plante Corp., 1978—; bd. dirs. Land of Lincoln Savs. and Loan, 1981-89, Home Title Svcs. of Am., Inc., 1981-89, Land of Lincoln Ins. Agy., Inc., 1981-89, Medema Builders, Inc., 1983-88, Ptnrs. of Ill., Inc., 1984-89, The Ill. Co., 1984-88, Ill. Co. Properties, Inc., subs. of Ill. Co., 1984-87, Ottawa Long Term Care, Inc., 1982—, Garrett Plante Corp., 1978—, St. Mary's Living Square, Chgo., 1985-92. Sr. boys' basketball coach Roselle Recreation Assn., Ill., 1981-83. Mem. ABA, Ill. Bar Assn., Nat. Assn. Realtors, Ill. Assn. Realtors, N.W. Suburban Bd. Realtors, Ill. Health Care Assn., Amateur Radio Club, No. Ill. DX Assn., Phi Alpha Delta. Republican. Episcopalian. Address: 9001 SW 122nd Ave Miami FL 33186

HAJIKANO, MAKI, artist; b. Tokyo, Apr. 11, 1965; came to U.S., 1992; d. Yasushi and Kinko Hajikano. BFA in Sculpture, U. Oreg., 1995, MFA in Sculpture, 1997. Emerging artist resident Pichuck Glass Sch., Wash., 1997; resident Bemis Ctr. Contemporary Arts, Omaha, 1999; artist in residence John Michael Kohler Arts Ctr., Sheboygan, Wis., 2002. Mem. Internat. Sculpture Ctr. Avocation: swimming.

HAJIM, EDMUND A. financial services executive; b. Los Angeles, July 26, 1936; s. Jack and Sophie H.; m. Barbara E. Melnick, Aug. 8, 1965; children: Geoffrey Blair, Jon Bradley, Corey Brooke. BS, U. Rochester, 1958; MBA, Harvard U., 1964. Rsch. analyst Capital Rsch. Co. subs. Capital Group, Inc., N.Y.C., 1964—66, office mgr., 1966-67; v.p., dir. Capital Mgmt. Svc., 1967-69; pres. Greenwich Mgmt. Co., Conn., 1969; pres., dir. Growth Fund Am., 1969-70, Income Fund Am., 1970; sr. v.p. E.F. Hutton, Nat. Instl. Equity, N.Y.C., 1974-77; dir., mng. dir. Lehman Bros., N.Y.C., 1977, pres. securities divsn., 1977-79; ptnr., mng. dir. Lehman Bros. Kuhn Loeb & Kuhn Loeb Lehman Bros. Internat., N.Y.C., 1977—83; chmn., CEO Lehman Mgmt. Co., N.Y.C., 1980-83, Furman, Selz L.L.C., N.Y.C., 1983-98; co-chmn. Ams., ING Barings, 1997—99; CEO ING Furman Selz Asset Mgmt. Inc., N.Y.C., 1998—2002; chmn., CEO ING Aeltus Group, 2001—02, MLH Capital, L.L.C., 2002—. Bd. dirs. Greenwich Technology Ptnrs., MLGA Holdings. Past chmn. bd. trustees Brunswick Sch., Greenwich; trustee Greenwich Hosp., HBS Alumni Assn., U. Rochester. Served with USN, 1958-61. Mem. Inst. Chartered Fin. Analysts, Chief Execs. Orgn., N.Y. Soc. Security Analysts (past dir.), Bond Club, Harvard Club, Wall St. Club, Stanwich Country Club, Nantucket Golf Club (founder). Office: MLH Capital LLC 600 Fifth Ave 25th Fl New York NY 10020

HAJOST, JAMES E. music educator, conductor, composer; b. Chgo., Feb. 22, 1956; s. Edward E. and Leona M. Hajost; m. Cynthia J. Moyes, June 9, 1979; children: Matthew C., Jennifer M., Kathryn L. BA in Edn., Northeastern Ill. U., 1981. Cert. H.S. tchr. Ill., spl. K-12 music tchr. Ill. Orch. tchr. grades 3-8 Cmty. Cons. Sch. Dist. 62, Des Plaines, Ill., 1985—. Musician numerous comty-.groups, 1974—. Composer: (composition) Elegy for Strings and Harp, 1991, Swing Set for Strings, 1994, Danse V, 1996, String Quartet No. 1, 1997, Swing Set for Vocal Group and Piano, 1999, (orchestral arrangements) numerous musical arrangements for young orchestras, 2002. Nominee Tchr. of Yr. award, Quinlan and Fabish Music Co., 2001, Golden Apple award, Golden Apple Found., 2002. Mem.: Music Educator's Nat. Conf., Ill. Music Educator's Assn. (dist. chairperson 1995—97), Ill. Music Educator's Assn. (dist. chairperson 1989—91), Ill. Educator's Assn.-NEA.

HAKALA, KAREN LOUISE, retired real estate administrator; b. Lansing, Mich., Dec. 8, 1941; d. Herod Maxson and Flora Belle (Barton) Mitchell; m. Paul Kenneth Hakala, June 24, 1959 (div. Nov. 1972); children: Chris, Craig. BS, No. Mich. U., Marquette, 1986. Real estate adminstr. The Cleve.-Cliffs Iron Co., Ishpeming, Mich., 1967-99; ret., 1999. Mediator Cmty. Resolution Resource Ctr., 2002—. Mem. devel. com. Planned Parenthood No. Mich., Marquette, 1996-99; bd. dirs. Marquette Symphony Orch., 1998-2000, treas. 1999-2000; mem. Planning Commn., City of Negaunee, 2001—, sec., 2001-02. Mem. AAUW (pub. policy rep. 1995-99, pres. 1999-2001), LWV Marquette County (bd. dirs. 2002—), Ret. Sr. Vol. Program.

HAKALA, REINO WILLIAM, mathematician, educator; b. Albany, NY, Aug. 25, 1923; m. Eunice Irma Kazanowski, June 17, 1950; children: Jonathan, Lisamaria, Christina. AB, Columbia U., 1946, MA, 1947; PhD, Syracuse U., 1965. Chemistry instr. Associated Coll. of Upper NY, Plattsburgh, 1947—48; atomic energy commn. fellow and grad. asst. Syracuse U., 1948—53; adj. prof. in chemistry Pa. State U., State Coll., Pa., 1953; assoc. prof. chemistry Fairfield (Conn.) U., 1954—57; asst. prof. of chemistry Earlham Coll., Richmond, Ind., 1957—59, Howard U., Washington DC, 1959—63; NSF sci. faculty fellow Syracuse U., 1963—64; prof. of chemistry and math. Mich. Tech. U., 1964—67; chmn. Depts. Math. and Physics Okla. City U., 1967—72; prof. of math. Wash. Tech. Inst., 1972—73; dean of the sch. of sci. and tech. Lake Superior State Coll., Sault Ste Marie, Mich., 1973—77, asst. to v.p. for acad. affairs, 1977, prof. of math., 1978—80, pres. faculty senate, 1978; dean of the coll. of arts and sci. Governors State U., U. Pk., Ill., 1982, spl. asst. to the provost, 1982, interim chair, divsn. of sci., 1983, prof. of math., 1984—. Pres. faculty senate Okla. City U., 1972; cons. Nat. Bur. Standards, 1962—63; mem. tech. com. pattern recognition IEEE. Contbr. articles to profl. jours. Fellow, Washington (D.C.) Acad. of Scis., 1961, Am. Inst. of Chemists, 1969, fellowships and grants, Atomic Energy Commn., NSF, NATO, Petroleum Rsch. Fund. Mem.: Internat. Assn. Pattern Recognition, Am. Math. Soc., Math. Assn. Am. Home: 2945 Chayes Pk Dr Homewood IL 60430 Office: Governors State University 1 University Pkwy University Park IL 60466 Office Fax: 708-534-1641.

HAKANSON, BRENT ERIC, composer, orchestra educator; b. Klamath Falls, Oreg., Jan. 26, 1962; s. James Rudolph and Stephanie Rose (Bonotto) H.; m. Darla Jolene Klein, Aug. 21, 1982; children: Joshua, Joli; m. Judith Lynn Watson, May 18, 1980 (div. Mar. 31, 1982); 1 child, Jaden. BS, So. Oreg. U., Ashland, Oreg., 1986; MusM, U. Oreg., Eugene, Oregon, 1990. Lic. License of Accomplishment. Instr. So. Oreg. U., Ashland, Oreg., 1990—91; orch. dir. Klamath Falls (Oreg.) City Schs., 1991—. Freelance musician, Klamath Falls, Oreg. Composer: (chamber music for voice, fl, vc, pno) Nine Events, 1987 (Coll. Divsn. Winner - OMTA Contest, 1987), (chamber music - flute, clarinet, piano) Interrupted Variations, 1988 (Ruth Lorraine Close Fellowship, 1988), (organ music) A Tribute In Thanksgiving, 1991 (Margaret R. Evans Commn., 1991), (orchestral suite) Suite of Six, 1998 (Youth symphony of So. Oreg. Commn., 1999), Soliloquy for Strings, 2000, Ceremony for Strings, 2002. Orch. chair So. Oreg. Music Educators Assn., Klamath Falls, Oreg., 2000—. Mem.: Music Educators Nat. Conf. D-Liberal. Lutheran. Avocations: fishing, bicycling, coffee roasting, Belgian ale. Office: Klamath Union High Sch 1300 Monclaire St Klamath Falls OR 97601

HAKANSSON, KJELL GEORG, business consultant; b. Simrishamn, Sweden, Dec. 19, 1929; s. John B. and Iris H. (Eneberg) H.; m. Britt M. Hedstroem, Mar. 24, 1952; children: Kristin, Lars-Goran. MBA, Gothenburg Sch. Econs., 1954. Asst. to pres. Konstharts AB, Trelleborg, 1954-57; v.p. fin. AB Linjebuss, Stockholm, 1957-62; v.p. fin., mktg. Forsheda AB, 1962-69; v.p., then pres. Kockums Industries AB, Soderhamn, 1969-79; pres., CEO Studsvik AB, Nykoping, Sweden, 1979-90; owner Hawk Internat. HB, Nykoping, Sweden, 1990—. Bd. dirs. Ostlänken AB, Nyköping. Capt. Swedish Air Force Res., 1948-84. Office: Hawk Internat Fruangsgatan 22 S-611 31 Nykoping Sweden E-mail: hawki@algonet.se.

HAKE, RALPH F. appliance manufacturing executive; b. Cin. BBA, U. Cin.; MBA, U. Chgo. V.p. adminstrn.l. Mead Corp., Escababa, Mich., 1980-84, dir. corp. devel. Dayton, Ohio, 1984-87; various fin. and ops. positions including corp. v.p., contr. Whirlpool Corp., Benton Harbor, Mich., from 1987, pres. Bauknecht appliance group, exec. v.p. N.Am. appliance group, sr. exec. v.p. ops., until 1997, sr. exec. v.p., CFO, 1997-1999; exec. v.p., CFO Fluor Corp., Aliso Viejo, Calif., 1999—2001; chmn., CEO Maytag Corp., 2001—. With U.S. Army, 1971-73. Mem. NAM (bd. dirs.).*

HAKE, THEODORE LOWELL, auction house owner; b. York, Pa., Aug. 30, 1943; s. Theodore Russell and Ethel Amanda (Towson) Hake; m. Jonell Ann Robison, Aug. 25, 1973; 1 child, Theodore James. BA in Polit. Sci., U. Pitts., 1965; MA in Comm., U. Pa., 1969. Owner, operator Hake's Americana & Collectibles, York, 1967—. Author: Ency. of Polit. Buttons, 3 vols., 1974—77, Hake's Guide to Character Toys, 2002, 12 other reference books for collectors of Am. popular culture. Mem.: Tin Container Collectors Assn., Token and Medal Soc., World's Fair Collectors Soc., Ephemera Soc. Am., Am. Polit. Items Collectors (bd. dirs. 1985—86, Hall of Fame 1985), Nat. Fantasy Fan Club. Office: Hake's Americana & Collectibles PO Box 1444 York PA 17405-1444 E-mail: hake@hakes.com.

HAKEEM, MUHAMMAD ABDUL, artist, educator; b. N.Y.C., Oct. 15, 1945; s. Cheveland and Ruby (Rountrea) Marshall; m. Sarah Sockarso, Feb. 9, 2003. Student of sculpture and painting, Pratt Inst., Pietrasanta, Italy, 1972; BFA, Pratt Inst., 1974; MA, Tchr. Coll., 1976; MEd, Columbia U., 1980. Artist N.Y. Daily News, 1976-78; asst. technician Bklyn. Mus., 1980-81, instr. African Art, 1981; tchr. Holy Rosary Sch., Bklyn., 1982-89; arts and crafts specialist Fresh Air Fund Camp, Fishkill, N.Y., summer 1983, Camp Merrimac, Contoo Cook, N.H., summers 1986-88; tchr. art Middle Sch. 319, Bronx, N.Y., 1997-98, Denver Sch. Dist., 2000—. Adj. prof. Naropa Inst., Boulder; part-time tchr. Boulder and Denver Pub. Schs., 2000—; workshop facilitator, lectr. Islamic culture and faith Arapahoe Ridge H.S., 2001—. One-man shows include Christ Hosp. Primary Care Ctr., Jersey City, N.J., 1997; exhibited in group shows at Bklyn. Mus., 1973, Lynn Kottler Galleries, 1974, Hansen Galleries, 1974, Galleries Internat., 1975, Cmty. Gallery, 1977, Waverly Gallery, Inc., 1977, Allan S. Park Gallery, 1978, Greenwich Bar and Restaurant, 1979, Macy Gallery, 1980, West Side Story, 1981, Lynn Kittler Galleries, 1981, World Trade Expo-Keane Mason Gallery, 1981, Tabor Gallery, 1982, Gallery II, St. George, Utah, 1984, Beaulahland, 1986, Morin-Miller Galleries, 1987, 89, Ednl. Alliance, 1988, Steamboat Springs (Colo.) Art Coun./Eleanor Bliss Ctr. for the Arts of the Depot (hon. mention), 1992, Boulder (Colo.) Art Ctr., 1993, Louisville (Colo.) Arts Ctr., 1993, Emmanuel Gallery-U. Colo., Denver, 1994, Cross Gallery, Boulder, 19955, Cross Gallery, Denver, 1995, Bklyn. Children's Mus., 1996, The Christ Hosp. Primary Care Ctr., 1997, Boulder Mus. Contemporary Art, 2000;, others works represented at Kearon-Hempenstall Gallery, Jersey City; multimedia exhbn. at Colo. History Mus., 1996, art exhibitions, Sovereign Gallery, 2003, Mia Trattoria Rest., 2003. Art tchr. Lower East Side Cmty Sch., N.Y.C., 1976-77, Urban League, Bklyn., 1969 summer; counselor Office of Cath. Edn., Bklyn., 1987-88; mem. customer panel Regional Transp. Divsn. Winner Cheekwood Nat. Contemporary Painting Competition, Cheekwood Mus. Art, Tenn., 1993. Mem. Kappa Delta Pi (Kappa chpt.). Home: 2950 Bixby Ln Apt A313 Boulder CO 80303

HAKEL, MILTON DANIEL, JR., psychology educator, consultant, publisher; b. Hutchinson, Minn., Aug. 1, 1941; s. Milton Daniel and Emily Ann (Kovar) H.; m. Lee Ellen Pervier, Sept. 1, 1962; children: Lane, Jennifer BA, U. Minn., 1963, PhD, 1966. Diplomate in Indsl. and Organizational Psychology Am. Bd. Profl. Psychology. Prof. psychology Ohio State U., Columbus, 1968-85, U. Houston, 1985-91, chmn. dept., 1987-91; Ohio Bd. Regents eminent scholar, prof. Bowling Green State U., 1991—; pres. Organizational Research and Devel., 1977—; ptnr. Applied Research Group, 1984-87. Trustee Am. Bd. Profl. Psychology, 1987-90; mem. com. on assessment and tchr. quality NRC, 1999-00; mem. bd. testing and assessment NRC, 1999-02, mem. U.S. nat. com. for Internat. Union for Psychol. Sci., 1997-01, chair, 2001-03. Co-author (sr.): Making It Happen: Doing Research with Implementation in Mind, 1982; author: Beyond Multiple Choice: Evaluating Alternatives to Traditional Testing, 1998; editor Current Directions in Psychol. Sci., 1998-99, Personnel Psychology, 1973-84, pub., 1984—; co-editor: Applying the Science of Learning to University Teaching and Beyond, 2002; contbr. 40 articles to profl. jours. Chair Human Capital Initiative Coordinating Com., 1991-99, co-chair Applying Sci. Learning to U. Edu. conf. steering com. Recipient James McKeen Cattell award, 1965; Fulbright-Hays Sr. scholar, 1978; NSF grantee, 1966-73; Distng. Svc. Contbrs. award, 1995. Fellow Am. Psychol. Soc. (founding bd. dir.); mem. Soc. for Indsl. and Orgnl. Psychology (pres. 1984), Internat. Assn. Applied Psychology, Summit Conf. Presbyterian. Home: 1435 Cedar Ln Bowling Green OH 43402-1476 Office: Bowling Green State U Dept Psychology Bowling Green OH 43403-0001 E-mail: mhakel@bgnet.bgsu.edu.

HAKES, JAY EDWARD, federal agency administrator; b. Gallipolis, Ohio; m. Anita Zervigon. Grad., Wheaton Coll., 1966; M, Duke U., 1968, PhD, 1970. Tchr. polit. sci. U. New Orleans, 1970-77; with AID, Dept. of Interior, Exec. Office of Pres., 1977-80; state energy dir. Fla. Gov. and U.S. Senator Bob Graham, 1980-93; adminstr. Energy Info. Adminstrn., U.S. Dept. Energy, Washington, 1993-2000; dir. Jimmy Carter Presdl. Libr. and Mus., Atlanta, 2000—. Office: Jimmy Carter Presdl Libr and Museum 441 Freedom Pkwy NE Atlanta GA 30307-1496 E-mail: jay.hakes@nara.gov.

HAKES, THOMAS BRION, manufacturing company executive, physician; b. Chgo., Dec. 27, 1944; s. L. Glenn and Vera M. (Brion) H.; m. Ellen D. Hallock, Apr. 6, 1990; children: Henrietta, John Bradford. BSEE, Rose-Hulman Inst. Tech., 1967; MD, Columbia U., 1973. Diplomate Am. Bd. Internal Medicine, Am. Bd. Oncology. Intern St. Luke's Hosp., N.Y.C., 1973-75; resident in medicine, fellow in oncology Meml. Hosp., N.Y.C., 1975-78; assoc. attending physician Meml. Sloan-Kettering Cancer Ctr., N.Y.C., 1978—; co-chmn. C/S Grp., Lebanon, N.J., 1994—. Office: C/S Group 3 Werner Way Lebanon NJ 08833-2223

HAKIM, BESIM SELIM, architecture and urban design educator, researcher and consultant; b. Paris, July 31, 1938; came to U.S., 1978; s. Selim D. and Meliha M. (Yamulki) H.; children: Omar, Lena, Sara, Malak. BArch, Liverpool (Eng.) U., 1962; MArch in Urban Design, Harvard U., 1971. Registered architect, Ariz. Asst. prof. Tech. U. of Nova Scotia, Halifax, Can., 1967-74, assoc. prof., 1974-80, adj. rsch. prof., 1980-83; adj. assoc. prof. U. N.Mex., Albuquerque, 1982-83; assoc. prof. King Fahd U. of Petroleum and Minerals, Dhahran, Saudi Arabia, 1984-85; assoc. prof. Coll. of Architecture and Planning King Faisal U., Dammam, Saudi Arabia, 1985-93. Ind. scholar and cons., 1994—; vis. prof. McGill U., Montreal, 1974, Tech. Inst. Architecture and Urbanism, Tunis, Tunisia, 1975, King Saud U., Riyadh, Saudi Arabia, 1982, 87, 89, 92, MIT, 1977; vis. scholar MIT, 1981, Cornell U., 1995; cons. to Skidmore, Owings and Merrill, Architects/Engrs., Chgo., Keith Graham & Assocs., Architects, Halifax, Nova Scotia, others; architect, engr. King Khaled Internat. Airport, Riyadh, Saudi Arabia, 1983-84; lectr. numerous univs. and profl. confs. in U.S., Can., Eng., Japan, Greece, Turkey, Tunisia, Jordan, United Arab Emirates, Saudi Arabia, Morocco. Prin. works include urban design downtown Halifax, N.S., Coors Corridor Study, Albuquerque, Hist. Old Town, Albuquerque, 11 custom-built houses, 8-story office bldg., hosp. renovations/additions, apt. bldgs. and a religious facility, U.S., Can., Mid-East; author: Arabic-Islamic Cities: Building and Planning Principles, 1986, 2d edit., 1988, Japanese edit., 1990; contbr. articles to profl. jours. Recipient citation for rsch. Progressive Architecture, 1987, Edn. Honors award AIA, 1990, Initiative for Architectural Rsch., 2002. Fellow Am. Inst. Cert. Planners; mem. AIA, Am. Planning Assn., Assn. Collegiate Schs. of Architecture, Middle East Studies Assn. N.Am. E-mail: arcan@sprynet.com.

HAKIM, CATHERINE, sociologist; b. May 30, 1948; BA with honors, U. Sussex, Eng., 1969; PhD, U. Essex, Eng., 1974. Sr. rsch. officer Office Population Censuses and Surveys, London, 1974-78; prin. rsch. officer Dept. Employment, London, 1978-89; prof. sociology U. Essex, Colchester, Eng., 1989-90; sr. rsch. fellow London Sch. Econs., 1993—. Author: Research Design: Strategies and Choices in the Design of Social Research, 1987, Key Issues in Women's Work: Female Heterogeneity and the Polarisation of Women's Employment, 1996, Social Change and Innovation in the Labour Market: Evidence from the Census SARs on Occupational Segregation and Labour Mobility, Part-Time Work and Student Jobs, Homework and Self-Employment, 1998, Research Design: Successful Designs for Social and Economic Research, 2000, Work-Lifestyle Choices in the 21st Century: Preference Theory, 2000, Models of the Family in Modern Societies: Ideals and Realities, 2003; co-author: (with W. R. Hawes) Labour Force Statistics, 1982; co-editor: (with H-P Blossfeld) Between Equalization and Marginalization: Women Working Part-Time in Europe and the USA, 1997; contbr. articles to profl. jours. Fellow Royal Statis. Soc. Office: London Sch Econs Houghton St London WC2A 2AE England Office Fax: 0207-955-7405. E-mail: c.hakim@lse.ac.uk.

HAKIMOGLU, AYHAN, electronics company executive; b. Erbaa, Turkey, Aug. 19, 1928; came to U.S., 1955; s. Mekki and Mediha H.; children by previous marriage: Zeynep B., Incigul R. O'Brien, Deborah A. Cueto, Leyla P.; m. Rachida Elmir, July 12, 1997. BSEE, Robert Coll., Istanbul, 1949; MSEE, U. Cin., 1950. Founder, pres., chmn. bd. Dynaplex Corp., Princeton, N.J., 1962-67; gen. mgr. Teledyne Telemetry Co., Los Angeles, 1966-67; founder, chmn. bd., pres. Aydin Corp., Horsham, Pa., 1967-96, Cons. Aydin Corp., Plymouth Meeting, Pa.; investor. Served to lt. Turkish Army, 1951-52. Named Turkish Am. of Yr. Assembly Turkish Am. Assn., 1985; recipient Outstanding Pub. Svc. award, Assembly Turkish Am. Assns., 1988, 89, Disting. Alumni award U. Cin., 1991. Moslem.

HAKKILA, EERO ARNOLD, retired nuclear safeguards technology chemist; b. Canterbury, Conn., Aug. 4, 1931; s. Jack and Ida Maria (Lillquist) H.; m. Margaret W. Hakkila; children: Jon Eric, Mark Douglas, Gregg Arnold. BS in Chemistry, Cen. Conn. State U., 1953; PhD in Analytical Chemistry, Ohio State U., 1957. Staff mem. Los Alamos (N.Mex.) Nat. Lab., 1957-78, assoc. group leader safeguard systems, 1978-80, dep. group leader, 1980-82, group leader, 1982-83, project mgr. internat. safeguards, 1983-87, program coord., 1987-95; ret., 1995. Editor: Nuclear Safeguards Analysis, 1978; contbr. numerous articles to profl. jours. Fellow Am. Inst. Chemists; mem. N.Mex. Inst. Chemists (pres. 1971-73), Am. Chem. Soc., Am. Nuclear Soc. (exec. com. fuel cycle and waste mgmt. div. 1984-86), Inst. Nuclear Materials Mgmt. Avocations: skiing, fishing, rockhounding, golf. E-mail: a_hakkila@msn.com.

HAKOSHIMA, SHIN-ICHI, business executive; b. Dec. 9, 1937; Grad., Kyushu U., 1962. With Asahi Shimbun, 1962—, assoc. editor econ. news dept., 1979-84, econ. editor, Nagoya Head Office, 1985-86, econ. editor Tokyo Head Office, 1987-89, dep. mng. editor Nagoya Head Office, 1990-91, mng. editor Seibu Head Office, 1991, mng. editor Tokyo Head Office, 1992-93, mng dir., adminstrn., 1996-97, mng. dir., CEO, 1998; sr. mng. dir., COO, 1998; pres., CEO, 1999—. Office: 5-3-2 Tsukiji Chuo-ku 104-8011 Tokyo Japan

HALABY, SAMIA ASAAD, artist, educator, computer artist; b. Jerusalem, Palestine, Dec. 12, 1936; s. Asaad Saba and Foutounie Assad (Atallah) H. BS in Design, U. Cin., 1959; MA in Painting, Mich. State U., 1960; MFA in Painting, Ind. U., 1963. Teaching asst. Ind. U., Bloomington, 1962-63, assoc. prof., 1969-72; instr. U. Hawaii, Honolulu, 1963-64, vis. lectr., summer 1966; asst. prof. Kansas City (Mo.) Art Inst., 1964-66, U. Mich., 1967-69; vis. lectr. art Yale U., 1972-73, assoc. prof., 1973-76, adj. assoc. prof., 1976-82. Lectr. in field; vis. prof. U. Hawaii, Honolulu, 1985-86, U. South Fla., 1990; adj. instr. Cooper Union, 1989-92; artist-in-residence Tamarind Lithography Workshop, Albuquerque, 1972; presenter 4th Internat. Symposium on Electronic Art, Mpls., 1993, 7th symposium, Rotterdam, 1996. One-man shows include Gima Gallery, Honolulu, 1964, The Gallery, Bloomington, 1970, Phyllis Kind Gallery, Chgo., 1971, Yale Sch. Art Gallery, 1972, Spectrum Gallery, N.Y.C., 1973, Marilyn Pearl Gallery, N.Y.C., 1978, 22 Wooster Gallery, 1982, 83, Tossan-Tossan Gallery, N.Y.C., 1983, 88, Housatonic Mus., Bridgeport, 1983, Galaria de arte Palace, Granada, Spain, 1986, Gallery II U. Mich., Kalamazoo, 1989, 911 Gallery, Indpls., 1993, Darat Al-Funun, Amman, Jordan, 1995, Galerie Atassi, Damascus, Syria, 1997, Galerie Le Porte, Halab, Syria, 1997, Agial Gallery, Beirut, 1999, SKOTO Gallery, N.Y.C., 2000, Sakakini Art Ctr., Ramallah, Palestine, 2000, Artim Gallery, Strasbourg, France, 2001; group shows include Solomon R. Guggenheim Mus., N.Y.C., 1975, Susan Caldwell Gallery, N.Y.C., 1977, Iraqi Cultural Ctr., London, 1979, Kunsternes Hus, Oslo, Norway, 1981, U. Art Mus., N.Mex., 1985, Hudson Ctr. Gallery, N.Y.C., 1985, Tercera Bienal de la Habana, Cuba, 1989, Prix Ars Electronica, Linz, Austria, 1990, Art and Algorithm, Mpls. Coll. Art, 1991, Hilo Internat. Exhbn. of Works on Paper, U. Hawaii, 1990, Digitized and Manipulated, Sangre De Cristo Arts Ctr., Pueblo, Colo., 1991, opening exhbn. Darat Al Funun of Shoman Found., Amman, Jordan, 1993, Fourth Internat. Symposium Electronic Art, Mpls., 1993, Arab Women, Nat. Mus. Women in the Arts, Washington, 1994, World Artist at the Millennium, Elizabeth Found., UN Lobby, 1999, Bradley U., Ill., 2001, Musee du Chateau DuFresne, Montreal, 2001, 13th Afro-Asian L.Am. exhbn. Tokyo Met. Mus, 2002, Williamsburg Bridges Palestine, WAH Ctr., Bklyn., 2002, Sta. Mus., Houston, 2003; performance art (computer abstractions) Bklyn. Mus., 1994, Poetry Project, N.Y.C., 1995, Lebanese Am. U., Beirut, 1995, HERE, N.Y.C., 1996; represented in permanent collections Solomon R. Guggenheim Mus., Inst. Du Monde Arab, Paris, Indpls. Mus. Art, Art Inst. Chgo., Nelson Rockhill Gallery Art, Kansas City, Ind. U. Mus., Mich. State U. Mus., Ft. Wayne (Ind.) Mus. Art, Detroit Inst. Art, Cleve. Mus. Art, Cin. Art Mus., Nat. Gallery Jordan, Amman, Yale U. Gallery, Tamarind Inst. Collection, Albuquerque, Alternative Mus., N.Y., Honolulu Acad. Arts, Ind. U. Mus., Bloomington, Mead Art Mus., Amherst, Conn., Palm Springs (Calif.) Desert Mus., Yale U. Gallery, New Haven, The Jane Voorhees Zimmerli Art Museum, New Brunswick, N.J., corp. collections, U.S. Steel, ATT Longlines, First Nat. Chgo, Kemper Ins. Chgo., S.E. Banking Corp. Fla., Witko Chem. Corp., Standard Oil Ohio, IBM, Arab Bank. Subject of Profl. Publs.; Kansas City Coun. for Faculty Devel. traveling fellow, 1965; Creative Artists Pub. Svc. Program grantee, 1978-79, UN grant UNDP cons., 1999. Studio: PO Box 965 New York NY 10013-0861 E-mail: samia@rcn.com.

HALAMANDARIS, HARRY, aerospace executive; b. Sunnyside, Utah, Sept. 26, 1938; s. Gust and Olga (Konakis) H.; m. Sandra Susan Hansen, Aug. 4, 1961; children: Chris Harry, Gina Lee. AS, Carbon Coll., 1958; BS in Math., Utah State U., 1960, BSEE, 1961, MSEE, 1962. Instr. West Coast U., L.A., 1964-68; mem. tech. staff Hughes Aircraft, Culver City, Calif., 1962-65; sr. mem. tech. staff Litton Guidance & Controls, Woodland Hills, Calif., 1965-69; gen. mgr., exec. v.p. Satellite Positioning Corp., Encino, Calif., 1969-72; pres., asst. group exec. Teledyne Systems, Northridge, Calif., 1972-89; dir. corp. tech. Teledyne Industries, Inc., L.A., 1989-94; group exec. Kaiser Aerospace and Electronics, Van Nuys, Calif., 1994-95; exec. v.p., COO Litton Industries, Inc., 1995-2000, sr. v.p., group exec., 2000—01, ret., 2001. Mem. adv. coun. Coll. Ea. Utah; industry adv. bd. U. So. Calif., Calif. State U., L.A.; bd. dirs. Econ. Devel. Corp., 1992-94. Contbr. over 30 articles to profl. jours. Mem. bd. govs. Pacific Boys Lodge, Woodland Hills, Calif., 1986-88; aerospace chmn. United Way, L.A., 1988-89. NSF fellow, 1961-62. Mem. Am. Electronics Assn. (bd. dirs., exec. com. 1984-94, pres. Roundtable exec. com. 1989-92), Utah State Alumni, Masons, Sigma Xi (officer, v.p. 1960-61), Phi Kappa Phi, Tau Beta Pi. Democrat. Greek Orthodox. Avocations: racquetball, gardening, sports, coaching youth sports. Home: 2204 Calle Opalo San Clemente CA 92673-5618

HALAMANDARIS, PHILL VICTOR, psychiatrist; b. L.A., Sept. 14, 1961; s. Philip Gus Halamandaris and Marilyn Anne Colombo. BA, Stanford U., 1983; MD, U. So. Calif., 1987. Attending psychiatrist NYU Med. Ctr./Bellevue Hosp., N.Y.C., 1992-99; priv. practice psychiatrist N.Y.C., 1993—; voluntary faculty

NYU Med. Ctr./Bellevue Hosp., N.Y.C., 1999—. Democrat. Avocations: physical fitness, travel, reading, film/theatre. Office: 455 W 23rd St Apt 1A New York NY 10011-2156 E-mail: p.halamandaris@att.net.

HALAMEK, LOUIS PATRICK, neonatologist; BS, Creighton U., 1981, MD, 1986. Diplomate Nat. Bd. Med. Examiners, Am. Bd. Pediats. Postdoctoral fellow Stanford (Calif.) U. Sch. Medicine, 1990-93, staff physician, 1992-94; acting asst. prof. dept. pediats. Stanford U., 1994-95, asst. prof. divsn. neonatology and devel. medicine, 1995—2000, assoc. prof., 2001—. Office: Divsn Neonatology 750 Welch Rd Ste 315 Palo Alto CA 94304-1510

HALAR, EUGEN MARIAN, physiatrist, educator; came to the U.S., 1965; m. Olga Katarina Svete, Aug. 19, 1961; children: Zeljko, Eugene. MD, Zagreb (Croatia) U., 1959. Diplomate Am. Bd. Phys. Medicine and Rehab. Intern Gen. Hosp. Karlovac, Croatia; resident in phys. medicine and rehab. Zagreb (Croatia) U., 1965, 1965—68, NYU, 1968—71; attending physician Univ. Hosp., 1968-69, Harborview Med. Ctr., 1971—97; chief svc. rehab. medicine VA Hosp., 1971-97; phys. medicine and rehab. attending physician Puget Sound Healthcare Sys., 1997-99, co-dir. cardiac rehab. program, 1997—99, prof. emeritus, 1999—. Prof. rehab. medicine U. Wash., Seattle, 1986—. Guest editor: Cardiac Rehabilitation, 1995, Stroke Mgmt. and Rehab., 1999. Fellow Am. Acad. Phys. Medicine and Rehab.; mem. Assn. Acad. Physiatrist, King County Med. Soc. Avocations: skiing, tennis, travel. Home: 817 179th Ct NE Bellevue WA 98008-4241 Office: U Wash Hsb Dept Rehab Medicine Ctr Seattle WA 98195-0001 E-mail: Halarem@msn.com.

HALAS, CYNTHIA ANN, business information specialist; b. Norristown, Pa., July 24, 1961; d. George and Maria (Mitrik) H. Student, Temple U., 1979-80; AS in Bus. Adminstrn., Montgomery County Coll., Blue Bell, Pa., 1993; student, Springhouse Computer Sch., Exton, Pa., 1994-95. Columnist, corr. The Recorder, Conshohocken, Pa., 1980-81; claims supr. Liberty Mut. Ins. Co., Blue Bell, 1980-84; claims svc. rep. Met. Property & Liability Ins. Co., Wayne, Pa., 1984-87; model Frank James Assocs., Phila., 1986-87; auditor/tng. coord. Coresource, Inc., Wayne, 1987-94; sys. support analyst Del. Valley Fin. Svcs., Inc., Berwyn, Pa., 1994-95; sys. support coord. Aetna-U.S. Healthcare, Blue Bell, Pa., 1995—. Active Nat. Arbor Day Found. Mem. NAFE, U.S. Fencing Assn. Byzantine Catholic. Avocations: golf, fencing, horseback riding, needle point, travel. Office: Aetna-US Healthcare 930 Harvest Dr Blue Bell PA 19422-1959

HALAS, PAUL ANTHONY, JR., business appraisal and valuation specialist, consultant; b. Chgo., June 27, 1933; s. Paul Aloysius and Elonia Bernidene (Zelinski) H.; m. Shirley Donna Willis, Aug. 17, 1957 (dec.); children: Julie, Vickie, Jon, Carl, Jim; m. Nina Romanenko, Feb. 19, 2000. Student, Columbia Sch. Broadcasting, 1951-53, Northwestern U., 1957-59. Cert. mgmt. cons., N.Y. Rep. Solar Chgo. divsn. USI's, 1957-60; rep. J. W. Bolton, Inc., Lawrence, Mass., 1960-62; gen. sales mgr. Schimanek, Internat., Chgo., 1962-63; v.p. mktg. Products Engring. Co., Tinley Park, Ill., 1963-68; gen. sales mgr. Vacudyne Corp., Chicago Heights, Ill., 1968-70; mktg. mgr. Fastron Co., Franklin Park, Ill., 1970-72, Scandura, Inc., Charlotte, N.C., 1972-78; mgmt. cons. Halas & Assocs., Charlotte, 1978-85, valuation specialist, 1985—. Contbr. numerous articles on bus. valuation and appraisal. Recipient Printed award Grain Age Mag., 1976. Mem. BBB, ASME (coord. ANSI A90 com. 1974-77), Nat. Ctr. for Employee Ownership, Inst. Bus. Appraisers, Inst. Mgmt. Cons., Charlotte C. of C. Republican. Roman Catholic. Avocations: music, photography, vacation. Office: Halas & Assocs 425 Roselawn Pl Charlotte NC 28211-4162 E-mail: hbvs@halas.com.

HALASKA, THOMAS EDWARD, academic administrator, director, engineer; b. Childress, Tex., Aug. 4, 1945; s. Howard Edward and Ruth Marie (Reinders) H.; m. Marilyn Jean Walenta, June 7, 1969; 1 child, Jean Ellen. BSEE, Milw. Sch. Engring., 1969; MBA, Ga. State U., 1975; EdD, U. Ga., 1992. Plant engr. Tom's divsn. Gen. Mills, Inc., Columbus, Ga., 1969-74; dir. mfg. Stuckey Stores div. Pet, Inc., Eastman, Ga., 1974-82; dir. mgmt. info. systems Mid. Ga. Coll., Cochran, 1982-87, dir. instnl. rsch., 1987—, CIO, 1992—. Mem. Soc. Coll. and Univ. Planning, Assn. for Instnl. Rsch., Univ. System Computer Network (regents adminstrv. com. info. tech.), Rotary (bd. dirs. Cochran chpt. 1986—). Republican. Roman Catholic. Avocation: pilot. Home: 2696 Chester Hwy Eastman GA 31023 Office: Mid Ga Coll 1100 2nd St SE Cochran GA 31014-1599 E-mail: thalaska@mgc.edu.

HALASZ, PIRI, columnist, writer; b. N.Y.C., Apr. 5, 1935; d. George and Ruth (West) Halasz. BA, Barnard Coll., 1956; MA, Columbia U., 1976, PhD, 1982. Rsch. asst. Time, Inc./Time mag., N.Y.C., 1956-63, contbg. editor, 1963-69; adj. asst. prof. L.I. U., Greenvale, NY, 1977-78, from adj. asst. prof. to adj. assoc. prof., 1985-86; adj. assoc. prof. Molloy Coll., Rockville Centre, NY, 1985-86; asst. prof. Bethany (W.Va.) Coll., 1990-94; online columnist From the Mayor's Doorstep, 1996—. Contbr. articles to profl. jours. Smithsonian Inst. fellow, 1980—81, Va. Ctr. Creative Arts fellow, 1986, 1989, 1997, 1998, 2001. Mem.: Authors Guild, Coll. Art Assn. Home: 520 E 76th St Apt 3A New York NY 10021-3162

HALASZ, ROBERT JOSEPH, editor; b. Budapest, Hungary, June 11, 1937; s. Nicholas and Piroska (Szenes) H.; m. Miriam Sonia Jackson, Oct. 2, 1965 (div. 1968). BA, U. Chgo., 1959; MA, Roosevelt U., 1967. Editor Standard Edn. Corp., Chgo., 1960-79, Funk & Wagnalls Inc., N.Y.C., 1980-83. Author: The U.S. Marines, 1993. Mem. Editl. Freelancers Assn. Avocations: painting, skiing, tennis. Home: 276 Riverside Dr New York NY 10025-5204

HALASZ, STEPHEN JOSEPH, retired electro-optical systems engineer; b. Eger-Csehi, Hungary; s. Sandor and Ilona (Huszák) H.; children: Stepehn S., Christopher L. Jacqueline R. BS, Columbia U., 1955. Test engr. J.A. Maurer, Inc., N.Y.C., 1955-56; project engr. GE Co., Utica, N.Y., 1956-58; sr. physicist Avion divsn. ACF Industries, Paramus, N.J., 1958-65; head IR and Display Lab. Aerojet Gen., 1965-72; sr. specialist Xerox Electro-Optical, Pasadena, Calif., 1972-75, Ford Aeronutronic, Newport Beach, Calif., 1975-83; chief scientist Hughes Aircraft, El Segundo, Calif., 1983-92. Contbg. author: (handbook) IR Handbook, 1969. With U.S. Army, 1945. NRA. Republican. Roman Catholic. Achievements include numerous designs and research projects including optical guidance for satellite interception; IR moving target tracker; handheld thermal imager; scanned matrix for IR pattern recognition; high speed target acquisition with fused senors; others; patentee in field. Home: 66887 San Carlos Rd Desert Hot Springs CA 92240-2622 E-mail: s_hal@msn.com.

HALAVAIS, ALEXANDER MICHAEL CAMPBELL, information scientist, educator; b. Washington, July 21, 1971; s. John Campbell and Mary Agnes Hoyt-Halavais; m. Jamie Lynne Atchison, June 27, 1993. BA in Polit. Sci., U. Calif., Irvine, 1993; PhD, U. Wash., 2001. Info. sys. cons. Halavais Consulting, Irvine, Calif., 1991—93; lead internat. instr. Odawara (Japan) City Bd. of Edn., 1993—95; sales fin. liaison Security Pacific/Bank Am., San Diego, 1995—96; lectr. U. Wash., Seattle, 1997—2001; asst. prof. SUNY, Buffalo, 2001—. Mem.: Am. Soc. Info. Sci. and Tech., Assn. Internet Rschrs., Internat. Communication Assn., U.S. Judo Assn. (life). Democrat. Avocations: Judo, travel, chess. Office: SUNY 359 Baldy Hall Buffalo NY 14260-1060 Personal E-mail: alex@halavais.net. Business E-Mail: halavais@buffalo.edu.

HALBACH, EDWARD CHRISTIAN, JR., law educator, educator; b. Clinton, Iowa, Nov. 8, 1931; s. Edward Christian and Lewella (Sullivan) H.; m. Janet Elizabeth Bridges, July 25, 1953; children: Kristin Lynn, Edward Christian III, Kathleen Ann, Thomas Elliot, Elaine Diane. BA, U. Iowa, 1953, JD, 1958; LLM, Harvard U., 1959; LLD, U. Redlands, 1973. Assoc. prof. Sch. Law, U. Calif. at Berkeley, 1959-62, prof., 1963—, dean, 1966-75. Co-author: Materials on Decedents' Estates and Trusts, 1965, 73, 81, 87, 93, 2000, Materials on Future Interests, 1977, Death, Taxes and Family Property, 1977, California Will Drafting, 1965, 77, 92; author: Use of Trusts in Estate Planning, 1975, 81, 84, 86, 91, Fundamentals of Estate Planning, 1983, 86, 87, 89, 91, 93, 95, Summary of the Law of Trusts, 1990, 1998, Principles and Techniques of Estate Planning, 1995; reporter Uniform Probate Code, 1969, Restatement 3d Trusts Prudent Investor Rule, 1991, Restatement of Law of Trusts, vols. 1 and 2, 2003; also articles. 1st lt. USAF, 1954-56. Mem. ABA (chmn. various coms. sect. individual rights and responsibilities and sect. real property probate and trust law, dir. probate and trust divsn., sect. chmn.), Iowa Bar Assn., Am. Law Inst. (reporter Restatement 3d Trusts, advisor Restatement 2d, 3d Property), Am. Acad. Polit. and Social Scis., Am. Bar Found., Am. Coll. Trust and Estate Counsel, Am. Coll. Tax Counsel, Internat. Acad. Estate and Trust Law (v.p., exec. com., pres.). Home: 679 San Luis Rd Berkeley CA 94707-1725 Office: U Calif Sch Law Boalt Hall Berkeley CA 94720

HALBERG, CHARLES JOHN AUGUST, JR., mathematics educator; b. Pasadena, Calif., Sept. 24, 1921; s. Charles John August and Anne Louise (Hansen) H.; m. Ariel Arfon Oliver, Nov. 1, 1941 (div. July 1969); children—Ariel (Mrs. William Walters), Charles Thomas, Niels Frederick; m. Barbro Linnea Samuelsson, Aug. 18, 1970 (dec. Jan. 1978); 1 stepchild, Ulf Erik Hjelm; m. Betty Reese Zimprich, July 27, 1985 BA summa cum laude, Pomona Coll., 1949; MA (William Lincoln Honnold fellow), UCLA, 1953, PhD, 1955. Instr. math. Pomona Coll., Claremont, Calif., 1949-50; assoc. math. UCLA, 1954-55; instr. math. U. Calif.-Riverside, 1955-56, asst. prof. math., 1956-61, assoc. prof. math., 1961-68, prof. math., 1968—, vice chancellor student affairs, 1964-65. Dir. Scandinavian Study Center at Lund (Sweden) U., 1976-78; docent U. Goteborg, Sweden, 1969-70; bd. dirs. Fulbright Commn. for Ednl. Exchange between U.S. and Sweden, 1976-79 Author: Aftermath, 1996, (with John F. Devlin) Elementary Functions, 1967, (with Angus E. Taylor) Calculus with Analytic Geometry, 1969. Served with USAAF, 1945-46. NSF fellow U. Copenhagen, 1961-62 Mem. Math. Assn. Am. (chmn. So. Calif. sect. 1964-65, gov. 1968), Am. Math. Soc., Swedish Math. Soc., Sigma Xi, Phi Beta Kappa. Home: PO Box 2724 Carlsbad CA 92018-2724 E-mail: doon@math.ucr.edu.

HALBERG, F. DAVID, principal; b. Toronto, Ont., Can., Sept. 18, 1943; s. Max and Esther (Sherman) H.; m. Georgette Greenberg, June 9, 1966; children: Michael, Jason, Eric. BEd, U. Miami, Coral Gables, Fla., 1966, MEd, 1967. Cert. tchr., adminstr., supr., Fla. Tchr. Dade County Schs., Miami, 1967-80, ESE placement specialist, 1980-81, asst. prin., 1981-89; prin. Fienberg Elem. Sch., Miami Beach, Fla., 1989-90, North Beach Elem. Sch., Miami Beach, 1990-96, Gloria Floyd Elem. Sch., West Kendall, 1996—. Named Elem. Prin. of Yr., Dade County Media Specialist Assn., 1993, Miami Beach Feeder Pattern Prin. of Yr., 1994; 1st runner-up Adminstr. of Yr., Coun. for Exceptional Children, 1999; recipient Cervantes Outstanding Educator award Nova Southea. U., 1999. Mem. Coun. for Exceptional Children, Dade County Sch. Adminstrs. Assn., ASCD, Am. Fedn. Sch. Adminstrs. Home: 16203 SW 108th Ct Miami FL 33157-2924

HALBERSTADT, ROBERT BILHEIMER, optometrist; b. Stockertown, Pa., Feb. 11, 1918; s. Joseph Victor and Lillian (Bilheimer) H.; O.D., No. Ill. Coll. Optometry, 1939; m. Mary Margaret Gassner, Nov. 9, 1940; children: Mary Diane Seip, Victoria Milou Mackenzie. Optometrist, Nazareth, Pa., 1940—; cons. Optometry Whitehall-Coplay Sch. Dist., 1966 78, Pathway Sch., Norristown, Pa. 1966-67, Miller Clinic, Stroudsburg, Pa., 1971-74, Learning Center, Scranton (Pa.) Pub. Schs., 1971-72; staff optometrist, cons. Allentown State Hosp., 1967-68; extern Gesell Inst., New Haven, 1967-68. Active Lehigh Valley Assn. for Brain Damaged Child, 1965-68; 2d Assn. for Brain Damaged Children, 1966-68; program chmn. Lehigh Valley Assn. for Children with Learning Disabilities, 1969-74, bd. dirs., 1971 74, 1st v.p., 1973-74, mem. Council Exceptional Children; with Friendship House, Scranton, 1973-75; mem. pres.'s club Ill. Coll. Optometry, 1973—, Century Club, 1976-88; mem. nat. pilot project team on formation fo spl. edn. model Intermediate Sch. Unit 20 of Pa., 1980-81; mem. Nazareth Area Residents for Clean Air, 1991. With USNR, 1944-46. Mem. Optometric Extension Program (state dir. 1950-58, regional dir. 1958-84, life mem. Pioneer Fund 1987—), Pa. Optometric Assn. (treas. 1948-57). Address: 116 S Broad St Nazareth PA 18064-2118

HALBERSTAM, DAVID, journalist, author; b. N.Y.C., Apr. 10, 1934; s. Charles A. and Blanche (Levy) H.; m. Elzbieta Tchizevska, June 13, 1965 (div. 1977); m. Jean Sandness Butler, June 29, 1979; 1 dau., Julia Sandness. AB, Harvard U., 1955; degree (hon.), CCNY, Colby Coll., Colorado State, Columbia Coll., Chgo., Dartmouth Coll., Drew Univ., Elizabethtown Coll., Ithaca Coll., Knox Coll., Lake Forest Coll., Lawrence Coll., Mercy Coll., Univ. Mich., Ann Arbor, Univ. New Haven, Niagara Coll., Tufts Univ., Tulane Univ., Univ. South, Sewance, Univ. South Carolina, Spartanburg, Wesleyan Univ. Reporter West Point Daily Times Leader, Miss., 1955—56, Nashville Tennessean, 1956—60; mem. staff N.Y. Times, 1960—67, corr., 1961—62, 1962—63, 1964—65, 1965—66; contbg. editor Harper's mag., 1967—71. Author: The Noblest Roman, 1961, The Making of a Quagmire, 1965, One Very Hot Day, 1968, The Unfinished Odyssey of Robert Kennedy, 1969, Ho (Ho Chi Minh), 1971, The Best and the Brightest, 1972, The Powers That Be, 1979, The Breaks of the Game, 1981, The Amateurs, 1985, The Reckoning, 1986, Summer of '49, 1989, The Next Century, 1991, The Fifties, 1993, October 1964, 1994, The Children, 1997, Playing for Keeps: Michael Jordan and The World He Made, 1998, The Children, 1998, War in a Time of Peace, 2001, Firehouse, 2002, The Teammates, 2003; co-editor: (with Glenn Stout) The Best American Sports Writing, 1991; editor: (with Glenn Stout) The Best American Sports Writing of the Century, 1999; author intro. for Requiem The Photographs of the Photographers Who Died in the Vietnam War, 1997. Trustee The Brearley Sch., 1993. Recipient Pulitzer prize for internat. reporting, 1964, George Polk Meml. award, 1964, Louis Lyons award, 1964, Page One award for Congo reporting, 1962, Overseas Press Club award, 1973, Elijah Lovejoy award Colby Coll., 1997, Bob Considine award St. Bonaventure Coll., 1999, Robert Kennedy Book award, 1999, Christopher award, 1999, Frederick Melcher Book award Unitarian Ch., 1999, Pres. Award, Trinity Coll., Jean Mayer Award, Tufts Univ., all for The Children, 1999. Mem. Soc. Am. Historians.

HALBERSTAM, HEINI, mathematics educator; b. Most, Czechoslovakia, Sept. 11, 1926; came to Eng., 1939, naturalized, 1998. s. Michael and Judith (Honig) H.; m. Heather M. Peacock, Mar. 11, 1950 (dec. 1971); children: Naomi Deborah, Judith Marion, Lucy Rebecca, Michael Welsford; m. Doreen Bramley, Sept. 28, 1972. BS with honours, Univ. Coll., London U., 1946, MS, 1948, PhD, 1952. Lectr. math. U. Exeter, 1949-57; reader Royal Holloway Coll., London U., 1957-62; Erasmus Smith prof. Trinity Coll., Dublin, Ireland, 1962-64; prof. Nottingham U., England, 1964-80; prof. math. U. Ill., Urbana-Champaign, 1980-96, prof. emeritus, 1996—. Vis. lectr. Brown U., 1955-56; vis. prof. U. Mich., 1966, U. Tel Aviv, 1973, U. Paris-South, 1972 Co-author: Sequences, 1966, 2d edit., 1983, Sieve Methods, 1975; co-editor math. papers of W.R. Hamilton, H. Davenport; contbr. articles to profl. jours. Mem. London Math. Soc. (v.p. 1962-63, 74-77), Am. Math Soc.

HALBERSTAM, MALVINA, law educator, lawyer; b. Kempno, Poland, May 2, 1937; came to U.S., 1947; d. Marcus and Pearl (Halberstam) H.; m. Wolf Z. Guggenheim (dec. 2002); children: Arye, Achiezer. BA cum laude, Bklyn. Coll., 1957; JD, Columbia U., 1961, MIA, 1964. Bar: N.Y. 1962, U.S. Dist. Ct. (so. dist.) N.Y. 1963, U.S. Ct. Appeals (2d cir.) 1965, U.S. Supreme Ct. 1966, Calif. 1968. Law clk. Judge Edmund L. Palmieri Fed. Dist. Ct. (so. dist.) N.Y., 1961-62; rsch. assoc. Columbia Project on Internat. Procedure, 1962-63; asst. dist. atty. N.Y. County, 1963-67; with Rifkind & Sterling, L.A., 1967-68; sr. atty. Nat. Legal Program on Health Problems of the Poor, L.A., 1969-70; prof. Sch. Law Loyola U., L.A., 1970-76; prof. Benjamin N. Cardozo Sch. Law Yeshiva U., N.Y.C., 1976—. Vis. prof. Gould Law Ctr., U. So. Calif., L.A., 1972-73, U. Va. Sch. Law, 1975-76, U. Tex. Sch. Law, summer 1974, Hebrew U., Jerusalem, 1984-85; counselor on internat. law U.S. State Dept. Office of Legal Adviser, 1985-86; cons., 1986-92. Author: (with De Feis) Women's Legal Rights: International Agreements An Alternative to ERA?, 1987; articles and rev. editor Columbia Law Rev., 1960-61; reporter Am. Law Inst. Model Penal Code Commentaries, 1977-81; contbr. articles, commentary, book revs. to profl. jours. Mem. Bklyn. Coll. Alumni Adv. Bd. on Women's Career Devel. and Leadership Program.; adv. com. to standing com. on law and nat. security, ABA; study group on shape Arab-Israeli settlement, humanitarian, and demographic issues Coun. on Fgn. Rels. Kent scholar (2x); Stone scholar; recipient Jane Marks Murphy prize. Mem.: Am. Assn. Law Schs. (chair sect. internat. law 2002—03), Am. Assn. Jewish Lawyers and Jurists (bd. govs.), Internat. Law Assn. (Am. br. exec. com., human rights com.), Assn. of the Bar City of N.Y. (coun. on internat. affairs), Am. Soc. Internat. Law, Am. Law Inst., Columbia Law Sch. Alumni Assn., Phi Beta Kappa. Home: 160 Riverside Dr New York NY 10024-2106 Office: Yeshiva U Benjamin N Cardozo Sch Law 55 Fifth Ave New York NY 10003-4391 E-mail: halbrstm@ymail.yu.edu.

HALBERSTEIN, JOSEPH LEONARD, retired associate editor; b. Piqua, Ohio, Mar. 10, 1923; s. David and Mollie (Oberferst) H.; m. Lillian Friedman, Aug. 9, 1964; children: Richard Martin, Howard Louis. BA in Journalism, Ohio State U., 1944; postgrad., Pa. State U., 1976. Sportswriter Columbus (Ohio) Citizen, 1943-44; sports editor Lima (Ohio) News, 1944-49; circulation mgr. Town and Village, N.Y.C., 1950-52; sports editor, mng. editor Wilmington (Del.) Sunday Star, 1952-54; wire editor, sports editor Gainesville (Fla.) Sun, 1955-71; mng. editor, assoc. editor Bucks County Courier Times, Levittown, Pa., 1971-93, ret., 1993. Lectr. various univs. Contbr. articles to profl. jours. Bd. dirs. ARC, Langhorne, Pa., 1971-80, Congregation Beth El, Levittown, 1978-85. Recipient 2d Pl. best column Nat. Newspaper Assn., 1961, 1st Pl. best column Keystone Press Assn., 1976, 2d Pl. best game story Basketball Writers Assn. Mem. Fla. Sportswriters Assn. (pres.), Pa. AP Mng. Editors Assn. (pres.), Soc. of Profl. Journalists (greater Phila. chpt. pres. 1981-82), Pa. Soc. of Newspaper Editors, Sigma Delta Chi. Avocations: walking, travel, computer study. Office: Bucks County Courier Times 8400 Route 13 Levittown PA 19057 E-mail: mrslfh@aol.com. *Newspapers bring information to people. Sometimes that information helps people make decisions that affect their lives or the lives of others. In journalism, one has to inform, to help, and, especially to care. Caring is what makes any endeavor a noble one.*

HALBERT, DAVID D. health management services executive; BS in Bus. Adminstrn., Abilene Christian U., 1978. Founder Halbert & Assocs., Inc.; founder, chmn. bd., CEO AdvancePCS, 1987—. Office: 750 W John Carpenter Frwy Ste 1200 Irving TX 75039

HALBOUTY, MICHEL THOMAS, geologist, petroleum engineer, petroleum operator; b. Beaumont, Tex., June 21, 1909; s. Tom Christian and Sodia (Manolley) H.; m. Billye Stevens, Dec. 27, 1981; 1 dau., Linda Fay. BS, Tex. A&M U., 1930, MS, 1931, Profl. Degree in Geol. Engring, 1956; D Eng. (hon.), Mont. Coll. Mineral Sci. and Tech., 1966; PhD in Geology (hon.), USSR Acad. Scis., 1990. Geologist, petroleum engr. Yount-Lee Oil Co., Beaumont, 1931-33, chief geologist, petroleum engr., 1933-35; v.p., gen. mgr., chief geologist and petroleum engr. Glenn H. McCarthy, Inc., Houston, 1935-37; owner firm cons. geologists and petroleum engrs. Houston, 1937-81; chmn., chief exec. officer Michel T. Halbouty Energy Co., 1981—; discoverer numerous oil and gas fields La. and Tex. Adj. prof. Tex. Tech U.; vis. prof. Tex. A&M U.; hon. prof. geology Nanjing (China) U., 1993. Author several books. Contbr. numerous papers on geology and petroleum engring. to profl. jours. Served as lt. col. AUS, 1942-45. Recipient Tex. Mid-Continent Oil and Gas Assn. disting. service award for an ind., 1965; named engr. of yr. Tex. Soc. Profl. Engrs. and Engrs. Council, 1968; recipient Disting. Alumni award Tex. A&M U., 1968; Michel T. Halbouty Geoscis. Bldg. named for him, 1977; recipient DeGolyer Disting. Service medal Soc. Petroleum Engrs. of Am. Inst. Mining, Metall. and Petroleum Engrs., 1971; hon. mem. Spindletop sect., 1972; hon. mem. inst., 1973, Anthony F. Lucas Gold medal, 1975; Pecora award NASA, 1977; Horatio Alger award Am. Schs. and Colls. Assn., 1978, Spirit of Life award City of Hope, 1978, Breath of Life award Cystic-Fibrosis Found., 1981, merit medal Circum-Pacific Council for Energy and Mineral Resources, 1982, Hoover medal Am. Assn. Engring. Socs., 1982, disting. service award Paul Carrington chpt. SAR, 1983, Tex. Heritage award Angleton C. of C., Tex., 1983 Mem. AAAS, Am. Assn. Petroleum Geologists (hon., pres. 1966-67, Human Needs award 1975, Sidney Powers Meml. medal 1977), Am. Soc. Oceanography, Internat. Assn. Sedimentology, Inst. Petroleum, London, Am. Petroleum Inst. (Gold medal for Dist. Achievement 2002), Am. Inst. Mining and Metall. Engrs., Soc. Econ. Paleontologists and Mineralogists, Soc. Econ. Geologists, Mineral. Soc. Am., Geol. Soc. Am., Soc. Exploration Geophysicists (hon.), Nat. Acad. Engring., Houston Geol. Soc. (hon.), N.Y. Acad. Sci., Tex. Acad. Sci. (Disting. Tex. Scientist of Yr. 1983), Am. Inst. Profl. Geologists, Am. Geol. Inst., Tex., Chinese Acad. Engring., Gulf Coast Assn. Geol. Socs. (hon.) Clubs: Ramada, Houston, Petroleum, River Oaks Country (Houston); Dallas Petroleum; Eldorado Country, Vintage (Palm Desert, Calif.); New Orleans Petroleum; Cosmos (Washington); Broadmoor, Kissing Camels (Colorado Springs). Episcopalian. Home: 2121 Kirby Dr Houston TX 77019-6035 Office: Halbouty Center 5100 Westheimer Rd Houston TX 77056-5596

HALBREICH, URIEL MORAV, psychiatrist, educator; b. Jerusalem, Nov. 23, 1943; came to U.S., 1978, naturalized, 1982. s. Mordechai and Zipora (Tennenbaum) H.; m. Judith Thadine, 1987; children: Jasmine, Bethany. MD, Hebrew U., 1969. Diplomate Tel Aviv U. Psychiatry and Psychotherapy. Intern gen. medicine Hadassah U. Hosp., Jerusalem, 1968; comdr., vice-chief med. officer Israeli Navy, 1970-72, chief psychiatrist, 1977-78; resident, 2d then 1st asst. Hadassah Hosp. Hebrew U., Jerusalem, 1972-78; temp. chief physician Hadassah U. Hosp., Jerusalem, 1978; asst. prof., rsch. psychiatrist Columbia U., N.Y.C., 1978-80; assoc. prof., dir. divsn. biol. psychiatry Albert Einstein Coll. Medicine, N.Y.C., 1982-85; prof. psychiatry, dir. biobehavioral rsch. SUNY, Buffalo, 1985—, prof. ob-gyn, 1988—. Vis. prof. Harvard U., 1996-98, exec. cons. dept. psychiatry; chmn. 1st Internat. Congress on Hormones, Brain and Neuropsychopharmacology, 1993, chmn. sect. on interdisciplinary collaboration World Psychiat. Assn., 1997—, others; chmn. 2d Congress on Hormones, Brain and Neuropsychopharmacology, 2000; chmn. bd. dirs. Internat. Inst. Edn. in Mental Health and Psychopharmacology, 1997—; cons. in field. Editor: Transient Psychosis, 1983, Resistance to Treatment with Antidepressant Drugs, 1986, Hormones and Depression, 1987, Multiple Sclerosis: A Neuropsychiatric Disorder, 1992, Psychopharmacology of Women, 1996, Psychiatric Issues in Women, 1996, Training in Psychiatry and Psychopharmacology, 1998, Psychopharmacology of Mood Anxiety and Cognition, 2000, Psychiatry and the Law in Eastern Europe, 2000, Womens Mental Health, 2002; contbr. articles to profl. jours., chpts. to books. Recipient Ben Gurion award Gen. Fedn. Labor, 1976, Yair Gon award Hebrew U. Hadassah Med. Sch., 1978, Nat. Rsch. Svc. award NIH, 1978; grantee NIMH, 1982—. Fellow: Am. Coll. Psychiatrists, Am. Psychiat. Assn. (disting.), Coll. Internat. Neuropsychopharmacology (co-chmn. edn. com. 1994—96), Am. Coll. Neuropsychopharmacology (chmn. rules and constitution com. 1996), Am. Psychopathology Assn.; mem.: Endocine Soc., Assn. Med. Psychiatry (chmn. edn. com. 1992—96, councilor 1992—96), Soc. Biol. Psychiatry (chmn. program com. 1992—93), Am. Coll. Psychiatrists, Internat. Assn. Womens Mental Health (pres. 2001—), Internat. Soc. Psycho. Neuro. Endocrinology (chmn. 21st congress 1990, pres. 1999—2002). Jewish. Office: SUNY Sch Med & Biomed Hayes C Ste 1 3435 Main St Bldg 5 Buffalo NY 14214-3016 E-mail: urielh@acsu.buffalo.edu.

HALBROOKS, JAMES RICHMOND (RICKY HALBROOKS), sheet metal mechanic; b. Decatur, Ala., Sept. 23, 1951; s. Marlen Kenneth Halbrooks Sr. and Carolyn Faye (Hogan) Halbrooks; m. Edna Ruth Whitten, Dec. 30, 1969; children: April Denise, Timothy Wayne. Journeyman in sheet metal. Recipient 1st pl. non-fiction award, Ala. Assn. Nat. League Am. PEN Women, 2001. Methodist.

HALDEMAN, CHARLES WALDO, III, aeronautical engineer; b. Phila., June 9, 1936; s. Charles Waldo Jr. and Anna Freemont (Douglass) H.; m. Louise Stephenson, June 27, 1959; children: Charles Waldo, George Stephenson. BS, MS, MIT, 1959, ScD, 1964. Rsch. asst. MIT Naval Supersonic Lab., Cambridge, Mass., 1959-64; staff engr. MIT Aerophysics Lab., Cambridge, Mass., 1964-79, assoc. dir., 1979-82; staff engr. MIT Lincoln Lab., Lexington, Mass., 1982-87, sr. staff engr., 1987-96, cons., 1996—; sr. scientist Quantum Energy Techs., Woburn, Mass., 1996—2002. V.p. engring., cons. Megatech Corp., Billerica, Mass., 1971-82. Contbr. numerous articles and rsch. papers to scientific jours.; patentee in field including Wavy Tube Heat Pumping, Vacuum Cleaning, Induction Heating, Materials Processing. Avocations: farming, hunting. Office: MIT Lincoln Lab 244 Wood St Lexington MA 02421-6426

HALDEMAN, JOE WILLIAM, novelist; b. Oklahoma City, June 9, 1943; s. Jack Carroll and Lorena (Spivey) H.; m. Mary Gay Potter, Aug. 21, 1965. BS in Physics and Astronomy, U. Md., 1967; MFA in Writing, U. Iowa, 1975. Assoc. prof. writing program MIT, 1983—. Author: War Year, 1972, The Forever War, 1975, Mindbridge, 1976, Planet of Judgment, 1977, All My Sins Remembered, 1977, Infinite Dreams, 1978, World Without End, 1979, Worlds, 1971, (with Jack C. Haldeman II) There Is No Darkness, 1983, Worlds Apart, 1993, Dealing in Futures, 1985, Tool of the Trade, 1987, Buying Time, 1989, The Hemingway Hoax, 1990, Worlds Enough and Time, 1993, 1968, 1995, None So Blind, 1996, Saul's Death and Other Poems, 1997, Forever Peace, 1997, Forever Free, 1999, The Coming, 2000, Guardian, 2002; editor: (with Martin H. Greenburg and Charles Waugh) Body Armor: 2000, 1986, Super-

tanks, 11987, Spacefighters, 1988; editor: Cosmic Laughter, 1974, Study War No More, 1977, Nebula Awards 17, 1983. Served with U.S. Army, 1967-69. Decorated Purple Heart; recipient Hugo award World Sci. Fiction Soc., 1976, 77, 91, 95, 98, Nebula award Sci. Fictions Writers Am., 1975, 91, 93, 98, 2001, Rhysling award Sci. Fiction Poetry Assn., 1984, 91, 2001, World Fantasy award, 1993, John W. Campbell award Sci. Fiction Rsch. Assn., 1998. Mem. Sci. Fiction Writers Am. (treas. 1970-73, chmn. grievance com. 1977-79, pres. 1992-94), Authors Guild, Writers Guild, Poets and Writers, Inc., Nat. Space Inst. E-mail: haldeman@mit.edu.

HALDEMAN, SCOTT, neurology educator; b. June 23, 1943; DC, Palmer Coll. Chiropractic, 1964; BS, U. Pretoria, 1968, MS, 1970; PhD, U. B.C., 1973, MD, 1976. Intern Vancouver Gen. Hosp., 1976-77; resident dept. neurology U. Calif., Irvine, 1977-80; fellow Long Beach (Calif.) VA Med. Ctr., 1980-81; clin. prof. dept. neurology U. Calif., Irvine, 1984—. Adj. prof. rsch. dept. So. Calif. U. Health Scis., 1985—; adj. prof. dept. epidemiology UCLA; pres. The Bone and Joint Decade 2000-2010 task force on neck pain and its assoc. disorders. Sect. editor: The Spine Jour. Mem. N. Am. Spine Soc. (past pres. 1988-89), World Fedn. Chiropractic (chmn. rsch. coun. 1990—). Office: 1125 E 17th St Ste W127 Santa Ana CA 92701-2228 E-mail: HaldemanMD@aol.com.

HALDOPOULOS, MARTHA A. psychologist; b. Gary, Ind., Jan. 15, 1941; d. Robert Burl and Dorothy Eva (Hoover) Miller; m. Peter Haldopoulos, June 13, 1964; children: Christiana Haldopoulos Staffin, Peter Andrew. BA in Psychology, Roosevelt U., 1964, MA in Psychology, 1968. Cert. sch. psychologist, Ill.; cert. instr. Adults and Children Together Against Violence (ACT), N.J. Sch. psychologist Sch. Assn. for Spl. Edn., DuPage County, Ill., 1968-75; clin. psychologist Family Enrichment Program Morristown Meml. Hosp., Morristown, N.J., 1979-90; co-coord., psychotherapist The Survivors Ctr., Morristown, 1990-2000; pvt. practice psychotherapist Psychotherapy Ctr. Morristown, 1990-2000; seminar developer presenter, cons. Family Seminar Svcs., Mendham, N.J., 1983—. Grad. sch. instr. psychology Nat. Coll. Edn., Evanston, Ill., 1970-75; psychologist-play therapist Little Friends Sch., Naperville, Ill., 1970-73, cons. psychologist, 1970-73; expert witness on child abuse/child devel. issues Morris, Sussex and EssexCounty Cts., N.J., 1979-92; dir., psychologist Assn. for the Devel. of Child Abuse Tng. and Edn., Mendham, 1985-98; co-coord., psychologist The Survivors Unit, Morristown, 1986-92; mem. Morris County Multi-Disciplinary Team on Child Abuse Issues, 1987-90; spkr. in field. Contbr. articles to profl. jours. Cons. Juvenile Conf. Com., Mendham, 1980-95. Named Outstanding Cmty. Worker of Yr. in Child Sexual Abuse, Divsn. Youth and Family Svcs., Morris County, 1986, Cmty. Child Care Champion, Children's Svcs. Morris County, Randolph, N.J., 1994. Avocations: sailing, gourmet cooking, gardening, traveling, playing musical instruments. Home: 6 Heather Hill Way Mendham NJ 07945 Office: FSS 6 Heather Hill Way Mendham NJ 07945 E-mail: fss.mah@verizon.net.

HALE, CECIL, communications educator, finance educator; b. St. Louis, Aug. 3, 1945; s. Cecil and Allean (Cunningham) H.; m. Brenda Kidd; children: Juanita, Tasha, Cecil-Jamil, Carolyn. Student, So. Ill. U., 1963-66; MA, Internat. U. of Comm., Washington, 1975; PhD, Union Inst., Cin., 1978; MPA, Harvard U., 1995. Lic. by FCC. Announcer, asst. gen. mgr. WMPP Radio, 1966—68; announcer XPRS Radio, L.A., 1972-74; announcer, asst. program/music dir. WNOV Radio, Milw., 1968-70, WVON Radio, Chgo., 1970-77; nat. dir., mgr. Phonogram/Mercury Records, Chgo., 1977-78; v.p. Capitol Records, Inc., Hollywood, Calif., 1978-81; prof. San Francisco State U., 1984-94, City Coll. San Francisco, 1986—; prof. Mass Media Inst. Stanford U., 1987-92. Cons. N.T.A., Lagos, Nigeria, 1982-83, Gallo Winery, Inc., Modesto, Calif., 1977, Capitol Records, Inc., Hollywood, 1981-82, Congl. Caucus, Washington, 1975. Author: The Music Industry, 1990; exec. producer phono records. Recipient Key to City and City Coun. Resolution, L.A., 1980, Outstanding Tchr. award Acad. Senate, City Coll. San Francisco, 1990, San Francisco State U. Faculty award, 1986; U. Calif. fellow, 1992; honored as Nat. African-Am. History Maker, 2002; fellow NATAS, 2000. Mem.: NEA, AAUP, ABA, NAACP, Kennedy Sch. Exec. Coun., Harvard Alumni Assn., Stanford Alumni Assn., Soc. Values in Higher Edn., Am. Fedn. Tchrs., Am. Fedn. TV and Radio Artists, Am. Fedn. Musicians, Nat. Acad. Recording Arts and Scis., Coun. Black Am. Affairs, Nat. Eagle Scout Assn., Harvard Club San Francisco (ex-officio bd. mem.), Harvard Club N.Y., Masons, Alpha Phi Alpha. Avocations: aviaton, computer science. Home: PO Box 26274 San Francisco CA 94126-2674 Office: City Coll San Francisco 50 Phelan Ave San Francisco CA 94112-1821

HALE, CYNTHIA LYNETTE, religious organization administrator; b. Roanoke, Va., Oct. 27, 1952; BA, Hollins Coll., 1975; MDiv, Duke U., 1979; D in Ministry, United Theol. Sem., Dayton, Ohio, 1991; DD (hon.), Bethany Coll., N.W. Christian Coll. Ordained Disciples of Christ Ch., Va., 1977. Head resident Hollins (Va.) Coll., 1975-76; intern to minister St. Mark's United Meth. Ch., Charlotte, N.C., 1976; undergrad. counselor Office of Minority Affairs Duke U., Durham, N.C., 1976-77; intern to minister Staunton Meml. Ch., Pittsboro, N.C., 1977-78; coordinating counselor summer transitional program Duke U., Durham, N.C., 1978; chaplain Fed. Correctional Instn., Butner, N.C., 1978-83; chaplain, instr. staff tng. acad. Fed. Prison System, Glynco, Ga., 1983-85; pastor, developer Ray of Hope Christian Ch., Decatur, Ga., 1986—; 1st vice moderator Christian Ch. (Disciples of Christ), U.S. and Can., 1993—. Bd. dirs. Coun. on Christian Unity, 1978-81; bd. trustees Disciples Nat. Convocation, 1980-86, pres. 1982-84, pres. ministers' fellowship, 1990—; task force on Renewal and Structural Reform, Disciples of Christ, 1980-87, adminstrv. com. 1982-87, gen. bd., 1982-88; bd. dirs. Disciples Divsn. Higher Edn., St. Louis, 1986-89; bd. trustees Lexington (Ky.) Theol. Sem., 1990—; bd. dirs. Disciples' Nat. Evangelic Assn., 1991—. Mem. Project Impact-Dekalb; bd. dirs. Beulah Heights Bible Coll., Destiny Atlanta.com; mem. governing bd. Nat. Coun. Chs., 1978—83, panel on bio-ethical concerns, 1980—82. Named Outstanding Ga. Citizen and Goodwill Amb., Sec. of State, 2001; recipient Liberation award, Disciples Nat. Conv., 1984, Religion award, DeKalb Br. NAACP, 1990, Religious award for dedicated svc., Ninety-Nine Breakfast Club, award, Martin Luther King's Bd. of Preachers, 1993, Chosen award, Atlanta Gospel Choice, 1998, Profiles of Prominence award, Nat. Women Achievement, 2000, Gospel Honor award, 2000. Mem. Christian Ch. Office: Ray of Hope Christian Ch 2778 Snapfinger Rd Decatur GA 30034-2439 E-mail: kingdominfo@rayofhope.org.

HALE, DANNY LYMAN, financial executive; b. Ft. Lauderdale, Fla., Mar. 23, 1944; s. Thomas Hatten and Marion June (Frizzell) H.; m. Reda Fay Kofahl, June 10, 1966; 1 child, Matthew Bryan. BA in Econs., Yale U., 1966. Cons. in fin. planning Gen. Electric Co., Fairfield, Conn., 1977-78, mgr. fin. stragety devel. Louisville, 1978-79, mgr. fin. ops., 1979-80; mgr. divsn. fin. ops. GE Credit Corp., Stamford, Conn., 1980-82, v.p., dept. gen. mgr., 1982-84; mng. dir., mgr. bus. devel. Kidder Peabody Group, N.Y.C., 1987-88; pres. chase Comml. Corp., Chase Manhattan Bank, Paramus, N.J., 1988-91; exec. v.p. U.S.F. & G. Corp., Balt., 1991, exec. v.p., CFO, 1993-98, Promus Hotel Corp., Memphis, 1999; sr. v.p., CFO Allstate Ins. Co., Northbrook, Ill., 2003—. With U.S. Army, 1967-69. Republican. Congregationalist. Home: 1071 Olmsted Dr Lake Forest IL 60045 Office: Allstate Ins co 2775 Sanders Rd F8 Northbrook IL 60062

HALE, DAVID FREDRICK, biotechnologist; b. Gadsden, Ala., Jan. 8, 1949; s. Millard and Mildred Earline (McElroy) Hale; m. Linda Carol Sadorski, Mar. 14, 1975; children: Shane Michael, Tara Renee, Erin Nicole, David Garrett. BA, Jacksonville State U. Dir. mktg. Ortho Pharm. Corp. divsn. Johnson & Johnson, Raritan, NJ, 1978-80; v.p. mktg. BBL Microbiology Sys. divsn. Becton Dickinson & Co., Cockeysville, Md., 1980-81, v.p., gen. mgr., 1981-82; sr. v.p. mktg. and bus. devel. Hybritech, Inc., San Diego, 1982, pres., 1983-86, CEO, 1986-87; pres., CEO Gensia Sicor, Inc., San Diego, 1987-97, Women First HealthCare, Inc., 1998-2000, also bd. dirs.; pres., CEO, dir. CancerVax Corp., Carlsbad, Calif., 2000—. Bd. dirs. LMA N.Am., Metabasis Therapeutics, Santarus, Inc., XCEL Pharms., Skin Medica, BIO Emerging Growth Sect. Bd., Children's Hosp., San Diego Econ. Devel. Corp., Biocom San Diego, Calif. HealthCare Inst.; founder CONNECT. Mem. World Pres.'s Orgn., Chief Exec.'s Orgn. Republican. Episcopalian. Home: PO Box 8925 17079 Circa del Sur Rancho Santa Fe CA 92067 Office: CancerVax Corp 2110 Rutherford Rd Carlsbad CA 92008

HALE, DEAN EDWARD, social services administrator; b. Balt., Aug. 4, 1950; s. James Russell and Marjorie Elinor (Hoerman) H.; m. Lucinda Hoyt Muniz, 1979; children: Christopher Deane, Lydia Alice JeeSoo. BA in Social Work, U. Pa., 1975; postgrad., U. London, 1974, U. Oreg., 1976; MSW, Portland State U., 2000. Dir. recreation Hoffman Homes for Children, Gettysburg, Pa., 1970; social worker Holt Adoption Program, Inc., Eugene, Oreg., 1975-78; supr. social svcs. Holt Internat. Children's Svcs., Eugene, 1978-84, Asia rep., 1984-90, program mgr., 1990-94, interim dir. internat. programs, 1994-95, dir. China, 1995-97, dir. social svcs. for India, 1997—. Guest lectr. U. Oreg.; cons. internat. child welfare, 1982—; co-founder Family Opportunities Unltd. Inc., 1981—. Author: Adoption, A Family Affair, 1981, When Your Child Comes Home, 1986, India Adoption Guidebook, 2003. Pres. Woodtique Heights Homeowners Assn., 1980-91, also bd. dirs.; pres. Our Saviour's Luth. Ch., 1981-85; bd. dirs. Greenpeace of Oreg., 1979-84; cons., campaign worker Defazio for Congress, 1988, 87-98; mem. Westside Neighborhood Quality Project, 1988. Named Outstanding New Jaycee, Gettysburg Jaycees, 1971. Mem.: NASW (bd. dirs. 1978—80, sec. 1979—80). Home: 2811 Tandy Turn Eugene OR 97401-5193 Office: PO Box 2880 1195 City View St Eugene OR 97402-3325 Fax: 541-683-4339. E-mail: deanh@holhntl.org.

HALE, FRANCIS JOSEPH, engineering educator, consultant, retired military officer; b. Manila, Philippines, Oct. 24, 1922; s. Harold Francis and Teresa Mary (Vaughan) H.; m. Frances Eugenia Keller, Apr. 23, 1949 (div.); children: Francis J. III, Olin T., Margaret Anne; m. Mary Alice Longcrier, July 19, 1980. BS, U.S. Mil. Acad., 1944; SM, MIT, 1952, ScD, 1963. Registered profl. engr., N.C. Commd. 2nd lt. USAF, 1944, advanced through grades to col., 1961; prof., head dept astronautics USAF Acad., Colo., 1962-63; ret. USAF, 1965; prof. mech. and aerospace engring. N.C. State U., Raleigh, 1965-89, prof. emeritus, 1989—. Vis. prof. mech. engring. Middle East Tech. U., Ankara, Turkey, 1973-74; vis. prof. mechanics U.S. Mil. Acad., West Point, N.Y., 1977-78; vis. prof. aerospace engring. U.S. Naval Acad. Annapolis, Md., 1990-91; tech. dir. Desalination Test Facility, Wrightsville Beach, N.C., 1981-82. Author: Introduction to Control System Analysis and Design, 2d edit., 1988, Introduction to Aircraft Performance, Selection and Design, 1984, Introduction to Space Flight, 1994; co-author: Thermodynamics for Engineers, 1984. Fellow AIAA (assoc.); mem. ASME, Soc. Automotive Engrs. (Ralph R. Teeter Ednl. award 1985), Order of Daedalians. Home: 2853 Rue Sans Famille Raleigh NC 27607-3048 Office: NC State U PO Box 7910 Raleigh NC 27695

HALE, HELENE H. state representative; b. Mpls., Mar. 23, 1918; children: Indira, William. BA, U. of Minn., 1938, MA, 1940. Supr. Hawaii County Bd. of Suprs., 1955—63; pres. Hawaii Isle Realty, Ltd., 1969—2000; rep. Hawaii State House, 2000—; tchr., lectr. Tenn. A&I State Coll., San Diego State Coll., Konawaena HS, U. of Hawaii-Hilo. Bd. suprs., mem. County of Hawaii, 1955—63, chmn., exec. officer, 1963—65; del. Hawaii State Constl. Conv., 1978; mem. Hawaii County Coun., 1980—84, 1988—92, 1992—94. Pres. Hawaii County YWCA Bd. of Dirs., 1973. Mem.: Hawaii County League of Women Voters (pres. 1995), Hawaii County Bd. of Realtors (pres. 1975), Hawaii State Fedn. of Women's Clubs (pres. 1999). Democrat. Office: State Capital Rm 331 415 S Beretania St Honolulu HI 96813 Fax: 808-586-6531. E-mail: rephale@Capital.hawaii.gov.*

HALE, JACK K. mathematics educator, research center administrator; b. Dudley, Ky., Oct. 3, 1928; s. James Marion and Cora Lee (Kelly) H.; m. Hazel Reynolds. BA in Math., Berea Coll., 1949; PhD in Math., Purdue U., 1953; DSc (hon.), Rijksuniveriteit-Gent, Belgium, 1983; doctor honoris causa, Stuttgart U., Federal Republic of Germany, 1988, Tech. U. Lisbon, 1991, Rostoch U., Federal Rep. Germany, 1999, Clark U., 2000. Instr. Purdue U., West Lafayette, Ind., 1949-54; with Sandia Corp., Albuquerque, 1954-57, Remington-Rand Univac, St. Paul, 1957-58, Rsch. Inst. for Advanced Study, Balt., 1958-64; prof. div. applied math. Brown U., Providence, 1964-89, chmn., 1973-76; Regents' prof. Ga. Inst. Tech., Atlanta, 1988-98, dir. Ctr. for Dynamical Systems and Nonlinear Studies, 1989-98, regents prof. emeritus, 1998—. Author: Oscillations in Nonlinear Systems, 1963, Functional Differential Equations, 1977, Ordinary Differential Equations, 1978, Methods of Bifurcate Theory, 1982, Introduction of Infinite Dimensional Dynamic Systems, 1984, Asymptomatic Behavior of Dissip. Systems, 1988, Dynamics and Bifurcation, 1992, Introduction to Functional Differential Equations, 1993; editor in chief Jour. Differential Equations, 1981—. Recipient Chauvenet prize Math. Assn. Am., 1965; Guggeheim fellow, 1979-80; disting. alumnus, Purdue, U., Berea Coll. Fellow Royal Soc. Edinburgh (hon.), Brazilian Acad. Sci. (corr.); mem. Polish Acad. Sci. (fgn.), Am. Math. Soc., Am. Acad. Mechanics, Brazilian Math. Soc. Home: 1480 Rainer Falls Dr NE Atlanta GA 30329-4104 Office: Dynamical Systems and Nonlinear Studies Ga Inst Tech Ctr Atlanta GA 30332-0001

HALE, JANE ALISON, French and comparative literature educator; b. Washington, Sept. 29, 1948; BA in French magna cum laude, Coll. William and Mary, 1970; MST in Edn., U. Chgo., 1974; MA in French, Stanford U., 1981; postgrad., Ecole Normale Supérieure de Jeunes Filles, Paris, 1981-82; PhD with distinction, Stanford U., 1984. Student tchg. supr., counselor Peace Corps Tng. Program, Ft. Archambault, Chad, 1971; tchr. French, cross-cultural coord. Peace Corps Tng. Ctr., St. Thomas, V.I., 1972; Peace Corps vol., tchr. English as fgn. lang. Lycée Franco-Arabe, Abéché, Chad, 1970-72; tchr. 2d grade Pleasant Grove Union Elem. Sch., Burlington, N.C., 1974-77; tchg. fellow in French Stanford U., 1982-83; tchr. French Inst. Intensive French, U. Fla., 1986-88; asst. prof. French and comparative lit. Brandeis U., Waltham, Mass., 1985-91, assoc. prof. French and comparative lit., 1991—. Presenter Internat. Conf. on TV Drama at Mich. State U., 1985, Samuel Beckett at 80 at U. Stirling, Scotland, 1986, Internat. Colloquium on Raymond Queneau, Thionville, France, 1990, Internat. Vian-Queneau-Prévert Colloquium at U. Victoria, Can., 1992, Internat. Symposium on Beckett in the 1990s, The Hague, 1992, MLA, N.Y.C., 1992, West Africa Rsch. Assn. Internat. Symposium, Dakar, Senegal, 1997, African Literature Assn., Fès, Morocco, 1999, Internat. Colloquium on Feminist Rsch. in French, Dakar, Senegal, 1999. Author: The Broken Window: Beckett's Dramatic Perspective, 1987, The Lyric Encyclopedia of Raymond Queneau, 1989; contbr. chpts. to books and articles to profl. jours. French Govt. scholar, 1981-82, Fulbright Sr. scholar, Senegal, 1993-94; Whiting fellow in the humanities, 1983-84, Dana faculty fellow Brandeis U., 1985-90, Bernstein faculty fellow Brandeis U., 1989, Marion and Jasper Whiting fellow, 1994-98; NEH travel grantee, 1988, Mazer grantee for faculty rsch. Brandeis U., 1990; recipient Lerman-Neubauer prize for excellence in tchg. and counseling, 2001. Mem. Samuel Beckett Soc. (exec. bd. dirs. 1989-92), Les Amis de Valentin Brû, Phi Beta Kappa. Office: Brandeis U Dept Romance & Comp Lit MS 024 Waltham MA 02454 E-mail: jhale@brandeis.edu.

HALE, JANET, federal agency administrator; b. Buffalo, Apr. 2, 1949; d. Herman Haltom and Rachel (Townes) H. BS, Miami U., Oxford, Ohio, 1971; M.P.A., Harvard U., 1980. Adminstrv. asst. State Rep. Tom Gallagher of Fla., Washington, 1974-76; research asst. House Republican Com., Washington, 1976-77; spl. asst. Senator Edward Brooke, Boston, 1977-79; spl. asst. to sec., dir. exec. secretariat HUD, Washington, 1981-82, dep. asst. sec. for policy, fin. mgmt. and adminstrn., 1982-86; asst. sec. Dept. of Transportation, Washington, 1986—89; Asst. Sec. Budget, Tech., and Finance Dept HHS, Washington, 2002—03; Under Sec. Mgmt. Dept. Homeland Security, 2003—. Bd. dirs. Big Sisters Boston, 1978-80 Avocation: tennis. Office: Navel Security Station Nebraska & Massachusetts Ave NW Washington DC 20393*

HALE, JOSEPH RICE, church organization executive; b. Texarkana, Tex., Mar. 25, 1935; s. Alfred Clay and Bess (Akin) H.; m. Mary Richey, June 2, 1964; 1 son, Jeffrey Glen. BA, Asbury Coll., Wilmore, Ky., 1957; BD, So. Methodist U., 1960; DD, Asbury Theol. Sem., 1978; LHD (hon.), Fla. So. Coll., 1994. Ordained to ministry Meth. Ch., 1958. Pastor Meth. Ch., Sunset, Tex., 1958-60; evangelist, 1960-66; assoc. dir. dept. evangelism Bd. Evangelism, Meth. Ch., 1966-68, dir. ecumenical evangelism, 1968-74; dir. evangelization devel. Bd. Discipleship, United Meth. Ch., 1975-76; gen. sec. World Meth. Coun., 1976—2001, gen. sec. emeritus, 2001. Exec. com. Key 73, 1970-73; sec. working group evangelism Nat. Coun. Chs., 1972; pres. Comm. Found., Inc., 1974-75; world amb. Internat. Prayer Fellowship, 1974; exec. com. Evangelization Forum, 1973-75; registrar World Meth. Evangelism Convocation, Jerusalem, 1974; mem. Conf. Secs. Christian World Communions, 1976—, chmn. Christian World Communions, 1983-86. Author: Design for Evangelism, 1970, Christ Matters!, 1971, God's Moment, 1972; contbr. articles to profl. jours.; producer: The Spirit is Moving, 1980 (video prodn.) Roots of Faith, 1979, To Live to God, 1984, Nairobi, 1986, Singapore, 1991, Rio de Janeiro,1996, Rio: Walking in the Spirit, 1996, One People In All the World, 1996; editor proc. 13th-17th World Meth. Confs. Decorated Great Cross of Merit, Equestrian Order of the Holy Sepulchre in Jerusalem; recipient Key to City of Daytona Beach Fla., 1963-64, Asbury Coll. Alumni award, 1977, Disting. Svc. award Christian Meth. Episcopal Ch., 1994, Gen. Commn. on Archives and History United Meth. Ch., 2002, Philip award Nat. Assn. United Meth. Evangelists, 1998; named Ky. col., 1977, Ecumenical Svc. award Gen. Commn. on Christian Unity United Meth. Ch., 2000, World Meth. Peace award World Meth. Coun., 2001; named Disting. Evangelist, United Meth. Ch., 2001, Disting. Alumnus, Perkins Sch. Theology So. Meth. U., 2002. Methodist. Home and Office: 34 Forest Park Dr Waynesville NC 28785

HALE, JUDSON DRAKE, SR., editor, writer; b. Boston, Mar. 16, 1933; s. Roger Drake and Marian (Sagendorph) H.; m. Sara Huberlie, Sept. 6, 1958; children: Judson Drake, Daniel, Christopher. BA, Dartmouth Coll., 1958; D Journalism (hon.), New Eng. Coll., 1984; LittD (hon.), Franklin Pierce Coll., 1987; LHD (hon.), Keene State Coll., 1989. Asst. editor Yankee, Inc., Dublin, N.H., 1958-61, assoc. editor, 1961-63, mng. editor, 1963-69; editor-in-chief Yankee Mag., Old Farmers Almanac; sr. v.p. Yankee Pub. Inc., Dublin, 1969—. Editor, v.p. Old Farmers Almanac. Author: Inside New England, 1982, The Education of a Yankee, 1987; editor: That New England, 1968; editor The Best of Yankee mag., 1985, The Best of the Old Farmer's Almanac, 1991, The Old Farmer's Almanac Book of Everyday Advice. Trustee MacDowell Colony. Served with AUS, 1955-57. Mem.: Mass. Hist. Soc., Cheshire County Dartmouth Alumni Club, Phi Kappa Psi. Democrat. Episcopalian. Home: Valley Rd Dublin NH 03444 Office: Yankee Pub Inc Main St Dublin NH 03444-0520 E-mail: judh@yankeepub.com.

HALE, KAYCEE, research marketing professional; b. Mount Hope, W.Va., July 18, 1947; d. Bernard McFadden and Virginia Lucille (Mosley) H. AA, Compton Coll., 1965; BS, Calif. State U., Dominguez Hills, 1981. Fashion model O'Bryant Talent Agy., L.A., 1967-77; faculty mem. L.A. Trade-Tech. Coll., 1969-71, Fashion Inst., L.A., 1969-77, 1975—; pres. The Fashion Co., L.A., 1970-75; co-host The Fashion Game TV Show, L.A., 1982-87; exec. dir. Fashion Inst. Design and Merchandising Resource & Rsch. Ctr., L.A., 1975—, Fashion Inst. Design and Merchandising Mus. and Libr., L.A., 1977-98. Lectr. in field, internat., 1969—. Author: (brochure) What's Your I.Q. (Image Quotient)?; (tape) Image Builders; contbg. editor Library Management in Review; columnist The Public Image, 1990; contbr. Bowker Annual 1990-91, (newsletter) Northeast Library System, 1991. Adv. bd. Calif. State U., Long Beach, 1988-91. Mem. ALA, Spl. Librs. Assn. (pres. elect 1986—, pres. 1987-88, bd. dirs. So. Calif. chpt. 1985—), Spl. Librs. Adv. Coun. (pub. rels. com. 1987-89), SLA Libr. Mgmt. Div. (chmn.-elect 1987-88, chmn. 1988-89, pres.'s task force on image of libr./info. profl.), Textile Assn. L.A. (bd. dirs. 1985-87), Calif. Media and Libr. Educators Assn., Am. Mktg. Assn., Western Mus. Conf., Am. Mus. Assn., Costume Soc. Am. Office: Fashion Inst Design & Merchandising 919 S Grand Ave Los Angeles CA 90015-1421

HALE, LOUIS DEWITT, lawyer; b. Caddo Mills, Tex., June 10, 1917; s. Ernest Louis and Ethel M. (Massay) H.; m. Carol Gene Moore, June 8, 1947; children: Janet Sue Hale Wilde, Nancy Carol Hale (dec.). BA, U. Tex., 1937, MA, 1940. Bar: Tex. 1940, U.S. Dist. Ct. (so. dist.) Tex. 1947, U.S. Ct. Appeals (5th cir.) 1974, U.S. Supreme Ct. 1946. Classification analyst Office Emergency Mgmt., Washington, 1941-42; classification officer Office Def. Transp., Washington, 1942-43; pvt. practice Corpus Christi, Tex., 1946—81, Austin, Tex., 1981—. State rep. Tex. Legislature, 1939-40, 53-62, 65-78, spkr. pro tempore, 1961-62, chmn. jud. com., 1961-62, 69-74; gen. counsel House Gen. Investigating Com., Austin, 1989-92, Tex. Assn. Builders, Austin, 1978-81. Author: Streamlining Texas Judiciary, 1972; contbr. articles to profl. jours. Mem. Tex. Jud. Coun., Austin, 1961-65, 69-81; chmn. jud. com. Tex. Constnl. Conv., Austin, 1974. With USAF, 1943-46, res. 1947-73, ret. lt. col. Recipient Disting. Svc. award Jr. C. of C., 1952. Mem. ABA, State Bar Tex. (Disting. Svc. award 1971, 73, 75), Tex. Assn. Builders (hon. life), Tex. State Tchrs. Assn. (hon. life, Disting. Svc. award 1961). Democrat. Baptist. Avocations; public speaking, historical research, coin collecting. Home: 7106 Montana Norte Austin TX 78731-2124 Office: 5808 Balcones Dr Ste 101 Austin TX 78731-4276

HALE, MARIE STONER, artistic director; b. Greenwood, Miss. Student in Piano, U. Miss., Hattiesburg; studied with Richard Ellis, Christine du Boulay, Jo-Anna Kneeland, David Howard. Tchr. Ellis/du Boulay Sch., Chgo., Jo-Anna Kneeland Imperial Studios, Palm Beach County, Fla.; co-founder Ballet Arts Found., West Palm Beach, Fla., 1973-86; co-founder, artistic dir. Ballet Fla., West Palm Beach, 1986—. Office: Ballet Fla 500 Fern St West Palm Beach FL 33401-5726*

HALE, MARSHA BENTLEY, real estate rehabilitator, song writer, mannequin historian; b. Santa Monica, Calif., Dec. 23, 1951; d. Marvin Addison Kempf and Margery Edith Hale; m. Douglas Eugene Marx. Student, UCLA, 1977-79; BFA in Film and Video, Calif. Inst. Arts, 1981. Co-owner Designer's Workshop, Beverly Hills, Calif., 1972-75, The Latticemakers, Westwood, Calif., 1975-76; owner Nat. Design Cons., 1976-86; mannequin historian, 1978—; CEO Vidi Vici, Inc., 1986-2003; contbg. writer FashionWindows.com, 2003--; animation archivist Amblin Entertainment, MCA Universal, 20th Century Fox, Dreamworks SKG, 1986-96; with Land Restoration & Design, Malibu, Calif., 1995—; songwriter Bentley Hale Prodns. (now Whirlwind Music LLC), 1996—; contbr. articles to profl. jours. Avocations: ocean, mountains, travel, cultural arts. Office: PO Box 97493 Las Vegas NV 89193-7493 E-mail: writingpen@aol.com.

HALE, MARTIN DE MORA, investor; b. N.Y.C., Jan. 29, 1941; s. Charles S. and Carmen Rosa (de Mora) H.; m. Deborah Campbell, Sept. 27, 1969; children: Charles, Martin de Mora Jr. Grad., Yale U., 1962; MBA, Harvard U., 1967. Chmn. bd. dirs. Great Lakes Chem. Corp., West Lafayette, Ind., 1994—2000; pres., CEO Putnam Mgmt. Co., Boston, 1981-83; exec. v.p., dir. Hellman, Jordan, Boston, 1983—2002. Bd. dirs. Octel Corp., Great Lakes Chem. Corp. Trustee Mus. Fine Arts, 1994—. 1st lt. U.S. Army, 1965. Avocations: contemporary art, contemporary crafts. Office: Hellman Jordan Mgmt Co 75 State St Boston MA 02109-1829 E-mail: mhale@hellmanjordan.com.

HALE, NATHAN CABOT, sculptor, artist, poet; b. L.A., July 5, 1925; s. Nathan Cabot Hale, Virginia Markoe Ferris; m. Alison Elizabeth Boothby, Dec. 27, 1964; children: Terri Dean, Lisa Jenny Rose. BS, Empire State Coll., 1973; PhD, The Union Inst., Cin., 1976. Instr. sculpture Pratt Inst., Bklyn., 1960; instr. anatomy and the elements of drawing Art Students League of N.Y., 1975—86; instr. sculpture Nat. Acad. Schulpture, N.Y.C., 1985. Dir. The Ages of Man Found., 1968—; lectr. in field; cons. in field; instr. drawing and anatomy Art Student's League, 1985—90; sr. editor Art World, 1985—89. Author: Creating Welded Sculpture, 1968, 1994, The Embrace of Life, 1969, Abstraction in Art and Nature, 1972, 1993, The Birth of a Family, 1979, The Spirit of Man, 1981, (book of poetry) Fox Tails, 1993, (book of fables) The Elephant's Peaceable Kingdom, On the Perception of Human Form in Sculpture, 2000; contbr. ; one-man shows include Felix Landau Gallery, L.A., 1957, Washington Irving Gallery, N.Y., 1960, Feingarten Gallery, Chgo., 1961, N.Y., 1961, Midtown Galleries, 1964, Hazelton Art League, Pa., 1966, Mus. of Ft. Wayne, Ind., 1966, Queens Coll., N.Y., 1966, NYU, 1967, Franklin and Marshall Coll., 1967, Midtown Galleries, N.Y., 1968, Quinata Gallery, Nantucket, 1968, Midtown Galleries, N.Y., 1973, exhibited in group shows at L.A. County Mus., Colo. Springs Fine Art Ctr., Norfolk Mus., Lehigh Univ., Philbrook Art Ctr., Ball State Univ., Hunterdon Art Ctr., Albright-Knox Art Gallery, Herron Mus. of Art, Davenport Mcpl. Art Gallery, Corcoran Gallery, Wayne State U., Pace Coll., Audubon Artists, Nat. Acad. Design, Columbus Gallery of Fine Art, Stamford Mus., Joslyn Mus., Springfield Mus. of Fine Art, Heckscher Mus., The Gallery of Modern Art. Dir. Ages of Man Found., 1969—. With USMC, 1941—42, with U.S. Merchant Marine, 1944—45. Recipient Purchase award in sculpture, L.A. County Mus., 1955, Silver medal, Audubon Soc. Sculpture, 1972. Fellow: Nat. Sculpture Soc.; mem.: Nat. Acad. Design (Gold medal in sculpture 1990), Century Assn. Avocations: sailing, fly fishing. Mailing: 57 Sheffield Rd Amenia NY 12501

HALE, NATHAN ROBERT, architect; b. Battle Creek, Mich., July 20, 1944; s. Nathan Shirley and Gertrude Anges (Barnes) H.; m. CarolAnn Purrington, May 28, 1966; children: Marilyce, Maile, Martha. BA, Syracuse U., 1967, BArch, 1971. Dir. Archs. Hawaii, Honolulu, 1971—. Served with AUS, 1968-70, Vietnam. Mem. AIA (bd. dirs. 1984, pres. 1992), Hawii C. of C. (exec. com. 1994-99), Econ. Devel. Corp. Honolulu (chair 1993-96, bd. dirs. 1982—), Rotary Club (bd. dirs. 1986-88), Friends of Children's Advocacy Ctr. (pres. 1991, 93, bd. dirs., 1986—). Office: Architects Hawaii Ltd Pacific Tower 300 1001 Bishop St Honolulu HI 96813-3429

HALE, RICHARD LEE, magazine editor; b. Formoso, Kans., Jan. 3, 1930; s. Glenn Becton and Ruby Tiarena (Johnson) H.; m. Nancy June Craig, Feb. 22, 1953; children— Steven Craig, Kristin Lee Hale Shurtz, Michael John, Sarah Johanna Hale Wilcher. BS in Journalism, U. Kans., 1952. Editor Bird City (Kans.) Times, 1955-58; editor, pub. St. Francis Herald, Kans., 1958-74; editor Golf Course Mgmt., Lawrence, Kans., 1974-76, PGA Mag., Palm Beach Gardens, Fla., 1976-80; dir. comm. GCSAA, Lawrence, 1980-82; editor Dental Econs., Penn Well Pub. Co., Tulsa, 1982-97, pub., 1989-97. Editor: (ann.) PGA Book of Golf, 1977-80; cons. editor Odontos Pub. Co., 1997-2002. Chmn. local com. Boy Scouts Am., St. Francis, 1970-74; trustee Trinity United Meth. Ch., Palm Beach Gardens, 1979-80, Am. Fund for Dental Health, 1989—. Spl. agt. CIC, U.S. Army, 1952-54. St. Francis Herald named Best Weekly Newspaper Kans. Press Assn., 1962. Mem. Am. Assn. Dental Editors, Am. Fund for Dental Health (trustee, advisor 1989-93), Kans. Press Assn. (bd. dirs. 1973-74), Golf Writers Assn. Am., Riverside Country Club (St. Francis; pres. 1971), Rotary (pres. local chpt. 1970), Alvamar Country Club (pres. 2003). Democrat. Methodist. Avocations: golf, travel, nature walks. Home: 5000 W 18th St Lawrence KS 66047 E-mail: dhale1@juno.com.

HALE, ROBERT FARGO, government consultant; b. Jan. 21, 1947; s. William David and Elizabeth (Wells) H.; m. Susan Kohn, June 23, 1973; children: Scott, Michael. BS with hons., Stanford U., 1968, MS, 1969; MBA, George Washington U., 1976. Cert. Def. Fin. Mgr., Am. Soc. Mil. Comptrollers. Analyst, study dir. Ctr. for Naval Analysis, Washington, 1972-75; analyst Congl. Budget Office, Washington, 1975-78, dep. asst. dir., 1978-81, asst. dir. def. issues, 1981-94; asst. sec. fin. mgmt. USAF, Washington, 1994-2001; program dir. and sr. fellow Logistics Mgmt. Inst., Washington, 2001—. Nat. pres. and v.p. Am. Soc. Mil. Comptrollers; mem. bus. practices implementation bd. Sec. Defense. Served to lt. (j.g.) USNR, 1969-72. Fellow: Nat. Acad. Pub. Adminstrn.; mem.: Nat. Contract Mgmt. Assn., Am. Soc. Mil. Comptrollers, Assn. Govt. Accts., Phi Beta Kappa. Jewish. Home: 3357 Taleen Ct Annandale VA 22003-1161 Office: LMI 2000 Corporate Ridge Rd Mc Lean VA 22102-7805 E-mail: rhale@lmi.org.

HALE, ROGER LOUCKS, manufacturing company executive; b. Plainfield, N.J., Dec. 13, 1934; s. Lloyd and Elizabeth (Adams) H.; m. Sandra Johnston, June 10, 1961 (div.); children: Jocelyn, Leslie, Nina, Deirdre; m. Eleanor L. Hall, Nov. 24, 1989. BA, Brown U., 1956; MBA, Harvard U., 1961. With Tennant Co., Mpls., 1961-99, pres., CEO, 1975-98, chmn., CEO, 1998-99, chmn., 1999, bd. dirs., VisionShare, Inc., 2001—. Bd. dirs. Walker Art Ctr., 1970—, pres., 1978-80, 2002—, bd. dirs. Ploughshares Fund, 1996—, vice chmn; Neighborhood Employment Network, 1980; bd. dirs., chmn. Pub. Radio Internat., 1990, 2003; chmn. Minn. Bus. Partnership, 1993-95; chmn. Gov.'s Workforce Devel. Coun. Named Exec. of Yr., Corp. Report mag., 1988, One of Minn.'s 5 Outstanding Corp. Dirs., Twin Cities Bus. Monthly, 1996; recipient Mpls. Spl. Recognition award for Svc. to City of Mpls., 1993. Office: Union Plz 333 Washington Ave N Ste 313 Minneapolis MN 55401-1364

HALE, ROGER W. utilities company executive; b. 1943; BA, U. Md., 1965; MS, Mass. Inst. Tech., 1979. V.p. mktg. southern region AT&T, Atlanta, 1966-86; group v.p. BellSouth Corp, 1986-89, exec. v.p., 1988-89; pres., CEO LG&E Energy Corp, 1989-92, bd. chmn., CEO, 1992—. With USAF, 1966. Office: LG&E Energy Corp 220 W Main St Louisville KY 40202-1395

HALE, THOMAS MORGAN, professional services executive; b. Syracuse, N.Y., Nov. 29, 1936; s. Thomas Morgan and Ruth Ingrid (Stangeland) H.; m. Marilyn Johnson, June 12, 1959 (div. Aug. 1980), m. Linda Diana Pappas, Feb. 12, 1981; Children: Rodney, Kenneth, Timothy, Marilee. BS, Fla. State U., 1959; MA, U. Houston, 1967; DPA, George Mason U., 1990; diploma, Nat. War Coll., D.C., 1980. Commd. ensign USN, 1959, advanced through the grades to capt., 1983; served on destroyers, ops. officer USS Sampson, 1963-65; assoc. prof. naval sci. Tex. A&M U., 1965-67; chief staff officer, comdr. Destroyer Squadron Five, 1967-71; with Bur. of Naval Personnel, 1971-74; comdg. officer USS Paul, 1974-76; staff, chief naval ops., chmn. Joint Chiefs of Staff, 1976-83; ret. USN, 1983; sr. mgr. RCI, Vienna, Va., 1983-87, v.p., 1987-96, divsn. gen. mgr., 1992-96, sr. v.p., 1996—. Qualified expert witness Federal Dist. Ct. System. Contbr to profl. jours. Recipient Legion of Merit award Sec. of the U.S. Navy, 1983. Mem. U.S. Naval Inst. (life), Assn. Career Mgmt. Firms N. Am. (bd. dirs. 1998-2003), The Retired Officer's Assn. (life), The Tower Club (life), Army Navy Country Club. Methodist. Home: 3783 Center Way Fairfax VA 22033-2602 Office: RCI 2650 Park Tower Dr Vienna VA 22180 E-mail: thomash463@aol.com.

HALE, THOMAS WALTER, emergency medicine physician; b. Scottsbluff, Nebr., Feb. 14, 1954; MD, U. Nebr., 1980. Cert. in emergency medicine. Intern UCLA Med. Ctr., Torrance, Calif., 1980-81, resident in emergency medicine, 1981-83; mem. hosp. governing bd. Twin Cities Cmty. Hosp., Templeton, Calif., pvt. practice, 1984—, mem. hosp. governing bd., 1991—, chmn., 1994-95, chief of staff, 1997-98. Mem. County Health Commn., San Luis Obispo, 2002—; mem. access to care task force Future Vision, 2003. Fellow Am. Coll. Emergency Physicians, Am. Acad. Emergency Med.; mem. Am. Acad. Emergency Medicine, Calif. Coll. Emergency Physicians, Calif. Med. Assn., San Luis Obispo County Med. Soc. Home: 8375 Los Osos Rd Atascadero CA 93422-4728 Office: PO Box 87 Templeton CA 93465-0087

HALE, TODD BENJAMIN, military officer, electrical engineer; b. Daytona Beach, FL, Sept. 23, 1971; s. Richard Wayne Hale, Sylvia Rose Hale. BSEE, Milw. Sch. Engring., 1993; MSEE, Air Force Inst. Tech., 1997, PhD in Elec. Engring., 2002. Commd. officer USAF, 1993, advanced through grades to capt., B-52 test engr. 513th Engring. and Test Squadron, 1993—96, radar signal processing rsch. engr. Air Force Rsch. Lab. Rome, NY, 1997—99; asst. prof. elec. engring. Air Force Inst. Tech., Wright-Patterson AFB, Ohio, 2002—. Mem.: IEEE.

HALE, WILLIAM BRYAN, JR., newspaper editor; b. Stephenville, Tex., Apr. 26, 1933; s. William Bryan and Gladys (Tittle) H.; divorced; children: Shandra Hale Reiss, Tamara Hale Cameron, Nicholas, Sabrina. Student, UCLA, 1953-54. Police beat/courts reporter Santa Monica (Calif.) Outlook, 1953-58; gen. reporter Ontario (Calif.) Daily Report, 1958-59; criminal court writer L.A. City News Service, 1959-60; gen. reporter L.A. Times, 1960-61; reporter Houston Chronicle, 1961-62; news editor Somerset (Pa.) American, 1962-63; night editor Elmira (N.Y.) Star-Gazette, 1963-64; copy editor, investigative reporter Milw. Jour., 1964-70; Tucson corr. Time mag./Time-Life Books, 1970-71; night city editor Tucson Citizen, 1970-71; nat. desk copy editor Los Angeles Times, 1971-90; sr. lectr. U. So. Calif., 1974-88; pres. Nat. Copy Editors Sch., Thousand Oaks, Calif., 1984-90; founder and dir. Australian Sub-Editors Sch., Sydney, Australia, 1989-94. Cpl. USMC, 1951-53. Avocations: horseback riding, hiking. Home: PO Box 35128 Tucson AZ 85740-5128

HALE, WILLIAM GRANT, veterinarian, educator; b. Princeton, W.Va., Sept. 26, 1959; s. William Grant and Barbara Ann Hale; children: Stefani Rochelle, Sherri Vanessa. MS in Mgmt., Troy State U., 1994; D in Bus. Adminstrn., Nova Southeastern U., 2003. Vet. br. supr. Ft. Meade Vet. Svcs., Fort Meade, 1994—98; chief enlisted instr. Amedd C&S, Dvs, Fort Sam Houston, Tex., 1998—; faculty bus. U. Incarnate Word, San Antonio, 1999—2000; master sgt. U.S. Army, 1986—. Editl. bd.: Outlook Jour. Decorated Meritorious Svc. Medal with one bronze oak leaf cluster US Army. Mem.: Acad. Mgmt. (assoc.). Home: 509 Olney Drive San Antonio TX 78209 Office: Department of Veterinary Science 2250 Stanley Road Suite 270 San Antonio TX 78234 Office Fax: 210-221-8127.

HALEN, WALTER JOHN, music educator, composer; b. Hamilton, Ohio, Mar. 17, 1930; s. John Martin and Gertrude Elizabeth (Zünndorf) Halen; m. Thalia Ruth Sims, Aug. 15, 1952; children: Eric John, David Walter. BMus, Miami U., Oxford, Ohio, 1952; M. Fine Art, Ohio U., 1953; PhD, Ohio State U., 1969; postgrad., Northwestern U., Evanston, Ill., 1958—61. Cert. tchr. Ohio. Dir. orch. and choir Celina Pub. Schs., Ohio, 1955—56; dir. orch. Bellevue Pub. Schs., Ohio, 1956—61; asst. prof. Drury Coll., Springfield, Mo., 1962—67; prof. music Ctrl. Mo. State U., Warrensburg, Mo., 1967—89, prof. emeritus, 1989—; pvt. tchr., cons. Lee's Summit, 1989—2000, Houston, 2000—. Concertmaster Springfield Symphony, 1962—66. Composer: (music ensemble) Two Poems of Dance, 1976, (string orch.) Two Tableaux, 1990; composer: (author) (method books) Etudes in Positions - Violin/Viola, 1996; composer: over 50 compositions including many commns. for large variety of media. Violist/violinist Toledo Orch., 1956—57; choir dir. United Ch. of Christ, Bellevue, Ohio, 1956—61; founder, dir. Bellevue String Ensemble, 1959—61. With U.S. Army, 1953—55. Named Composer of the Yr., Mo. Music Tchrs. Assn., 1976, recipient Achievement in Music award, Ohio U. Alumni Assn., Arts and Scis. Disting. Faculty award, Ctrl. Mo. State U., 1988, Byler Disting. Svc. award, 1989. Mem.: ASCAP, Music Educators Nat. Conf., Music Tchrs. Nat. Assn. (composition commn. chair 1986—2000, Tchr. Recognition award 1974, 1979), Am. String Tchrs. Assn. (state pres. Mo. 1969—71, Artist Tchr. 1992). Avocations: reading, investing, fitness. Home: 7726 Allegro Dr Houston TX 77040

HALES, ALFRED WASHINGTON, mathematics educator, consultant; b. Pasadena, Calif., Nov. 30, 1938; s. Raleigh Stanton and Gwendolen (Washington) H.; m. Virginia Dart Greene, July 7, 1962; children— Andrew Stanton, Lisa Ruth, Katherine Washington BS, Calif. Inst. Tech., 1960, PhD, 1962. NSF postdoctoral fellow Cambridge U., Eng., 1962-63; Benjamin Peirce instr. Harvard U., 1963-66; faculty mem. UCLA, 1966-92, prof. math., 1973-92, prof. emeritus, 1992—; dir. Inst. Def. Analyses, Ctr. Comms. Rsch., La Jolla, Calif., 1992—. Cons. Jet Propulsion Lab., La Canada, Calif., 1966-70, Inst. for Def. Analyses, Princeton, N.J. and LaJolla, Calif., 1964-65, 76, 79-92; vis. lectr. U. Wash., Seattle, 1970-71; vis. mem. U. Warwick Math. Inst., Coventry, Eng., 1977-78, Math. Sci. Rsch. Inst., Berkeley, 1986-87. Co-author: Shift Register Sequences, 1967, 82; contbr. articles to profl. jours. Bd. trustees Math. Sci. Rsch. Inst., Berkeley, 1995-99. Mem. Am. Math. Soc., Math. Assn. Am., Soc. Indsl. and Applied Math. (Polya prize in combinatorics 1972), Pasadena Badminton Club, Sigma Xi. Office: Ctr for Comm Rsch 4320 Westerra Ct San Diego CA 92121-1969 E-mail: hales@ccrwest.org.

HALES, CHARLES ALBERT, physician, educator; b. Greeley, Colo., Apr. 27, 1941; s. Charles A. and Dorothy G. (Henkel) H.; m. Mary Ann Little, June 12, 1965; children: Samuel, Christopher, John. BA, Emory U., 1962, MD, 1966. Diplomate Am. Bd. Internal Medicine, Am. Bd. Pulmonary Disease. Intern Boston City Hosp., resident I; resident II U. Calif., San Francisco, 1971—72; Harvard pulmonary fellow Mass. Gen. Hosp., Boston, staff physician, 1973—, chief pulmonary and critical care unit, 1999—; assoc. prof. Med. Sch. Harvard U., Boston, 1979-95, prof. medicine, 1995—. Lt. comdr. USNR, 1968-70. Mem. Am. Thoracic Soc., Am. Physiology Soc., Am. Soc. Clin. Investigation, Am. Heart Assn. (chmn. cardiopulmonary coun. 1991-93). E-mail: chales@partners.org.

HALES, DANIEL B. lawyer; b. Oak Park, Ill., Sept. 29, 1941; s. Burton W. and Marion (Jones) H.; m. Deborah J. Dorr, June 4, 1966; children, Daniel R.J., Marion P., George B. BA in Econs., U. Mich., 1963; Juris Doctorate, Northwestern U., 1966. Bar: Ill.1966, U.S. Dist. Ct. (no. dist.) Ill. 1967, U.S. Ct. Appeals (7th cir.) 1968, U.S. Supreme Ct. 1977. Ptnr. Peterson, Ross, Schloerb & Seidel, Chgo. Gen. counsel The Philadelphia Soc., Chgo.; dir. Chgo. Crime Commn. Pres., dir. Americans for Effective Law Enforcement Inc., Chgo.; bd. dirs. Duncan YMCA, Chgo.; chmn. Ill. Lawyers for Reagan and Bush, 1980; gen. counsel New Trier Twp., Winnetka, Ill. Republican Orgn.; mem. bd. govs. United Rep. Fund of Ill. Mem. Chgo. Bar Assn. (trust law com. 1975—), Law Club, N.E. Commonwealth Club, N.E. Federalist Soc. (advisor). Office: 711 Oak St # 102 Winnetka IL 60093

HALES, RALEIGH STANTON, JR., mathematics educator, academic administrator; b. Pasadena, Calif., Mar. 16, 1942; s. Raleigh Stanton and Gwendolen (Washington) Hales; m. Diane Cecilia Moore, July 8, 1967; children: Karen Gwen, Christopher Stanton. BA, Pomona Coll., 1964; MA, Harvard U., 1965, PhD, 1970. Tchg. fellow Harvard U., Cambridge, Mass., 1965—67; instr. math. Pomona Coll., Claremont, Calif., 1967—70, asst. prof., 1970—74, assoc. prof., 1974—85, prof., 1985—90, assoc. dean. coll., 1973—90; pres. Claremont Computations, 1983—90; prof. math. scis., v.p. acad. affairs Coll. Wooster, Ohio, 1990, pres., 1995—. Cons. Calif. Divsn. Savs. and Loan, 1968—70, Econs. Rsch. Assocs., L.A., 1969, Devel. Econs., L.A., 1971, Fed. Home Loan Bank Bd., Washington, 1971—72. Author: computer software; contbr. articles to profl. jours.; patentee calculator. Trustee Polytech. Sch., Pasadena, Calif., 1973—79, Foothill Country Day Sch., Claremont, 1985—90, chmn., 1989—90; coun. Internat. Badminton Fedn., 1989—99; bd. dirs. U.S. Badminton Assn., 1967—73, 1978—89, pres., 1985—88; mem. exec. bd. U.S. Olympic Com., 1989—90. Named Wig Disting. prof., Pomona Coll., 1971. Mem.: Wooster Country Club, Math. Assn. Am., Am. Math. Soc., Univ. Club N.Y., Pasadena Badminton Club (pres. 1978—85). Republican. Episcopalian. Home: 433 E University St Wooster OH 44691-2931 Office: Coll of Wooster 1189 Beall Ave Wooster OH 44691-2393

HALEVI, MARCUS, photographer; b. Croton-on-Hudson, N.Y., Jan. 17, 1942; s. Henry and Zelma (Brenner) H. BArch, U. Mich., 1965. Arch. The Archs. Collaborative, Cambridge, Mass., 1969-72; freelance photographer Somerville, Mass., 1972—. Resident artist MacDowell Colony, 1997. One person shows include Anchorage (Alaska) Fine Arts Mus., 1978, Peabody Mus., 1990, Carpenter Ctr. Arts Harvard U., 1995, Radcliffe Coll. Gallery, 2001, Sacramento St. Gallery, 2002; exhibited in group shows Inst. Contemporary Art, Boston, 1977, NYU Art Gallery, 1980, Cambridge Multicultural Art Ctr., 1990, Soka Gakkai Mus., Hiroshima, Japan, 1990, Howard Yezerski Gallery, Boston, 1991, Nat. Press Club, Washington, 1992, Aidekman Art Gallery, Boston, 1998, De Cordova Mus, Lincoln, Mass., 1998, PRC Gallery, Boston, 2002; prin. works include refugees of Mekong River, land mine clearing in Cambodia, st. children of Bangkok, child prostitution, Agent Orange poisoning of Vietnam vets., Cambodian refugee camps, asylums of Romania, Russian prison sys., urban India, environ. vigilantes, rural post offices; photographer: (book) Alaska Crude: Visions of the Last Frontier, 1977, portfolio pub., 2001. With USCG, 1967. Recipient Pulitzer Prize for gen. news, 1988, 1st prize Boston Photo-Arts, 1979, W. Eugene Smith Meml. Spl. Recognition award, 1989, 1st prize New Eng. Press Assn., 1991, 1st prize New Eng. AP awards, 1991, Picture of Yr. awards Nat. Press Photographers Assn. & U. Mo. Sch. Journalism including 2d prize for feature photograph, 1987, 3d prize for news picture story, 1990, 2d prize for spot news photography, 1990, judge's spl. recognition Canon photo-essayist, 1992; Nat. Endowment Arts photography grantee, 1992, Mass. Coun. for Arts and Humanities grantee, 1986, Mass. Cultural Coun. grantee, 1995. Home: 33 Cedar St Somerville MA 02143-2231 E-mail: haleviphoto@aol.com.

HALEY, DAVID ALAN, healthcare executive; b. St. Louis, Aug. 29, 1943; s. John David and Helen Ermyl (Richardson) H.; m. Donna Lee Davis, Nov. 21, 1965; children: Trisha Lynn, Jason Alan, Eric Nathan. BA, So. Ill. U., Edwardsville, 1966; MPH magna cum laude, UCLA, 1971. Adminstrv. asst. Kaiser Found. Hosp., Panorama City, Calif., 1971; assoc. adminstr. Our Lady of Lourdes Hosp., Pasco, Wash., 1971-74, Garfield Hosp., Monterey Park, Calif., 1974-75; assoc. exec. dir. Gen. Hosp., Ft. Walton Beach, Fla., 1976-79; v.p. ops. Our Lady of the Lake Regional Med. Ctr., Baton Rouge, 1979-88; pres. Phoenix Connection, Baton Rouge, 1988-89; CEO Gibson Gen. Hosp., Princeton, Ind., 1989-93; pres., CEO Four States Physicians Assn., Joplin, Mo., 1993-94; exec. dir. MedQuest Health Resources, Inc., 1995-96; pres., CEO, The Haley Group, Frankfort, Ill., 1996—. Mem. Four Rivers Comprehensive Health Planning Agy., Richland, Wash., 1972-74; treas. S.E. Wash. State Hosp. Coun., Pasco, 1973, v.p. 1974; corp. mem. Mid La. Health Systems Agy., Baton Rouge, 1979-82; gubernatorial appointee La. Statewide Health Coord. Coun., Baton Rouge, 1984, Ind. Healthcare Facility Adminstrn. Bd., Indpls., 1991-93; sec.-treas. S.W. Ind. Hosp. Coun., Evansville, 1992-93. Served with USNR, 1967-69. USPHS fellow, 1969-71. Fellow Am. Coll. Healthcare Execs.; mem. Healthcare Fin. Mgmt. Assn., La. Hosp. Assn. (council on planning, 1984-87), Ind. Hosp. Assn. (mem. coun. pub. rels. 1992-93), Vis. Nurse Assn. Southwestern Ind. (bd. dirs. 1992-93), La. Assn. Bus. and Industry (health care council 1987). Lodges: Kiwanis. Republican. Home and Office: The Haley Group 18142 S 66th Ct Ste 102 Tinley Park IL 60477

HALEY, DONALD ROBERT, health facility administrator; b. Tampa, Fla., Aug. 6, 1968; s. Donald M. and Linda G. Haley; m. Suzanne C. Connors, Aug. 16, 1971; children: Julia Suzanne, Connor Robert. BS in Natural Sci., U. of South Fla., Tampa, 1990; MBA, MHS, U. of Fla., Gainesville, 1993; PhD in Health Policy and Adminstrn., U. of N.C., 1999. Adminstrv. resident Martin Meml. Health Sys., Stuart, Fla., 1993—94, dir. decision support, 1994—95; dir. consumer devel. Blue Cross Blue Shield of Fla., Gainesville, 1999—, sr. policy analyst Jacksonville, 1999—2001; prof. U. of North Fla., Jacksonville, 2000—. Regent's adv. bd. Am. Coll. of Health Care Executives, Jacksonville, Fla., 2001—. Contbr. articles to profl. jours., ; author: (book chpt.) Managed Care and Public Health. Fellow Cecil G Sheps Ctr. for Health Svcs. fellowship, Nat. Rsch. Svc., 1998—99. Mem.: Assn. for Health Svcs. Rsch. (assoc.), Assn. of Managed Care Profls. (assoc.), First Coast Health Care Execs. (assoc.; bd. dirs. 2001), Regent's Adv. Coun. (assoc.; bd. dirs. 2001), Am. Coll. of Health Care Execs. (assoc.; regent's adv. bd. 2001—). Avocations: mountain biking, triathlons, cross country running, baseball. Home: 4198 Chelsea Harbor Dr W Jacksonville FL 32224 Office: U North Fl Dept Pub Health 4567 St Johns Bluff Rd S Jacksonville FL 32224 Home Fax: 904-565-6435.

HALEY, GEORGE, Romance languages educator; b. Lorain, Ohio, Oct. 19, 1929; s. George and Mary (Haley). AB, Oberlin Coll., 1948; MA, Brown U., 1951, PhD (Pres.'s fellow), 1956. Prof. U. Chgo., 1968—, chmn. dept. Romance langs., 1970-74. Author: Vicente Espinel and Marcos de Obregón, 1959, The Narrator in Don Quixote, 1965, Diario de un Estudiante de Salamanca, 1977, El Quijote de Cervantes, 1984, Vicente Espinel y Marcos de Obregon: Biografía, Autobiografía y Novela, 1994; mem. editl. bd. Modern Philology, 1967-95. Guggenheim fellow, 1962-63 Mem. Hispanic Soc. Am., MLA, Phi Beta Kappa. Home: 901 S Plymouth Ct Chicago IL 60605-2059 Office: 1050 E 59th St Chicago IL 60637-1559

HALEY, GEORGE BROCK, JR., retired lawyer; b. Atlanta, Feb. 9, 1926; s. George Brock and Naomi Esther (Alverson) H.; m. Marjorie Elizabeth Griffiths, June 24, 1950; children: Susan Haley Brumfield, Katherine Haley Herman, George Brock III, Victor Pearse. AB, Harvard U., 1948, LLB, 1951. Bar: Ga. 1951, D.C. 1976. Assoc. Kilpatrick & Cody (name changed to Kilpatrick Stockton), Atlanta, 1951-60, ptnr., 1960-93, of counsel, 1994—. Mem. Ga. Gov.'s Jud. Process Rev. Commn., Atlanta, 1988-89; v.p., trustee Frances Wood Wilson Found. Staff sgt. AUS, 1944-46, MTO. Mem. ABA, State Bar Ga., Atlanta Bar Assn., Atlanta Lawyers Club, Capital City Club. Methodist. Avocations: boating, hiking. E-mail: ghaley@kilpatrickstockton.com.

HALEY, GEORGE PATRICK, lawyer; b. Bad Axe, Mich., Sept. 23, 1948; s. Glen Kirk and Bernice (Cooper) H.; m. Theresa L. Thomas, Dec. 24, 1975. BS, U. Mich., 1970, MS, U. Calif., Berkeley, 1971; JD, Harvard U., 1974. Bar: Calif. 1974, U.S. Dist. Ct. (no. dist.) Calif. 1974, U.S. Dist. Ct. (ea. dist.) Calif. 1980. Assoc. Pillsbury Winthrop LLP, San Francisco, 1974-81, ptnr., 1982—. Prof. U. Shanghai, Shanghai-San Francisco Sister City Program, 1986-1989. Author numerous articles uniform commercial code, project fin. Dir. Calif. Shakespeare Festival, Berkeley, 1986-93; dir. Nat. Writing Project, 1996—. Mem. ABA (chmn. com. 1976-93), Am. Coll. Comml. Fin. Lawyers, State Bar Calif. (chmn. fin. instns. com. 1980, commercial code com. 1988). Republican. Methodist. Avocations: tai chi chuan, golf, cooking. Home: 1825 Marin Ave Berkeley CA 94707-2414 E-mail: ghaley@pillsburywinthrop.com.

HALEY, GEORGE W. ambassador; BS, Morehouse Coll.; JD, U. Ark., 1952. Bar: Ark., D.C., Kans., U.S. Supreme Ct. Pvt. practice law, Kansas City, Kans., 1952-69; dep. city atty. City of Kansas City, 1954-64; mem. senate State of Kansas, 1964-68; chief counsel of Fed. Transit Adminstrn. Washington, 1969-73; assoc. dir. EEOC, USIA, Washington, 1973-74, gen. counsel, congrl. liaison, 1975-76; ptnr. Obermayer, Rebmann, Maxwell & Hippel, Phila., 1976-81; legal advisor to Econ. Cmty. of West African States, 1978-84; sr. advisor to U.S. delegation, 22d Gen. Conf. UNESCO, 1983-84, U.S. del. 2d Internat. Conf. on Assistance to Refugees in Africa, 1984; del. to Centennial Celebration of Dakar, Senegal; chmn. Postal Rate Commn., 1990-94; vice chmn. Postal Rate Commn., 1995-98; U.S. ambassador to Republic of The Gambia U.S. Fgn. Svc., 1998—2001. Mem. NAACP (life).

HALEY, JOHN CHARLES, financial executive; b. Akron, Ohio, July 24, 1929; s. Arthur and Katherine (Moore) H.; m. Rheba Hopkins, June 11, 1951; children: Alyson, Susan, John, Thomas. AB, Miami U., Oxford, Ohio, 1950; MS, Columbia Grad. Sch. Bus., 1951; LL.D. (hon.), Pace U., 1984. With Chase Manhattan Bank, N.Y.C., 1953—, asst. treas., 1959-62, asst. v.p., 1962-64, v.p., 1964-70; exec. v.p. Chase Manhattan Corp, 1975-84; dep. chmn. Kissinger Assocs., 1984-85; chmn., chief exec. officer Bus. Internat. Inc., N.Y.C., 1986-87. Group pres. Orion Banking Group, London, 1970-73, dir. Armco Corp., chmn., bd. 1995-96. Trustee Siemens Found.; chmn. emeritus bd. trustees Pace U. Served with AUS, 1951-53. Mem. Beta Theta Pi. Home and Office: 8 Deer Run Path Rutland VT 05701-9654

HALEY, JOHN HARVEY, lawyer; b. Hot Springs, Ark., May 29, 1931; s. Harvey H. and Anne (Tanner) H.; m. Cynthia Martin, Sept. 7, 1997. AB, Emory U., 1952; LLB, U. Ark., 1955. Bar: Ark. 1955, U.S. Dist. Ct. (we. dist.) Ark. 1955, U.S. Ct. Appeals (8th cir.) 1955, U.S. Supreme Ct. 1971. Clk. Ark. Supreme Ct., Little Rock, 1955-56; ptnr. Rose Law Firm, Little Rock, 1956-71, Haley, Young, Bogard & Gitchell, Little Rock, 1971-73, Laser, Sharp, Haley, Young & Boswell, Little Rock, 1973-82, Haley, Polk & Heister, Little Rock, 1982—86, Arnold, Grobmyer & Haley, Little Rock, 1986—96; owner Haley Law Firm, Little Rock, 1996—2002; of counsel Eichenbaum, Liles & Heister, Little Rock, 2002—. Bd. dirs. North Ark. Telephone Co., Flippin, Ark.; Munro and Co., Hot Springs, Ark., Rose Creek Industries, Plaza Partnership, Talweg, LLC, Memphis; lectr. U. Ark. Law Sch., Little Rock, 1956-60, CLU instr., 1961-65; spl. counsel liquidation and rehab. Ark. Ins. Dept., 1967-71; pres. Combustion Technologies LLC, Little Rock, 1996—. Editor Ark. Law Rev., 1954-55. Chmn. Ark. State Bd. Correction, 1967-72, Ark. State Bd. Law Examiners, 1960-63, Election Rsch. Coun., Little Rock, 1961-64; dir. Wildwood Ctr. Performing Arts, Little Rock, 1994-99, Florence Crittenden Home, Little Rock, 1994-99; scoutmaster Second Presbyn. Ch. Troop, Little Rock, 1962-65. Methodist. Avocations: piloting, sailing, bicycling, underwater photography, skiing. Home: 3614 Doral Dr Little Rock AR 72212-2920 Office: Haley Companies PO Box 3730 Little Rock AR 72203-3730 Fax: 501-227-5628. E-mail: enginery@aol.com.

HALEY, JOHNETTA RANDOLPH, musician, educator, university official; b. Alton, Ill., Mar. 19; d. John a. and Willye E. (Smith) Randolph; children form previous marriage: Karen, Michael. MusB in Edn., Lincoln U., 1945; MusM, So. Ill. U., 1972. Cert. cons. 1995. Vocal and gen. music tchr. Lincoln High Sch., E. St. Louis, Ill., 1945-48; vocal music tchr., choral dir. Turner Sch., Kirkwood, Mo., 1950-55; vocal and gen. music tchr. Nipher Jr. High Sch., Kirkwood, 1955-71; prof. music Sch. Fine Arts So. Ill. U., Edwardsville, 1972—; dir. East St. Louis Campus, 1982—. Adjudicator music festivals; area music cons. Ill. Office Edn., 1977-78; prgram splst. St. Louis Human Devel. corp., 1968. Interim exec. dir. St. Louis Coun. Black People, summer, 1970; bd. dirs. YWCA, 1975-80, Artist Presentation Soc., St. Louis, 1975, United Negro Coll. Fund, 1976-78; bd. curators Lincoln U., Jefferson City, Mo., 1974-82, pres., 1978-82; chairperson Ill. Com. on Black Concerns in Higher Edn.; mem. Nat. Ministry on Urban Edn. Luth. Ch.-Mo. Synod, 1975-80; bd. dirs. Coun. Luth. Chs. Stillman Coll.; pres. congregation St. Phillips Luth. Ch.; bd. dirs. Girls, Inc.; mem. Ill. Aux. Bd., United Way; v.p. East St. Louis Cmty. Fund, Inc. Recipient Cotillion de Leon award for Outstanding Cmty. Svc., 1977, Disting. Alumnae award Lincoln U., 1977, Disting. Svc. award United Negro Coll. Fund, 1979; SCLC, 1981; recipient Cmty. Svc. award St. Louis Drifters, 1979, Disting. Svc. to Arts award Sigma Gamma Rho, Nat. Negro Musicians award, 1981, Sci. awareness award, 1984-85, Tri Del Federated award, 1985, Martin Luther King Drum Maj. award, 1985, Bus. and Profl. Women's Club award, 1985-86, Fred L. McDowell award, 1986, Vol. of Yr. award Inroads Inc., 1986, Woman of Achievement in Edn. award Elks, 1987, Woman of Achievement award Suburban Newspaper of Greater St. Louis and Sta. KMOX-Radio, 1988, Love award Greeley Cmty. Ctr., Sammy Davies Jr. award in Edn., 1990, Yes I

Can award in Edn., 1990, Merit award Urban League, 1994, Legacy award Nat. Coun. Negro Women, 1995, Diversity award Mo. ARC, 2001; named Disting. Citizen St. Louis Argus Newspaper, 1970, Dutchess of Paducah, 1973; the Johnetta Haley Scholars Acad. minority scholarship named in her honor So. Ill. U. Mem. AAUP, Music Educators Nat. Conf., Nat. Choral Dirs. Assn., Nat. Assn. Negro Musicians, Coll. Music Soc., Coun. Luth. Chs., Ill. Music. Educators, Jack and Jill, Inc., Women of Achievement in Edn., Friends of St. Louis Art Mus., The Links, Inc. (nat. parliamentarian, chair constnl. and by-laws com.), Las Amigas Social Club, Alpha Kappa Alpha (internat. parliamentarian, Golden soror award 1995, Grad Svcs. award 2001, nat. parliamentarian, 2002-), Mu Phi Epsilon, Pi Kappa Lambda. Lutheran. Home: 1926 Bennington Common Dr Saint Louis MO 63146-2555

HALEY, PRISCILLA JANE, artist, printmaker; b. Boston, June 22, 1926; d. Arthur Benjamin and Jessamy (Fountain) H.; m. Tadeusz Bilous, May 21, 1961. BA, Oberlin Coll., Ohio, 1948; postgrad., Bklyn. Mus. Sch., 1955. Resident artist Yaddo Found., Saratoga Springs, N.Y., 1957. One-man show Village Art Ctr., N.Y.C., 1960; 3-man show Islip Art Mus., 1975; represented in permanent collection N.Y. Pub. Libr., Nat. Acad. Galleries, Bklyn. Mus., Libr. of Congress, Bowdoin Coll. Art Mus., Oberlin Coll., Addison Gallery art, Wesleyan U. Libr., Portland (Oreg.) Mus. Art, others; portfolio of prints and poems by Maine poets, The Island, 1961. Recipient Medal of Honor Audubon Artists, 1957, 1st prize Bablyon Arts Coun. Juried Exhbn., 1992; Louis Comfort Tiffany Found. grantee, 1959. Mem. Soc. Am. Graphic Artists Home: 133 Livingston Ave Babylon NY 11702-1601

HALEY, ROGER KENDALL, librarian; b. Boston, Oct. 29, 1938; s. John F. and Rose (Walker) H.; m. Mary Hannon; 1 child, Michael J. AB, Georgetown U., 1960; M.L.S., U. Md., 1976. Reference asst. U.S. Senate Library, Washington, 1964-71, asst. librarian, 1971-73, librarian, 1973-97. Mem. Spl. Librs. Assn. (John Cotton Dana award 1993, Hall of Fame award, 2001). Office: 1243 Independence Ave SE Washington DC 20003-1445

HALEY, ROSLYN TREZEVANT, educational program director; b. Washington, July 23, 1955; d. Morti Trezevant and Sara Roslyn Kebe; m. Darrell D. Haley, July 30, 1988; children: Jessica, Darrell Jr., Donald, Anthony, Krystal. BA in History, S.C. State U., 1976; MPA, Calif. State U., L.A., 1983; EdD, UCLA, 1999. Faculty cert. U. Phoenix, 1996. Admissions evaluator UCLA, 1979-81, counselor Sch. Pub. Health, 1981-83, head counselor dept. theater, 1983-93; dir. student, counseling, and recruitment svcs. UCLA Sch. Theater, Film and TV, 1993—. Adult edn. tchr. L.A. Unified Sch. Dist., 1984-93; lectr. U. Phoenix, Woodland Hills, Calif., 1996—; bd. mem. Palmdale (Calif.) H.S., Visual and Performing Arts Acad., 1999. Author of poetry. March organizer March for Jesus, L.A., 1994, Antelope Valley, 1995-02; adminstr. Command Ctr., Convoy of Hope, Palmdale, 1998; sch. site coun. Palmtree Elem. Sch., Palmdale, 1998-99; recruiter Boy Scouts Am. Western L.A. Coun. Bd., 1998-99; campaign chair Antelope Valley YMCA, 2001. Recipient Outstanding Svc. award March for Jesus, L.A., 1994, Outstanding Svc. award First Missionary Bapt. Ch., Littlerock, Calif., 1997, Outstanding Svc. award Jesus Day, Antelope Valley. Mem. Am. Assn. Ednl. Rsch. Avocations: reading, swimming, horseback riding, cycling. Home: 37518 Larchwood Dr Palmdale CA 93550-6037 Office: UCLA Sch TFT 405 Hilgard Ave Los Angeles CA 90095-9000 Fax: 310-825-3383. E-mail: rhaley@ucla.edu.

HALEY, ROY W. finance company executive; b. 1947; BS, MIT, 1969. With Arthur Andersen & Co., Houston, 1969-71, 73-88, Ruhmann Mfg. Co., Schulenburg, Tex., 1971-73; pres. Am. Gen. Fin. Inc. (formerly Credithrift Fin. Inc.), 1989-91; also exec. v.p. adminstrn. Am. Gen. Corp., Houston; CEO Am. Gen. Fin. Inc., Evansville, Ind., 1989-91; pres. Am. Gen. Corp., Houston, 1991-93; pres., CEO Wesco Distbn., Pitts., 1994—; chmn., pres., CEO Wesco Internat., Inc., Pitts. Office: Wesco Internat Inc Commerce Ct Ste 700 Four Sta Sq Pittsburgh PA 15219*

HALEY, SALLY FULTON, artist; b. Bridgeport, Conn., June 29, 1908; d. John Poole and Elizabeth (Akers) H.; m. Michele Russo, June 29, 1935; children: Michael Haley, Gian Donato. BFA, Yale U., 1931. One-woman shows include Marylhurst Coll., 1965, Maryhill Mus. Fine Arts, Washington, 1975, Portland Art Mus., 1960, 75, Woodside Gallery, Seattle, 1971, 76, 79, Gov's. Office, Oreg. State Capitol, 1976, Wentz Gallery, Pacific N.W. Coll. Art, 1984, Fountain Gallery Art, Portland, 1962, 72, 77, 80, 81, 84, 86; exhibited in group shows Stewart Gallery, Boston, 1947, San Francisco Mus. Art, 1949, Walker Art Ctr., Mpls., 1954, Denver Art Mus., 1956, 57, 3d Pacific Coast Biennial Exhbn., 1960, Francis J. Newton's Collection, Bush House, 1964, Seattle Ctr. Art Pavilion, 1976, Womans Bldg., L.A., 1977, Laura Russo Gallery, 1993, 97, Oreg. Group Show, Expn. '86 World's Fair, Vancouver, B.C., Mus. N.W. Art, Conner, Wash., 1998; represented in permanent collections Fred Myer Trust, Wash. State U., State Capitol Bldg., Salem, Portland Art Mus., The Laura Russo Gallery, Portland, Lynn McAllister Gallery, Seattle, Barby Investment Co., AT&T, Kaiser Found., numerous others; retrospective, Marylhurst Coll., 1993, Mus. Northwest Art Ha Conner, Washington, 1998. Named Artist of Yr. Neighbor Newspaper Community, Portland, 1984; recipient Woman of Achievement award YWCA, 1988, Govs. award for the Arts, 1989, Poster award, 1982, Hubbard award Hubbard Mus., Ruidoso Downs, N.Mex., 1990-91.

HALEY, THOMAS JOHN, retired pharmacologist; b. Crosby, Minn., Nov. 4, 1913; s. Thomas Edward and Ida May (Young) H.; m. Edna Baker, June 1, 1944 (div. Sept. 1963); m. Jeanne Wall, Sept. 24, 1964; children: Kathyleen, Barbara. BS, U. So. Calif., 1938, MS, 1942; PhD, U. Fla., 1945. Lic. pharmacist, Calif., Nev. Grad. asst. instr. U. Fla., Gainesville, 1942-45; med. dir. E.S. Miller Labs Inc., L.A., 1945-47; chief pharmacology toxicologist Lab. Nuclear Medicine UCLA, 1947-66; prof. pharmacology U. Hawaii Med. Sch., Honolulu, 1966-69; leader pharmacology & toxicology Rsch. Triangle Inst., Research Triangle Park, N.C., 1969-71; adj. prof. pharmacology & toxicology U. N.C. Med. Sch., Chapel Hill, 1969-71; pharmacologist Food & Drug Adminstrn. Nat. Ctr. Toxicology Rsch., Pine Bluff, Ark., 1971-82; adj. prof. pharmacology U. Ark. Med. Ctr., Little Rock, 1971-82. Author: Clinical Toxicology, 1948, 1972, Respiratory Nervous System Ion Radiology, 1962, 1964, Manual of Toxicology, 1987. Sci. com. air pollution L.A. County, 1948-66. Mem. Inst. Strahlenhemat & Biol. (internat. mem.), L.A. C. of C. (clean air com. 1954-56), Oceanside City Coun. (hazard waste com. 1986-91). Democrat. Roman Catholic. Avocation: stamp collecting. Home: Oceanside, Calif. Died Mar. 19, 2003.

HALEY, USHA C.V. international business educator; b. Bombay, Nov. 9, 1957; arrived in U.S., 1977; d. Chandrasekara and Nandini Venkatesan; m. George Thomas Haley, June 12, 1984. BA, Elphinstone Coll., Bombay, 1977; MA, U. Ill., 1979; MPhil, NYU, 1987, PhD, 1990. Prof. mgmt. and internat. bus. Instituto Tecnologico y de Estudios Superiores de Monterrey, Mexico, 1993—94, Nat. U. Singapore, 1994—96, Queensland U. Tech., Brisbane, Australia, 1997—98, NJ Inst. Tech., Newark, 1998—2000, U. Tenn., Knoxville, 2000—03, U. New Haven, West Haven, Conn., 2003—. Rsch. assoc. Australian Nat. U., Canberra, 1998—2000; mem. grad. faculty mgmt. Rutgers U., 1999—2000; vis. prof. internat. bus. Purdue U., Singapore, 1996, Harvard U., Cambridge, Mass., 1999—2000; prin. Haley & Assocs., 1998—; bd. editors Mgmt. Decision, 1996—, Jour. Orgnl. Change Mgmt., 1996—, Jour. Internat. Mgmt., 2002—, Asia Pacific Bus. Rev., 2002—, Jour. Leadership and Leaders, 1998; internat. revs. editor Asia Pacific Bus. Rev., 2002—; presenter, cons. in field. Author: New Asian Emperors: The Overseas Chinese, their Strategies and Competitive Advantages, 1998, Strategic Management in the Asia Pacific: Harnessing Regional and Organizational Change for Competitive Advantage, 2000, Multinational Corporations in Political Environments: Ethics, Values and Strategies, 2001, Asian Post-crisis Management: Corporate and Governmental Strategies for Sustainable Competitive Advantage, 2002; contbr. articles to profl. jours.; guest editor: Management Decision, 1996, 1997, Jour. Orgnl. Change Mgmt., 1998, author, webmaster: www.asia-pacific.com, 1999—; author: behavior simluations; contbr. chapters to books. Recipient Friend of Emerald, Literati Club, 2002, Lifetime achievement award, 2003; grantee, Nat. Ctr. Sci. and Tech., Mexico, 1994, U. Tenn. Dept. Mgmt. and Coll. Bus. Adminstrn., 2001—03; scholar for higher edn., Govt. of India, 1974—77; Charles E. Merriam fellow, U. Ill., 1977—78. Mem.: Acad. Internat. Bus., Inst. Ops. Rsch. and Mgmt. Scis., Strategic Mgmt. Soc., Asia Acad. Mgmt., Acad. Mgmt., Beta Gamma Sigma. Office: U New Haven Sch Bus Dept Mgmt 300 Orange Ave West Haven CT 06516 Fax: 212-208-2468. E-mail: uhaley@asia-pacific.com.

HALEY, VINCENT PETER, lawyer; b. Phila., Oct. 6, 1931; s. Vincent Paul and Madeline R. (McCrystal) H.; m. Mary Ann Harron, Apr. 14, 1956; children— Paul V., Kevin G., Maureen T., Patricia Ann M., Kathleen A., Brian M., Regina E., Christopher P., Megan A. BS, Villanova, 1953, JD cum laude, 1959. Bar: Pa. 1960, Fla. 1979. Acct. Arthur Young & Co., CPAs, Phila., 1955-56; assoc. Schnader, Harrison, Segal & Lewis, Phila., 1959-67, ptnr., 1968-99, mem. exec. com., 1985-88, 89-94, sr. counsel, 2000—. Mem. bd. consultors Law Sch. Villanova U., 1985— ; lectr. in field. Sec. Mercy Health Sys., Bala Cynwyd, Pa., 1969—; mem. Archdiocese of Phila. Bd. Edn., 1973-79, pres., 1977-79; mem., bd. dirs. Police Athletic League of Phila., 1994-2001. With USNR, 1953-55. Mem. Pa. Bar Assn. (chmn. corp., banking and bus. law sect. 1979-81), Phila. Bar Assn., Villanova U. Law Alumni Assn. (pres. 1962-63), Huntingdon Valley Country Club, Roosevelt Racquet Club (Huntingdon Valley, Pa., bd. dirs. 1969-80, 91-94, 97-2000, treas. 1972-80), Order of Coif (chpt. v.p. 1962-63). Home: 305 Madison Rd Huntingdon Valley PA 19006-6713 Office: Schnader Harrison Segal et al 1600 Market St Ste 3600 Philadelphia PA 19103-7287

HALFACRE, ROBERT GORDON, ombudsman,landscape architect, horticulturist, educator; b. Newberry, S.C., June 22, 1941; s. Edwin Harvey and Lela (Ruff) H.; m. Carolyn F. Halfacre, Jan. 24, 1963 (div. Jan., 1980); children: Angela, Robert. BS, Clemson U., 1963, MS, 1965; PhD in Horticulture, Va. Poly. Inst., 1968; MLA, N.C. State U., 1973. Registered landscape architect, S.C. Asst. prof. N.C. State U., Raleigh, 1968-71, assoc. prof., 1971-74; assoc. prof. horticulture Clemson (S.C.) U., 1974-79, prof., 1979-90, Alumni disting. prof., 1990—, univ. ombudsman, 1998—. Landscape architect Landscape Archtl. Svcs., Clemson, 1977—; mem. Planning Commn. City of Clemson, 1990-93, pres. faculty senate, Clemson U., 1989-90, bd. visitors, 1992-94, chmn. grievance bd., 1996-98. Author: Carolina Landscape Plants, 1971, Keep 'em Growing, 1972, Fundamentals of Horticulture, 1975, Horticulture, 1979, Plant Science, 1987, Landscape Plants of the Southeast, 5th edit., 1989. Dir. Horticulture Gardens, Clemson U., 1974-77; pres. bd. dirs. Daniel H.S. P.T.A., Clemson, 1985-86; chmn. United Way Campaign, Clemson U., 1996-97. Recipient Silver Seal award Nat. Coun. State Garden Clubs, 1984, Helen S. Hull award, 1979, Sigma Xi Rsch. award, 1968, Outstanding Tchr. award N.C. State U., 1970, Outstanding Faculty award AAUP, 1997. award for Faculty Excellence, Clemson U. Bd. Trustees, 1997. Mem.: U. and Coll. Ombuds Assn., Am. Soc. Hort. Sci. (Julian C. Miller rsch. award 1968, L.M. Ware Outstanding Tchr. award So. region 1982), Am. Soc. Landscape Archs., Nat. Ombudsman Assn. Republican. Lutheran. Avocations: water skiing, writing, tennis, travel. Office: Clemson U 101 Clemson House 248 Palmetto Blvd Clemson SC 29631-5107 Fax: 864-656-4373. E-mail: ombudsman@clemson.edu.

HALFEN, DAVID, retired publishing executive; b. Newark, July 23, 1924; s. Abraham and Rachael (Sudit) H.; m. Geneviève Alberte Martin, Jan. 15, 1948; children: Daniel, William, Alexandre Anthony. BS with high honors, U. Wis., 1948; Diploma in French Civilization with high honors, U. Paris, 1949, PhD with highest honors, 1954. From asst. to chief cost acct. Atlas Constructors, Morocco, 1952-54; from asst. editor to editor-in-chief Hart Pub. Co., N.Y.C., 1954-56, 58-62; fgn. affairs editor Scholastic mag., N.Y.C., 1956-58; from field editor to v.p., gen. mgr. Coll. divsn. Scott, Foresman and Co., Glenview, Ill., 1962-78, v.p., gen. mgr. Lifelong Learning divsn., 1978-87, ret., 1987. Chmn. adv. com. USN Courses at Sea Program, 1987-92; sr. assoc. Middlesex Rsch. Ctr., Bethesda, Md., 1991-93; vol. exec. Internat. Exec. Svc. Corps, Zimbabwe, 1993, cons., 1994-96. Author: La Plume: Revue Symboliste 1889-1899, 1954. With AUS, 1943-46, PTO. Home: 1412 Queenscroft Keswick VA 22947

HALFERTY, FRANK JOSEPH, middle school music educator; b. Seattle, May 7, 1954; s. Edward A. and Eva Mae (Ellis) H.; m. Margaret A. Taylor, Mar. 17, 1979 (div. June 1991); children: Bryan W., Patrick Joseph; m. Melissa A. Rowland, July 31, 1992. BA in Music Edn., BA in Music Theory and Lit., Seattle Pacific U., 1976; MA in Music Composition, N.Mex. State U., 1982. Cert. tchr., Wash. Band and choral tchr. Raymond (Wash.) Sch. Dist., 1976-77; band and orch. tchr. Bellevue (Wash.) Sch. Dist., 1977-80; MA in Music Composition N.Mex. State U., Las Cruces, 1980-82; band tchr. Lake Washington Sch. Dist., Kirkland, Wash., 1982-93, Shoreline Sch. Dist., Seattle, 1993—, head music dept., 1994—2003, also dist. music specialist, coord., 2003—04. Mem. site-based mgmt. coun. Einstein Mid. Sch., Seattle, 1994-97; dir. Lake Washington All-Dist. Band, Kirkland, 1984-92; bd. dirs. Shoreline Arts Coun. Composer, arranger numerous musical works for band, instrumental ensembles, string orch. and choral groups. Crimson scholar, 1982; named Tchr. of Yr. by students, tchrs. and parents of Kirkland Jr. H.S., 1990; recipient Golden Acorn award Einstein Mid. Sch. PTSA, 1997. Mem. ASCAP (Writer award 1998-03), NEA, Music Educators Nat. Conf., Sno-King Music Edn. Assn. (sec. 1994-96), Shoreline Arts Coun. (bd. mem. 1997—), Phi Kappa Phi, Alpha Kappa Sigma. Avocations: camping, canoeing, woodworking, sailing. Home: 6155 NE 187th St Kenmore WA 98028-3221 Office: Einstein Mid Sch 19343 3rd Ave NW Seattle WA 98177-3012

HALFORD, RAYMOND GAINES, lawyer; b. Columbia, S.C., Apr. 10, 1925; s. Richard Eugene and Henrietta (Levy) H.; m. Wilma Eleazer, Dec. 31, 1960; children— Anne Lindsey, Richard Gaines. B.S., U. S.C., 1949, LL.B. cum laude, 1950. Bar: S.C. 1950, U.S. Dist. Ct. S.C. 1971, U.S. Ct. Appeals (4th cir.) 1978. Atty./advisor U.S. C.E., Aiken, S.C., 1950-52; account exec. Harris Upham & Co., Columbia, 1952-54; mortgage banker, Columbia, 1954-65; asst. atty. gen. Office Atty. Gen., Columbia, 1966— ; dep. atty. gen., gen. counsel S.C. Dept. Social Service, Columbia, 1983-84, S.C. Health and Human Services Fin. Commn., Columbia, 1984— . Div. chmn. United Fund, Columbia, 1958-59; Mem. YMCA; trustee United Community Services, Columbia, 1966-68. Served with U.S. Army, 1943-46. Named Outstanding Mem., Jr. C. of C., 1958; Disting. Service award Region IV, Nat. Welfare Fraud Assn., 1978. Mem. Clariosophic Literary Soc.., Order of Wig and Robe (chief justice), Delta Sigma Pi., Omicron Delta Kappa. Episcopalian. Home: 1162 Eastminister Dr Columbia SC 29204-3309 Office: SC Health and Human Services Fin Comm Jefferson Sq PO Box 8206 Columbia SC 29202

HALFORD, SHARON LEE, college administrator, advocate, educator; b. Clifton, Colo., July 22, 1946; d. Robert Lee and Florence V. (Kubly) Eighmy; m. Allen A. Dreher, Jan. 29, 1967 (div. Jan. 1979); children: Heidi Ann, Gretchen Christine, Kirsten Beth; m. Donald Gary Halford, May 23, 1986. BS in Edn., U. Colo., 1969; postgrad., U. Denver, 1981-83; M in Criminal Justice, U. Colo., 1987; postgrad., Colo. State U., 2000—. Legal asst. 1st Jud. Dist. Atty., Golden, Colo., 1979-81, legal rschr., 1981-83; victim svcs. dir. 18th Jud. Dist. Atty., Englewood, Colo., 1983-92. Mem. faculty Aurora (Colo.) C.C. Criminal Justice Dept., 1989-95, prof., chair pub. svc. dept., 1995-2001, dir. paralegal studies, 1995-2001, asst. v.p. instrn., 1999—, chair faculty senate, 1997-99, pres. faculty coun., 1997-99; mem. faculty Colo. Faculty Adv. Coun., 1993-99; project coord. Lowry Family Ctr.; cons. Svc. Learning, Colo. Campus Compact, 1997—, faculty devel. trainer, 1999—; lectr. Law Enforcement Tng. Acad., 1994—; cmty. educator Jr. Achievement, 2002--; project cons. WEPIC, U. Pa., 2000--; mem. Oxford (Eng.) 2000 Higher Edn. Law Round Table. Contbg. author, editor: Colorado Crime Victims Rights Contitutional Amendment Outreach Manual and Implementation Manual, 1992-93; author: (book) Connecting Colleges, Communities and Careers, 1998. Mem. Domestic Violence Task Force, Douglas County, Colo., 1985-92, Arapahoe County, Colo., 1985-94; trainer Rape Assistance and Awareness Program, Denver, 1985-91, MADD, 1990-92, Colo. Victim Witness Coord. Coalition, 1991; mem. 18th Judicial Dist. Child Advocacy Ctr. Com., 1990-99, Gov.'s Victims' Compensation and Assistance Coord. Com., 1991-95, Colo. Victim Asst. and Law Enforcement Bd., 1991-95, Criminal Justice Educators Task Force, 1992—, chair, 1995-98; mem. Colo. Corrections Consortium, 1992—, officer faculty senate, 1995-99; mem. Colo. Crime Victim Rights Constl. Amendment Com., 1990-99; com. chair Colo. PACT Project, 1993-95; mem. Colo. C.C. Diversity Com., 1997—. Fellow Nat. Orgn. for Victim Assistance, Nat. Victim Ctr.; mem. AAUW, LWV, ACLU, Anti-Defamation League, Colo. Orgn. for Victim Assistance (pres. 1992-95), Colo. Bar Assn. (co-chair paralegal com. 1999—), S.W. Criminal Justice Educators Assn., Acad. Criminal Justice Scis. (com. chair 1999—), Am. Assn. Paralegal Educators, Nat. Fedn. Paralegal Assns., Rocky Mountain Paralegal Assn., Nat. Criminal Justice Assn., So. Poverty Law Ctr., People-to-People Amb. Program, Am. Assn. Higher Edn., Am. Assn. Cmty. Colls.Am. Assn. Women in Cmty. Colls. Democrat. Methodist. Office: CC Aurora 16000 E Centretech Pky Aurora CO 80011-9057 E-mail: dshalford@aol.com., shar.halford@ccaurora.edu.

HALFVARSON, LUCILLE ROBERTSON, music educator; b. Petersburg, Ill., May 17, 1919; d. Harris Morton and Lucille (Fox) Robertson; m. Sten Gustaf Halfvarson, Aug. 8, 1946; children: Laura, Eric, Linnea, Mary. BA, Knox Coll., 1941; MusM, Am. Conservatory, 1969; DHL (hon.), Aurora U., 2000. Cert. tchr., Ill. Tchr. music and speech Freeman Elem. Sch., Aurora, Ill., 1941-44; choral dir. Galesburg (Ill.) Sr. H.S., 1944-46; dir. of music Our Savior Luth. Ch., Aurora, Ill., 1950-63; oratorio soloist, 1952-67; dir. of music Westminster Presbyn. Ch., Aurora, 1963-84; vocal instr. Merit Music Program, Chgo., 1982-93; ret., 1993. Choir dir. 1st Meth. Ch., Galesburg, 1944-46; choral-vocal instr. Waubonsee C.C., Sugar Grove, Ill., 1967-79; organizer Jr. Coll. Music Festival, Waubonsee Coll., Sugar Grove, 1972-73; pvt. vocal instrn., Aurora, 1979—. Conductor Messiah Concert Waubonsee Coll., Paramount Arts Ctr., 1968—, 25th Concert, 1992. Co-chair Citizens Adv. Com. Paramount Arts. Ctr., Aurora, 1977-78; founder United Arts Bd. Fox Valley, pres., 1977-82, Fox Valley Arts Hall of Fame, 2001; chair Paramount Celebration Arts, 1985-86; residency dir. Met. Life Affiliate Artist, Aurora, 1982-83; bd. dirs. YWCA, 1984-91, chair corp. award com., 1994-95; dir. New Eng. Congl. Ch. Bell Choir, 1997-99. Recipient Disting. Svc. award Cosmopolitan Club, Aurora, Ill., 1983; named Woman of Year YWCA, Aurora, 1976, Disting. Alumni Knox Coll., Galesburg, Ill., 1984; Paul Harris fellow Rotary Found. of Rotary Internat., 1999. Mem. AAUW, DAR, PEO, Music Educators Nat. Conf., Am. Choral Dirs. Assn., Aurora C. of C. (Image Maker 1992), Phi Beta Kappa. Avocations: needlecrafts, gardening, fishing, reading. Home: 1105 W Downer Pl Aurora IL 60506-4821

HALGREN, LEE A. academic administrator; Pres., v.p. acad. and student affairs State Coll. Colo., Denver, 1995—. Office: The State Coll Colo 1580 Lincoln St Ste 750 Denver CO 80203-1505 E-mail: halgrenl@mscd.edu.

HALICZER, JAMES SOLOMON, lawyer; b. Ft. Myers, Fla., Oct. 27, 1952; s. Julian and Margaret (Shepard) H.; m. Paula Fleming, Oct. 3, 1987. BA in English Lit., U. So. Fla., 1976, MA in Polit. Sci., 1978; JD, Stetson U., 1981. Bar: Fla. 1982. Assoc. Conrad, Scherer & James, Ft. Lauderdale, Fla., 1982-86, ptnr., 1988-92; assoc. Bernard & Mauro, Ft. Lauderdale, Fla., 1985-86; shareholder Cooney, Haliczer, Mattson, Lane, Blackburn, Pettis & Richards, Ft. Lauderdale, Fla., 1992-96, Haliczer, Pettis & White, P.A., Ft. Lauderdale, Fla., 1996—2002, Haliczer Pettis, P.A., Ft. Lauderdale, Fla., 2002—. Mem. ABA, Fla. Bar Assn., Broward County Bar Assn., Assn. Trial Lawyers Am., Def. Rsch. Inst., Am. Acad. Healthcare Attys., Phi Kappa Phi, Pi Sigma Alpha, Omicron Delta Kappa. Democrat. Methodist. Avocations: reading, jogging. Office: Haliczer Pettis PA 101 NE 3rd Ave Fort Lauderdale FL 33301-1162

HALIK, EUGENE EGON, engineering consultant; b. Prague, Czech Republic, Aug. 26, 1912; arrived in U.S., 1952, naturalized, 1957; s. Josef and Francis (Von Wallersberg) Halik; m. Rose Fremd Halik, Jan. 5, 1946 (dec. Apr. 27, 1996); 1 child, Michaela. ME, MS in Engring., Charles U., Prague, 1935. Engr. Lowy Hydropress Inc., N.Y.C., 1952—57; chief engr. Associated Univs. Inc. Nat. Radio Astronomy Obs., N.Y.C. and Greenbank, W.Va., 1957—62; rschr. Brookhaven Nat. Lab., 1962—73; rsch., cons. in electrohydraulics Princeton (N.J.) U., 1973—78; owner EEH Consulting Assocs., inc., McLean, Va. Presenter in field. Patentee in field. Mem.: N.Y. Acad. Scis., Am. Men and Women of Sci. Roman Catholic. Avocations: tennis, skiing, ice skating. Office: EEH Consulting Assocs Inc Regency Ste 714 1800 Old Meadow Rd Mc Lean VA 22102

HALILI, ANTONIO MARQUEZ, facilities maintenance mechanic; b. Caloocan City, Philippines, Jan. 9, 1951; s. Pedro Nosa Halili and Verginia Ileto Marquez; m. Brenda gotay Ferrer, Jan. 22, 1992; children: Jocelyn Jemeno, Anthony Bonifacio, Mark Solomon, Sara Virginia, Celina Marie. Diploma, Nat. Tech. Sch., L.A., 1983—85; postgrad., El Camino C.C., Torrance, Calif., 1986—88. Mechanic electrician USS Antietam CG 54, Long Beach, Calif., 1987—88. Vice-chair Asian pacific Islanders Employee Resource Group/Am. Airlines, 2003; participant, Saving Babies Lives March of Dimes, L.A., 2001—02; relief crew chief and leadman Go for Broke Found. Mem.: United Tondo Assn. (assoc.). Achievements include invention of a liquid hose clean up attachment. Home: 1318 E 55th St Long Beach CA 90805 Personal E-mail: tbhalili@hotmail.com.

HALIO, JAY LEON, language professional, educator; b. NYC, July 24, 1928; s. Samuel and Anna (Cohen) H.; children: Brian, Amy; m. Diane S. Isaacs. BA, Syracuse U., 1950; MA, Yale U., 1951, PhD, 1956. Instr. English U. Calif., Davis, 1955-57, asst. prof., 1957-63, assoc. prof., 1963-68, prof., 1968, U. Del., Newark, 1968—2003, assoc. provost for instrn., 1975-81, dir. Ctr. for Teaching Effectiveness, 1975-80, 86-87, dir. humanities semester, 1978-81; chmn. bd. editors U. Del. Press, 1985-97. Central exec. com. Folger Inst. Renaissance Studies, 1975-98; adv. bd. Ctr. for Renaissance and Baroque Studies, U. Md., mem. editl. adv. bd. Coll. Literature, Jour. Theatre and Drama Text; Fulbright-Hays sr. lectr. U. Malaya, 1966-67, Buenos Aires, Argentina, 1974. Author: Angus Wilson, 1964, Understanding Shakespeare's Plays in Performance, 1988, Philip Roth Revisited, 1992, Shakespeare in Performance: A Midsummer Night's Dream, 1994, 2d edit. 2003, Romeo and Juliet: A Guide to the Play, 1998, Understanding the Merchant of Venice, 2000, King Lear: A Guide to the Play, 2001, A Midsummer Night's Dream: A Guide to the Play, 2003; editor: Approaches to Macbeth, 1966, Twentieth Century Interpretations of As You Like It, 1968, Volpone, 1968, Macbeth, 1972, King Lear, 1973; (with David Bevington) Shakespeare: Pattern of Excelling Nature, 1978, British Novelists Since 1960: Dictionary of Literary Biography, vol. 14, 1983; (with Kenneth Muir, D.J. Palmer) Shakespeare, Man of the Theater, 1983; (with Barbara C. Millard) As You Like It: An Annotated Bibliography, 1985, Critical Essays on Angus Wilson, 1985, King Lear, 1992; (with Jerzy Limon) Shakespeare and His Contemporaries, 1992, The Merchant of Venice, 1993, The First Quarto of King Lear, 1994, Shakespeare's Romeo and Juliet: Texts, Contexts and Interpretation, 1995, Critical Essays on King Lear, 1996, (with Ben Siegel) Daughters of Valor: Contemporary Jewish American Women Writers, 1997, (with Hugh Richmond) Shakespearean Illuminations, 1998, Henry VIII, 1999, American Literary Dimensions, 1999 (with Ben Siegel), Comparative Literary Dimensions, 2000 (with Ben Siegel). Mem. MLA, Am. Lit. Assn., Assn. Lit. Scholars and Critics, Internat. Shakespeare Assn., Shakespeare Assn. Am., Phi Beta Kappa. Home: 8 Country Hill Dr Newark DE 19711-2526 Office: U Del Dept English Newark DE 19716 E-mail: jlhalio@yahoo.com.

HALITSKY, STEVE, application developer, researcher; b. Vinnitza, Ukraine, Aug. 31, 1943; s. Konstantyn and Olga Halitsky; m. Roxanne Bedzyk, July 7, 1975; children: Andrey Galitsky, Edward. MS in Applied Stats. and Computers, Cybernetics Inst., Kiev, Ukraine, 1975. C+ cert. Brainbench; cert. Russian transl. Wash. State Cert. Bd. Rschr. Cybernetics Inst., Kiev, 1972—80; sr. scientist Data Base Rsch. Inst., Kiev, 1982—91; translator Bible Socs. Printing Ho., Stockholm and Pasadena, Calif., 1990—93; tester and assembler Motorola, Inc., Schaumburg, Ill., 1994—95; quality technician Hydraforce, Inc., Lincolnshire, Ill., 1996—97, Quality TemPerm, Schaumburg, 1997—98; rsch. specialist Isomedix, Inc., Libertyville, Ill., 1997—98; tech. cons. SPR, Inc., Oak Brook, Ill., 1998—99; founder, CEO Theta Systems, Vernon Hills, Ill., 1999—; tech. cons. KFORCE, Inc., Oak Brook, 2000—01. Contbr. articles to profl. jours.; translator: The Practical Guide to Splines. Humanitarian aid organizer Former GULAG Prisoners Fellowship, Kiev, 1991—2003; rschr., organizer Studies of Anti-Nazi Resistance and Holocaust in Podolia,Ukraine), Vinnitza, 1991—2003; translator, interpreter, humanitarian aid helper several USA Christian Missions for former USSR, Kiev, 1988—91. Mem.: IEEE, ILAS (assoc.), SIAM (assoc.). Republican. Jewish. Achievements include development, formal description and implementation of new and more effective methods of analysis of multi-dimensional stochastic dynamic systems; establishment of specific boundaries for new methods of analysis of multi-dimensional systems. Avocations: jazz and classical music, herbal properties & remedies, humanitarian aid, history, reading. Home: 421 Grosse Pointe Cir Vernon Hills IL 60061 Office: Theta Systems 421 Grosse Pointe Cir Vernon Hills IL 60061 Personal E-mail: stevehalitsky@yahoo.com. E-mail: info@thetasystems.org.

HALIW, JEROME MICHAEL, civil engineer; s. Harry Jerome and Lillian Haliw; m. Kari Lynn Gagnon, May 20, 1989. BS, Colo. Sch. of Mines, 1991. Design engr. Isbill Associates, Inc., Aurora, Colo., 1992—97; project design engr. Raytheon Infrastructure, Inc., Englewood, Colo., 1997—2000; project mgr. Wash. Infrastructure Services, Inc., Littleton, Colo., 2000—02, chief discipline engr., airport design mgr. Denver, 2002—. Mem.: ASME, Colo. Sch. of Mines Alumni Assn., Order of the Engr. Office: Washington Group International Inc 7800 E Union Ave Ste 100 Denver CO 80237 Office Fax: 303-843-3133. E-mail: jerry.haliw@wgint.com.

HALKETT, ALAN NEILSON, lawyer; b. Chungking, China, Oct. 5, 1931; came to U.S., 1940; s. James and Evelyn Alexandrina (Neilson) H.; m. Mary Lou Hickey, July 30, 1955; children— Kent, James, Kate BS, UCLA, 1953, LL.B., 1961. Bar: Calif. 1962. Mem. firm Latham & Watkins, L.A., 1961-95, mem. exec. com., 1968-72, chmn. litigation dept., 1980-86, chmn. succession com., 1986-87. State chmn. Am. Coll., Calif., 1992-94; designee CPR panel Disting. Neutrals, 1994—. Served to lt. USN, 1954-58 Fellow Am. Coll. Trial Lawyers; mem. Calif. Bar Assn., Nat. Arbitration Forum, Def. Orientation Conf. Assn., Chancery Club, UCLA Law Alumni Assn. (pres. 1968), Order of Coif. Clubs: Jonathan (Los Angeles); Palos Verdes Country (Palos Verdes Estates, Calif.). Republican. Avocations: golf, old cars. Office: Latham & Watkins 633 W 5th St Ste 4000 Los Angeles CA 90071 2005 E-mail: halkett6@aol.com.

HALKIN, HUBERT, mathematics educator, research mathematician; b. Liege, Belgium, June 5, 1936; came to U.S., 1960; s. Leon E. and Denise (Daude) H.; m. Carolyn Mulliken, June 22, 1964 (div. 1971); children: Christopher, Sherrill-Anne; m. Katherine Hodges, Dec. 24, 1988 (div. 2001). Ingenieur, U. Liège, 1960; PhD, Stanford U., 1963. Tech. staff Bell Telephone Labs., Whippany, N.J., 1963-65; assoc. prof. math. dept. U. Calif., San Diego, 1965-69, prof., 1969—, dept. chmn., 1981-87. Editor Jour. Optimization Theory and Applications, 1968—, Revue Française d'Automatique de Recherche Operationnelle, 1973—. Guggenheim fellow, 1971-72. Mem.: Idyllwild, Club Aroma, Sierra Club. Office: U Calif San Diego Dept Math La Jolla CA 92093 E-mail: hhalkin@ucsd.edu.

HALL, ADAM STUART, lawyer; b. Atlanta, June 19, 1971; s. Andrew Clifford Hall and Patricia Ann Bursten. BA with honors, U. Fla., 1993, JD with honors, 1996. Bar: Fla. 1997, U.S. Dist. Ct. (so. dist.) Fla. 1997, U.S. Dist. Ct. (mid. dist.) Fla. 1998. Intern Supreme Ct. Fla., Tallahassee, 1995; assoc. Andrew Hall & Assocs., P.A., Miami, Fla., 1997-98, Hall, David and Joseph, P.A., Miami, 1998—. Chmn. unsecured creditor's com. Inre Telephone Co. Ctrl. Fla., Inc., Orlando, 1998-99. Mem. U. Fla. Coll. Law Alumni Coun., Gainesville, 1997—; mem. young leadership coun. United Way of Dade County, Miami, 1997—. Mem. ABA, ATLA, Acad. Fla. Trial Lawyers, Dade County Bar Assn. Avocations: scuba diving, skiing, football. Office: Hall David and Joseph PA 1428 Brickell Ave Penthouse Miami FL 33131

HALL, ALAN CRAIG, library director; b. Marietta, Ohio, Mar. 9, 1954; s. Harry Edward and Flossie June (Heddleston) H.; m. Barbara Ann Metzger, May 23, 1981; 1 child, Shawn Alan. BS in Edn., W.Va. U., 1976; MLS, Case Western U., 1977. With circulation dept. Washington County Pub. Libr., Marietta, Ohio, 1970-75; with govt. documents dept. Freiberger Libr., Cleve., 1976-77; dir. Delphos (Ohio) Pub. Libr., 1977-83, Pub. Libr. of Steubenville and Jefferson County, 1983—. Cons. Morgan County Libr., McConnellsville, Ohio, 1992-93, Barnesville (Ohio) Pub. Libr., 1991, Reed Meml. Libr., Ravenna, Ohio, 1997-98; chair Ohio Libr. Coun., Columbus, 1994, com. rev. bd. structure, 1999, co-chair Ohio statewide resource sharing com., 1998-99; pres. bd. dirs. SOLO Regional Libr. Sys., Ohio, 2002-2003; historic interpreter Ft. Steuben Project, 2000—. Author: Marietta's Innkeeper, 1991, The Mary Thompson Collection, 1997; editor: The Papers of A.T. Nye, 1975, Abandoned Underground Coal Mines of Jefferson County, 1991, Richmond, Ohio Cemetery Book, 1995; compiler Historic Pages Series, 1975-76; editor: Steubenville (Ohio) Bicentennial History Book, 1996-97; contbr. History of Ohio's Public Libraries, 2003; contbr. articles to profl. publs. Chairperson Ohio Humanities Coun., Steubenville, 1991; pres. Ret. Sr. Vol. Program, Steubenville, 1989-90; ruling elder Starkdale Presbyn. Ch., 1985-88, 94-96, 98-2000, chmn. pastor nominating com., 1996-97; mem. Cmty. Found. Jefferson County, 1999-2003, v.p., 2000—; mem. bicentennial com. Two Ridges Presbyn. Ch., 2002. Mem. ALA, Nat. Assn. Rd. Passengers, Jefferson County Hist. Soc., Steubenville Lions Club (pres. 1986-87), Ohio Libr. Assn. (pres. 1992-93, Libr. of Yr. 1989), Steubenville Rotary. Office: 407 S 4th St Steubenville OH 43952-2942 E-mail: alanh@oplin.org.

HALL, ALBERT L. retired lawyer; b. Chgo., June 17, 1926; s. Albert L. and Orpah (Starratt) H.; m. Catherine Ann Comstock, Sept. 27, 1947; children: Terry Lee, David M., Margaret Ruth, Diane Marie. Grad., Lake Forest Acad., 1944; BS, U. Ill., 1949, MS, 1950; JD, Northwestern U., 1955. Bar: Ill. 1955, U.S. Dist. Ct. (no. dist.) Ill. 1955. Tchr. Washington Park High Sch., Racine, Wis., 1950-52; ptnr. Hall, Roach, Johnston et al, Waukegan, Ill., 1958-91, of counsel, 1991-95, Bollman & Lesser, Lake Forest, Ill., 1996—. Arbitrator Am. Arbitration Assn., 1975-90, 19th Jud. Cir. Ct. Ill., 1990-98. Bd. dirs. Lake County Children's Orthopedic Clinic, Inc., 1966—, pres., 1979-81. With USNR, 1944-46. Mem. Lake County Bar Assn., Waukegan-Lake County C. of C. (pres. 1968-69), Delta Tau Delta, Phi Alpha Delta. Clubs: City Club of Waukegan (pres. 1970). Home: 2048 Hickory St Waukegan IL 60087-5019

HALL, ANDREW CLIFFORD, lawyer; b. Warsaw, Poland, Sept. 16, 1944; s. Edmund and Maria (Hahn) H.; came to U.S., 1949, naturalized, 1954; children: Michael Ian, Adam Stuart, Hilary Meyers Azrael, Katie Meyers; m. Gail Meyers, 1993. BA, U. Fla., 1965, JD with high honors, 1968. Bar: Fla. 1968, U.S. Dist. Ct. (so. dist.) Fla. 1968, U.S. Dist. Ct. (no. dist.) Ga. 1971, U.S. Ct. Appeals (5th cir.) 1971, Ga. 1973, U.S. Supreme Ct. 1974, U.S. Ct. Appeals (D.C. cir.) 1974, U.S. Ct. Appeals (11th cir.) 1981. Law clk. to judge U.S. Dist. Ct.; assoc., Haas, Holland, Levison, Gilbert, Atlanta, 1970-72, Frates, Floyd, Pearson, Stewart, Miami, 1972-75; ptnr. Storace, Hall & Hauser, Miami, 1975-79, Hall & Hauser, 1979-82, Hall & O'Brien, P.A., Miami, 1982-95, Andrew Hall and Assoc., Pa., 1995-99; Hall, David and Joseph, P.A., 1999—; instr. bus. law U. Fla.; Trustee U. Fla., Coll. of Law Found. Bd. dirs. Greater Miami Jewish Fedn.; chmn., bd. trustees, bd. dirs Cen. Agy. Jewish Edn., Ash Ha Torah; mem. coun. of 100 Fla. Internat. U. Mem. ABA, Hebrew Immigrant Aid Assn. (nat. bd. mem.), Fla. State Bar, Am. Judicature Soc., U. Fla. Coll. Law Alumni (coun.), Acad. Fla. Trial Lawyers (diplomate), Assn. Trial Lawyers Am., Phi Kappa Phi, Phi Alpha Delta, Order of Coif. Democrat. Jewish. Home: 3515 Bayshore Villas Dr Miami FL 33133 Office: Hall David and Joseph PA Att/Karen Fernandez 1428 Brickell Ave Ph Miami FL 33131-3411

HALL, ANNA CHRISTENE, retired government official; b. Tyler, Tex., Dec. 18, 1946; d. Willie B. and Mary Christine (Wood) H. BA in Polit. Sci., So. Meth. U., 1969. Clk.-stenographer Employment and Tng. Adminstrn., U.S. Dept. Labor, Dallas, 1970, fed. rep., 1970-80, program analyst Washington, 1980-84, div. chief, 1984-87, exec. asst., 1987-88, office dir. Dallas, 1988—2001; ret., 2002. Mem. Partnership for Employment and Tng., Nat. Honor Soc. Democrat. Presbyterian. Avocations: reading, theater, playing piano. Home: 603 Kingfisher Ln Arlington TX 76002-3456 E-mail: annachall@juno.com.

HALL, ANTHONY ELMITT, crop ecologist; b. Tickhill, Yorkshire, Eng., May 6, 1940; came to U.S., 1964; s. Elmitt and Mary Lisca (Schofield) H.; m. Bretta Reed, June 20, 1965; children: Kerry, Gina. Student, Harper Adams Agrl. Coll., Eng., 1958-60; student in agrl. engring., Essex Inst. Agrl. Engring., Eng., 1960-61; BS in Irrigation Sci., U. Calif., Davis, 1966, PhD in Plant Physiology, 1970. Farmer Dyon House, Austerfield, Eng., 1955-58; extension officer Ministry of Agr., Tanzania, 1961-63; research asst. U. Calif., Davis, 1964-70, asst. research scientist, 1971; research fellow Carnegie Inst., Stanford, Calif., 1970; prof. U. Calif., Riverside, 1971—, cons. agrl. devel., 1974—, chmn. dept botany and plant scis., 1994-97; prof. emeritus, 2003. Author: Crop Responses to Environment, 2001; editor: Agriculture in Semi-Arid Environments, 1979, Stable Isotopes and Plant Carbon-Water Relations, 1993; contbr. articles to profl. jours. Recipient BIFAD chair's award for scientific excellence, 2000, USDA Sec.'s Honor award plant breeding rsch., 2001. Fellow: Crop Sci. Soc. Am., Am. Soc. Agronomy; mem.: Phi Kappa Phi, Phi Beta Kappa, Gamma Sigma Delta (Disting. Achievement in Agr. award of merit 1999), Alpha Zeta. Achievements include design (with others) of a steady state porometer for measuring stomatal conductance; research on the physiology and breeding of heat and chilling tolerant, pest resistant and drought adapted cowpea cultivars including developing cowpea varieties CB27 and Ein El Gazal; patents in field, no6,501,006 B1, 2002. Office: U Calif Dept Botany & Plant Scis Riverside CA 92521-0124

HALL, BARRY G. evolutionary biologist; b. New York, July 17, 1942; m. Susan M. (Werlein), May 2, 1964; children: Steven, Scott, Rebecca Hathaway PhD, U. Wash., 1971. Asst. prof. Meml. U., Nfld. and Med. Sch., St. John's, Canada, 1974—77; asst. to assoc. to prof. U. Conn., Storrs, 1977—89; prof. U. Rochester, NY, 1989—2003, ret., 2003—. Author: (book) Phylo- genetics made easy: A how-to manual for molecular biologists, 2001; editor (editor in chief): Molecular Biology and Evolution, 1993—98. Recipient NIH Rsch. and Career Devel. Award, 1980; grantee, NIH, 1978—86, 1986—92, NSF, 1989—93, NIH, 1992—96, Am. Cancer Soc., 1996—98, NIH, 2000—03; scholar Fulbright Sr. Scholar, 1984. Mem.: Am. Soc. Microbiology. Achievements include patents for Determination of identity between two organisms by subjecting a restriction endonuclease digest of genomic DNA to electrophoresis and hybridization.

HALL, BENNETT FREEMAN, minister; b. Macon, Ga., Nov. 30, 1914; s. Charles McDonald and Mary Elizabeth (Lyon) H.; m. Mae Elizabeth Wells, June 2, 1937; children: Mari, Laura, Louise, Ben. Student, Bryan U., 1934-36; AB, Stetson U., 1938; ThM, So. Bapt. Theol. Sem., 1943; postgrad., Jewish Theol. Sem., 1968-71; ThM, Princeton Theol. Sem., 1975; DMin, Drew U., 1979. Ordained to ministry Bapt. Ch., 1936. Pastor, Sale Creek, Tenn., 1935-36, Sorrento, Fla., 1936-38, Union Gospel Mission, Louisville, Ky., 1938-39, Lucerne Park Ch., Orlando, Fla., 1939-41, Fayetteville and Williams, Ind., 1941-42, Falmouth (Ky.) Bapt. Ch., 1942-44, First Bapt. Ch., Titusville, Fla., 1944-49, Bay Haven Bapt. Ch., Sarasota, Fla., 1950-53, Southside Bapt. Ch., Bradenton, Fla., 1954-67, Somerset Hills Bapt. Ch., Bernardsville, N.J. (Now in Basking Ridge, N.J.), N.J., 1967-79, First Bapt. Ch., Lexington, Ky., 1982-85. Trustee Bapt. Bible Inst., Fla., 1949—59; mem. state mission bd. Fla. Bapt. Conv., Fla., 1957—59; dean, tchr. ext. dept. Stetson U., 1960—64; evangelist Jamaica Crusade, 1966; missions com. Met. N.Y. Bapt. Assn., 1968—72, chmn. constn. and credentials com., 1972—77; tchr., sem. ext. Met. N.Y. Assn., 1976—78; adv. bd. Cumberland Coll., Williamsburg, Ky., 1982—91; organizer seminars for ministers, Bradenton and Sarasota. Chmn. ARC, Titusville, 1944-46; mem. Mental Health Orgn., Bradenton, 1964-66 Home: 293 S Main St Winchester KY 40391-2471 *Two great statements, learned in college, have been the guiding principle of my life. The Socratic challenge: "Follow the truth wherever it leads." The other: "Learn to distinguish between the spiritual ointment and the spiritual receptacle."*

HALL, BEVERLY ADELE, nursing educator; b. Houston, Aug. 19, 1935; d. Leslie Leo and Lois Mae (Pesnell) H. BS, Tex. Christian U., 1957; MA, NYU, 1961; PhD, U. Colo., 1974. RN, Tex., N.Y. With Ft. Worth (Tex.) Dept. Health, 1957-59; asst. prof. U. Mass., Amhurst, 1961-65; chief nurse N.Y.C. Med. Coll., 1965-67; asst. prof. U. Colo., Denver, 1967-70; assoc. prof. U. Washington, Seattle, 1974-80; prof., chmn. dept. U. Calif., San Francisco, 1980-84; Denton Cooley prof. nursing U. Tex., Austin, 1984-2001, prof. emeritus, 2001—, mem. grad. faculty Sch. Biomed. Sci. Galveston; disting. prof. Coll. Art & Scis., Akachi, Japan, 1999-2000 Pres. med. svcs. Bd. Dir. Project Transitions; disting. prof. Coll. Nursing, Arts and Scis., Hyogo, Japan; mem. NIH Study Group; cons. HIV/AIDS Internat. Coun. fo Nurses. Author: Mental Health and the Elderly, 1985 (Book of Yr.); mem. editl. rev. bd. Advances in Nursing, Archives Psychiat. Nursing, Qualitative Health Rsch., Rsch. in Nursing and Health, Nursing Outlook, Jour. Profl. Nursing, Jour. of the Am. Psychiat. Nurses Assn.; contbr. articles to profl. jours., chpts. to books. Served to capt. U.S. Army, 1962-66. Recipient Tex. Excellence Teaching award U. Tex. Ex-Students Assn., 1994. Fellow Am. Acad. Nursing (governing bd., mem. fellowship selection com.), Am. Coll. Mental Health Adminstrn.; mem. ANA (divsn. gerontological practice), Coun. Nurse Rschrs., Am. Inst. Life Threatening Illness and Loss, So. Nursing Rsch. Soc. Home: 23 Jackson Ct San Antonio TX 78230-2569 Office: U Tex 1700 Red River St Austin TX 78701-1412

HALL, BEVERLY BARTON, librarian; b. Cin., July 15, 1918; d. Clarence Earl Barton and Maude Ethel Wedmore; m. Randolph Van Lew Hall, Apr. 26, 1947; children: Barton M., Martha H. Kern, Patricia H. Pellerin. BA, Middlebury Coll., 1940; BS, Columbia U., 1941; MS, So. Conn. State Coll., 1975. Cert. tchr./libr. grades K-12, Conn. Libr. Wellesley (Mass.) Coll., 1941-42, Great Neck (N.Y.) Pub. Libr., 1942-44, Yale U. Sch. Law, New Haven, 1944-50, Amity Regional H.S., Woodbridge, Conn., 1967-80. Author: Secret of the Lion's Head, 1995; also short stories. Founder, bd. dirs. Orange (Conn.) Pub. Libr., 1956-63; founder, head libr. St. John's Ch. Libr., Naples, Fla., 1993—; active Collier County Geneal. Soc., Collier County Hist. Soc., Collier County Friends of the Libr. Mem. Ch. and Synagoge Libr. Assn. (sec. 1999-2000). Republican. Episcopalian. Avocations: reading, water aerobics, counted cross-stitch, crocheting, music. Home: Apt 107 49 High Point Circle South Naples FL 34103

HALL, BEVERLY JOY, police officer; b. St. Paul, Minn., Dec. 31, 1957; d. Kenneth Ray and Harriet Kathleen (Fuller) H.; m. Charles Alan Neuman, Feb. 14, 1956. AAS in Law Enforcement, North Hennepin C.C., Brooklyn Park, Minn., 1977; grad., FBI Nat. Acad., 1993; BA in Law Enforcement Mgmt., Met. State U., St. Paul, 1999. Lic. peace officer, Minn. Community svc. officer Brooklyn Park Police Dept., 1977-79; police officer St. Paul Police Dept., 1979-86, police sgt., 1986-95, police lt., 1995-2000, police comdr., 2000—. Hostage negotiator, St. Paul Police Dept., 1991-92, hostage negotiating team coord., 1992-96. Mem. Internat. Assn. Women Police (regional coord. 1988-94, bd. dirs.), Nat. Assn. Women Law Enforcement Execs. (2d. v.p. 2000-01), Minn. Assn. of Women Police (pres. 1982-86), Assn. Tng. Officers of Minn., FBI Nat. Acad. Assocs. Avocations: gardening, jogging, reading. Office: Saint Paul Police Dept 100 11th St E Ste 1 Saint Paul MN 55101-2296

HALL, BLAINE HILL, retired librarian; b. Wellsville, Utah, Dec. 12, 1932; s. James Owen and Agnes Effie (Hill) H.; m. Carol Stokes, 1959; children: Suzanne, Cheryl, Derek. BS, Brigham Young U., 1960, MA, 1965, MLS, 1971. Instr. English, Brigham Young U., Provo, Utah, 1963—72, humanities libr., 1972—96. Book reviewer Am. Reference Book Ann., 1984-2000. Author: Collection Assessment Manual, 1985, Saul Bellow Bibliography, 1987, Jerzy Kosinski Bibliography, 1991, Jewish American Fiction Writers Bibliography, 1991, Conversations with Grace Paley, 1997; editor: Utah Libraries, 1972-77 (periodical award ALA 1977); contbr. articles to profl. jours. Bd. dirs. Orem (Utah) Pub. Libr., 1977-84; mem. Orem Media Rev. Commn., 1984-86; chmn. Utah Adv. Commn. on Librs. With U.S. Army, 1953-54, Korea. Mem. ALA (coun. 1988-92), Utah Libr. Assn. (pres. 1980-81, Disting. Svc. award 1989), Mountain Plains Libr. Assn. (bd. dirs. 1978-83, editor newsletter 1978-83, pres. 1994-96, grantee 1979, 80, Disting. Svc. award 1991), Phi Kappa Phi. Mem. Lds Ch. Avocations: writing, photography, carpentry, family history, reading. Home: 230 E 1910 S Orem UT 84058-8161 E-mail: bhall11@att.net.

HALL, BRIAN KEITH, biology educator, author, scientist; b. Port Kembla, N.S.W., Australia, Oct. 28, 1941; s. Harry J. and Doris (Garrad) Hall; m. June Denise Priestley, May 21, 1966; children: Derek Andrew, Imogen Elizabeth. BSc, U. New Eng., Australia, 1963, BSc with honors, 1965; PhD, U. New Eng., 1968, DSc, 1978. Teaching fellow U. New Eng., Armidale, 1965-68; asst. prof. biology Dalhousie U., Halifax, N.S., Can., 1968-72, assoc. prof., 1972-75, prof., 1975—, chmn. dept. biology, 1978-85, Killam rsch. prof., 1990-95, faculty sci., Killam prof. biology, 1996-2001, George S. Campbell prof. of biology, 2001—, univ. rsch. prof., 2002—; Killam rsch. fellow, 2003. Vis. prof. U. Guelph, 1975, U. Queensland, Australia, 1981, Southampton U., England, 1982; Rayne mem. vis. prof. U. Western Australia, 1993; mem. adv. com. on life scis. Natural Scis. and Engring. Rsch. Coun. Can., 1985; Turner-Newall lectr. U. Manchester, England, 1985; Frontiers in Biology lectr. Tex. A&M U., 1992; Von Hofsten lectr. Uppsala U., Sweden, 1993; Plenary lectr. Internat. Congress Vert. Morphol., 1994; Fry lectr. Can. Soc. Zoologists, 1994; Sarnat lectr. UCLA, 1994; Miller vis. res. prof. U. Calif., Berkeley, 1997; Landsdowne vis. prof. U. Victoria, 1998; Glaser Disting. vis. prof. Fla. Internat. U., 2000. Author: (book) Developmental and Cellular Skeletal Biology, 1978; author: (with N. MacLean) Cell Commitment and Differentiation, 1987; author: The Neural Crest, 1988, Evolutionary Developmental Biology, 1992, Evolutionary Developmental Biology, 2d edit., 1998, The Neural Crest in Development and Evolution, 1999; editor: Cartilage, 3 vols., 1983, Bone, A Treatise, 9 vols., 1990—94; editor: (with S. Newman) (book) Cartilage: Molecular Aspects, 1991; editor: (with J Hanken) The Vertebrate Skull, 3 vols., 1993, Homology: The Hierarchical Basis of Comparative Biology, 1994; editor: (with M. H. Wake) The Origin and Evolution of Larval Forms, 1999; editor: (with W. Olson) Keywords and Concepts in Evolutionary Development Biology, 2003; editor: (with W. R. Pearson and G. Muller) Environment, Development and Evolution, 2003. Recipient Young Scientist of Yr. medal, Atlantic Provinces Interuniv. Com. in Scis., 1974, Fry medal, Can. Soc. Zoologists, 1994, Craniofacial Biology Rsch. award, 1996, Alexander Kowalsky medal, 2001, award of excellence in rsch., Govt. of Can., 2002; fellow, Nuffield Found., 1982, Warwick James, London U., 1989, Ctr. Human Biology, U. Western Australia, 1993—; Killam Rsch. fellow, 2003—. Fellow: Royal Soc. Can.; mem.: Am. Acad. Arts and Sci. (hon. fgn.). Home: 2384 Armcrescent E Halifax NS Canada B3L 3C7 E-mail: BKH@is.dal.ca.

HALL, CARL WILLIAM, agricultural and mechanical engineer; b. Tiffin, Ohio, Nov. 16, 1924; s. Lester and Irene (Routzahn) H.; m. Mildred Evelyn Wagner, Sept. 5, 1949; 1 dau., Claudia Elizabeth. BS, B. in Agricultural Engring. summa cum laude, Ohio State U., 1948; M.M.E., U. Del., 1950; PhD, Mich. State U., 1952. Registered profl. engr., Mich., Ohio. Instr. U. Del., 1948-50, asst. prof., 1950-51, Mich. State U., 1951-53, assoc. prof., 1953-55, prof., 1955-70, chmn. dept. agrl. engring., 1964-70; dean, dir. research (Coll. Engring.); prof. mech. engring. Wash. State U., Pullman, 1970-82, pres. WSU Rsch. Found., 1973-82; dep. asst. dir. Directorate for Engring. NSF, 1982-90; ret., 1990. With ESCOE, Inc., Washington, 1979; dist. vis. prof. Ohio State U., 1991; rsch. con. U. P.R., 1957, 63; del. to USSR, 1958, 87; cons. U. Nacional de Colombia, 1960; cons. dairy engring., India, 1961, food engring., Taiwan, 1961, Mission to Ecuador, 1966, U. Nigeria, 1967, UNDP/SF Project 80 (higher edn. Latin Am.), 1964-70, world food and nutrition study Nat. Acad. Sci., 1976-77; mem. engring. edn. del. to People's Republic of China, 1978, Indonesia, 1978, 93, 94; co-chmn. NRC-India Nat. Sci. Acad. Workshop, New Delhi, 1979; with ACA, Inc. (cons. engring.), 1956-70, pres., 1962-70; chmn. Nat. Dairy Engring. Conf., 1953-66; mem. postgrad. edn. select com. USN, Monterey, Calif., 1975; rsch. fellow Jap. Soc. promotion Sci., 1991. Author: Drying Farm Crops, 1957, Agricultural Engineering Index 1907-60, 1961-70, 71-80, 81-90, (with others) Drying of Milk and Milk Products, 1966, 71, Agricultural Mechanization for Developing Countries, 1973; co-editor: Agricultural Engineers Handbook, 1960, Processing Equipment for Agricultural Products, 1963, 2d edit., 1979, Spanish edit., 1968, Milk Pasteurization, 1968, Ency. of Food Engineering, 1971, 86, Drying Cereal Grains, 1974, 2d edit., 1991, Dairy Technology and Engineering, 1976, Errors in Experimentation, 1977, Dictionary of Drying, 1979, Drying and Storage of Agricultural Products, 1980, Biomass as an Alternative Fuel, 1981, Dictionary of Energy, 1983, Food and Energy, 1984, Food and Natural Resources, 1988, Biomass Handbook, 1989, (with others) Drying and Storage of Grains, 1992, Literature of Agricultural Engineering, 1992, The Age of Synthesis, 1995, Laws and Models, 1999; editor, emeritus: Drying Technology: Marcel Dekker, Inc.; contbr. yearbooks, encys., handbooks, over 400 articles to profl. jours. Staff sgt. infantry U.S. Army, 1943—46, ETO. Decorated Bronze Star and CIB; recipient Disting. Faculty award Mich. State U., 1963, Centennial Achievement award Ohio State U., 1970, Massey-Ferguson Edn. medal, 1976, Max Eyth medal, Germany, 1979, Medal du Merite, France, 1979, Silver medal, Paris, 1980, Cyrus Hall McCormick medal, 1984, Disting. Svc. award and medal NSF, 1988, Excellence in Drying award IDS, 1990, Food Engring. award and medal, 1993; named Engr. of Yr. D.C. Coun. of Engrs. and Architects, 1999. Fellow AAAS (life), ASME (life, v.p. rsch. 1993-95), ASAE (life, pres. 1974-75), Am. Inst. Med. and Biol. Engring., NAE, Accreditation Bd. Engring. and Tech., Internat. Commn. Agrl. Engrs. (v.p. 1965-74); mem. Am. Soc. Engring. Edn. (life), Am. Inst. Biol. Scis., Wash. Soc. Profl. Engrs. (nat. dir. 1975-79), Va. Soc. Profl. Engrs. (pres. No. Va. chpt. 1987-88), Engrs. Coun. for Profl. Devel. (exec. com., bd. dirs., sec. 1973-74, chmn. engring. accreditation commn. 1979-80), 99th Inf. Divsn. Assn., VFW, Inst. Food Tech., Inst. Biol. Engring., Sigma Xi, Tau Beta Pi, Phi Kappa Phi, Gamma Sigma Delta, Phi Lambda Tau. Achievements include rsch. in energy, drying, food engring., properties of materials and biomass. Office: Engring Info Svcs 2454 N Rockingham St Arlington VA 22207-1033

HALL, CAROL ANN, music educator; b. Lamar, Colo., Dec. 22, 1952; d. Raymond Dewey and Hazel Vera Morrow; m. Charlie Merle Hall, Apr. 21, 1979 (dec. Oct. 10, 2001); 1 child, Charlie Walter. AA, Lamar C.C., 1972; BA in Elem. Edn., BA in Music Edn. K-12, Adams State Coll., Alamosa, Colo., 1974. 4th grade tchr. Springfield Elem. Sch., 1974—75, tchr. K-6 music, 1990—; tchr. K-6 music Parkview Elem. Sch., Lamar, 1975—78; tchr. K-12 music Vilas Sch., 1986—88. Piano tchr., Vilas, 1986—88; voice tchr., Pritchett, Vilas and Springfield, Colo.; performer, recorded composed song Goldband records, 2002—03. Music leader, mem. Tri Ch. Trio Springfield Bapt. Chapel. Recipient award, Am. Women of Who's Who, 2002—03. Mem.: Springfield Elem. Tchrs. Assn., Music Educators Nat. Conf. Baptist. Avocations: bowling, composing. Home: 429 Monroe Box 85 Pritchett CO 81064

HALL, CHARLES ALLEN, aerospace and energy consultant; b. Wichita, Kans., Oct. 11, 1933; s. J. Raymond and Nila Mildred (Allen) H.; m. Berneida K. Dechant, Nov. 29, 1940; children: Melissa Sue Smith, Charles A. Rowden. BS in Engring. and Mgmt., U. Denver, 1968; MSCE, U. Colo., 1972, PhD, 1978. With Martin Marietta Corp., Denver, 1959-64, mgr. mech. engring., 1964-78, dir. mech. engring., 1978-82, v.p. engring. Balt., 1982-84, dir. research, corp. Bethesda, Md., 1984-86, v.p. engring., corp., 1986-88; v.p. tech. activities Energy Systems, Oak Ridge, Tenn., 1988-92, pres. splty. components, 1992-96. Cons. in nuclear waste cleanup and aerospace fields, 1996—; program mgr. Hanford Nuclear Waste Treatment Plant for CH2M HILL, 2000-01. Inventor O-Leak Fuel Tubing, 1980; concept for solar energy chem. furnace, 1977. Mem. Colo. State Air Quality Control Commn., Denver, 1978-82. Mem. Fla. Def. Conversion and Transition Commn., Bayou Club (Largo, Fla.), Black Diamond Ranch (Lecanto, Fla.). Avocations: golf, Christian study. Died Oct. 1, 2002.

HALL, CHARLES P(OTTER), JR., educator consultant; b. Milw., Wis., July 7, 1932; s. Charles Potter Sr. and Myrtle P. (Pedersen) H.; m. Constance Nuzum, June 23, 1956; children: Peter C., Michael J., David E., Kristin E. BBA, U. Wis., 1954; PhD, U. Pa., 1961. CLU, CPCU. Spl. agt. Northwestern Mut. Life Ins. Co., Milw., 1955-58; asst. prof. U. Wash., Seattle, 1961-64; asst. dir. econ. rsch. AMA, Chgo., 1964-66; with Temple U., Phila., 1966—2001, assoc. dean, 1986-87, prof., dept. chair, 1968-75, 87-95, prof. emeritus, 2001—; dir. Internat. MBA, Paris, 1995-96, Phila., 1996—2001, cons., 2001—02. Cons. Pa. Healthcare Cost Containment Coun., Harrisburg, 1987, Math. Policy Rsch., Inc., Princeton, NJ, 1988—89; bd. dir. DE Valley Health Edn. Rsch. Found., Phila., 1983—89, cmty. svc., Vis. Nurse Assn. Ea. Montgomery Twp., Abington, Pa., 1985—91; nat. adv. bd. Am. Assn. for Partial Hospitalization, 1989—93; v.p. Internat. Ins. Soc.; mem. internat. visitors coun. Global Ind. Ctr., Phila. Mem. editl. bd.: Hospital Risk Control, 1994—2000; contbr. articles to profl. jours. Elder Carmel Presbyn. Ch., Glenside, Pa., 1968—71, 1982—87, 1996—2001, 2003—, trustee, 1974—80. Capt. USAFR, 1954—57. Fellow Am. Coll. Healthcare Exec. (regents adv. com. 1986-95, 96-2003); mem. Am. Risk and Ins. Assn. (pres. 1979-80), Am. Econ. Assn., Am. Pub. Health Assn., Am. Hosp. Assn., Internat. Ins. Soc. (v.p. 1991-2000), Nat. Acad. of Soc. Ins. Internat. Health Econ. Assn. (sec. 1994-96), Nat. Assn. Health Svc. Exec. (adv. com. to Phila. chpt. 1991-95). Republican. Presbyterian. Avocations: tennis, golf, travel. Home: 534 Custis Rd Glenside PA 19038-2012 Office: Temple U Fox Sch Bus And Mgmt Philadelphia PA 19122 E-mail: cphall4@comcast.net.

HALL, CHARLES WASHINGTON, lawyer; b. Dallas, June 30, 1930; s. Albert Brown and Eleanor Pauline (Hopkins) H.; m. Mary Louise Watkins, Aug. 3, 1957; children: Katherine Louise, Allison Ash, Charles Washington III. BA, U. of South, 1951; JD, So. Meth. U., 1954, LLM in Taxation, 1959. Bar: Tex. 1954. Ptnr. Storey, Armstrong & Steger, Dallas, 1954-57; sr. ptnr. Fulbright & Jaworski, Houston, 1957—. Mem. adv. com. on tax litigation Dept. Justice, 1979-80; dir. Friedman Ind., Inc., Tex. Med. Ctr., Inc. Houston; mem. Commr. Internal Revenue Adv. Group, 1990-91; mem. adv. coun. U.S. Claims Ct., 1988—. Pres., trustee Sarah Campbell Blaffer Found., Houston; dir. Goodwill Industry, Houston, 1977-84; trustee Inst. Religion, Houston, 1990-2000, Killson Found., Houston, M.D. Anderson Found., Houston, Allbritton Found., Houston, Allbritton Art Inst., Houston, John S. Dunn Rsch. Found., Houston, Houston Child Guidance Ctr., 1984-86, The Howell Family Found., Houston; trustee, treas. Ctr Am. Intrnat. Law (formerly Southwestern Legal Found.), Dallas; S.W.

Rsch. Inst., San Antonio; gov. Houston Forum, 1992-95. Recipient Disting. Alumni award, So. Meth. U., 1989. Fellow Am. Bar Found.; mem. ABA (chmn. sect. taxation 1987-88, ho. dels. 1991-95, nat. conf. lawyers and CPAs chmn. 1988-2000), Houston Bar Assn., Dallas Bar Assn., State Bar Tex. (chmn. sect. taxation 1970-71), Internat. Bar Assn., Am. Coll. Tax Counsel (regent 1982-91), Am. Law Inst., River Oaks Country Club, Petroleum Club, Coronado (pres. 1982-83), Houston City Club, Met. Club (Washington), Old Baldy Club, Order of St. Lazarus. Episcopalian. Office: Fulbright & Jaworski LLP 1301 Mckinney St Ste 5100 Houston TX 77010-3031

HALL, CHARLOTTE HAUCH, newspaper editor; b. Washington, Sept. 30, 1945; d. Charles Christian and Ruthadele Bertha (LaTourrette) H.; m. Robert Lindsay Hall, June 8, 1968; 1 child, Benjamin H. BA, Kalamazoo Co., 1966; MA, U. Chgo., 1967. Reporter, news editor The Ridgewood (N.J.) Newspapers, 1971-74; copy editor, news editor The Record, Hackensack, N.J., 1975-76; asst. mng. editor The Boston Herald Am., 1977-78; dep. met. editor The Washington Star, 1979-80; news editor, Nassau County editor, Washington news editor Newsday, Melville, N.Y., 1981-87, asst. mng. editor, 1988-94; mktg. dir. Newsday, Inc., Melville, 1994-96, mng. editor, 1997-99, v.p., mng. editor, 1999—. Trustee Kalamazoo Coll. Mem. Am. Soc. Newspaper Editors (bd. dirs.), Newspaper Assn. Am., Phi Beta Kappa. Office: Newsday Inc 235 Pinelawn Rd Melville NY 11747-4250

HALL, CLARA JEAN, special education educator; b. Dover, Del., Mar. 28, 1953; d. James Paris and Grace Helen (Neal) Mosley; m. Howard Ralph Hall, Aug. 12, 1978; children: Ilea Elizabeth Mosley, Karelle Ayita. BS, Del. State U., 1975; MEd, Western Md. Coll., 1976; PhD, Cleve. State U., 1994. Head resident - dorm Western Md. Coll., Westminster, Md., 1975—76; itinerent tchr. Sterck Sch. for the Deaf, Newark, Del., 1976—78, NJ Commn. for the Blind, Newark, 1978—80; instr. The Pa. State U., University Park, Pa., 1980—87; asst. prof. Cuyahoga CC, Parma, Ohio, 1999—. Adv. com. to develop certification Pa, Dept. of Edn., Harrisburg, Pa., 1986; adv. bd. - deaf interpretive services Cuyahoga CC, Parma, Ohio, 1999—; bd. of dir. Cleve. Hearing & Speech Ctr., Cleveland, Ohio, 2002—. Treas. Shaker Heights H.S. Band Boosters, Shaker Heights, Ohio, 2000—02. Recipient Outstanding Tchr. Award, Access Office Cuyahoga CC, 2002, Disting. Educator Award, Phi Delta Kappa, 1998, Commendation for Outstanding Svc., Ohio State Senate, 1997, Who's Who in Am. Teachers Award, Who's Who in Am. Teachers, 2002. Mem.: Hands That Bridge Sign lang. Club (advisor 2001—02), Am. Sign lang. Teachers Assn., Shaker Heights Dr. Martin Luther King Program. Liberal. Avocations: reading, singing, travel, doing voice overs, doing voice overs. Home: 16310 Parkland Dr Shaker Heights OH 44120 Office: Cuyahoqa Cmty Coll 11000 Pleasant Valley Rd Parma OH 44130 Home Fax: 216-987-5612. Personal E-mail: clara.hall@tri-c.edu.

HALL, CLARENCE ALBERT, JR., geologist, educator; b. L.A., Jan. 5, 1930; s. Clarence Albert and Margaret Olive (Fabrick) H.; children: Eric Robert, Kris Delorah. BS, Stanford U., 1952, MS, 1953, PhD, 1956. Instr. U. Oreg., Eugene, 1954-55; mem. faculty UCLA, 1956—, prof. geology, chmn. dept. geology, 1974-76, chmn. dept. geophysics and space physics, 1976, chmn. dept. earth and space scis., 1976-78, dean of phys. scis., 1983-94; dir. White Mountain Rsch. Sta. U. Calif. Systemwide, 1979-95. Contbr. articles to profl.jours.; editor Jour. Paleontology, 1971-71. Fulbright rsch. fellow in Italy, 1963-64, 70-71; recipient Dibblee medal, 1998. Fellow Geol. Soc. Am., Paleontol. Soc. Office: UCLA Dept Earth & Scis Los Angeles CA 90095-1567 E-mail: hall@ess.ucla.edu.

HALL, CLYDE MATTHEW, lawyer, advocate; b. Pocatello, Idaho, Apr. 8, 1951; s. William Mckinley and Charlotte Rose (Truchot) H. Student Idaho State U., 1968-75; Cert. in Broadcasting, Career Acad.-San Francisco, 1970; JD, Utah State U., 1980. Bar: Idaho 1981, Tribal 1981. Park ranger Grand Teton Nat. Park, Moose, Wyo., 1975-79; art instr. Sho-Ban High Sch., Ft. Hall, Idaho, 1979-80; chief judge Ft. Hall Tribal Ct., 1980-83; Indian art cons. Grant Teton Nat. Park, 1983— ; performer Am. Indian Art Exchange, Seattle, 1983— ; lawyer Ft. Hall Tribes, 1983— ; cons. D.T. Vernon Indian Arts Mus., Denver Mus. Natural History; others. Contbr. articles to profl. jours. Mem, New Alliance Party, Washington, Native Am. Ch.; chmn. bd. dirs. Alcohol Adv. Bd., Ft. Hall, 1981-88. Mem. Credit Assn. Idaho, Internat. Credit Assn., Shoshone Bannock Tribal Bar Assn., Am. Indian Broadcasters Assn., Imperial Gem. Ct. of Idaho (ambassador to native Ams.), G.A.I. Club. Democrat. Home: PO Box 135 West Agency Rd Fort Hall ID 83203 Office: Fort Hall Tribal Ct PO Box 306 Fort Hall ID 83203-0306

HALL, CYNTHIA HOLCOMB, federal judge; b. Los Angeles, Feb. 19, 1929; d. Harold Romeyn and Mildred Gould (Kuck) Holcomb; m. John Harris Hall, June 6, 1970 (dec. Oct. 1980). AB, Stanford U., 1951, JD, 1954; LL.M., NYU, 1960. Bar: Ariz. 1954, Calif. 1956. Law clk. to judge U.S. Ct. Appeals 9th Circuit, 1954—55; trial atty. tax div. Dept. Justice, 1960—64; atty.-adviser Office Tax Legis. Counsel, Treasury Dept., 1964—66; mem. firm Brawerman & Holcomb, Beverly Hills, Calif., 1966—72; judge U.S. Tax Ct., Washington, 1972—81, U.S. Dist. Ct. for central dist. Calif., Los Angeles, 1981—84; cir. judge U.S. Ct. Appeals (9th cir.), Pasadena, Calif., 1984—, sr. judge, 1997—. Lt. (j.g.) USNR, 1951—53. Office: US Ct Appeals 9th Cir 125 S Grand Ave Pasadena CA 91105-1621

HALL, CYNTHIA JEAN, music educator, author, composer, musician; b. Rossford, Ohio, July 29, 1950; MusB, Ohio Wesleyan U., 1972; MusM, MusMEd, Tex. Tech. U., 1979. Life Credential Music Edn., Calif. Lectr., cons. various founds. music edn., 1984—; music specialist Oak Park (Calif.) Unified Sch. Dist., 1989—; composer. Author children's, young adult and adult books. Vol. entertainer USO, Boys and Girls Clubs Am. Named one of 10 best music edn. tchrs. in Am., 1989. Mem. Romance Writers Am., Soc. Children's Book Writers and Illustrators, Alpha Xi Delta, Mu Phi Epsilon. Protestant. Home: 2109 Sanchez Dr Camarillo CA 93010-2517 Fax: 805-445-9211. E-mail: kybdkybd@earthlink.net.

HALL, DAVID, sound archivist, writer; b. New Rochelle, N.Y., Dec. 16, 1916; s. Fairfax and Eleanor Rayburn (Remy) H.; married, June 8, 1940 (widowed Mar. 24, 1992); children: Marion Hall Hunt, Jonathan, Peter, Susannah. BA, Yale U., 1939; postgrad., Columbia U., 1940-41. Advt. copy writer Columbia Records, Bridgeport, Conn., 1940-42; music program annotator NBC, N.Y.C., 1942-48; classics music dir. Mercury Record Corp., N.Y.C., 1948-56; music editor Stereo Rev., N.Y.C., 1957-62, contbg. editor, 1962-98; pres. Composers Rec., Inc., N.Y.C., 1963-67; curator Rodgers and Hammerstein Archives of Recorded Sound., N.Y. Pub. Library, N.Y.C., 1967-83, cons., 1983-85. Dir. Music Ctr. Am.-Scandinavian Found., N.Y.C., 1950-57; Fulbright vis. scholar Copenhagen U., 1956-57; free-lance writer, lectr.; classical recordings cons., 1967-98; mem. Commn. for the White House Record Libr., 1979. Author: The Record Book, 1940-48. Trustee Wilton Library Assn., Conn., 1975-79. Decorated knight Order of Lion, Finland. Mem. Nat. Acad. Rec. Arts and Scis. (trustee 1965-67), Nat. Music Council (dir. 1968-80), Assn. for Recorded Sound Collections (pres. 1980-82) Democrat. Home: PO Box 257 Castine ME 04421-0257 E-mail: dtdh@acadia.net.

HALL, DAVID, newspaper editor; b. Lebanon, Tenn., Mar. 7, 1943; s. Hal Turner Hall and Mildred (Durham) Hall Carson; m. Suzanne Lovell, Sept. 5, 1964; children: Carson, Matthew, Amanda. BS, U. Tenn., 1965, MA in Econs., 1966; postgrad., Northwestern U., 1995. Fin. news reporter, asst. fin. editor, Middle East corr., chief editorial writer, asst. mng. editor Chgo. Daily News, 1966-78; asst. mng. editor Chgo. Sun-Times, 1978; mng. editor St. Paul Pioneer Press, 1978-82; exec. editor St. Paul Pioneer Press and Dispatch, 1982-84; editor, v.p. The Denver Post, 1984-86, editor, sr. v.p., 1986-88; editor, v.p. The Record, Hackensack, N.J., 1988-92; editor The Plain Dealer, Cleve., 1992-99. Bd. dirs. Coun. on World Affairs. With U.S. Army, 1967-69, Vietnam. Recipient Disting. Alumni award Castle Heights Mil. Acad., Lebanon, 1984. Mem. Am. Soc. Newspaper Editors, Cleve. Com. on Fgn. Rels., Soc. Profl. Journalists, Scarabbean Soc., Cleve. City Club Found., Phi Gamma Delta. Presbyterian.

HALL, DAVID, law educator, dean, law educator, department chairman; b. Savannah, May 26, 1950; s. Levi and Ethel Hall; m. Marilyn Braithwaite-Hall; children: Sakile, Kiamsha, Rahsaan. BS in Polit. Sci., Kans. State U., 1972; MA in Human Rels., U. Okla., 1975, postgrad., 1975—78, JD, 1978; LLM, Harvard U., 1985, Doctor Juridical Scis., 1988. Bar: Ill. 1978, Mass. 1978, Okla. 1978. Profl. basketball player Spaidero Pallacanestro, Inc., Udine, Italy, 1972—74; grad. asst. human rels. dept. U. Okla., Norman, 1974—75; lawyer Chgo. regional office Fed. Trade Commn., 1978—80; assoc. prof. law Sch. Law U. Okla., Norman, 1983—85; asst. prof. law Sch. Law U. Miss., 1980—83; assoc. dean academic affairs Sch. Law Northeastern U., Boston, 1988—92, prof. law, 1985—, dean Sch. Law, 1993—99, provost, 1999—. Instr. ethnic studies dept. and law ctr. U. Okla., Norman, 1975—79; Robert D. Klien U. lectr. Northeast-eern U.; co-chair legal edn. forum Law Sch. Harvard U., Cambridge, Mass., 1984—85, co-coord. Nat. Symposium on the Constitution and Race, 1987; coord. law student outreach program Barron Assessment Ctr., Boston. Contbr. articles to profl. jours. Mem. bd. Mass. Civil Liberties Union, 1987—88, Inst. Affirmative action, Boston, TransAfrica Forum Scholars Adv. Coun., Washington, commn. on equal justice Mass. Legal Assistance Corp., 1995—, Nat. Consumer Law Ctr., 1993—; pres. African Cultural Soc. St. Paul A.M.E. Ch., Cambridge, Mass.; bd. dirs. Gang Peace Inc., 1995—. Named Professor of the Yr., NAACP, Outstanding Dean of Yr., Nat. Assn. Pub. Interset Lawyers, 1997; named to Savannah Athletic Hall of Fame; recipient African Am. 1st Oratory Competition, Black Rose award, Sigma Gamma Rho, Humanitarian award, Nat. Conf. Cmty. and Justice. Fellow: Am. Sociol. Assn.; mem.: ABA (standing com. lawyers' pub. svc. responsibility 1995—), Nat. Black Wholistic Soc. (pres. 1993, mem. bd. 1984—), Black Faculty and Staff Orgn., Nat. Conf. Black Lawyers (pres. Mass. chpt. 1986—), Okla. Bar Assn. (Outstanding Sr. award), Mass. Bar Assn. (mem. bd. minorities in the profession 1995—96), Boston Bar Assn., Assn. Law Sch. (diversity in legal edn. 1995—96), Order of the Coif. Office: Northeastern U Office of Provost 112 Hayden Hall 360 Huntington Ave Boston MA 02115-5005 E-mail: d.hall@nunet.neu.edu.

HALL, DAVID CHARLES, retired zoo director, veterinarian; b. St. Paul, Aug. 12, 1944; s. Wilhelm Frank and Estelle Elizabeth H.; m. Sandra Jean Prink, Oct. 2, 1945; children: Jason Wilhelm, Jeremy Marvin. BME, U. Minn., 1966, DVM, 1976. Sr. mktg. engr. Rosemount Engrng. Co., Eden Prairie, Minn., 1966-75; ptnr. Oregon (Wis.) Vet. Med. Clinic, 1976-86; dir. Henry Vilas Zool. Pk., Madison, Wis., 1986-2000; ret., 2000. Advisor Food divsn. Wis. Dept. Agrl. Trade and Consumer Protection, Madison, 1985-86, Exam. sect. Wis. Dept. Regulation and Licensing, Madison, 1981-82. Recipient Caleb Dorr acad. award, U. Minn., 1972-76. Mem. AVMA, Am. Assn. Zoo Vets., Am. Assn. Zool. Pks. and Aquariums, Phi Kappa Phi, Phi Zeta. Lodges: Optimists (pres. 1980). Lutheran. Avocations: skiing, swimming, hiking, hunting, other outdoor sports. Home: 3162 Waucheeta Trl Madison WI 53711-5952

HALL, DAVID MCKENZIE, business and management educator; b. Gary, Ind., June 21, 1928; s. Alfred McKenzie and Grace Elizabeth (Crimiel) H.; m. Jaqueline Virginia Branch, Apr. 30, 1960; children: Glen D., Gary D. BA, Howard U., 1951; MS, N.C. Agrl. Tech. State U., 1966; PhD, Kennedy Western U., 2002. Enlisted USAF, 1951; advanced through grades to brig. gen.; chief social actions Hdqrs. Mil. Airlift Command, Scott AFB, Il., 1972-1974; dep. base comdr. 375th Air Base Group, Scott AFB, 1974-75, base comdr., 1975-76; dir. data processing Air Force Logistics Command, Wright-Patterson AFB, Ohio, 1976-77, comptr., 1977-83; ret. USAF, 1983; dir. data processing Delco-Remy div. GM, Anderson, Ind., 1983-85; regional mgr. Electronic Data Systems, Anderson, 1985-88, Saginaw, Mich., 1988-93; prof. mgmt. and mktg. Northwood Univ., Midland, Mich., 1993-97; exec. in residence Saginaw Valley State U., University Center, Mich., 1997—. Brig. gen. USAF, 1951—83. Recipient Hon. Citizenship East St. Louis, Ill., 1975, Key to City Gary Ind., 1981, spirit of Saginaw award, 1999, Sagimore of the Wabash, 1999. Mem. NAACP, Saginaw Cmty. Outreach Found., Cmty. Affairs Com., Prince Hall Masons, Kappa Alpha Psi. Methodist. Avocations: reading, woodworking. Home: 49 W Hannum Blvd Saginaw MI 48602-1938 Office: Saginaw Valley State U Curtiss Hall 7400 Bay Rd University Center MI 48710 E-mail: dhall@svsu.edu.

HALL, DAVID WALTER, botanist, consultant; b. New Orleans, Sept. 6, 1940; s. Walter Knowlton and Lenna Anne (Guthrie) H.; m. Tiia Reet Karell, Nov. 25, 1981; children: Alexander, Elizabeth. BS, Ga. So. U., 1965, MS, 1967; PhD, U. Fla., 1978. Diplomate Am. Bd. Forensic Examiners; cert. expert in botany; registered profl. wetland scientist. Rsch. assoc. U. Fla., Gainesville, 1971-73, asst. in botany, 1973-81, dir. plant identification and info. svc., 1981-90; sr. scientist KBN Engring. and Applied Scis., Inc., Gainesville, 1990-96, Golder Assocs. Inc., Gainesville, 1996-97; pres. David W. Hall Cons., Inc., Gainesville, 1997—. Author: Illustrated Plants of Florida and the Coastal Plain, 1993, (with L.B. McCarty, J.W. Everett, J.R. Murphy and F. Yelverton) Color Atlas of Turfgrass Weeds--Golf Courses, Lawns, Roadside, Recreational Areas, Commercial Sod, 2001; co-author spl. publs. Inst. Food and Agrl. Scis., U. Fla., 1987, 88, 89, 92, dept. civil engring. U. Fla., 1989; contbr. or co-contbr. chpts. to: Aquatic Pest Control Applicator Training Manual, 1991, Turf Weeds and Their Control, 1994, Forensic Taphonomy: The Post-Mortem Fate of Human Remains, 1997. Bd. dirs., v.p. Fla. Tennis Found., 1992—; tennis coach Ga. So. U., 1966-67; profl. racket stringer, 1963-90; pvt. instr. tennis, 1965-90; umpire various tennis tournaments, 1963-85; dir. profl. tennis tournaments, 1964-85; condr. tennis clinics for area high schs. and coll. programs, leagues, underprivileged children; organizer, mem. City of Gainesville Tennis Adv. Bd.; founder U. Fla. Gator Tennis Boosters, 1968; bd. dirs. tennis program 300 Club, Gainesville, 1975-76, organizer, tennis chmn.; organizer, dir. Fla. intercity adult tennis league; mem. dist. 4 Cmty. Devel. Com., 1994-95; commr. tennis Gainesville Sports Coun., 1989-90. Named one of Outstanding Young Men of Am., 1973; NDEA Title IV fellow U. Fla., 1967-70; Mercer Rsch. fellow Harvard U., 1968; recipient Disting. Svc. award Fla. Assn. County Agrl. Agts., 1990, Nat. Assn. County Agrl. Agts., 1990, Disting. Alumni award dept. biology Ga. So. U., 1991, Svc. award Fla. Dept. Environ. Regulation, 1988, Svc. Leadership award Augusta Coll., 1963; ranked in various coll. and other tennis tournaments, 1960-94. Fellow Am. Coll. Forensic Examiners, Am. Acad. Forensic Scis.; mem. AAAS, Am. Soc. Plant Taxonomists, Exotic Plant Pest Coun.; Assn. Southea. Biologists, Soc. Wetland Scientists, Weed Sci. Soc. Am., So. Weed Sci. Soc., Fla. Acad. Scis., Fla. Native Plant Soc. (Green Palmetto Svc. award 1987), Nat. Assn. Environ. Profls., Fla. Assn. Environ. Profls., North Fla. Bot. Soc., Fla. Weed Sci. Soc. (pres. 1987-88, sec., treas. 1984-86, bd. dirs. 1984-90, Outstanding Weed Scientist 1999), Internat. Assn. for Identification (Fla. divsn.), Internat. Weed Sci. Soc., USTA (mem. exec. bd. 1991-93, mem. dels. assembly 1991-93, mem. pres.'s com. 1989-91, active other coms.), Fla. Tennis Assn. (pres. 1989-91, 1st v.p. 1985-87, chmn. adult tennis coun. 1986-89, mem. exec. bd. 1982-95, USTA del. 1991-93, mem. Fla. Tennis Assn./USTA league appeals com. 1985-86, Man of Yr. 1984), Gainesville Area Tennis Orgn. (pres., bd. dirs. 1994-2000), Swannee River Valley Cmty. Tennis Assn. (v.p., bd. dirs. 2000—). Achievements include definition of discipline of forensic botany. Home and Office: 3666 NW 13th Pl Gainesville FL 32605-4823

HALL, DENISE, special education educator; b. L.A., Sept. 15, 1960; d. Willie Mae and Curtis Coleman; children: Lanneau L. White Iv, Joshua L. White. BA, U. Tex., San Antonio, 1999. Cert. spl. edn. Com. officer U. Tex. at San Antonio Police Dept., San Antonio, 1995—98; tchr. sci. and english spl. edn. Northside Alternative HS, San Antonio, 1999—2002. Mentor Northside Ind. Sch. Dist., San Antonio, 1999—2002. Grantee Edn., U. Tex. at San Antonio, 1997—99. Home: 11218 Taylor Crest San Antonio TX 78249 Office: Northside Alternative HS 144 Hunt Ln San Antonio TX 78245-1102 Personal E-mail: Dhall915@aol.com.

HALL, DON ALAN, editor, writer; b. Indpls., Aug. 7, 1938; s. Oscar B. and Ruth Ann (Leak) H.; m. Roberta Louise Bash, Apr. 30, 1960; children: Alice Leigh, Nancy Elizabeth. BA, Ind. U., 1960, MA, 1968. News editor Rock Springs (Wyo.) Daily Rocket-Miner, 1960-63; mag. editor, picture editor Waukegan News-Sun, Ill., 1964-66; reporter, copy editor Salem Capital Jour., Oreg., 1966-70; free lance journalist Victoria, B.C., Can., 1970-74; copy editor, sci. writer, music reviewer Corvallis (Oreg.) Gazette-Times, 1974-78, copy desk chief, 1978-82, news editor, 1983-84, author weekly opinion column, 1985-87; author weekly nature column for Oreg. newspapers, 1976-85; instr. dept. journalism Oreg. State U., 1984-87. Author: On Top Of Oregon, 1975, Bird in the Bush, 1986; editor Mammoth Trumpet, Center for the Study of the First Americans, 1991-2001. Recipient Westinghouse-AAAS sci. writing award, 1977 Home and Office: 620 NW Witham Dr Corvallis OR 97330-6535

HALL, DONALD JOYCE, SR., greeting card company executive; b. Kansas City, Mo., July 9, 1928; s. Joyce Clyde and Elizabeth Ann (Dilday) H.; m. Adele Coryell, Nov. 28, 1953; children: Donald Joyce, Margaret Elizabeth, David Earl. AB, Dartmouth, 1950; LL.D., William Jewell Coll., Denver U., 1977. With Hallmark Cards, Inc., Kansas City, Mo., 1953—, adminstrv. v.p., 1958-66, pres., chief exec. officer, 1966-83, chief exec. officer, 1983-86, chmn. bd. only, 1983—. Dir. United Telecommunications, Inc., Dayton-Hudson Corp., William E. Coutts Co., Ltd.; past dir. Fed. Res. Bank Kansas City, Mut. Benefit Life Ins. Co., Business Men's Assurance Co., Commerce Bank Kansas City, 1st Nat. Bank Lawrence. Pres. Civic Council Greater Kansas City; past chmn. bd. Kansas City Assn. Trusts and Founds.; Bd. dirs. Am. Royal Assn., Friends of Art, Eisenhower Found.; bd. dirs. Kansas City Minority Suppliers Devel. Council, Kans. City Minority Suppliers Devel. Council,Kansas City Symphony; past pres. Pembroke Country Day Sch., Civic Council of Greater Kansas City; trustee, past chmn. exec. com. Midwest Research Inst.; trustee Nelson-Atkins Museum of Art. Served to 1st lt. AUS, 1950-53. Recipient Eisenhower Medallion award, 1973; Parsons Sch. Design award, 1977; 3d Ann. Civic Service award Hebrew Acad. Kansas City, 1976; Chancellor's medal U. Mo., Kansas City, 1977; Disting. Service citation U. Kans., 1980 Mem. Kansas City C. of C. (named Mr. Kansas City 1972, dir.), AIA (hon.) Office: Hallmark Cards Inc Office Chmn Bd 2501 Mcgee St Kansas City MO 64108-2600*

HALL, DONALD JOYCE, JR., consumer products company executive; BA in Econs. and Lit., Claremont Coll.; MBA, U. Kans. With Hallmark Cards, Inc., Kansas City, Mo., 1975—, various pos., including dir. splty. store devel., gen. mgr. Keepsake Ornaments, v.p.-creative, v.p. product devel., 1997—99, exec. v.p. strategy and devel., 1999—2002, pres., CEO, 2002—. Office: Hallmark Cards Inc 2501 McGee St Kansas City MO 64108*

HALL, DONALD ORELL, lawyer, rancher; b. Waco, Tex., Nov. 11, 1926; s. Ernest Orell and Thelma (Day) H.; m. Mary Ann Morgan, Sept. 1, 1951; children: Lisa Don, Brett Clayton. LLB, Baylor U., 1951, JD, 1969. Bar: Tex. 1951, U.S. Dist. Ct. (we. dist.) Tex. 1955, U.S. Ct. Appeals (5th cir.) 1983, U.S. Supreme Ct. 1983. Assoc. Koehne & Fulbright, Waco, 1951-54; judge Waco, 1954-56; dist. atty. Office of Prosecutor, Waco, 1956-67; ptnr. Hall & Kettler, Waco, 1968-87; pvt. practice Waco, 1988—. Guest columnist, newspapers, 1955—. With USN, 1943-46, PTO. Mem. ABA, Waco Bar Assn. (pres. 1955-56), Delta Theta Phi, Masons, Scotish Rite, York Rite. Republican. Baptist. Avocations: outdoors, sports, pilot, hunting, dog and horse breeding. Home and Office: 8208 Whippoorwill Dr Waco TX 76712-3412

HALL, DONALD VINCENT, social worker; b. Ft. Dodge, Iowa, June 13, 1955; s. John William and Helen Evelyn (Swanson) H.; m. Marla Jo Adamson, May 28, 1977; children: Lucas William, Jessica Lauren. BSW, U. Iowa, 1977; MSW, U. Kans., 1979. Cert. clin. social worker; lic. social worker, Iowa; diplomate bd. clin. social work; qualified clin. social worker. Social worker Heartland Edn. Agy., Johnston, Iowa, 1979-91, facilitator conflict resolution and concensus decision making, cons. long range planning, presenter workshops, 1989—; pvt. practice clin. social worker, psychotherapist children, individauls, couples, families, groups Counseling and Assessment Svcs., P.C., 1991—. Participant Des Moines Family Therapy Tng. Inst., 1991-92. Bd. dirs. Johnston (Iowa) Community Sch., 1984-90, pres. bd., 1987-90; chair Iowa Bd. for Treatment of Sexual Abuses, 2000-2001. Presbyterian (ordained elder). Avocation: private pilot. Home: 6845 NW Beaver Dr Johnston IA 50131-1245 Office: Counseling and Assessment Svcs PC 2404 Forest Dr Des Moines IA 50312-5400

HALL, DORIS SPOONER, educator; b. New Orleans, Dec. 27, 1949; d. Henry and Geneva (Battley) Spooner; m. Morris D. Hall, Aug. 4, 1973; 1 child, Amy Evon. B of Music Edn., La. State U., 1971, M of Music Edn., 1972, postgrad., ALA A&M U., 1991. Cert. tchr. Ala., La. Band dir. Shreveport (La.) City Schs., 1972-73; asst. band dir. Ala. A&M U., Normal, 1973-74, asst. prof. music, 1974-79, aux. coord. marching units, 1979-87, prof. music, 1980—. Lectr. music U. Ala., Huntsville, 1980-89, Oakwood Coll., Huntsville, 1980-90; clinician Ala. Sch. System, Birmingham, 1989-92; cons. in field. Active Huntsville Sympjony Orch., 1975-79, 86-92; recitals U. Ala. and Ala. A&M U., 1990-92. Named Outstanding Young Women, 1982; recipient Outstanding Achievers awards, 1983. Mem. AAUP, Nat. Flute Assn., Nat. Woodwinds Assn., Music Educators Nat. Conf., Ala. Edn. Assn., Tau Beta Sigma, ALpha Kappa Alpha. Roman Catholic. Avocations: dancing, reading, skating. Home: 12000 Bell Mountain Dr SW Huntsville AL 35803-3406 Office: Ala A&M U PO Box 258 Normal AL 35762-0258

HALL, DOROTHY SUSAN, nurse, educator; b. Lafayette, Ind., Apr. 18, 1959; d. Chester R. and Velma L. Hall; m. John Micheal Ott, Dec. 24, 1980 (div. Oct. 1990); children: Jennifer, Nicholas, Jacob. AAS in Surg. Tech., Ivy Tech. State Coll., Lafayette, 1994; BSN, Graceland Coll., Lamoni, Iowa, 1996; MSN, Purdue U., 2001. Cert. surg. technologist. Staff nurse Hi-Desert Med. Ctr., Joshua Tree, Calif., 1981-82; staff nurse-surgery Tri-City Med. Ctr., Oceanside, Calif., 1983-84, St. Elizabeth Med. Ctr., Lafayette, 1985-87, staff nurse emergency dept., 1987-89; instr. surg. tech. Ivy Tech. State Coll., 1987-95, assoc. prof., chair surg. tech. program, 1995—98. Treas., Crestview United Brethren Women's Missionary Fellowship, 1997-98. Mem. Assn. Surg. Technologists, Assn. Oper. Rm. Nurses. United Brethren. Avocations: gardening, reading. Home: 3441 Equinox Ter Lafayette IN 47909-7301 Office: Ivy Tech State Coll 3101 S Creasy Ln Lafayette IN 47903-6299 E-mail: dhall@ivytech.edu.

HALL, DOUGLAS ERSKINE, artist, educator; b. San Francisco, Apr. 25, 1944; s. Chaffee Earl Hall and Carolyn Erskine Andrews; m. Diane Andrews Hall; 1 child, Gannon C. BA, Harvard U., 1966; postgrad., Skowhegan (Maine) Sch. Painting and Sculpture, 1967; MFA, Rinehart Sch. Sculptire, Md. Inst. Art, 1969. Prof. San Francisco Art Inst., 1981—. Trustee San Francisco Art Inst., 1982—85, 1997—99; vis. artist Chgo. Art Inst., 1987, 94, U. Sao Paulo, Brazil, 1990; bd. dirs. Bay Area Video Coalition. Book, Doug Hall, Photographs, 2001, Beyond Boundaries: Contemporary Photography in California, The American Century: Art and Culture 1950-2000, one-man shows include Galerie Edition Kunsthandel, Essen, Germany, 2001, Bellvue (Wash.) Mus., 2001, Kunstwerke, Berlin, 1994, exhibited in group shows at The Aldrich Mus. Contemporary Art, Ridgefield, Conn., 2002, XXV Bienal de Sao Paulo, Brazil, 2002, Mary Boone Gallery, N.Y., 2001, Represented in permanent collections Berlinische Galerie, Martin Gropius Bau, Berlin, Mus. Modern Art, N.Y., Ctr. George Pompidou, Paris, Kunsthaus, Zurich, San Francisco Mus. Modern Art, Whitney Mus. Am. Art, N.Y., Mus. Contemporary Art, Chgo. Individual Artists' fellow, Nat. Endowment for the Arts, 1979—80, 1985—86, 1995—96, John Simon Guggenheim Meml. fellow, 1991—92. Fellow: Am. Acad. Rome (The Gilmore D. Clarke & Michael Rapuano Rome prize in visual arts 1995—96). Avocation: classical cellist.

HALL, DOUGLAS LEE, computer science educator; b. San Antonio, Feb. 5, 1947; s. Robert Arthur and Thelma (Stischer). AA in Foreign Lang., San Antonio Coll., 1967; BA in Spanish, U. Tex., 1969; MEd in Bilingual Edn., Pan Am. U., 1977; PhD, N. Tex. State U., 1987. Tchr. Edgewood Ind. Sch. Dist., San Antonio, 1969-73, Brownsville (Tex.) Ind. Sch. Dist., 1973-74, 76-78; precious metals specialist Nu-Metals, Inc., Dallas, 1974; tchr. DPC Am. Sch., Dubai, UAE, 1975-76; tng. dir. ABDick, San Antonio, 1978-79; bilingual tchr. Dallas Ind. Sch. Dist., 1979-82; computer cons. Taylor Mgmt. Systems, Dallas, 1982-83; lectr. in field N.Tex. State U., Denton, 1984-86; grad. advisor St. Mary's U., San Antonio, 1986—, chair dept. computer sci., 1990—2003, pres. faculty senate, 1992-93. Dir. Deutscher Volkstanzverein, San Antonio, 1987—; asst. dir. San Antonio Folk Dance Fest, 1986—; advisor St. Mary's U. Chpt. Assn. for Computing Machinery, 1989—; CEO Athens Solutions, 2000—, Xarism Multi Media, 2000—. Contbr. articles to profl. jours. Docent Inst. Texan Cultures, San Antonio, 1989—; pres. Crown Hill Pk. Homeowners, San Antonio, 1986-89; del. 1st U.S.-Japan Grassroots Summit, 1991. Named Tchr. of Yr., Brownsville Ind. Sch. Dist., 1974, 1977, Outstanding Elem. Tchr., 1974, Disting. Grad. Faculty Mem., U. North Tex., 1991—92, Disting. Computer Sci. Alumnus, 1998; recipient Disting. Alumnus award, San Antonio Coll., 2000, Tex. Folk Dance award, 2002. Mem. NEA, IEEE, ACM, Tex. State Tchrs. Assn., Am. Assn. Artificial Intelligence. Avocations: theology, genealogy, foreign languages. Home: 515 Marquis St San Antonio TX 78216-5217 Office: Saint Mary's U One Camino Santa Maria San Antonio TX 78228-8524

HALL, DOUGLAS SCOTT, astronomy educator; b. Lexington, Ky., May 30, 1940; s. William Scott and Catherine (Read) H.; m. Bonnie Schumacher, June 3, 1964 (div. 1978); children: Bruce Douglas, Brandon Scott; m. Mimi Kemp,

Aug. 1, 1981. BA in Chemistry, Swarthmore Coll., 1962; MA in Astronomy, Ind. U., 1964, PhD in Astronomy, 1967. Rsch. assoc. Dyer Obs., Nashville, 1967; asst. prof. Vanderbilt U., Nashville, 1967-71, assoc. prof., 1971-80, prof., 1980—. Dir. Dyer Obs., Nashville, 1986—; cons. Tenn. State U., Nashville, 1988—, adj. prof., 1991—; chair allocations com. Internat. Space Sta. Amateur Telescope, 2001--, chmn. proposal rev. com., 2001—. Co-author: Supernova 1987-A!, 1988, Photoelectric Photometry of Variable Stars, 1988; contbr. papers to profl. jours.; referee for various astron. jours. and rsch. found.; founder Internat. Amateur and Profl. Photoelectric Photometry Comms., 1980—, editor, 1984—; mem. edit. bd. Inf. Bull. Variable Stars, 1991—. Recipient U.S. Sr. Scientist award Alexander von Humbolt Found., Fed. Republic Germany, 1973-74; named Astronomer of Yr., Astron. League, 1984; rsch. grantee NSF, 1968-87, NASA, 1977-83, Rsch. Corp., 1979. Mem. Internat. Astron. Union, Am. Astron. Soc. (rsch. grantee 1988), Astron. Soc. of the Pacific (liaison), Internat. Amateur and Profl. Photoelectric Photometry (pres. 1980—), Am. Assn. Variable Star Observers (editl. bd. 1976—), Tenn. Acad. Sci. (editl. bd. 1972), S.E. Assn. for Rsch. in Astronomy (bd. dirs. 1992—), Barnard-Seyfert Astron. Soc. (bd. dirs. 1996—), Sigma Xi (pres. Vanderbilt chpt. 1987-89). Office: Arthur J Dyer Observatory Vanderbilt Univ Nashville TN 37235 E-mail: hall@astro.dyer.vanderbilt.edu.

HALL, ELEANOR WILLIAMS, public relations executive; b. Boston; d. James Murray and Julia Eleanor (Williams) H. AB cum laude, Radcliffe Coll., 1945. Exec. sec. Am. Express Co., N.Y.C., 1950-62, adminstrv. asst. corp. mktg., 1963-65, mgr. corp. mktg., 1965-69, mgr. corp. pub. rels., 1969-71; mgr. mktg. svcs. Am. Express Internat. Banking Corp. (now Am. Express Bank Ltd.), N.Y.C., 1971-72, asst. treas. advt. and pub. rels., 1972-76, asst. v.p. advt. and pub. rels., 1976-82; pres. Eleanor Hall Assocs., Inc., 1982-90. Mem. Harvard-Radcliffe Club. Address: 342 102d Ave SE Ste 218 Bellevue WA 98004-6165

HALL, ELLA TAYLOR, clinical school psychologist; b. Macon, Miss., Nov. 30, 1948; d. Essex and Mamie (Roland) Taylor; children: Banyikaai Monique (dec.), Motiqua Shante. BA, Fisk U., 1971, MA, 1973; PhD, George Peabody Coll., 1978. Mental health specialist behavioral sci. divsn. Meharry Med. Coll., Nashville, 1976-77; assoc. psychologist Bronx (N.Y.) Psychiat. tr., 1979; clin. psychologist Wiltwyck Residential Treatment Ctr., Ossining, N.Y., 1979-81; clin. cons. Abbott House, Irvington, N.Y., 1982-85; sch. psychologist Abbott Union Free Sch. Dist., 1985—. Cons. psychologist Youth Theater Interactions, Inc., N.Y., rschr in the field. Author: (poetry) Double Twister, Somebody, Clinging Tears, 1994, Maple Tree at Dawn, 1995, Down My Three Rows, 1995, Mama Sis, 1995, These Times, 1995, Ordinary, 1996, Young Wilted Flower, 2000, Secret Garden, 2000, Blood Silence, 2000; (art) In My Mind, 1994, Picking Cotton, 1995. Lay reader, acolyte Episcopal Ch.; mem. Com. on Spl. Edn. NIMH tng. grantee, Kendall grantee; Crusade fellow. Mem. Schomburg Ctr. for Rsch., N.Y. State Psychol. Assn., N.Y. Bot. Soc., Wildlife Conservation Soc., Delta Sigma Theta. Avocation: photography.

HALL, FLOYD, retired retail executive; b. Duncan, Okla., Sept. 4, 1938; m. Janet Hall; children: Larry, Karen. Student, Bakersfield Jr. Coll., So. Meth. U., Harvard U., 1977. Nat. sales mgr. Montgomery Ward, Chgo., 1966-70; v.p., regional v.p. The Singer Co., Dallas, Tex., 1970-73; pres., CEO B. Dalton Book Seller, Mpls., 1973-81; chmn., CEO Target Stores, Mpls., 1981-84, Grand Union Co., Wayne, N.J., 1984-89, also bd. dirs.; chmn., CEO The Museum Co., East Rutherford, N.J., 1989-95, also bd. dirs.; chmn., pres., CEO Kmart Corp., Troy, Mich., 1995-2000, also bd. dirs. Bd. dirs. Lynx Techs., Kenwood Prodns. Trustee Bklyn. Mus.; bd. dirs. Give Kids The World, Jundt Growth Fund. Served with U.S. Army.*

HALL, FRANKLIN PERKINS, lawyer, banker, state official; b. Amelia, Va., Dec. 12, 1938; s. Perkins Lee and Lois E. Hall; m. Phoebe Ann Poulterer, July 26, 1969; children: Kimberly Ann, Franklin P. Jr. BS, Lynchburg Coll., 1961; MBA, Am. U., 1964, JD, 1966. Bar: Va. 1966. Aide to U.S. Senate, Washington, 1964; asst. sec. Dept. HUD, Washington, 1968-69; sr. ptnr. Hall & Hall, Richmond, 1969—. Chmn. bd. Cardinal Savs. and Loan Assn., Richmond, Va., 1979-84; chmn. bd. Commonwealth Bank, Richmond, 1984— ; spl. counsel Va. Gen. Assembly, Richmond, 1970-75. Del. Va. House of Dels.; active Va. Gen. Assemly, 1976—; chmn. bd. Cen. Richmond Assn., 1974-75; pres. Richmond Jaycees, 1972-73. Recipient Disting. Svc. award Richmond Jaycees, 1972, Award Va. Jaycees, 1974, Disting. Citizen award Nat. Mcpl. League, 1976; named Outstanding Young Man of Va. award, 1973. Mem. Va. Trial Lawyers Assn. (bd. govs. 1982-84), Richmond Bar Assn. (exec. com. 1973-76), Soc. Advancement Mgmt., Newcomen Soc. Democrat. Presbyterian. Office: Hall & Hall 1401 Huguenot Rd Ste 100 Midlothian VA 23113-2662

HALL, FRED WILLIAM, JR., lawyer; b. Franklin, N.H., Sept. 22, 1920; s. Fred William and Grace Rachel (Canney) Hall; m. Jane Fell Coe, Sept. 23, 1950; children: Marcella, Susan, John. BS, U. N.H., 1941; JD, U. Mich., 1948; LLD (hon.), U. N.H., 1974. Mem. Govs. Judicial Selection Commn., 2000—. Bd. dirs. Jarvis Co., Inc., Rochester. Trustee U. N.H., 1966-73, chmn. bd., 1968-72; mem. N.H. Gov.'s Council, 1963-64, 2000-02, Gov.'s Judicial Selction Commn. Lt. col. U.S. Army, 1941-45, ETO. Decorated Silver Star with oak leaf cluster, Bronze Star with 2 oak leaf cluster; recipient Outstanding Civilian Service medal, Dept. Army, 1979, Civilian Aide to Sec. of the Army, 1970-78, U. N.H. Alumni Meritorious Service award, 1974, Charles Holmes Pettee medal, 1996; Paul Harris fellow, Rotary Found., 1984. Mem. ABA, N.H. Bar Assn. (pres. 1965-66), Rotary. Republican. Episcopalian. Home: 18 Eastern Ave Rochester NH 03867-1400 Office: Law Office Fred Hall Jr 59 S Main St PO Box 780 Rochester NH 03866-0780 Fax: 603-335-0946.

HALL, FREDERICK KEITH, chemist; b. Leeds, Eng., Jan. 3, 1930; naturalized, 1976; s. Frederick Stanley and Mary Elizabeth (Stocks) H.; m. Patricia Ellison, Aug. 25, 1956; children: Simon Keith, Stephanie Jane, Andrew Nicholas. BS with 1st class honors, U. Manchester, 1951; PhD, U. Leeds, 1954; grad. advanced mgmt. program, Harvard U., 1979. Rsch. chemist Courtaulds (Can.) Ltd., 1956-58, asst. tech. mgr., 1958-60, tech. mgr., 1960-63, plant mgr., 1963-66; dir. tech. svc. Internat. Paper Co., 1966-70, asst. dir. rsch. ctr., 1970-72, dir. primary process, 1972-75, corp. dir. rsch., 1975-77; dir. S & ED labs., 1977-79; chief scientist S & T labs., 1979-93, chief scientist, dir. rsch., 1994—; ret., 1995. With Brit. Army, 1953-55. Fellow TAPPI (pres. 1991-93), Royal Soc. Chemistry, Textile Inst., Am. Inst. Chemists; mem. Tuxedo Club. E-mail: fkhall@aol.com.

HALL, GARY, JR., Olympic athlete; b. Cin., Sept. 26, 1974; Recipient Gold medal 100 medly relay, Gold medal 100 free relay, Silver medal 50-meter freestyle and Silver 100-meter freestyle Atlanta Olympics, 1996; Gold medal 50-meter freestyle, Gold medal 100 medley relay, Silver medal 100 freestyle relay and Bronze medal 100-meter freestyle Sydney Olympics, 2000,; set Am. record for 50-meter freestyle. Office: USA Swimming 1 Olympic Plz Colorado Springs CO 80909-5746

HALL, GEORGANNA MAE, elementary school educator; b. St. Louis, June 4, 1951; d. George Winfred and Judith Lou (Wheatley) H. BS in Edn., Stephen F. Austin U., 1973; MS in Edn., U. Houston, 1979. Cert. elem., early childhood and kindergarten edn. tchr., Tex.; cert. mid mgmt. adminstr. Elem. educator Lamar Consol. Ind. Sch. Dist., Rosenberg, Tex., 1973-94; part-time campus coord. Houston C.C., 1994; regional dir. Sylvan Learning Ctrs. Pasadena (Tex.) Ind. Sch. Dist., 1994—. Mem. Smith Elem. Improvement Task Force, Richmond, Tex., summers 1988-90, active mem., summer 1991. Mem. choir St. John's Meth. Ch., Richmond. Mem. Tex. Classroom Tchrs. Assn., Nat. Assn. for the Edn. Young Children, Assn. Curriculum and Supervision, Celebration Ringers, Delta Kappa Gamma, Sigma Kappa. Avocations: needlework, crafts, doll collecting. Home: 4771 Sweetwater Blvd #147 Sugar Land TX 77479 Office: Sylvan Learning Ctrs 1020 E Thomas Pasadena TX 77506-2213

HALL, GEORGE ROBERT, economist; b. Pasadena, Sept. 30, 1930; s. George Jay and Anna Elizabeth (Turnbull) H.; m. Florence Ann Fray, Dec. 20, 1960; children: Elizabeth, Margaret, Andrew, George J. BA, Claremont McKenna Coll., 1951; MA, Harvard U., 1953, PhD, 1960. Asst. prof. U. Va., Charlottesville, 1959-63; economist Fed. Res. Sys., Washington, 1963-64; sr. economist Rand Corp., Santa Monica, Calif., 1964-73; dep. asst. sec. def. Dept. Def., Washington, 1974-76; sr. staff advisor Office of the Pres., Washington, 1976-77; commr. Fed. Energy Regulatory Commn., Washington, 1977-81; v.p. Charles River Assocs., Boston, 1981-87; cons. Putnam Hayes & Bartlett, Inc., Washington, 1987—2001; sr. cons. Charles River Assocs., Washington, 2001—. Home: 2010 Powhatan St Falls Church VA 22043-1860 Office: Charles River Assocs 1201 F St NW Ste 700 Washington DC 20004-1201

HALL, GLENN ALLEN, lawyer, state representative; b. Pekin, Ill., Oct. 22, 1955; s. Gerald Eugene and Vinetta Bell Hall; m. Mary Melodie Hall, Dec. 30, 1978; children: Kimberly, Jaired, Ellie, Chava, Justice. BS in Edn., U. Mo., 1980; JD, Regent U., 1989. Bar: Mo. 1989. Atty. Glenn Allen Hall, Atty. at law, Kansas City, Mo., 1989—2001; state rep. State of Mo., 1993-99; owner The Almond Branch, Salem, Mo., 2001—; atty. Glenn Allen Hall, Atty. at Law, Salem, Mo., 2001—. Author: No Justice in the Land, 1993, The Separation, 1999, When We Awake, 2003. Office: 115 W 4th St Salem MO 65560 Fax: 573-729-2344. E-mail: salemjustice@earthlink.net.

HALL, GRACE ROSALIE, physicist, educator, writer; b. Meriden, Conn., July 15, 1921; d. George John and Grace Cleora (Gleason) White; m. Eldon Conrad Hall, July 2, 1948; children: Brent Channing, Pamela Rosalie, Craig Gleason, Gordon Timothy. Spl. student, Pembroke Coll., 1940-41; BS in Chemistry, Ea. Nazarene Coll., 1946; MA in Physics, Boston U., 1946, postgrad., 1946-53; MA in English, Simmons Coll., 1975. Bookkeeper Cherry & Webb Co., Providence, 1939-42; sec. to registrar Eastern Nazarene Coll., Quincy, Mass., 1942-44, instr. physics, chemistry, 1945-46; teaching fellow physics Boston U., 1946-49; instr. physics lab. Northeastern U., Boston, 1956-57; instr. physics Simmons Coll., Boston, 1949; asst. prof. physics Eastern Nazarene Coll., Quincy, 1957-61, asst. prof. chemistry, 1969, asst. prof. phys. sci., 1974. Instr. Shakespeare Barrington (R.I.) Coll., 1984; tchr. Westwood (Mass.) Sem., 1975; ch. sch. dir. 1st Parish, Westwood, 1977—81; chair sem. U. Louisville, 1988. Author: The Tempest as Mystery Play: Uncovering Religious Sources of Shakespeare's Most Spiritual Work, 1999; contbg. author: Webs and Wardrobes, 1987; contbr. articles to profl. jours. Bd. dirs. South County Norfolk Assn. for Retarded Citizens, 1978—79; judge H.S. Sci. Fairs, North Quincy, Mass., 1960—64, 1969—76, Regional Sci. Fairs, Bridgewater, Mass., 1960—62; chair City-Wide Bookfair, Quincy, 1962; bd. dirs. Westwood Interfaith Coun., 1985—89; pres. Ch. Women United, 1959. Named R.I. Honor Soc.; recipient Libr. Family of Yr. award, City of Quincy, 1960; scholar faculty scholarship, Ea. Nazarene Coll., 1943—45. Mem.: MLA (session participant 1978, 1984), Shakespeare Inst. (spkr. 1999), Christianity and Lit. Assn. (conf. participant 1984, 1989—90, 1995, 2001), Shakespeare Assn. Am. (seminar participant 1988—96, 2000—01), Mythopoetic Soc., New Eng. Hist. Geneal. Soc., MIT Women's League (editor activities guide and newsletter 1989—2001, adv. group 1999—2001), Internat. Soc. Poets, Clarendon Soc., Munro Soc., Phi Delta Lambda. Avocations: children's literature, recycling, snorkeling. E-mail: grwhall@aol.com.

HALL, HANSEL CRIMIEL, communications executive; b. Gary, Ind., Mar. 12, 1929; s. Alfred McKenzie and Grace Elizabeth (Crimiel) Hall. BS, Ind. U., 1953; LLB, Blackstone Sch. Law, 1982. Officer IRS, 1959-64; gasoline svc. sta. operator, then realtor Chgo., 1964-69; program specialist HUD, Chgo., 1969-73; dir. equal opportunity St. Paul, 1973-75; dir. fair housing Indpls., from 1975; human resource officer U.S. Fish and Wildlife Svc., Twin Cities, Minn. Cons. in civil rights; pres. bd. dirs. Riverview Towers Cooperative Assn., Inc., 1984-87; pres., CEO Crimiel Comms., Inc., 1988-; pres. West Bank Cmty. Coalition, Inc., 2002-03; CFO, treas. Korean War Vets. Edn. Grant Corp., 1996-2001; del. U.S. parliamentarian to Russia and Czechoslovakia, 1992, to Cuba, 1999; bd. dirs. Nat. Korean War Vets. Assn., 1992. With USAF, 1951-53, Korea. Recipient Amb. for Peace cert. Korean Vets. Assn., 1991, Korean Svc. medal Rep. of Korea, 1991. Mem. Res. Officers Assn., Am. Inst. Parliamentarians, Nat. Assn. Parliamentarians, Minn. State Assn. Parliamentarians (pres. 1997-99), Toastmasters DTM, Ind. U. Alumni Assn., Omega Psi Phi.

HALL, HARLAN, federal agency administrator; b. Saddle Mountain, Okla., Aug. 11, 1932; s. Roy Fred and Ruby Hall; m. Francine Purdy, Dec. 2, 1956; children: Crystal Lael Charmana, LeRoye Wareagle. Dir. purchasing Circle Screw and Air Industry, L.A., 1957—74; adminstr. fed. program Indian Ctr. United Indian Devel., L.A., 1974—82; ret., 1982. Author: Remember We Are Kiowas (101 Kiowa Indian Stories), A Kothondo (101 Kiowa Indian Poems); co-author: Windows to Our Souls. Vol. Senator Paul Carpenter Calif. Senate, Garden Grove, 1979. Sgt. U.S. Army, 1950—53, Korea. Mem.: VFW, DAV. Democrat. Baptist. Home: 1630 Conifer Cir Corona CA 92879-3034

HALL, HAROLD ROBERT, retired computer engineer; b. Bakersfield, Calif., Feb. 7, 1935; s. Edward Earl and Ethel Mae (Butner) H.; m. Tenniebee May Hall, Feb. 20, 1965. BS, U. Calif., Berkeley, 1956, MS, 1957, PhD, 1966. Chief engr. wave-filter div. Transonic, Inc., Bakersfield, 1957-60; chief design engr. Circuit Dyne Corp., Pasadena and Laguna Beach, Calif., 1960-61; sr. devel. engr. Robertshaw Controls Co., Anaheim, Calif., 1961-63; research engr. Naval Command, Control and Ocean Surveillance Ctr., rsch. and devel. divsn. Navy Research Lab., San Diego, 1966-95. Webmaster for various not-for-profit orgns. including Calif. State Assn. of Parliamentarians, Friends of Ostomates Worldwide-U.S.A. Treas. Pacific Beach Town Coun., San Diego, 1996-98, Friends of Ostomates Worldwide-U.S.A., Akron, Ohio, 1992-2000. Recipient Thomas Clair McFarland award U. Calif., Berkeley, 1956, NSF fellow, 1957. Mem. IEEE, Acoustical Soc. Am., Phi Beta Kappa. Lic. amateur radio extra class. Home: 8585 Via Mallorca Unit 7 La Jolla CA 92037-2585 E-mail: bobn10ab@ieee.org.

HALL, HARRY H. agricultural economics educator; b. Cassville, Mo., Aug. 14, 1934; s. Bert L. and Cynthia Jane (Smith) H.; m. Betty Sue Dowler, June 4, 1961; children: Brian E., Janet Anne. BS, U. Mo., 1956; MS, Okla. State U., 1964; PhD, Iowa State U., 1969. Asst. county agt. U. Mo., Columbia, 1956-57, assoc. county agt., 1959-61; rsch. asst. Okla. State U., Stillwater, 1961-63, Iowa State U., Ames, 1963-65, rsch. assoc., 1965-69; prof. agrl. econs. U. Ky., Lexington, 1969—99; ret., 1999. Contbr. articles to profl. jours. With U.S. Army, 1957-59. Mem. Am. Agrl. Econs. Assn., So. Agrl. Econs. Assn., Phi Eta Sigma, Alpha Zeta, Gamma Sigma Delta, Phi Kappa Phi. Office: U Ky Dept Agrl Econs Lexington KY 40546-0001

HALL, HARVEY L. mayor, medical transportation company executive; m. Lavonne Hall; children: Amy, Shelly, Paul, Rochelle. Attended, Bakersfield Cmty. Coll., San Francisco City Coll. Pres. & founder Hall Ambulance Svc., Inc., 1971—; mayor City of Bakersfield, Calif., 2001—. Adv. coun. mem. Mount Elgon Corp., 1999—. Bd. mem. African Am. Network, 1999—, Coalition to Protect and Preserve Private Property Rights, 1991—; hon. bd. mem. Police Activities League, 2000—, bd. mem., 1998—2000, MARE Adv. Bd., 1997—2002, Bakersfield Firefighters' Burn Found., 1994—, Mexican Am. Opportunity Found., 1999—; trustee Kern County Network for Children, 1995—, Kern Cmty. Coll. Dist., 1996—2000; bd. mem. Bakersfield Coll. Found., 1994—2000, Downtown Bus. Assn., 1992—2000; pres., bd. mem. Kern County Law Enforcement Found., 1990—2000. Mem.: 15th Dist. Agr. Assn. (dir. 1998—), Boys and Girls Club of Bakersfield (pres. 1997—99). Office: 1501 Truxton Ave Bakersfield CA 93301 also: Hall Ambulance Svc 1001 21st St Bakersfield CA 93301 E-mail: mayor@ci.bakersfield.ca.us.*

HALL, HENRY LYON, JR., lawyer; b. Boston, July 23, 1931; s. Henry Lyon and Edith Page (Blanchard) H.; m. Jean Elizabeth Haring, Sept. 13, 1958; children: Henry Lyon, George B. AB, U. Mass., 1953; JD, George Washington U., 1962. Bar: Va. 1963, Mass. 1963. Assoc. Ropes & Gray, Boston, 1963-73, ptnr., 1973-97, of counsel, 1998—. Lectr., panelist seminars Mem. Mass. Gov.'s Commn. Sch. Dist. Orgn., 1971-73; mem. sch. com. Minuteman Reg. Vocat. Sch. Dist., 1971-83, chmn. 1971-75; mem. permanent audit com. town of Belmont, Mass., 1979—, chmn. 1982-92; chmn. by law rev. com. 1979-83, bylaw rev. com., 1983-91; town moderator, Belmont, 1991—; corporator, trustee Belmont Savs. Bank. Served in U.S. Army, 1953-56. Mem. ABA, Mass. Bar Assn., Mass. Moderators Assn. (bd. dirs. 1995—, 1st v.p. 1997-98, pres. 1998-99), Nat. Assn. Bond Lawyers, Va. State Bar, Boston Bar Assn., Mass. Taxpayers Found., Govt. Fin. Officers Assn., Mass. Charitable Soc., Mass. Mcpl. Assn., Order of Coif, Phi Delta Phi. Home: 22 Randolph St Belmont MA 02478-3540 Office: Ropes & Gray One International Place Boston MA 02110-2624 E-mail: hhall@ropesgray.com.

HALL, HOUGHTON ALEXANDER, electrical engineer, city official; b. Kingston, Jamaica, W.I., Aug. 17, 1936; arrived in U.S., 1985; s. James Alexander and Clarice Viola Hall; m. Grace Yvonne Anglin, Feb. 22, 1964; children: Andrew Geoffery, Christine Elizabeth. BS, U. W.I., Kingston, 1958, diploma in chem. tech., 1959, diploma in mgmt., 1977. Registered profl. engr., Fla.; chartered engr. Great Britain. Elec. engr. Jamaica Pub. Svc. Co., Kingston, 1960—84; dir. R&D Ministry of Sci., Tech. and the Environ., Kingston, 1984—85; elec. engr. electric dept. City of Tallahassee, 1985—90, supr., substation engring. electric dept., 1990—. Fellow Fla. Engring. Soc.; mem. IEEE (sr.), NSPE, Inst. Elec. Engrs., Tallahassee Sci. Soc. (charter pres. 1989-97, pres. 2000—), Fla. Acad. Scis. (chmn. engring. sect. 1994-97, 2000—, pres. 1997-99). Baptist. Avocations: electronics, scientific pursuits. Home: 4335 Sherborne Rd Tallahassee FL 32303-7607 Office: City of Tallahassee 2602 Jackson Bluff Rd Tallahassee FL 32304-4408 E-mail: halla@talgov.com.

HALL, HOWARD HARRY, lawyer; b. Syracuse, N.Y., Jan. 9, 1933; s. Harold Gibner and Mildred E. (Way) H. AB, Syracuse U., 1953, JD, 1959. Bar: N.Y. 1960, U.S. Ct. Appeals (2d cir.) 1960, U.S. Dist. Ct. (we., no., so.dists.) N.Y. 1960, U.S. Supreme Ct. 1963, Calif. 1978, U.S. Ct. Appeals (9th cir.) 1978, U.S. Dist. Ct. (we. dist.) N.Y., U.S. Dist. Ct. (cen. and so. dist.) Calif., 1978. Assoc. Hiscock, Cowie, Bruce, Lee and Mawhinney, Syracuse, N.Y., 1959-61; pvt. practice Syracuse, N.Y., 1961-74, Long Beach, Calif., 1978-82, Paramount, Calif., 1982—. Commr. of edn. Syracuse, N.Y., 1968-72. Capt. USMC, 1953-56. Mem. State Bar of Calif., Calif. Trial Lawyers Assn. Office: 15559 Paramount Blvd Paramount CA 90723-4330

HALL, HOWARD PICKERING, engineering and mathematics educator; b. Boston, July 8, 1915; s. George Henry and Elizabeth Isabel (McCallum) H.; m. Ellen Marguerite Ide, June 25, 1945 (dec. 1984); children: Charlotte McCallum, Stephanie Wilson, Lindsey Louise, Gretchen Elizabeth. AB, Harvard U., 1936, MS, 1937, DSc, 1951. Registered structural engr., Ill., 1953. Instr., civil engring. Brown U., Providence, 1937-38; structural analyst Mark Linenthal, Engr., Boston, 1938-39; instr., asst. prof., assoc. prof. civil engring. Northwestern U., Evanston, Ill., 1939-56; design engr, field engr. Porter, Urquart, Skidmore, Owings, Merrill, Casablanca, Fr. Morocco, 1951-53; dean, sch. engring., acad. v.p. Robert Coll., Istanbul, Turkey, 1956-68; dir. of studies, acting headmaster St. Stephen's Sch., Rome, 1968-72; prof. math. Iranzamin Internat., Tehran, Iran, 1973-80; math. tchr. Vienna Internat. Sch., 1980-83, Copenhagen Internat. Sch., 1983-86. Cons. S.J. Buchanan, Bryan, Tex., Eng., 1955. Contbr. articles to profl. jours. Served to Capt. U.S. Army, 1942-46, ETO. Recipient Clemens Herschel award Boston Soc. Civil Engrs., 1954. Mem. Sigma Xi. Home: 301 SW Lincoln St Apt 1401 Portland OR 97201-5033

HALL, HOWARD TRACY, chemist; b. Ogden, Utah, Oct. 20, 1919; s. Howard and Florence (Tracy) H.; m. Ida Rose Langford, Sept. 24, 1941; children: Sherlene, Howard Tracy Jr., David Richard, Elizabeth, Virginia, Charlotte, Nancy. A.S., Weber Coll., 1939; BS, U. Utah, 1942, MS, 1943, PhD, 1948; D.Sc. (hon.), Brigham Young U., 1971; HHD (hon.), Weber State U., 1987. Registered patent agt. Chemist U.S. Bur. Mines, Salt Lake City, 1942-44, 46; research asso. Gen. Electric Research Lab., Schenectady, 1948-55; dir. research, prof. chemistry Brigham Young U., 1955-67, disting. prof. chemistry, 1967-80, disting. prof. emeritus, 1980—. Chmn. Novatek Indsl. Diamond Mfg. Co., Provo. Contbr. articles to profl. jours.; patentee in field. Served as ensign USNR, 1944-46. Co-recipient Research medal Am. Soc. Tool Mfg. Engrs., 1962; Modern Pioneers Creative Industry award NAM, 1965; Engring. Materials Achievement award Am. Soc. Metals, 1973; Man of Yr. award Abrasive Engring. Soc., 1980; Alfred P. Sloan Found. research fellow, 1959-63 Fellow Am. Inst. Chemists (Chem. Pioneer award 1970), AAAS; mem. Am. Chem. Soc. (Creative Invention award 1972), Am. Phys. Soc. (co-winner Internat. Prize for New Materials 1977), Sigma Xi, Phi Kappa Phi. Achievements include pioneering in synthesizing of diamond. Home: 1711 Lambert Ln Provo UT 84604-1858 Office: Brigham Young Univ Dept Chemistry Provo UT 84602

HALL, JAMES ROBERT, secondary education educator; b. Salem, Ill., Dec. 24, 1947; s. James Wesley and Patricia Joyce (Ellis) H. BS, U. Ill., 1970. Cert. secondary tchr., Ill. Tchr. Murphysboro (Ill.) H.S., 1970—. Author, compiler (tng. manual) Key Club Faculty Advisors, 1975. Sunday sch tchr. United Meth. Ch., Murphysboro, 1973-76, youth dir., 1973-76, mem. coun. on ministries, 1984—, trustee, 1984—; founder, dir. Christian Lay Coun. Youth Coffeehouse, 1973-75; mem. Murphysboro Recreation Bd., 1974-76, pres. 1975-76; cmty. amb. So. Ill. U. Area Svcs., 1975—; bd. dirs. Murphysboro Heart Fund, 1973-76, co-chmn. 1975-76; chmn. Murphysboro Muscular Dystrophy Assn., 1971-74; counsellor Little Grassy Youth Ch. Camp, 1973; mem. steering com. Murphysboro Apple Festival, 1975—, exec. com., 1983—; bd. dirs. Murphysboro United Way, 1978-83, Murphysboro Sr. Citizens Coun., 1980-83, Resource Reclamation Inc., 1979-85; vice chmn. Murphysboro Swimming Pool Project Commn., 1983-84, chmn. 1984-88; active Murphysboro Tourism Commn., 1995—; chmn. Murphysboro Mainstreet Promotions Commn., 1998—. Named One of Outstanding Young Men of Am. 1975, 84; recipient Citizenship award Sta. WTAO Radio, 1983, 84, Ann. Cmty. Svc. award Modern Woodmen Am., 1982, Citizen of Yr. award Murphysboro C. of C., 1984, 2002, Disting. Educator award Phi Delta Kappa, 1991, Founder award Murphysboro Apple Festival, 2000, Joseph P. Whitehead Educator of Distinction award, 2002. Mem.: NEA, Murphysboro Edn. Assn., Ill. Edn. Assn., Key Club, Kiwanis (pres. 1977—78, chmn. spl. club svcs. Ill.-Ea. Iowa dist. 1984—85, Mid. sch. Builders Club advisor 1993—, cert. trainer 1993—, gov-elect 1995—96, Ill.-Ea. Iowa resolutions chmn. 2000—, counsellor 2001—, v.p. Internat. Conf. Key Club Adminstrs. 2003—, Kiwanis Internat. com. on Key Clubs 2003—, long range planning com. for Key Club, Target 2000, Key Club past dist. gov., Dr. Luis V. Amador medallion 1995, G. Harold Martin fellow 1996, Gerge F. Hixson fellow Diamond 2 Level I 1996—98), Key Club (advisor 1972—, lt. gov. dist. divsn. 1984—85, adminstr. Ill.-Ea. Iowa dist. 1985—96, 2002—, mem. com. of Key Clubs 2003—, I-I dist. Key Club James R. Hall achievement award named in his honor 1999). Avocations: collecting books and plates, bowling, tennis. Home: 28 Candy Ln Murphysboro IL 62966-2953 Office: Murphysboro H S 16 Blackwood Dr Murphysboro IL 62966-2937

HALL, JAMES ALAN, obstetrician-gynecologist; b. Indpls., Nov. 3, 1949; m. Kyle A. Carner, May 18, 1974; children: Audrey, Courtney, Lynly, Cassie. AB, Ind. U., 1972, MD, 1975. Cert. Am. Bd. Ob-Gyn. Staff Women's Health Ctr., Logansport, Ind., 1978—; assoc. clin. prof. Ind U., Indpls., 1978—. Fellow Am. Coll. Ob-Gyn., ACS; mem. Cen. Assn. Ob-Gyn., Wabash Valley Ob-Gyn (pres.). Home: 1025 Michigan Ave Ste 115 Logansport IN 46947-1585

HALL, JAMES BRYAN, gynecological oncologist; b. Dayton, Ohio, Nov. 24, 1946; s. Mitchell Z. and Moyne L. H.; m. Edith Miller, Mar. 22, 1975; children: James B. Jr., William B. AB, Taylor U., 1969; MD, Med. U. S.C., 1974. Diplomate Am. Bd. Ob-Gyn., Oncology. Rotating intern Miami Valley Hosp., Dayton, 1974-75; resident in ob-gyn. Wright State U.-Miami Valley Hosp., 1975-78, chief resident in ob-gyn., 1977-78; fellow in gynecologic oncology, asst. in gynecology Mass. Gen. Hosp., Boston, 1978-80; pvt. practice Charlotte, N.C., 1988-95. Instr. ob-gyn. Harvard U., Boston, 1978-80; dir. gynecologic oncology, dept. ob-gyn. Carolinas Med. Ctr., 1980—, dir. gynecology, Blumenthal Cancer Ctr., coord. med. student clerkship, 1982-87, acting dir. dept. ob-gyn., 1987-88, assoc. prof., 1986-88; asst. prof. U. N.C., Chapel Hill, 1980-86, assoc. prof., 1986-88, clin. prof., 1995—; spkr. at profl. confs. Contbr. numerous articles to med. jours. Fellow ACS, Am. Coll. Ob-Gyn.; mem. Am. Soc. Clin. Oncology, Soc.Gynecologic Oncology, Charlotte Gynecol. and Obstetrical Soc. (sec.-treas. 1984-86, v.p. 1986-87, pres. 1987-88, treas. 1998-2000), Am. Cancer Soc. (bd. dirs. Mecklenburg County chpt., chmn. profl. edn. com., exec. com.), AMA, N.C. Med. Soc., Assn. Profs. of Gynecologists and Obstetricians (pres.), James H. Nelson Jr. Oncology Soc. (pres.). Republican. Evang. nondenominational. Avocations: tennis, gourmet cooking. Office: Cancer Ctr Carolinas Med Ctr 1000 Blythe Blvd Charlotte NC 28203-5812

HALL, JAMES EVAN, lawyer; m. Anne Stewart Impink; 2 daughters. B, U. Tenn., 1967. Counsel U.S. Senate Subcommittee on Intergovernmental Rels.; staff U.S. Senator Al Gore, Sr.; pvt. practice Chattanooga; mem. cabinet staff Tenn. Gov. Ned McWherter; dir. Tenn. State Planning Office; chief of staff U.S. Senator Harlan Mathews; mem. Nat. Transp. Safety Bd., Washington, 1993—2001, vice-chmn., 1994, chmn., 1994—2001; mng. ptnr. Hall & Assoc. LLC, 2001—. With U.S. Army, Vietnam. Officer U.S. Army, 1967—73. Decorated Bronze Star.

HALL, JAMES FREDERICK, retired college president; b. Detroit, Dec. 30, 1921; s. Cortez Rogers and Bertha Wilhelmina H.; m. Betty Louise Stark, Sept. 17, 1949; children— Kristine Martha, Jay Charles. Student, U. Mich., 1939-41; BA, Wayne State U., 1947, MA, 1948; Ed.D., Tchrs. Coll., Columbia U., 1954. Instr. Highland Park Jr. Coll., 1948-49; adminstrv. asst., instr. N.Y.C. Community Coll., 1950-51; dir. student personnel services, dept. head Orange County Community Coll., Middletown, N.Y., 1952-55; dean collegiate tech. div., exec. asst. to pres. Ferris State U., 1955-57; founding pres. Dutchess Community Coll., 1957-72; pres. Cape Cod Community Coll., 1972-87. Trustee, Mass. rep., Gov.'s appointment New Eng. Bd. Higher Edn., 1975-87; chmn. Pres.'s Council of Regional Community Colls. in Mass., 1976-78; mem. Mass. Postsecondary Edn. Commn., 1978-85; trustee Middle States Assn. Schs. and Colls., 1966-72; mem. mgmt. team Labor Negotiations for Regional Bd. Community Colls., 1978; bd. incorporators Bass River Savs. Bank, 1979-85 Bd. dirs. Cape Code Conservatory, West Barnstable, Mass., 1973-87, Cape Code YMCA, 1991—, YMCA, 1991-2001; trustee Cape Cod Hosp., Hyannis, Mass., 1978-87; mem. Mass. Health Facilities Appeal Bd., 1988-91; mem. Gov. Oversight Com., Town of Yarmouth, Mass., 1992—; mem. Town of Yarmouth Appeals Bd., 1992-93; apptd. Town of Yarmouth Rep. to Steam Ship Authority, 1997-98, 99-2003; trustee Hist. Soc. Old Yarmouth, 1994—. Lt. (j.g.) USNR, 1942-46. Mem. New Eng. Assn. Schs. and Colls. (accreditation teams 1975-77), Southeastern Assn. Cooperation in Higher Edn. in Mass. (dir. 1972-79, pres. 1976, treas. 1978), Mass. Adminstrs. in Community Colls. (pres. 1974-75), Associated Colls of Mid-Hudson Area (chmn. bd. trustees 1963-64, 72, trustee 1963-72), Internat. Edn. Consortium (chmn. Coll. Consortium Internat. Studies, bd. dirs. 1985-87), Dutchess County Hist. Soc., South Yarmouth Lawn and Tennis Club (bd. dirs. 1991-93). Home: 29 Liverpool Dr Yarmouth Port MA 02675-1526

HALL, JAMES GRANVILLE, JR., history educator; b. Phila., Aug. 22, 1917; s. James Granville and Jane Margaret (Moorehead) H.; m. Eva Mae Woodruff, June 1946; 1 child, Evelyn Alison. AB, George Washington U., 1950; cert., Georgetown U., 1951; postgrad. U. Colo., Colorado Springs, 1965-67; MA, Va. State U., 1972. Commd. 2nd lt. U.S. Army, 1943; transferred to USAF, 1948, advanced through ranks to lt. col., 1961; aircraft controller U.S. Army, Panama, U.S., 1943-50; various assignments, 1950-64; comdr. dir. staff officer, weapons staff officer NORAD, 1964-67; comdr. MDC, King Salmon, 1968, Air Def. Sector, King Salmon, Alaska, 1967-68; dir. ops. 5th Tactical Control group, comdr. 605th Tactical Control Squadron, Clark Air Base, The Philippines, 1969-71; chief control & environ. 20th Air Div., Ft. Lee, Va., 1971-72; retired USAF, 1972; faculty history and govt. Austin (Tex.) C.C., Austin, 1973-93. Participant Mid. East Seminar, Fgn. Svc. Inst., U.S. Dept. State, Washington, 1953; lectr. civic and garden clubs, Tex., 1974—. Author: Men's Garden Club Show and Judges Handbook, 1980; contbr. articles to profl. jours. Polit. worker, Austin, 1974—2000; bd. dirs. Colorado Springs Opera Assn., 1967; organizer, leader Girl Scouts Am., Opheim, 1959—60; pres. Little League, Itazuke, Japan, 1961—63; mem. Austin Lyric Opera, 1987—90; guest expert TV and radio garden shows Austin, 1976—. Decorated Meritorious Svc. medal, Joint Svcs. Commendation medal, Air Force Commendation medal, Am. Campaign medal, World War II Victory medal, Nat. Def. Svc. medal with 1 Bronze Star, Vietnam Svc. medal with 1 Bronze Star, Armed Forces Expeditionary medal, Combat Readiness medal with 1 Bronze Oak Leaf Cluster, Air Force Reserve medal, Air Force Outstanding Unit Citation, Master Weapons Dir. Badge; recipient Philippine Presidential Unit Citation for Humanitarian Svc., 1970-71. Mem.: Heritage Found., Capitol Area Chrysanthemum Soc. (pres. 1975, 2000—03), Nat. Chrysanthemum Soc. (accredited judge 1976—85, awards chmn. 1986—91, master judge 1986—), S.W. Chrysanthemum Region Soc. (organizer, pres. 1981—82), VFW (life), Claremont Inst., Men's Garden Club of Am. (accredited judge 1976—, nat. schs. and judges chmn. 1979—81, judge emeritus 2000—), Men's Garden Club (pres. 1977). Republican. Anglican. Avocations: gardening, bridge, computers. Home and Office: JE Hall Family Partnership 12317 SE 89th St Oklahoma City OK 73150

HALL, JAMES H(ERRICK), JR., philosophy educator, writer; b. Houston, Oct. 20, 1933; s. James Herrick and Loula Ben (Vining) H.; m. Bonlyn Goodwin, 1957 (div. 1977); children: Christopher Vining, Jonathan Goodwin; m. Myfanwy Seaver Monroe, 1977; 1 child, Charles Trevor. AB, Johns Hopkins U., 1955; BD, Southeastern Sem., Wake Forest, N.C., 1958, ThM, 1960; PhD, U. N.C., Chapel Hill, 1964. Instr. philosophy U. N.C., Chapel Hill, 1960-62; asst. prof. Furman U., Greenville, S.C., 1963-65; assoc. prof. U. Richmond, Va., 1965-74, chmn. dept. philosophy, 1965-89, 94-96, 99—, prof., 1974—, The Thomas chair, 1982—, univ. quest dir., 1999-2001. Author: Knowledge Belief and Transcendence, 1975, Logic Problems, 1991; (with others) Biblical and Secular Ethics, 1988, Philosophy of Religion, 2003. Mem. vestry St. Paul's Episc. Ch., Richmond, 1988-91; profl. ch. musician, Chapel Hill, Raleigh, Balt., Washington, Richmond. NamedDisting. Educator, U. Richmond, 2001; Coun. for Philosophic Studies fellow, Grand Rapids, 1973, U. Warwick fellow, Coventry, U.K., 1989-90, Kenan fellow U. N.C., 1960-61; rsch. grantee Duke Found., Durham, 1964, Mednick Trust, 1973-74. Mem. AAUP (chpt. pres. 1991-92), Am. Philos. Assn., Soc. for Philosophy of Religion, So. Soc. for Philosophy and Psychology, Omicron Delta Kappa. Democrat. Episcopalian. Avocations: choral music, camping, computers, travel. Home: 209 Wood Rd Richmond VA 23229-7538 Office: U Richmond Dept Philosophy North Ct Richmond VA 23173 E-mail: jhall@richmond.edu.

HALL, JAMES RAYFORD, III, adult educator; b. Chgo., Sept. 4, 1946; s. James Rayford and Hortense Elizabeth (Jones) H. BA, Langston U., 1968; MA, Ball State U., 1970. History tchr. Chgo. Bd. Edn., 1968-86; history instr. Joliet (Ill.) Jr. Coll., 1970-71, Kennedy-King Coll., Chgo., 1987-91; instr. Gary (Ind.) Community Schs., 1987—, at-risk specialist, 1988-89; history instr. Calumet Coll., Whiting, Ind., 1989-91; polit. sci. and sociology instr. Ivy Tech State Coll., Gary, Ind., 1996—. Precinct Capt. 17th Ward Democratic Party, Chgo., 1978-81. Fellow Polit. Socialization of Disadvantage Youth, Ball State U. Office of Edn., 1969. Mem. Nat. Tchrs. Assn., Am.Fedn. Tchrs., Am. Polit. Sci. Assn., Am. Black Polit. Scientist Assn., TransAfrica. Democrat. Baptist. Avocations: photography, writing. Home: 584 Roosevelt St Gary IN 46404-1310 Office: Interplanetary Music BMI 584 Roosevelt St Gary IN 46404-1310

HALL, J(AMES) R(OBERT), English educator; b. Rochester, N.Y., Mar. 17, 1946; s. James Robert and Helen Grace (Schauseil) H.; m. Joan Marie Wylie, Aug. 17, 1974; children: Jennifer Joy Wylie Hall, Justin James Wylie Hall. BA, St. John Fisher Coll., 1968; MA, U. Notre Dame, 1970, PhD, 1973. Vis. lectr. U. Ill., Urbana, 1973-74; instr. English St. Mary-of-Woods (Ind.) Coll., 1975; asst. prof. U. Miss., University, 1978-84, assoc. prof., 1984-90, prof., 1990—. Scholarship reviewer Old English Newsletter Western Mich. U., 1976—2001; referee scholarly manuscripts; cons. Nat. Endowment Humanities, Washington, 1990—. Contbr. essays to profl. jours. Adviser Ole Miss Coll. Reps., University, 1995—; mem. exec. com. Lafayette County Rep. Party. Am. Coun. Learned Socs. rsch. fellow, 1981-82; Harvard U. tchg.-rsch. fellow, 1983-84, NEH rsch. fellow, 1993-94; Earhart Found. rsch. fellow, 2000. Mem. Medieval Acad. Am., Internat. Soc. Anglo-Saxonists, South Atlantic Modern Lang. Assn., Am. Friends Bodleian Libr., Assn. Lit. Scholars and Critics, Nat. Assn. Scholars. Roman Catholic. Home: 1705 Johnson Ave Oxford MS 38655-4725 Office: U Miss Dept English University MS 38677-1848 E-mail: jrhall@olemiss.edu.

HALL, JAMES STANLEY, jazz guitarist, composer; b. Buffalo, Dec. 4, 1930; s. Harold S. and Louella (Cowles) H.; m. Jane Susan Yuckman, Sept. 9, 1965; 1 dau., Debra Jean. Mus.B., Cleve. Inst. Music, 1955; PhD in Music (hon.), Berklee Sch. Music, Boston, 1995. Author: Exploring Jazz Guitar; joined chico Hamilton, 1955; mem. Jimmy Giuffre Trio, 1957, tour US and Europe with Jazz at Philharmonic, 1958, 59, Europe and S.A. with Ella Fitzgerald, 1959, 60; featured by Sonny Rollins, 1961-62; formed quartet with Art Farmer, 1962-64; leader own trio and quartet, 1962—; performed at White House, 1969; albums include Jazz Guitar, 1957, Undercurrent, All Across the City, Dedications & Inspirations, Diaglogues, Textures, 1997. By Arrangement, 1998, Jim Hall and Pat Metheny, 1999, Grand Slam, 2000, Jim Hall and Basses, 2001; motion picture appearance in Jazz on a Summer's Day, 1958; appearance on Ralph Gleason's TV Show, 1962-63, BBC, 1964, Jim Hall Invitational Concert, 1990, Tonite show, 1992; tour Europe, 1967, 69, 79-82, 86-87, 89—, Japan, 1970, 76, 79, 87, 90—; (documentary film) A Life in Progress. Recipient award Downbeat Critics Poll, 1963-65, 74, 76-80, 82-88, 89-90, 91-93, award Downbeat Readers' Poll, 1965-66, 2001, award Playboy Mag. All-Star Poll for Guitar, 1968-71; named Best Performer Jazz Mag., 1965-66, Best Composer-Arranger, Jazz Critics Circle NY, 1997; winner Jazz Times poll as Best Guitar, 1991, Jazzpar prize, Denmark, 1998, Disting. Alumni award Cleve. Inst. Music. Mem. BMI.

HALL, JANE ANNA, writer, model, artist; b. New London, Conn., Apr. 4, 1959; d. John Leslie Jr. and Jane Dezzie (Green) H. Grad. model, Barbizon Sch., 1976; grad., Westbrook H.S., 1977. Model Barbizon Agy., New Haven, 1977; employed by dir. of career planning Wesleyan U., Middletown, Conn., 1985-86; free lance writer, poet, 1986—; artist, 1989—. Poetry contest judge Saybrook 25th Anniversary Celebration, Acton Pub. Libr., 1992; group poetry reader Literacy Vols. Valley Shore, Westbrook, 1995, Russell Libr., Middletown, Conn., 1999, 2000. Author: Cedar and Lace, 1986, Satin and Pinstripe, 1987, Fireworks and Diamonds, 1988, Stars and Daffodils, 1989, Sunrises and Stone Walls, 1990, Mountains and Meadows, 1991, Moonlit and Water Lillies, 1992, Sunsets and Beaches, 1993, New and Selected Poems 1986-94, 1994, Under Par Recipes, 1994, New and Selected Poems for Children 1986-95, 1995, Butterflies and Roses, 1996, Hummingbirds and Hibiscus, 1997, Swans and Azaleas, 1998, Damsel Flies and Peonies, 1999, Egrets and Cattails, 2000, Doves and Rhododendron, 2001, Bluebirds and Mountain Laurel, 2002, Beach Poems, Vol. I, 2002, Cardinals and Maples, 2003, Spring Poems Vol. I, 2003, Summer Poems Vol. I, 2003, Autumn Poems Vol. I, 2003, Winter Poems Vol. I, 2003; cover designer (books), 1986—, founder, editor (newsletter) Poetry in Your Mailbox, 1989—; contbr. poetry The Bell Bouy, Expressions I and II, The Pictorial Gazette, Conn. chpt. Romance Writers of Am. Newsletter, others; (one-woman shows) Westbrook (Conn.) Pub. Libr., 1989—99, Russell Libr., Middletown, 2000, Guilford (Conn.) Free Libr., 2001, Russell Libr., Middletown, 2002;, author poems, The Full Moon Looks Like, 2002; contbr. articles Conn. chpt. Romance Writers Am. Newsletter; (one-woman shows), reader (group poetry), Conn. Sunday sch. tchr. 1st Congl. Ch., Westbrook, 1977-90, asst. supt., mem. bd. Christian edn., 1979-84; poetry reader Congl. Ch., Broad Brook, Conn., 1988; vol. ch. fair Westbrook Congl. Ch.; group poetry reader and displayer Westbrook Pub. Libr., 1989, 91, reader Night of Thousand Stars readathon, 1990, group poetry displayer Acton Pub. Libr., Old Saybrook, Conn., 1990, judge poetry contest 25th anniversary celebration, 1992; vol. 1st Congrl. Ch. Fair, Westbrook, Conn. Recipient 2d prize Conn. Poetry Soc., 1983-86, 3d hon. mention, 1996, chapbooks added to Soc. permanent archives at Housatonic Cmty. Tech. Coll., 1995; cert. of merit for disting. svc. to cmty., 1989, cert. world leadership, 1989. Mem. Internat. Platform Assn., Romance Writers Am. (book cover bd. designer Conn. chpt. 1991-93), Conn. Poetry Soc. (pres. Old Saybrook chpt. 1989-91, world poetry chmn. 1989; poetry reader 20th anniversary celebration at Russell Libr. Middletown, Conn. 1994, group poetry reader, Waterbury 2001). Avocations: interior decorating and design, fashion design, tennis, gardening, photography. Address: PO Box 629 Westbrook CT 06498-0629 *To help other human beings so that they may live a more wonderful life is the conduct of a true humanitarian.*

HALL, JAY, social psychologist; b. Houston, Oct. 18, 1932; s. Ernest James and Jamie (Clark) H.; m. Missy Hall; children: Kelly, Allison, Jeffrey. BA in Psychology, U. Tex., 1959, MA in Psychology, 1961, PhD in Psychology, 1963. Lectr. dept. psychology U. Tex., Austin, 1961-63, dir. S.W. Ctr. for Law and Behavioral Scis., 1964-66, assoc. prof. Grad. Sch. Bus., 1966-69; assoc. dir. Nat. Parole Insts., Austin, 1963-64; founder, chmn. bd. Teleometrics Internat., The Woodlands, Tex., 1969-93; CEO, chmn. Leadership Systems Internat., The Woodlands, Tex., 1996—. Author: Ponderables: Essays on Managerial Choice-Past and Future, 1982, The Competence Connection: A Blueprint for Excellence, 1988, Models for Management: The Structure of Competence, 1988, The Executive Trap, 1992, Why Some Leaders are Better than Others, 1995, Benchmarks: For a Thoughtful Journey, 2000; contbr. numerous articles and psychol. tests to profl. publs.; inventor Halford Grip sports/grip prosthesis. Trustee The Woodlands Med. Ctr., 1980-91, Community Life Found., 1985-88, The John Cooper Sch., The Woodlands, 1986-91; dir. Interfaith, The Woodlands, 1980-88. 1st lt. U.S. Army, 1955-58. Mem. Am. Psychol. Assn., AAAS, N.Y. Acad. Sci., Sigma Xi. Episcopalian. Avocation: golf.

HALL, JAY DE, finance educator, consultant; s. Orval Leonard and Erma LuEmma Hall. BA in Social Sci., U. Nebr., 1974; diploma, U. Stockholm, 1976; postdoctorate, U. Internat. Bus. and Econs., Beijing, 1995, U. Western Sydney, 1995. Program dir. u. ho. Internat. Ho.-U. Nebr., Lincoln, 1974—75; social worker Municipality of Danderyd, Sweden, 1975—77; educator, cons. ABF Coll., Solna, Sweden, 1977—90, asst. dean studies Stockholm, 1990—95; tchr. English as a fgn. lang. ACE U. Western Sydney, 1995; prof. bus. English U. Internat. Bus. and Econs., Beijing, 1995—97. Adv. lang. UN-World Food Program, Beijing, 1997—99. Mem. city election counting bd. Social Dem. Party, Solna, Sweden, 1994; sec. C. of C., Beaver City, Nebr., 2003—. Regents scholar, U. Nebr.-Lincoln, 1970. Democrat. Mem. Grace Brethren Ch. Achievements include organized study tours at ABF College-Solna, Sweden for groups going to England, Italy, Germany, The Netherlands, Australia, and the U.S. Avocations: travel, exotic foods, community service. Home: 100 South 8th St Plz #Cl Beaver City NE 68926 Office: C of C Box 303 Beaver City NE 68926 E-mail: jhall@swnebr.net.

HALL, JEROME WILLIAM, research engineering educator; b. Brunswick, Ga., Dec. 1, 1943; s. William L. and Frances K. H.; m. Loretta E. Hood, Aug. 28, 1965; children: Jennifer, Bridget, Bernadette. BS in Physics, Harvey Mudd Coll., 1965; MS in Engring., U. Wash., 1968, PhDCE, 1969. Registered profl. engr., D.C., N.Mex., Va. Asst. prof. civil engring. U. Md., College Park, 1970-73, assoc. prof., 1973-77, U. N.Mex., Albuquerque, 1977-80, prof., 1980—, dir. bur. engring. research, 1981-88, asst. dean engring., 1985-88, chmn. dept. of civil engring., 1990-97. Cons. in field. Contbr. articles to profl. jours. Recipient Teetor award Soc. Automotive Engrs., 1975; Pub. Partnership award Alliance For Transportation Rsch., 1997. Fellow Inst. Transp. Engrs. (pres. N.Mex. sect. 1985, pres. western dist. 1989, internat. bd. dirs. 1993-95); mem. Transp. Rsch. Bd. (chmn. com. 1986-92, chmn. group coun. 1992-95, panel chmn. 1990—), Am. Soc. Engring. Edn., Am. Rd. and Transp. Builders Assn. (pres. rsch. and edn. divsn. 2002-03), Nat. Assn. County Engrs. Republican. Roman Catholic. Office: Dept Civil Enging MSC01 1070 1UNM Albuquerque NM 87131-0001 E-mail: jerome@unm.edu.

HALL, JILL WATKINS, communications educator; b. Mobile, Ala., Sept. 4, 1946; d. William Woodrow and Otha Fyrn (Stephenson) W.; m. George Kennedy Hall Jr., Aug. 11, 1968; children: Judith Kennedy, William Stith, Katherine Stephenson. BA, Samford U., 1968; MA, U. Ky., 1970, PhD, 1998. Grad. asst. U. Ky., Lexington, 1968-70; instr. U. Louisville, 1973-75, Jefferson C.C., Louisville, 1975, 77-78, 80-81, Ind. U. S.E., New Albany, 1976-90; prof. comm. Jefferson C.C., 1990—; mediator Mediation Ctr. Ky., 1991-93, acad. program coord., 1998—2000, cons. tchg. consultation program, 2002—. Dir. Readers' Theatre for Bluegrass Invitational, Georgetown (Ky.) Coll., fall 1969. Den leader Boy Scouts Am., Anchorage, Ky., 1985-87. Named an Outstanding Young Woman of Am., 1970; fellow U. Ky., 1996. Mem. P.E.O. (Ky. state pres. 1982-83, pres. Louisville chpt. Q 1976-78). Democrat. Baptist. Avocations: antiques, gardening. Home: 2609 Anchor Way Anchorage KY 40223-1605 Office: Jefferson CC Divsn Humanities 109 E Broadway Louisville KY 40202-2005

HALL, JOAN TORRENS, lawyer; b. Belleville, NJ; d. Alfred and Margaret (Simpson) Torrens;m. John P. Hall Jr.; children: John P. III, James S. AB, Drew U., 1957; JD, Rutgers U., 1990. Bar: N.J. 1991, D.C. 1991. Tchr. Oliphant Sch., Middletown, R.I., 1958-59; psychology rschr. Princeton U., N.J., 1974-98; pvt. practice, 1990—; mediator Mediation Alternative Group, 1998—. Vis. lectr. Rutgers Law Sch., Camden, N.J., 1990. Contbr. articles to profl. jours. Bd. dir. LWV, Hopewell, NJ, 1972-87, 94-97; pres. PTO, Hopewell, 1979-80; chmn. ER Neighborhood Assn., Princeton, 1996-2002; chmn. MasterPlan Com., Hopewell Twp. Grantee NSF, 1996-97. Mem. ABA, Princeton Bar Assn., Stony Brook Millstone Watershed Assn. (bd. mem.). Avocation: tennis.

HALL, JOHN FRY, psychologist, educator; b. Phila., Apr. 24, 1919; s. Harry R. and Alta (Herner) H.; m. Jean Midlam, May 14, 1943; 1 son, John. BS, Ohio U., 1946; MA, Ohio State U., 1947, PhD, 1949. Mem. faculty Pa. State U., University Park, 1949—, prof. psychology, 1958—; prof. emeritus, 1985—; Program dir. psychobiology NSF, Washington, 1966-67. Vis. prof. U. Va., 1952, U. Wis., 1954, U. Calif. at Berkeley, 1962, U. Hawaii, 1968, Fla. State U., 1975-76 Author: Psychology of Motivation, 1961, Psychology of Learning, 1966, Readings in the Psychology of Learning, 1967, Verbal Learning and Retention, 1971, Classical Conditioning and Instrumental Learning, 1976, An Invitation to Learning and Memory, 1982, Learning and Memory, 1989; contbr. articles to profl. jours. Mem. Am. Psychol. Assn., Psychonomics Soc., A.A.A.S. Home: 334 Caloosa Palms Ct Sun City Center FL 33573-6938 E-mail: jejohall@aol.com.

HALL, JOHN HENRY, lawyer, historian, educator; b. Mound Bayou, Miss., Nov. 7, 1932; s. John and Icey M. (Roundtree) H.; m. Katie B. Green, Aug. 15, 1957. BS in Social Studies, Ind. U., 1970, MEd, 1971, MS in Secondary Sch. Adminstrn., 1972; JD, Southland U., 1981; EdD, Loyola U., Chgo., 1995; LLM comml. real estate, John Marshall Law Sch., Chgo., 2002. Bar: Ind. 1983, U.S. Supreme Ct. 1987. Foreman U.S. Reduction Co., East Chicago, Ind., 1957-62, shift supt., 1962-68; tchr. Gary (Ind.) Cmty. Schs., 1969-74, asst. prin., 1975—92; sole practice law Gary, 1983—; prof. law, racism and social change Ind. U., Gary, 1984. Legal resource Gary Community Sch. Corp., 1983-84; judge pro tem Lake County (Ind.) Superior Ct., East Chicago and Gary. Article writer Blacks in World History Information Newspaper (edn. and Cmty. Svc. awrd 1983), 1979—. Campaign mgr. Katie Hall State Rep., Indpls., 1976, Katie Hall Congress, Gary, 1984; Sunday sch., BTU tchr., served as chmn. deacon Van Buren (Miss.) Bapt. Ch., Served with USAF, 1952-57. Mem. ABA, Gary Secondary Prins. Assn. (sec./treas., v.p., pres., Outstanding Leadership award 1982), Lake County Bar Assn., Assn. Trial Lawyers Am., Phi Delta Kappa, Phi Alpha Delta. Democrat. Avocations: travel, creative writing, reading, walking, jogging. Office: PO Box 1498 Gary IN 46407-0498

HALL, JOHN HERBERT, lawyer; b. Orange, N.J., Dec. 5, 1942; s. Embert Brown Hall and Elizabeth (Sullivan) Carnahan; m. Suzanne Steeger, Aug. 21, 1965 (div. Apr. 1988); children: Christopher Evan, Jeremy Randall; m. Lisa Gersh, June 19, 1988; children: Samantha Gersh, Madeleine Gersh. BA, Wesleyan U., 1965; MBA, NYU, 1966; JD, Columbia U., 1969. Bar: N.Y. 1970, U.S. Dist. Ct. (so. dist.) N.Y. 1972, (ea. dist.) N.Y. 1981, U.S. Ct. Appeals (2d cir.) 1974, (10th cir.) 1977, (5th cir.) 1980, (11th cir.) 1981, (4th cir.) 1989, (D.C. cir.) 1982, U.S. Supreme Ct. 1981. Assoc. Debevoise, Plimpton, Lyons & Gates, N.Y.C., 1969-72, 73-78; grad. bus. Cmty. Law Offices, N.Y.C., 1972-73; ptnr. Debevoise & Plimpton, N.Y.C., 1979—, chair litigation dept., 1993—2002, mem. mgmt. com., 2003—. Bd. dirs. Community Law Offices, 1974-2000, Legal Aid Soc. N.Y., 1980-88. Co-author: Takeovers-Attack and Survival, 1987, 2d edit., 1993; panelist in field. Bd. dirs. Vols. Legal Svcs., 1990-96, Welfare Law Ctr. Mem. ABA (criminal, bus. law, litigation sects.), N.Y. Lawyers for Pub. Interest (bd. dirs. 1987-00), Am. Judicature Soc., Supreme Ct. Hist. Soc., Assn. of Bar of City of N.Y. (fed. cts. com. 1981-84), Prep for Prep Inc. (dir. 1974), U.S. Cycling Fedn., Nat. Legal Aid/Defenders Assn., Law Soc. Eng. and Wales, Global Counsel 3000. Avocations: bicycle racing, tennis. Home: 300 Central Park W Apt 19C New York NY 10024-1513 Office: Debevoise & Plimpton 919 3rd Ave 43rd Floor New York NY 10022-6225 E-mail: Jhhall@debevoise.com.

HALL, JOHN HOPKINS, retired lawyer; b. Dallas, May 10, 1925; s. Albert Brown and Eleanor Pauline (Hopkins) H.; m. Marion Martin, Nov. 23, 1957; children: Ellen Martin, John Hopkins II. Student, U. Tex., 1942, U. of South, Sewanee, Tenn., 1942-43; LL.B., So. Meth. U., 1949. Bar: Tex. bar 1949. Ptnr. Strasburger & Price, Dallas, 1957-93, ret., 1993. Served with U.S. Army, 1943-45. Fellow Tex. Bar Found., Am. Bar Found., Internat. Acad. Trial Lawyers, Am. Coll. Trial Lawyers; mem. Tex. Bar Assn., Tex. Assn. Def. Counsel, Internat. Assn. Def. Counsel, Fin and Feather Club. Episcopalian.

HALL, JOHN RAYMOND, JR., fire protection executive; b. Washington, Feb. 25, 1948; s. John Raymond and Elizabeth Florence (Lord) H.; m. Jean Baird Horky, Dec. 2, 1972. BA cum laude, Brown U., 1967; PhD, U. Pa., 1972. Rsch. analyst Resource Mgmt. Corp., Bethesda, Md., 1972-73; sr. rsch. assoc. Urban Inst., Washington, 1973-79; ops. rsch. analyst U.S. Fire Adminstrn., within Fed. Emergency Mgmt. Agy., Washington, 1979-82, Ctr. for Fire Rsch., within Nat. Bur. of Stds, Gaithersburg, Md., 1982-84; asst. v.p. fire analysis and rsch. Nat. Fire Protection Assn., Quincy, Mass., 1984—. Exec. sec. rsch. sect. Nat. Fire Protection Assn., 1990—; chair OR/MS Bd., Balt., 1994; past pres. Inst. for Ops. Rsch. and the Mgmt. Scis., Balt. and Providence, 1995, mem. fin. com. 1997-99; v.p. for mem. activities Inst. of Mgmt. Scis., Providence, 1983-86, sec. 1979-83, mem. at-large of coun., 1977-79, chmn. orgn. and bylaws com., 1979-94, pres. Washington chpt. 1978-79, v.p. for membership coll. on pub. programs and processes, 1982-85; trustee Washington Ops. Rsch./Mgmt. Sci. Coun., 1980-81, 83-84. Author: (with others) Procedures for Improving the Measurement of Local Fire Protection Effectiveness, 1976, How Effective Are Your Community Services?, 1977, 92, The SFPE Handbook of Fire Protection Engineering, 1988, 95, 2002, Fire Protection Handbook, 1986, 97; editor TIMS Chpts. Newsletter, 1976-79; columnist Mgmt. Sci. Update, 1980-81; columnist/editor Applications Rev., 1976-88; contbr. articles to profl. jours. Chmn. Fire Protection Commn., Norwood, Mass., 1986—. Recipient (4) Cert. of Outstanding Performance Fed. Emergency Mgmt. Agy., 1981-83, Cert. of Spl. Achievement, 1982, Cert. of Recognition Nat. Bur. of Stds., 1983-84, Leadership Giving award United Way of Neponset Valley, 1991. Mem.: ASTM (E5 exec. com. 1996—, 4th vice chair 1998—), AAAS, Combustion Inst., Inst. Mgmt. Scis., Am. Mgmt. Assn., Soc. for Risk Analysis, Ops. Rsch. Soc. Am. (tech. sects. com. 1972—76), Internat. Assn. for Fire Safety Sci. (exec. com. 1994—, chmn. arrangements com. 2000—02, program com. 1991—, newsletter editor 1994—), Sigma Xi, Phi Beta Kappa. Democrat. Achievements include rsch. on the modeling and conceptual framework innovations in fire risk analysis in the USA. Home: 10 Alden Dr Norwood MA 02062-5326 Office: Nat Fire Protection Assn PO Box 9101 1 Batterymarch Park Quincy MA 02269-9101

HALL, JOHN REGINALD, II, electronics company executive, retired army officer; b. Ft. Leavenworth, Kans., Aug. 8, 1944; s. John Reginald and Janet Markham (Cummins) H.; m. Emily Louise Moulton, June 24, 1967; 1 child, John Reginald III. Student, Dartmouth Coll., 1962-63; BS in Engring., U.S. Mil. Acad., 1967; MA in German, U. Conn., 1975. Commd. 2d lt. U.S. Army, 1967, advanced through grades to lt. col., 1988, ret., 1989; asst. prof., swim coach U. Conn., Storrs, 1971-75; sr. sys. engr. Joint STARS program ACS Def. (formerly Analytical Sys. Corp.), Burlington, Mass., 1979-82, project mgr. security sys. divsn., 1982-84, mgr. air traffic control sys. program, 1984-86, dir. European projects, 1986-95; dir. internat. bus. devel. ACS Def. (formerly Analytical Sys. Engring. Corp.), Burlington, Mass., 1995—. Author: U.S. Navy Commercial Security Systems Guide Specification, 1985, U.S. Navy Commercial Security Systems Design Manual, 1986; contbr. articles to profl. jours. Decorated Bronze Star medal, Meritorious Svc. medal with 2 oak leaf clusters. Mem. Am. Soc. for Indsl. Security, Armed Forces Comm.-Electronics Assn., Rye Beach Club (treas. 1990-91, v.p. 1991-93, pres. 1993-95), Masons (32 degree). Republican. Episcopalian. Avocations: swimming, golf, fly fishing, cross country skiing. Home: Straws Point PO Box 58 Rye NH 03870-0058 Office: ACS Def Inc 5 Burlington Woods Ste 100 Burlington MA 01803-4542 E-mail: jhall@acsdefense.com.

HALL, JOHN RICHARD, surgery educator, researcher; b. Tucson, Mar. 21, 1952; s. John Owen and Evelyn Myra (Lowe) H.; m. Mary Cecelia Dean, Apr. 27, 1991; children: Corey Evelyn, Mary Elizabeth, Katherine Irene. BS in Chemistry with honors, BS in Biology, Stanford U., 1974; MD, U. Ariz., 1977. Diplomate Am. Bd. Surgery. Dir. trauma svc. Amarillo (Tex.) Critical Care Svc., 1985-86; asst. prof. surgery La. State U., Shreveport, 1986-87; dep. dir. pediatric trauma svc. Cook County Hosp. and U. Ill., Chgo., 1987-95; dir. pediat. ICU Holston Valley Hosp., Kingsport, Tenn., 1995—, dir. trauma, 2000—; assoc. prof. surgery East Tenn. State U., Kingsport, 1996—99, prof. surgery, 2000—. Membership com. Ea. Assn. Surgery Trauma, 1993-94. Contbr. articles to profl. jours. Deacon Presbyn. Ch., Chgo., 1995. Recipient Nat. Leadership award, Hon. co-chmn. Tenn., 2001; grantee Rsch. grantee, U. Ill, 1988—94. Fellow Am. Coll. Surgeons; mem. Am. Assn. Surgery Trauma, Am. Trauma Soc., Am. Burn Soc., Western Trauma Assn., Ea. Trauma Assn. Avocation: computers. Office: Trauma Svc HVH 134 W Park Dr Kingsport TN 37660-3806

HALL, JOHN ROSS, educator; b. Louisville, Apr. 23, 1946; s. Edmund Kennard and Marian (Ross) H.; m. Janet C. Broome, Aug. 1, 1998. BA, Yale U., 1968; MA, U. Wash., 1972, PhD, 1975. Asst. prof. U. Mo., Columbia, 1976-89; prof. U. Calif., Davis, 1989—. Author: The Ways Out, 1978, Gone

From the Promised Land, 1987, Cultures of Inquiry, 1999, Apocalypse Observed, 2000, Sociology on Culture, 2003. Mem. Am. Sociol. Assn., Internat. Sociol. Assn., Soc. Scientific Study. Office: Univ Calif Dept Sociology 1 Shields Ave Davis CA 95616-5200

HALL, JOHN THOMAS, lawyer, educator; b. Phila., May 14, 1938; s. John Thomas and Florence Sara (Robinson) H.; m. Carolyn Park Currie, May 26, 1968; children: Daniel Currie, Kathleen Currie. AB, Dickinson Coll., 1960; MA, U. Md., 1963; JD, U. N.C., 1972. Bar: N.C. 1972. Chmn. dept. speech Mercersburg (Pa.) Acad., 1960-63, U. Balt., 1963-69; research asst. N.C. Ct. Appeals, Raleigh, 1972-73, dir. pre-hearing research staff, 1974-75, asst. clk., marshall, librarian, 1980-81; counsel Dorothea Dix Hosp., Raleigh, 1974; asst. dist. atty. State of N.C., Raleigh, 1975-80, 81-83; pvt. practice Raleigh, 1973-74, 83—. Mem. faculty King's Bus. Coll., Raleigh, 1973-75, N.C. Bar Assn., 1987—; undercover inmate Cen. Prison Duke Ctr. on Law and Poverty, Durham, N.C., 1970; vis. lectr. dept. comm. N.C. State U., 2000—; faculty U. Phoenix Online, 2003—. Mem. Raleigh Little Theatre, Theatre in the Park, Raleigh; charter mem. Wake County Dem. Men's Club, 1977—. Named Best Actor, Raleigh Little Theatre, 1975, 77, 80, 82, 85, 86, 93, 98. Mem.: Neuse River Valley Model R.R. (Raleigh), ABA, Wake County Acad. Criminal Trial Lawyers (v.p. 1986—87), 10th Jud. Dist. Bar Assn. (bd. dirs. 1986—89, chmn. grievance com. 1987—90), Wake County Bar Assn. (bd. dirs. 1986—89, vice chmn. exec. com. 1986—87), N.C. Bar Assn., Scottish Clan Gunn Soc. Avocations: model railroading, reading. Office: PO Box 1207 Raleigh NC 27602-1207

HALL, JOHNNIE CAMERON, pathologist; b. Nashville, Nov. 30, 1958; s. Johnnie Claiborne and Mary Pauline (Roark) H. BS in Biochemistry, David Lipscomb Coll., 1980; MD, U. Tenn., 1984. Diplomate Nat. Bd. Med. Examiners, Am. Bd. Pathology. Intern U. Tenn., Memphis, 1984-85, resident in pathology, 1986-88; surg. pathology fellow U. Tenn./Bapt. Meml. Hosp., Memphis, 1988; pathologist Pathology Group of Midsouth (formerly Midsouth Path. Group), Memphis, 1989—. Co-med. dir. Bapt. Regional Lab., Memphis, 1991-93; med. dir. Bapt. Regional Lab. Specialist Technologist Sch., Memphis, 1991-93; devel. coun. Freed-Hardeman U., 1993—, pres. Memphis Soc. of Pathologists, 1997-99, Tenn. Soc. of Pathology, 1999—; spkr. in field. Contbr. articles to profl. jours. Active Rep. Presdl. Task Force, Washington, 1990—, Nat. Taxpayers Union, Washington, 1990—, Heritage Found., Washington, 2000—. Fellow Coll. Am. Pathologists, Am. Soc. Clin. Pathologists; mem. AMA, Am. Soc. Microbiology, U.S. and Can. Acad. Pathologists, Tenn. Med. Assn., Memphis-Shelby County Med. Soc. (comms. com. mem.), Tenn. Soc. Pathologists (pres. 1999—). Republican. Mem. Church of Christ. Avocations: photography, fine art, books, movie memorabilia. Home: 8375 Westfair Dr Germantown TN 38139-3259 E-mail: jhall3@midsouth.rr.com.

HALL, JO(SEPHINE) MARIAN, newspaper editor, photographer; b. Aberdeen, S.D., July 12, 1921; d. Charles Martin Sykes and Deedie Mae (Keiser) Gruett; m. Winston Hall, Dec. 4, 1940 (dec.); children: Wendy Diane, Willis Edward. Student, U. Colo., 1958, U. S.D., 1976. With advt. dept. Mobridge (S.D.) Reminder, 1955-61, columnist, 1956-61; with advt. dept., columnist Mobridge Tribune, 1961-67, 93—, news editor, photographer, 1968-81, editor people page, 1981—. Airway observer U.S. Weather Bur., Mobridge, 1939-84; sec. bd. dirs. Klein Mus., Mobridge, 1976-80; chpt. pres. Am. Field Svc., 1972-82; vol. Mobridge Regional Hosp., 1990—; organist, dir. choir, sr. warden of vestry St. James Episcopal C., Mobridge; mem. S.D. Episcopal Diocesan Coun., 1993-99. Recipient numerous state and nat. awards for feature stories, news stories, columns, obituaries, photography, spl. sects. headlines, 1959—, including Herbert Bayard Swope award, 1978; 1st place award for newspaper editing Nat. Fedn. Press Women, 1979, for spl. edit., 1982; Golden Quill award S.D. Press Women, 1988; named S.D. State Homefront Hero of WW II, 2002. Democrat. Avocations: water aerobics, swimming, reading, cooking, gardening. Home: 910 3rd Ave W Mobridge SD 57601-1605 Office: Mobridge Tribune 111 3rd St W Mobridge SD 57601-2525

HALL, KATHRYN WALT, ambassador; m. Craig Hall; 2 children, 4 stepchildren. AB in Econs., JD, U. Calif., Berkeley. Asst. city atty., Berkeley, Calif.; with Safeway Stores; pres. Kathryn Hall Vineyards, Inc., Walt Mgmt., Inc.; mng. dir., ptnr. Hall Fin. Group, Inc.; amb. to Austria Vienna, 1997—. Mem. hunger adv. com. U.S. Ho. of Reps. Co-founder North Tex. Food Bank; mem. Nat. Adv. Coun. for Violence Against Women; trustee Woodrow Wilson Internat. Ctr. for Scholars; former bd. dirs., v.p. Tex. Mental Health Assn. Mem. Dallas Area C. of C., Comml. Real Estate Women, Tex. Retailers Assn. Office: The Honorable Kathryn Hall Amb Dept State 9900 Vienna Pl Washington DC 20521-9900

HALL, KATHY L. orchestra executive; b. Donnellson, Iowa; Prin. bassoonist Cedar Rapids (Iowa) Symphony Orch., exec. dir., 1992. Office: Cedar Rapids Symphony Orch 205 2nd Ave SE Cedar Rapids IA 52401-1213

HALL, KEITH R. retired federal official; b. Rockville Centre, N.Y., June 30, 1947; m. Linda Judith Merker, 1969; children: Jennifer, Jason. BA in History and Polit. Sci., Alfred U., 1969; MPA, Clark U., 1979. Commd. 2 lt. U.S. Army, 1970, advanced through grades to capt., chief intelligence collection mgmt., comdr. human source collection, 1970-74, commd. tactical signals intelligence co. Pyongtaek, Rep. Korea, 1974-75, supr. divsn. signals intelligence ops. tng. Army Intelligence Sch. Ft. Devens, Mass., 1976-79, resigned, 1979; budget examiner Office Mgmt. and Budget, Washington, 1979-83; dep. staff dir., budget dir. Senate Select Com. Intelligence, Washington, 1983-91; dep. asst. sec. defense intelligence Office of Sec. of Defense, Washington, 1991-95; exec. dir. for intelligence cmty. affairs Office of Dir. Ctrl. Intelligence/CIA, Washington, 1995-96; dep. dir., acting dir. Nat. Reconnaissance Office, Washington, 1996-97, asst. sec. of Air Force (space), dir., 1997—2001, ret., 2001—; v.p. Booz, Allen, Hamilton, 2002—. Presdl. mgmt. intern U.S. Office Personnel Mgmt., Washington, 1979-81. Mem. Security Affairs Support Assn., Nat. Milit. Intelligence Assn. (bd. dirs. 1988-97). Lutheran. Avocations: reading, baseball, hiking, bicycling, postal history. E-mail: hall_keith@bah.com.

HALL, KENNETH RICHARD, chemical engineering educator, consultant; b. Tulsa, Okla., Nov. 5, 1939; s. Snipes Webster and Selina Rose (Scarpin) H.; m. Janet Beulah Blood, June, 1964 (div. 1975); children: Tara Marie, Deirdre Rene; m. Frieda Maria Karner, Mar. 12, 1976; children: Kent Max, Keith Anton, Krysta Maria. BS ChemE, U. Tulsa, 1962; MS, U. Calif., Berkeley, 1964; PhD, U. Okla., 1967. Registered engr., Tex. Asst. prof. U. Va., Charlottesville, 1967-70, 71-74; asst. to pres. ChemShare Corp., Norman, Okla., 1970; sr. rsch. engr. AMOCO, Tulsa, 1970-71; vis. prof. U. Louvain, Belgium, 1971-72; assoc. prof. Tex. A&M U., College Station, 1974-78, prof., 1978—, dir. Thermodynamics Rsch. Ctr., 1979-85, 97-2000, asst. dir. Tex. Engring. Experiment Sta., 1985-88, assoc. dean engring., 1987—94, 2002—, from assoc. dir. to dep. dir., 1988—94, 2002—, assoc. dep. chancellor for engring., 1990—94, 2002—, interim head petroleum engring., 1991, interim head chem. engring., 1994; dir. CTS divsn. NSF, Va., 1994-96; GPSA prof. Tex. A&M U., College Station, 1997-2000, Jack E. and Frances Brown chair, 2001—, head dept. chem. engring., 2002—. Cons. OPC Engring., Houston, 1980-85, Quantum Tech., Houston, 1981-85; cons. Precision Measurement Inc., Duncanville, Tex., 1981-90; bd. dirs. Lorax Corp., Syn Fuels. U.S. editor Flow Measurement and Instrumentation; contbr. over 200 articles to profl. jours. Recipient numerous grants for research. Mem.: Am. Inst. Chem. Engrs. (chmn. ctrl. Va. chpt. 1969, chmn. cyrogenics 1977—79, exec. position II South Tex. sect. 1991—92, bd. dirs. fuels and petrochems. divsn. 1992—94), Am. Soc. Engring. Edn., Am. Chem. Soc., ASTM (chmn. D-3 1985—91, 1994—2001). Avocations: sports, reading. Home: 1401 Millcreek Ct College Station TX 77845-8352 Office: Tex A&M U Dept Chem Engring College Station TX 77843

HALL, KERMIT LANCE, academic administrator, historian, educator; b. Akron, Ohio, Aug. 31, 1944; s. Kermit Hall and Katherine Lois Galbraith; m. Phyllis Anne Moke, May 1, 1944. BA, U. of Akron, 1966; MA, Syracuse U., N.Y., 1967; PhD, U. of Minn., 1972; MSL, Yale U., 1980. Prof. of history Vanderbilt U., Nashville, 1972—76, Wayne State U., Detroit, 1976—81; prof. of law and history U. of Fla., Gainesville, 1981—92; dean and prof. of history and law U. of Tulsa, 1992—94, The Ohio State U., Columbus, 1994—99; provost, vice chancellor and prof. of history N.C. State U., Raleigh, 1999—2000; pres. and prof. of history Utah State U., Logan, 2000—. Dir. Am. Coun. on Edn., Washington, 2000—; adv. dir. Wells Fargo Bank of No. Utah, Salt Lake City, 2002—; mem. exec. adv. com. SCT Corp., Phila., 2001—; dir. Nat. Assn. State Univs. and Land Grant Colls., 2002—, Regence Blue Cross Blue Shield of Utah, 2003—. Author: (book) The Magic Mirror: Law in American History; editor: The Oxford Companion to the Supreme Court of the United States (Main Selection, History Book Club, 1992), The Oxford Guide To Supreme Court Decisions (Main Selection, History Book Club, 1999), The Oxford Companion to American Law. Mem. John F. Kennedy Assassination Records Rev. Bd., Washington, 1994—98; dir. Rsch. Triangle Inst., Raleigh, NC, 1999—2000, Utah Festival Opera, Logan, 2000. 1st lt. U.S. Army, 1968—69. Decorated Air Medal; named George E. Knepper Disting. Lectr., U. of Akron, 2000, Utah's Best Hands On Leader, Salt Lake Mag., 2001, Simon E. Sobeloff Lectr., U. of Md. Coll. of Law, 1996; recipient James Madison award, ALA, 1996, Outstanding Achievement award, Logan and Cahce Valley, Utah C. of C., 2003, Silver Gavel award, ABA, 1993, Outstanding Reference Work award, ALA, 1992, Hon. Fellow, Ctr. for Gt. Plains Studies, 1992; fellow Post-Doctoral fellow, Earhart Found., 1979—80, Legal History fellow, Am. Bar Found., 1980—81, Lectr. In Finland, Fulbright-Hayes Found., 1987; grantee Minority Scholars in History grantee, Pew Charitable Trust, 1991—94, Rsch. in Selection of Judges grantee, NSF, 1984—86, History Tchg. Alliance grantee, Rockefeller, Exxon, and Hewlett Founds., 1984—87, Defining the Core of Citizenship grantee, NEH, 1993—94, Native Ams. and Higher Edn. grantee, Coca Cola Found., 1994—96; vis. scholar Disting. Vis. Scholar, Am. Bar Found., 1986—87, U. of No. Iowa, 1996. Fellow: Am. Coun. Learned Socs.; mem.: ABA (com. on pub. edn. about the law 2001—, Silver Gavel award 1993), Am. Hist. Assn., Am. Soc. for Legal History (assoc.; bd. of directors 1994—97), Orgn. of Am. Historians (life), Rotary Internat. (assoc.). Democrat-Npl. Avocations: salt water fishing, hiking, reading, strength conditioning. Home: 1417 E 1300 North Logan UT 84341 Office: Utah State University 1400 Old Main Hill Logan UT 84322 Home Fax: 435-797-1173; Office Fax: 435-797-1173.

HALL, KIRSTINA J. humanities educator; b. Columbus, Ga., Aug. 22, 1944; d. Stanley William Eppihimer Jr. and Helen Jaynell Sanders; m. Millard Jackson Olds, May 15, 1964 (div. 1999); children: Marjorie J. Olds, Margaret J. Olds, Miriam J. Olds; m. Clifford Robert Hall, June 18, 1982. AA, Clayton State Coll., 1993; BA, Ga. State U., 1996, MA, 2003. V.p. P.C. & Co. Auto Sales, Inc., Jonesboro, Ga., 1982—; substitute tchr. Clayton County Sch. System, Clayton County, 1990—2001; prof. Ga. State U., Atlanta, 2001—. Mem.: ASCD, NCTE, MLA. Democrat. Avocations: painting, writing. E-mail: frachat@aol.com.

HALL, L. MICHAEL, psychologist, writer; b. Dec. 31, 1949; BS in Human Resources, Colo. Christian U., 1990; MA in Psychology, Regis U., 1993; PhD in Psychology, Union Inst., 1995. Internat. cons., trainer Neuro-Semantics, Clifton, Colo. Mailing: Neuro-Semantics PO Box 8 Clifton CO 81520 E-mail: michael@neurosemantics.com.

HALL, LARRY DEAN, energy company executive, lawyer; b. Hastings, Nebr., Nov. 8, 1942; s. Willis E. and Stella W. (Eckoff) H.; m. Jeffe D. Bryant, July 5, 1985; children: Scott, Jeff, Mike, Bryan. BA in Bus., U. Nebr., Kearney; JD, U. Nebr. Bar: Nebr. 1967, Colo. 1981. Ptnr. Wright, Simmons, Hancock & Hall, Scottsbluff, Nebr., 1967-71; atty., asst. treas. KN Energy Inc., Hastings, 1971-73, dir. regulatory affairs, 1973-76, v.p. law divsn. Lakewood, Colo., 1976-82, sr. v.p., 1982-85, exec. v.p., 1985-88, pres., COO, 1988-94, pres., CEO, 1994—99, also bd. dirs., 1988-94, chmn., CEO, pres., 1996-99; mng. dir. CPS Investments, 1999—. Bd. dirs. Colo. Assn. Commerce and Industry, Gas Rsch. Inst., Colo. Alliance for Bus., MLA, Magnum Techs.; chmn. Natural Gas Coun., 1998. Boy Scouts Am., Colo.; Marble Cmty. Ch.; Denver Police Officers Found. Mem. ABA, Colo. Assn. Commerce and Industry (bd. dirs.), Interstate Natural Gas Assn. Am. (chmn. 1997), CAB (bd. dirs.), Fed. Energy Bar Assn., Nebr. Bar Assn., Colo. Bar Assn., Midwest Gas Assn. (chmn.). Presbyterian. Avocations: skiing, golf, photography. Home: 329 Red Ridget Grand Junction CO 81503 Office: CPS Investments LLC 1400 16th St Ste 400 Denver CO 80202

HALL, LEE BOAZ, publishing company consultant, author; b. Little Rock, Oct. 8, 1928; s. Graham Roots and Louise (Boaz) H.; m. Mary Louise Reed, Nov. 29, 1951 (div.); children: Gwendolyn, Ann Valerie, Graham; m. Sarah Moore, Dec. 15, 1978. BA, Yale U., 1950. Reporter Ark. Gazette, Little Rock, 1950-51; officer Dept. Def., Washington, 1951-52, 1952-53; reporter Washington Post, 1953-55; with Life mag., 1955-70, bur. chief, 1958-59, 1963-66; editor Life en Espanol, 1966-69; editor internat. edits. Life, N.Y.C., 1970; pres. Tomorrow Pub. Co., N.Y.C., 1970-72; sr. v.p. internat. pub. Playboy Enterprises, Inc., Chgo., 1972-86; pres. Int Pub., Inc., 1986—, Donlee, Inc., Little Rock, 1986—. Author: International Magazine and Book Licensing, 1983. Served with U.S. Army, 1950-51. Mem. Federation Internationale de la Presse Periodique (liaison), Coral Casino, Montecito Country Club. Home and Office: 3 Hunt Dr PO Box 763 Summerland CA 93067-0763 E-mail: LeeBHall@aol.com. *Two words "fair play" define the principles and standards of conduct I try to adhere to in my life. Professionally, negotiating as I do with people of many cultures, fairness is of the essence. Too many Americans, isolated by oceans, guided by strict interpretation of the Puritan ethic and misled by the trappings of their power, lord their tastes, their customs and their wealth over those they perceive as less fortunate.*

HALL, LINDA SUE BOHANNON, special education educator; b. L.A., July 19, 1954; d. Hearold Eugene and Ruth Ella (Sanders) Paisley; divorced; children: David Eugene, Jamie Lyn; m. Roger J. Hall. AS, Mt. San Antonio C.C., Walnut, Calif., 1974; AA, Antelope Valley C.C., Lancaster, Calif., 1990; BA, Calif. State U., Northridge, 1992; MA, Chapman U., Orange, Calif., 1994. Cert. tchr. Calif., learning handicapped tchr., Calif.; cert. resource program specialist; recipient adminstrv. credential. Paraeducator L.A. County Office of Edn., Downey, Calif., 1987-93; tchr. Westside Sch. Dist., Lancaster, Calif., 1993-96, Lancaster Sch. Dist., Lancaster, 1996-2000, spl. edn. team mem., resource program chair, 1999—; program specialist, spl. edn. team Buena Park Sch. Dist., 2000—01; spl. edn. mgmt. Brea (Calif.) Olinda Unified Sch. Dist., 2001—. Dir. Awana Girls Club, Leona Valley, Calif., 1993-95; advisor Calif. Jr. Scholarship Fedn., Lancaster, 1994-96. Mem. Assn. Calif. Sch. Adminstrs., Calif. Educators Assn., Calif. Assn. Resource Specialists, Learning Disabilities Assn. Republican. Avocations: visual arts, sculpture, gardening, national parks. Office: Brea Olinda Unified Sch Dist 1 Civic Ctr Cir Brea CA

HALL, LOIS BREMER, retired educator, volunteer; b. Oak Park, Ill., July 27, 1923; d. Frederick Statler and Mabel (Forbes) Bremer; m. Bruce Hall, Sept. 9, 1955 (dec. Mar. 1981); children: Donald, Richard, Barbara. B in Music Edn., U. Mich., 1946. Cert. elem., secondary tchr. Mich., Ky.; ordained elder Presbyn. Ch. Tchr. handbell ringing Elm St. Recreation Ctr., Atlantic Recreation Ctr. Handbell ringer AARP, Osprey Village and Quality Health, Bapt. Hosp., 1st Presbyn. Ch. Fernandina Beach; dir. Amelia Handbell Choir; singer Amelia Island Chorale, Meml. United Meth. Ch., Amelia Plantation Chapel, Amelia Bapt. Ch., St. Peter's Episcopal Ch. Mem. com. Peck Ctr.; founding mem., vol. coord. CROP Walk, 1989—99; mem. exec. bd. Meml. United Meth. Ch.; vol. Church World Svc., Fernandina Beach, Synod of South Atlantic Coun., 1989; mem. Presbytery of St. Augustine Coun., 1984—97, music coord. of handbell and choral workshops, 1990—98; mem. hunger com. Presbyn. Gen. Assembly, 1992—96; vol.-in-mission New Hope Meth. Presbyn. Ch., N. Pole, Alaska, 1991—94, 1996; soloist, clarinet Ch. Choirs; bd. dirs. Amelia Arts Acad., 1994—2003, Ann. Fernandina Beach Talent Show, 2001—02. Recipient award for cultural enrichment, City of Fernandina Beach, 2001. Mem.: AARP (bd. dirs.), Woman's Club Fernandina Beach (pres. 1983—84, 1991—92, Outstanding New Mem. 1980—81, Cmty. Svc. award 1987—88), Rose Garden Club (treas. 1998—2002), Alpha Omicron Pi, Delta Omicron. Republican. Home: 607 Goldenrod Way Saint Marys GA 31558

HALL, MARCIA BROWN, art historian, educator; b. Washington, July 13, 1939; d. Charles Edward Brown and Frances Peebles Ocheltree; m. Charles Arthur Mann Hall, June 9, 1961 (div. May 1990); children: Christopher Martin, Brian Starbuck; m. Gerald Richard Hoepfner, Dec. 18, 1991. BA, Wellesley Coll., 1960; MA, Radcliffe Coll., 1962; PhD, Harvard U., 1967. Vis. lectr. Franklin & Marshall Coll., Lancaster, Pa., 1967-71; asst. prof., prof. Temple U., Phila, 1973—. Dir. NEH summer seminar, Rome, 1992. Author: Renovation and Counter-Reformation: Vasari and Duke Cosimo in Santa Maria Novella and Santa Croce, 1965-77, 1979, Color and Meaning: Practice and Theory in Renaissance Painting, 1992, Michelangelo: The Sistine Ceiling Restored, 1993, After Raphael: Painting in Central Italy in the Sixteenth Century, 1999, Michelangelo: The Frescoes of the Sistine Chapel, 2002; editor, contbr.: Color and Technique in Renaissance Painting, 1987, The School of Athens, 1997; co-editor: The Princeton Raphael Conference, 1990; contbr. articles to profl. jours. Fulbright found. fellow Villa I Tatti, 1963-64, Harvard Ctr. for Renaissance Studies, Florence, Italy, 1971-72, NEH fellow Univ. Profs., 1979-80, 95-96, Fulbright Sr. Rsch. fellow, 2002--. Mem. Coll. Art Assn., 16th Century Studies, Renaissance Soc. Am. Home: 720 Davidson Rd Philadelphia PA 19118-4302

HALL, MARCIA JOY, non-profit organization administrator; b. Long Beach, Calif., June 24, 1947; d. Royal Waltz and Norine (Parker) Stanton; m. Stephen Christopher Hall, March 29, 1969; children: Geoffrey Michael, Christopher Stanton. AA, Foothill Coll., 1967; student, U. Oreg., 1967-68; BA, U. Washington, Seattle, 1969. Instr. aide Glen Yermo Sch., Mission Viejo, Calif., 1979-80; market rsch. interviewer Rsch. Data, Framingham, Mass., 1982-83; adult edn. instr. Community Sch. Use Program, Milford, Mass., 1982-83; career info. ctr. coord. Milford High Sch., 1983-86; corp. rels. dir. Sch. Vols. for Milford, Inc., 1985-86; N.E. area coord, YWCA of Annapolis and Anne Arundel County, Severna Park, Md. 1987-89; exec. dir. West Anne Arundel County C. of C., Odenton, Md., 1989—2001, also exec. dir. Found., Inc., 1999—2001; coord. bus. and entrepreneurship continuing profl. edn. and outreach Anne Arundel C.C., Arundel Mills, Md., 2001—. V.p. Corridor Transp. Corp., 1997-99. Pres. PTO, Mission Viejo, 1979-80, Milford, 1981-84; consumer assistance vol., Calif. Pub. Interest Rsch. Group, 1977-78; chmn. grant com. 21st Century Edn. Found., Ann Arundel Pub. Schs., Leadership Anne Arundel. Mem.: Am. Assn. Women in C.C., Assn. Women in Comm., Md. Assn. C. of C. Execs. (pres. 1999—2000), Toastmasters (treas. 1988—, pres. 1989—). Avocations: piano, music composition, bridge, reading. Home: 507 Devonshire Ln Severna Park MD 21146-1017

HALL, MARIAN M. retired music educator; b. York, Pa., June 22, 1932; d. Thomas Adrian and Olive Murray Martin; m. John H. Hall, June 1, 1953; children: Debra Grey, Cindy Dolen, Michael, Daniel. BA, Western Md. Coll., 1953; M Equivalence, Towson State U., 1972. Music tchr. Balt. City Schs., 1971—95; ret., 1995. Organist, choir dir. Rocklin Meth. Ch.; with Beth Ifiloh Summer Camp, Pikesville, Md.; piano tchr. Jason's Music Store, 1990—. Mem.: Suzuki Assn., Music Educators Nat. Conf. Avocations: music, camping, hiking, boating, swimming. Home: 4600 Lincoln Dr Baltimore MD 21227

HALL, MARION TRUFANT, botany educator, arboretum director; b. Gorman, Tex., Sept. 6, 1920; s. Frank Marion and Nora Gertrude (Wharton) H.; m. Virginia Riddle, Nov. 9, 1944; children: Susan, Alan Lee, John Lane. BS, U. Okla., 1943, MS, 1947; PhD, Washington U., St. Louis, 1951; DSc (hon.), North Central Coll., Ill., 1977. Ranger Nat. Park Service, Dept. Interior, 1942; instr. botany U. Okla., 1946-47; curator Bebb Herbarium, 1949; field botanist, instr. Tex. Nature Camp, Nat. Audubon Soc., Kerrville, Tex., 1948; grad. asst. zoology, teaching fellow Washington U., 1948-50; spl. lectr. genetics and evolution Henry Shaw Sch. Botany, 1952; botanist Cranbrook Inst. Sci., Bloomfield Hills, Mich., 1950-56, acting dir., 1955-56; prof., head dept. botany Butler U., 1956-62; vis. prof. botany U. Okla., 1962; dir. Stovall Mus. Sci. and History, 1962-66, Morton Arboretum, Lisle, Ill., 1966-90, dir. emeritus, 1990—. Prof. botany, acting dir. U. Mich. Bot. Gardens, 1963-64; prof. horticulture U. Ill., Urbana; adj. prof. biology No. Ill. U.; cons. Mich. Dept. Conservation, Handbook Biol. Materials for Museums, also cons. on conservation issues, open space preservation & mgmt., vegetational analysis, land use rating. Contbr. numerous research articles to profl. jours. Bd. dirs. Joyce Found., Chgo. Henrietta Heerman scholar Washington U., 1951; recipient award for professionalism Am. Assn. Bot. Gardens and Arboreta Inc., citation for svcs. to U.S. govt. Inst. Mus. Svcs., Alumni Achievement award U. Okla., 1953, Liberty Hyde Bailey medal for outstanding achievement in Am. horticulture Am. Hort. Soc., 1990, Hutchinson medal for outstanding svc. to horticulture, 1990; NSF grantee. Fellow Ind. Acad. Sci., Cranbrook Inst. Sci.; mem. Ecol. Soc. Am., Asa Gray Meml. Assn., Mich. Natural Areas Coun., Okla. Acad. Sci., Mich. Bot. Club (past pres. Detroit), Phi Beta Kappa, Sigma Xi, Phi Sigma. Home and Office: 2016 Northwood Dr Maryville TN 37803-6365

HALL, MARK EVERETT, editor, writer; b. Gilroy, Calif, Nov. 20, 1951; s. Everett I. Hall and Evelyn L. Costa; m. Catherine Shank Hall, Sept. 21, 1977. BA, U. Calif., Santa Barbara, 1975; MA, U. Ky., 1978. Editor, pub. SunTech Jour., Mountain View, Calif., 1985-90; exec. editor Springer-Verlag, Santa Barbara, 1990-91; editor-in-chief LAN Tech., San Mateo, Calif., 1991-93, MacWeek, San Francisco, 1993-96; dir. Ziff Davis, Inc., Foster City, Calif., 1996-97; editor-in-chief Performance Computing, San Mateo, 1997-99; opinions editor, columnist Computerworld, Framingham, Mass., 1999—. Author: Sunburst, 1990; editor: SunTech Papers, 1991. Co-recipient Best News article Computer Press Assn., 1999, co-recipient Nat. award for News Am. Soc. Bus. Press Editors, 2001. Office: Computerworld PMB 299 4742 Liberty Rd S Salem OR 97302 E-mail: mark_hall@computerworld.com.

HALL, MARY ANN, English language educator; b. Pitts., Aug. 4, 1946; d. George G. and Helen K. (Summers) H. BA in Lit., U. Pitts., 1977, MFA in Writing, 1981, PhD in Lit., 1990. Tchr. asst., fellow U. Pitts., 1979-85, part-time instr., 1986-88, instr., 1988-93, asst. prof., 1993-98, assoc. prof., 1998—. Contbr. articles to profl. jours. Mem. Nat. Coun. Tchrs. of English (sec. Assembly for Tchg. of English Grammar 1992-94), Assn. Bus. Comm. Office: U Pitts at Titusville Brown St Titusville PA 16354

HALL, MARY HUGH, retired secondary school educator; b. Sumter, S.C., Apr. 15, 1937; d. Hughson Perry and Virginia Dare (Owens) Matthews; m. James Wallace Hall Sr., July 2, 1960; 1 child, James Wallace Jr. BA in Social Studies and French, Columbia Coll., 1959; postgrad., West Ga. Coll., 1975-79. Tchr. Arlington (Ga.) Schs., Inc., 1959-61; tchr., chair French dept. Douglas County H.S., Douglasville, Ga., 1965—97; ret., 1997. Mem. steering com. West Ga. Alliance, Carrollton, 1992—. Recipient Outstanding Officer award Jaycees, 1970, 71. Mem. NEA, Douglas County Assn. Educators, Ga. Assn. Educators. Avocations: dancing, reading, cooking, wood crafts. Home: 4679 Bedford Pl Douglasville GA 30135-1805

HALL, MARY TAUSSIG, professional volunteer; b. St. Louis, Feb. 21, 1911; d. Frederick Joseph and Florence (Gottschalk) Taussig; m. Louis Benoist Tompkins, June 17, 1941 (dec. Oct. 1950); children: Frederick Kingsbury Tompkins, Mary Waterman Tompkins (Mrs. Neil Houghton); m. Thomas Steele Hall, Oct. 21, 1952 (dec. 1990). BA, Bryn Mawr Coll., 1933; MSW, Washington U., St. Louis, 1938; LHD (hon.), Lindenwood Coll., 1979. Cert. social worker. Caseworker New England Home for Little Wanderers, Boston, 1938-39. Editor: Stones for Bread, 1940. Pres., Mo. Assn. Social Welfare, 1942-44, bd. dirs., 1942-48; bd. dirs., chair industry com. Urban League Greater St. Louis, 1943-52; bd. dirs. Family and Children's Svcs., St. Louis, 1944-57; apptd. by gov. state commr. Children's Code Commn., 1945, Bd. Children's Guardians, 1946-55; apptd. by mayor bd. dirs. City Hosp. # 2 during racial integration; founding bd. dirs. Washington U. Med. Ctr. Child Guidance Clinic, St. Louis, 1948-52; chmn. bd. Divsn. Children's Svcs., St. Louis, 1955-66; nat. com. policy Child Welfare League Am., 1955-57; nat. coun. Internat. Social Svc., 1968-88; mem. world coun. YWCA, N.Y.C., 1963—; pres. St. Louis chpt. bd. UN Assn., 1977-80, nat. steering com. coun. chpt. pres., 1979-82, nat. bd. govs. UN Assn. USA, 1980-90; mem. nat. coun. UN Assn. USA, 1991—. Recipient alumni award Washington U., 1956, Woman of Achievement award for Social Concern, City of St. Louis, 1979, Arnold Goodman Nat. Leadership award UN Assn. U.S.A., 1994, Humanitarian award Planned Parenthood Assn. St. Louis, 2001. Mem. Cosmopolitan Club (N.Y.C.). Avocations: garden, travel. Home: 4969 Pershing Pl Saint Louis MO 63108-1220

HALL, MARY THERESA, literature educator; b. Pitts., July 23, 1953; d. Edward and Mary Lydon Kyne; m. V. Donald Hall, Aug. 10, 1996. BA in English, Seton Hill U., 1975; MA in English, Carnegie Mellon U., 1987; PhD in English, Duquesne U., 1991. Permanent edn. cert. in English and French Pa. Elem. tchr. St. Pius X, Mt. Pleasant, Pa., 1975—76; tchr. English and French Seton-LaSalle H.S., Pitts., 1977—82, 1984—87; asst. dean of students Seton Hill U., Greensburg, Pa., 1982—84, instr. dept. English, 1987—91, asst. prof. English, 1991—96; assoc. prof. English Kutztown (Pa.) U., 1996—99, Thiel Coll., Greenville, Pa., 1999—. Sec. Western Pa. Symposium on World Lits.,

1991—96; advisor Alpha Iota Kappa chpt. Sigma Tau Delta, Pa., 2000—. Author: Country Parsons, Country Poets: Poetry and Prose as Spiritual Autobiography, 1992, Dylan Volume I, 1992, Catholic Women Writers: A Bio-Bibliographical Sketchbook, 2001, Teacher Commentary on Student Papers, 2002; contbr. articles to profl. jours. Mem.: MLA, English Assn. of Pa. State Univs., Pa. Soc. Tchg. Scholars, Pa. Coun. Tchrs. of English, Nat. Coun. Tchrs. of English. Democrat. Roman Catholic. Avocations: walking, reading. Home: 3510 Lee Run Rd Hermitage PA 16148 Office: Thiel Coll 75 College Ave Greenville PA 16125 E-mail: mthall@thiel.edu.

HALL, MICHAEL, disability processing specialist; b. N.Y.C., Sept. 20, 1947; s. Mark and Eva Hall; m. Karen Jane Klein; children: Ian D., Mitchell L. BA, CCNY, 1968; MA in Fgn. Affairs, U. Va., 1970; JD, Fordham U., 1975. Bar: N.Y. 1976, D.C. 1980. Disability processing specialist Social Security, Jamaica, NY. Home: 57 Florida Ave Commack NY 11725-5115 Office: NEPSC Proc Br 1 Jamaica Center Plz Jamaica NY 11432

HALL, MICHAEL L. obstetrician-gynecologist; b. Denver, Sept. 27, 1950; s. Louis Anthony and Jan Hall; children from previous marriage: Kevin, Kristyn, Nicholas; m. Martha Merrill, Nov. 23, 1989; children: Nathaniel, Michael, Mary, Emilie, Jorden. MD, U. Oreg./Health Scis. U., 1977. Diplomate Am. Bd. Ob-Gyn. Intern St. Joseph Hosp., Denver, 1977-78, resident in ob-gyn., 1978-81, mem. staff, 1981—; pvt. practice Denver. Mem. staff Swedish, Littleton, Colo. Fellow ACOG; mem. AMA, Am. Inst. Ultrasound in Medicine, Ctrl. Assn. Obstetricians and Gynecologists. Address: 499 E Hampden Ave Ste 210 Englewood CO 80110-2792 E-mail: mikeobg@msn.com.

HALL, MICHAEL LEE, federal government agency grants administrator; b. San Antonio, Jan. 2, 1946; s. John Edward and Lorraine Louise (Horn) Hall; m. Joy Lynn Schmidt, Aug. 28, 1966. BA, U. Tex., 1968, MA, 1972, Johns Hopkins U., 1974, PhD, 1977. Asst. prof. Centenary Coll. La., Shreveport, 1976-80, assoc. prof., 1980-87, chmn. dept. English, 1980-83; program officer Nat. Endowment for the Humanities, Washington, 1987-88, asst. dir. for seminars div. fellowships and seminars, 1988-95, sr. program officer collaborative rsch., 1996—. Humanities adminstr. NEH, Washington, 1985-87; program adminstr. LC/Ameritech Nat. Digital Libr. Competition Libr. of Congress, Washington, 1998-99; instr. (part-time) Georgetown U., Washington, 1989, U. Md., 1992, 94—; dir. summer seminar for secondary sch. tchrs. NEH, Centenary Coll. La., Shreveport, 1984. Co-editor: LIT: Literature and Interpretive Techniques, 1986; poetry editor Poet Lit. Mag., Oklahoma City, 1985-96; contbr. articles and revs. on Brit. and Am. lit. to profl. jours. Nat. Endowment for the Humanities fellow in residence U. Chgo, 1978-79. Mem. MLA, Nat. Coun. Tchrs. English, John Donne Soc. Democrat. Presbyterian. Avocations: traveling, swimming, photography, writing, computing. Office: NEH 1100 Pennsylvania Ave NW Washington DC 20004-2501 E-mail: mhall@neh.gov., mlhall@wam.umd.edu.

HALL, MICHAEL WAYNE, lawyer, judge; b. Walla Walla, Wash., Sept. 13, 1952; s. Charles Wayne and Laura Marie (Le Page) H.; m. Stephanie Francis Uberuaga, Dec. 18; children: Katherine, Alexandra, Annalise, Cameron. BA in Comms., Wash. State U., 1976; JD, Southwestern U., 1987. Bar: U.S. Dist. Ct. Wash. 1988. Founding ptnr. The Hall Law Firm, P.S., Edmonds, Wash., 1991—. Mediator, v.p. Puget Sound Christian Coll., judge pro tem Thurston County Superior Ct., also Edmonds Mcpl. Ct.; presdl. appt. bd. dirs. Wash. Selective Svc. Bd. dirs. Laser Project Found., Cybersch. Youth in Philanthropy Found. Recipient Nat. Leadership award, Nat. Republican Congrsl. com. Mem. Wash. State Bar Assn. (interprofl. com., mem. alternative dispute resolution sect.), Nat. Com. on Planned Giving. Avocation: fly fishing. Office: The Hall Law Firm PS 201 4th Ave N Ste 202 Edmonds WA 98020-3119 E-mail: michaelhall32@hotmail.com.

HALL, MIKE BURT (MARSHALL B. HALL), artist, educator; b. Ashland, Wis., June 18, 1932; s. Burt Carolus Hall and Ruby Alvina Bekken. Studied with Percy Mannser. Tchr. art Oreg. Soc. Artists, 1962; pvt. tchr. One man shows include Oreg. Soc. Artists, Portland, 1962, Maryhill (Wash.) Mus. Fine Arts, 1964, 66, Abbot Hall Gallery William Temple House, 1993; group shows include Soc. Western Artists De Young Mus., San Francisco, 1965, 67, 68, Charles and Emma Frye Mus. Art, Seattle, 1968, 69, Am. Artists Profl. League, 1982, 83, 84, 85, 86, Soc. Western Artists Rosicrucian Mus., San Jose, Calif., 1976, Morseburg Gallery, L.A., 1965, Qraz Gallery, Seattle, 1967, Husberg Fine Arts Gallery, Sedona, Ariz., 1970, First Ave Galleries, Scottsdale, Ariz., 1971, McAdoo Gallery, Santa Fe, N. Mex., 1971; permanent collections include Maryhill Mus. Fine Arts, West Coast Picture Frame Co., Concordia U., Mt. Hood C.C., The Halton Co., numerous pvt. collections Wash., Oreg., Calif., Ariz., Nev., N. Mex., Conn., others. Recipient Edmund Ayling award and degree of honor Soc. Western Artists, 1968, medal of honor Am. Artists Profl. League, 1984; Best of Show award Lake Oswego (Oreg.) Festival of Art, 1984, 2000, 03. Avocation: collecting art. Home: 2715 NE Saratoga St Portland OR 97211-5961

HALL, MILES LEWIS, JR., lawyer; b. Fort Lauderdale, Fla., Aug. 14, 1924; s. Miles Lewis and Mary Frances (Dawson) H.; m. Muriel M. Fisher, Nov. 4, 1950; children: Miles Lewis III, Don Thomas. AB, Princeton U., 1947; JD, Harvard U., 1950. Bar: Fla. 1951, U.S. Supreme Ct., 1972, U.S. Ct. Appeals (11th cir.), U.S. Dist. Ct. (so. and mid. dist.) Fla. Since practiced in, Miami; ptnr. Hall & Hedrick, Miami, 1953—. Dir. Gen. Portland, Inc., 1974-81. Author: Election of Remedies, Vol. VIII, Fla. Law and Practice, 1958. Pres. Orange Bowl Com., 1964-65, dir., 1950—, sec., treas. 1984-86; vice-chmn., dir. Dade County (Fla.) ARC, 1961-62, chmn., 1963-64, dir., 1967-73; nat. fund cons. ARC, 1963, 66-68, trustee, 1985—; pres. Ransom Sch. Parents Assn., 1966; chmn. South Fla. Gov.'s Scholarship Ball, 1966; mem. exec. bd. South Fla. council Boy Scouts Am., 1966-67; citizens bd. U. Miami, 1961-66; mem. Fla. Council of 100, 1961-97, vice chmn., 1961-62; mem. Coral Gables (Fla.) Biltmore Devel. Com., 1972-73; mem. bd. visitors Coll. Law, Fla. State U., 1974-77; bd. dirs. Coral Gables War Meml. Youth Ctr. Assn. Inc., 1967—, pres., 1969-72; bd. dirs. Salvation Army, Miami, 1968-83, Fla. Citizens Against Crime 1984-89; bd. dirs. Bok Tower Gardens Found. Inc., 1987—, sec., 1991—; trustee St. Thomas U., 1990-96, vice chmn., 1993-96; trustee Fla. Supreme Ct. Hist. Soc., 1988—, v.p., 1991-92, pres., 1993-95. 2d lt. USAAF, 1943-45. Fellow Am. Bar Found. (life), Fla. Bar Found. (life); mem. ABA (Fla. co-chmn. membership com. sect. corp. banking and bus. law 1968-72), Dade County Bar Assn. (dir. 1964-65, pres. 1967-68), Fla. Bar Assn., Am. Judicature Soc., Miami-Dade County C. of C. (v.p. 1962-64, dir. 1966-68), Harvard Law Sch. Assn. Fla. (dir. 1964-66), Cottage Club, The Miami Club (v.p., dir. 1989-91, pres. 1990-91), Princeton Club So. Fla. (past pres.), Miami Found. for Cancer Rsch., Inc. (pres. 1998—), Alpha Tau Omega. Methodist. Home: 2707 Alhambra Cir Coral Gables FL 33134 Office: Hall & Hedrick 25 SE 2nd Ave Ste 1105 Miami FL 33131-1605

HALL, MILTON REESE, retired oil company executive; b. Vicksburg, Miss., July 5, 1932; s. Alvin Howard and Adelle Vera (McKay) H.; m. Margaret Louise Bailey, Feb. 17, 1957; children: Mark Russell, Stacy Elaine. BS in Acctg., Miss. So. U., 1953; MBA in Acctg., U. Miss., 1956; postgrad., La. State U., 1958-62. CPA, Miss. Trainee, div. contr. Kaiser Aluminum & Chem. Co., various locations, 1956-66; analyst Tex. Instruments, Inc., Dallas, 1966-67; contr., v.p. Koch Industries, Inc., Wichita, Kans., 1967-92; retired, 1993. With U.S. Army, 1953-55. Republican. Baptist. Avocations: music, snow skiing.

HALL, MINA ELAINE, geriatrics nurse; b. Oakes, N.D., Sept. 22, 1953; d. Bryan J.W. Tyson and Emma Adelaide Durbin; m. Thomas Edward Hall, Feb. 23, 1979; children: John Joseph, Patrick Michael. BS, Winona State U., 1975; MS, S.D. State U., 1990; student, N.Am. Baptist Sem., 2001—03. Staff nurse, supr. Wadena (Minn.) Tri County Hosp., 1975-76; staff nurse Abbott-Northwestern Hosp., Mpls., 1976-79; lic. practice nursing instr. Worthington (Minn.) C.C., 1979-84; instr. nursing Augustana Coll., Sioux Falls, S.D., 1984-86; dir. nursing Luther Manor, Sioux Falls, 1990; instr. U. S.D., Vermillion, 1991-96; exec. dir. S.D. Nurses Assn., Sioux Falls, 1996—2001. Mem. S.D. Bd. Examiners Nursing Home Adminstrs., Sioux Falls, 1993—; assoc. project dir. Colleagues in Caring, Sioux Falls, 1998-2001. Chair S.D. Covering Kids Coalition, Sioux Falls, 2000-01. Grantee VA, 1989. Mem. S.D. Nurses Assn. (Dist. Nurse of Yr. 1989), Sioux Falls Sister Cities Assn. (pres. 1999-2001), S.D. League Women Voters (pres. 1995-99, natural resources chair 1986-91), Sioux Falls League Women Voters (pres. 1991, bd. dirs. 1992-96); Sigma Theta Tau. Avocations: reading, organic gardening, skiing, piano.

HALL, MONTY, television producer, actor; b. Winnipeg, Man., Can., Aug. 25, 1921; came to U.S., 1955; s. Maurice Harvey and Rose (Rusen) Halparin; m. Marilyn Doreen Plottel, Sept. 28, 1947; children: Joanna, Richard David, Sharon Fay. BS, U. Man., 1945, LLD (hon.), 1987; D Human Scis. (hon.), Hanneman U., 1988; PhD (hon.), Haifa U., 1989. TV personality, emcee, N.Y.C. and Hollywood, Calif., 1955—. Lectr. broadcasting and fund raising various charities. Actor, U. Man., Canadian Army shows; emcee: NBC-Radio, Monitor on NBC-TV, Keep Talking, Byline: Monty Hall, Video Village on CBS-TV, ABC-TV; host Let's Make a Deal, 1964-86, Split Second, 1986-87; Author: Emcee: Monty Hall, 1974; producer (TV show) Your First Impression; guest appearances numerous TV series: starring role (stage prodn.) High Button Shoes, 1978. Bd. dirs. numerous charitable orgns.; bd. govs. Cedars-Sinai Med. Ctr.; active numerous orgns. on behalf of Israel; hon. mayor, Hollywood, 1973-79. Decorated officer Order of Can., Order of Manitoba; recipient star on Hollywood's Walk of Fame, 1973, on Palm Springs Walk of Fame, 1996, on Can. Walk of Fame, 2002; Internat. Humanitarian award Variety Clubs, 1983, over 500 other awards, including Monty Hall floor at U. Calif./L.A. Hosp., Johns Hopkins U., Balt., Mt. Sinai Hosp., Toronto, Hahneman Hosp., Phila. Mem. AFTRA, Screen Actors Guild, Variety Clubs (internat. pres. 1975-77, internat. chmn. 1981—). Clubs: Hillcrest Country. Avocations: golf, tennis. *The longer I live, the more I am obsessed with man's inhumanity directed against his fellow man. Is there a basic flaw in man's makeup which prevents the good from overtaking and defeating the evil? I have spent my adult life dedicated to helping children around the world, the diseased, handicapped and underprivileged. The rewards tangible and intangible have shaped my life, have given me an inner peace with myself, and yet a frustration at what could be and is not. The same holds for nation against nation. What could be—and is not. Is this the order of things past and things to come? I pray with all my heart that the teachings of peace shall prevail.*

HALL, NANCY CHRISTENSEN, publishing company executive, author, editor; b. N.Y.C., Nov. 14, 1946; d. Henry Norman and Elvira (Dugan) Christensen; m. John R. Hall Jr., June 12, 1968; children: Jonathan Scott, Kirsten Marie. BA, Manhattanville Coll., 1968; postgrad., Old Dominion U., 1970-71. Sr. assoc. editor Cahners Pub. Co., N.Y.C., 1972-74; freelance editor N.Y.C., 1974-78; sr. editor Grosset and Dunlap, N.Y.C., 1978-81; exec. editor, asst. v.p. Macmillan Pub. Co., N.Y.C., 1981-84; assoc. pub., v.p. Simon & Schuster Pub. Co., N.Y.C., 1984-85; founder, prin. Nancy Hall, Inc., juvenile book devel co., N.Y.C., 1986—; founder, ptnr. Hall Assocs., Inc., 1996—. Author: Monsters: Creatures of Mystery, 1980, Macmillan Fairy Tale Alphabet Book 1983; editor: Platt and Munk Treasury of Stories for Children, 1981, Favorite Tales from Hans Christian Andersen, 1988; prodr. series: Macmillan Jumbo Seasonal Patterns, Macmillan Manipulatives, Sesame Street Early Learning Games, Mickey's Young Readers Libr., Disney's Small World Libr., My First Hello Readers, and others. Office: Nancy Hall Inc 23 E 22nd St New York NY 10010-5304

HALL, NECHIE TESITOR, advertising and public relations executive; b. May 10, 1946; d. Carl and Elsie Marie (Lenzini) Tesitor; m. James William hall, Nov. 25, 1967; 1 child, Meredith Elyse. BFA, U. Colo., 1967; postgrad., U. Colo., Colorado Springs, 1971. Asst. mktg. dir. Woodmoor Corp., Monument, Colo., 1968-69, dir. pub. rels., 1969-70; pres., ptnr. Praco, Ltd., Colorado Springs, 1970—. Cons. in field. Bd. dirs. fund raising chmn. Alcoholic Recovery Ctr., Colorado Springs, 1974-77, El Pomar Renewal Ctr., Colorado Springs, 1977-80; bd. dirs. Pauline Meml. Sch., Colorado Springs, 1980-82, Rocky Mountain Rehab. Ctr., Colo. Amateur Sports Corp., treas., 1990-91; bd. dirs. St. Francis Hosp., Endowment Found., Goodwill Industries, Myron Stratton Found.; asst. overall chmn. Nat. Sports Festival I & II U.S. Olympic Com., Colorado Springs, 1978-79; CASA chmn. bd., chmn. pub. rels. Nat. Sports Festival V, 1983; bd. dirs. Colorado Springs Fine Arts Ctr.; co-chmn. task force Olympic Hall of Fame; mem. bus. adv. coun. U. Colo., Colorado Springs; vice chmn. bd. dirs. Econ. Devel. Corp. Colorado Springs; trustee Pioneer's Mus.; mem. El Paso County Med. Soc. Found.; v.p., pres. bd. dirs. Ct. Appointed Spl. Advs.; vice chair, bd. dirs. Colorado Springs Fine Arts Ctr.; bd. dirs. United Mo. Banks, Colo., 1994-2000. Recipient Silver medal Am. Advt., 1987; named bus. Citizen of Yr. Colorado Springs C. of C., 1988. Mem. Pub. Rels. Soc. Am., Pikes Peak Ad Fedn. (Silver medalist 1987), Exec. Women Internat., Colorado Springs Press Club, Internat. Assn. Bus. Communicators, Country Club of Colo., Broadmoor Golf Club, C. of C. (bd. dirs.), Kappa Alpha Theta. Republican. Roman Catholic. Home: 100 Gardner Pl Colorado Springs CO 80906-3314 Office: Praco Ltd PO Box 387 Colorado Springs CO 80901-0387 also: Praco Ltd 5300 Dtc Pkwy Englewood CO 80111-3023

HALL, PAMELA ELIZABETH, psychologist; b. Jacksonville, Fla., Sept. 10, 1957; d. Gary Curtiss and Ollie (Banko) H. BA, Rutgers U., 1979; MS in Edn., Pace U., 1981, PsyD in Psychology, 1984. Lic. psychologist, N.Y., N.J., Calif., Conn. Psychology extern St. Vincent's Med. Ctr., N.Y.C., 1981-82; intern in clin. psychology Elizabeth (N.J.) Gen. Med. Ctr., 1982-83, staff psychologist, 1983-85, J.F.K. Med. Ctr., Edison, N.J., 1985-87; pvt. practice Summit and Perth Amboy, N.J., 1985—; sr. supervising psychologist Muhlenberg Med. Ctr., Summit, N.J., 1987-90. Rsch. affiliate, internat. lectr. NIMH field trials on assessment of dissociative disorders Yale U., New Haven, 1990—; adj. prof. psychology Pace U., N.Y.C., 1979-99; exec. bd. dirs. Nat. Coun. on Alcoholism and Drug Dependence of Middlesex County, 2000-02. Active Mayor's Com. on Substance Abuse, Perth Amboy, 1987; bd. trustees Nat. Coun. Alcoholism and Drug Dependence, 2000—. Named Henry Rutgers scholar, 1979. Mem. Am. Soc. Clin. Hypnosis, Internat. Soc. for Study of Dissociation (founder, pres. N.J. chpt. 1988—, dir. component socs.), Pace U. Alumni Assn., Rutgers U. Alumni Assn., Psi Chi. Avocations: crew, swimming, fine arts, weightlifting. Home: PO Box 1820 Perth Amboy NJ 08862-1820 Office: 12 Kent Place Blvd Summit NJ 07901-1907 Office Fax: 732-826-9392.

HALL, PAMELA S. environmental consulting firm executive; b. Hartford, Conn., Sept. 4, 1944; d. LeRoy Warren and Frances May (Murray) Sheely; m. Stuart R. Hall, July 21, 1967 (dec.). BA in Zoology, U. Conn., 1966; MS in Zoology, U. N.H., 1969, BS summa cum laude, 1982; student spl. grad. studies program, Tufts U., 1986-90. Curatorial asst. U. Conn., Storrs, 1966; rsch. asst. Field Mus. Natural History, Chgo., 1966-67; tchg. asst. U. N.H., Durham, 1967-70; program mgr. Normandeau Assocs. Inc., Portsmouth, N.H., 1971-79, marine lab. dir., 1979-81, programs and ops. mgr. Bedford, N.H., 1981-83, v.p., 1983-85, sr. v.p., 1986-87, pres., 1987—. Mem. Conservation Commn., Portsmouth, 1977-90, Wells, Estuarine Rsch. Res. Rev.Commn., 1986-88, Great Bay (N.H.) Estuarine Rsch. Res. Tech. Working Group, 1987-89; trustee Trust for N.H. Lands, 1990-93; trustee N.H. chpt. Nature Conservancy, 1991—, chair 1995-99, chair emeritus, 1999—, trustee, 2000—, incorporator N.H. Charitable Fund, 1991-99; bd. advisors Vivamos Mejor, USA, 1990—; bd. dirs. Environ. Bus. Coun. New England, 1995—, treas. 1997—; bd. emeritus Ecosystems Inst., 1997—; commr. N.H. Land and Heritage Commn., 1998-99. Graham Found. fellow, 1966; NDEA fellow, 1970-71. Mem. Women's Transp. Seminar, The Nature Conservancy, Soc. of the Protection of N.H. Forests, The Nat. Audubon Soc., Environ. Bus. Coun. New Eng. (Environ. Merit award 1998), Audubon Soc. N.H., Phi Sigma Soc. Home: 4 Pleasant Point Dr Portsmouth NH 03801-5275 Office: Normandeau Assocs Inc 25 Nashua Rd Bedford NH 03110-5500 E-mail: phall@normandeau.com.

HALL, PAUL J. lawyer; b. San Diego, Jan. 13, 1951; AB with highest honors, U. Calif., Santa Cruz, 1972; postgrad, Yale U.; JD, U. Calif., Berkeley, 1975. Bar: Calif. 1975. Mem. Manatt, Phelps & Phillips, L.A., 1975-94, Stein & Lubin LLP, San Francisco, 1995-98, Lillick & Charles LLP, San Francisco, 1998—. Bd. regents U. Calif., 1992-93, regent designate, 1991-92. Trustee U. Calif. Santa Cruz Found., 1986—. Mem. Calif. State Bar, Boalt Hall Alumni Assn. (bd. dirs. 1983-90, treas. 1985-86, sec. 1986-87, v.p. 1987-89, pres.-elect 1989-90, pres. 1990-91), U. Calif. Santa Cruz Alumni Assn. (bd. dirs. 1983-90, pres. 1986-90). Address: Lillick & Charles 2 Embarcadero Ctr Ste 2700 San Francisco CA 94111-3996

HALL, PENELOPE COKER, writer, magazine editor; b. Charlotte, N.C., Mar. 19, 1932; d. James Lide and Elizabeth (Boatwright) Coker; m. William Parmenter Wilson, Sept. 6, 1964 (div. 1971); 1 child, Eliza Wilson Ingle; m. Mortimer Waddhams Hall, Dec. 8, 1972; stepchildren: Dorothy, Margaret, Mary Howland, Matthew. Student, Sarah Lawrence Coll., Bronxville, N.Y., 1954. Sr. editor, biographer Cleveland Amory's Celebrity Register, N.Y.C.; prodr., commentator Wrap-Up with Mike Wallace, N.Y.C.; co-prodr., interviewer for series of hr. long spls. NBC-TV, N.Y.C.; co-host 10 Around Town Channel 10 TV, Phila.; co-host The New Yorkers Channel 5 TV, N.Y.C., 1968-70; reporter, Sunday anchor 10 O'Clock News, Channel 5, N.Y.C., 1970-73; host cable cooking show Millbrook, NY, 1976—; editor-in-chief Dutchess Mag., N.Y.C., 1993—99, editor-at-large, columnist, 1998—. Contbr. numerous articles to profl. jours.; author: Fancy and the Cement Patch, 1966, The Wish Bottle, 1967, Riding High, 1990. Bd. trustees Spoleto Festival, Charleston, S.C., 1997—, Coker Coll., Hartsville, S.C., 2000— Mem. Authors League, Nat. Trust for Hist. Preservation Nat. Trust Coun., Sandanona Beagles, Millbrook Hounds, Century Assn., Millbrook Golf and Tennis Club (bd. dirs. 1989-93), Cosmopolitan Club. Democrat. Episcopalian. Avocations: painting, horseback riding, boating. Home: PO Box 516 Millbrook NY 12545-0516

HALL, PETER C. lawyer, defender; b. Phila., Dec. 27, 1959; s. Charles Potter and Constance (Nuzum) H.; m. Kristin Anderson, Aug. 4, 1984; children: Charles, Nathan. AB, U. Miami, 1982; JD, Temple U., 1986. Bar: Pa. 1987, U.S. Dist. Ct. (ea. dist.) Pa. 1987. Asst. pub. defender Bucks County Pub. Defender, Doylestown, Pa., 1987-94, chief dep. pub. defender, 1994—. Democrat. Presbyterian. Office: Bucks County Pub Defender 55 E Court St 6th Fl Doylestown PA 18901 Home: 319 Hillside Ave Jenkintown PA 19046-2008 E-mail: petehallpd@hotmail.com.

HALL, PETER DOBKIN, historian, educator; b. N.Y.C., Feb. 22, 1946; BA, Reed Coll., 1968; MA, SUNY, Stony Brook, 1970, PhD, 1973. Postdoctoral fellow Instn. for Social and Policy Studies, Yale U., New Haven, 1973-77, rsch. assoc. program on non-profit orgns., 1977-83, rsch. scientist, 1973-97, dir., sr. rsch. scholar, 1996-99; Hauser lectr. nonprofit orgns. Harvard U. John F. Kennedy Sch. Govt., Cambridge, Mass., 2000—. Asst. prof. history Wesleyan U., Middletown, Conn., 1974—82; scholar-in-residence Rockefeller Archive Ctr., Rockefeller U., Tarrytown, NY, 1989—90; cons. Lilly Endowment, Inc., 1989—98. Author: The Organization of American Culture, 1900-1900: Institutions, Elites, and the Origins of American Nationality, 1982, Inventing the Nonprofit Sector and Other Essays on Philanthropy Voluntarism, and Nonprofit Organizations, 1992; co-author: The Lehigh Valley—An Illustrated History, 1982, Lives in Trust: The Fortunes of Dynastic Families in Late Twentieth Century America, 1992; co-editor: Sacred Companies: Organizational Aspects of Religion and Religious Aspects of Organizations, 1998; mem. editl. bd. History of Higher Edn. Ann., 1983—, History Edn. Quar., 1983-86; contbg. editor Philanthropy Monthly, 1989—; book rev. editor Nonprofit and Voluntary Sector Quar., 1992-98; contbr. articles on history of philanthropy, voluntarism, edn., social enterprise, nonprofits mgmt. and governnance to profl. jours. Recipient Grenzebach award for best pub. work in philanthropy and edn. Coun. for Advancement and Support Edn., 1993; Woodrow Wilson fellow, 1968, fellow Ctr. for Advanced Rsch. in Humanities, Wesleyan U., 1975, rsch. fellow Am. Coun. Learned Socs., 1987 Mem.: Conn. Acad. Arts and Scis., Internat. Soc. for Third Sector Rsch., Orgn. Am. Historians, Soc. for Sci. Study Religion, Social Sci. History Assn., Am. Hist. Assn., Assn. for Rsch. on Nonprofit Orgns. and Vol. Action (bd. dirs., v.p. membership and info. 1995—97). Office: Harvard U Kennedy Sch Govt Hauser Ctr Nonprofit Orgns 79 John F Kennedy St Cambridge MA 02138-5802

HALL, PETER FRANCIS, physiologist; b. Sydney, Australia, Dec. 12, 1924; s. William and Ruby Alice (Price) H.; m. Helen Ruth Godfrey, Nov. 10, 1968; children: Philip Charles, Warwick David. M.B.BS, U. Sydney, 1947, MD, 1956; PhD, U. Utah, 1962. Sr. med. officer Royal Prince Alfred Hosp., Sydney, 1947-50; registrar Guys Hosp., 1954-59; hon. med. officer Sydney Hosp., 1954-59; NIH fellow U. Utah, 1959-62; asst. prof. dept. physiology U. Pitts., 1962-64; prof. biochemistry Melbourne U., 1964-71; prof., chmn. dept. physiology U. Calif.-Irvine, 1971-78; prin. scientist Worcester Found. Exptl. Biology, Shrewsbury, Mass., 1978-86; chmn. endocrinology U. New South Wales and Prince Henry/Prince of Wales Hosps., Sydney, 1986—. Author: Gynaecomastia, 1959, Function of the Endocrine Glands, 1959; Contbr. articles to med. jours. Recipient Merck prize for chemistry, 1959 Fellow Royal Australian Coll. Physicians, Royal Coll. Physicians (London); mem. Am. Physiol. Soc., Am. Soc. Cell Biology, Am. Soc. Biol. Chemistry, Endocrine Soc. Mem. Ch. Of Eng. Home: 81 Ocean St Woollahra NSW 2025 Australia Office: Prince of Wales Hosp Dept Endocrinology High Street Randwick NSW 2031 Australia

HALL, SIR PETER GEOFFREY, urban and regional planning educator; b. London, Mar. 19, 1932; came to U.S., 1980; s. Arthur Vickers and Bertha (Keefe) H.; m. Carla Maria Wartenberg, Sept. 7, 1962 (div. 1967); m. Magda Mroz, Feb. 13, 1967. BA in Geography, Cambridge (Eng.) U., 1953, PhD, 1959; DDS (hon.), Birmingham (Eng.) U., 1991, 1991; PhD (hon.), Lund (Sweden) U., 1992; DLitt (hon.), Sheffield U., 1995, Newcastle U., 1995; DEng (hon.), Tech. U. Nova Scotia, Can., 1996; ArtsD (hon.), Oxford Brookes U., 1997; LLD (hon.), Reading U., 1999; DSc (hon.), U. West Eng., 2000; D Laws, U. Manchester, 2001; DLitt (hon.), Hemot Watt U., 2002, Guildhall U., London, 2002. Lectr. Birkbeck Coll., U. London, 1957-65; reader London Sch. Econs., 1966-67; prof. U. Reading, Eng., 1968-89, chmn., 1971-77, dean faculty urban and regional studies, 1975-78, bd. mgmt., 1983-86, prof. emeritus, 1989—; prof. dept. city and regional planning U. Calif., Berkeley, 1980-92, assoc. dir. Inst. Urban and Regional Devel., 1980-88, dir., 1989-92, prof. emeritus, 1993—. Prof. planning The Bartlett, Univ. Coll. London, 1992—, dir. sch. pub. policy, 1996—97; dir. Inst. of Cmty. Studies, 2001—; spl. advisor Dept. of Environ., London, 1991—94; mem. Urban Task Force, 1998—99. Author: The World Cities, 1966, 3d edit., 1984, Europe 2000, 1977 (Bentinck prize 1979), Great Planning Disasters, 1980, The Inner City in Context, 1981, Silicon Landscapes, 1985, Can Rail Save the City?, 1985, High-Tech America, 1986, Western Sunrise, 1987, Cities of Tomorrow, 1988, London 2001, 1989, Cities and Civilization, 1998; co-author: The Rise of the Gunbelt, 1991, Technopoles of the World, 1994, Sociable Cities, 1998, Cities in Civilization, 1998, Urban Future 21, 2000, Working Capital, 2002. Advisor Social Dem. party, 1983-85; active S.E. Econ. Planning Coun., 1966-79, Social Sci. Rsch. Coun., 1974-79. Fellow Brit. Acad., Royal Geog. Soc. (Gill Meml. prize 1968, Founder's medal 1991), St. Catharine's Coll. (hon.); mem. Royal Town Planning Inst. (hon.), Am. Planning Assn., Athenaeum Club, Brit. Acad. Avocations: reading, travel. Home: 12 Queen's Rd London W5 2SA England Office: Inst Cmty Studies 18 Victoria Park Sq London E2 9PF England E-mail: phall@icstudies.ac.uk.

HALL, PHOEBE JEAN, theater educator; b. Asheboro, N.C., Feb. 5, 1951; 1 child, Alicia Morris. MFA, U. of Louisville, 1989—92. Lectr. Meth. Coll., Fayetteville, NC, 1992—99; asst. prof. of speech and theatre Fayetteville State U., 1999—. Actor(performed in over 100 productions.): (actor, singer, dancer) Various Musicals, Comedies, And Straight Drama; dir.: (directed over 25 productions) Various Musicals, Comedies, And Straight Drama.; author: (plays) (educational touring production) Dueling Shakespeare. Entertainment chairperson for fund raisers Arts Coun., Fayetteville, 1995—2001; campaign mgr. US Senate Candidate, Sylva, 1985—89. Mem.: Actor's Equity Assn. (assoc.), Assn. of Am. Women in Academics (assoc.), Southeastern Theatre Conf. (assoc.), NC Theatre Conf. (assoc.), Black Theatre Network (hon.), Alpha Psi Omega (life; chpt. advisor 1999—2002). Office: Fayetteville State University Theatre 1200 Murchison Rd Fayetteville NC 28301 Home Fax: 910-672-1822; Office Fax: 910-672-1822. Personal E-mail: phall@uncfsu.edu. E-mail: phall@uncfsu.edu.

HALL, RALPH CARR, retired lawyer, real estate consultant; b. Chgo., Mar. 28, 1928; s. Rupert Irving and Pauline Martha (Prime) H.; m. Barbara Fordyce, Jan. 21, 1950; children: Brett C., Brian C., Judson P., Trudy A. JD, Tulsa U., 1952. Bar: Okla. 1952, Tex. 1974. V.P. Hall Investment Co., Tulsa, 1948-58; pres. Realty Constrn. Co., Tulsa, 1958-61; real estate investment rep. Am. Oil Co., Birmingham, Ala., 1961-63; div. real estate mgr. Kroger Co., Nashville and Charlotte, N.C., 1963-66; v.p., real estate counsel H.E.B. Properties, Corpus Christi, Tex., 1966-85; pvt. practice, Corpus Christi, 1985-97. Real estate cons., 1985-2000; mediator Nueces County Dispute Resolution Ctr., 1994-97. Pres., bd. dirs. Goodwill Ind. South Tex., Corpus Christi, 1969-88; planning commr. City of Corpus Christi, 1990-95. Mem. SCORE, Tex. Bar Assn., Nueces County Bar Assn., Corpus Christi Pistol and Rifle Club (pres. bd. dirs. 1980). Republican. Episcopalian.

HALL, RALPH MOODY, congressman; b. Fate, Texas, May 3, 1923; s. Hugh O. and Maude Hall; m. Mary Ellen Murphy, Nov. 14, 1944; children: Hampton, Brett, Blakeley. Student, U. Tex., Tex. Christian U., So. Meth. U., LLB, 1951. Bar: Tex. County judge Rockwall County, Tex., 1950-62; mem. Tex. Senate, 1962-72; pres., chief exec. officer Tex. Aluminum Corp., 1967—68; past gen. counsel Tex. Extrusion Co., Inc.; past organizer, chmn. bd. Lakeside Nat. Bank of Rockwall; chmn. bd. Bank of Crowley; past chmn. bd. dirs. Lakeside News, Inc.; chmn. bd. Linrock Inc.; pres. Crowley Holding Co., mem. U.S. Congress from 4th Tex. dist., Washington, 1981—; pres. pro tempore Texas Senate, 1968—69. Mem. energy and commerce com., mem. sci. com. Served with USNR, 1942-45. Mem. Am. Legion, VFW. Lodges: Rotary (past pres.). Democrat. Methodist. Office: US Ho of Reps 2405 Rayburn Ho Office Bldg Washington DC 20515-4304 E-mail: rmhall@mail.house.gov.*

HALL, RAYMOND, sociology educator; b. Marshall, Tex., Feb. 2, 1938; BA, Wiley Coll., 1962; MA, Stephen F. Austin State U., 1968; cert. in Ea. African Studies, Syracuse U., 1971, PhD, 1972; MA (hon.), Dartmouth Coll., 1993. Asst. prof. history and sociology Bishop Coll., Dallas, 1968-69, asst. prof. polit. sci. dept., 1971-72; asst. prof. sociology Dartmouth U., 1972-78, assoc. prof. sociology, 1978-86, prof. sociology, 1986, dir. dept. sociology, 1990, Orvil E. Dryfoos prof. of pub. affairs, 1994. Chmn. polit. sci. dept. Bishop Coll., Dallas, 1971-72; dir. Dartmouth MIT Urban Studies Program, 1975-77; chmn. Dartmouth-Talladega Title III Exch. com., 1973-78; dir. Dartmouth-Boston Urban Studies Program, 1978-80; chmn. urban studies program Dartmouth, 1981-84, acting chmn. dept. sociology, 1984, chmn. dept. sociology, 1985-91, 94-97; faculty adv. bd. The Beacon of Dartmouth, 1990—; cons. P.E.A.C.E., Inc., Syracuse 1969, Dallas Ind. Sch. Dist., 1968, 80, U.S. Dept. of Edn., 1992, field reader, sch. partnership program, 1988, field reader titles III & IX U.S. Dept. Edn., 1982—; field reader and tech. advisor title I and title III programs Dept. of Health, Edn. and Welfare, Dept. Human Svcs., 1975-81; cons. to curriculum com. Dallas Ind. Schs. Dist., 1969; spl. cons. NIH, Harvard Sch. of Pub. Health, 1993. Editl. bd. Gnosis, 1987—; contbr. numerous articles to profl. jours. Bd. trustees Wiley Coll., 1989-91, chair acad. programs com.; bd. dirs. The Forum for U.S.-Soviet Dialogue, 1983-86, A Better Chance, Hanover, N.H., 1973-75, Martin Luther King Recreation Ctr., Dallas, 1968-69, Dallas Opportunities Indsl. Coops., 1968-69. Served U.S. Army, 1962-64. Vis. scholar Social Sci. Rsch. Coun., 1975; Salzburg Seminar Presdl. fellow, 1994, 95; Jr. faculty fellowship Dartmouth Coll., 1977, IBM Faculty fellowship, 1971-73, Richard King Mellon fellowhip, The Maxwell Sch., Syracuse U., 1969-70; grantee Spencer Found., Hewlett Found., 1989, Dickey Endowment, 1988-89, Rockefeller Interdisciplinary, 1987-88, Sr. Faculty, Dartmouth Coll., 1981-82, Ford Found. Faculty, 1969-70. Mem. ACLU, Am. Sociol. Assn., Ea. Sociol. Assn., African Heritage Studies Assn., Soc. for the Study of Social Problems, Phi Beta Sigma. Home: 8 Pinewood Vlg West Lebanon NH 03784-3123 Office: Dept of Sociology Dartmouth Coll 106 Silsby Hall Hanover NH 03755

HALL, RICHARD CLAYTON, retired psychologist; b. Pitts., Apr. 29, 1931; s. Clayton LeClaire and Genevieve (Gorman) H.; m. Doris Margaret Bjorkland, Aug. 26, 1963; children: Karen, Janice, Dorothy. BS in Psychology with honors, Trinity Coll., 1952; MS, U. Pitts., 1959, PhD, 1963. Rsch. psychologist Polk (Pa.) Ctr., 1963-68, dir. behavior modification programs, 1968-75, chmn. subcom. human rights for behavior mgmt. procedures, 1987-89, staff psychologist, 1989-91; ind. researcher Key West, Fla., 1975-84, Polk, Pa., 1985-95; retired, 1995. Contbr. articles to profl. jours. With U.S. Army, 1953-55. NSF Coop. Grad. fellow, 1959. Mem. Sigma Xi, Pi Gamma Mu. Democrat. Presbyterian. Avocations: soloist at ch., civic operetta groups. Home: Polk, Pa. *Live so as to make a positive difference.* Died Oct. 18, 2002.

HALL, RICHARD CLYDE, JR., retired religious educational administrator; b. Florence, Ala., Apr. 13, 1931; s. Richard Clyde Sr. and Annie Hazel (Darrah) H.; m. Mildred Marie Denham, May 19, 1957; children: Richard Denham, Darralyn Marie, Kevin Clyde, Edward Earnest. AA, U. Fla., 1950, BA, 1953; MRE, Southwestern Bapt. Theol. Sem., 1958, DRE, 1966, EdD, 1975, MA, 1984. Ordained to gospel ministry So. Bapt. Conv., 1955. Youth dir. 1st Bapt. Ch., Miami, Fla., 1953; ednl. sec., youth dir. Ave. J Bapt. Ch., Ft. Worth, 1953-54; dir. Bapt. Student Union Fla. Bapt. Conv., Jacksonville, 1954-57; min. edn. Eastover Bapt. Ch., Ft. Worth, 1957-61; minister edn. 1st Bapt. Ch., Elizabethton, Tenn., 1961-63, Gambrell Street Bapt. Ch., Ft. Worth, 1963-65; assoc. ch. tng. dept. Bapt. Gen. Conv. Tex., Dallas, 1965-72, sec. ch. tng. dept., 1972-73; mgmt. cons. Pro, Inc., San Diego, 1973-74; cons. adult work ch. tng. dept. Bapt. Sunday Sch. Bd., Nashville, 1974-75, cons. gen. adminstrn. ch. tng. dept., 1975-76, mgr. youth sect. discipleship tng. dept., 1976-2000—. Teaching fellow religious psychology and drama Southwestern Bapt. Theol. Sem., Ft. Worth, 1960-61; del. Bapt. World Alliance, Tokyo, 1970; instr. youth edn. Sem. Extension, 1981—; discipleship workshop leader, family group leader Bapt. Youth World Conf., Buenas Aires, 1984; conf. leader, coord. numerous youth confs. Queensland, Australia, New South Wales, Australia, Auckland, New Zealand, Gaza City, Gaza, 1997-98, Victoria, Australia, Windhoek, Namibia, Gaza City, Gaza; conf. leader Caribbean Bapt. Fellowship, Montego Bay, Jamaica, 1986; sem. leader Bapt. Youth World Conf., Glasgow, Scotland, 1988, chaplain, Harare, Zimbabwe, 1993; del. Lausanne II-World Congress on Evangelism, Manila, Philippines, 1989; teaching fellow religious psychology and drama Southwestern Bapt. Theol. Sem., Ft. Worth, 1960-61; guest lectr. Southwestern Bapt. Theol. Sem., New Orleans Bapt. Theol. Sem., So. Bapt. Theol. Sem., Midwestern Bapt. Theol. Sem., Southeastern Bapt. Theol. Sem. and Golden Gate Bapt. Theol. Sem., 1985—; adj. prof. New Orleans Bapt. Theol. Sem., Golden Gate Bapt. Theol. Sem. and Midwestern Bapt. Theol. Sem., 1985—; instr. Okla. Bapt. U., 1991—. Author: Source, 1967-70, Church Training, 1970—; (cassette and workbook) The Work of the Associational Age Group Leader, 1980; (filmstrip) DiscipleLife: Training Youth in Discipleship, 1981, DiscipleLife, 1984; compiler: Youth Leadership Training Pak, 1982, DiscipleHelps: A Daily Quiet Time Guide and Journal, 1985; (with Joe Ford) DiscipleYouth I Kit, 1982, DiscipleYouth I Notebook, 1982, DiscipleYouth II Kit, 1985, DiscipleYouth II Notebook, 1985, DiscipleYouth Library, 1992, (with Dean Finley) The Notebook: A Disciple Youth Experience, 1996; (with Wesley Black) DiscipleNow Manual; (with Valerie Hardy) Mission Trip Administrative Manual. Trauma Center Plus, Handbook for Youth Discipleship, Basic Church Stuff: A Guide for Assimulating New Youth Church Members, Compiler. Recipient Career of Excellence award LifeWay Christian Resources, 1998. Mem. ASTD, Internat. Religious Edn. Assn., So. Bapt. Religious Edn. Assn. (sec.-treas. 1982-83), Ea. Bapt. Religious Edn. Assn. (sec.-treas. 1975-79, pres. 1980), Southwestern Bapt. Religious Edn. Assn., Adult Edn. Assn. Office: LifeWar Christian Resources 2720 Windemere Dr Nashville TN 37214-1733

HALL, RICHARD MURRAY, JR., finance executive, consultant; b. St. Joseph, Mo., Jan. 1, 1947; s. Richard Murray and Alice Elaine (Huff) H.; m. Joyce Ann Stearns, Mar. 28, 1971 (div. Nov. 1983). BBA in Econs., Wichita State U., 1969, MS in Fin., 1972; Grad. Degree in Banking, So. Meth. U., 1975. Asst. v.p. Fourth Nat. Bank & Trust, Wichita, Kans., 1969-75; v.p. Citizens Frost Bank, San Antonio, 1975-77, United Bank Denver, 1977-84; pres. Am. Nat. Bank/United Bank-City Ctr., Aurora, Colo., 1984-86; sr. v.p. Corp. Fin. Asocs., Denver, 1987-89; dir. Colo. Nat. Leasing, Inc., Denver, 1989-95, pres., 1989-95, chmn. bd. dirs., 1993-95; v.p. and gen. mgr. comml. banking divsn. Colo. Nat. Bank, Denver, 1992-94; pres., chmn. bd. dirs. Colo. Bus. Leasing, Inc., Denver, 1995—2001; pres. Alliance Capital Resources, Inc., 2000—03; regional pres. Cache Bank & Trust, Denver, 2003—. Dir. Am. Heart Assn. Colo., 1980—, pres., 1987-88; emeritus, 1998—; mem. Leadership Denver Assn., 1981, dir., 1990-95, pres. 1994-95; chmn. ArtReach, Inc., Denver, 1988, 89; bd. dirs. Colo. Spl. Olympics, 1994—, vice chmn., 1997, 99, chmn., 2000, dir. emeritus, 2001; bd. dirs. Health Agys. of Colo., 1997—, chmn., 1998-2000. Mem. Denver Athletic Club, Meridian Golf Club. Republican. Avocations: golf, skiing, writing. Office: Cache Bank & Trust 410 Seventeenth St Ste 100 Denver CO 80202

HALL, ROBERT ALAN, construction company executive; b. Montgomery, Ala., Oct. 30, 1958; s. Mack Luverne and Miriam (Johnston) H. BS in Commerce and Bus. Adminstrn., U. Ala., 1981. CPA, Ala., cert. internal auditor. Sr. acct. Jackson and Thornton, CPAs, Montgomery, 1981—83; sr. auditor Vulcan Materials Co., Birmingham, Ala., 1983—86, supr. internal audit, 1986—87; mgr., fin. and adminstrn. Saudi Arabian Vulcan Ltd., Jubail, Saudi Arabia, 1987—90; spl. assignments analyst Vulcan Materials Co., 1990—91; contr., treas., asst. sec. Bill Harbert Internat. Constrn. Inc., Birmingham, Ala., 1991—95, v.p., CFO, 1995—2000; sr. v.p., CFO, sec. B.L. Harbert Internat., LLC, 2000—. Presdl. appointee White House Conf. on Small Bus., 1995; mem. Pres.'s Bus. Adv. Coun., Washington, 1995-2001; mem. profl. adv. bd. Sch. Accountancy/U. Ala., 1991—. Charter mem. Rep. Presdl. Task Force, Washington, 1984-86; presdl. appointee White House Conf. Small Bus., 1995. Recipient Presdl. Achievement award Pres. Ronald Reagan, 1983, Cert. of Appreciation, Gov. of Ala., 1988; named hon. citizen City of L.A., 1984, hon. asst. atty. gen. State of Ala., 1984, hon. gov. of Tex., 1995, hon. lt. gov. of Ala., 1998. hon. col. State of Ala., 2001; named one of Outstanding Young Men of Am., 1986. Mem. AICPA, Ala. Soc. CPAs, Am. Businessmen's Assn. Saudi Arabia (bd. dirs. 1988-90), U. Ala. Sr. Execs. Club., Coll. Commerce, Hon. Order Ky. Cols. Baptist. Home: 416 Old Brook Cir Birmingham AL 35242-2658 Address: PO Box 531390 Birmingham AL 35253-1390

HALL, ROBERT EMMETT, JR., investment banker, realtor; b. Sioux City, Iowa, Apr. 28, 1936; s. Robert Emmett and Alvina (Faden) H.; m. De Phan. BA, U. S.D., 1958, MA, 1959; MBA, U. Santa Clara, 1976; grad., Am. Inst. Banking, Realtors Inst. Grad. asst. U. S.D., Vermillion, 1958-59; mgr. ins. dept., asst. mgr. installment loan dept. Northwestern Nat. Bank Sioux Falls, S.D., 1959-61, asst. cashier, 1961-65; asst. mgr. Crocker Nat. Bank, San Francisco, 1965-67, loan officer, 1967-69, asst. v.p., asst. mgr. San Mateo (Calif.) br., 1969-72; v.p., western regional mgr. Internat. Investments & Realty, Inc., Washington, 1972—; owner Hall Enterprises Co., San Jose, Calif., 1976—; pres. Alamaden Oaks Realtors, Inc., 1976—. Instr. West Valley Coll., Saratoga, Calif., 1972-82, Grad. Sch. Bus., U. Santa Clara (Calif.), 1981-82, Evergreen Valley Coll., San Jose, Calif. Treas. Minnehaha Leukemia Soc., 1963, Lake County Heart Fund Assn., 1962, Minnehaha Young Rep. Club, 1963. Mem. Am. Inst. Banking, Calif. Assn. Realtors (vice chmn.), Alamaden Country Club, Elks, Rotary (past pres.), KC, Beta Theta Pi. Home: 6951 Castlerock Dr San Jose CA 95120-4705 Office: Hall Enterprises 100A Crown Blvd San Jose CA 95120-2903 E-mail: rehall5257@aol.com.

HALL, ROBERT ERNEST, economics educator; b. Palo Alto, Calif., Aug. 13, 1943; s. Victor Ernest and Frances Marie (Gould) H.; m. Susan E. Woodward; children: Christopher, Anne, Jonathan, Andrew. BA, U. Calif.-Berkeley, 1964; PhD, MIT, 1967. Asst. prof., acting assoc. prof. U. Calif., Berkeley, 1967-70; from assoc. prof. to prof. MIT, Cambridge, 1970-78; prof., sr. fellow Stanford U. (Calif.), 1978—, Robert and Carole McNeil joint prof. and sr. fellow, 1998. Dir. econ. fluctuation program Nat. Bur. Econ. Research, Cambridge, 1978— ; adv. com. Congl. Budget Office, Washington, 1993—. Author: Macroeconomics, 1985, 5th rev. edit., 1997, Booms and Recessions in a Noisy Economy, 1990, The Rational Consumer: Theory and Evidence, 1990, Flat Tax, 1995, Economics, 1997, 2d rev. edit., 2000, Digital Dealing, 2001; editor: Inflation, 1983. Woodrow Wilson fellow, 1964; Ford Found. faculty rsch. fellow, 1969 Fellow Econometric Soc., Am. Acad. Arts and Scis.; mem. Am. Econs. Assn., Am. Statis Assn. Democrat. Office: Stanford U Hoover Instn Stanford CA 94305 E-mail: hall@hoover.stanford.edu.

HALL, ROBERT J. newspaper executive; b. Phila. BS in Acctg., Drexel U. CPA 1968. With Inquirer & Daily News, Phila., 1973—85; exec. v.p. & gen. mgr. Detroit Free Press, 1985, pub., chmn., Phila. Inquirer and Daily News, 1990—. Trustee Drexel U.; vice chmn. Greater Phila. First Corp.; chmn. Phila. Comm. for the 1994 World Cup Bid, Fairmount Pk. Historic Houses Project; bd. dirs. Police Athletic League, Greater Phila. C. of C., Phila. Conv. and Visitors Bur., Phila. Sports Congress, Met. Sunday Newspapers and Newspapers First Corp. Office: The Phila Inquirer PO Box 8263 400 N Broad St Philadelphia PA 19101*

HALL, ROBERT JOSEPH, physician, medical educator; b. Buffalo, June 4, 1926; s. Joseph M. and Florence C. (Kirst) H.; m. Dorothy Nowak, Aug. 28, 1948; children: Thomas R., Kathleen A. Hall Noble, Mary J. Hall Stuart, Michael F., Steven E. Student, Canisius Coll., Buffalo, 1943-45; MD, U. Buffalo, 1948. Diplomate Am. Bd. Internal Medicine, Sub Bd. Cardiovascular Disease (mem. cardiovascular disease sect. 1969-75). Intern Mercy Hosp., Buffalo, 1948-49; commd. 1st lt. M.C. U.S. Army, 1948, advanced through grades to col., 1966; resident in internal medicine Walter Reed Gen. Hosp., Washington, 1949-52, resident in cardiovascular diseases, 1956-57; asst. cardiovascular research Walter Reed Army Inst. Research, 1957-58; service in Korea and Japan, 1952-55; chief cardiology service Brooke Gen. Hosp., Ft. Sam Houston, Tex., 1961-66, Walter Reed Gen. Hosp., 1966-69; ret., 1969; clin. assoc. prof. medicine Georgetown U. Med. Sch., 1967-69; clin. prof. medicine Baylor U. Coll. Medicine, Houston, 1969—, U. Tex. Med. Sch., Houston, 1977—; med. dir. Tex. Heart Inst., Houston, 1969-93, chmn. exec. com. profl. staff, 1969-93; dir. div. cardiology St. Luke's Episcopal Hosp., Houston, 1969-95, assoc. chief med. service, 1970-83; dir. edn., cardiology Tex. Heart Inst. Tex. Heart Inst. and St. Luke's Episcopal Hosp., 1992—2002, dir. emeritus, 2002. Cons. Tex. Children's, VA, Brooke Gen. hosps., M.D. Anderson Hosp. and Tumor Inst.; mem. cardiovascular study sect. NIH, 1958-61; mem. phys. evaluation team Gemini project NASA, 1958-61; mem. nat. adv. heart counseil Dept. Def., 1966-69; adv. council Mended Hearts, 1970-78 Contbr. numerous articles med. jours. Mem. President's Adv. Panel Heart Disease. Decorated Legion of Merit; recipient Disting. Alumnus award Canisius Coll., 1995. Fellow A.C.P., Am. Coll. Cardiology (gov. 1968-71-74, chmn. bd. govs. and trustee 1973-74); mem. Am. Heart Assn. (fellow council clin. cardiology; pres. Houston chpt. 1974-75, advisor corp. cabinet 1980-86), Assn. Mil. Surgeons U.S., Assn. Advancement Med. Instrumentation, Pan Am. Med. Assn. (chmn. sect. cardiovascular diseases 1978-81), Assn. Univ. Cardiologists, Tex. Med. Assn., Tex. Cardiology Club, Harris County Med. Soc., Houston Cardiology Soc. (chmn. 1976-77), Houston Soc. Internal Medicine, Alpha Omega Alpha, 1948—. Home: 5504 Sturbridge Dr Houston TX 77056-1623 Office: 6624 Fannin St Ste 2480 Houston TX 77030-2309 E-mail: rjhall@wt.net.

HALL, ROBERT PAUL, social services administrator; b. Salisbury, Md., July 5, 1952; s. R. Paul and Elizabeth (Satterfield) H.; m. Conee Nelson, May 28, 1994. BA, U. Md., 1974; MDiv, Wesley Theol. Sem., 1977. Dir. planning Community Action of Greater Wilmington, Wilmington, Del., 1980-82; dir. devel. ARC, Wilmington, 1983-84; exec. dir. Delawareans United to Prevent Child Abuse, Wilmington, Del., 1984-96, Del. Assn. Home and Cmty. Care, Montchanin, 1997-98, Del. Ecumenical Coun. Children & Families, Wilmington, 1997—. Contbr. articles to profl. jours, Winner Commr's. award, 1991. Mem. NASW, ACA, Am. Psychotherapy Assn. (diplomate), Am. Mental Health Counselors Assn. (task force on childhood and adolescence), Am. Assn. Christian Counselors, Am. Pub. Health Assn. (governing coun., pres. Del. affiliate). Home: PO Box 260 Montchanin DE 19710-0260 E-mail: deccf@aol.com.

HALL, ROBERT WILLIAM, philosophy and religion educator; b. Arlington, Mass., Apr. 6, 1928; s. Samuel Harry and Agness (Babikian) H.; m. Mary Alice Starritt, Oct. 25, 1958; children— Christopher Allen, Jonathan Brooks, Pamela Leigh, Timothy Randall, Jennifer Lane, Nicholas Ramsay. AB, Harvard, 1949, MA, 1951, PhD, 1953. Vis. asst. prof. philosophy Vanderbilt U., 1955-57; asst. prof. philosophy and religion U. Vt., Burlington, 1957-63, assoc. prof., 1963-67, prof., 1967—, Marsh prof. intellectual and moral philosophy, 1985—2002, chmn. dept., 1963-72, prof. emeritus, 2002—. Author: Plato and the Individual, 1963, Studies in Religious Philosophy, 1969, Plato, 1981; editor: APEIRON, 1966-87. Served with CIC AUS, 1953-55. Shedd fellow in religion in higher edn., 1968-69 Mem. Am. Philos. Assn., Soc. Ancient Greek Philosophy (sec.-treas. 1963-72), Am. Soc. Aesthetics, Phi Beta Kappa. Home: 165 N Prospect St Burlington VT 05401-1607 Office: 70 S Williams St Burlington VT 05401-3404

HALL, ROGER LEE, musicologist, educator, composer; b. Glen Ridge, N.J., Nov. 13, 1942; Cert., Trinity Coll., London, 1967; BA, Rutgers U., 1970; MA, SUNY, 1972. Music cons. Nat. Geographic Soc., Washington, 1972; lectr. various colls., mus., 1974—; researcher, writer various jours., mags., 1975—; instr. Stonehill Coll., North Easton, Mass., 1979-82, Brookline (Mass.) Adult and Community Edn. Program, 1983-96; composer ASCAP, N.Y.C., 1985—; cable TV producer Pinetree Prodns., Stoughton, Mass., 1987—. Cons. Paul Revere House, Boston, 1981, The Shaker Seminar, Pittsfield, Mass., 1984-87. Editor: (music collection) The Happy Journey, 1982, Love is Little, 1992, Joy of Angels, 1995; composer: Piano Variations, 1984, Peace - A Patriotic Ode, 1989, A Little Theatre Music, 1990, Three Shaker Poems, 1996; feature writer: The World of Shaker, 1985—96; prodr., host Continental Cablevision, Stoughton, Mass., 1986; author: (pamphlet) Singing Stoughton, 1985, (booklets) Story of Simple Gifts, 1987, Music in Stoughton, 1989, The Stoughton Songster, 1991, A Guide to Film Music, 1997, 2d edit., 2002, A Guide to Shaker Music, 1997, 5th edit., 2002, New England Songster, 1997, A Guide to George Gershwin, 1998, Remembering Radio, 1998, A Guide to Christmas Music in America, 1999; radio tributes Sta. WBET-AM, 1985—93, Sta. WGBH-FM, 1981—98. Chmn. bd. Stoughton Arts Coun., 1980-84; mem. Town Hall Centennial Com., Stoughton, 1981. Served with U.S. Army, 1960-63. SUNY assistantship, 1971-72; Title IV fellow Case Western Res. U., 1972-74; Mass. Arts Lottery grantee, 1985-90. Mem.: Tune Lovers Soc. (pres. 2001—), Soc. For Am. Music, Old Stoughton Mus. Soc. (v.p. 1978—86), Shaker Study Group (pres. 1987—89). Lutheran. Avocations: collecting autographs, poetry, photography. Home and Office: 235 Prospect St Stoughton MA 02072-4163 E-mail: tunemaker3@aol.com.

HALL, SHANNON, marketing professional, public relations executive, writer, photographer; BA in Comm., Mills Coll. Pub. rels. mgr. Ingres; ptnr., mng. dir. Horn Group, Inc., 1994—. Contbr. SF Atty. Mag. ; freelance writer San Francisco mags., adv. assoc., photographer, San Francisco, 1999. Co-mgr. Calif. Minority Counsel program; mem. bd. dirs. Bay Area Video Coalition. Office: Horn Group Inc 612 Howard St San Francisco CA 94105 Office Fax: 415-905-4001. Business E-Mail: info@horngroup.com.

HALL, SHARON GAY, retired language educator, artist; b. Centralia, Ill., Oct. 2, 1942; d. Leon Lucene and Olyve Elizabeth Hall. BS, So. Ill. U., 1966, MS, 1984; postgrad., Ea. Ill. U., 1985—90. Cert. secondary tchr. Ill. English tchr. Webber Twp. H.S., Bluford, Ill., 1966—67, Mt. Vernon (Ill.) H.S., 1967—99, ret., 1999. Artist-in-residence Cedarhurst Art Guild, Cedarhurst Mus., 1974—. Treas. bd. dirs. Bus. and Profl. Women's Club, Mt. Vernon, 1966—76; mem. Jefferson County Hist. Soc., 2000—. Recipient Recognition award, Cedarhurst Mus., 2000. Mem.: NEA, AAUW, Ill. Edn. Assn., Mt. Vernon Edn. Assn. (sec., treas., bd. dirs. 1967—99), Phi Delta Kappa, Phi Theta Kappa, Alpha Delta Kappa. Republican. Avocations: raising exotic animals, handspinner, weaver, fiber artist, seamstress.

HALL, STEPHEN CHARLES, lawyer; b. Carmel, Calif., Sept. 14, 1948; s. Melvin Wiley and Dorothy Louise (Hoyt) H.; m. Kristi Lee Roberts, Feb. 23, 1983; children: Spencer Stephen Rodrigo, Rachel Genevieve Cristina, Trevor Charles. AB, Dickinson Coll., 1971; JD, Vt. Law Sch., 1977. Bar: Pa. 1978, Va. 1979, U.S. Dist. Ct. (ea. dist.) Va. 1982, U.S. Dist. Ct. (we. dist.) Va. 1990, U.S. Ct. Appeals (4th cir.) 1982. Title atty. Chgo. Title Inst. Co., Richmond, 1978-79; assoc. Edward E. Willey Jr., P.C., Richmond, 1979-82; ptnr. Willey & Hall, P.C., Richmond, 1983-88; assoc. Hazel & Thomas, P.C., Richmond, 1988-90, ptnr., 1990-94, Keith & Hall, Richmond, 1994—. Contbr. articles to profl. jours. Past chmn. bd. trustees St. Michael's Episcopal Sch. Mem. Richmond Bar Assn. (past chmn. publs. com.), Chesterfield County Bar Assn. (pres. 2003—), Bon Air Bus. and Profl. Assn. (past pres.), Salisbury Country Club. Episcopalian. Avocations: golf, photography. Office: Hairfield Morton Watson & Adams PLC 2800 Buford Rd Ste 201 Richmond VA 23235

HALL, SUSAN LAUREL, artist, educator, writer; b. Point Reyes Sta., Calif., Mar. 19, 1943; d. Earl Morris and Avis Mary (Brown) H. BFA, Calif. Coll. Arts & Crafts, Oakland, 1965; MA, U. Calif., Berkeley, 1967. Mem. faculty Sarah Lawrence Coll., Bronxville, NY, 1972—75, Sch. Visual Arts, NYC, 1981—92, Skowhegan Sch. of Painting and Sculpture, Maine, 1981, Univ. of Colo., Boulder Co., 1981, Art Inst. of Chgo., Chgo., 1981, Univ. of Tex., Austin, Tex., 1993, San Antonio, 1995, San Francisco Art Inst., San Francisco, 1996. One-woman shows include San Francisco Mus. Art, 1967, Quay Gallery, San Francisco, 1969, Phillis Kind Gallery, Chgo., 1971, 1998, 98 Greene St. Loft, N.Y.C., Whitney Mus., Henderson Mus. U. Colo., Boulder, 1973, Nancy Hoffman Gallery, N.Y.C., 1975, U. R.I. Gallery, Kingston, 1976, Harcus Krakow Rosen Sonnabend Gallery, Boston, 1976, Hal Bromm and Getler-Pall Galleries, N.Y.C., 1978, Helene Shlien Gallery, Boston, 1978, Hamilton Gallery, N.Y.C., 1978—79, 1981, 1983, Ovsey Gallery, L.A., 1981—82, 1984, 1987, 1989, 1991, Paule Anglim Gallery, San Francisco, 1975—83, Ted Greenwald Gallery, N.Y.C., 1986, Trabia Macafee Gallery, 1988—89, Wyckoff Gallery, Aspen, Colo., 1990—92, Milagros Contemporary Art, San Antonio, 1995, Brendan Walter Gallery, L.A., 1995, U. Tex., San Antonio, 1996, Jan Holloway Gallery, San Francisco, 1997, San Francisco Mus. Art Gallery, 1998, Gail Harvey Gallery, L.A., 1999, 2001, Frank Lloyd Wright Civic Ctr., San Rafael, 1999, Jernigan Wicker Gallery, San Francisco, 1999, exhibited in group shows at Whitney Mus. Am. Art, San Francisco Mus., Oakland Mus., Balt. Mus., Inst. Contemporary Art, Phila., Hudson River Mus., Bklyn. Mus., Nat. Mus. Women in the Arts, Mus. Fine Arts, Boston, Aldrich Mus. Contemporary Art, G.W. Einstein Gallery, Blum Helman Downtown, Leo Castelli Gallery Uptown, Graham Modern, N.Y.C., Kunstmus., Luzern, Switzerland, Landesmus., Bonn, Bolinas (Calif.) Mus., 2002, Represented in permanent collections pub. collections Whitney Mus., San Francisco Mus., Bklyn. Mus., Carnegie Inst., St. Louis Mus., Nat. Mus. Women in the Arts, others; author: Painting Point Reyes, 2002. Nat. Endowment Arts fellow, 1979-87, Adolph Gottleib Found. fellow, 1995; grantee: Pollack Krasner Found., N.Y. State Coun. on Arts; recipient Marin Arts Coun. Bd. Dirs. award, 1999.

HALL, TELKA MOWERY ELIUM, retired educational administrator; b. Salisbury, NC, July 22, 1936; d. James Lewis and Malissa (Fielder) Mowery; m. James Richard Elium III, June 20, 1954 (div. 1961); 1 child, W. Denise Elium Carr; m. Allen Sanders Hall, Apr. 15, 1967 (div. 1977). Student, Am. Inst. Banking, 1955-57, Mary-Hardin Baylor Coll., Waco, Tex., 1957; BA, Catawba Coll., Salisbury, 1967; MEd, Miss. U. for Women, Columbus, 1973; EdS, Appalachian State U., 1975; postgrad., U. N.C., Greensboro, 1977; EdD, U. N.C., Chapel Hill, 1990; postgrad., Ind. U., 1998. Cert. early childhood, intermediate lang. arts and social studies tchr., curriculum specialist, adminstr., supr., supt., NC; notary pub., NC; cert. in CPR and first aid and safety, ARC. Bookkeeper, teller Citizens & So. Bank, Spartanburg, SC, 1955-56; bookkeeper 1st Nat. Bank, Killeen, Tex., 1956-58; bookkeeper, savs. teller Exch. Bank & Trust Co., Dallas, 1958-61; acct. Catawba Coll., 1961-65; floater teller bookkeeping and proof depts. Security Bank & Trust Co., Salisbury, 1965-68, 71; tchr. Rowan County Sch. System, Salisbury, 1967-70, 71-72, 1973-82; asst. prin. North Rowan Elem. Sch., Spencer, NC, 1982-94, Rockwell Elem. and China Grove Elem. Sch., NC, 1994-96, ret., 1996; part-time asst. prin. of curriculum China Grove Elem., 1996-99, also part-time outside observer for Ctrl. Office, 1996, asst. prin. curriculum, 1996-99, ret., 1999. Receptionist H & R Block, Salisbury, 1979-83; Chpt. I reading tchr. Nazareth Children's Home, Rockwell, NC, 1979-81. Author: The Effect of Second Language Training in Kindergarten on the Development of Listening Skills. Mem. Salisbury Cmty. Chorus, 1951—52, Hist. Salisbury Found., Inc., Salisbury Concert Choir, 1981—83; foreperson Rowan County grand jury, 1991; cons. Dial HELP, Salisbury, 1981—83; charter mem. bd. dirs. Old North Salisbury Assn., 1980—2000; past mem. Children's Literacy Guild, YMCA, ARC; mem. YMCA; pianist Franklin Presbyn. Ch., 1952—55, choir dir., 1975—87, past pres. Women of Ch., adult class Sunday sch. tchr., 1979—80, nursery Sunday sch. tchr., 1996—99, deacon, 1980—83, elder, 1991—92, 1996—99, 2001—03, clk. of session, 1992, 1996—98, choir mem., 1947—, co-moderator women of ch., 1999—2003; mem. Magnify Christian Concert Choir, 1999—. Civitan Music scholar, 1954, Kiwanis Acad. scholar, 1966, Catawba Coll. Acad. scholar, 1965-67, Mary Morrow Ednl. scholar N.C. Assn. Educators, 1966. Mem. NEA, NCAE, AARP, AAUW (v.p. 1985-87, 91-93), AARP, ARC (vol.), NC Ret. Govtl. Employees' Assn., Rowan-Salisbury Ret. Pers., Salisbury Hist. Assn., Kappa Delta Pi, Theta Phi (pres. 1992-93). Avocations: photography, genealogy, calligraphy, singing, composing poetry, flowers. Home: 105 Sharon Ct Salisbury NC 28146-7241

HALL, TENNIEBEE M. editor; b. Bakersfield, Calif., May 21, 1940; d. William Elmer and Lillian May (Otis) Hall; m. Harold Robert Hall, Feb. 20, 1965. BA in Edn., Fresno State Coll., 1962; AA, Bakersfield Coll., 1960. Cert. tchr., Calif. Tchr. Edison (Calif.) Sch. Dist., 1962-65; substitute tchr. Marin and Oakland Counties (Calif.), Berkeley, 1965-66; engring. asst. Pacific Coil Co., Inc., Bakersfield, 1974-81; editor United Ostomy Assn., Inc., Irvine, Calif., 1986-91. Co-author: Treating IBD, 1989, Current Therapy in Gastroenterology, 1989; author, designer: Volunteer Leadership Training Manuals, 1982-84; editor: Calif. Parliamentarian, 1999-2003; contbr. articles to Ostomy Quar., 1973—. Mem. Pacific Beach Town Coun., San Diego, 1977—; campaign worker Maureen O'Connor (1st woman mayor of city), San Diego, 1986; mem. Nat. Digestive Diseases Adv. Bd., NIH, Washington, 1986-91; mem. planning

and devel. bd. Scripps Clinic and Rsch. Found. Inflammatory Bowel Disease Ctr., San Diego, 1993-2003; various vol. activities, 1966-74, 81-86. Recipient Outstanding Svc. award VA Vol. Svc., Bur. of Vets. Affairs, Washington, 1990. Mem. Nat. Assn. Parliamentarians, United Ostomy Assn. Inc. (regional program dir. 1980-84, pres. 1984-86, Sam Dubin award 1983, Industry Adv. award 1987), Crohn's and Colitis Found. Am. (nat. trustee 1986-95, nat. v.p. 1987-92). Avocations: travel, volunteerism. Home and Office: 8585 Via Mallorca Unit 7 La Jolla CA 92037-2585

HALL, TERRY L. aerospace executive; BA, Bemidji State U.; JD, U. Minn. Asst. city atty., chief prosecutor City of Rochester, 1978; with LeFevre, Lefler, et. al.; sr. corp. counsel Republic Airlines; pres., gen. mgr. Northwest Aircraft, Inc., 1986—90; v.p., treas. United Airlines, 1990-93; v.p., CFO Tyco Internat., 1993-95; v.p. fin., CFO Apogee Enterprises, Inc., 1995-97; sr. v.p. fin., CFO U.S. Airways, 1997-99; CFO Aerojet, Sacramento, 1999; treas. GenCorp Inc., 1999—2000, CFO, 1999—2001, sr. v.p., 1999—2002, COO, 2001—02, pres., CEO, 2002—. Office: GenCorp Inc PO Box 537012 Sacramento CA 95853-7012*

HALL, THOMAS EMERSON, economist, educator; b. Detroit, Jan. 31, 1954; s. Robert James and Jean M. (Ashley) H.; m. Christine Tippie, June 18, 1983; 1 child, Alexander E. BA, U. Colo., 1976; MA, U. Calif., Santa Barbara, 1978, PhD, 1982. Asst. prof. econs. Miami U., Oxford, Ohio, 1982-88, assoc. prof., 1989-93, prof. econs., 1993—. Vis. sr. economist Dept. State, Washington, 1988-89; cons. First Nat. Bank of Southwestern Ohio, 1991-95. Author: Business Cycles: The Nature and Causes of Economic Fluctuations, 1990, The Rotten Fruits of Economic Controls and the Rise from the Ashes, 1965-1989, 2003; co-author: The Great Depression: An International Disaster of Perverse Economic Policies, 1998. Named Outstanding Faculty Mem., Delta Gamma, Oxford, 1985, 86; recipient Richard T. Farmer Sch. Bus. Teaching Excellence award, 1992. Mem. Am. Econ. Assn., Midwest Econs. Assn., Delta Sigma Pi (acad. advisor 1984-89), Beta Gamma Sigma. Avocations: woodworking, writing. Home: 76 Oliver Rd Cincinnati OH 45215-2631 Office: Miami U Dept Econs Oxford OH 45056

HALL, THOMAS FORREST, federal agency administrator, naval officer; b. Barnsdall, Okla., Dec. 27, 1939; s. Oscar and Nelle Irene (Kellenberger) H.; m. Barbara Norman, June 22, 1963; 1 child, Thomas David. BS in Engring., U.S. Naval Acad., 1963; MBA, George Washington U., 1971; grad. with highest distinction, Naval War Coll., 1975; grad., Nat. War Coll., 1981. Commd. ensign USN, 1963, advanced through grades to rear adm. (two-star), 1991; naval aviator Patrol Squadron 8, 1965; co. officer, exec. asst. to comdt. of midshipmen U.S. Naval Acad., 1968; tng. officer, then officer in charge UNITAS XIV, Patrol Squadron 23, Brunswick, Maine, 1972; aviation tng. command placement officer, then aviation staffs placement officer, head air combat placement and asst. head of aviation Bur. Naval Pers., 1975; exec. officer Patrol Squadron 8, 1978, comdg. officer, 1979; staff, head Program Objective Memorandum Devel. Sect. Chief of Naval Ops., 1981; chief of staff to Comdr. Fleet Air, Keflavik, Iceland, 1982-85; comdr. Naval Air Sta. Bermuda, Bermuda ASW Sector, 1985-87; Chief of Naval Ops. Strategic Studies Group fellow, 1987; dep. dir. Naval Res., 1988-89; comdr. Iceland Def. Force, 1989-92; chief Naval Res., 1992-96, exec. dir., 1996—; asst. secy. defense reserve affairs U.S. Dept. Defense, Washington, 2001—. Decorated D.S.M., Defense Superior Svc. medal, Legion of Merit (2), Meritorious Svc. medal, Order of the Falcon Comdr's. Cross with Star Govt. Iceland. Methodist. Avocations: tennis, basketball, racquet ball, golf. Office: US Dept Defense Reserve Affairs 1500 Defense Pentagon Washington DC 20301-1500 Office Fax: 703-693-5371.

HALL, THOR, religion educator; b. Larvik, Norway, Mar. 15, 1927; came to U.S., 1957, naturalized, 1973; s. Jens Martin and Margit Elvira (Petersen) H.; m. Gerd Hellstrom, July 15, 1950 (dec.); 1 child, Jan Tore; m. Nancy Varnell, Mar. 12, 1999; 1 stepchild, Lindsay Whitaker. Diploma in theology, Scandinavian Methodist Sem., 1950; postgrad., Selly Oak Colls., Birmingham, Eng., 1950-51; M.R.E., Duke U., 1959, PhD, 1962. Ordained deacon Methodist Ch., 1952, elder, 1954. Minister Kongsvinger-Odal Meth. Ch., Norway, 1951-53; exec. sec. youth dept. Meth. Ch., Norway, 1953-57; minister Ansonville (N.C.) Meth. Ch., 1958-59; asst. minister 1st Presbyn. Ch., Durham, N.C., 1960-62; asst. prof. preaching and theology Duke U., 1962-68, assoc. prof., 1968-72; disting. prof. religious studies U. Tenn., Chattanooga, 1972-94, LeRoy A. Martin disting. prof. religious studies, 1987-94, prof. emeritus, 1994—. Vis. prof. Oslo U., 1977, Liberia, 1980, U. Copenhagen, 1984, 96; gen. bd. Evangelism, Meth. Ch., 1968-72; mem. Oxford Inst. Meth. Theol. Studies, 1982-92; cons. Ecumenical Prayer Seminars, 1967-80, Army, Navy, Air Force Chaplains Corps, 1967-68, 71-72; James Sprunt lectr. Union Theol. Sem., Richmond, Va., 1970; Voigt lectr. So. Ill. conf. United Meth. Ch., 1979; Goodson lectr. Va. conf., 1983, Stahley lectr. Ferrum Coll., Va., 1987; mem. Tenn. Com. for Humanities, 1978-82, chmn. subcom. on devel., exec. com., 1979-82. Author: A Theology of Christian Devotion, 1969, A Framework for Faith, 1970, The Future Shape of Preaching, 1971, Whatever Happened to the Gospel, 1973, (with others) Advent-Christmas (Proclamation B), 1975, Anders Nygren, 1978, Systematic Theology Today, Part I, 1978, The Evolution of Christology, 1982, Pentecost (Proclamation 4B), 1990; editor: Var Ungdom, 1953-57, The Unfinished Pyramid (Charles P. Bowles), 1967, A Directory of Systematic Theologians in North America, 1977; translator: A Political Dogmatic (Jens Glebe-Möller) 1987, Jesus and Theology (Glebe-Möller), 1989, Forgiveness (Carl-Reinhold Brakenhielm), 1993, The Story of Herman der Norweger (Herman Sachnowitz), 2002; contbr. articles to profl. jours. World Council Chs. scholar, 1950-51; Crusade scholar, 1957-59; Gurney Harris Kearns fellow, 1959-60; Angier Duke Meml. fellow, 1960-61; James B. Duke fellow, 1961-62; Am. Assn. Theol. Schs. faculty fellow, 1968-69; Fulbright-Hays travel grantee, 1984 Mem. AAUP, Soc. Sci. Study Religion, Am. Acad. Religion (v.p. Southeastern region 1984-85, pres. 1985-86), SE Commn. for the Study Religion (exec. dir. 1987-91), Soc. Philosophy of Religion. Home: 1102 Montvale Cir Signal Mountain TN 37377-2511 E-mail: thorhall@comcast.net. *The greatest factor contributing to personal growth and professional development is the full utilization of opportunities available at the present and the daily fulfillment of one's responsibilities, whatever they are.*

HALL, TIMOTHY COUZENS, biology educator, consultant; b. Darlington, Durham, Eng., Aug. 29, 1937; came to U.S., 1965; s. Gilbert Leslie and Dorothea Olive (Lindemann) H.; m. Sandra Severn, Aug. 20, 1960; children: Alexandra Vikki Anna, Liza Bryony, Peter Marcus Jeremy. BSc with honors, U. Nottingham, Eng., 1962, PhD in Plant Physiology, 1965. Louis W. and Maud Hill postdoctoral fellow dept. hort. sci. U. Minn., St. Paul, 1965-66; asst. prof. horticulture U. Wis., Madison, 1966-70, assoc. prof., 1970-75, prof., 1975-82, adj. prof. biophysics and genetics, 1982-84; dir. Agrigenetics Advanced Rsch. Div., Madison, 1980-84, Agrigenetics Rsch. Corp., Boulder, Colo., 1981-84; Disting. prof., head dept. biology Tex. A&M U., College Station, 1984-92, dir. Inst. Devel. and Molecular Biology, 1992-2000. Sr. biotech. cons. Rhône-Poulenc Agrochimie, Lyon, France, 1985-2000; chair, organizer Gordon Conf. on Plant Molecular Biology, 1987; cons. plant biotech. Novartis, 1997-98; mem. sci. adv. bd. Aventis Cropsci., 2000-01; mem. adv. com. Area of Excellence, Chinese U. Hong Kong, 2000—; co-chair, co-organizer Juan March Workshop on Chromatin and DNA Modification, 1998. Editor: (with J.W. Davies) Nucleic Acids in Plants, 2 vols., 1979, (with L. van Vloten-Doting and G.S.P. Groot) Molecular Form and Function of the Plant Genome, 1985; mem. editl. bd. Oxford Surveys Plant Molecular and Cell Biology, 1983-80, Transgenic Rsch., 1991-95, Plant Jour., 1991-99, Jour. Virology, 1996—; contbr. numerous articles to profl. jours., book chpts.; patentee in field. Pilot Royal Air Force, 1956-58. Grantee NIH, NSF, USDA, NATO, Dow Agro Scis., Rhône-Poulenc Agrochimie, Internat. Paper Co., Tex. Advanced Tech. Program, Rockefeller Found. Fellow Indian Virol. Soc.; mem. AAAS, RNA Soc., Am. Soc. for Biochemistry and Molecular Biology, Am. Soc. for Microbiology, Am. Soc. Plant Physiologists (organizer Juan March workshop on chromatin and DNA modification Madrid, 1998), Am. Soc. for Virology, Am. Phytopathol. Soc., Soc. Gen. Microbiology, Fedn. Am. Socs. Exptl. Biology, Biochem. Soc., Internat. Soc. for Molecular-Plant Microbe Interactions, Internat. Soc. Plant Molecular Biology, Soc. for In Vitro Biology, RNA Soc., Squash Club Tex. A&M U., Sigma Xi. Avocations: squash, racquetball, bridge, travel. Office: Tex A&M U Inst Devel Molecular Biol College Station TX 77843-3155 E-mail: tim@idmb.tamu.edu.

HALL, TONY P. ambassador, former congressman; b. Dayton, Ohio, Jan. 16, 1942; m. Janet Dick, 1973; 2 children. Student, Ohio State U.; AB, Denison U., 1964; LLD (hon.), Asbury Coll., Eastern Coll. Vol. Peace Corps, Thailand, 1966-67; mem. Ohio Ho. of Reps., 1969-72, Ohio Senate, 1973-78, U.S. Congress from 3d Ohio dist., Washington, 1979—2002; mem. rules com., ranking minority mem. subcom. tech. and the house; amb. U.N. Agencies for Food & Agr., 2002—. Founder, mem. steering com. Congl. Friends of Human Rights Monitors; mem. bd. mgrs. Air Force Mus. Found.; trustee Holiday Aid; mem. adv. com. Emergency Resource Bank; chmn. Dem. Caucus Task Force on Hunger. Recipient Disting. Svc. Against Hunger award Bread for the World, 1984, 87, Tree of Life award Jewish Nat. Fund, 1986, Golden Apple award Nat. Assn. Nutrition and Aging Svcs. Programs, 1986, Freedom award Asian Pacific Am. C. of C., 1986, Presdl. End Hunger award, 1988, Silver Anniversary award NCAA, 1989, Silver World Food Day medal Food and Agriculture Orgn. of UN, Ptnrs. award Oxfam Am., 1992; nominated for Nobel Peace prize, 1998, 99, 2001. Mem. Nat. Assn. Women, Infants & Children (Leadership award 1991). Democrat. Office: US Mission to UN Agencies for Food & Agr via V Veneto 119/A 00187 Rome Italy*

HALL, WANDA JEAN, mental health professional, consultant; b. Miami, Okla., July 3, 1943; d. Max Calvin Kinnaman and Dorothy D. (Peck) Fadler; m. James Marvin Hall, Apr. 10, 1964 (div. Feb. 1965); m. George Edward Hall, Mar. 21, 1973; children: Heather Renata, Samuel. AA, Stephens Coll., Columbia, Mo., 1963; BS, Kans. U., Pittsburg, 1965; MS, New Sch. for Social Rsch., N.Y.C., 1991. Asst. psychologist Parsons (Kans.) State Hosp., 1966-67; hosp. care investigator N.Y. Dept. Social Work, N.Y.C., 1968-70; social worker Drug Abuse Program, Amsterdam, The Netherlands, 1970-74; dir. Washington Park Co-op Presch., N.Y.C., 1974-75; project dir. Manhattan Devel. Ctr., N.Y.C., 1975-77; pvt. practice human devel. specialist human devel. specialist, N.Y.C., 1978-81; cmty. rels. coord. Orange County Dept. Mental Health, Goshen, N.Y., 1981-97, Flagler Coll., St. Augustine, Fla., 1998—. Parenting cons. Teens Exploring Parenting, Inc., Middletown, N.Y., 1990-94; instr. Orange County C.C., Middletown, 1990-97, Mt. St. Mary Coll., Newburgh, N.Y., 1993-96. Producer, host radio talk show Conversation on Epilepsy, Radio Sta. WGNY, 1981; dir, narrator mental health skits Forum Players, 1980; producer, host 6 TV series Love from the 26, 000 Club, 1983. Bd. dirs. Orange County Coalition for Choice, Warwick, N.Y., 1981-97, Orange County Task Force on Child Abuse/Neglect, 1981-89, Ct. Apptd. Spls. Accts., 1987-96, Bandwagon Cmty. Ctr., chair, 1990-95; mem. Planned Parenthood, Orange County, 1989-97, Safe Homes, Orange County, 1987-97, Middletown Coun. Cmty. Agys., 1980-96, Interagy. Coun. Child Sexual Abuse; co-founder Orange County Parenting Coalition., 1990-97. Recipient DWI Alcohol Safety award N.Y. State Alcohol Bur., Albany, 1986, Cmty. Svc. award Youth Bur. Goshen, 1987, Zonta scholar award, 1989, Cmty. Svc. award Otisville (N.Y.) State Correction, 1989, Nat. Assn. Counties award Confident Parenting Program, 1993, Hospice Orange Vol. award, 1993, The Gilbert award, 1995, Human Rights award Orange County Human Rights Commn., 1995, faculty award Assn. for Gerontology in Higher Edn., 2003. Mem. NAACP. Methodist. Avocations: swimming, piano, horseback riding.

HALL, WAYNE MICHAEL, management consultant; b. Fairbury, Nebr., Nov. 11, 1946; s. Frank Ehman and Bonnie Jean Hall; m. Sandra Kay Overby, Jan. 1, 1999; children: Jennifer E. Austin, Christopher M. BS, U. Nebr., 1969; MS, Kans. State U., 1977; M. Mil. Arts and Sci., U.S. Army Command and Gen. Staff Coll., 1985; EdD, George Washington U., 1985. Commd. 2d lt. U.S. Army, 1969, advanced through grades to brig. gen., 1997, G-2 intelligence officer 82d Airborn Divsn., 1987—89, comdr. 313d Mil. Intelligence Bn., 1989—91, comdr. 501st Mil. Intelligence Bn., 1994—96; J2 intelligence officer U. S. Forces Korea, Republic of Korea, 1996—98; dir. intelligence XXI study U.S. Army, Washington, 1998; dir. knowledge adv. Oak Ridge (Tenn.) BWXT, 1999—2001; ret. U.S. Army, 1999; cons. Hall & Assocs., Inc., Suffolk, Va., 2001—02; sr. exec. v.p., Homeland Security & Future Conflict MZM Inc., Washington, 2002—. Author: Stray Voltage: War in the Information Age, 2003; contbr. articles to profl. jours. Republican. Home: 5225 Regatta Pointe Rd Suffolk VA 23435

HALL, WILLIAM DARLINGTON, lawyer; b. Elkins, W.Va., Jan. 12, 1914; s. Nathan I. and Grace (Darlington) H.; m. Louise Brown, Aug. 3, 1949; children— Carolyn L., Dorothy K., Beverly G. B.E.E., W.Va. U., 1934, M.E.E., 1935, E.E., 1940; JD, George Washington U., 1946. Bar: D.C. 1945. Engr. Gen. Electric Co., Lynn, Mass., 1936-39; radio engr., patent adviser Signal Corps U.S. Army, Washington, 1939-47; chief patent sect., 1946-47; practiced in, 1947-74; partner firm Hall, Myers and Rose, 1974-89; of counsel Shlesinger & Myers, Bethesda, Md., 1989, Myers, Rose & Liniak, Bethesda, 1990-92, Myers, Liniak and Berenato, Bethesda, 1992-98, Hall, Priddy, Myers and Vande Sande, Potomac, Md., 1998—. Mem. Army-Navy Patent Adv. Bd., 1946-47 Home: 10850 Stanmore Dr Potomac MD 20854-1522 Office: Hall Priddy & Myers 10220 River Rd Potomac MD 20854-4916

HALL, WILLIAM EDWARD, JR., insurance agency executive; b. Roanoke, Va., Oct. 15, 1951; s. William Edward and Virginia (Moomaw) H.; m. Emily Ayers Rierson, May 27, 1972; children: Amanda Marie, John William. BA in Econs., U. N.C., Chapel Hill, 1973, MBA, 1977; MS in Fin. Svcs., Am. Coll., 1989. CPA, CLU, ChFC. Coll. agt. Northwestern Mut. Life, Chapel Hill, 1972-73, 75-77, spl. agt. Greensboro, N.C., 1973-75, 78—; staff acct. Price Waterhouse & Co., Charlotte, N.C., 1977-78; ptnr. Sprinkle & Assocs., Greensboro, 1978-87; sr. v.p., ptnr. Todd Orgn. of the Carolinas, Greensboro, 1987—. Bd. dirs. cen. N.C. chpt. Nat. Multiple Sclerosis Soc.; active Leadership Greensboro Alumni Assn. Bus. Found. fellow, 1977. Mem. AICPA, Nat. Assn. Accts., Estate Planning Coun., Am. Soc. CLUs, Greensboro CLU & ChFC (bd. dirs. 1980-83, sec.-treas. 1988-89, pres. 1990-91), Assn. Advanced Life Underwriters, Todd Nat. (legis. chmn. 1991—), Greensboro Country Club, Kiwanis, Phi Beta Kappa, Beta Gamma Sigma, Beta Theta Pi. Repubican. Presbyterian. Home: 1912 Lafayette Ave Greensboro NC 27408-7204 Office: Todd Orgn of The Carolinas Ste 300 620 Green Valley Rd Greensboro NC 27408-7725 E-mail: hall@toddcarolinas.com.

HALL, WILLIAM JACKSON, statistician, educator; b. Beltsville, Md., Nov. 13, 1929; s. Reginald Foster and Lily (Hambleton) H.; m. Helen Bloxom Cox, Mar. 27, 1954 (div. 1981); children: Jacqueline Arden, Rebecca Clayton, Bryan Hambleton, Kay Randall.; m. Nancy T. Hufsmith, Jan. 1, 1982. AB, Johns Hopkins U., 1950; MA, U. Mich., 1951; PhD, U. N.C., 1955; postgrad., Manchester (Eng.) U., 1953, Cambridge (Eng.) U., 1954. Statistician Bell Telephone Labs., N.Y.C., 1954-55; asst. chief Polio Surveillance Unit, Communicable Disease Center, USPHS, Atlanta, 1955-57; lectr. U. Calif. at Berkeley, 1957, vis. prof., 1969; asst. prof. U. N.C., 1957-61, assoc. prof., 1961-66, prof. stats., 1966-69; prof. dept. stats. and div. biostats. U. Rochester, N.Y., 1969—, chmn. dept. stats., 1969-81, acting dir. div. biostats., 1986-90. Vis. prof. stats. and biostats. Stanford (Calif.) U., 1967-69, U. Washington, 1982. Assoc. editor Annals of Math. Stats., 1968-73, Jour. Am. Statis. Assn., 1976-78. Fellow AAAS, Am. Statis. Assn., Inst. Math. Stats. (council 1973-76); mem. Royal Statis. Soc. Home: 75 Chelmsford Rd Rochester NY 14618-1729

HALL, WILLIAM JOEL, civil engineer, educator; b. Berkeley, Calif., Apr. 13, 1926; s. Eugene Raymond and Mary (Harkey) H.; m. Elaine Frances Thalman, Dec. 18, 1948; children: Martha Jane, James Frederick, Carolyn Marie. Student, U. Calif., Berkeley, 1943-44, Kings Point, 1944-45; BSCE, U. Kans., 1948; MS, U. Ill., Urbana, 1951, PhD, 1954. Teaching asst. U. Kans., 1947-48; engr. Sohio Pipe Line Co., 1948-49; mem. faculty U. Ill., Urbana, 1949-93, prof. civil engring., 1959-93, head dept. civil engring., 1984-91; prof. emeritus, 1993—. Cons. structural dynamics, seismic, materials to govt. orgns. and industry. Author books, articles, chpts. in books, revs. Recipient A. Epstein Meml. award U. Ill., 1958, Halliburton Engring. Edn. Leadership award, 1980, Disting. Engring. Svc. award U. Kans., 1985; Univ. scholar, U. Ill., 1986-89. Fellow AAAS; mem. NAE, ASME, ASTM, ASCE (hon., pres. Ctrl. Ill. sect. 1967-68, chmn. structural divsn. exec. com. 1973—, chmn. tech. coun. on lifeline earthquake engring. exec. com. 1982—, Kans. sect. award 1948, Walter L. Huber award 1963, Howard award 1984, Newmark medal 1984, C. Martin Duke award 1990, Norman medal 1992), Am. Concrete Inst., Am. Welding Soc. (Adams Meml. membership award 1967), Earthquake Engring. Rsch. Inst. (Housner medal 1998), Seismol. Soc. Am., Structural Engrs. Assn. Ill. (John Parmer award 1990), Sigma Xi, Tau Beta Pi (Daniel C. Drucker eminent faculty award 1993), Sigma Tau, Chi Epsilon (nat. honor mem. 1998), Phi Kappa Phi. Home: 3105 Valley Brook Dr Champaign IL 61822-6111 Office: U Ill Civil Engring 3103 Newmark Lab 205 N Mathews Ave Urbana IL 61801-2350 E-mail: w-hall3@staff.uiuc.edu., wj-efhall@worldnet.att.net.

HALL, WILLIAM KEARNEY, retired dermatologist; b. Springfield, Mo., Oct. 9, 1918; s. Edward Bennington and Mary Katharine (Kearney) H. BS, Yale U., 1939; MD, Harvard U., 1942. Commd. ensign USN, 1942, advanced through grades to capt., 1956, ret., 1962; intern U.S. Naval Hosp., Chelsea, Mass., 1942-43, resident Phila., 1953-56; pvt. practice St. Charles, Mo., 1962-83. Avocation: genealogy. Home: 33 Westmoreland Pl Saint Louis MO 63108-1227

HALL, WILLIAM SMITH, JR., land surveyor; b. Milford, Conn., Nov. 10, 1941; s. William Smith and Elizabeth (Brodeur) H.; m. Joy Collette Herrick, Sep. 13, 1969; children: William Smith 3d, Amber-Dawn. Student, U. Conn., 1959-60; AS in Civil Engring., Hartford State Tech. Coll., 1972. Lic. land surveyor, Conn.; cert. sr. civil engring. technician, notary public. Rodman-transitman Mcpl. Engring. Dept., Milford, 1960-67, road insp., survey party chief Trumbull, Conn., 1967-70; transitman, party chief Leonard Surveyors, Norwalk, Conn., 1970; transitman Donald Disbrow, P.E. & RLS, Hamden, Conn., 1970-72; lic. land surveyor Kasper Assocs., PE & LS, Bridgeport, Conn., 1972-77; owner, mgr., lic. land surveyor Hall Surveyors, Plymouth, Conn., 1973—. Mem. adv. com. civil dept. Capitol Commty. Tech. Coll., Hartford, Conn., 1984—, surveying instr., 1991—; Am. Congress Surveying and Mapping com. mem. film on land surveying A Matter of Degrees, 1983-86. Capt. Woodmont Vol. Fire Co. 5, Milford, 1969; chmn. bd. trustees Terryville Congl. Ch., Plymouth, 1986; mem. Plymouth Zoning Bd. Appeals, 1980—, vice chmn., 1985—, acting chmn., 1988. Mem. Conn. Assn. Land Surveyors (sec. 1979-82, pres. 1982-84, county bd. dirs. 1984—, code revision com. 1991-93, com. chmn. "Statute of Limitations" legis., Appreciation awards 1984), Surveyor's Proprietor's Coun. (sec.-treas. 1989, v.p. 1990, pres. 1991). Democrat. Avocations: bowling, sailing, swimming, boating, camping. Office: 350 Lake Plymouth Blvd Plymouth CT 06782-2703 E-mail: surveyor350@yahoo.com.

HALL, WILLIAM SPENCER, software engineer; b. Ancon, Republic of Panama, Oct. 9, 1935; parents Am. citizens; s. William Evens and Helena Spencer (Callaway) H.; m. Mary Helena Steketee, July 27, 1963 (div. 1984); children: Christopher Andrew, Mark Evens; m. Ewa Hanna Tarczynska, Dec. 19, 1987; 1 child, Katherine Anna. BEE, U. Va., 1958; MA with honors, Cambridge U., Eng., 1965; PhD in Applied Math., Brown U., 1968; MSE, U. Mich., 1985. Assoc. prof. math. U. Pitts., 1968-82; assoc. editor Math. Revs., Ann Arbor, Mich., 1982-85; mem. tech. staff AT&T Info. Systems, Lincroft, N.J., 1985-87; sr. engr. Olivetti Advanced Tech. Ctr., Cupertino, Calif., 1987-89, CONNECT Inc., Cupertino, 1989; sr. software engring. cons. Novell, Inc., San Jose, Calif., 1989-96; program mgr. Internat. NETCOM On-Line Comm. Svcs., Inc., San Jose, 1996—98; internationalization dir. SimulTrans LLC, 1998—2000; globalization cons. Convey Software, Inc., 2001—02; software cons. MLM Assoc., Inc., Santa Clara, 2002—. Contbr. articles to profl. jours. Election judge City of Pitts., 1973-82. 1st lt. USAF, 1958-63. Internat. Rsch. and Exchs. Bd. fellow 1975, 78, NAS fellow, 1978. Mem. Sigma Xi, Phi Eta Sigma, Tau Beta Pi. Democrat. Avocations: aviation, languages. Home and Office: 281 Hayes Ave Santa Clara CA 95051-6706 E-mail: billhall@mlm.assoc.com.

HALL, ZACH WINTER, academic administrator; b. Atlanta, Sept. 15, 1937; s. Dixon Winter and Marjorie Elizabeth (Owens) H.; m. Anne Browning, June 1958 (div. Aug. 1960); m. Marion Nestle, Dec. 1973 (div. June 1985); m. Julie Ann Giacobassi, Nov. 9, 1987. BA, Yale U., 1958; PhD, Harvard U., 1966. Asst. prof., then assoc. prof. Harvard Med. Sch., Boston, 1968-76; prof. U. Calif., San Francisco, 1976-94; dir. Nat. Inst. Neurol. Disorders and Stroke, Bethesda, Md., 1994-97; assoc. dean for rsch. U. Calif., San Francisco, 1997-98, vice chancellor rsch., 1998-2000, exec. vice chancellor, 2000—01; pres., CEO EnVivo Pharms., Inc., 2001—02; sr. assoc. dean for rsch. Keck Sch. Medicine, U. So. Calif., 2002—. Mem. Med. Adv. Bd., Chevy Chase, Md., 1995-99, Howard Hughes Med. Inst.; Alexander Forbes lectr. Grass Found., 1994; David Nachmanson lectr. Weizmann Inst., Rehovath, Israel, 1996. Author, editor: Molecular Neurobiology, 1992; editor jour. Neuron, 1988-94. Fellow AAAS; mem. Am. Acad. Arts and Scis., Inst. Medicine.

HALLA, BRIAN L. electronics company executive; b. Springfield, Ill., 1946; BSEE, U. Nebr., 1969. Applications engr. Control Data Corp., 1969—74; dir. mktg. Intel Corp., 1974—78; exec. v.p. LSI Logic, 1988—96; chmn. bd., pres., CEO Nat. Semiconductor Corp., Santa Clara, Calif., 1996—. Mem.: N.Y. Stock Exch. (adv. com.), Foveon Inc. (bd. dirs.), Tech. Network (bd. dirs.), Silicon Valley Mfg. Group, Semi-Conductor Indsl. Assn. (bd. dirs.,). Office: Nat Semiconductor Corp 2900 Semiconductor Dr Santa Clara CA 95051-0695*

HALLADAY, LAURIE ANN, public relations consultant, former franchise executive; b. Monroe, Mich., Aug. 18, 1945; d. Alvin John and Florence (Lowrey) Kohler; m. Edward L. Howell, Aug. 27, 1966; m. 2d Fredric R. Halladay, May 24, 1980. BJ, U. Mo., 1967. Reporter, staff writer Copley Newspapers, L.A., 1967-69; account exec. Furman Assocs., L.A., 1969-71, v.p., 1971-74; account supr. Bob Thomas & Assocs., L.A., 1974-76, v.p., 1976-78; v.p., sr. ptnr. Fleishman-Hillard, Inc., St. Louis, 1980-84; owner, operator McDonald's, Portland, Oreg., 1984-87, McDonald's McStop of Mid.-Mo., Kingdom City, 1988-92. Chmn. press ops. for Budweiser/G.I. Joe's Portland 200 Indy Car Race, 1984-87; mem. advt., promotions com. Hollywood Boosters, 1986. Bd. dirs. Waterman Place Assn., St. Louis, 1983; mem. pub. rels. com. Winston Churchill Meml., Fulton, 1988-92. Recipient Merit award Calif. Press Women, 1969, Lulu award Los Angeles Women's Ad Club, 1976, McDonald's Outstanding Store award, 1985, 86, 89, 90, 91. Mem. PRSA (Prism award 1977), Soc. Am. travel Writers (assoc. 1981-84), Women in Comm. (dir. St. Louis 1980-82), Nat. Tour Assn., Mo. Travel Coun., Delta Delta Delta (alumna adviser 1989, 90,, v.p. Delta Xi House Corp. 1991, collegiate dist. officer 1991, 94, regional program chmn. 1994, program resource team pub. rels. specialist 1995-96, nat. chmn. pub. rels. 1996, cons. pub. rels. chpt. 1998-2000). Home: 242 Hidden Bay Dr Unit 301 Osprey FL 34229-3107 E-mail: laurieh@comcast.net.

HALLAHAN, KIRK EDWARD, journalism educator; b. Cleve., Feb. 16, 1950; m. Jean Sheppard, Jan. 8, 1977. BA magna cum laude, UCLA, 1971; MA, U. Wis., Madison, 1974, PhD, 1995. Account supr. Harshe-Rotman & Druck, Inc., L.A., 1973-79; v.p. pub. rels. Calif. Fed. Savs. and Loan, L.A., 1979-84; sr. v.p. pub. affairs Calif. League of Savs. Instns., L.A., 1984-89; v.p. pub. affairs Coast Fed. Bank, L.A., 1989-91; asst. prof. U. N.D., 1993—96; assoc. prof. Colo. State U., Ft. Collins, 1996—. Sr. lectr. U. So. Calif. Sch. Journalism, 1977-84. Author: The Consequences of Mass Communication, 1997; founder, editor www.pr-education.org.; mem. editl. bd. Jour. Pub. Rels. Rsch., Pub. Rels. Review, Encyclopedia Pub. Rels. Mem. Pasadena Tournament Roses, Calif., 1979-93; adv. com. L.A. City Fire Dept., United Way Region V, Cen. City Assn. State dept. fellow Internat. Comm. Seminar, Yugoslavia, 1971. Recipient Jackson, Jackson & Wagner Behavioral Sci. prize, PRSA Found., 2001. Fellow PRSA (Silver Anvil award 1974, South Pacific dist. chmn. 1984, fin. svcs. sect. chmn. 1986, 87, L.A. Outstanding Profl. 1988); mem. Publicity Club L.A. (pres. 1978-79), Soc. Profl. Journalists, Phi Beta Kappa. Democrat. Presbyterian. Home: 3230 Pepperwood Ln Fort Collins CO 80525-2943 Office: Colo State U C-225 Clark Fort Collins CO 80523-1785

HALLAM, BEVERLY (BEVERLY LINNEY), artist; b. Lynn, Mass., Nov. 22, 1923; d. Edwin Francis and Alice (Linney) Hallam Murphy. BS in Edn, Mass. Coll. Art, 1945; postgrad., Cranbrook Acad. Art, Mich., 1948; MFA, Syracuse U., 1953. Chmn. dept. art Lasell Jr. Coll., Auburndale, Mass., 1945-49; assoc. prof. Mass. Coll. Art, 1949-62. Bd. dirs. Barn Gallery Assocs., Inc., Ogunquit, Maine. One-person shows include Joe and Emily Lowe Art Center, Syracuse U., 1953, DeCordova Mus., Lincoln, Mass., 1954, Shore Galleries, Boston, 1959, 62, 68, 73, 74, Witte Meml. Mus., San Antonio, 1968, U. Maine, 1969, Lamont Gallery, Exeter, N.H., 1969, Addison Gallery, Andover, Mass., 1971, Fitchburg Art Mus., 1972, Fairweather Hardin Gallery, Chgo., 1972, Hobe Sound (Fla.) Galleries, 1973, Inst. Contemporary Art, Boston, 1977, PS Galleries, Maine, 1981, Payson-Weisberg Gallery, N.Y.C., 1984, Farnsworth Mus., Rockland, Maine, 1984, 98, Midtown Galleries, N.Y.C., 1988, Francesca Anderson Gallery, Boston, 1988, Hobe Sound Galleries North, Portland, Maine, 1988, Evansville (Ind.) Mus. Arts and Sci., 1990,

Sheldon Swope Mus., Terre Haute, Ind., 1990, Art Mus. S.E. Tex., Beaumont, 1990, Bergen Mus. Art and Sci., Paramus, N.J., 1990, Polk Mus. Art, Lakeland, Fla., 1991, Farnsworth Art Mus., 1998, Ogunquit Art Assn., 1999, Mass. Coll. Art, Boston, 2000, Univ. New England, 2000, Berkshire C.C., Pittsfield, Mass., 2003, River Tree Ctr. for the Arts, Kennebunk, Maine, 2003; two-person show, Inst. Contemporary Art, Boston, 1956, numerous group shows including Barn Gallery, 1954-2003, Busch-Reisinger Mus., Harvard U., 1956, 59, 60, Portland Mus., 1959, 84, 92, 93, 97, Mus. Fine Arts, Boston, 1960, Inst. Contemporary Art, Boston, 1960, 63, 68, 77, Pace Gallery, Boston, 1962, DeCordova Mus., 1963, 64, 68, 69, 70, 71, 75, Ward-Nasse Gallery, N.Y.C., 1971-72, Ogunquit (Maine) Mus. Am. Art, 1964, 70, 71, 78, 80, 84, 89, 91-93, 95, 98, 2000, 2003, R.I. Arts Festival, 1966, Smithsonian Instn., Washington, 1966, Am. Water Color Soc. Traveling Exhibition, 1967, Watercolor U.S.A., Springfield, Mo., 1968, Maine State Mus., 1976, Maine Coast Artists, 1974, 75, 77, 83, 89, 92, 93, Joan Whitney Payson Gallery of Art, Maine, 1980, Farnsworth Art Mus., 1982, 87, 92, 95, 96, Bowdoin Coll. Mus. Art, 1984, 92, Midtown Payson Galleries, N.Y.C., 1985, 87, 90, 92, Expo '92, Seville, Spain, Barbara Scott Gallery, Bay Harbor Island, Fla., 1993, Fitchburg (Mass.) Art Mus., 1994, Monmouth (N.J.) Mus., 1995, Evansville Mus. Arts and Sci., 1996, U. New England, 2000, Francesca Anderson Fine Art, Lexington, Mass., 2002; represented in permanent collections Rose Art Mus. Brandeis U., Fogg Art Mus., Cambridge, Mass.; Corcoran Gallery Am. Art, Washington, Witte Meml. Mus., San Antonio, DeCordova Mus., Lincoln, Addison Gallery, Andover, Bowdoin Coll. Mus. Art, Fitchburg Art Mus., Ogunquit Mus. Am. Art, Portland Mus., Colby Coll., U. Maine, Currier Gallery Art, Manchester N.H., Farnsworth Library and Art Mus., Rockland, Maine, U. N.H. Art Galleries, Durham, Everson Mus., Syracuse, First Nat. Bank, Boston, Ernst and Ernst, Chgo., Carnegie Corp., N.Y., Nat. Mus. Women in the Arts, Washington, Gouws Capital Mgmt., Inc., Portland, Maine, Marion Koogler Art Mus., San Antonio, Tex., others, also, pvt. collections, U.S. Can., Paris, Switzerland; Publ. Beverly Hallam, Paintings, Drawings and Monotypes, 1956-71, 1971; subject of book and video Beverly Hallam: The Flower Paintings, 1990, Beverly Hallam: An Odyssey in Art, 1998, (by Carl Little) One Hundred Works From the 20th Century at Colby College Museum of Art, 1996, Maine In America, 2000, On Paper: Masterworks From The Addison Collection, 2003, others. Recipient Pearl Safir award Silvermine Guild Artists, New Canaan, Conn., 1955, Painting prize Boston Arts Festival, 1957, Blanche E. Colman Found. award, 1960, Hatfield awards Boston Soc. Watercolor Painters, 1960, 64, 1st prize Edwin Webster award, 1962, Am. Artist Achievement award, 1993, Disting. Alumna award Mass. Coll. Art, 2000, Maine Coll. Art award for Visual Artist Achievement, 2001. Mem. Ogunquit Art Assn. (past pres.), Archives Am. Art. Avocations: gardening, photography, digital abstractions. Home: 30 Surf Point Rd York ME 03909-5053

HALLARD, WAYNE BRUCE, retired economist; b. Plainfield, N.J., Dec. 28, 1951; s. Donald Jay and Patricia (Adelmann) H.; m. Grace Elizabeth Farrell, Apr. 29, 1972 (div. 1979); 1 child, Travis; m. Deborah Jane Russo, Aug. 16, 1987. Student, Brown U., 1970-71; AA in Bus., Union Coll., 1977; BS in Econs., Fairleigh Dickinson U., 1980, MBA in Econs., 1984; postgrad., N.Y.U., 1984-87. Store mgr. Wine Art of N.J., Watchung, 1972; mgr. Verizon, Newark, 1972—2003, ret. Cons. N.J. Coun. of Savs. Instns., West Orange, 1987-95, F.A. Russo Assocs., Scotch Plains, N.J., 1989—. Trustee, treas. Lehmen Found., Newark, 1979-84; bd. dirs., treas. Vol. Ctr. of Greater Essex County, 1990-97; mem. Mental Health Assn., East Orange, 1979-80, Newark Mus., 1987—; trustee, past sec., treas. Newark Jaycees Internat. Senators Scholarship Found., 1986-99; umpire Scotch Plains-Fanwood Youth Baseball Assn., 1982 ; trustee, past pres. Brotherhood Temple Sharey Tefilo Israel, South Orange, N.J., 1980—; trustee Fairleigh Dickinson U. With USAFR, 1971-80. Recipient Cert. of Appreciation Cts. and Corrections Assn. N.J. 1982; named One of Outstanding Young Men of Am., 1981, 83, 85, 86, 88. Mem. ACLU, Am. Econ. Assn., Greater Newark C. of C. (bd. dirs. 1980-82), Telephone Pioneers Am., Fairleigh Dickinson U. Alumni Assn. (bd. govs. 1997—, v.p. 1999-2001, pres.-elect 2001-2003, pres. 2003—), Am. Dog Show Judges, Ea. Pa. Stewards Assn., Am. Sealyham Terrier Club (past bd. dirs.), Garden State All Terrier Club (past treas., past corr. sec.), Mastiff Club Am., Aircraft Owners and Pilots Assn., Stewards Club Am., ARZA, Jewish Chatauqua Soc., Delta Mu Delta. Democrat. Jewish. Avocations: cooking, reading. Home: 518 Jerusalem Rd Scotch Plains NJ 07076-2011

HALLAUER, ARNEL ROY, geneticist; b. Netawaka, Kans., May 4, 1932; s. Roy Virgil and Mabel Fern (Bohnenkemper) H.; m. Janet Yvonne Goodmanson, Aug. 29, 1964; children: Elizabeth, Paul BS, Kans. State U., 1954; MS, Iowa State U., 1958, PhD, 1960. Rsch. agronomist USDA, Ames, Iowa, 1958-60, geneticist Raleigh, N.C., 1961-62, rsch. geneticist Ames, 1963-89; prof. Iowa State U., 1990—2002, C.F. Curtiss Disting. prof. agr. emeritus, 1991—. Author: (with J.B. Miranda) Quantitative Genetics in Maize Breeding, 1981, 2d edit., 1988; editor: Specialty Corns, 1994, 2d edit., 2000. 1st lt. U.S. Army, 1954-56. Recipient Applied Rsch. and Ext. award 1981, Henry A. Wallace award for disting.svc. to agr., 1992, Disting. Alumni Achievement citation, 1996, Iowa State U., Genetics and Plant Breeding award Nat. Coun. Plant Breeding, 1984, Gov.'s Sci. medal State of Iowa, 1990, Burlington No. Career Rsch. Achievement award Iowa State Found., 1991, Centennial medal Phi Kappa Phi, 1997, Verdent Plant Genetics award Verdent Ptnrs., Chgo., 2001; USDA grantee, 1982, 85, 87, 90; named to USDA/Agrl. Rsch. Sci. Hall of Fame, 1992. Fellow Am. Soc. Agronomy (Agronomic Achievement award for crops 1989, Agronomic Rsch. award 1992), Crop Sci. Soc. (Dekalb Pfizer Crop Sci. award 1981, Pres.'s award 2002), Iowa Acad. Sci. (disting. fellow 1985); mem. NAS, Nat. Agri-Mktg. Assn. (nat. award for excellence in rsch. 1993), Am. Genetic Assn., Am. Statis. Assn., Kans. State U. Alumni Assn. (alumni fellow 1997), Iowa State Alumni Assn. (faculty citation 1987, Disting. Achievement Citation 1995), Gamma Sigma Delta (Disting. Svc. to Agr. award 1990, Rsch. Award of Merit 1999, Verdant Ptnr.'s Crop Genetics award 2001). Pres. award, Crop Sci. Soc. Am., 2002. Republican. Lutheran. Home: 516 Luther Dr Ames IA 50010-4735 Office: Iowa State U 1505 Dept Agronomy Ames IA 50010

HALL-BARRON, DEBORAH, lawyer; b. Oakland, Calif., Oct. 7, 1949; d. John Standish Hall and Mary (Swinson) H.; m. Eric Levin Meadow, Feb. 1973 (div. June 1982); 1 child, Jesse Standish Meadow Hall; m. Richie Barron, 1997. Paralegal cert., Sonoma State U., Rohnert Park, Calif., 1984; JD, John F. Kennedy U., Walnut Creek, Calif., 1990. Bar: Calif. 1991. Paralegal Law Offices Marc Libarle/Quentin Kopp, Cotati, Calif., 1983-86, MacGregor & Buckley, Larkspur, Calif., 1984-86, Law Offices Melvin Belli, San Francisco, 1987-88, Steinhart & Falconer, San Francisco, 1988; mgr. Computerized Litigation Assocs., San Francisco, 1986; law clk. Morton & Lacy, San Francisco, 1989-91, assoc., 1991-96; atty. Law Offices of Charlotte Venner, San Francisco, 1996-97, Plastiras & Terrizzi, San Francisco, San Rafael, Calif., 1998, Bishop, Barry, Howe, Haney & Ryder, San Francisco, 1998-99, McLemore, Collins and Toschi, Oakland, Calif., 1999-2000, Nevin Levy, LLP, Walnut Creek, 2000—01, Curtis & Arata, Modesto, Calif., 2001—. Atty. Vol. Legal Svcs., San Francisco, 1991-96; judge San Francisco Youth Ct., 1995-97; com. chmn. Point Richmond (Calif.) coun., 1994-96. Recipient Whiley Manuel Pro Bono award State Bar Calif., 1993. Mem. Nat. Assn. Ins. Women, Def. Rsch. Inst., Bar Assn. San Francisco (del. 4th world conf. on women 1995, chair product liability com.), Internat. Com. Lawyers for Tibet (litigation com. 1991-97, co-chair women's com.), Ins. Claims Assn. (chmn. membership com. 1994-96), Hon. Order of Blue Goose Internat., Queen's Bench (chmn. employment com. 1994-97, bd. dirs. 1996—, newsletter editor and webmaster 1999), BASF intellectual property/entertainment law). Democrat. Avocations: sailing, playing guitar and saxophone, home brewing, mountain biking, human rights advocate. E-mail: deborahhallbarron@msn.com.

HALLBERG, BENGT O. systems strategy director, fiber optic specialist; b. Stockholm, Dec. 31, 1943; s. Olle E.S. and Anne-Marie K. H.; m. Lena M. Tengelin, June 13, 1975; children: Niklas O., Mattias A., Andreas E. MS in Physics, Royal Inst. Tech., Stockholm, 1978. Constrnl. engr. AB Svenska Bostäder, Stockholm, 1965-76; scientist Inst. of Optical Rsch., Stockholm, 1976-81; pres. Scan Fiber Opto AB, Stockholm, 1988-92, BOH Optical AB, Stockholm, 1981-95; dir. Fiber Network Application Lab, Ericsson, Stockholm, 1995-97; dir. sys. strategy Access Network, Ericsson Inc., N.Y.C., 1997—2000, BOH Strategy, Stockholm, 2000—. Inventor airborne multispectral radiometer, fiber optic communication system based on WDM; patentee frequency and output regulation in laser diodes. Mem. Optical Soc. Am., Internat. Soc. Optical Engring., European Optical Soc., Swedish Optical Soc. Office: Osterbink SE 13055 Orno Sweden

HALLBERG, BUDD JAYE, management consulting firm executive; b. Ottumwa, Iowa, Oct. 2, 1942; s. Melvin Kenneth and Janet Berina (Dowden) H.; m. Diana May Pierce, Dec. 30, 1962. BA, Parsons Coll., 1965; MA, Goddard Coll., 1980; BS, SUNY, 1981; diploma, Command & Gen. Staff Coll., 1981; cert., Wharton Sch., 1984, Yale U., 1996. Account exec. Francis I. duPont & Co., Moline, Ill., 1966-69, sales mgr. N.Y.C., 1969-70, br. mgr. Toledo, 1970-71; v.p. Dominick & Dominick, Inc., N.Y.C., 1971-72, Hornblower & Weeks, Inc., N.Y.C., 1972-74; mem. N.Y. Mercantile Exchange, N.Y.C., 1974-76; dir. U.S. Commodity Future Trading Commn., Washington, 1976-83; v.p. Heinold Commodities, Inc., N.Y.C., 1983-85; pres. SCAN Mgmt. Inc., Gettysburg, Pa., 1985—. Contbr. articles to profl. jours. Fund raiser Rep. party Old Greenwich, Conn., 1974, Gettysburg, Pa., 1995, St. Saviours Episc. Ch., Old Greenwich, 1975, Prince of Peace Episc. Ch., Gettysburg, 1985—. Lt. col. USAR, ret. Mem.: St. Nicholas Soc. of N.Y., Soc. of Colonial Wars, Friends of The Holland Soc. of N.Y., Sons of Union Vets of Civil War, The William Soc., Pa. Soc. Sons of the Revolution, Colonial Soc. Pa., Rotary, Franklin Inn Club (Phila.), Racquet Club Phila., Army and Navy Club Washington, Scottish Rite, York Rite, Masons (32 deg.). Avocations: fishing, hunting, tennis, jogging, golf. Home: 320 Spangler School Rd Gettysburg PA 17325-8639 Office: SCAN Mgmt Inc PO Box 4835 Gettysburg PA 17325-4835 E-mail: scanmngt@supernet.com.

HALLBERG, PARKER FRANKLIN, environmental company executive; b. Detroit, Nov. 21, 1939; s. Franklin Harold and Fae Marie (Parker) H.; m. Jane Birdwell Henderson, Nov. 28, 1964 (div. May 1976); 1 child, Thomas Stalworth Henderson. AB, U. Mich., 1961, MA, 1962. Procurement analyst NASA, Washington, 1964-67; budget officer USIA, Washington, 11967-68, fgn. svc. officer, 1968-92, asst. exec. officer Bangkok, 1968-70, br. pub. affairs officer Davao, The Philippines, 1970-73, pers. officer Washington, 1973-76, exec. officer Bangkok, 1976-78, Jakarta, Indonesia, 1980-82, Paris, 1987-91; ret., 1992; exec. dir. Internat. Vol. Svcs. Inc., Washington, 1996-97, bd. dirs., corp. sec., 1996—; exec. v.p. Enviro Tek Corp., Waterford, Va., 1997—, bd. dirs., corp. sec., 1996—. Bd. dirs. AgriCell.Com.Inc., Waterford. Treas., bd. dirs. Canterbury Sch., Accokeek, Md., 1965-68; vestryman St. Augustine's Episcopal Ch., Washington, 1965-67, Christ Ch., Bangkok, 1970, 78; bd. dirs., mem. exec. com. Episcopal Caring Response to AIDS, Washington, 1993-96; chmn. bd. trustees Internat. Art Found. Former Soviet States, Inc., N.Y.C., 2000—. Mem. Diplomatic and Counselor Officers Ret., Army and Navy Club, Arts Club Washington (bd. govs. 2001—). Democrat. Home: 2039 New Hampshire Ave NW Washington DC 20009 Office: Enviro Tek Corp PO Box 366 Waterford VA 20197 E-mail: pfhallberg@erols.com.

HALLBERG, THOMAS BOONE, education educator; b. Santa Rosa, Calif., Dec. 7, 1926; arrived in Mex., 1957; s. Oscar Albin and Mary Elizabeth (Barlow) Hallberg; m. Zenaida Ruíz-Martínez, July 22, 1961 (dec. 1994); children: María Elizabeth, Juana Esther, Oscar Boone, Thomas John. BA, Pomona Coll., 1949; MA, U. Mich., 1951. Investigator in botany Sec. Agr. Mex., Mexico City, 1960-63; founder, adminstr. Experiment Grounds, Ixtlan, Mexico, 1963—; fruitculture and forestry tchg. adminstr. Sec. Edn. Pub. Mex., Mexico City, 1972-79; rsch. adminstr. Sec. Edn. Pub. Del. Oaxaca, 1979-81; rsch. prof. Inst. Tech. Oaxaca Sec. Edn. Pub., 1981—. Avocations: hiking, camping, exploring traditional agricultural technology. Home: Rancho Teja 68725 Ixtlan de Juarez Oaxaca Mexico Office: Inst Tech Oaxaca Ave Victor Bravo Ahuja 125 68030 Oaxaca de Juárez Oaxaca Mexico Home: Apartado Postal 1461 Oaxaca de Juarez Oaxaca 68000 Mexico E-mail: hallberg@itoaxaca.edu.mx.

HALLECK, CHARLES WHITE, lawyer, photographer, former judge; b. Rensselaer, Ind., July 6, 1929; s. Charles Abraham and Blanche (White) H.; m. Carolyn L. Wood, Dec. 23, 1950 (div. Oct. 1969); children: Holly Louise, Charles White, Todd Alexander, Heather Leigh, Heidi Lynne, William Hemsley, Hope Leslie; m. Jeanne Wahl, May 16, 1970. AB, Williams Coll., 1951; JD, George Washington U., 1957; LL.D. (hon.), St. Joseph's Coll., 1971; AA in Photography, Foothill Coll., Los Altos Hills, Calif., 1996. Asst. U.S. atty. for D.C., 1957-59; assoc. Hogan and Hartson, Washington, 1959-65; judge Superior Ct. D.C., 1965-77; mem. firm Lamb, Halleck & Keats, Washington, 1977-80; sole practice, 1980-86; photojournalist, 1986-99; fine art photographer, 1999—. Served with USNR, 1951-55; to lt. Res. (ret.). Mem. Beta Theta Pi, Phi Delta Phi.

HALLECK, GEORGE THOMAS, marketing professional; b. Elizabeth, N.J., Mar. 9, 1948; s. Joseph George and Jean Constance Halleck; m. Jacquelyn Ann Halleck, Aug. 23, 1970 (div. Nov. 1994); children: Gregg Christopher, Robert George; m. Judith B. Halleck, Mar. 16, 1995; stepchildren: Vincent James Grillo, Julie Ann Grillo. AA, Union Coll., Cranford, N.J., 1968; BA, Lynchburg Coll., 1970; MS, Va. Commonwealth U., 1972. Tchr. St. Genevieve's Sch., Elizabeth, N.J., 1972-74; sales rep. Parke-Davis, Detroit, 1974-78, Johnson & Johnson, New Brunswick, N.J., 1978-84; sr. group product mgr. Howmedica-Pfizer, Rutherford, NJ, 1984-99; mktg. mgr. Internat. Technidyne Corp., Edison, N.J., 2000—. Roman Catholic. Achievements include patent for surgical instrument. Home: 27 Cornell Rd Cranford NJ 07016 E-mail: halleck3@aol.com.

HALLEGUA, DAVID SAMUEL, internist, rheumatologist, educator; b. Cochin, India, Oct. 2, 1963; arrived in U.S., 1988; s. Samuel H. and Queenie S. Hallegua; m. Sayareh F. Hallegua, Nov. 26, 1995. Med. diploma, Trivandrum Med. Coll., India, 1987. Diplomate Am. Bd. Internal Medicine, Am. Bd. Rheumatology. Clin. instr. UCLA Sch. Medicine, 2001—. Bd. dirs. Spondylitis Assn. Am., Burbank, Calif. Co-author: Dubois Lupus Erythematosus, 5th edit., 2001; contbr. articles to profl. jours. Recipient Intern of Yr. award, Sinai Hosp., Detroit, 1989—90; fellow, Cedars-Sinai Hosp., L.A., 1996—98. Mem.: ACP, Am. Coll. Rheumatology. Avocations: philately, philanthropy, public speaking. Office: 8737 Beverly Blvd #203 Los Angeles CA 90048

HALLEN, BARRY, philosopher, educator; b. Chgo., Apr. 5, 1941; s. George and Betty Hallen; m. Carla De Benedetti, Apr. 30, 1986; m. Patricia Slattery, Aug. 5, 1966 (div. Nov. 26, 1974). BA in Philosophy, Carleton Coll., 1963; MA in Philosophy, Boston U., 1968, PhD in Philosophy, 1970. Lectr. in philosophy U. Lagos, Lagos, Nigeria, 1970—75; from lectr. to reader in philosophy U. Ife, Ile-Ife, Nigeria, 1975—83, reader in philosophy, 1983—88; project dir. UNESCO, Milan, 1989—98; vis. prof. philosophy Morehouse Coll., Atlanta, 1997—2000, prof. philosophy, 2000—, chmn. dept. philosophy and Religionr, 2001—. Rschr. W.E.B. DuBois Inst. Harvard U., Cambridge, Mass., 1995—. Co-author: Knowledge, Belief & Witchcraft, 1997; author: The Good, The Bad & the Beautiful, 2000, A Short History of African Philosophy, 2002. Borden Parker Bowne fellow, Boston U., 1968—69. Mem.: Soc. African Philosophy in N.Am. (gen. sec. 1998—). Avocations: sailing, bicycling, writing detective stories. Office: Morehouse College 830 Westview Drive SW Atlanta GA 30314

HALLENBECK, ALFRED M. lawyer, corporation executive; b. 1930; married. B.A., Syracuse U., 1952; J.D., Yale U., 1957. Ptnr., Nixon, Hargrave, Devans & Doyle, 1957-81; v.p., gen. counsel Sybron Corp., Rochester, N.Y., 1982— . Trustee Syracuse U., Rochester Inst. Tech. Served to 1st lt. U.S. Army, 1952-54. Office: Sybron Corp 1100 Midtown Tower Rochester NY 14604-2009

HALLENBECK, KENNETH LUSTER, retired numismatist; b. Ann Arbor, Mich., Oct. 20, 1931; s. Kenneth Luster and Ethel (Apfel) Hallenbeck; m. June Eugenia Miekka, July 2, 1955; children: Kevin L., Thomas G., Scott A., Sheryl A. AB in Geography, U. Mich., 1955. Planning analyst Lincoln Nat. Life Ins. Co., Ft. Wayne, Ind., 1957-70, sr. planning analyst, 1970-72, asst. mgr. policy issue, 1972-77; bd. govs. Am. Numismatic Assn., Colorado Springs, Colo., 1971-87, mus. curator, 1977-82, v.p., 1987-89, pres., 1989-91; pres., dir. Hallenbeck Coin Gallery, Inc., Colorado Springs, 1983—; ret. Apptd. by Pres. Nixon to U.S. Assay Commn. 1974; testified before Congl. subcom. on coinage and consumer affairs for commemorative coinage, mem. design selection com. for Olympic coin designs, 1992, Focus group for design of Sacagawea dollar, 1999. Contbr. numerous articles to mags. Mem. Rep. Cen. Com., Ft. Wayne, 1972-77, Better Bus. Bur., Colorado Springs; del. to Rep. County and 5th Congl. Dist. Caucuses; sec. Pioneer Mus. Found. Bd.; mem. focus group Sacajewa Dollar design, 1998. With U.S. Army, 1955-57. Fellow Life Mgmt. Inst.; mem. Colorado Springs C. of C., Tokens and Medals Soc. (past pres.), Pioneer Mus. Found. Bd., Bd. Friends of the Pike's Peak Libr. Dist., Masons, Shriners, also numerous local, regional and nat. coin clubs. Republican. Congregationalist. Avocations: numismatics, western history. Office: Hallenbeck Coin Gallery Inc 711 N Nevada Ave Colorado Springs CO 80903-1007

HALLENBECK, POMONA JUANITA, artist; b. Roswell, N.Mex., Nov. 12, 1938; d. Cleve and Juanita Henriette (Williams) H.; children: Cheryl Ellis, Cynthia Ellis, Catherine Ellis. AA, Ea. N.Mex. U., 1965; BFA, Art Student's League, 1976; postgrad., Pan Am. Art Sch., 1976-77. Mgr. Paul Anderson Photography, San Antonio, 1951-54, tchr. Roswell (N.Mex.) Ind. Sch. Dist., 1960-64; dir., instr. Sketchbox Sch. Art, Galveston, Tex., 1965-71; monitor etching class Art Student's League, N.Y.C., 1975-77; dir., instr. Alleyworks Atlier, Austin, Tex., 1978-81; dir., proprietor, artist Sketchbox Studio, Roswell, 1982-94; instr. Elderhostel program Ghost Ranch, Abiquiu, N.Mex., 1984—2002, coord. Calender project, 1992—; owner, proprietor Pomona's Accent Line, Roswell, 1986-94, cons., 1988-94. Artist, demonstrator Roswell (N.Mex.) Mus. and Art Ctr., 1981-90, Roswell Ind. Sch., 1982-90, Wonder of Watercolor Workshops, Austin, Tex., 1997-2001, Art After Sch., Bastrop, Tex., 1997-2001, Watercolor by Design, U. Tex., Austin, 1999—, Fielding it with Watercolor, 2001-02, Watercolor for Beginners cont. edn. programs, Bastrop and Elgin, Tex., 1998—; creator Marathon Watercolor workshop, Stonypoint Conf. Ctr., N.Y., 2001; founder Elderhostels, Abiquiv and Santa Fe, 2002. Illustrator: (book covers) Julian of Norwich, Nachman, Pseudo Dionysius, Classics of Western Spirituality, Naming the Powers, Unmasking the Powers, Engaging the Powers, Walter Wink, Ghost Ranch Cookbook, Savoring the Southwest Again, The Human Being: The Enigma of the Son of Man; one-woman shows Ghost Ranch Trading Post and New Arts Bldg., 2000-02, Laughing at the Sun Gallery, Austin, 2001, Depot Gallery, Austin, 2001-02, Trail of Ponies, Santa Fe, N.Mex., 2001; (album cover) Smiling on the Inside; exhibited in Southwest Expressions Gallery, Chgo., 1990-91, Roswell Fine Art Mus., 1994, Artisan Gallery, Austin, 1995-, Cimmaron (N.Mex.) Art Gallery, 1995, Trading Post, 2001-02, Bitzer & Johnson, Roswell, 1997, 2001-02, Potter's Guild Sho, 1997, Gallery Bunkhouse, Cypress Mill, Tex., 2002, Laughing at the Sun Gallery, Austin, 1996-2003, Rose Minn Gallery, Elgin, Tex., 2001-02, Blaire Carnehan Gallery, Santa Fe, N.Mex., 2001-02. Mem. World Wildlife, 2000, Ghost Ranch Compadres, Santa Fe, 2000, People for the Ethical Treatment of Animals, 2000, 02, Recos River Project, 1990-2000; arts convener silent auction, Ghost Ranch, 1995, New Art Bldg., 1998. Recipient purchase award Am. Artist, 1975, 2nd Place award Austin Art Guild, 1999; named Best of Show, Ghost Ranch Compadre Show, 1990, ALTRUSA Fashion Show, 1990; scholar Altrusa Club, 1973; grantee Whitney Enterprises, 1990, artist-in-residence grantee Ghost Ranch, 1992, 93, 95-, McKee grantee, 1995-96. Mem. Am. Watercolor Soc. (assoc.), Soc. Illustrators, Nat. Watercolor Soc., Western Colo. Watercolor Soc., Supts. Salon of Paris (Bronze medal 1988), Ghost Ranch Found. Ctr., Roswell Mus. and Art Ctr., U.S. Humane Soc., Tex. Watercolor Soc., Tex. Fine Arts Assn., Austin Contemporary Art Assn., Mus. Women Artists, Washington. Democrat. Avocation: photography. Office: Sketchbox Studio of Art 130 Old Austin Trail Elgin TX 78621-5744 E-mail: sketchbox130@aol.com.

HALLENBERG, ROBERT LEWIS, lawyer; b. Oct. 21, 1948; s. Daniel Ward and Anna Mae (Lewis) H.; m. Susan Annette Shaffer, Nov. 29, 1980; children: Shea F., Jonathan E.R., Robert Lewis Jr. BA, U. Ky., 1970, JD, 1973; LLM in Taxation, U. Miami, Fla., 1974. Bar: U. Ky. 1970, U.S. Dist. Ct. (we. dist.) Ky. 1975, U.S. Tax Ct. 1986. Ptnr. Woodward, Hobson & Fulton, Louisville, 1974—. Adj. prof. U. Louisville Sch. Law, 1974-80. Bd. dirs. Louisville Theatrical Assocs., 1980-90, v.p., sec., 1985-90; bd. dirs. Goodwill Industries Ky., 1987-93, sec., 1988-91; pres. Louisville Estate Planning Coun., 1979-80; bd. dirs. Louisville Estate Planning Forum, 1986-93, sec., 1992-93; mem. Estate Planning Coun. of Louisville, bd. dirs., 1989-95, pres., 1993-94; Besy Lawyers in Am., Trust Estate. Named one of Best Lawyers in Am. Fellow Am. Coll. Trust and Estate Counsel, Best Lawyers in Am. (trusts and estates); mem. ABA (subchpt. com. 1974-77, real property, probate and trust com. 1985—), Ky. Bar Assn. (sec. tax com. 1984-85), Owl Creek Country Club (bd. dirs. 1988-91, pres. 1989-90, treas. 1990-91). Republican. Episcopalian. Office: Woodward Hobson & Fulton 2500 Nat City Tower Louisville KY 40202 E-mail: bhallenberg@WHF-law.com.

HALLER, ARCHIBALD ORBEN, sociologist, educator; b. San Diego, Jan. 15, 1926; s. Archie O. and Eleanor (Brizzee) Haller; m. Hazel Laura Zimmermann, Feb. 15, 1947 (dec. 1985); children: Elizabeth Ann, Stephanie Lynn Bylin, William John; m. Maria Camila Omegna Rocha, Apr. 12, 1986 (div. 1987); m. Maria Cristina Del Peloso, Sept. 16, 1989; stepchildren: Graziella, Camila. BA magna cum laude, Hamline U., 1950; MA, U. Minn., 1951; PhD, U. Wis., 1954. Assoc. prof., then prof. sociology Mich. State U., East Lansing, 1956-65; postdoctoral rschr. U. Wis., Madison, 1954-56, vis. prof., summer 1964, prof. sociology and rural sociology, 1965-94, emeritus prof., 1994—; affiliated faculty Indsl. Rels. Rsch. Inst., U. Wis., Madison, 1975-94; faculty in Latin Am. and Iberian studies U. Wis., Madison, 1965-94; affiliated faculty Inst. Environ. Studies, U. Wis., Madison, 1990-94. Fulbright prof. sociology Rural U. of Brazil, 1962; vis. prof. sociology Brigham Young U., Provo, Utah, 1973; Fulbright prof. sociology U. Sao Paulo, 1974; Fulbright travel grantee Univ. Sao Paulo, Brasilia, Pernambuco, Paraiba and Ceara, Brazil, 1979; vis. fellow Australian Nat. U., 1981; disting. vis. prof. rural sociology Ohio State U., 1982—83; Fulbright prof. sociology U. Sao Paulo, 1987—90; cons. UNESCO, 1989; cons. on Amazonian rsch. Govt. of Brazil, 1991—95; cons. Fed. U. Pernambuco, 1994; cons. for nat. social change to Pres. of Brazil, 1994—96; cons. on Amazonian rsch. Govt. of Brazil, 1997; cons. Faculty of Agrarian Sci. of Para, 1997—98, others; vis. prof. doctoral program in sociology and polit sci. Fed. U. Minas Gerais, Brazil, 1998; cons. Ind. U., Bangladesh, 1998; organizer symposia on Brazil; cons. on Amazonian rsch. Govt. of Brazil, 1999—2000; vis. prof. doctoral program in sociology and polit sci. Fed. U. Minas Gerais, Brazil, 2000—02; fellow Nat. Rsch. Coun. Brazil, 2000—02. Author: The Occupl. Aspiration Scale: Theory, Structure and Correlates, 1963, 71, The Socioeconomic Macroregions of Brazil--1970, 1983; co-editor (with R.M. Hauser et al) Social Structure and Behavior: Essays in Honor of William Hamilton Sewell, 1982; editor spl. issues Luso-Brazilian Rev.; author rsch. monographs and tech. articles; contbr. articles to profl. jour.; contbr. to theory of societal stratification, to processes of status allocation, to the demographic structure of societal inequality, to identifying the socioeconomic develop. regions of Brazil, and to the measurement of internat. devel. Mem. Mich. Com. on Mental Health Policies, 1961-62, Nat. Exec. Res., 1959-66; mem. sociology fellowship panel Coun. on Internat. Exch. Scholars, 1977-81, chmn., 1981. Decorated Grand Officer Order of Merit of Labor, Govt. of Brazil, 1981; univ. fellow U. Wis., 1953-1954; recipient John Luddy Phalen award in Latin Am. Studies U. Wis., 2000; Ann. Haller Disting. Lecture Series named in his honor U. Wis., 2000. Fellow AAAS, Am. Sociol. Assn.; mem. Internat. Rural Sociol. Assn., Internat. Sociol. Assn., Sociol. Rsch. Assn., NY Acad. Sci., Rural Sociol. Soc. (pres. 1970-71, rep. AAAS 1973-86, Disting. Rural Sociologist 1990), Univ. Club, Sigma Xi, Gamma Sigma Delta, Phi Beta Kappa. Home: 12928 Salt Cedar Dr Oro Valley AZ 85737 Office: U Wis 350 Agriculture Hall Madison WI 53706 Fax: 520-797-8444. Business E-Mail: haller@ssc.wisc.edu.

HALLER, CALVIN JOHN, banker; b. Buffalo, July 9, 1925; s. John Martin and Emelia (George) H.; m. Yvette Ann Hogrewe, June 12, 1948; children: Cary John, Darlene Ann Haller Kalfahs. BS in Bus. Adminstrn. with distinction, U. Buffalo, 1949. With Buffalo Savs. Bank (now Goldome), from 1949, now ret. pres. Western N.Y. Bd. dirs. Niagara Luth. Nursing Homes, Cerebral Palsy Assn., Buffalo, Children's Found., Erie County, Buffalo Fedn. of Neighborhood Ctrs.; bd. trustees Niagara Luth. Homes Found., Inc.; trustee, past pres. Met. YMCA Buffalo and Erie County; chmn. bd. trustees YMCA Greater Buffalo; trustee emeritus, past chmn. bd. Keuka Coll. Lt. (j.g.) USNR, 1943-46. Mem. N.Y. Soc. Security Analysts, Newcomen Soc. N.Am., Nat. Assn. Bus. Economists, U. Buffalo Alumni Assn., Beta Gamma Sigma. Clubs: Mason. Clubs (Buffalo), Country (Buffalo), Bond (Buffalo), Buffalo (Buffalo), Equality (Buffalo). Lutheran. Home: 235 Westfall Dr Tonawanda NY 14150-7136

HALLER, CHARLES EDWARD, engineering consultant; b. Fairfield, Conn., Sept. 5, 1924; s. William Charles and Gertrude Ida Mae (Belinski) H.; m. Eleanor Margret Hoffman, Oct. 11, 1950; children: Carolyn, Debra Lynn, Mark, Charles. Student, Yale U., 1943-44; BEE, Rensselaer Poly. Inst., 1947. Project engr. Western Union Telco., N.Y.C., 1948-56; assoc. lab. dir. ITT Labs., Nutley, N.J., 1956-62; v.p., dir. ops. ITT Worldcom, N.Y.C., 1962-67; pres. ITT Def. Communications, Nutley, N.J., 1967-74; mng. dir. I.O. ITT Telecom N.Am.,

Nutley, N.J., 1974-83; group gen. mgr., pres. ITT Asia Pacific, N.Y.C., 1983-87; cons. Internat. Enterprises, Kinnelon, N.J., 1987—. Author: Communications Switching Systems, 1964. With USN, 1943-46. Fellow IEEE (life). Republican. Avocations: politics, bowling, golf, reading, travel. Home and Office: 2 Summit Ter N Kinnelon NJ 07405-2436

HALLER, EUGENE ERNEST, materials scientist, educator; b. Basel, Switzerland, Jan. 5, 1943; s. Eugene and Maria Anne Haller; m. Marianne Elisabeth Schlittler, May 26, 1973; children: Nicole Marianne, Isabelle Cathrine. Diploma in Physics, U. Basel, 1967, PhD in Physics, 1970. Postdoctoral asst. Lawrence Berkeley (Calif.) Nat. Lab., 1971—73, from staff scientist to sr. staff scientist, 1973—80, faculty sr. scientist, 1980—; assoc. prof. U. Calif., Berkeley, 1980-82, prof. materials sci., 1982—. Co-chmn. Materials Rsch. Soc. Symposia, Boston, 1982, 89, Internat. Conf. on Shallow Levels in Semiconductors, Berkeley, 1984, 94; chair 20th Internat. Conf. on Defects in Semicondrs., 1999; adv. com. Paul Drude Inst., Berlin, 2001—; rev. com. instrument div. Brookhaven Nat. Lab., Upton, N.Y., 1987-93; mem. Japanese tech. panel on sensors NSF-Nat. Acad. Sci., Washington, 1988; vis. prof. Max-Planck-Inst. for Solid State Rsch., Stuttgart, 1986, Imperial Coll. Sci., Tech. and Medicine, London, 1991, German Aerospace Assn., Berlin, 1996. Mem. editl. bd. Jour. Phys. and Chem. Solids, 1993—, Material Sci. Founds., 1998—; contbr. articles to profl. jours. U.S. Sr. scientist award Alexander von Humboldt Soc., Germany, 1986, Max-Planck Rsch. award, 1994; rsch. fellow Miller Inst. Basic Rsch., Berkeley, 1990, 2001. Fellow Am. Phys. Soc. (James C. McGroddy prize in new materials 1999); mem. AAAS, Materials Rsch. Soc., Swiss Phys. Soc., Sigma Xi. Achievements include patents in surface passivation of semiconductors, synthesis of crystalline carbon nitride potentially a superhard material, and far infrared germanium laser. Office: U Calif Berkeley 328 Hearst Mining Meml Bldg Berkeley CA 94720-1760 Fax: 510-486-5530. E-mail: eehaller@lbl.gov.

HALLER, HAL MARTIN, JR., library director; b. Miami, Fla., Jan. 27, 1943; s. Hal Martin and Mary Ann Haller; m. Susanna Elizabeth Houseman, Aug. 6, 1965; children: Hal, Katie, Joy. AA, Miami-Dade C.C., 1963; BA, Fla. Bible Coll., 1966; BD, Luther Rice Sem., 1967; ThM, Dallas Theol. Sem., 1971; Master of Librarianship, Emory U., 1980; postgrad., Reformed Theol. Sem., 1989. Chmn. dept. biblical langs. Fla. Bible Coll., Hollywood, 1971-75, chmn. dept. systematic theology, 1975-79; asst. Pitts Theol. Libr. Emory U., Atlanta, 1980; min. theology Cmty. Bible Ch., Seminole, Fla., 1982-87; acad. dean Fla. Bible Coll., Kissimmee, 1987-96; min. on call First Bapt. Ch., Orlando, Fla., 1996-97; dir. libr. Southeastern Bible Coll., Birmingham, Ala., 1997-2000; assoc. prof., dir. libr. Luther Rice Sem., Lithonia, Ga., 2000—. Asst. libr. Clearwater (Fla.) Christian Coll., 1985-87; asst. prof. Grace Evang. Sch. Theology, Dallas, 1999—; accreditation team evaluator Accrediting Assn. B ible Colls., 2000, Transnat. Assn. Christian Colls. and Schs., 2001--. Mem. instrnl. materials coun. Sch. Bd. Pinellas County, St. Petersburg, Fla., 1985. Named Alumnus of Yr., Fla. Bible Coll., Kissimmee, 1994. Mem. Assn. Christian Librs., Evang. Theol. Soc., Grace Evang. Soc., Phi Theta Kappa. Republican. Baptist. Avocation: playing guitar. Home: 6526 Stewart Lake Ct Lithonia GA 30038- also: 7301 Aska Rd Blue Ridge GA 30513-5520 E-mail: hhaller@lrs.edu.

HALLER, IRMA TOGNOLA, secondary education educator; b. Bainbridge, N.Y., Aug. 25, 1937; d. Tullio and Margaretha (Fuchs) Tognola; m. Hans R. Haller, July 11, 1964. BA, SUNY, Albany, 1959; MEd in Teaching of Social Studies, Boston U., 1962. Tchr. social studies Chenango Valley Jr.-Sr. High Sch., Binghamton, N.Y., 1959-64; tchr. social studies and English Sidney (N.Y.) High Sch., 1964—, chair dept. social studies, 1986—. Mem. tchr. edn. adv. bd. SUNY, Oneonta, 1983-97, chair, 1985-88, 93-94; active local sch. improvement coms. Mem. steering com. Sidney Ctrl. Schs. Bus. Edn. Cmty. Partnership, 1992—. N.Y. State Electric and Gas Corp. grantee, 1985; Catskill Regional Tchr. Ctr. grantee, 1985, 87, 89. Mem. Nat. Coun. Social Studies, N.Y. State Social Studies Coun., N.Y. State United Tchrs., Catskill Area Social Studies Coun. (newsletter editor 1989-90), Sidney Tchrs. Assn., Phi Delta Kappa. Avocations: reading, walking. Office: Sidney H S 95 W Main St Sidney NY 13838-1601

HALLER, KAREN SUE, writer; b. St. Louis, Apr. 25, 1935; d. Frank Michael and Frieda Catherine (Hartmann) Kratoville; m. Albert John Haller; children: Christopher Karl, Debra Lynn. BS in Edn., U. Mo., 1956. Tchr. elem. sch. Ladue (Mo.) Sch. Dist., 1956-60; hearing testing tech. Spl. Sch. Dist. St. Louis County, 1975, 76. Author, photographer: Walking with Wildflowers, 1994; contbg. photographer: Wildflowers of Arkansas, 1984, Sensitive Plants of St. Francis National Forests, 1984, Wildflowers of North America, 1987. Asst. leader, leader brownie troop Girl Scouts Am., 1969, 70, jr. girl scouts troop, 1970, 71; advisor Co-ed explorer post Boy Scouts Am., 1976-80; bus tour guide, chmn. St. Louis Vis. Ctr., 1966-70; mem. mortar bd. U. Mo., Columbia, 1955; vol. interpreter Sophie M. Sachs Butterfly House, 1998-99, 2000-02; Earthwatch vol. Bees and Orchids of Brazil project, 1998, tchr., 2002-. Mem. Nat. Audubon Soc. (program chmn. 1987-90, awards chmn. 1990, Dorr scholar 1989), Mo. Native Plant Soc. (pres. 1991-93, Erna R. Eisendrath Edn. award 1994), Mo. Parks Assn. (bd. dirs. 2000, 01, 02—), Webster Groves Nature Study Soc. (pres. 1978-80, conservation chmn. 1983-86), Sierra Club, Naiads (v.p., pres., treas., sec.). Avocations: hiking, canoeing, camping, sewing, travel. Home and Office: 618 Spring Meadows Dr Ballwin MO 63011-3451 E-mail: karehaller@aol.com.

HALLER, ROBERT TERRENCE, marketing, advertising and public relations consultant; b. N.Y.C., May 20, 1930; s. Harry and Fay Haller; m. Charlotte Haller, Dec. 17, 1957; children: John D., William B. (dec.). BS, NYU, 1955; diploma, U.S. Army War Coll., 1980; MA, Cen. Mich. U., 1981. Account exec. BBDO, 1955-62; account supr. Interpub. Group: Pritchard Wood, 1962-65; advt. mgr. Savarin Coffee, 1965-66; account supr. McCaffrey & McCall, Inc., 1966-67; advt. mgr. Simplicity Pattern Co., 1967-69; pres. Fashion Scene, Inc., 1969-79; v.p., mgmt. supr. Ogilvy & Mather, Inc., N.Y.C., 1970-82; pres., creative dir. CFI Advt. & Pub. Rels., N.Y.C. and Lake Ariel, Pa., 1982-88; asst. prof., program dir. advt. and pub. rels. Marywood U., Scranton, Pa., 1988-95; chmn. Eagle Elite, Mktg., Advt. and Pub. Rels., Hamlin, Pa., 1995-97; with Leister & Sons Pub. Co., 1996—. Acct. exec. DuPont, Air France, Eagle Pencil, 1955—62; acct. supr. Smith Bros., Beck Beer, Caryl Richards, Faberge, 1962—65, Quaker Oats and Quaker Life cereal, 1966—67; mgmt. supr. Sears, Roebuck & Co., Panasonic, Matsushita Electric, Am. Express, Longines, Owens Corning Fiberglas, 1970—82; with Leister & Sons Pub. Co., 1996—. Author: Creative Firepower, 1987, Stinger Missile Conspiracy, 2000, The Coiled Serpent, 2001, Manchukuo Gold, 2002; contbg. newswriter Scranton Times, Wayne, Ind., contbg. author Broadcasting mag., Media Rev., Am. Mktg. Assn., North County News. Disaster assistance team vol. ARC, 2001—; vol. Am. Red Cross, Scranton, Pa., 2001—. With U.S. Army, col. inf. spl. ops. USAR, ret. Decorated Legion of Merit. Mem. Mystery Writers Am., Nat. Writers Assn., Am. Advt. Fedn., Pub. Rels. Soc. Am., Ad Club N.E. Pa., Civil Affairs Assn., 77th Army Res. Commd. Assn., NYU Vets. Alumni Assn. (pres. 1957-59), NE Pa. Advt. Club (bd. dirs. 1993-95), Mil. Officers of Am. Assn., NYU Club (bd. govs.), Alpha Delta Sigma (Nat. Adv. honor). Republican. Avocations: writer, photographer, travel. E-mail: eagleeliteone@aol.com.

HALLER, WILLIAM PAUL, analytical chemist, robotics and automation specialist; b. Orange, N.J., Nov. 23, 1957; s. William Charles and Patricia Marie (Scavone) Haller; children: Robert William, Alicia Ann. BS in Biochemistry, Fairleigh Dickinson U., 1980. Rsch. chemist Internat. Paint Co., Union, N.J., 1980-83; analytical quality assurance chemist Ortho-McNeil Pharm. Corp., Raritan, N.J., 1983-2000, quality assurance robotics specialist, 1985-2000; application cons. VelQuest Corp., Hopkinton, Mass., 2000—. Steering com. Johnson & Johnson Tech. Forum Group, 1995—2000. Co-author: Advances in Laboratory Automation-Robotics, 1986, 1990. Recipient Achievement award, Johnson & Johnson, 1991, Pioneer in Lab. Robotics award, 1995. Mem.: AAAS, Lab. Robotics Interest Group (steering com. 2002—, exec. com. 1992—2002), Am. Chem. Soc. Democrat. Achievements include development of protocols and criteria for the validation of robotic systems in the analytical lab; automate analytical methods to robotic systems; customized apparatus to help in automating analytical methods to robotic systems; standardized platforms and criteria for robotic systems to be used within the J&J family of companies worldwide. Office: VelQuest Corp 35 South St Hopkinton MA 01748 E-mail: haller1123@earthlink.net.

HALLERMAN, ERIC MICHAEL, geneticist, educator; b. N.Y.C., Apr. 17, 1955; m. Ester Foigel; children: Tamar, Simon. BS, U. Ill., 1977, MS, 1980; PhD, Auburn (Ala.) U., 1984. Postdoctoral fellow Hebrew U. of Jerusalem, 1984-87; rsch. assoc. U. Minn., St. Paul, 1987-89; asst. prof. Va. Poly. Inst. & State U., Blacksburg, 1989-95, assoc. prof., 1995—2003, prof., 2003—. Mem. adj. faculty U. Minn., 1988; mem. com. on agrl. biotech., health and the environ. NRC. Contbr. articles to profl. jours.; assoc. editor Aquaculture, Revs. in Fisheries Sci., N.Am. Jour. Aquaculture, Internat. Jour. Recirculating Aquaculture. Grantee USDA; Fulbright scholar 1998-99. Mem. Am. Fisheries Soc. (pres. genetics sect. 1992-93, faculty advisor Va. Tech. chpt. 1991-92, 2002-03, pres. introduced fishes sect. 1996-97). Office: Va Poly Inst and State U 150 Cheatham Hall Blacksburg VA 24061 E-mail: ehallerm@vt.edu.

HALLETT, CHARLES ARTHUR, JR., English and humanities educator; b. New Haven, July 19, 1935; s. Charles Arthur and Bridie D. (McIntyre) H.; m. Elaine Stewartson, Nov. 7, 1958. BA, The New Sch., 1961; MA, Columbia U., 1963; DFA, Yale U., 1967. Mem. faculty Fordham U., Bronx, N.Y., 1967—, assoc. prof. English, 1971-81, prof., 1981—. Asst. project dir. NEH Shakespeare Summerfest, N.Y.C., 1981; vis. prof. U. Warwick, Eng., 1978, Loyola U., New Orleans, 1994, Dartmouth Coll., 2001-03. Author: Middleton's Cynics, 1975, The Revenger's Madness, 1981, Analyzing Shakespeare's Action, 1991; (play) Aaron Burr, also articles; contbr. to Ency. Americana. Fellow Lawrence Langner Theatre Guild Found., 1965-66; Am. Coun. Learned Socs. grantee, 1981. Home: 116 E 91st St Apt 5 New York NY 10128-1667 Office: English Dept Fordham U Bronx NY 10458

HALLETT, E. BRUCE, III, publishing executive; b. Rochester, NY, Sept. 22, 1949; s. Bruce and Constance (Carpenter) Hallett; m. Deborah Ann Donahue, May 8, 1982; children: Cleary Carpenter, E. Bruce IV, Katherine Thrall, Thomas Henry Walker, Emma Brewster. BA, Princeton U., 1971; MBA, Columbia U., 1980. Writer, editor NY Daily News, NYC, 1971—79; fin. analyst Time Inc., NYC, 1980—81, asst. bus. mgr. Sports Illustrated, 1981—82, bus. mgr. Sports Illustrated, 1982—84, asst. to pub. Sports Illustrated, 1985—86, group dir. devel., 1986, internat. gen. mgr. TIME Mag., 1987—88, mng. dir. Time Inc. mags. Australia, 1988—95, pres. TIME Mag., 1995—2001; pres. Sports Illustrated Mag., 2002—. Mem.: Ekwanok Golf Club, Manchester, VT, Ballyliffin Golf Club (County Donegal, Ireland), Baltusrol Golf Club, Elanora Country Club (Narabeen, NSW, Australia). Office: Sports Illustrated Mag 135 W 50th St New York NY 10020-1393

HALLETT, JUDITH PELLER, classical studies educator; b. Chgo., Apr. 4, 1944; d. Leonard and Celia (Stern) Peller; m. Mark Hallett, June 26, 1966; children: Nicholas, Victoria. BA, Wellesley (Mass.) Coll., 1966; MA, Harvard U., Cambridge, Mass., 1967, PhD, 1971. Lectr. classics Clark U., Worcester, Mass., 1972-74; asst. prof. classical studies Boston U., 1974-82; Blegen vis. rsch. scholar Vassar Coll., Poughkeepsie, N.Y., 1980; Mellon vis. asst. prof. Brandeis U., Waltham, Mass., 1982-83; assoc. prof. classics U. Md., College Park, Md., 1983-92, prof. classics, 1993—, acting equity adminstr. Coll. Arts & Humanities, 1988-89, chair classics, 1996—. Asst. to assoc. editor The Classical World, 1980—; founder, mem. steerng com. Women's Classical Caucus, 1972—. Author: Fathers and Daughters in Roman Society, 1984; co-editor: The Personal Voice in Classical Scholarship and Roman Sexualities, 1997; contbr. more than 50 articles to scholarly jours. Mem. Md. Humanities Coun., 2001—; bd. trustees Balt. Hebrew U., 2002—. Recipient various fellowships and grants NEH. Mem. AAUP (pres. chpt. 1994—), Am. Philological Assn. (dir. 1997-99), Assn. Ancient Historians, Classical Assn. Atlantic States (2d v.p. 1997-98, pres. 1999-2000), Md. Humanities Coun., Phi Beta Kappa (pres. U. Md. College Park chpt. 1996-98). Democrat. Jewish. Home: 5147 Westbard Ave Bethesda MD 20816-1413 Office: Dept Classics U Md College Park MD 20742-0001

HALLETT, MARK, physician, neurologist, health researcher; b. Phila., Oct. 22, 1943; s. Joseph Woodrow and Estelle (Barg) H.; m. Judith E. Peller, June 26, 1966; children: Nicholas L., Victoria C. BA magna cum laude, Harvard U., 1965, MD cum laude, 1969. Diplomate Am. Bd. Psychiatry and Neurology. Resident in neurology Mass. Gen. Hosp., Boston, 1972-75; Moseley fellow Harvard U., London, 1975-76, lectr., assoc. prof. neurology Boston, 1976-84; head clin. neurophy. lab. Brigham and Women's Hosp., Boston, 1976-84; clin. dir. Nat. Inst. Neurol. Disorders and Stroke NIH, Bethesda, Md., 1984-2000, chief human motor control sect. NINDS, 1984—. Author: (with others) Entrapment Neuropathies, 1990, 3rd edit., 1998; editor: (with M.F. Brin and J. Jankovic) Scientific and Therapeutic Aspects of Botulinum Toxin, 2002; editor-in-chief: Clinical Neurophysiology, 2000—; contbr. numerous articles to profl. jours. Bd. dirs. Easter Seals Rsch. Found., Chgo., 1985-87; mem. med. adv. bd. Nat. Parkinson Found., Miami, 1985—, Dystonia Med. Rsch. Found., Chgo., 1989-93, 2000-03, Benign Essential Blepharospasm Rsch. Found., Beaumont, 1990—, Myoclonus Rsch. Found., Fort Lee, N.J., 1989—. Mem. Am. Assn. Electrodiagnostic Medicine (pres. 1991-92), v.p. Am. Acad. Neurology, 2001-2005. Am. Neurol. Assn., Am. Clin. Neurophysiology Soc., Soc. for Neurosci., Movement Disorder Soc. (pres. 1999-00), Phi Beta Kappa, Alpha Omega Alpha. Democrat. Jewish. Home: 5147 Westbard Ave Bethesda MD 20816-1413 Office: NINDS NIH Msc 1428 Bldg 10 Rm 5n226 10 Center Dr Bethesda MD 20892-1428 E-mail: hallettm@ninds.nih.gov.

HALLETT, WILLIAM JARED, retired nuclear engineer; b. Rock Springs, Wyo., Apr. 12, 1923; s. William Jared and Florence Myrtle (Miller) H.; m. Marjorie Louise Taylor, Dec. 25, 1942; children— Katherine O. Hallett Rembert (dec.), Carolyn R. Hallett Kortangen, Helen L. Hallett Warren, David William. BS in Chem. Engring., U. Colo., 1944; postgrad., UCLA, 1957-58, 62-70, No. Ill. U., 1973. Registered profl. nuclear engr., Calif. Engr. Tenn. Eastman Corp., Oak Ridge, 1944-47; sect. head Fairchild E & A Corp., Oak Ridge, 1947-50; project mgr. AI Div. Rockwell Internat., Canoga Park, Calif., 1950-66; div. dir., mgr. Argonne Nat. Lab., Ill., 1968-86; ret., 1986. Contbg. author: Nuclear Reactor Engineering, 1963; Nuclear Power and Its Environmental Effects, 1980 Bd. dirs. Simi Valley Unified Sch. Dist., Calif., 1965-68 Republican. Methodist. Avocations: photography, art collecting, travel.

HALLEY, DIANE ESTHER, artist; b. Jasper, Ind., May 14, 1939; d. John and Esther Margaret (Kruse) Darden; m. Norman B. Halley, May 21, 1966; 1 child, William Tull. BS in Elem. Edn., Ind. State U., 1961. Tchr. 4th grade, New Albany, Ind., 1961, Seymour, Ind., 1962-64, Westminster, Colo., 1964-68; portrait artist Arvada, Colo., 1979—. Juror fall exhbn. Colo. Watercolor Soc., 2002. Paintings included in books, Colo., 1990—, Denver Art Museum, Best of Watercolor-Painting Textures, 1997, Splash Six-The Magic of Texture, 2000; one-woman shows include Denver Nat. Bank, 1983, Foothills Art Ctr., Golden, Colo., 1984, Nat. Ctr. Atmospheric Rsch., Boulder, Colo., 1991, Colo. Christian U., 2000, exhibitions include Challenge of Champions, Watercolor Art Soc. Houston, 2003, one-woman shows include Lincoln Ctr., Ft. Collins, Colo., 2003. Pres. Clear Creek Valley Med. Aux., Lakewood, Colo., 1973—74, 1991—92. Recipient Founder's award, Colo. Watercolor Soc., 1992, Pres.'s award, 1994, Grumbacher award, Pikes Peak Watercolor Soc., 1995, Cash award, Lakewood Arts Coun., 2001, award of distinction, Mo. Nat. Watercolor Exhbn., 2003, Westminster Cmty. Artist Series award, 2003. Mem.: Kans. Watercolor Soc. (Am. artist cash award 1999), Rocky Mountain Nat. Watermedia Soc., Catherine Lorillard Wolf Art Club (Adriana Zahn award 1985, Cynthia Goodgal award 1986), Nat. Watercolor Soc. (Del Mar Coll. award 1982), Nat. Assn. Women Artists (Cecil Shapiro Meml. award 1998). Avocations: Bible study, bridge, gardening. Home: 6631 Osceola Ct Arvada CO 80003-6426

HALLEY, JAMES WOODS, physics educator; b. Chgo., Nov. 16, 1938; m. Merile Hobbs (dec. 2001); 2 children. BS, MIT, 1961; PhD, U. Calif., Berkeley, 1965. NSF predoctoral fellow U. Calif., Berkeley, 1963-65; NSF postdoctoral fellow Faculte des Scis., Orsay, France, 1965-66; asst. prof. U. Calif., Berkeley, 1966-68; assoc. prof. U. Minn., Mpls., 1968-77, prof. physics, 1977—, fellow Supercomputer Inst., 1989—, grad. faculty materials sci., 1989—. Vis. prof. Oxford U., 1973, Harwell AERE, 1973, U. Oreg., 1975, Yale U., 1976, Brookhaven N.L., 1976, 79, Harvard U., 1979, Mich. State U., 1980, Argonne, 1981—, Inst. for Theoretical Physics, Santa Barbara, 1983, 97, 98, chemistry dept. U. Calif., Santa Barbara, 1984, U. Calif., Berkeley, 1993; IBM Almaden Rsch. Ctr., 1987, Australian Nat. U., 1988; cons. 3M, 1985-89, UNESCO, 1986, GM Corp., 1989-90, Ednl. Testing Svc., 1989; mem. GRE bd. examiners Ednl. Testing Svc., 1991-96; physics bd. dirs. U.S. Com. for Sci. Coop. with Vietnam, 1985—. Author: Physics of Human Motion, 1981; editor 7 books; contbr. over 170 articles to profl. jours. Recipient George Taylor Tchg. award, 1979, McMillan professorship, 1979; Bush fellow, 1983-84; grantee NSF, 1972-79, 95—, Rsch. Corp., 1970-72, Corrosion Ctr., 1980-92, Ednl. Devel. Program, 1973, 79, 3M, 1982, IBM Advanced Edn. Project, 1985, Dept. Edn., 1986, IBM, 1988-90, Electric Power Rsch. Inst., 1988-90, Dept. Energy, 1990—, Sumitomo Metal Industries, 1992-93, NASA, 1992-95. Fellow Am. Phys. Soc.; mem. AAAS, Am. Chem. Soc., Materials Rsch. Soc. Achievements include research in theory of disorder in condensed matter, statistics and dynamics of polymers, physics of the fluid-solid interface, high temperature superconductivity, condensate fraction in bose superfluids. Office: Univ Minn Sch Physics and Astronomy Minneapolis MN 55455 E-mail: woods@woods1.spa.umn.edu.

HALLEY, SAMUEL HAMPTON, III, architect, architectural firm executive; b. Lexington, Ky., Feb. 8, 1941; s. Samuel Hampton and Mary Ford (Offutt) Halley; m. Suzanne Shelby Fish, Aug. 4, 1962; children: Samuel Hampton IV, Benjamin Helm, Elizabeth Simpson. BArch, U. Ky., 1966. Registered arch., Ky., Fla., Ohio, Ill., Ind., N.C., W.Va. Intern arch. Chrisman Miller & Wallace, Lexington, 1964-70; arch. McLoney & Tune, Lexington, 1970-71, Scruggs & Hammond, Lexington, 1974-75; ptnr. Hill-Halley Archs., Danville, Ky., 1971-74; pres. Omni Archs., Lexington, 1975—. Mem. adv. com. Lexington CC, 1982—88; chair adv. com. dept. landscape arch. U. Ky., Lexington, 1987—92, mem., 1992—. Author: (software) Project Management 1, 1981, Project Management 2, 1982. Pres. Gardenside Neighborhood Assn., Lexington, 1981—97, 2003; mem. Lexington Fayette Urban County Govt. City Coun., 1993; bd. dirs. Emerson Ctr., Lexington, 1986—, chmn., 2003. Recipient Disting. Svc. award, U. Ky., 1982. Mem.: AIA (E. Ky. chpt. pres. 1976, Student Medal award 1966), Ky. Soc. Archs. (pres. 1981, Disting. Svc. award 1986, Julian Oberwarth Svc. award 1992), C. of C. (CEO Roundtable 1990—94). Avocation: boating. Office: Omni Architects 212 N Upper St Ste 200 Lexington KY 40507-1001

HALLFORS, DENISE DION, research scientist, researcher; b. Fitchburg, Mass., Dec. 7, 1952; d. Alphonse Dion and Irene Judge; m. Eric John Hallfors, May 24, 1975; 1 child, Nicholas George. PhD, Brandeis U., 1992. Registered Nurse, NC, 2003. Sr. rsch. scientist Pacific Inst. for Rsch. and Evaluation, Chapel Hill, NC, 2002—; rsch. assoc. prof. U. of NC, Chapel Hill, NC, 1998—2002. Author: (jour. article) Will the Principles of Effectiveness Improve Prevention Practice? Early Findings from a Diffusion Study. (11th Ann. Douglas S. Leathar award, 2003). Vol. Orange United Meth. Ch., Chapel Hill, NC, 2002—03. Fellow Tng. Grant Fellowship, NIMH, 1998—2001; grantee FIRST award, Nat. Inst. on Drug Abuse, 1996, R01, 2001—02, Rsch. Grant, Robert Wood Johnson Found., 1999—2002. Mem.: Soc. for Prevention Rsch. (bd. of directors, treas. 1999—2003). Methodist. Achievements include research in Evaluation Of Drug Prevention Programs. Home: 8710 Seawell Schl Rd Chapel Hill NC 27516 Office: Pacific Inst for Rsch and Eval 1229 E Franklin St 2nd Fl Chapel Hill NC 27514 Office Fax: 919-968-1498. E-mail: hallfors@pire.org.

HALLGREN, RICHARD EDWIN, meteorologist; b. Kersey, Pa., Mar. 15, 1932; s. Edwin Leonard and Edith Marie Hallgren; m. Maxine Hope Anderson, Apr. 17, 1954; children: Scott, Douglas, Lynette. BS, Pa. State U., 1953, PhD, 1960; DSc (hon.), SUNY, 1989. Sys. engr. IBM Corp., 1960-64; sci. adv. to asst. sec. of commerce, 1964-66; dir. world weather sys. ESSA, Rockville, Md., 1966-69, asst. adminstrn., 1969-70; asst. adminstr. NOAA, Rockville, 1970-71, assoc. adminstr. environ. monitoring and prediction, 1971-73, asst. adminstr. for ocean and atmospheric scis., 1977-79; dep. dir. Nat. Weather Service, Silver Spring, Md., 1973-77, dir., 1979-88; exec. dir. Am. Meteorol. Soc., 1988-99, exec. dir. emeritus, 1999—. Permanent U.S. rep. World Meteorol. Orgn., 1980—88. Contbr. With USAF, 1954—56. Named Meritorious Sr. Exec., 1980, Disting. Sr. Exec., 1986; recipient Arthur S. Flemming award, U.S. C. of C., 1968, Gold medal, Dept. Commerce, 1969, Internat. Meteorol. Orgn. prize, Wold Meteorol. Orgn., 1990, Spl. Achievement award, NOAA, 2001, Charles L. Hosler medal, 2002; Alumni fellow, Pa. State U. Fellow: AAAS, Am. Meteorol. Soc. (pres., C.F. Brooks award, Cleveland Abbe award 2003); mem.: Am. Geogphys. Union, Oceanographic Soc., Sigma Xi. Lutheran. Home: 11428 Cedar Ridge Dr Potomac MD 20854-3761 Office: Am Meteorol Svc 1120 G St NW Ste 800 Washington DC 20005-6115 E-mail: hallgren@dc.ametsoc.org.

HALLIBURTON, JOHN ROBERT, lawyer; b. Shreveport, LA, July 31, 1934; s. Ralph Eloe and Mary Katherine (Smith) H.; m. Julia Ella Bateman, Dec. 17, 1955; children: Cherie Ann, John Robert II, RHonda Marie. BS in Math., Centenary Coll., LA, 1955; LLB/JD, So. Meth. U., 1964; postgrad., Grad. Sch. Am. and Fgn. Law, 1968-70; LLM in Internat. Law, George Washington U., 1974. Bar: Tex. 1964, D.C. 1972, U.S. Supreme Ct. 1967, U.S. Ct. Claims 1968, U.S. Ct. Appeals (former 5th cir.) 1968, U.S. Dist. Ct. (no. dist.) Tex. 1969, U.S. Dist. Ct. of D.C. 1970, D.C. Ct. Appeals 1973, U.S. Ct. Appeals (D.C. cir.) 1976, U.S. Dist. Ct. (we dist.) La. 1981, U.S. Ct. Appeals (5th and 11th cirs.) 1981, U.S. Ct. Claims 1982, U.S. Ct. Appeals (fed. cir.) 1987, U.S. Ct. Mil. Appeals, 1987, U.S. Ct. Vet. Appeals, 1993. Field support engr. Chrysler Corp., Huntsville, Ala., 1959—60; with Rockwell Internat. Corp. (merged into Rockwell Internat. Corp/Collins Radio Co. 1973), 1960—80; dir. govt. rels. and contract policy Collins Radio Co., Washington, 1969—74; gen. mgr. Collins Radio Limitada, Brazil; v.p. Collins Radio Internat., Inc., Collins Sys. Internat., Inc., 1974—75; mgr. contracts and dealer adminstrn., elecs. internat. ops. Rockwell Internat. Corp., Dallas, 1975—76, dir. govt. rels. elec. sys. group, 1976—80; asst. U.S. atty. for We. Dist. La. U.S. Dept. Justice, Shreveport, La., 1980—; instr. Atty. Gen.'s Adv. Inst., 1988—97, The Nat. Adv. Ctr., 1999—, U. Phoenix, Dallas, 2002—; chair Law Dallas/Ft. Worth Area, 2003—. Telecomm. tech. adv. com. Dept. Commerce, Wash., 1973-74. Author profl. reports. Composer, lyricist Absence, 1953. Mem. PAC good govt. com. Rockwell Internat. Corp., Dallas, 1978-80. 1st lt. U.S. Army, 1955-59. Fellow The State Tex. Bar Coll.; mem. State Bar Tex. (sec.-treas. internat. law sect. 1979-80, vice-chmn. 1980-81, prog. chmn. 1979-81), Rockwall County Bar Assn. (CLE lectr. 1987-97), State Bar of Tex. Pro Bono Coll., D.C. Bar Assn. (internat. law and transaction divsn. com. on transfer of tech. 1977-81, govt. contracts and litigation divsn. 1977-81), Nat. Aviation Club (Wash.), Chandlers Landing Yacht Club (Rockwall, Tex.), The Army and Navy Club (Wash.), K.C., Canyon Creek Country Club (Richardson, Tex.), Omicron Delta Kappa, Alpha Sigma Pi, Kappa Alpha (sec. 1954-55), Phi Delta Phi. Roman Catholic. Home: 7 Northcrest Cir PO Box 278 Rockwall TX 75087-0278 Office: US Ct House 300 Fannin St Ste 3201 Shreveport LA 71101-3068 also: US Ct Phoenix Churchill Tower 12400 Coit Rd Ste 200 Dallas TX 75251 also: Jones and Co 325 Massasoit Ave East Providence RI 02914 E-mail: jackh731@aol.com.

HALLIBURTON, LLOYD, Romance philology educator; b. Shreveport, La., July 31, 1934; s. Ralph Eloe and Mary Katherine (Smith) H.; m. Donna Lee Cavanagh, May 27, 1965 (div. Sept. 1976); children: Richard Lloyd, William Cavanagh de Tuite, Cristopher Lee, Manon Lee; m. María F. Sánchez, Jan. 6, 1993; children: Carlos David, Lawden Nerea. AB, Centenary Coll., 1955; MA, La. State U., 1961, PhD, 1970; C en F y L, U. de Valladolid, Spain, 1965; LittD (hon.), London Inst. for Applied Rsch., 1993. Instr. Spanish U. Notre Dame, Ind., 1962-63; asst. prof. Spanish Centenary Coll., Shreveport, 1963-66, Va. Mil. Inst., Lexington, 1966-69, assoc. prof. Spanish, 1970-80, asst. commandant, 1971-74; asst. prof. fgn. langs. La. Tech. U., Ruston, 1981-84, assoc. prof., 1984-91, prof., 1991—, dir. grad. program in romance langs., 1992-95. Vis. lectr. Romance langs. U. N.C., 1970; adj. prof. Spanish U. Va., Charlottesville, 1978—80; vis. prof. English Ga. Mil. Coll., Barksdale AFB, La., 1980—81, Grambling State U., 1986, 2001—03, U. Autonoma de Coahuila, Centro de Idiomas, Mexico, 2002; cons. USAF, U.S. Dept. Justice, Mosher Steel Co., Studebaker Internat., Irrigation Internat. de Mex., others; rsch. bd. advisors Am. Biog. Inst. Author: Colombia en la Poesía, 1967, Hendaye, 1990, Saddle Soldiers: General William Stokes and the 4th South Carolina Cavalry, 1993, The Cemaco Seed, 1996, García Lorca and Other Things Spanish: Critical Essays, 2002, John William Corrington: Reflections, 2003; contbr. articles to profl. jours. Mem. State Dem. Com., Lincoln Parish, La., 1984-94. Capt. U.S. Army, 1955-57. NDEA fellow, 1959-62; Fulbright fellow, 1965; NEH fellow, 1971; postdoctoral fellow La. State U., 1992; grantee VMI Found., La. Tech. U., 1967-92, La Tech summer rsch. grantee, Spain, 1998, 2001. Mem. Coun. for Devel. of Spanish in La., Phi Kappa Phi, Phi Sigma Iota, Sigma Tau Delta, Sigma Delta Pi, Alpha Chi, Omicron Delta Kappa. Roman Catholic. Avocations: gardening, hunting, deep-sea fishing. Office: Dept Fgn Langs La Tech U Ruston LA 71272-0001

HALLIDAY, IAN, astronomer; b. Lloydminster, Sask., Can., Nov. 10, 1928; s. Clarence Peter and Edith Victoria (Phillips) H.; m. Norma Lillian Mobley, July 7, 1951; children— John Douglas, Janet Elizabeth. BA, U. Toronto, 1949, MA, 1950, PhD, 1954. Sr. sci. officer Dominion Obs., Dept. Energy, Mines and Resources, Ottawa, 1952-70; sr. research officer Herzberg Inst. Astrophysics, Nat. Research Council Can., Ottawa, 1970-90, guest worker, 1990-96. Author research papers in field; editor: Jour. Royal Astron. Soc. Can, 1970-75; co-editor: Solid Particles in the Solar System, 1980. Recipient Queen's Silver Jubilee medal, 1977, Polish Medal of Merit, 1976 Fellow Royal Soc. Can.; mem. Internat. Astron. Union (pres. commn. 22 1976-79), Royal Astron. Soc. Can. (pres. 1980-82, hon. pres. 1989-93), Can. Astron. Soc., Am. Astron. Soc., Meteoritical Soc., Planetary Soc., Internat. Halley Watch (chmn. steering group 1985-90). Home: 825 Killeen Ave Ottawa ON Canada K2A 2X8 E-mail: ihalliday@idirect.com.

HALLIDAY, JOHN MEECH, investment company executive; b. St. Louis, Oct. 16, 1936; s. William Norman and Vivian Viola (Meech) H.; m. Martha Layne Griggs, June 30, 1962; children: Richard M., Elizabeth Halliday Traut. BS, U.S. Naval Acad., 1958; MBA, Harvard U., 1964. Dir. budgeting and planning Automatic Tape Control, Bloomington, Ill., 1964-66; dir. planning Ralston-Purina, St. Louis, 1966-67, v.p. subsidiary, 1967-68, dir. internat. banking, 1967-68; v.p. Servicetime Corp., St. Louis, 1968-70; assoc. R.W. Halliday Assocs., Boise, Idaho, 1970-87. V.p. Sawtooth Comm. Corp., Boise, 1970-73, Comdr. Corp., 1979-81; pres., CEO, bd. dirs. ML, Ltd., San Francisco, 1979—, H.W.L. Inc., San Francisco, 1985-93; pres. Halliday Labs., Inc., 1980-91; exec. v.p., bd. dirs. Franchise Fin. Corp. Am., Phoenix, 1980-85; bd. dirs., v.p. Harvard Bus. Sch. Assn. No. Calif., 1980-87; pres., CEO, bd. dirs. Cycletrol Diversified Industries, Inc., 1992—; guest lectr. U. Calif. Berkeley, 1991-2000, Calif. Bus.-Higher Edn. Forum, 1995-98; sponsor Halliday lectr. in astronomy, U. Calif. Santa Cruz, 2000—. Pres. Big Bros. San Francisco, 1978-81; trustee, pres. U. Calif.-Santa Cruz Found., 1988—, mem. Pres.Circle, U.S. Naval Acad., Annapolis, 1997—; mem. ad hoc com. on corrections Calif. State Senate, 1995-96; fellow bd. visitors and fellows viticulture and enology U. Calif., Davis, 1999—; sponsor undergrad. rsch. symposium U. Calif. Santa Cruz, 2002—; bd. dirs., charter dir. circle Seymour Marine Discovery Ctr., 2002—. Mem. Restaurant Assn. (v.p. 1969-70), Olympic Club (San Francisco), Scott Valley Tennis Club (Mill Valley, Calif.). Republican. Baptist. Home: 351 Corte Madera Ave Mill Valley CA 94941-1013 Office: 55 New Montgomery St Ste 317 San Francisco CA 94105-3426 E-mail: jhalli8835@aol.com.

HALLIDAY, JOSEPH WILLIAM, lawyer; b. N.Y.C., Aug. 9, 1938; s. Joseph John and Marie (Marro) H.; m. Vivian Ross Talbird, July 10, 1960; children: Katherine Ann Langan, Mary Allison Shaw. AB, Fordham U., 1960, LLB, 1963. Bar: N.Y. 1964, D.C. 1965. Assoc. White & Case, N.Y.C., 1965-72, ptnr., 1972-85, Skadden Arps Slate Meagher & Flom, LLP, N.Y.C., 1985—. Mem. tribar legal opinion com., lectr. Ctr. for Internat. Banking Studies, U. Va., Banking Law Inst., Inst. Internat. Rsch., Law and Bus., Euromoney, Practicing Law Inst. Editor-in-chief Fordham Law Rev., 1962-63. Served to 1st lt. U.S. Army, 1963-65. Mem. ABA, N.Y. State Bar Assn., Assn. of Bar of City of N.Y., N.Y. County Lawyers Assn., Larchmont Yacht Club (commodore 1985-86). Republican. Roman Catholic. Avocations: yachting, skiing, golf. Office: Skadden Arps Slate Meagher & Flom LLP 4 Times Sq Fl 24 New York NY 10036-6595 E-mail: jhallida@skadden.com.

HALLIDAY, STEPHEN MILLS, manufacturing company executive; b. Columbus, Ohio, Mar. 6, 1927; s. Ernest Raymond and Violet (Mills) H.; m. Elizabeth Reynolds, May 21, 1955; children: Elizabeth R., Tracy Halliday Williams, Stephanie Halliday Giroux. BA, Princeton U., 1950. Sales rep. Federal Glass Mfg. Co., Columbus, Ohio, 1950-57, Renite Co., Columbus, 1957-59, field engr., 1959-68, v.p. sales and engring., 1968-72, pres., 1972-87, pres., chmn. bd., 1987—. Past trustee, past mem. bldg. com. Broad Street Presbyn. Ch.; past trustee, past auction chmn. Columbus Ctr. Sci. and Industry; past trustee Columbus Sch. for Girls. Mem. Columbus C. of C., Columbus Club, Columbus Country Club, Rocky Fork Hunt and Country Club (past dir.), Princeton Club N.Y. Republican. Presbyterian. Office: 2500 E 5th Ave Columbus OH 43219-2700 E-mail: contact@renite.com.

HALLIDAY, WILLIAM JAMES, JR., lawyer; b. Detroit, Nov. 16, 1921; s. William James and Katherine Elizabeth (Krantz) H.; A.B. (scholar), U. Mich., 1943, J.D., 1948; m. Lois Jeanne Streelman, Sept. 6, 1947; children: Carol Lynn Halliday Murphy, Richard Andrew, Marcia Katherine, James Anthony. Admitted to Mich. bar, 1948; assoc. Schmidt, Smith & Howlett and successors, Grand Rapids, Mich., 1952-56, ptnr., 1956-66, counsel Varnum, Riddering, Schmidt & Howlett, 1984—; sec. Amway Corp. Ada, Mich., 1964-84, gen. counsel, 1966-71, v.p., 1970-79, exec. v.p., 1979-84, also dir.; asst. pros. atty., Kent County, Mich., 1949-51; twp. atty., Wyoming Twp., Mich., 1955-57; city atty., Wyoming, Mich., 1961-66. Bd. dirs. Met. YMCA of Grand Rapids. Served with M.I., U.S. Army, 1943-46, with JAGC, 1951-52. Decorated Bronze Star; recipient William Jennings Bryan award U. Mich., 1943. Mem. ABA, Mich. Bar Assn. (chmn. client protection fund com.), Grand Rapids Bar Assn., Phi Beta Kappa, Phi Kappa Phi, Delta Sigma Rho, Phi Eta Sigma. Republican. Presbyterian. Club: Kiwanis. Home: 3020 Uplands Dr SE Grand Rapids MI 49506-1933 Office: Varnum Riddering Schmidt & Howlett PO Box 352 Grand Rapids MI 49501-0352

HALLIDAY, WILLIAM ROSS, retired physician, speleologist, writer; b. Atlanta, May 9, 1926; s. William Ross and Jane (Wakefield) H.; m. Eleanore Hartvedt, July 2, 1951 (dec. 1983); children: Marcia Lynn, Patricia Anne, William Ross III; m. Louise Baird Kinnard, May 7, 1988. BA, Swarthmore Coll., 1946; MD, George Washington U., 1948. Diplomate Am. Bd. Vocat. Experts. Intern Huntington Meml. Hosp., Pasadena, Calif., 1948-49; resident King County Hosp., Seattle, Denver Children's Hosp., L.D.S. Hosp., Salt Lake City, 1950-57; pvt. practice Seattle, 1957-65; with Wash. State Dept. Labor and Industries, Olympia, 1965-76; med. dir. Wash. State Div. Vocat. Rehab., 1976-82; staff physican N.W. Occupational Health Ctr., Seattle, 1983-84; med. dir. N.W. Vocat. Rehab. Group, Seattle, 1984, Comprehensive Med. Rehab. Ctr., Brentwood, Tenn., 1984-87. Dep. coroner King County, Wash., 1964—66. Author: Adventure Is Underground, 1959, Depths of the Earth, 1966, 76, American Caves and Caving, 1974, 82, Floyd Collins of Sand Cave, 1998; co-author: (with Robert Nymeyer) Carlsbad Cavern: The Early Years, 1991; editor Jour. Spelean History, 1968-73; contbr. articles to profl. jours. Cons. Egyptian Environ. Affairs Agency; mem. North Cascades Conservation Coun., v.p., 1962—63; pres. Internat. Speleological Found., 1981—87, Internat. Union Speleol. Com. on Volcanic Caves, 1992—98, hon. pres., 1998—; asst. dir. Internat. Glaciospeleological Survey, 1972—76; mem. Gov.'s North Cascades Study Com., 1967—76; chmn. Hawaii Speleol. Survey, 1989—97; dir. We. Speleol. Survey, 1957—83, dir. rsch., 1983—96. Served to lt. USNR, 1949—50, served to lt. comdr USNR, 1955—57. Recipient medal Geol. Soc. China; named Alumnus of Yr., George Sch., 1992. Fellow Am. Coll. Chest Physicians, Nat. Speleological Soc. (hon. mem. 1965, bd. govs. 1950-2001), Explorers Club; mem. AMA, Internat. Assn. Hydrogeologists, Nat. Trust (Scotland), Geol. Soc. Am., Assn. Am. Geographers, Mars Soc., Mountaineers Club (past trustee), Seattle Tennis Club.

HALLIGAN, HOWARD ANSEL, investment management company executive; b. Glen Ridge, N.J., Aug. 11, 1937; s. Howard Kimball and Helen (Raymond) H.; m. Barbara Elyse McConchie, June 18, 1960; children— David, Barbara, Elizabeth BA, Williams Coll., 1959; MBA, Columbia U., 1961. Investment analyst Conn. Gen. Ins., Hartford, 1961-70; v.p. Conn. Gen. Investment Mgmt. Co., Hartford, 1970-78, Conn. Gen. Mut. Fund Group, Hartford, 1977 80; pres. CIGNA Investment Mgmt. Co., Hartford, 1978-87, CIGNA Mut. Fund Group, Hartford, 1980-87; sr. v.p. CIGNA Investment Group, Hartford, 1983-87; exec. v.p. Bigler Investment Mgmt. Co., Hartford, 1987-95, pres., 1996, Crossroads Investment Advisers, 1996-99; chmn. Fairview Venture Mgmt., Farmington, Conn., 1999—. Adv. bd. ABS Ventures, Battery Ventures, Brentwood Assocs., Domain Ventures, Edison Ventures, Highland Capital, Menlo Ventures, Morganthaler Ventures, Prince Ventures, RS & Co IV, U.S. Venture Ptnrs., 1989-99. Contbr. articles to profl. jours. Bd. dirs., chmn. fin. com. Simsbury Hist. Soc., Conn., 1973-75; pres. bd. Simsbury Little League, 1975-77; bd. dirs. Newington Children's Hosp., Conn., 1980-82. Mem. Hartford Soc. Fin. Analysts, Conn. Williams Alumni Soc. (pres. 1974-76), Alpha Delta Phi. Clubs: Hopmeadow Country (Simsbury); Dorset Field, Ekwanok (Vt.); Taconic Golf (Williamstown, Mass.). Republican. Congregationalist. Avocations: golf, tennis, skiing, piano. Office: Fairview Capital 10 Stanford Dr Farmington CT 06032-2451

HALLIGAN, JAMES EDMUND, university administrator, chemical engineer; b. Moorland, Iowa, June 23, 1936; s. Raymond Anthony and Margaret Ann (Crawford) H.; m. Ann Elizabeth Sorenson, June 29, 1957; children: Michael, Patrick, Christopher. MS in Chem. Engring, Iowa State U., 1962, MS, 1965, PhD, 1968. Registered profl. engr., Okla. Process engr. Humble Oil Co., 1962-64; mem. faculty Tex. Tech U., 1968-77; dean engring. U. Mo., Rolla, 1977-79, U. Ark., Fayetteville, 1979-82, vice chancellor for acad. affairs, 1982-83, interim chancellor, 1983-84; pres. N.Mex. State U., Las Cruces, 1984-94, Okla. State U., Stillwater, 1994—2003, pres. emeritus, 2003—. Mem. Gov. Tex. Energy Adv. Council, 1972-74; prof. achievement citation engr. Iowa State U. Coll. Engring., 1984. Served with USAF, 1954-58. Recipient Disting. Teaching award Tex. Tech U., 1972, Disting. Research award, 1975, 76; Disting. Teaching award U. Mo., Rolla, 1978, Disting. Achievement citation Iowa State U. Alumni Assn., 1996. Mem. AIChE, NSPE, Am. Chem. Soc., Am. Soc. Engring. Edn., Rotary, Tau Beta Pi, Phi Kappa Phi, Pi Mu Epsilon. Roman Catholic. Office: Okla State U 470 SU Stillwater OK 74078-1010

HALLILA, BRUCE ALLAN, welding engineer; b. Washington, D.C., Nov. 2, 1950; s. Esko Ensio and Gertrude Naomi (Tilley) H.; m. Pamela Joan Guerin, Dec. 18, 1982; children: Gregory Michael Decedue, April Patrice, Andrew Allan, Joshua Scott. BSME, BS in Welding Engring., LeTourneau U., 1974. Welding engr. Chgo. Bridge & Iron Co., Houston, 1975-77, Avondale Shipyards, Inc., New Orleans, 1977-80, asst. shipbuilding supt., 1980-82; steel supt. Halter Marine, Inc., New Orleans, 1982; welding supt. Bell Halter, Inc., New Orleans, 1982-84; sr. welding engr. Avondale Industries, Inc., New Orleans, 1984-86, chief welding engr., 1986-97; asst. plant sup. Pellerin Milnor Corp., Kenner, La., 1997—. Vice chmn. welding com. Ogden Corp., N.Y.C., 1984-86; welding cons. Gas Tech. Cons., Inc., Metairie, La., 1990—; CWI test proctor Am. Welding Soc., Miami, 1979-97; welding industry cons. State of La VoTech Welding Coun., Metairie, 1982—; panel mem. welding R & D, Maritime Adminstrn.; mem. adv. bd. La. Tech. Coll.-Jefferson Campus, 2002--. Mem. com. troop 33 Boy Scouts Am., 1991-97. Recipient Gov.'s award State of La., Baton Rouge, 1982. Mem. Am. Welding Soc. (dist. 9 dir. 1994-97, D3 com., 1997, CWI test supr. 1997—, chmn. sect. cert. 1997—, judge regional sci. and engring. fair 1997—, chmn. student scholarship award 1997—, Proposer award 1982, Dist. Meritorious award 1987, 92, named Disting. Mem. 1989, Sect. Educator award 2000), Am. Bur. Shipping (Silver mem., spl. com. on materials and welding 1997), Delta Sigma Psi. Republican. Avocations: woodworking, welding, photography. Home: 8725 Carriage Rd River Ridge LA 70123-3605 Office: Pellerin Milnor Corp PO Box 400 Kenner LA 70063-0400 E-mail: bahallila@aol.com.

HALLIN, DANIEL CLARK, communications educator; b. Palo Alto, Calif., June 11, 1953; BA in Polit. Sci. with honors, U. Calif., Berkeley, 1973, MA in Polit. Sci., 1974, PhD in Polit. Sci., 1980. Fellow Freedom Forum Media Studies Ctr., Columbia U., N.Y.C., 1991-92; prof. dept. comm., adj. prof. polit. sci. U. Calif., San Diego, 1980—, chairperson, 1994-97. Assoc. Ctr. for War, Peace and News Media; presenter, keynote spkr. various ednl. symposia and confs., most recently at Seoul Nat. U., 1997, Westminster U., London, 1998, Nat. U., Athens, Greece, 1998, Budapest, 2000, U. Leipzig, 2000, U. Munich, 2000, U. Calif. Berkeley, 2000, U. Perugia, 1999; Merkator prof. Inst. Medienwissenschaft U. Dusseldorf, 2000. Author: The "Uncensored War": The Media and Vietnam, 1989, The Presidency, The Press and the People, 1992, We Keep America on Top of the World: Television Journalism and the Public Sphere, 1994; contbr. chpt. to: Critical Theory and Public Life, 1985, Political Communication: Approaches, Studies, Assessments, 1987, Reading the News, 1986, Watching Television, 1986, Is the Cold War Over? Images of the USA and the USSR in Soviet and American Media, 1991, Comparatively Speaking, 1992, Viewing War: How the Media Handled the Persian Gulf, 1994; co-contbr. chpt. to: Taken by Storm: The Media, Public Opinion and U.S. Foreign Policy in the Gulf War, 1994, Mass Media and Society, 1996, Dewesternizing Media Studies, 2000, Tabloid Tales, 2000; mem. editl. bd. Polit. Comm.; contbr. articles and revs. to profl. publs. Pres. Binat. Assn. Schs. of Comm. of the Californias, 1997-99; bd. dirs. Internat. Comm. Assn. Recipient 1st prize media studies project essay contest Woodrow Wilson Internat. Ctr. for Scholars, 1990. Mem. Am. Polit. Sci. Assn., L.Am. Studies Assn., Internat. Comm. Assn., Union for Dem. Comm. Home: 3315 31st St San Diego CA 92104-4619 Office: Univ Calif San Diego Dept Comm 0503 La Jolla CA 92093 E-mail: dhallin@ucsd.edu.

HALLINAN, JOHN CORNELIUS, mechanical engineering consultant; b. Phila., Feb. 12, 1919; s. John Joseph and Ellen Bridget (Sullivan) H.; m. Eleanor Ruth Denny, July 7, 1945; children: Ann, Mary, Kathleen, Claire (dec.), Joan, John, Patricia, Mark, Michael, Joseph, William, Theresa. BSME, Villanova U., 1940. Design and lab. engr. Am. Bosch, Springfield, Mass., 1946-47; lab. mgr. Baldwin Lima Hamilton, Eddystone, Pa., 1947-54; rsch. engr. Caterpillar Inc., Peoria, Ill., 1954-62, lab. mgr., 1962-72, engring. mgr., 1972-85; engring. cons., Washington, Ill., 1985—. Contbr. articles to profl. jours. Trustee St. Patrick Parish, Washington, 1962-93, lector, 1978—. With USN, 1943-46. Named Engr. of Yr., Peoria Engring. Coun., 1975, Recipient Internal Combustion Engine award Am. Soc. of Mechanical Engineers, 1995. Mem. ASME (chmn. ctrl. Ill. sect. 1962-63, other sectional and regional offices, chmn. Soichiro Honda medal com., divsn. for disting. tech. svc. to diesel engine industry 1992, Internal Combustion Engine award 1995), Soc. Automotive Engrs., Submarine Vets. WWII. Achievements include direction and management of the design and development of large engines, turbocharging of engines, conversion of diesel to spark ignited engines. Home and Office: 700 Crestview Dr Washington IL 61571-1605 E-mail: moonbream@aol.com.

HALLINAN, JOSEPH THOMAS, journalist, author; b. Barberton, Ohio, Sept. 3, 1960; s. Neil Patrick and Judith Ann (Tonovitz) H.; m. Pamela L. Taylor, Sept. 10, 2000; children: Jack. BS magna cum laude, Boston U., 1984. Reporter The Indpls. Star, 1984-91; nat. corr. Newhouse News Svc., Washington, 1991-99; reporter Chgo. Tribune, 1999-2000; staff reporter The Wall St. Jour., 2000—. Author: Going Up The River: Travels in a Prison Nation, 2001. Recipient Pulitzer prize for investigative reporting, 1991; named Disting. Alumni, Boston U., 1992; Nieman fellow Harvard U., 1997-98. Roman Catholic. Avocations: fishing, travel. Home: 3750 Lake Shore Dr Chicago IL 60613

HALLISSEY, MICHAEL, strategic consultant; b. Southampton, England, Mar. 6, 1943; s. John Francis and Mary (Kendall) H. Grad., Magdalen Coll., Oxford U., Eng., 1964. Chartered acct., Eng. With Price Waterhouse, 1964-98, asst. mgr., 1968, Milan, 1969, ptnr. London, 1974-98, head practice devel., 1979-81, head strategic planning, 1981-82, head corp. fin. svcs., 1983-88; dir. strategy Price Waterhouse Europe, 1988-98, PricewaterhouseCoopers (formerly Price Waterhouse), 1998—2003; vis. fellow Imperial Coll. Sci. and Tech., London, 1998—2003. Contbr. articles to profl. publs. Fellow Royal Soc. of Arts; mem. Inst. Chartered Accts. Eng. and Wales. Mem. Conservative Party. Mem. Ch. of Eng. Avocations: politics, sailing, music, opera. Home: 66 Waterside Point Anhalt Rd London SW11 4PD England

HALLMAN, GARY L. photographer, educator; b. St. Paul, Aug. 7, 1940; s. Jack J. and Helen A. Hallman; 1 child, Peter J. BA, U. Minn., 1966, MFA, 1971. Mem. faculty dept. studio arts U. Minn., Mpls., 1970—, assoc. prof. photography, 1976—. Vis. adj. prof. R.I. Sch. Design, 1977-78; vis. exchange prof. U. N.Mex., 1984-85; vis. assoc. prof. The Colo. Coll., Colorado Springs, 1990; mem. visual arts adv. bd. Minn. State Arts Coun., 1973-76; bd. dirs. Minn. Artists Exhbn. Program, 1989-91. Exhbns. include Internat. Mus. Photography, George Eastman House, 1974, Light Gallery, N.Y.C., 1975, Balt. Mus., 1975, Mus. Modern Art, N.Y.C., 1978, Mpls. Inst. Arts, 1996, B. Gray Gallery East Carolina U., Greenville, N.C., 1997, Nat. Mus. of Am., Washington, 1984, Frederick R. Weisman Art Mus., Mpls., 1998, The State Russian Mus., St. Petersburg, 1998, Barg Gallery/Teheran Mus. Contemporary Art, 2001, Risk/Revisit: The Photography of Gary Hallman, PARTs Gallery, Mpls., 2002, McKnight Found. Open Spaces Project, 2002; represented in permanent collections Mus. Modern Art, N.Y.C., Internat. Mus. Photography, Rochester, N.Y., Nat. Gallery Can., Fogg Art Mus., Harvard U., Princeton U. Art Mus., Nat. Mus. Am. Art, Smithsonian Instn., Washington. Served with USN, 1958-61. Nat. Endowment Arts fellow, 1975-76; Bush Found. fellow, 1976-77; McKnight Found. fellow, 1982, 90, Artist Assistance fellowship grant, 1996. Mem. Soc. Photog. Edn., Coll. Art Assn. Am. Office: U Minn Dept Studio Arts Minneapolis MN 55455

HALLMAN, H(ENRY) THEODORE, JR., (TED HALLMAN), artist, textile designer; b. Bucks County, Pa., Dec. 23, 1933; s. H. Theodore and Mildred Eleanor (Brumbaugh) H. Cert., Fountainebleau Sch. Fine Arts, France, 1955; BFA, BS in Edn, Temple U., 1956; MFA in Painting, Cranbrook Acad. Art, 1957, MFA in Textiles, 1958; studied at, Bundestextilschule, Austria, 1962; PhD in Edn, U. Calif., Berkeley, 1974. Workshop tchr. in design, textiles, handweaving, color, U.S., Eng., Can.; lectr. in design, textile structures; chmn. Haystack Sch., Deer Isle, Maine, 1958-60, Penland (N.C.) Sch., summers 1963-70, 96, U. Calif., Berkeley, 1973-74, Calif. State U., San Francisco, 1970, Bklyn. Mus. Sch., 1973; lectr. teaching workshops Inst. Am. Indian Art, Sante Fe, No. N.Mex. C.C., El Rito, N.Mex., Nancy Block Studio, Sante Fe; head dept. textile design Moore Coll. Art, 1963-69; head of textiles, Ont. Coll. Art, Toronto, 1975-99, initiating summer programs in Florence, Italy, Como, Italy, Kyoto, Japan, Paris; bd. dirs. S.W. Craft Center, San Antonio; adv. bd. Pacific Basin Sch. Textile Arts, Berkeley, Calif.; bd. advisers Toronto (Ont., Can.) Mus. Textiles. One-man shows include Phila. Art Alliance, 1960, Loch Haven Art Center, Orlando, Fla., 1970, Woodmere Art Gallery, Phila., 1971, Royal Ont. Mus., Toronto, 1978, Renwick of Smithsonian, Washington, 1980, Centre des Arts Visuels, Montreal, Mendel Art Gallery, Saskatchewan, Moore Coll. Art, Phila., McMillan Meml. Gallery, Lincoln, Nebr., S.W. Craft Center, San Antonio, Tex., Fashion Inst. Tech., N.Y.C., 1983, Bklyn. Mus. Art, 1984, Tokyo Gallery Space '21, 1985, Kyoto Am. Ctr., 1985, Hamilton Art Gallery, 1985, Columbus Cultural Art Ctr., 1995, 97, Cambridge Gallery, Ont., 1994, Allentown Art Mus., 1998; two-man show Chgo. Art Inst., 1969, Disciples of Reenchantment, 1997, Art Expo at Javitz Ctr., N.Y.C., 1990, Allentown Art Mus., 1998; four-person show at Columbus Cultural Art Ctr.; group shows include Talkative Textiles, San Francisco and Sante Fe, 1992-93, opening show Barbara Okun Gallery, Santa Fe, 1992, Envision Gallery, Taos, N.Mex., 1993, Helen Drutt Gallery, Phila., 1994, Internationales Kunsthandwerk, Stuttgart, Germany, The Art Fabric: Mainstream; Miniature Weavings, London, Am. Fedn. Arts travelling exhbn., 1981-82, Milw. Art Mus., 1986, 5 Decades of Am. Fiber Art, Am. Craft Mus., N.Y.C., 1995, Ont. Craft Gallery, also numerous U.S. Govt. Agy. travelling shows; represented in permanent collections, Met. Mus. Art, N.Y.C., Victoria and Albert Mus., London, Royal Ont. Mus., Toronto, Bklyn., Mus. Art; represented in mus. collections: Cooper Hewitt Mus., N.Y.C., Smithsonian Inst., Washington, Phila. Mus. Art, Oakland (Calif.) Mus. Art, Cin. Art Mus., Utah Mus. Fine Arts, Mus. Contemporary Crafts, N.Y.C., Addison Gallery Am. Art, Andover, Mass., Mus. Decorative Arts, Chateau Dufresene, Montreal Que., Textile Mus., Toronto; exhbns.: N.Y. Art Expo '90, Fine Fiber, Chgo., 2001, Survey 2002, Snyderman Works Gallery, Phila.; invited show Helen Drutt Gallery, Phila.; work represented in numerous art, design and craft jours. and books. Adv. bd. Pacific Basin Sch., Berkeley, Calif. L.C. Tiffany grantee, 1962; Oscar D'Italia 85, Calvatore, Italy; elected Coll. of Fellows by Am. Craft Council, N.Y.C. Mem. Internat. Soc. Arts and Letters (hon. life), World Craft Council (invited lectr. conf., Mexico 1976), Ont. Craft Council (dir.). Home and Office: PO Box 281 Lederach PA 19450

HALLMAN, LEROY, lawyer; b. Grandview, Tex., July 16, 1915; s. Ernest L. and Willa (Prestridge) H.; m. Martha Booker, Nov. 12, 1944; children— Martha B., Willa Anne, Samuel John. Diploma Hillsboro Jr. Coll., 1934; LL.B. with highest honors, U. Tex., 1939. Ptnr. Phinney Hallman & Coke, Dallas, 1946-84, Storey, Armstrong, Steger & Martin, 1984— ; dir. Frozen Food Express Industries, Inc., Dallas, Hub Hill, Inc., Dallas. Contbr. articles to profl. jours. Mem. City of University Park Planning and Zoning Commn., Tex., 1972-80. Served to maj. USAAF, 1940-46, PTO. Fellow Tex. Bar Found.; mem. ABA, Dallas Bar Assn., State Bar Tex., Motor Carrier Lawyer Assn. (pres. 1970-71), Delta Theta Phi, Democrat. Baptist. Clubs: Northwood, Petroleum. Home: 3212 Southwestern Blvd Dallas TX 75225-7651 Office: 4600 1st Interstate Bank Tower 1445 Ross Ave Dallas TX 75202-2812

HALLMARK, DONALD PARKER, museum director, lecturer; b. McPherson, Kans., Feb. 16, 1945; s. Daniel Clell and Esther Ione (Hart) H.; m. Linda Lorraine Lego, June 10, 1967; m. Monica Lynn, Amy Kristen. BFA, U. Ill., 1967; MA, U. Iowa, 1970; PhD, St. Louis U., 1980. From asst. prof. to prof. Greenville (Ill.) Coll., 1970-81, chmn. art dept., 1976-81; dir. Richard W. Bock Sculpture Collection, Greenville, 1975-81, Frank Lloyd Wright's Dana-Thomas House Hist. Site, Springfield, Ill., 1981—. Founding bd. mem. Frank Lloyd Wright Bldg Conservancy, Chgo., 1988-96; adj prof. Sangamon State U., Springfield, 1986-90; lectr. FLW Bldg. Conservancy, Hollyhock House, L.A., The Gamble House, Pasadena, Calif., The High Mus., Atlanta, Decorative Arts Soc. SAH, Chgo., Indpls. Pub. Libr., The Natural Pattern of Structure Herberger Lectrs., Ariz. State U., Tempe, Art Inst. Chgo., FLW Bldg. Conservancy, Unity Temple, Oak Park, Ill., FLW Home and Studio Lectrs., Oak Park Pub. Libr., Mus. of Our Nat. Heritage, Lexington, Mass., The Chgo. Arch. Found., Santa Fe Bldg., Chgo., Nat. Bldg. Mus., Washington Author: (booklet) The Dana-Thomas House: Its History, Acquisition and Preservation, 1992, (catalogue) Paul Ashbrook, 1990 (illustrated book) The Natural Pattern of Structure, 1995; TV interview appearances Bob Vila's Guide to Historic Homes, The Dana-Thomas House, 1996, interview Frank Lloyd Wright and the Prairie School, Films for Humanities and Scis., 1999, Home and Garden TV, 2000; editor newsletter Guidelines for the Conservation of Frank Lloyd Wright Decorative Arts, 1996. Cons., sponsor Ill. Govt. Intern Program, Springfield, 1985—; libr. cons., vol. Michael Victor II Libr. Springfield Art Assn., 1988-93. Faculty grantee Shell Found., 1975; Grad. fellow St. Louis U., 1976. Mem.: Nat. Trust for Historic Preservation, The Frank Llyod Wright Bldg. Conservancy, Am. Assn. Mus. Presbyterian. Avocations: slide library collecting, antique collecting, travel, ground and garden maintenance. Home: 605 W Sheridan Rd Petersburg IL 62675-1359 Office: Ill Hist Preservation Agy 301 E Lawrence Ave Springfield IL 62703-2232

HALLO, WILLIAM WOLFGANG, Assyriologist; b. Kassel, Germany, Mar. 9, 1928; came to U.S., 1940, naturalized, 1946; s. Rudolf and Gertrude (Rubensohn) H.; m. Edith Sylvia Pinto, June 22, 1952 (dec. Oct. 10, 1994); children: Ralph Ethan, Jacqueline Louise; m. Nanette Stahl, Oct. 18, 1998. BA magna cum laude, Harvard U., 1950; candidatus Litterarum Semiticarum, U. Leiden, Netherlands, 1951; MA, U. Chgo., 1953, PhD, 1955; MA (hon.), Yale U., 1965; DHL (hon.), Hebrew Union Coll.-Jewish Inst. Religion, 1986. Rsch. asst. U. Chgo. Oriental Inst., 1954—56; from instr. to asst. prof. Bible and Semitic langs. Hebrew Union Coll.-Jewish Inst. Religion, Cin., 1956-62; asst. prof. Assyriology Yale U., 1962—65, prof. Assyriology, 1965-75, William M. Laffan prof. Assyriology and Babylonian lit., 1976—2002, emeritus prof., 2002—; curator Babylonian collection, 1963-2001, master Morse Coll., 1982-87; chmn. dept. Near Eastern langs. and civilizations, 1975-82, 85-89. Chmn. Univ. (now adv.) com. on Judaic Studies, 1979-84, acting chmn., 1998; vis. prof. Mid. Eastern civilization Columbia U., 1970-71, 80, Jewish Theol. Sem., 1981, 82-83, 2002; Franz Rosenzweig guest prof. U. Kassel, Germany, 1991. Author: Early Mesopotamian Royal Titles, 1957, Sumerian Archival Texts, 1973, The Book of the People, 1991, Origins: The Ancient Near Eastern Background of Some Modern Western Institutions, 1996; (with J.J.A. van Dijk) The Exaltation of Inanna, 1968; (with W.K. Simpson) The Ancient Near East: A History, 1971, 2d edit., 1998; (with Briggs Buchanan) Early Near Eastern Seals in the Yale Babylonian Collection, 1981; co-author: The Torah: A Modern Commentary, 1981, Heritage: Civilization and the Jews, 2 vols., 1984, The Tablets of Ebla, 1984; editor: Essays in Memory of E.A. Speiser, 1968; (with Carl D. Evans and John B. White) Scripture in Context: Essays on the Comparative Method, 1980; (with James C. Moyer and Leo G. Perdue) Scripture in Context II: More Essays on the Comparative Method, 1983; (with Bruce W. Jones and Gerald L. Mattingly) The Bible in Light of Cuneiform Literature: Scripture in Context III, 1990; (with K. Lawson Younger Jr. and Bernard F. Batto) The Biblical Canon in Comparative Perspective: Scripture in Context IV, 1991; (with K. Lawson Younger Jr.) The Context of Scripture, vol. I: Canonical Compositions from the Biblical World, 1997, Vol. II Monumental Inscriptions from the Biblical World, 2000, Vol. III Archival Documents from the Biblical World, 2002; (with Irene J. Winter) Seals and Seal Impressions, 2001; translator: The Star of Redemption, 1971; contbr. articles and book revs. to profl. jours.; mem. editl. bd. Yale Near Eastern Researches, 1967—2002; editor, 1970-2002; mem. editl. bd. Moment Mag., Bible Rev., Archaeology Odyssey. Mem. commn. Jewish edn. Union Am. Hebrew Congregations, 1967-71; co-founder, dir., mem. exec. com. Assn. Jewish Studies, 1970-71, v.p.,

1972-74. Fulbright scholar, 1950-51; fellow Guggenheim, 1965-66, Inst. Advanced Studies, Hebrew U., Jerusalem, 1978-79, Nat. Humanities Inst., 1987-88, Shelby Cullom Davis Ctr. for Hist. Studies, Princeton U., 1996-97; honored by an anniversary volume: The Tablet and the Scroll: Near Eastern Studies in Honor of William W. Hallo, 1993. Mem. Am. Oriental Soc. (assoc. editor, 1965-71, chmn. Ancient Near East sect. 1971-78, v.p. 1987-88, pres. 1988-89), World Union Jewish Studies, Fulbright Assn. (v.p. Conn. chpt. 2002-), Harvard Club (So. Conn.), Yale Club (N.Y.C.), Phi Beta Kappa. Home: 245 Blake Rd Hamden CT 06517-3324 Office: Yale Babylonian Collection PO Box 208240 New Haven CT 06520-8240 E-mail: william.hallo@yale.edu.

HALLOCK, C. WILES, JR., athletic official; b. Denver, Feb. 17, 1918; s. Claude Wiles and Mary (Bassler) H.; m. Marjorie Louise Eldred, Mar. 23, 1944; children: Lucinda Eldred Hallock Rinne, Michael Eldred. AB, U. Denver, 1939. Sports info. dir. U. Wyo., 1949-60, track coach, 1952-56; sports info. dir. U. Calif., Berkeley, 1960-63; dir. pub. relations Nat. Collegiate Athletic Assn., 1963-68; dir. Nat. Collegiate Sports Services, 1967-68; commr. Western Athletic Conf., 1968-71; exec. dir. Pacific-8 Conf. (now Pacific-10 conf.), San Francisco and Walnut Creek, Calif., 1971-83; historian Pacific 10 Conf., 1983. Mem. Laramie (Wyo.) City Council, 1958-60. Served to lt. comdr. USNR, World War II. Decorated Air medal; mem. Nat. Football Found. and Hall of Fame Honors Ct. Mem. Nat. Collegiate Athletic Assn., Nat. Assn. Collegiate Dirs. Athletics (Corbett award 1983), Collegiate Commrs. Assn., Coll. Sports Info. Dirs. Am. (Arch Ward award 1963), Football Writers Assn. Am. (past dir.), U.S. Basketball Writers Assn., Lambda Chi Alpha. Presbyterian. Home: 235 Western Hills Dr Pleasant Hill CA 94523-3167 Office: 800 S Broadway Walnut Creek CA 94596-5218 E-mail: i4claude@aol.com.

HALLOCK, JAMES ANTHONY, pediatrician, health facility administrator; b. Paterson, N.J., Oct. 28, 1942; s. Anthony E. and Alice S. (Dahab) H.; m. Jeanne LaRossa, June 27, 1965; children: James A. Jr., Jeffrey D., Julie E. AB, Seton Hall U., 1963; MD, Georgetown U., 1967. Diplomate Am. Bd. Pediatrics. Resident in pediatrics Children's Hosp. of Phila., 1967-69; chief resident in pediatrics Hosp. of U. Pa., 1969-70; asst. prof. pediatrics U. South Fla., Tampa, 1972-75, assoc. prof., 1975-80, prof., 1980-88, assoc. dean, 1978-83, dep. dean, 1983-85, exec. dean Tampa and St. Petersburg, 1985-88; prof. pediatrics, dean East Carolina U. Sch. Medicine, Greenville, NC, 1988—2001, vice chancellor for health scis., 1990—2001; pres., CEO ECFMG, Phila., 2001—. Contbr. articles to profl. jours. Maj. USAF, 1970-72. Fellow Am. Acad. Pediatrics; mem. N.C. Med. Soc., N.C. Biomed. Rsch. (bd. dirs. 1989), Pitt County Med. Soc., Pitt/Greenville C. of C. (bd. dirs. 1989), Rotary (St. Petersburg and Greenville chpts.). Office: ECFMG 3624 Market St Philadelphia PA 19104

HALLOCK, ROBERT BRUCE, physics educator; b. Washington, Dec. 9, 1943; s. Robert Frederick and Dorothy Hallock; m. Norma Evelyn Hayward, Jun 19, 1965; children: Robert William, Kevin Frederick. BS, U. Mass., 1965; MS, Stanford U., 1967, PhD, 1969, postdoctoral, 1969-70. Asst. prof. U. Mass., Amherst, 1970-74, assoc. prof., 1974-79, prof., 1979—2001, disting. prof., 2001—, dir. lab. low temp. physics, 1978—, head dept. physics and astronomy, 1985-93, interim dean Coll. Natural Scis. and Math., 2000—01. Vis. assoc. prof. Brown U., Providence, 1975, Cornell U., Ithaca, N.Y., 1977-78; co-chair Gordon Rsch. Conf. on Quantum Fluids and Solids, 1982; adj. prof. dept. polymer sci. and engring. U. Mass., 1985—; mem. five colls. Radio Astronomy Policy Bd., 1985-87; mem. Rsch. Corp. Grants Adv. Bd., 1989-96; mem. fundamental physics discipline working group NASA, 1997-2001; chair Quantum Fluids & Solids Internat. Conf., 1998-2000; bd. dirs. Rsch. Corp., 2003—. Author, editor: Superfluid Helium, 1983; contbr. articles to profl. jours. Leader Cub Scout Am., Hadley, Mass., 1975-80. Named Disting. Tchr. of Yr., U. Mass., 1998; Woodrow Wilson Found. fellow, 1965, Air Force Office of Sci. Rsch.-NRC fellow, 1969, A.P. Sloan Found. rsch. fellow, 1972-76, U. Mass. fellow, 1974, 93, J.S. Guggenheim Meml. fellow, 1992-93. Fellow Am. Phys. Soc. (exec. coun. New Eng. sect. 1986-89); mem. Phi Beta Kappa, Sigma Xi. Avocation: photography. Office: U Mass/Hasbrouck Lab Dept Physics Amherst MA 01003 E-mail: hallock@physics.umass.edu.

HALLOCK-BANNIGAN, SUZY, counselor, consultant, counselor educator; b. Moline, Ill., Mar. 26, 1942; d. Warren Arthur Hallock and Norma Anita (Ames) Nytes; m. Timothy Butterworth, June 26, 1966 (div. May 1976); children: Elizabeth Brook Newland, Benjamin Clark. AB, Mount Holyoke Coll., 1964; MEd, Lesley Coll., 1978; Cert. Advanced Grad. Studies, U. Vt., 1988. Lic. counselor, Vt.; cert. reality therapist. English tchr. MacDuffie Sch., Springfield, Mass., 1964-66; 2d grade tchr. Horton Pub. Sch., Pittsboro, NC, 1966-67, Elm Hill Sch., Springfield, Vt., 1967-68; tchr. adult basic edn. Bellows Falls HS, Vt., 1969-75; admissions counselor Hartford Coll. for Women, Conn., 1973-76; writer, reporter Keene Sentinel, NH, 1975; counselor Woodstock Union HS, Vt., 1976—; pvt. practice counselor Norwich & South Pomfret, Vt., 1978—; writer, reporter Keene Sentinel, Brattleboro, Vt., 1975. Dir. Dept. Counseling Svcs., Woodstock, Student Peer Counselor Program, Woodstock; sr. faculty assoc. William Glasser Inst., LA, 1985—; practicum supr., faculty assoc., 1978—; instr. William Glasser Inst., various; spkr. in field. Author: What Are You Doing?, 1980, Control Theory in the Practice of Reality Therapy, 1989; editor: A Thousand Words (How to Write An Effective Admissions Essay), 2001; contbr. articles to profl. jours. and newspapers. Mem. William Glasser Inst., Ireland, liasion, 1985—; mem. Woodstock Child Protection Team, 1990—; negotiator Woodstock Union Tchrs. Assn., 1986—91; mem. Local Stds. Bd., 1992—95; writer Vt.'s Common Core, Social Scis. Commn., 1993—94; evaluation com. Coun. on Stds. for Internat. Edn. and Travel, 1999—2001; keynote spkr.; profl. seminar instr. various, Ireland, 1985—; bd. dir. Pentangle Coun. on Arts, 1997—2000. Named Educator of Yr., Woodstock Community and Sch. Assn., 1983. Mem.: NEA, New Eng. Assn. Coll. Admissions Counselors (govt. rels. com. 2003, Outstanding Counselor 1986), Vt. Edn. Assn., Vt. Assn. Counseling & Devel. (Guzetta award 1991), Vt. Assn. Sch. Counselors (pres. 1993—94), Am. Psychotherapy Assn., Am. Assn. Sch. Counselors, North Chapel Soc. (welcoming com.). Democrat. Avocations: aerobic dancing, travel, irish things. Home: Donegal at 738 Old Stage Rd South Pomfret VT 05067 Office: Woodstock High Sch Woodstock VT 05091

HALLORAN, KATHERINE HESS, physician, consultant; b. New Haven, Aug. 14, 1929; d. Orvan Walter and Carol Woodruff (Maurer) Hess; m. Thomas Clifford Halloran, June 5, 1954; children: Charles, Priscilla, Peter. BA, Wellesley Coll., 1951; MD, Yale U., 1954. Diplomate Am. Bd. Pediats., Am. Bd. Pediat. Cardiology. Instr., asst. prof. Yale U. Med. Sch., New Haven, 1961-74; flight surgeon FAA, N.Y.C., 1974-85, regional flight surgeon Burlington, Mass., 1985-92; cons., 1992—. Contbr. articles to profl. jours. Meyer Berger fellow Columbia-Presbyn. Hosp., 1960. Mem. Am. Coll. Cardiology, Am. Acad. Pediats., Am. Heart Assn., Lexington Club, Wellesley Club, Sigma Xi. Avocation: watercolor painting. Home and Office: 9 Coach Rd Lexington MA 02420-1101 E-mail: thallo1210@aol.com.

HALLORAN, KATHLEEN L. financial executive, accountant; b. Sandwich, Ill., July 19, 1952; d. Oscar L. and Gertrude L. Huber; divorced. BA in Acctg., Lewis U., 1974; MBA, No. Ill. U., 1979. CPA, Ill. With NICOR, Inc., Naperville, 1974-84; asst. sec. No. Ill. Gas subs. NICOR, Inc., Naperville, 1983-84, asst. contr., 1984; sec., treas. NICOR Inc., Naperville, 1984-87; sec., contr. NICOR, Inc., Naperville, 1987-89, v.p., sec., contr., 1989-92, v.p. info. svcs. and gen. acctg., 1992-94; v.p. info. svcs. and rates No. Ill. Gas, Aurora, 1994-95, v.p. info. svcs., rates and human resources, 1995-96; sr. v.p. info. svcs., rates and human resources, 1996-98; sr. v.p. adminstrn., 1998-99; exec. v.p. fin. and adminstrn. No. Ill. Gas, Aurora, 1999—. Bd. dirs. Ctrl. DuPage Health, Voices for America's Children, Ill. Children's Healthcare Found.; mem. com. on dirs. Voices for Ill. Children; trustee Lewis U. Mem.: The Chgo. Network, Execs. Club Chgo., Econ. Club of Chgo., Am. Gas Assn. Office: Nicor Gas Co PO Box 190 Aurora IL 60507-0190 E-mail: khallor@nicor.com.

HALLORAN, M. ELIZABETH, statistician, educator; b. Wooster, Ohio, Aug. 19, 1951; d. John Connor Halloran and Julia Ann Shoolroy. BS, U. Oreg., 1972; postgrad., Freie U., West Berlin, 1983; M, Harvard U., 1985, DSc, 1989. Asst. to assoc. prof. Emory U., Atlanta, 1989—98, prof., 1998—. Assoc. editor: Am. Jour. Epidemiology, 1992—97, 2002—, mem. editl. bd.: Stats. in Medicine, 1994—; contbr. articles. Grantee, NIH, 1990, NSF, 1993. Fellow: Royal Statis. Soc., Am. Statis. Assn. (assoc. editor jour. 1996—2003). Avocations: piano, ballroom dancing, flying. Office: Emory Univ 1518 Clifton Rd Atlanta GA 30322

HALLORAN, MICHAEL JOHN, lawyer; b. St. Louis, June 4, 1951; s. Edward Anthony Halloran and Helen M. (Kickham) Phillips. BS in Commerce, St. Louis U., 1972, JD, 1975. Bar: Ill. 1975, U.S. Dist. Ct. (no. dist.) Ill. 1975, U.S. Ct. Appeals (7th cir.) 1975. Assoc. Seyfarth, Shaw, Fairweather & Geraldson, Chgo., Washington, 1975-78; atty. Beinhauer & Rouhana, N.Y.C., 1978-79; assoc. William B. Hanley & Assocs., Chgo., 1979-81, Bell, Boyd & Lloyd, Chgo., 1981-83, ptnr., 1983-86; pvt. practice, Chgo., 1987—. Home: 800 S Wells St Apt 552 Chicago IL 60607-4531 Office: 53 W Jackson Blvd Ste 319 Chicago IL 60604-3695

HALLORAN, MIKE, software company executive, music publishing executive; b. Anchorage, May 17, 1954; s. Thomas Orrey and Barbara (Long) H.; m. Sylvia Thayne Edwards, Apr. 28, 1979; children: Marjorie C., Julia C. Student, San Jose State U., 1972-75. Prin. artist/condr. Gilbert & Sullivan Soc., San Jose, Calif., 1973-92; prodr./dir. PFS Prodns., San Jose, Calif., 1974-85; rec. artist MBA Records, San Jose, Calif., 1975-89; owner PF Slow Pub. Co., San Jose, Calif., 1984—; prin. double bass Santa Clara (Calif.) Symphony, 1985-89; owner PPW Wholesale Comms., San Jose, 1986—; sales mgr. Distinct Corp., Saratoga, Calif., 1996—. Cons. vintage/antique musical instruments, San Jose, 1980—. Columnist IAMA Jour., 1990-91; prin. artist San Francisco Lyric Opera, 2000—. Active Santa Clara County Dem. campaign, 1994; music dir. Immanuel Luth. Ch., Los Altos, Calif., 1998—. Mem. Am. Fedn. Musicians, ASCAP. Roman Catholic. Avocations: music, cooking, film, san francisco opera. Home: PO Box 6840 San Jose CA 95150-6840 E-mail: halloranmichael@aol.com.

HALLORAN, RICHARD COLBY, writer, former research executive, former news correspondent, columnist, editor; b. Washington, Mar. 2, 1930; s. Paul James and Catherine (Lenihan) H.; m. Carol Prins, June 21, 1958; children: Christopher Paul, Laura Colby, Catherine Anne; m. Fumiko Mori, Nov. 11, 1978. AB with distinction, Dartmouth Coll., 1951; MA, U. Mich., 1957. Staff writer, then asst. fgn. editor Business Week mag., 1957-61; Tokyo bur. chief McGraw-Hill World News, 1962-64; Asia specialist Washington Post, Tokyo, 1965-66, bur. chief, 1966-68, Washington corr., 1968-69, N.Y. Times, 1969-72, Tokyo bur. chief, 1972-76, investigative reporter Washington Bur., 1976-78, energy corr., 1978-79, def. corr., 1979-84, mil. corr., 1984-89; dir. comm. and journalism East-West Ctr., Honolulu, 1990-94; ind. writer Honolulu, 1994—2000; editl. dir. Honolulu Star-Bull., 2001—02; columnist The Rising East, 2002—. Adj. fellow Pacific Forum-Ctr. Strategic and Internat. Studies; vis. instr. Asia Pacific Ctr. for Security Studies. Author: Japan: Images and Realities, 1969, Conflict and Compromise: The Dynamics of American Foreign Policy, 1973, To Arm a Nation: Rebuilding America's Endangered Defenses, 1986, Serving America: Prospects for the Volunteer Force, 1988, Sparky: A Portrait of Sentor Spark M. Matsunaga of Hawaii, 2002. Mem. Honolulu Com. Fgn. Rels., Pacific and Asian Affairs Coun., 1st lt. U.S. Army, 1952-55. Recipient citation for interpretation fgn. affairs Overseas Press Club, 1969, George Polk award for nat. reporting L.I. U., 1982, Gerald R. Ford prize for disting. reporting on nat. def. Gerald R. Ford Found., 1988, Outstanding Civilian Svc. medal U.S. Army, 1989, Japan's Order Sacred Treasure, Gold Rays with Rosette, 1998, Lifetime Achievement award Pacific and Asian Affairs Coun., 2000; Ford Found. fellow Columbia U., 1964-65, Woodrow Wilson nat. fellow Furman U., S.C., Luther Coll., Iowa, Union Coll., N.Y., U. Redlands, Calif., Linfield Coll., Oreg., Goucher Coll., Md., Ohio Wesleyan U., McMurry U., Tex., Trinity Coll., Vt., St. Mary's Coll., Calif., Wabash Coll., Ind., Pacific, Hawaii Pacific U., 2003. Mem. 100th Infantry Bn. Vet. Assn. (hon.), Japan-Am. Soc. of Hawaii. Fgn. Corrs. Club Japan. Roman Catholic. Home: 1065 Kaoopulu Pl Honolulu HI 96825-1364 E-mail: oranhall@hawaii.rr.com.

HALLOWELL, BURTON CROSBY, economist, educator; b. Orleans, Mass., May 2, 1915; s. William George and Sarah Frances (Crosby) H.; m. Pauline Russell, June 7, 1941 (dec.); 1 son, Robert Crosby; m. Joyce Glynn, Dec. 14, 2002. BA, Wesleyan U., Middletown, Conn., 1936, MA, 1938, LHD, 1969; PhD, Princeton, 1949; LHD, Boston U., 1969, Tufts U., 1976; LLD, Northeastern U., 1973, Am. Internat. Coll., 1975. Teller Windham County Nat. Bank, Danielson, Conn., 1936-37; Social Sci. Research Council pre-doctoral field fellow, 1940-41; instr. econs. Wesleyan U., 1941-42, asst. prof., 1946-50, assoc. prof., 1950-56, Andrews prof. econs., 1956-67, v.p. for planning and devel., 1962-65, exec. v.p., 1965-67; on leave for research on fed. debt mgmt. Merrill Found. for Advancement Fin. Knowledge, 1956-57; on leave as staff mem. N.Y.C. Commn. for Money and Credit, 1960-61; pres. Tufts U., Medford, Mass., 1967-76; vice chmn. Keystone Custodian Funds, Inc., 1976, chmn. bd., 1977-79, chief exec. officer, 1978-79, also dir., 1971-79. Econ. cons. Conn. Gen. Life Ins. Co., 1949-62, Com. Econ. Devel., N.Y.C., Washington, 1953-54; chmn. Mass. Housing Fin. Agy., 1968-71; Mem. exec. com. New Eng. Colls. Fund, 1968-71; mem. exec. com. Assn. Ind. Colls and Univs. in Mass., 1968-73, pres., 1972-73 Contbr. articles to profl. jours. Trustee Davis Ednl. Found., 1985—. With OPA and Civilian Supply, 1941, OSS, 1942; from. pvt. to capt. AUS, 1942-46. Mem. Am. Econ. Assn., Comml. Club of Boston, Phi Beta Kappa, Sigma Chi. Home and Office: PO Box 1545 North Eastham MA 02651

HALLOWELL SCHEMMER, SHANNON, nurse anesthetist; b. Orlando, Fla., Jan. 6, 1965; d. Albert Valentine and Ginger (Stanley) H. BSN, Clemson U., 1986; MSN, U. N.C., Charlotte, 1994. RN N.C., S.C., Utah, cert. critical care nurse, ACLS instr. Staff nurse III Greenville (S.C.) Meml. Hosp., 1986-89; asst. nurse mgr. PACU Carolinas Med. Ctr., Charlotte, 1989-91, staff nurse emergency dept., 1993, nurse anesthetist, 1994—2001, Heber Valley Med. Ctr., Heber City, Utah, 2001—. Cons. Nellcor, Inc., Pleasanton, Calif., 1991-92. Mem. AACN, Am. Assn. Nurse Anesthetists, Golden Key Honor Soc., Sigma Theta Tau, Phi Kappa Phi. Democrat. Avocations: water & snow skiing, cycling, running, hiking. Home: 2417 Fairway Village Dr Park City UT 84060-7018

HALLSTED, NANCY RUTH EVERETT, pianist, music educator; b. Reno, Nev., Dec. 28, 1938; d. Marion Kenneth and Ruth Elizabeth (Zollinger) Everett; m. Byron Leon Hallsted, June 10, 1962; children: Sheila Ann Hallsted-Baumert, John Edmond. BA, LaSierra U., Riverside, Calif., 1960; MA, U. So. Calif., L.A., 1965. Cert. permanent tchr. MTNA. Ind. pvt. tchr. piano, Bethesda, Md., 1971—; faculty piano, profl. studies The Levine Sch. of Music, Washington, 1988—. Presenter, performer internat. piano workshops; adjudicator for concerti, solo and piano ensemble competitions. Performer (chamber music): Gaithersburg Libr. Series, The Fairfax Symphony Musicales, The Chevy Chase Club; contbr. Arts adminstr., pres. Fri. Morning Music Club, Washington; bd. dirs. Washington Performing Arts Soc.; adv. planning bd. in music Strathmore Hall Arts Ctr., Rockville, Md. Recipient Fine Arts award, Bank of Am., Santa Fe award; scholar, U. So. Calif. Mem.: Md. State Music Tchrs. Assn., Montgomery County Music Tchrs. Assn. (past pres.). Home: 9212 Villa Dr Bethesda MD 20817-3310 E-mail: hallsted@erols.com.

HALLSTRAND, SARAH LAYMON, denomination executive; b. Nashville, Oct. 25, 1944; d. Charles Martin and Lillian Christina (Stenberg) Laymon; m. John Peter Hallstrand, July 6, 1974; 1 child, Lillian Johanna. BA cum laude, Fla. So. Coll., 1966; ThM, Boston U., 1971; D of Ministry, McCormick Theol. Sem., 1985; grad., Coll. for Fin. Planning, Denver, 1990. Ordained Am. Baptist Ch., 1976; cert. ret. counselor, fin. counselor; CFP. Dir. Christian edn. Trinity United Meth. Ch., Bradenton, Fla., 1968-70, Univ. United Meth. Ch., Syracuse, N.Y., 1971-73; assoc. min. First Bapt. Ch., Syracuse, 1973-78; pastor Oneida (N.Y.) Bapt. Ch., 1978-80; midwest rep. Mins. and Missionaries Benefit Bd., Am. Bapt. Chs., Oak Park, Ill., 1981—2002; pastor First United Meth. Ch., Tellico Plains, Tenn., 2002—; cons. MMBB, 2002—. Leader ret. planning seminars Am. Bapt. Assembly, Green Lake, Wis., 1985-2002, AutumnQuest Ret. Sems., Midwest Ministry Devel. Svc., 1994—, bd. dirs., 1987-2001, chair, 1993-96; mem. rep. Midwest Ministerial Leadership Commn., Valley Forge, Pa., 1985-2002; adj. prof., pastoral care McCormick Theol. Sem., Chgo., 1986-2001; adj. prof. retirement planning The Divinity Sch., Rochester, N.Y., 1994; vis. scholar Am. Bapt. Bd. Ednl. Ministries, Valley Forge, 1986-87; bd. dirs. The Gathering Place Retreat Ctr., Gosport, Ind., 1988-95; mem. program com. and women in ministry rep. Roger Williams Fellowship, 1988-95; mem. nat. continuing edn. team Am. Bapt. Chs., Valley Forge, Pa., 1991-98; conf. leader for women's spiritual renewal weekends; spkr. in field. Contbg. author: Songs of Miriam: A Woman's Book of Devotions, 1994; contbr. The Inclusive Pulpit Journ. Cmty. Ch. Press, 2003, contbr. articles to profl. jour. including The Inclusive Pulpit Jour., 2003. Mem. Fin. Planning Assn., Alpha Gamma Delta. Democrat. Home and Office: 126 Santee Way Loudon TN 37774 *The church has not been called to be successful as measured by the world's standards. It has always been and will always be that the true goal of the church is faithfulness as measured by the liberating and transforming gospel of Jesus Christ.*

HALLSTROM, LASSE, director; b. Stockholm, June 6, 1946; Dir. feature films, including A Lover and His Lass, 1975, Abba: The Movie, 1977, Father to Be, 1979, The Rooster, 1981, Happy We, 1983, My Life as a Dog, 1985, Children of Bullerby Village, 1987, Once Around, 1991, What's Eating Gilbert Grape, 1993, Something To Talk About, 1995, The Cider House Rules, 1999, Chocolat, 2000, The Shipping News, 2001. Office: ICM 8942 Wilshire Blvd Beverly Hills CA 90211-1934 also: Wayne Mejia de Blois de Blois Mejia & Co 9171 Wilshire Blvd Ste 541 Beverly Hills CA 90210-5515

HALLSTROM, ROBERT CHRIS, government actuary; b. Sacramento, June 8, 1953; s. Clifford Clarence and Billee June (Plunkett) H.; m. Pamela Jane Pracht, Apr. 25, 1987; 1 child, Kelsey Kathlene. BA in Math. with honors, Calif. State U., Sacramento, 1974, MS in Math., 1976. Cert. math. tchr. c.c., Calif. Asst. actuary Transam. Ins. Co., L.A., 1976-80; actuary Cal-Farm Ins. Co., Sacramento, 1980-84; instr. math. Sacramento City Coll., 1985, Sierra Coll., Rocklin, Calif., 1985; sr. casualty actuary Calif. Dept. Ins., San Francisco, 1985—. Fellow Casualty Actuarial Soc.; mem. Internat. Actuarial Assn. Avocations: mathematics, collecting books and phonograph records, reading. Office: Calif Dept Ins 45 Fremont St Fl 24 San Francisco CA 94105-2222 E-mail: hallstromr@insurance.ca.gov.

HALLUIN, ALBERT PRICE, lawyer; b. Nov. 8, 1939; children: Russell, Marcus. BA, La. State U., 1964; JD, U. Balt., 1969. Bar: Md. 1970, N.Y. 1985, Calif. 1991. Assoc. Jones, Tullar & Cooper, Arlington, Va., 1969-71; sr. patent atty. CPC Internat. Inc., Englewood Cliffs, N.J., 1971-76; counsel Exxon Rsch. & Engring. Co., Florham Park, N.J., 1976-83; v.p., chief intellectual property counsel Cetus Corp., Emeryville, Calif., 1983-90; ptnr. Fleisler, Dubb, Meyer & Lovejoy, San Francisco, 1990-92, Limbach & Limbach, San Francisco, 1992-94, Pennie & Edmonds, Menlo Park, Calif., 1994-97, Howrey, Simon, Arnold & White, LLP, Menlo Park, 1997—; pres., CEO, chmn. Halzyme Tech., Inc., 1995—. Contbr. articles to legal jours. Pres. Belle Roche Homeowners Assn., Redwood City, Calif., 1995—. Named One of Top 20 Intellectual Property Lawyers, Calif. Lawyer's mag., 1993. Mem. ABA, Am. Intellectual Property Law Assn. (chmn. chem. practice com. 1981-83, sec. 1984-85, bd. dirs. 1984-89, founding chmn. biotech. com. 1990-93), Licensing Exec. Soc., Assn. Corp. Patent Counsel, Bar Assn. San Francisco, San Francisco Patent Assn. Republican. Episcopalian. Office: Howrey, Simon, Arnold & White LLP 301 Ravenswood Ave Menlo Park CA 94025-3434 Fax: 650-463-8400. E-mail: HalluinA@Howrey.com., Halzym@Earthlink.net.

HALLWAS, JOHN EDWARD, English language educator; b. Waukegan, Ill., May 24, 1945; s. Emil Ferdinand and Ruth Edna (Wells) H.; m. Garnette Verna Stockstad, Jan. 3, 1966; children: John Darrin, Evan Bradley. BS in Edn., Western Ill. U., Macomb, 1967, MA, 1968; PhD, U. Fla., 1972. Grad. asst. Western Ill. U., Macomb, 1967-68, prof. English dept., 1970—. Author: Western Illinois Heritage, 1983, Illinois Literature: The 19th Century, 1986, Macomb: A Pictorial History, 1990, Spoon River Anthology: An Annotated Edition, 1992, The Bootlegger: A Story of Small-Town America, 1998, others; editor Western Ill. Regional Studies, 1978-92; co-editor: Tales From Two Rivers book series, 1981—, Prairie State Books, 1987—; columnist Macomb Jour., 1981-84, Jacksonville (Ill.) Jour. Courier, 1984-85, 87-88. NDEA fellow U. Fla., Gainesville, 1968-70; recipient Faculty Svc. award Nat. U. Continuing Edn. Assn., 1981, Alumni Achievement award Western Ill. U., Macomb, 1983, MidAm. award, Soc. for Study of Midwestern Lit., 1994; named faculty lectr. Western Ill. U., Macomb, 1983, Disting. prof., 1992. Mem. Soc. for Study Midwestern Lit., Ill. State Hist. Soc. (adv. bd. 1990-96), McDonough County Hist. Soc. (pres. 1981-83), Phi Beta Kappa, Phi Kappa Phi. Avocations: nature study, fitness walking, bicycling. Home: 31 Shorewood Dr Macomb IL 61455-9746 Office: Western Ill U Libr Macomb IL 61455

HALLWORTH, ROBERT EARL, anesthesiologist; b. Phila., Feb. 13, 1946; s. Robert Earl and Birdie Louise (Huppi) H.; m. Kathryn Celia Brown, Feb. 16, 1973; 1 child, Elizabeth Ann. BS in Pharmacy, Temple U., 1969; DO, Phila. Coll. Osteo. Medicine, 1979. Diplomate Nat. Bd. Med. Examiners, Am. Osteo. Bd. Anesthesiology, Am. Acad. Pain Mgmt. Staff pharmacists Albert Einstein Med. Ctr., Phila., 1973-75; intern Suburban Gen. Hosp., Norristown, Pa., 1979-80, anesthesia resident, 1980-82, Met. Hosp., Phila., 1982-83; anesthesiologist Group Anesthesia Svcs., Norristown, 1983-87, Cmty. Anesthesia Assocs., Ltd., Lancaster, Pa., 1987-99, Prime Care Desert Valley Hosp., Victorville, Calif., 1999—. Program dir. anesthesia residency Cmty. Hosp. of Lancaster, 1989-99. With U.S. Army, 1971-72. Mem. Internat. Soc. Spinal Endoscopy, Am. Osteo. Assn., Am. Soc. Regional Anesthesia, Am. Osteo. Coll. Anesthesiologists (examiner 1988—), Sigma Sigma Phi. Avocations: running, skiing, swimming, bicycling. Home: 19045 Elm Drive Apple Valley CA 92308 Office: Desert Valley Med Ctr 16850 Bear Valley Rd Victorville CA 92392-5794 E-mail: rhallworth@charter.net.

HALM, JAMES MAURICE, retired chemist, poet; b. Chgo., Oct. 11, 1930; s. James Albert and Sadie (Olejnick) H.; m. Carol Ann Wenzelburger, June 3, 1934; children: Cynthia, Jennifer, Rebecca, Elizabeth. BS in Chemistry, U. Ill., 1953; MS in Chemistry, St. Louis U., 1955; PhD in Chemistry, Va. Tech., 1972. Prof. chemistry Morton Coll., Cicero, Ill., 1957-67; rsch. asst. Va. Tech., Blacksburg, 1968-72; rsch. chemist Adressograph-Multigraph, Warrensville Heights, Ohio, 1972-74; rsch. assoc., project leader A.B. Dick Co., Chgo., 1974-81; sr. scientist St. Regis Paper Co., West Nyack, N.Y., 1981-85; prof. chemistry Norwich U., Northfield, Vt., 1986-90; scientist Internat. Paper, Tuxedo, N.Y., 1990-93, Erie, Pa., 1993-96. Adj. prof. chemistry William Rainey Harper Coll., Palatine, Ill., 1975-80; chemistry cons., Hendersonville, N.C., 1996—; vis. prof. chemistry Norwich U., 2000-01; adj. prof. chemistry U. NC, Asheville, 2001. Patentee in field; contbr. articles to sci. jours.; contbg. poet to numerous mags. and jours. With U.S. Army, 1954-56. Avocations: photography, classical music, gardening. Home: 3 Ridgestone Dr Hendersonville NC 28792-9488

HALMI, NICHOLAS, language educator; b. Iowa City, Iowa, Apr. 24, 1966; BA, Cornell U., 1988; MA, U. Toronto, 1989, PhD, 1995. Lectr. English U. Toronto, 1995—96, asst. prof. English, 1996—98, McMaster U., Hamilton, 1998—2001, U. Wash., Seattle, 2001—. Mem. adv. bd. Romanticism on the Net, 1996—. Editor: S.T. Coleridge & Opus Maximum, 2002; co-editor: Loveridge's Poetry and Prose, 2003; contbg. editor: Encyclopedia of the Romantic Era, 2003; asst. editor: Collected Works of Northrop Frye, 1998—2001. Mem.: Modern Lang. Assn. Office: U Wash Dept English Box 354330 Seattle WA 98195-4330

HALMI, ROBERT, film producer, television producer; b. Budapest, Hungary, Jan. 22, 1924; s. Bela and Sarah (Deri) H.; m. Esther Szirmay, Sept. 9, 1980; children: Kevin Gorman, Kim Gorman, Robert, Bill. Grad., U. Budapest, 1946. Mag. photographer, 1946-52; photographer Life mag., 1952-62; documentary producer, 1962-75; chmn. Hallmark Entertainment, N.Y.C., 1993—. Producer over 200 TV movies, miniseries and theatrical features including Nurse, 1980, Wilson's Reward, 1980, Nairobi Affair, 1984, Grand Larceny, 1987, Mayflower Madam, 1987, Pack of Lies, 1987, Best Friends, 1987, Cheetah, 1989, Ivory Hunters, 1990, Call of the Wild, 1993, The Yearling, 1994, Promise Kept: The Oksana Baiul Story, 1994, Getting Out, 1994, The Sunshine Boys, 1995, Kidnapped, 1995, Bye Bye Birdie, 1995, Gulliver's Travells, 1996, Captain Courageous, 1996, 20,000 Leagues Under the Sea, 1997, Moby Dick, 1998, Merlin, 1998, Crime & Punishment, 1998, Rear Window, 1998, Land of Oz, 1999, Don Quixote, 1999, Cleopatra, 1999, Arabian Nights, 1999, Alice in Wonderland, 1999, Noah's Ark, 1999, Mr. & Mrs. Bridge, Gypsy, 1993, The Incident in a Small Town, 1994, Lily in Love, Barnum, Prince Charming, 2001; exec. prodr.: Mother Teresa: In the Name of God's Poor, 1997, Mike Bassett: England Manager, 2001; exec. prodr.(TV): Izzy and Moe, 1985, Cook & Peary: The Race to the Pole, 1983, Spearfield's Daughter, 1986, Spies, Lies & Naked Thighs, 1988, The Josephine Baker Story, 1991, Mrs. Lambert Remembers Love, 1991, An American Story, 1992, Family Torn Apart, 1993, Scarlett, 1994, White Dwarf, 1995, Robinson Crusoe, 1996, Jakes Women, 1996, London Suite, 1996, Mary & Tim, 1996, In Cold Blood, 1996, For Love Alone: The Ivana Trump Story, 1996, Bridge of Time, 1997, Tidal Wave: No Escape, 1997, The Odyssey, 1997, Forbidden Territory: Stanley's Search for Livingstone,

1997, A Christmas Memory, 1997, The Long Way Home, 1998, Moby Dick, 1998, Merlin, 1998, Only Love, 1998, Animal Farm, 1999, Magical Legend of the Leprechauns, 1999, A Christmas Carol, 1999, The 10th Kingdom, 2000, Arabian Nights, 2000, Jason and the Argonauts, 2000, Voyage of the Unicorn, 2001, The Lost Empire, 2001, Infinite Worlds of H.G. WEIls, 2001, Snow White, 2001, Stranded, 2002, King of Texas, 2002, Dinotopia, 2002, Mr. St. Nick, 2002, The Snow Queen, 2002; author: Into Your Hands Are They Delivered, Animals of Africa, Animals of North America, Sports Cars of the World, How To Photograph Women, Zoos of the World, Recipient 15 Emmy awards, Peabody award, Christopher award, Genesis award, CINE Golden Eagle award, numerous Houston Film Festival awards. Address: Hallmark Entertainment 21st Fl 1325 Avenue of the Americas New York NY 10019-6026*

HALMOS, PAUL RICHARD, mathematician, educator; b. Budapest, Hungary, Mar. 3, 1916; came to U.S., 1929; s. Alexander Charles and Paula (Rosenberg) H.; m. Dorothy Moyer, Jan. 1, 1934 (div. Mar. 1945); m. Virginia Templeton Pritchett, Apr. 7, 1945. BS, U. Ill., 1934, MS, 1935, PhD, 1938; DSc (hon.), U. St. Andrews, Scotland, 1984; D Math. (hon.), U. Waterloo, Can., 1990. Instr. U. Ill., Urbana, 1938-39, assoc., 1942-43; fellow, asst. Inst. for Advanced Study, Princeton, N.J., 1939-42; asst. prof. Syracuse (N.Y.) U., 1943-46; from asst. prof. to prof. U. Chgo., 1946-61; prof. U. Mich., Ann Arbor, 1961-68; prof., chmn. dept. U. Hawaii, Honolulu, 1968-69; prof., then Disting. prof. Ind. U., Bloomington, 1969-85; prof. Santa Clara (Calif.) U., 1985-96, prof. emeritus, 1996—. Author: Finite Dimensional Vector Spaces, 1942, Measure Theory, 1950, A Hilbert Space Problem Book, 1967, I Want to Be a Mathematician, 1985, others. Mem. Math. Assn. Am. (Haimo award for Dist. Coll. & Univ. Teaching of Mat., 1994), Am. Math. Soc., others. Avocations: photography, walking. Home: 110 Wood Rd Apt I-203 Los Gatos CA 95030-6720 Office: Santa Clara U Dept Math Santa Clara CA 95053-0001

HALPAIN, SUE R. music educator, musician; b. Stephenville, Tex., Mar. 5, 1940; d. U.G. and Mae West Richards; m. Bill F. Halpain, June 17, 1961; 1 child, Philip W. MusB, U. Okla., 1962. Named Outstanding Oklahoman, Gov. David Boren, 1978; recipient Internat. Forest of Friendship award, City of Atchison, Kans. and Ninety Nines, 2001, winner, Okie Derby Proficiency Air Race, 1987. Mem.: Piano Guild Hall of Fame (adjudicator), Am. Coll. Musicians, Okla. Music Tchrs. Assn. (adjudicator 1964—, 1st v.p. 1972—74), Ctrl. Okla. Music Tchrs. Assn. (pres. 1969—71, 1988—90, 1999—2001, 2003—), The Ninety-Nines (chmn. Okla. 1977—79, gov. SCS 1988—90), Mu Phi Epsilon. Republican. Mem. Disciples Of Christ. Avocations: flying, camping, travel, skiing, reading. Home and Office: 8213 Brownsville Ln Bethany OK 73008 E-mail: shalpain99@aol.com.

HALPENNY, DIANA DORIS, lawyer; b. San Francisco, Jan. 18, 1951; d. William Frederick and Doris E. Halpenny. BA, Calif. State Coll., 1973; cert. elem. tchr., Calif. State U., Long Beach, 1976; JD, U. Pacific, 1980. Bar: Calif. 1980. Bookkeeper, sales clk. Farmers Empire Drugs, Santa Rosa, Calif., 1971-73; activity dir. Beverly Manor Convalescent Hosp., Anaheim, Calif., 1973-74; instrnl. aide LA County Supt. Schs., Downey, Calif., 1974-76, sub. tchr., 1976-77; assoc. Littler, Mendelson, Fastiff & Tichy, San Jose, Calif., 1980-82, Walters & Shelburne, Sacramento, 1982-84, Kronick Moskovitz Tiedemann & Girard, Sacramento, 1984-85; legal advisor Pub. Employment Rels. Bd., 1985-87; gen. counsel San Juan Unified Sch. Dist., 1987— Founding mem. In-house Sch. Attys. No. Calif.; past. pres. no. sect. Sch. Law Study Sect. Co. Counsels Assn., 1991—92; legal adv. com. Calif. Sch. Bd. Assn. Edn. Legal Alliance, chair, 2000—; mem. exec. bd. Calif. Edn. Mandated Cost Network, 1987—, chair, 1998—. Mem. Calif. Coun. Sch. Attys. (v.p. programs 1993, pres.-elect 1994, pres. 1995, exec. bd. dirs. 1993—), Order of the Coif. Office: San Juan Unified Sch Dist 3738 Walnut Ave Carmichael CA 95608-3099

HALPER, EMANUEL B(ARRY), real estate lawyer, developer, consultant, author; b. Bronx, N.Y., June 24, 1933; s. Nathan N. and Molly (Rabinowitz) H.; m. Ilona Rubinstein, Mar. 5, 1961; children: Eve Brook, Dan Reed. AB, CCNY, 1954; JD, Columbia U., 1957. Bar: N.Y. 1958, Minn. 1982; real estate broker, N.Y. House counsel Howard Stores Corp., Bklyn., 1960; ptnr. Zissu, Berman, Halper & Gumbinger, N.Y.C., 1965-87, of counsel, 1987-97; ptnr. Can. Pacific Realty Co., Fairfield, N.J., 1970—; v.p. devel. Chase Enterprises, Hartford, Conn., 1987-89; pres. Texam Horizon Ventures, 1989-93, Am. Devel. and Cons. Corp., Greenvale, N.Y., 1989—. Adj. prof. real estate NYU, 1973-83; spl. prof. law Hofstra U., 1998—. Author: Wonderful World of Real Estate, 1975 (republished as Conversations in Real Estate, 1990), Shopping Center and Store Leases, 1979, Ground Leases and Land Acqusition Contracts, 1988; columnist N.Y. Law Jour., 1982-1992; contbg. editor Real Estate Review, N.Y.C., 1973-99; chmn. editorial policy com. Internat. Property Investment Jour., Hempstead, N.Y., 1982-87. With USAR, 1957-63. Recipient Disting. Teaching award NYU, 1978, Dean's award Hofstra U. Law Sch., 1987. Mem. ABA (chmn. comml. leasing com. 1986-93, chmn. comml. and indsl. leasing group 1993-94, mem. supervisory coun. of real property, probate and trust law sect. 1994-2000, mem. standing com. on CLE, 1994-96, mem. standing com. pubs. 1997-98, Gavel award 1977, mem. standing com. on diversity 1999—), World Assn. Lawyers (chmn. internat. real estate com. 1982-90), Internat. Inst. for Real Estate Studies (chmn. bd. 1980-87), Am. Coll. Real Estate Lawyers. Jewish. Avocations: writing, painting, gardening, yoga, running. Office: PO Box 261 Greenvale NY 11548-0261 E-mail: e1h@aol.com.

HALPER, THOMAS, political science educator; b. Bklyn., Dec. 1, 1942; s. Albert and Pauline (Friedman) H.; m. Marilyn S. Snyder, Jan. 14, 1979; 1 dau., Pauline. AB, St. Lawrence U., 1963; MA, Vanderbilt U., 1967, PhD, 1970. Instr. Tulane U., 1967-68; asst. prof. polit. sci. Coe Coll., 1968-74, Baruch Coll., 1974-76, prof., chmn. dept., 1976—. Author: Foreign Policy Crises, 1971, Power, Politics and American Democracy, 1981, The Misfortunes of Others, 1989; contbr. articles to profl. jours. Mem. Am. Polit. Sci. Assn. Home: 75 Livingston St Brooklyn NY 11201-5054 Office: Baruch Coll Dept Polit Sci 1 Bernard Baruch Way New York NY 10010-5518

HALPERIN, BERTRAND ISRAEL, physics educator; b. Bklyn., Dec. 6, 1941; s. Morris and Eva (Teplitsky) H.; m. Helena Stacy French, Sept. 23, 1962; children: Jeffery Arnold, Julia Stacy. AB, Harvard U., 1961; A.M., U. Calif., 1963, PhD, 1965; vis. grad. student, Princeton U., 1964-65. NSF postdoctoral fellow U. Paris, 1965-66; mem. tech. staff Bell Labs., Murray Hill, N.J., 1966-76; lectr. Harvard U., 1969-70, prof. physics, 1976—, chmn. dept. physics, 1988-91, Hollis prof. maths. and natural philosophy, 1992—; sci. dir. Harvard U. Ctr. for Imaging and Mesoscale Structures, 1999—. Cons. Lucent Technologies, Schlumberger-Doll Rsch. Labs. Assoc. editor: Revs. Modern Physics, 1973-80. Recipient Wolf prize, Wolf Found., Herzlia, Israel, 2003. Fellow Am. Phys. Soc. (Oliver Buckley prize 1982, Lars Onsager prize 2001), Am. Acad. Arts and Scis.; mem. NAS, Am. Philos. Soc. Achievements include rsch. in solid state theory, statis. physics. Office: Harvard U Dept Physics Cambridge MA 02138

HALPERIN, GEORGE BENNETT, education educator, retired naval officer; b. N.Y.C., Aug. 7, 1926; s. George and Muryal (Lesser) H.; m. Ellen Elizabeth Barber, Dec. 18, 1957 (div. 1988); children: Gail Susan, Thomas Allyn; m. Kathleen Bourdon, Aug. 22, 2000. BS, U.S. Naval Acad., 1950; MBA, Stanford U., 1958; postgrad., Naval War Coll., Newport, R.I., 1965-66; MA in History, U. Vt., 1976; MEd, Harvard U., 1979; postgrad., Oxford U., 1987-88, St. Catherine's Coll., 1987-88. Commd. ensign U.S. Navy, 1950, advanced through grades to comdr., 1965; dir. systems and standards div. Naval Supply Ctr., Oakland, Calif., 1963-65; freight terminal officer Naval Support Activity, Danang, Vietnam, 1966-67; supply officer Naval Air Sta., Barbers Point, Hawaii, 1967-70; ret., 1970; tchr. history Stowe (Vt.) High Sch., 1972-80, asst. prin., 1975-76; tchr. John F. Kennedy Sch., Berlin, 1980-86. Chmn. Lamoille South Dist. Profl. Growth Com., 1977-78. Decorated Navy Commendation medal. Mem. U.S. Naval Acad. Alumni Assn., Army-Navy Country Club, Oxford Soc. Home: # 79 Apple Blossom Dr West Lebanon NH 03784

HALPERIN, JEROME ARTHUR, pharmaceutical executive; b. Paterson, N.J., Feb. 21, 1937; s. Harry Nathan and Frieda (Niestat) H.; m. Barbara Anne Hott, Sept. 1, 1963; children: Alicia Jennifer Odom, Rachel Elizabeth Halperin Montgomery. BS, Rutgers U., 1958; MPH, Johns Hopkins U., 1962; MS, MIT, 1974; DSc (hon.), Mercer U., 1993, Mass. Coll. Pharm., 1995, Phila. Coll. Pharmacy and Sci., 1996; DHL (hon.), Western U. Health Scis., 2000. Commd. officer USPHS, 1958, advanced through grades to rear admiral, 1983; staff pharmacist USPHS Hosps., Dept. HEW, Albuquerque and N.Y.C., 1958-61; radiol. health specialist Calif. Health Dept., Berkeley, 1962-65; agreement states coord. Bur. Radiol. Health, Rockville, Md., 1965-66; dir. indsl. radiation and air hygiene Kans. Dept. Health, Topeka, 1966-68; regional rep. Bur. Radiol. Health, Chgo., 1968-71; dir. Northeastern Radiol. Health Lab., FDA, HEW, Winchester, Mass., 1971-73; dep. assoc. dir. new drug evaluation Bur. Drugs, FDA, HEW, Rockville, Md., 1974-77, dep. dir., 1977-82; acting dir. Office of Drugs Nat. Ctr. for Drugs and Biologics FDA, Rockville, 1982-83; v.p. tech. CIBA Consumer Pharms., Edison, N.J., 1983-89; exec. dir. U.S. Pharmacopeial Conv., Inc., Rockville, Md., 1989-95, exec. v.p., CEO, 1995-2000. Chmn. Conf. on Pharmacy 21st Century Va., 1984; cons. WHO, 1979-2000; CEO Food and Drug Law Inst., Washington, 2001—; trustee Davis and Elkins Coll., 2003—. Contbr. articles to profl. jours. Mem. Bd. Health, Hoffman Estates, Ill., 1971; bd. dirs. Perspective Woods Citizen Assn., Olney, Md., 1977-80. Named Alumnus of Yr., Rutgers U. Coll. of Pharmacy, 1981, Disting. Person of Yr., Pharmaceutical Planning Svc., Inc., 1998; recipient Outstanding Svc. award, Federally Employed Women's Assn., 1983, Disting. Career award, Drug Info. Assn., 2001, Career Achievement award, Profl. Fraternities Assn., 2001, Disting. Alumni award, FDA, 2002. Fellow: Am. Pharm. Assn. (Remington Honor medal 2001), Am. Assn. Pharm. Scientists, APHA, AAAS; mem.: Internat.Pharm. Fedn. (expert mem. bd. pharm. scis.). Jewish. Office: FDLI Ste 200 1000 Vermont Ave NW Washington DC 20005 E-mail: jah@fdli.org.

HALPERIN, KRISTINE BRIGGS, insurance sales and marketing professional; b. Pocatello, Idaho, July 25, 1947; d. Fergus and Shirley (Tanner) Briggs; m. Michael Lauren Halperin, Aug. 5, 1995; children: Anthony Ted Rojas, Nancy Kristine Rojas. Student, Idaho State U., 1965-66. Tech. coord. Farmers Ins. Group, Pocatello, 1971-81; svc. rep. All Seasons Ins. Agy., Ventura, Calif., 1982; sr. comml. underwriting asst. Royal Ins. Co., Ventura, 1982-85; sr. comml. lines underwriter Andreini & Co., Ventura, 1985-88; large comml. account unit coord. Frank B. Hall, Inc., Oxnard, Calif., 1988-93; mgr. comml. lines dept. Fox Ins. Agy. Inc., Camarillo, Calif., 1993-2001; acct. mgt. Venbrook Ins. Svcs., Woodland Hills, 2001—02, Brown & Brown of Calif. DSD Ins. Agy., Thousand Oaks, 2002—03; self-employed ins. cons., 2003—. Editor (bulletin) News Waves, 1985—; artist various works specializing in charcoal portraits. Mem. NAFE, Ins. Women Ventura County (treas. 1987-88, v.p. 1988-90, 96-97, 2001, pres. 1990-91, 97-98, corr. sec. 1991-92, bd. dirs. 1986, Woman of Yr. 1989-90, 99-2000), Nat. Assn. Ins. Women. Republican. Baptist. Avocations: belly dancing, gardening, reading, hiking, carpentry. Home and Office: 2197 Brookhill Dr Camarillo CA 93010-2107

HALPERIN, MARK EVAN, journalist; b. Cambridge, Mass., Jan. 11, 1965; s. Morton H Halperin and Ina Young. AB, Harvard U., 1983—87. Polit. dir. ABC News, N.Y.C., 1997—. Office: ABC News 47 West 66th St New York NY 10023

HALPERIN, MICHAEL HOWARD, writer, educator; PhD, Union Inst. and U., Cin., 1993. Lectr. Loyola Marymount U. Story editor Universal TV, Universal City; exec. story cons. 20th Century-Fox TV, L.A.; writer-prodr. MCA-TV, Universal City; creative cons. Mattel, El Segundo, Hanna-Barbera, Hollywood; crea. cons. He-Man and the Masters of the Universe: The Begining, 2002. Author: Jacob's Rescue: A Holocaust Story, 1993, Writing Great Characters: The Psychology of Character Development in Screenplays, 1996, Writing the Second Act: Building Conflict & Tension in your Film Script, 2000, Writing the Killer Treatment: Selling your Story without a Script, 2002, Black Wheels, 2003. Recipient Screen & Entertainment Book Club Selection: Writing the Killer Treatment, 2002, Writers Digest Book Club Selection: Writing the Second Act, 2000, Movie/Entertainment Book Club Selection: Writing the Second Act, 2000, Writers Digest Book Club Selection: Writing Great Characters, 1998, Tchr.'s Choice award for Jacob's Rescue, Internat. Reading Assn., 1994, Notable Children's Trade Book award for Jacob's Rescue, Children's Book Coun./Nat. Coun., 1994, Cybie award for Voyeur, Acad. Interactive Arts & Scis., 1994, Best Book of 1993 for Jacob's Rescue, Am. Bookseller's Assn., 1993, Marcus Foster award, N.Y. Film and TV Festival, 1973, Chris award, Columbus Film Festival, 1966, Cert. Merit, Indsl. Photography, 1966; grantee Screenplay grantee, NEH, 1981. Mem.: Prodrs.s-Writers Guild Am. Pension Plan (dir. 1990—), Writers Guild-Industry Health Fund (trustee 1990—), Writers Guild of Am. West (bd. dirs. 1992—94, Svc. award 1999). Personal E-mail: michaelhalperin@sprintmail.com.

HALPERIN, MORTON H. political scientist; b. Bklyn., June 13, 1938; s. Harry and Lillian (Neubert) H.; m. Ina Elaine Weinstein, June 19, 1960 (div. Dec. 1979); children: David, Mark, Gary; m. Carol Pitchersky, Sept. 29, 1991. AB, Columbia U., 1958; MA, Yale U., 1959, PhD, 1961. Research assoc. Harvard U., 1960-66, asst. prof., 1963-66; dep. asst. sec. U.S. Dept. Def., Washington, 1966-69; sr. staff mem. Nat. Security Council, Washington, 1969; sr. fellow Brookings Instn., Washington, 1969-73; research project dir. Twentieth Century Fund, Washington, 1974-75; dir. Ctr. Nat. Security Studies, Washington, 1975-92; dir. Washington office ACLU, 1985-92; sr. assoc. Carnegie Endowment for Internat. Peace, 1992-94; Barer Prof. Internat. Rels. The George Washington U., Washington, 1992-94; spl. asst. to pres., sr. dir. for democracy Nat. Security Coun., Washington, 1994-96; sr. fellow Coun. Fgn. Rels., Washington, 1996-98; sr. v.p. Twentieth Century Fund/Century Found., Washington, 1997-98; dir. policy planning staff Dept. of State, 1998-2001; sr. fellow Coun. Fgn. Rels., Washington, 2001—; dir. Washington office Open Soc. Inst., 2002—. Author: Limited War in the Nuclear Age, 1963, Contemporary Military Strategy, 1967, Bureaucratic Politics and Foreign Policy, 1974, Top Secret, 1977, Nuclear Fallacy, 1987, Self-Determination in a New World Order, 1992. Recipient Meritorious Civilian Service award U.S. Dept. Def., 1969; recipient Hugh M. Hefner 1st Amendment Playboy Found., 1981, W. Lucius Cross medal Yale Grad. Sch. Alumni Assn., 1983, John Jay award Columbia Coll., 1986; MacArthur Found. fellow, 1981-85. Mem. ACLU, Coun. Fgn. Rels., Internat. Inst. Strategic Studies. Democrat. Jewish. Home: 2101 Connecticut Ave NW Washington DC 20008-1728

HALPERIN, RICHARD GEORGE, information technology executive; b. Chgo., Apr. 5, 1948; s. Robert Charles and Phyllis Dorothy (Jewel) H.; m. Carolyn A'Della Bacino, Oct. 5, 1974; children: Nicole, Heidi, Erik. BSBA, Northwestern U., 1970. Mktg. mgr. IBM, Des Plaines, Ill., 1970-79; nat. sales mgr. Kast Metals, Shreveport, La., 1979-83; area dir. Wang Labs., Rolling Meadows, Ill., 1983-85; v.p. sales and svcs. System Software Assoc., Chgo., 1985-89; sr. v.p. Software Group XL Datacomp, Hinsdale, Ill., 1989-91; pres. Ex, Inc., Chgo., 1991-92; pres., CEO JBA Internat., Inc., Birmingham, Eng., 1992-98; CEO Coherent Networks Internat., 1998-99. Bd. dirs. Genesis, Glenview, Ill., Advanced Graphical Applications, Schaumburg, Am. Indian Svcs., Phoenix, Alliance, Anderson Cons., Chgo., Made 2 Manage, Indpls.; partnership CADDO Petroleum, Shreveport, La., 1981-86, BLM, Shreveport, 1981—. Named Top Dist. Mgr., Wang, Chgo., and Rome, 1984. Mem. Internat. Soc. Philos. Enquiry, Data Processing Mgrs. Assn., Info. Tech. Assn. Am., Northwestern Club of Chgo., Delta Upsilon, N Club Mens. Address: 641 Golf Rd Crystal Lake IL 60014-5650

HALPERIN, ROBERT MILTON, retired electrical machinery company executive; b. Chgo., June 1, 1928; s. Herman and Edna Pearl (Rosenberg) H.; m. Ruth Levison, June 19, 1955; children: Mark, Margaret, Philip. Ph.B., U. Chgo., 1949; B.Mech. Engring., Cornell U., 1949; MBA, Harvard U., 1952. Locomotive prodn. engr. Electro-Motive divsn. Gen. Motors Corp., La Grange, Ill., 1949—50; trust rep. Bank of Am., San Francisco, 1954—56; adminstr. Dumont Corp., San Rafael, Calif., 1956—57; with Raychem Corp., 1957—94, pres., 1982—90, vice chmn., bd. dirs., 1990—94. Chmn. bd. dirs. Avid Tech. Inc.; bd. dirs. Vitria Tech. Inc. Bd. trustees U. Chgo.; bd. dirs. Harvard Bus. Sch. Pub. Co., Stanford U. Hosp. and Clinics; vice-chair, bd. dirs. Stanford U. Hosp. and Clinics. Lt. USAF, 1952-53. Mem. Harvard Club of N.Y.C. Office: 2929 Campus Dr Ste 400 San Mateo CA 94403

HALPERIN, SAMUEL, education and training policy analyst; b. Chgo., May 10, 1930; married; 2 children. Student (scholar), Ill. Inst. Tech., 1948-49; AB, A.M. (scholar 1950-52), Washington U., St. Louis, 1952, PhD in Polit. Sci. (fellow 1954-56), 1956; postgrad., Columbia U., 1953-54. Asst. prof. polit. sci. Wayne State U., 1956-60; Am. Polit. Sci. Assn. congl. fellow Com. on Edn. and Labor, U.S. Ho. of Reps., 1960-61; legis. asst. to Hon. Cleveland M. Bailey and Adam C. Powell, 1960-61; cons. to subcom. on edn. and Senator Wayne Morse, Com. on Labor and Public Welfare, U.S. Senate, 1961, subcom. on reorgn., research and internat. orgns., 1970-73; specialist, dir. legis. services br. U.S. Office Edn., Washington, 1961-64; asst. U.S. commr. edn. for legis. and dir. office legis. and congl. relations, 1964-66; dep. asst. sec. for legis. HEW, Washington, 1966-69; founder, dir. Ednl. Staff Seminar, Washington, 1969-73; dir. Inst. for Ednl. Leadership, George Washington U., 1973-81, pres., 1981, sr. fellow, 1981-86; fellow Jerusalem Ctr. Pub. Affairs, 1981-84; coordinator Relief Activities in South Lebanon, Am. Jewish Joint Distbn. Com., 1982; founder, dir. Am. Youth Policy Forum, Washington, 1993—. Professorial lectr. Am. U., 1962-63; adj. prof. Tchrs. Coll. Columbia U., 1966-68; lectr. in edn. policy Duke U. Inst. Policy Scis. and Public Affairs, 1974-75; mem. vis. com. Harvard Grad. Sch. Edn., 1973-79; mem. Urban Edn. Task Force, Nat. Urban Coalition; mem. profl. rev. panels; cons. speaker, guest lectr. in field; mem. nat. adv. bd. U.S. Peace Corps, Exec. High Sch. Internships Am., Nat. Sch. Vol. Program, HEW Steering Com. on Life-Long Learning, Nat. Student Ednl. Fund, Am. Council Edn.'s Nat. Identification Program for Advancement Women in Higher Edn. Adminstrn., United Student Aid Funds; mem. Sec. of Navy's Adv. Bd. on Edn. and Tng.; mem. adv. panel on human resources research Rand Corp. Author: The Political World of American Zionism, 1961, 2d edit., 1985, A University in the Web of Politics, 1960, Essays on Federal Education Policy, 1975, A Guide for the Powerless, 1981, 2d edit. 2000, Any Home a Campus: Open University of Israel, 1984, The forgotten Half Revisited, 1998; co-editor, contbg. author: Perspectives on Federal Educational Policy, 1976, Federalism at the Crossroads, Improving Educational Policymaking, 1976; contbr. numerous articles, revs. to profl. publs.; cons. Change mag.; mem. nat. adv. bd. Crossreference, Jour. Multi-Cultural Edn. Mem. nat. adv. bd. Am. Jewish Com.; founder, sec. D.C. Youth Svc. Corps.; mem. Nat. Adv. Coun. on Sch.-to-Work, D.C. Commn. on Nat. Svc.; mem. exec. bd. Coalition for Nat. And Cmty. Svc.; D.C. Pvt. Industry Coun., bd. dirs. Learning Matters: The Merrow Report on PBS, Ctr. for Youth as Resources, Assocs. for Renewal in Edn., Coun. for Advancement of Adult Lit., Alliance for Excellent Edn.; Maj. ROTC, 1948-52. Recipient Superior Svc. award HEW, 1964, 67, Disting. Svc. award, 1968; award of merit Nat. Assn. Pub. Sch. Adult Edn.; Disting. Svc. awards Nat. Assn. State Bds. Edn., 1977, Nat. Assn. of Svc. and Conservation Corps., 1990, 97, Jobs for the Future, 1994, Pres.'s medal George Washington U., 1994, Harry S. Truman award Am. Assn. C.C., 1995, Lewis Hine award Nat. Child Labor Com., 1999; AFL-CIO rsch. grantee, 1959-60, Wayne State U. faculty rsch. grantee, 1958-59; Rockefeller Found. fellow, Bellagio, 1981, 92. Mem. Phi Beta Kappa, Pi Sigma Alpha (pres.) Home: 3041 Normanstone Ter NW Washington DC 20008-2731 Office: Am Youth Policy Forum 1836 Jefferson Pl NW Washington DC 20036-2505 Fax: 202-775-9733. E-mail: shalperin18@comcast.net.

HALPERIN, STUART, entertainment company executive; b. Bklyn., June 20, 1963; Newswriter CNN; various mktg. positions New Line Cinema, 20th Century Fox Internat., Universal Pictures; co-founder, exec. v.p. Hollywood-.com, Santa Monica, Calif; exec. v.p. mktg. MovieTickets.com, Santa Monica, Calif., 2000—. Office: MovieTickets dot com 520 Broadway Ste 230 Santa Monica CA 90401

HALPERN, ABRAHAM LEON, psychiatrist; b. Warsaw, Feb. 2, 1925; came to U.S., 1957, naturalized, 1962; s. Rubin M. and Helen (Perelman) H.; m. Marilyn Lois Benjamin; children: Howard, Lon, Marnen, Heather Halpern Schneid, Mark, Emily Halpern Lewis, John. MD, U. Toronto, Ont., Can., 1952. Diplomate Am. Bd. Psychiatry and Neurology with cert. in forensic psychiatry, Am. Bd. Forensic Psychiatry; cert. mental hosp. adminstr.; cert. correctional health profl. Intern Toronto Western Hosp., 1952-53; resident Warren (Pa.) State Hosp., 1957-60, Ea. Pa. Psychiat. Inst., Phila., 1959; assoc. research scientist Mental Health Research Unit, Syracuse, N.Y., 1961-62; commr. mental health Onondaga County, 1962-67; practice medicine specializing in psychiatry Mamaroneck, N.Y., 1967—; dir. psychiatry United Hosp. Med. Ctr., Port Chester, 1967-91; attending psychiatrist Beth Israel Hosp., N.Y.C., 1968-73, Westchester County Med. Ctr., 1971—; cons. forensic psychiatry High Point Hosp., Port Chester, 1969-93; cons. St. Vincent's Hosp., Harrison, N.Y., 1973-93; clin. assoc. prof. psychiatry N.Y. Med. Coll., Valhalla, N.Y., 1973-80, clin. prof. psychiatry, 1980-94, prof. emeritus of psychiatry, 1994—; cons. Rye (N.Y.) Hosp. Ctr., 1994—; attending psychiatrist Kirby Forensic Psychiat. Ctr., Ward's Island, N.Y., 1994-95; attending psychiatrist dept. alcohol/substance abuse treatment Yonkers (N.Y.) Gen. Hosp., 1995-96; clin. dir. mental health svcs. Dept. Correctional Program, Westchester County, N.Y., 1996. Clin. asst. prof. SUNY, Syracuse, 1964-67; asst. clin. prof. Mt. Sinai Sch. Medicine, 1970-74; clin. assoc. prof. N.Y. Med. Coll., 1973-80, clin. prof. psychiatry, 1980-94, prof. emeritus, 1994—; clin. prof. forensic psychiatry, N.Y. Sch. Psychiatry, 1979-82; mem. med. adv. com. Vis. Nurse Assn., Syracuse, 1962-67; mem. N.Y. State Mental Hygiene Med. Rev. Bd., 1982-86; bd. govs. High Point Hosp., 1989-92. Assoc. editor Bull. Am. Acad. Psychiatry and the Law, 1982-88, Jour. Am. Acad. Psychiatry and the Law, 2002—; mem. editorial bd. Psychiat. Jour. of U. Ottawa, 1979-91; mem. exec. editorial com. Psychiat. Quar., 1982-90, assoc. editor, 1990—. Chmn. Syracuse chpt. Com. to Abolish Capital Punishment, 1962-65; mem. profl. adv. com. N.Y. State Assn. for Mental Health, 1964-67; mem. N.Y. State Law Revision Adv. Com. on the Insanity Def., 1979-80; mem. Westchester County Community Mental Health Bd., 1976-78, chmn., 1977-78; mem. Westchester County Hosp. Bd., 1992—; bd. visitors Harlem Valley Psychiat. Center, 1978-82; mem. N.Y. State Correction Med. Rev. Bd., 1980-87, N.Y. State Mental Hygiene Med. Rev. Bd., 1982-85; bd. dirs. Westchester Council on Alcoholism, 1980-85. Served to surgeon lt. comdr. Royal Can. Navy, 1942-45, 53-57. Recipient Citizenship award, NY State Bar Assn., 1966, Liberty Bell award, Onondaga County Bar Assn., 1966, Falun Dafa Appreciation award, 2000. Fellow ACP, Am. Acad. Forensic Scis., Am. Coll. Psychiatrists, Am. Psychiat. Assn. (com. psychiatry and law 1973-75, com. on abuse and misuse psychiatry and psychiatrists 1993—, Human Rights award 2000), Am. Assn. Psychoanalytic Physicians (dir. 1978-84, Sigmund Freud award 2002), Am. Pub. Health Assn., Academia, Medicinae and Psychiatriae Found. (charter); mem. AMA, N.Y. State Med. Soc. (com. on mental health, com. bioethical issues, com. on child abuse and domestic violence), Internat. Assn. Forensic Psychotherapy, Soc. Correctional Physicians, Pan Am. Med. Assn. (mem. council sect. on psychiatry 1983-85), Westchester County Med. Soc., Westchester Psychiat. Soc. (pres. 1973-74), Soc. Med. Jurisprudence (trustee 1980-85, 99—), Internat. Acad. Law and Mental Health (pres. 1983-87), Am. Acad. Psychoanalysis (sci. assoc. 1987), Am. Acad. Psychiatry and Law (councilor 1978-81, pres. elect 1981-82, pres. 1982-83, Golden Apple award 1987), Accreditation Coun. on Fellowships in Forensic Psychiatry (pres. 1990-93), Internat. Coun. on Prison Med. Svcs. (v.p. 1991—). Home and Office: 720 The Pky Mamaroneck NY 10543-4227 E-mail: ahalpern@att.net

HALPERN, ALEXANDER, lawyer; b. Tokyo, Aug. 13, 1948; came to U.S., Dec. 1948; s. Abraham Meyer and Mary (Fujii) H.; m. Carol Dreiling, May 12, 1973; children: Solomon J., Eve M., Peter N. BA in Sociology, Brandeis U., 1970; JD, U. Denver, 1976. Bar: Colo. 1976, U.S. Dist. Ct. Colo. 1976, U.S. Ct. Appeals (10th cir.) 1981, U.S. Supreme Ct. 1983. Ptnr. Caplan and Earnest, Boulder, Colo., 1976—. Pres. Ashoka Credit Union, Boulder, 1978—; bd. dirs. Shambhala Internat., 1991—; trustee Naropa U., Boulder, 1991—. Mem. ABA, Colo. Bar Assn., Asian Am. Bar Assn. Colo., Boulder County Bar Assn. Democrat. Buddhist. Office: Halpern Clancy LLC 1881 Canyon Blvd Ste 315 Boulder CO 80302 E-mail: ahalpern@halpernclancy.com.

HALPERN, ALVIN MICHAEL, retired physicist, educator, consultant; b. N.Y.C., July 17, 1938; s. Bernard and Gilda (Reiss) H.; m. Mariarosa Roffi, Dec. 2, 1966; children: Kenneth, Marc. AB, Columbia U., 1959, MA, 1961, PhD, 1965. Instr. Pratt Inst., N.Y.C., 1964-65; instr. physics Bklyn. Coll., 1965-66, asst. prof., 1966-69, assoc. prof., 1970-74, prof., 1975—, chmn. dept., 1980-90; exec. dir. Applied Scis. Inst., 1990-93; univ. dir. rsch. devel., v.p. rsch. found. CUNY, 1993-97, univ. dean rsch., interim pres. rsch. found., 1997-2000; retired. Contbr. articles to profl. jours. Recipient awards CUNY, 1976, 78, 80, 81, 84; Pfister fellow Columbia U., 1961-64, NSF predoctoral fellow Columbia U., 1959-61; NSF grantee, 1970, 72, 73, 78-80, 79-80, 80-82 Mem. AAAS, AAUP, Am. Phys. Soc., Am. Assn. Physics Tchrs., N.Y. Acad. Scis. E-mail: alvin_halpern@yahoo.com.

HALPERN, BARRY DAVID, lawyer; b. Champaign, Ill., Feb. 25, 1949; s. I.L. and Trula M. H.; m. Cynthia Ann Zedler, Aug. 4, 1972; children: Amanda M., Trevor H. BA, U. Kans., 1971, JD, 1973. Bar: Kans. 1973, Fla. 1975, Ariz.

1978, Colo. 1991, U.S. Dist. Ct. Kans. 1973, U.S. Dist. Ct. Ariz. 1978, U.S. Supreme Ct. 1976. Ptnr. Snell & Wilmer, Phoenix, 1978—. Mem. Gov.'s Task Force Edn. Reform, 1991, judge pro tem Maricopal County Superior Ct.; judge pro tem Maricopa County Superior Ct.; bd. dirs. Crisis Nursery, Phoenix, 1987, Friends of Foster Children, Phoenix, 1987, Phoenix Symphony, Combined Orgn. Met. Phoenix Arts and Scis., 1994—98, pres., 1996—97, mem. exec. com., 1998—2002. Mem. ABA, State Bar Ariz., State Bar, Fla., State Bar Kans., State Bar Colo., Maricopa County Bar Assn. (chmn. med.-legal com. 1995-96), Phoenix C. of C. (health care coun. 1993-96). Office: Snell & Wilmer 1 Arizona Ctr Phoenix AZ 85004-2202

HALPERN, BRUCE PETER, academic administrator, researcher, educator; b. Newark, Aug. 18, 1933; s. Leo and Thelma (Rubin) H.; m. Pauline Touber Anklowitz, June 9, 1956; children: Michael Touber, Stacey Rachael. AB, Rutgers U., 1955; M.Sc., Brown U., 1957, PhD, 1959. Asst. prof. physiology SUNY Upstate Med. U., Syracuse, N.Y., 1961-66; assoc. prof. psychology, neurobiology and behavior Cornell U., Ithaca, N.Y., 1966-73, prof., 1973-95, chmn. dept. psychology, 1974-90, 91-96, Susan Linn Sage prof. psychology, 1995—, prof. neurobiology and behavior, 1974—. Mem. Adv. Panel Sensory Physiology and Perception NSF, 1976-79; mem. adv. com. Nat. Inst. Neurol. and Communicative Disorders and Stroke, NIH, 1978-79, 85-87, Internat. Commn. on Olfaction and Taste, Union of Physiol. Scis., 1986-94; Fogarty sr. internat. fellow, vis. prof. oral physiology Osaka U., 1982-83; chmn. Gordon Conf. on Chem. Senses: Taste and Smell, 1987-90; PHS-NIMH postdoctoral fellow physiology, rsch. assoc., lect. psychology Cornell U., Ithaca, N.Y., 1959-61; vis. scientist Monell Chem. Senses Ctr., 1996-97. Exec. editor Chem. Senses, 1984-88; contbr. articles to profl. jours. NIMH grantee, 1958-62; NIH grantee, 1963-72; NSF grantee, 1972-90. Mem. Am. Physiol. Soc., Assn. Chemoreception Scis. (pres. 1982-83). Office: Cornell U Dept Psychology Dept Neurobiology/Behavior Uris Hall Ithaca NY 14853-7601 E-mail: bph1@cornell.edu. *For those with power: As one's ability to influence or control the actions of others increases, one must become increasingly unwilling to use that ability. For scholars: Any generally accepted scientific idea is an ideal area for creative research, since the idea is almost certainly incorrect.*

HALPERN, ERIC FRANKLIN, university publishing director; b. Portsmouth, N.H., Feb. 28, 1952; s. Stephen and Irene Sally (Needle) H.; m. Frances Jane Weatherburn; children: Helen Augusta, Ian Henry. BA, U. Calif., Santa Cruz, 1974, Oxford U., 1977; MA, Stanford U., 1980. Asst. editor Acquisitions Cornell Univ. Press., Ithaca, N.Y., 1981-84; editor Humanities Johns Hopkins Univ. Press., Balt., 1984-90, editor-in-chief, 1990-96; dir. Univ. Pa. Press, Phila., 1996—. Trustee Fairmount Park Art Assn. Mem. Assn. Am. Univ. Presses, Classical Assn. Atlantic States. Office: Univ Pa Press 4200 Pine St Philadelphia PA 19104-4011 E-mail: ehalpern@pobox.upenn.edu.

HALPERN, JACK, chemist, educator; b. Poland, Jan. 19, 1925; came to U.S., 1962, naturalized; s. Philip and Anna (Sass) H.; m. Helen Peritz, June 30, 1949; children: Janice Henry, Nina Phyllis. BS, McGill U., 1946, PhD, 1949, DSc (hon.), 1997, U. B.C., 1986. NRC postdoc. overseas fellow U. Manchester, England, 1949-50; instr. chemistry U. B.C., 1950, prof., 1961-62; Nuffield Found. traveling fellow Cambridge (Eng.) U., 1959-60; prof. chemistry U. Chgo., 1962-71, Louis Block prof. chemistry, 1971-83, Louis Block Disting. Svc. prof., 1983—. Vis. prof. U. Minn., 1962, Harvard, 1966-67, Calif. Inst. Tech., 1968-69, Princeton U., 1970-71, Max. Planck Institut, Mulheim, Fed. Republic Germany, 1983—, U. Copenhagen, 1978; Sherman Fairchild Disting. scholar Calif. Inst. Tech., 1979; guest scholar Kyoto U., 1981; Firth vis. prof. U. Sheffield, 1982, Phi Beta Kappa vis. scholar, 1990; R.B. Woodward vis. prof. Harvard U., 1991; numerous guest lectureships; cons. editor Macmillan Co., 1963-65, Oxford U. Press; cons. Am. Oil Co., Monsanto Co., Argonne Nat. Lab., IBM, Air Products Co., Enimont, Rohm and Haas; mem. adv. panel on chemistry NSF, 1967-70; mem. adv. bd. Am. Chem. Soc. Petroleum Rsch. Fund, 1972-74, Trans Atlantic Sci. and Humanities Program, 2001--; mem. medicinal chemistry sect. NIH, 1975-78, chmn., 1976-78; mem. chemistry adv. coun. Princeton U., 1982—; mem. univ. adv. com. Ency. Brit., 1985—; mem. chemistry vis. com. Calif. Inst. Tech., 1991—; chmn. German-Am. Acad. Coun., 1993-96, chmn. bd. trustees, 1996—. Assoc. editor: Inorganica Chimica Acta, Jour. Am. Chem. Soc.; co-editor: Collected Accounts of Transition Metal Chemistry, vol. 1, 1973, vol. 2, 1977; assoc. editor Procs. NAS; mem. editl. adv. bd. Oxford Univ. Press, Internat. Series Monographs on Chemistry; mem. editl. bd. Jour. Organometallic Chemistry, Accounts Chem. Rsch., Catalysis Revs., Jour. Catalysis, Jour. Molecular Catalysis, Jour. Coord. Chemistry, Gazzetta Chimica Italiana, Organometallics, Catalysis Letters, Kinetics and Catalysis Letters; contbr. articles to Ency. Britannica, rsch. jours. Trustee Gordon Rsch. Confs., 1968-70; bd. govs. David and Arthur Smart Mus., U. Chgo., 1988—; bd. dirs. Ct. Theatre. Recipient Young Author's prize Electrochem. Soc., 1953, award in catalysis Noble Metals Chem. Soc., London, 1976, Humboldt award, 1977, Richard Kokes award Johns Hopkins U., 1978, Willard Gibbs medal, 1986, Bailar medal U. Ill., 1986, Wilhelm von Hoffman medal German Chem. Soc., 1988, Chem. Pioneer's award Am. Inst. Chemists, 1991, Paracelsus prize Swiss Chem. Soc., 1992, Basolo Medal, Northwestern U., 1993, Robert A. Welch award, 1994, Henry J. Albert award Internat. Precious Metals Inst., 1995, award in Organometallic Chem. Am. Chem. Soc., 1995, Order of Merit Federal Republic of Germany, 1996. Fellow AAAS, Royal Soc. London, Am. Acad. Arts and Scis., Chem. Inst. Can., Royal Soc. Chemistry London (hon.), N.Y. Acad. Scis., Japan Soc. for Promotion Sci.; mem. NAS (fgn. assoc. 1984-85, mem. coun. 1990—, chmn. chemistry sect. 1991-93, v.p. 1993—, assoc. editor Proceedings NAS), Am. Chem. Soc. (editl. bd. Advances in Chemistry series 1963-65, 78-81, chmn. inorganic chemistry 1985, award in inorganic chemistry 1968, award for disting. svc. in advancement of inorganic chemistry 1985, award in organometallic chemistry 1995), Max Planck Soc. (sci. mem. 1983—), Art Inst. Chgo., Renaissance Soc. (bd. dirs.), New Swiss Chem. Soc. (Paracelsus prize 1992), Am. Friends of the Royal Soc. (bd. dirs.), Sigma Xi. Home: 5801 S Dorchester Ave Apt 4A Chicago IL 60637 Office: U Chgo Dept Chemistry Chicago IL 60637 E-mail: jhjh@midway.uchicago.edu.

HALPERN, JAMES BLADEN, lawyer; b. Buffalo, Apr. 20, 1936; s. Philip and Goldene P. (Friedman) H.; m. Jessie Malkoff, July 6, 1958 (div.); 1 child, Jennifer; m. Niesa N. Brateman, Aug. 26, 1979; 1 child, Sheri. BA, Harvard U., 1958, JD, 1961. Bar: NY 1961, D.C. 1970. Atty. corp. fin. div. SEC, Washington, 1961-64; chief counsel-instns., instl. investor study, 1969-70; assoc. firm Proskauer Rose Goetz & Mendelsohn, N.Y.C., 1964-69; assoc. Arent Fox Kintner Plotkin & Kahn, PLLC, Washington, 1971-73, mem., 1974—. Mem. ABA, D.C. Bar Assn., Am. Law Inst. Democrat. Jewish. Office: Arent Fox Kintner Et Al 1050 Connecticut Ave NW Washington DC 20036-5339

HALPERN, JOEL MARTIN, anthropologist, photographer; b. N.Y.C., Apr. 8, 1929; s. Carl M. and Nettie M. (Cantor) H.; m. Barbara D. Kerewsky, Oct. 26, 1952; children: Kay L., Susannah L. Cargill, Carla A. BA, U. Mich., 1950; PhD, Columbia U., 1956. Rsch. assoc. Human Rels. Area Files, Am. U., Washington, 1956; field svc. officer FSR/ICA/Dept. State, Laos, 1956-58; asst. prof. dep. anthropology UCLA, 1958-63; assoc. prof. dept. anthropology Brandeis U., Waltham, Mass., 1963-67; assoc. Russ Rsch. Ctr./Harvard U., Cambridge, Mass., 1965-67; assoc. prof. anthropology U. Mass., Amherst, 1967-69, prof., 1969-92, prof. emeritus, 1992—. Vis. prof. U. Freiburg, Germany, 1970-71; sr. rsch. assoc. Inst. Southeastern European Studies U. Graz (Austria), 1993—, vis. prof., 1994; resident fellow MIT-Harvard Joint Ctr. Urban Studies, Cambridge, 1969-70; cons. RAND Corp., 1959-61. Author: A Serbian Village, 1958, 2d edit., 1967, The Changing Village Community, 1967, Government and Politics in Laos, 1964; author, editor: The Far East Comes Near, 1989, Neighbors at War, Yugoslavia, 2000; featured in various exhibit catalogues. Chair Mekong com. Asia Soc./U.S. AID, 1968-70; legal cons. immigration cases, 1984—; cons. U.S. AID/Bosnia, 1996. NSF and NAS grantee, various yrs., 1960-87; NEH rsch. grantee, 1974-77, NIMH-NICHHD, 1974-77; IREX rsch. adv., 1993-94. Fellow Am. Anthrop. Assn.; mem. Am. Assn. for Advancement of Slavic Studies, Assn. for Asian Studies, Am. Assn. S.E. European Studies. Office: U Mass Dept Anthropology Amherst MA 01003 E-mail: jmhalpern@anthro.umass.edu.

HALPERN, JOSEPH ALAN, physician; b. Bklyn., Feb. 28, 1952; s. Lester A. and Adele Janet (Tax) H.; m. Cynthia Gould, Sept. 1, 1979; 1 child, Elyza. AB, Bard Coll., Annandale on Hudson, N.Y., 1974; MD, N.Y. Med. Coll., Valhalla, 1978. Diplomate ABEM, ABIM. Resident family practice SUNY, Buffalo, 1978-79; resident in medicine Norwalk (Conn.) Hosp., 1979-81, chief resident medicine, 1981-82; emergency physician Kent and Queen Anne Hosp., Chestertown, Md., 1982-83, North Arundel Hosp., Glen Burnie, Md., 1983-85; attending emergency physician John Hopkins Hosp., Balt., 1986-87; emergency physician Anne Arundel Med. Ctr., Annapolis, Md., 1987—; assoc. chief emergency medicine, 1994—99. Attending physician Bayview Med. Ctr., Balt., 1992-94. Fellow Am. Coll. Emergency Physicians; mem. ACP, Med. Chi. Md. Avocations: sailing, bicycling. Home: 2 Waters Rd Severna Park MD 21146-4642 Office: Anne Arundel Med Ctr 2001 Medical Pkwy Annapolis MD 21401 E-mail: jhalp228@aol.com.

HALPERN, JUDITH, social worker; b. N.Y.C., Aug. 2, 1936; d. Jay and Sarah (Simon) Golub; m. Sheldon W. Halpern, June 16, 1957 (div. Aug. 1987); children: Joel, Paul; m. David A. Berkenbilt, May 12, 1985; stepchildren: Jay Berkenbilt, Naomi Berkenbilt. BA, Cornell U., 1957; MSW, Hunter Coll. Sch. Social Work, 1969; Post-Master Cert. in Family Therapy, Cath. U., 1984. Cert. social worker N.Y., lic. Va. Social worker Jewish Community Svcs., N.Y., 1969-71; group therapist West Nassau (N.Y.) Mental Health Ctr., L.I., 1971-72; mental health clinic social worker Mercy Guidance Clinic, N.Y.C., 1972-73; mental health social worker Children's Health Ctr., Mpls., 1973-74, social worker, 1975-79; dir. clin. program Brown House Svcs., St. Paul, 1974-75; dir. therapeutic foster care program Crossroads Mental Health Svcs., Farmville, Va., 1979-80; social worker adolescent and child unit Chestnut Lodge, Rockville, Md., 1981-85; rsch. assoc. Chestnut Lodge Rsch. Inst., 1985-87; social worker No. Va. Psychiat. Group, Fairfax, Va., 1984-89, pvt. practice, Falls Church, Va., 1989—. Mem. task force on addictions Jewish Cmty., Washington; psychiat. cons. in field; bd. dirs. Southside Positive Parenting Ctr., Mpls. Bd. dirs., chmn. social action com. Congregation Olam-Tikvah. Mem.: NASW. Jewish. Avocations: photography, cooking, travel. Home: 4620 Linmar Ct Alexandria VA 22312-1534 Office: 6400 Arlington Blvd Ste 634 Falls Church VA 22042-2336

HALPERN, MARK, writer; s. William Maurice Halpern and Augusta Kershner; m. Phyllis Schutz, May 30, 1956; 1 child, Leda Brooke. BA, CCNY, 1951; MA, Columbia U., 1956. Editor-in-chief ann. rev. in automatic programming Pergamon Press, Oxford, Oxfordshire, England, 1969—74. Author: (non-fiction book) Binding Time: Six Studies in Programming Technology & Milieu, (monthly column, the vocabula review) The Critical Reader, (memoir (three parts) On the Heels of the Pioneers: A Memoir of the Not-quite earliest Days of Programming; contbr. articles to profl. jours. 1st lt. U.S. Army, 1951—53, PTO. Avocations: software design, exploratory travel, cartography & mapping. Office: Time-Binding Software 3309 Brunell Dr Oakland CA 94602 E-mail: markhalpern@iname.com.

HALPERN, MERRIL MARK, investment banker; b. Bayonne, N.J., May 4, 1934; s. Samuel and Belle (Schwartz) H.; m. Phyllis Goldstein, June 14, 1960 (div.); children: Belle Linda, Jennifer, Samuel, Isaac; m. Dolores M. Eckersley, Aug. 28, 1991. BS, Rutgers U., 1956; MBA, Harvard U., 1962. With Ernst & Ernst, N.Y.C., 1956-60, sr. acct., 1958-60; with McDonnell & Co., Inc., 1962-68, v.p., 1967-68; ptnr., dir. corp. fin. H. Hentz & Co., N.Y.C., 1969-70; prin. Merril M. Halpern & Co., N.Y.C., 1970-73; pres. Charterhouse Group Internat., Inc., N.Y.C., 1973-84, chmn. bd., 1984—. Trustee Nat. Humanities Ctr., 2000—, Continuum Health Ptnrs., 2001—. With U.S. Army, 1957—58. Office: Charterhouse Group Internat Inc 535 Madison Ave New York NY 10022-4212

HALPERN, PAUL G. history educator; b. N.Y.C., Jan. 27, 1937; s. Harry and Teresa (Ritter) H. BA with honors, U. Va., 1958; MA, Harvard U., 1961, PhD, 1966. Instr. Fla. State U., Tallahassee, 1965-66, asst. prof., 1966-70, assoc. prof., 1970-74; prof. dept. history, 1974—. Vis. prof. strategy dept. Naval War Coll., Newport, R.I., 1986-87. Author: The Mediterranean Naval Situation, 1908-14, 1971, The Naval War in the Mediterranean, 1914-18 1987, A Naval History of World War I, 1994, Anton Haus: Österreich-Ungarns Grossadmiral, 1998; editor: The Keyes Papers, 3 vols., 1972-81, The Royal Navy in the Mediterranean, 1915-1918, 1987. Mem. Naval Aviation Mus. Found., Pensacola, Fla., Naval War Coll. Found., Newport, R.I. 1st lt. U.S. Army, 1958-60. Fellow Woodrow Wilson Nat. Fellowship Found., 1958. Fellow Royal Hist. Soc.; mem. Am. Hist. Assn., The Navy Records Soc. (coun. 1968-72, 82-86), Naval Rev., U.S. Naval Inst., Royal United Svcs. Inst. Def. Studies, Friends of Imperial War Mus., Friends of Nat. Maritime Mus., Naval Hist. Found., Soc. for Mil. History, Phi Beta Kappa, Phi Eta Sigma. Avocations: model ship collecting, book collecting, model soldier collection. Home: 3103 Brandemere Dr Tallahassee FL 32312-2423 Office: Fla State U Dept History Bellamy Bldg Tallahassee FL 32306

HALPERN, PAUL HAROLD, physicist; b. Phila., Jan. 15, 1961; s. Stanley Joseph and Bernice (Finkler) H.; m. Felicia Hurewitz, 1994; children: Eli, Aden. BA, Temple U., 1982; PhD, SUNY, Stony Brook, 1987. Asst. prof. Hamilton Coll., Clinton, N.Y., 1987-88; from asst. prof. to assoc. prof. Phila. Coll. Pharmacy and Sci., 1988—99, prof., 1999—. Author: Time Journeys, 1990; Cosmic Wormholes, 1992, The Cyclical Serpent, 1995, Structure of the Universe, 1996, Quest for Alien Planets, 1997, Countdown to Apocalypse, 1998, The Pursuit of Destiny, 2000; contbr. articles to profl. jours. Mem. Am. Phys. Soc., Sigma Xi. Home: 345 Farwood Rd Wynnewood PA 19096-4014 Office: U of the Scis in Philadelphia 43D St Woodland Ave Philadelphia PA 19104

HALPERN, PEGGY LOUISE, social welfare researcher; b. Mpls., Sept. 12, 1942; d. Chester Calvin and Marian Rose (Nathanson) H. BA in Sociology, U. Minn., 1964; MSW, U. Pitts., 1966; PhD in Social Welfare, U. Md., 1981. Lic. ind. clin. social worker, D.C.; cert. ACSW; diplomate in clin. social work. Social worker Family and Children's Svcs., Mpls., 1967-71, Hennepin County Welfare Dept., Mpls., 1972-73; project mgr. Home Svcs. Assn., St. Paul, 1974-75; social worker Clin. Ctr., Bethesda, Md., 1976, Sachs Project, Balt., 1979; asst. prof. Sch. Social Work U. Hawaii, Honolulu, 1981-83; project mgr. Hawaii Dept. of Health, Honolulu, 1983-84; sr. rsch. analyst Am. Pub. Welfare Assn., Washington, 1985-88; long term care program assoc. Nat. Assn. State Units on Aging, Washington, 1989-90; sr. rsch. assoc., project dir. CSR, Inc., Washington, 1990-99; cons. Adminstrn. on Aging., Washington, Md., 2000; program analyst U.S. Dept. Health and Human Svcs., Washington, 2000—. Mem. NASW.

HALPERN, PHILIP MORGAN, lawyer; b. Derby, Conn., Apr. 17, 1956; s. Edwin Vincent and Carol Veronica (Gallagher) H.; m. Carolyn G. McElwreath, Mar. 11, 1989. BS magna cum laude, Fordham U., 1977; JD, Pace U., 1980. Bar: N.Y. 1981, U.S. Dist. Ct. (so. and ea. dists.) N.Y. 1981, U.S. Ct. Appeals (2d cir.) 1982, U.S. Tax Ct. 1984, U.S. Supreme Ct. 1985, U.S. Dist. Ct. Conn. 1989, Conn. 1989, U.S. Ct. Appeals (3d cir.) 1991; cert. trial adv. Nat. Bd. Trial Advocacy, 2002. Law clk. to sr. judge U.S. Dist. Ct. (so. dist.) N.Y., N.Y.C., 1980-82; assoc. litigation dept. Kimmelman, Sexter & Sobel, N.Y.C., 1982-83; ptnr. Collier, Halpern, Newberg, Nolletti & Bock, N.Y.C., 1983—; mng. ptnr. Collier, Haplern, Newberg, Nolletti & Bock LLP, White Plains, N.Y., 1996—. Arbitrator Civil Ct. City N.Y. and Am. Arbitration Assn., 1987-96; adv. coun. Bd. of Judges, So. Dist. of N.Y., 1995—; mediator U.S. Dist. (so. dist.) N.Y., 1998—, mem. office ct. adminstrn. adv. com. on civil practice, 1999—. Author: Age Discrimination in Employment Act: Employers Can Enforce Releases Too!, 1992, Fair Value Proceedings: Fixing Fair Value in New York, 1996; author, editor: Civil Pretrial Proceedings in New York, 2 vols., 1999, updated annually. Chmn. Young Reps., Tuckahoe, N.Y., 1975-77; chmn. taxi commn. Village of Mamaroneck, N.Y., 1986-87, mem. planning bd., 1987-89. Fellow Am. Bar Found. (life); mem. N.Y. State Bar Assn. (com. on lawyer competency, com. on fed. judiciary), Assn. of Bar of City of N.Y., ATLA, N.Y. Trial Lawyers Assn., N.Y. County Lawyers Assn., Fed. Bar Coun., Profl. Golfers Assn. (adv. coun. metro. sect. 1992—), Westchester Country Club. Roman Catholic. Office: Collier Halpern Newberg Nolletti & Bock LLP One N Lexington Ave White Plains NY 10601 also: 99 Park Ave New York NY 10016-1601

HALPERN, RALPH LAWRENCE, lawyer; b. Buffalo, May 12, 1929; s. Julius and Mary C. (Kaminker) H.; m. Harriet Chasin, June 29, 1958; children: Eric B., Steven R., Julie B. LL.B. cum laude, U. Buffalo, 1953. Bar: N.Y. 1953. Teaching assoc. Northwestern U. Law Sch., 1953-54; assoc. firm Jaeckle, Fleischmann, Kelly, Swart & Augspurger, Buffalo, 1957-58; asso. firm Raichle, Banning, Weiss & Halpern (and predecessors), 1958-59, ptnr., 1959-86, Jaeckle Fleischmann & Mugel LLP, Buffalo, 1986—. Pres. Buffalo Coun. World Affairs, 1972-74, Temple Beth Zion, Buffalo, 1981-83, Bur. Jewish Edn., 2000-02; chmn. Buffalo chpt. Am. Jewish Com., 1975-77; bd. govs. United Jewish Fedn., Buffalo, 1972-78, 91-97, 99—, v.p., 1992-95. Served to capt. JAGC U.S. Army, 1954-57. Mem. ABA (ho. dels. 1989-95, 97-99), N.Y. State Bar Assn. (chmn. com. profl. ethics 1971-76, chmn. com. jud. election monitoring 1983-86, chmn. spl. com. to consider adoption of ABA model rules of profl. conduct 1983-85, sec. internat. law and practice sect. 1992-93, vice chmn. 1993-95), Erie County Bar Assn., Am. Judicature Soc., Am. Law Inst. Home: 88 Middlesex Rd Buffalo NY 14216-3618 Office: Jaeckle Fleischmann & Mugel LLP 800 Fleet Bank Bldg Buffalo NY 14202-2292 E-mail: rlhalpern@compuserve.com., rhalpern@jaeckle.com.

HALPERSON, MICHAEL ALLEN, publishing executive; b. Boston, Sept. 11, 1946; s. Bertram David and Rose (Doolan) H. AB, Union Coll., 1968; MA in Teaching, U. Mass., 1970. Asst. to group v.p. Plymouth Rubber Co., Inc., Canton, Mass., 1972-73, corp. dir. pers. and indsl. rels., 1973-79, mgr. mktg., cons. products, 1979-81, dir. sales and mktg., 1981-85, v.p., 1985-92; v.p., gen. mgr. Plymouth Office Products a Hon Industries Co., Pawtucket, R.I., 1992-93; exec. v.p., COO Kryptonite Corp., Canton, Mass., 1994-95; exec. v.p. Dome Pub. Co. Inc., Warwick, R.I., 1995—, Data Binding, Inc., Warwick, R.I., 1995—; v.p. Parkway Realty, Inc., Warwick, R.I., 1995—, Dome Industries, Inc., Warwick, R.I., 1995—. Bd. dirs., v.p. Cape Cod Sea Camps, Inc., Capt. Del Assocs., Inc., Brewster, Mass.; treas. Camp Wono, Inc., Brewster, Mass. Bd. dirs. Canton Assn. Industries, Inc., 1977-92, Neponset Valley Nursing Assn., Inc., 1979-97, Southwood Cmty. Hosp., Norfolk, Mass., 1983-92, Neponset Valley Hospice, 1993-97, Norfolk-Bristol Homemakers Svc., Inc.; bd. dirs. Neponset Valley Health Sys., Inc., Norwood, Mass., 1985-92, chmn., 1990-92; bd. dirs. Norwood Hosp., Inc., 1983-92, chmn., 1988-90; bd. overseers Boston Ballet, 1992-93, Boston Symphony Orch., 1995—; trustee Boston Ballet Ctr. for Dance Edn., 1993-96, Boston Ballet, 1996-2002, sec. 1999-2000, Grant W. Koch Scholarship Trust, 1981—. With USAF, 1970-72. Mem. Bus. Products Industry Assn., (bd. dirs. 1996-99), Office Products Mfrs. Assn. (bd. dirs. 1985-92, 2000—, pres. 1989, chmn. 1990); St. Botolph Club, Boston, Williams Club, N.Y.C. Avocations: reading, swimming. Home: 78 Cannon Forge Dr Foxboro MA 02035-5217 Office: Dome Pub Co Inc PO Box 1220 Ten New England Way Warwick RI 02887-1220

HALPERT, DOUGLAS JOSHUA, lawyer; b. Bklyn., Nov. 9, 1962; s. Eugene and Miriam (Feigenbaum) H.; m. Yee-Wen Chen, July 22, 1989. BA in English Lit., U. Chgo., 1984; JD, Fordham Law Sch., 1988. Bar: N.Y. 1989, Ohio 1994. Immigration atty. Cohen, Swados, Wright, Hanifin, Bradford & Brett, Buffalo, 1988-94, Frost & Jacobs LLP, Cin., 1994-2000, Frost Brown Todd LLC, Cin., 2000—. Recipient Vol. Lawyer of Yr. award Cin. Bar Assn., 1998. Mem. Am. Immigration Lawyers Assn., Cin. Bar Assn., Alumni Schs. Com. of U. Chgo. Avocations: lit., writing, movies, sports. Office: Frost Brown Todd LLC 2200 PNC Ctr 201 E 5th St Cincinnati OH 45202-4182

HALPERT, LEONARD WALTER, retired editor; b. Bklyn., July 7, 1924; s. Daniel and Kate (Hollander) H.; m. Shirley Small, May 25, 1952; 1 child, Melinda BA, Bklyn. Coll., N.Y., 1947; MS in Journalism, Northwestern U., Evanston, Ill., 1948. Editorial writer Washington Times-Herald, Washington, D.C., 1950-51; reporter Buffalo Evening News, 1948-50, editorial writer, 1951-80, editorial page editor, 1980-89; ret., 1989. Served with AUS, 1943-45 Mem. Am. Soc. Newspaper Editors, Nat. Conf. Editorial Writers, Soc. Profl. Journalists. Home: 12 Neumann Pkwy Buffalo NY 14223-1429 E-mail: lenton42@aol.com.

HALPIN, ANNA MARIE, architect, writer; b. Murphysboro, Ill., July 24, 1923; d. John William and Anna Christina (Weilmuenster) H. BS in Architecture, U. Ill., 1948. Designer, project architect various firms, San Francisco, Rome, N.Y.C., 1948-67; editorial dir. Sweet's div. McGraw-Hill, Inc., N.Y.C., 1967-88, ret. Sweet's div.; freelance cons., 1988-98. Rep. to Constrn. Industries Coordination Com., Am. Nat. Metric Council, 1974-80 Mem. AIA (treas., dir. N.Y. chpt. 1974-78, coll. fellows 1976, nat. dir. 1977-79, nat. v.p. 1980, dir. Found. 1980, Richard Upjohn fellow 1991), Women's Equity Action League (pres. N.Y. state orgn. 1976-77), Constrn. Specifications Inst., Alliance Women in Architecture. Home: 519 E 86th St New York NY 10028-7541

HALPIN, DANIEL WILLIAM, civil engineering educator, consultant; b. Covington, Ky., Sept. 29, 1938; s. Jordan W. and Gladys E. (Moore) H.; m. Maria Kirchner, Feb. 8, 1963; 1 son, Rainer. BS, U.S. Mil. Acad., 1961; MSC.E., U. Ill., 1969, PhD, 1973. Research analyst Constrn. Engring. Research Lab., Champaign, Ill., 1970-72; faculty U. Ill., Urbana, 1972-73; mem. faculty Ga. Inst. Tech., Atlanta, 1973-85, prof., 1981-85; A.J. Clark prof., dir. Constrn. Engring. and Mgmt. U. Md., 1985-87; dir. div. Constrn. Engring. and Mgmt. Purdue U., 1987—, interim head Sch. Civil Engring., 2000—01; cons. constrn. mgmt. Vis. assoc. prof. U. Sydney, Australia, 1981; vis. prof. Swiss Fed. Inst. Tech., 1985, U. Karlsruhe, Germany, 1998; vis. scholar Tech. U., Munich, 1979; vis. lectr. Ctr. Cybernetics in Constrn., Bucharest, Romania, 1973; cons. office tech. assessment U.S. Congress, 1986-87; mem. JTEC Team to evaluate constrn. tech., Japan, 1990; juror emeritus Constrn. Innovation Forum, 1994; mem. rsch. com. Constrn. Industry Inst., 1995-2002. Author: Design of Construction and Process Operations, 1976, Construction Management, 1980, Planung und Kontrolle von Bauproduktionsprozessen, 1979, Constructo - A Heuristic Game for Construction Management, 1973, Financial and Cost Control Concepts for Construction Management, 1985, Planning and Analysis of Construction Operations, 1992, Construction Management, 2d edit., 1997. Served with C.E., U.S. Army, 1961-67. Decorated Bronze Star; recipient Walter L. Huber prize ASCE, 1979, Peurifoy Constrn. Rsch. award, 1992; grantee NSF, Dept. Energy. Mem. ASCE (past sect. pres. 1981-82, chmn. constrn. rsch. coun. 1985-86, Peurifoy Constrn. Rsch. award 1992), Am. Soc. Engring. Edn., Industry Inst. (rsch. com. 1996-2003), Juror Emeritus, Construction Innovation Forum, Nat. Acad. Constrn., Sigma Xi. Methodist. E-mail: halpin@ecn.purdue.edu.

HALPIN, MARY ELIZABETH, psychologist; b. Oak Park, ILl., June 4, 1951; d. Thomas Joseph and Rita Helen (Foley) H. BA, Marquette U., 1973, MEd, 1975, PhD, 1983. Lic. psychologist Ill., Calif., cert. sch. psychologist Ill. Staff psychologist Milw. Children's Hosp., 1975-83; postdoctoral intern El Dorado County Mental Health Ctr., Placerville, Calif., 1983-84; psychologist Inst. for Motivational Devel., Lombard, Ill., 1985-88; psychologist, founder, gen. ptnr. Assocs. for Adolescent Achievement, Deerfield, Ill., 1989-94; pvt. practice psychology, Deerfield, 1995—; sch. psychologist Winnetka (Ill.) Dist. 36, 2000—. Presenter Internat. Sch. Beijing, 1998. TV appearance Oprah Winfrey Show, 1995. Chmn., mem. peer rev. com. Charter Barclay Hosp., Chgo., 1991-93. Mem.: AAUW, APA, Ill. Psychol. Assn. (standing hearing panel ethics com. 1993, pub. rels. com. 1994, chair pub. rels. com. 1999—2002, area code rep. 1999—2002, pres.-elect 2002). Office: 420 Lake Cook Rd Ste 109 Deerfield IL 60015-4914

HALPIN, THOMAS S. military antiques dealer; b. Jamaica, N.Y., May 27, 1941; s. Thomas S. Halpin and Millicent May Shaw; m. Barbara Jean Kirk, May 20, 1982. BA in Econs., Tusculum Coll., 1964. Asst. mgr. F. W. Woolworth Co., Franklin Sq., N.Y., 1964-65; asst. mfr.'s rep. New Hyde Park, N.Y., 1965-66; sales rep. Gen. Binding Corp., Northbrook, Ill., 1966-72; proprietor Mil. & Naval Antiquities, Mineola, N.Y., 1972-98, Las Vegas, Nev., 1998—. Editor, 1975-87, 88-98; contbr. articles to profl. jours. Commiteeman N.Y. Conservative Party, 1978—. With USNR, 1962-65. Recipient Marie Moore award Grand Ctrl. Coin Conv., 1988. Mem. Navy League U.S. (life), N.E. Orders & Medals Soc. (pres. 1972-74, Best of Show 1967), L.I. Coin Club (v.p., sec. 1988-94, pres. 1994-98, Spl. Presentation plaque 1998). Episcopalian. Office: Mil and Naval Antiquities 7068 Valley Nails Ln Las Vegas NV 89110-2938 Fax: (702) 452-4676.

HALPRIN, ANNA SCHUMAN (MRS. LAWRENCE HALPRIN), dancer; b. Wilmette, Ill., July 13, 1920; d. Isadore and Ida (Schiff) Schuman; m. Lawrence Halprin, Sept. 19, 1940; children: Daria, Rana. Student, Bennington Summer Sch. Dance, 1938-39; BS in Dance, U. Wis., 1943; PhD in Human Services (hon.), Sierra U., 1987; PhD (hon.), U. Wis., 1994, Santa Clara U.; student, Calif. Arts Coll., Calif., 2003; PhD (hon.), Art Instit. of San Francisco, Calif., 2003. Presenter opening invocation STate of the World Forum by spl. invitation from Mikhail S. Gorbachev. Author: Moving Toward Life, Five Decades of Transformative Dance, Dance as a Healing Art, A Teachers' Guide and Support Manual for People with Cancer; performances at Kennedy Ctr., Washington,

Yerba Buena Ctr. for Arts, San Francisco, Joyce Theatre, NYC, 2001—; 80th yr. retrospective performance Cowell Theatre, Returning Home Video, 2003, Intensive Care, Reflections on Death and Dying, 2003, San Francisco, numerous other performances and publs. Bd. dirs. East West Holistic Healing Inst.; mem. Gov.'s Coun. on Phys. Fitness and Wellness. Recipient award Am. Dance Guild, 1980, Guggenheim award, 1970-71, Woman of Wisdom award Bay Area Profl. Women's Network, Tchr. of Yr. award Calif. Tchrs. Assn., 1988, Lifetime Achievement award in visual and performing arts San Francisco Bay Guardian newspaper, 1990, Women of Achievement, Vision and Excellence award, 1992, Balasaraswati/Joy Ann Dewey Bieneke chair for disting. tchg. Am. Dance Festival, 1996, Lifetime Achievement in Modern Dance award Am. Dance Festival, 1997, Lifetime Achievement award Calif. Arts Coun., 2000, Breast Cancer Watch, 2001; Person of Yr. in field of Dance award Ballet-ranz, Berlin; named to Isadora Duncan Hall of Fame, Bay Area Dance Coalition, 1986; Nat. Endowment Arts Choreographers grantee, 1976, NEA choreography grantee, 1977, San Francisco Found. grantee, 1981, Calif. Arts. Coun. grantee, 1990—; inductee Marin Women's Hall of Fame, 1998, lifetime achievement award Marin Arts Coun. Fellow Am. Expressive Therapy Assn.; mem. Assn. Am. Dance, Conscientious Artists Am., San Francisco C. of C. Home and Office: 15 Ravine Way Kentfield CA 94904-2713 *Today I am deeply involved in making a contribution as an artist to world peace. I'm interested in the development of public workshops and dance rituals to create harmony and understanding in social and healing interactions in communities. I am taking dances on a planetary scale.*

HALPRIN, HENRY STEINER, lawyer, educator; b. N.Y.C., May 5, 1924; s. Abraham J. and Julia (Steiner) H.; divorced; children: Karen K. Sims, Bruce S. LLD, U. Va., 1949, JD, 1970. Bar: N.Y. 1949, U.S. Dist. Ct. (ea. and so. dists.) N.Y. 1950, U.S. Supreme Ct. 1961, U.S. Dist. Ct. Conn. 1963, Conn. 1967. Asst. dir. spl. programs U.S. Housing and Homes Fin. Agy., N.Y.C., 1955-61; sr. assoc. Demov & Morris, 1961-62, ptnr., 1962-64; sole practice N.Y.C., 1965-68; ptnr. Halprin & Goler, N.Y.C., 1968—92; pvt. practice N.Y.C., 1992—. Adj. asst. prof. real estate NYU, 1979—; lectr. Baruch Coll., 1981-99. Bd. trustees Westport (Conn.) Libr., 1987-91. Home: 24 Buena Vista Dr Westport CT 06880-6603 Office: 60 E 42nd St New York NY 10165-0006 Fax: 212-490-3888.

HALQUIST, SHAWN A. music educator; b. Kane, Pa., July 30, 1960; s. Roger Allen and Jane Marie Halquist; m. Deanna Marie Halquist, June 17, 1989; children: Cody, Noah. MM, SUNY Binghamton, Binghamton, New York, 1983; BA, Edinboro U., Edinboro, Pennsylvania, 1982. Teaching Certificate Edinboro U., 1984. Band dir. Brockport H.S., Brockport, NY, 1997—, McDowell H.S., Erie, Pa., 1985—97. Cons. Empire Statesmen Drum Corps, Rochester, NY, 1998—. Mem.: Phi Beta Kappa, MENC, Phi Mu Alpha. Home: 18 Tearose Meadow Lane Brockport NY 14420 Office: Brockport High School 40 Allen Street Brockport NY 14420

HALSBAND, FRANCES, architect; b. N.Y.C., Oct. 30, 1943; d. Samuel and Ruth H.; m. Robert Michael Kliment, May 1, 1971; 1 child, Alexander H. BA, Swarthmore Coll., 1965; MArch, Columbia U., 1968. Registered architect, N.Y., N.J., Mass., Conn., Ohio, Va., N.H., Pa., D.C., N.C., Ill., Miss., La., Fla.; cert. Nat. Coun. Archtl. Reg. Bds. Arch. Mitchell/Giurgola Archs., N.Y.C., 1968-72; ptnr. R.M. Kliment & Frances Halsband Archs., N.Y.C., 1972—. Vis. critic archtl. design Columbia U., 1975-78, 87, N.C. State U., 1978, Rice U., 1979, U. Va., 1980, Harvard U., 1981, U. Pa., 1981, U. Calif., Berkeley, 1997; dean Sch. Architecture, Pratt Inst., 1991-94; Freidman prof. U. Calif., Berkeley, 1997; Emens Disting. prof. Ball State U., 1998; Kea prof. U. Md., 2000; mem. N.Y.C. Landmarks Preservation Commn., 1984-87; lectr. U. So. Calif., U. Va., Temple U., Washington U., Tulane U., Harvard U., U. Oreg., U. Washington. Projects include: computer Sci. Bldg., Columbia U. (AIA Nat. Honor award 1987), Gilmer Hall addition U. Va., Town Hall, Salisbury Conn., Computer Sci. Bldg., Princeton U. (AIA Nat. Honor award 1994), Case Western Res. Adelbert Hall restoration (AIA Nat. Honor award 1994), Alvin Ailey Am. Dance Theater Found., N.Y.C., hdqs. Marsh & McLennan Co., Ind. Bank Hdqs., Bklyn. Coll. Master Plan, Entrance Pavillion L.I. Rail Rd. Penn Sta. (AIA Nat. award), U.S. Courthouse and Post Office, Bklyn., Yale Div. Sch., Dartmouth Roth Ctr. for Jewish Life, U.S. Courthouse, Gulfport, Miss.; works exhibited in Cooper-Hewitt Mus., Bklyn. Mus., Nat. Acad. Design, Deutsches Architekturmuseum, Frankfourt; author: Annotated Bibliography of Technical Resources for Small Museums, 1983. Trustee Nat. Inst. Archtl. Edn., 1988-93; mem. archtl. rev. panel Fed. Res. Sys., 1993—; mem. U.S. Dept. State Office Fgn. Bldgs. Ops. Archtl. Adv. Bd., 1998—; U.S. Gen. Svcs. Adminstrn. Nat. Register Peer Profls., 1998—. Fellow AIA (exec. bd. N.Y.C. chpt. 1979, pres. N.Y.C. chpt. 1991-92), Century Assn.; mem. Archtl. League N.Y. (exec. bd. 1975—, v.p. arch. 1981-85, pres. 1985-89), Assn. Collegiate Schs. Architecture (N.E. regional dir. 1993-95). Office: RM Kliment & Frances Halsband 255 W 26th St New York NY 10001-8001

HALSCHEID, THERESE ANNE, poet; b. Phila., Pa., Mar. 14, 1958; d. Mary Halscheid. MA, Rowan U., 1989. Reading specialist, tchr. reading cert. Supervisory Certification. Vis. writer in schs. N.J. State Coun. on the Arts, Trenton, NJ, 1998—. Creative writing instr. various settings. Author: (poetry) Powertalk, 1995, (book of poetry) Without Home, 2001. Home: 1143 Mt Vernon Ave Haddonfield NJ 08033 Personal E-mail: thalscheid@hotmail.com.

HALSELL, GEORGE KAY, music educator; b. Bryan, Tex., 1956; s. Kay and Jo Inez (Wootten) H.; m. Melanie Lynn Marsh, 1984. MusB, Johns Hopkins Univ., 1979; MusM, U. Tex., 1980, DMA, 1989. Instr. music West Va. Univ., Morgantown, 1983-84; adj. instr. music Essex C.C., Balt., 1985-90, Frederick (Md.) C.C., 1985-90; asst. prof. music Adams State Coll., Alamosa, Colo., 1990-91; adj. instr. music Pikes Peak C.C., Colorado Springs, 1992-94, U. So. Colo., Pueblo, 1992-94; asst. prof. music Coll. So. Idaho, Twin Falls, 1994—2002, assoc. prof. music, 2002—. Freelance musician; lectr. Pueblo Symphony Orch., 1992-94. Office: Coll So Idaho PO Box 1238 315 Falls Ave Twin Falls ID 83303-1238 E-mail: ghalsell@csi.edu, gmhalsell@cableone.net.

HALSEY, ALBERT HENRY, sociologist; b. London, Apr. 13, 1923; s. William Thomas and Ada (Draper) H.; m. Gertrude Margaret Littler, Apr. 10, 1949; children: Ruth, Robert, Lisa, David, Mark. BSc, London Sch. Econs., U. London, 1950; PhD, U. London, 1954; MA, U. Oxford, Eng., 1962; D in Social Scis. (hon.), U. Birmingham, Eng., 1987; DLitt, Open U., Warwick, Leicester, Glamorgan, 1996. Research assoc. U. Liverpool, Eng., 1952-54; lectr. U. Birmingham, 1954-62; prof. U. Oxford, 1962—. Fellow Brit. Acad.; mem. Am. Acad. Arts and Scis. Mem. Labour Party. Anglican. Avocation: gardening. Home: 28 Upland Park Rd Oxford OX1 1NF England Office: Oxford U Nuffield Coll Oxford OX2 7RU England

HALSEY, ASHLEY, III, newspaper editor; b. Phila., Aug. 4, 1952; s. Ashley Jr. and Margaret (Woods) H.; m. Laura Jean Ketchum, Apr. 14, 1984; children: Graham Ketchum Halsey, Ellery Ketchum Halsey. BA, Temple U., 1974. Reporter Germantown Courier, Phila., 1972, sports editor, 1973, mng. editor, 1975-77; reporter Phila. Bull., 1977-79, Phila. Inquirer, 1980-81, nat. corr., 1982-85, asst. nat. editor, 1985-86, dep. nat. editor, 1986-88, dep. fgn. editor, 1989-91, nat. editor, 1991-96, travel editor, 1996-97; asst. city editor Washington Post, 1997-98, dep. Md. editor, 1999, Md. editor, 1999—. Avocations: sailing, running. Office: The Washington Post 1150 15th St NW Washington DC 20071-0002

HALSEY, DOUGLAS MARTIN, lawyer; b. Warwick, R.I., 1953; s. Donald Post Jr. and Marita H.; m. Amy Klinow, Sept. 5, 1976; children: Mark, Meredith. BA, Columbia U., 1976; JD cum laude, U. Miami, 1979. Bar: Fla. 1979, U.S. Ct. Appeals (11th cir.), U.S. Dist. Ct. (so. dist.) Fla. Assoc. Paul & Thomson, Miami, Fla., 1979-85; ptnr. Thomson, Bohrer, Werth & Razook, Miami, 1985-88, Douglas M. Halsey, P.A., Miami, 1989-97, Halsey & Burns, P.A., Miami, 1997-2000, White & Case LLP, Miami, 2000—. Rsch. editor U. Miami Law Review, 1978-79. Mem. Alexis de Tocqueville Soc., United Way of Miami-Dade County, 1995—; chmn.Children's Home Soc. Fla., 2000-2002; chmn. Foster Care Rev., Inc., Miami, Fla., 1998-2000. Mem. Fla. Bar (chmn. environ. and land use law sect. 1993-94, President's Pro Bono Svc. award 1991). Office: Wachovia Fin Ctr 200 S Biscayne Blvd Ste 4900 Miami FL 33131-2352

HALSEY, JAMES ALBERT, international entertainment impresario, theatrical producer, talent manager; b. Independence, Kans., Oct. 7, 1930; s. Harry Edward and Carrie Lee (Messick) H.; m. Minisa Crumbo; children: Sherman Brooks, Gina, Cris, Woody. Student, Independence Community Coll., 1948-50, U. Kans.; doctorate of Fine Arts honoris causa, Baker Univ., 1992. Pres. Thunderbird Artists, Inc., Independence, from 1950, Jim Halsey Co., Inc., Tulsa, from 1952, Norwood Advt. Agy., James Halsey Property Mgmt. Co., Tulsa Proud Country Entertainment, Stas. KTOW/KGOW, J.H. Radio Mgmt., Cyclone Records, Tulsa Records, J.H. Lighting and Sound Co., Singin' T Prodns.; v.p. Gen. Artists Corp., Beverly Hills, Calif., 1966; chmn., chief exec. officer Century City Artists Corp., Tulsa, Nashville; personal mgr. various entertainment personalities; pres. Internat. Fedn. Festival Orgns.; mgr. Oakridge Boys, 1975. Internat. jurist Golden Orpheus Festival, Bulgaria, 1981-82, 84, 88, 94; ptnr. Billboard Song Contest; cons. William Morris Agy., 1990-95; producer shows for auditoriums, fairs, rodeos, TV, internat. music fests also others in U.S. and internationally including Tulsa Internat. Music Festival, 1977-80, Neewollah Internat. Music Festival, 1981-83; gen. ptnr. Parker Ranch, Tulsa; bd. dirs. Merc. Bank and Trust, Tulsa, Citizens Nat. Bank, Independence, Farmers & Mchts. Bank, Mound City, Kans., Nashville Symphony; chmn. mus. bus. dept. Okla. City U., 1994—; lectr., speaker colls., univs., 1992—. Trustee Philbrook Art Ctr., Tulsa; bd. dirs. Thomas Gilcrease Mus. Assn., Tulsa Philharm. Assn., Roy Clark Celebrity Golf Classic, UNICEF, Nashville Symphony, Nat. Music Coun. Served with U.S. Army, 1954-56. Recipient Disting. Service award U.S. Jr. C. of C., 1959, Ambassador of Country Music award SESAC Corp., 1978, citation Cashbox Mag., 1980, citation Golden Orpheus Festival, 1982, Hubert Long award Wembley Festival, Eng., 1982, commendation Los Angeles Mayor Tom Bradley, Gov.'s medal Kans. Commn., 1986, Frederic Chopin medal Polish Artist Bur., 1987, Lifetime Achievement award Internat. Buyers Assn., 1997, Okla. Govs. award for excellence art and edn., 1998, Cherokee medal of honor Cherokee Hist. Soc., 1999; named Disting. Kansan Topeka Capital Jour.; inductee Okla. Music Hall of Fame, 2000. Mem. Country Music Assn. (bd. dirs. 1963-64, 70-71, v.p. 1979-80, Founding Pres.'s award 1985), Acad. Country Music (bd. dirs. 1969-70, 73-74, v.p. 1975-76, 78-79, 79-80, 88-89, Jim Reeves Meml. award 1977), Internat. Fedn. Festival Orgns. (Am. pres., Oscar Midem award 1982). Home: 720 N 136 Rd Mounds OK 74047-5275

HALSEY, MARTHA TALIAFERRO, Spanish language educator; b. Richmond, Va., May 5, 1932; d. James Dillard and Martha (Taliaferro) H. AB, Goucher Coll., 1954; MA, U. Iowa, 1956; PhD, Ohio State U., 1964. Asst. prof. Spanish, Pa. State U., Univ. Pk., 1964-70, assoc. prof., 1970-79, prof., 1979-95, prof. emeritus, 1995—. Vis. Olive B. O'Connor prof. lit. Colgate U., Hamilton, NY, 1983. Author: Antonio Buero Vallejo, 1973, Dictatorship to Democracy: the Recent Plays of Buero Vallejo (La Fundación to Música cercana), 1994; editor: Madrugada, 1969, Hoy es fiesta, 1978, Los inocentes de la Moncloa, 1980, El engañao, Caballos desbocaos, 1981, (with Phyllis Zatlin) The Contemporary Spanish Theater: A Collection of Critical Essays, 1988, Entre actos: Diálogos sobre teatro español entre siglos, 1999, Estreno, 1992-98; gen. editor Estreno Contemporary Spanish Plays, 1992-98, Estreno Studies in Contemporary Spanish Theater, 1998—; mem. editl bd. Modern Internat. Drama, 1968-75, Ky. Romance Quar., 1970-76, Annals Contemporary Spanish Lit., 1991—, Tesserae: Jour. Iberian and Latin Am. Studies, 1997—; contbr. articles to profl. jours. Grantee Am. Philos. Soc., 1970, 78, Inst. for Arts and Humanistic Studies, 1977, Program Cultural Coop. Between Spanish Ministry Culture and U.S. Univs., 1992, 94-95. Fellow Hispanic Soc. Am. (hon.); mem. MLA, N.E. MLA, Am. Assn. Tchrs. Spanish and Portuguese, Fellowship of Reconciliation, War Resisters League, Phi Beta Kappa, Phi Sigma Iota, Sigma Delta Pi. Democrat. Episcopalian. Home: 500 E Marylyn Ave Apt I 140 State College PA 16801-5248 Office: Pa State U Dept Spanish University Park PA 16802

HALSEY-BRANDT, GREG, mayor; m. Evelina Halsey-Brandt. BA in Geography, MA in Geography, U. B.C. Town planner; alderman, 1981-90; mayor City of Richmond, 1990—2001; min. state for intergovernmental affairs British Columbia, Canada, 2001—. Mem. Vancouver Regional Transit Commn. Mem. Planning Inst. B.C., Richmond C. of C. Office: PO Box 9061 Stn Prov Govt Victoria BC V8W 9E2 Canada*

HALSTEAD, THOMAS A. theology studies educator; b. Van Nuys, Calif., May 22, 1943; s. Dwight and Shirley Virginia Halstead; widowed; children: Holly, Christopher, Heather. BS, Calif. State U., Northridge, 1968, MS, 1970; MDiv, Talbot Theol. Sem., 1977; EdD, Nova S.E. U., 1994. Labor rels. and pers. Lockheed Calif. Co., Burbank, 1966—73; assoc. pastor Grace Cmty. Ch., Sunland, Calif., 1977—87; prof. Master's Coll., Newhall, Calif., 1985—. Office: Master's Coll 21726 Placerita Cyn Rd Newhall CA 91321 E-mail: thalstead@masters.edu.

HALSTRÖM, FREDERIC NORMAN, lawyer; b. Boston, Feb. 26, 1944; s. Reginald F. and Margaret M. (Graham) H.; divorced, 1989, m. Lena Strelnikova, 2001; children: Ingrid Alexandra, Reginald Frederic II, Mikhail Strelnikova. Student, Northeastern U., 1961-63, USAF Acad., 1963-65; AB, Georgetown U., 1967; JD, Boston Coll., 1970. Bar: Mass. 1970, U.S. Dist. Ct. Mass. 1971, U.S. Dist. Ct. R.I. 1981, U.S. Tax Ct., 1981, U.S. Ct. Appeals (1st cir.) 1971, U.S. Ct. Appeals (11th cir.) 1991. Assoc. Schneider and Reilly, P.C., Boston, 1970-73; ptnr. Parker, Coulter, Daley and White, Boston, 1973-78; prin. Halström Law Office, Boston, 1978—. Spl. prosecutor Dist. Atty., Norfolk County, 1969-70; spl. asst. city solicitor City of Quincy, 1980. Editor Mass. Law Quar., 1972; contbr. articles to profl. jours. Fellow Boston Coll. Law Sch., v.p. 1988-91, pres. 1991—, benefactor Frederic N. Halström Nat. Moot Ct. Team. Mem. ABA (chmn. products liability com. gen. practice sect. 1980-85, award of achievement young lawyers divsn. 1978, vice chmn. taxation on ins. cos. sect. 1986-88), Assn. Trial Lawyers Am. (gov. 1981-84, 87—), state del. 1976-78, 86-87, chair various coms.), Mass. Acad. Trial Attys. (co-chmn. tort law sect. 1980—, bd. of govs. 1976—, sec. 1987-88, pres.-elect 1995-96, pres. 1996-97), Mass. Bar Assn. (pres. young lawyers divsn. 1977-78, bd. dels. 1978-80), Middlesex County Bar Assn., Mass. Trial Lawyers Assn. (mem/ Bd. of Govs., 2001—), Trial Lawyers Pub. Justice (sustaining founder, v.p. 1989—), Thomas F. Lambert Jr. Endowed Chair Trust), Algonquin Club, Univ. Club (Boston). Home: 483 River Rd Carlisle MA 01741-1873 Office: 132 Boylston St Boston MA 02116-4616 Fax: 617-426-4791. E-mail: FHalstrom@aol.com.

HALT, JAMES GEORGE, advertising executive, graphic designer; b. Buffalo, Feb. 16, 1937; s. Clemens George Halt and Marion Helen Smith; m. July 6, 1963; children: Shannon, Kevin, Sean, Christopher. BFA, U. Buffalo, 1961. Artist, designer Thomas Lowes Assocs., Buffalo, 1961-63, art dir., 1963-69, creative dir., 1969-77; pres., owner James Halt Graphic Design, Buffalo, 1977—. Cons. Hammermill Paper Co., Erie, Pa. and Memphis, 1978—. Co-author, designer: Graphic Design USA, 1986, 89-90; designer: Trademarks USA, 1968, The Book of American Trademarks, vol. I, 1972, vol. II, 1973, Novum Gebruchsgraphik, 1980. Mem. Albright Knox Art Gallery, 1987—, Buffalo Mus. Sci., 1988—, Buffalo/Erie County Hist. Soc., 1993—, Zool. Soc. Buffalo, 1988—. Recipient Freedom Found. medal, Freedom Found. at Valley Forge, 1966, Creativity Certificate of Distinction, Art Direction Magazine Book/Show, N.Y.C., 1971, 73-79, 82-83. Mem. Art Dirs. Communicators of Buffalo (recipient over 75 awards 1961—). Democrat. Roman Catholic. Avocations: golf, woodworking, gardening. Home: 351 Springville Ave Amherst NY 14226-2857 Office: James Halt Graphic Design 166 Niagara Falls Blvd Buffalo NY 14223-3025

HALTER, H(ENRY) JAMES, JR., (DIAMOND JIM HALTER), retail executive; b. Fernandina, Fla., Feb. 28, 1947; s. Henry James and Grace (Bealey) H.; m. Wanda O'Quinn, Mar. 15, 1970; children: Jennifer, John, Elizabeth, Amelia. BS in Mgmt., Valdosta State Coll., 1970. Sales mgr. Southwestern Co., Nashville, 1969; collection mgr. Fla. Title & Mortgage Co., Jacksonville, 1970-72; appraiser Richard Hamilton & Assocs., Jacksonville Beach, 1972-74; exec. v.p. Developers Investors Svc. Corp., Jacksonville, 1975-78; pres. A-Coin and Stamp Gallery, Inc., Jacksonville, 1978-81; ptnr. Jacksonville Precious Metals, 1981, Sidetrack Video Arcade Chain, Ga., 1982-84; pres. Diamond House Corp., Valdosta, Ga., 1985—, J-Mart Jewelry Outlets, Inc., Tifton, Ga., 1988-91, chmn. bd., 1990-91; pres. K&H Ltd., Valdosta, 1992-94; exec. dir. Soc. for Legalization of Drugs, Valdosta, 1994-97. Bus. cons., 1996—. Author: May I Help You, 1988, LIZ, Inc., 1998; voice of Ernie Beaver for nationally syndicated TV cartoon spl. Coots and Critter, 1996. Bd. dirs. Park Ave. United Meth. Ch., Valdosta, 1986-88, Alapaha coun. Boy Scouts Am., 1982—; mem. Alumni Bd. Valdosta State U.; youth spkr. Atlanta Com. for the Olympic Games, selected local hero torch bearer Olympic Games, Atlanta, 1996; co-author Olympic Awareness Award for 1996 Olympic Games, 1994-95; mem. Ga. Small Bus. Task Force; bd. dirs. Redirecting Attitudes of Persons; pres. VHS Band Boosters Inc., 2002-03. Recipient Addy award, 1980, 83, God and Svc. nat. award Meth. Ch. and BSA, Cmty. Hero Torch Bearer, Coca Cola Olympic Torch Relay, 1996, Evangelism award King Solomon Missionary Bapt. Ch., 2000; named Adm. in Ga. Navy, 1983, Outstanding Ga. Citizen, 1990. Mem. Nat. Speakers Assn., Toastmasters, Sertoma, Vigil Honor, Order of the Arrow, Rotary, Sigma Iota (pres. charter), Alpha Phi Omega. Avocations: motivational speaking, antique paper money, Ga. history. Home and Office: 208 Breckenridge Dr Valdosta GA 31605-6402

HALTER, JON CHARLES, magazine editor, writer; b. Hamilton, Ohio, Nov. 24, 1941; s. Sam Lesher and Helen Louise (Olds) H.; m. Corina Garcia, Feb. 14, 1968; children: Jon Julian, Helen Margaret. BA, Syracuse U., 1964, MA, 1966. Vol. U.S. Peace Corps, Venezuela, 1966-68; asst. editor Nat. Petroleum News mag. McGraw-Hill Inc., N.Y.C., 1968-72; editor, writer Boys' Life mag. Boy Scouts Am., North Brunswick, N.J., 1972-79, Irving, Tex., 1979-90, exec. editor Scouting Mag., 1990-94; editor Scouting Mag., Exploring Mag., Irving, 1994—. Author: Bill Bradley: One to Remember, 1974, Reggie Jackson: All-Star in Right, 1975, Top Secret Projects of World War II, 1978, Their Backs to the Wall: Famous Last Stands, 1980 Mem. Soc. Profl. Journalists, Authors Guild. Democrat. Presbyterian. Avocations: reading, model building, tennis, running. Home: 505 E Huitt Ln Euless TX 76040-5532 Office: Boy Scouts Am Scouting Mag PO Box 152079 1325 W Walnut Hill Ln Irving TX 75015-2079 E-mail: jchalter@yahoo.com.

HALTIWANGER, ROBERT SIDNEY, JR., book publishing executive; b. Winston-Salem, N.C., Mar. 15, 1923; s. Robert Sidney and Janie Love (Couch) H.; m. Marguarite C. LaBelle, Aug. 23, 1994. AB, Harvard U., 1947. Coll. field rep. Prentice-Hall Inc., Atlanta, 1947-56, Southeast regional mgr., 1956-65, dir. Two Year div. Englewood Cliffs, N.J., 1965-71; v.p. sales Prentice-Hall Inc, Englewood Cliffs, N.J., 1971-80, exec. v.p. coll. div., 1980-85, pres. sales and mktg. coll. div., 1985—. Cons. Simon & Shuster, 1988-89. Served to 1st lt. USAF, 1943-46, PTO. Recipient Chmn. award Gulf and Western, 1985, Frank Enenbach award Prentice-Hall Coll. Div., 1987. Mem. Am. Assn. Pubs. (liason com. 1975-82), Harvard Club (N.Y.C. chpt.), Knickerbocker Club. Democrat. Presbyterian. Home: 1 Horizon Rd Fort Lee NJ 07024-6502 Office: Prentice Hall Inc Englewood Cliffs NJ 07632 E-mail: bobhalti@aol.com.

HALTOM, B(ILLY) REID, lawyer; b. Artesia, N. Mex., Sept. 9, 1945; s. Felix Tucker and Shirley Mae (Lucado) H.; m. Elizabeth Ann Berger, Dec. 25, 1964; 1 child, Robb Reid. BA in Philosophy, U. N.Mex, 1969; JD, Tex. Tech U., 1972. Bar: N.Mex. 1973, U.S. Dist. Ct. N.Mex. 1977, U.S. Ct. Appeals (10th cir.) 1980, U.S. Ct. Claims 1980, U.S. Supreme Ct. 1992, U.S. Dist. Ct. Ariz. 1992. Ptnr. Nordhaus, Haltom, Taylor, Taradash & Bladh, Albuquerque, 1980—. Fellow ABA, N.Mex. State BAr Assn., Albuquerque Bar Assn., Albuquerque Lawyers Club. Avocations: snow and water skiing, tennis, gourmet cooking. Office: Nordhaus Haltom Taylor Taradash & Bladh 405 MLK Jr Ave NE Albuquerque NM 87102-5310

HALTOM, MICHAEL FRED, religious studies educator, military officer; b. Dallas, June 22, 1950; s. Aubry Bennie and Margaret Tressie Haltom; m. Jean Anne Pressnall, Aug. 20, 1971; children: Michael David, Andrea Christina McGough. BA, Vennard Coll., 1977; MDiv, Western Evang. Sem., 1984. Ordained Assemblies of God, 1981. Asst. pastor First Evang. Meth. Ch., Duncanville, Tex., 1972—74; pastor Viola Cmty. Ch., Estacada, Oreg., 1974—78; prof. NT greek Eugene Bible Coll., Eugene, Oreg., 1978—85; v.p. World Evangelism Bible Coll. and Sem., Baton Rouge, 1985—88; chair bibl. studies divsn., prof. bibl. langs. Ctrl. Bible Coll., Springfield, Mo., 1988—. Chaplain USAFR, Travis Air Force Base, Calif., 1982—84, Kessler Air Force Base, Miss., 1985—88; wing chaplain Air N.G., Ft. Smith, Ark., 1989—. Editor: (editor) Beginner's New Testament Greek; author: (book) A Second Year Greek Grammar. Lt. col. USAF, 1982—2003. Decorated Air Force Commendation Medal with 3 oak leaf clusters USAF, Air Force Achievement Medal, Reserves Meritorious Svc. Medal with Hourglass and M device, Joint Meritorious Unit award U.S. Army, Armed Forces Svc. Medal USAF; named Outstanding Young Men Am., 1985; recipient Medal of Outstanding Merit, Soc. Mil. Orders World Wars, 1968. Mem.: N.G. Assn. (chaplain 1990—2002), Air Force Assn. (assoc.; chaplain 1982—88), Evang. Theol. Soc. (life). Republican. Mem. Assembly Of God Ch. Achievements include research in Text Types of Ancient Manuscripts. Avocations: travel, gardening, scuba diving. Office: Central Bible College 3000 North Grant Ave Springfield MO 65781

HALTON, DAVID CAMPBELL, journalist; b. Beaconsfield, Eng., May 28, 1940; came to U.S., 1991; s. Matthew Henry and Jean Joslyn (Campbell) H.; m. Zoya Titova, Sept. 17, 1968; children: Julian Alexander Halton, Daniel Andrew Halton. Diploma French Studies, Sorbonne, 1958; BA with honors in Modern History, U. Toronto, 1962; cert. polit. studies, Inst. D'Etudes Politiques, Paris, 1963. Contbg. editor Time Mag., Montreal, Quebec, Can., 1964-65; Paris correspondent CBC, 1966-67, 68-71, Moscow correspondent, 1967-68, Montreal correspondent, 1971-74, London correspondent, 1974-78, chief polit. correspondent, 1978-91, sr. Washington correspondent, 1991—. Mem. Nat. Press Club, Washington. Avocations: tennis, sailing. Office: CBC TV News 500 National Press Building Washington DC 20045-1501

HALTZEL, MICHAEL HARRIS, federal agency administrator, writer; b. N.Y.C., Mar. 28, 1941; s. Henry and Lillian (Feinberg) H.; m. Helen Scull Hitchman, June 12, 1966; children: Rebecca A. Haltzel-Haas, Andrew. BA, Yale U., 1963; MA, Harvard U., 1966, PhD, 1971. Asst. prof. history Hamilton Coll., Clinton, N.Y., 1971-75; dep. dir. Aspen Inst. Berlin, 1975-78; assoc. Russell Reynolds Assocs., Inc., N.Y.C., 1980-82; v.p. acad. affairs Longwood Coll., Farmville, Va., 1982-84; sr. v.p. Internat. Mgmt. and Devel. Inst., Washington, 1984-85; dir. West European studies Woodrow Wilson Internat. Ctr. Scholars, Washington, 1985-92; chief European divsn. Libr. Congress, Washington, 1992-94; dir. dem. staff, subcom. European Affairs U.S. Senate Foreign Rels. Com., Washington, 1994—; sec. U.S. Sen. NATO Parl. Assembly del., 2001—03. Mem. bd. com. Council Foreign Rels., Washington, 1997—, chmn. study group nationalities and ethnic conflict in Europe, 1992-93; election monitor Orgn. Security and Cooperation Europe, Bosnia and Herzegovina, 1996; mem. U.S. del. Conf. Security Coop. Europe Human Dimension, Copenhagen, 1990, Wehrkunde Security Conf., Munich, 1993, 2000; mem. review panel U.S. Info. Agency, Washington, 1992; mem. adv. com. Inst. World Affairs, 1990—; advisor Congl. Study Group Germany, 1989—; bd. dirs. World Affairs Coun. Greater Washington, 2000—; mem. bd. advisors, Am. Inst. for Contemporary German Studies, Johns Hopkins U., 2002—; mem. NATO-Russia Working Group, 2002—, German-Am. STrategy Group, 2003—. Author: Der Abbau der deutschen staendischen Selbstverwaltung in den Ostseeprovinzen Russlands, 1855-1905, 1977; co-editor: Between the Blocs: Problems and Prospects for Europe's Neutral and Nonaligned States, 1989, Northern Ireland and the Politics of Reconciliation, 1993; contbr. articles to newspapers and jours. Foreign Area fellow Am. Coun. Learned Socs., 1968-71; fellow Fulbright, 1963-64, Woodrow Wilson Nat., 1964-65, NDEA, 1965-66; recipient Order of Grand Duke Gediminas, 2002, Star of Romania, 2003. Democrat. Jewish. Avocations: hiking, tennis, canoeing, travel. Home: 2105 Wakefield St Alexandria VA 22308-2750 Office: Com Foreign Rels US Senate Washington DC 20510-6225 E-mail: haltzel@yahoo.com.

HALUSKA, BONNIE FRATI, rehabilitation nurse; b. Taylor, Pa., Sept. 4, 1950; d. Emilio and Ann (Anselmi) Frati; m. John Andrew Haluska, May 20, 1972. RN, Mercy Hosp. Sch. Nursing, 1971. Cert. rehab. nurse. Charge nurse Mercy Hosp., Scranton, Pa., 1971-72; staff nurse Allied Svcs. Rehab. Hosp., Scranton, Pa., 1972-79, asst. dir. nursing, 1979-89, dir. nursing, 1989-95; coord. Spinal Cord Injury Ctr., 1988-95; exec. dir. programs and nursing Allied Svcs. Rehab. Hosp., Scranton, Pa., 1995-99, asst. v.p. programs and nursing, 1999—. Mem. nursing community adv. bd. U. Scranton, 1992—. Recipient Florence Nightingale Recognition award Hosp. Assn. Pa., 1990, 91, 92, Pinnacle awards 1995 Innovation Recognition, Achievement award 1999, Nat. Rehab. Week Charles Luger award 1999. Mem. Assn. Rehab. Nurses (bd. dirs. Montage chpt. 1992), Pa. Orgn. Nurse Execs., Alpha Sigma Lambda.

HALVER, JOHN EMIL, nutritional biochemist; b. Woodinville, Wash., Apr. 21, 1922; s. John Emil and Helen Henrietta (Hansen) Halver; m. Jane Loren, July 21, 1944; children: John Emil, Nancylee Halver Hadley, Janet Ann Halver Fix, Peter Loren, Deborah Kay Halver Hanson. BS, Wash. State U., 1944, MS in Organic Chemistry, 1948; PhD in Med. Biochemistry, U. Wash., 1953. Plant chemist Assoc. Frozen Foods, Kent, Wash., 1946-47; asst. chemist Purdue U., 1948—49; instr. U. Wash., Seattle, 1949—50, affiliate prof., 1960—75; prof. U. Wash. Sch. Fisheries, 1978—92; prof. emeritus U. Wash., 1992—. Condr. research on vitamin and amino acid requirements for fish; identified aflatoxin B1 as specific carcinogen for rainbow trout hematoma ; identified vitamin C2 for fish ; dir. Western Fish Nutrition Lab. U.S. Fish and Wildlife Service, Dept. Interior, Cook, Wash., 1950—75, sr. scientist, nutrition, Seattle, 1975—78; cons. FAO, UNDP, Internat. Union Nutrition Scientists, Nat. Fish Research Inst., Hungary, World Bank, Euroconsult, UNDP, IDRC; affiliate prof. prof. U. Oreg. Med. Sch., 1965—69; vis. prof. Marine Sci. Inst. U. Tex., Port Aransas; pres. Fisheries Devel. Technology, Inc., 1980—90, Halver Corp., 1978—. Lay leader Meth. Ch., 1965—70. Capt. U.S. Army, World War II, col. USAR. Decorated Purple Heart, Bronze Star with oak leaf cluster, Meritorious Service Conduct medal. Fellow: Am. Inst. Nutrition, Am. Inst. Fishery Research Biologists; mem.: NAS, Hungarian Acad. Sci., World Aquaculture Soc., Am. Fishery Soc., Am. Chem. Soc., Am. Sci. Affiliation, Soc. Exptl. Biol. Medicine, Rotary, Alpha Chi Sigma, Pi Mu Epsilon, Phi Lambda Upsilon. Home: 16502 41st Ave NE Seattle WA 98155-5610 Office: U Wash Box 355100 Sch Fisheries and Aquatic Scis Seattle WA 98195-5100 E-mail: halver@u.washington.edu.

HALVERSON, LOWELL KLARK, lawyer, writer; b. Tacoma, May 4, 1942; s. Sidney Lawrence and Jeannette (Thompson) H.; m. Diane E. Vosburgh, June 13, 1964; children: Liana Kay, Ward Vosburgh. AB, Harvard U., 1964; JD, U. Wash., 1968. Bar: Wash. 1968, N.Y. 1981, U.S. Supreme Ct. 1979, Alaska 1989. Bd. dirs. Wash. Legal Found., 1984-87, pres. Wash. State Bar Assn., 1990-91. Author, editor: Washington Lawyer Practice Manual, 3 vols., 1972-78; author: (with others) Divorce in Washington-A Humane Approach, 1985, 2d edit., 1990, (with others) Divorce in New York, 1987. Fellow Am. Acad. Matrimonial Lawyers; mem. ABA, Wash. State Bar Assn. (gov. 7th congl. dist. 1977-80, merit award 1988, editor-in-chief Family Law Deskbook), Alaska State Bar Assn., N.Y. State Bar Assn., Seattle-King County Bar Assn. (trustee 1975-77, chmn. young lawyers sect. 1974-75, Disting. Service award 1980). Clubs: Harvard of Wash. (pres. 1974), Rainier. Home: 13721 Tastad Rd Arlington WA 98223-9413 Office: 3035 Island Crest Way Mercer Island WA 98040-2919

HALVERSON, STEVEN THOMAS, lawyer, construction executive; b. Enid, Okla, Aug. 29, 1954; s. Robert James Halverson and Ramona Mae (Ludke) Selenski; m. Diane Mary Schueller, Aug. 21, 1976; children: John Thomas, Anne Kirsten. BA cum laude, St. John's U., 1976; JD, Am. U., 1979. Bar: Va. 1979. Asst. project dir. ABA, Washington, 1977-79; with Briggs & Morgan, St Paul., Minn., 1980-83; sr. v.p. M.A. Mortenson Cos., Denver, 1984-99; pres., CEO Haskell Co., Jacksonville, Fla., 1999—. Chmn. Lowell Whiteman Sch.; bd. dir. U. North Fla. Co-author: Federal Grant Law, 1982, The Future of Construction, 1997; contbr. articles to profl. jour. Bd. dir. Jacksonville Symphony. Mem. Fla. Coun. 100, Constrn. Industry Roundtable. Republican. Roman Catholic. Office: Haskell Co Haskell Bldg 111 Riverside Ave Fl 1 Jacksonville FL 32202-4950 E-mail: sthalver@thehaskellco.com.

HALVERSTADT, DONALD BRUCE, urologist, educator; b. Cleve., July 6, 1934; s. Lauren Oscar and Lillian Frances (Jones) H.; m. Margaret Ann Marcy, Aug. 4, 1956; children: Donna, Jeffrey, Amy. BA magna cum laude, Princeton U., 1956; MD cum laude, Harvard U., 1960. Diplomate Am. Bd. Urology. Intern, then resident in surgery Mass. Gen. Hosp., Boston, 1960-62, resident in urology, 1964-67; pvt. practice medicine specializing in urology Oklahoma City, 1967—; chief pediatric urology svc. Okla. Children's Meml. Hosp., Oklahoma City, 1967—, chief staff, 1974-79; clin. prof. urology and pediatrics U. Okla. Med. Sch., 1970—, vice chair dept. urology, 1982—; interim provost U. Okla. for Health Scis., Oklahoma City, 1979-80; spl. asst. to pres. for hosp. affairs Oklahoma U., 1980-84; CEO State of Okla. Teaching Hosps., 1980-83, also bd. dirs.; CEO State Regents for Higher Edn., 1988-93. Mem. U. Okla. Bd. Regents, 1993-2000, chmn. 1999; founder, vice chmn., dir. Lincoln Nat. Bank, Oklahoma City; vice chair bd. govs. Okla. Med. Ctr. Hosp. Sys., 1998—; bd. dirs. Triad Hosps., Inc., chair compliance com., 2000—, nominating com. Contbr. articles to med. jours. Vice chair bd. govs. Univ. Health Ptnrs.; pres., chmn. bd. Okla. Ind. Phys. Svcs. Corp., 1986-96; trustee Columbia Presbyn. Hosp., 1990-96, chmn., 1995-96; bd. dirs. Nat. Assn. Basketball Coaches FDTN; athletic dir. adv. coun. U. Okla., 2003. Fellow ACS; mem. AMA (physicians recognition award 1969, 72, 79, 82, 85, 91, 94, 96, 99, 2002), Am. Urol. Assn., Am. Acad. Pediat., Soc. Pediat. Urology, Am. Soc. Nephrology, Soc. Univ. Urologists, So. Med. Assn., Okla. Med. Assn., Oklahoma County Med. Soc., Okla. State Regents for Higher Edn., Am. Coll. Physician Execs., Assn. Governing Bds. Colls. and Univs. (bd. dirs., sec. 1996-97, treas. 1997-98). Presbyterian. Home: 2932 Lamp Post Ln Oklahoma City OK 73120-6105 Office: # 707 711 Stanton L Young Blvd Oklahoma City OK 73104-5023

HALVERSTADT, ROBERT DALE, mechanical engineer, metals manufacturing company; b. Warren, Ohio, Jan. 25, 1920; s. Roscoe B. and Dorothy (Grubbs) Halverstadt; m. Maryella Green, Dec. 31, 1941; children: Marta Jean Halverstadt Carmen, Linda Anne Halverstadt Orelup, Sally Jo Halverstadt Ham. BS in Mech. Engring., Case Inst. Tech., 1951. Registered prof. engr., N.Y., Ohio. Journeyman machinist Republic Steel Corp., Cleve., 1939-51; design engr. GE, Evendale, Ohio, 1951-53; supr. Metalworking Lab., 1953-58; corp. cons. N.Y.C., 1958—63; mgr. Thomson Engring. Lab., Lynn, Mass., 1963—64; gen. mgr. engring. Continental Can Co., N.Y.C., 1964—73; group v.p. Booz, Allen & Hamilton Inc., N.Y.C., 1964-73; CEO Foster D. Snell Inc. subs., N.Y.C., 1964-73; pres. Design and Devel., Inc. subs., N.Y.C., 1966-73; mng. officer BA&H Environ. Resources Group (ERG), 1970—73; v.p. tech. Singer Co., N.Y.C., 1973-74; pres. Spl. Metals Corp. subs. Allegheny Ludlum Industries, Inc., New Hartford, N.Y., 1974-82, Materials Tech. Group, New Hartford, 1981-83; mng. dir. Allegheny Ludlum Industries Ltd., New Hartford; sr. staff v.p. Allegheny Internat., New Hartford, 1983-85; pres. AIMe Assocs., New Canaan, Conn., 1985—. Co-chmn. Titanium Metals Corp. Am., 1980—83; dir. Oneida Nat. Bank, 1979—83, Carus Corp., Centrex Lab., 1975—80; mem. adv. bd. Flexmedics, Inc., 1982—92; chmn. bd. Spl. Metals Corp., 1987—2000, chmn. bd. emeritus, 2000—01. Mem. editl. bd.: Internat. Jour. Turbo and Jet Engine Tech. Pres. industry, labor and edn. coun. Mohawk Valley, Inc., 1975—80. Lt (j.g.) USCGR, 1942—45. Recipient Jubilee of Victory medal, Govt. France, 1996, Cert. Recognition, Govt. France & Normandy, 2001. Fellow: Am. Soc. Metals (past treas., bd. dirs., Disting. Life mem. 2002); mem.: ASME, Univ. Club (N.Y.C.), Woodway Country Club, Theta Tau, Tau Beta Pi, Sigma Xi. Mem. United Ch. Of Christ. Achievements include patents in field. Home: 333 Oenoke Rdg New Canaan CT 06840-4114

HALVORSEN, HARALD WAYNE, electronics engineer; b. Big Sandy, Mont., May 20, 1927; s. Knute John and Gladys Alma (Fouts) Halvorsen. Cert., Capitol Radio Engr. Inst., Washington, 1950, U.S. War Coll. Def. Mgmt., 1964. Electronics technician Nat. Sci. Labs., Washington, 1951—52, electronics engr., 1952—57, sr. engr., 1957—60, project mgr., 1961—78. Writer tech. briefs Larry Brown Patent Lawyer, Washington, 1955; design electronics Electronics Vision Ind., Washington, 1957—60. With USN, 1945—46. Mem.: IEEE (sr.), Mensa. Achievements include patents in field; co-inventor flight simulator; invention of cryogenic blood thawer apparatus and process; method of transportation. Avocations: photography, electronic art, astronomy. Home: Apt 106 8600 16th Silver Spring MD 20910

HALVORSEN, PER HELGE, medical physicist, educator; b. Ostersund, Sweden, Dec. 23, 1966; came to U.S., 1984; s. Paul H. and Torbjörg (Brevik) H.; m. Yuan-Di Chang, Dec. 31, 1987; children: Stefan, Sonja. Student, U. Ky., Lexington, 1986-88; BS in Physics, U. Wis., 1988; MS in Radiol. Physics, U. Ky., 1990. Diplomate in therapeutic physics Am. Bd. Radiology. Clin. physicist Brown U./Roger Williams Med. Ctr., Providence, 1990-92; clin. physicist radiation therapy Harvard Med. Sch., Boston, 1992-94; chief physicist Moore Regional Hosp., Pinehurst, N.C., 1994-98; chief physicist Wake Radiology/U. N.C., Chapel Hill, 1998—2002; physicist Hosp. of St. Raphael, New Haven, 2003—. Adj. asst. prof. U. N.C., Chapel Hill, 1994-01. Mem. Am. Assn. Physicists in Medicine (profl. rels. com. 1995—, chmn. task group on solo practice physics 2000—), Am. Coll. Radiology (com. on accreditation 2000—), Norwegian Soc. Med. Physics. Avocations: tennis, soccer, boating. E-mail. Office: Hosp St Raphael Dept Radiation Onc 1450 Chapel St New Haven CT 06511 E-mail: per@halvorsen.com.

HALVORSON, ARDELL DAVID, soil scientist, researcher; b. Rugby, N.D., May 31, 1945; s. Albert F. and Karen Halvorson; m. Linda Halvorson; children: Renae, Rhonda. BS, N.D. State U., 1967; MS, Colo. State U., 1969, PhD, 1971. Soil scientist Agr. Rsch. Svc., USDA, Sidney, Mont., 1971-83, Akron, Colo., 1983-88, rsch. leader, 1988-94; lab. dir. USDA-Agr. Rsch. Svc., Mandan, N.D., 1994-97, soil scientist Ft. Collins, Colo., 1997—. Contbr. numerous articles to profl. publs. Fellow Am. Soc. Agronomy (assoc. editor 1983-87), Soil Sci. Soc. Am. (chmn. divsn. S-8 1989), Soil and Water Conservation Soc. (chpt. pres. 1991); mem. Crop Sci. Soc. Am. Office: USDA ARS 301 South Howes Rm 407 Fort Collins CO 80522-0470 E-mail: adhell.halverson@ars.usda.gov.

HALVORSON, DEBBIE DEFRANCESCO, state legislator; b. Steger, Ill., Mar. 1, 1958; d. Richard Lavern and Joyce Winifred DeFrancesco; children: Stephanie, Matthew. Degree, Robert Morris Coll., Prairie State Coll.; postgrad., U. Va., 1997, Harvard U., 1999. Twp. clk. Crete (Ill.) Twp., 1993-96; rep. 40th dist. Ill. State Senate, 1996—. Mem. appropriations commn., local govt. commn., minority spokesman commerce and industry com. Dem. Whip Ill. State Senate. Named Edn. Hero, Ill. Edn. Assn., 1997, Freshman Legislator of Yr., Ill. Health Care Assn., 1997, Statesman of Yr., Ill., 1998. Mem.: LWV (Homewood-Flossmoor chpt.), Nat. Orgn. Women Legislators (bd. dirs.), Profl. Womens Network, Chgo. Heights Bus. and Profl. Women, Chgo. Southland C. of C., Crete Womens Club, Altrusa. Office: 417 Capitol Bldg Springfield IL 62706-0001 Address: 241 W Joe Orr Rd Chicago Heights IL 60411-1744*

HALVORSON, GEORGE CHARLES, health care insurance company executive; b. Fargo, N.D., Jan. 28, 1947; s. George Charles and Barbara Theone (Paulson) H.; m. Mary Elizabeth Probst, June 27, 1986; children: Jonathan Dale, Seth Gregory, George Charles IV, Michael Thomas. BA, Concordia Coll., Moorhead, Minn., 1968. Cert. health cons., 1981. Successively mgr. market rsch., mgr. corp. planning, dir. planning and budget, v.p. planning and budget, sr. v.p. Blue Cross & Blue Shield, St. Paul, 1968-76; exec. dir. HMO Minn., St. Paul, 1976-83; pres. Sr. Health Plan, St. Paul, 1983-86, Health Accord, Inc., Mpls., 1983-86, Group Health, Inc., Mpls., 1986—2002; chmn., CEO Kaiser Permanente, 2002—. Ops. dir. HMO/Jamaica, Kingston, 1985-86; cons. AIG/Am. Internat. Health, Washington, 1987-88; lectr. in field. Author: How to Cut Your Company's Health Care Costs, 1987; contbr. articles to profl. jours. Chmn. Boy Scout Food Drive, St. Paul, 1988; fund raiser United Way, Mpls., 1987-88. Recipient Internship award Wall St. Jour. Newspaper Fund, 1968. Mem. Nat. Coop. Bus. Assn. (bd. dirs.), Minn. Bus. Partnership (bd. dirs.), Group Health Assn. Am., Minn. Council HMO's (bd. dirs.), Decathlon Club (Bloomington, Minn.), Mpls. Club. Avocations: writing, hunting, chess. Office: Group Health Inc 2829 University Ave SE Minneapolis MN 55414-3230 Address: Kaiser Permanente Oakland 1 Kaiser Plaza 94612

HALVORSON, JUDITH ANNE (JUDITH ANNE DEVAUD), elementary education educator; b. Bethesda, Md., Apr. 28, 1943; d. Henri J. and Mary L. (Baumgart) Devaud; m. Peter L. Halvorson, Feb. 4, 1964; 1 child, Peter Chase. BS in Edn., U. Cin., 1965; MA in Edn., U. Conn., 1974, Cert. Advanced Grad. Study in Edn., 1980, postgrad. in French, 2003—. Tchr. Greenhills-Forest Park (Ohio) City Schs., 1965-67, Weld County Schs., Greeley, Colo., 1969-70, Chaplin (Conn.) Elem. Sch., 1970-2000; ret., 2000. Mentor Beginning Educator Support program State of Conn. and Chaplin Elem. Sch., 1988-2000; supr. student tchrs. East Conn. State U., U. Conn., U. No. Colo., 1969-2000. Past vice-chmn., past chmn., past sec. Coventry (Conn.) Bd. Edn., 1981-95; chmn. Coventry Sch. Bldg. com., 1981-92, Coventry Parks and Recreation Com., 1980-82, chmn., 1982; mem. Dem. Town Com. Coventry, 1973-98. Grantee, Nat. Sci. Edn. project, 1977-78; named Outstanding Elem. Tchr. Am., 1974; recipient Citation for Cmty. Leadership, Nat. Women's History Month, 1991; recognized for svc. to pub. edn. in Conn., Conn. Assn. Bds. of Edn., 1993, 94, 95, for contbns. to Conn., Beginning Educator Support and Tng. program Conn. State Dept. Edn., 1991-93, for svc. to cooperating tchr. programs Ea. Conn. State U., 1993, 95, for Outstanding Svc. to Pub. Edn., State of Conn., 1995. Mem. NEA (life), Conn. Edn. Assn. (life), Chaplin Edn. Assn. (past pres., v.p., chmn. negotiations 1970-2000), Assn. Ret. Tchrs. Conn., Pi Lambda Theta (past pres., v.p., chmn. membership Beta Sigma chpt. 1974—), Phi Delta Kappa. Episcopalian. Avocations: swimming, skiing, golf, leisure travel, French language and culture. Home: 90 David Dr Coventry CT 06238-1320 E-mail: jandphalvorson@msn.com.

HALVORSON, MARJORY, opera director; Pvt. studies with, Sister Marietta Coyle, Jerry Daniels, Dolores Ravich. Dir. vocal studies Whitworth Coll., Spokane; artistic dir. Spokane Opera, Spokane. Dir. vocal master classes iwth Thomas Hampson, Richard Miller, Dale Moore, John Shirley-Quirk, James Maddalena, Armen Guzlimien; tchr. pvt. lesons in voice, vocal pedagogy, diction and lit.; director opera workshop. Named Woman of Achievement in Arts and Culture, City of Spokane, 1996; recipient outstaindng cmty. svc. award Westminster United Ch. of Christ. Office: Spokane Opera 643 S Ivory St Spokane WA 99202-2362

HALVORSON, MARY ELLEN, education educator, writer; b. Salem, Ohio, Apr. 23, 1950; d. Robert J. and Betty June (Bear) Batzli; m. Thomas Henry Halvorson, June 10, 1972; children: Christine Lynn, Matthew Thomas, Rebecca Lynn. BS in Edn. with distinction, No. Ariz. U., 1972, postgrad., 1973-92, U. Ariz., 1974-76, Ariz. State U., 1975-76, U. Phoenix, 1989-90; PhD in Edn., Calif. Coast U., 2001. Cert. Supt. Ariz., 2001, elem. tchr. libr. Ariz. Tchr. Prescott (Ariz.) Unified Schs., 1972-77, dir. community nature ctr., 1978, reading tutor, 1985-88, family math. tchr., 1989-90, part-time libr., 1991-92; dir. Prescott Study Ctr., 1987-90; writer ednl. materials Herald House, Independence, Mo., 1994—; instr. Yavapai C.C., 1994-96; edn. coord. Yavapai Prescott Indian Tribe, 1996-98; tchr. Prescott Unified Sch. Dist., 1998—99; supt. Tri-City Prep. H.S., 1999—. Guest speaker Abia Judd Young Authors, Prescott, 1992; math. enthusiast instr. Ariz. Dept. Edn., Prescott, 1989-92; asst. instr. outdoor edn. Ariz. State U., Prescott, 1977-78; tutor English grammar No. Ariz. U., Flagstaff, 1971-72; presenter, U. Oxford (Eng.) Round Table, 2003. Co-author: Arizona Bicentenial Resource Manual, 1975; contbr. book rev. column to Prescott Courier, 1993, also articles to profl. publs. Cert. adult instr. Temple Sch., Independence, Mo., 1985—; sec., bd. dirs. Whispering Pines, Prescott, 1989-93; music docent Prescott Symphony Guild, 1982-85; state Christian edn. dir. Cmty. of Christ. Ch., Ariz., 1977-82, elder, counselor to pastor, 1993—; spokesperson Franklin Heights Homeowners, Prescott, 1985; leader Prescott Pioneers 4-H Club, 1989—, Christian Youth Group, 1985—; fundraiser Graceland Coll., 1993; craft demonstrator Sharlott Hall Mus.; master of ceremonies Prescott Summer Pops Symphony, 1995, 97. Recipient 4-H Silver Clover Svc. award, 1995; named Outstanding Young Educator, Prescott Jaycees, 1976, Outstanding Young Women of Am., 1985. Mem. Phi Kappa Phi, Kappa Delta Pi, Sigma Epsilon Sigma. Avocations: teaching piano, sewing costumes for school musical groups, oil painting. Home: 2965 Pleasant Valley Dr Prescott AZ 86305-7116

HALVORSON, MILTON HUNTER, association administrator, retired; b. West New York, NJ, May 7, 1927; s. Ingar John and Isabella Mary Halvorsen; m. Lee Lillian Smith, May 15, 1950; children: Lori Lee, Glenn Milton, Gary Mitchell. Grad., Basic Engring. Sch., Biloxi, Miss., 1945; at, Ramapo Coll., Mahwah, NJ, 1998—. Cert. construction official NJ. Journeyman Iron Workers Local 45, Jersey City, 1947—57; project mgr. Interlake, Chgo., 1957—97; pres. We Must Care, Ridgefield, NJ, 1963—. Founder We Must Care Think Tank at Ramapo Coll., 1998—. Contbr. articles; public spkr. : (to civic groups). Founder Boys Club, Ridgefield, NJ, 1965. With USN, 1945—47, PTO. Grantee CEDA grant, U.S. govt., 1953. Mem.: Star Square Assoc. (pres. 1990—), NY State Masons (Master Mason 1948). Independent. Lutheran. Avocation: children's safety advocate. Home and Office: We Must Care PO Box 333 380 Shaler Blvd Ridgefield NJ 07657 Office Fax: 201-943-3145. E-mail: imustcare@aol.com.

HALVORSON, NEWMAN THORBUS, JR., lawyer; b. Detroit, Dec. 17, 1936; s. Newman Thorbus and Virginia Westbrook (Markle) H.; m. Sally Clark Stone, May 3, 1969; children: Christina English, Charles Burgess Westbrook. AB, Princeton U., 1958; LLB, Harvard U., 1961. Bar: Ohio 1962, D.C. 1963, U.S. Supreme Ct. 1965. Assoc. Covington & Burling, Washington, 1962-70; asst. U.S. atty. Office of U.S. Atty., Washington, 1983-85; assoc. ind. counsel (spl. prosecutor under Ethics in Govt. Act), 1987-90; ptnr. Covington & Burling, Washington, 1970—83, 1985—2002, sr. counsel, 2002—. Editor, Harvard Law Rev., 1960-61; author: Intermediate Sanctions Regs: Many Questions Remain, Tax Notes, 1998. Sr. warden, Jr. warden, vestryman Christ Ch. Georgetown, Washington, 1983-86, 89-92, chmn. fin. com., 1992-96; bd. dirs. Lupus Found. D.C., 1974-85; mem., bd. dirs. Eugene and Agnes E. Meyer Found., Washington, 1976-91, chmn., 1989-90, asst. sec./treas., 1990—; bd. mgrs. Hist. Soc. Washington, 1995—, chmn. investment com., 1999—, chmn. audit comm., 2001—; vice chmn. bd. dirs. Coun. for Ct. Excellence, Washington, 2003—; trustee Potomac Sch., McLean, Va., 1980-86, chmn., 1981-83; mem. com. of 100 on Federal City, 1970—, trustee, treas., 1975-79; bd. trustees, mem. exec. com. Greater Washington Rsch. Ctr., 1997-2001; trustee Cleveland Park Hist. Soc., 1997—, pres. 2002-03; dir. Rosedale Conservancy, 2002-03; bd. govs. Coord. Coun. Internat. Univs, 2001—. With USMCR, 1961-67. Mem. ABA, D.C. Bar. Clubs: Met. (Washington), Chevy Chase (Md.). Republican. Episcopalian. Home: 3500 Lowell St NW Washington DC 20016-5025 Office: Covington & Burling 1201 Pennsylvania Ave NW Washington DC 20004-2401

HALWIG, J. MICHAEL, allergist; b. Denver, Apr. 15, 1954; s. John Philip and Hilda (Fuggis) H.; m. Nancy Diane Graupman, June 14, 1975; children: Courtney Elizabeth, J. Christopher. BA, Johns Hopkins U., 1975; MD, Northwestern U., Chgo., 1980. Diplomate Am. Bd. Allergy and Immunology, Am. Bd. Internal Medicine. Intern in internal medicine Northwestern U. Meml. Hosps., Chgo., 1980-81, resident in internal medicine, 1981-83; allergy fellowship Northwestern U. Med. Sch., Chgo., 1983-85; practice medicine specilizing in allergy, asthma, immunology Atlanta, 1985—. Instr. Northwestern U. Med. Sch., Chgo., 1984-85, admissions amb., 1989—; clin. asst. prof. Emory U. Sch. Medicine, 1989—. Bd. dirs. Am. Lung Assn. Ga., 1996-2001. Fellow Am. Coll. Allergy, Asthma and Immunology (allergy practice and practice guidelines com. 1992—), Am. Acad. Allergy, Asthma and Immunology (Managed Care Key Contact Network 1996—); mem. AMA, Asthma and Allergy Found. of Am. (nat. chpt. bd. dirs., chpt. rels. and devel. com. 1997-99, mktg. and fundraising com. 1997-99, Ga. chpt. founder, bd. dirs., med. dir. 1995-99, chmn. med. adv. com. 1995-99), Joint Coun. on Allergy and Immunology, Med. Assn. Ga. (rep. Coun. on Legislation 1989-95), Allergy, Asthma and Immunology Soc. Ga. (pres. 1993-95, v.p. 1991-93, program chmn. 1991-93, co-chmn. third party payors com. 1992—, rep. Ga. medicare carrier adv. com. 1993—), So. Med. Assn., Cobb County Med. Assn., Cobb Area Pediat. Soc., Wellstar Health Care Sys. (pediat. asthma task force 1996-2001, asthma/COPD task force 1998-2001), Ga. Partnership for Caring. Presbyterian. Avocations: running, listening to jazz, golf. Office: 1700 Hospital South Dr Ste 404 Austell GA 30106-8116 E-mail: mhalwig@atlantaallergy.com.

HALWIG, NANCY DIANE, banker; b. Rochester, N.Y., Sept. 17, 1954; d. Norman Charles and Elizabeth Marie (Callemyn) Graupman; m. John Michael Halwig, June 14, 1975; children: Courtney Elizabeth, John Christopher. BA in Elem. Edn. with honors, Goucher Coll., 1975; M. Mgmt. in Fin., Northwestern U., 1979. Br. adminstrv. mgmt. trainee Md. Nat. Bank, Balt., 1975-76; comml. banking officer Am. Nat. Bank Chgo., 1976-80; v.p. relationship mgr. Citicorp USA-Chgo., 1980-85; v.p., team leader Citicorp N.Am., Atlanta, 1985-89, v.p. region credit officer, 1986-90; v.p., regional mgr. Kredietbank-Atlanta, 1990-95; regional v.p. Bank of Am., FSB, Atlanta, 1995-96, sr. v.p., 1996-98; regional mktg. mgr., sr. v.p. Congress Fin. Corp., a Wachovia Co., Atlanta, 1999—. Mem. contbns. com. Citicorp, Chgo., Atlanta, 1984-90; sec., bd. dirs. S.W. Cobb Allergy and Asthma, P.C., 1989-97. Mem. fin. com. Big Bros./Big Sisters, Atlanta, 1987-91; mem. leadership forum Scottish Rite Hosp., Atlanta, 1988-92; contbns. contact Scitrek Mus., Atlanta, 1988-90, mem. pres.'s coun., 1990-91; mem. steering com. N.W. Ga. Girl Scouts Friendship Circle, 1993-94, mem. Friendship Circle, 1993—, Juliette Low assoc., 1998—; troop treas. Girl Scouts U.S., 1994-96; sustainer Atlanta Women's Fund, 1995-2003; co-chair Atlanta Women in Fin., 1999. Named one of Atlanta Women to Watch, Atlanta Bus. Chronicle, 1988, Women Looking Ahead News Mag.'s WLA 100's List of Ga.'s Most Powerful Women in Banking & Fin., 1999, 2000, 2001. Mem. Fin. Women Internat. (Paragon Cir., futures com. 1996-97, nominating com. 1997-98), Nat. Assn. Bank Women (found. trustee 1984-85, treas. found. 1985-86, bd. dirs. and chmn. fin. com. 1987-88, chmn. task force on child care financing alternatives, restructuring task force 1988-89, nat. conf. program chmn. 1991-92), Aux. Am. Coll. Allergy, Asthma and Immunology, Women's Fin. Exch. (founding bd. dirs.), Atlanta C. of C. (bd. advisors), Atlanta Venture Forum, Assn. Corp. Growth (dir. 2000—, chpt. pres. 2003--), ACG Capital Connection Conf. (chair 2003), Turnaround Mgmt. Assn., Comml. Fin. Assn. (dir. 2002—), Northwestern Univ. Club of Atlanta, Vinings Village Women's Club (pres. 2000-01), Phi Beta Kappa. Republican. Avocations: strength training, swimming, running. Home: 4400 Woodland Brook Dr NW Atlanta GA 30339-5365 Office: Right Mgmt Cons 3290 Northside Pkwy Ste 700 Atlanta GA 30327 E-mail: ndhalwig@aol.com.

HALYARD, RAYMOND JAMES, aerospace engineer, mathematics educator; b. Evansville, Ind., Oct. 23, 1939; s. Ragon James and Leona (Barfield) H.; children: Debra Jo, Michael Travis, David James. BS in Aero. Engring., Purdue U., 1962; MCE, U. Houston, 1972. Registered profl. engr., Tex. Propulsion analysis engr. Rocketdyne Co., Canoga Park, Calif., 1963-65, McDonnell Douglas Corp., Houston, 1965-73, booster sys. flight contr., 1978-86; environ. engr. Lummus Co., Houston, 1973-75; avionics test engr. Rockwell Internat. Corp., Houston, 1975-78; engring. supr. shuttle booster sys. Rockwell Space Ops. Co., Houston, 1986-94; analysis engr. space sta. power sys. United Space Alliance, Houston, 1994—. Instr. math. San Jacinto Coll., Pasadena, Tex., 1991—. Author: The Quest for Water Planets, 1996; contbr. articles to sci. jours. Vol. youth mentor Crossroads Svc. Orgn., Houston, 1997—. Recipient Astronaut Silver Snoopy award NASA/Johnson Space Ctr., Houston, 1978, 88, cert. of appreciation for manned flight awareness from adminstr. NASA, 1988. Mem. Nat. Space Soc. Avocation: space futurist. Home: 16204 Diana Ln # 318A Houston TX 77062 Office: United Space Alliance 600 Gemini St Houston TX 77058-2783

HAM, KAREN, musician, music educator; b. Bklyn., Apr. 13, 1952; d. Irving and Eva (Walker) H. AA, Staten Island Coll., 1974; BA, CUNY, 1978; MA, NYU, 1983; student in piano, French Conservatory Music, N.Y.C., 19905. Tchr. Assn. Black Social Workers, Bklyn., 1978-85, Bklyn. Music Sch., 1985-87; tchr., condr. Holy Innocents Sch., Bklyn., 1985—. Dir. choir and music ensemble, keyboard classes. Roman Catholic. Avocations: research of american songwriters, american musical films. Office: Holy Innocents Sch 249 E 17th St Brooklyn NY 11226-4601

HAM, O(SCAR) EMERSON, JR., neurologist; b. Atlanta, Feb. 22, 1940; s. O. Emerson and Ruth Roan (McCurry) H.; m. Mary Little Schofield, Sept. 12, 1964; children: O. Emerson III, Stephen B. BA, Emory U., 1960, MD, 1964. Diplomate Am. Bd. of Psychiatry and Neurology; lic. M.D. Minn., Fla., Ga. Intern. in medicine U. Fla. Tchg. Hosp., Gainesville, 1964-65; fellow in neurology Mayo Clinic, Rochester, Minn., 1965-68; staff neurologist Wilford Hall USAF Hosp., San Antonio, Tex., 1968-70; pvt. practice neurology Neurol. Assn., Savannah, Ga., 1970-77; group practice neurology Neurol. Inst., Savannah, 1977—. Clin. instr. neurology U. Tex. Sch. Medicine, San Antonio, 1968-70; assoc. clin. prof. Med. Coll. Ga., Augusta, 1978-95. Contbr. articles to profl. jours. Grad. Leadership Savannah; bd. trustees, vice chmn. Ga. Infirmary, Savannah. Capt. USAF, 1968-70. Mem. AMA, Am. Acad. Neurology, Am. EEG Soc., Ga. Med. Soc. (past pres.), So. Med. Assn., Med. Assn. Ga., Ga. Neurol. Soc. (past pres.), Savannah Rotary, Alpha Omega Alpha. Episcopalian. Avocations: boating, hunting, hiking, skiing. Office: Neurol Inst Savannah 4 E Jackson Blvd Savannah GA 31405-5810

HAM, SOMMY L. publisher, writer; b. Houston, Sept. 12, 1953; 5. Robert Steele Jr. and Nellie (McGuinness) Gray; child by previous marriage: Laura Ann; m. Robert E. Ham Jr., Feb. 14, 1986 (div. June 1996); children: Mark, Katie, Jeffrey. AA with honors, Houston C.C., 1994; student, U. Houston, 1994-95. V.p. adminstrn. Cordovan Corp. Pubs., Houston, 1975-82; advt. rep. Golfer Mags., Inc., Houston, 1983-88, gen. mgr., 1996-97, pub., 1997—2001; editor Tomball-Magnolia Tribune, Magnolia, Tex., 2001—. Recipient scholarship Houston C.C., 1993, Alice B. Rogers scholarship award Advt. Fedn. Houston, 1995-96. Mem. Women in Comms., Exec. Women's Golf Assn., Romance Writers Am. (conf. co-chair N.W. chpt. 1995, treas.), Phi Theta Kappa. Avocation: journalism. Office: 517 W Main St Tomball TX 77375

HAMADA, DUANE TAKUMI, architect; b. Honolulu, Aug. 12, 1954; s. Robert Kensaku and Jean Hakue (Masutani) H.; m. Martha S.P. Lee, Dec. 22, 1991; children: Erin, Robyn, David. BFA in Environ. Design, U. Hawaii, 1977, BArch, 1979. Registered architect, Hawaii, Guam, Florida, Puerto Rico, Saipan. Intern Edward Sullam, FAIA & Assocs., Honolulu, 1979-80; assoc. Design Ptnrs., Inc., Honolulu, 1980-86; prin. AM Ptnrs., Inc., Honolulu, 1986-98, Design Ptnrs. Inc., Honolulu, 1998—. Chmn. 31st Ann. Cherry Blossom Festival Fashion Show, Honolulu, 1982, 32d Ann. Cherry Blossom Festival Cooking Show, 1983, mem. steering com., 1982, 83. Recipient Gold Key award for Excellence in Interior Design Am. Hotel and Motel Assn., 1990, Renaissance '90 Merit award Nat. Assn. Home Builder's Remodeler Coun., Merit award Honolulu mag., 1990, Cert. of Appreciation PACDIV USN, 1992, Gold Nugget award of Merit, 1997. Mem. AIA (jury student awards 1997, 98, jury profl. awards 1999), Constrn. Specifications Inst., Nat. Coun. Archtl. Registration Bds., Colegio de Arcquitectos de P.R., Japanese C. of C. Hawaii, Hawaiian Astron. Soc. Avocations: astronomy, music. Office: Design Ptnrs Inc 1580 Makaloa St Ste 1100 Honolulu HI 96814-3240 E-mail: dpinc@hawaii.rr.com.

HAMADA, HAROLD SEICHI, civil engineer, educator; b. Honolulu, Nov. 1, 1935; s. Kihachi and Tsuruyo (Hamada) H.; m. Lucy Tachiko Igawa, Aug. 24, 1958; children: Kyle Hideo, LeeAnn Hiroko. BS, U. Hawaii, 1957; MS, U. Ill., 1958, PhD, 1962. Registered profl. engr, Hawaii. Project officer Air Force Weapons Lab., Kirtland AFB, N.Mex., 1962-65; engr. Lawrence (Calif.) Radiation Lab., 1965-67; prof. civil engring. U. Hawaii, Honolulu, 1967-90, interim chmn. civil engring., 1990-92, chmn. civil engring., 1992—95, prof. civil engring., 1995—2000, prof. emeritus, 2000; with KSF, Inc., Honolulu, 2000—. Served with USAF, 1962-65. Fellow ASCE (pres. Hawaii sect. 1974), Am. Concrete Inst., Structural Engrs. Assn. Hawaii (pres. elect 1989, pres. 1990, past pres. 1991), Hawaii Soc. Profl. Engrs. (Engr. of Yr. 1993), Sigma Xi. Home: 2084 Alaeloa St Honolulu HI 96821-1021 Office: KSF Inc Ste 300 615 Piikoi St Honolulu HI 96814

HAMADA, OMAR LOUIS, physician; b. Tallahassee, June 10, 1966; s. Louis Bahjat and Ann Hanan (Souki) Hamada; m. Tara Lee Newton, Sept. 30, 1995; 1 child: Gabriella Maye. BS, Union U., 1986; MA, Columbia Bibl. Seminary, S.C., 1988; MD, U. Tenn., 1993. Diplomate Am. Bd. Family Practice, Nat. Bd. Med. Examiners, Am. Bd. Sports Medicine. Intern Bapt. Meml. Hosp., Memphis, 1992-93, resident in family practice, 1993 95, staff, 1995—, resident in ob-gyn., 1999—2002; staff LeBohneur Children's Hosp., Memphis, 1995—, U. Tenn. Bowld. Rsch. Hosp., Memphis, 1995—; asst. prof. U. Tenn., Memphis, 1997—; staff Regional Med. Ctr., Memphis, 1995—. Vis. prof./lectr. in field; peer reviewer Lebanese Med. Jour. Contbr. articles to profl. jours. Exec. dir. Hamada Evangelistic Outreach, Jackson, Tenn., 1988—; exec. bd. dirs. Youth For Christ, Memphis, 1995—. Flight Surgeon and Diving Med. Officer U.S. Spl. Forces. Recipient Golden Apple Excellence in Tchg. award 1997, 98, 99, 2000, Mead Johnson award for Grad. Med. Edn., 1994; named Top 40 under 40 Memphis Bus. Jour., 1998. Fellow Am. Acad. Family Physicians; mem. AMA, ACS, Am. Coll. Ob-Gyn., Am. Acad. Family Practitioners, Tenn. Med. Assn., Tenn. Acad. Family Physicians, Am. Lebanese Med. Assn., Undersea and Hyperbaric Med. Soc., Spl. Ops. Med. Assn., Assn. Mil. Surgeons U.S., Aerospace Med. Assn., U.S. Army Assn. Flight Surgeons, Am. Coll. Emergency Physicians, Am. Coll. Sports Medicine, Wilderness Med. Soc., Christian Med. and Dental Soc., Mensa, Internat. Mountain Med. Soc.

HAMADA, ROBERT S(EIJI), educator, economist, entrepreneur; b. San Francisco, Aug. 17, 1937; s. Horace T. and Maki G. Hamada; m. Anne Marcus, June 16, 1962; children: Matthew, Janet. BE, Yale U., 1959; SM, MIT, 1961, PhD, 1969. Economist Sun Oil Co., Phila., 1961—63; instr. U. Chgo., 1966—68, asst. prof. fin., 1968—71, assoc. prof., 1971—77, prof., 1977—89, Edward Eagle Brown prof., 1989—93, Edward Eagle Brown Disting. Svc. prof., 1993—, dir. Ctr. for Rsch. in Security Prices, 1980—85, dir. Ctr. Internat. Bus. Edn. and Rsch., 1992—94, dep. dean for faculty Grad Sch. Bus., 1985—90, dean, 1993—2001; CEO, dir. Merchants' Exchange, 2001—02. Vis. prof. univs. including London Bus. Sch., 1973, 79-80, UCLA, 1971, U. Wash., Seattle, 1971-72, U. B.C., Vancouver, Can., 1976; bd. dirs. A.M. Castle & Co., Fleming Cos., Inc., No. Trust Corp.; pub. dir. Chgo. Bd. Trade, 1989-2000; cons. numerous fin. instns., banks, mfg., mgmt. cons., acctg. and law firms. Past assoc. editor Jour. Fin., Jour. Fin. and Quantitative Analysis, Jour. Applied Corp. Fin.; cons. editor Scott, Foresman & Co. fin. series; contbr. numerous articles to profl. jours. Bd. dirs. numerous non-profit orgns., including Hyde Park Neighborhood Club, Chgo., Harper Ct. Found., Chgo., Hyde Park Co-op, U. Chgo. Lab. Schs., Window to the World Comms., Inc. (WTTW-TV), Terra Found. for the Arts. Named to 8 Outstanding Bus. Sch. Profs., fortune Mag., 1982; recipient 1st Outstanding Tchr. award, Grad. Sch. Bus., U. Chgo., 1970, McKinsey Tchg. prize, 1981; Sloan Found. fellow, 1959—61, Ford Found. fellow, 1963—65, Standard Oil Found. fellow, 1965—66, MIT scholar, 1959—61, Yale scholar, 1955—59. Mem. Am. Fin. Assn. (bd. dirs. 1982-85), Econometric Soc., Nat. Bur. Econ. Rsch. (bd. dirs., mem. investment and exec. coms.), Am. Econ. Assn. (investment com.), Inst. Mgmt. Scis. (investment com.), Tau Beta Pi. Office: U Chgo Grad Sch Bus 1101 E 58th St Chicago IL 60637-1511

HAMAI, JAMES YUTAKA, business executive; b. Oct. 14, 1926; s. Seizo and May (Sata) H.; m. Dorothy K. Fukuda, Sept. 10. 1954; children: Wendy A. BS, U. So. Calif., 1952; MS, 1955; postgrad. bus. mgmt. program ind. exec., UCLA, 1963-64. Lectr. chem. engring. dept. U. So. Calif., L.A., 1963—64; process engr., sr. process engr. Fluor Corp., L.A., 1954—64; sr. project mgr. ctrl. rsch. dept. Monsanto Co., St. Louis, 1964—67, mgr. rsch., devel. and engring. graphic sys. dept., 1967—68; mgr. comml. devel. New Enterprise, 1968—69; exec. v.p., dir. Concrete Cutting Industries, Inc., L.A., 1969—72; pres., dir. Concrete Cutting Internat. Inc., L.A., 1972—78, chmn. bd., 1978—; pres., CEO, dir. Techno Enterprises U.S.A., Ltd., L.A., 2000—. Cons. Fluor Corp., Los Angeles, 1970-72; dir. Intech Systems Co., Ltd., Tokyo, Cutting Industries Co., Ltd., Tokyo, Unity Five Industries, Ltd., Tokyo; internat. bus. cons. Served with AUS, 1946-48. Mem. Am. Inst. Chem. engrs., Am. Mgmt. Assn., Tau Beta Pi, Phi Lambda Upsilon. Club: Rotary (gov. dist. 1982-83). Home: 6600 Via La Paloma Rancho Palos Verdes CA 90275-6449 Office: PO Box 700 Wilmington CA 90748-0700

HAMAKER, RICHARD FRANKLIN, engineer; b. Lynchburg, Va., Jan. 10, 1924; s. John Irvin and Ray (Parker) H.; m. Marjorie Wrigley, Dec. 23, 1944 (div. 1974); children: Laurel Elisa, Lawrence Walter. BS in Mechanical Engring., MIT, 1946, MS in Mechanical Engring., 1953. Registered profl. engr., Va. Architect, engr., Lynchburg, Va., 1947-50; exec. officer MIT Dynamic Analysis Lab., Cambridge, Mass., 1951-53; magr. data processing Bendix Guided Missle div., Mishawaka, Ind., 1953-59; mgr. computer ctr. Mobil Oil, N.Y.C., 1960-61; systems engr. ITT, Huntsville, Ala., 1962 65; adv. engr. IBM, Research Triangle Park, N.C., 1965-74; owner Hamaker Woodcrafts, Durham, N.C., 1975—. Speaker Am. Mgmt. Assn. seminars, N.Y., 1958-62, IBM customer exec. seminars, N.Y., Calif., 1959. Author: A General Theory of Biological Architecture, 1995. Tech. dir. Durham Savovards, 1974-76; mill wright Friends West Point, Durham, 1975-77. Lt. (j.g.) USNR, 1943-46. Mem. Sigma Xi (pres.), Tau Beta Pi, Torch Club, MIT Club. Home: 1315 Morreene Rd G20 Durham NC 27705

HAMALAINEN, PEKKA KALEVI, historian, educator; b. Finland, Dec. 28, 1938; s. Olavi Simeon and Aili Aliisa (Laiho) H.; children: Kim Ilkka, Leija-Lee Louise Aili, Timothy Pekka Olavi, Kai Kalevi Edward. AB, Ind. U., 1961, PhD, 1966. Acting asst. prof. history U. Calif., Santa Barbara, 1965-66, asst. prof. history, 1966-70; assoc. prof. history U. Wis., Madison, 1970-76, prof., 1976—2001, prof. emeritus, 2001—, chmn. Western European area studies program, 1977—. Nat. screening com. Scandinavian area Inst. Internat. Edn., Fulbright Hays Program; cons. Dept. State., Washington, 1991—; chair grad. edn. coun. U. Wis., 1996—, Vilas assoc. Author: Kielitaistelu Suomessa 1917-1939, 1968, Nationalitetskampen och sprakstriden i Finland 1917-1939, 1969, In Time of Storm: Revolution, Civil War and the Ethnolinguistic Issue in Finland, 1978, Luokka ja Kieli Vallankumouksen Suomessa, 1978, Uniting Germany: Actions and Reactions, 1994; contbr. articles to profl. publs. and jours. Served to lt. Finnish Navy, 1957-58. Faculty research grantee U. Calif., 1966-69; faculty summer fellow, 1969; Ford Found. grantee, 1967; faculty research grantee U. Wis., Madison, 1970— ; Am. Philos. Soc. research grantee, 1973; Am. Council Learned Socs. fellow, 1976; research grantee, 1978 Mem. AAUP, Am. Hist. Assn., German Studies Assn., Soc. Advancement Scandinavian Study (adv. com. exec. coun.), Fin. Hist. Assn. (corr. emem.), Coun. European Studies, Paasikivi Seura, Ind. U. Alumni Assn. Office: U Wis 3211 Humanities 455 N Park St Madison WI 53706-1405

HAMAN, RAYMOND WILLIAM, lawyer; b. St. Maries, Idaho, Jan. 22, 1927; s. William and Eva Kate (Colliver) H.; m. Phyllis Maxine Garrett, June 24, 1948; children: Lorinda Ann, Bradley Lawrence (dec.). Student, Whitman Coll., 1947-49; JD, Washington and Lee U., 1952. Bar: Wash., 1952, U.S. Dist. Ct. (we. dist.) Wash. 1952, U.S. Ct. Appeals (9th cir.), U.S. Supreme Ct. Assoc. Evans, McLaren, Lane, Powell & Beeks, Seattle, 1952-59, ptnr., 1959-66, Lane Powell Moss & Miller, Seattle, 1966-89, Lane Powell Spears Lubersky, Seattle, 1989-91, of counsel, 1991-2001. Legal counsel Gov. Daniel J. Evans, Olympia, Wash., 1965, 67; mem. statute Law Com., 1966-95, chmn. 1988-95. Trustee, past pres. Lighthouse for the Blind, Inc., Seattle, 1964—; mem. vestry St. Augustine's Episcopal Ch., 1999—2002; bd. dirs. Mercer Island (Wash.) Sch. Dist., 1967—72, Island County (Wash.) United Way, 1993—, pres., 1997—98. With USMC, 1945—46, PTO. Mem. Wash. Bar Assn., Order of the Coif. Republican. Episcopalian. Home: PO Box 926 Langley WA 98260-0926 Office: Lane Powell Spears Lubersky 1420 5th Ave Ste 4100 Seattle WA 98101-2338

HAMANN, CHARLES MARTIN, lawyer; b. Greenwich, Conn., July 2, 1939; s. Edmund Henry and Mary (Foss) H.; m. Ethel McFarlan, July 11, 1964; children: Charles Franklin, Edmund Tappan. BA, Yale U., 1961; LLB, Harvard U., 1964. Bar: Mass. 1964. Law clk. Superior Ct., Boston, 1964-65; assoc. Nutter, McClennen & Fish, Boston, 1965-69, Herrick & Smith, Boston, 1969-74; ptnr. Casner & Edwards, LLP, Boston, 1974—. Mem. Belmont Town Meeting, 1970—; mem. Belmont (Mass.) Bd. Appeals, 1974-77; mem. Belmont Warrant (Fin.) Com., 1978-93, also chmn. 3 yrs.; mem. Belmont By-law Rev. Com., 1993—, now chmn. Fellow Am. Coll. Trust and Estate Counsel; mem. Boston Estate Planning Coun. (pres. 1987). Unitarian-Universalist. Avocations: tennis, hiking, swimming, reading. Home: 28 Temple St Belmont MA 02478-3545 Office: Casner & Edwards LLP 303 Congress St Boston MA 02210-1010 E-mail: hamann@casneredwards.com.

HAMANN, DERYL FREDERICK, lawyer, bank executive; b. Lehigh, Iowa, Dec. 8, 1932; s. Frederick Carl Hamann and Ada Ellen (Hollingsworth) Hamann Geis; m. Carrie Svea Rosen, Aug. 23, 1954 (dec. 1985); children: Karl F., Daniel A., Esther Hamann Brabec, Julie Hamann Bunderson; m. Eleanor Ramona Nelson Curtis, June 20, 1987. AA, Ft. Dodge Jr. Coll., Iowa, 1953; BS in Law, U. Nebr., 1956, JD cum laude, 1958. Bar: Nebr. 1958, U.S. Dist. Ct. Nebr. 1958, U.S. Ct. Appeals (8th cir.) 1958. Law clk. U.S. Dist. Ct. for Nebr., Lincoln, 1958-59; ptnr. Baird, Holm, McEachen, Pedersen, Hamann & Strasheim, Omaha, 1959—2003, sr. counsel, 2003—. Chmn. adv. com. Supreme Ct. Nebr., Omaha, 1986-95; chmn. bd. Great Western Bancorporation, Inc. Past pres. Omaha Estate Planning Coun. Mem. Nebr. Bar Found. (pres. 1981-86), Nebr. Assn. Bank Attys. (pres. 1985-86). Republican. Lutheran. Avocations: boating, reading. Office: Baird Holm McEachen Pedersen Hamann & Strasheim 1500 Woodmen Tower Omaha NE 68102

HAMARMAN, STEPHANIE, psychiatrist, educator; b. Phila., Jan. 23, 1964; d. Harry H. and Anne C. H.; m. Stuart Lee Goldberg, Aug. 16, 1998. BA, U. Pa., 1985, MD, 1993. Instr. psychiatry Hosp. U. Pa., 1993-96, Children's Hosp. Phila., 1996-98; med. dir. outpatient child & adolscent psychiatry N.J. Med. Sch., Newark, 1998—, asst. prof. psychiatry, 1998—. Co-author: (chpt.) Child Abuse, 2000; contbr. articles to profl. jours. Recipient Child Psychiatry award Group Advancement Psychiatry, 1997-98. Mem. Am. Acad. Child and Adolscent Psychiatry (prevention com. 2000—, task force child rsch. 1998-2000, Resident Leadership Achievement award 1995, scholar 1997-98, rsch. grantee for child rsch. 2001), Am. Acad. Psychiatry and Law (Rappeport com. 2000—), Am. Psychiat. Assn., Am. Profl. Soc. on Abuse of Children, Am. Assn. Acad. Psychiatry (Rappeport fellow 1996-97), Nat. Assn. Counsel for Children, N.J. Psychiat. and Child Psychiatris Assn. Office: NJ Med Sch 183 S Orange Ave UBHC C1404 Newark NJ 07103 E-mail: hamarmst@umdnj.edu.

HAMBARTSOUMIAN, EDUARD, obstetrician, researcher, embryologist; b. Erevan, Armenia, Sept. 29, 1955; arrived in U.S., 1995; s. Martin Andreas Hambartsoumian and Raya Magaki Stepanian; children: Lily, Vahakn. MD-(hon.), Erevan (Armenia) Sch. Medicine, 1981; cert. in fetal medicine, U. Paris, 1994. Chief ob-gyn. dept Aragats Dist. Hosp., Tsakhkahovit, Armenia, 1981—85; chief ob-gyn. dept. Erebouni Hosp., Erevan, Armenia, 1985—88, Maternity #3, Erevan, Armenia, 1988—93; scientist Hosp. Antoine Belcere, Paris, 1993—95; sr. scientist Boston U./Fertility Ctr. New England, 1995—. Embryologist Fertility Ctr. New England, Boston, 2000—01. Contbr. articles to profl. jours. Organist local ch. Named Honorary Inventor of USSR, Governement of USSR, 1978; grantee Travel grant, NIH, 1997. Mem.: Soc. Study Reprodn. (assoc.). Avocation: music. Home: 18 Wensley St Boston MA 02120 Office: Fertility Center New England 20 Pond Meadow Dr Reading MA 01867 Personal E-mail: hambartsoumian@hotmail.com.

HAMBEL, HENRY PETER, clinical hypnotherapist, forensic security consultant, educator; b. Bklyn., Apr. 11, 1951; s. Henry Thomas and Doris Ada (Mawhinney) H.; m. Carole Ann. AAS in Criminal Justice, Suffolk County Community Coll.; BS in Criminal Justice, PhD in Criminal Justice and Forensic Psychology, Pacific Western U.; postgrad., Newport U. Sch. Law; DSc, Clayton Col. Nat. Health, Ala. Diplomate Am. Bd. Law Enforcement Experts Adv. Bd., Am. Bd. Psychol.-Specialties in Hypnosis, Am. Coll. Forensic Examiners, Am. Psychotherapy Assn.; cert. hypnotherapist Nat. Guild Hypnotists, security guard instr. N.Y., Fla., chief liaison officer Am. Coll. Forensic Examiners, Bd. cert. Homeland Security. Former park police Suffolk County Park's Dept., Sayville, NY; deputy sheriff Suffolk County Sheriff's Dept.; police officer, undercover narcotics detective Suffolk County Police Dept.; pres., owner Pvt. Security Officer Agy.; expert witness, forensic security cons., pvt. practice Manorville. Clin. hypnotherapist, adminstr., security cons. Hambel Inst. Author: Last Call: The Party's Over: The Reality of Alcohol and Other Drug Use, 1990. Apptd. supr., mem. Olympic Games Security Team, Atlanta, 1996; mem. citizens police adv. coun. City of Port St. Lucie (Fla.) Police Dept.; mem. Smoke Free Alliance of St. Lucie County, Fla. Col. Fla. NG. Mem.: Nat. Sheriffs Assn., Nat. Assn. Chiefs of Police (Fla. State pres.), Soc. Police Black Belts, Am. Soc. Indsl. Security (cert. protection profl., bd. cert. security mgmt.), Internat. Police Assn. (life; assoc. sec. to Norway U.S. section), Fla. Guard Assn. (commisioned colonel, dir. civic affairs comdr.), Ret. Police Assn. N.Y., Ret. Detectives Assn. Suffolk County, Fraternal Order of Police. Avocations: animal rights advocacy, vegetarianism, anti-alcohol, drugs and tobacco, pistol shooting, archery. Office: 907 SW Lake Charles Cir Saint Lucie West FL 34986-3421 Fax: 722-878-1679. E-mail: HenryHambel@adelphia.net.

HAMBEL, JOHN JOSEPH, lawyer; b. Bklyn., Oct. 22, 1960; s. John J. and Jeanne Rose Doris (Tiberius) H.; m. Alesia Scott Walker, Nov. 14, 1993; children: Laura Caitlin, John Joseph III, Patricia Lynne. BS in Fgn. Svc., Georgetown U., 1983; postgrad., Hofstra U., 1983-84; JD, St. John's U., 1988. Bar: D.C., N.Y. Exec. asst. Rep. Norman F. Lent, Baldwin, N.Y., 1985-87; press sec. Nassau County Bd. Suprs., Mineola, N.Y., 1987-89; editor East Rockaway/Lynbrook Observer, Oceanside, N.Y., 1983-92; ptnr. Perferred Mktg. Inc., East Rockaway, N.Y., 1989-92; minority counsel, press sec. Energy and Commerce Commn. Ho. of Reps., Washington, 1989-95; counsel govt. affairs Nat. Assn. Life Underwriters, Washington, 1995-2000; mng. ptnr. Kehoe & Hambel, Washington, 2000-01; chief of staff Rep. Adam Putnam, Washington, 2001—, counsel subcom. on tech., info. policy, intergovtl. rels. and the census, 2003—. Mem. Am. Cancer Soc., S.W. Divsn., 1988—90, Kiwanis Club, Nassau County, 1983—91, Nassau County (N.Y.) Rep. Com., 1983—91, Fairfax County (Va.) Rep. Com., 1994—99, Vienna Presbyn. Ch., 1994—, trustee, 2001—. Recipient Friend of Edn. award N.Y. State Tchrs. Union, 1987. Republican. Avocation: music. Home: 8507 Redwood Dr Vienna VA 22180-6823 Office: Rep Adam Putman 506 Cannon HOB Washington DC 20515 E-mail: John.Hambel@mail.house.gov.

HAMBERG, DANIEL, economist, educator; b. Phila., Apr. 25, 1924; s. Isidor and Sophia (Kravitz) H.; m. Sylvia Gertrude Kaplan, July 1, 1949; 1 son, Kenneth. BS in Econs., U. Pa., 1945, MA, 1947, PhD, 1952. Instr. econs. U. Del., 1946-47, 48-52, Princeton (N.J.) U., 1947-48; from asst. prof. to prof. U. Md., College Park, 1952-61; leading prof. SUNY, Buffalo, 1961-85, prof. emeritus, 1985—, chmn. dept. econs., 1966-75. Cons. sec. labor, 1962-64 Author: Business Cycles, 1951, Economic Growth and Instability, 1956, Principles of a Growing Economy, 1961, Essays in the Economics of Research and Development, 1966, Models of Economic Growth, 1971, The U.S. Monetary System, 1981; contbr. numerous articles to profl. jours. Ford faculty research fellow, 1962-63; Fulbright prof., 1956-57, 65-66 Fellow Royal Econ. Soc.; mem. Am. Econ. Assn., Pi Gamma Mu, Phi Kappa Phi. Home: 4353 Marcott Cir Sarasota FL 34233-5035

HAMBERG, GILBERT LEE, lawyer; b. Phila., May 29, 1952; s. Marvin and Minnie (Bolnick) H.; m. Elizabeth G. Strulson, Dec. 6, 1981; children: Kayla, Adam, Carolyn. BA, Wesleyan U., Middletown, Conn., 1974; JD, Temple U., 1977. Bar: Pa. 1977, U.S. Dist. Ct. (we., mid. and ea. dists.) Pa. 1977, U.S. Dist. Ct. (ea. dist.) Mich. 1983, La. 1985, U.S. Dist. Ct. (ea., Mid. and we. dists.) La., N.Y. 1992, U.S. Dist. Ct. (so. dist.) N.Y. 1992. Atty. rates Pa. Pub. Utilities Commn., Harrisburg, 1977-80; asst. gen. counsel Laventhol & Horwath, Phila., 1980-82; counsel AAMCO Transmissions Inc., Bala Cynwyd, Pa., 1982-84; assoc. Monroe & Lemann, New Orleans, 1984-90, Milling, Benson, New Orleans, 1990-92, Bower & Gardner, N.Y.C., 1992-93; pvt. practice Yardley, Pa., 1993—. Mem. Pa. Bar Assn., La. Bar Assn. Avocations: tennis, gardening. Office: 1038 Darby Dr Yardley PA 19067-4519 E-mail: ghamberg@erols.com.

HAMBERG, MARCELLE ROBERT, retired urologist; b. Anderson, S.C., July 4, 1931; s. Robert Clark and Pauline Elizabeth H.; m. Cheryl Ann Jones, Dec. 14, 1961; children: Marcelle R. Hamberg Jr., Gabrielle C. Hamberg Buchanan. BS, Hampton U., 1953; MD, Meharry Med. Coll., 1957. Diplomate Am. Bd. Urology. Rotating intern Hubbard Hosp., Nashville, 1957-58, resident in surgery, 1958-59, resident in urology, 1959-62; Newman van Horne spl., fellow in cancer urology Mem. Sloan-Kettering Cancer Ctr., N.Y.C., 1962-63; pvt. practice in urology Louisville, 1963—69, Nashville, 1970—97; ret., 1997. Tchg. staff U. Louisville, 1968-69; sr. attending VA Hosp., Louisville, 1968-69; chief urology, assoc. prof. Meharry Med. Coll., Nashville, 1974—. 1st lt. U.S. Army Res., 1958-68. Mem. Am. Urol. Assn., Am. Urol. Assn. SE sect. Democrat. Avocations: woodworking, reading, lawn gardening. Home: 4474 Clarksville Pike Nashville TN 37218-1526

HAMBERGER, LARRY KEVIN, clinical psychologist, educator; b. Fond du Lac, Wis., June 4, 1953; s. Lawrence Edward and Hilda Ella (Kleberg) H.; m. Nancy Jean Albee, June 30, 1979; children: Heidi Jean, Alexander Michael. BS, U. Wis., Oshkosh, 1975; MA, U. Ark., 1979, PhD, 1982. Lic. psychologist, Wis. Internship Wood VA Med. Ctr., Milw., 1981-82; clin. instr. Med. Coll. Wis., Milw., 1982-83, asst. prof., 1983-89, assoc. prof., 1989-94, prof., 1994—; staff psychologist Mt. Sinai Med. Ctr., Milw., 1983; coordinator, dir. Men's Group Program Racine Family Practice Ctr., Racine, Wis., 1983—. Chair Kenosha Domestic Abuse Intervention Project, 1988-93; curriculum cons. Med. Coll. Wis., Milw., 1985—, stress mgmt. cons., 1982—; mem. Wis. Gov.'s Coun. on Domestic Abuse, 1994—; speaker various sci. meetings, 1979—. Author: Stress and Stress Manaagement, 1984 (Writer of Yr. award 1984); co-author: Making Collaborative Connections with Medical Providers, 1999; co-editor: Treating Men Who Batter: Theory, Practice and Program, 1989, Domestic Partner Abuse, 1996, Violence Issues for Health Care Educators and Providers, 1997; cons. editor Jour. Cons. and Clin. Psychology, 1989-90, Family Violence Bull., 1991—, Jour. Family Violence, 1995—, Jour. Interpersonal Violence, 1996—, Jour. Aggression, Maltreatment and Trauma, 1997—, Violence and Victims, 2000—; contbr. chpts. to books, articles to profl. jours. Mem. APA, Assn. Advancement Behavior Therapy, Wis. Batterers Treatment Provider Assn. (chair elect 2001), Wis. Psychol. Assn., Soc. Tchrs. Family Medicine, Jaycees (v.p. Franklin. Wis. club 1984-85). Lutheran. Avocations: gardening, exercise, rock and mineral collecting, woodworking. Office: Racine Family Practice Ctr 1320 Wisconsin Ave Racine WI 53403-1978 E-mail: lkh@mcw.edu.

HAMBIDGE, DOUGLAS WALTER, archbishop; b. London, Mar. 6, 1927; emigrated to Can., 1956; s. Douglas and Florence (Driscoll) H.; m. Denise Colvill Lown, June 9, 1956; children: Caryl Denise, Stephen Douglas, Graham Andrew. ALCD, London U., 1953, BD, 1958, DD, 1969. Ordained deacon Church of England, 1953, priest, 1954, consecrated bishop, 1969; asst. curate St. Mark's Ch., Dalston, London, 1953-55, priest-in-charge, 1955-56; incumbent All Saints Ch., Cassiar, B.C., Can., 1956-58; rector St. James Parish, Smithers, B.C., 1958-64, North Peace Parish, Ft. St. John, B.C., 1964-69; canon St. Andrew's Cathedral, 1965; lord bishop of Caledonia, 1969-80, New Westminster, B.C., 1980-81; lord archbishop of New Westminster and metropolitan of B.C., 1981-93; prin. St. Mark's Theol. Coll., Dar es Salaam, Tanzania, 1993-95; asst. bishop Diocese of Dar es Salaam, Dar es Salaam, 1993-95. Mem. Anglican Consultative Coun., 1985-93; chancellor Vancouver Sch. Theology, 1999. Anglican. E-mail: hambidge@vst.edu.

HAMBLEN, JOHN WESLEY, computer scientist, genealogist; b. Story, Ind., Sept. 25, 1924; s. James William and Mary Etta (Morrison) H.; m. Brenda F. Harrod, Mar. 1, 1947 (div. 1979); 1 son, James; m. Marianne Muhlbauer, Aug. 7, 1987. BA, Ind. U., 1947; MS, Purdue U., 1952; PhD, 1955. Tchr. math and sci. Kingsbury (Ind.) High Sch., 1946-48, Bluffton (Ind.) High Sch., 1948-51; asst. prof. math. Okla. State U., Stillwater, 1955-57; cons. in statis. methods for research staff Agrl. Expt. Sta., 1955-56, asso. prof. math., 1957-58; dir. Computing Center, 1957-58; asso. prof. stats., dir. Computing Center, U. Ky., Lexington, 1958-61; prof. math and technology Southern Ill. U., Carbondale, 1961-65; dir. Data Processing and Computing Center, 1961-65; project dir. computer scis. So. Regional Edn. Bd., Atlanta, 1965-72; prof. U. Mo., Rolla, 1972-87, prof. emeritus, 1987—, chmn. dept. computer sci., 1972-81; assoc. program. dir. NSF, 1985-86. Mem. tech. adv. com. Creative Application of Tech. to Edn., Tex. A&M U., 1966-68; mem. tech. adv. panel Western Interstate Commn. for Higher Edn., 1969-70; vis. scientist Ctr. for Applied Math. Nat. Bur. Standards, 1981-83; program chmn. World Conf. Computers in Edn., 1985, mem. program com. for 1990; cons. FTC, 1978-80, NSF, 1975-76, Nat. Bur. of Standards, 1986-88; compiler fed. land entries Brown County, Ind., 1994, Composite Index for Brown County, Ind. Family Studies, 1998. Editor, pub. The Hamblen Connector, 1989-98; pub. The Hamblen and Allied Families, 2d. edit., 1985; editor: Ednl. Data Processing Newsletter, 1964-65, Bartholomew County Family Histories Book, 1999 ; assoc. editor: Jour. Ednl. Data Processing, 1965-67; editor: Jour. Assn. Ednl. Data Systems, 1967-68; assoc. editor, 1968-87; mem. editorial bd. Jour. Computer Sci. Edn., 1987-97; computing editor T.H.E. Jour., 1980-88; contbr. articles to profl. jours. Historian Brown County (Ind.), 1992-94. Purdue Research Found. fellow, 1954-55; NSF grantee, 1966-81; recipient Disting. Svc. award Nat. Ednl. Computing Conf., 1988; decorated Order of Golden Shillelagh, SIGCSE award for outstanding contbns. to computer sci. edn., 1990. Fellow AAAS; mem. Assn. Ednl. Data Sys. (chmn. conv. adv. com. 1977-80, pres. 1968-69, sec. 1976-77, dir. 1965-70, 76-79, Aid to AEDS award 1971), Am. Fedn. Info. Processing Socs. (dir. 1981-86, chmn. edn. com. 1971-72, 79-84, edn. award 1985), Md. Geneal. Soc. (life), Brown County Hist. Soc. (life, 1st v.p. 1990-91, treas. 1992-95), Brown County Geneal. Soc. (life, v.p. 1992, pres. 1993-94), Bartholomew County Geneal. Soc. (founder, life, pres. 1990-92, treas. 1997-2000, chair family history book com. 1993-99), Ind. Geneal. Soc. (S.E. dist. dir. 1991-94, Disting. County Geneol. Svcs. award 1996), Jackson County Geneal. Soc. (life), Hamilton Twp. Alumni Assn. (v.p. 1993-94, pres. 1994-96), Sigma Xi, Pi Mu Epsilon, Theta Chi, Upsilon Pi Epsilon, Alpha Chi Sigma. E-mail: jwhamblen@vnetinc.net. *It is difficult to improve upon the popular version of the "Golden Rule" for a succinct guide in life. A clear conscience and a good insurance program contribute greatly to a good night's sleep. With moderation in food and drink plus a good night's rest we should be able to handle most anything that comes our way.*

HAMBLEN, LAPSLEY WALKER, JR., judge; b. Chattanooga, Tenn., Dec. 25, 1926; s. Lapsley Walker Sr. and Libby (Shipley) H.; m. Claudia Royster Terrell, Mar. 20, 1971; children by previous marriage: Lapsley Walker III, Allen M., William Shipley. BA, U. Va., 1949, LLB, 1953. Bar: W.Va. 1954, Ohio 1955, Va. 1957. Trial atty. IRS, Atlanta, 1955; atty. advisor U.S. Tax Ct., 1956; ptnr. Caskie Frost Hobbs & Hamblen and predecessor firms, Lynchburg, Va., 1957-82; dep. asst. atty. gen. tax divsn. U.S. Dept. Justice, 1982; judge U.S. Tax Ct., Washington, 1982-92, chief judge, 1992-94, 94-96, sr. judge, 1996-2000, ret., 2000. Former trustee So. Fed. Tax Inst.; former co-dir. ann. conf. on fed. taxation U. Va. Served with USN, 1945-46. Fellow: Am. Bar Found., Am. Coll. Trust and Estate Counsel, Am. Coll. Tax Counsel; mem.: Raven Soc., Phi Alpha Delta, Omicron Delta Kappa, Order of the Coif. Presbyterian.

HAMBLET, MICHAEL JON, lawyer, city official, former state official; b. Rapid City, S.D., Aug. 10, 1940; s. Herbert F. and Helen F. (Tice) H.; m. Maureen Anne Murphy, Nov. 26, 1966 (div. May 1986); children: Tracy Anne, Michael Jon; m. Mary K. Harvick, Aug. 12, 1995. B.A., U. Ill., 1962; m. Mary Katherine Harvick, Aug. 12, 1995; J.D., U. Mich., 1965. Bar: Ill. 1965. Assoc. Mayer, Brown, Chgo., 1965-69; ptnr. Herrick, McNeill, McElroy & Peregrine, Chgo., 1969-78, 82-83, Greenberg, Keele, Lunn & Aronberg, Chgo., 1979-81; Hamblet, Casey, Oremus, & Vacin (formerly Mathewson, Hamblet & Casey), Chgo., 1983—; mem. Ill. State Bd. Elections, Chgo. and Springfield, 1978—, chmn., 1979-81, 83-85, vice chmn., 1981-83; commr. Chgo. Bd. Elections, 1987-90, chmn. 1990—; mem. Ill. Bldg. Authority, Chgo., 1973-78, chmn., 1977-78. Mem. Cook County Econ. Devel. Adv. Com., 1982-87. Home: 1322 N Sutton Pl Chicago IL 60610-2008

HAMBLETON, GEORGE BLOW ELLIOTT, retired management consultant; b. Balt., Dec. 20, 1929; s. John Adams Hambleton and Margaret (Elliott) Carey; m. Janet Findlay MacLaren, Mar. 17, 1962 (dec. 1991); children: Anne Carey, Charles MacLaren, James Elliott; m. Diana Lea Walker, June 29, 1998. AB, Princeton U., 1952; program for mgmt. devel., Harvard U., 1964. Various positions with Latin American div. Pan Am, 1955-62, asst. div. service mgr., 1963-64, dir. USSR Moscow, 1966-70, dir. internat. affairs Washington, 1971-76, dir. comml. sales N.Y.C., 1977-80; v.p. mktg. N.Y. Airways, N.Y.C., 1976-77; exec. dir., vice chmn. Project Orbis, Inc., N.Y.C., 1980-83; pres. Andrews MacLaren, Inc., N.Y.C., 1983-86; dep. asst. sec., dep. dir. gen. U.S. and fgn. comml. svc. Dept. Commerce, Washington, 1986-88; sr. v.p. Mgmt. Internat. Inc., Westport, Conn., 1988—. Bd. dirs. Flight Found., Inc., Washington, Andrews MacLaren Ltd., Northants, Eng. Dir. Fgn. Policy Discussion Group, Washington, 1975-96; mem. N.J. Conservation Found.; mem. adv. com. East-West Trade, U.S. Dept. Commerce, 1973-79; mem. dist. export coun. U.S. Dept. Commerce, Conn., 1989-93; bd. dirs. River Blindness Found., Houston, 1990-95, Coll. of the Atlantic, Bar Harbor, Maine, 1996—. 1st lt. U.S. Army, 1952-55, Korea. Mem. Upper Raritan Watershed Assn., Brook Club (N.Y.), Met. Club (Washington), Naval and Mil. Club (London), Md. Club (Balt.), Princeton Club (N.Y.), Essex Hunt Club (Far Hills, N.J.), Union Club (N.Y.), Harvard Bus. Sch. Club (Washington, v.p. 1973-76), Wings Club (N.Y.), Soc. Colonial Wars (N.Y.). Republican. Episcopalian. Avocations: flying, fishing, skiing, running, hunting. Home: 280 Pleasant Valley Rd Mendham NJ 07945-2920 Office: Mgmt Internat Inc PO Box 943 Far Hills NJ 07931-0943

HAMBLEY, DOUGLAS FREDERICK, geological and environmental engineer; b. Toronto, Ont., Can., Jan. 14, 1950; s. Fredrick Armstrong and Gwendolyn Shannon (Plant) H.; m. Sherrie Kate Barham Hambley, May 24, 1992 (div. June 2000). BS in Mining Engring., Queen's U., 1972; MBA, Lewis U., 1986; PhD in Earth Scis., U. Waterloo, Ont., Can., 1991. Registered profl. engr., Can., Ill., Va., Pa., Md., Wis., profl. geologist, Pa., Wis., Ill. Jr. engr. Iron Ore Co. of Can., Schefferville, Que., 1972-73; mining engr. trainee Falconbridge (Ont.) Nickel Mines, Ltd., Can., 1974-75; mining engr. Harrison Bradford & Assocs., Ltd., St. Catharines, Ont., 1975-76; project engr. Denison Mines, Ltd., Elliot Lake, Ont., 1977-80; sr. mining engr. Engrs. Internat., Inc., Westmont, Ill., 1980-84; mining engr. Argonne (Ill.) Nat. Lab., 1984-88; rsch. asst. U. Waterloo, Ontario, 1988; sr. cons. Dunn Geosci. Corp., West Chicago, Ill., 1989; civil/geol. engr. Argonne (Ill.) Nat. Lab., 1990-91; mgr., geo-environtl. group Nova, Environtl. Svcs., Des Plaines, 1991; project mgr. Graef, Anhalt, Schloemer and Assocs., Inc., Chgo., Ill., 1992-2000; pvt. practice, 2000—; sr. cons. Practical Environ. Cons., Inc., Schaumburg, Ill., 2000—. Contbr. articles to profl. jours. Recipient Cert. of Appreciation, Office of Geologic Repositories, 1987, Ill. Dept. Profl. Regulation, 2000. Mem. Soc. Mining, Metallurgy and Exploration (chmn. Chgo. sect. 1987-88), Assn. Engring. Geologists (treas. N.C. sect. 1987-88), Can. Inst. Mining and Metallurgy, Assn. Groundwater Scientists and Engrs. (Brownfields task force, 2003—), Soc. Am. Mil. Engrs. (treas. Chgo. post 1996-97, 3rd v.p. 1998, 2d v.p. 1999, pres. 2000), Ill. Engring. Coun (dir. 1998, 2000—, v.p. 1999). Avocations: travel, cello, guitar, folk music. Home: 1404 Childs St Wheaton IL 60187-4607 Office: Practical Environtl Cons 919 N Plum Grove Rd Ste E Schaumburg IL 60173 E-mail: hambley@pec-inc.com.

HAMBLIN, MICHAEL R. biomedical researcher, educator; s. Richard and Edith Hamblin; m. Angela C. Edwards, Nov. 20, 1982. PhD, Trent Poly. Inst., Nottingham, England, 1977. Assoc. in surgery Ninewells Hosp. and Med. Sch., Dundee, Scotland, 1990—94; asst. prof. dermatology Harvard Med. Sch., Boston, 1994—. Asst. chemist Wellman Labs. Photomedicine, Mass. Gen. Hosp., Boston, 1994—. Contbr. articles to med. jours. Grantee, Nat. Cancer Inst.-NIH, 2002. Achievements include patents for acceleration of wound healing by photodynamic therapy; inhibition of fibrosis by photodynamic therapy; photosensitizer conjugates for pathogen targeting. Office: Wellman Labs Photomedicine BAR314B 55 Fruit St Boston MA 02114 Office Fax: 617-726-8566. E-mail: hamblin@helix.mgh.harvard.edu.

HAMBRICK, ERNESTINE, retired colon and rectal surgeon; b. Griffin, Ga., Mar. 31, 1941; d. Jack Daniel and Nannie (Harper) Hambrick Rubens. BS, U. Md., 1963; MD, U. Ill., 1967. Diplomate Am. Bd. Colon and Rectal Surgery, Am. Bd. Surgery. Intern in surgery Cook County Hosp., Chgo., 1967-68, resident in gen. surgery, 1968-72, fellow colon and rectal surgery, 1972-73, attending surgeon, 1973-74, part-time attending surgeon, 1974-80; pvt. practice colon and rectal surgery Chgo., 1974-97; pres. med. staff Michael Reese Hosp., Chgo., 1990-92, chief surgery, 1993-95; founder, chmn. STOP Colon/Rectal Cancer Found., 1997—. Mem. Nat. Colorectal Cancer Round Table, 1997—, steering com. 2000—. Contbr. articles to profl. jours. Trustee Rsch. and Edn. Found., Michael Reese Med. Staff, Chgo., 1994-98, treas., 1994-98. Mem. ACS, Am. Soc. Colon and Rectal Surgeons (v.p. 1992-93, trustee Rsch. Found. 1992-98), Am. Coll. Gastroenterology. Avocations: travel, photography, scuba diving, flying, writing. Office: PMB 133 47 W Division St Chicago IL 60610 E-mail: ehcrsone@aol.com.

HAMBURG, CHARLES BRUCE, lawyer; b. Bklyn., June 30, 1939; s. Albert Hamburg and Goldie (Blume) H.; m. Stephanie Barbara Steingesser, June 23, 1962; children: Jeanne M., Louise E. B.Chem. Engring., Poly. Inst. Bklyn., 1960; JD, Geroge Washington U., 1964. Bar: N.Y. 1964. Patent examiner U.S. Patent Office, 1960-63; patent atty. Celanese Corp. Am., N.Y.C., 1963-65, Burns, Lobato & Zelnick, N.Y.C., 1965-67, Nolte & Nolte, N.Y.C., 1967-75; prin. C. Bruce Hamburg, N.Y.C., 1976-79; ptnr. Jordan & Hamburg, L.L.P., N.Y.C., 1979—. U.S. corr. Patents and Licensing, Japan, 1986—. Author: Patent Fraud and Inequitable Conduct, 1972, 78, Patent Law Handbook, 1983-84, 84-85, 85-86, (in Japanese) Doctrine of Equivalents in U.S., 1995, 2nd edit. (in Korean), 1998; monthly columnist Patent and Trademark Rev., 1976-85; contbr. chpt. on U.S. patents: Patents Throughout the World, 1976—. Mem.: ABA, Internat. Fedn. Intellectual Property Attys., Licensing Execs. Soc., Internat. Assn. Protection Intellectual Property, NY Patent Trademark Copyright Law Assn., Am. Intellectual Property Assn., Masons. Office: 122 E 42nd St New York NY 10168-0002 E-mail: jandh@ipattorneys.com.

HAMBURG, DAVID A. psychiatrist, foundation executive; b. Evansville, Ind., 1925; MD, Ind. U., 1947, D.Sc. (hon.), 1976, Rush U., 1977, Mt. Sinai Sch. Medicine, 1980, U. Rochester, 1981, U. Ill., Chgo., 1984, Albert Einstein Sch. Medicine, 1985, U. Pitts., U. So. Calif., Hahnemann U., 1986; LHD (hon.), Ramapo Coll., 1991, Duke U., 1993, So. Indiana U., 2000. Diplomate Am. Bd. Psychiatry and Neurology. Intern Michael Reese Hosp., Chgo., 1947-48, resident in psychiatry, 1949-50, Yale U.-New Haven Hosp., 1948-49; staff psychiatrist Brooke Army Hosp., San Antonio, 1950-52; practice medicine specializing in psychiatry, 1950-75; research psychiatrist Walter Reed Army Inst. Research, Washington, 1952-53; assoc. dir. Psychosomatic and Psychiat. Inst., Michael Reese Hosp., Chgo., 1954-56; fellow Center for Advanced Study in Behavioral Scis., Palo Alto, Calif., 1957-58, 67-68; chief Adult Psychiat. Br. NIMH, Bethesda, Md., 1958-61; prof., chmn. dept. psychiatry Stanford U. Med. Sch., 1961-72, Reed-Hodgson prof. human biology, 1972-76; Sherman Fairchild Disting. scholar Calif. Inst. Tech., Pasadena, 1974-75; pres. Inst. Medicine Nat. Acad. Scis., Washington, 1975-80; dir. div. health policy research and edn., John D. MacArthur prof. health policy and mgmt. Harvard U., Cambridge, Mass., 1980-82; pres. Carnegie Corp., N.Y.C., 1983-97, pres. emeritus, 1997—. Adv. com. med. rsch. WHO, 1975-86; mem. exec. panel adv. com. Chief of Naval Ops, 1984-92; chmn. sci. adv. bd. NIMH, 1986-87; sec. Energy Adv. Bd., 1990-94; mem. Ctr. for Naval Analysis, 1990-93. Author: No More Killing Fields: Preventing Deadly Conflict, 2002, Learning to Live Together: Preventing Hatred and Violence in Child and Adolescent Development, 2003. Bd. dirs. Rockefeller U., 1979—, Mt. Sinai Med. Ctr., N.Y.C., 1984—; trustee Stanford U., 1988-94, Internat. Devel. Rsch. Ctr., Ottawa, Ont., Can., 1990-94, Am. Mus. Natural History, N.Y.C., 1990—; co-chmn. Carnegie Commn. on Preventing Deadly Conflict, 1994-99; mem. Pres.'s Com. of Advisors on Sci. and Tech., 1994-2001; dep. chmn. Fed. Res. Bank N.Y., Def. Policy Bd., U.S. Dept. Def., 1994-95. Recipient numerous awards including: Pres.'s medal Michael Reese Med. Ctr., 1974; A.C.P. award, 1977; MIT Bicentennial medal, 1976, Presdl. Medal of Freedom, 1996; Disting. Presdl. fellow for internat. activities Nat. Acads., 2002. Mem. Am. Psychiat. Assn. (Vestermark award 1977, Disting. Svc. award 1991, Pres.'s medal Bank St. Coll. 1994, Charter medallion Radcliffe Coll. 1994), Nat. Acad. Scis. (com. on internat. security and arms control 1981-86, Pub. Welfare medal 1998), AAAS (pres. 1984-85, chmn. bd. 1985-86), Assn. Rsch. Nervous and Mental Disease (pres. 1967-68), Am. Philos. Soc., Am. Acad. Arts and Scis., Phi Beta Kappa, Alpha Omega Alpha. Office: NY Presbyterian Hosp Dept Psych 525 E 68th St Box 171 New York NY 10021

HAMBURG, DAVID D. music educator; b. Madison, Wis., Sept. 10, 1952; m. Karin I. Hamburg; children: Erin, Alla. MusB, No. Ill. U., 1977; M in Tchg., St. Xavier U., 2001. Band tchr. Orion (Ill.) Sch. Dist. # 221, 1978—97, Rock Island (Ill.) Sch. Dist. #41, 1997—. Musician (composer). Bd. mem. Bettendorf (Iowa) Pk. Band, 2000—. Served with U.S. Army, 1970—73. Home: 2521 Brambleberry Ct Bettendorf IA 52722

HAMBURG, MARGARET ANN (PEGGY HAMBURG), public health administrator; b. Chgo., July 12, 1955; d. David Alan and Beatrix Ann (Mc Cleary) H.; m. Peter Fitzhugh Brown, May 23, 1992; children: Rachel Ann Hamburg Brown, Evan David Addison Brown. BA magna cum laude, Harvard/Radcliffe Coll., 1978; MD, Harvard, 1983. Diplomate Am. Bd. Internal Medicine, Nat. Bd. Med. Examiners. Intern, resident in internal medicine The N.Y. Hosp., Cornell Med. Coll., N.Y.C., 1983-86; spl. asst. to the dir., office of disease prevention and health promotion, office of the asst. sec. for health U.S. Dept. Health and Human Svcs., Washington, 1986-88; spl. asst. to the dir. Nat. Inst. Allergy and Infectious Diseases, NIH, Bethesda, Md., 1988-89, asst. dir., 1989-90; deputy commr. Family Health Svcs., N.Y.C. Dept. Health, N.Y.C., 1990-91; commr. of health N.Y.C. Dept. Health, 1991-97; asst. sec. planning and evaluation U.S. Dept. HHS, Washington, 1997—2001; v.p. biological programs Nuclear Threat Initiative, Washington, 2001—. Guest investigator The Rockefeller U., N.Y.C., 1985-86; clin. instr. dept. medicine Georgetown U. Sch. Medicine, Washington, 1986-90; asst. prof. clin. pub. health Columbia U. Sch. Pub. Health, N.Y.C., 1991-97; adj. asst. prof. medicine Cornell U. Med. Coll., N.Y.C., 1991-97; scholar Pub. Health Leadership Inst. Ctr. for Disease Control U. Calif., 1992; bd. dirs. N.Y.C. Health Systems Agy., Med. and Health Rsch. Assn., Health Hosps. Corp, Nat. Coun. on Women's Health, Primary Care Devel. Corp.; steering com. women and aids NIH, 1991; bd. govs. Greater N.Y. Hosp. Assn., 1991-97; mem. bd. sci. advisors. Nat. Pub. Radio, 1992-97; com. mem. on substance abuse mental health issues in aides rsch., 1993; advisory bd. mem. Medunsa Trust, Inc., Med. U. So. Africa, 1993-97; mem. defense sci. bd. task force on Gulf War Syndrome U.S. Dept. Defense, 1993—; mem. sci. counselors Nat. Ctr. Infectious Diseases, U.S. Ctrs. for Disease, 1994-97. Editorial bd. mem. Jour. N.Y. Acad. Sci., 1992-97, The Bull. of N.Y. Acad. Medicine, 1992-97, Current Reviews in Pub. Health, 1993-97; contbr. to numerous profl. jours. Vol. attending physician The Washington Free Clinic, Washington, 1988-90; coun. fgn. rels. bd. overseers Harvard U., 1999—. Recipient commendation Pub. Health Svc., 1988, 90, Spl. Recognition award Pub. Health Svc., 1990, cert. of Honor The Women's Club of N.Y., 1993, N.Y. Rotary Club award, 1993, Robert F. Wagner Pub. Svc. award NYU, 1993. Fellow AAAS (med. scis. section com. 1989—), ACP; mem. APHA, Am. Med. Women's Assn., Nat. Acad. Scis., Coun. on Fgn. Rels., Health Care Exec. Forum, N.Y. Acad. Medicine, Pub. Health Assn. N.Y.C., Inst. Medicine, Soc. Social Biology, Women in Health Mgmt., Med. Office: Nuclear Threat Initiative 1747 Pennsylvania Ave NW 7th Fl Washington DC 20006

HAMBURG, ROGER PHILLIP, retired political science and public affairs educator; b. Davenport, Iowa, June 19, 1934; s. Abe and Geraldine (Wolf) H.; m. Sally Schulman, Aug. 29, 1959; children: Phillip, Ruth, Joel. AB, U. Mich., 1956; AM, U. Chgo., 1958; PhD, U. Wis., 1965. Asst. prof. Eastern Wash. State Coll., Cheney, 1965-66, Marquette U., Milw., 1966-69, U. Wis.-Parkside, Kenosha, 1969-71; assoc. prof. dept. polit. sci. Ind. U., South Bend, 1971-79, prof., 1979-92, prof. sch. pub. and environ. affairs, 1992—99. Program dir. Michiana World Affairs Coun., South Bend, 1991-98; part-time tchr. Lake Mich. Coll., Niles; prof. emeritus polit. sci. Lake Mich. Coll., 1999—. With USAR, 1961-62. Avocation: playing piano. Home: 1922 Briarway South Bend IN 46614-1630 Office: Lake Michigan Coll Dept Polit Sci Niles MI 49120

HAMBURGER, BRIAN S. lawyer, consultant; b. Charlotte, N.C., 1972; s. Jeffrey A. and Linda Hamburger; m. KariAnn Hamburger. BS in Econs. and Fin. Mgmt., Quinnipiac U., 1994; JD, U. Miami, 1998. Bar: (NY), (NJ), (DC). Chief compliance officer New Century Fin. Group, Princeton, NJ, 1995—2000; jud. intern to Judge Linnea R. Johnson U.S. Dist. Ct. So. Dist. Fla., Miami, 1996; jud. intern to Judge David M. Gersten State Fla. 3rd Dist. Ct. Appeal, Miami, 1996-97; law clk. enforcement divsn. U.S. Securities and Exch. Commn., Miami, 1997; atty. securities practice group Stark & Stark, Princeton, N.J., 1998-2000; mng. dir. MarketCounsel, Princeton, 2000—; mng. mem. Hamburger Law Firm, Princeton, 2000—. Mem. arbitrators NASD Dispute Resolution; arbitrator N.Y. Stock Exch. Contbr. articles to profl. jours. Recipient Pres.'s Pinnacle award, 1998; scholar Dean's Svc. scholar, U. Miami, 1997—98. Mem.: ABA, Securities Industry Assn. (compliance and legal divsn.), NY County Lawyers Assn. (com. securities and exchs.), DC Bar Assn., NY State Bar Assn., Nat. Soc. Compliance Profls., Soc. Fin. Svc. Profls., Fin. Planning Assn. NJ (Gold Key mem.), NJ State Bar Assn.

HAMBURGER, JEFFREY ALLEN, financial planner; b. N.Y.C., Aug. 17, 1947; s. Erich G. and Inge J. (Kant) H.; m. Linda E. Dubow, May 29, 1969; children: Brian S., Rachael E. BS, Monmouth Coll., 1969. ChFC; registered investment advisor; cert. fund specialist, Pace qualifier; cert. fund specialist. V.p. Access Assn., Hackensack, N.J., 1976-80; pres. Fin. Roadmaps, Clifton, N.J., 1980-85; v.p. The Fin. Network, Clifton, 1986-87; pres. Access Fin. Planning, Clifton, 1987-95; mng. mem. New Century Fin. Group, L.L.C., Princeton, N.J., 1995—. Agt. coun. Lincoln Nat., Royal Alliance; mem. advisory bd. Royal Alliance Technology, Northeast Study Group, Royal Alliance Royal Ct., N.E. adv. bd. chmn., 2003. Mem. coun. Cub Scouts, Leonia, NJ, 1982—83; mem. state coun. Am. Diabetes Assn., 2001—; chmn. Tour de Cure Princeton, 2002—; fin. sec. Congregation Sons of Israel, 1985—86; bd. dirs. N.J. Easter Seals, 1997—2000. Sgt. NJNG, 1968—74. Named an Agt. of Yr., Mut. of N.Y., 1977-79, Life Underwriter of Yr., Passaic/Bergen Life Underwriters. Mem. Internat. Assn. for Fin. Planning, Nat. Assn. Life Underwriters (pres. 1977-86), Am. Soc. CLUs and ChFCs, N.J. Estate Planning Coun., Registry of Fin. Planning Practitioners. Jewish. Avocations: golf, sports, model trains, photography. Office: New Century Fin Group 118 Wall St Princeton NJ 08540-1522 E-mail: jhamburger@ncfg.com.

HAMBURGER, MARY ANN, medical management consultant; b. Newark, Aug. 25, 1939; d. Herman and Sylvia (Strauss) Marcus; div. June 1966; children: Bruce David, Marc Laurence. AA, U. Bridgeport (Conn.), 1960. Office mgr., Millburn, N.J., 1970-84; propr., mgr. Mary Ann Hamburger, Assocs., med. mgmt. cons. co., Maplewood, N.J., 1984-. Tchr. adult edn. South Orange Maplewood Bd. Edn., 1975-83; profl. physician recruiter, N.Y., N.J.; broker med. practices. Mem. NAFE. Democrat. Jewish. Avocations: reading, music, needlepoint, theatre, sports. Home and Office: 74 Hudson Ave Maplewood NJ 07040-1403

HAMBURGER, PHILIP (PAUL), writer; b. Wheeling, W. Va., July 2, 1914; s. Harry and Janet (Kraft) Hamburger; m. Edith Iglauer, Dec. 24, 1942 (div. 1966); children: Jay Philip, Richard Shaw; m. Anna Walling Matson, Oct. 27, 1968 (dec. Dec. 2, 2002). BA, Johns Hopkins U., 1935; MS, Grad. Sch. Journalism, Columbia, 1938. Mem. staff New Yorker mag., 1939—, writer Profiles, Talk of the Town, Reporter-at-Large articles, Notes for a Gazetteer, Letters from Fgn. Places, Casuals, music critic, 1948-49, TV critic, 1949-55; on leave from New Yorker as writer, Office of Facts and Figures and O.W.I., 1941-43. Frank R. Kent Meml. lectr., Johns Hopkins U., 1986; past mem. adv. bd. George Foster Peabody Radio and Television Awards; bd. dirs. Authors League Fund.; Condr. non-fiction workshop Ind. U. Writers' Conf., 1969, 75. Author (for govt.): Divide and Conquer, 1942, The Unconquered People, 1942, Tale of a City, 1942; Author: The Oblong Blur and Other Odysseys, 1949, J.P. Marquand, Esquire, 1952, Mayor Watching and Other Pleasures, 1958, Our Man Stanley, 1963, An American Notebook, 1965, Curious World: A New Yorker At Large, 1987, Friends Talking in the Night, 1999, Matters of State: A Political Excursion, 2000. Recipient 50th Anniversary Honors medal Grad. Sch. Journalism, Columbia U., 1963, N.Y. Pub. Libr. Lit. Lion award, 1986, George Polk career award, 1994, Columbia Journalism Alumni award, 1997. Fellow Am. Acad. Arts and Scis.; mem. Authors League Am., Authors Guild (quondam council), P.E.N., Nat. Press Club (Washington), Century Assn. (N.Y.C.). Home: 151 E 80th St New York NY 10021-0442 also: PO Box 1453 Wellfleet MA 02667-1453 Office: care The New Yorker 4 Times Sq New York NY 10036-6522

HAMBY, BARBARA JEAN, writer, poet; b. Chico, Calif., Apr. 20, 1929; d. Frank Llewellyn Fairfield and Grace Ellen Mann (deceased); children: Gail D. Wilson Anderson, Kurt E. Deutscher. Student, U. Wash., 1947-48, Clark Coll., 1990—. Author: My Muse Has Many Moods, 1995, Trilogy: Love Lines, Life Lines, Laugh Lines, 1998, Find Romance in Later Life, 2003. Named Golden Poet, World of Poetry, 1987, 91, Silver Poet, 1989, People to People Amb. to South Africa, Women Writers, 1998. Mem. Willamette Writers League, Oreg. State Poetry Assn. (2nd prize 1995), Wash. State Poets (3rd prize 1995), Columbia Poets (1st prize 1990), Sierra Club. Democrat. Unitarian Universalist. Avocations: swimming, walking, traveling. Office: Drummer Pub PO Box 65596 Vancouver WA 98665-0020 E-mail: musebjh@aol.com.

HAMBY, GENE MALCOLM, JR., lawyer; b. Florence, Ala., Mar. 23, 1943; s. Gene Malcolm Sr. and Katherine (Koonce) H.; m. Judy Priscilla Brown, Apr. 10, 1971; children: Mark Clifton, Anne Tyler. BS with great honor, U. North Ala., 1965; JD, U. Ala., Tuscaloosa, 1968. Bar: Ala. 1968, U.S. Dist. Ct. (no. dist.) Ala. 1972, U.S. Ct. Appeals (11th cir.) 1981. Assoc. Heflin & Rosser, Attys., Tuscumbia, Ala., 1968-70, ptnr. Pitts & Hamby, Sheffield, Ala., 1970-80, pvt. practice Sheffield, 1981-84; ptnr. Hamby & Baker, Attys., Sheffield, 1984-87, Jones, Hamby & Baker, Attys., Sheffield, 1987-89; pvt. practice, Sheffield, 1989—. Bd. dirs. Shoals Indsl. Devel. Authority, Sheffield, 1985-91, Law Sch. Found., U. Ala. Sch. Law, 1985—; past dist. v.p. U. Ala. Alumni, Tuscaloosa; past pres. U. North Ala. Alumni, Florence, Colbert County United Way, Sheffield; chmn. Sheffield Indsl. Devel. Bd., Sheffield, Sheffield Edn. Found., 1992-96; past bd. dirs. United Cerebral Palsy NW Ala., Sheffield, Shoals Indsl. Devel. Authority. With USAR, 1968-74. Recipient Kiwanis Citizen of Yr. award City of Sheffield, 1991, 2001. Mem. ATLA, ABA, Colbert County Bar Assn (past pres.), Ala. State Bar Assn., Ala. Trial Lawyers Assn. (past mem. exec. com.), Sheffield Bus. and Profl. Assn. (pres. 1999-2001), Kiwanis Club (past pres. Sheffield chpt.), Colbert County C. of C. (past pres.), Phi Kappa Phi. Democrat. Avocation: indian artifacts. Home: PO Box 328 Sheffield AL 35660-0328 Office: 406 N Nashville Ave Sheffield AL 35660-2938

HAMDAN, BARBARA BRUNET, preventive medicine physician; b. North Adams, Mass., June 23, 1932; d. Alphonse Paul and Ellen Mae (Andrews) Brunet; m. Hussein Mousa Hamdan, Oct. 1, 1957; children: Ziad, Nabil, Karim, Sharif, Amira, Khalil, Tarik, Rashid, Ghassan. BS, Coll. Our Lady of Elms, Chicopee, Mass., 1954; MD, U. Vt., 1958. Lic. physician, N.J.; specialization in preventive medicine/nutrition. Intern Seton Hall Med. Ctr., Jersey City, 1958, St. Francis Hosp., Trenton, N.J., 1959-60; resident in psychiatry N.J. Neuropsychiat. Inst., Princeton, 1960-64; resident in child psychiatry Union County Psychiat. Clinic, Plainfield, N.J., 1963-64; staff psychiatrist Cath. Charities Child Guidance Clinic, Trenton, N.J., 1965-67; cons. Willis Sch. for Psychoednl. Therapy, Plainfield, 1966; pvt. practice with emphasis in preventive medicine and nutrition, Princeton, 1965—. Mem. AMA, AAAS, Am. Med. Women's Assn., Am. Acad. Child Psychiatry, N.J. Med. Women's Assn., Acad. Orthomolecular Psychiatry (charter), Nat. Acad. Rsch. Biochemists (charter), N.Y. Acad. Scis., World Med. Assn., Eastern Holistic Health Assn., Am. Coll. Preventive Medicine, Internat. Acad. Med. Preventics. Roman Catholic. Avocations: ballroom dancing, cooking, reading, music.

HAMDY, MOSTAFA KAMAL, microbiologist, educator; b. Cairo, May 27, 1921; s. Hamed Alimobarik and Nefisa Mohamed (Sultan) H.; m. Kathryn Ann Russel, May 29, 1954; children: David Hamed, Kathryn Ann. BS, Cairo U., 1944, MS, 1949; PhD, Ohio State U., 1953. Instr. Alexandria (Egypt) U., 1944-48, Cairo U., 1944-49, lectr., 1948-49; Muelhaupt postdoctoral fellow Ohio State U., Columbus, 1953-54, postdoctoral fellow biochemistry dept., 1954-58; asst. prof. food sci. U. Ga., Athens, 1958-62, assoc. prof., 1962-65, prof., 1965—. Field sci. advisor FDA, 1975-96. Contbr. articles to profl. jours. V.p. Timothy Estate Assn., Athens, 1972-73. Recipient award Sears Roebuck Found., 1963, Creative Rsch. award, 1982, Disting. Rsch. Faculty award U. Ga. Coll. Agr., 1968, D.W. Brooks rsch. award, 1984, P.R. Edwards award, 1985, Dir.'s Rsch. award for High Achievement U. Ga., 1988; Commr.'s Spl. Citation FDA, 1991, Appreciation award 1996. Fellow Acad. Microbiology, Inst. Food Technologists (councilor 1975-78), Am. Soc. Microbiology; mem. Soc. Exptl. Biology and Medicine (pres. S.E. br. 1973-75), N.Y. Acad. Scis., So. Assn. Agrl. Scientists (sec.-treas. food sci. and tech. sect. 1972-74, Profl. Scientist award 1974, 88), Sigma Xi (Disting. Rsch. award 1967, 81), Phi Kappa Phi, Phi Sigma, Gamma Sigma Delta (Sr. Faculty award 1975), Stamp Club, Chess Club. Methodist.

HAMDY, RONALD CHARLES, geriatrician; b. Alexandria, Egypt, July 31, 1946; came to U.S., 1985; s. Charles and Mary Hamdy; m. Eleanor Gertrude Hamdy, Aug. 19, 1977; children: Conrad, Gerard, Ronan. MB, ChB with honours, U. Alexandria, 1968, DM, 1971. Rotating intern U. Alexandria, 1968-69; resident in internal medicine Al-Gomhouriya Gen. Hosp., Alexandria, 1969-70; resident registrar internal medicine U. Alexandria Main Teaching Hosp., 1970-72; sr. ho. officer geriatric and internal medicine Farnborough (Eng.) Hosp., Kent, 1972-73; registrar in geriatric medicine Bromley (Eng.) Group of Hosps., Kent, 1974; sr. registrar in geriatric medicine King's Coll. Group Hosps., London, 1975-77; consulting physician St. John's Hosp. Richmond (Eng.), Twickenham & Roehampton Health Authority, 1977-85, chmn. dept. clin. gerontology, ethics rsch. com., 1981-85; prof. internal medicine, Cecile Cox Quillen prof. geriatric medicine, head divsn. gerontology East Tenn. State U., Mountain Home, 1985—, Cecile Cox Quillen prof. geriatric medicine, head divsn. gerontology, 1990—; chief geriatrics VA Med. Ctr., Mountain Home, 1985-88, assoc. chief of staff geriatric and extended care, 1988—; dir. osteoporosis ctr. East Tenn. State U., 1997—. Hon. sr. lectr. geriatric medicine St. George's Hosp. Med. Sch., U. London, 1981-85; planning team for elderly Wandsworth Health Care, 1982-85; med. dist. initiated peer rev. orgn. VA Hosps., Dist. 8, 1986-89; vis. prof. Health Care for Elderly, U. London, 1991-93; Burroughs Wellcome vis. prof. geriatric medicine Royal Soc. Medicine, 1994-95; co-chmn. pharmacy and therapeutics com. VA Med. Ctr., Johnson City, Tenn., chmn. adverse drug reaction com.; chmn. program com. Coll. Medicine Continuing Med. Edn., East Tenn. State U.; mem. Gov.'s task force on Alzheimer's Disease, Tenn., task force on edn., prevention and detection of osteoporosis; mem. advisor to pub. guardian 1st Tenn. Devel. Dist.; adv. bd. Colonial Hill Health Care Ctr., Johnson City, Golden J-55, Johnson City Med. Ctr. Hosp., Inc.; sr. health adv. com. 1st Tenn. Regional Health Office; adj. clin. prof. divsn. clin. nutrition and psychiatry East Tenn. State U. Author: Diuretic Therapy in the Older Patient, 1978, Paget's Disease in Bone, Assessment and Management, 1981, Geriatric Medicine: A Problem Oriented Approach, 1984; editor: (with J. Turnbull, M. Lancaster, L. Norman) Alzheimer's Disease: A Handbook for Caregivers, 1990, 3d edit., 1998; mem. editl. adv. bd. Revs. Clin. Gerontology, South Med. Jour., Geriatria; reviewer for med. jours.; contbr. chpts. to books, articles to profl. jours. Fellow ACP (com. geriatrics 1987-90, chmn. com. geriatrics MKSAP IX 1991-94), Royal Coll. Physicians, Royal Soc. Medicine; mem. Internat. Soc. Clin. Densitometry, Am. Geriatrics Soc. (membership com., reviewer jour., ann. meeting planning com. 1993), Gerontol. Soc. Am., Royal Coll. Surgeons, So. Med. Assn. (vice-chmn. coun. 1995-96, chmn. coun. 1996-97, v.p. 1997-98, pres.-elect 1998-99, pres. 1999-2000, editor geriatric medicine sect. Dial-Access program, from assoc. councilor to councilor state Tenn., chmn. adv. com. sci. activities, reviewer jour., assoc. editor So. Med. Jour. 1995-2000, editor 2000—), So. Assn. Geriatric Medicine (pres. 1990-92), So. Assn. for Primary Care (editor clin. revs.), Tenn. Med. Assn. (reviewer jour.), Tenn. Geriatrics Soc. (founding), Brit.

Med. Assn., Brit. Geriatrics Soc., Bone and Mineral Soc., Alzheimer's Assn. (pres. bd. dirs. N.E. Tenn. chpt. 1990-91). Office: Ea Tenn State U Coll Medicine PO Box 70429 Johnson City TN 37614-1704 E-mail: hamdy@mail.etsu.edu.

HAMEKA, HENDRIK FREDERIK, chemist, educator; b. Rotterdam, Holland, May 25, 1931; came to U.S., 1960, naturalized, 1963; s. Dirk C. and Johanna (Mannebeck) H.; m. Charlotte C. Procacci, Aug. 3, 1972. Drs., U. Leiden, The Netherlands, 1953, DSc cum laude, 1956; MA (hon.), U. Pa., 1971. Rsch. assoc. U. Rome, Italy, 1956-57; fellow Carnegie Inst. Tech., 1957-58; rsch. physicist N. V. Philips Lamps, Eindhoven, The Netherlands, 1958-60; asst. prof. chemistry Johns Hopkins, 1960-62; assoc. prof. chemistry U. Pa., 1962-67, prof. chemistry, 1967—. Disting. vis. rsch. prof. USAF Acad., 1986-87. Author: Advanced Quantum Chemistry, 1965, Introductory Quantum Theory, 1967, Physical Chemistry, 1977, Chemistry, Fundamentals and Applications, 2002; contbr. numerous articles to sci. jours. Recipient Alexander von Humboldt prize, 1981; Alfred P. Sloan Research fellow, 1963-67. Achievements include research on theory of molecular structure and optical and magnetic properties of molecules; calculations of spin-orbit and spin-spin coupling; theory of resonance optical rotation, spectral predictions. Home: 1503 Argyle Rd Berwyn PA 19312-1905 Office: U Pa Dept Chemistry Philadelphia PA 19104

HAMEL, DANA BERTRAND, academic administrator; b. Rumford, Maine, Aug. 9, 1923; s. Donat H. and Louise (Kenison) H.; m. Shirley Elmeree Smith Knavel, Dec. 19, 1945; children— Dana Randolph, Michelle, April. AB, Ashland (Ohio) Coll., 1951; MA, Ohio State U., 1952; EdD, U Cin., 1962; AA in Humanities (hon.), Southside Va. C.C. Master watchmaker Thomas J. Apryle & Sons, Johnstown, Pa., 1946; owner Hamels, Jewelers, Conemaugh, Pa., 1946-48; mem. mgmt. dept. Gen. Motors Inst., Flint, Mich., 1955-57; dean adminstrv. affairs Ohio Coll. Applied Sci. and Ohio Mechanics Inst., Cin., 1957-63, acting pres., 1961-62, exec. v.p., dean of faculties, 1962-63; dir. Roanoke Tech. Inst., 1963-64; exec. dir. Va. Dept. Tech. Edn., Richmond, 1964-66; founding chancellor Va. Community Coll. System, Richmond, 1966-79, cons., 1979-80; cons. to pres., dir. spl. acad. programs Va. State U., Petersburg, 1980-961980—; exec. dir. Va. Ctr. Pub./Pvt. Initiatives; pres. Hamel & Assocs., Richmond, 1996—. Coord. for offices of Va. Sec. of Edn. and Dept. of Edn. for WorkForce 2000, V-Quest Programs, 1992-96; co-chair Metro Richmond 2000; acting dir. Adminstrv. Affairs, CEBAF. Gov.'s liaison SURA/Continuous Electron Beam Accelerator Facility, 1983—; trustee, v.p. 1983-99, Southeastern Univs. Rsch. Assn., Inc., 1981—; mem. Va. Adv. Coun. Vocat. Edn.; bd. dirs. Richmond Eye and Ear Hosp. Authority, 1989—, Ctr. of Excellence, Inc., Richmond Community High Sch., 1981—; chmn. bd. Va. Edn. Rsch. 1981-85, Network for Supercomputers, 1986—; sr. cons. 1986-93, So. Growth Policies Bd. Tech. Coun., 1987-95; Va. coord. Vamanuf Networking, 1990—; exec. dir. Mfg. Networking and Indsl. Modernization Project, 1992—; interim exec. dir. Va. Alliance Mfg. Competitiveness, 1993—; interim dir. Sch. to Work Program, 1994-95. Wth USAAF, 1942-45. Mem. So. Assn. Schs. and Colls. (former pres.), Am. Assn. Jr. Colls. (commn. on legis.), Nat. Coun. State Dirs. (former chmn.), Am. Soc. Engring. Edn., Am. Psychology and Guidance Assn., Nat. Assn. for Gifted Children, Am. Coll. Pers. Assn., Cin. Guidance and Pers. Assn., Va. League Nursing (pres. 1987), Forum Club, Masons, Kiwanians, Phi Delta Kappa, Psi Chi, Iota Lambda Sigma. Home and Office: Hamel & Assocs 300 Coalport Rd Richmond VA 23229-7019

HAMEL, ELIZABETH CECIL, volunteer, educator; b. Altoona, Pa., June 13, 1918; d. Francis Anthony and Charlotte Margaret (Devine) Murphy; m. William Rogers Hamel, Mar. 2, 1943; children: Michele Ferencsik, Deirdre, Anthony, Cecily Charlyn Houston. BArt, Villa Maria Coll., 1939; MA, Pa. State U., 1940; cert. approval, U. Cambridge, Eng., summer 1986. Tchr. English, head Spanish dept. East High Sch., Erie, Pa., 1940-43; prof. lit. Vernon Ct. Jr. Coll., Newport, R.I., 1966-69. Mem. Francestown (N.H.) Improvement Assn., 1958—, Peterborough (N.H.) Hist. Soc., 1987—, Art and Hist. Soc. East Martello Tower Mus., Key West, Fla., 1987—, Founders' Soc. Tennessee Williams Fine Arts Ctr., Key West, 1986—; bd. dirs. Old Island Restoration Found., Key West, 1990—; bd. dirs. Friends of Libr., 1985-86, 93—, sec., 1986-87, 92—; mem. White House Vol. Group, Washington, 1972-74; trustee Newport County Preservation Soc. Mem. Gen. Fedn. Women's Club (bd. dirs. Key West chpt. 1986—), Key West Woman's Club (bd. dirs., parliamentarian 1986—, del. state con. 1988—), Peterborough Woman's Club, Garden Club, Greenfield Woman's Club (pres. 1979-80). Republican. Roman Catholic. Avocations: antiques, sailing, swimming, travel, literature. Home: 10 Devon Dr Acton MA 01720

HAMEL, FRED MEADE, lawyer; b. Sheridan, Wyo., Nov. 26, 1943; s. Fred Herman and Marie (Kruger) H.; m. Michelle O'Bryan, Dec. 29, 1967; 1 child, Marc Steven. BSBA, U. Denver, 1965; JD, U. Colo., 1968. Bar: Colo. 1968, U.S. Dist. Ct. Colo. 1974, U.S. Ct. Appeals (10th cir.) 1977. Asst. sec. Union Investment Corp., Detroit, 1970—74; v.p. 1st Comml. Corp., Denver, 1970—74; prin. Fred M. Hamel Atty. At Law, Denver, 1974—. Pres. South Cen. Improvment Assn., 1978. Staff sgt. U.S. Army, 1968-70, Vietnam. Mem. Colo. Bar Assn., Denver Bar Assn. Avocation: golf. Office: 155 S Madison St Ste 206 Denver CO 80209-3013

HAMEL, LEE, lawyer; b. N.Y.C., Oct. 1, 1940; s. Herman and Jessie Blanche (Mapes) H.; m. Carole Ann Holmes, Dec. 30, 1965; children: Todd Leland, Stuart Russell. BA, Duke U., 1962; JD, U. Tex., 1967; postgrad., U. Houston, 1997—. Bar: Tex. 1967, U.S. Ct. Appeals (5th and 11th cirs.) 1968, U.S. Ct. Mil. Appeals 1968, U.S. Dist. Ct. (so. dist.) Tex. 1968, U.S. Supreme Ct. 1971, U.S. Tax Ct. 1979, U.S. Dist. Ct. (we. dist.) Tex. 1984, U.S. Dist. Ct. (ea. dist.) Tex. 1994. Asst. U.S. atty. U.S. Dist. Ct. (so. dist.) Tex., Houston, 1967—71, chief Corpus Christi divsn., 1970-71; owner Lee Hamel & Assocs., Houston, 1971-74, 90-99; ptnr. Dickerson, Hamel, Early & Pennock, Houston, 1974-88, Hamel & Rouner, Houston, 1988-89, Hamel Bowers & Clark, LLP, Houston, 2000—. Instr. Nat. Inst. for Trial Advocacy, 1986—. Editor (bd. of editors): Nat. Law Jour. Health Care Fraud and Abuse Newsletter, 1998—. Former trustee St. Luke's Hosp., Houston, St. James Home for Aged, Baytown; former dir. exec. bd. Episcopal Diocese of Tex.; pres. St. Francis Endowment Fund, 1993-94; former councilman Hunters Creek Village, Tex.; bd. dirs. Lone Star Legal Aid, 1999—. Comdr. USN, 1962-64, USNR, ret. 1993. Fellow Coll. of State Bar of Tex., Houston Bar Found., State Bar Tex.; mem. ABA (litig. sec., white collar crime com., bus. law sec., chair health care fraud subcomittee), FBA, Houston Bar Assn., Houston Vol. Lawyers Assn. (bd. dirs. 1998-99). Episcopalian. Avocation: backpacking. Office: Hamel Bowers & Clark LLP 5300 Memorial Dr Ste 900 Houston TX 77007-8201

HAMEL, LOUIS H., JR., lawyer; b. Haverhill, Mass., June 30, 1934; s. Louis H. and Dorothy A. (Berry) H.; m. Geraldine T. Griffin, Dec. 28, 1959 (div. 1977); children: Juliana, Louis III, Lucy, Paul, Mark J. BA, St. Paul's Coll., 1956; MA, Fordham U., 1959; JD, Harvard U., 1969. Bar: Mass. 1969, U.S. Dist. Ct. Mass. Instr. Manhattanville Coll., Purchase, N.Y., 1959-60; pres. Hamel Realty, Haverhill, Mass., 1961-69; assoc. Hale and Dorr, Boston, 1969-72, jr. ptnr., 1972-76, sr. ptnr., 1976-97, of counsel, 1998—. Contbr. articles to profl. jours. Bd. trustees Boston Chamber Music Soc., 1987—, pres., 1996-00. Office: Hale and Dorr LLP 60 State St Ste 25 Boston MA 02109-1816 also: 955 Main St Ste 202 Winchester MA 01890-4302 E-mail: louis.hamel@haledorr.com.

HAMEL, LOUIS REGINALD, systems analysis consultant; b. Lowell, Mass., July 23, 1945; s. Wilfred John and Angelina Lucienne (Paradis) H.; m. Roi Anne Roberts, Mar. 24, 1967 (dec.); 1 child, Felicia Antoinette; m. Anne Louise Staup, July 2, 1972 (div.); children: Shawna Michelle, Louis Reginald III; m. Melissa A. Truesdale, Sept. 24, 1999 (div.). AA, Kellogg C.C., 1978. Cert. worker's compensation profl. Retail mgr. Marshall Dept. Stores, Beverly, Mass., 1972-73; tech. svc. rep. Monarch Marking Systems, Framingham, Mass., 1973—74; employment specialist Dept. Labor, Battle Creek, Mich., 1977-78; v.p. corp. Keith Polygraph Cons. and Investigative Svc., Inc., Battle Creek, 1978-79; indsl. engr., engine components divsn. Eaton Corp., Battle Creek, 1979-82; tooling and process engr. Kelley Tech. Svcs., Battle Creek, 1983-84, Clark Equipment Inc., 1983-84; tooling and mfg. engr., mfg. mgr. Trans Guard Industries Inc., Angola, Ind., 1983-85; facilitator employee involvement, safety dir. Wohlert Corp., Lansing, Mich., 1985—, workers compensation adminstr., tng. dir., 1985—, system analysis cons., 1975—. Cons. in field. Mem. Calhoun County Com. on Employment of Handicapped, Battle Creek, Mich., 1977-78; mem. Capital Area Labor Mgmt. Com., 1986-91. With USN, 1963-71, Vietnam. Recipient Svcs. to Handicapped award Internat. Assn. Pers. in Employment Security, Mich. chpt. 1978. Mem. VFW, Nat. Geog. Soc., Mich. Assn. Concerned Vets. (dir.), Nat. Assn. Concerned Vets. Democrat. Roman Catholic. Home and Office: 12240 S M 66 Hwy Bellevue MI 49021-9639 E-mail: hamellm@prodigy.net. *Personal philosophy: A warm handshake, with a smile, will give more people a lift than all the elevators in the world.*

HAMEL, LOUISE, artist, writer, muralist; b. Boston, May 28, 1948; d. Raymond F. and M. Cecile (Dery) H.; m. Mattias M. Gould, Sept. 7, 1968 (div. July 1988); children: Rachel, Adrienne. Student, Decordova Museum Sch., 1976-79, Art Inst. Boston, 1978-79; grad. with honors, Ringling Sch. Art, 1989. Prodn. dir. Hamel Pub.Co., Natick, Mass., 1975-79; ptnr. Inner Space, Sudbury, Mass., 1979-84; indsl. designer Palm Rsch., Nokomis, Fla., 1984-97; pres. Louise Hamel Designs, Inc., Sarasota, 1987—2001; dir. art and mktg. Nat. Assessment Inst., Clearwater, Fla., 1990-91; v.p. design and devel. Nicholas James, Ltd., Sarasota, Fla., 1991-93; v.p. J&L Studio, LLC, 2001—. Mem. MMM Investments, 1996-97. One-woman shows include Emphasis Gallery, 1993, 95, 96, ARTarget, Sarasota, 1993; group shows include Selby Gallery, Sarasota, 1988, 89, 98, Voorhees Gallery, Sarasota, 1989, ARTarget, 1993, 96, 2000, ArtWerx Winterfest, Sarasota, 1994, Sarasota County Arts coun., 1995, 96, Art LEague Manatee Invitational, 1999, others; art. dir. (short film) Bad Guy, 1995; designer (feature film) Conspiracy of Weeds, 1997. Vol. Sarasota County Arts Coun., Fla., 1990-97. Mem. Sarasota Profl. Artists and Muralists Guild (charter), Artarget (bd. dirs. 1991-99).

HAMEL, MICHAEL A. career officer; BS in Aero. Engring., USAF Acad., 1972; MBA, Calif. State U., Dominguez Hills, 1974; grad., Squadron Officer Sch., 1975, Air Command and Staff Coll., 1980. Commd. 2d lt. USAF, 1972, advanced through grades to brigadier Maj. Gen.; staff devel. planner Space and Missile Sys. Orgn., L.A. AFB, 1972-75; missile analyst fgn. tech. divsn. Lowry AFB, Colo., 1975-77; mission dir. Aerospace Data Facility, Buckley Air N.G. Base, Colo., 1977-79; air staff tng. officer R&D Hdqs. USAf, Washington, 1979-80; project mgr., manned spaceflight engr. Office of Sec. of Air Force for Spl. Projects, L.A. AFB, 1980-86; program element monitor, exec. officer Hdqs. USAF, Washington, 1986-90; chief plans divsn. Hdqs. Air Force Space Command, Peterson AFB, Colo., 1991-94; comdr. 750th Space Group, Onizuka Air Sta., Calif., 1994-95; vice comdr. 21st Space Wing, Peterson AFB, 1995-96; mil. adviser to v.p. The White House, Washington, 1996-98; vice comdr. Space and Missile Sys. Ctr., L.A. AFB, 1998-99; dir. requirements Air force Space Command HQ, Peterson AFB, Colo., 1999—; dir. space ops. and intergradon HQ USAF, Pentagon, 2000—02; comdr. 14th AF Vanderberg AFB, Calif., 2002—. Decorated Def. Superior Svc. medal, Legion of Merit, Meritorious Svc. medal with 3 oak leaf clusters. Office: 14 AF/CC 747 Nebraska Ave Ste A300-8 Vandenberg Afb CA 93437-6268

HAMEL, PAUL BERNARD, ornithologist, researcher; b. Grand Rapids, Mich., Oct. 17, 1948; s. Bernard Charles and Mary Elizabeth (Ghering) Hamel; m. Lynda L. Wyant, July 1, 2000; m. Mary Catherine Kowalinski, July 13, 1968 (div. Mar. 4, 1992); children: Renée Danielle, Peter Damien, Patrick Steven. AS, Grand Rapids (Mich.) Jr. Coll., 1968; BS in Zoology, Mich. State U., 1970, MS in Zoology, 1972, MS in Park and Recreation Resources, 1973; PhD in Zoology, Clemson U., 1981. Master Bird Bander US Fish and Wildlife Svc., 1967. Instr. recreation and pk. adminstrn. Clemson (SC) U., 1972—75, rsch. asst. zoology, 1975—81, rsch. assoc. zoology, 1982—84; zoologist natural heritage program Tenn. Dept. Environment and Conservation, Nashville, 1984—93; rsch. avian ecologist USDA Forest Svc., Stoneville, Miss., 1993—95, rsch. wildlife biologist, 1995—. Author: Cherokee Plants and Their Uses, 1975, Bachman's Warbler: A species in peril, 1986 (Book of the Yr., Southeastern Sect., Wildlife Soc., 1987), Land Manager's Guide to the Birds of the South, 1992, Tennessee Wildlife Viewing Guide, 1993; contbr. articles to profl. jours. Recipient Taking Wing award, Ducks Unlimited, 1998. Mem.: Ecol. Soc. Am., Soc. Conservation Biology, Soc. Sigma Xi, Soc. Conservation Study Caribbean Birds, Assn. Field Ornithologists, Wildlife Soc., Cooper Ornithol. Soc., Wilson Ornithol. Soc. (life), Am. Ornithologists' Union (life), Miss. Ornithol. Soc. Achievements include research in forest management for nongame birds, threatened and endangered songbirds in forests of the southeastern United States. Avocations: reading, swimming, travel, foreign languages. Office: USDA Forest Svc PO Box 227 432 Stoneville Rd Stoneville MS 38776

HAMEL, RODOLPHE, pharmaceutical company executive, retired lawyer; b. Lewiston, Maine, June 3, 1929; s. Rodolphe and Alvina Melanie (Bilodeau) H.; m. Marilyn Vivian Johnsen, June 10, 1957; children: Matthew Edward, Anne Melanie. BA, Yale U., 1950; LLB, Harvard U., 1953. Bar: Maine 1953, D.C. 1953, N.Y. 1957. Assoc. firm Shearman & Sterling, N.Y.C., 1956-66; v.p., corp. sec., gen. counsel Macmillan Inc., N.Y.C., 1972-73; internat. counsel Bristol-Myers Squibb Co. (formerly Bristol-Myers Co.), N.Y.C., 1966-72, 73, v.p., counsel internat. div., 1974-81, assoc. gen. counsel, 1978-89, v.p., 1983-92, gen. counsel, 1989-94, sr. v.p., 1992-94, cons., 1995—. 1st lt. AUS, 1953-56. Mem. ABA, N.Y. State Bar Assn., Assn. of Bar of City of N.Y., Yale Club. Office: Bristol-Myers Squibb Co 345 Park Ave New York NY 10154-0004

HAMEL, WILLIAM JOHN, church administrator, minister; b. Marquette, Mich., July 30, 1947; s. John Peter and Jayne B. (Berklund) H.; m. Karen Margaret Holleen, Aug. 10, 1968; children: Krista Joy, Kari Elise. BS, Wheaton Coll., 1969; MDiv, Trinity Evang. Div. Sch., Deerfield, Ill., 1972; DD, Trinity Internat. U., 1998; DCM, Trinity Western U., 1998. Ordained minister Evang. Free Ch. Am., 1978. Pastor West Bloomington (Minn.) Evang. Free Ch., 1972-86; dist. supt. Midwest Dist. Evang. Free Ch. Am., Kearney, Nebr., 1986-90; exec. v.p. Evang. Free Ch. Am., Mpls., 1990-97, pres., 1997—. Mem. Evangelist Free Ch. Am. Office: Evang Free Ch Am 901 E 78th St Minneapolis MN 55420-1334

HAMELIN, JEAN-GUY, bishop; b. St.-Severin, Que., Can., Oct. 8, 1925; s. Bernard and Gertrude (Bordeleau) H. BA, Sem. Trois-Rivieres, Que., Can., 1945; Lic. Theology, Angelicum, Rome, 1953; Lic. Social Scis., Gregoriana, Rome, 1955. Ordained priest Roman Catholic Ch., 1949; consecrated bishop, 1974. Tchr. secondary sch., Trois-Rivieres, Canada, 1949—52; mem. faculty Sem. Trois-Rivieres, 1955—58; chaplain to various social orgns. Shawinigan, 1958—64; dir. social action dept. Bishop's Conf., Ottawa, Canada, 1964—68, gen. sec. Montreal, 1968—74; bishop Diocese of Rouyn-Noranda, 1974—2002; ret., 2002. V.p. Can. Conf. Cath. Bishops, 1983-85, 91-93, pres., 1993-95; ecclesiastical advisor Cooperation Internat. for Devel. and Solidarity, Brussels, 1988-94. Roman Catholic. Address: Office Chancery 515 Cuddihy Rouyn QC Canada J9X 4C5

HAMELIN, MARCEL, historian, educator; b. Saint-Narcisse, Que., Can., Sept. 18, 1937; m. Judy Purcell, Aug. 18, 1962; children— Danielle, Christine, Marc. Doctorat es Lettres, Universite Laval, Can. Faculty U. Ottawa, Ont., Canada, prof. history, 1966—2003, chmn. dept. history, 1968-70, vice dean sch. grad. studies, 1972-74, dean faculty of arts, 1974-90, rector, vice chancellor, 1990—2001, rector emeritus, 2001—; exec. dir. Interamerican Orgn. Higher Edn., 2002—. Chmn. Can.-Africa Cmty. Health Alliance, 2002—. Author: History of the Province of Quebec. Mem. Canadian Hist. Assn., Assn. Canadienne-francaise pour l'avancement des Scis. (pres. 1976-77), Royal Soc. Can. (Chevalier, Légion d'honneur). Fax: 613-562-5141. E-mail: mhamelin@uottawa.ca.

HAMELIN, PAUL ROBERT, pharmacist, pharmaceutical executive, consultant; b. Ann Arbor, Mich., Nov. 16, 1954; s. John and Edith Hamelin; m. Marty K. Hamelin, Dec. 1976; children: Geoff P., Ryan S. BS in Zoology, Mich. State U., 1976; BS in Pharmacy, Ferris State U., 1980. Registered pharmacist Mich. With Eli Lilly Co., Ind., 1980-89, Abbott Labs., Ill., 1989-95; group v.p. global med. mktg. Pharmacia/Searle, N.J. and Ill., 1995-2000; corp. officer, head comml. ops. Millennium Pharm., Cambridge, Mass., 2000—02; pres., CEO Elitra Pharms., 2002—. Bd. pharmacy Ferris State U., 2000. Home: PO Box 968 Leland MI 49654

HAMER, JEANNE MARIE HUNTINGTON, soprano, retired voice educator; b. Mar. 1, 1933; d. Edward Olney and Francine M. (Clavier) Huntington; m. Roger F. Hamer, Aug. 19, 1955; children: Michael Edward, Kathryn Louise. Mus.B with honors, U. Wyo., 1955, postgrad., 1976—82, MA with honors, 1984; postgrad., U. Denver, 1976. Grad. tchg. asst. U. Wyo., 1955—56; pvt. vocal tchr. Billings, Mont., 1957—58, Miles City, Mont., 1958—59, Grand Rapids, Mich., 1959—61, Torrington, Wyo., 1962—; instr. music Eastern Wyo. Coll., 1968—, chmn. dept. music, 1978—92, faculty emerita, 1992—. Part time instr., 1992—2001. Musician (lead role): (Operas) The Medium, The Telephone, Cavalleria Rusticana, I Pagliacci, Baby Doe; musician: (soloist) Billings Symphony, Casper (Wyo.) Symphony, Scottsbluff (Nebr.) Symphony, Nebr. Panhandle Symphony, U. Wyo. Symphony, Wyo. chorus for Wyo. Centennial at Teton Music Festival with Orch.; musician: (soprano) Barta Trio, 1972—89; musician: (mem.) Cheyenne Chamber Singers, 1992—; musician: (soloist, adjudicator for music festivals) ; musician: (organist, choir dir.) All Saints Episcopal Ch., 1974—82, 1986—98; musician: (dir.) Torrington Community Chorus, 1975—93. Mem.: Wyo. Am. Choral Dirs. (pres. 1988—91), Music Educators Nat. Conf., Am. Choral Dirs. Assn., Nat. Assn. Tchrs. Singing (gov. Wyo.), Order Eastern Star, PEO, Phi Kappa Phi. Episcopalian. Home: 515 E 23rd Ave Torrington WY 82240-2529

HAMER, MARTIN, retired chemist; b. Indpls., Ind., 1928; s. Irving and Sara Hamer; m. Joanne Kushner Hamer; children: Baian Hamer, Wax Sheila. BS in Chemistry, Indiane U.; MS in Organic Chemistry, Purdue U., 1951, PhD in Organic Chemistry, 1953. Cons. Bisco, INC, Schaumburg, 1993; sr. rsch. chemist Amoco Corp., Whiting, Ind., 1954—60; rsch. mgr. INTL. Minerals, Chemistry,Corp, Libertyville, 1960—82; rsch. dir. Bisoc, INC, Downers Grove, 1983—93. Enviroment Skokie Enviroment,Protection, 1973—78; enviromentalist Skokie Enviroment . Protection, Skokie, Ind., 1979—83; toastmaster Toastmaster, INTL., Skokie, Ill., 1979—83. Achievements include Many patents issued & several papers published. Home: 8423 Karlov Avenue Skokie IL 60076

HAMER, WALTER JAY, chemical consultant, science writer; b. Altoona, Pa., Nov. 5, 1907; s. Jesse James and Naomi Gertrude (Roland) H.; m. Alma Robinson, Mar. 19, 1941; 1 child, Margaret. BS, Juniata Coll., Huntingdon, Pa., 1929, DSc (hon.), 1966; PhD, Yale U., 1932. Asst. instr. Juniata Coll., 1926-29; fellow Yale U., New Haven, 1932-34; rsch. assoc. MIT, Cambridge, 1934-35; rsch. chemist Nat. Bur. Standards, Washington, 1935-50, chief electrochemistry, 1950-70, dir. Electrolyte Ctr., 1968-72; chem. cons. Washington, 1972—. Adj. prof. Georgetown U., Cath. U., govt. agys. commerce and agr., 1940-50; rsch. chemist Manhattan Project, Washington, 1943-45; adj. examiner Civil Svc. Commn., 1948-50; cons. U.S. Dept. Def., 1951-53; mem. electrochem. soc. Internat. Union Pure and Applied Chemistry, 1958-68; U.S. tech. advisor primary cells and batteries Internat. Electrotech. Commn., 1964; mem. vis. panel Electrochemistry Lab., U. Pa., Phila., 1962-63; U.S. tech. advisor primary cells and batteries Internat. Electrotech. Commn., 1964; lectr. in field. Contbr. articles to profl. jours.; editor: Electrochemical Constants, 1953, The Structure of Electrolytic Solutions, 1959. Recipient cert. of merit Manhattan Project, 1945, OSRD, 1945; Superior Accomplishment award U.S. Dept. Commerce, 1954, 62, 65, Disting. Svc. gold medal, 1966; 1st prize for paper IEEE, 1955. Fellow IEEE (life), AAAS (life), Am. Inst. Chemistry (life), N.Y. Acad. Sci. (life), Washington Acad. Sci. (life); mem. Am. Stds. Assn. (mem. com. primary cells and batteries 1952-62), The Electrochem. Soc., Inc. (hon., v.p. 1960-63, pres. 1963-64, Robert T. Foley award Nat. Capital sect. 1991), Yale Chemists Assn. (pres. 1958-61), Eisenhower Commn., Cosmos Club. Republican. Episcopalian. Achievements include discovery of the electromotive series of the elements in Molten Systems, of the primary pH Standard for Aqueous Systems from 0 to 60 degrees Celsius, of the ionization constant of water from 0 to 60 degrees Celsius; research in determining the Faraday Constant, method to set standards for electrolytic conductance, maintenance of U.S. national standard of voltage. Home and Office: Apt 220 333 Russell Ave Gaithersburg MD 20877-2833

HAMERLY, MICHAEL T. librarian, historian; b. Seattle, Sept. 23, 1940; s. James Charles Riley and Harriet Elinor (Jackson) H.; m. Carmen Victoria Flores Rosero, Jan. 19, 1963; 1 child, Michael Charles. BA, U. Wash., 1963, MA, 1965, M in Librarianship, 1979; PhD, U. Fla., 1970. From instr. to asst. prof. U. No. Colo., Greeley, 1970-74; dir. Archivo Arzobispal, Ecuador, 1975-78; rschr. Dept. Historia Maritima, Armada del Ecuador, 1975 77; vis. sr. lectr. dept. Spanish and Latin Am. studies Hebrew U., Jerusalem, 1981; cataloguer Pre-Columbian studies Dumbarton Oaks Rsch. Library and Collections, 1983-84; bibliographer, use a solidus cataloguer Latin Am. Bibliographic Found., Redlands, Calif., 1985-88; catalog librarian, assoc. prof. Pacific collection Micronesian Area Rsch. Ctr., U. Guam, Mangilao, 1988-91; collection devel. lib., assoc. prof. to prof. Robert F. Kennedy Meml. Lib. U. Guam, 1991-98, chmn. press coun., 1990-97, prof., curriculum resources ctr. coord., 1997; spl. project/catalogue libr. John Carter Brown Libr., Providence, 1998—. Andean area editor The Americas; a quar. rev. of Inter-Am. Cultural history, 1974-88; assoc. editor Revista del Archivo Historico del Guayas, 1975-90; contbg. editor Handbook of Latin Am. Studies, 1971—; editor Ecuadorian Studies/Estudios ecuatorianos, 2000—; contbr. articles to profl. jours. NDEA, Title VI, Doherty and Fulbright-Hays grantee, fellow; Am. Coun. Learned Socs. and Social Sci. Rsch. Coun. grantee. Mem. Latin-Am. Studies Assn., Conf. on Latin-Am. History, Centro de Investigaciones Historicas de Guayaquil, Acad. Arquidiocesana de Historia Eclesiastica, Asian-Pacific Am. Librs. Assn., Assn. Historiadores Ecuatorianos, Acad. Nat. Historia, Fulbright Assn., Guam Libr. Assn., Pacific Islands Assn. Librs. and Archives, Beta Phi Mu. Home: 9416 1st Ave NE Ste 113 Seattle WA 98115-2749 Office: John Carter Brown Libr PO Box 1894 Providence RI 02912-1894 Fax: 401-863-3477. E-mail: michael_hamerly@brown.edu.

HAMERMAN, DAVID JAY, gerontologist, educator; b. N.Y.C., Apr. 20, 1925; s. Joseph and Bertha (Broder) H. MD, NYU, 1948. Diplomate Am. Bd. Internal Medicine. Intern Mt. Sinai Hosp., N.Y.C., 1948-49, resident in medicine Montefiore, N.Y., 1949-51, chief resident in medicine N.Y.C., 1951-52; dir. arthritis program Albert Einstein Coll. Medicine, N.Y.C., 1956-68, prof. medicine, 1968—; chmn. dept. medicine Montefiore Hosp. Albert Einstein Coll. Medicine, N.Y.C., 1968-79, head div. geriatrics, 1983-89, dir. Resnick Gerontology Ctr., 1990—. Author: Primer on Connective Tissue, 1968; editor: Osteoarthritis: Public Health Implications for an Aging Society, 1997; contbr. articles to profl. jours. Capt. U.S. Army, 1953-55. Markle Found. scholar, 1957-62; Sinsheimer Found. fellow, 1963-68, Fogarty Inst. Internat. fellow, 1980-81; recipient Geriatric Leadership Acad. award Nat. Inst. on Aging, 1986-92. Fellow ACP; mem. Am. Soc. for Clin. Investigation, Assn. Am. Physicians. Office: Montefiore Med Ctr 111 E 210th St Bronx NY 10467-2401

HAMERMESH, DANIEL SELIM, economics educator; b. Cambridge, Mass., Oct. 20, 1943; s. Morton and Madeline (Goldberg) H.; m. Frances Witty, Dec. 18, 1966; children: David J., Matthew A. AB, U. Chgo., 1965; PhD, Yale U., 1969. Asst. prof. Princeton (N.J.) U., 1969-73; assoc. prof. Mich. State U., East Lansing, 1973-76, prof., 1976-93, chmn. dept., 1984-88; Edward Everett Hale centennial prof. econs. U. Tex., Austin, 1993—. Rsch. dir. ASPER-U.S. Dept. Labor, Washington, 1974-75, rsch. assoc. Nat. Bur. Econ. Rsch., 1979—; vis. prof. Harvard U., Cambridge, Mass., 1981, Latrobe U., Melbourne, Australia, 1987, Gadjah Mada U., Indonesia, 1990, Australian Nat. U., 1991, Rijksuniversiteit Limburg, The Netherlands, 1992, New Econ. Sch., Moscow, 1993, Hebrew U., Jerusalem, 1995, Erasmus U., The Netherlands, 1997, U. Bristol, Eng., 2000, U. Aberdeen, Scotland, 2002; mem. econ. adv. panel NSF, 1995-97; chmn. sci. adv. bd. German Inst. Econ. Rsch. Mem. bd. editors Am. Econ. Rev., 1990-94; co-editor Econ. Letters, 1994-98, Labour Econs., 1996-00, Jour. Population Econs., 2001-03. Pres. Congregation Kehillat Israel, Lansing, 1988-90. Recipient Best Article award Western Econ. Assn., 1987, Parents' Assn. Centennial Teaching fellow U. Tex., 1995-96; NSF rsch. grantee, 1980-82, 84-86, 86-91, 95—. Fellow Econometric Soc.; mem. Am. Econ. Assn., Midwest Econ. Assn. (pres. 1988-89), Soc. Labor Economists (pres. 2000-01). Jewish. Avocations: running, classical music. Office: U Tex Dept Econs Austin TX 78712 E-mail: hamermes@eco.utexas.edu.

HAMERMESH, MORTON, physicist, educator; b. N.Y.C., Dec. 27, 1915; s. Isador J. and Rose (Kornhauser) H.; m. Madeline Goldberg, 1941; children: Daniel S., Deborah R., Lawrence A. BS, City Coll. N.Y., 1936; PhD, N.Y.U., 1940. Instr. physics Coll. City N.Y., 1941, Stanford, 1941-43; research asso. Radio Research Lab., Harvard, 1943-46; asst. prof. physics N.Y.U., 1946-47, asso. prof., 1947-48; sr. physicist Argonne Nat. Lab., 1948-50, asso. dir. physics div., 1950-59, dir. physics div., 1959-63, assoc. lab. dir. basic research, 1963-65;

prof. U. Minn., Mpls., 1965-69, 70-86, prof. emeritus, 1986—; head Sch. Physics and Astronomy, 1965-69, 70-73; prof. physics, chmn. dept. physics State U. N.Y., Stony Brook, 1969-70. Translator: Classical Theory of Fields (by Landau and Lifshitz), 1951; numerous papers in field. Fellow Am. Phys. Soc.; mem. Research Soc. Am. Office: Univ Minn Physics Dept Minneapolis MN 55455 E-mail: mort@physics.spa.umn.edu.

HAMERS, ROBERT J. chemistry educator, researcher; Prof. chemistry U. Wis., Madison, Evan P. Helfaer chair, 1996—. Recipient Peter Mark Meml. award Am. Vacuum Soc., 1994, IBM Corp. Faculty award, 2002; NSF fellow, 1992-97, John Simon Guggenheim Found. fellow, 2000, S.C. Johnson Co. Disting. fellow, 2000—. Fellow Am. Vacuum Soc. Office: U Wisconsin Dept Chemistry 1101 University Ave Madison WI 53706-1322 Fax: 608-262-0453. E-mail: rjhamers@facstaff.wisc.edu.

HAMES, WILLIAM LESTER, lawyer; b. Pasco, Wash., June 21, 1947; s. Arlie Franklin and Nina Lee (Ryals) H.; m. Pamella Kay Rust, June 3, 1967; children: Robert Alan, Michael Jonathan. BS in Psychology, U. Wash., 1974; JD, Willamette U., 1981. Bar: Wash. 1981, U.S. Dist. Ct. (ea. dist.) Wash. 1982, U.S. Ct. Appeals (9th cir.) 1985, U.S. Dist. Ct. (we. dist.) Wash. 1985. Counselor Wash. Juvenile Ct., Walla Walla, Wash., 1974-76; reactor operator control rm. United Nuclear Inc., Richland, Wash., 1976-77; assoc. Sonderman, Egan & Hames, Kennewick, Wash., 1981-84, Timmons & Hames, Kennewick, 1984-86, Sonderman, Timmons & Hames, Kennewick, 1987-88; ptnr. Hames, Anderson & Whitlow, Kennewick, 1988—. Mem. Wash. State Bar Assn. (mem. exec. com. creditor, debtor sect.), Benton-Franklin County Bar Assn., Bankruptcy Bar Assn. (bd. dirs.), Fed. Bar Assn. (bd. dirs.), Am. Bankruptcy Inst. Democrat. Methodist. Home: 410 W 21st St Kennewick WA 99337 Office: Hames Anderson & Whitlow PO Box 5498 Kennewick WA 99336-0498 E-mail: billh@hawlaw.com.

HAMES-GARCIA, MICHAEL R. English language educator; b. Billings, Mont., Nov. 6, 1971; s. Alan and Helen Hames; life ptnr. Ernesto Martinez. BA, Willamette U., Salem, Oreg., 1993; MA, Cornell U., 1996, PhD, 1998. Asst. prof. Binghamton (N.Y.) U., 1998—; vis. Hewlett fellow Stanford U., Palo Alto, Calif., 2002—03. Editor: (collection of essays) Reclaiming Identity: Realist Theory and the Predicament of Postmodernism; author: (book) Crucibles of Freedom: Justice, Critical Race Theory, and Prison Praxis; editor: (collection of essays) Redefining Identity Politics. Prison educator Elmira (N.Y.) Maximum Security Correctional Facility for Men, 2001—02; peace and social justice activist. Recipient William and Flora Hewlett fellowship, Stanford U., 2002—03, Mellon Dissertation Completion fellowship, Cornell U., 1997—98, Sage fellowship, 1993—94, Irene Gerlinger Swindells scholarship, Willamette U., 1989—93, Stannus Music Talent Scholarship, 1989—93. Mem.: MLA, Radical Philosophy Assn., Am. Studies Assn., Nat. Assn. of Chicana and Chicano Studies (nat. sec. 1999—2001). Green Party. Avocation: pianist. Office: Binghamton U SUNY PO Box 6000 Binghamton NY 13902

HAMID, MICHAEL, electrical engineering educator, consultant; b. Dannaba, Tulkarm, Jordan, June 7, 1934; arrived in Can., 1958; m. Khetam Dahlah; Sept. 1, 1973; children: Rumsey, Sammy, Nady, Reema. BEE, McGill U., 1960, MEE, 1962; PhDEE, U. Toronto, 1966. Registered profl. engr., Ont., Man. Asst., assoc., full prof. U. Man., Winnipeg, Can., 1965; dean scholar's affairs Universite Internacional, Ann Arbor, Mich., 1972-75; chmn. grad. studies elec. engring dept. U. Man., Can., 1983-88; prof. elec. engring. U. South Ala., Mobile, 1990—, acting chair, 1999—. Mem. Can. Del. to Internat. Union of Radio Sci., 1965; pres., bd. dirs., treas. Internat. Microwave Power inst., 1969-73; adj. prof. Agrl. Engring., U. Man., 1970-77; vis. prof. U. Ctrl. Fla., Orlando, 1987-89; W.W. Clyde chair dept. elec. engring. U. Utah, 1987; mem. Man. Rsch. Coun., Prov. of Man., 1971-75; gen. chmn. Microwave Power Symposium, Monterey, Calif., 1971; vis. prof. Defence Rsch. Establishment, Dept. Nat. Defence Can., Ottawa, 1972; cons. Defence Rsch. Bd. Can., 1971-73; chmn. Internat. Conf. Biol. Effects of Microwaves and Ultrasound, U. Man., 1969; session organizer and chmn., invited speaker, Internat. Union Radio Sci. Gen. Assembly, Commn. VI., Warsaw, Poland, 1972; invited speaker Microwave State-of-the-Art Internat., IEEE Microwave Theory and Techniques Symposium, Chgo., 1972; ; mem. Man. Rsch. Counc. and chmn. of Elec. and Electronics Products Rsch. Com., 1971-75, Nat. Rsch. Coun. Can. Assoc. Com. on Bird Hazards to Aircraft, 1972-77, Policy Com. and Grants Selection com., Transp. Inst., U. Man., 1972-78; session organizer, invited speaker, Internat. URSI-IEEE-Antennas and Propagation Symposium, U. Colo., 1973; chmn. IEEE edn. activities bd., 1972; invited speaker Brazilian Soc. for Advancement Sci., 25th meeting, Sao Paulo, 1973; invited speaker, mem. Internat. Organizing Com., Colloquium on Microwave Communication, Hungarian Acad. Sci., 1970—; invited speaker NATO Adv. Group for Aerospace R&D E.M. Wave Propagation Panel, The Netherlands, 1974; adj. prof. Naval Postgrad. Sch., Monterey Calif., 1979-81; invited speaker Internat. Conf. on Communications Cirs. and Systems, India, 1981; invited speaker and mem. tech. program com., Internat. Symposium on Microwaves and Communication, Kharagpur, India, 1981; chmn. libr. and fin. coms., U. Man. Transport Inst., 1982-84; mem. Radar Subcom. of Radarsat, Can. Adv. Com. on Remote Sensing, Ottawa, 1983-88; mem. Grad. Studies Awards Com, U. Man., 1984-88; session chmn. URSI/IEEE-Antennas and Propagation Soc. Internat. Symposium, U. B.C., Vancouver, 1985; me. Antenna Tech. and Applied Electromagnetics Conf. Program Com., U. Man., 1986—; expert witness Andrew Antennas vs. Gabriel Electronics, patent infringement litigation, Portland, Maine, 1984-86; expert witness radio interference litigation WKRG, Inc. vs. State of Ala., 1990-91; invited speaker, 78th meeting of N.D. Acad. Sci., U. N.D., Grand Forks, 1986; vis. prof. U. Cen. Fla., dept. elect. engring., 1987—; gen. chmn. Symposium on Electromagnetic Detection of Latent Objects, 1989; me. Internat. Adv. and Tech. Program Com., Internat. Symposium on Recent Advances in Microwave Tech., Beijing, 1989, Reno, 1991, New Delhi, 1993. Author or co-author over 310 tech. articles, 7 monographs and book chpts., over 190 conf. papers, 26 rsch. reports, 25 patents; assoc. editor Jour. Microwave Power, 1969-77; mem. editorial bd. Microwave Jour., Jour. Microwave Power, IEEE Transactions on Microwave Theory and Techniques, 1969—. Fellow IEE, IEEE (life, award for contbns. to electromagnetic scattering and diffraction, devel. dielectric-loaded waveguides, resonators and antennas, life 2000—), Internat. Microwave Power Inst., Electromagnetics Acad. (invited mem.), U. South Ala. Alumni Assn. (Outstanding Scholar award 1998), Am. Assn. Engring Soc., Phi Eta Sigma, Tau Beta Pi, Phi Kappa Phi (scholar 1998). Office: U South Ala Dept Elec Engring Mobile AL 36688-0001 E-mail: mhamid@usouthal.edu.

HAMIEL, JEFF, airport executive; Lic. comml. pilot. With Met. Airports Commn., Mpls., 1977—, exec. dir., 1985—. Lt. col. USAFR. Office: Met Airports Commn 6040 28th Ave S Minneapolis MN 55450-2701*

HAMILL, FRANK ALEXANDER, biologist, researcher; b. Kansas City, Mo., Oct. 11, 1970; s. Robert Kim Hamill and Nancy Ann Craig, Russle R. Craig (Stepfather) and Jerryn Ann Hamill(Stepmother). PhD, U. of Ill., Chgo., 1995—2001. U. rsch. greenhouse mgr. Emporia State U., Kans., 1992—94, undergrad. tchg. asst., biology dept., 1993; grad. student coord. Makerere U., Kampala, Uganda, 1996—97; grad. tchg. asst. U. Ill., Chgo., 1996—97, grad. rsch. asst., 1997—2000; clin. projects mgr. Block Med. Ctr., Evanston, Ill., 2000—01; staff scientist S.W. Found. for Biomed. Rsch., San Antonio, 2001—, biosafety level 4 lab sci. mgr., 2002—. Editl. bd. Integrative Cancer Therapies, Thousand Oaks, Calif., 2001—; reviewer Jour. of Ethnopharmacology, Shannon, County Clare, Ireland, 1999—; referee Fitoterapia, Shannon, County Clare, Ireland, 2000—. Contbr. chpt. to book, articles to profl. jours. Alumni amb. U. of Ill. at Chgo., 2003—; clinic vol., pediatric infectious disease U. of Ill. Hosp., Ill., 1999—2001; vol. outreach educator S.W. Found. for Biomed.l Rsch., San Antonio, 2001—03. Recipient Hon. Tribal Affiliation (formal adoption), Buganda Kingdom, Baganda Tribe, Clan Ensenene, 1997; grantee, IIT Rsch. Inst., Chgo., 2002-2003, Signature Sci. LLC, 2002 and 2003, Edgewood Chem. and Biol. Ctr., U.S. Govt., 2003—, Conservation, Food and Health Found., 1999. Mem.: AASS, Internat. Soc. for Ethnopharmacology, Am. Soc. Pharmacognosy, NY Acad. Scis., Am. Soc. Tropical Medicine and Hygiene, Rho Chi (life). Achievements include discovery of antimicrobial chemicals for drug discovery from African plants; first to describe and comprehensively catalogue the medicinal plants used by the Baganda Tribe (Uganda) for first line health care; research in Novel techniques for rapid discovery of chemicals active against biowarfare agents, adapted for use in a Biosafety Level 4 (highest security containment level) environment. Avocations: orchid culture, snowboarding, skiing, music tchg. (violin), vol. interpreting for the deaf (am. sign lang.). Office: SW Found Biomedical Rsch 7620 NW Loop 410 San Antonio TX 78227 E-mail: ahamill@sfbr.org.

HAMILL, JOHN RICHARD, JR., physician; b. New Orleans, Oct. 16, 1943; s. John Richard and Sarah Jane H.; m. Michal Lorraine Sanyi, May 30, 1970; children: John, Paul. BA, Northwestern U., 1965; MD, Loyola U., 1969. Diplomate Am. Bd. Ophthalmology. Resident in ophthalmology Georgetown U. Med. Ctr., Washington, 1970—73; ophthalmologist The Washington Clinic, 1973—2002; pvt. practice Chevy Chase, Md., 2003—. Mem. clin. faculty ophthalmology Georgetown U. Sch. Medicine, 1974—. Fellow Am. Acad. Ophthalmology. Home: 12812 Deep Spring Dr Potomac MD 20854-2357 Office: 5454 Wisconsin Ave Ste 675 Chevy Chase MD 20815-6930

HAMILTON, ALLAN CORNING, retired oil company executive; b. Chgo., June 9, 1921; s. Daniel Sprague and Mildred (Corning) H.; m. Edith Johnson, June 3, 1950 (div. 1995); children: Kimball C., Scott W., Dean C., Gail W.; m. Geraldine C. Berndt, Jan. 27, 1996. BS in Econs., Haverford Coll., 1943; LLD (hon.), Union Coll., Schenectady, N.Y., 1979. With Standard Oil Co., N.J., 1946-51, Esso Export Corp., 1951-56; treas. Internat. Petroleum co. Ltd., Coral Gables, Fla., 1956-61, Esso Internat. Inc., 1961-66; with Exxon Corp. (formerly Standard Oil Co., N.J.), N.Y.C., 1966-83, treas., v.p., prin. fin. officer, 1970-83. Lt. USNR, 1943-46. Mem.: Met. Club (N.Y.C.), Explorers Club.

HAMILTON, ALLAN J. neurosurgeon; b. Kew Gardens, N.Y., Nov. 16, 1950; m. Jane Hamilton; children: Joshua, Tessa, Luke. BS, Ithaca Coll., 1972; postgrad., Hamilton Coll., 1975-77; MD, Harvard U., 1982. Diplomate Am. Bd. Neurol. Surgeons. Asst. in neurosurgery Mass. Gen. Hosp., Boston, 1989-90; asst. prof. neurosurgery U. Ariz., Tucson, 1990-96, clin. asst. prof. radiation/oncology, 1992-96, assoc. clin. prof. radiation/oncology, 1996—2000, clin. prof. radiation/oncology, 2000—, assoc. prof. surgery, 1996—2000, prof. surgery, 2000—, prof. psychology, 2001—, chief divsn. neurosurgery, 1995—, head dept. surgery, 1999—. Dir. wellness program Rehab. Inst. of Tucson, 1997—; student advisor, U. Ariz. Coll. of Medicine, 1992—, stereotactic neurosurgeon, 1992—; cons. State of Ariz. Bd. Med. Examiners, 1998—. Physician mem. Mex. Outreach planning com., Tucson, 1992-96; mem. legis. com. Ariz. head Injury Found., 1991—; team physician, med. cons. U. Ariz. collegiate Rodeo Team, Tucson, 1990-99. Maj. U.S. Army, 1987-88, 90-91. Albert Schseitzer fellow, 1981; recipient Lars Leksell award 10th European Congress of Neurosurgery, Berlin, 1995, Robert G. Ojemann award Upjohn Co., 1995-96, Presdl. Legion of Merit, 1999, Nat. Leadership award, 2002. Mem. ACS, Congress of Neurol. Surgeons (co.chmn. bus. adv. coun. 2002), Soc. Neurol. Surgeons, Internat. Stereotactic Radiosurgery Soc. (charter), Rocky Mountain Neurosurg. Soc., Am. Assn. Neorol. Surgeons, Am. Soc. Stereotactic and functional Neurosurgery, Soc. of Univ. Neurosurgeons, Western Neurosurgery Soc. Republican. Lutheran. Avocations: ranching, training quarter horses, skiing. Office: Univ Ariz Coll of Medicine Dept Surgery 1501 N Campbell Ave Tucson AZ 85724-5066 E-mail: louanne@u.arizona.edu.

HAMILTON, ALLEN PHILIP, financial advisor; b. Albany, Calif. s. Allen Philip Sr. and Barbara Louise (Martin) H.; m. Mary Williams, July 18, 1981 (div. Mar. 1987). BA in Bus. Mgmt., St. Mary's U., Moraga, Calif., 1961; AA, Contra Costa State Coll., 1957; AB, NW Mo. State U., 1969; postgrad., San Jose State U., 1959-61. CFP. Fin. advisor Consol. Investment Svcs., Kansas City, Mo., 1968-70; pres., CEO Balanced Mgmt. Assn., Mission, Kans., 1969-72, Advanced Svc. Assn., Overland Park, Kans., 1971-78; divisional mgr. Waddell & Reed, Inc., Kansas City, 1978-81; sr. v.p., regional dir. WZW Fin. Svcs., Kansas City, 1981-86; exec. v.p. Skaife & Co., Orinda, Calif., 1986-88; v.p., mktg. dir. Consol. Securities Corp., Walnut Creek, Calif., 1988; sr. dir. and cert. trainer Club Am., Inc., L.A., 1990—; fin. planner, prin. Hamilton Fin. Adv., Am. Investment Svcs., Pleasant Hill., Calif., 1989—; silver mktg. distbr., corp. trainer, Can. mktg. distbr. and trainer Nikken, Inc. Internat., various countries, 1991—; sales mgr., ind. distributor, sales trainer Alpine Industries, 1992—; prin. advisor Environ. Solutions Internat.; exec. dir., CEO Environ. Air Quality and Health Found. (Environ. Solutions Internat.), 1998—; sales, mktg. dir. Exthel Wireless Comm. Inc., 1998-99; trainer, presdl. dir. Builders Referral Inc., Orange County, Calif., 1998—; CEO Stage Coach Line Inc., Huntington Beach, Calif., 1999—, Fin. Enhancement Svcs. Inc., Newport Beach, Calif., 2000—. Sr. dir. Club Am. OTC Pink Shts., L.A., 1990-92; presdl. dir. FundAmerica, Irvine, Calif., 1988—; speaker in field. Author: (with others) The Financial Planner A New Profession, 1986. Asst. dist. commr. Boy Scouts Am., Kansas City, Kans., 1970-79; corp. dir. United Campaign, Overland Park, Kans., 1965-73; active TV show Kidney Found., Kansas City, Mo., 1969-70; sr. arbitrator San Francisco Bay Area Better Bus. Bur., 1986—. Lt. U.S. Army, 1963-65. Recipient Citation Nat. Campaign Re-election 1992, 1992m Senatorial Commn. Rep. Senatorial Inner Circle, 1991. Mem. Inst. Cert. Fin. Planners, Internat. Assn. for Fin. Planning (v.p., bd. dirs. 1982-87, practitioner div.), Registry of Fin. Planning Practitioners, Mt. Diablo Distbrs. Assn. Republican. Avocations: cars, outdoors, tennis, travel, boating. Office: 19744 Beach Blvd # 390 Huntington Beach CA 92648-2988 E-mail: aphamilton007@hotmail.com.

HAMILTON, AMELIA WENTZ (AMY WENTZ), elementary school educator; b. Elizabethtown, Ky., Mar. 31, 1970; d. Willard Mason and Judith Parr Wentz; m. Brian Joseph Hamilton; children: Clinton, Levi, Samuel Jewell. B in Music Edn., Morehead State U., 1993, BA in Edn., 1994; MA in Edn., Western Ky. U., 1997. Rank I in edn. adminstrn. (elem. principalship). Music tchr. Flaherty Elem. Sch., Ekron, Ky., 1995—, extended sch. svc. tchr., 1995—. Testing cons. Ky. Instrnl. Results Info. Sys. Stewart Pepper Mid. Sch., Brandenburg, Ky., 1995; substitute tchr. Meade County Bd. Edn., Brandenburg, 1995; test scoring Ky. Instrnl. Results Info. Sys. Advanced Sys., Lexington, 1993—94; mem. scholarship com. Flaherty Elem. PTO, Ekron, 2001—. Named to All-Collegiate Band, Ky. Music Educators Nat. Conv., 1992, 1993; recipient 18 Outstanding Salesperson awards, The Castle, 1993—95. Mem.: Mothers of Preschoolers, Am. Orff-Schulwerk Assn., Meade County Edn. Assn., Ky. Edn. Assn., Ky. Music Educators Nat. Conf., Ky. Orff-Schulwerk Assn., Meade County Women's Dem. Club, Pi Kappa Phi, Gamma Beta Phi, Sigma Alpha Iota (life), Chi Omega (life). Baptist. Avocations: vocal music, reading. Home: 326 Homeview Dr Brandenburg KY 40108 Office: Flaherty Elem Sch 2615 Flaherty Rd Ekron KY 40117 Personal E-mail: brianamy@bbtel.com.

HAMILTON, ANDREW DAVID, publishing company executive, writer; b. Providence, R.I., Aug. 18, 1959; s. David and Ann (Lownes) H.; children: A. Ryan Lownes, Jane Ann. BS in Mgmt., Roger Williams Coll., 1981; AS in Restaurant Mgmt., Johnson & Wales Coll., 1983. Store, dist. mgr. Tandy Corp., Ft. Worth, 1981-84; regional mgr. MicroSoft Corp., Redmond, Wash., 1984-86; pres., CEO Miles Mgmt., East Greenwich, R.I., 1986-90; exec. dir. Dome Pub. Co., Warwick, R.I., 1990—. Bd. dirs. Cliff Shoals Corp., Boston. Author, creator (software) Dome Home Software, 1992; author Virus Double Check, 1994; creator Calendar-Ease, 1995. Active R.I. Fund. Mem. Am. Jr. Entrepreneur Assn. (bd. dirs. 1991-92), Dunes Club, Point Judith Country Club. Avocations: golf, running, fencing. Home: PO Box 56 Jamestown RI 02835 Office: Dome Pub Co Inc 10 New Eng Way Warwick RI 02886

HAMILTON, ANN KATHERINE, artist; b. Lima, Ohio, June 22, 1956; d. Robert S. and Elizabeth B. H.; m. Michael John Mercil, Nov. 1993; 1 child, Emmett Moore Mercil. BFA in Textile Design, U. Kans., 1979; MFA in Sculpture, Yale Sch. of Art, 1985; PhD (hon.), R.I. Sch. of Design, 2002. Prof. Ohio State Univ., 2003—. Asst. prof. U. Calif., Santa Barbara, 1985-91. One woman shows include Santa Barbara Contemporary Arts Forum, Calif., 1985, The Mus. of Contemporary Art, L.A., 1988, San Diego Mus. of Contemporary Art, La Jolla, Calif., 1990, 21st Internat. São Paulo Bienal, 1991, Louver Gallery, N.Y.C., 1991, Tate Gallery, Liverpool, 1994, The Mus. of Modern Art, N.Y.C., 1994, Ruth Bloom Gallery, Santa Monica, Calif., 1994, Inst. Contemporary Art, Phila., 1995, Wexner Ctr. for the Arts, Columbus, Ohio, 1996, Veince Biennale, Italy, 1999, Akira Ikeda Gallery, Japan, 2001, Irish Mus. of Modern Art, Dublin., 2002, Wanas Found., Sweden, 2002 others. Exhibited in group shows at The Exit Gallery, Banff, Alberta, Can., 1981, The Walter Phillips Gallery, Banff, Alberta, Can., 1981, Twining Gallery, N.Y.C., 1983, 84, 90, The Oakland Mus., Cleveland Inst. of Art, 1987, Carl Solway Gallery, Cincinnati, 1987, Whitney Mus. of Am. Art, Philip Morris, N.Y., 1987, Santa Barbara Mus. of Art, Calif., 1988, The Nat. Mus. of Modern Art, Kyoto, 1990, The BMW Gallery, N.Y.C., 1990, New Orleans Mus. of Art, 1990, The Carnegie Mus. of Art, Pitts., 1991, Hayward Gallery, South Bank Centre, London, 1992, Stux Gallery, N.Y.C., 1992, Whitney Mus. of Am. Art at Equitable Ctr., N.Y., 1991, The Mus. of Modern Art, N.Y.C., 1993, Cleve. Ctr. for Contemporary Art, 1994, The Art Inst. of Chgo., 1995, others. Commissioned projects Mess Hall, Headlands Ctr. for the Arts, Sausalito, Calif., 1989-90, San Francisco Pub. Libr. Commn., The Arts Commn. of San Francisco, 1990-93; contbr. articles to profl. jours. Recipient Bessie award N.Y. Ann. award in the performing arts, creator category, 1988, Guggenheim Meml. Fellowship, 1989, Louis Comfort Tiffany Found. award, 1990, CAA Artist award, 1992, Skowhegan medal for Sculpture, 1992, NEA Visual Arts Fellowship, 1993, MacArthur Fellowship, 1993.

HAMILTON, ANTONIA WALLACE, foundation administrator; b. Phila., July 12, 1940; d. James Magee and Christine Ann (Klesius) Wallace; children: Jennifer W., Colin J. AB, Smith Coll., 1962; MA, U. VA., 1968; MLS, U. Mich., 1971. Program dir. mus. of art U. Iowa, Iowa City, 1975-77; pres. Back Room Graphics, Iowa City, 1977-79; dir. pub rels. Hansen Lind Meyer, Iowa City, 1982-86; corp. devel. dir. U. Iowa Found., Iowa City, 1987-91; dir. corp. and found. devel. Swarthmore Coll., 1991—92; dir. devel. Chester County Hst. Soc., 1992—98; exec. dir. Creative Artists Network, 1998—2002; dir. devel. Fleisher Art Meml., Phila., 2002—. Mem. Bd. Realtors, Ann Arbor, Mich. 1974; bd. dirs. Chester County Estate Planning Coun. 1994-98, Chester County Tourist Bur. 1995-97, Domestic Violence Ctr. of West Chester, 1996-98. Editor: Bonding, 1983, Parent-Infant Bonding, 1981, "Small Pleasures", 1980. Contbr. articles to profl. jours. Mem. Friends Devel. Coun., Mus. of Arts, Iowa City, 1985-87, Friends of Univ. Libr., Iowa City, 1979-84, Resources Conservation Commn., Iowa City, 1980-83, Airport Commn., Iowa City, 1990-91; dir. devel. Fleisher Art Meml., 2002—. Mem. AIA, Soc. Mktg. Profl. Svcs. (Ann. Design award, Washington, 1985, jury), Iowa City C. of C. (bd. dirs. 1989-91), Phi Beta Kappa, Beta Phi Mu. Avocations: reading, cooking, traveling. Home: 2206 Locust St Philadelphia PA 19103-5511 Office: Fleisher Art Meml 719 Catharine St Philadelphia PA 19147

HAMILTON, BOBBY, professional race car driver; b. Nashville, May 29, 1957; m. Debbie Hamilton; 1 child, Bobby Jr. Recipient NASCAR Winston Cup Series Rookie of Yr. award, 1991. Achievements include former Nashville Speedway track champion; NASCAR Winston Cup Series debut 1991; winner Dura-Lube 5000, Phoenix, 1996; 1997 season includes winner Rockingham, AC Delco 400; 1998 season includes winner Goody's 500, 2 top-5s, 8 top-10s, top 15 in points. Office: c/o Morgan-McClure Motorsports 26502 Newbanks Rd Abingdon VA 24210-7500

HAMILTON, BRUCE PETER MILBURN, endocrinologist, educator; b. Napier, New Zealand, Apr. 30, 1935; came to the U.S., 1968; s. Joseph Robert and Elizabeth Mary (Boult) H.; m. Jennifer Helen McLaren, Aug. 31, 1968; children: Simon Robert, James Peter, Matthew Joseph, Emily Jane. MBChB, Otago U., Dunedin, New Zealand, 1960. Intern, resident Wellington (New Zealand) Hosp., 1960-65; medical registrar St. Mary's Hosp., London, 1965-66; sr. med. registrar Radcliffe Infirmary, Oxford, Eng., 1966-67; postdoctoral fellow Yale U. Sch. Medicine, New Haven, Conn., 1968-71; asst. prof. sch. medicine U. Md., Balt., 1971-75, assoc. prof., 1975-84, prof., 1984—. Lt. Royal New Zealand Navy, 1955-60. Home: 4 St Johns Rd Baltimore MD 21210-2122 Office: VA Med Ctr 10 N Greene St Baltimore MD 21201-1524

HAMILTON, C. TODD, lobbyist; b. Pikeville, Ky., Jan. 19, 1975; s. Willard, Jr. and Lena Hamilton; m. Courtney Ann Blackburn, Apr. 1, 2000; 1 child, Halle R. BA, U. Ky., Lexington, 1994—97. Exec. dir. Holy Order of the Fellow Soldiers of Jacques DeMoly, Lexington, Ky., 1992—97; asst. dir., gov. & industry affairs Host Comm., Nat. Tour Assoc., Lexington, Ky., 1999—. Dir. Hamilton Properties, Adkins Properties, Pikeville, Ky., 1993—. Pres. U. Ky. Democrats, Lexington, 1995—97. Mem.: Pub. Affairs Coun., Jefferson Club, Lafayette Club, Soc. of Freemasonry. Protestant. Avocations: travel, history, politics. Office: Host Comms 546 E Main St Lexington KY 40504 Office Fax: 859-226-4263. Personal E-mail: chtoha@hotmail.com.

HAMILTON, CARL HULET, retired academic administrator; b. Morris, Okla., Sept. 30, 1934; s. Alva H. and Olah E. (Pryor) H.; m. Gloria Joyce Gore, Sept. 3, 1954; children: Ray, Carla Jo, Deanna Jean. ThB, Southwestern Coll., 1956; BA, Oklahoma City U., 1957; MA, U. Tulsa, 1962; PhD, U. Ark., 1968. English tchr. Southwestern Coll., Oklahoma City, 1957-60; editor Oral Roberts Evangelistic Assn., Tulsa, 1960-62; English tchr., editor Oral Roberts U., Tulsa, 1966-68; acad. dean, 1968-75; provost Oral Roberts U., Tulsa, 1975-84; adminstr. World Evangelism, San Diego, 1984-86; chief of staff Feed the Children, Oklahoma City, 1986-88; provost, chief acad. officer Oral Roberts U., 1989-98; ret., 2001. Min. of adminstrn. First United Meth. Ch., 1999-2001. Republican. Methodist. Avocations: fishing, water sports, motorcycling. Home: PO Box 488 Disney OK 74340-0488 E-mail: piscatore@brightok.net.

HAMILTON, CARLOS ROBERT, JR., internist, educator, university official; b. Houston, June 12, 1939; s. Carlos Robert and Berta (Denman) H.; m. Carolyn Burton, Aug. 12, 1961; children: Carlos R. III, Patricia Frances. BA, U. Tex., 1961; MS, MD with honors, Baylor Coll. Medicine, 1966. Diplomate Am. Bd. Internal Medicine, Am. Bd. Endocrinology and Metabolic Diseases. Intern in internal medicine Johns Hopkins Hosp., Balt., 1966-67, asst. resident in internal medicine, 1967-69, chief resident in medicine, 1970-71; clin. and rsch. fellow Harvard Med. Sch./Mass. Gen. Hosp., Boston, 1969-70; asst. prof. medicine Johns Hopkins U. and Hosp., Balt., 1971-72; staff endocrinologist Wilford Hall USAF Med. Ctr., San Antonio, 1972-74; clin. prof. medicine Baylor Coll. Medicine, Houston, 1974—; clin. prof. medicine Med. Sch. U. Tex., Houston, 1999-2000, prof. internal medicine, 2000—, exec. v.p. for clin. affairs Health Sci. Ctr., 2002—. Cons. endocrinology and internal medicine Med. Clinic of Houston, L.L.P., 1974—2000; med. advisor employee benefit com. Southwestern Bell Tel. Co., 1975—93; attending physician in endocrinology Ben Taub Gen. Hosp./Baylor Coll. Medicine, 1980—; attending physician, mem. active staff The Meth. Hosp./Meml.-Hermann Hosp., Houston, 1974—; mem. active staff St. Luke's Episcopal Hosp., 2000—, Meml. Hermann Hosp., 2000—; practicing physicians adv. coun. U.S. Dept. Health and Human Svcs., 2003—. Contbr. articles to profl. jours. Dist. and coun. chair, area pres., regional bd. dirs., v.p. Boy Scouts Am., Houston, Atlanta, Irving, Tex., 1980—; bd. regents Tex. Woman's U., 1999-2001. Recipient Dist. award of merit, Silver Beaver award, Silver Antelope award, Disting. Eagle Scout award, Silver Buffalo award Boy Scouts Am., 1982-99. Fellow ACP (bd. dirs. Tex. chpt., Mead-Johnson Residency scholar 1970, bd. dirs. Tex. Acad. Internal Medicine and ACP-ASIM health and pub. policy com.), Am. Coll. Endocrinology (trustee 1999-2000, sec.-treas. 2001-02); mem. SAR (bd. dirs. Paul Carrington chpt. 1992—, pres. 1993), Am. Soc. Internal Medicine (bd. dirs. polit. action com. 1995-98. Key Congl. Contact of Yr. 1996), Am. Assn. Clin. Endocrinologists (bd. dirs. 1995—, chair legis. and regulatory com. 1998-2000, sec. exec. com. 2000-01, treas. 2001-02, v.p. 2002-2003, pres.-elect 2003—), Tex. Med. Assn. (exec. com. polit. action com. 1989-01, chair 1995, 96), Harris County Med. Soc. (bd. dirs. 1992-99, pres.-elect 1998, pres. 1999), Kiwanis (bd. dirs. Houston chpt. 1986-95, pres. 1995), Alpha Omega Alpha, Sigma Xi. Office: U Tex Health Sci Ctr 7000 Fannin Rm 1535 Houston TX 77030 E-mail: carlos.r.hamilton@uth.tmc.edu.

HAMILTON, CAROL JEAN, retired English educator, writer, storyteller; b. Enid, Okla., Aug. 23, 1935; d. Clarence DeWitt and Ruby Raye (Settles) Barber; m. Joseph Jefferson Hamilton, Aug. 25, 1956 (div. May 1994); children: Debra Susan Hamilton Havenar, Christopher David, Stephen Anthony. BS, Phillips U., 1957; MA, U. Ctrl. Okla., 1978. Tchr. North Haven (Conn.) Schs., 1956-59, Indpls. Pub. Schs., 1970-71, Tinker Elem., Midwest-Del City Schs., Tinker AFB, Okla., 1971-82, Acad. Ctr. for Enrichment, Midwest City, Okla., 1982-93; Spanish tutor, tchr. Mid-Del Schs., Midwest City, 1985-88; instr. English and Spanish, Rose State Coll., Midwest City, 1988-98; prof. creative studies divsn. U. Ctrl. Okla., Edmond, 1996—2001. Artist-in-residence Contemporary Arts Found., Oklahoma City, 1971-79; instr. Okla. Quartz Mountain Arts Inst., 1993; instr., spkr. Okla. Writing Project, 1993, 2000; chmn. tchr. rights Mid-Del Schs., 1980-83; bd. dirs. Friends of Okla. Ctr. for the Book; chair Favorite Poems project Oklahoma City Arts Festival. Author: (children's novels) The Dawn Seekers, 1987 (S.W. Book award 1988), Mystery of Black Mesa, 1995 (Cherubim award 1995), (poetry) Once the Dust, 1992 (Okla. Book award 1992, Pegasus award), Daring the Wind, 1987, Legends of Poland, 1992, Legerdemain, 2000, (poetry) Breaking Bread, Breaking Silsnce, 2000 (Chiron Rev. Chapbook award 2000), Gold, Greatest Hits, I, People of the Llano, 2000. Bd. dirs. Okla. Friends Ctr. for the Book, 2001—. Recipient Byline lit. award Byline

mag., 1987-92, David Ray Poetry award Potpourri Mag., 2000, Walter Keith Wright award Green's mag., 2002; named Poet Laureate of Okla., 1995. Mem. Soc. Children's Book Writers, Acad. Am. Poetry, Am. Astron. League, Poetry Soc. Okla. (past pres., other offices), Mid-Okla. Writers (past pres.), Individual Artists Okla. (sec. bd. dirs. 1978-2002), Creative Writers Inst., Sierra Club. Democrat. Mem. Christian Ch. (Disciples Of Christ). Avocations: interpreting, storytelling. Home: 9608 Sonata Ct Midwest City OK 73130-6416 E-mail: hamiltoncj@earthlink.net.

HAMILTON, CHARLES HOWARD, metallurgy educator; b. Pueblo, Colo., Mar. 17, 1935; s. George Edwin and Eva Eleanor (Watson) H.; m. Joy Edith Richmond, Sept. 7, 1968; children: Curtis Gene, Krista Kathleen, Brady Glenn. BS, Colo. Sch. Mines, 1959; MS, U. So. Calif., 1965; PhD, Case Western Res. U., 1968. Research engr. Space div. Rockwell Internat., Downey, Calif., 1959-65, mem. tech. staff Los Angeles div., 1968-75; tech. staff, phys. metallurgy Sci. Ctr., Thousand Oaks, Calif., 1975-77, group mgr. metals processing, 1977-79, prin. scientist, 1979-81, dir. materials synthesis and processing dept., 1982-84; assoc. prof. metallurgy Wash. State U., Pullman, 1984-87, prof., 1987-2000, prof. emeritus, 2000—. Chmn. Rockwell Corp. tech. panel, materials research and engring; co-organizer 1st Internat. Symposium Superplastic Forming, 1982, Internat. Conf. on Superplasticity and Superplastic Forming, 1988. Sr. editor Jour. Materials Shaping Tech.; dep. editor Scripta Metallurgica et Materialia, 1989-94; contbr. tech. articles to profl. publs.; patentee advanced metalworking and tech. Bd. dirs. Snowdon Wildlife Sanctuary. Named Rockwell Engr. of Yr., 1979; recipient IR 100 award Indsl. Research mag., 1976, 80. Fellow Am. Soc. Metals; mem. AIME (shaping and forming com.), Sigma Xi. Home: PO Box 2064 Mc Call ID 83638

HAMILTON, CLYDE HENRY, judge; b. Edgefield, S.C., Feb. 8, 1934; s. Clyde H. and Edwina (Odom) Hamilton; children: John C., James W. BS, Wofford Coll., 1956; JD with honors, George Washington U., 1961. Bar: S.C. 1961. Reference asst. U.S. Senate Libr., Washington, 1958—61; Assoc. J.R. Folk, Edgefield, 1961—63; assoc., gen. ptnr. Butler, Means, Evins & Browne, Spartanburg, SC, 1963—81; judge U.S. Dist. Ct. S.C., Columbia, 1981—91, U.S. Ct. Appeals (4th cir.), Richmond, Va., 1991—. Gen. counsel Synalloy Corp., Spartanburg, 1969—80. Mem. editl. staff: Cumulative Index of Congl. Com. Hearings, 1935—58, bd. editors: George Washington Law Rev., 1959—60. Pres. Spartanburg County Arts Coun., 1971—73, Spartanburg Day Sch., 1972—74, sustaining trustee, 1975—81; past mem. steering com. undergrad. merit fellowship program and estate planning coun. Converse Coll., Spartanburg; trustee Spartanburg Meth. Coll., 1979—84; mem. S.C. Supreme Ct. Bd. Commrs. on Grievances and Discipline, 1980—81; del. Spartanburg County, 4th Congl. Dist. and S.C. Rep. Convs., 1976, 1980; mem., past chmn. fin. com. and adminstrv. bd. Trinity United Meth. Ch., Spartanburg, trustee, 1980—83. Capt. USAR, 1956—62. Recipient Alumni Disting. Svc. award, Wofford Coll., 1991, The Order of The Palmetto, Gov. Beasley, S.C., 1999. Mem.: S.C. Bar Assn., Piedmont Club (bd. govs. 1979—81). Office: US Ct Appeals 4th Cir 1901 Main St Columbia SC 29201-2443

HAMILTON, DAGMAR STRANDBERG, lawyer, educator; b. Phila., Jan. 10, 1932; d. Eric Wilhelm and Anna Elizabeth (Sjöström) Strandberg; m. Robert W. Hamilton, June 26, 1953; children: Eric Clark, Robert Andrew Hale, Meredith Hope. AB, Swarthmore Coll., 1953; JD, U. Chgo. Law Sch., 1956, Am. U., 1961. Bar: Tex. 1972. Atty. civil rights divsn. U.S. Dept Justice, Washington, 1965-66; asst. instr. govt. U. Tex., Austin, 1966-71; lectr. Law Sch. U. Ariz., Tucson, 1971-72; editor, rschr. Assoc. William O. Douglas U.S. Supreme Ct., Washington, 1962-73, 75-76; editor, rschr. Douglas autobiography Random House Co., 1972-73; staff counsel Judiciary Com. U.S. Ho. of Reps., 1973-74; asst. prof. L.B. Johnson Sch. Pub. Affairs U. Tex., Austin, 1974-77, assoc. prof., 1977-83, prof., 1983—, assoc. dean., 1983-87. Interdisciplinary prof. U. Tex. Law Sch., 1983—; vis. prof. Washington U. Law Sch., St. Louis, 1982, U. Maine, Portland, 1992; Godfrey Disting. vis. prof. U. Maine Law Sch., 2002; vis. fellow U. London, QMW Sch. Law, 1987—88; vis. prof. U. Maine, Portland, 2002; vis. fellow U. Oxford Inst. European & Comparative Law, 1998. Contbr. to various publs. Mem. Tex. State Bar Assn., Am. Law Inst., Assn. Pub. Policy Analysis and Mgmt., Swarthmore Coll. Alumni Coun. (rep.), Kappa Beta Phi (hon.), Phi Kappa Phi (hon.). Democrat. Mem. Soc. Of Friends. Home: 403 Allegro Ln Austin TX 78746-4301 Office: U Tex LBJ Sch Pub Affairs Austin TX 78713 E-mail: dagmar.hamilton@mail.utexas.edu.

HAMILTON, DANIEL STEPHEN, clergyman; b. Cedarhurst, N.Y., Jan. 7, 1932; s. Richard Samuel and Catherine Mary (Liston) H. BA, Cathedral Coll., 1954; S.T.B., Cath. U. Am., 1958; PhD, Greenwich U., 1991. Ordained priest Roman Catholic Ch., 1958; asst. pastor St. Anne's Ch., Garden City, N.Y., 1958-61; campus chaplain Adelphi U., Garden City, 1959-61; prof. St. Pius X Preparatory Sem., Uniondale, N.Y., 1961-68; campus chaplain Hofstra U., Hempstead, N.Y., 1961-66; columnist L.I. Catholic, Hempstead, 1962-85, editor, 1975-85; dir. Bur. Public Info., Diocese Rockville Centre, 1968-85; chmn. Ecumenical Commn., 1968-88; resident priest St. William the Abbot Parish, Seaford, N.Y., 1971-85; pastor Our Lady of Perpetual Help Parish, Lindenhurst, N.Y., 1985—. Named hon. papal prelate, 1980 Mem. Cath. Theol. Soc. Am., Fellowship Cath. Scholars. Home and Office: 210 S Wellwood Ave Lindenhurst NY 11757-4927

HAMILTON, DAVID F. judge; b. 1957; BA magna cum laude, Haverford Coll., 1979; JD, Yale U., 1983. Law clk. to Hon. Richard D. Cudahy U.S. Ct. Appeals (7th cir.), 1983-84; atty. Barnes & Thornburg, Indpls., 1984-88, 91-94; judge U.S. Dist. Ct. (so. dist.) Ind., Indpls., 1994—. Counsel to Gov. of Ind., 1989-91; chair Ind. State Ethics Commn., 1991-94. V.p. for litigation, bd. dirs. Ind. Civil Liberties Union, 1987-88. Fulbright scholar, 1979-80; recipient Sagamore of the Wabash, Gov. Evan Bayh, 1991. Mem.: Am. Inns. of Ct. (Sagamore chpt., pres. 2001—, criminal law com. jud. conf. 2000—). Office: US Dist Ct So Dist Ind 46 E Ohio St Rm 330 Indianapolis IN 46204-1921

HAMILTON, DAVID JOHN, information technology administrator; b. Bryn Mawr, Pa., Apr. 28, 1956; s. John A. and Eleanor N. H; m. Janet Ellen Gardner, Aug. 3, 1986; children: Sara Ashley, Sean Christopher. BME, U. Del., 1978; MBA, Widener U., Chester, Pa., 1981. Registered profl. engr., Del.; cert. in prodn. and inventory mgmt., cert. computer systems integrator. Prodn. engr. Stuart Pharms., Wilmington, Del., 1978-79, planning asst., 1979, planner, scheduler Newark, 1979-80, supr. inventory and materials control, 1980-83, plant systems coord., 1983-84; prodn. systems adminstr. ICI Pharms., Wilmington, 1984-85, materials mgr. Pasadena, Calif., 1985-88; mgr. bus. planning ICI Films, Wilmington, 1988-93; mgr. bus. reengineering ZENECA Inc., Wilmington, 1993-95; mgr. supply chain reengring. ICI Explosives, Inc., Dallas, 1995-96; bus. sys./tech. mgr. ICI Acrylics, Inc., Memphis, 1996-99; info. tech. dir. Ineos Acrylics, Inc., Memphis, 1999—2002, Lucite Internat., Inc., 2002—. Assoc. prof. Widener U., Chester, 1983-97; MRP II project leader Stuart Pharms., Wilmington, 1983-85. Author: Cycle Counting: An Approach to Inventory Record Accuracy, 1981; contbr. articles to profl. jours. Mem. Rep. Nat. Com., 1977-81; v.p. Woodside Pines, Arcadia, Calif., 1985-88. Mem. Am. Prodn. and Inventory Control Soc. (v.p. bd. dirs. 1984-85, 89—, instr., 1988, 89), Nat. Soc. Profl. Engrs., Inst. Indsl. Engrs., Am. Soc. Quality Control, Am. Assn. Artificial Intelligence, Del. Assn. Profl. Engrs., Coun. Logistics Mgmt. Republican. Lutheran. Home: 9879 Frank Rd Germantown TN 38139-8000 Office: The Lucite Ctr 7275 Goodlett Farms Pkwy Cordova TN 38016-4909

HAMILTON, DAVID LEE, sports association administrator, conservationist; b. Pitts., Mar. 26, 1937; s. James Arthur and Margaret (Kennett) H.; m. Molly Anne Wolford, June 27, 1959; children: David Scott, Bryan Lee, Timothy Drew. BSChemE, Bucknell U., 1957; MBA, U. Pitts., 1965. Various positions Exxon Co., USA, 1957-79; exec. asst. to pres. Exxon Corp., N.Y.C., 1979-80, dep. mgr. dept. petroleum products, 1983-85; v.p. supply and transp. Exxon Internat. Co., N.Y.C., 1980-82, sr. v.p., 1982-83; v.p. Esso Europe, London, 1985-86; v.p. mktg. Exxon Co., Internat., Florham Park, N.J., 1986-88; exec. v.p. OHM Corp., Findlay, Ohio, 1989-92; exec. dir., COO U.S. Tennis Assn., 2003—. Trustee Bucknell U., Lewisburg, Pa., 1984—, chair long-range planning com., 1997—2001, chair Presdl. Search com., 1999, chmn. bd. trustees, 2001—03; pres. Dallas Tennis Assn., 1994—97; treas. Tex. sect. U.S. Tennis Assn., 1997—99, pres., 1999—2000, chair comm. mktg. coun., 1999—2002, chmn. strategic planning com., 2003; bd. dirs. The Std. Steamship P&I Club, Bermuda, 1982—85, Concord Resource Group, Lawrenceville, NJ, 1989—91. Mem.: Canyon Creek Country Club (Dallas), TBarM Racquet Club (Dallas), Omicron Delta Kappa, Beta Gamma Sigma, Sigma Chi (Significant Sig award 1985). Avocations: grandparenting, tennis, travel, reading. Home: 12115 Elysian Ct Dallas TX 75230-2221 E-mail: kelcarchas@aol.com.

HAMILTON, DAVID MIKE, publishing company executive; b. Little Rock, 1951; s. Ralph F. and Mickey G. Hamilton; m. Carol N. McKenna, Oct. 25, 1975; children: Elisabeth M., Caroline E. BA, Pitzer Coll., 1973; MLS, UCLA, 1976. Cert. tchr. library sci., Calif. Editor Sullivan Assocs., Palo Alto, Calif., 1973-75; curator Henry E. Huntington Library, San Marino, Calif., 1976-80; mgr. prodn., mktg. William Kaufmann Pubs., Los Altos, Calif., 1980-84; pres. The Live Oak Press, LLC, Palo Alto, 1984—. Cons. editor, gen. ptnr. Sensitive Expressions Pub. Co., Palo Alto, 1985-98; consulting dir. AAAI Press, 1994—; mng. editor and pub. AI Mag. Author: To the Yukon with Jack London, 1980, The Tools of My Trade, 1986, Making A Digital Book, 1994; contbg. editor and webmaster AAAI world-wide web site, 1995—; contbg. author Small Press jour., 1986, Making a Digital Book, 1995, (books) Book Club of California Quarterly, 1985, Research Guide to Biography and Criticism, 1986. Sec. vestry Trinity Parish, Menlo Park, 1986, bd. dirs., 1985-87; trustee Jack London Ednl. Found., San Francisco; bd. dirs. ISYS Forum, Palo Alto, 1987-96; pres. site coun., mem. supt.'s adv. com. Palo Alto Unified Sch. Dist.; mem. Wellesley Coll. Parent's Coun., 1997—. Mem. ALA, Coun. on Scholarly, Med. and Ednl. Publs., Am. Assn. Artificial Intelligence (bd. dirs., dir. publs.), Authors Guild, Bookbuilders West (book show com. 1983), Author's Guild, Soc. Tech. Comm. (judge 1984), Assn. Computing Machinery (chmn. pub. com. 1984), Soc. Scholarly Pubs. (program com. 1999), Save the Redwoods League (life), Sierra Club (life), Commonwealth Club, Book Club Calif. Democrat. Episcopalian. Avocations: backpacking, camping, hiking, book collecting. Office: The Live Oak Press LLC PO Box 60036 Palo Alto CA 94306-0036

HAMILTON, DIANE BRONKEMA, nursing educator; b. Fulton, Ill., Sept. 24, 1946; d. Peter and Blanche (Hoogheem) Bronkema. Diploma, Northwestern U. Sch. Nursing, 1967; BSN, West Tex. State U., 1978; MA, U. Iowa, 1980; PhD, U. Va., 1987. RN. Instr. Mt. Mercy Coll., Cedar Rapids, Iowa, 1980-82; asst. prof. nursing U. Va., Charlottesville, 1985-87, Med. U. S.C., Charleston, 1988-92, U. Rochester, N.Y., 1992-94; prof. Western Mich. U., 1994—. Cons. in field. Author: Pharmacology in Nursing, 1998, 6th edit., 2003, Becoming a Presence in Nursing: The History of the University of Colorado 1898-1998, 1999, Visions of Partnership: A History of Midwest Nursing 1979-99, 2000; editl. bd. mem. Nursing History Review, 1991-2003, book rev. editor; image editor: Mind, Voice, Spirit, 1997; contbr. articles to profl. jours. Bd. dirs Heritage Coun., Cedar Rapids, 1980-82. Capt. USAF, 1970-75. Fellow U. Pa. 1991, Lillian Brunner post doc fellowship, 1992; grantee DuPont scholar, 1984, NIH, 1982; recipient Lavinia Dock award for hist. scholarship, 1991, Nat. Rsch. Svc. award NIH, 1983, Best of Image award, 1993, 97. Mem. ANA, Am. Assn. History Medicine, Am. Assn. History Nursing (bd. dirs. 1991-95), Women's Club, Sigma Theta Tau Internat. (heritage com.), Phi Kappa Phi. Avocation: gardening. Home: 2370 Mansfield St Kalamazoo MI 49009-1800 Office: Western Mich U Sch of Nursing Kalamazoo MI 49008

HAMILTON, DONALD DOW WEBB, publisher, freelance writer; b. Akron, Ohio, Feb. 6, 1940; s. Charles Bartow Webb and Grace Virginia (Crummet) H. Student, Kent State U., 1958—60; student of Lee Wyndham, NYU, 1961; diploma, U.S. Army Sch. of Info., Ft. Slocum, N.Y., 1963, U.S. Army Psywar Sch., Ft. Bragg, N.C., 1963. Asst. fashion editor N.Y. Times, N.Y.C., 1961; asst. prodn. mgr. Coll. Books, N.Y.C., 1961; pub. rels. mgr. Akron (Ohio) Goodwill Industry, 1971-73; pres. Akron Manuscript Club, Akron, 1980-82; freelance writer, 1959—; editor news report Two Edged Sword, 1986—2002; editor news svc. Rock Update, 1988—2002; editor news jour. Editor's Jour., 1990—2002. Key contbr. Messenger, 1995-2002. Mem. Presdl. Task Force, Washington, 1988—; judge adjutent VFW-Cuyahoga Falls, Ohio, 1990. With U.S. Army, 1962-65. Recipient Cert. of merit Broadcasting & Visual Activities, 1965, Congl. Order of Liberty, Washington, 1993. Mem. VFW. Avocations: speaking, music, walking. Home: 327 Portage Trl Cuyahoga Falls OH 44221-3233

HAMILTON, DOUGLAS WARREN, real estate executive; b. Sacramento, Calif., Feb. 21, 1947; s. Albert James and Maxene Ruth (Gergens) H.; m. Sara Binder, Jan. 19, 1992; children: Ethan A.S.W., Antonia K.R.R. BA in Math., U. Nebr., 1972; MBA, U. Pa., 1977. Asst. v.p. DLJ, N.Y.C., 1977-79; mng. dir. Merrill Lynch & Co., N.Y.C., 1979-93; CEO, chmn. Barker & Little, Inc., Rapid City, S.D., 1993—. With USMC, 1966-69. Office: 816 Saint Joseph St PO Box 2800 Rapid City SD 57709-2800

HAMILTON, ELWIN LOMAX, lawyer; b. Lubbock, Tex. Mar. 18, 1934; s. Elwin Louis and Mildred (Hunt) H.; children: Lauren, Karen. A.S., Arlington State Coll., 1954; B.A., North Tex. State Coll., 1956; LL.B., U. Tex., Austin, 1959. Bar: Tex. 1959, U.S. Dist. Ct. (no. dist.) Tex. 1961, U.S. Dist. Ct. (we. dist.) Tex. 1972, U.S. Ct. Claims 1972, U.S. Ct. Appeals (5th cir.) 1961. Atty. Humble Oil Co., Corpus Christi, Tex., 1959-60; mem. firm Morton & Brownfield, Tex., 1960-66; mcpl. judge, Morton, Tex., 1960-61; county dist. atty., Terry County, 1963-66; asst. exec. dir. State Bar Tex., 1966-69; asst. atty. gen., State of Tex., 1969-73; atty. Tex. Securities Bd., Austin, 1973-74; asst. gen. counsel to Gov. of Tex., Austin, 1974-82; ptnr. Senterfitt & Childress, Hamilton & Shook, San Saba, Tex., 1982-86, law practice, R. Mayo Davidson, San Saba Legal Services, 1987—; instr. Legal Asst. Studies, Austin Community Coll. Office: San Saba Legal Svcs PO Box 547 San Saba TX 76877-0547

HAMILTON, FRANK STRAWN, jazz musician, folksinger, composer and arranger, educator; b. N.Y.C., Aug. 3, 1934; s. Frank Strawn and Gladys (Bley) Hamilton; m. Sheila Lofton, Nov. 7, 1957 (div. Nov. 1971); children: Cameron Auguste (dec. 1998), Evan Baird, Liam Christopher (dec. Oct. 2001), Heather Alexa; m. Deeanne Lee Walter, May 5, 1972 (div. Oct. 1980); m. Mary Doyle, Jan. 15, 1983. Student, Los Angeles City Coll., 1952-53, Chgo. Mus. Coll., 1959-62, L.A. Valley Coll., 1963-64. Organizer, head teaching staff, v.p., co-founder Old Town Sch. Folk Music, Chgo., 1957-62; ho. musician Gate of Horn, Chgo., 1959-61; mem. The Weavers, 1962-63. Founder The Hot Club of Atlanta, 1995. Appeared Asheville (N.C.) Folk Festival, 1953, Newport Folk Festival, 1959; motion picture appearance in Subterraneans, 1958; performed with duo Meridian for spl. children's programs Young Audiences in Atlanta Pub. Sch. System, 1987-2003, with wife Mary; rec. artist Folkways, Vanguard records, Long Lonesome Home, ITR records; devel. method annotation folk guitar and 5 string banjo; film score: A Time Out of War, 1952; TV score: Survival; folk singer with wife Mary, The Hamiltons. Mem. Irish Arts Atlanta. Mem. ACLU, Fellowship of Reconciliation, UN Assn., Dramatist Guild, Chgo. Hist. Soc. (hon.), Tai Chi Health and Rsch. Assn. Home: 852 Cinderella Ct Decatur GA 30033-5812 E-mail: hamprod@mindspring.com.

HAMILTON, GEORGE HENRY, JR., energy consultant; b. Gary, Ind., Apr. 7, 1939; s. George Henry and Tina Lauree (Magee) H. BS in Geology, George Washington U., 1968. Dir., Andean Found., Washington, 1970-72; mem. profl. staff Gen. Electric Co., Washington, 1972-73; pres. Solar Energy Co., Washington, 1973-77; prin. devel. mgr. Pullman Corp., Houston, 1977-78; gen. mgr. no. hemisphere ops. Solar Energy Co., Washington; cons. in energy policy devel. and advanced energy systems, 1978—2003; cons. geologist Hamilton Exploration, Virginia Beach, Va., 2003—. Contbr. articles to profl. jours. Served with U.S. Army, 1962-65. Mem. Am. Assn. Petroleum Geologists, Am. Geol. Soc., AAAS, Biometrics Soc. Clubs: Nat. Aviation (Washington). Patentee solar energy heating module, power generating array. Home: PO Box 5381 Virginia Beach VA 23471-0381

HAMILTON, GILLIAN, geriatrician; b. N.Y.C., Feb. 23, 1946; PhD, U. Fla., 1971; MD, U. Ariz., 1981. Diplomat Am. Bd. Internal Medicine, Am. Bd. Geriat., Am. Bd. Hospice and Palliative Medicine. Intern/resident U. Ariz. Health Sci. Ctr., Tucson, 1981-83; fellowship Long Island Jewish Hosp., NY, 1983-85; assoc. med. dir. Maricopa County Long Term Care, 1986-92; adminstrv. med. dir. Hospice of the Valley, 1996—; dir. geriat. Samaritan Geriatric Ctr., 1992—2002. Recipient Geriatrician of Yr. Am. Geriatric Soc., 1999; named Best Doctor of Am. Best Doctors, 1999—, Best Doctors of Phoenix, Phoenix mag., 1996—. Office: Hospice of the Valley 1510 E Flower Phoenix AZ 85014

HAMILTON, HARRY LEMUEL, JR., educator; b. Charleston, S.C., May 26, 1938; s. Harry Lemuel and Velma Fern (Bell) H.; m. LaVerne McDaniel, June 26, 1965 (div. 1978); children: David M., Lisa L.; m. Mary MacIntyre, May 10, 1997. BA in Physics, Beloit Coll., 1960; MS in Meteorology, U. Wis., 1962, PhD in Meteorology, 1965. Asst. prof. atmospheric sci. SUNY, Albany, 1965-71, assoc. prof., 1971-90, dir. ednl. opportunity program, 1968-71, chairperson atmospheric sci., 1976-83, dean undergrad. studies, assoc. v.p. acad. affairs, 1983-88; rsch. scientist GE, Schenectady, N.Y., 1973-75; sr. v.p., provost Chapman U., Orange, Calif., 1990-2000, prof. atmospheric sci., 2000—. Trustee Beloit (Wis.) Coll., 1972—, Newport Beach Pub. Libr., 2001—, pres., 2003–; bd. dirs. Albany Med. Ctr., 1988-90, Mohawk Hudson Cmty. Found., 1988-90; pres. Empire State Inst. for Performing Arts, Albany, 1986-90; bd. dirs. world affairs coun. Orange County, 1995-2003; treas. Arts Orange County, 1995-2000; bd. dirs. Discovery Sci. Ctr., 1998–. Mem. Am. Meteorol. Soc., Am. Assn. for Higher Edn. Office: Chapman U 1 University Dr Orange CA 92866-1005 E-mail: hamilton@chapman.edu.

HAMILTON, J. LEONARD, collegiate basketball coach, former professional basketball coach; b. Gastonia, N.C., Aug. 4, 1948; m. Claudette Hale; children: Lenny, Allison. Student, Gaston (N.C.) C.C.; BS in Phys. Edn., U. Tenn., Martin, 1971; MA in Phys. and Health Edn., Austin Peay State U., 1973. Asst. coach Austin Peay State U., 1972-74, U. Ky., 1974-80, assoc. head coach, 1980-86; head coach Okla. State U. Cowboys, 1986-90, reached Big 8 Tournament, advanced to 2d round of Nat. Invitation Tournament, 1988-89, 89-90; head coach U. Miami Hurricanes, Fla., 1990-2000; played NCAA Tournament, 1998; ranked 12th in NCAA, 1998-99; head coach Washington Wizards NBA, 2000—01, Florida State U., 2002—. Charter mem. Hall of Fame, U. Tenn., Martin, 1983; named. Big East COnf. Coach of Yr., 1995, UPI Nat. Coach of Yr., 1995. Mailing: Florida State University Men's Basketball Florida State University Tallahassee FL 32306

HAMILTON, JACKSON DOUGLAS, lawyer; b. Cleve., Feb. 5, 1949; m. Margaret Lawrence Williams, Dec. 19, 1971; children: Jackson Douglas Jr., William Schuyler Lawrence. BA, Colgate U., 1971; JD, U. Pa., 1974. Bar: Calif. 1974, U.S. Dist. Ct. (cen. dist.) Calif. 1974, U.S. Tax Ct. 1978, U.S. Ct. Claims 1984, U.S. Ct. Appeals (6th and 11th cirs.) 1988, N.C. 1991, U.S. Supreme Ct. 1991. Ptnr. Kadison, Pfaelzer, Woodard, Quinn & Rossi, L.A., 1986-87, Spensley, Horn, Jubas & Lubitz, L.A., 1987-91, Roberts & Stevens, Asheville, N.C., 1991—. Adj. prof. law U. San Diego, 1981, Golden Gate U., San Francisco, 1981-85, U. N.C., Asheville, 1994; cons. Calif. Continuing Edn. Bar, 1983-84, select com. on sports Calif. Senate, 1983-85. Editor Entertainment Law Reporter, 1979—; contbr. articles to profl. jours. Mem. ABA (tax sect., internat. law sect.), N.C. Bar Assn. (tax. sect. coun.). Republican. Episcopalian. Office: Roberts & Stevens BB & T Bldg Asheville NC 28802

HAMILTON, JACQUELINE, art consultant; b. Tulsa, Mar. 28, 1942; d. James Merton and Nina Faye (Andrews) H.; m. Richard Sanford Piper, Jan. 2, 1968 (div. June 1976). BA, Tex. Christian U., 1965; grad., Stockholm U., 1967; postgrad., Harvard U., 1972-73, Tufts U., 1971, Rice U., 1982-83, Houston C.C., 1986-87. Art cons. for corps., pvt. collectors and mus., Houston, 1979—. Expert witness in lawsuits regarding art. Contbr. articles to profl. pubs. Bd. dirs. Opera in the Heights. Mem.: AIA (affiliate), Internat. Assn. Profl. Art Advisors, Rice Design Alliance, Assn. Corp. Art Curators, French-Am. C. of C., Swedish-Am. C. of C., Norwegian-am. C. of C., Swedish Club, L'Alliance Francaise, The Forum Club, The Houstonian Club. Presbyterian. Office: PO Box 1483 Houston TX 77251-1483

HAMILTON, JAMES ARTHUR, biomedical researcher, biophysics educator; b. Lewistown, Pa., Oct. 21, 1947; s. Joseph Arthur and Margaret (Gray) H.; m. Malinda Sue McLendon, May 28, 1983; 1 child, Lianna Renee. BS in Chemistry cum laude, Juniata Coll., 1969; PhD in Chemistry, Ind. U., 1974. Rsch. chemist Eastman Kodak, Rochester, N.Y., 1969; assoc. instr. Ind. U., Bloomington, 1969-71, rsch. asst., 1971-74, asst. prof. continuing edn. chemistry, 1975, postdoctoral fellow, 1976-78; asst. rsch. prof. medicine and biochemistry Boston U. Sch. Medicine, 1978-85, assoc. rsch. prof. medicine and biochemistry, 1986-91, prof. biophysics, 1991—. Founding mem. Obesity Rsch. Ctr., Boston Med. Ctr.; founder Adipagenix Inc.; co-organizer Internat. Workshop on Brain Uptake and Utilization of Fatty Acids, 2000. Assoc. editor Lipids, 1990—, Obesity Rsch., 2002—; editl. bd. Jour. Lipid Rsch., 1995—; contbr. over 100 articles to profl. jours. Recipient Nat. Rsch. Svc. award NIH, 1976; Shared Instrument grantee, 1990, 2003, prin. investigator grantee, 1991—. Mem. Biophys. Soc., Am. Chem. Soc. Democrat. Presbyterian. Office: Boston U Sch Medicine Biophysics 80 E Concord St Roxbury MA 02118-2307

HAMILTON, JAMES DOUGLAS, economics educator; b. Denver, Colo., Nov. 29, 1954; s. Warren Bell and Alcita Victoria Hamilton; m. Marjorie Ann Flavin, Aug. 6, 1983; children: Laura Diane, Richard Gregory. BA, Colo. Coll., 1977; MA, U. Calif., Berkeley, 1981, PhD, 1983. From asst. prof. to assoc. prof. to prof. econs. U. Va., Charlottesville, 1981-92; prof. econs. U. Calif., San Diego, 1992—. Vis. prof. U. Calif., San Diego, 1984-85; rsch. advisor Fed. Res. Bank, Richmond, Va., 1989-92; rsch. assoc. Nat. Bur. Econ. Rsch. Assoc. editor Jour. Econ. Dynamics and Control, 1988-2001, Jour. Bus. and Econ. Statistics, 1991—, Econometrica, 1992-95, Rev. Econs. and Statistics, 1993-2002, Jour. Money, Credit and Banking, 1993—. Grad. fellow NSF U. Calif., 1978-81; rsch. grantee NSF, 1988—. Fellow Econometric Soc.; mem. Am. Econ. Assn. Office: U Calif San Diego Dept Econs San Diego CA 92093-0508 E-mail: jhamilton@ucsd.edu.

HAMILTON, JEAN See CHAUDOIR, JEAN

HAMILTON, JEAN CONSTANCE, judge; b. St. Louis, Nov. 12, 1945; AB, Wellesley Coll., 1968; JD, Washington U., St. Louis, 1971; LLM, Yale U., 1982. Atty. Dept. of Justice, Washington, 1971-73, asst. U.S. atty. St. Louis, 1973-78; atty. Southwestern Bell Telephone Co., St. Louis, 1978—81; judge 22d Jud. Circuit State of Mo., St. Louis, 1982-88; judge Mo. Ct. Appeals (ea. dist.), 1988-90, U.S. Dist. Ct. (ea. dist.) Mo., 1990—, chief judge, 1995—2002. Office: US Courthouse 111 S 10th St Saint Louis MO 63102

HAMILTON, JERALD, musician; b. Wichita, Kans., Mar. 19, 1927; s. Robert James and Lillie May (Rishel) H.; m. Phyllis Jean Searle, Sept. 8, 1954; children: Barbara Helen, Elizabeth Sarah, Catharine Sandra. MusB, U. Kans., Lawrence, 1948, MusM, 1950; postgrad., Royal Sch. Ch. Music, Croydon, Eng., summer 1955, Union Theol. Sem. Sch. Sacred Music, N.Y.C., summer 1960; studies with, Laurel Everette Anderson, Andre Marchal, Catharine Crozier, Gustav Leonhardt. From instr. to asst. prof. organ and theory Washburn U., Topeka, 1949-59; dir. Washburn Singers and Choir, 1955-59; asst. prof. organ, dir. univ. singers and chorus Ohio U., Athens, 1959-60; asst. prof. organ and ch. music U. Tex., Austin, 1960-63; lectr. ch. music Episcopal Theol. Sem. S.W., Austin, 1961-63; mem. faculty U. Ill., Urbana-Champaign, 1963-88, prof. music, 1967-88, prof. emeritus, 1988—; organist, choirmaster Grace Cathedral, Topeka, 1949—59, St. David's Ch., Austin, 1960—63, St. John the Divine, Champaign, 1963—88, St. John's Cathedral, Albuquerque, 1988-93, organist-choirmaster emeritus, 1994—. Mem., chmn. commn. ch. music Episc. Diocese Kans., 1951-59; mem. bishop's commn. ch. music Episc. Diocese of Springfield, 1978-80, 82-88; concert organist, 1955-96. Author (with Marilou Kratzenstein) Four Centuries of Organ Music, Detroit Studies in Music Bibliography No. 51, 1984. Fulbright scholar, 1954-55 Mem. Assn. Anglican Musicians, Omicron Delta Kappa, Pi Kappa Lambda, Phi Mu Alpha. Episcopalian. Home: PO Box 3836 Edgewood NM 87015-3836

HAMILTON, JIMMY RAY, secondary education educator; b. McDowell, Ky., Mar. 4, 1949; s. Victor and Lola (Tackett) H.; children: Victor William, Madelin Mae Reinersmann; m. Christa Karin Weinkotz, Apr. 7, 1974; children: Margaret Ann Long, Nathaniel Ray. Student, Def. Info. Sch., 1969, 70, 72; BA in English and Secondary Edn., Ariz. State U., 1987; postgrad., U. Phoenix, 1994-95, Grand Canyon Coll., 1994-95. Cert. English and secondary edn. tchr., ESL and bilingual edn. Tchr. adult based edn. Marcos DeNiza H.S., Tempe, Ariz., 1987-89; tchr. English IV Red Mesa (Ariz.) H.S., 1989-90; tchr. English and drama, drama coach Many Farms (Ariz.) H.S., 1991-96. Head coach boys' varsity basketball, 1996-98; head coach girls' volleyball Ariz. Interscholastic Assn., Phoenix, 1993—. Contbg. editor: Writing For the Workplace, 1998; pub., editor: Come On, Act Navajo, 1998. Mem. Pres. Nixon Inaugural Com.,

Washington, 1973. Recipient Dir.'s award for best play Native Am. Drama Festival, Tuba City, 1991-92, 92-93, Dir.'s award Four Corners Classic Drama and Fine Arts Festival, 1994, 95, Big Fish of Tournament award Citgo Bassmasters Western Open, 2001; named Profl. Bass Masters Fisherman, 1999—. Avocations: guitar, writing, fishing, hunting. Home: PO Box 4028 Sun Valley AZ 86029

HAMILTON, JOHN J., JR., airport executive; b. Elizabethtown, N.Y., July 1, 1940; married; 2 children. BA, St. Michael's Coll., 1961. With USN; dir. ops. Burlington (Vt.) Internat. Airport, dir. aviation. With Vt. Air NG. Office: Burlington Internat Airport 1200 Airport Dr Ste 1 South Burlington VT 05403-6028

HAMILTON, JOHN MAXWELL, university dean, writer; b. Evanston, Ill., Mar. 28, 1947; s. Maxwell Millings and Elizabeth Curran (Carlson) H.; m. Regina Frances Nalewajek, Aug. 19, 1975; 1 child, Maxwell Janek. BA in Journalism, Marquette U., Milw., 1969; postgrad., U. N.H., 1971-73; MS in Journalism, Boston U., 1974; PhD in Am. Civilization, George Washington U., 1983. Reporter Milw. Jour., 1967-69; free-lance journalist Washington, 1973-75; fgn. corres., 1976-78; spl. asst., asst. adminstr. Agy. for Internat. Devel., Washington, 1978-81; staff assoc. House Fgn. Affairs Subcom. Internat. Econ. Policy/Trade, Washington, 1981-82; chief U.S. fgn. policy corres. Internat. Reporting Info. Sys., Washington, 1982-83; dir. Main St. Am. and the Third World, Washington, 1985-87; sr. counselor World Bank, Washington, 1983-85, 87-92; dean and prof. Manship Sch. Mass. Comm. La. State U., Baton Rouge, 1992—, Hopkins Breazeale found. prof., 1998; commentator MarketPlace Pub. Radio Internat., 1991—. Bd. dirs., treas. Internat. Ctr. for Journalists; bd. dirs. Pub. Affairs Rsch. Coun., Lamar Advt. Corp.; guest lectr. U.S. Info. Svc., Brazil, 1993, Pulitzer prize juror, 1999-2000; chair Roy W. Howard Award Jury, 2001; fellow Shorenstein Ctr. for the Press, Politics and Pub. Affairs, Kennedy Sch., Harvard U., 2002. Author: Main Street America and the Third World, 1986, 2d edit., 1989, Edgar Snow: A Biography, 1988, revised, 2003 (Critics Choice, L.A. Times, Frank Luther Mott-Kappa Tau Alpha Rsch. award 1988), Entangling Alliances: How the Third World Shapes Our Lives, 1990; co-author: (with George Krimsky) Hold the Press: The Inside Story on Newspapers, 1996, Casanova Was A Book Lover: And Other Naked Facts and Provocative Curiosities About Reading, Writing and Publishing, 2000; author chpts. in books; contbr. numerous articles to profl. jours. including Atlanta Constn., Balt. Sun, Bull. of Atomic Scientists, Boston Globe, Chgo. Tribune, Christian Sci. Monitor, Columbia Journalism Rev., Jour. Commerce, L.A. Times, N.Y. Times, The Nation, others. Officer USMC, 1969-73. Grantee Ford Found., Carnegie Inst., US AID, others, 1985-94; recipient By-Line award Marquette Coll. Journalism, 1993; named Journalism Adminstr. of the Yr., Freedom Forum, 2003. Mem. Assn. of Schs. of Journalism and Mass Comm. (chair task force on alliances 1992-94), Soc. Profl. Journalists. Democrat. Home: 3 Hidden Oak Ln Baton Rouge LA 70810 Office: La State Univ Manship Sch Mass Cmn Baton Rouge LA 70803-0001 E-mail: jhamilt@lsu.edu.

HAMILTON, JOHN RICHARD, lawyer; b. El Dorado, Kans., Jan. 8, 1940; s. Silas H. and Ora B. (Barker) H.; m. Shirley A. Tekamp, June 16, 1960 (div. July 1976); children: Michele L., Brian J.; m. Louise Brock, Dec. 22, 1984. BS, Union U., 1962; JD, Washburn Law Sch., 1965. Bar: Kans 1965, U.S. Dist. Ct. Kans. 1965, U.S. Ct. Appeals (10th cir.) 1969. Ptnr. Crane, Martin, Claussen, Hamilton & Forbes, Topeka, 1965—84, Hamilton & Hannah, Topeka, 1985—87, Hamilton, Gregg, Barker & Johnson, Topeka, 1988—. Mem. ATLA, ABA, Kans. Bar Assn., Topeka Bar Assn., Kans. Trial Lawyers Assn. (bd. dirs., v.p. 1982-83), Am. Bd. Trial Advs., Topeka Country Club. Democrat. Home: 2334 SW Mayfair Pl Topeka KS 66611-2054 E-mail: jhamilton@hamiltongregg.com.

HAMILTON, JUDITH HALL, computer company executive; b. Washington, June 15, 1944; d. George Woods and Jane Fromm (Brogger) Hall; m. Stephen T. McCellan, Oct. 29, 1988. BA, Ind. U., 1966; postgrad., Boston U., 1966-68, UCLA, 1980-81. Programmer Sys. Devel. Corp., Santa Monica, Calif., 1968-69, dir. programming, 1975-80; sys. analyst Daylin, Inc., Beverly Hills, Calif., 1969-71; sys. mgr. Audio Magnetics, Gardena, Calif., 1971-73; pres. Databasics, Inc., Santa Monica, 1973-75; v.p. Computer Scis. Corp., El Segundo, Calif., 1980-87; ptnr. Ernst & Young, L.A., 1987-89, N.Y.C., 1989-91; sr. v.p., gen. mgr. Locus Computing Corp., L.A., 1991-92; pres., CEO Dataquest, Inc., a Dun & Bradstreet Corp., San Jose, Calif., 1992-95, First Floor Software, Mountain View, Calif., 1996-98, Classrm. Connect, El Segundo, 1999—2002. Dir. Lante Corp. Classroom Connect; bd. dirs. R. R. Donnelley, Software.com, Lante, inc., Evolve, Inc., Artistic Media Ptnrs., Giga Info. Sys., Expression Ctr. for New Media, Com. for Econ. Devel. Bd. dirs. Nat. Pks. Found., 2002—, Wildlife Conservation Soc., 1994—, Cmty. Breast Helath Project, 1994—99. Recipient Herman Wells Visionary award, Ind. U., 2002. Mem.: Info. Tech. Assn. Am., Assn. Data Processing Svc. Orgns. (bd. dirs., chmn.), Women's Forum West, Com. of 200, Commonwealth Club Silicon Valley (bd. dirs. 1997—99), Kappa Alpha Theta. Office: Classroom Connect Ste 400 8000 Marina Blvd Brisbane CA 94005

HAMILTON, KIM RENEE, chiropractor, educator; b. Flint, Mich., Jan. 4, 1958; d. William G. and Joy Lou (Roberts) Groves; m. Terry J. Hamilton, June 12, 1976. D Chiropractic, Cleve. Chiropractic Coll., Kansas City, Mo., 1992. Diplomate Kans. State Bd. Healing Arts, cert. in acupuncture Kans. State Bd. Healing Arts, diplomate in chiropractic Mo. State Bd. Chiropractic Examiners. Pvt. practice, Kansas City, Mo., 1992—. Liaison Mo. State Bd. Chiropractic, Kansas City, 1997-98. Contbr. articles to profl. jours. Recipient Tchg. Excellence award Foot Levers Inc., 1995; named Dr. of Yr., Beta Chi Rho, 1997; Howe-Yochum diagnostic imaging fellow, 1995. Fellow Internat. Chiropractic Pediat. Assn.; mem. Internat. Chiropractic Assn., Am. Chiropractic Assn., Coun. of Diagnostic Imaging, Mo. State Chiropractic Assn., Cleve. Chiropractic Alumni Assn., Powers H.S. Alumni Assn. Avocations: art, writing, home remodeling.

HAMILTON, LEE HERBERT, educational organization administrator, former congressman; b. Daytona Beach, Fla., Apr. 20, 1931; m. Nancy Ann Nelson, Aug. 21, 1954; children: Tracy Lynn, Deborah Lee, Douglas Nelson. AB, DePauw U., 1952, hon. degree; scholar, Goethe U., Germany, 1952-53; JD, Ind. U., 1956; hon. degree, Hanover Coll., Detroit Coll. Law, Ball State U., U. S. Ind., Wabash Coll., Union Coll., Ind. U., Am. Univ., Marian Coll., Suffolk U. Mem. 89th-105th Congresses from 9th Dist. Ind., Washington, 1965-99; ranking minority mem. House com. internat. rels.; former chmn. select. com. to investigate covert arms transactions with Iran U.S. Congress, mem. joint econ. com., former chmn. fgn. affairs com., former co chair Joint com. Orgn. Congress, former chmn. Ho. intelligence com., former chmn. Ho. com. investigate Oct. surprise; dir. Woodrow Wilson Ctr. Internat. Scholars Smithsonian Instn., Washington, 1999—. Democrat. Office: Woodrow Wilson Ctr Internat Scholars One Woodrow Wilson Plz 1300 Pennsylvania Ave NW Washington DC 20523-0001

HAMILTON, LEONARD DERWENT, physician, molecular biologist; b. Manchester, Eng., May 7, 1921; came to U.S., 1949, naturalized, 1964; s. Jacob and Sara (Sandelson) H.; m. Ann Twynam Blake, July 20, 1945; children: Jane Derwent, Stephen David, Robin Michael. BA, Balliol Coll., Oxford U., Eng., 1943, BM, 1945, MA, 1946, DM, 1951; MA, Trinity Coll., Cambridge U., Eng., 1948, PhD, 1952. Diplomate Am. Bd. Pathology. USPHS rsch. fellow U. Utah, 1949-50; staff Sloan-Kettering Inst., N.Y.C., 1950-79, head isotope studies sect., 1957-64, assoc. scientist, 1965-79; staff Meml. Hosp., N.Y.C., 1950-65; faculty Sloan-Kettering div. Grad. Sch. Med. Scis. Cornell U., 1956-64; sr. scientist, head divsn. microbiology Med. Research Ctr. Brookhaven Nat. Lab., Upton, N.Y., 1964-76; head biomed. and environ. assessment divsn. Office. Environ. Policy Analysis, 1973-94. Attending physician Hosp. Med. Rsch. Ctr., 1964-85; dir. WHO Collaborating Ctr. for Assessment of Health and Environ. Effects of Energy Systems, 1983-97, WHO focal point on health and environ. effects of energy systems, 1983—, mem. WHO expert adv. panel on environ. hazards, 1983-98; prof. medicine Health Sci. Ctr., SUNY, Stony Brook, 1968—; adj. prof. biometry and epidemiology Med. U. S.C., Charleston, 1996—; cons. HEW, Ctr. Disease Control, Nat. Inst. Occupational Safety and Health, epidemiology study of Portsmouth Naval Shipyard, 1978-88; vis. fellow St. Catherine's Coll., Oxford U., 1972-73; internat. panel experts on fossil fuel UN Environment Programme, 1978, panel on nuclear energy, 1978-79, panel on renewable sources and comparative assessment of different sources, 1980; com. mem. Nat. Acad. Sci.-NRC, Washington, 1975-80; mem. N.Y.C. Mayor's Tech. Adv. Com. on Radiation, 1963-77, N.Y.C. Commr. of Health Tech. Adv. Com. on Radiation, 1978—; energy panel WHO Commn. on Health & Environment, 1990-91; mem. Interant. Expert Group 3, Comparative Environ. and Health Effects of Different Energy Systems for Electricity Generation, 1990-91; sr. expert Symposium on Electricity and the Environ., Helsinki, Finland, 1991. Editor: Gerrard Winstanley, Selections from His Works, 1944; Physical Factors and Modification of Radiation Injury, 1964; The Health and Environmental Effects of Electricity Generation-a Preliminary Report, 1974. Recipient Fed. Lab. Consortium award, 1990; Am. Cancer Soc. scholar, 1953-58; Commonwealth Fund grantee, 1955-62. Mem. AMA, Am. Assn. Cancer Rsch., Am. Soc. Clin. Investigation, Am. Soc. for Investigative Pathology, Soc. for Risk Analysis, Harvey Soc., Cosmos Club (Washington). Home: Childs Ln Old Field Setauket NY 11733 Office: Brookhaven Nat Lab Upton NY 11973

HAMILTON, LINDA HELEN, clinical psychologist; b. N.Y.C., Dec. 2, 1952; d. Peter and Helen (Casey) Homek; m. Terrence White, Aug. 10, 1974 (div. 1983); m. William Garnett Hamilton, Dec. 29, 1984. BA summa cum laude, Fordham U., 1984; MA, Adelphi U., 1986, PhD, 1989. Lic. psychologist, N.Y. Dancer N.Y.C. Ballet, 1969-88; clin. psychologist Fair Oaks Hosp., Summit, N.J., 1989-90, Miller Inst. for Performing Artists, N.Y.C., 1989-95; pvt. practice N.Y.C., 1991—. Rsch. assoc. Miller Inst. Performing Artists, N.Y.C., 1987-95; chair dance com. MedArt U.S.A., N.Y.C., 1990-92; cons. psychologist Sch. Am. Ballet, N.Y.C., 1991—, Alvin Ailey Am. Dance Ctr., N.Y.C., 1996—; advice columnist Dance Mag., 1992—, sr. editor, 1997—; adj. assoc. prof. Fordham U., 1998-2002; co-leader Performing Arts Medicine Delegation to Russia and Ea. Europe, 1992; cons. psychologist Wellness Program, N.Y.C. Ballet, 2001—. Author: The Person Behind the Mask: A Guide to Performing Arts Psychology, Advice for Dancers; featured in : (documentaries) by European Media Support; Dying to be Thin (Nova), 2001. Mem. exec. com. BFA Dance Program, Fordham U., 1997—. Miller Inst. Performing Artists grantee, 1987. Mem. APA (Daniel E. Berlyne award 1993), Internat. Assn. Dance Medicine and Sci., Performing Arts Medicine Assn., Dance Profls. Assocs. (bd. dirs. 1997—2002). Avocations: travel, reading, opera, ballet. Office: 2000 Broadway New York NY 10023-5028 E-mail: lindahamilton1@msn.com.

HAMILTON, LISA DAWN, secondary education educator; b. Enid, Okla., Feb. 17, 1972; d. Lowell James and Linda Lee (Smith) K. Student, Phillips U., Enid, 1990-91; BA, Northwestern Okla. State U., 1995, MEd, 2000. Cert. secondary tchr., Okla. Tchr. drama, debate and speech Ponca City (Okla.) H.S., 1995-98; prof. speech, forensics and debate Cowley County C.C., Arkansas City, Ark., 1998-2000; tchr., dept. chair drama, debate and speech Enid (Okla.) H.S., 2000—. Disciples of Christ scholar Phillips U., 1990, Phillips Acting Talent scholar, 1990, Acting Talent scholar Northwestern Okla. State U., 1991-94. Mem. Nat. Forensic League, Okla. Speech Theatre Comm. Assn., Okla. Edn. Assn., Great Plains Forensics Conf., Okla. Fine Arts Camp, Alpha Psi Omega. Democrat. Avocations: reading, crafting, watching movies, acting, directing. Office: Enid HS 611 W Wabash Enid OK 73701 E-mail: ld_2_17@yahoo.com.

HAMILTON, LISA GAY, actress; b. LA, Mar. 25, 1964; d. Ira and Tina. Grad., Juilliard Sch., 1988. Appeared in films: Reversal of Fortune, 1990, Naked in New York, 1994, Twelve Monkeys, 1995, Palookaville, 1995, Nick and Jane, 1997, Lifebreath, 1997, Jackie Brown, 1997, Drunks, 1997, Beloved, 1998, True Crime, 1999, The Sum of All Fears, 2002, The Truth About Charlie, 2002, Amanda America; TV appearances include Homicide, 1993, New York Undercover, 1994, Law & Order (Rebecca), 1995, Murder One, Chicago Hope, The Practice, 1997-2003, One Life to Live, 1996, The Defenders: Choice of Evils, 1998, Swing Vote, 1999, A House Divided, 2000, Hamlet, 2000; dir., prodr. Beah: A Black Woman Speaks, 2003; on Broadway plays include The Piano Lesson; (off Broadway) Measure for Measure, N.Y.C., Valley Song (Obie award, Clarence Derwent award, Drama Desk nominee). Office: Writers & Artists Agy 8383 Wilshire Blvd Ste 550 Beverly Hills CA 90211

HAMILTON, LYMAN CRITCHFIELD, JR., telecommunications industry executive; b. L.A., Aug. 29, 1926; s. Lyman Critchfield and Edna Lorraine (Gluck) H.; m. Mary W. Shepard, June 25, 1949 (div. 1984); children: William, Richard, Douglas, David; m. Beverly C. Lannquist, Nov. 17, 1984. Student, U. Redlands, 1944-45; BA, Principia Coll., 1947; MPA, Harvard U., 1949; LLD (hon.), Waynesburg Coll., 1979. Budget examiner U.S. Bur. of Budget, Washington, 1950-56; asst. adminstr. U.S. Civil Adminstrn. of Ryukyu Islands, Okinawa, Japan, 1956-60; investment officer World Bank & IFC, Washington, 1960-62; with Internat. Telephone & Telegraph Corp., N.Y.C., 1962-79, treas., 1967-76, v.p., 1968-73, sr. v.p., 1973-74, exec. v.p., 1974-77, pres., 1977-79, chief oper. officer, 1977, chief exec., 1978-79; chmn., pres. Tamco Enterprises, Inc., N.Y.C., 1980-89; chmn., pres., chief exec. officer Imperial Corp. of Am., 1989-90; pres., chief exec. officer Alpine Polyvision, Inc., 1991-93, chmn., 1993. Bd. dirs. Scan Optics, Inc., Manchester, Conn. Chmn. vis. com. Gerald R. Ford Sch. Pub. Policy, U. Mich.; adv. com. Monterey Inst. of Internat. Studies; trustee Monterey (Calif.) Symphony and York Sch.; Hartford (Conn.) Symphony. Lt. (j.g.) USNR, 1944—46. Mem. L.A. Country Club, Farmington Woods Country Club, Univ. Club, Old Capital Club (Monterey). Republican. also: 5485 Quail Meadows Dr Carmel CA 93923

HAMILTON, MALCOLM COWAN, librarian, editor, indexer, personnel professional; b. Bath, Maine, Jan. 29, 1938; s. Newell Cowan and Laura Emma (Munro) H. BA, U. Maine, 1961; MS, Simmons Coll., Boston, 1968. Cert. libr., tchr.; sr. profl. human resources cert. Tchr. English, Chelmsford (Mass.) H.S., 1961-67; libr. Harvard U. Grad. Sch. Edn., Cambridge, Mass., 1967-80, Harvard U. John F. Kennedy Sch. Govt., Cambridge, 1980-96, also univ. pers. libr., 1987—2002; project mgr. project adapt Harvard U., Cambridge, 1996-98, sr. cons. Office Human Resources, 1998-99; libr. Harvard U. Div. Sch., Cambridge, 1999—. Author: Travel Index, 1988; editor, indexer: Education Literature, 1907-1932, 11 vols., 1979; compiler: Directory of Educational Statistics; A Guide to Sources, 1974; assoc. editor Jour. Policy Analysis and Mgmt., 1981-87. Mem. ALA, Assn. Coll. and Rsch. Librs., Spl. Librs. Assn. (chmn. ednl. div. 1975-76, chmn. social scis. div. 1985-86, pres. Boston chpt. 1987-88), Soc. for Human Resources Mgmt. Democrat. Anglican. Home: 24 Elmore St Arlington MA 02476-5928 Office: Harvard Divinity Sch 45 Francis Ave Cambridge MA 02138-1911 E-mail: malcolm_hamilton@harvard.edu.

HAMILTON, MARK R. academic administrator; BS, U.S. Mil. Acad., 1967; Ma in English lit., Fla. State U., 1973; grad., Armed Forces Staff Coll., U.S. Army War Coll. Comdr. Division Artillery, Fort Richardson, 1988-90; chief staff Alaskan Command, Elmendorf AFB, 1992-93; dep. dir. force structure, resource and analysis Joint Staff, Washington, 1995-97; head recruiting U.S. Army, Fort Knox, Ky., 1997-98; pres. U. Alaska, Fairbanks, 1998—. Office: U Alaska PO Box 755000 Fairbanks AK 99775-5000

HAMILTON, MARTHA JEAN ANDERSON, media specialist; b. Greenville, S.C., May 15, 1946; d. Benjamin Mason and Gladys (Harling) Anderson; m. Leroy A. Hamilton Sr., July 3, 2001. BS, Appalachian State U., Boone, N.C., 1968; M.Librarianship, Emory U., Atlanta, 1974, Diploma Advanced Study Librarianship, 1983. Libr. Arlington Schs., Atlanta, 1968-70, Archer Public High Sch., Atlanta, 1970-74; media specialist Woodmont High Sch. Greenville County Sch. Dist., Piedmont, S.C., 1974-76, media specialist Berea High Sch. Greenville, S.C., 1976-80, media specialist Hillcrest High Sch. Simpsonville, S.C., 1980—. Chmn. Relay for Life in the Golden Strip Am. Cancer Soc., 2001, 2002. Recipient Citation award S.C. Occupational Info. Coord. Com., 1988. Mem. NEA, S.C. Assn. Sch. Librs., S.C. Edn. Assn., Greenville County Edn. Assn., Reidville (S.C.) Hist. Soc. (charter mem., historian, pres. 2002-03), Greenville County Coun. Media Specialists, Rotary, Iota Alpha Delta Kappa (historian 1978-80, 88-90, 92-94, v.p. 1980-82, pres. 1982-84, 94-96, sgt.-at-arms 1990-92, chaplain 1998-2000). Methodist. Avocations: reading, gardening, needlecrafts. Office: Hillcrest High Sch 3665 S Industrial Dr Simpsonville SC 29681-3299

HAMILTON, NANCY BETH, business executive; b. Lakewood, Ohio, July 22, 1948; d. Edward Douglas and Gloria Jean (Blessing) Familo; m. Thomas Woolman Hamilton, June 10, 1970; children: Susan Elizabeth, Catherine Anne. BA, Denison U., 1970. Cert. secondary edn. tchr., Fla. Tchr. Orange County (Fla.) Bd. Edn., 1970-71; registrar Jones Coll., Orlando, Fla., 1971-72; mgr. service dept. Am. Lawyers Co., Cleve., 1972-79, mgr. data processing dept., 1980-95, corp. sec.-treas., 1995—. Mem. bd. assoc. editors Comml. Law Jour., 1991—, vice chair, 2002—. Trustee, treas. Westshore Montessori Assn., Rocky River, Ohio, 1988—94; bd. dirs. Holly Lane PTA, Westlake, Ohio, 1988—94, treas., 1992—94; bd. dirs. Parkside PTA, Westlake, 1991—97, treas., 1994—96, Westlake Coun. PTAs, 1999—2001, Westlake H.S. PTA, 1995—98, pres., 1998—2000. Mem. Comml. Law League Am. (chmn. com. 1989-94, membership chmn. 1994-96, com. chair 1997—), Comml. Law League of Am. (Midwestern dist. rec. sec. 1997—), Assn. Law List Pubs. (treas. 1998—), Westwood Country Club, Alpha Phi (pres. Cleve. Westshore chpt. alumnae 1986-88). Republican. Methodist. Avocations: skiing, travel. Office: Am Lawyers Co 853 Westpoint Pky Ste 710 Cleveland OH 44145-1532

HAMILTON, PATRICIA ROSE, art dealer; b. Phila., Oct. 21, 1948; d. William Alexis and Lillian Marie (Sloan) Hamilton. BA, Temple U., 1970; MA, Rutgers U., 1971. Sec. to curator Whitney Mus., N.Y.C., 1971-73; sr. editor Art in Am., 1973; curator exhbns. Crispo Gallery, 1974-75; dir. Hamilton Gallery, 1976-84; artist's agt., 1984—. Democrat. Avocations: tennis, swimming, cooking. Home and Office: 6753 Milner Rd Los Angeles CA 90068-3214 E-mail: pathamilton@earthlink.net.

HAMILTON, PETER BANNERMAN, business executive, lawyer; b. Phila., Oct. 22, 1946; s. William George Jr. and Elizabeth Jane (McCullough) H.; m. Elizabeth Anne Arthur, May 8, 1982; children— Peter Bannerman, Jr., Brian Arthur. AB, Princeton U., 1968; JD, Yale U., 1971. Bar: D.C. 1972, Pa. 1972, Ind. 1985. Mem. staff Office Asst. Sec. Def. for Systems Analysis and Office Gen. Counsel, Dept. Def., Washington, 1971-74; mem. firm Williams & Connolly, Washington, 1974-77; gen. counsel Dept. Air Force, Washington, 1977-78; dep. gen. counsel HEW, Washington, 1979, exec. asst. to sec., 1979; spl. asst. to Sec. and Dep. Sec. Def., Washington, 1979-80; ptnr. Califano, Ross & Heineman, Washington, 1980-82; v.p., gen. counsel, sec. Cummins Engine Co., Inc., 1983-86, v.p. law and treasury, 1987-88, v.p., CFO, 1988-95; sr. v.p., CFO, Brunswick Corp., Lake Forest, Ill., 1996-98, exec. v.p., CFO, 1998-99; vice chmn., pres. Brunswick Bowling and Billiards, Lake Forest, 2000—. Bd. dirs. Brunswick Corp., The Kemper Ins. Cos., The Talbots, Inc. Articles editor: Yale Law Jour, 1970-71. Served to lt. USN, 1971-74. Home: 970 E Deerpath Rd Lake Forest IL 60045-2212 Office: Brunswick Corp 1 N Field Ct Lake Forest IL 60045-4811

HAMILTON, RANDY HASKELL, city manager; b. N.Y.C., Dec. 27, 1921; s. Harry and Adelaide Beatrice (Haskell) H.; m. Ruth Manning (div. May 1961); children: Sarah Beth, Leander Munhall III; m. Louanne McKernan, Apr. 29, 1962; children: Jill Katherine, Jennifer Sabrina. BA, U. N.C., 1943, MA in Pub. Adminstrn., 1947, MA in City and Regional Planning, 1949; PhD, U. Zurich, Switzerland, 1963. City mgr. City of Carolina Beach, N.C., 1949-52; dir., assoc. dir. Nat. League Cities, Washington, 1952-56; city mgr., mcpl. adv. Royal Govt. Thailand, Bangkok, 1956-64; dir. comparative urban studies project UN/IPA, N.Y.C., 1964-65; spl. project dir. League Calif. Cities, Berkeley, Calif., 1965-73; dean Grad. Sch. Pub. Adminstrn., Golden Gate U., San Francisco, 1973-90; vis. scholar Inst. Govtl. Studies, U. Calif., Berkeley, 1990—. Mem. editl. bd. Pub. Adminstrn. Rev., 1970-75, Internat. Jour. Pub. Adminstrn., 1977—, State and Local Govt. Rev., 1980-86; editor Western Govtl. Rsch. Jour., 1990-92, Jour. of E Govt., 2003—. Chmn. Gov.'s Adv. Coord. Coun. Pub. Personnel, Sacramento, 1973; chmn. adv. com. Calif. State Welfare Grant, Sacramento, 1972, State Calif., Sacramento, 1975; mem. Calif. Coun. on Criminal Justice, Sacramento, Calif., 1971-73; chmn. Highland Hosp. Found., Oakland, Calif., 1991-93. Capt. USAF, 1943-46. Decorated comdr. Royal Order of Crown (Thailand); named Man of Yr., N.C. Lion's Club, 1950; recipient spl. citation U.S. CSC, 1975. Fellow Nat. Acad. Pub. Adminstrn. (life); mem. Internat. City Mgmt. Assn. (Stephen B. Sweeney award 1980), Am. Soc. for Pub. Adminstrn. (nat. pres. 1976). Republican. Presbyterian. Office: U Calif Inst Govtl Studies 109 Moses Hall Berkeley CA 94720-2370

HAMILTON, RICHARD ALFRED, university administrator, marketing educator; b. Pitts., Dec. 22, 1941; s. Robert Curtis and Dorothy Katherine (Sexauer) Hamilton. BA, Otterbein Coll., 1965; MBA, Bowling Green State U., 1968; D in Bus. Adminstrn., Kent State U., 1973. Prodn, rate analyst dept. indsl. engring. RCA, Findlay, Ohio, 1966—67; computer sys. analyst dept. market rsch. Marathon Oil Co., Findlay, 1967—68; tchg. fellow Coll. Bus. Adminstrn. Kent State U., 1968—71; assoc. profl. direct mktg. U. Mo., Kansas City, 1971—; pres. Mission Woods Cons., Inc., 1977—. Cons. U.S. Senate Permanent Subcom. on Investigation, 1973—74, Midwest Rsch. Inst. and Office of Tech. Assessment of U.S. Congress, 1974—75; spkr. to profl. orgns. Author (with David R. Bywaters): How to Conduct Association Surveys, 1976; author: Tourism U.S.A.-Marketing Tourism, Vol. 3, 1978, Quantitative Direct Response Market Segmentation, 1989, Readings and Cases in Direct Marketing, NTC Business Books, Helzberg Diamonds-A Retailer's Use of Direct Marketing to Generate Store Traffic, 1995; contbr. articles to profl. jours. Recipient Cray Faculty award, U. Mo., 1987, Robert B. Clarke Outstanding Direct Mktg. Educator award, Direct Mktg. Ednl. Found., 1994, Disting. Rsch. in Mktg. award, Allied Acads., 2001; Univ. fellow, 1968—71, dissertation fellow, Marathon Oil Co., 1972. Mem.: Direct Mktg. Assn., Am. Mktg. Assn., Beta Gamma Sigma. Methodist. Home: 5306 Mission Woods Rd Shawnee Mission KS 66205-2008 Office: U Mo Bloch Sch Adminstrn Kansas City MO 64110 E-mail: hamiltonr@umkc.edu.

HAMILTON, RICHARD CLAY, basketball player; b. Feb. 14, 1978; Student, U. Conn., 2000. Profl. basketball player Washington Wizards, 1999—. Named one of 3 coll. players 1999 USA Basketball Sr. Men's Nat. Team . Office: Washington Wizards 601 F St NW Washington DC 20004

HAMILTON, ROBERT APPLEBY, JR., insurance company executive; b. Boston, Feb. 20, 1940; s. Robert A. and Alice Margaret (Dowdall) H.; m. Ellen Kuhlen, Aug. 13, 1966; children: Jennifer, Robert Appleby III, Elizabeth. Student, Miami U. (Ohio), 1958-62. CLU; chartered fin. cons. With Travelers Ins. Co., various locations, 1962-65, New Eng. Mut. Life Ins. Co., various locations, 1965-90, regional pension rep. Boston, 1968-71, regional mgr. Chgo., 1972-83, sr. pension cons., 1983-90; mktg. and fin. cons. Snowbeck Enterprises, Inc., Geneva, Ill., 1990-97, ret., 1997. Producer Sta. WCTV; mem. Rep. Town Com., Wenham, Mass., 1970-72, Milton Twp., Ill., 1973-75; mem. Wenham Water Commn., 1970-72. Mem. Midwest Pension Conf. (chmn. 1989-90), Am. Soc. Pension Actuaries (assoc.), Am. Soc. CLUs, Am. Assn. Fin. Planners, Profit Sharing Coun. Am., Chgo. Coun. Fgn. Rels., Alpha Epsilon Rho. Republican. Home: 110 Hamilton Ln Wheaton IL 60187-1807 also: 90 Shumaker Lane Tenants Harbor ME 04860-9709 E-mail: erisabob@aol.com.

HAMILTON, RONALD RAY, minister; b. Evansville, Ind., May 6, 1932; s. Floyd Ray Hamilton and Ruby Dixon (Chism) Hahn; m. Norma Jean Robertson, Mar. 25, 1956; children: Ronnetta Jean, Andrea, Robert Rae. BA, U. Evansville, 1955; BD, Garrett Theol. Sem., 1958, MDiv, 1972; PhD, Oxford Grad. Sch., Eng., Dayton, Tenn., 1989. Ordained elder United Meth. Ch. Minister Scobey (Mont.) Meth. Ch., 1958-61, St. Andrew Meth. Ch., Littleton, Colo., 1961-67; sr. minister First Meth. Ch., Grand Junction, Colo., 1967-75, Christ United Meth. Ch., Salt Lake City, 1975-80, Littleton United Meth., 1980-86, U. Park United Meth., Denver, 1986-91, First United Meth. Ch., Sun City, Ariz., 1992-98; chaplain Sun Health Corp., Sun City, 1998—. Author: The Way to Success, 1972, The Greatest Prayer, 1983, A Chosen People, 1986; editor jour., 1978. Recipient Spl. award Mental Health Assn., Mesa County, Colo., 1974, Goodwill Rehab. Inc., 1975. Mem. Lions Club, Rotary Club, Civitan (chaplain 1964-67). Republican. Avocations: acting, directing, travel, chess. Home: 20846 N 107th Dr Sun City AZ 85373-2388 Office: Boswell Meml Hosp 10401 W Thunderbird Blvd Sun City AZ 85351

HAMILTON, RUTH HELLMANN, design company owner; b. Millboro, S.D., Oct. 15; d. Walter Otto and Laura Ethel (King) Hellmann; m. Gordon Eugene Hamilton, June 11, 1950; children: Kristin Goodnight, Bret Hamilton, Lori O'Toole, Lynnelle Anderson. AB, Nebr. Wesleyan U., Lincoln, 1948; MEd and Humanities, So. Meth. U., 1952. Owner, chief exec. officer Sonoran Desert Designs, Tucson, 1976-98. Lectr. Ariz. Desert Mus., Tucson, 1985—86, Tohono Chul Mus., Tucson, 1986—2002, Prescott Coll., Tucson, 1987, Tucson Bot. Gardens, 1985—2002, Elderhostel, 1991—92; tchr. design student classes. Exhibited displays for Old Pueblo Mus. at Foothills Mall, 1987-90; demonstrations of desert designs Ariz. State Conv. Garden Clubs N.Mex., 1987, 89; one-woman shows at Tucson Garden Club, 1988, 90; original designs published

by Nat. Coun. Garden Clubs Calendars, 1984, 87, 89, 95, 98, 99, 2000, 02, 03, Sunset mag., Dec. 1999 Mem. pub. svcs. bd. KVOA-TV, 1969-74. Named Hon. Sr., St. Andrew's Presbyn. Ch. Mem.: Los Cerros Garden Club (pres. 1984—85, 1994—95). Avocation: flower arrangement and spacial design. Home: 7720 N Sendero De Juana Tucson AZ 85718-7517

HAMILTON, RUTH MILTON GREEN, retired college administrator, consultant; b. Sioux City, Iowa, Feb. 29, 1924; d. John and Myrtle Alma (Phipps) Milton; m. Robert Wood Green, Dec. 31, 1943 (dec. July 1989); children: Robert William, Sandra Lou Green Montignani; m. Gail B. Hamilton, Jr., May 30, 1999. Student, Morningside Coll., 1943-45. Registrar East H.S., Sioux City, 1943; acct. Buehler Bros., Iowa City, 1947-49; asst. dir. tchr. placement Morningside Coll., Sioux City, 1951-55, mem. staff registrar's office, 1960-65, asst. to registrar, 1965-70, dir. spl. project funding, 1971-81, dir. Title III Strengthening Devel. Instns. program, 1975-84, v.p. instl. rsch., planning and spl. projects, 1984-94; ret., 1994. Asst. to prin. Ames (Iowa) High Sch., 1955-59; pvt. cons. for edn. and non-profit agys. in spl. project funding. Pres. First Congregational Ch., Sioux City, 1980; co-chair City Hall Site Selection Com., Sioux City, 1991-93; mem. Main St. Energy Greenway Com., co-chair fundraising com.; bd. dirs. Siouxland Mental Health Agy., 1983-89; bd. dirs. Mary Treglia Cmty. Ho., 1989-99, v.p. bd. dirs., 1996-97, pres., 1998, Waco, bd. dirs., 1990-96, sec., 1994, v.p., 1995, pres., 1996. Named Woman of Excellence, Women Aware, 1986, woman of Yr., First Congregational United Ch. of Christ, 1999; awarded Order of Morningside for dedicated svc. to Morningside Coll., 1995. Mem. PEO, St. Luke's Med. Ctr. Aux., Omicron Delta Kappa (hon.). Democrat. Home: 4829 Robin Ln Sioux City IA 51106 E-mail: rutie630177408@yahoo.com.

HAMILTON, SHIRLEY SIEKMANN, arts administrator; b. South Bend, Ind., Aug. 31, 1928; d. George F. and Clarice B. (Rapp) Burdick; m. Max R. Siekmann, June 23, 1951; children: Sheryl, Pamela, David; m. Keith L. Hamilton, Sept. 3, 1983. Student St. Mary's Coll., 1946-47; BA, DePauw U., 1950; postgrad. Ind. U., South Bend. Tchr. public schs., St. Joseph County, Ind., 1950-51, Greencastle, Ind., 1951-52, Ft. Lauderdale, Fla., 1952-53; exec. dir. Michiana Arts and Scis. Council, Inc., South Bend, Ind., 1973-86; tech. asst. cons., adv. panelist Ind. Arts Commn.; treas. Ind. Alliance Arts Councils, 1982. Mem. St. Joseph County Parks and Recreation Bd., 1971-81, park found. bd., 1988-95; pres. Mental Health Assn. of St. Joseph County, 1972; St. Joseph County Scholarship Found., 1977-82; Cmty. Found. St. Joseph County, 1979-95, bd. dirs., grant chmn.; pres., bd. dirs. United Way St. Joseph County, 1981-82; bd. dirs., spl. events chmn. Internat. Summer Spl. Olympics Games, 1986-88; bd. dirs. Firefly, 1987—, Meml. Hosp. Found., 1990-97, South Bend Regional Mus. Art, 1988-95, Friends of Snite Mus. Art, Notre Dame Ind., 1989-95, Logan Ctr. Found., 1990-99, Morris Ctr. for the Performing Arts Bd., 1995—; cmty. adv. bd. Art Ctr., 2002—. Recipient Cmty. Svc. award Michiana Arts and Scis. Coun., 1968, Arts award, 1987, Arts Svc. award Ind. Assembly of Local Arts Agys., 1987. Mem. Ind. Arts Advs., Ind. Alliance Arts Councils, Nat. Assn. Arts Councils, Jr. League South Bend (pres.). Producer: (TV series) Inside Our Schools (Jr. League of South Bend Outstanding Cmty. Svc. award 1964).

HAMILTON, STANLEY RALPH, pathologist; b. Ft. Wayne, Ind., Dec. 2, 1948; s. Ralph Albert and Anita (Lunsford) H.; m. Cheryl Lynn (Fitzpatrick) Hamilton, Oct. 30, 1971; children: Brian, Kimberly, Mark. AB in Zoology, Ind. U., 1970, MD, 1973. From asst. prof. to prof. pathology & oncology Johns Hopkins U. Sch. Medicine, Balt., 1979—98; prof. and div. head pathology and lab. medicine M.D. Anderson Cancer Ctr. U. Tex., Houston, 1998—. Editor Clin. Cancer Rsch., Am. Jour. Pathology, Cancer Rsch., Br. Jour. Cancer. Mem. Am. Soc. Investigative Pathology, Am. Gastrointestinal Assn., U.S. & Can. Acad. Pathology, Gastrointestinal Pathology Soc., Am. Assn. Cancer Rsch., Arthur Purdy Stout Soc. Surg. Pathologists.

HAMILTON, SUSAN OWENS, transportation company executive, lawyer; b. Birmingham, Ala., Aug. 7, 1951; d. William Lewis and Vonnette (Wilson) Owens; m. M. Raymond Hamilton, June 8, 1974. BA, Auburn U., 1973; JD, Samford U., 1977. Bar: Ala., Fla. Claim agt. Seaboard System R.R. and predecessor cos., Birmingham, Ala., 1977-78, atty. Louisville, 1978-80, claims atty., 1980-81, asst. gen. atty. Jacksonville, Fla., 1981-83, asst. gen. solicitor, 1983-84, gen. mgr. freight claim services, 1984-85; asst. v.p. casualty prevention Chessie System R.R.'s, Balt. and Jacksonville, 1985-86; asst. v.p. freight damage prevention and claims CSX Transp., Jacksonville, 1986-87, asst. v.p. adminstrv. svcs., 1987-90, sr. asst. v.p. adminstrv. svcs., 1990-95; v.p., gen. counsel CTI, a Unit of CSX, 1995—; gen. mgr. Crew Mgmt. Ctr., CSX Transp., Jacksonville, Fla., 1997—, asst. v.p. labor rels., 2000—, asst. v.p. human resources, 2002—. Vice chair fund distbn. com., United Way of N.E. Fla., 1991-93, chmn., 1993-94, mem. exec. com., 1992-97, chmn. bd. dirs., 1996-97; mem. Gator Bowl Com., 1993—, Gator Bowl officer, 1995—, exec. com., 1998—, chmn.-elect, 2001—, chmn., 2002—. Mem. ABA, Jacksonville Bar Assn., Bus. and Profl. Women (pres. Jacksonville chpt. 1984-85), Fla. Bus. and Profl. Women (Outstanding Young Career Woman 1982), Uptown Civitan (bd. dirs. Jacksonville club 1982-84, v.p., pres. elect. 1993, pres. 1993-94). Methodist. Avocations: music, reading, sports. Home: 8224 Sabal Oak Lane Jacksonville FL 32256-7373 Office: J400 500 Water St Jacksonville FL 32202

HAMILTON, THOMAS ALLEN, independent insurance agent, securities representative; b. Oklahoma City, July 7, 1947; s. Vernon Carlton and Hazel (Margie) H.; m. Deborah; children: Travis Matthew, Heather Lynne. BBA Mktg. and Mgmt., Okla. U., 1969. Registered securities rep. Mass. Fin. Group, 1984, Sunesco, 1994, LifeMark Securities, Okla. City, 1995. Dept. mgr. J.C. Penney, Oklahoma City, 1969-71; spl. agt. CNA Ins., Oklahoma City, 1971-74; group cons. Mass. Mut. Ins. Co., Oklahoma City, 1974-79, qualified plan cons.; bus./estate ins. cons. Mass Mut. Ins. Co., Oklahoma City, 1979-93; ins. investment cons. Sun Fin. Group, Oklahoma City, 1993-95; ind. ins. agt. Hamilton Ins./Fin. Svcs.-licensed in property/casualty, life/health, disability, employee benefit plans, retirement and investment planning, 1996—; registered rep. Mass Mut., Oklahoma City, 1995—2002. Past chmn. troop 177 Boy Scouts Am., Oklahoma City, 1987-88; mem. Crossings Cmty. Ch. Mem. Nat. Assn. Ins. and Fin. Advisors, Nat. Assn. Health Underwriters, Oklahoma City Art Mus., Integris Med. Ctr. Okla. Found., Oklahoma City C. of C., Oklahoma City Ski Club, Oklahoma City Swing Dance Club. Republican. Protestant. Home: 6100 N Gun Hill Way Oklahoma City OK 73132 Office: 4334 NW Expressway Oklahoma City OK 73116

HAMILTON, THOMAS MICHAEL, marketing executive; b. Bronxville, N.Y., Jan. 8, 1947; s. Harold Thomas and Mary Theresa (Byrne) H.; m. Kathryn Borys, May 24, 1984. BS, SUNY, Buffalo. Sales mgr. Herk, Inc., N.Y.C., 1971-73; account exec. William Esty Co., Inc., N.Y.C., 1973-77, account supr., 1977-80, v.p., assoc. dir. sales promotion, 1980-83, sr. v.p., dir. sales promotion, 1983-88; pres. Hamilton Promotions, Inc., Katonah, N.Y., 1988-89; v.p. mktg. Harrington, Righter & Parsons Inc., N.Y.C., 1989-94; prin. The Hamilton Way, Katonah, N.Y., 1994—. Fundraiser United Way of Greater N.Y., 1976-84; council mem. HIP Consumer Council, N.Y.C., 1985; mem. North East Katonah (N.Y.) Community League, 1987—. Served to 1st lt. USAF, 1968-71. Mem. Mktg. Communications Execs. Internat. (bd. dirs. 1983-86), Promotion Mktg. Assn. Am. (bd. dirs. 1986-93, exec. com. 1987-93, vice-chmn. 1989-90, chmn.-elect 1990-91, chmn. bd. 1991-92, chmn. emeritus 1993-94). Avocations: golf, travel.

HAMILTON, THOMAS STEWART, physician, hospital administrator; b. Detroit, June 19, 1911; s. J.T. Stewart and Lucy (Safford) H.; m. Amy Washburn, June 30, 1937; children: Ann Washburn Hamilton Brainerd, Barbara Hamilton Almy, Jeanne. Grad., Philips Exeter Acad., 1930; AB, Williams Coll., 1934, D.Sc. (hon.), 1969; postgrad., Harvard, 1934-36; M.B., Wayne U., 1938, MD, 1939; D.Sc. (hon.), Trinity Coll., 1962, U. Hartford, 1975. Intern, asst. resident Harper Hosp., Detroit, 1938-40; gen. practice medicine Truro, Cape Cod, Mass., 1940-41; asst. dir. Mass. Gen. Hosp., Boston, 1941-42, 45-46; dir. Newton-Wellesley Hosp., Newton Lower Falls, Mass., 1946-54; exec. dir. Hartford (Conn.) Hosp., 1954-76, pres., 1969-76, pres. emeritus, 1976—; prof. U. Conn. Sch. Medicine, 1978-86, prof. emeritus, from 1986. Dir. Phoenix Mut. L.I.C., 1962-82. Contbr. articles to profl. jours. Trustee Soc. for Savs., 1961-70, McLean Fund, 1968-89; commr. Joint Commn. Accreditation Hosps., 1960-66; mem. cancer control com. USPHS, 1964-70, mem. liaison com. on med. edn., 1969-75; regent U. Hartford, 1962-68. Served to lt. col. M.C. AUS, 1942-45. Recipient Disting. Alumnus award Wayne State U. Sch. Medicine, 1970, Disting. Pub. Svc. award Conn. Bar Assn., 1975, Gold Medal award New Eng. Hosp. Assembly, 1975, Lifetime Achievement award Coll. Health Care Execs., 1999; inducted into Modern Health Care Hall of Fame, 1999. Fellow Am. Coll. Hosp. Adminstrs. (regent New Eng. 1953-57, Gold Medal award 1971); mem. AMA (mem. internship rev. com. 1958-68), Mass. Med. Assn., Conn. Med. Assn., Hartford County Med. Assn., Assn. Am. Med. Colls. (sec.-treas. 1968-70), Coun. Tchg. Hosps. (chmn. 1970), Am. Hosp. Assn. (pres., chmn. bd. trustees 1962-63, Disting. Svc. award 1969), Conn. Hosp. Assn. (pres. 1966, Disting. Svc. award 1970), Mass. Hosp. Assn. (pres. 1951), Soc. Med. Adminstrs. (pres. 1968-70), Med. Adminstrs. Conf., Marine Hist. Soc. Clubs: Masons Island Yacht. Home: Bloomfield, Conn. Died July 29, 2002.

HAMILTON, VIRGINIA VAN DER VEER, historian, educator; b. Kansas City, Mo., Sept. 7, 1921; d. McClellan and Dorothy (Rainold) Van der Veer; m. Lowell S. Hamilton, Aug. 4, 1946; children: Carol, David. AB, Birmingham (Ala.)-So. Coll., 1941, MA (Ford Found. Fund Adult Edn. fellow), 1961; PhD, U. Ala., Tuscaloosa, 1968; LittD, U. Ala., 1992. Staff writer AP, Washington, 1942—46, Birmingham News, 1948—50; asst. prof. history U. Montevallo, Ala., 1951—55; asst. prof., asst. to pres. pub. rels. Birmingham-So. Coll., 1955—56; lectr. in history U. Ala., Birmingham, 1965—68, asst. prof., 1968—71, assoc. prof., 1971—75, prof., 1975—87, prof. emerita, 1987—. Author: Hugo Black: The Alabama Years, 1972, Alabama: A History, 1977, The Story of Alabama, 1980, Your Alabama, 1980, Seeing Historic Alabama, 1982, rev. edit., 1996, Lister Hill: Statesman from the South, 1987, Looking For Clark Gable and Other 20th Century Pursuits, 1996; editor: Hugo Black and the Bill of Rights, 1978. Faculty Rsch. grantee U. Ala. at Tuscaloosa, 1969, U. Ala. at Birmingham, 1973-74, 74-75. Mem. So., Am. hist. assns., Orgn. Am. Historians, Soc. Am. Historians, Ala. Assn. Historians, Ala. Hist. Soc. Home: 2350 Montevallo Rd Apt 1602 Birmingham AL 35223-2342

HAMILTON, WARREN BELL, geologist, researcher, geophysicist, educator; b. L.A., May 13, 1925; s. Errett Campbell and Erva Laura (Bell) Hamilton; m. Alicita Victoria Koenig, Dec. 23, 1947; children: Lawrence C., Kathryn E., James D. BA, UCLA, 1945, PhD, 1951; MS, U. So. Calif., 1949. Asst. prof. U. Okla., Norman, 1951-52; from geologist to sr. scientist U.S. Geol. Survey, Denver, 1952-95, Pecora fellow emeritus, 1995-96; Disting. sr. scientist Colo. Sch. Mines, Golden, 1996—. Sr. exch. scientist Acad. Scis., USSR, 1967; vis. prof. Scripps Inst. Oceanography, San Diego, 1968, San Diego, 79, Calif. Inst. Tech., Pasadena, 1973, Yale U., New Haven, 1980, U. Amsterdam, Netherlands, 1981; mem. plate electronics del. to China and Tibet, 79; disting. lectr. Am. Assn. Petroleum Geologists, 1983—84; nominator MacArthur Found., 1984—85; vis. scholar We. Mich. U., 1984; Wilbert disting. lectr. La. State U., 1985, adj. prof., 2000—02; regents lectr. U. Calif., Santa Barbara, 1986, San Diego, 90, UCLA, 1988; Hooker disting. lectr. McMaster U., 1990; Ketin lectr. Istanbul (Turkey) Tech. U., 1998; adj. prof. U. Wyo., 2000—; Allday lectr. U. Tex., Austin, 2002; Disting. Alumni lectr. UCLA, 2003. Author: (book) Tectonics of the Indonesian Region, 1979; contbr. articles to profl. jours.; assoc. editor: Geology, 1973—82, Jour. Geophys. Rsch., 1974—76. With USN, 1943—46. Recipient Disting. Svc. award, U.S. Dept. Interior, 1981. Fellow: Geol. Assn. Can., Geol. Soc. Am. (chmn. Cordilleran sect. 1987—88, councilor 1995—98, Penrose medal 1989), Geol. Soc. London (hon.); mem.: NAS, Am. Geophys. Union, Colo. Sci. Soc. (hon.). Office: Colo Sch of Mines Dept of Geophysics Golden CO 80401

HAMILTON, WENDY, foundation administrator; Mem. Ind. chpt. MADD, 1984—, various positions, mem. Nat. Bd. Dirs., 1995—, nat. pres., 2002—. Office: PO Box 541688 Dallas TX 75354-1688

HAMILTON, WILLIAM BERRY, JR., retired shipping company executive; b. Birmingham, Ala., Apr. 4, 1929; s. William Berry and Nettie (Whatley) H.; m. Jean Lucile Patteson, Feb. 1, 1951; children: Jean Lucile, Ann Elizabeth, William Berry III. BA, Vanderbilt U., 1951. Accountant Hiwassee Constructors, Chattanooga, 1952; cert. pub. acct. O.E. Johnson & Assocs., Chattanooga, 1952-54; controller, gen. mgr. Spl. Products Co., Inc., Chattanooga, 1954-59; v.p., controller Ryder Truck Lines, Inc., Jacksonville, Fla., 1959-65, v.p. finance Chgo. Rawhide Mfg. Co., 1965-67; v.p., controller-treas. Sea-Land Service Inc., Elizabeth, N.J., 1967-69, exec. v.p. adminstrn., dir., 1969-75; v.p., treas., asst. sec. McLean Industries, Inc., Elizabeth, 1968-74; pres. Monterey Transp. Co., Inc. (subs. R.J. Reynolds Industries, Inc.), Winston-Salem, N.C., 1975-77; pres., dir. Security-First Corp., Jacksonville, Fla., 1977-82; chmn. bd., pres. St. John's Marine Fin. Co. Inc., 1979-95; chmn., chief exec. officer Port of Monmouth Devel. Corp., 1983-87; dir., mem. exec. com. J.J. Henry Co., Inc., N.Y.C., 1981-85; ret. Chmn. bd. Henry Laurel Co. Inc., 1983-87; dir. Henry Properties Ltd., L.I. Devel. Co. Ltd.; instr. acctg. U. Chattanooga, 1953-54 Served with USAF, 1951-52. Recipient Guest Lectr. award U. Fla., 1965 Mem. Am. Bur. Shipping, Soc. Naval Architects and Marine Engrs., Am. Inst. C.P.A.s, Financial Execs. Inst., Am. Trucking Assn. (nat. bd. dirs., chmn. methods and procedures nat. accounting 1959-65), Nat. Def. Transp. Assn., Nat. Assn. Accountants (named most valuable mem. Jacksonville 1959-60, chpt. v.p., bd. dirs. 1960-63), Tenn. Soc. C.P.A.s, Am. Accounting Assn., Nat. Officer Mgmt. Assn., Am. Mgmt. Assn., U.S. Power Squadron, USCG Aux., Propeller Club of U.S., Navy League, Phi Delta Theta, Pi Delta Epsilon. Episcopalian (vestryman). Clubs: Fla. Yacht, River (Jacksonville); Ponte Vedra, Sawgrass (Ponte Vedra Beach, Fla.); Sea Bright (N.J.) Beach; N.Y. Yacht, World Trade Center, Vanderbilt Alumni, Whitehall (N.Y.C.); Twin-City (Winston-Salem); Cat Cay (Bahamas). Lodge: Kiwanis. Home: 695B Ponte Vedra Blvd # 103 Ponte Vedra Beach FL 32082-2783 E-mail: bhamijr@aol.com.

HAMILTON, WILLIAM HOWARD, laboratory executive; b. Greenville, Pa., Apr. 2, 1918; s. Simeon Milo and Mary (Baer) H.; m. Ellinor Kistler, Feb. 9, 1944; children: William H. Jr., Nancy Hamilton Lopez. BS in Math. and Physics, Washington and Jefferson Coll., 1940; MS in Math. and Physics, U. Pitts., 1948. With Westinghouse Electric Corp., 1940-80; gen. mgr. Bettis Atomic Power Lab., West Mifflin, Pa., 1970-79; cons., 1979—. Chmn. Tech. Adv. Group TMI-2 Cleanup; chmn. tech. oversight com. Ft. St. Vrains; chmn. sr. ind. rev. panel Molten Salt Reactor Experiment, Oak Ridge; chmn. High Level Weste Rev. Com., Savannah River. Patentee continuous wave acoustic guidance system, 1965. Pres. Edgewood Council, Pitts., 1965-77. Served to lt. comdr. U.S. Navy, 1942-45. Recipient Westinghouse Order of Merit, 1958 Fellow IEEE. Clubs: Duquesne (Pitts.); Rolling Rock (Ligonier, Pa.). Republican. Presbyterian.

HAMILTON, WILLIAM MILTON, retired manufacturing executive; b. Phila., Feb. 5, 1925; s. Louis Valentine and Elsie Marie (Walter) H.; m. Edith Marie Busey, June 9, 1947; children: Barbara Marie, William Milton Jr., Patricia Ann. BS in Indsl. Mgmt., Ga. Inst. Tech., 1947. Asst. br. mgr. Swift & Co., Atlanta, 1947-48; treas. R.K. Price Co., Fayetteville, Ga., 1954-55; br. mgr. N.Y. Wire Cloth Co., Atlanta, 1955-56; from ops. mgr. to pres. Premier Indsl. Corp., Cleve., 1956-91, dir., cons., 1991-96, spl. asst. to chmn., 1998—, also bd. dirs.; CEO product mfg. group Premier Farnell, Cleve., 1996-98, spl. asst. to CEO, 1998—, pres., COO, 1998-99, spl. asst. to chief exec., 1999—2001, pres., 1999—2001. Served to lt. USN, 1943-46, 48-54. Mem.: Jonathan Landing Golf Club (Fla.), Elyria Country Club (Ohio). Methodist. Home: 2222 Pebblebrook Cleveland OH 44145-4378 Office: Premier Farnell 4500 Euclid Ave Cleveland OH 44103-3736 E-mail: hew1947@aol.com.

HAMILTON-KEMP, THOMAS ROGERS, organic chemist, educator; b. Lebanon, Ky., May 13, 1942; s. Thomas Rogers and Catherine Rose (Hamilton) K.; m. Lois Ann Groce, Sept. 13, 1980. AA, St. Catharine Coll., 1962; BA, U. Ky., 1964, PhD in Chemistry, 1970. Asst. prof. natural products chemistry U. Ky., Lexington, 1970-75, assoc. prof., 1975-85, prof., 1985—. Contbr. articles to profl. jours. Mem. SAR, Am. Chem. Soc., Am. Soc. Hort. Sci., Filson Club, Sigma Xi, Gamma Sigma Delta. Democrat. Roman Catholic. Home: 2025 Williamsburg Rd Lexington KY 40504-3015 Office: U Ky Agrl Sci Ctr N Rm N308 Lexington KY 40546-0001

HAMISTER, DONALD BRUCE, retired electronics company executive; b. Cleve., Nov. 29, 1920; s. Victor Carl and Bess Irene (Sutherl) H.; m. Margaret Irene Singiser, Dec. 22, 1946; children: Don Bruce, Tracy. AB cum laude, Kenyon Coll., 1947, LLD (hon.), 1989; postgrad., Stanford U., 1948-49, U. Chgo., 1957; LLD (hon.), Kenyon Coll., 1989. Application engr. S.E. Joslyn Co., Cin., 1947-48; regional sales mgr. Joslyn Mfg. and Supply Co., St. Louis, 1950-52, mktg. mgr. Chgo., 1953-55, asst. to pres., 1956-57, mgr. aircraft arrester dept., 1958-62, gen. mgr. electronic systems div., 1962-71, v.p., gen. mgr., dir. Goleta, Calif., 1973-78, group v.p. indsl. products, 1974-78, pres., chief exec. officer, 1978-85, chmn., 1979-94, ret. chmn., 1994; chmn. Joslyn Mfg. and Supply Co. named changed to Joslyn Corp., 1986; also bd. dirs. Joslyn Corp., 1973—; pres. Joslyn Stainless; chmn. emeritus Joslyn Corp., Goleta, 1995—; pres., dir. Joslyn Stamping Co.; pres., chmn., dir. Joslyn Def. Systems, Inc., 1981—; dir. Brewer Tichener Corp.; chief exec. officer Joslyn Corp., Chgo., 1991-94, ret., 1994. Served to lt. USNR, 1942-46. Mem. IEEE, Airline Avionics Inst. (pres., chmn. 1972-74) Clubs: Univ. (Chgo.). E-mail: dbh1141@aol.com.

HAMIT, FRANCIS GRANGER, freelance writer; b. N.Y.C., Oct. 6, 1944; s. Harold Francis and Ethel Cordelia (Granger) H.; m. Doris Elaine Pratt Kaesser, May 31, 1974 (div. Mar. 1978). B of Gen. Studies, U. Iowa, 1972, MFA in English, 1976. Freelance writer, Iowa City, Chgo., L.A., 1975—; area capt. RRS Security, Ill., 1977; assoc. editor Video Action Mag., Chgo., 1982; v.p. sales and mktg. EPIC Pvt. Security, West Covina, Calif., 1989-90. Author: Virtual Reality and the Exploration of Cyberspace, 1993; author, dir.: Marlowe: An Elizabethan Tragedy, 1988, contbg. editor: Security Technology and Design Mag., 1993—2000, Advanced Imaging Mag., 1994—2001, contbg. writer: 15th edit. Ency. Britannica, 1981—82. With U.S. Army, 1967-71, Vietnam, Germany. Mem.: Assn. Former Intelligence Officers, L.A. Sci. Fantasy Soc., Nat. Mil. Intelligence Assn. Democrat. Buddhist.

HAMLAR, PORTIA YVONNE TRENHOLM, lawyer, writer, educator; b. Montgomery, Ala. d. Harper Councill Sr. and Portia Lee (Evans) Trenholm; 1 child, Eric Lafayette. AB, Ala. State U., Montgomery, 1951; MA, Mich. State U., 1953; JD, U. Detroit, 1972; MPA, U. Mich., 2000. Bar: Mich. 1974, Ill. 1988. Atty. Chrysler Corp., Highland Park, Mich., 1973—80; asst. prof. law Widener U., Wilmington, Del., 1980—82; pvt. practice Southfield, 1982—2000; asst. to chancellor and dir. equity and affirmative action U. Wis., Stevens Point, 2001—. Editor DEOC Pub. Co., Rochester, Mich., 1977-81; mem. Orgn. Resources Counselors, Washington, 1974-80; exch. prof. Nat. Urban League, 1976-79. Author: Defending the Employer in OSHA Contests, 1977—82; mem. U. Detroit Law Rev., 1970—73; editor: Mich. Environ. Law Case Digest, 1990—2001. V.p. bd. dirs. Rochester Symphony Orch., 1983-86. Mem. ABA (chair subcom. labor law sect. 1975-80, spkr.), Mich. Women's Econ. Club (speaker), Alpha Kappa Mu, Mu Phi Epsilon, Kappa Beta Pi. Avocation: classical piano. Home: 3602 Yvonne Dr Stevens Point WI 54481 Office: U Wis-Stevens Point Rm 210 Old Main Stevens Point WI 54481 E-mail: phamlar@charter.net.

HAMLETT, JAMES GORDON, electronics engineer, management consultant, educator; b. Utica, N.Y. BSEE, Syracuse U., 1947-49; BSBA, SUNY, Syracuse, 1985; MBA, City U., Seattle, 1991. Cert. profl. cons.; chartered cons.; cert. vocat. edn. tchr., N.Y.; 1st class radiotel. lic. with ship radar endorsement, FCC. Engr.-writer Warner, N.Y., Inc., Syracuse, 1952-54; vocation edn. tchr. evenings adult edn. Syracuse Cen. Tech. H.S., 1956-62; project leader GE, Syracuse, 1966-90; mgmt. cons. Syracuse, 1990—. Adj. faculty City U., Seattle; pres., mgmt. cons. IntraGlobal Mgmt., Inc., Syracuse, N.Y., 1994—; lectr. City Univ. Trencin, Slovakia, 1995; steering com. Empire State Coll. SUNY, 1995—; spkr. in field. Author: Your Television Set, 1953, Engineering-Related Abbreviations, 1980-84 (VIP award 1980). Prin. Onondaga (N.Y.) Flood Control Com., 1962; tennis coach U.S. Jaycees, North Syracuse, N.Y., 1968; mem. steering com., sec., mem. exec. com. L.C. Smith Coll. Engring. and Computer Sci., Syracuse U., 1991, founding officer Alumni Assn., 1994—; keynote spkr. VA Regional Hosp., 1995. With U.S. Army, 1942-45, ETO. Recipient Cert. of Appreciation for Outstanding Dedication L.C. Smith Coll. Engring and Computer Sci. Syracuse U., 1993, Testimonial-Belgium Remembers (Battle of the Bulge), Ctr. Rsch. and Info. of Battle of Ardennes, Liége, Belgium, 1996, Citation for disting. svc. during Battle of Bulge, N.Y. State Senate Dist., 1996, N.Y. State Conspicuous Svc. medal, 1997; Bus. and Mgmt. Lectureship Ctrl. European grant, Slovakia, 1994-95. Fellow Soc. for Tech. Commn. (internat. stem mgr., mgmt. theory and practice 1980, exec. com.); mem. IEEE (life sr., exec. com. Cert. 1981, editor Syracuse Scanner 1959-69), VFW, N.Y. Acad. Scis. (cert. 1985), Am. Mgmt. Assn. Internat., Profl. Cons. Assn. Ctrl. N.Y., Am. Cons. League, Internat. Platform Assn., Syracuse GE Engrs. Assn., Greater Syracuse C. of C., Syracuse U. Alumni Assn., Am. Soc. Tng. and Devel., Empire State Coll. Alumni Assn. (pres. Syracuse area alumni/student assn.), City U. Alumni (life), Vets. Battle of the Bulge (life, historian, treas.), Order of the Engr. Avocations: tournament tennis (Wimbledon, Eng. 1969), reading management practice, music. Home: 330 Everingham Rd Syracuse NY 13205-3258

HAMLETT, ROBERT BARKSDALE, systems engineer; b. Richmond, Va., Nov. 3, 1949; s. Thomas Coleman and Kathleen Pendleton (Snow) H.; m. Linda Lane Moody, June 24, 1972 (div. Dec. 1982); 1 child, Sarah Barksdale; m. Karen Ann Carwile, Jan. 19, 1985; children: John Coleman, Robert Barksdale Jr. BS in Physics cum laude, Hampden-Sydney Coll., 1972. Programmer United Va. Bank, Richmond, 1972-74, systems programmer, 1975-78, systems programming officer, 1979-82, mgr. tech. support, 1983-84; account systems engr. IBM Corp., Richmond, 1984-87, adv. systems engr., 1987-93, advisory svcs. specialist, 1993-96, sr. I/T specialist, 1997—. Clk. Grace Bapt. Ch., Richmond, 1986-88, treas. 1997. Home: 5223 Willane Rd Glen Allen VA 23059-5352 Office: IBM Corp 9201 Arboretum Pkwy Richmond VA 23236-5402

HAMLIN, DON AUER, financial executive; b. Klamath Falls, Oreg., Oct. 6, 1934; s. Don Fessler and Margaret May (Auer) H.; m. Karen Ruth Wagner; children by previous marriage: Michael, Kathryn, Stephen, Mary, Mark, John, Matthew. BBA, Loyola U. of South, New Orleans, 1955; grad., USAF Command and Staff Coll., 1967; MS in Bus. Adminstrn., George Washington U., 1968. Commd. 2d lt. U.S. Army, 1955, advanced through grades to lt. col., 1975, served with inf., ordnance, M.P., 1955-64, inf. comdr. and staff officer Alaska, Hawaii, Vietnam, 1964-68, cost analyst and dep. agy. comdr. Pentagon Gen. Staff Washington, 1968-72, inf. adviser, 1972, comptr., 1972-75, ret., 1975; comptr. Severance & Assocs., San Antonio, 1975-81; sec.-treas., dir. Severance Reference Lab., Inc., San Antonio, 1981-82; co-founder, pres. Engring. Cybernetics, Inc., San Antonio, 1982-85; dir. fin. Whittaker Health Svcs., Austin, Tex., 1985-86; v.p. fin. Metlife Healthcare Network, 1986-88, Harris Meth. Health Plan, Ft. Worth, 1989-91, sr. v.p., CEO; pres. Harris Meth. Health Ins. Co., Ft. Worth, 1991-94; CEO Heritage Southwest Med. Group, Irving, Tex., 1994-96. Treas. San Vicente Artists, Silver City, N.Mex., 1996-2000; trustee Gila Regional Med. Ctr., Grant County, N.Mex., 1998—; bd. dirs. Mimbres Region Arts Coun., Silver City, 1997-99, Copper Crest Country Club, 1999-2002; pvt. investor, 1983—; dir. Data Terminal Corp., San Antonio, 1981; pres. Balance Point Youth Ranch, San Antonio, 1980-81. Pres. St. Pius X Bd. Edn., San Antonio, 1979. Decorated Legion of Merit with oak leaf cluster, Bronze Star with oak leaf cluster, Air medal with oak leaf cluster, Purple Heart with oak leaf cluster. Mem. San Antonio Med. Mgrs. Assn. (pres. 1982-84), Silver City C. of C. Home and Office: PO Box 5162 Silver City NM 88062-5162 Fax: 505-388-5821. E-mail: hamlin@silvercity-nm.com.

HAMLIN, GEORGE L. writer; b. Des Moines, Aug. 25, 1939; s. George L Hamlin and Marian E Haven; m. Betsy A. Hamlin, June 9, 1962. BS, Iowa State U., 1961. Tech. writer Naval Ordnance Lab., White Oak, Md., 1962-69, sr. tech writer, 1969-74, Naval Surface Weapons Ctr., White Oak, 1974-88, Naval Surface Warfare Ctr., White Oak, 1988-94, Advanced Tech. and Rsch., Burtonsville, Md., 1995—. Mem. stds. com. Soc Technical Comm., Washington, 1969—70; corp. planning group dir. Navy Labs., Washington, 1976—84; tech. manual stds. Naval Sea Sys. Command, Washington, 1982—89; mg.r White Oak Lab. Employees Assn., 1988—93. Co-author: (book) Packard: A History of the Motor Car and the Company, 1978 (Best History Book, 1979), Complete Handbook of Automobile Hobbies, 1981; editor (sr ed): The Packard Cormorant, 1975—; contbr. articles to profl jours. Police comnr Riverdale Police Dept, 1972—73; town councilman Riverdale Town Coun, Md., 1971—73; bd dirs Am's Packard Mus, Dayton, Ohio, 1996—97; trustee Packard Found, Dayton, 1998—. With U.S. Army, 1963. Recipient Excellence in Newspaper Writing Award, William Randolph Hearst Found, 1960. Mem.: Profl Car Soc (founder, chpts chmn 1985—, Appreciation Award 1999), Soc Automotive Historians, Theodore Roosevelt High Sch Found, Studebaker Drivers Club (regional mgr 1966—), Antique Automobile Club Am, Packard

Automobile Classics Inc (trustee, v.p. internat. 1991—, Weiss Trophy 1999). Avocations: automobile restoration, Pepsi collectibles. Office: PO Box 123 Fulton MD 20759-0123 E-mail: geohamlin@isualum.com.

HAMLIN, JAMES TURNER, III, university dean, physician; b. Danville, Va., Feb. 6, 1929; s. James T. and Nell (Davis) H.; m. Mary Caperton, June 9, 1955; children: Helen Austin, Mary Davis, James Turner. AB, Va. Mil. Inst., 1951; MD, U. Va., 1955. Intern Peter Bent Brigham Hosp., Boston, 1955; also resident; instr. medicine N.Y. Med. Coll., 1959-60; guest investigator Rockefeller Inst., N.Y.C., 1960-62; asst. prof. medicine Med. Coll. Ga., Augusta, 1962-64, asso. prof., 1964-66; asso. prof. medicine U. Va., Charlottesville, 1966-73, dir. clin. research center, 1966-71, asst. dean, 1970-71, acting dean sch. medicine, 1971-72, asso. dean, 1972-73; vice dean sch. medicine Tulane U., New Orleans, 1973-75, dean, 1975-88, dean emeritus, 1989—, prof. medicine, 1973-88, prof. emeritus, 1989—. Contbr. articles to med. jours. Mem. Am. Fedn. for Clin. Research, So. Soc. for Clin. Investigation, AAAS, AMA, Med. Soc. Va., Albemarle County, La. State, Orleans Parish med. socs., Sigma Xi, Alpha Omega Alpha. Republican. Presbyterian. Home: 199 Fairmont Cir Danville VA 24541-5210 Office: 1430 Tulane Ave New Orleans LA 70112-2699

HAMLIN, KENNETH ELDRED, JR., retired pharmaceutical company executive; b. Balt., Mar. 27, 1917; s. Kenneth Eldred and Julia (Gallup) H.; m. Janet Hoy, June 18, 1941; children: Kathleen Ann, Kenneth Thomas. BS, U. Md., 1938, PhD, 1941. Research assoc. U. Ill., Urbana, 1941-42; instr. U. Md., 1942-43; research chemist, asst. head organic research, head organic research, asst. dir. chem. research Abbott Labs., North Chicago, Ill., 1943-61, dir. research, 1961-66; v.p. research and devel. Cutter Labs., Inc., Berkeley, Calif., 1966-73, v.p. research and quality assurance, 1973-74, sr. v.p. sci. ops., 1974-81, vice chmn. bd. dirs., 1980-81, dir., 1968-81. Vol. tchr. gen. sci., computer sci. Author: (with Jenkins, Hartung, Hamlin and Data) The Chemistry of Organic Medicinal Products, 1957. Mem. Am. Pharm. Assn., Am. Chem. Soc., AAAS, Sigma Xi, Rho Chi, Alpha Chi Sigma. Republican. Home: 3270 Terra Granada Dr # 1A Walnut Creek CA 94595-3526 E-mail: kehamlin@silcon.com.

HAMLIN, ROBERT HENRY, public health educator, management consultant; b. Cambridge, Mass., Apr. 2, 1923; s. Howard E. and Margaret E. (Henry) H.; m. Beate Kraschewski, Dec. 16, 1960; 1 son, Andrew Werner. AB summa cum laude, Ohio State U., 1944; BSM., Northwestern Med. Sch., 1945, B.M., 1946, MD with honors, 1947; M.P.H. magna cum laude, Harvard, 1952, JD, 1953. Diplomate: Am. Bd. Preventive Medicine. Intern Johns Hopkins Hosp., Balt., 1946-47; cons. Mass. commn. reporting, preparing and promulgating legislation on pub. and mental health and pub. welfare, 1950-53; 1st asst. to commnr. pub. health, 1952-53; asst. prof. legal medicine Harvard Law Sch., 1952-57; lectr. pub. health law and adminstrn. Harvard Sch. Pub. Health, 1952-57, asso. prof. pub. health adminstrn., 1959-62, Roger Irving Lee prof. pub. health, 1962-65, chmn. dept. pub. health practice, 1963-65; v.p. Booz, Allen and Hamilton (mgmt. cons.), 1965-67; ind. mgmt. cons., 1968; chmn. bd. MACRO Systems, Inc. (mgmt. cons.), Washington, 1969-80; clin. prof. dept. comprehensive medicine Coll. Medicine, U. South Fla., 1980-83; acting dir., prof. pub. health program Coll. Pub. Health, U. South Fla., 1983; pres. United Health Techs., Inc. (mgmt. cons.), 1981—. Adj. prof. health adminstrn. Columbia U. Sch. Public Health and Adminstrv. Medicine, 1972-80; cons. Rockefeller Found., 1959-61; staff dir. spel. commn. Harvard health services, 1953-54; mem. U.S. Commn. for UNESCO, 1958-60; dir. pub. health, Brookline, Mass., 1953-57; cons. Hoover Commn. II, 1954-55; asst. to sec. health, edn. and welfare, 1957-59; vis. lectr. pub. health adminstrn. and law Harvard, 1957-59 Contbr. articles profl. publs. U.S. del. 10th session gen. conf. UNESCO, Paris, 1958, pub. health adminstrn. cons. to pvt. orgns., state and local govts. Served as apprentice seaman USN, 1943-46; lt. (j.g.) M.C. USNR, 1947-49. Fellow Am. Pub. Health Assn.; mem. Mass. Med. Soc., Phi Beta Kappa, Phi Eta Sigma, Alpha Epsilon Delta, Alpha Omega Alpha, Delta Omega. Office: United Health Techs 13300 Indian Rocks Rd-1904 Largo FL 33774-2010 Fax: (727) 595-5581.

HAMLIN, SONYA B. communications specialist; b. N.Y.C. d. Julius and Sarah (Saltzman) Borenstein; m. Bruce Hamlin (dec. 1977); children: Ross, Mark (dec. 1992), David. BS, MA, NYU; HLD (hon.), Notre Dame Coll., 1970. Host arts program Sta. WHDH-TV, Boston, 1963-65; host, prodr., writer (syndicated PBS program) Meet the Arts Sta. WGBH-TV, Boston, 1965-68; cultural reporter Sta. WBZ-TV, Boston, 1968-71, TV host, producer The Sonya Hamlin Show, 1970-75; host, producer Sunday Open House program Sta. WCVB-TV, Boston, 1976-80; host, producer, writer Speak Up and Listen program Lifetime Cable Network, N.Y.C., 1982-84; pres. Sonya Hamlin Communications, Boston and N.Y.C., 1977—, Different Drummer Prodns., N.Y.C., 1982-86. Pvt. comm. cons., U.S., Can., and Europe, 1977—; adj. lectr. Harvard Grad. Sch., Edn., Cambridge, Mass., 1974-76, Harvard Law Sch., 1977-81, Kennedy Sch. Govt., Harvard U., 1978-79; adj. asst. prof. Boston U. Med. Sch., 1977-80; mem. faculty Nat. Inst. Trial Advocacy, South Bend, Ind., 1977—, U.S. Dept. Justice, Washington, 1979-87, ABA, Chgo., 1979—; chmn. Law/Video Co., N.Y.C. and Waltham, Mass., 1987-92; comm. cons., weekly and weekend performer Today in NY (NBC), 1995—; daily panelist O.J. Today (Fox), 1995-96. Author: What Makes Juries Listen, 1985, How to Talk So People Listen, 1988, What Makes Juries Listen Today, 1998; prodr., dir., writer (films) China" Different Path, 1979 (Emmy nominee), Paul Revere: What Makes a Hero, 1976, others; contbr. articles to numerous profl. jours. Active Gov. Commn. Status of Women, Mass., 1973-83; campaign co-chair Mass. ERA Campaign, 1975-76; cons. Gov. Michael Dukakis, 1978, Dem. Nat. Party, Washington, 1979; bd. dirs. mem. Nat. Vol. Action com. United Way, Washington, 1986-91; bd. dirs. Taubman Ctr. Kennedy Sch. Harvard U., 1989-95; mem. Martha Graham Adv. Bd., 1997—; mem. Women's Leadership Bd., Kennedy Sch. Govt., Harvard U., 1999—. Recipient Best Program award for Meet the Arts Internat. Ednl. TV Assn., Tokyo, 1969, Ohio State Cultural Reporting award, 1970; named Outstanding Broadcaster New Eng. Broadcasters, Boston, 1973; Sonya Hamlin Day named in her honor Mayor of Boston, 1974.; archive of her works established Boston U. Library, 1983. Mem.: NATAS (two Emmy nominations), Internat. Women's Forum, Am. Fedn. TV and Radio Artists. Avocations: skiing, tennis, piano, dancing, museums.

HAMLIN, TOM, sportscaster; b. West Middletown, Ohio, Aug. 20, 1927; s. Harlin and Martha (Selby) H.; m. Phyllis Ann Hazelwood, June 20, 1953; children: Margo Ann, Thomas Charles. BA in Journalism, Ohio Wesleyan U., 1951. Sports dir. Sta. WLOK-AM-TV, Lima, Ohio, 1953-54, Sta. WMAN, Mansfield, Ohio, 1954-56, Stas. WAPI-AM and WABT-TV, Birmingham, Ala., 1956-60, Sta. WHIO-AM-TV, Dayton, Ohio, 1960-77, Sta. WKEF-TV, Dayton, 1979-85; freelance TV and radio announcer Voice Ohio State football network, 1973-75, Tampa Bay Bucs network, 1976-77; freelance TV and radio sports announcer, 1971-98, Ctrl. State U. Football, Ohio, 1987-96, N.A.I.A. Championship Games, 1990-92. Game analyst NCAA Basketball Final Four finals Sports Network Inc., 1963; Rose Bowl play-by-play announcer NBC Radio, 1974, 75. Bd. dirs. Greater Dayton Humane Soc., 1968-95, v.p., 1984-86. With USMC, 1945—46. Named Ala. Sportscaster of Yr. Nat. Sportswriters-Sportscasters Assn., 1959, Citizen of Yr., Dayton Jaycees, 1968; 6 nominations Ohio Sportscaster of the Yr. Mem. Ohio Sportscasters Assn. (pres. 1966-67), Agonis Club (pres. 1991-92). Presbyterian. Home: 401 Canterbury Dr Dayton OH 45429-1441

HAMLIN, WILFRID GARDINER, retired literature and philosophy educator; b. N.Y.C. s. Talbot Faulkner and Hilda Blanche Hamlin; m. Elizabeth Brett Hamlin, June 11, 1944 (dec. Apr. 1968); 1 child, Christopher Stone. BA, Wayne U.; MA, Antioch Coll., Yellow Springs, Ohio; PhD, Union Inst., Cin. Test psychologist Johnson O'Connor Rsch. Found., N.Y.C., 1940-42, 44-46, Adjutant Gen.'s Office, N.Y.C., 1945-46; mem. faculty Goddard Coll., Plainfield, Vt., 1948-99, coll. editor, 1975-98, mem. emeritus faculty, 1998—; student, asst. Black Mt. Coll. (N.C.), 1940—42. Edn. cons., 1950's and 60's. Author: To Start a School, 1971; editor: Teacher/School/Child, 1964. Avocations: photography, reading, theater, films, classical music. Home: PO Box 263 Plainfield VT 05667-0263

HAMLISCH, MARVIN, composer, conductor, pianist, entertainer; b. NYC, June 2, 1944; s. Max and Lilly (Schachter) Hamlisch; m. Terre Blair, 1989. Student, Juilliard Sch. Music, 1951—64; BA, Queens Coll., 1967. Prin. pops condr. Pitts. Symphony, 1994—, Balt. Symphony Orch., 1996—2000; prin. Pops condr. Nat. Symphony Orch., Washington, 2000—. Rehearsal pianist Broadway shows including Funny Girl, Fade Out-Fade In, (TV series) Bell Telephone Hour, early 1960's, first composition for film The Swimmer, 1968, film scores include Take the Money and Run, 1969, Bananas, 1971, Save the Tiger, 1973, Kotch, 1971, The Way We Were, The Sting, Same Time Next Year, 1979, Ice Castles, 1979, Chapter Two, 1979, Starting Over, 1979, Ordinary People, 1980, Sophie's Choice, 1982, Frankie and Johnny, 1991, Switched at Birth, 1991; composer: (films) Three Men and a Baby; popular songs include Sunshine, Lollipops and Rainbows, 1960, Nobody Does It Better, 1977, (Broadway musicals) A Chorus Line, 1975, They're Playing Our Song, 1979, The Goodbye Girl, 1993, theme song for Good Morning America, 1975; composer: symphonic work in one movement "Anatomy of Peace" (performed by Dallas Symphony Orch., London Symphony Orch., Symphony for UN at Carnegie Hall), 1991; composer: (lyrics by Alan and Marilyn Bergman) One Song (internat. debut at Barcelona Olympics), 1992; author: The Way I Was, 1992; musical dir. Barbra Steisand: The Concert (2 Emmy awards). Recipient Outstanding Music Direction & Music and Lyrics Emmy awards for Barbra Streisand: The Concert, 1994. Office: Nat Symphony Orch 2700 F St NW Washington DC 20566*

HAMM, AUROLYN MELBA, elementary school educator, writer; b. Elberton, Ga., June 14, 1956; d. Charles Augustus and MarieLouise Parker Hamm; children: April Michaela, Alan Mckenzie. BS, Emory U., 1978. Cert. tchr. Ga. Tchr. Benjamin E. Banneker H.S., Fairburn, Ga., 1986—93, Elbert County Mid. Sch., Elberton, 1995—. Author: (novel) A Moment In Time. Youth advisor NAACP, Elberton, 2002—03. Mem.: PAGE. Democrat. Roman Catholic. Personal E-mail: ahamm90159@aol.com.

HAMM, CHARLES JOHN, banker; b. Bklyn., May 11, 1937; s. Frank Coleman and Lisbeth (Higgins) H.; m. Irene Frail, Aug. 14, 1960; children: Charles William, Liza Higgins. BA, Harvard U., 1959; MBA, NYU, 1967. Vice pres., mgmt. supr. Wells Rich Greene Inc., N.Y.C., 1967-74; sr. v.p., mgmt. rep. Foote Cone & Belding Inc., N.Y.C., 1974-75; pres., chief operating officer F. William Free Inc., N.Y.C., 1975-77; exec. v.p. McCann-Erickson Inc., Atlanta, 1977-79, vice chmn. U.S.A., 1979-83; exec. v.p. McCann-Erickson World Wide, 1983-85, also dir.; pres. Independence Cmty. Bank, Bklyn., 1985-2001, chief exec. officer, 1986-2001, chmn., 1996—, dir., 1998—. Bd. dirs. Independence Cmty. Bank, N.Y.C., 1974-98; dir. Cmty. Preservation Corp., 1994-2002, N.Y. State Banking Bd., 1994-2002; bd. dirs., com. on econ. devel., com. on edn. N.Y.C. Partnership; bd. dirs., chmn. com. pub. affairs Savs. Banks Assn. N.Y. State, 1988-94; bd. dirs. N.Y. region Fed. Home Loan Bank, mem. exec. com., 1992-97, chmn. mktg. com., 1994-97; mem. exec. com., bd. dirs. Cmty. Banks Assn. N.Y. State, mem. long-range planning com., 1995-96; bd. dirs. N.Y. Investment Fund, Ind. Cmty. Bank, N.Y.C. Apptd. com. Bklyn. Waterfront Devel., 1995-96; mem. alumni coun. Phillips Exeter (N.H.) Acad., 1980-96, mem. fund raising adv. com., 1989-94; bd. dirs. Bklyn. Bur. Cmty. Svcs., 1985-98, chmn., 1989-98; bd. dirs. Bklyn. Hist. Soc., 1986-89, Bklyn. Botanic Garden, 1987—, mem. exec. com., 1994-99; bd. dirs. MSB fund Inc., 1987-90, Mason's Island Property Owners Assn., 1991-95, Pratt Inst. Bklyn., 1991—, chair fin. com., 1996-98; bd. dirs. Bklyn. Hosp. Ctr., 1985-93, Prospect Park Alliance, Bklyn., 1997—; chmn. devel. com. Pratt Inst., 1993-96; dir. The Friend Group, Cin., 1993—Mystic Seaport Mus., 2003—. 1st lt. C.E. U.S. Army, 1959-61. Recipient Robert E. Healey award Interpub. Group of Cos., 1979. Mem. Nat. Coun. Savs. Instns. (bd. dirs. 1991-92), Bklyn. C. of C. (bd. dirs. 1985-95, vice chmn. 1989-95, exec. com. 1989-95), Cmty. Banks Assn. N.Y. State (chmn. group IV/V, mem. exec. com. 1989-93), Univ. Club, Heights Casino Club (N.Y.C.), Bronxville Field Club (N.Y.), Mason's Island Yacht Club (Conn.), Hillsboro (Pompano Beach, Fla.). Office: Independence Cmty Bank 195 Montague St Brooklyn NY 11201-3631

HAMM, CLAIRE ROSE, development information services administrator; b. Trenton, NJ, Aug. 10, 1957; d. Daniel Michael and Rose Mary Serinaldi; m. Kim Edward Hamm, Apr. 25, 1981; children: Dana Rose, Kristopher Edward. Cert. in French, baccalaureate, U. Besançon, France, 1978; BA in French magna cum laude, Rider U., Lawrenceville, N.J., 1979, MA in Ednl. Adminstrn. and Supervision, 1985; MA in Counselor Edn., Coll. N.J., 2003. Cert. prin., supr., N.J. Office asst. devel. Princeton (N.J.) U., 1979-81, dir. grad. admissions, 1985-87, mgr. grad. programs, 1997-99; dir. rsch. and records Rider U., Lawrenceville, 1981-85; prin. elem. sch. St. Ann Sch., Lawrenceville, 1994-97; founding sch. adminstr. Princeton Acad., 1999-2000; dir. devel. info. svcs., career counselor Rider U., Lawrenceville, NJ, 2001—. Recipient award Outstanding Achievement in German Culture Studies, German Consulate, 1979. Mem.: Nat. Career Devel. Assn., N.J. Career Devel. Assn., N.J. Counseling Assn., Am. Counseling Assn., Pi Delta Phi. Roman Catholic. Avocation: exotic birds. Home: 23 Clover Hill Cir Ewing NJ 08638

HAMM, DAVID BERNARD, lawyer; b. Bklyn., Oct. 6, 1948; s. Isidore I. and Sarah (Lamm) H.; m. Margaret Weiss, June 20, 1971; children: Jennifer A. Maltz, Michael S. BA cum laude, CUNY, Bklyn., 1971; JD magna cum laude, N.Y. Law Sch., 1977. Bar: N.Y. 1978, U.S. Dist. Ct. (no. dist.) N.Y. 1978, U.S. Dist. Ct. (so. and ea. dists.) N.Y. 1979, U.S. Supreme Ct. 1981, U.S. Ct. Appeals (2d cir.) 1982, (3d cir.) 1988. Law clk. to presiding judges N.Y. State Ct. Appeals, Albany, 1977-79; assoc. Herzfeld & Rubin P.C., N.Y.C., 1979-85, mem., 1986—. Mem. Commn. Legis. and Civic Action Agudath Israel of Am., N.Y.C., 1979—. Recipient Community Service award Agudath Israel of Am., 1986. Mem. ABA, N.Y. State Bar Assn. (vice chair com. civil practice law and rules), N.Y. County Lawyers Assn. (torts law sect., appellate advocacy com.), Jewish Lawyers Guild, N.Y. Law Sch. Alumni Assn. (Prof. Vincent LoLordo award 1977). Democrat. Home: 2015 E 22nd St Brooklyn NY 11229-3615 Office: Herzfeld & Rubin PC 40 Wall St 53d Fl New York NY 10005-2301 E-mail: dhamm@herzfeld-rubin.com.

HAMM, MARIEL MARGARET, soccer player; b. Selma, Ala., Mar. 17, 1972; m. Christian Corry. BS in Polit. Sci., U. N.C., 1994. Forward U.S. Women's Nat. Soccer Team, Chgo., 1987—. Named U.S. Soccer Female Athlete of Yr., 1994—95, MVP, U.S. Women's Cup, 1995; recipient Gold medal, Atlanta Olympics, 1996, World Cup, 1999. Office: US Soccer Fedn US Soccer House 1801 S Prairie Ave Chicago IL 60616-1319

HAMM, RICHARD L. church administrator; b. Crawfordsville, Ind., Dec. 21, 1947; m. Melinda Ann Fishbaugh; children: David Lee, Laura Ann. Student, St. Petersburg Jr. Coll., 1966-67; BA in Religion, Butler U., 1970; D of Ministry, Christian Theol. Sem., 1974. Pastor Abington (Ind.) Christian Ch., 1968, Little Eagle Creek Christian Ch., Westfield, Ind., 1970; assoc. pastor Ctrl. Christian ch., Kansas City, Kans., 1974; founding pastor North Oak Christian ch., Kansas City, Mo., 1975-82; sr. pastor 1st Christian Ch., Ft. Wayne, Ind., 1982-90; regional min. Christian Ch. (Disciples of Christ) Tenn., 1990-93; gen. min., pres. Christian Ch. (Disciples of Christ) U.S. and Can., 1993—. Bd. dirs. mid-Am. region Christian Ch. (Disciples of Christ), 1977-81, bd. dirs. Kans. region, 1980-81, bd. dirs. Ind. region, 1983-90, chair area new ch. com. Ind. region, 1984-87, 89, mem. commn. ministry Ind. region, 1985-87, 89, mem. gen. bd., 1986-90, bd. dirs. divsn. overseas ministries, 1991—, commn. on ministry, 1991—; moderator, Christian Ch. Greater Kansas City, 1980-81; v.p. Nat. Coun. Chs., 1996; mem. ctrl. com. World Coun. Chs., 1998—. Author: From Mainline to Front Line, 1997, 2020 Vision for the Christian Church (Disciples of Christ), 2001. Mem. Mayor's Task Force Domestic Violence, 1990. Recipient Recognition award North Kansas City Edn. Assn., 1979, Recognition award Ft. Wayne, Ind., Edn. Assn. and Ft. Wayne Community Schs., 1984, Ind. Region's Model Ministry award, 1990; named Ecumenist of Yr. of Tenn., 1993. Mem. Tenn. Assn. Chs. (pres.-elect 1992), Clergy United Action (pres. 1984-86), Associated Chs. Ft. Wayne and Allen County (bd. dirs., officer 1982-90), Rotary. Mem. Christian Ch. Office: Christian Church (Disciples of Christ) PO Box 1986 Indianapolis IN 46206-1986

HAMM, VERNON LOUIS, JR., management and financial consultant; b. Mar. 14, 1951; s. Vernon Louis and Colleen Ann Hamm. BS, Murray (Ky.) State U., 1973; MBA, St. Louis U., 1975. Jr. exec. corp. accounts Brown Group, Inc., St. Louis, 1973-75; group supr. APC Skills Co., Palm Beach, Fla., 1975-77; account mgr. Inst. Mgmt. Resources, L.A., 1977-78; dir. mgmt. devel. Naus & Newlyn, Inc., Paoli, Pa., 1978-82; pres. Mgmt. Alternatives Ltd., Paoli, Pa., 1982—. Mgmt., fin. and energy cons., 1975— ; bd. dirs. Ryan's Family Steakhouses, Inc., Psychosystems Mgmt. Corp., N.Y.C., MAL Ventures, Detroit. Contbr. articles to profl. jours. Mem. Am. Soc. for Tng. and Devel., Am. Prodn. and Inventory Control Soc., Murray State U. Alumni Assn. E-mail: vhamm2@aol.com.

HAMMAKER, PAUL M. retail executive, business educator, author; b. Dayton, Ohio, Jan. 25, 1903; s. Wilbur Emory and Willamine (Weihrauch) H.; m. Patricia Curry, Sept. 5, 1929 (dec. 1955); children— Robert, John, David; m. Adrienne V. S. Stokes, June 15, 1956 (dec. 1970); m. Susan Ford, Nov. 24, 1989. B.C.S., U. Ill., 1925; LL.D., MacMurray Coll., 1957. With Marshall Field & Co., 1943-57, divisional v.p., 1948; gen. mdse. mgr., sr. v.p., asst. gen. mgr. Chgo. and suburban stores, until 1957; exec. v.p., gen. mgr. Montgomery Ward, 1957-59, mem. bd. dir., 1958-61, pres., 1959-61; dir. The Fair Store, Montgomery Ward Real Estate Corp., Montgomery Ward Credit Corp., Standard T Chem. Co., Inc.; Prof. bus adminstrn. Grad. Sch. Bus. Adminstrn., U. Va., 1962-73; sr. fellow Center for Study Applied Ethics, 1973—. Founder, partner Old Dominion Assos. (Mgmt. Cons.), 1964-89. Author: (with Louis T. Rader) Plain Talk About Managing. Mem. Alpha Tau Omega, Beta Gamma Sigma. Clubs: Farmington Country (Charlottesville, Va.) Home: 229 E Beverley St Apt 2 Staunton VA 24401-4380

HAMMAM, M. SHAWKY, electrical engineer, educator; b. Aug. 5, 1919; BSc, U. London, Eng., 1943, PhD, 1946. Registered profl. engr., N.Y. Sr. lectr. Alexandria U., Egypt, 1948-55; assoc. prof. Ein Shamus U., Egypt, 1955-63; vis assoc. prof. U. Kans., 1963-64; prof. Clarkson U., Potsdam, N.Y., 1964—. Niagara Mowhawk Power prof. Clarkson U., 1965. Fellow IEEE; mem. Inst. Elec. Engrs. (U.K.), Inst. Physics.

HAMMAN, RICHARD F. epidemiologist, educator; s. Lyle and Susan Hamman; m. Barbara Boyer, Aug. 15, 1970; children: Daniel Richard, Scott Robert. MD, Case Western Res., 1972; MPH, Johns Hopkins Sch. of Hygiene and Pub. Health, 1976, DrPH, 1979. Lic. gen. preventive medicine Am. Bd. of Preventive Medicine. Prof., chair U. Colo. Sch. of Medicine, Denver, 1989—. Recipient Kelly West award, Am. Diabetes Assn., 1996. Fellow: Am. Coll. of Preventive Medicine, Am. Coll. of Epidemiology; mem.: Delta Omega, Alpha Omega Alpha. Achievements include research in epidemiologic research to prevent Type 2 diabetes. Office: U Colo Health Sci ctr Dept Preventive Med & Biomed B-119 4200 E 9th Ave Denver CO 80262

HAMMAN, STEVEN ROGER, vocational rehabilitation specialist; b. Santa Monica, Calif., Nov. 2, 1946; s. Roy Ernest H. and Joan Barbara (Werner) Scott; m. Christine Frances Solomon, May 29, 1976; children: Zachary Charles, Tamara Edith, Bryan Joseph. AA, Northeastern Jr. Coll., 1967; BA, Colo. State Coll., 1970; MA, U. No. Colo., 1972; MS, Drake U., 1981. Cert. vocat. expert, rehab. counselor, ins. rehab. specialist. Social worker Poudre-Thompson Transp. Corps, Ft. Collins, Colo., 1974-78; placement specialist Missoula (Mont.) Rehab. Ctr., 1978-80; rehab. counselor Adolph Coors Co., Golden, Colo., 1981; rehab. counselor, br. mgr. Nat. Rehab. Cons., Duluth, Minn., 1981-82, Mont. case svcs. dir. Missoula, 1982-83, case svcs. dir. Northwest U.S. Spokane, Wash., 1983-86; rehab. cons., pres., chief exec. officer Vocability, Inc., Post Falls, Idaho, 1986—; pvt. practice as Social Security claimant's rep.; impartial hearings officer State of Idaho, Divsn. Vocat. Rehab., 1997—. Counselor, trainer Community Corrections Program, Ft. Collins, 1976. Cmty. organizer VISTA, Clay, W.Va., 1973-74; pres., bd. dirs. Mountain Van Spl. Transp., Missoula, 1980; bd. dirs. Heritage Place I and II, Coeur d'Alene Homes Inc., 1991-94; advanced master gardner Univ. Idaho Coop. Extention Ctr. Mem. Nat. Assn. Rehab. Practitioners in the Private Sector., Vocat. Evaluation and Work Adjustment Assn. (registered cons. Americans with Disabilities Act), Am. Bd. Disability Analysts (diplomate, sr. disability analyst), Nat. Orgn. Social Security Claimants Reps. Avocations: fly fishing, chess, cert. Kootenai county master gardener (Idaho). Office: Vocability Inc PO Box 772 Post Falls ID 83877-0772

HAMMAR, LESTER EVERETT, health care manufacturing executive, retired; b. Tillamook, Oreg., Dec. 15, 1927; s. Leo E. and Harriet L. (Parsons) H.; m. Margrit Steigl, May 9, 1964; children: Lawrence, Thomas, Stephanie. BS, Oreg. State U., 1950; MBA, Washington U., 1964. With Montsanto Co., 1952-69; controller Monsanto-Europe, 1966-69; v.p., controller Smith Kline & French Labs., Phila., 1969-72, Abbott Labs., North Chgo., Ill., 1972-88; ret. Bd. trustees Asia House Investments; project mgr. Exec. Svc. Corp. Chgo. Mem. audit com. City of Lake Forest; ruling elder, clk. of session 1st Presbyn. Ch. of Lake Forest; bd. dirs. Haven, Clara Abbott Fund; bd. dirs. Teton County Housing Authority. 1st lt. F.A., AUS, 1951-52. Mem. Fin Execs. Inst., Am. Mgmt. Assn. (former chmn. fin. coun., bd. mem.), 100 Club of Lake Country Club. Home and Office: 634 Academy Woods Dr Lake Forest IL 60045

HAMMARGREN, LONNIE L. former lieutenant governor; b. Dec. 25, 1937; married. BA, U. Minn., 1958, MA in Psychol., 1960, BS, MD, U. Minn., 1964, MS in Neurosurgery, 1974. Diplomate Am. Bd. Neurological Surgery; med. license Nev., Minn. Flight surgeon for the astronauts NASA Manned Space Craft Ctr.; former lt. gov., pres. of the senate State of Nev., 1995-98; med. pvt. practice Las Vegas, 1998—. Assoc. clin. prof. neurosurgery U. Nev. Sch. Medicine, Reno; clin. assoc. prof. surgery U. Calif., San Diego, 1982; chair Commn. Econ. Devel., Commn. Tourism; bd. dirs. Nev. Dept. Transp. Bd. regents U. and C.C. Sys. Nev., 1988-94; adv. bd. mem. Gov.'s com. for Employment of Handicapped; mem. State Bd. Edn., 1984-88; bd. mem. March of Dimes, Aid to Adoption of Spl. Kids. Mem. Spinal Cord Injury Program of Nev. (pres.), Cancer Soc., Aerospace Med. Assn., U Med. Ctr. Rehabilitation Unit (dir.), U. Med. Ctr. (chmn. neurosurgery dept.), Help Them Walk Again Found. (Nat. Dir.), Spina Bifida and Hydrocephalus Soc. (med. dir.), Internat. Ctr. for Rehabilitation Engring. (med. dir.), Pacific World Med. Found. (treas.), Paramed. and Emergency Care Bd. (adv.). Office: 3196 S Maryland Pkwy Ste 106 Las Vegas NV 89109-2312*

HAMMARSTEN, JAMES FRANCIS, internist, educator; b. Grey Eagle, Minn., Mar. 25, 1920; s. Francis Ragnar and Julia Linnea (Hammargren) Hammarsten; m. Dorothea Marie Jung, Apr. 15, 1944; children: Linnea, James Eric, Richard. BS, U. Minn., 1943, MB, 1944, MD, 1945. Diplomate Am. Bd. Internal Medicine (bd. dirs. 1967-73, various other offices). Intern U. Okla. Hosps., Oklahoma City, 1944-45; resident in internal medicine U. Minn. Hosps., VA Hosp., Mpls., 1947-49; asst. prof. medicine U. Minn., Mpls., 1949-53, prof., 1962-66; from asst. prof. to prof. U. Okla., Oklahoma City, 1953-62, prof., head dept. medicine, 1966-78, Carl Puckett prof. pulmonary diseases, vice-chmn. dept. medicine, 1967-77; prof. medicine U. Okla. Health Scis. Ctr., Oklahoma City, 1977-78; prof. U. Wash., Seattle, 1978-87; disting. vis. prof. health scis. Boise State U., 1978-87. Asst. chief med. svcs. VA Hosp., Mpls., 1949—53, chief med. svc., Oklahoma City, 1953—62, Boise VA Med. ctr., 1978—81; chief medicine St. Paul-Ramsey Hosp., 1962—66; cons. Internat. Union Against Tb; vis. prof. Laennec Hosp., Paris, 1977—78; clin. prof. med. U. N.D., 1987—. Contbr. articles to profl. jours. With U.S. Army, 1945—47, with USAF, 1953, col. USAR. Recipient Disting. Alumnus award, U. Minn. Master: ACP (re-certification com. 1971—73, Okla. Gov.'s coun. 1972—78); mem.: AAAS, AMA (alt. ho. dels. 1974—77, sec. coun. disease of chest 1974—77, counterpart dept. head Vietnam project 1967—75), So. Soc. Clin. Investigation, Soc. Exptl. Biology and Medicine, Minn. Thoracic Soc., Okla. Thoracic Soc., Okla. State Med. Assn., Okla. Soc. Internal Medicine, Okla. Heart Assn., Oklahoma County Med. Assn., N.Y. Acad. Scis., Minn. Soc. Internal Medicine, Idaho State Med. Assn., Idaho County Med. Soc., Am. Soc. Internal Medicine, Assn. Am. Physicians, Am. Fedn. Clin. Rsch., Am. Coll. Chest Physicians (hon. fellow), Am. Clin. and Climatological Assn., Am. Geriatric Soc., Assn. Am. Physicians (master and laurate), Ctrl. Soc. Clin. Rsch. (pres. 1968—69), Am.-Israel Med. Found. (trustee), Am. Heart Assn. (profl. edn. com. 1961—67, subcom. on pilot projects 1965—67, vice-chmn. profl. edn. com. 1963, others), Am. Thoracic Soc. (pres. 1969—70, councilor-at-large 1962—64, 1966—71, gen. med. sessions program com. 1963—65, chmn. med. sessions program com. 1963, subcom. on fellowship 1966—67, others), Am. Lung Assn. (bd. dirs. 1968—80, 1982—, various offices, Hall of Fame 1979), Lions, Sigma Xi, Alpha Omega Alpha. Democrat. Methodist. Home and Office: 30036 Loon Ln Melrose MN 56352-8000

HAMME, DAVID CODRINGTON, architect; b. York, Pa., Oct. 8, 1931; BA magna cum laude, Gettysburg Coll., 1952; BArch, U. Pa., 1960, MArch, 1962. Archtl. designer J. Alfred Hamme and Assocs., York, Pa., 1961-62; planner U.

Pa. Planning Office, Phila., 1962; sr. designer Phila. City Planning Commn., 1962-66; project dir. Wallace, McHarg, Roberts & Todd, Phila., 1966—81, sr. assoc., 1981—, Wallace Roberts & Todd, Phila., 1981—, ptnr., prin., 1981—2000, mng. prin., 1990—, dir. Phila. office, 2001—. Adj. prof. dept. architecture Drexel U., Phila., 1973—82, asst. dir. dept. architecture, 1985—86, Stanley J. Gwiazda prof., 2002—; lectr. dept. landscape architecture U. Pa., Phila., 1975—78, Phila., 1981—88, lectr. dept. plannint, 1996—. Theophilus Parson Chandler scholar; recipient Design award HUD, 1968, Honor award Am. Soc. Landscape Designers, 1973, Honor award for mgmt. approaches HUD, 1974, Arthur Spayd Brooke Gold medal for design, Charles Merrick Gay prize, Paul Philippe Cret medal for design, Warren Powers Laird medal for design. Mem.: AIA. Office: Wallace Roberts Todd 260 S Broad St Fl 8 Philadelphia PA 19102-5075

HAMMEL, ALICE MAXINE, music educator; b. Tampa, Fla., May 7, 1965; d. Nelson Dodge and Alice Maxine King; m. Bruce Ray Hammel, Feb. 6, 1993; children: Hannah Elizabeth, Hollie MaryAlice. BME, Shenandoah U., 1987; MME, Fla. State U., 1989; DMA, Shenandoah U., 1999. Band, choral dir. Trinity Cath. Sch., Tallahassee, 1987-89; choral dir. Hanover County Schs., Ashland, Va., 1990-93; ind. educator music Richmond, Va., 1989—; staff adjudicator Music Festivals, Birdsboro, Pa., 1989—; instr. U. Richmond, 1998—, dir. ednl. programs Musicate. Vis. asst. prof. U. Richmond; cons. and presenter in field; networking rsch. mentor Music Educators Nat. Conf., 2002—, nat. spokesperson. Musician (flutist): Music of Allan Blank, 1999; contbr. articles to profl. jours. Patriotic edn. chair Daus. Am. Colonists, Richmond, 1999—2001; dist. good citizens chair DAR, Richmond, 1998—2001, music chmn., 1997. Recipient Young Career Achievement award, Shenandoah U., 2000. Mem.: Coll. Music Soc., Va. Assn. Gifted, Am. Coun. Exceptional Children, Va. Music Educators Assn. (chamber music chair 1990—98, sight reading chair 1998—, spl. learners chair 1998—), Music Tchrs. Nat. Assn. (keynote spkr. 2001, woodwind rep. 2002), Music Educators Nat. Conf. (networking mentor rschr.), Sigma Alpha Iota (Nat. Leadership award 1987). Democrat. Baptist. Home: 5009 W Seminary Ave Richmond VA 23227-3407

HAMMEL, ERNEST MARTIN, medical educator, academic administrator; b. Ashtabula, Ohio, May 2, 1939; s. Eugene Christian and Etna Maria (Costas) H.; m. Martha Lorene Hertzer, Dec. 16, 1961; children: Eric John, James Martin. BS, Heidelberg Coll., 1962; MPH, U. Mich., 1966; PhD, 1976. Program develper Mich. Assn. Regional Programs, East Lansing, 1973-74; asst. dir. ops., 1975-76; exec. dir. OHEP Ctr. Med. Edn., Southfield, Mich., 1976—2002, dir. emeritus, 2002—. Adj. asst. dean Wayne State U. Sch. Medicine, Detroit, 1993-2002; adj. faculty health svcs. adminstr. extended degree programs Ctrl. Mich. U., Mt. Pleasant, 1980-99; adj. asst. prof. of cmty. and family medicine, Wayne State U. Sch. of Medicine, 1993—; co-dir. SAVE 100 Pharmacy Initiative of WSU-OHEP Consortium Quality, Cost-Effective Med. Care Program, 1995—; mem. task force Mich. Antibiotic Resistance Reduction Program, 1998-2002; task groups coord. OHEP Resource Ctr. on Gen. Competencies, 2002—. Editor several med. care orgns. publs. Contbr. articles to profl. jours. Trustee Kenny Mich. Rehab. Found., Rochester Hills, 1984-88; chmn. program consultation and cont. med. edn. devel. CME Accreditation com. Mich. State Med. Soc., Lansing, 1989—. Behavioral Sci. fellow U. Mich., 1969-70, Behavioral Sci. rsch. fellow, 1971-72; grad. student rsch. grantee Rackham Sch. Grad. Studies, U. Mich., 1972; Pub. Health svc. trainee U. Mich., 1965-66, 70-71, 72-73; contract Nat. Ctr. Health Svcs. R & D, 1973. Mem.: APHA, Mich. Pub. Health Assn., Mich. Assn. Med. Edn. (pres. 1995—97), Assn. Hosp. Med. Edn. (chmn. coun. med. edn. consortia 1997—99), U. Mich. Alumni Assn., Heidelberg Fellows. Office: OHEP Ctr for Med Edn 21415 Civic Center Dr Ste 301 Southfield MI 48076-3954

HAMMEL, HAROLD THEODORE, physiology and biophysics educator, researcher; b. Huntington, Ind., May 8, 1921; s. Audry Harold and Ferne Jane (Wiles) H.; m. Dorothy King, Dec. 29, 1948; children: Nannette, Heidi. BS in Physics, Purdue U., 1943; MS in Physics, Cornell U., 1950, PhD in Zoology, 1953; DSc (hon.), Huntington Coll., 1999. Jr. physicist Los Alamos (N.Mex.) Lab., 1944-46, staff physicist, 1948-49; from instr. to asst. prof. U. Pa., Phila., 1953-61; assoc. prof., fellow John B. Pierce Lab. Yale U., New Haven, 1961-68; prof. Scripps Instn. of Oceanography U. Calif., San Diego, 1968-88, emeritus prof., 1988—. Adj. prof. physiology and biophysics Ind. U., Bloomington, 1989—; fgn. sci. mem. Max Planck Inst. for Physiol. and Clin. Rsch., 1978—; U.S. sr. scientist Alexander von Humboldt Found., 1981. Author: (with Scholander) Osmosis and Tensile Solvent, 1976; contbr. over 200 articles to profl. jours. Fellow AAAS; mem. Am. Phys. Soc., Am. Chem. Soc., Am. Physiol. Soc. (Fifth August Krogh Disting. lectureship 1998, Honor award Environ. and Exercize sect. 1996), Am. Soc. Mammalogy, Norwegian Acad. Sci. and Letters. Democrat. Achievements include first measurement of phloem sap, and of xylem sap pressure in higher plants; research in osmosis and fluid transport in plants; thermal and metabolic responses to moderate cold exposure in Australian Aborigine, Kalahari Bushmen, Innuit, Alacalut Indians; explanation of freezing without cavitation in evergreen plants; extension and application of kinetic theory to Hulett's theory of solvent tension and to osmotic force in Starling's experiment; research in theory of adjustable set point and gain for regulation of body temperature in vertebrates, research in control of salt gland function in birds. Home: 1605 Ridgeway Dr Ellettsville IN 47429-9474 Office: Ind U Med Scis Program Bloomington IN 47405 E-mail: hhammel@indiana.edu.

HAMMER, ALFRED EMIL, artist, educator; b. New Haven, Jan. 11, 1925; s. Forrester L. and Eugenie (Bauer-Enquist) H.; m. Marian Valle, Aug. 14, 1948; children: Alfred Emil, Paul Forrester, Eric Valdemar, Eugenie Bauer; m. Jeanne Baker, Dec. 18, 1966; children: Stephen Drake, Rosamond Swan. BFA, R.I. Sch. Design, 1950, Yale U., 1951, MFA, 1952. From instr. to assoc. prof. painting and drawing R.I. Sch. Design, Providence, 1952-69, chmn. grad. studies, 1958-60, dean students, 1960-61; dean Cleve. Inst. Art, 1969-74; dir., prof. Sch. Art, U. Man., Winnipeg, Can., 1974-82; dir. Pacific N.W. Coll. Art, Portland, Oreg., 1982-83; prof. Hartford Art Sch., U. Hartford, Conn., 1983-88, dean, 1983-86; freelance artist, 1988—. Exhibited in group shows R.I. Ann. (1st prize award 1952), Providence Art Club Ann. (1st prize award 1953, 54, 55, 57), Newport Ann. (1st prize 1959), Boston Arts Festival, 1958, Shippee Gallery, N.Y.C., 1985, Joseloft Gallery U. Hartford, 1992, Conn. Watercolor Soc. (prize 1992, 97), New Britain Mus. Am. Art (1st prize for watercolor 1988); one-man shows include U. Maine, 1954, U. Man., 1980, Thomas Gallery, 1980, Melnyschenko Gallery, Winnipeg, 1981, Movie House Studio Gallery, Millerton, N.Y., 1992; represented in collections Agnes Gund, Jr. C. of C., Nat. Mus. Israel, R.I. Sch. Design Mus., Portland Art Mus., Conn. Bank and Trust Co., N.E. Savs., Hartford, Corp. Hdqrs. Otis Elevator Corp., Farmington, Conn., Bank of New Eng., Boston, Shawmut Bank, Hartford, Aenta Ins., Hartford, Govt. of Man., Gov.'s Coll. of Conn. Artists; represented in book Prize Winning Artists, 1960. Mem. Conn. Watercolor Soc., Lyme Art Assn. Home: 55 Bolton St Hartford CT 06114 E-mail: ballpeenhammer1@aol.com.

HAMMER, DAVID LINDLEY, lawyer, writer; b. Newton, Iowa, June 6, 1929; s. Neal Paul and Agnes Marilyn (Reece) H.; m. Audrey Lowe, June 20, 1953; children: Julie, Lisa, David. BA, Grinnell Coll., 1951; JD, U. Iowa, 1956. Bar: Iowa 1956, U.S. Dist. Ct. (no. dist.) Iowa 1959, U.S. Dist. Ct. (so. dist.) Iowa 1969, U.S. Ct. Appeals (8th cir.) 1996, U.S. Supreme Ct. 1977. Ptnr. Hammer Simon & Jensen, Dubuque, Iowa, Galena, Ill.; mem. grievance commn. Iowa Supreme Ct., 1973-85, mem. adv. rules com., 1986-92. Author: Poems from the Ledge, 1980, The Game is Afoot, 1983, For the Sake of the Game, 1986, To Play the Game, 1986, The 22nd Man, 1989, The Quest, 1993, My Dear Watson, 1994, The Before Breakfast Pipe, 1995, A Dangerous Game, 1997, The Vital Essence, 1999, A Talent for Murder, 2000, Yonder in the Gaslight, 2000, Straight Up with a Twist, 2001, A Deep Game, 2001, The Game is Underfoot, 2002, You Heard What Jesse Said, 2003, My Dear Holmes, 2003. Bd. dirs. Linwood Cemetery Assn., 1973—, pres., 1983-84; bd. dirs. Dubuque Mus. Art, 1998-2001, hon. dir.; bd. dirs., past pres. Finley Hosp., hon. dir.; bd. dirs. Finley Found., 1988-95; past campaign chmn., past pres. United Way; past bd. dirs. Carnegie Stout Pub. Libr. With U.S. Army, 1951-53. Fellow Am. Coll. Trial Lawyers; mem. ABA, Young Lawyers Iowa (past pres.), Iowa Def. Counsel Assn. (pres. 1991-92, del. to Def. Rsch. Inst. 1992-93), Assn. Def. Trial Attys. (exec. coun. 1983-86, past chmn. Iowa chpt.), Iowa State Bar Assn. (past chmn. continuing legal edn. com.), Iowa Acad. Trial Lawyers, Dubuque County Bar Assn. (past pres.), Baker St. Irregulars. Republican. Congregationalist. Office: 770 Main St Dubuque IA 52001

HAMMER, DEBORAH MARIE, librarian, paralegal; b. Bronx, N.Y., Nov. 16, 1947; d. Ben and Helen (Lorenz) Halprin; m. Mark Stewart Hammer, May 30, 1976; 1 child, Joshua Robert. BA, CCNY, 1968; MLS, Rutgers U., 1969. Cert. libr. N.Y. Gen. asst. info., tel. ref. div. Queens Borough Pub. Libr., 1969-71, gen. asst. popular libr., 1972-80, asst. div. head history, travel & biography, 1972-81, div. head history, travel & biography, 1981-92, div. mgr. social scis., 1992-98; fee conciliation coord., computer systems mgr. Nassau County Bar Assn., 1999—. Democrat. Avocations: reading, cooking, handcrafts, camping. Office: 15th and West Sts Mineola NY 11501

HAMMER, EMANUEL FREDERICK, clinical psychologist, psychoanalyst; b. N.Y.C., Aug. 15, 1926; s. Isadore and Rebecca (Lieberman) H.; m. Lila Maralyn King, June 4, 1950; children: Diane Robin, Cary Marc. Student, Bklyn. Coll., 1944-45, 46-47; BA magna cum laude, Syracuse U., 1948; PhD, NYU, 1951. Diplomate in clin. psychology Am. Bd. Profl. Psychology; cert. psychologist N.Y. Dir. intern tng. Lynchburg (Va.) State Colony, 1951-52; sr. research scientist N.Y. State Psychiat. Inst., 1952-55; dir. dept. psychology, Psychiat. Clinic N.Y.C. Criminal Cts., 1955-72; dir. Am. Projective Drawing Inst., N.Y.C., 1956—; chief psychologist Lincoln Inst. for Psychotherapy, N.Y.C., 1960-68; lectr. Bklyn. Coll., 1958-63, New Sch. for Social Research, 1972; adj. asso. prof. N.Y. U. Grad. Sch. Arts and Scis., 1966-76; psychiat. cons., therapist United Presbyn. Ch., 1966-80; prof. grad. art therapy dept. Pratt Inst., 1978-88; clin. prof. Postdoctoral Inst. Advanced Psychol. Studies, Adelphi U., 1980—. Author: The Clinical Application of Projective Drawings, 1958, Creativity, 1961, Use of Interpretation in Treatment, 1968, Antiachievement: Perspectives on School Drop-Outs, 1970, Creativity, Talent and Personality, 1984, Reaching the Affect: Style in the Psychodynamic Therapies, 1990, Advances in Projective Drawing Interpretation, 1997, also 75 profl. papers. Served with USAF, 1945-46, PTO. Fellow APA, Am. Anthrop. Assn. (liaison fellow); mem. Nat. Psychol. Assn. for Psychoanalysis (dir. admissions, sr. mem. and faculty), Soc. Personality Assessment (sec.), N.Y. Soc. Clin. Psychologists (pres. 1964-65). Home and Office: 381 W End Ave New York NY 10024-6104

HAMMER, HAROLD HARLAN, oil company financial executive; b. Chgo., May 23, 1920; s. B. James and Frances (Halbren) H.; m. Hannah Richmond, Mar. 1, 1956; children: John, Elizabeth. BS, Northwestern U., 1941; MBA, NYU, 1950, JD, 1955. Bar: N.Y. State 1955. Acct. U.S. Steel Corp., 1941-42; asst. sec.-treas. Duraloy Co., Scottdale, Pa., 1945-48; fin. analyst, asst. contr. Port of N.Y. Authority, 1948-50; investment counsel N.Y.C., 1950—; since practiced in; v.p. fin., dir. Control Data Corp., Mpls., 1966-72; chmn. fin. com., dir. Gen. Refractories Co., 1963-66; with Gulf Oil Corp., Pitts., 1972—, sr. v.p., 1972-73, exec. v.p., 1973-81, chief adminstrv. officer, 1981-85; chmn. MMC Group Inc., 1986—. Bd. dirs., chmn. J.C. Horne & Co., Standard-Thomson Corp. Author: Financing the Port of New York Authority, 1957, also articles in field. Bd. dirs. W. Penn Hosp. Served as lt. USNR, World War II. Mem. ABA, Fed., N.Y. Bar Assns., Phi Alpha Delta. Clubs: Fox Meadow Tennis (gov. 1966); Duquesne (Pitts.), Fox Chapel Golf (Pitts.); Rolling Rock (Liqonier, Pa.). Methodist. E-mail: hhhammer@earthlink.net.

HAMMER, JACOB MYER, physicist, consultant; b. N.Y.C., Sept. 14, 1927; s. Joseph Israel Hammer and Miriam Silverman; m. Rose Kizner (div. 1975); children: Daniel, Jonathan, Miriam; m. Katrina Schuyler, July 10, 1982; 1 stepson, David Reisberg. BS in Engring. Physics, NYU, 1950, PhD in Physics, 1956; MS in Physics, U. Ill., 1951. Mem. tech. staff Bell Telephone Labs., Murray Hill, N.J., 1956-59, RCA Labs., Princeton, N.J., 1959-68, David Sarnoff Rsch. Ctr., Princeton, 1970-87, photonics cons., 1987—. Sr. visitor Cavendish Lab., Cambridge U., 1968-69. Co-author: Integrated Optics, 1975, Fiber & Integrated Optics, 1979; co-editor: Surface Emitting Semiconductor Lasers and Arrays, 1993; contbr. numerous articles to profl. jours.; patentee in field. With AUS, 1946-47. Fellow IEEE (life, assoc. editor Jour. Quantum Electronics, 1987-90); mem. Am. Phs. Soc., Optical Soc. Am. Office: 42 City Gate Ln Annapolis MD 21401-2736 E-mail: jakehammer@ieee.org.

HAMMER, JANE AMELIA ROSS, advocate; b. Charlotte, N.C., Apr. 9, 1916; d. Otho Bescent and Lucy (Harris) Ross; m. Philip Gibbon Hammer, Aug. 27, 1937; children: Philip Jr., Thomas Ross, Michael Levering. AB, U. N.C., Chapel Hill, 1936, MA, U. N.C., 1937; postgrad., Radcliffe Coll., New Eng. Conservatory, 1938-39. Charter mem. N.C. Symphony, 1933-36; mem. faculty philosophy Spelman Coll., Atlanta, 1946-58. Bd dirs., PiPa Tag, Inc., Tarpon Springs, Fla., 1995—. Violinist Symphony String Quartet, N.C., 1933-36, Atlanta Symphony, 1947-52, Friday Morning Music Club Orch. at Kennedy Ctr., Washington, 1975-82; author: Protector: A Life History of Richard Cromwell, 1997; editor: Logic for Living, Lectures of H.H. Williams, 1951; editor, pub.: Origin of Belief (H.H. Williams), 1972; contbr. articles to profl. jours. Dir. tng. programs Overseas Edn. Fund U.S. LWV, Washington, 1962-63, mem. registration and voting projects staff Edn. Fund LWV, 1964-65, dir. Inner City Project in 10 U.S. cities, 1965-67, mem. spl. projects com., 1970-75, advisor natural resources com. LWV of Fla., Palm Harbor, 1990-92, bd. dirs. LWV Atlanta and State of Ga., 1942-61, pres. LWV of North Pinellas County, Fla., 1989-90; appointed pub. rep. mem. com. for feasibility study of health of residents of Pinellas County, U.S. Dept. Energy and Fla. Dept. Health and Rehab. Svcs., 1991-94; chmn. OASIS Coalition for Integration of Pub. Schs., Atlanta, 1960-61; mem. bd. overseers Dag Hammerskjold Coll., Columbia, Md., 1968-71; pres. FMMC Music Club Inc., Washington, 1973-76, trustee found., Washington Internat. Competition, 1968-71; treas. H.W. Philos. Soc., Washington and Fla., 1975—; mem. Pres. Clinton's Nat. Steering Com., 1995-2000; mem. Nat. Women's Dem. Club. Recipient Good Housekeeping Mag. award for Citizenship in Action, OASIS, 1962, named 500 Environ. Achiever, Friends of UN Environ. Programme, 1987; fellow Kenan, Univ. N.C., 1937. Mem. Friday Morning Music Club (Washington), The Social List (Washington), Jefferson Soc. (leadership circle 1996-2000), Cromwell Assn., Clan Ross Assn. (U.S.), Chi Omega (Epsilon Beta). Presbyterian. Avocations: gardening, swimming, research, writing. Home: 521 Holly Rd Edgewater MD 21037-3832 E-mail: hammerjaner@aol.com.

HAMMER, JOHN HENRY, II, hospital administrator; b. Bartlesville, Okla., Dec. 27, 1943; s. John Henry and Lucy (Macias) H.; children: John Henry, Erica, Megan. BBA, St. Joseph's Coll., 1966; student, U. Md. (Europe), 1968-69; MBA, U. Ill., 1984. Project mgr. Econ. & Manpower Corp., N.Y.C., 1971-73; asst. dir. human resources St. Catherine Hosp., East Chicago, Ind., 1974-80; pres. Employees Credit Union, East Chicago, Ind., 1974-80; dir. pers. Lakeview Med. Ctr., Danville, Ill., 1980-84, v.p., 1984-88, United Samaritans Med. Ctr., Danville, Ill., 1988-95; adminstrv. dir. U. Ill. Illini Union, Urbana, 1997—. Bd. dirs. East Cen. Ill. Health Systems Agy., East Cen. Ill. Health Planning Orgn., Vermilion Area Cmty. Health Ctr. Chmn. De La Garza Career Ctr. Program Com., 1974-80. bd. dirs. Jr. Achievement of Danville, 1990-95, vice chmn., 1991, chmn. 1993-95; mem. adv. bd. McKinley Health Ctr., 2002-. Capt. USAF, 1967-71, to lt. col. USAFR, 1974-93. Mem. Ind. Soc. Hosp. Personnel Adminstrn. (chmn. 1976-77, dir. 1977-79, pres. 1979-80), Am. Coll. Healthcare Execs., Rotary (bd. dirs. 1990-92, pres. 1991). Roman Catholic. Home: 218 W Ellsworth St Westville IL 61883-1232 E-mail: hammer2@uiuc.edu.

HAMMER, LINDA See LINDROTH, LINDA

HAMMER, MARION PRICE, association executive; b. Columbia, S.C., Apr. 26, 1939; 3 children. Exec. dir. Unified Sportsmen of Fla., Fairfax, Va., 1978—; pres. NRA, Fairfax, Va., bd. dirs. Tallahassee, Fla. Registered lobbyist for pro-gun issues. Recipient Harlon B. Carter Legis. Achievement award, 1992, SCOPE ann. 2d Amendment award, 1987, Roy Rogers Man of Yr. award, Outstanding Cmty. Svc. award Nat. Safety Coun., 1993, Nat. Edn. award Am. Legion, Sybil Ludington award. Mem. NRA (life, cert. firearm instr., chmn. legal policy com., chmn. task force on hunter safety legislation, vice chmn. women's policies com., mem. nominating com., pub. affairs com., ethics com., membership coms.). Office: Unified Sportsmen of FL PO Box 6565 Tallahassee FL 32314-6565

HAMMER, ROBERT EUGENE, psychologist; b. Faribault, Minn., Aug. 7, 1931; s. Rolf Walter and Verona (Bakken) H.; m. M. Kitti Nations, Apr. 30, 1967 (div. Jan. 1988); children: Gregory Clay, Cynthia Beth; m. Bonnie Jo French, Nov. 12, 1988. BS in Counseling Psychology, U. Houston, 1959, MA, 1963; PhD in Spl. Edn. Adminstrn., U. Iowa, 1970. Lic. psychologist, Iowa; cert. health svc. provider in psychology. Tchr. educable mentally retarded Houston Ind. Sch. Dist., 1961-63; testing supr. U. Houston Counseling Ctr., 1963-65; child psychologist Mental Health Inst., Independence, Iowa, 1965-67, dir. adolescent treatment unit, 1969-74, 89-93, dir. psychol. svcs., 1969-97, dir. activity therapies dept., 1994-97, dir. social svcs. dept., 1996-97; cons. psychologist part-time Duffy Psychology Assocs., Iowa City, Cedar Rapids, Iowa, 1997—. Rsch. dir. Iowa Div. State Mental Health Resources; pvt. practice counseling and cons. psychologist, 1974—; assoc. Duffy Psychology Assocs., 1997. Contbr. articles to profl. jours. Vol. fireman;; mem. men's gospel quartet United Parish Ch.; Meth. lay speaker; Bd. dirs. Iowa Nursing Found. Served with USAF, 1950—53. Mem. Am. Psychol. Assn., Nat. Assn. Rural Mental Health, Am. Soc. Quality Control, State Mental Health Dirs. Assn., Iowa Psychol. Assn., Houston TKE Alumni Assn., SPEBSQSA, U.S. Chess Fedn., Evaluation Network, Am. Legion, Lions, Masons. Home: PO Box 0257 120 2nd St S Coggon IA 52218-0257

HAMMER, TERENCE MICHAEL, physician; b. Chgo., May 7, 1946; s. Albert S. and Minnetta Elizabeth (Nichols) H.; 1 child, Kathryn Gyo Hammer. BS, U. Ill., 1968; MD, Stanford U., 1973. Diplomate Am. Bd. Family Practice. Intern L.A. County-U. So. Calif. Med. Ctr., 1973-74; med. dir. Long Beach (Calif.) Health Dept. Drug Program, 1974-75; resident in family medicine Contra Costa Med. Svcs., Martinez, Calif., 1975-77; pvt. practice in family medicine Redondo Beach (Calif.) Med. Group, 1977-81, Family Practice Assocs., Torrance, Calif., 1981-96, Med. Inst. Little Co. of Mary Hosp., Torrance, 1996—. Bd. dirs., treas. Med. Inst. of Little Co. of Mary Hosp.; lectr. in field. Bd. trustees Peninsula Edn. Found., Palos Verdes, Calif., 1991-99; bd. examiners Malcolm Baldridge Nat. Quality Awards, 1999, 2001. Named Calif. Rep. of Yr., 2001; named one of America's Top Family Drs., Consumers Rsch. Coun. Am., 2002. Mem. Am. Coll. Physician Execs., Premier Health Med. Group (pres. 1991—), South Bay Ind. Physicians Med. Group (pres. emeritus), Soc. Chief Med. Officers, Phi Beta Kappa. Lutheran. Avocations: fresh water fishing, modern art collecting, swimming, writing. Office: Med Inst Little Co Mary Hosp 20911 Earl St Ste 400 Torrance CA 90503-4355 Personal E-mail: hefish1@aol.com.

HAMMER, WADE BURKE, retired oral and maxillofacial surgeon, educator; b. Lakeland, Fla., Apr. 21, 1932; s. Orval Seown and Lilly Pearl (Wade) H.; m. Betty Dean Webb, June 22, 1956; children: Robert Burke Hammer, Joanna Wade Hammer Dykes. AA, U. Fla., 1956; D.D.S., Emory U., 1960. Diplomate Am. Bd. Oral and Maxillofacial Surgery. Pvt. practice dentistry, Orange Park, Fla., 1960-61; resident in oral and maxillofacial surgery U. Pa. Grad. Sch. Medicine, Phila., 1961-62, Grady Meml. Hosp., Atlanta and Emory U., 1962-65; practice dentistry specializing in oral and maxillofacial surgery Atlanta, 1965-68; mem. staff Med. Coll. of Ga. Hosp., Augusta; asst. prof. oral and maxillofacial surgery Med. Coll. Ga., Augusta, 1968-71, assoc. prof., 1971-75, prof., 1975-93, prof. emeritus oral and maxillofacial surgery, 1993. Staff VA Hosp. Complex, Augusta, 1969-99; cons. Ft. Gordon Army Med. Ctr., 1970-93, Univ. Hosp., Augusta, 1968-93. Contbr. articles to profl. jours. Chmn. exec. com. Gen. Faculty Orgn. Med. Coll. Ga., 1988; mem. USCG Auxiliary. With USN, 1950-54, col. USAR, 1976-92, ret. Decorated Legion of Merit, Meritorious Svc. medal, Army Commendation medal (5), Knight Hospitalar Order St. John of Jerusalem, Knight Sovereign Mil. Order of the Temple of Jerusalem. Fellow Am. Assn. Oral and Maxillofacial Surgeons (life), Am. Coll. Dentists, Am. Soc. Dental Anesthesiology; mem. ADA (life), Internat. Assn. Dental Rsch., Ga. Dental Assn., Ea. Dist. Dental Assn., Am. Assn. Dental Schs., Augusta Dental Soc., Ga. Soc. Oral and Maxillofacial Surgeons, Southeastern Soc. Oral and Maxillofacial Surgeons (pres. 1984-85), Res. Officers Assn. (Nat. Dental Surgeon 1990-92, Dept. of Ga. Pres. 1998-99), Interallied Confedn. of Res. Officers (US. del. 1992—), Assn. Mil. Surgeons, USCG Aux., Exptl. Aircraft Assn., Am. Legion, VFW, U.S. Army Order Mil. Merit, U.S. Sailing Assn., Boat-U.S., The Ret. Officers Assn., Sigma Xi, Omicron Kappa Upsilon (pres. Supreme chpt. 1980-81). Methodist. E-mail: wbhammer@aol.com.

HAMMERGREN, JOHN H. pharmaceutical company executive; BSBA, U. Minn.; MBA, Xavier U. With Baxter Healthcare Corp./Am. Hosp. Corp. and Lyphomed Inc., 1981-91; pres. med./surgical divsn. Kendall Healthcare Products Co., Mansfield, Mass., 1991-96; corp. exec. v.p., pres., CEO supply mgmt. bus. McKesson HBOC, Inc., 1996-99; now chmn., pres, CEO, dir. McKesson Corp. (formerly McKesson HBOC, Inc.). Office: McKesson Corp One Post St San Francisco CA 94104

HAMMERLE, FREDRIC JOSEPH, technical manufacturing executive; b. Newark, Jan. 2, 1944; s. Fredric Frank and Catherine G. (Wankmuller) H.; m. Nancy Elizabeth Looby, June 16, 1979; children: Oliver, Dora. BA, Rutgers U., 1966, MBA, 1967. Prodn. mgr. Engelhard Corp., Plainville, Mass., 1967-72, group v.p., 1978-86; v.p. mfg. Franklin Mint Corp., Franklin Center, Pa., 1972-78; exec. v.p., COO, sr. group exec. Cookson Precious Metals, Providence, 1986—2003; pres., CEO Precision Engineered Products, Inc., Attleboro, Mass., 2003—. Bd. dirs., treas. Internat. Precious Metals Inst. Referee Amateur Hockey Assn. U.S., 1980—; bd. dirs., sec. Sturdy Meml. Hosp., 1989—. Sgt. USMCR, 1966-72. Mem.: Silver Users Assn. (bd. dirs. 1985—, pres.), Gold Filled Assn. (bd. dirs. 1980—, sec., pres.), Mfg. Jewelers Silversmiths of Am. (bd. dirs. 1983—, pres.), Bass Anglers Sportsman Soc. (Montgomery, Ala.), Jewelry Info. Ctr., 24 Karat Club N.Y., Boston Jewelers Club (bd. dirs. 1995—, pres. 2001—). Roman Catholic. Avocations: ice hockey, restoring autos, fishing. Office: Precision Engineered Products Inc 110 Frank Mossberg Dr Attleboro MA 02703 E-mail: fhammerle@pep-corp.com.

HAMMERLINDL, DONALD JAMES, petroleum consultant; b. Milden, Sask., Can., July 31, 1944; came to U.S., 1968; s. Joseph Harold and Winnifred Jane (Adams) H. BS in Engring., U. Wyo., 1970. Ops. engr. ARCO Oil and Gas, Corpus Christi, Tex., 1970-73, reservoir engr. Dallas, 1973-80; chief engr. Triton Energy, Dallas, 1980-81; pres. Toltec Royalty, Dallas, 1981-82; v.p. DeGolyer and MacNaughton, Dallas, 1983—. Contbr. articles to profl. jours. Mem. Soc. Petroleum Engrs. (disting.), The Petroleum Soc., Assn. Profl. Engrs., Geologists and Geophysicists of Alta., Tex. State Bd. Registration of Profl. Engrs., Calgary Petroleum Club, The Hickory Creek Hunt. Avocation: horses. Home: Rte 1 Box 137A Forestburg TX 76239 Office: DeGolyer and MacNaughton Ste 400 4925 Greenville Ave Dallas TX 75206 E-mail: dhammerlindl@demac.com.

HAMMERMAN, EDWARD SCOTT, lawyer; b. Washington, Mar. 21, 1969; s. Murray Frederic and Marilyn (Hochberg) H. BA in English, Emory U., 1991; JD, Cath. U. Am., 1994. Bar: Pa. 1994, Fla. 1998, D.C. 1998. Staff atty. Venable, Washington, 1994-96; assoc. Leibowitz & Assocs., P.A., Miami, Fla., 1996-98, Collier Shannon & Scott, PLLC, Washington, 1998-99, Dickstein Shapiro Morin & Oshinsky, Washington, 1999—2002; founder Intermediary Copyright Royalty Svcs., 2002—; mng. mem. Hammerman, PLLC, Washington, 2002—. Editor newsletter Broadcasting and the Law, 1996-98, Ask the Expert, Office.com.; mng. editor newsletter Telecom Real Estate Advisor, 2002—. Bd. dirs. Am. Jewish Com., Miami, 1996-98. Mem. Fed. Comms. Bar Assn. (founder, co-chair 1992-94, law student com.), Assn. Emory Alumni (exec. com. 1998—), Masons. Democrat. Jewish. Office: Hammerman PLLC 5335 Wisconsin Ave NW Ste 440 Washington DC 20015-2052 E-mail: ted@copyrightroyalties.com.

HAMMERMAN, PAT JO, artist, educator; b. NYC, Oct. 15, 1954; d. Saul and Clara (Hollerer) Hammerman; m. Mark Krassner. BFA, Queens Coll., NY, 1976; MFA, Hunter Coll., NYC, 1979. Prof. fine art Queens Coll., NYC, 1980-82, St. John's Coll., Queens, NY, 1980-83, Queens Borough Cmty. Coll., NY, 1980—. Pres. 10/20 Art Space, NYC, 1986-2002, Real Art Inc., 1995—. One man shows include Key Gallery, NYC, 1981, Althea Via For a Gallery, NYC, 1982, Amarillo (Tex.) Art Ctr., 1983, Perceptions Gallery, Houston, 1984, Colby-Sawyer Coll., New London, NH, 1985, Jan Weiner Gallery, Kansas City, 1986, Forefront Gallery, LI, 1987, Carol Hasto Gallery, NYC, 1989, Interchurch Ctr., NYC, 1990, SUNY, Stony Brook, 1995, Queensboro C.C., Bayside, NY, 1996, Right Angle Gallery, Chgo., 1997, Peter Rose Gallery, NYC, 2001, Monroe Fine Art, Grand Rapids, Mich., 2002; exhibited in group shows at John

Szoke Gallery, NYC, 1988, Van Straaten Gallery, Chgo., 1988, The Queens Mus., Flushing, NY, 1989, Peter Rose Gallery, NYC, 1990, Michael Ingbar Gallery, NYC, 1991, and many more; represented in permanent collections. NY Found. for The Arts grantee, 1984. Mem. Women in the Arts, Phila. Printmakers, Coll. Art Assn., Queensborough Community Coll. Alumni Assn., Queens Coll. Alumni Assn., Jamaica Art Mobilization (treas. 1982-84). Home: 20724 27th Ave Flushing NY 11360-2403 Office: Queensborough Community Coll Flushing NY 11364

HAMMERSCHMIDT, JOHN ARTHUR, federal agency administrator; b. Harrison, Ark. Grad. with high honors, Dartmouth Coll., 1971; postgrad., Vanderbilt U., Harvard U., Cath U., Ecuador. Pres. Boone County Indsl. Devel. Corp., Ark.; CEO Hammerschmidt Lumber Co., 1974—83; staff mem. Office of V.P. U.S., Washington, 1984; spl. asst. to bd. chmn., mem. Nat. Transp. Safety Bd., 1985—91, mem., 1991—2001, 2001—. Office: NTSB 490 E L'Enfant Plz SW Washington DC 20594

HAMMERSCHMIDT, JOHN PAUL, retired congressman, lumber company executive; b. Harrison, AR, May 4, 1922; s. Arthur Paul and Junie (Taylor) H.; m. Virginia Sharp; 1 child, John Arthur. Student, The Citadel, U. Ark., Okla. State U. Chmn. bd. Hammerschmidt Lumber Co., Harrison, 1946-84; mem. 90th-102d Congresses from 3d Ark. Dist., 1967-93. Mem. Pub. Works and Transp. Com., 1967-93, ranking mem., 1987-93; mem. V.A. Com., 1967-93, ranking mem., 1973-86; bd. dirs. 1st Fed. Bank of Ark.; chmn. bd. 1st Fed. Bankshares of Ark.; bd. dirs. Dillard's Dept. Store, Southwestern Energy Co.; chmn. N.W. Ark. Coun.; nat. committeman Ark. Citizen of Yr. Com.; mem. Presdl. Commn. on Aviation Security and Terrorism; mem. Pres.'s task force on Vets. Health Care; mem. Claude and Mildred Pepper Found., 1989-90 (PVA Speedy award), bd. Met. Washington Airports Authority; chmn. bd., trustee Ark. State U., U. of the Ozarks; chmn. Ark. Rep. Com., 2000—. Chmn. Ark. Republican Com., 1964-66; mem. Rep. Nat. Finance Com., 1960-64, nat. Rep. committeeman from, Ark., 1976-80; mem. Harrison City Coun., 1948, 60, 62. Served as pilot USAAF, World War II, CBI. Decorated Air medal with 4 oak leaf clusters, D.F.C. with 3 oak leaf clusters, 3 Battle Stars, The China War Meml. medal, Meritorious Svc. award VFW Congl. award, Silver Helmet award, Nat. Order Trenchrats Legis. Svc. award, Award for Life Svc. to Vets.; named. Ark. Citizen of Yr., 1991, Ark. Aerospace Found. Hall of Fame, 1991. Mem. Ark. Lumber Dealers Assn. (past pres.), Midwest Lumbermens Assn. (past pres.), Harrison C. of C. (named Man of Yr. 1965), Am. Legion, Masons (33 degree-Grand Cross), Scottish Rite, Shriners, Jesters, Elks, Rotary (past pres. Harrison). Republican. Presbyterian (Ordained Elder, Deacon). E-mail: jph@northark.edu.

HAMMES, GORDON G. chemistry educator; b. Fond du Lac, Wis., Aug. 10, 1934; s. Jacob and Betty (Sadoff) H.; m. Judith Ellen Frank, June 14, 1959; children: Laura Anne, Stephen R., Sharon Lyn. AB, Princeton, 1956; PhD, U. Wis., 1959. NSF postdoctoral fellow Max Planck Inst. fur physikalische Chemie, Göttingen, Germany, 1959-60; from instr. to assoc. prof. Mass. Inst. Tech., Cambridge, 1960-65; prof. Cornell U., Ithaca, N.Y., 1965-88, chmn. dept. chemistry, 1970-75, Horace White prof. chemistry and biochemistry, 1975-88, dir. biotech. program, 1983-88; prof. U. Calif., Santa Barbara, 1988-91, vice chancellor, 1988-91; prof. Duke U., Durham, N.C., 1991—; vice chancellor Duke U. Med. Ctr., Durham, N.C., 1991-98; univ. disting. svc. prof. biochemistry Duke U., Durham, N.C., 1996—. Mem. physiol. chemistry sect., phys. biochemistry study sect., Tng. grant com. NIH; bd. counselors Nat. Cancer Inst., 1976-80; mem. adv. coun. chemistry dept., Princeton, 1970-75, Poly. Inst. N.Y., 1977-78, Boston U., 1977-92; mem. NRC, U.S. nat. com. for biochemistry, 1989-95. Author: Principles of Chemical Kinetics, 1978, Enzyme Catalysis and Regulation, 1982, (with I. Amdur) Chemical Kinetics: Principles and Selected Topics, 1966, Thermodynamic and Kinetics for the Biological Sciences, 2000; editor: Biochemistry, 1992-2003; also articles. NSF sr. postdoctoral fellow, 1968-69; NIH Fogarty scholar, 1975-76 Mem. NAS, Am. Acad. Arts and Scis., Am. Chem. Soc. (award biol. chemistry 1967, editl. bd. jours., exec. com. div. phys. chemistry 1976-79, exec. com. div. biol. chemistry 1977-88, com. profl. tng. 1985-92, task force on biotech. 1989-90), Am. Soc. Biochemistry and Molecular Biology (coun., editl. bd. jour. pres., William C. Rose award 2002), Phi Beta Kappa, Sigma Xi, Phi Lambda Upsilon. Home: 11 Staley Pl Durham NC 27705-2421

HAMMESFAHR, ROBERT WINTER, lawyer; b. Pittsfield, Mass., May 17, 1954; s. Frederick W. and Patricia Lue (Winter) H.; widowed; 1 child, Scott Gardner. BA, Colgate U., 1975; JD, Northwestern U., Chgo., 1978. Bar: Ill. 1978, U.S. Dist. Ct. (no. dist.) Ill. 1978, N.Y. 1991, U.S. Supreme Ct. 1989. Ptnr. Blatt, Hammesfahr & Eaton, Chgo., 1994-97, mng. ptnr., 1997-2000, chmn., 2000; mem. Cozen O'Connor, 2001—. Author: (with others) Punitive Damages: A Guide to the Insurability of Punitive Damages in the United States and Its Territories, 1988, Punitive Damages: A State-By-State Guide to Law and Practice, 1991, (pocket parts 1993, 96, Japanese edits., 1995, 99, 2000, 2001), 2d edit., 2002, The Law of Reinsurance Claims, 1994, Supplement 1997; editor, author: (with others) @Risk—Internet and E-commerce Insurance and Reinsurance, 2000, 2.0 version, 2002; contbr. articles to profl. jours. Mem. ABA, Chgo. Bar Assn. Avocations: tennis, skiing. Office: Cozen O'Connor 222 S Riverside Plz Ste 1500 Chicago IL 60606-6000 E-mail: rhammesfahr@cozen.com.

HAMMES-SCHIFFER, SHARON, chemist, educator; b. Ithaca, N.Y., May 27, 1966; d. Gordon G. and Judith (Frank) Hammes; m. Peter Ernest Schiffer, Apr. 1, 1990; children: Zachary J. Schiffer, Benjamin G. Schiffer. BA, Princeton U., 1988; PhD, Stanford U., 1993. Mem. tech. staff AT&T Bell Labs., Murray Hill, NJ, 1993-95; Clare Boothe Luce asst. prof. chemistry and biochemistry U. Notre Dame, Ind., 1995-2000; Shaffer assoc. prof. chemistry Pa. State U., State Coll., 2000—03, prof. chemistry State College, 2003—. Charter mem. study sect. NIH, 2002—; adv. bd. Theoretical Chemistry Accts., 2002—. Sr. editor: Jour. Phys. Chemistry, 2001—; contbr. articles to profl. jours. Recipient Career award, NSF, 1996, Camille Dreyfus Tchr.-Scholar award, 1999; NSF Grad. fellow, 1988—91, Alfred P. Sloan Rsch. fellow, 1998. Mem.: Am. Chem. Soc. Office: Dept Chemistry 152 Davey Lab Pa State U University Park PA 16802 E-mail: shs@chem.psu.edu.

HAMMETT, BENJAMIN COWLES, psychologist; b. L.A., Nov. 18, 1931; s. Buell Hammett and Harriet (Cowles) Graham; m. Ruth Finstrom, June 18, 1957; children: Susan Hood, Sarah, Carol Bress, John. BS, Stanford U., 1957; PhD, U. N.C., 1969. Lic. psychologist, Calif. Staff psychologist Children's Psychiat. Ctr., Butner, N.C., 1965-67; sr. psychologist, dir. rsch. VA Treatment Ctr. for Children, Richmond, Va., 1968-71; asst. prof. child psychiatry Va. Commonwealth U., Richmond, 1968-71; instr. psychology Western Grad. Sch. Psychology, 1980-87; pvt. practice clin. psychology Palo Alto, Calif., 1972-92; rsch. psychologist, 1992—; affiliate staff mem. O'Connor Hosp., San Jose, Calif., 1980-84. V.p. bd. dirs. Mental Rsch. Inst., Palo Alto, 1982-83, pres. bd. dirs., 1983-85, treas., 1990-92, mem. staff, 1992—, bd. dirs. emeritus, 1992—, rsch. affiliate, 1992-95, rsch. assoc., 1995—; bd. dirs. Western Grad. Sch. Psychology, 1993-97. Co-author chpts. two books. Scoutmaster Boy Scouts Am., 1952-54; 1st lt. Civil Air Patrol, 1969; vol. Bay Area Action and Peninsula Conservation Ctr., Palo Alto, 1983—, Calif. Acad. Scis., San Francisco, 1987—; treas. John B. Cary Sch. PTA, Richmond, Va., 1969-70; trustee Nat. Parks and Conservation Assn., 1995-98. Named Eagle Scout, 1947; grantee NIMH, 1970. Mem. AAAS, APA, Am. Psychol. Soc., Am. Group Psychotherapy Assn., Internat. Transactional Analysis Assn. (cert. clin. mem.), Assn. Applied Psychophysiology and Biofeedbck, Biofeedback Soc. Calif., Calif. Psychol. Assn., Assn. for the Advancement of Gestalt Therapy, El Tigre Club Stanford U. (sec. 1954). Democrat. Unitarian Universalist. Avocations: photography, computers, environmental volunteer, international ecological traveler. Home: 301 Lowell Ave Palo Alto CA 94301-3812

HAMMETT, LOUISE BARFIELD, community service volunteer, artist, historian, playwright; b. Columbus, Ga., Sept. 18, 1929; d. Grover C. and L. Louise Calhoun Barfield; m. Paul Lane Hammett, Jr., June 20, 1951; children: Constance Louise, Frances Pauline. BA, Auburn (Ala.) U., 1950; postgrad., LaGrange (Ga.) Coll., 1962-69; MA equivalent, U. Ga., 1982. Sch. tchr. LaGrange Pub. Schs., 1950-51; co-founder, art instr. Chattahoochee Valley Art Assn., LaGrange; founder art divsn., instr. LaGrange Acad.; art instr. Chattahoochee Valley C.C.; pvt. studio art instr., 1963—; founder, chmn. Friendship & Resources for Internat. Edification/Nurturing Zones, Inc., 1999—2002. Spkr. in field. Exhibited in group shows at Lamar Dodd Art Ctr., Chattahoochee Valley Art Assn., Columbus Art Mus., Internat. Club, Mobile, Ala., Chattahoochee Valley C.C., Columbus State U.; represented in permanent collections Bradley Meml. Libr., 1st Bapt. Ch., La Grange, Ga.; author: Who Are We? Where Are We Going? Why?, Soldiers-Patriots at Kettle Creek, 2d edit., 2003, Pinckney Barfield Walking Away from Death, documentary texts and performances; playwright, monologue presentations of A Valentine for Georgia, 1993—; editor: LCB's Tablet; pub.: History of Harris County, Georgia, 3d edit.; playwright, performer: A Colonial Dame, Anne Dutretré David, 1993—; rschr. History of First Bapt. Ch. of LaGrange, Ga.; contbr. articles to profl. jours. Advisor Harris County Libr., Ga.; advisor to bd. Mountain Hill Schoolhouse Restoration, Harris County, 1995—97; active Camp Viola; organizing mem. Tabard Book Club; organizing mem. 50th Anniversary celebrated charter Elms and Roses Garden Coun. of La Grange, 2003; organizing mem. Highland Country Club, Ladies Golf Assn.; vol. art dept. LaGrange Acad., 1970—71; brownie leader, girl scout leader Girl Scouts Am., 1957—61, 1972—73; founder, 1st pres. Ocfuskee Hist. Soc., LaGrange; chmn. Columbus Bd. Hist. and Archtl. Rev., 1988—90; liaison Zugdidi Nation of Ga., 1993—2001; charter and organizing mem. Talisman Garden Club; vice chmn. LaGrange Coun. of Ch. Women. Mem.: Nat. Soc. DAR (regent Button Gwinnett chpt. 1986—99, assoc. Kettle Creek chpt. 1999—, Oglethorpe chpt. 2000—). Presbyterian. Avocations: community service, historical research/writing, painting in oil.

HAMMETT, SETH, state legislator; b. Andalusia, Ala., June 24, 1946; m. Nancy Carmack Hammett; children: Merrill, Catherine. BS, MBA, Auburn U. Mem. 92nd dist. Ala. Ho. of Reps., Montgomery, 1978—, spkr. of the ho., legis. coun. chair, 1995—. Founding pres. SouthTrust Bank; pres. LBW Coll. Past chmn. Lurleen B. Wallace Cmty. Arts Coun.; chair Andalusia Inds. Devel. Bed., Andalusia Hist. Preservation Authority; mem. Ala. Bd. of Med. Scholarship awards, Ala. Emergency Med. Svc. Edn. Commn.; bd. trustees Andalusia Hosp. Served with USAF. Mem. Andalusia Area C. of C. Office: Ala State House Rm 519A 11 S Union St Montgomery AL 36130 Fax: 334-242-7668. E-mail: seth.hammett@alhouse.org.*

HAMMILLER, RUTH ELLEN, school official and psychologist; b. Burlington, Wis., May 6, 1952; d. Cyril Charles and Marion Frances (Rhodes) H. BS in Elem. Edn., U. Wis., Whitewater, Wis., 1974, MS in Edn. in Sch. Psychology, 1982, Sch. Psychologist Letter of Recognition, 1983; PhD in Ednl. Adminstrn., U. Wis., Madison, Wis., 1994. Cert. education, sch. psychologist, ednl. adminstr., Ind. Tour guide Nestle Co., Burlington, Wis., 1970-74; tchr. Brodhead (Wis.) Pub. Schs., 1974-82; vocat. guidance counselor U. Wis., Whitewater, 1982-83, grad. asst., 1982-83; tchr. Brodhead (Wis.) Pub. Schs., 1983-84; testing coord. Lake Mills (Wis.) Pub. Schs., 1989-91; program asst. U. Wis.-Edn. Adminstrns., Madison, 1992-93; sch. psychologist Lake Mills (Wis.) Pub. Schs., 1984-99; dir. pupil svcs. Palmyra (Wis.)-Eagle Area Sch. Dist., 1999—, testing & ATODA coord., 2000—, coord. gifted and talented program, 2003—. Psychol. cons. Divsn. on Ch. and Ministry-S.W. Assn. United Ch. of Christ, Madison, 1995-2001. Contbr. articles to profl. jours. Youth ministries mem., chair First Congl. Ch., Fort Atkinson, 1984-90, vice-moderator, 1992-93, 150th anniversary chairperson, 1991-92, long range planning chairperson, 1990-91, diaconate mem., 1994-99, vice moderator, 1999, moderator, 2000, long range planning com., 2001-, trustee, chairperson 2003, nominating com. Wisc. U.C.C. Conf. 2003—. Recipient Arvil S. Barr fellowship U. Wis., 1993-94, Netzer-Eye scholarship, 1992-93, UCEA Grad. Student Seminar award U. Coun. Ednl. Adminstrs., 1993, Mem. Am. Ednl. Rsch. Assn. (rsch. evaluator 1993—, Nat. Grad. Student Rsch. Seminar award 1993), Nat. Assn. Sch. Psychologists, Wis. Assn. Sch. Psychologist, Wis. Coun. of Adminstrn. of Spl. Svcs. (mem. exec. coun. 2002—), Phi Kappa Phi, Kappa Delta Phi, Psi Chi C Honor Soc. Avocations: music, golf, travel, writing, reading. Home: 1125 Seminole Dr Fort Atkinson WI 53538-1083 Office: Palmyra Eagle Area Sch Dist PO Box 901 Palmyra WI 53156-0901 E-mail: rhammiller@palmyra.k12.wi.us.

HAMMOND, ANTHONY, commissioner; Graduate, Southwest Mo. State U. Commr. Postal Rate Commn., Washington, 2002—; owner T. Hammond Co., Arlington, Va.; sr. vp Feather, Larson & Synhorst; sr. cons. Forbes 2000, Inc.; dir. of campaign ops. Rep. Nat. Com., 1988; exec. dir., fin. dir. Mo. Rep. Party, 1989—94; legis. dir. Mo. Congressman Gene Taylor, 1979—89. Office: Postal Rate Commn 1333 H St NW Ste 300 Washington DC 20268-0001*

HAMMOND, BENJAMIN FRANKLIN, microbiologist, educator; b. Austin, Tex., Feb. 28, 1934; s. Virgil Thomas and Helen Marguerite (Smith) H. BA, U. Kans., 1954; D.D.S., Meharry Med. Coll., 1958; PhD, U. Pa., 1962. Mem. faculty U. Pa. Sch. Dental Medicine, Phila., 1958—, prof. microbiology, 1970—, chmn. dept., 1972-85; Pres.'s lectr. U. Pa., 1981, assoc. dean acad. affairs, 1984, dir. periodontal microbiology lab., 1985—; prof. of medicine, dir. oral microbiology testing svc. lab. Med. Coll. Pa., 1995—; rsch. prof. periodontology Temple U., Phila., 1998—. Mem. oral biology and medicine study sect. NIH, 1972-75, 95-99; mem. Nat. Adv. Dental Rsch. Coun., 1975—; Ralph Metcalf disting. vis. prof. Marquette U., 1986; disting. lectr. U. Paul Sabatier, Toulouse, France, 1991. Trustee Atwater Kent Mus., 1999—, Arthur Ross Gallery, 2001, bd. dirs. Am. Poetry Soc., 2001, FIRE. Recipient USPHS Research Career Devel. award, 1965, Lindback award U. Pa., 1969; Silver medal City of Paris, 1978; NIH grantee, 1981—. Mem. Am. Soc. Microbiology, Internat. Assn. Dental Rsch. (E.H. Hatton award 1959), Am. Assn. Dental Rsch.(pres. 1978-79), Coll. Physicians of Phila., Phila. Mus. Art (trustee), The Phila. Club. Home: 560 N 23d St Philadelphia PA 19130-3132 E-mail: bhammond@dental.temple.edu.

HAMMOND, CHARLES AINLEY, clergyman; b. Asheville, N.C., Aug. 7, 1933; s. George Bradley and Eleanor Maria (Gantz) H.; m. Barbro Stigsdotter Laurell, July 16, 1960; children: Stig Bradley, Inga Allison. BA, Occidental Coll., Los Angeles, 1955; B.D., Princeton Theol. Sem., 1958; D.D., Missouri Valley Coll., 1981, Wabash Coll., 1982. Ordained to ministry United Presbyn. Ch., 1958; pastor chs. in Pa. and Calif., 1958-75; exec. presbyter Presbytery Wabash Valley, West Lafayette, Ind., 1975-87, Presbytery Phila., 1987-98; interim pastor Presbyn. Ch., New Providence, NJ, 1998-99, 1st Presbyn. Ch., Salt Lake City, 1999-2001, San Luis Obispo, Calif., 2002. Moderator 192d gen. assembly United Presbyn. Ch., 1980-81; chmn. Gen. Assembly Mission Coun., 1982-83. Author: Newtonian Polity in an Age of Relativity, 1977, Seven Deadly Sins of Dissent, 1979. Sec. Hallam (Pa.) Borough Planning Commn., 1962-64, Westchester Cmty. Plans, L.A., 1966-68, Pasadena (Calif.) Planning Commn., 1971-75; chmn. pvt. land use com., 1972-73, chmn. pub. land use com., 1973-74; mem. gen. assembly coun. Presbyn. Ch. (U.S.A.), 1983-91; bd. dirs. Met. Coun. Chs. of Phila., 1990-95; trustee Beaver Coll., 1991-99; gen. assembly Permanent Jud. Com., 1995-2001; mem. bd. corporators Pres. Min. Found. Recipient Disting. Alumnus award Princeton Theol. Sem., 1981. Mem. Assn. Presbyn. Ch. Educators, Friends of Old Pine (trustee). Republican. Presbyterian.

HAMMOND, CHARLES BESSELLIEU, obstetrician, gynecologist, educator; b. Ft. Leavenworth, Kans., July 24, 1936; s. Claude G. and Alice (Sims) H.; m. Peggy A. Hammond, June 21, 1958; children: Sharon L., Charles B. BS, The Citadel, 1957, Duke U., 1961. Diplomate Am. Bd. Ob-Gyn. Intern in surgery Duke U., 1961-62, resident in ob-gyn, 1962-63, 66-69, fellow in reproductive endocrinology, 1963-64, asst. prof. dept. ob-gyn, 1969-73, asso. prof., 1973-78, prof., 1978-81, E.C. Hamblen prof., 1981—, chmn., 1980—2002. Contbr. in field. Served with USPHS, 1964-66. Fellow (hon.) Royal Coll. Ob-gyn. (ad eundeum), Soc. Ob-gyn. Can. (hon.); mem. AMA, Am. Fertility Soc. (pres. 1985), ACOG (chmn. dist. IV 1997-2000, pres. 2002), Am. Assn. Ob-Gyn. Found. (pres. 1996-2002), Assn. Profs. Obstetrics and Gynecology, Am. Gynecol. and Obstet. Soc. (pres. 1993-94), Soc. Gynecol. Investigation, Am. Gynecol. Soc., Am. Assn. Obstet. and Gynecology, N.C. Med. Soc., N.C. Soc. Obstetricians and Gynecologists (pres. 1985), Am. Gynecol. Club (pres. 1994), Inst. of Medicine. Presbyterian. Home: 2827 McDowell Rd Durham NC 27705-5604 Office: Duke U Med Ctr PO Box 3853 Durham NC 27710 E-mail: hammo005@mc.duke.edu.

HAMMOND, CHARLES E, education educator; b. Tucson, Ariz., Aug. 21, 1954; s. Robert Morris and Marguerite Masius Hammond; m. Linda Cheng, Feb. 21, 1982. PhD, Columbia U., 1986. Asst. prof. of chinese lang. & lit. U. of Tenn., 1986—87; assoc. prof. of chinese lang. & lit. So. Ill. U., 1987—; sect. head East Asian Languages and Civilizations, So. Ill. U., 1987—. Rsch. grant, Ctr. for Chinese Studies, 1993. Mem.: Asian Studies Assn., Am. Assn. for Chinese Studies, Soc. for the Study of Chinese Religions, Am. Oriental Soc., T'ang Studies Soc., Chinese Lang. Teacher's Assn. Office: Southern Illinois University Dept of Fgn Languages Carbondale IL 62901

HAMMOND, CHARLES EDGAR, data processing executive; b. Kellogg, Idaho, Dec. 24, 1943; s. Charles William and Irene Elizabeth (Hoffman) H.; m. Jennifer Lee Giard, Aug. 12, 1967; children: Christa Lee, Robert Charles. BBA, Washington State U., 1967; MBA, Golden Gate U., 1973. Programmer, analyst Boeing Airplane Co., Seattle, 1967-68, Chevron Corp., San Francisco, 1969-70; div. mgr. Chevron Info. Tech. Co., San Ramon, Calif., 1980-2000; info. tech. mgr. U. Calif., Berkeley, 2000—. Mem. adv. com. Re-entry Program for Women and Minorities, Computer Sci. U. Calif., Berkeley, 1983—. Recipient Award of Merit Calif. Dept. Rehab., Sacramento, 1981. Mem. Beta Theta Pi. Clubs: Crow Canyon Country (San Ramon). Home: 2749 Tumwater Dr Walnut Creek CA 94598-4450 E-mail: ceha@onebox.com.

HAMMOND, DAVID ALAN, stage director, educator; b. NYC, June 3, 1948; s. Jack and Elizabeth Alida (Furno) H. BA magna cum laude, Harvard U., 1970; M.F.A., Carnegie-Mellon U., 1972. Mem. faculty Juilliard Theatre Center, N.Y.C., 1972-74; asst. conservatory dir. Am. Conservatory Theatre, San Francisco, 1974-81, assoc. stage dir., 1974-78; dir. Summer Tng. Congress, 1976-80, resident stage dir., 1979-81. Adj. assoc. prof. acting and directing Yale Sch. Drama, New Haven, 1981—85; adj. prof. dept. dramatic art U. N.C., Chapel Hill, 1985—88, prof., 1988—; artistic dir. PlayMakers Repertory Co., Chapel Hill, 1985—92, 1999—, assoc. producing dir., 1992—99; guest artist Pacific Conservatory Performing Arts, 1976, U. Wash., 1977, SUNY, Purchase, 1979, Tisch Sch. Arts/NYU, NYC, 1999—2003; guest dir. Aspen (Colo.) Music Festival, 1974—75, San Francisco Opera, 1978, Carmel (Calif.) Bach Festival, 1979—80, Sherwood Shakespeare Festival, Oxnard, Calif., 1981, Roundabout Theatre, N.Y.C., 1983, Valley Shakespeare Festival, Saratoga, Calif., 1984, 86, 88, Shakespeare Festival of Dallas, 1990, Teatro Alianza, Montevideo, 1992, Teatro Alianza, Montevideo, 1994, Teatro Alianza, Montevideo, Uruguay, 1997, Inst. Teatral El Galpun, Montevideo, 1995, Opera Co. N.C., 1998—99; resident dir. Yale Repertory Theatre, New Haven, 1981—85; Arts Am. cultural specialist U.S. Info. Svc., 1992, 94; guest prof. Escuela Mcpl. de Arte Dramatico, 2003, Escuela de Espresion Teatral Anglo-o.m.b.u., 2003, El Univ. del Plata, Montevideo, Uruguay, 2003. Recipient Drama-Logue Critics award, L.A., 1980, 81, Florencio award, Montevideo, Uruguay, 1992. Mem. Soc. Stage Dirs. and Choreographers, Actors' Equity, Am. Guild Mus. Artists, Dramatists' Guild, Nat. Theater Conf., Assn. for Theatre in Higher Edn. Office: PlayMakers Repertory Co Ctr For Dramatic Art cb 3235 Chapel Hill NC 27599-0001 E-mail: dhammond@email.unc.edu.

HAMMOND, DEANNA, educator; b. Terre Haute, Ind., Feb. 13, 1945; d. DeForest and Dorothy Illen (Spaulding) H. BS in Edn., U. Houston, 1970, MEd, 1983. Cert. tchr., reading specialist, TEx. Tchr. Gregg Elem. Sch., Houston, 1970, Fairchild Elem. Sch., Houston, 1970-77, Ctrl. Elem. Sch., Palacios, Tex., 1977-79, Foster Elem. Sch., Houston, 1979-90, also grade chmn.; magnet coord. John E. Codwell Elem. Sch., 1999—2002. Block capt. crime watch Huntington Village Civic Assn., Houston, 1982; exec. bd. PTA, Foster Sch.; dir. Vols. in Pub. Schs., Foster Sch. Mem. Tex. State Coun. Internat. Reading Assn., Greater Houston Area Reading Coun., Congress Houston Tchrs. (bldg. rep. 1983, 85-86), Assn. Children with Learning Disabilities, Am. Assn. Ret. Persons, Houston Area Ret. Tchrs. Assn., PTA, Young Homemakers Club (Palacios), Christian Womens Fellowship Club (Houston). Republican. Home: 12426 South Dr Houston TX 77099-2424

HAMMOND, FRANK JEFFERSON, III, lawyer; b. Moss Point, Miss., Sept. 18, 1953; s. Frank Jefferson Jr. and Jane (Laird) H.; m. Gale Ray, May 30, 1975; children: Katharine Blakeney, Benjamin Laird. BBA, U. Mis., 1974, JD, 1976; LLM, U. Fla., 1978. Bar: Miss. 1977, U.S. Dist. Ct. (no. dist.) Miss. 1977, U.S. Dist. Ct. (so. dist.) Miss. 1977, U.S. Ct. Appeals (5th cir.) 1977, U.S. Tax Ct. 1978, U.S. Ct. Appeals (11th cir.) 1980, U.S. Supreme Ct. 1989. Mem. Corlew, Krebs & Hammond, P.A., Pascagoula, Miss., 1978-84, Watkins & Eager, PLLC, Jackson, Miss., 1984—. Adj. prof. U. Ala. Sch. Law, Mobile, 1983; adj. faculty U. So. Miss., Gautier, 1983-84; bd. dirs. Merchants and Marine Bank, Pascagoula, Miss. Bd. trustees Dantzler Meml. Meth. Ch., Moss Point, 1981-84. U. Fla. Grad. Council fellow, 1977; Richard B. Stephens scholar, 1978. Mem. ABA, Miss. State Bar (chmn. sect. estates and trusts 1988-89), Phi Kappa Phi, Beta Alpha Psi, Beta Gamma Sigma, Omicron Delta Kappa. Home: PO Box 650 Jackson MS 39205-0650 Office: Watkins & Eager PLLC 400 E Capitol St Ste 300 Jackson MS 39201-2610

HAMMOND, GEORGE CHARLES, lawyer; b. Kenosha, Wis., Mar. 6, 1953; s. Eugene Raymond and Patricia Verda (Lawler) H.; m. Maria Elisabeth Hammond, Oct. 30, 1986; 1 child, Sophie Claire. BA, Dartmouth Coll., 1974; JD, U. Wis., 1985. Bar: Wis. 1985, N.Y. 1986, Calif. 2001. Assoc. Dewey Ballantine LLP, N.Y.C., 1984-93, LeBoeuf, Lamb, Greene & MacRae, LLP, N.Y.C., 1996-99, ptnr. San Francisco, 2000—, Haarmann, Hemmelrath & Ptnr., Frankfurt, Germany, 1999. Author: (fiction) The Morning Light, 2000, Mark Twain's Visit to Heaven, 1999, The Senior Partner, 1999, Bob and Charlie, 1999, (non-fiction) Conversations with Socrates, 1999, The Gospel According to Andrew, 1999, Even More Relativity, 1999, (computer program) The Syndicator's Delight, 1984. Avocations: philosophy, literature, travel, art, golf. Office: LeBoeuf Lamb Greene & MacRae LLP One Embarcadero Ctr #400 San Francisco CA 94111 E-mail: ghammond@llgm.com.

HAMMOND, GEORGE SIMMS, chemist, consultant; b. Auburn, Maine, May 22, 1921; s. Oswald Kenric and Marjorie (Thomas) Hammond; m. Marian Reese, June 8, 1945 (div. 1977); children: Kenric, Janet, Steven, Barbara, Jeremy; m. Eva L. Menger, May 22, 1977; stepchildren: Kirsten Menger-Anderson, Lenore Menger-Anderson. BS, Bates Coll., 1943; MS, PhD, Harvard U., 1947; DSc (hon.), Wittenberg U., 1972, Bates Coll., 1973; DHC (hon.), U. Ghent, 1973, Georgetown U., 1985, Bowling Green State U., 1990, Weizman Inst. Sci., 1993. Postdoctoral fellow UCLA, 1947—48; mem. faculty Iowa State Coll., 1948—58, prof. chemistry, 1956—58; prof. organic chemistry Calif. Inst. Tech., Pasadena, 1958—72, chmn. divsn. chemistry and chem. engring., 1968—72; Arthur Amos Noyes prof. chemistry; vice chancellor natural scis. U. Calif., Santa Cruz, 1972—74, prof. chemistry, 1972—78; exec. dir. for biosci., metals and ceramics Allied Corp., Morristown, NJ, 1978—88; cons., 1988—. Vis. assoc. prof. U. Ill., 1953; mem. chem. adv. panel NSF, 1962—65; fgn. sec. NAS, 1974—78, Author (with J.s. Fritz): Quantitative Organic Analysis, 1956; author: (with D.J. Cram) Organic Chemistry, 1958; author: (with J. Osteryoung, T. Crawford and H. Gray) Models in Chemical Science, 1971; co-editor: Advances in Photochemistry, 1961; editl. bd. Jour. Am. Chem. Soc., 1967—. Recipient James Flack Norris award, 1968, Nat. medal of sci., 1994, Othmer Gold medal, Chem. Heritage Found. Mem.: NAS (fgn. sec.), European Photochem. Soc., Inter-Am. Photochem. Soc., Materials Rsch. Soc., Am. Acad. Arts and Scis., Am. Chem. Soc. (award in petroleum chemistry 1960, Priestly medal 1976, Nat. medal of Sci. 1994, Seaborg medal 1994), Sigma Xi, Phi Beta Kappa. Home: 1414 SW 3rd Ave 2403 Portland OR 97201 E-mail: george@hammond.name.com.

HAMMOND, GLENN BARRY, SR., lawyer, electrical engineer; b. Roanoke, Va., Sept. 3, 1947; s. Howard Reichard and Billie (Cromer) Hammond; m. Elizabeth Wickham, Aug. 4, 2001; 1 stepchild, T. Rigsby Wickham;1 child from previous marriage, Glenn Barry. BA, Va. Mil. Inst., 1969; MBA, So. Ill. U., 1974; JD, U. Richmond, 1978; BSEE, Nova Coll., 1995. Bar: Va. 1979, U.S. Dist. Ct. (we. dist.) Va. 1979, U.S. Ct. Appeals (4th cir.) 1981, U.S. Ct. Mil. Appeals 1989, Air Force Ct. Mil. Rev. 1989, U.S. Supreme Ct., 1992. Assoc. Wilson, Hawthorne & Vogel, Roanoke, 1978-79; pvt. practice Roanoke, 1979-80, 86—; atty., advisor to chief adminstrv. law judge Social Security Adminstrn., HHS, Roanoke, 1980-86; ptnr. Wooten & Hart P.C., 1995-98; pres. R.F. Cons., Inc., Roanoke, Va., 1998—. Pres., bd. dirs. LCH Broadcasting Group, Inc. Roanoke. Editor: Psychiatry in Military Law, 1988. Sr. vice-comdr. Mil. Order World Wars, Roanoke, 1981. Col. JAGC, USAF, 1969-75, Res. 1975—. Mem. Air Commando Assn. (life), DAV (life), VFW (life), AFA (life), Nat. Mil. Intelligence Assn. (life), Armed Forces Comms. Electronics Assn., Nat. Orgn. Social Security Claimants Reps., Masons. E-mail: bluetig@earthlink.net.

HAMMOND, HAROLD LOGAN, pathology educator, oral and maxillofacial pathologist; b. Hillsboro, Ill., Mar. 18, 1934; s. Harold Thomas and Lillian (Carlson) H.; m. Sharon Bunton, Aug. 1, 1954 (dec. 1974); 1 child, Connie; m. Pat J. Palmer, June 3, 1986. Student Millikin U., 1953-57, Roosevelt U., Chgo., 1957-58; DDS, Loyola U., Chgo., 1962; MS, U. Chgo., 1967. Diplomate Am. Bd. Oral and Maxillofacial Pathology. Intern, U. Chgo. Hosps., Chgo., 1962-63, resident, 1963-66, chief resident in oral pathology, 1966-67; asst. prof. oral pathology U. Iowa, Iowa City, 1967-72, assoc. prof., 1972-80, assoc. prof., dir. surg. oral pathology, 1980-83, prof., dir., 1983—; cons. pathologist Hosp. Gen. de Managua, Nicaragua, 1970-90, VA Hosp., Iowa City, 1977—. Cons. editor: Revista de la Asociation de Nicaragua, 1970-71, Revista de la Federacion Odontologica de Centroamerica y Panama, 1971-77. Contbr. articles to sci. jours. Recipient Mosby Pub. Co. Scholarship award, 1962. Fellow AAAS, Am. Acad. Oral and Maxillofacial Pathology; mem. Am. Men and Women of Sci., N.Y. Acad. Scis., AAUP, Internat. Assn. Oral Pathologists, Internat. Assn. Dental Rsch., N.Am. Soc. Head and Neck Pathologists, Am. Dental Assn., Am. Assn. for Dental Rsch. Avocations: collecting antique clocks, collecting gambling paraphernalia, collecting toys. Home: 1732 Brown Deer Rd Coralville IA 52241-1157 Office: U Iowa Dental Sci Bldg Iowa City IA 52242-1001

HAMMOND, HERBERT J. lawyer, mediator, arbitrator; b. Santa Fe, May 19, 1951; m. Myra Hammond; children: Ariel, Jay. BS magna cum laude, U. N.Mex., 1973; JD, NYU, 1976. Bar: Tex. 1977, U.S. Patent and Trademark Office 1977. Sr. ptnr. Thompson & Knight, Dallas, 1994—. Contbr. articles to profl. jours. Mem. State Bar Tex. (vice-chmn. com. on computerization of the profession 1989-92, chair computer sect. 1994-95, newsletter editor computer sect.), Am. Intellectual Property Law Assn., Dallas Bar Assn. (chmn. intellectual property sect. 1998), Phi Beta Kappa, Phi Kappa Phi, Kappa Mu Epsilon. Office: Thompson & Knight 1700 Pacific Ave Ste 3300 Dallas TX 75201-4693 E-mail: hhammond@tklaw.com.

HAMMOND, HOWARD DAVID, retired botanist, editor; b. Phila., Feb. 10, 1924; s. Clarence Elwood Jr. and Myrtle Iva (Sprowles) H.; m. Sarah Lichtenberg, Apr. 30, 1955; 1 child, Julia Ethel. BS, Rutgers U., 1945, MS, 1947; PhD, U. Pa., 1952. Asst. prof. U. Del., Newark, 1957-58, Howard U., Washington, 1958-68; from asst. prof. to assoc. prof. SUNY, Brockport, 1968-83; assoc. editor N.Y. Bot. Garden, Bronx, 1984-92. Co-editor: Floristic Inventory Tropical Countries, 1989, Southwestern Rare and Endangered Plants: Proceedings of the Second Conference/USDA Forest Service, 1996; regional reviewer for Flora of North America, 1997—. Vol. Deaver Herbarium, No. Ariz. U., 1993—; mem. pub. art adv. com. City of Flagstaff, 1996-2002; adj. curator botany Mus. No. Ariz., 1998-2002. Mem. Am. Inst. Biol. Scis., Bot. Soc. Am., Torrey Bot. Soc.(editor 1976-82, 87-92, pres. 1992), Sigma Xi. Home: 4025 Lake Mary Rd Apt 33 Flagstaff AZ 86001-8608

HAMMOND, ISAAC WILLIAM, physician, epidemiologist; b. Cape Coast, Ghana, Mar. 17, 1951; s. Charles Williams and Beatrice Hammond; m. Marilyn Barker, June 11, 1977 (div. May 1981); 1 child, Allotey; m. Hoora Rahimi, Aug. 31, 1982; children: Mohammed, Mustafa, Reza, Mahjub, Sarah. BS, Calif. State U., 1976; MPH, Ind. State U., 1979; PhD, U. Okla., 1982; MD, U. Fla., 1989. Fellow U. Okla. Health Sci. Ctr., Oklahoma City, 1979-82; NIH fellow Cornell U. Med. Ctr., N.Y.C., N.Y., 1982-84; intern, resident Emory U. Med. sch., Atlanta, 1989-92; resident Tulane U. Med. Sch., New Orleans, 1992-93; staff physician, dir. hypertension clin. VA Med. Ctr., New Orleans, 1993-96; med. dir. Astra Zeneca, 2001—03; group med. dir. GlazoSmithKline, 2003—. Adj. assoc. prof. Tulane U. Sch. Pub. Health and Tropical Medicine, 1994-98; pres., dir. clin. rsch., dir. outcomes rsch. and disease state mgmt. Am. Rsch. Assocs., 1996—; reviewer FDA, 1996-98, Eli Lilly & Co., 1998-2001, AstroZeneca, 2001-03, GlaxoSmithKline, 2003—; assoc. prof. Ind. U., 1999-2001, U. North Tex., 1997—. Grantee NIH, Astra-Merck, Am. Heart Assn., WHO, Nat. Heart, Lung & Blood Inst. Mem. AMA, ACP, Am. Fedn. Clin. Rsch., Am. Soc. Hypertension, Am. Soc. Internal Medicine, Internat. Soc. Hypertension in Blacks, Nat. Med. Assn., N.Y. Acad. Sci., Royal Soc. Health, Soc. Epidemiol. Rsch., Soc. Gen. Internal Medicine, So. Med. Assn. Office: Am Rsch Assocs PO Box 7684 Wilmington DE 19803-0684

HAMMOND, JAMES M. endocrinologist; b. Temple, Tex., Feb. 3, 1941; s. Frederick Mathis and Helen (Mahoney) H.; m. Catherine Russell, Sept. 12, 1971; children: Christopher, Sarah. BA, Rice U., 1962; MD, Washington Sch. Medicine, 1966. Diplomate Am. Bd. Internal Medicine, Am. Bd. Endocronology and Metabolism. Resident Harvard unit Boston City Hosp., 1966-68; clin. assoc. Endocrine br. NCI, Bethesda, Md., 1968-71; fellow in endocrinology Washington U. Sch. Medicine, St. Louis, 1971-72, chief resident, 1972-73; asst. prof. medicine Pa. State U. Sch. Medicine, Hershey, 1973-79, assoc. prof. medicine, 1979-85, prof. medicine, 1985-2000, chief divsn. of endocrinology, 1991—2003, disting. prof., 2000—. Mem., chmn. biochem./endocrinology study sect. NIH, Bethesda, 1987-91; nat. rev. panel USDA, Washington, 1993, 95; mem. adv. bd. Ovarian Workshop. Editl. bd. Biology of Reproduction, 1995-97. Surgeon USPHS, 1968-71. Recipient UpJohn Achievement award Upjohn Corp., 1966; Fogarty Sr. Internat. rsch. fellowship Fogarty Found., 1980-81, Rsch. Career devel. NIH, 1981-86; faculty scholar medal Pa. State U., 1994. Mem. Endocrine Soc., Am. Fedn. for Clin. Rsch., Soc. for the Study of Reprodn., Am. Diabetes Assn., Am. Soc. for Clin. Investigation, Internat. Soc. Insulin-Like Growth Factors Rsch., Assn. Am. Physicians. Avocations: photography, scuba diving, literature, music. Office: Pa State Univ Coll Medicine Milton S Hershey Med Ctr PO Box 850 Hershey PA 17033-0850 E-mail: jhammond@psu.edu.

HAMMOND, JANE LAURA, retired law librarian, lawyer; b. nr. Nashua, Iowa; d. Frank D. and Pauline Hammond. BA, U. Dubuque, 1950; MS, Columbia U., 1952; JD, Villanova U., 1965, LHD, 1993. Bar: Pa. 1965. Cataloguer Harvard Law Libr., 1952-54; asst. libr. Sch. Law Villanova (Pa.) U., 1954-62; libr. Sch. Law, Villanova (Pa.) U., 1962-76; prof. law Sch. Law Villanova (Pa.) U., 1965-76; law libr., prof. law Cornell U., Ithaca, N.Y., 1976-93. Adj. prof. Drexel U., 1971-74; mem. depository libr. coun. to pub. printer U.S. Govt. Printing Office, 1975-78; cons. Nat. Law Libr., Monrovia, Liberia, 1989. Fellow ALA; mem. ABA (coun. sect. legal edn. 1984-90, mem. com. on accreditation 1982-87, mem. com. on stds. rev. 1987-95), PEO, Coun. Nat. Libr. Assn. (sec.-treas. 1971-72, chmn. 1979-80), Am. Assn. Law Librs. (sec. 1965 70, pres. 1975-76). Episcopalian. Office: Cornell U Sch Law Myron Taylor Hall Ithaca NY 14853

HAMMOND, JEREMY MARSHALL, engineer, educator; b. Portland, Maine, Aug. 10, 1973; s. Nancy Louise Jodrie; m. Kimberly Sue Burns, June 22, 1996. BS, Embry-Riddle Aero. Univ., Daytona Beach Florida, 1991—95; MS Engring. Physics, U. Maine, Maine, 1996—98, PhD Bio-Systems Engring., 1998—2001. Dir. of engring. Sensor R & D, Orono, Maine, 1997—2001; guest lectr. U. of Maine, Orono, Maine, 1998—98; sr. new product engr. IDEXX Laboratories, Westbrook, Maine, 2001—. Author: (journal articles) A semiconducting Metal Oxide Fish Freshness Sensor Array. Grantee SBIR Phase I and Phase II, NSF, 2000-2002. Achievements include patents pending for Gas sensors and sensor arrays. Office: IDEXX Laboratories 1 Idexx Dr Westbrook ME 04092 Office Fax: 207-856-8728. E-mail: jeremy-hammond@idexx.com.

HAMMOND, JOHN BAPTISTE, III, academic administrator; b. Baton Rouge, La., Aug. 18, 1962; s. John Batiste Hammond, Jr. and Shirley Jean (Kelly) Hammond; m. Yoko Kusumoto, Mar. 8, 1999; children: Therese Morgan, John Baptiste Hammond, IV. BS, MIT, 1984; MBA, Emory U., 1988; ABD, MIT, 1999. Assoc. dir. of admissions MIT, Cambridge, Mass., 1991—93; asst. dean Goizueta Bus. Sch., Atlanta, 1999—. Orgnl. cons. Hammond Consulting, Atlanta, 1999—; course dir. Goizueta Bus. Sch., 2000—. Author: The Physican Executive. Prin. for a day program Atlanta Pub. Schs., 2001—03; mentor Cambridge Pub. Schs., 1989—92. Mem.: Acad. of Mgmt., Alpha Phi Alpha Frat., Inc. (area dir. 1990—92). Achievements include research in co-author, Dept. of Labor monograph examining the status of african ams. in the workplace. Avocations: reading, travel, movies, cycling.

HAMMOND, JUDITH ANNE, family nurse practitioner; b. Newburgh, N.Y., Jan. 2, 1945; d. Barney and Violet (Cervoni) Carfarone; children: Michael, Teresa. Diploma, St. Francis Hosp. Sch. Nursing, Poughkeepsie, N.Y., 1966; BSN cum laude, Mt. St. Mary Coll., Newburgh, 1982; MS in Family Primary Care, Pace U., 1990. RN, cert. nurse practitioner in family health, sch. nurse-tchr. Staff nurse St. Luke's Hosp., Newburgh, 1966-69; pvt. duty nursing, 1974-75; sch. health nurse Mt. St. Mary Coll., Newburgh, 1976-79; occupational health nurse IBM Corp., Poughkeepsie, 1984-85, 87-88; nurse practitioner, sch. nurse-tchr. Newburgh Enlarged City Sch. Dist., 1989—. Adj. instr. Dutchess Community Coll., Poughkeepsie, 1988-89, coord nursing/health-related program, 1989. Mem. ANA, N.Y. State Nurses Assn., Nat. Assn. Sch. Nurses, N.Y. State Coalition of Nurse Practitioners, Am. Acad. Nurse Practitioners, Nurse Practitioner Assn., Sigma Theta Tau. Office: Heritage Jr High School 405 Union Ave New Windsor NY 12553 E-mail: jhammond@newburgh.k12.ny.us., cuffy1245@aol.com.

HAMMOND, JUDY MCLAIN, business services executive; b. Downey, Calif., June 24, 1956; d. Ernest Richard and Bernice Elaine (Thompson) McLain; m. Dennis Francis Hammond, Aug. 15, 1981. BS in Mgmt., Pepperdine U., 1982; MBA, U. So. Calif., 1986. Br. mgr. Kelly Svcs., Encino, Calif., 1978-81; mktg. mgr. Payco Am. Corp., Encino, 1981-83, GC Svcs. Corp., Santa Ana, Calif., 1983—; pres. Resource Mgmt. Svcs. Inc., Norwalk, Calif., 1986—; founder CEO The Debt Marketplace, Inc, 1994—. Cons., expert in collection and recovery. Author: Collect More From Collection Agencies. Mem.. Merchants Rsch. Coun. (bd. dirs.), LA Underwater Photographic Soc., Toastmasters. Avocations: scuba diving, underwater photography. Office: 10440 Pioneer Blvd Ste 2 Santa Fe Springs CA 90670-8235 E-mail: judy.hammond@debtmarketplace.com.

HAMMOND, KEN, newspaper magazine editor; Editor Texas Magazine, Houston Chronicle, Tex. Office: Houston Chronicle Pub Co 801 Texas Ave Houston TX 77002-2996 E-mail: ken.hammond@chron.com.

HAMMOND, LARRY AUSTIN, lawyer; b. Wichita, Kans., Sept. 17, 1945; BA, U. Tex., 1967, JD, 1970. Bar: Calif. 1971, Ariz. 1975. Law clk. to Hon. Carl McGowan U.S. Ct. Appeals (D.C. cir.), 1970-71; law clk. to Hon. Hugo L. Black U.S. Supreme Ct., 1971, law clk. to Hon. Lewis F. Powell Jr., 1971-73; asst. spl. prosecutor Watergate spl. prosecution force U.S. Justice Dept., 1973-74, dep. asst. atty. gen. office legal counsel, 1977-80; mem. Osborn Maledon P.A., Phoenix, 1995—. Adj. prof. law Ariz. State U., 1977, 85—, U. Ariz., 1983, U. Mex., 1983; judge pro tempore Ariz. Ct. Appeals, 1992. Editor-in-chief Tex. Law Rev., 1969-70. Mem. ABA, Order of Coif. Office: Osborn Maledon PO Box 36379 Phoenix AZ 85067-6379

HAMMOND, LINDA, artist; b. Dallas, Jan. 11, 1938; d. Rorie Emmitt and Mary Jane (Alexander) Cowden; m. Weldon Woolf Hammond, Aug. 3, 1963; children; Weldon Woolf III, Rory Cowden. BA magna cum laude, So. Meth. U., 1960. One-woman shows include San Antonio, 1984, 1986, 1993, exhibited in group shows at Rocky Mountain Nat., Golden, Colo., 1989, Western Fedn. Watercolor Socs., Corpus Christi, Tex., 1991, Sun City (Ariz.) Art Mus., 1994 (Best of Show award), U. Nev., Las Vegas, 2003, Mus. Tex. Tech U., Lubbock, 1998 (award), Soc. Layerists in Multi-Media, San Antonio, 1992, Bradford, Mass., 1994, 1998, San Miguel de Allende, 1996, U. Ark., Fayetteville, 1999, U. Colo., 2001, Represented in permanent collections San Antonio Art League; work pub. in Watercolor, 1996, 2000, others. Docent emeritus McNay Mus. Art, San Antonio, 1984—; patron San Antonio Art League, Hill Country Arts Found.; bd. trustees S.W. Sch. Art and Craft. Recipient Onderdonk award, 1991, Contbrs. award, 1993, Betty Maddux award, 1994, Artist of Yr. award, 1997. Mem.: San Antonio Art League, Soc. Layerists in Multi-Media, San Antonio Watercolor Group (signature mem., Bronze medal 1992, Silver medal 1993, 2000, Gold medal 1999), Tex. Watercolor Soc. (pres. 1990—92, signature mem., Purchase prize 1992, Best of Show award 1995, award of excellence 1997), Nat. Watercolor Soc. (signature mem.), Battle of Flowers Assn., Club Giraud, Zeta Tau Alpha. Home: 4 Lazy Ln San Antonio TX 78209-2833

HAMMOND, LOU RENA CHARLOTTE, public relations executive; b. Muenster, Tex. d. Louis Martin and Regina L. (Schoech) Wolf; m. Christopher Weymouth Hammond, Sept. 6, 1964; 1 child, Stephen. BA, U. Houston, 1962. Rep. pub. rels. Pan Am. Airways, N.Y.C., 1968-76, mgr. pub. rels., 1977-79, dir. pub. rels., 1980-81, dir. pub. affairs, 1981; pres., ptnr. Taylor and Hammond, N.Y.C., 1981-84; prin., pres. Lou Hammond and Assocs., N.Y.C., 1984—. Mem. adv. bd. Ctr. for Tourism and Travel at NYU. Editor: (calendar) Avenue mag., 1976-79. Mem. Women's Bd. of Madison Sq. Boys and Girls Club, N.Y.C. Recipient Matrix award in pub. rels., 1992, Winthrop W. Grice award Hotel Sales and Mktg. Assoc. Internat., 1992, Inside PR Mag.'s All-Star award, 1992. Mem. Soc. Am. Travel Writers, Fashion Group, Assn. Better N.Y., Les DAmes de Escoffier, Women's Forum, Women Execs. in Pub. Rels., Doubles Club. Roman Catholic. Avocations: bridge, tennis, 18th century antiques. Office: Lou Hammond & Assocs Inc 39 E 51st St New York NY 10022-5916 E-mail: louh@lhammond.com.

HAMMOND, MARIAN CORLEENE, retired literature educator; b. Ramage, W.Va., Dec. 8, 1919; s. Booker Shumate and Sadie Mearl Workman; m. John Elam Moore, July 7, 1942 (annulled Oct. 1945); children: Terry Colette Humphrey, Lisa Suzanne; m. Joseph Hammond, Nov. 17, 1945 (dec. Apr. 1998). AB in English, Berea Coll., 1941; EdM, Mills Coll., 1955; postgrad., Stanford U., 1958—76; adminstrv. credential, Calif. State U., Hayward, 1974; MA, San Francisco State U., 1976. Cert. prin. Calif. Tchr. English and drama Scott H.S., Madison, W.Va., 1941—42; children's libr. N.Y. Pub. Libr., N.Y.C., 1941; sci. tchr. Eccles (W.Va.) Jr. H.S., 1942—43; statistician, speech writer Del Monte Corp., San Francisco, 1946—53; tchr. English and drama San Lorenzo (Calif.) H.S., 1955—57; tchr. drama San Francisco State U., 1958—62; tchr. drama, Speech and English Chabot Coll., Hayward, Calif., 1962—70; prin., tchr. grades 7-12 Fremont (Calif.) Unified Sch. Dist., 1968—85; tchr. English, speech and tech. writing Heald Inst. Tech., Hayward, 1992—93; tchr. speech and English Western Career Coll., San Leandro, Calif., 2000—01; ret. Contbr. articles to mags Active Liberty Counsel, Orlando, Fla., 1999—2003, Am. Ctr. for Law and Justice, Atlanta, 1999—2003, Parents TV Coun., L.A., 2000—03. Mem.: AFTRA, Actor's Equity, Hayward ARts Coun., Castro Valley Mineral and Gem Soc. (life; dealer), Alpha Psi Omega (chair casting com.), Pi Gamma Mu, Tau Kappa Alpha. Republican. Baptist. Avocations: bead stringing, writing. Home: 27937 El Portal Dr Hayward CA 94542

HAMMOND, M(ARY) ELIZABETH HALE, pathologist; b. Salt Lake City, Jan. 5, 1942; d. Edward Girard and Ruth (Hansen) Hale; m. John Morgan Hammond, Dec. 30, 1964; children: Jonathan Hale, Thomas Hale, Kathleen Hale. BS, U. Utah., 1963, MD, 1967. Diplomate Am. Bd. Pathology. Intern U. Utah Sch. Medicine, Salt Lake City, 1967-68; USPHS fellow Karolinska Inst., Stockholm, 1968-69; resident, fellow Mass. Gen. Hosp., Boston, 1970-74, staff pathologist, 1974-77; instr. Harvard Med. Sch., Boston, 1974-76, asst. prof. of pathology, 1976-77; pathologist LDS Hosp., Salt Lake City, 1977—, dir. electron microscopy lab., 1978-92, chmn. dept. of pathology, 1992—, med. staff pres., 1995-97; prof. U. Utah Sch. Medicine, Salt Lake City, 1991—; dir. cardiac pathology Utah CARDIAC, Salt Lake City, 1986—, adj. assoc. prof. internal medicine, 1991, adj. prof. medicine, 2000—. Mem. Radiation Therapy-Oncology Group, 1986—, vice chmn. for translational rsch., 1995-99, chmn. pathology com., 1986-92, tumor repository com., 1993-; ad hoc reviewer Nat. Cancer Inst., 1986—. Author: Pathology of Mediastinum, 1990; editor: Solid Organ Transplant Pathology, 1994; mem. editl. bd. Jour. Heart Transplant, 1990-94, 2001-, Cardiovascular Pathology, 1991—, Jour. Radonocology Biology Physics, 1989—, assoc. editor, 1995; guest editor Ultrastructural Pathology, 1991-92; contbr. over 140 articles to profl. publs., chpts. to books. Bd. dirs. Deseret Found., Salt Lake City, 1977-94, chmn. rsch. com., 1985-94. Recipient Outstanding Achievement award YWCA, 1997; Rsch. scholar Am. Cancer Soc., 1974-77. Fellow Am. Coll. Chest Physicians, Am. Soc. Clin. Pathology, Coll. Am. Pathology (chmn. cancer com. 1997-2000, bd. govs. 2000—); mem. U.S. and Can. Acad. Pathology, Am. Assn. Pathology, Am. Assn. Immunology, Cardiovasc. Pathology Soc. (councillor 1988-91), Soc. for Ultrastructural Pathology (councillor 1989-91, pres. 1993-95), Soc. for Heart Transplantation, Utah Soc. Pathologists (pres. 1982-85), Utah Med. Ins. Assn. (bd. govs. 1987-92), Phi Beta Kappa, Alpha Omega Alpha. Democrat. Mem. Lds Ch. Achievements include pub. of first prospective series of humorally mediated cardiac transplant rejection. Office: LDS Hosp Dept Pathology 8th Avenue St Salt Lake City UT 84143-0001 Home: 970 Northcliffe Dr Salt Lake City UT 84103

HAMMOND, MARY SAYER, art educator; b. Bellingham, Wash., Oct. 1, 1946; d. Boyd James and Jacqueline Anna (Thurston) Sayer; m. Lester Wayne Hammond, Aug. 26, 1967 (div. Feb. 1977); m. Wiley Devere Sanderson, Jan. 13, 1983. BFA in Art Edn., U. Ga., 1967, MFA in Photo Design, 1977; PhD in History of Photo/Art Edn., Ohio State U., 1986. Art supr. Madison County Pub. Schs., Danielsville, Ga., 1968-71, art instr. U. Ga., Athens, 1971-73, instr. photo design, 1975-76; instr. in art edn. North Ga. Coll., Dalonega, 1975; instr. in art Valdosta (Ga.) State Coll., 1976-77, asst. prof. art, 1979-80; asst. prof. art, Am. Studies George Mason U., Fairfax, Va., 1980-87, assoc. prof. art, Am. Studies, 1987-94, prof. art, Am. studies, 1995-98, dir. divsn. art studio. Adminstrv. assoc. Ohio State U., Columbus, 1978-79, tchg. assoc., 1977-78; co-dir. Saturday program U. Ga., 1966-76, tchg. asst., 1974. Photographs represented in permanent collections at Ctr. for Creative Photography, Ariz., Internat. Mus. Photography, Rochester, N.Y., Nat. Gallery of Art, Washington, Nat. Mus. Women in Arts, Washington. Treas. Faculty Senate of Va., 1991-96. Grantee Fulbright Hays Commn., 1973-74; travel grantee Samuel H. Kress Found., 1986, George Mason U., 1991, 93, 96-98; photographer's fellow NEA, 1982-84. Mem. Soc. Photo Edn. (mid-Atlantic bd. dirs. 1990-98), Phi Kappa Phi (hon.). E-mail: mshammond@earthlink.net.

HAMMOND, NORMAN DAVID CURLE, archaeology educator, researcher; b. Brighton, Eng., July 10, 1944; BA, U. Cambridge, Eng., 1966, Diploma in Classical Archaeology, 1967, MA, 1970, PhD, 1972, ScD, 1987, DSc (hon.), 1999. Rsch. faculty Cambridge U., Eng., 1967-75; faculty Bradford U., Eng., 1975-77; vis. prof. Rutgers U., 1977-78, faculty, 1978-88, assoc. prof., 1978-84, prof., 1984-88; member staff Peabody Mus., Harvard U., 1988—, Willey lectr., 2000; prof. archaeology Boston U., 1988—. Vis. prof. U. Calif., Berkeley, 1977, Jilin U., China, 1981, Calif. Acad. Sci., 1984-85, U. Paris, 1987, Acad. Scis., USSR, 1991, U. Bonn, 1994; vis. faculty U. Cambridge, 1981-82, 91, 96-97, U. Oxford, 1989, 2004; archaeology corr. The Times, London (Press award, Brit. Archaeol. Awards 1994, 98), 1967—; field work in North Africa, Afghanistan, Greece, Guatemala, Belize, Ecuador, Spain; disting. lectr. Montana State U., 1996, Bushnell lectr. Cambridge U., 1997, Stone lectr. AIA, 1998, 2004, Brush lectr. AIA, 2001, Armand Brunswick disting. lectr. Met. Mus. Art, 2001. Author: (with F.R. Allchin) The Archaeology of Afghanistan, 1977, (with G.R. Willey) Maya Archaeology and Ethnohistory, 1979, Ancient Maya Civilization, 1982, 5th edit., 1994, various foreign edits., Cuello: An Early Maya Community in Belize, 1991; numerous monographs on excavations in No. Belize, 1973, 75, 76, Lubaantun, 1975, Nohmul, 1985; gen. editor: Procs., 44th Internat. Congress of Americanists, 1982-84. Dumbarton Oaks fellow, 1988; Rockefeller Found. scholar, 1997. Fellow Soc. Antiquaries London (medallist 2001), Brit. Acad. Office: Boston Univ Dept Archaeology 675 Commonwealth Ave Boston MA 02215-1406

HAMMOND, PAUL YOUNG, political scientist, educator; b. Salt Lake City, Feb. 24, 1929; s. James Thaddeus and Hortense Clair (Young) H.; m. Merylyn Felt Simmons, Aug. 29, 1950; children: Paul Brett, Wendy Simmons, Robyn Simmons, Spencer Blair, Clifford Simmons. BA, U. Utah, 1949; MA, Harvard U., 1951, PhD, 1953; postgrad. Fulbright scholar, London Sch. Econs., 1952-53. Instr. govt. Harvard U., Cambridge, Mass., 1953-55; lectr. Columbia U., N.Y.C., 1956-57; asst. prof. polit. sci. Yale U., New Haven, 1957-62; research asso. Washington Center Fgn. Policy Research, Johns Hopkins U., 1962-64; mem. research staff Rand Corp., Santa Monica, Calif., 1964-76, head social sci. dept., 1973-76; vis. research polit. scientist U. Calif., Berkeley, 1971-72; Edward R. Weidlein prof. environ. and pub. policy studies U. Pitts., 1976-83, disting. service prof. pub. and internat. affairs, 1983—; dir. Ridgway Ctr. of Internat. Security Studies, 1988-91, Energy and Environ. Center, 1979-81; Fulbright rsch. prof. Inst. of S.E. Asian Studies, Singapore, 1993—. Lectr. U. Tex., U. So. Calif., U. Calif., Santa Barbara and Los Angeles; cons. in field. Author: Organizing for Defense: The Administration of the American Military Establishment, 1961, The Cold War Years: American Foreign Policy Since 1945, 1969, Cold War and Detente: The American Foreign Policy Process Since 1945, 1975, NATO Strategic Planning: Preparations That Do No Harm, 1988, Fulfilling the Promise of the Goldwater-Nichols Act: Operational Planning and Command, 1989, NATO: The Infrastructure of Reassurance, 1989, What Future For the U.S. Military Presence in Europe, 1990, LBJ and the Presidential Management of Foreign Relations, 1992, Towards a Workable European Architecture: Political-Military Problems in the New Europe, 1994, Doing Without America?, 1996, On Taking Peacekeeping Seriously, 1997, Culture Versus Civilization: A Critique of Huntington, 1997; co-author: The American Civil-Military Decisions, 1963, Information System Applications for a High Level Staff, 1972, Social Choice and Soviet Strategic Decision Making, 1977, Regional Energy Policy Alternatives, 1977, Administration of Security Assistance: Systems and Process, 1978, Individual Energy Conservation Behaviors, 1980, The Reluctant Supplier, 1983, Alternative Organizational Structures for NATO, 1992; co-editor: Political Dynamics in the Middle East, 1971. Forrestal fellow in naval history, 1955, Stimson Fund fellow Yale U., 1959, Rockefeller fellow in internat. studies, 1963-64; Fulbright scholar London Sch. Econs., 1952-53. Mem. Am. Polit. Sci. Assn., Internat. Studies Assn., Internat Inst. Strategic Studies. Mem. Lds Ch. Office: Grad Sch Pub & Internat Affairs Posvar Hall University of Pittsburgh Pittsburgh PA 15260 E-mail: pyh@pitt.edu.

HAMMOND, R. PHILIP, chemical engineer; b. Creston, Iowa, May 28, 1916; s. Robert Hugh and Helen Hammond; m. Amy L. Farmer, Feb. 28, 1941 (div. 1969); children: Allen L., David M., Jean Phyllis, Stanley W.; m. Vivienne Fox, 1972. BSChemE, U. So. Calif., 1938; PhD in Phys. and Inorganic Chemistry (Naval Research fellow), U. Chgo., 1947. Registered profl. engr., Ill., Calif. Chief chemist Lindsay Chem. Co., West Chicago, Ill., 1938-46; group leader Los Alamos Sci. Lab., 1947-62, assoc. div. leader reactor devel. div., 1960-62; dir. nuclear desalination program Oak Ridge Nat. Lab., 1962-73; adj. prof. UCLA, 1972—80; head energy group R & D Assos. Corp., Santa Monica, Calif., 1973-83; desalination cons., 1987—; leader advanced sea water evaporator design Met. Water Dist. of So. Calif., L.A., 1989-98. Author articles on nuclear power reactors, nuclear wastes, reactor safety econs., energy centers, metallurgy of plutonium and refractory metals, rare earths, radiation chemistry, remote control engring.; contbr. to fusion energy concept using underground containment, to Ency. Brit. Mem. U.S. delegation Conf. on Peaceful Uses Atomic Energy, Geneva, Switzerland, 1955, 65, 71, IAEA Panel on Desalination, Vienna, Austria, 1964, 65, 66, 71; mem. U.S. team to USSR on desalination, 1964. Mem. Am. Nuclear Soc. (charter), Am. Chem. Soc., Am. Inst. Chem. Engrs., Sigma Xi, Phi Kappa Phi, Phi Lambda Upsilon. Achievements include patents for improved safety for high speed rail transport, for devices for preventing collisions at sea and for storing nuclear waste; origination of advanced concepts in sea water evaporator construction, and efficient coupling to nuclear energy sources; design (with others) of advanced reactor containment system capable of withstanding melt-down accidents with zero leakage, and of automotive engine using liquid air and liquid natural gas as fuel. Home and Office: PO Box 3971 Laguna Hills CA 92654-3971 *With our achievements in desalination, efficient agriculture, and nuclear power, it is now clear that the food producing ability of the earth is not limited by technology. But our political and social institutions have not kept up. Over a billion people live in hopeless poverty, and without hope, terrorism is an easy choice. Yet small investments by the rich countries in energy supply and clean water will create self-supporting communities with purchasing power. The war on terror is really a war on poverty.*

HAMMOND, RALPH CHARLES, real estate executive; b. Valley Head, Ala., Feb. 1, 1916; s. William Bleve and Alice Corina Jane (Holleman) H.; student Snead Jr. Coll., 1938-39, Berea Coll., 1940-41; AB, U. Ala., 1945; DLitt, Livingston U., 1992; m. Myra Leak, June 20, 1954; children— James, Ben. Press sec. to gov. Ala., Montgomery, 1946-50, exec. sec., 1955-59; gen. rep. ARC, Greensboro, N.C., 1950-54; mayor of Arab (Ala.), 1963-69; pres. City Ctr., Inc., Arab, 1959— . Commr. from Ala., U.S. Study Commn. S.E. River Basins, 1958-64; bd. dirs. Ala. Tb Assn., 1956-83, pres., 1972-74; hon. Christmas Seal chmn., Ala. Served with AUS, 1941-45. Commd. Poet Laureate of Ala., 1991-95; Paul Harris fellow Rotary Internat., 1992. Mem. Ky. Hist. Soc., Phillip Hamman Family Assn. Am. (pres. 1972-78), Ala. Poetry Soc. (pres. 1981-84, Ala. Poet of Yr. 1985), Ala. Writers' Conclave (pres. 1987-89), Nat. Fedn. State Poetry Socs. (treas. 1985-86, 2d v.p. 1990-92, 1st v.p. 1993-94, pres. 1994-96). Democrat. Methodist. Lodge: Masons. Author: My GI Aching Back, 1945; Ante Bellum Mansions of Alabama, 1951; Philip Hamman, Man of Valor, 1976; Song of Appalachia, 1982; How High the Stars, 1982; Upon the Wings of the Wind, 1982; One Golden Apple a Day, 1983; Collected Poems, 1983; Wisdom Is, 1984; Edging Through the Grass (Book of Yr. Ala. Poetry Soc.), 1985; editor: Alabama Poets: A Contemporary Anthology, 1989, A Blossoming of Sonnets, 1990, Upper Alabama-Poems Out of Light (George

Washington Honor medal Freedoms Found. Valley Forge 1993, Book of Yr. award Ala. Poetry Soc. 1993), Crossing Many Rivers-Poems Along the Way, 1995 (Book of Yr. award Ala. Poetry Soc. 1995), Vincent Van Gogh--A Narrative Journey, 1997, Personal Encounters, 2001; contbr. short stories and feature articles to jours., mags.; poems pub. in 40 jours. Home: 1280 Guntersville Rd Arab AL 35016-1618 Office: PO Box 486 Arab AL 35016-0486

HAMMOND, RAYMOND WILLIAM, pharmacotherapy specialist; b. Port Arthur, Tex., May 16, 1944; s. Woodrow Wilson and Anna Mary (Brockman) H.; m. Sandra Louise Borel, Feb. 1, 1964; children: Cynthia Lynn, Jeffrey Carl. BS in Pharmacy, U. Houston, 1973; PharmD, U. Tenn. Ctr. Health Scis., 1981. Lic. pharmacist, Tex.; cert. pharmacotherapy specialist. Staff pharmacist US-PHS Hosp., S.I., N.Y., 1974-75; dep. chief pharmacist Med. Ctr. Fed. Prisoners, Springfield, Mo., 1975-77, USPHS Outpatient Clinic, Savannah, Ga., 1977-78, chief pharmacist, 1978-79, 1981; pharmacist USPHS Indian Hosp., Whiteriver, Ariz., 1981-83; asst. chief inpatient clin. pharmacy services W.W. Hastings Indian Hosp., Tahlequah, Okla., 1983-91; chief customer svc. and quality assurance br. divsn. Supply Mgmt. Indian Health Svc., Albuquerque, 1991-94; asst. prof. pharmacy, experiential programs coord.; dir. drug utilization rev. program Coll. Pharmacy, U. N.Mex., 1994-97; clin. pharmacy corrd. Sierra Med. Ctr., El Paso, Tex., 1997-98; clin. assoc. prof. pharmacy coop. pharmacy program U. Tex., Austin and El Paso, 1998-99; assoc. dean practice programs Coll. Pharmacy U. Houston, 1999—. Clin. resource speaker SW Okla. State U. Sch. Pharmacy, 1984-91; adj. asst. prof. Northeastern State U. Coll. of Optometry, Tahlequah, Okla., 1986-90; adj. assoc. prof., 1991; mem. Pharmacotherapy Splty. Coun., 1994-2000; mem. adv. bd. Cherokee County Elder Care. Contbr. chpt. to book and articles to profl. jours. Mem. instl. rev. bd. NE State U., Tahlequah, 1985-91; bd. dirs. Cherokee County Hospice Assn., 1986-87. Capt. USPHS, 1974-94. Fellow Am. Coll. of Clin. Pharmacists; mem. Am. Soc. Health Systems Pharmacists, Tex. Soc. Health-Sys. Pharmacists, N.Mex. Soc. Hosp. Pharmacists (pres. 1997), Commd. Officers Assn. USPHS, Mensa, Rho Chi. Democrat. Roman Catholic. Avocations: photography, backpacking, computer science, fishing, beer and winemaking. Home: 3015 Marble Falls Dr Pearland TX 77584-7067 E-mail: rhammond@houston.rr.com.

HAMMOND, ROBERT LEE, retired feed company executive; b. Farmington, Minn., Oct. 23, 1926; s. Lee L. and Mae Francis (Kingston) H.; m. Helene Germaine Haven, May 8, 1948; children— Robert Lee, Jr., Jane Kay Kipling Student, U. Dubuque, 1944-45; student, Northwestern U., 1945-46. Co-owner Hammond Oil Co., Estherville, Iowa, 1952-60; asst. sales mgr. Golden Sun Feeds Inc., Estherville, Iowa, 1960-62, plant mgr. Des Moines, 1962-64, exec. v.p. sales mgr. Estherville, 1964-71, pres., 1971-88. Bd. dirs. Golden Sun Feeds Inc., chmn. bd. 1988-91; chmn. bd. Am. Feed Industry Ins., 1987-91. Pres. Indsl. Devel. Commn., Estherville, 1966-67. Served with USN, 1944-46 Am. Feed Industry Assn. (dir., com. chmn. 1971-74, nat. chmn. 1986-87), Iowa Grain and Feed Assn. (dir., treas. 1969-72), Estherville C. of C. (dir. 1958-60) Lodges: Elks, Masons, Rotary. Republican. Episcopalian. Avocations: hunting; golf; fishing; travel.

HAMMOND, ROBIE LEE, health science association administrator; d. Robert Lee Higginbotham and Claudia Elizabeth Elrod; widowed; children: Robby Lee, Gary Joe, Debra Lynn H. Olson. AA, Draughans Bus. Coll., Greenville, S.C., 1946. Cert. med. staff coord. Nat. Assn. of Med. Staff Svcs. Svc. rep. Bell Tel. & Telegraph Co., Greenville, SC, 1946—52, Chesapeake & Potomac Tel. Co., Norfolk, Va., 1953; sec. Portsmouth Psychiat. Ctr., Va., 1976—81; med. libr. Portsmouth Gen. Hosp., Va., 1981—82, med. staff coord., 1983—98; exec. dir. Portsmouth Acad. of Medicine, Va., 1998—, exec. dir. med. found., 1998—. Author. Mem. citizens adv. com. Educare for Seniors, Portsmouth. Mem.: Portsmouth Consortium of Founds., Va. Conf. of Med. Execs. Avocations: golf, gardening, reading, creative writing, decorating.

HAMMOND, ROY JOSEPH, reinsurance company executive; b. St. Louis, Jan. 9, 1929; s. Edward Herman and Alvera Ann (Herzog) H.; m. Donna LaSalle Perkins, Apr. 12, 1951 (div. July 2001); children— Douglas Edward, Donald Erwin, Laura Ann Hammond Budniakiewicz; m. Gloria June Kirkpatrick, Dec. 19, 2001. BS, Northwestern U., 1954; JD, DePaul U., Chgo., 1959. Bar: Ill. bar 1959. With Am. Mut. Reins. Co., Chgo., 1963-91, then sr. v.p., gen. counsel and sec., 1967-76, pres., chief exec. officer, bd. dirs., 1976-91; pres., chief exec. officer Whitehall Cons., Ltd., Camden, N.C., 1991—; pres. Wheeling (Ill.) Mcpl. Park Dist., 1963-65. Past mem. Reins. Assn. Am., bd. dirs., 1976—86. Served with AUS, 1946-48. Mem. ABA, Ill. State Bar Assn., Internat. Assn. Def. Counsel, Fedn. Ins. and Corp. Counsel, Chgo. Casualty Adjusters Assn. (pres. 1972-73), Chgo. Yacht Club. Republican. Presbyterian. Home and Office: Whitehall Shores 201 Azalea Dr Camden NC 27921-6991

HAMMOND, RUSSELL PAUL, music educator; b. Chgo., Oct. 30, 1959; s. John Edgar and Suzanne Louise Hammond; m. Michele Ann Smith. B Music Edn., Bradley U., Peoria, Ill., 1982; MMusic, U. Conns., Storrs, 1996. Chair dept. music Lyme/Old Lyme H.S., Old Lyme, Conn., 1987—2001, dir. choirs and theatre arts, 1987—2001; fine arts chair Ledyard H.S., Conn., 2001—, dir. choirs, 2001—. Mem.: Music Educators Nat. Conf., Am. Choral Dirs. Assn. (state pres. 1993—95, chair repertoire and stds. 1998—2001), Conn. Music Educators Assn. Roman Catholic. Avocations: running, rock-climbing, hiking, reading. Home: 93 Beech Tree Ridge PO Box 878 Killingworth CT 06419 Office: Ledyard High School 24 Gallup Hill Road Ledyard CT E-mail: hammond9@mindspring.com.

HAMMOND, TEENA GAY, editor; b. Louisville, Dec. 3, 1967; d. Jimmie Howard and Rosetta (Gay) H. Student, U. Louisville, 1985-87, Ariz. State U., 1989-93. Bus. reporter Bus. Jour., Phoenix, 1993-95; dir. mktg. and pub. rels. Murro Cons., Phoenix, 1995-96; bus. reporter Bus. Press, Ontario, Calif., 1996-97; West Coast retail editor Women's Wear Daily, Fairchild Publs., L.A., 1997-2000; with West Coast fashion and features dept. W mag., Fairchild Publs., L.A., 1997-2000; mng. editor Styleclick, L.A., 2000-01; entertainment editor MKA Mag., L.A., 2001; corr. People mag., 2002; sr. writer In Touch, 2002—; freelance writer, 2001—02. Recipient 1st place award for gen. reporting Ariz. Press Club, 1994, 1st place award for sustained coverage series, 1994, 3rd place award for gen. reporting, 1994; 2d place award for journalistic achievement Ariz. Newspaper Assn., 1994. Avocations: skydiving, scuba, hiking. E-mail: teenahammond@yahoo.com.

HAMMOND, WALTER EDWARD, aerospace engineer; b. Austin, Tex., Feb. 26, 1947; s. John Hays and Carmela Sierra (Abadiano) H.; m. Suzanne Scott Adams, Aug. 18, 1971; children: W. Scott, Anne E., David J., Michael C. BS, U. Tex., Arlington, 1971; MS, U. Tex., Austin, 1973; MBA, Tex. A&M U., 1982, MS in Indsl. Engring., 1983, D Engring., 1984. Registered profl. engr. Ala. Mem. tech. staff Rocketdyne Divsn. Rockwell Internat., Canoga Park, Calif., 1976-79; prin. sys. analyst Teledyne Brown Engring., Huntsville, Ala., 1983-86; level III assoc. Booz, Allen & Hamilton, Inc., Huntsville, 1987-88; sr. aerospace engr. Thiokol Corp., Huntsville, 1989; supr. Sys. Analysis Br. Sverdrup Tech., Inc., Huntsville, 1989-93; dir. coml. practices and partnerships Nat. Technology Transfer Ctr., Wheeling, W.Va., 1996; spl. projects engr. Hernandez Engring., Inc., Huntsville, 1999-2000; sr. engr. Pace & Waite, Inc., Huntsville, 2000—02; sr. sys. engr. Jacobs Engring./Sverdrup, Huntsville, 2002—. Mem. sci. adv. bd.USAF, Washington, 1999—. Author 2 books on space transp. systems; contbr. articles to profl. jours. Corr. sec. Hispanic Heritage Assn. of North Ala., Huntsville, 2000. Decorated Commendation medal USAF, Meritorious Svc. medal (USAF, assoc. 2002. Fellow AIAA (assoc., bd. dirs. 1976—, Spl. Svc. award 1986), Brit. Interplanetary Assn.; mem. Res. Officers' Assn. (life). Republican. Methodist. Avocations: jogging, snow skiing. Office: Jacobs Engring/Sverdrup MailStop SD42/Sverdrup Huntsville AL 35812 E-mail: Walter.E.Hammond@msfc.nasa.gov.

HAMMOND, WELDON WOOLF, JR., hydrogeologist; b. San Antonio, May 17, 1937; s. Weldon Woolf and Thelma Evangeline (Vandever) H.; m. Linda Lou Cowden, Aug. 3, 1963; children: Weldon Woolf III, Rory Cowden. BA, U. Tex., 1960, MA, 1969, PhD, 1984. Geologist, dist. mgr. Tex. Water Devel. Bd., Austin, San Antonio, 1964-71; ecologist Alamo Area Coun. Govt., San Antonio, 1971-77; from lectr. to assoc. prof. U. Tex. San Antonio, 1977-90, dir. divsn. earth and phys. scis., 1993-99, dir. ctr. water rsch., 1986—; cons. San Antonio, 1979—. McNutt Disting. prof. geology, U. Tex. San Antonio, 1999—, Dean Coll. of Scis. and Engrg., UTSA, 1999-2000, dir. divsn. earth and phys. scis., 2000-01, chair dept. earth and environ. sci., 2002-03; dir. Inst. for Rsch. in Water and Environl. Resources, 2003—. Capt. USN, 1960-63, 90-91. Mem. Assn. Engring. Geologists, Geol. Soc. Am., Assn. Ground Water Scientists and Engrs., Internat. Assn. Hydrogeologists. Home: 4 Lazy Ln San Antonio TX 78209-2833 Office: Univ Tex San Antonio 6900 N Loop 1604 W San Antonio TX 78249-0663

HAMMOND, WILLIAM MICHAEL, historian, educator; b. Pasadena, Calif., Jan. 1, 1943; s. Paul Chester Hammond and Mary Ethel Champieux; m. Lillamaud Munsell Leike, Apr. 28, 1973; children: Michael Anthony, Elizabeth Anne. STB, Cath. U. Am., 1967, MA, 1968, PhD, 1973. Lectr. in univ. honors U. of Md., College Park, Md., 1991—; chief, gen. histories br. U.S. Army Ctr. Mil. History, Washington, 2001—. Author: The U.S. Army in Vietnam: Public Affairs: The Military and the Media, 1963 - 1968 (Notable Govt. Docs., ALA, 1989), Public Affairs: The Military and the Media, 1968-1973, Reporting Vietnam, Military and Media at War (Richard W. Leopold award, Orgn. Am. Historians, 2000), Black Soldier, White Army: The 24th Infantry in Korea. Editor, web master, bd. dirs. Strathmore - Bel Pre Civic Assn., Silver Spring, Md., 1986—. Rsch. fellow, Joan Shorenstein Ctr. for the Press and Pub. Policy, Harvard U., 1999. Fellow: Interuniv. Seminar on Armed Forces and Soc.; mem.: Orgn. Am. Historians (Disting. Lectr. 2002—), Soc. Mil. History. Roman Catholic. Avocations: photography, watercolor painting, travel. Home: 2604 Bainbridge Ln Silver Spring MD 20906 Office: US Army Ctr Mil History Fort Lesley J McNair Washington DC 20319-5058

HAMMONDD, CHARLOTTE CLAREN, writer, researcher; b. Atlanta, Ga., Sept. 2, 1951; d. William Rogers Frederick and Frances Estelle Hammond. MA Psychology, U. of West Ga., Carrollton Georgia, 1991—93; BA History, Ga. State U., Atlanta Georgia, 1969—73. Writer Charlotte Hammond, Decatur, Ga.; educator Emory U., Atlanta, 2001—01, Friends Sch., Atlanta, 1995—97. Poet, Ga. Author: (novels) The Other Side of the Door, Compassion's War, The Six Lessons of Alpha Centouri, Six Lessons and Mirrors are out of print, (poetry) Mirrors of Serenity. Avocations: paranormal research, therapy for abused animals, past life investigation.

HAMMOND-KOMINSKY, CYNTHIA CECELIA, optometrist; b. Sept. 1, 1957; d. Andrew and Angeline (Laorno) Kominsky; m. Theodore Glen Hammond, Sept. 21, 1985. Student, Oakland U., Rochester, Mich., 1976—77; OD magna cum laude, Ferriss Coll. Optometry, 1981. Lic. optometrist Mich., cert. diagnostic and therapeutic pharm. agt. Intern Optometric Inst. and Clinic of Detroit, 1980, Ferris State Coll., Big Rapids, Mich., 1980, Jackson (Mich.) Prison, 1981; assoc. in pvt. practice Warren, Mich., 1981—82; optometrist Pearle Vision Ctr., Sterling Heights, Mich., 1982—87, K-Mart Optical Ctr., Sterling Heights, 1982—87, Royal Optical, Sterling Heights, 1988—. Provided eye care to nursing homes, Mt. Clemens, Mich. Head vol. caregivers and organ donation programs St. Therese of Lisieux Ch., Shelby Twp., Mich. Achievements include invention of binocular low vision aid device. Avocations: music, sports, decorative painting, gardening, antique crystal. Home: 47626 Cheryl Ct Shelby Township MI 48315-4708 Office: Royal Optical Lakeside Mall 14300 Lakeside Cir Sterling Heights MI 48313-1326

HAMMONDS, JAY A. retired secondary education educator, administrator; b. Conshohocken, Pa., July 18, 1943; s. Sidney E. and Grace E. Hammonds; m. Susan A. Earl, June 25, 1966; 1 child, Elizabeth A. BS in Edn., West Chester State Coll., 1965, MEd, 1971; postgrad. in Edn., U. Del., 1980—. Cert. Social Studies tchr. Del. Tchr. social studies Felton (Del.) Pub. Schs., 1965-67, P.S. du Pont High Sch., Wilmington, Del., 1967-78, Glasgow High Sch., Newark, Del., 1978-96, dept. chair, 1980-96; G.H.S. restructuring com. Network Adminstr. (MAC). Tchr. clin. studies coop. U. Del., Newark, 1985—86, curriculum cons., 1989. Author (multimedia software): Historic Atlas of South Asia, Historic Atlas of East Asia. Merit badge counselor Chester County Coun. Boy Scouts Am., West Chester, 1963—70, neighborhood commr., 1970—73; asst. coord. Amateur Radio Emergency Svc., Chester County, 1980—89; Del. rep. Internat. Credit Assn., Edn. Found. Seminar, 1992. Named G.H.S. Tchr. of Yr., 1987, Christina Dist. H.S. Tchr. of Yr., 1987, Del. Tchr.-Historian of Yr., 1992; Am. Studies fellow, Ea. Coll., 1987, Robert A. Taft fellow, U. Del., 1989, Dewitt Wallace-Reader's Digest fellow, Woodrow Wilson Inst., Princeton, 1991, Keizai Koho Ctr. fellow, Japan, 1992. Avocations: amateur radio, photography, genealogy, computing. Home: 1314 Sherwood Dr West Chester PA 19380-1607

HAMMONDS, TIMOTHY MERRILL, association executive, economist; b. Cortland, N.Y., June 5, 1944; s. Robert Merrill and Helen Marie (Conrad) H.; m. Karen Stein, June 17, 1966; 1 child, Lynn Vanessa. MBA, Cornell U., 1967, PhD, 1970. Assoc. prof. agrl. econs. Oreg. State U., Corvallis, 1970-75; sr. v.p. Food Mktg. Inst., Washington, 1975-93, pres., CEO, 1993—. Mem. bd. on agr. NAS, 1988-91; bd. dirs. Nat. Minority Supplier Devel. Coun., Bratton Woods Com., Acad. Food Mktg., St. Joseph's U., 1996—, Sloan Found. Ctr. for Retail Food Industry, U. Minn., 1995—; mem. adv. bd. Cornell U. Sch. Agrl. Econs., 1994—. Editor Agribus Jour., 1985-93; mem. editl. bd. Am. Jour. Agrl. Econs., 1978-80; contbr. articles to profl. jours. Recipient Rainbow/PUSH Coalition Ptnrs. award, 1998. Mem. Am. Agrl. Econs. Assn., Phi Kappa Phi. Republican. Methodist. Office: Food Mktg Inst 800 Connecticut Ave NW Washington DC 20006-2709

HAMMONS, BRIAN KENT, lawyer, business executive; b. Wurzburg, Federal Republic Germany, Mar. 6, 1958; arrived in U.S., 1958; s. R. Dwain and Donna G. (Carender) H.; m. Kimberly M. Pflumm, July 26, 1980; children: April Michelle, David Dwain, Adam Carender. BS summa cum laude, S.W. Mo. State U., Springfield, 1980; JD cum laude, So. Meth. U., Dallas, 1985. Bar: Mo. 1985. Exec., treas., v.p. Hammons Products Co., Stockton, Mo., 1980-86, exec. v.p., sec., 1987-96, pres., COO, CEO, 1997—; assoc. Stinson, Mag & Fizzell, Kansas City, Mo., 1986-87. Mem. Stockton Airport Bd., 1987-89, Stockton City Coun., 1989-91; pres. Stockton Cmty. Found., Stockton Cmty. Develop., 2002—; cub scout leader Boy Scouts Am.; Sunday sch. and Bible study tchr.; soccer coach. Mem. Mo. Bar Assn., springfield Area C. of C. (bd. dirs.) 2003—), Mo. Chamber Commerce and Industry (bd. dirs. 2003—), Masons (sec. 1980-81), Lions (pres. 1990-91), Leadership Mo., Young Presidents Orgn., Phi Delta Phi. Republican. Methodist. Avocations: running, flying, tennis, golf, hunting. Office: Hammons Products Co 105 Hammons Dr PO Box 140 Stockton MO 65785

HAMMONS, ELLA, consumer products company executive; b. Ringling, Okla., May 29, 1934; d. William E. Folsom and Dollie M. Morris; m. Bob J. Hammons, Apr. 10, 1967; 1 child, Frieda Surratt. Grad., Ringling H.S. Owner antique shop, Ringling. Chmn. Ringling Cemetery Com.; bd. trustees Hist. Soc., 1990—2003; co-chmn. Rep. Com., 1986. Recipient Svc. award, City of Ringling, 2001. Mem.: Ringling C. of C. (past pres.). Avocation: antiques. Home: PO BOX 15 Ringling OK 73456

HAMNER, EUGENIE LAMBERT, English educator; b. Darlington, Ala, May 24, 1936; d. Robert Eugene Jr. and Helen (Burford) Lambert; m. Gustavus O. Hamner, 1966 (div. 1988); children: Helen Gaussen, Nicholas Feagin. BA in English & history, Huntingdon Coll., 1958; MA in English, U. N.C., 1959, PhD in English, 1965. Instr. English, Winthrop Coll., Rock Hill, SC, 1959-60; instr. U. NC, Chapel Hill, NC, 1963-64; asst. prof. Huntingdon Coll., Montgomery, Ala., 1964-65, U. Ga., Athens, Ga., 1965-66; from asst. prof. to prof. U. So. Ala., Mobile, Ala., 1969-96, prof. emeritus, 1996. Co-editor: Ways of Knowing: Essays on Marge Piercy, 1991, (children's book) A Kitten for Julie and Christopher, 1997. Bd. dir. Mobile Mus. Art, 1984-88; mem. Mobile Hist. Devel. Commn., 1987-92; elem. sch. vol. Rolling Readers USA. Alpha Beta scholar, 1958, Sigma Sigma Sigma scholar, 1958. Mem. South Atlantic Modern Lang. Assn., Habitat for Humanity (pres.'s cir.), Mobile Opera Guild, Nat. Soc. Colonial Dames of Am., Omicron Delta Kappa. Democrat. Episcopalian. Avocations: reading, gardening, travel, children. Home: 3764 Mordecai Ln Mobile AL 36608-2007

HAMNER, LANCE DALTON, prosecutor; b. Fukuoka, Japan, Sept. 18, 1955; parents Am. citizens; s. Louie D. and Mary Louise (Sloan) H.; m. Karla Jean Cleverly, Sept. 22, 1980; children: Lance Dalton Jr., Nicholas James, Louie Alexander, Samuel Sean, Victoria Jean. BS summa cum laude, Weber State Coll., 1984; JD magna cum laude, Ind. U., 1987. Bar: Ind., US Dist. Ct. (no., so. dist.) Ind. 1988. Atty. Barnes & Thornburg, Indpls., 1988-89; dep. prosecuting atty. Marion County Prosecutor's Office, Indpls., 1989-90; pros. atty. Johnson County, Franklin, Ind., 1990—. Legal corr. WGGR Radio News, Indpls., 1995; adj. prof. law Sch. Law Ind. U., Indpls., 1995—96, Bloomington, 1996—98; frequent spkr. on legal topics including search and seizure and interrogation law; lectr. Ind. Continuing Legal Edn. Forum, Indpls., 1992; mem. faculty Newly-Elected Pros. Sch. Ind. Pros. Attys. Coun., 1999; mem. faculty Indpls. Police Acad., 1999, Ind. Police Corps, 2000—. Author: Indiana Search & Seizure Courtroom Manual, 2001, 2002; editor: Ind. Law Jour., 1987. Scoutmaster Boy Scouts Am., Franklin, Ind., 1999—. Mem. Nat. Dist. Attys. Assn., Assn. Govt. Attys. in Capital Litigation, Ind. Prosecuting Atty.'s Coun., Nat. Eagle Scout Assn., Order of the Coif. Republican. Mem. Lds Ch. Avocations: family, fitness, writing. Office: Prosecutor's Office Courthouse Annex N 80 S Jackson St Franklin IN 46131-2353

HAMNER, REGINALD TURNER, lawyer; b. Tuscaloosa, Ala., June 4, 1939; s. Raiford Samuel and Ellie Wells (Turner) H.; m. Anne Ellen Young, Nov. 8, 1969; children: Patrick Turner, William Christian. BS, U. Ala., 1961, JD, 1965. Bar: Ala. 1965, U.S. Dist. Ct. (mid. dist.) Ala. 1966, U.S. Ct. Appeals (5th cir.) 1966, U.S. Ct. Mil. Appeals 1968, U.S. Supreme Ct. 1968, U.S. Ct. Appeals (11th and 5th cirs.) 1981. Law clk. Supreme Ct. Ala., Montgomery, 1965; dir. legal-legis. affairs Med. Assn., State of Ala., 1968-69; sec., exec. dir. Ala. State Bar, Montgomery, 1969-94; ct. project coord. U.S. Dist. Ct. for Mid. Dist.) Ala., Montgomery, 1995—. Bd. dirs. S.E. br., YMCA, Montgomery, 1978-81; former legal counsel govtl. adv. panels investigating Ala. Prison System; vice chmn. State Child Welfare Com.; dir. Attys. Ins. Mut. of Ala., Inc.; sec., treas. Ala. Law Found., 1987-93; chmn. Ala. Rhodes Scholarship Com., 1989-94. With JAG, USAF, 1965-68, col. USAFR, ret. Fellow Am. Bar Found. (life, state chmn. 1994-95); mem. ABA (com. mem., mem. ho. of dels. 1972-76, 85-89, 93, 96—), Am. Judicature Soc., Nat. Assn. Bar Execs. (pres. 1978-79), Am. Soc. Assn. Execs. (commr. certification com. 1991-94), Ala. Coun. Assn. Execs. (pres. 1984), Ala. Law Inst. (council), Jud. Conf. U.S. Ct. Appeals (11th cir. 1981-95), U. Ala. Nat. Alumni Assn. (pres. 1989-90), Montgomery Country Club, Omicron Delta Kappa, Alpha Epsilon Delta, Phi Alpha Delta, Delta Tau Delta. Episcopalian. Home: 7518 Wynford Cir Montgomery AL 36117-7498 Office: US Courthouse One Church St Ste C-563 Montgomery AL 36104

HAMOLSKY, MILTON WILLIAM, physician; b. Lynn, Mass., May 25, 1921; s. Israel and Sophie (Cremer) H.; m. Sandra Oelbaum, Feb. 18, 1979; children— Deborah Lynne, John Stephen, David James, Joy, Robin. AB, Harvard U., 1943, MD, 1946; Ad Eundum, Brown U., 1964. Diplomate Am. Bd. Internal Medicine. Intern Beth Israel Hosp., Boston, 1946-47, resident, 1947-48, 50-51, asst. physician, dir. endocrine clinic, 1957-63; instr. Harvard U. Med. Sch., 1951-55, asst. prof. medicine, 1955-63; prof. med. sci. Brown U., 1963-87, prof. emeritus, 1987—; physician-in-chief R.I. Hosp., Providence, 1963-87, W&I Hosp., Providence, 1981-87, U.S. Vets. Adminstrn. Hosp., 1981-87. Vis. asst. prof. biochemistry Brandeis U., 1958-59; vis. Commonwealth fellow Coll. de France, 1960-62; chief adminstrv. officer R.I. Bd. Med. Licensure and Discipline, 1987-2001; bd. govs. Lifespan Hosps., 2003—; exec. com. Diet Counseling Svc. Obstet. Health Care Com.; pres. Zlinkoff Found. Med. Edn. and Rsch., 1989-95; pres. Dolen Found., 1989-95; chmn. adv. com. Comty. Health Ctrs., 1990—; bd. trustees R.I. Hosp., 1986-97; cons. Roger Univ. Bradley Hosps.; acting dir. R.I. Dept. Health, 1995. Author: Thyroid Testing, 1968; contbr. numerous articles on endocrinology to profl. publs. Trustee Planned Parenthood, Providence, R.I. Child Guidance Clinic, Camp Jori, Providence, R.I. Hosp., 1986-97; mem. Bd. Pub. Schs. Edn. Com., 2003—. Served as capt. M.C., U.S. Army, 1948-50. Recipient Henry A. Christian award Harvard U. Med. Sch., 1946, Mallinckrodt award as founder nuclear medicine, 1977, W.W. Keen disting. svc. award Brown U., Am. Heart Assn. Hon. John Chafee award Cmty. Svc., 2002; named to R.I. Heritage Hall of Fame, 1996; tchg. fellow Tufts U., 1950-51, Harvard Univ., 1950-51, rsch. fellow 1951-52, Damon Runyon rsch. fellow 1951-52. Mem. A.C.P. (master gov. R.I. chpt., Milton W. Hamolsky lifetime svc. award 1999), AMA, Am. Thyroid Assn., Endocrine Soc., Am. Physiol. Soc., Soc. Clin. Investigation, Am. Fedn. Clin. Research, R.I. Diabetes Soc. (pres.), R.I. Heart Assn. (pres.) Home: 150 Arlington Ave Providence RI 02906-2330 Office: RI Dept Health 3 Capitol Hl Ste 1 Providence RI 02908-5097 E-mail: MiltonH@DOH.State.ri.us.

HAMOND, KAREN MARIE KOCH, secondary education educator; b. Arlington, Mass., Dec. 12, 1954; d. James Walter and Dorothy Mary (Buchanan) Koch; m. Norman Roy Hamond, Oct. 9, 1976; children: Jeremy Michael, Jason Matthew, Jillian Marie, Jennifer Margaret. BA, Salem (Mass.) State Coll., 1976; MS, Lowell (Mass.) U., 1983; Cert. Advanced Studies, Harvard U., 1992. Cert. secondary math. tchr. Mass., NH, secondary maths. tchr. N.H. Tchr. St. Mary's High Sch., Lawrence, Mass., 1976-77, Peabody (Mass.) Vets. Meml. High Sch., 1977-78, Triton Regional High Sch., Byfield, Mass., 1978—99, math. team advisor, 1980-91; prof. math. Western New Eng. Coll., Springfield, Mass., 1992—99; head math. dept. Timberlane Regional HS, Plaistow, NH, 1999—2001; head math and bus. dept., head math./tech. dept. Everett (Mass.) HS, 2001—; math dept. coord., 1995—99. Tchr. summer sch. Gov. Dummer Acad., Byfield, Mass., 1993-99. Mem ASCD, Nat. Coun. Tchrs. of Maths., Math. Assn. Am., NEA, Mass. Tchrs. Assn.. Am. Math. Soc. Avocations: camping, skiing, travel. Home: 14 Riverview Dr Newbury MA 01951-1807

HAMORI, ÉVA LYDIA, economist; b. Törökszentmiklós, Hungary, May 25, 1939; d. Paul Heffner and Agnes Csillag. Tchr. diploma, 1966; cert. acctg., Econ. Secondary Sch., 1975; cert. fgn. trade, Ministry of Fgn. Trade, 1979; diploma, U. Econ. Scis., 1983; cert. econ. law, U. of Law Scis., 1990; Doctor Univ. (hon.), U. Econs. Scis., 1996; Dipl.econ., Budapest, 2001. Tchr. local schs., Budapest, 1957-70; acct. Bldg. Co., Budapest, 1970-73; exec. on fin. and comml. dept. Metrimpex Fgn. Trade Co., Budapest, 1974-79; inside contr., analyser economist at indsl. cos. Budapest, 1979-88; analyser economist Comml. and Credit Bank, OKHB, Budapest, 1988-90; mgr. Hungarian Nat. Bank Fgn. Exch. Regulation Dept., 1991-94, ret., 1994; enterpreneur, 1999—. Author, editor: A Pocketful of Economics, 1998, Zseb-Közgazdasag, 2000; contbr. articles to profl. jours. Mem.: Hungarian Econ. Assn. Avocations: music, reading, gardening, travelling, cooking. Office: PO Box 696 H-1535 Budapest Hungary

HAMOS, JULIE E. state representative; b. Budapest, Hungary, Jan. 29, 1949; m. Alan Greiman. BA, Wash. U., 1972; JD, George Washington U., 1975. Legis. dir. AFSCME Ill., 1979—81; legis. liaison Cook County State's Atty.'s Office, 1981—84; atty. child support divsn., 1984—88; pres. Julie E. Hamos & Assocs., Ltd., 1988—; mem. Ill. Ho. of Reps., 1998—. Resource bd. Met. Planning Coun., 1998—; adv. bd. Trilogy, 2001—; bd. dirs. Planned Parenthood, Chgo., 1995—. Democrat. Jewish. Office: 246-W Stratton Office Bldg Springfield IL 62706 Address: 820 Davis St Ste 103 Evanston IL 60201*

HAMOVITCH, WILLIAM, university official; b. Montreal, Que., Can., Sept. 1, 1922; came to U.S., 1946, naturalized, 1953; s. Abraham and Tillie (Weisenfeld) H.; m. Mitzi Berger, May 30, 1946 (dec. Dec. 31, 1992); children: Alan, Susan. B.Com., McGill U., 1943; M.P.A. (Adminstrn. fellow), Harvard, 1945, MA, 1946, PhD, 1949. Lectr., asst. prof. U. Buffalo, 1946-53; asst. prof., assoc. prof., prof. Queens Coll. City U. N.Y., Queens, 1953-86, chmn. dept. econs., 1965-76, provost, acad. v.p., 1976-84, acting pres., 1985; v.p. acad. affairs William Paterson Coll. N.J., Wayne, 1986-92, ret., 1992. Research scientist N.Y.C. Temp. Commn. on City Finances, 1965; Chmn. Commn. on Off-Track Betting in Nassau County, 1970 Author: Conflict and Stability in Labor Relations: A Case Study, 1952; Editor: The Federal Deficit: Fiscal Imprudence or Policy Weapon?, 1965, Monetary Policy: The Argument From Keynes' Treatise to Friedman, 1966, Employment and Occupation Projections for Nassau-Suffolk to 1985, 1968. Fellow Royal Econ. Soc.; mem. Am. Econ. Assn. Home: 12 Birch Hill Rd Great Neck NY 11026

HAMOY, CAROL, artist; b. N.Y.C., May 22, 1934; d. Morris David and Selma (Essex) Cohen. Student, Newark (N.J.) Sch. Fine Art, 1952-54, Art Students League, N.Y.C., various yrs. Lectr., spkr. in field. One-woman shows include USMA/West Point, N.Y., 1978, Katonah (N.Y.) Gallery, 1983, Lower Manhattan Cultural Coun., N.Y.C., 1986, May Mus./Lawrence, N.Y. Ceres, N.Y.C., 1992, MTA-Arts for Transit, N.Y.C., 1993, Robert Kahn Gallery, Houston, 1993, Temple Judea Mus., Elkins Park, Pa., 1993, Univ. Art Ctr., Shreveport, La., 1994, Ceres, N.Y.C., 1995, 98-99, 2001, Goldman Art Gallery, Rockville, Md., 1996, Nat. Mus. Am. Jewish History, Phila., 1996, Broadway Windows, N.Y.C., 1997, Ellis Island Immigration Mus., N.Y.C., 1997, Mizel Mus., Denver, 1997, Breman Heritage Mus., Atlanta, 1998, Eldridge St. Project,

N.Y.C., 1998, Inter-Am. Gallery, Miami, Fla., 1998, Skirball Mus., Cincinnati, 1999, Franklin Marshall Coll., Lancaster Pa., 1999, Margolis Gallery, Houston, 1999, Lower East Side Tenement Mus., N.Y., 2000, The Neuberger Mus., Purchase, N.Y., 2000, Ceres, N.Y.C., 2001, Dacotah Prarie Mus., Aberdeen, S.D., 2002, Azarian/McCullough Gallery, Sparkill, N.Y., 2002, Futernick Gallery, Miami, 2003; exhibited in group shows at Pelham (N.Y.) Art Ctr., 1988, U. Ky., Lexington, 1989, HUC, N.Y.C., 1989, Kentuck Mus., Northport, Ala., 1989, Clough Hansen Gallery, Memphis, 1989, JRC Gallery, Evanston, Ill., 1992, Soho 20, N.Y.C., 1993, Charach-Epstein Mus., West Bloomfield, Mich., 1994, 97, Nat. Jewish Mus., Washington, 1995, Fine Arts Rosen Mus., Boca Raton, Fla., 1995, Right Brain Gallery, Atlanta, 1999, Miss. Univ. for Women, 1999, Skirball Mus., Cin., 1999, Neuberger Mus., Purchase, N.Y., 2000, Ellipse Arts Ctr., Arlington, Va., 2000, Contemporary Crafts, Pitts., 2000, Ceres, 2000, The Joseph Gallery Mus, N.Y.C., 2000-01, Moving On/Frauen Mus., Bonn, Germany, John Jay Coll., 2001—, Joseph Gallery, N.Y., 2000-01, Frauen Mus., Bonn, Germany, 2001-02, Detritus Show John Jay College, N.Y., 2001-02, Judaica Mus., Riverdale, N.Y., 2001-02, Kommunale Galerie Wilmersdorf, Berlin, 2001-02, Ctr. for Visual Art & Culture, Stamford, Conn., 2002, Am. Craft Mus., N.Y., 2002-03, Joseph Gallery, N.Y.C., HUC Mus., N.Y.C., 2003—, others; permanent collections include Nat. Mus. Women in the Arts, Nat. Jewish Mus., Washington, Frauen Mus., Bonn, others. Nominee, Joan Mitchell Found., 2000; grantee Va. Ctr. for Creative Arts, Sweet Briar, Va., 1980, Artists' Space, N.Y.C., 1981, Hillwood Art Mus., N.Y. State Coun. for Creative Arts, 1992, MTA-Arts for Transit, N.Y.C., 1993, Lucius N. Littauer Found. Bessemere Trust Co. N.A., 1997, Meml. Found./Jewish Culture fellow, Artists' Fellowship, Inc. of N.Y.C., 1999. Studio: 340 E 66th St New York NY 10021-6821 E-mail: hamoycar@aol.com.

HAMPER, ROBERT JOSEPH, marketing executive; b. Chgo., May 20, 1956; s. Robert William and Barbara Jean Hamper. BSBA with honors, Ill. State U., 1977, MBA with honors, 1979; ABD, Northern Ill. U., 1999. Fin. mgr. Ill. Bell, Chgo., 1979-82; staff mgr. AT&T, Basking Ridge, N.J., 1982-84; mem. tech. staff Bell labs., Homedale, N.J., 1983-84; sr. staff. mgr. market analysis Ameritech Svcs., Schaumburg, Ill., 1985-87; dir. strategic planning Ameritech Corp., Chgo., Ill., 1987-90; pres. R.J. Hamper Bus. Cons., River Forest, Ill., 1981—, mgr. investment fund, 1990—. Asst. prof. fin. and mktg. Dominican U., River Forest, 1983-98; adj. prof. fin. Loyola U., Chgo., 1988—; seminar presenter in field; career counselor, 1985—. Author: Developing a Profitable Marketing Plan: Text and Cases, 1987, Marketing and Planning Forms, 1987, Strategic Market Planning, 1990, 92, 94, 95, 97, 99, 2003, Handbook for Proposal Writing, 1995, 97, 98, 2000; contbg. author: College Business Math, 1995, 97, 99; contbr. articles to profl. jours. Leader Boy Scouts Am., Park Forest, Ill., 1979-83. Mem. Am. Mktg. Assn. (exec.), Am. Mgmt. Assn., Fin. Mgmt. Assn., Am. Fin. Assn., Am. Hosp. Assn. Home and Office: 730 Clinton Pl River Forest IL 60305-1914

HAMPLE, HENRY, music educator, musician; b. New Rochelle, NY, Jan. 26, 1960; s. Stuart Hample and Amie Block Herscovici. BA, NYU, 1988; MA, Brown U., 1998. Copy coord. Money Mag., N.Y.C., 1991—93; copy chief Premiere Mag., N.Y.C., 1993; assoc. editor VIBE Mag., N.Y.C., 1994—96; mng. editor Nat. Multiple Sclerosis Soc., N.Y.C., 1999—2000, Fairchild Pubs., N.Y.C., 2000—02; music tchr. Hands On!, New York, NY, 2002—. Pvt. music tchr., 1980—. Musician: (CD) The Wash Cycle (Washboard Jungle), The Brown Album (Washboard Jungle), Sleep (Drink Me), Life Is Pasted On My Eyes (Scapegoats), My Big Apple Pie (Y'ALL); fiddler, vocalist (bluegrass band) The Linemen, 1999—, Back Porch Rockers Cajun Dance Band, 2002—, fiddler, guitarist, vocalist (folk duo) Buffalo and Starboy, 2001—, multi-instrumentalist, vocalist (postmodern jug band) Washboard Jungle, 1989—94, bassist, vocalist (punk rock band) Scapegoats, 1980—83. Scholar, Brown U., 1996—99. Home: 520 E 12th St New York NY 10009 Personal E-mail: hample@rcn.com.

HAMPSON, THOMAS MEREDITH, lawyer; b. Ann Arbor, Mich., Feb. 18, 1929; s. Harold Snover and Louise Susan (Goetchius) H.; m. Margaret H. Clark, Nov. 24, 1951 (div. Dec. 1969); children: Melissa Clark, Douglas Meredith; m. Zena Collier, Dec. 30, 1969. BA, Cornell U., 1951, LLB with distinction, 1955. Bar: N.Y. 1955, U.S. Dist. Ct. (we. dist.) N.Y. 1955, U.S. Supreme Ct. 1964. Assoc. Harris, Beach, Wilcox, Rubin & Levey, Rochester, N.Y., 1955-62; ptnr. Harris Beach, LLP, Rochester, 1962—. Vis. instr. Cornell Law Sch., Ithaca, N.Y., 1969-75. Radio broadcaster The Jazz Scene, 1960-80, Jazz Notes, 1979-81, Mostly Jazz, 1985--; newspaper columnist, 1985-88. Chmn. Monroe County Fair Campaign Practices Com., Rochester, 1977-91; trustee Rochester Pub. Libr., 1976-98; dir. Cornell Lab. Ornithology, Ithaca, N.Y., 1984-90, Hawk Mountain Sanctuary Assn., 1990-98, Rundel Libr. Found., 1995—; bd. dirs. N.Y. State Civil Liberties Union, N.Y.C., 1963-69; commr. Rochester Civil Svc. Commn., 1997—, chmn. 2000—. 1st lt. USAF, 1951-53. Recipient Civil Liberties award N.Y. Civil Liberties Union, Genesee Valley chpt., 1987. Mem. ABA, N.Y. State Bar Assn., Monroe County Bar Assn., City Club (pres. 1965-66), Philosophers' Club (pres. 1985-88). Democrat. Unitarian Universalist. Avocations: birding, jazz. Home: 83 Berkeley St Rochester NY 14607-2207 Office: Harris Beach LLP 99 Garnsey Rd Pittsford NY 14534

HAMPTON, ANITA, artist, writer; Student, Fresno City Coll., Saddleback Coll., El Toro, Calif., Laguna Beach Sch. Art, Ventura (Calif.) Coll., Calif. Poly State U., San Luis Obispo, Cuesta Coll. Art program instr., Mission Viejo, Calif.; instr. in landscape, portrait and still life painting; instr. Cuesta Coll., San Luis Obispo, Mission Art Gallery, El Toro, Calif. Exhibited works in shows at Oil Painters Am Regional Show, Oil Painters Am. Nat. Show, San Luis Obispo Art Mus., Calif. Art Club Gold Medal Show, San Juan Capistrano Mission, R. Weisman Mus. Art/Pepperdine U., Carmel Ann. Painting Festival, others. Recipient numerous major awards. Mem Calif. Art Club, Oil Painters Am., Laguna Plein Air Painters Assn. Home: PO Box 6134 Los Osos CA 93412-6134

HAMPTON, BENJAMIN BERTRAM, brokerage house executive; b. N.Y.C., Aug. 3, 1925; s. max and Pauline (Weinberger) H.; m. Elizabeth Golub-Cohen, Oct. 16, 1975; 1 child by previous marriage, Roger Neil; stepchildren: Laurence, James, Lisa. B Aero. Engring., NYU, 1947; cert. in mech. engring., Pa. State Coll., 1945; MBA, Harvard U., 1949. Sales mgr. Carew Products, Inc., N.Y.C., 1949-51; project mgr. Emerson Radio & TV Corp., 1951-52; div. mgr. Paragon Oil Co., Mineola, N.Y., 1952-55; mgmt. cons. E.N. Kagan & co., N.Y.C., 1955-60; exec. asst. to pres. mktg. sect. Fed. Pacific Electric co., Newark, 1960-62; asst. to pres. Seagrave Corp., N.Y.C., 1962-63; v.p. Swingline Inc., Long Island City, N.Y., 1963-68, exec. v.p., 1968-71, bd. dirs., 1970-71; exec. v.p., bd. dirs. Poloron Products Inc., New Rochelle, N.Y., 1971-73, pres., CEO, bd. dirs., 1973-74; exec. v.p., bd. dirs. West Chem. Products, Inc., Long Island City, 1975-78; prin. Hampton Assocs., 1979-82; v.p. Merrill Lynch Pierce Fenner & Smith, Great Neck, N.Y., 1982—. Co-chmn. N.Y. State fin. com. J.F. Kennedy presdl. campaign, 1960. With AUS, 1944-46. Mem. Harvard Club, Pi Lambda Phi. Home: 339 E Shore Rd Kings Point NY 11023-1707 Office: Merrill Lynch 1010 Northern Blvd Great Neck NY 11021-1134 E-mail: ben_hampton@ml.com.

HAMPTON, CAROL MCDONALD, priest, educator, historian; b. Oklahoma City, Sept. 18, 1935; d. Denzil Vincent and Mildred Juanita (Cussen) McDonald; m. James Wilburn Hampton, Feb. 22, 1958; children: Jaime, Clayton, Diana, Neal. BA, U. Okla., 1957, MA, 1973, PhD, 1984; cert. individual theol. study, Episcopal Theol. Sem. of S.W., 1998; MDiv summa cum laude, Phillips Theol. Sem., 1999. Ordained to Episcopal Transitional Diaconate, 1999, ordained priest, 1999. Tchg. asst. U. Okla., Norman, 1976—81; instr. U. Sci. and Arts Okla., Chickasha, 1981—84; coord. Consortium for Grad. Opportunities for Am. Indians U. Calif., Berkeley, 1985—86; trustee Ctr. of Am. Indian, Oklahoma City, 1981. Vice chmn. Nat. Com. on Indian Work, Episc. Ch., 1986; field officer Native Am. Ministry of Episc. Ch. (Nat.), 1986-94, sec., co-chmn., advising elder, prin. elder coun., 1994-96; field officer for Congl. Ministries of Episc. Ch. (Nat.), 1994-97; mem. nat. coun. Chs. Racial Justice Working Group, 1990-97, co-convenor, 1991-93, convenor, 1993-95; officer Multicultural Ministries of Episc. Ch. (Nat.), 1994-97. Mem. editl. bd.: First Peoples Theology Jour.; contbr. articles to profl. jours. Trustee Western History Collections, U. Okla., Okla. Found. for the Humanities, 1983-86; mem. bd. regents U. Sci. and Arts Okla., 1989-95; bd. dirs. Okla. State Regents for Higher Edn., mem. adv. com. on social justice; mem. World Coun. of Chs. Program to Combat Racism, Geneva, 1985-91; bd. dirs. Caddo Tribal Coun., Okla., 1976-82; accredited observer Anglican Consultative Coun. UN 4th World Conf. on Women, 1995; v.p. Nat. Conf. Cmty. Justice, 1999-2002; bd. dirs. Ctrl. Okla. Human Rights Alliance, 1999—, Planned Parenthood, Oklahoma City, 2002—. Recipient Okla. State Human Rights awatrd, 1987; Francis C. Allen fellow Ctr. for the History of Am. Indian, 1983. Mem.: Okla. Conf. Chs. (bd. dirs. 2000—), Indigenous Theol. Tng. Inst. (bd. dirs. 2000—), Jr. League (Oklahoma City), Am. Assn. Indian Historians (founding mem. 1981—), Okla. Hist. Soc., Am. Hist. Assn., Orgn. Am. Historians, Western Social Sci. Assn., Western History Assn. Democrat. Episcopalian. Avocation: travel. Home: 1414 N Hudson Ave Oklahoma City OK 73103-3721 E-mail: cjchampton@aol.com., champton@stpaulscathedralokc.org.

HAMPTON, CHARLES EDWIN, lawyer, mathematician, computer programmer; b. Oct. 22, 1948; s. Roy Mizell and Hazel Lucretia (Cooper) H.; m. Cynthia Torrance, Sept. 14, 1968; children: Charles Edwin Jr., Adam Ethan. Student, Baylor U., 1967, Rice U., 1967-68; BA with highest honors, U. Tex., 1971, JD with high honors, 1977; MA, U. Calif., Berkeley, 1972, Candidate in Philosophy in Math., 1975. Bar: Tex. 1977, U.S. dist. Ct. (we. dist.) Tex. 1979, U.S. Dist. Ct. (no. dist.) Tex. 1980, U.S. Ct. Appeals (5th cir.) 1986. Rsch. asst. U. Calif., 1974-75; briefing atty. to justice Tex. Supreme Ct., 1977-78; assoc. Law Offices Don L. Baker, PC, Austin, Tex., 1978—81; legal counsel Office Ct. Adminstrn., Tex. Jud. Coun., Austin, 1981; staff atty. Supreme Ct. Tex., Austin, 1981-96; assoc. Rinehart & Nugent, 1984-87. Vis. comm. dept. math. U. Tex., Austin, 1987-95. NSF fellow, 1971-74; Moody Found. scholar. Mem. ABA, State Bar Tex., Travis County Bar Assn., Chancellors, Order of Coif, Lions, Phi Beta Kappa, Phi Kappa Phi, Phi Delta Phi.

HAMPTON, CLYDE ROBERT, lawyer; b. Worland, Wyo., May 10, 1926; s. Clyde E. and Mabel L. (Lasley) H.; m. Dorothy Laura Gaebelein, June 3, 1949; 1 dau.: Dorothy Norma. B.A., Columbia Coll., 1949; LL.B., U. Colo., 1952. Bar: Colo. 1952. Atty., then counsel, sr. counsel and now gen. atty. Conoco, Inc., Denver, 1952-85, ret., 1985—, sole practice, 1985—; lectr., educator in field. Republican committeeman; bd. dirs. Denver Theol. Sem.; ch. officer Presbyterian ch. Served to capt. USNR. Recipient numerous awards in energy-related fields. Mem. Am. Petroleum Inst. (past chmn. environ. law com.; Disting. Merit award 1982), ABA (past chmn. Natural Resources Law Sect.), Aurora Bar Assn., Colo. Bar Assn., Sigma Chi, Phi Alpha Delta. Clubs: Petroleum, Columbia U. Alumni (Denver). Author: Landman's Legal Handbook, 1970; contbr. numerous articles on environ. law, natural resources to profl. jours. Home and Office: 14830 E Jefferson Ave Aurora CO 80014-4070

HAMPTON, DANIEL OLIVER, professional football player; b. Oklahoma City, Sept. 19, 1957; m. Terry H. Student, U. Ark. Profl. football player Chgo. Bears, 1979—2000. Named to Pro Football Hall of Fame, 2002. Participant NFL Pro Bowl All-Star Game, 1980, 82, 84, 85; mem. NFL Super Bowl Championship Team, 1985. Office: Chgo Bears 250 Washington Rd Lake Forest IL 60045-2459

HAMPTON, JAMES WILBURN, hematologist, medical oncologist; b. Durant, Okla., Sept. 15, 1931; s. Hollis Eugene and Ouida (Mackey) H.; m. Carol McDonald, Feb. 22, 1958; children: Jaime, Clay, Diana, Neal. BA, U. Oklahoma, 1952, MD, 1956. Int. U. Okla. Hosps., 1956-57, res.; instr. to prof. U. Okla., Oklahoma City, 1959-77; clin. prof. med., 1977—. Mem. admissions bd., 1965—, subcom., 1985-95, bd., 1995-, head hematology/oncology, 1972-77; head hematology, mem. Okla. Med. Rsch. Found., Okla. City 1972-77; dir. cancer prog. and med. oncology Bapt. Med. Ctr., 1977-85; med. dir. Cancer Ctr. S.W., 1985-94; Troy and Dollie Smith Cancer Ctr., 1994—; mem. Internat. Com. on Thrombosis and Hemostasis; cons. NIH, Biomed. and Nat. Cancer Inst., Stockholm; vis. scientist NHLBI, 1966-67; vis. prof. U. N.C., Chapel Hill, 1966; founder, pres. Stewart Wolf Soc., 1990-92; founder Robert Montgomery Bird Soc., 1973-74, pres. 1996-98. Contbr. over 100 articles to profl. jours. Chmn. network Cancer Prevention and Control for Am. Indians/Alaska Natives Nat. Cancer Rsch. Inst., 1990-99; mem. Intercultural Cancer Coun., 1996—, chair-elect 2000-01, chair 2001-02; bd. dirs. Heritage Hills, Oklahoma City, 1972-90, initiator Hospice of Ctrl. Okla., 1982-89; initiator Hospice of Okla. County, 1990—; bd. dirs. Am. Cancer Soc., mem. at large, nat. bd. dirs., 1990-96, mem. com. task force on Cancer in the Socio-economically Disadvantaged, 1990-2000, chmn. Okla. divsn. svc. and rehab. com., collaborating ptnr. Dialogue on Cancer (Pres. Bush), 1999—; chmn. Okla. Pain Initiative, 1996; co-chmn. Save St. Paul's Episcopal Cathedral com., 1983, chmn. bishop's Okla. Com. on Indian work, mem. province VII Indian com., alt del. Diocesan conv. for Okla., 1991-95, mem. adv. com. Office of Minority Health NIH, 1996-99, mem. Coun. on Combating Racism, Epis. Ch. of Am., 1995-97, others. Recipient ACS Humanitarian awd., 1999, NIH Career Devel. awd. 1966-76, Physician of the Yr. (pvt. prac.), Univ. Okla. Alumni Assocs.; honored by Lakota Tribe at Mayo Clinic, 1999. Fellow ACP; mem. AMA (mem. minority affairs consortium, steering com. 1997-2000), Am. Fedn. Clin. Rsch. (pres. midwest sect. 1970-71), Ctrl. Soc. Clin. Rsch. (assoc. editor Jour. Lab. and Clin. Med. 1975-76), Okla. County Med. Soc. (editor bull. 1981—, bd. dirs. 1982-85, 1989-91), Internat. Soc. Thrombosis and Hemostasis, Assn. Am. Indian Physicians (pres. 1978-79, 88-89, Indian Physician of Yr. award 1987, 2000); Am. Physiol. Soc., Assn. Am. Pathologists, Am. Soc. Hematology, Am. Soc. Clin. Oncology, So. Soc. Clin. Investigation, Am. Pscyhosomatic Soc., English Speaking Union, Oklahoma City Golf and Country Club, Blue Cord Club, Faculty House Club, Chaine des Rotisseurs. Home: 1414 N Hudson Ave Oklahoma City OK 73103-3721 Office: US Oncology Lake Hefner Campus 11100 Hefner Pointe Dr Oklahoma City OK 73120-5049

HAMPTON, JOHN LEWIS, retired newspaper editor; b. Verda, Ky., Jan. 13, 1935; s. John Lewis and Ruby Lillian (Slagle) H.; m. Lillian Valls; children from previous marriage: Rachel, Jessica Hampton Fazio, Jonathan Hugh. AB in Journalism (Outstanding Journalism Grad. award 1959), U. Ky., 1959; MA in Communications and Journalism (grad. fellow 1960), Stanford U., 1960. Staff writer AP, Lexington, Ky., 1960-61; bur. chief Louisville (Ky.) Courier-Jour., 1961-67; staff writer Nat. Observer, Washington, 1967-71, sr. editor, then asst. mng. editor, 1971-77; mem. editorial bd. Miami (Fla.) Herald, 1977, editor, 1978-99. Served with AUS, 1953-56. Named to Hall Disting. Alumni U. Ky., Ky. Journalism Hall of Fame, 2000; recipient Pulitzer prize in editorial writing, 1983 Mem. Am. Soc. Newspaper Editors, Inter Am. Press Assn. (bd. dirs. 1987-99), Fla. Soc. Newspaper Editors. Office: Miami Herald 1 Herald Plz Miami FL 33132-1693 E-mail: jhampton@herald.com.

HAMPTON, JOHN PHILIP, systems engineer, retired naval officer; b. Atlanta, Jan. 14, 1948; s. John Philips and Barbara Louise (Hampton) P.; m. Frances Hunter, Sept. 12, 1988; children: Philip Jr., Travis. BA in Math., Baylor U., 1970; MA in Personnel Supvr., Central Mich. U., 1982; MA in Computer and Space Sys. Mgmt., Webster U., Colorado Springs, 1991. Analyst Shell Oil Co., Houston, 1970-71, Western Geophys. Co. Am., Houston, 1971-73; commd. ensign USN, 1973, advanced through grades to commdr., 1973-95, ret., 1995; sys. engr. Titan/ACSS, Inc., Chesapeake, Va., 1995—. Comdr. USN, 1973-95. Mem. AIAA, Armed Forces Comms. and Electronics Assn., Kiwanis (sec. Va. Beach club 1997). Avocations: jogging, racquetball. Office: Titan/ASCC Inc 825 Greenbrier Cir Ste M Chesapeake VA 23320-2639 E-mail: jhampton@acstsc.com.

HAMPTON, KYM, basketball player; b. Louisville, Nov. 3, 1962; Grad., Ariz. State U., 1984. Forward, Vigo, Spain, 1985—87, Barcelona, 1987—89, Valencia, Spain, 1989—91, Avellino, Italy, 1994—95, Pavia, Italy, 1995—97, Aix-en-Provence, France, 1993—94, Chanson, Japan, 1992—93, N.Y. Liberty, N.Y.C., 1997—. Named to, Italian League All-Star Team, 1992, 1995, 1996; recipient Street & Smith Hon. Mention, 1982, 1983, 1984. Avocations: jazz, R&B, travel, water sports, singing. Office: NY Liberty 2 Penn Plz New York NY 10121-0101

HAMPTON, LEROY, retired chemical company executive; b. Ingalls, Ark., Apr. 20, 1927; s. Ed Levi and Kitty Annie (Larry) H.; m. Anne Neris Herndon, July 11, 1954; children: Mary Louise, Gloria, Stanley Lamar, Cedric Leroy, Candice La Neris. BS, U. Colo., 1950; MS, Denver U., 1960. Registered pharmacist, Colo., Mich. Registered pharmacist Rocky Mountain Drug Co., Denver, 1950-53; scientist-chemist Dow Chem. Co., Golden, Colo., 1953-58, profl. scientist-chemist in charge, 1958-61, devel. chemist, 1961-63, devel. leader, 1963-67, recruiting supr., 1967-68; recruiting mgr. N.E. Region, 1968-70, mgr. minority employee relations, 1970-75; dir. Dow Chem. Employees Credit Union, 1975-95, pres., 1979, 85, v.p., 1991, pres., chmn., 1992; mgr. issue analysis Dow Chem. Co., 1976-80, rsch. assoc., 1981-86. Owner, operator hardware store, Denver, 1965-67; mem. cmty. adv. panel Do Chem. Co., Mich. Ops. V.p. Midland Bd. Edn., 1981—82, sec., 1979—80; dir.affirmative action Saginaw Valley State U., Univ. Ctr., Mich., 1987—90; v.p. Midland Assn. Retarded Citizens, 1985—86, treas., 1986—87; mem. Midland/Dow Comty. advisory panel, 2001—; deacon Meml. Presbyn. Ch., Midland, 1985—87, 1995—97; Bd. dirs. Midland Kiwanis Club Found., Mich., 1973—74, 1990—95; v.p., 1990—92; pres., 1994—95; bd. dirs. ARC, Midland, 1974—76; mem. Midland Bd. Edn., 1978—82; bd. dirs. Midland Assn. Retarded Citizens, 1982—88. Mem. Am. Chem. Soc., Am. Pharm. Assn., Mich. Pharmacists Assn., Kiwanis (pres. Midland club 1976-77), Alpha Phi Alpha. Democrat. Presbyn. Home: 2206 Burlington Dr Midland MI 48642-3895

HAMPTON, MARK GARRISON, architect; b. Tampa, Fla., July 17, 1923; s. Ham Stonewall and Laura (Bingenheimer) H. BS, B.Arch., Ga. Inst. Tech., 1949. Owner Mark Hampton, Architect, Tampa, 1952-65, Miami, Fla., 1974—; partner Herbert H. Johnson Assocs., Miami, 1966-73. Prin. works include Chemistry and Life Sci. bldgs, U. So. Fla., Tampa, 1961, First Fed. Office Bldg, Sarasota, 1973. Bd. dirs. Lannan Found., Palm Beach, Fla., 1972-88; pres. Tampa Art Inst., 1958, 64. Served with inf. AUS, 1943-46. Decorated Bronze Star, Purple Heart; recipient award Homes for Better Living competition, 1957, 62; Nat. Design award Horizon Home program, 1963 Fellow AIA (juror Nat. Honor awards 1963, 64, medal of honor for design Fla. Central chpt. 1974, award of honor for design 1987, test of time award 1987). Episcopalian. Office: Mark Hampton Architect FAIA 3900 Loquat Ave Miami FL 33133-5622

HAMPTON, NANETTE DAVINA, private school educator, writer; b. Chgo., Feb. 9, 1968; d. Joenell Long and Darene Leynell Ajibona Hampton; m. Corillis Anderson (div. Nov. 8, 1989); children: Nadina, Janay;children: Eugene, Lashon, Chanté Liddell. Student, St. Paul Tech. Coll., 1994. Cert. home health aide, CNA and LPN Minn., 1994. Disc jockey Columbia Broadcasting SCH, Chgo., 1989; home health aide St. Paul (Minn.) Tech. Coll., 1994; instr. St. Paul (Minn.) Pub. Schs., 2000, tchg. asst., 1996—2002. Author: The Art of Making Love, 1996, Queen Sheeba, 2002, Garden of Eden, 2002, (poem) A Mother's Love, 2000. Master: Cooking Club of Am.; mem.: NAACP, Nat. Writers Union, Nat. Assn. Female Execs. Avocations: reading, singing, writing, shopping, cooking.

HAMPTON, PHILIP MICHAEL, consulting engineering company executive; b. Asheville, N.C., Sept. 5, 1932; s. Boyd Walker and Helen Reba (Smith) H.; m. Wilma Christine Gross, July 7, 1951; children: Philip Michael, Deborah Lynn, Gregg Ashley. AB in Geology, Berea Coll., 1954. Draftsman-designer Johnson & Anderson, Inc., Pontiac, Mich., 1955-57, designer, also project mgr., 1957-59, dir. bus. devel., 1962-76, v.p., 1966-74, exec. v.p., 1974-76; v.p. Spalding G. DeDecker & Assos., Inc., Madison Heights, Mich., 1976-84; founder, pres. Hampton Engring. Assocs., Inc., 1985—; pres. HMA Consultants Inc., 1977—, Geo Internat., Inc., 1978—. V.p. JAVLEN Internat., 1971-73, Micuda-Hampton Assocs., Inc., 1985-86; co-founder, owner My World Shops and Hampton Galleries, Ltd., 1976-90; co-owner Hampton-Tyedten Galleries Ltd., 1979-81; mem. public adv. panel GSA, 1977-78; chmn. task force of com. fed. procurement of architect/engr. svcs. ABA, 1977-79. Editor: Total Scope, 1963-71. Pres. Waterford Bd. Edn., 1969-71; mem. state resolution com. Democratic Conv., 1972; exec. com. Oakland County Dem. Com., 1973-74; precinct del., 1972-76, 80—; trustee Environ. Research Assocs., sec.-treas., 1969-71, pres., 1971-73; chmn. Waterford Cable Communications Commn., 1981-88; mem. Cultural Council Pontiac, 1987-90; bd. dirs. Oakland C. of C., 1972-74, Readings for the Blind, Inc., 2002-; chmn. utilities com. Oakland Bus. Roundtable, 1993—; vice chmn. Pontiac Urban League, 1996—. Named to Honorable Order Ky. Colonels. Fellow Am. Cons. Engrs. Coun. (internat. engrng. com. 1971-76, vice chmn. pub. rels. com. 1970-72, chmn. publs. com. 1972-74, chmn. ABA model procurement code com. 1977-79, nat. dir. 1986-89, mem. com. fellows 1988—, Pres. award 1990); ASCE, AAAS, mem. Nat. Water Well Assn. (chmn. tech. div. 1969-71), Cons. Engrs. Coun. Mich. (awards com. 1970-74), Am. Arbitration Assn. (comml. panel 1977—), Pontiac C. of C. (co-founder 1989), Oakland Bus. Roundtable (charter). Clubs: Pontiac Exchange, Pontiac-Detroit Lions Quarterback Club (co-founder). Presbyterian. Home and Office: 2440 Ostrum St Waterford MI 48328-1829 Office: 35 W Huron St Ste 801 Pontiac MI 48342-2128 *My first employment, at age 13, was as a janitor. The superintendent of facilities taught me to pay attention to detail. He advised, "clean under the stairwells and the entrance will take care of itself." I understood his meaning and adopted the philosophy as my own in many areas of my life and career.*

HAMPTON, PHILLIP JEWEL, artist, educator; b. Kansas City, Mo., Apr. 23, 1922; s. Cordell Bernard Daniels and Goldie Kelley Powell; m. Dorothy Louise Smith, Sept. 28, 1946 (dec. Oct. 1986); children: Harry James, Robert Keith. Student, Drake U., 1947-48; BFA, Kans. City U., Kan. City Art Inst., 1951; MFA, Kans. City Art Inst., 1952. Dir. art program Savannah State Coll., Ga., 1952-69; prof. art So. Ill. U., Edwardsville, Ill., 1969-92, emeritus prof. fine arts, 1992—; artist, spl. projects Hampton Studio, Edwardsville, Ill., 1992—. Dir. day camp City of Kansas City Recreation, 1952; art cons. US GSA, East St. Louis, Ill., 1995-98; curator 2 spl. exhbns. St. Louis Artists' Guild, 1998—; judge Watercolor Mo. Nat., Winston Churchill Meml., Fulton, Mo., 2001; lectr. St. Louis Ar Mus., 2001. Author: (catalogs) 3d World Drawings, 1979, Schemata of Ethnic Minority Artists, 1980; artist book/promotional materials Symphony Kids, KFUO-99FM, 1996; exhibited in one-man show at So. Ill. U., Edwardsville Gallery, 2000; represented in permanent collection at St. Louis Art Mus. Mem. adv. bd. West Broad YMCA, Savannah, 1966-69; bd. dir. United Fund, Edwardsville, 1971-74; mem. Citizens Adv. Coun. Dist. 7, Edwardsville, 1973-75. Recipient Gov.'s award for best-in-show Ill. State Fair Profl. Art Exhbn., 1990 (Salute to Black Men award, Omicron Eta Omega chpt. 2001), others. Mem. St. Louis Art Mus., Art St. Louis, St. Louis Artists' Guild. Presbyterian. Avocations: reading, writing, chess, market studies. Home: 832 Holyoake Rd Edwardsville IL 62025-2315

HAMPTON, REX HERBERT, former mining executive, director; b. Chgo., Aug. 3, 1918; s. John William and Alice Grace (Melling) H.; m. Ruth Lorraine Gibbons, Sept. 30, 1940 (dec. May 1994); children: Hope, Rex Herbert, Robin Virgil, Maryalice. BS in Forest Mgmt, Utah State U., 1942; MA in Internat. Affairs, George Washington U., 1963; Grad., U.S. Air Force War Coll., 1973. Real estate broker, Colo. Commd. 2d lt. U.S. Army, 1942, advanced through grades to brig. gen., 1968; ret., 1972; mgr. Bennett Shellenberger Realty, Colorado Springs, Colo., 1975-80; chmn. bd., pres., CEO Golden Cycle Gold Corp., Colorado Springs, 1980-93, ret., 1993. Dir. Golden Cycle Gold Corp.; cons. ATE Enterprises Liquidating Trust, Cin. Decorated D.S.M., Legion of Merit with cluster, Bronze Star, others Mem. DAV, VFW, Ret. Officers Assn. (past pres. chpt.), El Paso Club, Peterson Field Officers Club, Broadmoor Golf Club (Colorado Springs), IOOB. Clubs: Peterson Field Officers, Broadmoor Golf (Colorado Springs). Republican. Mem. Lds Ch.

HAMPTON, SHELLEY LYNN, hearing impaired educator; b. Muskegon, Mich., Nov. 27, 1951; d. Donald Henry and Ruth Marie (Heinanen) Tamblyn; m. John Pershing Hampton Jr., Aug. 10, 1985; 1 child, Sarah Elizabeth. BA, Mich. State U., 1973, MA, 1978. Cert. tchr., Wash., Mich., N.Y. Tchr. presch. thru 3d grade N.Y. State Sch. for Deaf, Rome, 1973-78; cons. Ingham Intermediate Sch. Dist., Lansing, Mich., 1978-81; hearing impaired coord. Shoreline Sch. Dist., Seattle, 1981—. N.W. rep. Bur. of Edn. Handicapped, N.Y.C., 1978; N.Y. del. Humanities in Edn., 1977; adv. bd. State Libr. for the Blind, Lansing, 1980-81; adj. prof. Mich. State U., 1979-81, Seattle Pacific U., 1984-86; participant World Cong. Edn. and Tech., Vancouver, B.C., 1986; computer resource technician Spl. Programs, 1988-92, collegial team leader, 1992-95; rep. Site-Based Mgmt. Coun., Seattle, 1992-95. Writer: Social/Emotional Aspects of Deafness, 1983-84. Del. N.Y. State Assn. for Edn. of Deaf, N.Y.C., 1974-78; N.Y. del. Humanities in Edn., 1977; mem. bd. Plymouth Congl. Ch., Seattle, 1983-87; coord., Kids on the Block puppet troupe, 1999-2003. Recipient Gov.'s Plaque of Commendable Svc., State of Mich., 1981; grantee State of Wash., 1979, 82, Very Spl. Arts Festival, 1979-81; recipient Outstanding Svc. award Mich. Sch. for the Blind, 1980. Mem. NEA, Wash. State Edn. Assn., Shoreline Edn. Assn., Alexander Graham Bell Assn., Regional Hearing Impaired Coop. for Edn., Internat. Orgn. Educators of the Hearing Impaired, Auditory-Verbal Internat., Kiwanis Club, Caucus, Conf. Ednl. Adminstrs. Serving the Deaf. Home: 14723 62nd Dr SE Everett WA 98208-9383 Office: Shoreline Hearing Program 16516 10th Ave NE Seattle WA 98155-5904

HAMPTON, VERNE CHURCHILL, II, lawyer; b. Pontiac, Mich., Jan. 5, 1934; s. Verne Churchill and Mildred (Peck) H.; m. Stephanie Hall, Oct. 5, 1973; children: J. Howard, Timothy H., Julia C. Thibodeau. BA, Mich. State U., 1955; LLB, U. Va., 1958. Bar: Mich. 1958. Since practiced in, Detroit; ptnr. firm Dickinson Wright, 1967—. Bd. dirs., sec. Carhartt, Inc., R & R Radio Corp. Former mem. Mich. Rep. Fin. Com.; bd. dirs. Detroit Bus./Edn. Alliance; corp. mem. Boys' Clubs Met. Detroit. Mem. ABA, State Bar Mich. (chmn. bus. law sect. 1980-84), Detroit Athletic Club, Country Club Detroit, Yondotega Club, Sigma Alpha Epsilon, Phi Alpha Delta. Republican. Episcopalian. Home: 360 Provencal Rd Grosse Pointe Farms MI 48236-2959 Office: Dickinson Wright PLLC 500 Woodward Ave Ste 4000 Detroit MI 48226-3416 E-mail: vhampton@dickinson-wright.com.

HAMPTON, WILLIAM PECK, lawyer; b. Pontiac, Mich., Jan. 24, 1938; B, Mich. State U., 1960; JD, Wayne State U., 1963. Bar: Mich. 1964. Rep. Mich. Ho. of Reps., 1964-70; cir. judge, presiding judge Oakland County Cir. Ct., 1970-77; sr. ptnr. Secrest, Wardle, Lynch, Hampton, Truex & Morley, Farmington Hills, Mich., 1977—. Spl. counsel County of Oakland, Oakland County Drain Commr.; twp. atty. Charter Twp. of Bloomfield, Charter Twp. of West Bloomfield; atty. City of Auburn Hills, City of Bloomfield Hills. Chmn. Mich. State Officers' Compensation Commn., 1994-98; co-chmn. State Bar Com. on Judicial Qualifications, 1990-96; atty. discipline bd. State of Mich., 2001—, vice-chmn., 2002—. Fellow Am. Coll. Trial Lawyers; mem. State Bar of Mich., Oakland County Bar Assn., Mich. Judges Assn., Mich. Soc. Planning Ofcls. Republican. Office: Secrest Wardle Lynch Hampton Truex & Morley 30903 Northwestern Hwy Farmington Hills MI 48334-2556 E-mail: hamptonw@secrestwardle.com.

HAMRE, GARY LESLIE WILLIAM, entrepreneur; b. Mpls., July 28, 1939; s. Hiram O. and Mayme R. (Sorensen) H.; m. Margaret Ann Renshaw, July 14, 1958 (div. 1981); children: Jeffrey A.C., Cheryl L., Dayna L.; m. Karen Sue Link, Nov. 30, 1984. BA, U. Minn., 1966; postgrad., Ohio State U., 1978. Lic. real estate sales cons. Area mgr. Union Oil Co. Calif., Mpls., 1963-71, Columbus, Ohio, 1971-78; pres. G.L.W.H. Ent., Inc., Ohio, 1978—; owner 76 Halfway House Truck Stop, 1978-90; sales cons. comml. real estate, 1990—. Dep. sheriff Franklin Country Sheriff's Office, Columbus, 1977—, sgt., 1999—; sustaining mem. Rep. Nat. Com., Washington, 1981—; bd. dirs., com. chmn. Am. Diabetes Assn., 1988—91. Mem. NRA (life), Fraternal Order of Police, Nat. Restaurant Assn., Ohio Restaurant Assn., Ctrl. Ohio Restaurant Assn. (bd. dirs. 1984-92, pres. 1990, chmn. bd. 1991), Nat. Assn. Truckstop Operators (assignment com. 1986-90), Sales Execs. Club, Lions (pres. Powell, Ohio 1986-87, Lion of Yr. 1985-86, zone chmn. 1987-88, Melvin Jones fellow 1991, dist. 13F gov. 1990-91, chmn. state constn. and by-laws 1993-96), Masons, Shriners (provost), Moose. Lutheran. Avocations: golf, boating, snowmobiling, hunting, fishing. Home: 22 Barrhill Dr Delaware OH 43015-7608

HAMREN, NANCY VAN BRASCH, bookkeeper; b. L.A., Feb. 2, 1947; d. Milton Carl and Winifred (Taylor) Van Brasch; m. Jerome Arthur Hamren, Feb. 14, 1981; children: Emily Allison, Meredith Ann. Student, Pasadena City Coll., 1964-65, San Francisco State Coll., 1966-67, U. Oreg., 1975-79. Bookkeeper/office mgr. Springfield Creamery, Eugene, Oreg., 1969—, also bd. dirs. Originator Nancy's Yogurt, Nancy's Cultured Dairy Prodcuts. Active mem. Oreg. Shakespearean Festival, Ashland, 1986, Planned Parenthood, Sta. KLCC-PBS Radio; bd. dirs. BRING Recycling, sec. bd. dirs. Mem. Oreg. Dairy Assn., Audubon Soc., N.Am. Truffling Soc., The Wilderness Soc., Oreg. Pub. Broadcasting, Buhl (Idaho) Arts Coun., Conservation Internat, Provender Alliance (bd. dirs.), The Slow Food Movement. Democrat. Avocations: gourmet cooking, gardening, walking, wine tasting. Home: 1315 Ravenwood Dr Eugene OR 97401-1912 Office: Springfield Creamery 29440 Airport Rd Eugene OR 97402-9524

HAMRICK, JOSEPH EUGENE, JR., information services specialist; b. Chapel Hill, N.C., Feb. 4, 1954; s. Joseph Eugene Sr. and Emily Southerland (Cole) H.; m. Elaine Kay Metcalf, Oct. 2, 1982 (div. 1998); children: Aubrie Nicole, Allison Laurel, Wendy-Anne Alisa, Claire Elise; m. Julia Warren Rogers, May 31, 1999. BS in Computer and Mmt. Sci, Met. State Coll., Denver, 1989. Cert. system profl. Inst. for Cert. Computer Profls. Programmer, analyst Aviation Mgmt. Systems, Denver, 1980-83; mgr., AVsoft devel. PHH Aviation Systems, Golden, Colo., 1983-86; programmer, analyst Columbine Systems, Inc., Golden, 1986-88; dir., info. svcs. Property Asset Mgmt., Denver, 1988—. Cons., pres. Bridgeware, Denver, 1985—. Cons. Terry Considine U.S. Senate Campaign, Denver, 1985-86. Sgt. USAF, 1975-79. Avocations: golf, bowling, reading. Office: Aimco 4582 S Ulster St Ste 1100 Denver CO 80237 E-mail: rhamrick@aimco.com.

HAMRICK, LINDA L. educator; b. Fort Wayne, Ind., Feb. 14, 1954; BS in Edn., Ball State U., 1977; MS in Edn., Ind. U., 1980; EdD in Ednl. Leadership, Ball State U., 1991. Cert. tchr., sch. adminstr., supt., Ind. Tchr. Fort Wayne (Ind.) Cmty. Schs., 1978—; adminstrv. intern Ft. Wayne (Ind.) Cmty. Schs., 1997—; educator-YIC Whitley County Probation, Columbia City, Ind., 1997—. Assoc. faculty Ind. U., 1987, 88; sch. supt. internship N.W. Allen County Schs., Fort Wayne, 1990-91. Site dir. youth basketball Ft. Wayne YMCA, 1982-86; site supr. Ft. Wayne Park Dept., 1980-85. Mem. AAPHERD, Ind. Middle Level Educators Assn., Internat. Reading Assn., Am. Endurance Ride Conf., Internat. Arabian Horse Assn., Upper Midwest Endurance Ride Conf. Avocations: horse riding endurance, snowmobiling, downhill skiing, boating, water skiing. Office: South Side HS 3601 S Calhoun St Fort Wayne IN 46807-2006

HAMRLIK, ROMAN, professional hockey player; b. Gottwaldov, Czechoslovakia, Apr. 12, 1974; Hockey player Tampa Bay Lightning, 1992—98, Edmonton Oilers, 1998—2000, NY Islanders, 2000—. Named to play in NHL All-Star Game, 1996. Office: New York Islanders Nassau Veterans Memorial Coliseum Uniondale NY 11553

HAMROCK, MARGARET MARY, retired educator, writer; d. Louis Francis and Mary (Augustin) H. BS in Edn., Kent State U., 1946. Tchr. Campbell (Ohio) Bd. Edn., 1927-75; ret., 1975. Author: Tell Me I'm Somebody, 1994; composer of songs; over 100 letters to editor pub. in Cleve. Plain Dealer, Youngstown Vindicator, nat. mags. Mem. Ohio Ret. Tchrs. Assn. (life), Kent State U. Alumni Assn. Avocations: reading, writing.

HAMROFF, MICHAEL SCOTT, archives executive; b. Queens, N.Y., Mar. 12, 1963; s. Sheldon and Zelda (Lurie) H.; m. Iris Eden, Mar. 29, 1987; children: Samantha, Brooke, Brandon. BA cum laude, Hofstra U., 1985. Exec. Comprehensive Archives, Richmond Hill, N.Y., 1985—. Mem. Assn. Record Mgrs., Profl. Records and Info. Svc. Mgrs. Avocation: golf. Office: Comprehensive Archives Inc 87-46 123d St Richmond Hill NY 11418 E-mail: mhamroff@erols.com.

HAMSCHER, ALBERT NELSON, history educator; b. Phila., Aug. 19, 1946; s. Albert Nelson Hamscher Jr. and Florence May Wagner; m. Claire Louise Dehon, Aug. 9, 1997. BA, Pa. State U., 1968; MA, Emory U., 1970, PhD, 1973. Instr. Kans. State U., Manhattan, 1972-73, asst. prof., 1973-76, assoc. prof., 1977-85, prof., 1986—. Mem. Inst. for Advanced Study, Princeton, N.J., 1988-89. Author: The Parlement of Paris After the Fronde, 1653-1673, 1976, The Conseil Privé and The Parlements in the Age of Louis XIV, 1987; mem. bd. editors French Hist. Studies, 1989-92, Regents Press Kans., 2001—; contbr. numerous articles to profl. jours. Grantee NEH, Washington, 1976, 80-81, 87, 88-89, Am. Philos. Soc., Phila., 1979, Am. Coun. Learned Socs., 1988. Office: Kans State Univ Dept History Eisenhower Hall Manhattan KS 66506 E-mail: aham@ksu.edu.

HAMSTRA, CHRISTINE JOSEPHINE, social worker; b. Wyandotte, Mich., July 28, 1953; d. Joseph and Stefania (Karolczyk) Baran; m. Jeffrey William Hamstra, July 18, 1987; children: Kathryn, Stephan. BA, Ea. Mich. U., 1975; MSW, U. Mich., 1983. Lic. social worker, Tex. Mental health worker Ypsilanti (Mich.) Area Community Svcs., 1975-76; program assoc. 4-H Youth Programs, Wayne, Mich., 1978-79; child care worker Yorkwood's Ctr., Ypsilanti, 1979-81; youth therapist Bridgeway Ctr., Inc., Jackson, Mich., 1983-84; adolescent therapist Care Unit Hosp. of Dallas/Ft. Worth, Ft. Worth, 1984-88; chem. dependency therapist Psychiat. Inst. of Ft. Worth, 1988-89; pvt. practice, prin. Daigle & Assocs., Hurst, Tex., 1989-91; pvt. practice Dr. Saleem & Assocs., Hurst, 1991—. Mem. NASW. Avocations: outdoors, aerobics, reading, travel. Office: Dr Saleem & Assocs 500 Goldhawk Bedford TX 76022

HAMZAEE, REZA GHOLI, economics educator; b. Arak, Iran, July 5, 1951; arrived in U.S., 1974; s. Gholamali and Nosrat Hamzaee; m. Diana Riazi, Sept. 21, 1979; 1 child, Maanie. BS, Nat. U. Iran, 1973; MA, U. Calif., 1977; PhD, Arizona State U., 1985. Tchr. Varjavand High Sch., Tehran, 1971-72; acct. Pars Indsl. Group, Tehran, 1973-74; econs. instr. Ariz. State U., Tempe, 1981-84; asst. prof. econ. Mo. Western State Coll., St. Joseph, 1984-88, assoc. prof. econs., 1988-92, prof., 1992—, chair dept. bus. and econs., 1990, 2003—, post-professorial rank Faculty Active Career Program, 2003—. Prof. Walden U., 1992—; cons. editor Nat. Social Sci. Jour., 1991; cons. and spkr. in field; vis. profl. Indsl. Mgmt. Inst. Iran; sr. assoc. Aviation Cons. Group LLC, Ormond Beach, Fla., 2001—. Mem. nat. bd. referees Nat. Social Sci. Jour., cons. editor, 1991-95; mem. editl. bd. Iran Econ. Jour., 1999—; contbr. articles to profl. jours. Grad. scholar Ariz. State U., 1984; recipient Jesse Lee Myers Excellence in Tchg. award, 1990, Burlington No. Faculty Achievement award 1991. Mem. Western Econ. Assn., Ea. Econ. Assn., Atlantinc Econ. Soc., Assn. Global Bus., Western Regional Sci. Assn. Avocations: swimming, racquetball, classical music, reading, guitar playing. Office: Mo Western State Coll Dept Econ 4525 Downs Dr Dept Econ Saint Joseph MO 64507-2246

HAN, CHIEN-PAI, statistics educator; b. Hunan, China, Dec. 17, 1936; came to U.S., 1960; s. Chung-Shih and Pei-Wen Han; m. Maria Han, Aug. 28, 1965; children: Richard, Julie. BA, Nat. Taiwan U., Taipei, 1958; MA, U. Minn., 1962; PhD, Harvard U., 1967. Asst. prof. stats. Iowa State U., Ames, 1967-69, assoc. prof., 1970-75, prof., 1975-82; prof. math. U. Tex.-Arlington, 1982—. Statis. cons. Mus. N.Mex., Santa Fe, 1965; vis. asst. prof. Harvard U., Cambridge, Mass., 1970 Author: (with T.A. Bancroft) Statistical Theory and Inference in Research, 1981; mem. editl. bd. Comms. in Stats. Theory and Methods, 1975-92, Jour. Statis. Rsch., 1994; assoc. editor Comms. in Stats., 1993—. Fellow Am. Statis. Assn. (pres. Iowa chpt. 1971-72); mem. Internat. Statis Inst. (elected), Inst. Math. Stats., Internat. Assn. Survey Statisticians, Internat. Chinese Statis. Assn. (bd. dirs. 1987-92, pres. 2000), Sigma Xi, Mu Sigma Rho. Office: U Tex Dept Math PO Box 19408 Arlington TX 76019-0408

HAN, CHINGPING JIM, industrial engineer, educator; b. Shanghai, People's Republic China, Aug. 24, 1957; came to U.S., 1983; s. Bao-San Zhang and Xiao-xian Han; m. Marie Han; children: George, Elaine. PRC, BSME, Dalian Inst. Tech., Dalian, 1982; MS in Indsl. Engring., Pa. State U., 1985, PhD, 1988. Asst. prof. mfg. systems engring. Fla. Atlantic U., Boca Raton, 1988-93, assoc. prof. and assoc. dir. mfg. systems engring., 1993-2000, prof. computer sci., 2001—. Contbr. articles to profl. jours., procs. Avocations: classical music, travel. Home: 20208 Back Nine Dr Boca Raton FL 33498 Office: Fla Atlantic Univ Dept Computer Sci and Engring 777 Glades Rd Boca Raton FL 33431-6498 E-mail: han@fau.edu.

HAN, DEGUANG, mathematician, educator; b. Weifang, Shandong, P. R. China, Sept. 10, 1959; m. Xiaohong Dong; 1 child, Tony. PhD in Math., Texas A&M U., 1998. Postdoctoral McMaster U., Hamilton, Canada, 1998—2000; asst. prof. U. Crl. Fla., Orlando, Fla., 2000—. Author: Frame, Bases and Group Representations, 2000. Recipient PDF award, NSERC, 2000; grantee Chinese NSF, NSF China, 1991, 1994, 1998. Mem.: Chinese Math. Soc., Math. Assn. Am., Am. Math. Soc. Office: Dept Math U Ctrl Fla Orlando FL 32816 Office Fax: (407) 823-6253. Business E-Mail: dhan@pegasus.cc.ucf.edu.

HAN, JIAHUAI, medical researcher; BS in Biochemistry, Beijing U., 1982, MS in Protein Biochemistry, 1988; PhD in Molecular Biology, U. Brussels, 1990. Rsch. fellow Dept. Internal Medicine and Howard Hughes Med. Inst., U. Tex. Southwestern Med. Ctr., Dallas, 1987—92; rsch. assoc. Dept. Immunology, The Scripps Rsch. Inst., La Jolla, Calif., 1992—93, sr. rsch. assoc., 1993—96, asst. mem., 1996—. Contbr. articles to profl. jours. Recipient Established Investigator award, Am. Heart Assn., 1995. Office: Scripps Rsch Inst IMM-9 10550 N Torrey Pines Rd La Jolla CA 92037-1000

HAN, JIAWEI, computer scientist, educator; b. Shanghai, Aug. 10, 1949; came to U.S., 1979; arrived in Can., 1987; s. Yu-chang Han and Jia-zhi Wang; m. Yandong Cai, July 3, 1979; 1 child, Lawrence. BSc, USTC, Beijing, China, 1979; MSc, U. Wis., 1981, PhD, 1985. Asst. prof. Northwestern U., Evanston, Ill., 1986-87, Simon Fraser U., Burnaby, B.C., Can., 1987-91, assoc. prof., 1991-95, prof., 1995-2001, U. Ill., Urbana-Champaign, 2001—. Editor Jour. Intelligent Info. Sys., Jour. of Knowledge Discovery and Data Mining; author: Data Mining: Concepts and Techniques, 2001. Mem. IEEE, ACM, Spl. Interest Group on Mgmt. of Data, Spl. Interest Group on Knowledge of Discovery and Data Mining. Office: U Ill Dept Computer Sci Urbana IL 61801

HAN, KE, materials scientist, metallurgy consultant; b. Jinan, Shandong, China, Jan. 1, 1956; s. Sizheng Han and Ma Jin; m. Min Tian. PhD, Oxford U., Eng., 1992. Postdoct. Los Alamos (N.Mex.) Nat. Lab., 1995—99; asst. scientist, project leader Nat. High Magnetic Field Lab., Tallahassee, 1999—2002, assoc. scientist, project leader, 2002—. Contbr. articles. Grantee In House Research Program rsch. grant, 2002. Office: Nat High Magnetic Filed 1800 E Paul Dirac Dr Tallahassee FL 32306 Business E-Mail: han@magnet.fsu.edu.

HAN, LORI COX, political science educator; b. Vallejo, Calif., May 3, 1966; d. Nancy Jane Cox; m. Tomislav Han; children: Taylor Ann NyBlom, Davis Anthony. BA, U. Calif., Davis, 1988; MA, Calif. State U., Northridge, 1993, U. So. Calif., L.A., 1995, PhD, 1997. Assoc. prof. polit. sci. Austin Coll., Sherman, Tex., 1998—. Governing coun. Presidency Rsch. Group, 1999—; vis. asst. prof. UCLA, 1997—98. Author: (book) Governing From Center Stage: White House Communication Strategies During the Television Age of Politics, 2001. Mem.: Ctr. for the Study of the Presidency, Western Polit. Sci. Assn., Am. Polit. Sci. Assn. Office: Austin Coll St 61649 900 N Grand Ave Sherman TX 75090 Business E-Mail: lhan@austincollege.edu.

HAN, NONG, artist, sculptor, painter; b. Seoul, Korea, Oct. 10, 1930; came to U.S., 1952, naturalized, 1958; Commr. Asian Art Commn. Asian Art Mus. San Francisco, The Avery Brundage Collection, City and County of San Francisco, 1981-84. One-man exhbns. paintings and/or sculpture include Ft. Lauderdale (Fla.) Mus. Arts, Santa Barbara (Calif.) Mus. Art, Crocker Art Mus., Sacramento, Calif., 1965, Ga. Mus. Art, Athens, 1967, El Paso (Tex.) Mus. Art, 1967, Nat. Mus. History, Taiwan, 1971, Nihonbashi Gallery, Tokyo, Japan, 1971, Shinsegye Gallery, Seoul, Korea, 1975, Nat. Mus. Modern Art, Seoul, 1975, San Francisco Zool. Garden, 1975, Tongin Art Gallery, Seoul, 1978, Consulate Gen. Republic of Korea, L.A., 1982, Choon Chu Gallery, Seoul, 1982, Mee Gallery, Seoul, 1984, 86, Leema Art Mus., Seoul, 1985, Tong-A Dept. Store, Taegu, Korea, 1986, Tongso Gallery, Masan, Korea, 1986, Han Kwang Art Mus., Pusan, Korea, 1986, Union de Arte, Barcelona, Spain, 1987, Acad. de Belles Arts, Sabadell, Spain, 1987, Nong Hyup Art Mus., Ft. Lee, N.J., 1995, The Info. Ctr. Korean Embassy, Washington, 1997; Gallery Art Exchange, N.Y.C., 1998, Korean Cultural Ctr., Annandale, Va., 1999, Paeksang Meml. Hall The Korea Times, Seoul, 2000, The Korea Central Daily, Vienna, Va.; numerous group exhibits Mus. and Art Ctr., Douglaston, N.Y., 1961, Nat. Collection Fine Arts, Smithsonian Instn., Washington, 1961, Mus. Fine Arts, Springfield, Mass., 1961, Conn. Acad. Fine Arts, Hartford, Conn., 1962, Charles and Emma Frye Art Mus., Seattle, 1962, The Denver Art Mus., 1965, Jersey City Mus., 1967, U. Santa Clara (Calif.) Mus., 1967, U. Calif., Berkeley, 1968, Maison de la Culture du Havre, Le Havre, France, 1970, Oakland (Calif.) Art Mus., 1971, Gallerie des Champs Elysees, Paris, 1971, Nat. Sculpture Soc., Lever House, N.Y.C., 1971, Taipei Provincial Mus., Republic of China, 1971, San Francisco Mus. Modern Art, 1972, Galerie Hexagramme, Paris, 1975, Galeria de Arte Misrachi, Mexico City, 1979, The Mun Ye Art Ctr., Seoul, 1986, Salon de Artistes Francais, Paris, France, 1971, Salon d'Automne, Paris, 1969-71, Salon Grands et Jeunes d'Aujourd'hui, Paris, 1971-77, The Jane Voorhees Zimmerli Art Mus. Rutgers, New Brunswick, N.J., 1997, Chgo. Cultural Ctr., 1997, Mus. Contemporary Art, Washington D.C., 1997, Taipei Gallery Taiwanese Cultural Ctr., N.Y.C., 1998, Fisher Gallery U. So. Calif., L.A., 1998, Japanese Am. Nat. Mus., L.A., 1998, Bedford Gallery, Dean Lesker Regl. Ctr. for the Arts, Walnut Creek, 1998, The Kaohsing Museum of Fine Art, 1998, Taipei Museum of Fine Arts, 1998, Marugame Genichiro Inokuma Mus. of Contemporary Art, Japan, 1999, Fukuoka Asian Art Mus., Fukuoka City, 1999, Akita Senshu Mus. Art, Akita City, 1999; represented in numerous permanent collections including, Santa Barbara Mus. Art, Anchorage (Alaska) Hist. and Fine Art Mus., Museo de Arte, Lima, Peru, Govt. Peru, Nat. Mus. History, Govt. of Republic of China, Oakland (Calif.) Art Mus., Ga. Mus. Art, Athens, Korean Embassy, Lima, Peru, Nat. Mus. of Modern Art, Nat. Mus. Korea, Govt. of Republic of Korea, Seoul, Nat. Gallery of Modern Art, New Delhi, India, Asian Art Mus. San Francisco, Govt. of People's Republic China, Beijing and Shanghai, Palacio de la Zarzuela, Madrid, Palacio de la Moncloa, Madrid, The Korean Embassy, Madrid, Mus. Art de Sabadell, Spain, Mus. Nat. des Beaux-Arts, Monte Carlo, Monaco, The Philatelic Mus. Palais des Nations, Geneva, Korean Embassy, Wash., Nat. Mus., Manila, Philippines, others; author: Nong Questions, 1982. Chmn. San Francisco-Seoul Sister City Com., City and County San Francisco, 1981-84. Served with U.S. Army, 1956-59; Served with USAF, 1959-60. Recipient numerous awards including citations from Republic of Korea, Cert. Disting. Achievement State of Calif., 1982, Proclamation City and County of San Francisco, 1982; Nong Stamp issued in his honor UNISEF, 1996. Office: Nong Gallery 7057 N Seminole Trl Leon VA 22725 E-mail: Robert_338@msn.com. *Beauty and ugliness, good and bad, right and wrong. Which test should I choose to measure these? Then, how long can I rely on the test I choose?.*

HAN, OKSOO, pianist, music educator; b. Seoul, Korea, June 18, 1938; d. Kyung-Seok H. and Young-Hwan Kim; m. Won-Hoon Park, Sept. 25, 1971; children: Suzanne, Thomas. BA, Ewha Women's U., Seoul, Korea, 1960; MA, Cin. Conservatory Music, 1962; DMA, William Penn Coll., 1983. Artist Eric Semon Mgmt., N.Y.C., 1965-72; prof. L.I. U., 1966-75, Kyunghee U., Seoul, Korea, 1976-78, Dankook U., Seoul, Korea, 1983—; dir. Korean chpt. World Piano Competition, Cin., 1987—; chmn. Han Romanson Internat. Piano Competition, Seoul, 1994—. Jury Tchaikovsky, Prokofiev, Cin. Internat. Competitions, others, 1987—. Soloist Carnegie Recital Hall, 1964, European Debut Recitals, 1964 (recording) My Favorite Chopin, 1991. Recipient Cultural Merit citation Korean Govt., 1967; named Musician of Yr., Seoul, 1982. Mem. Am. Music Scholarship Assn. (bd. dirs. 1987—). Home: 17-29 Kookee-Dong Chongroku Seoul 110-011 Republic of Korea Office: Dankook U San 8 Hannam-Dong Seoul 140-210 Republic of Korea

HAN, QIWEN, research scientist; s. Zhongfa Han and Hongwei Guan; m. Kun Hu; children: Steven Anthony children: Shelley Xue, Matthew Eric. PhD, ND State U., 1995—2000. Sr. scientist Rhodia, Inc., Cranbury, NJ, 2000—02; project supr. Nat. Starch and Chem. Co., Bridgewater, NJ, 2002—. Vice chair Chinese Student and Scholar Assn. at ND State U., Fargo, ND, 1996—97. Mem.: Phila. Soc. for Coatings Tech., Fedn. of Societies for Coatings Tech., Internat. Union of Pure and Applied Chemistry, Chinese Chem. Soc., Am. Chem. Soc., NY Acad. of Sciences. Achievements include patents for synthesis of liquid hydroxy terminated polybutadiene; anti-blistering coatings; fast-cure polyurethanes; invention of cast tires; environementally benign coatings; research in waterborne and solvent-based coatings and adhesives; molecular-level study of polymer films; material surfaces and interfaces; development of high-performanc low-cost polymers.

HAN, RUI, pharmacologist, educator; b. Teiling, China, Mar. 8, 1929; s. Chang-he and G.C. (Chou) H.; m. Su-de Zhou, 1956; children: Hong, Tao. MD, Sheng Yang Med. Coll., China, 1951; PhD, Chinese Union Med. Coll., China, 1960; PhD (hon.), Toyama Med. & Pharm. U., Japan, 1995. Assoc. prof. Inst. Materia Medica, China, 1978-80, 82-85, prof., 1985—. Vis. assoc. prof. Mt. Sinai Sch. Medicine, 1980-82; vis. prof. Toyama Med. & Pharm. U., Japan, 1994-95; dep. dir. Inst. Materia Medica, 1978-83; ad hoc cons. WHO, Geneva, 1978; sci. cons. Nanking Inst. Materia Medica, 1984-88; prin. investigator new anticancer drug studies N-formyl sarcolusin, harringtonine, homoharringtonine, taxol, retinamide RII, glyciphosphoramide Ministry Pub. Health Award, China, 1978-86. Editor: Cancer Chemoprevention & Drug Treatment, 1991; mem. editl. bd. Chinese Jour. Cancer, Chinese Jour. Cancer Rsch., Chinese Med. Sci. Jour. Recipient Outstanding Scientist award Ministry Pub. Health, 1990, State Coun., 1991. Mem. Soc. Exptl. Biology & Medicine, Cell Kinetic Soc., N.Y. Acad. Scis., Am. Assn. Advancement Sci. Office: Chinese Acad Med Scis Inst Mt Md Xian Nong Tan St Beijing 100050 China E-mail: ruihan@public.east.cn.net.

HAN, SYUNG D. international trade consultant, financier; b. Seoul City, Republic of Korea, Mar. 3, 1943; U.S. citizen; s. Young and Kum J. Han. PhD (hon.), Oddessa (USSR) U., 1991; PhD, KW U., 1993; postgrad., Harvard U., 1994, 96, George Washington U., 1994, Columbia U., 1997. Pres. Sunnyland Ent., Inc., Westminster, Calif., 1972-74; CEO, chmn. Global Economies Analysis, Inc., Falls Church, Va., 1974—; pres. S.D. Sunnyland Ent., Inc., Falls Church, 1974—, Sunnyland Holding Inc., Falls Church, 1994—. Recipient medal of peace Peace Found., USSR, 1991, medal of freedom Rep. Party, Washington, 1993. Mem. Nat. Def. Preparation Assn., Acad. Polit. Sci., Washington Internat. Trade Assn., Commonwealth of Va. (public notary). Roman Catholic. Office: SD Sunnyland Ent Inc 6231 Leesburg Pike Falls Church VA 22044-2102

HAN, XIANLIN, education educator, consultant; s. Wuxiang Han and Xinxian Huang; m. Hongping Ye, Sept. 22, 1959; children: Rowland Hua, Rachel Jing. PhD, Wash. U., St. Louis, 1990. Instr. Wash. U. Sch. of Medicine, St. Louis, 1992—97, rsch. asst. prof., 1997—2000, asst. prof. medicine, 2000—. Achievements include patents pending for Early Alzheimer's disease diagnosis. Office Fax: 314-362-1402. E-mail: xianlin@pcg.wustl.edu.

HAN, YIJIE, information technology educator; b. Hangzhou, Zheijiang, China, Nov. 28, 1959; arrived in U.S., 1982; s. Changjin and Jianru (Shi) Han; m. Shiming Zhan; 1 child, Lichy. BE, Univ. of Sci. and Tech. of China, Hefei, 1982; MA, Duke U., 1984, PhD, 1987. Asst. prof. U. Ky., Lexington, 1987—92; lectr. Hong Kong U., 1992—93; info. specialist Electronic Data Systems, Inc., Troy, Mich., 1993—99; assoc. prof. U. Mo., Kansas City, 1999—. Contbr. chapters to books. Grantee, U. Ky., 1987, 1990, U Mo., Kansas City, 2002. Mem.: Assn. Computing Machinery. Office: U Mo Kansas City 5100 Rockhill Rd Kansas City MO 64110 Office Fax: 816-235-5159.

HANABUSA, COLLEEN, state legislator, lawyer; b. Honolulu, 1952; m. June and Isao Hanabusa. BA in Econs. and Sociology, U. Hawaii, 1973, MA in Sociology, 1975, JD, 1977. Labor atty., Honolulu; legal rschr. Madison, Wis., 1978; mem. Hawaii Senate, Dist. 21, Honolulu; chair water, land and Hawaiian affairs com. Hawaii Senate, Honolulu, mem. commerce and consumer protection com., mem. govt. ops. and housing com. Advisor Arnold Morgado for Mayor Canmpaign, 1994. Recipient 2d runner-up Hawaii Jr. Miss Pageant, 1969. Avocation: reading murder mysteries. Office: State Capitol 415 S Beretania St Honolulu HI 96813-2407 Fax: (808) 586-7797.*

HANAHAN, DONALD JAMES, biochemist, educator; b. Springfield, Ill., May 13, 1919; s. James Francis and Clara (Schiller) H.; m. Lillian Marie Larsen, June 21, 1947; children: Douglas A., Laura J., Timothy J., Colleen J., Carolyn M. BS, U. Ill., 1941, PhD, 1944. Rsch. assoc. Manhattan Project, 1944-45; fellow U. Calif., Berkeley, 1945-47; faculty U. Wash., Seattle, 1948-67, prof. biochemistry, 1958-67; prof., head dept. biochemistry U. Ariz., Tucson, 1967-76; prof. biochemistry U. Tex. Health Sci. Center, San Antonio, 1976—, chmn. dept., 1976-84, prof. emeritus, 1994-98. Author: Lipid Chemistry, 1960, A Guide to Phospholipid Chemistry, 1997; contbr. articles to profl. jours. Guggenheim Found. fellow, 1955; NIH spl. fellow, 1965-66; Macy faculty scholar, 1974 Mem. Am. Chem. Soc., Am. Soc. Biol. Chemists. Home: 25 Arroyo Ln Novato CA 94947 E-mail: donald.hanahan@verizon.net.

HANAHAN, JAMES LAKE, retired insurance executive; b. Burlington, Iowa, Aug. 27, 1932; s. Thomas J. and Clarice P. (Lorey) H.; m. Marilyn R. Lowe, Dec. 27, 1952; children: Bridget Sue Bahlke, Erin Rose Savage. BS, Drake U., 1955; postgrad., George Williams Coll., 1956. Phys dir. Monmouth (Ill.) YMCA, 1955-56; cmty. rels. staff Caterpillar Tractor Co., Peoria, Ill., 1956-57; rep. Conn. Gen. Life Ins. Co., Des Moines, 1957-59, asst. mgr., 1959-63, mgr. group ins. ops. Tampa, Fla., 1963-80; pres., chief exec. officer WHP, First In Employee Benefits Inc., 1980-91, J&H Cons. Group Inc., 1980-91; v.p. AON Cons., 1991-2000; ret., 2000. Instr. C.P.C.U. courses; seminar leader C.L.U. workshop; cons. ins. seminar Fla. State U.; guest instr. U. South Fla., Hillsborough County Schs. Great Am. Teach-In. Bd. dirs. West Coast Employee

Benefit Coun., Tampa Sports Found., Jr. Achievement, Tampa Bay Acad.; chmn. joint bd. trustees Town and Country Hosp. and Meml. Hosp, Tampa; past pres. Pinellas Emergency Mental Health Svcs.; mem. Hillsborough County Health Coun. Recipient Double D award Drake U., PEMHS Cmty. Svc. award. Mem. Sales Mktg. Execs. Tampa (past pres., Exec. of Yr. 1982), Nat. Risk Mgmt. Soc., Greater Tampa C. of C., Mineret Soc. Tampa U., Tampa Sports and Recreation Coun. (bd. dirs.), Self Ins. Assn. Am., Pinellas Econ. Devel. Coun. (chmn.), Health Ins. Inst. Am., Profl. Benefit Adminstrs. Assn., Com. of 100, Nat. D Club (Drake U.; dir.), Timber Greens Country Club, Pres.'s Assn., Phi Sigma. Democrat. Roman Catholic. Home: 6659 Garden Palm Ct New Port Richey FL 34655-5117 E-mail: jim_l_hanahan@aoncons.com.

HANAMEY, ROSEMARY T. nursing educator; b. Detroit, May 16, 1937; d. Albert Edward and Catherine Margaret (Shaheen) Hanamey. BSN, Mercy Coll., Detroit, 1959; MS, Boston Coll., 1963; postgrad., U. Mich., 1982. RN Mich., 1959. Staff nurse Mt. Carmel Mercy Hosp., Detroit, 1959—60, Mass. Gen. Hosp., Boston, 1960—63; instr. nursing Mercy Coll., Detroit, 1963—65, asst. prof., 1967—69; asst. exec. sec. Mich. Nurses Assn., Lansing, 1965—67; exec. sec. Mich. Conf. AAUP, Detroit, 1969—70; instr. nursing Madonna Coll., Livonia, Mich., 1972—76; asst. prof. nursing Ea. Mich. U., Ypsilanti, 1976—80; vol. parish nurse St. Joseph Cath. Ch., Dexter, Mich., 1997—. Mem. careers com. Mich. League Nursing, Detroit, 1977—97; cons. Detroit Practical Nurse Ctr., 1980—85; mem. parish nurse partnership St. Joseph Mercy Health Sys., Ann Arbor, Mich., 1997—. Author: (videotape) Intravenous Therapy: Monitoring and Problem Solving, 1977 (2nd place, 1978), Intravenous Therapy: Basic Concepts, 1977 (3rd place, 1978). Precinct del. Dem. Party, Detroit, 1966—69. Grantee, USPHS, 1961—62; scholar, Marygrove Coll., Detroit, 1955—56. Mem.: AAUP, Cath. Med. Assn. Avocations: swimming, walking. Home: 8074 Huron St Unit I Dexter MI 48130-1053

HANAN, LAURA MOLEN, artist; b. Ft. Monmouth, N.J., Jan. 30, 1954; d. Richard Eugene Molen and Agnes Arlene (Stahlhacke) Rose; m. John Morris Hanan, Apr. 26, 1985 (div. July 15, 2003); 1 child, Whitney Anne. BS, U. Calif. Berkeley, 1978; BA in Journalism, Humboldt State U., 1980; AOS in Visual Comm., Northwest Coll. Art, 1992. Reporter, city editor Contra Costa Sun, Moraga, Calif., 1980-81; sports reporter, photographer The Canby (Oreg.) Herald, 1981-82; sr. tech. writer MDS Qantel Bus. Computers, Hayward, Calif., 1982-84; bus. mgr., owner, designer Hanan Constrn. and Design Co., Inc., Alameda, Calif., 1986-90; dir. admissions Northwest Coll. Art, Poulsbo, Wash., 1992-93; fine artist, graphic artist Laura Hanan Art, Gig Harbor, Seattle, Wash., 1993—; owner, renovator Sage Equities, 2000; founder gallery Brick & Mortar, Tacoma, 2001. Creative dir. Pacific Pipeline, Kent, Wash., 1992-93; co-owner The Watermark Gallery, Village Art Gallery, Freighthouse Gallery, Gig Harbor, Tacoma, 1993-96; art dir., cons. Exec. Office Svcs., Gig Harbor, Beaverton, Oreg., 1996-97; owner, artist Brick & Mortar Gallery, Tacoma, 2001—; sponsor, artist 6th Ann. Arts & Crafts Benefit for Prison Pet Partnership Program, 2002. Exhibited in group shows Emerald City Fine Art Gallery, Seattle, 1996-97, Nicholas Joseph Fine Art, N.Y.C., 1997-98, Hastings-Ray Gallery, Southern Pines, N.C., 1997-2000, Peninsula Br. Libr., Gig Harbor, 1994, 95, 96, Tacoma Art Mus., 2000; represented in permanent collection Pierce County Libr., also pvt. collections. Art donor 5th Ann. Wild West Showdown supporting Tacoma Actors Guild, 2002. Recipient First Place prize Peninsula Art League, 1995, 2d place, 1996, 3d place, 1997, Peoples Choice award Peninsula Art League, 1997; accepted for 1999 Tacoma Art Mus. juried fundraiser, for 25th anniversary "The Night Tacoma Danced", 2001, 03. Achievements include Bought and restored 100 yr. bldg. received local landmark status, opened gallery (Brick & Motar Gallery), June 2001. Avocations: graphic art, weight lifting, sewing, computers, walking.

HANAN, PATRICK DEWES, foreign language professional, educator; b. New Zealand, Jan. 4, 1927; s. Frederick Arthur and Ida Helen (Dewes) H.; m. Anneliese Drube, July 1951; 1 son, Rupert Guy. BA, Auckland U., 1948, MA, 1949; BA, U. London, 1953, PhD, 1960. Lectr. Sch. Oriental and African Studies, 1954-63; assoc. prof., then prof. Stanford U., 1963-68; prof. Chinese lit. Harvard U., Cambridge, Mass., 1968-89, Victor S. Thomas prof. Chinese lit., 1989-98, Victor S. Thomas rsch. prof. Chinese lit., 1998—. Dir. Harvard-Yenching Inst., 1987-95. Author: The Chinese Short Story, 1973, The Chinese Vernacular Story, 1981, The Invention of Li Yu, 1988; transl.: The Carnal Prayer Mat, 1990, Silent Operas, 1990, A Tower for the Summer Heat, 1995, The Sea of Regret, 1995, The Money Demon, 1999. Named Officer of New Zealand Order of Merit. Fellow Am. Council Learned Socs., Guggenheim Found.; Mem. Am. Acad. Arts and Scis. Office: 2 Divinity Ave Cambridge MA 02138-2020

HANARD, PATRICIA ANN, family nurse practitioner; b. Searcy, Ark., Dec. 19, 1943; d. Claudis E. and H. Frances (Stringfellow) Byrum; m. Marcel Roger-Andre Hanard II, Apr. 19, 1964; children: Marcel III, Samantha, Brendan, Dominic. AAS, Ill. Cen. Coll., 1971; BS with honors, Coll. St. Francis, Joliet, Ill., 1985; MLS, Bradley U.; MSN in Pub. Health Nursing, U. Ill., 1996. RN, Ill. cert. family nurse practitioner; cert. in reproductive endocrinology and infertility; registered med. lab. technician. Nurse emergency rm. Proctor Hosp., Peoria, Ill., 1972-78; head nurse, mgr. office Midwest Med. Svcs., Peoria, 1978-87; head nurse ob/gyn Coll. Medicine U. Ill., Peoria; clin. nurse specialist, office mgr. Fertility and Reproductive Medicine Ctr. of Ctrl. Ill., 1987-97; family nurse practitioner Midwest Urol. Assn., 1997-99. Maj. U.S. Army, 1991—. Mem. AWHONN, Am. Fertility Soc., Am. Med. Technologists, Ill. State Assn. Med. Technologists, ANA, Ill. Nurses Assn., Soc. Urologic Nurses Assn., Alpha Chi Omega, Phi Theta Kappa, Phi Kappa Phi, Sigma Theta Tau. Home: 28 Palma Ln Hot Springs Village AR 71909 E-mail: patricia.hanard@il.ngb.army.mil.

HANAUER, JOE FRANKLIN, real estate executive; b. Stuttgart, Fed. Republic Germany, July 8, 1937; came to U.S., 1938; s. Otto and Betty (Zurndorfer) H.; m. Jane Boyle, Oct. 20, 1972; children: Jill, Wendy, Jason, Elizabeth. BS, Roosevelt U., 1963. Pres. Thorsen Realty, Oak Brook, Ill., 1974-80; sr. v.p. Coldwell Banker, Newport Beach, Calif., 1980-83, pres., 1984, chmn. bd., CEO, 1984-88; prin. Combined Investments LP, Laguna Beach, Calif., 1989—; chmn. bd. dirs. Grubb & Ellis Co., San Francisco, 1993-97. Bd. dirs. MAF Bancorp, Chgo.; chmn. bd. Homestore.com., Calamos Mutual Funds; chmn. policy adv. bd. Joint Ctr. for Housing Studies Harvard U., 1995-96. Bd. dirs. Chgo. Chamber Orch., 1976—; trustee Roosevelt U. Home: 179 E Lake Shore Drive Chicago IL 60611 Office: Combined Investments LP 361 Forest Ave Ste 200 Laguna Beach CA 92651-2146

HANAUER, STEPHEN BRETT, medical educator; b. Chgo., Jan. 1, 1952; s. Richard A. Hanauer and Doree J. (Newton) Cohn; m. Jayne Susan Rosenthal, Aug. 27, 1972; children: Benjamin, Jeffrey, Richard. BA, U. Mich., 1973; MD, U. Ill., 1977. Diplomate Am. Bd. Internal Medicine, Am. Bd. Gastroenterology. Intern in internal medicine U. Chgo., 1977-78, resident in internal medicine, 1978-80, fellowship in gastroenterology, 1980-82, asst. prof. medicine, 1982-87, assoc. prof. of medicine, 1988-92, prof. medicine and clin. pharmacology, 1993, dir. inpatient gastroenterology, 1982-85, dir. The Logan Ctr. for G.I. clin. rsch., 1983—, co-dir. outpatient gastroenterology clinic, 1984—, co-dir. inflammatory bowel disease rsch. ctr., 1993—, dir. sect. gastroenterology/nutrition, 2000—. Mem. housestaff evaluation com. U. Chgo., 1983-85, housestaff selection com., 1984-89, continuing med. edn. com. 1984—, physician's credentials and privileges com., 1984-86, patient/guest rels. com., 1985-91, strategic planning subcom. for hosp. restructuring, 1986, com. on clin. pharmacology, 1992, ambulatory care adv. coun., 1994; mem. FDA ad hoc cons. on new drug devel., 1986; mem. gastrointestinal drugs adv. com., 1987-93. Reviewer Gastroenterology, Annals of Internal Medicine, New Eng. Jour. Medicine; edtl. bd. Alimentary Tract Pharmacology and Therapeutics; contbr. articles to profl. jours. Chmn. FDA Adv. Panel for Gastrointestinal Drugs, 1996-2000 Named Hon. Ky. Col., Commonwealth of Ky. Mem. ACP (fellowship 1986), Am. Gastroenterol. Assn. (nominating com. 1991, abstract rev. com. 1991—, soc. for mucosal immunology 1994—, rsch. com. 1995, chmn. immunology and inflammatory disorders sect. 1996), Chgo. Soc. Gastroenterology (pres.), Am. Coll. Gastroenterology (ad hoc com. on FDA rels., endl. affairs com., rsch. com., fellowship 1988), Alpha Omega Alpha. Office: U Chgo Med Ctr 5841 S Maryland Ave #MC4076 Chicago IL 60637-1426

HANAWALT, PHILIP COURTLAND, biology educator, researcher; b. Akron, Ohio, Aug. 25, 1931; s. Joseph Donald and Lenore (Smith) H.; m. Joanna Thomas, Nov. 2, 1957 (div. Oct. 1977); children: David, Steven; m. Graciela Spivak, Sept. 10, 1978; children: Alex, Lisa. Student, Deep Springs Coll., 1949-50; BA, Oberlin Coll., 1954; MS, Yale U., 1955, PhD, 1959; ScD (hon.), Oberlin Coll., 1997. Postdoctoral fellow U. Copenhagen, Denmark, 1958-60, Calif. Inst. Tech., Pasadena, 1960-61; rsch. biophysicist, lectr. Stanford U., Calif., 1961-65, assoc. prof., 1965-70, prof., 1970—, Howard H. and Jessie T. Watkins univ. prof., 1997—, chmn. dept. biol. scis., 1982-89; faculty dept. dermatology Stanford Med. Sch., 1979—. Mem. physiol. chemistry study sect. NIH, Bethesda, Md., 1966—70, mem. chem. pathology study sect., 1981—84; mem. sci. adv. com. Am. Cancer Soc., N.Y.C., 1972—76, Coun. for Extramural Grants, 1998—2001; chmn. 2d ad hoc senate com. on professoriate Stanford U., 1985—90; mem. NSF fellowship rev. panel, 1985; mem. carcinogen identification com. Calif. EPA, 1995—98; mem. toxicology adv. com. Burroughs-Welcome Fund, 1995—2001, chmn., 1997—2000; mem. sci. adv. bd. Fogarty Internat. Ctr., NIH, 1995—99; chmn. Gordon Conf. on Mutagenesis, 1996, Gordon Conf. on Mammalian DNA Repair, 1999; mem. bd. on radiation effects rschr. NAS Commn. on Life Scis., 1996—98; trustee Oberlin Coll., 1998—; Sonnebonn lectr. Ind. U., 2002. Author: Molecular Photobiology, 1969; author, editor: DNA Repair: Techniques, 1981, 83, 88, Molecular Basis of Life, 1968, Molecules to Living Cells, 1980; mng. editor DNA Repair Jour., 1982-93; sr. editor Cancer Rsch., 2003—; assoc. editor Jour. Cancer Rsch., Molecular Carcinogenesis, Environ. Health Perspectives, Biotechniques; bd. rev. editors Sci.; mem. editl. bd. Procs. of NAS, 2003—; contbr. more than 400 articles to profl. jours. Recipient Outstanding Investigator award Nat. Cancer Inst., 1987-2001, Excellence in Tchg. award No. Calif. Phi Beta Kappa, 1991, Environ. Mutagen Soc. Ann. Rsch. award, 1992, Peter and Helen Bing award for Disting. Tchg., 1992, Am. Soc. for Photobiology Rsch. award, 1996, Internat. Mutation Rsch. award, 1997, Ellison Found. Sr. scholar award, 2001—, John B. Little award in radiation scis. Harvard Sch. Pub. Health, 2002; Hans Falk lectr. Nat. Inst. Environ. Health Scis., 1990, Severo Ochoa Meml. Hons. lectr. NYU, 1996, IBM-Princess Takamatsu lectr. Japan, 1999; Fogarty sr. rsch. fellow, 1993. Fellow: AAAS, Am. Acad. Microbiology; mem.: NAS, European Molecular Biology Orgn. (fgn. assoc.), Radiation Rsch. Soc., Environ. Mutagen Soc. (pres. 1993—94, Student Mentoring award 2001), Am. Soc. Biochemistry and Molecular Biology, German DNA Repair Network (hon.), Biophys. Soc. (exec. bd. 1969—71), Genetics Soc., Am. Soc. for Photobiology, Am. Assn. Cancer Rsch. (bd. dirs. 1994—97), Radiation Rsch. Soc. Achievements include co-discovery of DNA excision-repair and transcription-coupled DNA repair; research on role of DNA change in human genetic disease and aging. Home: 317 Shasta Dr Palo Alto CA 94306 4542 Office: Stanford U Dept Biol Scis Herrin Biology Labs 371 Serra Mall Stanford CA 94305-5020

HANBERY, DONNA EVA, lawyer; b. Framingham, Mass.; d. Donald Taylor and Jacqueline Joyce (LaVine) H. B.A. summa cum laude, Hamline U., 1974; J.D. magna cum laude, U. Minn., 1977. Bar: Minn. 1977, U.S. Dist. Ct. D.C. 1977. Ptnr., Curtin, Mahoney & Cairns, P.A., Mpls., 1976— ; chmn., lectr. Advanced Legal Edn. Seminar on Landlord Tenant Law, 1982, 83, 84. Columnist New Homes mag., 1979—, Multi Housing mag., 1978— . Co-author: Why Cucumbers Are Better Than Men, 1983. Fundraiser, performer Law Revue for Family Plus, Mpls., 1982-83, bd. dirs., sec., counsel Crime Stoppers Minn., 1979— . Mem. ABA, Minn. Bar Assn., Hennepin County Bar Assn., Loring Mall Bus. Assn. (chmn. 1980-84), Minn. Multi-Housing Assn. Republican. Lutheran.

HANBEY, TERESA, healthcare executive, consultant; b. Vancouver, B.C., Can., Mar. 17, 1951; d. Anthony Timmons and Olga Jane Buchkowsky; m. Gregory Hanbey; 1 child, Michael Timmons Hanbey. BSW, Calif. State Poly. U., 1974; postgrad., U. B.C., Vancouver, 1980. Calif. state tchg. credential in adult edn. Mgmt. cons., 1990 ; founder, exec. dir. Hepatitis C Outreach Project, Washington, 1992—. Mem. HIV work group Wash. State Dept. Alcohol and Substance Abuse, 1999—; mem. nat. PCR adv. bd. Roche Diagnostics, Indpls., 1999; organizer Conf. for Patient Leaders, Orlando, Fla., 1999, Pub. Forum, Portland, 1999, Appalachian Outr3each S.E. Ky. AHEC, 1999. Mem. Bloodborne Illnesses Task Force, Bellingham, Wash., 1998-99; organizer Hepatitis C; the Quite Explosion Health Support Ctr., Bellingham, 1993, Hepatitis C, Continuing Med. Edn. for Physicians, St. Joseph Hosp., Bellingham, 1998, Cmty. Program: The ABC's of Hepatitis, St. Luke Found., Bellingham, 1999; mem. Minority Outreach Project, Houston, 1999, Biker Outreach, Nev., 1999. Mem. Soc. for Women's Health Rsch. (sci. adv. bd. 1999—). Avocations: gardening, home remodeling and design. Office: Hepatitis C Outreach Project PO Box 248 Vancouver WA 98666 0248 E-mail: thanbey@hcop.org.

HANBURY, GEORGE LAFAYETTE, II, academic administrator; b. Norfolk, Va., Sept. 20, 1943; s. Emmette Cecil and Adah Christine (Nelligar) H.; m. Jana Hanbury; 1 stepchild, Jia; children from previous marriage: George Lafayette III, Melissa Lee. BS in Pub. Adminstrn, Va. Poly. Inst., 1965; MPA, Old Dominion U., 1977; postgrad., Sr. Exec. Inst. Govt., U. Va., 1985; PhD, Fla. Atlantic U., 2001. Asst. to city mgr., Norfolk, 1967-70; asst. city mgr. Virginia Beach, Va., 1970-74; city mgr., 1974-82, Portsmouth, Va., 1982-90, Ft. Lauderdale, Fla., 1990-98; exec. v.p. Nova Southeastern U., Ft. Lauderdale, 1998—. Mem. Internat. City Mgmt. Assn., Am. Soc. Pub. Adminstrs., Pi Alpha Alpha. Home: The Four Seasons 333 Sunset Dr Apt 807 Fort Lauderdale FL 33301-2655 Office: Nova Southeastern Univ 3301 College Ave Fort Lauderdale FL 33314-7796 E-mail: hanbury@nova.edu.

HANBURY, KEVIN M. dean, priest; b. Jersey City, N.J., June 25, 1946; s. Raymond F. and Roseann Hanbury. BA, Seton Hall U., 1968; MDiv, Immaculate Conception Seminary, 1976; MA, Forham U., 1978; EDS, Seton Hall U., 1979, EdD, 1985. Priest Holy Family Parish, Nutley, NJ, 1972—75; H.S. tchr. Seton Hall Prep. Sch., West Orange, NJ, 1975—85; from asst. dean for enrollment to assoc. dean Seton Hall U., South Orange, NJ, 1987—97, assoc. dean for coll. human svcs., 1997—. Asst. dir. campus ministry Seton Hall U., 1958—87; rep. Resources in Christian Living, Allen, Tex., 1998—2001; cons. Silver-Burdett Pub. Co., 1985—90, Tabor Pub. co., 1982—97; dir. retreat Newark Archdiocese, Newark, 1995—2000; dir. master degree program Cath. Sch. Leadership, 1998, Edn. Ptnrs. in Cath. Schs., 2000. Contbr. articles to mags. and profl. jours. Grantee, RASKOB Found. for Cath. Activities, 2001, Alliance in Cath. Edn. grant, Notre Dame U., 2000—06, Our Sunday Visitor grant, Our Sunday Visitor Pub. Inc., 2001, 2002. Mem.: Kappa Delta Pi. Roman Catholic. Home and Office: Seton Hall University 400 South Orange Ave South Orange NJ 07079 Fax: 973-275-2187. E-mail: hanburke@shu.edu.

HANCE, ANTHONY JAMES, retired pharmacologist, educator; b. Bournemouth, Eng., Aug. 19, 1932; came to U.S., 1958; s. Walter Edwin and Jessie Irene (Finch) H.; m. Ruth Anne Martin, July 17, 1954; children: David, Peter, John. BSc, Birmingham (Eng.) U., 1953, PhD, 1956. Rsch. fellow in electrophysiology Birmingham U., 1957-58; rsch. pharmacologist UCLA, 1959-62; rsch. assoc. in pharmacology Stanford U., Palo Alto, Calif., 1962-65, asst. prof., 1965-68; assoc. prof. pharmacology U. Calif., Davis, 1968-94, prof. emeritus, 1994—. Contbr. articles to profl. jours. Mem. Am. Soc. for Pharmacology and Exptl. Therapeutics, Biomed. Engring. Soc., Assn. for Computing Machinery. Home: 1103 Radcliffe Dr Davis CA 95616-0944

HANCE, DARWOOD B. radiologist; b. Thief River Falls, Minn., Feb. 29, 1932; s. Alphie N. and Nora J. Hance; m. Helene M. Hance, Jan. 2, 1999; children: Joseph, Jeffrey, Julie, Richard, Kristina, Derek. Student, U. Miami, 1950-53; MD, U. Tenn., Memphis, 1956. Diplomate Am. Bd. Radiology, Am. Bd. Nuclear Medicine. Intern City of Detroit Receiving Hosp., 1956-57; resident in radiology Wayne State U., Detroit, 1957-60; chief of radiology 32d USAF Hosp., Minot, N.D., 1960-62, St. Jude Hosp., Memphis, 1962-63, Reid Meml. Hosp., Richmond, Ind., 1963-68, Kern Med Ctr., Bakersfield, Calif., 1968-83, Greater Bakersfield Meml. Hosp., 1968-97; fellow in neuroradiology UCLA, 1977, fellow in ultrasound, 1985, vis. assoc. prof.; radiologist UCLA Med. Ctr., 1997—. Capt. USAF, 1956-62. Fellow: Coop. of Am. Physicians (pres. 1985—), Am. Coll. Radiology (counselor 1974—76), Am. Coll. Nuc. Medicine (pres. 1987, chmn. bd. 1991—2001, Gold medal 1999). Roman Catholic. Avocations: sailing, swimming. Office: 100 Ucla Med Plz Ste 100 Los Angeles CA 90095-6970

HANCE, JAMES HENRY, JR., bank executive; b. St. Joseph, Mo., Sept. 16, 1944; s. James Henry Sr. and Kathryn (Lichty) H.; m. Beverly Vaughan Smith, May 20, 1960; children: Samantha, Lindsay, Meredith, Blair. BA in Econs., Westminster Coll., Fulton, Mo., 1966; MBA in Fin., Washington U., St. Louis, 1968. CPA. Ptnr. Price Waterhouse, Phila. and Charlotte, N.C., 1968-85; chmn. bd. Consolidated Coin Caterers Corp., Charlotte, 1985-86; exec. v.p., chief acctg. officer NCNB Corp., Charlotte, 1987-88; CFO, co-vice-chmn. Bank of Am. (formerly NationalBank), Charlotte, N.C., 1988—. Bd. dirs. Nationsbank of Tenn., D.C., Md., Charlotte, N.C. Bd. dirs. Microelectronis Ctr. N.C., Research Triangle Park, 1988; trustee Presbyn. Hosp. and Presbyn. Hosp. Health Svcs. Corp., Charlotte, 1989, Charlotte Country Day Sch., 1990; mem. acctg. and fin. commn. Bank Adminstrn. Inst., Rolling Meadows, Ill., 1989. Fellow Soc. Internat. Bus. Fellows. Republican. Presbyterian. Office: Bank of Am 100 N Tryon St Fl 58 Charlotte NC 28202-4000

HANCOCK, ALBERT SIDNEY, JR., engineering executive; b. Chickasha, Okla. s. Albert Sidney and Grace Ora (Liles) H.; m. Lillian May Shields; children: Craig Sidney, Curt Eric, Kevin Jay. Chief engr. Silent Sioux Mfg. Corp., Orange City, Iowa; pres. B&M Mfg. Corp., Orange City; pres., founder Hi-Precision Mfg. Co., Inc., Orange City; ops. mgr., projectile and tool design divsn. S&W Ammunition Co., Orange City; owner Hancock Engring., Orange City, 1958—. Cons. small arms ammunition. Inventor in field. Chmn. Planning and Zoning Com., Orange City; dir. Orange City Devel. Corp. Mem. ASM, ASTM, ARA (life), Soc. Mfg. Engrs. (sr.), Nat. Def. Indsl. Assn. (life), Nat. Reloading Mfrs. Assn., VFW, Elks, Shriners, Flying Fez. Avocation: flying. Home: 501 3rd St NE Orange City IA 51041-2123 Office: Hancock Engring PO Box 226 Orange City IA 51041-0226 E-mail: ahancock@frontiernet.net.

HANCOCK, CHARLES CAVANAUGH, JR., scientific association administrator; b. Riverside, Calif., Oct. 19, 1935; s. Charles Cavanaugh and Mary Elizabeth (Riordan) H.; children: Christopher Alan, Stephen Edward. BS in Chem. Engring, Stanford U., 1958; MS in Indsl. Engring, Tex. Tech U., 1967. Commd. 2d lt. U.S. Air Force, 1958, advanced through grades to lt. col., 1974; worldwide locations in research and devel. and logistics, to, 1979; ret., 1979; exec. officer Am. Soc. Biochem. and Molecular Biology, Bethesda, Md., 1979—; also mgr. Jour. Biol. Chemistry. Gen. sec. 17th Congress of Biochemistry and Molecular Biology; bd. dirs. Chem. Heritage Found., 1993-94. Decorated Meritorious Service medal with 3 oak leaf clusters. Mem. AAAS, Inst. Indsl. Engrs. (sr.), Coun. Engring. and Sci. Soc. Execs., Conv. Liaison Coun. (chmn. 1991-92), Profl. Conv. Mgmt. Assn., Coun. Sci. Editors, Soc. Scholarly Pub., Sigma Xi, Alpha Pi Mu, Univ. Club San Diego. Clubs: Univ. Club. Office: Am Soc Biochem & Molecular Biology 9650 Rockville Pike Bethesda MD 20814-3998 E-mail: chancock@asbmb.faseb.org.

HANCOCK, DIANE KERR, research chemist; b. Mpls., Feb. 6, 1941; d. John Charles and Anena (Hansen) Kerr; m. Kenneth George Hancock, June 27, 1964 (dec. Sept. 1993); children: Kenneth S., John A., Catherine Y. BA, Harvard U., 1963; MA, U. Wis., 1966; PhD, U. Md., 1991. Lectr. environ. toxicology U. Calif., Davis, 1975-77; lab. coord. U. Md., College Park, 1979; rsch. chemist Nat. Inst. Standards and Tech., Gaithersburg, Md., 1980—. Mem. Internat. Com. for Uniform Methods of Sugar Anal, 1983-2000, Washington Editorial Rev. Bd., Nat. Inst. Standards & Tech., Gaithersburg, 1990-91. Patentee in field. Recipient Nat. scholarship Radcliffe Coll., Harvard, 1959, Rsch. assistantship NIH, 1964-66, Women in Sci. award NSF, 1978. Mem. AAAS, Am. Chem. Soc. Home: 15229 Manor Lake Dr Rockville MD 20853-1562 Office: Nat Inst Stds and Tech B254 Bldg 227 Gaithersburg MD 20899-8311 E-mail: diane.hancock@nist.gov.

HANCOCK, DON RAY, researcher; b. Muncie, Ind., Apr. 9, 1948; s. Charles David and June Lamoine (Krey) H. BA, DePauw U., 1970. Cmty. worker Fla. Meth. Spanish Ministry, Miami, 1970-73; seminar designer United Meth. Seminars, Washington, 1973-75; info. coord. S.W. Rsch. and Info. Ctr., Albuquerque, 1975—. Cons. State Planning Coun. on Radiactive Waste Mgmt., Washington, 1980-81; task force mem. Gov.'s Socioecon. Com., Santa Fe, 1983; pub. adv. bd. WIPP Socioecon. Study, Albuquerque, 1979-81. Contbr. articles to profl. jours. Bd. chmn. Roadrunner Food Bank, Albuquerque, 1981-92, N.Mex. Coalition Against Hunger, 1978-85; bd. dirs. Albuquerque Housing and Neighborhood Econ. Devel. Com., 1994-2001, United Meth. Bd. of Ch. and Soc., Washington, 1976-80. Mem. Univ. Heights Assn. (bd. dirs. 1977-82, 85, 88-89, 90-2003). Democrat. Office: SW Rsch and Info Ctr PO Box 4524 Albuquerque NM 87196-4524 E-mail: sricdon@earthlink.net.

HANCOCK, ELLEN MARIE, communications executive; b. N.Y.C., Apr. 15, 1943; d. Peter Joseph and Helen Gertrude (Houlihan) Mooney; m. W. Jason Hancock, Sept. 17, 1971. BA, Coll. New Rochelle, 1965; MA, Fordham U., 1966. With IBM, 1966—, programmer, 1966-81, dir. communications programming sect., communication products div. Raleigh, N.C., 1981-83, v.p. communications programming sect., communication products div., 1983-84, asst. group exec. systems devel. info. systems and storage group Armonk, N.Y., 1985, v.p. telecommunication systems communication prodn. div., 1985-86, pres. communications products div., 1986-88, v.p., gen. mgr. communication system Somers, N.Y., 1988-91, v.p., gen. mgr. networking systems Staines, Eng., 1991-92, sr. v.p., group exec. networking systems, 1992—; v.p. technology Apple Computers, Cupertino, Calif., 1996-97. Bd. dirs. ARDIS Co., Lincolnshire, Ill., Colgate-Palmolive Co., N.Y.C., ROLM Co., IBM UK Holdings Ltd., London, Integrated Systems Solutions Corp.; adv. bd. Fireworks Ptnrs, IBM. Trustee Coll. of New Rochelle, N.Y., 1986—, Marist Coll., Poughkeepsie, 1988—. Roman Catholic. Home: PO Box 169 Ridgefield CT 06877-0169

HANCOCK, GERRE EDWARD, musician, educator; b. Lubbock, Tex., Feb. 21, 1934; s. Ervin Edward and Flake (Steger) H.; m. Judith Duffield Eckerman, July 22, 1961; children: Deborah, Lisa. MusB, U. Tex., 1955; diploma, U. Sorbonne, Paris, 1956; M in Sacred Music, Union Theol. Sem., N.Y.C., 1961; MusD, Nashotah House Episcopal Sem., 1986, U. South, 1999. Asst. organist St. Bartholomew's Ch., N.Y.C., 1960-62; organist, choirmaster Christ Ch. Cathedral, Cin., 1962-71; mem. artist faculty Coll.-Conservatory Music, U. Cin., 1964-71; organist, master choristers St. Thomas Ch., N.Y.C., 1971—; faculty Juilliard Sch., N.Y.C., 1971—, Inst. Sacred Music, Yale U., New Haven, 1974—2002, Eastman Sch. Music, U. Rochester, NY, 1995—2000. Concert organist McFarlane Mgmt., Cleve., 1964—; condr. choral festivals, U.S. and Europe, 1964—; clinician organ and choral workshops, Australia and Republic of South Africa, 1964—. Author: Organ Improvisations, 1976, Improvising: How to Master the Art, 1994; composer: (cantata) Plum Line and City, 1967, (choral works) Missa Resurrectionis, 1979; performer concerts throughout U.S., Can., Europe, South Africa, Australia, Japan. Served with U.S. Army, 1956-58. Fellow Royal Sch. Ch. Music, Am. Guild Organists (past mem. coun.), Royal Coll. Organists (hon.); mem. Assn. Anglican Musicians (founder, past pres.), Phi Mu Alpha Sinfonia (past pres.), Pi Kappa Lambda. Clubs: St. Wilfrid (N.Y.C.) (pres. 1973-74). Independent. Episcopalian. Avocation: tennis. Office: St Thomas Ch 1 W 53rd St New York NY 10019-5496

HANCOCK, HERBERT JEFFREY (HERBIE HANCOCK), composer, pianist, publisher; b. Chgo., Apr. 12, 1940; s. Wayman Edward and Winnie (Griffin) Hancock; m. Gudrun Meixner, Aug. 31, 1968. Student, Grinnell (Iowa) Coll., 1956-60, Roosevelt U., Chgo., 1960, Manhattan Sch. Music, 1962, New Sch. Social Research, 1967. Owner-pub. Hancock Music Co., 1962—; founder Hancock and Joe Prodns., 1989—; pres. Harlem Jazz Music Center, Inc. Performer: Chgo. Symphony Orch., 1982, Coleman Hawkins, 1960, Donald Byrd, 1960—63, Miles Davis Quintet, 1963—68; recorded with Chick Corea, scored (films) The Spook Who Sat By the Door, 1973, Death Wish, 1974, A Soldier's Story, 1984, Jo Jo Dancer, Your Life is Calling, 1986, Action Jackson, Colors, 1988, Harlem Nights, 1989, Livin' Large, 1991, scored and appeared 'Round Midnight, 1986 (Academy award best original score, 1986), albums Takin' Off, 1963, Succotash, Speak Like a Child, 1968, Fat Albert Rotunda, 1969, Mwandishi, 1971, Crossings, Sextant, 1972, Headhunters, 1973, Thrust, The Best of Herbie Hancock, 1974, Man-Child, 1975, The Quintet, V.S.O.P., 1977, Sunlight, 1978, An Evening with Herbie Hancock and Chick Corea in Concert, Feets Don't Fail Me Now, 1979, Monster, Greatest Hits, 1980, Lite Me Up, 1982, Future Shock, 1983, (with Foday Musa Suso) Village Life, 1985, (with Dexter Gordon) The Other Side of 'Round Midnight, 1987, Perfect Machine, 1988, Jamming, 1992, Cantaloupe Island, Tribute to Miles, 1994, Dis Is Da Drum, 1995, The New Standard, 1996, 1 + 1, 1997, Gershwin's World, 1998 (Grammy). Named top jazz artist Black Music mag., 1974; recipient citation of achievement Broadcast Music, Inc., 1963, Jay award Jazz mag., 1964, critics poll for talent deserving wider recognition Down Beat mag., 1967, 1st place piano category, 1968, 1969, 1970, composer award, 1971, All-Star

Band New Artist award Record World, 1968, Grammy award for best rhythm and blues instrumental performance, 1983, 1984, Grammy award for best jazz instrumental composition (co-composer), 1987, Grammy award best jazz instrumental performance, 1995. Mem.: Nat. Acad. TV Arts and Scis., Nat. Acad. Rec. Arts and Scis., Broadcast Music, Jazz Musicians Assn., Pioneer (Grinnell Coll.). Address: Hancock Music # 1600 1880 Century Park E Ste 1600 Los Angeles CA 90067-1661

HANCOCK, JAMES BEATY, interior designer; b. Hartford, Ky. s. James Winfield Scott and Hettie Frances (Meadows) H. BA, Hardin-Simmons U., 1948, MA, 1952. Head interior design dept. Thornton's, Abilene, Tex., 1945-54; interior designer The Halle Bros. Co., Cleve., 1954-55; v.p. Olympic Products, Cleve., 1955-56; mgr., interior designer Bell Drapery Shops of Ohio, Inc., Shaker Heights, 1957-78, v.p., 1979—. Lectr. interior design; works include 6 original murals Broadway Theater, Abilene, 1940, mural Skyline Outdoor Theatre, Abilene, 1950, cover designs for Isotopics mag., 1958-60. With AUS, 1942-46. Recipient 2d place award of oil painting West Tex. Expn., 1940, honorable mention, 1940, Diploma for being an Am. vet. of WWII who liberated France, Govt. of France. Mem. Abilene Mus. Fine Arts (charter), Western Res. Hist. Soc., Cleve. Cir. of the Decorative Arts Trust (charter), Trideca Soc. Cleve Mus. Art, English Speaking Union. Home and Office: 1 Bratenahl Pl Apt 103 Cleveland OH 44108-1152 E-mail: hancockjb@aol.com.

HANCOCK, JOHN COULTER, telecommunications company executive; b. Martinsville, Ind., Oct. 21, 1929; s. Floyd A. and Catherine (Coulter) H.; m. Betty Jane Holden, Feb. 6, 1949; children: Debbie, Dwight, Marilyn, Virginia. BSEE, Purdue U., 1951, MEE, 1955, PhD, 1957. Engr. Naval Avionics Facility, Indpls., 1951-57; asst. prof. elec. engring. Purdue U., West Lafayette, Ind., 1957-60, assoc. prof. elec. engring., 1960-63, prof. elec. engring., 1963-65, head Sch. Elec. Engring., 1965-72, dean Schs. Engring., 1972-84; exec. v.p., chief tech. officer Sprint, Inc., Kansas City, Mo., 1984-86; exec. v.p. corp. devel. and tech. United Telecommunications, Inc., Kansas City, Mo., 1986-88, cons., 1988—. Mem. Nat. Sci. Bd., 1986—; bd. dirs. Hillenbrand Industries, Batesville, Ind. Author: An Introduction to the Principles of Communications Theory, 1961 Fellow IEEE, AAAS, Am. Soc. Engring. Edn. (pres. 1983-84, Lamme award 1980); mem. Nat. Acad. Engring., Sigma Xi, Eta Kappa Nu, Tau Beta Pi.

HANCOCK, JOHN WALKER, III, banker; b. Long Beach, Calif., Mar. 8, 1937; s. John Walker and Bernice H.; m. Elizabeth Hoien, June 20, 1959; children: Suzanne, Donna, Randy, David. BA in Econs, Stanford U., 1958, MBA, 1960. With Security Pacific Nat. Bank, L.A., 1960-92, v.p., 1968-77, sr. v.p., 1977-84, exec. v.p., 1984-92; pres. Bancap Investment Group, Long Beach, Calif., 1992—. Bd. dirs. Harbor Bank; chmn. Meml. Med. Ctr.; commr. Port of Long Beach. Bd. dirs. Long Beach Symphony, Meml. Hosp., Long Beach City Coll. Found. Mem. Stanford U. Alumni Assn., Calif. Club (L.A.), Va. Country Club, Balboa Bay Club, Pacific Club, Bohemian Club, Thunderbird Country Club. Republican. Home: 258 Roycroft Ave Long Beach CA 90803-1717 Office: Bancap Investment Group 192 Marina Dr Long Beach CA 90803-4613

HANCOCK, N(EWELL) LES(LIE), accountant; b. Pitts., Apr. 13, 1943; s. Newell Francis and Mildred Helen (Bouverot) H.; m. Margaret Ann Kendrick, Nov. 30, 1968; children: Michelle Lynn, Jennifer Ann, Marie Noelle. BSBA, U. Denver, 1966; postgrad., various schs., 1969—. CPA, Colo. Supr. Pannell, Kerr, Forster, Denver and Atlanta, 1969-78; mgr. Wolf & Co. of Colo., Inc., Denver, 1978-79, 83-84; supr. Kafoury, Armstrong & Co., Reno, 1979-82; pvt. practice acctg. Arvada, Colo. and Reno, 1982—; mgr. Ashby, Armstrong & Co., Denver, 1984-87; asst. contr. 1st Resorts Inc. and Great Am. Mgmt. Group Inc., Lakewood, Colo., 1987-89; team leader subcontract audit Nat. Renewable Energy Lab., Golden, Colo., 1989—2002. Served to 1st lt. U.S. Army, 1966-69. Mem. AICPA, Colo. Soc. CPAs (report rev. com. 1984-90, pvt. co. practice com. 1990-93, accountancy regulation com. 1993-94, mem. rels. com. 1994-96, mem. svcs. com. 1996-97), Nev. Soc. CPAs (bd. dirs. Reno chpt. 1982-83, auditing stds. com. 1981-82, vice chmn. acctg. principles com. 1981-83), Hospitality Accts. Assn. (sec. 1976-77). Republican. Baptist. Avocations: summer sports, collections. Office: PO Box 740535 Arvada CO 80006-0535

HANCOCK, S. LEE, business executive; b. Knoxville, Tenn., Aug. 11, 1955; s. Melton Donald and Alma Helen (McDaniel) Hancock; m. Kathleen Ann Koll, July 26, 1986. BS summa cum laude, Southwest Mo. State U., 1975; JD cum laude, So. Meth. U., 1979. CPA Mo.; bar: Mo. 1979, U.S. Dist. Ct. (we. dist.) Mo. 1979, U.S. tax Ct. 1982, U.S. Ct. Claims Calif. 1983, Calif. 1988, U.S. Supreme Ct. 1992. Assoc. Blackwell, Sanders, Matheny, Weary & Lombardi, Kansas City, Mo., 1979-83, ptnr., 1984-88, Allen, Matkins, Leck, Gamble & Mallory, Newport Beach, Calif., 1988-98, of counsel, 1998-99; chmn., CEO, Go2 Directory Systems, Newport Beach, Calif., 1998—2001, CEO, 1998—. Bd. dirs. Calif./Orange County Venture Forum, Orange County Cmty. Found., sec., 1994—95, pres., 1995—97; mem. Young Pres. Orgn., 2000—. Mem.: ABA, Lawyers Assn. Kansas City (pres. young lawyers sect. 1986—87, bd. dirs. 1986—87), Orange County Bar Assn., Mo. Bar Assn., Calif. Bar Assn., Young Execs. Am. (bd. dirs. Orange County chpt. 1992—96, pres. Orange County chpt. 1994—95), Order of Coif. Republican. Avocations: flying, sailing, skiing, photography. Home: 4 Hampshire Ct Newport Beach CA 92660-4933 Office: Go2 Directory Systems Ste 320 18400 Von Karman Ave Irvine CA 92612-1514

HANCOCK, SANDRA OLIVIA, secondary school educator, elementary school educator; b. Jackson, Tenn., Oct. 22, 1947; d. Carthel Leon and Thelma (Thompson) Smith; m. Jerome Hancock, Aug. 1, 1969; children: Casey Colman, Mandy Maria. BS, U. Tenn., 1969, MS, 1973; grad. safety seminar, Universal Cheerleaders Assn., 1989. Cert. educator. Educator Lexington (Tenn.) H.S., 1969-70, Clarksburg (Tenn.) H.S., 1970-78, 83-90, Dresden (Tenn.) Jr. H.S., 1994-95; instr. Camden (Tenn.) Elem. Sch., 1995—. Instr. Very Spl. Arts Festival, Carroll County, Tenn., 1994; GED instr. Contbr. poetry to various publs. Cub scout leader Boy Scouts Am., Clarksburg, 1982—84; assoc. mem. St. Labre Indian Sch. and Home Arrow Club, Ashland, Mont., 1988—89; vol. March of Dimes, Leukemia Soc. Am.; mem. fund raising com. Project Graduation Huntingdon H.S., 1992—95; art edn. asst. Huntingdon Spl. Sch. Dist., 1993—94; sec. Harbor Town Property Owners' Assn., 2001—; dir. presch. 1st United Meth. Ch., Huntingdon, 1992—93. Recipient various poetry awards. Mem.: NEA, Tenn. Reading Assn., Haiku Soc. Am., Benton County Tenn. Arts Coun., Poetry Soc. Tenn. (rec. sec 1993—94, spkr. 1994), Am. Assn. Cheerleading Coaches and Advisors, Nat. Cheerleaders Assn. (Superior Advisor Performance award 1988), U.S. Olympic Assn., Tenn. Writers' Alliance, Nat. Fedn. State Poetry Socs., Benton County Reading Assn., Benton County Edn. Assn., Tenn. Edn. Assn., Phi Delta Kappa (N.W. Tenn. chpt. sec. 1993—94). Republican. Avocations: travelling, water skiing, snorkeling. Home and Office: 250 Branch Loop Rd Big Sandy TN 38221 also: Camden Elem Sch 208 Washington Ave Camden TN 38320-1130

HANCOCK, STEWART F., JR., law educator, judge; b. Syracuse, N.Y., Feb. 2, 1923; s. Stewart F. and Marion (MCLennan) H. BS, U.S. Naval Acad., 1945; LLB, Cornell U., 1950; LLD (hon.), Syracuse U., 1993, Le Moyne Coll., 1999. Corp. counsel, chief legal officer City of Syracuse, 1961-63; justice 5th judicial dist. N.Y. Supreme Ct., 1971-77, assoc. justice appellate divsn. 4th judicial dept., 1977-86; assoc. judge N.Y. Ct. Appeals, Albany, 1986-93; disting. vis. prof. law, jurist in residence Syracuse U., 1994—; counsel Hancock & Estabrook, Syracuse, 1994—. Mem. N.Y. State Com. on Profession and the Cts., 1994—. Rep. chmn. Onondaga County, 1964-66; Rep. candidate for Congress, 1966; former mem. Onondaga County Met. Water Bd.; mem. Syracuse Bd. Edn., ARC, Dunbar Ctr., Pebble Hill Sch., Crouse-Irving Meml. Hosp., Syracuse Symphony; mem. First Presbyn. Ch., Cazenovia. Line officer USN, 1945-47, lt. (s.g.) USNR, 1950-51. Fellow Am. Bar Found., New York State Bar Found.; mem. ABA, N.Y. State Bar Assn. (com. on jud. selection, com. on jud. independence, steering com. on commerce and industry, Gold medal for disting. svc. in law 2000), Onondaga County Bar Assn, dir. Frank H. Hiscock Legal Aid Soc. Office: Hancock & Estabrook 1500 Mony Tower 1 PO Box 4976 # 1 Syracuse NY 13221-4976 E-mail: shancock@hancocklaw.com.

HANCOCK, TAPP, elementary school educator; b. Sept. 17, 1958; d. Alexander Hamilton and Tapp Latta Hancock. BA in Elem. and Spl. Edn., Converse Coll., 1980, M Elem. Edn., 1981; specialist in early childhood edn., U. SC, Spartanburg, 1985; MA in Counseling, Calif. Luth. U., 1990. Cert. tchr., counselor Calif. Elem. tchr. Spartanburg City Schs., 1981—86, Granville County Schs., Creedmoor, NC, 1986—87, Bakersfield (Calif.) City Schs., 1987—. Cons. Han-5 Math., Bakersfield, 1995—2002; presenter, spkr. in field. Mem. adv. bd.: McGraw Hill 2002 Math Textbook, 2002, adv. chmn.: Standards for Excellence in Math. and Language Arts, 1997, contbg. editor: C.M.C. Jour., 1999, inventor: math. kits, books/manipulatives Han-5, An Innovative System Teaching Mathematics, 2000. Regional coord. San Joaquiin Valley Math. Project, Bakersfield, 1996—2001; chmn. elem. math. events Bakersfield Math. Coun., 1996—2000; mem. Calif. History-Social Sci. Project, Santa Barbara, 2000—02; master tchr. CBET, Bakersfield, 2001—02. Named Outstanding Tchr. for Kern County, Bakersfield Math. Coun., 1999; recipient regional Presdl. Excellence award in math., NSF, Washington, 1997; scholar, Fulbright Found., 2000—01. Mem.: Nat. Coun. Tchg. Math., Calif. Math. Coun. Avocations: sailing, reading, travel, wine. Office: Han5 Math 8000 Kroll Way Condo # 2 Bakersfield CA 93311

HANCOCK, TERRY BLACKMON, psychologist, educator; b. Houston, Feb. 27, 1954; d. Janice Merle Roberts; m. James David Hancock, Dec. 1, 1979; children: Lindsey Kathleen, William Thomas, James Hunter. BS, Abilene Christian U., 1975; MS, Tex. Woman's U., 1979; PhD, Vanderbilt U., 1988. Cert. psychologist Tenn., 1994. Rsch. assoc. Vanderbilt U., Nashville, 1989—2000, rsch. asst. prof., 2000—. Investigator Kennedy Ctr., Vanderbilt U., Nashville, 1996—; mem. Instl. Rev. Bd., Vanderbilt U., Nashville. Contbr. chapters to books, articles to profl. jours. Grantee Early Identification and Prevention of Conduct Disorders in Head Start Children, Adminstrn. on Children, Youth and Families and Nat. Inst. of Health, 1997—2002, Bldg. Social Communication Skills During Peer Interactions, Adminstrn. on Children, Youth, and Families, 2001—. Mem.: APA (licentiate), Assn. for Play Therapy, Soc. for Prevention Rsch. Achievements include research in with parents and young children and young children's mental health. Home: 6437 Brownlee Dr Nashville TN 37205 Office: Vanderbilt Univ Box 328 GPC Nashville TN 37203 Office Fax: 615-343-1570. Personal E-mail: terry.hancock@vanderbilt.edu. E-mail: terry.hancock@vanderbilt.edu.

HANCOCK, WILLIAM FRANK, JR., management consultant; b. Richmond, Va., Jan. 4, 1942; s. William Frank and Gladys Elizabeth (George) H.; m. Donna G. Hosmer, May 18, 1968; children: Peter James, Jeffrey William, Jennifer Beth. BBA, U. Iowa, 1964; MBA, U. Pa., 1966; postgrad., Capella U. CPA, CLU, CPCU, CMA, CDP. Exec. asst. to exec. v.p. John Hancock Mutual Life Ins. Co., Boston, 1966-69; mgmt. cons. Keane Assocs., Boston, 1969-74, regional mgr., 1974-75; v.p., gen. mgr. comml. sys. SofTech, Inc., Waltham, Mass., 1975-79; dir. internat. sales and field ops. Nixdorf Computer Co., Burlington, Mass., 1979-80; mgr. mktg. Digital Equipment Corp., 1980-84, electronic commerce mgr., 1984-97; mgmt. cons. electronic commerce Grant Thornton LLP, 1997—98; mgmt. cons., nat. electronic commerce practice Ernst & Young, LLP, 1998—2000; prin. IBM, 2000—02; mng. dir. Three Rivers Assocs., Sherborn, Mass., 2002—. Adj. prof. acctg. and fin. Grad. Sch. Bus., Northeastern U., Boston, 1966—, sr. instr. acctg. Grad. Sch. Bus. Babson Coll., Wellesley, Mass, 1985—; vis. prof. Cambridge Coll., 2002—. Treas. Pilgrim Ch.; trustee Sherborn Libr.; chmn. Sherborn coun. Boy Scouts Am. With U.S. Army, 1967-72. Recipient Outstanding Teacher of Yr. Awd., Northeastern Univ., 1989. Mem. AICPA, Data Processing Mgmt., Nat. Assn. Accts., Assn. Computing Machinery, Boston C. of C., Exec. Club Boston, Wharton Alumni Club, U. Iowa Alumni Assn. Congregationalist. Home and Office: Three Rivers Assocs 24 Dexter Dr Sherborn MA 01770-1124 E-mail: whancock@attbi.com.

HANCOX, DAVID R(OBERT), audit administrator, educator; b. Albany, N.Y., Aug. 1, 1951; s. Robert F. and Elaine C. (Morgart) H.; m. Judith A. Gaylord, Jan. 17, 1975; children: Robert, Bradford, Ryan D. AS, Hudson Valley Community Coll., 1973; BBA, Siena Coll., 1975. Cert. internal auditor; cert. govt. fin. mgr. State auditor N.Y. State Comptr., Albany, 1974—; lectr. Albany Bus. Coll., 1982-83, Schenectady (N.Y.) Community Coll., 1988, Siena Coll., Loudonville, N.Y., 1991—, Sage Coll., Albany, 1992-97; dir. state audits N.Y. State Comptr., 1989—. Co-author: State and Local Government, Program Control and Audit: Handbook for Managers and Auditors, 1997, Small Government Finance Library: Accounting, Reporting, Auditing, 1999, Government Performance Audit in Action, 2001. Chair adminstrn. com., v.p. parish coun. St. James Ch., 1994-98, pres. parish coun., 1998-99; cluster leader Albany Diocese, 1995-96. Mem. Assn. Govt. Accts. (pres. N.Y. Capital chpt. 1986-87, bd. dirs. 1987-89, Arlington, Va. regional v.p. 1990—, Gold award 1991), Inst. Internal Auditors (Albany chpt. bd. govs. 1988-90, 93-96, pres. 1996-97), Bd. Dirs., Homeless and Travelers Aid Soc., 1999. Roman Catholic. Avocations: reading, computers, exercising. Home: 21 Magnolia Ter Albany NY 12209-1714 Office: N Y State Comptr 110 State St Albany NY 12236-0001 E-mail: dhancox@nycap.rr.com., dhancox@osc.state.ny.us.

HANCU, ILEANA, research scientist; b. Bucharest, Romania, Dec. 17, 1972; d. Ion Florian and Mariana Cretu; m. Dan Hancu, July 8, 1995; 1 child, Maria Christina. BS, U. Bucharest, Bucharest, Romania, 1995; MS, U. Pitts., Pitts., 1998, PhD, 2001. Rsch. asst. U. Pitts., Pitts., 1996—2001; rsch. scientist GE Global Rsch. Ctr., Niskayuna, NY, 2001—. Reviewer Jour. of Magnetic Resonance, San Diego, 2001—02. Contbr. scientific papers to profl. jour. (Andrew Mellon pre-doctoral fellowship, 2000, Mary Warga pre-doctoral fellowship, 1996). Mem.: Optical Soc. of Am., Internat. Soc. for Magnetic Resonance in Medicine. Achievements include patents pending for Invention Describes Systems And Methods For High Resolution, In Vivo Imaging Of Functional Activity. Office: GE Global Rsch Ctr One Rssch Cir Niskayuna NY 12309 Office Fax: 518-387-6923. E-mail: hancu@research.ge.com.

HAND, BENNY CHARLES, JR., lawyer, judge; b. Valley, Ala., Sept. 12, 1964; s. Benny Charles Sr. and Nelda Lee (Knight) H.; m. Martha Lynne Reynolds, May 29, 1988; children, Hannah Elisabeth, Abigail Faith, Ester Aliyn. BS in Bus. Mgmt., Auburn U., 1987; JD, Cumberland Sch. Law, 1990. Bar: Ga. 1990, Ala. 1990, U.S. Dist. Ct. (mid. dist.) 1990. Account mgr. Shamrock Rentables, Opelika, Ala., 1984-85; owner, pres. Suburban Pro, Opelika, 1985-87; pres. Premier Car Care, Opelika, 1991-94; pvt. practice Opelika, 1990—; judge Wedowee (Ala.) Mcpl., 1995—; city atty. City of Uniontown, Ala., 1995—; bd. dirs. Sim-Ptnrs., East Ala. Sickle Cell. Vice chmn. bd. Beacon Coll., Columbus, Ga., 1995—. Bd. dirs. East Ala. Mental Health Human Rights, Opelika, 1994—; deacon Believers Bapt. Ch., Auburn, 1995—; Rep. nominee U.S. Ho. of Reps., 1994; mem. Lee County Rep. Club. Recipient Rutherford Inst. for Outstanding Svc., 1994. Office: 114 Nth 8th Opelika AL 36801-6040

HAND, BRUCE GEORGE, lawyer; b. Oak Park, Ill., Apr. 11, 1942; s. Robert David and Dorothy Marie (Riedel) H.; m. Carolyn Jeanne Coleman, July 9, 1966; children: Keith John, Tracey Ellen, Katherine Anne. BA in Liberal Arts & Scis., U. Ill., 1964; JD, U. Oreg., 1969. Bar: Wash. 1969, U.S. Dist. Ct. (we. dist.) Wash. 1970. Assoc. Brumbach & Lamb, Seattle, 1969-74; pvt. practice Bellevue, Wash., 1974—. Trustee St. Thomas Sch., Medina, Wash., 1975-85, pres., 1985; trustee, pres. Hamlin Robinson Sch., Seattle, 1986-87. 1st lt. U.S. Army, 1964-66. Mem. Washington State Bar Assn., King County Bar Assn., East King County Bar Assn., Estate Planning Coun. Seattle. Republican. Episcopalian. Avocations: securities investment, reading. Home: 2639 82nd Ave NE Medina WA 98039-1507 Office: 845 106th Ave NE Ste 200 Bellevue WA 98004-4308 E-mail: bhand52@aol.com.

HAND, CADET HAMMOND, JR., marine biologist, educator; b. Patchogue, N.Y., Apr. 23, 1920; s. Cadet Hammond and Myra (Wells) H.; m. Winifred Werdelin, June 6, 1942; children: Cadet Hammond III, Gary Alan. BS, U. Conn., 1946; MA, U. Calif. at Berkeley, 1948, PhD, 1951. Instr. Mills Coll., 1948-50, asst. prof., 1950-51; research biologist Scripps Inst. Oceanography, 1951-53; mem. faculty U. Calif. at Berkeley, 1953—, prof. zoology, 1963-85, prof. emeritus, 1985—; dir. Bodega Marine Lab., 1961-85; Cons. NIH, 1964-66, NSF, 1964-69; mem. atomic safety and licensing bd. panel Nuclear Regulatory Commn., 1971-92, adminstrv. judge atomic safety and licensing bd. panel, 1980-92. NSF sr. postdoctoral fellow, 1959-60; Guggenheim fellow, 1967-68 Contbr. articles to profl. jours. Fellow Calif., Wash. acads. scis.; mem. No. Calif. Malacozool. Soc. (pres. 1963-87), Soc. Systematic Zoology, Ecol. Soc. Am., Ray Soc. (Gt. Britain), Am. Soc. Zoologists (chmn. div. invertebrate zoology 1977-78), Am. Soc. Limnology and Oceanography. Home: PO Box 1016 Bodega Bay CA 94923-9769 Office: Bodega Marine Lab Bodega Bay CA 94923

HAND, CHRISTOPHER MICHAEL, cancer research scientist, medical consultant, therapeutic medical physicist, educator; b. Phila., Jan. 14, 1963; s. Walter Richard Sr. and Mary Anne (Hartzell) H.; m. Patricia Ann Tucci, Oct. 11, 1986; 1 child, Michael David. BA in Biology, Holy Family Coll., 1985; PhD in Radiation Biology, Hahnemann U., 2000. Lab. supr. Hahnemann U., Phila., 1985-94, rsch. scientist, 1994-2000; therapeutic med. physics resident dept. radiation oncology U. Chgo. Hosps., 2000—02; therapeutic med. physicist Dept. Radiation Oncology Abington Meml. Hosp., Abington, Pa., 2002—. Field rschr. Office Naval Rsch., 1991-98; part-time instr. Gwynedd-Mercy Coll., Gwynedd Valley, Pa., 2000—; presenter in field. Contbr. articles to profl. jours. Head basketball coach Mayfair Youth Orgn., Phila., 1989-96. comdr. USNR, 1986—. Bondi fellow, 1996. Mem.: Radiation Rsch. Soc., Am. Assn. Pharm. Scientists (Outstanding Paper award 1994), Am. Assn. Physicists in Medicine, Naval Res. Assn., Beta Beta Beta. Roman Catholic. Avocations: skeet shooting, unicycling, martial arts. Office: Abington Meml Hosp Dept Radiation Oncology 1200 Old York Rd Abington PA 19001- E-mail: cdrradiation@comcast.net.

HAND, HERBERT HENSLEY, finance educator, writer, entrepreneur; b. Hamilton, Ohio, July 11, 1931; s. Herbert Lawrence and Berta Elizabeth (Hensley) H.; m. Katharine Harris Gucker, July 26, 1952; children: Stephen Harris, Herbert Gucker. BS, Ind. U., 1953; MSEE, ABT, MIT, 1955; MBA, U. Miami, 1966; PhD, Pa. State U., 1969. V.p. Hand Oil Co., 1955-65; instr. Pa. State U., 1968-69; asst. and assoc. prof. Ind. U., Bloomington, 1969-73, assoc. prof., 1973-76; disting. prof. entrepreneurship U. S.C. Coll. Bus. Adminstrn., Columbia, 1976-95. State dir. Small Bus. Devel. Ctr. S.C., 1968-69; exec. v.p. Carter-Miot Engring. Co., Columbia, S.C., 1981, also bd. dirs.; pres. Carolina Consultants, 1973-84; chmn., CEO, pres. Phronesis, Inc., 1985-92, Alternative Control Sys. Corp., 1993-99; cons. to numerous cos., 1973—. Author: (with H.P. Sims, Jr.) Managerial Decision Making in the Business Firm-A Systems Approach, 1972, The Profit Center Simulation, 1975; (with A.T. Hollingsworth) A Guide to Small Business Management, 1979, Practical Readings in Small Business, 1979; contbr. over 90 research articles and papers in field to profl. jours.; mem. editorial bd. Bus. Horizons, 1971-73, Acad. of Mgmt. Review, 1975-79; holder numerous U.S. and fgn. patents in field of biotech. Served to 1st lt. USAF, 1953-55. Recipient Western Electric award for most innovative bus. course, 1971, 23 other teaching awards; Small Bus. Inst. Regional award SBA, 1976, 80, 81, Small Bus. Inst. Nat. award, 1980; Office Naval Research grantee, 1976, 77, 78. Mem. Acad. Mgmt., So. Mgmt. Assn., Am. Inst. Decision Scis., Internat. Coun. for Small Bus., Rotary. Presbyterian. E-mail: hekat@bellsouth.net.

HAND, JAMES STANLEY, lawyer; b. Mt. Kisco, N.Y., Mar. 14, 1949; m. Gail Stewart; children: Jordan, Alison. BA, UCLA, 1971; JD, U. N.D., 1980. Bar: N.D. 1980, U.S. Dist. Ct. N.D. 1980, U.S. Ct. Appeals (8th cir.) 1983. Assoc. Anderson and Assocs., Grand Forks, N.D., 1980-82; pvt. practice law Grand Forks, 1982-84; ptnr. Hand & Triplett, Grand Forks, 1984-87; state rep. for U.S. Senator Kent Conrad, 1987—. Adj. grad. faculty Embry-Riddle Aeronautical U., Grand Forks AFB, 1983; lectr. U. N.D., 1985-86. Pub. mem. N.D. Bd. Nursing, Bismarck, 1986-87; mem. Grand Forks County Child Care Resource and Referral Adv. Bd., 1991-96, Grand Forks Fed. Exec. Assn. Bd., 1996—. Recipient Hammer award Nat. Partnership for Reinventing Govt., 1998. Mem.: N.D. Bar Assn. Office: 102 N 4th St Grand Forks ND 58203-3738

HAND, JOHN OLIVER, museum curator; b. N.Y.C., Aug. 17, 1941; s. John Osborn and LaBelle (Bridges) H. BA, Denison U., Granville, Ohio, 1963; MA, U. Chgo., 1967; M.F.A. (Samuel Kress Found. fellow 1969-72), Princeton U., 1971, PhD (Belgian Am. Found. fellow 1972-73), 1978. With edn. dept. Nat. Gallery Art, Washington, 1965-69, curator No. Renaissance painting, 1973—. Preceptor Princeton U., 1971 Author papers in field. Office: Nat Gallery Art Washington DC 20565-0001

HAND, MARY JANE, artist; b. St. Cloud, MN, Oct. 3, 1947; d. Lloyd Arvid and Delores Cecelia (Hand) Wahlberg; children: Amy Beth, Emily Jane, Chelsea Jo. BS in Art edn., U. Minn., 1972; MA in Human Devel., St. Mary's U., 2000. Cert. tchr. art edn., K-12 Minn. Adminstrv. asst. L.J. Graham Advt., N.Y.C., 1984—85, Augsburg Pub., Mpls., 1986, Inst. Cultural Affairs; CNA Augsburg, Ebeneezer, Fairview, Mr. & Mrs. James Kelley, Margaret Hamm Estate. Cons. in field. Fundraiser Mpls. Pk. and Recreation, Mpls. Pub. Schs., Minn. Project Leon, Nicaragua, Pine Range Reservation, Children's Theatre Co., Minn. Orch., Minn. Sinfonia; vol. Minn. Hist. Soc., Mpls. Inst. Art; vol. battered women and children's mental health issues Wasburn Child Guidance Ctr. Home: 2110 Clinton Ave Apt 1 Minneapolis MN 55404-2649

HAND, MARYANNE KELLY, artist, educator; b. Augusta, Ga., Apr. 15, 1955; d. Issac Marvin and Dorothy Whaley Kelly; children: Jill Estes Tatum, Micah Kelly. AA in Graphic Design/Visual Comm., Art Inst. Atlanta, 1974. Tchr. Episcopal Day Sch., Augusta, 1984—91; tchr. art Augusta State U., 1993—2000; pvt. tchr. Transatlantic Antiques, Augusta, 2002—; freelance artist. Represented in pub. and pvt. collections. Named to Nat. Archives Women Artists; recipient Hon. Mention, Manhattan Arts. Mem.: S. Ea. Pastel Soc. Avocations: interior decorating, painting, dancing, woodcarving. Office: Transatlantic Antiques 3309 Washington Rd Augusta GA 30904 E-mail: makart@bellsouth.net.

HAND, PAUL DESAUTELS, SR., social work educator; b. New Bedford, Mass., May 31, 1931; s. Samuel Joseph and Lauretta (Desautels) H.; m. Gloria Elizabeth Zarrella, July 4, 1958; children: Mary E., Michele M., Annette M., Suzanne M., Paul D., Denise M., Joseph W. BA cum laude, Assumption Coll., Worcester, Mass., 1956; MSW, Boston U., 1959; MBA, Anna Maria Coll., Paxton, Mass., 1985. Caseworker ARC, Boston, 1957-58, Worcester (Mass.) Children's Friend Soc., 1959-72; mem. faculty social work Anna Maria Coll., Paxton, 1965-99, ret., 1999; social wk. cons. Mill Hill Nursing Home, Worcester, 1976-93, Mass. Dept. Youth Svcs., Worcester, 1974-96, Notre Dame Long-Term Care Ctr., Worcester, 1985-94, Spring Valley Nursing Home, Worcester, 1988-95; clin. social worker Elmwood Counseling, Worcester, 1989-96. Chmn. Worcester Human Rights Commn., 1985-88; chmn. human rights com. Mass. Dept. Mental Health, 1986-91; mem. affirmative action com. United Way, Worcester, 1986-90; bd. dirs. Y.O.U., Inc., Cath. Charities Diocese of Worcester, Mass. Recipient Key of the City of Worcester, 1976, Appreciation award, City Mgr., Worcester, 1988. Mem. NASW (Lifetime Achievement award Ctrl. Mass. com. Mass. chpt. 2001), Coun. on Social Wk. Edn., Am. Legion, Internat. Fedn. Mental Health, Internat. Critical Incident Stress Found., Inc., Delta Epsilon Sigma. Democrat. Roman Catholic. Avocations: sailing, photography, fishing, tropical fish. Home and Office: 71 Morningside Rd Worcester MA 01602-2545

HAND, PETER JAMES, neurobiologist, educator; b. Oak Park, Ill., Jan. 5, 1937; s. James Harold and Edna Mae (Watson) H.; m. Mary Minnis, Sept. 16, 1958; children: Katherine Patricia, Carol Jane, Margaret Anne, Robin Lynn, Stephen Douglas, Peter James; m. Carol Louise Corson, Oct. 23, 1976; m. Christine L. Arnold, Sept. 19, 1986. VMD, U. Pa., 1961, PhD, 1964. Mem. faculty U. Pa., Phila., 1964—, prof. anatomy, 1979-99, head dept. anatomy, 1980-87, 91-97, emeritus prof., 1999—. Mem. NIH rev. com. Regional Primate Ctrs., 1985-89; mem. nominating com. Lifu Acad. award in Chinese Medicine; adj. faculty Indian River C.C., 2003—. Contbr. articles to profl. jours. Pres. coun. USO, Cape May, NJ, 1972—73, nat. del.; mem. ch. coun. Jupiter First Ch., 2002—; trustee Mid-Atlantic Ctr. for Arts, Cape May, NJ, 1973—74; bd. dirs. Cape May Taxpayers Assn., 1972—74, University City Hist. Soc., Phila., 1978—80; v.p. bd. dirs. Arbors Village Assn., 2002—. NIH grantee, 1970-82, 86-92, 95—. Mem. Am. Assn. Anatomists, Am. Assn. Vet. Anatomists, Soc. Neurosci. (pres. Phila. chpt. 1984-85), Internat. Brain Rsch. Orgn., World Assn. Vet. Anatomists, Internat. Assn. for Study of Pain, Am. Coll. Acupuncture (pres. 1997-98), Internat. Coll. Acupuncture and Electro-Therapeutics, Sigma Xi, Alpha Psi (trustee 1965-87). Republican. Home: 5290 SE Joshua Tree Ter Hobe Sound FL 33455-7891 E-mail: chand33455@adelphia.net., handpain@adelphia.net .

HAND, RANDALL EUGENE, lawyer; b. Temple, Tex., Oct. 26, 1956; s. Robert E. and Ellen M. (Collier) H.; m. Debra S. Spitzer, Nov. 14, 1982. MPA, JD, So. Meth. U., 1981; BA, U. Notre Dame, 1978. Bar: Tex. 1981, U.S. Dist. Ct. (no. dist.) Tex. 1982, U.S. Ct. Appeals (5th cir.) 1986; cert. civil trial lawyer Tex. Bd. Legal Specialization. Assoc. Brutsche & Clements, Dallas, 1981-82, Weil, Brutsche & Clements, Dallas, 1982, Law Offices of Mark C. Clements,

Dallas, 1982-86; shareholder Clements, Allen & Warren, P.C., Dallas, 1986-89; pvt. practice Dallas, 1989-95; bus. svcs. mgr. Tex. Instruments Software, Plano, Tex., 1995-97; contracts mgr. Sterling Software, Plano, Tex., 1997-2000; sr. counsel Allegiance Telecom, Dallas, 2000—. Author (computer program) mediation document system for WordPerfect 5.0, 1989. Mem. North Dallas C. of C., Dallas, 1989. Mem. ABA, Dallas Bar Assn. (computer use and tech. sect., bus. litigation sect.), Am. Arbitration Assn. Office: Allegiance Telecom 9201 N Ctrl Expressway Dallas TX 75231

HAND, VIRGINIA SAXTON, home health nurse; b. Phila., July 21, 1956; d. John Grant and Grace Marie (Palermo) Saxton; m. Arthur L. Hand III, June 2, 1979; children: Arthur IV, Katherine, Ryan, Sean. RN, St. Agnes Med. Ctr. Sch., Nursing, Phila., 1977. RN, Pa. Staff nurse St. Agnes Med. Ctr., Phila., 1977-78, head nurse, 1979-81; staff nurse Frankford Hosp., Phila., 1985-93; home health nurse Phila., 1993—. Mem. Parent's Guild Immaculata Coll., 1999—, v.p., 2000, pres., 2001—; vol. meals to shut-ins St. Matthew Outreach, Phila., 1989—; group facilitator St. Mathew's Mothers of PreTeens, Phila., 1994—2003; mem. Precana team St. Matthew's Ch., 2003; mem. St. Matthew Sacramental Prep Team, 2003. Mem. Father Judge Mother's Assn. (coord. St. Matthew health and wellness 1999—). Roman Catholic. Home: 3212 Cottman Ave Philadelphia PA 19149-1511 E-mail: visnurse@aol.com.

HANDA, Y. PAUL, research scientist, engineering executive; b. Lucknow, Uttar Pradesh, India, Dec. 9, 1950; PhD, U. of Otago, Dunedin, New Zealand, 1975. Postdoctoral fellow UCLA, 1975—76, Wright State U., Dayton, Ohio, 1976—77; rsch. assoc. NRC of Can., Ottawa, Canada, 1977—81; rsch. chemist Allied Chem. Co., Buffalo, 1981—82; assoc. rsch. officer NRC of Can., Ottawa, 1982—87, sr. rsch. officer, 1987—2000; sr. scientist Pactiv Corp., Canandaigua, NY, 2000—. Bd. dirs. TPM&F, SPE, Brookfield, Conn., awards chair, 2000—; mem. editl. bd. Cellular Polymers, Shawbury, Shropshire, England, 2000—; mem.,adv. bd. Jour. Chem. Thermodynamics, London, 1992—98. Contbr. more than 120 articles to profl. jours. Mem.: Am. Chem. Soc., Soc. of Plastics Engrs. Achievements include patents for cellular polymers. Home: 16 Coddington Grove Pittsford NY 14534-4772 Office: Pactiv Corp 2651 Brickyard Rd Canandaigua NY 14424-7990 E-mail: phanda@pactiv.com.

HANDAL, EPHREM I. (IHSAN HANDAL), theology studies educator, deacon; b. Bethlehem, Palestine, Dec. 7, 1950; arrived in U.S., 1979; s. Ibrahim A. and Nijmeh A. Handal; m. Judy C. Handal, Jan. 7, 1989; children: Cyril, Jose Antonio. BA, U. Steubenville, 1983, MA, 1987; D Sacred Theology, Romano-Byzantine Sch. Theology, Duluth, Minn., 2000. Lectr. Bethlehem Bible Coll., 1984—85; rsch. asst. Dominican House of Studies, Washington, 1986—87; pvt. lectr. Missionaries of Charity, Washington, 1992—94; lectr. theology and spirituality Notre Dame Grad. Sch. Christendom Coll., Alexandria, Va., 1988—96; asst. prof. of theology & spirituality Notre Dame Grad. Sch. Christendom, Alexandria, Va., 1996—. Mem. students adv. coun. Evangelizing Islam, 2002; mem. permanent diaconate program Archdiocese of Washington, 2001; del. theol.-pastoral congress and 2d world meeting Holy Father with Families, Rio de Janeiro, 1997. Scholar Pres.'s, U. Steubenville, 1979-1983. Mem.: Fellowship Cath. Scholars, Cath. Bibl. Assn. (assoc.). Office: Notre Dame Grad Sch 4407 Sano St Alexandria VA 22312 Personal E-mail: ephrem1950@hotmail.com.

HANDEL, BERNARD, accountant, actuarial and insurance consultant, lawyer; b. N.Y.C., Sept. 25, 1926; s. Louis and Sarah (Brody) H.; m. Shirley M. Krom. BBA, CUNY; JD, Pace U. With Eisner & Lubin, CPAs, N.Y.C., 1946-52; v.p. Davis Assocs., N.Y.C., 1952-56; pres. Handel Group divsn. H.D.L. Assocs., Inc., Poughkeepsie, N.Y., 1956—, Hudson Valley Planning, Poughkeepsie, 1961—81. Sr. cons. Milliman & Robertson, Inc., 1992-94; bd. dirs. First Ameritas Life Ins. Co. Author books and articles in field; editl. bd. Benefits Quarterly, Pension Mgmt., Corp. Health Care Report, Health and Welfare Benefits Alert. Bd. dirs. Hudson Valley Health Sys. Agy., pres. 1982-84; bd. dirs. Dutchess County Health Planning Coun., 1976-96, Dutchess County chpt. ARC, Am. Health Planning Assocs., 1982-85, Bardavon Opera House, 1985-92; bd. dirs. Dutchess C.C. Found., 1998—, chmn., 2003—; treas. Dutchess County Assn. Sr. Citizens, 1976; past insp. N.Y. State Athletic Commn.; mem. N.Y. State Hosp. Rev. and Planning Coun., 1978-92; trustee Vassar Bros. Hosp., 1986—, vice-chmn., 1991-92, chmn., 1993-95; trustee, sec. Mid-Hudson Health, 1993-2000; chmn. Human Resources Dutchess County Econ. Zone, 1996—; v.p. World Affairs Coun. of Mid-Hudson Valley, 2003—. With U.S. Army, 1945—46. Recipient Americanism award ADL, 1995, Franciscan award St. Francis Hosp., 1994, Chancellor's medal SUNY, 2000. Mem. Internat. Found. Employee Benefit Plans (chmn. cons. actuaries com., chmn. health care svc. com. 1980-83, 88-90, chmn. health care data base com., 1986-87, dir. 1981-83, 85-87, 90-91, 94-96, 99-2001), Acad. of Employee Benefit Authors, IS-CEBS (fellow, gov. coun. 1982-84), N.Y. State Soc. CPAs, ABA, N.Y. State Bar Assn., Rotary, Poughkeepsie Tennis Club. Office: 75 Washington St Poughkeepsie NY 12601

HANDEL, DARRELL DALE, composer, retired music educator; b. Lodi, Calif., Aug. 23, 1933; s. Emil A. and Lenore (Mettler) Handel; m. Marlyn Mainard, May 1, 1955; children: Aaron, Roger, Susan, Jennifer. MusB, U. of the Pacific, 1955, MusM, 1956; PhD, U. Rochester, 1969. Prof. U. Kans., Lawrence, 1966-71, U. S.C., Columbia, 1971-76; prof. composition U. Cin., 1976-2000; ret., 2000. Invited guest composer Kiev Music Fest, 1996. Composer: (mezzo soprano and orch.) Acquainted with the Night, 1981, (soprano and chamber group) The Poems of Our Climate, 1977, (orch.) Kyushu, 1992, (chamber group) Barge Music, 1994, (harp solo and string orch.) Orpheus Left His Heart, 1997, (flute and harp) Vignette, 2003, (albums) Vienna Modern Masters. Recipient numerous awards, ASCAP, 1980—; fellow, Ohio Arts Coun., 1983, 1984. Mem.: Soc. Composers, Am. Music Ctr. Home: 824 Pamplona Ave Davis CA 95616-0149

HANDEL, DAVID JONATHAN, health care administrator; b. NYC, Jan. 2, 1946; s. Milton M. and Ruth (Stamer) H.; m. Julia Elizabeth Noll, June 26, 1971; children: Daniel, Jennifer. BS, Cornell U., 1966; MBA, U. Chgo., 1968. Assoc. planning coordinator for health scis. Northwestern U., Chgo., 1970-73, adminstr. Northwestern U. Med. Clinics and Med. Assocs., 1973-76; dir. planning and implementation Mid-Ohio Health Planning Fedn., Columbus, Ohio, 1976-79; assoc. hosp. adminstr. Vanderbilt U. Hosps., Nashville, 1979-82, assoc. dir. ops., 1982-85; dir. Ind. U. Hosps., Indpls., 1985-96; exec. v.p., COO Clarian Health Ptnrs., Inc., Indpls., 1997—. V.p. United Hosp. Svcs., Indpls., 1986-88, pres., 1989-90, Bedford Reg. Med. Ctr., 1997—, La Porte Regional Health Sys., Inc., 1998—; vice-chmn. Rehab. Hosp. Ind., 2002—; v.p. Goshen Health Sys., 2000—. Contbr. articles to profl. jours. Sr. asst. health svcs. officer USPHS, 1968-70. Fellow Am. Coll. Health Care Execs.; mem. Ind. Hosp. Assn. (bd. dirs. 1994-97). Office: Clarian Health 550 University Blvd Indianapolis IN 46202-5149

HANDEL, MARK DAVID, atmospheric scientist; b. N.Y.C., June 20, 1957; s. Morton E. and Irma Carol (Ruby) H. AB in Physics with honors, U. Chgo., 1979; MS in Oceanog., MIT, 1984, ScD in Atmospheric Physics, 1991. Rsch. meteorologist Hurricane Rsch. Divsn., NOAA, Miami, Fla., 1987; geophysics scholar Phillips Lab., USAF, Bedford, Mass., 1991-92; sr. staff officer Bd. on Atmospheric Sci. and Climate NRC, Washington, 1993-97. Cons. NOAA Disaster Survey for Hurricane Andrew, 1992-93, for Hurricane Iniki, 1992-93; sr. cons. Tigger Co., 1974— Guest editor Climatic Change; contbr. articles to profl. jours. and to Ency. of Weather and Climate. Facilities coord. Nat. Rugby Referees Conf., 1992; chair USA Rugby Conf. on Game, 2002. Hertz Found. fellow, 1979-85. Mem. AAAS, Internat. Hazards Soc., Am. Meteorol. Soc., Am. Geophys. Union, Am. Phys. Soc., New Eng. Rugby Referees (bd. dirs. 1988-92), Potomac Rugby Referees, Ct. Theater of U. Chgo. (bd. dirs. 1977-78). Avocations: stunt kite flying, hiking, rugby football. Home and Office: 2355 Nebraska Ave NW Washington DC 20016-3317 E-mail: tigg@erols.com.

HANDEL, MORTON EMANUEL, management consultation executive; b. N.Y.C., Apr. 12, 1935; s. Benjamin and Mollie (Heller) H.; m. Irma Ruby, Aug. 5, 1956; children: Mark, Gary, Karen. BA, U. Pa., 1956; postgrad., NYU, 1957-59; DHum (hon.), U. Hartford, 2002. V.p. Dale Plastic Playing Card Corp., N.Y.C., 1955-57; gen. mgr. Handel Nets & Fabrics Corp., N.Y.C., 1957-62; pres. A.M. Industries, Inc., Farmingdale, N.Y., 1962-68, Allan Marine, Inc., Deer Park, N.Y., 1969-71; chmn. bd. Marlow Yacht Corp., Deer Park, 1969-71; v.p. fin., sec.-treas. Aurora Products Corp. (subs. Nabisco Inc.), 1971-73, sr. v.p., chief fin. officer, 1973-74; v.p. Rowe Industries Inc., 1971-74; v.p., dir. Aurora Nederland N.V., 1971-74, Aurora Plastics Can. Ltd., 1971-74; v.p. fin., chief fin. officer Coleco Industries Inc., 1974-78, sr. v.p., chief fin. officer, 1978-82, exec. v.p. fin. and adminstrn., 1982-83, exec. v.p. corp. com., 1983-85, exec. v.p. corp. devel., 1985-88, chmn., dir., chief exec. officer, 1988-90; pres., dir. S&H Cons., Ltd, Bloomfield, Conn., 1990—. Bd. dirs. Linens 'N Things, Clifton, N.J.; pres. and dir. Ranger Industries, Inc., Bloomfield, Conn., 1997-2001; chmn. bd. dirs. Marvel Enterprises, Inc., N.Y.C., 1997—; trustee Aurora Products Profit Sharing Trust, 1971-74, Coleco Industries Inc. Pension Plan, 1975-90. Pres. Rochdale Village Civic Assn., 1964-65; pres. bd. dirs. Hartford Symphony Orch., 1976—; bd. dirs. Jewish Children's Svc. Corp., 1976-78; corporator St. Francis Hosp., 1982—; bd. dirs. One Thousand Corp., 1983-95, Greater Hartford Arts Coun., Inc., 1987-89, Hebrew Home for the Aged, 1989—; vice chmn. bd. regents U. Hartford, 1992-2000; trustee, vice chmn. Hartt Sch. Music, 1991—; bd. dirs. Jewish Fedn. of Greater Hartford, 1996-2000, Hartford Dispensary Inc., 1996-2002; bd. overseers Bushnell Ctr. for Performing Arts, 2002—. Mem. Am. Mgmt. Assn., Fin. Execs. Inst., Alpha Epsilon Pi. Home: 41 Ranger Ln West Hartford CT 06117-3040 Office: S&H Cons Ltd One Regency Dr Bloomfield CT 06002-2404 E-mail: morthandel@aol.com.

HANDEL, PETER H. physics educator; b. Hermannstadt, Siebenbuergen, Transylvania, Oct. 16, 1937; came to U.S., 1969; s. Peter and Anna (Broneske) H.; children: Susanne C., Christine D., Peter F. MS in Physics, U. Bucharest, Romania, 1959; PhD in Physics, U. Bucharest, 1965. Scientist Hydroetechnic Rsch. Inst., Bucharest, 1959; rsch. scientist Physics Inst. of Romanian Acad., Bucharest, 1960-66, Physics Inst. Max von Laue-Paul Langevin, Munich, Fed. Republic Germany, 1967-69; assoc. prof. physics dept. U. Mo., St. Louis, 1969-72, prof. physics, 1972—. Cons. Emerson Electric Co., St. Louis, 1975-81; sr. scientist, cons. McDonnell Douglas Rsch. Labs., St. Louis, 1982-83; 16 prestigious vis. prof. appointments, various univs. in Europe, Australia, Japan, and U.S., 1970—; mem. internat. program com. of conf. series on noise in phys. systems and head conf. series on quantum 1/f noise. Author quantum 1/f noise theory and of the polarization catastrophe theory of cloud electrification; contbr. over 190 articles to profl. jours.; patentee in field. Grantee NSF, 1971-77, 90—; rsch. grantee USAF, 1984—. USN, 1978-82, 90—, Ultra-low Phase Noise MURI, 2001—. Office: U Mo Dept Physics 8001 Natural Bridge Rd Saint Louis MO 63121-4901 E-mail: handel@umsl.edu.

HANDEL, RICHARD CRAIG, lawyer; b. Hamilton, Ohio, Aug. 11, 1945; s. Alexander F. and Marguerite (Wilks) H.; m. Katharine Jean Carter, Jan. 10, 1970. AB, U. Mich., 1967; MA, Mich. State U., 1968; JD summa cum laude, Ohio State U., 1974; LLM in Taxation, NYU, 1978. Bar: Ohio 1974, S.C. 1983, U.S. Dist. Ct. (so. dist.) Ohio 1975, U.S. Dist. Ct. S.C. 1979, U.S. Tax Ct. 1977, U.S. Ct. Appeals (4th cir.) 1979, U.S. Supreme Ct. 1979; cert. tax specialist. Assoc. Smith & Schnacke, Dayton, Ohio, 1974—77; asst. prof. U. S.C. Sch. Law, Columbia, 1978—83; ptnr. Nexsen, Pruet, Jacobs & Pollard, Columbia, 1983—87, Moore & Van Allen, Columbia, 1987—88, Nexsen Pruet Jacobs & Pollard, Columbia, 1988—89; chief tax policy and appeals S.C. Tax Commn., Columbia, 1989—95; chief coun. Policy S.C. Dept. of Revenue, Columbia, 1995—2003, sr. adminstr., gen. counsel, 2003—. Adj. prof. U. S.C. Sch. Law, 1990—2001. Contbr. articles to legal jours. Bd. dirs. Friends of Richland County Pub. Libr., 1993-99. With U.S. Army, 1969-70, Vietnam. Recipient Outstanding Law Prof. award, 1980-81; Gerald L. Wallace scholar, 1977-78. Mem.: ABA (com. state and local taxes, chmn. membership com. 1997—, vice-chmn. com. tax procedures 1993—94, com. stds. tax practice, sec. 2003—), Order of Coif., S.C. Bar Assn. Office: SC Dept Revenue PO Box 125 301 Gervais St Columbia SC 29214-0702 E-mail: rickch@aol.com., handelr@sctax.org.

HANDELMAN, ALICE SAMUELS, public relations professional, writer; b. Bklyn., Mar. 17, 1943; d. Ned Harlan and Margaret (Isaacs) Samuels; m. Howard Talbot Handelman, Aug. 29, 1965; children: Karen, Patricia Handelman Bloom, Marjorie Lynn. BJ, U. Mo., 1965. Intern reporter Miami (Fla.) News, summer 1964; staff feature writer St. Louis Blues hockey club, 1968-77; freelance writer St. Louis, 1967—; cmty. rels. assoc. Jewish Ctr. for Aged of Greater St. Louis, Chesterfield, Mo., 1981-85, dir. cmty. rels., 1985-2000. Pub. rels. cons. Jewish Family and Children's Svc., St. Louis, 1983, 89; guest lectr. Maryville U., 1997. Author, photographer: LaSalle Street--A History of the St. Louis Wholesale Flower market, 1987; freelance writer, contbr. to St. Louis Globe-Dem., St. Louis Post-Dispatch, N.Y. Times, St. Louis Jewish Light, St. Louis Blues Goal Mag., Hockey News, Hockey World, Ladue News, Sporting News, Nat. Hockey League, Hockey Pictorial, Suburban Jour. Newspapers; writer copy for Knight's Catalogue, 1983. Instr. hockey for women Meramec C.C., St. Louis, 1976—77; adv. com. vis. prof. program JCA Assocs., 1981—83, Gerontol. Inst., St. Louis, 1981—83; pres. Weber Sch. PTA, Creve Coeur, Mo., 1982; mem. Women's Am. ORT, 1965; mem. ctrl. advancement team Pkwy. Ctrl. H.S., 1985—89; photographer Tour de Cure bicycle ride to benefit Am. Diabetes Assn., 1992, 1993; sec., bd. dirs. Gateway Elder Svcs., 1998—, pres., 1999—; chair devel. com. Mideast Area Agy. on Aging, 2001—03; pub. rels. chmn. Nat. Coun. Jewish Women, 1981—83, publicity chmn. fashion sale, 1985; life mem. Jewish Hosp. Aux., 1965—, Jewish Ctr. for Aged Aux., 1986—, Nat. Coun. Jewish Women; pres. Young Women's Coun. on Edn. of Jewish Fedn. St. Louis, 1969; mktg./pub. rels. com. Reform Jewish Acad. St. Louis, 2000—01, Jewish Family and Children's Svc., 2000; mem. pub. rels. com. Temple Israel, 2000, 2001; bd. dirs. Am. Jewish Com., 2001—03; bd. dirs. women's divsn. Jewish Fedn. St. Louis; bd. dirs. Mideast Area Agy. on Aging, 1997—. Recipient William Randolph Hearst award Hearst Found., Columbia, Mo., 1965, United Way Graphic Design award, 1986, United Way Photography award, 1987, 89, 2d place award Guide to Jewish Life in St. Louis photo contest, 1989, 2d place award Jewish Hosp. St. Louis Generations of Women photo contest, 1989, Star Communicator comm. program award United Way Greater St. Louis, 1990, Bronze Photography award, 1995, 15 Yr. Svc. award Jewish Ctr. for Aged, 1997, Fred Goldstein Communal Svc. award Jewish Fedn. St. Louis, 1998; named St. Louis Woman of Achievement, 2002; Besse Marks Meml. scholar, 1964-65. Mem. Nat. Fedn. Press Women (1st place award comm. contest, 3d place photo feature 1989, 3d place award advt. photography 1993, hon. mention advt. photo, 2d place mktg. new svc. award, 2d place mag. advt., 1996, 3d place direct mail mktg. fundraising lit., 2d place direct mail advt.-fund raising Ann. NFPW Comm. Contest 1996, 3d place Color mag. advt. 1996, St. Louis chpt. Quest award for disting. achievement in comm. 2000, 1st place award for personality profile 2002), Jewish Ctr. for Aged Aux., Fellows of Jewish Hosp., Mo. Press Women (1st place corp. newsletter category state feature writing comm. contest 1988, 93, 1st place advt. photography, 2d place feature article, 3 1st place awards 1994, 1st place not for profit newsletter 1994, 5 1st place comm. awards 1995, 2d pl. feature writing, 1st place newsletter award Mo. Assn. of Homes for the Aging 1994, planning com. Fair St. Louis Srs. Day 1995-98, planning com. Srs. Day VP Fair 1994), Mo. Assn. Homes for the Aging (publicity com., Outstanding 1st Place Newsletter award), Mo. Press Women (pub. chmn. 1994, 2000—), Women in Comm. (Ruth Philpott Collins award 1984, Best in the Midwest 2d place feature writing 1992), Press Club Met. St. Louis (bd. dirs. 2002, 1st v.p. 2003), Westwood Country Club. Jewish. Home: 12 Terry Hill Ln Saint Louis MO 63131-2422

HANDELSMAN, LAWRENCE MARC, lawyer; b. N.Y.C., Jan. 17, 1945; s. David and Ruth (Litner) H.; m. Sara Pruzan, June 10, 1967; children: Sharon, Carolyn. BBA, CCNY, 1965; JD, NYU, 1968. Bar: N.Y. 1968, U.S. Ct. Mil. Appeals 1969, U.S. Dist. Ct. (so. and ea. dists.) N.Y. 1973, U.S. Ct. Appeals (2d cir.) 1973, Fla. 1978. Assoc. Stroock & Stroock & Lavan, N.Y.C., 1973-78, ptnr., 1979—. Served to capt. JAGC, U.S. Army, 1969-73. Mem. ABA (bus. bankruptcy com. 1969—), Assn. of Bar of City of N.Y. (bankruptcy com. 1974-77, 1985—). Home: 22 Scarsdale Farm Rd Scarsdale NY 10583-1919 Office: Stroock & Stroock & Lavan 180 Maiden Ln Fl 36 New York NY 10038-4937 E-mail: lhandelsman@stroock.com.

HANDELSMAN, YEHUDA, endocrinologist, internal medicine physician; b. Tel Aviv, Aug. 22, 1947; came to U.S., 1969; s. Jacob and Zahava (Lewin) H.; m. Nava Dina Pedazur, Feb. 22, 1986; children: Tomer Lee, Roy Gil. AA with honors, San Joaquin Delta Coll., Stockton, Calif., 1973; BA summa cum laude, U. of the Pacific, Stockton, Calif., 1975; MD, Tel Aviv U., 1984; postdoctoral fellow, U. So. Calif., 1988-89. Diplomate Am. Bd. Internal Medicine. Intern Beekman Downtown Hosp., N.Y.C., 1985-86, resident in internal medicine, 1986-88; clin. fellow in diabetes and endocrinology L.A. County-U. So. Calif. Med. Ctr., L.A., 1988-89; attending physician Midway Hosp., L.A., 1990-93, Granada Hills (Calif.) Cmty. Hosp., 1991—, Encino-Tarzana (Calif.) Med. Ctr., 1991—, head sect. endocrinology, dir. med. edn. Diabetes Care Ctr. Cons., bd. dirs. Dynamic Home Care, L.A., Las Vegas, 1991—; cons. Yad B'yad-Human Saving Fund, L.A., 1991—; clin. instr. medicine U. So. Calif. Med. Sch., 1988-90; dir. endocrine quar. conf. Encino-Tarzana Med. Ctr., dir. monthly diabetes edn. seminars, 1995—, head of sect. 1998—; mem. diabetes edn. faculty Bristol Myers Squibb, 1997—; mem. spkrs. bur. Parke-Davis, 1997—; co-chmn. Internat. Com. for Insulin Resistance, 2003. Med. columnist Israel Shelanu, 1992-94, L.A. News, 1989-91, L.A. Health News, 2001-03. Bd. dirs. Diabetes Care Ctr. Encino-Tarzana Hosp., 1994—; dir. Israeli Spl. Olympic Games, 1968-82. Fellow ACP, Am. Coll. Endocrinology (co-chmn. nat. task force for insulin resistance 2001-02); mem. AMA (Physician Recognition award 1988, 95, 98), Am. Assn. Clin. Endocrinologists (bd. dirs. 2002—), Calif. Med. Assn. (Physician Recognition award 1995, 98), N.Am. Menopause Soc., Nat. Osteoporosis Found., Am. Diabetes Assn., Am. Israeli Med. Soc., L.A. County Med. Assn., Calif. Med. House Staff Assn., Am. Med. Student Assn., Coun. Israel Cmty. (pres.), Phi Kappa Phi, Theta Alpha Phi, Alpha Gamma Sigma, Delta Sy Omega. Avocations: talk show host, theater, basketball, politics, music. Office: 18372 Clark St #212 Tarzana CA 91356-2804

HANDFORD, MARTIN JOHN, illustrator, author; b. London, Sept. 27, 1956; s. Ruth Winter. BA, Maidstone Art Coll., 1980. Author, illustrator: Where's Waldo?, 1987, Find Waldo Now, 1988, The Great Waldo Search, 1989, Where's Waldo? The Ultimate Fun Book, 1990, Where's Waldo? The Magnificent Poster Book, 1991, Fun With Waldo, 1992, More Fun With Waldo, 1992, Where's Waldo? In Hollywood, 1993, Where's Waldo? The Dazzling Deep-Sea Divers Sticker Book, 1994, Where's Waldo? The Wildly Wonderful Activity Book, 1995, Where's Waldo? The Simply Sensational Activity Book, 1995, Where's Waldo? The Completely Crazy Activity Book, 1997, Where's Waldo? The Wonder Book, 1997, Plundering Pirates: A Where's Waldo? Fun Fact Book, 2001, Fighting Knights: A Where's Waldo? Fun Fact Book, 2001, Where's Waldo? With Free Magnifying Lens, 2002, Where's Waldo Now?, 2002. Office: care Candlewick Press 2067 Massachusetts Ave Cambridge MA 02140-1340

HANDLEMAN, AARON L. lawyer; b. Bridgeport, Conn., Mar. 31, 1946; s. Howard W. and Beatrice (Kaplan) H.; m. Sandra R. Landow, Aug. 31, 1969; children: Michelle, Jessica. BA, Marietta Coll., 1968; JD, George Washington U., 1971. Bar: D.C. 1971, U.S. Dist. Ct. D.C. 1971, Md. 1972, U.S. Supreme Ct. 1978. Ptnr. Danzansky, Dickey, Tydings et al, Washington, 1971-81, Finley, Kumble, Wagner, Heine, Underberg, Manley & Casey, Washington, 1981-87, Laxalt, Washington, Perito & Dubuc, 1988-90, Eccleston & Wolf, Washington, 1990—. Gen. counsel, bd. dirs. Cultural Alliance Greater Washington, 1981-89; trustee Marietta Coll., Ohio, 1985-90, 92—. Named Outstanding Young Alumni Marietta Coll., 1981. Mem. Marietta Coll. Alumni Assn. (pres. 1990-92). Democrat. Jewish. Home: 11713 Le Havre Dr Potomac MD 20854-3175 Office: Eccleston & Wolf 2001 S St NW Washington DC 20009

HANDLER, ARTHUR M. lawyer; b. N.Y.C., Feb. 16, 1937; BS, Queens Coll., 1957; LLB, Columbia U., 1960. Bar: N.Y. 1960, U.S. Dist. Ct. (ea. dist.) N.Y. 1960, U.S. Dist. Ct. (so. dist.) N.Y. 1963, U.S. Tax Ct. 1971, U.S. Ct. Appeals (2d cir.) 1971, U.S. Supreme Ct. 1965. Staff counsel SEC, Washington, 1960-61; law clk. to Judge Richard H. Levet, U.S. Dist. Ct. for So. Dist.N.Y., N.Y.C., 1961-62; asst. U.S. atty. So. Dist. N.Y., N.Y.C., 1962-65; assoc. Proskauer, Rose, Goetz & Mendelsohn, N.Y.C., 1965-67, Golenbock and Barell, N.Y.C., 1967-70, ptnr., 1970-89, Whitman & Ransom, N.Y.C., 1990-93, Burns Handler & Burns, N.Y.C., 1993-99, Handler & Goodman, N.Y.C., 1999—. Arbitrator Am. Stock Exchange, N.Y.C., 1986—. Vol. atty. Pres.'s Com. for Civil Rights under Law, Jackson, Miss., 1966. Mem. ABA, N.Y. State Bar Assn., Bar Assn. of City of N.Y., Fed. Bar Council, Am. Arbitration Assn. (arbitrator 1969—). Clubs: University (N.Y.C.); Lords Valley Country (Hawley, Pa.) (bd. govs. 1977-80). Avocations: golf, skiing, theatre, travel. Office: Handler & Goodman LLP 805 3d Ave New York NY 10022

HANDLER, HAROLD ROBERT, lawyer; b. Jersey City, Aug. 24, 1935; s. Morris Sidney and Fan (Krieger) Handler; m. Lynne Tishman Handler; children from previous marriage: Maren, Jeremy, Jolyon. BS, Lehigh U., 1957; LLM, Columbia U., 1961. Bar: N.Y. 1961, U.S. Tax Ct. 1963, U.S. Ct. Appeals (2d cir.) 1980. Atty., advisor U.S. Tax Ct., Washington, 1961-63; assoc. Simpson Thacher & Bartlett, N.Y.C., 1963-69, ptnr., 1970-97, of counsel, 1998—. Adj. assoc. prof. law NYU, 1978-80. Chmn. fin. com., citizens adv. com. Met. Transp. Authority, N.Y.C., 1975—79; trustee Citizens Budget Commn.; chmn. bd., chmn. exec. com. Jewish Cmty. Ctr. in Manhattan, N.Y.C., 1992—2001; trustee Jewish Communal Fund, 1997—. Fellow Am. Coll. Tax Counsel; mem. ABA, N.Y. State Bar Assn. (chmn. subcom. tax sect. 1979-83, mem. exec. com. tax sect. 1990—, officer 1996-2000, chair 1999-20000), Assn. of Bar of City of N.Y. (chmn. tax com. 1983-86, mem. tax coun. 1990-98), Am. Law Inst., Inst. Fed. Taxation (panelist), Inst. Securities Regulation (panelist).

HANDLER, JEROME SIDNEY, anthropology educator; b. N.Y.C., Sept. 3, 1933; s. Sam and Sara (Wieder) H.; children— Joshua Martin, Lisa Frances. BA, UCLA, 1956, MA, 1959; PhD, Brandeis U., 1965. From asst. prof. to prof. anthropology So. Ill. U., Carbondale, 1964-93, prof. Black Am. studies, 1993-95, prof. emeritus, 1995—. Olive B. O'Connor vis. prof. Am. instns. Colgate U., Hamilton, N.Y., 1971-72; hon. rsch. asst. Univ. Coll., London, 1966-67; staff archaeologist New World Archaeol. Found., Chiapas, Mex., 1957; cons. AID, fall, 1964, Peace Corps, summer 1969; cons. Libr. of Congress, 1998, 99, 2000, 01, panelist NEH, 1977-79, 82; mem. adv. com. African Burial Ground, N.Y.C., GSA, 1991-93. Author: A Guide to Source Materials for the Study of Barbados History, 1627-1834, 1971, The Unappropriated People: Freedmen in the Slave Society of Barbados, 1974, Supplement to A Guide to Source Materials for the Study of Barbados History, 1991; co-author: Plantation Slavery in Barbados: An Archaeological and Historical Investigation, 1978, Searching for a Slave Cemetery in Barbados: A Bioarcheological and Ethnohistorical Investigation, 1989 Vis. Rsch. fellow U. W.I., Jamaica, 1969-70, Barbados, 1983; research assoc. Research Inst. for Study of Man, N.Y.C., 1978-79; vis. scholar Center for Afro-Am. Studies, UCLA, 1980, Dept. Afro-Am. Studies, Harvard U., summer 1992; Rsch. grantee NSF, 1966-67, 71-73, Wenner-Gren Found. Anthrop. Rsch., 1971-72, 87, Rsch. Inst. Study Man, 1962, 70, NIH, 1965, Am. Philos. Soc., 1968, Nat. Geographic Soc., 1987, Nat. Endowment for Humanities Inst. for Coll. Tchrs., 1997-98; Nat. Endowment for Humanities fellow, 1969-70, 75-76, 79; Travel grant Am. Coun. Learned Socs., 1977, grantee Social Sci. Rsch. Coun. and Am. Coun. Learned Socs. Joint Com. on Latin Am. Studies, 1983; Nat. Humanities Ctr. fellow, 1982-83, John Carter Brown Library fellow, 1985, 88, 2002, DuBois Inst. Afro-Am. Rsch. fellow Harvard, 1989 90; fellow Va. Found. Humanities, 1995-99, sr. fellow, 2002; Va. Found. sr. fellow, 2002—; fellow Libr. Co. Phila., 2002. Fellow Am. Anthrop. Assn. (rep. to Am. Coun. Learned Socs. 1985-90); mem. Caribbean Studies Assn. (past mem. exec. council) Home: 120 Blithe Ct Charlottesville VA 22901 Office: Va Found Humanities 145 Ednam Dr Charlottesville VA 22903-4629

HANDLEY, GERALD MATTHEW, lawyer, educator; b. Phila., Dec. 7, 1942; s. John F. and Helen E. (Gerdelman) H.; m. Sandra I. Martin, June 13, 1970; children: Christopher, Elizabeth. BS, La Salle Coll., Phila., 1965; JD, U. Mo., Kansas City, 1972. Bar: Mo. 1972, U.S. Dist. Ct. (we. dist.) Mo. 1972, U.S.Supreme Ct., 1976, U.S. Ct. Appeals (8th and 10th cirs.) 1980, U.S Dist. Ct. Kans. 1998. Asst. pub. defender Office Pub. Defender, Kansas City, Mo., 1972-73, 1st asst. pub. defender, 1973-75, interim pub. defender, 1975-76; ptnr. Speck & Handley, Kansas City, 1980-90; pvt. practice Law Offices of G. Handley, Kansas City, 1991-92, 93—; ptnr. Handley Larsen, Kansas City, 1992-93. Lectr. Rockhurst Coll., Kansas City, 1976-78; instr. U. Mo. Sch. Law. Contbr. chpts. to law books. Pres., Home Owners Assn., Kansas City, 1980. Served with U.S. Army, 1966-67, Vietnam. Fellow Am. Bd. Criminal Lawyers; mem. ABA, NACDL, Fed. Bar Assn., Mo. Bar Assn., (Lon Hocker Trial Lawyer award 1977), Mo. Assn. Criminal Def. Lawyers (pres. 1980, hon. bd. dirs.), U.S. Supreme Ct. Bar Assn., 8th Cir. Bar Assn., Kansas City Met. Bar Assn. Roman Catholic. Avocations: golf, gardening. Home: 22 W 54th St Kansas City MO 64112-2816 Office: 1100 Main Ste 2800 Kansas City MO 64105 E-mail: ghandley@swbell.net.

HANDLEY, LEON HUNTER, lawyer; b. Lakeland, Fla., Sept. 9, 1927; s. Driskle Hubert and Mamie (Denmark) H.; m. Mary Virginia Wolfe, May 2, 1953; children: Leon Hunter, Mary Ellen, Laura Catherine, Leann Virginia. BSBA with honors, U. Fla., 1949, JD, 1951. Bar: Fla. 1951, U.S. Dist. Ct. (so. dist.) Fla. 1952, U.S. Dist. Ct. (mid. dist.) Fla. 1962, U.S. Supreme Ct. 1956, U.S. Ct. Appeals (5th cir.) 1960, U.S. Ct. Appeals (11th cir.) 1981. Pres. Gurney & Handley, Orlando, Fla., 1951—. Bd. dirs. Orlando/Tampa Cracker Groves, Inc., Orlando, 1964—; v.p., bd. dirs. So. Indsl. Savs. Bank, Orlando, Claude H. Wolfe, Inc., Orlando, 1969—; pres., chmn. bd. dirs. Mine & Mill Supply Co., Lakeland, 1966—; gen. counsel, life dir., past pres. Cen. Fla. Fair; chmn. bd. trustees Sta. WMFE-TV. Pres. Chesley Magruder Charitable Trust; elder Presbyn. Ch.; trustee Lake Highland Prep. Sch., Orlando. Warrant officer U.S. Maritime Svc., 1945-46, ETO; sgt. U.S. Army, 1946-48, Korea; capt. USAFR, 1949-59. Named one of Best Lawyers in Am.; named to U. Fla. Hall of Fame. Fellow Am. Coll. Trial Lawyers; mem. ABA, Am. Bd. Trial Advocates (Fla. Trial Lawyer of Yr. 1966, advocate), Orange County Bar Assn. (past pres.), Fla. Bar Assn. (past pres. sta. jr. bar sect., bd. govs. 1959-60), Fedn. Ins. and Corp. Counsel, Internat. Assn. Def. Counsel, Assn. Def. Trial Attys., Trial Attys. Am., Am. Judicature Soc., Pres.'s Coun. (founder U. Fla. chpt.), Citrus Club, Orlando Country Club, Univ. Club, Masons (grand orator Fla. 1982, 86), K.T., Shriners, Scottish Rite (33d degree, insp. gen. hon. 1979), Rotary (pres. Orlando chpt. 1984, Paul Harris fellow), Travelers' Century Club, Fla. Blue Key (pres. 1951), Phi Delta Phi, Alpha Tau Omega (pres. U. of Fla. chpt. 1951), Phi Kappa Phi, Alpha Kappa Psi, Beta Gamma Sigma. Republican. Avocations: jogging, handball. Home: 1800 Turnberry Ter Orlando FL 32804-6015 Office: Gurney & Handley 225 E Robinson St Ste 450 Orlando FL 32801-1905

HANDLIN, JOSEPH JASON, lawyer; b. NYC, Feb. 21, 1952; s. Nathan and Beatrice (Greenberg) H.; m. Laura Sara Ellin, Aug. 18, 1985. AB magna cum laude, Harvard U., 1973; JD, NYU, 1976. Bar: N.Y. 1977, U.S. Dist. Ct. (so. and ea. dists.) N.Y. 1977. Gen. counsel Muzak Corp., N.Y.C., 1977-78; assoc. Estroff, Frankel & Waldman, N.Y.C., 1978-80, Guggenheimer & Untermyer, N.Y.C., 1980-84, Dahan & Nowick, N.Y.C., 1984-86, Epstein, Becker, Borsody & Green P.C., N.Y.C., 1986-87; ptnr. Surkin & Handlin, N.Y.C., 1987-98; prin. Law Offices of Joseph J. Handlin, N.Y.C., 1998—. Adj. instr. Cardozo Law Sch., N.Y.C., 1983—88; asst. prof. NYU, 1988—2002, assoc. prof., 2002—. Recipient Lewis F. Powell, Jr. Medal for Excellence in Adv. Am. Coll. Trial Lawyers, 1975. Mem.: ABA, N.Y. County Lawyers Assn., Assn. of Bar of City of NY (sec. com. on small law firm mgmt. 1993—96, chair 1996—99, com. on real property law 1999—2002, com. on land use planning and zoning 2002—), N.Y. State Bar Assn. (ho. of dels. 1999—2003), Harvard Club (sec. admissions com. 1986—87, chmn. admissions com. 1990—92, bd. mgrs. 1992—95, sec. club 1996—2000, v.p. 2000—02, pres. 2002—). Home: 345 S End Ave Apt 4N New York NY 10280-1064 Office: Law Offices of Joseph J Handlin 75 Maiden Ln Fl 3 New York NY 10038-4810 E-mail: jhandlin@ksi.com.

HANDMAN, BOBBIE (BARBARA HANDMAN), foundation executive; V.p., N.Y. regional dir. People for the Am. Way Found., Washington. Organizer A Quiet Walk for the First Amendment. Recipient Nat. Medal of Arts, 1998. Office: People for the Am Way 2000 M St NW Ste 400 Washington DC 20036-3397 E-mail: pfaw@pfaw.org.

HANDS, ERIC WILLIAM, civil engineer, general engineer, researcher; b. Oakland, Calif., Sept. 27, 1943; s. Richard Ford Hands and Esther Mae (Larson) Hazelet; m. Monica Louise Ulery, 1968 (div. 1973); 1 child, Lars Michael Foxen; m. Sherrill Ann Gardner, 1977 (div. 1985); 1 child, Lief Forrest. Student, U. Calif., Davis, 1975-80, U. Wash., DC, 1981-82, 84, Griffin Bus. Coll., 1983; BS Regents Coll., U. State NY, Albany, 1984; student, West Coast U., 1988. Engr.-in-tng., Calif., 1985, EPA universal type, EPA; cert. advanced marine firefighter 2002, marine firefighter. Engring. technician, software developer Naval Undersea Warfare Engring. Sta., Keyport, Wash., 1980-81; engr., carpenter, sales profl. various orgns., 1984—; real estate/ins. sales staff Channel Islands Real Estate/Met. Ins., Port Hueneme, Camarillo, Calif., 1985; civil engr. Martin, Northart & Spencer, Santa Barbara, Calif., 1985-86, Dept. Pub. Works, County of Santa Barbara, Santa Barbara, Calif., 1986-87; owner, tech. cons. Winters Soldiers Cons., Seattle, 2001—. Author, editor: Energy and Resources, 1976. Sr. team leader, sustaining mem. Rep. Nat. Com., 2000—; contbg. mem. Dem. Nat. Com., 1993; hon. mem. Rep. Nat. Com., 1992; sr. team leader Nat. Rep. Congl. Com., 2001, sr. del., mem. bus. adv. coun.(EPA Universal Tech.), 2002—03. Named one of 2000 Outstanding Scientists of 20th Century, 2001, 2000 Outstanding Scientists of 21st Century, 2002; recipient Cert. of Appreciation, Nuc. and Plasma Sci. Soc., 2000. Mem.: NSPE, ASCE, IEEE (cons. AICN 2000 database), Internat. Brotherhood of Elec. Workers, Sailors Union of the Pacific, NY Acad. Sci., Wash. Soc. Profl. Engr. (rec. sec. Seattle chpt. 1998—2001), United Brotherhood Carpenters and Joiners (Shipwrights and Joiners), Am. Legion (asst. adj. Queen Anne Post 170) (Winter Soldier Cons., 2001) (asst. adj. Queen Anne Post 170). Home and Office: 5035 15th Ave NE Apt 205 Seattle WA 98105-4335 Address: Winter Soldier Cons Ste 1339 4739 University Way NE Seattle WA 98105-4412 E-mail: eds2@seanet.com.

HANDS, TERENCE DAVID (TERRY HANDS), theater and opera director; b. Jan. 9, 1941; s. Joseph Ronald and Luise Berthe (Kohler) H.; m. Josephine Barstow, 1964 (div. 1967); m. Ludmila Mikaël, 1974 (div. 1980); 1 child; ptnr. Julia Lintott, 1988-1996; 2 children; m. Emma Lucia, 2002. BA in Eng. Lang. and Lit. with honors, Birmingham (Eng.) U., 1962, DLitt (hon.), 1988; diploma with honors, RADA (Royal Acad. of Dramatic Art), 1964; DLitt (hon.), Middlesex U., 1997. Founder, artistic dir. Liverpool (Eng.) Everyman Theatre, 1964-66; artistic dir. RSC Theatreground, 1966-67; from assoc. dir. to artistic dir. Royal Shakespeare Co., England, 1967-91, dir. emeritus, 1991—. Cons. Comedie Francaise, 1975-80, Clwyd Theatr Cymru, dir., 1997— contbr. to Theatre 72, Playback pubs.; translator of plays. Dir.: (plays) Hamlet, 1994, Merry Wives of Windsor, 1995, The Pretenders, 1996, The Royal Hunt of The Sun, 1996, The Importance of Being Ernest, 1997, A Christmas Carol, 1997, Equus, 1997, The Journey of Mary Kelly, 1998, The Seagull, 1998, The Norman Conquests, 1998, Macbeth, 1999, 12th Night, 1999, Under Milk Wood, 1999, Macbeth (Broadway), 2000, Private Lives, 2001, King Lear, 2001, Bedrom Farce, 2001, The Rabbit, 2001, Rosencrantz and Guildenstern Are Dead, 2002, Betrayal, 2002, Romeo and Juliet, 2002, The Four Seasons, 2002, Blithe Spirit, 2003. Decorated chevalier des Arts et des Lettres, 1975; recipient Pragnell Shakespeare award 1991; fellow Welsh Coll. Music and Drama. Fellow Shakespeare Inst. (hon.), Royal Welsh Coll. Music & Drama, North East Wales Inst. Office: Clwyd Theatr Cymru Mold Flintshire North Wales CH7 1YA England

HANDSCHUMACHER, ROBERT EDMUND, biochemistry educator; b. Abington, Pa., Oct. 16, 1927; m. Joan A. Goddard; children: Kurt, Mark. BSChemE, Drexel Inst., 1949; MS in Biochemistry, U. Wis., 1951, PhD in Biochemistry, 1953. Postdoctoral fellow Lister Inst., 1953-54; postdoctoral fellow pharm. Yale U. Sch. Medicine, New Haven, 1955-56, asst. prof. pharm., 1956-60, assoc. prof. pharm., 1960-64, dir. div. biol. scis., 1969-72, chmn. dept. pharm., 1974-77, prof. pharm., 1964-95, prof. emeritus, 1996—. Chmn. Eleanor Roosevelt Internat. Fellowship Com., 1966-73, Am. Cancer Soc. Coun. Rsch. Grants, 1977-78, sci. rev. com. Ludwig Cancer Unit, Brussels, 1980-84, health and med. care com. Commn. Acad. Sci., 1984—; sec., treas. Am. Assn. Cancer Rsch., Phila., 1982-88; rsch. prof. Am. Cancer Soc., 1977-95; Philips Meml. lectr. Meml. Sloan-Kettering, N.Y.C., 1985; chmn. exp. therap. adv. bd. B-W Fund, 1990-93; coun. mem. Nat. Inst. Environ. Health Scis., 1987-91. Author 250 articles, book chpts., etc. Sci. dir. Anna Fuller Fund, Yale U. Sch. Medicine, 1973-88; chmn. Samuel Roberts Noble Found. Adv. Bd., Okla., 1982-90; mem. bd. govs. Yale U. Press, New Haven, 1989-93; bd. dirs. Lutherans in Mission, 1999—. Fellow AAAS; mem. Conn. Acad. Sci. & Engring. (charter). Democrat. Lutheran. Achievements include development of new cancer treatments involving Asparaginase, 5-Fluorouracil; initial purification of the Lymphokine IL-1; discovery of receptor for the transplantation drug Cyclosporin. Home: 97 Great Harbor Rd Guilford CT 06437-3036 E-mail: handschu@att.net.

HANDY, CAROLYN, nonfiction writer; b. Bennington, Vt., Dec. 20, 1950; d. Herbert Lewis and Barbara (Lindsay) Handy; m. William R. Goodloe, Aug. 27, 2002; 1 child, Hannibal Lloyd. AA, Greenfield (Mass.) C.C., 1972; B in English, Sch. Lifelong Learning, Lee, N.H., 1991; M in English, U. N.H., 1995. Staff reporter Tri-Town Transcript, Dover, N.H., 1989-93, editor, 1993-98; staff reporter Shipyard News, Portsmouth, N.H., 1992-93, editor, 1993-95; reporter Granite State Vacationer, Dover, 1992-94; editor U. N.H. student guide, Durham, 1993-98. Online faculty Comms. dept. U. Phoenix, 2002—. Mem.: Toastmasters Internat. (chpt. v.p. pub. rels. 1996—2000, chpt. v.p. edn. 2000—01, chpt. pres. 2001—02, Competent Toastmasters recognition 1997, Advanced Toastmaster Bronze recognition 1999, Competent Leader 1999, Advanced Toastmaster Silver recognition 2002), Mensa.

HANDY, CHARLES BROOKS, accountant, educator; b. Coffey, Mo., Apr. 26, 1924; s. Herbert Franklyn and Laura Ada Margaret (Mueller) H.; m. Donna Jean Peters, June 29, 1958 (dec.); children: William Mark, Karen Lynne; m. Mary C. O'Brien McGrane, Nov. 5, 1994. BA, Westminster Coll., Fulton, Mo., 1947; MA, U. Iowa, 1956; PhD, Iowa State U., 1970. C.P.A., Iowa. Staff acct. McGladrey, Hansen, Dunn & Co. (now McGladrey & Pullen), Davenport, Iowa, 1955-58; instr. acctg. Iowa State U., Ames, 1958-60, asst. prof., 1960-70, assoc. prof., 1970-75, prof., 1975-92, chmn. supervisory com. bus. adminstrv. scis., 1975-78, acctg. coordinator, 1977-78, chmn. dept. indsl. adminstrn., 1978-80, dir. Sch. Bus. Adminstrn., 1980-84, dean Coll. Bus. Adminstrn., 1984-89, ret. dean emeritus, 1992. Served to lt. (j.g.) USNR, 1943-46. Mem. AICPA's, Iowa Soc. CPA's, Beta Alpha Psi, Omicron Delta Epsilon. Republican. Presbyterian. Home: 57 High Point Cir W Unit 205 Naples FL 34103-4246 E-mail: chandyflia@aol.com.

HANDY, EDWARD OTIS, JR., retired financial services executive; b. Akron, Ohio, Jan. 9, 1929; s. Edward Otis and Alice (Saalfield) H.; m. Susan Eastabrooks, May 12, 1951; children: Susan Littlefield, John E., Edward O. III, Seth H. AB, Harvard U., 1951, LLB, 1956. Bar: R.I. 1956, U.S. Dist. Ct. R.I. 1956. Assoc. Edwards & Angell, Providence, 1956-59; staff atty. Textron Inc., Providence, 1960-74, asst. gen. counsel, 1974-76, v.p. employee benefits, 1976-87, v.p., sec., 1987-91; ret., 1991. Bd. dirs. ERISA Industries Com., 1982-91, vice chmn., 1990-91; pres., bd. dirs. Providence Athenaeum, 1972-78; trustee various orgns. Capt. USMC, 1951-53, Korea. Mem. Providence Art Club, Hyannisport Club. Republican. Unitarian Universalist.

HANDY, JOHN W. career officer; b. Raleigh, NC, Apr. 29, 1944; BS in History, Meth. Coll., 1966; Diploma, Squadron Officer Sch., 1972, Air Command and Staff Coll., 1979; MS in Systems Mgmt., U. So. Calif., 1979; Diploma, Air War Coll., 1982, Nat. War Coll., 1984; postgrad., Harvard U., 1993. Commd. 2d lt. USAF, 1967, advanced through ranks to gen., 2000; various assignments to dir. of programs and evaluations Hdqtrs. USAF, Washington, 1995-97; comdr. 21st Air Force, McGuire AFB, N.J., 1997-98; dep. chief of staff for installations and logistics Hdqtrs. USAF/The Pentagon, Washington, 1998-2000; vice chief of staff USAF/The Pentagon, Washington, 2000—01; comdr. U.S. Transportation Command, Scott AFB, Ill., 2001—. Decorated Def. Disting. Svc. medal, Disting. Svc. medal, Legion of Merit with oak leaf cluster, Meritorious Svc. medal with three oak leaf clusters, Air medal with oak leaf cluster, Antarctica Svc. medal, Vietnam Svc. medal with three svc. stars, Republic of Vietnam Gallery Cross with Palm, others.*

HANDY, MARY THOMAS, retired elementary school educator; b. Marion, Md., Apr. 9, 1936; d. Monroe Henry Thomas and Agnes Elizabeth Mack; m. William Thomas Handy, Dec. 23, 1961 (div. Feb. 1972); children: Andrew Eltonio Thomas, William Thomas Jr. BS, Bowie State U., 1958; MEd, U. Va., 1971; grad., U. Md., 1988. Tchr. elem. sch. Withams Elem. Sch., Va., 1963—64, North Accomack Elem. Sch., Mappsville, Va., 1964—70, Prince St Elem Sch, Saisbury, Md., 1970—85; tchr. mid. sch. Wicomico Mid. Sch., Salisbury, 1985—98, ret., 1998—. Counselor dormitory U. Va., Charlottesville, 1971—. Parent adv. bd. mem. Carter G. Woodson Mid. Sch., Crisfield, 2003—; mem. Ea. Shore chpt. Bowie Alumni Assn., 1970—2003; mem. Somerset County br. #7026 NAACP, Westover, Md., 2000—; mem., sec. Ea. Shore chpt. Crisfield-Woodson Alumni Assn., 1997—2003; sec. edn. com. Somerset County Br. #7026 NAACP, 2001. Recipient Cert. of Appreciation, Wicomico County Bd. Edn., Salisbury, Md., 1995, McCready Found., Inc. Jr. Aux. Bd., Crisfield, Md., 2000, Letter of Appreciation dedication, Wicomico County Bd. Edn., Salisbury, 1998, Ret. Tchr. award, Crisfield-Woodson Alumni Assn., 1999. Mem.: Wicomico County Ret. Tchr.'s Assn. (Top Vol. award 2003), Md. Ret. Tchr.'s Assn. Avocations: bicycling, exercising, walking, singing, travel. Home: 28152 Holland Crossing Rd Marion Station MD 21838

HANDY, RICHARD LINCOLN, civil engineer, educator; b. Chariton, Iowa, Feb. 12, 1929; s. Walter Newton and Florence Elizabeth (Shoemaker) H.; married, Apr. 18, 1964 (div. 1980); 1 child, Beth Susan.; m. Kathryn Etona Claussen, Feb. 13, 1982. BS in Geology, Iowa State U., 1951, MS, 1953, PhD in Soil Engring. and Geology, 1956. Asst. prof. civil engring. Iowa State U., Ames, 1956-59, assoc. prof., 1959-63, prof., 1963-87, disting. prof., 1987-91, disting. prof. emeritus, 1991—; prof.-in-charge Spangler Geotech. Lab., 1963-91; cons. in soil engring., soil and rock testing, landslide stabilization; v.p. research W.N. Handy Co., 1958-91, chmn. bd., 1986-90; pres. Handy Geotech. Instruments, Inc., 1980-93, 1999—, chmn. bd. dirs., 1993—; mem., chmn. bd. dirs. Geopier Found. Co., L.C., 1993-95. Author: The Day the House Fell, 1995; co-author: (with M.G. Spangler) Soil Engineering 3rd edit., 1972, 4th edit. 1982, 5th edit. 1993; contbr. articles to profl. jours. Recipient faculty citation Iowa State U., 1976; named Anson Marston Disting. Prof. Engring., Iowa State U., 1987. Fellow AAAS, Geol. Soc. Am., Iowa Acad. Sci.; mem. ASCE (Thomas A. Middlebrooks award 1986), Soil Sci. Soc. Am., Internat. Soc. Soil Mech. and Found. Engrs. Achievements include patents in soils field. Home and Office: 1502 270th St Madrid IA 50156-7522 E-mail: rlhandy@iowatelecom.net.

HANDY, ROBERT MAXWELL, lawyer; b. Buffalo, Apr. 1, 1931; s. John Abner and Yvonne Fernande (Blaise) H.; m. Berniece Emily Reist, July 2, 1955; children: Mary, Robert, David. BS, Trinity Coll., 1953; MS, Northwestern U., 1958, PhD, 1962; JD, Ariz. State U., 1984. New product devel. research mgr. Westinghouse Electric Co., Pitts., 1961-69; product mgr. Semiconductor div. Motorola, Inc., Phoenix, 1969-72, corp. dir. research, 1972-75; exec. dir. Ariz. Solar Energy Research Commn., 1975-76; dir. bus. and tech. planning Integrated Circuits div. Motorola, Inc., Mesa, Ariz., 1976-80, sr. patent counsel, 1980-88, group patent counsel, 1988-94; intellectual property counsel Ea. Europe, Mid. East, and Africa Motorola GmbH, Weisbaden, Germany, 1995-98; pvt. practice Gilbert, Ariz., 1999—2002; patent atty. Ingrassia Fisher & Lorenz, Scottsdale, Ariz., 2002—. Fgn. expert instr. Quingdao U., China, 2001-02; instr. Carnegie Mellon U., 1967. Served to lt. (j.g.) USNR, 1954-57. Royall A. Cabell fellow, 1959-60 Mem.: IEEE, Phi Beta Kappa. Office: Ingrassia Fisher & Lorenz 7150 E Camelback Rd Ste 325 Scottsdale AZ 85251

HANDY, ROLLO LEROY, b. Kenyon, Minn., Feb. 20, 1927; s. John R. and Alice (Kispert) H.; m. Toni Scheiner, Sept. 17, 1950 (dec. July 1997); children: Jonathan, Ellen, Benjamin. BA, Carleton Coll., Northfield, Minn., 1950; MA, Sarah Lawrence Coll., 1951; postgrad., U. Minn., 1951-52; PhD, U. Buffalo, 1954. Mem. faculty U. S.D., 1954-60, prof. philosophy, head dept., 1959-60; assoc. prof. Union Coll., Schenectady, N.Y., 1960-61; mem. faculty SUNY, Buffalo, 1961-76, prof. philosophy, 1964-76, chmn. dept., 1961-67, chmn. divsn. philosophy and social scis., 1965-67, provost faculty edn. studies, 1967-76; pres. Behavioral Rsch. Coun., Great Barrington, Mass., 1976-84, Am. Inst. Econ. Rsch., Great Barrington, Mass., 1977-91, pres. emeritus, 1991—. Author: Methodology of the Behavioral Sciences, 1964, Value Theory and the Behavioral Sciences, 1969, The Measurement of Values, 1970, (with Paul Kurtz) A Current Appraisal of the Behavioral Sciences, 1964; (with E.C. Harwood) rev. edit., 1973, (with E.C. Harwood) Useful Procedures of Inquiry, 1973; co-editor: Philosophical Perspectives on Punishment, 1968, The Behavioral Sciences, 1968, The Idea of God, 1968. With USNR, 1945-46. Mem. AAUP (chpt. pres. 1964-65), Am. Anthrop. Assn., Am. Philos. Assn. Home: 750 Weaver Dairy Rd Apt 159 Chapel Hill NC 27514-1440 E-mail: rhandy4728@aol.com.

HANDY, VIRGINIA MAE, writer; b. Benton Harbor, Mich., July 21, 1935; d. C. Russell Handy and Mary Charlotte Edwards. AA, Benton Harbor Jr. Coll., 1954; BA cum laude, Western Mich. U., 1956. Cert. libr. Mich. Bd. Librs. Cataloger Detroit Pub. Libr., 1956—62, Lakehead U. Libr., Thunder Bay, Canada, 1964—67, Sodus Twp. Libr., Sodus, Mich., 1968—72; med. records abstractor Mercy-Meml. Med. Ctr., Benton Harbor and St. Joseph, Mich., 1972—91; Log cabin day coord., editor Log Cabin Soc. Mich., Sodus, 1987—; fiber arts instr. Salvation Army Ctr. for the Arts, Benton Harbor, 1997—. Spinning and weaving demonstrator, 1975—; profl. cons. for log cabins Mich. Humanities Coun., East Lansing, 2002—; columnist Mich. Mag., 1992—96. Author: The Palmer Park Log Cabin: A Souvenir History, 2001, Best Photos of 2000, 2001, Flax Craft, a Collection of Newsletters, 1993-1999, 2002; editor: Log Cabin News, the Quar. Newsletter of the Log Cabin Soc. Mich., 1989—. Founder Log Cabin Day in Mich., 1987; leader 4-H, 1975—85; mem. Blossomland Arts and Cultural Coun., St. Joseph, Mich., 1993—94; organizer Detroit 300 Event and Log Cabin Day, 2001; lobbyist for Log Cabin Day bill Mich. Legis., Lansing, 1988—89. Recipient Award of Merit for founding Log Cabin Soc. Mich., Hist. Soc. Mich., 1991, 1st Place for linen curtin, Fiberfest, 1992; Artist-in-Residence grantee, Arts Coun. of Greater Kalamazoo, 2003. Mem.: Mich. League of Handweavers, Mich. Festivals and Events Assn., Mich. Centennial Farm Assn., Pioneer Amm. Soc., Log Cabin Soc. Mich. (co-founder 1988, sec.-treas. 1988—, 10th Log Cabin Day plaque 1996). Avocations: photography, piano, genealogy, restoring old garden and farm buildings, book collecting. Home: 3503 Rock Edwards Dr Sodus MI 49126-8700

HANDZEL, STEVEN JEFFREY, accountant; b. Phila., Nov. 9, 1954; s. Joseph Leo and Dori Lou (Kistler) H.; m. Beth Ann Barrick, Apr. 20, 1985; children: Samantha Nicole, Patrick Ryan, Daniel Joseph. BBA, Coll. of William and Mary, 1976; MBA, West Chester U., 1991. CPA, Pa. Staff auditor Peat, Marwick, Mitchell & Co., Phila., 1976-79, supr. sr., 1979-80; mgr. fin. reporting U.S. Cold Storage, Inc., Phila., 1980-83, treas. fed. credit union, 1982-83; audit mgr. Barbacane, Thornton & Co., Wilmington, Del., 1983-86; audit supr. Chester County, West Chester, Pa., 1986-88, acctg. mgr., 1988-92; pvt. practice Steven J. Handzel, CPA, West Chester, Pa., 1993—; CFO Graphic Arts Sales Found., Inc., 1997—. Bd. dirs., treas. J.L. Handzel Marine Engring. Svcs., Inc., Pa.; exec. dir. Safe Harbor Greater West Chester, Inc., 2000-01, W.C. Atkinson Meml. Cmty. Svc. Ctr., Inc., 2002—. Rep. committeeman Chester County, 1977-94; mem. coun. West Chester Borough, 1980-88, v.p. couns., 1980-81; mem. sch. bd. West Chester Area Sch. Dist., 1989-93, 95-99, pres. 1997-98; treas. West Chester Recreation Commn., 1987-88, Chester County Assn. Boroughs, 1983, sec., 1984, v.p., 1985, pres., 1986-87; mem. Chester County Intermediate Unit Sch. Bd., 1991-93, 95-99, v.p., 1997-98, pres. 1999; pres. West Chester Jaycees, 1990-91, dist. dir. Pa. Jaycees, 1991-92, regional dir., 1992-93, state v.p., 1993-94, state treas., 1994, Eyreman award, 1990, Statesman award, 1991. Mem. AICPA, Pa. Inst. CPAs (local gov. auditing and acctg. com., non-profit orgns. com. 1994-96), Govt. Fin. Officers Assn. (spl. rev. com. 1990-99), Lions. Methodist. Avocations: skiing, sailing, gardening. Home: 302 N High St West Chester PA 19380-2614 Office: PO Box 3492 West Chester PA 19381-3492

HANDZLIK, JAN LAWRENCE, lawyer; b. N.Y.C., Sept. 21, 1945; s. Felix Munso and Anna Jean Handzlik; children: Grant, Craig, Anna. BA, U. So. Calif., 1967; JD, UCLA, 1970. Bar: Calif. 1971, U.S. Dist. Ct. (ctrl. dist.) Calif. 1971, U.S. Ct. Appeals (9th cir.) 1971, U.S. Supreme Ct. 1975, U.S. Dist. Ct. (no. dist.) Calif. 1979, U.S. Tax Ct. 1979, U.S. Dist. Ct. (ea. dist.) Calif. 1981, U.S. Dist. Ct. (so. dist.) Calif. 1982, U.S. Ct. Internat. Trade 1984, U.S. Ct. Appeals (2d cir.) 1984. Law clk. to Hon. Francis C. Whelan, U.S. Dist. Ct. (ctrl. dist.) Calif., L.A., 1970-71; asst. U.S. atty. fraud and spl. prosecutions section criminal divsn. U.S. Dept. Justice, L.A., 1971-76; assoc. Greenberg & Glusker, L.A., 1976-78; ptnr., prin. Stilz, Boyd, Levine & Handzlik, P.C., L.A., 1978-84; prin. Jan Lawrence Handzlik, P.C., L.A., 1984-91; ptnr. Kirkland & Ellis, L.A., 1991—. Counsel to Ind. Christopher Commn. Study of L.A. Police Dept., 1991; dep. gen. counsel to Hon. William H. Webster L.A. Police Commn. response to urban disorders, 1992; mem. adv. com. Office Los Angeles County Dist. Atty., 1994—96; mem. standing com. discipline U.S. Dist. Ct. (ctrl. dist.) Calif., 1997—2001; dep. gen. counsel ind. rev. panel Rampart investigation police corruption L.A. Police Commn., 2000; blue ribbon rev. panel L.A. Police Dept. handling Rampart corruption incident, 2003. Mem. editl. adv. bd. DOJ Alert, 1994—95. Bd. dirs. Friends Child Advs., L.A., 1987—91, Inner City Law Ctr., L.A.; mem. bd. judges Nat. and Calif. Moot Ct. Competition Teams, UCLA Moot Ct. honors program. Mem.: ABA (sect. criminal justice nat. com. white collar crime 1991—, west coast white collar crime com., vice chair 1998—2000, criminal justice sect. nominating com. 2000—01, chair 2000—02, gov. coun. 2002—, mem. sect. litig.), Los Angeles County Bar Assn. (coms. on fed. cts. 1988—2001, chair criminal practice subcom. 1989—90, fed. appts. evaluation 1989—93, white collar crime com. 1991—97, exec. com. criminal justice sect. 1997—2002, fed. cts. coord. com. 2001—), State Bar Calif. (sects. on criminal law and litigation), Fed. Bar Assn. (exec. com. 1997—), Chancery Club. Office: Kirkland & Ellis 777 S Figueroa St Ste 3700 Los Angeles CA 90017-5835 E-mail: jan_handzlik@la.kirkland.com.

HANE, JEFFREY W. lawyer; b. Brainerd, Minn., Jan. 31, 1963; s. Thomas Loren and Donna Jean Hane; m. Linda Rae Bradseth, Aug. 14, 1993. BA in Polit. Sci., Bemidji State U., 1986; MA in Religion, So. Calif. Coll., 1992; JD, U. N.D., 1993. Bar: Minn. 1993, N.D. 1993, U.S. Dist. Ct. (no. dist.) Minn. 1993, U.S. Dist. Ct. N.D. 2001, U.S. Ct. Appeals (8th cir.) 1994. Atty. Brink, Sobolik, Severson, Malm, Hallock, Minn., 1992—; asst. county atty. Kittson County, Minn., Hallock, Minn., 1994—. Mem. Minn. State Bar Assn., N.D. State Bar Assn., Minn. Trial Lawyers Assn., Nat. Lawyers Assn., Christian Legal Soc., Order of the Coif, Order of Barristers. Avocations: carpenter, cross-country skiing. Office: Brink Sobolik Severson Malm 217 S Birch Ave Hallock MN 56728

HANE, MIKISO, history educator; b. Hollister, Calif., Jan. 16, 1922; s. Ichitaro and Hifuyo (Taoka) H.; m. Rose Michiko Kanemoto, Sept. 19, 1948; children: Laurie Shizue, Jennifer Kazuko. BA, Yale U., 1952, MA, 1953, PhD, 1957. Asst. prof. history U. Toledo, Ohio, 1959-61, Knox Coll., Galesburg, Ill., 1961-66, assoc. prof. history, 1966-72, prof. history, 1972-92, prof. emeritus, 1993—. Author: Japan, A Historical Survey, 1972, Peasants, Rebels and Outcasts, 1982, Emperor Hirohito and His Chief Aide, 1982; editor, translator: Reflections on the Way to the Gallows, 1988, Eastern Phoenix: Japan Since 1945, 1996, Japan, A Short History, 2000. Fulbright grantee, 1957-58, Japan Found. grantee, 1973, NEH grantee, 1979-80. Mem. Assn. for Asian Studies (bd. dirs. 1985-88), Am. Hist. Assn. (teaching div. 1980-83), Midwest Conf. on Asian Affairs (pres. 1988), Nat. Coun. on Humanities. Buddhist. Home: 2285 N Broad St Galesburg IL 61401-1454 Office: Knox Coll History Dept South St Galesburg IL 61401 E-mail: mhane@knox.edu.

HANEKE, DIANNE MYERS, retired education educator; b. San Francisco, Feb. 23, 1941; d. Wayne and Dorothy (Johnson) Myers; m. John Paul Haneke, Apr. 10, 1965; children: Mark, Debra, Julie. BA in Social Sci., Edn., So. Calif. Coll., 1964; MS in Edn., SUNY, Albany, 1971, cert. advanced studies, 1990, PhD in Reading, 1998. Cert. elem., social studies and reading tchr. N.Y. Reading specialist Greenville (N.Y.) Elem. Sch., 1971-72, 84-85, Durham (N.Y.) Elem. Sch., 1972-74, Cairo (N.Y.) Durham Schs., 1979-82, 86-89; counselor Capital Area Christian Counseling, Delmar, NY, 1980-81; instr. psychology Columbia Greene CC, Hudson, NY, 1982-83; reading specialist Hunter (N.Y.)-Tannersville Schs., 1985-86; instr. edn. and reading Mt. St. Mary Coll., Newburgh, NY, 1990-92; assoc. prof. reading edn. Concordia U., Austin, Tex., 1993—2001, dir. field work experiences, 1993—2001, prof. emeritus, 2001—. Author: A Woman After God's Own Heart, 1982, A View From the Inside: An Action Plan for Gender Equity in New York State Educational Administration, 1990, Improve Your Writing: A Workshop and Desktop Reference, 2001. Instr. water safety ARC, 1978—91; host parents Youth for Understanding, 1984—85, 1988—89; leader, resource person Girl Scouts U.S., 1978—90. Recipient Alumnus of the Yr. award, So. Calif. Coll., 1979, Disting. Contbr. award, 1988, Disting. Svc. award, So. Calif. Coll. Alumni Assn., 1994; Myers-Haneke Edn. endowed scholar, So. Calif. Coll., 1971—. Mem.: ASCD, Tex. State Reading Assn., Internat. Coun. Tchrs. English, Nat. Reading Conf., Coll. Reading Assn., Christian Educators Assn. Internat., Capital Area Reading Coun., Assn. Tchr. Educators, Am. Ednl. Rsch. Assn., Phi Delta Kappa, Delta Kappa Gamma. Republican. Avocations: swimming, tennis, music, travel, Special Olympics. E-mail: d.haneke@prodigy.net.

HANEL, DOUGLAS PAUL, orthopedist, surgeon; b. Great Falls, Mont., July 26, 1950; s. Edward B. and Hazel J. Hanel; m. Margaret Mary Phelps, Mar. 31, 1978; children: Marnie E. children: Maggie M. BA in Zoology, U. Wash., 1973; MD, St. Louis U., 1977. Diplomate Am. Bd. Orthopaedic Surgery, cert. added qualification in hand surgery Am. Bd. Orthopaedic Surgery, re-cert. orthopaedic surgery Am. Bd. Orthopaedic Surgery, re-cert. hand surgery Am. Bd. Orthopaedic Surgery. Intern St. Louis U., 1977—78, resident orthopaedic surgery, 1978—82, asst. prof. orthopaedics, 1985—88; fellow hand surgery U. Louisville, 1982—83, fellow microvascular surgery, 1983—84; asst. prof. orthopaedics Med. Coll. Wis., Milw., 1988—91, assoc. prof. orthopaedic surgery,

1991—92; assoc. prof. orthopaedics U. Wash., Seattle, 1992—2001, prof. orthopaedics, 2001—. Dir. hand fellowship Med. Coll. Wis., Milw., 1998—2002; dir. orthopaedic edn. U. Wash., Seattle. Fellow: Am. Acad. Orthopaedic Surgeons (assoc.); mem.: AMA (assoc.), Am. Orthopaedic Assn. (assoc.), Acad. Orthopaedic Soc. (assoc.), Am. Soc. for Surgery of the Hand (assoc.), Orthopaedic Trauma Assn. (assoc.). Office: Orthopaedic Surgery 325 Ninth Ave Seattle WA 98104-2499 Personal E-mail: dhanel@u.washington.edu.

HANELINE, DOUGLAS LATHAM, literature educator; b. Greenwich, Conn., Sept. 14, 1948; m. Ellen J. Bilstein, Sept. 2, 1983; children: Joellen, Elizabeth. AB, Middlebury Coll., 1970; MA, U. Del., 1972; PhD, Ohio State U., 1978. Assoc. prof. English Dakota State U., Madison, S.D., 1979-84; prof. English Ferris State U., Big Rapids, Mich., 1984—, asst. v.p. for acad. affairs, 1999—2001. Dir. Mich. Humanities Coun., Lansing, 1996-2000. Fellow Am. Med. Writers Assn. (editl. rev. bd. AMWA Jour. 1997—, awards adminstr. 1998-2000). Home: 20182 12 Mile Rd Big Rapids MI 49307-8805 Office: Ferris State U Languages and Literature 820 Campus Dr Big Rapids MI 49307-2281 E-mail: douglas_haneline@ferris.edu.

HANEMAN, VINCENT SIERING, JR., consulting engineer, educator, university dean; b. Orange, N.J., Feb. 19, 1924; s. Vincent Siering and Helen (Harris) H.; m. Adelaide Russell, Oct. 3, 1961 (dec.); children: Vincent Siering III, Charles Frederick, Rosalyn Tullos, Kaye Kavísic; m. Barbara Gilliam, June 1, 2002. S.B., MIT, 1947; MS in Aero. Engring, U. Mich., 1950, PhD, 1956. Registered profl. engr., Ohio, Okla., Tex., Ala., Alaska. Asst. head flight research Project Meteor, Mass. Inst. Tech., 1947-49; project head automatic wind tunnel data reduction U. Mich., 1949-51; project officer analogue computer research Wright Air Devel. Center, Ohio, 1951-52; assoc. prof., asst. dept. head aero. engring. Air Force Inst. Tech., Wright Patterson AFB, Ohio, 1955-59; chief spl. projects div. guidance and control directorate Air Force Ballistic Missile Div., 1959-60; pres., sr. asso. Haneman Assos., Richardson, Tex., 1960-66, Stillwater, Okla., 1967-72, Auburn, Ala., 1972-73; chmn. bd. Haneman Assos., Inc., Richardson, Stillwater and Auburn, 1961-73, exec. v.p. Stillwater, 1966-67; prof. mech. engring., dir. engring. research, asso. dean Coll. Engring., Okla. State U., 1966-72; prof. aeros. engring., dean Sch. Engring., Auburn U., 1972-80; prof. mech. engring., dean sch. engring. U. Alaska, Fairbanks, 1980-91, prof. emeritus, dean emeritus sch. engring., 1991—. Cons. flight simulator project U. Mich., 1952-55, Gen. Electric Co., Gen. Dynamics, Space Tech. Labs., Chance Vought Corp., Ling Temco-Vought, Nat. Acad. Scis., Union Carbide, Auburn U., State of Ark., U. Tex. Pan-Am., Brownsville, others. Contbr. articles on instrumentation, control and guidance, aircraft performance, engring. edn. to tech. jours. Mem. Army Sci. Adv. Panel, 1967-77; chmn. night low level com. Project Master, Point of Contact Airmobile. Served to 1st lt. USAAF, 1943-45, MTO; to maj. USAF, 1951-60; to maj. gen. Res., moblzn. asst. to dep. chief staff for research and devel. Decorated D.S.M., Legion of Merit with oak leaf cluster, D.F.C. with oak leaf cluster, Air medal with 7 oak leaf clusters, Air Force Commendation medal. Assoc. fellow Am. Inst. Aeros. and Astronautics; fellow Am. Soc. Engring. Edn. (past sec. mech. and aero. divs., past nat. chmn. aero. div., past mem. gen. council, past mem. exec. com., past chmn. engring. research council, past 1st v.p., chmn. dean's inst. 1978, chmn. planning factors com. Engring. Coll. Council 1976-80, pres. 1980-81), Am. Astronautical Soc. (sr.), Am. Helicopter Soc., IEEE, Nat. Soc. Profl. Engrs. (ethics com. 1974-75, nat. chmn. Engring. Week 1977, 78, chmn. cost of engring. edn. com., nat. dir. 1979-80), Ala. Soc. Profl. Engrs. (state chmn. Engring. Week 1973-76), Alaska Soc. Profl. Engrs. (pres. 1985-86, pres. Fairbanks chpt. 1982-83, gov. 1974—, exec. com. Sustaining U. Program com.), Nat. Conf. Advancement Research (ad hoc mem. exec. com. 1977-79), Sigma Xi, Tau Beta Pi, Sigma Tau, Phi Kappa Phi, Pi Epsilon Gamma, Sigma Nu. Address: 1365 Burke Ln Auburn AL 36830-5140

HANES, DARLENE MARIE, marketing professional; b. St. Mary's, Pa., Mar. 24, 1956; d. Donald Frank and Martha Mary (Krug) H. CLU degree, Am. Coll., Bryn Mawr, Pa., 1986, chartered fin. cons. degree, 1988. CLU. Underwriter N.Y. Life Ins. Co., Concord, Calif., 1980-87; v.p. East Bay Fin. Ctr., Concord, 1987-96, v.p. agy. devel., 1988-91; v.p. brokerage ops. Ruckart Assocs., Murfreesboro, Tenn., 1990-96; with Allstate Life Inst., Nashville, 1996-99; fin. planner Nat. Brokerage Co., Nashville, 2000—. Pres. Am. Cancer Soc. League, 1984-86, bd. dirs.; bd. dirs. Airport Commn., St. Mary's, 1975, Nashville Assn. CLU and ChFC Soc., Hosp. Hospitality House, 1995-96, Friends of Watkins Inst., 1996-97; active Jr. League. Named Person of Day, Am. Heart Assn., 1985. Mem. Nat. Assn. Life Underwriters (Nat. Quality award 1985, 86, 87, Pres.'s Trophy 1986), Mt. Diable Assn. Life Underwriters (bd. dirs. 1982—, pres. 1986-87), East Bay CLU Soc. (v.p. 1989), Calif. Assn. Life Underwriters (regional coord. 1987—), Gen. Agts. and Mgrs. Assn., Hosp. Guild (sec. 1989-90), Jr. League. Republican. Roman Catholic. Avocations: water-skiing, skydiving, water skiing, para sailing.

HANES, DONALD KEITH, cooperative communications executive; b. Oregon, Ill., Apr. 4, 1933; s. Harold Samuel and Ruth Lucille (Burke) H.; m. Patricia Elsberg, July 30, 1960; children: Deborah Ann, Dawn Michele, Katherine Elizabeth BS in Journalism and Comm., U. Ill., 1955. Publs. advt. mgr. Watt Pub. Co., Mt. Morris, Ill., 1957-61; agrl. promotion specialist Portland Cement Assn., Chgo., 1961-65; asst. dir. advt. and pub. rels. Am. Breeders Svc., DeForest, Wis., 1965-68; dir. info. and edn. Farm Electrification Coun., Oakbrook, Ill., 1968-71; from dir. to v.p. pub. rels. Nat. Coun. Farmer Coops., Washington, 1971-82, v.p. comm., 1982-90, v.p., mem. instnl. rels., 1990-96; ret., 1996. Bd. dirs. Coop. Devel. Found., Washington, 1986-94, United Coop. Svcs., Washington, 1980-81, 89, vice chmn. bd., 1981-83, 84-85, 90-2000, del.-at-large, 1983-84, 88, chmn. bd., 1985-87, United Coop Appeal, 1995; chmn. Md. Coop. Law Coalition, 1983-88. Producer (film) From This Land, 1979 (Cine Golden Eagle award 1979, Gold Camera U.S. Indsl. Film Festival 1980), (video) Cooperative Benefits, 1992; co-producer: (video) The Cooperative Spirit, 1994. Served to capt. USAR, 1955-65. Recipient Coop Communications award, 1984, Coop Career award Nat. Planning com. for Coop Month, 1996. Mem. Coop Communicators Assn. (hon. mem., pres. 1975-76, H.E. Klinefelter award 1979), Agrl. Rels. Coun. (Founders award 1977, pres. 1982-83), Advt. Coun. Coops. (pres. 1982-84, Leadership award 1984), Nat. Agrimktg. Assn. (co-founder Chesapeake chpt. 1982, bd. dirs. 1982-84). Clubs: Nat. Press (Washington). Lodges: Masons. Republican. Methodist. Avocations: Am. hist., fishing, swimming, horseback riding, travel. Home: 1100 Cedrus Way Rockville MD 20854-5534 E-mail: hanesnpat@aol.com.

HANES, FRANK BORDEN, author, farmer, former business executive; b. Winston-Salem, N.C., Jan. 21, 1920; s. Robert March and Mildred (Borden) H.; m. Barbara Mildred Lasater, Dec. 3, 1942 (dec. Feb. 1990); children: Frank Borden, Nancy Hanes White, Robin March; m. Jane Craig, July 3, 1991. BA, U. N.C., 1942; DHL, St. Andrew's Presbyn. Coll., 1992. Columnist, feature writer, reporter, copy editor Winston-Salem Jour. and Sentinel, 1946-49; vice chmn., dir. Mchts. Devel. Co., shopping center, Winston-Salem, 1956-64. Dir. Chatham Mfg. Co., Elkin, N.C., Hanes Cos., Winston-Salem. Author: Abel Anders, 1951, The Bat Brothers, 1953, The Fleet Rabble, 1961, Journey's Journal, 1958, Jackknife John, 1964, The Seeds of Ares, 1977, The Garden of Nonentities, 1983. Chmn. com. for endowed professorships U. N.C., 1965-67; chmn. Friends of U. N.C. Libr., 1966-68, Old Salem, Inc., 1968-70, Summit Sch., 1959-62; pres. Winston-Salem Operetta Assn., 1949-50, Winston-Salem Arts Coun., 1955-56, N.C. Lit. and Hist. Assn., 1973-74; mem. bd. visitors U. N.C., 1980-86; chmn. Arts and Sci. Found., 1976-90; vice chmn., trustee John Motley Morehead Found.; chmn. John W. and Anna Hodgin Hanes Found.; bd. govs. U. N.C. Press; mem. bd. N.C. Soc.; bd. dirs. N.C. Children's Home Soc., N.C. Zool. Soc. With USNR, 1942-45 Recipient Roanoke Chowan award for poetry N.C. Lit. and Hist. Assn., 1953, award Winston-Salem Arts Coun., 1957, Cum Laude Soc. award Woodberry Forest Sch., 1961, Sir Walter Raleigh award for fiction, 1961, Disting. Alumnus award U. N.C., 1975, Disting. Svc. medal U. N.C., Alumni Assn., 1978, Ragan award for contbns. to fine arts, 1985, William R. Davie award U. N.C. Bd. Trustees, 1989, Fortner award for contbns. to writers and cmty. St. Andrew's Presbyn. Coll., 1995, Frederic W. Marshall disting. svc. award, 2002, N.C. Soc. award for contbns. to N.C. culture, 2002. Mem. PEN, N.C. Writers Conf. (chmn. 1951-52), N.C. Quarter Horse Assn. (pres. 1963-64), Order of Gimghoul (pres. 1940-42), Order of Minotaur (pres. 1940-41), Sigma Alpha Epsilon. Clubs: Rotarian. (Winston-Salem), Old Town (Winston-Salem); Rancheros Visitadores (Santa Barbara, Calif.); Roaring Gap (N.C.) (pres. 1976-78); Rainbow Springs (Macon County, N.C.). Home: 1057 W Kent Rd Winston Salem NC 27104-1131

HANES, JOHN GRIER, lawyer, state legislator; b. Cheyenne, Wyo., 1936; s. Harold H. and Mary Elizabeth H.; m. Liv Paul; children: Greg, Clint. BS in Bus. Adminstrn., U. Wyo., 1958, JD, 1960. Bar: Wyo. 1960, U.S. Ct. Appeals (10th cir.) 1960, U.S. Ct. Mil. Appeals, 1960, U.S. Supreme Ct. 1964. Dep. sec. of state State of Wyo., 1963-65; prin. Burke Woodard & Bishop, Cheyenne, 1965-90, of counsel, 1990—; atty. Wyo. Senate, 1967-71; mcpl. judge City of Cheyenne, 1970-73; mem. Burke, Woodard & O'Donnell, Cheyenne, Wyo., until 1990; of counsel Woodard & O'Donnell, P.C. and predecessor firms, Cheyenne, Wyo., 1990—; mem. Wyo. Ho. of Reps., 1993-99, Wyo. Senate, 1999—. Chmn. Senate Jud. Com. Vol. Cheyenne Frontier Days; mem. Heels; Rep. precinct committeeman, 1976-94. With U.S. Army JAGC. Mem. C. of C., Rotary (pres. 1982-83, dist. gov. 1990-91), Sigma Nu. Avocations: outdoor sports, travelling. Home: 848 Creighton St Cheyenne WY 82009-3231 Office: 1720 Carey Ave 600 Boyd Bldg Cheyenne WY 82001-4429

HANES, JOHN WARD, sculptor, civil engineer consultant; b. San Francisco, June 5, 1936; s. Ward Herbert and Ruth Florence (Jacks) H.; m. Virginia Rae Meadows, Nov. 27, 1957 (div. Feb. 1966); children: Derek S., Kim R., Mark A.; m. Meda Lee Walter, June 29, 1968; 1 child, Ward W. BS in Engring., U. Calif., Davis, 1979. Registered civil engr., Calif. From engr. technician to civil engr. Soil Conservation Svc., USDA, Berkeley, Calif., 1960-79, civil engr. Davis, 1979-83, hydraulic engr., 1983-90; sculptor, consulting civil engr. Boonville, Calif., 1990—; CEO Hanes Ranch, Inc., Boonville, 1999—. Pres. Santa Rosa (Calif.) Ski Club, 1971. Mem. Gualala Arts Ctr., Mendocino Arts Ctr., Nat. Sculpture Soc. Avocations: private pilot, multi media art, hunting, fishing. Home: Box 510 29000 Mountain View Rd Boonville CA 95415

HANES, RALPH PHILIP, JR., former textiles executive, arts patron, cattle farmer networker; b. Winston-Salem, N.C., Feb. 25, 1926; s. Ralph Phillip and Dewitt H (Chathan); m. Joan Audrey Humpstone, Jan. 14, 1950 (dec. Jan. 1983); m. Mary Charlotte Metz, Dec. 23, 1984. Grad., Woodberry Forest Sch., 1944; student, U. N.C., 1944-46; BA, Yale U., 1949; L.H.D. (hon.), St. Andrews Coll., Laurinburg, N.C., 1981; DFA (hon.), N.C. Sch. of Arts, 1987; HHD (hon.), Wake Forest U., 1990. With Hanes Cos., Inc. (formerly Hanes Dye and Finishing Co.), Winston-Salem, N.C., 1950-93; pres. Hanes Dye and Finishing Co., 1965-68, chmn. bd., 1968-88, chmn. emeritus, 1988-93; chmn. bd. Ampersand, Inc., 1976-85. Mem. coun. of sr. fellows Salzburg Seminars in Am. Studies. Editor (cons. editor): (other) Performing Arts Rev., 1981—85, Jour. Arts Mgmt. and Law, 1981-86; editorial adv. bd. Art Economist, 1982-86., 1981—86, editorial adv. bd. Art Economist, 1982—86. Mem. (appt. by Pres. L. B. Johnson) Nat. Council Arts, 1965—70; mem. Moravian Music Found., 1963—65; founder/mem. bd. visitors N.C. Sch. Arts, 1985—; bd. visitors Barter Theatre State Theatre of Va., 1967—75; trustee exec. com. N.C. Sch. Arts, 1966—78; assoc. fellow Jonathan Edward Coll., Yale U., 1971—74; mem. Spoleto Festival, 1979—86, Nat. Mus. Am. Art, Renwick Gallery, 1976—89, Alliance for Arts Edn., 1976—79; mem. exec. com. Nat. Coun. for Arts and Edn., 1976—79; mem. adv. coun. for arts Fed. res. Bank of Richmond (Va.), 1977—78; Bus. Com. for Ars Arena Stage, Washington, 1980—86; mem. Gov.'s Coun. Bus., Arts and Humanities, 1977—85; mem. fine arts com. Fed. res. bank of Washington, 1979—81; mem. adv. bd. Pauline Koner Dance Consort, 1977—80; mem. Arts Resources Corp., 1981—83; chmn. Am. Art Forum, 1986—87, bd. dirs., 1986—90, Arena Stage, 1990—92; com. mem. State of N.C. award, 1993; Yr. of Mountains Commn. N.C., 1995—96; corp. mem. Woods Hole Oceanog. Inst., 1994—98; mem. coun. advisors Blue Ridge Pky., 1998—; exec. com. Ambs. for the Arts, NEA, 1999—; mem. Art Based Elem. Schs., 2000; commr. Winston-Salem Cultural Affairs, 2001—; co-chair Artsignite Fest., 2002; initiator New River Blue Way, N.C., Va., W.Va., 2002; mem. adv. bd. Blue Ridge Rural Land Trust, 2003—; arts cons. govts. of, Austria, 1978; bd. dirs. Nat. Coun. Friends of Kennedy Ctr., 1975—80; mem. founding com. Agri-Rsch. Extension Network of N. Am., 1995—97; chmn. cabinet Spl. Olympics World Games, 1999; bd. dirs. (appt. by Pres. J.F. Kennedy) Nat. Cultural Ctr. for Performing Arts, 1962—65; mem. adv. music panel, 1970—72; bd. dirs. Am. Symphony Orch. League, 1958—61; trustee Salem Coll., 1961—64; bd. dirs. Jargon Soc. Inc., 1968—69, pres., 1968—75; founder N.C. State Arts Coun., chmn., 1964—66; founder/bd. dirs. Ams. for the Arts (formerly Am Coun. Arts), 1960—69; pres. Ams. for the Arts, 1964—66, vice chmn., 1967—69; mem. nat. adv. com. Brevard Sch. Music, 1969—74, Am. Crafts Coun., 1970—72, Appalachian Trail Conf., 1973—76; chmn. Yale U. Coun. com. on Music, 1970—73; bd. dirs. Nat. Audubon Soc., 1972—78, John. W. and Anna H. Hanes Found., 1974—, So. Appalachian Highlands Conservancy, 1974—78; Old Salem Inc., 1974—77; bd. dirs. Isaak Walton League Am., 1974—78, Nature Conservancy, 1975—79; bd. dirs. (apptd. by Pres. Gerald Ford) Kennedy Ctr. for the Performing Arts, 1975—80; bd. dirs. Salzburg Seminar of Am. Studies, 1978—82, Am. Land Trust, 1976—93; bd. dirs. Arts Internat., 1981—85; adv. com. Am. Farmland Trust, 1983—97; mem. internat. coun. N.Y.C. Ballet, 1984—86; trustee emeritus Kennedy Ctr. for the Arts, DC, 1999—; bd. govs. Nat. Com. for the New River, N.C., Va., W. Va., 1999—2001; mem. internat. coun. Mus. Modern Art, 1978—83. Named Young Man of Yr. Winston-Salem Jaycees, 1958, Young Man of Yr. N.C. Jaycees, 1958, Hon. Comdr., USS N.C., 1998; recipient Chmn.'s award NEA, 1966, Gov.'s award for preservation of natural area, 1969, pub. svc. award State of N.C., 1976, Morrison award for the Arts, 1977, Swan award, Tenn., 1970, N.C. Soc. of N.Y.C. award, 1979, Cmty. Svc. award Winston-Salem Urban League, 1979, Conservation award Isaac Walton League Am., 1982, award for disting. svc. to arts Nat. Gov.'s Assn., 1982, N.C. Gov.'s award in fine arts, 1982, awards Winston-Salem chpt. NAACP, 1983, Nat. Medal of Arts Amb. for the Arts presented by Pres. George Bush, 1991, award Piedmont Opera Theatre, 1992, tribute Nat. Arts Club, N.Y.C., 1995, Southeastern Ctr. for Contemporary Arts Leadership award, 1998, Winston-Salem Arts Coun. Young Leadership award, 2000, Charlotte & Philip Hanes Art Gallery award, Wake Forest U., 2001, Excellence award, Downtown Winston-Salem, 2003, award, Phil and Charlotte Hanes Student Commons Bldg., NCSA, 2003. Mem.: Century Assn. (N.Y.C.), Walpole Soc., Wilderness Soc., Royal Soc. Arts, Ut Prosim Soc., Pa. Acad. Fine Arts, N.Am. Mycological Assn., Nat. Wildlife Fedn., East African Wildlife Soc., Appalachian Consortium, World Bus. Coun., Trout Unltd., S.E. Coun. on Founds., Peale for Visual Arts (Phila.), Potomac Appalachian Mountain Club, Am. League Anglers, Isaac Walton League, Appalachian Trail Conf., Currituck, Bohemian Club, Cane River Club, Twin City Club, Piedmont Club, Met. Club (Washington), Lotos Club (N.Y.C.), Yale Club (N.Y.C.). Home and Office: PO Box 1704 Winston Salem NC 27102-1704

HANESIAN, DERAN, chemical engineer, chemistry and environmental science educator, consultant; b. Niagara Falls, NY, Sept. 26, 1927; s. Vahan and Anna (Kabasakallian) H.; m. Eva Hanesian. BChE, Cornell U., 1952, PhD, 1961. Registered profl. engr., N.Y., N.J. Prodn. engr. E.I. duPont de Nemours, Niagara Falls, 1952-57, research engr. Deepwater, N.J., 1960-63; prof. dept. chem. engring., chemistry and environ. sci. N.J. Inst. Tech., 1963—, chmn. dept. chem. engring., chemistry and environ. sci., 1975-88; research engr. E.I. duPont, 1964-66, Exxon, Florham Park, N.J., 1967-70. Tchr. Celanese, 1977, 80, Algerian Petroleum Inst., 1978; vis. prof. U. Edinburgh, 1981, Yerevan Poly. Inst., Armenia, USSR, 1983; acting dep. dir., vis. prof. Ctr. for Plastics Recycling Rsch., Rutgers U., Piscataway, N.J., 1989-93. Served with U.S. Army, 1945-46. Recipient Robert Van Houten award N.J. Inst. Tech., 1977, 2001, Outstanding Profl. Devel. by Tenured Faculty Mem. award, 1994, Excellence in Tchg. (lower divsn. undergrad.) award, 1998, Bd. Overseers Pub. and Inst. Svc. award, 1999, Newark Coll. Engring. Innovation in Engring. award, 2000; designated Master Tchr., N.J. Inst. Tech., 2000; grantee NSF, 1967, 72, 91, German Acad. Exch. Svc., 1982, Fulbright grantee Yerevan Poly. Inst., 1982. Fellow: AIChE (emeritus), Am. Chem Soc., Am. Soc. Engring. Edn. (life Chester F. Carlson award 2003), Mid-Atlantic AT& T Found. (award 1986, Centennial cert. award 1993, John Fluke award 1994, Mid Atlantic Disting. Tchg. award 1997, Mid Atlantic Outstanding Campus Rep. award 1999, Zone 1 Outstanding Campus Rep. award 1999, Mid Atlantic Outstanding Campus Rep. award 2001, Chester F. Carlson award 2003); mem.: AAUP, Armenian Students Assn. Am. (Prof. Dicran H. Kabakjian award 1998), Sigma Xi, Alpha Chi Sigma, Omega Chi Epsilon, Omicron Delta Kappa, Tau Beta Pi, Order of Engrs., Fulbright Assn. Armenian Apostolic. Home: 51 Shepard Pl Nutley NJ 07110-2730 Office: NJ Inst Tech 323 Dr ML King Blvd Newark NJ 07102 E-mail: hanesian@adm.njit.edu.

HANES-STEVENS, LAVERNE E. minister, social services administrator; b. Pitts., Apr. 22, 1959; m. Stephen A. Stevens, July 3, 1982. BS, Syracuse U.; MSEd, Duquesne U.; PhD, South Fla. Bible Coll. and Theol. Sem., 2001. Nat. bd. cert. counselor, cert. master addictions counselor 1999. Exec. dir. Lydia's Pl., Pitts., 1996—98; women's substance abuse clin. supr. Chesterfield (Va.) County Mental Health Svcs., 1998—2000; dir. Renewal Ministries, Midlothian, Va., 2000—; substance abuse grants mgr. Richmond (Va.) Behavioral Health Authority. Elder Remnant of Faith Worship Ctr., Midlothian, 2000—. Author: (book) The Fruit of Your Pain: Experiencing Spiritual Renewal Through Seasons of Struggle, 2002. Mem.: Am. Assn. Christian Counselors. Office: Renewal Ministries P O Box 4874 Midlothian VA 23112 E mail: lhs@renewalmin.com.

HANEY, DONALD CLAY, geologist; b. Ferguson, Ky., July 2, 1934; married, 1956; 2 children. BS, U. Ky., 1960, MS, 1962; PhD in Geology, U. Tenn., 1966. Instr. geology Campbellsville Coll., 1960-62; from instr. to assoc. prof. geology Ea. Ky. U., 1962—78, chmn. dept., 1968—78, prof., 1978—99; mem. faculty, dir., state geologist Ky. Geol. Survey U. Ky., Lexington, 1978—99, dir. emeritus, 1999—. Mem. Geology Soc. Am. Achievements include research in structural geology of east Tennessee; Pennsylvania sediments in ea. Ky., including structure, sedimentology and coal resources. Office: Univ Kentucky Kentucky Geological Survey 228 Mining & Mineral Rscs Bldg Lexington KY 40506-0001 E-mail: haney@kgs.mm.uky.edu.

HANEY, EDWARD FRANCIS, social studies educator, educator; b. Pitts., Mar. 24, 1947; BS, Ind. (Pa.) U., 1969; MEd, Duquesne U., 1976. Cert. Tchr. Pa., Mediator. Tchr. Pitts. Pub. Schs., 1969—, also peer coach coord. Design team New Am. Schs. Team-Oliver, Pitts., 1995—; team leader Personalize Academic Learning Strategies Team-Oliver, Pitts., 1989-95; curriculum chmn. Brentwood Sch. Dist., health, safety & transp. chair; vol. Meals on Wheels; peer coach facilitator Oliver High.; fgn. exch. student host 15 times. Vol. CCD instr., ch. coun. mem., pastoral coun., Pitts.; committeeman Boro of Brentwood, Pa., inspector of Elections; v.p. Threnhauser Civic Assn., Brentwood, market day vol.; dir. Brentwood Sch. Dist., 1996-97; active New Am. Schs. Com., Parent Tchr. Student Orgn., Crime Watch. Recipient vol. cert. USAF Recruiting, 1985-86, Vol. Svc. award Jr. Achievement, Pitts., 1987-93, Nat. Bronze Leadership award Jr. Achievement, 1998, Educator of Yr. award S.W. Pa., 1999, Tchr. Excellence award, 1999, Tchr. of Distinction S.W. Pa. award, 2000, Thanks to Tchr. Impact award, 2000-01, Innovation award Jr. Achievement of S.W. Pa., 2001. Mem. Pa. Fedn. Tchrs., Pitts. Fedn. Tchrs., World Affairs Coun. (Pitts. Recogntion award 2002). Democrat. Roman Catholic. Avocations: travel, reading. Home: 247 Wainwright Ave Pittsburgh PA 15227-3324

HANEY, MARLENE CAROL, music educator; b. Spokane, Wash., Dec. 10, 1952; d. Edward Nishan and Myrtle Anne (Jenkins) Getoor; m. Dennis Lee Haney, June 14, 1975, children: Mark Phillip, Stephanie Ann. BA, Whitworth Coll., 1975. Cert. Music Tchrs. Nat. Assn., 97, Wash. State Music Tchrs. Assn., 1998. Prin., owner Grand M Studio, Spokane, 1980—. Adv. bd. Music Fest N.W., Spokane, 1995—; adjudicator sonatina/sonata festival Ctrl. Wash. U., 2003. Adjudicator Sonatina/Sonatina Festival Ctrl. Wash. U., 2003. Mem.: Spokane Music Tchrs. Assn. (pres. 1995—97), Wash. State Music Tchrs. Assn., Music Tchrs. Nat. Assn., Mu Phi Epsilon. Nazarene. Avocations: rose gardening, travel.

HANEY, PETER MICHAEL, pediatrics educator; b. Bklyn., Aug. 30, 1958; s. Thomas Bernard and Eileen Cronin Haney; m. Helen Marie Haney, Aug. 7, 1982; children: Eileen, Ann Marie, Karen, Maria, Teresa, Thomas. Student, U. Konstanz, Germany, 1978; BS, U. Scranton, 1979; PhD, Case Western Res. U., 1984, MD, 1986. Diplomate Am. Bd. Pediat. subboard for neonatal-perinatal medicine. Intern pediat. Johns Hopkins U., Balt., 1986-87, resident pediat., 1987-89; fellow newborn medicine Washington U., St. Louis, 1989-92, instr. pediat., 1992-93, asst. prof. pediat., 1993-97, asst. prof. cell biology, 1995-97; asst. prof. pediat. Baylor Coll. Medicine, Houston, 1997—. Dir. Neonatal-Perinatal Medicine Fellowship, Washington U., St. Louis, 1993-97. Contbr. articles to profl. jours. Recipient Nat. Rsch. Svc. award NIH, 1992-94, New Investigator award Dept. Def. Breast Cancer Rsch. Program, 1996—, First award NIH, 1998—. Fellow: Am. Acad. Pediat.; mem.: Am. Soc. Cell Biology, Soc. for Pediat. Rsch., Acad. Breastfeeding Medicine, Biochem. Soc., Internat. Soc. for Rsch. in Human Milk and Lactation. Roman Catholic. Office: Baylor Coll Medicine 1100 Bates Ave Houston TX 77030-2600 E-mail: phaney@neo.bcm.tcm.edu.

HANEY, ROBERT LOCKE, retired insurance company executive; b. Morgantown, W.Va., June 14, 1928; s. John Ward and Katherine Eugenia (Locke) H. BA, U. Calif., Berkeley, 1949. Sr. engr. Pacific Telephone Co., San Francisco, 1952-58; mgmt. analyst Lockheed Missiles & Space Co., Sunnyvale, Calif., 1958-64; sr. cons. John Diebold, N.Y.C., 1964-65; sr. indsl. economist Mgmt. & Econs. Research, Inc., Palo Alto, Calif., 1965-67; prin. economist Midwest Research Inst., Kansas City, Mo., 1967-69; dir. mktg. coordination Transam. Corp., San Francisco, 1969-73; staff exec. Transam. Ins. Corp., L.A., 1974-82; 2d v.p. Transam. Life Cos., L.A., 1982-93; ret., 1993. Cons. in field. Co-author: Creating the Human Environment, 1970. Lt. (j.g.) USN, 1949-52. Mem. Scabbard & Blade. Republican. Episcopalian. Avocations: photography, gardening, cycling. Home: The Ariz Sr Acad Village 7709 S Vivaldi Ct Tucson AZ 85747 E-mail: bhan83@cs.com.

HANEY, THOMAS DWIGHT, lawyer, educator; b. St. Paul, May 17, 1948; s. Thomas Dwight and Helen Elizabeth (Johnson) H.; m. Barbara Jeanne Tozer, Aug. 23, 1969. Student Kans. State U., 1966-69; B.A., Washburn U., 1970, J.D., 1973. Bar: Kans. 1973, U.S. Dist. Ct. Kans. 1973, U.S. Ct. Appeals (10th cir.) 1973, U.S. Supreme Ct. 1980. Asst. dist. atty., chief consumer protection and career criminals Shawnee County Dist. Attys. Office, Topeka, 1973-78; chief counsel enforcement dir. Kans. Securities Commn., Topeka, 1978; chief criminal div. Kans. Atty. Gen.'s Office, Topeka, 1979-82; asst. U.S. atty., supr. U.S. Atty. Dist. Kans., Topeka, 1982-84; ptr. firm Eidson, Lewis, Porter & Haynes, Topeka, 1984-89; ptnr. Porter, Fairchild & Haney, Topeka, 1989—2001, of counsel Wright, Henson, Somers, Clark & Baker, LLP, 2001—; adj. instr. Washburn U. Law Sch.; internat. legal adv. Delta Chi; lectr. in field. Author: Civil Liability for Police, 1982; A Guide for the Kansas Peace Officer, 1982. Mem. adv. bd. Indian Ctr., Topeka, 1982, Shawnee Court Jail Constrn. Com., Topeka, 1983— ; bd. dirs. Campfire; parliamentarian 2d Dist. Republican Com., Topeka, 1981-82. Named Alumnus of the Year Kans. State U. Delta Chi, 1995. Mem. ABA, Am. Judicature Soc., Kans. Bar Assn., Topeka Bar Assn., Kans. Assn. Def. Counsel. Office: Commerce Bank Bldg 2d Floor 100 SE 9th Street Topeka KS 66601-3555

HANFLING, SUE CAROL (SUKI HANFLING), social worker; b. N.Y.C., Dec. 22, 1945; d. Seymour Leonard and Arline Jocelyn (Marcus) H.; 1 child, Michael Ian. BA magna cum laude, U. Rochester, 1968; BA, U. Chgo., 1969; MSW, Boston Coll., 1973. Cert. sex therapist Am. Assn. Sex Educators, Counselors, and Therapists. Dir. Walnut St. Ctr. for Retarded Adults, Somerville, Mass., 1970-71; pvt. practice Belmont, Mass., 1976—; adminstrv. social worker McLean Hosp. Adult Outpatient Clinic, Belmont, 1977—2002. Founder, dir. Human Sexuality program McLean Hosp., Belmont, 1985—, co-founder, dir. McLean Inst. for Couples and Families, 1985—; cons. Watertown Multi-Svc., 1980-90, founder/dir. The Inst. for Sexuality and Intimacy, 2002—; lectr. in field. Mem. Am. Assn. for Sex Educators, Am. Assn. Sex Therapists (cert.), Phi Beta Kappa. Democrat. Jewish. Avocations: photography, piano, working out. Home: 4A Locust Ln Watertown MA 02472-1733 Office: 73 Trapelo Rd Belmont MA 02478-1048

HANFORD, AGNES RUTLEDGE, retired financial adviser; d. Warren Day and Agnes Beatrice (Kane) H. Grad., Convent of Sacred Heart Prep. Sch., N.Y.C.; BA in English, French, Newton Coll., 1950. Asst. clk. rules com U.S. Ho. of Reps., Washington, 1953-56; account exec. W.E. Hutton & Co., N.Y.C., 1956-74; fin. cons. Thomson McKinnon Securities, N.Y.C., 1974-80, Tampa, Fla., 1980-89; fin. adviser Prudential Securities, Inc., Tampa, 1989-94; ret., 1994. Mem. Hillsborough County Rep. Exec. Com., Tampa, 1980-93, Women's Econ. Coun., N.Y., 1979-80, Tampa Mus. Art, 1980—, Tampa Bay History Ctr., 1995—; mem. Friends of Plant Park, 1995—, bd. dirs., 1997—; mem. adv. coun. U. South Fla. Contemporary Art Mus., 1996—. Mem. Women's Nat. Rep. Club (mem. bd. govs. 1970-75, v.p. 1975-76), Tampa Yacht and Country Club, Lawrence Beach Club. Roman Catholic.

HANFORD, GEORGE HYDE, retired educational administrator; b. Cambridge, Mass., July 29, 1920; s. Alfred Chester and Ruth Hyde H.; m. Elaine Halstead, Sept. 15, 1942; children: Anne Catherine, Mary Lee Hanford Wile. BA, Harvard U., 1941, MBA, 1943; L.L.D. (hon.), W.Va. Wesleyan Coll.; EdD (hon.), Thomas Edison State Coll. Asst. dean Harvard Grad. Sch. Bus. Adminstrn., 1946-48; treas., bus. mgr., tchr., coach N. Shore Country Day Sch., Winnetka, Ill., 1948-55; treas., then v.p., exec. v.p. Coll. Entrance Exam. Bd., N.Y.C., 1955-79, pres., 1979-86, pres. emeritus, 1987—. Author: Life with the SAT, 1991, A Tale of Three Cities in One, 1996, For the Entertainment of Strangers, 1997. Former trustee Nat. Scholarship Svc. and Fund Negro Students, Dwight Sch., Ednl. Testing Svc., Am. Coun. on Edn., Ea. Ednl. Consortium, United Bd. Coll. Devel., Thomas A. Edison State Coll., N.J. Inst. Collegiate Tchg. and Learning, Nat. Coun. for Excellence in Critical Thinking. With USNR, 1943-46. Recipient disting. or spl. svc. awards Am. Sch. Counselors Assn., Nat. Assn. Coll. Admissions Counselors, Nat. Assn. Secondary Sch. Prins., Nat. Assn. Student Fin. Aid Adminstrs., Johnson C. Smith Univ.; inducted into Harvard Varsity Club Hall of Fame, 1997. Mem. Exec. Svc. Corps of New Eng., Hawaiian Mission Children's Soc., Cambridge Hist. Soc. (pres. 1995-97), Canterbury Soc. (symposiarch 1993—), Belmont Hill Club, Cambridge Boat Club, Tenafly Tennis Club. Episcopalian. E-mail: symposiarch@earthlink.net.

HANFORD, GRAIL STEVENSON, writer; b. Far Rockaway, N.Y., Apr. 10, 1932; d. Warren Day and Agnes Beatrice (Kane) Hanford. BA, Smith Coll., 1954. Reporter Tustin (Calif.) News, 1955; newspaper editorial asst. The Register, Santa Ana, Calif., 1955; assoc. editor Am. Mercury Mag., N.Y.C., 1956-59; freelance writer N.Y.C., 1959-60; editor Royal Ins. Cos., N.Y.C., 1960-62; book editor/copy editor Am. Legion Mag., N.Y.C., 1962-75, sr. editor Washington and Indpls., 1976-82, asst. editor Indpls., 1982-83; sr. writer Writers For Bus., Indpls., 1983-88, Tampa, Fla., 1988—. Contbr. articles to profl. jours. Bd. dirs. Cathedral Sch. of St. Mary, Garden City, N.Y., 1967-71, pres. Alumna Assn., 1967-69; bd. dirs. Hort. Soc. Indpls. Mus. of Art, 1981-86; pres. Smith Coll. Club Indpls., 1982-84. Mem. Fla. Motion Picture and TV Assn., Nat. Book Critics Cir., Indpls. Press Club (bd. dirs. 1980), Am. News Women's Club, West Fla. Smith Coll. Club (v.p. 1992-94. pres. 1996-99), Ivy League Club of Tampa Bay (bd. dirs. 1989-96, sec. 1990, v.p. 1991). Republican. Roman Catholic. Office: Writers For Bus 4141 Bayshore Blvd Tampa FL 33611 1803

HANFORD, JOHN V., III, federal agency administrator; Grad., U. N.C., Gordon-Conwell Theol. Sem. Pastoral asst. West Hopewell Ch., Hopewell, Va.; exec. dir. congl. fellows program Internat. Religious Freedom, 1986—2001; congl. fellow internat. religious freedom Office of Senator Richard Lugar, 1987; amb. at large for internat. religious freedom U.S. Dept. of State, Washington, 2001—. Office: US Commn Internat Religious Freedom 800 N Capitol ST NW Ste 790 Washington DC 20002 Office Fax: 202-523-5020. E-mail: communications@uscirf.gov.

HANFORD, PAT, performing company executive; Exec. dir. Tulsa Ballet, Ballet Internationale, 2002—. Office: Ballet Internationale 502 N Capitol Ave Ste B Indianapolis IN 46204 Office Fax: 317-637-1637.

HANFT, RUTH S. SAMUELS (MRS. HERBERT HANFT), health care consultant, economist; b. N.Y.C., July 12, 1929; d. Max Joseph and Ethel (Schechter) Samuels; m. Herbert Hanft, June 17, 1951; children: Marjorie Jane, Jonathan Mark. BS, Cornell U., 1949; MA, Hunter Coll., 1963; PhD, George Washington U., 1989; ScD (hon.), U. Osteo. Med & Health Scis., 1993. Cons. Urban Med. Econs. Project, Hunter Coll., N.Y.C. and D.C. Dept. Health, 1962—63; health economist Office of Rsch. and Stats., Social Security Adminstrn., Washington, 1964—66; chief grants mgmt. health div. Office Econ. Opportunity, Washington, 1966—68; sr. health analyst Office of Asst. Sec. Planning and Evaluation HEW, Washington, 1968—71, spl. asst., asst. sec. health, 1971—72, dep. asst. sec. for health policy, rsch. and stats. Office of Asst. Sec. for Health, 1977—79, dep. asst. sec. for health rsch., stats. and tech., 1979—81; health care cons., 1981—88; cons., rsch. prof. dept. health svcs. mgmt. and policy George Washington U., Washington, 1988—91, prof., 1991—95; cons., 1995—. Vis. prof. Dartmouth Med. Sch., 1976—; sr. rsch. assoc. Inst. Medicine NAS, Washington, 1972—76; adj. Ctr. for Bioethics, U. Va., 1999—. Contbr. articles to profl. jours. Mem. Med. Assistance Svc. Bd. Commonwealth Va., 1984—89; trustee Meharry Med. Coll., 1989—94. Fellow: Acad. Health Svcs. Rsch., Hastings Ctr., Nat. Acad. of Social Ins. (charter mem.); mem.: NAS, Inst. Medicine, Cosmos Club. Jewish. Home: 3340 Brookside Dr Charlottesville VA 22901-9566

HANGEN, WILLIAM J. retired business executive; b. St. Louis, Mar. 28, 1931; s. William M. and Mabel Josephine (Jinkerson) H.; m. Shirley Mae Diebal, June 13, 1953; children: William Eric, Lori Jean Young, Jill Marie Mask, Kurt David. Student, Washington U., St. Louis, 1948-51; BS, U. Mo., 1953; postgrad., Wayne State U., 1957-62. Chemist, pigments dept. E.I. duPont de Nemours & Co., Newark, 1955-56; materials engr. missle divsn. Chrysler Corp., Detroit, 1956-64; engring. and mgmt. positions elec. products and advanced products divsns. Sheldahl, Inc., Northfield, Minn., 1964-83, v.p., gen. mgr. elec. products divsn., 1970-76, sr. v.p., gen. mgr. indsls. group, 1976-80, exec. v.p., 1980-83; dir. exec. search, bd. dirs. Moli-D Cos., Inc., 1983-91, chief fin. officer, 1986-91; gen. mgr. food products divsn. Ryt-Way Industries, Northfield, Minn., 1991-94. Contbr. to profl. jours. Corp. rep. Inst. Printed Circuits, 1970—83, bd. dirs., 1974—76, treas., 1976—78, v.p., 1978—80, pres., 1980—82, mem. program com., 1975—79, chmn., 1977—79, chmn. fin. com., 1978, chmn. long range planning com., 1978—80. Served with Ordnance Corps AUS, 1953—55. Mem. Am. Chem. Soc., Walter's Lake Property Owners Assn. (pres. 1962-64), Alpha Chi Sigma, Optimist Club (v.p. Waterford, Mich. 1963-67), Northfield Golf Club, Northfield Hockey Assn., Am. Legion. Republican. Lutheran. Home: 4992 90th St E Northfield MN 55057-4347

HANGLEY, WILLIAM THOMAS, lawyer; b. Long Beach, N.Y., Mar. 11, 1941; s. Charles Augustus and Faustine Charmillot H.; m. Mary Dupree Hangley, July 24, 1965; children: Michele Dupree, William Thomas, Katherine Charmillot. BS in Music, SUNY-Coll. at Fredonia, 1963; LLB cum laude, U. Pa., 1966. Bar: Pa. 1966, U.S. Ct. Appeals (3d cir.) 1966, U.S. Dist. Ct. (ea. dist.) Pa. 1966. Assoc. Schnader, Harrison, Segal & Lewis, Phila., 1966-69; mem., CEO, Hangley Connolly Epstein Chicco Foxman & Ewing, Phila, 1969-94, CEO Hangley Aronchick Segal & Pudlin, 1994—; judge protem Phila. Ct. of Common Pleas, 1991—; mem. adv. bd. Pub. Interest Law Ctr. Phila. Contbr. articles to profl. publs. Bd. dirs. Ams. for Dem. Action, 1972-81. Fellow Am. Coll. Trial Lawyers (chmn. Com. on Fed. Rules of Evidence, 2001-02, mem. Pa. state com. 1999—, comms. com. 2002—), Am. Bar Found.; mem. ABA (co-chmn. litigation sect. com. on fed. procedure 1990-95—, co-chair task force on merit selection of judges 1995-97, mem. task force on discovery 1997-98, task force on judiciary 1998—), Pa. Bar Assn. (ho. of dels. 1989-92), Am. Law Inst., Phila. Bar Assn., Legal Club (v.p. 2001—), Jr. Legal Club, Order of Coif, U. Pa. Inns of Ct. (master of the bench). Roman Catholic. Office: Hangley Aronchick Segal & Pudlin 1 Logan Sq Fl 27 Philadelphia PA 19103-6995 E-mail: whangley@hangley.com.

HANHILA, MATT OSCAR, JR., orthodontist; b. Kingman, Ariz., May 8, 1940; s. Matt Oscar and Merna (Ellis) H.; m. Jennifer Kagel, June 28, 1963; children: Matt O. III, Hillary, Leeann, Christo. BS in Phys. Sci., U. Ariz., 1962; DDS, U. So. Calif., L.A., 1966; MS, Loyola U., Chgo., 1970. Diplomate Am. Bd. Orthodontics. Pvt. practice, Glendale, Ariz., 1970—. Bd. examiner Ariz. Ortho Study Club, Phoenix, 1985—, pres., 1999—; peer rev. dental Ariz. Dental Soc., 1994—. Mem. U. Ariz. Alumni (bd. dirs.), Rotary (bd. dirs. Glendale chpt.). Office: 5406 W Glenn Dr Ste 2 Glendale AZ 85301-2662

HANI, ANTOINE GEORGE, psychiatrist, psychoanalyst; b. Beirut, May 1, 1925; came to U.S., 1953; s. George Antoine Hani and Marie Haddad; m. Virginia Helen Ahlstrom; children: George, Valerie, Stephaine; m. Thea Jeitani Hani, Oct. 6, 1984. MD, St. Joseph U., Beirut, 1953. Bd. cert. Adult Psychoanalysis and Child and Adolescent Psychoanalysis. Tchg. analyst Washington Psychoanalytic Inst., 1969, supervising and tng. analyst, 1981—, dir., 1996-99; pvt. practice Chevy Chase, Md., 1958—. Contbr. articles to profl. jours. Cross fertilizing rels. Fedn. European Psychoanalysts, Fedn. Latin Am. Psychoanalysts. Recipient cert., Washington Psychoanalytic Soc., Inst. and Found., 2002. Fellow: Am. Coll. Psychoanalysts (honor 1999), APA (honor 1973); mem.: Washington Psychoanalytic Soc. (pres. 1987—89, honor and recognition for disting. career in psychoanalysis), Am. Psychoanalytic Assn. (fellow bd. on profl. stds. 1993—99), Internat. Psychoanalytic Assn. (mem. new groups com. 1995—, chmn. com. to develop psychoanalysis in Mid. East 1995—). Roman Catholic. Home: 8501 Thornden Ter Bethesda MD 20817 Office: 5480 Wisconsin Ave # 1619 Chevy Chase MD 20815 E-mail: antoinehani@aol.com.

HANIFEN, RICHARD CHARLES, retired bishop; b. Denver, Colo., June 15, 1931; s. Edward Anselm and Dorothy Elizabeth (Ranous) H.. BS, Regis Coll., 1953; STB, Cath. U., 1959, MA, 1966; JCL, Pontifical Lateran U., Italy, 1968. Priest Roman Cath. Ch., 1959. Asst. pastor Cathedral Parish, Denver, 1959—66; sec. to archbishop Archdiocese Denver, 1968—69, chancellor, 1969—76; aux. bishop Denver, 1974—83; 1st bishop Colorado Springs, 1984—2003. Office: Bishop Colo Springs 29 W Kiowa St Colorado Springs CO 80903-1403*

HANIGAN, LAWRENCE, retired railway executive; b. Notre-Dame-de, Stanbridge, Can., Apr. 3, 1925; s. John Henry and Alice (Lareau) H.; m. Anita Martin, July 20, 1946; children: Carmen, Doris, Guy, Patricia, Michael. Sales mgr. Boisse Lumber Co., Montreal, 1950-52; regional mgr. Cooper-Widman Ltd., Montreal, 1952-70; mem. City of Montreal Exec. Com., 1970-78; chmn. Montreal Urban Community Exec. Com., 1972-78; chmn., gen. mgr. Montreal Urban Community Transit Commn., 1974-85; chmn. VIA Rail Canada Inc., 1985-93. Home: 358 du Baron St Sain -Sauveur QC Canada J0R IR4

HANIN, ISRAEL, pharmacologist, educator; b. Shanghai, Mar. 29, 1937; s. Arie and Rebecca (Lubarsky) Hanin; m. Leda Toni, June 12, 1960; children: Adam, Dahlia. BS, UCLA, 1962, MS, 1965, PhD in Pharmacology, 1968. Vis. scientist dept. toxicology Karolinska Inst., Stockholm, 1968; staff pharmacologist Lab. Preclin. Pharmacology, NIMH, Washington, 1969-73; from asst. prof. to assoc. prof. psychiatry and pharmacology U. Pitts. Sch. Medicine, 1973-81, prof., 1981-86; prof., chmn. dept. pharmacology and exptl. therapeutics Loyola U. Chgo. Stritch Sch. Medicine, Maywood, Ill., 1986—2003, dir. Inst. Neurosci. and Aging, 1986—2000, dir. MD/PhD program, 1992—2003. Rsch. grant rev. com. NIMH, 1979—82, Nat. Inst. Aging, 1987—92, NIH Res., 1991—95; pharmacology test com. Nat. Bd. Med. Examiners, 1987—90; sci. adv. bd. Interneuron Pharms., Inc., Lexington, Mass., 1991—2000; cons. UCB Pharm., Brussels, 1981—98; Alzheimer's disease rsch. fund panel Ill. Dept. Pub. Health, 1995—2000; AMVETS rsch. initiative com. Hines VA Hosp., 1996—. Editor 15 books; contbr. articles to profl. jours. Served to 2d lt. Armored Corps, Israeli Army, 1955-58 NIMH, NIH, Nat. Inst. Aging grantee, 1965—. Mem.: Assn. Med. Sch. Pharmacology (treas. 1998—2002, pres. 2002—), Am. Coll. Neuropsychopharmacology, Am. Soc. Neurochemistry, Am. Soc. Pharmacology and Exptl. Therapeutics (co-founder Great Lakes chpt. 1987, pres. 1990—92), Am. Chem. Soc., Neurosci. Soc. (pres. Pitts. chpt. 1982—83, pres. Chgo. chpt. 1990—91). Address: Loyola U Chgo Stritch Sch Medicine Pharmacol Rm 3621 Bldg 102 Maywood IL 60153 E-mail: ihanin@lumc.edu.

HANISKO, JOHN-CYRIL PATRICK, electronics engineer, physicist; b. Detroit, Mar. 17, 1937; s. John Joseph and Pauline Victoria (Vrabel) H. BEE, U. Detroit, 1963, MSEE, 1965; MA, Wayne State U., 1972, PhD in Physics, 1988. Engr. Burroughs, Detroit, 1962-65; rsch. engr. Boeing, Seattle, 1965-67; sr. engr. Eastman Kodak, Rochester, N.Y., 1967-68; staff engr. Kent-Moore Corp., Warren, Mich., 1971-73; rsch. engr. Udylite, Warren, 1973-75; cons. Southfield, Mich., 1975-76; project engr. Bendix, Troy, Mich., 1976-80; staff engr. TRW, Farmington Hills, Mich., 1980-94; tech. specialist Eaton Corp., Southfield, Mich., 1994—. Contbr. articles to profl. jours. Mem. Cath. League for Civil and Religious Rights, N.Y., Nat. Tax Limitation Com., Washington, Nat. Right to Life Com., Washington. Named Design of Yr. EDN Mag., 1977. Mem. IEEE (sr.). Roman Catholic. Achievements include 15 patents for Electrical Control Apparatus for Internal Combustion Engines, for Sequential Injection Timing Apparatus, for Voltage Controlled Oscillator Having Ratiometric and Temperature Compensation, for Automotive Anti-theft Device, for brake-sensor signal processing, for resistive brake lining wear and temperature sensing system, for method and apparatus for trimming gain of an accelerometer, for method and apparatus for detecting operational failure of a digital accelerometer, for single-wire brake sensing system, for apparatus and method for testing an acceleration sensur, for brake actuator service limit sensor for single-lamp brake status indicator systems, parallel resistor array for progressively detecting brake lining wear. Home: 21888 Murray Crescent Dr Southfield MI 48076-1619 Office: Eaton Corp 26201 Northwestern Hwy Southfield MI 48076-3926 E-mail: john-cyrilhanisko@eaton.com.

HANKENSON, E(DWARD) CRAIG, JR., performing arts executive; b. Mankato, Minn., Apr. 12, 1935; s. Edward Craig and Ethel Irene (Favre) H.; m. Francis Joyce Hall, Mar. 23, 1957 (div. 1978); 1 child, Meridith Joyce.; m. Catherine Ann Donaldson, 1981; 1 child, Jennifer Leigh, MusB, Eastman Sch. Music, 1957, MusM, 1959. Head voice and opera dept. Auburn U., Ala., 1959-62; bus. mgr. Chautauqua Opera Assn., N.Y., 1958-61, stage mgr., 1957-59, stage dir., 1962; mgmt. intern San Francisco Opera Co., 1962-65; assoc. dir. Brevard Mus. Center, N.C., 1965-68; gen. mgr. Saratoga Performing Arts Ctr., N.Y., 1968-75, dir., 1975—78; exec. dir. Wolf Trap Found. Performing Arts, Vienna, Va., 1978-81; pres. Producers, Inc., 1980; dir., chmn. dept. arts mgmt. and events U. South Fla., Tampa, 1983-86; pres. KiddyCart Inc., 1987—, Producers, Inc., 1981—; chmn. bd. PICASTAR, 1985—. Dir. Rochester Comty. Opera, N.Y., 1957-59; mem. Title III adv. coun. N.Y. Dept. Edn., 1969-75, N.Y. Gov.'s Commn. on Arts in Edn., 1978; cons. N.Y. Coun.on Arts; coun. bd. Rensselaer Poly. Inst.; cons. theater constrn. and mgmt. Concord Pavillion, Calif., Blossom Music Ctr., Cleve., Art Park, Buffalo, Mud Island, Memphis, Tampa Bay Performing Arts Ctr., Tampa, Robin Hood Dell, Phila. Prodr.: (TV spls.) Snow White, PBS, 1973, Al Hirt and Pete Fountain Together, PBS, 1979, Great Jazz Pianists, PBS, 1979-81, Brigadoon, Majestic Theatre, N.Y.C., 1980-81, Lionel Hampton's Return to the Paradise, PBS, 1988, Thames Live Cinema, Radio City Music Hall, 1988; nat. tour of Show Boat, 1980, Kiss Me Kate and Taming of the Shrew, Washington Internat. Jazz Festival, 1980, nat. tour Pete Fountain, Jerry Mulligan and Al Hirt, 1982, 83, Tom Paxton, Dab O' Dixie, 1987, translator: Haydn's Lo Speziale, 1958, Smetana's Bartered Bride, 1964; creator Ticket Reservation Systems, 1968, prodr. of Glenn Miller, Artie Shaw, Woodie Herman, Helen O'Connell, Warren Covington, Don Cornell, Pied Pipers BigBand Nat. Tour Show, 1993; prodr.: (tours) Midnight in the Garden of Good and Evil, 1999, Last Swing of the Century, 1999, Irish Christmas, 1999. Bd. dirs. Capitol Area Resident Opera Co., 1969-71; mem. alumni adv. bd. Eastman Sch. Music, 1974-78; mem. com. performing arts Leukemia Soc. Am., Inc.; mem. spl. adv. com. on spl. projects and presenting orgns. Nat. Endowment for the Arts, 1979-80; elder, mem. ruling session Temple Ter. Presbyn. Ch., 1990—, chmn. rsch. and planning, 1992—; bd. dirs., sec. Ter. Landings Assn.; youth group leader H.S., 1996—, Terrace Presbyn. Ch., 1996—; small group leader, Montreat, NC, Youth Conf., 2000, 01, leader 12-step program, 2001; pres. Univ. Cmty. Civic Assn., 1997—; mem. adv. bd. Tampa Habitat for Humanity, 2000—, mem. com., 2001; bd. dirs. Parents Coun. Hollins U., 2001-, vice chmn., 2003—; co-chair Hollins U. Parents Coun., 2003—. Recipient citation Central Theaters, Moscow, 1973. Mem. Internat. Assn. Concert and Festival Mgrs. (dir.), Performing Arts Assn. N.Y. (pres. 1972-78), Orgn. Summer Festival Mgrs. (moderator 1971-79, dir), N.Y. Fedn. Music Clubs (dir.), Saratoga Springs C. of C. (dir. 1969-72, chmn. promotion com. 1970-72), Council of Pres.'s, Albany League Arts, Saratoga Springs PTA (pres. 1972-73), Temple Terrace C. of C. (spl. events com., bd. dirs., bd. dirs. Farmer's Market), Univ. Cmty. Civic Assn. (pres.), Rotary (chair programming com.), Hollins U. Parents' Coun. Bd., Temple Terrace Police (adv. coun., 2000, 01), Temple Terrace Rotary (bd. dirs. 2001—). Achievements include conceiving the process of computerized event tickets and consulted for Ticketron ticket system. Office: Producers Inc 11806 N 56th St Ste B Tampa FL 33617-1652 Personal E-mail: chanken1@tampabay.rr.com. Business E-Mail: craig@producersinc.com.

HANKIN, JOSEPH NATHAN, college president; b. N.Y.C., Apr. 6, 1940; s. Harry and Beatrice H.; m. Carole G. Hankin, Aug. 20, 1960; children— Marc, Laura, Brian. BA in Social Scis. (N.Y. State Regents scholar), CCNY, 1961; MA in History, Columbia U., 1962, Ed.D. in Adminstrn. Higher Edn. (Kellogg fellow), 1967; postgrad. seminar, Harvard U. Grad. Sch. Bus., 1979; Litt.D. (hon.), Mercy Coll., 1979; DHL (hon.), Coll. New Rochelle, 1996; D Pedagogy (hon.), Manhattan Coll., 2000; DHL (hon.), Lehman Coll., 2002. Cert. large complex case arbitrator Am. Arbitration Assn. N.Y. State Regents coll. teaching fellow, 1961-63; fellow dept. history CCNY, 1962-63, lectr., 1963-65; lectr. history Bklyn. Coll. CUNY, summer 1963, lectr. history Queens Coll., summer 1964; course asst. dept. higher and adult edn. Tchrs. Coll., Columbia U., spring 1965, occasional lectr., 1965—, adj. prof. higher and adult edn., 1976—; dir. evening div. and summer session Harford Jr. Coll., Bel Air, Md., 1965-66, dean continuing edn. and summer session, 1966-67, pres., 1967-71, Westchester C.C., Valhalla, N.Y., 1971—. Mem. vis. team Md. State Bd. Cmty. Colls., Annapolis, 1976; bd. dirs. Mut. Funds Trust, 1988—; mem. task force on study higher edn. in D.C., 1966-67; spkr., panelist and cons. in field; condr. workshops and seminars. Contbr. articles and revs. to profl. publs. and newspapers. Mem. adv. com. Columbia U. Tchrs. Coll. C.C. Ctr., 1970—; bd. dirs., mem. exec. com. Westchester C.C. Found., 1971—; mem. Tri-State Coll. Consortium (now Eastern Ednl. Consortium), 1975—, pres., 1977-89, fin. com., 1982-87; mem. adv. com. SUNY Ednl. Opportunity Ctr., 1975—; mem. Coun. for Arts in Westchester, N.Y., 1971—, mem. coll. adv. com., 1971, mem. arts action plan for Westchester com., 1974-75, mem. Friends of Arts, 1976—, mem. benefit com., 1983-86, trustee, 1983-85; mem. Westchester Rockland Newspapers Lend-A-Hand Adv. Bd., 1974-90; mem. Friends Harrison Pub. Libr., 1980—, Friends Neuberger Mus., 1979—; bd. advisors Hudson River Mus., 1985—; mem. adv. bd. Westchester County Hist. Soc., 1981-84; trustee Westchester Econ. Understanding Found., 1979, Hartford Family Found., 1984—. Recipient Disting. Service award Bel Air (Md.) Jaycees, 1968, Brotherhood award Westchester region NCCJ, 1975, Arabic Soc. plaque, 1977, Plaque Pres. Ea. Ednl. Consortium, 1978, Championship of Youth award Youth Services div. B'nai B'rith, 1978, Community Svc. award Soc. Italian-Am. Orgns., 1986, plaque Alpha Beta Gamma and Drucker Mgmt. Soc., 1983, plaque Italian Club, 1984, plaque French Club, 1977, Honor award AIA, 1983, Cert. Vol. Services United Way Westchester, 1986, Cert. Appreciation Westchester 2000, 1988; Kellog fellow in C.C. adminstrn. Columbia U., 1965. Mem. Am. Assn. Jr. Colls. (v.p. 1971-74, bd. dirs. 1971-74, pres.'s acad. 1976—, various coms., Cert. Recognition 1981), Am. Assn. Higher Edn. (charter, life), Assn. Pres.'s Public C.C.s (legis. com. 1974-76, 86—, exec. com., mem.-at-large 1987-88), Faculty Student Assn. Westchester C.C. (dir. 1971—), Coll. Consortium for Internat. Studies (exec. com. 1974-88, sec.-treas. 1984-88, mem. ad hoc com. on by-laws 1983), Middle States Assn. Colls. and Schs. (ad hoc com. centennial celebration 1985—, pres. 1999) N.Y. State Assn. Jr. Colls., Young Presidents Orgn. (pres.'s forum 1979-90, founding dir. 1979-80, 84-85, day chairperson 1977-89), CEO Orgn., World Pres. Orgn., Westchester County C. of C. (bd. dirs. 1981-85, chmn. 1988, reaccreditation task force com. on staff 1982-83, chmn. nomination com. 1983-85), Phi Delta Kappa, Alpha Beta Gamma (hon.), Phi Theta Kappa. Home: 4 Merion Dr Purchase NY 10577-1302 Office: Westchester Community Coll 75 Grasslands Rd Valhalla NY 10595-1636 E-mail: joseph.hankin@sunywcc.edu. *In order to succeed, to do the best we can at whatever level on whatever path we choose, we do not need brilliance, nor money, nor luck, nor successful parents, nor benign climate, nor even perfect health. We do need belief and hope, imagination and inventiveness, foresight, preparation, and also motivation and perseverance, as well as hard work.*

HANKIN, LAWRENCE ALAN, actor; b. N.Y.C., Dec. 7, 1937; s. Ruben Robert and Phyllis Pearle Hankin. BA, Syracuse U., 1960. Lifeguard N.Y.C. Dept. Beaches, 1955—59; short order cook The Orange Diner, Syracuse, 1957—58; postman U.S. Post Office Dept., Farrockaway, NY, 1957—59; stand-up comedian various night clubs, 1960—69; actor Plattsburgh (N.Y.) Summer Stock, 1960—61, The Compass Players, St. Louis, 1961, Second City, Chgo., 1961, The Com., San Francisco, 1961—70; actor various films and tv shows Hollywood, Calif., 1978—. Filmmaker Solly's Diner Prodn., Hollywood, 1980, Sometimes Jones Prodn., Santa Monica, 1990—. Writer, dir., performer : (film short) Solly's Diner, 1979 (Acad. award nomination, 1979); The Last Tape, 2002. Mem.: SAG, AFTRA. Avocations: bicycling, drawing, painting.

HANKIN, MITCHELL ROBERT, lawyer; b. Phila., May 16, 1949; s. Samuel and Harriet (Cohen) H. BA, Trinity Coll., Hartford, Conn., 1971; JD, Columbia U., 1974. Bar: Pa. 1974, U.S. Dist. Ct. (ea. dist.) Pa. 1975, U.S. Ct. Appeals (3d cir.) 1975. Assoc. Blank, Romeklaus, Comisky, Phila., 1974-75; asst. U.S. atty. U.S. Atty.'s Office, Phila., 1975-76; ptnr. Hankin Enterprises, Willow Grove, Pa., 1976—. Bd. dirs. Bank of Old York, Bank of King of Prussia (Pa.), Royal Bank of Pa. Mem. ABA, Pa. Bar Assn., Montgomery County Bar Assn., Phila. Bar Assn., Phi Beta Kappa. Home: 1115 Barberry Rd Bryn Mawr PA 19010-1907

HANKINS, PATRICIA L. ceramic artist, educator; b. Sharon, Pa., Apr. 26, 1944; d. George Brinton and Jean (McFadden) Lykens; m. Frank Chapin Hankins, June 8, 1968; children: Charlotte Chapin, Katherine Brinton. BA, Swarthmore Coll., 1966; MA in Art History, Bryn Mawr Coll., 1967; MFA in Ceramics, Ga. State U., 1995. Asst. prof. art gordon Coll., Barnesville, Ga., 1983-99; ceramic artist Clay Path Studios, Meansville, Ga., 1995—. Vis. prof. Ga. State U., Atlanta, 2000-2003. Contbr.: Best of Pottery, 1996, Modern Ceramic Design, 1998, Wheel Thrown Ceramics, 1998; contbr. articles t o Clay Times; one-woman shows include Ga. State U., Atlanta, 1995, Birmingham (Ala.) So. Coll., 1996, U. S.C., Beaufort, 1996, Bare Hands Gallery, Birmingham, 1997, 621 Gallery, Tallahassee, 1998, Pennebaker Gallery, Jackson, Miss., 1999, 2002, Warren Wilson Coll., Asheville, N.C., 2000. Pres. Arts Coun. Pike County, Ga., 1983-86, Friends of Libr., Pike County, 1990-92. Kress fellow Bryn Mawr Coll., 1967, Bryn Mawr fellow, 1968. Mem. Nat. Coun. for Edn. in Ceramic Arts (moderator Ft. Worth 1997, Columbus, Ohio 1998), Coll. Art Assn., Archaeol. Inst. Am., Am. Crafts Coun. Avocations: travel, sailing, tennis, golf, computer graphics. Home: 155 Dunn Rd Meansville GA 30256-2129 E-mail: claypath@earthlink.net.

HANKINS, PHILLIP R. music educator; b. Ironton, Ohio, June 22, 1945; s. Carl Wilson and Nellie Marie Hankins; m. Deidre May, June 14, 1973; 1 child, Sean. MusB in Edn., U. Tampa, 1972. Cert. Tchr. Music K-12 1972. Dir. band Hillsborough County Sch. Sys., Tampa, Fla., 1972—. Music dir. Keystone United Meth. Ch., Odessa, Fla., 1995—. Staff sgt. USAF, 1967—71. Mem.: Fla. Band Master Assn. (n/a). Democrat-Npl. Methodist. Avocation: tournament bass fishing. Home: 604 Speck Ct Tampa FL 33613 Office Fax: 813-872-5359. Personal E-mail: hankins604@aol.com.

HANKINSON, DEBORAH G. former state supreme court justice; BS with distinction, Purdue U.; MS, U. Tex., Dallas; JD, So. Meth. U. Bar: Tex., U.S. Ct. Appeals (5th cir.) 1995; cert. civil appellate law Tex. Bd. Legal Specialization. Spl. edn. tchr. Plano (Tex.) Ind. Sch. Dist.; assoc. Thompson and Knight, Dallas, 1983-95; judge U.S. Ct. Appeals (5th cir.), Dallas, 1996, Tex. Supreme Ct., Dallas, 1997—2003. Liaison Gender Bias Reform Implementation Com., family law sect. Dallas Bar. Editor-in-chief Southwestern Law Jour. Fellow Tex. Bar Found., Dallas Bar Found. Mem. ABA (litigation sect., com. appellate practice, judicial sect.), State Bar Tex. (judicial, litigation, appellate sects.), Dallas Bar Assn. (apellate law sect.), 5th Cir. Bar Assn., Coll. of State Bar Tex., Order of the Coif.*

HANKINSON, TIM, soccer coach; b. Feb. 18, 1955; BS in Athletic Adminstrn., U. S.C., 1977. Lic. coach U.S. Soccer Fedn. Head coach Oglethorpe U., Atlanta, 1978-80, Ala. A&M, 1980-81, De Paul U., 1982, Datagraphic Soccer Club, 1984, Syracuse U., 1985-90, UMF Tindastol, Iceland 2nd Divsn., 1991; head coach, gen. mgr., owner Charleston Battery, USISL, 1992-94; gen. mgr. Raleigh Flyers, USISL, 1995; dir. player devel. Major League Soccer, 1996-98; head coach Tampa Bay Mutiny, 1998—. Former coach U.S. Pro-40 Select team; former chmn. mktg. com. USISL. Named Big East Conf. Coach of Yr., 1986, Nat. Coach of Yr., USISL, 1994. Achievements include leading Ala. A&M to NCAA Final Four, 1980, 81, Datagraphic Soccer Club to U.S. Amateur Cup semifinals, 1984, Syracuse U. to Big East Conf. Tournament Championship, 1985. Office: care Tampa Bay Mutiny 4042 N Himes Ave Tampa FL 33607-6653

HANKS, ALAN R. chemistry educator; b. Balt., Nov. 30, 1939; s. Raymond Hanks and Lillian (Simon) Miller; m. Beverly Jean Hinson, Jan. 17, 1961; children: Craig, Denise, Leta. BS in Physics, West Tex. State U., 1962; MS in Biophys. Chemistry, N. Mex. Highlands U., 1964; PhD in Biophysics, Pa. State U., 1967. Nuclear med. sci. officer Armed Forces Inst. Pathology, Washington, 1967-69; from asst. to prof. biochemistry, biophysics Tex. A&M U., Coll. Sta., Tex., 1969-82; state chemist, seed commnr., prof. Purdue U., West Lafayette,

Ind., 1982—. Corr. mem., liaison Collaborative Internat. Pesticide Analytical Coun., 1988—; mem. FAO panel on pesticides UN, 1991—, mem. WHO panel on pesticides, 2001—. Contbr. articles to profl. jours. Fellow Assn. Ofcl. Analytical Chemists (chmn. methods bd. 1986-89, bd. dirs. 1990-96, sec.-treas. 1992-93, pres.-elect 1993-94, pres. 1994-95, chmn. liaison com. 1997-2001); mem. Assn. Am. Feed Control Ofcls. (chmn. minerals com. 1985-96, pres. 1999-2000, lab. methods and svc. com. 1988-93, bd. dirs. 1996-2001, codex observer mem. to codex com. on methods of analysis and sampling 2000—), Assn. Am. Plant Food Control Ofcls. (chmn. Magruder check sample com. 1988-90, bd. dirs. 1989-94, chmn. environ. affairs com. 1990-99, pres.-elect 1991-92, pres. 1992-93). Avocations: fishing, gardening, sports, travel. Home: PO Box 2627 West Lafayette IN 47906-2627 E-mail: hanksa@purdue.edu.

HANKS, CLAY DAVID, academic administrator; b. Luling, Tex., Oct. 27, 1959; s. Edgar Earl and Laura Ann Hanks, Laura Ann Hanks; m. Cheryl Lynn Otte; children: Clayton, Cole. BA, Tex. A&M U., 1988, MPA, 1989, PhD, 2000. Sr. acad. bus. adminstr. Tex. A&M Sys. Health Sci. Ctr., College Station, 1999—2001, dir. adminstrn., 2001—02. Survey coord. Tex. schs. Pub. Policy Rsch. Inst., College Station, 1993—96. Author: (instr. manual) An Introduction to Political Science Methods, 1992; contbr. articles to profl. jours. Mem. Easterwood Airport Zoning Bd., College Station, 1992—93. Home: 711 Honeysuckle College Station TX 77845 Office: Tex A&M Sys Health Sci Ctr 1716 Briarcrest Dr Bryan TX 77802 Office Fax: 979-845-7929. Personal E-mail: brazosinvest1@hotmail.com. Business E-Mail: chanks@medicine.tamu.edu.

HANKS, EUGENE RALPH, land developer, rancher, forester, retired military officer, investor; b. Corning, Calif., Dec. 11, 1918; s. Eugene and Lorena B. Hanks; m. Frances Elliot Herrick, Mar. 4, 1945; children: Herrick, Russell, Stephen, Nina. Student, Calif. Poly. Coll., 1939-41, U. So. Calif., 1949-50, Am. U., 1958-59; grad., Command and Staff Coll., Norfolk, Va., 1960. With Naval Aviation Flight Tng.,V-5 Program USN, 1941-42, commd. ensign, 1942, advanced through ranks to capt., 1963; carrier fighter pilot, Am. Ace, six victories, 1942-45; test pilot Naval Air Test Ctr., 1946-48; mem. Navy Flight Exhbn. Team Blue Angels, 1950; commdg. officer 3 jet fighter squadrons including Navy's 1st squadron of F4 Phantoms, Mach II Missile Fighters, Miramar, Calif., 1952-61; 1st ops. officer U.S.S. Constellation, 1961-62; dir. ops. Naval Air Missile Test Ctr., 1963—66; test dir. Joint Task Force Two, Albuquerque, 1966-69; ret., 1969; owner, mgr., developer Christmas Tree Canyon, Cebolla Springs and Mountain River subdivs., Mora, N.Mex., 1967—. Decorated Navy Cross, DFC with star (2), Air medal (7), Legion of merit; named Citizen of Yr., Citizen's Com. for Right to Bear Arms, 1987, 93. Mem.: NRA, Am. Forestry Assn., Assn. Naval Aviation, Mora C. of C., Blue Angels Assn., Combat Pilots Assn., Ret. Officers Assn., Am. Fighter Aces Assn., Am. Aviation Mus., Naval Aviation Mus. Found., Dun and Bradstreet's Million Dollar Club, Oxford Club (chmns. cir.), Am. Legion, Gt. Britain Legion of Valor. Republican. Home and Office: Christmas Tree Canyon Box 239 Mora NM 87732-0239 E-mail: rhanks@nnmt.net.

HANKS, GARY ARLIN, psychology educator; b. Salt Lake City, July 2, 1944; s. John D. and Erva (Wright) H.; m. Diana Twelves, 1968 (div. 1978); m. Suzanne Warnock Ostler, Dec. 20, 1984 (div. 1985); m. Ecaterina Manolache, 1998; 1 child, Sara Elena. BS, U. Utah, 1968, MSW, 1972; clin. cert. Washingtonian dept. psychiat., Harvard U., 1973; PhD in Psychology, Calif. U., L.A., 1977. Cert. social worker; diplomate Am. Psychotherapy Assn. Asst. prof. U. South Fla., Tampa, 1973-74; clinician LDS Ch. Social Svcs., L.A., 1975-77; chief psychiat. social worker William Beaumont Army Med. Ctr., El Paso, Tex., 1977-78; chmn. dept. psychology Internat. Relative Psychology Inst., Salt Lake City, 1984—; pres. Relative Analysis Assocs., Salt Lake City, 1994—, Mate Selection Internat., Salt Lake City, 1994—. Author: Maturity Analysis Test, 1985, 2002, Spirituality Analysis Test, 1986, 2002, Relative Psychology, 1991, Relative Religion, 1991, Relative Analysis, 1991, Relationship Maturity, 1994, Emotional Maturity Test Battery, 1994. Missionary LDS Ch., Fed. Republic Germany, 1963; polit. activist. Capt. U.S. Army, 1968-78. Rsch. grantee NIMH, 1973. Mem. Am. Fedn. Socs. Clin. Social Workers. Avocations: outdoor life, travel, disco dancing. *The basis of emotional maturity is that the more emotionally independent one becomes, the more others will oppress him.*

HANKS, GEORGE CAROL, JR., state judge; b. Breaux Bridge, La., Sept. 25, 1964; s. George Carol and Quenola Reese Hanks; m. Stacey L. Hanks, Apr. 29, 1995. JD, Harvard U., 1989; BA summa cum laude, La. State U., 1986. Bar: Tex. 1989, U.S. Dist. Ct. (so. dist.) Tex. 1992, U.S. Ct. Appeals (5th cir.) 1993, U.S. Dist. Ct. Ariz. 1994, U.S. Supreme Ct. 2003, U.S. Ct. Internat. Trade 2003. Jud. law clk., Houston, 1989-91; assoc. atty. Fulbright & Jaworski, Houston, 1991-96; shareholder Wickliff & Hall PC, Houston, 1996-2001; judge 157th Dist. Ct., State of Tex., 2001—02; justice Tex. Ct. Appeals (1st cir.), Houston, 2003—. Panel chmn. grievance com., spl. disciplinary counsel State Bar Tex., Houston, 1993-99. Contbr. articles to profl. jours. Bd. dirs. Big Bros. and Big Sisters, Houston, 1995-97, Houston chpt. ARC, 2001—. Fellow Houston Bar Assn.; mem. Fed. Bar Assn., Nat. Bar Assn., Am. Judges Assn., Houston Bar Assn. Avocations: aviation, scuba diving. Home: 12035 Circle Dr E Houston TX 77071 Office: 1037 San Jacinto Fl 10 Houston TX 77002 E-mail: ghanks@prodigy.net., george.hanks@1stcoa.courts.state.tx.us.

HANKS, JAMES JUDGE, JR., lawyer; b. Washington, Jan. 31, 1943; s. James Judge and Dorothy (Teeple) H. AB, Princeton U., 1964; LLB, U. Md., 1967; LLM, Harvard U., 1969. Bar: Md. 1967. Law clk. to judge U.S. Ct. Appeals (D.C. cir.), 1967—68; assoc. Weinberg and Green Law Firm, Balt., 1969—74; ptnr. Weinberg and Green, Balt., 1975—93, Ballard Spahr Andrews & Ingersoll, LLP, Balt., 1993—2003, Venable, LLP, Baltimore, 2003—. Vis. prof. of law Cornell Law Sch., 1993, adj. prof. law 1994—, adj. prof. mgmt., Cornell Bus. Sch., 1999—; adj. prof. law Northwestern Law Sch., 1997, 2002-; lectr. various profl. orgns. and law schs.; Commerzbank vis. prof. law Bucerina Law Sch., 2003. Author: Maryland Corporation Law; co-author: Legal Capital, 3d edit.; contbr. articles to profl. jours. Fellow Am. Bar Found.; mem. ABA, Am. Law Inst., Md. State Bar Assn. (chmn. bus. law sect. 1982-83), Md. Club. Democrat. Episcopalian. Home: 1159 Riverside Ave Baltimore MD 21230-4119 Office: Venable LLP Two Hopkins Plz Ste 1800 Baltimore MD 21201

HANKS, LAWRENCE JULIUS, SR., management consultant, researcher; s. James Jethro Hanks; m. Diane Gordon, Aug. 7, 1982; children: Shonda Latrice, Lawrence Julius II, Latoysha Joy Brown, Mahogany Arlette. BS, Morehouse Coll., Atlanta, 1976; PhD, Harvard U., 1984. Chair dept. of polit. sci. Tuskegee U., Ala., 1984—93; dean office of African am. affairs Ind. U., Bloomington, 1993—98. Dir. The African Am. Documentation Project, Bloomington, Ind., Project Particpate/ Ala. State U., Montgomery, 1990—93. Author: (book) Black Political Empowerment in Three Georgia Counties; editor: Black and Multiracial Politics; author: 365 Days of Kwanzaa, Daily Fruit; contbr. book. Mem. Nat. Urban League's Nat. Bd. of Trustee's, N.Y.C., 1980—83; bd. mem. The Ala. Adv. Com. to the U.S. Commn. on Civil Rights, Montgomery, Ala. Recipient Christmas Parade Grand Marshal, City of Ft. Gaines, Ga., 2002. Mem.: Nat. Conf. of Black Polit. Scientist, So. Polit. Sci. Assn. (sect. chair for the so. politics sect. 1994—95), Am. Polit. Sci. Assn. (mem. com. on the status of blacks 1996—98), NAACP (life), Kappa Alpha Psi Frat. Avocations: travel, collecting memorabilia, personal empowerment, reading. Office: Dept of Polit Sci 1100 Et 7th Str Bloomington IN 47405 Office Fax: 812-855-2027. E-mail: lhanks@indiana.edu.

HANKS, TOM, actor, producer, director; b. Concord, Calif., July 9, 1956; m. Samantha Lewes, 1978 (div. 1985); 2 children; m. Rita Wilson, Apr. 1988; children: Chester, Truman Theodore. Student, Calif. State U., Sacramento. Motion picture appearances include He Knows You're Alone, 1980, Splash, 1984, Bachelor Party, 1984, Volunteers, 1985, The Man with One Red Shoe, 1985, The Money Pit, 1986, Nothing in Common, 1986, Every Time We Say Goodbye, 1986, Dragnet, 1987, Big, 1988, Punchline, 1988, Turner and Hooch, 1989, The 'Burbs, 1989, Joe Versus the Volcano, 1990, Bonfire of the Vanities, 1990, Radio Flyer, 1992, A League of Their Own, 1992, Sleepless in Seattle, 1993, Philadelphia, 1993 (Golden Globe for Best Actor - Drama 1994, Academy Award for Best Actor 1994), Forrest Gump, 1994 (Academy Award for Best Actor 1995), Apollo 13, 1995, Celluloid Closet, 1995, Toy Story (voice), 1995, Saving Private Ryan, 1998 (nominated Acad. awards), You've Got Mail, 1998, Toy Story 2 (voice), 1999, The Green Mile, 1999, Cast Away, 2000 (Golden Globe for Best Actor 2001), Road to Perdition, 2002, Catch Me If You Can, 2002; actor, dir., writer That Thing You Do!, 1996; prodr. My Big Fat Greek Wedding, 2002; TV movie appearances include Mazes and Monsters, 1982, I Am Your Child, 1997, (TV series) Bosom Buddies, 1980-82, (TV mini-series) dir., prodr., writer From the Earth to the Moon, 1998 (Emmy award for best mini-series, 1999), Band of Brothers, 2001 (Emmy awards for best directing and best mini-series, 2002); guest star (TV shows) Saturday Night Live, 1985, The Tonight Show, Late Night with David Letterman, Tales from the Crypt (None But the Lonely Heart, also dir.), Fallen Angels (I'll Be Waiting), also dir., 1993. Recipient Louella O. Parsons Awd., Hollywood Women's Press Club, 1994, Golden Globe award, 1995, People's Choice award, 1995, 99; named Man of the Yr., Harvard's Hasty Pudding Theater Club, 1995. Mem. Actors' Equity Assn., Screen Actors Guild, AFTRA. Office: Creative Artists Agy c/o Richard Lovett 9830 Wilshire Blvd Beverly Hills CA 90212-1804*

HANLE, PAUL ARTHUR, museum administrator; b. Newark, N.J., Oct. 27, 1947; s. John Edward and Claire (Kane) Hanle; m. Joan Burroughs, Oct. 1979. AB in Physics, Princeton U., 1969; MS in Physics, MPhil, Yale U., 1972, PhD in History of Sci, 1975. Research fellow Smithsonian Instn., Washington, 1973-74; assoc. curator Nat. Air and Space Mus., Smithsonian Instn., Washington, 1974-78, curator of sci. and tech., 1978-80, acting chmn. space sci. and exploration dept., 1980-81, chmn. dept., 1981-84, assoc. dir. for research, 1984-86; assoc. dir. acad. affairs, 1987; exec. dir. Md. Sci. Ctr., Balt., 1987-96; pres. Acad. Natural Scis., Phila., 1996-2000, Biotechnology Inst., Washington, 2000—. Mem. Inst. Advanced Study, Princeton, 1983—84. Co-author (with Paul Forman): Einstein. A Centenary Exhibition, 1979; author: Bringing Aerodynamics to America, 1982; editor: High Technology on Earth, 1979; co-editor (with Von Del Chamberlain): Space Science Comes of Age, 1981; co-author (with Robert W. Smith): The Space Telescope: A Study of NASA Science Technology, 1989. Recipient Rsch. award, Smithsonian Instn., 1978, Robert H. Goddard Hist. Essay award, 1979; NSF intern, 1971, NSF traineeship, 1971—72. Mem.: AAAS, Soc. History Tech., Am. Assn. Mus., Assn. Sci. & Tech. Ctrs., Sigma Xi. Office: Biotechnology Inst Ste 202 1840 Wilson Blvd Arlington VA 22201-3000 E-mail: phanle@biotechinstitute.org.

HANLEY, DANIEL F., JR., neurologist, educator; b. Portland, Maine, May 17, 1949; s. Daniel F. and Mara (Benoit) H.; m. Christine Marie Wright, 1982; children: Christina, Daniel, Margaret, William Thomas. BA, Williams Coll., 1971; MD, Cornell U., 1975. Diplomate in neurology Am. Bd. Neurology and Psychiatry; diplomate Am. Bd. Internal Medicine, Nat. Bd. Med. Examiners. Dir. neuroscis. CCU, Johns Hopkins Med. Instns., Balt., 1983-99, prof. dept. neurology, 1996—, prof. dept. neurosurgery, 1996—, prof. anesthesia and critical care medicine, 1996—, prof. Sch. Nursing, 1999—, Jeffrey and Harriet Legum chair, 1999—, dir. brain injury outcomes, 1999—. Cons. neurol. ICU planning Mayo Clinic, N.Y.C., 1990, Sinai Hosp., Balt., 1994-95, UCSF, 1992, Columbia Presbyterian, 2000. Author: Neurocritical Care, 1989, Neurocritical Care, 1997, Update in ICU and Emergency Medicine, 1997; contbr. more than 200 articles to profl. jours. Recipient Alexander Humboldt rsch. prize, 1996-97; grantee NIH, 1984-98, 99—, FDA, 1999—, France-Merrick Found., 2000—. Fellow, Am. Acad. Neurology, Am. Heart Assn. (stroke coun.); mem.: AMA, Stroke (sect. editor 1999—), Soc. Critical Care Medicine (edn. bd. 1990—2003), Nat. Stroke Assn. (exec. bd., NINR coun. 2000—), Am. Soc. Neurologic Investigation (pres.). Roman Catholic. Avocations: tennis, skiing, swimming. Home: 1204 Berwick Rd Ruxton MD 21204-6504 Office: Johns Hopkins Med Instn Dept Neurology 600 N Wolfe St Jefferson 1-109 Baltimore MD 21287 0001 E-mail: dhanley@jhmi.edu.

HANLEY, FRANK, labor union official; b. N.Y.C., July 5, 1930; s. Simon P. and Sally Hanley; m. Patricia Healy, 1959; 6 children. Student, U. Notre Dame, 1954-58, trade union program, Harvard U., 1959. Mem. Internat. Union Oper. Engrs., Washington, 1948—, asst. to gen. pres., 1959-74, v.p., 1974-79, sec.-treas., 1979-89, gen. pres., 1990—. Mem. exec. coun. AFL-CIO; bd. dirs. Union Labor Life Ins. Co. Mem. VFW, Notre Dame Club. Office: Internat Union Operating Engrs 1125 17th St NW Washington DC 20036-4707

HANLEY, FRED WILLIAM, librarian, educator; b. Booneville, Miss., May 13, 1939; s. John Martin and Ethel May (Robertson) H.; m. Bethany Nell Holt, June 21, 1971; children: Seth Patrick, Cassandra May. BS, Lambuth Coll., Jackson, Tenn., 1961; MDiv, Meth. Theol. Sch., Delaware, Ohio, 1964; MA in History, Ariz. State U., 1966, MA in Counseling, 1968. Cert. secondary tchr., Ariz. Assoc. pastor Prospect Street Meth. Ch., Marion, Ohio, 1961-64; tchr. history Phoenix Union High Sch. Dist., 1965-74, curriculum coord., 1974-78, chmn. English dept., 1978-89, varsity cross country coach, 1978-80, chmn. libr. dept., 1989—, chmn. tech. com., 1991—, varsity golf coach, 1980-89, 99—, varsity tennis coach, 2001—. Editor Ariz. Health Svcs. jour., 1965. Bd. dirs. Wesley Found., Tempe, Ariz., 1964-69; vol. Am. Cancer Soc., Phoenix, 1985-91; chmn. Phoenix Symphony Guild Symphonette Orch., 1993—; mem. exec. com. Phoenix Symphony Guild Orchestral Tng. Program, 1994—; libr. Phoenix Symphony Guild, 1998—. Recipient Tchr. of Yr. award West High Sch., Phoenix, 1969, Disting. Alumnae award Lambuth Coll., 1979. Mem. ALA, NEA, Ariz. Edn. Assn., Ariz. Libr. Assn., N. Cen. Assn. of Sec. Schs. Accreditation Team for Ariz., Nat. Coun. Tchrs. English., Phi Alpha Theta. Democrat. Avocations: marathon running, golf, hiking. Home: 10411 W Flower St Avondale AZ 85323-4403 Office: Alhambra High Sch 3839 W Camelback Rd Phoenix AZ 85019-2598 E-mail: fhanley@phxhs.k12.az.us.

HANLEY, HENRY GORMAN, cardiologist; b. Providence, Feb. 11, 1941; s. James Lawrence and Mary Rose (Gorman) H.; m. Linda Ellis, June 20, 1970 (div. Jan. 1989); children: Tara, April; m. Kathy Davis, Nov. 18, 1989; children: Eric, Alan. AB, Harvard U., 1962; MD, Yale U., 1966. Diplomate in internal medicine and cardiovascular diseases Am. Bd. Internal Medicine. Asst. prof. Baylor Coll. Medicine, Houston, 1971-76, asst. prof. dept. cell biophysics, 1974-76; assoc. prof. medicine U. Ky. Coll. Medicine, Lexington, 1976-80; prof. medicine, chief sect. cardiology La. State U. Med. Ctr., Shreveport, 1980—2002; cardiologist Freedman Meml. Cardiology LLC, Alexandria, La., 2002—. Contbr. articles to profl. jours. Mem. Am. Heart Assn. (pres. La. chpt. 1988-90), Am. Coll. Cardiology (mem. exec. coun. La. chpt. 1997-98, gov. La. chpt. 2000-2003), Shreveport Country Club. Roman Catholic. Avocations: golf, travel. Home: 5667 Mirador Cir Shreveport LA 71119-4009 Office: Freedman Meml Cardiology LLC Doctors Bldg Ste 112 3311 Prescott Rd Alexandria LA 71301

HANLEY, HILDA CHRISTINA, endocrinologist; b. Dundalk, Ont., Can., 1939; MD, U. Toronto, 1963. Intern Wellesley Hosp., Toronto, 1963-64; resident in internal medicine St. Vincents Hosp., Bridgeport, Conn., 1964-67; fellow in endocrinology Yale-New Haven (Conn.) Hosp., 1967-68; pvt. practice Bridgeport. Chief divsn. endocrinology St. Vincents Med. Ctr. Fellow Am. Assn. Clin. Endocrinologists; mem. AMA, ACP, Am. Diabetes Assn., Conn. State Med. Soc., Conn. Endocrine Soc. Office: 3715 Main St Ste 202 Bridgeport CT 06606-3611

HANLEY, JODI ANN, mathematician, educator; b. Green Bay, Wis., May 19, 1968; d. Richard Thomas Terrien and Jacquelynn Marie Franz; m. William Gary Hanley, Nov. 13, 1987. AS in Drafting and Engring. Tech., San Bernardino Valley Coll., San Bernardino, Calif., 1996, AS in Math., 1998; BA in Math., Calif. State U., San Bernardino, 1999, MA in Math., 2002. Enlisted, rank of E2 USMC, 1986, rose through ranks to Sgt. E5; adj. faculty, math. instr. San Bernardino Valley Coll., 2001—, Chaffey C.C., Rancho Cucamonga, Calif., 2001—, Crafton Hills Coll., Yucaipa, Calif., 2003—. Avocations: sewing, philately, gardening, math. tutor.

HANLEY, KEVIN LANCE, maintenance manager; b. Oil City, Pa., Nov. 25, 1961; s. Harold Edward and Helen Louise (Banta) H.; m. Patricia Yolanda DeLeon, Sept. 29, 1984 (div. Feb. 2001); children: Jennifer Jessica, Kevin Lance Jr; m. Carolyn Jean Rydman, May. 18, 2002; 1 adopted child, Jessica Joy Rydman. Grad. high sch., Titusville, Pa.; diploma, McDonald's Regional Hdqs., L.A., 1986. Maintenance supr. Paschen Mgmt. Corp. McDonald's, Camarillo, Calif., 1980-86, asst. mgr., 1986-88, 95, maintenance cons., 1988-89; mgr. phys. plant Westmont Coll., Santa Barbara, Calif., 1988—; apartment mgr. Bartlein & Co., Ventura, Calif., 1990-97. Gen. cons. "R" Cleaning Maintenance, Santa Paula, Calif., 1989-91; owner Custodial-Plus Svcs., Montecito, Calif., 1996—. Sec.-treas. Ch. of God of Prophecy, Carpinteria, Calif., 1987—95, 1997—2000, co-pastor, 1988—95. 1st class petty officer USNR, 1994—. Recipient Navy and Marine Corp Achievement medals, 1998, 2000. Republican. Avocations: backpacking, bowling, camping. Office: Westmont Coll 955 La Paz Rd Santa Barbara CA 93108-1023 E-mail: khanley@westmont.edu.

HANLEY, MARK YOUNG, historian, educator, researcher; b. Pueblo, Colo., Oct. 18, 1953; s. Harold Gordon Hanley and Winifred Haskell Snyder; m. Janet Susan McCormick, Aug. 7, 1976; children: Matthew Mark, Kelly Suzanne. BA, Western State Coll., 1976; MA, U. Ill., 1984; PhD, Purdue U., 1989. Vis. asst. prof. history Ind. U.-Purdue U., Indpls., 1991—91; asst. prof. history N.E. Mo. State U., Kirksville, 1991—96; assoc. prof. history Truman State U., Kirksville, Mo., 1997—. Editl. bd. mem. Truman State U. Press, Kirksville, 2000—03. Author: (book) Beyond a Christian Commonwealth: The Protestant Quarrel with the American Republic, 1830-1860; contbr. book, reference book. Grantee, Pew Charitable Trust and Nat. Assn. for the Study Am. Evangelicals, 1997. Mem.: Nat. Assn. for the Study Am. Evangelicals, Soc. for Historians the Early Am. Republic, Am. Soc. Ch. History, Orgn. Am. Historians, Rotary Internat. Avocations: antiques, skiing. Home: 22535 Harrison Trail Kirksville MO 63501 Office: Truman State Univ 100 E Normal St Kirksville MO 63501 Personal E-mail: ss04@truman.edu. E-mail: ss04@truman.edu.

HANLEY, MARY ANN, music educator, pianist, writer; b. St. Paul, Dec. 21, 1922; d. John Francis and Sophia Magdalena (Wicynska) H. BA, Coll. St. Catherine, 1953; MusM, Cinn. Conservatory, 1957; DMA, U. Cinn., 1969. Joined Sisters of St. Joseph of Carondelet, 1944. Head music dept. Holy Redeemer H.S., Marshall, Minn., 1953-55, St. Joseph's Acad., St. Paul, 1956-61; faculty mem. Coll. St. Catherine, St. Paul, 1961-95, prof., 1978-95, prof. emerita, 1995—, chair music dept., 1973-74, 76-79; faculty Internat. Music Session, Grenoble, France, 1985, 86. Music judge various orgns., 1963—; lectr. in field. Piano soloist, 1962—; contbr. articles to profl. jours. Fellow NEH, 1972, 81, Blandin Found., 1988, 89; grantee Hill Family Found., 1963, 70. Mem. Music Tchrs. Nat. Assn. (exec. bd. 1991-94, master tchr. cert.), Minn. Music Tchrs. Assn. (pres. 1989-91), Soc. Ethnomusicology, Internat. Coun. Traditional Music, Thursday Musical. Roman Catholic. Avocations: theater, swimming, plants. Home and Office: 2004 Randolph Ave #4172 Saint Paul MN 55105-1794 E-mail: mahanley@stkate.edu.

HANLEY, THOMAS PATRICK, obstetrician-gynecologist; b. St. Louis, Apr. 16, 1951; s. Thomas P. and Virginia Barbara (Lydon) H.; m. Patricia Ann McHargue, Dec. 27, 1975; children: Colleen, Thomas III, Timothy, Matthew. BA, St. Louis U., 1973, MD, 1977. Diplomate Am. Bd. Ob-gyn. Intern St. Louis U., 1977-78, resident, 1978-81; practice medicine specializing in ob-gyn St. Louis, 1981—; pres. med. staff St. Mary's Health Ctr., 1993; mem. staff Mo. Bapt. Hosp., St. Luke's Hosp.; clin. prof. St. Louis U. Med. Sch., 1983—. Mem. exec. com. St. Louis Med. Group, 1995-2000. Mem. AMA (Physicians Recognition award 1981—), Am. Coll. Ob-Gyn. (Physicians Excellence award 1986—), Md. State Med. Soc., St. Louis Gynecol. Soc. (pres. 1989-90), St. Louis Met. Med. Soc. Republican. Roman Catholic. Avocation: golf. Office: 1035 Bellevue Ave Ste 208 Saint Louis MO 63117-1846

HANLEY, THOMAS RICHARD, engineering educator; b. Logan, W.Va., July 26, 1945; s. Thomas Jesse and Dorothy Louise (Hay) H.; m. Norma Kathryn Decker, Dec. 27, 1979; children: Thomas Jeffrey, Alan Michael, Andrew Richard, Caitlin Marisa. BSChemE, Va. Poly. Inst., 1967; MSChemE, Va. Poly. Inst. and State U., 1971, PhDChemE, 1972; MBA in Mgmt., Wright State U., 1975. Registered profl. engr., Ky. Devel. engr. AF Materials Lab., Wright Patterson AFB, Ohio, 1972-75; asst. prof. Tulane U., New Orleans, 1975-79; assoc. prof. Rose-Hulman Inst. Tech., 1979-83; prof., dept. head La. Tech. U., Ruston, 1983-85; prof., chmn. dept. Fla. State U., Fla. A&M U., Tallahassee, 1985-91; dean Speed Sci. Sch. U. Louisville, 1991—. Bd. dirs. Plasticolors, Ashtabula, Ohio; divsn. advisor NSF, Washington, 1987-93; presenter at numerous nat. and internat. profl. confs. Contbr. articles to profl. jours. Capt. USAF, 1972-75. Recipient award Soc. Am. Mil. Engrs., 1966, 67, Acad. award Am. Legion, 1967, Ralph R. Teetor Ednl. award SAE, 1989, Outstanding Engr. in Edn. award Ky. Soc. Profl. Engrs., 1994; grantee NSF, Nat. Renewable Energy Lab., GE, Colgate-Palmolive, United Catalysts, IKA Works, Swan Biomass, Toro, Olin, Stone and Webster. Fellow AIChE (profl. devel. recognition cert. 1980, student chpt. advisor award 1979); mem. Am. Soc. Engring. Edn., Nat. Assn. Basketball Coaches, Sigma Xi, Phi Kappa Phi, Tau Beta Pi, Phi Lambda Upsilon, Omega Chi Epsilon. Office: U Louisville Speed Sci School Louisville KY 40292-0001 E-mail: tom.hanley@louisville.edu.

HANLEY, WILLIAM HERBERT, association executive; b. S.I., N.Y., July 12, 1942; s. John J. and Norma M. (Freeman) H.; m. Irene A. Petrou, June 28, 1969; children: Matthew D., Elizabeth A. BA, Manhattan Coll., 1964; MA, Marquette U., 1966. Instr. Manhattan Coll., Riverdale, N.Y., 1966-68; assoc. prof. Rockland Community Coll., Suffern, N.Y., 1968-79; exec. adminstr. Soc. Cosmetic Chemists, N.Y.C., 1979-88; exec. v.p. Illuminating Engring. Soc. N.Am., N.Y.C., 1988—. Mem. Am. Soc. Assn. Execs. (cert.), N.Y. Soc. Assn. Execs. (bd. dirs. 1990—), Coun. Engring. and Sci. Soc. Execs. Roman Catholic. Office: Illuminating Engring Soc NAm 120 Wall St Ste 17 New York NY 10005-4001 E-mail: whanley7007@aol.com., whanley@iesna.org.

HANLIN, TODD CAMPBELL, education educator; b. Buchanan, Mich., Nov. 9, 1941; s. Philip R. and Doris Evelyn (Campbell) H.; children: Rob-Phillip, Carrie Elizabeth. AB, Wabash Coll., 1964; MA in German, U. Kans., 1967; PhD in German, Bryn Mawr Coll., 1975. Instr. German The Coll. of Wooster, Ohio, 1967-71; asst. prof. of German U. Pa., Phila., 1975-81; asst. prof. to prof. U. Ark., Fayetteville, 1981—. Cons. numerous scholarly pubs., 1978—. Author: Franz Kafka: Kunstprobleme, 1977; translator: Anton Fuchs, The Deserter, 1991, Gerald Szyszkowitz, On The Other Side, 1991, Gustav Ernst, Springtime on the Via Condotti, 1997, Gerald Szyszkowitz, Murder at the Western Wall, 2000, The Best of Austrian Science Fiction, 2001. Danforth Assoc. award Danforth Found., St. Louis, 1979; recipient Fulbright award for German Civilization, Bonn, Germany, 1982, 95. Mem. Am. Assn. Tchrs. of German (pres., v.p. 1973—), German Studies Assn. (session dir. 1983 conf.), Modern Austrian Lit. and Culture Assn., Deutsche Schillergesellschaft. Office: Univ Ark 425 Kimpel Hall Fayetteville AR 72701 E-mail: thanlin@uark.edu.

HANLON, JAMES ALLISON, confectionery company executive; b. Oak Park, Ill., Nov. 27, 1937; s. James Graves and Frances (Allison) H.; m. June Weiland, May 30, 1959; children: Perian, Loretta, Jill, James. BA, U. Notre Dame, 1959; postgrad., U. London, 1979, U. Pa., 1980. Mgr. accounts Needham Harper Steers Advt., Chgo., 1959-67; mgr. mktg. L.S. Heath & Co., Inc., Robinson, Ill., 1967-70; v.p. mktg. Peter Paul Cadbury, Naugatuck, Conn., 1970-79, pres., chief exec. officer, 1983-86; pres. Cadbury Can., Toronto, Ont., 1979-83, also bd. dirs.; pres., chief exec. officer Leaf N.Am., Bannockburn, Ill., 1988-95; chmn., CEO, pres. Harmony Foods, Santa Cruz, Calif., 1996—. Nat. trustee Boy's Clubs of Am. With USMCR, 1956-59. Named Mktg. Warrior of Yr., AMR, Inc., 1979, Most Motivated Exec., 1992; recipient Kettle award Confectionary Industry, 1992. Mem. New Haven Country Club. Roman Catholic. Home: 403 Estancia Ct Monterey CA 93940 *Life unfolds itself at it's own pace...Any grand plans should be tempered by the unaticipated events.*

HANLON, LODGE L. lawyer, insurance agency executive, accountant; b. Barnesville, Ohio, Apr. 30, 1931; s. Kenneth K. and Sara (Lodge); m. Suzanne Hanlon, July 15, 1961; children: Elizabeth, Thomas, Fred. BSBA in Acctg., Kent (Ohio) State U., 1953; JD, Ohio State U., 1958. Bar: Ohio 1958; CPA, Ohio. Tax acct. Arthur Andersen & Co., Cleve., 1958-63; ptnr. Kinder Kinder & Hanlon, St. Clairsville, Ohio, 1963-84; officer Hanlon Duff & Paleudis Co., St. Clairsville, Ohio, 1984—2003, Hanlon Duff Estadt & McCormick Co. LPA, St. Clairsville, Ohio, 2003—. Assoc. instr. Ohio U., Belmont County, 1968-84. Founder, sec. Barnesville Area Edn. Found., 1980—; pres. Barnesville Exempted Village Bd. of Edn., 1978, Barnesville C. of C., 1964; chmn. Belmont County Bd. Mental Retardation/Devel. Disabilities, St. Clairsville, 1985-86. Capt. USAF, 1954-56. Mem. Estate Planning Coun. Upper Ohio Valley (bd. dirs., pres. 1991), Am. Legion, Moose, Elks (past exec. ruler Barnesville lodge 1973), Belmont Hills Country Club (trustee, officer 1985-90). Republican. Presbyterian. Avocations: golf, stamp collector. Office: Hanlon Duff Estadt & McCormick Co LPA 46457 National Rd W Saint Clairsville OH 43950-9721

HANMER, STEPHEN READ, JR., retired government executive; b. Denver, Aug. 15, 1933; s. Stephen Read and Mary Virginia (Marchant) H.; m. Lois Eileen Boteler, June 25, 1955; children: Susan Eileen Hanmer Alexander, Stephen Read III, Sara Lynn. BS in Phys., Va. Mil. Inst., Lexington, 1955; MS in Aerospace Engring., MSME, U. So. Calif., 1964. Commd. 2d lt. U.S. Army, 1956, major, 1965, lt. col., 1968, comdg. 6th bn., 32d Artillery, 1968, col., 1975, retired, 1977; assoc. prof. dept. mechanics U.S. Mil. Acad., 1964-67; def. plans div. staff mem. U.S. Mission to NATO, Brussels, 1978-81; dir. theater nuclear force policy Office of Sec., Dept. Def., Washington, 1981-84; prin. dep. asst. sec. Internat. Security Policy Dept. Def., Washington, 1984-85; amb., dep. head U.S. del. Strategic Arms Reduction Talks, 1985-87, amb., chief U.S. del., 1988-89; dep. dir. ACDA, 1989-93; asst. to pres. Kaman Scis. Corp., Alexandria, Va., 1993-98; ret., 1998. Mary Moody Northen chair dept. internat. studies Va. Mil. Inst., 2002. Decorated Legion of Merit, Bronze Star; recipient Meritorious Civilian Svc. medal U.S. Dept. Def., 1981, Sec. of Def. medal, 1987, Sr. Exec. Svc. Disting. Exec. award, 1988, Sec. State Superior Honor award, 1993, Disting. Honor award ACDA, 1993. Mem. St. Andrews Soc. Washington (sec. 1995, 96, v.p. 1997), Sertoma Club (bd. dirs. 1977), Internat. Inst. for Strategic Studies, Am. Def. Preparedness Assn. Republican. Episcopalian.

HANN, ROY WILLIAM, JR., civil engineer, educator; b. Oklahoma City, Mar. 21, 1934; s. Roy W. and Irene (Billups) H.; m. Ann Mullman, Dec. 27, 1960 (div. Apr. 1983); children: Kimberly Anne, Sharon Irene, Roy Lee, Karen Bea; m. Martha D'Anne Metting, June 23, 1984; children: Tyson Orion, Heather Eileen. BS, U. Okla., 1956, M.C.E., 1957, PhD, 1963. Registered profl. engr., Okla., Tex. lic. real estate broker, Tex. lic. comml. pilot. Engr. C.H. Guernsey and Assos., Oklahoma City, 1959-60; asst. prof. civil engring U. S.C., Columbia, 1962-64; asst. prof. civil engring. dept. environ. engring. div. Tex. A&M U., College Station, 1965-67, assoc. prof., 1967-71, prof., rsch. engr., 1971—, head environ. engring. div., 1970-75, 81-86, dir. sea grant program, 1976-77; dir. Inst. for Oil Spill Tech. Tex. Engring. Experiment Sta., 1991—. Pres. Civil Engring. Systems, Inc., Internat. Spill Tech. Corp., Hann Investments; owner, operator Spring Valley Ranches; cons. in field. Author: Fundamental Aspects of Water Quality Management, 1972; contbr. articles on computer methods, oil pollution control and water supply, water pollution to profl. jours. With USPHS, 1957-59. Recipient Palladium medal Nat. Audubon Soc. and Am. Assn. Engring. Socs., 1983. Mem. ASCE (Paper award 1970-72), Am. Soc. Engring. Edn., Tex. Soc. Profl. Engrs. (Named Outstanding Young Engr. Brazos chpt. 1969), Am. Water Works Assn. (Outstanding Paper award 1969), Sigma Xi, Sigma Chi, Chi Epsilon, Bryan-College Station Apt. Assn. (pres. 1975-76, dir. 1977-84), Omicron Delta Kappa, Tau Beta Pi. Home: 1300 Walton Dr College Station TX 77840-2529 Office: Tex A&M Univ Dept Civil Engring College Station TX 77843-3136 E-mail: r.hann@civil.tamu.edu.

HANN, WILLIAM MATHIS, chemist, researcher; b. Pittman, N.J., Apr. 15, 1945; s. William Mathis Hann and Helen Scott (King) Watts; m. Christina Freeburger, Aug. 1, 1981; children: Marlene A., Matthew A., Cynthia A. BS in Chemistry, LaSalle U., Phila., 1974. Sr. rsch. technician Rohm and Haas Co., Spring House, Pa., 1973-75, rsch. scientist, 1976-85, sr. rsch. scientist, 1985-88, group leader water treatment, 1988-01; principal scientist Indsl. Specialities, 2001—. Mem. steering com. Understanding Asia, Spring House, 1996-98; symposium co-chair Corrosion 97, 1996-97, Corrosion 98, 1997-98; symposium vice-chair Corrosion 93, 1992-93, chmn. corrosion 89, 1988-89. Contbr. articles to profl. jours. Recipient V.P.'s award and Otto Haas award Tech. Achievement. Mem. Nat. Assn. Corrosion Engrs. Achievements include development of immunoassay detection technique for ppm levels of water soluble polymers; developed well-known Acumer and Optidose dispersant product lines, which are sold world wide; primary inventor of ten U.S. patents covering dispersants, oilfield chemicals, ceramics, oil production and corrosion inhibitors. Office: Rohm and Haas Co 727 Norristown Rd Spring House PA 19477

HANNA, COLIN ARTHUR, county official, management and computer consultant; b. Abington, Pa., Dec. 3, 1946; s. Arthur and Jean Victoria (McClure) H.; m. Anne Price Hemphill, Dec. 28, 1967; children: Jean Price, Colin Alexander. AB, U. Pa., 1968. With CBS, Inc., 1969-76; account exec. CBS Radio Spot Sales, N.Y.C., 1969-70, 71-72, sales mgr. Phila., 1974-76; mgr. creative svcs. CBS-Viacom Group, N.Y.C., 1970-71; acct. exec. WCAU Radio, Phila., 1972-74; dir. sales devel. WCAU-TV, Phila., 1976; pres. Hanna & Wile Advt., Wayne, Pa., 1976-77, Tri-State Trade Exch., Inc., West Chester, Pa., 1978-80, Hanna Enterprises Ltd., 1980—. Prin. Whittlesey and Assocs., West Chester, 1980-85; pres. The Cheshire Group, West Chester, 1985-91, The Bank Execs. Network, Inc., 1988-90, PC Helper, 1991-95 Vestryman Ch. of Good Samaritan, Paoli, Pa.; mem. bd. overseers Sch. Arts and Scis. U. Pa.; elected mem. Chester County Rep. Com., 1992—; county commr. Chester County, 1995—, chmn. bd. commrs., 1998, 99, 2001, 03; bd. mem. Delaware Valley Regional Planning Commn., 1996—, chmn., 1996-97, 98—; apptd. co-chmn. Pa. Census 2000 advisory panel; apptd. mem. Human Resources Investment Coun., Sound Land Use Adv. Panel. With USNR, 1968-69. Mem. Shakespear Soc. Phila., Newcomen Soc. N.Am., Coll. Alumni Soc. U. Pa. (pres.), Gen. Alumni Soc. U. Pa. (v.p.), Alumni Assn. U. Pa. (pres.), County Commrs. Assn. Pa., Mensa, Racquet (Phila.), Radley Run Country (West Chester), Tred Avon Yacht (Oxford, Md.). Republican. Episcopalian. Home and Office: 603 Fairway Dr West Chester PA 19382-2013

HANNA, DUKE ELLSWORTH, neurological surgeon; b. Indpls., July 24, 1923; s. Duke Ellsworth and Alice Roosevelt (Morehouse) H.; m. Eleanor Jane Myron, Mar. 10, 1945; children: Anita, Cheryl, Robert. BS, Ind. U., 1944, MD, 1946. Diplomate Am. Bd. Neurol. Surgery. Resident in neurol. surgery U. Chgo., 1951-54, instr. neurol. surgery, 1954-55; asst. clin. prof. neurol. surgery UCLA, 1972-83, assoc. clin. prof. neurosurgery, 1983—. Chief neurol. surgery St. John's Hosp., Santa Monica, Calif., 1976-79, Santa Monica/UCLA Med. Ctr., 1965-75. Author: Illustrative Cranial Neuroradiology, 1967; contbr. articles to profl. jours. Coroner Jay County Ind., Redkey, 1950-51. Lt. (j.g.) USN, 1946-48. Mem. AMA, Calif. Med. Assn., Am. Soc. of Neuroimaging, Congress of Neurol. Surgery, Calif. Assn. Neurol. Surgery, Am. Assn. Neurol. Surgery. Republican. Avocations: aviation, photography. E-mail: DukeHanna@cs.com.

HANNA, EMMA HARMON, architectural designer, business owner, official; b. Sharpsville, Pa., Apr. 29, 1939; d. James McKarney Supplee and Anne (Woods) Thompson; m. William Hayes Harmon, Sept. 1, 1962 (div. 1984); 1 child, James McKarney Harmon; m. Hugh Allen Hanna, Mar. 21, 1992. BArch, Kent (Ohio) State U., 1962. Drafter W.H. Harmon Architects, Orlando, Fla., 1970-73; pres., owner The Plan Shop, Inc., Orlando and Palm Bay, Fla., 1973-87, The Plan Place, Inc., Palm Bay, 1987-97; pres. Engring. & Design Concepts, Palm Bay, 1986-97; owner, pres. The Hanna Studio, Inc., 1997—. Vice chmn. Palm Bay Utility Corp.; vice chmn. substance abuse program Broken Glass, Valkaria, Fla. Mem. coun. City of Palm Bay, 1989-91, dep. mayor, 1991-92; treas. League of Cities, Brevard County, Fla., 1989-92, East Ctrl. Fla. Planning Coun., Orlando, 1989-90; mem. Federated Rep. Women, South Brevard County, 1989-91; mem. exec. com. Brevard County Reps.; mem. Panther Athletic Assn. bd. Fla. Inst. Tech., 1990—, pres., 1995-96, women's locker room bd., 1997-2000; mem. open campus adv. coun. Brevard C.C., Holmes Regional Hosp. Devel. Coun., 1991—, bd. dirs. 1998—; bd. dirs. Holmes Regional Found., 2002--; mem. Health First Women's Adv. Coun. Bd., 1997-2000, pres., 1999, found. bd. dirs. 2002—; mem. Brevard County Commn. on Aging, 2000—; chair devel. coun. Palm Bay Hosp., 2001-03; bd. dirs. Fla. Inst. Tech. Sch. Psychology, 2002—. Mem.: Greater South Brevard C. of C. (mem. govt. affairs com., bd. dirs. 1991—93, 1998—2001), Palm Bay C. of C., Bldg. Ofcls. Assn. Brevard County (assoc., Assoc. of Yr. 1989), Home Builder and Contractors Brevard County (assoc., bd. dirs. 1993—97, 2nd v.p. 1994—95, Assoc. of Yr. 1995), Drafters Guild (organizer), Zonta Club Melbourne (bd. 1997—2001, sec. 1999—2001, Zontian of Yr. 1998), Exch. Club (chpt. pres., charter pres.). Avocations: bridge, walking. Home and Office: The Hanna Studio 1482 Meadowbrook Rd NE Palm Bay FL 32905-5007 E-mail: hannastudio@telsurf.net.

HANNA, FRANK JOSEPH, JR., credit company executive; b. Apr. 20, 1939; s. Frank Joseph and Josephine (Nahoom) Hanna; m. Vail Deadwyler, Sept. 15, 1960; children: Frank, Lisa, David. BBA, U. Ga., 1961. Credit mgr. Sears, Roebuck & Co., Atlanta, 1961—63, GM, Atlanta, 1963—65; gen. mgr. Rollins Acceptance Corp., Atlanta, 1965—81; with Credit Claims & Collections, 1981—90, First Fin. Mgmt. Corp., 1990—93, Worldwide, Inc., Atlanta, 1993—. Real estate investor, 1968. Office: 245 Perimeter Center Pky Ste 300 Atlanta GA 30346

HANNA, GEORGE VERNER, III, lawyer; b. Shelby, N.C., Mar. 2, 1943; s. George and Mildred Mae (McSwain) H.; m. Linda Faye Tyndall, May 4, 1982 (div.); children: George Verner IV, Mark W., Elizabeth P.; m. Deborah Henson Hannon, Apr. 14, 1984. AB, U. N.C., 1965, JD, 1968. Bar: N.C. 1968, U.S. Dist. Ct. (we. dist.) N.C. 1969, U.S. Dist. Ct. (ea. dist.) N.C. 1972, U.S. Dist. Ct. (mid. dist.) 1974, U.S. Ct. Appeals (4th cir.) 1976, U.S. Supreme Ct. 1976. Law clk. N.C. Supreme Ct., Raleigh, 1968-69; assoc. Moore & Van Allen, PLLC, Charlotte, N.C., 1969-73, ptnr., 1974—. Arbitrator Am. Arbitration Assn. Former com. chmn. Mecklenburg Coun. Boy Scouts Am.; past vice-chair bd. mgrs. Harris YMCA, Charlotte; past chmn. bd. mgrs. McCrorey YMCA, Charlotte; past pres., bd. dirs. So. Piedmont Legal Svcs., Charlotte, Children's Law Ctr., Charlotte. Fellow: Am. Bar Found.; mem.: Mecklenburg Bar Found. (past pres.), Mecklenburg County Bar (pres.), N.C. Bar Assn. (past bd. govs.), ABA, Charlotte Tower Club, Quail Hollow Club. Methodist. Home: 244 Hempstead Pl Charlotte NC 28207-1922 Office: Moore & Van Allen PLLC Bank of Am Corp Ctr 100 N Tryon St Ste 4700 Charlotte NC 28202-4003 Fax: 704-378-2030. E-mail: georgehanna@mvalaw.com.

HANNA, HARRY MITCHELL, lawyer; b. Portland, Oreg., Jan. 13, 1936; s. Joseph John and Amelia Cecelia (Rask) H.; m. Patricia Ann Shelly, Feb. 4, 1967; 1 child, Harry M. Jr. BS, U. Oreg., 1958; JD, Lewis and Clark Coll., 1966. Bar: Oreg. 1966, U.S. Tax Ct. 1967, U.S. Dist. Ct. Oreg. 1970, U.S. Supreme Ct. 1971, U.S. Ct. Appeals (9th cir.) 1973, U.S. Ct. Claims 1973. Airport mgr. Port of Portland, 1964-66; mng. ptnr. Hanna & Purcella, Portland, 1966-80, Niehaus, Hanna, Murphy, Green, Holloway & Connolly, Portland, 1980-88; shareholder, v.p. Hanna Strader, P.C., Portland, 1988—. Judge pro-tempore U.S. Dist. Ct. Oreg., 1973-78; adj. prof. N.W. Sch. Law, Lewis and Clark Coll., Portland, 1976-77. Trustee Emanuel Med. Ctr. Found., 1989-94; pres. Ctrl. Cath. H.S. Bd., 1992-95; vice chair Life Flight Devel. Bd., 1994-97, chair 1997—, Mem. ABA, Fed. Bar Assn., Oreg. State Bar Assn., Multnomah Bar Assn., Rotary (pres. East Portland club 1989-90). Avocations: tennis, hunting, fishing, coaching youth athletics. Office: Hanna Strader PC 1300 SW 6th Ave Ste 300 Portland OR 97201-3461

HANNA, JAMES CURTIS, state official; b. Takoma Park, Md., July 14, 1935; s. Frederick G. Hanna and Seona E. (Shenk) Young; m. Carol Patche, 1956 (div. 1973); children: Laurie Jane, Daniel Frederick; m. Janet M. Reese, 1985. AA, U. Fla., 1956; BA, U. Miami, 1964. Registered architect, Fla., Md. Draftsman Philpott, Ross & Saarinen, Ft. Lauderdale, Fla., 1964-74; constrn. mgr. Enterprise Developers, Ft. Lauderdale, 1974-75; engring. mgr. Bailey & Assoc., Ft. Lauderdale, 1975-77; staff arch. Md. Dept. Housing and Comty. Devel., Annapolis, 1977-84, adminstr. arch. and constrn., 1984-90, dir. codes adminstrn. Crownsville, 1990—. Dept. of Housing and Comty. Devel. rep. Md. Emergency Mgmt. Agy.; Dept. Housing and Comty. Devel. subject matter expert Ams. with Disabilities Act., mem. Gov.'s Emergency Mgmt. Adv. Coun., task force on energy efficiency, 2001--; mem. steering com., co-chair ea. region Coun. of State Adminstrv. Agys., mem. steering com. North East Energy Partnership, 1999-2003. Bd. dirs. Sylvan Shores Svcs. Corp., Riva, Md., 1987-93, sec.-treas., 1993; mem. Nat. Trust for Hist. Preservation, 1986-91; appted. Gov.'s Mgmt. Adv. Coun., 1996-2003. Mem. Nat. Conf. State Bldg. Codes and Stds. (del., bd. dirs., past pres., so. regional dir.), Coun. of State Adminstrv. Agys. (steering com., co-chair ea. region, apptd. mem. Md.'s Green Bldg. Coun., apptd. Md.'s task force on energy efficiency), Nat. Inst. Bldg. Scis., Nat. Fire Protection Assn., N.Am. Fireman's Assn., Md. Bldg. Ofcls. Assn. (bd. dirs., sec. 1997, 98, 91-2003), Industrialized Bldg. Commn. (rules devel. com.). Avocations: water sports, antiques, computers. Office: State of Md Dept Housing Comty Devel 100 Community Pl Crownsville MD 21032-2022

HANNA, JOHN, JR., lawyer, educator, arbitrator, mediator; b. Dec. 19, 1934; m. Jane Merchant, Dec. 27, 1958; children: Elizabeth Hanna Morss, Katharine Hanna Morgan, John M. AB, Princeton U., 1956; LLB, Harvard U., 1959. Bar: N.Y. 1960, Mass. 1964, U.S. Dist. Ct. Mass. 1965, U.S. Dist. Ct. (ea. and so. dists.) N.Y. 1963, U.S. Dist. Ct. (no. dist.) N.Y. 1976, U.S. Dist. Ct. (we. dist.) N.Y. 1983, U.S. Ct. Appeals (1st and 2d cirs.) 1963. Assoc. Root, Barrett, Cohen, Knapp & Smith, N.Y.C., 1959-61; asst. U.S. atty. So. Dist. N.Y., 1961-63; assoc. Ropes & Gray, Boston, 1963-69; counsel N.Y. State Office Employee Rels. Govs. Office, Albany, 1969-73; dep. commr., gen. counsel N.Y. State Dept. Environ. Conservation, Albany, 1973-75; ptnr. Whiteman, Osterman & Hanna, Albany, 1975—. Adj. prof. Rensselaer Poly. Inst., Troy, NY, 1988—98; adj. prof. internat. environ. law John Marshall Law Sch., 2001—; NY panel disting. neutrals CPR Inst. Alternative Dispute Resolution, 2003—; mem. adv. bd. Inst. Transnat. Arbitration. Co-author: New York State Bar Association Environmental Handbook, 1987, New York Treatise on Environmental Law, 1992. Adv. bd. Inst. for Transnat. Arbitration; active Town of Chatham Planning Bd., NY, 1976—, Princeton U. Alumni Schs. Comm. No. NY, 1982—, co-chmn., 1982—2003; treas., trustee Shaker Mus. Found., Old Chatham, NY, 1978—96; trustee ea. N.Y. chpt. The Nature Conservancy, 1994—2002, chair conservation com., 1996—2002; trustee N.Y. State Archives Partnership Trust, 1995—, chair, 1996—; trustee Olana Partnership, 2002—; mem. commn. on environ. law Internat. Union for Conservation of Nature, 1999—; vol. arbitrator VIS Internat. Comml. Moot, Pace U. Law Sch., 1998—2000; adv. coun. Ctr. for Internat. Bus. and Trade Law, John Marshall Law Sch. Mem.: ABA (internat. law sect., practice sect., natural resources and environ. sect.), N.Y. State Bar Assn. (1st vice chmn. 1981—83, chmn. 1983—84, ho. of dels. 1984—85, 2003—), Cert. Inst. of Arbitrators London. Office: Whiteman Osterman & Hanna One Commerce Plz Albany NY 12260 E-mail: jhanna@woh.com.

HANNA, LEE ANN, critical care nurse; b. Little Rock, June 16, 1961; d. David Lee and Betty Lou (Pope) Redmond; m. Anthony Warren Hanna, June 18, 1986; children: Thomas Dale, Katherine Elizabeth. AS in Nursing, Belmont Coll., 1980; BSN, Union U., 1983; MSN, Vanderbilt U., 1993. RN, Tenn. Critical care nurse Bapt. Hosp., 1980-85, Vanderbilt U., 1985-94; mgr. CQI/edn. Am. Transitional Hosp., Nashville, 1995-99; dir. edn. Centennial Med. Ctr., 1999—. Instr.: ACLS, BCLS and PALS; lectr. in field. Mem. AACCN (cert.), Nat. Assn. Healthcare Quality (cert.). E-mail: leeann.hanna@hcahealthcare.com.

HANNA, MICHAEL GEORGE, JR., immunologist, pharmaceutical executive; b. Cleve., July 7, 1936; s. Michael George and Camella (Karem) Hanna; m. Barbara Ann Pearson, Sept. 6, 1958; children: Michael George, Christina Louise, Suzanne Kathleen. BS in Biology, Baldwin-Wallace Coll., 1958; MS in Biology, Notre Dame U., 1960; PhD, U. Tenn., 1964; DSc (hon.), Baldwin-Wallace Coll., 2000. Rsch. biologist biology div. Oak Ridge Nat. Lab., 1964-68, dir. immunology carcinogenesis group, 1968-75; dir. cancer biology, head host tumor interaction sect. cancer biology program Nat. Cancer Inst. Frederick (Md.) Cancer Rsch. Facility, 1975-79, dir., 1979-82, Litton Inst. Applied Biotech., Rockville, Md., 1982-85; sr. v.p., COO Biotech. Rsch. Inst., Rockville, Md., 1985-94; pres., CEO PerImmune, Inc., Rockville, Md., 1994-98; chmn., pres., chief sci. officer Intracel, Frederick, Md., 1998—2002; chmn. emeritus, chief sci. officer Intracel Resources, Frederick, Md., 2002—. Cons. NASA Lunar Receiver Lab., 1968—70; chmn. tech. adv. com. biotech. U.S. Dept. Commerce, 1985—90; mem. working group biotech. U.S. Dept. Def., 1985—90; mem. bd. overseers Ctr. Advanced Rsch. Biotech., 1984—88; commencement spkr. Baldwin-Wallace Coll., 2000. Gen. editor: Contemporary Topics in Immunobiology, 1971—85, Vaccine Rsch., 1991—96, mem. editl. bd.: Immunopharmacology, 1978—2003, Cancer Rsch., 1978—92, Jour. Biol. Response Modifiers, 1982—2002, Cancer Metastasis, 1984—; contbr. articles of 300 to profl. jours. Chmn. local emergency planning com. homeland security Frederick County, 2002—; trustee Baldwin-Wallace Coll., 1998—. Recipient Charles Thornton award, Litton Industries, 1984. Mem.: Internat. Soc. Imunopharmacology (coun. 1991—), Am. Assn. Immunologists, Am. Assn. Cancer Rsch., Soc. Exptl. Pathology. Achievements include patents for (with others) for Tumor Specific Monoclonal Antigodies; (with others) Tumor Associated Monoclonal Antibodies Derived from Human B-Cell Line; (with others) Active Specific Immunotherapy of Carcinomas. Office: 93 Monocacy Blvd Frederick MD 21701 E-mail: hannam@intracel.com.

HANNA, NESSIM, marketing educator; b. Assiut, Egypt, Apr. 30, 1938; came to U.S., 1961, naturalized, 1973; s. Yanni and Lulu Shehata (Oweda) H.; m. Dana Lascu, Aug. 28, 1987 (div. 1988); m. Margaret Ann Curzan, 1996. BS in Commerce, Cairo U., 1958; MS in Mktg., U. Ill., 1964, PhD in Mktg, 1969. Asst. prof., chmn. dept. mktg. W.Va. Inst. Tech., Montgomery, 1968-69; asso. prof. bus. adminstrn. Mid. Tenn. State U., Murfreesboro, 1969-70; prof. mktg. No. Ill. U., De Kalb, 1970—; mktg. cons. Arab Rsch. and Adminstrn. Ctr., 1975-77, Investments Cons. Internat., 1974-77. Vis. prof. mktg. U. Petroleum and Minirals, Dharan, Saudi Arabia, 1980-81, Norwegian Sch. Mgmt., Oslo, 1988; chmn. dept. mktg., dir. research inst. King Saud U., Kassim, Saudi Arabia, 1983-84; vis. scholar Hong Kong Bapt. U., fall 1991. Author: Marketing Opportunities in Egypt: A Business Guide, 1977, Principles of Marketing, 1985, Pricing Policies and Procedures, 1995, Winning Strategies, 1991, Consumer Behavior: An Applied Approach, 2001; contbr. articles to profl. jours. Named Outstanding Citizen Citizenship Council Met. Chgo., 1974 Mem. Southwestern Social Sci. Assn., Am. Mktg. Assn., Midwest Bus. Adminstrn. Assn., Assn. Egyptian-Am. Scholars (treas.), Acad. Mktg. Sci., Am. Inst. Decision Scis., Phi Beta Lambda, Beta Gamma Sigma, Phi Kappa Phi, Alpha Mu Alpha. Republican. Christian Orthodox. Avocation: overseas travel. Home: Ste 2402 5415 N Sheridan Rd Apt 2402 Chicago IL 60640-1939 Office: No Ill U Dept Mktg Dekalb IL 60115 E-mail: nessimh@aol.com.

HANNA, SUZANNE LOUISE, nurse; b. Mankato, Minn., Aug. 31, 1953; d. Frank Edward and Phyllis Ruth (Moeller) Wilkins; m. Thomas Ray Hanna, Sept. 15, 1973; children: Elizabeth Amy, Joseph Ryan, Thomas Wilkins. Diploma in nursing with highest honors, Iowa Western C.C., Council Bluffs, 1991. RN, Iowa; cert. provider ACLS, Am. Heart Assn. Exec. sec. First Nat. Bank, Mpls., 1971-72, Nat. Bank of Am., Salina, Kans., 1972; receptionist The Evening Sentinel, Shenandoah, Iowa, 1972-73; ins. sec. Wilson Ins. Agy., Shenandoah, 1973-79; med./surg. staff nurse Shenandoah Meml. Hosp., 1980-81; office nurse Dr. Floyd A. Jones, Shenandoah, 1983-95; clin. nurse Great Plains Physician Group, Omaha, Nebr., 1995-98; emergency rm. nurse Shenandoah Meml. Hosp., 1992-95; clin. nurse Nebr. Health Sys., 1998—. Bd. dirs. Ag-Pro Corp., Shenandoah; co-chairperson family life com., 1989-90. Alt. rep . Page County Convs., 1988—92; commr. Park Bd. Shenandoah, 1998—; active Ladies Guild St. Mary Ch., Shenandoah, 1986—; mem. parish coun. St. Mary Ch., Shenandoah, Iowa, pres. parish coun., 1989—92, instr. religious edn., 1988—90, mem. choir, 1991—93, organist, song leader, 1992—, dir. choir, 2001—, liturgy planning com., 1996—; bd. dirs. Des Moines Diocesan Pastoral Coun., 2002—. Mem.: Am. Legion Aux.(local post), Shenandoah Music Assn. (pres. 2000—), Beta Sigma Phi (pres. 1979—80). Roman Catholic. Avocations: volleyball, aerobics, swimming. Home: 1302 Johnson Dr Shenandoah IA 51601-2606 Office: 1 Jack Foster Dr Shenandoah IA 51601-4586 E-mail: sueh@heartland.net.

HANNA, TERRY ROSS, lawyer, small business owner; b. Wadsworth, Ohio, May 17, 1947; s. Harry Ross and Geraldine (Frensley) H.; m. Max Anna Hindes, Jan. 20, 1968; children: Travis, Taylor, Molly. BBA, U. Okla., 1968, JD, 1972; LLM, NYU, 1973; MA in Bibl Studies, Dallas Theol. Sem., 1988. Bar: Okla. 1972, U.S. Tax Ct. 1974, U.S. Ct. Appeals (10th cir.) 1979, U.S. Supreme Ct. 1989; CPA, Okla. Mem. McAfee & Taft, Oklahoma City, 1972-80; pres. P 356 Inc., Oklahoma City, 1980—; of counsel Crowe & Dunlevy, Oklahoma City, 1987—. Owner Mo Jo Video, 1995—; spl. lectr. Oklahoma City U. Sch. Law, 1974-75. Editor Okla. U. Law Rev., 1970-72. Mem. internat. com. Boy Scouts Am., 1988—; dir. U.S. Found. for Internat. Scouting, Irving, 1989—. Baden-Powell fellow World Scout Found., 1988—; recipient Silver Beaver award Boy Scouts Am., 1988. Mem. Okla. Bar Assn. (pres. taxation sect. 1978-79), Sports Lawyers Assn., Order of Arrow (lodge advisor 1989—), Kappa Sigma (chpt. advisor 1974-75), Phi Delta Phi (magister 1972). Republican. Mem. Christian Ch. Avocations: coach, patch collector, fishing, golf, computers. Home: 2600 W Coffee Creek Rd Edmond OK 73003-3326 Office: Crowe & Dunlevy 1800 Mid America Towers Oklahoma City OK 73102 E-mail: HANNAT@crowedunlevy.com., thanna@ionet.net.

HANNA, WILLIAM BROOKS, literary agent; b. Montreal, Feb. 22, 1936; s. George Spencer and Phyllis Edith (Brooks) H.; children: Catherine Frances, Philip Spencer; m. Frances Ann Gerhardt, Nov. 20, 1982. Grad., Upper Can. Coll., 1954; BA in Modern History, U. Toronto, 1958. Successively coll. sales mgr., sch. sales mgr., editor-in-chief Collier-Macmillan-Can., Ltd., 19S8-65; pres. Pergamon of Can., Ltd., also dep. chmn. bd., 1967-68; exec. v.p., dir. Pergamon Press, Inc., 1966-68; v.p., dir. Burns & MacEachern, Ltd., Toronto, 1968-70; pres., dir. GLC Pubs., Toronto, 1970-75; pres., chief exec. officer, dir. Holt Rinehart & Winston of Can., Ltd., Toronto, 1975-78; pub. joint UNICEF/Red Cross Com. for 1979 Internat. Yr. of Child, 1978-79; v.p. Gen. Pub. Co. Ltd., Toronto, 1979—84, Stoddart Pub. Co. Ltd., Toronto, 1984—2000, Acacia House Pub. Svcs. Ltd., 2001—. Chmn. convocation Trinity Coll., U. Toronto, 1994-96, trustee 1996-2002; chmn. export com. Can. Book Publ. Coun., 1993-95. Mem. Assn. Can. Pubs. (rep. to 25th Congress of Internat. Assn. Can. Pubs. (dir. CANCOPY 1997-98), co-chmn. copyright com. 1998-2000, Arbor award U. Toronto 1998), Faculty Club U. Toronto. Home and Office: 51 Acacia Rd Toronto ON Canada M4S 2K6 E-mail: bhanna.acacia@rogers.com.

HANNA, WILLIAM JOHNSON, electrical engineering educator; b. Longmont, Colo., Feb. 7, 1922; s. William Grant and Anna Christina (Johnson) H.; m. Katherine Fagan, Apr. 25, 1944 (dec. 1993); children: Daniel August, Paul William; m. Helen Yeager McCarty, Sept. 19, 1996. BSEE, U. Colo., 1943, MS, 1948, D in Elec. Engring., 1951. Registered profl. engr., Colo., Kans. Mem. faculty U. Colo., 1946-91, prof. elec. engring., 1962-91, prof. emeritus, 1991—. Cons. in field; mem. Colo. Bd. Engring. Examiners, 1973-85; with Ponderosa Assocs., Lafayette, Colo. Author articles, reports. Served to 1st lt. AUS, 1943-46. Recipient Faculty Recognition award Students Assn. U. Colo., 1956, 61, Alfred J. Ryan award, 1978, Archimedes award Calif. Soc. Profl. Engrs., 1978, Outstanding Engring. Alumnus award U. Colo., 1983, Faculty Service award, 1983; named Colo. Engr. of Yr. Profl. Engrs. Colo., 1968; named to Hon. Order of Ky. Cols. Mem. IEEE, Am. Soc. Engring. Edn., Nat. Soc. Profl. Engrs. (pres. Colo. 1967-68), Nat. Coun. Engring. Examiners (pres. 1977-78, Disting. Svc. award with spl. commendation 1990), AIEE (chmn. Denver 1961-62) Clubs: Masons. Republican. Presbyterian. Home and Office: 27 Silver Spruce Nederland Star Rt Boulder CO 80302-9604 *Honors and awards I have received are but a reflection of the character of my friends and associates. To them and my family go the accolades.*

HANNAFORD, JANET KIRTLEY, software administrative manager; b. Seattle, June 25, 1940; d. Vernon Augustus and Dorothy Kathryn (Jenns) Kirtley; m. Norman Kenneth Christie, July 1, 1960 (div. 1978); children: Linda Jean, Norman Bruce; m. Robert John Hannaford, Dec. 26, 1981. BA magna cum laude, U. Wash., 1984. Adminstrv. sec. Baylor Coll. of Medicine, Houston, 1976-78; asst. to pres. Weems & Co., Inc., Houston, 1978-79; adminstrv. asst. Seattle Trust & Savs. Bank, 1979-82; cons. Fred Hutchinson Cancer Rsch. Ctr., Seattle, 1985-88. Mktg. cons. Lifetime Learning Ctr., seattle, 1987. Editor newsletter AAUW Bull., 1987. Site dir., chmn. Expanding Your Horizons in Math. and Sci., Seattle Cen. Community Coll., 1990-92; founder, 1st pres. SMARTgirls, Inc., 1996-99. Mem. AAUW (1st v.p. 1989-90, task force chmn. 1990-92), Beta Gamma Sigma, Phi Beta Kappa. Avocations: creative needlework, folk dancing, reading, volunteering, electronic puzzles and card games. Home: 7550 40th Ave NE Seattle WA 98115-4926 E-mail: janhanna2@aol.com.

HANNAFORD, PETER DOR, public relations executive, writer; b. Glendale, Calif., Sept. 21, 1932; s. Donald R. and Elinor (Nielsen) H.; m. Irene Dorothy Harville, Aug. 14, 1954; children: Richard H., Donald R. II. AB, U. Calif., 1954. Acct. exec. Helen A. Kennedy Advt., 1956; v.p. Kennedy-Hannaford, Inc., San Francisco and Oakland, Calif., 1957-62, pres., 1962-67, Pettler & Hannaford, Inc., Oakland, Calif., 1967-69; v.p. Wilton, Coombs & Colnett, Inc., 1969-72; pres. Hannaford & Assoc., Oakland, Calif., 1973; asst. to Gov. of Calif., Calif.; dir. pub. affairs Gov. Office, Calif., 1974; chmn. bd. Hannaford Co., Inc. (formerly Deaver & Hannaford, Inc.), 1975-95; pub. Ferndale Enterprise, Calif., 1996-98; pres. Hannaford Enterprises Inc., Calif., 1998—; sr. cons. APCO Worldwide, 2001—. Vice chmn. Calif. Gov. Consumer Fraud Task Force, 1972-73; bd. dir. Eberle Comms. Group Inc. Author: The Reagans: A Political Portrait, 1983, Talking Back to the Media, 1986 (Japanese edit. 1990); co-author: Remembering Reagan, 1994, Recollections of Reagan, 1997, My Heart Goes Home: A Hudson Valley Memoir, 1997, The Quotable Ronald

Reagan, 1998, The Essential George Washington, 1999, The Quotable Calvin Coolidge, 2000, Ronald Reagan and His Ranch, 2002. Mem. Alameda County Rep. Ctrl. Com., Rep. State Ctrl. Com. Calif., 1968-74, The Commonwealth Fund's Commn. on Elderly People Living Alone, 1986-91; Rep. nominee for U.S. Congress, 1972; governing bd. Tahoe Regional Planning Agy., 1973-74; trustee White House Preservation Fund, 1981-89, pub. rels. adv. com. USIA, 1981-92; mem. adv. com. Mt. Vernon 1991-96. 1st lt. Signal Corps, U.S. Army, 1954-56. Shapiro fellow, George Washington U. Sch. Media and pub. affairs, 2002. Mem.: Author's Guild, Potomac Polo Club, Cosmos Club, U. Club, Theta Xi. Presbyterian. Office: 9th Fl 1615 L St NW Washington DC 20036-5610

HANNAH, JANELLYN BENDER, public health nurse; b. Shelby, Mich., Jan. 2, 1947; d. George Washington Bender and Vada Elnor (Reid) McDade; m. Wayne V. LeCompte (div.); 1 child, Nicole Renee; m. Robert A. Hannah, July 1, 1984. BSN, Calif. State U., Sacramento, 1971; nurse educator, U. Calif., Irvine, 1989. RN Calif., cert. gerontol. nurse, diabetes educator, trauma response specialist. Pub. health nurse Houma County Health Dept., Warner Robbins, Ga., 1971-73; staff nurse Sacramento Health Dept., 1974-75; public health nurse Preventive Health Care for Aging, Santa Ana, Calif., 1980—; diabetes health educator HealthPrep, Westminster, Calif., 1996—. Recipient Disting. Woman of Yr. in Health, Soroptimist Internat., 1998. Mem.: So. Calif. Pub. Health Assn., Orange Assn. Diabetes Educators, Am. Assn. Diabetes Educators, Nat. Gerontol. Nursing Assn. (dir.-at-large), Am. Soc. on Aging, Am. Diabetes Assn. (mem. we. region leadership coun.), Sigma Theta Tau. Avocations: reading, gardening. Home: 9611 Jonquil Ave Westminster CA 92683-6922 E-mail: hprep@socal.rr.com.

HANNAH, JOHN ROBERT, SR., accountant; b. Monroe, La., Aug. 11, 1939; s. Robert Ruskin Hannah and Berta (Gilliland) Nelson; m. Elizabeth Girdner, Dec. 26, 1965; children: Allison, John Robert Jr. BS, La. State U., 1960. CPA, Tex. Acct. Arthur Young & Co., Houston, 1960-70, Peters & Smith, Midland, Tex., 1970-71; ptnr. Hannah & Trott, Midland, 1971-72; contr. Western States Producing Co., San Antonio, 1972-73; v.p. fin. Sommers Drug Stores Co., San Antonio, 1973-77; pvt. practice acctg. San Antonio, 1987—; ptnr. Peters, Anders & Hannah, San Antonio, 1978-86. Seminar speaker Bexar County Med. Soc., San Antonio, 1981. Fin. chmn. YMCA, San Antonio, 1975-82, chmn., 1982-83; adminstr. Bible Study Fellowship, San Antonio, 1977-83; bd. dirs. Morningside Ministries, 1991, Christian Ministry Assistance, 1992, treas.; chmn. bd. trustees Alamo Heights United Meth. Ch., 1998. Lt. USN, 1961-65. Mem. Am. Inst. CPA's, Tex. Soc. CPa's, Fin. Execs. Internat., Execs. Internat. Club (San Antonio, pres. 1975-76). Methodist. Home: 102 Castleoaks Dr San Antonio TX 78213-2303 Office: 800 Navarro St Ste 210 San Antonio TX 78205-1725

HANNAH, JUDY CHALLENGER, private education tutor; b. Balt., Oct. 8, 1948; d. John Thomas and Doris Rose (Etherington) Diehl; m. Brian Challenger, Apr. 15, 1968 (div. Dec. 1994); children: John Joseph, Jennifer Elizabeth; m. W. P. Hannah, Oct. 6, 2001. AA, Arlington Bible Coll., 1985; BS, Liberty U., 1991; M in Edn., Mt. St. Mary's Coll., 1996; Diploma, Inst. of Children's Lit., 1997. Cert. elem. tchr., Md., 1996. Tchr., K-4 Mill Valley Sch., Owing Mills, Md., 1984-85, Arlington Bapt. Sch., Balt., 1985-86, Mill Valley Sch., 1986-87; bookkeeper, sec. Challenger Engr., Inc., Finksburg, 1987-92; dir. B/A child care ABC Care Inc., 1992-95; tchr. internship Thurmont Elem. Sch., Md., 1995-96; tutor/office mgr. Learning Resources, Westminster, Md., 1996-97; pvt. tutor, owner A Lesson Learned, Inc., Union Bridge, Md., 1997—. Mem. delegation People to People Amb. Programs, China, 2001. Vol. Crisis Hotline, Balt., 1972, leader/tchr. Pioneer Girls Internat., Arlington Bapt. Ch., 1975-78; mem. profl. women's adv. bd. Am. Biog. Inst. Mem. Md. Emmaus, Internat. Dyslexia Assn., Smithsonian Inst., Vol. in Missions, Pi Lamba Theta, People To People Internat. Republican. Avocations: writing, hiking. Home: 48 Bucher John Rd Union Bridge MD 21791-9527

HANNAH, LAWRENCE BURLISON, lawyer; b. Urbana, Ill., Aug. 5, 1943; s. Lawrence Hugh and Margaret Alene (Burlison) H.; m. Kathleen O'Hara, Nov. 8, 1969; 1 child, Scott David. BA, Dartmouth Coll., 1965; JD cum laude, U. Pa., 1968. Bar: Wash. 1971, U.S. Dist. Ct. (we. dist.) Wash. 1971, Ct. of Appeals (9th cir.) 1971, U.S. Supreme Ct. 1990. Analyst U.S. Central Intelligence Agency, Langley, Va., 1969-71; ptnr. Perkins Coie, Bellevue, Wash., 1971—. Contbr. articles to profl. jours. Mem. King County Personnel Bd., Wash., 1984-90; mem. fin. com. Mcpl. Gov. Candidates, King County, 1972—. 1st lt. USAF, 1968-69. Mem. ABA, Wash. State Bar Assn., Seattle-King County Bar Assn. Methodist. Avocations: jogging, boating, tennis. Home: 1610 W Lake Sammamish Pky SE Bellevue WA 98008-5229 Office: Perkins Coie 411 108th Ave NE Ste 1800 Bellevue WA 98004-5584

HANNAH, WAYNE ROBERTSON, JR., lawyer; b. Freeport, Ill., Aug. 18, 1931; s. Wayne Robertson and Edith (Biene) H.; m. Patricia Anne Matthews, June 1, 1957; children— Tamara Lee, Wendy, Wayne Robertson III BA, Ill. Coll., 1953; JD, NYU, 1957. Bar: Ill. 1957, U.S. Dist. Ct. (no. dist.) Ill., U.S. Supreme Ct. Ptnr. Sonnenschein, Nath & Rosenthal, Chgo., 1965—. Dir. Checker Motors Corp., N.Y.C. and Kalamazoo, 1982-86; lectr. Ill. Inst. Continuing Edn. Sec. 7th cir. Root-Tilden Scholarship Program NYU, 1967-94; chmn. Root-Tilden-Kern scholarship com., 1981-86, trustee law ctr., 1985—; pres. bd. Firman Cmty. Svcs, Chgo., 1972-75; trustee, pres., chmn. bd. Chgo. City Ballet, 1982-86. 2d lt. USMC, 1951-54. Root-Tilden scholar NYU, 1954-57; Fulbright scholar, 1953-54 Mem. ABA (real estate com.), Chgo. Bar Assn. (chmn. condominium subcom. real estate com. 1977-78, sec., dir. condominium assn. 1991—), Ill. Bar Assn. (real estate com.), Econ. Club (Chgo.), Skokie Country Club (Glencoe, Ill.). Presbyterian. Avocations: tennis, golf. Office: Sonnenschein Nath and Rosenthal 233 S Wacker Dr Ste 8000 Chicago IL 60606-6491 E-mail: wrh@sonnenschein.com.

HANNAMAN, ALBERTA ANNA, artist; b. Passaic, N.J., Dec. 11, 1932; d. Henry George and Alice Edith Hannaman. Student, Newark Sch. Fine & Indsl. Art, 1950-53. Offset stripper Screenline Photo, N.Y.C., 1956-84, Verilen Graphics, N.Y.C., 1984-87; offset stripper inhouse printing dept. DDB Needham Worldwide, N.Y.C., 1987-88, Screen Images, N.Y.C., 1988-91. Poet, artist: Prince of Flowers, 1987; contbr. articles to poetry anthologies; exhibited in group shows at Del Bello Gallery, Toronto, Ont., Can., 1988-91, The Miniature Painters, Sculptors and Gravers Soc., Washington, 1990, 91, 98-02, Long Beach Island Art Gallery, Surf City, N.J., 1990, 91, 98.

HANNAM-OOSTERBAAN, MARIA GERTRUDE, educator; b. The Netherlands, July 28, 1916;, U.S., 1948,arrived in U.S., 1948; d. Jan and Anna Geertruida (Vanderweg) O.; m. Aug 12, 1940. Tchr. Degree, Christian Coll., Amsterdam, 1936, Bachelor, Whittier Coll., 1953. Elem. tchr. Batavia Christian Sch. Dist., Java, Indonesia, 1937-38; tchr. Palembang, Sumatra, Indonesia, 1938-41; clandestine tchr. Concentration Camp, Semarang, Indonesia, 1942—46; tchr. Ranchito Sch. Dist., Pico., Calif., 1953—55, L.A. City Sch. Dist., 1955-77. Mem. Westminster Presbyn. Ch. Mem. AAUW, Calif. Ret. Tchrs. Assn., Order Eastern Star. Presbyn. Home: # G222 710 W 13th Ave Escondido CA 92025-5511

HANNAN, BRADLEY, educational publishing consultant and executive; b. Rochester, N.Y., Apr. 24, 1935; d. Jack Seymour MacArthur and Alice E. (Knapp) Staley; m. William J. Hannan, Jr., June 15, 1957 (div. 1977); children: Megan, Timothy, Patrick, Moira. BA, Ariz. State U., 1957. Tchr. various sch. dists., Ariz., 1957-62; English language cons. Evanston (Ill.) Twp. High Sch., 1963-65; editor, then sr. editor Harper & Row Pubs., Evanston, 1965-75; sr. reading text editor Scott, Foresman & Co., Glenview, Ill., 1975-78, sr. editor lang. arts, 1982-87; dir. reading McDougal Littell & Co., Evanston, 1978-81; project dir. spelling Ednl. Challenges, Alexandria, Va., 1981-82; dir. curriculum and product mgmt. for reading and lang. arts texts Open Court Pub. Co., Chgo. and Peru, Ill., 1987-88; cons., project dir. lang. arts texts Harcourt Brace, Orlando, Fla., 1988-89; sr. mng. editor reading, lang. arts, social studies Sci. Rsch. Assocs., Chgo., 1989; cons. ednl. pub. Chgo., 1989-90; dir. reading, lang. arts, social studies Proof Positive/Farrowlyne Assocs., Chgo., 1990-98; editor ALA, Chgo., 1998; editl. cons., writer ednl. materials, 1998—. Speaker Internat. Reading Assn., New Orleans, 1981, Chgo. Women in Publishing, 1981, Childrens' Reading Roundtable, Chgo., 1985; developer reading textbook series. Mem. Internat. Reading Assn., Chgo. Book Clinic, Chgo. Women in Pub. Avocations: language acquisition and development, reading competence, book production, phonics. Home and Office: 800 Judson Ave Apt 301 Evanston IL 60202-2451

HANNAN, MOHAMMAD A. physicist, educator; b. India, Oct. 21, 1940; came to U.S., 1995; s. Mohammad A. Shahid and Amena Khatun; m. Syeda M., Sept. 10, 1968. BSc, Dhaka U., 1966; MSc, U. London, 1974, PhD, 1978. Lectr., asst. prof. Dhaka U., Bangladesh, 1968-78; lectr. U. Ife, Nigeria, 1978-84; asst. prof. Fed. U. Technology, Onda State, Nigeria, 1984-87; rschr. Atomic Energy Inst., Tripoli, Libya, 1987-92; instr. S. Tex. C.C., 1996-98; lectr., asst. prof. U. Tex. Pan-Am., Edinburg, 1998—. Contbr. numerous sci. articles to internat. and nat. jours. Mem. Am. Phys. Soc., Am. Inst. Physics, Am. Solar Energy Soc., Am. Nuclear Soc. Home: 515 S Sugar Rd Apt 90 Edinburg TX 78539-5291

HANNAN, MYLES, lawyer, banker; b. Rye, N.Y., Oct. 14, 1936; s. Joseph A. and Rosemary (Edwards) H.; m. Phyllis Wiley, Oct. 12, 2002; children from previous marriages: Myles Jr., Paul F., Thomas J., Kerry E. BA, Holy Cross Coll., 1958; LLB, Harvard U., 1964. Bar: N.Y. 1964, Mass. 1970, Md. 1994, D.C. 1996, U.S. Dist. Ct. (so. and ea. dists.) N.Y. 1966, U.S. Dist. Ct. Md. 1995. Assoc. Cadwalader, Wickersham & Taft, N.Y.C., 1964-69; v.p., gen. counsel, sec. High Voltage Engring. Corp., Burlington, Mass., 1969-73; v.p., sec. Stop & Shop Cos., Inc., Boston, 1973-79; group v.p. law and adminstrn. Del. North Cos., Inc., Buffalo, 1979-81; v.p., fin., gen. counsel, sec. Anacomp, Inc., Indpls., 1981-84; exec. v.p. Empire of Am. FSB, Buffalo, 1984-89; adminstrv. v.p. Berkeley Group Inc., Buffalo, 1990-91; ptnr. Linowes and Blocher LLP, Washington, 1992—. Trustee Studio Arena Theatre, Buffalo, 1986-89; bd. dirs. Buffalo Philharm. Orch., 1987-89. Lt. USNR, 1958-61. Home: 12108 Whippoorwill Ln North Bethesda MD 20852 Office: Linowes and Blocher LLP 1010 Wayne Ave Ste 1000 Silver Spring MD 20910-5615 E-mail: mh@linoweslaw.com.

HANNAN, ROBERT EMMET, business development consultant; b. Pitts., Dec. 7, 1946; s. William Michael and Mary Virginia (Lydon) H.; m. Karen Lee Flanagan, Aug. 29, 1971; children: Sean, Ryan, Tara. BS in Psychol. and Philosophy honors, John Carroll U., 1968; MBA in Econs. honors, Rutgers U., 1980. Account mgr. BBDO Adv., N.Y.C., 1968-70, William Esty Advt., N.Y.C., 1970-72; mktg. mgr. Block Drug Co., Jersey City, 1972-75; mem. mktg. and strategic mgmt. staff Becton Dickinson, Orangeburgh, N.J., 1975-81; prin. Ctr. for Concept Devel., N.Y.C., 1981-85, also bd. dirs.; founder, mng. ptnr., bd. dirs. The Genesis Group, Montclair, N.J., 1981-99; pres. Genesis divsn. Wolters Kluwer, Montclair, 1999-2000; pres. Adis Bus. Intelligence divsn. Wolters Kluwer, Montclair, 2000—02; CEO, The Genesis Group, 2002—. Bd. dirs., chmn. exec. com. ViRxys, Maryland Gene Therapy Firm, DEMEGEN, Pitts. Cancer Therapy Firm; lectr. in field. Contbr. papers to profl. jours.; mem. editoral bd. Jour. of Consumer Mktg., 1983—; founder, exec. editor newsletters: The Genesis Report Rx, The Genesis Report Dx, The Genesis Report MCx and The Genesis Report Molecular and Genetic Medicine. Del. Civic Conf. Com., Glen Ridge, 1987-89; capt. Neighborhood Watch, Glen Ridge, 1986-89; mem. North Side Assn., 1986-89, Glen Ridge; mgr. Glen Ridge Jr. Wrestling, 1985-90; bd. dirs., com. chair and mem. bd. devel. com. YMCA, 1995—. Mem. AAAS, Am. Assn. Clin. Chemists, N.Y. Acad. Scis., Martial Arts Assn. (N.Y.), Montclair Golf Club, Amateur Comedy Club (N.Y.C., com. mem. 1972—), DeBordieu Club. Roman Catholic. Avocations: biking, golf, music, reading. Home and Office: 99 Rice Bluff Rd Pawleys Island SC 29585 Home: Point at Crystal Lake 38 Whalen Ct West Orange NJ 07052 E-mail: rhannan@sc.rr.com.

HANNAY, WILLIAM MOUAT, III, lawyer; b. Kansas City, Mo., Dec. 3, 1944; s. William Mouat and Gladys (Capron) H.; m. Donna Jean Harkins, Sept. 30, 1978; children: Capron Grace, Blaike Ann, William Mouat IV. BA, Yale U., 1966; JD, Georgetown U., 1973. Bar: Mo. 1973, D.C. 1974, N.Y. 1975, Ill. 1980. Law clk. to Judge Myron Bright, U.S. Ct. Appeals, 8th Cir., St. Louis, 1973-74; law clk. to Justice Tom Clark U.S. Supreme Ct., Washington, 1974-75; assoc. Weil Gotshal & Manges, N.Y.C., 1975-77; asst. dist. atty. New York County Dist. Atty.'s Office, N.Y.C., 1977-79; ptnr. Schiff Hardin & Waite, Chgo., 1979—. Adj. prof. IIT/Chgo.-Kent Law Sch., 1983—. Author: International Trade: Avoiding Criminal Risks, 1994, Designing an Effective Antitrust Compliance Program, updated 2002, Tying Arrangements, updated 2002, International Antitrust Enforcement, updated 2002; contbr. articles to profl. jours. Chmn. bd. dirs. Gilbert and Sullivan Soc. Chgo., 1984-87, Served with U.S. Army, 1967-68, Vietnam. Mem. ABA (chair sect. internat. law and practice 1998-99, chair Africa law initiative coun. 2000-02, mem. ho. of dels. 2002-), Chgo Bar Assn. (chmn. antitrust com. 1986-87), Yale Club (pres. 1987-89), Chgo. Yacht Club, Union League Club (Chgo.). Democrat. Episcopalian. Home: 591 Plum Tree Rd Barrington IL 60010-2329 Office: Schiff Hardin & Waite 7200 Sears Tower Chicago IL 60606 E-mail: whannay@schiffhardin.com.

HANNEMAN, ELAINE ESTHER, salesperson; b. Waupaca, Wis., Aug. 28, 1928; d. Martin Fred Strey and Laura Rucks; m. Alfred Adam Hanneman, Feb. 14, 1948; children: Karen, Dale, Sally, Sandra. High sch. grad., 1946. Acct. AAL Life Ins. Co., Appleton, Wis., 1946-48; salesperson Cinderella Cosmetics, 1948-60; sales Artex Paint, Milw., 1960-74, Car Ins. and Memberships (AAA), Appleton, Wis., 1974-78, Am. Family Life, Columbus, Ga., 1979—. Mem. Gold Century Club, Pres. Club, Am. Family Life. Lutheran. Avocations: travel, reading, swimming, crafts. Home: 103 West St Weyauwega WI 54983 also: 8742 Edgewater Dr Amherst Junction WI 54407-9510

HANNEMAN, RODNEY ELTON, metallurgical engineer; b. Spokane, Wash., Mar. 14, 1936; s. Christie Luther and Viva Helen (Sugrue) H.; married; 3 children. BS in Phys. Metallurgy, Wash. State U., 1959; MS in Metallurgy, MIT, 1961, PhD, 1964; grad., GE Mgmt. Devel. Inst., 1979. With GE Co., Schenectady, 1963-81, mgr. materials characterization lab., 1977-80, mgr. materials programs, 1980-81; v.p. research, devel. and energy resources Reynolds Metals Co., Richmond, Va., 1981-85, v.p. quality assurance and tech. op., 1985-98; pres. Mgmt. and Tech. Consultants, Richmond, Va., 1998—2002. Mem. vis. com. dept. materials sci. and engring. MIT, 1975—80, mem. adv. bd. Materials Processing Ctr, 1980—97; mem. adv. bd. U. Va., 1982—87, chmn. indsl. adv. bd. grad. engring. program, 1983—86; chmn. rsch. coordinating coun. Gas Rsch. Inst., 1985—87, adv. coun., 1988—2001; bd. dirs. Materials Properties Coun., 1982—90; mem. adv. com. Va. Ctr. for Innovative Tech., 1999—2002; adv. bd. Commonealth Grad. Enging., Richmond, 2003—. Exec. v.p. found. bd. Sci. Mus. Va., 1989—; v.p. Civic Assn., 1990-92. Recipient Alumni Achievement award Wash. State U., 1978; Joint Engring. Council award, 1984 Mem. AIME, MAPI, SAE, Am. Soc. Metals (Geisler award 1971, Engring. Materials Achievement award 1973), Am. Chem. Soc. (Chem. Innovator award 1970, Edison medallion 1979), Indsl. Rsch. Inst., Aluminum Assn. (chmn. tech. com. 1989-97), Sigma Xi. Achievements include patents in field.

HANNERS, G(ARY) DALE, retired psychological mental health professional; b. Leachville, Ark., Sept. 16, 1942; BS, Memphis State U., 1966; MS, Ark. State U., 1968; PhD, U. Memphis, 1995. Lic. psychol. examiner, Ark.; cert. sch. psychologist. Tchr. Memphis Pub. Schs., 1964-65; with personnel dept. Sears, Roebuck and Co., Memphis, 1965-66; supr. client svcs. Abilities Unltd., Jonesboro, 1966-70; rehab. counselor State of Ark., Jonesboro, 1970-74, psychol. examiner, 1979—; psychologist, human resources cons., 1994—. Pvt. practice cons. human svcs., Ark., 1970-79; cons. Little People Am., Calif. Mem. Am. Psychol. Assn. (assoc.), Ark. Psychol. Assn., Ark. Sch. Psychol. Assn., Civitan (sec.-treas. Jonesboro chpt. 1967-70). Republican. Baptist. Avocations: music, reading, farming, landscaping. Home: 2113 Club Cv Jonesboro AR 72401-6100 E-mail: d0916@webtv.net.

HANNETT, FREDERICK JAMES, healthcare consulting company executive; b. Seattle, Sept. 12, 1950; m. JoAnne Thompson, May 10, 1980; children: Tom, Emily. Pres., COO The Jefferson Group, Washington, 1987-96; mng. prin. The Capitol Alliance, Washington, 1997—. Mem. Va. Bd. Health; bd. advisors Dem. Leadership Coun., Washington. Avocations: tennis, skiing, golf. Office: The Capitol Alliance 1350 I St NW Ste 870 Washington DC 20005-3386 Home: 4949 Rock Spring Rd Arlington VA 22207-2705

HANNI, GERALDINE MARIE, retired therapist; b. Salt Lake City, Nov. 14, 1930; d. John Henry and Theresa Justine (Keirce) Gold; m. Kenneth J. Hanni, Mar. 14, 1951; children: Debra, Valerie, Kathleen, Cynthia, Kristine. BS, U. Utah, 1951, MSW, 1983. Lic. clin. social worker. Tchr. Hillside Jr. High Sch., Salt Lake City, 1970-73; intern Davis County Schs., Farmington, Utah, 1981-82, Westside Mental Health, Salt Lake City, 1982-83; group leader LDS Social Services, Salt Lake City, 1985; therapist ISAT, Salt Lake City, 1983-90, clin. dir., 1987-90; clin. instr. U. Utah, Salt Lake City, 1986-90; pvt. practice, 1990-97; ret., 1997. Mem. bd. Salt Lake County Sexual Abuse Task Force, Salt Lake City; cons. LDS Social Services, Salt Lake City, 1984-86. Contbg. author: Abuse and Religion; Confronting Abuse—an LDS Perspective. Sect. dir. Mortar Bd. Honor Soc., western U.S., 1970; pres. Highland High PTA, Salt Lake City, 1980; chairperson Highland High Community Sch. Orgn., Salt Lake City, 1981. Mem. Nat. Assn. Social Workers (Utah chpt.). Democrat. Mem. Lds Ch.

HANNIBAL, EDWARD LEO, copywriter; b. Manchester, Mass., Aug. 24, 1936; s. Joseph Leary and Loretta Louise (McCarthy) H.; m. Margaret Adele Twomey, June 14, 1958; children: Mary Ellen, Edward J., Eleanor, John, Julia. BA, Boston Coll., 1958. Copywriter Kenyon & Eckhardt, N.Y.C., 1962-63, Norman, Craig & Kummel, N.Y.C., 1963-64; v.p. assoc, creative dir. Benton & Bowles, Inc., N.Y.C., 1965-68; exec. v.p., creative dir. Wayne Jervis Assocs., N.Y.C., 1968-1970, v.p., creative supr. Grey Advt., 1975-79; exec. v.p., co-creative dir. Hannibal Figliola Advt., N.Y.C., 1980-83; sr. v.p., group creative dir. Grey Worldwide, N.Y.C., 1985—. Adj. assoc. prof. Sch. Continuing & Profl. Studies N.Y. U. Author: Chocolate Days, Popsicle Weeks, 1970, Dancing Man, 1973, Liberty Square Station, 1977, (with Robert Boris) Blood Feud, 1979, A Trace of Red, 1982. Mem. PEN. Democrat. Roman Catholic. Avocations: reading, running. Office: Grey Worldwide 777 3rd Ave New York NY 10017-1401

HANNIG, GARY L. state representative; b. Litchfield, Ill., July 22, 1952; m. Elizabeth Helen Hannig. BS, U. Ill., 1974. CPA. Mem. Ill. Ho. of Reps., 1978—, asst. majority leader, 1997—. Mem. Holy Family Cath. Ch., Task Force Chgo. Sch. Reform. Mem.: Lichtfield C. of C., Nat. Rifle Soc., Macoupin County Hist. Soc., Wolfpack Antique Car Club, K. of C., Moose, Benld Croation Lodge. Democrat. Office: 300 Capitol Bldg Springfield IL 62706 Address: 225 S Macoupin St Gillespie IL 62033*

HANNIGAN, JOHN DENNIS, logistics engineer; b. Boston, Apr. 19, 1935; s. John Joseph and Catherine Rita (Donahue) Hannigan; m. Joanne Clark, Aug. 5, 1955 (dec. 1963); children: John Clark, Catherine Mae, David Brian, Debra Jo; m. Jo Ann Hansen, Nov. 13, 1964 (div. 1978); children: David Anthony, Denice Michelle; m. Karen Sue Stanberry, Dec. 2, 1978; children: Stacey Nicole, Bridget Marie. Student, Am. U., 1964—66, Ind. U./Purdue U., Ft. Wayne, 1970—72. Cert. configuration mgr. Supply cataloguer U.S. Govt., Vinthill Farms Sta., Va., 1964—66; mgr. engring. svcs. Wells Industries, Springfield, Va., 1966—68; sr. logistics analyst Magnavox, Ft. Wayne, 1968—76, mgr. configuration mgmt., 1986—; supr. tech. pubs. ESystems, Huntington, Ind., 1976—78, mgr. logistics support engring. St. Petersburg, Fla., 1980—82; logistics program mgr. Northrop DSD, Rolling Meadows, Ill., 1978—80; sr. logistics engr. Sperry Gyroscope, Clearwater, Fla., 1982—86. Served with U.S. Army, 1953—64. Mem.: Armed Forces Commn. and Electronics Assn., Electronics Industries Assn., Nat. Mgmt. Assn., Soc. Logistics Engrs., Am. Def. Preparedness Assn., Soc. Old Crows. Republican. Mem. Ch. Of The Nazarene. Home: 5523 Sable Ct Fort Wayne IN 46835-4192 Office: 1313 Production Rd Fort Wayne IN 46808-1164 E-mail: naginna@gte.net.

HANNIGAN, PAMELA S. economist, educator; b. Indpls., Aug. 12, 1955; d. Michael L. Hannigan and Bette J. Anderson. BS, MIT, 1975; MS, NYU, 2002; cert. appraiser fine art and antiquities, U. Md., 2001. Rschr. Harvard Inst. Econ. Rsch.-Martin Felstein, Cambridge, Mass., 1977—78; econ. analysis mgr. AT&T Anti-Trust Task Force, N.Y.C., 1977—78; energy economist Chase Manhattan Bank, N.Y.C., 1980—85; pres. Strategic Devel. Assn., N.Y.C., 2001—; asst. prof. Real Estate Inst. NYU, N.Y.C., 2002—. Cons., rschr. Euopean Union, Brussels, 2001—02; adv. bd. Energy Independence Inst., N.Y.C., 1983—87; chair IPAA-Supply/Demand Com., Houston, 1986—87. Author: Retrospective Silhouette: One Century of Lithographic Posters, 1996, Rembrandt the Etcher, 1995, Policy Analysis and Crisis Management in New York City, 2002. Mem.: Internat. Soc. Appraisers, Wagner Rev. (editor 2000—), Am. Assn. Mus. (advocate, curator com. 1991—). Avocations: ballet, ancient civilizations, collecting art. Home: 1 Lincoln Plz New York NY 10023 Office: NYU Real Estate Inst 11 W 42d St New York NY 10036

HANNING, GARY WILLIAM, utility executive, water company executive, consultant; b. Sherman, Tex., Aug. 30, 1942; s. William Homer and Mary Maxine (Harshbarger) H.; m. Robin Dale Smith, June 8, 1974; children: TJ, Lorissa Diane. BS, Rollins Coll., 1974; MBA, Stetson U., 1976. Mgr., co-owner Hanning Water Systems, Denison, Tex., 1963-66; engring. technician Gen. Dynamics, Ft. Worth, 1966-67; engr. supr. Bendix Field, Pasadena, Calif., 1967-70; engr. Philco-Ford Corp., Cape Kennedy, Fla., 1970-73, Jet Propulsion Lab., Pasadena, Calif., 1973-74; sect. mgr. Planning Rsch. Corp., Kennedy Space Ctr., 1974-77; pres. S.S.S. Water Systems, Inc., Denison, 1978-83, Texoma Svcs. Corp., Pottsboro, Tex., 1980-99, Tanglewood Water Co., 1994-99; exec. Tecon Water Cos. Inc., 1999—. Bd. dirs. Ind. Water and Sewer Co. Tex. Inc., Austin, Boy Scouts Am., Circle Ten, Dallas; entrepreneur Bells Discount Supply, Tex., 1983-87; adv. bd. Expresiv Technologies, Austin, 2000-03. Contbr. articles to profl. jours. Mem. City Coun., Pottsboro, Tex., 1992-98. With USN, 1960-63. Mem. State Bar of Tex. (grievance com. 2000-02), Tanglewood Golf Assn. (sec.-treas. 1992-96), Am. Legion, C. of C. Mem. Ch. of Christ. Avocations: inventing, camping, reading, golfing, boating, hunting. Office: PO Box 1144 Pottsboro TX 75076

HANNON, BRUCE MICHAEL, engineer, educator; b. Champaign, Ill., Aug. 14, 1934; s. Walter Leo and Kathleen Rose (Phalen) H.; m. Patricia Claire Coffey, Aug. 11, 1956; children: Claire, Laura, Brian. BSCE, U. Ill., 1956, MS in Engring. Mechanics, 1966, PhD in Engring. Mechanics, 1970. Engr. with chem. industry, 1957-66; instr. U. Ill., Urbana, 1966-71, assoc. prof. energy rsch., 1974-83, prof. regional sci., 1983—, Jubilee prof. liberal arts and scis., 1991—. Vis. prof. Nat. Ctr. for Supercomputing Applications; cons. NSF, NAS, NAE, chem. industry, various fed. energy agys; patentee in field. Contbr. articles to profl. jours. 1st lt. C.E. AUS, 1956-57. Named Engring. Tchr. of Yr., U. Ill., 1970, Man of Yr., Sierra Club, 1971; recipient 1st prize Mitchell Award Club of Rome, 1975. Home: 1208 W Union St Champaign IL 61821-3229 Office: U Ill 220 Daven Hall Urbana IL 61801

HANNON, GERARD V. lawyer; b. London, Oct. 9, 1951; s. Charles Stephen and Mary (McHugh) Hannon; m. Anne Theresa Murtagh, July 30, 1988; children: Charles Patrick, Martin James, Erin Mary. BA, Queen's Coll., N.Y.C., 1974; JD, Fordham U., 1977. Bar: N.Y. 1978, U.S. Dist. Ct. (ea. dist.) N.Y. 1978, U.S. Dist. Ct. (so. dist.) N.Y. 1978, U.S. Supreme Ct. 1987. Assoc. Milbank Tweed Hadley & McCloy, N.Y.C., 1977—82, Parker Chapin EW, N.Y.C., 1982—84, Coudert Bros., N.Y.C., 1984—. Adj. prof. Columbia U. Grad. Sch. Bus., N.Y.C., 1989; mem. adv. bd. Fordham U. Sch. Law, N.Y.C., First Am. Title Ins. Co. N.Y., N.Y.C. Mem. adv. bd. St. Anglia Merci Sch., N.Y.C. Mem.: ABA, Assn. Bar City N.Y., N.Y. State Bar Assn., Cornell Club N.Y., Phi Beta Kappa. Avocations: tennis, travel.

HANNON, LEO FRANCIS, retired lawyer, educator; b. Boston, June 29, 1926; s. Bernard Francis and Elsie A. (Byrne) H.; m. Marion Ryan, June 7, 1958 (dec.); children: Elizabeth, James, Patricia, Jane. BS, Boston Coll., 1951; LLB, Georgetown U., 1958. Bar: D.C. 1958, U.S. Dist. Ct. D.C. 1958. Spl. agt. Office of Naval Intelligence, Washington, 1953-59; sr. atty. Nat. Labor Rels. Bd., Phila., 1960-69; mng. counsel labor security and benefits E.I. DuPont Co., Wilmington, Del., 1969-90; tchr. U. Del., Newark, 1991-95. Mem. Bus. Roundtable Litig. Com., N.Y., Washington, 1980-90. Author: Legal Side of Private Security, 1992; contbr. articles to profl. jours. Bd. mem. Contact USA, Harrisburg, Pa., 1993-96; bd. dirs., vol. Seamen's Ctr., Wilmington, Del. With USN, 1944-46, 51-53. Avocations: writing, travel, golf. Home: 1211 Hilltop Ave Wilmington DE 19809-1625

HANNON, PATRICIA, literature educator, writer; MS, Georgetown U., Washington, 1979; PhD, NYU, N.Y.C., 1990. Instr. French NYU, N.Y.C., 1985—88; assoc. prof. French Cath. U., Washington, 1989—97; guest faculty French Sarah Lawrence Coll., Bronxville, NY, 1998—2000. Author: Fabulous Identities: Women's Fairy Tales in Seventeenth-Century France, 1998; contbr. articles to profl. jours. Seminar grantee, Folger Shakespeare Libr., 1995, Rsch. grantee, NEH, 1994, French Govt., 1984. Mem.: MLA, Simone de Beauvoir Soc., Soc. for Seventeenth-Century French Lit.

HANNON, PATRICIA ANN, library director; b. Passaic, N.J., Jan. 1, 1947; d. L. Robert and Frances Laurent Hannon. BA in Math., Caldwell Coll., 1968; MLS, L.I. U., 1972. Libr. Hackensack (N.J.) Pub. Libr., 1968-75; dir. Wood-Ridge (N.J.) Pub. Libr., 1975-81, Wanaque (N.J.) Pub. Libr., 1983-84, Oakland (N.J.) Pub. Libr., 1984-88, Emerson (N.J.) Pub. Libr., 1988—. Pres. St. Joseph's Parish Coun., E. Rutherford, N.J., 1979, Regency Pk. Condominium Assn., Ramsey, N.J., 1990-91. Named Outstanding Young Women of Am., 1977. Mem.: Highlands Regional Libr. Coop. (pres. 1999—2001), Bergen County Libr. Coop. Sys. (pres. 1997, 1988), N.J. Libr. Assn. (pres. 2003—), Emerson C. of C. (sec. 1992—94, 1997—), Beta Phi Mu. Avocations: guitar, needlepoint houses. Office: Emerson Pub Libr 20 Palisade Ave Emerson NJ 07630-1822 E-mail: Hannon@bccls.org.

HANNOUM, ABDELMAJID, historian, educator, anthropologist, researcher; b. Meknes, Morocco, Dec. 25, 1960; arrived in U.S., 1991; s. Hamani Hannoum and Tamou Adib. BA, U. Fez, Morocco, 1983, MA, 1985; PhD with hons., U. of Paris, 1991; PhD, Princeton (N.J.) U., 1995. Rsch. asst. Inst. for Advanced Study, Princeton, 1996—98; vis. asst. prof. New Sch. for Social Rsch., N.Y.C., 1998—99; fellow Harvard U., Cambridge, Mass., 1999—2000; asst. prof. Simon's Rock Coll., Great Barrington, Mass., 2000—; vis. scholar Columbia Univ., NYC, 2003—04. Author: Colonial Histories, Post-colonial Memories; contbr. articles to profl. jours. Recipient William H. Rea' 34 Student award, Princeton U., 1992; fellow, 1995, Harvard U., 1999—2000; grantee, Ctr. for Regional Studies, Princeton, 1994, Program in Near Ea. Studies, Ctr. for Internat. Studies, Princeton, 1994. Mem.: Am. Anthrop. Assn. Office: Simons Rock College 84 AlfordRoad Great Barrington MA 01230 Home Fax: 413-528-7365; Office Fax: 413-528-7365. Personal E-mail: hannoum@yahoo.com. E-mail: hannoum@yahoo.com.

HANNUM, DAVID LAWRENCE, business consultant, training specialist, educator; b. Detroit, May 6, 1945; s. John Andrew and Ruth (Life) H.; m. Mary Ellen Oltesvig, Apr. 19, 1968; children: James K., Charles M. BS, Regis Coll., Denver, 1982; MBA, Fairleigh Dickinson U., 1984; M cert. in project mgmt., George Washington U., 1991. Instr. Mich. Bell., Detroit, 1971-78, mgr. tng., 1978-80; with course devel. dept. AT&T, Denver, 1980-82, systems test mgr. Parsippany, N.J., 1982-84, project mgr. Morris Plains, N.J., 1984-89, mgr. tng. South Plainfield, N.J., 1989-91; networking cons. AT&T GIS, Atlanta, 1991-96; owner, chief cons. DLH Cons., 1996-97; cons. eB Networks, 1997-2000; prin. cons. Network Solutions, Inc., 2000—02; CEO Damar Enterprises, 2002—. Co-owner Pocono Craft Loft, Tannersville, Pa., 1986-92; trainer Engring. Soc. Detroit, 1979; assoc. prof. County Coll. of Morris, Dover, N.J., 1984-85; tech. editor Addison-Wesselly, Premier Pub. Author various computer tng. courses. Leader, trainer, commr. Boy Scouts Am., Mich., Colo., N.J., Pa., 1975-90. With USNR, 1962-63. Mem. IEEE, IEEE Computer Soc. (assoc. editor, columnist Micro mag. 1982-86), Profl. Picture Framers Assn. (cert. picture framer), Mastergardeners, Am. Assn. Woodturners. Avocations: handcrafts, woodworking, fishing, travel, community activities. Home and Office: 100 Marthas Cv Fayetteville GA 30215-5137

HANOVER, R(AYMOND) SCOTT, tennis management professional; b. Des Moines, June 10, 1964; s. Norman E. and Jo Ann (Taylor) H.; m. Marla J. Boicourt, Apr. 23, 1988. BA, Grand View Coll., 1986. Staff writer, news asst. Des Moines Register, 1985-90; sch. dir. Missouri Valley sect. U.S. Tennis Assn., Kansas City, Mo., 1990-96; mgr. Plaza Tennis Ctr., Kansas City, Mo., 1996—. Dir. 73d Nat. Pub. Parks Tennis Championships, USTA Men's Futures Profl. Tournament, 1998-00; mem. exec. com. Big 12 Collegiate Tennis Conf. Championships, 2000; mem. USTA Mo. Valley bd. dirs., 2000-02, NCAA Divsn. II nat. exec. com., 2002. Editor U.S. Profl. Tennis Assn. Missouri Valley divsn. newsletter, 1992-95. Dir. Heart of Am. Dist. Tennis., 1996-98, sec., 1999-2000, pres., 2000-02; co-founder, bd. dirs. Kansas City Met. Tennis Assn., sec., 2000—. Recipient Svc. award Nebr. AHPERD, 1991, Missouri Valley Tennis Assn. and Heart of Am. Tennis Assn. Facility of Yr. award, 1997. Mem. U.S. Tennis Assn. (NRPA Excellence in Tennis award, life, referee 1997—, liaison to Club Mgrs. Assn. 1998—, Mo. Valley nominating com. 1998, nat. com. USA Sch. Tennis 2001-02, nat. SERV com. 2003—, nat. com. cmty. tennis 2001—, Outstanding Pub. Facility award 1998, Heart of Am. Orgn. of Yr. award 1998, dir. Heart of Am. Tournament of Yr. 1999, 2001), Missouri Valley Tennis Assn. (chmn. pub. rels. com. 1989-90, chmn. cmty. devel. com. 1996-98), U.S. Profl. Tennis Registry, Grand View Alumni Coun. (pres. 1988-90). Office: Kansas City Parks/Recreation 4747 JC Nichols Pkwy Kansas City MO 64112-1627

HANRAHAN, JOYCE YANCEY, educational consultant, antiquarian bookseller; b. Fyffe, Ala., Sept. 29, 1933; d. Wallace Odell and Nellie Lee (Raughton) Yancey; m. Edward John Hanrahan, Nov. 12, 1960. BA, U. Ala., University, 1955; MEd, U. N.H., 1964, 68; postgrad., Boston U., U. Calif., Boston U., Harvard. Cert. tchr., prin., N.H., N.J., Maine, Wis. Tchr. pub. schs., Madison, Wis., Durham, N.H., 1960-68; prin. Little Harbour Sch., Portsmouth, N.H., 1969-72, York (Maine) Elem. Sch., 1978-84; ednl. field agt. New Eng. Program in Tchr. Edn., Durham, 1972-75; exec. dir. Community Day Care Ctr., Portsmouth, 1975-76; cons. N.H. Child and Family Svcs., Concord, N.H., 1976-78; headmistress lower sch. Internat. Sch., Brussels, 1984-87; head lower sch. Shady Side Acad., Pitts., 1987-89; asst. head, prin. The Pingry Sch., Short Hills, N.J., 1989-2000. Mem. accrediting com. European Coun. Internat. Schs., 1984-87; cons. on early childhood edn. and child care related issues, New Eng., 1970-84; participant numerous TV panels on edn. related issues, 1970-84; ptnr. J & J Hanrahan, rare books. Author: Works of Maurice Sendak: 1947-1994, 1995, Maurice Sendak, Revised and Expanded to 2001, 2001; writer, dir. TV program on child care as polit. issue. Mem. Portsmouth City Coun., 1972-76, C. of C., N.H. Gov.'s Task Force on Mental Health of Children, 1976-80, N.H. Early Childhood Task Force, Concord, 1972-80; bd. dirs. N.H. Charitable Trust, Concord, 1974-84, United Fund, Children's Mus., SPNEA, AAA-NH, numerous others. Fellow U.S. Govt., U. N.H., 1968-69, NEH, Ga. Inst. Tech., 1980, Prin.'s Ctr., Harvard U. Sch. Edn., 1984, Aspen Inst., 1990; grantee to study European publ. history of Maurice Sendak, 1998. Mem. ASCD, Nat. Assn. Ind. Schs., Harvard Prin.'s Ctr., Antiquarian Booksellers Assn. AM., Nat. Assn. Edn. Young Children. Avocations: book and antique collecting, travel, reading. Home: 120 Salt Marsh Cir Wells ME 04090-3862 E-mail: hanrahan@maine.rr.com.

HANRAHAN, LAWRENCE MARTIN, healthcare consultant; b. Cin., Mar. 9, 1961; s. Robert Donald and Mary Francis (Doran) Hanrahan, Barry Wright and Kathryn Regina Kinkaid; m. Madeleine Carol Routon. AB in Chemistry, Miami U., 1983; MD, U. Cin. Coll. Medicine, 1988; MBA, U. Tex. Grad. Sch. Bus., Austin, 1992. Founder, owner Landscaping group, Cin., 1975-85; chief ultrasound tech., instr., rsch. assoc. The Good Samaritan Hosp. Peripheral Vascular Lab., Cin., 1983-84; instr., technologist The Christ Hosp. Clin. Vascular Lab., Cin., 1986; tech. cons., instr. Biosound, Inc., Indpls., 1983-89; surg. rsch. fellow divsn. surgery Boston U. Sch. Medicine; peripheral vascular technologist, instr. Seton Med. Ctr., Austin, 1991; summer assoc. health care ops. Deloitte & Touche, Houston, 1991, cons. health care ops., 1991-92, sr. cons., 1992-94, mgr. health care ops., 1994—; sr. assoc. healthcare provider cons. William M. Mercer, Inc., Houston, 1995-97; co-founder Hanrahan Williams LLC, Houston, 1997-2000; dir. Genesis Healthcare Internat., Inc., Houston, 2000—; co-founder, pres., CEO IQHPC, L.P., Houston, 2001—. Founder, chmn., pres. CORE Med. Techs., Inc., Houston, 1992—; treas. Miami Med. Edn. and Devel., Miami U., 1975-79; com. mem. Disting. Lecture Series, U. Tex. Sch. Bus., Austin; founding pres. Tex. Bus. Hall of Fame Found. Scholarship Alumni Assn., 1992-93; bd. dirs., exec. com., 1992-93. Contbr. articles to profl. jours. Finalist ACS resident competition, 1990, San Diego State U. Entrepreneurship competition; winner New Eng. Surg. Soc. resident competition, 1990; Tex. Bus. Hall of Fame Found. scholar, 1991, Abell-Hanger Endowed presdl. scholar, 1991. Mem. AMA, Soc. for Vascular Tech., Mass. Med. Soc., Harris County Med. Soc., Med. Student Surg. Soc., Tex. Med. Assn. (com. on physician access 1999—, alt. del. 2003-2004), Harris County Med. Soc. (alternate del.), Beta Theta Pi. Achievements include patents in field. Avocation: jazz music. Office: 4888 Loop Central Drive Ste 401 Houston TX 77081 E-mail: LHanrahan@iqhpc.com.

HANRAHAN, MARGARET VILLAR (PEGGI HANRAHAN), oil company executive; b. Pensacola, Fla., Mar. 1, 1953; d. William Edward and Betty Sue (Cimiotti) Villar; m. E. T. Kevin Hanrahan, Sept. 16, 2002. Sec., treas. Major Oil Co., Jackson, Miss., and Mobile, Ala., 1973-75, v.p., 1975-77, The Jeffreys Co., Inc., Mobile, 1977-91, pres., 1991-99; sec.-treas. Koala Energy Co., LLC, 1995-99; adminstr. Miller, Hamilton, Snider & Odom, L.L.C. Attys., 1995-96; ind. cons., 1996; exec. asst. Sen. Jeff Sessions of Ala., Washington, 1997—. Pres. Art Patrons League, Mobile, 1982-83, 1st v.p., 1981-82, treas., 1979-81, allied arts coun. rep., 1982-83; bd. dirs. Mobile Mus. Art, 1983-84; pres. Freedoms Found. at Valley Forge, Mobile, 1983-84, v.p. for awards, 1982-83, v.p. for edn., 1980-82; pres. Midtown Mobile Assn., 1980-91; treas. Women of Trinity Episcopal Ch., Mobile, 1982-84, pres. 1989-90; dir. Wilmer Hall Children's Home, Mobile, 1990-93. Mem. Ala. Petroleum Landmen's Assn. (sec. 1983-84, bd. dirs. 1986-89), Am. Assn. Petroleum Landmen, Assn. Legal Adminstrs. Episcopalian. Home: 3612 Rose Ln Annandale VA 22003-1934

HANRAHAN, PATRICIA LEE, healthcare educator, researcher; b. Nev. d. Mary and William Hanrahan; m. Leon N. Sarantos, July 6, 1974; 1 child, Chris Hanrahan Sarantos. BA, Coll. of New Rochelle, N.Y., 1966; MEd, Goddard Coll., Plainfield, Vt., 1975; MA, U. of Chgo., Sch. of Social Svc. Adminstrn., 1979, PhD, 1990. Rsch. assoc. (asst. prof.) U. of Chgo., 1993—98, rsch. assoc. (assoc. prof.), 1998—. Co-dir. U. of Chgo. Ctr. for Pub. Mental Health Svcs. and Policy Rsch., 1997—. Author (rsch. dir.): (50 jour. articles and book chpts.) Mental Health Svcs. Rsch. (NIMH Pre-Doctoral Fellowship, 1986); author: (rsch. fellow) (mental health svcs. rsch.) Hospice Care for Persons with Dementia (Ill. Dept. of Pub. Health Rsch. Scholar, 1990), Supportive Housing for Persons with Mental Illnesses (NIMH Nat. Rsch. Svc. Post-Doctoral Fellowship, 1991). Rsch. grants, NIMH, SAMHSA, Robert Wood Johnson, U. of Chgo. Home Health Care Rsch. Com., Ill. Office of Mental Health, Alzheimer's Assn., 1989—2003. Mem.: Unv. of Chgo. Ctr. on Memory Disorders, Chgo. Consortium for Stigma Rsch. Avocations: travel, bicycling.

HANRAHAN, PAUL THADDEUS, marketing executive; b. Phila., Nov. 10, 1957; s. Paul and Mary (Walsh) H.; m. Rodanthe Nichols, July 30, 1988; two children. BS in Mech. Engring., U.S. Naval Acad., 1979; MBA, Harvard Bus. Sch., 1986. Submarine officer USS Parche, San Francisco, 1979-84; project dir. AES Corp., Washington, 1986-89, pres., CEO, 2002—; mng. dir. AES Transpower, London, 1990-93; pres., CEO AES China, Hong Kong, 1993—2002. Office: AES China 26/F 30 Queen's Rd Central Central Hong Kong Hong Kong

HANRAHAN, ROBERT JOSEPH, chemist, educator; b. Chgo., Jan. 7, 1932; s. James Richard and Lucille Florence (Granger) H.; m. Mary Ellen Hogan, Oct. 28, 1957; children: Ann Marie, Sheila Frances, Robert Joseph, Margaret Evyleen. BS, Loyola U., Chgo., 1953; PhD, U. Wis., Madison, 1957. Research chemist Pure Oil Co., Crystal Lake, Ill., 1953; teaching asst., research asst. Monsanto research fellow U. Wis., Madison, 1953-57; NSF postdoctoral fellow Leeds (Eng.) U., 1957-58; asst. prof. phys. chemistry U. Fla., 1958-64, assoc. prof., 1964-71, prof., 1971—, chmn. phys. chemistry div., 1977-86. Vis. sci. Hahn-Meitner Inst. Nuclear Research, Berlin, 1976; cons. in field. Patentee in field; contbr. articles to profl. jours. AEC rsch. grantee, 1963-74; ERDA grantee, 1975-77; Dept. Energy grantee, 1977-88, 2001—; Dreyfus Found. grantee, 1983. Mem. Am. Chem. Soc., Am. Phys. Soc., Radiation Research Soc., AAAS, Am. Soc. Mass Spectrometry, Inter-Am. Photochem. Soc. Democrat. Roman Catholic. Achievements include rsch. in chem. effects of nuclear radiation and on solar energy systems. Home: 3730 NW 16th Pl Gainesville FL 32605-4848 Office: U Fla Dept Chemistry Gainesville FL 32611 E-mail: hanrahan@chem.ufl.edu.

HANRATH, LINDA CAROL, librarian, archivist; b. Chgo., Aug. 22, 1949; d. John Stanley and Victoria (Fraint) Grzesiakowski; m. Richard Alan Hanrath, Nov. 1, 1980; 1 child, Emily. BA in History, Rosary Coll., 1971, MA in Library Sci., 1974. Tchr. social studies Notre Dame High Sch., Chgo., 1971-75; outreach libr. Indian Trails Pub. Libr., Wheeling, Ill., 1975-76, Arlington Heights (Ill.) Meml. Libr., 1976-78; corp. libr. William Wrigley Jr. Co., Chgo., 1978—. Mem. Spl. Librs. Assn. (chmn. libr. jobline com. 1981-83, 86-87, food agrl. and nutrition divsn. 1988-89, sec. Ill. chpt. 1984-86, pres.-elect 1993-94, pres. Ill. chpt. 1994-95, conf. bd. info. svcs. adv. coun. 1990—, winner outstanding achievement award 1997), Assn. Records Mgrs. and Adminstrs., Soc. Am. Archivists, Midwest Archives Conf., Beta Phi Mu. Avocations: needlework, skiing, reading, gourmet cooking. Home: 715 E Devon Ave Roselle IL 60172-1461 Office: William Wrigley Jr Co 410 N Michigan Ave Chicago IL 60611-4213 E-mail: lhanrath@wrigley.com.

HANRATTY, CARIN GALE, pediatric nurse practitioner; b. Dec. 31, 1953; d. Burton and Lillian Aleskowitz; m. Michael Patrick Hanratty, May 22, 1983; children: Tyler James, Alison Erin. BSN, Russell Sage Coll., 1975; postgrad., U. Calif., San Diego, 1980, St. Joseph's Cool., 2002—. Cert. CPR instr.; cert. NALS; cert. specialist ANA. PNP day surgery unit Children's Med. Ctr., Dallas, 1981-85; clin. mgr. pediatrics Trinity Med. Ctr., Carrollton, Tex., 1985-86; pediatric drug coord. perinatal intervention team for substance abusing women and babies Parkland Meml. Hosp., Dallas, 1990-97; sch. nurse practitioner Dallas Ind. Sch. Dist., 1997-98; head nurse Lewisville Ind. Sch. Dist. Colony H.S., 1998—2002. Guest talk show Morning Coffee, Sta. KPLX-FM, various TV programs. Rep. United Way, 1988-97, blood donor chair Parkland Hosp., 1990-97, chair March of Dimes, 1992-97; bd. dirs., med. cons. KIDNET Found. Mem. ARC (profl., life), Nat. Assn. PNPs (v.p. Dallas chpt. 1982-83), Tex. Nurses Assn. Avocations: sewing, swimming.

HANRATTY, THOMAS JOSEPH, chemical engineer, educator; b. Phila., Nov. 9, 1926; s. John Joseph and Elizabeth Marie (O'Connor) H.; m. Joan L. Hertel, Aug. 25, 1956; children: John, Vincent, Maria, Michael, Peter. BS Chem. Engring., Villanova U., 1947; hon. doctorate, 1979; MS, Ohio State U., 1950; PhD, Princeton U., 1953; PhD (hon.), Polytechnic INst. Toulouse, 1999; doctorate (hon.), Tolouse Poly. Inst., 1999. Engr. Fischer & Porter, 1947-48; research engr. Battelle Meml. Inst., 1948-50; engr. Rohm & Haas, Phila., summer 1951; research engr. Shell Devel. Co., Emeryville, Calif., 1954; faculty U. Ill., Urbana, 1953—, assoc. prof., 1958-63, prof. chem. engring., 1963—, James W. Westwater prof. chem. engring., 1989-97. Cons. in field; vis. assoc. prof. Brown U., 1962-63 Contbr. articles to profl. jours. NSF sr. postdoctoral fellow, 1962; recipient Curtis W. McGraw award Am. Soc. Engring. Edn., 1963, Sr. Research award, 1979; Disting. Engring. Alumnus award Ohio State U., 1984; Shell Disting. prof., 1981-86; 1st winner Internat. prize for rsch. in multiphase flow, 1998; Sr. Univ. Scholar, U. Ill., 1987, Lamme award Ohio State Univ., 1997. Fellow Am. Phys. Soc.; mem. NAE, Am. Acad. Arts and Scis., NAS. AIChE (Colburn award 1957, Walker award 1964, Profl. Progress award 1967, Ernest Thiele award Chgo. sect. 1986), Serra Internat. Club. Roman Catholic. Home: 1019 W Charles St Champaign IL 61821-4525 Office: U Ill 205 Roger Adams Lab 600 S Mathews Ave Urbana IL 61801-3602 E-mail: hanratty@scs.uiuc.edu.

HANSBURY, STEPHAN CHARLES, judge; b. Mt. Holly, NJ, Nov. 3, 1946; s. Charles Clark and Kathryn Irene (Meyer) H.; m. Sharon Buckley; children: Elizabeth Kathryn, Jillian Judith, Stephanie Clark. BA, Allegheny Coll., 1968; MBA, Fairleigh Dickinson U., 1973; JD, Seton Hall U., 1977; cert. civil trial atty., Supreme Ct. N.J., 1989. Bar: N.J. 1977, U.S. Dist. Ct. (no. dist.) N.J. 1977, U.S. Supreme Ct. 1982. Dir. spl. programs Bloomfield (N.J.) Coll., 1968-71; dir. fin. aid Monmouth Coll., West Long Branch, N.J., 1971-72; asst. adminstr. Morris View, Morris Plains, N.J., 1972-78; assoc. Hansbury, Martin & Knapp, Morris Plains, 1978-87, pres., 1987-92; ptnr. Kummer Knox, Naughton & Hansbury, Parsippany, N.J., 1992-99, pres., 1996-97; ptnr. Cooper, Rose & English, LLP, 2000-2001; judge Superior Ct. of N.J., 2001—. Gen. counsel Cheshire Home, Florham Park, NJ, 1978-2000, Ciba-Geigy Corp., Summit, NJ, 1980-92; com. on complimentary dispute resolution NJ Supreme Ct., 2002—. Legis. aide Assemblyman Arthur Albohn, Morristown, NJ, 1980-83; active Morris County Bd. Social Svcs., 1989-96, chmn. 1992-94; bd. dirs. Colonial Symphony. Mem. ABA, N.J. Bar Assn., Morris County Bar Assn. (trustee 1987-90), Rotary (pres. 1998-99), Morristown Club, Worrall F. Mountain Inn of Ct. (master). Republican. Episcopalian. Avocations: tennis, golf, reading. Office: Courthouse PO Box 910 Morristown NJ 07963-0910

HANSCHEN, PETER WALTER, lawyer; b. San Francisco, July 7, 1945; s. Walter A. and Dorothy E. (Watkins) H.; m. Brenda C. Hanschen, Feb. 7, 1987. BA, San Francisco State U., 1967; JD, U. Calif.-Berkeley, 1971. Bar: Calif. 1972, U.S. Supreme Ct. 1985, U.S. Ct. Appeals D.C. Cir. 1975. Assoc. Lawler, Felix & Hall, L.A., 1971-73; atty. Pacific Gas Transmission Co., San Francisco, 1973-76, Pacific Gas & Elec. Co., San Francisco, 1976-79; gen. counsel Pacific Gas Transmission, San Francisco, 1979-83; asst. gen. counsel Pacific Gas & Elec. Co., San Francisco, 1983-88; ptnr. Graham & James, San Francisco, 1988-99, Morrison & Foerster, San Francisco, 1999—. Mem. ABA, Internat. Bar Assn., Fed. Energy Bar Assn., Counsel of Calif. Pub. Utilities. Avocations: golf, gardening, sports. Office: Morrison & Foerster LLP Ste 450 101 Ygnacio Valley Rd PO Box 8130 Walnut Creek CA 94563-8130 E-mail: phanschen@mogo.com.

HANSEL, GREGORY PAUL, lawyer; b. Glen Cove, N.Y., Feb. 21, 1960; s. Paul George and Helen (Stephens) H. BA magna cum laude, Harvard U., 1982; JD, U. Va., 1986. Bar: Fla. 1986, U.S. Ct. Appeals (11th cir.) 1986, U.S. Dist. Ct. (mid. dist.) Fla. 1987, D.C. Ct. Appeals 1988, U.S. Supreme Ct. 1992, Maine 1997. Sr. legis. asst. Atty. Gen. Fla., Tallahassee, 1984; ptnr. Shackleford, Farrior, Stallings & Evans, P.A., Tampa, Fla., 1986-96, Holland & Knight, Tampa, 1996-97, Preti, Flaherty, Beliveau, Pachios & Haley, LLC, Portland, Maine, 1997—. Co-author: Business Litigation in Florida, 1995. Mem. ABA, Fla. Bar (chmn. Fla. Bar conv. 1995), Maine State Bar Assn. Greek Orthodox. Office: Preti Flaherty Beliveau Pachios & Haley LLC 1 City Ctr Portland ME 04101-4004 E-mail: ghansel@preti.com.

HANSEL, JAMES GORDON, engineer, educator; b. N.Y.C., Oct. 17, 1937; s. Gordon Franklin and Edith (Bradshaw) H.; m. Sarah Elizabeth Martin, Dec. 27, 1964; 1 child, Claire E. BS in Engring. with high honors, Stevens Inst. Tech., 1959, MSME, 1960, ScD, 1964. Mem. rsch. faculty Princeton (N.J.) U., Guggenheim Labs., 1964-69; rsch. engr. Exxon Rsch., Linden, N.J., 1969-72; mgr. new catalyst devel. Engelhard Corp., Menlo Park, N.J., 1972-81; sr. engring. assoc. Air Products and Chems., Inc., Allentown, Pa., 1981—. Adj. assoc. prof. Columbia U., N.Y.C., 1976-80; vis. lectr. mech. engring. Stevens Inst. Tech. Hoboken, N.J., 1970-76, cons. on engring. safety to major corps., 1987—; adj. prof. chem./mech. engring. Pa. State U., State Coll., 1992-2000. Author: Theory of Experiments, 1967; contbr. author Book of Knowledge encyc., 1979, Encyclopedia of Chemical Technology, 1994; contbr. articles to profl. jours. Bd. dirs. Am. on Wheels Mus., 1998—; indsl. and profl. adv. coun. Pa. State U., Coll. of Engring., 1998—. Mem. Am. Inst. Chem. Engrs. (tech. com. on reactive chems.), Internat. Standards Orgn. (tech. com. on hydrogen vehicles), N.Y. Acad. Sci., Sigma Xi, Tau Beta Pi. Achievements include patents for on applications of oxygen; development of Three Way Conversion catalyst and automotive engine control system used in over 400 million automobiles worldwide; safety practices for hydrogen powered vehicles. Home: 829 Frank Dr Emmaus PA 18049-1505 Office: Air Products & Chems Inc 7201 Hamilton Blvd Allentown PA 18195-1526 E-mail: hanseljg@acpi.com.

HANSEL, PAUL GEORGE, physicist, consultant; b. Grand Island, Nebr., June 22, 1917; s. Arthur Hiram and Wilma D. (Amick) H.; m. Helen Stephens; children: Stephen, James, Gregory. BS in Engring. Physics, U. Kans., 1946. Engr. Signal Corps Labs., Ft. Monmouth, N.J., 1941-47; chief radio engr. Servo Corp. Am., Hicksville, NY, 1947-61; v.p. rsch. and engring. Electronic Communications, Inc., St. Petersburg, Fla., 1961-79; cons. Advanced Tech. Cons.'s, St. Petersburg, from 1979. Contbr. articles, reports to sci. and tech. jours.; patentee radio direction finding, navigation. Mem. adv. coun. U. Fla. Coll. Engring., Gainesville, 1965-89; pres. adv. coun. U. Fla., 1976-86. Recipient Apollo award NASA, 1972, citation for inventions War Dept. (now Dept. Def.), 1946. Fellow IEEE (Pioneer award 1970); mem. AAAS, N.Y. Acad. Scis., Fla. Acad. Scis. Avocations: writing, lecturing, flying. Home: Saint Petersburg, Fla. Died Mar. 11, 2003; St. Petersburg, Fla..

HANSEL, WILLIAM, biology educator; b. Vale Summit, Md., Sept. 16, 1918; s. John W. and Helen M. (Sperlein) H.; m. Milbrey Downey, Aug. 16, 1942; children: Barbara, Kay. MS, Cornell U., 1947, PhD, 1949. Asst. prof. Cornell U., Ithaca, N.Y., 1949-52, assoc. prof., 1952-61, prof., 1961-90, Liberty Hyde Bailey prof., 1983-90, chmn. physiology dept., 1978-83; Gordon D. Cain prof. La. State U., Baton Rouge, 1990—. Scientific adv. Merck, Sharp and Dohme, Rahway, 1980-85, Smith, Kline, Beecham, Westchester, Pa., 1986-91. Author: Genetic Engineering of Animals, 1990, Nutrition and Reproduction, 1998; contbr. over 300 articles to profl. jours. Maj. U.S. Army, 1941-46, ETO. Recipient 13 nat. or internat. rsch. and svc. awards including first Pharmacia and Upjohn Internat. award for life time rsch. in ruminant reproduction, 1998. Fellow AAAS; mem. Soc. Study Reprodn. (pres. 1976), Am. Physiol. Soc., Endocrine Soc., Soc. Exptl. Biology and Medicine (treas. 1975), Gamma Sigma Delta, Sigma Xi, Phi Kappa Phi. Achievements include isolation and identification of cusative agent of bovine x-disease; development of successful technique for estrous cycle regulation in cattle; pioneered development of assays for hormones in blood of animals; discovery of control mechanisms for corpus luteum function in cattle; demonstrated the relationships between nutrition and reproduction in cattle; development of successful targeted treatment for human prostate and breast cell tumors grown in test mice. Office: Pennington Biomed Rsch Ctr 6400 Perkins Rd # B1047 Baton Rouge LA 70808-4124 E-mail: hanselw@mhs.pbrc.edu.

HANSELL, DEAN, lawyer; b. Bridgeport, Conn., Mar. 24, 1952; BA, Denison U., 1974; JD, Northwestern U., 1977. Bar: Ill 1977, US Dist Ct (no dist) Ill 1977, US Ct Appeals (7th cir) 1978, US Ct Appeals (DC cir) 1979, US Ct Appeals (9th cir) 1979, Calif 1980, US Dist Ct (cent dist) Calif 1981, US Dist Ct (so dist) Calif 1989, US Supreme Ct 1998, US Ct Appeals (8th cir) 2001. Asst. atty. gen. for environ. control State of Ill., Chgo., 1977-80; atty. FTC, L.A., 1980-83; assoc. Donovan Leisure Newton & Irvine, L.A., 1984-86; ptnr. LeBoeuf, Lamb, Greene & MacRae, L.A., 1986-01, mng. ptnr., 2001—. Mem. Ill Solar Resources Adv Panel, 1978—80; adj assoc prof Southwestern Univ Sch Law, Los Angeles, 1982—86; judge pro tem Los Angeles County Munic Ct, 1987—97, Los Angeles County Superior Ct, 1989—; mem adv bd Fayette Haywood Legal Servs, Tenn., 1979—83; mem. adv. bd. Nat. Inst. Citizen Edn. in Law, 1989—94, Asian Pacific Am. Legal Ctr., 1996—. Mem. editl. bd.: Los Angeles Lawyer Mag., 1995—, Internat. Reins. Dispute Reporter, 1996—2001; contbr. articles to profl. jours. Commr. L.A. Bd. Police Commrs., 1997—2001, v.p., 2001; commr. L.A. Bd. Info. Tech., 2001—, v.p., 2003—; bd. dirs. Jewish Fedn. Coun. Met. L.A. Region, 1984—87, Project LEAP, Legal Elections All Precincts, Chgo., 1976—80, Martin Luther King Jr Ctr Nonviolence, L.A., 1991—95, L.A. Pub. Libr. Found., 1997—. Mem.: Am. Bar Assn., Calif Bar Asn, Los Angeles County Bar Asn (mem exec comt antitrust sect 1982—92, chair 1989—90), Phi Beta Kappa, Omicron Delta Kappa. Office: LeBoeuf Lamb Greene & MacRae 725 S Figueroa St Ste 3100 Los Angeles CA 90017-5404 E-mail: dhansell@llgm.com.

HANSELL, EDGAR FRANK, lawyer; b. Leon, Iowa, Oct. 12, 1937; s. Edgar Noble and Celestia Delphine (Skinner) H.; m. Phyllis Wray Silvey, June 24, 1961; children— John Joseph, Jordan Burke AA, Graceland Coll., 1957; BBA, U. Iowa, 1959, JD, 1961. Bar: Iowa 1961. Assoc. Nyemaster, Goode, McLaughlin, Voigts, West, Hansell & O'Brien, P.C., Des Moines, 1964-68, ptnr., shareholder, 1968—. Bd. dirs. The Vernon Co., Greater Des Moines Partnership, Downtown Cmty. Alliance, Inc., Des Moines Internat. Airport; mem. adv. com. to bd. dirs. The Lauridson Group, Inc.; adj. prof. law Drake U., Des Moines, 1990—98. Mem. editorial adv. bd. Jour. Corp. Law, 1985—. Bd. dirs. Des Moines Child Guidance Ctr., 1972-78, 81-87, pres., 1977-78; trustee Iowa Law Sch. Found., 1975-90, pres., 1983-87; bd. dirs. Iowa Natural Heritage Found., 1988-93, Iowa Sports Found., 1986-97; bd. dirs. Iowa State Bar Found., 1991-2000, pres., 1996-98. With USAF, 1961-64. Mem. ABA, Iowa Bar Assn. (pres. young lawyers sect. 1971-72, bd. govs. 1971-72, 85-87, mem. grievance commn. 1973-78, Merit award young lawyers sect. 1977, 98, chmn. corp. and bus. law com. 1979-85, pres. 1989-90), Polk County Bar Assn., Des Moines Club (pres. 1979-80). Home: 139-37th Des Moines IA 50312-4303 Office: Nyemaster Goode Voigts West Hansell & O'Brien PC 700 Walnut St Ste 1600 Des Moines IA 50309-3800 E-mail: efh@nyemaster.com.

HANSELL, JOHN ROYER, retired physician; b. Phila., June 30, 1931; s. Henry Lewis and Elizabeth (Campbell) H. AB, U. Pa., 1953; MD, Jefferson Med. Coll., 1957. Diplomate Am. Bd. Pathology, Am. Bd. Nuclear Medicine (chmn. 1988-89). Intern Germantown Hosp., Phila., 1957-58, resident, pathologist, 1956-61, Bryn Mawr (Pa.) Hosp., 1961-62; pathology fellow New Eng. Deaconess Hosp., Boston, 1962-63; resident Mayo Clinic, Rochester, Minn., 1966-67; chief nuclear medicine VA Med Ctr., Phila., 1967-93. Contbr. chpts. to books and articles to profl. jours. Comdr. USPHS, 1963-66. Fellow Soc. Nuclear Medicine, Coll. Am. Pathologists. Republican. Avocations: antiques, gardening.

HANSELL, PHYLLIS SHANLEY, nursing educator, administrator, researcher, consultant; b. N.Y.C., Jan. 3, 1947; s. Peter James and Jewell Mae (Altis) S.; m. Robert Lewis Hansell, June 16, 1984; children: Benjamin, Christopher. BS, Fairleigh Dickinson U., 1972; MEd, Columbia U., 1975, EdD, 1981. RN. Staff nurse Mountainside Hosp., Montclair, N.J., 1967-69; head nurse N.Y. Med. Coll., N.Y.C., 1970-72, clin. instr., 1972-75; instr. Seton Hall U., South Orange, 1975-77, asst. prof., 1977-79, prof. nursing, 1986-94, 96—, dir. nursing rsch., 1986-94, dept. chair, 1996-99, acting dean, 1999-2000, dean Coll. Nursing, 2000—; dir. nursing rsch. Meml. Sloan-Kettering, N.Y.C., 1984-86; dean, prof. Coll. Nursing Seton Hall U., 2000. Chair N.J. Assn. of Baccalaureate and Higher Degree Programs in Nursing. Contbr. articles to profl. jours., chpt. to book. Bd. dirs. Jr. League, Montclair, 1992-94, chair grants and corp. devel., chair Newark Teen Arts Festival, Montclair and Newark, 1994-95. Recipient Gov.'s merit award Gov. N.J., 1994. Fellow: Am. Acad. Nursing; mem.: ANA (chair rsch., Gov.'s award 1994), N.J. State Nurses Assn. (mem. coun., rsch. award 1994), Am. Acad. Practice (Disting. Practitioner 2000), Sigma Theta Tau (v.p. Gamma Nu chpt. 1994—96, rsch. award 1983). Avocations: opera, ballet, skiing, tennis, golf. Office: Seton Hall U 400 S Orange Ave South Orange NJ 07079-2697

HANSELL, RICHARD STANLEY, obstetrician, gynecologist, educator; b. Indpls., Nov. 18, 1950; s. Robert Mathey and Jewell (Martin) H.; m. Cathy C., Oct. 7, 1995; children: Elizabeth, Victoria. BA, DePauw U., 1972; MD, Ind. U., 1976. Cert. Am. Bd. Obstetrics and Gynecology. Practice medicine specializing in ob-gyn Cedarwood Med. Ctr., St. Joseph, Mich., 1980-86; asst. prof. ob-gyn. Ind. U., Indpls., 1986-93, assoc. prof., 1993—2002, prof., 2002—. Instr. Western Mich. U., Kalamazoo, 1980-86; med. bd. Planned Parenthood, Benton Harbor, Mich., 1980-86; med. dir. Planned Parenthood of Ctrl. Ind., 1991-95; examiner Am. Bd. Ob-gyn., 1994—. Mem. AMA, Am. Coll. Ob-Gyn, Assn. of Profs. of Gynecology and Obstetrics, Ind. State Med. Soc., Ctrl. Assn. Ob/gyn., Indpls. Med. Soc. Lodges: Kiwanis. Presbyterian. Avocations: golf, fishing. Office: Ind U Med Sch Dept Ob-Gyn 1001 W 10th St Indianapolis IN 46202-2859

HANSELL, SUSAN, writer, educator; b. Stockton, Calif., May 8, 1956; d. Jack Aaron Smuck and Jane Hansell Lewis; m. Anthony Generalao Baguinat, Mar. 1991 (div. Apr. 1995). BA with high honors, U. Calif., Berkeley, 1981; MA, San Francisco State U., 1987; MFA, CUNY, 1996. Lectr. San Francisco State U., 1987-88, Calif. State U., Northridge, 1989-92, Loyola Marymount U., L.A., 1990-91, Bklyn. Coll.-CUNY, 1994—2000, Calif. State U., Long Beach, Calif., 2000—. Author: (plays) Am. Rose, 1997, Rollover Othello, 1996, Affair on the Air, 1998, My Medea, 1995, Drop It, 1988, 14 Ladies in Hats, 1988, Pink Rope, 1986, Mary Mary, 1996, Little Kings, 2001, What Do We Have Here?, 2002, We Are All Dick 3, 2003. Recipient E.A. Biderman poetry prize Grey Panthers, 1985. Mem. Dramatists Guild, Theatre Comms. Group. Avocation: swimming. Office: CSULB Dept English 1250 Bellflower Blvd Long Beach CA 90840

HANSELMAN, RICHARD WILSON, entrepreneur; b. Cin., Oct. 8, 1927; s. Wendell Forest and Helen E. (Beiderwelle) H.; m. Beverly Baker White, Oct. 16, 1954; children: Charles Fielding, II, Jane White. BA in Econs, Dartmouth Coll., 1949. V.p. merchandising RCA Sales Corp., Indpls., 1964-66, v.p. product planning, 1966-69, v.p. product mgmt., 1969-70; pres. luggage div. Samsonite Corp., Denver, 1970-73, pres. luggage group, 1973-74, exec. v.p. ops., 1974-75, pres., 1975-77; sr. v.p. Beatrice Foods Co., Chgo., 1976-77, exec. v.p., 1977-80; pres., chief operating officer, dir. Genesco Inc., Nashville, 1980-86, chief exec. officer, 1981-86, pvt. investor, corp. dir., 1986—. Chmn. bd. dirs. Found. Health Sys. (now Health Net Inc.), 1999; bd. dirs. Brass Eagle Inc., Metal Powder Products Co., Arvin Meritor; chmn. Titan Plastics (formerly Wollin Products). Hon. trustee Com. for Econ. Devel. Served with U.S. Army, 1950-52. Mem. Belle Meade Country Club, Union League, Chgo. Club, Golf Club of Tenn., Phi Kappa Psi. Office: 104 Westhampton Pl Nashville TN 37205

HANSELMANN, FREDRICK CHARLES, lawyer; b. Phila., Sept. 1, 1955; s. Helmuth Fredrick and Maria Elizabeth (Dougherty) H.; m. Mary Nina Johnson, May 7, 1983; children: Elizabeth Ryan, Peter Cornelius, Kevin Andrew, Charlotte Mary. BA magna cum laude, La Salle Coll., 1977; JD, U. Notre Dame, 1980. Bar: Pa. 1980, U.S. Dist. Ct. (ea. dist.) Pa. 1981, U.S. Dist. Ct. (mid. dist.) Pa. 1987, U.S. Ct. Appeals (3d cir.) 1981. Assoc. German, Gallagher & Murtagh, P.C., Phila., 1981-85, Wilson, Elser, Moskowitz, Edelman & Dicker, Phila., 1985-90; ptnr. Mylotte David & Fitzpatrick, Phila., 1990-99; of counsel McBreen and Kopko, Phila., 1999—. Mem. ABA, Pa. Bar Assn., Phila. Bar Assn., Def. Rsch. Inst., Profl. Liability Underwriting Soc., Lawyers Club Phila., Notre Dame Club Phila., Avalon Yacht Club, Glen Lake (Mich.) Assn. Republican. Roman Catholic. Home: 118 Azalea Way Flourtown PA 19031-2008 Office: McBreen & Kopko 8 Penn Ctr 1628 John F Kennedy Blvd Ste 1400 Philadelphia PA 19103 Fax: 215 864-2610. E-mail: fchlaw2@aol.com.

HANSEN, ANDREW MARIUS, retired library association executive; b. Storm Lake, Iowa, Mar. 25, 1929; s. Andrew Marius and Margaret Mary (Van Wagenen) H.; m. Rina M. Smith, Feb. 24, 1967; 1 child, Neil S. BA, U. Omaha, 1951; postgrad., U. Md., 1955; MA, U. Minn., 1962; postgrad, U. Iowa, 1968-71. Librarian Bismarck (N.D.) Public Library, 1957-63, Sioux City (Iowa) Public Library, 1963-67; instr. Sch. of Library Sci., U. Iowa, Iowa City, 1967-71; exec. sec. ALA, Chgo., 1971-80, exec. dir. reference and adult services div., 1980-94. Vis. asst. prof. Ind. State U., Terre Haute, 1966; adj. faculty Dominican U., River Forest, Ill., 2001. Pres. Friends of Wilmette Pub. Libr., 1984-85; mem. Village of Wilmette Transp. Commn., 1995—2003. Served with USAF, 1951-55. Mem. ALA (Mudge-Bowker award 1993), N.D. Libr. Assn. (pres. 1958-59, sec.-treas. 1962-63), Iowa Libr. Assn. (pres. 1967-68), Coalition Adult Edn. Orgns. (bd. dirs. 1972-93), Ch. and Synagogue Libr. Assn. (treas. Northeastern Ill. chpt. 1985-91), Chgo. Libr. Club (sec. 1983-84), Rotary. Presbyterian. Home: 314 Skokie Blvd Wilmette IL 60091-3002 E-mail: andy_hansen@msn.com.

HANSEN, BARBARA CALEEN, physiologist, science educator; b. Boston, Nov. 24, 1941; d. Reynold L. and Dorothy (Richardson) Caleen; m. Kenneth Dale Hansen, Oct. 8, 1976; 1 child, David Scott. BS, UCLA, 1964, MS, 1965; PhD, U. Wash., 1971. Asst. prof. then assoc. prof. U. Wash., Seattle, 1971—76; prof., assoc. dean U. Mich., Ann Arbor, 1977—82; assoc. v.p. acad. affairs and research, dean grad. sch. So. Ill. U., Carbondale, 1982—85; v.p. for grad. studies and research U. Md., Balt. and Balt. County, 1985—90, prof. physiology, dir. obesity and diabetes rsch. ctr., 1990—. Mem. adv. com. to dir. NIH, Washington, 1979—83; mem. joint health policy com. Assn. Am. U., Washington, 1982—86, Nat. Assn. State U. and Land-Grant Colls., Washington, 1982—86, Am. Coun. on Edn., Washington, 1982—86; mem. nutrition study sect. NIH, 1979—83; mem. program com. Inst. Medicine-NAS, Washington, 1982—84; mem. Armed Forces Epidemiology Bd., 1991—95; mem. bd. sci. counselors NIEHS, 1992—94, NIH, 1992—94, mem. nat. toxicology bd., 1992—94, NIEHS, 1992—94; mem. search com. Office of Rsch. Integrity, NIH, 1992—93. Author: The Commonsense Guide to Weight Loss for People with Diabetes, 1998, The Metabolic Syndrome X, 1999; co-editor: Controversies in Obesity, 1983, editor chpts. on physiology; contbr. articles to profl. jours.; co-editor: Insulin Resistance and Insulin Resistance Syndrome, 2002. Mem. adv. com. Am. Bur. Med. Advancement China, NYC, 1982—85; mem. adv. bd. African-Am. Inst., 1987—91; mem. adv. com. Robert Wood Johnson Found., Princeton, NJ, 1982—91. Fellow Nueroscis. fellow, U. Pa., 1966—68. Mem.: Internat. Assn. Study of Obesity (pres. 1986—90), Nat. Assn. State U. and Land Grant Colls. (chmn. coun. on rsch. policy and grad. edn. 1986—87), N.Am. Assn. Study of Obesity (pres. 1984—85, 1986—), Am. Soc. for Clin. Nutrition (pres.-elect 1994—95, pres. 1995—96, v.p.), Am. Soc. for Nutritional Scis., Inst. Medicine of NAS, Am. Physiol. Soc., Phi Beta Kappa (Arthur Patch McKinley scholar 1964). Republican. Presbyterian. Achievements include discovery of of periodic (10-14 min.) cycling pattern of pancreas insulin secretion; identification of the pattern of progressive defects in insulin secretion and insulin action preceeding overt clinical type 2 diabetes mellitus; showed prevention of obesity prevents most type 2 diabetes. Office: U Md-Balt Sch Medicine Obesity-Diabetes Rsch Ctr 10 S Pine St MSTF 600 Baltimore MD 21201-1116

HANSEN, BEVERLY ANNE, environmental policy educator; b. Johnson City, N.Y., Jan. 12, 1955; d. Robert Charles and Doris Therese Frankis; m. Emerson Wade Hansen, June 19, 1982; children: Katie, Alyssa, Erin. BS in Biology, Niagara U., 1977; MS in Environ. Sci., SUNY, Syracuse, 1984; MBA, Syracuse U., 1984; PhD in Environ. Sci., SUNY, Syracuse, 2003. Cert. tchr., N.Y. Microbiologist Syracuse Rsch. Corp., 1979-82, Packaging Cons. Internat., Inc., Syracuse, 1984-86, 92-94, 1997-98; rschr. Randolph G. Pack Environ. Inst., Syracuse, 1996, 98, 99; part-time prof. SUNY, Oswego, 1994-99; biology tchr. Fayetteville-Manlius H.S., Manlius, N.Y., 1999—. Part-time instr. SUNY Coll. Environ. Scis. and Forestry, Syracuse, 1998—. Co-editor jour. Adirondacks and Beyond, 1998. Mem.: Am. Polit. Sci. Assn. Democrat. Roman Catholic. Home: 3306 Tuccamore Cir Baldwinsville NY 13027-9016 E-mail: bhanson2@twcny.rr.com.

HANSEN, BRUCE LYNN, retired music educator; b. Brigham City, Utah, Oct. 17, 1951; s. Rulon Han and Edith Irene Hansen; m. Dora Marie Jones, Aug. 28, 1976; children: Nicole Irene, Joelyn Marie, Donnelle Caroline, Bruce Robert, Taylor Ashley. BA, Utah State U., 1973; MA, U. Wash., 1980. Cert. tchr. Wash., 1974. Tchr. music St. John Sch. Dist., Wash., 1973—76, Napavine Sch. Dist., Napavine, 1976—77, Port Townsend Sch. Dist., 1977—83, Centralia Sch. Dist., 1983—2003; ret., 2003. Priesthood leader Ch. of Jesus Christ of Latter-day Saints, Centralia, 1983—2003. Conservative. Achievements include Centralia MS Band selected to participate in Washington DC Independence Day Parade; The band was selected in 1986. Avocations: travel, backpacking, music. Office: Centralia School District 901 Johnson Rd Centralia WA 98531

HANSEN, CARL R. management consultant, b. Chgo., May 2, 1926; s. Carl M. and Anna C. (Roge) H.; m. Christia Marie Loeser, Dec. 31, 1952; 1 child, Lothar. MBA, U. Chgo., 1954. Dir. market rsch. Kitchens of Sara Lee, Deerfield, Ill., Earle Ludgin & Co., Chgo.; svc. v.p. Market Rsch. Corp. Am., 1956-67; pres. Chgo. Assoc. Inc., 1967—. Chmn. Ill. adv. coun. SBA, 1973-74; mem. exec. com. Ill. Gov.'s Adv. Coun., 1969-72; resident officer U.S. High Commn. Germany, 1949-52; vice chmn. Rep. Cen. Com. Cook County; chmn. Cook County Young Reps., 1957-58, 12th Congl. Dist. Rep. Orgn., 1971-74, 78-82, Suburban Rep. Orgn., 1974-78, 82-86, del. Rep. Nat. Conv., 1968, 84, 92; chmn. Legis. Dist. Ill., 1964—; del. Rep. State Conv., 1962-96; Elk Grove Twp. Rep. committeeman, 1962-2002; pres. John Ericsson Rep. League Ill., 1975-76; Rep. presdl. elector Ill., 1972; chmn. Viking Ship Restoration Com., mem. Cook County Bd. Commrs., 1970, 74—, chmn. legis. com., adminstrn. com.; mem. bd. dirs. Nat. Assn. Counties; mem. Am. Scandinavian Found. 1st lt. AUS, 1944-48, maj. Res. Mem. Am. Mktg. Assn., Am. Statis. Assn., Nat. Assn. Counties (dir.), Res. Officers Assn., Chgo. Hist. Soc., Planning Forum, Am. Legion, VFW, Dania Soc., Sons of Norway, Swedish Am. Hist. Soc., Lions, Masons, Shriners. Home: 110 S Edward St Mount Prospect IL 60056-3414 Office: 118 N Clark St Chicago IL 60602-1304

HANSEN, CAROL LOUISE, English language educator; b. San Jose, Calif., July 17, 1938; d. Hans Eskelsen and Thelma Josephine (Brooks) Hansen; m. Merrill Chris Davis, July 17, 1975 (div.). BA in English, San Jose State U., 1960; MA in English Lit., U. Calif., Berkeley, 1968; PhD in English Lit., Ariz. State U., 1975. Asst. prof. English City Coll. San Francisco, Calif., 1985—, Coll. San Mateo, Calif., 1987—, De Anza Coll., 1998-99; lectr. expository writing U. San Francisco, 2001. Writing coord. Calif. State U., Monterey Bay, 1996; mem. rsch. com. Conf. on Coll. Composition and comm., 2001; presenter in field. Author: Woman as Individual in English Renaissance Drama, 1993, 2d edit., 1995, 3d edit., 2000, The Life and Death of Asham: Leonard and Virginia Woolf's Haunted House, 2000, Beyond Evil: Cathy and Cal in East of Eden, 2002; contbr. articles to profl. jours. Active Grace Cathedral, San Francisco. Fellow NDEA. Mem.: MLA (chair exec. com. discussion group on two-yr. colls. 1999), Virginia Woolf Soc. Episcopalian. Avocation: animal welfare. Office: City Coll San Francisco 50 Phelan Ave San Francisco CA 94112-1821 E-mail: carhansen1@aol.com.

HANSEN, CHARLES, lawyer; b. Jersey City, May 23, 1926; s. Charles Henry and Katherine (Bensch) H.; m. Carolyn P. Smith, Sept. 26, 1953; children: Mark, Melissa. BS, U. Mich., 1946; JD, Mich. Law Sch., 1950. Bar: N.Y. 1951, Wis. 1961, Mo. 1980. Engr. Westinghouse Electric Co., 1946; assoc. Mudge, Stern, Williams & Tucker, 1950-53; chief labor counsel, div. counsel Sylvania Electric Products, 1953-61; sec., gen. counsel Trane Co., La Crosse, Wis., 1961-69, exec. v.p., 1968-73; pres. Cutler-Hammer World Trade, Inc., 1973-77; v.p. Cutler-Hammer, Inc., 1973-77, exec. v.p., 1977-79; sr. v.p. law Emerson Electric Co., 1979-84, sr. v.p., sec., gen. counsel, 1984-89; ptnr. Bryan Cave, 1989-95, of counsel, 1995—. Adj. prof. Sch. Law St. Louis U., 1987-99. Served to lt. (j.g.) USNR, 1943-46. Mem. ABA, Wis., Mo. bar assns., Am. Law Inst., Order of Coif, Tau Beta Pi. Home: 8 Wydown Ter Saint Louis MO 63105-2217 Office: 211 N Broadway 1 Metropolitan Sq Ste 3600 Saint Louis MO 63102-2750 E-mail: hansencih@aol.com.and., chansen@bryancave.com.

HANSEN, CHARLES MORTON, editor, retired military officer; b. Huntington Park, Calif., Sept. 27, 1933; s. Andrew Hansen and Lena S. Andrew. BA in History, UCLA, 1955; MA in History, San Francisco State U., 1985. Commd. 2d lt. U.S. Army, 1955, advanced through grades to col., 1977, platoon leader, 1957-59, bn. comdr., 1969-70, co-comdr., 1962—63, sr. adv., 1965-66, ret., 1982; contbg. editor Am. Genealogist, 1988—; editor The Genealogist, 1996—. Contbr. articles to profl. jours. Decorated Legion of Merit, Bronze Star, Combat Infantry Badge, Cross of Gallantry Republic of Vietnam; recipient Coddington award for Merit, New Eng. Hist. Geneal. Soc., 1995. Fellow: Am. Soc. Genealogists; mem.: Soc. Heraldica Scandinavia (Denmark), Heraldy Soc. (London), Soc. Genealogists (London), Ninth Infantry Rgt. Assn., Harbor Point Racquet Club. Methodist. Avocation: tennis. Home: 25 Rodeo Ave Apt 22 Sausalito CA 94965-1783

HANSEN, CHRISTIAN ANDREAS, JR., plastics and chemical company executive; b. New Braunsfels, Tex., Sept. 12, 1926; s. Christian Andreas and Velma Arbeda (Ivy) H.; m. Emily Dann; B.S., Rice U., 1948; Exec. With Exxon, 21 years, last position gen. mgr., Linden, N.J.; dir. mfg. chem. div. G.A.F. Corp., N.Y.C., 1969-71; chmn. bd., chief exec. officer, pres., founder Hanlin Group, Inc., Linden Chlorine Products, Inc., 1971-93; LCP/Nat. Plastics, Inc., 1977-93; retired, 1993.; chmn. Chem. Industry Council N.J., Trenton, 1977-82; mem. N.J. Gov.'s Commn. on Hazardous Waste Disposal. Founder, chmn., CEO, pres. Pathways, Inc., 1994-98; Hansen Plastics, Inc., 1994-98; co-founder Ultrapure Products, Inc., 2000-; real estate agt. Weichert Realtors, N.J.; pres. Union County (N.J.) United Fund, 1967-69; councilman City of Baytown (Tex.), 1961-63; leader Boy Scouts, Sea Scouts. Served to lt. USNR, 1943-46. Named Man of the Year, Union County United Fund, 1970. Mem. Am. Inst. Chem. Engrs., Chlorine Inst. (past pres., past bd. dirs.), Eastern Union County C. of C. (v.p. 1968-69). Pub.: God's Bible and Jesus' Papers, 1994; patentee in field. Home and Office: 1 Scenic Dr Highlands NJ 07732-1329

HANSEN, CHRISTOPHER AGNEW, lawyer; b. Yakima, Wash., Dec. 10, 1934; s. Raymond Walter and Christine F.M. (Agnew) H.; m. Sandra Ridgely Pindell, Aug. 4, 1959; Anne Ridgely, Christopher Agnew Jr., Eric Bruce. BS, Cornell U., 1957; JD, U. Md., 1963. Bar: Md. 1963, U.S. Supreme Ct. 1973, U.S. Ct. Appeals (4th cir.) D.C. 1978. Law clk. Cir. Ct. for Balt. County, Towson, Md., 1960-63; assoc. Piper & Marbury, Balt., 1963-74; of counsel Casey, Scott, Canfield & Heggestad PC, Washington, 1982-93; ptnr. Constable, Alexander & Skeen, Towson, 1984-86, Parks, Hansen & Ditch, Towson, 1986-94; of counsel Heggestad & Weiss, PC, Washington, 1993—2001; pvt. practice Towson, 1974-83, 95—. With U.S. Army, 1957-60. Mem. ABA, D.C. Bar, Md. State Bar Assn., Bar Assn. Balt. County, Balt. City Bar Assn., Phi Alpha Delta. Episcopalian. Home: 800 Hatherleigh Rd Baltimore MD 21212-1614

HANSEN, CLAIRE V. financial executive; b. Thornton, Iowa, June 3, 1925; s. Charles F. and Grace B. (Miller) H.; m. Renee C. Hansen, Aug. 17, 1946; children: Charles James, Christopher David, Peter Chrissis. BSc, U. Notre Dame, 1947; MBA, Harvard U., 1948. Chartered fin. analyst. With Salk, Ward & Salk, Inc.; v.p. Salk Inst. Agency, 1954-59; with Duff, Anderson & Clark, Chgo., 1959-67, v.p., dir., 1967-71; dir. Duff and Phelps, Inc., 1972-88; exec. v.p. Duff & Phelps, 1973-75, pres., chief exec. officer, 1975-84, chmn., chief exec. officer, 1984-87; chmn. bd. dirs. Duff & Phelps Utilities Income, Inc., Chgo., 1987—2001, CEO, 2000—01; chmn. bd. dirs. Duff & Phelps Select Income Fund, Inc., Chgo., 2002—. Bd. dirs. Chgo. Lung Assn., 1962-80, pres. 1973-75; bd. dirs. Am. Lung Assn., 1971-83, Ctr. Religion and Psychotherapy in Chgo., 1979-83; trustee Glenwood Sch., 1974-95, chmn., 1983-87; bd. dirs. Auditorium Theatre Coun., 1983-88, treas., 1987-88; bd. dirs. Schwab Rehab. Hosp., 1978-82, pres., 1980-82; bd. dirs. Pelican Bay Found. Inc., 1993-99, treas., 1993-96, pres., 1996-97. Mem. Inst. Chartered Fin. Analysts, Mid-Am. Club, Univ. Club, Chgo. Club, Olympia Fields Country Club, Club Pelican Bay, Hole-in-the-Wall Golf Club. Republican. Episcopalian. Home: 5601 Turtle Bay Dr Apt 2001 Naples FL 34108-2703 Office: 55 E Monroe St Ste 3600 Chicago IL 60603-5026

HANSEN, CURTIS LEROY, federal judge; b. 1933; BS, U. Iowa, 1956; JD, U. N.Mex., 1961. Bar: N.Mex. Law clk. to Hon. Irwin S. Moise N.Mex. Supreme Ct., 1961-62; ptnr. Snead & Hansen, Albuquerque, 1962-64, Civerolo, Hansen & Wolf, P.A., 1964—92; dist. judge U.S. Dist. Ct., N.Mex., 1992—2003, sr. dist. judge, 2003—. Mem. State Bar N.Mex., Albuquerque Bar Assn., Am. Coll. Trial Lawyers, Am. Bd. Trial Advocates, Albuquerque Country Club. Office: US Courthouse Chambers Ste 660 333 Lomas Blvd NW Albuquerque NM 87102-2272

HANSEN, DAVID RASMUSSEN, federal judge; b. Exira, Iowa, 1938; BA, N.W. Mo. State U., 1960; JD, George Washington U., 1963. Asst. clk. to minority House Appropriations Com. Ho. of Reps., 1960—61; adminstrv. aide 7th Dist. Iowa, 1962—63; pvt. practice Jones, Cambridge & Carl, Atlantic, Iowa, 1963—64; capt., judge advocate General's Corps U.S. Army, 1964—68; pvt. practice Barker, Hansen & McNeal, Iowa Falls, Iowa, 1968—76; ptnr. Win-Gin Farms, Iowa Falls, 1971—; judge Police Ct., Iowa, 1969—73, 2d Jud. Dist. Ct., Iowa, 1976—86, U.S. Dist. Ct. (no. dist.), Cedar Rapids, Iowa, 1986—91, U.S. Ct. Appeals (8th cir.), Cedar Rapids, 1991—2002, chief judge, 2002—03, sr. judge, 2003—. Office: US Courthouse Rm 304 101 1st St SE Cedar Rapids IA 52401-1202*

HANSEN, DONALD MARTY, journalist, retired accountant; b. Elmhurst, Ill., July 6, 1935; s. Donald Joseph Hansen and Vivian Leona (Bourgart) Guthrie; m. Rose Ann Baumeister, Aug. 12, 1961 (div.); children: Teresa Lynn, Donna Louise, David Lawrence, Daniel Leonard. Assoc. in Acctg., Racine Tech., 1970. Drill press operator J.I. Case Co., Racine, Wis., 1964-70; acct. Scott Petersen Meat Co., Chgo., 1974-95, Crosby Freezer, Inc., Chgo., 1995-2000; editor, pub. Don Hansen's Nat. Weekly Football and Basketball Gazettes, Westmont, Ill., 1987—; columnist USA Today Online, 1998—; editor, pub. Don Hansen's Ann. 52-page Football Schedules Booklet, 2000—. Stringer Football News, Miami, 1981—, The Sporting News, St. Louis, 1987—, USA Today, Arlington, Va., 1987—; mem. Melberger award selection com. Downtown Wilkes-Barre Touchtown Club, 1993—; mem. com. for NCAA Divsn. III Player of the Yr., John Gagliardi award, 1993—. Editor, pub. Don Hansen's Annual 52-Page Football Schedules Booklet, 2000—; contbr. articles to profl. jours. Originator, promoter, operator annual summer wrestling tournament Oak Park-River Forest (Ill.) H.S., 1978-80; mem. selection com. Farm All-Am. Football Team, 1999 ; mem. selection com. NCAA Divsn. II Hall of Fame Football, 1999—. With USN, 1952-54. Recipient Leadership trophy Chase Park (Chgo.), 1947, Celebrity Cert. of Appreciation ARC, 1992, Statistician of the Yr. Oak Park-River Forest H.S., 1981. Mem. CO-SIDA Coll. Sports Info. Dirs. Am., Knucklers Card Club (sgt. at arms and host 2001). Republican. Mem. Assembly of God Ch. Home: Apt 10 5613 King Arthur Ct Westmont IL 60559-2269 Office: Don Hansen's Nat Weekly Football Gazette PO Box 305 Westmont IL 60559-0305 E-mail: fbgazette@thc.to., don@donhansen.com.

HANSEN, DONALD W. insurance and financial services executive; b. Chgo., June 9, 1924; s. Chris M. and Violet Louise (Anderson) H.; m. Nancy SanRoman, Dec. 21, 1944; children: Donald W. II, Scott D., Debra Anne. BS in Bus. and Econs, Ill. Inst. Tech., 1948; postgrad., U. Chgo. Grad. Sch. Bus., 1957. Fin. rep., mgr. bank relations Comml. Credit Co., Chgo., 1948-57; pres. Sears Roebuck Acceptance Co., Wilmington, Del., 1957-63; v.p. fin. services Allstate Ins. Co., 1963-75, v.p. money center and banking adminstrn., 1971-76; pres. Allstate Fin. Corp., 1964-74; chmn. bd. Allstate Savs. & Loan Assn., 1963-66; pres., chief exec. officer Allstate Enterprises Mortgage Corp., Anaheim, Calif., 1972-74, First Farwest Corp., Portland, Oreg., 1976-78, Midwestern United Life Ins. Co., Ft. Wayne, Ind., 1978-83, United Equitable Corp., Lincolnwood, Ill., 1983-86, Am. Warranty Corp., 1983-86. Active Young Pres. Orgn., 1959-73. Served to 1st lt. AUS, 1943-46, aide-de-camp to Brig. Gen. W. A. Brederlinden 44th Div. Mem. Scottsdale Country Club. Republican. Presbyterian. Home: 11040 N 77th St Scottsdale AZ 85260-5564 E-mail: hansen069@webtv.net.

HANSEN, DONNA LAUREN, court reporting educator; b. Concordia, Kans., Dec. 25, 1939; d. Peter August and Lynda Bernice (Carlson) H. BA, Bethany Coll., 1961; MS, Kans. State U., 1986. Cert. tchr., Kans., notary pub., Kans. Tchr. Munden (Kans.) High Sch., 1961-64; instr. typing Brown Mackie Coll., Salina, Kans., 1964-74, instr. ct. reporting, 1974-77, chair ct. reporting, 1977-88, 96-98, cons., instr., 1989—, chair med. office dept., 1998—. Instr. shorthand workshop Pittsburg (Kans.) State U., 1978, Emporia (Kans.) State U., 1978; adminstr. social work spl. project City of Camden, N.J., summers 1962, 63. Compiler (books) Court Reporting Procedures, 1981, Court Reporting Theory Review Books 1, 2, 3, 1983, Court Reporting Advanced Theory Review, Vols. I, II, III, 1984. Bd. dirs. YWCA, Salina, 1991-93, membership chair, 1992-93; mem. alumni bd. Bethany Coll., Lindsborg, Kans., 1979-81. Mem. AAUW (pres 1995-97, numerous offices, Outstanding Mem. 1980), Kans. Bus. Tchrs. Assn., Nat. Bus. Tchrs. Assn., Kans. Shorthand Reporters Assn., Nat. Shorthand Reporters, Delta Kappa Gamma (numerous offices). Republican. Lutheran. Avocations: reading, swimming, cooking, sewing. Office: Brown Mackie Coll 2106 S 9th St Salina KS 67401-2810

HANSEN, ELAINE T. academic administrator; AB with greatest distinction cum laude, Mt. Holyoke Coll., 1969; MA, U. Minn., 1972; PhD, U. Wash., 1975. Asst. editor Mid. English dictionary U. Mich., 1975-77, assoc. rsch. editor, 1977—78; asst. prof. Haverford (Pa.) Coll., 1978—80, assoc. prof., 1980—90, dept. chair, 1989-92, prof. dept. English, 1991—, provost, 1995—2002; pres. Bates Coll., 2002—. Lectr. in field. Author: The Solomon Complex: Reading Wisdom in Old English Poetry, 1988, Chaucer and the Fictions of Gender, 1992, Mother Without Child: Contemporary Fiction and the Crisis of Motherhood, 1997; mem. editl. bd. Coll. Lit.; reader manuscripts for jours. and univ. presses; contbr. articles to profl. jours., also revs. and papers. NEH Summer stipendee, 1981; Mellon grantee for faculty devel. in humanities, 1983-84, Whitehead grantee for faculty in the humanities, 1987-88; Am. Coun. Learned Socs. fellow, 1993-94. Mem. MLA (mem. Chaucer divsn. exec. com. 1995-99, divsn. rep. to del. assembly 1996-99, com. on acad. freedom and profl. rights and responsibilities 1997-2000), Am. Coun. Learned Socs. (prescreener Cen. Fellowship Program), Medieval Acad., New Chaucer Soc., Nat. Women's Studies Assn., Soc. for Feminist Medieval Scholarship (pres. 1993-95). Office: Bates College Office of the Pres Lane Hall Rm 204 Lewiston ME 04240 E-mail: president@bates.edu.

HANSEN, ERIC PETER, lawyer; b. Mpls., June 12, 1951; s. Donald Arthur and Florence (Paulsen) H.; m. Janet G. Bostrom, Mar. 21, 1981; children: Lindsey Elizabeth, Jessie Johanna. BA, St. Olaf Coll., 1973; JD, Duke U., 1976. Bar: Minn. 1976, .S. Dist. Ct. Minn. 1979, U.S. Ct. Appeals (8th cir.) 1979. Atty. 3M Co., St. Paul, 1976-80, divsn. atty., 1980-83, sr. atty., 1983—2002, asst. gen. counsel, 2002—. Mem. Minn. Bar Assn. Republican. Office: 3M Co PO Box 33428 3M Center Saint Paul MN 55144-1001 E-mail: ephansen@mmm.com.

HANSEN, FLORENCE MARIE CONGIOLOSI (MRS. JAMES S. HANSEN), social worker; b. Middletown, N.Y., Jan. 7, 1934; d. Joseph James and Florence (Harrigan) Congiolosi; m. James S. Hansen, June 16, 1959 (dec. Nov. 1989); 1 child, Florence M. BA, Coll. of New Rochelle, 1955; MSW, Fla.

State U., 1960; PhD, Union Inst., 1992. Caseworker Orange County Dept. Pub. Welfare, N.Y., 1955-57, Cath. Welfare Bur., Miami, Fla., 1957-58, supr. Spokane, Wash., 1960, Cuban Children's Program, Spokane, 1962-66; founder, dir. social svc. dept. sacred Heart Med. Ctr., Spokane, 1968-85, dir. Kidney Ctr., 1967-91; caseworker Cath. Welfare Bur., Miami, Fla., 1957-58. Asst. in program devel. St. Margaret's Hall, Spokane, 1961-62; trustee Family Service Spokane, 1981—, also bd. dirs.; mem. budget allocation panel United Way, 1964-76, mem. planning com., 1968-77, mem. admissions com., 1969-70, chmn. projects com. 1972-73; mem. kidney disease adv. com. Wash.-Alaska Regional Med. Program, 1970-73. Mem. Spokane Quality of Life Commn., 1974-75; vol. primary health care Nangoma Mission Hosp., Mumbwa Dist., Zambia, 1992—; cons. CARE Internat., Zambia, 1993-95. Recipient Ursula Laurus citation Coll. of New Rochelle, 1990, Angela Merici medal, 1995. Mem. NASW (pres. Wash. chpt. 1972-74, Wash. State Social Worker of Yr. award 1991, Nat. Social Worker of Yr. award 1991), Acad. Cert. Social Workers (charter). Roman Catholic. Home: 5609 W Northwest Blvd Spokane WA 99205-2039 Office: Nangoma Mission Hosp Mumbwa Dist PO Box 1 Nangoma Zambia

HANSEN, GLEN ARTHUR, scientist, researcher; b. Thermopolis, Wyo., June 28, 1961; s. Glen Arthur and Ilene Lois (Haynes) H.; m. Paula Dee Rathbun, May 23, 1998. AAS in Petroleum Engring. Tech., Casper Coll., 1982; BS in Petroleum Engring., U. Wyo., 1985; MS in Mech. Engring., U. Nebr., 1991; PhD in Computer Sci., U. Idaho, 1996. Rsch. asst. U. Nebr., Lincoln, 1989-90, tchg. asst., 1990-91; sr. engr. Idaho Nat. Engring. Lab., Idaho Falls, 1991-95, engring. specialist, 1995-96; tech. staff mem. Los Alamos Nat. Lab., 1996—, project leader, 1997—; prin. investigator Los Alamos (N. Mex.) Nat. Lab., 1998—. Mem. IEEE, ASME, Am. Nuclear Soc. (Idaho chpt.), Soc. Indsl. Applied Math., Assn. Computing Machinery. Home: 945 San Ildefonso Rd # 57 Los Alamos NM 87544-2849 Office: Los Alamos National Lab PO Box 1663 Los Alamos NM 87545-0001

HANSEN, GRANT LEWIS, retired aerospace and information systems executive; b. Bancroft, Idaho, Nov. 5, 1921; s. Paul Ezra and Leona Sarah (Lewis) H.; m. Iris Rose Heyden, Apr. 21, 1945; children: Alan Lee, Brian Craig, Carol Margaret, David James, Ellen Diane. BS in Elec. Engring., Ill. Inst. Tech., 1948; postgrad. engring. and mgmt., UCLA, Calif. Inst. Tech.; D.Sc., Nat. U., 1978. With Douglas Aircraft Co., 1948-60; v.p., program dir. for Centaur (Convair div.), 1960-65; v.p. launch vehicle programs Convair div. Gen. Dynamics Corp., 1965-69, v.p., gen. mgr., 1973-78; asst. sec. air force for research and devel., 1969-73; v.p. Gen. Dynamics Corp., San Diego, 1974-78; exec. v.p. System Devel. Corp., Santa Monica, Calif., 1978-86; also pres. SDC Systems Group, 1978-84. U.S. del. NATO (Adv. Group for Aerospace Research and Devel.), 1969-73; U.S. mem. sci. com. for nat. reps. SHAPE Tech. Center, The Hague, Netherlands, 1969-73; mem. research and tech. adv. council NASA, 1971-73; mem. sci. adv. bd. Dept. Air Force, 1976-86. Served with USNR, World War II. Decorated Purple Heart; recipient Pub. Service award NASA, 1966, Disting. Pub. Service award NASA, 1975, Alumni Recognition award Ill. Inst. Tech., 1967, USAF Exceptional Civilian Service medal, 1973, 83; inducted Ill. Inst. Tech. Hall of Fame, 1984. Fellow AIAA (nat. pres. 1975), Am. Astronautical Soc., AAAS, Internat. Acad. Astronautics; mem. IEEE (sr.), German Soc. Air and Space Travel (corr.), Nat. Acad. Engring., NRC, Eta Kappa Nu, Tau Beta Pi. Home: 10737 Fuerte Dr La Mesa CA 91941-5740 *I've given my whole self to each challenge I've accepted, believing that what's best for my future is an honest day's effort today. I have great faith in my God and my country.*

HANSEN, H. JACK, management consultant; b. Chgo., Mar. 28, 1922; s. Herbert Christian John and Laura Elizabeth (Osterman) Hansen; m. Joan Dorothy Norum, Nov. 28, 1980; children: Marilyn Joan, Gail Jean, Mark John, Jacquelyn Lee. BSME, Ill. Inst. Tech., 1944. Cert. mgmt. cons. Mech. and indsl. engr. Harper Wyman Co., Chgo., 1944-51; chief indsl. engr. Shakeproof divsn. Ill. Tool Works, Des Plaines, 1951-53; cons., prin. A.T. Kearney & Co., Chgo. and N.Y.C., 1953-71; pres. H.J. Hansen Co., Elburn, Ill., 1971—2000. Acting mfg. engring. mgr. European Ops., Hobart Corp., 1974—78; owner, mgmt. cons. Hansen Mgmt. Search Co., Mt. Prospect, Ill., 1980—93; active turnaround cons., 1992—2000; apptd. by Kane County States Atty. Second Chance Panel, 2001—; apptd. to Kane County Chronicle's Readers adv. bd., 2002. Mem. Planning Commn. Village of Elburn, 1995—97, trustee, 1997—2001, chmn. Pers. Commn., mem. Fin. Commn., mem. Pub. Works Commn.; pres. Men's Club, 1987—90, Good Shepherd Luth. Ch., Des Plaines, Ill., 1988—90; active mem. mcpl. legis. com. DuKane Valley Coun., 1997—2001. With U.S. Army, 1945—46. Inductee Tilden Tech. Alumni Assn. Hall of Fame, 2000. Mem. Inst. Mgmt. Cons. (founding), Methods-Time Measurement Assn. (bd. dirs. 1964-70, pres. 1967-68), Am. Arbitartion Assn., Soc. Advancement Mgmt. (past bd. dirs.), coun. for Internat. Progress in Mgmt. (past bd. dirs.), Found. Internat. Progress in Mgmt. (past bd. dirs.), Econ. Devel. Com. (tech. com., membership com.), Elburn C. of C. Office: H J Hansen Co 317 Prairie Valley St Elburn IL 60119-8977

HANSEN, H. REESE, dean, educator; b. Logan, Utah, Apr. 8, 1942; s. Howard F. and Loila Gayle (Reese) H.; m. Kathryn Traveller, June 8, 1962; children: Brian T., Mark T., Dale T., Curtis T. BS, Utah State U., 1964; JD, U. Utah, 1972. Bar: Utah, 1974. Atty. Strong, Poelman & Fox, Salt Lake City, 1972-74; from asst. prof. to assoc. prof. Brigham Young U., Provo, Utah, 1974-79, prof., 1979—, from asst. dean to assoc. dean, 1974-89, dean, 1989—. Commr. ex officio Utah State Bar, Salt Lake City, 1989—; commr. Nat. Conf. Commrs. on Uniform State Laws, 1988-95. Co-author: Idaho Probate System, 1977, Utah Probate System, 1977, Cases and Text on Laws of Trusts, 7th edit., 2001; editor: Manual for Justices of Peace--Utah, 1978; contbr. articles to profl. jours. Mem. Lds Ch. Office: Brigham Young U 348A Jrcb Provo UT 84602-1029

HANSEN, HAL T. retired investment company executive; Pres. Cargill Investor Svcs., Chgo., ret. 1998. Founder Viking Investors Svcs., Lake Forest, Ill., 1998—; exec. cons. CP Risk Mgmt. (subs. Chgo. Ptnrs.), 1998—. Nat. Futures Assn. (former chmn.).

HANSEN, HAROLD B., JR., principal; b. Sewickley, Pa., July 3, 1955; s. Harold B. and Mary Clara (VanderVort) H.; m. Patty Jo Gabhart, Sept. 19, 1976; children: Jeremiah James, Joshua Andrew, Esther Beth, Christopher Seth. BA in Elem. Edn., Purdue U., 1980; MA in Sch. Adminstrn., Western N.Mex. U., 1987. Cert. secondary lang. arts and spl. edn. tchr., TESL tchr., instrnl. leader, sch. adminstr., elem. tchr., coach, N.Mex. Resource rm. tchr. Flossmoor/Homewood (Ill.) Pub. Schs., 1981, Newcomb (N.Mex.) H.S., 1981-82; tchr. self-contained spl. edn. Chester (Mont.) Pub. Schs., 1982-84; adminstr., prin., tchr. Bennett (Colo.) Bapt. Ch. Sch., 1984; propr., tutor Hemispheric Learning Tutorial Svcs., 1982—; tchr. resource room, coach cross county, wrestling, track and field Gallup-McKinley County Pub. Schs., Tohatchi/Navajo Reserv., N.Mex., 1985-90, elem. tchr. phys. edn. and health, at-risk tchr. Tohatchi Elem. Sch. Tohatchi, 1990-98, 5th grade track & field head coach, 1991-98, 5th grade boys' and girls' basketball asst. coach, 1995-98; prin. Smith Lake Elem. Sch., Gallup-McKinley County Pub. Schs., 1998—. Mem. various sch. coms. Gallup-McKinley County Pub. Schs., 1990—98, 2001—; seminar leader on hemispherecity; dep. registration officer McKinley County, N.Mex., 1986—98; mem. Prins.' Leadership Inst. with RE: Learning NM, Prins.' Leadership Acad. with Success for All Found. Past pres. Village of Hope, substance abuse tng. ctr.; co-founder, past bd. dirs. Christian Home Educators Assn.; dir. Approved Workmen Are Not Ashamed; past coord. Jump Rope for Heart, Am. Heart Assn.; past mem. Coun. for Curricular Excellence, McKinley County; pst TESOL rep. for Western N.Mex. U.'s Gallup Grad. Ctr.'s Advd. Coun., 1997—99. Named to Outstanding Young Men of Am., 1987. Mem. N.Mex. Assn. Health, Phys. Edn., Recreation and Dance, Christian HomeEducators Assn., Aesthetic Realism Found. Home: PO Box 100 Smith Lake NM 87365-0100 Fax: 888-391-4847; 505-786-5542. E-mail: hbchansen@citilink.net., chansen@sle.gmcs.k12.nm.us.

HANSEN, HAROLD JOHN (HARRY HANSEN), artist, educator; b. Chgo., June 18, 1942; s. Harold Melbourne and Florence Marion (O'Connell) H.; m. Martha Dianne Lyon, May 8, 1965; children: Daniel Charles, Susan Elizabeth. BFA, U. Ill., 1964; MFA, U. Mich., 1966. Instr. Kendall Sch. Design, Grand Rapids, Mich., 1966-69; asst. prof. art Ferris State Coll., Big Rapids, Mich., 1969-70, U. S.C., Columbia, 1970-75, assoc. prof. art, 1975-86, prof. art, 1986—. Guest curator S.C. State Mus., Columbia, 1997, Columbia Mus. Art, 2002. Exhibited watercolors and other works at more than 100 solo and maj. exhbns. including 100 Artists/100 Yrs. of S.C., S.C. State Mus., 1999-2000; exhibited in group shows at S.C. State Mus., Columbia, 1999-00. Recipient more than 40 awards for art work; grantee S.C. Humanities Coun., 1994-95, S.C. Arts Commn. and NEA, 1975. Mem. S.C. Watercolor Soc. (bd. dirs. 1989—). Office: U SC Dept Art Columbia SC 29208-0001

HANSEN, JACK WINSOR, musician, educator; b. Seward County, Nebr., Dec. 5, 1927; s. Grant Elbert Hansen and Ruby Gertrude Winsor. MusB, Roosevelt U., 1950, MusM cum laude, 1952; studied with, Rudolph Ganz and Mollie Margolies; pvt. studies with Marguerite Long, Paris; pvt. studies with Maurice Dumesnil, pvt. studies with William Walton. Mem. piano faculty Chgo. Mus. Coll., 1952—54; tchr. piano Sherwood Sch. Music, Chgo., 1954—56; instr. piano and composition N.D. State Coll., Minot, 1956—57; concert pianist various U.S. cities, 1957—87. Musician: NBC Artist Showcase Symphony, WGN Symphony, CBS Beethoven Bicentennial celebration with Chgo. Chamber Orch., numerous radio shows throughout U.S.; contbr. ; musician (soloist): Am. premiere of Haydn G Major Concerto, 1955, Can. premiere of Haydn G Major Concerto, 1968, world premiere of Markaitis Concerto for piano and woodwinds, 1966, Am. TV premiere of Beethoven post. Rondo for piano and orch., 1970. Recipient Richard Strauss award, 1949, Midwest Young Artists award, Soc. Am. Musicians, 1949, Allied Arts award, 1956—57. Mem.: N.W. Ind. Music Tchr.'s Assn., South Suburban Music Tchr.'s Assn., Chgo. Area Music Tchr.'s Assn., Nat. Music Tchr.'s Assn., Massenet Soc. (former bd. dirs.). Avocations: writing, poetry, collecting antiques, Egyptology. Home: Ft Deaborn Sta PO Box 10692 Chicago IL 60610

HANSEN, JAMES LEE, sculptor; b. Tacoma, Wash., June 13, 1925; s. Hildreth Justine and Mary Elizabeth Hansen; m. Annabelle Hair, Aug. 31, 1946 (dec. Sept. 1993); children: Valinda Jean, Yauna Marie; m. Jane Lucas, May 13, 1994. Grad., Portland Art Mus. Sch. Faculty Oreg. State U., Corvallis, 1957-58, U. Calif., Berkeley, 1958, Portland State U., 1964-90. One-man shows include Fountain Gallery, Portland, Oreg., 1966, 69, 77-81, U. Oreg. Art Mus., Eugene, 1970, Seligman (Seders Gallery), Seattle, 1970, Portland Art Mus., 1971, Cheney Cowles Meml. Mus., Spokane, Wash., 1972, Polly Freidlander Gallery, Seattle, 1973, 75-76, Smithsonian Instn., Washington, 1974, Hodges/Banks Gallery (now Linda Hodges Gallery), Seattle, 1983, Abanté Gallery, Portland, 1986, 88, 92, Maryhill Mus. of Art, Goldendale, Wash., 1997-98, Bryan Ohno Gallery, Seattle, 1997, 99, 2002, Mus. Northwest Art, La Conner, Wash., 1999; exhibited in group shows at N.W. Ann. Painters and Sculptors, Seattle, 1952-73, Oreg. Ann. Painters and Sculptors, Portland Art Mus., 1952-75, Whitney Mus. Am. Art, N.Y.C., 1953, Santa Barbara (Calif.) Mus. Art, 1959-60, Denver Art Mus., 1960, San Francisco Art Mus., 1960, Smithsonian Instn., Washington, 1974, Wash. State U., Pullman, 1975, Benton County Hist. Mus., 1998; represented in permanent collections Graphic Arts Center, State Capitol, Olympia, Wash., U. Oreg., Eugene, Salem (Oreg.) Civic Center, Clark Coll., Vancouver, Wash., Portland Art Mus., Transit Mall, Portland, Seattle Art Mus., Gresham Town Fair (Oreg.), Oreg. Health Scis. U., Portland, Vancouver Sculpture Park, others; represented by Hansen Studio, Vancouver, Peter Bartlow Gallery, Chgo., Bryan Ohno Gallery, Seattle. Address: 28219 NE 63rd Ave Battle Ground WA 98604-7107

HANSEN, JAMES VEAR, former congressman; b. Salt Lake City, Aug. 14, 1932; s. J. Vear and Sena H.; m. Ann Burgoyne, 1958; children: Susan, Joseph James, David Burgoyne, Paul William, Jennifer. BS, U. Utah, 1960. With Framington City Coun., 1960-72, Utah State Legis., 1972-80; mem. Utah Ho. of Reps., 1973-80; spkr. of the house U.S. Ho. of Reps., 1979-80; mem. U.S. Congress from 1st Utah dist., Washington, 1981—2002; mem. nat. security com., resource com. Pres. James V. Hansen Ins. Agy., Woodland Springs Devel. Co. Republican. Office: Ho of Reps 242 Cannon Ho Office Bldg Washington DC 20515-0001*

HANSEN, JAMES VERNON, computer science, information systems educator; b. Idaho Falls, May 31, 1936; s. Heber Lorenzo and Myrtle Jane (Simmons) H.; m. Diane Lynne Bradbury, Sept. 18, 1963; children: Tamsin, Jeffrey, Dale, Peter. BS, Brigham Young U., 1963; PhD, U. Wash., 1973. Systems analyst TRW, Redondo Beach, Calif., 1966-69; sr. rsch. scientist Battelle Meml. Inst., Richland, Wash., 1972-74, also cons.; asst. prof. Ind. U., Bloomington, 1974-77, assoc. prof., 1977-81; Glen Ardis prof. Brigham Young U., Provo, Utah, 1982—. Instr. EDI Group, Chgo., 1987-91. Author: Controls in Microcomputer Systems, 1984, Data Communications: Concepts and Controls, 1987, Database Management and Design, 1992, 2d edit., 1995, Machine Learning and Multiagent Systems. Served with U.S. Army, 1959-62. Grantee Peat, Marwick, Mitchell Found., 1982, 83, 84. Mem. Assn. Computing Machinery, Inst. for Ops. Rsch. and Mgmt. Sci., IEEE Computer Soc., Am. Assn. Artificial Intelligence, Sierra Club. Mem. Lds Ch. Office: Brigham Young U Dept Comp Sci Provo UT 84602

HANSEN, JANET M. bank executive; b. Sioux Falls, S.D., June 5, 1943; d. Edward Woodrow and Ruth Lillian Hansen. Student, Nettleton C.C., Sioux Falls, 1961; BS, U. Minn., 1983; JD, William Mitchell Coll. Law, 1987. Bar: Minn. 1988. Tchr. Nettleton Coll., 1961-65; dep. clk. U.S. Dist. Ct., Sioux Falls/Rapid City, S.D., 1965-78; paralegal East River Legal Svcs., Vermillion, S.D., 1978-80; legal sec. Faegre & Benson, Mpls., 1980-86, law clk., 1986-87; trust acct. mgr. Norwest Bank Minn., Mpls., 1987-91, trust dept. mgr., 1991-97; regional trust mgr. pvt. client svcs. Wells Fargo, Las Vegas, 1997—99; regional trust mgr. Wells Fargo Pvt. Client Svcs. Ctr., 1999—. Team capt. United Way, Mpls., 1996, Las Vegas, 1997-98. Recipient Leader Lunch award YWCA, 1986. Mem. Minn. Bar Assn., Hennepin County Bar Assn., Minn. Women Lawyers, Fin. Women Internat., So. Nev. Estate Planning Coun., Nev. Planned Giving Roundtable, So. Nev. Golf Assn. for Bus. Women (pres. 1999-2000), Women's So. Nev. Golf Assn. (v.p., 2002-03). Avocations: golf, reading, theater, movies, fishing. Office: Wells Fargo Ste 200 3300 W Sahara Ave Las Vegas NV 89102 E-mail: Hansenjm@wellsfargo.com.

HANSEN, JANICE ELIZABETH, psychologist; b. Wyandotte, Mich., Oct. 31, 1948; d. Robert Lewis and Wanda Elizabeth (Janice) Rutt; m. Lawrence Lee Lippitt, Jan. 1, 1980 (div.); 1 child, Eric Robert; m. Mark Allan Hansen, June 17, 1994. BA, Ea. Mich. U., 1971, MS, 1973; PhD, Kent State U., 1978. Lic. psychologist, Mich. Staging psychologist coord., staging psychologist ACTION, Peace Corps., Washington, 1973-74; univ. counselor U. Akron Counseling and Testing Ctr., 1977-79; psychologist for oncology program Akron Gen. Med. Ctr., 1979-81; clin. psychologist, dir. rehab. psychology Boulder (Colo.) Meml Hosp. PM&R, 1981-85; pvt. practice Sullivan, Nolan & Assocs., Ann Arbor, 1988-97; neuropsychologist, rehab. psychologist, phys. medicine/rehab Chelsea (Mich.) Cmty. Hosp., 1986-99; neuropsychologist, pvt. practice Saline, Mich., 1997—. Vol. fund raising Am. Cancer Soc., 1995, March of Dimes, Ann Arbor, 1997; den leader Cub Scouts/Boy Scouts Am., 1991-95. Mem. Am. Psychol. Assn., Mich. Psychol. Assn. Methodist. Avocations: bicycling, snow skiing, family history. Home: 3295 Rumsey Dr Ann Arbor MI 48105-1467 Office: 101 S Ann Arbor St Ste 203A Saline MI 48176-1360

HANSEN, JEAN MARIE, math and computer educator; b. Detroit, Mar. 8, 1937; d. Harvey Francis and Ida Marie (Hay) Chapman; m. Donald Edward Hansen, Aug. 29, 1968; children: Jennifer Lynn, John Francis. BA, U. Mich., 1959, MA, 1960. Cert. Secondary Sch. Tchr. Tchr. Detroit Pub. Schs., 1959-60, Newark (Calif.) Sch. Dist., 1960-65, Dept. Def., Zweibruken, Germany, 1965-67, Livonia (Mich.) Pub. Schs., 1967-69; instr. Ford Livonia Transmission Plant, 1990—. Trustee/pres. Northville (Mich.) Bd. Edn., 1981-97; trustee Northville Dist. Libr., 1999—, pres. bd., 2003. Author: California People and Their Government, 1965, Voices of Government, 1969-70. Named Disting. Bd. Mem., Mich. Assn. Sch. Bds., 1991, Citizen of Yr., Northville C. of C., 1991. Mem. AAUW (v.p. Northville bd. 1982-86, pres. 1987-89, Mich. chpt. Agt. of Change award, edn. area 1985), LWV, Kiwanis, Northville Women's Club. Republican. Avocations: weaving, basket weaving, skiing, golf, travel. Home: 229 Linden St Northville MI 48167-1426 E-mail: jhansen@comcast.net.

HANSEN, JOHN MARK, political scientist; b. Colby, Kans., Feb. 17, 1959; s. John G. and Joyce E. Hansen; m. Dana Saowalak, June 18, 1989; children: Ary, Maya. BA in Polit. Sci. and Econs., U. Kans., 1981; PhD in Polit. Sci., Yale U., 1987. From asst. prof. to assoc. prof. polit. sci. U. Chgo., 1986—94, prof. polit. sci., 1994—, chair dept. polit. sci., 1995—98, assoc. provost for rsch. and edn., 1998—2001, dean divsn. social scis., 2002—; prof. govt. Harvard U., Cambridge, Mass., 2001—02. Author: Gaining Access: Congress and the Farm Lobby, 1919-1981, 1991, Mobilization, Participation and Democracy in America, 1993 (Outstanding Book award Nat. Conf. Black Polit. Scientists 1994); contbr. articles to profl. jours. Fellow Ctr. for Advanced Study in the Behavioral Scis., 1993-94, rsch. fellow in govt. studies Brookings Instn., 1985-86. Fellow: Am. Acad. Arts and Scis.; mem.: Am. Polit. Sci. Assn. (chair endowments com. 2000—01, coun. 1993—95, exec. com. centennial campaign 1997—, Heinz Eulau award 1999), Phi Beta Kappa. Home: 5642 S Dorchester Ave Chicago IL 60637 Office: Univ Chgo 1126 E 59th St Chicago IL 60637 E-mail: j-hansen@uchicago.edu.

HANSEN, JOHN HERBERT, university administrator, accountant; b. Milw., Mar. 20, 1945; s. John Herbert and Elsie F. (Patri) H.; m. Christina Ann Laniey, Sept. 5, 1970. BBA, U. Wis., 1969; M in Acctg., U. Ill., 1973. CPA, Wis. Dir. treas. svcs. Marquette U., Milw., 1973—. With USAF, 1970-73. Mem. AICPA, Milw. Bond Club. Clubs: Merrill Hills Country. Republican. Avocations: golf, gardening. Office: Marquette U PO Box 1881 Milwaukee WI 53201-1881 E-mail: john.hansen@marquette.edu.

HANSEN, JOHN JOSEPH, lawyer; b. San Anselmo, Calif., Sept. 7, 1961; s. Joseph G. and Barbara M. H.; m. Marjorie Ann Walker, Feb. 18, 1995. BA, Coll. Idaho, 1983; JD, U. Idaho, 1987. Bar: Idaho 1987, U.S. Dist. Ct. Idaho 1987, Wash. 1994. Staff atty. Idaho Legal Aid Svcs., Caldwell, 1987-88; trial atty. Ada County Pub. Defender, Boise, 1988-92; dep. atty. gen. Idaho Atty. Gen., Boise, 1992-93; asst. Open Soc. Fund, Vilnius, Lithuania, 1994; dep. pros. atty. Yakima County Prosecutor, Wash., 1994-97; assoc. Wiebe & Fouser P.A., Caldwell, 1997-98; chief pub. defender Twin Falls County Pub. Defender, Idaho, 1998—. Vol. Ctrl. Wash. chpt. Nat. Multiple Sclerosis Soc., Yakima, 1994-97; vol. atty. ABA-CEELI, Brcko, Bosnia, 2002, Sarajevo, Bosnia, 2003. Roman Catholic. Avocations: music, books, travel. Office: Twin Falls County Pub Defender PO Box 126 Twin Falls ID 83303-0126 E-mail: jhansen@co.twin-falls.id.us.

HANSEN, JOHN PAUL, retired metallurgical engineer; b. Bain, Minn., Feb. 11, 1928; s. Charles George and Henrietta Eva (Taylor) H.; m. Doris Alma Dropps, Sept. 9, 1950; children: Steven Michael, Bradley Paul, Kurt Lewis. BS, U. Minn., 1954, MS, 1955, PhD, 1958. Registered profl. engr., Ala. Metall. engr. U.S. Bur. Mines, Mpls., 1958-63, chief Tuscaloosa Metallurgy Rsch. Lab. Tuscaloosa, 1967-70; prof. metall. engring. U. Ala., University, 1963-67, head chem. and metall. engring. dept., 1970-73, prof. emeritus metall. engring. Tuscaloosa, 1988—. Lectr. U. Ala.; cons. Army Missile Command, Ala. Geol. Survey. Served with AUS, 1946-49, 50-52. Mem. AIME, Sigma Xi, Tau Beta Pi, Alpha Sigma Mu, Omega Chi Epsilon. Clubs: University Faculty (pres. 1973). Lutheran. Achievements include research reduction of iron ores and prereduced iron ore pellets. Home: 1245 E Highpoint St Springfield MO 65804-7605 E-mail: johnphans@aol.com.

HANSEN, KAREN THORNLEY, accountant; b. Chgo., June 1, 1945; BA, Marycrest Coll., Davenport, Iowa, 1967. CPA, N.Y.; cert. med. technologist. Med. staff tech. Mercy Hosp., Davenport, Iowa, 1967-68, St. Joseph Hosp., Chgo., 1968, Spl. Hematology, Wilford Hall, USAF Hosp., Lackland AFB, Tex., 1973-78; staff acct. Lewittes & Co., Poughkeepsie, N.Y., 1980-81; sr. acct. Urbach, Kahn & Werlin, Poughkeepsie, 1981-82; ptnr. Hansen & Dunn, CPA's, Poughkeepsie, 1982-94, Hansen & Arnold, Poughkeepsie, 1995-2000, Sedore & Co., CPA, 2001—. Bd. dirs., sec. United Way Dutchess County, Poughkeepsie, 1988—94; mem. Jr. League Poughkeepsie, 1979—; mem. membership com. and econ. devel. com. Poughkeepsie Partnership, Inc.; trustee St. Martin de Porres Ch.; bd. dirs. YMCA Dutchess County, Girl Scouts U.S.A., 1983—87, Mid-Hudson Civic Ctr., Inc., 1993—95, Civic Properties, Inc., 1992—, Poughkeepsie Inst., 1999—. Mem. AICPA, N.Y. State Soc. CPAs, Greater Poughkeepsie Area C. of C. (bd. dirs. 1986—, 1st vice chair 1996, chair, 1997, sec. exec. com. 1991, Amrita Club (bd. dirs. 1982-92, pres. 1990), Poughkeepsie Tennis Club. Republican. Roman Catholic. Office: Sedore & Co CPA 309 Main St Poughkeepsie NY 12601-3116

HANSEN, KATHRYN GERTRUDE, editor, former state official; b. Gardner, Ill., May 24, 1912; d. Harry J. and Marguerite (Gaston) Hansen. BS with honors, U. Ill., 1934, MS, 1936. Sec. U. N.C., 1936-37, U. High Sch., U. Ill., 1937-44; personnel asst. U. Ill., Urbana, 1944-46, supr. tng. and activities, 1946-47, personnel officer, instr. psychology, 1947-52; exec. sec. U. Civil Service System, Ill.; also sec. for merit bd., 1952-61; adminstrv. officer, sec. merit bd., 1961-68; dir. system, 1968-72; lay asst. firm Webber, Balbach, Theis and Follmer, P.C., Urbana, Ill., 1972-74. Author: (with others) A Plan of Position Classification for Colleges and Universities: A Classification Plan for Staff Positions at Colleges and Universities, Grundy-Corners, 1982, Sarah, A Documentary of Her Life and Times, 1984, Ninety Years with Fortnightly, Vols. I and II, an historical compilation, 1986, Vol. III, 1995, Whispers of Yesterday, 1989, Through the Years with the Champaign-Urbana Business and Professional Women's Club, 1912-33, 1993, My Heritage, 1995, Presbyterian Women of First Presbyterian Church, Champaign, Illinois, An Historical Documentary, 1870-1995, 1996, (with Patricia Phillips) Fifty Golden Years, Altrusa International of Champaign-Urbana, Illinois, 1950-2000, 2001; editor: The Illini Worker, 1946-52, Campus Pathways, 1952-61, This is Your Civil Service Handbook, 1960-67; author, cons., editor publs. on personnel practices. Bd. dirs. U. YWCA, 1952-55, chmn., 1954-55; bd. dirs. Champaign-Urbana Symphony, 1978-81; mem., sec. Presbyn. Women 1st Presbyn Ch., Champaign, 1986-90, mem. coordinating team, 1986-91, hon. life mem., 1999. Mem. Coll. and Univ. Personnel Assn. for Human Resources (hon., life mem., editor jour. 1955-73, newsletter, internat. pres. 1967-68, nat. publs. award named in her honor 1987, Ill. State award 1996), Annuitants Assn. State Univs. Retirement System Ill. (state sec.-treas. 1974-75), U. Ill. Found., Pres.'s Coun. (life), Laureate Cir., U. Ill. Alumni Assn. (life), Friends of the Library (bd. dirs. 1987-91), Nat. League Am. Pen Women, AAUW (state 1st v.p. 1958-60, hon., life), Secretariat U. Ill. (life, named scholarship 1972—), Grundy County Hist. Soc. (life), Altrusa Internat., Fortnightly Club (Champaign-Urbana), Eastern Star, Delta Kappa Gamma (state pres. 1961-63), Phi Mu (life), Kappa Delta Pi, Kappa Tau Alpha. Presbyterian. Home: 1004 E Harding Dr Apt 307 Urbana IL 61801-6346

HANSEN, KENNETH D. lawyer, ophthalmologist; b. Seattle, Mar. 26, 1947; s. George R. and Elaine D. (Jacobsen) H.; m. Barbara Caleen, Oct. 8, 1976; 1 son, David Scott. BS in Psychology, U. Wash., 1969, JD, 1972, MD with honors, 1976. Bar: Wash. 1972, Mich. 1977, Ill. 1984, D.C. 1986, U.S. Supreme Ct. 1981; diplomate Am. Bd. Ophthalmology. Legal counsel Assn. Wash. Bus., Olympia, 1972-73; asst. atty. gen. State of Wash., Seattle, 1973-74; v.p., gen. counsel N.W. Med. Rsch. Found., Seattle, 1976-86; pres. Internat. Health Found., 1986—; intern medicine U. Mich. Hosp., Ann Arbor, 1977, resident in ophthalmology, 1978-80; sr. med. staff Henry Ford Hosp., Detroit, 1981-82; dir. ophthalmology Carbondale (Ill.) Clinic, 1983-86, chmn. dept. surgery, gen. counsel, 1984-86; clin. asst. prof. ophthalmology and med. humanities So. Ill. U., Carbondale, 1983-86; clin. asst. prof. ophthalmology U. Md., Balt., 1986—; gen. counsel Internat. Inst. for Biomed. Rsch., 2002—. Med.-legal adv. com. U. Mich. Hosp. System; cons. Nat. Def. Med. Coll., China; charter coun. mem. practicing physicians adv. coun. to Sec. of U.S. Dept. Health and Human Svcs., 1992-97; internat. med.-legal lectr. Assoc. editor Trauma, 1995—, Wash. Law Rev., 1971-72; contbr. articles to legal and med. profl. jours., publs. Recipient U. Wash. Med. Thesis Award, Gold Medal Egyptian Med. Syndicate, 1986; William Wallice Wilshire Meml. scholar; Anna C. Dunlap Meml. scholar; Grad. Rsch. fellow, 1975—; recipient Red Rose award Soc. Rsch. Adminstrs., 1989. Fellow Am. Coll. Legal Medicine (jud. coun., model statutes com., Pres.'s award 1989), Internat. Coll. Surgeons; mem. ABA, AMA, Wash. State Bar Assn., Mich. Bar Assn., Ill. Med. Soc. (med.-legal coun.), Ill. Bar Assn., Mich. Med. Schs. Coun. Deans (med.-legal adv. com.), Mich. Ophthalmology Soc. (Rsch. award 1981), Am. Acad. Ophthalmology, D.C. Bar Assn., Phi Delta Pi, Phi Eta Sigma, Pi Sigma Epsilon. Baptist. Home: 6501 Bright Mountain Rd Mc Lean VA 22101-1701 Office: 901 N Stuart St Ste 210 Arlington VA 22203

HANSEN, KENT FORREST, nuclear engineering educator; b. Chgo., Aug. 10, 1931; s. Kay Frost and Mary (Cummins) H.; m. Katherine Elizabeth Kavanagh, June 13, 1959 (dec. Dec. 1975); children: Thomas Kay, Katherine Mary; m. Deborah Lea Hill, June 26, 1977, (div. Aug. 1991); 1 child, Gordon Benedict; m. Léonie Andrews Work, June 11, 1992. S.B., Mass. Inst. Tech., 1953, Sc.D., 1959. Sr. engr. Sylvania Electric Products, Waltham, Mass.,

1957-58; asst. prof. nuclear engring. MIT, Cambridge, Mass., 1960-64, assoc. prof., 1964-68, prof., 1968—, assoc. dean engring., 1979-81, assoc. dir. energy lab., 1984-90. Bd. dirs. EG&G, Inc., Stone & Webster, Inc.; cons. to industry. Co-author: Numerical Methods of Reactor Analysis, 1964, Advances in Nuclear Science and Technology, Vol. 8, 1975. Ford postdoctoral fellow, 1960-61 Fellow Am. Nuclear Soc. (dir., Arthur Holly Compton award 1978); mem. Am. Nuclear Soc., Nat. Acad. Engring., Sigma Xi, Sigma Chi. Home: 23 Phillips Pond Rd Natick MA 01760-5643 Office: MIT Energy Lab Massachusetts Ave Cambridge MA 02139-4325 E-mail: kfhansen@mit.edu.

HANSEN, LELAND JOE, communications executive; b. Spokane, Wash., Mar. 26, 1944; s. Herman Johnny and Emma Irene (Borth) H.; m. Jonni Krajeski, Apr. 15, 1979 Creative dir., dir., producer Mel Blanc and Assocs., Beverly Hills, Calif., 1971-73; creative dir., writer, producer, dir. nat. TV and radio commls. and entertainment programs ABC Watermark, Universal City, Calif., 1973-80; pres., chief exec. officer, writer, producer, dir. film and TV GDE Prodns. Inc., Sherman Oaks, Calif., 1980-87; sr. writer, dir. video svcs. Rockwell Internat., Canoga Park, Calif., 1987-95; ind. film, video and multimedia audio prodr. specializing in mktg. videos for corps., 1995—. Voice-over artist nat. TV and radio. Dir. American Top Forty, 1973-77, The Elvis Presley Story, Soundtrack of the Sixties; creator, producer, dir. Alien Worlds, 1973-80. Founding mem. Am. Forces Radio, Saigon, Socialist Republic of Vietnam, 1963-64. Served with U.S. Army, 1962-65, Vietnam. Recipient Belding award The Advt. Club Los Angeles, 1977. Mem. AFTRA. Avocations: pilot, architectural design, model builder.

HANSEN, LEONARD JOSEPH, writer, journalist, editor, communications executive; b. Aug. 4, 1932; s. Einar L. and Margie A. (Wilder) H.; m. Marcia Ann Rasmussen, Mar. 18, 1966 (div.); children: Barron Richard, Trevor Wilder. AB in Radio-TV Prodn. and Mgmt., San Francisco State U., 1956, postgrad., 1956-57; cert., IBM Mgmt. Sch., 1967. Jr. writer Sta. KCBS, San Francisco, 1952-54; assoc. prodr., dir. Ford Found. TV Rsch. Project San Francisco State U., 1955-57; crew chief live and remote broadcasts Sta. KPIX-TV, San Francisco, 1957-59, air promotion dir., writer, 1959-60; pub. rels. mgr. Sta. KNTV-TV, San Jose, Calif., 1961; radio and TV promotion mgr. Seattle World's Fair, 1962; pub. rels. and promotion mgr. Century 21 Ctr., Inc., Seattle, 1963-64; pub. rels. dir. Dan Evans for Gov. Com., Seattle, 1964; propr., mgr. Leonard J. Hansen Pub. Rels., Seattle, 1965-67; campaign mgr. Walter J. Hickel for Gov. Com., Anchorage, 1966; exec. cons. to Gov. of Alaska Juneau, 1967; gen. mgr. No. TV Inc., Anchorage, 1967-69; v.p. mktg. Sea World, Inc., San Diego, 1969-71; editor, pub. Sr. World Publs., inc., San Diego, 1973-84; chmn. Sr. Pubs. Group, 1977-89; pres., editor-in-chief WriteRight, Inc., 1999—. Spkr., mktg. cons. to sr. citizens, 1984-92; panelist pub. affairs radio programs, 1971-92; lectr. journalism San Diego State U., 1975-76; pres., pub. Mature Market Editl. Svcs., 1991-98. Writer weekly syndicated column Mainly for Seniors, 1984-99, Travel for Mature Adults, 1984-99; writer, journalist The Mature Market; contbg. editor Mature Life Features, news/feature syndicate, 1987-90; chmn. Mature Market Seminars, 1987-90; author: Life Begins at 50—The Handbook for Creative Retirement Planning, 1989. Founding mem. Housing for Elderly and Low Income Persons, San Diego, 1977-78; mem. Mayor's Ad hoc Adv. Com. on Aging, San Diego, 1976-79; vice chmn. Housing task Force, San Diego, 1977-78; bd. dirs. Crime Control Commn., San Diego, 1980; del. White House Conf. on Aging, 1981. With U.S. Army, 1953-55. Nat. Press Found. fellow, 1994, 97, 98, fellow in journalism Alicia Patterson Found., 1999; recipient numerous svc. and citizenship awards from clubs. and cmty. orgns., Long Term Achievement in Nat. Media award Am. Soc. on Aging, 1999. Fellow Nat. Press Found.; mem. Soc. Profl. Journalists (Best Investigative Reporting award 1979), San Diego Press Club (Best Newswriting award 1976-77, Headliner of Yr. award 1980), Nat. Press Club, Am. Soc. Journalists and Authors, Nat. Soc. Newspaper Columnists, Am. Soc. on Aging. Home and Office: Ste E-11 1901 18th St Bellingham WA 98225-8033 E-mail: len@lenhansen.com.

HANSEN, MARILYN SCHOOLEY, interior designer; b. Yankton, S.D., July 25, 1947; d. Dale Louis and Eleanor (Logsdon) Schooley; m. Robert Lowell Hansen, July 7, 1977; children: Peter, Christiana. BS, Iowa State U., 1969. Mem. interior design staff Reynold's Furniture, Sioux Falls, S.D., 1969-70, J.C. Penney, Omaha, 1970-72, J.L. Brandeis, Omaha, 1973-75, Davidson's Furniture, Omaha, 1975-79; dir. interior design J.L. Brandeis, Omaha, 1979-80; owner, designer The Designers, Omaha, 1980—. Owner Designer's Furniture Gallery, 1998—. Bd. dirs. YWCA, Omaha, 1990-93; mem. G.R.O.W. St. Margaret's Ch., dir. children's choir; mem. Omaha Symphony Guild, Omaha Opera Guild; chairperson Omaha Cmty. Playhouse, 1970—, bd. dirs., 1994—; chairperson Opera Omaha, 1976-91, bd. dirs., 1986-92. Named Entrepreneur of 1991 YWCA. Fellow Am. Soc. Interior Design (pres. Nebr./Iowa chpt. 1989, 90, 91, medalist 1986, cert., ASID Symphony Showhouse Designer, 1975—, restoration dir. Nebr. Gov.'s manion, 1996, 97, 98, Nebr. Interior awards 1991-2003). Avocations: artist, singer, actress. Home: 101 N 39th St Omaha NE 68131-2306 Office: The Designers 12123 Emmet St Omaha NE 68164-4264

HANSEN, MARK CHARLES, lawyer; b. N.Y.C., Aug. 13, 1956; s. Charles and Carolyn (Smith) H.; m. Anne Samuels, June 28, 1986; children: Elisabeth Bayard, Caroline Alexandra, Charles McLean. AB, Dartmouth Coll., 1978; JD, Harvard U., 1982. Bar: D.C. 1990, Mass. 1983, Md. 1996. Law clk. to Hon. William H. Timbers U.S. Ct. Appeals (2d cir.), Bridgeport, Conn., N.Y.C., 1982-83; assoc. Hill & Barlow, Boston, 1983-85; asst. U.S. atty. U.S. Dist. Ct. (so. dist.) N.Y., 1986-89; shareholder Johnson & Gibbs, P.C., Washington, 1990-93; ptnr. Kellogg, Huber, Hansen, Todd & Evans PLLC, Washington, 1993—. Faculty Nat. Inst. Trial Advocacy, Georgetown U., Washington, 1991-95. Recipient Spl. Commendation U.S. Dept. of Justice, 1988. Mem. ABA. Office: Kellogg Huber Hansen Todd & Evans PLLC Sumner Sq 1615 M St NW Ste 400 Washington DC 20036 E-mail: mhansen@khhte.com.

HANSEN, MARK S. food marketing and distribution company executive; Various merchandising, mktg. and procurement positions Gt. Atlantic & Pacific Tea Co. and Nat. Tea Co., 1971-79; various mgmt. positions Jewel Cos., Inc., Arlington Heights, Ill., 1979-84; exec. v.p., COO, Federated Foods, Inc., Arlington Heights, 1984-89; pres., CEO, PetsMart, Phoenix, 1989-97, Sam's Club divsn. Wal-Mart Stoes, Inc., Bentonville, Ark., 1997-98; chmn. bd. dirs., CEO, Fleming Cos. Inc., Oklahoma City, 1998—2003. Office: 6301 Waterford Blvd Oklahoma City OK 73118-1157*

HANSEN, MATILDA, former state legislator; b. Paullina, Iowa, Sept. 4, 1929; d. Arthur J. and Sada G. (Thompson) Henderson; m. Robert B. Michener, 1950 (div. 1963); children: Eric J., Douglas E.; m. Hugh G. Hansen (dec.). BA, U. Colo., 1963; MA, U. Wyo., 1970. Tchr. history Englewood (Colo.) Sr. High Sch., 1963-65; dir. Albany County Adult Learning Ctr., Laramie, Wyo., 1966-78, Laramie Plains Civic Ctr., 1979-83; treas. Wyo. Territorial Prison Corp., Laramie, 1988-93, also bd. dirs. Bd. dirs. Wyo. Territorial Park. Author: (textbooks) To Help Adults Learn, 1975, Let's Play Together, 1978, Clear Use of Power, A Slice of Wyoming Political History, 2002. Legislator Wyo. Ho. of Reps., Cheyenne, 1975-95, minority whip, 1987-88, asst. minority leader, 1991-92, 93-94; mem. mgmt. coun. Wyo. State Legislature, Cheyenne, 1983-84; chair Com. for Dem. Legislature, Cheyenne, 1990-94, Wyo. State Dems., 1995-99. GE fellow in econs. for high sch. tchrs., 1963; named Pub. Citizen of Yr., Wyo. Assn. Social Workers, 1980-81. Mem. LWV Wyo. (v.p. 1966-68), LWV Laramie (bd. dirs. 1966-72, Nat. Conf. State Legislators (vice chair human resources 1983, nat. exec. com. 1990-94), Laramie Area C. of C., Laramie Women's Club, Faculty Women's Club. Democrat. Mem. Soc. Of Friends. Avocations: gardening, quilting, mountaineering. Home and Office: 1306 E Kearney St Laramie WY 82070-4142

HANSEN, MORTEN T. management educator; m. Helene Hansen. PhD, Stanford U. Prof. Harvard Bus. Sch., Boston, Mass., 1996—. Office: Harvard Business Sch Soldiers Field Boston MA 02163

HANSEN, NICK DANE, lawyer; b. Detroit, June 19, 1938; s. Nick F. and Ellen (Adelorn) H.; m. Susan Fox Cohee, Aug. 23, 1963; children: Todd Erik, Dana E. BA, Albion Coll., 1960; JD, Wayne State U., 1964; LLM, Georgetown U., 1970. Bar: Mich. 1964, Ill. 1970, Wis. 1975, Tex. 1985. Law clk. to assoc. justice Mich. Supreme Ct., Lansing, 1964-66; atty. Office of Chief Counsel IRS, Washington, 1966-70; ptnr. McDermott, Will & Emery, Chgo., 1970-74; sr. tax atty. Kimberly-Clark Corp., Neenah, Wis., 1975, tax counsel, 1975-76, staff v.p., 1976-80, v.p., tax counsel Dallas, 1980-98; cons., 1998—. Bd. dirs. ithought.com Mem. bd. advisor Jour. Internat. Taxation. Sec., bd. dirs. Bergstrom-Mahler Mus., Neenah, 1982-85. Mem. ABA (chmn. com. fgn. activities tax sect. 1991-92, article editor The Tax Lawyer), Tex. Bar Assn., Wis. Bar Assn., Tax Execs. Inst. E-mail: ndhans2000@aol.com.

HANSEN, NILES MAURICE, economics educator; b. Louisville, Jan. 2, 1937; s. Kristian and Alma (Jensen) H.; m. Josephine Drescher, Aug. 22, 1959; children: Karen, Eric, Laura; m. Koren Sherrill, Feb. 9, 1979; 1 child, Stephen. BA, Centre Coll. Ky., 1958; MA, Ind. U., 1959, PhD, 1963. Asst. and assoc. prof. U. Tex., 1963-67; prof. econs., assoc. dir. Ctr. for Devel. Change U. Ky., 1967-69; prof. econs., dir. Ctr. for Econ. Devel. U. Tex., Austin, 1969-75; head urban and regional systems, acting chmn. human settlements and svcs., rsch. scholar Internat. Inst. for Applied Systems Analysis, Laxenburg, Austria, 1975-77; vis. fellow Can. Inst. for Rsch. on Regional Devel., Moncton, New Brunswick, 1987; vis. scholar Regional U. d'Aix-Marseille, Aix-en-Provence, France, 1988; Leroy G. Denman Jr. regents prof. econs. U. Tex. Author: French Regional Planning, 1968, France in the Modern World, 1969, Rural Poverty and the Urban Crisis, 1970, Intermediate-Size Cities as Growth Centers, 1971, Growth Centers and Regional Development, 1972, Location Preferences, Migration and Regional Growth, 1973, The Future of Nonmetropolitan America, 1973, Public Policy and Regional Development, 1974, The Challenge of Urban Growth, 1975, Improving Access to Economic Opportunity, 1976, The Border Economy, 1981; co-author: Regional Policy in a Changing World, 1990; editor: Human Settlement Systems: International Perspectives on Structure Change and Public Policy, 1977, The Border Economy: Regional Development in the Southwest, 1981, Regional Policy and Regional Integration, 1996; contbr. articles to profl. jours. NSF fellow U. Paris, 1965-66, Fulbright 40th Ann. Disting. fellow, Turkey, 1987. Mem. Am. Econ. Assn., So. Regional Sci. Assn. (pres. 1979, elected fellow 1993), Western Regional Sci. Assn. (pres. 1982), French Speaking Regional Economists, N.Am. Regional Sci. Assn. (pres. 1992). Home: 807 Rock Creek Dr Austin TX 78746-4529 Office: U Tex Dept Econs Austin TX 78712

HANSEN, ORVAL, lawyer, former congressman, think tank executive; b. Firth, Idaho, Aug. 3, 1926; s. Farrel L. and Lily (Wahlquist) H.; m. June Duncan, Dec. 31, 1955; children: Margaret, Elizabeth, James, Katherine, John, Mary, Sarah. BA, U. Idaho, 1950, LLD (hon.), 1988; JD, George Washington U., 1954, LLM, 1973, PhD, 1986. Bar: Idaho 1954, D.C. 1954. Practice law, Idaho Falls, 1956-68; staff asst. to Senator Henry Dworshak, 1950-54; mem. Idaho Ho. of Reps., 1956-62, 64-66, house majority leader, 1961-62; mem. Idaho Senate, 1966-68, 91st 93d congresses from 2d Idaho Dist.; former mem. Cook, Purcell, Hansen & Henderson, Washington; of counsel Hopkins, Roden, Crockett, Hansen & Hoopes, PLLC, Washington. Trustee John F. Kennedy Ctr. for Performing Arts, 1976-86; pres. Columbia Inst. for Polit. Rsch. With USNR, 1944-46; lt. col. USAFR, ret. Rotary Found. fellow U. London (Eng.) Sch. Econs., 1954-55 Mem. D.C. Bar Assn., Am. Legion, V.F.W., Phi Beta Kappa, Sigma Chi, Phi Alpha Delta. Republican. Mem. Lds Ch. Home: 5555 Little Falls Rd Arlington VA 22207-1525

HANSEN, PER BRINCH, computer scientist, researcher; b. Copenhagen, Nov. 13, 1938; came to U.S., 1970, naturalized, 1992; s. Jorgen Brinch and Elsebeth (Ring) H.; m. Milena Marija Hrastar, Mar. 27, 1965; children: Mette, Thomas. MS, Tech. U. Denmark, Copenhagen, 1963, Dr.techn., 1978. Sys. programmer Regnecentralen, Copenhagen, 1963-70, mgr. software devel., 1967-70; rsch. assoc. Carnegie-Mellon U., Pitts., 1970-72; assoc. prof. Calif. Inst. Tech., Pasadena, 1972-76; chmn. dept. computer sci. U. So. Calif., L.A., 1976-77, prof., 1976-84, Henry Salvatori prof., 1982-84; prof. U. Copenhagen, 1984-87; disting. prof. Syracuse (N.Y.) U., 1987—. Cons. Burroughs, Honeywell, IBM, JPL, Mostek, TRW, others. Author: Operating System Principles, 1973, The Architecture of Concurrent Programs, 1977, Programming a Personal Computer, 1982, On Pascal Compilers, 1985, Studies in Computational Science, 1995, The Search for Simplicity, 1996, Programming for Everyone, 1999, Classic Operating Systems, 2001, The Origin of Concurrent Programming, 2002; mem. editl. bd. Acta Informatica, Annals of the History of Computing, Concurrency, Software, Lecture Notes in Computer Sci.; contbr. articles to profl. jours.; inventor programming langs. Concurrent Pascal, Edison, Joyce, SuperPascal. Recipient Chancellor's medal Syracuse U., 1989; grantee NSF, Army Rsch. Office, Office Naval Rsch., Rome Air Devel. Ctr. Fellow IEEE (Computer Pioneer award 2002). Avocations: history, photography, jazz. Home: 5070 Pine Valley Dr Fayetteville NY 13066-9723 Office: Syracuse U 2-175 CST Syracuse NY 13244-0001 E-mail: pbh@top.cis.syr.edu.

HANSEN, PETER HOLGER, history educator, historian; b. New Haven, Oct. 31, 1961; s. G. Holger and Anne Hansen; m. Allison Chisolm, June 25, 1988; children: Katherine, William. BA, Carleton Coll., 1984; MA, Harvard U., 1986, PhD, 1991. Urban fellow City of N.Y., 1984-85; tchg. fellow Harvard U., Cambridge, Mass., 1986-88; vis. mem. Inst. for Hist. Rsch., London, 1988-90; adj. asst. prof. history Lehman Coll., CUNY, 1991-92; asst. prof. history Worcester Polytech Inst., Mass., 1992-98, assoc. prof. history, 1998—. Dir. internat. studies, 1995—; vis. fellow Clare Hall, Cambridge U., Eng., 1995-96, Australian Nat. U., 1998; cons. to BBC. Assoc. editor new dictionary of Nat. Biography; contbr. articles to profl. jours.; webmaster N.Am. Conf. on Brit. Studies. Bd. dirs. Elm Park Ctr. Early Childhood Edn., Worcester, pres., 2002-03. Fellow NEH, 1995-96, grantee, 1993; fellow Krupp Found., Harvard U., 1988-89. Fellow Royal Geog. Soc., Royal Hist. Soc.; mem. Am. Hist. Assn., N. Am. and N.E. Conf. Brit. Studies, World History Assn., Soc. for Cinema Studies. Democrat. Office: Worcester Polytechnic Inst Dept Humanities 100 Institute Rd Worcester MA 01609-2280 E-mail: phansen@wpi.edu.

HANSEN, PETER JACOB, chemistry educator; b. Willmar, Minn., Feb. 27, 1939; BA in Chemistry, St. Olaf Coll., Northfield, Minn., 1961; PhD in Phys. Chemistry, Iowa State U., 1966. Peace Corps vol., lectr. chemistry U. Ife, Ibadan, Nigeria, 1966-68; prof. chemistry Northwestern Coll., Orange City, Iowa, 1969-99; vis. asst. prof. chemistry U. Iowa, Iowa City, 1999—. Mem. Am. Chem. Soc., Phi Beta Kappa. Home: 1203 Cambria Ct Iowa City IA 52246-4530 Office: U Iowa Dept Chemistry Iowa City IA 52242-1294 E-mail: peter-j-hansen@uiowa.edu., pjhansen@ia.net.

HANSEN, REX COSSEY, mechanical engineer; b. Salt Lake City, Dec. 23, 1952; s. Alvin Leo and Norma Dean (Cossey) H.; m. Gloria Lyn Haslam, May 18, 1978; children: Karen, Angela, Staci, Kayla. AA, Snow Coll., 1975; BS, Brigham Young U., 1977. Mech. engr., gas res. engr. Pacific Gas & Electric Co., San Francisco, 1977-81; sr. reservoir engr. Northwest Pipeline Corp., Salt Lake City, 1981-93; sr. petroleum engr. Williams Prodn. Co., Salt Lake City, 1993 95; compression engr. Northwest Pipeline Co., Salt Lake City, 1995-98; sr. petroleum engr. Wexpro Co., Salt Lake City, 1998—. Mem. gas storage steering com. Gas Rsch. Inst., Chgo., 1990-98; mem. natural gas res. com. Am. Gas Assn., Chgo., 1979-88. Mem. Soc. Petroleum Engrs. (tech. com. chair 1993-94, sect. chair 1990-91). Avocations: sailing, snow skiing, gardening.

HANSEN, RICHARD OLAF, geophysicist, educator; b. Ottawa, Ont., Can., Oct. 4, 1946; came to U.S., 1968; s. Hyllard Olaf and Muriel Lenora (Helson) H.; m. Kathleen Jean Thoms, June 15, 1968. BSc with honors, Carleton U., 1968; MS, U. Chgo., 1969, PhD, 1973. Research assoc. U. Pitts., 1973-75; postdoctoral research asst. U. Oxford, Oxford, Great Britian, 1975-76; lectr. U. Calif., Berkeley, Calif., 1976-78; staff scientist EG&G Geometrics, Sunnyvale, Calif., 1979-85; prof. Colo. Sch. of Mines, Golden, Colo., 1985-95; prin. geophysicist Pearson, de Ridder and Johnson, Inc., Lakewood, Colo., 1995—. Assoc. editor Geophysics, 1987-91, 95-99. Mem. Soc. Exploration Geophysicists, Am. Geophys. Union, Am. Physical Soc., European Assn. Geoscientists and Engrs. Office: Pearson de Ridder and Johnson Inc Ste 100 12640 W Cedar Dr Lakewood CO 80228-2032

HANSEN, ROBERT CLINTON, electrical engineering consultant; b. St. Louis, 1926; m. 1952; 2 children BS, U. Mo., 1949, D of Eng. (hon.), 1975; MS, U. Ill., 1950, PhD, 1955. Rsch. assoc. antenna lab. U. Ill., 1950-55; sr. staff engr. microwave lab. Hughes Aircraft Co., 1955-59; sr. staff engr. telecomm. lab. Space Technol. Labs., 1959-60; dir. test mission analysis office Aerospace Corp., Calif., 1960-67; head electronics divsn. KMS Technol. Ctr., 1967-71; pres., cons. R.C. Hansen, Inc., Tarzana, Calif., 1971—. Mem. commn. B, Internat. Sci. Radio Union Editor: Microwave Scanning Antennas, 1964-65, Significant Phased Array Papers, 1973, Geometric Theory of Diffraction, 1981, Moment Methods in Antennas and Scattering, 1990; author: Phased Array Antennas, 1998. Recipient Disting. Alumnus award U. Ill. Elect. Engring. Dept., 1981, Disting. Alumnus Svc. medal, 1986. Fellow IEEE (pres. antennas and propagation soc. 1964, 80), Aerospace & Electronic Sys. Soc. (Barry Carlton award 1991, AP Disting. Achievement award 1994, Electromagnetics award 2002), Inst. Elec. Engrs. (London); mem. NAE, Am. Phys. Soc. Office: RC Hansen Inc PO Box 570215 Tarzana CA 91357

HANSEN, ROBERT JOSEPH, civil engineer; b. Tacoma, May 27, 1918; s. Joseph and Olaug (Axness) H.; m. Eleanor Swaim Welch, Dec. 26, 1948; children: Eric Charles, Karen Welch. BS, U. Wash., 1940; Sc.D., MIT, 1948. Research engr. NRC, 1940-43; Princeton U., 1943-45; Arthur D. Little Co., Cambridge, Mass., 1945; NRC predoctoral fellow, 1946-47; research asso. MIT, 1947-48, mem. faculty, 1948—, prof. civil engring., 1957—, dep. dir. Project Transp., 1964-67. Ptnr. Hansen, Holley & Biggs, Inc. (cons. engrs.), Cambridge, 1955-88, prin., 1975-88; ptnr. Newmark, Hansen & Assos., Cambridge and Urbana, Ill., 1958-68; cons. biomechanics Mass. Gen. Hosp., 1956-60; mem. security resources panel Exec. Office of Pres., 1957; mem. sr. adv. panel Air Force Ballistic Div., USAF, 1958-60; mem. exec. com. Adv. Com. CD, Nat. Acad. Scis., 1959— Author: (with others) Structural Design for Dynamic Loads, 1959; also articles, chpts. in books.; editor: Seismic Design for Nuclear Power Plants, 1970. Recipient Army-Navy cert. of appreciation, 1948; Disting. Service citation Dept. Def., 1969 Fellow ASCE (Moisseiff award 1974, Raymond C. Reese research prize 1975, Innovation Civil Engring award 1989); mem. Boston Soc. Civil Engrs., Sigma Xi, Tau Beta Pi. Home: 25 Cambridge St Winchester MA 01890-3703

HANSEN, ROBERT WILLIAM, artist, educator; b. Osceola, Nebr., Jan. 1, 1924; s. William Otto and Gladys Marie (Miller) H.; m. Margaret Helen Kuhlman, Mar. 21, 1948; children: Eric Pat, Fritz Gerald. AB, BFA, U. Nebr., 1948; Maestro de Bellas Artes, Escuela U. de Bellas Artes, San Miguel de Allende, Mex., 1949; postgrad., U. de Michoacan, Morelia, Mex., 1952-53. Asst. prof. art Bradley U., 1949-55, U. Hawaii, 1955-56; asst. prof. Occidental Coll., 1955-60, assoc. prof., 1960-67, prof., 1967-87, prof. emeritus, 1987—. One-man shows include Ferus Gallery, L.A., 1957, Comara Gallery, L.A., 1964, 66, 68, 70, 72, 75, Castellane Gallery, N.Y.C., 1964, L.A. Mcpl. Gallery, 1973, Brand Gallery, 1976, Mich. State U. Gallery, 1980, Oranges/Sardines Gallery, L.A., 1981-82, Occidental Coll., 1987; group shows include, Mus. Modern Art, N.Y.C., 1961, Carnegie Internat., Pitts., 1961, 64, The New Vein Show, Europe and S. Am., 1969-71; represented in permanent collections, Mus. Modern Art, N.Y.C., Whitney Mus., N.Y.C., Fine Arts Gallery of San Diego; translator: Curvilinear Perspective, 1988. Founder (1989), pres. Carpinteria Creek Com. With U.S. Army, 1943-46. Guggenheim fellow, India, S.E. Asia, 1961-62; Fulbright sr. rsch. grantee, India, 1961-62; Tamarind lithographic fellow, 1964-65. Mem. ACLU, Phi Beta Kappa. Home: 1498 Santa Ynez Ave Carpinteria CA 93013-1312 E-mail: bobmighansen@earthlink.net.

HANSEN, ROBYN L. lawyer; b. Terre Haute, Ind., Dec. 2, 1949; d. Robert Louis and Shirley (Nagel) Wieman; m. Gary Hansen, Aug. 21, 1971 (div. 1985); children: Nathan Ross Hansen, Brian Michael Hansen; m. John Marley Clarey, Jan. 1, 1986; 1 child, John Zender Clarey. BA, Gustavus Adolphus, 1971; JD cum laude, William Mitchell Coll. Law, 1977. Bar: Minn. 1977, U.S. Dist. Ct. Minn. 1977. Atty. Briggs and Morgan P.A., St. Paul, 1977-93, Leonard, Street and Deinard, St. Paul, 1993—. Trustee Actors Theatre, St. Paul, 1980—88, Minn. Mus. Am. Art, 1994—97; mem. Minn. Inst. Pub. Fin., 1987—93, bd. dirs., 1993—95, pres., 1995; bd. dirs. St. Paul Downtown Coun., 1985—93, Met. State U. Found., 1993—2003, chair, 2000—02; bd. dirs. St. Paul Area Conv. and Vis. Bur., 1995—, chair, 1999—2001; bd. dirs. Capital City Partnership, 1997—. Mem. ABA, Minn. Bar Assn., Ramsey County Bar Assn., Nat. Assn. Bond Lawyers, St. Paul Area C. of C. (bd. dirs., exec. com. 1997-99). Office: Leonard Street and Deinard 380 St Peter St Ste 500 Saint Paul MN 55102 E-mail: robyn.hansen@leonard.com.

HANSEN, SALLY JO, educational consultant; b. San Fernando, Calif., Sept. 8, 1937; d. Kenneth Morris Sr. and Carmen (Woods) High; m. Mark Herman Hansen, June 14, 1958; children: Laurie Jo, Mark. BA, U. Redlands, 1959. Cert. lang. devel. specialist, Calif., cert. crosscultural lang. and acad. devel. specialist, Calif. Tchr. remedial reading Newport-Mesa Unified Sch. Dist., Newport Beach, Calif., 1965-80, tchr. ESL, 1980-88, title VII coord., 1988-97, ESL bilingual project coord., 1990-97, coord. Healthy Start, 1990-97, coord. staff devel., 1992—97; ednl. cons. Costa Mesa, Calif., 1997—; external evaluator Sch. Reform, State of Calif., 2001—. Mem. Sch. Intervention Audit team State of Calif.; adj. prof. tchr. tng. program U. Calif., Irvine, 2001—; presenter and staff trainer in field. Author and editor: ESL Guide for Classroom Teachers, 1992. Pres. PTA, Newport Beach/Costa Mesa, 1965-70 (bd. dirs. 1965-80); legis. rep. Orange County Tchr. of Speakers of Other Langs., 1985-87. Mem. Nat. Assn. Bilingual Edn., Calif. Assn. Bilingual Edn., Nat. Charity League (officer), Rep. Women, U. Redlands Alumni Assn., Assistance League Newport-Mesa (officer). Presbyterian. Avocations: travel, reading, camping, fishing.

HANSEN, STEPHEN CHRISTIAN, banker; b. N.Y.C., July 3, 1940; s. Norbert C. and Harriet C. H.; m. Ethel Olmsted, June 12, 1971; 1 son, Lee Christian. AB, Princeton U., 1962; LL.B., U. Va., 1966; postgrad., Brown U. Grad. Sch. Banking. Bar: N.Y. 1966. Assoc. Alexander & Green, N.Y.C., 1966-68; mem. N.Y. State Legislature, 1968-70; spl. asst. to undersec. HUD, Washington, 1970-73; spl. asst. to chmn. FDIC, Washington, 1973-76; sr. v.p. Dollar Bank, Pitts., 1976-78, pres., 1978—, pres., CEO, 1982—. Chmn. Regional Indsl. Devel. Corp. Bd. dirs. Pitts. Regional Alliance; trustee Carnegie Inst.; bd. dirs. Carnegie Sci. Ctr.; bd. dir. Cleve. Dist. Pitts. Fed. Res. Mem. N.Y. State Bar Assn. Office: Dollar Bank PO Box 987 Pittsburgh PA 15230-0987

HANSEN, STEVEN ALAN, construction executive; b. Key West, Fla., July 5, 1949; s. Baron Lewis Hansen and June Marie (Ferree) Correll; m. Sally Jo Cooper, Nov. 13, 1976; children: Blake, Carter, Reid. BA in Govt. and Religion, Ind. U., 1972. V.p. Hansen-Haberman Constrn., Aspen, Colo., 1978-82; pres. Hansen Constrn. Inc., Aspen, 1982—. Avocations: oil painting, sketching. Office: Hansen Constrn Inc PO Box 10493 Aspen CO 81612-7329

HANSEN, THOMAS EDWARD, physician, educator; b. Portland, Oreg., May 12, 1953; s. John Robert and Evelyn Sidney (Thompson) H.; m. Kim Anisa Manley, Dec. 26, 1973; children: Evan Christopher, Kara Joanne. BA with distinction, Stanford U., 1975; MD cum laude, U. Oreg., Portland, 1979. Bd. cert. in psychiatry with added qualifications in geriat. psychiatry. Resident psychiatry Yale U. Sch. Medicine, New Haven, 1983; asst. prof. dept. psychiatry Oreg. Health Scis. U., Portland, 1983-95, assoc. prof. dept. psychiatry, 1995—; staff physician Portland VA Med. Ctr., 1983—, co-mgr. acute psychiatry, 1996—. Contbr. articles to profl. jours. Soccer coach, vol. S.E. Soccer Club, Portland City United, 1985-95; treas. Lincoln H.S. Boosters, Portland, 1998-01. Rsch. grantee VA Rsch. Svc., Portland, 1985-95. Fellow Am. Psychiat. Assn.; mem. Am. Assn. for Geriat. Psychiatry, Am. Soc. Clin. Psychopharmacology, Soc. Biol. Psychiatry, Assn. for Convulsive Therapy, Oreg. Psychiat. Assn. (various coms., com. chair 1984-96), Phi Beta Kappa, Alpha Omega Alpha. Avocations: running, gardening, home brewing. Office: Portland VAMC 3710 SW US Vets Hosp Portland OR 97201 E-mail: than_kman@msn.com.

HANSEN, W. LEE, economics educator, author; b. Racine, Wis., Nov. 8, 1928; s. William R. and Gertrude M. (Spillum) H.; m. Sally Ann Porch, Dec. 26, 1955; children— Ellen J., Martha L. BA, U. Wis., Madison, 1950, MA, 1955; PhD, Johns Hopkins U., 1958. Asst. prof. econs. UCLA, from 1958, assoc. prof., to 1965; assoc. prof. econs. U. Wis., Madison, from 1965, prof., prof. emeritus, 1996—. Sr. staff economist Pres.'s Coun. Econ. Advisers, Washington, 1964-65; trustee Nat. Coun. on Econ. Edn., N.Y.C., 1976-2000, sec., 1996-2000; mem. bd. founders NCEE, 2000—. Author: Benefits, Costs, and Finance of Public Higher Education, 1969, Education, Income, and Human Capital, 1970, The Labor Market for Scientists and Engineers, 1973, Perspectives on Economic Education, 1977, A Framework for Teaching Basic Economic Concepts, 1984, The End of Mandatory Retirement, 1989, Unemployment Insurance: The Second Half-Century, 1990, Academic Freedom on Trial: 100 Years of Sifting and Winnowing at the University of Wisconsin, 1998; contbr. articles to profl. jours. Sgt. U.S. Army, 1951-53. Recipient Amoco Disting. Tchg. award U. Wis., 1982, Hilldale award, 1988, Disting. Svc. award Nat. Coun. on Econs. Edn., 1991, Marvin Bower award, 1994,, Henry H Villard Rsch. award, 2000, Tchr.

Acad. U. Wis., 1994, Outstanding Postsecondary Educator award nat. Fedn. Ind. Bus. Found., 1992, Leavey award for excellence in pvt. enterprise edn. Freedoms Found., 1996; Guggenheim fellow, 1969-70; Fulbright sr. scholar, Australia, 1988. Mem. AAUP (chair com. on the econ. status of the profession 1979-86, mem. nat. coun. 1980-82, retirement com. 1985-95), Am. Econ. Assn. (chmn. com. on econ. edn. 1983-88, exec. sec. commn. grad. edn. econs. 1988-91), Indsl. Rels. Rsch. Assn., Midwest Econs. Assn. (pres. 1987), Phi Beta Kappa. Unitarian Universalist. Office: U Wis Dept Econs 1180 Observatory Dr Madison WI 53706-1320 E-mail: wlhansen@facstaff.wisc.edu.

HANSEN, WALTER EUGENE, insurance executive; b. Woodland, Wash., May 15, 1929; s. August Hans and Esther Johanna (Johnson) H.; m. Barbara Inez Cowart, Oct. 1950; m. Donna Carol Phillips, Aug. 1, 1953; children: Larry, Monty, Gena, Martin, Lori, Bradley, Walter Eugene Jr. Grad. high sch. Farmer, logger, 1943-51; svc. mgr. Sears Roebuck & Co., L.A. and Portland, Oreg., 1951-57; agt. various ins. cos., 1957-63; dist. mgr. Bankers Life & Casualty Co., 1960-61; state mgr. Protective Security Life Ins. Co., 1963-65; regional mgr. Amn. Pacific Life Ins. Co., 1963-72; owner Pacific N.W. Ins. Svc., Portland, 1963—, Am. Pacific Agys., Portland, 1970—, N. Fork Motors, Woodland, Wash., 1987—, 1989—. Owner Nat. Rsch. Assocs., Seattle, 1968—, N. Fork Ranch, 1962—. Mem. editl.bd. Longview Daily News, 1999-00. Past Boy Scouts Am.; chmn. Community USA Bicentennial Commn., 1976; mem. Wash. State Centennial Com., 1989; commr. Woodland Recreation Dist., 2000—; mem. Woodland Urban Growth Com., 1999-00. Mem. Internat. Platform Assn., Nat. Assn. Life Underwriters, Nat. Trust Hitoric Preservation, Libr. Congress, Accident and Health Underwriters Assn., Smithsonian Assocs., Navy League of U.S. Home: PO Box 2000 Woodland WA 98674-1900

HANSEN, WAYNE W. lawyer; b. Clintonville, Wis., June 7, 1942; s. William W. and Berniece M. (Kuehn) H.; m. Carolyn M. Lemke, Dec. 21, 1969; children: Drew D., Janna J. BBA, U. Wis., 1965, JD, 1967. Bar: Wis. 1967, U.S. Dist. Ct. (we. dist.) Wis. 1971, U.S. Ct. Appeals (7th cir.) 1972, U.S. Dist. Ct. (ea. dist.) Wis. 1975, Wash. 1979, U.S. Dist. Ct. (we. dist.) Wash. 1979, U.S. Ct. Appeals (9th cir.) 1982, U.S. Dist. Ct. (ea. dist.) Wash. 1986. Atty. NLRB, Mpls., 1967-70, Schmitt Nolan Hansen & Hartley, Merrill, Wis., 1970-79; ptnr. Lane Powell Spears Lubersky, Seattle, 1979-98; mng. ptnr. Seattle office Jackson Lewis LLP, 1998—. Contbg. author: Developing Labor Law, 1971, Doing Business in Washington State*Guide for Foreign Business, 1989. Office: Jackson Lewis LLP 1420 5th Ave Ste 2000 Seattle WA 98101-1348

HANSEN, WELLS STEVENSON, language educator, researcher; s. Donald Charles and Jill M. Hansen. BA, Boston Coll., 1983—87; MA, U. of Chgo., 1987—88; EdD, U. of Mass., 2000—. Author: (profl. papers) Classical Jour., New Eng. Classical Jour., Salem Press. Fellow Klingenstein Fellowship, Columbia U., 1994; grantee Fulbright, USIA, 1998. Mem.: Am. Ednl. Rsch. Assn., Am. Classical League, Classical Assn. of Mass., Classical Assn. of New Eng., Am. Philol. Assn. E-mail: wells_hansen@milton.edu.

HANSEN, WIDMER CASE, retired weapons systems engineer, analyst; b. Aug. 1, 1913; s. William Carl and Ada Margaret (Nelson Borg) Hansen; m. Blanche Davis, July 13, 1946 (div. 1981); children: June Hansen Butkas, Jacqueline Hansen Conlon, Widmer Case Jr.(dec.); m. Colombe Martha Schultz, Dec. 28, 1983 (dec. 1995); 1 stepchild, Carol Colombe Schultz Cross. BSEE, U.S. Naval Acad., 1937; postgrad., Naval Postgrad. Sch., 1946—47, Indsl. Coll. of Armed Forces, 1956—57; MEngring., Johns Hopkins U., 1949. Cert. naval ordnance engr. Commd. ens. U.S. Navy, 1937, advanced through grades to capt., 1963, ret., various assignments, 1937—52; comdr. and capt. Bur. Ordnance, Bur. Naval Weapons, Washington, 1952—60; capt. Spl. Projects Office Tech. Rep., Syosset, NY, 1960—63; weapons sys. analyst Air-Air Grumman Corp., Bethpage, NY, 1963—76; ret. Mem. human investigations subcom., R&D com. VA Med. Ctr., Canandaigua, NY, 1985—97. Mem.: NRA, Sigma Xi. Republican. Achievements include first to prodn. of naval missiles for service use. Avocations: travel, photography, marksmanship. Home: 35 Yacht Club Dr Canandaigua NY 14424-2483

HANSEN, WILLIAM, federal agency administrator; b. Pocatello, Idaho; BS in Econs., George Mason U. Legis. asst. Dept. Edn., Washington, 1981, acting asst. sec. legis. and congl. affairs, dep. asst. sec. elem. and secondary edn., acting dep. under sec. for planning, budget, and evaluation, 1990—91, asst. sec. mgmt. and budget, CFO, 1991—93, dep. sec. edn., 2001—; dep. dir. pub. affairs Dept. Commerce; head Office Intergovtl. and Industry Affairs Dept. Energy; pres., CEO Edn. Fin. Coun. Mem. nat. bds. and commns. on sch. reform; mem. Nat. Commn. on Cost of Higher Edn. Office: Dept Edn Office Deputy Sec 400 Maryland Ave SW Washington DC 20202-0500

HANSEN, WILLIAM FRANK, hydrologist; s. Frank August and Betty Lucille Hansen; m. Lynda Lee Hagerich, June 21, 1947; children: Eric William, David Allen Rash, Jared Paul, Andrea Suzanne Johnson, Heather Lee Rash. BS in Forestry, U. of Mo., 1971, MS in Forest Hydrology, 1975. Forest hydrologist Siskiyou Nat. Forest, Grants Pass, Oreg., 1975—83, Francis Marion and Sumter Nat. Forest, Columbia, SC, 1983—. Rsch. specialist U. of Mo., Columbia, 1971—75. Recipient Numerous Certs. of Merit, U.S. Dept. of Agr., 1975—2003. Home: 100 Warner Woods Rd Lexington SC 29072 Office: USDA Forest Svc 4931 Broad River Rd Columbia SC 29212 Office Fax: 803-561-4004. E-mail: wfhansen@fs.fed.us.

HANSEN-CARTER, MARILYN RAY, nurse; b. Galveston, Tex., May 25, 1931; d. Raymond J. and Elizabeth E. (Weyer) Hansen; m. Wade V. Carter, Jr., Feb. 21, 1957; children: Renee, Wade, Kim, Vanette. R.N., St. Mary's Sch. Nursing, 1951. Head nurse VA Hosp., Houston, 1953-56; psychiat. nurse Panama Canal Co., Balboa, C.Z., 1956-79; charge nurse Starlight Hosp., Center Point, Tex., 1982-96; reporter Canal Record, 1981-82. Founder, chmn. Hill Country Zonian's Assn., Kerrville, 1979-82; chmn. Hill Country Youth Ranch Charity Ball, 1977; poll clk. local, fed. elections, 1981-83. Contbr. to cookbooks. Vol. Salvation Army, 1979-82, Cowboy Artists Am. Mus. Named Nurse of Yr., VA Hosp., Houston, 1954; recipient Outstanding Job Performance award U.S. Civil Service, 1968. Mem. Native Plant Soc. Tex., Tex. Nurses Assn., Panama Canal Soc. Fla., Am. Assn. Ret. Persons. Lutheran. Club: Hill Country Zonians.

HANSEN-FLASCHEN, JOHN HYMAN, medical educator, researcher; b. Hamilton, Ohio, June 25, 1950; s. Steward Samuel and Joyce (Davies) Flaschen; m. Susan Lauretta Hansen, Aug. 22, 1951; children: Lynn, Lauren. AB, Brown U., 1972; MD, NYU, 1976. Diplomate in internal medicine, pulmonary medicine, critical care medicine Am. Bd. Internal Medicine. Resident in medicine U. Pa., Phila., 1976-79, chief resident in medicine, 1980-81, pulmonary fellow, 1979-80, 81-82, attending physician, 1982—, asst. prof. medicine, 1982-87, assoc. prof., 1988-98, prof., 1999—, dir. edn. and tng. programs in pulmonary and critical care, 1983-90, dir. pulmonary and critical care divsn., 1990-98, chief pulmonary, allergy and critical care divsn., 1998—, dir. Penn Lung Ctr., 1996—. Mem. editl. bd. Clin. Pulmonary Medicine, Respiratory Medicine, UpToDate; editor Pulmonary and Critical Care MKSAP 13, ACP; contbr. articles to profl. jours. Mem. steering com. Nat. Emphysema Treatment Trial, 1997—. Recipient Spl. Investigator award Am. Heart Assn., 1982-84, Lindback Tchg. award U. Pa., 1999, 3 other tchg. awards; Measey Found. fellow, 1982-83. Fellow ACP, Am. Coll. Chest Physicians, Coll. Physicians Phila.; mem. Am. Thoracic Soc. (chmn. postgrad. edn. com. 1995—, clin. problems long range planning com. 1997-99), Soc. for Critical Care Medicine, Soc. for Bioethics Consultation, Laennec Soc. Phila. (pres. 1990-91), Drinker Soc. for Critical Care in Phila. (founder, 1st pres. 1988-90), Sigma Xi, Alpha Omega Alpha. Democrat. Home: 365 Penn Rd Wynnewood PA 19096-1401 Office: Hosp of U Pa 873 Mahoney Bldg 3400 Spruce St Philadelphia PA 19104-4206

HANSER, PHILIP, econometrician; b. Ft. Lauderdale, Fla., Jan. 8, 1951; s. Edward and Nettie (Ornstein) H.; m. Jane Ivy Boris, June 25, 2000; children—Leora B., Samuel B., Raviva S. BA, Fla. State U., Tallahassee, 1972; MPhil, PhD, Columbia U., 1975. Rsch. asst. in econometrics Bur. Applied Social Rsch., Columbia U., 1972-74, cons. Center for Computing Activities, 1974-75; lectr. dept. math. U. Pacific, 1975-77; asst. prof. dept. econs. and math, 1977-80; econometrician resource planning dept. Sacramento Mcpl. Utility Dist., 1980-86; project mgr. Electric Power Research Inst., 1986-92, program mgr., 1992-1995; principal, Putnam, Hayes, & Bartlett, 1995-96; principal, The Brattle Group, 1996-; vis. lectr. dept. econs. U. Calif., Davis, 1982-83; guest lectr., MIT, 1997, 1999; industry cons. Electric Power Rsch. Inst. NSF fellow, 1972-74; recipient Tchg. Incentive award U. Pacific, 1979; Outstanding Young Men of Am. award Jr. C. of C. Am., 1980. Mem. Econometric Soc., Am. Statis. Assn., Internat. Assn., Energy Economists, Inst. Math. Stats., Internat. Soc. Forecasters. Author: (with D. Christianson and D. Hughes) Statistics Through Laboratory Experiences, 1977; contbr. articles to profl. jours. Home: 106 Hartman Rd Newton MA 02459-2854 Office: The Brattle Group 44 Brattle St Cambridge MA 02138-3736 Personal E-mail: pqhanser@comcast.com. Business E-Mail: philip.hanser@brattle.com.

HANSFORD, NATHANIEL, academic administrator, lawyer; b. Columbia, S.C., Oct. 16, 1943; s. Bradley Richard and Ernestine (Stokely) H.; m. Frances Fincher, Sept. 19, 1970; children: Nathaniel F., Mary Frances. BS, U. Ga., 1965, JD, 1968; LLM, U. Mich., 1980. Bar: Ga. 1967, Ala., 1979. Law clk. Judge Lewis R. Morgan U.S. Ct. Appeals, Newnan, Ga., 1968-70; assoc. Mitchell & Mitchell, Dalton, Ga., 1973-75; dean, prof. Sch. Law U. Ala., Tuscaloosa, 1975-88; pres. North Ga. Coll. and State U., Dahlonega, Ga., 1999—. Bd. dirs. Synovus Fin. Corp., Columbus, Ga., Cohulta Bank, Chatsworth, Ga. Author: Alabama Equity, 1984, UCC Transaction Guide, 1988, Sales, Leases & Bulk Sales, 1989. Bd. vis. U. Ga. Sch. Law. Capt. U.S. Army, 1970-73, col. USAR, 1973-94. Fellow Am. Bar Found., Ala. Bar Assn.; mem. Order of Coif, Kiwanis (treas. Tuscaloosa chpt. 1976-82), Rotary, Phi Beta Kappa. Office: North Ga Coll and State U 32 College Cir Dahlonega GA 30597-0001

HANSHAW, JAMES BARRY, physician, educator; b. Scarsdale, N.Y., Dec. 23, 1928; s. George Lee and Kathryn Frances (Reilly) H.; m. Marian Christine Kernan, Aug. 14, 1954; children: Thomas, Lee, Elizabeth, John, Margaret. AB, Syracuse U., 1950; MD, SUNY, Syracuse, 1953, DSc (hon.), 1991. Intern Cin. Gen. Hosp., 1953-54; resident pediatrics U. Rochester Med. Center, 1956-58; Nat. Found. postdoctoral fellow virology Harvard U. Sch. Pub. Health, 1958-60; academic medicine, specializing in pediatrics Rochester, N.Y., 1960-75; instr. to prof. pediatrics and microbiology U. Rochester Sch. Medicine, 1960-75; prof., chmn. dept. pediatrics U. Mass., Worcester, 1975-85, interim vice chancellor, acad. dean, 1985-86; interim chancellor, 1987; provost, dean U. Mass., 1986-89, dean emeritus, prof. pediatrics, 1989—, interim chmn. dept. pediatrics, 1997-98; chmn. dept. pediatrics Meml. Health Care, 1993-98. Lectr. pediatrics Harvard U. Med. Sch., 1975-2002; vis. prof. Inst. Child Health, London U. and Hosp. for Sick Children, London, 1971-72; coll. health physician WPI, 1990—. Author: (with J.A. Dudgeon) Viral Infections Fetus and Newborn, 1978, 2d edit. (with Dudgeon and W.C. Marshall), 1985. Served with USAF, 1953-56. Buswell fellow U. Rochester, 1960-62; NIH grantee, 1962-75 Mem. AMA, Am. Pediatric Soc., Soc. Pediatric Research, Am. Acad. Pediatrics, Infectious Diseases Soc. Am., New Eng. Pediatric Soc., Sigma Xi, Alpha Omega Alpha. Home: 18 Baypath Dr Boylston MA 01505-1427 E-mail: jhans76271@aol.com.

HANSHAW, LEANN VIALA, counseling administrator; d. Paul Edward and Marilyn Goodbar Viala; m. Lance Lamar Hanshaw, June 11, 1965; children: Hastings children: Holly Huckabee, Heath. BSE, Ouachita Bapt. U., 1964. Cert. counseling edn. Tchr. Hardin Bale Elem., Little Rock, 1964—65, Brady Elem. Sch., Little Rock, 1968—70, Pulaski Acad., Little Rock, 1971—72; sch. counselor Westside Elem. Sch., Cabot, Ark., 1985—. Lectr. in field, spkr. Author: Sealed With series, 1998 (Writer of the Yr., Ark. Counselors, 1998). Vol. Open Arms Shelter, Lonoke, Ark., 1986—2002. Named Woman of Yr., Cabot C. of C., 1998; recipient award for outstanding career edn. project in state, Ark. Dept. Career Edn., 1988. Mem.: Ark. Sch. Counselors Assn. (State Treas., 1993-1994) (vice-president 1991—92, Ark. Sch. Elem. Counselor of Yr. 1991—92), Ark. Edn. Assn. Methodist. Avocations: antiques, travel, reading, Bible study.

HANSHE, JOHN, musicologist, writer; b. Tehran, Iran, Oct. 13, 1971; arrived in U.S., 1974; s. John Henry Hanshe and Bernadette Naso. Student, New Sch Social Rsch., 2002—. Amanuensis James Purdy, Brooklyn Heights, NY, 1997—; artist asst. Nan Goldin Photographer, N.Y.C., 2000—01. Author: (plays) Midnight Ruby, The Fool's Tribunal, The Savage Exile, Kabuki Hysterics, Prince Vogelfrei, The Sawdust Ring, A Soldier's Things, Bright Desolation, Always the Moon, Coronation of a King, The Wolves' Lair, (novels) Arabesque, (poetry) Spirits of Exile (Internat. Poet of Merit, 2002); contbr. music. Mem.: Friedrich Nietzsche Soc. Avocations: jazz, travel, theater, mountaineering, swimming. Personal E-mail: romanexile@hotmail.com.

HANSLEY, LEE, art gallery owner, curator; b. Roanoke Rapids, N.C., Jan. 11, 1948; s. Lonnie L. and Kathleen (Crumpler) H. Student, U. N.C., 1966-70. City editor The Daily Herald, Roanoke Rapids, 1970-73; editor The Northampton News, Jackson, N.C., 1973-75, Roanoke-Chowan News-Herald, Ahoskie, N.C., 1976, Halifax (N.C.) County This Week, 1976-78, The Suburbanite Newspaper, Winston-Salem, N.C., 1978-80; exhbns. curator Southeastern Ctr. Contemporary Art, Winston-Salem, 1980-86; pub. rels. dir. WUNC Radio, Chapel Hill., N.C., 1986-91; ind. cons. Durham (N.C.) Arts Coun., 1992; proprietor Lee Hansley Gallery, Raleigh, N.C., 1993—. Cons. art exhibits Duke U. Law Sch., Durham, 1995—. Curator: Edith London: A Retrospective, 1992; editor: (exhbn. catalogs) Award in Visual Arts, 1981, 83, 84, 85, 86, Durham Art Guild 50th Anniversary Catalogue, 1998. Mem. Raleigh Arts Commn., 1989-95, chmn., 1991-93; mem. Durham Art Guild, 1991-97; bd. dirs. City Gallery, Raleigh, 1989-93, Theatre Devel. Bd., N.C. State U., 1986-91, 99—, N.C. State U. Gallery of Art and Design, 2003—; pub. rels. bd. Nat. Pub. Radio, Washington, 1989-91; mem. City of Raleigh Pub. Art Com., 1989-2003; founder, chmn. bd. Mus. Contemporary Art of N.C., 2003—. Recipient Gen. Excellence award N.C. Press Assn., Chapel Hill, 1978, Investigative Reporting award, 1978, Lee Hansley Gallery Scholarship N.C. Sch. Arts award. Mem. N.C. Mus. Art., Mus. Modern Art, Smithsonian Instn., Gianini Soc. N.C. Sch. Arts, Weatherspoon Gallery, Ackland Art Mus. Democrat. Avocations: gardening, non-fiction, art collecting, music. Home: 804 N King Charles Rd Raleigh NC 27610-1628 Office: Lee Hansley Gallery 225 Glenwood Ave Raleigh NC 27603-1404 E-mail: leehansley@aol.com.

HANSMAN, CATHERINE ANN, adult education educator, researcher; b. Springfield, Mass., Aug. 21, 1957; d. Henry Joseph Hansman and Nina Leah Bartsch; m. Joseph Martin Ferguson, Jr., July 3, 1980 (div. July 17, 1997); children: Sean Kendrick Ferguson, Julia Leah Ferguson. MusB, U. of Cin., 1979; MS, Ind. U., Ft. Wayne, 1990; EdD, Ball State U., 1995. Band dir. Growing with Music, Cin., 1978—80; pvt. music tchr. Ft. Wayne, 1978—95; computer analyst/trainer USAF, Wright Patterson AFB, Ohio, 1980—85; English/devel. studies instr. Ind. U./Purdue U., Ft. Wayne, Ind., 1990—95, dir. Ctr. for Women and Returning Adults, 1995; asst. prof., program coord. MEd in adult edn. Ga. So. U., Statesboro, 1995—98; asst. prof., program coord. MEd in adult learning and devel. Cleve. State U., 1998—2001, assoc. prof., coord. programs - leadership and lifelong learning and adult learning and devel., 2001—. Author, editor: monograph Critical Perspectives on Mentoring: Trends & Issues, author, editor (with Peggy Sissel): book Understanding and Negotiating the Political Landscape of Adult Education, author, rschr.(with helen graf): rsch. Exploring the Connection of Literacy and health in the democratization of a society (U. of Ga. Sys. Rsch. grant, 1997); author: (book chpt.) Mentoring and Women's Career Development, Context Based Adult Learning. Planning com. mem. Shaker Heights (Ohio) PTO Drug/Alcohol Abuse Com., 2001; exec. coun. mem. Commn. of Profs. of Adult Edn., 1999—2002; mem. scholarship selection com. Jeannette Rankin Found., Athens, Ga., 2002; tech. subcom. Greater Cleve. Adult Edn. Assn., Cleve., 1999; editl. bd. mem. Adult Edn. Quar. Jour., Cornell U., Ithaca, NY, 2000, N.Y. Jour. of Adult Edn., N.Y.C., 2003. Recipient Kellogg Found. grant, Cyril O. Houle Emerging Scholars in Adult and Continuing Edn., 2000—02, Faculty Rsch. Challenge grant, Cleve. State U., 1998—2000. Mem.: Am. Edn. Rsch. Assn., Am. Assn. for Adult and Continuing Edn. Avocations: music, walking, gardening, cooking, theater. Office: Cleve State U Rte 1419 2121 Euclid Ave Cleveland OH 44115-2214 Office Fax: 216-687-5378. E-mail: c.hansman@csuohio.edu.

HANSMAN, ROBERT G. art educator, artist; BFA, U. Kans., 1970. Asst. prof. Washington U., St. Louis. Instr. dept. parts and recreation Project Artspark, 1993, Arts Connection/City Faces, 1994—; instr. juvenile detention program Children's Art Cir., 1995; established Jermaine Lamond Roberts Meml. Art Studio, clinton-Peabody Pub. Housing, 1997. One-man shows include St. Louis C.C. at Forest Park, 1988, MJF Arts Studio Gallery, 1990, University City Pub. Libr., 1992, 1995, Bonsack Gallery, 1995. Mem. pub. housing revitalization focus group Darst-Webbe, 1995. Named Reader's Poll Best Local Artist, The Riverfront Times, 1995; recipient First Pl. award/Best of Show, St. Louis Artists Guild, 1988, 1992, Componere Gallery, 1990, Not Just An Art Dirs. Club, 1990, The Gallery Connection, 1991, Art St. Louis Gallery, 1991, World of Difference award City Faces, 1996, Mo. Arts award, Mo. Arts Coun., 1997, Excellence in Tchg. award, Emerson Electric, 2000, Disting. Faculty award, 2001, honoree, Colin Powell's Am. Promise, 1999, Mo. Ho. of Reps., 1997; grantee, Bi-State Arts in Transit Project, 1995, 1996, 1999. Office: Washington U Sch Arch Campus Box 1079 One Brookings Dr Saint Louis MO 63130 E-mail: hansman@architecture.wustl.edu.

HANSMAN, ROBERT JOHN, JR., aeronautics and astronautics educator; b. Brockton, Mass., Oct. 13, 1954; s. Robert John and Sally Jean (Power) H.; m. Laura Ann Wernick, Aug. 13, 1983; children: Heather Ann, Christopher John. Student, U. Mass., 1972-73; AB, Cornell U., 1976; MS, MIT, 1980, PhD, 1982. Comml. pilot, flight instr. ratings. Pilot numerous ops., New England, 1970-76, Schweizer Aircraft Co., Elmira, N.Y., 1976; rsch. asst. dept. of physics MIT, Cambridge, Mass., 1976-82, lectr. dept. astronautics and aeronautics, 1982-83, prof. dept. astronautics and aeronautics, 1995—, head divsn. humans and automation, 1993—; dir. Internat. Ctr. Air Transp., Cambridge, 1995—. Cons. pvt. practice Cambridge, Mass., 1982—. Contbr. numerous articles to profl. jours. Mem. U.S. Congressional Aero. Adv. Com., Washington, 1987-89; rsch. and devel. adv. com. FHA, 1997--; mem. Fed. Transp. Adv. Group, 1999-2000. Named astronaut finalist, NASA, 1984; recipient Gold C with 3 diamonds, Fedn. Aeronatique Internat., 1980, Presdl. Young Investigator award, NASA, 1980, Excellence in Aviation award, FAA, 1997. Fellow AIAA (assoc., atmospheric environ. tech. com., best paper in thermophysics award 1986, Losey Atmospheric Scis. award 1994); mem. Am. Meteorol. Soc., Am. Phys. Soc., Human Factors Soc., Soaring Soc. Am. (bd. dirs., Exceptional Svc. award 1989), Air Traffic Control Assn., Soaring Safety Found. (bd. dirs.), Phi Beta Kappa, Sigma Xi. Achievements include patents for global positioning satellite applications, ice prevention, ice measurement, liquid monitoring in tanks. Avocations: competition sailplane pilot, running, triathalons. Office: MIT 33-305 Dept Aero and Astro 77 Massachusetts Ave Cambridge MA 02139 E-mail: rjhans@mit.edu.

HANSMANN, HENRY BAETHKE, law educator; b. Highland Park, Ill., Oct. 5, 1945; s. Elwood Hansmann and Louise Frances (Baethke) Moore; m. Marina Santilli, 1992; 1 child, Lisa Santilli. BA, Brown U., 1967; JD, Yale U., 1974, PhD, 1978. Asst. prof. law U. Pa. Law Sch., Phila., 1975-81, assoc. prof. law, econs. and pub. policy, 1981-83; prof. law Yale U., New Haven, 1983-88, Harris prof., 1988—2003; prof. law NYU, N.Y.C., 2003—. Author: The Ownership of Enterprise, 1996. John Simon Guggenheim Found. fellow, 1985-86. Mem. Am. Econs. Assn., Am. Law and Econ. Assn. Home: 240 Mercer St # 1603 New York NY 10012-1507 Office: NYU Sch Law 40 Washington Sq S New York NY 10012 E-mail: henry.hansmann@nyu.edu.

HANSMANN, RALPH EMIL, investment executive; b. Utica, N.Y., May 25, 1918; s. Emil C. and Friedericka (Fuchs) H.; m. Doris Macdonald, Oct. 16, 1943; children: Robert E., Jane C. AB, Hamilton Coll., 1940, LLD, 1992; MBA, Harvard, 1942. Investment assoc. Harold F. Linder, William T. Golden, N.Y.C., 1945-48, 53—; staff Gen. Am. Investors Co., Inc., 1949-52. Emeritus trustee Inst. Advanced Study, Princeton, N.J.; life trustee Hamilton Coll., Clinton, N.Y.; trustee, treas. N.Y. Pub. Libr. Served as lt. USNR, 1942-45. Mem. Ridgewood (N.J.) Country Club, Harvard Club (N.Y.C.), Phi Beta Kappa. Home: 385 Manchester Rd Ridgewood NJ 07450-1212 Office: 500 Fifth Ave New York NY 10110

HANSON, ARNOLD PHILIP, JR., lawyer, publishing company executive; b. Boston, Nov. 24, 1949; s. Arnold Philip Sr. and Della Ann (Lavernoich) H.; m. Barbara Jean Davis, Oct. 19, 1974; children: Christopher Davis, Stephanie Ann, Jonathan Robert. AB, Dartmouth Coll., 1971; JD, Boston U., 1974; M in Mgmt., Yale U., 1982. Bar: N.H. 1974, U.S. Dist. Ct. N.H. 1974. Assoc. Bergeron & Hanson, Berlin, N.H., 1974-79, ptnr., 1979-80; mgmt. teaching asst. Yale U., New Haven, 1980-82; internal cons. Insilco Corp., Meriden, Conn., 1981, asst. to chmn. bd. dirs., 1982-83; dir. pub. Taylor Pub. Co. subs. Insilico Corp., Dallas, 1984-88, vp. publ., new product devel., 1988— ; cons. Hanson and Assocs., Plano, Tex., 1983—. Pres., drive chmn. United Way, Berlin, 1976-80; pres., v.p., bd. dirs. Androscoggin Valley C. of C., Berlin, 1977-80. Mem. ABA, N.H. Bar Assn. (bd. govs. 1979-80), Am. Mktg. Assn., Assn. MBA Execs. Republican. Clubs: Androsloggin Valley Country (Gorham, N.H.) (pres., bd. dirs. 1978-80); Canyon Creek Country (Richardson, Tex.). Avocations: golf, tennis. Home: PO Box 186 Berlin NH 03570-0186 Office: Taylor Pub Co PO Box 597 Dallas TX 75221-0597

HANSON, ARNOLD PHILIP, retired lawyer; b. Berlin, N.H., July 11, 1924; s. Arnold H. and Evelyn (Renaud) H.; m. Della Ann Lavernoich, June 26, 1948; children: Arnold Philip, Caryl Hanson Brensinger, Julie E. Hanson Mook. BA, U. N.H., 1948; JD, Boston, 1951. Bar: N.H. 1951. Pvt. practice, Berlin, N.H., 1951-60; ptnr. Bergeron & Hanson, Berlin, 1960-80, Bergeron & Hanson, P.A., Berlin, 1980-87, Bergeron, Hanson & Bornstein, P.A., Berlin, 1988-91; county atty. Coos County, N.H., 1952-56; ret. Mem. ct. accreditation com. State of N.H., 1970-77, Regional Criminal Justice Planning Coun., 1978-88; ptnr. North Country TV Cable Co., Groveton, N.H., 1962-89; chmn. bd., chmn. exec. com. Berlin City Bank, 1975-87. Chmn. city Republican Conv., Berlin, 1952-54; bd. dirs. Rep. State Com., 1958-60; del. Rep. Nat Com., 1964; trustee A.V. Hosp., 1976-85, mem. coms., 1976-86; area chmn. fundraising campaigns including ARC, U. N.H. Centennial Fund, Crippled Children, N.H. Children's Aid Soc., Boy Scouts Am., Boston U. Law Sch. Centennial Fund, St. Paul's Sch. Advanced Studies Program, A.V. Hosp. Bldg. Fund maj. gifts program, Frank Kenison Fund Boston U. Law Sch.; mem. U. N.H. 50th Reunion Fund Raising Class of 1948, 1996-98. Served with USN, 1943-46. Recipient Silver Shingle award Boston U. Sch. Law, 1977, Alumni Meritorius award U. N.H., 1986. Fellow Am. Bar Found.; mem. N.H. Bar Assn. (pres. 1974-75, bd. govs. 1973-76), Coos County Bar Assn. (pres. various yrs.), Tri-Legal County Svcs., N.H. Alumni Assn. (bd. dirs. 1974-77), Boston U. Alumni Assn., Am. Legion (post judge adv. 1952-64), VFW (post judge adv. 1952-93), Nashua Country Club (Nashua, N.H.), Seven Lakes Country Club (Ft. Myers, Fla.), Kiwanis (pres. 1966). Lutheran. Home: 55 Hawthorne Village Rd Nashua NH 03062-2271 also: 13190 Oakmont Drive #8 Fort Myers FL 33907-8020 E-mail: dahanson@aol.com.

HANSON, ARTHUR STUART, physician, consultant; b. Mpls., Mar. 10, 1937; s. Arthur Emanuel and Frances Elenor (Larson) H.; m. Gail Joan Taylor, June 16, 1963; children: Marta Eileen, Peter Arthur. BA, Dartmouth Coll., 1959; MD, U. Minn., 1963. Diplomate Am. Bd. Internal Medicine, Am. Bd. Pulmonary Disease. Intern Hennipen County Med. Ctr., 1963-64; resident in internal medicine U. Minn., 1964-65, 68-70, fellow pulmonary disease, 1970-71; cons. Park Nicollet Clinic, Mpls., 1971—, med. dir., 1975-82, v.p. legis. and cmty. affairs, 1982-86; dir. med. edn. Park Nicollet Med. Found., Mpls., 1982-86; pres., CEO Park Nicollet Inst., Mpls., 1986—2002, cons. pulmonary medicine, 2002—. Bd. dirs. Minn. Health Data Inst., 1993-03. Pres., bd. chair Minn. Smoke Free Coalition, 1985-88, 96-98; chmn. bd. Smoke Free Generation Minn., 1984-90. Recipient Cmty. Leadership award, Am. Lung Assn. Hennepin County, 1987, Harvey H. Rogers Meml. award, Minn. Pub. Health Assn., 1988, award for excellence in health promotion, Minn. Health Commr., 1989, Physician of Excellence award, Park Nicollet Health Svcs., 2000, Lynn Smith 25-Yr. award, Am. Cancer Soc., 2001. Fellow ACP, AMA (del., chmn.), Am. Coll. Chest Physicians; mem. Minn. Med. Assn. (pres. 1992-93, Stop the Violence award 1994, Disting. Svc. award 1998), Minn. Healthcare Coalition on Violence, Hennepin County Med. Soc. (pres. 1990-91, Charles Bolles Bolles-Rogers award 1998). Unitarian Universalist. Avocations: birding, gardening, physical fitness, reading, traveling. Office: Park Nicollet Clinic Ste 300 6490 Excelsior Blvd Minneapolis MN 55426

HANSON, AVARITA LAUREL, lawyer; b. N.Y.C., July 21, 1953; d. Earle L. and Gloria (Troupe) H.; m. William A. Alexander, June 14, 1975; children: Justin, Colin. AB, Radcliffe Coll., 1975; JD, U. Pa., 1978. Bar: Tex. 1979, U.S. Ct. Appeals (5th cir.) 1980, U.S. Dist. Ct. (so. dist.) Tex. 1980, U.S. Dist. Ct. (no. dist.) Ga. 1981, U.S. Ct. Appeals (11th cir.) 1981, Ga. 1983. Assoc. Fulbright & Jaworski, Houston, 1978-82; pvt. practice Houston and Atlanta,

1982—; judge Fulton County Juvenile Ct., 1995-97; exec. dir. examining bds. divsn. Ga. Sec. of State, 1997-99; prof. John Marshall Law Sch., 2000—, acad. dean, 2001—. Ptnr. Secret & Assocs., Atlanta, 1983-84; dir. pro bono project Ga. Bar Assn. and Ga. Legal Svcs. Program, 1985-89; clk. Fulton County Commn., 1990-95; bd. dirs. Atlanta Legal Aid Soc., 1986—, Ga. Legal Svcs. Program, 1995—. Exec. producer TV show Legally Speaking, 1983-90. Candidate coun. City of College Park, Ga., 1985; trustee Ben Hill United Meth. Ch., 1985-88; bd. dirs. YWCA Greater Atlanta, 1989-92. Mem. Ga. Assn. Black Women Attys. (pres. 1985), Atlanta Bar Assn. (adv. bd. 1989—), Gate City Bar Assn. (pres. 1991), Leadership Atlanta, Leadership Ga. (bd. trustees), Radcliffe Coll. Alumnae Assn. (bd. dirs.), Atlanta Women's Network, Ga. Women's Polit Caucus, Harvard Club Ga. (pres. 1994, v.p. 1987-90), Harvard Alumni Assn. (bd. dirs. 1990-93, 95—), Leadership Am. Democrat. Avocation: gourmet cooking. Office: John Marshall Law Sch 1422 W Peachtree St Atlanta GA 30309 E-mail: avarita@aol.com.

HANSON, BRUCE EUGENE, lawyer; b. Lincoln, Nebr., Aug. 25, 1942; s. Lester E. and Gladys (Diessner) H.; m. Peggy Pardun, Dec. 25, 1972 (dec. Nov. 1989). BA, U. Minn., 1965, JD, 1966. Bar: Minn. 1966, U.S. Dist. Ct. Minn. 1966, U.S. Tax Ct. 1973, U.S. Ct. Appeals (8th cir.) 1973, U.S. Ct. Appeals (fed. cir.) 1983, U.S. Supreme Ct. 1970. Shareholder Doherty, Rumble & Butler, P.A., St. Paul, 1966-99; ptnr. Oppenheimer, Wolff & Donnelly, LLP, Mpls., 1999—. Dir., sec. Am. Saddlebred Horse Assn.; bd. trustees, chair United Hosp., 1996-98. Mem. ATLA, Hennepin County Bar Assn., Minn. State Bar Assn., Am. Health Lawyers Assn., Minn. Soc. Hosp. Attys., North Oaks Golf Club, Order of Coif, Phi Delta Phi. Home: 23 Evergreen Rd Saint Paul MN 55127-2077 Office: Oppenheimer Wolff & Donnelly LLP 45 S 7th St Ste 3300 Minneapolis MN 55402-1614 E-mail: BHanson@Oppenheimer.com.

HANSON, C. WILLIAM, III, anesthesiologist, educator; b. Harrisburg, Pa., June 5, 1955; s. Clarence William and Ann Morgan Hanson; m. Beth M. Hanson, Sept. 24, 1993; children: Addison, Watson, Callaghan. BA, Yale U., 1977; MD, U. Pa., 1983. Anesthesiologist Hosp. of U. Pa., Phila.; prof. U. Pa., Phila. Office: Hospital of the Univ of Pa 3400 Spruce St Philadelphia PA 19104-4283

HANSON, CARL MALMROSE, financial company executive; b. Boston, Aug. 25, 1941; BA, U. Mass., 1963; MBA, Dartmouth Coll., 1969. CPA, Mass. Acct. Coopers Lybrand, Boston, 1969-73; chief fin. officer South Shore Bank, Quincy, Mass., 1973-76; v.p. Multibank Fin. Corp., Quincy, Mass., 1976-79; pres. Multibank Leasing Corp., Quincy, Mass., 1979-80; contr. State St. Boston Corp., 1980-84; chief fin. officer Chase Bank Fla., St. Petersburg, 1984-87; contr. Bank New England, Boston, 1987-89; chief fin. officer Amoskeag Bank Shares, Manchester, N.H., 1989-92; exec. v.p. Kirchman Corp., Orlando, Fla., 1992-94, Globex Techknowledge Corp., Heathrow, Fla., 1994-95; pvt. practice fin. cons., 1995—; pvt. practice money mgr. Lt. USN, 1964-68. Mem. Fin. Execs. Inst. (treas. 1989-91).

HANSON, CURTIS JAMES, music educator, composer; b. Duluth, Minn., Oct. 3, 1953; s. Arthur Ferdinand and Mary Eileen Hanson; m. Brenda Jean Maertens; children: Eric, Evan. BS in Edn., Bemidji State U., 1975, MS in Edn., 1980; D in Musical Arts, U. Colo., 1990. Vocal music dir. grades K-12 Cottonwood (Minn.) Pub. Schs., 1978—87; grad. part-time instr. music U. Colo., Boulder, 1987—89; adj. instr. music U. Minn., Duluth, 1994—98; instr. voice, asst. dir. John Duss Music Conservatory, Duluth, 1995—. Adj. instr. music S.W. State U., Marshall, Minn., 1982—86; sr. choir dir. Christ the Servant Luth. Ch., Louisville, 1990—94, Our Savior's Luth. Ch., Duluth, 1996—2001, Pilgrim Luth. Ch., Superior, 2001—. Composer: (choral music) Silent Night, 1995, Beautiful Savior, 1995, numerous other choral works, (major choral work with orch.) Missa Millennia in Honor of St. Francis, 2000, Dona nobis pacem, 2001. Mem.: Music Educators Nat. Conf., Am. Choral Dirs. Assn., Nat. Assn. Tchrs. of Singing, Pi Kappa Lambda. Office: John Duss Music Conservatory 2211 Greysolon Rd Duluth MN 55812

HANSON, DANA W. dermatologist; b. Saint John, NB, Canada; m. Phyllis Hanson; children: Anthony, Julie, Natasha, Marc. BSc, U. New Brunswick, 1970; MD, Dalhousie U., 1974, postgrad. internal medicine; postgrad. dermatology, McGill U. Pvt. practice, Medicine Hat, Saint John, Canada; dermatologist Fredericton, Canada, 1980—. Chair bd. dirs. Beaverbrook Art Gallery, Fredericton. Fellow: Royal Coll. Physicians; mem.: Regional Health Corp., New Brunswick Med. Soc. (pres. 1992—93, chair bd. dirs.), Can. Dermatology Assn. (sec.-treas.), Can. Med. Assn. (dep. spkr. of gen. coun. 1994—98, spkr. gen. coun. 1998—2001, pres.-elect 2001—02). Avocation: Avocations: camping, bicycling, hiking, cross-country skiing, singing. Office: 1015 Regent Fredericton NB E3B 3Y9 Canada Address: Can Med Assn 1867 Alta Vista Dr Ottawa ON K1G 5W8 Canada

HANSON, DAVID ALAN, music educator; b. Bryan, OH, Dec. 6, 1945; s. Chester Adams and Mary Adele (Daenitz) Hanson; m. Lori Ray Stelzer, Aug. 16, 1960. MusB, Bowling Green State Univ., Bowling Green, OH, 1968; MusM, Univ. of Mich., Ann Arbor, Mich., 1972. Cert. Permanent Tchng. Certificate Ohio. Music ed. Findlay City Sch., Findlay, Ohio, 1968—2003, Heidelberg Coll., Tiffin, Ohio, 1974—2003, Bluffton Coll., Bluffton, Ohio, 2000—03. Prin. double Bass Lima Symphony, Lima, Ohio, 1968—74. Author: (7 music articles) Triad, (4 music articles) The Instrumentalist; composer: (compositions) 18 for brass, full orchestra, choir, guitar, double Bass- two publ. Recipient Outstanding Young Educator Award, Findlay Jaycees/ Findlay, OH, 1977, Tchr. Golden Apple Award, Findlay Rotary Club/Findlay, OH, 1996, D. Robert Baker Award, Findlay City Sch./Findlay, OH, 1999. Mem.: Am. String Tchr. Assoc., Ohio Music Ed. Assoc. (NW Region Chair), Music Ed. Nat. Conf., Findlay Arts Coun. Avocations: lepidoptera study, reading, photography, bicycling. Home: 1709 Forest Pk Findlay OH 45840

HANSON, DAVID JAMES, lawyer; b. Neenah, Wis., July 20, 1943; s. Vernon James and Dorothy O. Hanson; m. Diana G. Severson, Aug. 25, 1965 (div. Sept. 1982); children: Matthew Vernon, Maja Kirsten, Brian Edward; m. Linda Hughes Bochert, May 28, 1983; children: Scott Charles, Sarah Katherine. BS, U. Wis., 1965, JD, 1968. Bar: Wis. 1968, U.S. Dist. Ct. (we. dist.) Wis. 1968, U.S. Dist. Ct. (ea. dist.) Wis. 1969, U.S. Ct. Appeals (7th cir.) 1970, U.S. Supreme Ct. 1971. Asst. atty. gen. State of Wis. Dept. of Justice, Madison, 1968-71, dep. atty. gen., 1976-81; asst. chancellor, chief legal counsel U. Wis., Madison, 1971-76; ptnr. Michael, Best & Friedrich LLP, Madison, 1981—. Lectr. Law Sch., U. Wis., Madison, 1972-75; chair govt. law sect. State Bar Wis., Madison, 1979-88. Contbr. articles to profl. jours. Bd. dirs. Sand County Found., Madison, 1988—, Wis. Ctr. for Academically Talented Youth, Madison, 1991-94, trustee Edgewood Coll., Madison, 1997—. Mem. ABA, Madison Club, Blackhawk Country Club. Democrat. Unitarian Universalist. Avocations: canoeing, skiing, golf, biking, hunting. Office: Michael Best & Friedrich PO Box 1806 Madison WI 53701-1806 E-mail: djhanson@mbf-law.com.

HANSON, DAVID JUSTIN, sociology educator, researcher; b. Orlando, Fla., Aug. 10, 1941; s. George Dewey and Clair (Cameron) H.; m. Carol Ann Wenger, Aug. 1,1 964; 1 child, Cynthia Denice. BA cum laude, Fla. State U., 1963; MA, Syracuse U., 1967, PhD, 1972. Asst. prof. sociology SUNY Coll Arts & Sci., Potsdam, 1968-76, assoc. prof., 1976-82, chair dept. sociology, 1977-85, prof. sociology, 1982—, dir. MA program in human svc., 1983-88, dir. of assessment, 1989-95. Alcohol and alcohol abuse cons. for 3d edit. Books for Coll. Libis., ALA, Chgo., 1985-86; alcohol cons. Health Can., Ottawa, 1996. Author: Preventing Alcohol Abuse: Alcohol, Culture and Control, 1995, Alcohol Education: What We Must Do, 1996; editor: Current Social Research, 1993; contbr. articles to profl. jours. V.p. Alcohol and Substance Abuse Coun. of St. Lawrence County, Inc., Canton, N.Y., 1987-95. Recipient Award for Excellence, N.Y. State Sociol. Assn., 1987; grantee Rsch. Found. of SUNY, Albany, 1984. Mem. Phi Kappa Phi (pres. Potsdam chpt. 1991—), Alpha Kappa Delta, Phi Eta Sigma. Office: SUNY Potsdam Coll of Arts & Scis Pierrepont Ave Potsdam NY 13676 Home: 112 Breckenridge Pl Chapel Hill NC 27514-3253 E-mail: hansondj@potsdam.edu.

HANSON, DENNIS MICHAEL, medical imaging executive; b. Cleve., Aug. 20, 1943; s. John Joseph and Victoria (Tucholski) H. BBA, Cleve. State U., 1971; MPH, U. Pitts., 1974. Asst. adminstr. Huron Rd. Hosp., Cleve., 1974-76; adminstr. asst. Mt. Sinai Med. Ctr., Cleve., 1976-80; dir. radiology U. Louisville, Ky., 1980-84, assoc. prof., 1982-86; sr. cons. Honeywell, Mpls., 1986-87; mgr. radiology U. N.C., Chapel Hill, 1987-90; mgr. diagnostic imaging Kaiser Hosp., Honolulu, 1990-97. Cons. Dowdy Mgmt. and Consulting, Cocoa Beach, Fla., 1999-2000; radiol. tech. Norton Healthcare, Louisville, Ky. Councilman City of Meadowbrook Farm, Ky., 1982-86. With USAF, 1961-65. Named Ky. Colonel, 1984. Fellow Am. Coll. Healthcare Execs.; mem. Am. Hosp. Radiology Adminstrs. E mail: dmhansonmph@aol.com.

HANSON, DIANE CHARSKE, management consultant; b. Cleve., May 15, 1946; d. Howard Carl and Emma Katherine (Lange) Charske; m. William James Hanson, June 30, 1973. BS, Cornell U., 1968; MS, U. Pa., 1989. Home service rep. Rochester Gas and Electric, N.Y., 1968-70; home economist U. Conn., Storrs, 1970-72; job analyst personnel dept. State of Conn., Hartford, 1972-73; sales rep. Ayerst Labs., Waterbury, Conn., 1973-80, sales trainer, 1979-80; dist. sales mgr. Phila., 1980-87; pres. Creative Resource Devel., W. Chester, Pa., 1986—. Developer, pres. Womens Referral Network, West Chester, 1987-89. Vice-pres., bd. dirs., aux. pres. Chester County Soc. for Prevention Cruelty to Animals, 1986-97, pres. bd. dirs., 1992-94, mem. exec. com., 1994-95. Mem. ASTD (v.p. comm. Phila./Delaware Valley chpt. 1991-92, pres. Del. chpt. 1999-2002), Internat. Soc. for Performance Improvement (v.p. programs Great Valley chpt. 1993-94, pres.-elect 1995, pres. 1996), Pa. State Tech. Devel. Ctr. (bd. dirs. 1991-92), Assn. Quality and Participation, Phila. Soc. for Human Resources, Phila. Human Resources Planning Group, Phila. Orgn. Devel. Network, Chester County Human Resources Assn. (program chair 1991-92), Greater Valley Forge Human Resources Assn. (bd. dirs. 1993-94). Avocations: skiing, tennis, gardening, sailing, exercise. Home and Office: 824 W Strasburg Rd West Chester PA 19382-1927 E-mail: hanson@team-doctor.com.

HANSON, DORENE KAY, engineering draftsman; b. Lemmon, S.D., Jan. 22, 1960; d. Donald Patrick Hanson and Joyce E. Van Cleave. Assoc. Degree in Tech. Drafting, Black Hills State Coll., 1981. Rodman U.S. Geol. Survey, Independence, Mo., 1978-79, 81-83; janitor Bison (S.D.) Sch. Dist., 1979-80; transp. aide S.D. Transp. Dept., Belle Fourche, 1980-81; engring. draftsman III Western Area Power Adminstrn., Watertown, S.D., 1983—. Vol. Spl. Olympics, Watertown, Kampeska Days Com., Watertown, 1985—94; co-chair Watertown Ladies Ducks-Ducks Unltd. Vol. Recipient Cert. of Excellence, Source One Mgmt., Inc., Watertown, 1990, Kampeska Day Spirit award Kampeska Day Com., Watertown, 1991. Avocations: stamps, arts and crafts, volleyball, bowling. Office: Western Area Power Adminstrn 1330 41st St SE Watertown SD 57201 Fax: 605-882-7409. E-mail: fireworksfrun@wat.midco.net., dhanson@wapa.gov.

HANSON, FLOYD BLISS, applied mathematician, computational scientist, mathematical biologist; b. Bklyn., Mar. 9, 1939; s. Charles Keld and Violet Ellen (Bliss) H.; m. Ethel Louisa Hutchins, July 27, 1962; 1 child, Lisa Kirsten BS, Antioch Coll., 1962; MS, Brown U., 1964, PhD, 1968. Space technician Convair Astronautics, San Diego, 1961; applied mathematician Arthur D. Little, Inc., Cambridge, Mass., 1961; physicist Wright-Patterson AFB, Dayton, Ohio, 1962; assoc. research scientist Courant Inst., N.Y.C., 1967-68; asst. prof. U. Ill., Chgo., 1969-75, assoc. prof., 1975-83, prof., 1983—, assoc. dir. Lab. for Advanced Computing, 1990—, assoc. dir. Lab. for Control & Info., 1993—. Faculty rsch. participant Argonne (Ill.) Nat. Lab., 1985-87, faculty rsch. leave, 1987-88, rsch. assoc., 1988; vis. prof., divsn. applied math. Brown U., 1994; mem. vis. faculty Sch. Civil and Environ. Engring., Cornell U., 1995. Assoc. editor-in-chief Applied and Computational Control Signals and Circuits, 1996—; author: (with others) Control and Dynamical Systems: Advances in Theory and Applications, 1996; contbr. articles in field to profl. jours. Recipient UIC CETL Tchr. Recognition award, 1999, Premiere UIC award for excellence in Tchg., 2001—02; grantee rsch. grantee, NSF, 1970—83, 1988—, NSF equipment grantee, 1973, computer grantee, Nat. Ctr. Supercomputer Applications, 1986—, supercomputer grantee, Los. Alamos Nat. Lab., 1990—97, Cornell Theory Ctr., 1993—96, Pitts. Supercomputer Ctr., 1993—98, 2003—, San Diego Supercomputer Ctr., 1998—. Mem. IEEE (sr., tech. com. on control edn. appointment, 2002), Soc. Indsl. and Applied Math., Computer Soc. of IEEE, Control Sys. Soc. of IEEE, Resource Modeling Assn. Home: 5435 S East View Park Chicago IL 60615-5915 Office: U Ill Dept Math Stats and Computer Sci M/C 249 851 S Morgan St Rm 322 Chicago IL 60607-7042 E-mail: hanson@uic.edu.

HANSON, GARY A. lawyer, legal educator, university administrator; b. Santa Fe, Sept. 30, 1954; s. Norman A. Hanson and Mary Gene (Moore) Garrison; m. Tracey J. Tannen, Mar. 11, 1982; children: Paul, Carly, Sean. BS magna cum laude, U. Utah, 1976; JD, Pepperdine U., 1980. Bar: Calif. 1980, U.S. Dist. Ct. (cen. dist.) Calif. 1980, U.S. Ct. Appeals (9th cir.) 1980. Pvt. practice, Westlake Village, Calif., 1980-82; assoc. gen. counsel Pepperdine U., Malibu, Calif., 1982-83, acting gen. counsel, 1983-84, univ. gen. counsel, 1984—2000, v.p., gen. counsel, 2000—. Adj. prof. law Pepperdine U., Malibu, 1982—, lectr. bus. law, 1986—; pro bono atty. San Fernando Valley Christian Sch., L.A., 1982-83; mem. Pro Bono Estate Adv. Svc., San Diego, 1983-86; cons. West Ednl. Pub. Co., 1988. Contbr. articles to profl. jours.; pres. Ind. Colls. and Univs. jour., 1989. Recipient Pres.'s award San Diego Christian Found., 1984. Mem. ABA, L.A. County Bar Assn., Nat. Assn. Coll. and Univ. Attys. Republican. Office: Pepperdine U 24255 Pacific Coast Hwy Malibu CA 90263-4607

HANSON, GERALD EUGENE, oral and maxillofacial surgeon; b. Lincoln, Nebr., July 18, 1947; s. Gerald Stephen and Ferne Althea (Russell) H. DDS, MPH, Loma Linda U., 1973; oral & maxillofacial surgery cert., U. Minn., 1976. Diplomate Am. Bd. Forensic Dentistry. Pvt. practice, Palm Desert, Calif., 1976-78, Las Vegas, Nev., 1978—. Mem. com. edn. & rsch. Eisenhower Med. Ctr., Rancho Mirage, Calif., 1977, dir. continuing dental edn. program, 1977-78; chief divsn. oral & maxillofacial surgery Sunrise Hosp., 1984-94, Columbia Mountain View Hosp., 1995—. Rep. environ. reference com. joint policy coun. APHA, Washington, 1977; bd. dirs. Clark County chpt. Am. Cancer Soc., 1979-83; chmn. oral cancer screening clinics Jaycees State Fair & Annual Health Fair, Las Vegas, 1981; adv. bd. Clark County C.C., Las Vegal, 1979; mem. Nev. State Bd. Health, 1990-95; treas., bd. dirs. Am. Assn. Oral and Maxillofacial Surgery Found., 1995—. Fellow Pierre Fauchard Acad., Internat. Coll. Dentists, Western Soc. Oral & Maxillofacial Surgeons (bd. dirs. 1981-83, 91-97, pres. 1995-96), Am. Assn. Oral & Maxillofacial Surgeons (trustee Dist. VI 1984-88, Nev. del. 1979-83, sec.-treas. 1988-91), Am. Coll. Dentistry; mem. ADA (chmn. sci. session 1982, mem. coun. hosp. affairs 1985-89, AAOMS rep. interprofl. rels. com. 1987), Nev. Dental Assn. (co-chmn. group care & hosp. svcs. com. 1979-84, Clark County del. Ho. Dels. 1980-84, pres. 1987), Am. Coll. Oral & Maxillofacial Surgeons, Nev. Soc. of Oral and Maxillofacial Surgeons (pres. 1983-85), Am. Assn. Oral and Maxillofacial Surgery Found. (bd. dirs. 1995—), Las Vegas Execs. Assn., Clark County Aviation Assn. (pres. 1999), Clark County Dental Soc. (pres. 1982-83). Avocations: flying, antique airplane collecting, music, diving, skiing. Office: 2585 S Jones Blvd Ste 1A Las Vegas NV 89146-5604

HANSON, GERALD WARNER, retired county official; b. Alexandria, Minn., Dec. 25, 1938; s. Lewis Lincoln and Dorothy Hazel (Warner) H.; m. Sandra June Wheeler, July 9, 1960; 1 child, Cynthia R. AA, San Bernardino Valley (Calif.) Coll., 1959; BA, U. Redlands (Calif.), 1979; MA, U. Redlands, 1981; EdD, Pepperdine U., 1995. Cert. advanced metrication specialist. Dep. sealer San Bernardino (Calif.) County, 1964-80, div. chief, 1980-85, dir. weights and measures, 1985-94; CATV cons. City of Redlands, 1996—, City of Yucaipa, 1998-99. Substitute tchr. Redlands Unified Sch. Dist., 1996—. Chmn. Redlands Rent Rev. Bd., 1985-99; bd. dirs. House Neighborly Svc., Redlands, 1972-73, Boys Club, Redlands, 1985-86, mem. Redlands Planning commn., 1990-98. With USN. Fellow U.S. Metric Assn. (treas. 1986-88, 92—); mem. NRA (life), Nat. Conf. on Weights and Measures (life, asst. treas. 1986-94), Western Weights and Measures Assn. (life, pres. 1987-88), Calif. Assn. Weights and Measures Ofcls. (life, 1st v.p. 1987), Calif. Rifle and Pistol Assn. (life), Masons, Shriners, Kiwanis (treas. Redlands club 1983-95), Over the Hill Gang (San Bernardino, newsletter editor 1998-2000). Avocations: golf, digital photography, mechanics, microcomputers. Home: 225 E Palm Ave Redlands CA 92373-6131 E-mail: doctorjer@hotmail.com.

HANSON, GLEN R. federal agency administrator; DDS, UCLA; PhD, U. Utah. Fellow Nat. Inst. Health Pharmacology Rsch. Assocs. Tng. Program, 1978—80; prof., dept. pharmacology and toxicology U. Utah; dir., divsn. neuroscience and behavioral rsch. Nat. Inst. Drug Abuse, 2000—, acting dir., 2001—. Mem. editl. bd. Jour. Pharmacology and Experimental Therapeutics. Office: 6001 Executive Blvd Rm 5274 Bethesda MD 20892-9581

HANSON, HAROLD PALMER, physicist, government official, editor, academic administrator; b. Virginia, Minn., Dec. 27, 1921, s. Martin Bernhard and Elvida Elaine (Paulsen) H.; m. Mary Jean Stevenson, June 22, 1944; children: Steven Bernard, Barbara Jean. BS, Superior (Wis.) State Coll., 1942; MS, U. Wis., 1944, PhD, 1948. Mem. faculty U. Fla., 1948-54, dean grad. sch., 1969-71, v.p. acad. affairs, 1971-74, exec. v.p., 1974-78, exec. v.p. emeritus, 1990—; mem. faculty U. Tex., Austin, 1954-69, prof. physics, 1961-69, chmn. dept., 1962-69; provost Boston U., 1978-79; exec. dir. Com. on Sci. and Tech., U.S. Ho. of Reps., Washington, 1979-82, 84-90; provost Wayne State U., Detroit, 1982-84. Summer rsch. physicist Lincoln Labs., MIT, 1953, Gen. Atomic Co., San Diego, 1964; summer vis. lectr. U. Wis., 1957; Fulbright rsch. scholar, Norway, 1960-61. Editor DELOS, 1991—. Bd. dirs. N. Central Fla. Health Planning Coun.; mem. steering com. Fla. Ednl. Computer Network. With USNR, 1944-46. Decorated St. Olav's medal Norway, Order of North Star 1st class Sweden; U. Fla. presdl. scholar, 1976 Fellow Am. Phys. Soc.; mem. Sigma Xi, Sigma Pi Sigma, Omicron Delta Kappa. Clubs: Town and Gown (Austin); Rotary. Office: U Fla 118 440 2346 NPB Gainesville FL 32611-2085 E-mail: hanson@phys.ufl.edu.

HANSON, HEIDI ELIZABETH, lawyer; b. Portsmouth, Ohio, Nov. 13, 1954; BS, U. Ill., 1975, JD, 1978. Bar: Ill. 1978, U.S. Dist. Ct. (no. dist.) Ill., U.S. Ct. Appeals (7th cir.). Atty. water, air and land pollution divs. Ill. EPA, Springfield, Ill., 1978-85, atty. water pollution div. Maywood, Ill., 1985-86; assoc. Ross & Hardies, Chgo., 1987-89, ptnr., 1990-94; founder H.E. Hanson Law Offices, Western Springs, Ill., 1994—. Named hon. Ky. Col., 2000. Mem.: Indsl. Water, Waste and Sewer Group, Air and Waste Mgmt. Assn., Chgo. Bar Assn., Chicagoland C. of C. Avocation: gardening. Office: 4721 Franklin Ave Ste 1500 Western Springs IL 60558-1720

HANSON, J. DONALD, retired diversified financial services company executive; Chartered acct. With Arthur Andersen & Co., 1958—, mng. ptnr., 1968-82, London, 1982-89, mng. ptnr. strategic affairs and comm. London, N.Y., Chgo., 1989-93, mng. ptnr. ptnr. matters and comm. N.Y.C., 1993-98; ret, cons. to London office, 1998—. Pres. Profl. Svcs. Ins. Co., Bermuda; bd. dirs., chmn. investment com. Profl. Asset Indemnity Ltd., Bermuda. Mem. ct., chmn. superannuation fund Manchester U.

HANSON, JANICE CRAWFORD, artist, financial analyst; b. Norwalk, Conn., Oct. 8, 1952; d. Arthur James and Jean Alice (MacKinnon) Crawford; m. Jeffrey Becker Hanson, May 29, 1976; children: Forrest James, Shane Crawford. BA, Wellesley Coll., 1974; MBA, U. Denver, 1979. CFA. Sec. to assoc. dean Yale Sch. of Music, New Haven, Conn., 1975-76; adminstrv. asst. to dir. of internships Inst. Policy Scis. Duke U., Durham, N.C., 1976-78; fiscal analyst Denver Water Bd., 1979-84; fin. analyst Englewood, Colo., 1984; part-time fin. analyst Jeffrey B. Hanson M.D., P.C., Granger, Ind., 1989-92; part-time watercolorist Englewood, Colo., 1989—. Exhibitions include group shows Watercolor West Exhbn., Riverside, Calif., 1995, 1999, Western Colo. Watercolor Soc. Nat. Juried Exhbn., Grand Junction, Colo., 1994, 1995, 1996, 2000, Rocky Mountain Nat. Watermedia Exhbn., Golden, Colo., 1996, 1998, 2002, Pikes Peak Watercolor Soc. Internat. Exhbn., Colo. Springs, Colo., 1997, 1998, 2000, Am. Women Artists Nat. Juried Competition, Taos, N.Mex., 1999, Nat. Watercolor Soc. Annual Exhbn., Brea, Calif., 2001, exhibitions include group show Pikes Peak Watercolor Soc. Internat. Exhbn., Colo. Springs, 2003, We. Fedn. Watercolor Soc., 2002, 2003. Vol. Denver Dumb Friends League, 1986-88, Cherry Creek Schs., Englewood, Colo., 1992—. Recipient Best of Show award Nat. Greeley Art Mart, 1994, Platinum award, Nat. Greeley Art Mart, 1995, Dean Witter award for originality Colo. Watercolor Soc. State Juried Exhbn., 1996, WinsorNewton Merchandise award, 1999, Daler-Rowney award Pikes Peak Watercolor Soc. Internat. Exhbn., 2000, Betty Simpson award Rocky Mountain Nat. Watermedia Exhbn., 2002; Am. Women Artists scholar, 1999. Mem.: Denver Soc. Security Analysts, Western Colo. Watercolor Soc. (signature), Colo. Watercolor Soc. (signature), Watercolor West (juried assoc.), Assn. for Investment Mgmt. and Rsch., Nat. Watercolor Soc. (signature). Avocations: running, fiber arts, needlework, photography.

HANSON, JASON DAVID, lawyer; b. L.A., Feb. 14, 1969; s. William Dean and Merrilyn Ethyl (Coleman) H. BS, Cornell U., 1991; JD, Duke U., 1994. Bar: Md. 1994, D.C. 1995. Assoc. Arnold & Porter, Washington, 1994-97; trial atty. anti trust divsn. U.S. Dept. Justice, Washington, 1997-99; global litigation counsel GE Med. Sys., Milw., 1999—2001, gen. counsel Americas, 2001—. Staff editor: Duke Law Jour., 1993-94. Mem. ABA. Office: Dept of Justice Anti Trust Divsn 1401 H St NW Ste 3700 Washington DC 20005-2110

HANSON, JEAN ELIZABETH, lawyer; b. Alexandria, Minn., June 28, 1949; d. Carroll Melvin and Alice Clarissa (Frykman) H.; m. H. Barndt Hauptfuhrer, May 15, 1982; children: Catherine Jean, Benjamin Colman (twins). BA, Luther Coll., 1971; JD, U. Minn., 1976. Bar: N.Y. 1977, U.S. Dist. Ct. (so. dist.) 1977. Probation officer Hennepin County, Mpls., 1972-73; law clk. Minn. State Pub. Defender, Mpls., 1975-76; assoc. Fried, Frank, Harris, Shriver & Jacobson, N.Y.C., 1976-83, ptnr., 1983-93, 94—. Gen. counsel U.S. Treasury, Washington, 1993-94; mem. bd. regents Luther Coll.; mem. bd. visitors Law Sch. U. Minn. Recipient Disting. Svc. award Luther Coll., 1991, Outstanding Achievement award U. Minn., 1999. Mem. ABA, N.Y. State Bar Assn., Assn. of Bar of City of N.Y. (securities regulation com. 1991-98, mem. task force women in the profession 1995-98), U. Minn. Law Alumni Assn. Democrat. Lutheran. Office: Fried Frank Harris Shriver & Jacobson One New York Plaza New York NY 10004 E-mail: jean.hanson@ffhsj.com.

HANSON, JEANNE SUTLEY, accountant; b. Jackson, Miss., Mar. 29, 1946; d. Cecil C. and Ella Jane (Inman) Sutley; m. Thomas C. Hanson, Feb. 13, 1970; (div. Dec. 1987); children: Molly, Clayton. BS, U. Ark., Little Rock, 1980. CPA, Ark. Proof clk. First Nat. Bank, Little Rock, Ark., 1966-68; programmer, analyst Commercial Nat. Bank, Little Rock, 1968-73, Poly-Tech Systems, Inc., Little Rock, 1974-77, staff acct. E. L. Gaunt & Co., Little Rock, 1980-82, Patricia Fletcher, CPA, Little Rock, 1982-83; pvt. practice, acctg. Little Rock, 1983-87; ptnr. Wm. R. Kremer, Ltd., Little Rock, 1987-88; tax mgr. IDS Tax Svcs., Little Rock, 1988-92; pvt. practice Little Rock, 1993—. Mem. AICPA, Ark. Soc. CPA's, Am. Soc. Women Accts., Civitan (gov. Ozark dist. 1997-98). Methodist. Avocations: needlecrafts, reading, dancing, swimming, walking. Home: 2221 Wentwood Valley Dr Apt 35 Little Rock AR 72212-3627 Office: 5800 A St Little Rock AR 72205-3302

HANSON, JO, artist, lecturer, writer; b. Carbondale, Ill. d. Thomas A. and Carrie M. H. MA in Art, San Francisco State U.; MA in Edn, U. Ill. Past instr. sculpture U. Calif., Berkeley, Calif. Coll. Arts and Crafts, Oakland. Participant art panels Women's Caucus for Art and Coll. Art Assn., 1979, 81, 89, 91, 93, 99, Exploratorium Symposium, "Rising Above Our Garbage", San Francisco, 1994; co-curator Living in Balance, San Francisco Internat. Airport and Richmond Art Ctr., 1993, 94, Dear Mother Earth, Marin County Civic Ctr., 1998; moderator Bioneers Conf. panels on art and ecology, 1999-2002; presenter Soc. for Ecol. Restoration, 1999; subject of "Life Messages" book by Josephine Carleton, Andreus McMeel, 2002. Author: Artists' Taxes, The Hands-on Guide, 1987; co-prodr. Women Environment Artists Directory, 1996—; one-woman shows of sculpture and installations include, Corcoran Gallery Art, Washington, 1974, Pa. Acad. Fine Arts, Phila., 1976, Utah Mus. Fine Arts, Salt Lake City, 1977, San Francisco Mus. Modern Art, 1976, 80, Internat. Sculpture Conf., San Francisco, 1982, Internat. Conf. Healthy Cities, San Francisco, 1993, Dublin (Calif.) Civic Ctr., 1994, Fresno Art Mus., 1998; exhibited in group shows at San Francisco Mus. Modern Art, 1978, Museau de Arte Contemporanea da U. de São Paulo, Brazil, 1980, Pratt Manhattan Center, N.Y.C., 1981, Auckland City Art Gallery, N.Z., 1985, Municipal Art Soc., N.Y. 1990, John F. Kennedy U., San Francisco, 2001, Yerba Buena Ctr., San Francisco, 2002; represented in permanent collections including Herbert F. Johnson Mus. Cornell U., Fresno (Calif.) Art Mus., Mills Coll., Oakland, Calif., Oakland Mus. of Art, San Francisco Arts Commn., San Francisco Mus. Modern Art, numerous pvt. collections. San Francisco Arts commn., 1982-89; adv. bd. artist-in-residence Exploratorium, San Francisco, 1983-91; originator, advisor artist-in-residence program San. Fill Co., San Francisco, 1989—; advisor art and ecology Bioneers Conf., 1999—, EarthLight Mag., 1999—. Recipient citation San Francisco Bd. Suprs., 1980,

San Francisco mayor, 1989, Honor award Bioneers Conf., 2000; named Disting. Woman Artist of Yr., Fresno (Calif.) Art Mus., 1998; Nat. Endowment for Arts fellow, 1977, grantee, 1980. Mem. Coll. Art Assn. (co-chair panel art and ecology 1999), Women's Caucus for Art (Regional Lifetime Achievement award 1992, Nat. Lifetime Achievement award 1997), Pacific Rim Sculptors Group.

HANSON, JOHN M. civil engineering and construction educator; b. Brookings, S.D., Nov. 16, 1932; m. Mary Josephson, Jan. 16, 1960 (dec. 1999). BSCE, S.D. State U., 1949; MS in Structural Engring., Iowa State U., 1957; PhD in Civil Engring., Lehigh U., 1964. Profl. engr. Ill., N.C., Colo., Oreg., Mich. Structural engr. J.T. Banner & Assoc., Laramie, Wyo., 1957-58, Phillips, Carter, Osborn, Denver, 1958-60; research inst. prof. Lehigh U., Bethlehem, Pa., 1960-65; engr., asst. mgr. structural devel. Portland Cement Assn., Skokie, Ill., 1965-72; rsch. dir., v.p., pres. Wiss, Janney, Elstner Assocs., Northbrook, Ill., 1972-92; disting. prof. civil engring. and constrn. N.C. State U., Raleigh, 1993-2000, cons. engr., 2000—. Contbr. articles to profl. jours. Served to lt. USAF, 1953-55, Korea Recipient Disting. Engr. award S.D. State U., 1979; Profl. Achievement citation Iowa State U., 1980 Fellow Prestressed Concrete Inst. (bd. dirs. 1977-80, 93-95, Korn award 1978); mem. ASCE (hon., State of Art award 1974, Reese award 1976, 88, T.Y. Lin award 1979, Boase award 1995, Forensic Engring. award 1999), Am. Concrete Inst. (hon., bd. dirs. 1981-84, 88-94, v.p. 1988-89, pres. 1990, Bloem award 1976, Henry Crown award Ill. chpt. 1993), Internat. Assn. Bridge and Structural Engring. (hon., pres. 1993-97), Internat. Concrete Repair Inst. Lutheran. E-mail: jmhanson@nc.rr.com.

HANSON, JOHN C. investment company executive; Ltd. ptnr. Brown Bros. Harriman & Co., N.Y.C.

HANSON, JOHN J. lawyer; b. Aurora, Nebr., Oct. 22, 1922; s. Peter E. and Hazel Marion (Lounsbury) H.; m. Elizabeth Anne Moss, July 1, 1973; children from their previous marriages— Mark, Eric, Gregory. AB, U. Denver, 1948; LL.B. cum laude, Harvard U., 1951. Bar: N.Y. bar 1952, Calif. bar 1955. Asso. firm Dewey, Ballantine, Bushby, Palmer & Wood, N.Y.C., 1951-54; ptnr. firm Gibson, Dunn & Crutcher, L.A, 1954—, mem. exec. com., 1978-87, adv. ptnr., 1991—. Contbr. articles to profl. jours. Trustee Palos Verdes (Calif.) Sch. Dist., 1969-73. Served with U.S. Navy, 1942-45. Fellow Am. Coll. Trial Lawyers; mem. Am. Bar Assn., Los Angeles County Bar Assn. (chmn. antitrust sect. 1979-80), Bel Air Country Club. Home: 953 Linda Flora Dr Los Angeles CA 90049-1630 Office: Gibson Dunn & Crutcher 333 S Grand Ave Ste 4400 Los Angeles CA 90071-3197

HANSON, JOHN MARK, ecologist, researcher; b. Ottawa, Ont., Can., Apr. 14, 1955; s. Albert John and Mary Margaret (Pender) H.; m. Catherine Mary Merlin, May 31, 1980; children: Margaret Anne, Jennifer Theresa, Brian Joseph. MSc, U. Ottawa, 1980; PhD, McGill U., 1985. Postdoctoral fellow U. Alta., Edmonton, Can., 1985-89; vis. fellow Halifax (N.S.) Fisheries Rsch. Lab., 1989-90; rsch. scientist Dept. Fisheries and Oceans, Moncton, Canada, 1990—, editor secondary publs. div. marine and anadromous fish, 1991-93, co-editor secondary publs. sci. br., 2001—02. Referee numerous jours. in fisheries and aquatic scis. in N.Am. and Europe; mem. groundfish subcom. Can. Atlantic Fisheries Sci. Adv. Com., Dartmouth, N.S., 1990-93, mem. groundfish com. and marine mammals stock assessment com., 1993-96; mem. molluscan subcom. of Com. on the Status of Endangered Wildlife in Can. Co-author: Atlas of Alberta Lakes, 1990; contbr. articles to jours. in field. Postgrad. fellow Natural Scis. and Engring. Rsch. Coun. Can., 1981-83, postdoctoral fellow, 1986-88, vis. fellow, Halifax, 1989-90. Mem. Can. Soc. Zoologists, Ecol. Soc. Am. (cert. sr. ecologist), Am. Fisheries Soc. (cert. fisheries scientist), Can. Coun. for Fisheries Rsch., N.Am. Benthological Soc., Estuarine Rsch. Found. Achievements include research in aquatic ecology, ecology of fishes, bivalve molluscs, and crustaceans in freshwater and marine habitats, marine invasive species. Office: Gulf Fisheries Ctr PO Box 5030 Moncton NB Canada E1C 9B6 E-mail: hansonm@dfo-mpo.gc.ca.

HANSON, KAREN, philosopher, educator; b. Lincoln, Nebr., Apr. 11, 1947; d. Lester Eugene and Gladys (Diessner) H.; m. Dennis Michael Senchuk, Aug. 22, 1970; children: Tia Elizabeth, Chloe Miranda. BA summa cum laude, U. Minn., 1970; MA, PhD, Harvard U., 1980. Lectr. to assoc. prof. Ind. U., Bloomington, 1976-91, prof. philosophy, 1991—, Rudy prof., 2001—, adj. prof. Am. studies, gender studies & comparative lit., 1991—, chair philosophy, 1997—2002, dean Honors Coll., 2002—. Mem. governing bd. Ind. U. Inst. for Advanced Study, Bloomington, 1992-95, Ind. U. Soc. for Advanced Study, 2001-02; mem. editl. bd. Peirce Edition Project, Indpls., 1982-89, 90—. Author: The Self Imagined, 1986; co-editor: Romantic Revolutions, 1990; assoc. editor Jour. Social Philosophy, 1982-86; mem. editl. bd. Philosophy of Music Edn. Rev., 1992—, Notre Dame Philosophical Reviews, 2001-, Essays in Philosophy, 2000-, Symploke, 1998-; editl. cons. Am. Philos. Quar., 1995-99; contbr. articles to profl. books and jours. Del. Am. Coun. Learned Socs., 1993-98 (exec. com., 1994-98); officer John Dewey Found., 1989—. Scholar Disting. scholar, Office Women's Affairs, 1995. Mem. Am. Philos. Assn. (exec. officer 1986-91, 2000-03, program com. 1984-91, nominating com. 1993-94, 95-96, chair com. priorities and problems 1998-2000), Am. Soc. for Aesthetics (program com. 1989-90, 98-2000, trustee 1997-2000), Soc. for Women in Philosophy, Phi Beta Kappa (exec. com. Gamma of Ind. chpt. 1993-97, 2002—, officer 1995-97, 2002—, pres. 1996-97). Home: 1606 S Woodruff Ln Bloomington IN 47401-4448 Office: Ind U Dept of Philosophy Sycamore 026 Bloomington IN 47405

HANSON, KAREN LYNN, editor; b. Danville, N.J., Dec. 1, 1977; d. George Dewey and Harriet Mae Hanson. BS in Journalism, Ohio U., 2000. Regional sales coord. OBIE Media, Cleve.; assoc. editor Eastword Publs. Devel., Cleve. Author (mag.) Southest Ohio, 1999. Mem.: Severance Athletic Club. Presbyterian. Avocations: exercise, writing. Home: 2027 Lee Rd # 302 Cleveland Heights OH 44118 Office: Eastword Publs Devel Cleveland OH 44115

HANSON, KENT BRYAN, lawyer; b. Litchfield, Minn., Sept. 17, 1954; s. Calvin Bryan and Muriel (Wessman) H.; m. Barbara Jane Elenbaas, Aug. 24, 1974; children: Lindsay Michal, Taylor Jordan, Chase Philip. AA with high honors, Trinity Western Coll., 1974; BA, U. B.C., Vancouver, 1976; JD magna cum laude, U. Minn., 1979. Bar: Minn. 1979, U.S. Dist. Ct. Minn. 1980, U.S. Ct. Appeals (8th cir.) 1980, U.S. Dist. Ct. (we. dist.) Wis. 1983, Wis. 1985, U.S. Ct. Appeals (9th cir.) 1989, U.S. Dist. Ct. Ariz. 1992, Ohio 1993, Calif. 1994. Assoc. Grossman, Karlins, Siegel & Brill, Mpls., 1979-81, Gray, Plant, Mooty, Mooty & Bennett, Mpls., 1981-85; ptnr. Bowman & Brooke, Mpls., 1986-95; CEO Hanson, Marek, Bolkcom & Greene, Ltd., Mpls., 1996—. Bd. dirs. Inner City Boys Club, Ctrl. Free Ch., Mpls., 1979-81; 12th ward del. Mpls. Dem. Farmer Labor Com. Conv., 1982; mem. exec. bd. Ctrl. Free Ch., Mpls., 1986; chair exec. bd. Ctrl. Community Ch., 1993-96. Mem. ABA, State Bar Assn. Wis., Minn. Def. Lawyers Assn., Minn. State Bar Assn., Hennepin County Bar Assn., Calif. State Bar Assn., State Bar of Ohio, Def. Rsch. Inst. Avocations: classical music, golf, tennis, computers, motorcycles. Office: Hanson Marek Bolkcom & Greene Ltd 2200 Rand Tower 527 Marquette Ave Minneapolis MN 55402-1302

HANSON, KERMIT OSMOND, business administration educator, university dean emeritus; b. Troy Twp., Iowa, May 14, 1916; s. Gerhard Severin and Sunniva Fosmark (Borge) H.; m. Jane Elizabeth Haugen, Aug. 17, 1940; children: James Stephen, Katherine Jane, Paul Richard, Daniel Gerhard. AB cum laude, Luther Coll., Decorah, Iowa, 1938; MS, Iowa State U., 1940, PhD, 1950; D.Sc. (hon.), Luther Coll., 1981. Ops. analyst Fed. Land Bank, Omaha, 1941-43; chief statis. service sect. VA br. office, Seattle, 1946-47; mem. faculty Sch. Bus. Adminstrn., U. Wash., Seattle, 1948-81, prof. acctg., finance and statistics, 1954-81, chmn. dept. accounting, finance and statistics, 1955-60, assoc. dean, 1959-64; dean Sch. Bus. Adminstrn., U. Wash. (Grad. Sch. Bus. Adminstrn.), 1964-81, dean emeritus, 1981—; John F. Mee Disting. prof. Sch. Bus. Adminstrn. Pacific Luth. U., 1985-86. Instr., ednl. dir. Pacific Coast Banking Sch., 1948-81, also mem. bd. dirs.; exec. dir Pacific Rim Bankers Program, 1977-89, vice chmn. bd. dirs., 1979-98, chmn. emeritus, 1998—; bd. dirs. Pacific Horizon Funds, Inc., 1982-98, Wash. Fed. Savs. & Loan Assn., 1966—, Seafirst Retirement trust, 1993-97, Safeco Corp., 1976-81; cons. GAO, 1970-78; chmn. Wash. Gov.'s Adv. Coun. on Productivity, 1974-75; mem. bd. adv. Naval Postgrad. Sch., Monterey, Calif., 1976-84. Author: Managerial Statistics, 1955, 2d edit. (with G. Brabb), 1961, (with M. Tomich) (monograph) Pacific Rim Bankers Program—A Brief History—The First Ten Years 1977-1986, 1987, The Pacific Coast Banking School—The First 50 Years, 1988. Mem. adv. com. Chief Seattle coun. Boy Scouts Am., 1958—, pres., 1967-69; bd. trustees Horizon House, 1990-96, pres., 1994-96; mem. adv. bd. U. Miami (Fla.) Sch. Bus., 1983-88, Pacific Luth. U. Sch. Bus., Tacoma, 1987-90, Seattle Pacific U. Sch. Bus., 1985-90; bd. dirs. Journey for Perspective Found., 1964-76. Lt. USNR, 1943-46. Recipient Silver Beaver award Seattle council Boy Scouts Am., 1963, Disting. Service award U. Wash., 1981, Pioneer Meml. award Luther Coll., 1997. Mem. Am. Assn.. Collegiate Schs. Bus. (pres. 1971-72), Am. Accounting Assn., Am. Finance Assn., Financial Execs. Inst., Beta Gamma Sigma, Beta Alpha Psi, Alpha Kappa Psi. Lutheran. Home: 17760 14th Ave NW Shoreline WA 98177-3207

HANSON, LEE CRAIG, physician; b. Duluth, Minn., Aug. 12, 1952; s. LeRoy Charles Hanson and Joann Isabel Brochman; m. Debbie Lynne Larson, June 18, 1983; children: Kristina, Tristan, Kaylee. BS in Biology magna cum laude, Calif. State U. Stanislaus, Turlock, 1986; PhD in Botany, U. Calif., Davis, 1991; MD, Saba (Netherlands Antilles) U., 1998. Rsch. assoc. dept. botany U. Vt., Burlington, 1991-94; asst. prof. genetics Saba U. Sch. Medicine, 1994-96; resident internal medicine St. Mary's Health Ctr., St. Louis, 1998-2001; hospitalist Alliance In-patient Medicine, Inc., St. Louis, 2001—. Staff sgt. USAF, 1970-82. Avocation: adult hockey. Office: St Marys Health Ctr 6420 Clayton Rd Saint Louis MO 63117-1872 E-mail: lchanson@bigfoot.com.

HANSON, LINDA N. academic administrator, educator; d. Pierce R. Nesbitt and Miriam B. Brinson; m. J. Laird Hanson; 1 child, J. Pierce Hanson. B English, Speech, So. Nazarene U.; M Ednl. Adminstrn., EdD Ednl. Leadership, Seattle U. Tchr. Savannah Christian Prep. Sch.; English tchr. secondary sch. Atlanta pub. schs.; tchr. Sch. Edn. and Inst. Pub. Svc. Seattle U.; asst. provost exec. edn. Seattle U.; v.p. U. Rels. Seattle U.; pres. Coll. Santa Fe, 2001—. Pres. Ind. Colls. Wash.; v.p. devel. Tex. A&M U., Corpus Christi. With Assn. of Coll. and Cmty. Arts Adminstrs., Tex. Commn. on Arts Peer Rev., Rotary IV, others; mem. Santa Fe Chamber Music Festival's Adv. Bd., Santa Fe C. of C., Pres.'s Leadership Group, Higher Edn. Ctr. Alcohol and other Drug Prevention; exec. dir. Paramount Theatre for Performing Arts. Mem.: N.Mex. Women's Forum, Nat. Assn. Ind. Colls. and Us., Roundtable. Office: Coll Santa Fe 1600 St Michael's Dr Santa Fe NM 87505

HANSON, MARTIN PHILIP, mechanical engineer, farmer; b. Watseka, Ill., Feb. 4, 1937; s. Philip Andrew and Mary Jane (Martin) H.; m. Virginia Ann Garfield, Jan. 2, 1960; children: Martin Philip Jr., Adam Gunnar. BS, U.S. Naval Acad., 1959. Registered profl. engr., Mich., Ill. Commd. ensign USN, 1959, advanced through grades to lt. comdr., 1968; reactor mech. asst. USS Enterprise (CVAN-65), Alameda, Calif., 1968-69; resigned, 1969; project engr. Consumers Power Co., Jackson, Mich., 1969-74; project engring. mgr. United Engrs. and Constructors Inc., Phila., 1974-77, Seabrook, N.H., 1977-82, Glen Rose, Tex., 1982-83, Washington, 1983-87; project control specialist Systematic Mgmt. Svcs., Argonne, Ill., 1987-92; project engr. Mac Tech. Svcs. Co., Argonne, 1992-95; sr. project mgmt. specialist Aguirre Engrs., Inc., Argonne, 1995-97; v.p. RERC Environ., Inc., Chgo., 1997-99. Sec. repository coordination group Dept. Energy, Washington, 1983-85, sec. repository change control, 1985-87. Capt. USNR, 1969-92, comdr. res. regts. Mem. ASME (past chmn. New England sect.), Organ Transplant Support (past dir.-at-large), Nat. Soc. SAR. Achievements include organizing new programs for continuous fiber ceramic composites and other technologies. Home: 1009 Troutlilly Ln Darien IL 60561-8819 E-mail: navy59@comcast.net.

HANSON, MARY LOUISE, retired social services administrator; b. Walsenburg, Colo., Nov. 8, 1928; d. Norman Francis and Ellen Matilda (Peterson) Kastner; m. Peter R. Hanson, Sept. 1, 1951 (dec. Dec. 1991); children: Sherod Day, Janell Marie, Kari Annette. BA, U. Wyo., 1951, MA, 1958. Bookkeeper Rawlins Nat. (Wyo.) Bank, 1948-49; scholarship sec. U. Wyo., Laramie, 1962-64; dist. counselor Vocational Rehab., Laramie, 1964-71; exec. dir. Laramie Sr. Ctr., 1973-92; ptnr. First St. Gallery, Laramie, 1996—. Pres. Laramie Sr. Housing, Inc., 1982-92, Laramie Housing, Inc., 1988—. Developed 1st counseling and tng. programs for vocat. rehab. Albany and Platte Counties, Wyo., 1964-71; dir. renovation hist. bldgs., Laramie, 1973-92. Fed. and Wyo. State grantee, 1964-71, Divsn. Aging., 1973-92. Mem. Albany County Hist. Soc., Laramie Plains Mus., U. Wyo. Alumni Assn. Achievements include developing 24 units of Regency Apartments for seniors in 1996. Home: 710 Ivinson Ave #4 Laramie WY 82070-2001 E-mail: alpine@partae.com.

HANSON, MONIQUE SHIRAZ, not-for-profit fundraiser; d. Shafi Ul and Dorothy Evelyn Hossain; m. Torrey Hanson, Dec. 15, 1997; m. Jonathan Duncan (div.). BA, U. Wis., 1986. Asst. to dir. membership and spl. events Sci. Mus. Minn., St. Paul, 1987—89; performance supr. St. Paul Chamber Orch., St. Paul, 1989—92; asst. dir. devel. then dir. devel. Milw. Repertory Theater, Milwaukee, 1992—96; dir. devel. Intiman Theatre, Seattle, 1996—98; dir. corp. and found. rels. Newberry Libr., Chgo., 1998—2000; exec. dir. corp., found. and govt. rels. Roosevelt U., Chgo., 2000—01; dir. corp. and found. rels. Alzheimer's Assn., Chgo., 2001—. Mem. women with vision com. Chgo. Found. Women, Chgo., 1999—2000. Mem. Leadership Tomorrow, Seattle, 1998; bd. dirs. Cmty. Advs. Inc., Milw., 1995—96. Mem.: Assn. Fundraising Profls. (chair profl. devel. workshops annual midwestern regional conf. 1999—2000), Nat. Assn. Female Execs. D-Liberal. Unitarian. Office: Alzheimers Assn 225 N Michigan Ave 17th Fl Chicago IL 60601 Office Fax: 866-741-5530. E-mail: monique.hanson@alz.org.

HANSON, MURRAY, minister; b. Albert Lea, Minn., May 26, 1948; s. Palmer J. and Betty L.; m. Mary Ann, Dec. 26, 1970; children: Andrew, Rebecca. BA, Mankato State U., 1970; MDiv, Dubuque Theol. Sem., 1973, D Ministry, 1980. Ordained to ministry Presbyn. Ch. (U.S.A.), 1973. Intern Sunnyside Presbyn. Ch., South Bend, Ind., 1972; supply pastor Hazelton (Iowa) Presbyn. Ch., 1973; assoc. pastor Lakeside Presbyn. Ch., Storm Lake, Iowa, 1973-77; pastor 3d Presbyn. Ch., Rockford, Ill., 1977—. Supr. field edn. McCormick/Dubuque Sems., Chgo., Dubuque, 1979-92; commr. Gen. Assembly, Presbyn. Ch. (U.S.A.), No. Ill., 1989. Author: An Examination of the Influence of the Roman Catholic Religious Affiliation of Alfred Smith and John Kennedy in the Presidential Elections of 1928 and 1960, 1970, 71, A Self-Assessment Manual for Local Congregations, 1980, Self-Assessment Study of Third Presbyterian Church, 1980. Bd. dirs. Protestant Community Svcs., Rockford, 1985-87, Regional "For Kids' Sake), No. Ill./So. Wis., 1990-95; tour organizer, host to Eng., Scotland, Jordan, Israel, Egypt, Greece, Turkey, Denmark, Norway, Sweden, 1985—. Recipient U. Dubuque Theol. Sem. Alumni award, 1992. Mem.: Greater Rockford Clergy Assn. (pres. 1984—86, 2002—). Office: 3d Presbyn Church 1221 Custer Ave Rockford IL 61103-4667

HANSON, NORMA LEE, farmer; b. Brainerd, Minn., Feb. 3, 1930; d. Fred Christian Kruckow and Lena Belle Sawyer; m. Lynn Curtis Hanson; 1 child, Michael Lynn. Student, Mpls. Sch. Bus., 1949—50; grad., Northland C.C., 1972. File clk. and predetermining mortgage payments Investors Diversified Svcs., Mpls., 1949—53; social reporter Thief River Falls Times, 1954—63; office mgr. Kiewel Products Co., 1963—70; lobbyist Minn. Farmers Union, St. Paul, 1970—72, columnist, 1973—76; asst. farm mgr. Good-Vue Ayr Farms, Goodridge, 1976—. Chmn. Senate Dist. 1, Minn., 1990—, Northwest Minn. Women's Fund, 2001—. Mem.: NW Minn. Dairy Assn. (sec., treas. 2000—), Am. Dairy Assn. (pres. 1986—2001), Midwest Dairy Assn. (bd. dirs. 1995—2000, sec., treas. N.W. Minn. chpt. 2000—), Am. Agrl. Women (chmn. dairy com. 1999—), Hort. Soc. (pres. 13th dist. 2000—), Goodridge Area Hist. Soc. (pres. 1980—, founder). Democrat. Lutheran. Avocations: horticulture, horseback riding, reading, writing, snowmobiling. Home: 21625 330th Ave NE Goodridge MN 56725

HANSON, PATTI LYNN, human resources specialist; b. Kennewick, Wash., Apr. 21, 1953; d. Lyle Harry and Ellene Lavonne (McGrath) Morgan; m. Dale R. Hanson, Jan. 18, 1995. AS, El Paso C.C., Colorado Springs, Colo., 1972; BS, Regis Coll., 1982; M in Human Resources Devel., Webster U., 1994. Sec. Adams County Sch. Dist., Thornton, Colo., 1972-73, Montgomery Ward & Co., Denver, 1973-77, computer operator, 1977-79, sec., 1979-83, pers. supr., 1983-84, pers. mgr. Shawnee Mission, Kans., 1984-86, govt. funds coord. Kansas City, Mo., 1986, divsn. tng. mgr., 1986-88; regional human resource mgr. KFC Nat. Mgmt. Co., Irving, Tex., 1988-90; human resources dir. Businessland, Inc./JWP, Lenexa, Kans., 1990-91; v.p. human resources tech. acquisition svcs. divsn. Entex Info. Svcs., Overland Park, Kans., 1992-99; sr. human rels. cons. FBD Consulting, Overland Park, 2000—02, ind. cons., writer, 2002—; rsch. and evaluation mgr. Sprint, 2002—. Adj. instr. Ottawa U., Kansas City, 2000—. Author: (book) The M&A Transition Guide: A 10-Step Road Map to Workforce Integration, 2001; articles published in Employemnt Mgmt. Today, Kansas City Business Jour., Greater Kansas City Mag.. Mem. Human Resource Mgmt. Assn. of Johnson County (bd. dirs., dir. comms.), Soc. Human Resources Mgmt. Republican. Avocations: golf, jogging, writing. Home: 11978 Connell Dr Shawnee Mission KS 66213-2514 E-mail: Patti.L.Hanson@mail.sprint.com.

HANSON, PAUL RICHARD, historian, educator; b. Seattle, Feb. 26, 1952; s. Kermit Osmond and Jane Elizabeth (Haugen) H.; m. Betsy Ann Lambie, May 28, 1977; children: Timothy S., Christopher B., Laura E. BA, Stanford U., 1974; MA, U. Calif. Berkeley, 1976, PhD, 1981. Vis. asst. prof. Ariz. State U., Tempe, 1981-83, Linfield Coll., McMinnville, Oreg., 1984; asst. prof., assoc. prof., prof. Butler U., Indpls., 1984—, dean coll. of liberal arts and sciences, 2002—. Author: Revolutionary France, 1987, Provincial Politics in the French Revolution, 1989, Phi Alpha Theta award, 1990. Fellow NEH, 1985, Am. Coun. Learned Soc., 1990, Am. Philos. Soc., 1991. Mem. Am. Hist. Assn., Soc. French Hist. Studies, We. Soc. French History (exec. coun.), Ind. Assn. Historians (pres. 1998-99). Avocations: tennis, hiking, camping, wine tasting. Office: Butler Univ Dept Liberal Arts & Scis 4600 Sunset Ave Indianapolis IN 46208 E-mail: phanson@butler.edu.

HANSON, RICHARD EDWIN, civil engineer; b. Sioux City, Iowa, July 22, 1931; s. Gustav Edwin and Delia Thelma (Horton) H.; m. Joann Gager Terhune, Nov. 6, 1954 (div. Jan. 1971); children: Richard Edwin Jr., John William, Tamara Terhune; m. Lillie Gwenette Capitanio, Feb. 21, 1987. BSCE, Iowa State U., 1953; postgrad., U.S. Army Gen. Staff Coll. Registered profl. engr., Iowa. Engr.-in-tng. U.S. Army Corps Engrs., Washington, 1957-58; sr. co. engr. Dickinson Constrn. Co., Chgo., 1959-62; asst. chief constrn. mgmt. Goddard Space Flight Ctr., NASA, Greenbelt, Md., 1963-69; chief project mgmt. U.S. Postal Svc., Washington, 1969-70; chief Air Force project mgmt. U.S. Army Corps Engrs., Washington, 1971-77, chief of constrn. Balt., 1977-81, chief of constrn. South Atlantic div. Atlanta, 1982-85, chief of constrn. Washington, 1986-91, dir. constrn. ops. Pacific Ocean div. Honolulu, 1991-96; cons. in engring. and constrn. mgmt., 1996—. Editor: Corps Engrs. Constrn. Newsletter, 1988-91. Pres. Walbrooke Manor Citizens Assn., Lanham, Md., 1963-64. 1st lt. C.E., U.S. Army, 1953-57. Mem. ASCE, NSPE, Army Engr. Assn., Soc. Am. Mil. Engrs. (bd. dirs. Washington chpt. 1988-91), Beta Theta Pi. Republican. Avocations: flying, golf, skiing, fishing, sailing. Home: 44-125 Kahinani Way Kaneohe HI 96744-2569 E-mail: hanson0731@aol.com.

HANSON, RICHARD JAMES, art educator, artist; b. Ft. Dodge, Iowa, Dec. 11, 1948; s. Carl August and Mary Margaret Hanson; m. Mary Ann Mori, Aug. 15, 1972; 1 child, Robby. BA in Art Edn., U. No. Iowa, 1971; MA in Studio Art (Painting), Minn. State U., 1976. Art instr. Chariton (Iowa) C.C., 1971—74, Ft. Dodge Cmty. Schs., 1974—. Exhibited in group shows at Nat. Arts for the Pks. Exhbn., Jackson Hole, Wyo., 2001, Nat. Watercolor Soc. Internat. Exhbn., Brea, Calif., 2001. Recipient Jurors award, Iowa Art Salon, Des Moines, 1997, Blanden Art Mus., Ft. Dodge, 1997, Butler Inst. Am. Art, Youngstown, Ohio, 1999, San Diego Watercolor Soc., 2000. Mem.: Profl. Educators of Iowa, Iowa Watercolor Soc., Nat. Watercolor Soc. Home: 1120 Wraywood Dr Fort Dodge IA 50501

HANSON, RICHARD JOSEPH, computer scientist, consultant; s. James William and Irene Rose Hanson; m. Karen Haskell, Oct. 20, 1977; children: Joseph Haskell, Frederick Richard, Christina Carrie, Eric Norman. PhD, U. Wis., 1964. Prin. scientist Visual Numerics, Inc., Houston, 1989—98; rsch. scientist Rice U., Houston, 1999—. Cons. Visual Numerics, Inc., Houston, 2002—. Author: (book) Solving Least Squares Problems. Democrat. Episcopal. Avocation: walking.

HANSON, RICHARD WINFIELD, biochemist, educator; b. Oxford, N.Y., Nov. 10, 1935; s. John Vincent and Agatha Helen H.; m. Gloria M. Lucchesi, June 10, 1961; children: Paul, Benjamin, Daria. BS, Northeastern U., 1959; MS, Brown U., 1961, PhD, 1963. Asst. prof to prof. biochemistry Temple U. Sch. Medicine, Phila., 1965-78; prof., chmn. dept. biochemistry Case Western U. Sch. Medicine, Cleve., 1978-99, Leonard and Jean Sheggs prof. biochemistry, 1993—. Cons. USPHS, FDA. Assoc. editor Jour. Biol. Chemistry; contbr. articles to profl. jours. Served to capt. Med. Service Corps, U.S. Army, 1963-65. Recipient Mead-Johnson award, 1971, Kaiser Permenante award, 1982, Maurice Saltzman award, 1991, Osborne Mendel award, 1995, William C. Rose award, 1999; named 250th Anniversary Disting. Tchg. Prof., Princeton U., 2001-02; named to Cleve. Med. Hall of Fame, 2002. Mem. AAAS, Inst. Medicine NAS, Am. Soc. Biochemistry and Molecular Biology (pres. 1999-2000). Office: Case Western Res U Dept of Biochemistry, Rm W405 10900 Euclid Ave Cleveland OH 44106

HANSON, RICK, psychologist; b. Stillwater, Okla., Oct. 21, 1952; s. William Roderick and Helen Louise Hanson; m. Jan Hanson, Feb. 14, 1982; children: Forrest, Laurel. BA summa cum laude, UCLA, 1974; MA in Psychology, Rosebridge Inst., 1986; PhD in Psychology, Wright Inst., 1991. Lic. psychologist, Calif. Pres. Together Seminars, L.A., 1977; seminar leader, mgr. Earthplay, Inc., L.A., 1978-80; risk analyst Stan Kaplan Assocs., Newport Beach, Calif., 1980-81; pvt. practice bus. cons. Sausalito, Calif., 1981-82; pres. Body of Knowledge, Mill Valley, Calif., 1983-85; mgmt. cons., prin. Peak Mgmt., San Rafael, Calif., 1985-92; pvt. practice psychology San Rafael, 1992—. Columnist Family Matters, 1992—; Author: Mother Nurture: A Mother's Guide to Health in Body, Mind, and Intimate Relationships, 2002. Pres., bd. dirs. Family Works, San Rafael, 1995; spkr. Marin county Mother's Clubs, schs., 1992—; mem. bd. dirs. Spirit Rock Meditation Ctr., 1995—. U. Calif. Presdl. scholar, 1973; named Best Family Therapist Pacific Sun Poll, 1995. Mem. APA, AAAS, Soc. for Exploration of Psychotherapy Integration, Phi Beta Kappa. Avocations: rock climbing, hiking, reading. Office: 610 D St San Rafael CA 94901-3708

HANSON, ROBERT DELOLLE, lawyer; b. Harrisburg, Pa., Dec. 13, 1916; s. Henry W. A. and Elizabeth (Painter) H.; m. Barbara Esmer, Apr. 22, 1949 (dec. Mar. 2000). BA, Gettysburg Coll., 1939; LLB, Dickinson Law Sch., 1942. Bar: Pa. 1942. Practice in Harrisburg, 1946-98; solicitor Dauphin County, 1958-76, Dauphin County Redevel. Authority, 1959-98. Pres. coun. of congregation Luth. Ch., 1953-55, 57-59; pres. Family and Children's Svc. of Harrisburg, 1956-57; mem. Harrisburg Sch. Bd., 1952-57, Dauphin County Housing Authority, 1960-98; gen. chmn. Tri-County United Fund, 1969, pres., 1971-72; trustee Gettysburg Coll., 1974—, sec., 1980, vice chmn., 1983-86; pres. Keystone area coun. Boy Scouts Am., 1980-82. Maj. inf. AUS, 1942-46, ETO. Decorated Bronze Star, Purple Heart; recipient Silver Beaver award Boy Scouts Am., 1980, Eagle award Boy Scouts Am., 1990, Alexis de Tocqueville award United Way of Am., 1991, Others award Salvation Army, 1992, Lavern Brenneman award Gettysburg Coll., 1996, Wisdom award of honor The Wisdom Soc. for the Advancement of Knowledge, Learning and Rsch. in Edn., 1999. Mem. ABA, Pa. Bar Assn. (sec., treas. taxation sect. 1948-59), Dauphin County Bar Assn. (dir. 1958-59), Gettysburg Coll. Alumni Assn. (treas. 1958-59, v.p. 1968-71, pres. 1971-72), Masons (33 deg., past master, pres. bd. trustees 1982-85), Execs. Club (pres. 1953), Harrisburg Rotary (pres. 1979). Lutheran. Home: 2500 N 2nd St Harrisburg PA 17110-1106 Office: 119 Locust Street Harrisburg PA 17101-1426

HANSON, ROBERT DUANE, civil engineering educator; b. Albert Lea, Minn., July 27, 1935; s. James Edwin and Gertie Hanson; m. Kaye Lynn Nielsen, June 7, 1959; children: Craig Robert, Eric Neil. Student, St. Olaf Coll. Northfield, Minn., 1953-54; BSE, U. Minn., 1957, MS in Civil Engring., 1958 PhD, Calif. Inst. Tech., Pasadena, 1965. Registered profl. engr., Mich., N.D. Design engr. Pitts.-Des Moines Stel, Des Moines, 1958-59; asst. prof. U. N.D. Grand Forks, 1959-61; rsch. engr. Calif. Inst. Tech., 1965; asst. prof. U. Calif.-Davis, 1965-66; from asst. prof. to prof. civil engring. U. Mich., Ann Arbor, 1966—2001, prof. emeritus, 2001—, chmn. dept. civil engring., 1976-84; sr. earthquake engr. Fed. Emergency Mgmt. Agy., 1994-2000. Vis. prof., dir Earthquake Engring. Rsch. Ctr., U. Calif., Berkeley, 1991; dir. BCS divsn. NSF Washington, 1989-90; cons. NSF, 1979-88, 92-94; cons. Bechtel Corp., Ann Arbor, 1976-87, Sensei Engrs., Ann Arbor, 1977-90, Bldg. Seismic Safety Coun., 1988-94, Fed. Emergency Mgmt. Agy., 1992-94, 2000—. Contbr.

articles to profl. jours. Recipient Reese Rsch. award ASCE, 1980; recipient Disting. Svc. award U. Mich., 1969; tchg. award Chi Epsilon, 1985, Attwood Engr. Excellence award, 1986. Mem. NAE, ASCE (life; com. chmn. 1975-94), Earthquake Engring. Rsch. Inst. (hon., v.p. 1977-79, bd. dirs. 1976-79, 88-92, pres.-elect 1988, pres. 1989-91, past pres. 1991-92). Lutheran. Home: 2926 Saklan Indian Dr Walnut Creek CA 94595-3911 E-mail: rdhanson2@aol.com.

HANSON, ROBERT JOHN, retired environmental engineer, consultant; b. Amherst, Wis., Feb. 2, 1924; s. Leslie Adolph and Grace Alice (Ludvigson) H.; m. Donna Marie Nelson, Oct. 17, 1945; children: Robert J. Jr., Brian N., Barry T., Sandra McGuire, Lauri Bisignani. BS in Civil Engring., U. Wis., 1948, MS in Civil Engring., 1949. Diplomate: Am. Acad. Environ. Engr. Sanitary engr. Ind. State Bd. Health, Indpls., 1949-51, USAF, Wright-Patterson, AFB, 1951-55; mgr. environ. quality ICI Americas, Inc. and predecessor co. Atlas Powder Co., Wilmington, Del., 1955-87. Vol. executive Internat. Exec. Svc. Corps., Stamford, Conn., 1989—; pro-bono cons. to developing countries; cons. World Environ. Ctr., N.Y.C., 1992—. Mem. adv. com. water use data, USGS, 1974-84; dir. Del. Solid Waste Auth., 1986-94; dir., pres. Water Resources Assn. Del. Basin, Valley Forge, Pa., 1972-87. Cpl. U.S. Army (POW), 1943-45, ETO. Mem. Mfg. Chemists Assn. (chmn. water resources commn.), Water Environment Fedn. (life), Masons, Chi Epsilon (Wis. chpt.). Avocations: woodworking, choral singing, swimming, golf, skiing. Home: 2707 Point Breeze Dr Wilmington DE 19810-1117 E-mail: stalag4b@aol.com.

HANSON, RONALD WILLIAM, lawyer; b. Aug. 3, 1950; s. Orlin Eugene and Irene Agnes Hanson; m. Sandra Kay Cook, Aug. 21, 1971; children: Alec Evan, Corinn Michele. BA summa cum laude, St. Olaf Coll., 1972; JD cum laude, U. Chgo., 1975. Bar: Ill. 1975, U.S. Dist. Ct. (no. dist.) Ill. 1975, U.S. Ct. Appeals (7th cir.) 1978, U.S. Ct. Appeals (10th cir.) 1989. Assoc. Sidley & Austin, Chgo., 1975-83, ptnr., 1983-88, Latham & Watkins, Chgo., 1988—, chmn. audit com., 1998—. Ofcl. advisor to Nat. Conf. of Commrs. on Uniform State Laws; lectr. Ill. Inst. Continuing Legal Edn., Springfield, Am. Bankruptcy Inst., Washington, Banking Law Inst., Practicing Law Inst., Am. Law Inst. Contbr. articles to profl. jours. Mem. ABA, Ill. Bar Assn., Chgo. Bar Assn., Order of Coif, Met. Club, Phi Beta Kappa. Republican. Lutheran. Home: 664 W 58th St Hinsdale IL 60521-5104 Office: Latham & Watkins Sears Tower Ste 5800 Chicago IL 60606-6306 E-mail: ronaldhanson@lw.com.

HANSON, THOR, retired health agency executive and naval officer; b. Amarillo, Tex., May 7, 1928; s. Carl Joseph Emanuel and Lillian (Nelson) H.; m. Charlotte Ann Edens, Oct. 6, 1956; children: Inge Rew, Erica Karen, Ivor Carl, Lars Jon, Ursula Edens. BS, U.S. Naval Acad., 1950; MA, Oxford U., Eng., 1954. Commd. ensign U.S. Navy, 1950, advanced through grades to vice adm., 1979, service in Korea and Vietnam, naval aide, exec. asst. to sec. Navy, 1970-72, comdg. officer Naval Sta., 1973-74; chief U.S. Naval Mission to Brazil, 1974-76; comdr. Cruiser-Destroyer Group 8; also comdr. Attack Carrier Striking Group 2, U.S. 6th Fleet, 1976-77; mil. asst. to Sec. of Def., 1977-79; dir. joint staff Office Joint Chiefs Staff, 1979-82, ret., 1982; mil. analyst Cable News Network, 1982; pres., CEO Nat. Multiple Sclerosis Soc., 1982-92, pres. emeritus, 1992—. Chmn. Nat. Health Coun., 1991-93; hon. bd. dirs. Resch.! Am. Bd. dirs. North Fork Environ. Coun.; pres. Southold Citizens for Safe Roads. Decorated Def. D.S.M. with oak leaf cluster, Legion of Merit, Bronze Star with combat V, Meritorious Service medal, Joint Service Commendation medal; Vietnam Navy Distinguished Service medal; Brazilian Naval Order of Merit; Rhodes scholar, 1951-54 Mem. Am. Assn. Rhodes Scholars, Coun. on Fgn. Rels., U.S. Naval Inst., U.S. Naval Acad. Alumni Assn., Am. Fedn. Musicians (hon. life), Century Assn., N.Y. Yacht Club, Orient Yacht Club, Leander Rowing Club (England), Ends of the Earth Club, Digressionists Club. Episcopalian. Home: Interwellen PO Box 112 900 Birdseye Ln Orient NY 11957-0112

HANSON, TRUDY L. speech professional, educator; b. Magnolia, Miss., June 12, 1950; d. Truett Carr and Marie (Green) Lewis; m. Michael D. Hanson, Aug. 19, 1972; children: Leah, Chad, Ashley, Tori. BS in Speech/English Edn., La. State U., 1971, MA Speech, 1973; EdD Higher Edn., Tex. Tech U., 1994. Tchg. asst. La. State U., Baton Rouge, 1971-73; prof. West Tex. A&M, Canyon, 1989—. Instr. Thomas Nelson C.C., Hampton Roads, Va., 1974, Amarillo Coll., 1981-89. Dir. West Tex. A&M U. Storytelling Festival, 1991—; parent chair Amarillo Coll. Suzuki Strings, 1985—, Amarillo Coll. Symphony Youth Orch., 1993-96, Amarillo Symphony Youth Orch., 1993-96. Mem. Nat. Comm. Assn., So. States Comm. Assn. (pres. 2000-01), Tex. Speech Comm. Assn. (pres. 1998), Tejas Storytelling Assn., Tex. Assn. Comm. Adminstrn. (pres. 1994-95), Storytellers of the High Plains (pres. 2000—). Democrat. Mem. Lds Ch. Home: 6209 Estacado Ln Amarillo TX 79109-6922 Office: WTAMU Box 60747 ACT Dept Canyon TX 79016

HANSON, VICTOR ARTHUR, surgeon; b. Syracuse, N.Y., May 5, 1933; s. Victor Arthur Sr. and Dorothy (Burns) H.; m. Mary Diane Nadijcka, Sept. 13, 1985. AB, Princeton U., 1955; MD, U. Pa., 1959. Diplomate Am. Bd. Surgery. Intern then resident, instr. surgery U. Pa. Hosp., Phila., 1964-69, chief resident, 1968-69; instr. surgery SUNY, Syracuse, N.Y., 1969-71, asst. prof. surgery, 1971-78, clin. asst. prof. surgery, 1978-80; asst. prof. surgery Thomas Jefferson U., Phila., 1980-88; pvt. practice Syracuse, 1969-80; dir. rsch. VA Med. Ctr., Wilmington, Del., 1983-87; pvt. practice Wilmington, Del., 1987-90; staff surgeon HMO, Atlanta, 1990-96; pvt. practice Atlanta, 1996—. Contbr. articles to profl. jours. Lt., naval flight surgeon, USN, 1961-64, Vietnam. Grantee Am. Heart Assn., 1975, FDA, 1988, Merit Rev. X Z Vets. Adminstn. Hosp. System. Fellow ACS; mem. AMA, Med. Assn. Ga., Med. Assn. Atlanta, Soc. Surgery of the Alimentary Tract, So. Med. Assn. Avocations: tennis, model railroading. Home: 3875 W Nancy Creek Ct NE Atlanta GA 30319-4803 Fax: 404-255-3726. E-mail: vahanson@mindspring.com.

HANSON, VICTOR HENRY, II, newspaper publisher; b. Augusta, Ga., Aug. 17, 1930; s. Clarence Bloodworth, Jr. and Elizabeth (Fletcher) H.; m. Elizabeth Stallworth, Dec. 29, 1953; children: Clarence Bloodworth III, Victor Henry III, Elizabeth Mickel, Mary Fletcher, Robert Stallworth. Grad., Choate Sch., 1949; student, U. Va., 1949-51; BA, U. Ala., 1954. With Birmingham (Ala.) News & Post Herald, 1946-54, 57—, gen. mgr., 1963-83; with advt. and prodn. dept. WAPI-TV, Birmingham, 1954-55; v.p. Birmingham News Co., 1960-79, pres., 1979-2000, pub., 1983-2000. Trustee Birmingham Mus. of Art; bd. dirs. Grace House Ministries; elder Presbyn. Ch. Served to capt. USAF, 1955-57. Recipient Tree of Life award, Nat. Jewish Fund, 1991. Mem. SAR, Birmingham C. of C., Soc. of Cincinnati, N.C. Soc. of Cincinnati, Birmingham Country Club, Summit Club, Mountain Brook Club, Kappa Alpha. Home: 3910 Hunters Ln Birmingham AL 35243-5920 Office: 402 Office Park Dr Ste 100 Birmingham AL 35223 Business E-Mail: vhanson3@bhamnews.com.

HANSON, WENDY KAREN, retired chemical engineer; b. Mpls., May 29, 1954; d. Curtis Harley Hanson and Patricia Lou (Vogler) Schweiger. BS, U. Minn., 1976; BA, U. Colo., Denver, 1984; postgrad., U. Calif., La Jolla, 1984-87. Chem. technician Shasta Beverages, Mpls., 1977-78, Conwed, Roseville, Minn., 1978-80; geologist Century Geophys. Corp., Grand Junction, Colo., 1980, Tooke Engring., Grand Junction, 1980-82; sr. scientist Sci. Ventures, San Diego, 1987-96; engr. Parker-Hannifin Corp., San Diego, 1996-97, ret., 1997. Patentee magnesium separation from Dolomitic phosphate by sulfuric acid leaching. Judge San Diego (Calif.) Sci. and Engring. Fair, 1987-96; leader, publs. editor San Diego (Calif.) Wilderness Assn., 1989-97. Avocations: backpacking, gardening, spitoon collecting. E-mail: packerwendy92117@yahoo.com., wkhanson@prodigy.net.

HANSON, LORD (LORD JAMES EDWARD HANSON), industrialist; b. Jan. 20, 1922; s. Robert and Louisa Ann (Rodgers) H.; m. Geraldine Kaelin, 1959; 2 children: Robert William, John Brook, 1 stepchild, Karyn. Exec. chmn. Hanson PLC, London, 1965-97. Office: 28 Old Brompton Rd Box 164 London SW7 3SS England Fax: (011.44.020) 7245 9900.

HANSOTTE, LOUIS BERNARD, retired lawyer; b. Atlantic City, Oct. 3, 1927; s. Marcel Alfred and Bertha (Goldsmith) H.; m. Wilma Sleeper, Dec. 29, 1955; children: Beth Marcelle, Jeffrey Ronal. BS in Engring., U.S. Mil. Acad., 1950; LLB, LaSalle Extension U., 1961. Bar: Calif. 1962, U.S. Dist. Ct. (so. dist.) Calif. 1962; CLU. Commd. 2d lt. U.S. Army, 1950, advanced through grades to capt., 1953; served in Korea; resigned, 1955; agt., supr., then mgr. Pacific Mut. Life and Union Central Life, 1956-64; sr. ptnr. Hansotte, Nostrand & Lange, San Diego, 1964-94, ret., 1994—. Instr. bus. law, coord. real estate program and paralegal studies program Grossmont C.C., El Cajon, Calif., 1964-94. Author: Legal Aspects of California Real Estate, 1983; California Probate Real Estate Sales, 1983; A Whistleblower's Handbook, 2000, The Medi-Cal Enigma, 2001, Stop "It"-Identity Theft, 2002; contbr. articles to profl. jours. Mem. Calif. State Bar Assn., San Diego County Bar Assn., Nat. Assn. Life Underwriters, Am. Coll. of Life Underwriters, Calif. Assn. of Real Estate Tchrs., West Point Alumni Assn., Army Athletic Assn., West Point Soc. of San Diego (co-founder, past pres.). Home: PO Box 19324 San Diego CA 92159-0324 E-mail: lhansotte@earthlink.net., medcal@earthlink.net., whistleblower@earthlink.net., mygoodname@earthlink.net.

HANSRAJ, KENNETH KARAMCHAND, surgeon, research scientist; b. Georgetown, Guyana, Oct. 28, 1961; arrived in U.S., 1974; s. Augustus and Anjanie Hansraj; m. Marcia Dee Griffin, Aug. 1, 1998; 1 child, Jonathan. BS, Fairleigh Dickinson U., 1982; grad., Columbia U. Sch. General Studies; MD, Hahnemann U., 1987. Cert. Am. Bd. Minimally Invasive Spinal Medicine and Surgery, 1999, Am. Bd. Orthopedic Surgeons, 2001, Nat. Bd. Med. Examiners, 1989, lic. N.Y. 1996, Calif., 1991. Fellow in biomechanics Hosp. for Special Surgery, N.Y.C., 1987—88; gen. surgery tng. Mt. Sinai Hosp., N.Y.C., 1988—90; resident orthopaedic surgery King/Drew Med. Ctr., L.A., 1990—95; fellow in minimally invasive spinal surgery Calif. Ctr. for Minimally Invasive Spine Surgery, Thousand Oaks, Calif., 1995; fellow in scoliosis and spinal surgery Hosp. for Special Surgery, N.Y.C., 1995—96; spinal surgeon, dir. The Special Spine Inst., Poughkeepsie, NY, 1997—. Attending orthopaedic surgeon St. Francis Hosp., Poughkeepsie, NY, 1997—, St. Vincent's Hosp., Staten Island, NY, 1997—, Bailey Seton Hosp., Staten Island, NY, 1997—; jr. attending orthop. surgeon Hosp. for Special Surgery, N.Y.C., 1995—96, New York Hosp., N.Y.C., 1995—96, Meml.-Sloan Kettering Med. Ctr., N.Y.C., 1995—96; presenter in field. Editor: Surgical Techniques International; contbr. articles to profl. and med. jours. Fellow: Am. Acad. Orthopaedic Surgeons. Office: The Spl Spine Inst Ste 202 243 North Rd Poughkeepsie NY 12601 Office Fax: 845-471-1551.

HANTGAN, GEORGE, social services administrator; s. Nathan and Eva H.; m. Ida Hantgan, Nov. 27, 1949; children: Jeffrey Clyde, Roberta Elise, Richard Selden. BA, Bklyn. Coll., 1940; MPA, NYU, 1943; MSW, Columbia U., 1948. Exec. dir. United Jewish Fund, Jewish Community Ctr., 1950-81; endowment cons. United Jewish Community of Bergen County, 1950-81; exec. cons., endowment cons. United Jewish Fund of Englewood, 1981-83; pvt. practice United Jewish Fund, Jewish Community Coun., Englewood, N.J., 1983—. Recipient Medal United Jewish Appeal and Govt. Israel, Disting Svc. award Yeshiva U. Wurzweiler Sch. Social Work, Spl. Lifetime Achievement award, Jewish Cmty. Ctr. on the Palisades, Mayor LaGuardia award. Mem. Acad. of Cert. Social Workers, Nat. assn. of Social Workers (past state chmn.), Bergen County Health and Welfare Coun., assn. of Jewish Community Orgn. Profls. Home: 158 St Nicholas Ave Englewood NJ 07631-1639

HANTGAN, ROY RUSSELL, biomedical researcher, educator; b. Washington, June 11, 1946; s. Samuel and Margaret Hantgan; m. Julie Beth Edelson, Dec. 19, 1971; children: Abbie Edelson, Aaron Edelson. PhD, Cornell U., 1968—74. Asst. prof. of biochemistry U. of NC, Chapel Hill, NC, 1977—83; assoc. prof. of biochemistry Wake Forest U. Health Sci., Winston-Salem, NC, 1983—2003. Nato-supported vis. scientist U. Hosp. Utrecht, Utrecht, Netherlands, 1989—93. Contbr. chapters to books, articles to profl. jours. Rsch. grant, NIH, 1982—90, NSF, 1998—2002, Established Investigatorship, Am. Heart Assn., 1982—87. Mem.: AAAS, Fedn. of Am. Societies for Exptl. Biology, Biophysical Soc., Internat. Soc. for Thrombosis and Hemostasis. Achievements include contributed to understanding the molecular and cellular bases of cardiovascular disease. Avocations: international travel, camping, hiking. Office: Wake Forest University Health Sciences Medical Center Blvd Winston Salem NC 27157-1019 Home Fax: 336-716-7671; Office Fax: 336-716-7671. E-mail: rhantgan@wfubmc.edu.

HANTHO, CHUCK, retired metal products executive; Bd. dirs. Dofasco., Inc., 1989—2002; chmn. bd. Dofasco, Inc., 1995—2002; ret., 2002; former chair policy bd. Can. Industry Program Energy Conservation. Office: Donfasco Inc PO Box 2460 Hamilton ON L8N 3J5 Canada

HANTON, E. MICHAEL, public and personnel relations consultant; b. Gary, Ind. s. Zachary and Maria (Suciu) H. AB, Ind. U., 1951, MA, 1955; grad., USAF Air War Coll., 1968. Various prodn. positions U.S. Steel Corp., Gary, 1940-41, 50; prodn. contr. Douglas Aircraft Corp., Santa Monica, Calif., 1946-47; classified advt. mgr Weaver Pub. Co., Santa Monica, 1947-48; reporter Muncie (Ind.) Evening Press, 1952, Gary Post-Tribune, 1952-53; head cashier Office Lake County Treas., Gary, 1955-60; pub. and pers. rels. cons. Gary, 1960—, Plattsburgh, N.Y., 1968—. Asst. prof. State U. Coll. Arts & Scis., Plattsburgh, 1966-67; cons. community rels. and fund raising. Author: The New Nurse, 1973. With USAAF, 1941-45, USAF active res. 1945-69, ret. Decorated Air medal, Purple Heart. Mem. Am. Med. Writers Assn., Assn. Edn. in Journalism and Mass Communications, Health Scis. Comm. Assn., Am. Acad. Advt., Nat. League Nursing, Gary C. of C., Plattsburgh C. of C., Air Force Assn., Res. Officers Assn., Nat. Arts Club, Steel Club, Caterpillar Club, Flying Boot Club. Office: PO Box 872 Chico CA 95927

HANTUSH, MOHAMED M. hydrologist, researcher; b. Baghdad, Iraq, Mar. 5, 1962; came to U.S., 1985; s. Mahdi S. Hantush and Iqbal A.S. Hantush; m. Dina A. Mustafa, Feb. 28, 2000. BSCE, Kuwait U., Kuwait City, 1985; MSCE, U. Calif., Davis, 1988, PhD in Civil Engring., 1993. Postdoctoral rschr. U. Calif., Davis, 1993-97; hydrologist EPA, Ada, Okla., 1997-2001, Cin., 2001—. Contbr. articles to profl. jours. Mem. ASCE (Best Referee award 2000), Am. Geophys. Union, Nat. Groundwater Assn. Moslem. Office: EPA 26 W Martin Luther King Dr Cincinnati OH 45268 E-mail: hantush.mohamed@epa.gov.

HANUS, JEROME GEORGE, archbishop; b. Brainard, N.E., May 26, 1940; Student, Conception Sem., Mo., St. Anselm U., Rome, Princeton Theol. Sem., Princeton U. Ordained priest Roman Cath. Ch., 1966. Abbot Conception Abbey, 1977—87, pres. Swiss Am. Benedictine Congregation, 1984—87; bishop Diocese of St. Cloud, Minn., 1987—94; co-adjuctor archbishop Dubuque, Iowa, 1994—95; archbishop, 1995—. Office: Archdiocese of Dubuque 1229 Mt Loretta Ave Dubuque IA 52004*

HANUSHEK, ERIC ALAN, economics educator; b. Lakewood, Ohio, May 22, 1943; s. Vernon F. and Ruth (Hostetler) H.; m. Nancy L. Keleher, June 11, 1965 (div.); children: Eric Alan, Megan E. BS, U.S. Air Force Acad., 1965; PhD in Econs., MIT, 1968. Sr. staff economist Coun. Econ. Advisers, Washington, 1971-72; assoc. prof. USAF Acad., Colo., 1972-73; sr. economist Cost of Living Coun., Washington, 1973-74; assoc. prof. econs. Yale U., New Haven, 1975-78; dir. pub. policy analysis U. Rochester, N.Y., 1978-83, prof. econs. and polit. sci., 1978-2000, chmn. dept. econs., 1982-87, 88-90, dir. W. Allen Wallis Inst. Polit. Economy, 1992-99; rsch. assoc. Nat. Bur. Econ. Rsch., 1996—; Hanna sr. fellow Hoover Instn. Stanford (Calif.) U., 2000—; sr. rsch. fellow Green Ctr. U. Tex., Dallas, 2000—. Dep. dir. Congl. Budget Office, Washington, 1984-85; mem. com. nat. stats. Nat. Rsch. Coun., 1992-98, adv. coun. on Edn. Statistics, 2002; cons. World Bank 1984-95, U.S. Com. on Civil Rights, 1986-89. Author: Education and Race, 1972, (with J. Jackson) Statistical Methods for Social Scientists 1977, (with C. Citro) Improving Information for Social Policy Decisions, 1991, (with R. Harbison) Education Performance of the Poor, 1992, Making Schools Work, 1994, (with J. Banks) Modern Political Economy, 1995, (with N. Maritato) Assessing Knowledge of Retirement Behavior, 1996, (with Dale W. Jorgenson) Improving America's Schools, 1996, (with Constance F. Citro) Assessing Policies for Retirement Income, 1997, The Economics of Schooling and School Quality, 2003. Served to capt. USAF, 1965-74. Disting. vis. fellow Hoover Instn., Stanford U., 1999-2000. Fellow Internat. Acad. Edn. (bd. dirs. 2002—), Assn. Pub. Policy Analysis and Mgmt. (v.p. 1986-87, pres. 1988-89), Am. Econ. Assn., Econometric Soc., Soc. Labor Economists. E-mail: hanushek@hoover.stanford.edu.

HANVIK, JAN MICHAEL, arts promoter, writer; b. Mpls., Nov. 9, 1950; s. William Joseph and Geneva Margaret (Dicks) H. BFA in Dance, CUNY, 1982; MA in L.Am. and Caribbean Studies, NYU, 1985. Exec. dir. Pan Am. Musical Art Rsch. Inc. (PAMAR), N.Y.C., 1987—2001, Clemente Soto Velez Cultural Ctr., 2001—03, Columbia County Coun. of Arts, 2002—. Cons. Ford Found., N.Y.C., 1995-96, NEA, 1995-97, Compton Found., 1997, N.Y. State Coun. Arts, 1982—, Nat. Inst. Fine Arts, Mexico City, 1995-96. Contbr. articles to Dictionary of 20th Century Cultures, 1996, International Encyclopedia of Dance, 1996, also to mags. Bd. dirs. World Dance Alliance Ams., N.Y.C., 1997—. Fulbright Sr. scholar, El Salvador, 1990-91, Uruguay Arts Adminstrn., 1999, Argentina, 2001, Am. Cultural Specialist, Bolivia, 1988; Ford Found. grantee Cuba Dance Rsch., 2000. Mem.: Alliance of N.Y. Art Orgns. Mem. Soc. Of Friends. Avocations: gardening, travel, kayaking. Office: CCCA 209 Warren St Hudson NY 12502 E-mail: americasarts@yahoo.com.

HANWAY, DONALD GRANT, retired agronomist, educator; b. Broadwater, Nebr., Aug. 6, 1918; s. Frank Pierce and Emma Terrissa (Twist) H.; m. Blanche Elizabeth Larson, Sept. 26, 1942 (dec. Aug. 1996); children: Donald Grant, Wayne Edward, Janice Kay; m. Susanne Ruth Pennington, Apr. 10, 1999. BS, U. Nebr., 1942, MS, 1948; PhD, Iowa State Coll., 1954. Tchr. rural schs., Morrill County, Nebr., 1936-40; mem. faculty dept. agronomy U. Nebr., Lincoln, 1947-84, chmn. faculty dept. agronomy, 1955-76, prof. emeritus, 1984—, also extension agronomist, chief of party univ. mission to Ataturk U. Erzurum, Turkey, 1965-67. Agronomic cons., Nigeria, Columbia, Morocco, Tunisia; mem. Plant Variety Protection Adv. Bd., 1987-90. Contbr. articles to profl. jours. Mem. Nebr. Commn. on Status of Women, 1986-89. With USAAF, 1942-46. Honoree Nebr. Hall of Agrl. Achievement, 1988. Fellow AAAS, Am. Soc. Agronomy, Crop Sci. Soc.; mem. Soil Sci. Soc. Am., Soil and Water Conservation Soc., Am. Inst. Biol. Scis., Phi Beta Kappa, Sigma Xi, Alpha Zeta, Gamma Sigma Delta. Episcopalian. Home: 5600 Pioneers Blvd Apt 215 Lincoln NE 68506-5175

HANWAY, H. EDWARD, insurance company executive; BA, Loyola Coll., Balt., 1974; MBA, Widener U., 1984. CPA Pa. With CIGNA and predecessor companies, 1978—; v.p. opers. CIGNA Corp., 1986-88; pres. CIGNA Internat., 1989—96, CIGNA Healthcare, Phila., 1996—99; pres., CEO CIGNA Corp., Phila., 1999—2000, chmn., CEO, 2000—. Chmn. bd. dirs. MedUnite; past chmn. Coun. Affordable Quality Healthcare. Trustee Loyola Coll. Balt., Eisenhower Exch. Fellowships; mem. bd. advisors March of Dimes Found. Mem.: Pa. Inst. CPAs, AICPA. Office: Cigna Corp 1 Liberty Place Philadelphia PA 19192

HANZEL, MIMI S. psychotherapist; b. Asheville, N.C., Aug. 28, 1941; d. James Andrew and Mary Athalinda (Wilmerding) Sutton; m. Charles J. Hanzel, June 1, 1963; children: Charles J., Mary Athalinda. BA, Calif. State U. L.A., 1984, MS, 1987; PhD, The Fielding Inst., 1995. Dual diagnosis coord. Pacific Clinics-El Camino, Santa Fe Springs, Calif., 1995—. Vol. Nat. Charity League, 1982-88, Assistance League of Pasadena, Calif., 1980-88. Recipient Outstanding Student Yr., The Fielding Inst., 1990-91; grantee L.A. Dept. Mental Health, 1997. Mem. San Gabriel Valley Psychol. Assn. (gov. affairs chair 1997), Am. Psychol. Assn., Calif. Psychol. Assn., Calif. Assn. Marriage and Family Therapists. Episcopal. Avocations: walking, reading, traveling. Office: Pacific Clins-El Camino 11721 Telegraph Rd Ste A Santa Fe Springs CA 90670-6835

HANZELKA, RICHARD LOUIS, education educator; b. Belle Plaine, Iowa, Aug. 8, 1939; s. Louis Bernard and Agnes Lucille (Stoklas) H.; m. Mylene Glee Millhollin, Aug. 8, 1964; children: Kristine Marie, Susan Lynette, Marci Joelle, Amy Katherine. BA, U. Iowa, 1961, MA, 1964, PhD, 1974. Permanent profl. cert., Iowa; cert. supt., Iowa. Tchr. jr. h.s. lang. arts Cedar Rapids (Iowa) Comty. Schs., 1961-64; asst. prof. SUNY, New Paltz, 1964-69; cons. K-12 lang. arts Muscatine-Scott Co. Sch. Sys., Davenport, Iowa, 1969-74; staff devel. coord. K-12 lang. arts Miss. Bend Area Edn. Agy., Davenport, 1974-88, acting dir. edn. svcs. Bettendorf, Iowa, 1988-89, dir. gen. edn., 1989—99, dir. orgnl. strategic planning, 1999—2001; head edn. dept. Marycrest Internat. U., Davenport, Iowa, 2001—02; dir. Ea. Iowa Writing Project St. Ambrose U., Davenport, Iowa, 2002—. Mem. steering com., co-dir. Iowa Writing Project, Cedar Rapids, 1978—; dir. orgnl., strategic planning Miss. Bend Area Edn. Agy., Bettendorf, 1992—; Franklin Flex Trainer instr. Franklin Quest, Salt Lake City, 1994—. Contbr. articles to profl. jours. Coord. pre-Cana program Diocese of Davenport, 1979-82, deacon evaluation team, 1990-92; bd. dirs. 90 Miles Off Broadway, New Paltz, N.Y., 1968-69; pres. parish coun. St. John Vianney Ch., Bettendorf, 1989-91. Recipient Disting. Svc. award Miss. Valley Coun. Tchrs. of English, 1981; Drew Meml. scholar U. Iowa, 1957-60; NDEA Title IV fellow U. Iowa, 1972-73. Mem. ASCD (bd. dirs. 1991-99, nominating com. 1996, exec. coun. 2000—), Nat. Coun. Tchrs. of English (State Lit. Mag. leader 1984-87), Ednl. Svcs. Dirs. (chmn. 1991-92), Sch. Adminstrs. Iowa, Iowa Coun. Tchrs. of English (pres. 1979-81, disting. svc. award 1984), Iowa Assn. for Supervision and Curriculum Devel. (pres. 1991-92, exec. dir. 1995—). Roman Catholic. Avocations: singing, acting, woodworking, walking, reading. Home and Office: 2580 New Lexington Dr Bettendorf IA 52722-2115

HANZLIK, RAYBURN DEMARA, lawyer; b. L.A., June 7, 1938; s. Rayburn Otto and Ethel Winifred (Membery) H.; children: Kristina, Rayburn N., Alexander, Geoffrey. BS, Principia Coll., 1960; MA, Woodrow Wilson Sch. Fgn. Affairs, U. Va., 1968; JD, U. Va., 1974. Bar: Va. 1975, D.C. 1977. Staff asst. to Pres. U.S., Washington, 1971-73; assoc. dir. White House Domestic Council, 1975-77; atty. Danzansky Dickey Tydings Quint & Gordon, Washington, 1977-78, Akin Gump Strauss Hauer & Feld, Washington, 1978-79, Darling, Rae & Gute, L.A., 1979-81; adminstr. Econ. Regulatory Adminstrn., Dept. Energy, Washington, 1981-85; ptnr. Heidrick and Struggles, Inc., 1985-91, McKenna & Hanzlik, Irvine, Calif., 1991-92; chmn. Lanxide Sports Internat., Inc., San Diego, 1992-95, Stealth Propulsion Internat., Ltd., San Diego, Calif. and, Melbourne, Australia, 1994-97; exec. v.p. Commodore Corp., N.Y.C. and McLean, Va., 1997-98; atty. Trainum, Snowdon & Deane, Washington, 1999—; mng. dir. Washington Technology Strategies, 2002—. Contbg. author: Global Politics and Nuclear Energy, 1971, Soviet Foreign Relations and World Communism, 1965. Alt. del. Republican Nat. Conv., 1980; dir. Calif. Rep. Victory Fund, 1980; candidate U.S. Senate, 1980. Served to lt. USN, 1963-68, Vietnam. Republican. Christian Scientist. E-mail: rayburn.hanzlik@verizon.net.

HAPGOOD, ROBERT DERRY, English educator; b. Lompoc, Calif., Dec. 11, 1928; s. Arthur Richard and Elsie Rachel (Brown) H.; m. Marilyn Janelle Oliver, July 16, 1950; children— Miranda Kristin, Susanna Elizabeth. BA with highest honors, U. Calif., Berkeley, 1950, MA, 1951, PhD, 1955. Instr. English Ind. U., 1955-57; vis. prof. Am. lit. and civilization Dijon (France) U., 1957-58; instr. U. Calif., Berkeley, 1958-59, asst. prof. Riverside, 1959-65; mem. faculty U. N.H., Durham, 1965—, prof. English, 1969-95; prof. emeritus English, 1996—; chmn. dept. U. N.H., 1972-75, dir. London program, 1986-89; dir. U. N.H./Cambridge U. summer program, 1982-85; exchange prof. Osaka (Japan) U., 1977-79. Vis. prof. Shoin Women's U., Japan, 1992; dir. Shakespeare Workshop, Bowdoin Coll., summers 1972-75. Author: Shakespeare the Theatre-poet, 1988; editor: Hamlet - Shakespeare in Production, 1999; mem. editorial bd. Univ. Press New Eng., 1975-77. Served with AUS, 1953-55. Recipient essay prize English Inst., 1968, Lindberg award for Outstanding Scholar-Tchr., 1990; fellow Inst. Renaissance Studies, Ashland, Oreg., 1961; Mellon postdoctoral fellow, 1964-65; fellow Southeastern Inst. Medieval and Renaissance Studies, Chapel Hill, N.C., 1969; Am. Coun. Learned Socs. fellow, 1979-80, Folger Inst. fellow, 1987, NEH summer fellow, 1994. Mem. MLA. Home: Cove Rd PO Box 451 Cape Neddick ME 03902-0451 Office: U NH English Dept Hamilton Smith Hall Durham NH 03824 E-mail: HapgoodR@aol.com.

HAPNER, MARY LOU, securities trader and dealer; b. Fort Wayne, Ind., Nov. 9, 1937; d. Paul Kenneth Brooks and Eileen (Summers) H. BS with honors, Ariz. State U., 1966, MS, 1967. Stockbroker Young, Smith & Peacock, Phoenix, Ariz., 1971-76, v.p., 1976-89, Peacock, Hislop, Staley & Given, Phoenix, 1989-90, 1st v.p., 1990—. Author: Career Courage, 1984; (poems) The Power of Forgiveness, 1995, Take Someone's Hand, 1997, Cherubs, 1997, Self Portrait, 1998, Vision, 1999, Millenium, 2000, Walk with Me, 2001. Chmn. March of Dimes, Sun City, Ariz., 1983; trustee St. Lukes, Phoenix, 1978; mem. fin. com. YWCA, Phoenix, 1975; mem. dean's coun. of 100, Ariz. State U. Coll. Bus., 2000-03; chair budget com. Ch. of Beatitudes, Phoenix, mem. exec. coun., 1991; bd. dirs. Ariz.'s Children Found., 1998; founder Ariz. Biltmore Country Club Women's Orgn., 1976, champion 1976-83. Recipient Spirit of Philanthropy award, 1997, Impact award for Enterprising Women, 2001, Arthritis Angel award, 2002, Rookie of Yr. award Arthritis Found., 2003. Mem. Charter

100 (chair membership 1979-81, pres. 1980, pres. 1982, v.p. 1981, treas., membership chair 1995, v.p. 2003—). Republican. Lutheran. Avocations: golf, singing with concert choirs, writing poetry.

HAPP, HARVEY HEINZ, electrical engineer, educator; b. Berlin, June 27, 1928; came to U.S., 1947, naturalized, 1953; s. Harry and Hertha (Friedmann) H.; m. Ruth Hollander, Nov. 17, 1951; children: Deborah Ann, Sandra Eva. BS in Elec. Engring, Ill. Inst. Tech., 1954; M.E.E., Rensselaer Poly. Inst., Troy, N.Y., 1958; D.Sc., U. Belgrade, Yugoslavia, 1962. Registered profl. engr., N.Y. With Gen. Electric Co., 1954-88, sr. application engr., 1968-72, mgr. analytical engring. services, 1972-77, mgr. advanced system tech., 1977-82, mgr. system analysis, 1982-87, cons., 1987-88, also mem. faculty power system engring. course; with N.Y. State Dept. Pub. Service, 1988—. Lectr. colls. Author: Diakoptics and Networks (translated into Russian and Romanian), 1971, Piecewise Methods and Applications to Power Systems (translated into Chinese), 1980; editor: Gabriel Kron and Systems Theory, 1973; mem. editorial bd. Procs. IEEE, 1979-84; contbr. numerous articles and book revs. to profl. jours., chpts. to tech. books. Fellow IEEE (life; Prize Paper award Region 5 1962, power sys. engring. com. 1977, Region 1 award 1980); mem. Tensor Soc. Gt. Britain (v.p. 1972-82), Conf. Internat. des Grands Reseaux Electrique a Haute Tension, Internat. Power Sys. Computations Conf. (co-founder 1962), Gen. Electric Co. Engrs. and Scientists Assn. (chmn. policy com. 1968-70), Ill. Inst. Tech. Alumni Assn., Sigma Xi, Tau Beta Pi, Eta Kappa Nu. Home: 2211 Webster Dr Niskayuna NY 12309-3930 Office: NY State Dept Pub Svc 3 Empire State Plz Albany NY 12223-1000 E-mail: harvey_happ@dps.state.ny.us.

HAPPEL, DOROTHY, violinist, concertmaster; b. Winfield, Kans., Jan. 5, 1927; d. William Shields and Halo (Wilson) Merriam; m. John Happel, May 26, 1951; children: Jill, George Syms, Ruth Emilie. Studies with Jacques Gordon, Music Mountain, Conn., 1939-42; MusB, Eastman Sch. Music, 1948; postgrad., Juilliard Sch. Music, 1949-53. Ind. recital violinist, U.S. and Europe, 1935—; soloist various symphony orchs., 1948—; mem. Lake Placid (N.Y.) Sinfonietta, 1948—, concertmaster, 1975—, Greenwich (Conn.) Symphony, 1967-93; violinist, bd. dirs. Chamber Players, 1971—93; concertmaster Greenwich (Conn.) Choral Soc., 1967—93; recital on 1st plastic violin Weill Hall, N.Y., 1990. Pres. bd. dirs. Downtown Music at Grace, White Plains, NY, 2002—. Recipient Young Artist award Mus. Fund Soc. Phila., 1946, Naftzger award Wichita (Kans.) Symphony, 1948, Am. Artists award Bklyn. Acad. Music, 1952, Artist award Concert Artists Guild, 1955. Episcopalian. Home: 69 Tompkins Ave Hastings On Hudson NY 10706-3944 E-mail: happel@bestweb.net.

HAPPEL, STEPHEN P. university dean; b. Indpls., Aug. 18, 1944; s. Hermann Ernst and Jane Rita (Connor) H. BA, St. Meinrad (Ind.) Coll., 1966; MA, Ind. U., 1969; PhL, Higher Inst. Philosophy, Leuven, Belgium, 1973; PhD, Cath. U. Louvan, Leuven, Belgium, 1977, STD, 1979. Assoc. prof. dept. religion St. Meinrad Sch., 1978-83, Cath. U. Am., Washington, 1983-99, chair dept. religion, 1994-99, dean Sch. Religious Studies, 1999—. Cons. Dept. Def., Washington, 1985-87, Drexler Assocs., Annapolis, Md., 1987-89. Author: Coleridge's Religious Imagination, 1984, A Catholic Vision, 1984, Conversion and Discipleship, 1984, Metaphors for God's Time in Science and Religion, 2002. Named Flannery Prof., Gonzaga U., 1992-93, Rsch. Prof., Vatican Obs. Rsch. Group, Rome, 1989-99, Am. Coun. Learned Socs. Travel awardee, 1991. Fellow Soc. Arts Religion and Contemporary Culture; mem. MLA, Am. Acad. Religion, Cath. Theol. Soc. Am. Avocations: jogging, piano. Office: Catholic Univ of America Sch Theology and Religious Studies Office of Dean Washington DC 20064-0001 E-mail: happel@cua.edu.

HAQ, BILAL UL, national science foundation program director, researcher; came to U.S., 1968; s. Fazli and Sorraya (Rabbani) H.; m. Nazli Azam, June 11, 1975. MSc, U. Panjab, 1963; PhD, U. Stockholm, 1967, DSc, 1972. UNESCO scholar U. Vienna, Austria, 1964-65; Swedish Internat. Devel. Authority rsch. scholar U. Stockholm, 1965-68; rsch. scientist Woods Hole (Mass.) Oceanographic Inst., 1968-82, Exxon Prodn. Rsch. Co., Houston, 1982-88; program dir. marine geology and geophysics NSF, Washington, 1988—. Rsch. assoc. Smithsonian Inst., Washington, 1988-92; vis. prof. U. Copenhagen, Geol. Survey of Denmark, 1991; keynote spkr. Bur. Mineral Resources, Canberra, Australia, 1988, Internat. Geol. Congress, Washington, 1989, Kyoto, Japan, 1992, Linnean Soc. Conf. on the Indus River and Its Civilization, London, 1994, Intergovt. Oceanographic Commn. Conf. on Integrated Coastal Zone Mgmt., Karachi, Pakistan, 1994, Internat. Sedimentol. Congress, Alicante, Spain, 1998; vis. com. for Brit Geol. Survey, U.K. Nat. Environ. Rsch. Coun., Swindon, 1990-91; mem. panel U.S., Japan Coop. Program Natural Resources, Tokyo, 1991-92; on assignment White House Office Mgmt. and Budget, 1992, World Bank environ. dept., 1993; hon. prof. Tongji U., Shanghai, China, 1997—, Qingdao Inst. Oceanology, China, 2000—. Author, editor: Introduction to Marine Micropaleontology, 1978, 98, Marine Geology and Oceanography of Arabian Sea, 1984, Ocean Drilling on Exmouth Plateau, 1990, Calcareous Nannoplankton, 1984, Nannofossil Biostratigraphy, 1984, Sequence Stratigraphy and Facies Association, 1993, Sequence Stratigraphy and Depositional Response to Eustatic, Tectonic and Climatic Forcing, 1995, Sea Level Rise and Coastal Subsidence: Causes, Consequences and Strategies, 1995, Coastal Zone Management Imperative for Developing Maritime Nations, 1997; prodr., host, author video film Sequence Stratigraphy and the Danian Succession, 1993. Recipient 1998 Francis P. Shepard medal Soc. for Sedimentary Geology, Antarctic svc. medal NSF, 1999. Fellow AAAS, Geol. Soc. Am.; mem. Am. Assn. Petroleum Geologists (disting. lectr. 1989), Am. Geophys. Union. Achievements include research in global sea level and environmental change. Office: NSF 4201 Wilson Blvd Arlington VA 22230-0001

HAQUE, MALIKA HAKIM, pediatrician; b. Madras, India; came to U.S., 1967; d. Syed Abdul and Rahimunisa (Hussain) Hakim; m. C. Azeez Haque, Feb. 5, 1967; children: Kifizeba A.H. Akbar, Masarath N.H. Badar, Asim Zayd Haque. MBBS, Madras Med. Coll., 1967. Diplomate Am. Bd. Pediatrics. Rotating intern Miriam Hosp. Brown U., Providence, 1967-68; resident in pediatrics N.J. Coll. Medicine Childrens Hosp., 1968-70; fellow in devel. disabilities Ohio State U., 1970-71; acting chief pediat. Nisonger Ctr., 1973-74; staff pediatrician Children and Youth Project Children's Hosp., Columbus, Ohio; clin. asst. prof. pediatrics Ohio State U., 1974-80, clin. assoc. prof. pediatrics, 1981-99, clin. assoc. prof. dept. internat. health Coll. Medicine, 1993-99, clin. prof. pediatrics and internat. health Coll. Medicine, 1999—. Pediatrician in charge Cmty. Children's Hosp. Cmty. Health Ctrs. Children's Hosp., Columbus, 1982—; dir. Pediat. Academic Assn., 1992-2002; cons. Ctrl. Ohio Head Start Program, 1974-79; med. cons. Bur. Rehab. and Devel. Disabilities for State of Ohio, 1990—. Contbr. articles to profl. jours. and newspapers. Charter founder Ronald Reagan Rep. Ctr.; trustee Asian Am. Health Alliance Network, Columbus, 1994-2001. Recipient Physician Recognition award, AMA, 1971—86, 1988—99, 2002—, 2003—, Gold medals in surgery, radiology, pediat. and ob-gyn., Presdl. medal of Merit, Pres. Ronald Reagan, 1982, Nat. Leadership award, Nat. Rep. Congl. Com., 2001, Physician of the Yr. award, 2003. Fellow Am. Acad. Pediatrics; mem. Islamic Med. Assn., Am. Assn. of Physicians of Indian Origin, Pediat. Acad. Assn. (dir. 1992-2002), Ambulatory Pediat. Assn., Ctrl. Ohio Pediatric Soc. Muslim. Achievements include research on enuresis and tumors caused by human papilloma viruses. Home: 5995 Forestview Dr Columbus OH 43213-2114 Office: 700 Childrens Dr Columbus OH 43205-2664

HARAD, GEORGE JAY, manufacturing company executive; b. Newark, Apr. 24, 1944; m. Beverly Marcia Harad, June 12, 1966; children: Alyssa Dawn, Matthew Corde. BA, Franklin and Marshall Coll., 1965; MBA with high distinction, Harvard Bus. Sch., 1971. Staff cons. Boston Cons. Group, 1970-71; asst. to sr. v.p. housing Boise Cascade Corp., 1971, asst. to v.p., 1971; fin. mgr. Boise Cascade Realty Group, Palo Alto, Calif., 1972-76; mgr. corp. devel. Boise Cascade Corp., Boise, Idaho, 1976—80, dir. retirement funds, risk mgmt., 1980—82, v.p., contr., 1982—84, sr. v.p., CFO, 1984—89, exec. v.p., CFO, 1989—90, exec. v.p. paper, 1990—91, pres., COO, 1991—94, pres., CEO, 1994—95, chmn., bd. dirs., 1995; chmn., dir. Boise Cascade Office Products Corp.; CEO, chmn. Boise Cascade Corp., 1995—. Bd. dirs. FmGlobal Ins. Co.; bd. govs. Nat. Coun. for Air and Stream Improvement Inc. Founder, pres. Boise Coun. for Gifted and Talented Students, 1977—79; bd. dirs. Boise Philharm. Assn., 1983—84; dir. bd. trustees Coll. Idaho, 1986—91. Recipient George F. Baker scholar, 1970—71; Grad. Prize fellow, Harvard Grad. Sch. Arts and Scis., 1965—69, Frederick Roe fellow, Harvard U. Sch. Bus., 1971. Mem.: Am. Forest and Paper Assn. (bd. dirs., mem. exec. com. 1984—94), NAM (bd. dirs), Century Club (Boston), Arid Club, Crane Creek Country Club. Office: Boise Cascade Corp PO Box 50 Boise ID 83728-0050

HARADA, NORIO, software engineer, researcher, educator; b. Aichi, Japan, Feb. 12, 1945; s. Iwao and Tomiko Harada; m. Reiko Harada, Oct. 31, 1971; children: Shin, Satoshi. BS, Nagoya U., Nagoya-Shi, Japan, 1967, MS, 1969; D Engring., Kyoto U., Kyoto-Shi, Japan, 1979. Rschr. Nippon Electric Co. Ltd., Kawasaki-Shi, Kanagawa, Japan, 1969-82, rsch. supr., 1982-84; rsch. mgr. NEC Corp., Kawasaki-Shi, 1984-87, mgr. Minato-Ku, Tokyo, 1987-91, chief engr., 1991-96; prof. computer sci. Takushoku U., Tokyo, 1996—. Contbr. articles to profl. jours. Recipient Yonezawa Meml. Paper award, 1985. Mem. IEEE, AAAS, Assn. Computing Machinery, Math. Soc. Japan, Inst. Electronics, Info. and Comm. Engrs. Japan (Excellent Paper award 1985, 88), Info. Processing Soc. Japan, N.Y. Acad. Scis. Buddhist. Avocations: mathematics, tennis, reading, research. Home: 18-5 Yokoyamadai 1-Chome Sagamihara-Shi Kanagawa 229-1121 Japan Office: Takushoku U 815-1 Tatemachi Hachioji Shi Tokyo 193-0985 Japan E-mail: nharada@cs.takushoku-u.ac.jp.

HARAGAN, DONALD ROBERT, university administrator, geosciences educator; b. Houston, Apr. 15, 1936; s. Donald William and Mary (Thompson) H.; m. Willie Mae O'Berry, July 2, 1966; children— Shannon Lea, Shelley Jo. BS, U. Tex., 1959, PhD, 1969; MS, Tex. A & M U., 1960. Registered profl. engr., Tex. Research asst. Tex. A & M U., College Station, 1959-60; research scientist U. Tex., Austin, 1960-66, instr., 1966-69; asst. prof. Tex. Tech. U., Lubbock, 1969-72; assoc. prof. Tex. Tech U., Lubbock, 1972-78, prof. geosci., 1978—, dept. chmn., 1972-77, 80-83, interim dean, 1985, interim v.p., 1985-86, v.p. for acad. affairs and research, 1986-88, exec. v.p., provost, 1988—; interim pres. Tex. Tech. U., Lubbock, 1996, pres., 1996-2000, pres. emeritus, 2000—. Contbr. articles in field to profl. jours. Mem. Am. Soc. Civil Engrs., AAAS, Am. Meteorol. Soc., Am. Water Resources Assn., Tex. Acad. Sci. Home: 6914 Nashville Dr Lubbock TX 79413-6002 Office: Tex Tech U Honors Coll Lubbock TX 79409 E-mail: don.haragan@ttu.edu.

HARA-ISA, NANCY JEANNE, graphic designer, county official; b. San Francisco, May 14, 1961; d. Toshiro and Masaye Hara; m. Stanley Takeo Isa, June 15, 1985. Student, UCLA, 1979-82, BA in Art and Design, Calif. State U., L.A., 1985. Salesperson May Co., L.A., 1981; svc. rep. Hallmark Cards Co., L.A., 1981-83; prodn. artist Calif. State U., L.A., 1983, Audio-Stats Internat. Inc., L.A., 1983; prodn. asst. Auto-Graphics Inc., Pomona, Calif., 1984-85, lead supr., 1985-86; art dir., contbg. staff writer CFW Enterprises, Burbank, Calif., 1987-88; graphic designer, prodn. mgr. Bonny Jularbal Graphics, Las Vegas, Nev., 1988-90; graphic designer Weddle Caldwell Advt., Las Vegas, 1990-92; owner Nancy Hara-Isa Designs, 1992—; graphic artist Regional Transp. Commn. of Clark County, Las Vegas, 1993-98; mgmt. analyst Clark County Dept. Aviation, Las Vegas, 1998—. Freelance designer Caesars Palace. Writer Action Pursuit Games mag. Parade asst., mem. carnival staff Nisei Week., L.A., 1980-84; asst. mem. Summit Orgn., L.A., 1987—; mem. selection com. United Way; alumni grad. Clark County Leadership Forum, 1996; mem. pub. policy com. Alzheimers Assn. So. Nev. Mem. NAFE, Women in Profl. Graphic Svcs. (acting 1st v.p. 1990, 2d v.p. 1991), Women in Comms., Green Valley Rep. Women's Club (1st v.p. 2000, treas. 2003), Am. Soc. Pub. Adminstrs. (coun. mem. 1998-99). Avocations: photography, swimming, horseback riding, shooting. Home: 1803 Dalton Dr Henderson NV 89014

HARALAMPU, GEORGE STELIOS, electric power engineer, former engineering executive electric utility company; b. Lynchburg, Va., Mar. 20, 1925; s. Stelios P. and Thelxiope (Hagipalaiologous) H.; m. Helen Avtges, June 14, 1953; children: Evelyn, Stephen. BSEE, Tufts U., 1952; MSEE, Northeastern U., 1960. Registered profl. engr., Mass. Successively jr. engr., asst. engr., engr., protection engr. New Eng. Electric System, Boston, 1952-69, protection and planning engr. Westborough, Mass., 1969-73, asst. chief engr., 1973-75, dir. elec. engring., 1975-84, dir. engring., 1984-91, v.p. engring., 1988-91, ret., 1991. Mem. steering com. Edison Electric Inst., Washington, 1968-73; chmn. system protection T.F., N.E. Power Coordinating Coun., N.Y.C., 1978-83; mem. system design task force New Eng. Power Pool, Springfield, Mass., 1969-70, chmn. transient voltage analysis, 1971-77. Contbr. articles to profl. jours. Sgt. U.S. Army, 1943-46, ETO. Fellow IEEE (chmn. surge protective devices com. 1979-80, com. award 1988); mem. IEEE Power Engring. Soc. (Laurence Cleveland award 1987), Power Engring. Soc. Boston (sr., chmn. 1967-68), Masons. Republican. Greek Orthodox. Avocations: furniture making, gardening, traveling, symphony. Home: 60 Long Ave Belmont MA 02478-2963

HARALICK, ROBERT MARTIN, electrical engineering educator; b. N.Y.C., Sept. 30, 1943; s. David and Yetta (Stier) H.; m. Joy Gold, Aug. 20, 1967 (div. July 1977); 1 child, Tammy-Beth; m. Linda G. Shapiro, Feb. 12, 1978 (div. Aug. 1992); 1 child, Michael Aaron; m. Ihsin T. Phillips, Dec. 1993. BA, U. Kans., 1964, BS, 1966, MS, 1967, PhD, 1969. Asst. prof. elec. engring. U. Kans., Lawrence, 1969-71, assoc. prof., 1971-75, prof., 1975-78, Va. Poly. Inst. and State U., 1979-84; v.p. rsch. Machine Vision Internat., Ann Arbor, Mich., 1984-86; Boeing Clairmont Egtvedt prof. elec. engring., adj. prof. computer sci. U. Wash., Seattle, 1986-2000; pres. Mnemonics Inc., 1979—; disting. prof. computer sci. Grad. Ctr. CUNY, 2001—. Co-dir. NATO Advanced Study Inst. Image Processing, 1978; co-chmn. NATO Advanced Study Inst. on Image Processing, 1980, Robust Computer Vision Workshop, 1990, 92, 94; vice chmn. 5th Internat. Conf. on Pattern Recognition, Miami, 1980; dir. NATO Advanced Study Inst. on Pictorial Data Analysis, 1982; adj. prof. Ctr. Bioengring. U. Wash., Seattle, 1988—; program chmn. 10th annual ICPR Conf. on Pattern Recognition Systems and Applications, 1990; program co-chmn. Internat. Conf. on Document Analysis and Recognition, 1991, vice chmn., 1997; co-chmn. Evaluation and Validation of Computer Vision Algorithm, 1998, chmn., 2001. Author: (with T. Creese) Differential Equations for Engineers, 1977; Pictorial Data Analysis, 1983, (with L. Shapiro) Computer and Robost Vision, Vol I and II, 1992, The Inner Meaning of Hebrew Letters, 1995, (with M. Glazerson) The Torah Codes and Israel Today, 1996; editor: (with J. C. Simon) Issues in Digital Image Processing, 1980, Digital Image Processing, 1981; assoc. editor Computer Vision, Graphics and Image Processing, 1975-93, Pattern Recognition, 1977-93, Communication of the ACM, Image Processing, 1982-92, IEEE Transactions on Systems, Man and Cybernetics, 1979-88, IEEE Transactions on Image Processing, 1992-96, Jour. of Electronic Imaging, 1994—; mem. editl. bd. IEEE Transactions on Pattern Analysis and Machine Intelligence, 1981-84, IEEE Expert, 1986-90, Machine Vision and Applications, 1987—, Real Time Imaging, 1994—, mem. adv. bd.; mem. adv. program com. Structural & Syntactic Pattern Recognition, 1990; contbr. over 525 articles to profl. jours.; digital computer art exhbns. include William Rockhill Nelson Gallery, Kansas City, Mo., 1971, Nat. History Mus., U. Kans., 1971, Dulin Gallery Art, 1971 (2 purchase awards), Nat. Invitational Print Show, U. R.I., 1972, Fla. State U., 1972, San Diego State Coll., 1972; author of over 550 books, book chpts., others. Recipient Dow Chem. Young Outstanding Faculty award Am. Soc. Engring. Educators, 1975, Outstanding Young Elec. Engrs. Honorable Mention award Eta Kappa Nu, 1975, Best Paper award 5th Ann. Symposium on Automatic Imagery Pattern Recognition, 1975, Best Paper award Pattern Recognition Soc., 1989; NSF faculty fellow, 1977-79. Fellow IEEE, IAPR; mem. IEEE Computer Soc. (chmn. pattern analysis and machine intelligence tech. com. 1975-82, acoustics, signal and speech processing, sys., man and cybernetics, pattern recognition tech. subcom. 1975-81, data structures and pattern recognition subcom. 1975-81, biomed. pattern recognition subcom. 1975-81, internat. assn. for pattern recognition gov. bd. 1986-2000, pres. 1996-98, program com. pattern and image processing conf. 1978, 4th internat. joint conf. on pattern recognition 1978, conf. B-pattern recognition methods and sys. program com. 11th internat. conf. on pattern recognition 1992, structural and syntactic pattern recognition 1992, 2d internat. conf. on document analysis and recognition 1993, chairperson various workshops and confs., Cert. Appreciation award 1978, 84), Pattern Recognition Soc., Internat. Assn. for Pattern Recognition (pres. 1996-98), Am. Assn. Artificial Intelligence, Assn. Computing Machinery. Avocation: hammered dulcimer. Home: 207 Woodside Dr Hewlett NY 11557 E-mail: haralick@ptah.cuny.edu.

HARALSON, LINDA JANE, communications executive; b. St. Louis, Mar. 24, 1959; d. James Benjamin and Betty Jane (Myers) N.; married. BA summa cum laude, William Woods Coll., 1981; MA, Webster U., 1982. Radio intern Stas.-KFAL/KKCA, Fulton, Mo., 1981; paralegal Herzog, Kral, Burroughs & Specter, St. Louis, 1981-82; staffing coord. then mktg. coord. Spectrum Emergency Care, St. Louis, 1982-85, mktg. mgr., 1985-87; dir. mktg. and recruitment Carondelet Rehab. Ctrs. Am., Culver City, Calif., 1987—. Mktg. dir. outpatient and corp. svcs. Calif. Med. Ctr., L.A., 1987-88; mktg. dir. Valley Meml. Hosp., Livermore, Calif., 1988-89; account exec. Laurel Comm., Medford, Oreg., 1989-91; cmty. rels. dir. Rogue Valley Med. Ctr., Medford, 1991-95; cmty. pub. rels. dir. Rogue Valley Manor, Medford, 1995-97; pvt. practice in comms. and mktg., 1997—. Party chmn. Heart Assn., St. Louis, 1982—; bd. dirs. Am. Lung Assn. Oreg. Recipient Flair award Advt. Fedn. St. Louis, 1984, Hosps. award Hagen Mktg. Rsch. and Hosps. mag., 1984; Presdl. Acad. scholar William Woods Coll., Fulton, 1977-81. Mem. AAUW, Britt Music Festivals, Alpha Phi Alumnae Assn. (pres. chpt. 1985-87). Republican. Avocations: running, travel, sports, french, needlepoint. Home and Office: 1550 NW Patrick Ct Albany OR 97321

HARAMUNDANIS, KATHERINE LEONORA, information scientist, writer, astronomer; b. Boston, Jan. 25, 1937; d. Sergei Illarionovich and Cecilia Helena (Payne) Gaposchkin; m. John Haramundanis, Mar. 6, 1958; children: George John, Sergei Edward. BA, Swarthmore Coll., 1958; MS in Computer Sci., Boston U., 1997. Rsch. assoc. Smithsonian Astrophys. Obs., Cambridge, Mass., 1958-74; tech. writer Wang Labs., Lowell, Mass., 1974-77; cons. writer Digital Equipment Corp., Nashua, NH, 1977-98; sr. mem. tech. staff Compaq Computer Corp., 1998—2000, Hewlett-Packard Co., 2000—. Judge Soc. for Tech. Comm., 1989, 92, 2000. Author: Cecilia Payne-Gaposchkin: An Autobiography and Other Recollections, 1984, 2nd edit., 1996, The Art of Technical Documentation, 1992, 97, Exploring Workstation Applications, 1996; (with C. Payne-Gaposchkin) Introduction to Astronomy, 1970; contbr. articles to profl. jour. Recipient Spl. Svc. award Smithsonian Instn., 1966, Merit award Smithsonian Astrophys. Obs., 1972. Mem.: History of Sci. Soc., Am. Soc. Oriental Rsch., Am. Archeol. Soc., Am. Astron. Soc., Linguistic Soc. Am., Assn. Computational Linguistics, Soc. for Tech. Commn. (exec. coun. 1993—95), IEEE Profl. Comm. Soc., Assn. for Computing Machinery (treas. Spl. Interest Group for Design of Comm. Interest (SIGDOC) 1993—96, chair 1997—2003, SIG gov. bd. exec. com. 2001—), IEEE Computer Soc., AAAS. Home: PO Box 1365 Westford MA 01886-4865

HARARI, CARMI, clinical psychologist, psychoanalyst; b. N.Y.C., Dec. 4, 1920; s. Ezra and Dina (Katz) H.; m. Clara Soshen, June 19, 1942 (div.); children: Karen Tarnofsky, Michelle Kelly; m. Sarah Zaraleya Kurzweil, Dec. 31, 1979. BSS in Psychology, CCNY, 1946; MA in Clin. Psychology, NYU, 1947; EdD in Psychology of Family Life, Columbia U., 1968; cert. in psychoanalysis, 1978. Lic. psychologist, N.Y.; cert. psychologist, N.Y. State Dept. Mental Hygiene. Sch. psychologist, N.Y.C., 1946-47; clin. psychologist VA Hosps. and Clinics, N.Y.C., 1947-50; lectr., asst. prof. NYU, Columbia U., CUNY, Met. Inst. Psychoanalytic Studies, N.Y.C., 1948-82; pvt. practice N.Y.C., 1950—; staff psychologist N.Y.C. Children's Ct., 1950-52, chief psychologist, 1953-57; dir. Community Consultation Svcs., N.Y.C., 1957-75; staff psychologist, 1957-70; exec. dir. Humanistic Psychology Ctr. of N.Y., N.Y.C., 1973—; dir. Interactions: Psychol. Svcs. for the Whole Family, New City, N.Y., 1990—. Cons. various schs., N.Y.C., 1956-75, Ministry Social Welfare, Israel, 1961, Office Disability Determinations, N.Y. State Dept. Social Svcs., 1970—, others; adj. prof. various N.Y. colls.,1975-82; dir. internat. devel., mem. exec. bd. Assn. Humanistic Psychology, 1969-80; exec. sec. N.Y. Soc. Clin. Psychologists, 1967-69, pres. 1970-72; NGO rep. Internat. Coun. Psychologists, UNESCO, 1980-84, bd. dirs. internat. liaison, 1982-92; treas. Psychologists for Social Responsibility, Washington, 1982-88; rep. UNESCO, 1980-86. Author book chpts.; contbr. articles to profl. jours. and newsletters. Organizer, leader Group Psychotherapy Found., N.Y.C. Around the World Study Tour, 1966; chair adv. bd. Women's Ctrs. for Occupational Devel., N.Y.C., 1969-71; trustee Psychol. Svc. Ctr. N.Y., Soc. Clin. Psychologists, N.Y.C., 1969-72; organizer, leader internat. confs. humanistic psychology, Denmark, Eng., France, Iceland, Ger., India, Israel, Japan, Mex., Netherlands, Norway, Sweden, USSR, 1969-76; bd. dirs. Assn. for Humanistic Psychology, Humanistic Psychology Inst., San Francisco, 1970-76; adv. bd. Identity House, N.Y.C., 1972-73. With USAF, 1942-45. Recipient War Svc. scholarship, N.Y. State, 1952. Fellow APA (divsn. pres. humanistic psychology found. 1971-73, coun. rep. 1974-77, 78-81, 85-88, 91—, pres. proposed divsn. transpersonal psychology 1982-83, chmn. subcom. on psychology of peace making, 1988-90, mem. com. on internat. rels. in psychology, fellow divsn. social issues, clinical, ind. practice, mem. group psychology and group psychotherapy); mem. Assn. Interam. Psychology Soc., Internat. Assn. for Cross Cultural Psychology, Internat. Assn. Applied Psychol (pres. divsn. polit. psychology 1998), Phi Delta Kappa, Kappa Delta Pi. Home and Office: 10 Wyndham Ln New City NY 10956-4527 Office: 19 W 34th St New York NY 10001-3006

HARARI, ZARALEYA KURZWEIL, psychologist, psychotherapist; b. Bklyn., Dec. 30, 1926; d. Phillip and Goldie (Simon) Kurzweil; m. Lawrence H. Strear, Aug. 24, 1947 (div. Sept. 1969); children: Peter Mark, Marcy Jana De Luca, Karen Jody Cucolo; m. Carmi Harari, Dec. 31, 1979; stepchildren: Karen Tarnofsky, Michelle Chino. BA, Bklyn. Coll., 1948; MS, CUNY, 1961; EdD, Yeshiva U., 1969. Lic. psychologist, sch. psychologist; nat. cert. sch. psychologist; nat. cert. health svc. provider psychology. Psychologist Wyandanch (N.Y.) Pub. Schs., 1961-63, Uniondale (N.Y.) Pub. Schs., 1963-69; pvt. practice N.Y.C. and Rockland County, 1969—; asst. prof. CUNY, 1970-75; mem. field faculty grad. program Goddard Coll., N.Y.C., 1977-78; consulting psychologist Greer-Woodycrest Children's Svcs., Pomona, NY, 1980-82; psychologist East Ramapo Ctrl. Sch. Dist., Spring Valley, NY, 1982-91. Lectr. Nassau C.C., Garden City, N.Y., 1967-69, Coll. of New Rochelle, N.Y., 1977-78, Rockland C.C., Suffern, N.Y., 1977-80; lectr. spkr.'s bur. Rockland County Mental Health Assn., Pomona, 1977—; cons. drug rehab. Topic House, L.I., N.Y., 1965-69; clin. dir. homosexual walk-in ctr. Identity House, N.Y.C., 1972-76; bd. dirs. women's issues divsn. Humanistic Psychology Ctr. of NY, N.Y.C.; pres. Women Unltd.; med. staff Nyack (N.Y.) Hosp., 1974—; presenter in field over 50 countries, 1972—. Editor: (Bklyn. Coll. Yr. Book) Brocklundian, 1947; contbr. articles to profl. jours., chapters to books; creator Zaraleya Psychoenergetic Technique, 1972, Zaraleya Semester Based Self-Actualization Psychotherapy; Exhibited in group shows at Arts Coun. Rockland (NY), 1997, 1999, Rockland Ctr. for Arts, 1998. Parent seminar leader New City (N.Y.) Libr., 1981; conf. presenter E. Ramapo Ctrl. Sch. Dist., 1982, 1984, 1987; newsletter editor Rockland Ctr. for the Arts, Nyack, NY, 1986—88. Recipient Gold Key award Bklyn. Coll., 1947. Mem.: APA (exec. bd. divsn. humanistic psychology, newsletter editor 1977—79, svc. award 1977), Internat. Assn. Cross-Cultural Psychology, Internat. Assn. Applied Psychology, Internat. Coun. Psychologists (chair com. libr. subscription devel.), Nat. Register Health Svc. Providers in Psychology, Nassau and Suffolk Psychol. Assn., Rockland County Psychol. Soc. (chairperson clin. com. 1981, 1982), N.Y. Soc. Clin. Psychologists, Nat. Assn. Sch. Psychologists. Avocations: writing, drawing, painting, travel. Office: 10 Wyndham Ln New City NY 10956-4527

HARARY, KEITH, research scientist, writer, science journalist; b. N.Y.C., Feb. 9, 1953; s. Victor and Lillian (Mazur) H.; m. Darlene Moore, Oct. 22, 1985. BA in Psychology, Duke U., 1975; PhD, Union Inst., 1986. Crisis counselor Durham (N.C.) Mental Health Ctr., 1972-76; rsch. assoc. Psychical Rsch. Found., Durham, 1972-76; rsch. assoc. dept. psychiatry Maimonides Med. Ctr., Bklyn., 1976-79; dir. counseling Human Freedom Ctr., Berkeley, Calif., 1979; rsch. cons. SRI Internat., Menlo Park, Calif., 1980-82; design cons. Atari Corp., Sunnyvale, Calif., 1983-85; pres., rsch. dir. Inst. for Advanced Psychology, San Francisco, 1986—; freelance sci. journalist, 1988-98; editor-at-large Omni Mag., 1996-98; sr. v.p., rsch. dir. Capital Access, 1996—2001. Invited lectr. Duke U., 1995; lectr. in field; adj. prof. Antioch U., San Francisco, 1985, 86; guest lectr. Lyceum Sch. for Gifted Children, 1985-89; vis. rschr. USSR Acad. Scis., 1983; rsch. cons. Am. Soc. for Psychical Rsch., 1971-72, sci. applications Internat. Corp., 1991-93 ; psychol. cons., nat. media spokespers on Budget Rent A Car Corp., 1997-99; psychol. cons., media spokesperson Sears Corp., 1997; psychol. cons. Microsoft Corp., 1998-99. Co-author: The Mind Race, 1984, 85, 30-Day Altered States of Consciousness Series, 1989-91, rev. edits., 1999, Who Do You Think You Are? Explore Your Many-Sided Self With the Berkeley Personality Profile, 1994, CD-ROM edit., 1996; featured monthly columnist in The Omni Mind Brain Lab in Omni Mag., 1995-98; contbr. over 100 articles to profl. jours., other publs. Mem. APA, Am. Psychol. Soc., Assn. for Media Psychology, Am. Soc. for Psychical Rsch. (bd. dirs. 1994—). Achievements include first to develop reflective approach to personality profiling; development of advanced human perception research, including original training methodologies in altered states induction, and extended perception; development of original scientific terminology in specialized

theoretical areas in advanced perceptual research, including extended perception, extended human abilities, mental noise, paranormal hysteria, stress apparitions, others; development of original clinical approaches to crisis intervention. Home and Office: PO Box 2190 Portland OR 97208-2190

HARATUNIAN, MICHAEL, engineering company executive; b. 1933; Various positions STV Group, Inc., Douglasville, Pa., 1972—, pres., COO, 1988—, chmn. bd. dirs., CEO, 1991-99, chmn. bd., 1999—2002, chmn. emeritus, 2002—. Office: STV Group Inc 225 Park Ave S New York NY 10003-1604 E-mail: Haratunm@stvinc.com.

HARAZIN, WILLIAM DENNIS, lawyer; b. Berwyn, Ill., Aug. 24, 1953; s. Robert John and Mary Ann H.; m. Becky R. French, Mar. 13, 1981. BS, Ill. State U., 1974, postgrad., 1975, JD, 1978. Bar: Ill. 1978, U.S. Dist. Ct. (no. dist.) Ill. 1978, N.C. 1981, U.S. Dist. Ct. (ea. and mid. dists.) N.C. 1981, U.S. Ct. Appeals (4th cir.) 1982. Lectr. So. Ill. U., Carbondale, 1977-78; assoc. Abramson & Fox, Chgo., 1978-79; instr. Durham (N.C.) Tech. Inst., 1979; atty. Ind. Legal Svcs., Raleigh, N.C., 1980-81; ptnr. Barringer, Allen & Pinnix, Raleigh, 1981-88; ptnr. property co. Harazin, French & Pinnix, Raleigh, 1982-95; instr. N.C. State U., Raleigh, 1982-95, vis. asst. prof., 1995—; owner Law Office of William D. Harazin, Raleigh, 1988—. Mem. legal adv. group World Trade Ctr. N.C., RTP, N.C., 1990-95; vis. asst. prof. N.C. State U., 1995—. Mem. Raleigh Housing Appeals Bd., 1983-86, chmn., 1986-89; mem. Carbondale Fair Housing Bd., 1977-78; exch. mem. to Japan, Rotary Internat., Raleigh, 1986. Mem.: ABA (mem. com. internat. bus. law), N.C. Dist. Export Coun., N.C. Bd. Sci. and Tech. (internat. com. 1995—2000), World Trade Ctr. N.C. (bd. dirs. 1992—, chmn. 2001—), Wake County Bar Assn., N.C. Dist. Export Coun., N.C. World Trade Assn. (treas. 1985—90, Triangle chpt. pres. 1990—92, statewide pres. 1992—94), Ill. Bar Assn., N.C. Bar Assn. internat. law sect. (coun. mem. 1992—, treas. 1994—95, sec. 1995—96, vice-chair 1996—98, chair 1998—99, mem. bus. law sect.), Internat. Visitors Ctr. (bd. dirs. 1999—), N.C. Ctr. for World Langs. and Culture (bd. dirs. 1994—96), Nat. Assn. Eagle Scouts. Office: 434 Fayetteville Street Mall Raleigh NC 27601-1701

HARB, MAC, Canadian government official; BS, U. Ottawa, Ont., Can., 1979, M in Elec. Engring., 1983. Alderman City of Ottawa, 1985-88, dep. mayor, 1987-88; mem. of parliment Ho. of Commons, Ottawa, 1988—, sec. to min. for internat. trade, 1993-95, chmn. internat. trade com., vice chair pub. account com. Former vice-chmn. Ottawa Non-Profit Housing Corp, Ottawa Econ. Affairs Com.; bd. mgmt. Preston St. bus. improvement bd. Mem. Assn. Profl. Engrs. on Ont. Avocations: cooking, gardening, travel. Office: Ho of Commons Ctr Block Rm 552D Ottawa ON Canada K1A 0A6

HARBAUGH, DANIEL PAUL, lawyer; b. Wendell, Idaho, May 18, 1948; s. Myron and Manuelita (Garcia) Harbaugh. BA, Gonzaga U., 1970, JD, 1974. Bar: Wash. 1974, U.S. Dist. Ct. (ea. dist.) Wash. 1977, U.S. Ct. Appeals (9th cir.) 1978. Asst. atty. gen. State of Wash., Spokane, 1974-77; ptnr. Richter, Wimberley & Ericson, Spokane, 1977-83, Harbaugh & Bloom, P.S., Spokane, 1983—. Bd. dirs. Spokane Legal Svcs., 1982—86; bd. govs. LAWPAC, Seattle, 1980—92. Bd. dirs. Spokane Ballet, 1983-88; chpt. dir. Les Amis du Vin, Spokane, 1985-88; mem. Spokane County Civil Svc. Commn., 1991-2003, chmn., 1999-2003, Gonzaga U. Pres'. Coun., 1991-2000. Mem. ATLA, Wash. State Bar Assn. (spl. dist. counsel 1982-95, mem. com. rules for profl. conduct 1989-92, mem. legis. com. 1995-96), Spokane County Bar Assn. (chair med.-legal com. 1991), Wash. State Trial Lawyers Assn. (v.p. 1988-89, co-chair worker's compensation sect. 1992, 93, spl. select. com. on workers' corp. 1990—, forum 1994—, vice-chmn. 1994-97, mem. legis. com. 1995-98), Nat. Orgn. Social Security Claimants Reps., Internat. Wine and Food Soc. (pres. local chpt. 1989-91, cellar master 1994-96, cellar com. 2001—), Spokane Enol. Soc., Spokane Club, Spokane Country Club (adminstrv. com. 1995-98, chmn. 1997-98, trustee 1996-99, sec.-treas. 1997-98, pres. 1998-99, ex-officio 1999-2000, long range planning com. 1999-2001), Alpha Sigma Nu, Phi Alpha Delta. Roman Catholic. Office: Harbaugh & Bloom PS PO Box 1461 Spokane WA 99210-1461 E-mail: dan@hblaw2.com.

HARBAUGH, JAMES JOSEPH, former professional football player; b. Toledo, Ohio, Dec. 23, 1963; Degree in comm., U. Mich., 1987. Quarterback Chgo. Bears, 1987-93, Indpls. Colts, 1994-98, Balt. Ravens, 1998-99, San Diego Chargers, 1999—2000, Carolina Panthers, 2001; offensive asst. Oakland Raiders, 2002—. Selected to Pro Bowl, 1995. Office: 1220 Harbor Bay Pkwy Alameda CA 94502 Office Fax: 510-864-5134.

HARBAUGH, JOHN WARVELLE, geologist, educator; b. Madison, Wis., Aug. 6, 1926; s. Marion Dwight and Marjorie (Warvelle) H.; m. Josephine Taylor, Nov. 24, 1951 (dec. Dec. 25, 1985); children: Robert, Dwight, Richard; m. Audrey Wegst, Oct. 21, 2000. BS, U. Kans., 1948, MS, 1950; PhD, U. Wis., 1955. Prodn. geologist Carter Oil Co., Tulsa, 1951-53; prof. geol. sci. Stanford U., 1955-99, prof. emeritus, 1999—. Author: (with G. Bonham Carter) Computer Simulation in Geology, 1970, (with D.M. Tezlaff) Simulating Clastic Sedimentation, 1989, (with P. Martinez) Simulating Nearshore Environments, 1993, (with R. Slingerland and K. Furlong) Simulating Clastic Sedimentary Basins, 1994, (with J.C. Davis and J. Wendebourg) Computing Risk for Oil Prospects: Principles and Programs, 1995, (with J. Wendebourg) Simulating Oil Entrapment in Clastic Sequences, 1997. Recipient Haworth Disting. Alumni award U. Kans., 1968, Krumbein medal Internat. Assn. Math. Geologists, 1986, U. Wis.-Madison Disting. Alumni award, 2003. Fellow Geol. Soc. Am.; mem. Am. Assn. Petroleum Geologists (Levorsen award 1970, Disting. Svc. award 1987, Disting. Edn. award Pacific sect. 1999, 2001, Disting. alumni award, U. Wis. 2003). Republican. Home: 683 Salvatierra St Stanford CA 94305-8539 E-mail: harbaugh@pangea.stanford.edu.

HARBAUGH, JOSEPH DELBERT, legal educator, consultant; b. June 15, 1939; s. Kenton E. and Giovanna D. (Fusco) H.; m. Leona R. Noon, June 17, 1961; children: Regina, Denise, Laurie, Wendolyn; m. Barbara J. Britzke, July 23, 1982; children: Elizabeth, Andrew, Nicholas. BS in Polit. Sci., St. Joseph's Coll., 1961; LLB, U. Pitts., 1964; LLM, Georgetown U., 1967. Bar: D.C. 1965, Conn. 1965, U.S. Ct. Appeals (2d cir.) 1967, U.S. Supreme Ct. 1968, Pa. 1979. Chief pub. defender Conn. Cir. Ct., 1965-68; assoc. prof. Sch. Law U. Conn., 1968-72; with Sch. Law Duke U., 1972-74; prof. Sch. Law Temple U., Phila., 1974-82; vis. prof. Law Ctr. Georgetown U., 1982-84; prof. Sch. Law Am. U., 1984-87; dean T.C. Williams Sch. Law U. Richmond, Va., 1987-95; dean Shepard Broad Law Ctr. Nova Southeastern U., Ft. Lauderdale, Fla., 1995—. Majority chief counsel Pa. Senate Judiciary Com., 1978-80, minority chief counsel, 1980-85; cons. to continuing legal edn. orgns. Author: (with McDonald) Task Analysis of the Criminal Justice Attorney, 1977; editor: Comparative Analysis of ABA Standards for Criminal Justice with Connecticut Law, Rules and Practice, 1973, Lawyer Negotiation Training Materials, 1988, (with Bastress) Interviewing, Counseling and Negotiating: Skills for Effective Representation, 1990; videotapes include: (with Britzke) Basics of Interviewing, 1982, Basics of Negotiating, 1984, (with Guernsey and Zwier) The Negotiator, 1995; contbr. articles to profl. jours. Mem. ABA (ho. of dels., pres.'s task force on profl. competency 1981-83, 92—, mem. accreditation com. 1982-88, chmn. legis. com. criminal justice sect. 1982-83), Pa. Bar Assn., Assn. Am. Law Schs. (del. to ABA Ho. of Dels. 1983-86, 92—, mem. exec. com. 1980-82). Democrat. Office: Nova Southeastern U Shepard Broad Law Ctr Leo Goodwin Sr Hall 3305 College Ave Fort Lauderdale FL 33314-7721 Home: 9801 NW 35th St Hollywood FL 33024-8003 E-mail: harbaughj@nsu.law.nova.edu.

HARBERGER, ARNOLD CARL, economist, educator; b. Newark, July 27, 1924; s. Ferdinand C. and Martha (Bucher) H.; m. Ana Beatriz Valjalo, Mar. 15, 1958; children: Paul Vincent, Carl David. Student, Johns Hopkins U., 1941-43; MA, U. Chgo., 1947, PhD, 1950; Doctor honoris causa, U. Tucuman, 1979, Cath. U. Chile, 1988, Tech. U. Cen. Am., 1989. Asst. prof. polit. economy Johns Hopkins U., 1949-53; asso. prof. econs. U. Chgo., 1953-59, prof., 1959—, chmn. dept., 1964-71, 75-80, Gustavus F. and Ann M. Swift disting. svc. prof., 1977-91, prof. emeritus, 1991—, dir. Ctr. Latin Am. Econ. Studies, 1965-92. Vis. prof. MIT (Ctr. Internat. Studies), New Delhi, 1961-62, Econ. Devel. Inst., IBRD, 1965, Harvard U., 1971-72, Princeton U., 1973-74, UCLA, 1983, 84, U. Paris, 1986; prof. econs. UCLA, 1984—; cons. IMF, 1950, 89, 2002—, U.S. Pres.'s Materials Policy Commn., 1951-52, U.S. Treasury Dept., 1961-75, Com. Econ. devel., 1961-78, Planning Commn., India, 1961-62, 73, Pan Am. Union, 1962-76, Dept. State, 1962-76, Cen. Bank, Chile, 1965-70, Dominican Republic, 1989, China, 1995, Ecuador, 1996, Planning Dept., Panama, 1963-77, Colombia, 1969-71, Nicaragua, 1990, Indonesia, 1997—; cons. Ford Found., 1967-77, Planning Commn., El Salvador, 1973-75, Budget and Planning Office, Uruguay, 1974-75, Can. Dept. Regional Econ. Expansion, 1975-77, Econ. Min. Argentina, 1994-2000, Fin. Ministry, Bolivia, 1976, Mex., 1976—; cons. Can. Dept. Employment and Migration, 1980-82, Indonesian Ministry Fin., 1981-82, 86, 97-2000, Can. Dept. Fin., 1982-88, Can. Dept. Industry, Sci. and Tech., 1991-99, Chinese Ministry Fin., 1983; ministry fin., Malawi, 1988, Venezuela, 1989, Colombia, 1991, 94, 2002, Dominican Republic, 1996, 97, Egypt, 2002; mem. internat. adv. coun. Inst. Internat. Studies, Stanford U., 1991-99; v.p., chmn. adv. coun. Inst. for Policy Reform; cons. Office Econ. Adviser to the Pres. Russia, 2000—. Author: Project Evaluation, 1972, Taxation and Welfare, 1974; editor: Demand for Durable Goods, 1960, The Taxation of Income from Capital, 1968, Key Problems of Economic Policy In Latin America, 1970, World Economic Growth, 1985, (with Glenn P. Jenkins) Cost-Benefit Analysis, 2002; contbr. sci. papers to profl. jours. and govt. publs. With AUS, 1943-46. Guggenheim fellow; Fulbright scholar; faculty rsch. fellow Social Sci. Rsch. Coun., Ford Found. faculty rsch. fellow, 1968-69. Fellow Econometric Soc., Am. Acad. Arts and Scis., Am. Econ. Assn. (mem. exec. com. 1970-72, v.p. 1992, pres.-elect 1996, pres. 1997, disting. fellow 1999), Western Econ. Assn. (v.p. 1987-88, pres. 1989-90), Royal Econ. Soc., Nat. Tax Assn. (Holland medal 2001), NAS, Phi Beta Kappa. Home: 136 Buckskin Rd Bell Canyon CA 91307-1125 Office: UCLA PO Box 951477 405 Hilgard Ave Los Angeles CA 90095-1477 E-mail: harberger@econ.ucla.edu.

HARBERT, BILL LEBOLD, retired construction corporation executive; b. Indianola, Miss., July 21, 1923; s. John Murdock and Mae (Schooling) H.; m. Mary Joyce Patrick, June 28, 1952; children— Anne Harbert Moulton, Elizabeth Harbert Cornay, Billy L., Jr. BS, Auburn U., 1948; Advanced Mgmt. Program, Harvard U., 1966. Lic. profl. engr. and land surveyor, Ala. Exec. v.p. Harbert Constrn. Corp., Birmingham, Ala., 1948-79, pres., 1979-81; pres., COO Harbert Internat., Inc., Birmingham, 1981-90, vice-chmn., 1990-91, pres., chmn. bd., 1991-98; pres., chmn. bd. dirs. Bill Harbert Internat. Constrn., Inc., 1992—, chmn., CEO, 1998-99; ret., 1999. Trustee, co-chmn. Laborers Nat. Pension Fund, Dallas, 1968—; bd. dirs. U. Ala. Health Service Found., Birmingham, 1983-95, Met. Devel. Bd. of Birmingham, 1980-83, AMI Brookwood Med. Ctr., 1990—, Internat. Pipe Line Contractors Assn., 1980, 88, 93-94, 98, 2d v.p., 1999-2000, Comprehensive Cancer Ctr.-U. Ala., Birmingham, 1999-2000. Sgt. U.S. Army, 1943-46 Mem. Birmingham Area C. of C. Clubs: Vestavia Country (pres. 1971), Riverchase Country (pres. 1980). Methodist. Home: 205 Vestavia Cir Birmingham AL 35216-1351

HARBERT, CHARLES ARMON, medicinal chemist; b. Indpls., Apr. 7, 1940; s. Charles Homer and Ruth Laura (Griffey) H.; m. Kay Louise Strode, Sept. 9, 1961; children: Kelle Harbert Moley, Jennifer Ruth. BS, U. Colo., 1962; PhD, U. Mo., 1967. NIH postdoctoral fellow Stanford U., 1967—69; rsch. scientist Pfizer Ctrl. Rsch., Groton, Conn., 1969-72, project leader, 1972-76, mgr., 1976-81, dir., 1981-84, exec. dir., 1984-91, sr. exec. dir., 1991-93, v.p., 1993—99; ret., 1999. Co-chair Keystone Symposium, 1995; mem. adv. com. U. Mo. Chemistry Dept., Columbia, Mo., 1992—; mem. vis. com. Conn. Coll., New London, 1986, 93; chair medicinal chemistry Gordon Rsch. Conf., New London, 1990. Mem. Bd. Edn., Waterford, Conn., 1979-81, Bd. Fin. Waterford, 1977-78, Bd. Tax Review, Waterford, 1975-77. NIH Postdoctoral fellow NIH, Stanford, 1967-69; recipient Disting. Alumni award U. Mo., 1993. Mem. Am. Chem. Soc. (awards com. med. chem. divsn. 1994-99), Sigma Xi, Phi Lambda. Achievements include inventor/patents including conformational mapping of dopmaine receptor for antagonists; co-inventor Zoloft.

HARBERT, KENNETH RAY, health care educator, physician; b. McKeesport, Pa., Feb. 2, 1947; s. Stephen Ray and Dorothy (Floyd) H.; m. Peggeen Owings, June 2, 1983; children: Renee, Dedra. AS, Community Coll. Allegheny City, Pitts., 1972; BS, SUNY, 1975; MHA in Hosp. Adminstrn., Cen. Mich. State U., 1982; PhD in Health Edn., Pa. State U., 1993. Physician asst. U. Pitts., 1975-77; with psychiatry dept. George Washington U., Washington, 1980-82; co-founder, co-dir. Stress Adaptability Response Group, Washington, 1979-83; coordinator edn. Greater S.E. Community Hosp., Washington, 1978-80, dir. med. edn., 1980-83; dir. physician extender services Geisinger Med. Ctr., Washington, 1983-93. Cons. Nat. Med. Advt. Group, Bethesda, Md., 1982—83, Washington Occupl. Health Svcs., Washington, 1980—82; prof. Phila. Coll. Osteo. Medicine, chair, 1996—2000; project dir. CERMUSA Office Naval Rsch., 1995—96. Editor: Physician Assistants Present and Future Models, 1986; author: Procedural Manual for the Utilizations of PA's, 1992; exec. producer: (video) Lifesavers Then... Caregivers Now, 2000. Mem. Mayor's Health Council, Washington, 1981-83, Emergency Cardiac Care Council, Cen. Pa., 1986-87; com. mem. Vietnam Women's Meml. Project, Washington, 1986. Served with USN, 1966-72, USCGR, 1978-92, USPHS Res. 1992-2000. Recipient cert. appreciation U.S. Senate, Washington, 1982. Mem. Vets. Caucus of Am. Acad. Physicians Assts. (chmn. 1982-86, founder 1982-2000, Nat. Humanitarian award 1997, Lifetime Achievement award 2001, VA Spl. Appreciation award 2001), Am. Hosp. Assn. (mem. health tng. edn. com. 1985-87), Am. Mktg. Assn., Alliance Continuing Med. Edn., Am. Acad. Physicians Assts. (winner clin. photo contest 1984), Res. Officers Assn., Assn. Mil. Surgeons of U.S. (life), 1st Marine Divsn. (life), Naval Assn. of PA's (life). Lodges: Rotary. Avocations: sailing, swimming, reading. Office: U St Francis 4401 Silver Ave SE Ste B Albuquerque NM 87108

HARBERT, SUSAN RANDALL, administrator; b. Apr. 25, 1957; BS in Home Econs. Edn., U. Conn., 1979; MBA, Boston U., 1982. Tchr. Fairfield (Conn.) Woods Jr. High Sch., 1979-80; mgr. Filenes, Boston, 1982-83; officer State St. Bank & Trust Co., Boston, 1985-88; ptnr. Grantham, Mayo, Van Otterloo & Co., Boston, 1988—. Home: 19 Isaac Sprague Dr Hingham MA 02043-2670

HARBESON, JOHN WILLIS, political science educator; b. New Brunswick, NJ, Sept. 14, 1938; s. Robert Willis and Gladys (Evans) H.; m. Ann Elizabeth Warmoth, Aug. 25, 1963; children: Eric John, Kristen Lynne. BA cum laude, Swarthmore (Penn.) Coll., 1960; MA, U. Chgo., 1962; PhD, U. Wis., 1970. From asst. prof. to prof. polit. sci. U. Wis.-Parkside, Kenosha, 1967-85; prof. polit. sci. CUNY, 1985—. Lectr. U. Nairobi, Kenya, 1966 67; vis. prof. Addis Ababa U., Ethiopia, 1973-75; prof. Land Tenure Ctr., U. Wis., Madison, 1976-85; sr. social sci. analyst Agy. Internat. Devel., 1979-82; professorial lectr. Johns Hopkins U., Washington, 1980-82; adj. prof. Columbia U., N.Y.C., 1990-91; sr. adv. Agy. for Internat. Devel. for Democracy and Governance Issues in Ea. and So. Africa, 1993-95; Jennings Randolph sr. fellow U.S. Inst. of Peace, 1998-99; vis. fellow Princeton U. Ctr. Internat. Studies, 2001-02; chmn. divsn. social scis., U. Wis., 1975-79, dir. internat. studies, 1977-79, 82-85; dir. internat. studies, CUNY, 85-88, chmn. dept. polit. sci., 1999-2001. Author: Nation Building in Kenya, 1973, Ethiopian Transformation, 1988; author, editor: Military in African Politics; author, co-editor: Africa in World Politics, 1991, 3d edit., 2000, Civil Society and the State in Africa, 1993, Responsible Government: The Global Challenge, 1993; contbr. over 75 articles to profl. jours. Chairperson Congl. campaigns, Racine, Wis., 1970, 72, Dem. Party, Croton On-Hudson, N.Y., 1989-91, 2000-01; elected village trustee Croton-on-Hudson, 1991-93; pres.'s coun. U. Ill., 1992—. Recipient Meritorious Svc. award Agy. of Internat. Devel., 1980, Rsch. award J.D. and C.T. MacArthur Found., 1991; fellow Am. Coun. of Learned Socs., 1989, Rockefeller Found., 1966. Mem. ACLU (sec. Racine-Kenosha chpt. 1972-74), Am. Polit. Sci. Assn. (governing coun. 2003-, chmn. comparative democratization sect., gov. coun., area studies liaison com., chair African politics conf. group), African Studies Assn., Nat. Urban League (bd. dirs. Racine chpt. 1971-73), Swarthmore Coll. Alumni Coun., Am. Polit. Sci. Assn. Episcopalian. Avocations: tennis, organ and piano playing, reading, singing. Home: 5 Valley Trl Croton On Hudson NY 10520-2213 Office: Convent and 138th Cuny New York NY 10031 E-mail: jwharbeson@aol.com.

HARBIN, CALVIN EDWARD, retired educator; b. Puxico, Mo., Mar. 26, 1916; s. Samuel Wesley and Ada Maria (Shelton) H.; m. Dorothy Comoh, June 26, 1947; chilren: Maria, Ruth, Charles. BS, S.E. Mo. State U., 1949; MA, Peabody-Vanderbilt U., 1949; EdD, U. Mo., 1952; LLD (hon.), Rio Grande Coll., 1976. Prof., dean Ft. Hays State U., Hays, Kans., 1952-81; cons. faculty mem. U.S. Army Command and Gen. Staff Coll., Ft. Leavenworth, Kans., 1968-72. Counselor Hansen Found., Logan, Kans., 1981—. Author: Teaching Power, 1967; co-author (with Dane and Polly Bales): Kate Hansen, Beloved Teacher, America's Cultural Ambassador to Japan, 1999, Grandest Mission on Earth, 2000; contbr. articles to profl. jours.; composer hymns. Col. U.S. Army, 1941-76, ETO. Mem. SAR. Republican. Presbyterian. Avocations: gardening, writing, senior citizen's organizations. Home: 303 W 19th St Hays KS 67601-3116

HARBIN, MICHAEL ALLEN, religion educator, writer; b. Vincennes, Ind., May 24, 1947; s. Hugh Allen and Norma June (Palmer) H.; m. Esther Marie Rinas, May 31, 1971; children: Athena Colleen, Heidi Elizabeth, Douglas Allen. BS, U.S. Naval Acad., 1969; ThM, Dallas Theol. Sem., 1980, ThD, 1988; MA, Calif. State U., Carson, 1993. Instr. Dallas Bible Coll., 1984-86; freelance writer Garland, Tex., 1986-93; prof. Taylor U., Upland, Ind., 1993—, chair biblical studies, 1999—. Mem. elder bd. South Garland Bible Ch., Garland, Tex., 1981-93, chmn. elder bd., 1982-86; mem. elder bd. Upland Cmty. Ch., 1995—; del. nat. conv. Evangel. Mennonite Ch., 1996, 99, 2002, 03. Author: To Serve Other Gods, 1994, The Promise and the Blessing, 2003; contbr. Del. 16th Senatorial Dist. Rep. Conv., Dallas, 1990, 92; alt. del. State Rep. Conv., Ft. Worth, 1990. Capt. USNR, ret. Fellow Inst. of Bibl. Rsch.; mem. Soc. Bibl. Lit., Bibl. Archaeol. Soc., Evang. Theol. Soc., Near Ea. Archaeol. Soc. Home: 629 W South St Upland IN 46989-0673 *I owe whatever success I have achieved to the fact that I have always tried to take God and his Word seriously and apply the implications to my life.*

HARBISON, JAMES WESLEY, JR., lawyer; b. Mooresville, N.C., Aug. 30, 1934; s. James Wesley and Ola Mae (Bonney) H.; m. Margaret Geddes Morgan, Apr. 15, 1961; children: Anne, James. AB, Duke U., 1956; LLB, Yale U., 1959. Bar: N.C. 1959, N.Y. 1960, U.S. Dist. Ct. (so. and ea. dists.) N.Y. 1961, U.S. Ct. Appeals (2d cir.) 1962, U.S. Supreme Ct. 1968, U.S. Ct. Appeals (7th cir.) 1970, U.S. Ct. Appeals (5th cir.) 1975. Assoc. Simpson, Thacher & Bartlett, N.Y.C., 1960-73; ptnr. Wickes, Riddell, Bloomer, Jacobi & McGuire, N.Y.C., 1973-78, Morgan, Lewis & Bockius LLP, N.Y.C., 1979—. Served to capt. USAF, 1959-60, N.Y. A.N.G., 1960-68. Mem. ABA, N.C. Bar Assn., N.Y. State Bar Assn., Assn. of Bar of City of N.Y., Fed. Bar Council, Am. Judicature Soc. Clubs: Met., Yale (N.Y.C.). Democrat. Methodist. Home: 30 E End Ave New York NY 10028-7053 Office: Morgan Lewis & Bockius LLP 101 Park Ave Fl 44 New York NY 10178 0060

HARBOTTLE, GARMAN, chemist; b. Dayton, Ohio, Sept. 25, 1923; s. William Edwin and Susan (Garman) Harbottle; m. Naomi Perkiss, June 10, 1949; 1 child, Laura. BS, Calif. Inst. Tech., 1944; PhD, Columbia U., 1949. Chemist Brookhaven Nat. Lab., Upton, N.Y., 1949—; dir. Internat. Atomic Energy Agy., Vienna, Austria, 1965-67; rsch. collaborator Met. Museum of Art, 1990—. Adj prof SUNY, Stony Brook, 1985—93, Stony Brook, 1999—; guest prof Univ Sci Technology China, Hefei, 1997. Editor (assoc ed): Archaeometry Jour, 1981—96, Jour Radioanalytical Chemistry, 1982—2001. Trustee Vanderbilt Mus, Centerport, NY, 1979—87, Inc Village of Old Field, NY, 1980—86. Recipient George von Hevesy Medal, 1983, Glenn T Seaborg Medal, Am Nuclear Soc, 1995, Roald Fryxell medal, Soc. Am. Archaeology, 1994, Pomerance medal, Am. Inst. Archaeology, 2002; fellow Postdoctoral, Atomic Energy Comn, 1951—52, Guggenheim, 1957—58. Mem.: Soc Archaeological Scis (pres 1987). Office: Brookhaven Nat Lab Upton NY 11973-5000 E-mail: garman@bnl.gov.

HARBOUR, JAMES WILLIAM, theater educator; s. David Frank and Selma K. Harbour; m. Maureen Patricia Fennessy, Dec. 19, 1961. BFA in Classic Theatre, So. Oreg. Coll., 1971; MFA, U. of Calif., Riverside, California, 1975. Asst. prof. Ga. So. U., Statesboro, Ga., 1995—, dir. of theatre, 2001—. Chairman grad. auditions com. Southeastern Theatre Conf., 2002—, chmn. acting and directing com., 1998—2002; assoc. artistic dir. Maui Acad. of Performing Arts, Kahului, Hawaii, 1990—91. Actor: (plays) Appear and Show Cause (Disting. Performance by a Supporting Actor award Detroit (Mich.) News, 1984); dir.: (over 36 plays); actor: (over 120 plays). Mem.: Actor's Equity Assn., Am. Theatre Assn. (chmn. directing com. 1978—82). Office: CommArts - Georgia Southern University P O Box 8091 Statesboro GA 30460 Office Fax: 912-681-0822. E-mail: jharbour@gasou.edu.

HARBOUR, NANCY CAINE, lawyer; b. Cleve., July 30, 1949; d. William Anthony and Bernadette (Frohnapple) Caine; m. Randall Lee Harbour, Sept. 29, 1979. BA magna cum laude, U. Detroit, 1970; JD, Cleve. State U., 1978. Bar: Mich. 1978. Writer Project Map, Inc., Washington, 1971-72; newspaper reporter Alexandria (Va.) Gazette, 1972-73, Times Herald Record, Goshen, N.Y., 1973-75; atty. Conklin, Benham, et al., Detroit, 1978-82, Martens, Ice & Geary, P.C., Detroit, 1982-90; ptnr. Martens, Ice, Geary, Detroit, 1990—2001; dir. profl. edn. Butzel Long, 2002—. Mem. Mich. Bar Assn., State Bar Mich. (compensation coun. 1983-85), Gamma Pi Epsilon. Office: Butzel Long PC 150 W Jefferson St Detroit MI 48226 E-mail: harbour@butzel.com.

HARBOUR, ROBERT RANDALL, state agency administrator; b. Oklahoma City, Dec. 13, 1949; s. Robert Roy and Anna Belle (Boatner) H.; m. Patti Rae Levine, Apr. 4, 1981; children: Ann Joelle, Robert Daniel. BA in Pub. Adminstrn., U. Ctrl. Okla., 1975. Clk. Okla. Dept. Human Svcs., Oklahoma City, 1974-76; interviewer Okla. Employment Security Commn., Oklahoma City, 1976-80, sr. interviewer, 1980-89, local office mgr. I, 1989-93, trainer, mgr. I, 1993—, tng. program writer, presenter, 1993—. Job search workshop presenter, employment svc. programs presenter Okla. Employment Security Commn., Oklahoma City, 1987-93; facilitator job fair Gov.'s Coun. Small Bus., Oklahoma City, 1990, Mayor's Employer Adv. Coun., Oklahoma City, 1992, Oklahoma City C.C., 1991. Contbr: (workbook) Job Search Workshop Workbook, 1989; writer: (tng. programs) State-Mandated Manager Training Program, 1993, Non-Supervisory Employee Training Program, 1993, New Employee Training Program, 1993. Recipient Spl. Merit award Mil. Order Purple Heart, Oklahoma City, 1991, Career Day Program Appreciation award Pvt. Industry Coun., Oklahoma City, 1991, Honorable Mention award ASTD Tng. Manual, 1994. Mem. ASTD (Honorable Mention for tng. manual ctrl. Okla. chpt. 1994, Honorable Mention award for program design ctrl. Okla. chpt. 1995), Internat. Assn. Pers. in Employment Svc., Nat. Forensic League, Internat. Platform Assn. Democrat. Avocations: public speaking, writing, reading, bowling, tennis. Home: 5705 NW 102d St Oklahoma City OK 73162-6900 Office: Okla Employment Security Commn 2401 N Lincoln Blvd Rm 200 Oklahoma City OK 73105-4495

HARBUCK, EDWIN CHARLES, insurance agent; b. Shreveport, La., Mar. 5, 1934; s. Charles Adam and Elsie (Owens) H.; m. Delores Threlkeld, June 10, 1955; children: Jonathan S., Edwin Seth, Christopher L., Charles Adam II. BS, Centenary Coll., 1956. CLU. Vice pres., gen. mgr. Harbuck Sporting Goods, Inc., Shreveport, 1958-63; agt. Prudential Ins. Co. of Am., Shreveport, 1963—. Chmn. bd. trustees First Bapt. Ch. Sch., Shreveport, 1978, 98-99; mem. La. State Civil Svc. Commn., 1981-93; chmn. Centenary Coll. Gt. Tchrs. Scholar Campaign, Shreveport, 1992-93; campaign chmn. United Way N.W. La., Shreveport, 1989, pres., 1993; trustee Centenary Coll. La., 1990, vice chmn. bd. trustees, 1999—; v.p. La. Civil Svc. League, 1994—. Recipient Monte M. Lemann Pub. Svc. award La. Civil Svc. League, New Orleans, 1985, Clyde E. Fant Meml. award for Cmty. Svc., 1994; named Shreveport Outstanding Young Man, Jaycees, 1962, Outstanding Young Men in Am., U.S. Jaycees, Washington, 1970. Mem. Chartered Life Underwriters (pres. Shreveport chpt. 1976), Tax Inst. Arklatex, Estate Planning Coun., Million Dollar Roundtable (life), Shreveport Club, Pierremont Oaks Tennis Club. Baptist. Avocations: tennis, hunting, fishing, scuba diving. Home: 4364 Richmond Ave Shreveport LA 71106-1418 Office: Harbuck & Ridley LLC 400 Travis St Ste 808 Shreveport LA 71101-3112 E-mail: edharbuck@harbuckridley.com.

HARBUS, RICHARD, arbitrator, mediator; b. N.Y.C., Sept. 15, 1940; children: Jonathan, Alexandra. BA, Columbia U., 1961; JD, Yale U., 1964. Bar: N.Y. 1965. Law clk. U.S. Ct. Appeals (2d cir.), N.Y.C., 1964-66; assoc. Leibman, Eulau, Robinson & Perlman, N.Y.C., 1966-67; atty. Met. Life Ins. Co., N.Y.C., 1967-74; from asst. prof. law to prof. N.Y. Law Sch., N.Y.C., 1974-81; gen. counsel Rsch. Found., CUNY, N.Y.C., 1981-82; prof. law Sch. Law, Touro Coll., Huntington, N.Y., 1982-92; trial officer N.Y.C. Housing Authority, 1992—. Hearing officer N.Y.C. Bd. Edn., 1978—; adminstrv. law judge Taxi and Limousine Commn., N.Y.C., 1983-87, Parking Violations Bur., N.Y.C., 1988—; arbitrator N.Y. Civil Ct., N.Y.C., 1975—, Nat. Assn. Securities Dealers, 1992—, N.Y. Stock Exch., 1992—; lectr. Office Ct. Adminstrn., N.Y.C., 1982, Suffolk County Acad. Law, Hauppauge, N.Y., 1987. Contbr.

articles to legal publs. Mem. ABA (various coms.), Assn. Arbitrators Civil Ct. N.Y., Am. Arbitration Assn. (comml. mediator). Democrat. Jewish. Avocations: playing piano and cello, reading, travel, photography.

HARBUSCH, KARIN MARIA, education educator, researcher; b. Saarlouis, Germany, July 30, 1959; d. Norbert and Maria Harbusch; m. Matthias Hecking, June 11, 1991; children: Jesko Hecking-Harbusch, Jascha Harbusch-Hecking. Diploma, U. of the Saarland, 1978—83, D, 1984—89. Freelancer Dialogika GmbH, Saarbruecken, Germany, 1984—86; sr. rschr. German Rsch. Ctr. for Artificial Intelligence GmbH, Saarbruecken, Germany, 1989—95. Temp. prof. U. of Hamburg, Germany, 1990—91. Mem.: Gesellschaft fuer Informatik. Home: Marienstr 20 Rheinland-Pfalz Lahnstein D-56112 Germany Office: University of Koblenz-Landau Universitaetsstr 1 Rheinland-Pfalz Koblenz D-56070 Germany Office Fax: +49 261 287 100 2604. E-mail: harbusch@uni-koblenz.de.

HARBUTT, SARAH, photographer, director; d. Charles Harbutt. Dir. of photography Newsweek, 2000; staff New York Times, NY, 1989—92, dep. picture editor, 1992—2000. Creator (exhibitions) "Our Grandmothers", collection, Parsons Sch. of Design and Maine Photographic Workshops, 1997. Recipient Publishers Award, New York Times, 1993, Mag. Picture Editor of the Yr., NPPA, 1999, Mag. of the Yr., Soc. of Mag. Designers, Editing Team of the Yr., World Press Photo, Canon Prize for Picture Editor of the Yr., Via Pour L'Image Internat. Photojournalism Festival at Perpignan, 2000. Office: Newsweek Dir of Photography 251 W 57th St New York NY 10019*

HARCLERODE, HOWARD CHARLES, II, (SKIP HARCLERODE), chemical engineer; b. Cumberland, Md., Jan. 20, 1947; s. Howard Charles and Marjorie Marlyn (Frankfort) H.; m. Judith Dianne Lonnholm, Sept. 18, 1971; children: Kristin Anne, Brent Garrett, Drew Matthew. BS in Chem. Engring., U. Md., 1970, MS in Chem. Engring., 1971. Registered profl. engr., Md., Del., D.C., Va., Ohio; lic. master plumber, Md. Project engr. Allied Chem. Corp., Morristown, N.J., 1971-72, sr. project engr., 1972-75; project engring. mgr. Lever Bros. Co., Balt., 1975-77, maintenance mgr., 1977-78, project mgr. Sulfonation Plant, 1978-79; project mgr. ctrl. engring. Davison Chem. divsn. W.R. Grace & Co., Balt., 1979-84; facilities and engring. mgr. Rsch. divsn. W.R. Grace & Co., Columbia, Md., 1984-86; v.p. Harwel Constrn. Co., Inc., Phoenix, Md., 1983-90, pres., owner, 1990-92, KBD Engring. Co., Phoenix, Md., 1986—. Pres. Jack Dale Assocs., Inc., 1989-90, v.p., owner Alpha & Omega Engring. Co., Inc., 1995—; bd. dirs. Md. State Bd. Profl. Engrs. Legis. asst. to U.S. Senator Pete Domenici, Washington, 1981-82; Rep. candidate for 8th dist. Md. Ho. of Dels., Baltimore County, 1986; trustee Ctrl. Presbyn. Ch., pres., 1988-92; scoutmaster Boy Scouts Am. Mem. AIChE, NSPE (vice chmn. 1983-85, Congl. fellow 1981-82), Md. Soc. Profl. Engrs. (treas. 1984-85), Order of Engr. Presbyterian. Office: KBD Engring Co Inc 1 Country Club Ln Phoenix MD 21131-1835 E-mail: kbdeng@aol.com., skipharclerode@comcast.net.

HARCOURT, MICHAEL FRANKLIN, retired premier of Province of British Columbia, lawyer, educator; b. Edmonton, Alta., Can., Jan. 6, 1943; s. Frank Norman and Stella Louise (Good) H.; m. Mai-Gret Wibecke Salo, June 26, 1971; 1 son, Justen Michael. BA, U. B.C., 1965, LLB, 1968. Bar: B.C. 1969. Founder dir. Vancouver Cmty. Legal Assistance Soc., 1969-71; ptnr. firm Lew, Fraser & Harcourt, 1971-79; pres. Housing and Econ. Devel. Cons. Firm, Vancouver, from 1977; alderman City of Vancouver, 1972-80, mayor, 1980-86; mem. Legis. Assembly, 1986-96; leader New Dem. Party of B.C., 1987-96; premier Province of B.C., 1991-96, ret., 1996; former leader of opposition, leader of govt.; sr. assoc. Sustainable Devel. Inst., Vancouver, 1996—, L.I.U. Ctr. for Studies of Global Issues, U. B.C. Asst. dir. Justice Devel. Commn., Vancouver; dir. Housing Corp. B.C.; adj. prof. faculty grad. studies U. B.C., 1996—; bd. dirs. Vancouver Internat. Airport, Vancouver Port Authority; fed. commr. B.C. Treaty Commn.; chair Internat. Ctr. for Sustainable Cities. Bd. dirs. Asia-Pacific Found. Mem. Law Soc. B.C., Nat. Rountable Environ. and Economy (chmn. fgn. rels. com.), Jericho Tennis Club. New Democrat. Mem. United Ch. Can. Avocations: tennis, golf, skiing, jogging, basketball. Office: HU B5-2202 Main Mall Vancouver BC Canada V6T1Z4

HARCOURT, ROBERT NEFF, educational administrator, journalist, genealogist; b. East Orange, N.J., Oct. 19, 1932; s. Stanton Hinde and Mary Elizabeth (Neff) H. *Son of Stanton Hinde Harcourt, U.S. Naval Academy 1925, Harcourt shares a great grandfather with publisher Alfred Harcourt, one of founders of Harcourt, Brace & Co. Thru direct lineal descent from John Howland and John Tilley, both signers of the November 11, 1620 "Mayflower Compact", he shares ancestors with American Presidents Franklin Roosevelt, Gerald Ford, Richard Nixon, both George Bushes, and with Theodore Roosevelt through his Thomas Jansen Van Dyke lineage. He is additionally a consanguined cousin of Sir Winston Churchill and the American presidents Stephen Grover Cleveland and Millard Fillmore. Prince William and Prince Harry of Great Britain are distant cousins through common consanguinal family ties with their mother, Lady Diana Frances Spencer, the Princess of Wales. He is descended from John Hobby, one of the founders of Greenwich, CT., who served for several terms in Connecticut's general assembly. On mother's side (Neff family), he is descended from Swiss hero Adam Näf who, in 1531, saved the Banner of Zurich at the Battle at Kappel Am Albis. The Näf sword is today on display at Zurich's Swiss National Museum. Harcourt is the grandson of John Peter Neff, former Vice-President of American Arch & Co. of NYC, whose patented locomotive was displayed at the 1939 New York World's Fair. His mother, Mary E. Neff Harcourt served for forty-five years as a Westfield, N.J. Red Cross volunteer.Appointed by the college president as a member of IAIA's 40th anniversary(2002-2003) events committee specifically focused on the production of a 40 year college history video plus the 40th anniversary celebratory booklet.* BA, Gettysburg Coll., 1958; MA, Columbia U., 1961. Cert guidance, secondary edn., career and vocational guidance, N.Mex. Social case worker N.J. State Bd. Child Welfare, Newark and Morristown, 1958-61; asst. registrar Hofstra U., 1961-62; asst. to evening dean of students CCNY, 1961-62; housing staff U. Denver, 1962-64; fin. aid and placement dir. Inst. Am. Indian Arts (IAIA), Santa Fe, 1965-95, contract cons., 1999, apptd. by coll. pres. to steering com., 2000, nat. capital campaign steering com.; appointed by corp. pres. to adv. bd. Genre Ltd. Art Pubs., L.A., 1986—; nat. color ad participant The Bradford Exchange, Chgo., 1986—. Truman scholar coord. *In 1955-56, Mr. Harcourt was the personnel and public relations specialist with the U.S. Army's first Atomic Cannon Unit in Neckarsulm, Germany. He presented his research paper, "Cyclic Regeneration" to the International Conference on General Semantics in Denver, Colorado, in August, 1968, S.I. Hayakawa Honorary Chairman. Using photographic works, he participated in the spring 1973 Institute of American Indian Arts Faculty Exhibit at the Kennedy Center, Washington D.C. Mr. Harcourt took selected graduate courses at the University of Denver (Post Master's Fellowship), Northern Arizona University, San Francisco State University, University of Hawaii, Rutgers University and Worcester College of Oxford University in England.* Donor Am. Indian Lib. collection Gettysburg (Pa.) Coll., active Santa Fe Civic Chorus, 1977-78, art judge, 3d and 4th ann. Aspen Fundraiser Nat. Mus. Am. Indian, 1993, 94, vol. Inst. for Preservation Original Langs. Am. (IPOLA). With U.S.Army, 1954-56. Decorated Nat. Def. medal, 1970; named Hon. Okie, Gov. Dewey F. Bartlett; postmasters fellow U. Denver, 1962-64, col. a.d.c. to N.Mex. Gov. David F. Cargo, 1970; recipient disting. Alumni award Gettysburg Coll. Alumni Assn., 1995. Mem. Am. Contract Bridge League (exec. bd., Santa Fe unit, life master, ACBL dist. 17 rep.), SAR, Santa Fe Coun. Internat. Rels., Am. Assn. Counseling and Devel., New England Historic Geneal. Soc., Assn. Specialists in Group Work (charter), Adult Student Pers. Assn. (charter), Southwestern Assn. Indian Affairs, Neff Family Hist. Soc., St. Andrew Scottish Soc. of N.Mex., Gen. Soc. Mayflower Descs. (bd. assts. N.Mex. chpt.), Pilgrim John Howland Soc., Upson Family Assn., Order of the Founders and Patriots of Am. (regional counselor), Mil. Order of the Loyal Legion of the U.S., Mil. Order Fgn. Wars of U.S., Gen. Soc. of War of 1812, Nat. Soc. Sons and Daus. of the Pilgrims, Soc. Descs. Washington's Army at Valley Forge, Presdl. Families Am. (charter, N.Mex. regent), Decs. Colonial Physicians and Chirurgiens, Phi Delta Kappa (past mem. exec. bd. local chpt.), Alpha Tau Omega, Alpha Phi Omega, Safari Club Internat. Home: 2980 Viaje Pavo Real Santa Fe NM 87505-5344

HARCROW, E. EARL, lawyer; b. Carrizozo, N.Mex., Mar. 4, 1954; s. James Earl and Nettie (McInnes) H.; m. Julie A., Apr. 16, 1987; children: Ashley Nicole, James Earl. BS, Tex. Tech. U., 1976, JD, 1979. Bar: Tex. 1979, U.S. Dist. Ct. (no. dist.) Tex., U.S. Ct. Appeals (5th cir.) 1979. Asst. dist. atty. Lubbock (Tex.) Dist. Atty. Office, 1979-80, Tarrant Dist. Atty. Office, Ft. Worth, 1980-83; ptnr. Shannon, Gracey, Ratliff & Miller, Ft. Worth, 1985-99, mng. ptnr., 1995-96, ptnr. in charge of tech., 1996-99; ptnr. Haynes & Boone, Ft. Worth, 1999—; gen. counsel Dallas Ft. Worth Med. Ctr., 1990—. Bd. dirs. Planned Parenthood North Tex., 1987-92; fellow Tex. Bar Found., 1991—. Office: Haynes and Boone LLP 201 Main St Ste 2200 Fort Worth TX 76102-3126

HARD, BRIAN, truck leasing company executive; b. Sept. 6, 1946; m. Jan Hard; children: Tyler, Ashley. BSBA, Belknap Coll. CEO Penske Truck Leasing Co., Reading, Pa., pres., COO. Bd. dirs. Penske.*

HARDAGE, DARWIN "DAR" HENRY, animal technologist; b. Caddo, Okla., June 24, 1941; s. William Harry Hardage and Pauline Harbour; m. Darla June Gibson, Sept. 3, 1962 (div. Dec. 1978), remarried, Jan. 26, 1980 (dec. 2003); children: Bryce Keelan, Elizabeth Kathleen, Tifford Andrish, Joshua Hunter. Student, U. Calif., Davis, 1976-78. Field radio operator, mil. policeman USMC, 1959-63; animal caretaker San Diego Zoo, 1964-66; animal technician U. Calif., Davis, 1966-68; animal technologist Shell Devel. Co., Modesto, Calif., 1968-79; animal control officer, poundmaster City of Turlock, Calif., 1981-83; meetinghouse custodian Modesto Facilities Mgmt. Group, Turlock, 1984-99; custodian Stanislaus County, 2001—. Contbr. poetry to profl. publs. Scoutmaster Boy Scouts Am., Modesto, 1981-87; rsch. specialist Cherokee genealogy LDS Ch., Modesto, 1984—; spkr. geneal. socs., 1984—. Recipient Scouters' Key, Boy Scouts Am., 1985, award of merit Boy Scouts Am., 1985, On My Honor Religious award LDS Ch., 1985. Avocations: genealogy, camping, hiking, fishing, target shooting. Home: 1336 Monterey Ave Modesto CA 95354-4246

HARDAGE, PAGE TAYLOR, elementary education educator; b. Richmond, Va., June 27, 1944; d. George Peterson and Gladys Odell (Gordon) Taylor; 1 child, Taylor Brantley. AA, Va. Intermont Coll., Bristol, 1964; BS, Richmond Profl. Inst., 1966; MPA, Va. Commonwealth U., Richmond, 1982. Cert. tchr., Va. Competent toastmaster, dir. play therapy svcs. Med. Coll. Va. Hosps., Va. Commonwealth U., Richmond, 1970-90; dir. Inst. Women's Issues, Va. Commonwealth U., U. Va., Richmond, 1986-91; adminstr. Scottish Rite Childhood Lang. Ctr. at Richmond, Inc., 1991-99. Bd. dirs. Richmond Bus. Coun. Math. and Sci. Ctr. Found., Richmond, Emergency Med. Svcs. Adv. Bd., Richmond. Treas. Richmond Black Student Found., 1989—90, Leadership Metro Richmond Alumni Assn.; group chmn. United Way Greater Richmond, 1987; bd. dirs. Maggie L. Walker Hist. Found., Richmond YWCA, 1989—91, Capital Area Health Adv. Coun.; commr. Mayors Commn. of Concerns of Women, City of Richmond. Mem.: ASPA, NAFE, Va. Assn. Fund Raising Execs., Va. Recreation and Park Soc. (bd. dirs.), Internat. Mgmt. Coun. (exec. com.), Adminstrv. Mgmt. Soc., Rotary Club of Hanover. Unitarian Universalist. Avocations: bridge, target shooting, aerobics, pub. speaking.

HARDAWAY, ERNEST, II, oral and maxillofacial surgeon, public health official; BS, Howard U., 1957, DDS, 1966, cert. in oral and maxillofacial surgery, 1972; MPH, Johns Hopkins U., 1973. Intern, then chief resident oral and maxillofacial surgery Howard U. Med. Ctr., Washington, 1969-72; asst. prof., mem. attending staff Howard U. Coll. Medicine and Med. Ctr., Washington, 1974—; with Bur. Quality Assurance, HHS, Washington, 1974-77; various adminstrv. positions Bur. Med. Services and Health Services Adminstrn., USPHS, 1977-80; dep. commr., then commr. pub. health City of Washington, 1982-84; acting v.p. fin. and adminstrv. affairs Mile Sq. Health Ctr., Inc., 1984; asst. to regional health adminstr. Fed. Employee Occupl. Health Program, 1985, dir., 1986—89, Chgo. and Kansas City, 1989—90; mem. CFO coun. com. on entrepreneurial govt. Office Mgmt. and Budget, Washington, 1991—2001; chmn. com. on acad. affairs Coll. Bus. U. Ill., 2001—. Mem. profl. staff Com. on Ways and Means, U.S. Ho. of Reps., 1972; spl. asst. to dir. Office Policy Planning and Evaluation, HEW, 1973; presenter at numerous profl. meetings. Contbr. articles to dental jours. Mem. D.C. Emergency Med. Care Adv. Com., D.C. Long-Term Planning Group, 1983, D.C. Health Coordinating Council, D.C. Commn. on Homelessness, 1984; mem. adv. bd. Rosemont Health Ctr., 1984; sec. D.C. Commn. on Licensure to Practice Healing Art, 1983; bd. dirs. United Black Fund, 1984, Potomac Valley Myastenia Gravis Found., 1984; mem. com. human rsch. Instnl. Rev. Bd., Chgo., 1994-2001; chmn. com. acad. affairs U. Ill., 2002. Global Community Health fellow HEW, 1971, Louise C. Ball fellow, 1969; recipient Meritorious Service award USPHS, 1982, J.B. Johnson Nursing Ctr. award, 1983, Outstanding Service placque D.C. Village Choir, 1984, Disting. Service cert. Concerned Citizens for Alcohol Abuse, 1984, Whitman-Walker award for AIDS effort, 1984, Exceptional Accomplishment award Regional Health Adminstr., 1987. Fellow Am. Assn. Oral and Maxillofacial Surgeons (ho. of dels. 1977-80), Internat. Coll. Dentistry, Royal Soc. Health, Acad. Dentistry Internat., Am. Coll. Dentistry; mem. ADA (cons. council hosp. dental care 1976-77), D.C. Soc. Oral and Maxillofacial Surgeons (sec.-treas. 1979-81), Nat. Dental Assn. (Dentist of Yr. 1983, 1st ann. Disting. Service award 1984), Omicron Kappa Upsilon, Chi Delta Mu, Sigma Pi Phi. Home: 88 W Schiller St Apt 1204 Chicago IL 60610-2037

HARDAWAY, PENNY (ANFERNEE DEON HARDAWAY), professional basketball player; b. Memphis, July 18, 1972; Grad., Memphis State U. Guard, forward Orlando Magic, Fla., 1993—99, Phoenix Suns, 1999—. Mem. Ea. Conf. Champions Orlando Magic, 1994—95, Dream Team III, 1996. Actor: (films) Blue Chips, 1994. Named to 1st team, All Am. Memphis State U., 1992—93, Newcomer of Yr. in the BMC, 1992—93, NBA All-Rookie 1st team, 1993, All-Star team, Ea. Conf., 1994—95, 1995—96, All-NBA 1st team, 1995; recipient Nat. H.S. Player of Yr. award, Paracle Mag., 1990—91. Achievements include being honored by retiring of Jersey at Memphis State U., 1994. Office: Phoenix Suns 201 E Jefferson St Phoenix AZ 85004-2412

HARDAWAY, ROBERT MORRIS, III, retired physician, educator, retired army officer; b. Camp John Hay, Philippines, Jan. 9, 1916; s. Robert Morris and Olive (Gray) H.; m. Lee H. Harkey, June 12, 1939; children— Robert Morris IV, Elizabeth J., Thomas G. II, Christopher L. AB, U. Denver, 1936; postgrad., U. Colo. Med. Sch., 1935-37; MD, Washington U., St. Louis, 1939. Diplomate Am. Bd. Surgery. Commd. 1st lt., M.C. U.S. Army, 1939, advanced through grades to brig. gen., 1970; ward officer, surg. service Fitzsimons Gen. Hosp., Denver, 1940-41, N. Sector Gen. Hosp., Hawaii, 1941-43; tchr. Med. Field Service Sch., Carlysle Barracks, Pa., 1943-45; surg. trainee Nichols Gen. Hosp., Louisville, 1945-46; resident surgery Madigan Gen. Hosp., Tacoma, 1946-47, Fitzsimons Gen. Hosp., 1949-50; chief surg. service 34th Gen. Hosp., Korea, 1947-49, Sta. Hosp., Ft. Belvoir, Va., 1950-54, 97th Gen. Hosp., Frankfurt, Germany, 1954-58, Martin Army Hosp., Ft. Benning, Ga., 1958-60; dir. div. surgery Walter Reed Army Inst. Research, Washington, 1960-67; comdg. officer 97th Gen. Hosp., Frankfurt, Germany, 1967-70; comdg. gen. William Beaumont Army Med. Ctr., El Paso, 1970-75; prof. surgery Tex. Tech U. Sch. Medicine, El Paso, 1976—2002; staff R.E. Thomason Gen. Hosp., El Paso, 1975—2002. Author: Syndromes of Disseminated Intravascular Coagulation, 1966, Clinical Management of Shock, Surgical and Medical, 1968, Capillary Perfusion in Health and Disease, 1981, Shock— the Reversible Stage of Dying, 1988, Treatment of Wounded in Vietnam, 1988, Blood Problems in Critical Care, 1989; contbr. articles on intravascular coagulation and hemorrhagic shock to jours. and books. Decorated Army Commendation medal with oak leaf cluster, Legion of Merit with oak leaf cluster, D.S.M.; recipient 2d prize for exhibit A.M.A., 1964; Silver award exhibit Am. Soc. Clin. Pathologists-Coll. Am. Pathologists, 1964; certificate of outstanding achievement U.S. Army Sci. Conf., 1964 Fellow ACS, Am. Coll. Angiology, Am. Assn. for Surgery Trauma, Microcirculation Assn.; mem. Assn. Mil. Surgeons U.S., AMA, Alpha Omega Alpha. Episcopalian. *Nothing we know, (or think we know) is the ultimate truth.*

HARDAWAY, TIMOTHY DUANE, basketball player; b. Chgo., Sept. 1, 1966; Grad., U. Tex. at El Paso, 1989. With Golden State Warriors, 1989—95, Miami Heat, 1995—. Named to NBA All-Rookie team, 1990, All-Star team, 1991, 1992, 1993. Office: Denver Nuggets 1000 Chopper Circle Denver CO 80204

HARDBERGER, PHILLIP DUANE, judge, lawyer, journalist; b. Morton, Tex., July 27, 1934; s. Homer Reeves and Bess (Scott) H.; m. Linda Morgan, May 1968; children: Amy, Kimberlea Jones BA, Baylor U., 1955; MS, Columbia U., 1960; LL.B., Georgetown U., 1965. Reporter Waco (Tex.) News Tribune, 1952-54; press rep. Tex. Baptist Conv., 1958-59; assoc. editor Mil. Pub. Inst., N.Y.C., 1961; exec. sec. Peace Corps, 1962-66; spl. asst. to dir. OEO, 1967-68; trial lawyer, 1968-94; chief justice Fourth Ct. of Appeals, State of Tex., San Antonio, 1994—. Author: Texas Courtroom Evidence, Texas Workers' Compensation Trial Manual; contbr. articles to profl. jours. Served to capt. USAF, 1955-58. Home: 319 W Hollywood Ave San Antonio TX 78212-2211 Office: Fourth Ct of Appeals 300 Dolorosa Ste 3200 San Antonio TX 78205-3037

HARDCASTLE, KENNETH IRVIN, crystallographer, researcher; b. San Jose, Calif., Jan. 2, 1931; m. Gladys E. Hardcastle, June 25, 1960; children: Kenneth C., Elizabeth, Geoffrey. AB, San Jose State Coll., 1952; MS, U. Miss., 1954; PhD, U. So. Calif., 1961. Rsch. assoc. Tufts U., Medford, Mass., 1961-63; prof. Calif. State U., Northridge, 1963-99; staff crystallographer Emory U., Atlanta, 1999—. Recipient Fulbright Assn. award, Parma, Italy, 1983. Mem. Am. Chem. Soc., Am. Crystallographer Soc., Sigma Xi. Avocation: tennis. Office: Emory U Chem Dept 1515 Pierce Dr NE Atlanta GA 30322-1003

HARDEE, LEWIS JEFFERSON, JR., theater educator; b. Wilmington, N.C., Jan. 17, 1937; s. Lewis Jefferson and Dorothy (Dosher) H. BA, U. N.C., 1959, MA, 1971. Instr. Am. Acad. Dramatic Arts, N.Y.C., 1970-84; asst. prof. theatre Wagner Coll., S.I., N.Y., 1984-89, assoc. prof., 1989-95, prof., 1995-2000, prof. emeritus, 2000—, head theatre dept., prodr., 1995-99. Music dir., composer in residence Penny Bridge Players, Bklyn., 1981-84, music dir. Wagner Coll. Theatre, S.I., 1984-94. Author: A Brief History of the Lambs, 1997; composer Revolution!; composer, author, lyricist The Prince and the Pauper, 1978, revised, 1992, Treasure Island, 1979, Christopher Columbus, 1981, 92, Christopher Columbus His Story, 1991, Hansel and Gretel, 1981, Nothing to Hide, 1983, Robin Hood, Build Me A Bridge, 1983, Goldilocks, 1983, Sweet Land of Liberty, 1986, The Little Prince, 1987, Three Southern Families, A History, 1994; editor, The Lambs' Script, 1997—; co-author: Nothing to Hide, 1983; compiler: The Lambs' Consolidated Membership Roster, 1874-2001. Bd. dirs. The Lambs, N.Y.C., 1987—95, historian, 1996—, corr. sec., 1998—2001; v.p. The Lambs, Inc., 2002—, The Lambs Found., Inc., 2002—; bd. dirs. Inter-Cities Performing Arts, Inc., Union City, NJ, 1988—89, Brunswick Performing Arts Ctr., Inc., Southport, NC, 1989—94, Hampden-Booth Theatre Libr., N.Y.C., 2000—. With U.S. Army, 1960—62. Grantee Meet the Composer, Inc., 1982, N.C. Coun. for Arts, 1976; recipient Award of Merit Eleanor Gay Lee Gallery Found., 1983; Parade Grand Marshall, N.C. Fourth of July Festival, 1998. Mem. ASCAP, Dramatists Guild, Assoc. Artists Southport (hon. life), Omicron Delta Kappa. Avocation: history. Home: 320 E 57th St New York NY 10022-2948

HARDEGREE, GLORIA JEAN FORE, health services administrator; b. Atlanta, Ga., July 18, 1940; d. Lee Harrison and Corine Joan (Atkinson) Fore; m. Guy H. Hardegree Jr., Jan. 23, 1960; children: Pamela Jean Reas, Sherrie Etta Drew. Diploma in nursing, Crawford W. Long Hosp., 1971; BS, Coll. St. Francis, 1982; M in Counseling, Liberty U. RN Ga., cert. occupl. health nurse, case mgr. Occupl. health nurse Dobbs House Inc., Dallas, 1974-75, AT&T, Atlanta, 1974, Ga. Power Co., Atlanta, 1976—, coord. Wellness Program. Recipient Schering award, 1987, Nurse of Yr. award, Med. Products S.E., 1991, Mayor's work award, 1995, Promina Cup for Wellness Program, 1999—2002, 1st Pl. in chronic disease mgmt., Disease Mgmt. Assn. Am., 2000—02. Mem.: Atlanta Ga. Assn. Occupl. Health Nurses, Inc. (Hero award 2002, 2003), Am. Assn. Occupl. Health Nurses Inc. (Innovations award 2002, 2003), Ga. Assn. Occupl. Health Nurses Inc. (recording sec., pres. 1988—92, Nurse of Yr. award 1987, 2000). Office: Southern Co Bin 10013 241 Ralph Mcgill Blvd NE Atlanta GA 30308-3374

HARDEN, ANITA JOYCE, nurse; b. Jackson, Tenn., May 17, 1947; d. Percy Lawrence and Marjorie (Robinson) H.; 1 child, Brian Robinson Weir. BSN, Ind. U., 1968, MBA, 1989; MSN, Ind. U.-Purdue U., Indpls., 1973. Staff nurse Indpls. Hosps., 1968-71; instr. Ind. U. Sch. Nursing, 1973-75; dir. continuing care Gallahue Mental Health Ctr., Indpls., 1975-80; mgr. psychiatry Cmty. Hosp., Indpls., 1980-87, product line mgr. for psychiat. and mental health svcs., 1986—; dir. psychiat. svcs. Cmty. Hosp. North, 1987-89, v.p., 1990-94; exec. dir. mental health svcs. Cmty. Hosps. of Ind., Inc., 1989-90; exec. dir. mental health St. Vincent-Cmty. Health Network, 1994-96; exec. dir. behavioral care svcs. Cmty. Hosps. Indpls., 1996-2001, v.p. behavioral health, 2001—. Clin. asst. prof. Ind. U., 1977-82, clin. assoc. prof., 1982—; clin. assoc., trainer Suicide Prevention Svc., Indpls., 1974-77; chmn. adv. bd. de-institutionalization project Cen. State Hosp., Indpls., 1978-79; bd. dirs. Safe Sitter, Behavioral Sys. LLC, InteCare Contbr. articles to profl. jours. Mem. Ind. County Cmty. Mental Health Ctr., 1979-80; bd. dirs. Marion County Mental Health Assn., Indpls. Zoo; bd. dirs. Alternatives in Madison County, Jackson-Peoples Living Ctr. Recipient Outstanding Achievement in Professions award Ctr. Leadership Devel., 1981, Clin. Excellence award Ind. U. Sch. Nursing, 1989. Mem. Ind. U. Alumni Assn., Christian Women's Fellowship, 500 Festival Assocs., Greater Indpls. Orgn. Nurse Execs. (v.p.), Coalition 100 Black Women (bd. dirs.), Neal-Marshall Aumni Club, Alpha Kappa Alpha, Sigma Theta Tau, Chi Eta Phi. Mem. Christian Ch. Home: 7607 Newport Bay Dr Indianapolis IN 46240-3370 Office: 7150 Clearvista Dr Indianapolis IN 46256-1695 Business E-Mail: aharden@ecommunity.com.

HARDEN, DANIEL ALEXANDER, JR., chemical engineer; b. Nov. 9, 1946; s. Daniel and Jewel Mae (Pouncil) H. BSChE, Wayne State U., 1978, postgrad. Engr. Exxon Co., USA, Linden, N.J., 1978-82; instr. Metro Youth Found., Detroit, 1984-85. Served with U.S. Army, 1963-66, Vietnam. Mem. Engring. Soc. Detroit. Avocations: reading, marksmanship, music, modern art. Home: 3904 Mount Elliott St Detroit MI 48207-1841

HARDEN, JON BIXBY, publishing executive; b. Fitzgerald, Ga., Mar. 7, 1944; s. William Harmon and Mary Bixby (Brewster) H.; m. Lynne Ann Lumsden, May 3, 1986; children: Gregory Ross, Heather Lynne. AAS, Rochester Inst. Tech., 1965; BS, Univ. Rochester, 1967; MBA, U Pa., 1969. Research analyst Doubleday & Co., Inc., N.Y.C., 1969-72, mgr. corp. research, 1972-74, pub. group mgr., 1974-77; dir. bus. devel. McGraw-Hill Book Co., N.Y.C., 1977-80, dir. planning and devel. Internat. div., 1980-84; v.p. corp. devel. and strategic planning Simon & Schuster, Inc., N.Y.C., 1984-85; pres. Dodd, Mead & Co., Inc., N.Y.C., 1985-88; gen. mgr. Romaine Pierson Pubs., Inc., Port Washington, 1988-89; pres. JBH Communications, Inc., 1989—; editor, pub. The Hartford News, Conn., 1989—; pub. Greater Hartford mag., 1996—. Bd. dirs. SCAN Vol. Parents Aids Assn., Inc., 1980—89, v.p., 1985—89; treas. Ancient Burying Ground Assn., 2000—02, v.p., 2002—; bd. dirs. Cmty. Ptnrs. in Action, 2000—; bd. mgrs. West Side YMCA, 1985—89, vice-chmn., 1987—89. Mem. The Hartford Club, The Hartford Golf Club. Home: 16 Oak Ridge Ln West Hartford CT 06107-3505 Office: JBH Comms Inc 99 Hanmer St Ste A Hartford CT 06114-3071

HARDEN, MARVIN, artist, educator; b. Austin, Tex. s. Theodore R. and Ethel (Sneed) H. BA in Fine Arts, UCLA, 1959, MA in Creative Painting, 1963. Prof. art Calif. State U., Northridge, 1967-97, prof. emeritus, 1997—; Tchr. art Santa Monica City Coll., Calif., 1968; mem. art faculty UCLA Extension, 1964-68; instr. art LA Harbor Coll., Calif., 1965—68. Mem. visual arts fellowship, painting panel NEA, 1985. One-man shows include Ceeje Galleries, LA, 1964, 66, 67, LA City Coll., 1968, Occidental Coll., LA, 1969, Whitney Mus. Am. Art, NYC, 1971, Eugenia Butler Gallery, LA, 1971, Rath Mus., Geneva, Switzerland, 1971, Irving Blum Gallery, LA, 1972, LA Harbor Coll., 1972, David Stuart Galleries, LA, 1975, Coll. Creative Studies, U. Calif., Santa Barbara, 1976, James Corcoran Gallery, LA, 1978, Newport Harbor Art Mus. Survey, 1979, LA Mcpl. Art Gallery, Major Retrospective, 1982, Conejo Valley Art Mus., 1983, Simard Gallery, LA, 1985, The Armory Ctr. for the Arts Pasadena, Calif., 1994, Ventura (Calif.) Coll. Art Gallery, 1997, Louis Stern Gallery, LA, 1998; group shows include US State Dept. Touring Exhbn., USSR, 1966, Oakland (Calif.) Mus. Art, 1966, UCLA, 1966, Mpls. Inst. Art, 1968, San Francisco Mus. Art, 1969, Phila. Civic Ctr. Mus., 1969, Mus. Art, RI Sch. Design, 1969, NJ State Mus., 1969, Everson Mus. Art, Syracuse, 1969, La Jolla (Calif.) Mus., 1969, 70, High Mus. Art, Atlanta, 1969, Flint (Mich.) Inst. Arts, 1969, Ft. Worth Art Center Mus., 1969, Contemporary Arts Assn., Houston, 1970, U. N.Mex., 1974, U. So. Calif., 1975, Bklyn. Mus., 1977, LA County Mus. Art, 1977, 95, Newport Harbor Art Mus., 1977, Frederick S. Wight Gallery, UCLA, 1978, Cirrus Editions, Ltd., LA, 1979, 81, 82, Franklin Furnace, NYC, 1980, Art Ctr. Coll. Design, LA, 1981, Alternative Mus., NYC, 1981, Laguna Beach Mus. (Calif.), 1982, Cirrus, 1982, LA Inst. Contemporar

Art, 1983, Mus. Contemporary Art, Chgo., 1983, Mint Mus., Charlotte, NC, 1983, DeCordova and Dana Mus. and Park, Lincoln, Mass., 1983, Equitable Gallery, NYC, 1984, LA Municipal Art Gallery, 1984, 1985, Cirrus, LA, 1986, 1990, Heal the Bay, Surfboard Art Invitational, 1990, Pasadena Armory Ctr. for the Arts, 1992, Claremont Coll. West Gallery, LA, 1992, Grolier Club, NYC, 1993, Calif. State U., San Luis Obispo, 1994, Cheney Cowles Mus., Spokane, Wash., 1995, Louis Stern Fine Art, LA, 1995, Porter Troup Gallery, San Diego, 1995, Armory Ctr. for the Arts, Pasadena, 1996, 97, Tel Aviv Mus. Art, 1998, Gail Harvey Gallery, Santa Monica, Calif., 1998, Palos Verdes Art Ctr., 1999, LA City Coll., 1999, Davis and Cline Gallery, Ashland, Oreg., 2002, Hunsaker/Schlesinger Fine Art, Santa Monica, 2002, Glendale Coll. Art Gallery, 2002, Davis and Cline, Ashland, Oreg., 2003; others; represented in permanent collections include Whitney Mus. Am. Art, NYC, Mus. Modern Art, NYC, NY Pub. Libr. Spence Collection, Getty Ctr. for Arts and Humanities, LA County Mus. Art, Atlantic Richfield Co. Corp. Art Coll., Grunwald Ctr. Graphic Arts UCLA, City of LA, Metromedia, Inc., LA, San Diego Jewish Cmty. Ctr., Berkeley (Calif.) U. Mus., Home Savs. & Loan Assn., LA, also pvt. collections. Bd. dir. Images & Issues, 1980-86; mem. artists adv. bd. LA Mcpl. Art Gallery Assn., 1983-86. Recipient UCLA Art Coun. award, 1963, Disting. Prof. award Calif. State U. Northridge, 1984, Exceptional Merit Svc. award Calif. State U. Northridge, 1984; Nat. Endowment Arts fellow, 1972; Awards in Visual Arts fellow, 1983; Guggenheim fellow, 1983. Mem. LA Inst. Contemporary Art (co-founder 1973). Home: Inwardness Ranch PO Box 1793 Cambria CA 93428-1793

HARDEN, MARY LOUISE, human resources consultant, real estate agent, real estate appraiser; b. Natchez, Miss., Mar. 27, 1942; d. John Charles and Dorothy Louise (Reynolds) Brown; m. Billy Gene Redd, Mar. 12, 1957 (div. 1961); children: Andre Ranier, Allison Lawanda, Robin Yvette; m. Percy Lawrence Harden Jr., Aug. 31, 1968; children: Darrell Lawrence, Craig Robison. Student, Ball State U., 1975-76, Ind. U., Purdue U., 1983-88; BSBA, Ind. Wesleyan U., 1989; postgrad., U. S.C., 1990; MA, Ball State U., 1995. Editor-in-chief U.S. Army Fin. and Acctg. Ctr., Indpls., 1974-81, pers. mgmt. specialist, 1981-87, pub. affairs officer, 1987-91; personnel mgmt. specialist Def. Fin. and Acctg. Svc., 1991-99; fed. women's program mgr. U.S. Army Fin. and Acctg. Ctr., Indpls., 1981-85. Minority advisor United Way of Ctrl. Ind., Indpls., 1985—2000; active Ind. Fever Adv. Team, 2001—; bd. dirs. Nat. Coalition of 100 Black Women, Indpls., 1986—, pres., 2002—; bd. dirs. Indpls. YWCA, 1989—, Urban Mission YMCA, 2002—, C.J. Walker Theatre Ctr., 2001—. Named Madame C.J. Walker Outstanding Woman of Yr., Ctr. for Leadership Devel. and Indpls. C. of C., 1988. Fellow: Dept. Def. Exec. Leadership Program; mem.: Am. Soc. Mil. Comptrs., Federally Employed Women. Presbyterian. Avocations: photography, real estate, flea markets, reading. Office: 6025 Crows Nest Dr Indianapolis IN 46228-1409

HARDEN, OLETA ELIZABETH, English educator, university administrator; b. Jamestown, Ky., Nov. 22, 1935; d. Stanley Virgil and Myrtie Alice (Stearns) McWhorter; m. Dennis Clarence Harden, July 23, 1966. BA, Western Ky. U., 1956; MA in English, U. Ark., 1958, PhD, 1965. Teaching asst. U. Ark., Fayetteville, 1956-57, 58-59, 61-63; instr. S.W. Mo. State Coll., Springfield, 1957-58, Murray (Ky.) U., 1959-61; asst. prof. English Northeastern State Coll., Tahlequah, Okla., 1963-65; asst. prof. Wichita (Kans.) State U., 1965-66; asst. prof. English Wright State U., Dayton, Ohio, 1966-68, assoc. prof., 1968-72, prof., 1972-93, asst. chmn. English dept., 1967-70, asst. dean, 1971-73, assoc. dean, 1973-74, exec. dir. gen. univ. services, 1974-76, pres. of faculty, 1984-85, prof. emerita, 1993—. Author: Maria Edgeworth's Art of Prose Fiction, 1971, Maria Edgeworth, 1984; editor: The Extension, 1999—. R & D grantee Wright State U., 1969, 78, Ford Found. grantee, 1971, Wright State U. sabbatical grantee Oxford U., Eng., 1978-79, 86-87; recipient Presdl. award for outstanding svc. Wright State U., 1986, Alumni Teaching Excellence award, 1993. Mem. MLA, AARP (impact alliance leader Ohio, 2001—), Coll. English Assn., AAUP, Women's Caucus for Modern Langs., Am. Conf. for Irish Studies (presenter 1989, 91, 94, 95). Office: Wright State U Dept English 7751 Colonel Glenn Hwy Dayton OH 45431-1674 Home: 2618 Big Woods Trl Dayton OH 45431-8704 E-mail: oharden@aol.com.

HARDEN, PATRICIA KEEGAN, financial aid officer; b. Rye, N.Y., May 18, 1937; d. Vincent L. and Eleanor C. Keegan; m. David O. Harden, Apr. 15, 1978. BS, Simmons Coll., 1958. Dir. fin. aid Simmons Coll., Boston, 1970-78; asst. mgr. Capt.'s Quars. Inn, Saba, Netherlands Antilles, 1977-81; dir. fin. aid Endicott Coll., Beverly, Mass., 1981-84, Emmanuel Coll., Boston, 1984-96, Urban Coll. Boston, 1997—. Cons. Mass. Higher Edn. Assistance Group, Newton, 1998—, Butera Sch. Art, Boston, 1999—. Vol. asst. Beacon Hill Civic Assn., Boston, 1992-94; treas. Iona Cornerstone Found., Inc., 1995-2000. Mem. Mass. Assn. Student Fin. Aid (pres. 1992-95), Ea. Assn. Student Fin. Aid (comm. chair 1975-82). Office: Urban Coll Boston 178 Tremont St Boston MA 02111-1006

HARDEN, PATRICK ALAN, journalist; b. Twickenham, Eng., Aug. 13, 1936; s. Ernest William and Annie Ceridwen (Jones) H.; m. Connie Marie Graham, Nov. 2, 1963; children: Marc Graham, Ceri Marie. Cert. in journalism, Ealing (Eng.) Tech. Coll., 1957. With UPI, 1960-78, regional exec., 1968-69, European picture mgr. London and Brussels, 1969-72, regional exec. Detroit, 1973-75; gen. mgr. UPI Can. Ltd., Montreal, 1976-78, UP Can., Toronto, 1979-82, dir., sec., 1979-82; treas. UPI Can. Ltd.; gen. mgr. Edmonton (Alta.) Sun, 1982-84, pub., 1984-92; v.p. Toronto Sun Pub. Corp., 1989-94; v.p., bur. chief Washington, 1992-94; Washington columnist Toronto Sun Pub. Corp., 1994-97; freelance writer, 1997-98; Washington bur. chief LRP Pubs., Alexandria, Va., 1998—. E-mail: pharden@lrp.com.

HARDEN, RICHARD RUSSELL, lawyer; b. Oak Park, Ill., Apr. 22, 1958; s. James Edward Harden and Patricia Gilkison Murphy; m. Kathryn Diane Knosher, June 21, 1980; childen: Jeffrey Joseph, Colleen Elizabeth. BA, Knox Coll., 1980; JD, U. Ill., 1983. Bar: Ill. 1983. Assoc. Robert P. Moore & Assocs., Champaign, Ill., 1983-86, Thomas, Mamer & Haughey, Champaign, 1986-90, ptnr., 1990—. Spkr., mem. faculty Ill. Inst. for CLE, Champaign, 1997—, Carle Found., Champaign, 1998, Ill. Primary Healthcare Assn., 2001. Contbg. author: Medical Evidence, 1997, (supplement) 2000, Carle Selected Papers, 2000. Various positions, including scoutmaster, cubmaster, asst. scoutmaster, advisor, commr. Boy Scouts Am., Champaign, 1992—, advisor law exploring, learning for life divsn.; elder Westminster Presbyn. Ch., Champaign, 1989-92, 1998-2001. Mem. Ill. Bar Assn., Ill. Assn. Def. Trial Counsel, Champaign County Bar Assn., Def. Rsch. Inst., Phi Beta Kappa. Avocations: camping, hiking, canoeing, golf, climbing. Office: Thomas Mamer & Haughey PO Box 560 30 E Main St Champaign IL 61824-0560 E-mail: Rharden@tmh-law.com.

HARDER, HEATHER ANNE, education educator; b. Henderson, Tenn., Mar. 2, 1948; d. Wendell Anderson and Anne (Gibbs) Stack; children: Kerri Anne, Stacie Elizabeth. BS, Ind. U., 1970, MS, 1974, PhD in Elem./Early Childhood Edn., 1988. Tchr., reading specialist Crown Point (Ind.) Community Schs., 1970-79; mem. adj. faculty Ball State U., Muncie, Ind., 1977-79, Purdue U.-Calumet, Hamond, Ind., 1981-82, Gov.'s State U., University Park, Ill., 1985-93; coord. edn. programs U. Chgo. Owner, exec. dir. Small World Child Care Ctr., Merrillville, Ind., 1980-2000. Author: Perfect Power in Consciousness, Exploring Life's Last Frontier, Interdimensional Communication, Many Were Called-Few Were Chosen. Mem. Ind. Assn. Edn. Young Children, Midwest Assn. Edn. Young Children, Ind. State Reading Assn., Internat. Reading Assn., Phi Delta Kappa. Avocations: reading, painting, old movies, gardening, reading. Home: 1187 W 132nd Ln Crown Point IN 46307-9282 E-mail: heatherharder@aol.com.

HARDER, KELSIE BROWN, retired language professional, educator; b. Pope, Tenn., Aug. 23, 1922; s. Prince William and Belle (MaGee) H.; m. Louise Maron, Oct. 9, 1960; children: Kelsie Terry, Gerald William, Dennis Prince, Frank Maron, Thomas Brown, Ann Leslie, Marcia Louise. BA magna cum laude, Vanderbilt U., 1950, MA, 1951; PhD, U. Fla., 1954. Asst. prof. English Youngstown U., 1954-58, assoc. prof., 1958-60, prof., 1960-64; Fulbright lectr. India, 1962-63; prof. English SUNY, Potsdam, 1964-89, chmn. English and drama depts., 1964-78, chmn. faculty, 1985-89, chmn. governance com. SUNY faculty senate, 1988-91, Disting. Teaching prof., 1989-94, Disting. Prof. English Emeritus, 1994—. Chair Symposium on Contemporary American Fiction, 1995; Fulbright vis. prof. U. Lodz, Poland, 1971-72; cons. Office Edn., Washington, summers 1966, 67, Random House Dictionary of the English Lang., Dictionary of American Reg. English; mem. Com. on Place Name Survey of U.S., SUNY Awards Com., 1976-81; dir. Place Name Survey of U.S., 1988-91. Guest appearances: Cable News Network, stas. WXYZ, WEWS.; Editor: Names, 1966-68, 81-87, Illustrated Dictionary of Place Names: Canada and the United States, 1976, 2d edit., 1985, Favorite Baby Names, 1985, Names and Their Varieties: A Collection of Essays in Onomastics, 1986; mem. adv. bd.: American Speech, 1960-61, 80-81, Unusual and Most Popular Baby Names, 1988; co-editor: A Dictionary of Am. Proverbs, 1992; co-author: Claims to Name, 1993; contbr. articles to profl. jours. Served with AUS, 1944-46. Recipient SUNY Best award, 1989. Mem.: MLA, Eta Sigma Phi, Am. Dialect Soc. (proverbs chmn., usage com.), Internat. Ctr. Onomastics (Belgium), N.Y. Folklore Soc. (exec. com.), Miss. Folklore Soc., Tenn. Folklore Soc., Ohio Folklore Soc. (past pres.), Am. Name Soc. (past exec. sec.-treas., v.p., pres.), Publ. MLA, St. Lawrence County Hist. Assn. (past pres., trustee), Milton Soc. (life), Spenser Soc. (life), Phi Kappa Sigma (counselor), Phi Kappa Phi (chpt. pres. 1993), Sigma Delta Pi, Sigma Phi Epsilon (counselor, dist. gov. 1965—66, chpt. pres. alumni bd. 2000—02), Phi Beta Kappa. Home: 5 Lawrence Ave Potsdam NY 13676-1815

HARDER, KELSIE T. artist, educator; b. Trenton, Tenn., Mar. 8, 1942; s. Kelsie Brown Harder and Geneva Lee (Tomlin) Carlson; m. Kumiko Tanaka, Oct. 2, 1991; children: Michon Skyler, Samuel Armstrong (dec.), Tsunami Tomlin and Tanaka Solomon (twins). Student, Claremont (Calif.) Men's Coll., 1960-61, Escuela de Bellas Artes, Morelia, Mex., 1961, Ventura (Calif.) Coll., 1961-62; BA, U. Nev., 1973-75, candidate Masters of Edn., 1977—78. Cert. inventory mgmt. specialist USAF, illustrator technician USAF. Artist self-employed, 1957—; prof. Truckee Meadows C.C., Reno, 1978—. Chmn. art dept. Truckee Meadows C.C., 1982—91; art exhibit judge 34 regional exhbns. Contbr. art and articles to profl. jours., mags., textbooks; 30 one-man shows, including Sierra Nev. Mus. of Art, 1969, 81, Rush-Presbyn.-St. Luke's Art Gallery, Chgo., 1973, Blue Cross Art Corp., Oakland, Calif., 1982, Alan Short Gallery, Stockton, Calif., 1991; represented in over 100 collections. Recipient numerous regional and nat. awards including Nev. Centennial Eight Western State Drawing and Painting Competition, 1st Pl. award for drawing and 1st Pl. award for painting Nev. Mus. Art, 1964, YWCA Silver cert. for Outstanding Cmty. Svc., No. Nev., 1972, 88. Office: Truckee Meadows CC 7000 Dandini Blvd Reno NV 89512-3901

HARDER, ROBERT CLARENCE, state official; b. Horton, Kans., June 4, 1929; s. Clarence L. and Olympia E. (Kubik) H.; m. Dorothy Lou Welty, July 31, 1953; children: Anne, James David. AB, Baker U., Baldwin, Kans., 1951; MTh, So. Meth. U., 1954; ThD in Social Ethics, Boston U., 1958; LHD (hon.), Baker U., 1983, Ottawa U., 1991. Ordained to ministry Meth. Ch., 1959; pastor East Topeka Meth. Ch., 1958-64; mem. Kans. Ho. of Reps., 1961-67; rsch. assoc. Menninger Found., Topeka, 1964-65; instr. Washburn U., Topeka, 1964, 68, 69; dir. Topeka Office of Econ. Opportunity, 1965-67; tech. asst. coordinator Office of Gov. of Kans., 1967-68; dir. community resources devel. League of Kans. Municipalities, 1968-69; dir. Kans. Dept. Social Welfare, Topeka, 1969-73, sec., 1973-87; projects adminstr. Topeka State Hosp., 1987-89. Adj. prof. pub. adminstrn. Kans. U., 1987-95, instr. Sch. Social Welfare, 1971-87; cons. Menninger Topeka, 1991-92; sec. Kans. Dept. Health and Environment, 1992-95. Contbr. articles to profl. jours. Recipient Disting. Svc. award East Topeka Civic Assn., 1963, Romana Hood award, 1965, Cert. of Recognition, State of Kans., 1979, 87, Spl. Commendation award Kans. Senate, 1987, Spl. Commendation, Kans. Ho. of Reps., 1987, Outstanding Alumnus award Perkins Sch. Theology, So. Meth. U., 1994, Disting. Svc. award Kans. Children's Svc. League, 1998; named Outstanding Pub. Ofcl. of the Yr., 1987. Mem. Am. Soc. Public Adminstrs. (Public Adminstr. of Yr. Kans. chpt. 1980), Am. Public Welfare Assn., Kans. Health Care Commn., Kans. Conf. Social Welfare (Outstanding Person of Yr. 1987). Democrat.

HARDER, ROLF PETER, graphic designer, painter; b. Hamburg, Germany, July 10, 1929; came to Can., 1955; s. Henry and Henriette (Loeffler) H.; m. Maria-Inger Rumberg, May 3, 1958; children— Christopher, Vivian Student, State Art Sch. (Acad. Fine Arts), Hamburg, 1948-52. Designer Rolf Ruehle Werbung, Hamburg, 1952-55; designer Schneider Cardon Ltd, Montreal, Que, Can, 1955-56; art dir. George Ferguson Assocs., Montreal, 1956-57; visualizer Lintas GmbH, Hamburg, 1957-59; designer, owner Rolf Harder Design, Montreal, 1959-65; co-founder, designer Design Collaborative, Montreal, 1965-77; pres., designer Rolf Harder & Assocs., Montreal, 1977—. Mem. internat. adv. bd. Typos Mag., London, 1979— ; co-organizer exhibition The Visual Image of the Munich Games, Mus. Fine Arts, Montreal, 1972 Published: works and exhibited in U.S., Can., Europe, Japan, South Korea, S. Am, USSR; Represented in permanent collections Nat. Archives of Can., Ottawa, Libr. of Congress, Washington, Musee de La Publicité, Palais du Louvre, Paris, Die Neue Sammlung, Munich, AGI Archives, Essen, Germany, Mus. Arts and Crafts, Hamburg, Germany, Mus. Modern Art, San Francisco, Design Austria, Vienna, U. Reading, Eng., U. Que., Musee De Quebec. Coach Beaconsfield Soccer Assn., Montreal, 1966-70. Recipient over 100 nat. and internat. design awards, including World Logo Design award, Internat. Trademark Ctr., Belgium, 1998. Fellow Soc. Graphic Designers of Can.; mem. Royal Canadian Acad. Arts, Alliance Graphique Internationale (past pres. Can. group). Clubs: Clearpoint Tennis, West-Island Tennis (Montreal). Avocations: tennis, music. Home: 43 Lakeshore Rd Beaconsfield QC Canada H9W 4H6

HARDER, VIRGIL EUGENE, business administration educator; b. Ness City, Kans., July 19, 1923; s. Walter J. and Fern B. (Pausch) H.; m. Dona Maurine Dobson, Feb. 4, 1951; children— Christine Elaine, Donald Walter. BS, MA, U. Iowa, 1950; PhD, U. Ill., 1958. Instr. bus. adminstrn. U. Ill., Urbana, 1950-55; asst. prof. U. Wash., Seattle, 1955-59, assoc. prof., 1959-67, prof., 1967-86, prof. emeritus, 1986—, asso. dean sch. bus. adminstrn., 1966-74; dir. Inst. Fin. Edn. Sch. for Exec. Devel., Seattle, 1974-83. Served with AUS, 1943-45. Fellow Am. Bus. Communications Assn. (pres. 1965) Clubs: Trail Blazers. Office: U Wash Sch Bus Adminstrn Seattle WA 98195-0001

HARDER, WENDY WETZEL, communications executive; b. Oceanside, Calif., Feb. 14, 1951; d. Burt Louis and Marjorie Jean (Evans) W.; m. Peter N. Harder, Dec. 1, 1984; 1 child, Jonathan Russell. AA, Palomar Coll., 1971; BA in Communications, U. So. Calif., 1973; MBA, Pepperdine U., 1988. Pub. rels. dir. Orange County Community Devel. Coun., Santa Ana, Calif., 1975-76; assoc. producer Sta. KOCE-TV, Huntington Beach, Calif., 1976-77, reporter, 1977-79, anchor, assoc. producer, 1979-82; sr. adminstr. communications Mission Viejo (Calif.) Co., 1983-84, mgr. corp. affairs, 1984-85, dir. corp. affairs, 1985-91, v.p. corp. affairs, 1991-93, v.p. mktg. and corp. comm., 1993-97; dir. cmty. rels. Soka Univ. Am., 1998—. 1st v.p. Aliso Viejo (Calif.) Cmty. Found., 1988-93, 2003—, pres., 1993-97, Saddleback Coll. Found., Mission Viejo, 1989-91; co-chmn. The Ctr. on Tour-Schs. Com., Orange County, Calif., 1989-92; v.p. Found. for Vocat. Visions, 1996-2002, pres., 2000-2003; bd. dirs. Dunaj Internat. Dance Ensemble, Orange County, 1985—2000; pres. pack com. Pack 709 Cub Scouts, 2001—, Mt. Olives Found. Bd., 2003—. Recipient Golden Mike award Radio & TV News Assn., 1981; co-recipient Best Spl. Event award, Pub. Rels. Soc. Am., 1986, Golden Mike award Radio & TV News Assn., 1979. Mem. Pub. Rels. Soc. Am., Aliso Viejo C. of C. (bd. dirs. 2002—), Orange County Press Club (Best Feature Release award 1983), Phi Beta Kappa. Republican. Lutheran. Avocations: folk dancing, reading. Office: Soka Univ Am 1 University Dr Aliso Viejo CA 92656 E-mail: wwharder@soka.edu.

HARDERSEN, PAUL SCOTT, planetary scientist; b. Davenport, Iowa, May 10, 1965; s. Edwin Christian and Barbara Hardersen. BA in Polit. Sci., BS in Geology, Iowa State U., 1997; M in Geology, Rensselaer Poly. Inst., 2001, PhD in Geology, 2003. Asst. prof. space studies U. N.D., Grand Forks, 2003—. Assoc. mem. Com. for the Sci. Investigation of Claims of the Paranormal. Author: The Case for Space, 1996. With USN, 1983—88. Mem.: AAAS, Am. Astron. Soc., Geol. Soc. Am., Meteoritical Soc. Avocations: astronomy, hiking, cooking, travel. Office: Univ of North Dakota Space Studies Dept Room 526 Box 9008 Grand Forks ND 58202 Office Fax: 701-777-3711. Business E-Mail: Hardersen@volcano.space.edu.

HARDESTY, DAVID CARTER, JR., university president; b. Philadelphia, Miss., Sept. 20, 1945; m. Susan B. Hardesty, 1968; children: Ashley, D(avid) Carter III. AB, W.Va. U., 1967; MA, Oxford (Eng.) U., 1969; JD, Harvard U., 1973. Bar: W.Va. 1973. Tax commr., sec. Econ. Devel. Authority, State of W.Va., Charleston, 1977-80, chmn. Mcpl. Bond Commn., 1977-80; assoc. Bowles Rice McDavid Graff & Love, Charleston, 1973-77, ptnr., 1981-95; pres. W.Va. U., Morgantown, 1995—. Chmn. W.Va. Tax Study Commn., 1982-84; mem. W.Va. Asian Trade Missions, 1978-79, 95; chmn. W.Va. Roundtable, Inc., 1994-95; frequent speaker at bus. group meetings. Chancellor United Meth. Ch., W.Va., 1986-95; trustee Univ. Sys., 1989-95, 1st chmn., 1989-91; trustee W.Va. Wesleyan Coll., 1986-94, Nat. 4-H Coun., 2000--; mem. Gov.'s Energy Task Force, 2001--; mem. W.Va. Rhodes Scholar Selection Com., 1980-2000, sec., 1991-98; bd. advisors W.Va. U., 1980-89, chmn. bd. advisors, 1987-89; bd. dirs. United Meth. Charities W.Va., 1978-94; bd. dirs. Greater Kanawha Valley Found., 1980-89, chmn., 1988-90. Rhodes scholar, 1969. Mem.: ABA, Nat. Assn. State Univs. and Land Grant Colls., Nat. Assn. Coll. and Univ. Attys., Am. Coun. on Edn., 4th Cir. Jud. Conf., W.Va. Bar Assn. Office: WVa U Office of Pres PO Box 6201 Morgantown WV 26506-6201 E-mail: dhardest@wvu.edu.

HARDESTY, LARA ANN, radiology educator; b. Pitts., Dec. 3, 1966; d. Robert Lynch and Catherine (Steward) H. BS, Carnegie Mellon U., 1988; MD, U. Pa., 1993. Diplomate Am. Bd. Radiology. Resident in radiology Pa. State U. Coll. Medicine, Hershey, 1993-97; fellow in women's imaging dept radiology U. Pitts. Sch. Medicine, 1997-98, asst. prof. radiology, 1998—. Contbr. articles to med. juors., including Radiology, Am. Jour. Roentgenology, chpt. to book. Mem. Radiol. Soc. N.Am., Soc. for Advancement Women's Imaging, Am. Assn. Women Radiologists, Am. Roentgen Ray Soc., Soc. for Breast Imaging, Pitts. Mammography Soc. Avocations: biking, skiing, gardening, furniture building. Office: Magee Womens Hosp Dept Radiology 300 Halket St Pittsburgh PA 15213 E-mail: lhardesty@mail.magee.edu.

HARDESTY, LARRY LYNN, librarian; b. Hyannis, Nebr., Aug. 8, 1947; s. George Kenton and Enid LaVon (Cotton) H.; m. Carol Jean Weaver, June 6, 1970. BA in Edn., Kearney State Coll., 1969, MS in Edn., 1971; MLS, U. Wis., 1974; MS in Edn., Ind. U., 1978, PhD, 1982. Tchr. Cen. Cath. High Sch., Grand Island, Nebr., 1969-70; social worker Adams County Welfare Office, Hastings, Nebr., 1971, Hall County Welfare Office, Grand Island, 1972; reference libr. Kearney State Coll., 1973-75; head reference dept. DePauw U., Greencastle, Ind., 1975-83; dir. of libr. svcs. Eckerd Coll., St. Petersburg, Fla., 1983-95; coll. libr. Austin Coll., Sherman, Tex., 1995—. Cons. Office of Mgmt. Studies, Washington, 1979-81; organizer libr. confs. Eckerd Coll., 1984-92; spkr. in field. Author: Faculty and the Library, 1991; editor: Book, Bytes and Bridges, 2000; co-editor: User Instruction in Academic Libraries, 1986, Bibliographic Instruction in Practice, 1993; mem. several editl. bds. profl. jours.; contbr. numerous articles to profl. jours. With USAR, 1970-76. Recipient Disting. Alumnus award Ind. U.-Bloomington, Sch. Libr. and Info. Sci., 2000, Disting. Alumnus award U. Wis.-Madison, 2002, U. Nebr., Kearney, 2002; Coun. on Libr. Resources grantee, 1975-77, 84, 88, 92, 94. Mem. ALA (life, chairperson coll. librs. sect. 1995-96), Assn. Coll. and Rsch. Librs. (bd. dirs. 1987-91, 1999-2001, chair bd. dirs. Fla. chpt. 1986-87, pres. 1999-2000, chair nat. conf. 2003, Acad./Rsch. Libr. of Yr. 2001), So. Accreditation Assn. (reaffirmation team 1991—), Fla. Libr. Assn. (bd. dirs 1988-1990), Beta Phi Mu, Phi Alpha Theta. Democrat. Methodist. Avocations: antique collector, aquariums, model and full size farm tractor collector. Home: 4089 Gibbons Rd Sherman TX 75092 6324 E mail: lhardesty@austincollege.edu.

HARDGROVE, JAMES ALAN, lawyer; b. Chgo., Feb. 20, 1945; s. Albert John and Ruth (Noonen) H.; m. Kathleen M. Peterson, June 15, 1968; children: Jennifer Anne, Amy Kristine, Michael Sheridan. BA, U. Notre Dame, 1967; cert. English law, U. Coll. Law, 1969; JD, U. Notre Dame, 1970. Bar: Ill. 1970, U.S. Ct. Appeals (7th cir.) 1970, U.S. Dist. Ct. (no. dist.) Ill. 1970, U.S. Dist. Ct. (cen. dist.) Ill. 1978, U.S. Supreme Ct. 1980. Law clk. to presiding justice U.S. Ct. Appeals (7th cir.), Chgo., 1970-71; assoc. Sidley & Austin, Chgo., 1971-76, ptnr., 1977—. Mem. ABA, Ill. Bar Assn., Chgo. Bar Assn., Legal Club. Home: 948 Ridge Ave Evanston IL 60202-1720 Office: Sidley Austin Brown & Word Bank One Plz 10 S Dearborn St Chicago IL 60603-2000 E-mail: jhardgro@sidley.com.

HARDIE, JAMES CARL, college administrator, consultant; b. Pitts., June 10, 1922; s. Stanley Frank and Helen Katherine (Wassel) H.; m. Emma Kathryn Cepko, Jan. 28, 1956; children: James Matthew, Lynn Anne. BA, U. Pitts., 1943, ML, 1948. Counselor U. Pitts., 1946; dir. housing, head men's dormitories Carnegie Inst. Tech., Pitts., 1946-47; dir. athletic publicity U. Pitts., 1947-48; dir. campaign Ketchum, Inc., Pitts., 1948-57; dir. devel., v.p. Case Inst. Tech., Cleve., 1957-67; v.p. Case We. Res. U., Cleve., 1967-69; cons. to more than 60 non-profit instns. Cleve., 1969—. Chmn. bd. Jennings Found. Yardstick Project, 1968-81; founder Corp. 1% Program for Higher Edn., 1961-69; trustee George S. Dively Found., 1985-97. Lt. U.S. Army, 1943-45. Decorated Purple Heart; recipient Disting. Svc. award Ohio Coun. Fund-Raising Execs., 1988, Citation Coun. Fin. Aid to Edn., 1979; named Outstanding Profl. Nat. Soc. Fund-Raising Profls., 1991. Mem. Union Club Cleve., Grand Harbor Country Club (Fla.), Grenelefe Country Club (Fla.), Omicron Delta Kappa, Delta Sigma Rho. Republican. Avocations: golf, reading, gardening, piano, writing. Home and Office: 245 Springdale Lane Moreland Hills OH 44022 also: 1508 Ocean Dr Apt 103 Vero Beach FL 32963-5346

HARDIE, JAMES HILLER, lawyer; b. Pitts., Dec. 1, 1929; s. James H. and Elizabeth Gillespie (Alcorn) H.; m. Frances P. Curtis, Dec. 5, 1953; children: J. Hiller, Janet Hardie Harvey, Andrew G., Michael C., Rachel Hardie Share. AB, Princeton U., 1951; LL.B., Harvard U., 1954. Bar: Pa. 1955. Assoc. Reed Smith LLP, Pitts., 1954-62, ptnr., 1962-99, of counsel, 1999—. Mem. ABA, Am. Law Inst., Pa. Bar Assn. Office: Reed Smith LLP PO Box 2009 Pittsburgh PA 15230-2009 E-mail: jhardie@reedsmith.com.

HARDIE, THOMAS GARY, journalist, editor, business executive; b. New Orleans, June 17, 1921; s. Harry and Agnes Thornton (George) H.; m. Ruth Carol Dion, Dec. 23, 1950; children: Todd D., Louise Hardie Isaacs, Elizabeth Hardie Nelson. BA, Princeton U., 1943; postgrad., Harvard U., 1946-47. Reporter Washington Post, Washington, D.C., 1947-48; mem. staff Marshall Plan, Paris, 1948-49; corr. Internat. News Svc., Paris, 1950-52, UPI, Paris, 1952-53; v.p. Nobelt Co., Cockeysville, Md., 1953-58, pres., 1958-86, Butler, Md., 1986—; editor weekly column Universal Press Syndicate, Kansas City, Mo., 1992—. Vestry, St. John's Episc. Ch., Glyndon, Md., 1969-72, 1986-89. Capt. field arty. U.S. Army, 1943-46, PTO. Decorated Air medal. Mem. Maryland Club, Nantucket Yacht Club. Republican. Episcopalian. Avocations: sailing, golf. Home: Thornhill Farm Butler MD 21023 Office: Nobelt Co PO Box 34 2620 Butler Rd Butler MD 21023-0034 E-mail: tghardie@aol.com.

HARDIES, MICHAEL JOHN, medical educator, internist; b. Amsterdam, N.Y., May 9, 1948; s. Edwin K. and Nora Mae (Koch) H.; m. Arlene Dolores Radlowski, Jan. 24, 1970; 1 child, Kimberly Raegan. BA, Colgate U., 1970; MD, Union U., 1974. Diplomate Am. Bd. Internal Medicine. Intern Albany (N.Y.) Med. Ctr. Hosp., 1974-75, resident in internal medicine, 1975-77; founder, pres. Capital Healthcare Assn. P.C., Troy, N.Y., 1978-92, Occupl. Health Resources, Troy, 1986—; founder, chmn., CEO Corp. Health Dimensions, Troy, 1988-2000; pres. Healthworks Med. Group, 1992—; asst. prof. medicine Albany Med. Coll., 1988—; chmn., chief med. officer CHD Meridian, 2000—. Fellow ACP; mem. Am. Coll. Physician Execs., Am. Coll. Occupl. and Environ. Medicine, Am. Soc. Internat. Medicine, Rensselaer County Acad. Medicine, Med. Soc. State of N.Y. Avocations: skiing, travel, hockey, theatre, music. Office: CHD Meridian Healthcare 40 British American Blvd Latham NY 12110-1464 E-mail: mjhardies@chdmeridian.com.

HARDIMAN, JOSEPH RAYMOND, securities industry executive; b. Salisbury, Md., May 27, 1937; s. Leonard Roy and Virginia Mildred (Darden) H.; m. Katherine McCampbell, Mar. 23, 1963; children: Katherine Hughes, Elizabeth Gore. BA, U. Md., 1959, LLB, 1962. Bar: Md. 1962. Law clk. to Hon. Hall Hammond Md. Ct. of Appeals, 1962-63; assoc. Miles & Stockbridge, Balt., 1963-68; exec. v.p., sec., dir. Robert Garrett & Sons, Inc., Balt., 1968-75; gen. ptnr. Alex. Brown & Sons, 1975-87, mng. dir., COO, 1984-87; pres., CEO, dir. Nat. Assn. Securities Dealers, Inc., 1987-97, Nasdaq Stock Market, Inc., 1987-97. Bd. dirs. Corvis Corp., Bridge Learning Sys., Inc., Deutsche Scudder Funds, ISI Funds, Nevis Fund, Soundview Technology Group, Inc., Brown Investment Adv. and Trust Co. Bd. dirs. Arthritis Found., Md., 1975-79, pres., 1976-78; bd. dirs. Balt. Urban Coalition, 1975-78, U. Md. Med. Sys., 1980-86, Fund for Ednl. Excellence, 1984-91, Ctr. for the Study of the Presidency,

1992-97, U. Md. Found., 1992-2000, U. Md. Balt. Found., 2000—; steering com. Baltimore County Charter Rev. Commn., 1977-78; trustee St. Paul's Sch. for Girls, 1978-86, Securities Industry Found. Econ. Edn., 1988-96; adv. bd. U. Calif. Securities Regulation Inst., 1988-97; bd. visitors U. Md. Sch. Law, 1990—; active Am. Bus. Conf., Con. on Competitiveness, 1994-97. Mem. Md. Club, Elkridge Club (Balt.), Met. Club (D.C.), Links Club (N.Y.C.), Gulfstream Club (Fla.), Order of Coif, Phi Delta Theta, Omicron Delta Kappa. Home: 8 Bowen Mill Rd Baltimore MD 21212-1053

HARDIN, ADLAI STEVENSON, JR., judge; b. Norwalk, Conn., Sept. 20, 1937; s. Adlai S. and Carol H. BA, Princeton U., 1959; LLB, Columbia U., 1962. Bar: N.Y. 1963, U.S. Dist. Ct. (so. and ea. dists.) N.Y. 1965, U.S. Supreme Ct. 1967, U.S. Ct. Appeals (2d cir.) 1965, U.S. Ct. Appeals (5th cir.) 1974, U.S. Ct. Appeals (3d cir.) 1977, U.S. Ct. Appeals (9th cir.) 1982, U.S. Ct. Appeals (4th and D.C. cirs.) 1985, U.S. Ct. Appeals (7th cir.) 1988. Assoc. Milbank, Tweed, Hadley & McCloy, N.Y.C., 1963, ptnr., 1971; judge U.S. Bankruptcy Ct., 1995—. Judge Bankruptcy Appellate Panel for 2d Circuit, 1996-2000. Trustee Spence Sch., 1981-87; former elder, trustee Madison Ave. Presbyn. Ch. With USAR, 1962-68. Mem. ABA (past chmn. N.Y. State membership com., antitrust sect., litigation sect.), Fed. Bar Coun. (trustee 1983-92, v.p. 1986-88, chmn. bd. dirs. 1990-92), Fed. Bar Found. (pres. 1992-94), N.Y. State Bar Assn. (mem. com. on profl. ethics, mem. jud. election monitoring com., mem. internat. litigation com.), Assn. of Bar of City of N.Y. (sec. 1979-82, chmn. com. on profl. and jud. ethics 1970-73, mem. spl. com. on lawyers role in securities transactions, mem. spl. com. to cooperate with ABA in revision of Canons of Ethics, mem. nominating com., mem. com. on membership, mem. com. on profl. discipline), Nat. Conf. Bankruptcy Judges, Am. Bankruptcy Inst., Westchester County Bar Assn. Office: US Bankruptcy Ct US Courthouse 300 Quarropas St White Plains NY 10601-4150

HARDIN, BRYAN DAVID, occupational safety and health specialist; b. Clinton, Okla., July 4, 1944; s. Everett Tirey and Alma Jewell (Carmichael) H.; children: Bryan David Jr., Erin Elizabeth; m. Mary Victoria Broun, Sept. 30, 1996. BS in Math., Okla. U., 1966, BS in Zoology, 1970, MS in Zoology, 1972; PhD in Environ. Health Sci., U. Cin., 1983. Commd. officer USPHS, 1972, advanced through grades to asst. surgeon gen., 1999, grad. trainee, 1975-77; criteria document mgr. Nat. Inst. for Occupl. Safety and Health, Rockville, Md., 1972-75, rsch. biologist (toxicologist) Cin., 1977-86, sr. reviewer divsn. standards devel. and tech. transfer, 1986-87, br. chief, 1987-90, acting AIDS coord. Atlanta, 1988, dep. dir divsn. stds. devel. and tech. transfer Cin., 1990-92, asst. dir. Washington, 1992—93; spl. asst. to asst. Sec. of Labor for Occpl. Safety & Health, Washington, 1993—94; sr. scientist Office of Dir. Nat. Inst. Occupl. Safety and Health, Washington, 1994-95, acting dep. dir. Atlanta, 1996, lead sr. scientist Office of Dir. Washington, 1996-98, dep. dir. Atlanta, 1998-2000. Mem. reproductive and devel. toxicology work group Nat. Toxicology Program, 1980—86; mem. Toxic Substances Control Act Interagy. Testing Com., 1987—89; mem. task group for environ. health criteria documents Internat. Program on Chem. Safety, WHO, 1989; chmn. Toxic Substances Control Act Interagy. Testing Com., 1989; mem. working group Internat. Program on Chem. Safety, WHO, 1990, chmn. expert consultation, 91; mem. endocrine disruptor screening and testing adv. com. USEPA, 1996—98; adv. bd. for the risk edn. project Am. Chem. Soc., 1997—2000; cons. occupl. and environ. health, Hilton Head, SC, 2000—; adj. asst. prof. environ. and occupl. health Rollins Sch. Pub. Health, Emory U., Atlanta, 2000—01; sr. cons. Global Tox, toxicology and indsl. hygiene cons., Redmond, Wash., 2001—. Contbr. articles and abstracts to profl. jour. 1st lt. U.S. Army, 1966—68, capt. USAR, 1968—72. Decorated Distinguished Svc. Medal (DSM); named Sci. Fed. Employee of Yr., Greater Cin. Fed. Exec. Bd. and Fed. Bus. Assn., 1983; recipient Surgeon Gen.'s Exemplary Svc. medal, 1993, 1997, Career Scientist of Yr. award, USPHS, 1999, Disting. Svc. award, Internat. Safety Equipment Assn., 2001. Mem.: AAAS, Am. Coll. Occupl. and Environ. Medicine, Soc. Toxicology, Am. Indsl. Hygiene Assn., Teratology Soc. (pub. affairs com. 1985—88, constn. and bylaws com. 1993—96), Sigma Xi. Avocation: vocal music. Office: 33 Office Park Rd 4 A Box 344 Hilton Head Island SC 29928 E-mail: bhardin@adelphia.net.

HARDIN, CLIFFORD MORRIS, retired university chancellor, cabinet member; b. Knightstown, Ind., Oct. 9, 1915; s. James Alvin and Mabel (Macy) H.; m. Martha Love Wood, June 28, 1939; children: Susan Carol (Mrs. L.W. Wood), Clifford Wood, Cynthia (Mrs. Robert Milligan), Nancy Ann (Mrs. Douglas L. Rogers), James. BS, Purdue U., 1937, MS, 1939, PhD, 1941, DSc (hon.), 1952; Farm Found. scholar, U. Chgo., 1939-40; LLD, Creighton U., 1956, Ill. State U., 1973; Dr. honoris causa, Nat. U. Colombia, 1968; DSc, Mich. State U., 1969, N.D. State U., 1969, U. Nebr., 1978, Okla. Christian Coll., 1979. Instr. U. Wis., 1941-42, asst. prof. agrl. econs., 1942-44; assoc. prof. agrl. econs. Mich. State Coll., 1944-46, prof., chmn. agrl. econs. dept., 1946-48, dir. expt. sta., 1949-53, dean agr., 1953-54; chancellor U. Nebr., 1954-69; sec. U.S. Dept. Agr., Washington, 1969-71; vice chmn. bd., dir. Ralston Purina Co., St. Louis, 1971-80; dir. Center for Study of Am. Bus., Washington U., St. Louis, 1981-83, scholar-in-residence, 1983-85; cons., dir. Stifel, Nicolaus & Co., St. Louis, 1980-87. Bd. dirs. Gallup, Inc., Lincoln, Nebr., 1980-99; bd. dirs. Omaha br. Fed. Res. Bank of Kansas City, 1961-67, chmn., 1962-67. Editor: Overcoming World Hunger, 1969. Trustee Rockefeller Found., 1961-69, 72-81, Winrock, Internat., Morrilton, Ark., 1984-94, Am. Assembly, 1975—, U. Nebr. Found., 1975—; mem. Pres.'s Com. to Stregthen Security Free World, 1963. Mem. Assn. State Univs. and Land-Grant Colls. (pres. 1960, chmn. exec. com. 1961).

HARDIN, DALE WAYNE, retired lawyer, federal official; b. Peoria, Ill., Sept. 9, 1922; s. James P. and Lucille Maureen (Elgin) H.; m. Sandra L. Gorzen, July 3, 1939; children: Bradley J., Stacy Keaton, Rebecca M., J. Scott Keaton. AB in Polit. Sci., George Washington U., 1949, JD, 1951. Bar: Va. 1951, D.C. 1951, U.S. Dist. D.C. 1951, U.S. Ct. Appeals (D.C. cir.) 1951. Assoc. Mills & Partridge, Washington, 1951; spl. agent FBI, Washington, 1951-54; fin. counsel ICC, Washington, 1954-55, legis. counsel, 1955-64, presdl. appointee as commr., 1967-77, vice chmn., acting chmn. agy., 1971-73, chmn. rates divsn., 1975-77; Presdl. appointee, mem. Adminstrv. Conf. U.S., 1969-72; dir. dept. transp. and comm. U.S. C. of C., Washington, 1964-66; v.p. govt. affairs Overmeyer Co., Washington, 1966-67; spl. counsel Am. Trucking Assn., Washington, 1967; assoc. prof. polit sci. S.W. Tex. State U., San Marcos, Tex., 1977—, assoc. prof. emeritus, 1989-00, acting dean sch. liberal arts., 1986-87, chmn. dept. home econs., 1990-92; ret. law educator, 2000. Gen. counsel Transp. Assn. Am., Washington, 1959; moderator 14th Ann. Seminar, State Bar Tex., 1982, moderator profl. devel. program gen. paralegal skills, 1988, standing com. on legal assts., 1988-00; chmn. Tex. forum IV Conf. Legal Asst. Educators, 1985, chair forum VII, 1988; presenter papers in field. Bus. sec. George Washington U. Sch. Law Rev., 1951. With USMC, 1942—46, PTO. Mem. Soc. Former Spl. Agents FBI. Fed. Bar Assn., Va. State Bar., D.C. Bar, Phi Delta Phi. Avocation: golf. Home: 10829 River Plantation Dr Austin TX 78747-1490

HARDIN, DAVID JESSE, application developer; b. Washington, D.C., Aug. 11, 1952; s. Jesse Elbert and Alice (Lewis) Hardin; m. Linda Ann Gordon, June 1, 1974; children: Bonnie, Dorothy, Evan, Joseph, Rachel. BS in Music Edn., U. Md., 1974, BS in Math., 1977; MS in Computer Sci., Johns Hopkins U., 1981. Software engr. ORI, San Jose, Calif. and Denver, Colo., 1980—88; mgr. software engring. Hughes Aircraft/Raytheon, Denver and Washington, D.C., 1988—2000, QSS Group Inc., Washington, 2000—. Dir. Colo. Mormon Chorale Ch. Jesus Christ Latter-Day Saints, Denver, 1983—93, asst. dir., Mormon Choir, Washington, 1998—. Arranger choral music, performed in pub., 1987—. Office: QSS Group 4500 Forbes Blvd # 200 Lanham MD 20706

HARDIN, EUGENE BROOKS, JR., retired banker; b. Wilmington, N.C., Oct. 18, 1930; s. Eugene Brooks Hardin and Roberta Gilmour (Sterling) Demme; m. Olivia Lynch, Aug. 16, 1958; children: John Haywood II, Olivia Cary. BS, U. N.C., 1952. With Wachovia Bank & Trust Co., Wilmington, 1956—, asst. v.p., 1957-60, v.p., 1962-68, sr. v.p., 1969-72, sr. v.p., regional exec. Raleigh, 1972-79, regional v.p., 1979-95; cashier Burlington, N.C., 1961-62; ret., 1995. Bd. dirs. Wachovia Bank, Raleigh, N.C. Pres., bd. dirs. Babies Hosp., Wilmington, 1968-72; pres. United Fund, 1970; treas., trustee Episcopalian Diocese East Carolina, 1965-72; chmn. Raleigh Civic Center Authority, 1978-81; chmn. Raleigh-Durham Airport Authority, 1981-82; chmn. bd. trustees St. Mary's Coll., 1979-85; bd. dirs. Children's Home Soc. N.C. Served with USNR, 1948-49; to 1st lt. USAF, 1952-56. Mem. Robert Morris Assos. Clubs: Civitan (pres. Wilmington 1971-72); Carolina Yacht (Wrightsville Beach); Carolina Country (Raleigh); Cape Fear Country (Wilmington); Land Fall (Wilmington). Home: 404 Drummond Dr Raleigh NC 27609-7006

HARDIN, GARRY JOE, II, music educator; b. Elizabethton, Tenn., June 29, 1966; s. Garry Joe and Janet Kathy Hardin; m. Paige Lynette Bass, June 11, 1994; children: Luke Alexander, James Daniel. D of Musical Arts, U. Cin., 2000, MusM, 1997, Appalachian State U., 1990; MusB, Dallas Bapt. U., 1988. Asst. prof. music Coll. of Ozarks, Point Lookout, Mo., 2000—; adj. prof. Cedarville Coll., Cedarville, Ohio, 1999—99. Dir. instrumental music Liberty Heights Ch., West Chester, Ohio, 1999—2000; music dir. Landmark Bapt. Temple, Glendale, Ohio, 1995—98, Fairfield First Bapt. Ch., Fairfield, Ohio, 1993—95; min. music Grace Bapt. Ch., Elizabethton, Tenn., 1990—92. Composer: (orchestral composition) The Vagrant's Dance (CCM World Premier, 1999), (instrumental solo) Scenes Metallic (Premiere at CCM Music Ninety-Eight, 1998), (solo piano) Four Countryside Memoirs (Premiere at CCM Music Ninety-Seven, 1997), (chamber music) Ponderings on an Afternoon Commute (Premiere at CCM Music Ninety-Six, 1996), Fanfare Perpetuo (Premiere at Internat. Trumpet Guild Conf., 1994). Scholar Full Tuition Grad. Student Award, College-Conservatory of Music, 1995—2000. Mem.: Mo. Music Educators Assn., Internat. Assn. for Jazz Edn. Baptist. Avocations: home improvement, hiking, computers, camping, weightlifting. Home: 239 Sunset Inn Rd Branson MO 65616 Office: College of Ozarks P O Box 17 Point Lookout MO 65726 Personal E-mail: cofojoe@yahoo.com.

HARDIN, GERALD LARSON, city planner and community developer, educator; b. Gladstone, Mich., Nov. 13, 1947; s. James Abraham and Constance Emma (Edson) H.; m. Nancy Ahlbin, 1972 (div. Mar. 1986); m. Teresa Marquerite Grindstaff, Apr. 12, 1990; children: Joanna, Joseph, Jennifer Oaks. BS in Sociology, East Tenn. State U., 1974, BS in Art, 1978, MA in Geography and Urban Planning, 1992, postgrad. in ednl. leadership and policy, 2000—. Cert. Am. Inst. Cert. Planners; lic. bldg. insp., Tenn. Cmty. devel. mgr. City of Bristol, Tenn., 1988-96; adj. prof. East Tenn. State U., Johnson City, 1997-99; cmty. devel. rehab. specialist City of Johnson City, 1999-2001; adj. instr. N.E. State Tech. C.C., 2001—, East Tenn. State U., 2001—. Adj. prof. Va. Intermont Coll., Bristol, 1993-96, King Coll., Bristol, Tenn., 1998—, N.E. State Tech. C.C., Blountville, Tenn. Contbr. articles, columnist series on edn. The Tennessean, 1999. Mem. planning com. Bristol unit Am. Cancer Soc., 1996-99; bd. dirs. Bristol Heart Assn., 1998-99, also pres.; bd. dirs. Theatre Bristol, 1989-99. With USN, 1966-69; with USNR, 1982-86, 89-96, Persian Gulf, 1990-91. Mem. Am. Planning Assn. (bd. dirs. Tri-Cities Tenn. chpt. 1993—, pres. 1995-96), Upper East Tenn. Bldg. Ofcls. Assn. Avocations: boating, hiking, fishing. Home: 208 Cloverdale Pl Bristol TN 37620-6115 E-mail: gernter@3wave.com.

HARDIN, GREGORY, rehabilitation services professional; b. Chgo., Nov. 29, 1953; s. Meritte and Sarah Hardin; m. Marilyn Hardin, June 30, 1972 (div. Apr. 1996); children: Gwen, Jamol, Malik, Lashabia, Sarah, Gregore'. BS in Psychology and Addictionology, Calumet Coll. St. Joseph, 1996. Cert. alcohol and drug abuse counselor. Crisis specialist Christian Haven Homes, Wheat Field, Ind., 1996—98; counselor Camelot Care Ctrs., Inc., Schearville, Ind., 1997—2000; program dir. Semoran Treatment Ctr., Gary, Ind., 1999—. Mem. treatment and intervention com. Partnership for a Drug Free Ind., Crown Point, 1997—. Roman Catholic. Avocations: chess, magic, reading, computers, macramé. Office: Semoran Treatment Ctr 8060 Melton Rd Gary IN 46403

HARDIN, HAL D. lawyer, judge, federal official; BS, Middle Tenn. State U. (MTSY); JD, Vanderbilt U., 1968. Bar: Tenn., U.S. Supreme Ct., D.C., U.S. Ct. Claims, U.S. Tax. Ct., U.S. Ct. Mil. Appeals, Tex., Ky. Fingerprint technician FBI; dir. St. Louis Job Corps Ctr.; vol. Peace Corps; asst. dist. atty.; pvt. practice; presiding judge Nashville Trial Cts., 1976-77; spl. judge Ct. of Appeals, 1977; U.S. atty. Middle Dist. Tenn., 1977-81; practice law Nashville, 1981—. Adj. prof. Aquinas Coll., Tenn. State U., 1975—76; adj. instr. fed. sentencing, criminal practice and procedure Nashville Sch. Law, 1994—. Bd. dirs. Nat. Assn. Former U.S. Atty., 1993—96, Leadership Nashville, 1983, Capital Case Resource Ctr., 1988—95, Leadership Alumni Assn., 1985. Master: Inns of Ct.; fellow: Tenn. Bar Found.; mem.: Washington D.C. Bar Assn., Ky. Bar Assn., Nat. Peace Corps Assn. (bd. dirs. 2001—), Am. Bd. Trial Advs. (sec. Tenn. chpt. 1987, nat. bd. dirs. 1988—89, pres. Tenn. chpt. 1990), 6th Cir. Jud. Con. (life), Tenn. Criminal Def. Attys. Assn., Nat. Criminal Def. Attys. Assn., Tex. Bar Assn., Tenn. Bar Assn. (gen. counsel 1982—90), Nashville Bar Assn. (bd. dirs. 1983—85, v.p. 1985). Office: 218 3d Ave N Nashville TN 37201

HARDIN, JAMES CARLISLE, III, lawyer, educator; b. Charlotte, N.C., Sept. 12, 1948; s. James Carlisle Jr. and Mary Gene (Roberts) H.; m. Sally M. Drennan, June 6, 1968 (div. Dec. 1973); 1 child, Christine M.; m. Caryle Wilson (dec. June 1986); 1 child, James Carlisle IV; m. Katharine C. Harrison, May 2, 1992. AB, Wofford Coll., 1969; MA in History, U. Va., 1970, postgrad., 1970-71; JD, Duke U., 1974. Bar: S.C. 1974, U.S. Dist. Ct. S.C. 1976, N.C. 1989; U.S. Dist. Ct. (we. dist.) N.C. 1989. Ptnr. Roddey, Carpenter & White, P.A., Rock Hill, S.C., 1974-86, Kennedy Covington Lobdell & Hickman, Charlotte & Rock Hill, S.C., 1986—. Chmn. specialization adv. bd. S.C. Supreme Ct., 1988-90; mem. S.C. Commn. on Continuing Lawyer Competence and Specialization, 1990-97; instr. Winthrop Univ., Rock Hill, 1979-91; mem. sect. coun. Probate Estate Planning and Trust Sect. S.C. Bar, 1997—, chmn., 1981, 91, chmn. elect. 2002; bd. dir. Rock Hill Econ. Devel. Corp., chmn. 1998-2000. Mem. bd. dirs. Rock Hill YMCA, 1986-89, S.C. Meth. Found., 1986—; bd. dirs. St. John's United Meth. Ch., Rock Hill, 1997—; bd. dirs. Piedmont Med. Ctr., 1994—2000, chmn., 1996. Fellow Am. Coll. Trust and Estate Coun. (state chmn. 1991-); mem. Rock Hill C. of C. (bd. dirs. 1991-95), Kiwanis (bd. dirs. Rock Hill 1978-80), Rock Hill Country Club, Phi Beta Kappa. Avocations: golf, swimming. Office: Kennedy Covington Lobdell & Hickman First Union Ctr 113 E Main St Rock Hill SC 29730-4539

HARDIN, JAMES NEAL, German and comparative literature educator, publisher; b. Nashville, Tenn., Feb. 17, 1939; s. James N. and Ina M. (Anderson) H.; m. Anne Farr. AB, Washington and Lee U., 1960; postgrad., U. Berlin, 1960-61; PhD, U. N.C., 1967. Prof. German lit. U. S.C., Columbia, 1969—98. Pres. Hardin Pub. Inc. Author: Co-founder, Camden House, imprint published by Boydell & Brewer Ltd., Johann Beer, 1983, Johann Beer Bibliographie, 1984, Christian Gryphius Bibliographie, 1985, J.C. Ettner Bibliographie, 1988; editor: Der Vielgeliebte Oesterreicher, 1977; editor/co-editor: Dictionary of Lit. Biography, Vols. 59, 66, 69, 81, 85, 90, 94, 97, 118, 124, 129, 133, 138, 148, 194 and 168, Goethe's Wilhelm Meister's Travels, 1991; founder, co-editor: Studies in German Language, Literature and Linguistics, Works of Christian Gryphius, 2 vols., 1985; contbr. articles to profl. jours. and mags. Capt. U.S. Army, 1967-69. Decorated Army Commendation medal; recipient Alexander von Humbolt award, 1974-75, Russell award for scholarship, 1979; Fulbright scholar, 1960-61 Mem. MLA, South Atlantic MLA. Office: PO Box 4088 Spring Island SC 29910 E-mail: jameshardin@direcway.com.

HARDIN, JAMES W. botanist, herbarium curator, educator; b. Mar. 31, 1929; BS, Fla. So. Coll., 1950; MS, U. Tenn., 1951; PhD, U. Mich., 1957. Instr. U. Mich., 1956-57; from asst. prof. to prof. N.C. State U., Raleigh, 1957-68, prof., 1968-96, emeritus prof., 1996—, curator herbarium, 1957-96. Vis. prof. Mountain Lake Biological Sta. U.Va., summers 1962, 64, 83, U. Okla. Biological Sta., summers 1967, 70; mem. exec. com. Flora Southeastern U.S., 1966-97; endangered species com. N.C. Dept. Natural & Econ. Resources, 1973-74, natural areas adv. com., 1973-79; mem. plant conservation sci. com. N.C. Dept. Agriculture, 1980-97, chmn. 1987-97; mem. endangered species com. N.C. Wildlife Resources Commn., 1976-78, N.C. State Mus. Natural Hist., 1975-78; pres. Highlands Biological Station, Inc., 1963-69, trustee, 1958-69, sec., 1960-63; invited symposium speaker. Author: Human Poisoning, 1974, Textbook of Dendrology, 2001; editor ASB Bull., 1980-86; mem. editorial com. Am. Jour. Botany, 1964-66; mem. editorial bd. Brittonia, 1964-67, Brimleyana, 1975-97; reviewer jours. in field. Trustee Highlands Biol. Found., 1976-. Mem. Am. Soc. Plant Taxonomists (pub. policy com. 1976-78, editorial bd. 1964-67, editor-in-chief Systematic Botany 1985-91, pres. elect 1991-92, pres. 1992-93, past pres. 1993-94, Cooley award 1958), Southern Appalachian Botanical Club (v.p. 1959-60, pres. 1964-65, Bartholomew award 1994), Botanical Soc. Am. (editorial com. 1964-66, chair southeastern sect. 1968-69), Assn. Southeastern Biologists (Meritorious Teaching award 1991, chmn. local arrangements 1966, 77, v.p. 1968-69, pres. 1979-80, editor 1980-86), Soc. Economic Botany (chmn. local arrangements 1979), Phi Kappa Phi, Sigma Xi (exec. com. N.C. chpt. 1962-63, sec. 1965-66, treas. 1966-67, v.p. 1967-68, program chmn. 1968-69, pres. 1969-70). Home: 204 Furches St Raleigh NC 27607-4056 Office: 204 Furches St Raleigh NC 27607

HARDIN, JOAN ROTHCHILD, psychologist, artist; b. Rochester, N.Y., Feb. 6, 1944; d. Harold and Rhoda (Stone) Rothchild; m. Russell Hardin, May 18, 1972; 1 child, Joshua. Student, Sheffield (Eng.) U., 1964; BA, U. Mich., 1965; MEd, Boston U., 1972; PhD, U. Pa., 1975. Diplomate Internat. Acad. Behavioral Medicine, Counseling and Psychotherapy, lic. psychologist N.Y. Project dir. youth leadership in smoking control project Lung Assn. Mid-Md., Rockville, 1977-78; staff psychotherapist D.C. Inst. Mental Hygiene, Washington, 1977-79; asst. professorial lectr. George Washington U., Washington, 1979; lectr. psychology Roosevelt U., Chgo., 1980-85; pvt. practice, Chgo., 1980-93, N.Y.C., 1995—; co-owner Bklyn. Artisans Gallery, N.Y.C., 1995—2003, pres., 1997—2003. Cons. Blue Gargoyle Youth Svc. Ctr., Chgo., 1979-80. Exhibited in group shows at AquaSource Art Gallery, N.Y.C., 1994, Freeport (Ill.) Art Mus., 1994, Gallery South Orange, N.J., 1994, Fired Up About Clay, A Festival of Tiles at Oakland (Calif.) Mus., 2001, Karpeles Mus., Newburgh, N.Y., 2001, Pence Gallery, Davis, Calif., 2001, Tiles in America, Clay Fine Arts Gallery, N.Y., 2002, 21st Century Tiles, Minn. Crafts Coun., 2002, prin. works include tiles commd. Battery Park Vet. Hosp., N.Y.C., 2000, tiles commd. West Village Vet. Hosp., 2000, works featured in Handbuilt Ceramics, 1997, works featured in Ceramic Art Tile for the Home, 2001, tiles featured on www.GUILD.com, 2000, tiles featured on www.GUILD.com, 2001, 2002, 2003. Bd. dirs. 393 West Broadway Corp., N.Y.C., 1994—2002, pres., 1997; founding mem. Hyde Park Psychotherapy Assoc., Chgo., 1982—84; active Tile Heritage Found. Recipient architecture award 4th Ann. Silverhawk Fine Craft Competition, 1999. Mem. APA, N.Y. State Psychol. Assn., Internat. Soc. for Study Dissociation, Am. Acad. Experts in Traumatic Stress, Voices in Action, Bklyn. Potters Group (treas. 1995-99), N.Y. Artists Equity.

HARDIN, LOWELL STEWART, retired economics educator; b. nr. Knightstown, Ind., Nov. 16, 1917; s. J. Fred and Mildred (Stewart) H.; m. Mary J. Cooley, Sept. 21, 1940; children: Thomas Stewart, Joyce Ann, Peter Lowell. BS, Purdue U., 1939, DAgr (hon), 1990; PhD, Cornell U., 1943. Grad. asst., instr. Cornell U., 1939-43; instr., asst. and assoc. prof., prof. Purdue U., 1943-65, adj. prof. agrl. econs., 1965-66, prof., 1981-84, emeritus prof., asst. dir. internat. programs, 1984—, acting head dept. agrl. econs., 1954-57, head dept., 1957-65; also dir. Purdue Work Simplification Lab. Program adviser agr. Ford Found., 1965-66, program officer agr., 1966-81; former trustee Internat. Food Policy Rsch. Inst., Washington, Internat. Ctr. for Agrl. Rsch. in Dry Areas, Aleppo, Syria, Internat. Svc. for Nat. Agrl. Rsch., The Hague, The Netherlands, Winrock Internat. Inst. for Agrl. Devel., Morrilton, Ark. Author: (with L.M. Vaughan) Farm Work Simplification, 1949. Fellow AAAS, Am. Agrl. Econ. Assn. (pres. 1963-64); mem. Internat. Assn. Agrl. Economists, Sigma Xi, Alpha Gamma Rho, Phi Kappa Phi, Alpha Zeta, Sigma Delta Chi. Federated Church. Home: 2628 Calvin Ct W Lafayette IN 47906-1402

HARDIN, MARTHA LOVE WOOD, civic leader; b. Muncie, Ind., Aug. 13, 1918; d. Lawrence Anselm and Bonny Blossom (Williams) Wood; m. Clifford Morris Hardin, June 28, 1939; children: Susan Hardin Wood, Clifford Wood, Cynthia Hardin Milligan, Nancy Hardin Rogers, James Alvin. Librarian U. Chgo., 1939-40. Co-author Genealogy: Ancestors of Lawrence Anselm Wood, Genealogy Ancestors of Bonny Williams Wood; contbr. articles to profl. jours. Chmn. Nebr. Heart Fund, 1967; vol. worker Lincoln Gen. Hosp., 1965, Clarkson Hosp., 1966; hon. chmn. Symphony Ball, Washington, 1970; mem. met. bd. YWCA, Washington, 1969-71, St. Louis, 1973-95; mem. Women's Com. of Pres.'s Com. on Employment of Handicapped, 1970-91, permanent mem. bd., 1970—; bd. dirs. St. Louis Speech and Hearing Clinic, St. Louis Met. YWCA, Cen. Inst. Deaf, St. Louis, 1986-92; co-chmn. nat. fund-raising campaign U. Nebr. Found., 1977-80. Mem. DAR, PEO, St. Louis Geneal. Soc., Mortar Bd., Old Warson Country Club, St. Louis Club, Wednesday Club, Phi Beta Kappa, Pi Beta Phi.

HARDIN, PAUL, III, law educator; b. Charlotte, NC, June 11, 1931; s. Paul and Dorothy (Reel) Hardin; m. Barbara Russell, June 8, 1954; children: Paul Russell, Sandra Mikush, Dorothy Holmes. AB, Duke U., 1952, JD, 1954; LHD (hon.), Clemson U., 1970, Coker Coll., 1972; LittD (hon.), Nebr. Wesleyan U., 1978; LLD (hon.), Adrian Coll., 1987, Monmouth Coll., 1988; HHD (hon.), Wofford Coll., 1989; LLD (hon.), Rider Coll., 1990; LHD (hon.), Duke U., 1994. Bar: Ala. 1954. Practiced in Birmingham, 1954, 1956—58; asst. prof. Duke Law Sch., 1958—61, assoc. prof., 1961—63, prof., 1963—68, univ. trustee, 1969—74, 1995—2001; pres. Wofford Coll., Spartanburg, SC, 1968—72, So. Methodist U., Dallas, 1972—74, Drew U., Madison, NJ, 1975—88; chancellor U. NC, Chapel Hill, NC, 1988—95, chancellor emeritus, prof. law, 1995—; interim pres. U. Ala., Birmingham, Ala., 1997. Vis. prof. U. Tex., 1960, U. Pa., 1962—63, U. Va., 1974; dir. Smith Barney mut. funds. Author (with Sullivan, others): The Administration of Criminal Justice, 1966; author: (with Sullivan) Evidence, Cases and Materials, 1968; contbr. articles to profl. jours., law revs. Chmn. Human Rels. Com., Durham, NC, 1961—62; pres. Nat. Assn. Schs. and Coll. of United Meth. Ch., 1984; mem. gen. conf. United Meth. Ch., 1968, 1976, 1980, 1984; chmn. Nat. Commn. on United Meth. Higher Edn., 1975—77. Served with CIC U.S. Army, 1954—56. Mem.: Order of Coif, Carnegie Found. for Advancement Tchg. (bd. dirs. 1990—98), Phi Beta Kappa. Office: University of North Carolina School of Law Chapel Hill NC 27599-3380 E-mail: phardin1@bellsouth.net.

HARDIN, SHERRIE ANN ASFOURY, commercial photographer; b. Saratoga Springs, May 28, 1950; d. Edward Asfoury and Olivia Dorethea (Rehm) Melrose; m. Lin Hardin, Feb. 13, 1972. Student, Polk Community Coll., Winter Haven, Fla., 1968-69, 77, LA Harbor Coll., Wilmington, Calif., 1984-85, El Camino Coll., Hawthorne, Calif., 1985-87. Dep. Polk County Sheriff's Office, Bartow, Fla., 1975-78; freelance comml. artist Winter Haven, Fla., Sacramento, 1978-84; photographer Nissan Motor Corp. in USA, Gardena, Calif., 1985-86; gen. mgr. Awards-Rex Group, Hawthorne, Calif., 1986-88; photog. coord. Meisel, Atlanta, 1988-89; owner, mgr. Sherrie Hardin, Photographer, 1985—; ptnr. LS Advt. & Graphics, Inc., 1998—, v.p., CFO, 2002—. Mentor Cartersville Md. Sch., 1996-98. Photog. work includes stock, indsl., environ. and nature photography, restorations of old damaged photographs and fine art photography. Chair 7th Dist. Ann. Congl. H.S. Art Comp., 1998—2001; grad. Jedco-Polk Leadeership XI; chmn. Leadership XII; downtown Christmas com., city playspace and Halloween downtown coms. City of Rockmart, 2000—; mem. Rotary Internat. Recipient Polk County Small Bus. of Yr. award, 2000. Mem.: Polk County Home Builders Assn. (charter), Am. Bus. Women's Assn., Nat. Assn. Photoshop Profls., Greater Rome C. of C., Paulding County C. of C., Nat. Trust for Hist. Preservation, Etowah Creative Art Coun. (bd. dirs.), Rockmart Civic Arts Commn. (bd. dirs.), High Mus. of Art, Polk County C. of C., Haralson County C. of C., Rotary (sgt. at arms 2000, v.p. 2001, pres. 2002—). Avocations: golf, fishing, sculpting, painting, gardening. Office: 219 S Marble St Rockmart GA 30153 E-mail: lsadvertising@direcway.com.

HARDIN, WILLIAM DOWNER, retired lawyer; b. Newark, Sept. 27, 1926; s. Charles R. and Emma (Downer) H.; m. Rosemarie Koellhoffer, Jan. 19, 1952 (dec. Mar. 1996); m. Ruth M. Johnson, May 29, 1999; children: William Downer, David Gerth, Peter Roe. AB, Princeton, 1948; LL.B., Columbia, 1951. Bar: N.J. 1951. Law clk. N.J. Superior Ct., 1951-52; assoc. firm Pitney, Hardin, Kipp & Szuch, Newark and Morristown, 1952—57, mem. firm, 1957—96. Mem. N.J. Bd. Bar Examiners, 1964-68, chmn., 1968; mem. local draft bd. SSS, 1953-74, chmn., 1970-74; mem. Family Svc. Bur., Newark, 1953-75, pres., 1960-66; mem. Family Svc. Morris County, 1976-85, 87-98, pres., 1979-82, 95-97, v.p., 1992-95; mem. membership com. Family Svc. Assn. Am., 1965-78, dir., 1971-79, 89-95; mem. Nat. Budget and Consultation Com., 1966-71, Coun. on Accreditation Svcs. for Families and Children, 1978-80. Trustee Newark Acad., 1952-85, pres., 1969-72, chmn., 1976-78; mem. Legal Svcs. of N.J. 1983-2002, chmn., 1990-96; mem. Legal Aid Soc. of Morris County, N.J. 1984-93, pres., 1989-90. With USNR, 1944-46. Mem. ABA, Fed. Bar Assn. N.J. Bar Assn., Essex County Bar Assn., Morris County Bar Assn., Morristown Club, Nassau Club, Coral Beach and Tennis Club, Short Hills Club, Princeton Club of N.Y., Morris County Golf Club. Episcopalian. Home: 15 Gapview Rd Short Hills NJ 07078-2077 Office: 200 Campus Dr Florham Park NJ 07932-1007

HARDING, BRUCE ALAN, engineering technology educator; b. Buffalo, Mar. 8, 1947; s. E. Albert and Marion E. (Ulrich) H.; m. Martha Jane Holmes, Aug. 31, 1968; 1 child, Seth Mathes. AAS, Purdue U., 1970, BS, 1971, MS, 1973; postgrad., U. Va., 1979-82. Adminstrv. asst. Olin Mathieson Chem. Corp., Charlestown, Ind., 1967-68; technologist Westinghouse Rsch., W. Lafayette, Ind., 1968-73; coord. learning resources Rappahannock Community Coll., Warsaw, Va., 1974-82; instr. Purdue U., W. Lafayette, 1982-85, asst. prof., 1985-88, assoc. prof. mech. engring. tech., 1988-93, prof., 1993—. Vis. prof. engring. adminstrn. U. Cinn., 1993; adj. faculty Ind. U., South Bend, 1988—; partner Potomac Media Cons., Warsaw, 1978-83; cons. CTS Electronics, Rochester, Ind., 1985, Aluminum Corp. Am., Lafayette, Ind., 1985, Am. Soc. for Quality Control, Lafayette, 1985, Revere Copper & Brass, Inc., Peoria, Ill., 1987, Computerland, W. Lafayette, 1987-90, Talbert Mfg., Rensselaer, Ind., 1988, Sealed Power, Inc., Rochester, 1989, AM Gen. subs. LTV, Elkhart, Ind., 1989, Hudson Inst., N.Y.C., 1989, State of Ind., Indpls., 1989, IBM Corp., Rochester, Minn., 1989, Diamet Corp. subs. Mitsubishi Metal, Columbus, Ind., 1990—, various others; reviewer John Wiley & Sons, N.Y.C., 1987, Prentice-Hall, Inc., N.Y.C., 1987, Soc. of Mfg. Execs., 1992, West Publishers, 1992, Houghton Mifflin, 1993; software tester Versacad Corp., Orange County, Calif., 1987-88, Intergraph Corp., Huntsville, Ala., 1988-89; mem. com. Am. Soc. Mech. Engrs., 1992—; speaker in field; chair ISO tech. com. 10-tech. product documentations stds. (engring. drawings), 1999—. Contbr. numerous articles to profl. jours.; editor Second Ann. Roundtable on Ind./Edn. Mix. Dist. commr. Boys Scouts Am., New Albany, Ind., 1966—; bd. dirs. Richmond County Relief Fund, Warsaw, 1976-80; pres. Richmond County C. of C., Warsaw, 1978-79. Rsch. grantee IBM Corp., 1990-93, Purdue U., 1987, software grantee Automated Engring., Inc., 1987, Versacad Corp., 1986-87, Bridgeport Machine Tools, Inc., 1986, Autodesk, Inc., 1985, Computervision, Inc., 1994—, equipment grantee Apple Computer, 1985, Partnership in Engring. Edn. grantee Digital Equipment Corp., 1984-85. Fellow Am. Soc. Engring. Edn. (sec. svc. award 1989, campus rep. Purdue U. 1984—, bd. dirs. 1992-94, coord. campus reps. Ill.-Ind. sect. 1989—, mem. Nat. Coun. Campus Rep. Coords., 1990-92, mem. and chmn. various coms.); mem. ASME (ANSI 14.5M standards com. 1992—, chmn. Y14.40 ANSI com. writing stds. on graphics symbols 1995—, Y14 ANSI main com. on engring. drawings and related practices 1995—, bd. on standardization 2003—), Am. Tech. Edn. Assn. (state rep. Gt. Lakes coun. 1987-92), Instrument Soc. Am., Soc. Mfg. Engrs. (faculty devel. grant 1983, svc. award 1986, pres.'s award 1988, mem. editl. bd. Electronics in Mfg. 1990-93, mem. exec. bd. Ind. chpt. 1988-93), Assn. Electronics Mfg. (bd. advisors 1990—, bd. chmn. 1992), Rotary (bd. dirs. 1991-93), Kappa Delta Pi. Avocations: golfing, woodworking. Home: 445 Maple St West Lafayette IN 47906-3066 Office: Purdue U 136 Knoy Hall West Lafayette IN 47907-1417

HARDING, ENOCH, JR., clothing executive; b. Greenville, SC, Apr. 7, 1931; s. Enoch and Nell (Evans) H.; m. Sarah Tomlinson, Dec. 26, 1953 (div. 1978); children: Enoch III, Earle T., David H., Elizabeth W.; m. Virginia Black, Sept., 1978. BS, Presbyn. Coll., Clinton, S.C., 1953. Div. mgr. Stone Mfg. Co., Columbia, SC, 1955-62, Oxford Industries, Columbia, 1962-71; div. pres. Kellwood Co., NYC, 1971-77, 83-95, corp. exec. v.p. oper., 1995-2000, ret., 2000; pres. Vanity Fair Mills, Reading, Pa., 1977-83, ret., 2000. Vice chmn. Midlands Tech. Coll., Columbia, 1961-71. 1st lt. US Army, 1953-55. Mem. Union League Club NYC Avocation: sailing. Home: 36 Harleston Pl Charleston SC 29401-1268

HARDING, FANN, health scientist, administrator; b. Henderson, Ky., Jan. 29, 1930; d. James Hilary and Lucy (Caldwell) H. Student, Western Coll., Oxford Ohio, 1947-48; AB in Biology, Coker Coll., Hartsville, S.C., 1951; MS in Anatomy, Med. U. S.C., Charleston, 1954, PhD, 1958. Research and teaching asst. dept. anatomy Med. U. S.C., 1951-53, teaching fellow, 1953-55, research fellow, 1955-58; analyst pub. health research program, research and tng. grants br. Nat. Heart Inst., Bethesda, Md., 1958-61, scientist adminstr. research and tng. grants br., 1961-64, chmn. nat. adv. heart council statements com., 1961-64, sr. health scientist adminstr. research grants br. (sect. chief), 1964-69, sr. health scientist adminstr. thrombosis and hemorrhagic diseases br. (acting chief), extramural program, also arteriosclerosis program, 1969-72; mem. Nat. Heart Inst. (Fellowship Bd.), 1966-68; sr. health scientist adminstr. thrombosis and hemorrhagic diseases program (acting chief), div. blood diseases and resources Nat. Heart and Lung Inst. (name changed to Nat. Heart, Lung and Blood Inst. 1976), Bethesda, 1972-74; asst. to dir. div. blood diseases and resources Nat. Heart, Lung and Blood Inst., 1974—, program dir. extramural research tng. and career devel. in blood diseases and transfusion medicine, exec. sec. blood diseases and resources adv. com., 1974-95; asst. coordinator U.S.-USSR Health Exchange Program, 1974-95; ret., 1996; sculptor, 1996—. Mem. Women's Action Program Adv. Coun., HEW, 1971-72; cons. James H. Mitchell Found., Washington, 1962-67, Washington VA Hosp., 1968-70; environ. cons. Henderson (Ky.) Citizens Com., 1974-76; bd. dirs. Lupus Found. Am., 1985-88; initiated and implemented concept of transfusion medicine, 1982—. Editorial bd.: Lupus News, 1988—. Organizer NIH Orgn. for Women, 1970; bd. dirs. Assn. Women in Sci. Edn. Found., 1973-77; bd. visitors Coker Coll., 1974-78; bd. dirs., sec., treas. Nat. Children's Choir, Washington, 1981-91; mem. bd. advisors Psychoceramie Found., 2002 Recipient Ruth Patrick award, 1951, NIH sustained performance award, 1973, Nat. award Fedn. Orgns. for Profl. Women, 1977, Disting. Svc. award Transfusion Medicine Acad. Award Program, Am. Assn. Blood Banks, 1990, Disting. Alumni award Coker Coll., 1992, award of Merit for Transfusion Medicine, NIH, 1993, Founder's award for Pioneering Contbns. to Advance Women in the Professions, Fedn. Orgns. for Profl. Women, 1995. Fellow Sigma Delta Epsilon; mem. AAAS (panel on women in sci. 1973-77), Nat. Women's Polit. Caucus (charter), Assn. Women in Sci. (founding mem. 1971, exec. bd. 1973-75), Fedn. Orgn. Profl. Women (founding pres., exec. bd. 1972—), Nat. Womans Party (bd. dirs. 1981—, corr. sec. 1989-91, rec. sec. 1991-96), Microcirculatory Soc. (charter), Reticuloendothelial Soc. (charter), Am. Assn. Blood Banks, Internat. Soc. Thrombosis & Haemostasis, Internat. Soc. Blood Transfusion, Internat. Soc. Lymphology. Home: 2119 S Street NW Washington DC 20008-4011 Fax: (202) 265-3267. E-mail: ffharding@aol.com.

HARDING, JAMES WARREN, retired finance company executive; b. Montoursville, Pa., Nov. 9, 1918; s. James John and Alda (Edkin) H.; m. Emily Sue Landes, Mar. 22, 1941 (dec. Mar., 1992); 1 child, Connie Sue Harding; m. Mary Briand, Jan. 15, 1994. BA, Lycoming Coll., 1938, LL.D. (hon.); MA, U. Chgo., 1940. With Kemper Cos., Chgo., 1940-84, accountant, 1940-50, comptroller, 1960-68, exec. v.p., 1969; chmn. bd. Bank of Chgo., from 1969; pres. Kemper Corp., 1969-84, ret.; pres. Am. Underwriting Corp., Central Mortgage Co., Nat. Agts. Service Co., 1969—, also bd. dirs. Bd. dirs. Kemper Fin. Svcs. Contbr. articles to ins. and trade mags. Finance chmn. Crusade of Mercy, Chgo., 1964-65; trustee James S. Kemper Found., Mundelein Coll.; adv. bd. U. Chgo., Brigham Young U. Served with USNR, 1943-44. Recipient Hardy award Ins. Inst., 1946 Mem Fin. Execs. Inst., Phi Kappa Sigma. Clubs: Chgo. University, Indian Wells Country Club. Republican. Methodist. Home: 46610 Quail Run Dr Indian Wells CA 92210-9012

HARDING, JOHN HIBBARD, retired insurance company executive; b. Plainfield, N.J., Jan. 12, 1936; s. Ernest Reginald and Emily (Hibbard) H.; m. Joan Edith Tarro, Nov. 29, 1973; children— David, Philip, Robert, Brooke, Ashley. BA, Princeton U., 1958. Asst. actuary Nat. Life Ins. Co., Montpelier, Vt., 1965-67, assoc. actuary, 1967-69, actuary R&D, 1969-72, v.p., actuary, 1972-80, sr. v.p., chief actuary, 1980-83, exec. v.p., 1983-85, vice chmn. bd., dir., 1985-87, pres., COO, 1987-96; v.p., chief actuary Blue Cross-Blue Shield of Vt., 1997-2000. Chmn., CEO Adminstrv. Svcs., Inc.; dir. Equity Svcs., Inc., Nat. Life Investment Mgmt. Co., Sentinel Advisors, Inc., 1987-96. Fellow Soc. Actuaries (bd. govs. 1993-95); mem. Am. Acad. Actuaries (bd. dirs. 1982-85, v.p. 1988-90, pres.-elect 1991-92, pres. 1992-93, immediate past pres. 1993-94). Home: PO Box 180 East Calais VT 05650-0180 E-mail: hardingcalais@aol.com.

HARDING, KAREN ELAINE, chemistry educator; b. Atlanta, Sept. 5, 1949; d. Howard Everett and Ruth Evangeline (Lund) H.; m. Bruce Roy McDowell, Aug. 30, 1975. BS in Chemistry, U. Puget Sound, Tacoma, 1971; MS in Environ. Chemistry, U. Mich., 1972; postgrad., Evergreen State Coll., 1972, 84, Yale U., 1986, Columbia U., 1991. Chemist Environ. Health Lab., Inc., Farmington, Mich., 1972—73, U. Mich. Med. Sch., Ann Arbor, 1973—75; instr. chemistry Schoolcraft Coll., Livonia, Mich., 1975—77; chair chemistry dept. Pierce Coll., Lakewood, Wash., 1977—. Adj. prof. U. Mich., Dearborn, 1974-77; instr. S.H. Alternative Learning Ctr., Tacoma, 1980-83, Elderhostel, Tacoma, 1985-89; mem. exec. com. Chemlinks project NSF. Mem. County Solid Waste Adv. Com., Tacoma, 1989—, Superfund Adv. Com., Tacoma, 1985-89, Sierra Club, Wash., 1989—; mem., past pres. Adv. Com. Nature Ctr., Tacoma, 1981-87. Faculty Enhancement grantee Pierce Coll., 1990; recipient Nat. Teaching Excellence award, 1991. Mem. NW Assn. for Environ. Studies (treas. 1985—), Am. Chem. Soc., Ft. Steilacoom Running Club (race dir. 1986—). Avocations: running, skiing, backpacking, bicycling, reading. Office: Pierce Coll 9401 Farwest Dr SW Lakewood WA 98498-1999

HARDING, LAURA J. music educator; b. Montevideo, Minn., Aug. 11, 1977; d. Steven L. and Karen E. Kling; m. Wade A. Harding, Apr. 24, 1999. BA, Luther Coll., 1999; postgrad., U. St. Thomas. Tchr. music, Minnetonka, Minn., 1999—, Shakopee, Minn., 2001—. Mktg. comm. staff Berqquist Co., Chanhassen, Minn., 2000—01; tchr. music Pre-Sch. Ramalynn Montessori, Bloomington, Minn., 2001—02. Mem.: Minn. Music Tchrs. Assn., Music Tchrs. Nat. Assn., Assn. Profl. Piano Instrs. Avocations: bicycling, reading, music.

HARDING, LINDA OTTO, gerontological nurse, diabetes educator; b. Calicoon, N.Y., Apr. 30, 1944; d. Max Hermann and Leona (Kleb) Otto; m. Bruce Nelson Harding, June 4, 1966; children: Jonathan, Linette. Diploma, Robert Packer Hosp. Sch. of Nursing, Sayre, Pa., 1965; student, Phillips U., Enid, Okla., 1967-68. RN, N.Y., Pa.; cert. personal care home administr.; cert. gerontol. nurse; cert. diabetes educator. Psychiat. nurse Meth. Hosp., Indpls., 1969-71; Tb control nurse Madison County Dept. Health, Anderson, Ind., 1971-73; charge nurse Milford (Pa.) Valley Convalescent Home, 1974-83; office nurse Tri State Med. Assocs., Matamoras, Pa., 1983-91; dir. resident health svcs. Twin Cedars Assisted Living Ctr., Shohola, Pa., 1990—. Founder Tri State Alzheimer's Support Group; dir. Diabetes Support Group, Bon Secoures Cmty. Hosp.; welcome sec. Bethany Christian Fellowship. Named Vol. of Yr., Mercy Cmty. Hosp., 1997. Mem. ANA, Nat. Gerontol. Nurses Assn., Pa. State Nurses Assn. (past newsletter editor, treas., v.p., nominating com., Kathryn J. Grove Nursing Advocacy award 2003), Am. Assn. Diabetes Educators, N.E. Pa. Assn. Diabetes Educators. Home: 360 Little Walker Rd Shohola PA 18458

HARDING, MAJOR BEST, former state supreme court chief justice; b. Charlotte, N.C., Oct. 13, 1935; m. Jane Lewis, Dec., 1958; children: Major B. Jr., David L., Alice Harding Sanderson. BS, Wake Forest U., 1957, also LLD; LLM in Jud. Process, U. Va., 1995; LLD, Stetson U., 1991, Fla. Coastal Sch. Law, 1999. Bar: N.C. 1959, Fla. 1960. Staff judge adv. hdqrs., Ft. Gordon, Ga., 1960-62; asst. county solicitor Criminal Ct. of Record, Duval County, Fla., 1962-63; pvt. practice law, 1964-68; judge Juvenile Ct., Duval County, 1968-70, 4th Jud. Cir. of Fla., 1970-74, chief judge, 1974-77; justice Supreme Ct. of Fla., Tallahassee, 1991—2002, chief justice, 1998-2000. Supervisory judge Family Mediation Unit, 1984-90; mem. Matrimonial Law Commn. and Gender Bias Study Commn.; chair Fla. Ct. Edn. Coun., past mem. Jud. Conf.; 1st dean New Judges Coll., 1975, faculty mem. in probate and juvenile areas, until 1979; dean Fla. Jud. Coll., 1984-92, faculty mem., 1984—, mem. bench-bar commn.; chmn. Supreme Ct. com. on law-related edn., 1997—. Bd. dirs. Legal Aid Assn., Family Consultation Svc., Daniel Meml. Home; mem. bd. visitors Wake Forest Sch. Law, Winston-Salem, N.C., Reformed Theol. Sem., Orlando, Fla.; past pres. Rotary Club of Riverside, Jacksonville, Fla., Rotary Club of Tallahasee; chmn. U.S. Constn. Bicentennial Commn., Jacksonville; past mem., deacon, elder St. John's Presbyn. Ch.; commr. Gen. Assembly Presbyn. Ch. U.S., 1971. Recipient Award for Outstanding Contbn. to Field of Matrimonial Law Am. Acad. Matrimonial Lawyers, 1986, Disting. Svc. award Nat. Ctr. State Cts., 2001, William A. Dugger Profl. Integrity award Capital Rotary Club. Mem. ABA (mem. bar admission com., Commn. Lawyer Assistance Programs Jud. Recognition award), Am. Bd. Trial Advocates (Jurist of Yr. Jacksonville chpt. 2000), The Fla. Bar, N.C. State Bar Assn., Chester Bedell Inn of Ct. (past pres., ex-officio bd. mem., master emeritus Chester Bedell), Dade County Trial Lawyers Assn. (Justice Harry Lee Anstead professionalism award 1998), Scabbard and Blade, Tallahassee Am. Inn of Ct. (ex officio trustee), Tallahassee Bar Assn., Econ. Club of Fla. (treas.), Sigma Chi (Significant Sig award 1997), Phi Delta Phi. Episcopalian.

HARDING, MARIE, ecological executive, artist; b. Glen Cove, N.Y., Nov. 13, 1941; d. Charles Lewis and Marie (Parish) H.; m. John P. Allen, Jan. 29, 1965 (div. Oct., 1991); 1 child, Eden A. Harding. BA, Sarah Lawrence Coll., 1964; postgrad., Arts Students League, N.Y.C., 1965. Founder Synergia Ranch Ctr. for Wellness, Innovation, Retreats and Confs., Santa Fe, 1969; founding mem., actress Theater of All Possibilities, Santa Fe, 1971-86; founding mem., dir. Inst. Ecotechnics, Santa Fe, also London, 1974—; bd. dirs. Synopco Corp., N. Mex., 1974-81; bd. dirs., founding mem. Savannah Systems Pty., Ltd., Kimberly region, Australia, 1976—, Outback Sta. Pty. Ltd., Kimberly region, Australia, 1976-94; chair, dir. EcoWorld, Inc., Santa Fe, 1982-94; dir., founding mem., CFO Space Biospheres Ventures, Biosphere 2, Ariz., 1984-94; chair, CEO Oceans Expdns., Inc., 1986-92; pres. ecol. and biosphere R&D/implementation project Global Ecotechnics Corp., Santa Fe, 1994—; pres. Decisions Team, Inc. Ecol. Project Mgmt., Ariz., 1994—; pres., mng. mem. Synergia Ranch, LLC, retreats and confs., Santa Fe. Particpant in constrn. and fin. Capt. R. Heraclitus rsch. vessel, Oakland, Calif., 1974; bd. dirs. Hotel Vajra, Kathamdu, Nepal, 1976-94, Caravan of Dreams Performing Arts Ctr., Ft. Worth, 1983-94, Synergetic Press, London and Ariz., 1984—. Artist: paintings shown in exhibitions San Francisco, London, Ft. Worth, Santa Fe, Biosphere 2, Ariz., 1979-93, Berlin, London, 2003, Biosphere 2 Paintings Exhbn., London, 1996, San Marcos Studio Tour shows, 1999-2002, London, 2003, Berlin, 2003; project dir., artist mural project History of Jazz, Dance, Theater, Ft. Worth, 1982-83, San Marcos Studio Tours, 1999-2002; prodr., dir. (films) Bryon Gysin Loves ya, Project Charlie, The Search, Synergia History, Planet Earth Conf. Vol. Swallows, Madras, India, 1964, Project Concern, Vietnam, Hong Kong, 1964-65; artist, founder, trustee October Gallery Trust, internat. artists forum, London, 1979; mem. Planetary Coral Reef Found., Inc., 1993—. Avocations: ecological project implementation, endangered lifestyles/cultures, painting, landscape gardening, retreat facilitation. Home and Office: 26 Synergia Rd Santa Fe NM 87508-4438

HARDING, ROBERT WILLIAM, academic administrator; b. Dec. 24, 1947; s. Robert Baselt and Dorothy Elaine (Brown) Harding; m. Cielo Violante Fajardo, Oct. 6, 1974; 1 child, Michael. AB, Stanford U., 1970; MA, UCLA, 1980, PhD, 1990. Instr. Calif. State U., Northridge, 1981—2003, mgr. acad. resources Coll. Bus. and Econs., 1995—2003. Lt. USN, 1971—78, comdr. USNR, 1978—93. Mem.: NRA, Phi Beta Kappa. Republican.

HARDING, SUSAN KATHLEEN, early childhood and elementary school educator, writer, poet; b. Mpls., Mar. 2, 1947; d. Stanley Herbert and Ruth Evelyn (Swedberg) Johnson; m. Lawrence David Harding, Apr. 8, 1978; children: Jonathan David, Robin Susan, Rachelle Ruth. BS in Elem. Edn., U. Minn., 1969; cert. grad., Inst. Bibl. Studies, San Bernardino, Calif., 1975. Cert. elem. tchr., Minn., Calif. Elem. sch. tchr. Ind. #833 South Washington County Schs., Cottage Grove, Minn., 1970-75; curriculum coord. Campus Crusade for Christ, San Bernardino, Calif., 1976-78; elem. sch. tchr. San Bernardino, Calif., 1978-80; lead tchr. Hope Nursery Sch., Richfield, Minn., 1989-96, Mt. Olivet Day Svcs., Mpls., 1999—2003. Contbr. poetry to anthologies and CDs. Sunday sch. tchr. Crosstown Covenant Ch., Mpls., 1993-97. Republican. Evangelical. Avocations: swimming, gardening, walking, needlework, reading.

HARDING, TERESA J. interior designer, property management; b. L.A. d. Edward Joseph Harding and Jane Elizabeth (Gunter) Kruse; divorced. BA, U. Okla. Cert. interior designer, Calif. Buyer lamps and accesories W & J Sloane, San Francisco, interior designer Beverly Hills, Calif.; interior designer, owner Harding Interior, L.A. Mem. Brentwood Homeowners Assn., L.A., 1994; treas. Nat. Charity League, 1994—. Mem. Nat. Charity League (treas. 1994-96), Colleagues Helpers in Philanthropic Svcs. (hon.), Am. Soc. Interior Design, Calif. Coun. for Interior Design Cert.

HARDING, WAYNE MICHAEL, sociologist, researcher; b. Boston, Jan. 10, 1947; s. Lawrence Robert and Genevieve Ruth (Ewell) H.; m. Kathleen Mary Fraser, Sept. 27, 1971; 1 child, Alexander Fraser. AB in Sociology magna cum laude, Brandeis U., 1970; EdM, Harvard U., 1971; PhD, Brandeis U., 1992. Evaluation cons. to exemplary program in occupational edn. Cardinal Cushing Ctr. for the Spanish Speaking, Boston, 1970-71; asst. dir. edn. The Sanctuary, Inc., Cambridge, Mass., 1971-73; rsch. asst. analytical studies and planning group Mass. Inst. Tech., Cambridge, 1974; rsch. assoc. The North Charles Mental Health Rsch. and Tng. Found., Cambridge, 1974—. Dir. projects, officer, co-founder Social and Behavioral Rsch., Inc., Cambridge, 1980-85, Social Sci. Rsch. and Evaluation, Inc., Lincoln, Mass., 1984—; lectr. on psychiatry Harvard Med. Sch., Cambridge, 1984—; ptnr., co-founder Social Sci. Rsch. Enterprises, Lincoln, 1987—; sr. rsch. scientist Gemini Industries, Inc., Burlington, Mass., 1989-81, Rainbow Tech., Inc., Olney, Md., 1994—2000. Bd. dirs., treas. Rogers Pierce Children's Ctr., Arlington, Mass., 1980-84; mem. Burlington bd. Appeals. Avocations: gardening, skiing. Home: 16 Chadwick Rd Burlington MA 01803-3604 Office: Social Sci Rsch Evaluation 21-C Cambridge St Burlington MA 01803-4990

HARDIS, STEPHEN ROGER, retired manufacturing company executive; b. N.Y.C., July 13, 1935; s. Abraham I. and Ethel (Krinsky) H; m. Sondra Joyce Rolbin, Sept. 15, 1957; children: Julia Faye, Andrew Martin, Joanna Halley. BA with distinction, Cornell U., 1956; M.P.A. in Econs., Woodrow Wilson Sch. of Pub. and Internat. Affairs Princeton U., 1960. Asst. to controller Gen. Dynamics, 1960-61; fin. analyst Pfaudler Permutit Inc., 1961-64; staff asst. to controller, 1964; mgr. corp. long-range planning Ritter Pfaudler Corp., 1965-68, dir. corporate planning, 1968; treas. Sybron Corp., Rochester, N.Y., 1969—, v.p. fin., 1970-77, exec. v.p. fin. and planning, 1977-79; vice chmn., chief fin. and adminstrv. officer Eaton Corp., Cleve., 1979—, vice chmn., CEO, 1995, chmn., CEO, 1996-2000; ret., 2000; chmn. Axcelis Techs., 2000—. Bd. dirs. Progressive Corp., Nordson Corp., Lexmark Corp., Marsh & McLennan, Axcelis Techs., Inc., Steris Corp, Apogent Techs., Inc. Past mem. Gov.'s Task Force on High Tech. Industry; past mem. bd. dirs. Rochester Area Hosp. Corp., Rochester Area Edn1. TV Sta., Genesee Hosp.; trustee Cleve. Clinic, Inc., Playhouse Square Found., Musical Arts Assn. (Cleve. Orchestra). With USNR, 1956-58. Mem. Phi Beta Kappa. Office: Eaton Corp 1111 Superior Ave E Cleveland OH 44114-2507

HARDISON, DEE, former mayor; Tchr. spl. edn. Torrance Unified Sch. Dist., 1980-89, program specialist, 1989-94; mem. Torrance City Coun., 1986-94; mayor City of Torrance, 1994—2002. Office: Arc South Bay 1735 W Rosecrans Ave Gardena CA 90249

HARDISON, DONALD LEIGH, retired architect; b. Fillmore, Calif., Mar. 23, 1916; s. Leigh Winter and Myrtle Glenn (Thorpe) H.; m. Betty Jane Decker, June 14, 1942; children— Stephen Decker, Janet Leigh Hardison Brown AB, U. Calif.-Berkeley, 1938. Lic. architect, Calif. Prin. Hardison & Assocs., Richmond, Calif., 1948-56; ptnr. Hardison & Komatsu, Richmond, 1956-61, pres. San Francisco, 1965-78; chmn. bd. Hardison Komatsu Ivelich & Tucker, San Francisco, 1978-87, ret., 1987. Prin. works include Sonoma State Coll. Residence Hall, 1972 (AIA award 1977), Chevron Cafeteria-Tech. Ctr., Richmond, 1981, McAllister Tower, San Francisco, 1982, (co-architect) U. Calif.-Berkeley Student Ctr. Complex, 1970 (AIA award 1970) Mem. Richmond Planning Commn., 1952-55; mem. Calif. Commn. on Housing and Cmty. Devel., 1969-74; bd. dirs. Art Ctr., Richmond, 1965-70, Richmond Mus. of History, 1990-2003. Fellow AIA (bd. dirs. 1978-80, chancellor Coll. Fellows 1985, pres. East Bay chpt. 1954, pres. Calif. council 1965, Calif. council Disting. Service citation 1984) . Clubs: Commonwealth (San Francisco). Lodges: Rotary (pres. Richmond, Calif. 1986-87). Republican. Presbyterian.

HARDISTY, WILLIAM LEE, English language educator; b. Creston, Iowa, Feb. 14, 1946; s. Ernest Dale and Velda Marie (Schaffer) H.; m. Bernadine Maxine Reimers, July 30, 1967; children: Lance William, Chad Eugene. AA, Creston (Iowa) C.C., 1965; BS, N.W. Mo. State U., Maryville, 1967, MA, 1972; postgrad., U. No. Iowa, Cedar Falls, 2003. Cert. tchr., Iowa, Mo. Instr. Iowa Western Coll., Council Bluffs, 1987—; chmn. lang. arts A-H-S-T H.S., Avoca, Iowa, 1967—; drama dir. A-S-T High Sch., Avoca, Iowa, 1967-92; instr. U. No. Iowa Workshops. Presenter Iowa Tchrs. English, Des Moines, 1991-95, Iowa Conservation Edn. Coun., Ames, 1995, Iowa State Edn. Assn., 1982-99, others. Contbr. articles to profl. and popular publs. Dist. chmn. Mid-Am. coun. Boy Scouts Am., 1984-2000, trustee; chmn. Rep. Party Knox Twp., Avoca, 1988—; pres. Iowa Assn. County Conservation Bds., Des Moines, 1990; pres. Pott count R.E.A.P. Bd. Council Bluffs, 1992; elder Presbyn. Ch., 1969—; mem. Sheriff's Dept. Citizens Adv. Bd., 1994—. Mem. NRA (life), NEA (life), Nat. Coun. Tchrs. English (life), Pheasants Forever (bd. dirs. 1990-91), Iowa State Edn. Assn., Southwest Uniserv Unit (exec. bd. 1994—, UNIeiicadre 1998—), Phi Delta Kappa. Avocations: writing, hunting, hiking, canoeing, travel. Home: 317 E Jaycee St Avoca IA 51521-5104 Office: A-H-S-T High Sch 768 S Maple Avoca IA 51521

HARDMAN, HAROLD FRANCIS, pharmacology educator; b. East Orange, N.J., Aug. 2, 1927; s. Harold Maine and Agnes Lillian (McGovern) H.; m. Jean Ely Dettmer, June 27, 1950; children— David, Timothy, John, Susan. B.Sc. (Am. Found. Pharm. Edn. scholar), Rutgers U., 1949; M.Sc. (Am. Found. Pharm. Edn. fellow), U. Ill. at Chgo., 1951; PhD (Am. Found. Pharm. Edn. fellow), U. Mich., 1954, MD, 1958. Asst. prof. pharmacology U. Mich., 1958-60; assoc. prof. pharmacology Marquette U., Milw., 1960-62; prof. pharmacology, chmn. dept. Med. Coll. of Wis. at Milw., 1962—, chmn. dept., 1962-88, assoc. dean basic scis., 1968-70; prof. emeritus, 1992—; chmn. retirees, 1993-95. Bd. dirs. Med. Coll. Wis., 1980-82; trustee Biosis, 1988-91 Served to sgt. AUS, 1946-47. John and Mary Markle scholar acad. medicine, 1958-62; recipient Outstanding Alumni award U. Mich., 1989, Disting. Svc. award Med. Coll. Wis., 1985, Med. Alumni recognition award, 1995, Pharmacology Grad. Student Recognition award, 1995; Citation Esteem, Dean and Bd. Dirs. Med. Coll. Wis., 1988. Mem. Am. Soc. Pharmacology and Exptl. Therapeutics (chmn. program com. 1973-76, councillor 1976-79, pres.-elect 1981-82, pres. 1982-83), Fedn. Am. Socs. Exptl. Biology (pres. 1983-84), Assn. Med. Sch. Pharmacology Chairmen (sec. 1970-72, pres. 1978-80), Milw. Acad. Medicine (pres. 1974-75) Achievements include rsch. in cardiovascular pharmacology with continuous support from NIH for 32 yrs. Studied the effect of drug and receptor ionization upon pharmacological activity with emphasis upon beta adrenergic receptor agonists and antagonists. Also conducted studies on the behavioral and cardiovascular actions of marijuana and derivatives. Home: 1120 Indianwood Dr Brookfield WI 53005-5705 E-mail: jhardman7@worldnet.att.net.

HARDMAN, JAMES CHARLES, lawyer, motor carrier executive; b. Chgo., Sept. 22, 1931; s. William Pryor and Mary Margaret (O'Donnell) H.; children: James Pryor, Katie Maura. BS in Bus., Quincy Coll., 1953; MBA, Northwestern U., 1958, JD, 1961. Bar: Ill. 1961, Minn. 1984, U.S. Dist. Ct. (no. dist.) Ill. 1962, U.S. Ct. Appeals (7th cir.) 1968, U.S. Dist. Ct. D.C. 1971, U.S. Supreme Ct. 1971, U.S. Ct. Appeals D.C. Cir. 1978. Gen. atty. Swift & Co., Chgo., 1961-62; sole practice Chgo., 1962-83; v.p. adminstrn., gen. counsel Dart Transit Co., St. Paul, 1984-94; atty. Law Offices James C. Harman, St. Paul, 1994—. Vis. prof. law U. Denver, 1978-79; lectr. small bus. mgmt. Northeastern Ill. U., Chgo., 1982 Author: Fair Labor Standard Act and Motor Carrier Operations, 1974, Motor Carriage: The Interstate Commerce Commission, 1976, Welcome to the Wonderful World of Political Action, 1990; contbr. articles to profl. jours. V.p. Sauganash Cmty. Assn., Chgo., 1980-83; chmn. bd. govs. Transp. Law Jour., Denver, 1976-78. Served to lt. (j.g.) USN, 1953-55. Recipient Am. Jurisprudence Labor Law award, 1961, award of Merit Transp. Law Inst., 1968, 72, Lifetime Achievement Award, Transportation Lawyers Assn., 1999, Minnesota Trucking Assn., 2001, Truckload Carrier Assn., 2003. Mem. Transp. Lawyers Assn. (pres. 1980, chmn. 1982, Lifetime Achievement award 1999, 2001), Minn. Trucking Assn. (chmn., Disting. Svc. award 1998), Minn. Bar Assn., Ill. State Bar Assn., Chgo. Bar Assn. (Legal Writing award 1970), Elks. Roman Catholic. Home: 753 Carla Ln Saint Paul MN 55109-1925 Office: Law Offices James C Hardman 753 Carla Ln Little Canada MN 55109-1925 E-mail: jchardman@att.net.

HARDMAN, JOEL GRIFFETH, retired pharmacologist; b. Colbert, Ga., Nov. 7, 1933; s. Joel Carlton and Ruby Lee (Griffeth) Hardman; m. Georgette Johnson, July 16, 1955; children: Pamela Hope, Frances Leigh, Mary George, Joel Carlton. BS in Pharmacy, U. Ga., 1954, MS in Pharmacy, 1959; PhD in Pharmacology, Emory U., 1964. Instr. pharmacy U. Ga., Athens, 1957-60; predoctoral fellow dept. pharmacology Emory U., Atlanta, 1960-64; instr. physiology Vanderbilt U., Nashville, 1964-67, from asst. prof. to assoc. prof., 1967—72, prof., 1972-75, prof., chmn. dept. pharmacology, 1975-90, assoc. vice chancellor health affairs, 1991-97, prof. pharmacology emeritus, 1998. Francqui fgn. vis. prof. Free U. Brussels, 1974; mem. pharmacology study sect.

NIH, 1975—79, chmn., 1977—79; mem. rsch. com. Tenn. Heart Assn., 1976—79; mem. adv. bd. Advances Cyclic Nucleotide Rsch. Mem. editl. bd. Jour. Biol. Chemistry, 1975—80, Jour. Cyclic Nucleotide Rsch., 1974—94, Circulation Rsch., 1980—86; editor: Molecular Pharmacology, 1983—85; co-editor-in-chief (book) The Pharmacological Basis of Therapeutics, 10th edit., 2001; contbr. scientific papers to profl. publs. Recipient H. B. Van Dyke award, Columbia U., 1981. Mem.: AAAS, Am. Heart Assn. (mem. rsch. com. 1979—84), Am. Soc. Pharmacology and Exptl. Therapeutics (pres. 1993—94), Alpha Omega Alpha.

HARDS, RICHARD CHARLES, artist; b. Logan, UT, Aug. 18, 1961; BFA, Utah State U., 1985; MFA, U. Wis., Madison, 1989. Artist Carl Hammer Gallery, Chgo., 1993—, Lisa Sette Gallery, Scottsdale, Ariz., 1996—, Jackson Fine Arts, Atlanta, 2000—. Home: 1951 S Canalport Ave Chicago IL 60616-1044

HARDTNER, QUINTIN THEODORE, III, lawyer; b. Shreveport, La., Mar. 5, 1936; s. Quintin Theodore and Jane (Owen) H.; m. Susan Mayer, June 30, 1962; children: Susan Owen, Quintin Theodore IV, George Jonathan. BBA, Tulane U., 1957, JD, 1961. Bar: La. 1961; cert. tax atty., estate planning and adminstrv. specialist. Assoc. Jones, Walker, Waechter, Poitevent, Carrere & Denegre, New Orleans, 1961-62; ptnr. Hargrove, Guyton, Ramey and Barlow, Shreveport, 1962-94; pres. Barlow & Hardtner L.C., Shreveport, 1994-2000; ptnr. Lemle & Kelleher, LLP, Shreveport, 2000—. Past dir. and chmn. Community Found. Shreveport-Bossier; past dir. Sci-Port Discovery Ctr.; mem., past pres. Com. of 100; past dir. Biomed. Rsch. Found. N.W. La. Past mem. adv. bd. Salvation Army; past trustee, past chmn. bd. All Sts. Episcopal Sch., Vicksburg, Miss.; past trustee, past chmn. St. Mark's Day Sch.; past trustee Southfield Sch.; past vestryman St. Mark's Episcopal Ch.; past bd. dirs., v.p. Shreveport Assn. for Blind; past bd. dirs. Family and Children's Svcs.; past co-chmn. Centenary Coll. Fund. Served to lt. USMC, 1957-59. Fellow Am. Coll. Trust and Estate Counsel, Am. Bar Found., La. Bar Found.; mem. ABA, La. State Bar Assn. (past mem ho. of dels., cert. tax atty., cert. estate planning and adminstrn. specialist), Ark.-La.-Tex. Tax Inst. (past bd. dirs.), Shreveport Bar Assn. (past pres.), Estate Planning Coun. Shreveport (past dir., past pres.), Shreveport Club, Cambridge Club, Rotary (past pres., bd. dirs.). Home: 525 Southfield Rd Shreveport LA 71106 Office: 10th Fl Louisiana Tower 501 Edwards St Shreveport LA 71101-3537 E-mail: qhardtner@lemle.com.

HARDWAY, WENDELL GARY, retired academic administrator; b. Bolair, W.Va., Mar. 5, 1927; s. Ressie Bruce and Elsie Clennen (Miller) H.; m. Hannah Lou Garrett, July 12, 1950. BS, W.Va. U., 1949, MS, 1953; PhD, Ohio State U., 1959. Tchr. Troy (W.Va.) High Sch., 1949-54; asst. prof. sci. Glenville (W.Va.) State Coll., 1954-57, assoc. prof. edn., 1959-61, prof., chmn. div. edn., dir. student teaching, 1961-66; pres. Bluefield (W.Va.) State Coll., 1966-73, Fairmont (W.Va.) State Coll., 1973-88, ret., 1988. Pres. United Way, Fairmont, 1976; mem. Glenville City Council, 1958-64; pres. W.Va. Intercollegiate Athletic Conf., 1977-78. Served with AUS, 1945-46. Named Man of Yr., Bluefield Jaycees, 1969, Disting. Pioneer, Glenville State Coll., 1985, Outstanding Alumnus, W.Va. U. Coll. Agr., 1987. Hardway Libr. at Bluefield State Coll. and Hardway Hall (adminstrn. bldg.) at Fairmont State Coll. named in his honor. Mem. Phi Delta Theta, Gamma Sigma Delta, Phi Delta Kappa, Kappa Delta Pi. Methodist. Home: 4 Bel Manor Dr Fairmont WV 26554

HARDWICK, CHARLES LEIGHTON, pharmaceutical company executive, state legislator; b. Somerset, Ky., Nov. 8, 1941; s. Joseph Fulton and Lucy Belle (Simpson) H.; m. Patricia Ruth Johnson, Mar. 30, 1959 (div. July 1993); children: Virginia Lee, Charles Jr; m. Sheilagh Mylott, Aug. 10, 2002. BS, Fla. State U., 1962, MBA, 1964. Sales supr. Continental Baking Co., Detroit, 1964-66; sales rep. Pfizer, Inc., N.Y.C., 1966-70, regional mgr., 1970-73, dir. mktg., 1973-77, dir. civic info., 1977—; v.p. govt. and pub. affairs Pfizer Inc., N.Y.C., 1977—2002, sr. v.p. worldwide govt. and pub. affairs, 2002—, mem. Pfizer Leadership Team; Rep. Assembly minority leader, Gen. Assembly State of N.J., 1985-87, speaker of assembly, 1986-89, N.J. Assembly minority leader emeritus, 1989-91. Vice chmn. U.S. Trade Adv. Commn., Washington, 1983-85; mem. Presdl. Federalism Adv. Commn., Washington, 1981-83. Mem. Am. Legis. Exchange Council (bd. dirs. 1986—, named Legislator of Yr. 1986), Nat. Rep. Legislators Assn. (pres. 1982-84). Avocation: tennis. Office: 235 E 42d St New York NY 10017

HARDWICK, DAVID FRANCIS, pathologist; b. Vancouver, B.C., Can., Jan. 24, 1934; s. Walter H. W. and Iris L. (Hyndman) H.; m. Margaret M. Lang, Aug. 22, 1956; children: Margaret F., Heather I., David J. MD, U. B.C., 1957, LLD (hon.), 2001. Intern Montreal (Que., Can.) Gen. Hosp., 1957-58; resident Vancouver Gen. Hosp., 1958-59, Children's Hosp., Los Angeles, 1959-62; research assoc. U. So. Calif., 1961-62; clin. instr. U. B.C., Vancouver, 1963-65, asst. prof. pathology, 1965-69, assoc. prof., 1969-74, prof., 1974—, head dept. pathology, 1976-90, assoc. dean rsch. and planning, 1990-96; dir. labs. Children's Hosp., Vancouver, 1969-92, Vancouver Gen. Hosp., 1976-90; chmn. M.A.C., Children's Hosp., 1970-87; interinstitutional planning U. B.C. Medicine, 1996-98, spl. advisor on planning, 1999—. Adj. prof. Chinese U. Hong Kong; mem. U. B.C. Senate, 1966-71. Author: Acid Base Balance and Blood Gas Studies, 1968, Intermediary Metabolism of Liver, 1971, Directing the Clinical Laboratory, 1990, Laboratory Supervision and Management, 2d edit., 2002; contbr. numerous articles to profl. publs. Bd. dirs. Children's and Women's Rsch. Inst., B.C., 1998—, Women's Hosp. Found., 1997—, B.C. Transplant Found., 1993—. Recipient Queen's Centennial medal Govt. Can., 1978, U. B.C. Faculty Citation Teaching award, 1987, Wallace Wilson Leadership award, 1990, William Boyd Lectureship award Canadian Assn. Path, 1994, Sydney Israels Founders award B.C. Rsch. Inst. Children and Family, 1997, Univ. medal for Outstanding Svc., U. B.C., 1997; Sydney Farber lectr., Soc. Ped. Path., 1998. Fellow Royal Coll. Physicians (Can.), Coll. Am. Pathologists; mem. Internat. Acad. Pathology (pres. 1996, v.p. N.Am. 1998—, Gold medal 2002), Can. Med. Assn., B.C. Assn. Lab. Medicine, B.C. Med. Assn., N.Y. Acad. Sci., Soc. Pediat. Pathology, Internat. Acad. Pathology (Disting. Svc. award 1994), U.S. Acad. Pathology, Can. Assn. Pathology, B.C. Transplant Found. (chmn. bd. 2000—), Med. Student & Alumni Ctr. Soc. (chair 2001—), Alpha Omega Alpha. Home: 727 W 23rd Ave Vancouver BC Canada V5Z 2A7 Office: U BC Dept Pathology 2211 Wesbrook Mall Vancouver BC Canada V6T 1W5 E-mail: david.f.hardwick@ubc.ca.

HARDWICK, ELIZABETH, writer; b. Lexington, Ky., July 27, 1916; d. Eugene Allen and Mary (Ramsey) H.; m. Robert Lowell, July 28, 1949 (div. Oct. 1972); 1 child, Harriet. AB, U. Ky., 1938, MA, 1939; postgrad., Columbia U., 1939-41. Adj. assoc. prof. Barnard Coll. Author: (novels) The Ghostly Lover, 1945, The Simple Truth, 1955, Sleepless Nights, 1979, (essays) A View of My Own, 1962, Seduction and Betrayal, 1974, Bartleby in Manhattan, 1983, Sight Readings, 1998, Herman Melville, A Life, 2000; editor: The Selected Letters of William James, 1960; adv. editor: N.Y. Rev. Books. Recipient George Jean Nathan award for dramatic criticism, 1966, Gold medal for criticism Am. Acad. Arts and Letters, 1993; Guggenheim fellow, 1947. Mem. Am. Acad. and Inst. Arts and Letters, Acad. Arts and Scis. Home: 15 W 67th St New York NY 10023-6226

HARDWICK, KEVIN DALE, retired protective services official; b. Cin., Feb. 16, 1960; s. Clyde U. Jr. and Marian D. (Seichrist) H.; m. Cynthia Susan Sunderman, Oct. 19, 1985; children from previous marriage: Kevin, Andrew, Adam, Patrick. Student, U. Cin., 1978-82. Emergency med. tech., Ohio, Ky.; fire inspector, Ohio, Ky.; paramedic, Ky.; fire investigator, Ohio, Ky. Fire inspector, capt. New Burlington Fire Dept., Cin., 1978-82; fire safety officer, lt. Cin./No. Ky. Internat. Airport, 1982—2002; regional mgr. Ferra Fire Apparatus, Inc., Holden, La., 2002—. Fire investigator, coord. Boone County (Ky.) Fire Investigation, 1994-2001; instr. Fire Dept. Instrs. Conf., Indpls., 1995, 96; mem. adv. com. Fire Dept. Safety Officer, Quincy, Mass., 1995—. Author: The Voice, 1994, 95, 96, 97; contbr. articles to profl. jours. Recipient Appreciation award Cin. FBI Agts., 1988, Ferrara Firefighting, 1994. Mem. Masons, Scottish Rite, Shriners. Avocations: softball, motorcycles, travel, golf, fire truck design. Home and Office: 1568 Covered Bridge Rd Cincinnati OH 45231-2425

HARDY, ASHTON RICHARD, lawyer; b. Gulfport, Miss., Aug. 31, 1935; s. Ashton Maurice and Alice (Baumbach) H.; m. Katherine Ketelsen, Sept. 4, 1959; children: Karin H. Wood, Katherine H. Foster. BBA, Tulane U., 1958, JD, 1962. Bar: La. 1962, FCC, 1976. Ptnr. Jones, Walker, Waechter, Poitevent, Carrere & Denegre, New Orleans, 1962-74, 76-82; gen. counsel FCC, Washington, 1974-76; ptnr. Fawer, Brian, Hardy, Zatzkis, New Orleans, 1982-86, Hardy & Popham, 1986-88, Walker, Bordelon, Hamlin, Theriot & Hardy, New Orleans, 1988-92, Hardy, Carey & Chautin, New Orleans, 1992—. Gen. counsel La. Assn. Broadcasters, 1976-86, Greater New Orleans Assn. Broadcasters, 1976—, La. Assn. Advt. Agys., 1982-86; lectr. in field; advance rep. to Pres. U.S., 1971-74. Bd. dirs. New Orleans Mission, 1989—, Met. Crime Commn. New Orleans, 1993—, vice-chmn., 1997-2002, United Christian Charities, 1993-99, Prison Fellowship/La., 1976—. Lt. USN, 1958-60. Named to Hall of Fame, Greater New Orleans Broadcasters Assn., 2001. Mem. La. Bar Assn. (del. ho. of dels. 1987-92), FCC Bar Assn., Nat. Religious Broadcasters (nat. bd. dirs. 2003— bd. dirs. S.W. chpt. 2003—), Christian Legal Soc., Metairie Country Club (pres. 1986), Comm Club. Home: 306 Cedar Dr Metairie LA 70005-3902 Office: Hardy Carey & Chautin LLP Ste 300 110 Veterans Memorial Blvd Metairie LA 70005-4960 E-mail: arhardy@bellsouth.net.

HARDY, CHARLES ASHLEY, III, historian, educator, film producer; b. Norwalk, Conn., Dec. 31, 1951; s. Charles Ashley Hardy Jr. and Mary McCulloch Hardy-Roberts; m. Doreen Ruth Price, June 14, 1975; children: Nathaniel Bates, Eliza Makepeace. BA, Temple U., 1976, PhD, 1989. Prodr. WHYY-FM, Pa., 1980—84; prof. West Chester (Pa.) U., 1990—. Prodr.: (radio documentary) The Popular Culture Show, 1980—84, I Remember When:Times Gone But Not Forgotten (Corp. for Pub. Broadcasting, Pub. Radio Program Award, 1983), (with Alessandro Portelli) (audio essay) I Can Almost See the Lights of Home (Oral History Assn. Nonprint Media Award, 1999); author: Philadelphia All the Time: Sounds of the Quaker City, 1896 to 1947, 1992; editor: (video documentary series) United States History Video Collection, 1996; prodr.: (video documentary) All Aboard for Philadelphia, 1989, (radio documentary series) Goin' North: Tales of the Great Migration, 1985. Recipient The Forrest C. Pogue award, Oral History in the Mid. Atlantic Region, 2001; fellow The Salzburg Seminar in Am. Studies, 1995. Mem.: Orgn. Am. Historians, Oral History Assn. (coun. 2001—03). Home: 985 East Penn Dr West Chester PA 19380 Office: West Chester Univ Main Hall West Chester PA 19383 Personal E-mail: chardy@wcupa.edu. E-mail: chardy@wcupa.edu.

HARDY, CHARLOTTE B. insurance agent; b. Springhill, La., Sept. 23, 1943; d. Willis Bevil and Vivian Ernestine (Britt) Burns; m. Barry Wayne Hardy, Aug. 18, 1963; children: Pamela H. Davis, Jason W. AA, So. Ark. U., 1978, BS, 1980. Mem. office staff Nickerson Ins. Agy., Springhill, La., 1961-62; exec. sec. Berry Petroleum, Magnolia, Ark., 1963-66; piano tchr. El Dorado, Ark., 1969-79; tchr. El Dorado Pub. Schs., 1980-85; ins. agt. State Farm Ins., El Dorado, 1985—. Recipient Pub. Rels. award NALU, 1995, 97, Nat. Sales Achievement award, 1995-2001, Nat. Multiline Sales award, 1997, 99-2001. Mem. Nat. Assn. Ins. Fin. Advisors, Ark. State Life Underwriters (Pub. Rels. award 1994, 95), El Dorado Life Underwriters Assn. (sec.-treas. 1988-89, v.p. 1989-90, Pres.'s Leadership award 1998), El Dorado-Camden Life Underwriters Assn. (pres.-elect 1992-93, pres. 1993-94), Golden Triangle Life Underwriters Assn., El Dorado C. of C. (bd. dirs. 1990-93). Baptist. Avocations: music, fishing. Home: 200 Meadow Hills Dr El Dorado AR 71730 Office: State Farm Ins Cos 600 W Main El Dorado AR 71730 E-mail: hardy.b3ep@statefarm.com.

HARDY, CHESTER ALFRED, engineer; b. El Paso, Tex., Nov. 17, 1929; m. Evelyn Anne Moore, June 22, 1955; 1 child, Clinton Alfred (dec.). BS in Engring., U. Tex., El Paso, 1955; MS in Engring., So. Meth. U., 1959, MS in Engring. Adminstrn., 1961. Registered profl. engr., Tex. Mgr. Gen. Dynamics, Fort Worth, Tex., 1980-87; dir. Lockheed Martin, Fort Worth, 1987—. Chmn. corp. R&M panel Gen. Dynamics, 1976; lectr. Agard Nato, Munich, London, N.Y., 1976; tchr. bus. sch. Tex. Christian U., Ft. Worth, 1968. Contbr. articles to profl. jours. With USN, 1948-52. Named to, Lockheed Martin Aero. Hall of Fame. Mem. Tex. Soc. Profl. Engrs., Moslah Shrine, Colonial Country Club, Soc. Mayflower Desces., Jamestowne Soc., Ancient and Hon. Arty. Co. of Mass., SAR, Flagon and Trencher, Colonial Order of the Crown, Magna Charta Barons, Soc. Knights of the Garter, Soc. Descs. of Colonial Clergy, Nat. Huguenot Soc., Nat. Soc. Sons and Daus. of Pilgrims, Plantagenet Soc. Episcopalian. Avocations: tennis, skiing.

HARDY, CLARENCE EARL, JR., government, nonprofit and corporate sector executive; b. Edenton, N.C., July 2, 1944; m. Mae A. Brewer; children: Clarence, Melva. BA in Polit. Sci. and Econs., N.C. Ctrl. U., 1967; MPA in Pub. Adminstrn., Syracuse U., 1969; diploma in sr. mgrs. in govt. program, Harvard U., 1990. Pers. mgmt. analyst Atomic Energy Commn., 1971-73; pers. officer, mgmt. analyst Atomic Energy Commn. Energy Rsch. and Devel. Adminstrn., 1973-75, sr. mgmt. analyst, program evaluation officer, 1975-76, chief hqrs. pers. ops. br., 1976-77; pers. officer Fed. Energy Regulatory Commn., 1978; chief pers. mgmt. svcs. Dept. Energy Hqrs., 1977-78, dep. dir. hqrs. pers. ops. divsn., 1978-79; chief pers. divsn. Nat. Bur. Standards, 1979; dir. pers. mgmt. EPA, 1979-88, dep. dir. Office of Human Resources Mgmt., 1988-97; dir. Office Cooperative Environ. Mgmt., 1997—2001; exec. dir. Combined Fed. Campaign of Nat. Capital Area, 2001—03; pres. & CEO DQC Consultants, 1994—. Prof. George Mason U., 1998—99. Recipient Disting. Fed. Career award, 2001; N.C. Ctrl U. Polit. Sci. scholar, 1966, 67, Presdl. rank award, 1998; Maxwell fellow, 1968, 69, Congl. fellow Brookings Instn., 1996. Mem. Internat. Pers. Mgmt. Assn., Internat. Platform Assn., Am. Soc. Pub. Adminstrn., Am. Mgmt. Assn., Am. Judicature Soc., Acad. Polit. and Social Sci., Am. Polit. Sci. Assn., World Future Soc., Acad. Mgmt., Nat. Assn. Environ. Profls. E-mail: cehardy44@aol.com.

HARDY, DORCAS RUTH, business and government relations executive; b. Newark, N.J., July 18, 1946; d. C. Colburn and Ruth (Hart) H.; m. Samuel V. Spagnolo. BA, Conn. Coll., 1964-68; MBA, Pepperdine U., 1976. cert. sr. advisor. Legis. rsch. asst. U.S. Senator Clifford P. Case, Washington, 1970; spl. asst. White House Conf. Children and Youth, Washington, 1970-71; exec. dir. Health Svcs. Industry Commn., Cost of Living Coun., Washington, 1971-73; asst. sec. Calif. Dept. Health, Sacramento, 1973-74; assoc. dir. U. So. Calif. Ctr. Health Svcs. Rsch., 1974-81; asst. sec. human devel. svcs. HHS, Washington, 1981-86; commr. Social Security Washington, 1986-89; pres. Dorcas R. Hardy & Assocs., Spotsylvania, Va., 1989—; exec. v.p. Pub. Issue Mgmt., Washington, 2001—03. Chmn. bd. dirs., and CEO Work Recovery, Inc., Tucson, 1996-98; bd. dirs. First Coast Svc. Options, Inc., Options Clearing Corp., Wright Investors Svc. Managed Funds; Social Security Advisory Bd.; bd. visitors Mary Washington Coll.; VA Bd. of Rehabilitative Services. Author: Social Insecurity: The Crisis in America's Social Security System and How to Plan Now for Your Own Financial Survival, 1992. Mem. Girl Scouts USA, Va. Bd. Rehab. Svcs.; bd. dirs. Com. on Developing Am. Capitalism; former chmn. Pres.'s Task Force on Legal Equity for Women. Mem. Soc. Cert. Sr. Advisors. Office: Washington Metro Office 11407 Stonewall Jackson Dr Spotsylvania VA 22553-4608 E-mail: drhardy@worldet.att.net.

HARDY, HARVEY LOUCHARD, retired lawyer; b. Dallas, Dec. 2, 1914; s. Nat L. and Winifred F. (Fouraker) H.; m. Edna Vivian Bedell, Feb. 14, 1948; children: Victoria Elizabeth Hardy Pursch, Alice Anne Hardy Gannon. Bar: Tex. 1936, U.S. Dist. Ct. (so. and we. dists.) Tex. 1946, U.S. Ct. Appeals (5th cir.) 1946, U.S. Supreme Ct. 1949. First asst. dist. atty. Bexar County, San Antonio, 1947-50, acting dist. atty., 1950-51; city atty. San Antonio, 1952—53, Castle Hills, Tex., 1967—96, Helotes, Tex., 1984-96, Fair Oaks Ranch, Tex., 1973-96; legal adviser bd. trustees Fireman and Policemen's Pension Fund of San Antonio, 1956-96; ret. Legal advisor Grey Forest Utilities, 1986-96. Author: A Lifetime at the Bar: A Lawyer's Memoir, 1999. 1st lt. inf. U.S. Army, 1941-45. Decorated Bronze Star with cluster. Fellow Tex. Bar Found.; mem. Tex. Bar Assn., San Antonio Bar Found., Tex. Assn. City Atts., San Antonio Bar Assn. Methodist. Home: 215 Atwater Dr San Antonio TX 78213

HARDY, JAMES CHESTER, speech pathologist, educator; b. Salina, Kans., Apr. 14, 1930; s. James Chester and Mary Ellen (Baker) H.; m. Dolores Nadine McFarland, May 23, 1953 (div. Dec. 1988): children: Allan James, Charles Thomas, Matthew Hurt. BS, N.E. Mo. State U., 1951; MA, U. Iowa, 1957, PhD, 1962. Speech correctionist Pub. Schs., Poplar Bluff, Mo., 1954-55; grad. asst. dept. speech pathology & audiology U. Iowa, Iowa City, 1955-56, grad. asst. U. Hosp. Sch., 1956, speech therapist, 1956-57, supr. speech and hearing dept. U. Hosp. Sch., 1967, asst. prof. dept. speech pathology and audiology, 1961-64, assoc. prof., 1964-69, assoc. prof. dept. pediatrics, 1966-69, prof. dept. speech pathology and audiology, 1969-97, prof. dept. pediatrics, 1969-97, dir. speech and hearing clinic, 1972-79, dir. profl. svcs. div. devel. disabilities, dept. pediatrics, 1979-97, dir. Iowa program for assistive tech., 1990-97, ret., 1997. Cons. Iowa Newborn Hearing Evaluation Referral Project, 1998, Iowa Sch., 1999-2001. Author: Cerebral Palsy: Remediation of Communication Problems, 1983; contbr. articles to profl. jours., chpts. to textbooks. Bd. dirs. Optimist Club of Iowa City, 1966-67, pres., 1966-67; scout master Boy Scouts Am., Iowa City, 1973-78, chmn., troop com., 1977-78. With U.S. Army, 1952-54. Recipient Disting. Alumnus award Dept. Speech Pathology and Audiology/U. Iowa, 2000. Fellow Am. Acad. for Cerebral Palsy and Devel. Medicine, Am. Speech-Language-Hearing Assn.; mem. Iowa Speech and Hearing Assn. (pres. 1963, Louis DiCarlo award 1987, Honors of the Assn. 1997).

HARDY, JANE ELIZABETH, communications educator; b. Fenelon Falls, Ont., Can., Mar. 27, 1930; came to U.S., 1956, naturalized, 1976; d. Charles Edward and Augusta Miriam (Lang) Little; m. Ernest E. Hardy, Sept. 3, 1955; children: Edward Harold, Robert Ernest. BS with distinction, Cornell U., 1953. Garden editor and writer Can. Homes Mag., Maclean-Hunter Pub. Co., Ltd., Toronto, Ont., 1954-55, 56-62; contbg. editor Can. Homes, Southam Pub. Co., Toronto, Ont., 1962-66; instr. Cornell U., 1966-73, sr. lectr. in comm., 1979-96. Mem. Cornell U. Provost's Adv. Com. on Status of Women, 1977-81, Cornell U. Coun., 2003—; lectr., condr. workshops on writing. Author: Writing for Practical Purposes, 1996; editor pro-tem Cornell Plantations Quar., 1981-82; author numerous publs. including brochures, slide set scripts, contbr. numerous articles in mags. Mem. coun. Cornell U., 2003—; chmn. bd. dirs. Matrix Found, 1998—2003, bd. dirs., 1998—. Mem. Women in Comms. Inc. (faculty advisor 1977-95, liaison 1986-94, chair, adv.mem. 1988-90), Assn. for Women in Comms. (nat. bd. dirs. 1997-2000), Cornell U. Assn. Class Officers (bd. mem. 1997-2003), Royal Hort. Soc., Ithaca Garden Club, Ithaca Women's Club, Pi Alpha Xi, Phi Kappa Phi, Alpha Omicron Pi. Home: 215 Enfield Falls Rd Ithaca NY 14850-8797

HARDY, JOHN CHRISTOPHER, physicist, educator; b. Montreal, Que., Can., July 10, 1941; s. Noel Woodburn and Ethel May (Collins) H.; m. Lynn Helen Frederick, June 3, 1964 (div.); children: Ericka, Kirsten, Bruce, Alana; m. June Dennie, July 5, 1997; stepchildren: Benjamin, Samantha. BSc, McGill U., Montreal, 1961, MSc, 1963, PhD (D.W. Ambridge prize 1965), 1965. NRC Can. postdoctoral fellow Oxford (Eng.) Nuc. Physics Lab., 1965—67; Miller rsch. fellow Lawrence Radiation Lab., Berkeley, Calif., 1967—69, staff physicist, 1969—70; assoc. rsch. officer Atomic Energy Can. Ltd., Chalk River, Canada, 1970—74, sr. rsch. officer, 1975—83, head nuc. physics br., 1983—86, asst. v.p., 1986—89, dir. tandem accelerator superconducting cyclotron divsn., 1989—97; prof. physics Tex. A&M U., College Station, 1997—. Sci. assoc. CERN, Geneva, 1976-77; program adv. coms. Oak Ridge Nat. Lab., UNISOR, 1979-85, HHIRL, 1991-92, HRIBF, 1999—, chmn., 2000—; program adv. coms. Lawrence Berkeley Lab., Super HILAC, 1983-86, Cyclotron, 1994-99, chmn., 1995-99; program adv. com. Nat. Superconducting Cyclotron Lab., 1990-93; mem. adv. bd. TRIUMF, 1992-98, U. Chgo. rev. com. for physics divsn. Argonne Nat. Lab., 1999—; mem. sci. polcy com. HRIBF, Oak Ridge Nat. Lab., 2002—. Contbr. articles to profl. jours. and books; editor North Renfrew Times, 1972-97; mem. editl. bd. Nuc. Physics News Internat., 1995-97, Phys. Rev. C. Jour., 1980-82, 95-97. Chmn. bd. dirs. Deep River Sci. Acad., 1986-97, trustee 1997—. Fellow: Am. Phys. Soc. (DNP program com. 1999—2001, exec. com. DNP 2002—), Royal Soc. Can. (v.p. acad. III 1992—95, chmn. fundraising com. 1994—97, Rutherford medal in physics 1981); mem.: Can. Assn. Physicists (Herzberg medal 1976). Office: Tex A&M U Cyclotron Inst College Station TX 77843-3366 E-mail: hardy@comp.tamu.edu.

HARDY, JOHN EDWARD, English language educator, author; b. Baton Rouge, Apr. 3, 1922; s. Roger Barlow and Mary (McCoy) H.; m. Marie Elam, Dec. 30, 1942 (div.); children: Margot (Mrs. Timm Ferguson), Leonore (Mrs. David Dvorkin), Catherine, Laura, Anne, Eve; m. Willene Schaefer, June 25, 1969. BA, La. State U., 1944; MA, State U. Iowa, 1946; PhD, Johns Hopkins U., 1956. Mem. English faculties U. Detroit, 1945-46, Yale U., 1946-48, U. Okla., 1948-52, Johns Hopkins U., 1952-54; mem. faculty U. Notre Dame, 1954-66, prof. English, 1964-66, mem. acad. council, 1963-66, grad. council, 1963-66; prof. English, chmn. dept. U. South Ala., 1966-69; prof. English U. Colo., Boulder, 1969-70; prof. English, chmn. dept. U. Mo., St. Louis, 1970-72; dir. grad. studies in English U. Ill.-Chgo., 1972-75, prof. English, 1972-92; prof. emeritus, 1992—; head dept. English U. Ill.-Chgo., 1984-89, mem. grad. coll. exec. com., 1974-76, 81-82. Author: (with Cleanth Brooks) Poems of Mr. John Milton, 1951, The Curious Frame, 1962, Man in the Modern Novel, 1964, Katherine Anne Porter, 1973, Certain Poems, 1958, The Fiction of Walker Percy, 1987; Editor: The Modern Talent, 1964, (with Seymour L. Gross) Images of the Negro in American Literature, 1966. Fulbright prof. Am. lit. U. Munich, Germany, 1959-61; Ford Faculty Study fellow, 1952-53; Rockefeller fellow poetry, 1954; fellow Inst. for Humanities U. Ill. Chgo., 1989-90. Mem. MLA, Phi Beta Kappa. Home: 6033 Riverbend Lakes Dr Baton Rouge LA 70820-5050

HARDY, JOSEPH A., SR., wholesale distribution executive; b. 1923; Founder Green Hills Lumber, 1952—56; retail jeweler Hardy & Hayes Corp., Pitts., 1946-56; founder, chmn., CEO 84 Cash & Carry Inc. (now 84 Lumber Co.), Eighty Four, Pa., 1956—, pres., 1956-93. With U.S. Army, 1942-46. Office: 84 Lumber Co 1019 Rt 519 Eighty Four PA 15330*

HARDY, JULIA IRENE, elementary school educator; b. Montrose, Iowa, Aug. 11, 1917; d. Carl Alfred Peterson, Achsa Leah LaDuke; m. Francis William Hardy, Oct. 12, 1940; children: Judith (Jeudi) Kay Vitale Eblin, Bruce William. BS in Edn., We. Ill. U., 1965; MS in Edn., Colo. State U., 1965; postgrad., Nat. Coll. Edn., U.S. Internat. U., U. Hawaii; MS in Edn., We. Ill. U., 1970. Cert. Permanent profl. cert. Iowa, 1976. Tchr., counselor, reading specialist Keokuk Cmty. Sch. Dist., Keokuk, Iowa, 1957—81. Tchr. Lee County Pub. Schs., Montrose, Iowa, 1936—48; grad. asst. We. Ill. U., Macomb, 1967—68; bd. dirs., chmn. credit com. Keokuk Cmty. Sch. Employees Credit Union, 1986—2001; pvt. tutor, Keokuk, Iowa, 1969—89; presenter poetry programs and readings. Author: (inspirational poetry) The Wonder of It All, 1996; composer: poems set to music for Emerald Records, 2000—. Tchr. Bethel Bible, 1970. Mem.: Internat. Soc. Poets (life Internat. Poetry Hall of Fame 1997), Internat. Reading Assn. (life Outstanding Achievement in Poetry award), Am. Legion Auxiliary, Order Ea. Star #40 (past matron, Grand page 1952), Kappa Delta Pi, Delta Kappa Gamma (com. mem. Alpha Epsilon chpt., Scholarship 1960), Beta Sigma Phi. Democrat. Lutheran. Avocations: art, reading, poetry. Home: 2720 McKinley Ave Keokuk IA 52632-2250

HARDY, KEVIN LAMONT, football player; b. Evansville, Ind., July 24, 1973; Degree in Bus., U. Ill., 1995; postgrad. Wide line backer Jacksonville Jaguars, 1996—2001; linebacker Dallas Cowboys, 2002—. Active Boys & Girls Club, Leukemia Soc.; founder Youth Inst. for Edn., Leadership and Devel. Found., 1997; supporter charity golf tournament; spkr. area schs. and sports banquets; spokesman Jaguars Cool Cats Club presented by NIKE. Named All-Pro AP, Pro Football Writers/Pro Football Weekly, Coll. & Pro Football Newsweekly, Football News, USA Today, Football Digest, 1999, All-Style team ESPN Mag., 2000; named to All-Rookie teams Pro Football Writers of Am./Pro Football Weekly, Football News, Football Newsweekly, 1996, Pro Bowl, 1999; recipient Honorable Mention All-Pro, AP. Avocation: collecting baseball cards. Office: 2401 E Airport Frwy Irving TX 75062

HARDY, LINDA LEA STERLOCK, media specialist; b. Balt., Aug. 15, 1947; d. George Allen and Dorothy Lea (Briggs) Sterlock; m. John Edward Hardy III, Apr. 25, 1970; 1 child, Roger Wayne. BA in History, N.C. Wesleyan Coll., 1969; MEd in History, East Carolina U., 1972, MLS, 1990. Cert. tchr., N.C. History tchr. Halifax (N.C.) County Schs., 1972-83, learning lab tchr., 1983-91, computer lab tchr., 1990-95; media specialist Nash-Rocky Mount (N.C.) Schs., 1995—. Part-time history instr. Nash C.C., 1993. Mem. AAUW (pres. Rocky Mount br. 1993-95, sec. 1997-99, Named Gift award 1987), Bus. and Profl. Women (pres. Rocky Mount chpt. 1986-87, 90-91, 2003—, treas. 1992-97, 2000-03, sec.-treas. dist X 1989-90, state election chmn. 1989-90, 93-95, state credentials chmn. 1997-98, sec.-treas. dist. 6 1997-98, Girl Friday award 1981, 98, Woman of Yr. award 1986, 97, 2002, state found. fin. chair 1996-97, state treas. 1999-2001, state sec. 2001-02, dist. VI dir. 2002-03, state membership chair 2003—, trustee 2003—), Nat. Assn. Educators, N.C. Assn. Educators, Nash/Rocky Mount Assn. Educators (faculty rep. 1995—), Phi Delta

Kappa, Pi Gamma Mu. Methodist. Avocations: reading, travel, needlepoint, computers. Office: Red Oak Middle School 3170 Red Oak Battleboro Rd Battleboro NC 27809-9284 E-mail: llshardy@netscape.net.

HARDY, MICHAEL C. performing arts administrator; b. Durham, N.C., July 14, 1945; s. William Marion Hardy and Eloise Frances (Carrington) Schipke; children: Miranda, Christopher. AB, Duke U., 1966; MA, U. N.C., 1968; PhD, U. Mich., 1971. Gen. mgr. drama dept. East Carolina U., 1971-73; prodr. Krannert Ctr. Performing Arts at U. Ill., 1973-79, dir., 1979-83; pres., CEO Snug Harbor Cultural Ctr., Inc., N.Y.C., 1983-88; ind. cons., 1988-91; exec. dir. Internat. Soc. for the Performing Arts, Grand Rapids, Mich., 1991-98; pres. Ky. Ctr. for the Arts, Louisville, 1998—2002; pres., CEO Miami Ctr. for the Arts, 2002—. Contbr. articles to profl. jours. With N.Y. Cultural Inst. Group, 1984-88; CIG chair Mayor Ed Koch's Commn. Cultural Affairs, N.Y.C., 1987-88; bd. dirs. Leadership Louisville, 1999—, Regional Leadership Coalition, 2001—, Louisville Bach Soc., 2001—; vice chair Collaborative for Tchg. and Learning, 1998—. Recipient Carolina Playmaker's Mask award U. N.C., 1968, Commendation for Achievement award N.Y. State Legis., 1988, Dept. Parks and Recreation citation N.Y.C., 1988. Mem.: Internat. Soc. for Performing Arts. Office: Miami Ctr for the Arts 1444 Biscayne Blvd Ste 202 Miami FL 33132

HARDY, MICHAEL LYNN, lawyer; b. St. Louis, Aug. 28, 1947; s. William Frost and Ruth (Shea) H.; m. Martha Bond, Sept. 2, 1972; children: Brian M., Kevin S. AB, John Carroll U., 1969; JD, U. Mich., 1972. Bar: Ohio 1972. Assoc. Guren, Merritt, et al, Cleve., 1972-77, ptnr., 1977-84, Thompson Hine LLP and predecessor, Cleve., 1984—, ptnr.-in-charge Cleve. office, 2003—. Editor-in-chief Ohio Environ. Monthly, 1989-94, Ohio Environ. Law, 1992; bd. advisors Harvard Environ. Law Rev., 1976-78, The Environ. Counselor, 1988—. Trustee Nature Ctr. at Shaker Lakes, 2001—; bd. dirs. Nat. Club Assn., 2002—. Capt. U.S. Army, 1969—74. Mem. ABA (nat. resources sect.), Ohio State Bar Assn. (sec. environ. law com. 1983-84, vice-chmn. 1984-86, chmn. 1987-91), Def. Rsch. Inst. (chmn. industrywide litig. com. 1989-91), Canterbury Golf Club. Home: 30649 Summit Ln Cleveland OH 44124-5836 Office: Thompson Hine LLP 3900 Key Ctr 127 Public Sq Cleveland OH 44114-1216 E-mail: mike.hardy@thompsonhine.com.

HARDY, PAUL DUANE, lawyer; b. N.Y.C., Nov. 7, 1936; s. Reginald Sayre and Mae Estelle (Sculthorp) Hardy; m. Jacqueline Hardy, June 8, 1971; children: Valerie, Christopher. BA, U. Pa., 1958; LLB, U. Va., 1961. Bar: Pa. 1963, DC 1972, Fla. 1974. Ptnr. Rawle & Henderson Law Firm, Phila., 1963-70, Holland & Knight Law Firm, Tampa, Fla., 1973-86, Stagg Hardy Law Firm, Tampa, 1986-93, Akerman Senterfett Law Firm, Tampa, 1993—. Chief trial counsel U.S. Maritime Adminstrn., Washington, 1970—73. With U.S. Army, 1961—63. Mem.: Maritime Law Assn. U.S. (bd. dirs. 1983—86). Office: Akerman Senterfett Law Firm 100 S Ashley Dr Tampa FL 33602-5360 E-mail: PaulHardy1617@aol.com.

HARDY, RALPH W. F. biochemist, biotechnology executive; b. Lindsay, Ont., Can., July 27, 1934; s. Wilbur and Elsie H.; m. Jacqueline M. Thayer, Dec. 26, 1954; children: Steven, Chris, Barbara, Ralph (dec.), Jon. BSA, U. Toronto, 1956; MS, U. Wis.-Madison, 1958, PhD, 1959; DSc (hon.), U. Guelph, 1997. Asst. prof. U. Guelph, Ont., Can., 1960-63; research biochemist DuPont deNemours & Co., Wilmington, Del., 1963-67, research supr., 1967-74, assoc. dir., 1974-79, dir. life scis., 1979-84; pres. Bio Technica Internat., Inc., Cambridge, Mass., 1984-86; pres., CEO Boyce Thompson Inst., Inc., Ithaca, NY, 1986-95, pres. emeritus, 2000—, dep. chmn. Bio Technica Internat., Inc., 1986-90, cons., bd. dirs., 1990-99; pres. Nat. Agrl. Biotech. Coun., Ithaca, 1996—. Mem. exec. com. bd. agr. NRC, 1982—88, mem. commn. life scis., 1984—90, bd. biology, 1984—90, mem. com. on biotech., 1988—95, chmn. com., 1993—94, bd. sci. technol. internat. devel., 1990—93, chmn. com. on biol. control, 1992—95, chmn. com. on biol. nitrogen fixation, 1992—94, chmn. com. on natural products, 1996—97; mem. com. genetic experimentation Internat. Coun. Sci. Union, 1981—95; chmn., founder Nat. Agrl. Biotech. Coun., 1988—93; mem. sci. adv. com. U.S. Dept. Energy, 1991—95; mem. alt. agr. rsch. comml. bd. USDA, 1992—96, mem. and corp. sec. alt. agrl. rsch. comml. corp., 1996—2000; mem. Can. reallocations com. NSERC, 1997—98; mem. sci. adv. bd. Foragen, Guelph, Ont., Canada, 1999—; bd. dirs. BioCap, Canada, BioProducts, Can. Author: Nitrogen Fixation, 1975, A Treatise on Dinitrogen Fixation, 3 vols., 1977-79; contbr. over 150 articles to sci. jours. Mem. biotech. exec. bd. Cornell U., 1986-95, adv. coun. Vet. Coll., 1989-96; mem. gov. bd. Cornell Ctr. for Environment, 1991-95. Recipient Gov. Gen.'s Silver medal, 1956, Sterling Henricks award 1986; WARF fellow, 1956-58; DuPont fellow, 1958-59 Mem. Indsl. Biotech. Assn. (bd. dirs. 1986-89), Agr. Rsch. Inst. (bd. govs. 1988-91), Am. Chem. Soc. (exec. com. biol. chemistry divsn. 1978-81, Del. award 1969), Am. Soc. Biol. Chemists and Molecular Biologists, Am. Soc. Plant Biology (exec. com., treas. 1974-77), Am. Soc. Agronomy, Am. Soc. Microbiology. Episcopalian.

HARDY, RICHARD EARL, rehabilitation counseling educator; b. Victoria, Va., Oct. 11, 1938; s. Clifford E. and Louise (Hamilton) H.; 1 son, Jason Elliott. BS, Va. Poly. Inst. and State U., 1960, MS, 1962, EdD, 1966. Rehab. counselor State of Va., Richmond, 1961-63; rehab. advisor HHS, Washington, 1964-66; chief psychologist S.C. Dept. Rehab., Columbia, 1966-68; prof. chmn. dept. rehab. counseling Med. Coll. Va., Richmond, 1968-96, chmn., prof. emeritus, 1996—. Former bd. mem. S.C. State Bd. Psychology, former ABPP candidate examiner; internat. cons. to numerous countries including Turkey, Iraq, Peru, Uruguay, South Africa, Brazil, Thailand Author, editor: International Rehabilitation: Approaches and Programs, Hemingway: A Psychological Portrait, 1988, Gestalt Psychotherapy, 1991, Hispaniola Episode: A Mental Health Allegory, 1992, (with J.G. Cull) The Brass Chalice: Drug Prevention Stories and Information for Children and Youth, 1994, Counseling in the Rehabilitation Process, 1999, Woodpeckers Don't Get Headaches: The Psychology of Stress, Relationships, and Addiction, 2001, numerous others. Recipient Nat. award Nat. Rehab. Assn., 1976; recipient Nat. award Am. Assn. Workers for Blind, 1976, Outstanding Grad. award Med. Coll. Va./Va. Commonwealth U., Dept. Rehab. Counseling, 1997, Richard E. Hardy endowed scholarship Med. Coll. Va., 1998. Fellow Am. Psychol. Soc., Assn. Allied & Preventive Psychology; mem. Am. Assn. Vol. Action Scholars, Phi Kappa Phi. Office: Va Commonwealth U 6962 Forest Hill Ave Richmond VA 23225 E-mail: richardehardy@cs.com.

HARDY, ROBERT PAUL, lawyer; b. San Francisco, Apr. 30, 1958; s. David John Hardy and Constance Catherine (Parrette) Morris; m. Mary Louise Stevens, Aug. 6, 1988; children: Nicholas Paul, Jackson Robert. BA, UCLA, 1981; JD, U. So. Calif., 1984. Bar: Calif. 1984, U.S. Dist. Ct. (ctrl. dist.) Calif. 1984, U.S. Ct. Appeals (9th cir.) 1984, N.Y. 1995. Assoc. Kindel & Anderson, L.A., 1984-86, Jones, Day, Reavis & Pogue, L.A., 1986-91, N.Y., 1991-93, ptnr., 1994-97, Brown & Wood, N.Y.C., 1997—2001, Sidley Austin Brown & Wood, N.Y.C., 2001—. Recipient Am. Jurisprudence award The Lawyers Co-operative Pub. Co. and Bancroft-Whitney Co., 1982. Mem. ABA. Democrat. Episcopalian. E-mail: rhardy@sidley.com.

HARDY, ROMAYNE ADAMS, music educator; b. Danville, Va., Jan. 12, 1937; d. James Lee Adams and Shirley Marie Breedlove-Adams; m. Robert Raymond Hardy, Aug. 12, 1961 (dec. Nov. 21, 1996). MusB, Peabody Conservatory, 1960. Co-owner, mem. faculty Marsh Sch. Music, Virginia Beach, Va., 1960—. Mem.: Music Tchrs. Nat. (news editor 1990), Nat. Guild Piano Tchrs., Nat. Fedn. Music Clubs. Mem. Foursquare Gospel Ch. Avocations: dogs, cats, goats. Home: 5085 Indian Trail Rd Suffolk VA 23434-7322 Office: Marsh Sch Music 328 Office Square Ln Virginia Beach VA 23462

HARDY, RUSSELL WILLIS, neurosurgeon; b. Orange, N.J., Mar. 30, 1940; s. Russell Willis and Myrtle Ward H.; m. Judith Markus Hardy, Dec. 14, 1968; children: Jennifer Lynn, Caroline Frances. AB, Dartmouth Coll., 1962, B Med. Sci., 1963; MD, Harvard U., 1965. Diplomate Am. Bd. Neurological Surgery. Intern, resident Boston City Hosp., 1965-67; rsch. assoc. NIH, Bethesda, Md., 1967-69; with USPHS, 1969; resident neurosurgery U. Hosps. of Cleve., 1969-73; staff surgeon Cleve. Clinic, 1973-88, U. Hosps. Cleve., 1988—; prof. neurosurgery Case Western Res. U. Sch. Medicine, Cleve., 1988—. Cons. Gliatech Corp., Cleve., 1995—; chmn. Health Tech. Cons., Cleve., 1998—; chmn. Fedn. for Internat. Edn. in Neurosurgery, Chgo. Editor: Lumbar Disc Disease, 1982, 2nd edit., 1993. Fellow Am. Coll. Surgeons; mem. Am. Assn. Neurol. Surgeons, Congress of Neurol. Surgeons, Soc. Neurol. Surgeons, Acad. Medicine Cleve. (pres. 1996-97), Neurosurgical Soc. Am. (pres. 1993-94). Republican. Presbyterian. Avocations: tennis, fly fishing, antique sports cars. Office: U Neurosurgeons Cleve 11100 Euclid Ave Cleveland OH 44106-1736

HARDY, THOMAS CRESSON, insurance company executive; b. Hoisington, Kans., 1942; s. C.C. and Delia Hardy; children— Jay C., Glenn W. BA, U. Kans., 1963; MBA, Wharton Sch., U. Pa., 1965. CLU, CPCU, FLMI. With Exxon Corp., N.Y.C., 1965-69; treas. Keene Corp., N.Y.C., 1969-73; exec. v.p. fin. Fidelity Union Life Ins. Co., Dallas, 1973-79; (co. acquired by Allianz of Am. 1979); v.p. Allianz of Am.; pres. Allianz Investment Corp., Dallas, 1979-82; pres., chief exec. officer Gt. Am. Res. Ins. Co., 1983-88; exec. v.p., CFO Provident Life & Accident Ins. Co., Chattanooga, 1988-94; pres., CEO, bd. dirs. Loewen Life Ins. Group, 1997—2000, Mayflower Nat. Life Ins. Co., 1997—2000, Unity Fin. Life Ins. Co., 2001—. Chmn. bd. dirs. Security Instnl. Co., 1997-2000; pres., CEO, bd. dirs. Nat. Capitol Life, 1997-2000. Bd. dirs., pres. Chattanooga Symphony & Opera Assn., 1989-97; bd. dirs. exec. com. Chattanooga Allied Arts, 1992-97; mem. U. Kans. Bus. Sch. Adv. Bd., bd. dirs. 1994—; bd. visitors Berry Coll., 1992-99; bd. dirs. La. Philharm. Orch., 1999-2001. Mem. Fin. Execs. Inst. (chpt. pres., nat. bd. dirs.). E-mail: thardy@uflife.com.

HARDY, VICKI, elementary school principal; b. Dallas, Dec. 12, 1949; d. Charles Preston and Bertha Frances (Wynne) Sheldon; m. Howard Lawrence Hardy, Jan. 22, 1972; children: Shane, Travis, Erin. BS, U. Tex., 1971; MEd, U. North Tex., 1977, 81. Tchr. Pearland (Tex.) Ind. Sch. Dist., 1972-73; tchr., asst. prin. Hurst Euless Bedford Ind. Sch. Dist., Bedford, Tex., 1973-86; curriculum cons. Irving (Tex.) Ind. Sch. Dist., 1986-89; prin. Schertz-Cibolo-Universal City Sch. Dist., Schertz, Tex., 1989-92, Cedar Hill (Tex.) Ind. Sch. Dist., 1992-96, Northwest Ind. Sch. Dist., Trophy Club, Tex., 1996—. Evaluator So. Assn. of Schs., 1987; TSII mem. Tex. Edn. Agy., Austin, 1990—. Mem. ASCD, Internat. Reading Assn., Nat. Coun. Tchrs. English, Tex. Elem. Prins. and Suprs. Assn., Ex-Students Assn. of U. Tex., Women in the Major Leagues, Delta Kappa Gamma (v.p. 1985-86, Friendship award 1985), Phi Delta Kappa (2d v.p. 1988-89, pres. 1989-90) Avocations: travel, crafts, sports, photography, sewing. Office: Lakeview Elem Sch 100 Village Trl Trophy Club TX 76262-5201 E-mail: vhardynisd@yahoo.com.

HARDY, VICTORIA ELIZABETH, management educator; b. Marion, N.C., Feb. 26, 1947; d. Milton Victor Roth and Bertha Jean (Norris) R.; m. Michael Carrington Hardy, June 19, 1983 (div. 1993); 1 child, Christopher. BS in Edn., U. Mo., 1970; postgrad., So. Ill. U., 1974-75; postgrad. Mgmt. Devel. Program, Stanford U., 1980-81; MA in Mgmt., Aquinas Coll., 1999. Cert. facility mgr. Pub. sch. tchr. English and Theater, 1970-75; gen. mgr. Miss. River Festival, Edwardsville, Ill., 1975-77; dir. events and svcs. Stanford (Calif.) U., 1977-83; exec. dir. Meadowlands Ctr. for the Arts, Rutherford, N.J., 1983-87; pres., chief exec. officer Music Hall Ctr. for the Arts, Detroit, 1987-89; prin. AMS Planning & Rsch., Conn., 1989-94; tenured prof. facility mgmt. Ferris State U., Big Rapids, Mich., 1994—. Mem. faculty CUNY, 1986-88. Contbr. to various publs. Mem. USICA study team to China, 1981; state bd. dirs. Arts Found., Mich., 1987-95; bd. dirs. Internat. Facility Mgmt. Assn., 1994-97, standing coms. recognition and profl. devel.; mem. People to People facilities del. to Australia and New Zealand, 1996, bd. dirs., chair IFMA Found., 1998—. Named Disting. Educator of Yr., IFMA, 2001; named to Creativity in Business Doubleday, 1986; recipient Gold medal for Cmty. Programs, Coun. for Advancement and Support of Edn., Stanford, 1985. Mem. League of Hist. Am. Theaters (pres. bd. dirs. 1987-89), Arts Presenter Assn. (exec. bd. dirs. 1977-83). Democrat. Avocations: skiing, gardening. Office: Ferris State Univ Coll of Tech Swan 312 915 Campus Dr Big Rapids MI 49307-2291

HARDY, WALTER NEWBOLD, physics educator, researcher; b. Vancouver, B.C., Mar. 25, 1940; s. Walter Thomas and Julia Marguerite (Mulroy) H.; m. Sheila Lorraine Hughes, July 10, 1959; children: Kevin James, Steven Wayne. BSc in Math and Physics with honors, U. B.C., 1961; PhD in Physics, Univ. B.C., 1965. Postdoctral fellow Centre d'Etudes Nucleaires de Saclay, France, 1964-66; mem. tech. staff N.Am. Rockwell, Thousand Oaks, Calif., 1966-71; assoc. prof. physics U. B.C., 1971-76, prof., 1976—. Vis. scientist Ecole Normale Superieure, Paris, 1980-81, 85, 95. Contbr. articles to sci. jours.; patentee precision microwave instrumentation. Recipient Stacie prize NRC of Can., 1978, Gold medal B.C. Sci. Coun., 1989, Killam prize Can. Coun., 1999, Fritz London Prize, 2002; Rutherford Meml. scholar, 1964; Alfred P. Sloan fellow, 1972-74; Can. Coun. Rsch. fellow, 1984-86. Mem. Can. Assn. Physicists (Herzberg medal 1978, gold medal for achievement in physics, 1993, Brockhouse medal 1999), Am. Phys. Soc. Office: U BC Dept Physics Astronomy Vancouver BC Canada V6T 1Z1

HARDY, WAYNE RUSSELL, insurance and investment broker; b. Denver, Sept. 5, 1931; s. Russell Hinton and Victoria Katherine (Anderson) H.; m. Carolyn Lucille Carvell, Aug. 1, 1958 (July 1977); children: James Russell Hardy, Jann Miller Hardy. BSCE, U. Colo., 1954; MS in Fin. Svcs., Am. Coll., 1989. CLU; chartered fin. cons. Western dist. mgr. Fenestra, Inc., San Francisco, 1956-63; ins. and investment broker John Hancock Fin. Svs., Denver, 1963—, Wayne R. Hardy Assocs., Denver, 1963—. Speaker convs. and sales seminars, 1977, 81, 84, 85, 89; v.p. CLU assn. John Hancock, 1979-80, chmn. agt.'s adv. com., 1983-84; active State of Colo. Ins. Adv. Bd., 1991-93; profl. model, actor J.F. Images Agy., Denver, 1964-89. Chmn. Colo. Coun. Camera Clubs, Denver, 1962; bd. dirs. Porter Charitable Found., Denver, 1983-85; deacon, class pres. South Broadway Christian Ch., 1961-65; mem. Denver Art Mus., Denver Botanic Gardens, Rocky Mountain Estate Planning Coun., Mensa, Alliance Francaise. Capt. U.S. Army, 1954-56, Korea, USAR, 1956-80. Mem. Am. Soc. CLU and ChFC (pres. Rocky Mountain chpt. 1990-91), Nat. Assn. Life Underwriters (pres. Denver chpt. 1983-84, Nat. Quality award 1968—, expert witness ins. litigation, Disting. Life Underwriters award 1970-83), Screen Actors Guild, Million Dollar Round Table (life), U. Colo. Alumni (bd. dirs. 1990-92), U. Colo. Alumni C Club (bd. dirs. 1972-74), Univ. Club, Greenwood Athletic Club, Village Tennis Club, Rocky Mountain Optimist Club (pres. 1984-85). Republican. Avocations: tennis, photography, foreign languages, art, travel. Home and Office: 6178 E Hinsdale Ct Englewood CO 80112-1534

HARDY, WILLIAM ROBINSON, lawyer; b. Cin., June 14, 1934; s. William B. and Chastine M. (Sprague) H.; m. Leslie Warrington Bailey, Apr. 16, 1999; children from previous marriage: Anita Christina, William Robinson Jr. AB magna cum laude, Princeton U., 1956; JD, Harvard U., 1963. Bar: Ohio 1963, U.S. Supreme Ct. 1975. Life underwriter New Eng. Mut. Life Ins. Co., 1956-63; assoc. Graydon, Head & Ritchey, Cin., 1963-68, ptnr., 1968-98. Mem. panel comml. arbitrators Am. Arbitration Assn., 1972—, mem. panel large complex case program, 1993—, panel of mediators, 1993—, comml. arbitrator tng. faculty, 1998—; reporter joint com. for revision of rules of U.S. Dist. Ct. for So. Dist. Ohio, 1975, 80, 83, mem., 1990—. Bd. dirs. Cin. Union Bethel, 1968-82, pres., 1977-82, emeritus, 1982—; bd. dirs. Ohio Valley Goodwill Industries Rehab. Ctr., Cin., 1970—, pres., 1981-92; mem. Cin. Bd. Bldg. Appeals, 1976-2001, vice chmn., 1983, chmn., 1983-2001; pres. Hamilton County (Ohio) Alcohol and Drug Addiction Svcs. Bd., 1990-92; trustee Substance Abuse Mgmt. and Devel. Inc., 1998-99. Capt. USAR, 1956-68; maj. gen. Ohio Mil. Res., comdr., 1996-2001. Recipient award of merit Ohio Legal Ctr. Inst., 1975, 76, Ohio Commendation medal, 1999. Mem. ABA, AAAS, Ohio Bar Assn., Cin. Bar Assn., Ohio Acad. Trial Lawyers, Am. Arbitration Assn., Assn. for Conflict Resolution, 6th Cir. Jud. Conf. (life), Ohio Soc. Colonial Wars (gov. 1979), Princeton (N.Y.C.) Club, Interlachen Country Club (Winter Park, Fla.), Edgartown (Mass.) Yacht Club, Phi Beta Kappa. Mem. Ch. Of Redeemer. Office: 432 Walnut St Ste 206 Cincinnati OH 45202-3909

HARDY-BRAZ, STEVEN THOMAS, psychologist; b. Rockville, Conn., Dec. 22, 1966; s. Milton Bradford and Ellen Blake Hardy; m. Liza Hardy Braz, Aug. 12, 1995. Cert. mgmt. substance abuse treatment, South Ctrl. C.C., New Haven, 1990; BA in Clin. Counseling Psychology, BS in Criminal Justice, U. New Haven, 1990; MA in Devel. Psychology, Gallaudet U., 1991, specialist in psychology, 1995, cert. instr. instrumental enrichment, 1996; cert. dynamic assessment, Tuoro Coll., 1996. Sch. psychologist Ea. N.C. Sch. for the Deaf, Wilson, 1996-99; ednl. specialist Ctr. for Devel. and Learning U. N.C., Chapel Hill, 1998—. Asst. to dir. re-entry Elan One Corp., 1986; logistics coord. Family Life Program/Learning Vacation, 1990-91; instr. psychology dept. Gallaudet U., 1991-92, staff mem. personal discovery program, 1992—, rsch. instr. Rsch. Inst./Mental Health, 1993-94; asst. boys basketball coach Scranton State Sch. for the Deaf, 1994-95; sign lang. interpreter, 1994—; contract sch. psychologist, 1995—; psychol. assoc. Dr. William Kachman, Md., 1995—; adv. bd. mem. N.C. State Mental Health Svcs. for the Deaf, Raleigh, 1997—; presenter in field. Mem. editl. bd. The Ednl. Forum, 1995—; contbr. chpt. to book. Mem. APA, Nat. Assn. Sch. Psychologists (nat. cert. sch. psychologist), Wilson Assn. Sch. Deaf, Mensa. Avocations: Aikido, rock climbing. Office: 104 N Green St Farmville NC 27828 1315 E mail: hardybraz@coastalnet.com.

HARDYMON, DAVID WAYNE, lawyer; b. Columbus, Ohio, Aug. 22, 1949; s. Philip Barbour and Margaret Evelyn (Bowers) H.; m. Monica Ella Sleep, Mar. 13, 1982; children: Philip Garnet, Teresa Jeanette. BA in History, Bowling Green State U., 1971; JD, Capital U., Columbus, Ohio, 1976. Bar: Ohio 1976, U.S. Dist. Ct. (so. dist.) Ohio 1976; U.S. Supreme Ct. 1980, U.S. Ct. Appeals (6th cir.) 1982, Ky. 1999, U.S. Dist. Ct. (no. dist.) Ohio 1999, W.Va. 2000, U.S. Dist. Ct. (so. dist.) W.Va. 2000. Asst. prosecuting atty. Franklin County Prosecuter's Office, Columbus, Ohio, 1976-81; assoc. Vorys, Sater, Seymour & Pease, Columbus, 1981-86, ptnr., 1987—. Mem. Chmn's. Club Franklin Country Rep. Orgn., 1983. Fellow Columbus Bar Found.; mem. Ohio State Bar Assn., Columbus Bar Assn. Avocations: sailing, archery. Office: Vorys Sater Seymour & Pease PO Box 1008 52 E Gay St Columbus OH 43215-3161

HARDY-PARCELL, CATHY KAY, music educator, department chairman; d. R. Keith and Beverly Louise Hardy; m. John Cleo Parcell, Sept. 30, 1990. MusB Edn., Wheaton Coll., Ill., 1980; MM in Vocal Performance, U. of Mo., 1987. Opera express dir. Lyric Opera of Kans. City, Kans .City, Mo.; voice instr. U. of Mo., Kans. City, 1983—93, Mo. Western State Coll., St. Joseph, 1986—89; role singer Lyric Opera, Kans. City, Mo., 1986—89; music dept. head Longview C.C., Lee's Summit, Mo., 1989—. Guest conductor-choral festival Ctr. Pl. Restoration Sch., Independence, Mo., 2003. Singer: (competition) Operatic Arias (Competions Winner, 1984). Keyboard player Various Bapt. Chs., Kans. City, Mo., 2000—03. Mem.: Mo. Chpt. of Music Educators Nat. Conf., Music Educators Nat. Conf., Coll. Music Soc., Am. Coral Dirs. Assn. Conservative. Avocations: computer technology, carpentry, sewing. Office: Longview C C 500 SW Longview Rd Lees Summit MO 64081-2100 Office Fax: 816-672-2078. E-mail: hardy@kcmetro.edu.

HARE, A(LEXANDER) PAUL, sociology educator; b. Washington, June 29, 1923; arrived in Israel, 1980; s. Alexander Paul and Lulu Irene (Waters) H.; m. Rachel Diana Thies, 1947 (div. 1972); children: Sharon E., Diana S., Mally M., Christopher P.; m. June Sara Rabson, 1974; children: Simon L., Andrew G. BA, Swarthmore Coll., 1947; BS, Iowa State U., 1948; MA, U. Pa., 1949; PhD, U. Chgo., 1951. Instr. Harvard U., Cambridge, Mass., 1955-60; assoc. prof. Haverford (Pa.) Coll., 1960-66, prof., 1966-73, U. Cape Town, Republic of South Africa, 1973-81, Ben-Gurion U. of the Negev, Beer Sheva, Israel, 1982-91. Author: Handbook of Small Group Research, 1962, (2d edit.), 1976, Creativity in Small Groups, 1982, Social Interaction as Drama, 1985, Groups, Teams, and Social Interactions, 1992; co-author: (3d edit.) The Small Group, 1978, Dramaturgical Analysis of Social Interaction, 1988, Small Group Research, 1994, J.L. Moreno, 1996, Symlog Field Theory, 1996, Small Groups, 1996, Individuals and Groups in Organizations, 1998, The Hebrew Israelite Community, 1998, Israel as Center Stage, 2001; author, editor: 28 books; contbr. over 100 articles to profl. jours., chapters to books. Served to 1st lt. U.S. Army, 1943-46, ETO. Univ. Cape Town fellow, 1979. Mem. Am. Sociol. Assn. (cert.), Soc. Exptl. Social Psychology. Mem. Soc. Of Friends. Office: Ben-Gurion U Dept Behavioral Scis Beer Sheva 84105 Israel E-mail: paulhare@bgumail.bgu.ac.il.

HARE, ESTER ROSE, physician; b. St. Catherine, Jamaica, Apr. 15, 1952; came to U.S., 1979; d. Emcle and Lovina (Lee) H. BSc with honors, U. West Indies, Jamaica, 1975; PhD in Biochemistry, Dalhousie U., Halifax, Can., 1984; MD, U. Conn., 1990. Diplomate Am. Bd. Internal Medicine. Intern U. Hosp. Cleve., 1990-91; resident Med. U. Hosp., Charleston, S.C., 1992-94; pvt. practice Orangeburg (S.C.) Med. Assn., 1994—. Mem. bd. health Women's Christian Orgn., Orangeburg, 1995—. Mem. ACP, AMA, Nat. Med. Assn., Am. Soc. Internal Medicine, S.C. Med. Assn., Sigma Psi. Avocations: gardening, aerobics. Office: Orangeburg Med Assocs 1291 Glen Gloria Orangeburg SC 29118

HARE, FRANCES HUTCHESON, JR., lawyer, educator; b. Birmingham, Ala., Jan. 31, 1936; s. Francis Hutcheson and Isabelle (Corr) H.; m. Suzanne Balliet; children— Francis, Catherine, Amelia. B.S., U. Ala., 1956; J.D., U. Va., 1959. Bar: U.S. Ct. Appeals (5th cir.), U.S. Ct. Appeals (11th cir.), U.S. Supreme Ct. Ptnr. firm Hare, Wynn, Newell & Newton, Birmingham; assoc. prof. Cumberland Sch. Law, Samford U., Birmingham, 1975—; chief legal officer Attorney Info. Exch. Group, Birmingham, 1999—; bd. editors Jour. Product Liability. Elder, Covenant Presbyn. Ch. Fellow Internat. Acad. Trial Lawyers, Internat. Soc. Barristers, Am. Bar Found., Am. Bd. Trial Advocates (pres. Ala. chpt. 1983-84); mem. ABA, Ala. Bar Assn., Birmingham Bar Assn., Ala. Law Inst., Ala. Trial Lawyers Assn. (pres. 1971-72), Assn. Trial Lawyers Am. (gov. 1975-76), Nat. Adv. Bd. Christian Legal Soc., 11th Cir. Ct. Appeals Lawyers Adv. Com., Am. Judicature Soc., Inner Circle of Advocates, Scribes. Co-author: Anatomy of a Personal Injury Lawsuit, 1981; The Preparation of a Products Liability Case, 1981.

HARE, NORMA Q. retired school administrator; b. Dadeville, Mo., July 10, 1924; d. James Norma and Mary Delia (Blakemore) Quarles; m. John Daniel Hare, June 27, 1944 (dec.); children: J. Daniel, Thomas C. BA, Calif. State U. Fresno, 1958, MA, 1963. Cert. tchr., sch. adminstr. Elem. tchr. Parlier Sch. Dist., Calif., 1956-57, Sanger Sch. Dist., Calif., 1958-66, S. San Francisco Schs., 1966-67, elem. edn. specialist, 1967, elem. sch. principal, 1967-81. Dir. Title I, Spruce Sch. ESEA, El Rancho Sch. Early Childhood edn. program, sch. dist. mgmt. negotiator, S. San Francisco Schs., 1977-79. Author: (books) Who is Root Beer, 1977, Wish Upon A Birthday, 1979, Mystery at Mousehouse, 1980, Puritans, Pioneers and Planters, 1995; co-author: (book) The Magatagans, 1998. Mem.: DAR, AAUW, Colonial Dames XVII Century (treas. 1995—98), Soc. Mayflower Descendants (gov. San Francisco/Peninsula colony 1983—86, pres. Sierra de Santa Lucia chpt. 2003—, govs. award 1988, 1992). Avocations: genealogy, travel. E-mail: nghare@aol.com.

HARE, PETER HEWITT, philosophy educator; b. N.Y.C., Mar. 12, 1935; s. Michael Meredith and Jane Perry (Jopling) H.; m. Daphne Joan Kean, May 30, 1959 (dec. Aug. 1995); children: Clare Kean, Gwendolyn Meigs; m. Susan Howe, Nov. 1, 2000. BA, Yale U., 1957; MA, Columbia U., 1962, PhD, 1965. Lectr. philosophy SUNY, Buffalo, 1962-65, from asst. prof. to prof., 1965-97, disting. svc. prof., 1997—, asst. chmn. dept., 1965-68, chmn. dept., 1971-75, 85-94, assoc. dean divsn. undergrad. edn., 1980-82, prof. emeritus, 2001—. Vis. prof. Moscow State U., 1989; bd. advisors, Peirce Edition Project, Ind. U./Purdue U., 1998—. Author: A Woman's Quest for Science, 1985; (with others) Evil and the Concept of God, 1968, Causing, Perceiving and Believng, 1975; editor: Doing Philosophy Historically, 1988, (with others) History, Religion and Spiritual Democacy, 1980, Naturalism and Rationality, 1986, (series) Frontiers of Philosophy, Prometheus Books, 1986—; photo illustrations in Susan Howe, Kidnapped, 2002, The Midnight, 2003; mem. editl. bd. Am. Philos. Quar., 1978-87, Jour. Speculative Philosophy, 1987—. Mem. Am. Philos. Assn. (nominating com. ea. divsn. 1990-92, program com. 1993-95, chmn. program com. 1994-95, mem. nat. bd. officers 1996-99, chmn. com. career opportunities, 1996-99, ombudsman 1996-99, chair Romanell lectr. com. 2000-2001), Peirce Soc. (editor Transactions 1974—), pres. 1975-76), N.Y. State Philos. Assn. (pres. 1975-77), Soc. for Advancement Am. Philosophy (exec. com. 1977-80, pres. 1988-90, Herbert W. Schneider award 1996), Josiah Royce Soc. (mem. exec. com. 2003—), Elizabethan Club. Home: 115 New Quarry Rd Guilford CT 06437-1621 Office: SUNY Dept Philosophy Park Hall Buffalo NY 14260 E-mail: phhare@acsu.buffalo.edu.

HARE, ROBERT YATES, music history educator; b. McGrann, Pa., June 14, 1921; s. Robert Deemar and Beulah (Yates) H.; m. Constance King Rutherford, Mar. 31, 1948; children: Stephen, Beverly, Madeleine. Mus.B., U. Detroit, 1948; MA, Wayne State U., 1950; PhD, U. Iowa, 1959. Instr. Marietta (Ohio) Coll., 1949-51, Del Mar Coll., Corpus Christi, Tex., 1951-55; prof., chmn. grad. studies San Jose (Calif.) State U., 1956-65; prof., dean Eastern Ill. U. Music, 1965-74; prof. music history and lit. Ohio State U., Columbus, 1974-86, prof. emeritus, 1986—, dir. Sch. Music, 1974-78, dir. audio-rec. engring., 1979-82, arts adminstr. research and faculty devel., 1982-86. Cons. in field; Mem. council

music edn. in higher edn. Ill. Music Educators Assn., 1969-74. Condr. coll. symphony band, 1956-63, San Jose Youth Symphony, 1957-59, univ. symphony, 1968-74, Ea. Ill. U. Symphony, 1968-74; French horn recitals, Carnegie Music Hall, Pitts., 1940, 42; French hornist, Pitts. Symphony Orch., 1941-43, 44-45, Buffalo Philharmonic, 1943-44, Cin. Summer Opera Co., 1945, Indpls. Symphony Orch., 1945-46, San Antonio Symphony Orch., 1947-49; orchestrator, San Antonio Symphony Orch., 1947-49; recs. include Pitts. Symphony Orch., Indpls. Symphony Orch. (as French hornist), San Jose State U. Symphonic Band (as condr.); contbr. articles to profl. jours. Mem. com. grad. and profl. edn. in arts and humanities Ill. Bd. Higher Edn., 1969-70; mem. performing arts commn. Ill. Sesquicentennial, 1967; mem. exec. bd. Greater Columbus Arts Council, 1974-76, Ohio Alliance for Arts in Edn., 1974-76; trustee Columbus Symphony Orch., 1975-79. Profl. Promise scholar Carnegie-Mellon U., 1939 Mem. Music Educators Nat. Conf. (publs. planning com. 1970-76), Am. Musicol. Soc., Coll. Music Soc., Phi Mu Alpha, Sinfonia (hon.), Pi Kappa Lambda (hon.), Delta Omicron (hon.). Lodges: Masons; Shriners. Home: 2624 SW Ashworth Pl Topeka KS 66614-2507 Office: Ohio State U Coll Arts 305 Mershon Auditorium Columbus OH 43210

HAR-EL, GADY, surgeon; b. Tel-Aviv, Israel, June 21, 1954; came to U.S., 1986; s. Ovadia and Helen (Hakim) H.; m. Rivi Belach, Sept. 20, 1983; children: Amir, Ila. MD, Ben Gurion U., Beer-Sheva, Israel, 1983. Prof., vice chmn. dept. otolaryngology State U. Health Sci. Ctr., Bklyn., 1994—, prof. neurosurgery, 1994—; dir. skull base ctr. Atate U. Health Sci. Ctr., Bklyn., 1994—. Author of 3 books and 30 chpts. to books; contbr. 150 articles to profl. jours. Recipient Internat. Cancer Tech. Transfer award Internat. Union Against Cancer, Geneva, Switzerland, 1998. Fellow Am. Acad. Otolaryngology (Hon. award 1995), Am. Coll. Surgeons (assoc.), Am. Rhinologic Soic.; mem. AMA, Am. Laryngological, Rhinological & Otological Soc., Am. Acad. Facial Plastic & Reconstructive Surgery, Am. Soc. Head & Neck Surgery, N.Am. Skull Base Soc., N.Y. Laryngological Soc., N.Y. Head & Neck Soc., Med. Soc. State of N.Y., Kings County Med. Soc. (otolaryngology sect.), Soc. Head & Neck Surgery, Soc. Univ. Otolaryngologists. Office: 134 Atlantic Ave Brooklyn NY 11201-5502

HARELL, GEORGE S. radiologist; b. Vienna, Apr. 27, 1937; came to U.S., 1940; s. Isidore and Zinaida (Hilferding) Silbermann; m. Carol Deane Wright, Mar. 21, 1970, children: Mark, Ben. AB, Oberlin Coll., 1959, MD, Columbia U., 1963. Resident in radiology Med. Sch., Stanford (Calif.) U., 1967-71, asst. prof., 1971-78, assoc. prof., 1978-82; radiologist dept. radiology East Jefferson Gen. Hosp., Metairie, La., 1982-84, chmn. dept. radiology, 1984-94. Clin. prof. radiology Tulane U., New Orleans, 1987—; project officer NIH, Washington, 1965-67. Contbr. chpt. to: The Oesophagus, 1986, 92, 97. Lt. comdr. USPHS, 1963-65. James C. Picker Found. grantee, 1972-74, NIH grantee, 1977-80, 82-85, Am. Heart Assn. grantee, 1981-83. Mem. Soc. Computed Body Tomography/Magnetic Resonances, Soc. Gastrointestinal Radiologists, Phi Beta Kappa. Home and Office: 1283 Chickanut Creek Ln Bellingham WA 98229 E-mail: geode@sprintmail.com.

HAREZI, ILONKA JO, medical technology research executive; b. Princeton, Ind., Jan. 17, 1949; d. Joseph and Helen Marie Fullop; m. John O. Schofield, Dec. 14, 1971 (div. Dec. 1982); 1 child, Franceska; m. Courtland Reeves, Nov. 26, 1986; children: Bryan, Katharine. PhD, Chgo. Sch. Design, 1969. Mktg. ptnr. Fullop and Assocs., 1983-85; founder, sec., treas. Kinetic Energy Ltd., 1985-90; freelance set designer Ilonka Creative Environments, 1974-84; founder, v.p. Harezi Internat., 1980-84; founder, sec., treas. Elf Cocoon Corp., 1984-86; founder, pres., chmn. Elf Cocoon Internat. Ltd., 1985-92; founder, pres. Elfworks, Inc., 1991-94, Elfworks, Nev., 1994-96; pres., dir. Allied Fund for Capital Appreciation, Inc., 1994—98. Interviewed by radio, TV, and newspapers on design and extremely low frequency electromagnetic tech.; presenter tech. sems. on ELF and scalar phenomena. Author: The Resonance in Residence; contbr. articles to profl. jours. Bd. dirs. Inst. for Higher Human Learning Potential, Phila., 1979. Fellow N.Y. Acad. of Sci.; mem. NAFE, ACLU, AAAS, Am. Inst. Interior Designers, Women's Internat. League for Peace and Freedom, Nat. Assn. Against Health Fraud, Nat. Narcotics Officers Assns. Coalition, N.Y. Acad. Sci., UN-USA Bus. Coun., Knights of Malta (dame), Knights of Africa (dame), U.S. Acad. Polit. Sci., Am. Craft Coun. Achievements include patents pending for ST8 Bulb for delivery of ozone into body. Office: ELF Tesler St Rt 1 Saint Francisville IL 62460

HARFF, CHARLES HENRY, lawyer, retired diversified industrial company executive; b. Wesel, Germany, Sept. 27, 1929; s. Philip and Stephanie (Dreyfuss) H.; m. Marion Haines MacAfee, July 19, 1958; children— Pamela Haines, John Blair, Todd Philip BA, Colgate U., 1951; LL.B., Harvard U., 1954; postgrad., U. Bonn, Fed. Republic Germany, 1955. Bar: N.Y. 1955. Assoc. Chadbourne & Parke, N.Y.C., 1955-64, ptnr., 1964-84; sr. v.p., gen. counsel, sec. Rockwell Internat. Corp., Pitts., 1984-94, sr. v.p., spl. counsel, 1994-96, ret., 1996. Cons., 1996—2001; bd. dirs. Arvin Meritor, Inc. Trustee Christian A. Johnson Endeavor Found., N.Y.C., 1984-2001; bd. dirs. Atlantic Legal Found., 1989-98, Fulbright Assn., 1995-2002, pres., 2001. Fulbright scholar U. Bonn, Germany, 1954-55. Mem. ABA, N.Y. State Bar Assn., The Assn. Gen. Counsel, Harvard Club of N.Y.C., Duquesne Club, Allegheny Country Club, Farm Neck Golf Club (Martha's Vineyard, Mass.).

HARFORD, JAMES JOSEPH, writer; b. Jersey City, Aug. 19, 1924; s. Thomas William and Jane Hume (Henderson) H.; m. Mildred Rita Waters, Apr. 19, 1952; children: Susan Gately, James Joseph, Peter Benedict (dec.), Jennifer, Christopher. BSME, Yale U. 1945W. Sales engr. Worthington Corp., 1946-49; assoc. editor Modern Industry, 1950-52; free-lance writer Europe, 1952-53; exec. sec. Am. Rocket Soc., 1953-63; exec. dir. Am. Inst. Aeros. and Astronautics, 1963-88, exec. dir. emeritus, 1988—. V.p. Internat. Astronautical Fedn., 1988-90. Author: Korolev (How One Man Masterminded the Soviet Drive to Beat America to the Moon), 1997, (with others) China Space Report, 1979. Mem. 1945W class coun. Yale U.; trustee Friends of Princeton Pub. Libr., 1996—2002. Lt. (j.g.) USNR, 1945—46. Recipient NASA Pub. Svc. award, 1985, Air Force Exceptional Svc. award, 1987, Nat. Space Club Robert Goddard Hist. Essay prize, 1995, Internat. Astron. Fedn. award, 1997; Verville fellow Nat. Air and Space Mus., 1989-92. Fellow AIAA (Disting. Svc. award 1988, Internat. Coop. Aerospace award 1995), AAS, Brit. Interplanetary Soc., Royal Aero. Soc. (assoc.); mem. Internat. Acad. Astronautics, Cosmos Club, Nassau Club. Home and Office: 601 Lake Dr Princeton NJ 08540-5634 E-mail: jimharford@msn.com.

HARGADON, BERNARD JOSEPH, JR., retired consumer goods company executive; b. Ardmore, Pa., Dec. 27, 1927; s. Bernard Joseph and Anna Mendenhall (Lancaster) H.; m. Jill Dinwiddie, Dec. 15, 1990; children from previous marriage: Geoffrey, Robert, Louise, Lawrence (dec.), David. BS, Drexel U., 1952, MBA, 1959; PhD (hon.), Golden Gate U., 1995. Auditor Gen. Motors Corp., 1955-57; prof. acctg. Drexel U., 1957-59; with AID, Colombia, 1960-63, McKesson, San Francisco, 1964—; pres. McKesson Internat., 1980-95, ret., 1995. Adj. prof. internat. bus. Golden Gate U. Author: in Spanish Principles of Accounting, 1964, Principles of Cost Accounting, 1971. Trustee Golden Gate U., Oakland Mus. of Calif.; bd. dirs. World Affairs Coun. No. Calif.; mem. Pacific Coun. Internat. Policy. With USN, 1945-48. E-mail: bhargadon@aol.com.

HARGAN, CHARLES JAMES, retired lithographer, village official; b. Clarion, Iowa, June 24, 1941; s. Vernon Garney and Olive Lucile (Tourtelotte) H.; m. Carol Ann Moze, Nov. 25, 1961 (div. June 1981); children: Robert, James, Susan; m. Inga Lynn Johnson, Oct. 6, 1984 (dec. July 2002); 1 child, David. Lithographer W.A. Krueger Co. (now Quebecor World Inc.), Brookfield, Wis., 1962—2001, ret., 2001—. Pres. Village of Germantown, wis., 1993—, trustee, 1986-93. With U.S. Army, 1958-62. Mem. Am. Legion. Republican. Lutheran. Avocations: bowling, fishing, writing, travel, history. Office: Village of Germantown PO Box 337 Germantown WI 53022-0337

HARGENS, CHARLES WILLIAM, III, electrical engineer, consultant; b. Phila., Oct. 21, 1918; s. Charles William Jr. and Marjorie (Garman) H.; m. Mary K. Johnson, June 14, 1941; children: William Garman, Mary Van Deusen, Roger Snow. SB, MIT, 1941. Registered profl. engr., Pa. Design engr. Lockheed Aircraft, Burbank, Calif., 1941-42; group engr. Gilfillan Bros., L.A., 1942-43; vis. staff mem. MIT Radiation Labs., Cambridge, 1942-44; group engr. RCA, Camden, N.J., 1945-47; sr. engr., tech. dir., inst. fellow Franklin Inst. Labs., Phila., 1947-88; assoc. prof. Temple U., Phila., 1976-77, Drexel U., Phila., 1978-87; noise control cons. air mgmt. div. City of Phila., 1978—. Rsch. assoc. Wills Eye Hosp., 1970; cons., prof. acoustics; invited lectr. U. Wis., 1962, 63, 64. Co-author: Studies in Medicine, Physics and Voice, 1968, (chpts.) Bioengineering and the Skin, 1981, Handbook of Noninvasive Methods and the Skin, 1994; contbr. articles to Jour. Ophthalmic Surgery, Jour. Acoustical Soc. Am., Investigative Dermatology, Indsl. Rsch., Electronics Jour. Instrument Soc. Am., Jour. Franklin Inst., IEEE Transactions. Mem. adv. com. Spring Garden Coll., Phila., 1972-76; rsch. assoc. Bd. of City Trusts, 1970. Recipient Diploma, War Manpower Commn., 1944, Citation Mayor City of Phila., 1974. Fellow IEEE (Phila. Sect. Appreciation award 1972, Benjamin Franklin Key award 2003); mem. ASTM (Citation 1982), Franklin Inst. (com. sci. and arts 1981), MIT Alumni Assn. (life, Bronze Beaver award 1976), Numerical Control Soc. (founder), Sigma Xi. Episcopalian. Achievements include 12 patents for radio, electronics, computation, instrumentation optics and measurement; development of specialized instruments for dermatologists, brain tissue and other researchers. Home and Office: 1006 Preston Rd Glenside PA 19038-7333 *Never retire completely from your profession, unless health forces it upon you. It is foolish to give up all the experience, knowledge, and associations acquired over a productive lifetime.*

HARGESHEIMER, ELBERT, III, lawyer; b. Cleve., Jan. 4, 1944; s. Elbert and Agnes Mary (Heckman) H.; children: Heather Leigh, Elbert IV, Jon-Erik, Piper Elizabeth, Kevin R. Cross, Mark R. Dziob. AB, Cornell U., 1966; JD, SUNY, Buffalo, 1969. Bar: N.Y. 1970, U.S. Dist. Ct. (we. dist.) N.Y. 1971. Assoc. Miller, Bouvier, O'Connor & Cegielski, Buffalo, 1970-73, ptnr., 1973-74, Godinho & Hargesheimer, Hamburg, N.Y., 1974-84; pvt. practice law Hamburg, 1984—. Chief counsel Joint Legis. Commn. to Revise Bus. and Corp. Law, N.Y. State Assembly and Senate, 1974-75; prosecutor Village of Blasdell (N.Y.), 1978-80, 83-87, village atty. 1980-82; fund chmn. South Towns Hosp. Found., Inc., 1973-76, fin. chmn., bd. dirs., 1976-77, v.p., 1978-82; chmn. Hamburg Town Rep. Com., 1978-88; coord. Erie County Pretrial Svcs. Program, 1987-88; counsel Erie County Rep. Com., 1980-92; mem. Erie County Bd. Ethics, 1979-89, chmn. 1983.; charter mem., counsel S.W. Hamburg Taxpayers Assn. Named Mr. Rep., Town of Hamburg Rep. Club, 1982, Rep. of Yr., Hamburg Town Rep. Com., 1988. Mem. Western N.Y. Trial Lawyer's Assn., Theta Chi. Methodist. Home and Office: 22 Buffalo St Hamburg NY 14075-5002

HARGIS, BARBARA LOUISE, artist; b. Painesville, Ohio, May 28, 1930; d. Ralph Frances and Claire Louise (Marquis) Fetterly; m. Henry Joseph Hargis Jr., June 4, 1955; children: Ben William, William John, Glenn D. AA, Citrus Coll., 1985. Artist Art Gallery, La Puente, Calif., 1984-94; gallery owner Hargis Gallery, Pomona, Calif., 1994—. Grantee Millennium Prodn., Cambridge, Mass., 1995. Mem. Carlsbad Oceanside Art League (life), DA Gallery Non Profit, Pomoma Valley Art (dir. 1988, life), Corona Art Assn. (life), Women in Arts Mus. (charter mem.), Covina Arts and Crafts, Parks and Recreation (life). Republican. Baptist. Avocations: amateur radio, tennis, swimming, sewing, pool. Studio: 20121 Winton St El Cerrito CA 92881 E-mail: www.puaa.net//Hargisfineart28@aol.com.

HARGIS, DAVID MICHAEL, lawyer, writer; b. Warren, Ark., Feb. 10, 1948; s. James Von Hargis and Noma Lee (Anderson) Watkins; m. Carolyn Jane Sangster (div. 1981); children— Michelle Leigh, Michael Bradley; m. Linda Jane Huckelbury, Jan. 8, 1981; 1 child, Christopher Key. B.S.B.A. with honors, U. Ark., 1970, J.D., 1973. Bar: Ark. 1973, U.S. Dist. Ct. (ea. and we. dists.) Ark. 1974. Assoc. Williamson Law Firm, Monticello, Ark., 1973-74; asst. U.S. atty. Eastern Dist. Ark., Little Rock, 1974-75; assoc. House, Holmes & Jewell, Little Rock, 1975-79; ptnr. House, Holmes & Jewell, P.A., Little Rock, 1979-85; founder Wilson, Wood & Hargis, 1985—; atty. Legal Services Corp., Little Rock, 1977; county atty. Pulaski County, Ark., 1980-82; atty. Pulaski County Quorum Ct., 1980-82; spl. circuit judge Pulaski County Circuit Ct., 1982; atty. Office of Spl. Prosecutor, Pulaski County Grand Jury, 1983-84; spl. counsel Ark.Ins. Dept., 1984. Editor-in-chief Ark. Law Rev., 1972-73; guest columnist Ark. Gazette, 1984. Contbr. articles to legal jours. Co-author: Quality Assurance in Health Test, American College of Pathologists, 1986. Recipient spl. commendation Legal Services Corp., 1977, Ark. Edn. Assn., 1984. Mem. ABA (legal edn. sect., corp. sect.), Ark. Bar Assn., Omicron Delta Kappa, Beta Gamma Sigma. Methodist. Home: 10 Durance Dr Little Rock AR 72223-9106 Office: 807 W 3rd St Little Rock AR 72201-2103

HARGRAVE, JAMES LEE, editor, consultant; b. Granite City, Ill., Sept. 19, 1951; s. Donald Jean and Doris Jean Hargrave; m. Sharon Kay Chapman, Sept. 9, 1972; 1 child, Jane Elizabeth. BS, So. Ill. U., 1976; MA, So. Bapt. Theol. Sem., Louisville, 1985. Ordained min. to Bapt. Ch., 1986. Art supr. Madison (Ill.) Pub. Sch. Sys., 1976-78; advt. mgr. Dicor Photographic Co., Belleville, Ill., 1978-82; children's ministry St. Matthews Bapt. Ch., Louisville, 1982-85; children's min. First Bapt. Ch. Ferguson, St. Louis, 1985-89; state Sun. sch. assoc. Ala. Bapt. Conv., Montgomery, 1989-93; editor-in-chief Lifeway Christian Resources, Nashville, 1993—. Author: Children's Sunday School for a New Century, 1999, Teaching Children: Laying Foundations for Faith Leader Training Pack, 2000; co-author: Towards 2000: Leading Chidlren in Sunday School, 1995, Crayons, Computers, and Kids, 1996. Mem. adv. bd. Nat. Presch. Children's Conv., Nashville, 1996—; mem. steering com. Nat. Leadership Summit, Nashville, 1995-97. Mem. Soc. Am. Magicians, Internat. Brotherhood Magicians, Baptist Assn. Christian Educators. Avocations: magic, music, art, cooking, drama. Office: Lifeway Christian Resources MSN 172 One LifeWay Plz Nashville TN 37234-0002 E-mail: James.Hargrave@lifeway.com.

HARGRAVE, ROBERT WARREN, retired hair styling salon chain executive; b. Meridian, Miss., Sept. 15, 1944; s. George Herbert and Clara (Gibson) H.; m. Janeice Stodghill, Dec. 23, 1967; 1 child, Jennifer Lyn. Student, Tyler Jr. Coll., 1963-65; BS, Baylor U., 1967; postgrad., East Tex. State U., 1968. Lic. nursing home adminstr., Tex. Nursing home adminstr. ARA-Nat. Living Ctrs., Waco, Tex., 1969-71, dir. personnel and spl. programs Houston, 1971-75; exec. v.p. ARA-Geriatrics, Colo., Tex, 1975-79; founder, owner 16 hair styling salons San Antonio Enterprises, Inc., 1979—2000. Tchr. nursing home adminstrn., McLennan Community Coll., Waco, 1970, mem. steering com. to establish nursing home license program, 1970; mem. Nat. Bd. Salon Franchises, Cutco Insustries, Inc., N.Y.C., 1985-87, pres. Direct Licensees' Assn., 1991-92; adv. com. Tex. Cosmetology Commn., 1994-2000. Mem. adv. bd. cosmetology dept. South San High Sch., 1987-2000, adv. coun. for career and tech. edn. N. East Ind. Sch. Dist., 1994-2000. Mem. Am. Salon Assn., Tex. Salon Assn., San Antonio Salon Assn., Tex. Nursing Home Assn. (chpt. pres. 1970), Colo. Health Care Assn. (del. for nat. fire safety 1978), Am. Health Care Assn., Nat. Parks and Recreation Assn., Nat. Therapeutic Recreational Soc., Gideons Internat. Avocations: boating, fishing. Home and Office: 2400 Legend Dr Heath TX 75032

HARGRAVE, RUDOLPH, state supreme court chief justice; b. Shawnee, Okla., Feb. 15, 1925; s. John Hubert and Daisy (Holmes) H.; m. Madeline Hargrave, May 29, 1949; children: Cindy Lu, John Robert, Jana Sue. LLB, U. Okla., 1949. Bar: Okla. 1949. Pvt. practice, Wewoka, Okla., 1949; asst. county atty. Seminole County, 1951-55; judge Seminole County Ct., 1964-67, Seminole County Superior Ct., 1967-69; dist. judge Okla. Dist. Ct., Dist. 22, 1969-79; justice Okla. Supreme Ct., Oklahoma City, 1978—, former vice chief justice, chief justice, 1989—. Mem. Seminole County Bar Assn., Okla. Bar Assn., ABA Lodges: Lions; Masons. Democrat. Methodist. Office: Okla Supreme Ct State Capitol Bldg Room 202 Oklahoma City OK 73105*

HARGRAVE, SARAH QUESENBERRY, consulting company executive; b. Mt. Airy, N.C., Dec. 11, 1944; d. Teddie W. and Lois Knight (Slusher) Quesenberry. Student, Radford Coll., 1963-64, Va. Poly. Inst. and State U., 1964-67. Mgmt. trainee Thalhimer Bros. Dept. Store, Richmond, Va., 1967-68; Cen. Va. fashion and publicity dir. Sears Roebuck & Co., Richmond, 1968-73, nat. decorating sch. coord. Chgo., 1973-74, nat. dir. bus. and profl. women's programs, 1974-76; v.p., treas., program dir. Sears-Roebuck Found., Chgo., 1976-87, program mgr. corp. contbns. and memberships, 1981-84, dir. corp. mktg. and pub. affairs, 1984-87; v.p. personal fin. svcs. and mktg. Northern Trust Co., Chgo., 1987-89; pres. Hargrave Consulting, 1989—. Spkr., seminar leader in field. Bd. dirs. Am. Assembly Collegiate Schs. Bus., 1979-82, mem. vis. com., 1979-82, mem. fin. and audit com., 1980-82, mem. task force on doctoral supply and demand, 1980-82; mem. Com. for Equal Opportunity for Women, 1976-81; chmn., 1978-79, 80-81; mem. bus. adv. coun. Walter E. Heller Coll. Bus. Adminstrn., Roosevelt U., 1979-89; co-dir. Ill. Internat. Women's Yr. Ctr., 1975. Named Outstanding Young Women of Yr. Ill., 1976; named Women of Achievement State Street Bus. and Profl. Woman's Club, 1978 Mem. ASTD, Eddystone Condominium Assn. (v.p. 1978-86), Profl. Women's Network. Home and Office: 34 Fairlawn Ave Daly City CA 94015-3425

HARGRAVE, VICTORIA ELIZABETH, librarian; b. Ripon, Wis., Aug. 22, 1913; d. Alexander Walter and Estelle Winifred (Swanson) H. AB, Ripon Coll., 1934; library diploma, U. Wis., 1938; MA, U. Chgo., 1947; postgrad., U. Cal. at Los Angeles, 1970. Tchr. Brandon (Wis.) High Sch., 1934-37; extension librarian Ia. State Coll. Library, 1938-44; librarian Ripon Coll., 1944-46, MacMurray Coll., 1947-78. Mem. adv. council librarians U. Ill. Grad. Sch. Library Sci., 1962-64 Mem. A.L.A., AAUW. Home: 4650 54th Ave S Apt 416 Saint Petersburg FL 33711-4637

HARGRAVES, ORIN KNIGHT, lexicographer; b. Denver, Sept. 14, 1953; s. Orin K. and Barbara Magness H. BA, U. Chgo., 1977. Dir. Internat. Meditation Ctr. Author: Culture Shock! Morocco, 1995, London At Your Door, 1997, Chicago At Your Door, 1999, Mighty Fine Words and Smashing Expressions, 2002; Contbg. editor: Numerous dictionaries, 1990—. Theravada Buddhist. Home: 5130 Band Hall Hill Rd Westminster MD 21158-1406 E-mail: orinkh@carr.org.

HARGRAVES, WILLIAM FREDERICK, II, mathematics and computer science educator; b. Cin., Aug. 18, 1932; s. William Frederick and Annie Leona (Thomas) H.; m. Maurine Collins, July 5, 1957; children: William Frederick III, Jock Frederick, Charles Frederick. BS in Edn. with honors, Miami U., Oxford, Ohio, 1954, MA in Physics, 1961. Commd. 2d lt. USAF, 1954, advanced through grades to col., ret., 1982, comdr. 20th mil. airlift squadron, 1955-59, air liaison officer, 1959-61; rsch. scientist USAF, Weapons Rsch. Ctr., Kirtland AFB, N.Mex., 1961—65; aircraft comdr., instr. pilot 22 mil. airlift command USAF, Tachikawa, Japan, 1965-70, air liaison officer 1st ARVAN Divsn., 1970-71, asst. prof. air sci., AFROTC program, Miami U., 1971-74, chief flight deck devel., R&D Wright Patterson AFB, 1978, dep. divsn. chief, US Pentagon Washington, 1978-82, ret., 1982; asst. prof., asst. dean arts and scis. Cen. State U., Wilberforce, Ohio, 1982—. Asst. track and field coach Cen. State U., 1993— Founder Pilgrim Bapt. Chr. Men's Choir, Hamilton, Ohio, 1980, Grant Chapel Ave. Ch., Albuquerque, 1962; trustee Bethel AME Ch., 2002—. Decorated Dist. Flying Cross 72, Air medal, Air Force commendation medal with 2 oak leaf clusters, Vietnam Service medal with 5 bronze stars, Nat. Def. Svc. medal; named to Covington (Ky.) Black Hall of Fame, 1992; Rhodes scholar candidate, Ky., 1950. Mem. Phi Beta Kappa, Omicron Delta Kappa, Kappa Delta Pi, Pi Mu Epsilon, Sigma Pi Sigma. Methodist. Home: 123 W Walnut St Oxford OH 45056-1721 Office: Cen State U 1400 Brush Row Rd Wilberforce OH 45384 E-mail: whargraves@csu.ces.edu.

HARGREAVES, DAVID WILLIAM, communications company executive; b. Akron, Ohio, May 4, 1943; s. William B. and Helen Grace (Slusser) H.; m. Sandra Jean Tessier, Sept. 4, 1965; children: Kristen Elizabeth, Cinda Anne, Gregory David. BSEE, U. Maine, Orono, 1965; MBA, U. Rochester, 1967. Sales engr. Mobile Communications div. Gen. Electric, Lynchburg, Va., 1970-74, mgr. systems projects, 1974-75, mgr. systems bids/proposals, 1975-78; mgr. internat. mktg. Gen. Electric Powerline Carrier Bus., Lynchburg, 1978-80; gen. mgr. Gen. Electric Microwave Link Operation, Owensboro, Ky., 1980-84; mng. dir. Alpha Telecom div. Alpha Industries, Methuen, Mass., 1984-86; pres. Dynatech Tactical Comms. Inc. (formerly Controlonics Corp.), Nashua, N.H., 1986-97; pres., CEO DTC Comms. Inc., Nashua, 1997—. Condr. seminars in field. Contbr. articles to profl. jours. Chmn. bd. Gen. Electric United Way Pacesetter campaign, Lynchburg, 1978; advisor Jr. Achievement project bus., Owensboro, 1982, 83. Served to capt. U.S. Army, 1968-70, Vietnam. Decorated Bronze Star, D.S.C., 1970. Mem.: Am. Mktg. Pres.'s Assn., Massibesic Yacht Club, Tau Beta Pi, Eta Kappa Nu. Republican. Avocations: sailing, skiing, amateur radio. Home: 191 Buttrick Rd Hampstead NH 03841-2183 Office: DTC Comm Inc 486 Amherst St Nashua NH 03063

HARGREAVES, GEORGE HENRY, civil and agricultural engineer, researcher; b. Chico, Calif., Apr. 2, 1916; s. Carey and Luella May (Raymond) H.; m. Elizabeth Ann Gardner, Aug. 9, 1941 (dec. Dec. 1948); 1 child, Margaret Ann Hargreaves Stolpmann; m. Sara Etna Romero, Jan 6, 1951; children: Mark Romero, Sonia Maria Hargreaves Hart, George Leo. BS in Soils, U. Calif., Berkeley, 1939; BSCE, U. Wyo., 1943. Civil engr. U.S. Bur. Reclamation, Sacramento, 1946-48; reclamation engr. U.S. Army C.E., Greece, 1948-49; engr. AID, Greece, Peru, Haiti, Philippines, Brazil and Colombia, 1950-68; chief civil engr. engring. br. Natural Resources divsn. Inter-Am. Geodetic Survey, Ft. Clayton, 1968-70; rsch. engr. in irrigation Utah State. U., Logan, 1970-86; rsch. Internat. Irrigation Ctr., 1980-86, rsch. prof. emeritus, 1986—. Author: World Water for Agriculture, 1977; co-author: Irrigation Fundamentals, 1998, Fundamentos Del Riego, 2000; contbr. numerous articles to profl. jours. Lt. (j.g.) USNR, 1943-46, PTO. Recipient Royce J. Tipton award, 1997. Mem.: Internat. Commn. Irrigation and Drainage (chmn. U.S. Com. on crops and water use 1992—96, drainage and flood control 1999—2003, chmn. U.S. com. on history of irrigation), Am. Soc. Agrl. Engrs. (chmn. Rocky Mountain sect. 1974). Achievements include development of methodology used by the International Water Management Institute in the IWMI World Water and Climate Atlas, providing worldwide climate data and an index of rainfall adequacy for agricultural production. Home: 1660 E 1220 N Logan UT 84341-3040 Office: Utah State U Internat Irrigation Ctr Dept Biol Irrigation Engring Logan UT 84322-4150

HARGROVE, ERWIN CHARLES, JR., political science educator; b. St. Joseph, Mo., Oct. 11, 1930; s. Erwin Charles and Gladys Lenore (France) H.; m. Lynne Douglas, Apr. 10, 1961 (div. Jan., 1991); children: John, Amy, Sarah; m. Julia Mosher, Sept. 21, 1991. BA, Yale U., 1953, PhD, 1963. From asst. prof. to prof. polit. sci. Brown U., Providence, 1960—76, prof., dept. chair polit. sci., 1973—75; sr. fellow Urban Inst., Washington, 1976—85; prof. polit. sci., dir. Inst. for Pub. Policy Studies Vanderbilt U., Nashville, 1976-85, chmn. dept. polit. sci., 1992-96, prof. polit. sci. emeritus, 2000—. Author: Presidential Leadership, Personality and Political Style, 1966, Professional Roles in Society and Government: The English Case, 1972, The Power of the Modern Presidency, 1974, The Missing Link: The Study of Implementation of Social Policy, 1975, Jimmy Carter as President, Leadership and the Politics of the Public Good, 1988 (Richard E. Neustadt award, 1988), Prisoners of Myth: Leadership of the Tennessee Valley Authority, 1933-1990, 1994, The President as Leader: Appealing to the Better Angels of Our Nature, 1998; co-author (with Michael Nelson): Presidents, Politics and Policy, 1984; co-editor (with Paul Conkin): TVA, Fifty Years of Grass Roots Bureaucracy, 1983; co-editor: (with Samuel Morley) The President and the Council of Economic Advisers: Interviews with CEA Chairmen, 1984; co-editor: (with Jameson Doig) Leadership and Innovation: A Biographical Perspective on Entrepreneurs in Government, 1987; co-editor: (with John Glidewell) Impossible Jobs in Public Management, 1990 editor spl. edit. Politics and Policy, 2002. With U.S. Army, 1954-56. Democrat Episcopalian. Home: 662 Timber Ln Nashville TN 37215-1120 E-mail Erwin.C.Hargrove@Vanderbilt.edu.

HARGROVE, JAMES WARD, financial consultant; b. Shreveport, La., Oct 31, 1922; s. Reginald H. and Hallie (Ward) H.; m. Marion Elizabeth Smith, Aug 25, 1942; children: James W., Florence, Thomas M., William H. Grad., Sewanee Mil. Acad., 1939; BA, Rice U., 1943. Sec., treas. Caddo Abstract Co., 1946-47 with Tex. Eastern Transmission Corp., 1947-69, sr. v.p., 1967-69; asst postmaster gen. finance and adminstrn. U.S. Postal Service, Washington 1969-71, sr. asst. postmaster gen. support, 1971-72; fin. cons. Houston 1972-76; U.S. ambassador, 1976-77; chmn. Vaughan, Nelson & Hargrove, Inc (investment counselors), 1977— 83. Gov.-adviser Rice U.; chmn. Entrix Inc 1989—. Mem. Phi Beta Kappa. Home: 60 Tiel Way Houston TX 77019-151 E-mail: james@hargrove.org.

HARGROVE, JOHN RUSSELL, lawyer; b. Chgo., Jan. 20, 1947; s. John Francis and Dolly (Arzich) H.; m. Mary Cheryl Fuller, Feb. 12, 1972; children John Ashby, James Fuller. BS, Butler U., 1969; JD magna cum laude, Ind. U. 1972. Bar: Ind. 1972, Fla. 1974, U.S. Tax Ct. 1975, U.S. Supreme Ct. 1976 Law clk. to Hon Roy L. Stephenson U.S. Ct. Appeals Ind., 1971-72, U.S. Ct Appeals (8th cir.), 1972-74; mng. dir. and shareholder Heinrich, Gordon

Hargrove, Weihe & James, P.A., Ft. Lauderdale, Fla., 1985-91. Lead articles and book rev. editor Ind. Law Rev., 1971-72. Bd. visitors Ind. U. Sch. Law, 1995—; bd. dirs. EV Ready Broward, 1996-98; nat. co-chair Franciscan Games, 1996. Schofield scholar. Recipient Faculty award Ind. U. Sch. of Law, 1972. Fellow Fla. Acad. Probate and Trust Litigation; mem. ABA, Fed. Bar Assn. (Broward County Fla. chpt., exec. com. 1979-80, v.p. 1980-81, pres. 1981-82), Fla. Bar Assn., Ind. Bar Assn. (mem. bd. vis. Sch. of Law 1995—). Roman Catholic. Office: 500 E Broward Blvd Ste 1000 Fort Lauderdale FL 33394-3087

HARGROVE, LINDA, professional basketball coach; m. Ed Hargrove; children: Brian, Tara. BS magna cum laude, Southwestern Coll., 1975; MEd, Wichita State U., 1985. Head coach Cowley County C.C. Tigers, 1972-89, Wichita State U. Shockers, 1989-98; head coach, dir. player pers. Colo. Xplosion, Am. Basketball League, Denver, 1998—; head coach Portland Fire, WNBA, 1999—. Asst. coach 1990 U.S. Sr. Nat. Women's Team, 1989, 1992 U.S. Olympic Team; cons. WNBA Orlando Miracle; mem. USA Basketball Sr. Nat. Team Com. Inductee Southwestern Coll. Athletic Hall of Fame, 1992. Mem. Women's Basketball Coaches Assn. (bd. dirs., Midwest divsn. I rep.). Office: Portland Fire One Center Ct Ste 150 Portland OR 97227

HARGROVE, MIKE (DUDLEY MICHAEL HARGROVE), former professional baseball team manager; b. Perryton, Tex., Oct. 26, 1949; m. Sharon Rupprecht, Dec. 12, 1970; children: Kimberly Denise, Melissa Kathryn, Pamela Christine, Andrew Michael, Cynthia Michelle. BS in Phys. Edn. and Social Scis., Northwestern Okla. State U. Baseball player Tex. Rangers, 1974-78, San Diego Padres, 1979, Cleve. Indians, 1979-85, coach minor league team, 1986, mgr. minor league team, 1987-89, coach, 1990-91, mgr., 1991-99; mgr. Am. League championship team, 1995, 97; mgr., coach Balt. Orioles, 1999—2003. Named Am. League Rookie of Yr. Baseball Writers' Assn. Am., 1974, Am. League Rookie Player of Yr. Sporting News, 1974; named to All-Star team, 1975, Am. League Mgr. of Yr. Sporting News, 1995.

HARGROVE, WADE HAMPTON, lawyer; b. Clinton, N.C., Mar. 6, 1940; s. Wade Hampton and Susan (Baker) H.; m. Sandra Dunaway, June 7, 1969; children: Wade Hampton III, Andrew D. AB with honors, U. N.C., 1962, JD, 1965. Bar: N.C. 1965, D.C. 1967. Ptnr. Brooks, Pierce, McLendon, Humphrey, Leonard, Raleigh, NC, 1995—; gen. counsel, exec. dir. N.C. Assn. Broadcasters, 1970—, N.C. CATV Assn., 1980—; chmn. bd. dirs. 1st Union Nat. Bank, Raleigh, 1989-93. Mem. N.C. Gov.'s Coun. on State Policy, 1974—79; chmn. N.C. News Media Adminstrn. Justice Coun., 1976; commr. N.C. Milk Commn., 1976—78, chmn., 1988—2000; commr. N.C. Agy. Pub. Telecom. ; spl. advisor to U.S. at Internat. Conf. on Direct Satellite Broadcasts, Geneva, 1983; mem legis. study Commn. on Open Govt., 1993; chair N.C. Ctr. Pub. Policy Rsch., 1994—; bd. visitors U. N.C., 1991—, U. N.C. Sch. Journalism, 1993—. Named to N.C. Assn. Broadcasters Hall of Fame, 1998; recipient Disting. Svc., N.C. Assn. Broadcasters, 1973, N.C. CATV Assn., 1985. Mem. ABA, N.C. State Bar, D.C. Bar, Fed. Comms. Bar Assn., U. N.C. Law Alumni Assn. (pres. 1991-94), Capital City Club (bd. govs. 1983-91), Figure Eight Yacht Club, Cardinal Club (bd. govs. 1992—), Order of the Long Leaf Pine. Presbyterian. Home: 1005 Marlowe Rd Raleigh NC 27609-6971 Office: Brooks Pierce McLendon Humphrey Leonard 1600 First Union Bank Capitol Ctr Raleigh NC 27601-1309

HARGROVE, WALTER CLARK, III, cardiothoracic surgeon; b. Greenville, NC, May 24, 1947; s. Walter Clark, Jr. and Alice Leigh (Blow) H.; m. Claudia Liane Ludwig, Aug. 20, 1991; children: Nelson, Nicholas, Saskia. BS, U. N.C., 1969; MD, Bowman Gray Sch. Medicine, 1973. Resident in surgery Hosp. U. Pa., Phila., 1974-75, fellow in vascular surgery, 1981, resident in thoracic surgery, 1982-83; from asst. prof. to assoc. prof. surgery U. Pa., Phila., 1984-96, clin. prof. surgery, 1998—; prof. cardiothoracic surgery Allegheny U. Health Scis., Phila., 1996-98. Maj. U.S. Army, 1979-81. Fellow ACS; mem. Am. Assn. Thoracic Surgery, Soc. Thoracic Surgery. Episcopalian. Avocation: golf. Office: Phila Heart Inst Ste 2 D 39th and Market St Philadelphia PA 19104 Business E-Mail: clark.hargrove@mail.med.upenn.edu.

HARHUT, CHET, judge; BS in Acctg. and Bus., Bethell Coll.; JD, U. Pitts., 1972; M of Judicial Studies, U. Nev., 1995. Judge Lackawanna County Ct., 1987-96, judge family ct., 1996-2001, pres. judge, 2000—. Office: Lacka County Ct House 200 N Washington Ave Scranton PA 18503-1524

HARI, KENNETH STEPHEN, painter, sculptor, writer; b. Perth Amboy, N.J., Mar. 31, 1947; s. Stephen John and Jeannette Anna (Matuszewsky) H. Diploma, Newark Sch. Fine and Indsl. Arts, 1966; BFA, Md. Inst. Art, 1968, Yale U., 1970; postgrad., NYU, 1988. Cons. various cos. One man exhbns. include ctrl. Ala., 1996, Beijing, 1996; group exhbns. include Md. State Mus., 1967, Union Coll., Schenectady, 1969, Monmouth (N.J.) Coll., 1970, Newark Mus., 1971, Trenton State Coll., 1972, one-man exhbns. include C.C. Price Gallery, N.Y.C., H.S. Graphics, Ltd., Keasbey, N.J.; represented in permanent collections of over 390 mus. throughout world, including Vatican, Lincoln Center Gallery for Performing Arts, N.Y.C., Va. Poly. Inst., Blacksburg, N.J. State Mus., Trenton, Grand Ole Opry House, Nashville, Xiaoyi Liu collection, Mus. Kenneth Hari, Beijing, China, established 1991, other pub. and pvt. collections; Important works include portraits of, W.H. Auden, N.Y.C., 1969, M. Moore, N.Y.C., 1969, Pablo Casals, Marlboro, Vt., 1970, Andres Segovia, N.Y.C., 1972, James Michener, Piperville, Pa., 1973, Marcel Marceau, N.Y.C., 1973, Donald Delue, N.Y.C., 1973, Dr. Allan Callow, Boston, 1973, Kurt Vonnegut, Jr., 1973, Buckminster Fuller, 1973, Lord Hailsham, London, 1978, Dr. Linus Pauling for Pauling Inst., Menlo Park, Calif., 1979, Paul Robeson for Paul Robeson Center, Rutgers U., Newark, 1979 (Hay award recipients.); Zhao Peng Fei, Beijing, Philip Johnson, N.Y.C., Paul Roache, Spain, Chen Chi, N.Y.C., Liu Zongyu, Beijing, Zhongguo Shengj, Living Treasure of China, 1999, Hiroko Seta, Tokyo, Japan, 1999, Rosemary Clooney, Beverly Hills, Calif., 1999, Paul Robeson exhbn. Rutgers U., 2003; exhibited at Johnson & Johnson, New Brunswick Travel Exhibition, The Angel of Revelation Mural, N.J., 1990; Original lithographs pub. Prophet, 1971, Lovers of Our Time, 1971, Vermont, 1972, Folk Singer, Marcel Marceau, 1973, Abraham, 1973, Ernest Hemingway, 1978, Homage to Virginia, 1980, Tropical Ladies, 1981, The Pearl, 1999. Bd. dirs. N.J. Art Festival, 1973— . Office: Eastman & John Watson Art Galleries Care John Eastman PO Box 243 Keasbey NJ 08832-0243 *Art is the soul of man, and without it he is lost.*

HARIANAWALA, ABIZER I. pharmacologist, researcher; b. Morvi, India, Feb. 12, 1967; arrived in U.S., 1992; s. Ismail A. and Mefuza I. Harianawala; m. Nisreen Abizer Lokhandwala, Dec. 27, 1994; 1 child, Arif. BPharm, L.M. Coll. Pharmacy, Ahmedabad, Gujarat, India, 1989, MPharm, 1991; PhD in Pharmaceutics, U. Conn., 1998. Rsch. investigator II Bristol Myers-Squibb, New Brunswick, NJ, 1998—2001; sr. scientist II Geltex a divsn. of Genzyme, Waltham, Mass., 2001—. Contbr. articles to profl. jours. Mem.: Am. Assn. Pharm. Scientists (awards com. 2000—01, grad. symposium award 1998, outstanding poster award 1994). Achievements include invention of low-dose entecavir formulation and use. Avocations: reading, cricket, travel, cooking. Office: GelTex 153 Second Ave Waltham MA 02451

HARIJAN, RAM, technology transfer researcher; b. Keecheri, Kerala, India, June 3, 1938; s. Narayanan and Devaki (Amma) Nambiar; m. Lakshmi VP, Aug. 19, 1977; 1 child, Pooja Devi. BA with honors, Madras U., India; MA with award, Southampton U., Eng.; PhD, Reading U., Eng. Lectr. Kerala (India) U.; mining officer Singareni Collieries, India; sch. tchr. Barnstaple Grammar Sch., Eng.; lectr. Bosworth Coll., Eng.; tutor cons. Open U., Eng.; researcher Centre for Studies in Tech. Transfer, Eng. Involved in rsch. which influenced the computerisation policies of Indian Govt., 1985-89; vis. prof. U. Madras, 1982, Calicut U., 1985. Chmn. North Devon Dist. Labour Party, 1972-77, North Devon Assn. Racial Equality, 1978-80; vol. social worker Helping the Disabled and Disadvantaged. Avocations: bridge, chess. Home: 30 Norfolk Rd Desford Leicester LE9 9HR England E-mail: DrRamOfIndia@msn.com.

HARIK, VASYL MICHAEL, research scientist; b. Chernivtsi, Ukraine, USSR, Oct. 5, 1964; came to US, 1988; s. Michael Emmanuel and Maria H.; m. Pauline, Sept. 7, 1993. Diploma, Moscow State U., 1990; MS, U. Del., 1993, PhD, 1997. Tchg. fellow U. Del., Newark, 1992-93, I-Harima rsch. asst., 1993-94, project coord., 1994-96, ICI rsch. asst., 1997; rsch. fellow Johns Hopkins U., Balt., 1997-98; low cycle fatigue program coord. U.S. Army Rsch. Lab., Aberdeen, Md., 1998-99, Army Rsch. Lab. rsch. fellow, 1998—. Tchg. fsst. Author: Hydrodynamics, 1989. Tchr. for children with ADD Remedial Math Project I.H.M. Sch., Wilmington, Del., 1991. Rsch. fellow NASA, 1997-98, Johns Hopkins U. fellow, 1997; recipient J. F. Lincoln Arc Welding Found. award for design project, 1995. Mem. Am. Acad. Mechanics, ASME, Am. Soc. Composites, Am. Soc. Materials, Am. Soc. Engring. Edn. (nat. fellow 1998, 99), Soc. Indsl. and Applied Math., Golden Key. Avocations: graphic design, history and archives, writing. Office: U Del ARL Composites Group Newark DE 19716

HARING, ELLEN STONE (MRS. E. S. HARING), philosophy educator; b. L.A., 1921; d. Earl E. and Eleanor (Pritchard) Stone; m. Philip S. Haring, Dec. 1942 (div. June 1951). BA, Bryn Mawr Coll., 1942; MA, Radcliffe Coll., 1943, PhD (AAUW fellow), 1959. Adminstrv. worker ARC, Boston, 1943; mem. faculty Wheaton Coll., Norton, Mass., 1944-45, Wellesley Coll., 1945-72, assoc. prof., 1958-64, prof. philosophy, 1964-72, U. Fla., Gainesville, 1972-93, prof. emerita, 1993—, chmn. dept., 1972-80. Mem. Am. Philos. Assn., Metaphys. Soc. Am.

HARING, EUGENE MILLER, lawyer; b. Washington, May 16, 1927; s. Horace E. and Edith (Miller) H.; m. Janet K. Marshall, Apr. 10, 1971. AB summa cum laude, Princeton U., 1949, A.M. (Woodrow Wilson fellow), 1951; LL.B., Harvard U., 1955. Bar: N.J. 1955, N.Y. 1983, U.S. Dist. Ct. N.J. 1955, U.S. Dist. Ct. (so. and ea. dists.) N.Y. 1992, U.S. Ct. Appeals (3d cir.) 1962, U.S. Supreme Ct. 1969. Asst. in instrn. Princeton U., 1950-52; assoc. McCarter & English, Newark, 1955-61, ptnr., 1961-97, chmn. exec. com., 1982-97, of counsel, 1997—. Cert. mediator U.S. Dist. Ct., 1994—; mediator CPR Inst. for Dispute Resolution, N.J. Panel, 1994—; mem. roster of mediators Judiciary of State of N.J.; mem. civil justice reform act adv. com. U.S. Dist. Ct. N.J., 1997-2000. Contbr. articles to profl. jours. Chmn. Princeton Twp. Zoning Bd. Adjustment, 1979-80, mem. bd., 1975-79; vestryman Trinity Episc. Ch., Princeton, 1975-79, 97-2000, warden, 1980-84; mem. com. on constn. and canons Episc. Diocese of N.J., 1980-87, chancellor, 1983-94, 99—, hon. life canon, 2001—; trustee Gen. Theol. Sem., N.Y., 1987-90; mem. vis. com. Rutgers U. Law Sch., 1994-2000; trustee N.J. Jersey Shore Found., 1988-92. Served with USNR, 1945-46. Fellow Am. Bar Found. (life), Lawyers Adv. Com. (U.S. Ct. Appeals 3d cir. 1990-93, U.S. Dist. Ct. N.J. 1997—); mem. ABA, N.J. State Bar Assn. (emeritus), N.J. State Bar Found. (trustee 1986-87, v.p. 1987-88, chmn. 1988-90), Essex County Bar Assn. (Spl. Merit award 1998), Mercer County Bar Assn., Am. Law Inst. (life), Harvard Law Sch. Assn. N.J. (pres. 1971-72, nat. v.p. 1972-73), Hist. Soc. U.S. Dist. Ct. for Dist. N.J. (trustee 1987-90, 97—), Hist. Soc. 3d Cir. Ct. Appeals (bd., dirs. 1993-2000), Nassau Club, Princeton, Springdale Golf Club, Princeton, Monmouth Hunt Club, Phi Beta Kappa. Avocation: golf. Home: 75 Rosedale Ln Princeton NJ 08540-2417 Office: McCarter & English Gateway 4 100 Mulberry St Newark NJ 07102-4004 E-mail: eharing@mccarter.com.

HARING, HOWARD JACK, newsletter editor; b. Boyertown, Pa., Aug. 7, 1924; s. Howard and Beulah (Rose) H.; m. Rosalind Kenyon Hoyle, Dec. 10, 1949; children: Christopher, Jeffrey, Douglas, Andrea, Eric. AB, Muhlenberg Coll., 1948; MJ, Columbia U., 1949. Reporter Providence Jour.-Bull., 1949; editor Boyertown (Pa.) Times, 1950; reporter Allentown (Pa.) Morning Call, 1951-53; sports columnist, TV mag. editor Washington Star, 1954-58; assoc. editor Saturday Evening Post, Phila., 1958-62; copy chief Ladies Home Jour., N.Y.C., 1963-69; exec. editor Boy's Life mag., North Brunswick, N.J., 1970-71; editor Exploring mag., 1972-74; sr. editor Guideposts mag., N.Y.C., 1975-81, mng. editor, 1982-88, contbg. editor, 1989-95; editor newsletter South County (R.I.) Ctr. for Arts, 1991-99, Richmond (R.I.) Sr. Citizens, 1995—. Instr. editing newspapers and periodicals Am. U., Washington, 1955-58; mem. Am. Soc. Mag. Editors, 1972-90. Editor numerous books for Curtis Pub. Co., Scribner's and Reader's Digest Books; revised and edited: Pete Martin's Jerry Giesler, 1959. Vice-chmn. Indsl. Commn. West Windsor Twp., N.J., 1970-72, chmn., 1973-74. With AUS, 1942-46. Decorated Purple Heart. Home and Office: 87 Beaver River Rd West Kingston RI 02892-1135

HARING, ROBERT WESTING, newspaper editor; b. Salem, Mo., Nov. 13, 1932; s. Arthur S. and Martha I. (Westing) H.; m. Jo M. Houser, June 1, 1957 (dec. Nov. 1991); children: Robert A., Joel B., Jon G.; m. Carolyn Scudder, May 20, 1995. AA, Kansas City (Mo.) Jr. Coll., 1951; BJ, BA in History, U. Mo., 1954. Reporter So. Illinoisan, Carbondale, Ill., 1954-55, city editor, 1957-59; writer AP, Little Rock, 1959-61, corr. Tulsa, 1961-64, asst. bur. chief Columbus, Ohio, 1964-67, bur. chief Newark, 1967-71, exec. N.Y.C., 1971-75; Sunday editor Tulsa World, 1975-81, exec. editor, 1981-95; ret., 1998. Chmn. Goodwill Industries, Tulsa, 1990-94; bd. dirs. River Parks Authority, Tulsa, 1985-93; pres. Tulsa Zoofriends, 1994-96; chmn. Tulsa Mentoring Coun., Tulsa Lit. Coalition, 1996-98; initiated price earnings ratio in newspaper stock tables, 1973. With U.S. Army, 1955-57. Avocations: running, tennis, bicycling. Home: 1620 S Detroit Ave Tulsa OK 74120-6214 E-mail: harings@msn.com.

HARINGTON, CHARLES RICHARD, vertebrate paleontologist; b. Calgary, Alta., Can., May 22, 1933; s. Charles Frederic and Florence Katherine (Shillington) H.; m. Gail Doreen Rice, Sept. 15, 1994. BA, U. Alta., 1954, BSc, 1957, PhD, 1977; MSc, McGill U., 1961. Wildlife biologist Can. Wildlife Svc., Ottawa, Ont., 1960-65; vertebrate paleontologist Can. Mus. Nature, Ottawa, 1965—98; coord. climate change in Can. program Nat. Mus. Natural Scis., Ottawa, 1977—92; curator quaternary zoology emeritus, rsch. assoc. Can. Mus. Nature, Ottawa, 1998—. Chmn. Can. Com. on Climatic Fluctuations and Man, Ottawa, 1985-90. Author: Quaternary Vertebrate Faunas of Canada and Alaska, 1978; editor: Climatic Change in Canada, 5 vols., 1980-85, Canada's Missing Dimension: Science and History in the Canadian Arctic Islands, 1990, The Year Without a Summer?: World Climate in 1816, 1992; contbr. articles to profl. jours., popular publs. and revs. Named Officer, Order of Can., 2001; recipient Can. Assn. Geographers prize, 1957, Meritorious Svc. award, Yukon Govt., 1998, Lifetime Achievement Heritage award, Yukon Hist. and Mus. Assn., 2002, The Queen's Golden Jubilee medal, 2002. Fellow Royal Geog. Soc. (Eng.), Royal Can. Geog. Soc. (Massey medal 1987), Arctic Inst. N.Am. Avocations: travel, camping, reading, canoeing, bicycling. Office: Paleobiology Can Mus of Nature Ottawa ON Canada K1P 6P4 E-mail: dharington@mus-nature.ca.

HARIRI, GISUE, architect, educator; b. Abadan, Iran, May 16, 1956; came to U.S., 1974; d. Karim Hariri and Behjat (Isphahani) Saboonchi. BArch, Cornell U., 1980. Apprentice Jennings and Stout, San Francisco, 1980-82; Paolo Soleri, Arcosanti, Ariz., 1982-83; apprentice Paul Segal Assocs. Architects, N.Y.C., 1983-85; ptnr. Hariri & Hariri, N.Y.C., 1986—. Lighting and furniture designer, 1993—; participant in Urban Housing Festival, The Hague, The Netherlands, 1991; lectr. in field. Work exhibited in Mus. Modern Art, 1999, Storefront for Art and Architecture, N.Y.C., 1988, Parson Sch. Design, N.Y.C., 1988, Princeton (N.J.) U., 1988, Archtl. League N.Y., 1990, Kent (Ohio) State U., 1991, Richard Anderson Gallery, N.Y.C., 1993, Cornell U., Ithaca, N.Y., 1993, Contemporary Arts Ctr., Cin., 1993, others, also in various profl. publs.; Monograph: Hariri & Hariri Work in Progress, 1996, Kliczkowski Casas Internat., 1997. Recipient Young Architects Forum award Archtl. League N.Y., 1990. Mem. Internat. Interior Design Assn. Media Stars, 1998. Office: Hariri & Hariri 18 E 12th St New York NY 10003-4458

HARIRI, V. M. arbitrator, mediator, lawyer, educator; BS, Wayne State U.; JD, Detroit Coll. Law; LLM, London Sch. Econs. and Polit.Sci.; diploma arbitration, Reading (Eng.) U. Pvt. practice internat. and U.S. bus. law, Detroit. Drafting com. Republic of Kazakhstan Code on Arbitration Procedure, Free Econ. Zone Legislation, Republic of Belarus; instr. internat. comml. arbitration Chartered Inst. Arbitrators, Am. Arbitration Assn. Fellow Chartered Inst. Arbitrators (exec. com. N.Am. br., founding com. and expert advisor); mem. ABA, Internat. Bar Assn., Am. Soc. Internat. Law, Am. Arbitration Assn., London Ct. Internat. Arbitration, World Jurist Assn., Mich. Trial Lawyers Assn. Office: 143 Cadycentre Ste 352 Northville MI 48167-1244

HARISDANGKUL, VALEE, physician; b. Bangkok, June 20, 1941; came to U.S., 1976; s. Sin Fong Wong and Samandsri Harisdangkul. MD, Siriraj Hosp., Bangkok, 1966; PhD, Columbia U., 1971. Diplomate Am. Bd. Internal Medicine and Rheumatology. Fellow in rheumatology Hosp. for Spl. Surgery, N.Y.C., 1971-73; asst. prof. Mahidol U., Bangkok, 1973-75, assoc. prof., 1975-76; fellow in rheumatology Michael Reese Med. Ctr., Chgo., 1976-77; resident in internal medicine U. Miss. Med. Ct., Jackson, 1977-79, asst. prof., 1979-85, assoc. prof., 1985-94, prof., 1994—, dir. rheumatology lab., 1982-90, chief. div. rheumatology, 1983-92, dir. fellowship tng. program divsn. rheumatology, 1993—. Contbr. articles to profl. jours. Rockefeller Found. scholar, 1967-71; recipient Gold medal Siriraj Med. Sch., 1966, nominated Best Doctor in U.S.A.,2002. Fellow ACP, Am. Coll. Rheumatology; mem. Thai Med. Assn., Thai Rheumatology Assn. Office: Univ of Miss Med Ctr 2500 N State St Jackson MS 39216-4500 E-mail: harisdangk@aol.com.

HARITOS, GEORGE KONSTANTINOS, engineer, educator, military officer; b. Athens, Greece, Nov. 29, 1947; came to the U.S., 1964; naturalized, 1970; s. Konstantinos G. and Maria K. (Yiakoumakis) H.; m. Mary Jeannette Martell, June 20, 1971; children: Konstantinos, Marika. BS in Engring., U. Ill., Chgo., 1969, MS in Mechanics and Materials, 1970; PhD in Structural Mechanics, Northwestern U., 1978. Commd. 2d lt. USAF, 1971, advanced through grades to col., 1993; ret., 2001; aero. structures engr. aero. systems divsn. USAF, Dayton, Ohio, 1971-75; asst. prof. engring. mechanics USAF Acad., Colorado Springs, 1978-82; assoc. prof. engring. mechanics Air Force Inst. Tech., Dayton, 1982-85; program mgr. mechanics of materials Air Force Office Scientific Rsch., Washington, 1986-89, dir. aerospace scis., 1989-90, assoc. dir., 1990-91, dep. dir. and comdr., 1993-95; chief flight vehicles divsn. Hdqrs. Air Force Systems Command, Washington, 1991-92; chief air vehicles br. Hdqrs. Air Force Materiel Command, Dayton, 1992-93; assoc. dean Grad. Sch. Engring. Air Force Inst. Tech., Dayton, Ohio, 1995-98, vice comdt., 1998-99, comdt., 1999—2001, prof. engring. mechanics, 2001—03; dean, prof. Coll. Engring. U. Akron, 2003—. Mem. Def. Com. on Rsch., Washington, 1993-95, OSR Rsch. Coun., Washington, 1993-95. Editor: Damage Mechanics in Composites, 1987, Smart Structures and Materials, 1991; assoc. editor: Internat. Jour. Damage Mechanics, 1990—; contbr. articles to profl. jours. Decorated Legion of Merit, Meritorious Svc. medal with five oak leaf clusters, Air Force Commendation medal with oak leaf cluster, nat. def. svc. medal with svc. star; Walter P. Murphy fellow Northwestern U., 1975. Fellow AIAA (assoc.); mem. Am. Acad. Mechanics, Am. Soc. for Engring. Edn., ASME (materials and structures com. 1986—). Achievements include research in fracture mechanics; fatigue at elevated temperature; engineering mechanics and materials; initiated international research thrusts in mesomechanics for connecting the behavior of materials to their microstructural makeup, and in biomimetics for synthesizing multifunctional materials that imitate biological materials. Office: U Akron Auburn Sci & Engr Center 201 Akron OH 44325-3901

HARITOS, MARY J. language educator, interpreter; b. Chgo., May 9, 1948; d. Victor and Eileen Martell; m. George K. Haritos, June 20, 1971; children: Konstantinos G, Marika G. BA with honors, U. Ill., Chgo., 1970; MA, U. Ill., 1973; PhD, Northwestern U., 1985. Tchr. Bennet Hill Acad., Colorado Springs, Colo., 1978-79; adj. prof. Wright State U., Dayton, Ohio, 1984-85, Am. U., Washington, Va., 1986-88, George Mason U., Fairfax, Va., 1987-92; tenured lectr. Wright State U., Dayton, Ohio, 1992—. Author: Las Novelas de Pedro Jorge Vera, 1989. Mem. ch. coun. The Annunciation Greek Orthodox Ch., Dayton, 1999—. Mem.: Wright-Patterson AFB Officers Wives' Club (advisor 1999—2002, bd. govs. 1999—2002). Avocations: musician (piano), choir, rollerblading, gourmet cooking. Office: Wright State U 3460 Colonel Glenn Way Dayton OH 45435-0001 E-mail: maryharitos@wright.edu.

HARK, WILLIAM HENRY, medical executive, retired military officer; b. Charleston, W.Va., Nov. 1, 1932; s. Zundel and Esther Sylvia (Henry) H.; m. Claudette Berkley Watson, Apr. 14, 1961; 1 child, William Tucker. AB, W.Va. U., 1954, BS, 1955; MD, Med. Coll. Va., 1957; MPH, Harvard U., 1963. Diplomate Am. Bd. Preventive Medicine. Intern Walter Reed Gen. Hosp., Washington, 1957-58; resident in aerospace medicine U.S. Army, 1962-65, advanced through grades to col., physician, aviation med. cons., 1957-76, ret., 1976; mgr. med. specialties divsn. FAA, Washington, 1980-92, dep. fed. air surgeon, 1992-99. Adv. group for aerospace R&D, NATO, Brussels, 1969-71; mem. joint com. on aviation pathology Dept. of Def., Washington, 1969-71. Decorated Legion of Merit, Air medal, Bronze Star, Vietnam Campaign medal U.S. Army, 1968. Fellow Am. Coll. Preventive Medicine, Aerospace Med. Assn.; mem. Assn. Mil. Surgeons U.S. Avocations: photography, computers. Home: 4317 Southwood Dr Alexandria VA 22309-2822

HARKAVY, IRA BAER, Supreme Court justice; b. Bklyn., Apr. 13, 1931; s. Morris Abraham and Esther (Brown) Harkavy; m. Roberta Susan Firsty, Aug. 11, 1957; children: Steven Jeffrey, Daniel Joseph, Elliot Glenn. AB, Bklyn. Coll., 1951; JD, Columbia U., 1954. Bar: N.Y. 1954, U.S. Dist. Ct. (ea. and so. dists.) N.Y. 1957, U.S. Supreme Ct. 1960. From assoc. to ptnr. Harkavy, Tell & Mendelson, N.Y.C., 1954-67; ptnr. Harkavy & Tell, N.Y.C., 1967-70; sr. ptnr. Delson & Gordon, N.Y.C., 1970-81; judge Civil Ct. N.Y.C., Kings County, 1982-92; acting justice Supreme Ct., Kings County, 1992-2000, justice, 2000—. Chmn. Planning Bd. 14, Bklyn., 1967—81; mem. Bklyn. Bicentennial Com., 1975—77, Bklyn. Borough Bd., 1976—81, Bklyn. Civic Coun., 1975—82; chmn. Anti-Defamation League of B'Nai B'Rith, Bklyn., 1966—70; mem. N.Y. Regional Bd., 1985—90; bd. dirs. Bklyn. Coll. Found., 1958—81, sec., 1959—64, 1971—81; mem. adv. bd. Am. Jewish Congress, 1972—75; 1st v.p. YM-YWHA, Kingsbay, 1975—76, pres., 1997—2001; pres. Madison Jewish Ctr., 1978—81; trustee Bklyn. Coll. Hillel Found., 1975—, v.p., 1976—77, pres., 1977—81, chmn. bd., 1983—88, Midwood Devel. Corp., 1976—81; v.p. bd. judges Civil Ct., N.Y.C., 1979—83, pres. bd. judges, 1993—96; pres. Jewish Cmty. Coun. Kings Bay, 2001—; bd. trustees Bklyn. Pub. Libr., 1975—, pres., 1982—85. Recipient Pres.'s medal, Bklyn. Coll., 1975, Cert. of Merit, Bklyn. Borough, 1976, 1981, award, N.Y. State Assn. Libr. Bds., 1991. Mem.: ALA (Trustee of Yr. 1995), N.Y. State Trial Lawyers Assn., Bklyn. Bar Assn., N.Y. State Bar Assn., Assn. of Bar of City of N.Y., Am. Judges Assn., Am. Arbitration Assn. (arbitrator 1968—81), Am. Libr. Trustee Assn. (sec. 1988—89, regional v.p. 1989—), B'nai B'rith (pres. King County Lodge 1965—67, pres. Bklyn. Unity Lodge 1985—89), Bklyn. Coll. Alumni Assn. (bd. dirs., pres. 1973—83), ABA, Phi Alpha Delta. Avocation: Avocations: reading, golf, computers. Office: Supreme Ct 360 Adams St Brooklyn NY 11201

HARKAVY, OSCAR, writer, consultant; b. N.Y.C., May 28, 1923; s. Jacob and Anna (Schultz) H.; m. Frances Hoffman, Dec. 23, 1950; children: Stephen James, John Brooks. AB, Columbia Coll., 1944; MBA, Syracuse U., 1948, PhD, 1952. From instr. to asst. prof. Syracuse U. Coll. Bus. Adminstrn., 1946-53; from asst. to dir. to chief program officer The Ford Found., N.Y.C., 1953-88; vis. sr. assoc. The Population Coun., N.Y.C., 1988-90; writer, cons. New Rochelle, N.Y., 1990—. Author: Curbing Population Growth, 1995; co-author, co-editor: Fair Start for Children, 1992. Chmn. Population Resource Ctr., Princeton, N.J., 1992-99, bd. dirs., 1988—; adv. coun. Nat. Ctr. for Children in Poverty, 1988-96. 1st lt. US Army Air Force, 1943-46. Fellow AAAS; mem. Phi Beta Kappa, Beta Gamma Sigma. Avocations: painting, writing. Home and Office: 15 Split Rock Ln New Rochelle NY 10804-3413 E-mail: budfran@aol.com.

HARKAVY-FRIEDMAN, JILL MARTINE, psychologist; BA, U. Pa., Phila., 1978; PhD, U. Fla., 1984. Asst. prof. clin. psychology in psychiatry Columbia U., N.Y.C., 1989—; rsch. scientist N.Y. State Psychiat. Inst., N.Y.C., 1989—. Mem. bus. adv. bd. League for the Hard of Hearing, N.Y.C., 2000, co-chair comedy night, 1994. Fellow, USPHS, 1980—83; grantee, NIMH, 1997—2002, Am. Found. for Suicide Prevention. Mem.: APA, Am. Found. for Suicide Prevention (mem. rsch. adv. coun. 1999). Achievements include research in suicidal behavior, schizophrenia and psychiatric diagnosis and assessment. Office: NYSPI/ Columbia Univ 1051 Riverside Dr New York NY 10032

HARKES, JOHN, professional soccer player; b. Kearny, N.J., Mar. 8, 1967; m. Cindy Harkes; children: Ian, Lauren. Student, U. Va. With U.S. Nat. Team, 1987—, capt.; midfielder West Ham United English Premier League, 1995—96; midfielder, capt. D.C. United Team, 1996—99; midfielder Derby County Football Club, New England Revolution, Foxboro, Mass., 1999—. Named Player of Yr., Mo. Athletic Club, 1987, Atlantic Coast Conf., 1987, Most Valuable Player, U.S. Cup, 1990, Co-Most Valuable Player, Copa Am., 1995. Achievements include first American to play in F.A. Cup Final, 1993; first American to score goal in Coca-Cola League Cup Final, 1993; captaining D.C. United to first-ever MLS Championship, 1996; scoring English League's Goal of Yr., 1990. Office: New England Revolution Foxboro Stadium Rte 1 Foxboro MA 02035

HARKEY, JOHN NORMAN, judge; b. Russellville, Ark., Feb. 25, 1933; s. Olga John and Margaret (Fleming) H.; m. Willa Moreau Charlton, May 24, 1959; children— John Adam, Sarah Leigh. AS, Marion (Ala.) Inst., 1952; LLB, BS, BSL, U. Ark., 1959, JD, 1969. Bar: Ark. 1959. Since practiced in, Batesville; pros. atty. 3d Jud. Dist. Ark., 1961-65; ins. commr. Ark., 1967-68; chmn. Ark. Commerce Commn., 1968-69; spl. justice Ark. Supreme Ct., 1988; judge juvenile divsn. Ark. 16th Dist., 1989-90; sr. ptnr. Harkey, Walmsley and related firms, Batesville, 1970-92; chancery and probate judge 16th Jud. Dist., Batesville, Ark., 1993-98, circuit and chancery judge, 1999-2001, circuit judge, 2001—. 1st lt. USMCR, Korea. Mem. Ark. Bar Assn., Am. Bar Register, U.S. Marine Corps League. Home: 490 Harkey Rd Batesville AR 72501-9294 Office: PO Box 2656 Batesville AR 72503-2656

HARKEY, ROBERT SHELTON, lawyer; b. Charlotte, N.C., Dec. 22, 1940; s. Charles Nathan and Josephine Lenora (McKenzie) H.; m. Barbara Carole Payne, Apr. 2, 1983; 1 child, Elizabeth McKenzie. BA, Emory U., 1963, LLB, 1965. Bar: Ga. 1964, U.S. Dist. Ct. (no. dist.) Ga. 1964, U.S. Ct. Appeals (1st, 5th, 7th, 9th and 11th cirs.) 1964-86, U.S. Supreme Ct. Assoc. Swift, Currie, McGhee & Hiers, Atlanta, 1965-68; atty. Delta Air Lines, Atlanta, 1968-74, gen. atty., 1974-79, asst. v.p. law, 1979-85, assoc. gen. counsel, v.p., 1985-88; gen counsel, v.p., 1988-90; gen. counsel, sr. v.p. Delta Air Lines, Atlanta, 1990-94, gen. counsel, sr. v.p., sec., 1994—. Mem. coun. Emory U. Law Sch., 1997—. Unit chmn. United Way, Atlanta, 1985; trustee Woodruff Arts Ctr., 1995—; bd. visitors Emory U., 1996-99. Mem. ABA (com. gen. counsels), Air Transport Assn. (chmn. law coun. 1996-98), State Bar Ga. (chmn. corp. counsel sect. 1992-93), Atlanta Bar Assn., Corp. Counsel Assn. Greater Atlanta (bd. dirs. 1990), Commerce Club, Lawyers Club of Atlanta, Cherokee Town and Country Club. Presbyterian. Avocations: tennis, reading. Office: Delta Air Lines Hartsfield Atlanta Internat Airport Atlanta GA 30320

HARKEY, VERNA RAE, piano, educator; b. Ft. Worth, Nov. 20, 1928; d. Verne and Rachel Isabelle (Beam) Morrill; m. Kenneth L. Harkey, Sept. 21, 1951; children: Karl M., Kevin L. BA, George Pepperdine Coll., 1950. Tchr. piano, Long Beach, Calif., 1950—. Mem. Crippled Children Soc. Mem. Nat. Music Tchrs. Assn., Music Tchrs. Assn. Calif., Southwestern Youth Music Festival, Epsilon Eta, Mu Phi Epsilon (founder Long Beach alumnae chpt., vice chmn. 1986-87). Republican. Mem. Ch. of Christ. Home: 1562 Merion Way Seal Beach CA 90740-4957

HARKIN, ANN WINIFRED, elementary school educator, psychotherapist; b. Glasgow, Scotland, Oct. 14, 1951; came to US, 1956; d. John Joseph and Mary W. Leavy H.; 1 child, Julia A. Wilkinson. BA in Psychology cum laude, Immaculata Coll., 1973, MA in Counseling Psychology summa cum laude, 1999. Instrnl. II permanent cert. elem., secondary sch. tchr., Pa. Tchr. grade 3 St. Anastasia, Newtown Square, Pa., 1973-78; tchr. grade 1 Mother of Divine Providence, King of Prussia, 1979-89, St. Aloysius Acad., Bryn Mawr, Pa., 1989—; legal asst. Elizabeth R. Howard, Esquire, 2001—. Counselor Paoli Addictions Ctr., Pa. Mem. APA, ACA, Nat. Cath. Educators Assn., Diamond Rock Schoolhouse Assn., Donegal Soc. Phila., Chi Sigma Iota. Avocations: horticulture, animals, hiking, swimming, drawing. Home: 738 Cedar Dr Phoenixville PA 19460-3606

HARKIN, DANIEL JOHN, controller; b. Bradenton, Fla., Mar. 29, 1955; s. John Lewis and Stella Marie H.; m. Theresa Ann Ford; children: Erin Kathleen, Shaun Ford. BBA, Fla. Atlantic U., 1975. CPA, Fla. Controller Vis. Home Health Svc., Boca Raton, Fla., 1975-78; CPA Cherry Bekaert & Holland, Ft. Lauderdale, Fla., 1978-85; controller Griffin Bros. Co., Inc., Davie, Fla., 1985-90, L.W. Rozzo, Inc., Pembroke Pines, Fla., 1990—. Contbr. articles to profl. jours. Fla. univ. faculty scholar Fla. Atlantic U., 1972-75. Mem. AICPA, Fla. Inst. CPAs (mem. com. 1980-91, adv. com. MAS 1990-91, speaker 1984), Nat. Assn. Accts., Nat. Inst. Tax Profls., Inst. Mgmt. Accts., Greenpeace, Roscicrucian Order AMORC. Roman Catholic. Avocations: computer systems and programming, gardening, boating, philosophy, teaching. Home: 1834 SW 21st St # 2 Fort Lauderdale FL 33315-1833 Office: L W Rozzo Inc 17200 Pines Blvd Hollywood FL 33029-1505

HARKIN, THOMAS RICHARD, senator; b. Cumming, Iowa, Nov. 19, 1939; s. Patrick and Frances H.; m. Ruth Raduenz, 1968; children: Amy, Jenny. BS, Iowa State U., 1962; JD, Cath. U. Am., 1972. Mem. staff Ho. of Reps. Select Com. U.S. Involvement in S.E. Asia, 1970; mem. 94th-98th Congresses from 5th Iowa Dist., mem. sci. and tech. com., mem. agr., nutrition and forestry coms.; U.S. Senator from Iowa, 1984—. Mem. Dem. Steering Com., com. labor and human resources; chmn. Appropriations Subcom. on Labor, Health and Human Svcs and Edn.; ; chmn. Agr., Nutrition, and Forestry subcom. on Rsch., Nutrition, and Gen. Legis.; mem. Small Bus. Com.; prin. author Ams. with Disabilities Act. Co-author: (with C.E. Thomas) Five Minutes to Midnight: Why the Nuclear Threat is Growing Faster than Ever, 1990. Dem. candidate for Presidency of U.S., 1992. Served with USN, 1962-67. Named Outstanding Young Alumnus Iowa State U. Alumni Assn., 1974 Democrat. Office: US Senate 731 Hart Senate Bldg Washington DC 20510-0001*

HARKINS, DANIEL CONGER, lawyer; b. Akron, Ohio, Aug. 9, 1960; s. Daniel Drury and Marjorie Helen (Conger) H. BA in Econs., Coll. of Wooster, 1982; JD, Case Western Res. U., 1985; LLM in Taxation, NYU, 1986. Bar: Ohio 1985, D.C. 1986. Assoc. Williams, Zumkehr & Welser, Kent, Ohio, 1985-88; assoc. Martin, Browne, Hull & Harper, Springfield, Ohio, 1988-93, ptnr., 1993-96; pvt. practice Springfield, 1996-98; prin. Harkins & Assocs., 1998—. Mem. Bd. Bldg. Appeals, Springfield, 1990-98, vice chmn., 1991-92, chmn., 1995-97,; trustee Springfield Family YMCA, 1991-95, treas., 1991-94, pres., 1994-96; v.p., sec. Jr. Achievement, 1991-94; trustee Clark County Mental Health Found., 1991-98; chmn. fin. com., mem. ctrl. and exec. coms. Clark County Rep. Com., 1992-97; vice chmn. Clark County Rep. Ctrl. Com., 1994-97; chmn. Clark County Rep. Party, 1997—; coach wrestling team Cath. Ctrl. H.S., Springfield, 1992-93; pres. elect Tecumseh Coun., Boy Scouts Am., 1996—, pres. 1998-2000, pres.-elect 1996-98, pres. & v.p., area 5; mem. Clark County Bd. of Elections, 1998—; bd. dirs. Clark State Cmty. Coll. Found., 1999—; mem Florida Presidential Vote Recount Team, 2000. Mem. Ohio State Bar Assn. (chmn. mcpl. income tax com., taxation com. 1995—), D.C. Bar Assn., Clark County Bar Assn. (exec. com. 1991—, treas. 1993—), Clark County Law Libr. Assn. (treas. 1996—). Congregationalist. Avocations: running, swimming, skiing, amateur wrestling. Office: 333 N Limestone St Ste 104 Springfield OH 45503-4250

HARKINS, JOHN GRAHAM, JR., lawyer; b. Phila., May 9, 1931; s. John Graham and Elizabeth Taylor (Bowers) H.; m. Beatrice Gibson McIlvain, June 30, 1955; children: John Graham III, Alida McIlvain. BA with honors, U. Pa., 1953, LL.B. summa cum laude, 1958. Bar: Pa. 1959, U.S. Supreme Ct. 1971. Assoc. firm Pepper, Hamilton & Scheetz, Phila., 1958-63, partner, 1963-92, co-chmn., 1982-86, chmn., 1986-92; ptnr. Harkins Cunningham, Phila., 1992—. Instr. U. Pa., 1956-58, lectr. Law Sch., former bd. overseers-law, 1981-95; mem. adv. com. Inst. Law and Econs., 1981—, com. chmn., 1981-91. Editor-in-chief: U. Pa. Law Rev, 1957-58. Supr. Easttown Twp., Pa., 1972-77; past bd. dirs. Chester County Hosp.; past trustee Curtis Inst. Music; trustee U. Pa., 1987-97, trustee emeritus, 1998—; trustee U. Pa. Health Sys., 1988-2001, vice chmn., 1991-2001; mem. bd. overseers U. Pa. Med. Sch., 1990-2001, chmn., 1991-2001; dir. Citizens for Pa.'s Future, 2001--. With U.S. Army, 1953-55. Fellow Salzburg Seminar in Am. Studies, 1961 Mem. Am. Coll. Trial Lawyers, Am. Law Inst., Am. Bar Assn., Pa. Bar Assn., Phila. Bar Assn., Jud. Conf. U.S. Ct. of Appeals for 3d Circuit, Order of Coif, Phi Beta Kappa. Clubs: Merion Cricket, Radnor Hunt. Home: Lowbrook PO Box 813 Devon PA 19333-0813 Office: Harkins Cunningham 2800 One Commerce Sq 2005 Market St Philadelphia PA 19103-7075

HARKINS, PATRICK NICHOLAS, III, lawyer; b. Jackson, Miss., Apr. 27, 1941; s. Patrick Nicholas and Mary Ruth (Gammon) H.; m. Mary Elizabeth Wilson, Apr. 12, 1969; children: Elizabeth Glenn, DeMatt Henderson. BBA, U. Notre Dame, 1963; JD, U. Miss., 1965. Bar: Miss. 1965, U.S. Dist. Ct. (no. and so. dists.) Miss. 1965, U.S. Ct. Appeals (5th cir.) 1965, U.S. Supreme Ct. 1968. Legis. asst. U.S. Congressman G.V. Montgomery, 1967-68; assoc. atty. Watkins, Pyle, Ludlam, Winter & Stennis, Jackson, 1969; atty. Watkins & Eager PLLC, Jackson, 1970—, ptnr., 1973—. Served to capt. U.S. Army, 1965-67. Fellow Am. Coll. Trial Lawyers, Miss. Bar Found. (pres. 1992-93); mem. ABA, DRI (pres.2001-2002), Miss. Bar Assn., Miss. Def. Lawyers Assn. (bd. dirs. 2003—), Internat. Assn. Def. Counsel (chair products liability 1995-97, dir. def. counsel trial acad. 1998), Hinds County Bar Assn., Jackson Country Club. Roman Catholic. Home: 2060 Sheffield Dr Jackson MS 39211-5848

HARKINS, RICHARD WESLEY, marine engineer, naval architect; b. Duluth, Minn., Oct. 11, 1946; s. Wesley Ray and Vivian G. (LaBrosse) H.; m. Deborah Ann deGonzaque, Apr. 11, 1954; children: Ryan Wesley, Blair Ashley, Danielle Ashley. BS, U.S. Mcht. Marine Acad., Kings Point, N.Y., 1971; MSE in Naval Architecture and Marine Engring., U. Mich., 1976. Registered profl. engr., Ohio. 3d asst. engr. Hanna Steamship Corp., Cleve., 1971; 1st asst. engr. Poling Transp. Corp., N.Y.C., 1971-72; engr. Ingalls Shipbuilding Co., Pascagoula, Miss., 1972-74; fleet supt. Interlake Steamship Co., Cleve., 1976-94; v.p. ops. Lake Carriers' Assn., Cleve., 1994—. Author: (tech. paper) Investigation of Fuel Injection Cavitation, 1985 (Best Paper of 1985 Soc. Naval Architects and Marine Engrs.). Mem. Soc. Naval Architects and Marine Engrs. (ship machinery com. 1985, chmn. diesel panel 1985—, chmn. papers com. 1985-87, local sect. rep. 1985-87). Roman Catholic. Avocations: cross-country skiing, running, antique autos, golf. Home: 2771 Hampton Rd Cleveland OH 44116-2548 Office: 614 W Superior Ave Ste 915 Cleveland OH 44113-1306 E-mail: harkins@lcaships.com.

HARKLEROAD, JO-ANN DECKER, special education educator; b. Wilkes-Barre, Pa., Oct. 22, 1936; d. Leon Joseph Sr. and Beatrice Catherine (Wright) Decker; m. A. Dwayne Harkleroad; 1 child, Leon Wade. AS, George Washington U., 1960, BS in Health, Phys. Edn. and Recreation, minor in Spl. Edn., 1968, MA in Spl. Edn. and Ednl. Diagnosis and Prescription, 1969, postgrad., 1997-99. Recipient Appreciation cert. Fairfax County (Va.) Police Dept., 1987, Meritorious Svc. medal Pres. Com. on Employment of People with Disabilities, 1988. Instr. Cath. U. Am., Washington, 1960-61; tchr. Bush Hill Day Sch., Franconia, Va., 1961-63; ednl. diagnostician Prince William County Schs., Manassas, Va., 1969-71, supr. title I, 1971-72; writer, editor Sta. WNVT-TV, Fairfax, Va., 1980-82; dir. spl. edn. Highland County Schs., Monterey, Va., 1987-90. Author: (novel) Horse Thief Trail, 1981, 83, 86; columnist op-ed page The Recorder; radio broadcaster Sta. WVMR, Frost, W.Va. Ruling elder Presbyn. Ch., McDowell, Va., Clifton, Va.; mem. divsn. of Faith in Action Hunger com. Shenandoah Presbytery; dir. McDowell Presbyn. Ch. Choir; rotating dir. Highland County Cmty. Choir; past pres. Highland County Pub. Libr. Bd. Avocations: hiking, camping, rifleshooting, reading, gardening. Home: Windy Ridge Farm HC 33 Box 60 Mc Dowell VA 24458-9704

HARKLESS, ANGELA, lawyer, publishing executive; b. Jackson, Miss., Oct. 7, 1964; d. Wesley and Julia L. (Murrell) H. BA in Comm., Loyola U., Chgo., 1986; JD, Ind. U., 1995; postgrad., London Law Consortium, 1995. Bar: Ill. 1995. Rsch. asst. WFYR-FM, Chgo., 1983-86; editl. asst. Chgo. Tribune, 1987-88; adminstrv. exec. asst. CBS, Inc., N.Y.C., 1989-90; atty. Harkless Law Firm, Chgo., 1996—; editor, pub. Cachét Mag., Chgo., 1999—. Notes editor Fed. Comm. Law Jour., 1993-95, Law News Ctr. Mem. amb. com. Chgo. Sister Cities Internat., 1990-92; bd. dirs. Young Adult Bd. DuSable Mus., Chgo., 1996—. Scholar RKO Broadcast, Inc. Black Media Coaliton, 1985, Journalism scholar McGraw-Hill, 1986; law fellow Coun. on Legal Edn., 1992-95. Mem. ABA, Ill. State Bar Assn., Chgo. Bar Assn., Fed. Comm. Bar Assn. (mem. planning com. Chgo. chpt.), Chgo. Assn. Black Journalists (pres. 1999—), Multicultural Journalism Consortium (pres. 1994—), Alpha Kappa Alpha Sorority Inc. Avocations: learning foreign languages, golf, tennis, collecting antiques.

HARKNESS, JOHN CHEESMAN, architect; b. N.Y.C., Nov. 30, 1916; s. Albert and Sara Arden (Cheesman) H.; m. Sarah Pillsbury, June 14, 1941 (separated); children: Sara Harkness Super, Joan Harkness Hantz, Nell, Timothy, Alice, Frederick, John Pillsbury. BFA cum laude, Harvard U., 1938, BArch, MArch, 1941. Registered architect Maine, Mass., R.I. Architect Saarinen and Swanson, Birmingham, Mich., Harrison, Fouilhoux and Abramovitz, N.Y.C., Skidmore, Owings and Merrill, N.Y.C., prior to 1945; prin. The Architects Collaborative, Cambridge, Mass., 1945-95, pres., 1966-67, 77-84, also bd. dirs., chmn. bd. prins., 1984-86. Mem. design faculty Harvard Grad. Sch. Design, 1946-50, mem. vis. com.; mem. vis. com. R.I. Sch. Design; mem. capitol area planning bd., Minn. State; archtl. advisor Boston Redevel. Authority for Park Pla., Mass. Design Competition. Author: Encycolpedia of Architecture, 1989; prin.-in-charge projects Martin County Libr., Fla., Creative Arts Ctr., master plan, Squires addition Student Activities Ctr., Biology Bldg., all at Va. Poly. Inst. and State U., Blacksburg, Univ. Ctrs., Coll. William and Mary, Va., Sci. Bldg. Middlebury (Vt.) Coll., Hillside Office Bldg., Waltham, Mass., CBS Office Bldg., Mt. Pleasant, N.Y., master plan and 6 med. bldgs. Children's Hosp. Med. Ctr., Boston (Harleston Parker medal Boston Soc. Architects, Honor award AIA), hdqrs. CIGNA, Bloomfield, Conn. (award N.Eng. Regional Coun. AIA, award excellence Am. Inst. Steel Constrn. 1985), Hoffman Lab. Exptl. Geology (Boston Arts Festival award 1964), athletic facilities, addition Mus. Comparative Zoology, med. sch. Lab. Reprodn. and Reproductive Biology, all at Harvard U., master plan indsl. complex, Jubail, Saudi Arabia, master plan and office bldg. Summit at Westchester, Mt. Pleasant, Cen. Nat. Mus., Riyadh, Saudia Arabia, hdqrs. Shawmut Bank Boston, Amoskeag Bank, Manchester, N.H., Montego Bay (Jamaica) Hosp., Ainsworth Gymnasium Smith Coll., Northampton, Mass. (honor award N.Eng. Regional Coun. AIA), U. Tunis Libr. and Sch. Law, Econs., and Bus. Adminstrn., Tunisia, James L. Hanley Edn. Ctr., Providence (award), New Trier Twp. High Sch., Winnetka, Ill, Blue Hills Regional Vocat. Sch., Canton, Mass., Wayland (Mass.) High Sch. Ambulance driver Am. Field Svc., 1943-44. Pvt. U.S. Army, 1945, ETO, NATOUSA, bronze cross of merit with swords from Polish Rep. for action at the Battle of Casino, Italy. Recipient various competition and archtl. design awards including 6 awards Am. Assn. Sch. Adminstrs., 1960-67, William Ware award, Boston Soc. Architects honor award, 1993; named Harvard Athletic Hall of Fame, NCAA Wrestling champion, 1938, lifetime svc. to wrestling award Mass. and Nat. Wresting Hall of Fame, 1999. Fellow AIA (archtl. juror various design programs, 2d award alt. to Appleton Travelling fellowship); mem. NAD, Boston Soc. Architects (past pres., 1st prize 1940), Mass. State Assn. Architects (past pres.), Archtl. League N.Y., Harvard Grad. Sch. Design Alumni Assn. (past pres.), Harvard U. Alumni Assn. (former dir. 1988), Phi Beta Kappa. Home: 223 Oakland Ave Arlington MA 02476-7253 Office: Fletcher Harkness Cohen Moneyhun Inc 46 Waltham St Boston MA 02118-2436

HARKNESS, MABEL GLEASON, retired librarian; b. Oil City, Pa., Jan. 20, 1913; d. Charles Wilcox and Mabel Amy (Fulton) Gleason; m. Benjamin Olney, Mar. 23, 1946 (dec. 1963); m. Bernard Emerson Harkness, Sept. 5, 1964 (dec. 1980). AB, U. Rochester, 1935, MA, 1962; LHD (hon.), Keuka Coll., 2003. Cert. libr., N.Y. Libr. Stromberg-Carlson Co., Rochester, N.Y., 1942-51, Garden Ctr. Rochester, 1953-67, Monroe County (N.Y.) Bookmobile, 1952-53; now ret. Vol. cataloger Geneva (N.Y.) Hist. Soc.; editor Gleam mag., Rochester Poetry Soc., 1945, Engr.'s Notebook, Stromberg-Carlson Co., 1946-50, Garden Ctr. Bull., 1955-67; co-founder, past pres. Western N.Y. chpt. Spl. Librs. Assn., 1945. Compiler: Harkness Seedlist Handbook 1986 (Worth award for bot./hort. writing Am. Rock Garden Soc.), 2d edit., 1993; contbr. articles on horticulture and local history to various publs. Trustee Keuka Coll., Keuka Park, N.Y., 1971-80, now emeritus. Mem. AAUW (life), Am. Rock Garden Soc. (life), Alpine Garden Soc. (Eng.), Scottish Rock Garden Club (life). Republican. Episcopalian. Avocations: musicology, architectural history. Home: 5169 Pre Emption Rd Geneva NY 14456-9736

HARKNESS, MARY LOU, librarian; b. Denby, S.D., Aug. 19, 1925; d. Raleigh Everette and Mary Jane (Boyd) Barker; m. Donald R. Harkness, Sept. 2, 1967. BA, Nebr. Wesleyan U., 1947; AB in L.S, U. Mich., 1948; MS, Columbia U., 1958. Jr. cataloger U. Mich. Law Library, 1948-50; asst. cataloger Calif. Poly. Coll., 1950-52; asst. cataloger, then head cataloger Ga. Inst. Tech., 1952-57; head cataloger U. South Fla., Tampa, 1958-67, dir. libraries, 1967-87, dir. emeritus, 1987—. Cons. Nat. Library Nigeria, 1962-63. Bd. dirs. Southeastern Library Network, 1977-80. Recipient Alumni Achievement award Nebr. Wesleyan U., 1972 Mem. ALA, Fla. Library Assn., Athena Soc. Democrat. Presbyterian. Home: 13511 Palmwood Ln Tampa FL 33624-4409 E-mail: mharkne2@helios.acomp.usf.edu.

HARKNESS, PETER ANTHONY, editor, publisher; b. Washington, July 31, 1943; s. Richard Long and Gladys (Suiter) H.; m. Patricia French, Apr. 10, 1971; children: Wyeth Long, Rollin Charles. Student, U. N.C., 1961-63, 64-65; BA in Journalism, Am. U., 1966. Mng. editor Congl. Quar., Washington, 1980-84, exec. editor, 1984-87; editor, pub. Governing Mag., Washington, 1988—. Author: China and U.S. Far East Policy, 1945-1966, 1967. Bd. dir. Ptnrs. for Livable Cmtys., Washington, 1993—, Nat. Bicycle Fedn., 2000. With U.S. Army, 1969—75. Recipient Raymond Clapper award for investigative reporting White House Corr. Assn., 1974. Fellow Nat. Acad. Pub. Adminstrn. Avocations: biking, skiing, sailing.

HARKNESS, R. KENNETH, restaurant chain executive; b. Warren, Ohio, Aug. 22, 1949; s. Roy K. and Yvonne D. (Howitt) H.; m. Marianne Loprete, Sept. 28, 1974 (div. Apr. 1999); 1 child, Austin Blaine; m. Valerie Joy Hollenbach, June 24, 2001. BS in Bus., Rutgers U., 1972, MBA in Acctg., 1973. Pres., chief exec. officer N.Y. Sub Inc., Dallas, 1974-81, 85—, Fox Hunt Realty, Inc., Far Hills, N.J., 1981-85, Kenco Restaurants, Inc., Dallas, 1987—. Mem. University Park Master Plan Com. Mem. Nat. Restaurant Assn., Tex. Restaurant Assn., Rep. Inner Circle. Episcopalian. Office: NY Sub Inc 3411 Asbury St Dallas TX 75205-1844

HARKNESS, S. SUZAN JANE, political scientist, educator; b. La Crosse, WI, June 8, 1961; d. James Francis Sobkowiak, Doris Louise Lord; m. Stephen Brian Harkness; 1 child, Sebastian. BS, U. Wis.; MA, U.S. Internat. U.; PhD, U. Hawaii, Manoa, 2001. Adj. prof. U. Hawaii, Honolulu, 1998—2000; Congl. postdoc. fellow U.S. Congress, Washington, 2002; asst. prof. polit. sci. U. D.C., Washington, 2002—. Adj. prof. Hawaii Pacific U., Honolulu, 2000—00.

HARKRADER, ALAN DALE, JR., photojournalist; b. Chgo., June 27, 1928; s. Alan Dale and Barbara Ann (Fiedler) H.; m. Mary Ellen Wheeler, July 17, 1954; children: Alan Dale III, Mark Eugene. BS in Journalism, Bradley U., 1954, MA in Fine Art, 1974. Staff photographer Morning Star, Peoria, Ill., 1952-54, Herald and Rev., Decatur, Ill., 1954-56, Jour. Star, Peoria, 1956-91, ret., 1991. With U.S. Army, 1946-47, Japan, 1950-52, Korea. Mem. Nat. Press Photographers Assn. (regional bd. dirs. 1965, Mellor award 1965, McLaughlin award 1969), Ill. Press Photographers Assn. (life, pres. 1960, Ill. Photographer of Yr. award 1958, 60, 62, 63, 65). Democrat. Roman Catholic. Home: 1712 E Shady Oak Dr Peoria IL 61614 E-mail: aharkrader@aol.com.

HARKRADER, MILTON KEENE, JR., corporate executive; b. Cranford, N.J., Apr. 8, 1939; s. Milton Keene and Elizabeth Dyer (Evans) H.; m. Nina B. Salo, June 25, 1960; children: Nina Elizabeth, Milton Keene III, Eric Scott. AB, Hamilton Coll., 1958; MBA, U. Pa., 1960. Account exec. Dancer Fitzgerald Sample, Inc., N.Y.C., 1960-63; product mgr. Colgate Palmolive Co., N.Y.C., 1963-65; account exec. Foote Cone & Belding, Inc., N.Y.C., 1965-66; v.p., account supr. Young & Rubicam, Inc., N.Y.C., 1966-73; exec. v.p. Isidore Lefkowitz Elgort, Inc., N.Y.C., 1973-79; group v.p. DDB Needham Worldwide, N.Y.C., 1979-91; v.p. comm. and devel. Hamilton Coll., Clinton, N.Y., 1991-94; exec. v.p. Nordico Mktg. Devel. Inc., N.Y.C., 1994—. Dir. Good Friends Film Prodns., Inc.; pres. Meadows Assocs., Inc. Mem. DKE Club, Univ. Club, Weston Field Club. Home: 81 Field Point Dr Fairfield CT 06824-6329

HARL, NEIL EUGENE, economist, lawyer, educator; b. Appanoose County, Iowa, Oct. 9, 1933; s. Herbert Peter and Bertha Catherine (Bonner) H.; m. Darlene Ramona Harris, Sept. 7, 1952; children: James Brent, Rodney Scott. BS, Iowa State U., 1955, PhD, 1965; JD, U. Iowa, 1961. Bar: Iowa 1961. Field editor Wallace's Farmer, 1957-58; research assoc. U.S. Dept. Agr., Iowa City and Ames, Iowa, 1958-64; assoc. prof. econs. Iowa State U., Ames, 1964-67, prof., 1967—, Charles F. Curtiss Disting. prof., 1976—, dir. Ctr. Internat. Agrl. Fin., 1990—. Mem. adv. group to commr. IRS, 1979-80; mem. adv. com. Heckerling Inst. on Estate Planning, Miami, Fla., 1983-96; mem. adv. com. Office Tech. Assessment, U.S. Congress, 1988-95, vice chair, 1992-93, chair, 1993-94; mem. exec. bd. U.S. West Comms., Iowa, 1989-90; mem. adv. com. on agrl. biotech. USDA, 2000-02; mem. Fed. Commn. on Payment Limitations, 2002-03; lectr. in field. Author: Farm Estate and Business Planning, 1973, Farm Estate and Business Planning, 15th edit., 2001, Legal and Tax Guide for Agricutural Lenders, 1984, Legal and Tax Guide for Agricutural Lenders, supplement, 1987, Agricultural Law, 15 vols., 1980—81, Agricultural Law Manual, 1985, rev. edit., 2003, The Farm Debt Crisis of the 1980s, 1990; co-author: Farmland, 1982, Principles of Agricultural Law, 1997, 3d edit., 2003, Taxation of Cooperatives, 1999, Reporting Farm Income, 2000, Family Owned Business Deduction, 2001, Arrogance and Power: The Saga of WOI-TV, 2001, The Law of the Land, 2002; author, actor films and videotape programs; contbr. articles to profl. jours. Trustee Iowa State U. Agrl. Found., 1969-85. 1st lt. AUS, 1955-57. 1st lt. U.S. Army, 1955—57. Recipient Outstanding Tchr. award Iowa State U., 1973, Disting Svc. to Agr. award Am. Soc. Farm Mgrs. and Rural Appraisers, 1977, Iowa sect. 1996, Faculty Svc. award Nat. Univ. Ext. Assn., 1980, Disting. Svc. award Am. Agrl. Editors Assn., 1984, Disting. Achievement citation Iowa State U., 1985, Disting. Svc. to State Govt. award Nat. Gov.'s Assn., 1986, Disting. Svc. award Iowa State U., 1986, Farm Leader of Yr. award Des Moines Register, 1986, Henry A. Wallace award, 1987, Superior Svc. award USDA, 1987, Disting. Svc. to Iowa Agr. award Iowa Farm Bur., 1992, Faculty Excellence award, Iowa Bd. Regents, 1993, Charles A. Black award Coun. Agrl. Sci. Tech., 1997, Excellence in Internat. Agr. award Iowa State U., 1999, Disting. Svc. to Agr. award Chgo. Farmers Club, 1999, Exceptional Svc. to Agr. award Iowa Master Farmers, Wallaces Farmer, 2000, Pres.'s award for disting. svc. Iowa State U., 2002; named Seminar Leader of Yr. Nat. Assn. Accts., 2000. Fellow Am. Coll. Trusts and Estates Counsel, Am. Agrl. Econs. Assn. (exec. bd. 1979-85, pres. 1983-84), Am. Agrl. Econs. Found. pres. 1993-94, Outstanding Ext. Program award 1970, Excellence in Communicating Rsch. Results award 1975, Disting. Undergrad. Tchr. award 1976), ABA Rsch. Found., Iowa State Bar Found.; mem. ABA, Iowa Bar Assn. (Pres. award 1991), Am. Agrl. Law Assn. (pres. 1980-81, Disting. Svc. award 1984); bd. dirs. Iowa Barn Found. (v.p. 1999-2001). Home: 2821 Duff Ave Ames IA 50010-4709 also: 3001 Kanaloa 78-261 Manukai St Kailua Kona HI 96740 Office: Iowa State U Dept Econs Ames IA 50011-1070 E-mail: harl@iastate.edu.

HARLAN, JOHN MARSHALL, construction company executive; b. Detroit; s. Campbell Allen and Ivabell Lucile (Campbell) H.; m. Elizabeth Henninger, Feb. 18, 1956; children: Patricia G. Harlan Schumacher, Diana L. Harlan Stein, Sandra S. Harlan McAndrews. BSEE, U. Mich., 1956. Electrician Harlan Electric Co., Detroit, 1956-60, estimator, then contract mgr. and v.p., 1960-63, pres., bd. dirs. Southfield, Mich., 1963-72, pres., chmn., 1972-94; dir. MYR Group Inc., 1995-2000, PPC Holdings, Inc., 2001—. Pres., bd. dirs. Federated Elec. Contractors, 1968-73; chmn., bd. dirs. Contractors Mut. Assn., Washington, 1973-81; bd. dirs. Nat. Constrn. Employers Coun., Washington, 1978-82; fellow, bd. dirs. Engring. Soc. Detroit, 1982-88. Pres., bd. dirs. Sci. and Engring. Fair Met. Detroit, 1964-95; trustee Lawrence Tech. U., Southfield, 1981-98. Fellow Acad. Elec. Contracting; mem. Nat. Elec. Contractors Assn. (bd. dirs., pres. Southeastern Mich. chpt. 1968-95), Constrn. Assn. Mich. (chmn. bd. dirs. 1990-98), Tau Beta Pi, Eta Kappa Nu. Home: 7769 Clearwater Dr Williamsburg MI 49690-9579 E-mail: jmh@gtii.com.

HARLAN, KATHLEEN TROY (KAY HARLAN), management consultant; b. Bremerton, Wash., June 9, 1934; d. Floyd K. and Rosemary (Parkhurst) Troy; m. John L. Harlan, Feb. 16, 1952 (div. 1975); children: Pamela Kay Myles, Kenneth Lynwood, Lianna Sue Collinge. Chair Kitsap-North Mason United Way, 1968-70; owner, operator Safeguard N.W. Sys., Tacoma, 1969-79; devel., mgr. Poulsbo (Wash.) Profl. Bldg., 1969-75; pres. Greenapple Graphics, Inc., Tacoma, 1976-79; owner, mgr. Iskrem Hus Restaurant, Poulsbo, 1972-75; pres. Bus. Seminars, Tacoma, 1977-82; owner, mgr. Safeguard Computer Ctr., Tacoma, 1982-91; owner Total Sys. Ctr., Tacoma, 1983-88. Assoc. mem. Effectiveness Resource Group, Inc., Tacoma, 1979—80; pres. New Image Confs., Tacoma, 1979—82; mem. Orgnl. Renewal, Inc., Tacoma, 1983—88; CEO Manage Ability, Inc., 1991—97; exec. dir. Another Door to Learning, 1996—97; CEO Read, Inc., 1997—; sprk. on mgmt. and survival in small bus. Contbg. author: book Here is Genius!, 1980; author: small bus. manuals. Mem. Wash. State br. Boundary Rev. Kitsap County, 1970—76, Selective Svc. Bd. 19, 1969—76; trustee Clover Pk. Tech. Coll., 1999—, chair, 2001—; co-chair Wash. State Small Bus. Improvement Coun., 1986—91; del. White Ho. Conf. on Small Bus., 1986; chair Wash. State Conf. on Small Bus., 1987; founder, mem. exec. bd. Am. Leadership Forum, 1988—94, bd. dirs., 2001—; dir. Bus. Leadership Week, Wash., 1990—96; chair Pro-Tech Pierce County, 1992—94, Allenmore Hosp., 1993—96; founding mem. Multicare Health Found., 1995—98. Named Woman Entrepreneur of the Yr., Wash., 1986, 1987; recipient Nellie Cashman award. Mem.: Tacoma-Pierce County C. of C. (lifetime exec.

bd. 1985—, chair spl. task force on small bus. Pierce County 1986—89, treas. 1987—88, chair-elect 1988—90, chair 1990—91, chmn. spl. task force edn. 2001—). E-mail: nkatie1952@aol.com.

HARLAN, LEONARD MORTON, merchant banker; b. Newark, June 1, 1936; s. Harold Robinson and Doris Harriet (Siegler) H.; children: Joshua, Noah. BME, Cornell U., 1959; MBA with distinction, Harvard U., 1961, DBA, 1965. Lic. real estate broker, N.Y., N.J. V.p. Donaldson, Lufkin & Jenrette, Inc., 1968-69; founder, chmn. bd. The Harlan Co., Inc., N.Y.C., 1969-96; bd. dirs. Ryland Group, Inc., 1984—; pres. Castle Harlan, Inc., 1987—; gen. ptr. Legend Capital Group, 1987—; pres. Castle Harlan Ptnrs. II, 1992—, Castle Harlan Ptnrs. III, 1997—. Bd. dirs. Tradesco Molding, Inc., Matrix Global Investments, Inc.; guest lectr. Harvard U. and Columbia U. Grad. Schs. Bus. Adminstrn., 1968—; adj. prof. banking and real estate NYU Real Estate Inst., 1968-93, Grad. Sch. Bus. Adminstrn., 1976-80; adj. prof. bus. adminstrn. Columbia U. Grad. Sch. Bus. Adminstrn., 1980-93; trustee North Country Sch./CTT, 1989 95. Mem. editl. bd. Real Estate Rev. Jour., 1971-84; mem bd advisors Jour. Pvt. Equity, 1997—; contbr. articles to profl. jours. Mem. Pres.'s Com. on Indsl. Innovation, 1978; mem. Urban Devel. Action Grant Task Force, HUD, 1984; mem. nat. leadership coun. Am. Jewish Com., 1993—, mem. exec. com. Ctrl. N.J. chpt., 1980—, treas., 1988-96, bd. govs., 1996—, nat. budget com., 1986-87; trustee N.Y.C. Citizens Budget Commn., 1988—; mem. Cranbury (N.J.) Mcpl. Planning Bd., 1987-93; mem. vis. com. Harvard Bus. Sch., 1992—. Recipient Charles B. Shatuck Meml. award Am. Inst. Real Estate Appraisers, 1967, 72; Disting. Tchr. award NYU, 1979; Ford Found. fellow, 1964-65; Zurn fellow, 1962-63. Mem. Harvard Bus. Sch. Alumni Assn. (v.p. 1991-93, bd. dirs. 1989-93), Harvard Club N.Y. (admissions com. 1973-75), Harvard Bus. Sch. Club Greater N.Y. (v.p. N.Y.C. chpt. 1977-79, bd. dirs. 1989-98), Harvard Club of Princeton, Cornell Club of Princeton. Office: Castle Harlan Inc 150 E 58th St Fl 37 New York NY 10155-3799

HARLAN, LINDA CAROL, epidemiologist; b. Glasgow, Mont., Feb. 24, 1950; d. Norman Joseph Mavencamp and Bernice Audrene Klingler; m. William Robert Harlan, Aug. 23, 1980; 1 child, Nicole Porter. BSN, Mont. State U., 1972; MPH, U. Mich., 1981, PhD, 1985. RN Calif., 2002. Project coord. U. Calif., Davis, 1973—80; sr. rsch. analyst Westat, Inc., Rockville, Md., 1981—82; rsch./tchg. asst. U. Mich., Ann Arbor, 1983—84, post-doctoral fellow, 1985—87; biostatistician, epidemiologist Henry Ford Hosp., Detroit, 1984—85; cancer epidemiologist Nat. Cancer Inst., Bethesda, Md., 1987—. Mem. editl. bd.: Jour. Clin. Oncology, 2003—; contbr. articles to profl. jours. Office: Nat Cancer Inst Ste 4005 6130 Executive Blvd Bethesda MD 20892-7344 E-mail: lh50w@nih.gov.

HARLAN, MARY JANE, nursing administrator; b. Knoxville, Tenn., Nov. 22, 1948; d. Robert Beardslee and Gladys Luray (Waller) Spence; m. Larrie Harlan, May 20, 1967 (div. Apr. 1971); 1 child, Katherine; m. Richard S. Ticknor, July 9, 1972; 1 child, Julian Lucille Spence. BS, U. Tenn., 1970, MS in Nursing, 1985. RN. Area mgr., sales rep. Beecham Products, Atlanta, 1978-83; team leader Planned Parenthood, Oak Ridge, Tenn., 1986-92; dir. nursing Vol. Med. Clinic, Knoxville, Tenn., 1987—; dir. clin. ops. Health Solutions, Knoxville, Tenn., 1992-98; dir. clin. svcs. Cmty. Health Care Clinics, Knoxville, 1998—. Adj. faculty U. Tenn., Knoxville, 1997; spkr. in field. Mem. AIDS Regional Adv. Com. Sect., Knoxville, 1994—; pres. bd.dirs. AIDS Prevention Edn. Coalition, Knoxville, 1995. Mem. Phi Kappa Phi, Sigma Theta Tau. Avocation: theatre. Home: 1900 Maplewood Dr Knoxville TN 37920-2749 Office: 1601 Western Ave Knoxville TN 37921

HARLAN, NANCY MARGARET, lawyer; b. Santa Monica, Calif., Sept. 10, 1946; d. William Galland and Betty M. (Miles) Plett; m. John Hammack, Dec. 1, 1979; children: Laryssa Maria Rebello, Leea Elyce. BS magna cum laude, Calif. State U., Hayward, 1972; JD, U. Calif., Berkeley, 1975. Bar: Calif. 1975, Fed. Bar, U.S. Dist. Ct. (ctrl. dist. 9th cir.) 1976. Assoc. Poindexter & Doutr+248, L.A., 1975—80; residential counsel Coldwell Banker Residential Brokerage Co., Fountain Valley, Calif., 1980—81; sr. counsel for real estate subs. law dept. Pacific Lighting Corp., Santa Ana, Calif., 1981—87; sr. v.p., gen. counsel The Presley Cos., 1987—. Bd. dirs. La Casa; exec. v.p. student body U. Calif., Berkeley, 1974—75. Mem.: NAFE, ABA, Bus. and Profl. Women, L.A. Women Lawyers Assn., Orange County Women Lawyers Assn., Calif. Women Lawyers Assn., Orange County Bar Assn. (dir. corp. counsel sect. 1982—), L.A. County Bar Assn., State Bar Calif. Office: William Lyon Homes Inc 4490 Von Karman Ave Newport Beach CA 92660-2008

HARLAN, NEIL EUGENE, retired healthcare company executive; b. Cherry Valley, Ark., June 2, 1921; s. William and Mary Nina (Ellis) H.; m. Martha Almlov, Sept. 27, 1952; children: Lindsey Beth, Neil Eugene, Sarah Ellis. Student, U. Edinburgh, Scotland, 1946; BS, U. Ark., 1947, LLD, 1969; MBA, Harvard U., 1950, DBA, 1956. Mem. faculty Grad. Sch. Bus. Adminstrn. Harvard U., 1951-62, asst. prof., 1954-58, assoc. prof., 1958-61, prof., 1962; asst. sec. Air Force Washington, 1962-64; exec. v.p. Anderson, Clayton & Co., 1964-67; dir. McKinsey & Co., Inc., 1967-74, McKesson Corp., San Francisco, 1974-93, chmn., CEO, 1984-86, 89-90. Author: Management Control in Air Frame Subcontracting, 1956; (with R.H. Hassler) Managerial Economics, 1962. Chmn. San Francisco Ballet, 1982-85; trustee exec. com. World Affairs Coun. No. Calif., 1983—; vice-chmn., dir. Nat. Park Found., 1986-92; bd. govs. San Francisco Symphony, 1985-88; mem. Calif. Com. on Campaign Fin., Calif. Bus. Roundtable, 1984-87; vis. com. Harvard Bus. Sch., 1984-87. Served with AUS, 1943-46. Mem. Webhannet Golf Club, Edgecomb Tennis Club (Kennebunk Beach, Maine), Bohemian Club, Pacific Union Club (San Francisco), Links Club (N.Y.C.). Home: 4816 St Margarets Dr Vero Beach FL 32967 Office: McKesson Corp 1 Post St Ste 3200 San Francisco CA 94104-5292

HARLAN, NORMAN RALPH, construction executive; b. Dayton, Ohio, Dec. 21, 1914; s. Joseph and Anna (Kaplan) H.; m. Thelma Katz, Sept. 4, 1955; children: Leslie, Todd. Indsl. Engring. degree, U. Cin., 1937. Chmn. Am. Constrn. Corp., Dayton, 1949, Harlan, Inc., realtors. Mem. Dayton Real Estate Bd., Ohio Real Estate Assn., Nat. Assn. Real Estate Bds., C. of C., Pi Lambda Phi. Home: 303 Glenridge Rd Kettering OH 45429-1631 Office: Am Constrn Corp 2451 S Dixie Dr Dayton OH 45409-1861

HARLAN, RAYMOND CARTER, retired communication executive, writer, educator; b. Shreveport, La., Nov. 13, 1943; s. Ross E. and Margaret (Burns) H.; m. Nancy K. Munson, 1966 (div. 1978); children: Kathleen Marie, Patrick Raymond; m. Sarah J. Kinzel, 1979 (div. 1982); m. Linda Frances Gerdes, Mar. 30, 1985; stepchildren: Kimberly Jo Gillis, Kellie Leigh Raffa, Ryan William Gerdes. BA in Speech and Drama cum laude, Southwestern U., 1966; MA in English, U. Tex., 1968; MA in Speech & Theatre Arts, Bradley U., 1976. Commd. 2d lt. USAF, 1968, advanced through grades to maj., 1980, ret., 1988. Asst. prof. Bradley U., Peoria, Ill., 1972-76; instr., asst. prof., course dir. Air Force Acad., Colorado Springs, 1976-81; asst. prof. Air Force Inst. Tech., Dayton, Ohio, 1987-88; pres. ComSkills, Aurora, Colo., 1988-2000; internat. trainer Inst. for Internat. Rsch., London, 1990-92; mgr. doc and tng. AT&T Broadband, 2000-01; instr. Afloat Coll. Edn. Program, 2002—; presenter in field. Author: The Confident Speaker, 1993; co-author: Telemarketing That Works, 1991, Interactive Telemarketing, 1995; contbr. articles and revs. to profl. jours. Decorated Air Force Commendation medal with three oak leaf clusters, Air Force Meritorious Svc. medal with one oak leaf cluster; recipient George Washington Honor Medal Freedom Found., 1983, Leo A. Codd award Am. Def. Preparedness Assn., 1975, 1st Prize ann. poetry contest Ariz. State Poetry Soc., 1979. Mem. Soc. for Tech. Comm., Assn. Air Force Missileers. Lutheran. Avocations: skiing, cycling, gardening. E-mail: rayha2@comcast.net.

HARLAN, ROBERT DALE, information studies educator, academic administrator; b. Hastings, Nebr., Aug. 4, 1929; s. Hugh Allan and Madge Keister (Newmyer) H. BA, Hastings Coll., 1950; MA in Library Sci., U. Mich., 1956, MA, 1958, PhD, 1960. Head book order sect. Library U. Mich., Ann Arbor, 1956-58, lectr., 1960; asst. prof. Sch. Library Sci. U. So. Calif., Los Angeles, 1960-63; asst. prof. library and info. studies U. Calif., Berkeley, 1963-70, assoc. prof., 1970-76, prof., 1976-94, prof. emeritus, 1994—; assoc. dean Sch. Library and Info. Studies, 1971-74, 77-82; acting dean Sch. Library and Info. Studies U. Calif., Berkeley, 1985-86. Vis. assoc. prof. Sch. Libr. Sci. UCLA, summer 1973; cons. NEH, Washington; proprietor Park Hills Press. Author: John Henry Nash, 1970, Bibliography of the Grabhorn and Grabhorn-Hoyem Presses, 1977, George L. Harding, 1978, The Colonial Printer: Two Views, 1978, Chapter Nine, 1982, William Doxey's Publishing Venture: At the Sign of the Lark, 1983, The Two Hundredth Book, 1993; chmn. edit. bd. catalogues and bibliographies series U. Calif. Press, 1982-99; contbr. numerous articles and revs. to profl. jours. Rackham pre-doctoral fellow, U. Mich., 1958-60, summer faculty fellow U. Calif., Berkeley, 1964; grantee Assn. Coll. and Research Libraries, 1960, 63. Mem. Bibliog. Soc. Am., Bibliog. Soc. U. Va., Am. Soc. 18th Century Studies, Will Cather Pioneer Meml. Soc., Fine Press Book Assn., Book of Calif. Club (bd. dirs. 1982-88, sec. bd. 1987-88). Office: U Calif Sch Info Mgmt Berkeley CA 94720-0001

HARLAN, ROBERT ERNEST, professional football team executive; b. Des Moines, Sept. 9, 1936; m. Madeline Harlan; children: Kevin, Bryan, Michael. BJ, Marquette U., 1958. Former gen. reporter UPI, Milw.; sports info. dir. Marquette U., Milw., 1959; dir. community rels. St. Louis Cardinals baseball team, 1966-68, dir. pub. rels., 1968-71; asst. gen. mgr. Green Bay (Wis.) Packers, 1971-75, corp. gen. mgr., 1975-81, corp. asst. to pres., 1981-88, exec. v.p. adminstrn., 1988-89, pres., chief exec. officer, 1989—. Bd. dirs. Firstar Bank, Green Bay. Mem. exec. bd. Packer 65 Roses Sports Club. Served with U.S. Army. Mem. bd. of trustees, St. Norbert Coll., Wis. Avocation: golf. Office: Green Bay Packers 1265 Lombardi Ave Green Bay WI 54304-3997 also: Green Bay Packers Lambeau Field PO Box 10628 Green Bay WI 54307-0628

HARLAN, ROSS EDGAR, retired utility company executive, writer, lecturer, consultant; b. Poteau, Okla., July 11, 1919; s. Edgar Leslie and Leola (Carter) H.; m. Margaret Burns, May 31, 1942; children: Raymond Carter, Rosemary, Marvin Allen, Scott Lee. Student, Southeastern Okla. State U., 1937-38, Eastern Okla. State Coll., 1938-39; BSBA, Okla. State U., 1941; postgrad., Harvard U., 1942. Mem. faculty, coach Poteau High Sch., 1945-46, Poteau Jr. Coll., 1945-46; with Okla. Gas & Electric Co., Oklahoma City, 1946-85, mgr. rates and contracts dept., 1954-64, v.p., 1964-78, sr. v.p. div. mgmt., 1978-80, sr. v.p. adminstrn. and public affairs, 1980-85; ret.; ind. cons., writer, 1985—. Cons. spl. books div. Reader's Digest, 1985—. Author: Strikes, 1946, Frontier Oklahoma-The Twin Territories, 1994 Pres. Okla. Council on Econ. Edn., 1977-79; pres. alumni bd. Ea. Okla. State Coll., 2000-03; bd. govs. Nat. Wrestling Hall of Fame, 1977-85; pres. adv. bd. Okla. State U. Coll. Bus. Assos.; adv. bd. Okla. State U. Tech. Inst.; bd. govs. Okla. State U. Found., bd. govs. Ea. Okla. State Coll. Devel. Found. With Army N.G., 1937-38; to lt. col. USAAF, 1941-46, Res. 1946-79. Named to Okla. State U. Coll. Bus. Hall of Fame, 1980, Ea. Okla. State Coll. Hall of Fame, 1992; recipient George Washington Honor medal Freedoms Found. Am., 1970, 2002, Disting. Alumnus award Okla. State U., 1979; named Boss of Yr., Nat. Secs. Assn., 1977; charter mem. Poteau (Okla.) Athletic Hall of Fame. Mem. Oklahoma City C. of C., Ea. Okla. State Coll. Alumni Assn. (pres. 2001-03), Toastmasters Internat. (comm. and leadership award 1985), Am. Legion, VFW, Mil. Order of World Wars (Silver Patrick henry medallion 2000), Disabled Am. Vets., Beta Gamma Sigma. Methodist. Home and Office: 2639 N Eagle Ln Oklahoma City OK 73127-1166

HARLAN, WILLIAM ROBERT, JR., physician, educator, researcher; b. Richmond, Va., Nov. 1, 1930; s. William Robert and Helen J. (Weaver) H.; m. Linda Carol Mavencamp, Aug. 23, 1980; children: Elizabeth, William, Christopher, Nicole. BA, U. Va., 1951; MD magna cum laude, Med. Coll. Va., 1955. Diplomate Am. Bd. Internal Medicine, Am. Bd. Family Practice. Intern U. Wis., Madison, 1955-56; resident in medicine Duke U. Hosp., Durham, N.C., 1958-62; dir. Clin. Research Center, Med. Coll. Va., 1963-70; asso. dean U. Ala. Med. Sch., 1970-72; prof. medicine and community health scis. Duke U., 1972-74; prof. medicine and postgrad. medicine U. Mich., Ann Arbor, 1974-88, asst. dean Med. Sch.; dir. div. epidemology and clin. applications Nat. Heart, Lung and Blood Inst., 1988-91; assoc. dir. for disease prevention NIH, Bethesda, 1991—2002; expert NIMH, 2001—, sr. advisor, 2001—. Cons. World Bank; mem. sci. adv. bd. U.S. Air Force; mem. Armed Forces Epidemiology Bd., NIH study sects. and adv. councils. Contbr. articles to med. jours. Served with M.C. USN, 1956-58. Fellow ACP, Am. Coll. Preventive Medicine, Am. Acad. Family Practice, Am. Heart Assn.; mem. N.Y. Acad. Sci., Sigma Xi, Alpha Omega Alpha. Episcopalian. Home: 3503 Windsor Pl Chevy Chase MD 20815-4001 also: 155 N Sea Pines Dr Hilton Head Island SC 29928-5804 E-mail: wharlan@starpower.net.

HARLASS, FREDERICK E. obstetrician, gynecologist, perinatologist; b. Butte, Mont., Feb. 14, 1947; s. June Rena and Edward Gustave Harlass; m. Penny M. Wylie, Feb. 22, 1952; children: Steven Bruce, Scott Alexander, Sarah Lynn. MD, U. of Wash., 1980. Maternal-Fetal Medicine Am. Bd. of Obstetrics & Gynecology, 1996. Obstetrician, gynecologist U.S. Army, Ft. Wainwright, Alaska, 1984—86, chief, ambulatory care Ft. Lewis, Wash., 1986—87, fellow perinatal medicine, 1987—89, chief divsn. of obstetrics El Paso, 1989—91; residency dir. Tex. Tech U., El Paso, 1991—95, chmn., dept. of obstetrics & gynecology, 1995—2000, prof., 2000—. Chief dept. obstetrics, and gynecology, med. dir. for labor and delivery Del Sol Med. Ctr., El Paso, 2000—. Author numerous textbooks. Bd. mem. Lay Midwifery Commn., El Paso, 1993—97. Lt. col. U.S. Army and USN, 1966—99. Decorated 14 awards U.S. Army and USN. Fellow: FACOG (assoc.). Achievements include research in Diabetes in pregnancy. Avocations: golf, travel. Home: 5637 Buckley Dr El Paso TX 79912 Office: Tex Tech U 4800 Alberta El Paso TX 79912 Home Fax: 915-545-6946. Personal E-mail: frederick.harlass@ttuhsc.edu.

HARLEM, SUSAN LYNN, librarian; b. L.A., Oct. 1, 1950; d. Frank Joseph and Esther Frances (Bomell) H.; m. Anthony Stephen Hacsi, Aug. 31, 1990. BA, UCLA, 1972, MLS, 1976. Libr. U. Md., College Park, 1976-79, U.S. Dept. Edn., Washington, 1979-82, GSA, Washington, 1982-87, NLRB, Washington, 1988—. Tutor Washington Lit. Coun., 1992—. Co-author: Washington on Foot, 1984. Office: NLRB Libr 1099 14th St NW Washington DC 20570-0001 E-mail: susan.harlem@nlrb.gov.

HARLEMAN, DONALD ROBERT FERGUSSON, environmental engineering educator; b. Palmerton, Pa., Dec. 5, 1922; s. Robert Roy and Nora (Curry) H.; m. Martha Havens, Oct. 21, 1950; children: Kathleen T., Robert I.H., Anne C. BSCE, Pa. State U., 1943; MS, MIT, 1947, DSc, 1950. Design engr. Curtiss-Wright Corp., Columbus, Ohio, 1944-45; from research asst. to research assoc. Hydrodynamics Lab. MIT, Cambridge, Mass., 1945-50, asst. prof. hydraulics, 1950-56, assoc. prof., 1956-62, prof. civil engring., 1963-75, Ford prof. engring., 1975-91, Ford prof. engring. emeritus, 1991—, head water resources and environ. engring. div., 1972-83, dir. R.M. Parsons Lab., 1973-83. Vis. prof. Calif. Inst. Tech., 1962-63; del. U.S.-Japan Joint Sci. Seminar on Coastal Engring., 1964, 74;; sr. visitor applied math. and theoretical physics Cambridge (Eng.), 1968-69; vis. scientist Internat. Inst. Applied Systems Analysis, Vienna, 1977-78; mem. Water Pollution Control Fedn.; mem. U.S. nat. com. Internat. Assn. Water Pollution Research. Mem. bd. editors Jour. Hydraulic Research. Guggenheim fellow, 1968-69; named Outstanding Alumnus Coll. Engring., Pa. State U., 1979. Mem. ASCE (Research prize 1960, Karl Hilgard Hydraulic prize 1971, 73, J.C. Stevens award, 1973, W.W. Horner award 1983, hon. 1989), Boston Soc. Civil Engrs. (Desmond Fitzgerald medal 1967, hon. mem. 1987), Am. Geophys. Union, Internat. Assn. for Hydraulic Research, Am. Soc. Limnology and Oceanography, Nat. Acad. Engring. Home: 100 Memorial Dr Cambridge MA 02142-1314 Office: MIT Dept Civil Engring Cambridge MA 02139

HARLEY, COLIN EMILE, lawyer; b. Columbia, S.C., Mar. 27, 1940; s. William Hummel and Caroline (Monteith) H.; m. Emilia Saint Amand, June 5, 1965; children: Emile, Gray; m. Anita H. Laudone, May 20, 1978; children: Clayton, Victoria. AB, Dartmouth Coll., 1962; LLB, U. S.C., 1965; LLM, NYU, 1967. Bar: S.C. 1965, N.Y. 1968. Sole practice, Laurens, S.C., 1965; assoc. Davis Polk & Wardwell, N.Y.C., 1967-72, ptnr., 1973—; adj. asst. prof. taxation NYU Sch Law, 1970-75. Trustee Greenwich (Conn.) Country Day Sch., 1987-96, pres., 1994-96. With USMCR, 1961-67. Office: Davis Polk & Wardwell 450 Lexington Ave Fl 31 New York NY 10017-3982 E-mail: colin.harley@dpw.com.

HARLEY, HALVOR LARSON, banker, lawyer; b. Atlantic City, N.J., Oct. 7, 1948; s. Robison Dooling and Loyde Hazel (Gochnauer) Harley. BSc, U. S.C., 1971, MA, 1973; JD, Widener U., 1981. Bar: Pa. 1982, D.C. 1989, U.S. Ct. Appeals (3d cir.) 1987, U.S. Dist. Ct. (ea. dist.) Pa. 1987, U.S. Supreme Ct. 1988, U.S. Ct. Appeals D.C. 1989. Staff psychologist Columbia Area Mental Health Ctr., S.C., 1971-73; dir. Motivational Rsch. Cons., Columbia, 1973-79; psychologist Family Ct. Del., Wilmington, 1979; pvt. practice law Phila., 1982; v.p. investment banking Union Bank, L.A., 1982-88; v.p., mgr. Tokai Bank, Newport Beach., Calif., 1988-94; first v.p., regional mgr. Mellon Pvt. Asset Mgmt., Newport Beach, 1994-97, first v.p., 1994—; regional sales mgr. So. Calif. Pvt. Asset Mgmt., 1994—. Contbr. ; author: Help for Herpes, 1982; cinematographer:. Fundraiser Orange County Performing Art Ctr., 1983—84; trustee, exec. com. Orange County Mus. Arts; vol. Hosp. Ship HOPE, Sri Lanka, 1968—69; bd. dirs., v.p. exec. com. Alzheimers Assn. Orange County; bd. dirs. Lido Sands Homeowners Assn., Newport Beach, 1984—85, So. Calif. Entrepreneurship Acad., pres./bd. dirs.; bd. dirs. United Cerebral Palsy of Orange County; chmn. Bastile Day Com. Mem.: ATLA, World Trade Ctr. Assocs. Orange County (directing com. 1983—85), Indsl. League Orange County (membership com. 1983—84), Calif. Bankers Assn., Am. Bankers Assn., Am. Judicature Soc., Orange County Performing Arts Fraternity (trustee), Psi Chi (chpt. pres. 1971—73). Home: 5015 Lido Sands Dr Newport Beach CA 92663-2403 Office: Mellon Pvt Wealth Mgmt 4695 Macarthur Ct Ste 240 Newport Beach CA 92660-8851

HARLEY, NAOMI HALLDEN, radiation specialist, environmental medicine educator; b. N.Y.C., Aug. 4, 1932; d. Carl Edward and Ida Wilson (Palmer) Hallden; m. John Henry Harley, Sept. 11, 1964. BS, Cooper Union U., N.Y.C., 1959; MS, NYU, 1967, PhD, 1971, Advanced Profl. Cert., 1983. Phys. scientist U.S. AEC, N.Y.C., 1951-65; rsch. prof. environ. medicine NYU, 1965—; coun. mem., sci. com. chmn. Nat. Coun. on Radiation Protection and Measurement, Washington, 1982—. Contbr. articles to profl. jours. Adviser to UN Sci. Com. on Effects of Atomic Radiation (UNSCEAR), 1989—. USPHS fellow, 1988. Fellow: AAAS, Health Physics Soc. Democrat. Office: NYU Sch of Medicine Dept Environ Medicine 550 1st Ave New York NY 10016-6402 E-mail: naomi.harley@med.nyu.edu.

HARLEY, RAFAEL EMANUEL, secondary school educator; b. N.Y.C., Mar. 31, 1967; s. Randolph Emanuel and Shela Francina Harley; children: Rashad, Jacquelyn. BS in Criminal Justice, BA in Pub. Adminstrn. / Polit. Sci., Fla. Meml. Coll., 2002. Cert. bookkeeper Am. Inst. Profl. Bookkeepers. Accounts mgr. Network Svcs., Inc., Coral Gables, Fla., 1993—97; project mgr. NPD Group, Uniondale, NY, 1997—99; tchr., coach Miami (Fla.)-Dade County Pub. Schools, 2000—. Author: (poetry) Hands of Time, 2001 (Editor's Choice award, 2001). Founder, CEO, chmn. Harley Found., Inc., Miami, 1997—, co-founder, COO Harley-Benjamin Found., Miami, 2001—. Ops. specialist USNR, 1988—2002. Mem.: AFL-CIO, NAACP, ASPA, Acad. Polit. Sci., Naval Enlisted Res. Assn., Am. Fedn. Tchrs., United Tchrs. Dade, Am. Polit. Sci. Assn., Golf Soc. U.S., Masons (sec., treas. 1996—2002, Man of the Yr. 2000), Omega Psi Phi (editor, keeper peace, keeper fin. 1995—2002, scholar 1996, award Perseverance 2001). Office: Harley Foundation Inc 19132 NW 33rd Ave Opa Locka FL 33056 Personal E-mail: scarrdogg1@hotmail.com. Business E-Mail: REH Enterprises@AOL.com.

HARLEY, ROBISON DOOLING, JR., lawyer, educator; b. Ancon, Panama, July 6, 1946; s. Robison Dooling and Loyde Hazel (Goehenauer) Harley; m. Suzanne Purviance Bendel, Aug. 9, 1975; children: Arianne Erin, Lauren Loyde. BA, Brown U., 1968; JD, Temple U., 1971; LLM, U. San Diego, 1985. Cert.: Calif. Bd. Legal Specialization (criminal law specialist since 1981) 1981, Nat. Bd. Trial Advocacy (criminal trial adv. since 1981) 1982, bar: Pa. 1971, Calif. 1976, NJ 1977, DC 1981, US Dist. Ct. (cen. and so. dists.) Calif. 1976, US Dist. Ct. NJ 1977, US Dist. Ct. (ea. dist.) Pa. 1987, US Ct. Appeals (9th cir.) 1982, US Ct. Appeals (3rd cir.) 1986, US Supreme Ct. 1980, US Ct. Mil. Appeals 1972. Asst. agy. dir. Safeco Title Ins. Co., LA, 1975—77; ptnr. Cohen, Stokke & Davis, Santa Ana, Calif., 1977—85; prin. prin. Harley Law Offices, Santa Ana, 1985—. Adj. prof. Orange County Coll. Trial Advocacy; adj. prof. paralegal program U. Calif.; instr. trial adv. programs US Army, USN, USAF, USMC; judge pro-tem Orange County Cts. Author: Orange County Trial Lawyers Drunk Driving Syllabus; contbr. articles to profl. jours. Trial counsel, def. counsel, mil. judge, asst. staff judge adv. USMC, 1971—75, regional def. counsel Western Region, 1986—90; bd. dirs. Orange County Legal Aid Soc. Lt. col. JAGC USMCR. Decorated Nat. Def. Svc. medal, Res. medal. Mem.: ATLA, ABA, Orange County Criminal Lawyers Assn. (found. com.), Orange County Trial Lawyers Assn., Orange County Bar Assn. (judiciary com., criminal law sect., adminstrn. of justice com.), Assn. Specialized Criminal Def. Advs., Nat. Assn. for Criminal Def. Attys., Calif. Pub. Defenders Assn., Calif. Attys. for Criminal Justice, Calif. Trial Lawyers Assn., Marine Corps Assn., Marine Corps Res. Officers Assn., Res. Officers Assn. Republican. Avocations: sports, physical fitness, reading. Home: 31211 Paseo Miraloma San Juan Capistrano CA 92675-5505 Office: Harley Law Offices 825 N Ross St Santa Ana CA 92701-3419

HARLEY, ROBISON DOOLING, physician, educator; b. Pleasantville, N.J., Feb. 27, 1911; s. Halvor L. and Alice (Robison) H.; children— Robison Dooling, Ardee R., Heather L., Halvor L. II, William W. B.Sc., Rutgers U., 1932; MD, U. Pa., 1936; PhD, U. Minn., 1949. Diplomate Am. Bd. Ophthalmology. Intern Phila. Gen. Hosp., 1936-38; fellowship Mayo Clinic, Rochester, Minn., 1938-41, jr. staff cons., 1941-42; pvt. practice as ophthalmologist and ophthalmic surgeon Atlantic City and Phila., 1947-67; attending surgeon, dir. ophthalmology St. Christopher's Hosp. for Children, Phila., 1958-70; chief surgeon Atlantic City Hosp., 1950-67; cons. Shore Meml. Hosp., Somers Point, 1958-67; attending surgeon Temple U. Hosp., Phila., 1947-87; also Wills Eye Hosp. and Research Inst. Cons. Betty Bacharach Home for Children; cons. surgeon Wills Eye Hosp.; attending surgeon, dir. dept. pediatrics and motility; formerly prof., chmn. ophthalmology, prof. pediatrics Temple U. Health Sci. Ctr., Phila.; now prof. emeritus; dir. Overseas Eye Programs: Project Hope, Care-Medico, Internat. Eye Surgeons, Project Orbis; adj. prof. Thomas Jefferson U.; A.L. Morgan lectr., Toronto, 1972, Antonio Navas lectr., P.R., 1979, Frank Costenbader lectr., Washington., 1979. Author 152 med. publs. indluding book chpts. and 4 textbooks; contbg. author: Textbook of Pediatrics, 1975, 77, 79, 98; contbr. chpt. Pediatric Ophthalmological Surgery; editor: Pediatric Ophthalmology, 1975, Pediatric Opthalmology textbook, 2 vols., 1983, 4th edit., 1999; contbr. articles to profl. jours., chpts. to books; mem. editorial bd.: Jour. Pediatric Ophthalmology and Strabismus. Mem. exec. bd. Atlantic area coun. Boy Scouts Am., 1949—; mem. Fight for Signt Inc., N.Y.C., Retinitis Pigmentosa Found. Served to lt. col. AUS, 1942-47. Decorated Legion of Merit from Panama (Vasco Nunez de Balboa); recipient Outstanding Humanitarian award Am. Acad. Ophthalmology, Dallas, 2000, Hero of Medicine, Pride of the Profession award AMA, 2001. Fellow ACS (gov. 1959-62), Am. Acad. Ophthalmology (assoc. sec. continuing edn., Outstanding Humanitarian award 2000); mem. Assn. Rsch. Ophthalmology, Pan-Am. Congress Ophthalmology, Am. Ophthal. Soc., Del. Assn. Blind. (pres.), Phi Beta Kappa, Sigma Xi. Clubs: Explorers N.Y.C., Brigantine (N.J.) Yacht (commodore); Union League (Phila.); Corinthian Yacht (Cape May, N.J.). Home: 2401 Pennsylvania Ave Apt 704 Wilmington DE 19806-1410

HARLEY, RUTH, artist, educator; b. Phila. children: Peter Wells Bressler, Victoria Angela. Student, Pa. State U., 1941; BFA, Phila. Coll. Art, 1945; postgrad., U. N.H., 1971, Hampshire Coll., 1970. Former instr. Phila. Mus. Art, 1946-59; former art supt. Ventnor (N.J.) City Bd. Edn., 1959-61. Art tchr. The Print Club, Phila., Allens Lane Art Ctr., Phila., Suburban Ctr. Arts, Lower Merion, Pa., Radner (Pa.) Twp. Adult Ctr., 1949-59, Atlantic City Adult Ctr., 1959-60. One-woman shows include Dubin-Lush Galleries, Phila., 1956, Contemporary Art Assn., Phila., 1957, Vernon Art Exhbns., Germantown, Pa., 1958, Detroit Inst. Arts, 1958, Phila. Mus. Art, 1957, 59, Moore Inst., Phila., 1962-68, Greenhill Galleries, Phila., 1974, Phila. Civic Ctr., 1978, Natal Rio Grande du Norte, Brazil, 1979, Galerie Novel Esprit, Tampa, Fla., 1992-95, Mind's Eye Gallery, St. Petersburg, Fla., 1993, Ga. Tech. Art Ctr., 1998, Robert Ferst Ctr. for the Arts Ga. Inst. Tech., 1998-99; exhibited in group shows, including Group 55, Phila., 1955, Print Club, Phila., 1955, Nat. Tours 1956-59, Pa. Acad. Fine Arts, 1957, Vernon Art Exhbns., 1958, Detroit Inst. Arts, 1958, Phila. Mus. Art, 1959, Moore Inst., 1962, Phila. Civic Ctr. Mus., 1975, Galerie Nouvel Esprit Assemblage Russe, 1992, Kenneth Raymond Gallery, Boca Raton, 1992-93, Mind's Eye Gallery, 1993, Polk Mus. Art, Lakeland, Fla., 1993, Don Roll Gallery, Sarasota, Fla., 1994-95, Las Vegas (Nev.) Internat. Art Expo, 1994, Heim Am. Gallery, Fisher Island, Fla., 1996, McLean Gallery, Malibu, Calif., 1997, 98, 99, Robert Ferst Ctr. Arts, Ga. Tech. U., 1998, 99, Christina Gallery, Atlanta, 1999, 2000, Adrian Howard Gallery, St. Petersburg, 2000, 2001, 2002, Melrose Bay Art Gallery, Melrose, Fla., 2001, Red River Valley Mus., Vernon, Tex., 2001, Kirkpatrick Mus., Okla., 2001, Airport,

Gainesville, Fla., 2001; represented in permanent collections at U. Villanova (Pa.) Mus., TemplU. Law Sch., Pa., Woodmere Mus., Phila.; included in Art in America Ann. Guide, 2000-01, 2002; photo sculpture commd. through Phila. Re-Devel. Authority. Contbr. art prize to Ventnor N.J. Sch. Sys. Address: PO Box 433 Melrose FL 32666-0433 E-mail: harleyruth@aol.com.

HARLOW, CAROL JEAN, prospect researcher; b. New Haven, Conn., Apr. 12, 1952; d. Frank J. and Aileen W. H.; children: Anna, Lydia. BA, U. Conn., Storrs, 1974; MS, Southern Conn. State U., New Haven, 1978. Circulation librarian Atlanta Coll. of Art, Atlanta, 1980-83; registrar, 1983-85; admissions coord. Emory Univ. Sch. of Nursing, Atlanta, 1985-88; tech. writer TechData, Clearwater, FL, 1995-96; dir. prospect rsch. Univ. Tampa, Tampa, FL, 1996—. Mem. vestry St. Catherine's Episcopal Ch., 1999—. Democrat. Avocations: reading, opera. Office: University of Tampa 401 W Kennedy Blvd Tampa FL 33606-1450 Fax: 813-258-7297. E-mail: charlow@ut.edu.

HARLOW, EDWARD E., JR., oncologist; BS in Microbiology, U. Okla., 1974, MS, 1978; PhD, U. London, 1982. Rsch. microbiologist McDonnell Douglas Aerospace, St. Louis, 1974-75; fellow of the Lady Tata Meml. Trust Imperial Cancer Rsch. Fund Labs., London, 1978-81, vis. fellow, 1982; prof. genetics, dir. rsch. Mass. Gen. Hosp. Cancer Ctr., Charlestown; now prof., chmn. biological chemistry and molecular pharmacology Harvard Med. Sch. Mem. selection jury Lasker Prize; mem. awards assembly GM Cancer Rsch. Found.; mem. new investigator rsch. adv. com. Med. Found.; mem. external adv. bd. UCLA Jonsson Comprehensive Cancer Ctr., Washington U. Cancer Ctr.; mem. sci. adv. bd. Children's Hosp., Boston, Found. for Advanced Cancer Studies; Eppley vis. prof. U. Nebr. Med. Ctr., 1991; Ralph R. Braund vis. prof. Forum on Cancer Rsch., 1993; Richard C. Parker meml. lectr. Columbis U., 1993; Charles L. Spurr prof. oncology Wake Forest U., 1994; William Sokolow vis. lectr. U. Calif., San Francisco, 1995; Eudoxia Dutkevich meml. lectr. U. Toronto, Can., 1996; Charles B. Smith vis. rsch. prof. Meml. Sloan-Kettering Cancer Ctr., 1996; Howard Hughes lectr. MIT,1996. Author: (with D. Lane) Antibodies: A Laboratory Manual, 1988, Using Antibodies: A Laboratory Manual, 1998; editor: (with F. Alt and E. Ziff) Current Communications in Molecular Biology, Nuclear Oncogenes, 1987, (with J. Brugge, T. Curran and F. McCormick) Origins of Human Cancer, 1992; contbr. articles to profl. jours. Trustee Cold Spring Harbor Lab. Recipient Alfred P. Sloan, Jr. medal GM Cancer Rsch. Found., 1995. also: Harvard Med Sch Dept Molecular Pharmacology 240 Longwood Ave # C1-213 Boston MA 02115-5701

HARLOW, ELIZABETH MARY, retired music educator; b. Boston; d. William Joseph and Elizabeth Frieda (Binnig) H.; 1 child, William Harlow Gunn. MusB, Danbury State Tchrs. Coll., Conn., 1959. Music tchr. Guilford Bd. Edn., Conn., 1959-62, North Haven Bd. Edn., Conn., 1962-65, Hamden Bd. Edn., Conn., 1976-99; ret., 1999. Mem. Conn. Ednl. Assn., Nat. Music Educators, Am. Choral Dirs. Assn. Hamden Edn. Assn.

HARLOW, JOAN BEVERLEY, writer; b. Malden, Mass. d. Albert Ernest and Marguerite Wells (Small) Hiatt; m. Richard Lee Harlow; children: Deborah, Lisa, Kristan, Scott, Jennifer. Cert., Stenotype Inst., Boston. Lectr. in field. Author: (children's books) Poems Are for Everything, 1973, Shadow Bear, 1981, The Mysterious Dr. Chen, 1996, Star in the Storm, 2000, The Dark Side of the Creek, 2000, The Wishing Sky, 2001, Joshua's Song, 2001, Creatures of Sand Castle Key, 2001. Mem. Soc. Children's Book Writers and Illustrators, Authors Guild

HARMAN, CAROLE MOSES, retired art educator, artist; b. Bklyn. BA in Art Edn., R.I. Sch. Design, 1965, MA in Art Edn., 1969; PhD of Pedagogy (hon.), R.I. Coll., 2002. Tchr. art Fairfield (Conn.) Pub. Schs., 1965-68; chair dept. art Hope H.S., 1969—78, Central H.S., 1978—99; critic tchr., dept. art edn. R.I. Sch. Design, Providence, 1969—99; ret., 1999. Lectr. R.I. Inst. Secondary Edn., Brown U., 1989—; adj. tchr. art edn. dept. R.I. Coll., 1999—, coll. supr. art student tchrs., 1999—; cons. to the arts Providence Sch. Dept., 2000—; bd. dirs. New Urban Arts; trustee R.I. Sch. Design, 2002—. Exhibited in shows at Providence Art Club, Diva Gallery, Providence, R.I. Sch. Design, R.I. Art Educators, Salon de Refuse AS220, Providence, others. Active John Hope Settlement House; co-chair bus. edn. partnership Citizens Bank and Central H.S., 1989—; trustee R.I. Sch. Design, 2002. Recipient Proclamation citation and Key to the City awarded by Mayor Vincent Cianci for Outstanding Svc. to schoolchildren of Providence, Tchr. of Yr. award Providence Sch. Dept., 1982-83, Milken Family Found. Nat. Edn. award, 1993, Excellence in Edn. tchr. award Pub. Edn. Fund, 1998; grantee Pub. Edn. Fund, 1992-96. Mem. R.I. Sch. Design Alumni Assn. (pres. 1994-96, v.p. 1992), coun. exec. com. 1984—. Address: 158 10th St Providence RI 02906-2922

HARMAN, CHARLES MORGAN, mechanical engineer; b. Cannonsburg, Pa., July 25, 1929; s. Charles Nash and Mildred (Barker) H.; m. Althea Ann Ashton, June 12, 1956 (div.); children: Ruth Ann, Charles Morgan, Samuel Stuart. BS, U. Md., 1954; MS, U. N.D., 1957; PhD, U. Wis., 1961. Registered profl. engr., Wis., N.C. Asst. prof. mech. engring. Duke U., Durham, N.C., 1961-70, prof. mech. engring., 1970—, assoc. dean Grad. Sch., 1970-80, dir. grad. studies, 1986—2001; pres. Synergy Rsch. Corp., 1983-84. Engring. cons. Douglas Aircraft Co., 1961-64, Army Research Office, Durham, 1964— Contbr. articles to profl. jours.; editor: Jour. Advanced Transp, 1976— . Served with USN, 1949-51. Ford Found. fellow, 1960-61; recipient Profl. Achievement citation Douglas Aircraft Co., 1964 Mem. ASME. Home: 1701 Tisdale St Durham NC 27705-5631 Office: Duke U Dept Mech Engring Durham NC 27708-0301

HARMAN, DONALD LEE, nurse, educator, consultant; b. Titusville, Pa., Mar. 22, 1948; s. William Ceska and Eva Louise (Matha) H. BS in Edn., Edinboro U., Pa., 1970, MEd, 1972; AD in Nursing, Ohio U.-Zanesville, 1977; MSN, U. Wis., 1993. RN, Ohio, Ill., Wis. Dir. out-patient svcs. Spencer Hosp., Meadville, Pa., 1974; in-svc. instr. Guernsey Meml. Hosp., Cambridge, Ohio, 1974-77; instr. in med., surg., and pediat. nursing Blessing Hosp., Quincy, Ill., 1977-79; relief. staff nurse Rush Presbyn. St. Luke's Hosp., Chgo., 1979; camp nurse Young Men's Jewish Coun., Chgo., 1979; emergency rm. nurse Henrotin Hosp., Chgo., 1979, intravenous therapist, 1980; head instr. med. surg. nursing Sch. Nursing Madison (Wis.) Gen. Hosp., 1980-81, dir. nursing Edn., 1981-86; dir. mktg. and sales Epic Sys. Corp., 1986-88; tng. and devel. coord. Hazleton Labs. Am., Inc., Madison, Wis., 1988-89, asst. mgr. clin. rsch. unit, 1989-90; instr. Madison Area Tech. Coll., 1988-92; staff nurse U. Wis., Madison, 1990-94; charge nurse Mendota Mental Health Inst., 1990-94; clin. nurse specialist Citation Computer Sys. Inc., 1993—96; sr. clin. sales cons. Health-VISION Corp., 1996—98; clin. cons., instr. Eclipsys Corp., 1999—2001; clin. nurse specialist Oakwood Nursing Home, 2001—03; employee health nurse Dept. of Corrections, 2001—03; with Corner Computer Company, 2003—. Pres., bd. dirs. CommonHealth Co.; del. to China U.S. Healthcare Systems, 1987; cons. HMDS Computer Systems, 1994-95. Author: Energy--For All Reasons Facilitator's Guide. Recipient Copper Cup award, Madison Gen. Hosp., 1983. Mem. NEA (life). Methodist.

HARMAN, DONNA A. lawyer; b. Elkhart, Kans., Aug. 6, 1959; d. Donald E. and Pearl Duvall Akers; m. John R. Harman III, Aug. 20, 1988; children: Caitlin, Caroline. BA in Pub. Affairs and Econs., Anderson U., 1981; JD, Am. U., 1988. Bar: D.C. 1989. Fin. dir. Rep. Party La., Baton Rouge, 1981-83; legis. aide U.S. Rep. W. Henson Moore, Washington, 1983-85; mgr. govt. rels. The Dow Chem. Co., Washington, 1985-89; dir. govt. rels. Champion Internat., Washington, 1989-99, counsel govt. affairs, 1999—. Chairperson Alternative Minimum Tax Coalition, Washington, 1993—; bd. co-chair Tax Coalition, Washington, 1996. Bd. dirs. Nat. Presbyn. Ch., Washington, 1998—; leader Girls Scouts Am. Avocation: girls soccer. Office: Champion Internat Corp 1875 I St NW Ste 540 Washington DC 20006-5425

HARMAN, GEORGE GIBSON, physicist, consultant; b. Norfolk, Va., Dec. 7, 1924; s. George Gibson and Annie Wall (Baldwin) Harman; m. Ann Worischek, Jan. 31, 1953 (div. 1985); children: Joyce Catherine, Arthur Lawrence, Stewart Thomas; m. Donna K. Williamson, 1986. BS in Physics, Va. Poly. Inst., 1949; MS in Physics, U. Md., 1959. With Nat. Inst. Stds. and Tech. (formerly Nat. Bur. Stds.), Washington, 1950—, sr. rsch. scientist, 1976-93, fellow, 1993—2003, dean of staff, 2001—. Rsch. fellow Reading U., England, 1962—63. Author: 2 books; contbr. With U.S. Army, 1943—46. Recipient Silver medal, U.S. Dept. Commerce, 1973, Gold medal, 1979, Achievement award, Internat. Electronics Packaging Soc., 1988. Fellow: IEEE (chmn. fellows and awards com. 1989—, Centennial medal 1984, Outstanding Contbns. award 1992, 1993, 15-Yr. Outstanding Contbns. to ECT Conf. 1993, Harry Diamond Meml. award 1996, Third Millennium medal 2000, Outstanding Sustained Tech. Contbns. award 2001), Soc. Mfg. Engrs. (Excellence in Electronic Mfg. award 2001), Internat. Microelectronics Packaging Soc. (chpt. pres. 1980—82, regional dir. 1698—1987, chmn. found. grants com., chmn. nat. tech. program com. 1990—92, nat. pres. 1995, Tech. Achievement award 1981, Lewis F. Miller award 1984, Disting. Svc. award 1986, 1987, Daniel C. Hughes award 1989, DVS European Electronic Packaging award 1998); mem.: ASTM, Am. Phys. Soc., Cosmos Club Washington, Sigma Pi Sigma, Sigma Xi. Achievements include patents in field. Home: 4719 Dorset Ave Bethesda MD 20815-5445 Office: Nat Inst Standards and Tech Div # 812 Gaithersburg MD 20899-0001

HARMAN, GILBERT HELMS, philosophy educator; b. East Orange, NJ, May 26, 1938; s. William Henry and Marguerite Variel (Page) H.; m. Lucy Newman, Aug. 14, 1970; children: Elizabeth, Olivia. BA, Swarthmore Coll., 1960; PhD, Harvard U., 1964. With dept. philosophy Princeton (N.J.) U., 1963—, prof., 1971—, acting chair, 2001—02, chair cognitive studies program, 1992-97. Author: Thought, 1973, The Nature of Morality, 1977, Change in View, 1986, Skepticism and the Definition of Knowledge, 1990, (with Judith Jarvis Thomson) Moral Relativism and Moral Objectivity, 1996, Reasoning, Meaning, and Mind, 1999, Explaining Value and Other Essays in Moral Philosophy, 2000; editor: On Noam Chomsky, 1974, (with Donald Davidson) Semantics of Natural Language, 1971, (with Donald Davidson) The Logic of Grammar, 1975, Conceptions of the Human Mind, 1993. Mem.: Philosophy Sci. Soc., Am. Psychol. Soc., Cognitive Sci. Soc., Am. Philos. Assn. Home: 106 Broadmead St Princeton NJ 08540-7216 Office: Princeton Univ Dept Philosophy Princeton NJ 08544-1006 E-mail: harman@princeton.edu.

HARMAN, JANE, congresswoman; b. N.Y.C., June 28, 1945; d. A. N. and Lucille (Geier) Lakes; m. Sidney Harman, Aug. 30, 1980; children: Brian Lakes, Hilary Lakes, Daniel Geier, Justine Leigh. BA, Smith Coll., 1966; JD, Harvard U., 1969. Bar: D.C. 1969, U.S. Ct. Appeals (D.C. cir.) 1972, U.S. Supreme Ct. 1975. Spl. asst. Commn. of Chs. on Internat. Affairs, Geneva, 1969-70; assoc. Surrey & Morse, Washington, 1970-72; chief legis. asst. Senator John V. Tunney, Washington, 1972-73; chief counsel, staff dir. Subcom. on Rep. Citizen Interests, Com. on Judiciary, Washington, 1973-75; adj. prof. Georgetown Law Ctr., Washington, 1974-75; chief counsel, staff dir. Subcom. on Constl. Rights, Com. on Judiciary, Washington, 1975-77; dep. sec. to cabinet The White House, Washington, 1977-78; spl. counsel Dept. Def., Washington, 1979; ptnr. Manatt, Phelps, Rothenberg & Tunney, Washington, 1979-82, Surrey & Morse, Washington, 1982-86; of counsel Jones, Day, Reavis & Pogue, Washington, 1987-92; mem. U.S. Ho. of Reps. 103rd-105th, 107th-108th Congresses from 36th Calif. dist., 1992-98, 2001—; mem. nat. security com., intelligence com. 103rd-105th Congresses; mem. energy and commerce com., intelligence com. 107th Congress, 2001—; mem. Nat. Commn. on Terrorism, 1999—2000. Regents prof. UCLA, 1999-2000; mem. vis. coms. Harvard Law Sch., 1976-82, Kennedy Sch. Govt., 1990-96. Vice-chmn. Ctr. for Nat. Policy, Washington, 1981—90; trustee Smith Coll.; counsel Dem. Platform Com., Washington, 1984; chmn. Dem. Nat. Com. Nat. Lawyers' Coun., Washington, 1986—90; bd. dirs. Planned Parenthood, 1998—2000, Venice (Calif.) Family Clinic, 1998—2000. Mem. Phi Beta Kappa. Democrat. Office: 811 N Catalina Ave Ste 1302 Redondo Beach CA 90277 also: 2400 Rayburn HOB Washington DC 20515-0536*

HARMAN, JOYCE ELIZABETH, humanities educator; d. Harold Lagar and Elizabeth Luella (Moore) Harman. BA, Ohio State U., 1960, MA, 1962; postgrad., Case Western Res. U., 1964—66. Editl. asst. Charles E. Merrill, Columbus, 1967; manuscript specialist Ohio Hist. Soc., Columbus, 1967—69; historian Hist. St. Augustine, Fla., 1969—74; adj. prof. Edison C.C., Ft. Myers, Fla., 1986—96; substitute tchr. Lee County Schs., Ft. Myers, 1997—2002; intake screener Juvenile Svcs. Program, Ft. Myers, 1999—2000; adj. prof. Barry U., Ft. Myers, 2002—. Author: Trade & Privateering in Spanish Florida, 1732-1763, 1969. Recipient Cert. of Commendation, Am. Assn. for State & Local History, 1970. Mem.: Fla. Hist. Soc., Nat. Writers Assn. (Gulf Coast chpt.), Ohio State U. Alumni Assn. Republican. Methodist. Avocations: reading, writing, music, theater. Home: 13809 Heronwood Ln #21 Fort Myers FL 33919-8147 Office: Barry Univ 10100 Deer Run Farms Rd #200 Fort Myers FL 33912-1045

HARMAN, ROBERT JOHN, retired religious organization administrator; b. Elmhurst, Ill., Oct. 10, 1937; s. Clifford Martin and Anna Elizabeth (Johnson) H.; m. Marcia Bornemeier, Aug. 1, 1959; children: Scott, Michael. BA, North Ctrl. Coll., 1959; BD, Garett Evang. Theol. Sem., 1962; postgrad., Union Theol. Sem., 1973-74, 69-72; MPA, NYU, 1975. Ordained to ministry Evang. United Brethren Ch., 1962; (merged with United Meth. Ch. 1968). Sr. pastor Cmty. United Meth. Ch., Naperville, Ill., 1968-73; planner, nat. divsn. Gen. Bd. Global Mins., N.Y.C., 1975-84; dist. supt. No. Ill. Conf. Meth. Chs., Chgo., 1984-85; dir. planning United Meth. Ch. Gen. Bd. of Global Mins., N.Y.C., 1985-89, dep. gen. sec., world divsn., 1989-2000; retired, 2000. Unit dir. Nat. Coun. Chs., N.Y.C., 1978-83, 89-96; del. World Coun. Chs., Geneva, 1991, mem. unit II commn. on chs. in mission; health, edn. and witness, 1992—; mem. exec. com. World Meth. Coun., 1991. Mem. editl. bd., pres. Christianity and Crisis Jour., 1982-84; contbr. articles to profl. jours. Dep. gen. sec. Cmty. and Instl. Mins., Evangelization and Ch. Growth. Recipient numerous fellowships.

HARMAN, TERRIE, lawyer; b. Williamsport, Pa., May 23, 1953; d. Lyle Eugene H. and Phyllis Ann Stuart; m. Thomas David McCarron, Oct. 5, 1989. AB, Wilson Coll., 1975; JD, Franklin Pierce Law Ctr., 1978. Bar: N.H. 1978, Maine 1978. Staff atty. Pine Tree Legal Assistance, Bangor, Maine, 1978—79; assoc. Myers & Laufer, Concord, NH, 1979—82; atty. pvt. practice, Portsmouth, NH, 1982—2001; ptnr. Watson, Bosen, Harman, Venci and Lemire, Portsmouth, 2001—. Bd. dirs. Children and Family Svcs. of N.H., Friends of the Kotzschmar Organ, Portland, Maine. Bd. dirs. Feminist Health Ctr., Portsmouth, 1997—. Mem. N.H. Bar Assn., Maine Bar Assn., Portsmouth Men's Chorus (founder, exec. dir. 2000—), Young Organists Collaborative. Avocations: church organist, piano and organ teacher, auctioneer. Home: PO Box 463 New Castle NH 03854-0463 Office: 75 Congress St Ste 211 Portsmouth NH 03801

HARMAN, THOMAS, state official; m. Dianne Harman; children: Michael, Michelle. BS in Bus. Adminstrn., Kans. State U.; JD, Loyola U. Businessman; coun. mem. Huntington Beach City Coun., 1994—2000; state assembly mem. Dist. 67 Calif. State Assembly, 2000—. Mem. budget com.; vice-chair govtl. orgn. judiciary com.; mem. natural resources com.; mem. revenue and taxation com.; mem. VA com. Mem.: Orange County Local Agy. Found. Commn., Bolsa Chica Land Trust, Huntington Beach C. of C. Republican. Mailing: Rm 5158 PO Box 942849 Sacramento CA 94249 Office: Ste 570 17011 Beach Blvd Huntington Beach CA 92647

HARMAN, WALLACE PATRICK, lawyer; b. El Paso, Tex., Jan. 22, 1949; s. Wallace Irvin and Dorothy Louise (Pearson) H.; m. Gina Marie Ries, Dec. 31, 1988; children: Loren Patrick, Claire Marie. BA, Stanford U., 1972; JD, U. Calif., 1977. Bar: Calif. 1977, U.S. Ct. Appeals (9th cir.) 1977, N.Mex. 1978, U.S. Dist. Ct. N.Mex. 1978, U.S. Ct. Appeals (10th cir.) 1978. Zone adminstrn. mgr. Am. Motors Corp., Burlingame, Calif., 1972-74; atty., shareholder Sutin, Thayer & Browne, APC, Albuquerque, N.Mex., 1977-87, group leader comml. group, 1985-87; atty., shareholder, mng. ptnr., leader bus. group The Payne Law Firm, P.C., Albuquerque, 1987-91; atty., ptnr. Hisey & Wainwright, P.A., Albuquerque, 1991-92; atty., pres., chief exec. officer The Harman Law Firm, P.C., Littleton, CO, 1992—. Mem. N.Mex. Supreme Ct. Med.-Legal Panel, Albuquerque, 1978-80, 91—; mem. N.Mex. Supreme Ct. Lawyers Assistance Com., Albuquerque, 1991—; area rep. The Taft Sch., Watertown, Conn., 1992—; mem. mentorship program Hatings Coll. Law. Co-author: Recent Developments in Commerical Law, University of New Mexico Law Review, 1989. Bd. advisors Lovelace Med. Ctr., Albuquerque, 1980-89; mem. state bd. trustees The Nature Conservancy, N.Mex., 1984-88; adv. bd. Assistance League Albuquerque, 1982-89, Jr. League Albuquerque, 1984-87, Make-a-Wish Found. of N.Mex., Inc., 1996-97. Recipient AV Rating award Martindale-Hubbell, 1990. Mem. ABA, Albuquerque Bar Assn. Democrat. Avocations: photography, sports, computers, landscaping, writing. E-mail: wpatnickharmon_@msn.com.

HARMAN, WILLARD NELSON, malacologist, educator; b. Geneva, NY, Apr. 20, 1937; s. Samuel Willard and Mary Nelson (Covert) H.; m. Susan Beth Mead, June 12, 1968 (div. 1980); children: Rebecca Mary, Willard Wade; m. Barbara Ann Stong, June 8, 1981; children: Jessica Mary, Samuel Willard. Student, Hobart Coll., 1954-55; BS, Coll. Environ. Sci. and Forestry, SUNY, 1965; PhD, Cornell U., 1968; postgrad., Marine Biol. Lab., Woods Hole, Mass., 1968. Asst. prof. SUNY, Oneonta, 1968-69, assoc. prof., 1969-76, prof. biology, 1976—2002, chmn. dept. biology, 1981-89, dir. Biol. Field Sta., 1989—, disting. svc. prof., 2002—. Resource advisor N.Y. State Dept. Environ. Conservation, Albany, 1980—. Contbr. articles to profl. jours. Rep. Otsego County Republican Com., N.Y., 1973-76; chmn. planning bd., Springfield, N.Y., 1984-96. Served with USN, 1956-61. Recipient Chancellor's award SUNY, 1974-75, Quality award EPA, 1989, Excellence award SUNY, 1990. Mem. Soc. Limnology and Oceanography, N.Am. Benthological Soc., Soc. for Exptl. and Descriptive Malacology, Am. Malocological Union, Otsego County Conservation Assn. (bd. dirs. 1970—, pres. 1974-78, 80-81, chmn. lake com. 1981—). Episcopalian. Avocations: sailing, fishing, scuba diving, skiing. Home: RR 2 Box 829 Cooperstown NY 13326-9327 Office: Biol Field Sta 5838 St Hwy 80 Cooperstown NY 13326-9330

HARMAN, WILLIAM BOYS, JR., lawyer; b. Newport News, Va., June 5, 1930; s. William Boys and Helen (Conner) H.; children: Susan Carol, Thomas Scott, Ann Carrington. AB, Coll. William and Mary, 1951, JD, 1956; LLM, Georgetown U., 1960. Bar: Va. 1956, D.C. 1961. Tax atty. Gen. Motors Corp., Detroit, 1956-58; atty. Office Chief Counsel, IRS, Washington, 1958-59, Office of Tax Legis. Counsel, U.S. Treasury Dept., Washington, 1959-61; atty. firm Cummings & Sellers, Washington, 1961-62; asso. gen. counsel Am. Life Conv., Washington, 1962-67, gen. counsel, 1968-72; v.p. law Am. Life Ins. Assn., 1973-75; exec. v.p. Am. Council Life Ins., 1976-78; partner firm Sutherland, Asbill & Brennan, Washington, 1978-85, Davis & Harman, Washington, 1985—. Served with USCGR, 1952-54. Mem. ABA, Va. State Bar, D.C. Bar Assn., Assn. Life Ins. Counsel, Am. Law Inst., SAR, William and Mary Law Sch. Assn., Order of Coif, Washington Golf and Country Club, Metropolitan Club, Phi Beta Kappa, Phi Alpha Delta, Sigma Alpha Epsilon. Home: 3839 N Tazewell St Arlington VA 22207-4568 Office: Davis & Harman Ste 1200 1455 Pennsylvania Ave NW Washington DC 20004-1008 E-mail: wbharman@davis-harman.com.

HARMAN, WILLIAM P. religious studies educator; b. Elkins, W.Va., 1946; s. Fred Dove Harman and Bessie Pulliam. AB, Oberlin Coll., 1968; MA, U. Chgo., 1981, PhD. Lectr. Loras (Iowa) Coll., 1979; chair, dept. religion Depauw U., Greencastle, Ind., 1981—2002; head, dept. philosophy & religion U. Tenn., Chattanooga, 2002—. Cons. Nat. Endowment Humanities, Washington, 1998; pres., Midwest Am. Acadamy Religion, Chicago, 1999—2001; bd. mem. Am. Inst. Indian Studies, Chicago, Ill., 2000—. Author: (book) Religion in Tamilnadu, The Sacred Marriage of a Hindu Goddess; contbr. articles to profl. jours. Fellow, Nat. Endowment Humanities, 1986, Am. Inst. Indian Studies, 1989. Mem.: Am. Anthrop. Assn. (assoc.), Am. Acad. Religion (assoc.; panel coord. 2001). Office: U Tenn Philosophy and Religion Dept 615 McCallie Ave Chattanooga TN 37403 E-mail: william-harman@utc.edu.

HARMEL, HILDA HERTA See PIERCE, HILDA

HARMEL, MEREL HILBER, anesthesiologist, educator; b. Cleve., May 19, 1917; s. Louis and Hermine (Greenbaum) H.; m. Armide Chilcoat, July 2, 1944 (dec. 1988); children: Nancy Armide, Ruth Courtney, Priscilla Gover, Mary Louise; m. Ernestine Friedl Levy, Dec. 27, 1990.. BA, Johns Hopkins U., 1938, MD, 1943. Diplomate Am. Bd. Anesthesiology. Fellow in anesthesiology NRC; anesthesiologist-in-chief Albany Med. Ctr., 1948-52, Kings County Med. Ctr., Bklyn., 1952-68, pres. med. bd., 1958-62, chmn. exec. com., 1964-65; cons. L.I. Jewish, St. Albans Naval, Maimonides, St. John's Episcopal, VA hosps., N.C. Eye and Ear Hosp., Durham; assoc. prof. anesthesiology (surgery) Albany Med. Coll., 1948-52; prof., chmn. dept. anesthesiology SUNY Downstate Med. Ctr., 1952-68, Pritzker Sch. Medicine, U. Chgo., 1968-71; prof. anesthesiology Duke Med. Ctr., Durham, N.C., 1971—, chmn. dept. anesthesiology ctr., 1971-83, prof. anesthesiology, 1983-87, Merel H Harmel prof. in anesthesiology, 2002, prof. emeritus, 1987—; prof. canesthesiology Duke U. Med Ctr., 2002—. Vis. prof. dept. anesthesiology Sch. Medicine, Johns Hopkins U., 1985—. Contbr. articles to profl. jours. Commonwealth fellow Oxford U., 1961-62, hon. mem. Sr. Common Rm., Pembroke Coll., 1961, Disting. Alumnus award Johns Hopkins Sch. Medicine, 2003; Merel Harmel vis. lectureship established Duke U. Med. Ctr., 1983. Fellow Am. Coll. Anesthesiology (bd. govs.), Royal Coll. Anaesthesia Faculty; mem. AMA, Am. Soc. Anesthesiologists (Living History Series), Assn. Univ. Anesthetists, Duke U. Med. Ctr. Founders Soc., Johns Hopkins U. Soc. Scholars, Japan Soc. Anesthesiologists (hon.), Assn. Anesthesiologists Français (hon.), Oxford Soc. Carolinas (hon. sec. 1990—, W.G. Anlyan Lifetime Achievement award 1999). Office: Duke U Med Ctr Dept Anesthesiology PO Box 3094 Durham NC 27715-3094 E-mail: harme001@mc.duke.edu.

HARMEL, WARREN, marketing professional; married; 3 children. Degree in bus. adminstrn., mktg. cum laude, U. Cape Town, South Africa. Founding ptnr., gen. mgr. Mortimer Tiley/BBDO, 1979; dir. Phillips Petroleum Acct. Tracy-Locke, Dallas, 1986, promoted to v.p. strategic planning; sr. v.p. bus. devel. and strategy Orneles & Assocs., 1990—95; pvt. practice as founder, mng. ptnr., 2002—. Recipient 4 Effie awards, David Ogilvy Rsch. award, Adv. Rsch. Found. Mem.: Assn. Hispanic Adv. Agys. (founder). Office: 3102 Oak Lawn Ste 109 Dallas TX 75219

HARMELIN, STEPHEN JOSEPH, lawyer; b. Phila., May 7, 1939; s. Louis M. and Ethel (Katz) H.; m. Julia Tose, June 18, 1995; children: Alison Kate, Melina Alexis. BA cum laude, U. Pa., 1960; LLB, Harvard U., 1963. Bar: Pa. 1964, U.S. Supreme Ct. 1968. Atty. broadcast bur. FCC, Washington, 1964; aide White House, Washington, 1964-65; assoc. Dilworth, Paxson, Kalish & Dilks (name now Dilworth Paxson LLP), Phila., 1965-70; ptnr. Dilworth, Paxson, Kalish & Dilks, Phila., 1970-86; co-chmn. corp. dept. Dilworth, Paxson, Kalish & Dilks (now Dilworth Paxson LLP), Phila., 1986-91; mng. ptnr. Dilworth Paxson LLP, Phila., 1991—. Bd. dirs., chmn. CONFAB, Inc., King of Prussia, Pa., 1996-97; chmn. Publicker Industries, Greenwich, Conn., 1980-84; lectr. Phila. Coll. Art, 1970-72. Spl. asst. dist. atty. City of Phila., 1970; commr. Pa. Conv. Ctr. Authority, Phila., 1989-2002; gen. counsel Pa. Legis. Reapportionment Commn., 1982-98; chmn. Thomas Skelton Harrison Found., sec., gen. counsel Nat. Constitution Ctr., Phila., 1982, Found. of the Phila. Heart Inst., 1988; trustee The Barnes Found., 2002; dir. Greater Phila. First Found., 2002; bd. dirs. Phila. divsn. Am. Cancer Soc., 1986, crusade chmn., 1987-88. With USCGR, 1963-69. Mem. ABA, Phila. Bar Assn., Union League Club. Republican. Jewish. Office: Dilworth Paxson LLP 1735 Market St Philadelphia PA 19103-7501

HARMELINK, HERMAN, III, clergyman, author, educator, ecumenist; b. Sheldon, Pa., Dec. 26, 1933; s. Herman II, and Thyrza (Eringa) H.; m. Barbara Mary Conibear, Aug. 11, 1959; children: Herman IV Alan, Lindsay Alexandra (Mrs. Richard L. LeMay, Jr.). BA cum laude, Central Coll., 1954; MA, Columbia U., 1955; postgrad., U. London, 1955; MDiv, New Brunswick Theol. Sem., 1958; World Coun. Chs. scholar, U. Heidelberg, 1959; STM magna cum laude, Union Theol. Sem., N.Y.C., 1964, MPhil, 1978. Ordained to ministry Reformed Ch. Am., 1959. Min. Cmty. Ch., Glen Rock, N.J., 1959-64, Woodcliff Cmty. Ch., Woodcliff-on-Hudson, N.J., 1964-71, Reformed Ch., Poughkeepsie, N.Y., 1971—; ecumenical officer Internat. Coun. Cmty. Chs., 2000—. Adj. faculty in philosophy SUNY, Marist Coll.; chaplain Holland-Am. Line; mem. faith and order commn. Nat. Coun. Chs., 2000—, vice chmn., 1976-79, mem. commn. on regional and local ecumenism, 1981-84, mem. exec. bd., 2000—, del. Gen. Assembly, 1999—; pres. Synod of N.J., 1969; chmn. interch. rels. Ref. Ch. Am., 1964-71; chmn. Ecumenical Rels. Commn. Internat. Coun. of Cmty. Chs., 1994—; del. 18th Plenary Consultation on Ch. Union, St. Louis, 1999; mem. steering com. Reconciliation of Ministries task force Chs. Uniting in Christ, 2002—; pres. Dutchess Interfaith Coun., 1977-78, devel. retirement cmty. com., 1989—, bd. dirs.; del. gen. coun. World Alliance Ref. Chs., Frankfurt, 1964, Nairobi, 1970; adv. Gen. Assembly World Coun. Chs.,

Uppsala, Sweden, 1968; U.S. del. 50th Anniversary Faith and Order Commn., Lausanne, Switzerland, 1977. Author: Ecumenism and the Reformed Church, 1968, The Reformed Church in New Jersey, 1969, Another Look at Ferlinghuysen and His Awakening, 1969; contbg. author: Piety and Patriotism, 1976, Vision from the Hill, 1984, The Livingston Legacy, 1987; author: Concord Makes Strength, 2002. Trustee Peter A. Lindsay Trust Imperial Coll. U. London; trustee St. Francis Hosp., exec. com. of bd., joint conf. com., chmn. planning com.; bd. dirs. Dutchess County Arts Coun., 1976-80, Bardavon 1869 Opera House, 1978-79; mem. allocation and planning divsn. United Way of Dutchess County; mem. Dutchess County Execs. Com. on Med. Ethics; sec. bd. dirs. Rehab. Programs, Inc., 1977-79; bd. dirs. Anderson Ednl. Found., Collingwood Repertory Theatre, 1978-80, Mid-Hudson Meml. Soc., 1981-84; pres. Poughkeepsie Generating Cmty., 1974—; bd. dirs. Literacy Vol. of Dutchess County, pres. 1987-89; bd. dirs. Literacy Vols. Am., N.Y., chmn. pers. comm., mem. program com., pres.-elect, 1992-93, pres. 1993-96, bd. dirs. nat. bd. Lit. Vols. Am.; Poughkeepsie Rural Cemetery, chmn. fin. com.; pres. Ranfurly Library Svc. of N.Y. Inc., Town of Poughkeepsie Dem. Com., Dutchess County Dem. Com.; participant U.S.-S. African Leader Exchange Program, 1971; adv. bd. Wartburg Luth. Svcs., 1993—; chmn. Anderson Sch. Wine Showcase; ecumenical adv. del. Presbyn. Ch. Gen. Assembly, Long Beach, Calif., 2000. Lt. USNR, 1957-61. Fulbright Travel grant to Germany, 1958-59. Mem. N Am. Acad. Ecumenists, Am. Soc. Ch. History, Presbyn. Hist. Soc., Poughkeepsie C. of C., Dutchess Interfaith Coun., Dutchess County Clergy Club, Dutchess County Hist. Soc. (life, bd. dirs. 1974-78), Poughkeepsie Rotary (pres. 1977-79, sec. 1979—, sec. Dist. 721, 1980-81, gov. 1982-83, chmn. World Community Svc., Rotary Internat. Coun. on Legis., Monte Carlo, 1983, Rotary Internat. pres.'s rep. to dist. confs. 1984, 88, Paul Harris fellow, sect. leader internat. conv., Portland, 1990), Lumanites (sec.-treas.), 251, Poughkeepsie Social Reading Club (past pres.), Circumnavigators Club (N.Y.C.), The Club, Travelers Century Club (life mem.), Fjord Club, Mil Order Fgn. Wars of U.S. (life vet. companion, chaplain, mem. coun. N.Y. commandery), Fulbright Assn. (life), St. George's Soc. N.Y. (life), Chevalier du Tastevin (France), Royal Overseas League (London), Friends of St. George's and Descendants of the Knights of the Garter (life, Windsor), The English Speaking Union, The Co. of Pastors, Witherspoon Soc., Ctr. for Lifetime Study. Office: 70 Hooker Ave Poughkeepsie NY 12601 *In the words of John Bunyan, "He who would valiant be 'gainst all disaster, let him in constancy follow the Master. There's no discouragement shall make him once relent his first avowed intent to be a pilgrim."*

HARMER, DON STUTLER, physicist, educator, nuclear engineer; m. Carolyn Wood, 1952 (div. 1964); children: Diana H. Brown, Katherina H. Lucey, Nancy H. Wiggers; m. Lee DeLoache, Dec. 22, 1965; children: David Stutler, Muffin Louise Blakeney, Jonathan Aubrey. Student, USN Electronics Schs., Great Lakes, Ill. and Washington, 1946-47; BS in Chemistry cum laude, George Washington U., 1952; PhD in Nuclear Chemistry, UCLA, 1956; postgrad., N.C. State U., 1960. Postdoctoral fellow Brookhaven Nat. Labs., Upton, N.Y., 1956-59; prof. physics and nuclear engrng. Ga. Inst. Tech., Atlanta, 1959—. Cons. on solar neutrino experimental physics rsch. Brookhaven Nat. Labs., 1959-67; cons. computer systems design Digital Equipment Corp., Maynard, Mass., 1967-76; cons. hardware and software design, systems tng. CompuCom Inc., Atlanta, 1986-89; performed experimental rsch. on blood coagulation and in vitro tagging Ferst Rsch. Ctr., Atlanta, 1960-67; designed and implemented numerous on-line computer data acquistion and control systems. Contbg. author (textbook) Introduction to Computer Technology and Interfacing, 1970; contbr. more than 80 articles on physics and computer systems to profl. jours.; patentee in field. With USN, 1946-48, USNR, 1948-53. Recipient Outstanding Mentor award, 1992; named Faculty Mem. of Yr., 1992-93. Fellow Am. Inst. Chemists, Am. Inst. Physics, Am. Nuclear Soc., Southeastern MGT Register (past pres.), Peachtree MG Registry, MG Car Club, Sigma Nu. Episcopalian. Home: 3926 Harts Mill Ln NE Atlanta GA 30319-1854 E-mail: don.harmer@physics.gatech.edu.

HARMLESS, J. WILLIAM, theologian, educator; b. Kansas City, July 30, 1953; s. Roy and Mary Louise H. PhD, Boston Coll., Chestnut Hill, Mass., 1990. Ordained priest Roman Cath. Ch., 1987. Thomas R. Caestecker prof. liberal arts dept. theology Spring Hill Coll., Mobile, Ala., 1990—2003; vvis. prof., Touhy chmn. for interreligious studies John Carroll U., Cleve., 2003—. Author: Augustine and the Catechumenate, 1995; contbr. articles to profl. jours. Trustee Loyola U., New Orleans, 1996-2003, Spring Hill Coll., Mobile, Ala., 1992-02. Mem. N.Am. Patristic Soc. Roman Catholic. Avocations: running, music. Office: Creighton U 2500 California Plz Omaha NE 68178-0522

HARMON, ANGIE (ANGIE SEHORN), actress; b. Dallas, Aug. 10, 1972; d. Larry and Daphne Harmon; m. Jason Sehorn, 2001. Actress starring in TV series: Baywatch Nights, 1995, C-16: FBI, 1997, Law & Order, 1998-2001; appeared in Lawn Dogs, 1997; TV guest appearances include Renegade, 1995; TV films include Batman Beyond, (voice) 1999, Batman Beyond: Return of the Joker (voice), 2000, Video Voyeur: The Susan Wilson Story, 2002, Sudden Fear, 2002; appeared in films including Lawn Dogs, 1997, Good Advice, 2001, Agent Cody Banks, 2003. Office: c/o CAA 9830 Wilshire Blvd Beverly Hills CA 90212*

HARMON, BARBARA SAYRE, artist; b. Yerington, Nev., Aug. 8, 1927; d. Ruth (Barker) and Fred Grayson Sayre; m. Cliff Franklin Harmon, July 7, 1948; 1 child, Jonathan Henry. *Her father, pioneer western landscape painter Fred Grayson Sayre, was a member 1909-1915 of the Palette & Chisel Club of Chicago, many of whose members became the Taos, Santa Fe and California art founders. Sayre was a charter member of the California Watercolor Society, and co-founder with artist Joseph Klietch of the Painter's and Sculptor's Club of Los Angeles. Barbara's early travels with him on sketching trips to remote areas of the Southwest, and the magical fairy tale he used to tell her have been her lifelong inspiration. She married fellow artist Cliff Harmon in 1948, and one son Jonathan Henry born in 1951 has joined in the Harmon's continuing creative projects since childhood.* Student, Bisttram Sch. Fine Art, 1945—48, Black Mountain Coll., 1950; studied bookbinding with Johanna Jalowitz, studied etching with Lawton Parker, 1951. Founder, mgr. Children's Gallery, Taos, N.Mex., 1963—, Children's Gallery Press, 1967—; co-dir. Torreon Gallery, Taos, 1980—. *She attended Bisttram School of Fine Arts 1945-48; studied bookbinding with Johanna Jalowitz at Black Mountain College in 1950; etching with Lawton Parker 1951; founded Children's Gallery, Taos 1963; joined Stables Gallery, Taos, where exhibited still life, ethnic portraits and original graphics, 1963-1987; founded Children's Gallery Press 1967; presented original paintings, graphics and book art, such as Tabbigall's Garden 1967, and Thimbly Hill 1980 at Baker Gallery, Lubbock, TX, 1963-1995; Blair Galleries, Santa Fe, NM, 1971-1979. Co-director Torreon Gallery, Taos 1980 to present.* Exhibitions include paintings, graphics and book art Southwestern galleries, 1963—; author, illustrator Tabbigail's Garden, 1967, Little People's Counting Book, 1968, This Little Pixie, 1969, Monday's Mouse, 1970, The Tumpfee Wood Acorn Book, 1977, Thimbly Hill, 1980, cover designer, illus. N.Mex. mag. Christmas story, 1981; Represented in permanent collections Harwood Found., U. N.Mex., Stanford U. Libr., Palo Alto, U. N. Mex. Libr., Taos Pub. Libr., Taos Art Mus., numerous pvt. collections; works appear in numerous mags. and books. Home: PO Box 202 Taos NM 87571-0202 E-mail: cfharmon@laplaza.org.

HARMON, CHRISTOPHER C. international relations educator, writer; b. Olympia, Wash., Apr. 29, 1954; s. Charles Robert Harmon and Virginia Connolly; m. Laura, Sept. 10, 1989. BA, Seattle U., 1977; MA in Govt., PhD in Internat. Rels. and Govt., Claremont (Calif.) Grad. Sch., 1984. Pub. affairs fellow Hoover Instn., Stanford, Calif., 1984; legis. aide for fgn. policy U.S. Ho. of Reps., Washington, 1985-88; assoc. prof. strategy U.S. Naval War Coll., Newport, R.I., 1988-92; prof. internat. rels. Command & Staff Coll. Marine Corps U., Quantico, Va., 1993—. Author: Terrorism Today, 2000; co-author, co-editor: Statecraft & Power, 1994; contbr. articles to profl. jours. Fellow Earhart Found., 1981-82, Publius fellow Claremont Inst. for Study of Statesmanship and Polit. Philosophy, 1980; Disting. Pub. Svc. award, U.S. State Dept., 2001. Republican. Roman Catholic. Office: Command & Staff Coll Marine Corps U 2076 South St Quantico VA 22134-5068

HARMON, CLARENCE, former mayor, law educator; m. Janet Kelley; 4 children. BS, Northeast Mo. State U.; MA in Criminal Justice Administrn. and Pub. Administrn., Webster U.; past postgrad., Harvard U. Past sec. to bd. commrs. City of St. Louis; with St. Louis Police Dept., 1969-95, chief, 1991-95; dir. bus. devel., dir. dept. mkt. rsch. and analysis United Van Lines, Inc., 1995-97; mayor City of St. Louis, 1997—2001; tchr. So. Ill. U., Carbondale. Bd. dirs. United Way, St. Louis, St. Louis Symphony, Mo. Bot. Garden, Fair St. Louis; trustee Webster U., St. Louis Sci. Ctr. Fanforth Found. fellow; recipient Reach Out award St. Vincent Home, 1992, Dr. Martin Luther King, Jr. Life and Legacy award, 1992; named Mo. Police Chief of Year Mo. Police Chiefs' Assn., 1995. Mem. Am. Assn. Indsl. Mgmt. (bd. dirs.). Address: 1920 Virginia Ave Saint Louis MO 63104-6899 Fax: 314-622-4061.*

HARMON, DANIEL PATRICK, classics educator; b. Chgo., May 3, 1938; s. Bernard Leonard and Dorothy Mildred (Lesser) H. AB, Loyola U., Chgo., 1962; MA, Northwestern U., 1965, PhD, 1968; postdoctoral, Am. Sch. Classical Studies in Athens, 1975. Acting asst. prof. U. Wash., Seattle, 1967-68, asst. prof. classics, 1968-75, assoc. prof., 1975-76, assoc. prof. classics and comparative lit., 1976-84, prof. classics, 1984—, chmn. classics, 1976-91; dir. U. Wash. Rome Ctr., 1992-2000. Contbr. articles and revs. to profl. jours. Mem. Am. Philol. Assn., Archaeol. Inst. Am., Société des Études Latines, County Louth (Ireland) Archaeol. and Hist. Soc., Classical Assn. Pacific Northwest (pres. 1974-75). Avocations: painting, photography, music. Home: 3149 NE 83rd St Seattle WA 98115-4751 Office: U Wash Dept Classics PO Box 353110 Seattle WA 98195-3110 E mail: dph@u.washington.edu.

HARMON, DAVID, finance company executive; b. 1938; MBA, Mich. State U., 1965. With Electronic Memories and Magnetics, Hawthorne, Calif., 1965-78; CEO El Camino Resources Ltd., Woodland Hills, Calif., 1978—; with El Camino Resources Internat., Woodland Hills, 1986—. Office: 6233 Varel Woodland Hills CA 91367*

HARMON, DEBRA MAE, journalist; b. Bagley, Minn., Apr. 4, 1968; d. Alvin Eugene and Betty Ann (Dahl) H. BS, Bemidji (Minn.) State U., 1989. Editor Warroad (Minn.) Pioneer, 1990-91, Page One Publ, Warroad, 1991-92; asst. editor Farmers Pub., Bagley, 1992-98; freelance editor Bagley Pub. Sch., 1992—, Kids' Place; tech. coord. Bagley Elem., 1999—2002; technologist Bagley Sch. Dist., 2002—. Spl. publ. editor Farmers Independent, Bagley, 1994-98. Treas. Berean Bapt. Ch., Bagley, 1989-98. Mem. Soc. Profl. Journalists, Bagley Jaycees. Avocations: photography, writing, skiing, biking.

HARMON, GEORGE MARION, academic administrator; b. Memphis, Aug. 12, 1934; s. George Marion and Madie P. (Foster) H.; m. Bessie W. Porter, Dec. 27, 1958; children: Nancy R., Mary K., Elizabeth T., George Marion III. BA, Rhodes Coll., 1956; MBA, Emory U., 1957; DBA, Harvard U., 1963. Market rsch. analyst Continental Oil Co., Houston, 1957; rsch. assoc. Harvard U., 1960-63; asst. prof. Coll. Bus. Adminstrn., dir. Salzberg Meml. Transp. Program Syracuse U., N.Y., 1963-66; sr. assoc. sys. econs. divsn. Planning Rsch. Corp., Washington, 1966-67; prof., chmn. dept econs. and bus. adminstrn., dir. continuing edn. program in econs. and bus. adminstrn. Rhodes Coll. (formerly Southwestern at Memphis), Memphis, 1967-74; prof., dean divsn. bus. and mgmt. W.Va. Coll. Grad. Studies, Charleston, 1974-75; prof., dean Sch. Bus. and Mgmt. Saginaw Valley State Coll., University Center, Mich., 1975-78; pres. Millsaps Coll., Jackson, Miss., 1978-2000, pres. emeritus, sr. counsel spl. projects, 2000—; mem. faculty fin. Sch. Banking of the South, La. State U., 1968-72; dir. Audio Visual Sys., Inc., Tenn., 1970-72; v.p., treas. Allen Industries, Inc., Tenn., 1970-72; co-founder, v.p. Computer Survey Sys., Inc., Tenn., 1972-73. Bd. dirs., chmn. exec. compensation com. MacCarty Farms, Inc., Magee, Miss., 1982-93, bd. dirs. Entex, Inc., Houston, 1981-99; mem. So. Regional Edn. Bd., Atlanta, 1994-98; bd. dirs. Union Planters Bank of Miss. Contbr. articles on bus. adminstrn. to profl. jours. Bd. dirs. Fayetteville-Manlius Cen. Sch. Dist., N.Y., 1961-63, John Houston Wear Found., Jackson, 1979-2000, Endora Welty Found., 1999—; trustee, chmn. pers. and labor rels. com. Saginaw Osteo. Hosp., 1977-78; bd. dirs. Jackson Symphony Orch. Assn., 1981-85, Miss. Opera Assn., 1981-86; chmn. So. Colls. and Univs. Union, 1983-88, Miss. Found. Ind. Colls., 1982; univ. senate United Meth. Ch., 1990-2000; comm. and sec. Jackson Internat. Airport Authority, 1991-97; chmn., bd. dirs. Jackson Med. Edn. Dist., 1998-2000; bd. dirs. Cath. Charities of Miss., 2002—, Madison County Libr. Found., 2002—, St. Catherine's Village Retirement Ctr. Found., 2002—. Mem. NCAA (coun. 1986-92), Jackson C. of C. (bd. dirs. 1981-84), Newcomen Soc. Miss. (pres. 2001-, chmn. 2001-), Soc. Internat. Bus. Fellows, Jackson Country Club, Univ. Club, Capitol City Club, Harvard Club (N.Y.C.), Rotary, Phi Beta Kappa, Beta Gamma Sigma, Omicron Delta Kappa, Kappa Sigma (Pres.'s Commn. 2000—). Roman Catholic. Home: 104 Adderbury Ct Ridgeland MS 39157-8709 Office: 210 E Capitol St Ste 1088 Jackson MS 39201-2306 Fax: 601-914-3783. E-mail: harmon@millsaps.edu.

HARMON, HARRY WILLIAM, architect, former university administrator; b. San Francisco, Feb. 8, 1918; s. Harry A. and Isabel (Quagelli) A.; m. Lois Anna Holtin, July 28, 1953; children: Bruce Gregory, Mark Brian, Patricia Andree. B.Arch., U. So. Calif., 1941. Draftsman Kaufmann, Lippincott & Eggers (architects), Los Angeles, 1945-48; project architect UCLA, 1948-50, sr. architect, 1952-62; chief coll. facilities planning Calif. State Colls., Inglewood, Calif., 1962-67, asst. vice chancellor Los Angeles, 1967-69; vice chancellor phys. planning, devel. Calif. State Univs., 1969-75; exec. vice chancellor Calif. State Colls., 1975-83, exec. vice chancellor emeritus, 1983—. Spl. cons. FAO; mem. Nat. Panel Arbitrators. Chmn. bd. visitors USAF Installation Devel. for USAF Directorate of Engrng. Svcs., 1989—. Lt. USNR, 1942-45; lt. comdr. 1950-51; capt. Res. ret. Fellow AIA (nat. dir. 1977-80, sec. 1981-85, Disting. Svc. award Calif. coun. 1985, Edward C. Kemper award 1986, chair nat. jud. coun. 1986-88, mem. coun. 1986-93), Assn. Univ. Architects; mem. Coun. Ednl. Facility Planners Internat., Soc. Coll. and U. Planners, Am. Arbitration Assn., U. So. Calif. Alumni Assn., Blue Key, Alpha Rho Chi. Home: 1408 La Plaza Dr San Marcos CA 92069-4712 E-mail: hharmon@mailhost2.csusm.edu.

HARMON, JACQUELINE BAAS, librarian, infosystems specialist; b. Kalamazoo, Oct. 23, 1934; d. Jacob and Ethyl (Zuidema) Baas; m. Robert E. Davis, Aug. 21, 1955 (div. July 1979); children: Robert J., Sarah Jane, James E.; m. W. R. Harmon, Jan. 5, 1985 (dec. Nov. 2001). BS, Western Mich. U., 1955; postgrad., U. Iowa, 1961; MLS, U. Tex., Austin, 1978; MDiv, Asbury Theol. Sem., 1997. Cert. tchr., Mich., Tex., Iowa. Dir. info. svcs. Motorola, Inc., Austin, 1978-83; mgmt. and systems specialist Lockheed Missiles and Space Corp., Austin, 1983-84; corp. librarian Microelectronics and Computer Tech. Corp., Austin, 1984-98; pastor Lone Oak (Tex.) United Meth. Ch., 1998—2000, Keltys United Meth. Ch., Lufkin, Tex., 2001—. Contbr. articles to profl. jours. Pres. Austin Library Comm., City of Austin, 1978-89, Cen. Tex. Library Systems Bd., Austin, 1986-88, Sta. KLRN Adv. Bd., Austin, 1979; v.p. Internat. Hospitality Commn., Austin, 1976-88; mem. U. Tex. Adv. Coun. Library Sch., 1984-89. Mem. IEEE, Am. Assn. for Artificial Intelligence, ALA, Tex. Library Assn. Home: 508 McMullen St Lufkin TX 75904 E-mail: j_wr_harmon@juno.com.

HARMON, JAMES ALLEN, bank executive; b. N.Y.C., Oct. 12, 1935; s. Bert and Belle (Kirschner) H.; m. Jane Elizabeth Theaman, Aug. 11, 1957; children: Deborah Lynn, Douglas Lee, Jennifer Ann. BA, Brown U., 1957; MBA, Wharton Grad. Sch., U. Pa., 1959. With N.Y. Hanseatic Corp., N.Y.C., 1959-74, sr. v.p., 1969-74; gen. ptnr. Wertheim & Co., Inc., N.Y.C., 1975-97, vice chmn., 1980-86; chmn. and CEO Schroder Wertheim & Co., Inc., N.Y.C., 1986-96, sr. chmn. N.Y.C., London, 1996-97; pres., chmn. Export-Import Bank U.S., 1997—2001; founder, chmn. Harmon & Co., N.Y.C., 2001—. Trustee emeritus Barnard Coll., Brown U. Address: 43 Kettle Creek Rd Weston CT 06883

HARMON, JANE, producer; With Jane Harmon Assocs., N.Y.C. Prodr. The Last Night of Ballyhoo (by Alfred Uhry), Tony award Best Play, Driving Miss Daisy (by Alfred Uhry, Pulitzer prize), also nat. and internat. tours and Broadway, Buried Child (by Sam Shepard), A Life in the Theatre (by David Mamet), The Robber Bridegroom (by Waldman/Uhry); co-prodr. Asinamali!, Beloved Friend. Bd. dirs. Young Playwrights Inc.; mem. League of Am. Theatres and Prodrs. Inc., Off Broadway Theatre League, League of Profl. Theatre Women. Office: Jane Harmon Assocs One Lincoln Plaza Ste 28-0 New York NY 10023

HARMON, JEANNE ANN, writer; b. Eau Claire, Wis., Dec. 16, 1948; d. Gordon Elmer Buckli and Eunice Elaine Ebert, Raymond Glenna (Stepfather); m. Patrick Eugene Harmon, Sept. 15, 1973; children: Amy Renee Batron, Micheal Christopher. Diploma in Theology, Liberal Arts, Apostolic Bible Inst., St. Paul, 1970; BA in Human Rels., Psychology (with hons.), Judson Coll., 1982. Layout artist, keyliner Myles McDonough Studios, St. Paul, 1970—72; curriculum writer Word Aflame Publs., St. Louis, 1977—80; tchr. ESL Elgin (Ill.) C.C., 1985—91; sr. editor Cook Comm. Min., Colorado Springs, Colo., 1985—2000; owner, writer, editor Harmony Creative Svcs., Colorado Springs, Colo., 2002—. Presenter in field. Co-author: Become a Children's Book Author; author: (children's book) A Rooster Reminds Peter, Moses Leads God's People, God's Promise to Abraham, Joshua's New Job, Breakfast on the Beach, (picture book) Little Gray Donkey, David and the Giant, Jesus and the Big Catch, (children's book) Esther, the Beautiful Queen, Prayer; editor: (children's devotional book) Awesome Real-life Devotions; author: (children's book) Paul Sees the Light, Peter Follows Jesus. Mentor Big Brother/Big Sister, St. Paul, 1970—71; foster parent Luth. Social Svcs., Elgin, 1986—89; sunday sch. tchr. Jubilee Christian Ctr., Elgin, 1980—95; leader ladies auxillary Jubilee Christian Centre, Elgin, 1983—85. Mem.: Front Range Writers, Christian Writers Fellowship, Soc. Children's Book Writers Illustrators. Republican. Pentecostal. Avocations: reading, cooking, doll collecting, movies. Home and Office: Harmony Creative Svcs 6815 Meadowwood Pl Colorado Springs CO 80918-6305

HARMON, JOHN WATSON, surgeon, educator; b. White Plains, N.Y., Apr. 22, 1943; m. Gail McGreevy; children: James Milton, Eve Page. BA, Harvard U., 1965; MD, Columbia U., 1969. Prof. surgery Johns Hopkins Sch. Medicine; dir. surg. rsch., staff surgeon Johns Hopkins Bayview Med. Ctr. Fellow ACS; mem. Am. Surg. Assn., Am. Physiological Soc., Cosmos Club, Alpha Omega Alpha. Office: Johns Hopkins Bayview Med Ctr Dept Surgery A Bldg 5C 4940 Eastern Ave Baltimore MD 21224-2735 E-mail: jharmon@jhmi.edu.

HARMON, KAY MADELON, occupational therapist; b. Galveston, Tex., Feb. 5, 1949; d. Roger Q. and Alma Faye (Hall) H.; m. Stanley Davis Mitchell, June 24, 1967 (div. Nov. 1968). BA in Sociology, East Tex. Bapt. U., Marshall, 1980; advanced cert. in Occupational Therapy, Tex. Woman's U., Denton/Dallas, 1989. Lic. occupational therapist, Tex., Ark. Staff occupational therapist N.E. Ark. Rehab. Hosp., Jonesboro, 1989-91; dir. clin. svcs. Marshall (Tex.) Phys. Therapy, 1991-93; staff occupational therapist Pro Care Rehab., Mountain Home, Ark., 1993, Premier Rehab., Texarkana, Ark., 1994-95, CMS Therapies Rehab., Longview, Tex., 1995-96; Rehab Works, Longview, Gladwater, Tex., 1996; regional occupational therapy supr. Sundance Rehab., Northeast, Tex., 1996; outpatient occupational therapist and home health Marshall (Tex.) Regional Med. Ctr., 1996-99. Cons. Rehab. Choice in local nursing homes, Marshall, 1997-99, Vencare Rehab Svcs. in nursing homes Mena, Mt. Ida, Hot Springs, Ark., 1999-2000, Smith McGrew Clinic, Hot Springs, Glenwood, Hope and Murphreesboro, Ark., 2000—. Mem.: Am. Soc. Hand Therapists (assoc. Tex. chpt.), Ark.. Occupational Therapy Assn., Am. Occupational Therapy Assn. (alt. rep. from Ark. to representative assembly), Shreveport Orchid Soc., Am. Orchid Soc., Phi Theta Epsilon. Baptist. Avocations: growing orchids, performance poetry. Home: 108 Old Brundage #25 Hot Springs National Park AR 71913 Office: 10121 N Rodney Parham Rd Little Rock AR 72227-5549 E-mail: kaymadelon@aol.com.

HARMON, KAY YVONNE, elementary education educator; b. Albert Lea, Minn., Dec. 12, 1942; d. Melvin Harold and Bertha Loretta (Sorensen) Vogelsang; m. Perry Dean Harmon, Aug. 14, 1971; children: Kristine Kay, Phillip Dean. BA, Luther Coll., 1963; BS, U. Minn., 1966. Tchr. elem. Grand Meadow (Minn.) Pub. Sch., 1963-65; tchr. secondary art edn. Little Falls (Minn.) Pub. Sch., 1966-68; secondary art tchr. Robinsdale Pub. Sch., New Hope, Minn., 1968-73; arts and crafts leader Crystal (Minn.) Park and Recreation, summer 1969; dir. chpt. I, art secondary tchr. Ulen (Minn.)-Hitterdal Pub. Sch., 1982—. Instr. Community Edn., Ulen, 1986-88, Hawley, Minn., 1987-88, 91. Adult leader Eglon Hawks 4-H Club, 1984-93; mem. Hawley Art Show Com., 1987—, treas., 1999—; mem. Hawley Friends of Fine Arts, 1989-99, sec.-treas., 1991-96. Mem. ASCD, NEA, Nat. Art Educators Assn., Minn. Edn. Assn., Art Educators Minn., Minn. Alliance for Arts, Ulen-Hitterdal Edn. Assn. (pres. 1990, treas. 1996—, membership chair 1997—), Alpha Delta Kappa (chpt. chaplain 1996-98, chpt. rec. sec. 1994-96). Methodist. Avocations: reading, drawing, bowling, golf, painting. Home: 26258 28th Ave S Hawley MN 56549-9161 Office: Ulen-Hitterdal Pub Sch PO Box 389 Ulen MN 56585-0389

HARMON, MARIAN SANDERS, writer, sculptor; b. Detroit, Jan. 16, 1916; d. Joseph and Anne (Stern) Sanders; m. Edward Stein, Jan. 15, 1950 (dec. 1960); m. Leonard Byron Harmon, 1963. BA, U. Mich., 1937. Dir. radio and TV Simons Michelson, Detroit, 1948-60; editor Table Talk Bridge Newspaper, 1954-62; writer ABC-TV, N.Y.C., 1960-65. Organizer, pres. Visual Arts Forum, 1981-93. Author: (poems) The Hourglass, 1982, East of Morning, 1998, Widows' Walk, 1999; editor AAUW, East Hampton, 1984-87, various newspapers, 1945-65; first editor Northwest Detroiter, 1947; freelance writer for newspapers and mags.; computer art in invitational art shows, 1995, 96, 97. Recipient Best Sculpture in Show award Guild Hall East Hampton, 1989. Home: PO Box 1547 East Hampton NY 11937-0795

HARMON, PATRICK, historian, sports commentator; b. St. Louis, Sept. 2, 1916; s. Jack and Laura (Duchesne) H.; m. Anne M. Worland, Aug. 31, 1940; children— Michael, Timothy, Kathleen, Daniel, John, Sheila, Peggy, Brigid, Kevin, Teresa, Christopher. AB, U. Ill., 1939. Sports editor News-Gazette, Champaign, Ill., 1942-47, Gazette, Cedar Rapids, Iowa, 1947-51, Post, Cin., 1951-85; ret., 1985; sports commentator Sta. WCPO-TV, 1953-56, Sta. WKRC, 1958, Sta. WLW-TV, 1958-68; curator, historian Coll. Football Hall of Fame, Kings Island, Ohio, 1986-95; historian, 1995—2003. Contbg. sports editor: World Book, 1959—2003. Recipient Fred Hutchinson Meml. award for community service, 1969; named Internat. Churchmen's Sports Writer of Year, 1973 Mem. Sigma Chi. Home and Office: 608 Maple Trace Cincinnati OH 45246

HARMON, PHYLLIS DARNELL, mortgage banker; b. Kingsport, Tenn., May 24, 1937; d. Kelly R. Darnell and Leah Viola Denny; m. John L. Harmon, Sept. 26, 1958; 1 child, Mark Darnell. Credit mgr. Givner's, Inc., Lorain, Ohio, 1955-59; traffic mgr. Sta. WQTE-AM-FM, Monroe, Mich., 1959-61; accounts receivable mgr. Dundee (Mich.) Cement Co., 1961-65; owner, operator Grosse Pointe (Mich.) Mortgage Co., 1984—. Prospects and clerical chmn. United Found., Detroit, 1965-68; bd. dirs. Wayne County (Mich.) Spl. Edn. Adv. Bd., 1978-87, State Mich. Bd. Licensing and Regulation, Lansing, 1980-85; dir. corp. bd. dirs. United Cerebral Palsy Assn., Detroit, 1984-89. Office: Grosse Pointe Mortgage Co 1263 Berkshire Rd Grosse Pointe Park MI 48230-1034 Fax: 313-884-3131.

HARMON, RICHARD WINGATE, management consultant; b. Exeter, N.H., July 16, 1958; BS in Adminstrn., U. N.H., 1981; MBA in Adminstrn., N.H. Coll., 1986. Lic. comml. pilot and flight instr. Owner, pres. Harmon-Waters, Exeter, 1982—, Harmon Realty Investments, Exeter, 1985—; founder, owner Harmon Aviation, Exeter, 1988—, Exeter Storage Depot, Inc., 1989—. Venture capital cons., constrn. mgmt. cons., bus. turnaround cons., bus. start-up cons. Mem. Aircraft Owners and Pilots Assn., Exptl. Aircraft Assn., Seaplane Pilots Assn., N.H. Coll. Alumni Assn., U. N.H. Alumni Assn., Sigma Alpha Epsilon. Avocations: music, golf, skiing, travel, aviation. Office: Harmon-Waters 95 High St Exeter NH 03833-2927

HARMON, ROBERT GERALD, health company executive, educator; b. Barnsdall, Okla., Mar. 20, 1944; s. Thomas Frederick and Eleandor Virginia (Colley) H.; m. Carol Louise Kalnitsky, Aug. 22, 1971; children: Rex, Susan. BA, Washington U., St. Louis, 1966, MD, 1970; MPH, Johns Hopkins U., 1977. Diplomate Am. Bd. Preventive Medicine. Intern, then resident U. Colo. Med. Ctr., Denver, 1970-73; asst. prof. health svcs. and internal medicine U. Wash., Seattle, 1977-80; chmn. dept. community medicine Maricopa Med. Ctr., Phoenix, 1980-85; dep. dir. Maricopa County Divsn. Pub. Health, Phoenix, 1980-82, dir., 1983-85; dir. Dept. Health State of Mo., Jefferson City, 1986-90; clin. prof. U. Mo. Sch. Medicine, Columbia, 1986-90; administr. Health Resources Svcs. Adminstrn. USPHS/HHS, Rockville, Md., 1990-93; sr. v.p. MetraHealth Ctr. for Corp. Health Inc., Oakton, Va., 1994-95; v.p., nat. med. dir.

Optum divsn. UnitedHealth Group, McLean, Va., 1996—. Adj. assoc. prof. sch. medicine U. Ariz., Tucson, 1981-85; cons. community medicine Project Health Opportunity for People Everywhere, Jamaica, 1973, 76; Pan Am. Health Orgn., Carribean, 1979, U.S. AID, Africa, 1978, 79. Contbr. articles to profl. jours. With USPHS, 1974-75. Fellow Am. Coll. Preventive Medicine (bd. regents 1983-88, 96-2000, pres.-elect 2001—03, pres. 2003—); mem. Nat. Assn. County Health Ofcls. (pres. 1983-85), Am. Pub. Health Assn. (gov. councilor 1984-88), Assn. State and Territorial Health Ofcls. (exec. com. 1987-90), Ariz. County Health Ofcls. (pres. 1984-85), Omicron Delta Kappa. Avocation: sports. Office: Optum Divsn UnitedHealth Group 1925 Isaac Newton Sq Ste 300 Reston VA 20190 E-mail: bob_g_harmon@uhc.com.

HARMON, ROBERT JOHN, child psychiatrist; b. Cleve., June 7, 1946; s. William Clare and Roberta (Held) Harmon; m. Darlene K. Harmon, July 11, 1969; children: Jaeda, Ian. AB magna cum laude, Miami U., Oxford, Ohio, 1967; MD summa cum laude, U. Colo., Denver, 1971. Lic. physician, Colo., Md.; diplomate Am. Bd. Psychiatry and Neurology. Psychiatry resident U. Colo. Sch. Medicine, Denver, 1971-73, child psychiatry resident, 1976-78; rsch. assoc. social and behavioral scis. NIMH, Bethesda, Md., 1973-76; postdoctoral faculty developmental psychobiology rsch. grp. U. Colo. Sch. Medicine, Denver, 1979—, asst. prof. child psychiatry, 1978-82, assoc. prof. child psychiatry, 1982-92, prof., 1992, dir. child psychiatry tng., 1985-88, head Div. Child Psychiatry, 1984—2002; dir. Kempe Therapeutic Presch., 1992—, dir. Irving B. Harris Program, 1996—; psychiat. dir. women's and children's residential svcs. The Haven, 2001—. Examiner Am. Bd. Psychiatry and Neurology, Evanston, Ill., 1988—; mem. diagnostic classification task force Zero to Three, Washington, 1987—, bd. dirs., 1986—. Co-editor: The Development of Attachment, 1982, Continuities and Discontinuities in Development, 1984; contbr. articles to profl. jours. Grantee John D. and Catherine T. MacArthur, 1984-86, NIMH, 1980-83, Harris Found., 1996—; Rsch. Scientist Devel. awardee, 1980-85. Fellow Am. Acad. Child and Adolescent Psychiatry; mem. Colo. Child and Adolescent Psychiatric Soc. (exec. com. 1983-87), Devel. Psychobiology Rsch. Grp., Soc. for Rsch. in Child Devel., Am. Psychiatric Assn. (disting.fellow), World Assn. for Infant Mental Health, Soc. of Profs. in Child and Adolescent Psychiatry, Am. Acad. Addiction Psychiatry, Am. Coll. Psychiatrists. Office: U Colo Sch Medicine 4200 E 9th Ave # C286-52 Denver CO 80262-0001 Fax: 303-315-5040.

HARMON BROWN, VALARIE JEAN, hospital laboratory director, information systems executive; b. Peoria, Ill., June 21, 1948; d. Donald Joseph and Frances Elizabeth (Classen) Harmon; m. James Roger Brown, Aug. 21, 1982 (dec. May 1994). BSMT, Northwestern U., Chgo., 1970. Med. tech. Evanston (Ill.) Hosp., 1970-71, chief tech., 1971-75; med. tech. II M.D. Anderson Hosp., Houston, 1975-76; dir. lab. Physicians Ref. Lab., Houston, 1978-81, Med. Ctr. Hosp., Conroe, Tex., 1981-91, Palo Pinto Gen. Hosp., Mineral Wells, Tex., 1993-94; sales mgr. Long Beach (Calif.) Meml. Med. Ctr., 1995-96; quality assurance/regulatory affairs mgr. Consol. Med. Labs., Lake Bluff, Ill., 1996-97; admissions dir. Bio-Diagnostics Labs., Torrance, Calif., 1997-2000; asst. dir. lab. Parkview Cmty. Hosp. Med. Ctr., Riverside, Calif., 2000—01; regional mgr. Memphis Antech Diagnostics, Southaven, Miss., 2001—03. Lab. cons. Texaco Chem. Wellness Program, Conroe, 1989; health career sponsor Willis Ind. Sch. Dist., Tex., 1989, 90; mem. adv. bd. Med. Lab. Technician program Weatherford Coll., 1994. Coord. blood drive Gulf Coast Region Blood Ctr., 1986-91; sponsor colon cancer screening Montgomery County Health Fair, 1986; sponsor Camp Sunshine/Lions Club, 1988; sponsor cholesterol screening Med. Ctr. Hosp. Health Fair, 1989. Mem. NAFE, Am. Soc. Clin. Pathologists, Am. Soc. Med. Technologists, Clin. Lab. Mgmt. Assn. Republican. Roman Catholic. Avocations: embroidery, reading, antiques. Home: 7697 Rigmoore Pt Olive Branch MS 38654

HARMOND, RICHARD PETER, historian, educator; b. NYC, Mar. 19, 1929; s. William and Violet (Makein) H. BA, Fordham U., 1951; MA, Columbia U., 1954, PhD, 1966. Assoc. prof. history St. John's U., N.Y.C., 1957—. Co-author: Long Island as America, 1977, A History of Memorial Day: Unity, Discord and the Pursuit of Happiness, 2002; co-editor: Technology in the 20th Century, 1983, Biographical Dictionary of American and Canadian Naturalists and Environmentalists, 1997; assoc. editor L.I. Hist. Jour., 1989—2003, mem. editl. bd., 2003—; contbr. articles to profl. jours. With U.S. Army, 1951-53. Mem. Orgn. Am. Historians, Soc. History of Tech., Theodore Roosevelt Assn. (trustee 1994-97), Phi Alpha Theta (paper prize com. 1994-97). Office: St John's U Hist Dept Jamaica NY 11439-0001

HARMON-WEISS, SANDRA RHOADS, physician administrator; b. Norristown, Pa., Feb. 23, 1943; d. G. Lewis and Martha M. (Flyte) Rhoads; m. Richard C. Weiss, Sept. 20, 1986; children: Jennifer, Eric, Christopher, Richard. BA, Temple U., 1971, MD, 1974. Resident Thomas Jefferson U. Hosp., 1974-77; physician, pres. Conshohocken (Pa.) Family Practice, 1977-92; med. dir. U.S. Healthcare, Blue Bell, Pa., 1990-95, head of govt. programs, 1995-96, Aetna U.S. Healthcare, Blue Bell, 1996—. Mem. com. on Medicare managed care Inst. of Medicine, Washington, 1995—; mem. adv. com. for standards revision for adult day care Nat. Coun. on Aging, Washington, 1996. Author: The Role of Nutrition in Chronic Disease Care, 1997; contbr. articles to profl. jours. Bd. dirs. Ret. Sr. Vol. Program, Plymouth Meeting, Pa., 1993-95; trustee Delmarva Found., Easton, Md., 1996-99. Recipient Mead Johnston award for family practice, 1976-77, Dir.'s citation HCFA Office of Managed Care, Balt., 1996; named to Hall of Fame, Norristown Area H.S., 1989. Fellow Am. Acad. Family Physicians; mem. APHA, Am. Geriatrics Soc., Am. Coll. Physician Execs., Pa. Acad. Family Physicians. Avocations: walking, antique silver, travel. Office: Aetna US Healthcare 980 Jolly Rd # 13S Blue Bell PA 19422-1904

HARMONY, MARLIN DALE, chemistry educator; b. Lincoln, Nebr., Mar. 2, 1936; s. Philip and Helen Irene (Michal) H. AA, Kansas City (Mo.) Jr. Coll., 1956; BS in Chem. Engring., U. Kans., 1958; PhD in Chemistry, U. Calif.-Berkeley, 1961. Asst. prof. U. Kans., Lawrence, 1962-67, assoc. prof., 1967-71, prof., 1971-98, chmn., 1980-88, prof. emeritus, 1998—. Panel mem. NRC-Nat. Bur. Standards., 1969-78; mem. review panel NSF, 1977, 92. Author: Introduction to Molecular Energies and Spectra, 1972; contbg. editor: Physics Vade Mecum, 1981; mem. editorial bd. Structural Chemistry, 1989-98; contbr. articles to profl. jours.; patentee in field. Postdoctoral fellow NSF Harvard U., 1961-62. Fellow AAAS; mem. Am. Chem. Soc., Am. Phys. Soc., Sigma Xi, Alpha Chi Sigma, Phi Lambda Upsilon, Tau Beta Pi Democrat. Home: 1033 Avalon Rd Lawrence KS 66044-2505 Office: U Kans Dept Chemistry Lawrence KS 66045-0001

HARMS, ALLAN L. patent lawyer; b. Auburn, Nebr., Feb. 14, 1945; m. Sally L. Lucas, Aug. 31, 1968; 2 children. BSEE, U. Nebr., 1968; MBA, U. Iowa, 1973, JD, 1974. Bar: Iowa 1974, U.S. Patent Office 1975. Lawyer White & Wenzel, Cedar Rapids, Iowa, 1974-75; patent lawyer Eells, Blackstock, Affeldt & Harms, Cedar Rapids, 1975-87, Wenzel, Piersall & Harms, P.C., Cedar Rapids, 1987-95, Wenzel & Harms, P.C., Cedar Rapids, 1995—. Asst. Linn County Atty., Cedar Rapids, 1975-83. Treas. Kennedy H.S. Choral League, 1992—93; bd. dirs. Invent Iowa, Iowa City, 1998—. Mem. ABA, Iowa State Bar Assn., Linn County Bar Assn. (tech. comm. 2000—), Iowa Intellectual Property Law Assn. (pres. 1990), SPEBSQSA Internat. (Harmony Hawks Chorus chpt. 1980—, treas. 1986-96, pres. Cedar Rapids chpt. 1997-98), Cedar Rapids Noon Lions Club (pres. 1992-93, Lion of the Yr. 1993). Avocations: barbershop quartet singing, band membership, volunteering. Office: Wenzel & Harms PC 2750 1st Ave NE Cedar Rapids IA 52402-4831 Fax: 319-363-8906. E-mail: wenzelharms@aol.com.

HARMS, DONALD C. lawyer; b. Detroit, May 27, 1941; s. Herbert R. and Elsa J. (McClelend) H.; m. Sue J. Kingsley, June 15, 1963; children: Kristin, Sharon, Melissa. BA, U. Mich., 1963; JD cum laude, Wayne State U., 1967. Bar: Mich. 1967, U.S. Dist. Ct. (ea. dist.) Mich. 1967. Ptnr. Larson & Harms, P.C., Farmington Hills, Mich., 1968—. Arbitrator Am. Arbitration Assn., Detroit, 1975—; bd. dirs. McKenzie Bay Internat., Ltd. Clk., Ward Evangel. Presbyn. Ch., Livonia, Mich., 1979-80, moderator Evang. Presbyn. Ch., 1984-85. Mem. State Bar of Mich. (pres. gen. practice sect. 1975-77), Farmington Hills C. of C. (pres. 1979), Kiwanis. Office: Larson & Harms PC 37899 W 12 Mile Rd Ste 300 Farmington MI 48331-3026 Business E-Mail: dharms@larsonharms.com.

HARMS, ELIZABETH LOUISE, artist; b. Milw., May 26, 1924; d. Frederick George and Veva (Sanderson) H.; m. Douglas Derwood Craft, Sept. 8, 1951. Diploma, Sch. Art Inst. Chgo., 1950, BFA, 1963, MFA, 1964. One-man shows: 55 Mercer St., N.Y.C., 1980, Fischbach Gallery, N.Y.C., 1975, Carnegie Inst. Mus. Art, 1969, Condeso/Lawler, 1982, 84, 85, 86, 90, 93, Gallery Jupiter, Little Silver, N.J., 1987, Jersey City Mus., 1988, Paul McCarron, N.Y.C., 2001, DVA, Narrowsberg, N.Y., 1996, 2002; group shows include Moravian Coll., Bethlehem, Pa., 1978, Jersey City Mus., 1980, 86, North of New Brunswick, South of N.Y., Rutgers-Newark, 1981, Coll. of New Rochelle, 1982, T. Bell Invitational, Condeso/Lawler, 1985, Montclair (N.J.) Art Mus., 1984, 86, Robeson Mus., Rutgers, Newark, 1988, Invitational Acad. & Inst. for Arts & Scis., N.Y.C., 1992, Skidmore Coll., Saratoga Springs, N.Y., 1993, So. Allegheny Mus. Art, Loretto, Pa., 1994. Recipient Armstrong prize Art Inst. Chgo., 1962; Tiffany Found. grantee, 1977 Home: PO Box 245 Jeffersonville NY 12748-0245

HARMS, JOHN KEVIN, lawyer; b. Bitburg Air Base, Germany, Oct. 19, 1960; s. William Robert and Catherine Dorothy (Heslin) H.; m. Pamela Tinkham, 1988; children: William Cameron Harms, Wade Devlin Harms. Student Wash. Seminar in Econ. Policy, Am. U., 1981; BPA magna cum laude, Loyola U., New Orleans, 1982; JD, Northwestern U., 1985; MBA, Western New Eng. Coll., 1989, U.S. Army Command & Gen. Staff Coll., 1997, U.S. Air War Coll., 1997; postgrad., Am. U., Washington, 1981, U.S. Army Command and Gen. Staff Coll., 1997, USAF Air War Coll., 1997, U.S. Navy Coll. Continuing Edn. Bar: Ill. 1985, U.S. Army Ct. Mil. Review 1986, U.S. Ct. Mil. Appeals 1991, Mass. 1994. Commd. 2d lt. USAR, 1982, advance through grades to lt. col., 2001; aide-de-camp to comdg. gen. 33d Inf. Brigade, Ill. Army Nat. Guard, 1983-85; rsch. asst. Am. Bar Found., Chgo., 1985; legal assistance atty. Office of Staff Judge Advocate, Ft. Devens, Mass., 1986; trial def. counsel U.S. Army Trial Def. Svc., Ft. Devens, Mass., 1986-87, sr. def. counsel, 1987-90; deputy staff judge adv. Office of Staff Judge Adv. Mil. Traffic Mgmt. Command Ea. Area, Bayonne, N.J., 1990-92; internat. ops. law atty. Third Mil. Law Ctr., U.S. Army Res., Boston, 1992-95; atty.-adv., environ. law specialist Office of the Staff Judge Adv., Fort Devens, 1992-95; chief counsel Devens Res. Forces Tng. Area, Devens, Mass., 1995-96; atty., advisor govt. contracts and chief, environ. law Electronic Sys. Ctr., Hanscom AFB, Mass., 1996—; adminstrv. and contract law atty. 94th Regional Support Command, USAR, Devens, 1996—2000; dep. staff judge adv. 94th Regional Support Command, Ft. Devens, 2000—. Mem. North Western Law Review, 1985; mem. 1st del. of Am. criminal lawyers to the Peoples Rep. of China as part of Citizen Amb. Program, People to People Internat., 1987. Cubmaster Cub Scout Pack 50, 1999—2001, Boy Scouts Am., 1999—2001; leader den Weblos/Boy Scouts Am., 2001—03; bd. trustee North Ctrl. Charter Essential Sch., Fitchburg, Mass., 2002—, sec., 2003—. Named Outstanding Young Man Am., 1988. Mem. ABA, Boston Bar Assn. (mem. environ. law sect.), Bluekey Nat. Honor Fraternity, Alpha Sigma Nu, Delta Sigma Pi, Beta Gamma Sigma. Avocations: racewalking, novel writing, Kindai Inazuma Ryu karate (green belt). Office: Office Staff Judge Advocate Attn ESC/JAS 35 Hamilton St Hanscom AFB MA 01731-2010 E-mail: john.harms@us.army.mil.

HARMS, ROBERT THOMAS, linguist, educator; b. Peoria, Ill., Apr. 12, 1932; s. Wilbert Erwin and Mildred Matilda (Thomas) H.; m. Sirpa Helina Aaltonen, July 1, 1956; children: Kirsti Maria, Ritva Helena, Eerik Thomas, Timo Kalevi. AB, U. Chgo., 1952, A.M. in Slavic Langs, 1956, PhD in Linguistics, 1960; postgrad. (Fulbright scholar), U. Helsinki, Finland, 1954-56; U.S.-Soviet exchange, Leningrad State U., 1962-63. Instr. U. Tex., Austin, 1958-61, asst. prof. linguistics, 1961-64, asso. prof., 1965-67, prof., 1967—, chmn. dept. linguistics, 1973-77. Vis. asst. prof. Columbia U., 1960, vis. asso. prof., 1965; vis. asso. prof. Ohio State U., 1964; U.S.-Hungary exchange prof. U. Szeged (Hungarian Acad. Scis.), Budapest, 1967-68 Author: Estonian Grammar, 1962, Finnish Structural Sketch, 1964, Introduction to Phonological Theory, 1968; Editor: (with Emmon Bach) Universals in Linguistic Theory, 1968. Fulbright research grantee Finland, 1968; Nat. Acad. Scis. exchange prof. Acad. Scis. USSR and Estonian Acad. Scis. Mem. Linguistic Soc. Am., Finno-Ugrian Soc., Phi Beta Kappa. Lutheran. Home: 2609 Deerfoot Trl Austin TX 78704-2715 Office: U Tex Dept Linguistics Austin TX 78712

HARMS, STEVEN ALAN, lawyer; b. Detroit, Feb. 15, 1949; s. Herbert Rudolph and Elsa Jane (McClelland) H.; m. Nancy Gayle Banta, June 26, 1971; children: Jennifer Elizabeth, Heather Lynn, Robin Ann. BA, Hope Coll., 1970; JD, Detroit Coll. Law, 1975. Bar: Mich. 1975, U.S. Dist. Ct. (so. dist.) Mich. 1975, U.S. Ct. Appeals (6th cir.) 1982; bd. cert. creditors rights specialist. Ptnr. Muller, Muller, Richmond, Harms, Myers & Sgroi, P.C., Birmingham, Mich.; sec. gen. practice session State Bar Mich., 1982-83; mediator Oakland County Cir. Ct., 1990—. Lectr. in field; adj. prof. Bus. Law Walsh Coll., Troy, Mich., 1990—. Author: Successful Collection of a Judgement, 1981, Post Judgement Collection, 1988, Handling the Collection Case in Michigan, 1989, rev. edit., 2003, Collection Law, 2003, A Credit Manager's Guide to Collection Law, 2003; co-author: Attorney Fee Agreements, 1995; contbg. editor: Michigan Civil Procedure, 1997, rev. edit., 2002. Bd. dirs. fin. com. YMCA, North Oakland County, Mich., 1987—, chmn. bd., 1990-91. Mem.: Pearson Yacht Owners Assn. (commodore 1988-90), Hunter Sailing Assn. (vice commodore 1985-86, commodore 1987-88). Republican. Office: Muller Muller Richmond Harms Myers & Sgroi PC 33233 Woodward Ave Birmingham MI 48009-0903 E-mail: steve@mullerfirm.com.

HARMSEN, DOROTHY, food products executive; b. Minneapolis; m. William Harmsen, 1939; children: William Jr., Robert, Michael. Student, U. Minn. Co-founder Jolly Rancher Candies, Wheatridge, Colo., 1942. Author: Two Comprehensive Western Art Volumes, 1972-79. Bd. dirs. Denver Art Mus., Arthritis Found., Salvation Army, Harmsen Mus. Art, Habitat for Humanity. Home: 3131 E Alameda Ave Denver CO 80209-3409

HARMSEN, MARK SPAULDING, legislative aide; b. Pasadena, Calif., Apr. 28, 1956; s. Tyrus George and Lois (Spaulding) H. AA, Pasadena C.C., 1976; BSBA, San Diego State U., 1978. Rsch. dir. Rep. Assocs., Glendale, Calif., 1979-85; dist. dir. Hon. David Dreier, Glendora, Calif., 1985—. Mem. Pasadena Tournament of Roses Assn., 1982—. Presbyterian. Office: Congressman David Dreier Ste 225 2220 E Rte 66 Glendora CA 91740 Fax: 626-963-9842. E-mail: mark.harmsen@mail.house.gov.

HARMSEN, TYRUS GEORGE, librarian; b. Pomona, Calif., July 24, 1924; s. Fred H. and Hazel H.; m. Lois Spaulding, Apr. 15, 1955; children: Mark Spaulding, Caroline Lora. AB, Stanford, 1947, MA, 1950; AB in L.S, U. Mich., 1948. Cataloguer dept. manuscripts Henry E. Huntington Library, San Marino, Calif., 1948-49, 50-59; coll. librarian Occidental Coll., Los Angeles, 1959-86, dir. book arts program, prof. bibliography, 1986-91. Vis. lectr. Sch. Library Sci., U. So. Calif., 1958, 68. Author: The Plantin Press of Saul and Lillian Marks, 1960, Joseph Arnold Foster, Printer, 1998. Served with AUS, 1943-46. Council on Library Resources fellow, 1969 Mem.: Zamorano, Rounce and Coffin (Los Angeles) (treas. 1956-91). Presbyterian. Home: 1300 Medford Rd Pasadena CA 91107-1603

HARMUTH, HENNING F. electrical engineer, educator; b. Vienna, July 27, 1928; arrived in U.S., 1969; s. Adolf Alois Harmuth and Margarete Beckert; m. Anna Elisabeth Hoene-Harmuth, June 21, 1957 (div. 1978); 1 child, Ursula; m. Anne Blackshear Spragins-Harmuth, June 27, 1979. Diploma in Engring., Tech. U., Vienna, Austria, 1951; D of Tech. Scis., Tech. U., 1953. Registered Md., 1980. Cons. engr. pvt. practice, Karlsruhe, Germany, 1965—71; prof. Cath. U. Am., Washington, 1971—96; ret. Cons. UN/UNESCO, Warangal, India, 1972. Author: Transmission of Information by Orthogonal Functions, 1969, Transmission of Information by Orthogonal Functions, 2d edit., 1972, Sequency Theory - Foundations and Applications, 1977, Acoustic Imaging with Electronic Circuits, 1981, Autennas and Waveguides for Nonsinusoidal Waves, 1984, Propagation of Nonsinusoidal Electromagnetic Waves, 1986, Information Theory Applied to Space-Time Physics, 1989, Radiation of Nonsimusoidal Electromagnetic Waves, 1990, Propagation of Electromagnetic Signals, 1994, Electromagnetic Signals - Reflection, Focusing, Distortion, and Their Applications, 1999, Interstellar Propagation of Electromagnetic Signals, 2000, Modified Maxwell Eduations in Quantum Electrodynamics, 2001, Calculus of Finite Differences in Quantum Electrodynamics, 2003; contbr. articles to profl. jours. Mem.: IEEE (life). Home: 758 Bayou Dr Destin FL 32541 E-mail: harmuth@gnt.net.

HARNACK, BARBARA WOOD, artist, sculptor; b. N.Y.C., Oct. 9, 1957; d. William and Phyllis Claire (Mitchell) H.; m. Michael N.J. Dean Lancaster; 1 child, Amrit Ringling Lancaster. Cert. of graduation, Parson's Sch. Design, N.Y.C., 1980. Co-founder Malden Bridge (N.Y.) Pottery, 1979-86; co-founder, sec. bd. dirs. Historic Malden Bridge Playhouse Soc., 1983-86; owner Woods Gallery, Malden Bridge, N.Y., 1982-86; curator exhibits Malden Bridge Arts Ctr., 1979-86. Adv. bd. Internat. Friends Transformative Art, Scottsdale, Ariz., 1991-92; bd. dirs. Children's Workshop, Cerrillos, N.Mex., 1995; exhibits coord. N.J. Lancaster Fine Art, Madrid, N.Mex., 1997. Vol. Meals on Wheels, Westchester County, 1972; founder Scarecrow Day, Malden Bridge, 1984-85; vol. flood victim support ARC, Elmira, N.Y., 1973; vol. Holiday Project Internat., N.Y., N.Mex., 1990—, Amnesty Internat., 2002, Santa Fe Bot. Garden, 2003; vol. child tchr. Hudson River Mus., N.Y., 1973. Recipient Macy's Merit award Albany (N.Y.) Inst. History and Art, 1978, Purchase prize Feats of Clay Lincoln Arts, 1998. Mem. Am. Craft Coun. Avocations: gardening, backpacking, birding, building adobe home. Home: 98 B Gold Mine RD Cerrillos NM 87010

HARNACK, DON STEGER, retired lawyer; b. Milw., June 19, 1928; s. Benjamin John and Katherine (Steger) H.; m. Rose Marie Ball, Oct. 17, 1959; children: Christopher Wallen, Gretchen Marie, Pamela Ann. BS, U. Wis., 1950; LLB, Harvard U., 1953. Bar: Wis. 1953, U.S. Dist. Ct. (ea. dist.) Wis. 1955, U.S. Tax Ct. 1957, Ill. 1959, U.S. Dist. Ct. (no. dist.) Ill. 1962, U.S. Ct. Appeals (6th and 7th cirs.) 1963, U.S. Ct. Claims 1966, U.S. Ct. Appeals (8th cir.) 1971, U.S. Supreme Ct. 1972. Assoc. Quarles, Spence & Quarles, Milw., 1955-57; trial atty. regional counsel IRS, Chgo., 1957-61; assoc. Dixon, Todhunter, Knouf & Holmes, Chgo., 1961-65; ptnr. McDermott, Will & Emery, Chgo., 1965-96, of counsel, 1997-98; ret., 2001. Contbr. articles to profl. jours. Active Winnetka (Ill.) Zoning Bd., 1971-75; park bd. atty. Winnetka Park Dist., 1978-83; pres. N.E. Ill. coun. Boy Scouts Am., 1982-83; life trustee ULC Boys and Girls Club, Chgo., UL Civic and Arts Found.; trustee Village of Winnetka, 1984-88. Served with U.S. Army, 1953-55, USNR, 1959-69. Recipient Silver Beaver award Boy Scouts Am., 1984, named distinguished Eagle Scout, 1996. Mem. ABA, Ill. Bar Assn., Wis. Bar Assn., Union League Club (bd. dirs., officer, v.p. 1981-87, pres. 1987-88). Republican. Avocations: fishing, golf, reading, flying. E-mail: bigcoho2@aol.com.

HARNDEN, EDWIN A. lawyer; BA Columbia U., 1969, JD Columbia U., 1972. Mng. ptnr. Barran Liebman LLP, Portland, Oreg.; pres. Oreg. State Bar, 2001—02. Past pres. Profl. Liability Fund. Fellow Am. Bar Found. (life) Office: ODS Tower 601 SW 2d Ave Ste 2300 Portland OR 97204-3159 Office Fax: 503-274-1212. E-mail: eharnden@barran.com.

HARNED, ROGER KENT, radiology educator; b. Madison, Wis., June 19, 1934; s. Lewis Boyer and Ermil Amelia (Caldwell) H.; m. Jacquelyn Sue Heal, Aug. 29, 1959; children: Roger Kent II, Jennifer M. Harrison. BS, U. Wis., 1956; MD, U. Va., 1961. Am. Bd. Radiology. Intern Milw. County Gen. Hosp., 1961-62; resident in radiology Deaconess Hosp., Milw. Children's Hosps., 1964-67; instr. dept. radiology Sch. Medicine U. Va., Charlottesville, 1967-68; from asst. to assoc. prof. radiology Sch. Medicine U. Nebr., Omaha, 1969-79, prof. radiology, 1979-96, prof. emeritus, 1996—. Cons. physician Omaha Vets. Hosp., 1969-96; grad. faculty U. Nebr., Omaha, 1972-96; peer rev. various med. jours. Contbr. articles on gastrointestinal radiology to profl. jours. Fellow Am. Coll. Radiology (emeritus), Armed Forces Inst. Pathology (disting. scientist 1987-88); mem. Radiol. Soc. N.Am., Nebr. Radiol. Soc. (pres. 1982-83, Silver medal award 2001), Soc. Gastrointestinal Radiologists (pres. 1987-88), Am. Roentgen Ray Soc. Presbyterian. Avocations: western art and history, photography, fly fishing. Home: 12624 Martha St Omaha NE 68144-2626

HARNER, JAMES LOWELL, English language educator; b. Washington, Ind., Mar. 24, 1946; s. Thomas Lloyd and Ruth Ellen (Clark) H.; m. Darinda Jane Wilson, Aug. 26, 1967; 1 child, Lenée Francais. BS magna cum laude, Ind. State U., 1968; MA, U. Ill., 1970, PhD, 1972. Prof. English Bowling Green (Ohio) State U., 1971-88, Tex. A&M U., College Station, 1988—. Author: Literary research Guide, 1989 (Choice Mag. Outstanding Acad. Book 1990), 4th edit., 2002, English Renaissance Prose Fiction, 1978, 3d edit., 1992, On Compiling an Annotated Bibliography, 1983-2000, Samuel Daniel and Michael Drayton, 1980, Directory of Scholarly Presses, 1991, (online database) World Shakespeare Bibliography Online, 1996—, (Besterman medal 1997, Besterman/McColvin medal, 2001); editor World Shakespeare Bibliography, 1988—, Essential Bibliographies Series, 1985-96; mem. editl. bd. Seventeenth-Century News, 1973—, Lit. Rsch., 1984—, Shakespeare Yearbook, 1992—, Shakespeare Quar., 1993—. Mem. MLA, The Bibliog. Soc., Shakespeare Assn. of Am., Internat. Shakespeare Assn., Bibliog. Soc. of Am. Democrat. Presbyterian. Avocations: book collecting, travel, manuscript collecting. Home: 4736 Stonebriar Cir College Station TX 77845 Office: World Shakespeare Bibliog Tex A&m U Dept English College Station TX 77843-4227

HARNER, MICHAEL JAMES, anthropologist, educator, author; b. Washington, Apr. 27, 1929; s. Charles Emory and Virginia (Paxton) H.; m. June Knight (Kocher), 1951; children: Teresa J., James E.; m. Sandra Ferial (Dickey), 1966. AB, U. Calif., Berkeley, 1953, PhD, 1963, Calif. Inst. of Integral Studies, 2003. Asst. prof. Ariz. State U., 1958—61; from sr. mus. anthropologist to assoc. rsch. anthropologist and asst. dir., Hearst Mus. Anthropology U. Calif., Berkeley, 1961—66; from vis. assoc. prof. to assoc. prof. Columbia U., N.Y.C., 1966—70; from assoc. prof. to prof. grad. faculty New Sch. Social Rsch., N.Y.C., 1970—87, chmn. dept. anthropology, 1973—77; internat. tchr. shamanism, 1977—; founder, dir. Ctr. for Shamanic Studies, Norwalk, Conn., 1979—87; founder, pres., trustee Found. for Shamanic Studies, Mill Valley, Calif., 1985—. Field rsch. Harvard U. Upper Gila expdn., 1948, Upper Amazon Basin, 1956-57, 60-61, 64, 69, 73, Western North Am., 1951-53, 59, 65, 76, 78, Lapland, 1983, 84, Can. Arctic, 1987; vis. assoc. prof. U. Calif., Berkeley, 1971, 72, vis. prof., 1975; vis. assoc. prof. Yale U., 1970; co-organizer first Internat. Congress on Shamanism, Moscow, 1999. Author: Population Pressure and the Social Evolution of Agriculturalists, 1970, The Jivaro: People of the Sacred Waterfalls, 1972, 2d edit., 1984, Music of the Jivaro of Ecuador, 1972, The Ecological Basis for Aztec Sacrifice, 1977, The Way of the Shaman, 1980, 3d edit., 1990; co-author: Cannibal, 1979, Core Practices in the Shamanic Treatment of Illness, 1999; editor: Hallucinogens and Shamanism, 1973. Fellow Social Sci. Rsch. Coun., Doherty Found., Am. Mus. Nat. History fellow. Fellow AAAS, Am. Anthrop. Assn., Royal Anthrop. Inst. G.B. and Ireland; fellow N.Y. Acad. Scis. (life, co-chmn. anthropology sect. 1980-81); mem. Am. Ethnol. Soc., Soc. Am. Archaeology, Soc. Ethnohistory, Internat. Transpersonal Assn. (bd. dirs. 1982-85, 89-91), Assn. for the Anthropology of Consciousness, Xat Medicine Men's Soc., Inst. Andean Studies, Explorers Club. Office: Found Shamanic Studies PO Box 1939 Mill Valley CA 94942-1939 E-mail: michaelharner@shamanism.org.

HARNESS, GREGORY C. Senate librarian; b. Fargo, N.D., Aug. 11, 1949; s. Wayne Lawrence and Lois Lenora (Baumgarten) Harness. BS, Moorhead (Minn.) State Coll., 1972, MS in History, 1977; MLS, U. Md., 1979. Ref. libr. U.S. Senate Libr., Washington, 1975—79, head of info. svc., 1979—95, asst. libr., 1995—97, libr. of the Senate, 1997—. Instr. Cath. U. Am., Washington, 1983—89. Office: US Senate Libr Russell Bldg Rm B-15 Washington DC 20510-7112

HARNESS, WILLIAM EDWARD, tenor; b. Pendleton, Oreg., Nov. 26, 1940; s. Edward Cleo and Edna Margaret (Senn) H.; m. Anna Marie Ward, Jan. 11, 1964; children— Janine Kay, Heidi Maurine, William Edward, Shaana Marie, Shane Michael. Student pub. schs., Spokane, Wash. Gen. carpenter Rainway Mfg. Co., Spokane, 1958-61; with Wash. Water Power Co., Spokane, 1961-62; tech. service rep. Nat. Cash Register Co., Seattle, 1962-73. Concert and opera tenor various opera cos. and symphonies, 1973—; released e secular rec., 12 sacred recs., U.S. and Can.; profl. debut, San Francisco Opera Co., 1973, debut with N.Y.C. Opera, 1976, Met. Opera, N.Y.C., 1977, Hamberg (West Germany) Opera, 1978, maj. symphony debuts include Vancouver (B.C., Can.), Seattle, Los Angeles Philharm., San Francisco, Minn., Milw. Symphonies, sacred concert artist, 1978—; roles include: Edmondo in Manon Lescaut, Tonio in Daughter of the Regiment, Alfredo in La Traviata, Rodolfo in La Boheme, Count Almaviva in The Barber of Seville, Tamino in The Magic Flute, Faust in Faust, Cauaradossi in Tosca, Prince Calof in Turandot, Riccardo in Un Ballo in Maschera; sacred concert artist, U.S. and Can., South Africa, Latvia, Romania, Croatia. Recipient V.I.P. award Nat. Cash Register Co., 1970; Florence Bruce

award San Francisco Opera, 1972; Enrico Caruso award, 1973; Cecilia Schultz award Seattle Opera, 1972; Distinguished Citizen award State of Wash., 1974; Nat. Opera Inst. fellow, 1973-74; Martha Baird Rockefeller grantee, 1974-76 Address: PO Box 328 Washougal WA 98671-0328 E-mail: whsc@pobox.com.

HARNESS, WILLIAM WALTER, lawyer; b. Ottumwa, Iowa, Apr. 14, 1945; s. Walter W. and Mary E. (Bukowski) H.; m. Carolyn Margaret Barnes, Jan 4, 1969; children: Matthew William, Michael Andrew. BA, U. Iowa, 1967; JD, Cleve. State U., 1974. Bar: Ohio 1975, U.S. Dist. Ct. (no. dist.) Ohio 1975, D.C. 1976, U.S. Dist. Ct. D.C. 1976, U.S. Ct. Appeals (D.C. cir.) 1976, U.S. Ct. Appeals (5th cir.) 1981, U.S. Dist. Ct. (we. dist.) N.C. 1979, U.S. Ct. Appeals (1st cir.) 1980, U.S. Ct. Appeals (4th cir.) 1981, U.S. Ct. Appeals (11th cir.) 1981. Mem. labor rels. staff Monogram Industries, Cleve., 1970-75; asst. counsel Nat. Treasury Employees Union, Washington, 1975-77, nat. counsel, Atlanta, 1977—; lectr. Emory U., Atlanta, 1978—; participant various seminars Ga. State U. Pres. Spring Mill-Kingsborough Ct. Corp., Atlanta. Served to 1st lt. U.S. Army, 1967-70. Mem. ABA (com. on fed. labor-mgmt. 1981-84), D.C. Bar Assn. (bd. dirs.), Soc. Fed. Labor Relations Profls., Indsl. Relations Research Assn. Home: 1285 Mile Post Dr Atlanta GA 30338-4756 Office: Nat Treasury Employees Union 2801 Buford Hwy NE Ste 430 Atlanta GA 30329-2137

HARNETT, JOSEPH DURHAM, oil company executive; b. Paterson, N.J., Aug. 23, 1917; s. James Harold and EMily (Steele) H.; m. Wilhelmina Nordstrom, June 21, 1941 (dec. July 1958); children: Gordon D., Linda C., Ralph H., David S.; m. Nancy Beam. BS, Purdue U., 1939. With Consol. Edison Co., N.Y.C., 1939, Worthington Pump & Machinery Corp., 1940, Standard Oil Co., Cleve., 1941-80, v.p., 1957-68, sr. v.p., 1968-70, exec. v.p., 1970-77, pres., 1977-80. Mem. Am. Petroleum Inst. (bd. dirs.), Country Club Cleve., Pepper Pike Club, Everglades Club, Lost Tree Club. Presbyterian. Home: 11090 Turtle Beach Rd # 204 North Palm Beach FL 33408-3423 Office: Moore and Ellrich 4400 P G A Blvd Ste 400 Palm Beach Gardens FL 33410-6557

HARNETT, LILA, retired publisher; b. Bklyn., Oct. 4, 1926; d. Milton Samuel and Claire S. (Merahn) Mogan; m. Joel William Harnett. BA, CUNY, 1946; postgrad., New Sch. for Social Rsch., 1950. Pers. exec. Walter Lowen Agy., N.Y.C., 1947-52; pub. Bus. Atomics Report, N.Y.C., 1953-63; weekly columnist N.Y. State Newspapers, 1964-74; fine arts editor Cue Mag., N.Y., 1975-80; founder, contbg. editor Phoenix Home & Garden mag., 1980—, assoc. pub., 1988—, editor, 1996-99. Pub. Scottsdale (Ariz.) Scene mag., 1992-98. Trustee Phoenix Art Mus., 1999—. Mem.: ArtTable, Inc. (founder 1979—). Home: 4523 E Clearwater Pkwy Paradise Valley AZ 85253 E-mail: lila.harnett@prodigy.net.

HARNEY, KATHRYN ANN, opera singer; b. Lincoln, Nebr., Sept. 8, 1955; d. Herman and Sylvia (Korbel) H. Fellowship Artist, Hochschule fur Musik, Munich, 1979; Diploma in Opera, Hartt Coll. of Music, Hartford, Conn., 1975; BMus, U. Nebr., 1972, MMus, 1973. Faculty U. So. Miss., Hattiesburg, 1975-77, Shepherd Sch. of Music/Rice U., Houston, 1977; opera singer/mezzo-soprano various roles in Europe, 1977—; opera singer/debut Conn. Opera, Hartford, 1974. Opera roles include: Charlotte in Werther, Baba the Turk in Rakes Progress, La Principessa di Bouillon in Adriana Lecouvreur, Der Komponist in Ariadne Auf Naxos, Venus in Tannhausser, Dorabella in Cosi Fan Tutte. Mem. Sigma Alpha Iota. Methodist. Avocations: cooking, interior decorating. Home: PO Box 15374 Hattiesburg MS 39404-5374 Office: Artist Mgmt Owen-Evans Ltd London England

HARNEY, PATRICIA RAE, enviromental technical supervisor; b. Oklahoma City, Sept. 8, 1960; d. Donald R. Thompson and Donaleen L. (Turner) Robinson; m. Timothy D. Harney, Dec. 2, 1997; 1 child, Adrian. AAS in Ct. Reporting, Mile Hi Coll. Ct. Reporting, 1985; AS in Environ. Sci., Front Range C.C., Westminster, Colo., 1999; BS in Environ. Sci., Americus U., 2003. Cert. in hazardous materials; cert. Dept. Transp.; cert. indsl. emergency responder. Pvt. practice ct. reporter, Denver, 1985-91; facility adminstr. Allen Bradley Co., Englewood, Colo., 1990-91; nuc. analyst Rocky Flats Environ. Tech. Site, Golden, Colo., 1991-95; tech. writer/analyst Y-12 Nuc. Plant, Oak Ridge, Tenn., 1995-96; nuc. safety sys. engr. Rocky Flats Environ. Tech. Site, Golden, 1996-99, tech. supr., 1999—2001, shift mgr., 2001—. Com. mem. Pro Bono Com., Denver, 1989-91. Mem. Non-Profit Orgn. for Abused Children, Denver, 1984-86; vol. fundraiser Leukemia Soc., 2003. Recipient Productivity Improvement award for centralized waste storage facility EG&G Rocky Flats, 1994, 1st Pl. award Picasso Mgmt. Tng., 2000. Mem. Am. Nuc. Soc., Phi Theta Kappa. Avocations: reading, skiing, scuba diving, biking. Home: 8722 W Ute Dr Littleton CO 80128-6964

HARNIK, HANS, lawyer; b. Vienna, July 2, 1918; arrived in USA, 1940; s. Manuel and Bertha (Friedman) Harnik; m. Edith Bettelheim, July 6, 1944; children: Peter J., Stephen M. Student, U. Vienna Law Sch.; BA, Bklyn. Coll., 1945; LLB, Bklyn. Law Sch., 1945; JSD, 1948. Bar: NY, US Supreme Ct., US Ct. Appeals (2d cir.), US Dist. Ct. (so. dist.)/NY, US Dist. Ct. (ea. dist.)/NY. Assoc. Wachtell Manheim & Frouf, NYC, 1945—53, ptnr., 1953. Contbr. articles. Recipient Grand Medal of Honor, Austria. Mem.: Am. Fgn. Law Assn., NY County Lawyers Assn., Assn. Bar City NY, Consular Law Soc. Home: 520 E 86th St New York NY 10028-7534

HARNISCH, LAWRENCE M. editor; b. Chgo., July 22, 1951; s. Lawrence E. Harnisch and Ruth Wilson. BMus, U. Ariz., 1971. Music critic Ariz. Daily Star, Tucson, 1981-85, copyeditor, 1985-88, L.A. Times, 1988—. Recipient staff/group Pulitizer prizes L.A. Times, 1992, 94, 97. Office: Los Angeles Times 202 W 1st St Los Angeles CA 90012 E-mail: lmharnisch@spamcop.net.

HARNOIS, MARION C. toxicologist, consultant; b. Ware, Mass., Oct. 16, 1936; d. Edward Harnois and Edwardina Bonin. BA, St. Joseph Coll., 1958; MS, U. Pitts., 1960, SD of Hygiene, 1965; postdoctoral, Baylor U., 1965—68. Diplomate Am. Bd. Toxicology. Geneticist Willowbrook State Sch., S.I., NY, 1968—71; rsch. scientist Hosp. for Joint Disease, N.Y.C., 1971—72; rsch. microbiologist, toxicologist Lederle Labs., Pearl River, NY, 1972—81; toxicologist Gulf Oil Co., Pitts., 1981—84; fellow Japan Found. Cancer Rsch., Tokyo, 1985—87; toxicologist Calif. Food and Agr., Sacramento, 1987—88; environ. analyst Mass. Dept. Environ. Protection, Boston, 1989—2002; cons. toxicologist Worcester, Mass., 2002—. Mem.: Environ. Mutagen Soc., Soc. for inVitro Biology, N.Y. Acad. Scis., Soc. for Risk Analysis (pres. New Eng. chpt. 2002—03), Soc. Toxicology. Avocations: photography, flower arranging, travel, genealogy. Home: 321 Plantation St Apt 104 Worcester MA 01604*

HARNSBERGER, RICHARD STEPHEN, law educator; b. Omaha, Dec. 14, 1921; s. Carl Wesley Harnsberger and Lillian Lucille Coppersmith; children: Richard Stephen, Robert Scott. BS, U. Nebr., 1943, MA, 1951, JD cum laude, 1949; D in Juridicial Sci., U. Wis., 1959. Bar: Nebr. 1949. Assoc. Stewart and Stewart, Lincoln, Nebr., 1949—55; dep. county atty. Lancaster County, Lincoln, 1955—56; faculty mem. U. Nebr. Coll. Law, Lincoln, 1956—. Mem. adv. bd. Nebr. State Dept. Environ. Control, Lincoln, 1973—77; trustee Groundwater Found., Lincoln, 1983—96, Govs. Water Coun., Lincoln, 1996; spkr. in field. Co-author: Nebraska Water Law, 1984; contbr. articles to profl. jours. Trustee Family Svcs. Assn., Lincoln, 1952—58; mem. citizens adv. group City of Lincoln Street Action Plan, 1976—78; bd. dirs. Legal Svcs. S.E. Nebr., Lincoln, 1982—86, Water Com. Nebr. Legis., Lincoln, 1998. Capt. U.S. Army, 1943—46, ETO. Recipient Maurice Kremer Groundwater Achievement award, Groundwater Found., 1999, Outstanding Educator award, Nebr. State Bar Found., 2002. Mem.: ABA (mem. standing com. on environ. law 1973—79), Nebr. State Bar Assn., Order of the Coif, Beta Gamma Sigma. Avocation: reading. Home: 1919 S 48th St Lincoln NE 68506 Office: U Nebr Coll of Law Lincoln NE 68583-0902

HAROLD, TOM, advertising executive; Former CEO iPares (formerly Dillon New Media), Mpls.

HARON, DAVID LAWRENCE, lawyer; b. Detroit, Sept. 24, 1944; s. Percy Hyman and Bess (Holland) H.; m. Pamela Kay Colburn, May 25, 1969; children: Eric, Andrea. BA, U. Mich., 1966, JD, 1969. Bar: Mich. 1969, U.S. Dist. Ct. (ea. dist.) Mich., 1969, U.S. Supreme Ct. 1974, U.S. Ct. of Appeals (6th cir.) 1996. Law clk. to chief judge Mich. Ct. Appeals, Detroit, 1969-70; assoc. Barris, Sott, Denn & Driker, Detroit, 1970-74; sr. ptnr. Josephson, Tennen, Haron and Bennett, Southfield, Mich., 1974-90; prin., shareholder, sr. v.p. Frank, Stefani, Haron and Weiner, Troy, Mich., 1990—; arbitrator Mich. Prudential Securities, Inc. Expedited Arbitrations, 1994-96. Cons. Universe Computer Software, 1985; pres., bd. dirs. S&H Licensing Corp., Southfield; panelist Ct. TV Law Ctr. Bar Assn. Mem. editorial bd. Prospectus Jour. Law Reform, 1969, (newsletter) Atty.'s Mktg. Report, 1986-88; contbr. articles to profl. jours. Mem. Farmington Hills Planning Commn., 1996—, vice-chair, 2000-01, chair, 2001-02, 03—; vol. handicap parking enforcement officer Farmington Hills Police Dept., 1990-93; bd. dirs. Forest Elem. Sch. PTO, 1983, 87-88; v.p. North Farmington Baseball for Youth, 1984; mem. Sta. WTVS Auction, Detroit, 1985-88; trustee C.A.T.C.H., 1996—, Temple Israel, West Bloomfield, Mich., 1987-93, tchr. Sunday Sch., 1986-88, chmn. Ritual com., 1988-93, advisor youth group, 1987-90; chmn. Farmington Hills Com. to Increase Voter Participation, 1987-89; bd. dirs. Met. Detroit chpt. Zionist Orgn. Am., 1987-90; pres. North Farmington H.S. Parent Club, 1989-95; mem. bd. advisors Farmington Hills Corps.-Salvation Army, 1997-2000; mem. site selection com. South Oakland County Habitat for Humanity; chair Cardozo Law Soc. of the Jewish Fedn. Met. Detroit, 1999 2002. Recipient Outstanding Alumnus award Mumford H.S., Detroit, 1985, Cert. recognition City of Farmington Hills, 1986. Fellow The Roscoe Pound Found., Mich. State Bar Found.; mem. ABA (mem. com. on comml. leasing 1987-91, real property, probate and trust law sect., mem. bus. law sect. com. on fed. regulation of securities, mem. subcom. on alternative dispute resolution, SEC enforcement matters), ASTM (mem. com. on environ. assessment 1992—), ATLA, Nat. Arbitration Forum (arbitrator), Assn. Health Lawyers Am. (co-chmn. fraud & abuse SISLC false claims/qui tam working group), Mich. Trial Lawyers Assn., Am. Soc. Writers on Legal Subjects, Internat. Assn. Jewish Lawyers and Jurists, Million Dollar Advocates Forum, State Bar Mich. (mem. pro bono com. real property sect. 1996-98, mem. professionalism com. 1994-2002, chmn. professionalism com. 1996-98, chmn. unauthorized practice of law com. 1990-92, mem. unauthorized practice of law com. 1999-2002, chmn. Ct. Appeals com. 1977-78, mem. rep. assembly 1999—), Nat. Assn. Securities Dealers (mediator, arbitrator), Am. Arbitration Assn. (arbitrator, mediator, spkr.), Comml. Law League Am., Detroit Bar Assn., Jewish Fedn., Oakland County Bar Assn. (participant Mich. law-related edn. project 1988-89, real estate com. 1990—, environ. law com. 1992-95, lawyer dispute conciliator, spkr. 1993, chmn. professionalism com. 1995-97, Cir. Ct. facilitator, master Inn of Ct. 1997—; recipient Professionalism award, 2003), Oakland County Bar Found. (trustee, treas. 2003-), U. Mich. Alumni Assn., U. Mich. Victor's Club, Zionist Orgn. (bd. dirs. Detroit 1987-90), Tau Epsilon Rho, Tau Delta Phi. Jewish. Home: 34685 Old Timber Rd Farmington Hills MI 48331-1436 Office: Frank Stefani Haron and Weiner 5435 Corporate Dr Ste 225 Troy MI 48098-2624 Fax: 248-952-0890. E-mail: dharon@fsh-law.com.

HAROON, NASREEN, artist; b. Karachi, Pakistan, Dec. 10, 1952; came to U.S., 1980; d. Ahmad and Amina (Dada) Adaya; m. Haroon Haji Husein, Apr. 29, 1972; children: Omar, Sana. BA in Psychology, Philosophy and History, St. Josephs Coll., Karachi, 1972. Design cons. Shangri-La Hotel, Santa Monica, Calif., 1983—; spkr. on cultural, ethnic, religious diversity, 1991—. Exhibited oil paintings in numerous exhbns., 1992—; featured in premier issue Zarposh Mag., 1997; appears regularly on Adelphia Cable TV program God Squad; participant Muslim Jewish Dialogue; paintings selected for Art In Embassies program, displayed at U.S. Embassy, Pakistan. Bd. dirs. Islamic Ctr. So. Calif., 1999-2002, pres. women's assn., 1991, Pakistan Arts Coun. of Pacific Asia Mus., Pasadena, Calif., 1994-96, v.p., 1997-99, Devel. in Literacy, L.A., 1996-97, Santa Monica (Calif.) Bay Interfaith Coun., 1994—; chmn. Muslim Jewish Dialogue. Recipient award for planning Youth Day, Westside Interfaith Coun., 1998. Democrat. Moslem. Avocations: reading, gardening, jewelry design, photography, travel. Office: Shangri-La Hotel 1301 Ocean Ave Santa Monica CA 90401-1010

HARP, CHADWICK ALLEN, lawyer, author, educator; b. Norristown, Pa., Mar. 24, 1969; s. Leroy Allen Jr. and Judith Ann (Beck) H. BA cum laude, George Washington U., 1991; JD, Dickinson Sch. Law, Carlisle, Pa., 1996. Bar: Pa. 1996. Various positions George Washington U. Med. Ctr., 1988-93, asst. to dean, 1990-93; law clk. Breidenbach, Breidenbach & Troncellitti, Norristown, Pa., 1994-96; atty. Fox, Differ, Callahan, Sheridan & McDevitt, Norristown, Pa., 1999-2000, Fox, Rothschild, O'Brien & Frankel, LLP, 2000; pvt. practice East Norriton, Pa., 2000—. Adj. prof. Montgomery County C.C., 1996—; facilitator U. Phoenix, 2001—; mem. faculty bus. edn. dept. Reading H.S., Pa., 2001—; pub. affairs intern Sec. Def., 1987—88. Author: Estate Planning For Individuals With Disabilities, 2002, Young Warriors, 2002, Return to the Lake, First Who You Are, Second What You Know: The Ten Habits of the Effective Teacher, 2002; contbr. articles to profl. jours. Bd. dirs. Pa. Children's Aid Soc., 1995—. Mem. ABA, Pa. Bar Assn., Montgomery Bar Assn., Nat. Acad. Elder Law Attys., Inc., Sigma Nu. E-mail: chadwickharp@aol.com.

HARP, GILLIS JOHN, history educator; b. Ames, Iowa, June 16, 1956; s. Bernard John Harp and Thelma Eileen Wiebe; m. Barbara Judith Tychsen, June 4, 1983; children: Caroline, Anna, Eleanor. BA, Carleton U., 1979; MA, U. Va., 1980, PhD, 1986. Instr. U. Toronto, Ont., Can., 1984-86; asst. prof. history McGill U., Montreal, Can., 1986-88; assoc. prof. history Acadia U., Wolfville, NS, 1992-99; prof. history Grove City (Pa.) Coll., 1999—. Author: Positivist Republic, 1995. Mem. Evang. Fellowship Anglican Communion. Office: Grove City Coll 100 Coll Dr Grove City PA 16127

HARP, JOHN ANDERSON, lawyer; b. Helena, Ark., Nov. 30, 1950; s. Bert Seth and Mary Eleanor (Jolley) H.; m. Jane Van Cleave, Apr. 26, 1980; children: Anderson, Elizabeth, William, Hamilton. BA, Am. U., Washington, 1973; JD, Mercer U., Macon, Ga., 1980. Bar: Ga., Ala. Ptnr. Taylor, Harp & Callier, Columbus, Ga., 1985—. Co-author: Litigating Head Trauma Cases, 1991; bd. editors Neurolaw Letter, 1991—, Topics in Spinal Cord Injury Rehab., 1994—; issues editor Topics in Spinal Cord Injury Rehabilitation, vol. 6, no. 4, 2001; contbr. articles to profl. jours. Reservist USMCR with Office of Asst. Sec. of Def., The Pentagon, 1996-2001. Col., USMCR, 1995-2000, Marine Forces Pacific G-3, 2000-02. Mem. ABA, ATLA, Ga. Bar Assn., Ala. Bar Assn., Nat. Spinal Cord Assn. (bd. dirs. 1987-95), Marine Corps Res. Officers Assn. (bd. dirs. 1995-98, nat. pres. 1997-98, vice-chmn. bd. dirs. 1998-99, Non Sibi Sed Patriae award), Mercer U. Law Sch. Alumni Assn. (nat. v.p. 1997-98, nat. pres.-elect 1998-99, nat. pres. 1999—). Avocations: running, skiing. Office: Taylor Harp & Callier 233 12th St Ste 900 Columbus GA 31901-2449

HARPEL, GERALD ROBERT, obstetrician and gynecologist; b. Boston, Mar. 25, 1946; s. Aaron and Dorothy (Goldring) H.; m. Cassie M. Lemaster, Nov. 4, 1989; children: Crystal L. Lemaster, Aaron B. (dec.), Michael A. BA, Boston U., 1967; MPH, Yale U., 1969; MD, Boston U., 1973. Diplomate Am. Bd. Ob Gyn. Intern R.I. Hosp.-Brown U., 1973-74; resident in ob-gyn. Good Samaritan Hosp., Phoenix, 1974-77; chief of staff Harrison Meml. Hosp., Cynthiana, Ky., 1995-2000, chmn. ob-gyn., 1995—; pvt. practice Just for Women-Ob-Gyn., Cynthiana, Ky. Clin. prof. emeritus ob-gyn. U. So. Calif., 1995; vis. prof. Harrison County Dept. Edn., Cynthiana, 1995—. Chmn. Cmty. Health Partnership, 1998—. Fellow ACS, Am. Coll. Ob-Gyn., Internat. Coll. Surgery, L.A. Ob-Gyn. Soc.; mem. APHA, Am. Assn. Gynecol. Laproscopists, Am. Soc. Reproductive Medicine, Ky. Med. Assn., Ky. Pub. Health Assn., Calif. Med. Assn., L.A. County Med. Assn., Am. Coll. Phys. Execs. Office: Just for Women-Ob-Gyn 1210 Ky Hwy 36 E Ste 1A Cynthiana KY 41031

HARPEN, MICHAEL DENNIS, physicist, educator; b. Toledo, July 6, 1949; s. Walter John and Jeanne (Beaber) H.; m. Lydi Hong, July 24, 1981; children: Dennis, Mary. BS, MS, Xavier U., 1971; PhD, U. Cin., 1979. Postdoctoral scholar UCLA, 1979-81; prof. radiology U. South Ala., Mobile, 1981—. Cons. NIH, Washington, 1989—, Radiol. Physics, 1981—. Contbr. articles to profl. publs. Mem. Am. Assn. Physicists in Medicine (Outstanding Publ. award), Am. Coll. Radiology, Soc. Magnetic Resonance in Medicine, Assn. Univ. Radiologists. Republican. Roman Catholic. Achievements include patent for improved method for assessment of free thyroxine and thyroxine binding globulin. Home: 9255 Lake Woods Dr Semmes AL 36575-4445 Office: U South Ala Dept Radiology 2451 Fillingim St Mobile AL 36617-2238

HARPER, ALFRED JOHN, II, lawyer; b. El Paso, Tex., Aug. 11, 1942; s. Mosely Lloyd and Marion M. (McClintock) H.; m. Cynthia Newkam; children— A. John, Leslie J. BA, North Tex. State U., 1964; LLB cum laude, So. Meth. U., 1967. Bar: Tex. 1967, U.S. Dist. Ct. (so. dist.) Tex. 1967, U.S. Dist. Ct. (no. dist.) Tex. 1975, U.S. Dist. Ct. (we. dist.) Tex. 1976, U.S. Dist. Ct. (ea. dist.) Tex. 1995, U.S. Ct. Appeals (5th cir.) 1968, U.S. Ct. Appeals (9th cir.) 1976, U.S. Ct. Appeals (11th cir.) 1982, U.S. Ct. Appeals (10th cir.) 1984, U.S. Ct. Appeals (6th cir.) 1990, U.S. Ct. Appeals (1st cir.) 1991, U.S. Ct. Appeals (2d cir.) 1995, U.S. Ct. Appeals (8th cir.) 2002, U.S. Supreme Ct. 1971. Assoc. Fulbright & Jaworski, L.L.P., Houston, 1967-74, ptnr., 1974—. Cert. labor and employment law specialist State Bar Tex. bd. legal specialization. Editor Jour. Air Law and Commerce, 1966-67; contbr. articles to profl. jours. With USMCR, 1960-66. Fellow Coll. Labor and Employment Lawyers; mem. ABA (past coun., labor and employment law sect., past mgmt. co-chmn. com. on devel. law under Nat. Labor Rels. Act, past mgmt. co-chmn. meetings and insts. com., labor law sect.), Tex. Bar Assn., Order of Coif, Houston Country Club. Republican. Methodist. Office: Fulbright & Jaworski 1301 Mckinney St Houston TX 77010-3031 E-mail: ajharper@fulbright.com.

HARPER, BARBARA CLARA, counselor, educational program administrator, counselor; b. NYC, Aug. 9, 1932; d. James Gullins and Irene Christine (Robinson) H.; m. William C. Booth, Apr. 24, 1951 (div. 1958); 1 child, James Alan; m. Washington Mays, Jan. 1, 1959 (div. 1987). AA, Mattaluck Community Coll., 1978; BS, N.H. Coll., 1987, MS, 1989. Cert. profl. counselors inc. Conn. Bd., lic. profl. counselor, foster mother. Gen. office staff Avnet Electronics, Bronx, NY, 1955-59; sec., gen office staff PHA, Waterbury, Conn., 1959-64; pers. interviewer Scovill Mfg. Co., Waterbury, 1964-66; caseworker, ctr. dir. New Opportunities for Waterbury, 1966-68; coord. Waterbury Cmty. Sch., 1969-94; clinician Child Guidance Clinic Greater Waterbury, Inc., 1963—. Part-time instr. Displaced Housewives and Work Incentive Programs, 1975-80; mem. clerical staff Mattaluck C.C., Waterbury, 1974-80. Mem. Drug Free Sch., 1984; vol. leader Coop. Ext. Svc., USDA 4-H, 1984-91; com. leader Boy Scouts Am., 1974-76, Girl Scouts, 1962; sec. Northeastern Heights Coun., 1971, The Promoters Club of Wilson Sch., 1980; bd. dir. NOW Inc., 1964; vol. organist, choir dir. St. Cecilia's Ch., 1960. With USAF, 1950-52. Recipient Silver Clover award Coop. Extension Svc., U. Conn. 1989, Cert. of Appreciation award Youth Svc. Bur., Dedicated Svc. Appreciation award Boy Scouts of Am. Troop 223, 1975. Mem.: Conn. Assn. Marriage and Family Counselors (past pres. 2002—03, sec. 1998—99, pres. 2001—02), Nat. Polit. Congress of Black Women (sec. 1998—99, pres.-elect 1999—2001, pres. 2001—02), Long Hill Cmty. Club (sec.), Waterbury Black Dem. Club. Democrat. Home and Office: 165 Traverse St Waterbury CT 06704-3229

HARPER, CATHERINE B. primary school educator; d. William Joseph and Mariam Bradley; m. Robert T. Harper, July 4, 1982. BS in Elem. Edn. summa cum laude, L.I. U., 1974; MS in Edn., Hofstra U., 1975. Educator educably mentally retarded William Floyd UFSD, Beach, NY, 1975—86, 2nd grade educator, 1986—. Presenter in field. Contbr. chapters to books. Vol. Bellport (N.Y.) Housing Alliance, 1993—97; organizer, coord. North Fork (N.Y.) Parish Outreach, 1991—. Named torchbearer, 2002 Olympic Winter Games, 2002; recipient Am. Tchr. award, Walt Disney Co., 1996; scholar, Fulbright Meml. Fund, Japan, 2002. Roman Catholic. Avocations: preservation, restoring 19th century textiles, reed organ. Office: Woodhull Elem Landau Pl Shirley NY 11967

HARPER, CHARLES H. columnist, reporter; b. Rehoboth, Mass., Mar. 9, 1928; s. Almon Lewis Harper, Bessie Belle Harper; m. E. Jean Aird, June 27, 1959; children: Daniel children: Nancy, Patricia Enzien. BS in Edn., Boston U., 1952. Small bus. cons. Harper Assocs., Westborough, Mass., 1981—87; columnist-reporter The Westborough (Mass.) News, Mass., 1988—. Dir. Mass. Assn. for Mental Health, Boston, 1978—84. Author: (novels) The Sexual Harrassment of Laura Lovejoy, 1997. Metro chmn. Nat. Alliance Bus., Worcester, 1980—81. Recipient Presdl. citations, Ronald Reagan --Jimmy Carter, 1980, 1982.

HARPER, CHARLES MICHEL, food company executive; b. Lansing, Mich., Sept. 26, 1927; s. Charles Frost and Alma (Michel) Harper; m. Joan Frances Bruggema, June 24, 1950; children: Kathleen Harper Wenngatz, Carolyn, Charles Michel, Elizabeth Harper Murphy. BS in Mech. Engring, Purdue U., 1949; MBA, U. Chgo., 1950; LHD (hon.), U. Nebr., 1986; hon. (hon.), Coll. St. Mary, 1986; JD (hon.), Law Coll. of St. Mary, 1986; DEng (hon.), Purdue U., 1989; LHD (hon.), Kearney State U., 1990, Bellevue Coll., 1993, Creighton U., 1993. Supr. methods engring. Oldsmobile divsn. Gen. Motors Corp., Detroit, 1950—54; indsl. engr. Pillsbury Co., Mpls., 1954—55, dir. indsl. engring., 1955—60, dir. engring., 1961—66, v.p. rsch., devel. and new products, 1965—70, group v.p.-poultry, food svc. and venture bus., 1970—74; exec. v.p., COO, dir. ConAgra Inc., Omaha, 1974—76, pres., CEO, 1976—81, chmn. bd., CEO, dir., 1981—93; chmn. bd., CEO RJR Nabisco Holdings Corp., N.Y.C., 1993—95, chmn. bd., 1995—96, ret., 1996. Bd. dirs. Valmont Industries, Inc., Peter Kiewit Sons, Inc., ConAgra, Inc.; mem. exec. com. Nat. Commn. on Agrl., Trade and Export Policy, 1984—86. Pres. Mid-Am. Coun. Boy Scouts Am., 1983—84; mem. coun. Village of Excelsior, Minn., 1965—70, mayor, 1974. Served U.S. Army, 1946—48. Named Alumnus of Yr., U. Chgo. Grad. Sch. Bus., 1991. Mem.: U. Nebr. Lincoln Coll. Bus. Adminstrn. Alumni Assn. (hon. life mem.), Ak-Sar-Ben (gov.), Omaha C. of C. (chmn. 1979), U.S. C. of C. (bd. dirs., chmn. food and agrl. com.), Beta Theta Pi.

HARPER, CHRISTINE JOHNSON, psychiatric clinical nurse, administrator; b. Tyler, Tex., June 26, 1952; d. Reinhold P. and Alice G. (Levingston) Johnson; m. James H. Harper, Sept. 4, 1982; 1 child, Timothy Wright. BSN, U. Tex., 1974; MS, U. Tex., Tyler, 1981; MSN, Tex. Woman's U., 1992. RN, Tex.; cert. clin. nurse specialist in psychiat. mental health. Instr. Tyler Jr. Coll., 1976-87; sr. lectr. U. Tex., Tyler, 1987-91, adj. nursing faculty, 1994—; clin. specialist Rusk (Tex.) State Hosp., 1992-94, dir. nursing svcs., 1994—. Mem. nurse practice orgn. exec. com. Tex. Dept. Mental Health/Mental Retardation, 1995-97; bd. dirs. nurse examiners State of Tex. Adv. Com. on Edn. Mem. Tex. Nurses Assn. (bd. dirs. dist. 19, ho. of dels., past pres., Exemplary Leadership in Tex. Nursing award 1988), Tex. Bd. Nurse Examiners (adv. com. edn. 1996-97), Tex. Mental Health Mental Retardation Nurse Practice Orgn. (exec. com. 1995-97), Am. Psychiat. Nurses Assn. (Tex. rep. 1995), Sigma Theta Tau (chmn. nominations Iota Nu chpt.), E-mail: cjharper@lcc.net.

HARPER, CONRAD KENNETH, lawyer, former government official; b. Detroit, Dec. 2, 1940; s. Archibald Leonard and Georgia Florence (Hall) H.; m. Marsha Louise Wilson, July 17, 1965; children: Warren Wilson, Adam Woodburn. BA, Howard U., 1962; LLB, Harvard U., 1965; LLD (hon.), CUNY, 1990, Vt. Law Sch., 1994. Bar: N.Y. 1966. Law clk. NAACP Legal Def. and Ednl. Fund, N.Y.C., 1965-66, staff lawyer, 1966-70; assoc. Simpson Thacher & Bartlett, N.Y.C., 1971-74, ptnr., 1974—93, 1996—2002, of counsel, 2003—; legal adviser U.S. Dept. of State, Washington, 1993-96. Lectr. law Rutgers U., 1969-70; vis. lectr. law Yale U., 1977-81; cons. HEW, 1977; chmn. admissions and grievances com. U.S. Ct. Appeals, 2d cir., 1987-93; co-chmn. Lawyers' Com. for Civil Rights Under Law, 1987-89; mem. Permanent Ct. of Arbitration, The Hague, 1993-96, 98—, Adminstrv. Conf. U.S., 1993-95, Harvard Corp., 2000—; bd. dirs. N.Y. Life Ins. Co., Pub. Svc. Enterprise Group. Trustee Inst. Internat. Edn., 1992-93, N.Y. Pub. Libr., chmn. exec. com., 1990-93, vice-chmn. bd. trustees, 1991-93; trustee William Nelson Cromwell Found., 1990—, Met. Mus. of Art, 1996—; bd. mgrs. Lewis Walpole Libr., 1989-93; bd. visitors Fordham Law Sch., 1990-93, CUNY, 1989-93; vestryman Ch. of St. Barnabas, Irvington, N.Y., 1982-85; bd. dirs. Phi Beta Kappa Assocs., 1992-93; chancellor The Episc. Diocese of N.Y., 1987-92; bd. legal advisors Martindale-Hubbell, 1990-93. Fellow Am. Bar Found., N.Y. Bar Found., Am. Coll. Trial Lawyers, Am. Acad. Arts and Scis.; mem. Am. Philos. Soc., ABA (bd. editors jour. 1980-86), Nat. Bar Assn., N.Y. State Bar Assn., Assn. of Bar of City of N.Y. (chmn. exec. com. 1979-80, pres. 1990-92), Am. Law Inst. (mem. coun. 1985—, 2nd v.p. 1998-2000, 1st v.p. 2000—), Am. Assn. for Internat. Commn. Jurists (bd. dirs. 1988-93), Am. Soc. Internat. Law (mem. exec. coun. 1997-2000, exec. com. 1998-2000, counselor 2000—), Met. Black Bar Assn., Acad. Polit. Sci. (bd. dirs. 1998—), Coun. Fgn. Rels., Grolier Club (coun. mem. 1993, 97—), Century Assn., Harvard Club (mem. bd. mgrs. 1993), Phi Beta Kappa. Democrat. Episcopalian.

HARPER, DAVID TAYLOR, civilian military employee; b. L.A., Feb. 3, 1959; s. Clarence Bluford Harper and Myrtle Marie Sparks, Dwain Sparks (Stepfather); m. Joyce Lee Van Leuvan; m. Barbara Christine Jecz (div. Sept. 1,

1990); 1 child, Benjamin;stepchildren: Donald Drorbaugh, Deborah Drorbaugh. AAS, C.C. of the Air Force, Maxwell AFB, Ala., 1984; AA, U. Md., 1985; BS with honors, Calif. State U., Sacramento, 1988; MPA, Calif. State U., Carson, 1999. Spl. agt. Air Force Office Spl. Investigations, N.Y.C., 1988—89, El Segundo, Calif., 1989—; instr. criminal justice U. Phoenix, 2002—. Tech., sgt. USAF, 1976—85. Mem.: ASPA, Acad. Polit. Sci., Am. Polit. Sci. Assn. (assoc.), Pi Alpha Alpha. Avocations: computers, writing, travel. Office: AFOSI Detachment 110 Ste 1467 2420 Vela Way El Segundo CA 90245 Office Fax: 310-363-2170. Personal E-mail: dtharper@sbcglobal.net.

HARPER, DIANE MARIE, retired communications retailer; b. Harrisburg, Pa., Oct. 22, 1938; d. Paull Harry Rineard and Berneice Marie (Westhafer) Gerhardt; m. William Irvin Harper, Nov. 17, 1957 (div. Aug. 1981); children: Dawn Michelle, Steven Lee, William Madison; 1 stepson: William Lee. Telephone operator United Telephone Pa., Carlisle, 1956-59, keypunch operator Harrisburg, 1960-61, Safety Sales & Svc., Harrisburg, 1967-70; keypunch operator, lead data entry operator Kinney Shoe Corp., Camp Hill, Pa., 1970-84; data entry operator First Health, Harrisburg, 1984-92; resolution analyst Electronic Data Systems, Camp Hill, 1992-97; comms. retailer Electronic Data Sys., Rossmoyne, 1997-99, ret., 1999. Part-time cashier KMart, 2000-01; Stephen min. of Evang. Luth. Ch., Stephen min. tng. leader, 2003; reporter, writer pubs. com. Electronic Data Systems, 1996-97, human resources coord. corrective action com., 1993-96, social coord. 2d shift Pa. XIX staff, 1993-96. Committeeperson 4th Ward, Carlisle, Pa., 1959-61, 1st Ward, Mechanicsburg, 1997—; minority insp. polls, Carlisle, 1959-61; pres. Mothers of DeMolay, Carlisle, 1976-78, Mechanicsburg Area Dem. Club, 1998-99, pres. emeritus, 1999, v.p., 2000; Halloween parade assoc. City of Mechanicsburg; mem. coun., chair witness and outreach com. St. Paul's Evang. Luth. Ch., Carlisle, Pa., 2000-, also lay minister, mem. choir. Mem. NOW, Nat. Abortion and Reproductive Rights Action League, Nat. Pks. and Conservation Assn., Nat. Resources Def. Coun., Nat. Arbor Day Found., Pa. Sheriff's Assn. (hon.), Pa. Chiefs of Police Assn., Mechanicsburg Mus. Assn., Legal Assts. Club, Friends Dauphin County Libr., Friends Mechanicsburg Libr., Little Theatre Mechanicsburg (v.p. 1962-63, pres. 1963-67), Nat. Trust for Hist. Preservation, Carlisle Women's Dem. Club, Blues Soc. Ctrl. Pa. Democrat. Avocations: theatre, reading, travel, cooking. Home: 306 S Market St Mechanicsburg PA 17055-6326

HARPER, DONALD VICTOR, retired transportation and logistics educator; b. Chgo., Mar. 27, 1927; s. Victor Rudolph and Mildred Victoria (Safbom) H.; children: Christine Ann, Diane Elizabeth, David Victor. Student, Wright Jr. Coll., 1945, 46-47; BS in Journalism, U. Ill., Urbana, 1950, PhD in Econs., 1957. Instr. Coll. Commerce and Bus. adminstrn. U. Ill., Urbana, 1953-56; lectr. Carlson Sch. Mgmt. U. Minn., Mpls., 1956, asst. prof. Carlson Sch. Mgmt., 1956-59, assoc. prof., 1959-65, prof. transp. and logistics, 1965-97, chmn. dept. mgmt. and transp., 1967-70, dir. MBA and PhD programs, 1970-79, dir. PhD program, 1979-80, chmn. dept. mktg. and logistics mgmt., 1991-96; prof. emeritus, 1997—; cons. to bus. and govt. agys. Author: Economic Regulation of the Motor Trucking Industry by the States, 1959, Price Policy and Procedure, 1966, Transportation in America: Users, Carriers, Government, 2d edit, 1982; contbr. articles to profl. jours. Served with USNR, 1945-46. Mem. Am. Econ. Assn. (Disting. Mem. award transp. and pub. utilities group 1988), Am. Mktg. Assn., Transp. Research Forum, Am. Soc. Transp. and Logistics, Transp. Club Mpls. and St. Paul, Assn. Transp. Law, Logistics and Policy. Home: 2451 Sheldon St Saint Paul MN 55113-3138 Office: U Minn Carlson Sch Mgmt 321 19th Ave S Minneapolis MN 55455-0438 E-mail: dharper@csom.umn.edu.

HARPER, DOUGLAS ALBERT, sociologist, researcher; b. St. Paul, Jan. 27, 1948; s. Herbert H. and Norman Maxine (Schmuck) H.; m. Suzan Carol Fritz, Sept. 18, 1977; children: Molly, Colter. BA, Macalester Coll., 1970; PhD, Brandeis U., 1976. From asst. to full prof. sociology, chair SUNY, Potsdam, 1975-91; prof. sociology, chair U. of South Fla., Tampa, 1991-95; prof., chair dept. sociology Duquesne U., Pitts., 1995—. Part-time vis. prof. anthropology U. Amsterdam, The Netherlands, 1990-94; vis. prof. U. Bologna, Italy. Author: Good Company, 1982, Working Knowledge, 1987, Changing Works, 2001; editor: Cape Breton 1952: The Photographic Vision of Timothy Asch, 1994; co-editor: Eyes Across the Water, 1993; co-dir.: (film) Ernie's Sawmill, 1982; founding editor: (jour.) Visual Sociology, 1985—. Ford Found. grantee, 1990. Mem. Am. Sociology Assn., Soc. for Study of Symbolic Interaction. Democrat. Avocations: photography, jazz guitar. Office: Duquesue U Pittsburgh PA 15282-0001

HARPER, ELIZABETH A. retired occupational therapist; b. Rochester, Minn., Feb. 15, 1935; d. Ephraim John Koeneman and Margaret Richman; m. Gordon E. Harper, Dec. 28, 1957; children: William Jacque, James Walter. BS, Ohio State U., 1957. Staff occupl. therapist VA Hosp., Long Beach, Calif., 1957—59; dir. occupl. therapy Palo Alto (Calif.) Stanford Hosp. Ctr., 1959—63; basic motor skills specialist Portola Valley Sch. Dist., 1974—76; occupl. therapist sensory integration specialist Children's Hosp. Stanford, Palo Alto, 1976—78, Children's Health Coun., Palo Alto, 1978—89; occupl. therapist Santa Clara County Dept. Edn., 1989—91; occupl. therapy cons. pvt. practice Santa Clara, San Mateo, Calif., 1991—96; ret., 1996—. Sensory integration faculty mem. Sensory Integration Internat., Torrance, Calif., 1976—, sensory integration faculty mem. emeritus, 1986—. Mem.: Calif. Occupl. Therapy Assn., Am. Occupl. Therapy Assn. (registered occupl. therapist, alt. del.). Libertarian. Avocations: hiking, walking, swimming, gardening. Home: 50 Joaquin Rd Portola Valley CA 94028

HARPER, EMERY WALTER, lawyer; b. Hackensack, NJ, Feb. 25, 1936; s. Walter Van Saun and Dorothy Charlotte (Schmidt) H.; m. Judith Van Nest Hover, Sept. 9, 1961 (div. 1991); 1 child, Caroline Curry BA cum laude, Amherst Coll., 1958; LLB, Yale U., 1961. Bar: N.Y. 1962. Assoc. Lord Day & Lord, Barrett Smith, N.Y.C., 1961-69, ptnr., 1970-93, Schnader, Harrison, Segal & Lewis, N.Y.C., 1993-96, chmn. internat. maritime group, 1993-95; pres. Harper Cons., Inc., N.Y.C., 1997—; of counsel Inman Deming LLP, 1998—. Bd. dirs. The Shipping Network, Inc.; bd. dirs., founding mem. The Admiralty/Fin. Forum, Inc.; lectr. on maritime law Dalian, PRC, 1984; advisor U.S. del. to joint working group on liens and mortgages Internat. Maritime Orgn., 1st, 2d, 5th and 6th sessions UN Conf. on Trade and Devel., 1986-89; lectr. on admiralty and maritime financing; lectr. on ship fin. topics, Mex., Panama, Chile, Thailand, 1993-95; course dir. practice and techniques Financing Marine Assets and Ops., N.Y., 1995; organizer, pres. Am. Corps. in Coastwise Trade; participant U.S. Delegation to IMO/UNCTAD Joint Diplomatic Conf. on Maritime Liens and Mortgages, Geneva, 1993; cons. Inman Deming Internat., LLC, Washington, 1998—; del. to diplomatic conf. arrest of ships Internat. C. of C., 1999. Co-author: Essays on Maritime Liens and Mortgages and on Arrest of Ships, 1985; contbr. articles to profl. publs. Trustee The Gateway Sch., N.Y., 1975-83; deacon Brick Presbyn. Ch., 1970-76, elder, 1976-82, trustee, corp. sec., 1982-88; mem. legal adv. com. Liberian Shipowners Coun., 1988-2000; chmn. Subcom. on Liberian Maritime Law Revision, 1993-99; chmn. Marshall Islands Roundtable, 1999-2001; mem. Seatransport com. U.S. Coun. for Internat. Bus., 1987-91; dir. Cmty. Living Corp. Found., Inc., 2002—; bd. dirs. CLC Found., Inc., 2002—. With USAFR, 1961-67. Mem. ABA (chmn. admiralty and maritime law com., sect. internat. law and practice), Assn. of Bar of City of N.Y. (mem. admiralty com. 1974-80, 90-93, 98-2000, chmn. 1977-80), Maritime Law Assn. (founding chmn. com. on Marine financing 1978—), Com. Maritime Internat. (internat. subcom. on maritime liens and mortgages), N.Y. Amherst Alumni Assn. (pres. 1975-77), Pilgrims Soc., Union Club, Down Town Club. Office: 18 E 48th St Fl 10 New York NY 10017 also: East Tower 1301 K St NW Ste 800 Washington DC 20005-3373 E-mail: eharper974@aol.com.

HARPER, GEORGE MILLS, English language educator; b. Linn Creek, Mo., Nov. 5, 1914; s. Charles Avery and Grace (Shipman) H.; m. Mary Jane Hughes, June 15, 1944; children: Margaret Mills, Ann Christian. AB, Culver-Stockton Coll., 1940; MA, U. Fla., 1947; PhD, U. N.C., 1951; D.Litt. (hon.), Trinity Coll., Dublin, 1980. From instr. to prof. English, U. N.C., 1950-66, asso. dean arts and scis., 1955-60, chmn. English dept., 1962-66, chmn. faculty, 1961-64, chmn. humanities, 1962-65; prof., chmn. English dept. U. Fla., 1966-69; dean arts and scis., Univ. prof. Va. Poly. Inst., 1969-70; chmn. English dept. Fla. State U., Tallahassee, 1970-73, prof., 1970-90, Disting. prof., 1978-90, ret. Cons. U.S. Office Edn., 1967, 68, 69; lectr. Yeats Internat. Summer Sch., Ireland, 1964, 65, 68, 72, 74, 75, Internat. Congress Comparative Lit., Fribourg, Switzerland, 1964 Author: Neoplatonism of William Blake, 1961, Yeats's Quest for Eden, 1966, Yeats's Golden Dawn, 1974, Yeats's Theory of Theatre, 1975, W. B. Yeats and W. T. Horton, 1980; editor: (with Kathleen Raine) Thomas Taylor the Platonist, 1969 (with others), Yeats and the Occult, 1975, (with others) Letters to W.B. Yeats, 1977, (with W. K. Hood) A Critical Edition of Yeats's A Vision (1925), 1978, The Making of Yeats's "A Vision," 1987; gen. editor Yeats's "Vision" Papers, 1992; contbr. articles to profl. jours. Pres. Chapel Hill (N.C.) C. of C., 1965; bd. govs. Chapel Hill Pub. Library, 1959-65. Served to lt. comdr. USNR, 1942-46; comdr. Res. Mem. MLA (chmn. Celtic group 1967, 75), South Atlantic MLA (v.p. 1985, pres. 1986-87), Coll. English Assn. (pres. 1975-76) Democrat. Methodist. Home: 407 Plantation Rd Tallahassee FL 32303-4205 E-mail: Maryjaneharper@mindspring.com.

HARPER, GERARD EDWARD, lawyer; b. N.Y.C., Feb. 2, 1953; s. Eugene Walter and Muriel (Drumgoole) H.; children: Amanda, Julia. BA, Rutgers U., 1975; JD, NYU, 1978. Bar: N.Y. 1980, U.S. Supreme Ct. 1986, D.C. 1989, U.S. Ct. Appeals (9th cir.) 1988), U.S. Ct. Appeals (2d cir.) 1991, U.S. Dist. Ct. (so. and ea. dists.) 1980, N.Y. 1985, U.S. Dist. Ct. (no. dist.) Calif., U.S. Dist. Ct. (D.C. cir.). Law clk. to Justice George MacKinnon U.S. Cir. Ct., Washington, 1978-79; assoc. Paul, Weiss, Rifkind, Wharton & Garrison, LLP, N.Y.C., 1979-86, ptnr., 1986—. Editor-in-chief NYU Law Rev., 1977-78. Gen. counsel, chmn. law com., mem. exec. com. N.Y. Dem. State Com., N.Y.C., 1987—. Mem. ABA, N.Y. State Bar Assn., N.Y. County Lawyers' Assn., Assn. of Bar of City of N.Y., Order of Coif. Roman Catholic. Office: Paul Weiss Rifkind Wharton & Garrison LLP 1285 Avenue Of The Americas Fl 21 New York NY 10019-6028 E-mail: gharper@paulweiss.com.

HARPER, HARLAN, JR., lawyer; b. San Antonio, Sept. 15, 1928; s. Harlan and Julia Viola (Kelley) H.; m. Linda A. Steere, July 16, 1960; children: Anne Elizabeth, David Harlan. BA, So. Methodist U., Dallas, 1953, JD, 1957. Bar: Tex. 1957, U.S Dist. Ct. (no., ea. and we. dists.) Tex. 1957. Assoc. McNees & McNees, 1957, John Harrison, 1958-61; sr. ptnr. Fanning, Harper, Martinson, P.C. and predecessors, Dallas, 1961-97; semi-ret., 1997—. Served with USAF, 1953-55. Mem. Tex. Bar Assn., Pi Kappa Alpha. Baptist.

HARPER, HENRY H. retired military officer; b. Ft. Benning, Ga., Aug. 24, 1934; s. H.M. and Frances Louise (Hearn) Harper; m. Helen Harpe, Apr. 2, 1960; children: Cynthia Jane, Linda Leigh BE, U. Md., 1964; MA, George Washington U., 1965; Disting. grad., Indsl. Coll. Armed Forces, 1973. Commd. officer U.S. Army, 1954, advanced through grades to maj. gen., 1980, dep. comdg. gen. Armaments Command, 1977-79, dir. logistics U.S. European Command Stuttgart, Fed. Republic Germany, 1979-82, comdg. gen. Depot System Command Chambersburg, Pa., 1982-86, ret., 1986; corp. sr. v.p. Synovus Fin. Corp., Columbus, Ga., 1986-95; ret., 1995. Dir. Ga. State Golf Assn., 1999—. Chmn. bd. dirs. Easter Seals West Ga., Inc.; chmn., bd. dirs. Goodwill Industries, Springer Opera House; bd. dirs. Universal Bank. Mem. Assn. U.S. Army (bd. govs., dir. Chambers Fort chpt. 1982-85), Columbus C. of C. (bd. dirs.). Episcopalian. Avocations: golf, jogging.

HARPER, JAMES ROBERT, graphic designer, sculptor; b. Chgo., Oct. 15, 1954; BFA, No. Ill. U., 1976; MA, Gov.'s State U., 1979; AAS, Tompkins Cortland C.C., Dryden, N.Y., 1985; postgrad., Cornell U., 1987-89. Instr. metalsmithing NCU Craft Studio Cornell U., Ithaca, N.Y., 1979-81; art dir. Shepard Advt., Inc., Ithaca, 1981-82; computer cons. Advt. Assocs., Inc., Ithaca, 1984-86; computer analyst, cons. Cornell U., Ithaca, 1989-95; pres. Jim Harper Designs, Ithaca, 1980—. Sec. IthacaNet, Inc., 1996-98. E-mail: jimh@jhdesigns.com.

HARPER, JAMES WELDON, III, finance consultant; b. Frederick, Md., Mar. 3, 1937; s. James Weldon Jr. and Mildred Mary (Conaway) H. Student, Duke U. Coll. rep. Time, Inc., 1955-59; jr. exec. trainee Merrill Lynch Pierce Fenner and Smith, N.Y.C., 1959-60; v.p. fin. planning Haight and Co., Inc., Washington, 1961-72; pres. fin. cons. Weldon Enterprises Ltd., Washington, 1973-95; founder, chmn., CEO Enviro Tek Corp. Internat., Waterford, Va., 1994—; founder, CEO Argicell.com, Inc., 2000—02. Former pres. U.S. Energy Conservation Service, Inc.; cons. Aries Corp.; nat. coord. Nat. Planned Giving Assocs., Inc., 1983-92; bd. dirs. 6 cos., 1962-91; involved with 115 corps., 98 partnerships; conservator Nat. Real Estate Trust for Health Care, Inc., 1987-92. Author 3 manuals. With U.S. Army, 1959. Methodist. Office: Enviro Tek Corp PO Box 366 Waterford VA 20197-0366 E-mail: jwhetc@erols.com.

HARPER, JANET SUTHERLIN LANE, retired educational administrator, writer; b. La Grange, Ga., Apr. 2, 1940; d. Clarence Wilner and Imogene (Thompson); m. William Sterling Lane, June 28, 1964, (div. Jan. 1981); children: David Alan, Jennifer Ruth; m. John F. Harper, June 9, 1990. BA in English and Applied Music, LaGrange Coll., 1961; postgrad., Auburn U., 1963; MA in Journalism, U. Ga., Athens, 1979. Music and drama critic The Brunswick News, Brunswick, Ga., 1979-99; info. asst. Glynn County Schs., Brunswick, 1979-82; adj. prof. Brunswick Coll., Ga., 1981-87; dir. pub. info. and publs. Glynn County Schs., Brunswick, 1982-99, dir. grant writing and rsch., 1999-2000; ret., 2000. Contbg. editor Ga. Jour., 1981-84; editor, writer GAEL Conf. Jours., 1987-89. Mem. Golden Isles Arts and Humanities Bd., 1997—2000, sec., 1998—2000; organist St. Simons United Meth. Ch., 1981—; bd. dirs. Jekyll Island Music Theatre, 1994—2001, pres., 1994—97; bd. dirs. Am. Cancer Soc., 1998—2001. Recipient award of excellence in sch. and cmty. rels. Ga. Bd. Edn., 1984, 92, Edn. Leadership award, Ga., 1989, disting. svc. award Ga. Sch. Pub. Rels. Assn., 1991. Mem.: Ga. Sch. Pub. Rels. Assn. (exec. bd. 1981—87, pres. 1985—86, exec. bd. 1996—2000), Brunswick Press-Advt. Club (award of excellence in pub. rels. 1992), Ga. Assn. Ednl. Leaders (media rels. 1983—2001), Nat. Sch. Pub. Rels. Assn. (Golden Achievement award 1985, 2 awards 1988, 1990, 3 awards 1991, 1992, 1994, 1998), Mozart Soc. E-mail: harperss@bellsouth.net.

HARPER, JENNIFER, journalist, entertainer; b. Elizabeth, N.J. d. Bertram Jacob and Kathleen Handley Sauerbrunn; m. Eric L. Harper, (div. July 1986); 1 child, Christina Elizabeth. BFA, Syracuse U.; diploma in Theol. Studies, Va. Theol. Sem., 2003. Writer Washington Star, 1978-80, San Antonio (Tex.) Express News, 1980-81, Dallas Morning News, 1982-84; media analyst, reporter Washington Times, 1984—. Commentator on-air analysis CNN, 1998—, CNBC, 1998, PBS, 1998, America's Voice, 1998—, C-SPAN, 2001, MSNBC, 2001—, Fox News, 2001—, Sinclair Broadcasting, 2003—. Bandleader, vocalist Peaches O'Dell & Her Orch., Washington, 1990—. Vol. counselor Am. Cancer Soc., Washington, 1990—; emergency snow driver Suburban Hosp., Bethesda; mem. lay cert. program Va. Theol. Sem., 2000-03. Recipient Nat. Writing award Md.-Del.-D.C. Press Assn., 1998, Page Design award Soc. Newspaper Design, 1995, Gen. Excellence award Penney-Mo. Lifestyle Journalism Awards, 1994, Best Rev. award Nat. Newspaper Assn., 1991. Mem. SAG, AFTRA, Washington Area Music Assn. (Best Swing Vocalist 2002). Episcopalian. Avocations: swing music, herbal gardening. Office: Washington Times 3600 New York Ave NE Washington DC 20002 E-mail: jharper@washingtontimes.com., peaches@peachesodell.com.

HARPER, JEWEL BENTON, pharmacist; b. Springfield, Tenn., Nov. 14, 1925; s. William Henry and Violet Irene (Benton) H.; m. Josephine Cook, Feb. 12, 1953; children: Pamela Jewel, Karen Jo. BS, Austin Peay State U., 1948, Samford U., 1950; diploma, U.S. Army Med. Field Svc. Sch., 1964, Command and Gen. Staff Coll., 1968, U.S. Army Logistics Mgmt. Ctr., 1977. Pharmacist Battlefield Pharmacy, Nashville, 1950-52, VA Hosp., Nashville, 1952-63, Lexington, Ky., 1963-67, Durham, N.C., 1967-76, Manchester, N.H., 1976-82, Vanderbilt U., Nashville, 1982-86, Nashville Meml. Hosp., 1986-91. Served to col. Med. Svc. Corps, USAR, 1944-85. Fellow Am. Coll. Apothecaries (emeritus); mem. Assn. Mil. Surgeons U.S., Am. Pharm. Assn., Tenn. Pharmacists Assn., Res. Officers Assn. U.S. (pres. chpt. 1962-63, sec. 1970-73, dept. surgeon 1977-82), Mil. Order of the World Wars (mem. in perpetuity, charter Screaming Eagles chpt. 2003), Mil. Officers Assn. Am., Assn. U.S. Army, Am. Legion, VFW, The Gideons Internat., Lambda Chi Alpha, Kappa Psi. Republican. Baptist. Avocations: country music, deep sea fishing, horticulture. Home and Office: 503 Cunniff Ct Goodlettsville TN 37072-3003

HARPER, JOANNALEE O. dietician; b. Phila., Oct. 20, 1941; d. Robert Stanley and Margaret Charlotte (Moore) Oberlander; m. Charles Edwin Harper, Sept. 7, 1968; 1 child, Charles Edwin Jr. BS, Albright Coll., 1963; MS, Drexel U., 1966. Registered dietitian Walter Reed Army Med. Ctr., lic. Dir. food svcs. Walkens Glen, 1964-65, Temple U. Hosp., Phila., 1967-69; clin. dietitian DeWhit Army Hosp., Ft. Belvoir, Va., 1965; nutrition instr. Abington (Pa.) Sch. Nursing, 1969-72; clin. dietitian GlenOaks Hosp., Glendale Heights, Ill., 1988—. Cons. Butterball Turkey Talk Line, Downers Grove, 1983—; tchr. Wheaton (Ill.) Sch. Dist. 200, 1991—. Chmn. children's corner Ctrl. DuPage Hosp. Women's Aux., Winfield, Ill., 1988. 1st lt. U.S. Army, 1963—65. Avocation: golf. Home: 25w700 Red Maple Ln Wheaton IL 60187-7927 E-mail: momharper@aol.com.

HARPER, JOHN FRANK, cardiologist; b. Akron, Ohio, July 21, 1946; s. Frank E. and Jean E. (Sigmond) H.; m. Laurie Spencer, Dec. 20, 1969; children: David, Jonathan, Andrew, Anne. BA, So. Meth. U., 1968; MD, U. Tex. Dallas, 1972. Diplomate Am. Bd. Med. Examiners, Am. Bd. Internal Medicine, Cardiovascular Diseases. Intern Parkland Meml. Hosp., Dallas, 1972-73; resident, cardiology fellow VA Hosp., Dallas, 1973-75, 77-79; cardiologist Presby. Hosp. Dallas, 1979-92, chief cardiology sect., 1992-2000. Sr. ptnr. North Tex. Heart Ctr., Dallas, 1991—; med. dir. Finley Ewing Cardiovascular Rehab. Ctr., Dallas, 1985-95. Maj. USAF, 1975-77. Fellow Am. Coll. Cardiology, Am. Heart Assn. (clin. coun. cardiology); mem. Tex. Med. Assn., Tex. Club Internists, Dallas County Med. Assn. Republican. Avocations: golf, running. Home: 4305 Lorraine Ave Dallas TX 75205-3707

HARPER, JUDSON MORSE, university administrator, consultant, educator; b. Lincoln, Nebr., Aug. 25, 1936; s. Floyd Sprague and Eda Elizabeth (Kelley) H.; m. Patricia Ann Kennedy, June 15, 1958; children: Jayson K., Stuart H., Neal K. BS, Iowa State U., 1958, MS, 1960, PhD, 1963. Registered profl. engr., Minn. Instr. Iowa State U., Ames, 1958-63; dept. head Gen. Mills, Inc., Mpls., 1964-69, venture mgr., 1969-70; prof., dept. head agrl. and chem. engring. Colo. State U., Ft. Collins, 1970-82, v.p. rsch. and info. tech., 1982-2000, interim pres., 1989-90, spl. asst. to the pres., 2000—. Cons. USAID, Washington, 1972-74, various comml. firms., 1975—; Lady Davis scholar Technion, Haifa, Israel, 1978-79. Author: Extrusion of Foods, 1982, Extrusion Cooking, 1989; editor newsletter Food, Pharm. & Bioengring. News, 1979-83, LEC Newsletter, 1976-89; contbr. articles to profl. publs.; patentee. Mem. sch. bd. St. Louis Park, Minn., 1968-70. Recipient Disting. Svc. award Colo. State U., 1977, Fulbright-Hayes scholar, 1978, Svc. award Centro de Investigaviones y Asistencia Technologica de Estado de Chihuahua, Chichuahua, Mex., 1980, Food Engring. award Dairy and Food Industry Supply Assn. and Am. Soc. Agrl. Engrs., 1983, Cert. of Merit, USDA Office Internat. Coop. and Devel., 1983, Cert. of Merit, Consejo Nacional de Ciencia y Technologie en Mexico, Mexico City, 1984, Profl. Achievement Citation Iowa State U., 1986, Cert. Appreciation Chinese Inst. of Food Tech., 1987, Charles Lory Pub. Svc. award, 1993, Hammer award The Nat. Performance Rev., 1994. Fellow Inst. Food Technologists (Internat. award 1990), AAAS; mem. Am. Inst. Chem. Engring. (dir. 1981-84), Am. Soc. Agrl. Engrs. (com. chmn. 1973-78, hon. engr. Rocky Mountain region), Am. Chem. Soc., Am. Soc. Engring. Edn. (com. chmn. 1976-77). Mem. Ind. United Methodist Ch. Home: 1818 Westview Rd Fort Collins CO 80524-1891 Office: Colo State U Spl Projects Office Fort Collins CO 80523-2046 E-mail: judson.harper@colostate.edu.

HARPER, KENNETH FRANKLIN, retired state legislator, real estate broker; b. Covington, Ky., Jan. 15, 1931; s. Kenneth Wellington and Elizabeth Mary (Brickler) H.; m. Eileen Ann Kathman, May 16, 1953; children: Gregory, Scott, Glenn, Bryan, Lesley. Student, U. Ky. Mem. Ky. Ho. of Reps., 1964-68; asst. commr. Ky. Dept. Child Welfare, 1969-70; commr. Ky. Dept. Pub. Info., 1970; sec. of state Commonwealth of Ky., 1971; broker, owner, pres. Harper Realty, 1986—; mem. from 63d dist. Ky. Ho. of Reps., 1963-68, 82-94, minority caucus chmn., 1989—92, vice-chmn. tourism and energy com. Adv. bd. U.S. Bank, No. Ky.; bd. dirs. Harper Group LLC. Pres. Nat. Repub. Legislators Assn., 1991-92; exec. com. Kenton County Rep. Party, No. Ky.; chmn. emeritus No. Ky. Univ. Found.; past mem. Rep. State Ctrl. com.; commr. emeritus No. Ky. Conv. and Visitors Bur., chmn., 1991-92; mem. Southbank Ptnrs.; past state co-chmn. Am. Legis. Exch. Coun.; mem. No. Ky. Assn. for the Retarded; past mem. Exec. Task Force on Hist. Preservation; mem. Greater Cin. Tall Stacks Commn.; past mem. No. Ky. U. Small Bus. Incubator; v.p. The Southbank Fund. Recipient numerous Jaycee awards, Boss of Yr. award Nat. Secs. Assn., 1971, Walter L. Pieschel award No. Ky. C. of C., 1980, KMI Alumni Spirit of Excellence award, 1993, others; Paul Harris fellow Rotary Internat., 1989; named one of Outstanding Young Men of Am., 1964. Mem. Nat. Assn. Realtors, Ky. Assn. Realtors, No. Ky. Assn. Realtors (life), Nat. Rep. Legislators Assn. (past pres.), Pi Kappa Alpha (Omega Chpt. Outstanding Alumni). Roman Catholic. Home and Office: Harper Group LLC PO Box 17717 2700 Main Chase Ln Crestview Hills KY 41017-4707

HARPER, KIMBALL TAYLOR, ecologist, educator; b. Oakley, Idaho, Feb. 15, 1931; s. John Mayo and Mary Ella (Overson) H.; m. Caroline Frances Stepp, June 7, 1958; children: Ruth L., James K., Gay A., Denise C., Karla D., Steven S.. BS, Brigham Young U., 1958, MS, 1960; PhD, U. Wis., 1963. Range technician U.S. Forest Svc., Moab and Moticello, Utah, 1957-58, range scientist Ogden, Utah, 1958-59; rsch. asst. U. Wis., Madison, 1959-63; asst. prof., then assoc. prof. U. Utah, Salt Lake City, 1963-73; prof. Brigham Young U., Provo, Utah, 1973—, chmn. dept. botany and range sci., 1973-76. Vis. scholar U. Calif., Berkeley, 1984-85; mem. Mono Lake com. NRC, Washington, 1986-87. Editor, co-author: Intermountain Biogeography, 1978, Ecological Impacts of Weather Modification, 1981, Natural History of the Colorado Plateau and Great Basin; mem. editorial bd. Great Basin Naturalist, 1977-87; contbr. numerous articles to profl. jours. Ward bishop LDS Ch., Spanish Fork, Utah, 1978-83. Served as cpl. U.S. Army, 1953-55, Korea. Grantee NSF, U.S. Forest Svc., U.S. Bur. Land Mgmt., U.S. Army., 1965—. Fellow AAAS; mem. Am. Bot. Soc., Ecol. Soc. Am. (editor, mem. editorial bd. jour. 1965-67, 1975-79), Soc. for Range Mgmt., Am. Inst. For Biol. Scis., Soc. for Study Evolution, Brit. Ecol. Soc., Phi Kappa Phi. Republican. Avocations: photography, gardening. Home: 410 S 300 E Spanish Fork UT 84660-2422 Office: Brigham Young U Dept Botany And Range Provo UT 84602

HARPER, MARY SADLER, financial advisor; b. Farmville, Va., June 15, 1941; d. Edward Henry and Vivien Morris (Garrett) Sadler; m. Joseph Taylor Harper, Dec. 21, 1968; children by previous marriage: James E. Hatch III, Mary Ann Hatch Czajka. Cert., Fla. Trust Sch., U. Fla., 1976. Registered securities rep., Fla., gen. securities prin., fin. and ops. prin., options prin., mcpl. securities prin., investment mgmt. advisor. Dep. clk. Polk County Cts., Bartow, Fla., 1964-67; rep. Allen & Co., Lakeland, Fla., 1967-71; with First Nat. Bank, Palm Beach, Fla., 1971-89, sr. v.p., 1984-86, S.E. Bank N.A., Palm Beach, 1986-89, 1st United Bank, 1997-98; pres., CEO Palm Beach Capital Svcs., Inc., 1986-88; mng. dir. Investment Svcs., Palm Beach Capital Svcs. Divsn., 1988; v.p. investments, trustee J.M. Rubin Found, Palm Beach, 1983—; v.p. sec., sr. v.p. investment divsn. Island Nat. Bank & Trust Co., 1989-97; chair, dir., pres., CEO Island Investment Svcs., Inc. (A Wachovia Co.), Palm Beach, 1989-98; also bd. dirs., mng. exec., sr. v.p. Wachovia Investments, Palm Beach, 1998-2000; sr. v.p. Wachovia Bank N.A., 1999-2000; sr. v.p., investment mgmt. advisor Wachovia Securities, Inc., 2000—; sr. v.p. investments Legg Mason, Wood, Walker, Inc., 2000—. Adv. coun. Nuveen, 1987-99, pres., 2001, chmn., 2002. Adv. panel Palm Beach County YWCA, 1985, mem. endowment com., 1990—93; mem. Jupiter Hosp. Found.; life mem. Juno Beach Civic Assn.; profl. endowment com. Rehab. Ctr. for Children and Adults, 1998—2002; chmn. Palm Beach adv. bd. Palm Beach Nat. Bank & Trust Co., 2000—01; dir., v.p. Friends of Abused Children, 2001—03; mem. Fla. History Mus.; dir. Ctr. for Family Svcs., 2003—; mem. adv. bd. Biomotion Found., 2002—. Mem. Inst. CFPs (assoc.), Nat. Assn. Securities Dealers (dist. com. mem. 1995-98), Fin. Planners Assn., Fin. Women Internat., Fla. Securities Dealers Assn., Exec. Women of Palm Beaches (fin. com. 1985-92), Internat. Soc. Palm Beach (treas., trustee 1986—), Jupiter Hosp. Med. Assn. (pres.'s club 1989—), Loxahatchee Hist. Soc. (bd. dirs. 1991-93, chair devel. com. 1992-93), Sebring, Fla. Hist. Soc. (life), Jupiter/Tequesta C. of C. (assoc.), United Daus. of Confederacy, Gov.'s Club, Pub. Securities Assn. (exec. rep.), Jonathans Golf Club, Rotary (Palm Beach Found. com. 1990—, bd. dirs. 1992-94, co-chair, 1997, bd. dirs. 2000—, chair Rotary Internat. Found., Palm Beach 1998-2001, dir. ctr. for family svcs. 2003.), Lighthouse Ctr. for the Arts (life), Norton Art Mus. (patron), Old Port Yacht Club, Palm Beach Yacht Club. Democrat. Baptist. Avocations: reading, history. Home: 800 Ocean Dr PH 4 Juno Beach FL 33408-1730 Office: Legg Mason 324 Royal Palm Way Ste 100 Palm Beach FL 33480 Fax: 561-626-7978. E-mail: msharper@leggmason.com.

HARPER, MICHAEL JOHN KENNEDY, obstetrics and gynecology educator; b. London, Feb. 25, 1935; arrived in U.S., 1964; s. John Kennedy and Helen Malvina (Koeller) Harper; m. Marian Wedd, July 23, 1960 (div. Feb. 1982); children: Charlotte G. K., Tristram J. K., Felicity W. K.; m. Ann Carlene Vandeventer, Feb. 16, 1985; 1 child, Helen H. K. BA in Agr., U. Cambridge, Eng., 1957, MA, 1961, PhD in Reproductive Physiology, 1962, ScD, 1979; diploma, U. Reading, Eng., 1958; MBA, U. Tex., San Antonio, 1984. Tech. officer pharm. divsn. Imperial Chem. Industries Ltd., Cheshire, Eng., 1960-64, 65-66; vis. scientist Worcester Found. for Exptl. Biology, Shrewsbury, Mass., 1964-65, staff scientist, 1966-68, sr. scientist, 1968-72; med. officer Human Reproduction Sect. WHO, Geneva, 1972-75; assoc. prof. U. Tex. Health Sci. Ctr., San Antonio, 1975-81, prof. ob-gyn. and physiology, 1981-93; prof. ob-gyn. and cell biology Baylor Coll. Medicine, Houston, 1993-95; prof. ob-gyn Eastern Va. Med. Sch., Arlington, 1995—, dir. Consortium for Indsl. Collaboration in Contraceptive Rsch./ CONRAD Program, 1995—, dir. Global Microbicide Project, 2001—. Lectr. Clark U., 1971; cons. NIH, Bethesda, Md., 1970—, WHO, Geneva, 1974—87, USAID, Arlington, Va., 1988—95, Andrew W. Mellon Found., N.Y.C., 1991—; mem. com. reporting on contraceptive R&D looking to the future Inst. Medicine, 1996; mem. 107 com. "Contraceptive Rsch. and Devel.: Looking to the Future.", 1996, "New Frontiers in Contraceptive Rsch.", 2003. Author: (book) Birth Control Technologies, 1983, Birth Control Technologies, paperback edit., 1985; contbr. articles to profl. jours. Recipient Woodman prize, U. Cambridge, 1956, Agr. Food Products prize, U. Reading, Eng., 1958, Rsch. Career Devel. award, NIH, 1968—72. Fellow: Inst. Biology (Eng.); mem.: Am. Physiol. Soc., Soc. Gynecologic Investigation, Soc. Study of Reproduction, Am. Assn. Anatomists, Endocrine Soc., Soc. Study of Fertility (Eng.), Soc. Endocrinology (Eng.). Achievements include invention of alkene/alkanol derivatives (Tamoxifen), alkene derivatives. Avocations: classical music, reading, hunting, automobiles, genealogy. Office: Conrad Program E Va Medical Sch 1611 N Kent St Ste 806 Arlington VA 22209-2111 E-mail: mjkharper@msn.com., mharper@conrad.org. *Honesty, integrity and the fortitude to withstand disappointment are key ingredients for a career in life science. Progress in biological research is slow and often imperceptible. By encouraging one's juniors to grow professionally, one's own growth is enhanced.*

HARPER, ODENA IRENE, retired communications educator; b. Brazil, Ind., July 21, 1938; d. James Jacob and Hazel Irene Miller; m. Glenn Everett Harper, Jan. 18, 1958 (dec. Feb. 16, 2000); children: Judy Jo Harper Kemp, William Wade. BS in Edn., Ind. State U., Terre Haute, 1969, MS in Edn., 1972. Cert. tchr. Ind. Elem. educator Clay Cmty. Schs., Knightsville, Ind., 1969—80, media specialist, 1975—80, media supr., 1980—2003. Recipient Clay County Focus award in Edn., Clay County C. of C., 1988. Mem.: Ind. Libr. Fedn., Ind. State Tchrs. Assn., Alpha Delta Kappa, Phi Kappa Phi. Avocations: reading, computer activities. Office Fax: 812-442-0204. E-mail: odenah@aol.com.

HARPER, PATRICIA NELSEN, psychiatrist; b. Omaha, July 25, 1944; d. Eddie R. and Marjorie L. (Williams) Nelsen. BS, Antioch Coll., Yellow Springs, Ohio, 1966; MD, U. Nebr., 1975; grad., Topeka Inst. Psychoanalysis, 1997. Cert. psychiatrist. Psychiatric residency Karl Menninger Sch. of Psychiatry, Topeka, 1975-78; staff psychiatrist The Menninger Clinic, Topeka, 1978-98. Faculty mem. Karl Menninger Sch. of Psychiatry, Topeka, 1982-98. Program dir. Addictions Recovery Program C.F. Menninger Meml. Hosp., Topeka, 1987-97. Mem. Am. Psychiatric Assn., Am. Med Women Assn., Am. Psychoanalytic Assn. Office: Pk Nicollet Clinic Health Sys Minn 3800 Park Nicollet Blvd Minneapolis MN 55416-2527

HARPER, RICHARD HENRY, film producer, director; b. San Jose, Calif., Sept. 15, 1950; s. Walter Henry and Priscilla Alden H.; m. Ann Marie Morgan, June 19, 1976; children: Christine Ann, Paul Richard, James Richard. Show designer Walt Disney Imagineering, Glendale, Calif., 1971-76; motion picture producer, dir. Harper Films, Inc., La Canada, Calif., 1976—. Producer, dir. (films) Impressions de France, Disney World, Fla., 1982, Magic Carpet Round the World, Disneyland, Tokyo, 1983, American Journeys, Disneyland, Calif., 1985, Collecting America, Nat. Gallery Art, Washington, 1988, Hillwood Mus., Washington, 1989, Journey Into the 4th Dimension for Sanrio World, Journey Into Nature for Sanrio World, Japan, 1990, Masters of Illusion, Nat. Gallery of Art, Washington, 1992. Recipient more than 150 awards world-wide for outstanding motion picture prodn. including Silver trophy Cannes Internat. Film Festival, 2 Gold awards Internat. Festival of the Ams., 1981, 82, 14 Golden Eagle C.I.N.E. awards, 1977-92, Emmy award Nat. Acad. TV Arts and Scis., 1993-. Mem. Acad. of Motion Picture Arts and Scis.

HARPER, ROB, secondary school educator; b. Seattle, Wash., Feb. 16, 1961; s. Robert Chester and Florence Agnes Harper; m. Chris Evans, July 21, 1984; children: Ashley, Grant. BA Music Edn., Ea. Wash. U., 1983; MA in Edn. in Curriculum and Instrn., Gonzaga U., Spokane, Wash., 1997. Cert. continuing edn. Wash., 1983. Music and German tchr. Columbia Sch. Dist. #206, Hunters, Wash., 1983—86; music tchr. Davenport (Wash.) Sch. Dist. #207, 1986—. Mem.: Wash. Music Educators Assn. Avocations: model railroading, hunting. Home: 1210 Jefferson St P O Box 1032 Davenport WA 99122 Office: Davenport Sch Dist #207 1101 Seventh St Davenport WA 99122

HARPER, ROB MARCH, artist, educator; b. Chico, Calif., Oct. 5, 1942; s. Robert Wreathal and Lorene Marie (March) Harper; m. Georgia Lee Schiller, May 31, 1971. BFA, San Francisco Art Inst., 1971; MFA, Washington U., St. Louis, 1974. Artist/illustrator, Oakland, Calif., 1974-88; tchr. adult edn. Alameda County Pub. Schs., Oakland, Hayward, 1988—. Tchr., artist Oakland Pks. and Recreation Dept., 1988—. One-man shows include Lucien Labaudt Art Gallery, San Francisco, 1974, exhibited in group shows at Nelson Gallery Art, Kansas City, Mo., 1974, St. Louis Art Mus., 1974, Butler Inst. Am. Art, Youngstown, Ohio, 1975, Cooperstown (N.Y.) Art Assn., 1975, 1977, E. B. Crocker Art Gallery, Sacramento, 1976, Civic Arts Gallery, Walnut Creek, Calif., 1976, Marrietta (Ohio) Coll., 1976, Chautauqua (N.Y.) Art Assn., 1977, Miniature Painters, Sculptors and Gravers Soc., Washington, Arts Club Washington, 1977, 1979, Nat. Soc. Painters Casein and Acrylic, Inc., Am. Acad. and Inst. Arts and Letters, N.Y.C., 1979, Lynn Ho Gallery, Antioch, Calif., 1994, Chico (Calif.) Art Ctr., 1994, Sarratt Gallery, Vanderbilt U., Nashville, 1996, Maude Kerns Art Ctr., Eugene, Oreg., 1996, Spartanburg (S.C.) County Mus. Art, 1996, Rosewood Arts Centre Gallery, Kettering, Ohio, 1999, San Francisco Mus. Modern Art Rental Gallery - Group Show, 1999, Laguna Art Mus., Laguna Beach, Calif., 2000, Oakland Mus. Calif., 2002, Represented in permanent collections O.K. Harris Gallery, N.Y.C., also pvt. collections. Recipient Hallmark award-purchase, 1973—74, Butler Inst. Am. ARt purchase prize, 1975. Home: 3099 California St Oakland CA 94602-3907 E-mail: robingeo@juno.com.

HARPER, ROBBIE JANE, critical care nurse, administrator; b. Midwest City, Okla., Sept. 14, 1967; d. Billey Kent and Robbie Jo (McGruder; m. Danny Scott Harper I, June 19, 1987; children: Christina Krichelle, Danny Scott II. BSN, U. Okla., 1990. CCRN; CMC. NICU nurse Children's Hosp., Oklahoma City, 1990-91; charge nurse Marshall County Hosp., Madill, Okla., 1991-92; MICU nurse VA Hosp., Oklahoma City, 1992-97, case mgr., 1997-99, utilization rev. coord., 1999—2001, quality improvement specialist, 2001—. Named Critical Care Nurse of the Yr., Am. Assn. Critical Care Nurses, 1996. Mem.: Am. Inst. Outcomes-Case Mgmt. Presbyterian. Avocations: swimming, sewing. Office: VA Med Ctr 921 NE 13th St Oklahoma City OK 73104

HARPER, ROBERT, actor; b. N.Y.C., May 19, 1951; BA in English with high distinction, Rutgers Coll., 1974. Mem. repertory co. Arena Stage, Washington, 1974-76. Guest artist Rutgers U., New Brunswick, N.J., 1977, 84. Actor: Long Wharf Theater, 1978, 1984, Theater for a New City, 1981; (Broadway plays) Once in a Lifetime, 1978, The Inspector General, 1978, The American Clock, 1980; (TV films) J. Edgar Hoover, The Wrong Man, Not Quite Human, Payoff, Running Mates, The Story of Bill W, Paper Angels, Ruby Ridge; (TV series) Newhart, Roseanne, Murphy Brown, Wiseguy, L.A. Law, NYPD Blue, Law and Order, Philly, Frank's Place; (films) Creepshow, 1982, Once Upon a Time in America, 1984, Amazing Grace and Chuck, 1987, Twins, 1989, Final Analysis, 1992, Deconstructing Harry, 1997, The Insider, 1999. Advisor charity events The Laugh Factory, Hollywood, 1981—. Regents fellow U. Calif., 1974, Kennedy Ctr. award Am. Coll. Theater Festival, 1974. Mem. MLA (spkr. conv. 1996), ACLU (sponsor Garden Event 1994), Acad. Motion Picture Arts and Scis., Acad. TV Arts and Scis., Am. Soc. Aesthetics, Screen Actor's Guild, Actor's Equity Assn. Office: 8721 Santa Monica Blvd West Hollywood CA 90069-4507

HARPER, ROBERT ALLAN, retired consulting psychologist; b. Dayton, Ohio, Apr. 25, 1915; s. Earl Paull and Mary (Belden) H.; m. Flora Mie Bridges; children: Robert Belden, John Paull. Student, U. Dayton, 1934-36; BA, Ohio State U., 1938, MA, 1939, PhD, 1942. Instr. Kent State U., 1942-43; analyst War Manpower Commn., 1943; assoc. prof. Wagner Coll., 1943-45; psychiat. social worker U.S. Army, 1945-46; asst. prof. Ohio State U., 1946-50, dir. marriage counseling clinic, 1949-50; chmn. family life dept., dir. marriage counseling service Merrill-Palmer Inst., Detroit, 1950-53; pvt. practice psychotheraphy Washington, 1953-92. Author: (with John F. Cuber) Problems of American Society, 1948, Marriage, 1949, Psychoanalysis and Psychotherapy: 36 Systems, 1959, (with Albert Ellis) Creative Marriage, 1961, A Guide to Rational Living, 1961, 75, 98, How to Stop Destroying Your Relationships, 2001, (with Walter R. Stokes) 45 Levels to Sexual Understanding and Enjoyment, 1971, The New Psychotherapies, 1975; cons. editor: Jour. Sex Edn. and Therapy, Psychotherapy, Jour. Rational-Emotive Therapy, Jour. Contemporary Psychotherapy, Internat. Jour. Family Therapy Fellow Am. Psychol. Assn. (pres. div. psychotherapy 1978-79, pres. div. cons. psychology 1980-81, pres. div. humanistic psychology 1983-84, exec. bd. div. ind. practice, coun. reps. 1978-84, 90-96), Am. Assn. Marriage Counselors (sec. 1954-58, pres. 1960-62), Nat. Coun. Family Rels. (dir. 1951-55), Am. Acad. Psychotherapists (pres. 1961-63), Am. Group Psychotheraphy Assn., Eastern Psychol. Assn., D.C. Psychol. Assn. (dir. 1982-85); mem. Am. Soc. Psychologists in Pvt. Practice (exec. com.), Soc. Sci. Study Sex, Interam. Soc. Psychologists, Am. Soc. Group Psychotherapy and Psychodrama, Internat. Council Psychologists (exec. bd. 1971-74), N.Y. Acad. Scis., Internat. Soc. Gen. Semantics, Inst. Rational Living (bd.), ACLU, Washington Soc. Clin. Psychologists (exec. com.), Nat. Acads. Practice (treas. 1982-88), Phi Beta Kappa. Clubs: Cosmos. Home: 4903 Potomac Ave NW Washington DC 20007-1541

HARPER, S. BIRNIE, business brokerage company owner; b. Ft. Smith, Ark., June 8, 1944; s. S. Birnie and Margaret (Marshall) H.; m. Fern Dodson, 1969; children— Eliza, Sam, Dodson, Sara BS in Commerce, Washington and Lee U., 1966; MBA, Harvard U., 1968. With Mid-Am. Industries Inc., Ft. Smith, 1968-88, v.p. fin., 1975-79, exec. v.p., 1979-82, CFO, 1982-95, exec. v.p., COO, 1985-86, pres., 1986-88, also bd. dirs.; pres. Wortz Co., Poteau, Okla., 1989—95, pres., CEO, 1990-95, also bd. dirs.; pres., owner Sunbelt Bus. Brokers, Ft. Smith, 1995—. Bd. dirs. Ft. Smith Boys and Girls Club, 1982—, pres., 92, 93; trustee Sparks Regional Med. Ctr., 1978-84, 94-2000, 02—, treas., 1999-2000, 02—; bd. dirs. Old Ft. Mus., 1982-85, 86-90, pres., 1983, 89; sr. warden St. John's Episcopal Ch., 1982-83, 2000-01; bd. dirs. United Way Ft. Smith, 1976-78, 2000-2002, Ft. Smith C. of C., 1976-79, 81-84. Home: 2502 Greenridge Dr Fort Smith AR 72903-5104 Office: Sunbelt Bus Brokers 423 Rogers Ave Fort Smith AR 72901-1911

HARPER, SANDRA STECHER, university administrator; b. Dallas, Sept. 21, 1952; d. Lee Roy and Carmen (Crespo) Stecher; m. Dave Harper, July 6, 1974; children: Justin, Jonathan. BS in Edn., Tex. Tech. U., 1974; MS, U. N. Tex., 1979, PhD, 1985, grad. mgmt. devel. program, Harvard U., 1992. Speech/reading tchr. Nazareth (Tex.) High Sch., 1974-75; speech/English tchr. Collinsville (Tex.) High Sch., 1975-77, Pottsboro (Tex.) High Sch., 1977-79; instr. comm. Austin Coll., Sherman, Tex., 1980-82; rsch. asst. U. N. Tex., Denton, 1982-84; vis. instr. comm. Austin Coll., Sherman, 1985; from asst. prof. to assoc. prof. comms. McMurry Coll., Abilene, Tex., 1985-95; dean Coll. Arts and Scis. McMurry U., Abilene, Tex., 1990-95; v.p. for acad. affairs Oklahoma City U., 1995-98; asst. dir. NEH univ. core curriculum project McMurry U., Abilene, Tex.; provost, v.p. for acad. affairs Tex. A&M, Corpus Christi, 1998—, prof. comms., 1998—. CIES mentor for Russian adminstr. from Moscow State U., Ulyanovsk, 1995-96; mem. adv. bd. Coll. Am. Indian Devel., 1995-98; critic judge Univ. Interscholastic League, Austin, 1980-93; mem. adv. bd. Univ. Rsch. Consortium, Abilene, 1990-95; mem. formula adv. com., mem. instrn. and operation formula study com. Tex. Higher Edn. Coordinating Bd., 1999—, mem. adv. com. AA in Tchg., 2003—; mem. working group Am. Assn. State Colls. and Univs. Am. Democracy Project, 2002—. Contbr. articles to profl. jours.; author: To Serve the Present Age, 1990; co-author U.S. Dept. Edn. Title III Grant; editl. bd. Soc. for the Advancement of Mgmt. Jour., 1999—. Planner TEAM Abilene, 1991; del. Tex. Commn. for Libr. and Info. Svcs., Austin, 1991; chair Abilene Children Today: Life and Cmty. Skills Task Force, 1994-95; del. Oklahoma City Edni. TV Consortium, 1997-98; bd. dirs. South Tex. Pub. Broadcasting, 1998—, Leadership Corpus Christi; mem. gov.'s exec. devel. program class XVIII, LBJ Sch. Pub. Affairs, U. Tex., Austin, 1999, S. Tex. Regional Leaders Forum, 2001-02. Named Outstanding Faculty Mem., McMurry U., 1988, Outstanding Adminstr., 1993; Media Rsch. scholar Ctr. for Population Options, 1989; recipient Corpus Christi YWCA Women in Careers Secondary Edn. award, 2000. Mem. Nat. Comm. Assn., Am. Assn. Higher Edn., Tex. Pub. Univ. Chief Acad. Officers Assn. (v.p. 2003—). Democrat. Roman Catholic. Office: Tex A&M 6300 Ocean Dr Corpus Christi TX 78412-5503 E-mail: sharper@falcon.tamucc.edu.

HARPER, SHIRLEY FAY, nutritionist, educator, consultant, lecturer; b. Auburn, Ky., Apr. 23, 1943; d. Charles Henry and Annabelle (Gregory) Belcher; m. Robert Vance Harper, May 19, 1973 (dec. Mar. 2000); children: Glenda, Debra, Teresa, Suzanna, Cynthia. BS, Western Ky. U., 1966, MS, 1982. Cert. nutritionist and lic. dietitian, Ky. Dir. dietetics Logan County Hosp., Russellville, Ky., 1965-80; cons. Western State Hosp., Hopkinsville, Ky., 1983-84, instnl. dietetic adminstr., 1984-88; dietitian Rivendell Children's Psychiat. Hosp., Bowling Green, Ky., 1988-90; instr. nutrition Western Ky. U., Bowling Green, 1990-92. Cons. Auburn (Ky.) Nursing Ctr., 1976-95, Belle Meade Home, Greenville, Ky., 1980—, Brookfield Manor, Hopkinsville, Ky., 1983—, Sparks Nursing Ctr., Central City, Ky., 1983—, Muhlenberg Cmty. Hosp., Greenville, 1989-2000, Russellville (Ky.) Health Care Manor, 1978-83, 92—, Westlake Cumberland Hosp., Columbia, Ky., 1993—, Franklin-Simpson Meml. Hosp., Franklin, Ky., 1993—, Lakeview Health Care Ctr., Morgantown, Ky., 2001-02, Trigg County Personal Care Home, Cadiz, 2002--, Gainsville Manor, Hopkinsville, 2002--; nutrition instr. Madisonville (Ky.) Cmty. Coll., 1995-98. Mem. regional bd. dirs. ARC of Ky., Frankfort, 1990-96; vice chair ARC of Logan County, 1992-93, chmn., 1993-96, 97—; bd. dirs. Logan County ARC United Way, 1993—; co-chair adv. coun. devel. disabilities Lifeskills, 1992-93, adv. coun. Lifeskills Residential Living Group Home, 1993-2000, human rights adv. coun., 1994-2000; chair Let's Build our Future Campaign; nutrition del. Citizen Am. Program to USSR, 1990; adv. chair for vocat. edn., Russellville; mem. adv. coun. for home econs. and family living, We. Ky. U., 1990-93; bd. dirs. ARC of Logan County for United Way, 1993—; del. 24th Internat. Congress on Arts and Comm., Oxford (Eng.) U., 1997. Recipient Outstanding Svc. award Am. Dietetic Assn. Found., 1993, Outstanding Svc. award Barren River Mental Health-Mental Retardation Bd., 1987, Svc. Appreciation award Logan-Russellville Assn. for Retarded Citizens, 1987, Internat. Woman of Yr. award for contribution to Nutrition and Humanity, Internat. Biographical Assn., 1993-94, World Lifetime Achievement award Am. Biographical Inst., 1995; inaugurated Lifetime Dep. Gov., Am. Biographical Rsch. Bd., 1995, Pres.'s award ARC of Logan County, 1996, award of excellence Oxford, Eng. Internat. Congress on Arts and Comm., Internat. Sash of Acad., Am. Biograph. Inst., 1997. Mem. Am. Dietetic Assn., Nat. Nutrition Network, Ky. Dietetic Assn. (pres. Western dist. 1976-77, Outstanding Dietitian award 1984), Bowling Green-Warren County Nutrition Coun., Nat. Ctr. for Nutrition and Dietetics (charter), Ky. Nutrition Coun., Logan County Home Economist Club (sec. 1994-95, 1999-2000, v.p. 1995-96, 2000-01, pres. 1996-97, 2001—), Internat. Biog. Assn., Internat. Platform Assn., Diabetes Care and Edn., Dietitians in Nutrition Support, Cons. Dietitians in Health Care, Phi Upsilon Omicron (pres. Beta Delta alumni chpt. 1994-96, Outstanding Alumni award 1997). Avocations: music, drawing and art, poetry, reading, cake decorating. Home and Office: 443 Hopkinsville Rd Russellville KY 42276-1286 E-mail: shirleyfharper@aol.com.

HARPER, STEVEN JAMES, lawyer; b. Mpls., Apr. 25, 1954; s. James Henry and Mary Margaret H.; m. Kathy Joseph Loeb, Aug. 21, 1976; children: Benjamin James, Peter William, Emma Suzanne. BA with distinction, MA in Econs., Northwestern U., 1976; JD magna cum laude, Harvard U., 1979. Bar: Ill. 1979, U.S. Dist. Ct. (MNo. Dist.) Ill. 1979, U.S. Dist. Ct. (W.D.) Wisc. 1988, U.S. Ct. Appeals (10td Cir.) 1989, U.S. Dist. Ct. (E.D.) Mich. 1997, U.S. Ct. Appeals (5th Cir.) 2001, U.S. Ct. Appeals (3rd Cir.) 2002, U.S. Ct. Appeals (7th Cir.) 2002. Assoc. Kirkland & Ellis, Chgo., 1979-85, ptnr., 1985—; adj. prof. of law Northwestern U., Evanston, Ill., 1997—. Mem. ABA, Bd. of Visitors Northwestern U. 1999-; fellow Am. Coll. of Trial Lawyers 1999-. Office: Kirkland & Ellis 200 E Randolph Dr Fl 54 Chicago IL 60601-6636

HARPER, W(ALTER) JOSEPH, financial consultant; b. Columbus, Ohio, Apr. 6, 1947; s. Joseph and Patricia A. (Whetzle) Harper; m. J. Lynn Rutherford, Aug. 1, 1970; children: Tracy, Kelly, Brett. BS in Edn., Ohio State U., 1970. CFP, registered investment advisor Ohio. Tchr., coach Lake Wales (Fla.) Schs., 1970-71, Westerville (Ohio) Pub. Schs., 1971-74; securities salesman, fin. planner Investors Diversified Svcs., Columbus, 1974-83; fin. planner, investment mgr. Harper Assocs., Columbus, 1983—. Mem. golf team Ohio State U., 1966—69. Mem.: Inst. Cert. Fin. Planners (bd. dirs., pres. Cul. Ohio Soc.), Internat. Assn. Fin. Planning, Nat. Assn. Personal Fin. Advisors, Scioto Country Club, Rotary. Republican. Avocations: sports, children's activities, duck hunting. E-mail: harps@jadeinc.com.

HARPHAM, EDWARD JOHN, political science educator, dean, writer, research; b. Montreal, Que., Can., June 16, 1951; arrived in U.S.A., 1952, naturalized, 1957; s. John and Jean Harpham; m. Wendy Schlessel, Oct. 18, 1954; children: Rebecca, Jessica, William. BA in Polit. Sci., Pa. State U., 1973; MA in Govt., Cornell U., 1976, PhD in Govt., 1980. Vis. asst. prof. polit. sci. U. Houston, 1978-81; asst. prof. govt. and polit. economy U. Tex. at Dallas, Richardson, 1981-86, coll. master Sch. Social Scis., 1986-89, assoc. prof. govt. and polit. economy, 1986-2001, prof., 2001—. Dir. Collegium V Honors Program, U. Tex. at Dallas, 1998—, assoc. dean undergrad. edn., 1998—, Andrew R. Cecil lectr., 1994. Author: Disenchanted Realists, 1985, Rhythms of American Politics, 1998, We the People: Texas Edition, 2001, 2d edit., 2003; editor: Political Economy of Public Policy, 1982, Attack on the Welfare State, 1984, Texas at the Crossroads, 1987, John Locke's Two Treatises of Government: New Interpretations, 1992, Texas Politics: A Reader, 1997, 2d edit., 1998; contbr. articles to profl. jours. Coach youth soccer Dallas North Soccer Assn., Richardson, 1992-98; coach youth softball Spring Valley Athletic Assn., Richardson, 1993-2000, coach youth basketball, 1995-98; coach youth volleyball Garland Volleyball Assn., 2003. Fellow Ctr. for Study of Am. Polit. Economy, 1977, resident fellow Inst. for Humane Studies, 1977-78. Mem. Am. Polit. Sci. Assn., History of Econ. Thought Soc., David Hume Soc., Southwestern Polit. Sci. Assn. (v.p. 1993-94, pres. 2001-02), Golden Key (hon.), Phi Eta Sigma, Phi Kappa Phi, Phi Beta Kappa. Avocations: music, history. Office: U Tex-Dallas PO Box 830688 Richardson TX 75083-0688

HARPHAM, HEATHER ELISE, educator; b. Oakland, Calif., May 16, 1967; d. Howard Charles Harpham and Jessica Flynn; m. Brian Morton; children: Amelia-Grace, Gabriel. BA, World Coll. West, 1989; Masters Degree, NYU, 1998, MFA, 2000. Actor, tchr. creative arts team NYU, N.Y.C., 1994—2000. Editor: The Gallatin Rev., NYU, author short stories. Home: PO Box 762 San Anselmo CA 94979

HARPHAM, VIRGINIA RUTH, violinist; b. Huntington, Ind., Dec. 10, 1917; d. Pyrl John and Nellie Grace (Whitaker) Harpham; m. Dale Lamar Harpham, Dec. 25, 1938; children: Evelyn, George. AB, Morehead State U., 1939. Violinist Nat. Symphony Orch., Washington, 1955-90, prin. of second violin sect., 1964-90; mem. Lywen String Quartet, 1960-69, Nat. Symphony String Quartet, 1973-82. Named to Hall of Fame, Morehead State U., 2003. Episcopalian. Home: 5354 43d St NW Washington DC 20015-2008 E-mail: veeharp@tidalwave.net.

HARP-JIRSCHELE, MARY, communications executive; Grad., St. Norbert Coll., 1976. Writer, reporter The Post-Crescent, Appleton, Wis.; media rels. specialist in corp. rels. Aid Assn. for Lutherans, Appleton, Wis., 1984-87, dir. pub. info., 1987-93, asst. v.p. media and mem. rels., 1993-95, 2d v.p. comms. products and svcs., 1995-97, v.p. comms., 1997-99, v.p. comms. and facilities mgmt., 1999—2001; v.p. comm. Aid Assn. for Lutherans/ Luth. Brotherhood, Mpls., 2001—02, Thrivent Fin. for Lutherans, 2002—. Mem. Pub. Rels. Soc. Am., Internat. Assn. Bus. Communicators. Office: Thrivent Fin for Luth 625 Fourth Ave S Minneapolis MN 55415

HARPOLE, DAVID HAROLD, JR., thoracic surgeon; b. New Orleans, Apr. 5, 1958; s. David Harold Sr. and Ann (Martin) H.; m. Linda Heskerstad, July 17, 1993. BS summa cum laude, Washington & Lee U., 1980; MD, U. Va., 1984. Diplomate Am. Bd. Surgery, Am. Bd. Thoracic Surgery. Staff thoracic surgeon The Carney Hosp., Boston, 1995-96, VA Med. Ctr., West Roxbury, Mass., 1993-96; thoracic oncology team Dana Farber Cancer Inst., Boston, 1993-96; assoc. thoracic surgeon Brigham and Womens Hosp., Boston, 1993-96; instr. in surgery Havard Med. Sch., Boston, 1993-96; assoc. prof. surgery Duke U. Med. Ctr., Durham, 1996—; chief of cardiothoracic surgery VA Med. Ctr., Durham, 1996—. Mem. ACS, Am. Coll. Chest Physicians; mem. Assn. for Acad. Surgery, Soc. for Surg. Oncology, Am. Assn. for Cancer Rsch., Am. Soc. of Clin. Oncology. Office: Divsn of Thoracic Surgery DUMC 3627 Duke U Med Ctr Durham NC 27710-0001

HARPOOTLIAN, RICHARD ARA, lawyer; b. Bklyn., Jan. 23, 1949; s. Harold C. and Joan (Williams) H.; m. Pamela McCreery, Jan. 1, 1972. BS, Clemson U., 1971; JD, U. S.C., 1974. Bar: S.C. 1974. Asst. solicitor Solicitor's Office (5th cir.), Columbia, S.C., 1975-77, dep. solicitor, 1977-83; ptnr. Swerling & Harpootlian, Columbia, 1983-90; solicitor Solicator's Office (5th cir.), Cola, S.C., 1991-95; pvt. practice, 1995—. Chmn. S.C. Dem. Party, 1998-2003. Methodist. Home: 1721 Enoree Ave Columbia SC 29205-2907 Office: 1410 Laurel St Columbia SC 29201-2516 E-mail: ratt@harpootlianlaw.com.*

HARPSTER, ROBERT EUGENE, engineering geologist; b. Olney, Ill., Sept. 25, 1930; s. Christian Edward and Margaret (Tatum) H.; m. Carol Ann Dewald, Nov. 25, 1977; step-children: Larry Britt, Charla Britt. BS, Beloit Coll., 1952; MA, U. Tex., 1957. Registered geologist Calif.; cert. engring. geologist Calif., cert. quality assurance lead auditor. Petroleum geologist Geo Svc. Co., Abilene, Tex., 1952; engring. soil instr. Corp Engrs., Ft. Belvoir, Va., 1952-54; project geologist Bechtel Corp., Vernon, Calif., 1956-57; sr. project engr. geologist dept. water resources State Calif., Sacramento, 1957-73; sr. project engr. geologist Woodward-Clyde Cons., San Francisco, 1973-80, mgr. and implementor for internat. engring. projects, v.p. quality assurance/applied sci., 1980-88; quality assurance, organizer and implementor Woodward-Cyde Coms., Las Vegas, Nev., 1988-93; sr. quality assurance specialist, design rev. MACTEC, CER/SAIC, Las Vegas, Nev., 1993—. Mem. tech. rev. bds. U.S. Gov. and pvt. industries, San Francisco, 1972--; instr. Antelope Community Coll., Lancaster, Calif., 1969-72; del. People to People, USSR, 1991. Author: Selected Clays used for Dam/Fills Construction, 1979, Methods of Investigating Faults, 1979. Coach swimming Antelope Valley YMCA, Lancaster, 1969-72. Sgt. U.S. Army, 1952-54. Fellow Geological Soc. Am., Assn. Engring. Geologist (mem. chmn., v.p. 1961-63, vice chmn. 1959-62), Am. Soc. Civil Engrs., Am. Soc. for Quality Control, Earthquake Engr. Rsch. Inst., Interanl Clay Mineral Soc. Achievements include field methods for investigating faulting, and development of x-ray diffraction studies for relative age dating of paleosoils. Home: 5735 Buena Vista Ave Oakland CA 94618-2120

HARR, JEFFREY ALAN, secondary school educator; b. Lakewood, Ohio, Nov. 13, 1968; s. William John and Sharon Ruth Harr; m. Pamela Sue Motz, June 29, 1991; 1 child, Zoe Catherine. BA in Secondary Edn., U. Akron, 1991, MA in Lit., 1996. Cert. tchr. Ohio. Tchr. Kent (Ohio) City Schs., 1991—. Basketball coach Kent City Schs., 1996—99, drama dir., 1998—99, curriculum leader, 2000—. Author: (young adult novel) Phobia, 2003. Recipient Outstanding Educator award, MEO/SERRC, 1999. Mem.: Kent Edn. Assn. Avocations: writing, baseball. Home: 528 Allen Ave Cuyahoga Falls OH 44221

HARR, KARL GOTTLIEB, JR., retired lawyer; b. South Orange, N.J., Aug. 3, 1922; s. Karl Gottlieb and Mildred (Reid) H.; m. Patricia Stratton Adams, Oct. 11, 1947; children: Timothy Adams, Karl Gottlieb III, Catherine Anne, Amy. AB, Princeton, 1943; LL.B., Yale, 1948; D.Phil. (Rhodes scholar), Oxford U., 1950. Bar: N.Y. 1951, D.C. 1988. Assoc. firm Sullivan & Cromwell, N.Y.C., 1950-54; spl. asst. to under-sec. state for adminstrn., staff dir. sec. state's pub.

com. on personnel, 1954-55; dir. spl. project Richardson Found., 1955; dep. asst. sec. def. for NSC affairs and plans, alt. def. mem. NSC Planning Bd., 1956-57; spl. asst. to Pres. of U.S.; vice chmn. Ops. Coordinating Bd.; adviser NSC Planning Bd., 1958-61, mem. Pres. of U.S. com. on U.S. info. activities abroad, 1960-61; counsel to Rogers, Hoge, Hills, N.Y.C., 1961-63; pres. Aerospace Industries Assn. Am., Inc., Washington, 1963-87; of counsel Baker and Hostetler, Washington, 1988-89; sr. fellow Eisenhower World Affairs Inst., Washington, 1982-90. Bd. dirs. 1st Am. Bank, Washington; bd. dirs., mem. exec. com. Eisenhower World Affairs Inst., 1982-92. Author: The Genesis and Effect of the Popular Front in France, 1987. Chmn. emeritus bd. dirs. Expt. in Internat. Living; alumni trustee Princeton, 1968-72; bd. dirs. Freedom House, 1980-90; mem. Pres. of U.S. Coun. on Internat. Youth Exchange, 1982-84. With AUS, 1943-46. Mem. Am. Bar Assn., Phi Beta Kappa, Phi Delta Phi. Home: Chevy Chase, Md. Died Mar. 5, 2002.

HARR, LUCY LORAINE, public relations executive; b. Sparta, Wis., Dec. 2, 1951; d. Ernest Donald Harr and Dorothy Catherine (Heintz) Harr Vetter BS, U. Wis., Madison, 1976, MS, 1978. Lectr. U. Wis., Madison, 1977-82; from asst. editor to editor Everybody's Money Everybody's Money Credit Union Nat. Assn., Madison, 1979-84, mgr. ann. report, 1984-92, v.p. pub. rels., 1984-93, sr. v.p. credit union devel., 1993-96, sr. v.p. consumer rels. and corp. responsibility, 1996-97; owner Providing Solutions, Stoughton, Wis., 1997—; ptnr. Fourth Lake Comm., LLP. Dir. consumer appeals bd. Ford Motor Co., Milw., 1983-87. Author: Credit Union Basic Guide to Retirement Planning, 1998. Bd. dirs. Madison Area Crimestoppers, 1982-84; Midwest coord. of ofcls. USA Triathlon, 2003. Recipient Clarion award, 1982. Mem. Women in Comm. (pres. Madison profl. chpt. 1982-83, nat. v.p. programs 1986-87, vice-chair/sec. nat. interim bd. 1996-97, chair nat. bd. dirs. 1997-2001), Internat. Assn. Bus. Communicators (program chair dist. meeting 1981), Am. Soc. Assn. Execs. (Gold Circle award 1984) Avocations: bicycling, reading. E-mail: lharr@providing-solutions.com.

HARRAN, MARILYN JEAN, historian, educator, consultant; b. Westfield, Mass., July 22, 1948; d. Eugene Daniel and Barbara (Bigelow) Harran. B.A., Scripps Coll., Claremont, CA, 1966—70; MA, Stanford U., 1972, PhD, 1979. Instr. Barnard Coll., Columbia U., N.Y.C., 1976—79, asst. prof. of religion, 1979—85; assoc. prof. religious studies and history Chapman Coll., Orange, Calif., 1985—92, dir., freshman seminar program, 1987—91; prof. religious studies and history Chapman U., Orange, Calif., 1992—; assoc. dean Wilkinson Coll., Chapman U., Orange, Calif., 1997—98; dir., Rodgers ctr. for holocaust edn. Chapman U., Orange, Calif., 2000—, Stern chair in holocaust edn., 2000—. Cons.; spkr.; vis. scholar Inst. fuër Spaetmittelalter und Reformation U. Tuebingen, Germany, 1974—76. Author: (history) Luther on Conversion: The Early Years; editor: Luther and Learning: The Wittenberg University Luther Symposium; author: Martin Luther-Learning for Life; contbr. history, encyclopedia, reference work. Recipient Graves Award, Pomona Coll. and ACLS, 1988-89, Tchr. of the Holocaust award, The 1939 Club, 2000; fellow Fellowship for archival rsch., Internat. Rsch. & Exchanges Bd., 1990, 1989; grantee Rsch. grant, NEH, 1980-81, Travel to Collections grant, 1990. Mem.: Am. Soc. of Ch. History (coun. mem. 1979—81), Am. Hist. Assn. Avocation: travel. Office: Chapman Univ One University Dr Orange CA 92866 Office Fax: 714-532-6072.

HARRAN, SUSAN R. small business owner, writer; b. Buffalo, Nov. 16, 1942; d. Gilbert Pitzl and Esther Emma (Pfleger); m. Lee Morse, Sept. 23, 1965 (div. Feb. 14, 1973); m. James J. Harran, Jan. 23, 1987; stepchildren: Michael, Jeffrey, Edward, Maxine Krauza. AB in liberal arts, U. Tenn., Knoxville, 1964. Cert. tchg. U. Tenn., 1964, speech and drama U. Chattanooga, 1959. Eng. tchr. Melbourne (Fla.) High Sch., 1964—65; pers. coord. Northrup Space Labs, Huntsville, Ala., 1965—66; tchr. grade 5 Tinker Elem. Sch., Tampa, Fla., 1967; ops. mgr. tng. spur United Air Lines, NYC, 1968—86; co-owner antique bus. A Moment in Time, Neptune, NJ, 1985—. Columnist Antique Week, Knightstown, Ind., 1997—; lectr. various clubs, 2000—; appraiser E-Appraisal, Chgo., 2001. Author: (books) Collectible Cups and Saucers, 1997, Collectible Cups and Saucers Book II, 2000, Dresden Porcelain Studios, 2002, Collectible cups & Saucers, 2004. Mem.: Antique Appraisal Assn. Am. Avocations: collecting porcelains, travel, swimming, reading, food. Home and Office: 208 Hemlock Drive Neptune NJ 07753 E-mail: antique208@msn.com.

HARRAWOOD, PAUL, civil engineering educator; b. Akin, Ill., Aug. 28, 1928; s. Raymond E. and Verdie Alma (Galbraith) H.; m. June Anne Harris, Nov. 28, 1953; 1 child, Laura Anne. BS, U. Mo.-Rolla, 1951, MS, 1956; PhD (NSF fellow), N.C. State U., 1967. Instr. civil engring. U. Mo., Rolla, 1954-56; asst. prof. Duke U., Durham, N.C., 1956-67, asst. dean engring., 1961-62; assoc. prof. Vanderbilt U., Nashville, 1967-70, dir. engring. sci. div., 1967-71, prof., 1970—, assoc. dean engring., 1967-79, acting dean engring., 1970-71, dean engring., 1979-86; prof. emeritus civil engring, dean emeritus Sch. of Engring., Vanderbilt U., Nashville, 1997—. Test engr. McDonnell Aircraft Corp., 1957; constrn. mgmt. engr. U.S. Army C.E., 1958 Served with USNR, 1951-54. Named Engr. of Year Tenn. Soc. Profl. Engrs., 1986. Mem. ASCE, Sigma Xi, Tau Beta Pi, Chi Epsilon. Home: 178 Slat Mill Ln Fairfield VA 24435-2237

HARRE, ALAN FREDERICK, academic administrator; b. Nashville, Ill., June 12, 1940; s. Adolph Henry and Hilda (Vogt) Harre; m. Diane Carole Mack, Aug. 9, 1964; children: Andrea Lyn, Jennifer Leigh, Eric Stephen. BA, Concordia Sr. Coll., 1962; MDiv, Concordia Sem., St. Louis, 1966; MA, Presbyn. Sch. Christian Edn., Richmond, Va., 1967; PhD, Wayne State U., 1976. Ordained to ministry Luth. Ch. Asst. pastor St. James Luth. Ch. Grosse Pointe, Grosse Pointe Farms, Mich., 1967-73; asst. prof. theology Concordia Tchrs. Coll., Seward, Nebr., 1973-78, assoc. prof., 1978-84, asst. to pres., 1981, dean student affairs, 1982-84, acting pres., 1984; pres. Concordia Coll., St. Paul, 1984-88, Valparaiso (Ind.) U., 1988—. Author: (book) Close the Back Door, 1984. Bd. dirs. Associated New Am. Colls., Cmty. Found. N.W. Ind., Inc., N.W. Ind. Forum, Ind. Campus Compact, Independent Coll. Ind. Found., Luth. Ednl. Conf. Am., Luther Inst., Christmas in April, Porter County Cmty. Foun., Cmty. Devel. Corp., Quality Life Coun., Gary Accord; mem. adv. bd. YMCA; mem. Pres.'s Coun. Mid-Continent Conf. Recipient Disting. Cmty. Leader award, 1998, Sam Walton Bus. Leader award, 1999, Crystal Globe award, 1999. Mem.: Ind. Soc. Chgo., Ind. Conf. Higher Edn., Am. Assn. Higher Edn., Union League Club Chgo. Home: 3900 Hemlock Dr Valparaiso IN 46383-1814 Office: Valparaiso U Office of the President Valparaiso IN 46383-9978 E-mail: alan.harre@valpo.edu.

HARRELD, JAMES BRUCE, information technology executive; b. Gallipolis, Ohio, Dec. 12, 1950; s. James Baldwin and Ann Elizabeth (Lascu) Harreld; m. Mary E. Gillilan; children: Sara Elisabeth, Kelly Lynn, James Christopher, Matthew Parker. BS, Purdue U., 1972; MBA, Harvard U., 1975. Asst. to exec. sec. Sigma Chi, Evanston, Ill., 1972—73; asst. to pres. Epsilon Data Mgmt., Boston, 1973—74; v.p., dir. Boston Cons. Group, Boston, Munich, Chgo., 1975—82; v.p. Dart & Kraft, Northbrook, Ill., 1982—84; sr. v.p. strategy and devel. Kraft, Inc., Glenview, Ill., 1984—89, sr. v.p., chief info. officer, 1988—89, Kraft Gen. Foods, Glenview, 1989—92, sr. v.p. mktg. svcs. and info. systems, 1992—93; pres. and dir. Boston Chicken, Inc., Golden, Colo., 1993—95; sr. v.p., chief strategist IBM, White Plains, NY, 1995—. Adj. prof. mgmt. Kellogg Grad. Sch. Bus. Adminstrn. Northwestern U., 1993—95. Co-author: Survival Manual, 1973. Recipient Balfour Province award, Sigma Chi, 1972, Significant Sig award, 1989, recipient Disting. Engring. Alumnus award, Purdue U., 1991. Mem.: Stanwich Club, Amelia Island Plantation Club, Amelia Island Club, Hot Springs Club, Denver Country Club, Harvard Club (Boston), Alpha Pi Mu, Tau Beta Pi. Republican. Presbyterian. Avocations: reading, golf. Office: IBM New Orchard Rd Armonk NY 10504

HARRELD, KAREN L. jewelry designer, photographer; b. Long Beach, Calif., Mar. 1, 1949; d. Erik Donald Flamer and Mae Elizabeth Estep-Flamer; m. Charles Vincent Harreld, June 19, 1970; children: Shane Elizabeth Harreld-Grimes, Chad Erik. BS Communication Studies, Oreg. Inst. Tech.; student in Comms., Klamath C.C., Oreg. Inst. Tech. Tel. operator Gen. Tel., Long Beach, Calif., 1967—69; PBX operator US Nat. Bank, Long Beach, 1969—70, Downey, Calif., 1970—72; temp. PBX operator Kelly Girl, Sacramento, 1970; correspondant Herald and News, Chiloquin, Oreg., 1978; sole-proprietor/owner-operator Chuck's Repair (a Napa AutoCare Ctr.), Chiloquin, 1987—96; sole-proprietor/artist, jewelry designer, photographer,writer Silver Buffalo of the Cascades, Chiloqin, 1997—. Exhibition-mixed media, Purple Indian, Klamath County Fair, Oreg. (1st Pl., 2000), exhibition-original oil painting, Arizona Desert (1st Pl., 2000), Crater Lake (1st Pl., 2000). Foster parent Children's Svcs., Klamath Falls, Oreg., 1979—83; leader in art, cooking, geology, and sewing 4-H, Chiloquin, 1984—86; ofcl. scorekeeper at internat. shooting events including the jr. olympics, world cup, and U.S. shooting team selection matches NRA, Olympic Tng. Ctr., US Shooting Team, Colo., 1990—96. Mem.: Soc. for Tech. Communication Oreg. Inst. of Tech. (v.p. 2002—03), Two Rivers Village Arts (assoc.; artist in residence 2000—02), Sons of Norway (asst. sec. 2002—, v.p. 2003), Alpha Chi, Phi ThetaKappa. Republican. Avocations: glass fusion, specializing in dichroic glass, gardening. Home: 25985 Modoc Point Rd Chiloquin OR 97624 Office: Silver Buffalo of the Cascades 25959 Modoc Point Rd Chiloquin OR 97624 E-mail: silverbuff@aol.com.

HARRELL, CARLTON (BENJAMIN CARLTON HARRELL), writer, retired editor; b. Mamie, N.C., Oct. 1, 1929; s. Taylor Smith Jr and Nellie Augusta (Gallop) Harrell; m. Audrey Jeanine Tarkenton, Apr. 26, 1952; children: Melissa Ann, Sheila Lynn. Student, U. N.C., 1947-49. Reporter Daily Advance, Elizabeth City, N.C., 1950-52, 53-56, Goldsboro (N.C.) News-Argus, 1956-57, Durham (N.C.) Sun, 1957-64, state editor, 1964-65, asst. city editor, 1965-69, city editor, 1969-72, mng. editor, 1972-90; assoc. editor Herald-Sun, Durham, 1991-96, editor emeritus, columnist, 1996—. 2d lt U.S. Army, 1952—53. Mem.: Hist Preservation Soc Durham, Res Officers Assn, Am Soc Newspaper Eds. Office: Herald Sun 410 Argonne Dr Durham NC 27704-1428

HARRELL, CAROLYN HARDISON, nursing home administrator; b. Feb. 25, 1942; d. Dewey Jasper and Emma Blanche (Lilley) Hardison; m. Jerry W. Harrell, Apr. 18, 1979; children from previous marriage: Natalie Dawn, John Michael Cameron. B in Nursing, Pacific Western U., 1981, DSc in Health Care Adminstrn., 1982. RN Va. Staff nurse Petersburg Gen. Hosp., 1963—66; staff nurse, supr., insvc. dir. Cen. State Hosp., Petersburg, 1963—73; owner, oper. Cameron's Day Care Ctr., Colonial Heights, Va., 1973—74; dir. nurses Guardian Corp., Petersburg, 1974—76; adminstr. Am. Health Care Corp., Richmond, Va., 1976—77, Beverly Enterprises, Greenville, NC, 1977—83, Pitt County Meml. Hosp., 1983—85, Britthaven, Inc., Kinston, NC, 1985—86, regional dir., 1986—94, v.p. ops., 1994—2001; ret., 2001. Vocat. adv. com. Martin C.C., 1979. Recipient Citizenship award, 1960. Mem. N.C. Health Care Facilities Assn., Va. Health Care Facilities Assn., Am. Coll. Nursing Home Adminstrs., Bus. and Profl. Women Club. Republican.

HARRELL, CHARLES LYDON, JR., lawyer; b. Norfolk, Va., Oct. 22, 1916; s. Charles Lydon Sr. and Ethel Theresa (Toone) H.; m. Martha de Weese Guild, Feb. 5, 1943 (dec. March 1991); children: Charles Lydon III, John Morgan, Marshall Guild, deWeese Toone; m. Lynn Aikens Johnson, July 13, 1993. BA, Randolph-Macon Coll., 1938; LLB, U. Richmond, 1941. Bar: Va. 1940, U.S. Dist. Ct. (ea. dist.) Va. 1946, U.S. Bankruptcy Ct. (ea. and we. dist.) Va. 1946, U.S. Ct. Appeals (4th cir.) 1947, U.S. Ct. Internat. Trade 1950, U.S. Supreme Ct. 1952. Ptnr. Harrell & Landrum, Norfolk, 1947-76; pvt. practice, Norfolk, 1987—. Commr. in chancery Cir. Ct. Princess Anne County, 1950-76, City of Norfolk, 1955-77; spl. justice Princess Anne County, 1952-65. Mem. health care consumer coun. Naval Hosp., Portsmouth, 1980-90; mem. coun. of ch. Ghent United Meth. Ch., 1950—, tchr. Bible class, 1966—, master, mem. com. Boy Scouts of Am., Sea Scouts; mem. Coun. of Ministries, 1955-88, chmn. commn. on Christian concerns Meth. Ch., 1971-76; co-founder, chmn., pres. bd. dirs. Ghent Venture, Inc.; v.p. Norfolk Seaman's Soc., 1970-80, bd. dirs., 1990—, v.p.; bd. dirs. Handicaps Unltd. of Va., legis. chmn., legal advisor; vol. prayer counsellor Christian Broadcast Network, 1977-93; co-founder, bd. dirs. Va. Assn. of Blind, 1981—; dir. Norfolk Interfaith Coalition for the Elderly, Tidewater Christian Outreach Project; pres. Mobility on Wheels, Inc., 1980-83, bd. dirs., 1977—, v.p. 2000—; mem. com. for therapeutic recreation of handicapped people City of Norfolk, 1991-98; co-founder, v.p., dir. New Life Devel.; pro bono counsel Tidewater Legal Aid Soc., 1989—. Comdr. USN, to 1962. Decorated 9 campaign medals, 4 combat stars; recipient Cross Mil. Svc., UDC. Mem. ABA, Norfolk-Portsmouth Bar Assn., Va. State Bar Assn. (Lawyers Helping Lawyers), Va. Bar Assn., Jud. Soc., Christian Legal Soc., Am. Legion, VFW (past comdr.), Jr. C. of C., Jesus to the World Evangelistic Assn. (co-founder, bd. dirs., v.p., chmn. bd.), Christian Legal Soc., Gideons, Masons, Shriners, Kiwanis, Ret. Officers Assn., The Fleet Res., Tin Can Sailors Assn., Mine Warfare Assn., The Caine Mutineers, McNeil Law Soc., Phi Beta Kappa, Omicron Delta Kappa (sec. Tidewater Alumni chpt.), Tau Kappa Alpha. Avocations: swimming, scuba diving, spear fishing. Home and Office: 4464 Ocean View Ave Virginia Beach VA 23455

HARRELL, DAVID EDWIN, JR., history educator; b. Jacksonville, Fla., Feb. 22, 1930; s. David Edwin and Marilyn Mildred (Lee) H.; m. Adelia Francis Roberts, Sept. 6, 1955; children— Mildred Susan, David Edwin III, Elinor Elizabeth, Marilyn Lee, Harold Robert. BA, David Lipscomb Coll., 1954; MA, Vanderbilt U., 1958, PhD, 1962. Asst. prof. East Tenn. State U., 1961-64, assoc. prof., 1964-66, U. Okla., 1966-67, U. Ga., 1967-70; prof. U. Ala. at Birmingham, 1970-75, univ. scholar, 1975-81, 85-90, chmn. dept. history, 1970-74, 85-87; disting. prof. U. Ark., 1981-85; dir. Am. Studies Rsch Ctr., Hyderabad, India, 1993-95; Daniel F. Breeden eminent scholar Auburn U., 1990—. Disting. USIA lectr., Bangladesh, 1993, 96, Sri Lanka, 1994, 95, Indonesia, 1994, Nepal, 1995, Egypt, 1995, Nigeria, 2001. Author: Quest for a Christian America, 1966, White Sects and Black Men in the Recent South, 1971, The Social Sources of Division in the Disciples of Christ, 1973, All Things Are Possible: The Healing and Charismatic Revivals in Modern America, 1975, Oral Roberts: An American Life, 1985, Pat Robertson: A Personal Religious and Political Portrait, 1987, The churches of Christ in the Twentieth Century, 1999; editor: Varieties of Southern Evangelicalism, 1981, Indian Jour. Am. Studies, 1993-95; contbr. articles to profl. jours. Recipient author's awards for best articles East Tenn. Hist. Soc., 1966, author's awards for best articles Mo. Hist. Soc., 1969, ambassadorial citation, India, 1995; sr. Fulbright scholar, Hyderabad, India, 1993-95, Allahabad, India, 1976-77. Fellow Inst. for Ecumenical and Cultural Research; mem. Am. Hist. Assn., Orgn. Am. Historians, So. Hist. Assn., Am. Acad. Religion, Am. Soc. Church History, Disciples of Christ Hist. Soc., Indian Assn. Am Studies. Home: PO Box 704 Auburn AL 36831-0704 Office: Auburn U History Dept 310 Thatch Hall Auburn AL 36849-5207 E-mail: harrede@auburn.edu.

HARRELL, EDWARD HARDING, newspaper executive; b. Richmond, Va., Dec. 1, 1939; s. Emmett Livingston Harrell and Martha Mason (Harding) Harrell Owen; m. Diane Greer Dickerson, July 18, 1965 (dec.); children: Sara Wesley, Katherine Harding Cole. BA, U. Va., 1962. Advt. salesman Richmond Newspapers, 1963-68, asst. advt. dir., 1975-82; gen. mgr. Westover Pub., Richmond, 1968-71; mktg. dir. Media Gen. Fin., Richmond, 1971-74; asst. gen. mgr. Pitts. Press, 1982-86; pres. Harrell Assocs., 1986-89, Tribune Rev., 1989—. Bd. dirs. Conv. and Vis. Bur., Pitts., 1985—87, Pitts. Dance Coun., 1985—2000; pres., bd. dirs. Sweetwater Arts Ctr., Sewickley, Pa., 1985—94, Va. Mus. Natural Hist., 1987—94, City Theatre, 1994—, Pitts. Downtown Partnership, 1994—, Pitts. Cultural Trust Bd., 1994—, Phipps Conservatory, 1997—, Opportunities Made Equal Bd., 1997—99, Press Club Western Pa., 1995—. Capt. U.S. Army, 1962—66. Mem. Newspaper Assn. Am., Duquesne Club (Pitts.), Edgeworth Club (Sewickley). Democrat. Episcopalian. Avocations: sailing, reading. Office: 503 Martindale St Pittsburgh PA 15212-5746 E-mail: edharrell@aol.com.

HARRELL, FRANK WILLIAM, family physician; b. Ocala, Fla., Sept. 28, 1949; s. Henry Lytle and Frances Louise (Allen) H.; m. Linda S. Armstrong, Dec. 27, 1971 (div.); children: Christopher Thomas, Elizabeth Ann; m. Claudia Elaine Robinson Shrake, Feb. 14, 1997. BA, Vanderbilt U., 1971; MD, U. Miami, Fla., 1975. Family practice residency U. Louisville, 1975-78; staff physician Family Health Ctr., Louisville, 1978-81, med. dir., 1981-83; pvt. practice Louisville, 1983—. Mem. Am. Acad. Family Practice, Ky. Med. Soc., Thoroughbred Chorus. Independent. Presbyterian. Office: 1170 E Broadway Ste 302 Louisville KY 40204-1744 E-mail: fwharrell@pol.net.

HARRELL, GARY PAUL, lawyer; b. Texas City, Tex., July 8, 1952; s. James Eugene Jr. and Mary Alice Harrell; m. Leigh Evans, May 27, 1978. BS, U. Tex., 1977, MA, 1979; cert. mgmt. healthcare facilities, UCLA, 1984; JD cum laude, Lewis & Clark Coll., 1991. Bar: Oreg. 1991, U.S. Dist. Ct. (fed. dist.) Oreg. 1991; diplomate Am. Coll. Healthcare Execs. Staff/charge nurse Healthcare Facilties, Austin, Tex., 1972-78; gen. mgr. Nursing Support Svcs., Austin, 1978-80; dir. edn. Downey (Calif.) Cmty. Hosp., 1980-84; v.p. patient care Grande Ronde Hosp., La Grande, Oreg., 1984-88; assoc. Lane Powell Spears Lubersky, Portland, Oreg., 1990-94; ptnr. Harrell & Nester, LLP, Portland, 1994—. Adj. prof., asst. prof. Calif. State U., Long Beach, 1980-84; pres. Oreg. State Bd. Nursing, Portland, 1987-90. Contbr. chapters to books. With USNR, 1970-74. Recipient Am. Jurisprudence award, 1989. Fellow: Am. Coll. Health Care Adminstrs. (past pres. Oreg. chpt.), Healthcare Fin. Mgmt. Assn. (past pres. Oreg. chpt.); mem.: Oreg. Health Care Assn., Oreg. Health Lawyers Assn. (sec.), Am. Health Lawyers Assn., Oreg. Assn. Nurse Attys. (treas., past pres.), Oreg. State Bar (sec. exec. com. health law sect.). Avocations: flying, sailing, motorcycling. Office: Harrell & Nester LLP 1515 SW 5th Ave Ste 1022 Portland OR 97201-5445

HARRELL, INA PERRY, maternal/women's and medical/surgical nurse; b. Gates County, N.C., Dec. 26, 1930; d. Willie Lee and Willa Maris (Tinkham) Perry; m. Reuben Brooks Harrell, Dec. 19, 1954; children: Brooks Lee, David Austin. Diploma in nursing, Norfolk Gen. Hosp., 1952; diploma in obstetrics, Providence Lying-In Hosp., 1953. RN, N.C., Va.; cert. obstet. labor and delivery nurse, in CPR, admissions assessment nurse. Staff nurse obstetrics unit, labor and delivery room Norfolk (Va.) Gen. Hosp., N.C., 1953-54; head nurse labor and delivery room and obstetrics unit Meml. Mission Hosp., Asheville, 1956-67; office nurse Dr. Bruce J. Franz, Asheville, N.C., 1967-77; staff nurse St. Joseph's Hosp., Asheville, 1977-95, ret., 1995. Mem. Nat. Bapt. Nurses Fellowship, N.C. Nurses Assn., Norfolk Gen. Hosp. Alumni Assn. E-mail: inaharrell@aol.com.

HARRELL, LIMMIE LEE, JR., lawyer; b. Jackson, Tenn., Aug. 15, 1941; s. Limmie Lee Sr. and Mary Benthal (Nowell) H.; m. Betsy D. Harrell; children: Limmie Lee III, Mary Kimberley. BS, Memphis State U., 1963, JD, 1966. Bar: Tenn. 1966, U.S. Dist. Ct. (we. dist.) Tenn. 1968, U.S. Supreme Ct. Ptnr. Harrell & Harrell, Attys., Trenton, Tenn., 1966—. Bd. dirs. Bank of Commerce, Trenton. Pres. Gibson County Young Dems., Trenton, Tenn., 1968. Named one of Outstanding Young Men in Am. Mem. ABA, Tenn. Bar Assn., Gibson County Bar Assn., Assn. Trial Lawyers Am., Tenn. Trial Lawyers Assn., Memphis State Alumni Assn. (pres. 1984-85). Clubs: Pinecrest Country Club (Trenton, Tenn.) (pres. (3) terms). Lodges: Elks (exalted ruler 1971-72), Moose. Baptist. Avocations: golf, fishing, hunting, water skiing. Home: 300 Rosemont Dr Trenton TN 38382-3116 Office: Harrell & Harrell Attys Court Sq Trenton TN 38382-1862

HARRELL, MARGARET ANN, writer, educator, researcher, photographer; b. Greenville, NC, Sept. 25, 1940; d. John Henry and Rosa Lee Harrell; m. Jean-Marie Mensaert, Feb. 25, 1970 (dec. 1990). BA in History with honors and distinction, magna cum laude, Duke U., 1962; MA in Contemporary Brit. and Am. Lit., Columbia U., 1964; postgrad., U. N.C., 1976, Carl Jung Inst., Zurich, Switzerland, 1984-87; cert. practitioner of basic applications of psychodynamic systems, Inst. Human Devel., Ghent, 1992; tchg. diploma, Light Body Internat., Ter Duinen, Belgium, 1999. Moderator Ford Found. summer courses in Greek classics Columbia U., N.Y.C., 1963; copy editor, asst. editor Random House Pubs., N.Y.C., 1965-68; dance instr., 1969; sec. Euro-clear, Brussels, 1972-75; asst. to psychologist, dream rschr., 1983-84; co-organizer US and Indian workshops and lectrs., 1993—; editor, 1968—. Contbr. poetry reading Am. Book Week, Leuven, Belgium, 1992; participant Internat. Poetry Festival, Belgium and Romania, 1992; del. Culture Building Stone for Europe, 2002, Brugge, Belgium, 1993, Athens, 1994; mem. computer parapsychology project U. Amsterdam, 1994, 2000-01; contbr. Internat. Drama Festival, Sibiu, Romania, 1995-96; guest lectr. Sibiu U., 1995; editing coord. internat. Mus. Exhbn. on Life of Jan Mensaert, 1995-2001; pvt. tchr. LuminEssence, 2002—, Awakening Your Light Body, 2002—; presenter, panelist Internat. Parapsychol. Assn., 1995. *After thirty years of work, in 1996 in Romania, the first three volumes of Love in Transition: Voyage of Ulysses--Letters to Penelope were published. Coffee table-size volumes, Space Encounters, sprang out of the series. The final result is experimental not only verbally but visually--it incorporates fragmented poetical sound, photography that captures subtle images, sometimes appearing to be superimposed, and computer PK (that is, as defined to her by Dr. J.B. Rhine, founder of research parapsychology, mental participation in creating a physical effect: "mind through matter"). Making demonstrations of a metaphysical nature, the implications for consciousness (and human potential) are conceivably revolutionary.* Author: Marking Time with Faulkner: A Study of the Symbolic Importance of the Mark and of Related Actions, 1999, Love in Transition: Voyage of Ulysses--Letters to Penelope, Vol. I, II, III, 1996, Vol. IV, 1998, Space Encounters: Chunking Down the 21st Century, Vol. I and II, 2002, Vol. III, Inserting Consciousness into Collisions, 2003; author numerous poems; contbr. Exceptional Human Experience News, 2000—, Exceptional Human Experience Jour., 2003; jour. coord. editor Life, Page One, 2001, 2music CD-roms, 2001. Sponsor Save the Children, 1985—; co-organizer Introduction of South Indian Tamil Siddha tradition into Belgium. Fellow MacDowell Colony, 1969, 1970, 1973. Mem. Am. Soc. for Psychical Rsch., Nat. Arbor Day Found., Romanian Cure Hist. Archeological Soc. (hon.), Save the Children, Kayumari (co-founder), various wildlife orgns. Avocations: t'ai chi, energy studies, art, computers. E-mail: marharr@bellsouth.net.

HARRELL, ROY G., JR., lawyer; b. Norfolk, Va., Sept. 14, 1944; s. Roy G. and Winifred B. H. BS with honors, The Citadel; LLB cum laude, Washington & Lee. Bar: Fla.; cert. in real property. Assoc. Jennings, Watts, Clarke & Hamilton, Jacksonville, Fla., 1971-75, Greene, Mann, Rowe, Stanton, Mastry & Burton, St. Petersburg, Fla., 1975-76, ptnr., 1976-83; founding ptnr. Baynard, Harrell, Ostow & Ulrich (formerly Baynard, Harrell, Mascara & Ostow), St. Petersburg, 1983-94; of counsel Carlton, Fields, Ward, Emmanuel, Smith & Cutler, P.A., St. Petersburg, 1994-98; ptnr. Holland & Knight LLP, St. Petersburg, 1998—. Coun. Am. Lawyer's Auxiliary, 1992-93. Notes editor Washington & Lee Law Review. Past chmn. governing bd. S.W. Fla. Water Mgmt. Dist., 1985-98; past co-chair Pinellas Anclote River Basin Bd.; former mem. policy com. Tampa Bay Nat. Estuary Program; former mem. Tampa Bay Water Coordinating Coun.; pres. United Way, Pinella County, 1986; grad. leadership St. Petersburg, 1976, Leadership Tampa Bay; past chmn. campus adv. bd. U. South Fla. Bayboro Campus; former bd. dirs. Bayfront Ctr. Found.; mem. Citizens Vision 2000; former bd. dirs. 1000 Friends of Fla.; immediate past chmn. bd. dirs. St. Anthony's Devel. Found.; former mem. bd. dirs. ARC, Tampa. Capt. U.S. Army, 1969-71. Recipient Leadership award Leadership St. Pete, 1986, Leadership award Nat. Assn. Leadership Orgn., 1986, PACE award Pinellas Emergency Mental Health Svcs. 1986, Human Svcs. award, 1987. Mem. ABA (mem. various coms.), Am. Coll. Mortgage Attys., Va. Bar Assn., Fla. Bar, St. Petersburg Bar Assn., Greater St. Petersburg C. of C. (Mem. of Yr. award 1981, pres. 1986-87), Leadership St. Pete Alumni Assn. (former chair bd. dirs.), Dragon Club, St. Petersburg Yacht Club, Suncoasters, Suncoast Tiger Bay Club, Anthonians (former pres.), Phi Sigma Alpha, Phi Alpha Delta. Office: Holland & Knight LLP 200 Central Ave Ste 1600 Saint Petersburg FL 33701-3326

HARRELL, ROY HARRISON, JR., minister; b. San Angelo, Tex., July 13, 1928; s. Roy Harrison and Melinda (Garza) H.; m. Iris Ann Keeton, Dec. 15, 1951 (div. Aug. 1982); children: Amy Sue Reiwe, Patrick Roy, Paula Ann Hahn; m. Iva Helen Odeen Dunton, Apr. 21, 1990. BA, Hardin Simmons U., 1949; MDiv, SW Bapt. Theol. Sem., 1956. Ordained to ministry So. Bapt. Conv., Aug. 1946. Campus min. Draughns Bus. Coll., Ft. Worth, 1952-53; youth min. Polytechnic Bapt. Ch., Ft. Worth, 1953-56; campus min. Tex. Wesleyan Coll., Ft. Worth, 1953-56; instr., asst. prof. Religion, campus min. Baylor U., Med. Ctr., Dallas, 1956-62; campus min. Baylor U., Waco, Tex., 1962-68; asst. pastor U. Bapt. Ch., Abilene, Tex., 1969, Pk. Cities Bapt. Ch., Dallas, 1970-82; pastor Ross Ave. Bapt. Ch., Dallas, 1983-95, pastor emeritus, 1995—. Pres. East Dallas Coop. Parish, 1991-92. Contbr. articles to profl. jours. Mem. Youth Crime Commn. of Greater Dallas Crime Commn., 1990—99, Dallas Pub. Schs. Religious Cmty. Task Force, 1989—; chair Dallas Observance of Nat. Day of Prayer Breakfast, 1996; hon. supporter Dallas Obersvance Israel Indendence Day, 1998; mem. chapel com. Thanks-Giving Sq., 1991—98, chair, 1995—98, cons., 1997—, v.p., chaplain, 2000—; mem. adv. bd. East Dallas Cmty. Orgn., 1995—2001, bd. dirs., 2001—, United Way Met. Dallas, 1992—2000, mem. faith com., 1994—2000, co-chair, 1994—95, exec. com., 1996—97, mem. nominating com., 1998—99; pres. East Dallas Coop. Parish Coun., 1993—94; founding bd. mem. Dallas-Our Kids, 1998, pres., 2001—02; bd. dirs. Interfaith Garden of Prayer, Baylor U. Med. Ctr. Mem.: Dallas Pastors Assn. (sec.-treas. 1990—91, v.p. 1991—92, pres. 1992—94), Dallas Mus. of Art, Rotary Internat.

(dist. 5810 chair ethics in bus. and govt. com. 1998—99, chair literacy com. 1999—2002), Rotary Club Dallas (chair literacy com. 1997—99, bd. dirs. 1999—2002, v.p. cmty. svc. 2000—01). Home: 3521 Villanova St Dallas TX 75225-5008 E-mail: royhharrell2@cs.com. *The church is the only institution dedicated to changing the lives of people at their very heart. A minister therefore has the gravest of responsibility.*

HARRELL, SAMUEL MACY, agribusiness executive; b. Indpls., Jan. 4, 1931; s. Samuel Runnels and Mary (Evans) H.; m. Sally Bowers, Sept. 2, 1958 (div.); children: Samuel D., Holly Evans, Kevin Bowers, Karen Susan, Donald Runnels, Kenneth Macy. BS in Econs., Wharton Sch., U. Pa., 1953. Pres., chmn. bd., chief exec. officer, chmn., exec. com. Early & Daniel Industries, Cin., 1971—; chmn. bd., chmn. exec. com. Early & Daniel Co., Cin., 1971—; chmn. bd., chief exec. officer, chmn. exec. com. Tidewater Grain Co., Phila., 1971—. Dir. Harriman Inst. Columbia U.; bd. dirs. Wainwright Bank & Trust Co., Wainright Abstract Co., Nat. Grain Trade Council, U.S. Feed Grains Council; mem. Chgo. bd. Trade Contbg. author: The Status of Agribusiness in Russia and the CIS. Dir. Harriman Inst., Columbia U. With AUS, 1953-55. Mem. Nat. Assn. Cert. Valuation Analysts, Inst. Bus. Appraisers, Am. Soc. Farm Mgrs. & Rural Appraisers, Am. Soc. Agrl. Cons., Internat. Bus. Brokers Assn., Young Pres.'s Orgn., U. Pa. Alumni Assn. (past pres.), Terminal Elevator Grain Mchts. Assn. (dir.), Millers Nat. Fedn. (dir.), Assn. Operative Millers, Am. Soc. Bakery Engrs., Am. Fin. Assn., Council on Fgn. Relations, Fin. Exec. Inst., N.Am. Grain Export Assn. (dir.), Mpls. Grain Exchange, St. Louis Mchts. Grain Exchange, Buffalo Corn Exchange, Delta Tau Delta (Past prs. Ind. alumni) Clubs: Columbia, Indpls. Athletic, Woodstock, Traders Point Hunt, Dramatic, Players, Lambs (Indpls.); Racquet (Phila.); University (Washington and N.Y.C.). Lodges: Masons, Rotary. Presbyterian. Office: EDI Internat Inc 3200 Teton Pines Dr Wilson WY 83014 Home: 15787 Imperial Point Ln Wellington FL 33414-7114

HARRELL, STEVEN JEFFREY, lexicographer; b. Highland, Ill., June 18, 1965; s. Dallas Thomas and Agnes Louise (Ax) H. BA, U. Ill., 1989; AAS, Southwestern Ill. Coll., 1994; MA, Calif. State U., 1999; Lang. cert., Berlitz Lang. Ctr., 1999; Tech. cert., EEI Comm., 2001. Lexicographer Mc Neil Techs., Inc., Hyattsville, Md., 1995—. Albanian interpreter Linguistics, Internat., Balt., 1995—. Author: Albanian-English Military Dictionary, 2000, Georgian-English Dictionary, 2001; creator (comics): Viper-man. Mem. Dictionary Soc. N.Am., Pi Delta Phi, Phi Eta Sigma, Alpha Lambda Delta.

HARRELL, WILLIAM RODNEY, electronics engineer; b. Lebanon, Ky., Aug. 5, 1959; s. Wayland S. and Margaret A. (Johnson) H.; m. Janet Lee Bryant, Sept. 29, 1984; children: Tyler Matthew, Courtney Nicole, Chad Michael. BSEE, U. Ky., 1981, MSEE, 1983; PhD in elec. engring., U. Md., 1994. Rsch. asst. Wenner-Gren Biomed. Rsch. Lab., Lexington, Ky., 1982; tchg. asst. U. Ky., Lexington, 1982-83; microwave engr. U.S. Dept. Def., Ft. Meade, Md., 1984-85, microelectronic rsch. engr., 1985-89; sr. microelectronic engr. Microelectronics Rsch. Lab., Columbia, Md., 1990—97; asst. prof. Clemson U., SC, 1997—. Contbr. articles to profl. jours, including Jour. Microelectronic Engring., IEEE Transactions on Electron Devices, Thin Solid Films, Jour. of Electronic Materials, Synthetic Metals, Electrochem. and Solid State Letters, Jour. of Vacuum Sci. and Tech. Acad. fellowship U.S. Dept. Def., U. Md., College Park, 1989-90. Mem. IEEE. Baptist. Achievements include demonstration of 2-photon lithography for the first time; experiments observing saturation of the Poole-Frenkel effect for the first time; theoretical and experimental explanation of the temperature variation of the Poole-Frenkel effect over a wide range of electric fields; demonstration of polymers/carbon nanotube composite electronic device. Home: 114 Knollwood Dr Clemson SC 29631-2062

HARRELSON, CLYDE LEE, retired secondary school educator; b. Baton Rouge, Nov. 20, 1946; s. Hezzie Clyde and Marguerite Lucille (Tucker) Harrelson. BA, Southeastern La. U., 1968; MA, La. State U., 1974, EdS, 1980, postgrad., 1981, So. U., 1982. Cert. social studies and English tchr., prin., supr. La. Tchr. English East Baton Rouge Parish Sch. Bd., 1970—2003, McKinley Mid. Magnet Sch., Baton Rouge, 1982—2001, dean of students, 1998—2001; tchr. social studies Ctrl. HS, 2002—03; ret., 2003. Mem. Arts Coun. Greater Baton Rouge, Found. Hist. La., La. Preservation Alliance, Nat. Trust Hist. Preservation, Colonial Williamsburg Found., NCCJ, La. Dem. Com., Nat. Dem. Com.; mem. exec. com. East Baton Rouge Parish Dems., 1981—85, 1996—. Mem.: Smithsonian Instn., Mus. Modern Art, Met. Mus. Art, New Orleans Mus. Art, Baton Rouge Gallery, La. Endowment for the Humanities, Old State Capitol Assocs., La. Arts and Sci. Ctr., La. State U. Mus. Art, Kiwanis, Phi Delta Kappa. Episcopalian. Home: 12418 Lake Sherwood Ave S Baton Rouge LA 70816-4454

HARRELSON, WALTER JOSEPH, minister, religion educator emeritus; b. Winnabow, N.C., Nov. 28, 1919; s. Isham Danvis and Mabel (Rich) H.; m. Idella Aydlett, Sept. 20, 1942; children: Marianne McIver, David Aydlett, Robert Joseph. Student, Mars Hill (N.C.) Coll., 1940-41, Litt.D. (hon.), 1977; AB, U. N.C., 1947, Litt.D. (hon.), 1994; B.D., Union Theol. Sem., 1949, Th.D., 1953; postgrad., U. Basel, Switzerland, 1950-51, Harvard, 1951-53; D.D. (hon.), U. of South, 1974, Christian Theol. Sem., 1992. Instr. philosophy U. N.C., 1947; ordained to ministry Baptist Ch., 1949; tutor asst. Union Theol. Sem., 1949-50; prof. Old Testament Andover Newton Theol. Sch., 1951-55; dean, assoc. prof. Old Testament U. Chgo. Div. Sch., 1955-60; prof. Old Testament Div. Sch., Vanderbilt U., Nashville, 1960-75, chmn. grad. dept. religion, 1962-67, dean, 1967-75, Disting. prof. Hebrew Bible, 1975-90, prof. emeritus, 1990—, dir. Lilly Ministry Project, 1990-94; interim dean Disciples Div. House, 1993-94; prof. Wake Forest U., 1994-96, adj. univ. prof. Divinity Sch., 1996—. Dir. Ecumenical Inst. Advanced Theol. Studies, Jerusalem, 1977-78, 78-79; chmn. transl. com. Rev. Standard Version of the Bible, 2000; vis. prof. Brite Div. Sch. Tex. Christian U., 1992, Boston Coll., 1991, 93; mem. ch. rels. com. U.S. Holocause Meml. Mus. Author: Jeremiah, Prophet to the Nations, 1959, Interpreting the Old Testament, 1964, From Fertility Cult to Worship, 1969, 80, The Ten Commandments and Human Rights, 1980, rev. edit., 1997, (with Rabbi R.M. Falk) Jews and Christians: A Troubled Family, 1990, (with Bruce M. Metzger and Robert C. Dentan) The Making of the New Revised Standard Version of the Bible, 1991, (with Rabbi R.M. Falk) Jews and Christians: In Pursuit of Social Justice, 1996, Festschrift, Passion, Vitality, and Foment: The Dynamics of Second Temple Judaism, 2001; co-author, editor: Teaching the Biblical Languages, 1967, New Interpreter's Study Bible, 2003; editor, contbr.: Israel's Prophetic Heritage, 1962; editl. chmn. Religious Studies Rev., 1974-80; assoc. editor Mercer Dictionary of the Bible, 1990; assoc. editor Mercer Commentary on the Bible, 1995. Dir. project to film Ethiopian Manuscripts, NEH, 1972-84; bd. dirs. Dead Sea Scrolls Found., 1991—, Planned Parenthood Assn., Nashville; active ch. rels. com. U.S. Holocaust Meml. Coun. Traveling fellow Union Theol. Sem., 1949; Am. Coun. Learned Socs. fellow, 1950-51, 70; exch. fellow U. Basel, 1950-51; fellow Inst. Internat. Edn., 1950-51; Fulbright rsch. scholar, Rome, 1962-63; Harvie Branscomb Disting. prof. Vanderbilt U., 1977-78, Alexander Heard Disting. Svc. prof., 1985-86; NEH fellow, Rome, 1983-84; recipient Thomas Jefferson prize, 1987-88, Alumni/ae award Vanderbilt U., 1989, Festschrift, Justice and the Holy, 1989, Union Theol. Sem., N.Y.C., 2003. Mem. NAS (mem. ethics com. Inst. Medicine), Soc. for Values in Higher Edn. (pres. 1972-74), Soc. Bibl. Lit. (pres. 1972), Am. Acad. Religion, Cath. Bibl. Assn., Phi Beta Kappa. Home and Office: 708 E Moore St Southport NC 28461-4029 E-mail: wharrelson@ec.rr.com.

HARRIBANCE, SEAN LALSINGH, parapsychologist; b. Fyzabad, Trinidad and Tobago, Nov. 11, 1939; arrived in U.S., 1969; s. Harribance Singh and Sampatia Batchasingh; m. Christine Ann Comyn, Feb. 28, 1971; children: Linnea Christine, Sean Lalsingh Jr. Cashier Trinidad Bus Svc., San Fernando, 1959—69; part-time rsch. subject Parapsychology Lab., Dr. Hamlyn Dukhan, Trinidad, 1966—69; parapsychol. rsch. subject Found. for Rsch. on Nature of Man, Durham, NC, 1969—73; part-time rsch. subject Psychical Rsch. Found., Durham, NC, 1969—73, 1980; pres. Sean Harribance Inst. for Parapsychology, Inc., 1980—. Part-time parapsychology rsch. subject Laurentian U., Sudbury, Ont., Can., 1996, 97, 2000; hon. dir. Sean Harribance Inst. for Parapsychology Rsch., Inc., Tex., Sean Harribance Inst. Parapsychology Found., Trinidad; affiliated with engring. dept. Duke U., 1975. Co-author: This Man Knows You, 1976; contbr. articles to profl. jours. including Internat. Jour. Psychophysiology, Internat. Jour. Neuroscience, Perceptual and Motor Skills, Jour. Parapsychology, Jour. Am. Soc. for Psychical Rsch., Jour. Neuropsychiatry and Clin. Neuroscience, Procs. Parapsychol. Assn., Rsch. in Parapsychology. Named Hon. Citizen, recipient key to city, City of Baton Rouge, 1975; named hon. lt. col. aide-de-camp Ala. State Militia, 1975. Home: PO Box 908 Sugar Land TX 77487-0908 E-mail: harribance@yahoo.com.

HARRICE, CY (NICHOLAS PSIHARIS), commercial radio and television announcer; b. Chgo., Mar. 1, 1915; s. Peter and Vasiliki (Anargyros) Psiharis; child by previous marriage, Lincoln Peter; m. 2d, Helena Seroy, Dec. 12, 1959; 1 child, Melanie Samantha. Student Sch. Commerce, Northwestern U., 1934-38. Concession barker Chgo. World's Fair, 1934; with Samuel Insull ABC Network, 1935; announcer, copywriter, newsman, programmer Sta. WLS, Chgo., 1936-42; news broadcaster Sta. WGN, Chgo., 1942-45; freelance comml. announcer NBC, CBS, ABC and Mutual, N.Y.C., 1945—. Contract comml. announcer "and, they are mild!" segment Pall Mall cigarette advt. campaign for radio and TV, 1946-70; product spokesman for GM, Proctor & Gamble, DuPont Co., Miller Brewing Co., Alka-Seltzer, Kaiser-Fraser; host Adventures Sherlock Holmes, 1947-49; announcer radio programs for Walter Winchell, Grand Cen. Sta., Cavalcade of Am., The Big Story, H.V. Kaltenborn, Wednesday Night Fights, William L. Shirer, RCA Victor Show, The Thin Man, Quick as a Flash; producer What's the Good Word; co-starred with Ginger Rogers in Seven Hundred Boiled Shirts, Cavalcade of Am., NBC, 1951; pres. Stair Mountain Prodns. Recipient Sargent Oratorical award, 1935; Clio award, 1962; 1st place Gold medal sabres Ill. Fencers League, 1936; mem. champion sabre team Amateur Fencers League Am., 1935. Mem. SAG (bd. dirs. 1966-69), AFTRA (bd. dirs. 1956-60), Friars Club, Lambs Club, Deru Club, Lynx Club. Address: PO Box 189 Kelly WY 83011-0189

HARRIES, JAMES THEODORE, psychologist; b. Buffalo, N.Y., June 25, 1930; s. James Theodore Harries and Lula Anna Willer-Harries; m. Karen Louise Davies, June 27, 1964 (dec. June 1997). Student, Art Inst. Buffalo, 1948-50, Albright-Knox Art Sch., 1955-58; BFA, U. Buffalo, 1958; MEd, SUNY, Buffalo, 1960, PhD, 1970. Lic. psychologist, ednl. psychology, Mass.; health svc. provider cert. Mass. Bd. Registration Psychologists. Cert. sch. psychologist Amherst (N.Y.) Sch. Sys., 1966-67; adj. prof. Canisius Coll. Grad. Sch., Buffalo, 1968-69; dir. doctoral program sch. psychology Boston U., 1969-73; dir. Mental Health Ctr. Salem (Mass.) Coll., 1973-77, coord. grad. studies in counseling, 1977; pres. Behaviorl Devel. Assocs., P.C., Brookline, Boston, 1977—. Pres. Western N.Y. Pers. and Guidance Assn., Buffalo, N.Y., 1966-68; vis. prof. U. Heidelberg, Germany, 1971; resident prof. U.S. Dept. Def., Boston U., Karlsruhe, Germany, 1971. Author: Psychological Dimensions of Prostate Cancer, 1999; editor: 38 Psychological Measures: A Reference for Counselors, 1969; editor The Counselor, 1964-65, Jour. N.Y. State Counselors Assn., 1967-68. Active Buffalo Soc. Artists, 1954-69; bd. mem. Mental Health Assn. Erie County, Buffalo, 1966; co-founder N.Y. State Sch. Counselors Assn., 1966. Recipient George E. Hutcherson Hon. award State N.Y. Counselors Assn., 1968. Mem. APA, Am. Coll. Forensic Examiners, Inc., Am. Assn. Clin. Counselors, Nat. Assn. Sch. Psychologists (nat. dir. New Eng. region 1975-77, nat. bd. mem. 1975-77), Prescribing Psychologists' Register Inc. (charter), Mass. Sch. Psychologists Assn. (pres. 1974-76, Presdl. award 1976), Phi Delta Kappa (life). Avocations: organizational structure, anxiety research, watercolor painting, travel, architecture. Home: Sea Cliff Walk Folly Point Rd Gloucester MA 01930 Office: Behavioral Devel Assocs PO Box 389 Rockport MA 01966-0489

HARRIES, KARSTEN, philosophy educator, researcher; b. Jena, Thuringia, Germany, Jan. 25, 1937; came to U.S., 1951; s. Wolfgang and Ilse (Grossmann) H.; m. Elizabeth Wanning, July 4, 1959; children: Lisa, Peter, Martin; 2d m., Elizabeth L. Langhorne, Mar. 14, 1991. BA, Yale U., 1958, PhD, 1962. Instr. Yale U., New Haven, 1961-63, asst. prof. philosophy, 1965-66, assoc. prof., 1966-70, prof., 1970—, Mellon prof., 1986-91; asst. prof. U. Tex., Austin, 1963-65. Lectr. U. Bonn, Fed. Republic Germany, winters 1965-66, 68-69. Author: The Meaning of Modern Art, 1967, The Bavarian Rococo Church, 1983, The Broken Frame, 1989, The Ethical Function of Architecture, 1996 (Winner of 8th Ann. AIA Internat. Architecture Book award for criticism), Infinity and Perspective, 2001; editor: (with Christoph Jamme) Martin Heidegger: Kunst, Politik, Technik, 1992, Martin Heidegger: Politics, Art, and Technology, 1994; contbr. numerous articles and revs. to profl. jours. Recipient Disting. Teaching Effectiveness award U. Tex., 1964; Morse fellow Yale U., 1965-66, Guggenheim fellow, N.Y.C., 1971-72. Mem. Am. Philos. Assn., Soc. for Eighteenth Century Studies, Cusanus Soc. Home: 16 Morris St Hamden CT 06517-3423 Office: Yale U Dept Philosophy New Haven CT 06520 E-mail: karsten.harries@yale.edu.

HARRIFF, SUZANNA ELIZABETH (BAHNER), advertising consultant; b. Vicksburg, Miss., Dec. 30, 1953; d. David S. and F. Suzanna (McElwee) Bahner; m. James R. Harriff, Sept. 10, 1977; 1 child, Michael James. BA summa cum laude, SUNY-Fredonia, 1976; postgrad., Cornell U. Law Sch., 1981; MDiv with distinction, Colgate Rochester Div. Sch., 1995. Ordained to ministry Am. Bapt. Chs. USA, 1995. Media asst. Comstock Advt., Syracuse, N.Y., Buffalo, 1976-77; media buyer/planner G. Andre Delporte, Syracuse, 1979-81; media dir. Roberts Advt., Syracuse, 1982; dir. media svcs. Signet Advt., Syracuse, 1982-84; owner, pres. MediaMarCon, Syracuse, 1984—. Interim dir. mktg. and comm. Onondaga C.C., 1998—99; pub. rels. cons. Syracuse Symphony Orch., 2000—01; adj. prof. Newhouse Sch. at Syracuse U., 2001—02. Pheresis donor ARC, 1987—; vol. pub. TV auction drive, chair media divsn. Sta. WCNY-TV, 1986—97, gen chair, 1994; accompanist musicals and chorus Manlius-Pebble Hill Sch., 1991—96; resource devel. chair Winterfest, Syracuse, 1992; lead female vocalist Aspen Dreams, 1996—; cmty. liason Cmty. United Way, 2000—01; music dir., pianist Manlius United Meth. Ch., NY, 1983—92, youth dir., 1983—85; dir. music First Bapt. Ch., Manlius, 1993—96; assoc. pastor Andrews Meml. United Meth. Ch., 1996—99; interim pastor Oswego First United Meth. Ch., 2000; pastor Apulia and Onativia United Meth. Chs., 2000—02; tchr. Am. Bapt. Chs. N.Y. state lay studies program Bethel Bible Inst., Syracuse; co-chair St. Nicholas Ecumenical Festival, 1992—98, Am. Bapt. Ch. Nat. Biennial Conf., 1995; workshop leader United Meth. Ch., 1997—; interim pastor Hannibal Cmty. Ch., 2003—. Recipient 500 Hour Svc. pin WCNY, 1996, Women in Bus. award, 2001, Bronze and Silver Paragon awards Nat. Coun. for Mktg. and Pub. Rels., 2000, Gold Medallion of Excellence, Upstate N.Y. dist., 1999. Mem. NAFE, Syracuse Advt. Club (dir. 1985-88, program chair 1986-88, pres. 1988-89), Nat. Coun. for Mktg. and Pub. Rels. (Dist. Gold medallion for radio spot 2000, Nat. Bronze Paragon award 2000, Nat. Silver Paragon award 2000), Irish-Am. Cultural Inst. Syracuse, Phi Beta Kappa. Democrat. Avocations: music, theatre. Home: 8180 Bluffview Dr Manlius NY 13104-9740 E-mail: mediamarco@aol.com.

HARRIGAN, ANTHONY HART, author; b. N.Y.C., Oct. 27, 1925; s. Anthony Hart and Elizabeth Elliott (Hutson) H.; m. Elizabeth McP. Ravenel, Aug. 16, 1950; children: Anthony Hart, Elizabeth Chardon, Elliott McP., Mary Ravenel. Student, Bard Coll., Kenyon Coll., Gambier, Ohio, U. Va. Reporter Virginian-Pilot, Norfolk, 1953-55, Charleston (S.C.) News & Courier, assoc. editor, 1957-70; exec. v.p. U.S. Indsl. Coun., Nashville, 1970-78, pres., 1978-90. Pres. U.S. Bus. and Indsl. Coun. Ednl. Found., 1978-90; trustee, rsch. fellow Nat. Humanities Inst.; lectr. Harvard U., Nat. War Coll., Vanderbilt U., U. Colo.; past mem. rsch. com. S.C. Commn. Higher Edn. Author: Ten Poets Anthology, 1947, The Editor and the Republic, 1952, Red Star Over Africa, 1964, The New Republic, 1965, Defense Against Total Attack, 1966, A Guide to the War in Vietnam, 1965, American Perspectives, 1974, American Perspectives II, 1977; co-author: The Indian Ocean and the Threat to the West, 1976, The Southern Oceans and the Security of the Free World, 1978, Putting America First, 1987, American Economic Pre-eminence, 1989; co-author or editor other works, 1978; editl. adv. bd. Modern Age, 1955—, author newspaper column, 1970-90, also numerous articles in nat. jours. Trustee Nat. Humanities Inst. Served with USMCR, World War II. Recipient Mil. Rev. award U.S. Army Command and Gen. Staff Coll., 1965; grantee Relm Found., 1966, Wilbur Found., 1992, 95, Earhart Found., 1993. Mem. Soc. Colonial Wars in S.C., Nat. Press Club, Carolina Yacht Club. Anglican.

HARRIGAN, EDMUND PATRICK, physician, researcher; b. Springfield, Mass., Jan. 31, 1953; s. Edmund Lawrence and Kathleen Marie (Griffin) H.; m. Julie Marie Burghardt, Apr. 22, 1950; children: Eamon Patrick, David Russell, Jeffrey Conor, Paul William. BA in Chemistry magna cum laude, St. Anselm Coll., Manchester, N.H., 1974; postgrad., UCLA, 1975; MD, U. Mass., 1979. Diplomate Am. Bd. Psychiatry and Neurology. Intern in internal medicine Berkshire Med. Ctr., Pittsfield, Mass., 1979-80; resident in neurology Boston U., 1980-83, teaching fellow in neurology, 1980-83; pres. Coastal Neurology Svcs., Inc., Somersworth, N.H., 1985-90; with CIBA Geigy Pharm., Summit, N.J., 1990-92, Pfizer Ctrl. Rsch., Groton, Conn., 1992—. Contbr. articles to profl. jours., chpt. to book. Mem. AMA, Am. Acad. Neurology, Am. Soc. Exptl. Neuro-Therapeutics (mem. exec. com.). Office: Pfizer Ctrl Rsch Eastern Point Rd Groton CT 06340

HARRIGAN, JOHN THOMAS, JR., physician, obstetrician-gynecologist; b. Perth Amboy, N.J., Apr. 20, 1929; s. John T. and Mary E. (Czapp) H.; m. Marlene Lulka, Apr. 14, 1961 (div.); children: John, Alisa, Edmund; m. Karen Tiejen, Aug. 23, 1992. Student, U. Va., 1946-49; MD, George Washington U., 1953. Diplomate Am. Bd. Ob-Gyn. Intern Doctors Hosp., Washington, 1953-54; resident in ob-gyn Luth. Hosp., Balt., 1954-55, Providence Hosp., Washington, 1957-58, Free Hosp. for Women, Boston, 1958-59; practice medicine specializing in ob-gyn, sub specialist in maternal-fetal medicine Jersey City, 1960-65, Colonia, N.J., 1962-70, Madison Twp., N.J., 1965-70; asst. attending in ob-gyn Margaret Hague Hosp., Jersey City, 1960-65; attending physician in ob-gyn Rahway Hosp., N.J., 1962-70, South Amboy Hosp., N.J., 1965-73, sec. to med. staff, 1970; attending in ob-gyn Maitland Hosp. Unit, Newark, 1970-74; dir. dept. ob-gyn Monmouth Med. Ctr., Long Branch, N.J., 1974-76, dir. regional perinatal edn. program, 1975-78; dir. Monmouth Perinatal Ctr., Long Branch, 1975-78; sr. attending in ob-gyn St. Peter's Med. Ctr., 1978—; assoc. prof. ob-gyn Hahnemann Med. Coll., Phila., 1975-78; prof. dir. div. maternal-fetal medicine Rutgers Med. Sch., Piscataway, N.J., 1978—, prof. ob-gyn., dir. div. maternal-fetal medicine, 1978-86, U. Medicine and Dentistry N.J., Robert Wood Med. Sch., 1986—. Cons. in maternal-fetal medicine to physicians, Eastern N.J.; mem. maternal and infant care services com. N.J. Dept. Health, 1975— ; dir. statewide premature delivery prevention project; med.-legal expert cons.; tech. adv. panel Healthstart program, N.J. Health Dept. Contbr. articles to med. jours.; reviewer med. jours. Mem. task force on biomed. causes and pub. rels. Gov.'s Coun. on Prevention Mental Retardation, N.J., task force on genetics and fetal defects, 1984—; mem. pub. affairs com. MOD Birth Defects Found.; pres. Perinatal Assn. N.J., 1991-93; mem. N.J. Commn. of Health and Parental and Child Health adv. Com., 1993—, vice chair, 1995—. Capt. M.C. U.S. Army, 1955-57. Fellow ACOG (vice chmn. N.J. sect. 1979-82, chmn. N.J. sect. 1982—, nat. adv. coun. 1982—, legis. rep., treas. dist. III 1986); mem. AMA, Med. Soc. N.J. (maternal infant care com. 1988—), Am. Inst. Ultrasound in Medicine (legis. com. 1994), Am. Fertility Soc., N.J. Perinatal Assn. (v.p. 1980-90, pres. 1990), N.J. Perinatal Tech. adv. Com. Baker channing Soc., N.J. Ob-gyn. Soc. (coun.), N.J. Maternal Fetal Medicine Soc. (pres. 1994-95). Democrat. Roman Catholic. Home: 301 Sussex Ave Spring Lake NJ 07762-1231 Office: Jersey Shore Med Ctr Perinatal Inst 301 Sussex Ave Spring Lake NJ 07762-1231

HARRIMAN, GERALD EUGENE, retired business administrator, economics educator; b. Dell Rapids, S.D., May 30, 1924; s. Roy L. and Margaret (Schrantz) H.; m. Eileen Bernadine Bensman, June 10, 1950; children— G. Peter, Mary K., Margaret C., Elizabeth A. BS, U. Notre Dame, 1947; A.M., U. S.D., 1949; PhD, U. Cin., 1957. Expediter Minn. Mining & Mfg. Co., 1947-48; from instr. to asst. dean, chmn. dept. bus. adminstrn. and finance Xavier U., 1949-66; prof. bus. adminstrn., chmn. div. bus. and econs. Ind. U. at South Bend, 1966-75, prof. bus. adminstrn. and econs., 1975-89, prof. emeritus, 1989—, dean faculties, 1975-87, acting chancellor, 1979, vice chancellor acad. affairs, 1987-89; ret., 1989. Vis. prof. fin. U. S.D., 1962; chmn. acad. deans Ind. Conf. Higher Edn., 1981-82; cons. in field. Mem. citizens adv. coun. long range fin. planning Coun. of City of Cin., 1963; mem. Community Edn. Roundtable, 1984—; mem. Scholarship Found. of St. Joseph County, Inc., 1992. Served with USNR, 1942-45. Mem. Am. Econs. Assn., Am. Finance Assn., Beta Gamma Sigma. Home: 16600 Gerald St Granger IN 46530-9579 Office: 1700 Mishawaka Ave South Bend IN 46615-1408

HARRIMAN, JOHN HOWLAND, retired lawyer; b. Buffalo, Apr. 14, 1920; s. Lewis Gildersleeve and Grace (Bastine) H.; m. Barbara Ann Brunmark, June 12, 1943; children— Walter Brunmark, Constance Bastine, John Howland. AB summa cum laude, Dartmouth, 1942; JD, Stanford U., 1949. Bar: Calif. 1949. Assoc. firm Lawler, Felix & Hall, Los Angeles, 1949-55; asst. v.p., then v.p. Security Pacific Nat. Bank, Los Angeles, 1955-72, sr. v.p., 1972-85. Sec. Security Pacific Corp., 1971-85; dir. Master Metal Works; mem. nat. adv. coun. The Pub. Svc., 1992-93. Mem. L.A. adv. coun. Episcopal Ch. Found., 1977-79; mem. Republican Assocs., 1951-72, trustee, 1962-72; mem. Calif. Rep. Central Com., 1956-69, 81—, exec. com., 1960-62, 81-84; mem. L.A. County Rep. Central Com., 1958-70, exec. com., 1960-62, vice chmn., 1962; chmn. Calif. 15th Congl. Dist. Rep. Central Com., 1960-62, Calif. 30th Congl. Dist. Rep. Central Com., 1962; treas. United Rep. Fin. Com. L.A. County, 1969-70; chmn. L.A. County Reagan-Bush campaign, 1980, co-chmn., 1984; exec. dir. Calif. Rep. Party, 1985-86. With USAAF, 1943-46. Mem. Am. Bar Assn., State Bar Calif., Phi Beta Kappa, Theta Delta Chi, Phi Alpha Delta. Clubs: California (Los Angeles); Lincoln, Breakfast Panel (pres. 1970-71).

HARRIMAN, MALCOLM BRUCE, investment advisor, financial consultant; b. Sandusky, Ohio, Feb. 25, 1950; s. Robert Byron and Catherine (Nicholson) Harriman; m. Carla J. Holgren, Sept. 19, 1971 (div. Mar. 1980); m. Susan Gwen Alexander, June 27, 1980 (div. Jan. 1985); 1 child, Sasha Bryn; m. Alysa Ellen Gelband, Apr. 19, 1986; children: Sarah Ashley, Catherine Nicole. BA, Antioch Coll., 1976; MA, U. Md., 1980. Lic. ins. agent Fla., N.C., Ga., Mass., Tenn., Va.; registered rep. Nat. Assn. Securities Dealers, N.Y. Stock Exch., Chgo. Bd. Options Exch., Am. Stock Exch., Phila. Stock Exch. Child care worker Ft. Wayne (Ind.) Children's Home, 1971-72; adolescent program supr. Taylor Manor Hosp., Ellicott City, Md., 1972-76; program coord. child and adolescent svcs. Horizon Hosp, Clearwater, Fla., 1981-82, mktg. specialist, 1983-86; v.p., prin. ptnr. Am. Residential Ctrs., Tampa, Fla., 1986-89; pres., prin. ptnr. Continuum Psychiat. (formerly Am. Residential Ctrs.), 1989-95; exec. dir., COO Tampa Bay Acad., Riverview, Fla., 1988-94, chmn. bd., 1994-96; pres., chief exec. officer HealthExpert Sys., Inc. (formerly HealthWare, Inc.), 1989-97; chief clin. officer Echo Mgmt. Group, Tampa, 1997; fin. advisor, retirement plan cons. Raymond James & Assocs., Inc., Tampa, 1997—. Bd. dirs. Sr. Care Group, Inc., vice chmn., 2000—; assoc. dept. psychiatry U. South Fla. Med. Sch., Tampa, 1980—81; mem. severely emotionally disturbed network project adv. coun. Pinellas County, Fla., 1985—86. Gubernatorial appointee Project Freeway task force HRS Dist. V, Fla., 1985—86; mem. adv. bd. Behavioral Informatics Tomorrow, Inst. Behavioral Healthcare, San Francisco, 1993—98; mem. adv. com. Cognitive Rehab. Inst., Tampa, Fla., 1993—94; bd. dirs. Friends of Rsch. Psychiatry, Coll. Medicine, U. South Fla., pres., 2000—; mem. adv. coun. Personal Enrichment Through Mental Health Svcs., 1998—99, bd. dirs., 2000—. Mem.: Fla. West Coast Employee Benefits Coun., Assn. for Ambulatory Behavioral Healthcare (outcome task force 1993—94, cons. bd. dirs. 1994—98), Nat. Assn. Psychiat. Treatment Ctr. for Children (bd. dirs. 1989—95), Fin. Planning Assn., Suncoast C. of C. (edn. com., del. youth svcs. adv. coun. 1982—86), Brandon C. of C. Republican. Presbyterian. Office: Raymond James & Assoc 100 S Ashley Dr Tampa FL 33602-5360 Fax: 813-221-5576. Business E-Mail: malcolmharriman@raymondjames.com.

HARRIMAN, RICHARD LEE, performing arts administrator, educator; b. Independence, Mo., Sept. 10, 1932; s. Walter S. and M. Eloise (Faulkner) H.; AB, William Jewell Coll., 1953, LittD (hon.), 1983. MA, Stanford U., 1959. Instr., asst. prof. English U. Dubuque, Iowa, 1960-62; asst. prof. English, William Jewell Coll., Liberty, Mo., 1962, acting head English dept., 1965-69, dir. fine arts program, 1965—, asso. prof., 1966—. Treas. Kansas City Arts Council, 1980, sec., 1981; sec. Kansas City Am. Arts Festival, 1988-89. Served with, AUS, 1953-55. Woodrow Wilson fellow, 1957. Mem. MLA, AAUP, Internatl. Soc. of Performing Arts, Shakespeare Assn. Am., Assn. Performing Arts Presenters (nat. exec. bd. 1975-78), Lambda Chi Alpha, Sigma Tau Delta, Alpha Psi Omega. Methodist. Home: 1043 E Highway H Apt 3 Liberty MO 64068-4303

HARRINGER, OLAF CARL, architect, museum consultant; b. Hamburg, Germany, Apr. 29, 1919; came to U.S., 1927; s. Henry Theodore and Anke (Berger) H.; m. Helen Ehrat Hedges, Dec. 20, 1975; children— Carla, Brita, Eric. Student, Evanston Acad. Fine Arts, The New Bauhaus, 1937-38, Ill. Inst. Tech., 1942-45. Designer Raymond Loewy Assos., Chgo., 1946-49, H. Allan Majestic Assos., Chgo., 1949-51, Dickens, Inc., Chgo., 1951-52, Olaf Harringer and Assos. (architects/designers), Chgo., 1952-62; account exec. several exhibit

firms Chgo., 1962-68; dir. exhibits Mus. Sci. and Industry, Chgo., 1957-60, 68-80; prin. Olaf Harringer Assos., Chgo., 1981-95. Mem. AIA (emeritus). Home: 3650 N 36th Ave # Villa5 Hollywood FL 33021-2543 E-mail: hharringer@aol.com.

HARRINGTON, ANNE WILSON, medical librarian; b. Phila., June 18, 1926; d. Edgar Myers and Jean Gould (DeHaven) Wilson; m. James Paul Harrington, June 11, 1948; children: Barbara Gould Harrington Murphy, Ian Edgar, Eric Bradley. BA, U. Pa., Phila., 1948; MS in Libr. Sci., Villanova U., 1977. Clk. Princeton U., 1948-51; CEO, ptnr. Teesdale Co., West Chester, Pa., 1954—; libr. asst. Franklin Inst., Phila., 1974-76; med. staff libr. The Chester County Hosp., West Chester, 1977-99. Mem., treas., chmn. sub-com. Consortium Health Info., Chester, 1977-99. Trustee, sec., com. chmn. Wilmington (Del.) Friends Sch., 1963—72, 1989; bd. dirs., subcom. chmn. cmty. bd. Kendal Corp. CCRC, Kennett Square, Pa., 1973—98; treas. com. on edn. Phila. Yearly Meeting Soc. Friends, 1980—91; mem., rep. Friends Coun. on Edn., Phila., 1991—96; overseer Quaker Info. Ctr., Phila., 1992—96, Phila. Yearly Meeting Soc. Friends, libr. svcs. group, 1999—, publ. working group, 2000—. Mem. Acad. Health Info. Profls. (sr.), Phila. Area Med. Library Assn., Lake Paupac Club (chmn. environ. com., bd. dirs. 1990-96), Friends Med. Soc. Democrat. Avocations: music, reading, walking, sailing, tennis. Home: 234 Crosslands Dr Kennett Square PA 19348

HARRINGTON, ANTHONY ROSS, radio announcer, educator; b. Sanford, N.C., Feb. 18, 1958; s. Refus Roy and Pauline (Kelly) H. Diploma, Cen. Carolina Tech. Coll., 1977; AGE, Cen. Carolina C.C., 1983; BS summa cum laude, Campbell U., 1985, MEd, 1988, EdS, 1993; EdD, N.C. State U., 1995-2000. Cert. tchr., N.C.; lic. FCC radiotelephone operator. News announcer Sandhills Community Broadcasters, Southern Pines, N.C., 1977-78; announcer, engr. Harnett Broadcast, Inc., Lillington, N.C., 1978-88; bus driver Harnett County Schs., Lillington, 1974-76, instr. social studies, 1985—; mgr. radio sta., instr. radio-TV, mem. transfer adv. bd. Ctrl. Carolina C.C., 1988-99, lead history instr., 1999—, chmn. dept. pub. svcs., 2000. Campus rep. Ctrl. Carolina C.C. Found., 2002—. Mem. Cen. Carolina C.C. Tri-County English Alliance, 1989—; support N.C. Dems., Raleigh, 1986—; pres. Campbell U. Friends of Libr., 2003—. Pres.'s scholar Campbell U., 1983-85, Coates-Rodgers History scholar Campbell U., 1983-85. Mem. ASCD, NEA, Nat. Assn. Secondary Sch. Prins., N.C. Assn. Educators, N.C. C.C. Faculty Assn., N.C. Assn. Historians, N.C. Distance Learning Assn., N.C. Assn. Broadcasters, Nat. Coun. Social Studies, Century Club (N.C.), Campbell U. Century Club, Masons (chaplain 1983, jr. steward 1984, sr. steward 1990, sec. 1991-97), Ctrl. Carolina C.C. Century Club, Profl. Educators of N.C., Masons, Shriners. Presbyterian. Avocations: photography, singing popular and religious music. Home: 4224 Mount Pisgah Church Rd Broadway NC 27505-8506 Office: Ctrl Carolina CC 1105 Kelly Dr Sanford NC 27330-9059

HARRINGTON, ANTHONY STEPHEN, lawyer, diplomat; b. Taylorsville, N.C., Mar. 9, 1941; s. Atwell Lee and Louise (Chapman) H.; m. Hope Reynolds, Sept. 25, 1971; children: Adam Reynolds, Michael Addison. AB, U. N.C., 1963; LLB, Duke U., 1966. Bar: N.C. 1966, D.C. 1968, U.S. Supreme Ct. 1970. Asst. dean Duke Law Sch., Durham, N.C., 1966-68; assoc. Hogan & Hartson, Washington, 1968-73, ptnr., 1974-99; U.S. amb. to Brazil Am. Embassy Brasilia, 2000-01; pres. Stonebridge Internat. LCC, 2001—. Bd. dirs. Ovation, Inc., Ctr. for Democracy, SouthernNet Inc., Southeastern Metal Products, Rosemount Ctr., PRE Solutions Inc., Kenan Inst. Pvt. Enterprise; co-chair Nat. Alliance to End Homelessness; vice-chmn. Pres. Fgn. Intelligence Adv. Bd., 1993-99; mem. Commn. on Roles and Capabilities of Intelligence Cmty., 1995; chmn. Pres.'s Intelligence Oversight Bd., 1994-99. Gen. Counsel Dem. Nat. Com., Washington, 1981-85. Episcopal. Club: Met. Avocations: politics, reading, gardening, tennis. Home: Ratcliffe Manor 7768 Ratcliffe Manor Ln Easton MD 21601-7432 also: 701 Pennsylvania Ave NW Washington DC 20004-2608 Office: Stonebridge Internat 555 13th St NW Washington DC 20004-1109

HARRINGTON, BETTY BYRD, entrepreneur; b. Longview, Tex., July 11, 1936; d. William Henry Byrd and Minnie Lee Tidwell; 1 child, Randy Lee Harrington. AA, Cedar Valley DCCCD, Dallas, 1988. Actress, model, entertainer Kathy King Entertainment Agy., DeSoto, Tex., 1956—; owner Gateway to Success/Career Devel. & Outplacement Svc., DeSoto, Tex., 1981—, Resume Writing, Career Counseling & Outplacement Svc., DeSoto, 1987—. Author: The Dallas Dazzler, Job Search and Interview Techniques, (poetry) She Has Been Faithful, 1996, Pity the Children, 1996, My Dad, A Firm But Gentle Soul, 1999. Mem.: AGVA, SAG, AFTRA, Lions, Order of Eastern Star (past matron). Republican. Baptist. Home and Office: 1338 E Parkerville Rd Desoto TX 75115-6421 E-mail: resumewriting@aol.com.

HARRINGTON, BRUCE MICHAEL, lawyer, investor; b. Houston, Mar. 12, 1933; s. George Haymond Harrington and Doris (Gladden) Maginnis; m. Anne Griffith Lawhon, Feb. 15, 1958; children: Julia Griffith, Martha Gladden, Susan McIver BA, U. Tex., 1960, JD with honors, 1961. Bar: Tex. 1961, U.S. Dist. Ct. (so. dist.) Tex. 1962, U.S. Ct. Appeals (5th cir.) 1962, U.S. Supreme Ct. 1973. Assoc. Andrews & Kurth and predecessor firm, Houston, 1961-73, ptnr., 1973-84. Dir. Offenhauser Co., Houston, Allied Metals, Inc., Houston Trustee St. John's Sch., Houston, 1981-92, chmn. bd., CEO, 1986-92; chmn. bd. Covenant House, Tex., 1991-95; trustee St. Luke's Episcopal Hosp., Tex. Med. Ctr., Houston, 1983-86; bd. dirs. YMCA Bd. Mgmt., Am. Cancer Soc., 1992-94, Ctr. for Hearing and Speech, 1993, chmn. bd., 1995-98; vice chmn. Gateway Found., 1993-95; mem. adv. com. Assn. Governing Bds. of Colls. and Univs. Mem. ABA, Nat. Assn. Ind. Schs. (chmn. trustee com.), Ind. Schs. Assn. S.W. (chmn. trustee com., bd. exec. com.), Tex. Bar Assn., Houston Bar Assn., The Mil. and Hosp. Order of St. Lazarus (chancellor), The Venerable Order of St. John (U.K.), The Order of Saints Maurice and Lazarus (Savoy), Houston Country Club, Petroleum Club, Houston Club, Phi Delta Phi, Order of Coif. Republican. Episcopalian. Home: 3608 Overbrook Ln Houston TX 77027-4128

HARRINGTON, CAROL A. lawyer; b. Geneva, Ill., Feb. 13, 1953; d. Eugene P. and M. Ruth (Bowersox) Kloubec; m. Warren J. Harrington, Aug. 19, 1972; children: Jennifer Ruth, Carrie Anne. BS summa cum laude, U. Ill., 1974, JD magna cum laude, 1977. Bar: Ill. 1977, U.S. Dist. Ct. (no. dist.) Ill. 1977, U.S. Tax Ct. 1979. Assoc. Winston & Strawn, Chgo., 1977-84, ptnr., 1984-88, McDermott, Will & Emery, 1988—. Speaker in field. Co-author: Generation-Skipping Tax, 1996, Generation-Skipping Transfer Tax, Warren, Gorham & Lamont, 2000. Fellow Am. Coll. Trusts and Estate Coun. (bd. regents 1999—); mem. ABA (chmn. B-1 generation skipping transfer com. 1987-92, coun. real property, probate and trust law sect. 1992-98), Ill. State Bar Assn., Chgo. Bar Assn. Chgo. Estate Planning Coun. Office: McDermott Will & Emery 227 W Monroe St Ste 3100 Chicago IL 60606-5096

HARRINGTON, CHARLENE ANN, sociology and health policy educator; b. Concordia, Kans., Sept. 28, 1941; d. Lyman K. and Maxine (Boucher) Harrington; m. Ben Yerger, Aug. 28, 1976. BSN, U. Kans., Kansas City, 1963; MA in Cmty. Health, U. Wash., 1968; PhD in Sociology and Higher Edn., U. Calif., Berkeley, 1975. Staff nurse Good Samaritan Hosp., Portland, Oreg., 1963-64; sch. nurse U.S. Army Dependent Schs., Heilbronn, Germany, 1964-65; pub. health nurse Seattle King County and Group Health, Seattle, 1966-68; asst. prof., nursing program U. Kans., Kansas City, 1968-70; dep. dir., spl. asst. Calif. State Dept. Health, Sacramento, 1975-78; dir. Golden Empire Health Planning Agy., Sacramento, 1978-80; sr. rschr. Inst. for Health and Aging, U. Calif., San Francisco, 1980-83, asst. prof. Sch. Nursing, 1983-85, assoc. prof. dept. social and behavioral scis. Sch. Nursing, 1985-89, prof., vice chair dept. social and behavioral scis., 1989-93; chair dept. social and behavioral scis. U. Calif., San Francisco, 1994-96, prof. social and behavioral scis., 1997—. Assoc. dir. Inst. for Health and Aging, U. Calif., San Francisco, 1981-94; cons. Nat. Coalition for Nursing Home Reform, Washington, 1987—; com. on regulation nursing homes Inst. Medicine, 1984-86, com. on nursing staff, 1994-96. Author: Health Policy and Nursing, 3d edit., 2001; contbr. over 125 chpts. to books, articles to profl. jours. Fellow Am. Acad. Nursing (chair commn. on health policy 1991-93); mem. ANA, APHA, Nursing Econs. (bd. dirs. 1985-93), Inst. Medicine (com. nurse staffing 1995-96, roundtable of quality 1997-98, com. on quality in long-term care 1997—), Am. Sociol. Assn. (sect. coun. mem. 1992-94), Elected Inst. of Medicine (com. on longterm care quality 1998-2001, round table on quality 1997-98), Sigma Theta Tau. Democrat. Avocation: gardening. Office: U Calif Sch Nursing 3333 California St San Francisco CA 94143-0001

HARRINGTON, DONALD FRANCIS, lawyer; b. Cleve., June 24, 1929; s. Willis James and Dorothy Virginia (Hoose) H.; m. Nancy F. Overton, July 26, 1956; 1 child, Donald Francis Jr. BBA, Western Res. U., 1955; LLB, Cleve. State U., 1961, LLM, 1964, JD, 1968. Bar: Fla. 1961, Ohio 1963. Gen. counsel spl. disability fund State of Fla., Tallahassee, 1965-66; indsl. claims judge Dade County, State of Fla., Miami, 1966-70; ptnr. Henry, Stroemer & Harrington, Miami, 1970-76; pvt. practice Coral Gables, Fla., 1976—; sr. trial atty. Fireman's Fund Ins. Co., Miami, 1987-92. With U.S. Army, 1951-53. Mem. VFW, Am. Legion, Fla. Bar Assn. (bd. cert.), Emerald Soc. (past pres.), Elks Club (exalted ruler). Democrat. Roman Catholic.

HARRINGTON, DONALD JAMES, university president; b. Bklyn., Oct. 2, 1945; s. John Joseph and Ruth Mary (Cummings) H. BA, Mary Immaculate Sem., Northampton, Pa., 1969, MDiv, 1972, ThM, 1973; LLD (hon.), St. John's U., 1985; postgrad., U. Toronto, 1980-82; PhD (hon.), Fu Jen U., Taipei, Taiwan, 1994; DHum (hon.), Am. U. Rome, 1994, Dowling Coll., 1996; D of Pedagogy (hon.), St. Thomas Aquinas Coll., Sparkhill, N.Y.; STD (hon.), Niagara U., 2000. Ordained priest Roman Catholic Ch., 1973. Instr. Niagara U., Niagara University, N.Y., 1973-80, dir. student activities, 1974-77, dean student activities, 1977-80, exec. v.p., 1981-84, pres., 1984-89, St. John's U., Jamaica, N.Y., 1989—. Bd. dirs. The Bear Stearns Cos., Inc., 1993—, Commn. Ind. Colls. and Univs., Albany, N.Y., 1987-89; mem. bd. Cath. edn. Diocese of Buffalo, 1987-89. Trustee Niagara U., 1984—, St. John's U., 1986—, DePaul U., 1988-91, Sem. Immaculate Conception, 1990-97, Res. Group, 1988—, Sisters Hosp., Buffalo, 1988-89; chair adv. com. Love Canal Land Use, 1988-89; bd. dirs., mem. exec. com. Commn. Ind. Colls. and Univs., 1991—; chair Big East Athletic Conf., 1994-97; mem. sanctity of life com. Diocese of Bklyn., 1990-96; chair Western N.Y. Consortium for Higher Edn., 1988-89, mem. exec. com., 1985-89; mem. adv. bd. New Yorkers Caring for N.Y.-N.Y. Med. Coll., 1998—; mem. Commr.'s Coun. on Higher Edn., 1998—. Recipient Pro Ecclesia et Pontifice, Pope John Paul II, 1989. Mem. Assn. Cath. Colls. and Univs. (bd. dirs. 1997—). Office: St John's U Office of Pres 800 Utopia Pkway, Newman Hall Rm 318 Jamaica NY 11439-0001

HARRINGTON, ELLIS JACKSON, JR., lawyer; b. Barnesville, Ga., Aug. 10, 1944; s. Ellis Jackson Sr. and Inez (Dixon) H.; m. Elizabeth Gray, Dec. 23, 1965; children: Lisa Jackson, Sara Christine. AB, U. N.C., 1966, JD, 1969. Bar: N.C. 1969, U.S. Ct. Mil. Appeals 1970, U.S. Dist. Ct. (mid. dist.) N.C. 1976, Asst. pub. defender 18th Jud. Dist. of N.C., Greensboro, 1973-75; ptnr. Booth, Fish, Simpson & Harrison, Greensboro, 1975-79, Booth, Harrington Johns & Campbell, Greensboro, 1979-95, Booth, Harrington Johns & Toman, L.L.P., Greensboro, 1995—2002, Booth Harrington & Johns LLP, Greensboro, 2002—. Bd. dirs. Child Care Ministries, Greensboro, 1980-86, Greensboro Commn. of Status of Women, 1992-97. Recipient Cert. of Appreciation, ARC, 1987. Mem. ABA, Am. Bd. Trial Advocates, N.C. Bar Assn., Assn. Trial Lawyers Am., 18th Jud. Dist. Bar Assn. (pres. 1986-87), N.C. Acad. Trial Lawyers, Phi Beta Kappa, Phi Delta Phi. Democrat. Presbyterian. Avocations: travel, fishing, photography. Office: Booth Harrington & Johns LLP 239 N Edgeworth St Greensboro NC 27401-2217

HARRINGTON, GARY BURNES, retired controller; b. Parkville, Mo., Nov. 8, 1934; s. George Burnes and Ethel Mae (Burge) H.; m. Doris Ann Scott, Oct. 28, 1953; children: Gary Burnes Jr., Sherri Ann, Michael Scott, John Patrick, Heather May. Student, Oklahoma City U., 1962-67. Acctg. supr. CIT Fin. Svcs., Oklahoma City, 1952-76; sr. auditor CIT Fin. Corp., N.Y.C., 1976-83, sr. supervising auditor Livingston, N.J., 1983-86; audit officer Mfrs. Hanover Corp., N.Y.C. and Atlanta, 1986-88, The CIT Group/Sales Fin., Livingston and Oklahoma City, 1988-89; asst. contr. The CIT Group/Sales Financing, Livingston and Oklahoma City, 1989-95, ret., 1995. Various positions from Webelo leader to dist. commr. Boy Scouts Am., Oklahoma City and Norman, Okla., 1967—. Staff sgt. USAF, 1947-48, USAFR. Mem. Inst. Internal Auditors (1st v.p. 1979-80, pres. 1980-81, bd. chmn. 1981-82, Dist. Svc. award 1982), Am. Legion. Republican. Baptist. Avocations: woodworking, fishing, camping, hunting. Home: 13609 Calistoga Dr Oklahoma City OK 73170-5111

HARRINGTON, GEORGE FRED, aviation consultant; b. Killingly, Conn., July 29, 1923; s. George Whitman and Beatrice Evelyn (Sheldon) H.; m. Ruth Lydia Saarinen, June 7, 1947; children: Joanne Ruth, George Lauri, Julie Ann. BS, U.S. Mil. Acad., 1947; MBA, Harvard U., 1957; grad., Armed Forces Staff Coll., 1961, Indsl. Coll. of Armed Forces, 1967. Commd. 2d lt. USAF, 1947, advanced through grades to col., 1968, ret., 1977; mgr. market devel. Beech Aircraft, Washington, 1978-81, gen. mgr. internat. div. Wichita, 1981-82, v.p., 1982-85; cons. Gen. Aviation, Arlington, Va., 1986—. Cons. in field. Pres. Collingwood Libr. & Mus. on Americanism, Mt. Vernon, Va.; overseer Plimoth (Mass.) Plantation. Decorated D.S.M., Legion of Merit with oak leaf cluster. Mem. Air Force Assn., Ret. Officers Assn., Harvard Bus. Sch. Club of Washington (pres. 1988-89), Masons, Shriners, Nat. Sojourners (past nat. pres.). Republican. Methodist. Avocations: gardening, music. Home and Office: 1300 Crystal Dr # 304 Arlington VA 22202-3234

HARRINGTON, GERARD, III, marketing and communications executive, business consultant; b. N.Y.C., Nov. 13, 1956; s. Gerard Jr. and Sue Leah (Sayer) Harrington Salomon; m. Kristen Overman; children: David Gerard, Esther Elise. BS, Northwestern U., 1978; postgrad., Westbrook U., 2002—. News writer Ind. TV News Assn., N.Y.C., 1978—79, mng. editor, 1979—80; news writer, producer Cable News Network, Atlanta, 1980—83, exec. prodr., 1983—84; news dir. Sta. WTZA-TV (now Regional News Network), Kingston, NY, 1984—86; contbg. editor Crain's N.Y. Bus., N.Y.C., 1986—88; bus. reporter Poughkeepsie (N.Y.) Jour., 1987—88; pres., CEO Harrington Assocs. Inc., Kingston, 1988—2001, 2003—; copy editor Daily Freeman, Kingston, 1999—2001; account dir. John Mallen Comms. Inc., Kingston, 2001—02; dir. mktg., pub. relations Humanity's Team U.S., Ashland, Oreg., 2003—. Mem. adv. coun. Krissler Bus. Inst., 1990-92; adj. prof. communications Marist Coll.; instr. mktg. communications Inst. Internat. Bus., SUNY-New Paltz; mng. editor The Trends Jour., 1992-98; founder Hudson Valley Health, Fitness & Nutrition Expo, N.Y., 1997. Co-editor: Problems in Law of Mass Communications, 1978; writer TV documentary A Finite World, 1982 (Best TV program award Populaton Action Coun. 1982); producer TV documentary Parricide: The Saddest Murder, 1983; developer Hudson ValleyOpoly bd. game, 1991; co-editor, contbr. Trends 2000, 1997; editor, cons. Coaching Tips for Job Seekers: Keys and Secrets for Success, 2003; contbr. articles to profl. jours. Bd. dirs. Ulster Performing Arts Ctr., Kingston, 1988-98, pres. bd. dirs., 1994-96; bd. dirs. Ulster County Arts Coun., 1996—, v.p., 1999—. Recipient award for outstanding prodn. of major breaking news event CNN, 1983, Outstanding News Programming award N.Y. State Broadcasters Assn., 1986, Gold Eclat awards for pub. rels. excellence Hudson Valley Area Mktg. Assn., 1991, 93, 95. Mem. Am. Mktg. Assn., Pub. Rels. Soc. Am., Internat. Assn. Bus. Communicators, Soc. Profl. Journalists, Profl. Communicators Hudson Valley, Regional Plan Assn., Hudson Valley Direct Mktg. Assn. Avocations: writing, newspaper and coin collecting, tennis, bicycling, swimming. Home: 57 Fairmont Ave Kingston NY 12401-5221 E-mail: gerryharrington@mindspring.com.

HARRINGTON, HERBERT H. accountant; b. Meadville, Pa., Sept. 19, 1946; s. Herbert H. and Sara R. (Rogers) H. BA, Kent State U., 1969; postgrad., Memphis State U., 1975; MS in Criminal Justice, Dyersburg State U., 1977. CPA, Tenn. Transp. dir. West Tenn. Easter Seal Soc., 1972-75; compt. So. Trucking, Inc., 1976-77; acct. Cen. So., Inc., 1978-79; compt. Wonder div. ITT Baking Corp., 1980-84; contr. N. Fla. Transport, 1985-86; fin. con. Computa-Tax, Inc., 1986—; pres. H&H Enterprises, Inc., Covington, 1989—; CEO Tenco, Inc., Burlison, Tenn., 1995—. Cons. computer and acctg. software, Covington, 1973—. Author 3 textbooks on acctg. procedures and practice. Served with USN, 1963-81. Mem. Covington C. of C. Lodges: Lions, Good Fellows, Optimists, Rotary. Episcopalian. Home and Office: PO Box O Munford TN 38058-1914

HARRINGTON, JAMES TIMOTHY, lawyer; b. Chgo., Sept. 4, 1942; s. John Paul and Margaret Rita (Cunneen) H.; m. Roseanne Strupeck, Sept. 4, 1965; children: James Timothy, Roseanne, Maris Zajdela. BA, U. Notre Dame, 1964, JD, 1967. Bar: Ill. 1967, Ind. 1968, U.S. Dist. Ct. (no. dist.) Ill. 1967, U.S. Dist. Ct. (no. and so. dists.) Ind. 1968, U.S. Ct. Appeals (7th cir.) 1969, U.S. Ct. Appeals (4th cir.) 1977, U.S. Ct. Appeals (8th cir.) 1979, U.S. Ct. Appeals (3d cir.) 1981, U.S. Supreme Ct. 1979, U.S. Ct. Appeals (D.C. cir.) 1993. Law clk. U.S. Dist. Ct. (no. dist.) Ind., 1967-69; assoc. Rooks, Pitts & Poust, Chgo., 1969-75, ptnr., 1976-87, Ross & Hardies, Chgo., 1987—2003, McGuiness, Woods, Ross & Hardies LLP, 2003—. Lectr. environ. law, fed. procedures, adminstrv. law, 1960—. Vice chmn. Mid Am. Legal Found.; chmn., bd. dirs. Ill. Safety Coun. Fellow Am. Bar Found.; mem. Ill. Bar Assn., Ind. Bar Assn., Chgo. Bar Assn. (environ. law com., real estate com.), Indsl. Water Waste and Sewer Group (past chmn.), Air and Waste Mgmt. Assn. (bd. dirs. Lake Mich. sect.), Assn. Environ. Law Inst., Lawyers Club Chgo., Exec. Club Chgo., Union League Club Chgo. Roman Catholic. Home: 746 Foxdale Ave Winnetka IL 60093-1908 Office: Ross & Hardies 150 N Michigan Ave Ste 2500 Chicago IL 60601-7567 E-mail: jharrington@mcguinewoods.com.

HARRINGTON, JEAN PATRICE, college president; b. Denver; d. James Michael and Katherine Ann (Holl) H. BA, Coll. Mt. St. Joseph, 1953; MA, Creighton U., 1958; PhD, U. Colo., 1967; LHD (hon.), Xavier U., 1983, Ohio Dominican Coll., 1988; LLD (hon.), St. Thomas Inst., Cin., 1985, Coll. Mt. St. Joseph, 1988, Hebrew Union Coll., 1990; D. Tech. Studies (hon.), Cin. Tech., 1988; LLD (hon.), No. Ky. U., 1996, U. Dayton, 1999. Joined Sisters of Charity of Cin., 1940; prin. St. Rose of Lima, Denver, 1953-56; tchr. Cathedral H.S., Denver, 1956-58, prin., 1958-68; dir. instl. rsch. Coll. Mt. St. Joseph, Cin., 1968-69, pres., 1977-87; exec. dir. Cin. Youth Collaborative, 1988-90; interim pres. Cin. State Coll., 1997. Bd. dirs. Penrose Hosp., Colorado Springs, 1976-86, St. Mary Corwin Hosp., Pueblo, Colo., 1972-80, Cin. Bicentennial Commn., 1982-89, Samaritan Health Resources, Inc., 1983-96, St. Rita Sch. for Deaf, 1983-86, United Appeal Cabinet, 1983, Cin. Cmty. Chest, 1988-95, Dan Beard coun. Boy Scouts Am., 1988-91; trustee Good Samaritan Hosp. and Health Ctr., Dayton, Ohio, 1978-80, 89-97, bd. dirs., 1989-96; trustee Miami U., 1989-97, chmn. 1994-97; bd. dirs. Coll. of Mt. St. Joseph, 1995-2002; trustee U. Dayton, 1999-2002. Recipient Disting. Svc. citation NCCJ, 1987, Women Helping Women award Soroptimist Internat., 1990, Statesman award Cin. Assn. Execs., 1988, St. Francis award Friars Club, 1994, Daniel Ransahoff Initiative award, 1994, Lincoln award No. Ky. U., 1994, Gt. Living Cincinnatian award C. of C., 1996, Svc. to Edn. award Ohiana Libr. Assn., 1998, Children's Advocate award Beech Acres; named Career Woman of Achievement YWCA, 1981, Disting. Bus. and Profl. Woman of Yr., 1982; inductee Hall of Excellence of Ohio Fedn. of Ind. Colls., 1990, Ohio Women's Hall of Fame, 2000, Pres.' award Children's Def. Fund, 2003. Mem. Nat. Assn. Ind. Colls. and Univs., Assn. Cath. Colls. and Univs. (bd. dirs.), Ohio Found. Ind. Colls., Greater Cin. Consortium Colls. and Univs. (vice chmn. 1980-82), Coun. Ind. Colls. (bd. dirs. 1981-85), Cin. C. of C. (bd. dirs. 1978-84, trustee 1981-85, sec. 1979-85). Roman Catholic. E-mail: jphsc@juno.com.

HARRINGTON, JEFFREY MICHAEL, military officer; b. Mansfield, Ohio, Sept. 26, 1962; s. Paul Owen and Lois Ruth Harrington; m. Susan Marie Pangrass, May 11, 1960; children: Elizabeth, Meghan, Patric. BS, U. of State of N.Y., 1994; MPA, U. Okla., 1995; postgrad., Nova Southeastern U., 1999—. Cert. journeyman legal sec., shorthand legal reporter. Commd. 2d. lt. USMC, advanced through grades to capt., 1980—, adj., 1998—. Adj. prof. Strayer U., Washington, 1996—. Trustee KC, Quantio, 1997-98. Mem. ASCD, Am. Soc. Pub. Adminstrn. (Eastern N.C. chpt. 1996-97), Nat. Assn. Scholars, Am. Statis. Assn., Acad. Polit. Sci., Army-Navy Club, Quantico Sharks Swim Club (pres. 2000-02). Democrat. Roman Catholic. Home: 4515 B Quantico VA 22134 E-mail: ssgt4429@comcast.net.

HARRINGTON, JEREMY THOMAS, priest, publishing executive; b. Lafayette, Ind., Oct. 7, 1932; s. William and Ellen (Cain) H. BA, Duns Scotus Coll., 1955; postgrad., U. Detroit, 1955, Marquette U., 1961; MA, Xavier U., Cin., 1965; MS in Journalism, Northwestern U., 1967; LHD (hon.), St. Bonaventure U., 1999. Ordained priest Roman Cath. Ch., 1959. Joined Order Friars Minor, 1950; tchr. Roger Bacon High Sch., Cin., 1960-64; assoc. editor St. Anthony Messenger, Cin., 1964-66, editor, 1966-81, pub., 1975-81, pub., CEO, 1991—; mem. bd. Franciscan Province Cin., 1969-72, 75-81, chief exec. bd., 1981-90. Author: Your Wedding: Planning Your Own Ceremony, 1974; Editor: Conscience in Today's World, 1970, Jesus: Superstar or Savior?, 1972. Mem. Catholic Press Assn. (pres. 1975-77, dir.), Kappa Tau Alpha. Home: 1615 Vine St Cincinnati OH 45202 Office: St Anthony Messenger 28 W Liberty St Cincinnati OH 45202 E-mail: JeremyH@AmericanCatholic.org. *My success has been made by others. As a priest, as well as an editor and publisher, my challenge is to discover, recognize, encourage and make available to others the talents of authors and artists. To me, that's a parable of life. The more we can discover, appreciate and foster the good qualities and strengths of others, the more "successful" we are. Success in life is realizing how many gifts are made available to us by God and our fellow human beings.*

HARRINGTON, JOHN LEO, former baseball company executive; b. Boston, July 12, 1936; s. John Joseph and Catherine (Quinn) H.; m. Maureen Helen Fitzgibbon, Oct. 3, 1959; children: Debra, Brian, Sean. BS in Bus. Adminstrn., Boston Coll., 1957, MBA, 1966. CPA, Mass. Asst. prof. Boston Coll., 1965-69; treas. Boston Red Sox, 1970-78; sr. v.p. Kaler, Carney Ins. Group, Boston, 1979-80; v.p. JRY Corp., 1981-86, pres., 1987-2002; gen. ptnr. of Boston Red Sox, 1981-2002, CEO; exec. dir., trustee Yawkey Found., Dedham, Mass., 1981—; cons. NASA, Cambridge, 1966-69; bd. dirs. Computer Systems of Am., Boston, 1969-75, Fleet Bank NA, Health and Retirement Properties Trust, 1990-95, N.E. Sports Network, Inc., Hospitality Properties Trust, 1995—. Trustee Dana Farber Cancer Ctr.,-Jimmy Fund, Boston, 1970—, U.S. Little League Baseball Found.; treas. Town of Westwood, Mass., 1979-83; pres., bd. dirs. Boston Coll. Alumni, 1973-77, bd. dir. Nat. Baseball Hall of Fame, 1992—; trustee John F. Kennedy Libr. Found., 1997—. Served to lt. USNR, 1958-65. Recipient Presdl. award Boston Coll., 1976. Mem. AICPAs, Mass. Soc. CPAs, Beta Gamma Sigma. Avocations: sailing, skiing, tennis. Office: 400 Centre St Newton MA 02458-2076

HARRINGTON, JOHN MICHAEL, JR., lawyer; b. Boston, July 5, 1921; s. John Michael and Marie Bernadine (Ratchford) H.; m. Ellen Patricia White, May 12, 1951; children— John Michael III, Marc W., Francis X. B., Ellen M., Matthew J., Patrick W. AB, Harvard U., 1943, LL.B., 1949. Bar: Mass. 1949, U.S. Dist. Ct. (Mass.) 1950, U.S. Ct. Appeals (1st cir.) 1956, U.S. Supreme Ct. 1968. Law clk. Supreme Jud. Ct. Mass., Boston, 1949-50; assoc. Ropes & Gray LLP, Boston, 1950-55, 57-61, ptnr., 1961-93, counsel, 1994—; asst. U.S. atty. Dist. of Mass., Boston, 1955-57. Trustee Winchester Sav. Bank, Mass., 1966-91; mem. Mass. Jud. Conduct Commn., Boston, 1978-81. Trustee Roxbury Latin Sch., Boston, 1962-67, St. Sebastian's Country Day Sch., Needham, Mass., 1973-86; mem. fin. com. Town of Winchester, 1959-62. Served to capt. field arty. U.S. Army, 1943-46, ETO Fellow Am. Coll. Trial Lawyers, Am. Bar Found.; mem. ABA (standing com. on fed. judiciary 1st cir. 1978-84), Boston Bar Assn. Clubs: Union (v.p. 1982-86, pres. 1986-88), Curtis, Harvard (Boston). Democrat. Roman Catholic. Home: 19 Cabot St Winchester MA 01890-3501 Office: Ropes & Gray LLP One International Pl Boston MA 02110-2624

HARRINGTON, JOHN NORRIS, ophthalmic plastic and reconstructive surgeon, educator; b. Dallas, Oct. 1, 1939; s. Marion Thomas and Ruth Evelyn (Norris) H.; m. Elizabeth Hunt, June 20, 1964; children: Thomas Wesley, Clinton Hunt. BA, Tex. A&M U., 1961, BS, 1964; MD, U. Tenn., Memphis, 1966. Diplomate Am. Bd. Ophthalmology. Intern Letterman Gen. Hosp., San Francisco, 1966-67; resident in ophthalmology Scott and White Clinic, Temple, Tex., 1970-73; fellow in ophthalmic plastic and reconstructive surgery U. Calif., San Francisco, 1973-74; plastic and reconstructive surgeon Tex. Ophthal. Plastic, Reconstructive & Orbital Surg. Assoc., Dallas, 1974—. Clin. prof. ophthalmic plastic and reconstructive surgery U. Tex. Southwestern Med. Ctr., Dallas, 1974—, chair faculty svc. bd., 2003; chief staff Mary Shiels Hosp., Dallas, 1986-88; active staff, dir. ophthalmic plastic and reconstructive surgery Baylor U. Med. Ctr., Dallas; active staff dept. oncology Baylor-Sammons Cancer Ctr.; team physician NHL Dallas Stars, NBA Dallas Mavericks. Mem. editl. bd. Ophthalmic Plastic and Reconstructive Surgery Jour.; contbr. chpts. to textbooks, articles to med. jours. Mem. Univ. Park Citizens League, Dallas, 1976-82; pres. Highland Park High Sch. Dads Club, Dallas, 1982-83; sec. bd. deacons Park Cities Bapt. Ch., Dallas, 1981. Maj. M.C., U.S. Army, 1966-70, Vietnam. Decorated Bronze Star. Fellow ACS, Am. Soc. Ophthalmic Plastic and Reconstructive Surgery (sec. 1991-93, v.p. 1994, pres.-elect 1995, pres. 1996, del. to AMA 1995—), Am. Acad. Ophthalmology (bd. counselors 1991-94, Honor award 1989, Sr. Achievement award 2003); mem. AMA (house of dels.

1995—), Tex. Med. Assn., Dallas Acad. Ophthalmology (pres. 1986). Avocations: music, skiing, water sports. Office: 2731 Lemmon Ave E Ste 304 Dallas TX 75204-2866 E-mail: jnhoplsurg@aol.com.

HARRINGTON, JOHN TIMOTHY, retired lawyer; b. Madison, Wis., May 26, 1921; s. Cornelius Louis and Emily (Chisholm) H.; m. Deborah Reynolds, May 23, 1948; children— Elizabeth Chisholm, Samuel Parker, Hannah Quincy, Jane McRae BS, Harvard U., 1942, LL.B., 1948. Bar: Wis. 1949. Assoc. Quarles & Brady and predecessor firms, Milw., 1948-58, ptnr., 1958-91; ret., 1991—. Served to lt. comdr. USNR, 1942-46, PTO Home: 924 E Juneau Ave Milwaukee WI 53202-2748 Office: Quarles & Brady 411 E Wisconsin Ave Ste 2550 Milwaukee WI 53202-4497 E-mail: jtharrington@webtv.net.

HARRINGTON, JOHN TOLAN, medical educator, dean, physician; b. Fall River, Mass., Dec. 30, 1936; s. John J. and Elizabeth C. (Tolan) H.; m. Gertrude Rose Hargraves, Aug. 27, 1960; children: Gertrude, Kathleen, Daniel, Ann, John, Mark, Timothy. BA magna cum laude, Coll. of the Holy Cross, 1958; MD cum laude, Yale U., 1962. Diplomate Am. Bd. Internal Medicine. Intern, resident in internal medicine N.C. Meml. Hosp., Chapel Hill, 1962-65; clin. and rsch. fellow in nephrology Tufts-New Eng. Med. Ctr., Boston, 1965-68; nephrologist, dir. hemodialysis unit New Eng. Med. Ctr., Boston, 1971-81, chief gen. medicine divsn., 1981-86; chmn. dept. medicine Newton (Mass.)-Wellesley Hosp., 1986-94; dean academic affairs Tufts U. Sch. Medicine, Boston, 1994-95, asst. prof. medicine, 1971-75, assoc. prof. medicine, 1975-79, prof. medicine, 1979—, dean ad interim, 1995-96, dean, 1996—2002, dean emeritus, 2002—. Author: Acid-Base, 1982; editor (monthly jour. feature) Nephrology Forum in Kidney Internat., 1979—; contbr. articles to profl. jours. Pres. Hummocks Cmty. Orgn., Portsmouth, RI, 1978—80, Nat. Kidney Found., Mass., 1988. Master ACP (gov. Mass. chpt. 1989-93); fellow Royal Irish Coll. Physicians (hon.); mem. Internat. Soc. Nephrology, Am. Soc. Nephrology, Holy Name Soc. Democrat. Roman Catholic. Avocations: sailing, swimming, irish poetry and drama, baseball.

HARRINGTON, JOHN VINCENT, retired communications company executive, engineer, educator; b. N.Y.C., May 9, 1919; s. John Joseph and Dorothy (Neisel) H.; m. Frances Cullinane, Jan. 23, 1943; children: John F., Nancy Harrington Higgins, Jeffrey, Richard, Brian. B.E.E., Cooper Union, 1940; M.E.E., Poly. Inst. Bklyn., 1948; Sc.D., Mass. Inst. Tech., 1957. Research engr. U.S. Air Force Cambridge Research Lab., Mass., 1946-51; leader data transmission group Lincoln Lab., M.I.T., Cambridge, 1951-56, asso. div. head aircraft control and warning, 1956-58, head radio physics div., 1958-63; prof. aeros., astronautics and elec. engring., 1st dir. Center Space Research, M.I.T., 1963-73; v.p. research and engring. Communications Satellite Corp., Washington, 1973-79; sr. v.p. research and devel., dir. COMSAT Labs., Clarksburg, Md., 1979-84. Dir. Epsco, Inc., 1964-72, Shawmut County Bank, Cambridge, 1964-73, COMSAT Gen. Telesystems, Inc., Washington, 1973-81, Environ. Research and Tech., Inc., Concord, Mass., 1981-82; mem. Space Applications Bd., NRC, 1975-81 Contbr. articles to profl. jours. Lt. USNR, 1942-46. Recipient Exceptional Civilian Service medal U.S. Air Force, 1952, Exceptional Profl. Achievement citation Cooper Union, 1965, Gano Dunn award Cooper Union, 1983. Fellow IEEE, AAAS, AIAA. Home: 3730 Cadbury Cir # C721 Venice FL 34293-2207

HARRINGTON, JOSEPH FRANCIS, educational company executive, history educator; b. Boston, Oct. 24, 1938; s. Joseph Francis and Mary Virginia (Lynch) H.; m. Brenda Marie Crowley, Sept. 3, 1966; children: Megan Marie, Christopher Joseph John. BS, Boston Coll., 1960; MA, Georgetown U., 1963, PhD, 1971. Instr. Framingham (Mass.) State Coll., 1966-68, asst. prof., 1968-70, assoc. prof., 1970-72, prof., 1972—2003, bd. chmn. dept. history, 1972—82; pres. Learning, Inc., Stoughton, 1979—2003, also bd. dirs.; pres. J.C. Ednl. Enterprises, 2003—, Treas. The East European Rsch. Ctr., 1990—. Author: Masters of War, Makers of Peace, 1985, Powers, Pawns and Parleys, 1978, Tweaking the Nose of the Russians: American-Romanian Relations, 1940-90; editorial bd. dirs. New England Jour. of History, 1991—, editor, 1995—; editor: The Creative Child and Adult Quarterly, 1991-94; contbr. articles to profl. jours. Mem. Stoughton, Mass. Sch. Com., 1971-77, 82-87, 91-94. With U.S. Army, 1962-65. Tchg. fellow Georgetown U., Washington, 1960-62, 65-66, hon. fellow Kennedy Presdl. Libr., 1986-93. Mem. Mass. Assn. for Advancement of Individual Potential (bd. dirs., pres. 1987-89, 90-92, v.p. for R&D 1989), Nat. Assn. Creative Children and Adults (bd. dirs. 1985-92, editor The Creative Child and Adult Quar. 1991-93), New Eng. Slavic Assn. (v.p. 1990-91, treas. 1991-98), Soc. for Romanian Studies (pres. 1994-97, bd. dirs. 1997-2000), Kennedy Libr. Acad. Adv. Coun. Roman Catholic. Avocations: reading, racquetball. Home: 119 Holmes Ave Stoughton MA 02072-1926 Office: Framingham State Coll State St Framingham MA 01701

HARRINGTON, KATHLEEN M. federal agency administrator; BA, Colgate U.; MA in Psychology, The Cath. U. Am. Asst. adminstr. pub. affairs Fed. Aviation Adminstrn.; asst. sec. labor congrl. and intergovtl. affairs Sec. of Labor Elizabeth Dole; v.p. govt. rels. Aetna, Inc.; sr. v.p. pub. affairs and advocacy Health Ins. Assn. Am.; asst. sec. pub. affairs U.S. Dept. Labor, Washington. Office: US Dept Labor 200 Constitution Ave NW Washington DC 20210

HARRINGTON, KAY LORRAINE, executive secretary; b. Stockton, Calif., Jan. 27, 1947; d. Hal Hubert Van Da Griff, Ellen Louise (Carlson) Van Da Griff; m. Fredric T. Harrington, Aug. 23, 1987; children: Shannon Eckels, Christopher Eckels, Jennifer Eckels, Derek Eckels. BA in English, Regis Coll., 2003. Adminstrv. asst. Babson Coll., Wellesley, Mass., Regis Coll., Weston, Mass. Recipient Grand prize, Poetry Guild, 1998, Editor's Choice award for Outstanding Achievement in Poetry, Nat. Libr. Poetry, 1998, Pres.'s award for Lit. Excellence, Iliad Press, 2002. Home: 5 Glen Rd Wayland MA 01778

HARRINGTON, LAMAR, curator, museum director; b. Guthrie Center, Iowa, Nov. 2, 1917; d. Arthur Sylvester and Anna Mary (Landkamer) Hannes; m. Stanley John Harrington, Jan. 1, 1938 (div. Jan. 1972); 1 child, Linda Harrington Chace. Student, Cornish Sch. Fine Arts, Seattle, 1945-50; BA in History of Art, U. Wash., 1979. Staff Henry Art Gallery, U. Wash., Seattle, 1957-75, assoc. dir., 1969-75; curator, rsch. assoc. Archives Northwest Art, U. Wash. Libr., 1975-77; dir., chief curator Bellevue Art Mus., Wash., 1983-90; cons. in arts, 1977—; founding curator art Univ. Ho., Seattle, 1997—2002. Mem. panel visual arts divsn. NEA, 1976—78; juror fellowship We. States Arts Fedn., 1989, Flintridge Found., Pasadena, 2001; pres. We. Assn. Art Mus., 1973—75; trustee Pacific NW Arts Ctr., 1971—74; exec. com. Living Treasures video series NW Designer-Craftsmen, 1996—99, Pacific NW Arts Coun. of Seattle Art Mus., 1976, mem. steering com. Photography Coun., 1977—78; participant 1st Symposium on Scholarship and Lang. Nat. Endowments for Humanities and Arts, 1981; mem. adv. com. NW Oral History Project Archives Am. Art, 1981; mem. adv. coun. Pilchuck Glass Sch., 1992—95, trustee, chmn. archives, 1981—87; v.p. Pottery Northwest, 1977—78; trustee, chmn. archives Internat. Coun., 1987—92; trustee Seattle bd. Santa Fe Chamber Music Festival, 1981—87, adv. bd. Santa Fe, 1988—89; trustee Puget Sound Chamber Music Soc., 1987—88; lectr. in field; organizer exhbns.; leader seminars; mem. art juries; appearances KCTS-TV, 1963—73, founder Archives of NW Art U. Wash., 1969; curator 3d Wyo. Biennial Exhbn., 1988 -89; curator James W. Washington Jr.: The Spirit in the Stone Bellevue Art Mus., 1989, resident curator, mgr. Frank Lloyd Wright: In the Realm of Ideas, 1989—90; curator art collection, quar. exhbns. NW art Univ. House, Wallingford, 1995—2002; curator Between Night and Morning Work of Guy Anderson, 1990; curator Eternal Laughter: A Sixty-Yr. Retrospective of George Tsutakawa Bellevue Art Mus., 1990; founder changing exhbn. program Univ. House U. Wash., Wallingford, 1997, curator changing exhbn. program U. House, 1997—2002, founder experiments in art and tech. Seattle chpt. Henry Art Gallery, 1968. Author: Ceramics in the Pacific Northwest: A History, 1979, Washington Craft Forms: an Historical Perspective, 1981. Named LaMar Harrington Endowment, Bellevue Art Mus., 1991; recipient Friends of Crafts award, Seattle, 1972, Woman of Achievement award, Women in Comm., 1974, Gov. Writer's award, 1980, Arts Svc. award, King County Arts Commn., 1987, Arts award, Bellevue Art Commn., 1989, Cmty. Svc. award, Am. Inst. Interior Designers, 1990, Pyramid award, Corp. Coun. Arts, 1990. Fellow: Am. Crafts Coun. (hon.); mem.: AIA (hon.), Japan-Am. Soc. Wash. (trustee 1986—88), Allied Arts Seattle (trustee 1962—81), Pacific NW Arts and Crafts Assn. (pres. 1957—59), U. Wash. Retirement Assn. (exec. com. 1992—94). Home: 4400 Stone Way N Apt 319 Seattle WA 98103-7492

HARRINGTON, LORI LYNN, social services administrator; b. Jackson, Mich., May 31, 1970; d. Patrick John and Sharon Ann Nagy; m. David Charles Harrington, Jr., July 31, 1993. BA in Psychology, St. Mary's Coll., Notre Dame, Ind., 1992; MSW, We. Mich. U., 1996. lic. LSW, 2000. Profl. child interviewer Child & Family Advocacy Ctr., Elkhart, Ind., 1992-96, program coord., 1996-99; exec. dir. Mental Health Assn., Elkhart, Ind., 1999—. Adv. bd. midwest region Children's Advocacy Ctr., St. Paul, 1999; treas., bd. dirs. Creative Expressions, 2001-03; treas., bd. dirs. Local Coordinating Coun., 2003—. Mem. NASW, Am. Profl. Soc. Abuse of Children (founding bd. mem., treas., v.p. 1996-98), Elkhart C. of C. (leadership academy 1999-2000), Kiwanis. Democrat. Roman Catholic. Avocations: reading, dancing, cultural events, wine tasting, skydiving. Office: Mental Health Assn in Elkhart County 116 South Main St Elkhart IN 46516 E-mail: llharrington@hotmail.com.

HARRINGTON, MARION RAY, ophthalmologist; b. Dallas, Sept. 20, 1924; s. Silas Fredrick and Mary Katherine (Ray) H.; m. Nan Puckhober, Oct. 1, 1942; 1 child, Nan Katherine Kern. Student, U. Tex., 1942, MD, 1947. Diplomate: Am. Bd. Ophthalmology. Intern St. Paul Hosp., Dallas, 1941-48; chief ophthalmology Portsmouth (Va.) Naval Hosp., 1950-52; practice medicine specializing in ophthalmology Dallas, 1952—; mem. faculty U. Tex., Southwestern Med. Sch., Dallas, 1952-2001, clin. prof., 1975-2001; ret. Served with USN, 1947-48, 50-52. Fellow ACS, Internat. Coll. Surgeons; mem. AMA, Tex. Med. Assn., Dallas County Med. Soc., So. Med. Soc., Am. Acad. Ophthalmology, Am. Assn. Ophthalmology, Tex. Acad. Ophthalmology and Otolaryngology, Tex. Ophthalmologic Assn., Dallas Acad. Ophthalmologists, Royal Soc. Medicine, Internat. Lens Implant Soc., Contact Lens Soc. Episcopalian. Home: 3620 Overbrook Dr Dallas TX 75205-4327

HARRINGTON, MARY EVELINA PAULSON (POLLY HARRINGTON), religious journalist, writer, educator; b. Chgo. d. Henry Thomas and Evelina (Belden) Paulson; m. Gordon Keith Harrington, Sept. 7, 1957; children: Jonathan Henry, Charles Scranton. BA, Oberlin Coll., 1946; postgrad., Northwestern U., Evanston, Ill., Chgo., 1946-49, Weber State U., Ogden, Utah, 1970s, 80s; MA, U. Chgo.-Chgo. Theol. Sem., 1956. Publicist Nat. Coun. Chs., N.Y.C., 1950-51; mem. press staff 2d assembly World Coun. Chs., Evanston, Chgo., 1954; mgr. Midwest Office Communication, United Ch. of Christ, Chgo., 1955-59; staff writer United Ch. Herald, N.Y.C., St. Louis, 1959-61; affiliate missionary to Asia, United Ch. Bd. for World Ministries, N.Y.C., 1978-79; freelance writer and lectr., 1961—; corr. Religious News Svc., 1962—. Prin. lectr. Women & Family Life in Asia series to numerous librs., Utah, 1981, 1981—82; pub. rels. coord. Utah Energy Conservation/Energy Mgmt. Program, 1984—85; tchr. writing Ogden Cmty. Schs., 1985—89; adj. instr. writing for publs. Weber State U., 1986—; instr. Acad. Lifelong Learning, Ogden, 1992—95, Eccles Cmty. Art Ctr., Ogden, 1993—94; dir. comm. Shared Ministry, Salt Lake City, 1983—97; chmn. comm. Intermountain Conf., Rocky Mountain Conf. Utah Assn. United Ch. of Christ, 1970—78, 1982—, Ind. Coun. Chs., 1960—63, United Ch. of Christ, Ogden, 1971—; dir. comm. United Chs., 1971—78, Christ Congl., Ogden, 1980—; chmn. comm. Ch. Women United Utah, 1974—78, Ogden rep., 1980—, hostess Northern Utah, 1998. Editor: Sunshine and Moonscapes: An Anthology of Essays, Poems, Short Stories, 1994, (booklet) Family Counseling Service: Thirty Years of Service to Northern Utah, 1996; contbr. numerous articles and essays to religious and other publs. Pres. T.O. Smith Sch. PTA, 1976-78, Ogden City Coun. PTA, 1983 85; assoc. dir. Region II, Utah PTA, Salt Lake City, 1981-83, mem. State Edn. Commn., 1982-87; chmn. state internat. hospitality and aid Utah Fedn. Women's Clubs, 1982-86; v.p. Ogden dist., 1990-92, pres. Ogden dist., 1992-96, state resolutions com., 1996—; trustee Family Counseling Svc. No. Utah, Ogden, 1983-95, emeritus trustee, 1995—; Utah rep. to nat. bd. Challenger Films, Inc., 1986—; state pres. Rocky Mountain Conf. Women in Mission, United Ch. of Christ, 1974-77, sec., 1981-84, vice moderator Utah Assn., 1992-94; chair pastor-parish rels. com. United Ch. of Christ Congl., Ogden, 1999-2003, chmn. search com., 1995-96, Mission com., 2002-. Recipient Ecumenical Svc. citation Ind. Coun. Chs., 1962, Outstanding Local Pres. award Utah PTA, 1978, Outstanding Latchkey Child Project award, 1985, Cmty. Svc. award City of Ogden, 1980, 81, 82, Celebration of Gifts of Lay Woman Nat. award United Ch. of Christ, 1987, Excellence in the Arts in Art Edn. award Ogden City Arts Commn., 1993, Spirit of Am. Woman in Arts and Humanities award Your Cmty. Connection, Ogden, 1994, Heart and Hand award United Ch. of Christ, Ogden, 2001; Utah Endowment for Humanities grantee, 1981, 81-82. Mem. Nat. League Am. Penwomen (chmn. Utah conv. 1973, 11 awards for articles and essays 1987-95, 1st pl. news award 1992, 1st pl. short stories 1997, 3d pl. articles 1997), AAUW (state edn. rep. 1982-86, parliamentarian Ogden br. 1997—, membership v.p. Ogden br. 2003—), League of Utah Writers (Publ. Quill award 1998). Democrat. Avocation: building miniature world of peace each Christmas by family in the home. Home and Office: 722 Boughton St Ogden UT 84403-1152 E-mail: gkHarrington1@comcast.net.

HARRINGTON, NANCY O'CONNOR, volunteer; b. Chgo., Oct. 28, 1928; d. John Roland and Ethel Catherine (Constable) O'Connor; m. James Edward Harrington, Sept. 8, 1951; children: Mary Beth Grayson, Janet Gaines, Gail, Nancy Chartier-Jackson. BA in art edn., Rosary Coll., River Forest, 1946-50. Cert. art tchr., Ill. Artist Chgo. Park Dist., 1949; art tchr. Chgo. elem. schs., 1951-52; color coord. homes Palos Park (Ill.) Builder, 1957-58; vol. Art Inst. of Chgo., 1980-86. Exhibited in Loyola Ramble, 1970s, Wilmette, 1960s, Palos Park, Ill., Evergreen Park, Ill., Chgo., Osprey, Fla., 1990s, Glenview, Ill., 1980s, 1990s. Bd. mem. Acad. Our Lady H.S. Alumni Bd., 1960's; pres. Mothers Club, v.p. Parents Club Regina Dominican H.S., Wilmette, Ill., 1972-73; vol. Judge Robert Downing Dem. Party, Glenview, Ill., 1974; 1st forelady of criminal ct. Cook County Ct. Sys., Chgo., 1980s; assoc. mem. Art Inst. Chgo., 1990—; vol. Resurrection House Daycare Ctr. for Homeless, Sarasota, Fla., 1993-98, Juvenile Diabetes Found., 1998—; colleague Ringling Mus. Art, Sarasota, 1994—; gen. chair Beaux Arts Festival, The Oaks C.C., 1996; mem. women's bd. Rosary Coll., 1990-98; hostess Hist. Spanish Pointe Fla. Luncheon, 1998, 99; mem. women's bd. dirs. Dominican U., 1997—; decorating chmn., Bishop's Charity Ball at Chelsea Ctr., 2002, Bishop's Garnet Ball for Charity at St. Anne's Hall, Sarasota, 2003. Recipient medallion Regina Dominican H.S. Mothers Club, 1972-73, Kemeny Lion medallion Art Inst. Chgo., 1980s, Resurrection House medallion, 1999; Honored vol. Sarasota Arts Coun., 1992; named Artist of Class of 1950, Rosary Coll. Mem. AAUW, Natl. Heritage Soc., North Shore Country Club (gen. chairperson 9-hole golf 1986, gen. chairperson art festival, 1996), Oaks Country Club (mem. garden club, 1991—, ad hoc archtl. rev. bd., 1991-92, women's bd., 1993, Dominican Univ. Women's Bd., 1997—, vol. Juvenille Diabetes Found., Sarasota, Fla. 1998, 99, Hostess of Mrs. Potter Palmer Luncheon Historic Spanish Pointe, Osprey, Fla., Ringling Sch. of Art and Design Libr.; chair Art Seminar of 25th Internat. Congress on Arts and Comm., New Orleans, 1998; attendee, singer choir 26th Internat. Congress Arts and Commn., Lisbon, 1999; gen. chairperson art festival, 1995—, gen. chairperson Oaks Celebrates Arts, 1994, chairperson Art Club, 1993-94; founder Art Appreciation Club, 1993, Artist of Month Column (author) 1994—); founding mem. Nat. Women's Art Museum. Roman Catholic. Avocations: travel, reading, aquacize, opera, bridge. Home: 210 Saint James Park Osprey FL 34229-9065

HARRINGTON, RICHARD J. information business executive; b. 1947; BA CPA, Univ. Rhode Island. Pres., CEO Thomson Newspapers, Inc., Des Plaines, Ill., 1993—; now pres., CEO The Thomson Corp., Stamford, Conn., 1997 . Mem. adv. com. U. R.I. Adv. bd. William F. Achtmeyer Ctr. Global Leadership; mem. bus. adv. coun. U. R.I.; bd. dirs. Norwalk C.C. Found. Office: Thomson Corp The Metro Center One Station Pl 6th Fl Stamford CT 06902

HARRINGTON, ROBERT DUDLEY, JR., retired printing company executive; b. Worcester, Mass., Dec. 19, 1932; s. Robert Dudley and Anne Victoria Harrington; m. Melissa Banks Hubner, Mar. 25, 1978 (div.). AB, Brown U., 1955; MBA, Columbia U., 1957. With Morgan Guaranty Trust Co., N.Y.C., 1957-59; v.p. Faulkner, Dawkins & Sullivan, N.Y.C., 1959-69; pres. Printers Express Co., Inc., Greenwich, Conn., 1976—. Trustee, mem. Woods Hole Oceanographic Instn. Corp., pres. Assocs. Mem. N.Y. Yacht Club, Edgartown Yacht Club, Round Hill Club, Edgartown Reading Rm., Holland Lodge, Athelstan Lodge, The Pilgrims. Office: 333 Greenwich Ave Greenwich CT 06830-6505

HARRINGTON, ROGER FULLER, electrical engineering educator, consultant; b. Buffalo, Dec. 24, 1925; s. Henry Bassett and Emilie (Fuller) H.; m. Juanita L. Crawford, Aug. 7, 1954; m. Sandra, Judith, Alan, Laura. BS, Syracuse U., 1948, MS, 1950; PhD, Ohio State U., 1952. Instr. Syracuse U., N.Y., 1948-50, asst. prof., 1952-56, assoc. prof., 1956-60, prof., 1960-94, dir. Electromagnetics Ctr., 1982-94. Vis. prof. U. Ill., Urbana, 1959-60, U. Calif., Berkeley, 1964, E. China Normal U., 1983, Ecole Poly. Fédéral de Lausanne, Switzerland, 1991; guest prof. Tech. U. Denmark, Lyngby, 1969; cons. in field. Author: Introduction to EM Engineering, 1956, Time-Harmonic EM Fields, 1961, Field Computation by Moment Methods, 1968. Served with USN, 1944-46. Rsch. fellow Ohio State U., Columbus, 1950-52; Fulbright lectr., Denmark, eng., 1969; named Disting. Alumni Ohio State U., 1970; recipient Chancellor's Citation Syracuse U., 1984, URSI van der Pol Gold medal, 1996, jubilee medal Nicola Tesla Found., 1998. Mem. IEEE (Centennial medal 1984, Disting. Achievement award 1989, Electromagnetics award 2000, Third Millennium medal 2000), AAUP, Sigma Xi, Sigma Nu. Home: 5424 N Strada De Rubino Tucson AZ 85750 6061 Office: U Ariz Dept Elec Computer Engring Tucson AZ 85721-0001

HARRINGTON, ROY EDWARDS, agricultural engineer, author; b. Atlanta, Mo., Oct. 23, 1925; s. Quincy K. and Sally Ethel (Edwards) H.; m. Dorose Oleta Zink, Sept. 6, 1953; children: Ellen Joyce Thompson, Janet Lisa Fish, Linda Carol Timmons. BS in Agrl. Engring., U. Mo., 1950. Registered profl. engr., Ill. Product devel. mgr. Deere & Co., Moline, Ill., 1950-66, mgr. product planning, 1971-86, ret., 1986; agrl. engr. Ford Found., New Delhi, 1966-71. Cons. farm mechanization WinRock Internat., Ill., 1992,, New Delhi, 1987, Vols. in Tech. Asst., Peshawar, Pakistan, 1989, World Bank, Hungary, 1986; spkr. in field. Author: A Tractor Goes Farming, 1995, Grandpa's John Deere tractors, 1996, How John Deere Tractors & Implements Work, 1997; co-author: John Deere Tractors and Equipment, 1991; author: (booklet) Agricultural Mechanization in India, 1973; contbr. Genuine Value, The John Deere Journey, 2000 (Timeline Products); holder 21 tractor and farm implement patents, 1953-68; contbr. articles to profl. jours. Pres. Quad Cities World Affairs Coun., Moline, 1981-82; farm equipment mgr. Great Collections of Quad Cities, Moline, 1993; vol. exec. Internat. Exec. Svcs. Corps., Ludhiana, India, 1997. Served to sgt. inf. U.S. Army, 1944-46. Fellow Am. Soc. Agrl. Engrs. (v.p. 1987-90), Indian Soc. Agrl. Engrs.; mem. Soc. Automotive Engrs. Baptist. Avocations: photography, bulldozer operation. Home: 3500 27th Avenue Ct Moline IL 61265-5366

HARRINGTON-LLOYD, JEANNE LEIGH, interior designer; b. L.A. d. Peter Valentine and Avis Lorraine (Brown) Harrington; m. James Wilkinson, Dec. 17, 1966 (div. Mar. 1976); m. David Lloyd, Nov. 27, 1985. BS in Psychology, U. Utah, 1984; cert., Salt Lake Sch. Interior Design, 1985; MS in Mgmt., Marylhurst Coll., 1990. With Mary Webb-Davis Agy., L.A., 1970; model, actress McCarty Agy., Salt Lake City, 1983-85; contract designer Innerspace Design, Salt Lake City, 1985-89; space planning and utilization mgr. U.S. Bancorp, Portland, Oreg., 1991-99. Mem. ASID, Internat. Interior Design Assn., Internat. Facilities Mgmt. Assn. Democrat. Avocations: travel, art history, reading, weight training, riding dressage. Home: 7077 Surfbird Cir Carlsbad CA 92009-4018

HARRIOTT, PETER, chemical engineering educator; b. Ithaca, N.Y., July 21, 1927; s. John Frederick and Stella (Fahl) H.; m. Mary Louise White, Oct. 24, 1953; children— George, James, John, Paul, Douglas. B.Ch.E., Cornell U., 1949; Sc.D., MIT, 1952. Engr. Gen. Elec. Co., Waterford, N.Y., 1952-53; Mem. faculty Cornell U., 1953—, asst. prof., 1953-54, assoc. prof., 1954-65, prof. chem. engring., 1965—, Fred Hoffman Rhodes prof. chem. engring., 1975—. Author: Process Control, 1964, Chemical Reactor Design, 2003; co-author: Unit Operations of Chemical Engineering, 1984, 6th edit., 2000. NSF Postdoctoral fellow, 1966 Mem. Am. Chem. Soc., Am. Inst. Chem. Engrs., Sierra Club, Nature Conservancy, Sigma Xi, Tau Beta Pi, Phi Kappa Phi, Alpha Chi Sigma. Clubs: Adirondack Mountain. Home: 139 Ellis Hollow Creek Rd RD 2 Ithaca NY 14850 Office: Cornell U Dept Chem Engring Ithaca NY 14853 E-mail: PH@cheme.cornell.edu.

HARRIS, AARON, management consultant; b. Birmingham, Ala., Oct. 27, 1930; s. Moses and Fannie (Williams) H.; m. Edna Mabel Turner, May 13, 1954; children: Kevin Brian, Edwin Maurice. BA, Talladega Coll., 1952; MS, Columbia U., 1959; postgrad., Princeton U., 1961. Trainee Bklyn. Pub. Library, 1956-59; asst. librarian Burroughs Wellcome Co., Tuckahoe, N.Y., 1959-64; assoc. librarian IBM Corp., East Fishkill, N.Y., 1964-66; library mgr. IBM Research Lab., San Jose, Calif., 1966-73; personnel exec. IBM Corp., San Jose, 1973-77; v.p. Discovery Sys., Inc., 1974—; data processing mgr. IBM, 1977-80, mgr. tng. and devel., 1980-84, mgr. human resources info. systems, 1985-88; program mgr. mgmt. devel. Rolm Systems, Santa Clara, Calif., 1988-91. Adv. instr. IBM Mgmt. Inst., 1992; cons.; pres. Amistad Assocs. Gen. chmn. Citizens Com. on Schs., San Jose, 1969-71; mem. San Jose CSC, 1974-78; foreman pro tem Santa Clara County Grand Jury, 1979-80; candidate San Jose Sch. Bd., 1969, 73; past bd. dirs. Santa Clara chpt. ARC, Mus. Art, San Jose; bd. dirs. Opera San Jose, 1986-92, Santa Clara County Urban League, 1984-87. San Jose Planning Commr., 1989-92; bd. dirs. Am. Civil Liberties Union Ala., 1996-99; conf. pres. laymen's coun. AME Zion Ch. With AUS, 1952-55. Recipient Citizen of Year award Omega Psi Phi, 1970, Outstanding Contbn. award Omega Psi Phi, 1991. Mem. Talladega Coll. Alumni Assn. (pres. Birmingham chpt. 1995-2000, Outstanding Contbn. award 2000). Mem. AME Zion Ch. Home and Office: 341 Turnberry Rd Birmingham AL 35244-3291 E-mail: aaron_harris@prodigy.net. *Those who have presented obstacles for failure have been overwhelmed by my confidence. Those who longed for my success have been supportive with encouragement and opportunity. The principles embodied in the golden rule are my constant aim.*

HARRIS, ALICE CARMICHAEL, linguist, educator; b. Columbus, Ga., Nov. 23, 1947; d. Joseph Clarence and Georgia (Walker) H.; m. James Vaughan Staros, Aug. 7, 1976; children: Joseph Vaughan, Alice Carmichael. BA, Randolph-Macon Woman's Coll., 1969; MA, U. Essex (Eng.), 1972; PhD, Harvard U., 1976. Tchg. fellow linguistics Harvard U., Cambridge, Mass., 1972-74, 75-76, lectr. linguistics, 1976-77, rsch. fellow linguistics, 1977-79; rsch. asst. prof. linguistics Vanderbilt U., Nashville, 1979-84, assoc. prof. linguistics, 1985-91, assoc. prof. anthropology, 1986-92, prof. linguistics, 1991—2002, prof. anthropology, 1992—2002, chair dept. Germanic, Slavic langs., 1993—2002; prof. linguistics SUNY, Stony Brook, 2002—. Chair faculty coun. Coll. Arts and Scis., 1995-96; vice chair grad. faculty coun., 1993-94, sec. faculty senate, 1993-94; assoc. rsch. U. Tbilist, USSR, 1974-75; tutor linguistics Dunster House, Harvard U., Cambridge, 1975-77; cons. to Simon and Schuster; Erskine vis. prof. U. of Canterbury, Christchurch, New Zealand, 1999. Author: (book) Georgian Syntax, 1981, Diachronic Syntax, 1985, The Indigenous Languages of the Caucasus, 1991, Endoclitics and the Origins of Udi Morphosyntax, 2002; co-author: Historical Syntax in Cross-Linguistic Perspective, 1995 (Leonard Bloomfield book award, 1998); mem. editl. bd. (book) Natural Language and Linguistic Theory, 1987—90, assoc. editor (jour.) Language, 1988—89, mem. editl. bd. Diachronica, 1994—, mem. adv. com. Publs. MLA, 1995—98; contbr. Sinclair Kennedy fellow Harvard U., 1974-75, NSF Nat. Needs Postdoctoral fellow, 1978-79; grantee Internat. Rsch. and Exch. Bd., 1973, 74-75, 77, 81, 89, 92, Linguistic Soc. Am., 1981, NSF 1980-83, 81-83, 83-85, 85-89, 97-99, 2001-03, NEH, 1990-91, Deutscher Adademischer Austausch Dienst, 1994; scholar Harvard U. 1972-73, Georgetown U., 1973; recipient Mellon Found. Regional Faculty Devel award 1981, ACLS travel award, 1988, venture fund Vanderbilt U., 1987, 92, 94. Mem. Internat. Soc. Hist. Linguistics (mem. exec. com. 1995-01), Linguistic Soc. Am. (cons., com. status women in linguistics, nominating com.), Southeastern Conf. Linguistics, Soc. for Study of Caucasia (exec. coun. 1990-98), Societas Caucasologica Europaea (v.p. 1990-92, exec. com. 1992-94, 1994-2000), Phi Beta Kappa (Earl Sutherland prize for rsch. Vanderbilt U. 1998). Office: SUNY Dept Linguistics Stony Brook NY 11794-4376

HARRIS, ANDREW MICHAEL, director; b. Olean, NY, Jan. 10, 1967; s. David Joseph and Yvonne Anne H.. BS in Bus. Adminstrn., Boston U., 1989, MBA, 1995. Commd. U.S. Army, 1989, advanced through grades to maj.; asst. to the sr. v.p. Boston U., 1991—94, mgr. of fin. and adminstrn., 1994—96, dir. fin. planning and budget, 1998—2003, assoc. dir. analytical svcs., 1998—. Cmty. task force mem. Boston U. Cmty. Task Force, Boston, 2002—03; philanthropic support Boston Briefing Series, Boston, 2002—03. Decorated Army Commendation Medal US Army, Overseas Svc. Ribbon, Army Achieve-

ment Medal; recipient Pi Lambda Phi Alumni award, Pi Lambda Phi Nat. Hdqs., 1989-1998, Hon. Scarlet Keyaward, Boston Unversity Alumni Assn., 2002; ROTC 4 Yr. Academic Scholarship, US Army, 1985. Mem.: N.G. Assn. U.S., Boston Briefing Series (life; founder and bd. mem. 2002—03), Soc. Preservation Audubon Circle, Algonquin Club of Boston (com. mem. 1999—2003), Army and Navy Club, Pi Lambda Phi Alumni Assn. (life). Republican. Roman Catholic. Avocations: travel, book collecting, politics, wine, fitness. Office: Boston U Med Campus 715 Albany St 560 Boston MA 02118 Office Fax: 617-638-4949. Personal E-mail: amh@bu.edu.

HARRIS, ANN, elementary school teacher; b. Eden, Miss., Aug. 20, 1946; d. Tommie L. and Rosetta (Tolbert) H. BS in Edn., Jackson (Miss.) State Coll., 1968, MS, 1972, EdS, 1974; EdD, Ind. U., 1983. Cert. elem. tchr., Miss. Elem. tchr. Jackson Pub. Schs.; asst. prof. edn. Ky. State U., Frankfort, Western Ky. U., Bowling Green; elem. tchr. Atlanta Pub. Schs. Guest lectr. home econs. dept. Indiana U., Bloomington, 1982-83; elem. tchr. Atlant Pub. Schs. Former leadership team chairperson E.L. Connally Sch., Olympics Com.; chair Red Cross and March of Dimes; rep. Am. Heart Fund; mem. PTA. Fundraiser chairperson, program chairperson Tchr.'s Awards Banquet, 1998, 99, 2000; v.p. Wesley Sunday Sch. Class, Atlanta First United Meth. Ch., 2001. Recipient Outstanding Elem. Tchr. Am. award, 1975, Finer Womanhood award Nat. Coun. Negro Women, 1980, Disting. Svc. citation United Negro Coll. Fund, 1979-80, Ky. Amb. Goodwill award, 1986, Atlanta Asssn. Educators cert. for Tchr. of Yr., 1996-97, Achievement cert. Atlanta Fedn. Tchrs., 1996-97, Spl. Congrl. Recognition for Edn. cert. Rep. John Lewis, 1997, Spl. Recognition in Edn. cert. Phi Delta Kappa, 1997, John Herkiotz award for outstanding contbns. of tchg. democracy for work in mock election NASSP, 1997, Cert. of Appreciation Am. Red Cross Mem. Enrollment Campaign, 1997-98, Rotary Red Apple for Reading award Apple Corps, 2002; named Tchr. of Yr., Connally Elem. Sch., 1996-97, Coca-Cola, 1996-97; cert. Red Cross, 1997-98, 99-2000; named to Hon. Order Ky. Cols., 2001. Mem. NEA, Ga. Assn. Educators, Atlanta Assn. Educators.

HARRIS, ANN BIRGITTA SUTHERLAND, art historian; b. Cambridge, Eng., Nov. 4, 1937; came to U.S., 1965, naturalized, 1996; d. Gordon B.B.M. and Gunborg Elizabeth (Wahlström) Sutherland; m. William Vernon Harris, July 13, 1965 (div. Oct. 1999); 1 son, Neil William Orlando Sutherland. BA with 1st class honours, Courtauld Inst., U. London, 1961, PhD, 1965. Asst. lectr. U. Leeds, 1964-65; asst. prof. art history Columbia U., N.Y.C., 1965-71, Hunter Coll., N.Y.C., 1971-73; asso. prof. SUNY, Albany, 1973-77; chmn. for acad. affairs Met. Mus. Art, N.Y.C., 1977-80; part-time faculty Juilliard Sch., N.Y.C., 1978-84; prof. U. Pitts., 1984—. Founder, 1st pres. Women's Caucus for Art, 1973-76; disting. vis. prof. U. Tex.-Arlington, fall 1982; Mellon prof. history of art U. Pitts., spring 1984; vis. prof. history of art So. Meth. U., Dallas, fall 1993. Author: Andrea Sacchi, 1977, Selected Drawings of Gian Lorenzo Bernini, 1977; co-author: Die Zeichnungen von Andrea Sacchi und Carlo Maratta, 1967, Women Artists: 1550-1950, exhbn. catalogue, 1977, Landscape Painting in Rome, 1575-1675, exhbn. catalogue, 1985; coauthor: Italian, French, English and Spanish Drawings and Watercolors in the Detroit Institute of Arts, 1992. Fellow Guggenheim Found., 1971, Ford Found., 1975-76, NEH, 1981-82, rsch. fellow Getty Mus. Art, 1988. Mem. Coll. Art Assn., Women's Caucus for Art. Office: U Pittsburgh Dept History of Art Pittsburgh PA 15260

HARRIS, ANN MARIE, mathematician, educator; b. Cambridge, Cambridgeshire, Eng., Apr. 30, 1956; d. Drew Warren Tomberlin and Jeanne Esther Britney; m. Laurence Earl Harris, May 30, 1980 (div.); children: Britney Jeanne, David Earl, Christen Marie. BA, Miss. U. for Women, Columbus, 1978; MS, Utah State U., 1996. Tchg. asst. U. of Mo., Rolla, 1978—79; h.s. math tchr. Cuba Sch. Dist., Cuba, Mo., 1979—80; jr. high math tchr. Edinburg Sch. Dist., 1980—81; tchg. asst. Utah State U., Logan, 1993—96; instr. Idaho State U., Pocatello, 1996—99; prof. math. Brigham Young U. - Idaho, Rexburg, 1999—. Contbr. Recipient Achievement in Writing award, Nat. Coun. of Tchrs. of English, 1974, Rollins award, Utah State U., 1996; scholar Nat. Merit scholar, Miss. U. for Women, 1974—78. Mem.: Math. Assn. of Am. (sec.-treas. Intermountain sect. 2000—). Avocations: reading, sewing, cooking, snowboarding, biking. Home: 152 South 2nd East Rexburg ID 83440 Office: Brigham Young University - Idaho 239 Romney Bldg Rexburg ID 83460 E-mail: harrisa@byui.edu.

HARRIS, BARBARA HULL (MRS. F. CHANDLER HARRIS), social agency administrator; b. L.A., Nov. 1, 1921; d. Hamilton and Marion (Eimers) Baird; m. F. Chandler Harris, Aug. 10, 1946; children: Victoria, Randolph Boyd. Student, UCLA, 1939-41, 45-47. Ptnr. J.B. Assocs., cons., 1971-73; statewide dir. vols. Children's Home Soc. Calif., 1971-75. Heart Sunday chmn. Los Angeles County Heart Assn., 1965, bd. dirs., 1966-69; mem. exec. com. Hollywood Bowl Vols., 1966-84, chmn. vols., 1971, 75; chmn. Coll. Alumni of Assistance League, 1962; mem. exec. com. Assistance League So. Calif., 1964-71, 72-80, 83-89, pres., 1976-80; bd. dirs. Nat. Charity League, L.A., 1965-69, 75, sec., 1967, 3d v.p., 1968; ways and means chmn., dir. L.A. Am. Horse Show, 1969; dir. Coronet Debutante Ball, 1963, chmn. ball bd., 1969-70, 75, 84, 96—, mem. ball bd., 1969—; pres. Hollywood Bowl Patroness Com., 1976; v.p. Irving Walker aux. Travelers Aid, 1976, 79, pres., 1988-89; pres. So. Calif. alumni coun. Alpha Phi, 1961, fin. advisor to chpts. U. So. Calif., 1961-72, UCLA, 1965-72; benefit chmn. Gold Shield, 1969, 1st v.p., 1970-72; chmn. Golden Thimble III Needlework Exhbn., Hosp. of Good Samaritan, 1975; bd. dirs. UCLA Affiliates, 1976-78, KCET Women's Coun, 1979-83, Region V United Way, 1980-83; pres. Jr. Philharm. Com., 1981-82; bd. dirs. L.A. Founder chpt. Achievement Rewards for Coll. Scientists, 1980-91, pres., 1984-85; pres. L.A. County chpt. Freedom Found. Valley Forge; mem. com. Hollywood Bowl 75 Yr. HIstory, 1994-96. Recipient Outstanding Svc. award L.A. County Heart Assn., 1965. Outstanding Alumni award for cmty. svc. UCLA, 1978, Mannequin's Eve award, 1980, Outstanding Bd. Mem. of Yr. award Assistance League So. Calif., 1989-90, Golden Eve award Mannequins of Assistance League, 2000, Western Divsn. Freedoms Found. at Velley Forge Freedoms award, 2002. Mem. Hollywood C. of C. (bd. dirs. 1980-81). Home: 7774 Skyhill Dr Los Angeles CA 90068-1232

HARRIS, BARBARA S. publishing executive; BS in Phys. Edn., Fla. State U., 1978; Masters, N.E. Mo. State U. Editor-in-chief Shape mag. Weider Publ., Woodlands Hills, Calif., 1986—2003; exec. v.p. Am. Media, Woodlands Hills, Calif., 2003—. Past adviser Calif. Gov.'s Coun. on Phys. Fitness and Sports; past chmn. bd. dirs. Am. Coun. Exercise; mem. adv. bd. L.A. Commn. on Assaults Against Women, Melpomene Inst.; mem. adv. bd. Fitness Cert. program U. Calif., L.A.; instr. Omega Inst.; presenter in field. Appearances on Oprah, Today Show, CNN, MSNBC, Access Hollywood, Entertainment Tonight. Achievements include climbing 20,000 foot mountain in the Bolivian Andes, Mt. Rainier and Mt Kilimanjaro. Avocations: running, weightlifting, kayaking, photography, rock climbing. Office: Am Media 21100 Erwin St Woodland Hills CA 91367-3712

HARRIS, BAYARD EASTER, lawyer; b. Washington, July 22, 1944; s. Edward Bledsoe and Grace (Childrey) H.; m. Rebecca Bond Jeffress, June 10, 1967; children: Nicholas Bayard, Nathan Bedford (dec. 1989), Ellen Coley. AB in History, U. N.C., 1966; JD cum laude, U. S.C., 1973. Bar: Va. 1974, U.S. Dist. Ct. (we. dist.) Va. 1974, U.S. Ct. Appeals (4th cir.) 1974, U.S. Supreme Ct. 1982. Assoc. Woods, Rogers, Muse, Walker & Thornton, Roanoke, Va., 1973-79, ptnr., 1979-85, Woods, Rogers & Hazlegrove, Roanoke, 1985-90; pres. Ctr. for Employment Law, Roanoke, 1991-98; of counsel Woods, Rogers and Hazlegrove, PLC, 1998—; tchg. assoc. Roanoke Coll., Salem, Va., 2003—. Mem. Transp. Safety Bd., 1992-96. Comments and rsch. editor U. S.C. Law Rev., 1972-73. Chpt. chmn. ARC, Roanoke Valley, 1985-87, chmn. ea. ops. hdqrs., 1988-91; pres. Nathan's Gift Found. Lt. USNR, 1966-70. Recipient Clara Barton award ARC Roanoke Valley chpt., 1986. Mem. ABA (labor and employment sect. 1974—), Va. Bar Assn. (labor and employment com. and sect. 1974. Republican. Episcopalian. Avocations: golf, gardening. Office: Woods Rogers & Hazlegrove 10 S Jefferson St Ste 1400 Roanoke VA 24011-1331 E-mail: bharris@woodsrogers.com.

HARRIS, BEN M. education educator; b. Chgo., Feb. 8, 1923; s. Eva Mae (Barber) Sands; m. Mary Lee Christian, Sept. 28, 1948; children: Kim Christian, Tamara Lee. AA, Glendale Coll., 1943; BA, UCLA, 1948, MEd, 1951; EdD, U. Calif., Berkeley, 1958. Cert. elem. tchr., secondary tchr., prin., sch. adminstr., Calif. Chemist Desert Chem. Co., Twenty Nine Palms, Calif., 1943-44; tchr. Burbank (Calif.) Jr. High Sch., 1948-51; curriculum coordinator Inyo County Schs., Independence, Calif., 1951-54; tchr. Lafayette (Calif.) Elem. Sch., 1954-55; dir. curriculum Lafayette Sch. Dist., 1955-56, dir. pers., 1956-57; acad. asst. dept. edn. U. Calif., Berkeley, 1957-58; asst., then assoc. prof. U. Tex., Austin, 1958-68, prof. edn. adminstrn., 1968-87, M.K. Hage Centennial prof. edn., 1987, prof. emeritus, 1988—. Cons. Ministry Edn., Venezuela, 1973, Bahrain, 1985, Effective Border Schs. R&D Initiative, 1995-96, U. Sch. Collaborative project, Austin Pub. Schs., 1995-97; vis. prof. U. Wash., Seattle, 1976, U. Tex., San Antonio, 1989, U. Tex. Pan Am., Edinburg, 1992, 1997-2002; planning cons. Ministry of Edn., Egypt, 1987, Venezuela, 1973, 75, Malaysia, 1989, 91; UNESCO advisor U. Cordoba, Spain, 1971, U. Petroleum and Minerals, Dharan, 1979; advisor Lagoven, S.A. Venezuela Petroleum, 1991-92, Am. 2000 New Generation Schs. Project, Austin, 1991-92; vis. lectr. Taiwan Tchrs. Coll., Taichung/Kaochsfungand, 1994; dir. evaluation effective schs. border project, Edinburgh, 1995-97. Author: Supervisory Behavior in Education, 1963, 3d edit., 1985, Developmental Teacher Evaluation, 1986, Inservice Education for Staff Development, 1980, 2d edit., 1989; (with others) Inservice Education: A Guide to Better Practice, 1969, Personnel Administration in Education, 1980, 3d edit., 1992, Invention*Developmental Teacher Evaluation Kit; co-developer Diagnostic Executive Competency Assessment System, 1988, Performance Criteria for School Executives, 1991, Summary Report on Formative Evaluation of Partner School Progress, 1997; mem. editl. bd. Handbook of Rsch. on School Supervision, 1998. Served with USNR, 1944-46. Fulbright scholar U. Teheran, Iran, 1962-63, Bahrain, 1985. Mem. ASCD (nat. bd. dirs. 1973-75, 80-82), Am. Edn. Rsch. Assn., Coun. Profs. of Instrnl. Supervision (pres. 1976-77), Sam Bass Theatre Assn., Trad. Jazz Club, Fulbright Alumni Assn., Phi Delta Kappa. Avocations: country and western dancing, singing, gardening. Office: U Tex Austin Dept Ednl Adminstrn George Sanchez Bldg # 310 Austin TX 78712 Fax: 512-471-5975.

HARRIS, BENJAMIN HARTE, JR., lawyer; b. Sept. 12, 1937; s. Ben H. and Mary Cade (Aldridge) H.; m. Martha Elliott Lambeth, Aug. 26, 1961; children: Benjamin Harte, Wayt. AB, Davidson Coll., 1959; JD, U. Ala., 1962. Bar: Ala. 1964, U.S. Dist. Ct. (so. dist.) Ala. 1965, U.S. Ct. Appeals (5th cir.) 1981, U.S. Supreme Ct. 1971, U.S. Ct. Appeals (11th cir.) 1981. Assoc. Johnstone, Adams, Bailey, Gordon & Harris (formerly Johnstone, Adams, May, Howard & Hill, LLC), Mobile, Ala., 1964-70; mem. Johnstone, Adams, Bailey, Gordon & Harris, Mobile, 1971. Chmn. Atty's Ins. Mut. Ala., bd. dirs. Past bd. dirs., past pres. Boys' Club, 1989-95; past chmn., past trustee UMS Prep Sch.; v.p., bd. dirs. Gordon Smith Ctr.; mem. stds. com. United Way. Fellow: Ala. Bar Found. (past. pres., past trustee, past pres.), Am. Bar Found. (life); mem.: Nat. Conf. Bar Pres. (past exec. coun.), 11th Cir. Ct. Appeals Hist. Soc. (trustee, v.p.), Ala. Jud. Commn., Am. Arbitration Assn., Am. Judicature Soc., Ala. Def. Lawyers Assn., Ala. Law Sch. Found. (past pres., trustee, Pipes Disting. Alumnus award 2003), Ala. Law Inst., Ala. State Bar (bd. commrs. 1978—87, mem. exec. com., trustee bar found., past chmn. disciplinary commn., past pres.), Mobile County Bar Assn. (exec. com. 1980—87), ABA (past ho. of dels., past bd. govs.), Athelstan Club, Murray House (pres. 2003—, dir.), Mobile Rotary Club (Paul Harris fellow), Brock Inn of Ct. (pres. 1996—98). Episcopalian. Office: PO Box 1988 Mobile AL 36633-1988

HARRIS, BENJAMIN LOUIS, chemical engineer, consultant; b. Savannah, Ga., Aug. 1, 1917; s. Raymond Branson and Edith (Kontner) H.; m. Janet Diekmann, Oct. 4, 1942; children: Benjamin S., Stefanie Harris Hunt, Deborah Harris Kommalan, Penelope Harris Clifton, Rebecca Harris Gutin. BE, Johns Hopkins U., 1938, PhD, 1941; diploma, Indsl. Coll. Armed Forces, Washington, 1965. Registered profl. engr., Md. Asst. prof. Johns Hopkins U., Balt., 1946-53; with R & D Command U.S. Army, Edgewood Arsenal, Md., 1952-66; dep. asst. dir. def. R & D U.S. Office Sec. Def., Alexandria, Va., 1966-70; tech. dir. U.S. Army Chem. Rsch., Devel. and Engring. Ctr., Aberdeen, Md., 1970-81; pres. Engring. Rsch. Co. of Glenarm, Md., 1981-83. Cons. in field, 1981—; pres. Profl. Engrs. Bd., Md., 1987-88, v.p., 1988-98. Editor St. George Philatelic Soc. Newsletter, 1988-96; patentee in field, contbr. articles to profl. jours. Mem. Gov.'s Exec. Adv. Coun., Md., 1988-95; mem. exec. bd. Balt. Area coun. Boy Scouts Am., 1964—; mem. adv. com. USCG, NRC, Washington, 1967-77; mem. com. ethics and professionalism Nat. Coun. Examiners Engring. and Surveying. Maj. U.S. Army, 1941-46, Res., 1938-41, 46-77, ret. col., 1977. Recipient Silver Beaver award Boy Scouts Am., 1952, Silver Antelope award, 1987, Disting. Eagle award, 1976, Lamb award Luth. Ch., 1964, St. George award Cath. Ch., 1983; named Ky. Col. Fellow AAAS, AIChE; mem. SAR (past pres. Col. Nicholas Ruxton Moore chpt.), Am. Chem. Soc., Order Founders and Patriots Am. (gov. gen. 1996-98), Sons and Daus. of Pilgrims (gov. Md. br. 1996-98), Soc. Boonesborough, Nat. Congress Patriotic Orgns., Descendants of Ancient Planters, Sons of Confederate Vets., Soc. of Colonial Wars State of Md., Order of the Crown of Charlemgne USA, Huguenot Soc. Md., Order Honorable Arty. Co., St. George Soc. Balt., St. Andrews Soc. Balt., Ancient and Honorable Mech. Co. of Balt., Nat. Gavel Soc., Mil. Order World Wars (past comdr. Balt.-Devereaux chpt.), Ret. Officers Assn., Res. Officers Assn., Chem. Corps Regtl. Assn., Soc. of War of 1812 in State of Md., Corps. of the U.S. (charter mem., sr. exec., 1978), Democrat. Lutheran. Avocations: genealogy, philately, crafts, gardening. Home and Office: 11630 Glen Arm Rd Apt U44 Glen Arm MD 21057-9486 E-mail: benlharris@juno.com.

HARRIS, BERNARD, statistician, mathematician, educator; b. N.Y.C., N.Y., June 20, 1926; s. Samuel S. and Ella L. Harris; m. Anita Belle Greenberg, May 19, 1929 (dec. Sept. 2, 1977); children: Shelley Anne, Mark Bruce, David Brian, Susan Elizabeth; m. Susan Stephens Burns, Sept. 24, 1983; stepchildren: Laura Burns, Erin Burns. BBA, CCNY, 1946; MA, George Washington U., 1953; PhD, Stanford U., 1958. Statistician U.S. Census Bur., Suitland, Md., 1950—52; mathematician Nat. Security Agy., Ft. Meade, Md., 1952—58; assoc. prof. U. Nebr., Lincoln, 1958—64; prof. Math. Rsch. Ctr. U. Wis., Madison, 1964—85, prof. stats. dept., 1966—. Chmn. stats. task force FAA/DOD Com. on Material Properties, 1986—90, 1981—82; mem. PRA Procedures Rev. Bd., 1981—82, PRA Rev. Bd., U.S. Nuclear Regulatory Commn., 1992—95; lectr. in field; vis. prof. U. Lund, Lund, Sweden, 1990, U. So. Calif., 1992; vis. rsch. prof. Math. Inst. Steklova, Moscow, 1991, Moscow, 92, Moscow, 96, U. Muenster, Germany, 1993, Heinrich Heine U., Duesseldorf, Germany, 1994, Duesseldorf, 95, Duesseldorf, 96, Kungliska Techniska Hogskolan, 1998, 99; cons. to various govt. and indsl. orgns., 1958—63. Mem. editl. bd.: Statistics and Decisions, 1983—2002; author: (books) Theory of Probability, 1966; editor: Spectral Analysis of Time Series, 1967, Graph Theory and Its Applications, 1970; contbr. articles and revs. to profl. publs. Fellow: Am. Statis. Assn. (bd. dirs. 1978—80, mem. coun. 1996—, pres. Nebr. chpt. 1958—60, chmn. sect. risk analysis 1994—95), Inst. Math. Stats. (program chair 1996); mem.: AAAS, Classification Soc. N.Am. (bd. dirs. 1991—2001, Univ. Faculty award 1999), Math. Assn. Am., Am. Math. Soc., Internat. Statis. Inst. Office: U Nebras Math Dept Lincoln NE 68588-0323

HARRIS, BRETT ROSENBERG, lawyer; b. Livingston, NJ, Nov. 24, 1966; s. Paul Irwin and Edith Rosenberg; m. Mitchell Paul Harris, Nov. 16, 1996; children: Alicia Rose, Cooper James. BA cum laude, Washington & Jefferson Coll., 1988; JD, NYU, 1991. Summer intern Ctr. for Law and Social Policy, Washington, 1989; summer assoc. Winthrop Stimson Putnam & Roberts, NYC, 1990; assoc. Fox & Fox, Newark, 1991-95, Wilentz, Goldman & Spitzer, P.A., Woodbridge, NJ, 1995—2000, ptnr., 2000—. Exec. editor NYU Rev. Law and Social Change, 1990-91. Mem. NJ State Bar Assn. (chair Internet and computer law com., dir. corp. and bus. law sect.), trustee of Temple Emanu-el of Westfield "I have a Dream" Foundation, Inc.; mem. of Medical and profl. advisory Coun. of the Arnold P. Gold Found. Avocation: baseball scorer. Home: 423 Everson Pl Westfield NJ 07090-3229 Office: Wilentz Goldman & Spitzer PA 90 Woodbridge Ctr Dr Ste 900 Woodbridge NJ 07095-0958 E-mail: bharris@wilentz.com.

HARRIS, CARL G. music educator; b. Fayette, Mo., Jan. 14, 1935; s. Carl G. Harris Sr. and Frances M. (Harris) Harris. BA, Philander Smith Coll., 1956; MA, U. Mo., 1964; Mus D, U. Mo., Conservatory of Music, 1964. Dir. of choirs Philander Smith Coll., Little Rock, 1959—69; prof., chair, dir. of choirs Va. State U., Petersburg, Va., 1971—84, Norfolk State U., Norfolk, Va., 1984—97; prof. of music, organist Hampton U., Hampton, Va., 1997—. Min. of music Bank St. Meml. Bapt. Ch., Norfolk, 1984—; organist Gillfield Bapt. Ch., Petersburg, Va., 1971—84, Centennial United Meth. Ch., Kans. City, Mo., 1968—71. Contbr. articles various profl. jours. Recipient Disting. Alumnus award, U. Mo., 1980, Alumnus award, Philander Smith Coll., 1975. Mem.: Lions, Kappa Delta Pi in Edn., Alpha Kappa Mu Nat., Tau Beta Sigma Hon. Band Soc., Phi Delta Kappa Edn., Kappa Kappa Psi Hon. Band, Phi Mu Alpha Sinfonia Music, Omega Psi Phi Fraternity, Inc. Democrat. Episcopal. Home: 171 Atlantic Ave A Hampton VA 23664 Office: Hampton U Dept of Music Hampton VA 23668 E-mail: charris54@cox.net.

HARRIS, CARLOS ORTEZ, elementary school educator; b. Atlanta, Ga., May 5, 1971; s. John Arnold and Deborah Person. Grad. in bus. edn., Clark Atlanta U., 1994; MA in Speech Comm., Calif. State U., Hayward, 2001. Tchr. Fulton County Bd. Edn., Atlanta, 1995—96, Atlanta Job Corp., 1996—97. Author: (book) The Rhetoric of Tupac Shakur vol. 1, 2003. Christian. Avocations: reading, writing, music, astrology, Religion. Home: 1243 Bell Avenue East Point GA 30344 Personal E-mail: carlosharris29@hotmail.com.

HARRIS, CASPA, JR., lawyer, educator, association administrator; b. Washington, May 20, 1928; BS in Acctg., Am. U., 1958, JD, 1967. CPA Va.; bar: Va. 1967, D.C. 1968, U.S. Supreme Ct. Staff pub. rels. NIH, Bethesda, Md., 1955-58; sr. auditor KPMG Peat Marwick, Washington, 1958-62; chief internal auditor Howard U., Washington, 962-65, comptroller, 1965-71, v.p. bus. and fiscal affairs, treas., 1971-87; pres. Nat. Assn. Coll. and Univ. Bus. Officers, Washington, 1987-95; lawyer, cons. pvt. practice, Waterford, Va., 1995—. Prof. sch. of law Howard U., Washington, 1968-87, Kaufman-Cades CPA Rev. Sch., 1978-87, U. Ky., 1976—, U. Calif. Santa Barbara, 1984—.; chmn., bd. dirs. Coll. Constrn. Loan Assn., Coll. Constrn. Loan Ins. Co.; bd. dirs. Nat. Harmony Meml. Park, The Common Fund; adv. coun. Met. Life Pension dept., Systems & Computer Tech. Corp.; treas. bd. State of Va., 1982-86, mem. Civil Rights Appellate Rev. Divsn. U.S. Dept. Edn., 1988-90; adv. bd. on colls. and univs. IRS, 1984-95; Presdl. adv. bd. on Historically Black Colls. and Univs., 1990-93; cons. Cassidy & Assocs., Washington, Nat. Heart Inst. Past chmn. of bd. Nat. Assn. Coll. & Univ. Bus. Officers Assns., also other offices; past pres. Ea. Assn. Coll. and Univ. Bus. Officers; bd. dirs. Salvation Army Met. Washington, 1970-76; mem. USO Fin. Com., 1970-71, Health Welfare Coun. and United Givers Fund D.C., 1970-72, nat. scholarship com. Lone Star Industries, Inc., 1983-90; treas. and dir. Nat. Capital Area Health Care Coalition, 1983-84; bd. dirs., vice chmn. D.C. chpt. ARC, 1981-86; chmn. fin. com., dir., The College Bd., 1983-88; bd. visitors Norfolk State U., 2000—. Recipient Am. Univ. Disting. Alumni award 1968, Ea. Assn. Coll. & Univ. Bus. Officers, KPMG Peat Marwick award 1995, Nat. Assn. Coll. Stores, Earl Kintner award, 1995, Disting. Bus. Officers award Nat. Assn. Coll. and Univ. Bus. Officers, 1996. Mem. AICPA (minority recruitment com. 1969-72), Va. Soc. CPAs, Va. State Bar Assn., Bar Assn. D.C., Reston Lions Club (pres. 1978-79). Home: 39109 John Wolford Rd Waterford VA 20197-1616

HARRIS, CHARLES DAVID, music educator; b. Mpls., Jan. 6, 1939; children: Laura Kathleen, Mary Louise, Caroline Ruth. MusB, Northwestern U., 1960, MusM, 1961; PhD, U. Mich., 1967. Levitt prof. music history and harpsichord Drake U., Des Moines, 1965—2003. Editor: (critical editions) Johann Caspar Kerll: The Collected Works for Keyboard, Johann Friedrich Doles, Jr., Johann Kuhnau; contbr. articles to profl. jours. Grantee, Fulbright Commn., 1964—65, 1971—72. Mem.: Am. Musicological Soc. Democrat. Avocation: hiking. Home: 1536 SE 74th Ave Portland OR 97215 Personal E-mail: dh1376@comcast.net.

HARRIS, CHARLES E. marketing professional; b. Chgo., Nov. 29, 1965; s. Jerrold and Carol Ann (Block) H. BA in Psychology, U. Calif., Irvine, 1987. Pub. rels. asst. Calif. Angels, Anaheim, 1985-86; asst. sports info. dir. U. Calif., Irvine, 1986-88, sports mktg. & promotions dir., 1988—. Guest speaker 11th Annual NCAA Profl. Devel. Seminar, Nashville, 1990. Editor (basketball game program) Courtside, 1987-88. Bd. mem. Jewish Sports Hall Fame, Orange County, Calif., 1988-90. Mem. Beta Theta Pi (bd. dirs. housing corp. 1990—). Address: 7914 Gleason Dr #1060 Knoxville TN 37919-5475

HARRIS, CHARLES EDGAR, retired wholesale distribution company executive; b. Englewood, Tenn., Nov. 6, 1915; s. Charles Leonard and Minnie Beatrice (Borin) H.; m. Dorothy Sarah Wilson, Aug. 20, 1938; children: Charles Edgar, William John. Pres., chmn., CEO H.T. Hackney Co., Knoxville, Tenn., 1972-83; ret. Former chmn. bd., chief exec. officer, dir. various corps. in Tenn., Ky., N.C., and Ga.; former bd. dirs. Park Nat. Bank, 1st Am. Nat. Bank Knoxville; dir. U.S. Indsl. Coun. Former bd. dirs. Downtown Knoxville Assn., Greater Knoxville Smoky Mountain coun. Bou Scouts Am., Met. YMCA, Knoxville, United Way Knoxville; mem. budget com. 1982 World's Fair, Knoxville; deacon, trustee Ctrl. Bapt. Ch., Knox County Assn. Bapt.; mem. exec. bd. Tenn. Bapt. Conv., Nashville; assoc. chmn. Layman's Nat. Bible Week, Washington; trustee Carson Newman Coll., Jefferson City, Tenn.; dir. Tenn. Taxpayers Assn.; dir. Religious Heritage of Am., St. Louis; bd. dirs. Tenn. Bapt. Children's Homes. Recipient Outstanding Community Leadership award Religious Heritage Am., Red Triangle award and Silver Triangle award YMCA. Mem. Greater Knoxville C. of C. (bd. dirs., Outstanding Corp. Citizenship award), Nat. Assn. Wholesalers-Distbrs., LeConte Club (charter), Knoxville Execs. Club (bd. dirs.), Rotary (officer, bd. dirs.). Home: 7914 Gleason Rd Apt 1060 Knoxville TN 37919-5475

HARRIS, CHARLES ELMER, lawyer; b. Williamsburg, Iowa, Nov. 26, 1922; s. Charles Elmer and Loretto (Judge) H.; m. Marjorie Clark, Jul. 9, 1949 (div. June. 1969); m. Linda Rae Slaymaker, Nov. 25, 1992; children: Martha Ann, Julie Ann, Charles Elmer III. Student, St. Ambrose Coll., 1940-42; BSC., U. Iowa, 1946, JD, 1949. Bar: Iowa 1949. Mem. firm Brody, Parker, Roberts, Thoma & Harris, Des Moines, 1949-66, Herrick, Langdon, Belin Harris, Langdon & Helmick, Des Moines, 1966-78, Belin Harris Helmick, P.C., Des Moines, 1978-91, Belin, Harris, Lamson, McCormick, P.C., Des Moines, 1991-96; pvt. practice, Des Moines, 1997-99; ret., 1999. Lectr. tax schs., meetings, 1951, 55, 67, 69, 77-84, 90, 91. Comments editor: Iowa Law Rev., 1948-49. Bd. dirs. NCCJ, 1964-67, Iowa Bar Found., 1977-92, Iowa Law Sch. Found., 1977-90, United Way Found., 1981-89. Lt. (j.g.) USNR, 1943-46. Fellow Am. Coll. Trust and Estate Counsel; mem. ABA, Iowa Bar Assn. (bd. govs. 1973-80, Merit award 1980), Polk County Bar Assn. (pres. 1972-73), Polk County Jr. Bar Assn. (pres. 1952-53), Order of Coif, Sigma Chi, Delta Theta Phi. Roman Catholic. Home: 5141 Robertson Dr Des Moines IA 50312-2170 E-mail: Harris5141@aol.com.

HARRIS, CHARLES GEORGE, research scientist, consultant; b. Indpls., Ind., Aug. 17, 1955; s. Charles George and Frances Barge Harris; m. Mary Louise Smith, Nov. 24, 1989; children: Nicholas Lawrence, Jeremy Francis Harrissmith. Field svcs. mgr. Hydropro, Inc., Lake Park, Fla., 1984—99; tech. mgr. Energy Recovery, Inc., Chesapeake, Va., 1999—2000; sys. mgr. Advanced Membrane Sys., Newport News, Va., 2000—. Contbr. articles to profl. jours. Actor ArtsEnter of Cape Charles, Va., 2001—03. Mem.: S.E. Desalting Assn., Internat. Desalination Assn., Am. Membrane Tech. Assn., Am. Water Works Assn. Avocations: motor racing, acting. Home: PO Box 1064 Cheriton VA 23316 Office: Advanced Membrane Sys 9286A Warwick Blvd Newport News VA 23607 Home Fax: 757-331-8222; Office Fax: 757-595-5531. Personal E-mail: chipdad@aol.com. E-mail: charris@ams-water.com.

HARRIS, CHARLES MARCUS, lawyer; b. Orange, N.J., July 5, 1943; s. Roger Kennedy and Margaret Louise (Adams) H.; m. Jean Ellen Redding, July 6, 1968; children: Charles Redding, Anna Dean. AB, Duke U., 1965, JD, 1972; MA, U. Ariz., 1966. Bar: N.C. 1972, U.S. Dist. Ct. (we. dist.) N.C. 1972, U.S. Dist. Ct. (ea. dist.) N.C. 1976, U.S. Dist. Ct. (mid. dist.) N.C. 1977. Field examiner NLRB, Winston-Salem, N.C., 1966-69; ptnr. Smith Helms Mulliss & Moore, Charlotte, N.C., 1972-93; ptnr. Poyner & Spruill, Charlotte, 1993—. Mem. editorial bd. Duke Law Jour., 1971-72. Jr. warden Christ Episc. Ch., Charlotte, 1983-84, 89-90; pres. United Family Svcs., Charlotte, 1986; pres. Friendship Trays Bd., Charlotte, 1991-93. Mem. ABA, N.C. Bar Assn., Duke U. Alumni Assn. (pres. Mecklenburg chpt. 1979-81, gen. alumni bd. 1993—), Charlotte City Club, Charlotte Country Club. Republican. Home: 4733 Cambridge Crescent Dr Charlotte NC 28226-3324 Office: Poyner & Spruill 100 N Tryon St Ste 4000 Charlotte NC 28202-4010

HARRIS, CHARNEY ANITA, painter, sculptor; b. Chgo. Student, Phila. Coll. Art, Phila. Mus. Art, 1964-68, New Sch. Social Rsch., N.Y.C., 1970-73. One-woman shows include Phila. Art Alliance, 1965, 73, Revsin Art Gallery, Phila., 1973, Kling Gallery, Phila., 1976, Allentown (Pa.) Art Mus., 1981,

Gallery K, Washington, 1984, Hudson River Mus., N.Y., 1985, Mangel Gallery, Phila., 1982, 91; exhibited in group shows at Cheltenham Art Ctr., Phila. (hon. mention), 1964, 69, 77, Allens Lane Art Ctr. (Painting prize), 1964, Pa. Acad. Fine Arts, Phila., 1964, Phila. Art Alliance, 1964, 72, Moore Coll. Art, Phila., 1966, 67, 68, 85, 86, Phila. Civic Ctr. Mus. (Painting prize), 1967, 71, 74, Hobson Pittman-Young Philadelphians Show, 1968, Marian Locks Gallery, Phila., 1970, 74, New Sch. Social Rsch., N.Y.C. (Painting prize), 1970, William Penn Meml. Mus., Harrisburg, Pa., 1975, U. Del., Newark, 1976, Allentown Art Mus., 1977, Woodmere Art Gallery, Phila., 1977, 78, Constructs Show, N.Y., 1978, Samuel S. Fleisher Art Meml., Phila., 1979, Carnegie-Mellon U., Pitts., 1980, Phila. Mus. Art, 1982, Mangel Gallery, 1985, 90-93, 95, 96, 98, 2001-03, City Hall, Phila., 1985, West/Art and the Law, 1985-86, Cleve. Ctr. for Contemporary Art, 1985-86, Shippensburg U., Pa., 1987, 97, Woodmere Art Mus., Phila., 1989, Ednl. Alliance, N.Y., 1991, Soho Gallery, N.Y.C., 1991, 92, Nicholas Alexander Gallery, N.Y.C., 1994, Millicent Roger Mus., Taos, N.Mex., 1996, James A. Michener Art Mus., 1997; represented in permanent collections Phila. Mus. Art, Allentown Art Mus., Hobson Pittman Mus. House, Bryn Mawr Coll., First Ronald McDonald House, also corps., univs., colls., and pvt. collections. Recipient painting prize Pa. Gallery Fine Arts, New Sch. Social Rsch., 1970, Pa. Acad. Fine Arts, 1964. Mem. Am. Artists Equity Assn. Home: 2 Sunnyside Ln Yardley PA 19067-2616

HARRIS, CHAUNCY DENNISON, geographer, educator; b. Logan, Utah, Jan. 31, 1914; s. Franklin Stewart and Estella (Spilsbury) H.; m. Edith Young, Sept. 5, 1940; 1 child, Margaret (Mrs. Philip A. Straus, Jr.). AB, Brigham Young U., 1933; BA, Oxford U., 1936, MA, 1943, DLitt, 1973; postgrad., London Sch. Econs., 1936-37; PhD, U. Chgo., 1940; DEcon (honoris causa), Catholic U., Chile, 1956; LLD (honoris causa), Ind. U., 1979; DSc (honoris causa), Bonn U., 1991, U. Wis., Milw., 1991. Instr. in geography Ind. U., 1939-41; asst. prof. geography U. Nebr., 1941-43, U. Chgo., 1943-46, assoc. prof., 1946-47, prof., 1947-84, prof. emeritus, 1984—, dean social scis., 1955-60, chmn. non western area programs and internat. studies, 1960-66, dir. ctr. for internat. studies, 1966-84, chmn. dept. geography, 1967-69, Samuel N. Harper Disting. Svc. prof., 1969-84, spl. asst. to pres., 1973-75, v.p. acad. resources, 1975-78. Del. Internat. Geog. Congress, Lisbon, 1949, Washington, 1952, Rio de Janeiro, 1956, Stockholm, 1960, London, 1964, New Delhi, 1968, Montreal, 1972, Moscow, 1976, Tokyo, 1980, Paris, 1984, Sydney, Australia, 1988, Washington, 1992, The Hague, 1996; v.p. Internat. Geog. Union, 1956-64, sec.-treas., 1968-76; mem. adv. com. for internat. orgns. and programs Nat. Acad. Scis., 1969-73, mem. bd. internat. orgns. and programs, 1973-76; U.S. del. 17th Gen. Conf. UNESCO, Paris, 1972; exec. com. div. behavioral scis. NRC, 1967-70; hon. cons. geography Libr. of Congress, 1974-80, mem. coun. of scholars, 1980-83, Conseil de la Bibliographie Géographique Internationale, 1986-94. Author: Cities of the Soviet Union, 1970; editor: Economic Geography of the U.S.S.R, 1949, International List of Geographical Serials, 1960, 71, 80, Annotated World List of Selected Current Geographical Serials, 1960, 64, 71, 80, Soviet Geography: Accomplishments and Tasks, 1962, Guide to Geographical Bibliographies and Reference Works in Russian or on the Soviet Union, 1975, Bibliography of Geography, Part I, Introduction to General Aids, 1976, Part 2, Regional, vol. 1, U.S., 1984, A Geographical Bibliography for American Libraries, 1985, Directory of Soviet Geographers 1946-87, 1988; contbr. Sources of Information in the Social Sciences, 1973, 86, Encyclopedia Britannica, 1989, Columbia Gazetteer of the World, 1998; contbg. editor: The Geog. Rev., 1960-73, Soviet Geography, 1987-91, Post-Soviet Geography and Economics, 1992-99, emeritus 2000—; hon. editor Urban Geography, 1984—; contbr. articles to profl. jours. Life mem. vis. com. U. Chgo. Libr.; pres. coun. Residents Assn., Montgomery Place, Chgo., 2000-01. Recipient Alexander Csoma de Körösi Meml. medal Hungarian Geog. Soc., 1971, Lauréat d'Honneur Internat. Geog. Union, 1976; Alexander von Humboldt Gold Medal Gesellschaft für Erdkunde zu Berlin, 1978; spl. award Utah Geog. Soc., 1985; Rhodes scholar, 1934-37. Fellow Japan Soc. Promotion of Sci.; mem. Assn. Am. Geographers (sec. 1946-48, v.p. 1956, pres. 1957, Honors award 1976), Am. Geog. Soc. (coun. 1962-74, v.p. 1969-74; Cullum Geog. medal 1985), Am. Assn. Advancement Slavic Studies (pres. 1962, award for disting. contbns. 1978), Am. Acad. Arts and Scis., Social Sci. Rsch. Coun. (bd. dir. 1959-70, vice-chmn. 1963-65, exec. com. 1967-70), Internat. Coun. Sci. Unions (exec. com. 1969-76), Internat. Rsch. and Exchs. Bd. (exec. com. 1968-71), Nat. Coun. Soviet and East European Rsch. (bd. dir. 1977-83), Nat. Coun. for Geog. Edn. (Master Tchr. award 1986); hon. mem. Royal Geog. Soc. (Victoria medal 1987), Geog. Socs. Berlin, Frankfurt, Rome, Florence, Paris, Warsaw, Belgrade, Japan, Chgo. (Disting. Svc. award 1965, bd. dir. 1954-69, 82-90), Polish Acad. Scis. (fgn. mem.). Home: 5550 S South Shore Dr Apt 906 Chicago IL 60637-5033 Office: U Chgo Com on Geog Studies 5828 S University Ave Chicago IL 60637-1583

HARRIS, CHRISTINE, dance company executive; b. Milw. Mktg. dir. Milw. Symphony Orch., 1984-90, head Arts in Cmty. Edn. program, 1990-95; with Inst. Music, Health and Edn., Mpls., 1996-97; exec. dir. Milw. Ballet, 1997—. Office: Milw Ballet 504 W National Ave Milwaukee WI 53204-1746

HARRIS, CHRISTOPHER, publisher, designer, editor; b. Plainfield, N.J., June 7, 1933; s. Maynard Lawrence and Edith Johnson (Bushnell) H.; m. Linda Martin Robinson, Oct. 8, 1955 (dec. 1967); children— Katherine Hamilton, Stephen Christopher, Andrea Lawrence; m. Sarah Pickett Hargrove Sullivan, Aug. 18, 1977. BA, Yale U., 1955. Book mfg. coordinator Rand McNally & Co., Hammond, Ind., and N.Y.C., 1955-60; mng. editor Studio Books div. Viking Press, N.Y.C., 1960-70; editor, pres. Chatham Press, Riverside and Old Greenwich, Conn., 1970-76; dir. design and prodn. Yale U. Press, New Haven, 1977-88; dir. Summer Hill Books, 1978—; editor Proctor Libr. Newsletter, Weathersfield, Vt., 1996—; auditor Town of Weathersfield, 1996-97. Chmn., Weathersfield Dem. Town Com., 2000—; trustee Proctor Libr., 2003—. Democrat. Home and Office: 304 Beaver Pond Rd Perkinsville VT 05151-9558

HARRIS, CHRISTOPHER J. state legislator, lawyer; b. Arlington, Tex., Feb. 22, 1948; m. Tammy Harris, Feb. 22, 1948. Student, Tex. Christian U.; JD, Baylor U., 1974. Rep., Dist. 93 Tex. Ho. of Reps., 1985—91; rep., Dist. 10 Tex. State Senate, 1991—2002, pres. pro tempore, 2001, rep., Dist. 9, 2003—, chmn. adminstrn. com., mem. jurisprudence, state affairs, nominations coms.; pvt. practice law Arlington, Tex. Mem. Human Svcs. Com., 1999; vice chair Jurisprudence Com., 1999; chmn. Senate Adminstrn. Com., 1999; vice chair Senate Fin. Com., 2001; mem. Senate Health and Human Svcs. Com., 2001, Senate State Affairs Com., 2001; vice chair Tex. Sunset Commn., 2001. Honored by Nat. Child Support Enforcement Assn., Tex. Civil Justice League, Tex. State Bar family law sect., Tarrant County Family Bar Assn., Fort Worth and Dallas C. of C., Ret. Tchrs. Assn., Humane Soc. North Tex., Future Farmers Am., Tex. Mpcl. Officers League, Am. Subcontractors Assn., Tex. Assn. Alcoholism and Drug Abuse Counselors, Tex. State Troopers Assn. Mem.: Tex. State Bar Assn., Arlington Bar Assn., Tarrant County Family Law Bar Assn., Tarrant County Bar Assn. Republican. Episcopalian. Address: 4108 Amon Carter Blvd Ste 210 Fort Worth TX 76155

HARRIS, CHRISTOPHER KIRK, lawyer; b. Aluquerque, July 6, 1951; s. Paul and Margureite (Kirk) H. BA, Yale U., 1973; MSc, London Sch. Econs., 1974; JD, Boston Coll., 1977. Bar: Mass. 1977, D.C. 1980, Mont. 1986, U.S. Supreme Ct. 1981. Atty. GAO, Washington, 1977-78; chief counsel U.S. Senate Judiciary Subcom., 1979; atty. land and natural resources divsn. U.S. Dept. Justice, Washington, 1979-83; counsel Ho. of Reps. Energy and Commerce Com., Washington, 1983-84; ptnr. McCutchen Doyle Brown & Enersen, 1991-94, Harris, Tarlow & Stonecipher, Bozeman, Mont., 1994-2000; mem. Mont. Ho. of Reps., 2001—. Mem. Mont. Environ. Quality Coun.; gen. counsel Nat. Oil Recyclers Assn., 1985—. Author: Hazardous Waste: Confronting the Challenge, 1987, Report That Spill!, 1990, Environmental Crimes, 1992, Hazardous Chemicals and the Right to Know, 1993, Used Oil: Management Practices and Potential Liability, 1988, (with others) Environmental Litigation, 1999. Recipient Cert. of Merit energy and minerals divsn. GAO, 1978, Spl. Achievement award U.S. Atty. Gen., 1981. Office: 519 N Black Bozeman MT 59715

HARRIS, CHRISTY FRANKLIN, lawyer; b. Greensboro, N.C., Dec. 8, 1945; s. Luther Franklin and Rebecca Ann (Bluster) H.; children: Stacey Lynn, Aubrey Leigh. AA, Oxford Coll., Emory U.; BA, U. Fla., 1967, JD with honors, 1970. Bar: Fla. 1970, U.S. Dist. Ct. (mid. dist.) Fla. 1970, U.S. Ct. Mil. Appeals 1971, U.S. Ct. Appeals (11th cir.) 1984. Assoc. Holland & Knight, Lakeland, Fla., 1970, 1973-74; pres. Canan & Harris P.A., Lakeland, Fla., 1974-76; pres., sr. atty. Harris, Midyette & Clements P.A., Lakeland, Fla., 1976-89, Harris & Midyette, P.A., Lakeland, Fla., 1989-91, Harris, Midyette, Geary, Darby & Morrell, P.A., Lakeland, Fla., 1991-98, Harris, Midyette & Darby, P.A., Lakeland, Fla., 1998-2000; shareholder Peterson & Myers, P.A., Lakeland, Fla., 2000—. Mem. 10th cir. Grievance Com., Lakeland, 1976-79, 83-86, chmn. 1979, vice chmn., 1986; mem. Unauthorized Practice of Law Com., 1983-86; bd. dirs. Internat. Speedway Corp., 1984—. Bd. dirs. Program to Aid Drug Abusers, Lakeland, 1975-76, Campfire, 1979-85. Served to capt. USMCR, 1968-73, mil. judge, 1972-73. Named to Hon. Order of Ky. Cols., 1974. Mem. Lakeland Bar Assn., Attys. Title Ins. Fund, Grand Am. Rd. Racing Assn., LLC (founding mem.), Order of Coif, Phi Beta Kappa, Phi Kappa Phi. Republican. Avocations: motor sports, sport fishing. Home: 1335 Longoak Dr N Lakeland FL 33811-2146 Office: Peterson & Myers PA 225 E Lemon St Ste 300 PO Box 24628 Lakeland FL 33802-4628 E-mail: charris@petersonmyers.com.

HARRIS, CURTIS C. physician; MD, U. Kans. Intern and resident in internal medicine and oncology; chief Lab. Human Carcinogenesis Nat. Cancer Inst., NIH, Bethesda, Md., also head molecular genetics and carcinogenesis sect. Deichmann lectr. VII Internat. Congress of Toxicology, 1995. Editor: 10 books; exec. editor Carcinogenesis; contbr. articles. Recipient Alton Ochsner Relating Smoking and Health award, 1993, Walter Hubert award lectr., Brit. Assn. Cancer Rsch., 1995. Mem.: Am. Assn. Cancer Rsch., Chem. Industry Inst. Toxicology (mem. sci. adv. panel, chmn. 1989—94, Founder's award 1995), Internat. Soc. Gastroentergol. Carcinogenesis (Charles Heidelberger award 1999). Office: NIH Nat Cancer Inst Lab Carcinogenesis Rm 2C01 37 Convent Dr Bldg 37 Bethesda MD 20892-0001

HARRIS, CYRIL MANTON, physicist, engineering and architecture educator, consulting acoustical engineer; b. Detroit; s. Bernard O. and Ida (Moss) H.; m. Ann Schakne; children: Nicholas Bennett, Katherine Anne. BA, UCLA, 1938, MA, 1940; PhD, MIT, 1945; Sc.D. (hon.), N.J. Inst. Tech., 1981, Northwestern U., 1989. Rsch. asst. Carnegie Instn. Washington, 1941; mem. staff Bell Telephone Labs., 1945-51; cons. Office Naval Research, London, Eng., 1951; Fulbright lectr. Tech. U., Delft, Holland, 1951-52; Charles Batchelor prof. elec. engring., prof. architecture and past chmn. div. archtl. tech. Columbia U.; now prof. emeritus. Vis. Fulbright prof. U. Tokyo, 1960; acoustical cons. Met. Opera House, N.Y.C., John F. Kennedy Ctr. Performing Arts, Washington, Krannert Ctr. Performing Arts, U. Ill., Powell Symphony Hall, St. Louis, Nat. Acad. Scis. Auditorium, Washington, Minn. Orch. Hall, Mpls., Nat. Ctr. Performing Arts, Bombay, Avery Fisher Hall, N.Y. State Theater reconstructions, Lincoln Ctr., N.Y.C., Symphony Hall, Salt Lake City, Benaroya Hall, Seattle; past dir. Inst. Theatre Tech.; mem. noise control group, mem. com. on undersea warfare NRC, 1955-57, mem. bldg. adv. bd., 1977-79; mem. coun. hearing and bio-acoustics Armed Forces-NRC, 1953-55; mem. adv. panel 213 to Nat. Bur. Standards, 1966-69, chmn., 1969-71. Author: (with V.O. Knudsen) Acoustical Designing in Architecture, 1950, rev., 1980, Handbook of Noise Control, 1957, 2d edit., 1979, 3d edit retitled Handbook of Acoustical Measurements and Noise Control, 1991, Dictionary of Architecture and Construction, 1975, 2d edition 1993; Historic Architecture Sourcebook, 1977, Illustrated Dictionary of Historic Architecture, 1983; Handbook of Utilities and Services for Buildings, 1990, Noise Control in Buildings, 1993, American Architecture: An Illustrated Encyclopedia, 1998, Shock and Vibration Handbook 5th edit., 2002; mem. editl. adv. bd.: Physics Today, 1955-66; contbr. articles to profl. jours. Hon. trustee St. Louis Symphony Soc., 1977—; mem. nat. adv. bd. Utah Symphony Orch., 1976-85. Recipient Franklin medal, 1977; Emile Berliner award, 1977; Hon. award U.S. ITT, 1977; Wallace Clement Sabine medal, 1979; AIA medal, 1980; Gold Medal Audio Engring. Soc., 1984; award of honor for sci. and tech. City of N.Y., 1985; Alumni award UCLA, 1989, Pupin medal Columbia U., 1998. Fellow IEEE, Acoustical Soc. Am. (pres. 1964-65, assoc. editor jour. 1959-70, Gold medal), Audio Engring. Soc. (hon.); mem. NAS, NAE, Am. Inst. Physics (governing bd. 1965-66), N.Y. Acad. Scis. (pres. 1991-93, chmn. bd. 1992-94), Am. Philos. Soc., Century Assn., Sigma Xi, Tau Beta Pi. Office: Columbia U Mudd Bldg New York NY 10027

HARRIS, DALE HUTTER, judge, lecturer; b. Lynchburg, Va., July 10, 1932; d. Quintus and Agnes (Adams) Hutter; m. Edward Richmond Harris Jr., July 24, 1954; children: Mary Fontaine, Frances Harris Russell, Jennifer Harris Haynie, Timothy Edward. BA, Sweet Briar Coll., 1953; MEd in Counseling and Guidance, Lynchburg Coll., 1970; JD, U. Va., 1978; LLD (hon.), Wilson Coll., 1988. Bar: Va. 1978, U.S. Dist. Ct. (we. dist.) Va. 1978, U.S. Ct. Appeals (4th cir.) 1978. Admissions asst. Sweet Briar Coll. (Va.), 1953-54; caseworker Winchester/Frederick Dept. Welfare, Va., 1954-55; vis. lectr. Lynchburg Coll., Va., 1971; assoc. Davies & Peters, Lynchburg, 1978-82; substitute judge 24th Dist. Gen. Dist., Juvenile and Domestic Rels. Dist. Ct., Va., 1980-82; judge Juvenile and Domestic Rels. Dist. Ct., Lynchburg, 1982—2003. Judge Family Ct. Pilot Project, Va., 1990—91; lectr. law U. Va. Law Sch., 1986—98; pres. Va. Coun. Juvenile and Family Ct. Judges, 1994—96; mem. panel of experts and adv. com. Child Protection and Custody Resource Ctr., 1994—2001; mem. Commn. on Future of Va.'s Jud. Sys., 1987—89; mem. adv. bd. Hilton Project on Model State Laws about Family Violence. Vice chmn. bd. dirs. Sweet Briar Coll., 1976-86; vol. coord. vols. in probation with Juvenile and Domestic Ct., 1971-73; chmn. steering com. for establishment Youth Svc. Bur., Lynchburg, 1972-73; chmn. bd. dirs. Lynchburg Youth Svcs., 1973-75; mem. adv. bd. Juvenile Ct., 1957-60, 62-68, sec., 1966-68; bd. dirs. Family Svc. Lynchburg, 1967-69; Lynchburg Fine Arts Ctr., 1965-67, Seven Hills Sch., 1966-73, Greater Lynchburg United Fund, 1963-65, Lynchburg Assn. Mental Health, 1960-61, Miller Home, 1980-82, Lynchburg Gen.-Marshall Lodge Hosps., Inc., 1980-82; v.p. Lynchburg Mental Health Study Commn., 1966; bd. dirs. Lynchburg Sheltered Workshop for Mentally Retarded Young Adults, 1965-69; bd. dirs. Lynchburg Guidance Ctr., 1959-61, v.p., 1970, pres., 1961; bd. dirs. Hist. Rev. Bd. Lynchburg, 1978-82; adv. bd. study of effectiveness of civil protection orders Nat. Ctr. State Cts., 1994-97. Mem.: ABA, Am. Prosecutors Rsch. Inst., Nat. Coun. Juvenile and Family Ct. Judges (mem. child custody edn. com. 1993—98, chair family violence commn. 1998—2000, trustee 1998—2001, chair custody com. 1999—2001), Lynchburg Bar Assn., Va. State Bar (bd. govs. criminal law sect. 1988—90, bd. govs. family law sect. 1989—91), Va. Bar Assn., Phi Beta Kappa. Office: Juvenile and Domestic Relations Dist Ct PO Box 757 Lynchburg VA 24505-0757

HARRIS, DALE RAY, lawyer; b. Crab Orchard, Ill., May 11, 1937; s. Ray B. and Aurelia M. (Davis) H.; m. Toni K. Shapkoff, June 26, 1960; children: Kristen Dee, Julie Diane. BA in Math., U. Colo., 1959; LLB, Harvard U., 1962. Bar: Colo. 1962, U.S. Dist. Ct. Colo. 1962, U.S. Ct. Appeals (10th cir.) 1962, U.S. Supreme Ct. 1981. Assoc. Davis, Graham & Stubbs, Denver, 1962-67, ptnr., 1967—, chmn. mgmt. com., 1982-85. Spkr., instr. various antitrust and comml. litig. seminars; bd. dirs. Lend-A-Lawyer, Inc., 1989-94. Mem. campaign cabinet Mile High United Way, 1986—87, chmn., atty. adv. com., 1988, sec., legal counsel, trustee, 1989—94, 1996—2001, mem. exec. com., 1989—2001, chmn. bd. trustees, 1996, 1997; trustee The Spaceship Earth Fund, 1986—89, Legal Aid Found. Colo., 1989—95, 2000—01; mem. devel. coun. U. Colo. Arts and Scis. dept., 1985—93; area chmn. law sch. fund Harvard U., 1978—81; bd. dirs. Colo. Jud. Inst., 1994—2003, vice chair, 1998; bd. dir. Colo. Lawyers Trust Account Found., 1996—2001; steering com. Youth-At-Work, 1994, School-To-Work, 1995; mem. jud. adv. coun. Colo. Supreme Ct., 2001—; bd. dirs. Rocky Mountain Arthritis Found., 2002—, Qualife Wellness Cmty., 2002—. With reserves USAR, 1962—68. Recipient Williams award, Rocky Mountain Arthritis Found., 1999. Fellow: Am. Bar Found. (Colo. state chmn. 1998—); mem.: Colo. Assn. Corp. Counsel (pres. 1973—74), Denver Bar Assn. (chmn. centennial com. 1990—91, bd. trustees 1992—95, pres. 1993—94, Merit award 1997), Colo. Bar Assn. (coun. corp. banking and bus. law sect. 1978—83, chmn. antitrust com. 1980—84, bd. govs. 1991—95, chmn. family violence task force 1996—2000, pres.-elect 1999—2000, co-chair multi-disciplinary practice task force 1999—2000, bd. govs. 1999—2002, pres. 2000—01, chmn. profl. reform initiative task force 2001—, chmn. transitions com. 2002—03, 2001—03), Colo. Bar Found. (award of merit 2002), ABA (antitrust and litigation sects.), Rotary (Denver), Denver Law Club (pres. 1976—77, Lifetime Achievement award 1997), Univ. Club, Colo. Forum, The Two Percent Club (exec. com. 1994—), Citizens Against Amendment 12 Com. (exec. com. 1994), Phi Beta Kappa. Home: 2032 Bellaire St Denver CO 80207-3722 Office: Davis Graham & Stubbs 1550 17th St Ste 500 Denver CO 80202-1202 E-mail: dale.harris@dgslaw.com.

HARRIS, DANA BOUND, software company executive; b. Pomona, Calif., Dec. 29, 1957; s. Warren and Beverly June (Bound) Harris; m. Tammy S. Lake, July 9, 1983; children: Danielle Katherine, Brittany Sue, Zachary Bound. BA in Computer Sci., BA in Physics, SUNY, Potsdam, 1981. Software engr. E-Systems, Inc., Falls Church, Va., 1981-83; sr. engr. Computer Scis. Corp., Falls Church, 1983-84; software engring. supr. Presearch, Inc., Fairfax, Va., 1984-85, asst. program mgr., 1985-87, program mgr. Liverpool, N.Y., 1987-92; sr. computer scientist Computer Scis. Corp., Liverpool, 1992-94; pres., chmn. bd., chief info. officer Systems Made Simple, Inc., Liverpool, 1991-2000; dir. info. tech. Philips Broadband Networks, Inc., Manlius, NY, 2000—01; pres. Scientific Bus. Gear, 2001—. Mem. SUNY-Potsdam Computer Sci. Bd. Advisors, 2000—. Mem.: IEEE, Planetary Soc., Assn. Computing Machinery. Republican. Mem. Christian Ch. Avocations: swimming, reading science fiction, building computers, watching 49er's football, technical writing. Home: 4256 Orion Path Liverpool NY 13090 1942 Office: Scientific Bus Gear LLC 4256 Orion Path Liverpool NY 13090

HARRIS, DARLENE, judge, lawyer, county legislator; d. Robert and Novella Harris. BA, U. Pa., 1986; postgrad., U. London, 1988; JD, Hofstra U., 1989. Bar: N.Y. 1989. Staff atty. Juvenile Rights divsn. Legal Aid Soc., N.Y.C., 1989-90, Appeals Bur. Legal Aid Soc., Hempstead, N.Y., 1990; sr. ct. atty. Dist. Ct. of Nassau County, Hempstead, 1991-95; atty. Atty.'s Office Town of Hempstead, 1995-97, Law Offices of Elliot Bloom, Mineola, NY, 1996—97; pvt. practice Uniondale, NY, 1997—99. Mem. R.E.A.C.H. Project, Hempstead. Mem. NAACP (exec. bd.), Women in Cts. (Nassau county jud. com.), Nassau County Bar Assn., N.Y. State Bar Assn., Black and Hispanic Bar Assn., Kiwanis Club, 100 Black Women. Republican.

HARRIS, DARRYL WAYNE, publishing executive; b. Emmett, Idaho, July 29, 1941; s. Reed Ingval and Evelyn Faye (Wengreen) H.; m. Christine Sorenson, Sept. 10, 1965; children: Charles Reed, Michael Wayne, Jason Darryl, Stephanie, Ryan Joseph. BA, Brigham Young U., 1966. Staff writer Deseret News, Salt Lake City, 1965, Post-Register, Idaho Falls, 1966-67; tech. editor Idaho Nuclear Corp., Idaho Falls, 1967-68; account exec. David W. Evans & Assos. Advt., Salt Lake City, 1968-71; pres. Harris Pub., Inc., Idaho Falls, 1971—; pub. Potato Grower of Idaho mag., 1972—, Snowmobile West mag., 1974—, Sugar Producer mag., 1974—, Blue Ribbon mag., 1987-90, Modstock mag., 1992—, SnowAction mag., 1987—2000, Western Guide to Snowmobiling, 1988—, Houseboat Mag., 1990—, Pontoon and Deck Boat Mag., 1995—, Mountain Turf mag., 2001—, Idaho Falls mag., 2001—, SnoWest Canada mag., 2001—, Presspective mag., 2001—, Today's Playground mag., 2001—, SkatePark mag., 2001—, Sledheads Mag., 2001—. Campaign mgr. George Hansen for Congress Com., 1974, 76; campaign chmn. Mel Richardson for Congress Com., 1986; 1st counselor to pres. Korean Mission, Ch. Jesus Christ of Latter-day Saints, Seoul, Korea, 1963, area public communications dir., Eastern Idaho, 1976-86; pres. Korea Seoul Mission, 1997 2000; High Priest, LDS Ch., 1987-2002, Bishop BYU, Idaho 27th Ward, 2003—, high coun. Idaho Falls Ammon Stake, 1987-91, Ammon 8th Ward Bishopric, 1991-96; founder Blue Ribbon Coalition, 1987; v.p. Teton Peaks coun. Boy Scouts Am., 1987-92; publicity chmn. Upper Snake River Scout Encampment, 1988; founder, pres. Our Land Soc., 1989-92. Mem. Agr. Editors Assn., Internat. Snowmobile Industry Assn. (Best Overall Reporting journalism award 1979, 80), Western Publs. Assn., World Champion Cutter and Chariot Racing Assn. (historian 1966-80), Nat. Snowmobile Found. (founder 1988), Kappa Tau Alpha. Clubs: Pres. award 1978). Lodges: Idaho Falls Kiwanis (pres. 1978, Disting. Office: Harris Pub Inc 360 B St Idaho Falls ID 83402

HARRIS, DAVID ALAN, not-for-profit organization executive; b. Santa Monica, Calif., Sept. 23, 1949; s. Eric Albert and Nelly (Chender) H.; m. Giulia Boukhobza, Jan. 14, 1979; children: Daniel, Michael, Joshua. BA, U. Pa., 1971; MS, London Sch. Econs., 1972, postgrad., 1975-77, Oxford (Eng.) U., 1977-78. Dir. govt. and internat. affairs Am. Jewish Com., N.Y.C., 1987-90, exec. dir., 1990—. Nat. coord. Freedom Sunday for Soviet Jewry rally, Washington, 1987; pub. mem. U.S. Del. to Conf. on Security and Coop. in Europe; vis. scholar Johns Hopkins U., 2000-02. Author: The Jokes of Oppression, 1988, Entering a New Culture, 5th edit., 1989, The Jewish World, 1989, In The Trenches, Vol. 1, 1999, Vol. 2, 2002; contbr. over 100 articles to mags. and newspapers. Trustee Conn. Coll., 1999-2002. Cited by Lifestyles mag., Avenue mag., and Jewish monthly as Jewish leader; honored by govts. of Bulgaria, Germany and Poland. Mem.: Coun. Fgn. Rels. Office: Am Jewish Com 165 E 56th St New York NY 10022-2709 E-mail: harrisd@ajc.org.

HARRIS, DAVID FORD, management consultant, retired government official; b. Hillsboro, Mo., Feb. 14, 1931; s. Walter Dunklin and Nelle (Landrigan) H.; m. Erna Beckmann, Mar. 5, 1964; children: Christopher Beckmann, Stefanie Ford. BS, U.S. Mil. Acad., West Point, 1954; MBA, Stanford U., 1961. Budget officer Post Office Dept., Washington, 1964-68, spl. asst. postmaster gen., 1968-70; chief adminstrv. officer, sec. Postal Rate Commn., Washington, 1970-83; sec. to bd. govs. U.S. Postal Svc., Washington, 1983-95; ret., 1995; mgmt. cons. representing N.Am. for CB Group, Santiago, Chile, 1996—. Capt. U.S. Army, 1954-64. Mem. West Point Alumni Assn., Stanford Alumni Assn., Alexandria Sportsman's Club. Roman Catholic. Home and Office: 3643 Trinity Dr Alexandria VA 22304-1840

HARRIS, DAVID FREDERICK, pathologist; b. Doylestown, Pa., July 21, 1944; s. William Brisbane Dick and Harriet Washburn (Miller) H.; m. Helen Louise Staats, June 13, 1970; children: Enon, Noah, Morgan. BA, Dartmouth Coll., 1966; MD, Cornell U., 1970. Diplomate Am. Bd. Clin. Pathology, Am. Bd. Anatomic Pathology. Intern Northwestern U., Chgo., 1970-71; resident Walter Reed Army Hosp., Washington, 1971-73, rsch. fellow, 1973-75, Staats Hosp., Charleston, W.Va., 1975-76; resident in pathology Blodgett Meml. Hosp., Grand Rapids, Mich., 1976-79; pathologist Hays (Kans.) Pathology Lab., 1979-80, Med. Ctr. Hosp., Odessa, Tex., 1980-82, Lee M. Hosp., Giddings, Tex., 1982-90, Ctrl. Tex. Med. Ctr., San Marcos, Tex., 1983-90, Upson Regional Med. Ctr., Thomaston, Ga., 1990—. Maj. U.S. Army Med. Corps, 1971-75. Fellow Coll. Am. Pathologists; mem. Ga. Assn. Pathologists, Ga. Med. Assn. Mem. Soc. Of Friends. Avocations: gardening, skiing, swimming. Home: 236 Peachbelt Rd Thomaston GA 30286-4062 Office: Upson Regional Med Ctr PO Box 1059 Thomaston GA 30286-0013 E-mail: dfharris@urmc.org.

HARRIS, DAVID HENRY, retired life insurance company executive; b. N.Y.C., May 7, 1924; s. Julian A. and May L. (Wilenski) H.; 1 child, Jean Harris Haig; m. Cassandra Sturman, Feb. 20, 1987. Student, Sherborne (Eng.) Sch., 1937-40. With Prudential Ins. Co. Am., 1940-43, Equitable Life Assurance Soc. U.S., N.Y.C., 1946-86, exec. v.p., 1973-77, exec. v.p., chief adminstrv. officer, 1977-80, exec. v.p., chief staff, 1981-86, bd. dirs., 1977-86; pres. Equitable Found., 1986-88. Chmn. bd. Equimatics, Inc., 1971-73, Informatics, Inc., 1974-75; vice chmn. Equitable Variable Life Ins. Co., 1975-76, chmn., 1976-77. Bd. dirs. Can. Life of Am. Series Fund, 1989-2000; trustee Chappaqua Libr., 1991-94. With AUS, 1943-46. Fellow Soc. Actuaries. Home: 130 E 67th St New York NY 10021-6136

HARRIS, DAVID JACK, artist, painter, educator; b. San Mateo, Calif., Jan. 6, 1948; s. Jack McAllister and Audrey Ellen (Vogt) H. BA, San Francisco State U., 1971, MA, 1975. Dir. Galerie de Tours, San Francisco, 1971-72; lectr. Chabot Coll., Hayward, Calif., 1975-80; interior designer David Harris Assocs., San Mateo, 1975-85; freelance artist, painter San Mateo, 1975—; ptnr. Harris & Kasten, Archs. & Designers, 1990—. Art cons. David Harris Assocs., Belmont, Calif., 1980—; v.p. Coastal Arts League Mus., Half Moon Bay, Calif., 1988—; ptnr., art dir. Fine Art Pub., Palo Alto, Calif., 1989—; bd. dirs. 1870 Gallery and Studios, Belmont, 1978—, gallery dir., 1989—, owner, partner HSW Gallery, San Francisco. Painter murals Chartered Bank of London, 1979, Caesar's Hotel, Las Vegas, 1984, Pacific Telephone, San Francisco; author mus. catalog California Concepts, 1988; represented in permanent collections at Ask Computer, Palo Alto, shared Fin., Harris Corp., Bain and Co., San Francisco, Verilink, Litton Industries, Foothill Bank, Los Altos, Chartered Bank of London, San Francisco, Stanford U., Palo Alto, Golden Nugget Hotel, Atlantic City, Nat. Bank of Detroit, Crisafi, Sciabica, Woodward, D.J. Crisafi and Co., Sheraton Grande, L.A., 1st am. Title Guaranty Co., Walt Disney, Voysys Corp., Spieker Pntrs., Storm & Co., Menlo Park, Calif., Royal family, Saudi Arabia, others. Recipient Purchase award North Cen. Washington Mus., 1988. Mem.

Internat. Soc. Interior Designers, Coastal Arts League Mus. (v.p. 1988—, Zoe Tierny award 1988). Avocations: travel, photography, hiking. Home and Office: 485 Miramar Dr Half Moon Bay CA 94019-1372 E-mail: davidharris@legacysolutions.net.

HARRIS, DAVID PHILIP, crisis management executive; b. Boston, June 23, 1937; s. David Henry and Edith Endicott (Young) H.; m. Judith Ann Brown, Oct. 23, 1999; children from previous marriage: Kristian Alexander, Thomas Cameron. BS in Sci., U. Rochester (N.Y.), 1959; MBA, U. Pa., 1963. Auditor Touche, Ross et al, Boston, 1960-61; asst. contr. Kendall Co., Chgo., Charlotte, N.C., 1963-65; mgr. internal cons. Dart Industries, Stamford, Conn., 1965-67; asst. contr. Achushnet Co., New Bedford, Mass., 1967-70; asst. treas. Bell & Howell Co., Chgo., 1970-73; v.p., treas. CFS Continental, Inc., Chgo., 1973-78; pres., chief exec. officer Harris Devel. Co., Lake Forest, Ill., 1975—. Chmn., CEO Amtec Devel. Co., Highland Park, Ill., 1978-83; affiliate Morris Andersen & Assocs., Glenview, Ill., 1984-93; bd. dirs. Juvenile Shoe Corp., Aurora, Mo., Intellimedia Corp., Benton Harbor, Mich.; exec. v.p., dir. STS Cons. Ltd., Deerfield, Ill., 1995-98. Treas., dir. Lake Forest Symphony Assn., 1983-88, Touchstone Theatre, Chgo., 1987-90; mem. engring. com. Beach Restoration Project, Lake Forest, 1987-88, long term plan com., Lake Forest, 1991—; bd. dirs. Zoning Bd. Appeals, Lake Forest, 1988-93, ARS Viva Symphony Orch., 1998—; fin. planning advisor bd. edn. Lake Forest Sch. Dist. 67, 1992-99, mem. sch. bd. edn., 2001—; dir. rsch. Lake Forest Civic Fedn., 1992-98; trustee advisory coun. Univ. Rochchester, 2002— With U.S. Army and USAR, 1959-65. Mem. Fin. Mgrs. Assn. Chgo. (sec. 1972-91, pres. 1988-89), Tower Club. Republican. Presbyterian. Avocation: sailing.

HARRIS, DAVID THOMAS, immunology educator; b. Jonesboro, Ark, May 9, 1956; s. Marm Melton and Lucille Luretha (Buck) H.; m. Francoise Jacqueline Besencon, June 24, 1989; children: Alexandre M., Stefanie L., Leticia M. BS in Biology, Math. and Psychology, Wake Forest U., 1978, MS, 1980, PhD in Microbiology and Immunology, 1982. Fellow Ludwig Inst. Cancer Rsch., Lausanne, Switzerland, 1982-85; rsch. asst. prof. U. N.C., Chapel Hill, 1985-89; assoc. prof. U. Ariz., Tucson, 1989-96, prof., 1996—. Cons. Teltech, Inc. Mpls., 1990—, Advanced Biosci. Resources, 1991-95; bd. sci. advisors Cryo-Cell Internat., 1992-95; bd. dir. Ageria, Inc., Tuscon; dir. Cord Blood Stem Cell Bank, 1992—; mem. Ariz. Cancer Ctr., Steele Meml. Children's Rsch. Ctr., Ariz. Arthritis Ctr. Program, sci. adv. bd. Cord Blood Registry, Inc., chief sci. div. Cord Blood Registry, Inc.; founder ImmuneRegen BioScis., Inc., 2002. Co-author chpts. to sci. books, articles to profls. jour.; reviewer sci. jour.; co-holder 7 scientific patents. Grantee numerous grants, 1988—. Mem. AAAS, Am. Assn. Immunologists, Reticuleondothelial Soc., Internat. Soc. Hematotherapy and Graft Engring., Internat. Soc. Devel. and Comparative Immunology, Scandanavian Soc. Immunology, Sigma Xi, Democrat. Mem. Ch. of Christ. Avocations: tennis, hiking, jogging, skiing, travel. Office: U Ariz Dept Microbiology Bldg 90 Tucson AZ 85721-0001 E-mail: davidh@U.Arizona.edu.

HARRIS, DELMARIE JONES, elementary education educator; b. New Orleans, Mar. 16, 1947; d. Ralph and Ruth Lena (Ackerson) Jones; m. Hosey W. Williams (div. 1974); children: Hosey Willie, Sabrena Michelle; m. Ronald Andrew Harris, Mar. 7, 1978; 1 child, Rene Andrea. Student, Southern U., New Orleans, 1967-70; BA, Southern U., 1971. Tchr. St. Mary of Angels, New Orleans, La., 1971-73, J.F. Gauthier Elem. Sch., Poydras, La., 1973—. Grade chmn. J.F. Gauthier steering com. bull. 741, 1987, language arts textbook adoption rep., 1992-93; recorder St. Bernard Parish Discipline Dress Code Adoption Com., 1988-90, math. rep., 1990, primary tchr.; mem. com. to rewrite curriculum for math. State of La., 1996. Mem. NEA, Nat. Coun. Tchrs. Math., Internat. Reading Assn., La. Assn. Educators, St. Bernard Assn. Educators. Democrat. Roman Catholic. Avocations: interior decorating, dancing.

HARRIS, DENISE MICHELLE, advertising account executive; b. Stockton, Calif., Sept. 7, 1970; d. Overton Thomas Harris Sr. and Evelyn Jean Harris. BA, CSU Hayward, Hayward, CA, 1998. Advt. account exec. ANG Newspapers, Hayward, Calif., 1996—98, The San Jose Mercury News, San Jose, Calif., 1998—99; advt. account mgr. The Weather Channel, Atlanta, Ga., 1999—2001. Recipient Academic Senate's Student of the Month, San Joaquin County Academic Senate, 1993, Advt. Excellence Tng. Award, Knight Ridder, Effective Presentation Tng., Mandel Comm., Profl. Selling Skills Tng., Achieve Global. Mem.: Alpha Kappa Alpha Sorority Inc. (connection chair 1999—2001). Avocations: skiing, reading, writing, travel, yoga.

HARRIS, DIANA KOFFMAN, sociologist, educator; b. Memphis, Aug. 11, 1929; d. David Nathan and Helen Ethel (Rotter) Koffman; m. Lawrence A. Harris, June 24, 1951; children: Marla, Jennifer. Student, U. Miami, 1947-48; BS, U. Wis., 1951; postgrad., U. Oxford (Eng.), 1968-69. Advt. and sales promotion mgr. Wallace Johnston Distbg. Co., Memphis, 1952-54; welfare worker Tenn. Dept. Pub. Welfare, Knoxville, Tenn., 1954-56; instr. sociology Maryville (Tenn.) Coll., 1972-75, Fort Sanders Sch. Nursing, Knoxville, 1971-78, U. Tenn., Knoxville, 1967—; series editor Garland Pub., Inc., 1989—. Author: Readings in Social Gerontology, 1975, (with Cole) The Elderly in America, 1977, The Sociology of Aging, 1980, 2d edit., 1990; co-author: Sociology, 1984, Annotated Bibliography and Sourcebook: Sociology of Aging, 1985, Dictionary of Gerontology, 1988, Teaching Sociology of Aging, 1991, 4th edit., 1996, 5th edit., 2000; aging series editor Garland Pub., Inc., 1989—; contbr. articles to profl. jours. Chmn. U. Tenn. Coun. on Aging, 1979—; organizer Knoxville chpt. Gray Panthers, 1978; mem. Govnr.'s Task Force on Preretirement Programs for State Employers, 1973, White Ho. Conf. on Aging, 1981; bd. mem. Knoxville-Knox County Coun. on Aging, 1976, Sr. Citizens Info. and Referral, 1979, Sr. Citizens Home-Aide Svc., 1977; del. E. Tenn. Coun. on Aging, 1977. Recipient Meritorious award Nat. U. Continuing Edn. Assn., 1982, Pub. Svc. award Nat. Alumni Assn., 1992, Appreciation award Assn. Gerontology in Higher Edn., 1994, Appreciation award for excellent scholarly contbn. to ednl. gerontology lit. Ednl. Gerontology jour., 1996; grantee Retirement Rsch. Found., 1997—. Mem. Am. Sociol. Assn., AAAS, Gerontol. Soc. Am., Popular Culture Assn., So. Sociol. Soc., So. Gerontol. Soc. (pres.'s award 1984), N. Central Sociol. Assn., London Competitor's Club, Nat. Contest Assn., Knoxville Kontestars. Home and Office: U Tenn Dept Sociology PO Box 50546 Knoxville TN 37950-0546

HARRIS, DIANE CAROL, merger and acquisition consulting firm executive; b. Rockville Centre, N.Y., Dec. 25, 1942; d. Daniel Christopher and Laura Louise (Schmitt) Quigley; m. Wayne Manley Harris, Sept. 30, 1978. BA, Cath. U. Am., 1964; MS, Rensselaer Poly. Inst., 1967. With Bausch & Lomb, Rochester, N.Y., 1967-96, dir. applications lab., 1972-74, dir. tech. mktg. analytical systems divsn., 1974-76, bus. line mgr., 1976-77, v.p. planning and bus. programs, 1977-78, v.p. planning and bus. devel. Soflens divsn., 1978-80, corp. dir. planning, 1980-81, v.p. corp. devel., 1981-96; v.p. RID-N.Y. State, 1980-83; pres. Hypotenuse Enterprises, Inc., 1994—. Mem. adv. bd. Merger Mgmt. Report, 1986—92; internat. bd. dirs. Assn. Corp. Growth, v.p. corp. mem. affairs, 1993—94, v.p. internat. expansion, 1994—95, pres.-elect, 1996—97, pres., 1997—98, immediate past pres., 1998—99; bd. dirs. Flowserve Corp., chair audit com., 2001—; bd. dirs. Monroe Fund, Venture Capital Group. Contbr. articles to profl jours. Pres Rochester Against Intoxicated Driving, 1979—83, chmn polit action comt, 1983, 1986; bd dirs, chmn long range planning comt Rochester area Nat Coun Alcoholism, 1980—84; mem Stop DWI Adv Panel to Monroe County Legis, 1982—87, NY State Coalition for Safety Belt Use, 1984—85; mem. key exec. group Rensselaer Poly. Inst., 1993—96; mem. Com. 200, 1993—2002; mem ACG Speakers Bur, 1993—; mem adv comt Catalyst, 1995; bd dirs Rochester Rehab Ctr, 1982—84, Friends of Bristol Valley Playhouse Found, 1983—87. Named one of 50 Women to Watch in Corp Am, Bus Week Mag, 1987, 1992, 100 Women to Watch, Duns Bus Rev, 1988; recipient Distinguished Citizen's Award, Monroe County, 1979, Tribute to Women in Indust and Serv Award, YWCA, 1983, Pres's 21st Century Leadership Award, Women's Hall of Fame, 1995; grantee NSF, 1963. Mem.: Assn. Corp. Growth (Meritorious Svc. award 1995), Internat. Alliance Com. and Rochester Women's Network (com. of 200 1993—2002), Nat. Assn. Women Bus. Owners, Fin. Execs. Inst., Am. Mgmt. Assn., C. of C. (pub safety com. Rochester area chpt, task force on hwy safety and legi 1981—86, high technology Rochester adv. panel 1989—91, 1999—2000), Phi Beta Kappa, Delta Epsilon Sigma, Sigma Xi. Home: 60 Mendon Center Rd Honeoye Falls NY 14472-9363 Office: Hypotenuse Enterprises Inc 1545 East Ave Rochester NY 14610-1614 E-mail: harris@hypot.com.

HARRIS, DOLORES M. academic administrator; b. Camden, N.J., Aug. 5, 1930; d. Roland Henry Sr. and Frances Anna (Gatewood) Ellis; m. Morris E. Harris Sr., 1948 (div. 1987); children: Morris E. Jr., Sheila Davis, Gregory M. Sr. BS, Glassboro (N.J.) State Coll., 1959, MA, 1966; EdD, Rutgers U., 1983. Tchr. and reading specialist Glassboro Bd. Edn., 1958-68, dir. aux. svcs., 1968-70; supr. adult edn. Camden Welfare Bd., summer 1968; head state dir. Glassboro SCOPE, summer 1969-70; assoc. dir. Jersey City State Coll., summer 1971; dir. adult edn. Glassboro State Coll., 1970-74, dir. continuing edn. dept., 1989-90, acting assoc. v.p. acad. affairs, 1989-91; ret., 1991. Chmn. adv. bd. Women's Ednl. Equity Comms. Network project, San Francisco, 1977-78; bd. dirs. Glassboro State Coll. Mgmt. Inst.; cons. crossroads project Temple U., Phila., 1977; cons. corrections project Va. Commonwealth U., Richmond; cons. Mich. State Dept. of Edn., Lansing, 1973; examiner N.Y. State Civil Svc. Commn., 1976—; mem., vice-chmn. comm. Accrediting Coun. for Continuing Edn. and Tng., Richmond, 1985-89, chmn., 1989—; workshop/seminar chair Eastern Montgomery County chpt. SCORE, 1991—. Author: (with others) Black Studies for ABE and GED Programs in Correction, 1975; author: guide How to Establish ABE Programs, 1972; founding editor: newsletter For Adults Only, 1970; contbr. articles to profl. jours. Founder, mem. bd. trustees, chair bd. Glassboro Child Devel. Ctr., 1974-87; bd. dirs. Gloucester County (N.J.) United Way, 1977—, sec. bd., 1980, pres. bd., 1983-85; charter mem., bd. dirs. Glassboro Glass Mus., 1979-87; vice chair, chair, mem. Gloucester County Commn. on Women, 1983-87; mem., chair edn. subcom. Gloucester County REACH, 1987—; trustee Frederick Douglas Meml. and His. Assn., 2000—; counselor, seminar/workshop chair SCORE. Recipient Disting. Svc. award Holly Shores Girl Scouts Am., 1979, Disting. Alumnae award Glassboro State Coll., 1971, Disting. Svc. award Camden County, 1974; named to Legion of Honor, Chapel of Four Chaplains, 1983; named Women of Yr., Gloucester County Bus. and Profl. Women's Club, 1985; named Woman of Achievement, Gloucester County Commn. on Women, 1987; named one of Outstanding Citizens, Holly Shores Girl Scouts Am., 1987; named one of 100 Most Influential Black Ams., Ebony mag., 1989; NJ Woman of Achievement award, 1991. Mem. NEA, AAUW (v.p. membership com. Gloucester County chpt. 1986-87), N.J. Assn. (life, pres. 1973-74), Soc. Docta (charter, bd. dirs. 1987—), N.J. Edn. Assn., N.J. State Fedn. Colored Women's Clubs (pres. 1976-80), Northeastern Fedn. Women's Clubs (v.p.-at-large 1983-85, parliamentarian 1985—), Nat. Assn. Colored Women's Clubs, Inc. (pres. 1988-92, Ebony 100 Influential Black Am. 1988-92), Links Club, Women for Greater Phila. (bd. dirs.), Ea. Montgomer County SCORE (chair seminars, workshop prorams 2001—). Presbyterian. Avocations: reading, fitness exercises.

HARRIS, DON VICTOR, JR., lawyer; b. Nottingham Twp., Ind., Jan. 16, 1921; s. Don Victor and Nellie Florence (Dukes) H.; m. Joan Elliott Haffler, Aug. 15, 1959; children: Leigh Elliott (Mrs. John A. Hay), Meghan St. Clair (Mrs. Michel P. Zeisser). AB, DePauw U., 1943; JD, Harvard U., 1945. Bar: D.C. 1947. Law clk. to judge U.S. Ct. Appeals 2d Circuit, 1945-46; assoc. firm Covington & Burling, Washington, 1946-57, ptnr., 1957—. Lectr. in law George Washington U., 1963-64; lectr. tax insts.; mem. IRS Commr.'s Adv. Group, 1976 Contbr. articles to law jours.; Case editor: Harvard Law Rev. Bd. dirs. Oak Hill Cemetery Co.; bd. dirs. Found. for Preservation Historic Georgetown. Fellow Am. Coll. Tax Counsel, Am. Bar Found. (life); mem. Am. Law Inst. (life), ABA (chmn. sect. taxation 1976-77), D.C. Bar Assn., Fed. Bar Assn., Phi Beta Kappa, Beta Theta Pi, Am. Camellia Soc. (judge), Met Club, Chevy Chase Club, John's Island Club (Fla.). Episcopalian. Home: 2803 P St NW Washington DC 20007-3067 also: John's Island 777 Sea Oak Dr No 715 Vero Beach FL 32963-3541 Office: Covington & Burling 1043-C 1201 Pennsylvania Ave NW Washington DC 20004-2401 E-mail: dharris@cov.com., ursa1921@aol.com.

HARRIS, DONALD, composer; b. St. Paul, Apr. 7, 1931; s. Barney William and Hattie (Paper) H.; m. Marilyn Hackett, 1983; children: Daniel, Jeremy. Mus.B., U. Mich., 1952, Mus.M., 1954. Music cons. Am. Cultural Center, USIS, Paris, 1965-67; asst. to pres. for acad. affairs New Eng. Conservatory Music, Boston, 1967-71, v.p., 1971-74, exec. v.p., 1974-77, mem. teaching faculty depts. composition and music lit., 1967-77; composer-in-residence, prof. music, chmn. composition and theory Hartt Sch. of Music, U. Hartford, Conn., 1977-80, dean, 1981-88; dean Coll. of the Arts The Ohio State U., 1988-97, prof. composition, 1997—. Vis. prof. music George Washington U., 1998; pres. Internat. Coun. Fine Arts Deans, 1994-96. Composer: Piano Sonata, 1956, Fantasy for Violin and Piano, 1957, Symphony in Two Movements, 1961, String Quartet, 1965, Ludus for 10 Instruments, 1966, Ludus II for 5 Instruments, 1973, Charmes for Voice and Orchestra, 1977, On Variations, 1976, For the Night to Wear (Hortense Flexner), mezzo-soprano and 7 instruments, 1978, Balladen for solo piano, 1979, Of Hartford in a Purple Light (Wallace Stevens) for soprano and piano, 1979, Prelude to a Concert in Connecticut, 1981, Les Mains (Marguerite Yourcenar) for mezzo-soprano and piano, 1983, Meditations for Solo Organ, 1984, Three Fanfares for Four Horns, 1984, Canzona & Carol for Double Brass Quintet and Timpani, 1986, Pierrot Lieder (soprano & 5 instruments), 1988, Mermaid Variations (chamber orch.), 1993, Second String Quartet, 2002; recs., CRI, Delos, Golden Crest Records; co-editor: The Correspondence Between Arnold Schoenberg and Alban Berg, 1986. Recipient commns. from Serge Koussevitzky Music Found., 1977, Elizabeth Sprague Coolidge Found., 1977, Goethe Inst., 1978, Conn. Commn. Arts, 1979, French Nat. Radio, 1972, Festival Contemporary Am. Music at Tanglewood, 1965, Boston Musica Viva, 1973, Cleve. Orch., 1975, Arnold Schoenberg Inst., 1988, Cleve. Chamber Orchestra, 1991, Jefferson Acad., 2001; recipient Louisville Orch. award, 1954, Prince Rainier of Monaco Composition prize, 1960, award Am. Acad. and Inst. Arts and Letters, 1991; grantee-in-aid Rockefeller Found., 1969; grantee-in-aid Chapelbrook Found., 1970; fellowship grantee Nat. Endowment for Arts, 1974; Fulbright scholar, 1956; Guggenheim fellow, 1965. Mem. ASCAP (Deems Taylor award 1989, others 1973—). Address: 5257 Courtney Pl Columbus OH 43235-3474 E-mail: harris.27@osu.edu.

HARRIS, DONALD RAY, lawyer; b. Lake Preston, S.D., Apr. 21, 1938; s. Raymond H. and Nona (Trousdale) H.; children: Beverly, Scott, Bradley, Lindi; m. Sharon K. Brown, Sept. 4, 1982. BA, State U. Iowa, 1959; JD, U. Iowa, 1961. Bar: Ill. 1963, U.S. Dist. Ct. (no. dist.) Ill. 1963, U.S. Ct. Appeals (3d, 4th, 6th, 7th, 9th and fed. cirs.) 1966-95, U.S. Dist. Ct. (we. dist.) Tex. 1989, U.S. Supreme Ct. 1977, U.S. Ct. Fed. Claims 1995, U.S. Dist. Ct. (ea. dist.) Wis. 1997. Assoc. Jenner & Block, Chgo., 1963-70, ptnr., 1970—. Lt. inf. U.S. Army, 1961-63. Mem. ABA, Ill. Bar Assn., Chgo. Bar Assn., Bar Assn. 7th Cir., Chgo. Coun. Lawyers, Am. Coll. Trial Lawyers, ITC Trail Lawyers Assn., Lawyers Club of Chgo. Office: Jenner & Block One IBM Plz Chicago IL 60611-3586 E-mail: dharris@jenner.com.

HARRIS, DONALD WAYNE, research scientist; b. Ft. Scott, Kans., Sept. 23, 1942; s. Carl Raymond Harris and Kathryn Francis (Peare) Hayes; m. Louisa Dudley Beisser, Aug. 1, 1998; children: Daniel Duane (dec. 1994), Sheila, Lynette, Crystal Ann, Rebecca Braden, Maude Miller, John Cole Painter, Hannah Painter. BS, U. Mo., 1966, PhD, 1974. From scientist to mgr. carbohydrate polymer rsch. Clinton (Iowa) Corn Processing Co., 1974-84; sr. rsch. scientist AE Staley Mfg. Co., Decatur, Ill., 1984-92; rsch. fellow AE Staley Mfg. Co. divsn. Tate & Lyle N.Am., Lafayette, Ind., 1992—. Patentee in field; contbr. articles to profl. jours. With U.S. Army, 1968-70. Mem. Am. Chem. Soc., Am. Assn. Cereal Chemists, Phi Lambda Upsilon. Avocations: hiking, hunting, fishing. Home: 5208 Cameron Ln Lafayette IN 47905-7581 E-mail: dwharris@tlna.com.

HARRIS, DORIS ANN, medical/surgical nurse; b. Sayre, Pa., Mar. 5, 1947; d. Allan N. and Ruth E. (Stafford) H. Student, RPH Sch. Nursing, Sayre, 1968; BSPA, St. Joseph's Coll., Windham, Maine. RN, Conn. Staff nurse Conn. Hospice, Inc., Branford, 1980-88; spl. procedures nurse Yale Gynecology-Oncology Clinic, New Haven, 1988-90; nurse oncology unit Middlesex Hosp., Middletown, Conn., 1990-94; staff nurse The Madison (Conn.) House, 1994-98, Middlesex Hosp. Home Care, Clinton, Conn., 1998—. Mem. Nat. League for Nursing, Ind. Assn. Hospice Caregivers (co-founder, co-dir. 1987-2000). Home: 131 Liberty St Clinton CT 06413-1739

HARRIS, DOUGLAS CLAY, retired newspaper executive; b. Owensboro, Ky., Oct. 9, 1939; s. Marvin Dudley and Elizabeth (Adelman) H. BS, Murray State U., 1961; MS, Ind. U., 1964, EdD, 1968; grad. advanced mgmt. program, Harvard U., 1987. Counselor, asst. to dean of students Ind. U., Bloomington, 1965-68; mgmt. appraisal specialist United Air Lines, Elk Grove Village, Ill., 1968-69; dir. manpower div. Computer Age Industries, Washington, 1969; area personnel dir. Peat Marwick Mitchell & Co., N.Y.C., 1969-72; v.p. personnel Knight-Ridder, Inc., Miami, Fla., 1972-85, v.p., sec., 1986-98. Served to capt. U.S. Army, 1961-62. Republican. Home and Office: 30730 Watson Blvd Big Pine Key FL 33043-5009

HARRIS, DUCHESS, social sciences educator; b. Newport News, Va., May 16, 1969; d. Frank and Miriam Mann Harris; m. Jon Vincent Thomas, Nov. 26, 1994; 1 child, Austin Harris Thomas. BA in Am. History and African-Am. Studies, U. Pa., 1991; PhD in Am. Studies, U. Minn., 1997. Constituent adv. Sen. Paul Wellstone, St. Paul, 1993—94; rsch. fellow U. Minn. Law Sch., Mpls., 1996—97; asst. prof. African-Am. studies and polit. sci. Macalester Coll., St. Paul, 1997—; policy fellow Hubert H. Humphrey Inst. Pub. Affairs, 1998—99. Contbr. articles and book revs. to profl. jours., chapters to books. Commr. Mpls. Commn. Civil Rights, 1996—98; bd. dirs. Genesis II for Women, St. Paul, 1996—99, Model Cities Family Devel., St. Paul, 1994—99, Minn. Women's Found., Mpls., 2000—. Named one of 30 Leaders under 30, Ebony Mag., 1997; fellow, Woodrow Wilson Found., 2001—02; grantee, Bush Course Devel., 2000, 2001. Mem.: Am. Studies Assn. (minority scholars com.), Nat. Conf. Black Polit. Scientist (exec. coun., chair women and politics sect.), Mensa. Democrat. Home: 401 Vadnais Lake Dr Saint Paul MN 55127 Office: Macalester Coll 1600 Grand Ave Saint Paul MN 55105

HARRIS, EARL DOUGLAS, state agency administrator; b. Athens, Ga., Apr. 9, 1947; s. Roland Russell and Martha Sue (Davis) H.; m. Jean Wright, Dec. 26, 1975; cchildren: Jeannette, Stephanie. BSAE, U. Ga., 1970, MBA, JD, 1973. Bar: Ga. 1973, U.S. Dist. Ct. (mid. dist.) Ga. 1973, U.S. Ct. Appeals (5th cir.) 1973, U.S. Ct. Claims 1977, U.S. Tax Ct. 1977, U.S. Patent Office 1977, U.S. Customs Ct. 1977, U.S. Supreme Ct. 1977, U.S. Ct. Customs and Patent Appeals 1980, U.S. Ct. Internat. Trade 1981, U.S. Ct. Appeals (5th, 11th and federal cir.) 1981. Sole practice of law and patent law, Watkinsville, Ga., 1973-76, 86-92; city atty. Town of Bogart, 1974-75, 85-90; sr. ptnr. Harris & Rice, Watkinsville, 1977-79; mem. Harris, Rice & Alford, P.A., Watkinsville, 1978-80; ptnr., pres. Harris & Alford, P.A., 1980-85; Ga. asst. commr. agr., 1992—. Mem. Ga. State Olympic Law Enforcement Commd., 1996; pres. Fed. Title Corp., 1978—90; county atty. Oconee County, Ga., 1978—80; atty. Town of Bishop, 1980—89; corp. sec. Lawlog Corp., 1980—90. Contbr. over 250 articles to profl. publs. Bd. dirs. The Oconee Enterprise, Inc., 1987-93, Clarke County unit Am. Cancer Soc., 1970-72, Ga. Fed. State Shipping Point Inspection Svc., Inc., 1995—; mem. Oconee County Dem. Exec. Com., 1976-94, treas., 1976-82; pres., trustee N.E. Ga. Presbytery, 1987-91; trustee Masonic Children's Home Ga., 1985-89; trustee, gen. counsel Ga. Scottish Rite Found., Inc., 1989-2000, chmn. bd., 2000—; pres., chmn. bd. dirs. Ga. Masonic Charities Found., Inc., 1996-98; active Boy Scouts Am. Served with USMC, 1965-68; with USAF, 1968. Mem. State Bar Ga., Alcovy Cir. Bar Assn., Western Cir. Bar Assn., Sphinx Soc., Gridiron Secret Soc., AGHON Soc. (past pres.), U. Ga. Agrl. Alumni Assn. (pres. young alumni div. 1975-76, dir. at Large, 1996-97, sec.-treas., 1997-99), Oconee County C. of C. (dir., sec. 1976-78), Masons (Past Grand Master of Masons in Ga., Wollstein award, Ga. Lodge of Rsch. Calloway award), Scottish Rite (33 degree, sovereign grand insp. den. Ga., mem. supreme coun. USA So. Jurisdiction), Order of Eastern Star (past patron), Societas Rosicruciana in Civitatibus Foederatis (IX grade, Chief Adept for Ga.), Shriners, KT (grand comdr. Ga., knight comdr. of the Templar nat. award), Tall Cedars of Lebanon, Royal Order of Scotland (Ga. screener), Red Cross of Constantine (Pussiant sovereign), Knights of York Grand Cross of Honor (past prior), York Rite Coll. (past gov.), Knight Templar Priests (past preceptor), Philathes Soc., Blue Key (past pres.), Omicron Delta Kappa, Sigma Iota Epsilon, Alpha Zeta, Phi Alpha Delta. Presbyterian (ruling elder). Home: 31 Meadow Way Covington GA 30014-1642

HARRIS, ED(WARD ALLEN), actor; b. Englewood, N.J., Nov. 28, 1950; s. Bob L. and Margaret Harris; m. Amy Madigan. Student, Columbia U., 1969-71, U. Okla., Norman, 1972-73; BFA, Calif. Inst. of Arts, Valencia, 1975. Appeared in plays A Streetcar Named Desire, Sweet Bird of Youth, Julius Caesar, Hamlet, Camelot, Are You Lookin?, Time of Your Life, Learned Ladies, Kingdom of Earth, Grapes of Wrath, Present Laughter, Balaam, Killers' Head, Fool for Love (Obie award 1983), Prairie Avenue (L.A. Drama Critics Circle award 1981), Scar, 1985 (San Francisco Critics award), Precious Sons, 1986 (Theater World award), Simpatico, 1994, 95, Taking Sides, 1996; (repertory plays) Servant of Two Masters, Ohio, Claptrap, Cambridge, Mass., 1985, Pirates of Penzance at N.Y. Shakespeare Festival, Glass Menagerie, Long Wharf, New Haven, 1986, Bobby Gould in Hell, 1989; appeared in films including Come, 1978, Borderline, 1978, Knightriders, 1980, Creepshow, 1981, The Right Stuff, 1982, Swing Shift, 1982, Under Fire, 1982, A Flash of Green, 1983, Places in the Heart, 1983, Alamo Bay, 1984, Sweet Dreams, 1985, Code Name: Emerald, 1985, Walker, 1987, To Kill a Priest, 1988, Jacknife, 1989, The Abyss, 1989, State of Grace, 1990, Paris Trout, 1991, Glengarry Glen Ross, 1992, Needful Things, 1993, The Firm, 1993, China Moon, 1994, Milk Money, 1994, Apollo 13, 1995 (Acad. award nominee for best supporting actor 1996, SAG award 1996), Just Cause, 1995, Eye for an Eye, 1995, Nixon, 1995, The Rock, 1996, (TV movie) Riders of the Purple Sage, 1996 (also exec. prodr.), Absolute Power, 1997, Stepmom, 1998, The Truman Show, 1998 (Golden Globe award, 1999), The Third Miracle, 1999, Waking the Dead, 2000, The Prime Gig, 2000, Pollock, 2000 (aslo prodr., dir.), Enemy at the Gates, 2001, Buffalo Soldiers, 2001, A Beautiful Mind, 2001, Just a Dream, 2002, The Hours, 2002, Masked and Anonymous, 2003, The Human Stain, 2003; TV movies include The Amazing Howard Hughes, 1977, The Seekers, 1979, The Aliens Are Coming, 1980, The Last Innocent Man, 1987, Running Mates, 1992, The Stand, 1994 (unbilled cameo). Trustee Calif. Inst. of Arts, Valencia, 1985—. Mem. Screen Actors Guild, Equity. Address: 22031 Carbon Mesa Rd Malibu CA 90265-5008*

HARRIS, EDWARD DAY, JR., physician; b. Phila., July 7, 1937; children: Ned, Tom, Chandler. AB, Dartmouth Coll., 1958, grad. with honors, 1960; MD cum laude, Harvard U., 1962. Diplomate Am. Bd. Internal Medicine and Rheumatology (chmn. subsplty. bd. in rheumatology 1986-88). Intern Mass. Gen. Hosp., Boston, 1962-63, asst. resident, 1963-64, sr. resident, 1966-67, clin. research fellow arthritis unit, 1967-69; asst. prof. Harvard Med. Sch., Boston, 1970; from asst. prof. to prof. Dartmouth Med. Sch., Hanover, N.H., 1970-83, Eugene W. Leonard prof., 1979-83, chief connective tissue disease sect., 1970-83; mem. staff Mary Hitchcock Meml. Hosp., 1970-83; chief med. service Middlesex Gen. U. Hosp., New Brunswick, N.J., 1983—; asst. prof. Harvard U. Med. Sch., Boston, 1970; prof., chmn. medicine U. Medicine and Dentistry N.J.-Rutgers U. Med. Sch., New Brunswick, 1983-88; Arthur L. Bloomfield prof. medicine Stanford U. Sch. Medicine, 1988-95, chmn. dept. medicine, 1988-95, George DeForest Barnett prof. medicine, 1988—. Chief med. svc. Stanford U. Hosp., 1988-95; dir. Ctr. for Musculoskeletal Diseases, Stanford, 1996—; pres. med. staff, Stanford U. Hosp., 1997-99; med. dir. Internat. Med. Svc., 1997—. Master: Am. Rheumatism Assn. (numerous coms. 1967—, pres. 1985—86); fellow: ACP (gov. No. Calif. chpt. ACP-Am. Soc. Internal Medicine 2000—01), Royal Soc. London, Am. Soc. Internal Medicine; mem.: Alpha Omega Alpha (exec. sec. 1997—, editor The Pharos 1997—). Office: Stanford U 1000 Welch Rd Ste 203 Palo Alto CA 94304-1808 E-mail: madera@stanford.edu.

HARRIS, EDWARD FREDERICK, orthodontics educator; b. San Jose, Calif., Oct. 2, 1947; s. Roy Hayward and Bonnie (Keeble) H.; m. Karen J. Morse, May 29, 1970 (div. July 1983); children: Jeremy T., Emily J.; m. Betsy D. Barcroft, Jan. 24, 1990. BA, San Jose State U., 1969; MA, Ariz. State U., 1972, PhD, 1977. Asst. prof. orthodontics U. Conn., Farmington, 1978-80; prof. orthodontics Coll. Dentistry U. Tenn. Ctr. for Health Scis., Memphis, 1980—. Contbr. articles to profl. jours. NIH fellow, 1973-80. Mem. Am. Assn. Phys. Anthropologists, Internat. Assn. Dental Rsch., Sigma Xi. Republican. Methodist. Office: 875 Union Ave # 301S Memphis TN 38163-0001 E-mail: eharris@utmem.edu.

HARRIS, ELAINE K. medical consultant; b. N.Y.C., Mar. 17, 1924; d. Julius and Bertha (Wecker) Kirschbaum; m. Herbert Harris, Aug. 1, 1948; children: Gail, Linda, Geoffrey. AB Bus. Economics cum laude, Hunter Coll.; AM Bus. Edn., Columbia U. Lic. tchr. bus., N.Y. Founder, pres. Sjogren's Syndrome Found., 1983-91, exec. dir., 1991-94. Cons. in field; v.p. exec. bd. Nat. Alliance for Oral Health; developer Sjogren's Syndrome Ednl. Symposia for lay and profls., nat. and internat. support group network. Editor: Moisture Seekers

Newsletter, 1984-94, Sjogren's Syndrome Handbook: An Authoritative Guide for Patients, 1989; editor: The New Sjogren's Syndrome Handbook, 1998; contbg. author: Sjogren's Syndrome: Clinical and Immunologic Aspects, 1987, Self-Help, Concepts and Applications, 1992; contbr. articles to profl. jours. Founded Nassau-Suffolk Chpt. Hunter Coll. Alumni Assn., 1949; treas. Youth Employment Svc., Great Neck (N.Y.) Pub. Schs., former chair of Broader Horizons Com., PTO, Great Neck Pub. Sch., others; active Jewish communal field. Recipient Women's Living Legacy, Women's Internat. Ctr., 1994, Third Internat. Conf. on Sjogren's Syndrome, Greece, 1991; elected to Hunter Coll. Hall of Fame, 1989. Mem. Pi Lambda Theta. Avocations: gardening, baking, photography, grandparenting.

HARRIS, E(LEANOR) LYNN(E), religious studies educator, literature educator, minister, writer; b. Villa Park, Ill., July 07; d. Robert Carl and Karin Elizabeth (Peterson) Karlström. BA, MA, U. Chgo.; MDiv, No. Bapt. Theol. Sem., 1975; D of Ministry, Chgo. Theol. Sem., 1980; PhD, NYU, 1980. Ordained min. United Ch. of Christ, 1987. Prof. U. Ill. Chgo., 1970—. Interim min. Union Congl. Ch., Moline, Ill., 1997; min. Glen Ellyn (Ill.) Congl. Ch., 1987-89; night ministry, Chgo., 1999, 2000, 01; adj. faculty religious studies Loyola U., Chgo., U. St. Francis; adj. faculty English Ind. U. Northwest, DePaul U., Ill. Benedictine U.; sec. Bd. Christian Witness in Soc., 1984 88; mem. seminaries com. Chgo. Met. Assn., United Ch. Christ, 2000-03; active Night Ministry, Chgo., summers 1999, 2000, 01; presenter, cons. adult edn. St. Pauls Ch., 2002; contbr. poetry to Kavya Bharati; presenter in field. Author: The Mystic Spirituality of A.W. Tozer, A Twentieth Century American Protestant, 1992; contbr. poems and articles to profl. jours. Recipient Lucia Queen of Light award City of Chgo., 1970. Mem. MLA, Am. Acad. Religion, Soc. Sci. Study Religion, Am.-Scandinavian Found., Chgo. Metro. Assn. (seminaries com.), Mensa. Avocations: art, music, travel, folk dancing, camping. Home: PO Box 412 Wheaton IL 60189-0412

HARRIS, ELISABETH TAMLYN, psychiatric social worker; b. Bklyn., Aug. 10, 1919; d. Walter Irving and Ethel Annie (Bishop) Tamlyn; divorced; 1 child, John. BA magna cum laude, Wilson Coll., 1941; postgrad., Brown U., 1941-42; MS, Columbia U., 1944; cert. paralegal with distinction, Manhattanville Coll., 1987. Cert. ACSW, lic. clin. social worker N.Y., Vt., Conn., diplomate Am. Bd. Examiners in Clin. Social Work. Social worker foster home dept. Children's Aid Soc., N.Y.C., 1944-46; field dir. ARC Mil. Hosp. Svc., 1946-51; psychiat. social worker San Mateo (Calif.) Adult Psychiat. Clinic, 1954-55; psychiat. social worker ARC chpt. San Jose (Calif.) Home Svc. Dept., 1955-56; resource cons., psychiat. social worker N.Y. Presbyn. Hosp., Cornell Med. Ctr. Westchester div., White Plains, NY, 1959-89, resource cons. emerita, 1989—; pvt. practice in psychiat. social work and psychotherapy Port Chester, N.Y., 1964—. Cons., nat. conf. workshop leader Parents Without Ptnrs., 1962-65; panel speaker, workshop leader Mental Health Assn., Westchester County, N.Y.; speaker various community groups, profl. confs. in field. Contbr. numerous articles to jours. Mem. team Med. Com. for Human Rights, Selma, Ala., summer 1965. Fellow: Am. Orthopsychiat. Assn., Soc. Clin. Social Workers; mem.: NASW, Am. Assn. Sex Educators, Counselors and Therapists (cert. sex. therapist). Democrat. Unitarian Universalist. Avocations: reading, swimming, music, repairing antiques. Home and Office: 29 Mitchell Pl Port Chester NY 10573-1804

HARRIS, EMILY LOUISE, special education educator; b. New London, Conn., Nov. 16, 1932; d. Frank Sr. and Tanzatter (McCleese) Brown; m. John Everett Harris Sr., Sept. 10, 1955; children: John Everett Jr., Jocelyn E. (dec.). BS, U. Conn., 1955; MEd, Northeastern U., 1969. Cert. tchr, elem. spl. subject sci., Mass., spl. subject reading, secondary prin., elem. prin. Tchr. New Haven Sch. Dept., 1957-59, Boston Sch. Dept., 1966-68, Natick (Mass.) Sch. Dept., 1969-72; cert. nurse's asst. The Hebrew Rehab. Ctr., Roslindale, Mass., 1973-75; spl. edn. educator Boston Sch. Dept., 1975-76, 78—, support tchr., 1976-78. Site coord. Tchr. Corps., 1977-81; leader, co-leader Harvard U. Student Tchrs. at Dorchester H.S. Sem., 1995—; tchr. adviser Future Educators Am. Dorchester H.S. Editor, compiler: Cooking With the Stars, 1989. Mem.-del. Mass. Fedn. Tchrs., Boston, 1993-96; elected rep. AFL-CIO (Boston Tchrs. Union), 1986-96; registrar of voters Dorchester (Mass.) H.S., 1986—; adv. bd. New England Assn. Schs. and Colls., 1980-93; 1st v.p., bd. dirs. League of Women for Comty. Svcs., Boston, 1976-80, Cynthia Sickle-Cell Anemia Fund, Boston, 1976-80. Recipient Tchg. award Urban League Guild Mass., 1993. Mem. AAUW, Zeta Phi Beta (Zeta of Yr. 1994), Alpha Delta Kappa, Kappa Delta Pi, Order Ea. Star (past worthy matron Prince Hall chpt. 1983-84), Delta Omicron Zeta, Phi Delta Kappa. Baptist. Avocations: reading, sewing. Home: 36 Dietz Rd Hyde Park MA 02136-1134

HARRIS, EON NIGEL, dean, rheumatologist, internist; b. Georgetown, Guyana, S.Am. came to U.S., 1987; s. T. Wilson and Cicely H.; m. Yvette Williams, 1981; children: Zaman Rashid, Tamia Alisha, Sandhya Caroline. BS, Howard U., 1968; MPhil, Yale U., 1970; MD, U. Pa., 1976; PhD in Medicine, U. West Indies, Kingston, Jamaica, 1982. Diplomate Am. Bd. Internal Medicine, Am. Bd. Rheumatology. Intern U. of the West Indies, Kingston, Jamaica, 1977, resident, 1978-81; lectr. U. West Indies, Kingston, 1981-83; rheumatology fellow Hammersmith Hosp., London, 1983-85; dir. Lupus rsch. lab. St. Thomas Hosp., London, 1985-87; asst. prof. U. Louisville, Ky., 1987-91, assoc. prof., 1991-96; dean, v.p. acad. affairs Morehouse Sch. of Medicine, Atlanta, prof. dept. medicine, 1996—. Chief div. rheumatology U. Louisville; med. adv. bd. Lupus Found. Am. Editor: Phospholipid Binding Antibodies, 1991; contbr. articles to profl. jours. Recipient Internat. League Against Rheumatism prize Ciba-Geigy, 1993. Fellow Am. Coll. Rheumatology (chmn. antiphospholipid study group 1993—); mem. Phi Beta Kappa, Alpha Omega Alpha. Office: Morehouse Sch of Medicine 720 Westview Dr SW Atlanta GA 30310-1458

HARRIS, F. CHANDLER, retired university administrator; b. Neligh, Nebr., Nov. 5, 1914; s. James Carlton and Helen Ayres (Boyd) H.; m. Barbara Ann Hull, Aug. 10, 1946; children: Victoria Williams, Randolph Boyd. AB, UCLA, 1936. Assoc. editor Telegraph Delivery Spirit, L.A., 1937-39; writer, pub. svc. network radio programs Univ. Explorer, Sci. Editor, U. Calif., 1939-61; pub. info. mgr. UCLA, 1961-75, dir., 1975-82, dir. emeritus, 1982—. Mem. pub. rels. com., western region United Way, 1972-75; bd. dirs. Am. Youth Symphony, L.A., 1978-98, v.p., 1983-98; bd. dirs. Hathaway Home for Children, 1982-88. Recipient 1st prize NBC Radio Inst., 1944; Harvey Hebert medal Delta Sigma Phi, 1947, Mr. Delta Sig award, 1972; Adam award Assistance League Mannequins, 1980, Univ. Service award UCLA Alumni Assn., 1986; bd. dirs. Western L.A. Regional C. of C., 1976-80. Mem. U. Calif. Retirees Assn. L.A. (pres. 1985-87), Sigma Delta Chi, Delta Sigma Phi (nat. pres. 1959-63), UCLA Faculty Club (sec. bd. govs. 1968-72). Editor Interfraternity Rsch. Adv. Coun. Bull., 1949-50, Carnation, 1969-80, Royce Hall, 1985. Home: 7774 Skyhill Dr Los Angeles CA 90068-1232

HARRIS, FRED, prosthetist; b. Bklyn., Sept. 29, 1941; s. Fred and Eva H.; m. Sheila, Sept. 1966; children: Freddie, Jeffrey, Ted. AAS, N.Y.C. C.C., 1974; BS, CUNY, 1980. Orthotist, prosthetist VA Med. Ctr., N.Y.C., 1963—. With U.S. Army, 1960-62. Mem. AAAS, NAACP, Am. Congress Rehab. Medicine, Am. Acad. Orthotics & Prosthetics, N.Y. Acad. Scis., N.Y. Orthotic & Prosthetic Assn., N.Y. State Am. Acad. Orthotist & Prosthetists, Lower Limb Orthotics Soc., Cad/Cam Soc., Upper Limb Soc., Internat. Soc., N.Y. State Rifle Pistol Assn., Prescription Footwear Assn., Prosthetics & Orthotics, Sierra Club, Libr. of Congress Assn. Baptist. Avocations: reading, music, softball, basketball, bowling. Home: 633 Hegeman Ave Brooklyn NY 11207-7103

HARRIS, FRED R. political scientist, educator, retired senator; b. Walters, Okla., Nov. 13, 1930; s. Fred Byron and Alene (Person) Harris; m. LaDonna Crawford, Apr. 8, 1949 (div. 1981); children: Kathryn, Byron, Laura; m. Margaret S. Elliston, Sept. 5, 1982. BA, U. Okla., 1952, JD, 1954. Bar: Okla. 1954. Founder, sr. partner firm Harris, Newcombe, Redman & Doolin, Lawton, Okla., 1954-64; mem. Okla Senate, 1956-64, U.S. Senate from Okla., Washington, 1964-73; prof. polit. sci. U. N.Mex., Albuquerque, 1976—. Author: (book) Alarms and Hopes, 1969, Now is the Time, 1971, The State of the Cities: Report of the Commission on Cities in the 70's, 1972, Social Science and National Policy, The New Populism, 1973, Potomac Fever, 1977, America's Democracy, 1980, America's Democracy, 3d edit., 1985, Readings on the Body Politic, 1987, Deadlock or Decision, 1993, In Defense of Congress, 1994, Coyote Revenge, 1999, Easy Pickin's, 2001; co-author: America's Legislative Processes, 1983, Understanding American Government, 1988, Quiet Riots, 1988, America's Government, 1990, Locked in the Poor House, 1998. Mem. Nat. Adv. Commn. Civil Disorders, 1967—68; chmn. Dem. Nat. Com., 1969—70. Mem.: Order of Coif, Phi Beta Kappa. Office: U New Mexico Dept Polit Sci Albuquerque NM 87131-0001 E-mail: fharris@unm.edu.

HARRIS, FREDERICK HOLLADAY DEBROSCHE, business educator; b. Durham, NC, Feb. 16, 1949; s. Frederick Holladay and Rose (deBrosche) H.; m. Nancy Taylor Steed, Sept. 12, 1970; children: Taylor Drake, Sarah Elizabeth. AB, Dartmouth Coll., 1971; PhD, U. Va., 1981. From asst. to assoc. prof. econs. U. Tex., Dallas-Fort Worth, 1982—90; assoc. dean of faculty affairs, McKinnon prof. econ. and fin. Babcock Sch., Wake Forest U., Winston-Salem, NC, 1991—. Cons. in field. Contbr. articles to profl. jours.; assoc. editor Jour. Indsl. Econs., 1988-93. Mem. Am. Econ. Assn., Fin. Mgmt. Assn., Am. Fin. Assn. Office: Babcock Grad Sch Mgmt PO Box 7659 Winston Salem NC 27109-7659 E-mail: rick.harris@mba.wfu.edu.

HARRIS, FREDERICK JOHN, foreign language and literature educator; b. N.Y.C., July 29, 1943; s. Frederick and Anna (Guttmann) H. BA, Fordham U., 1965; MA, Columbia U., 1966, PhD, 1969. Asst. prof. Fordham U., N.Y.C., 1970-79, assoc. prof., 1979-84, prof. French and comparative lit., 1984—, chmn. divsn. humanities, 1979-85, chmn. dept. modern langs. and lits. (bi-campus), 1995-99. Bd. dirs. Fordham U. Press, N.Y.C.; mem. adv. com. Krieg und Literatur/War and Literature. Author: André Gide-Romain Rolland: Two Men Divided, 1973, Encounters with Darkness: French and German Writers on World War II, 1983, Friend and Foe: Marcel Proust and André Gide, 2002; contbr. articles to profl. jours. Mem. MLA, PEN Am. Ctr. (translation com.), Am. Assn. Tchrs. French, Internat. Comparative Lit. Assn., Am. Comparative Lit. Assn., Coll. English Assn., Assn. des Amis d'André Gide, Société des Professeurs Français et Francophones d'Amérique (bd. dirs. 1995-98), Stewart Hall (v.p. 1989-90, bd. dirs.). Roman Catholic. Office: Rose Hill Campus Lincoln Center Campus Fordham U New York NY 10023 E-mail: fharris@fordham.edu.

HARRIS, GERALD WAYNE, retired radio advertising sales executive; b. Durham, N.C., Oct. 21, 1933; s. Erskine Owen Harris and Lora (Poole) Bryant; m. Shirley Eileen Cheek, July 10, 1954 (div. 1979); children: Ann, John, Guy, Sammy. Spl. corr. News-Leader, Richmond, Va., 1960-69; ops. mgr., news dir. WINA AM-FM, Charlottesville, Va., 1962-67; news reporter WSVA-TV, Harrisonburg, Va., 1967-69; gen. mgr. WTHO AM-FM, Thomson, Ga., 1969-71; news reporter WSPA AM-FM-TV, Spartanburg, S.C., 1971-77; advt. rep. WKDY Radio, Spartanburg, S.C., 1977-88, WNNC-WIRC-WXRC, Newton, Hickory, NC, 1988—98; ret., 1998. Republican. Baptist. Home: 19 N Davis Ave Newton NC 28658-2328

HARRIS, GLENDA STANGE, medical language specialist, proofreader, writer; b. Jacksonville, Fla., Jan. 11, 1954; d. Robert Lee and Wynelle (Jowers) S.; m. David Michael Harris Sr., Aug. 11, 1973; children: David Michael Jr., Mason Andrew. Asst. adminstr. Primary Health Care Ctr., Orange Park, Fla., 1980-83; med. lang. specialist Ctr. for Plastic and Reconstructive Surgery, Orlando, Fla., 1984-90, Fayette Med. Clinic, Fayetteville, Ga., 1991—. Freelance proofreader. Author: (newspaper column) Grand Slam News, 1991-94. Vol. mentor/tutor Fayette County Sch. System. Republican. Methodist. Avocations: reading, hiking, gardening, wildlife/nature photography, collecting books. Home: 135 Mark Ln Fayetteville GA 30214-7202 Office: Fayette Med Clinic 101 Yorktown Dr Fayetteville GA 30214-1568 E-mail: glen7297@aol.com.

HARRIS, GORDON H. lawyer; b. Atlanta, May 7, 1938; s. Huie H. Harris and Elizabeth (McBrayer) Stroud; m. Dorothy Laing, Dec. 6, 1960; children: Sarah Overmeyer, Bruce McBrayer. BA in Math., U. Fla., 1961, JD with honors, 1965. Bar: Fla. 1966, U.S. Dist. Ct. (mid. dist.) Fla., U.S. Ct. Appeals (5th and 11th cirs.), U.S. Supreme Ct. 1966. Instr. legal writing and research U. Fla. Law Sch., Gainesville, 1965-66; assoc. Holland and Knight, Bartow, Fla., 1966-69; ptnr. Gray, Harris & Robinson, Orlando, Fla., 1969—; asst. atty. Orange County, 1978-84. Guest instr. Valencia Community Coll., 1978-80; atty. Tourist Devel. Council, 1977-84; asst. prosecutor Orange County, 1969-71. Exec. editor U. Fla. Law Rev., 1964-65. Mem. East Ctl. Fla. Regional Planning Council, Orlando, 1976-77; sr. warden St. Michael's Episc. Ch., 1980, lay reader 1966—; chmn. bd. trustees Trinity Prep. Sch., 1984—; exec. com. Fla. Citrus Bowl, 1982-85, bd. dirs. 1980-85; bd. dirs. March of Dimes 1977-82, Parents Anonymous of Fla., Inc., 1982-92, Valencia Community Coll. Found., 1978-90. Mem. ABA, Fla. Bar Assn., Orange County Bar Assn., Assn. Trial Lawyers Am., Acad. Fla. Trial Lawyers, U. Fla. Alumni Assn. (nat. pres. 1981, chmn. bd. 1982, dir. Gator boosters 1973-83, province comdr. 1993—, life), Am. Judicature Soc., Fla. Shrine Assn. (pres. 1982-83), Order of Coif, Fla. Blue Key, Phi Kappa Phi, Phi Delta Pi, Kappa Alpha, Kappa Alpha Order Found. (bd. trustees 1999). Clubs: Touchdown, Country, University (Orlando); Citrus. Lodges: Shriners (potentate 1983), Masons. Republican. Office: Gray Harris & Robinson PA PO Box 3068 Orlando FL 32802-3068

HARRIS, GREGORY SCOTT, municipal official; b. Denver, June 5, 1955; s. Herbert E. and Marcia Jean (Raabe) H. BS in Journalism with honors, U. Colo., 1977; MBA, Loyola U., Chgo., 1981. Dir. public relations IMPACT Internat., Inc., Chgo., 1977-78; dir. edn. Nat. Home Furnishings Assn. (NHFA), Chgo., 1978-79, v.p. industry affairs, 1981-87, exec. v.p., chief operating officer, 1987-88; exec. dir. Interior Design Soc., Chgo., 1979-82; sec. NHFA Service Corp., 1986-87, v.p., 1986-87, pres., 1987-91, also bd. dirs.; pres. Open Hand: Chgo. Found., 1988-91; chief of staff Chgo. City Coun., 1992—. Mem. Devel. Adv. Coun. City of Chgo., 1990-92; bd. dirs. Nonprofit Fin. Ctr.; mem. advocacy and pub. policy com. AFC. Trustee Design Found., Chgo., 1980-88; chmn. bd. dirs. AIDS Walk Found., 1990-91; bd. dirs. AIDS Legal Coun., 1992-94, Heartland Alliance for Human Needs and Human Rights; fin. dir. Simpson for Congress Com., 1991-92; mem. adv. bd. The Neofuturists, 2000. Recipient Leadership in Mktg. award Newspaper Pubs. Assn., 1983, Outstanding Young Chicagoan award Chgo. Jaycees, 1992, Outstanding Svc. to Immigrant and Refugee Cmty. award, 1996, Uptown C. of C. Ann. award, 1996, Voice of People Cmty. award, 1994, Equality award Human Rights Campaign, 1997, W. Clement Stone award, 1998, Biggest Heart award Hearts Found., 1999, Food For Life award, Florence Bezazian Citizenship award, 1999, Greater Chgo. Com. Humanitarian Efforts award, 2000, Inst. Cultural Affairs USA cert. of appreciation, 2000, Svc. award Cambodian Buddhist Assn., 2002, Chgo. House Pub. Svc. award, 2002; named to City of Chgo. Hall of Fame, 1996. Office: Chgo City Coun City Hall 121 N La Salle St Chicago IL 60602-1202

HARRIS, HAZEL LYNN, medical/surgical nurse; b. Taylor, Tex., Apr. 29, 1953; d. L.B. Clark, Doris Evelyn Clark; m. James Paul Harris; 1 child, Jonathan. BSN, Tex. Woman's U., 1974. RN Tex., cert. orthopedic nurse. Student nurse Parkland Health & Hosp. Sys., Dallas, 1973—74, staff nurse, 1974—80, unit mgr., 1982—, Clin. instr. Am. Tng. Ctr., Dallas, 1988—90; mem. nursing peer rev. Parkland Health & Hosp. Sys., Dallas, 1999—99. Contbr. Book. Polit. action com. Am. Heart Assn., Dallas, 2000—03. Finalist Tex. Nurses Excellence award Cmty. Svc., Nurseweek, 2000; named one of Great 100 Nurses, Dallas/Ft. Worth Hosp. Coun. and Dists. Three and Four of Tex. Nurses Assn., 1998. Mem.: ANA, Tex. Nurses Assn., Nat. Assn. Orthopedic Nurses (treas. Dallas chpt. 1982—90), Nat. Coun. Negro Women (life; rec. sec. Greater Trinity sect. 1999—2003), Chi Eta Phi Sorority- Xi Phi Chapter (Tamiochus 2001—03, Basileus 2003). Methodist. Avocations: shopping, travel, walking. Home: 5606 Shady Crest Trail Dallas TX 75241-1803 Office: Parkland Health & Hosp Sys 5201 Harry Hines Blvd Dallas TX 75235 Home Fax: 214-374-0823; Office Fax: 214-590-7596. Personal E-mail: hazelharrisrn@aol.com. Business E-Mail: hlharr@parknet.pmh.org.

HARRIS, HENRY WILLIAM, physician; b. Catawba, N.C., Jan. 6, 1919; s. Henry William and Katie (Coulter) H.; m. Margaret Ann Roberts, Nov. 29, 1950; children: Henry William, John R., James P. BA, U.N.C., 1940; MD cum laude, Harvard U., 1943. Diplomate: in pulmonary disease Am. Bd. Internal Medicine. Intern Harvard Med. Service, Boston City Hosp., 1944-45, asst. resident medicine, 1945-46; resident fellow Thorndike Meml. Lab., 1944, 46; resident chest service Bellevue Hosp., N.Y.C., 1947; staff physician Gunderson Clinic, LaCrosse, Wis., 1948-53; asst. prof. medicine U. Utah Coll. Medicine, 1955-59, asso. prof., 1959-60; chief pulmonary disease service VA Hosp., Salt Lake City, 1955-60; prof. chmn. dept. medicine Woman's Med. Coll. of Pa., 1960-67; chmn. dept. medicine Catholic Med. Center Bklyn. and Queens, 1967-70; asso. prof. clin. medicine N.Y.U. Sch. Medicine, 1969-70, prof., 1970—. Acting dir. chest svc. Bellevue Hosp., N.Y.C., 1983-89, attending; with Tisch-Univ. Hosp., N.Y..C., Gouveneur Hosp., N.Y.C.; cons. VA Hosp., N.Y.C.; med. coord. Bur. Tuberculosis, Dept. of Health, N.Y.C. Mem. editorial bd.: Annals of Internal Medicine, 1976-80; Contbr. articles to profl. publs. Bd. dirs. Am. Lung Assn., 1961-79, v.p., 1972-73; bd. dirs. N.Y. Lung Assn., 1974-95, v.p., 1983—, pres. 1987-90; bd. dirs. Am. Bur. Med. Advancement in China., 1978—, v.p., 1983-87, pres. 1987-92, chmn. H. Wm. Harris vis. prof. com., 1986-96. Served to capt., M.C. AUS, 1953-55. Fellow ACP; mem. Am. Thoracic Soc. (pres. 1962-63). Home: 4 Birchwood Ct Apt 3L Mineola NY 11501-4513 Office: Chest Service Bellevue Hosp 1st Ave New York NY 10016

HARRIS, HOLTON EDWIN, plastics machinery manufacturing executive; b. N.Y.C., Aug. 24, 1923; s. David William and Mildred (Stoutenborough) H.; m. Jeanne Deming, Feb. 22, 1963; children: Walter Deming, Dorothy Stoutenborough. BSEE, MIT, 1947, MSEE, 1948. Engr. GE, Syracuse, N.Y., 1948-49, sect. sales mgr. Schenectady, N.Y., 1949-52; asst. to pres. R.W. Cramer Co., Centerbrook, Conn., 1952-53; sales mgr. Ea. Air Devices, Dover, N.H., 1953-54; mgr. comml. products Reeves Instrument Corp., Carle Place, N.Y., 1954-58, pres. Harrel, Inc., Norwalk, Conn., 1958—. Lectr. in field. Contbg. author: Modern Plastics Ency., 1990, Blow Molding Handbook, 1989; patentee in field; contbr. numerous articles to profl. jours. Mem. Representative Town Meeting, Westport, Conn., 1965-75, 93-97, 19-2001, dep. moderator, 1973-75, chmn. fin. com.; chmn. Rep. Town. Com., Westport; mem. Charter Revision Com., Westport. 1st lt. U.S. Army Signal Corp., 1943-46, South Pacific. Recipient award in recognition of meritorious svc., Town of Westport, Conn. Mem. IEEE (life), Soc. Plastics Engrs. (sr.), Instrument Soc. Am. (sr.). Avocation: amateur radio. Home: 5 Newtown Tpke Westport CT 06880-1802 Office: Harrel Inc 16 Fitch St Norwalk CT 06855-1392 E-mail: info@harrel.com., harrish@harrel.com.

HARRIS, HOWARD HUNTER, oil company executive; b. Cushing, Okla., Dec. 7, 1924; s. Oscar Hunter and Gertie Lee (Stark) H.; m. Gwendolyne J. Moyers (died July 26, 2003), Dec. 31, 1945; children: Howard Sidney, Rodney Craig. BS in Bus. Adminstrn., JD, U. Okla., 1949; postgrad. in advt. mgmt., Stanford U., 1971. Atty. Emery & Harris, Cushing and Stillwater, Okla., 1949-50; staff atty. Sun Oil Co., Tulsa, 1950-54; div. atty. Marathon Oil Co., Tulsa, 1954-63; staff atty Marathon Internat. Oil Co., Findlay, Ohio, 1963-65; mgr. legal affairs Deutsche Marathon Petroleum Gmbh., Frankfurt and Munich, 1965-70; mktg. aty. and assoc. gen. counsel Marathon Oil Co., Findlay, Ohio, 1970-74, v.p. corp. external affairs, 1974-86, ret. Pres. Gainey Ranch Cmty. Assn., 1995-98. Served with AUS, 1943-45. Decorated Bronze Star Mem. Am. Petroleum Inst., ABA, Ohio Bar Assn., Okla. Bar Assn., Order of Coif, Beta Gamma Sigma. Lodges: Masons. Republican. Episcopalian.

HARRIS, IRA STEPHEN, secondary education educator, administrator; b. Bklyn., July 13, 1945; s. Simon and Vera (Vichness) H.; m. Arlene Cramer, Dec. 25, 1971; children: Elliot, David, Sara. BS, Fairleigh Dickinson U., 1968; MS, L.I. U., 1970, Profl. Diploma magna cum laude, 1978. Sci. educator 158Q Marie Curie H.S., Bayside, N.Y., 1968-76; tchr. math., sci. and social studies, media specialist Campbell Jr. H.S. 218Q, Flushing, N.Y., 1976-79, Beard Jr. H.S. 189Q, Flushing, 1979-86; tech. specialist Carson Intermediate Sch. 237Q, Flushing, 1986—; asst. prin. Carr Jr. H.S. 194Q, Flushing, 1995-2001; ret. Commodore Newbridge Boat Club, Bellmore, N.Y.; v.p., edn. chmn. Bellmore Jewish Ctr.; pres. East Bay Civic Assn., Bellmore. Mem. N.Y. Acad. Scis. (judge sci. fair N.Y.C. 1985—). Republican. Home: 2729 Claudia Ct Bellmore NY 11710-4740 E-mail: captainira@aol.com.

HARRIS, IRVING, lawyer; b. Cin., May 23, 1927; s. Albert and Sadye H.; m. Selma Schottenstein, June 18, 1950; children: Jeffrey Philip, Jonathan Lindley (dec.), Lisa Ann Hollister. Undergrad. degree, U. Cin., 1948, LLB, 1951. Ptnr. Cors, Hair & Hartsock, 1954-81, Hartsock, Harris & Schneider, Cin., 1981-82, Porter, Wright, Morris & Arthur, Cin., 1982-89; ptnr. firm Harris, Harris, Field Schacter & Bardach Ltd., Cin., 1989-2000. Mem. Ohio Trade Mission to Orient, 1973, to Eng. and Germany, 1974; spl. counsel to Atty. Gen. Ohio, 1963-71; life mem. 6th Cir. Jud. Conf.; lectr. Advising, Oper. and Rebuilding the Financially Distressed Co., 1991; bd. dirs. Bank One, Cin., 1993-2000, HRC Ltd. Partnership (Hyatt Regency (Cin.) Cin. Mem. Ohio Devel. Financing Commn., 1974—84, vice-chmn., 1978—79; spl. counsel Ohio Atty. Gen.'s Office for the Police and Firemen's Disability and Pension Fund, 1994—97; trustee Skidmore Coll., 1976—90, trustee emeritus, 1991—, Big Bros.; trustee Cin. Symphony Orch., 1989—96; bd. overseers U. Cin. Law Sch., 1998—; arbitrator Ct. of Common Pleas of Hamilton County, 2001—; mediator U.S. Dist. Ct. (so. dist.) Ohio Western divsn., 1999—. Mem. ABA (Sherman Act com., sect. on antitrust and bus. law 1969—, subcoms. on derivative actions, bankruptcy, litigation of bus. and corp. litigation 1992—), Ohio Bar Assn., Cin. Bar Assn., Am. Judicature Soc., Potter Stewart Inn of Ct. (master of the bench), Queen City Club, Univ. Club, Camargo Hunt Club, Cin. Tennis Club, Snowmass Country Club, Ocean Reef Club. Home: 18 Grandin Ln Cincinnati OH 45208-3365 Office: Harris Interests 3801 Carew Tower 441 Vine St Cincinnati OH 45202-2806

HARRIS, IRVING BROOKS, investor, director; b. St. Paul, Aug. 4, 1910; s. William and Mildred (Brooks) H.; m. Joan White; children: Roxanne, Virginia, William. AB, Yale U., 1931, hon. degree, 1990, Loyola U., 1976, Kenyon Coll., 1986, Columbia Coll., 1987, Lesley Coll., 1988, Bank Street Coll. Edn., 1988, De Pauw U., 1989; hon. deg., U. Ill., 1992, Roosevelt U., 1996; hon. degree, Gov.'s State U., 1997; Hon. Degree, Erikson Inst., 2002. Exec. in finance business, 1931-42; aircraft part bus., 1944-46; exec. Toni Home Permanent Co., after 1946; (sold stockholdings in Toni Co. to Gillette Safety Razor Co.), 1948; dir. Gillette Safety Razor Co., 1948-60; exec. v.p. Toni Co., 1946-52; chmn. bd. Sci. Research Assos., 1953-58; pres. Michael Reese Hosp. and Med. Center, Chgo., 1958-61, Harris Group, Inc., 1959-76. Chmn. exec. com. Pittway Corp., 1962—2000; chmn. William Harris Investors, 1987—2000. Trustee U. Chgo., Nat. Ctr. Clin. Infant Programs, Chgo. Ednl. TV Assn.; chmn. emeritus Family Focus; chmn. Irving Harris Found.; pres. emeritus Erikson Inst.; pres., co-founder The Ounce of Prevention Fund, 1982—, chmn. emeritus, 1997—; trustee Am. Jewish Com.; former chmn. adv. bd. Ill. Dept. Children and Family Svcs. Tng. Inst., Ill. Competitive Access and Reimbursement Equity Program; vice chmn. Gov.'s Task Force on Future of Mental Health in Ill.; spl. counselor to select com. on children Ill. Gen. Assembly; served with Bd. Econ. Warfare OPA, 1942-44. Recipient Chgo. UNICEF World of Children award, 1985, hon. membership award Chgo. Pediatric Soc., 1986, Am. Orthopsychiat. Assn. award, 1986, Salesman of Yr. award Harvard Club Chgo., 1989, Disting. Svc. to State Govt. award Nat. Gov.'s Assn., 1990, Amicus Certus award Luth. Soc. Svcs. of Ill., 1990, Cmty. Partnership award United Neighborhood Orgn., Chgo., 1990, As They Grow award Parents, 1991, Citizen fellow Inst. Medicine Chgo., 1990, Service to Young Children award Chgo. Met. Assn. for Edn. of Young Children, 1995; Clifford Beers lectr. Yale U., 1987. Fellow Am. Acad. Pediatrics (hon.), Am. Acad. Arts and Scis.; mem. NAS (pres.'s circle 1989), Am. Orthopsychiatric Assn. (award 1986, Marian F. Langer award 1995), Chgo. Pediatric Soc. (hon.), Standard Club, Midday Club. Home: 209 E Lake Shore Dr Chicago IL 60611-1307 Office: William Harris Investors Inc 2 N La Salle St Ste 400 Chicago IL 60602-3703

HARRIS, ISAAC RON, lawyer; b. Haifa, Israel, Oct. 1, 1954; came to U.S., 1955; s. Lee B. and Leah (Jacobson) H.; m. Shari E. Shapiro, Sept. 6, 1981; children: Jessica Sara, Emma Rachel. BA, Brown U., 1976; JD, Georgetown U., 1980. Bar: N.Y. 1981, U.S. Dist. Ct. (so. and ea. dists.) N.Y. 1981. Asst. dist. atty. Kings County, Bklyn., 1980-84; assoc. Hall, Dickler, Lawler, Kent & Friedman, N.Y.C., 1984-85; ptnr. Smith & Harris, Mt. Kisco, NY, 1995—2000; prin. I. Ron Harris, Esq., Mt. Kisco, N.Y., 2000—. Mem. N.Y. State Bar Assn., Westchester County Bar Assn., No. Westchester Bar Assn. Home: 44 North Way Chappaqua NY 10514-2214 Office: I Ron Harris Esq 69 S Bedford Rd Mount Kisco NY 10549

HARRIS, JACK HOWARD, II, consulting firm executive; b. Chgo., Mar. 22, 1945; s. Jack Howard and Myrtice Geneva (Dickson) Harris; m. Barbara Beck Czika, Jan. 1, 1983; children: Jack, William, Thomas P.stepchildren: Joseph C Czika, Brad D. Czika. AB, U. Chgo., 1966; MPh, George Washington U., 1984. Chief China desk Air Force Intelligence, USAF, Washington, 1971—74; dir. policy studies BDM Corp., Washington, 1974—78; sr. assoc. Booz-Allen and Hamilton, Washington, 1979; corp. v.p. govt. ops. Sci. Applications, Inc.,

Washington, 1980—85; exec. v.p., CFO The Harris Group, Inc., Washington, 1985—95; with Ctr. for Nat. Program Evaluation, Washington, 1988—94; v.p. Corp. and Polit. Comms., Inc., Melbourne Beach, Fla., 1995—. With USAF, 1967—71. Mem.: VFW, DAV, Internat. Platform Assn., Air Force Assn., Mensa, Am. Legion, Triple Nine Soc., Phi Gamma Delta. Home and Office: 2009 Neptune Dr Melbourne Beach FL 32951-2707 E-mail: jack@theharrises.cc.

HARRIS, J(ACOB) GEORGE, health care company executive; b. Kings Mountain, N.C., Sept. 5, 1938; s. James A. and Carolyn (Hord) H.; m. Sondra Gilbert, Mar. 29, 1959; children: Cynthia, Susan, David. BA in Math., Duke U., 1960. With Am. Hosp. Supply Corp., 1960-84, region mgr., 1964-67, pres. Port Credit, Ont., Can., 1967-70, v.p. ops. Evanston, Ill., 1970-71, pres. dietary products div. McGaw Park, Ill., 1971-74, corp. v.p. Evanston, 1974-78, exec. v.p., 1978-84; chmn., chief exec. officer Health Group Inc., Nashville, 1984-85; founder, pres., CEO Pinnacle Care Corp. (merged Mariner Health Group), 1985-94; pres., COO Mariner Health Group, 1994; ret., 1994; formerly bd. dirs. Mariner Health Group. Bd. dirs. Union Spl. Corp., Chgo., Monoclonal Antibodies, Inc., Mountain View, Calif., Electro Neucleonics Inc., Health Group, Electro-Biology Inc., Dialogic Comm. Corp. Bd. dirs. Highland Park (Ill.) Hosp., 1981-84; trustee McCormick Sem., Chgo. Mem. Scientific Apparatus Mfrs. Assn., Richland Country Club. Home: 1204 Beddington Park Nashville TN 37215-5810 E-mail: bocaj1938@aol.com.

HARRIS, JAMES BRAXTON, retired humanities educator, freelance/self-employed writer; b. Reidsville, NC, Apr. 30, 1929; s. Whitelaw Reid and Willie Zoie (Kelly) Harris; m. Gertrude Lawrence, Dec. 24, 1950; children: Lorraine, Helen, Joseph, Kelene, Lawrence. BA, Lenoir-Rhyne Coll., 1949; MA, Appalachian State U., 1956; EdD, Ind. U., 1960. Tchr. English and history Pub. Schs., Hildebran, Francisco and Hickory, NC, 1949—50, 1953—57; prof., vice chancellor Appalachian State U., Boone, NC, 1958—64, 1970—90, prof. emeritus, 1991—; dean Brevard (NC) Coll., 1964—68; dir. pre-svc. tchr. edn. NC Dept. Pub. Instrn., Raleigh, 1968—70; freelance writer Hendersonville, NC, 1991—. Tech. tng. cons. Naval Sea Sys. Command USN, Washington, 1985—89; cons. to colls., univs. and profl. orgns. Author: Lyrics for Three Julies: Song Lyrics for Three Musical Plays, 1992, Lyrics for Three Lovers: Song Lyrics for Three Musical Plays, 1993, Bittersweet Lyrics: Song Lyrics for Three Musical Plays, 1994, The Bolejack Chronicle, 2000, The Stokesburg Trilogy, 2000, The Dorian Chronicle, 2000, The Boldorian Chronicle, 2000, The Trinity Trilogy, 2000, The Chronicle of Seals, 2000, The Technics Trilogy, 2000, The C (sic) cycle: Precis and Personae, 2000, Dalton's Folly, 2003, Bay's Book: Being Benign Bagatelles Befitting Beneficent Bards, 2003; contbr. articles to profl. jours. Bd. dirs. Western Carolina Cmty. Action, Hendersonville and Brevard, 1966—68. 1st lt. USAF, 1950—53. Grantee, Appalachian State U., 1972—73. Avocation: designing houses and small buildings. Home: 37 Jeter Mountain Rd Hendersonville NC 28739

HARRIS, JAMES CAROL OVERTON, JR., psychiatrist, pediatrician; b. Birmingham, Ala., Nov. 6, 1940; s. James Carol and Mary Virginia (Respess) H. BS, Univ. Md., 1962; MD, George Washington U., 1966. Cert. Am. Bd. Pediatrics, Am. Bd. Psychiatry, Am. Bd. Child Psychiatry. With Peace Corps, Thailand, 1967-70; dir. developmental neuropsychiatry Johns Hopkins U., Balt., 1976—; pres. med. staff Kennedy Krieger Inst., Johns Hopkins U., Balt., 1986-88; asst. prof. The Johns Hopkins U., Balt., 1976-82, interim dir. divsn. of child and adolescence psychiatry, 1978-82, dir. consultation/ liason svc., 1978-82, dir. edn. divsn. of child and adolescence psychiatry, 1982-89; assoc. prof. psychiatry, metal hygiene, pediat. Johns Hopkins U., Balt., 1982—97, prof., 1997—; co-dir. autism clinic The Johns Hopkins U., Balt., 1983—, co-dir. sleep disorder clinic, 1983—, joint appointment dept. of mental hygiene, 1985—. Adj. scientist Ctr. for Brain Evolution and Behavior, Poolesville, Md., 1978—84, Lab. Comparative Ethology, 1984—93; mem. White House conf. on Mental Health, 1999; cons. Joseph P. Kennedy Jr. Found., 2000—; mem. Pres.'s Com. on Mental Retardation, 2001—02; vis. scholar dept. psychiatry U. Chgo., 2001—02, vis. rsch. scientist Inst. for Mind and Biology, 2001—02. Author: Developmental Neuropsychiatry Fundamentals, 1995, Developmental Neuropsychiatry: Assessment, Diagnosis and Treatment, 1995 (Med. Book of Yr. 1995); mem. editl. bd. Jour. Child Neurology, 2001—, Archives of Gen. Psychiatry, 2002—; contbr. more than 100 articles and abstracts to profl. jours. Recipient NIMH Trainee award, 1964—65, Pollen award, 1965—66, R-01 Rsch. award, Nat. Inst. Child Health and Human Devel.; Fgn. fellow, Assn. Am. Med. Colls.-Smith Kline & French, 1965. Fellow: Am. Acad. Child and Adolescent Psychiatry, Am. Psychiat. Assn. (Disting.); mem.: Soc. Profs. Child and Adolescent Psychiatry (pres. 1998—2000), Soc. Study Behavioral Phenotypes, Am. Assn. Psychiatry and the Law, Soc. Neurosci., Am. Assn. Dirs. Psychiat. Residency Tng., Md. Psychiat. Soc., Am. Coll. Neuropsychopharmacology. Avocation: foreign travel. Home: 200 Tuscany Rd Baltimore MD 21210-3010 Office: Johns Hopkins U Sch Medicine CMSC 341 600 N Wolfe St Baltimore MD 21287-0005 : 400 N McClurg Ct Apt 3203 Chicago IL 60611 Fax: 410-889-5623. E-mail: jamesharris@erols.com.

HARRIS, JAMES HERMAN, pathologist, neuropathologist, consultant, educator; b. Fayetteville, Ga., Oct. 19, 1942; s. Frank J. and Gladys N. (White) H.; m. Judy K. Hutchinson, Jan. 30, 1965; children: Jeffrey William, John Michael, James Herman. BS, Carson-Newman Coll., 1964; PhD, U. Tenn.-Memphis, 1969, MD, 1972. Diplomate Am. Bd. Pathology; sub-cert. in anatomic pathology and neuropathology. Resident, fellow NYU-Bellevue Med. Ctr., N.Y.C., 1973-75; adj. asst. prof. pathology NYU, N.Y.C., 1975-83; asst. prof. pathology and neuroscis. Med. Coll. Ohio, Toledo, 1975-78, assoc. prof., 1978-82, dir. neuropathology and electron microscopy lab., 1975-82; cons. Toledo Hosp., 1979-82, assoc. pathologist/neuropathologist, dir. electron microscopy pathology lab., 1983-91, mem. courtesy staff, 1991—, mem. overview com., credentials com., appropriations subcom. medisgroup, interqual task force. Chmn. clin. support svcs. com., vice chmn. med. staff quality rev. com. Toledo Hosp.; cons. neuropathologist Mercy Hosp., 1976—93, mem. courtesy staff, 1993—; cons. neuropathologist U. Mich. Dept. Pathology, 1984—93; cons. med. malpractice in pathology and neuropathology; mem. AMA Physician Rsch. and Evaluation panel; mem. ednl. and profl. affairs commn., exec. coun. Acad. Medicine; mem. children's cancer study group Ohio State U. Satellite; chmn. tech. and issues subcom. of adv. com. Blue Cross; mem. Task Force on Cost Effectiveness N.W. Ohio; chmn. med. necessity appeals com. Blue Cross/Blue Shield; adv. bd. PIE Mut. Ins. Co. Author med., sci. papers; reviewer Jour. Neuropathology and Exptl. Neurology. Chmn. fin. com., dir. bldg. fund campaign First Bapt. Ch., Perrysburg, Ohio; chmn. steering com. Pack 198 Boy Scouts Am.; faculty chmn. Med. Col. Ohio United Way Campaign; mem. adv. com. Multiple Sclerosis Soc. N.W. Ohio; chmn. alumni scholarship fund Carson-Newman Coll., 1994—95; alumni exec. com. Truett McConnell Coll., 1995—2001; chmn. Loyalty Fund Campaign for 50th Ann., 1996—98. Recipient Outstanding Tchr. award Med. Coll. Ohio, 1980; named to Outstanding Young Men Am., U.S. Jaycees, 1973; USPHS trainee, 1964-69, postdoctoral trainee, 1973-75; grantee Am. Cancer Soc., 1977-78, Warner Lambert Pharm. Co., 1978-79, Miniger Found., 1980, Toledo Hosp. Found., 1985, Promedica Health Care Found., 1986. Mem. Am. Profl. Practice Assn., Am. Pathology Found., Am. Soc. Law and Medicine, Am. Coll. Physician Execs., Lucas County Acad. Medicine (bar acad. liaison com.), Ohio State Med. Assn. (fed. key contact), Med. Assn. Ga., Am. Asn. Neuropathologists (profl. affairs com., awards com., program com., constn. com.), Internat. Acad. Pathologists, Ohio Soc. Pathologists, Truett McConnell Coll. Alumni Assn. (pres. 1998-2001, mem. steering com. capital campaign), EM Soc. Am., Sigma Xi. Republican. Avocations: tennis, real estate rehabilitation, building developer, gardening, white water rafting. Home and Office: 9105 Nesbit Lakes Dr Alpharetta GA 30022-4028

HARRIS, JAMES RIDOUT, retired communications executive; b. Apr. 14, 1920; s. Walter Karl and Hortense (Ridout) H.; m. Frances Elizabeth Wiley, June 23, 1943; children: Richard Wells, Betty Anne, Beverly Jean. BS, U. Richmond, 1941; MEE, Poly. U., 1948; postgrad., Williams Coll., 1959. Engr. Chesapeake & Potomac Telephone Co., Richmond, 1941-42; with Bell Telephone Labs., N.Y. and N.J., 1942-82, dir. data comms., 1961-65, dir. customer switching and govt. comm., 1965-71, dir. customer equipment studies ctr., 1971-81, dir. data network spl. studies ctr., 1981-82; dir. spl. studies ctr. AT&T Info. Systems Labs., 1983. Developer pioneer solid state computing equipment, 1950, world's earliest transistor-based computing equipment; supr. devel. world's earliest high speed transistor-based computer, Bell Labs., 1953; patentee computing, communications and solid state cirs.; dir. preparation Engring. Ops. Bell System, 1977. Elder, trustee, pres. corp. Presbyn. Ch. Recipient George R. Stibitz Computer Pioneer award, 1999. Mem. IEEE (sr., adminstrv. com. of computer soc. 1962-65), Am. Phys. Soc., Soc. Automotive Engrs., Phi Beta Kappa, Sigma Xi. Home: 8 Dogwood Ln Rumson NJ 07760-1412 E-mail: jharris@monmouth.com.

HARRIS, JAMES THOMAS, III, college administrator, educator; b. Findlay, Ohio, July 31, 1958; s. James Thomas II (dec.) and Carolyn Sue (Cairns) H.; m. Mary Catherine Kurdila, June 27, 1981; children: Zachary James, Braden Gerald. BE in Secondary Edn., U. Toledo, 1980; MEd in Ednl. Adminstrn., Edinboro U., 1983; D in Edn. in Higher Edn. Adminstrn., Pa. State U., 1988; postgrad. Inst. Ednl. Mgmt., Harvard U., 1993. Secondary tchr., dept. chair Highland H.S., Sparta, Ohio, 1980-81, Ctrl. Cath. H.S., Toledo, 1981-82; grad. asst., acad. advisor Edinboro (Pa.) State U., 1982-83; fin. aid adminstr. Pa. State U., University Park, 1983-86, assoc. dir. Corp. and Found. Rels. dept., 1986-88; v.p. Coll. Mt. St. Joseph, Cin., 1988-91, Wright State U., Dayton, Ohio, 1991-94; pres. Defiance (Ohio) Coll., 1994—2002, Widener U., 2002—. Faculty mem. 10 CASE Confs., 1986—; spkr., workshop presenter in field. Contbr. articles to profl. jours. Chair Vol. Connection of Defiance County, 1995-2002; vol. Leadership Defiance, Dayton, vice chair, 1992-94; bd. dirs. Defiance County United Way, 1998-2001; vol. ARC, Cin., 1988-91; bd. trustees Ohio Found. of Indep. Colls., 1994-2002; exec. com. Ohio Campus Compact, 1998-2002; vol. advisor St. Joseph Ch. and Elem. Sch., 1988-91; grad. Leadership Dayton, 1992; coach Nat. Collegiate Boxing Assn., Brunei, 1985, USSR, 1988. Recipient fellowship Am. Assn. Higher Edn. Edn. Resource and Index Ctr., 1997, Excellence in Edn. award Pa. State U., 2000, Alumni Leadershiip and Svc. award Pa. State U., 1996, Disting. Alumni award U. Toledo, 1999, Cmty. Leadership award NAACP Northwest Ohio chap., 1999; named to Top 50 Coll. and Univ. Presidents Templeton Found, 1999; Alumni Fellow, Pa. State U., 2003. Mem. NAACP, Am. Assn. Higher Edn., Pa. Assn. of Indep. Colls. and Univs., Rotary, Young President's Orgn., Alpha Kappa Delta, Pi Lambda Theta. Roman Catholic. Avocations: reading, blues music, walking. Office: Widener U 1 University Pl Chester PA 19013

HARRIS, JAN CAPLAN, health care administrator; b. Ithaca, N.Y., Jan. 15, 1944; d. Frank and Shirley Ellen (Rickard) Caplan; m. Sonny G. Harris, Mar. 23, 1990; children: Josh, Greg, Irene, Mike, Ginger, Morgan, J.B. BSN, Cornell U., 1966; MA in Liberal Studies, Dartmouth Coll., 1974; MS in Healthcare Adminstrn., U. Colo., 1989. Cert. profl. in healthcare quality. Coord. fed. programs, dir. instrn., tech. ctr. Northwest Arctic Sch. Dist., Kotzebue, Alaska, 1976-82; dir. planning and devel., interim pres., ops. exec. Maniilaq Assn., Kotzebue, 1985-93; adminstr., v.p. health svcs. Maniilaq Health Ctr., Kotzebue, 1993-97; sr. health care quality improvement coord. PRO-West, Anchorage, 1998—2001, mgr. Medicare ops., 1998—2001; sr. health sys. specialist Alaska Ctr. for Rural Health/Inst. for Circumpolar Health Studies U. Alaska, Anchorage, 2001—03, dir. health workforce devel., 2003—. Cons. Walrus Works, Anchorage, 1982-85, Harris Consulting, 1986—. Bd. dirs. Anchorage Neighborhood Health Ctr., 1999—, chair, 2000—02. Recipient Svc. award PHS/Indian Health Svc. Fellow: Am. Coll. Healthcare Execs.; mem.: Alaska Pub. Health Assn., Nat. Rural Health Assn., Nat. Assn. Healthcare Quality, Alaska Healthcare Quality Consortium (pres. 2000—02), Alaska Healthcare Execs. Network (pres. 2001—), Am. Soc. Quality. Home and Office: 6900 Oakwood Dr Anchorage AK 99507

HARRIS, JANINE DIANE, lawyer; b. Akron, Jan. 12, 1948; d. Russell Burton and Ethel Harriett (Smith) H.; m. Robert I. Coward, Sept. 14, 1968 (div. 1977); m. John Richard Ferguson, Feb. 1, 1980; children: Brigit Grace, Rachel Anna. AB, Bryn Mawr Coll., 1970; JD, Georgetown U., 1975. Bar: Va. Supreme Ct. 1975, U.S. Dist. Ct. D.C. 1976, U.S. Ct. Appeals (D.C. cir.) 1976, D.C. Ct. Appeals 1976, U.S. Supreme Ct. 1978, U.S. Ct. Appeals (6th cir.) 1981, U.S. Ct. Appeals (8th cir.) 1981. Assoc. Baker & Hostetler, Washington, 1975-78, Pettit & Martin, Washington, 1978-79, Peabody, Lambert & Meyers, Washington, 1979-82, ptnr., 1983-84; sole practice, Washington, 1984—. pres. bd. trustees Burgundy Farm Country Day Sch., 1993-96; mediator and mentor/evaluator D.C. Superior Ct. Multi-Door Dispute Resolution Prog. Contbr. articles to legal jours. Mem. Nat. Conf. Women's Bar Assns. (bd. dirs. 1984-87, pres.-elect 1987-88, v.p. 1986-87, pres. 1988-89), Nat. Found. for Womens' Bar Assn. (pres. 1985-88, dir. 1988-2001), Women's Bar Assn. D.C. (pres. 1984-85), D.C. Bar (bd. govs. 1984-88), ABA (com. on specialization), Va. Women Attys. Assn. Club: Bryn Mawr.

HARRIS, JAY STEPHEN, lawyer, producer; b. L.A., May 2, 1938; s. Nathan and Leah (Spector) H.; m. Fredda Stoll, June 20, 1981; m. Marie Masters, Apr. 15, 1967 (div. 1976); children: Jenny, Jesse. AB, Cornell U., 1961; LLB, NYU, 1965. Bar: N.Y. 1966, U.S. Dist. Ct. (so. dist.) N.Y. 1967. Asst. dist. atty. New York County, 1965-67; assoc. Phillips, Nizer, Benjamin, Krim & Ballon, N.Y.C., 1967-68, Weissberger & Frosch, N.Y.C., 1969-73; ptnr. Weissberger & Harris, N.Y.C., 1973-81, Gottlieb Schiff Ticktin & Harris, N.Y.C., 1981-85; pvt. practice N.Y.C., 1985—89, 2001—; of counsel Hall, Dickler, Kent, Friedman & Wood, N.Y.C., 1991-2000. Exec. producer NBC spls. Ann. TV Guide Spls., 1979-82. Author: TV Guide: The First 25 Years, 1978; prodr. Weissberger Theater Group. Bd. dirs. Am. Theatre Wing, N.Y.C., 1977—, Williamstown Theatre Festival, 1993—. Recipient Tony award for Best Play for Side Man, 1999. Mem. N.Y. State Bar Assn. E-mail: jayharrisnyc@aol.com.

HARRIS, JAY TERRENCE, communications educator; b. Washington, Dec. 3, 1948; s. Richard James and Margaret Estelle (Burr) H.; m. Eliza Melinda Dowell, June 14, 1969 (div.); 1 child, Taifa Akida; m. Anna Christine Harris, Oct. 25, 1980; children: Jamarah Kai, Shala Marie. BA, Lincoln U., 1970, LHD (hon.), 1988. Reporter Wilmington (Del.) News-Jour., 1970-73, spl. project editor, 1974-75; instr. journalism and urban affairs Medill Sch. Journalism, Northwestern U., Evanston, Ill., 1973-75, asst. prof., 1975-82, asst. dean, 1977-82; nat. corr. Gannett News Service, Washington, 1982-84, columnist Gannet newspapers and USA Today, 1984-85; exec. editor Phila. Daily News, 1985—88; v.p. Phila. Newspapers, Inc., 1987—94; chmn., pub. San Jose Mercury News, 1995—2001; Annenberg prof. journalism & comm. Annenberg Sch. for Comm., USC, 2001—. Asst. dir. Frank E. Gannett Urban Journalism Ctr., Northwestern U., 1977-82; founder, exec. dir. Consortium for Advancement of Minorities in Journalism Edn., Evanston, 1978-81; dir. Dow Jones Newspaper Fund, Princeton, N.J., 1980— ; bd. visitors John S. Knight Profl. Journalism Fellowships, Palo Alto, Calif., 1982— ; head Minorities and Communication Div. Assn. for Edn. in Journalism, 1982-83; journalist in residence Notre Dame, 2002-03; bd. mem. Deep River Assocs., 2002—. Author: (annual census) Minority Employment in Daily Newspapers, 1978-82; co-author series articles on drug trafficking in Wilmington, 1972 (Pub. Service awards AP Mng. Editors Assn. 1972, Greater Phila. chpt. Sigma Delta Chi 1973) Past mem. bd. advisors Sch. Journalism U. Mo. Frank E. Gannett Urban Journalism fellow, 1973-74; recipient Pub. Service award Greater Phila. chpt. Sigma Delta Chi, 1973; Pub. Service award AP Mng. Editors Assn., 1972; Spl. Citation Nat. Urban Coalition, 1979; Par Excellence Disting. Service in Journalism award Operation PUSH, 1984; Drum Maj. for Justice award Southern Christian Leadership Conf., 1985; Robert C. Maynard Fellow, 2001—. Mem. Am. Soc. Newspaper Editors (chmn. readership and rsch. com.), Women in Communication, Nat. Assn. Black Journalists, Omega Psi Phi Office: San Jose Mercury News 750 Ridder Park Dr San Jose CA 95190-0001

HARRIS, JEFFREY, lawyer; b. Bklyn., Mar. 20, 1944; s. Herman and Pearl (Herman) H.; m. Joyce Rosa Meckler, June 22, 1975; 1 child, Daniela Rose. BS, NYU, 1965; JD, Syracuse U., 1968. Bar: N.Y. 1969, U.S. Supreme Ct. 1976, D.C. 1977, Va., 1990. Asst. U.S. atty. So. Dist. N.Y., U.S. Dept. Justice, N.Y.C., 1972-76; chief investigation rev. unit. U.S. Dept. Justice, Washington, 1976-77; dep. chief counsel U.S. Ho. of Reps., Korean Investigation, Washington, 1977-79; asst. dir. FTC, Washington, 1979-81; exec. dir. Atty. Gen.'s Task Force on Violent Crime, U.S. Dept. Justice, Washington, 1981; dep. assoc. atty. gen. U.S., Washington, 1981-83; sr. v.p. Capital Bank N.A., Washington, 1983-85; sr. v.p., counsel Capital Bancorp, Miami, Fla., 1983-85; ptnr. Sachs, Greenebaum & Tayler, Washington, 1985-90, Rubin, Winston, Diercks, Harris & Cooke, LLP, Washington, 1990—. Instr. Advocacy Inst., U. Calif. Hastings Coll. Law, San Francisco, 1979-83; adj. asst. prof. George Washington U., Washington, 1980 Lt. (j.g.) USN, 1968-71. Named Meritorious Exec. Pres. of U.S.; recipient Spl. Commendation, Att. Gen. of U.S.; decorated Navy Commendation medal, Vietnam Cross of Gallantry. Mem. ABA Office: Rubin Winston Diercks Harris & Cooke LLP 6th Fl 1155 Connecticut Ave NW Washington DC 20036-4306 E-mail: jharris@rwdhc.com.

HARRIS, JEFFREY MARK, lawyer, educator; b. Chgo., Mar. 11, 1946; s. Al J. and Sylvia (Ruskin) H.; m. Laura Elizabeth Fitzgerald, July 13, 1975; children: Michael, Brian, Andrea. BA, So. Ill. U., 1967; JD, DePaul U., 1971. Bar: Ill. 1972, Fla. 1975, U.S. Dist. Ct. (no. dist.) Ill. 1975, U.S. Dist. Ct. (so. dist.) Fla. 1976, U.S. Supreme Ct. Asst. state atty. State Atty.'s Office, Chgo., 1974-76, Ft. Lauderdale, Fla., 1976-78; pvt. practice, Ft. Lauderdale, 1978—. Adj. prof. Nova U. Law Ctr., Ft. Lauderdale, 1982-97. Mem. ABA, Fla. Bar Assn. (cert. in criminal law, chmn. grievance com. 1990, mem. law cert. com. 1990-93, evidence com. 1999), Nat. Assn. Criminal Def. Attys., Broward County Criminal Def. Bar Assn. (bd. dirs. 1989—, treas. 1991, v.p. 1992, pres. 1994), Broward County Bar Assn. (vice-chmn. 1998, chmn. bar/bench com. 1999), Fla. Criminal Def. Bar Assn. (bd. dirs. 1992—, sec. 2002), B'nai B'rith. Office: One E Broward Blvd Fort Lauderdale FL 33301

HARRIS, JEFFREY SAUL, physician, executive, consultant; b. Pitts., Mar. 13, 1949; s. Aaron Wexler and Janet Mary (Wexler) Harris; m. Mary V. Anderson, Jan. 2, 1981; children: Sarah Ariel, Noah Aaron, Susannah Leia. BS in Molecular Biophysics/Biochemistry, Yale U., 1971; MD, U. N.Mex., 1975; MPH, U. Mich., 1982; MBA, Vanderbilt U., 1988. Diplomate Am. Bd. Preventive Medicine in Occupl. Medicine and Gen. Preventive Medicine, Am. Bd. Emergency Medicine, Am. Bd. Medicine Quality, Am. Bd. Ind. Med. Exam. Gen. med. officer USPHS, Juneau, Alaska, 1976-78; clin. dir. S.E. Alaska Native Health Corp, Juneau, 1978-79; asst. to commr. Tenn. Dept. Health and Environ., Nashville, 1980-83; dir. health care mgmt. Northern Telecom Inc., Nashville, 1983-88; pres. HDM, Inc., Nashville, 1988-90; med. dir. Aetna Health Plans of Tenn., Nashville, 1990-91; nat. practice leader, health strategy Alexander & Alexander Cons. Group, San Francisco, 1991-94; chief prevention, health and disability officer Indsl. Indemnity, San Francisco, 1994-97; pres. J. Harris Assocs., Inc., Mill Valley, Calif., 1979—; CEO, Med-Fx, Inc., 1999—; physician The Permanente Med. Group, San Rafael, Petaluma, Calif., 2001—. Author: Best Practices in Occupational Medicine, 2003; author, co-editor Occupational Medicine Practice Guidelines: Evaluation and Management of Common Health Problems and Functional Recovery in Workers, 1997, 2004; author, co-editor: Integrated Health Management, 1998; author, editor Managed Care in Occupational Medicine, 1998, Quick Reference to Practice Guidelines in Occupational Medicine, 1999, author, co-editor Managing Employee Health Care Costs, 1992, Manual of Occupational Health and Safety, 1992, 1996, 2003, Health Promotion in the Work Place, 1994, 2001, author-co-editor, 2003; co-author: Strategic Health Management, 1994; mem. editl. bd. Am. Jour. Health Promotion, 1985—, Occupl. Environ. Med. Report, 1988—; contbg. editor: JAMA, Am. Jour. Public Health, Internat. Jour. Occupl. Environ. Health, Jour. Occupl. and Environ. Medicine; contbr. articles to profl. jours., chapters to books. Fellow Am. Coll. Occupl. Environ. Medicine (dir., chmn. practice guidelines com. 1992-98, Presdl. award 1996), Am. Coll. Preventive Medicine, Am. Coll. Med. Quality, Am. Bd. Ind. Med. Examiners. Avocations: skiing, running, playing music, painting, writing. Home: 386 Richardson Way Mill Valley CA 94941-4053 E-mail: jharrismvl@aol.com., jeff_harris@medfx.net.

HARRIS, JERALD DAVID, lawyer; b. July 14, 1947; s. Donald W. and Dorothy (Botwin) H.; m. Carol Sue Fohlen, Mar. 25, 1972; children: Alyse, Jeffrey, Danielle. BA, Miami U., Oxford, Ohio, 1969; JD, U. Cin., 1972. Bar: Ohio 1972, U.,S. Dist. Ct. (so. dist.) Ohio 1972, U.S. Ct. Appeals (6th cir.) 1977, U.S. Dist. Ct. (ea. dist.) Ky. 1978, U.S. Supreme Ct. 1978. Assoc. Kondritzer, Gold & Frank, Cin., 1972-75; ptnr., 1975-79; sole practice, 1979-81; sr. ptnr. Harris and Katz Co. LPA, Cin., 1982-88, Harris, Bella & Burgin A Legal Profl. Assn., 1988—. Lectr. U. Cin. Coll. Law, 1986—, adj. prof., 2002-03. Author: Ohio Workers' Compensation Act. 1986; editor Workers' Compensation Jour. Ohio. Co-chmn. young profl. div. Jewish Welfare fund; bd. dirs. Hillel; vice chmn. Isaac M. Wise Temple Bldg. Fund campaign; mem. Young Leadership Coun. of Jewish Fedn. of Cin.; v.p., bd. dirs. Bonds for Israel; mem. Jewish Cmty. Rels. Coun.-WCET; active Jerry Springer for Gov. campaign; county chmn. Supreme Ct. campaign; bd. dirs. ARC, 1975-79; founding sponsor Civil Justice Found.; adv. Atty. General's Workers' Compensation Coun.; mem. Indsl. Commn. Ohio. Mem. Cin. bar Assn. (past chmn. workers compensation com. 1983-86, other coms.), Ohio Bar Assn. (workers compensation com.), Assn. Trial Lawyers Am., Ohio Acad. TrialLawyers (chmn. social security and adminstrv. law sect. 1981-85, chmn. workers compensation edn., com., 1985, vice chmn., regional coord. workers compensation com., chmn. workers compensation sect. 1992-93, legis. coord. com. 1993, Service to legal Profession award 1981, Cert. of Appreciation 1983, Disting. Svc. award, 1985, 87, Hall of Fame award, 1998, trustee), Nat. Orgn. Social Security Claimants Reps. (Ohio chmn. 1981-83), Am. Soc. Law and Medicine, Ohio State Bar Assn. Coll. Cuyahoga bar Assn.) worker's compensation com.), Phi Alpha Theta. Home: 10592 Cinderella Dr Cincinnati OH 45242-4909 Office: Harris & Burgin A Legal Profl Assn 9545 Kenwood Rd Ste 301 Cincinnati OH 45242-6100

HARRIS, JEREMY, mayor; s. Ann Harris; m. Ramona Sachiko Akui. BA, BS in Biology, U. Hawaii, 1972; MS in Population and Environ. Biology, U. Calif., Irvine, 1973. Lectr. oceanography, biology Kauai C.C.; del. Hawaii Constl. Conv., 1978; chmn. Kauai County Council; exec. asst. to mayor City and County of Honolulu, 1985-86, mng. dir. of Honolulu, 1986-94, mayor, 1994—. Founder, chair Mayors' Asia-Pacific Environ. Summit, 1999. Mem.: Am. Planning Assn. (Disting. Leadership award 2002), Internat. Downtown Assn. (Merit award), Am. Soc. Pub. Adminstrn. (Pub. Adminstr. of Yr. 1993, 1994), Am. Inst. Archs. (hon.). Office: Office Mayor Honolulu Hale 530 S King St Honolulu HI 96813

HARRIS, JEROME SYLVAN, pediatrician, pediatrics and biochemistry educator; b. N.Y.C., Feb. 27, 1909; s. Mark and Mary (Marcus) H.; m. Jacqueline Cato Hijmans, Oct. 23, 1958. AB summa cum laude, Dartmouth Coll., 1929; MD cum laude, Harvard U., 1933. Intern U. Chgo. Clinics, 1934; resident Boston Children's Hosp., 1935-36; mem. faculty Duke Sch. Medicine, Durham, N.C., 1937-79, J. Buren Sidbury prof. pediatrics, also prof. biochemistry, 1950-79; chmn. dept. pediatrics Duke Med. Center, 1954-68. Cons. Nat. Bd. Med. Examiners, 1956-60; mem. human embryology and devel. study sect. NIH, 1959-63 Contbr. articles to profl. jours. Bd. dirs. Durham Child Guidance Clinic, 1950-54. Served to lt. col. M.C. AUS, 1942-46. Mem. Am. Soc. Clin. Investigation, Soc. Pediatric Research, Am. Acad. Pediatrics, Am. Pediatrics Soc., So. Soc. Pediatric Research, Phi Beta Kappa, Sigma Xi, Alpha Omega Alpha. Office: Box 3916 Duke Med Ctr Durham NC 27710

HARRIS, JEWELL BACHTLER, social worker; b. Aug. 30, 1948; BA, Skidmore Coll., 1970; MSW, Simmons Sch. Social Work, 1973; D of Social Work, U. Ala., 1990. Cert. social worker, Idaho. Psychiat. social worker Philbrook Ctr. for C&Y Svcs., Concord, N.H., 1973-78, Community Coun. of Nashua, NH, 1978-79, dir. of C&Y Svcs., 1979-84, 87-90; social work cons. Rolfe and Rumford Home, Concord, 1974-81; social worker Pierre O. Durand, M.D., P.A., Bedford, N.H., 1990-91, Family and Children's Mental Health Svcs., Pocatello, Idaho, 1991-93, pvt. practice, Pocatello, Idaho, 1993—; clin. supr., clin. social worker Valley Med. Shoppe, Pocatello, Idaho, 2001—03; adj. prof. social work Idaho State U., Pocatello, 2003—. Mem. N.H. Project on the Health Care of Foster Children, Manchester, 1988—90, N.H. div. Mental Health Task Force Mental Health of Children, Concord, 1977—84; Bd. dirs. Big Bros./Big Sisters, Nashua, 1988—91, sec., 1991. Scholarship Simmons Coll. Sch. Social Work, 1971-72. Mem. NASW, Acad. Cert. Social Workers (diplomate), Network.

HARRIS, JOE FRANK, former governor; b. Cartersville, Ga., Feb. 16, 1936; s. Grover Franklin and Frances (Morrow) H.; m. Elizabeth Carlock Harris, June 25, 1961; 1 son. Joe Frank, Jr. BBA, U. Ga., 1958; LLD (hon.), Woodrow Wilson Coll. Law, 1981, Asbury Coll., 1983, Morris Brown Coll., 1983, LaGrange Coll., 1987, Mercer U., 1987. Sec.-treas. Harris Cement Products, Inc., Cartersville, 1958-79; pres. Harris Georgia Corp., Cartersville, 1979-83; mem. Ga. Gen. Assembly, 1965-83; gov. State of Ga., 1983-91; prof., Disting. Exec. fellow Ga. State U., Atlanta, 1993—. Bd. regents Univ. Sys. Ga., 1999—. Served with U.S. Army, 1958. Democrat. Methodist. Home: 712 West Ave Cartersville GA 30120-3441

HARRIS, JOEL B(RUCE), lawyer; b. N.Y.C., Oct. 15, 1941; s. Raymond S. and Laura (Greene) H.; m. Barbara J. Rous, June 13, 1965 (div.); 1 child, Clifford S.; m. Deborah Sherman, Apr. 1, 1986 (div.); children: Sydney Anne, Cassidy Raye. AB, Columbia U., 1963; LLB, Harvard U., 1966; LLM, U. London, 1967. Bar: N.Y. 1968, U.S. Dist. Ct. (so. dist.) N.Y. 1970, U.S. Ct. Appeals (2d cir.) 1970, U.S. Dist. Ct. (ea. dist.) N.Y. 1975, U.S. Supreme Ct. 1976, U.S. Ct. Appeals (3d cir.) 1980, U.S. Dist. Ct. (we. dist.) N.Y. 1981. Assoc. Simpson, Thacher & Bartlett, N.Y.C., 1967-70; asst. U.S. atty. So. Dist. N.Y., 1970-74, chief civil rights unit, 1973-74; assoc. Weil, Gotshal & Manges, N.Y.C., 1974-76, ptnr., 1976-86, Thacher, Proffitt & Wood, N.Y.C., 1986—; chmn. litigation dept., Latin Am. practice group. Speaker, panelist, moderator confs. Contbr. articles to profl. jours. Knox Meml. fellow, 1966-67. Fellow Am. Bar Found.; mem. ABA (chmn. com. internat. litigation 1981-84, chmn. com. personal rights litigation 1984-87), N.Y. State Bar Assn. (mem. internat. law and practice sect., sect. chair 1997-98, mem. exec. com. 1990—, chmn. internat. dispute resolution com. 1990-93, chmn. seasonal meeting 1993, 2001), Assn. Bar City N.Y., Inter-Am. Bar Assn., Fed. Bar Coun., Am. Soc. Internat. Law, Internat. Law Assn., Am. Judicature Soc. Home: 40 Prince St New York NY 10012-3426 Office: Thacher Proffitt & Wood 11 West 42nd St New York NY 10036 E-mail: jharris@tpwlaw.com.

HARRIS, JOHN D., II, electronics executive; BA, Boston U. Contracts adminstr. for missile programs Raytheon Co., 1983—, v.p. ops. and contracts for electronic systems, v.p. contracts for govt. and def. segment, 2002—03, contracts, 2003—. Office: Raytheon Co 141 Spring St Lexington MA 02421*

HARRIS, JOHN H., JR., radiologist; b. Great Falls, Mont., Oct. 16, 1925; s. John Harold and Nancy Catherine (Hamilton) H.; m. Catherine Connell, Aug. 31, 1972; children: John H. III, Robert D. BSc, Dickinson Coll., 1948; MD, Jefferson Med. Coll., 1953; MSc, U. Pa., 1955, DSc, 1957. Diplomate Am. Bd. Radiology. Radiologist Carlisle (Pa.) Hosp., 1957-79; prof. radiology Mich. State U., East Lansing, 1979-80, U. Tex. Med. Sch., Houston, 1980—. Assoc. prof. radiology Milton S. Hershey Med. Sch., Hershey, Pa., 1972-79; prof. radiology Jefferson Med. Coll., Phila., 1977-79; prof. emergency medicine U. Tex. Med. Sch., 1992-2001, prof. emeritus, 2001--; adj. prof. radiology Baylor Coll. Medicine, Houston, 1985-2001. Author: Radiology of Emergency Medicine, 4th edit., 2000, Radiology of Acute Cervical Spine Trauma, 3d edit., 1996; editl. bd. Contemporary Diagnostic Radiology, Diagnostic Radiology, Current Problems in Diagnostic Radiology; assoc. editor Emergency Radiology; assoc. editor Radiology, 1999—. Fellow Am. Coll. Radiology (bd. chancellors 1976-79, vice chair bd. chancellors 1979-80, chair bd. chancellors 1980-82, pres. 1982-83), Am. Soc. Emergency Radiology (co-founder 1988, pres. 1988-90), Royal Australasian Coll. Radiologists (hon.), Am. Acad. Orthop. Surgeons (assoc.); mem. Am. Coll. Emergency Physicians (hon.). Avocations: choral music, swimming, biking, tennis.

HARRIS, JOHN WILLIAM, hematologist, educator; b. Boston, Mar. 30, 1920; s. Ulysses Sylvester and Lillian (Dennett) H.; m. Stephanie Jean Bunting, Apr. 7, 1951; children: Wendy Alexandra, Alison Dennett, Stephen Bunting. BS, Trinity Coll., Hartford, Conn., 1941; MD, Harvard, 1944. Intern Boston City Hosp., 1944-45, resident, 1947-48; research fellow medicine Thorndike Meml. Lab., Harvard Med. Sch., 1948-51, research assoc., 1951-52; sr. instr. medicine Western Res. U., Cleve., 1952-54, asst. prof., 1954-57, assoc. prof., 1957-62, prof., 1962-99, prof. emeritus, 1999—. Hematologist, vis. physician Cleve. Met. Gen. Hosp., 1952-99, assoc. dir. dept. medicine, 1967-81; attending physician VA Hosp., Cleve., 1953-58, sr. attending physician hematology, 1959-99; cons. staff Lutheran Hosp., 1965-99; mem. hematology study sect. NIH, 1962-66, chmn., 1983-85, mem. hematology tng. grants com., 1969-73; mem. com. blood and transfusion Nat. Acad. Scis.-NRC, 1963-65; chmn. Merit Rev. Bd. in Hematology, Med. Research Service, VA, 1977-80 Served to capt. U.S. Army, 1945-47. Recipient USPHS Research Career award, 1962, Martin Luther King, Jr. award for outstanding research in sickle cell anemia, 1972; Alfred Stengel Research fellow ACP, 1951-52; Markle scholar in medicine, 1955-60; named to Cleve. Med. Hall of Fame, 1998. Fellow ACP, Internat. Soc. Hematology (nat. counselor, Interam. div. 1986); mem. AAAS, Am. Fedn. Clin. Research, Am. Soc. Clin. Investigation (past v.p.), Central Soc. Clin. Research, Soc. Exptl. Biology and Medicine, Am. Soc. Hematology (pres. 1981-82), Acad. Medicine Cleve., Assn. Am. Physicians, Phi Beta Kappa, Alpha Omega Alpha. Home: Bruening Health Ctr Rm 603C 2181 Ambleside Dr Cleveland OH 44106 Office: 2500 Metrohealth Dr Cleveland OH 44109-1900

HARRIS, JOSEPH C. education educator; b. Columbus, Ga., Sept. 18, 1940; s. Joseph Clarence and Georgia (Walker) H.; m. Nancy Flowers; children: Alice Kittrell, Elizabeth Whiting Flowers; m. Monika Maria Totten; 1 child, Sonja Sophia Totten-Harris. BA, U. Ga., 1961; BA with honors, Cambridge (Eng.) U., 1967; MA, Harvard U., 1963, PhD, 1969. Asst. prof. Harvard U., Cambridge, Mass., 1969-72, prof., 1985—; from asst. prof. to prof. Stanford (Calif.) U., 1972-82; prof. Cornell U., Ithaca, N.Y., 1982-85. Vis. prof. Bonn U., 1992. Editor: The Ballad & Oral Literature, 1991; contbr. articles to profl. jours. Jr. fellow Soc. for the Humanities, 1971-72, Guggenheim Found. fellow, 1985-87, Am. Coun. Learned Soc. fellow, 1975-76; recipient Elliott prize Medieval Acad., 1972. Office: Harvard Univ Dept English 12 Quincy St Cambridge MA 02138-3902

HARRIS, JOSEPH LAMAR, state official; b. Pensacola, Fla., Mar. 26, 1951; s. Joseph Erlis and Mazie Lois (Plant) H.; m. Elizabeth Gail Golden, Dec. 15, 1973; children: Heather Brooke, Brandon Lamar. AA in Bus., Pensacola Jr. Coll., 1971; BA in Acctg. magna cum laude, U. West Fla., 1973. CPA, Fla., Ala.; cert. govt. fin. mgr., govt. fin. officer. Staff acct. Touche Ross and Co., Atlanta, 1974-75; divsn. acct. Gulf Power Co., Pensacola, Fla., 1975; field auditor Audit Agy., HEW, Montgomery, Ala., 1975-77; budget analyst II Ala. Budget Office, Montgomery, 1977-82, budget analyst III, 1982-85, budget analyst IV, 1985-87; acting budget officer, dep. state budget officer State of Ala., Montgomery, 1987-88, dep. state budget officer, 1988-96; exec. dir. Ala. Bd. Pub. Accountancy, Montgomery, 1996—. Bd. dirs. Ala. Gov.'s Legis. First Reading Com., Montgomery, 1984-96; bd. dirs. Ala. Bd. Pub. Accountancy, sec.-treas. 1989-94; chmn. state adv. group Ala. Mgmt. Improvement Program, Montgomery, 1987-89; mem. adv. coun. to govtl. acct. and auditor tng. program Auburn U., Montgomery, 1992-97. Named to Troy State U. Acctg. Hall of Honor, 2003; recipient Cert. of Appreciation, Office of the Gov. State of Ala, 1987. Mem. AICPA (CPA exam. content oversight task force 1999-2001), Ala. Soc. CPA (state legis. com. 1981-2002, Outstanding CPA in Govt. award 1997-98), Assn. Govt. Accts. (chpt. treas. 1975-77, chpt. programs dir. 1996-97, chpt. scholarships com. 1997-98, programs com. 1998-2000), Govt. Fin. Officers Assn. Ala. (legis. com. 1995-96), Ala. State Employees Assn., Nat. Assn. State Bds. Accountancy (govt. rels. com. 1990-93, strategic initiatives com. 1997-99, 2002—, exec. dirs. com. 1998-2001, examinations com. 1999-2000, ethics com. 2001-02), Ala. Assn. Accts. Mem. Assembly of God Ch. Avocations: hunting, sports card collecting. Home: 6032 Meridian Ln Montgomery AL 36117-2789 Office: Ala Bd Pub Accountancy 770 Washington Ave Ste 236 Montgomery AL 36130-0375 E-mail: lharris@asbpa.state.al.us.

HARRIS, JOSEPH MCALLISTER, retired chemist; b. Pontiac, Ill., July 27, 1929; s. Fred Gilbert and Catherine Marguerite (McAllister) H.; m. Margot Jeanette L'Hommedieu, Feb. 17, 1952; children: Timothy, Kaye, Paula, Bruce, Anne, Martha, Rebecca. BA, Blackburn Coll., Carlinville, Ill., 1952; postgrad., So. Ill. U., 1953-54, U. Ill., 1956-61. Technician Olin Ind., Inc., Energy, Ill., 1953-54; quality control staff Union Starch and Refining Co., Granite City, Ill., 1954; rsch. asst. Ill. State Geol. Survey, Urbana, 1954-61; chemist II Water Pollution Control Bd., Annapolis, Md., 1961-63; phys. chemist Ball Bros. Rsch., Inc., Muncie, Ind., 1963-66; engr. Radio Corp. Am., Marion, Ind., 1966-70; chemist OA Labs., Inc., Indpls., 1973-86, OA Labs. & Rsch., Inc., Indpls., 1986-93, cons., 1993—. Bd. dirs. Tri-County Hearing Assn. for Children, Muncie, 1967-70. Mem. Am. Chem. Soc., AAAS, Soc. Applied Spectroscopy. Republican. Presbyterian. Avocations: gardening, camping. Home: 800 E Washington St Muncie IN 47305-2533

HARRIS, JUDITH ANN WHITE, health occupations vocational educator, nurse; b. Springfield, Ohio, Mar. 6, 1939; d. Willis and Tennessee Belle (Poole) Martin; m. Allen G. Harris, Mar. 21, 1986; 1 child by previous marriage, Denise Marian Womble. Student, U. South Fla., 1978-85, BS/MS in Psychology, 2000. RN, Fla.; cert. tchr., Fla. Nurse Dr. Robert Tapogna, Springfield, Ohio, 1960-62, Springfield City Hosp., 1962-65, Dr. Robert Beam, Springfield, 1965-75; ednl. coord., instr. med. assisting Sarasota Vocat. Ctr., Fla., 1977-82, instr. med. assisting program, chmn. dept., 1982-84, 89-91, instr. health svc. oocupations, placement coord. health occu, 1985-88; dept. chmn. Allied Health, 1989-95. Bd. dirs. Fla. Bd. Inc.; pres. J.W. Harris Pub. Co.; cruise ship lectr. for Princess, Royal Caribbean and Celebrity Cruise Lines; v.p., sec. Al Harris Pest Control, Inc. 1996-; dir. adv. & mktg., 2000-. Author: J.W. Harris Medical Assisting Review Manual, 1995, Templin, 2002; contbr. articles to profl. jours. Vol. Children's Breath Clinic, Sarasota, 1977-79, Kidney Found., Sarasota, 1982, ARC, Sarasota, 1976-88; dir. Spl. Care Unit, 1984-88; v.p. Sons of Norway, 1993-95; choir soloist Beneva Christian Ch., 1989—, deaconess, 1993-96, elder 1997—, chmn. Health Care Svcs. Dept., 1996—, vice chmn. bd. dirs., 2001-02, chmn. bd., 2002—; asst. state dir. Fla. Good Sons, 1993-94; bd. dirs. Fla. Bd. Camping Assn., Inc., sec., 1999--, newsletter editor, 1996—; chmn. FVA Leadership Forum, 1992—; parish nurse and chmn. health svcs. dept. Beneva Christian Ch., 1995—; pres. FVA Post Pres.'s Club, 1999—; 1st v.p. Sarasota Bay Republican Women's Club Federated, 1998-2001; mem. Sarasota Tiger Bay Club, 1999—, Sarasota Homebuilders Assn., 1999—; sec. Acorn Glass Bowling League, 2000—. Named Outstanding Vocat. Tchr. Sarasota County Sch. Bd., 1985, Woman of Impact for Edn., Sarasota County Commn. on the Status of Women, 1995. Mem. Am. Vocat. Assn. (Outstanding Vocat. Tchr. region II 1985, Vocat. Tchr. Yr. 1987), Health Occupations Educators (vice chmn. policy com. 1985-86), Nat. Assn. Health Occupations Tchrs. (v.p. region II 1984-86, pres. elect 1988, pres. 1989-91), Fla. Vocat. Assn. (bd. dirs. 1983-85, pres. 1987-88, Pres. award 1984, Outstanding Vocat. Educator region 23 award 1982, Sarasota Mayors award 1984, Gov.'s Proclamation for Outstanding Tchg. 1987, chmn. leadership forum 1993—), Health Occupations Educators Assn. Fla. (pres. 1983-84, chmn. legis. com. 1985-93, Outstanding Tchr. 1983), Sarasota County Vocat. and Adult Edn. Assn. (pres. 1978-80, editor newsletter 1978-83), Am. Assn. Med. Assts., Good Sams Inc. Fla. (asst. state dir. dist. 12 1993-95), Fraternal Order of Eagles Aux. (dist. 3 auditor 1995-96, eagle nurse 1995-97, chair health care dept. 1995—, condr. 1996—), Sarasota Bay Republican Women's Club (life; v.p. 1998—), Women's Coun. Realtors (ways and means chair 2002-, corr. sec. 2003, rec. sec. 2004), Sarasota Assn. Realtors, Sunrise Rotary Club (Paul Harris fellow, 2002-, Rotary Internat. Sustaining Mem. 2002-), Tiger Bay Club, Delta Kappa Gamma, Phi Kappa Phi. Avocations: swimming, camping, knitting, sewing, biking. Home: PO Box 7278 Sarasota FL 34278 Office: 6100 Palmer Blvd Sarasota FL 34232 E-mail: alharrispestcontrol@netzero.net.

HARRIS, JUDITH RICH, writer; b. NYC, Feb. 10, 1938; d. Sam L. and Frances (Lichtman) R.; m. Charles S. Harris, Dec. 24, 1961; children: Nomi L., Elaine R. Valk. BA, Brandeis U., 1959; MA, Harvard U., 1961. Freelance sci. writer, 1979—. Author: The Child: Development from Birth through Adolescence, 1984, 87, 91, Infant and Child: Development from Birth through Middle Childhood, 1992, The Nurture Assumption, 1998; contbr. articles to profl. jours. Recipient George A. Miller award APA, 1997; finalist Pulitzer prize General Non-Fiction, 1999. Mem. Soc. for Rsch. in Child Devel., Am. Psychol. Soc., Human Behavior & Evolution Soc., Phi Beta Kappa. E-mail: 72073.1211@compuserve.com.

HARRIS, JULIE (JULIE ANN HARRIS), actress; b. Grosse Pointe Park, Mich., Dec. 2, 1925; d. William Pickett and Elsie (Smith) H.; m. Jay I. Julien, Aug. 12, 1946 (div. 1954); m. Manning Gurian, Oct. 21, 1954 (div. 1967); 1 child, Peter; m. Erwin Carroll, Apr. 1977, (div. 1982). Student, Perry Mansfield Theatre Work Shop, 1941-43, Yale Drama Sch., 1944-45. Theater debut in It's a Gift, N.Y.C., 1945; appeared in plays Playboy of the Western World, 1946, Oedipus, 1946, Henry IV-Part II, 1946, Alice in Wonderland, 1947, We Love A Lassie, 1947, Macbeth, 1948, Sundown Beach, 1948 (Theatre World award 1949), The Young and Fair, 1948-49, Magnolia Alley, 1949, Montserrat, 1949, The Member of the Wedding, 1950-51 (Donaldson award 1950), I Am a Camera, 1951-52 (Tony award 1952, Donaldson award 1952, Variety-N.Y. Drama Critics Poll 1952), Mademoiselle Colombe, 1954, The Lark, 1955 (Tony award 1956), The Country Wife, 1957, The Warm Peninsula, 1959, Little Moon of Alban, 1960, Romeo and Juliet, 1960, King John, 1960, A Shot in the Dark, 1961, Marathon 33, 1964 (Tony nomination 1964), Hamlet, 1964, Ready When You Are, C.B, 1964, The Hostage, 1965, Skyscraper, 1965 (Tony nomination 1969), A Streetcar Named Desire, 1967, Forty Carats, 1968 (Tony award 1969), The Women, 1970, And Miss Reardon Drinks A Little, 1971-72, Voices, 1972, The Last of Mrs. Lincoln, 1972 (Tony award 1973), The Au Pair Man, 1973 (Tony nomination 1974), In Praise of Love, 1974, Break a Leg, 1979, On Golden Pond, 1980, Mixed Couples, 1980, Under the Ilex, 1983, Tusitala, 1988, (nat. co.) Driving Miss Daisy, Love Letters, 1989, The Belle of Amherst, 1977 (Grammy award 1977, Tony award 1977), Currier Bell, Glass Menagerie, 1994, Ellen Foster, 1997, Love is Strange, 1999, Fossils, 2001; one-woman theater presentations include Lucifer's Child, 1991; film debut in The Member of the Wedding, 1952 (Acad. award nomination); other films include The East of Eden, 1955, I Am A Camera, 1955, The Truth About Women, 1958, Poacher's Daughter, 1960, Requiem for a Heavyweight, 1962, The Haunting, 1963, The Moving Target, 1966, You're a Big Boy Now, 1966, Reflections in a Golden Eye, 1967, The Split, 1968, Journey into Midnight, 1968, The People Next Door, 1970, The Hiding Place, 1975, Voyage of the Damned, 1976, The Bell Jar, 1979, The Prostitute, 1980, The Nutcraker: The Motion Picture, 1986, Gorillas in the Mist, 1988, Housesitter, 1992, The Dark Half, 1993, Little Surprises, 1995, Carried Away, 1996; TV series include Thicker Than Water, 1973, The Family Holvak, 1975, Knots Landing, 1979-87; TV movies include Wind From the South, 1955, The Good Fairy, 1956, The Lark, 1957, Johnny Belinda, 1968, Little Moon of Alban, 1958 (Emmy award 1959), A Doll's House, 1959, Victoria Regina, 1961 (Emmy award 1962), The Power and the Glory, 1961, Pygmalian, 1964, Hamlet, 1964, The Holy Terror, 1965, Anastasia, 1967, The House on Green Apple Road, 1970, How Awful About Alan, 1970, Home for the Holidays, 1972, The Greatest Gift, 1974, Backstairs at the White House, 1979, The Gift, 1979, The Christmas Wife, 1979, Too Good To Be True, 1988, Single Women, Married Men, 1989, They've Taken Our Children: The Chowchilla Kidnapping Story, 1993, When Love Kills: The Seduction of John Nearn, 1993, One Christmas, 1994, Scarlett, 1994, The Christmas Tree, 1996, James Dean: A Portrait, 1996, Carried Away, 1996, Bad Manners, 1997, Ellen Foster, 1997, The First of May, 1998, (voice) Frank Lloyd Wright, 1998; author: (with Barry Tarshis) Julie Harris Talks to Young Actors, 1971. Recipient Antoinette Perry award for best actress in Forty Carats, 1969, The Last of Mrs. Lincoln, 1973; Nat. Medal of the Arts, 1994, Tony award for lifetime achievement in Theater, 2002. Office: William Morris Agy c/o Samuel Liff 1325 Avenue of the Americas New York NY 10019*

HARRIS, K. DAVID, senior state supreme court justice; b. Jefferson, Iowa, July 29, 1927; s. Orville William and Jessie Heloise (Smart) H.; m. Madonna Theresa Coyne, Sept. 4, 1948; children: Jane, Julia, Frederick. BA, U. Iowa, 1949, JD, 1951. Bar: Iowa 1951, U.S. Dist. Ct (so. dist.) Iowa, 1958. Sole practice Harris & Harris, Jefferson, 1951-62; dist. judge 16th Judicial Dist., Iowa, 1962-72; justice Iowa Supreme Ct., Des Moines, 1972-99, sr. justice, 1999—. Served with U.S. Army, 1944-46, PTO. Mem. VFW, Am. Legion, Rotary. Roman Catholic. Avocation: writing poetry. Office: Iowa Supreme Ct State Capitol Bldg Des Moines IA 50319-0001

HARRIS, KATHERINE, congresswoman; b. Key West, Fla., Apr. 5, 1957; m. Anders Ebbeson. Student, U. Madrid, 1978; BA in History, Agnes Scott Coll., 1979; MPA in Internat. Trade, Harvard U., 1996. Senator 24th dist. Fla. State Legislature, 1994—98; sec. of state State of Fla., 1999—2002; mem. U.S. Ho. of Reps from 13th Fla. dist., 2003—. Vice chmn. banking and ins. com. Fla. State Senate, vice chmn. govtl. reform and oversight com., chmn. commerce and econ. opportunities com. Congl. intern U.S. Senate and U.S. Ho. of Reps., 1978; vice chmn. Sarasota County Legis. Del.; mem. Supreme Ct. Gender Bias Commn.; vice chmn. Fla. Am. Legis. Exch. Coun.; mem. arts and tourism com. Nat. Conf. State Legislators; former mem. adv. coun. Mote Marine Lab., Women's Resource Ctr., Sarasota County Arts Coun.; mem. Leadership Sarasota, Leadership Tampa; former vice chmn. bd. trustees Ringling Mus.; mem. nominating com. Pub. Svc. Commn.; active Habitat for Humanity, New Coll., Fla. Rep. Exec. Com. Recipient Disting. Leadership Alumni award, Leadership Sarasota, 1994, Arts Advocacy award, Sarasota County Arts Coun., 1995, Best Govt. Ofcl. award, Sarasota Mag., 1995—2002, Legislator of Yr. award, Sarasota Opera, 1996, Ind. Funeral Dirs. of Fla., 1996, Fla. Optometric Assn., 1996, Legis. Appreciation award, Dept. Labor and Employment Security, 1996. Mem. Sarasota C. of C. (Disting. Leadership Alumni award 1994), Englewood C. of C., Charlotte C. of C., Venice C. of C., Jaycees. Republican. Presbyterian. Avocations: reading, sailing, painting, skiing, skeet shooting, painting, skiing, skeet shooting, reading. Office: 116 Cannon Ho Office Bldg Washington DC 20515-0913*

HARRIS, KATHERINE SAFFORD, speech and hearing educator; b. Lowell, Mass., Sept. 3, 1925; d. Truman Henry and Katherine (Wardwell) Safford; m. George Harris, Oct. 2, 1952; children: Maud White, Louise. BA, Radcliffe Coll., 1947; PhD, Harvard U., 1954. Rsch. assoc. Haskins Labs., New Haven, 1952-85, v.p., 1985—; prof. CUNY, N.Y.C., 1970—, disting. prof., 1982—. Active U.S./Israeli Speech Program Littauer Found., N.Y.C., 1986. Author: (with Borden and Raphael) Speech Science Primer, 1970, 4th edit., 2002, (with Baer and Sasaki) Phonatory Control, 1986. Active U.S./Israeli Speech Program Littauer Found., N.Y.C., 1986. Nat. Inst. Deafness and Other Comm. Disorders grantee. Fellow AAAS, Acoustical Soc. Am. (pres. 2000-01), Am. Speech Hearing Assn., N.Y. Acad. Scis. Office: CUNY Grad Sch 415 5th Ave New York NY 10016

HARRIS, KATHLEEN RENEE, information technology supervisor, fashion designer; b. L.A., Nov. 30, 1954; d. William Rogiere Harris and IdaBelle (Norman) Rivers. AA in Data Processing, Chabot Coll., 1980; BS in Bus. Mgmt., U. Phoenix, 2001. Gen. clk. sec. Western Girl Temp. Agy., San Leandro, Calif., 1973-75; mag card II operator Bechtel Inc., San Francisco, 1975-76, data entry operator, 1976-79, office asst., 1979-80; adminstrv. asst. II Bechtel Power Corp., Walnut Creek, Calif., 1980-82; computer programmer I Bechtel Corp., San Francisco, 1982-86; ind. programmer/analyst, 1987—; project mgr. Clorox Co., 1998-99, info. systems super., 1999—. Database analyst Wollborg-Michelson; sys. support analyst Kraft Foods, 1990-92; LAN adminstr. So. Pacific Lines, 1992-93; sr. help desk specialist Triad Sys/Geoworks/Concord Gen., 1994-95; PC support tech. EDS/Blue Shield, 1995-96; LAN support mgr., Pacific Bell, 1996-97; project coord. Charles Schwab, 1997-98; project mgr., Clorox Co., 1998-99; designer, seamstress, owner Feline Fit, Etc., Calif.; co-owner Next Generation Model Mgmt. Co., 1984. Mem. Better Bus. Bur. Avocation: licensed private pilot. Home: 894 Shelborne Dr Tracy CA 95377-8228 E-mail: kathleen.harris@clorox.com.

HARRIS, KRISTINE, historian, educator; b. New York, July 10, 1964; d. Robert and Ingrid H.; m. Robert Polito, June 27, 1987. BA, Wellesley Coll., 1986; MA, PhD, Columbia U., 1997. Instr. New Sch. Social Rsch., N.Y.C., 1995; asst. prof. history SUNY, New Paltz, 1996—, dir. Asian studies program, 2000—. Contbr. articles to profl. jours. and books, collections. Fulbright Found. fellow, 1992-93, Am. Coun. Learned Socs. fellow, 1993, 98; grantee Pacific Cultural Found., 1994-95. Mem. Am. Hist. Assn., Assn. Asian Studies. Office: Dept History State U New York New Paltz NY 12561 E-mail: harrisk@newpaltz.edu.

HARRIS, LOUIS, public opinion analyst, columnist; b. New Haven, Jan. 6, 1921; s. Harry and Frances (Smith) H.; m. Florence Yard, June 16, 1943; children: Susan, Peter, Richard. AB in Econs., U. N.C., 1942. With Elmo Roper and Assocs., 1946-56, ptnr., 1954-56; chmn., CEO Louis Harris and Assocs., Inc. (marketing and pub. opinion research), N.Y.C., 1956-92; CEO LH Rsch. Inc., N.Y.C., 1992-94; cons. CBS News, 1962-68, ABC News Nat. Polling Day, 1971-72; dir. polling ABC News, 1976-80; columnist Washington Post, also Newsweek mag., 1963-68, Chgo. Tribune-N.Y. Daily News Syndicate, 1969-88, Creators Syndicate, 1988-92; dir. Time mag.-Harris Poll, 1969-72; guest analyst, commentator Nat. Pub. Radio, 1983-91; dir. Bus. Week-Harris Poll, 1982—. Polled extensively in John F. Kennedy Presdl. campaign, 1960; mem. Kennedy Strategy Com., 1960; dir. Life Poll, 1969-71; faculty assoc. Columbia U., N.Y.C., 1953-64; adj. prof. polit. sci. U. N.C., 1964—; bd. dirs., mem. compensation com. Donaldson, Lufkin & Jenrette, N.Y.C. Author: Is There a Republican Majority?, 1964, (with William Brink) The Negro Revolution in America, 1964, Black and White, 1967, Black-Jewish Relations in New York City: The Anguish of Change, 1973, Inside America, 1987, Americans and the Arts, No. VI: Nationwide Survey of Public Opinion, 1992, No. VII, 1996; also numerous articles. Chmn. bd. dirs. Am. Councils for Arts, 1975-82; chmn. Nat. Research Center Arts, 1971—; bd. dirs., v.p. Franklin and Eleanor Roosevelt Inst., 1983—; bd. dirs. Nat. Ctr. on Edn. and the Economy, 1987-97, Recruiting New Tchrs., 1987—, chmn., 1998—; hon. trustee Am. Archtl. Found., 1996—; exec. com. legal def. fund NAACP, 1990—; bd. dirs. First Book, 1995—, Get Am. Working, 1998—, Youth Venture, 1997—, Found. for Island Health, Found. for Island Health, 2000—. Served as officer USNR, World War II. Mem. Am. Assn. Pub. Opinion (dir.), Am. Sociol. Assn., Am. Statis. Assn., Am. Mgmt. Assn., Am. Mktg. Assn., Am. Polit. Sci. Assn., Fgn. Policy Assn. (bd. govs. 1986-91), Century Assn. *To make those in power confront the facts is critically important for the sake of progress of any kind, but to get people with power to act upon the facts to better the lot of the human race is by far more important.*

HARRIS, LOUIS SELIG, pharmacologist, researcher; b. Boston, Mar. 27, 1927; s. Max Selig and Pearl (Oppochinski) H.; m. Ruth Irma Schaufus, Aug. 22, 1952; 1 child, Charles Allan. BA, Harvard U., 1954, MA, 1956, PhD, 1958. Sect. head, sr. rsch. biologist Sterling-Winthrop Rsch. Inst., Rensselaer, N.Y., 1958-66; lectr. in pharmacology Albany (N.Y.) Med. Coll., 1959-66; from assoc. prof. to prof. U. N.C., Chapel Hill, 1966-73; Harvey Haag prof. Med. Coll. Va./Va. Commonwealth U., Richmond, 1972—, chmn. pharmacology, toxicology dept., 1972-92, assoc. v.p. health scis., 1996—2003; acting assoc. dir. Nat. Inst. on Drug Abuse, Rockville, Md., 1987-88. Sterling Drug vis. prof., 1983; mem. com. on problems of drug dependence NAS/NRC, 1973-77; bd. dirs. Com. on Problems of Drug Dependence, Inc., 1977-93, 1998-2002, chmn., 1990-92, pres., 2001-03; hon. prof. U. Puerto Rico Sch. Medicine, 1972—, Beijing Med. U., People's Republic of China, 1990—. Editor: (monograph) NIDA Monographs, Proceedings, Committee on Problems of Drug Dependence, 1979-2002; author chpts. in books. Chmn. bd. dirs. Found. for Pharmacology, Harris Family Found.; bd. dirs. Human Resources Inc., VCU Intellectual Property Found., Med. Coll. Va. Found., 1999-2003. Recipient Hartung Meml. award U. N.C., 1981, Univ. Excellence award Med. Coll. Va./Va. Commonwealth U., 1984, Disting. Svc. award, 1999, Outstanding Faculty award, 1984, Nathan B. Eddy award Com. on Problems of Drug Dependence, 1985, Abe Wikler award Nat. Inst. on Drug Abuse, 1991, Gov.'s award on Drug Abuse Rsch., 1992, Presdl. medallion Va. Commonwealth U., 1993, Life Achievement award in Sci. and Industry, Commonwealth of Va., 1997. Fellow Am. Coll. Neuropsychopharmacology, Coll. Problems Drug Dependence, Collegium Internationale Neuro-Psychopharmacologicum; mem. AAAS, Am. Soc. Pharmacology and Exptl. Therapeutics, Am. Chem. Soc., Am. Assn. for Med. Sch. Pharmacology, Am. Pain Soc. (charter 1977), Am. Pharm. Assn., Am. Soc. for Clin. Pharmacology and Therapeutics, Assn. Harvard Chemists, Elisha Mitchell Sci. Soc., Internat. Narcotic Enforcement Officers Assn., Soc. for Neurosci., Internat. Soc. Biochem. Pharmacology, Internat. Soc. for Study of Pain, Mex. Pharmacology Soc. (hon.), Va. Acad. Sci., Harvard Club Boston, Cosmos Club Washington. Achievements include research in field. Home: 7830 Rockfalls Dr Richmond VA 23225-1049 Office: Va Commonwealth U PO Box 980027 Richmond VA 23298-0027 E-mail: harris@hsc.vcu.edu.

HARRIS, LUCY BROWN, accountant, consultant; b. Ft. Smith, Ark., Feb. 25, 1924; d. Joseph Real and Lucy (McDonough) Brown; m. Clyde B. Randall, June 10, 1944 (div. Aug. 1970); children: Clyde B. III, Bradford, Sara, Lucy, Mark R.; m. Mack C. Harris, Aug. 1, 1980. Student, Holton Arms Jr. Coll., 1943, U. Mo., 1944; BA, U. Ark., 1970; grad., U. Tex., 1982. CPA. Comptroller Rebmar, Inc., Dallas, 1974-78; acctg. mgr. Republic Bank, Dallas, 1978-80; ptnr. Lucy B. Harris Ltd. Co., CPAs, Dallas, 1981—. Cons. Discipleship Counseling Svcs., Dallas, 1987-90. Mem. Better Bus. Bur.; bd. dirs. Ethel Daniels Found., Dallas, 1987-90, NAWBO. Mem. AICPA, Nat. Assn. Women Bus. Owners, Tex. Soc. CPAs, CPA Club, Jr. League of Dallas, Brookhollow Golf Club, Kappa Alpha Theta. Episcopalian. Avocation: painting. Office: 3710 Rawlins St Ste 810 Dallas TX 75219-4237 E-mail: lbrownh24@earthlink.net.

HARRIS, LYTTLETON TAZWELL, IV, property management-investment company executive; b. Baton Rouge, Aug. 7, 1940; s. Lyttleton Tazwell and Marjorie Fleming (Windsor) H.; m. Venita Walker VanCaspel, Dec. 26, 1987. BBA, U. Miss., Oxford, 1962; MS, La. State U., 1963. Product mgr. Scott Paper Co., Phila., 1968-71; mktg. mgr. Wm. B. Reily & Co., New Orleans, 1971-72; mktg. dir. Blue Plate Foods, Inc., New Orleans, 1972-74, Dallas Fed. Savs., 1974-77; v.p. First Magnolia Fed. Savs., Hattiesburg, Miss., 1977-81; pres. S.W. Mgmt. & Mktg. Co., Houston, 1982—2001; v.p. Innerview Pub. Co., Houston,

1984-86; mng. editor Money Dynamics Letter Pub. Co., Houston, 1985-91; gen. mgr. Diamond V Ranch of Bernardo, Tex., 1990-99; mng. ptnr. Harris Investment Partnership, 1998—; chmn. The John Quincy Adams Found., 2003—. V.p. Nat. Kidney Found. Miss., Jackson, 1980-82; bd. dirs. Nat. Kidney Found. S.E. Tex., Houston, 1983-88, Boy Scouts Am., Hattiesburg, 1980-82; vol. Big Bros. of Dallas, 1975-77; trustee Crystal Cathedral Ministries, 1998—, Northwood U., 1999—. With USAR, 1963-68. Mem. Am. Mktg. Assn., Sales and Mktg. Execs. (pres. 1982), Nat. Gavel Soc., Nat. Congress of Patriotic Orgns. (regional v.p. 1997-2001), Soc. Colonial Wars (lt. gov. Tex. soc. 1997-98, dep. gov. 1998-99, gov. 1999-2000), Mil. Order Stars and Bars, Order of Three Crusades, Huguenot Soc., Order Founders and Patriots of Am. (gov. Tex. chpt. 1987-91, gov. gen. 1992-94, Meritorious Svc. award 1990, Disting. Svc. award 1996), U. Miss. Alumni Assn., Sons of Confederate Vets., Soc. Ams. of Royal Descent, Sons of the Revolution (v.p. Tex. soc. 1997-98, pres. 1998-2000), Soc. of the War of 1812, Royal Soc. St. George, Houston Racquet Club, Univ. Club, Sigma Alpha Epsilon, Delta Sigma Pi. Republican. Methodist. Avocations: snow skiing, international travel, genealogy. Office: Southwest Mgmt & Mktg 6524 San Felipe St Ste 102 Houston TX 77057-2611 E-mail: LTHIV@aol.com.

HARRIS, MARCELITE JORDAN, retired career officer; b. Houston, Jan. 16, 1943; d. Cecil Oneal and Marcelite Elizabeth (Terrell) Jordan; m. Maurice Anthony Harris, Nov. 29, 1980 (dec. Jan. 1996); children: Steven Eric, Tenecia Marcelite. BA, Spelman Coll., 1964; postgrad., Ctrl. Mich. U., 1973-75, crwa. State U., 1975-76, Chapman Coll., 1979-80; BS, U. Md., Okinawa, Japan, 1986. Tchr. Head Start, Houston, 1964-65; commd. 2d lt. USAF, 1965, advanced through grades to maj. gen., 1965-97; student Squadron officers Sch., 1975; with Hdqrs. USAF, Pentagon, 1975; comdr. 39 Cadet Squadron, USAF Acad., Colorado Springs, Colo., 1978, Air Refueling Wing, McConnell AFB, Kans., 1980, Avionics Maintenance Squadron, McConnell AFB, 1981, Field Maintenance Squadron, McConnell AFB, 1982; dir. maintenance Pacific Air Forces Logistics Support Ctr., Kadena Air Base, Japan, 1982; student Air War Coll., 1983; dep. chief maintenance Tech. Tng. Ctr., Keesler AFB, Miss., 1986, wing comdr., 1988; student Harvard U.Sr. Officers Course, 1988, Capstone Flag and Gen. Officers Course, 1990; vice comdr. Oklahoma City Air Logistics Ctr., Tinker AFB, 1990-97; dir. tech. tng. USAF, Randolph AFB, Tex., 1993-97, dir. of maintenance, 1994, ret., 1997. Cabinet mem. United Way, Oklahoma City, 1991; mem. adv. bd, Salvation Army, Oklahoma City, 1991—; bd. dirs. U.S. Automobile Assn., 1993—, 5 Who Care, 1992, Urban League. Decorated Bronze star, D.S.M.; named one of Top 100 Afro-Am. Bus. and Profl. Women, Dollars and $ense Mag., 1989, named Most Prestigious Individual, 1991, One of Top 100 Most Influencial People, City News, N.J., 1997; recipient Ellis Island Medal of Honor award, 1996, Living Legacy award 1998. Mem. AAUW, Air Force Assn. (life), Tuskegee Airmen Inc. (life), Maintenance Officer Assn., Retired Officer Assn., Ret. Officer Assn., Delta Sigma Theta. *Life is a miracle, but you have to give it meaning, shape and value. Choose what you can contribute to make society better. My sister and I got our strength from our parents. We learned to keep trying until we succeeded. That's perseverance.*

HARRIS, MARIE, writer; b. N.Y.C., Nov. 7, 1943; d. Basil and Marie Harris; m. William Matthews, May 4, 1963 (div.); children: William Matthews, Sebastian Matthews; m. Charter Weeks, Nov. 4, 1977; 1 child, Manuel Weeks. BA, Goddard Coll., 1971. Co-owner Isinglass Mktg., Barrington, NH, 1978—. Author: Weasel in the Turkey Pen, 1993, Your Sun, Manny, 1999, G is for Granite, 2002. Fellow NEA, 1976-77; named poet laureate State of N.H., 1999—. Mem.: Acad. Am. Poets, Poetry Soc. Am., Nat. Writers Union. Avocations: birding, sailing. Home: PO Box 203 Barrington NH 03825 E-mail: marie@isinglasmarkting.com.

HARRIS, MARTHA JANE, retired librarian; b. Milton, W.Va., Dec. 29, 1926; d. Dolphus Marshall and Julia Esther (Seabright) Martin; m. Byron Stanley Harris Sr., Dec. 1, 1944; 1 child, Byron Stanley. Student, Indian River Community Coll., Ft. Pierce, Fla., 1972-73; BS, Fla. State U., 1974, MA, 1975. Cert. tchr., Fla. Libr. Henrico County Sch. Bd., Richmond, Va., 1959-64; children's libr. Martin County Pub. Libr., Stuart, Fla., 1964-65, St. Lucie-Okeechobee Regional Libr. System, Ft. Pierce, 1965-70; dir. youth svcs. St. Lucie County Libr., Ft. Pierce, 1975-76; high sch. libr. Sch. Bd. St. Lucie County, Ft. Pierce, 1976-90. Mem. AAUW (br. pres. 1982-84), ALA, Fla. Libr. Assn., Order Ea. Star (chaplain 1957-58), Beta Phi Mu. Methodist. Avocations: writing, collecting, geology, travel, gardening. Home: 6710 Samba St Fort Pierce FL 34945-3069

HARRIS, MARY EMMA, art historian, landscape designer; b. Kinston, N.C., July 11, 1943; d. Aubrey Eugene and Dorothy (Rouse) H. BA, Greensboro Coll., 1965; MA, U. N.C., 1974; cert. landscape design & comml. hort., N.Y. Bot. Garden, 1991. Mem. edn. dept. Detroit Inst. Art, 1969-70; rsch. dir. Black Mountain Coll. Rsch. N.C. Mus. Art, Raleigh, 1970-73; ind. scholar N.Y.C., 1973—; pvt. practice landscape designer and horticulturist, 1992—; chair, project dir. Black Mountain Coll. Project, Inc., N.Y.C., 1999—. Author: The Arts at Black Mountain College, 1987, Remembering Black Mountain College, 1996. Named Disting. Alumna Greensboro Coll., 1988; recipient Cmty Svc. award Pks. Coun., 1999; Ind. Scholar grantee NEH, 1973, 79. Mem. Assn. Ind. Historian Art (treas.). Home: 42 Grove St Apt 33 New York NY 10014-5390 Office: Black Mountain Coll Project Inc Village Sta PO Box 607 New York NY 10014-0607

HARRIS, MATTHEW NATHAN, surgeon, educator; b. N.Y.C., Dec. 20, 1931; s. Saul and Deborah (Moskowitz) H.; m. Frances Wicentowski, June 27, 1954; children: Amy Rachel, Julie Rebecca, Daniel Charles. BA, NYU, 1952; MD, Chgo. Med. Sch., 1956. Diplomate Am. Bd. Surgery, Nat. Bd. Med. Examiners; lic. physician, N.Y. Intern Bellevue Hosp. Ctr., N.Y.C., 1956-57, resident in gen. surgery, 1957-58, 60-63; sr. clin. trainee in cancer USPHS, N.Y.C., 1963-64; instr. anatomy NYU, N.Y.C., 1966-68, dir. elective surg. anatomy, 1973-74; prof. surgery, dir. surg. oncology NYU Sch. Medicine, N.Y.C., 1979—. Vis. surgeon Bellevue Hosp. Ctr.; attending surgeon Tisch Hosp.; cons. and lectr. in field.; cons. surgeon Manhattan V.A. Hosp. Contbr. articles to Jour. ACS, Breast Disease, Cancer, Annals Surgery, Radiology, N.Y. State Jour. Medicine, Cancer Rsch., Surgery, Jour. Lab. Investigations, others. Capt. USAR, 1958-60, Korea. Chgo. Med. Sch. scholar, 1955. Fellow ACS (cancer liaison fellow, N.Y. state chmn.); mem. AMA, Am. Soc. Clin. Oncology, Am. Assn. Clin. Anatomists, Am. Radium Soc., N.Y. Cancer Soc., N.Y. Surg. Soc. (pres. 1991-92), N.Y. Med. Soc., N.Y. Met. Breast Cancer Group, Soc. Surg. Oncology, N.Y. Cancer Programs Assn., Inc., Pan-Am. Med. Soc., Soc. Cons. Armed Forces, 38th Parallel Med. Soc. (Korea), Pan Pacific Surg. Assn., Internat. Pigment Cell Soc., Assn. Cancer Edn., Assn. Academic Surgery, So. Alumni Bellevue Hosp., Chgo. Med. Sch. Alumni Assn., Alpha Omega Alpha, Sigma Xi, Beta Lambda Sigma. Achievements include research in cytologic evaluation breast diseases by stereoactic aspiration, malignant melanoma vaccine, primary surgical management malignant melanoma. Office: NYU Med Ctr 530 1st Ave New York NY 10016-6402

HARRIS, MEL, broadcast executive; b. Arkansas City, Kans., 1942; married; 1 child. PhD in Mass Comm., Ohio U. Pres. TV Group Paramount Pictures, 1978—92, Sony Pictures Entertainment, Culver City, Calif., 1992—95, co-pres., COO, 1999—. Former radio announcer; formerly with Kaiser and Metromedia broadcast groups; co-founder Paramount Home Video, CIC Home Video. With U.S. Army, Vietnam. Decorated Bronze Star; named one of 20 most influential studio execs., Video Store mag., 1999; named to Video Hall of Fame, 1986. Mem.: Acad. TV Arts and Scis., Motion Picture Assn. Am. (bd. dirs.). Office: Sony Pictures Entertainment Inc 10202 Washington Blvd Culver City CA 90232-3119

HARRIS, MERLE WIENER, college administrator, educator; b. Hartford, Conn., July 25, 1942; d. Irving and Leah (Glasser) Wiener; m. David R. Harris, June 23, 1963; children: Jonathan, Rebecca. BS, Ctrl. Conn. State U., 1964, MS, 1973; EdD, U. Mass., 1988. Clk., edn. com. Conn. Gen. Assembly, Hartford, 1971-72; career edn. coordinator Bloomfield (Conn.) Pub. Schs., 1973-78; asst. to commr. Dept. of Higher Edn., Hartford, Conn., 1978-82, asst. commr., 1982-88, deputy commr., 1988-89; pres. Charter Oak State Coll., Newington, Conn., 1989—; exec. dir. Bd. for State Acad. Awards, Hartford, Conn., 1989—; interim pres. Cen. Conn. State U., 1995-96. Cons.on career edn. U.S. Dept. Edn., Washington, 1974; fellow Inst. for Ednl. Leadership, 1980; bd. dirs. Old State House, 1996—, Conn. Literacy Vols., 1991—98, Conn. Humanities Coun., 1991—97, Conn. Acad. for Edn. in Math., Sci. and Tech., 2000—, vice chmn., 2002—; chmn. Joint Com. Ednl. Tech., 1991—98; mem. Conn. Commn. Ednl. Tech., 2000—. Mem. New Eng. Assn. Schs. and Colls. (bd. dirs. 1997—), Am. Coun. on Edn. (commr. on ednl. credit and credentials 1995-98). Democrat. Jewish. Avocations: gardening, cooking, teaching. E-mail: mharris@charteroak.edu.

HARRIS, MICALYN SHAFER, lawyer, educator, arbitrator, mediator; b. Chgo., Oct. 31, 1941; d. Erwin and Dorothy (Sampson) Shafer. AB, Wellesley Coll., 1963; JD, U. Chgo., 1966. Bar: Ill. 1966, Mo. 1967, U.S. Dist. Ct. (ea. dist.) Mo. 1967, U.S. Supreme Ct. 1972, U.S. Ct. Appeals (8th cir.), 1974, N.Y. 1981, N.J. 1988, U.S. Dist. Ct. N.J., U.S. Ct. Appeals (3d cir.) 1993. Law clk. U.S. Dist. Ct., Mo., 1967-68; atty. The May Dept. Stores, St. Louis, 1968-70, Ralston-Purina Co., St. Louis, 1970-72; atty., asst. sec. Chromalloy Am. Corp., St. Louis, 1972-76; pvt. practice St. Louis, 1976-78; atty. CPC Internat., Inc., 1978-80; divsn. counsel CPC N.Am., 1980-84, asst. sec., 1981-88; gen. counsel S.B. Thomas, Inc., 1983-87; corp. counsel CPC Internat., Englewood Cliffs, NJ, 1984-88; assoc. counsel Weil, Gotshal & Manges, N.Y.C., 1988-90; pvt. practice, 1991; v.p., sec., gen. counsel Winpro, Inc., 1991—. Arbitrator Am., Arbitration Assn., NYSE, NASD; adj. prof. Lubin Sch. Bus. Pace U.; mediator. Mem.: ABA (Ctr. Profl. Responsibility, bus. law sect., past chair corp. counsel com., past chair subcom. counseling the mktg. function, mem. securities law com., tender offers and proxy statements subcom., chair task force on e-mail privacy, task force on electronic contracting, task force on conflicts of interest, ad hoc com. on tech., profl. responsibility com.), Am. Law Inst. (mem. consultative groups, restatement of agy. 3d, UCC Arts. 1 & 2, internat. jurisdiction & judgements projects), Computer Law Assn., N.J. Gen. Coun., Am. Corp. Counsel Assn. N.Y. (mergers and acquisitions com., corp. law com.), Mo. Bar Assn. (past chmn. internat. law com.), Bar Assn. Metro St. Louis (past chair TV com.), Assn. Bar City N.Y., N.J. Bar Assn. (computer law com.), N.Y. State Bar Assn. (exec. com. bus. law sect., securities regulation com., chair internet and technology law com., past chair subcom. on licensing, task force on shrink-wrap licensing, electronic comm. task force). Address: 625 N Monroe St Ridgewood NJ 07450-1206

HARRIS, MICHAEL DAVID, lawyer; b. Cleve., Mar. 16, 1946; s. Harold E. and Belle (Silver) H.; m. Amy L. Jacobson, July 3, 1971; children— Jeffrey Marshall, Andrew Jay. B.S. in Engring., Purdue U., 1969; J.D., Am. U., 1972. Bar: D.C. 1972, U.S. Patent Office 1972, Calif. 1973, U.S. Dist. Ct. (cen. dist.) Calif. 1973, U.S. Ct. Appeals (9th cir.) 1974, U.S. Ct. Customs and Patent Appeals 1981. Examiner U.S. Patent Office, Washington, 1969-72; assoc. then ptnr. Poms, Smith, Lande & Rose, Los Angeles, 1972-82, 87—; ptnr. Koppel & Harris, Westlake Village, Calif., 1982-87; judge pro tem Los Angeles Mcpl. Ct., 1976-84; instr. So. Calif. Inst. Law, Ventura, 1984. Editor Century City Bar Jour., 1977. Mem. Century City Bar Assn. (pres. 1983-84, bd. govs. 1976-86), Los Angeles County Bar Assn. (trustee 1984-85), Los Angeles Patent Law Assn., Ventura County Bar Assn. Libertarian. Jewish. Home: 5025 Jacobs Ct Oak Park CA 91377-4716 Office: Best & Krieger PO Box 2710 Palm Springs CA 92263-2710

HARRIS, MICHAEL GENE, optometrist, educator, lawyer; b. San Francisco, Sept. 20, 1942; s. Morry and Gertrude Alice (Epstein) H.; m. Dawn Block; children: Matthew Benjamin, Daniel Evan, Ashley Beth, Lindsay Meredith. BS, U. Calif., 1964, M in Optometry, 1965, D in Optometry, 1966, MS, 1968; JD, John F. Kennedy U., 1985. Bar: Calif., U.S. Dist. Ct. (no. dist.) Calif. Assoc. practice optometry, Oakland, Calif., 1965-66, San Francisco, 1966-68; instr., coord. contact lens clinic Ohio State U., 1968-69; asst. clin. prof. optometry U. Calif., Berkeley, 1969-73, dir. contact lens extended care clinic, 1969-83, chief contact lens clinic, 1983—, assoc. clin. prof., 1973-76, asst. chief, then assoc. chief contact lens svc., 1970—, lectr., then sr. lectr., 1978—, vice chmn. faculty Sch. Optometry, 1983-85, 95—, prof. clin. optometry, 1984-86, clin. prof., 1986—, dir. residency program, 1993-95, asst. dean, 1994-95, assoc. dean, 1995—, acting dean, 2000, dir. policy and planning, 2003—; lectr. Peter's Meml. U. Calif. Sch. Optometry, 2000. Peter's Meml. lectr. U. Calif. Sch. Optometry, 2000; vis. prof. City U., London, 1984; vis. rsch. fellow U. NSW, Sydney, Australia, 1989; sr. vis. rsch. scholar U. Melbourne, Victoria, Australia, 1989, Victoria, 92; mem. ophthalmic devices panel med. device adv. com. FDA, 1990—, interim chmn., 1994; lectr., cons. in field; mem. regulation rev. com. Calif. Bd. Optometry; cons. hypnosis Calif. Optometric Assn., Am. Optometric Assn.; cons. Nat. Bd. Examiners in Optometry, Soflens divsn. Bausch & Lomb, 1973—, Barnes-Hind Hydrocurve Soft Lenses, Inc., 1974—87, Pilkinton-Barnes Hind, 1987—94, Contact Lens Co., 1977—2001, Palo Alto, Va., 1980, Primarius Corp., Cooper Vision Optics, 1979—, Alcon, 1980—, CIBA, 1976—, Vistakon, 1980—2000; co-founder Morton D. Sarver Rsch. Lab., 1986. Editor current comments sect. Am. Jour. Optometry, 1974-77; editor Eye Contact, 1984-86; assoc. editor The Video Jour. Clin. Optometry, 1988-92; cons. editor Contact Lens Spectrum, 1988—; author: Contact Lenses: Treatment Options for Ocular Disease, Contact Lenses for Pre & Post-Surgery; editor: Problems in Optometry, Special Contact Lens Procedures; Contact Lenses in Ocular Disease, 1990; mem. editl. bd. Contact Lens and Anterior Eye Jour.; contbr. chpts. to books, articles to profl. jours. Planning commnr. Town of Moraga, Calif., 1986, vice-chmn., 1987—88, chmn., 1988—90; mem. Town Coun., Moraga, 1992—96; mem. adv. planning commn. Medi-Cal., 1993—95, chmn., 1994—96, with managed care commn., 1995—, chmn. managed care commn., 1996—98; life mem. Bay Area Coun. for Rescue & Recovery, 1976—; grantor Michael G. Harris Family Endowment Fund U. Calif., Dr. Michael G. Harris Tchg. award U. Calif.; commr. Sunday Football League Contra Costa County, 1974—78; planner, fin. advisor College Pk. HS Track Project; mem. Pleasant Hill C. of C., Friends of Rodgers Ranch, Friends of Libr.; vice-mayor Town Coun., Moraga, 1994—95; city county rels. com. Contra Costa County, Calif.; planning commr. City of Pleasant Hill, Calif., 1999—2002, coun. mem., 2002—; vice chair Redevel. Agy., Pleasant Hill, 2002—; founding mem. Young Adults divsn. Jewish Welfare Fedn., 1965—69, chmn., 1967—68; charter mem. Jewish Cmty. Ctr. Contra Costa County; founding mem. Jewish Cmty. Mus. San Francisco, 1984; para-rabinnic Temple Isaiah, Lafayette, Calif., 1987, bd. dirs., 1990, Jewish Cmty. Rels. Coun. Greater East Bay, 1979—83, Campolindo Homeowners Assn., 1981—85. Named Alumnus of Yr., U. Calif. Sch. Optometry, 1999; U. Calif. fellow, 1971; Calif. Optometric Assn. scholar, 1965, George Schneider meml. scholar, 1964. Fellow: AAAS, Prentice Soc. (pres.-elect 1994—96, pres. 1996—98), Assn. Schs. and Colls. Optometry (coun. on acad. affairs), British Contact Lens Assn., Am. Acad. Optometry (diplomate cornea and contact lens sect., chmn. contact lens papers, mem. contact lens com. 1974—, vice-chmn. contact lens sect. 1980—82, chmn. sect. 1982—84, immediate past chmn. 1984—86, chmn.jud. com. 1989—2001, chmn. bylaws com. 1989—, ethics taskforce 1999—, Eminent Svc. award 2003); mem.: ABA, Contra Costa Bar Assn., Calif. Acad. Sci., Calif. State Bd. Optometry (regulation rev. com.), Internat. Soc. Contact Lens Rsch., Mex. Soc. Contactology (hon.), Nat. Coun. on Contact Lens Compliance, Am. Optometric Found., Internat. Assn. Contact Lens Educators, Assn. Optometric Contact Lens Educators, Calif. Optometric Assn., Am. Optometric Assn. (proctor 1969—79, cons. on hypnosis, mem. contact lens sect., position papers com., mem. com. on opthalmic stds., subcom. on testing and certification, cons. editor Jour.), Internat. Assn. Contact Lens Educators, Robert Gordon Sproul Assn. U. Calif., Mensa, Benjamin Ide Wheeler Soc. U. Calif., JFK U. Sch. Law Alumni Assn., U. Calif. Optometry Alumni Assn. (life), Pleasant Hill C. of C. Democrat. Office: U Calif Sch Optometry Berkeley CA 94720-0001 E-mail: mharris@uclink.berkeley.edu.

HARRIS, MICHAEL JAMES, software engineer; b. Pocatello, Idaho, Feb. 6, 1951; s. James Vernon and Connie Rachel (Williams) H.; m. Colette Jilene Card, June 5, 1984; children: Gregory, Kristen, Jason, Jennifer, Jonathan, Connie. BS, U.S. Naval Acad., 1973; MSCS, Naval Postgrad. Sch., 1974. Commd. ens. USN, 1973, advanced through grades to lt., 1976, resigned, 1979; computer sci. instr. Brigham Young U., Provo, Utah, 1979-82; software engr. Eyring Rsch. Inst., Provo, 1982-84, Hewlett-Packard, Boise, Idaho, 1984-92, Word Perfect, Orem, Utah, 1992-98, Novell Inc., Orem, 1995-96, 97—, Datalogics, Orem, 1996. Software engr., pres. HMC, Inc., Boise, 1979-84. Co-patentee software, printers. Republican. Mem. Lds Ch. Avocations: tennis, jogging, guitar, home remodeling, gardening. Home: 1396 N 725 W Orem UT 84057-5903 E-mail: mharris@novell.com.

HARRIS, MILDRED STAEGER, retired broadcast executive; b. Newark, Oct. 18, 1917; d. Henry Ernest and Louise Sheffick Staeger; m. William Finlaw Harris, Oct. 20, 1945 (dec. Nov. 1963); children: Steven Alan, Sandra Louise, Douglas William. Prof. designation in bus. mgmt., UCLA, 1980. Mgr. fixed assets ABC, L.A., 1971-76, mgr. adminstrn., 1976-80, tech. mgr., 1980-85. Children's libr. counselor Kings County Literacy Coun., Hanford, Calif., 1990, bd. dirs., 1991—; coord. Am. Women in Radio and TV, L.A., 1979-84. Named Businesswoman of Yr., YWCA Coun., 1973; recipient Emmy award for Summer Olympics, NATAS, 1985. Mem. Calif. Sheriffs Assn., Literacy Vols. Am., Libr. of Congress. Avocations: history, language, reading, genealogy. Office: Kings Literacy Coun 505 W Cameron St Hanford CA 93230-3615

HARRIS, MORTON ALLEN, lawyer; b. Columbus, Ga., Mar. 13, 1934; s. Alvin L. Harris and Harriett (Berman) Wolpin; m. Judye Rose Spielberger, Aug. 11, 1957; children: Alvin L., Wendy H., Tracy A., S. Beth. BBA, Emory U., 1956; JD, Harvard U., 1959. Bar: Ga. 1959, U.S. Ct. Appeals (5th and 11th cirs.) 1981, U.S. Tax Ct. 1981, U.S. Supreme Ct. 1981. With Page, Scrantom, Harris & Chapman, Columbus, 1959-93, Hatcher, Stubbs, Land, Hollis & Rothschild, Columbus, 1993—. V.p., bd. dirs. Small Bus. Coun. Am., pres., 1980—86; trustee Ga. Fed. Tax Conf., pres., 1988—89; trustee City of Columbus Pension Bd., 1993—2001, 2002—, vice-chair, 1996—2001. Contbg. author: Journal of Taxation, 1976, Business Organizations, 1976; dept. editor: The Tax Times, 1986-87; mem. editorial adv. bd. Practical Tax Lawyer, 1986—, Estate Planners Quarterly. Mem. Columbus Estate Planning Coun., 1964--, pres., 1973, Temple Israel, Inc., 1997-99, 2002--; trustee Inst. for Study Am. Cultures, 1983—, pres. 1997—; spl. advisor Muscogee County Sch. Dist. Health Improvement Program, Columbus, 1983—; trustee Resource One Found.; trustee Columbus State U. Found. Recipient Ann. Vol. award State of Ga., 1985. Fellow Am. Coll. Tax Counsel, Am. Coll. Employee Benefits Counsel, Am. Coll. Trust and Estate Counsel; mem. ABA (chmn. tax sect. personal svc. orgn. com. 1978-80, chmn. tax sect. membership com. 1983-86, counsel tax sect. 1989-96, asst. sec. 1989-91, sec. 1991-93, task force on alt. tax sys. 1996-98, task force tax code simplification 2000-02, divsn. coord. liaison to IRS divsn. samll bus./self employed 2000-02), State Bar Ga. (chmn. tax sect. 1981-82), Jaycees (pres. Columbus chpt. 1966), Kiwanis Club Greater Columbus (pres. 1971-72). Fax: 706-322-7747. E-mail: mah@hatcherstubbs.com

HARRIS, NEIL, historian, educator; b. Bklyn., 1938; s. Harold and Irene Harris. AB, Columbia U., N.Y.C., 1958; BA, Cambridge U., Eng., 1960; PhD, Harvard U., 1965. From instr. to asst. prof. history Harvard U., Cambridge, Mass., 1965-69; assoc. prof. U. Chgo., 1969-72, prof., 1972-90, Preston and Sterling Morton prof. of history, 1990—, dir. Nat. Humanities Inst., 1975-77, chmn. dept. history, 1985-88. Mem. adv. bd. Temple Hoyne Buell Ctr., Columbia, 1984-89; mem. adv. com. dept. architecture Art Inst. Chgo., 1982—; mem. Smithsonian Council, 1978-84, chmn. 1984-92; visiting prof. Yale U., 1974; dir. d'etudes Ecole des Hautes Etudes en Sci. Sociales, Paris, 1985. Author: Artist in American Society, 1966, Humbug: The Art of P.T. Barnum, 1970, Cultural Excursions, 1990, Building Lives, 1999; editor: Land of Contrasts, 1970, the WPA Guide to Illinois, 1983; bd. editors New Eng. Quar., 1982—, Winterthur Portfolio, 1978-80, 85-88, Frederick Law Olmsted Papers, 1973, Am. Scholar, 1994-2000; mem. editorial adv. bd. History Today, 1978-86. Trustee H.F. DuPont Winterthur (Del.) Mus., 1978-87, Newberry Libr.; mem. Nat. Mus. Svcs. Bd., Washington, 1977-84; vis. com. J. Paul Getty Mus., 1995—; bd. dirs. Nat. Mus. Am. History, 1997-2000, Terra Found. for Arts, 2002—. Named Am. Coun. Learned Socs. fellow, 1972-73, NEH fellow, 1980-81, Guggenheim fellow, 1999-2000; Getty scholar, 1991, Nat. Mus. Am. Art scholar, 1995-96; Boucher lectr. Johns Hopkins U., 1971, Cardozo lectr. Yale U., 1974, Tandy lectr. Whitney Mus. Am. Art, 1982, Kemper lectr. Pitzer Coll., 1980, Buell lectr. Columbia U., 1993; recipient Joseph Henry medal Smithsonian Instn., 1991. Fellow Am. Acad. Arts and Scis.; mem. Am. Antiquarian Soc., Am. Coun. Learned Socs. (vice chmn. N.Y. 1978-89, chmn. 1989-93), Orgn. Am. Historians, Phi Beta Kappa (senator united chpts. 1985-97, vis. lectr. 1985-86). Home: 4950 S Chicago Beach Dr Chicago IL 60615-3207 Office: U Chgo Dept History 1126 E 59th St Chicago IL 60637-1580

HARRIS, NICHOLAS GEORGE, publisher; b. Salisbury, Eng., Sept. 8, 1939; s. George Ivan and Phyllis Dorothy (Porter) H.; m. Margaret Jane Darling, Feb. 3, 1968; children: Nicola, Gregory. Sales rep. Collins Pubs., London, 1963-67, Montreal, 1967-72, sales dir. Toronto, 1972, exec. v.p., 1973; pres. William Collins Sons & Co., Can. Ltd., 1974-87; chmn., pres. Collins Pubs. N.Am., 1986-87; mng. dir. McClelland & Stewart, 1988-89; pres. Wright Harris, Inc., 1990; v.p., gen. mgr. Grolier, Ltd., 1990-92; pres. Nick Harris Assocs., 1993—. Trustee Markham Pub. Lib., 1994-2000. Served to 1st lt. Brit. Army, 1958-63. Mem. Donalda Club (Toronto). Anglican. Office: 3080 Yonge St Ste 5000 Toronto ON Canada M6N 3N1

HARRIS, PATRICIA ANNE, manufacturing executive, physical therapist; b. Galveston, Tex., June 18, 1961; d. Lloyd C. Harris and Frances Teresa Jensen; m. C. Delius, Feb. 21, 1986; children: Claire, Jensen. BS in Biology, Stephen F. Austin U., 1983; BS in Phys. Therapy, U. Tex. Med. Br. Galveston, 1985; MBA, Colo. Tech. U., 2003. Lic. phys. therapist Colo. Phys. therapist Meml. Hosp., Nacogdoches, 1985—87; dir. phys. therapy AMI Med. Ctr., Nacogdoches, 1987—89; phys. therapist Bd. Coop. Edn. Svc., Colorado Springs, 1989—94; clinic mgr. H&W Therapy, Woodland Park, 1994—98; owner SWING Golf Catalog, Colorado Springs, 1998—2001; v.p. Walker Wear, Colorado Springs, 2001—. Parent vol. Manitou Springs Pub. Sch., Colo., 2001; coach Spl. Olympics, Nacogdoches, 1986; Big Sister Big Bros./Big Sisters, Nacogdoches, 1980; coach Tee Ball, Pks. and Recreation, Colo., 1994; golf instr. LPGA Girls Golf Program, Colorado Springs, 1999. Mem.: C. of C., Exec. Women's Golf Assn. (sec. 2000—01). Avocations: golf, bicycling, reading, woodworking. Office: Walker Wear 2845 Janitell Colorado Springs CO 80906

HARRIS, PATRICIA FLORA, epidemiologist; b. Sacramento, Nov. 8, 1959; d. James Madison and Flora Frances Harris; m. Richard K. Green, Jan. 7, 1984; children: Morgan Harris Green, Hannah Harris Green. BA, Radcliffe Coll., 1982; MA, U. Wis., 1989, MD, 1995, MA, 2000. Diplomate Am. Bd. Internal Medicine, 1998, Am. Bd. Geriatrics, 2002. Intern and resident U. Wis., Madison; faculty physician Washington Hosp. Ctr., 2002—. Office: Washington Hosp Ctr 110 Irving St NW Rm 2B39 Washington DC 20010 Office Fax: 202-877-0544. Personal E-mail: patriciapfh@hotmail.com. E-mail: patricia.f.harris@medstar.net.

HARRIS, PATRICIA SKALNY, lawyer; b. Detroit, Mar. 28, 1949; d. John Francis and Sophie Skalny. B.A., U. Mich., 1970, J.D., 1974. Bar: Mich. 1974, U.S. Dist. Ct. (ea. dist.) Mich. 1976. Atty. Gen. Motors Corp., Detroit, 1974— . Mem. ABA, Mich. Bar Assn., Women Lawyers Assn., Soc. Automotive Engrs. Office: Gen Motors Corp 3044 W Grand Blvd Detroit MI 48202-3037

HARRIS, PAUL, sculptor; b. Orlando, Fla., Nov. 5, 1925; Student, U. N.Mex., New Sch. Social Research, Hans Hofmann Sch. Fine Arts. Fulbright prof. sculpture Universidad Catolica de Chile, 1961-62; later faculty San Francisco Art Inst., Calif. Coll. Arts and Crafts, Oakland; artist-in-residence Rinehart Sch. Sculpture, Md. Inst. Art, 1981, U. Ariz., Tucson, 1986. Vis. critic, lectr. U.S.F.S. Ctrs., Valparaiso and Concepcion, Chile, 1962, Rinehart Sch. Sculpture, spring 1981, Md. Inst. Art, (9 times) 1963-86, U. Oreg., Eugene, 1968, Newark (N.J.) State U., 1970, Mont. State U., Bozeman, 1970, 74, State U. N.Mex., Las Cruces, 1971, Montclair (N.J.) State U., 1973, Commonwealth U. Va., 1975, 76, 95, Clemson U., 1975, Haverford Coll., 1977, Phila. Coll. Art, 1977, R.I. Sch. Design, 1977, U. Ariz., Tucson, 1986. One-man shows include Poindexter Gallery, N.Y.C., 1957, 1960, 1963, 1967, 1970, Lanyon Gallery, 1965, Berkeley Gallery, 1965, William Sawyer Gallery, San Francisco, 1986, 1969, 1971, 1987, Galerie Thelen, Essen, 1970, San Francisco Mus. Art, 1972, U. Calif., Santa Barbara, 1972, U. N.Mex., 1973, Ark. Arts Ctr., 1973, Loch Haven Art Ctr., Orlando, 1981, Stanford U. Art Mus., Calif., 1982, Greenville County Mus. Art, S.C., 1982, Iannetti-Lanzone Gallery, San Francisco, 1989, Fuller Goldeen Gallery, 1983, C. Grimaldis Gallery, Balt., 1989, Galerie Redmann, Berlin, 1990, 1995, Michael Himowitz Gallery, Sacramento, 1993, Bolinas (Calif.) Mus., 1999, Fresno (Calif.) Art Mus., 1999, 2003, The Coll. of Marin Gallery, Kentfield, Calif., 2000, Yellowstone Art Mus., Billings, Mont., 2001, exhibited in group shows at Mus. Modern Art, N.Y.C., 1958, 1963, N.Y. World's Fair, 1965, Art Inst. Chgo., 1965, Md. Inst. Art, 1966, Mus. Contemporary Crafts, 1966, 1973, São Paulo Bienal, 1967, Crocker Art Gallery Assn., Sacramento,

1968, Smithsonian Instn. Traveling Exhibn., 1969, Phila. Inst. Art., San Francisco Mus. Art, N.J. State Mus., L.A. County Mus., 1973, Brandeis U., A.C.A. Gallery, 1972, Contemporary Art Ctr. Cin., 1973, Coll. Marin Galleries, 1974, JPL Gallery, London, 1975, Yellowstone Art Ctr., Billings, Mont., 1976, Renwick Gallery, Nat. Coll. Fine Arts, Washington, 1976—77, Falkirk Ctr., San Rafael, Calif., 1980, Transam. Bldg. Gallery, San Francisco, 1982, San Francisco Mus. Modern Art, 1983, Otis Art Inst. Parsons Sch. Design, 1984, Fendrick Gallery, 1984, William Sawyer Gallery, San Francisco, 1985, 1993, Iannetti Lanzone Gallery, 1987, Meml. Union Art Gallery, U. Calif., Davis, 1988, Civic Arts Gallery, Walnut Creek, Calif., 1988, Constantine Grimaldis Gallery, 1987, Balt., 1988, Gallery, San Francisco, 1989, Cologne (Germany) Art Fair, 1989, 1992, 1995, 1997, Galerie Redmann, Berlin, 1990, 1993, 1994, Bolinas Mus., Calif., 1990, Wolk Gallery, St. Helena, Calif., 1993, 1994, Oliver Art Ctr., Calif. Coll. Arts and Crafts, Oakland, Calif., 1993, Orlando (Fla.) History Mus., 1994, Sheldon Meml. Art Gallery, U. Nebr., 1996, Western Book Exhibit, San Francisco, 1996, The Woodson Art Mus., Wausaw, Wis., 1997—98, Wrongtree Press, 1973, on aspects of ballet A False Alarm on the Nightbell Once Answered-It Cannot Be Made Good, Not Ever, Art in Am. Illus. Torso (Dorothy Schmidt), 1974, Paul Harris (Dennis Leon, Harry Abrams), 1975, drawings, for Pas d'Une, 1979; writer, artist (drawings) Phases of the Moon, 1995, designer (book) Motives and Cues by Marguerite Harris, 1993; lithographs, Paradise: Variations, 1996, Paul Harris, drawings, 1998, sculpture, 1999. Recipient Longview Found. grant, 1960, Neallie Sullivan award, 1967; Tamarind fellow, 1969-70; named Miembro Academico de la Facultad de Bellas Artes Universidad Catolica de Chile, 1962; resident Macdowell Colony, 1977; grantee Lebovitz Fund, 1978; Guggenheim fellow 1979. Address: PO Box 930 Bolinas CA 94924-0930

HARRIS, PAUL LYNWOOD, retired aerospace transportation executive; b. Richmond, Va., May 30, 1945; s. Paul Lynwood Sr. and Marjorie (Southward) H.; m. Susan Lee, Sept. 20, 1969; children: Meredith Lynn, Joanna Lee. AA, Ferrum Coll., 1965; BS, U. Richmond, 1967. CPA, Va. Staff acct. Price Waterhouse & Co., Washington, 1967-71, sr. acct., 1971-73; v.p. fin. Universal Restoration Inc., Washington, 1973-76; treas. Hawker Siddely Aviation Inc., Washington, 1976-78, Brit. Aerospace Inc., Herndon, Va., 1978-81, v.p. fin., 1981-86, sr. v.p. fin., 1986-88; fin. dir. Brit. Aerospace Comml. Aircraft, Hatfield, Eng., 1988-92; sr. v.p. adminstrn. Brit. Aerospace, Inc., Herndon, Va., 1992-93; sr. v.p., gen. mgr. Brit. Aerospace N.Am., Inc., Herndon, Va., 1993-99; ret., 2000; vice-chmn. Ferrum Coll., 2002—. Bd. trustees Ferrum Coll., 1999-2000. Bd. dirs. Reflectone, Inc., Cheshire Homes No. Va., Arlington, 1986, Washington Dulles Task Force, 1993-2001, Dulles Area Transport Assn., 1993-95; chmn. fin. com. United Christian Parish, Reston, Va., 1979. Mem. AICPA, Nat. Aviation Club (pres. 1995-96), Fin. Execs. Inst. Methodist. Home: 2525 Heath Pl Reston VA 20191-4224 E-mail: paulsusan2000@yahoo.com.

HARRIS, PAUL SMITH, human resources professional; b. Santa Monica, Calif., Nov. 29, 1935; s. Wallace Albert and Henrietta (Smith) H.; m. Jill B. Hall, Sept. 15, 1956 (div. June 1974); children: Gregory A., Geoffrey A.; m. Nancy Lynn Cherry, Sept. 9, 1975; 1 child, Doug B. BA in Psychology, U. Utah, 1958; postgrad., UCLA, 1961-63. Mgr. employment Western Airlines Inc., L.A., 1956-64, mgr. selection Am. Airlines Inc., N.Y.C., 1964-66; mgr. adminstrn. IBM, Princeton, N.J., 1966-72; dir. orgn. planning and devel. CNA Fin. Corp., Chgo., 1972-76; v.p. human rsch. developer W.E. Walker Stores Inc., Jackson, Miss., 1976-80; pres. Harris Cons., Inc., Salt Lake City, 1980-83; dir. pers. Americas divsn. Intercontinental Hotels, Washington, 1983-88; v.p. human rsch. devel. Showboat Casino and Hotel, Atlantic City, 1988-93; exec. v.p. Showboat Devel. Co., Atlantic City, 1993-98; ret., 1998. Bd. dirs. C. of C., Middlesex County, N.J., 1970-71, Chgo. Alliance of Businessman, 1974-75. Mem. Masons (master mason Mt. Moriah # 2 Utah, 32 degree). Republican. Christian Scientist. Avocations: tennis, skiing, flying.

HARRIS, PENNY SMITH, fundraising consultant; b. Old Town, Maine, Apr. 6, 1941; d. Owen Halbert and Louise Marion (Whitten) Smith; m. Parker Fred Harris, June 22, 1963 (div. 1992); children: Susan Leslie, Nancy Lynne. BS in Sociology, U. Maine, 1963; MS in Bus. Mgmt., Husson Coll., 1984. Cert. fund raising exec. Social worker Elizabeth Lund Home, Burlington, Vt., 1964-65; pub. sch. tchr. Essex Junction, Vt.; asst. dir. devel., corp. support mgr. Maine Pub. Broadcasting Network, Bangor, 1985—89; dir. devel. Eastern Maine Healthcare, Bangor, 1989—94; dir. healthcare campaign N.E. Health, Rockland, Maine, 1994-97; sr. assoc. Copley Davenport Co., Inc., Wenham, Mass., 1997-98, M. Davenport Assocs., 1998—; pres. PS Harris Assocs., Portland, Maine, 2001—. Trustee Maine Pub. Broadcasting Corp., 1991—95, Ctr. for Maine Contemporary Art, 1993—, U. Maine Sys., 1991—2001; mem. task force on campaign fin. Senator George Mitchell, Augusta, Maine, 1983; mem. All Am. City selection award jury, Nat. Civil League, N.Y.C., 1987; chmn. bd. dirs. Ctr. for Maine Contemporary Art, 2003—; bd. dirs. Greater Bangor United Way, 1990—93. Mem. LWV (pres. Bangor-Brewer chpt. 1979-81, state pres. 1982-85, nat. bd. dirs. 1986-88, sec. nat. bd. dirs. 1988-90, project dir. TV polit. debates Bangor 1982, project dir. Nat. Security and You Conf., Portland, Maine 1983), U. Maine Alumni Assn. (v.p. bd. dirs. 1991-93), Greater Portland C. of C. Democrat. Methodist. Avocations: skiing, travel, hiking, biking. Home and Office: PO Box 2862 South Portland ME 04116

HARRIS, PETER C. molecular biologist, educator; b. Honiton, Devon, Eng., July 11, 1957; arrived in US, 1999; s. Gerald C. and Myrtle F. Harris; m. Gail A. D'Souza, Aug. 25, 1984; children: Catherine, Sarah. BSc, U. E. Anglia, Norwich, Eng., 1981; PhD, U. Glasgow, Scotland, 1984. Fellow Harvard Med. Sch., Boston, 1984—87, U. Oxford, England, 1987—90, prof., 1999; scientist Med. Rsch. Coun., Oxford, 1990—94, sr. scientist, 1994—99; prof. Mayo Clinic, Rochester, Minn., 1999—. Contbr. articles to prof. jours. Recipient Inaugural Winner Kaplan Internat. prize, Polycystic Kidney Disease Rsch. Mem.: Human Genome Orgn., Jour. Am. Soc. of Nephrology, Internat. Soc. of Nephrology, Am. Soc. of Nephrology (mem. program com. 1998). Achievements include patents for polycystic kidney disease. Avocations: reading, walking, philately. Office: Mayo Clinic 200 First St SW Rochester MN 55905 Business E-Mail: harris.peter@mayo.edu.

HARRIS, PHILIP JOHN, engineering educator; b. Montreal, Que., Can., Mar. 22, 1926; s. Thomas Percival and Gladys Marion (Gillett) H.; m. Norma Joyce Maynard, May 23, 1953; children: Elizabeth Joyce Harris Richardson, Janet Constance. B.Sc., U. Man., 1948; M.Eng., McGill U., 1949, PhD, 1964. Structural designer Dominion Bridge Co. Ltd., Lachine, Que., 1949-51; chief civil engr. C.D. Howe Co., Ltd., Montreal, 1951-58; asst. prof. dept. civil engring. McGill U., Montreal, 1958-59, assoc. prof., 1959-73, prof. dept. civil engring., 1973-91, chmn. dept., 1977-84, bd. govs., 1975-82, prof. emeritus, 1993—; prof. dept. civil engring. McMaster U., Hamilton, Ont., 1991-95. Cons. structural and found. engring., 1958-91, cons. engr., 1991-99. Contbr. articles to profl. jours. NRC Can. grantee, 1965-79; Natural Scis. and Engring. Research Council grantee, 1979-87. Fellow Can. Soc. Civil Engring., Engring. Inst. Can.; mem. ASCE (life). Anglican. Home: 408 Swanson Ct Burlington ON Canada L7R 4G6

HARRIS, PHILIP ROBERT, management and space psychologist; b. Bklyn., Jan. 22, 1926; s. Gordon Roger and Esther Elizabeth (Delahanty) H.; m. Dorothy Lipp, July 3, 1965 (dec. 1997); m. Janet Belport, Feb. 14, 2001. BBA, St. John's U., 1949; MS in Psychology, Fordham U., 1952, PhD, 1956; spl. student, NYU, 1948-49, Syracuse U., 1961. Lic. psychologist U. of State of N.Y., 1959, N.Y. Dir. guidance St. Francis Prep. Sch., N.Y.C., 1952-56; dir. student personnel, v.p. St. Francis Coll., N.Y.C., 1956-63; exec. dir. Assn. Human Emergency-Human Murray Tng. Program, 1964-66; vis. prof. Pa. State U., 1965-66; vis. prof., cons. Temple U., sr. assoc. Leadership Resources Inc., 1966-69; v.p. Copley Internat. Corp., La Jolla, Calif., 1970-71; pres. Mgmt. and Orgn. Devel. Inc. (now Harris Internat. Ltd.), La Jolla, 1971—; edn. dir. Air/Space Am., 1988; sr. scientist Netrologic, Inc., La Jolla, Calif., 1990-93. Rsch. assoc. Calif. Space Inst., U. Calif., San Diego, 1984-90; adj. prof. Pepperdine U., U. No. Colo.; acad. adv. Command Coll., Commn. on Peace Officers Stds. and Tng. State of Calif., Dept. Justice, 1986-94; past cons. Westinghouse, N.V. Philips, I.B.M., Computer Sci. Corp. Control Data, govt. agys.; chmn. bd. dirs. United Socs. in Space, Inc., 1993-97. Author: Effective Management of Change, 1976, Improving Management Communicatio Skills, 1978, Managing Cultural Differences, 1979, 5th edit., 2000, New Worlds, New Ways, New Management, 1983, Managing Cultural Synergy, 1982, Management in Transition, 1985, Living and Working in Space, 1992, 2d edit., 1996, High Performance Leadership, 2d edit., 1994, New Work Culture, 1998, Launch Out, 2003; co-author: Transcultural Leadership, 1993, Developing Global Organizations, 1993, 2d edit., 2001, Multicultural Management 2000, 1998, Multicultural Law Enforcement, 1995, 2nd edit., 2001; editor: Innovations in Global Consultation, 1980, Global Strategies in Human Resource Development, 1983; author (series) New Work Culture, 3 vols., 1994-98; co-editor Manging Cultural Differences Series Butterworth-Heinemann, 1979—; mem. editl. bd. European Bus. Rev.; founding editor emeritus Space Governance Jour., 1993-98; contbr. 225 articles to profl. jours. V.p. Bklyn. Downtown Renewal Effort, 1957-59. Named to Gulf Pub. Author Hall of Fame, 1999; Fulbright prof. to India U.S. State Dept., 1962; NASA faculty fellow, 1984. Fellow AIAA (assoc.); mem. ASTD (Torch award 1975), Aviation Space Writers Assn. (journalism awards 1986, 88, 89, 93), World Bar Assn. (Space Humanitarian award1992), Nat. Space Soc., United Socs. in Space (dir. emeritus), Soc. for Human Performance in Extreme Environments, La Jolla Beach and Tennis Club. Independent. Home and Office: 2702 Costebelle Dr La Jolla CA 92037-3524 E-mail: philharris@aol.com.

HARRIS, RALPH WILLIAM, religious journalist; b. Detroit, Sept. 1, 1912; s. Charles and Georgia Alice (Stilwell) H.; m. M. Estelle Overton, Apr. 16, 1938; children: Carole Estelle, Sharon Beth Snyder. Diploma, Ctrl. Bible Inst., 1937, BA, 1961, MA, 1969. Pastor Faith Tabernacle, Clio, Mich, 1938-43; nat. youth leader Assemblies of God, Springfield, Mo., 1943-48; pastor Fremont-Tabernacle, Seattle, 1948-54; editor-in-chief ch. sch. lit. Assemblies of God, Springfield, Mo., 1954-76, exec. editor Complete Biblical Libr., 1983-91; semi-ret. Founder Speed-the-Light program Assemblies of God youth program, 1944; faculty South Pacific Bible Coll., Fiji, 1980; originator Founds. for Faith study course for 6th graders, 1967, 68. Author: (book) Now What, 1964, Spoken by the Spirit, 1973, Acts Today, 1994; producer column Assembly Lines, 1956-86; contbr. numerous articles to profl. jours. Founder Langston Neighborhood Watch, Springfield, 1983; ad hoc chmn. for Ozarks Crime Prevention Coun., Springfield, 1989; occasional column News-Leader, Springfield, 1993—; alumni pres. Ctrl. Bible Coll., 1946, 47, 54-68; rep. U.S. Armed Forces lesson selection com. Assemblies of God, 1963-68; co-founder Jr. Bible Quiz for ages 9 to 11, 1975. Named hon. mem. Evang. Press Assn. Avocation: directing more than 30 tours to middle east. Home: #208 1601 S Fort Ave Springfield MO 65807 E-mail: rwhstl@axs.net.

HARRIS, RANDY JAY, university official, finance executive; b. Provo, Utah, Nov. 6, 1946; s. Robert Jay and Odessa Webster (Hill) H.; m. Donna Clara Dodge, Aug. 29, 1969; children: Chad Randy, Tiffiny Lyn, Kimberly Dawn, Christopher Jay, Matthew Scott, Heather Anne. BS, Brigham Young U., 1971, MPA, 1988. CPA; cert. real estate appraiser; ordained bishop LDS Ch. Tax acct. Price Waterhouse & Co., CPA's, L.A., San Diego, 1971-72; tax mgr. Dodge & Dodge, CPA's, Orem, Utah, 1972-73; from sr. auditor to fin. mgr. Latter Day Saints Ch., Salt Lake City, 1973—79, fin. mgr., 1979—80; contr. Weber State U., Ogden, Utah, 1980-90; mng. ptnr. Dodge, Evans & Harris CPA, P.C., Orem, Utah, 1990-92; contr., CFO, asst. v.p. fin. Fla. State U., Tallahassee, 1992-95; assoc. v.p. for fin. U. Mich., Ann Arbor, 1995-97; pres. Veritas Ins. Co., Burlington, Vt., 1995-97; vice chancellor adminstrn. and fin. U. Houston Sys., 1997—2002; v.p. adminstrn. and fin. U. Houston, 1997—2002; pres. Guatamala Norte mission The Ch. of Jesus Christ of Latter Day Saints, 2002—. Instr. pub. mgmt. Grad. Sch. Bus., Brigham Young U., 1988-91; adj. instr. acctg. Weber State U., 1980-90; chmn. bd. Screendesign, Inc., 2000-01. Councilman City of Layton, Utah, 1973-81; bd. dirs. Heritage Mus., Layton, 1984-86, Utah Children's Aid Soc., 1991-92, Ann Arbor Summer Festival, 1996-97; bd. dirs. Humana Hosp. Davis North, Layton, chmn., 1987-92; mem. Layton Parks and Recreation Commn., 1973-75, Utah Layton and Recreation Comm., Layton, 1974-76; mem. exec. com. Western Assn. Coll. and Univ. Bus. Officers, 1989-90; bd. suprs. Latter-Day Saints Credit Union; treas. Bonneville coun. Boy Scouts Am., 1984-85, v.p. Suwannee River Area Coun., 1994-95; Davis County Reps., 1984-85. Mem. AICPA, Nat. Assn. Coll. and Univ. Bus. Officers, Utah Assn. CPAs (chmn. strategic planning com. 1989-92, pres. No. chpt. Ogden 1984-85, chmn. ann. conv. cpm., vice-chmn. practice rev. com. 1982-83, chmn. personal fin. planning com. 1984-85), Ctrl. Assn. Coll. and Univ. Bus. Officers, Fin. Affairs Tax Com. (chmn. Fla. interinstitutional coun. 1992-95), U. Mich. Musical Soc. (bd. dirs. 1997), Nat. Assn. of State Univs. and Land-Grant Colls. (coun. on bus. affairs 1998—, pres. 2000-01). Avocations: marathon running, cross country skiing. Home: 382 West 1750 South Kaysville UT 84037 Office: 5a Avenida 5-55 Edificio Euro Plaza Torre 2 15 Nivel Oficina 1504 Zona 14 Guatemala City Guatemala E-mail: rjharrisd@hotmail.com.

HARRIS, RAY KENDALL, lawyer; b. Tucson, July 9, 1957; s. Ray Fisher and Mary Jane (Lewis) H.; m. Patricia Ellen Gallogly, Oct. 10, 1986; children: Ellen Rose, Austin William. BSBA, U. Ariz., 1979, JD, 1982. Bar: Ariz. 1982, U.S. Dist. Ct. Ariz. 1982, U.S. Ct. Appeals (9th cir.) 1985, U.S. Ct. Appeals (10th cir.) 1988, U.S. Ct. Appeals (fed. cir.) 2000. Assoc. Fennemore Craig PC, Phoenix, 1982-88, dir., 1988—. Bd. dirs. Ariz. Innovation Network, Phoenix, 1996-98, High Tech. Industry Cluster, Phoenix, 1998—, Ariz. Tech. Incubator, Scottsdale, 1998-2002; mem. Ariz. Tech. Coun., 2002—. Exec. editor Ariz. Law Rev., 1981-82. Mem. Friends of Sci. and Tech./Ariz. Sci. Ctr., Phoenix, 1994—. Mem. State Bar Ariz. (chair intellectual property sect. 1995-97), Computer Law Assn., Am. Intellectual Property Law Assn., Ariz. Software Assn. (bd. dirs. 1995-2001), Ariz. Technology Coun. (bd. dirs. 2001—). Home: 1410 W Ruth Ave Phoenix AZ 85021-4449 Office: Fennemore Craig PC 3003 N Central Ave Ste 2600 Phoenix AZ 85012-2913 E-mail: rharris@fclaw.com.

HARRIS, RAYMOND JESSE, retired government official; b. Van Buren, N.Y., Dec. 28, 1916; s. Francis Elbert and Anna Marie (Selinsky) H.; m. Rosalba Emilia Prestianni, Jan. 7, 1950 (dec. 1989). AB, Harvard U., 1940, postgrad., 1940-42, U. Pa., 1952-54, 59-60. Corr. drafter U.S. State Dept., Washington, 1947; vice consul Am. consulate palermo, Italy, 1947-50, Munich, Germany, 1950-51; personnel technician, information officer City of Phila., 1952-59, administrv. asst. to water commr., 1959-79; ret., 1979; Republican committeeman 59th ward City of Phila., 1986-98. Served with USAAF, 1942-45; ETO. Named Water Dept. Supr. of Year, 1971, 72, 73, 76; recipient Ted Moses award Pa. Water Pollution Control Assn., 1978. Mem. Am. Water Works Assn., Archeol. Inst. Am., Amnesty Internat. USA, Nat. Trust Historic Preservation, Pa. Hist. Soc., Acad. Polit. Sci., Am. Anti-Vivisection Soc., Planetary Soc., Harvard of Phila. Club, Germantown Rep., Preservation Alliance Greater Phila. Home: 275 W Tulpehocken St Philadelphia PA 19144-3209

HARRIS, REGINALD MERVYN, JR., librarian, writer; b. Annapolis, Md., June 25, 1960; s. Reginald Mervyn and Ellen Felicia (Powell) H. BA, Randolph-Macon Coll., 1982. Mgmt. trainee Tandy Corp./Radio Shack, Balt., 1987-89, mgr., 1989; credit liaison Balt. Mag., 1989; part-time libr. circulation asst. Soper Libr., Morgan U., Balt., 1992-93; libr. assoc. Enoch Pratt Free Libr., Balt., 1990-97, info. tech. support specialist, 1997-99, info. tech. tng. mgr., 1999—2001, mem. program planning guideline com. PC supportingsubcom., 1993, head info. tech. support dept., 2001—; rep. to Balt. mayor's web page subcom., 1996. Mem. program planning guildeline com., PC support and tng. subcom., 1993. Author: Ten Tongues: Poems, 2002. Mem. cmty. adv. bd. Study to Help the AIDS Rsch. Effort, Johns Hopkins Hosp., Balt., 1989-92. With USCG, 1983-87. Recipient Individual Artist award in fiction Md. State Arts Coun., 2000, Individual Artist award in poetry, 2001; nominee Gay Men's Poetry Category Lambda Lit. award, 2003. Mem. Pratt Staff Assn. (bd. govs. 1991-93). Home: 907 Homestead St Baltimore MD 21218-3608 Office: Enoch Pratt Free Libr Info Tech Support Dept 400 Cathedral St Baltimore MD 21201 E-mail: RmHarris2001@hotmail.com.

HARRIS, RENNIE, choreographer; b. Phila. Choreographer Rennie Harris Puremovement, Phila. Recipient City of Phila. Cultural Fund award; fellow Pew fellow, Arts for Choreography; grantee, Pa. Coun. Arts, Nat. Dance Project, NEA, Pew Repertory Devel. Initiative. Office: Rennie Harris Puremovement 624 S 4th St Philadelphia PA 19147-1525

HARRIS, RICHARD ANTHONY SIDNEY, trust company executive; b. Bklyn., Dec. 22, 1940; s. Stanley Sidney and Rose (Franquelli) H.; m. Sharon Lynne Harvey, Dec. 21, 1975 (div. 1998); 1 child, Aaron Nathaniel Graeme. Student St. John's U., Jamaica, N.Y., 1958-61. Adminstr. Harris Trust, N.Y.C., 1972—, trustee, 1972— ; adminstr. Beehive Trading Co., Provo, Utah, 1980—, Aaron Reseda Med., Calif., 1976— ; pres. Reseda Mgmt., 1976—, also dir.; pres. World Perspective, 1995—. Mem. Am. Assn. Individual Investors, Internat. Platform Assn., Heritage Found. Roman Catholic. Office: PO Box 2194 Los Angeles CA 90078-2194

HARRIS, RICHARD EUGENE VASSAU, lawyer; b. Detroit, Mar. 16, 1945; s. Joseph S. and Helen Harris; m. Milagros A. Brito; children: Catherine, Byron. AB, Albion Coll., 1967; JD, Harvard U., 1970; postdoctoral, Inst. Advanced Legal Studies, London, 1970-71. Bar: Calif. 1972. Assoc. Orrick, Herrington, Rowley & Sutcliffe, San Francisco, 1972-77; ptnr. Orrick, Herrington & Sutcliffe, San Francisco, 1978-98; pvt. practice Richard E. V. Harris Law Office, Oakland, Calif., 1998—. Faculty Calif. Tax Policy Conf., 1987, 95; spkr. univ., govtl. and profl. groups. Knox fellow, Harvard U., 1970—71. Mem.: ABA (litigation sect. corp. counsel com., subcom. chmn. 1980—82, antitrust law sect. state action com. 1981—, vice chmn. 1982—83, vice chmn. govt. liability com. 1982—84, co-chmn. Nat. Insts. Antitrust Liability 1983, Boulder task force 1983—84, coun. urban state and local govt. sect. 1983—88, litigation sect. corp. counsel com., subcom. chmn. 1983—, co-chmn. Nat. Insts. Antitrust Liability 1985, bus. law sect., SEC investigation atty.-client privilege waiver task f 1988, profl. conduct com., tax sect., state and local taxes com. 1989—, tax litigation com. 1992—, conflicts of interest task force 1993—96, internat. com. 1994—, corp. counsel com. 1995—, conflicts of interest com. 1996—2000, ad hoc com. on ethics 2000, com. profl. conduct 2001—, Ctr. Profl. Responsibility, ABA Ethics 2000 adv. group), Bar Assn. San Francisco (ethics com. 1980—, state bar conf. del. 2003, 2003), Am. Law Inst. (cons. restatements of law unfair competition 1991—94, governing lawyers com. 1991—2000, torts com. 1993—, agy. com. 1996—, trusts com. 1996—).

HARRIS, RICHARD FOSTER, JR., insurance company executive; b. Athens, Ga., Feb. 8, 1918; s. Richard Foster and Mai Audli (Chandler) H.; m. Virginia McCurdy, Aug. 21, 1937 (div.); children: Richard Foster (dec.), Gaye Karyl Harris Law; m. Kari Melandso, Dec. 29, 1962. BCS, U. Ga., 1939. Bookkeeper, salesman 1st Nat. Bank, Atlanta, 1936-40; agt. Vol. state Life Ins. Co., Atlanta, 1940-41; asst. mgr. N.Y. Life Ins. Co., Atlanta and Charlotte, N.C., 1941-44; mgr., agt. Pilot Life Ins. Co., Charlotte and Houston, 1944-63; mgr., agt. bus. planning divsn., city agy. Am. Gen. Life Ins. Co., Houston, 1963—. Bd. dirs. Fidelity Bank & Trust Co., Houston, 1965-66, mem. bd. bus. devel. Sterling Bank, Upper Kirby Br., 1996. Chmn. fund dr. Am. Heart Assn., Charlotte, Mecklenburg County, 1958-59, chmn. bd., 1959-61; gen. chmn. Shrine Bowl Promotion, Charlotte Shriners, 1955; v.p., bd. dirs. Myers Park Meth. Ch. Men's Class, 1956-59, bd. stewards, Charlotte, 1959-61; bd. dirs. Houston Polit. Action Com., 1982—; charter mem. Rep. Presdl. Task Force, pres., 1981-90; at large del. Rep. Nat. Conv. Planning Platform, Houston, 1992; co-chmn. Christian Cmty. Svc. Ctr., 1984-90; mem. 1st Tuesday Group, Houston, 1985—; tchr. Men's Bible class St. John the Divine Ch., 1963-93; founder Episcopal H.S., Houston, 1984. Recipient Pres.'s Cabinet award Am. Gen. Life Ins. Co., 1964-67, 69, 71, 77-83, Disting. Salesman award Charlotte Sales Exec. Club, 1955, 57-59, Bronze Medallion award Am. Heart Assn., 1959, Nat. Quality awards, 1965-92, The Rep. Presdl. Legion of Merit award, 1992; named Adm. of Tex. Nav. Gov. of Tex., 1989. Mem. Assn. Advanced Life Underwriters, Am. Soc. CLUs, Nat. Assn. Life Underwriters, SAR (Good Citizenship award 1991), Life Underwriters Polit. Action Com. (life), Houston Estate and Fin. Forum, English Speaking Union, Mensa Internat., Houston Assn. Life Underwriters, Lone Star Leaders Club, Tex. Leader's Round Table (life), Million Dollar Round Table (life), Tex. Assn. Life Underwriters, Am. Security Coun. (nat. adv. bd. 1979—), Houston Intown C. of C. (charter mem.), Houston Club, 100 Club, Forum Club of Houston, Pachyderm Club, Houston Intown C. of C., Kiwanis (bd. dirs. 1979—), Masons (32 degree), Shriners, Sertoma (life, v.p. bd. dirs. Charlotte chpt.), Royal Order Jesters. Episcopalian. Home: 2701 Westheimer Rd Houston TX 77098-1243 Office: Am Gen Life Ins Co Wortham Tower 2727 Allen Pkwy Ste 104 Houston TX 77019-2100

HARRIS, RICHARD LEE, engineering executive, retired army officer; b. Bellevue, Pa., Dec. 26, 1928; s. Everett Lee and Marjorie Anna (Messer) H.; m. Patricia Ann Walton, Dec. 12, 1953; children: Sandra Jo, Carole Jill, William Walton, Robert Lee. BS, U.S. Mil. Acad., West Point, N.Y., 1951; student, Army Engr. Sch., 1951, 59; MS, MIT, 1956; grad., Oak Ridge Sch. Reactor Tech., 1957, Command and Gen. Staff Coll., 1963, Nat. War Coll., 1967. Designated sr. parachutist, nuclear reactor comdr. registered profl. engr., Pa., Tex. Commd. 2d lt. U.S. Army, 1951, advanced through grades to maj. gen., 1973; with (32d Engrs. Combat Bn.), 1951; co-comdr. (13th Engrs. Combat Bn., 7th Inf. Divsn.), Korea, 1952-53; res. engr. (Phila. Engrs. Dist.), 1953-54; engrs. supply officer Columbus Depot, 1954-55; tech. ops. officer AEC, N.Y.C., 1957-59; officer in charge (SM-1A Nuclear Power Plant), Alaska, 1960-62; with (U.S. STRIKE Command), 1963-65; bn. comdr. (20th Engrs. Combat Bn.), Vietnam, 1965-66; with Office Chief of Staff, U.S. Army, 1967-68, Hdqrs. U.S. Army Pacific, 1968-70; comdr. divsn. support command (1st Cav. Divsn.), Vietnam, 1970-71; asst. comdt. Army Engrs. Sch., 1971-73; dir. mgmt. info. sys. Office Chief Staff Army, Hdqrs. Dept. Army, 1973-76; comdr. U.S. Army Tng. Ctr.-Engr. and Ft. Leonard Wood, Mo., 1976-78; divsn. engr. North Ctrl. Engr. Divsn., 1978-80; ret., 1980; v.p. Radian Corp., Austin, 1980-93; ret., 1993. Decorated D.S.M., Legion of Merit with 4 oak leaf clusters, Bronze Star with 2 oak leaf clusters, Air medal with 4 numerals, Joint Services Commendation medal, Purple Heart. Fellow: Soc. Am. Mil. Engrs.; mem.: Mil. Officers Assn., Assn. U. S. Army, Phi Kappa Phi. Home: 8817 Balcones Club Dr Austin TX 78750-3042

HARRIS, RICHARD W. law educator, lawyer; b. Arlington, Va., Aug. 4, 1952; s. Glendal W. and Jean K. Harris; m. Deborah Lynn Weber, Nov. 22, 1987; children: Lindsey, Taylor, Cameron. BS in acctg., U. Md., Coll. Pk., 1974, MBA, 1976; JD with honors, U. Md., Balt., 1981; LLM tax, Georgetown Law Ctr., Washington, 1989. CPA Md., 1975; bar: Md. 1982. Mem. Levitan, Ezrich, West & Kaxton, Bethesda, Md., 1981—84; pvt. practice Lanham, Md., 1984—89; asst. prof. taxation Am. U., Washington, 1989—95, prof. taxation Grand Valley State U., Grand Rapids, Mich., 1995—. Dir. grad. tax program Grand Valley State U., 1995—2002, L. William Seidman chair of acctg. and taxation, 1995—, chair MST adv. bd., 1995—2002; chair West Mich. Tax Symposium, Grand Rapids, Mich., 1995—. Contbr. articles to profl. jours. Co-founder and dir. Grand Rapids Vol. Income Tax Assistance Program, 1997—. Mem.: Mich. Assn. of CPA's, Md. State Bar Assn. Avocations: pvt. pilot, basketball coach, motorhome travel. Home: 3751 Oak Creek Ct Grand Rapids MI 49546 Office: Grand Valley State Univ 401 W Fulton Grand Rapids MI 49504 Office Fax: 616-975-7973. Business E-Mail: harrisr@gvsu.edu.

HARRIS, RICKY E. music educator; b. Thomasville, N.C., Mar. 3, 1964; s. Walter E. and Hilde Harris; m. Michelle D. Dalton, Apr. 30, 1993; children: James, Emma. MusB, Appalachian St. U., 1987. Cert. tchr. 1987. Band dir. N.W. Ashe HS, West Jefferson, NC, 1987—92, Ctrl. Davidson Mid. Sch., Lexington, NC, 1993—. Adjudicator Ctrl. Dist. Bandmasters, Asheboro, 1998; condr. Iredell County Schs., Statesville, NC, 2000—01, Mt. Airy (N.C.) City Schs., 1997; adjudicator Forsyth County Schs., Winston Salem, NC, 2002—02; condr. Surry County Schs., Dobson, NC, 1999—99. Scout master Cub Scouts of Am., Winston Salem, NC, 2001—02. Nominee Disney Am. Tchr. award, 2002; grantee, Bryan Found., 1990. Mem.: Nat. Band Assn., Music Educators Nat. Conf., Am. Sch. Band Dirs. Assn., Profl. Educators of N.C., N.W. Dist. Bandmasters (auditions chmn. 1997—2002), N.C. Bandmasters Assn., Phi Mu Alpha Sinfonia (chpt. pres. 1986). Baptist. Avocations: hiking, camping, fishing. Office: Central Davidson Middle School 2591 NC Hwy 47 Lexington NC 27292 Home Fax: 336-357-5965; Office Fax: 336-357-5965.

HARRIS, ROBERT A. retired music educator; b. Rich Hill, Mo., May 8, 1928; s. Archie L. and Edith Jeannette (Bailey) H. AA in Music, Joplin Jr. Coll., 1948; MusB, Kans. State Tchrs. Coll., 1950, MS in Edn., 1953; student, Rosina Lhevinne. Pianist, organist 1st United Meth. Ch., Carthage, 1946—; pvt. tchr. piano Carthage, Mo., 1947—; tchr. music, choir dir. Coll. Our Lady of the Ozarks, Carthage, 1949-53, 55-57; prof. music Mo. So. State Coll., Joplin, 1971-95. Piano adjudicator; presenter piano and organ recitals. Cpl., chaplain's asst. U.S. Army, 1953-55. Mem. Nat. Guild Piano Tchrs., Nat. Fedn. Music Clubs (local v.p.), Fellowship of United Methodists in Music and Worship Arts, Music Tchrs. Nat. Assn., Am. Coll. Musicians, Mo. State Tchrs. Assn., Mo. Federated Music Club (ch. musician yr. 1993). Avocation: collectibles.

HARRIS, ROBERT BLYNN, civil engineer, educator; b. Dec. 31, 1918; m. Jean Margaret; children: William R., James F., David B., Peter S. BS, U. Colo., 1940; MS, Calif. Inst. Tech., 1947. Prof. engr., Mich. From instr. to prof., assoc. chmn. civil engring. U. Mich., Ann Arbor, 1947-87. Vis. prof. Nat. Inst. Constrn. Mgmt. and Rsch., Bombay, 1987-88, U. Utah, 1986, Calif. Inst. Tech., 1946-47, U. Conn., 1943-44, U. Colo., Boulder, 1972. Author: Precedence and Arrow Networking Techniques for Construction, 1978, Two Structural Theories — The Influence Line and Moment Distribution, 1971; contbr. articles to profl. jours. Mem. ASCE (Richard R. Torrens award 1996), Am. Soc. Engring. Edn., Tau Beta Pi, Chi Epsilon, Pi Mu Epsilon, Kappa Kappa Psi, Phi Kappa Phi. Home: 325Wilkinson St Apt 217 Chelsea MI 48118-1524 Office: 2350 GG Brown Lab U Mich Ann Arbor MI 48109-2125 E-mail: harris@engin.umich.edu.

HARRIS, ROBERT DALTON, history educator, researcher, writer; b. Jamieson, Oreg., Dec. 24, 1921; s. Charles Sinclair and Dorothy (Cleveland) H.; m. Ethel Imus, June 26, 1971. BA, Whitman Coll., Walla Walla, Wash., 1951; MA, U. Calif., Berkeley, 1953, PhD, 1959. Tchg. asst. U. Calif., Berkeley, 1956-59; instr. history U. Idaho, Moscow, 1959-61, asst. prof., 1961-68, assoc. prof., 1968-74, prof. history, 1974-86, prof. emeritus, 1986—. Author: (Book) Necker, Reform Statesman of Ancient Regime, 1979, Necker & Revolution of 1789, 1986. 1st lt., U.S. Army, 1942-46; Ballet Folk of Moscow, Idaho, (bd. dirs., 1971-73), Historian, First United Methodist Church, Moscow, Idaho, 1989—. Mem. Am. Hist. Assn., Am. Assn. of U. Prof. Democrat. Methodist. Avocations: social dancing, violinist. Home: Apt 318 640 N Eisenhower St Moscow ID 83843-9588

HARRIS, ROBERT GAYLEN, art director, graphic designer, illustrator; b. Tacoma, Nov. 29, 1960; s. Gaylen Amon and Janelle Lee (Hinton) H.; m. Chelene Hope Ward, Sept. 24, 1988 (div. Nov. 1995). AD, Tacoma C.C., 1981; student, Brigham Young U., 1981-84. Graphic artist Phone Directories, Provo, Utah, 1983-84; graphic designer Clark Pub., Tacoma, 1984-89; art dir. Bringhurst Corp., Tacoma, 1989-98; owner Images, Tacoma, 1987—, Art Haus Harris Gallery, Tacoma, 1997—; art dir. Web-X, Tacoma, 1998—; pres. Art Haus, Inc., Tacoma. Curator The Pierce County Playwrights Festival, Tacoma, 1995-97; cons. in field. Designer holiday poster Tacoma C. of C., 1991-97; designer fire safety poster Tacoma Fire Dept., 1992; designer food safety awareness posters Domani Labs., Tacoma, 1997; mem. Tacoma Art Mus., Seattle Art Mus., Bellevue Mus. Art. Named regional winner Corel/Egghead Software Nat. Design Contest, 1995, 2nd place original concept-digital PIP Corp. Masters Competition, 1998; winner Corp. Identification Corel World Design Contest, 1996, 2001, Grand prize winner abstract category Dec.-Jan. Corel 10th World Design Contest, 2000, cover art/article Corel User, May 2000; featured artist Reader Gallery, Corel Mag., Mar. 1996, June 1998. Mem. Allied Artists Am. Avocations: painting, writing, reading, computing, travel. Home and Office: 1119 E 53d St Apt D Tacoma WA 98404-2720

HARRIS, ROBERT LAIRD, minister, theology educator emeritus; b. Brownsburg, Pa., Mar. 10, 1911; s. Walter William and Ella Pearl (Graves) H.; m. Elizabeth Krugar Nelson, Sept. 11, 1937 (dec. 1980); children: Grace Sears, Allegra Smick, Robert Laird; m. Anne Paxson Krauss, Aug. 1, 1981. BSChemE, U. Del., Newark, 1931; postgrad, Washington U., 1931-32; ThB, Westminster Theol. Sem., 1935, ThM, 1937; MA in Oriental Studies, U. Pa., 1941; PhD, Dropsie Coll., 1947. Ordained to ministry Presbyn. Ch. Am., 1936; instr. Faith Theol. Sem., Phila., 1937-43, asst. prof. Bibl. Exegesis, 1943-47, prof. Bibl. Exegesis, 1947-56; prof. Covenant Theol. Sem., St. Louis, 1956-81, dean, 1964-71, prof. emeritus, 1981—; prof. Winona Lake Summer Sch. of Theology, 1964, 66-67, Near East Sch. Archaeology and Bible, Jerusalem, 1962; vis. prof. China Grad. Sch. Theology, Hong Kong, 1981, Freie Theologische Akademie, Giessen, Fed. Republic Germany, 1982-85, Tyndale Theol. Sem., Amsterdam, The Netherlands, 1986-2000, Bibl. Theol. Sem., Hatfield, Pa., 1992, J. Manoel Conceicao Presbyn. Sem., Sao Paulo, Brazil, 1995. Vis. lectr. Wheaton Coll., Ill., 1957-61; lectr. Japan, Korea, 1965, India, 1981, Australia, 1989; moderator Presbyn. Ch. in Am., 1982. Author: Introductory Hebrew Grammar, 1950, Inspiration and Canonicity of the Bible, 1957, 2d edit., 1995, Man-God's Eternal Creation, 1971, You and Your Bible, 1990; editor: Theological Wordbook of the Old Testament, 2 vols., 1981, Leviticus in Expositor's Bible Commentary, Vol. 2, 1990; mem. editorial bd. New Internat. Version of Bible, 1965-2000, chmn., 1970-74; contbg. author various books. Trustee Bibl. Theol. Sem., Hatfield, Pa., 1985-2000. DuPont fellow U. Del., 1930-31; recipient first prize Zondervan Textbook Contest, 1955; Foxwell Lecture lectureship Tokyo Christian Theol. Sem., 1981. Mem. Evang. Theol. Soc. (pres. 1961), Tau Beta Pi, Phi Kappa Phi Republican. Home: 625 Robert Fulton Hwy Quarryville PA 17566 *In my ministry of over 60 years I have seen a distressing erosion of national morals and decency. But there has also been a counter-resurgence of evangelical faith. As part of this movement, I am gratified to have had a part in producing the New International Version of the Bible.*

HARRIS, ROBERT LEE, JR., history educator; b. Chgo., Apr. 23, 1943; s. Robert L. Sr. and Ruby L. (Watkins) H.; m. Anita B. Campbell, Nov. 14, 1964; children: Lisa M., Leslie S., Lauren Y. BA, Roosevelt U., 1966, MA, 1968; PhD, Northwestern U., 1974. Tchr. 6th grade St. Rita Elem. Sch., Chgo., 1965-68; instr. Miles Coll., Birmingham, Ala., 1968-69; asst. prof. U. Ill., Urbana, 1972-75, Cornell U., Ithaca, N.Y., 1975-82, assoc. prof. history, 1982—, dir. Africana studies, 1986-91, vice provost, 2000—. Mem. tech. adv. com. Grad. Record Exam., Princeton, N.J., 1988-94; cons. Cicada Films, N.Y.C., 1988-89, Cin. Pub. Sch. System, 1990-91; chair adv. com. for U.S. history Coun. for Internat. Exch. of Scholars, Washington, 1992-94; mem. N.Y. State adv. com. U.S. Commn. on Civil Rights, 1999-2002. Author: Black Studies in the United States, 1990, Teaching African-American History, 1992; also articles. Bd. dirs. N.Y. Coun. for the Humanities, N.Y.C., 1983-87; trustee DeWitt Hist. Soc., Ithaca, 1994-99. NEH fellow, 1974-75, Ford Found. fellow, 1983-84; W.E.B. DuBois Inst. fellow Harvard U., 1983-84; Rockefeller Humanities fellow SUNY, Buffalo, 1991-92. Mem. Am. Hist. Assn. (life, chmn. program com. 1995), Assn. for Study of Afro-Am. Life and History (life, pres. 1991-92), Orgn. Am. Historians (life, chair com. on minority history and historians 1999)), Soc. for History of Edn. (bd. dirs. 1996—), Alpha Phi Alpha (nat. historian 1999—). Avocations: music, gardening, jogging, basketball. Office: Cornell U Africana Studies Rsch Ctr Ithaca NY 14850

HARRIS, ROBERT L(EE), judge; b. Spokane, Wash., Oct. 3, 1934; s. Roy L Harris, Celia A Reed; m. Mary Jo Bourke; children: Joanna, Marie, Robert. BA, Wash. State U., 1954; JD, U. Wash., 1958. Bar: Wash. 1958. Judge Superior Ct. of Wash., Vancouver, 1979—. Mem. Project 2001, Supreme Ct. Task Force, Bd. Jud. Adminstrn., trial ct. funding Supreme Ct. Task Force 2003, chmn. Pres. St. Joseph Cmty. Hosp., Vancouver, 1967—74. Mem.: Superior Ct. Judges Assn. (pres. 2001—02). Achievements include one of first judges to use therapists to debrief jurors following their trial to help provide psychological assistance in gruesome trials. Avocation: youth sports. Office: Superior Court PO Box 5000 Vancouver WA 98666 Office Fax: 360-397-6078.

HARRIS, ROBERT NORMAN, advertising and communications educator; b. St. Paul, Feb. 11, 1920; s. Nathan and Esther (Roberts) H.; m. Paula Nidorf, May 2, 1992; children: Claudia, Robert Norman, Randolph B. BA, U. Minn., 1940. A founder Toni Co., div. Gillette Co., 1940-55; exec. v.p. Lee King & Ptnrs., Chgo., 1955-60, Allen B. Wrisley Co., Chgo., 1960-62, North Advt., Chgo., 1962-72; pres. Robert Piguet, Ltd., Chgo., 1972-73, Westbrook/Harris, Inc., Chgo., 1973-77; exec. v.p., gen. mgr. Creamer Inc., Chgo., 1977-81; pres. The Harris Creative Group, Inc., 1981—; prof. advt. and mass communications San Jose State U. (Calif.), 1983-92. Bd. dirs. KTEH Pub. Broadcasting Sys. Found., San Jose, 1987-99, CHM Villages Golf and Country Club CATV Sys., 1995-99. Mem. NATAS, Am. Mktg. Assn., Am. Advt. Fedn., Am. Assn. Advt. Agys., Sons in Retirement (bd. dirs. 1986-90).

HARRIS, ROBERT T. internist; b. Sumter, S.C., Feb. 11, 1948; s. Thomas A. and Marinel S. Harris; m. Holly Ann Fox, Aug. 14, 1971; children: Jonathan, Laurel. BS, Duke U., 1970; M of Health Sci., Johns Hopkins U., 1975; MD, Emory U., 1978. Diplomate Am. Bd. Internal Medicine, Am. Bd. Med. Mgmt. Intern in internal medicine Ga. Bapt. Med. Ctr., Atlanta, 1978—79, resident in internal medicine, 1979—81, chief resident, 1980—81; fellow in psychosomatic medicine Duke Med. Ctr., Durham, NC, 1981—82, assoc. in medicine; physician Blue Ridge Intenal Medicine, Raleigh, NC, 1985—91; med. dir. Carolina Physicians Health Plan, Raleigh, NC, 1991—94; sr. med. dir. Healthsource N.C., Raleigh, 1994—98; v.p. med. svcs. Blue Cross Blue Shield N.C., Durham, 1998—99, chief med. officer, sr. v.p. health care svcs., 1999—. Contbr. articles to profl. jours. Bd. dirs. Theatre in the Park, Raleigh, 2001; mem. numerous coms. Pullen Meml. Bapt. Ch., Raleigh, 1986—. Fellow: Am. Coll. Physician Execs., Am. Coll. Physicians; mem.: N.C. Med. Soc., Raleigh Soc. Internal Medicine (pres. 1992—93). Avocations: fishing, sailing, singing/theater. Office: Blue Cross Blue Shield NC PO Box 2291 Durham NC 27702

HARRIS, ROBERT VAIL, JR., research scientist, information scientist; b. Danbury, Conn., Jan. 27, 1947; s. Robert Vail Sr. and Lucile Matthew Harris; m. Meredith Newbury, May 28, 1966; children: Geoffrey Schaffer-Harris, Miranda Bachman, Morgen Lefeber. BS in Physics, U. Wis., 1968; MS in Applied Math., Cornell U., 1970, PhD in Applied Math., 1972. Asst. prof. math. Davis and Elkins (W.Va.) Coll., 1972-74; computer programming cons. Psi-Tran Corp., Arlington, Va., 1974; ultrasonics engr. Harisonic Lab., Stamford, Conn., 1975-78; computer ultrasonics engr. Pratt and Whitney Aircraft, West Palm Beach, Fla., 1978-85; computer cons. Cotonou, Benin, 1985-86; mgr. info. svcs. Soc. Togolaise de Sidérurgie, Lomé, Togo, 1986-91; sr. rsch. scientist Battelle, Richland, Wash., 1992—. Sec. Spiritual Assembly Bahá'ís Jupiter, Fla., 1983-84; mem. tchg. com. Bahá'ís of Lomé, Togo, 1989; officer Spiritual Assembly Bahá'ís of Pasco, Wash., 1996—. Rsch. grantee Dept. Energy, 1998, 99. Mem.: Phi Eta Sigma. Achievements include co-patent Ultrasonics Testing Device. Office: Battelle PO Box 999 Richland WA 99352-0999

HARRIS, ROBIE H. writer; b. Buffalo, N.Y., Apr. 3, 1940; d. Norman and Evelyn Sarah Heilbrun; m. William Wolpert Harris, Sept. 7, 1962; children: Benjamin H., David B. AB, Wheaton Coll., 1962; MAT, Banks St. Coll. Edn., 1972; PhD, Lesley Coll., 2000. Dir. After Sch. Program Bank St. Coll. Early Childhood Ctr., N.Y.C., 1965—67; writer Bank St. Coll. Media Lab., N.Y.C., 1967—69. Spkr. in field. Author: It's Perfectly Normal, Changing Bodies, Growing Up, Sex and Sexual Health, 1994, Happy Birth Day!, 1996, 2002, It's So Amazing! A Book About Eggs, Sperm, Birth, Babies, and Families, 1999, Hi New Baby!, 2000, Goodbye Mousie, 2001, Hello Benny! What It's Like To Be A Baby, 2002, I Am Not Going To School Today, 2003, Don't Forget to Come Back!, 2003, I Hate Kisses, Hot Henry and Messy Jessie, Rosie's Rock 'N' Riot, Rosie's Secret Spell, Rosie's Double Dare, Rosies' Razzle Dazzle Deal; co-author: Before You Were Three. Adv. Planned Parenthood Fedn. Am., N.Y.C., 1995—. Recipient Disting. Alumni award for leadership in edn., Bank St. Coll. Edn., N.Y.C., 2002. Mem.: PEN New Eng. (co-chair children's book caucus 1988—2003). Office: 80 Trowbridge St Cambridge MA 02138

HARRIS, ROGER CLARK, psychiatrist, consultant; b. Washington, Aug. 27, 1938; s. Lester Wilbur and Margaret Elizabeth (Gilligan) H.; m. Ann Marie Dorman, Sept. 22, 1962; children: Laura Colleen, Gregory Scott Henry. BS, U. Md., 1961; postgrad., U. Md., College Park, 1961-62; MD, U. Md., Balt., 1964-68. Diplomate Am. Bd. Med. Examiners, Am. Bd. Psychiatry and Neurology. Intern Washington Hosp. Ctr., 1968-69; resident in psychiatry U. Md. Med. Sch., 1969-72; staff psychiatrist Portsmouth (Va.) Psychiat. Ctr., 1972-73, Larry H. Dizmang and Assoc., Annapolis, Md., 1973-74; pvt. practice Annapolis, 1974-75; prin. Roger C. Harris Group Practice of Psychiatry and Assocs., Annapolis, 1975—; pres. Chesapeake Comprehensive Counseling Ctrs., Inc., Washington and Balt., 1988-96. Co-founder Psychiatry Consultation Svc. of Baltimore City Police Dept., 1970-72; chief psychiatry svc. Anne Arundel Gen. Hosp., Annapolis, 1978-81; asst. clin. prof. psychiatry U. Md. Sch. Medicine, 1973—; acting dir. of outpatient clinic U. Md. Emergency Psychiat. Svcs., 1971-72, chief resident, 1971-72; primary founder psychiatry dept. Anne Arundel Gen. Hosp. Mem. Disability Rev. Bd. for Anne Arundel County, 1985-87, Orgn. of Physicians for Social Responsiblity, 1985—. Recipient Cert. Appreciation Arundel Lodge, Inc., Annapolis, 1988, Mitchell Scholarship, Alpha Tau Omega Social Fraternity, College Park, Md., 1960. Mem. Chesapeake Bay Psychiat. Soc., Am. Psychiat. Assn., Md. Psychiat. Soc., Anne Arundel County Med. Soc., Am. Group Psychotherapy Assn., Orthopsychiat. Assn., Epping Forest Boat Club, Young Foresters Orgn., Alpha Tau Omega (sec. 1958-60). Democrat. Presbyterian. Avocations: boating, swimming, body surfing, bodyboard surfing, classical music. Home: 212 Eareckson Ln Stevensville MD 21666-3040 Office: 1511 Ritchie Hwy Ste 201 Arnold MD 21012-2410

HARRIS, ROGERS SANDERS, bishop; b. Anderson, S.C., Feb. 22, 1930; s. Wilmot Louis and Sarah Elizabeth (Sanders) H.; m. Anne Marshall Stewart, Mar. 28, 1953; children: Katherine Anne, Frances Elizabeth, Rebecca Susan. BA, U. of South, 1952, MDiv, 1957, DD (hon.), 1986; D Ministry, Va. Theol. Sem., 1977, DD (hon.), 1986. Ordained deacon Episcopal Ch., 1957, priest, 1958, bishop, 1985. Vicar Grace Episcopal Ch., Ridge Spring, S.C., 1957-59, St. Paul's Episcopal Ch., Batesburg, S.C., 1957-59; rector Ch. of Good Shepherd, Greer, S.C., 1959-69, St. Christopher's Ch., Spartanburg, S.C., 1969-85; suffragan bishop Diocese of Upper S.C., Columbia, S.C., 1985-89; bishop Diocese of S.W. Fla., St. Petersburg, 1989-97. V.p. Province IV of Episcopal Ch., 1991-94, pres., 1994-97; mem. Presiding Bishop's Coun. of Advice, N.Y.C., 1994-97. Trustee U. of South, Sewanee, Tenn., 1985—; trustee, v.p. Bishop Gray Inn, Davenport, Fla., 1989-97. 1st lt. USMC, 1952-54, Korea. Mem. Order of Holy Cross (assoc.). Episcopalian.

HARRIS, ROLAND ARSVILLE, JR., director program or activities, sociologist; b. Portsmouth, Va., July 25, 1930; s. Roland Arsville Sr. and Odelle (Thomas) H.; m. Helen Beatrice Johnson, Oct. 12, 1956; children: Roland Arsville III, Benjamin Christopher. BA, Paine Coll., 1971; MEd, U. Ga., 1972; PhD, U. Tenn., 1981. Enlisted U.S. Army, 1948, advance through grades to sgt. 1st class, 1968; from instr. to asst. prof. Knoxville (Tenn.) Coll., 1972-76, dir. instl. rsch. and planning, 1976-85, Title III coord., 2nd officer-in-charge, 1985-87, chief adminstrv. officer, 1987-88; exec. v.p., COO, 1995-96; acting pres., 1996-97; exec. dir. instnl. advancement Stillman Coll., Tuscaloosa, Ala., 1988-92. Hearing examiner U.S. Civil Svc. Merit award, Knoxville, 1985; mem. Tuscaloosa Tourism Adv. Com., 1989; loaned exec. United Way, Tuscaloosa, 1990, team capt., 1991. Mem. Am. Sociol. Assn., Optimists Internat., Phi Beta Sigma, Sigma Pi Phi. Democrat. Baptist. Avocations: reading, golf, travel, walking. Home: 802 Wildview Way Knoxville TN 37920-7605

HARRIS, RONALD DAVID, chemical engineer; b. Norman, Okla., Apr. 9, 1938; s. Loyd Ervin and Maurine Cora (Dill) H.; m. Judith Anne Wright, July 28, 1962 (div.); children: Todd David (dec.), Scott Howard, Susanna Katherine. B.Chem. Engring., M.Sc., Ohio State U., 1961; MBA, U. Cin., 1970; student, Chase Law Sch., Cin., 1970-71. Chem. engr. Procter & Gamble Co., Cin., 1961-62, process devel. group leader, 1964-71; mgr. food product devel. Clorox Co., Oakland, Calif., 1971-73, dir. R & D Pleasanton, Calif., 1973-77; v.p. R & D Anderson Clayton Foods, Dallas, 1977-87; v.p. tech. Kraft Inc., Glenview, Ill., 1987-90; v.p. Kraft U.S.A. Tech., 1990-94; v.p. sci. rels. Kraft Foods, Inc., 1994-96; exec. v.p. R & D, Nabisco, Inc., Hanover, N.J., 1999-2001; mng. gen. ptnr. Harris Mgmt. LLC, 1998—. Instr. Keller Grad. Sch. Mgmt., 1995—; assoc. dir. exec. edn., sr. lectr. Ohio State U., 1996-99, 2001—; adj. prof. food sci., lectr. mgmtm. sci. Ohio State U., 1996—. Patentee process for adsorbent bleaching oils, dry prepared fluffy frosting mixes. Trustee San Ramon Valley Unified Sch. Dist., 1977; mem. Richardson City Planning Commn., 1980-83, Richardson City Coun., 1983-87, Lake Forest Bldg. Rev. Bd., 1993-99; bd. dirs. Richardson Symphony Orch., 1982-85, Heard Natural Sci. Mus., 1985-87, Richardson br. YMCA, 1984-87, 1st United Meth. Ch., Richardson, 1986-87, Chilled Foods Assn., 1988-94, 1st Presbyn. Ch., Lake Forest, 1988—; bd. dirs. Hull House Assn., 1988-96, vice chmn., 1993-96; mem. citizens adv. com. North Tex. Mcpl. Water Dist., 1980; mem. adv. com. doctorate in chemistry program U. Tex., Dallas, 1983-89; mem. adv. bd. dept. food sci. U. Minn., 1984-96; mem. adv. bd. dept. chem. engring. Ohio State U., 1991—, pres. Chem. Engring. Alumni Soc., 1998-99, alumni adv. coun. Ohio State U., 2000—, mem. Pres.' Club; mem. adv. bd. Masters in Ops. and Tech. Ill. Inst. Tech., 1995-99; mem. Leadership Richardson, 1984-87; life mem. Julian C. Hyer Youth Camp; mem. Littlefield Soc., U. Tex., Austin, 1991—. Officer U.S. Army, 1962-64. Named Disting. Alumnus, Ohio State U., 1992, Meritorious Svc. award, 2000. Mem. Am. Chem. Soc., Inst. Food Technologists, Am. Oil Chemists Soc., Richardson C. of C. (1st v.p., dir., pres. 1982), Richardson Hist. Soc., Tex. Mcpl. League, Columbus Athletic Club, Lake Forest Club, Lions (bd. dirs., pres. 1982-83), Columbus Rotary, Tau Beta Pi, Phi Eta Sigma (past chpt. pres.), Phi Lambda Upsilon, Delta Mu Delta, Kappa Sigma (past chpt. pres., alumnus advisor 1996-99). Home: 1051 Urlin Ave Columbus OH 43212 E-mail: hiyoron@aol.com.

HARRIS, ROXANNA MARIE, emergency room nurse; b. Kansas City, Kans., July 16, 1950; d. Alvin Thomas Harris and Emilia Frances (Scigliano) Harris-Douthat. Lic. paramedic, Med. Ctr., Independence, Mo., 1985; ADN, Fort Scott (Kans.) C.C., 1991. RN, Kans.; cert. ACLS, PALS instr., CPR, BLS, advanced life support obstetrics. Paramedic Sac-Osage Hosp., Osceolo, Mo., 1988-91, Mercy Hosp., Fort Scott, Kans., 1991-92; emergency rm. travel nurse Am. Home Health, Kans., 1993-94, Yukon Kuskokwim Delta Regional Hosp., Bethal, Alaska, 1994-96; in-patient and obstet. nurse Nome (Alaska) Emergency Nurses, 1996-99; corrections nurse Anvil Mountain, Nome, 1997-99; hospice nurse Kailua-Kona, Hawaii, 1999-2000; travel nurse Native Am. Hosps., 2000; nurse Mayo Regional Hosp., Dover-Foxcroft, Maine, 2000-01; ER nurse Kaiser-Permanente Hosp., Walnut Creek, Calif., 2001; travel nurse emergency rm. Valley Hosp., Palmer, Alaska, 2002—03. Triage nurse Alaska Bush Hosp., Nome, Bethel; nurse State of Alaska Correctional Facility, 2003—. Vol. Res. Police Officer and Rescue Squad. Mem.: Emergency Rm. Nurses Assn. Avocations: scuba diving, photography, reading, cross country skiing, snow mobiling. Office: 10158 Locust St Kansas City MO 64131-4222

HARRIS, ROY JAY, JR., editor, business journalist; b. St. Louis, Oct. 2, 1946; s. Roy Jay and Ruth Dorothy (Schofer) H.; m. Andrea McKenna (dec.); children: David McKenna Harris, Roy Jay Harris III; m. Eileen Carol McIntyre. BS in Journalism, Northwestern U., 1968, MS in Journalism, 1971. Staff reporter The Wall Street Jour., Pitts., 1971-74, L.A., 1974-88, dep. bur. chief, 1988—94; sr. editor CFO Mag., Boston, 1996—. With U.S. Army, 1969-70. Mem. Soc. Am. Bus. Editors and Writers, Soc. Profl. Journalists, Am. Soc. Bus. Publ. Editors (nat. v.p. 2003—). Office: CFO Mag 253 Summer St Fl 3 Boston MA 02210-1118 E-mail: royharris@cfo.com.

HARRIS, RUBY LEE, real estate agent; b. Booneville, Miss., Mar. 5, 1939; d. Carl Jackson and Gladys (Downs) Hill; m. Lee Kelly Harris, Apr. 21, 1962; children: Lee Kelly Jr., Bradford William. Student, N.E. Miss. Jr. Coll., Booneville, 1957-58, U. Ala., Tuscaloosa, 1958-59. Lic. real estate agt., Calif. Agt. Forest E. Olson, El Toro, Calif., 1974-76, Coldwell Banker, Mission Viejo, Calif., 1976-78, Associated Realtors, Mission Viejo, 1978—. Mem. Children's Home Soc. Calif., Mission Viejo, 1985-88, Boys and Girls Club Am., San Clemente, Calif., 1989-91, Capistrano, 1994-95; mem. election com. Orange County, Mission Viejo, 1974—. Mem. Nat. Assn. Realtors, Calif. Assn. Realtors, Saddleback Valley Bd. Realtors (bd. dirs. 1989). Republican. Avocations: bicycling, gardening. Office: Associated Realtors 25350 Marguerite Pkwy Ste B Mission Viejo CA 92692-2993

HARRIS, RUTH HORTENSE COLES, retired accounting educator; b. Charlottesville, Va., Sept. 26, 1928; d. Bernard Albert and Ruth Hortense (Wyatt) Coles; m. John Benjamin Harris, Sept. 2, 1950; children: John Benjamin Jr., Vita Michelle. BS, Va. State U., 1948; MBA, NYU, 1949; cert. advanced study, EdD, Coll. William and Mary, 1977; LHD, Va. Union U., 1998. CPA, Va. Instr. commerce dept. Va. Union U., Richmond, 1949-53, asst prof., 1953-64; head dept., 1956-69; assoc. prof., head dept. Va. Union U., Richmond, 1964-69, prof., dir. div. commerce, 1969-73, dir. Sydney Lewis Sch. Bus. Adminstrn., 1973-81, prof. acctg., 1981-85, 87—, chmn. dept., 1987-97, mem. mgmt. team Sch. Bus., 1985-87, disting. prof. emeritus, 1997. Bd. dirs. Am. Assembly Collegiate Schs. Bus., St. Louis, 1976-79; mem. adv. bd. Intercollegiate Case Clearing House, 1976-79; mem. state adv. coun. Cmty. Svc. and Continuing Edn. (Title I) Agy., Charlottesville, 1977-81. Chmn. Interdeptl. Com. on Rate-Setting for Children's Facilities, Richmond, 1983-85; bd. dirs. Richmond Urban League; mem. agy. evaluation comn. United Way Greater Richmond; mem. fin. sec. Va. Commonwealth chpt. Nat. Coalition 100 Black Women; participant Va. Heroes, Inc., Richmond, 1991-94, 96. Recipient tchg. excellence award Sears Roebuck Found., 1990, Outstanding Faculty award Va. Coun. for Higher Edn., 1992, Eboné Image award No. Va. chpt. Nat. Coalition of 100 Black Women, 1993, Serwa award Va. Commonwealth chpt., Nat. Coalition 100 Black Women, 1989, Tenneco Excellence in Tchg. award United Negro Coll. Fund, 1995; named Belle Ringer of Richmond--1992 Richmond br. Nat. Assn. Univ. Women. Mem. AICPA (Outstanding Va. Educator award), Va. Soc. CPA's (com. mem., Outstanding Va. Educator award, Disting. Career in Acctg. Edn. award). Baptist. Avocations: ringing handbells, reading, playing piano. Home: 2816 Edgewood Ave Richmond VA 23222-3518 E-mail: hortense2@aol.com.

HARRIS, RUTH JENSEN, lawyer; b. Mpls., Mar. 8, 1920; d. Anton and Edith Cecilia (Axtell) J.; m. Reginald Albright Harris, Nov. 25, 1966 (dec. Oct. 1995). BS, U. Minn., 1941, JD, 1943. Bar: Minn. 1944. Democrat. Unitarian Universalist. Home: 400 Selby Ave Apt 327 Saint Paul MN 55102-4511

HARRIS, SAMUEL Y. architect, educator; BA (cum laude), Amherst Coll.; MArch, MS in Engring., U. Pa.; JD, U. Md. Project engr. Keast & Hood Co.; assoc. Venturi, Rauch and Scott Brown; ptnr. Kieran, Timberlake & Harris; proprietor S. Harris & Co.; instr. sch. architecture U. Pa. Vis. prof. Yale U., 1994; adj. assoc. prof. Goucher Coll.; faculty Harvard Sch. Design; bd. dirs. Ctr. Conservation Art and Historic Artifacts, Cliveden; advisor Phila. Preservation Alliance, Highlands. Author: Building Pathology: Deterioration, Diagnostics and Intervention, 2000. Bd. dirs. Friends of Lemon Hill. Fellow: AIA; mem.: Carpenters' Co. Office: S Harris & Co 2601 Pennsylvania Ave Philadelphia PA 19130 also: Univ of Pennsylvania Department of Architecture 115 Meyerson Hall Philadelphia PA 19104-8311*

HARRIS, SCOTT BLAKE, lawyer; b. N.Y.C., June 18, 1951; s. Stanley Robert and Adele Jean (Ganger) Harris; m. Barbara Straughn, Aug. 5, 1978. AB magna cum laude, Brown U., 1973; JD magna cum laude, Harvard U., 1976. Bar: DC 1977, U.S. Ct. Appeals (DC cir.) 1978, U.S. Supreme Ct. 1983. Law clk. to presiding justice U.S. Dist. Ct., Washington, 1976-77; assoc. Williams & Connolly, Washington, 1977-84, ptnr., 1984-93; chief counsel Bur. Export Adminstrn., U.S. Dept. Commerce, Washington, 1993-94; chief internat. bur. FCC, 1994-96; ptnr. Gibson, Dunn & Crutcher, Washington, 1996-98; mng. ptnr. Harris, Wiltshire & Grannis LLP, Washington, 1998—. Mem. adv. bd. Ctr. Wireless Tech., Va. Tech. U., 1996—, Satellite Comm. Mag., 1996—2000, Critical Infrastructure Fund, LLP, 1999—2000, Telecom. Reports Internat., 2000—02, Morphics Tech., Inc., 2000—02; adj. prof. Georgetown U. Law Ctr., 1996, 2001—02. Columnist: Aviation Week, 2000—01, Space News, 2001—. Trustee Fed. Comm. Bar Assn. Found., 1997—2000. Mem.: ABA (co-chair telecom. com., sect. internat. law 1999—2002), US ITU Assn. (bd. dirs. 1999—), Fed. Comm. Bar Assn. (co-chair online comm. com. 2000—02), Phi Beta Kappa. Home: 3409 Fulton St NW Washington DC 20007-1436 Office: Harris Wiltshire & Grannis LLP 1200 18th St NW Washington DC 20036-2506 E-mail: sharris@harriswiltshire.com.

HARRIS, SIDNEY EUGENE, dean, management educator; b. Atlanta, Ga., July 21, 1949; s. Nathaniel and Marian (Johnson) H.; m. Mary A. Styles, July 24, 1971; 1 child, Savaria Brandy Harris. BA in Mathematics, Morehouse Coll., 1971; MS in Ops. Rsch., Cornell U., 1975, PhD, 1976. Mem. tech. staff Bell Telephone Labs., Holmdel, N.J., 1973-78; asst. prof. Ga. State U., Atlanta, 1978-82, assoc. prof., 1982-87; prof. mgmt. Claremont (Calif.) Grad. Sch., 1987-97, dean, 1991-96. Bd. dirs. Svc. Master Corp., Chgo. (cons.); bd. dirs. Family Savs., L.A., chair audit com., 1991-97, compensation com.; bd. dirs. Total System Svcs., Macon, Ga., AirGate PCS, Atlanta, Coca-Cola Co., Atlanta, 1991—, AT & T, IBM, Xerox Corp. Hewlett Packard, BellSouth, Svc. Master, Chgo. Editor MIS Quar., 1991; contbr. articles to profl. jours.; author, co-author to several books; lectr. in field. Bd. dirs. Peter F. Drucker Non-Profit Found., N.Y.C., 1991—; vice chmn. L.A. County Productivity Commn., L.A., 1991; bd. trustees Menlo Coll.; mem. Family Support Adv. Bd., 1990. Recipient Vol. Svc. award Nat. Computer Com. Bd., 1985. Mem.: Soc. Internat. Bus. Fellows, Beta Gamma Sigma, Sigma Xi. Avocations: tennis, jogging, sailing. Office: Ga State U J Mack Robinson Coll Bus University Plaza Atlanta GA 30303

HARRIS, STANLEY S. retired judge, arbitrator, mediator; b. Washington, Oct. 19, 1927; s. Stanley Raymond and Elizabeth (Sutherland) H.; m. Rebecca Ashley, Aug. 1, 1964; children: Scott Sutherland, Todd Ashley, Mark Ashley.

BS, U. Va., 1951, JD, 1953. Bar: D.C. 1953, U.S. Supreme Ct. 1964. Assoc., then ptnr. Hogan & Hartson, Washington, 1953-70; judge Superior Ct. D.C., 1971-72, D.C. Ct. Appeals, 1972-82; U.S. atty. for D.C. Dept. Justice, 1982-83; judge U.S. Dist. Ct. D.C., 1983—, sr. judge, 1996—2001; ret., 2001; arbitrator, mediator. Mem. com. on criminal law Jud. Conf. U.S., 1988-94, chmn. com. intercircuit assignments, 1994-2000. Served with U.S. Army, 1945-47. Recipient Judiciary award Assn. Fed. Investigators, 1982. Mem. Bar Assn. D.C. (bd. dirs. 1970-72, Lawyer of Yr. award 1982, Disting. Career award 1996), Lawyers' Club of Washington (pres. 1998-99). Republican. Home: 4982 Sentinel Dr Apt 406 Bethesda MD 20816-3579

HARRIS, STEPHEN ERNEST, electrical engineering and applied physics educator; b. Bklyn., Nov. 29, 1936; s. Henry and Anne (Alpern) H.; m. Frances Joan Greene, June 7, 1959; children: Hilary Ayn, Craig Henry. BS, Rensselaer Poly. Inst., 1959; MS, Stanford U., 1961, PhD, 1963. Mem. tech. staff Bell Telephone Labs., Murray Hill, N.J., 1959-60; coop. student Sylvania Electric Systems, Mountain View, Calif., 1961-63; prof. elec. engring. Stanford U., Calif., 1963-79, prof. elec. engring. and applied physics, 1979—, dir. Edward L. Ginzton Lab., 1983-88, Kenneth and Barbara Oshman prof., 1988—. Chair Dept. Applied Physics, Stanford U., 1993-96. Recipient Alfred Noble prize ASCE, 1965, Curtis McGraw rsch. award Am. Soc. Engring. Edn., 1973, Davies medal for engring. achievement Rensselaer Poly. Inst., 1984, Einstein prize, 1991, Optical Soc. Am. Teaching award, 1992, Frederic Ives medal Optical Soc. Am., 1999, IEEE/LEOS Quantum Electronics award, 1994. Fellow: IEEE (David Sarnoff award 1978), AAAS (Arthur L. Schawlow prize in laser sci. 2002), Am. Phys. Soc., Optical Soc. Am. (Charles Hard Townes award 1985), Am. Acad. Arts and Scis.; mem.: Nat. Acad. Scis., Nat. Acad. Engring. Office: Stanford Univ Edward L Ginzton Lab 450 Via Palou Mall Stanford CA 94305-4085

HARRIS, STEVEN BROWN, lawyer; b. 1947; s. Sam and Madelyn Harris; married; 2 children. BA with honors, Dartmouth Coll., 1969; LLB, George Washington U., 1973. Bar: D.C. 1974; U.S. Ct. Appeals 1974. With Time Inc., 1969-70; atty. Office of Gen. Counsel, Office of Econ. Opportunity, 1973-75, Legal Svcs. Corp., 1975-77; asst. gen. counsel Mcpl. Securities Rulemaking Bd., 1977-78; staff rep. Nat. Commn. for Rev. of Antitrust Laws and Procedures, 1979; legis. counsel Rep. Barbara Jordan, 1979, Senator Donald W. Riegle Jr., 1979-81; counsel U.S. Senate Com. on Banking, Housing and Urban Affairs, 1981-86, staff dir., chief counsel, securities subcommittee, 1986-88, chief counsel to full com., 1989-90, staff dir., chief counsel, 1990-94, minority staff dir., chief counsel, 1994—2001, staff dir., chief counsel, 2001—. Office: Banking Housing & Urban Affairs US Senate Commn 534 Dirksen Bldg Washington DC 20510-0001

HARRIS, STUART FRANCIS, educator, researcher; b. London, Mar. 14, 1931; s. Henry Bevan and Frances (Page) H.; m. Pamela Anne Manning, Feb. 1, 1958; children: Jan Lesley, David Bevan, Michael Stuart, Richard Miles, Jeremy Cartwright. B of Econs., Sydney U., 1955; PhD, Australian Nat. U., 1964. Dir. Bureau of Agrl. Econs., Canberra, Australia, 1967-72; dep. head dept. overseas trade Australian Govt., Canberra, 1972-75; prof. ctr. resource and environ. studies Australian Nat. U., Canberra, 1975-81, ctr. dir., 1981-84; head. dept. fgn. affairs. Australian Govt., Canberra, 1984-87, head. dept. fgn. affairs and trad., 1987-88; prof. dept. internat. rels. Australian Nat. U., Canberra, 1988—. Chair Remuneration Tribunal, Canberra, 1993-98, Australia China Coun., Canberra, 1991-97; mem. Trade Policy Adv. Coun, Canberra, 1992-97; mem. Fgn. Affairs Coun., 1997—. Author: (with others) Principles of Rural Policy in Australia, 1974, Processes of Economic Policy Making in Australia, 1975, European Interests in Asean, 1982, Japan and Greater China, 2001; author: Review of Australia's Overseas Representation, 1991; joint editor: The End of the Cold War in East Asia, 1991, China as A Great Power, 1995, Asia-Pacific Security, 1997; contbr. articles to profl. jours. Officer Order of Australia, 1989. Mem. Acad. Social Scis. in Australia (hon. treas. 1983-97, fellowship 1979). Office: Australian Nat U Dept Internat Rels Canberra 2601 Australia E-mail: stuart.harris@coombs.anu.edu.au.

HARRIS, SYDNEY MALCOLM, retired judge; b. Toronto, Ont., Can., June 23, 1917; s. Samuel Aaron and Rose (Geldzaeler) H.; m. Enid Harriet Perlman, Nov. 9, 1949; children: Mark, David. BA, U. Toronto, 1939; Barrister-at-Law, Osgoode Hall, Toronto, 1942; LLB, York U., Toronto, 1991. Bar: Ont. 1942, created Queen's Counsel 1962. Barrister, solicitor firm Harris & Rubenstein, Toronto, 1950-76; judge criminal div. Ont. Provincial Ct., Toronto, 1976-90; judge provincial divsn. Ont. Ct., Toronto, 1990-92. Mem. Assessment Rev. Bd., 1993-99; dep. judge Small Claims Ct., 1993-99. Pres. Canadian Jewish Congress, 1974-77. Recipient Centennial medal, 1967, Queen's Jubilee medal, 1977 Mem. Am. Judges assn., Can. Bar Assn., Ont. Conf. Judges, Assn. of Ont. Land Surveyors (exec. com. coun. and complaints rev. councillor 1995-2001). Home: 3303 Don Mills Rd Apt 2006 Toronto ON Canada M2J 4T6

HARRIS, T. GEORGE, editor; b. Simpson County, Ky., Oct. 4, 1924; s. Garland and Luna (Byrum) Harris; m. Sheila Hawkins, Oct. 31, 1952 (dec. Jan. 1977); children: Amos, Anne, Crane, Gardiner; m. Ann Rockefeller Roberts, Mar. 3, 1979 (div. Apr. 1993); children: Clare, Joseph, Mary Louise, Rachel Pierson; m. Jeannie Pinkerton, Sept. 12, 1998; 1 child, A. J. Clancy. Student, U. Ky., 1946; BA, Yale U., 1949. Reporter Clarksville (Tenn.) Leaf-Chronicle, 1942; corr. Time, 1949-55; Chgo. bur. chief Time-Life-Fortune, 1955-58, San Francisco bur. chief, 1960-62; sr. editor Look mag., 1962-68; editor in chief Psychology Today mag., 1969-76, 88-90, US, 1977; founding editor Am. Health mag., AH Fitness Bull., Spirituality and Health, Beliefnet.com, 1980-90; exec. editor Harvard Bus. Rev., Boston, 1992-93; editor UCSD-Connect Hi-tech. Weekly Online, 2000—. Sci. adv. ABC's 20/20 Program, Inst. Advancement of Health. Editor: Bodywatch. Bd. dirs. Am. Health Found., Nat. Vol. Ctrs., Rockefeller Bros. Fund, Go Code Corp.; med. adv. com. Nat. YMCA; regent Cathedral of St. John the Divine. 1st lt. battlefield Commn. at Bastogne, F.A. AUS, WWII. Mem.: Century Assn., Yale Club N.Y.C., La Jolla Beach and Tennis Club, Phi Beta Kappa. Episcopalian. Home and Office: 8115 Paseo Del Ocaso La Jolla CA 92037-3140 Fax: 858-459-0838.

HARRIS, TERESA ANN, retired social services executive, social worker; b. Youngstown, N.Y. BA, Elms Coll., 1956; MEd, Springfield Coll., 1961; MSW, U. Conn., 1963. Cert. social worker. Psychiat. social worker Area Mental Health Clinic, Holyoke, Mass., 1963-66, Children's Study Home, Springfield, Mass., 1966-69, social work supr., 1969-88, asst. exec. dir., 1988-98. Cons. social work, Springfield, 1969—. Bd. dirs. Springfield Day Nursery, 1991-94, Gandara Mental Health Ctr. Recipient Disting. Svc. to Community award Child and Family Svc., Springfield, 1990, Woman of Achievement award YWCA, Springfield, 1993; named Child Adv. of Yr., Springfield Coun. for Children, 1991. Fellow Am. Orthopsychiat. Assn.; mem. NASW, Acad. Cert. Social Workers.

HARRIS, THEODORE CLIFFORD, songwriter, music publisher; b. Lakeland, Fla., Aug. 2, 1937; s. Thomas Carl and Rhoda Keen (Sutton) H.; m. Jackie Ann Thompson, Dec. 20, 1967; children: Bradley Carlton, Joshua Chandler. Grad. high sch., Lakeland. Staff songwriter Silver Star Music, Nashville, 1958-62; co-owner Harbot Music, Nashville, 1965-67; owner Contention Music, Nashville, 1967-97. Guest instr. U. Tenn., Nashville, 1975-76. Rec. artist country music field, 1958-66. Recipient 70 composer, pub. award, 1965-90, Named to the Nashville Songwriter's Assn. Internat. Hall of Fame, 1990. Mem. Country Music Assn. (bd. dirs. Nashville chpt. 1972-73), Nashville Songwriters Assn. Internat. Republican. Baptist. Avocations: fishing, metal detecting, lapidary arts.

HARRIS, THEODORE EDWARD, mathematician, educator; b. Phila., Jan. 11, 1919; s. Julius and Hazel (Rosenfield) H.; m. Constance Ruth Feder, June 29, 1947; children: Stephen Joel, Marcia Faye. Student, So. Meth. U., 1935-37; BA, U. Tex., Austin, 1939; MA, Princeton U., 1946, PhD, 1947; D of Tech. (hon.), Chalmers Inst. of Tech., Gothenburg, Sweden, 1989. With Rand Corp., 1947—66, chmn. dept. math., 1959—66; prof. math. U. So. Calif., 1966—89, prof. emeritus, 1989—. Vis. asst. prof. UCLA, 1949-50; vis. assoc. prof. Columbia, 1953; vis. prof. Stanford U., 1963; lectr. U. So. Calif., 1989-97. Author: The Theory of Branching Processes, 1963; Editor: Annals of Math. Statistics, 1955-58. Served to maj. USAAF, 1942-45. Recipient Albert S. Raubenheimer disting. faculty award, 1985, disting. emeritus award U. So. Calif., 1990. Fellow AAAS, Inst. Math. Stats. (pres. 1966-67); mem. Am. Math. Soc., Nat. Acad. Scis., Phi Beta Kappa, Sigma Xi. Jewish. Fax: 213-740-2424.

HARRIS, THOMAS L. public relations executive; b. Dayton, Ohio, Apr. 18, 1931; s. James and Leona (Blum) H.; m. JoAnn K. Karch, Apr. 14, 1957; children: James Harris, Theodore Harris. BA, U. Mich., 1953; MA, U. Chgo., 1956. Exec. v.p. Daniel J. Edelman Inc., Chgo., 1957-67; v.p. pub. rels. Needham Harper & Steers, Chgo., 1967-72; pres. Foote Cone & Belding Pub. Rels., Chgo., 1973-78, Golin-Harris Communications Inc., Chgo., 1978-89, also vice chmn.; adj. prof. Medill Sch. Journalism, Northwestern U., Evanston, Ill., 1987—; mng. ptnr. Thomas L. Harris & Co., Highland Pk., Ill., 1992—. Served with U.S. Army, 1953-55. Mem. Public Relations Soc. Am. (Gold Anvil award 2000). Home: 241 Melba Ln Highland Park IL 60035-1904 Office: Thomas L Harris & Co 600 Central Ave Highland Park IL 60035-3211 E-mail: ttlhco@aol.com.

HARRIS, THOMAS RAYMOND, biomedical engineer, educator; b. San Angelo, Tex., Feb. 19, 1937; s. Loyd Franklin and Rubye Harris; m. Alene Blythe Hawes; children: Calvin Thomas, Andrew Mitchell. BS, Tex. A&M U., 1958, MS, 1962; PhD, Tulane U., 1964; MD, Vanderbilt U., 1974. Design engr. Standard Oil Co. Calif., 1958-60; mem. faculty Vanderbilt U., Nashville, 1964—, prof. biomed. engring. and chem. engring., 1976—; assoc. prof. medicine Vanderbilt U. Sch. Medicine, 1980-85, prof. medicine, 1985—; dir. biomed. engring. program Vanderbilt U. Sch. Engring., 1977-88, chair dept. biomed. engring., 1988—, Orrin Henry Ingram Disting. prof. engring., 2002—. Cons. in field. Author articles in field; mem. editorial bds. profl. jours. Served as 2d lt. AUS, 1958-59. Grantee Nat. Heart, Lung and Blood Inst., NSF. Mem. Am. Physiol. Soc., Am. Inst. Chem. Engrs., Am. Soc. Engring. Edn., Am. Heart Assn. (sci. councils), Biomed. Engring. Soc. (pres. 1985-86), Soc. Engring. in Medicine and Biology, Microcirculatory Soc. Baptist. Office: Vanderbilt U Dept of Biomed Engring PO Box 1724 Nashville TN 37235 Business E-Mail: thomas.r.harris@vanderbilt.edu.

HARRIS, VENITA VAN CASPEL, retired financial planner; b. Sweetwater, Okla. d. Leonard Rankin and Ella Belle (Jarnagin) Walker; m. Lyttleton T. Harris IV, Dec. 26, 1987. Student, Duke, 1944-46; BA, U. Colo., 1948, postgrad., 1949-51, N.Y. Inst. Fin., 1962. CFP. Stockbroker Rauscher Pierce & Co., Houston, 1962-65, A.G. Edwards & Sons, Houston, 1965-68; founder, pres., owner Van Caspel & Co., Inc., Houston, 1968—, Van Caspel Wealth Mgmt.; owner, mgr. Van Caspel Planning Svc., Van Caspel Advt. Agy.; sr. v.p. investments Raymond James and Assocs., 1987-95; ret., 1995. Moderator PBS TV show The Money Makers and Profiles of Success, 1980; 1st women mem. Pacific Stock Exchange. Author: Money Dynamics, 1978, Money Dynamics of the 1980's, 1980, The Power of Money Dynamics, Money Dynamics for the 1990's, 1988; editor: Money Dynamics Letter. Bd. dirs. Horatio Alger Assn., Robert Schuller Ministries; trustee Northwood U.; founding mem. Com. of 200. Recipient Matrix award Theta Sigma Phi, 1969, Horatio Alger award for Disting. Americans, 1982, Disting. Woman's medal, Northwood Univ., 1988, George Norlin award U. Colo. Alumni Assn., 1987. Mem. Internat. Assn. Fin. Planners, Inst. Cert. Fin. Planners, Phi Gamma Mu, Phi Beta Kappa. Methodist. Home: 4 Saddlewood Estates Dr Houston TX 77024-6841 Office: 6524 San Felipe St Ste 102 Houston TX 77057-2611

HARRIS, VERA EVELYN, human resources specialist; b. Watson, Sask., Can., Jan. 11, 1932; came to U.S., 1957; d. Timothy and Margaret (Popoff) Harris; children: Colin Clifford Graham, Barbara Cusimano Page. Student, U. B.C., Vancouver, Can. Office mgr. Keglers, Inc., Morgan City, La., 1964-67; office mgr., acct. John L. Hooper & Assocs., New Orleans, 1967-71; office mgr. Elite Homes, Inc., Metairie, La., 1971-73; comptroller Le Pavillon Hotel, New Orleans, 1973-74; contr. Waguespack-Pratt, Inc., New Orleans, 1974-76; adminstrv. contr. Sizzler Family Steak Houses of So. La., Inc., Metairie, 1976-79; dir. adminstrn. Sunbelt, Inc., New Orleans, 1979-82, sec., dir., 1980—; exec. v.p. Corp. Cons., Inc., 1980-83, pres., 1984-86, Harris Pers. Resources, Arlington, Tex., 1986—, Harris Enterprises, Arlington, 1986—, Harris Pers. Resources Health Staff, Arlington, 1990—. Mem.: Soc. Exec. Recruiting Cons. (pres. 1997—99), Ind. Recruiters Group, La. Assn. Pers. Cons. (treas. 1985—86). Home: 4915 Arborgate Dr Arlington TX 76017-1049 Office: Harris Personnel Resources 1600 E Pioneer Pkwy Ste 340 Arlington TX 76010-6564 E-mail: vharris@iamerica.net.

HARRIS, VIRGINIA SYDNESS, religious studies educator; b. Fargo, N.D., Oct. 24, 1945; d. Kenneth Jeffries and Jeanette Lucille Sydness; m. Granville Reed Harris, Dec. 29, 1966; children: G. Richard, Donald Thomas, Steven Jeffrey. BS in Polit. Sci. and Edn., Moorhead State U., 1967; CSB (hon.), Mass. Metaphysical Coll., 1982; postgrad., Principia Coll., Elsah, Ill., Mills Coll. Owner Edgewater Inn & Marina, Detroit Lakes, Minn., 1966-70; asst. to presdl. interpreter U.S. Dept. State, Washington, 1967-68; sec. sch. tchr. Fargo (N.D.) Pub. Schs., 1968-70; TV host, prodr. Pub. Broadcast Sys., Fargo, 1968-70; Christian Sci. tchr., 1982—; Christian Sci. lectr., 1983-89. Faculty mem. Healing & Spirituality Symposium Harvard Med. Sch. and New Eng. Deaconess Hosp., Boston, 1995—. Contbr. articles to profl. jours.; spkr. in field. Bd. dirs. LWV, 1968-73, YWCA, 1969-73; clk. Christian Sci. Ch., Boston, 1986-90, bd. dirs., chair, 1990—; treas., bd. dirs. Nat. Found. Women Legislators, Inc., Washington, 1994—. Mem. AAUW, PEO, Jr. League Boston, Wellesley Coll. Club, City Club Washington. Avocations: jogging, skiing, reading, needlepoint. Home: 111 Bogle St Weston MA 02493-1056 Office: The First Ch of Christ Scientist 175 Huntington Ave # A253 Boston MA 02115-3117

HARRIS, WALTER EDGAR, chemistry educator; b. Wetaskiwin, Alta., Can., June 9, 1915; s. William Ernest and Emma Louise (Humbke) H.; m. Phyllis Pangburn, June 14, 1942; children: Margaret Anne, William Edgar. BS, U. Alta., 1938, MS, 1939; PhD, U. Minn., 1944; DSc (hon.), U. Waterloo, 1987, U. Alta., 1991. Research fellow U. Minn., 1943-46; prof. analytical chemistry U. Alta., Edmonton, 1946-80, chmn. dept. chemistry, 1974-79, chmn. Pres.'s Adv. Com. on Campus Revs., 1980-90. Author: (with H.W. Habgood) Programmed Temperature Gas Chromatography, 1965, (with B. Kratchovil) Chemical Separations and Measurements, 1974, Teaching Introductory Analytical Chemistry, 1974, An Introduction to Chemical Analysis, 1981, Risk Assessment, 1997, (with H.A. Laitinen) Chemical Analysis, 1975; contbr. numerous articles to profl. jours. Decorated Order of Can., 1998; recipient Outstanding Achievement award U. Minn., 1973; Govt. Alta. Achievement award, 1974 Fellow AAAS, Royal Soc. Can., Chem. Inst. Can. (hon., Fisher Sci. Lecture award 1969, Chem. Edn. award 1975, hon. fellow, 2001); mem. Am. Chem. Soc., Sigma Xi. Home: Ste 515 11148-84 Ave Edmonton AB Canada T6G 0V8 Office: U Alta Dept Chem Edmonton AB Canada T6G 2G2 E-mail: Walter.Harris@ualberta.ca.

HARRIS, WARREN LYNN, computer engineer; b. Albuquerque, May 8, 1966; s. Jerry Dale and Viola Guadalupe (Gutierrez) H., m. Clarissa Cosgrove, Apr. 1, 1998, 1 child: Tiffany Bellan. BS, Ariz. State U., 1988. Programming mgr. I.P.C. Computer Svcs., Inc., Tempe, Ariz., 1985-89; software sys. engr. Intel Corp., Chandler, Ariz., 1990; dir. software R & D Pics, Inc., Tempe, 1990-91; dir. software R & D parics divsn. Ansoft Corp., Tempe, 1991-94, devel. engr. Phoenix, 1994—2002; software engr. Neolinear, Inc., Tempe, 2002—. Mem. IEEE, Assn. for Computing Machinery, Mortar Bd., Golden Key, Upsilon Pi Epsilon. Avocations: racquetball, model building, chess, pool, star trek collecting. Office: Neolinear Inc 4801 S Lakeshore Dr Ste 201 Tempe AZ 85283

HARRIS, WARREN WAYNE, lawyer; b. Houston, Nov. 5, 1962; BBA, U. Houston, 1985, JD, 1988. Bar: Tex. 1988, U.S. Ct. Appeals (5th cir.) 1989, U.S. Ct. Appeals (fed. cir.) 1995, U.S. Ct. Appeals (8th, 10th and 11th cirs.) 1996, U.S. Dist. Ct. (so., no., ea. and we. dists.) Tex. 1990, U.S. Supreme Ct. 1991; bd. cert. civil appellate law Tex. Bd. Legal Specialization. Briefing atty. Tex. Supreme Ct., Austin, 1988-89; assoc. Porter & Hedges, L.L.P., Houston, 1989-95, ptnr., 1996, Bracewell & Patterson, L.L.P., Houston, 1996—. Editor-in-chief: Houston Lawyer mag., 1991-92; assoc. editor: The Appellate Advocate, 1992-97; editor: Pocket Parts, 1993-95, The Appellate Lawyer, 1994-96; chair editl. bd. Tex. Bar Jour., 2002—. Fellow: Houston Young Lawyers Found. (vice-chair 1996—98), Houston Bar Found., Tex. Bar Found. (co-chair dist. 4 nominating com. 1994—2000); mem.: ABA (litigation sect. appellate practice com. 1990—, tort and ins. practice sect. appellate advocacy com. 1990—, chair 2000—01), Houston Lawyer Referral Svc. (trustee 1994—95), Houston Young Lawyers Assn. (pres. 1999—2000), Houston Bar Assn. (coun. appellate practice sect. 1993—, chair appellate practice sect. 1998—99, Pres.'s award 1993—94), Tex. Young Lawyers Assn. (bd. dirs. 1994—98, outstanding dir. 1995—96, Pres.'s award 1996—97), State Bar Pro Bono Coll., State Bar Coll. (bd. dirs. 1994—95), State Bar Tex. (appellate sect. 1988—, coun. 1997—2000, sec. 2002—), Stages Repertory Theatre (pres. 1994—95, chair 1994—95, bd. dirs. 1994—96, WineFest com. chair 1994—96), Order of Barons, Order of Barristers, Phi Delta Phi. Republican. Office: Bracewell & Patterson LLP 711 Louisiana St Ste 2900 Houston TX 77002-2781 E-mail: warren.harris@bracepatt.com.

HARRIS, WAYNE MANLEY, lawyer; b. Dec. 28, 1925; s. George H. and Constance M. Harris; m. Diane C. Quigley, Sept. 30, 1978; children: Wayne, Constance, Karen, Duncan, Claire. LLB, U. Rochester, 1951. Bar: N.Y. 1952, U.S. Supreme Ct. 1958. Ptnr. Harris, Chesworth & O'Brien (and predecessor firms), Rochester, NY, 1958—. Drafter 5 laws passed in State of N.Y. Pres. Adopt-A-Stream program Delta Labs, Inc., 1971—; pres. Friends Bristol Valley Playhouse Found., 1984—87, Monroe County Conservation Coun., Inc., 1956—61, v.p., 1984—87, Powder Mills Pk. Hatchery Preservation, Inc., 1993—95, pres., 1995—2002. With U.S. Army, 1944—46, Germany. Decorated Bronze Star; named Vol. Conservationist of the Yr., N.Y. State Conservation Coun. Inc., 2000; recipient Sportsman of the Yr. award, Genesee Conservation League, Inc., 1960, Conservationist of the Yr. award, Monroe County Conservation Coun., Inc., 1961, N.Y. State Conservation Coun. Nat. Wildlife Fedn. Water Conservation, 1967, Kiwanian of the Yr. award, Kiwanis Club, 1965, Livingston County Fedn. Sportsmen award, 1967, Hon. Fellowship award, Rochester Acad. Sci., 1970, Meritorious Leadership in Civic Devel. award, Rochester C. of C., 1972, Svc. award, Rochester Against Intoxicated Drivers, 1989, Conspicuous Svc. cross, N.Y. State, 2000, N.Y. Senate Resolution 241 award, 2001. Mem.: ATLA, Indsl. Mgmt. Coun., AIDA Reins. and Arbitration Soc., N.Y. State Trial Lawyers Assn., Wild Turkey Fedn. Home: 60 Mendon Center Rd Honeoye Falls NY 14472-9363 Office: Harris Chesworth & O'Brien 1820 East Ave Rochester NY 14610-1829

HARRIS, WESLEY L. aeronautical engineer, educator; b. Richmond, Va., Oct. 29, 1941; s. William M. and Rosa P. (Minor) Harris; m. Myrtle Ann Satterwhite, June 14, 1960 (div. Mar. 1985); children: Wesley Jr., Zelda, Marcus, Kamau, kalomo, Eletha; m. Sandra Maria Butler, Sept. 21, 1985; 1 child, Tosha. B in Aeronautical Engring. with honors, U. Va., 1964; MA in Aeronautical Scis., Princeton U., 1966, PhD in Aeronautical Scis., 1968; LHD (hon.), Lane Coll., 1994; DEng (hon.), Milw. Sch. Engring., 1994; DSc (hon.), Old Dominion U., 1995. Asst. prof. aerospace engring. U. Va., 1968-70, assoc. prof., 1971-72; assoc. prof. physics Southern U., 1970-71; dir. office min. edn., 1975—78; assoc. prof. aeronautics & astronautics/ocean engring. MIT, Cambridge, 1973-79, assoc. prof. aeronautics and astronautics, 1980-81, prof., 1981-85, 1996—2001, Charles Stark Draper prof. of aeronautics and astronautics, 2001—, head dept. aeronautics and astronautics, 2003—; mgr. computational methods Office Aeronautics & Space Tech. NASA Hdqs., Washington, 1979-80, assoc. administr. Office of Aeronautics, 1993-96; dean sch. engring. U. Conn., Storrs, 1985-90; v.p. U. Tenn. Space Inst., Tullahoma, 1990-93. Mem. adv. groups Nat. Rsch. Coun. Commn. Engring. and Tech. Sys., Bd. Engring. Edn., Bd. Army Sci. and Tech., Air Force Studies Bd., Com. Aero. Techs.; mem. adv. com. NSF, U.S. Army Sci. Bd.; advisor univs.; nat. adv. com. dept. engring. Hampton U., 1989—96. Contbr. scientific papers to profl. jours. Trustee Sci. Mus. Conn., 1985—90, Princeton (N.J.) U., 2001—; adv. bd. dirs. Am. City Bank, Tullahoma, 1990—93; bd. vis. sch. engring. Duke U., 1991—99; vis. com. dept. aeronautics and astronautics MIT, 1988—95. Named Milton Pikarsky Meml. lectr., CCNY Sch. Engring., 1990, Barry Goldwater chair, Am. Instns. Ariz. State U., 2000—01; recipient Herbert S. and Jane Gregory Disting. Lectr. award, Coll. Engring. U. Fla., 1992, Dr. Martin Luther King Leadership award, MIT, 2001. Fellow: AIAA, Am. Helicopter Soc.; mem.: NAE, AAAS, Nat. Tech. Assn., Math. Assn. Am., Am. Phys. Soc. Democrat. Avocation: squash. Office: MIT Dept Aeronautics 33-410 77 Mass Ave Cambridge MA 02139-4307 E-mail: weslhar@mit.edu.

HARRIS, WHITNEY ROBSON, lawyer, educator, military officer, philanthropist; b. Seattle, Aug. 12, 1912; s. Olin Whitney and Lily Harris; m. Jane Freund Foster, Feb. 14, 1964 (dec.); 1 child, Eugene Whitney; m. Anna Galakatos, Jan. 8, 2000. AB magna cum laude, U. Wash., 1933; JD, U. Calif., 1936; LHD (hon.), McKendree Coll., 1999; LHD (hon.), U. Mo., 2001. Bar: Calif. 1936, U.S. Supreme Ct. 1945, Tex. 1953, U.S. Ct. Mil. Appeals 1955, Mo. 1964. Pvt. practice, L.A., 1936-42; trial counsel at trial of maj. German war criminals, Nuremberg, Germany, 1945-46; chief legal advice br. U.S. Mil. Govt. for Germany, 1946-48; prof. law So. Meth. U., 1948-54; staff dir. legal service and proc. Com. Orgn. Exec. Br. Govt., 1954; exec. dir. ABA, 1954-55; solicitor for Tex. Southwestern Bell Telephone Co., Dallas, 1955-63, gen. solicitor St. Louis, 1963-65; pvt. practice St. Louis, 1965-89; arbitration judge, 1993—. Sr. counselor Mo. Bar Assn., 1987—; lectr. UCLA, Stanford U., Washington U., Wellesley Coll., U. Denver, Reed Coll., U. Wash., Claremont Coll., Boston Coll., Williams Coll., So. Meth. U., U. Mo., McKendree Coll., Ga. State Coll., Slippery Rock U., others; trustee McKendree Coll. Author: Family Law, 1953, Tyranny On Trial, 1954, 3rd. edit., 1999, Legal Services and Procedure, 1955; author: (with others) Law, Culture and Values, 1989; contbr. articles to profl. jours. Capt. USN, 1942—46, WWII. Decorated Legion of Merit, Order of Merit Officer's Class (Germany), Medal of the War Crimes Commn. (Poland); named nat. outstanding fund raising vol. Nat. Soc. Fund Raising Execs., 1985. Mem. ABA (chmn. internat. law sect. 1953-54, chmn. adminstrv. law sect. 1960-61), Naval War Coll. Found. (grad. level), Order of Coif, Phi Beta Kappa, Phi Kappa Psi, Delta Theta Phi. Achievements include establishment of Whitney Robson Harris Collection on Third Reich of Germany, Washington U., 1980; Whitney R. Harris Inst. Global Legal Studies, Wash. U., 2002; Whitney R. and Anna Harris Spkrs. Series on Ethics Leadership and Pub. Responsibility, Fontbonne U., 2003. Home: 2818 Stonington Pl Saint Louis MO 63131-3417 *Tyranny leads to inhumanity, and inhumanity is death. Let us resolve that tyranny shall not extend its sway, nor war become its game— placing our faith in the cause of justice, in the freedom of man, and in the mercy of God.*

HARRIS, WILEY LEE, financial services executive; b. Lynchburg, Va., Jan. 15, 1949; s. Willie M. Harris; m. Thelma E. Thomas, June 28, 1991. BS in Indsl. Sociology, Yale U., 1971. Human resources trainee GE, Lynchburg, 1972-74, equal employment opportunity mgr., 1974-77; human resources mgr. GE Info. Svcs. Co., Chgo., 1977-79, Rockville, Md., 1979-87; compensation mgr. GE Capital, Stamford, Conn., 1987—. Mem. NAACP, Lynchburg, 1980—. Recipient Civic Achievement award NAACP, Lynchburg, 1986, Employment Achievement, State of Va., Richmond, Va., 1980. Mem. Internat. Assn. for Employee Benefits, Am. Compensation Assn., Am. Soc. for Personnel Adminstrn. Republican. Office: GE 3135 Easton Turnpike Fairfield CT 06828

HARRIS, WILLIAM JAMES, JR., research administrator, educator; b. South Bend, Ind., June 17, 1918; s. William James and Elizabeth M. (Scott) H.; m. Ruth Laubinger, Aug. 26, 1944 (dec. 1977); children: June Elizabeth Sherren, William James III, Debbie Shafer Hayden, Britta Shafer Kreuger, Barkley Shafer.; m. Elizabeth Dotten Shafer, June 24, 1978. BS in Chem. Engring; MS in Engring, Purdue U., 1940, D.Engring. (hon.), 1978; Sc.D., M.I.T., 1948. Head ferrous alloys br. metallurgy div. Naval Research Lab., 1947-51; exec. sec. materials adv. bd. Nat. Acad. Sci.-NRC, 1951-54, exec. dir., 1957-60, asst. sec., planning div. engring., 1960-62; asst. to dir. Battelle Meml. Inst., 1954-57, asst. to v.p., 1962-67; asst. dir. tech. Columbus Labs., 1967-69; v.p. research and test dept. Assn. Am. Railroads, 1970-85; E.B. Snead and Disting. prof. transp. engring. Tex. A&M U., 1985-95; assoc. dir. Tex. Transp. Inst., 1987-95, sr. rsch. engr., 1995—97; disting. prof. emeritus/Snead prof. emeritus Tex. A&M U., 1995-97; commr. Pres.'s Commn. on Critical Infrastructure Protection, 1997-98, sr. exec., 1998-99; cons. CIAO, 1999—2002. Hon. prof. China Acad. Ry. Scis., 1987; pres. W. J. Harris, Inc., 1985-98; pres., chmn. bd. Piscataway Co., Accokeek, Md., 1958-63; mem. Nat. Exec. Res. Dept. Transp., 1983—; sr. tech. advisor UN Devel. Orgn., 1987-91. Editor: (with others) Perspectives in Materials Research, 1963; co-author: Guildelines for Best Heavy Haul Practices, 2002; contbr. (with others) articles to tech. publs. Mem. nat. materials adv. bd. Nat. Acad. Sci., 1967—, chmn., 1969-70; sec. Pres.'s Com. on Hwy. Safety, 1969; mem. high speed ground transp. adv. com. U.S. Dept. Transp., 1972-74, Md. Gov.'s Sci. Adv. Com., 1972-76, Md. Gov.'s Energy Council, 1974-76; pres. Moyoane Assn., 1951-53, 58; pres., chmn. bd. Alice Ferguson Found.,

1966-68; chmn. exec. com., disting. profs. Tex. A&M U. Served to lt. comdr. USNR, 1941-45. Decorated Naval letter of commendation; recipient Disting. Svc. award (Carey award) Transp. Rsch. Bd., NRC, 1977, Roy Crum award for disting. rsch., 1989; Disting. Rsch. award Transp. Rsch. Forum, 1986; named R.R. Man of Yr., 1976; inducted into Cooperstown Conf. R.R. Hall of Fame, 1993, Batteile Meml. Inst. Transp. Hall of Fame, 1994, Internat. Heavy Haul of Fame, 1999. Fellow Am. Soc. Metals, ASME, Metall. Soc. (pres. 1970), Nat. Acad. Engring., elected 1977, (chair program com. 1995-98, chmn. audit com. 1982, fin. com. 1995-98); mem. Intelligent Transp. Soc. Am. (hon. mem., coord. coun. 1990-97, bd. dirs. 1997—, chmn. N.Am. steering com. 1993-95, chmn. clearinghouse and publ. speech com., world congress bd. dirs., Spl. award for Internat. Congress Leadership 1995), Am. Inst. Mining, Metall., and Petroleum Engrs. (dir. 1964-69, v.p. 1964-67, chmn. inst. metals divsn. 1960, Mathewson medal 1950), Engrs. Joint Coun. (bd. dirs. 1965-70, pres. 1968-70), Engring. Found. (chmn. rsch. conf. com. 1964-67, bd. dirs. 1968-70), Am. Ordnance Assn. (chmn. materials divsn. 1966-68), Nat. Security Indsl. Assn. (chmn. exec. planning com. 1965-67, chmn. rsch. and devel. adv. com. 1967-69), Transp. Rsch. Bd. (exec. com. 1977-85, 87-90, chmn. coun. 1989-95, emeritus internat. transp. sys. com. of transp. rsch. bd. com.), Nat. Def. Transp. Assn. (life, chmn. com. on engring. tech.), Found. on Engring. Techs. (chmn. 1990-97), Internat. Heavy Haul Assn. (chmn. 1982-89), Alice Ferguson Found. (hon. life mem.), Sigma Xi, Alpha Sigma Mu, Tau Beta Pi, Phi Lambda Upsilon, Sigma Delta Chi. Home: 1200 N Nash St Apt 1140 Arlington VA 22209-3682

HARRIS, WILLIAM JOHN, retired management holding company executive, consultant; b. Hamilton, Ont., Can., Feb. 6, 1928; s. William Frederick and Leila Matilda (Rodway) H.; m. Grace Edna Paddock, Oct. 12, 1957; children: Jeffrey Louis, Susan Marie, Laura Ann. Student, Wash. U., St. Louis, 1949-51. Sales and advt. mgr. Tuckett Ltd. (subs. Imperial Tobacco), Hamilton, 1951-64; mktg. mgr. Imperial Tobacco divsn. Imasco Ltd., Montreal, Que., Can., 1965-75, corp. sec., 1976-79; sr. v.p. Imasco Ltd., Montreal, 1980-89, ret., 1989. Cons. in field, 1990—. Recipient Gold Medal award Assn. Can. Advertisers Inc., 1979. Roman Catholic. Avocations: music, gardening, carpentry, golf.

HARRIS, WILLIAM NORMAN, music educator; b. Washington, Sept. 8, 1952; s. Clarence Norman and Helen Lucy (Holsey) H. BMEd, Millikin U., 1974; postgrad., various univs. Elem. gen. music tchr. Montgomery County Pub. Schs., Rockville, Md., 1974—. Prodr., dir. spring musical theatre, Poolesville (Md.) Jr./Sr. High Sch., 1986-91; leader, tenor/baritone soloist St. John's Episc. Ch., Bethesda, Md., 1995, U. Md. Chorus; baritone soloist Montgomery Coll. Chorus, 1995. Former mem. Montgomery County Masterworks Chorus, U. Md. Chorus; actor, singer Montgomery Coll., Summer Dinner Theatre, Rockville, 1988, 89, 90; artistic dir., choral master Damascus (Md.) Theatre Co.; singer U.S. Postal Svc. (Black History Month's Observances) Hdqrs., Washington, 1986-88; dir. children's chorus for PYE Panda Earth Day Expo '90. Fellow NEA, Music Educators Nat. Conf.; mem. Md. Music Educators Assn. (pres. south ctrl. region), Phi Mu Alpha Sinfonia, Beta Theta chpt. (treas. 1972-74). Democrat. Methodist. Avocations: tour narrator for Tourmobile, Washington Sightseeing Shuttle Svc., interior decorating, white water rafting. Home: 19256 Misty Meadow Ter Germantown MD 20874-5367 E-mail: billharristernor@aol.com., bill_harris@fc.mcps.k12.md.us.

HARRIS, WILLIAM STACY, physics educator; b. Richmond, Va., Apr. 25, 1947; s. James Calvin and Josephine (Henry) H. BS in Physics, Norfolk State U., 1969; MA in Physics Edn., Va. Tech., 1972. Instr. math., project Upward Bound, Va. Tech., Blacksburg, Va., summer 1973; instr. Mountain Empire C.C., Big Stone Gap, Va., 1984—, equal employment opportunity/affirmative action officer, 1990-99, assoc. prof. physics, 1972—. Bd. dirs. Wise County (Va.) C. of C., 1990-92; chair Libr. Gallery Bd., Wise County Pub. Libr., 1994—. Recipient fellowship Ford Found., 1969-71. Mem. Am. Assn. Physics Tchrs., Va. C.C. Assn. Avocation: photography. Home: PO Box 772 Big Stone Gap VA 24219-0772 Office: Mountain Empire CC PO Box 700 Rt 23 South Big Stone Gap VA 24219 E-mail: bharris@me.vccs.edu.

HARRIS, WILLIAM VERNON, history educator; b. Nottingham, Eng., Sept. 13, 1938; naturalized; 1982; s. K. W. F. and Elizabeth H.; m. Silvana Patriarca; 1 child, Neil BA, Oxford U., 1961, MA, 1964, D.Phil., 1968. Instr. history Columbia U., N.Y.C., 1965-68, asst. prof., 1968-71, assoc. prof., 1971-76, prof., 1976—, William R. Shepherd prof. history, 1995—, chmn. history dept., 1988-94. Mem. adv. council Am. acad. in Rome, 1976—, resident, 1978, 82; dir. NEH summer seminars, 1979, 81; mem. Inst. Advanced Study, Princeton, N.J., 1970-71, 78; Gray lectr. Cambridge U., 1998. Author: Rome in Etruria and Umbria, 1971, War and Imperialism in Republican Rome, 1979, Ancient Literacy, 1989, Restraining Rage: The Ideology of Anger-Control in Classic Antiquity, 2002 (James Henry Breasted prize Am. Hist. Assn.); editor: (series) Columbia Studies in the Classical Tradition, 1976—, The Imperialism of Mid-Republican Rome, 1984—, The Inscribed Economy, 1993—, The Transformations of Urbs Roma in Late Antiquity, 1999—. Fellow, NEH, 1978, Guggenheim Found., 1982—83, Nat. Humanities Ctr., 1998, vis. fellow, All Souls Coll., Oxford U., Eng., 1983, St. John's Coll., Oxford U., 2002. Fellow AAAS, Soc. Antiquaries (London), Finnish Soc. Scis.; mem. Academia Europaea (fgn.), Archaeol. Inst. Am., Am. Philol. Assn., Am. Hist. Assn., Assn. Ancient Historians, Century Assn. Office: Columbia U 624 Fayerweather Hall New York NY 10027 E-mail: wvh1@columbia.edu.

HARRIS, WILLIAM WOLPERT, b. St. Paul, Mar. 11, 1940; s. Irving Brooks and Rosetta (Wolpert) H.; m. Robie Heilbrun, 1968; 2 children. BA, Wesleyan U., 1961; PhD, MIT, 1977. Exec. Conley Electronics, 1961-63; exec. v.p. G. Barr Co., div. Pittway Corp., 1963-66; asst. to pres. North Advt., Inc., 1966; dir. Janus Films, Inc., 1966-77; asst. to dir. Fordham U. Ctr. for Communications, 1967-68. Founder, exec. dir. Pub. Interest Communication Svcs., Inc., 1976-88; instr. urban media MIT, 1977; lectr. urban media Boston U. Met. Coll., 1974, 75, 78; adj. assoc. prof. media and communications policy Tufts U., 1981-82; vis. prof. sociology Wesleyan U., 1993; vis. prof. Brandeis U., 1997-98; sr. fellow Tufts U. Coll. Citizenship and Pub. Svc., 2000—; founder, treas. KIDSPAC, 1981—; founder, chmn. Children's Rsch. and Edn. Inst., Inc., 1984—; mem. Presdl. Mission on AIDS to Africa, 1999. Ind. producer documentaries; contbr. articles to profl. jours. Pres. Coydog Found. Recipient Outstanding Children's Leader award Statewide Adv. Coun., Office for Children, Commonwealth of Mass., 1992, Spl. Pub. Recognition award, Mass. Psychol. Assn., 1990, Award for Disting. Contbn. to Child Advocacy, Am. Psychol. Assn., 1989, Dale Richmond award Am. Acad. Pediats., 1997, Leadership award for pub. svc. Zero to Three, 2000, Disting. Alumnus award Wesleyan U., 2001, Pub. Advocacy award Internat. Soc. for Traumatic Stress Studies, 2002; hon. DHL, Lesley Coll., 1988 Office: 80 Trowbridge St Cambridge MA 02138-3102

HARRIS, WILSON, psychiatrist, research scientist; b. Arroyo, PR, Mar. 30, 1952; widower. Grad., S.W. Sch. Hypnotherapy, La.; PhD in Law, Columbia U., 1970, MD, 1972; ThD, Am. Bapt. Sem., W.Va., 1974. Co-dir., rsch. scientist, psychiatrist, tchr. US Indsl. Rsch. Labs., Washington, 1972-78, 85—, legal cons., 1972-78, 85—; dir. World Industries Internat. Rsch. Facilities, Washington, 1982-90, legal cons., 1996—; pres. Nat. Cons. Network, Sacramento, 1993—. Host Do It With Dr. Harris, TV and radio program, 1985—, DownTowners (variety show); staff Carolina Christian U., Linwood, NC; prodr. Liberty Christian Records, 1999—. Prodr. Open Forum, 1980-82; prodr. (mus. TV programs) Heaven's Paradise, 1994-96, Living Free, 1998, (TV/radio prodn.) The Coming Hour, 1999—, (comedy series) Night Vision, 1998-2001. Dir., founder Haven Home for Children, dir. childrens devel. programs; overseer United Full Gospel Ministries and Ch., Calif., state overseer, bishop; founder, dir. Children's Consortium Network for Rights in Am., 1988—; developer Shepherds House I Learn Inst. for Abused Children, Calif., 1996—; bishop Ch. of God in Christ, Emmanuelle Temple Ch. of God in Christ, SE Jurisdiction, Calif., 1978—. Recipient Charles Neville Humanitarian award, 1979, 84, 89, Piedmont Humanitarian award, 1985, 90, Nat. Journalist award Owens Sci. Acad. Collegiate Assn., 1995, Amoco Humanitarian award, 2001. Mem. ASCAP, Am. Guild Hypnotherapists, Am. Assn. Nutritional Counselors Therapists, Internat. Assn. Christian Pastoral Counselors, Am. Guild Variety Artists, Investigators, Reporters, Editors Assn., Am. Fedn. Fed. Investigators Reporters, Am. Soc. Rsch. Scientists, NC Assn. Christian Counselors Therapists (diplomate), Nat. Chaplains Assn. (juvenile officer). Democrat. Avocations: art, archeology, watersports, inventing, karate (7th degree black belt tirakuando karate). Office: Nat Cons Network PO Box 340792 Sacramento CA 95834-0792

HARRIS-JONES, YVONNE, national trainer, human resources consultant; b. West Palm Beach, Fla., Sept. 15; d. Albert Thomas Simpson and Mary (Lightfoot) Thomas Simpson. BA, CCNY, 1970; MA, New Sch. Social Rsch., N.Y.C., 1977. Tng. specialist N.Y. Life Inst. Co., N.Y.C., 1970-72; sr. tng. specialist Fed. Res. Bank N.Y., N.Y.C., 1972-76; mng. dir. employee rels. Am. Stock Exch., N.Y.C., 1976-96. Mem. adv. bd. Career Opportunities in the Acctg. Profession, chair, 1993-95. Mem. Nat. Assn. Negro Bus. and Profl. Women's Clubs, Inc. (gov. N.E. Dist., Corp. award 1985, officer), Women's Ctr. Edn. and Career Advancement (adv. bd.), Soc. Human Resource Mgmt. (bd. dirs. 1991-94), Coalition 100 Black Women, Zeta Delta Phi. Avocations: reading, jogging, tennis, travel. Office: Yvonne Harris-Jones Enterprises PO Box 20 Mohegan Lake NY 10547-0020

HARRIS-LOPEZ, TRUDIER, language educator, researcher, consultant, writer; b. Mantua, Ala., Feb. 27, 1948; d. Terrell Harris Sr. and Unareed (Burton) Harris; m. Hunnell James Lopez. BA, Stillman Coll., 1969; MA, Ohio State U., 1972, PhD, 1973. Tchg. asst. Ohio State U., Columbus, 1970—73; asst. prof. English, Coll. William and Mary, Williamsburg, Va., 1973—79; assoc. prof. English, U. N.C., Chapel Hill, 1979—84, prof. English, 1984—88, J. Carlyle Sitterson prof. English, 1988—93, 1996—; Augustus Baldwin Longstreet prof. Am. lit. Emory U., Atlanta, 1993—96. William Grant Cooper vis. dist. prof. Eng. U. Ark., Little Rock, 1987; vis. dist. prof. Ohio State U., 1988; mem. com. Lillian Smith Awards, 1983—84, 1994—95; resident Rockfeller Study and Conf. Ctr., Bellagio, Italy, 1994. Mem. editl. bd.: Melus, 1980—82, Black Am. Lit. Forum, 1982—86, Jour. Am. Folklore, 1995—2000, S. Atlantic Rev., 1997—2000, contbg. editor: Callaloo: A Black South Jour. of Arts and Letters, 1982—85; editor (book rev.): Callaloo, 1984—85; fiction book rev.:, 2000—01, mem. adv. bd.: Black Periodical Lit. Project, 1990—, Dictionary of Literary Biography, 1993—; author: From Mammies to Militants: Domestics in Black American Literature, 1982, Exorcising Blackness: Historical and Literary Lynching and Burning Rituals, 1984, Black Women in the Fiction of James Baldwin, 1985, Fiction and Folklore: The Novels of Toni Morrison, 1991, The Power of the Porch: The Storyteller's Craft in Zora Neale Hurston, Gloria Naylor and Randall Kenan, 1996, Saints, Sinners, Saviors: Strong Black Women in African American Literature, 2001, South of Tradition: Essays on African American Literature, 2002, Summer Snow: Reflections from a Black Daughter of the South, 2003; co-editor: Afro-American Fiction Writers After 1955, 1984, Afro-American Writers After 1955: Dramatists and Prose Writers, 1985, Afro-American Poets After 1955, 1985, The Oxford Companion to Women's Writing in the United States, 1995, The Oxford Companion to African American Literature, 1997, Call and Response: The Riverside Anthology of the African American Literary Tradition, 1998, The Literature of the American South: A Norton Anthology, 1998, The Concise Oxford Companion to African American Literature, 2001; editor: Afro-American Writers Before the Harlem Renaissance, 1986, Afro-American Writers Before the Harlem Renaissance to 1940, 1987, Afro-American Writers, 1940-1955, 1988, Selected Works of Ida B. Wells-Barnett, 1991, New Essays on Baldwin's Go Tell It on the Mountain, 1996. Mentor Blue Ribbon Mentor/Adv. Program Chapel Hill/Carrboro Sch. Sys., 1998—. Recipient Dist. Alumni award, Ohio State U., 1994, Brown-Hudson Folklore award, N.C. Folklore Soc., 1997, Bill Hogarth AIDS Svc. award, Triangle AIDS Interfaith Network, 1998, Eugene Current-Garcia award, Ala. Dist. Literary Scholar, 2002; fellow, Bunting Inst., 1981—83, Ford Found. and Nat. Rsch. Coun., 1982—83, Ctr. Advanced Study in Behavioral Sci., 1989—90, Nat. Humanities Ctr., 1996—97, Inst. Arts and Humanities, 2002, U. N.C., 2002; Humanities fellow, NEH, 1988—89. Mem.: S.E. Women's Studies Assn., Am. Lit. Assn., Zora Neale Hurston Soc., Toni Morrison Soc., Richard Wright Cir., Langston Hughes Soc., Coll. Lang. Assn. (v.p. 1980—81, creative scholarship award 1987), S. Atlantic Modern Lang. Assn. (tchg. award 1987), Am. Folklore Soc., Modern Lang. Assn. (exec. com. divsn. black Am. lit. and culture 1984—89, com. lit. and lang. of Am. 1994—96, del. assembly 1994—96, elections com. 2002—03), George Moses Horton Soc. Study African Am. Poetry (founder, pres. 1996—), St. George Tucker Soc. (exec. coun. 1995—), Zeta Phi Beta. Avocations: travel, bicycling, walking, tennis, sports. Office: Univ NC Chapel Hill Dept English CB #3520 Greenlaw Chapel Hill NC 27599-3520

HARRIS-OLAYINKA, VERDA (LORRAINE HARRIS-OLAYINKA), health agency administrator, cultural consultant; b. Bklyn., Jan. 19, 1949; d. Warren Linwood and Mattie (Noonan) Harris; m. Ade Olayinka, July 16, 1988; children: Khalebo Harris, Khalim Harris. BA, Bklyn. Coll., 1975; M of Profl. Studies, Cornell U., 1985. Coord., supr. FAMUS Artists-St. Petersburg (Fla.) Arts Comsn., 1977-78; project dir. NAACP-APETS, St. Petersburg, 1978-79; intake coord. Vocat. Found., Inc., N.Y.C., 1979-80; job developer Westside Cluster Ctrs. and Settlements, Inc., N.Y.C., 1980-82; instr. continuing edn. York Coll., Jamaica, N.Y., 1984-86; project dir. Paul Robeson Theatre, Bklyn., 1987; program dir. Latimer-Woods Econ. Devel. Assn., Bklyn., 1987-89; cultural cons. Rsch. and Devel., Bklyn., 1989—; rsch. coord. East Fulton Street Group, Bklyn., 1991-92; project coord. HEALTH WATCH Info. and Promotion Svcs., Inc., Bklyn., 1992—96; city rsch. scientist III N.Y.C. Dept. Pub. Health, 1996—2001, pres., dir. office correction AIDS prevention, 2001—. Bd. dirs. 40 Greene Avenue Cultural Ctr., Inc., Bklyn., 1988-90, East Fulton Street Group, 1991-97; facilitator Nat. Conf. Artists, N.Y.C., 1987, Ednl. Summit: Linking Culture and Edn., N.Y.C., 1992. Author: (booklet) African American Studies for the Adult Basic Reader, 1986; (book) Advancing the Mission of Education, 1992, AIDS & African-Americans: It's Time for Action, 1996, Internat. Jour. Africana Studies, 2000. Grantee CUNY/Mcpl. Assistance Corp./Adult Edn. Act literacy project. Avocations: classical piano, blues/jazz bassoon, traditional african flutes, expounding african culture and the arts. Home: 400 Marion St Brooklyn NY 11233-2716

HARRISON, ALONZO, construction company executive; b. Forrest City, Ark., Aug. 16, 1952; s. Walter James and Doris Nell (Burnett) H.; children: Aliah T., Alona A. BA, Washburn U., 1974; postgrad., Harvard U., 1977; MPA, Kans. U., 1978; postgrad., U. Pa., 1980; grad. minority bus. exec. program, Dartmouth Coll., 1995; postgrad., Ga. Tech. U., 1992, Tex. A&M U., 1996. Sys. engr. IBM, Topeka, Kans., 1974-75; pub. svc. employment mgr. Dept. Labor Svcs., Topeka, 1975-79; mgmt. coord. The Menninger Found., Topeka, 1979-84; pres., CEO H.D.B. Constrn., Inc., Topeka, 1984—. Fin. seminars instr.; mgmt., investment and tax cons; mem. adv. com. Gen. Motors Corp. Fairfax Constrn. Project, Kansas City, Kans., 1984-86; chmn. region regulatory fairness Bd. U.S. Small Bus. Adminstrn. Contbr. articles to profl. jours. Fin. advisor Topeka Alcoholic Info. Ctr., 1977, White House Conf. Small Bus., 1995; mgr. Women's Slow Pitch Softball, 1974-78; sponsor Girls AAU Basketball, 1977-79; mem. E. Topeka Neighborhood Improvement Assn., 1981-82, East Topeka Cmty. Devel. Bd., Shawnee County Cmty. Devel. Corp.; mem. adv. com. Kans. Dept. Transp., 1985-86; youth counselor Upward Bound Program, 1970-74; minority committeeman Dem. Party, 1979-82; mem. Cmty. Housing Resource Adv. Coun., Cmty. Resource Coun. Bank IV of Kans., 1993—, WIBW TV Adv. Coun., 1989-93; exec. bd. dirs. Go-Topeka, 1999—. Recipient Cert. of Achievement, Harvard U., 1977, Outstanding Minority Bus. in Kans., award, 1987; named Outstanding Contractor, 1987, 89-91, Gov.'s Martin Luther King, Jr. Man of Yr., Kans., 1993, K.C. Small Bus. Person of Yr., SBA, 1998; named African Am. Entrepreneur of Yr., 2003; inductee W.U. Athletic Hall of Fame, 2001. Mem. Assn. Disadvantaged Bus. Enterprises (sec., treas.), Omega Psi Phi (pres.). Baptist.

HARRISON, ALVIN, Olympic athlete; b. Orlando, Fla., Jan. 20, 1974; 2 children. Student, Hartnell Coll. Winner Gold Medal 4X400 meter relay U.S.A. Track and Field Team, Sydney, 2000. Owner Arrowhead Entertainment. Author (with twin brother Calvin): Go to Your Destiny, 2000. Office: USA Track and Field One RCA Dome Ste 140 Indianapolis IN 46225

HARRISON, ANGELA EVE, manufacturing executive; b. Little Rock, Apr. 9, 1967; d. Stephen E. and Donie E. (Brown) H.; m. Petey King, Sept. 19, 1998; children: Haven Harrison King, Ashton Harrison King. BA in Psychology, U. Ark., 1989. Clin. specialist Nutri-Sys., Little Rock, 1990-91; sec., trea. Welsco, Inc., Maumelle, Ark., 1991-94, pres., CEO, 1994—. Co-chairperson Humane Soc., Pulaski County, Ark., 1996-98. Recipient Ark. Bus. Exec. Yr. Ark. Bus., 1997, named Top 100 Women Ark., 1996, 97, 98, 99, Top 500 Women Owned Cos. Working Women Mag., 1998, 99, 2000, 2001. Mem.: Internat. Oxygen Mfg. Assn. (bd. dirs. 1996—2000), Nat. Welding Supply Assn. (regional chmn. 1996—2000), Nat. Assn. Women Bus. Owners (Woman Bus. Owner of Yr., Ark. chpt. 1998), Young Pres.'s Assn. Avocation: golf. Office: Welsco Inc 9006 Crystal Hill Rd North Little Rock AR 72113-6693 E-mail: mail@welsco.com.

HARRISON, BENJAMIN LESLIE, retired army officer; b. Trumann, Ark., July 23, 1928; s. Benjamin Leslie and Ruth Venetta (Blackshare) H.; m. Carolyn Wright Algee, Sept. 29, 1951; children: Benjamin Leslie, III, Laura Louise. BA, U. Miss., 1951; MA, U. Mo., Kansas City, 1963; MBA, Auburn U., 1969; grad., Advanced Mgmt. Program, Harvard U., 1971. Enlisted U.S. Army, 1946, commd. 2d lt., 1951, advanced through grades to maj. gen., 1977; served as troop comdr. and staff officer, various locations, 1951-73; dep. comdt. U.S. Army Command and Gen. Staff Coll., Ft. Leavenworth, Kans., 1973-76; dep. comdg. gen. U.S. Army Aviation Center and Ft. Rucker, Ala., 1976-77; dir. rev. officers edn. and tng. U.S. Army, Washington, 1977-78; comdg. gen. U.S. Army Adminstrn. Center and Ft. Benjamin Harrison, Ind., 1978-79; ret., 1979. Decorated D.S.M., Silver Star with oak leaf cluster; named to U. Miss. ROTC Hall of Fame, 1992, U.S. Army Aviation Hall of Fame, 1992. Home: 221 E 21st Ave Belton TX 76513-2017 *My philosophy of life: Work and study as though you are going to live forever; enjoy life as though you are going to die tomorrow.*

HARRISON, BETTINA HALL, retired biology educator; b. Foxboro, Mass. d. Malcolm Bridges and Rita Louise (Busiere) Hall; m. John W. Harrison, July 12, 1941 (dec.); children: John W., Deborah, Christine. BS, U. Mass., 1939; AM, Radcliffe Coll., 1940; PhD, Boston U., 1968. Faculty Lasell Jr. Coll., Auburndale, Mass., 1940-41, 52-56, Maine Mills Lab., 1941-43, 49-51; with Cen. Main Hosp., 1943-45; faculty biology U. Mass., Boston, 1965—96; ret., 1996. Contbr. Life corporator Boston Mus. Sci. Mem.: AAAS, N.Y. Acad. Sci., New Eng. Soc. Electron Microscopy (pres. 1963—64). Home: 299 Cambridge St Winchester MA 01890-

HARRISON, BROOKS TALTON, law firm official; b. Pasadena, Tex., Sept. 5, 1971; s. Ben Talton and Suzanne Marie (Brannon) H. BS in Polit. Sci., U. Houston, 1999. Environmentalist Environomentalist, Inc., Pasadena, 1994-96; client coord. Foster and Sear, LLP, Pasadena, 1996-2000; adminstr. Internat. Union Oper. Engrs. 347, Texas City, Tex., 2000-01; exec. adminstr. Harrison and Assocs., Pasadena, 2001—. Dir. BTH Consulting, Deer Park, Tex., 1996—. Writer/cons. Dem. Party of Tex., 1993—. Mem. Harris County Labor Coun. (del.), Galveston County Labor Coun. (del.). Judaism. Avocations: fast pitch softball, reading, volunteering. Home: 1619 Maywood Pasadena TX 77503 E-mail: brooksharrison@hotmail.com.

HARRISON, CALVIN, Olympic athlete; b. Orlando, Fla., Jan. 20, 1974; Student, Hartnell Coll. Winner Gold Medal 4x400 meter relay U.S.A. Track and Field Team, Sydney, 2000; USA jr. champion, 1993; Pan Am. jr. champion, 1993; USA outdoor championships 400 m runner up. Author (with twin brother Alvin): Go To Your Destiny, 2000. Office: USA Track and Field One RCA Dome Ste 140 Indianapolis IN 46225

HARRISON, CAROL L. music educator; b. Topeka, Kans., Feb. 28, 1941; d. Myrl Charles Moore and Grace Elaine Jenks; m. Richard Martin Moore, Sept. 1, 1963 (div. Apr. 1984); children: Eric Christian Moore, Kristin T. Moore; m. James Bentley Harrison, June 29, 1984; 1 child, Aaron Lynn. MusB with highest distinction, U. Kans., 1963; MA, U. Iowa, 1969. Cert. libr., K-12 instrumental music and vocal tchr., learning disabilities music tchr., mentally handicapped and behavior disordered tchr. Tchr. Newport News Pub. Schs., Va., 1963—65; pvt. violin/piano tchr. Iowa City, 1966—69; Suzuki specialist Klamath Falls, Oreg., 1970—84; string specialist Klamath County Schs., Klamath Falls, 1977—81; orch. spl. edn. tchr. S.W. Mo. Pub. Schs., 1984—2003; string instr. S.W. Bapt. U., Bolivar, Mo., 1984—; mem. 1st violin sect. springfield Symphony, Mo., 1984—; h.s. transition tchr. Marionville R-9 Sch., Mo., 2000—. Mem. 1st violin sect. Ft. Smith Symphony, Ark., 1999—, North Ark. Symphony, Fayetteville, 1999—, Springfield Regional Opera, Mo., 1986—, Little Theater, Springfield, 2003; violinist Joyful Sounds, Springfield, 1995—; recording and backup instrumentalist Branson Artists, 1990—; violinist S.W. Bapt. U. Faculty Trio, 1995—. Mem. Klamath Arts Coun., 1977—80; founder Klamath Youth Symphony, 1976; mem. Britt Festival Orch., Jacksonville, Oreg., 1976—83; bd. dirs. Cmty. Concert, Klamath Falls, 1977—80, Bolivar, 1984—86. Mem.: Learning disabilities Assn. of Am., Sigma Alpha Iota, Pi Kappa Lambda. Home: HC 77 Box 783 Pittsburg MO 65724 Office: Southwest Baptist Univ Music Dept 1600 University Dr Bolivar MO 65613

HARRISON, CHARLES MAURICE, lawyer, former communications company executive; b. Anderson, SC, Aug. 30, 1927; s. Emmitte Smallwood and Jessie Maysel (Hawkins) H.; m. Lorna Jean Tomalty, June 27, 1970; children: Suzanne Elizabeth, Linda Jean. AB, Marshall U., 1949; JD, W.Va. U., 1952. Bar: W.Va. 1952, D.C. 1958, N.Y. 1965, N.J. 1972. Legal asst. W.Va. Dept. Ins., Charleston, 1952-54; hearing examiner Pub. Svc. Commn., Charleston, 1954-57; atty. Chesapeake and Potomac Tel. Co., Washington and Charleston, 1957-64, Western Electric Co., N.Y.C., 1964-69; gen. atty., sec., treas. Bellcomm, Inc., Washington, 1969-71; asst. gen. counsel, asst. sec. Bell Tel. Labs., Murray Hill, N.J., 1971-75, gen. atty., sec., 1975-76, sec., gen. counsel corp. matters, 1976-84; asst. sec., asst. gen. counsel AT&T Bell Labs, 1985-87; gen. atty. AT&T, Berkeley Heights, N.J., 1987-89; of counsel Ventantonio & Wildenhain, Warren, NJ. Bd. dirs. Somerset County C. of C. (chmn. 1990-92). Trustee Family Counseling Svcs. Somerset County, N.J., 1976-94, pres., 1978-81; chmn. R&D Coun. N.J., 1985-87, Bridgewater (N.J.) Commn. Substance Abuse, 1986-89, Bridgewater Mcpl. Facilities Commn., 1988-89, Bridgewater Twp. Alliance Com. on Alcoholism, 1989-99; bd. dirs. Martin Luther King Youth Ctr., 1984-90, Somerset Alliance for Future, 1992, N.J. affiliate Am. Heart Assn., 1991-94, Somerset County Coalition on Affordable Housing, 1995—; bd. dirs., pres. Somerset Treatment Svcs., 1992-99, bd. dirs., 2002--; mem. Bridgewater-Raritan Youth Svcs. Commn., chmn., 1989-90; mem. Bridgewater Planning Bd., 1989-94, chmn., 1992-94; mgmt. com. Ridewise Traffic Mgmt. Assn., 1992-96; mem. Somerset County Local Adv. Com. on Alcohol and Drug Abuse, 1992-99, Bridgewater Twp. Operation (police-pub.) Cooperation, 1992—, 200 Club of Somerset County, 1990—; trustee Henderson Meml. Scholarship Fund, 1993-99; mem. Twp. Coun., 1994-2001, con. pres., 1996, 2000; mem. Bridgewater Zoning Bd. of Adjustment, 2002--. With AC, U.S. Army, 1945-46, W.Va. Air N.G., 1955-57, UsAFR, 1955-62. Named Somerset County Citizen of Yr., 1996. Mem. Rotary (pres. Somerville 2000—), Somerville Elks, Am. Legion. Republican. *Regardless of profession, career, occupation, or trade, success in life can only be achieved if a significant part of one's effort includes the gift of one's personal talent, energy, and time to his or her community. In this part of one's life, financial reward, public recognition, or even results, do not count as much as dedication and sincerity, but the opportunities for creativity and personal satisfaction are enormous.*

HARRISON, CHARLES WAGNER, JR., applied physicist; s. Charles Wagner and Etta Earl (Smith) H.; m. Fern F. Perry, Dec. 28, 1940; children: Martha R., Charlotte J. Student, U.S. Naval Acad. Prep. Sch., 1933-34, U.S. Coast Guard Acad., 1934-36; BS in Engring., U. Va., 1939, EE, 1940; SM, Harvard U., 1942, M of Engring., 1952, PhD in Applied Physics, 1954; postgrad., MIT, 1942, 52. Registered profl. engr., Va. Engr. Sta. WCHV, Charlottesville, Va., 1937-40; commd. ensign U.S. Navy, 1939, advanced through grades to comdr., 1948; research staff Bur. Ships, 1939-41, asst. dir. electronics design and devel. div., 1948-50; research staff U.S. Naval Research Lab., 1944-45, dir.'s staff, 1950-51; liaison officer Evans Signal Lab., 1945-46; electronics officer Phila. Naval Shipyard, 1946-48; mem. USN Operational Devel. Force Staff, 1953-55; staff Comdg. Gen. Armed Forces Spl. Weapons project, 1955-57; ret. U.S. Navy, 1957; cons. electromagnetics Sandia Nat. Lab., Albuquerque, 1957-73. Instr. U. Va., 1939-40; lectr. Harvard U., 1942-43, Princeton U., 1943-44; vis. prof. Christian Heritage Coll., El Cajon, Calif., 1976. Author: (with R.W.P. King) Antennas and Waves: A Modern Approach, 1969; contbr. numerous articles to profl. jours. Fellow IEEE (Electronics Achievement award 1966, best paper award electromagnetic compatibility group 1972); mem. Internat. Union Radio Sci. (commn. B), Electromagnetics Acad., Famous Families Va., Sigma Xi. Home: 2808 Alcazar St NE Albuquerque NM 87110-3516 *Research is like saving - if postponed until needed, it is too late to start. One should keep expanding his mind.*

HARRISON, CHRISTINE DELANE, company executive; b. Dearborn, Mich., July 22, 1947; d. Walter Frederick and Marguerite Elaine (Champagne) Hancock; m. Charles Richard Bashawaty, Aug. 31, 1968 (div. 1972); 1 child, Brett Charles; m. Andrew David Harrison, June 14, 1980; 1 child, Andrew David II. BS, Eastern Mich. U., 1969. Cert. early elem. tchr., Mich. Tchr. Westland Schs., Mich., 1969-71, Dept. Army, Ansbach, Germany, 1971-72; prin. sec. chemistry dept. U. Mich., Ann Arbor, 1973-78; word processing mgr. Great Copy Co., Ann Arbor, 1978-79; dir., v.p. Great Lakes Sch., Madison Heights, Mich., 1979-92; v.p. adminstrv. asst. Good Herbs, Inc., Troy, Mich., 1992—. Editor: Thorne's Guide to Herbal Extracts, 1992, A Practical Guide to Herbal Extracts, 1995-2002; mem. editl. bd. Herbal Extracts, 1984, Bull. Thermodynamics and Thermochemistry, 1973-78. Bd. dirs. Perry Nursery Sch., Ann Arbor, 1976-77. Recipient Prodn. award and Dedication award Los Feliz Apple Sch. Mem. Nat. Trust for Hist. Preservation, Greenpeace, Sierra Club. Avocations: reading, bicycling, aerobics, sailing. Office: Good Herbs Inc 1465 Combermere Dr Troy MI 48083-2745

HARRISON, CLIFFORD, chef, small business owner; Grad., Calif. Culinary Inst., San Francisco, 1987; postgrad, U. Hawaii. Chef, co-owner Bacchanalia, Atlanta, Float Away Cafe, Ga.; chef with Judy Rogers Zuni Cafe, San Francisco; chef with Bob Kinkead 21 Federal, Nantucket Island, Mass.; chef Bimini Twist, NY, La Petite Ferme, NY, Grolier Club, NY. Elected mem. James Beard Found. Office: 1198 Howell Mill Rd Atlanta GA 30301

HARRISON, CLIFFORD JOY, JR., banker; b. Nashville, Feb. 21, 1925; s. Clifford Joy and Rosa Lee (Bennett) H.; m. Saralu Fondren, May 3, 1957; children: Julia Lee, Clifford Joy III, John Fondren. BA, Vanderbilt U., 1949; postgrad., Law Sch., 1949-50, Nashville Sch. Law, 1950-53; LLB, Stonier Grad. Sch. Banking, Rutgers, 1963; student, Advanced Mgmt. Program, Harvard U., 1975. With 3d Nat. Bank, Nashville, 1950-88, ret. vice chmn. in charge trust divsn., retail divsn. and mktg., 1988. Past pres. Estate Planning Coun.; past pres. trust divns. Tenn. Bankers Assn. Past pres. YMCA Found. Bd.; past chmn. bd. trustees Tenn. Nature Conservacy. 1st lt. USAAF, 1943-46. Decorated Air medal with oak leaf cluster. Mem. Exch. Club, City Club (past pres.), Belle Meade Country Club, Beta Theta Pi, Phi Alpha Delta. Episcopalian. Home: 102 Abbottsford Nashville TN 37215-2437 E-mail: cjharrison@mindspring.com.

HARRISON, DAVID GEORGE, lawyer; b. Albany, Oreg., Apr. 6, 1945; s. Russell Benjamin and Altha Edna (Green) H.; m. Katherine Scott Crockett, Jan. 2, 1971; children— Elizabeth, Scott. B.S., Oreg. State U., 1967; M.B.A., Am. U., 1973; J.D., U. Oreg., 1973. Bar: Oreg. 1973, D.C. 1974, Tenn. 1975, Va. 1978, U.S. Dist. Ct. (ea. dist.) Tenn. 1975, U.S. Dist. Ct. (we. dist.) Va. 1978, U.S. Dist. Ct. (ea. dist.) Va. 1982, U.S. Ct. Appeals (4th cir.) 1978. Legal counsel, sec. Tenn. Forging Steel Corp., Harriman, Tenn., 1974-77; atty. Martin, Hopkins & Lemon, Roanoke, Va., 1977-81, Wetherington & Melchionna, Roanoke, 1981— . Bd. dirs. Family Service of Roanoke Valley, 1982-84, mem. exec. com., 1983-84. Served with U.S. Army, 1968-71. Mem. ABA (mem. antitrust and labor relations com. of labor and employment law sect. 1978), Va. State Bar, Va. Bar Assn., Roanoke Bar Assn., D.C. Bar, Oreg. State Bar. Presbyterian. Club: Kiwanis. Office: Weatherington & Melchionna 1100 United Va Bank Bldg Roanoke VA 24011

HARRISON, DAVID MICHAEL, finance educator, consultant; b. Ottawa, Kans., Oct. 26, 1970; s. C. Michael and Sharon Ann (Knopp) Harrison; m. Amy Marie Rosenbaum, July 18, 1992; children: Aaron Michael, Katarina Rose. B in Bus. Adminstrn., Pittsburg State U., Kans., 1992; MBA, Wichita State U., 1994, PhD, U. Fla., 1998. Fin. prof. U. Vt., Burlington, 1998—. Rschr. U.S. Dept. Housing & Urban Develop., Washington, 1997—2000, Fed. Deposit Ins. Corp., Washington, 1998—2000; cons. Dwight Asset Mgmt., Burlington, 2001. Contbr. articles. Mem.: Fin. Mgmt. Assn., Am. Real Estate Soc. (Best Paper in Real Estate Fin. award 2001, Best Paper in Real Estate Valuation awarad 2000, Best Paper in Real Estate Investment award 1999), Am. Real Estate and Urban Econ. Assn. Office: Univ Vt Sch Bus 205 Kalkin Hall Burlington VT 05405

HARRISON, DEAN THOMAS, physician assistant; b. Balt., Oct. 1, 1951; s. Adron Calvin and Mary June (Tarlton) H. AA, Exxex Cmty. Coll., Balt., 1976; BS, Johns Hopkins U., 1982; MSPA, U. Nebr., 2002. Clin. physician's asst. oncology Johns Hopkins Sch. Medicine, Balt., 1977-80; chief physician asst. bone marrow transplantation Johns Hopkins Hosp. Oncology Ctr., Balt., 1980-88; asst. dir. Creative Med. Mgmt., Columbia, Md., 1988-90; from asst. med. dir. to regional med. dir. In Phynet Med. Mgmt., Balt., 1990-2001; emergency med. physician U. Md., 1998-2001; asst. clin. prof. medicine Duke U. Sch. Medicine, Durham, N.C., 2001—; dir. MLP/Emergency Dept., asst. med. dir. observation unit Duke U. Med. Ctr., Durham, 2001—. Clin. faculty George Washington U., 1994—, Essex C.C., 1992-95, Johns Hopkins Oncology Ctr., 1979-82. Author: Graft versus Host Disease Exa Hematology, 1981, Bone Marrow Transplantation Guide, 1980; contbr. articles to profl. jours. Fellow: Am. Acad. Physician Assts., M. Acad. Physician Assts. (pres. 1997—99). Home: 506 Edburton Ct Hillsborough NC 27278 Office: Duke Univ Hosp Durham NC 27703 E-mail: deanharr@aol.com.

HARRISON, DONALD, lawyer; b. N.Y.C., Mar. 2, 1946; s. David and Arlene Beverly (Johnson) H. BA magna cum laude, Harvard U., 1967, JD magna cum laude, 1971. Bar: D.C. 1973, U.S. Ct. Internat. Trade 1975, U.S. Ct. Appeals (Fed. cir.) 1982, U.S. Supreme Ct. 1979. Law clk. to judge Francis L. Van Dusen U.S. Ct. Appeals 3d circuit, Phila., 1972-73; ptnr. Gibson, Dunn & Crutcher, 1988—. Editor Harvard Law Rev., 1969-71. Office: Gibson Dunn & Crutcher Washington Sq 1050 Connecticut Ave NW Ste 900 Washington DC 20036-5306 E-mail: dharrison@gibsondunn.com.

HARRISON, DONALD, newspaper editor; b. Phila., May 14, 1928; s. Martin and Diana (Feinstein) H.; m. Grace Wagner, Sept. 7, 1952; children— Eric Ethan, Lori Ann, Ellen Wendy. BA, U. Pa., 1949. City editor Phila. Jewish Times, 1949-51; mng. editor News of Delaware County, 1954-63; asst. city editor Phila. Bull., 1963-69, city editor, 1969-72, editorial writer, 1972-73, editor arts and culture, 1973-79, regional editor, 1979-81, asst. mng. editor, 1981-82; assoc. editor editorial pages Phila. Daily News, 1982-87, dep. editor editorial pages, 1987—2001; editor Milestones, 2001—. Lectr. journalism U. Pa., 1960 Editor: From the Letters of Robert S. Gerdy (1942-45), 1969. Served with AUS, 1951-53. Recipient Lowell Mellett award for critical evaluation of journalism, 1985 Mem. Nat. Conf. Editl. Writers (past bd. dirs.), Franklin Inn Club (past bd. dirs.), Soc. Profl. Journalists (past pres. Greater Phila. profl. chpt.). Home: 1434 Westwood Ln Wynnewood PA 19096-3839 E-mail: donharrison@att.net.

HARRISON, DONALD CAREY, university official, cardiology educator; b. Blount County, Ala., Feb. 24, 1934; s. Walter Carey and Sovola (Thompson) H.; m. Laura Jane McAnnally, July 24, 1955; children— Douglas, Elizabeth, Donna Marie. BS in Chemistry, Birmingham So. Coll., 1954; MD, U. Ala., 1958. Diplomate Am. Bd. Internal Medicine (cardiovascular disease). Intern, asst. resident Peter Bent Brigham Hosp., 1958-60; fellow in cardiology Harvard U., 1961, NIH, 1961-63; mem. faculty Stanford U. Med. Sch., 1963-86, chief div. cardiology, 1967-86, prof. medicine, 1971-86; chief cardiology Stanford U. Hosp., 1967-86, William G. Irwin prof. cardiology, 1972-86; sr. v.p., provost for health affairs U Cin. Med. Ctr., 1986—2003; sr. v.p., provost for health affairs, emeritus U. Cin. Med. Ctr.; prof. medicine, cardiology U. Cin. Coll. Medicine; CEO U. Cin. Med. Ctr., 1987—2003. Cons. to local hosps., industry and govt.; bd. dirs. Novoste, Inc., Med. Edn. and Consultation, AtriCure Med., Venturi, LLP., Uterine Muscle Dysfunction, Inc., Kendle Industries, Emerging Concepts Inc., Am. Heart Assn., U. Cin. Physicians. Mem. editorial bd. Brit. Jour. Clin. Practice, 1993—; mem. editorial bd. Drugs, 1980—, Am. Jour. Cardiology, 1984—, Health, 1988—, Inpharma, 19926; contbr. articles to med. jours., chpts. to books. Served with USPHS, 1961-63. Fellow Interam. Soc. Cardiology (v.p. 1980-86), Am. Coll. Cardiology (mem. chmn., v.p. 1972-73, sec. 1969-70, trustee 1972-78), Am. Heart Assn. (fellow coun. circulation, clin. cardiology and basic sci., chmn. program com. 1972-76, nat. chmn. publs. com. 1976-81, pres.-elect 1980-81, pres. 1982-83); mem. Am. Soc. Clin. Investigation, Am. Fedn. Clin. Rsch., Am. Assn. Physicians, ACP, Assn. U. Cardiologists, Am. Clin. and Climatol Assn., Brit. Cardiac Soc., Acad. Medicine Cin., Assn. Acad. Health Ctrs. (past chmn.). Home: 9250 Old Indian Hill Rd Cincinnati OH 45243-3438 Office: U Cin Med Ctr ML 0669 G11 Wherry Hall Cincinnati OH 45267-0669 Fax: 513-558-6399. E-mail: don.harrison@uc.edu.

HARRISON, EARL DAVID, lawyer, real estate executive; b. Bryn Mawr, Pa., Aug. 25, 1932; divorced; 1 child, H. Jason. BA, Harvard U., 1954; JD, U. Pa., 1960. Bar: D.C. 1960. Pvt. practice, Washington; exec. v.p. Washington Real Estate Corp., Washington, 1986-94; pres. EDH Assocs., Inc., 1994—. Capt. U.S. Army, 1954-57. Decorated Order of Rio Branco (Brazil); Order of Merit (Italy). Mem.: ABA, Coun. Internat. Restaurant Real Estate Brokers Ltd. (v.p., gen. coun.), Met. Washington Restaurant Assn., Nat. Restaurant Assn., Nat. Assn. Realtors, Greater Washington Comml. Assn. Realtors, Washington Assn. Realtors, D.C. Bar Assn., Internat. Coun. Shopping Ctrs., U. Pa. Club, Nat. Press Club, Harvard Club. Office: 1077 30th St NW Ste 706 Washington DC 20007-3834 E-mail: david@edhlaw.com.

HARRISON, EARL GRANT, JR., educational administrator; b. Media, Pa., Oct. 10, 1932; s. Earl Grant and Carol Rogers (Sensenig) H.; m. Jean Spencer Young, July 6, 1957; children: Colin Young, Dana How. BA, Haverford Coll., 1954, LLD (hon.), 1991; BDiv, Yale U., 1959; MA in Social and Philos. Founds. Edn., Columbia U., 1965. Instr. Religion and Philosophy Antioch Coll., 1956-58; dir. Coun. Religion Ind. Schs., N.Y.C., 1959-64; tchr. Bklyn. Friends Sch., 1964-65; dir. religious edn. William Penn Charter Sch., Phila., 1965-68; headmaster Westtown (Pa.) Sch., 1968-78; head of sch. Sidwell Friends Sch., Washington, 1978-98. Interim exec. dir. Friends Coun. on Edn., Phila., 2000-01; bd. mgrs. Haverford Coll., 1973-85; mem. instl. rev. bd. Nat. Eye Inst., 1987—03; trustee The Kendal Corp., 1999—. Trustee Good Hope Sch., St. Croix, 1974-80, 82-88. Mem. The Headmasters Assn. (v.p. 1986-87), Country Day Headmasters Assn. (pres. 1992-93), Assn. Ind. Schs. Greater Washington (pres. 1989-90). Democrat. Avocations: tennis, travel.

HARRISON, EDWARD ROBERT, physicist, educator, science administrator; b. London, Jan. 8, 1919; came to U.S., 1965; s. Robert and Daisy (White) H.; m. Photeni Marangas, June 23, 1945; children: John Peter, June Zoe. Student, Sir John Cass Coll., London U., 1937-40. With Atomic Energy Rsch. Establishment, Harwell, Eng., 1948-64; vis. scientist CERN, Geneva, 1959-60; prin. scientist Rutherford High Energy Lab., Harwell, 1961—65; sr. rsch. assoc. Nat. Acad. Sci., Washington, 1965-66; prof. dept. physics and astronomy U. Mass., Amherst Coll., Mt. Holyoke, Smith, Hampshire Coll., 1966-96, head five coll. astronomy depts., 1973-74. Vis. prof. Astronomy Ctr., U. Sussex, Eng., 1974, U. Va., Charlottesville, 1976; staff mem. Nat. Radio Astronomy Obs., 1976; vis. astronomer Carter Obs., N.Z., 1981; Disting. vis. scholar U. N.C., 1987, Disting. Univ. prof. physics and astronomy, 1987-96; adj. prof. U. N.Mex., 1996-98, U. Ariz., 1998—; lectr. various fgn. univs. Author: Cosmology: The Science of the Universe, 1981, Masks of the Universe, 1985, Darkness at Night: The History of a Cosmological Riddle, 1987; contbr. articles and book revs. to profl. jours. With Brit. Army, 1940-47. Named Disting. Univ. Prof. of Physics and Astronomy, U. Mass., 1986. Fellow Inst. Physics (Eng.), AAAS, Royal Astron. Soc., Am. Phys. Soc.; mem. Internat. Astron. Union, Am. Astron. Soc., Sigma Xi. Home: 7529 S Eliot Ln Tucson AZ 85747

HARRISON, ELZA STANLEY, medical association executive; b. Akron, Ohio, Apr. 10, 1938; d. Marshall Clayton and Elsie Helen Stanley; m. Ronald L. Davis, Feb. 4, 1961 (div. June 1979); children: Mark Davis, Lesley Davis; m. William Harrison II, May 29, 1989 (dec.); m. Michael Dunning, May 12, 2001. BA in English, U. Akron, 1963. Cert. assn. exec. Acting exec. dir., dir. pub. affairs, legis. rep. Med. & Chirurg. Facility, Balt., 1975-86; v.p. industry affairs Med. Mut. Liability Ins. Co., Hunt Valley, Md., 1986-87; exec. dir. Md. Dental Assn., Columbia, 1987—. Bd. dirs. Md. Found. Dentistry for Handicapped, Columbia, Dental Assn. Co., Columbia; mem. bd. visitors Nat. Mus. Dentistry, President Cir. for Oral Health Studies. Mem. Am. Soc. Assn. Execs., Am. Soc. Constituent Dental Execs., Md. Soc. Assn. Execs. (pres. 1985-86). Democrat. Episcopalian. Office: Maryland Dental Assn 6410 Dobbin Rd Columbia MD 21045-5824 E-mail: elza@msda.com.

HARRISON, ERIC JAY, construction executive, consultant; b. Pitts., Mar. 8, 1936; s. Max Clark and Helen Rigg Harrison; m. Sharon Stricker Hamburg, Sept. 1, 1962 (div. Dec. 16, 1977); children: Todd, Mark; m. Judith Lee Casteel, Sept. 22, 1984; children: Todd, David. BA, Haverford Coll., 1958; MA, Columbia U., 1961; cert., East Asian Inst., 1961, Wayne State U., 1968. Constrn. mgr. St. Marys (Pa.) Area Sch. Dist., 1991—95, CCI Constrn., Mechanicsburg, Pa., 1995—96, Slippery Rock (Pa.) Area Sch. Dist., 1996—97, City of Pitts. Sch. Dist., 1997—98, Hayes Large Architects, Altoona, Pa., 1998, NJ Cunzolo and Assocs., Bellevue, Pa., 1998—99, STV Inc., Douglassville, Pa., 1999—2003. Founder, mem. supervisory com. Citizens E. Credit Union, Pitts., 2000—; cons. St. David's Soc., Pitts., 2002—, TTI; bd. dirs. TBSI, Pitts. Exhibitions include Pitts. Opera Verbena Gala; author: (poetry) The Marginal Review, 1980. Founder Greentree Hist. Soc., Pa., Fishers of Men, Upper St. Clair, Pa., 1997. With USCG, 1961—62. Mem.: AIA, Assn. for Corp. Growth, Pitts. History and Landmarks. Republican. Presbyterian. Avocation: photography. Home and Office: 1591 Pinehurst Dr Pittsburgh PA 15241-3201 Fax: 412-392-3501.

HARRISON, FRANK, former university president; b. Dallas, Nov. 21, 1913; s. Frank and Ruby (Davison) H.; m. Elsie Claire Redfearn, June 26, 1946; children— Frank, Susan Claire, James Redfearn. BS, So. Methodist U., 1935; MS, Northwestern U., 1936, PhD, 1938; MD, U. Tex. Southwestern Med. Sch., 1956. Mem. faculty U. Tenn. med. units, Memphis, 1938-51, prof., 1946-51, chief divsn. anatomy, 1946-51; prof. anatomy U. Tex. Southwestern Med. Sch., Dallas, 1952-68, assoc. dean, 1956-68; assoc. dean grad. studies U. Tex. at Arlington, 1965-68, acting pres., 1968-69, pres., 1969-72, Health Sci. Ctr., San Antonio, 1972-85, dir. Inst. Biotech., 1985, pres. emeritus. Named Distinguished Alumnus So. Meth. U., 1971 Mem. Am. Assn. Anatomists, Am. Physiol. Soc., Tex. Philos. Soc., Biophys. Soc., IEEE, Soc. Exptl. Biology and Medicine, Phi Beta Kappa, Alpha Omega Alpha, Kappa Sigma, Alpha Kappa Kappa. Home: 4168 Valley Ridge Rd Dallas TX 75220-1924

HARRISON, FRANK J. retired bishop; b. Syracuse, N.Y., Aug. 12, 1912; Ed., Notre Dame U., St. Bernard's Sem. Ordained priest Roman Catholic Ch., 1937; apptd. titular bishop of Aquae in, Numidia; and aux. bishop of Syracuse, 1971-76; appt. bishop of, 1976; installed, 1977; retired, 1987. Roman Catholic. Office: PO Box 511 Syracuse NY 13201-0511

HARRISON, GEORGE BROOKS, research engineer, retired career officer; b. Greenville, S.C., July 30, 1940; s. William Henry and Mary Carter (Ogburn) H.; m. Pennie Maria Jenkins, Nov. 29, 1963; children: Taylor Leigh, Todd Henry, Tracy Elizabeth. BS in Pub. Policy, USAF Acad., 1962; MBA, U. Pa., 1970. Cert. flight instr. single and multi-engine instrument glider (6800 accident-free flying hours, 540 combat hours). Commd. 2d lt. USAF, 1962, advanced through grades to maj. gen., 1989; fighter pilot, forward air contr. and instr. 557th and 436th Tactical Fighter Squadron, Florida and Vietnam, 1963-69; joint exercise planner U.S. Readiness Command, MacDill AFB, Fla., 1971-74; grad. Armed Forces Staff Coll., Norfolk, Va., 1974; ops. officer 13th and 25th Tactical Fighter Squadron, Udorn, Thailand, 1974-75; comdr. 4485th Test Squadron, Eglin AFB, Fla., 1975-78; grad. Air War Coll., Montgomery, Ala., 1979; wing comdr. 479th Tactical Tng. Wing, Holloman AFB, N.Mex., 1982-86; chief joint ops. divsn. Orgn. of Joint Chiefs of Staff, Washington, 1984-86; dept. chief of staff, plans U.S. Air Forces in Europe, Ramstein AFB, Fed. Republic Germany, 1986-89; asst. chief of staff, studies and analyses Hdqrs. USAF, Washington, 1989-91; dep. chief of staff for ops. U.S. Air Forces in Europe, Ramstein AFB, 1991-92; comdr. Air Warfare Ctr., Eglin AFB, Fla., 1992-93; comdr. combined/joint task force USAF, S.W. Asia, 1993; comdr. Air Force Operational Test and Evaluation Ctr., Kirtland AFB, N.Mex., 1994-97; prin. rsch. engr., dir. rsch. ops. Ga. Tech Rsch. Inst., 1997—; mil. affairs cons. CNN, 1997—. Mem. USAF Sci. Adv. Bd., Washington, 1998—; sponsor Mil. Ops. Rsch. Soc., 1989-91; U.S. del. NATO Adv. Group on Aerospace R&D, Paris, 1989-91; lectr. to mil., tech. and civic groups, 1982-2003. Contbr. articles to mil. jours. Mem., lt. col. CAP, S.C., N.Mex. and Ga., 1978—; dist. commr. Boy Scouts Am., Fed. Republic Germany, 1986-89, coun. commr., 1991-92, exec. coun. N.M., 1995-97; exec. v.p., bd. dirs. Air Warrior Courage Found., 1998—; bd. dirs. Nat. Mus. Aviation, 1998—. Decorated D.S.M. with oak leaf cluster, D.F.C., Air medal with eleven oak leaf clusters, Legion of Merit with one oak leaf cluster, Def. Superior Svc. medal. Fellow Beta Gamma Sigma; mem. Order of Daedalians (flight capt. 1987-89, 2003), Air Force Assn., Quiet Birdmen. Baptist. Avocation: general aviation. Office: Ga Tech Rsch Inst 400 10th St CRB 225 Atlanta GA 30318-5712 E-mail: georgeharrison@gtri.gatech.edu.

HARRISON, GEORGE HARRY, III, (HANK HARRISON), publishing executive, author; b. Monterey, Calif., June 17, 1940; s. Edith Cooke; 1 child, Courtney Love. BA in Psychology, San Francisco State Univ., 1965; postgrad., Univ. London, 1978-81. Mgr. Grateful Dead (formerly Warlocks), Palo Alto, Calif., 1965-66, 70-73; founder, counselor LSD rescue founder Inst. Contemporory Studies, San Francisco, 1967; pvt. practice counselor San Francisco, 1967-78; pub., founder Arrives Press, San Francisco, 1979—. Writer-in-residence Montalvo Ctr. Arts, Saratoga, Calif., 1974; founder Media Assocs., Los Altos, Calif., 1991—; presenter, expert witness, lectr. in field; co-owner Sacramento Equestrian Ctr., Riverglades, 1998; story cons., contbg. editor NBC prodn. The Search for the Unicorn Killer, 1999; co-developer Adobe Acrobat, ANCO Labor; cons. in field; lectr. in field. Author: The Dead Trilogy, 1972-97, Quest for Flight, 1975, 2nd edit., 1995, The Cauldron and the Grail, 1992, The Stones of Ancient Ireland, 1996, Ace of Cups: The Grail in Tarot, 1998, The Beekeeper, 2001, The Grail in the Troubadour World, 2003, Crown of Stars, 2003; contbr. VSD (Paris), San Francisco Oracle, The Berkeley Barb, The Ga. Straight and L.A. Free Press, Dragon's Quest, True Hollywood Story: Courtney Love, 2003; editor emeritus Doctor Dobb's Jour.; tech., staff writer Info World Apple Plus Mag., radio, TV guest including Geraldo, Am. Jour., Inside Edition, Hard Copy, Maury Povitch Show, America's Most Wanted, Fox News Contribution, 1998; editor: Vancouver Mag., 1974-75, Las Vegas Sun, 1976-77, Jour. Psychedelic Drugs, 1967; contbg. editor High Times, 1996-97; prodr. (CD) Garcia: The Lost Concert, 1999; commentator Mystery of the Holy Grail Sacred Mysteries (The Learning Channel); editor: (book and CD) A Guide to Fractional and Civil War Currency, 2003. With M.C., USN, 1958-61. Rocky Mountain Writers Conf. scholar, 1968, Frances Yates scholar Warburg Inst. U. London, 1976-81. Mem. Press Club, Ind. Pub. Assn., San Francisco Press Club, Las Vegas Press Club, Sacramento Press Club, Masons. Democrat. Avocations: motorcycle repair, horse breeding, dog breeding, animal rescue. Home and Office: PO Box 46 Wilton CA 95693-0046 Office Fax: 916-687-8711. E-mail: riverglade@hotmail.com.

HARRISON, GILBERT WARNER, investment banker; b. N.Y.C., Dec. 25, 1940; s. Daniel and Trese (Warner) Harrison; m. Shelley Danien, Dec. 18, 1965; children: Edward D., Robin G. Kaplan, Nancy L. Lascher. BS, U. Pa., 1962, JD, 1965. Bar: Pa. 1968, N.Y. 1965, Conn. 1965, Fla. 1969. Practice law, N.Y.C. and Phila., 1965—71; dir., fin. officer Precision Plastics Co., Phila., 1965—71; mng. dir. Shearson Lehman Bros Inc., N.Y.C. and Phila., 1985—89; chmn. Financo, Inc., N.Y.C. and Phila., 1971—; founding ptnr. Mercantile Capital Ptnrs., LLC, N.Y.C., 2000—. Mng. ptnr. Financo Investor's Fund L.P.; gen. ptnr. Financo Investors Mgmt. Partnership L.P.; mem. undergrad. bd. The Wharton Sch., U. Pa., 1984—; bd. dirs. Am. Eagle Outfitters, Warrendale, Pa., 1996—, Fashion Inst. Tech. Ednl. Found., N.Y.C., 1995—, Peggy Guggenheim Collection, Venice, 1996—, Penn Club N.Y.C., 1995—; cons., lectr. in field. Mem.: ABA, Am. Arbitration Assn., Fla. Bar, Phila. Bar Assn., Pa. Bar Assn., Assn. Corp. Growth, Wharton Entrepreneurial Ctr., Am. Mgmt. Assn., Trump Internat. Golf Club (Fla.), Breakers Club (Fla.), Noyac Golf Club (N.Y.), Harmonie Club (N.Y.C.), Locust Club (dir., Phila.), Philmont Country Club (Huntingdon Valley, Pa., dir.). Office: Financo Inc 535 Madison Ave New York NY 10022-4212 Fax: 212-593-0309. E-mail: gharrison@financo.com.

HARRISON, GLENNON JOSEPH, economist; b. Mobile, Ala., Aug. 27, 1952; s. Edward Tyler and Elizabeth Caroline (George) Harrison; m. Mary Ann Saour, Sept. 6, 1986, children: Michael, Peter. BA, Tulane U., 1974; MA in Econs., Manchester U., Eng., 1977, PhD, 1986. Research analyst fed. research div. Libr. of Congress, Washington, 1982—86, sr. research specialist fed. research div., 1986, analyst in internat. trade and fin. Congl. Rsch. Svc., 1987—90, specialist in internat. trade and fin., 1990—99, sect. head labor and industry sect., 1997—99, specialist in industry and transp., sect. head transp. and industry analysis sect., 1999—. Author numerous reports for U.S. Congress. Active Rockville (Md.) Traffic and Transp. Commn., 1982-86, chmn., 1985-86; active Rockville Planning Commn., 1986-91, 94-95, chmn., 1990; mem. coun. City of Rockville, 1995-2001; active transp. infrastructure and svcs. steering com., Nat. League of Cities, 1998-2001, transp. infrastructure and svcs. policy com., 1996-2001; active met. devel. policy com. Met. Washington Coun. of Govts., 1996-97; mem. Nat. Capital Region Transpl Planning Bd., Washington, 1998-2001. Named one of Outstanding Young Men of Am., 1987; Doherty Found. fellow, Sao Paulo, Brazil, 1979-80. Home: 115 Upton St Rockville MD 20850-1837 Office: Congl Rsch Svc Libr Of Congress Washington DC 20540-0001

HARRISON, GORDON RAY, engineering executive, consultant, research scientist; b. Wister, Okla., Dec. 14, 1931; s. Trannie Gordon and Isah Lee (Ray) H.; m. Barbara Ann Herndon, June 22, 1957; children: William Andrew, Melissa Leigh, Lori Jeanne, Amanda Ray. BS in Physics, U. Central Ark., 1952; MS, Vanderbilt U., 1954, PhD, 1958. Sr. staff engr. and engring. mgr. Sperry Microwave, Clearwater, Fla., 1957-71; prin. research scientist to lab. dir. Engring. Expt. Sta., Ga. Inst. Tech., Atlanta, 1971-83; v.p. Electromagnetic Scis., Inc., Atlanta, 1983-91; ind. cons. tech., bus., 1991—. Contbr. chpt. to book, numerous articles to profl. jours.; patentee microwave ferrimagnetic garnets. Fellow IEEE; mem. Soc. Microwave Theory and Techniques, Magnetics Soc., Mustang Club Am., Sigma Xi. Democrat. Methodist. Office: Electromagnetic Scis Inc PO Box 7700 Norcross GA 30091-7700

HARRISON, GUY NEWELL, lawyer; b. Longview, Tex., Dec. 14, 1946; s. Guy Franklin and Margaret Louise (Newell) H.; m. Lucinda Dodson, July 5, 1969; children: Parker Trigg Harrison, Worth McKinley Harrison. BBA, So. Meth. U., 1968, JD, 1974. Bar: Tex., U.S. Dist. Ct. Tex., U.S. Supreme Ct. Ptnr. Green & Harrison, Longview, Tex., 1974—. Pres. Longview YMCA, 1976-78; bd. dirs. YMCA of the USA, 1990-91, Good Shepherd Hosp. Found., Longview, 1989-91. Sgt. U.S. Army, 1968-70, Vietnam. Recipient Lowell Linnes award YMCA of the Midwest, 1979; named Atty. of Yr. Longview Legal Secs. Mem. Gregg Bar Assn., Tex. Trial Lawyers Assn., Tex. State Bar Assn. (bd. dirs. 1995-, chmn. 1997-98, pres.-elect 2001-02, pres. 2002-03); fellow (life) Tex. Bar Found. (trustee 1998-). Home: 1901 Warwick Cir E Longview TX 75601-3134 Office: 217 Center Longview TX 75601

HARRISON, HAROLD HENRY, SR., physician, scientist, educator; b. Oak Park, Ill., Mar. 18, 1951; s. Orlow Harold and Wanda Odell (Olesczynski) H.; m. Brenda E. Naccari, 1993; children: Amelia, Margaret, Harold Henry Jr.. BS in Biochemistry with honors, U. Ill., 1972; MD, PhD, U. Ill., Chgo., 1979. Diplomate Nat. Bd. Med. Examiners, Am. Bd. Pathology. Resident in internal medicine U. Ill. Hosps., Chgo., 1979-80; resident lab. medicine Northwestern U. Hosp., Chgo., 1980-83; asst. prof. U. Chgo. Med. Sch., 1984-92; asst. dir. clin. chemistry U. Chgo. Hosps., 1984-86, dir. spl. chemistry, toxicology and molecular pathology, 1986-90, dir. protein and genetic chemistry, 1990-92, staff physician, 1984-92, United Blood Svcs., Chgo., 1981-84; dir. clin. pathology, med. dir. Phoenix Labs., 1992-97, Genetrix, Inc., Scottsdale, Ariz., 1992-97; assoc. dir. Southwest Biomed. Rsch. Inst., Scottsdale, 1992-97; med. dir. S.W. Genetics and Lab. Medicine, Phoenix, 1997—, Quest Diagnostics, Teterboro, N.J., 1998-2000, HEMEX Labs., Phoenix, 2000—. Chair workshop program Genetics Task Force Ill., Chgo., 1988; sr. clin. lectr. pathology Med. Sch., U. Ariz., Tucson, 1993—; lectr. in field. Contbr. articles to profl. publs. Adelmann Fund scholar, 1976, T. B. Sachs scholar, 1975, V. S. Yarros scholar, 1974, Edmund J. James scholar, 1969-72. Fellow Coll. Am. Pathologists (inspector 1992), Am. Soc. Clin. Pathologists; mem. Am. Coll. Med. Genetics, Am. Coll. Physician Execs., Am. Soc. Human Genetics, Am. Assn. Clin. Chemistry, Sigma Xi, Phi Eta Sigma. Achievements include discovery of XRD image process, prealbumin Chicago, serum protein polymorphism M-158, low-Z expressor phenotype, CDGS diagnosis with 2DE-immunogloblin chain microheterogeneity and clonality analysis; research in clinical and genetic applications of two-dimensional electrophoresis.

HARRISON, HENRY STARIN, real estate educator, entrepreneur; b. New Haven, June 19, 1930; s. Julius and Helen (Starin) H.; m. Minna Snyder, Apr. 16, 1960 (div. 1970); children: Julie, Eve; m. Ruth Lambert, May 30, 1976; children: Kate, H. Alex. BS in Econs., U. Pa., 1952; MA, Goddard Coll., 1974. Asst. to pres. Charlton Press, Derby, Conn., 1954-56; assoc. Harris Weissbuck Co., New Haven, 1956-57; pres. Harrison Appraisal Co., New Haven, 1958-90, H & R Ins. Agy., 1975-88, Health Care Mmgt. Co., 1964-86, The H2 Co., New Haven, 1986-95, H Squared Co., 1995—, A&A World Travel, New Haven, 1989-94; treas., v.p. Forms & Worms, Inc., 1989-97; pub. NAFFA, Inc., New Haven, 1985—. Appraisal cons. Nat. Assn. Environ. Risk Auditors, Blooming-

ton, Ind., 1989-94. Author: Houses, Houses, Houses, 1974, URAR-Illustrated Guide, 1975, Appraising Single Family Residences, 1978, Home Buying - The Complete Illustrated Guide, 1980, Small Income Property-Illustrated Guide, 1980, Dictionary of Real Estate Appraisal, 1982, Condominium-Illustrated Guide, 1984, Review Appraisers Handbook, 1987, Appraising Residences and Income Properties, 1989, ARIP Student Workbook, 1989, NAERA Environmental Manual, 1989, Environmental Risk Screening, 1990, 1001 Q & A Appraisal Exam Preparation, 1990, Standards of Professional Appraisal Practice and Ethics, 1991, ARIP General Property Supplement, Real Estate Evaluation Illustrated Guide, 1993, Real Estate Principles and Practices Plus, 1994, Russian Appraisal Textbook, 1994, Advanced Appraisal Methods, 1994, Guide to New Haven, Connecticut, 1995, How To Make an FHA Single Family Appraisal, 1999, How To Pass the HUD/FHA Appraisal Qualification Examination, 1999, Spanish and English Dictionary of Real Estate and Appraisal, 2000, Hopkins History and Chronicles (1660-2000), 2002; pub. Real Estate Valuation Mag., 1985—; also articles, book chpts., audio-visual materials; patentee Perpetual Birthday and Anniversary Reminder Calendar. Alderman City of New Haven, 1961-63; pres. Young GOP, New Haven, 1960, Real Estate Edn. Found., 1980—, Greater New Haven Arts Coun., 1989-91; trustee Goddard Coll., 1976-78. 1st lt. USAF, 1952-54. Recipient Real Estate Educators Assn. award, 1995. Fellow Am. Coll. Health Care Adminstrs. (award 1984); mem. Am. Inst. Real Estate Appraisers (pres. Conn. chpt. 1975-76, Profl. recognition award 1976, 78, MAI award 1980), Am. Soc. Appraisers (award 1987), Soc. Real Estate Appraisers (nat. vice gov. 1980), Columbia Soc. Appraisers (award 1959), Greater New Haven Real Estate Bd. (Realtor of Yr. award 1976, Educator of Yr. 1992), Lawn Club. Jewish. Avocations: water sports, travel. Home: Carriage House 315 Whitney Ave New Haven CT 06511-3715 Office: Harrison Cos Carriage House 315 Whitney Ave New Haven CT 06511-3772 E-mail: henryhsq@aol.com.

HARRISON, JAMES WILBURN, gynecologist; b. Martin, Tenn., Mar. 23, 1918; s. Woodie and Georgia Harrison; m. Babs Wise Dudley, Jan. 29, 1948; children: James Wilburn Jr., James Michael, Babs Suzanne, Linda Denise. Student, U. Tenn., Martin, 1936-37, U. Tenn., Knoxville, 1937-38; MD, U. Tenn., Memphis, 1941; grad., U.S. Army Command and Gen. Staff Coll., Ft. Leavenworth, Kans., 1952. Diplomate Am. Bd. Ob-gyn. Asst. resident Brooke Gen. Hosp., Ft. Sam Houston, Tex., 1947; chief surgery Station Hosp., Clark AFB, Philippines, 1948-49; resident, sr. resident Letterman Gen. Hosp., San Francisco, 1949-51; advanced through grades to col. U.S. Army; ret., 1954; chief staff St. Michael Hosp., Texarkana, Ark., Wadley Regional Med. Ctr., Texarkana, Tex., So. Clinic, Texarkana, Ark.; chief ob-gyn. Ft. Polk, La., 1953—54. Asst. clin. prof. ob-gyn. U. Ark. Coll. Medicine, Little Rock. Chmn. Bowie County Child Welfare Bd.; mem. NE Tex. Mental Health Bd. With USAR, 1955—78. Decorated Legion of Merit. Fellow: VFW (life), ACOG (life), ACS (life), Tex. Soc. Ob-gyn. (life), Assn. Mil. Surgeons U.S. (life), Internat. Coll. Surgeons (life); mem.: AMA (life), AMA Sr. Physicians, Tri-State Med. Soc. (pres. 1960), Tex. Med. Assn., Alumni Assn. U.S. Army Command and Gen. Staff Coll. (founding mem.), Tex. 50 Yr. Club, Northridge Country Club (founding mem.), Am. Legion. Methodist. Avocations: collecting, travel, military history. Home: 4009 Pecos St Texarkana TX 75503-2857

HARRISON, JEREMY THOMAS, dean, law educator; b. San Francisco, Dec. 23, 1935; s. James Gregory and Agnes Johanna (Patrick) H.; m. Roseanne E. Thomas, Dec. 29, 1962 (dec. Oct. 1983); children: James, Amelia, Roseanne, Jeremy, Alexandra, Nadya, Rachel; m. Laura Ellen Marrack, Apr. 28, 1990; children: Robert, Peter, Paul, Philip, John. BS, U. San Francisco, 1957, JD, 1960; LLM, Harvard U., 1962. Bar: Calif. 1961, Hawaii 1987. Assoc. Brobeck, Phleger & Harrison, San Francisco, 1960-61; law clk. to assoc. justice U.S. Ct. Claims, Washington, 1962-63; lectr. law U. Ghana, Accra, 1963-64, U. Ife, Ibadan, Nigeria, 1964-66; prof. law U. San. Francisco, 1966-85; dean Sch. Law U. Hawaii, Honolulu, 1985-94; dean Mich. State U. Detroit Coll. Law, East Lansing, 1996-98, prof. law, 1998—. Vis. prof. law Haile Sellassie I U., Addis Ababa, Ethiopia, 1971-74, U. Hawaii, 1977-79; Elips Disting. prof. law Gadjah Mada U., Yogyakarta, Indonesia, 1995-96. Author: Cases and Materials on Evidence, Africa, 1967, Cases and Materials on Ethiopian Civil Procedure, 1974. Counsel citizen's panel Hawaii's Jud. Adminstrn., Honolulu, 1985-86; bd. dirs. Straub Found., Honolulu; pres. Pacific Health Rsch. Inst., Honolulu, 1993-95. Mem. ABA, Am. Bar Found., Calif Bar Assn., Hawaii Bar Assn. Office: Mich State U Detroit Coll Law 465 Law College Bldg East Lansing MI 48824-1300

HARRISON, JOHN ALEXANDER, financial executive; b. Lakeland, Fla., Jan. 22, 1944; s. William Henry and Aileen Helen (Jarvi) H.; m. Susan Leigh Smart, May 9, 1970; children: Kathryn Leigh, Jane Elizabeth. B.I.E. with highest honors, Ga. Inst. Tech., 1966; MBA (J. Spencer Love fellow 1966-68), Harvard U., 1968. With Baxter Travenol Labs., Inc., Deerfield, Ill., 1968-78, v.p. fin. and adminstrn. internat., 1977-78; v.p. fin. Tiger Leasing Group, 1980-82, N.Am. Car Corp., subs. Tiger Internat., Inc., Chgo., 1978-81; pres. Tiger Fin. Services, Inc., 1981-82; exec. v.p. Merrill Lynch Leasing Inc., N.Y.C., 1982-85; mng. dir. Merrill Lynch Capital Markets, N.Y.C., 1982-87, real estate fin. group investment banking div., 1985-87; CFO U.S. Consumer Banking Group Citibank, N.A., N.Y.C., 1987—91; CFO, mng. dir. Fin. Security Assurance Holdings Ltd., N.Y.C., 1991—2002; ret., 2002. Bd. dirs. Fairbanks Capital Holdings Corp., Salt Lake City, adv. bd. Sch. of Indsl and Sys. Engring., Ga. Inst. of Tech., 2003-. Bd. dirs. 1998-2002, Youth Guidance, Chgo., 1979-80. Mem. Harvard Bus. Sch. Club Chgo. (dir. 1970-71), Tau Beta Pi, Phi Kappa Phi, Phi Eta Sigma, Tau Kappa Epsilon. E-mail: jah122@aol.com.

HARRISON, JOHN, III, music educator; b. New Bedford, Mass., Oct. 13, 1951; s. John, Jr. and Jean Rita Harrison; m. Roberta Katherine Harrison, June 23, 1985; children: John IV, Alexander Paul. BMus, Berklee Coll. Music, Boston, 1969—73. Prof. U. Mass., Dartmouth, 1991—. Musician: (jazz piano trio) Going Places - Roman Sun, 1994—2002. Home: 830 Tradewind St New Bedford MA 02740 E-mail: John.Harrison@att.net.

HARRISON, JOHN RAYMOND, foundation executive, retired newspaper executive; b. Des Moines, June 8, 1933; s. Raymond Harrison and Dorothy (Stout) Harrison Cohen; m. Lois Cowles, June 24, 1955 (div. Apr. 1981); children: Gardner Mark, Kent Alfred (dec.), John Patrick, Lois Eleanor; m. Mary Gee MacQueen, Sept. 5, 1981 (div. 2000). Grad., Phillips Exeter Acad., 1951; AB, Harvard U., 1955, postgrad. Sch. Bus., 1955-56; DHL (hon.), Fla. So. Coll. With various papers throughout the U.S.; vice pres. N.Y. Times Co., ret.; chmn. Harrison Charitable Found., Atlanta. Dir. Internat. Herald-Tribune, Paris, 1974-91. Bd. dirs. Ft. Pierce (Fla.)-St. Lucie County Indsl. Devel. Coun., 1959-62, Ft. Pierce Meml. Hosp., 1959-62, Lincoln Pk. Child Care Ctr., Ft. Pierce, 1959-62, Gainesville United Fund, 1965, Boys Club Gainesville, 1965, U. Fla. Found., 1967, YMCA Greater Lakeland, 1967-69, Human Rels. Coun. Lakeland, 1967-69, Boys Club Lakeland, ARC, 1967-69; trustee Robert H. Anderson Found., Ridge Sch., Bartow, Fla., High Mus., 1988-94; mem. Pres.'s Resources Coun. Wellesly (Mass.) Coll.; mem. bd. counsellors Fla. So. Coll., 1974; mem. bd. visitors Emory U., 1984, pres., 1986; trustee Westminster Schs., 1989-92, Kennesaw State Coll. Found.; mem. bd. councillors Carter Presdl. Ctr.; mem. bd. overseers Harvard U., 1995—. Recipient Pulitzer prize for editl. writing, 1965, Nat Headliners award for pub. svc. editl. writing, Nat. Headliners Club, 1972, Walker Stone award for editl. writing Scripps-Howard Found., 1974, 76, Silver Gavel award for pub. svc. editls. ABA, 1977, Sigma Delta Chi Bronze medal, 1970, 73. Mem. Greater Lakeland C. of C. (dir. 1966-67), Associated Harvard Alumni (dir. 1979-82), Spee Club, Hasty Pudding Inst. 1770 (grad. dir.), Capital City Club, Commerce Club, Knickerbocker Club, Harvard Club (N.Y.C., Boston, Ga. bd. dirs.), Kennebunk River Club, Piedmont Driving Club (Atlanta).

HARRISON, JOHNNIE SHEPPARD, religious organization administrator; b. Jacksonville, Fla., Oct. 16, 1947; d. John and Sarah Sheppard; m. Augustine Richard Harrison, Sr., Aug. 11, 1969; children: Rezella Delourse, Augustine Richard Harrison, Jr.;children: Kyle Harold Taylor, Deltris Quinn Sheppard. AA, Brevard C.C., Melbourne/Cocoa, Fla., 1983; AS, BA, Living Word Bible Coll. & Sem., Maryland Heights, MO, 1986; BS, Orlando Coll., 1996; MBA, Nova Southeastern U., 1999; postgrad. Nova Southeastern U., 2003—. Resources control clk. NASA, Kennedy Space Ctr., Fla., 1978—85; postal worker USPS, Melbourne, Fla., 1985—90; dir. KAPS ministry Bahamas Mission Internat. Ministry, Melbourne, Fla., 2002—. Author: InnerCity Ministry (Cert. of Appreciation, 1997), (poem) I Am A Woman; composer: (peom) Celebration; author: (poem) Life is a Celebration, Strategies for Constructive Leadership (Cert. of Achievement, 2001). Supr. of women Ch. of God in C!hrist, Inc., Memphis, 1998. Mem.: So. Brevard Ministerial Alliance, Inc. (assoc.; parliamentarian 2002—03). Home: 626 Reddick Street Melbourne FL 32901-7112 Office: Church of God In Christ Inc P O Box SS 6281 Np Nassau The Bahamas also: 2712 S Main Street Melbourne FL 32901 Home Fax: 425-977-8463; Office Fax: (242) 324-2819. Personal E-mail: harrisoj@sbe.nova.edu. E-mail: johnnie_harrison714@hotmail.com.

HARRISON, JOSEPH HEAVRIN, lawyer; b. Evansville, Ind., July 23, 1929; s. Homer William and Lillie Isabelle (Heavrin) H.; m. Sharon Jeanene Miller, June 30, 1957 (div. 1976); children: Joseph Heavrin, Sara Ann; m. Julie Anne Gerard, Dec. 10, 1976; 1 child, Meghann. BA in Econs., U. Notre Dame, Ind., 1952; JD cum laude, U. Notre Dame, 1953. Bar: Ind. 1953, U.S. Dist. Ct. D.C. 1953, U.S. Dist. Ct. (so. dist.) Ind. 1953, U.S. Ct. Appeals (7th cir.) 1968, U.S. Tax Ct. 1984. Mng. ptnr. Bowers Harrison and predecessors, Evansville, Ind., 1955. Pres. Sandy's Assocs., Inc. (18 Hardee's franchised restaurants). Dir. Vanderburgh County Legal Aid Soc., Evansville, 1958—68, pres., 1964—65; Ind. counsel Bush Presdl. campaign, 1988; co-chair Ind. Lawyers for G.W. Bush, 2000—; chmn. Vanderburgh County Election Bd., 1979—90, Vanderburgh Rep. Fin. Com., 1982—89; mem. Evansville Econ. Devel. Commn., 1991—, pres., 1995—2001; Ind. commr. Ohio River Valley Water Sanitation Commn., 1982—, chmn., 1987; commr. Vanderburgh County Conv. & Vis. Bur., 1997—2001; bd. dirs. Arbor Hosp., 1991—94. With U.S. Army, 1953—55. Fellow Ind. Bar Found.; mem. ABA, Evansville Bar Assn., Ind. Bar Assn., Am. Judicature Soc., Evansville Country Club (pres. 1976), Oak Meadow Country Club. Republican. Roman Catholic. Avocations: golf, flying. Office: Bowers Harrison LLP PO Box 1287 25 NW Riverside Dr Evansville IN 47708-1255

HARRISON, JOSEPH WILLIAM, state legislator; b. Chgo., Sept. 10, 1931; s. Roy J. and Gladys V. (Greenman) H.; m. Ann Hovey Gillespie, June 9, 1956; children: Holly Ann, Tracy Jeanne, Thomas Joseph, Amy Beth, Kitty Lynne, Christy Jayne. BS, U.S. Naval Acad., 1956; postgrad., Ind. U. Law Sch., 1968-70. Asst. to pres. Harrison Steel Castings Co., Attica, Ind., 1960-64, sales rsch. engr., 1964-66, asst. sec., 1966-69, sec., 1969-71, v.p., 1971-84, dir., 1968-74; mem. Ind. Senate, 1966—, majority leader, 1980—. Mem. Attica Consol. Sch. Bd., 1964-66, pres., 1966-67. Served with USN, 1956-60. Mem. Am. Legion, Sigma Chi. Lodges: Elks, Eagles. Republican. Methodist. Home: 504 E Pike St Attica IN 47918-1524 Office: PO Box 409 Attica IN 47918-0409 also: State Senate State Capitol 200 W Washington St Indianapolis IN 46204-2728

HARRISON, JUDITH ANNE, human resources executive; b. N.Y.C., Aug. 15, 1954; d. William Russell and Lucille Kathlene Harrison; m. Brian Taylor Jarvis, Sept. 18, 1993. BA, CCNY, 1976. Bus. mgr. creative svcs. Burson-Marsteller, N.Y.C., 1976-80; creative ops. mgr. mktg. and comm. Arthur Young, N.Y.C., 1981-84; dir. collateral svcs. advt. and promotion CBS, N.Y.C., 1984-86; dir. mktg. comm. Media Gen., N.Y.C., 1986-87; pres. J.A. Harrison Comm., N.Y.C., 1988-92; v.p. The Fry Group, N.Y.C., 1992-96; v.p. human resources Ruder Finn, N.Y.C., 1997-99, s.r. v.p., 1999; chairwoman HR Roundtable/Coun. of Pub. Rels. Firms, 2000—. Mem.: World Studio Found. (bd. dirs. 1998—), Am. Women in Radio and TV (bd. dirs. N.Y. chpt. 1990—91), Soc. Human Resource Mgmt., Pub. Rels. Soc. Am., Women in Comms. Office: Ruder Finn 301 E 57th St New York NY 10022-2900

HARRISON, KEITH MICHAELE, law educator; b. Washington, Nov. 6, 1956; s. Charles Thomas Harrison Sr. and June Earlene (Bell) Harrison-Russ; m. Karen Marie Anderson, Aug. 21, 1982; children: Michaele Marie, David Tyler. BA, St. John's Coll., Santa Fe, N.Mex., 1977; JD, U. Chgo., 1981. Bar: Ill. 1981, D.C. 1982, N.Y. 1985. Clin. teaching fellow Antioch Sch. Law, Washington, 1985-86; asst. prof. law No. Ill. U., DeKalb, 1986-89, U. Denver, 1989-94, assoc. prof. law, 1994-2001; pres.-elect faculty senate, 1995-96; pres. faculty senate, 1996-98; assoc. dean Coll. Law, 1998-2000; vice dean, prof. law Franklin Pierce Law Ctr., Concord, New Hampshire, 2001—. Vis. prof. Syracuse U. Coll. Law, 1993; vis. lectr. Escuela de Relaciones Internacionales, Universidad Nacional, Heredia, Costa Rica, 1993. V.p. Sam Cary (Colo.) Scholarship Endowment Fund, 1991. Served to lt. USCG, 1981-85. Mem. D.C. Bar Assn., Sam Cary Bar Assn. (treas. 1991), Multiplikatoren Group (Germany). Office: Franklin Pierce Law Ctr 2 White St Concord NH 03301

HARRISON, LOIS SMITH, hospital executive, educator; b. Frederick, Md., May 13, 1924; d. Richard Paul and Henrietta Foust (Menges) Smith; m. Richard Lee Harrison, June 23, 1951; children: Elizabeth Lee Boyce, Margaret Louise Wade, Richard Paul. BA, Hood Coll., 1945, MA, 1993, Columbia U.; LHD (hon.), Hood Coll., 1993. Counselor CCNY, 1945-46; founding adminstr., counselor, instr. psychology and sociology Hagerstown (Md.) Jr. Coll., 1946-51, registrar, 1946-51, 53-54, instr. psychology and orienta, 1954-56; registrar, instr. psychology, Balt. Jr. Coll., 1951-54; bus. mgr., acct. for pvt. med. practice Hagerstown, 1953-2000; trustee Washington County Hosp., Hagerstown, 1975-97, chmn. bd., 1986-88, 95—; mem. bd. Washington County Health Sys. Inc., 1997—. Chmn. Home Fed. Savs. Bank, Hagerstown, 1997-99; chmn. acute care Health Sys. Bd., 1997—; chmn. bd. dirs. Home Fed. Savs. Bank, 1998-2000, emeritus, 2001—; spkr. ednl. panels, convs. hosp. panels and seminars. Author: The Church Woman, 1960-65. Trustee Hood Coll., Frederick, 1972—, chmn. bd., 1979-95; mem. Md. Gov.'s Commn. to Study Structure and Ednl. Devel. Commn., 1971-75; pres. Washington County Coun. Ch. Women, 1970-72; appointee Econ. Devel. Commn., County Impact Study Commn. Bd.; bd. dirs. Md. Hosp. Assn., 1988-98, Md. Chs. United, 1975—; chmn. bd. dirs. Md. Hosp. Edn. Inst., 1978-98; mem. Christ's Reformed Ch., 1935—; pres. Ch. Consistory; chmn. Chesapeake Healthcare Forum, 1995-97. Recipient Alumnae Achievement award Hood Coll., 1975, Washington County Woman of Yr. award, AAUW, 1984, Md. Woman of Yr. award, 1984, Md. Woman of Yr. award Francis Scott Key Commn. for Md.'s 350th Anniversary, 1984; named one of top 10 women Tri-State area, Herald-Mail Tri-State newspaper, 1990, Zonta Internat. Woman of Yr., 1994, Outstanding Woman of the Yr., Woman At the Table award, 2002. Mem. Hagerstown C. of C. Republican. Home: 12835 Fountain Head Rd Hagerstown MD 21742-2748 Office: Washington Cty Hosp Off Chmn Bd Hagerstown MD 21740 E-mail: lorichco@aol.com.

HARRISON, MARION EDWYN, lawyer; b. Phila., Sept. 17, 1931; s. Marion Edwyn and Jessye Beatrice (Cilles) H.; m. Carmelita Ruth Deimel, Sept. 6, 1952; children: Angelique Marie (Mrs. Kevin B. Bounds), Marion Edwyn III, Henry Deimel. BA, U. Va., 1951; LLB, George Washington U., 1954, LLM, 1959. Bar: Va. 1954, D.C. 1958, Supreme Ct. 1958. Spl. asst. to gen. counsel Post Office Dept., 1958-60, assoc. gen. counsel, 1960-61, mem. bd. contract appeals, 1958-61; ptnr. firm Harrison, Lucey & Sagle (and predecessors), Washington, 1961-78, Barnett & Alagia, 1978-84; ptnr. Scott, Harrison & McLeod, 1984-86, Law Offices Marion Edwyn Harrison, Washington, 1986—; pres. Free Congress Rsch. and Edn. Found., Inc., 2002—. Mem. coun. Adminstrv. Conf. U.S., 1971—78, sr. conf. fellow, 1984—88; mem. D.C. Law Revision Commn., 1975—92; lectr. Nat. Jud. Coll., Reno, 1979, La. State U. Law Sch., Aix-en-Provence, 1987, 89, Tulane U. Law Sch., Crete, 1997, Hofstra U. Law Sch., Nice, 1999, Nice, 2003, Pa. State U. Dickinson Law Sch., Vienna, 2000, Tulane U. Law Sch., Thessalonika, 2001, St. Mary's U. Law Sch., Innsbruck, 2002; adv. dir. NationsBank, N.A., 1987—93. Contbr. articles to profl. publs.; editor-in-chief Fed. Bar News, 1960-63; mem. editorial bd. Adminstrv. Law Rev., 1976-89. Trustee AEFC Pension Fund, Chgo., 1986-92; pres. Young Rep. Fedn. Va., 1954-55; mem. Va. Rep. Cen. Com., 1954-55; bd. visitors Judge Adv. Gen. Sch., Charlottesville, Va., 1976-78; chmn. Wolf Trap Assn., 1984-87; bd. dirs. Wolf Trap Found., 1984-88; pub. mem. USIA Mission, Argentina, 1971. Officer AUS, 1955-58. Decorated Commendation medal. Fellow: Am. Bar Found. (life); mem.: FBA (nat. coun. 1966—82), ABA (chmn. sect. adminstrv. and reg. law 1974—75, ho. of dels. 1978—88, chmn. lawyers in govt. com. 1980—82, bd. govs. 1982—86, chmn. com. on fgn. and internat. orgns. 1986—87), Bar Assn. D.C. (chmn. adminstrv. law sect. 1970—71, bd. dirs. 1971—72), Inter-Am. Bar Assn., Supreme Ct. Hist. Soc., Federalist Soc., George Washington U. Law Assn. (pres. 1974—77), Smithsonian Instn. (nat. bd. dirs. 1991—97), Soc. Mayflower Desc., Gainey Ranch Golf Club (Scottsdale, Ariz.), Met. Club, Washington Golf and Country Club, Knight of Malta. Republican. Roman Catholic. Home: 4111 N Ridgeview Rd Arlington VA 22207-4617 Address: 7222 E Gainey Ranch Rd Scottsdale AZ 85258-1529 Office: 717 Second St NE Washington DC 20002 Address: Dufourstrasse 32 8008 Zurich Switzerland

HARRISON, MARK ISAAC, lawyer; b. Pitts., Oct. 17, 1934; s. Coleman and Myrtle (Seidenman) H.; m. Ellen R. Gier, June 15, 1958; children: Lisa, Jill. AB, Antioch Coll., 1957; LLB, Harvard U., 1960. Bar: Ariz. 1961, Colo. 1991. Law clk. to justices Ariz. Supreme Ct., 1960-61; ptnr. Harrison, Harper, Christian & Dichter, Phoenix, 1966-93, Bryan Cave, LLP, Phoenix, 1993—. Adj. prof. U. Ariz. Coll. Law, 1995-97, Ariz. State Coll. Law, 2001—; nat. bd. visitors, 1996—. Co-author: Arizona Appellate Practice, 1966; editorial bd. ABA/BNA Lawyers Manual on Profl. Conduct, 1983-86; contbr. articles to profl. jours. Chmn. Phoenix City bond Adv. Commn., 1976—79; pres. Valley Commerce Assn., 1978, Ariz. Friend of Talking Books, Inc., 2000—01; vice chmn. Maricopa County Dem. Cen. Com., 1967—68, Ariz. Dem. Com, 1969—70, legal counsel, 1970—72; del. Dem. Nat. Conv., 1968; bd. dir. Careers for Youth, 1963—67, pres., 1966—67; bd. dir. Planned Parenthood of Cen. and No. Ariz., 1992—98, pres., 1995; bd. dir. Ariz. Policy Forum, 2000—. Recipient Peggy Goldwater award, Planned Parenthood, 2003, Planned Parenthood of Ctrl. and No. Ariz., 2003. Fellow: Am. Acad. Appellate Lawyers (pres. 1993—94), Am. Bar Found.; mem.: ABA (standing com. profl. discipline 1976—84, chmn. 1982—84, chmn. commn. pub. understanding law 1984—87, chmn. coord. com. on professionalism 1987—89, com. on women in the profession, ethics com. 1999—2002, Michael Franck Profl. Responsibility award 1996, Peggy Goldwater award 2003, Disting. Hon. Alumnus award), Lawyers Com. for Civil Rights Under Law (bd. dirs.), Law Coll. Assn. U. Ariz. (bd. dir. 1999—, pres. 2002—), Am. Law Inst. (nat. coun., lawyers com. for human rights), Harvard Law Sch. Assn. (nat. exec. coun. 1980—84), Ariz. Civil Liberties Union, Am. Judicature Soc. (exec. com. 1983—86, bd. dir. 1983—87), Western States Bar Conf. (pres. 1978—79), Nat. Conf. Bar Pres., Am. Inns of Ct. (master, pres. Sandra Day O'Connor chpt. 1993—94), Ariz. Bar Found. (pres. 1991, Walter E. Craig Disting. Svc. award 2002), State Bar Ariz. (bd. govs. 1971—77, pres. 1975—76), Am. Bd. Trial Advocates, Maricopa County Bar Assn. (pres. 1970), Assn. Profl. Responsibility Lawyers (pres. 1992—93). Office: Bryan Cave 2 N Central Ave Ste 2200 Phoenix AZ 85004-4406 E-mail: ellenmark@aol.com., mharrison@bryancave.com.

HARRISON, MARVIN, football player; b. Phila., Pa., Aug. 25, 1972; Degree in retailing, Syracuse Univ. Wide receiver Indpls. Colts, 1996—. Office: Indpls Colts 7001 W 56th St Indianapolis IN 46254

HARRISON, MICHAEL, opera company executive; b. Augusta, Ga., June 22, 1940; s. Oscar T. and Helen (Harrison) Smith. BA, Vanderbilt U., 1962; postgrad., Yale U., 1962-64. Actor, singer Broadway, Regional Opera and Theatres, 1964-80; gen. dir. Providence Opera Theatre, 1979-81, Opera/Columbus, Columbus, Ohio, 1983-89, Balt. Opera Co., 1989—. Pres. Harrison/Connor Consultants, L.A., 1981—83. Mem.: Md. Club., Rotary, Ctr. Club. Episcopalian. Office: Balt Opera Co Inc 110 W Mount Royal Ave Ste 306 Baltimore MD 21201-5732*

HARRISON, MICHAEL GREGORY, judge; b. Lansing, Mich., Aug. 4, 1941; s. Gus and Jean D. (Fuller) H.; m. Deborah L. Dunn, June 17, 1972; children: Abigail Ann, Adam Christopher, Andrew Stephen. AB, Albion (Mich.) Coll., 1963; JD, U. Mich., 1966; postgrad., Hague Acad. of Internat. Law, George Washington U. Bar: Mich. 1966, U.S. Dist. Ct. (ea. and we. dists.) Mich. 1967, U.S. Ct. Appeals (6th cir.). Asst. pros. atty. County of Ingham, Lansing, 1968-70, corp. counsel, 1970-76; judge 30th Jud. Cir. State of Mich., Lansing, 1976-2000; chief judge 30th Jud. Cir. State of Mich., Lansing, 1980-91; judge Ct. of Claims, 1979-2000; of counsel Foster, Swift, Collins and Smith, Lansing, 2000—. Counsel Capital Region Airport Authority, Lansing, 1970-76, Ingham Med. Ctr., Lansing, 1970-76; chmn. Ingham County Bldg. Authority, Mason, Mich., 1971-76; adj. prof. Thomas M. Cooley Law Sch., Lansing, 1976—. Editor Litigation Control, 1996; contbr. chpt. to Michigan Municipal Law, Actions of Governing Bodies, 1980; contbr. articles to profl. jours. Mem. shared vision steering com. United Way-C. of C.; mem. adv. bd. Hospice of Lansing, 1989—; pres. Greater Lansing Urban League, 1974-76, Lansing Symphony Assn., 1974-76; chmn. Mid. Mich. chpt. ARC, Lansing, 1984-86; bd. dirs., sec. St. Lawrence Hosp., Lansing, 1980-88; bd. dirs. ARC Gt. Lakes Regional Blood Svcs., 1991-95, Lansing 2000, 1987—, Greater Lansing Symphony, 2002—; mem. exec. bd. Chief Okemos coun. Boy Scouts Am., pres., 2003—; mem. criminal justice adv. com. Olivet Coll.; hon. bd. dirs. Lansing Area Safety Coun.; mem. State Bar Bd. Commrs., 1993-96; chair State Bar Rep. Assembly; mem. felony sentencing guidelines steering com., chmn. caseflow mgmt. coordinating com., mem. juror use and mgmt. task force Mich. Supreme Ct. Recipient Disting. Citizens award Boy Scouts Am., Disting. Vol. award Ingham County Bar Assn., award of judicial excellence ABA, Disting. Alumni award Albion Coll. Fellow: Mich. Bar Found., Am. Bar Found.; mem.: ABA (coun. mem. judicial divsn., coun. mem. tort and ins. practice sect., Fund for Justice and Edn. coun. 2003, award of jud. excellence), Mich. State Bar Found. (pres. 1991—2000), Nat. Conf. State Trial Judges (exec. com. 1991—94, vice chmn. 1995—96, chmn. 1997—98), Mich. Judges Assn. (treas. 1991, sec. 1992, 2d v.p. 1993, 1st v.p. 1994, pres. 1995), Mich. State U. Am. Inn of Ct. (pres. 2001—, master), Am. Judicature Soc. (bd. dirs. 1996—2002), Rotary Club, Lansing (pres. 2001—02), Country Club, Lansing. Republican. Congregationalist. Avocations: skiing, golf, tennis, travel, photography. Office: 313 S Washington Sq Lansing MI 48933-2193 E-mail: mharrison@fosterswift.com.

HARRISON, MICHAEL JAY, physicist, educator; b. Chgo., Aug. 20, 1932; s. Nathan J. and Mae (Nathan) H.; m. Ann Tukey, Sept. 1, 1970. AB, Harvard, 1954; MS, U. Chgo., 1956, PhD, 1960. Fulbright fellow and H. Van Loon fellow in theoretical physics U. Leiden, Netherlands, 1954-55; NSF fellow U. Chgo., 1957-59; research fellow math. physics U. Birmingham, Eng., 1959-61; asst. prof. Mich. State U., East Lansing, 1961-63, assoc. prof., 1963-68, prof., 1968—, faculty grievance officer, 1972-73, dean Lyman Briggs Coll., 1973-81, adj. prof. community health scis., 1988-93, adj. prof. epidemiology, 1993—. Vis. research physicist Inst. Theoretical Physics, U. Calif., Santa Barbara, 1980-81; with Air Force Cambridge Research Center, summer 1953, M.I.T. Lincoln Lab., summer 1954, RCA Sarnoff Lab., summers 1961-63; physicist Westinghouse Labs., summer 1956; cons. RCA Lab., 1961-64, United Aircraft Co., 1964-66, U.K. Atomic Energy Authority, Harwell Lab., summer 1960, Thailand project in Bangkok, Mich. State U.-AID, summer 1968; vis. research affiliate theoretical biology and biophysics, Los Alamos Nat. Lab., 1987-88. Contbr. articles to U.S., fgn. profl. jours. Am. Council on Edn. fellow U. Calif., Los Angeles, 1970-71. Fellow Am. Phys. Soc.; mem. AAUP (chpt. treas. 1966-67), N.Y. Acad. Scis., Harvard Club of Ctrl. Mich. (pres. 1988-93), Rotary, B'nai B'rith, Phi Beta Kappa, Sigma Xi. Jewish. Avocations: hiking, travel, photography. Home: 277 Maplewood Dr East Lansing MI 48823-4746 Office: Mich State U Physics Dept East Lansing MI 48824 E-mail: harrison@pa.msu.edu.

HARRISON, MONIKA EDWARDS, business development executive; b. Waiblingen, Federal Republic of Germany, July 31, 1949; came to U.S., 1957; d. Donnie Everette and Irmgard E. BA, Fla. State U., 1970, MS, 1977. Cabinet aide State Treas. Fla., Tallahassee, 1971-73; advisor to Pres. Fla. Senate, Tallahassee, 1973-74; legis. analyst U.S. Dept. Agr., Washington, 1975-76; dir. policy and planning U.S. Dept. Edn., Washington, 1976-85; dep. dir. Inst. Mus. Svcs., Washington, 1985-86; assoc. adminstr. U.S. SBA, Washington, 1986-89; assoc. dir. bus. devel. COLSA, Inc., Arlington, Va., 1989-92; assoc. adminstr. for small bus. devel. ctrs. U.S. SBA, Washington, 1992-93, assoc. adminstr. for bus. initiatives, 1993-2000, dep. ADA for entrepreneurial devel., 2000—02, chief human capital officer, 2002—. Commr. Cen. European Small Bus. Enterprise Devel. Commn., 1992-95; lectr. George Mason U., Fairfax, Va., 1985-86. Recipient Sr. Exec. Svc. award U.S. SBA, 1992-95, Presdl. Meritorious Exec. award, 2000. Office: US SBA 409 3rd St SW Washington DC 20024-3212

HARRISON, MOSES W., II, state supreme court chief justice; b. Collinsville, Ill., Mar. 30, 1932; m. Sharon Harrison; children: Luke, Clarence. BA, Colo. Coll.; LLB, Washington U., St. Louis. Bar: Ill. 1958, Mo. 1958. Pvt. practice, 1958-73; judge 3d Jud. Cir., Ill., 1973-79, 5th Dist. Appellate Ct., Ill., 1979-92; chief justice Ill. Supreme Ct., 1992—2003. Mem. ABA, Am. Judicature Soc., Ill. State Bar Assn. (former bd. govs.), Madison County Bar Assn. (former pres.), Tri-City Bar Assn., Met. St. Louis Bar Assn., Justinian Soc.*

HARRISON, ORRIN LEA, III, lawyer; b. Dallas, July 1, 1949; s. Orrin Lea Jr. and Annie Bell (Lassig) H.; m. Paula Diane Wagnon, May 29, 1971; children: Orrin IV, Erin, Lindsey. BA cum laude, U. of South; JD with honors, So. Meth. U. Bar: Tex. 1974, U.S. Dist. Ct. (no., so., ea. and we. dists.) Tex., U.S. Ct. Appeals (5th and 11th cirs.), U.S. Supreme Ct. From assoc. to ptnr. Locke, Purnell, Boren, Laney & Neely, Dallas, 1974-87; shareholder Locke, Purnell, Rain & Harrell, Dallas, 1987-92; ptnr. Vinson & Elkins, Dallas, 1992—2003, Akin Gump Strauss Haner & Feld, Dallas, 2003—. Sec. 500 Inc., 1981, treas., 1982; chancellor Ch. of Incarnation, Dallas, 1985-97; bd. dirs. Dallas Econ. Devel. Coun., 1986-92, Medisend Internat., 1997-2000; mem. Leadership Dallas, 1988l mem. Dallas Bus. Com. for the Arts, 2001—; mem. Dallas Country Heritage Soc., 2001—. Lt. JAGC, USN, 1971-75. Fellow Am. Bar Found., Tex. Bar Found. (life); mem. ABA, State Bar of Tex. (bd. dirs. 1993-96), Dallas Bar Found. (trustee 1993-01), Am. Bd. of Trial Advocates (Dallas pres., 1989), Internat. Soc. of Barristers, Dallas Bar Assn. (bd. dirs. 1983-97, pres. 1992), Tex. Young Lawyers Assn. (bd. dirs. 1981-83), Dallas Young Lawyers Assn. (pres. 1980-81), Tower Club, Univ. Club, Jeremy Golf and Country Club, Lakewood Country Club. Republican. Episcopalian. Avocations: skiing, swimming, mountain biking. Home: 3624 Normandy Ave Dallas TX 75205-2103 Office: Akin Gump Strauss Hauer & Feld 1700 Main St Ste 4100 Dallas TX 75201-2975 E-mail: oharrison@akingump.com.

HARRISON, PATRICIA ANN, educational association administrator; d. Nathaniel and Ernestine Harrison. BS in Biol. Sciences, Ill. State U., 1975—79; MS in Ednl. Adminstrn. and Supervision, So. Ill. U. Edwardsville, 1989—92. Counselor/tutor, upward bound program So. Ill. U. Edwardsville, Ill., 1981—83, asst. coord., upward bound program, 1988—88, coord., upward bound programs, 1988—95, asst. dir., east St. Louis ctr. Edwardsville/East Saint Louis, 1995—2000, acting dir., east St. Louis ctr., 2000—01, dir., east St. Louis ctr., 2001—. Participant Harvard U., Grad. Sch. Edn., Inst. Higher Edn., Mgmt. Devel. Program, Cambridge, Mass., 2002—02; conf. spkr., achieving ednl. and career goals Kujenga African Am. Youth Leadership Conf., Belleville, Ill.; mentor, emerging leaders program Mid-America Assn. Ednl. Opportunity Program Pers.; field reader, trio proposals US Dept. Edn., Washington DC, 2000—01; mem., sexual harassment adv. com. So. Ill. U. Edwardsville, 1997—2000; chair, edn. found. com. Ill. Assn. Ednl. Opportunity Program Pers., Ill., 1991, exec. bd. mem., Ill., 1986—90, chair, resource devel., Ill., 1988—90, treas., Ill., 1986—87, chair, concerns in secondary edn., Ill., 1986—86; workshop presenter - integrating sci. and math. for motivational curricula Mid-America Assn. Ednl. Opportunity Program Pers. Profl. Staff Conf. V.p. Greater East St. Louis Cmty. Fund, East Saint Louis/Brooklyn, 2002—03; mem. Girls Scouts River Bluffs Coun., Ill., 2002, nominating com. mem., 2001—02; mem., even start bd. Adult Edn. Program, County Regional Office Edn., Ill., 2000—01; mem., fundraising and registration com. East St. Louis Jackie Robinson Khoury League, East Saint Louis, 1992—98. Recipient Yes I Can Spl. Achiever, St. Louis Sentinel, 1993, Woman Achievement, YWCA, 1990. Mem.: Phi Kappa Phi (chair 1991), Alpha Kappa Alpha (life; chair 1988—90). Catholic. Achievements include Wrote/developed proposals, secured funding and implemented start-up for seven (7) of the currently operating programs at the Southern Illinois University Edwardsville East Saint Louis Center; Initiated, planned and implemented first local SIUE East St. Louis Center TRIO Programs Science Fair Competition for pre-school through 12th grade youth; Successful grant proposal writer for programs including Upward Bound, Upward Bound Math and Science, Talent Search, GEAR UP, and Youth Tech computer programs while at the SIUE East St. Louis Center. Avocations: sewing, reading, shopping for home, crafts. Office: Southern Ill U Edwardsville 411 E Broadway East Saint Louis IL 62201 Office Fax: 618-482-6935. E-mail: pharris@siue.edu.

HARRISON, PATRICIA DE STACY, federal agency administrator; b. N.Y.C. m. Emmett Bruce Harrison; 3 children. BA, Am. U., 1968; MA, George Mason U. V.p. Holly Realty Co., Arlington, Va., 1965-69; co-founder, ptnr. E. Bruce Harrison Co., Washington, 1973—96; former pres. AEF/Harrison Internat., Washington; asst. sec. for educ. and cult. affairs U.S. Dept. State, Washington, 2001—. Keynote spkr. U.S. Dept. Labor del. to Israel and Greece, Indsl. Devel. Authority of Ireland Conf./Women Execs. in Mgmt., U.S. Info. Agy./WorldNET program for entrepreneurs via satellite to 7 countries, Export Expo '90, Seattle, Nat. Govs. Conf., U.S. SBA Fin. Mgmt. Conf. in 9 states, mgmt. and tng. program for women entrepreneurs Budapest, Hungary (Alliance Decade for Democracy series); guest lect. Thomas Colloquium on Free Enterprise, 1989; trustee Guest Svcs., Inc.; mem. adv. coun. Avon Products, Inc. Author: Inside and Out: The Story of a Hostage, 1981, (with Margaret Mason, editor) The Washington Post Pocket Style Plus, 1983-84, America's New Women Entrepreneurs, 1986. Bd. dirs. Med. Coll. Pa. Recipient Librs.' and Tchrs.' award for play produced at Kennedy Ctr., 1980, Del. award Insieme per La Pace, Rome, 1988, Disting. Woman award Northwood Inst., 1991; named Washington Woman of Yr., Washington Women Mag., 1985, Entrepreneur of Yr., Washington, Arthur Young Co. and Venture mag., 1988, Women of Enterprise award. Mem. Nat. Women's Econ. Alliance Found., Pres.'s Export Coun., SBA Nat. Adv. Coun. (co-chmn., exec. com.), SBA Women's Network for Entrepreneurial Tng. (adv. coun.), Nat. Coal Coun. (exec. com.), Women in Internat. Trade, Nat. Fedn. Press Women (ex-officio, communication award 1979, bus. communicator of yr. 1988), Capital Press Women (ex-officio, named bus communicator of yr. 1988, journalist award for non-fiction 1988), Pub. Rels. Soc. Am. (counsellors acad.), Internat. Pub. Rels. Assn. Office: US Dept State Educ & Cult Affairs Bureau 2201 C St NW Washington DC 20520 Office Fax: 202-203-5115.

HARRISON, PATRICK WOODS, lawyer; b. St. Louis, July 14, 1946; s. Charles William and Carolyn (Woods) H.; m. Rebecca Tout, Dec. 23, 1967; children: Heather Ann, Heath Aaron. BS, Ind. U., 1968, JD, 1972. Bar: Ind. 1973, U.S. Dist. Ct. (so. dist.) Ind. 1973, U.S. Dist. Ct. Nebr. 1982, U.S. Supreme Ct. 1977. Assoc. Goltra, Cline, King & Beck, Columbus, Ind., 1972-73; ptnr. Goltra & Harrison, Columbus, 1973-78; pvt. practice Columbus, 1979-80; ptnr. Cline, King, Beck and Harrison, Columbus, 1980-85, Beck, Harrison & Dalmbert, Columbus, 1985—. Ind. Jud. Nominating Commn. nominee Ind. Supreme Ct., 1984. With U.S. Army, 1968-70. Fellow Ind. Trial Lawyers Assn. (bd. dirs. 1984, emeritus dir. 1999, Co-Trial Lawyer of Yr. 1999); mem. Am. Trial Lawyers Assn. Republican. Baptist. Avocation: golf. Home: 14250 W Mount Healthy Rd Columbus IN 47201-9309 Office: Beck Harrison & Dalmbert 320 Franklin St Columbus IN 47201-6732 E-mail: pharrison@direcway.com., woodyh@bhdatty.com.

HARRISON, PAULA JEAN, music educator; b. Kansas City, Mo., May 9, 1949; d. Lester Irving and Isabelle Marie (Entsminger) Mast; m. Gerald Wayne Waltz, Aug. 23, 1970 (div. Nov. 1992); children: Matthew Amos Waltz, Amy Elizabeth Waltz McGee; m. Paul Douglas Harrison, Dec. 20, 1997. Student, Ind. U., 1970. Piano, flute tchr. Paula Waltz Music Studio, Houston, 1982—92; music tchr. The Kinkaid Sch., Houston, 1983—89; accompanist Houston Bapt. U., 1989—90; dir. of music Richmond Plaza Bapt. Ch., Bellaire, Tex., 1990—92; choir accompanist Conroe HS, Tex., 1992—98; piano tchr. Paula Harrison's Music Studio, Conroe, 1992—2003; organist, chirldrens choir dir. First United Meth. Ch., Conroe, 1996—2003; rehearsal pianist Montgomery County Choir Soc., Conroe, 1998—2003. Musician (flutist): Webster Groves Symphony Orch., 1966—67; performer (accompanist): St. Louis All-County Double Woodwind Quintet, 1966—67, Annie - Class Act Productions, 1998, Gypsy - Crighton Theater, 1996, Nunsense - Crighton Theater, 1995. Fl. gov. Ind. U. Wilkie Dorm, 1968—69, female v.p., 1969—70; chaplain Sigma Alpha Iota, Ind. U., 1968—69; organist Grace Luth. Ch., Conroe, Tex., 1992—95. Recipient Am. Band Master's award, Phi Beta Mu-Lambda Chpt., 1966. Mem.: Houston Chorister Guild, Huntsville Music Tchrs Assn. (pres. 2001—03), Am. Assn. of English Handball Ringers, Federated Music Club of Navasota, Sigma Alpha Iota, Ind. U. (pres. 1969—70). Republican. Methodist. Avocations: reading, needlecrafts, walking, swimming. Home: 202 Pine Shadow Dr Conroe TX 77301

HARRISON, RICHARD WAYNE, lawyer; b. Marfa, Tex., June 23, 1944; AA, Schreiner U., 1964; BBA, U. Tex. Austin, 1966; JD, U. Tex. Sch. Law, 1968. Ptnr. Florence & Harrison, Hughes Springs, Tex., 1968-69; pvt. practice Hughes Springs, Tex., 1969-73; asst. atty. gen. Atty. Gen.'s Office of Tex., Austin, 1973-74, chief tax divsn., 1974-76, spl. asst. atty. gen., 1976-78; ptnr. McGinnis, Lochridge & Kilgore, Austin, 1978-87, Jones, Day, Reavis & Pogue, Austin, 1987-94; mng. ptnr. Harrison & Rial LLP, Austin, 1994—2000; owner Rick Harrison & Assocs., Austin, 2000—02; ptnr. Fritz, Byrne, Head & Harrison LLP, Austin, 2002—. Trustee, treas. St. Andrew's Episcopal Sch., Austin; precinct chmn. Cass County Dem. Com., 1969-73; pres. Hughes Springs Indsl. Found., 1970; Cass County chmn. Salvation Army, 1970-72; area coord. Lloyd Bentsen for Senate Com., 1970; chmn. Hughes Springs United Fund Drive, 1972; mem. Austin Convocation Cursillo Steering Com., 1983-86, chmn., 1985-86; sr. warden St. Luke's-on-the-Lake Episcopal Ch., 1984. Fellow: Tex. Bar Found.; mem.: Schreiner Coll. Former Student Assn. (bd. dirs. 1984—88), Cass County Bar Assn. (past pres.), Travis County Bar Assn., State Bar of Tex. (fed. jud. com. 1980—83, bar jour. com. 1980—83), Barton Creek Country Club, Masons. Democrat. Home: 1730 Camp Craft Rd Austin TX 78746-7317 Office: Fritz Byrne Head & Harrison LLP 98 San Jacinto Blvd Ste 2000 Austin TX 78701

HARRISON, ROBERT ALLEN, retired aerospace transportation executive; b. Omaha, Sept. 15, 1929; m. Joyce Eleanor Amirikian, Sept. 9, 1961; children: Lynda Joy, Robert Amirikian. AB, Harvard U., 1951; MS, George Washington U., Washington, 1982. Pres. Harrison and Co., Fairfax, Va., 1990—97, Harrison Aerospace Corp., Fairfax, 1997—2001. Dir. Am.-Russian Tech. Exch. Ctr., Moscow, 1991—93. Author: (book) Probabilistic Distribution Analysis; editor: Handbook of Reliability Engineering. Mem.: Inst. for Ops. Rsch. and Mgmt. Sci., Cavalier Golf and Yacht Club, Harvard Club of Washington (vice-president 1994—95). Home: 8909 Glenbrook Rd Fairfax VA 22031 Home (Summer): 303 Atlantic Ave Virginia Beach VA 23451 Home Fax: 703-280-2202. Personal E-mail: jharrison31@cox.net.

HARRISON, ROBERT WILLIAM, zoologist, educator; b. Napoleon, Ohio, Nov. 3, 1915; s. Charles Foster and Goldie Della (Fahrer) H.; m. Marion Murlless Billings, May 30, 1943 (div. 1973); children: Suzanne Harrison Marchetti, Elizabeth A. Harrison Greene, Barbara A. Harrison DiOrio; m. Ruth Lightner Hastings, July 31, 1974 (div. Nov. 1980). AB, Oberlin Coll., 1938; postgrad., Springfield (Mass.) Coll., 1938-39; cert., Marine Biology Lab., Woods Hole, Mass., summer 1939, 41; MA, Wesleyan U., Middletown, Conn., 1941; MS, Yale U., 1942, PhD (Nat. Cancer Inst. rsch. fellow), 1949; cert., U.S. Naval War Coll., Newport, R.I., 1969, U.S. Naval Med. Sch. Asst. in biology Springfield Coll., 1938-39; asst. Wesleyan U., 1939-41, vis. assoc. prof., 1957; asst. in zoology Yale U., New Haven, 1941-42, 46-48, rsch. asst. pathology Med. Sch., 1942; instr. zoology U. R.I., Kingston, 1949-50, asst. prof., 1950-56, assoc. prof., 1956-65, prof., 1965-77; vis. extension prof. physiology R.I. Hosp. Sch. Nursing, Providence, 1966, 67, 70; prof. emeritus U. R.I., Kingston, 1977—, assoc. dean divsn. univ. extension, 1968-69, acting dean, 1969-70, acting chmn. dept. zoology, 1974-75; cons. Crime Lab., Wakefield, R.I. Chmn. Faculty Senate, U. R.I., Kingston, 1963-64; advisor to health professions, 1970-74; vis. spl. instr. Brown U., 1958. Author: An Analysis of a Random Sample of Navy Air-Sea Rescues, 1945. Bd. dirs. Animal Rescue League So. R.I.; mem. Rep. Town Com. of South Kingstown, R.I., 1962-66, chmn. bipartisan com. on town adminstr. Town Coun., 1966; pres. Friends of U. R.I. Libr.; scoutmaster, commr. Boy Scouts Am.; choir Kingston Congl. Ch., 1952—. Cpl. Ohio N.G., 1932-40, sgt. temporary, 1938-39; lt. USNR, active duty, 1942-46; capt. USNR, Med. Svc. Corps, 1953-70, ret. AEC grantee, 1962; Physiol. Soc. rsch. fellow U. Ill., 1959. Mem. AAUP, AAAS, Nat. Ret. Tchrs. Assn., Am. Inst. Biol. Scis., R.I. Assn. Health, Phys. Edn. and Recreation (hon. life), N.Y. Acad. Scis., Am. Soc. Zoologists, Am. Coll. Sports Medicine, Fleet Res. Assn., Ret. Officers Assn., Am. Assn. Ret. Persons, Commodore Point Judith Yacht Club, South County Chamber Singers Club, Tavern Hall Club of Kingston, U.S. Sailing Assn., Sierra Club, Oberlin Coll. Heisman Club, Smithsonian Assocs., River Bend Athletic Club, YMCA South County, Yale Assn. R.I., U. R.I. Faculty Ctr. Assn. Congregationalist. Home: 40 Dockray St Wakefield RI 02879-3915 Office: U RI Dept Zoology Kingston RI 02881

HARRISON, RONALD O. association administrator; m. Mysie Harrison; children: Kim, Raymond 1 stepchild, Mysie S. Saulsbury. LLD(hon.), Flagler Coll.; BSBA, Fla. State U.; grad., Command and Gen. Staff Coll.; grad. Sr. Res. Officer Course, U.S. Army War Coll. Commd. 2d lt. USNG, 1961, advanced through grades to; various positions including platoon leader Fla. Army N.G., 1963, adj. gen.; pres. N.G. Assn. of U.S., 2000—. Past pres. Adjs. Gen. Assn. of U.S.; former mem. policy bd. DOD Res. Forces, Dept. of Army Res. Forces. Trustee Heart of the City Found., Orlando; past dir. Rotary Club, Orlando; ordained ruling elder First Presbyn. Ch. Orlando. Named to Athletic Hall of Fame, Fla. State U. Mem.: Assn. U.S. Army, N.G. Officers' Assn. Fla., AGAUS, N.G. Assn. of U.S., Greater Orlando C. of C. Office: Nat Guard Assn US 1 Massachusetts Ave NW Washington DC 20001

HARRISON, ROSLYN SIMAN, lawyer; b. Phila., Mar. 6, 1935; d. Max and Stella (Shapiro) Siman; m. Saul E. Harrison, June 12, 1955 (div. Mar. 1990); children: Dana Lynn, Julia Anne, Michael E. BA summa cum laude, Bryn Mawr Coll., 1956; LLB with honors, Rutgers U., Newark, 1977. Bar: N.J. 1977, U.S. Dist. Ct. N.J. 1977, U.S. Ct. Appeals (3rd cir.) 1981, N.Y. 1985, U.S. Dist. Ct. (ea. dist.) N.Y. 1985, U.S. Dist. Ct. (so. dist.) N.Y. 1987, U.S. Supreme Ct. 1987, U.S. Dist. Ct. (ea. dist.) Pa. 1988, U.S. Ct. Appeals (fed. cir.) 1994. Tchr. history Longmeadow (Mass.) High Sch., 1957-59; instr. polit. sci. Webster Coll., Webster Groves, Mo., 1964-66; assoc. McCarter & English, LLP, Newark, 1977-85, ptnr., 1986-2000, of counsel, 2000—. Social Sci. Rsch. Coun. grantee, 1955. Mem. ABA, N.Y. State Bar Assn., Assn. Fed. Bar State of N.J., N.J. Bar Assn. (mem. curriculum adv. com. Inst. for Continuing Legal Edn. 1990-96, chmn. N.J. bar intellectual property law sect. 1993-95), N.J. Intellectual Property Law Assn. (chmn. copyright com. 1993, chmn. trademark com. 1994-95), Internat. Trademark Assn. (internat. com., meetings com., ADR com. panel of neutrals), Am. Arbitration Assn., John J. Gibbons Am. Inn. of Ct. (mem. com. 1993—). Office: 4 Gateway Ctr 100 Mulberry St Newark NJ 07102-4056 E-mail: rharrison@mccarter.com.

HARRISON, RUSSELL SAGE, political science educator, consultant; b. Southport, N.C., Feb. 24, 1944; s. Russell S. and Julia (Grayson) H. BA, Duke U., 1966; PhD, U. N.C., 1971. Asst. prof. polit. sci. Rutgers U., Camden, N.J., 1971-77, assoc. prof. polit. sci., 1977—, chmn. dept. polit. sci., 1997-99. Project dir. Camden County Mgmt. Audit, 1995-96, Professionalization of County Govt., Camden, 1991-92. Author: Inequality of Public School Finance, 1977. Cons. South Jersey Port Authority, Salem (N.J.) Port Authority, N.J. Dept. Transp., Fed. Econ. Devel. Adminstrn., N.J.; trustee Cadbury Retirement Cmty., Camden, 1995-98, asst. sec., 1995-98; active Soc. of Friends, clk., 1998—. Mem. Am. Polit. Sci. Assn., Am. Soc. Pub. Adminstrn., Northeastern Polit. Sci. Home: 301 Plantation Dr Cinnaminson NJ 08077-4308 Office: Rutgers U Dept Political Sci Camden NJ 08101-0020

HARRISON, RUTH FEUERBORN, retired literature and writing educator; b. Garnett, Kans., Aug. 23, 1930; d. Vincent Herman and Mary Jane (Weaver) Feuerborn; m. Bryce Robert Howard, Sept. 14, 1949 (div. Aug. 1973); children: Sam Bryce Howard, Bryan Jeffrey Howard, Gregory Robert Howard; m. Frederick Charles Harrison, Sept. 13, 1973. BA in English, Portland State U., 1966, MA in English, 1968; PhD in Medieval Comparative Lit., U. Oreg., 1974. Asst. prof. English dept. Portland (Oreg.) State U., 1969-74; freelance editor, cons. Editing, Inc., 1974-77; adj. prof. English dept. Linfield Coll., McMinnville, Oreg., 1977-82; tech. writer, tech. editor Bendix (aka UNC Geotech), Grand Junction, Colo., 1983-87; adj. prof. English dept. Oreg. Coast C.C., Newport, Oreg., 1987-93. Textbook reviewer Prentice-Hall, 1974-77; poetry workshop leader Moon Fish, Yachats (Oreg.) Lit. Festival, others; judge nat. student chapbook contest Nat. Fedn. State Poetry Socs., 2000; contest judge Chapparal Poets, League Minn. Poets, Utah State Poetry Soc., 1999—. Author: (textbooks) Punctuation: A Programmed Text, 1969, English 101: Survey of English Literature, 1972, hist. booklet for Little Log Ch. Hist. Mus., Yachats, 1994, Quite Unreasonable, 2001; (poems) Bone Flute, 1996. Joint honor scholar, 1947; NEH grantee, 1981; grad. assistantships Portland State U., 1966-68, U. Oreg., 1968-69. Mem. NOW, Oreg. State Poetry Assn. (spring and fall contest coord. 2002, 03, recipient more than 30 awards), South County Tuesday Writing Group, Acad. Am. Poets, Nat. Fedn. State Poetry Socs. Democrat. Avocations: herb garden, writing poetry. Home: 2710 NW Bayshore Loop Waldport OR 97394-9515 E-mail: rfharrison@newportnet.com.

HARRISON, S. DAVID, lawyer; b. N.Y.C., Jan. 29, 1930; s. Louis and Molly (Ginsburg) Harrison; m. Joan S. Horowitz, Mar. 23, 1958 (dec. May 1993); children: Andrew L., Rachel E.; m. Roberta S. Karmel, Oct. 29, 1995. AB, Harvard U., 1951, LLB, 1954; LLM, NYU, 1959. Bar: NJ 1955, NY 1968. Law sec. to Hon. William J. Brennan, Jr. N.J. Supreme Ct., 1954-55; from assoc. to ptnr. Platoff, Platoff & Heftler, Union City, NJ, 1955-65; corp. counsel Beaunit Corp., N.Y.C., 1965-71, corp. sec., 1966-71; asst. sec. Tyrex, Inc., 1969-71; dir. Man-Made Fibers Prodrs. Assn., 1970-71; pvt. practice law N.Y.C., 1971—; of counsel Rosen & Livingston. Bd. dirs. various corps.; mem. panel arbitrators N.Y. Stock Exch. Chmn. zoning bd. Village Hastings-on-Hudson, 1988—98; bd. dirs. Am. Friends Sarah Herzog Hosp. Jerusalem, 1992—; trustee Gallery at Hastings, NY, 1993—97. Mem.: ABA, Am. Arbitrators Assn., Nat. Panel Arbitrators, N.Y. State Bar Assn., Harvard Club Westchester, Harvard Club N.Y., Masons. Home: 66 Summit Dr Hastings Hdsn NY 10706-1215 Office: 275 Madison Ave New York NY 10016

HARRISON, SAUL ISAAC, child psychiatrist, medical educator; b. N.Y.C., Nov. 4, 1925; MD, U. Mich., 1948. Diplomate Am. Bd. Psychiatry and Neurology, Am. Bd. Child and Adolescent Psychiatry. Prof./dir. child/adolescent psychiatry edn. U. Mich., Ann Arbor, 1956-83; prof./dir. child/adolescent psychiatry Harbor UCLA, Torrance, 1984-92. Author/editor 9 books; contbr. over 100 articles to profl. jours., chpts. to books. Lt. USNR, 1943-45, 48-50, 52-54. Commonwealth Fund Fellow, London, 1966; recipient McGavin award Am. Psychiat. Assn. for career accomplishment in child/adolescent psychiatry, 1992. Fax: 310 822-2373.

HARRISON, SIMON M. mediator, lawyer, arbitrator; b. Miami, Aug. 20, 1954; s. Raymond and Doris (Harris) H.; m. Susan Marie Landefeld, Oct. 20, 1979; 1 child, Robert. BA, U. Fla., 1975, JD, 1978. Bar: Fla. 1978, Colo. 1992. Ptnr. Perch and Harrison, P.A., Lehigh Acres, Fla., 1978-93; pvt. practice Ft. Myers, Fla., 1993—. Bd. dirs. Gulf Abstract and Title Co., Ft. Myers. Mem. ABA, Fla. State Bar Assn., Colo. Bar Assn., Lee County Bar Assn. Democrat. Jewish. Avocations: scuba diving, golf. Office: PO Box 07372 Fort Myers FL 33919-0361 E-mail: simon@smharrison.com.

HARRISON, SUE ANN MCHANEY, writer; b. Lansing, Mich., Aug. 29, 1950; d. Charles Robert and Patricia Ann (Sawyer) McHaney; m. Neil Douglas Harrison Sr., Aug. 22, 1969; children: Koral(dec.), Neil Jr., Krystal. BA, Lake Superior State U., 1971. Author: Mother Earth Father Sky, 1990 (Best Book for Young Adults award Am. Libr. Assn., 1991), Cry of the Wind, 1998, Call Down the Stars, 2001. Methodist.

HARRISON, THEODORE JOEL, otolaryngologist, facial plastic surgeon; b. Phila., 1951; BA, U. Pa., 1972; MD, Jefferson Med. Coll., 1976. Diplomate Am. Bd. Otolaryngology. Pvt. practice, N.Y.C. Mem. staff Beth Israel Med. Ctr., N.Y.C., Cabrini Med. Ctr., N.Y.C., N.Y. Eye and Ear Infirmary, Orthop. Inst. Hosp. for Joint Diseases, N.Y.C.; clin. instr. dept. otolaryngology-head and neck surgery Mt. Sinai Sch. Medicine, N.Y.C. Fellow Am. Acad Otolaryngology-Head and Neck Surgery; mem. Med. Soc. State of N.Y., N.Y. County Med. Soc. Address: 2 Fifth Ave # 1 New York NY 10011-8855

HARRISON, THOMAS FLATLEY, lawyer; b. N.Y.C., Jan. 11, 1942; s. John P. and Mary F. (Flatley) H.; m. Lorraine Brereton, Aug. 16, 1969; children: John J., Jane C., Ann B., Peter T. AB, Holy Cross Coll., 1963; JD, Fordham U., 1966. Bar: N.Y. 1967, Ill. 1979, Ohio 1981, D.C. 1988, Conn. 1989. Asst. counsel N.Y.C. Dept. Rent and Housing, 1966-69; asst. atty. gen. N.Y. State Dept. Law, 1969-74; chief enforcement N.Y. region U.S. EPA, 1974-76, regional counsel Chgo., 1976-80; sr. corp. counsel B.F. Goodrich Co., Akron, Ohio, 1980-87; ptnr. Manatt, Phelps, Rothenberg & Evans, Washington, 1987-88; ptnr., co-chmn. environ. and land use dept. Day, Berry & Howard LLP, Hartford, Conn., 1988—. Faculty Practising Law Inst. Contbr. articles to profl. jours. Mem. 49th Assembly Dist. Rep. Orgn., N.Y.C., 1963-73, bd. govs., 1969-73; active Silver Lake, Ohio, Rep. Orgn., 1981-87; mem. Rep. Town Com., Avon, Ct., 1991—, Inland Wetlands Commn., Avon, 1992-95; mem. bd. Fin. 1995—, chmn., 2002–; mem. Conn. Coun. on Environ. Quality, 1997—; mem. Conn. Small Bus. Compliance Adv. Panel, 1996—; bd. dirs. Conn. League of Conservation Voters, 2000—, Natl. Audobon Conn. 2001—. Recipient Outstanding Performance award EPA, 1976. Mem. Conn. Bar Assn. (exec. com. environ. law sect. 1989—, sect. chair 1998-99). Roman Catholic. Home: 51 Briar Hill Rd Avon CT 06001-4007 Office: Day Berry & Howard LLP City Place Hartford CT 06103-3499 E-mail: tfharrison@dbh.com.

HARRISON, THOMAS JAMES, electrical engineer, educator; b. Wausau, Wis., May 13, 1935; s. Glenn M. and A. Laura (Barclay) H.; m. Carol H. Harrison; children: Nancy E., Kristine A. BS in Elec. Engring, Carnegie Inst. Tech., 1957, MS in Elec. Engring, 1958; PhD, Stanford U., 1964. Registered profl. engr., Calif. Design engr. IBM, Poughkeepsie, N.Y., 1958-59, assoc. engr. Peekskill, N.Y., 1960, staff engr., adv. engr. San Jose, Calif., 1960-68, sr. engr. Boca Raton, Fla., 1968-78, mem. corp. tech. com. Armonk, N.Y., 1979, program mgr., mgr. advanced software engring. tech. Boca Raton, 1980-83; cons. acad. specialist Tallahassee, Fla., 1984-87; prof. elec. engring. Fla. A&M U., Fla. State U., Tallahassee, 1987-99, chmn. elec. engring., 1988-95. Mem. U.S. Nat. Com. for Internat. Electrotech. Commn., 1972-82; U.S. expert Internat. Orgn. Standardization Comns., 1975-84; mem. engring. com. U. Fla., 1972-87, Fla. Atlantic U., 1971-83; alternate mem. bd. dirs. Accreditation Bd. for Engring. and Tech., 1995—. Author, editor: Handbook of Industrial Control Computers, 1972, Minicomputers in Industrial Control, 1978; contbr. articles to tech. handbooks and jours.; patentee analog-to-digital converters, sampling filter. With AUS, 1959. Fellow IEEE, Instrument Soc. Am. (bd. dir. standards and practices bd. 1971-84, v.p. 1980-81, soc. pres. 1985-86), Am. Nat. Standards Inst. (standard mgmt. bds.), Am. Soc. Engring. Edn., Rotary, Sigma Xi, Tau Beta Pi, Delta Upsilon, Omicron Delta Kappa, Eta Kappa Nu, Phi Kappa Phi. Home: 2967 Giverny Circle Tallahassee FL 32309-8200 Office: Fla A&M U Fla State U Dept Elec & Computer Engrin 2525 Pottsdamer St Tallahassee FL 32310-6046 E-mail: harrison@eng.fsu.edu.

HARRISON, THOMAS R. music educator; s. Clyde and Cathey Harrison; m. Kay Walsh, Sept. 1, 1995; 1 child, Natasha. PhD, U. Salford, 2002. Dir. music engring. tech. Elizabeth City State U., Elizabeth City, NC, 1998—. Office: Elizabeth City State University 1704 Weeksville Rd Elizabeth City NC 27909

HARRISON, THOMAS SAMUEL, IV, small business owner; b. Portland, Oreg., Sept. 24, 1952; s. Thomas Samuel Jr. and Margaret (Lindsay) H.; m. Karen Anne Hammelman, Oct. 25, 1975; children: Thomas V., Michael, Elizabeth, Anna, John. AB in Math., Dartmouth Coll., 1975. Owner, mgr. TS4, Oregon City, Oreg., 1979—; pres. TS4 Media Svcs. Corp., Oregon City, 1989—; gen. ptnr. Harrison Interests, Oregon City, 1994—. Republican. Avocations: robotics, woodworking, model trains. Home: 15011 S Forsythe Rd Oregon City OR 97045-9463 Office: TS4 Media Svcs Corp 15011 S Forsythe Rd Oregon City OR 97045-9463 Fax: 877-691-0535. E-mail: tomh@ts4.com.

HARRISON, WALTER ASHLEY, physicist, educator; b. Flushing, N.Y., Apr. 26, 1930; s. Charles Allison and Gertrude (Ashley) H.; m. Lucille Prince Carley, July 17, 1954; children: Richard Knight, John Carley, William Ashley, Robert Walter. B. Engring. Physics, Cornell U., 1953; MS, U. Ill., 1954, PhD, 1956. Physicist Gen. Elec. Research Labs., Schenectady, 1956-65; prof. applied physics Stanford (Calif.) U., 1965-2001, prof. emeritus, 2001—, chmn. applied physics dept., 1989-93, prof. emeritus, 2001—. Scientific adv. bd. Max Planck Inst., Stuttgart, Germany, 1989-92. Author: Pseudopotentials in the Theory of Metals, 1966, Solid State Theory, 1970, Electronic Structure and the Properties of Solids, 1980, Elementary Electronic Structure, 1999, Applied Quantum Mechanics, 2000; editor: the Fermi Surface, 1960, Proceedings of the International Conference on the Physics of Semiconductors, 1985, Proceedings of the International Conference on Materials and Mechanisms of High-Temperature Superconductivity, 1989. Guggenheim fellow, 1970-71; recipient von Humboldt sr. U.S. scientist award, 1981, 89, 94; vis. fellow Clare Hall, Cambridge U., 1970-71. Fellow Am. Phys. Soc. Home: 817 San Francisco Ct Stanford CA 94305-1021 Office: Stanford U Dept Applied Physics Stanford CA 94305-4045 E-mail: walt@stanford.edu.

HARRISON, WALTER LEE, university president; b. Pitts., May 15, 1946; s. Lester Maurice and Alice Hagedorn (Cohen) H.; m. Dianne Ellen Mintz, June 22, 1970. BA, Trinity Coll., 1968; MA, U. Mich., 1969; PhD, U. Calif., Davis, 1980. Lectr. Johannes Gutenberg U., Mainz, Fed. Republic of Germany, 1976-77; instr. Iowa State U., Ames, 1978-80, Colo. Coll., Colorado Springs, 1980-82, dir. coll. rels., 1982-85; pres. Gehrung Assocs., Keene, N.H., 1985-89; exec. dir., v.p. univ. rels. U. Mich., Ann Arbor, 1989-98; pres. U. Hartford, West

Hartford, 1998—. Vis. prof. Colo. Coll., 1988-91; adj. prof. U. Mich., 1991-98. Contbr. articles to profl. jours. Trustee Fountain Valley Sch., 1990-99; bd. dirs. Univ. Musical Soc., 1990—98, Mich. Journalism Fellow Program, 1991-98; bd. fellows Trinity Coll., 1994-96; dir. St. Francis Hosp. and Med. Ctr., 1998—, Hartford Stage Co., 2000—, Hartford Symphony Orch. 1998-; trustee Suffield Acad., 2002—; bd. dirs. divsn. I NCAA, 2002—. Mem. Coun. Advancement and Support Edn., Phi Kappa Phi. Avocations: baseball, recreational sports. Office: Univ of Hartford 200 Bloomfield Ave West Hartford CT 06117-1599 E-mail: horky@hartford.edu.

HARRISON, WENDY JANE MERRILL, insurance company executive; b. Waterbury, Conn., Dec. 4, 1961; d. David Kenneth and Jane Joy (Nevius) Merrill; m. Aidan T. Harrison (div. Nov. 1998); children: Christopher, Charlotte, Ryan; m. Michael G. Kelly, Oct. 2, 1999. BA in Journalism, George Washington U., Washington, 1981; MBA in mgmt., Cornell U., 1992. Intern in edn. HEW, Washington, summer 1978, writer, summer 1979; rsch. asst. dep. health svcs. adminstrn. George Washington U., Washington, 1979-81; sec. Nat. Assn. Beverage Importers, Washington, 1981; account exec. Staff Design, Washington, 1982; adminstrv. aide Internat. Food Policy Rsch. Inst., Washington, 1983-86; program assoc. Acad. for Ednl. Devel., Washington, 1986-87; pvt. practice cons. Washington, 1987-88; adminstrv. mgr. food and nutrition policy program Cornell U., Ithaca, 1988-92; cons. in mgmt. of med. practices Med. Bus. Mgmt., Ithaca, 1994-95; realtor Century 21 Alpha, 1995-97; compensation mgr. Santa Clara (Calif.) U., 1996-98; sr. compensation analyst Stanford (Calif.) U., 1998-99; human resources cons. Siemens Info. and Comm. Networks, 2000; compensation and benefits mgr. Kana Comms., 2000-2001; U.S. compensation mgr. KLA-Tencor, 2001—02; pres. The Benefits Source Ins. Svcs. Inc., Calif., 2003—. Cons., editor George Washington U., 1986; cons., rapporteur Internat. Food Policy Restaurant Inst., Washington and Copenhagen, Denmark, 1987; cons., adminstr. Hansell & Post, Washington, 1987-88, Cornell U., Washington and Ithaca, 1988; pvt. practice cons., 2001—. Sponsor Worldvision, Tanzania, 1988-91. George Washington U. scholar, 1979-81. Mem. AMA, Soc. for Human Resources Mgmt., Sigma Delta Xi (scholar 1980). Democrat. Episcopalian. Avocations: piano, hiking, swimming. Home: 39 Starlite Ct Mountain View CA 94043-1937 E-mail: wendy@benefits-source.org.

HARRISON, WILLIAM BURWELL, JR., bank executive; b. Rocky Mount, N.C., Aug. 12, 1943; s. William Burwell and Katherine (Spruill) H.; m. Anne MacDonald Stpehens, Dec. 7, 1985; children Katherine Adams, Anne Stephens. AB in Econs., U. N.C., Chapel Hill, 1966, spl. student in bus. adminstrn., 1966-67; Sr. Mgmt. Program, Harvard Bus. Sch., Vevey, Switzerland, 1979. Trainee Chem. Bank, N.Y.C., 1967-69, Mid-South corp. and corr. banking group, 1969-74, West Coast corp. and corr. banking group, 1974-76, dist. head, Western regional coord. San Francisco, 1976-78, regional coord., sr. v.p. London, 1978-82, sr. v.p., divsn. head Europe, 1982-83, exec. v.p. U.S. corp. divsn. N.Y.C., 1983-87, group exec. banking and corp. fin. group, 1987-90, vice chmn. instl. banking, 1990—; vice chmn. Global Bank, 1992—, Chase Manhattan Corp., N.Y.C., 1995—2000, chmn., CEO, 2000; CEO, pres. J.P Morgan Chase & Co., N.Y.C., 2000—. Bd. dirs. Merck & Co., Inc., Whitehouse Station, NJ, Banco Gen. Negocious, Buenos Aires; mem. bd. advisors N.C. Outward Bound Sch., Asheville; mem. Bretton Woods Com. Trustee Carnegie Hall; bd. dirs. United Negro Coll. Fund, Inc.; trustee Central Park Conservancy; mem. bd. visitors Kenan Flagler Bus. Sch.; mem. bd. overseers Sloan-Kettering Cancer Ctr., 1999—. Mem.: Nat. Golf Links Am., Golf Club Purchase, Field Club Greenwich, Links Club, Racquet Club, Bus. Coun., Bus. Roundtable, Fin. Svcs. Roundtable, Augusta Nat. Golf Club, Blind Brook Club, Round Hill Club. Episcopalian. Avocations: athletics, traveling.

HARRISON, WILLIAM D. humanities educator; b. Newark, Oct. 10, 1942; s. David J. and Anna R. Harrison; m. Penny Ligier Harrison, Dec. 29, 1973 (div. Mar. 1986); 1 child, Kristin R. Wildsmith. AA, Daytona Beach C.C., Fla., 1965; BA, U. South Fla., 1968; MS, Rollins Coll., Winter Park, Fla., 1978. Dist. counselor Youth Svcs., Daytona Beach, 1973—77; instr. Bethune Cookman Coll., Daytona Beach, 1978—81, asst. prof., 1988—; instr. Orange County C.C., Middletown, NY, 1982—85. Author: Silverfoots Second Dance, 2001, Reuben + John, 2003. With U.S. Army, 1969—71. Mem.: Soc. Music of S.W., Moose. Democrat. Avocation: choreography. Home: 309 Riverside Dr #205 Holly Hill FL 32117 Office: Bethune Cookman Coll 640 MM Bethune Blvd Daytona Beach FL 32114

HARRISON, WILLIAM WRIGHT, b. Kingston, N.Y., Aug. 6, 1915; s. James Burwell and Isabella (Clarke) H.; m. Janet Phillips, Apr. 6, 1940; children: Janet P. (Mrs. Richard Rea Hinch), Susan F. (Mrs. Glassell Slaughter Fitz-Hugh Jr.), William Wright Jr. Student, U. Va., 1933-34. With Va. Nat. Bank (formerly Peoples Nat. Bank Charlottesville), 1942-81, chmn., chief exec. officer, 1969-80, dir., cons., 1980-85. Former chmn. Allied Bank Internat.; dir. Royster Co., Norfolk, Shennandoah Life Ins. Co.; chmn. Minbanc Capital Corp., Washington. Former chmn. Mcpl. Bond Commn., Norfolk; chmn. Va. Found. Ind. Colls.; bd. dirs. Gen. Hosp. Virginia Beach, pres.; bd. dirs. U. Va. Patent Found., Va. Opera, Old Dominion U. Rsch. Found., Gov.'s Commn. on Indsl. Devel.; trustee Norfolk Found., Ea. Va. Med. Sch. Found., Chrysler Mus., Norfolk; former bd. visitors U. Va.; former commr. Va. Port Authority. Mem. Norfolk C. of C. (pres. 1971) Clubs: Princess Anne Country, Harbor. Episcopalian. Home: Virginia Beach, Va. Died Mar. 28, 2001.

HARRISON-SCOTT, SHARLENE MARIE, elementary school educator; b. Fresno, Calif., Dec. 5, 1949; d. Philip B. and Geraldine Marie (Doucette) German; m. Russell Albert Harrison, Aug. 29, 1970 (div. June 1991); children: Nicholas Benjamin, Christopher Ryan; m. Jeffrey Brian Scott, Dec. 11, 1993. BA, Calif. State U., Fresno, 1971; cert. in libr. media tchg., Fresno Pacific Coll., 1996. Tchr. kindergarten Modesto (Calif.) City Schs., 1972-90, tchr., libr. K-6th grades, 1991—. Master tchr. Demonstration Sch. for Calif. State, Stanislaus, 1974-76; instr. Fresno Pacific Coll., 1985-91, Ottowa U., Phoenix, 1990; cons. Archdiocese L.A., 1986-91; mem. recommended reading lit. list revision com. Calif. Dept. Edn. Author: Bear Necessities, 1987-93. Recipient Disting. Educator in Tech. award Computer Using Educators Region VI, 1998, Profl. Svc. award Calif. Sch. Libr. Assn., 2001, Disting. Sch. award winner, 1999. Mem. ALA, Calif. Reading Assn. (symposia spkr. 1989-93), Calif. Sch. Libr. Assn. (pres. 1997-98, chair sch. libr. stds. for K-6 info. skills sect. 2002—), Phi Delta Kappa, Omega Nu. Democrat. Roman Catholic. Avocations: gardening, decorating, antique collecting, reading. Home: 3501 Sagewood Ct Modesto CA 95356-1724 E-mail: bks4me@thevision.net.

HARROD, DANIEL MARK, lawyer; b. Peoria, Ill., Sept. 23, 1945; s. Samuel Glenn and Dorothe Grace (White) H.; m. Amy Lynn Moore, June 4, 1993; children: Maggie, Emily. BA, Eureka (Ill.) Coll., 1967; JD, John Marshall Law Sch., 1975. Bar: Ill., U.S. Dist. Ct. Ill., U.S. Supreme Ct. Pub. defender Woodford County, Eureka, 1980-90; prin. Harrod Law Firm, Eureka. Chmn., bd. dirs. Peoria Area Civic Chorale, Peoria, 1990—. Lt. col. Ill. Air N.G., 1967-88. Mem. Rotary (sgt. at arms 1985—). Avocations: tennis, racquetball. Home: 206 Moody St Eureka IL 61530-1705 Office: Harrod Law Firm 107 E Eureka Ave Eureka IL 61530-1239

HARROD, LOIS MARIE, secondary school educator, poet; b. Dec. 7, 1942; Supr. creative writing N.J. Gov. Sch. of Arts; tchr. English high sch. Author: (poetry books) Every Twinge A Verdict, 1987, Crazy Alice, 1991, (chapbook) Green Snake Riding, 1994, Part of the Deeper Sea, 1997, Spelling the World Backwards, 2000; contbr. poems to Am. Poetry Rev., The Carolina Quarterly, Southern Poetry Review, American Pen, Prairie Schooner, The Literary Rev., Zone 3, Green Mt. Rev. Fellow N.J. Coun. Arts, 1998. E-mail: lmharrod@worldnet.att.net.

HARROLD, BERNARD, lawyer; b. Wells County, Ind., Feb. 5, 1925; s. James Delmer and Marie (Mounsey) H.; m. Kathleen Walker, Nov. 26, 1952; children— Bernard James, Camilla Ruth, Renata Jane. Student, Biarritz Am. U., 1945; AB, Ind. U., 1949, LLB, 1951. Bar: Ill. 1951. Since practiced in, Chgo.; assoc., then mem. firm Kirkland, Ellis, Hodson, Chaffetz & Masters, 1951-67; sr. ptnr. Wildman, Harrold, Allen & Dixon, 1967—. Note editor: Ind. Law Jour, 1950-51; contbr. articles to profl. jours. Served with AUS, 1944-46, ETO. Fellow Am. Coll. Trial Lawyers, Acad. Law Alumni Fellows Ind. U. Sch. Law; mem. ABA, Ill. Bar Assn. (chmn. evidence program 1970), Chgo. Bar Assn, Lawyers Club, Univ. Club, Order of Coif, Phi Beta Kappa, Phi Eta Sigma. Home: 809 Locust St Winnetka IL 60093-1821 Office: Wildman Harrold Allen & Dixon 225 W Wacker Dr Fl 28 Chicago IL 60606-1229 *I try to see people and events for what they really are, apply my talents, work hard, and pay good attention to fairness.*

HARROLD, DENNIS EDWARD, lawyer; b. Los Angeles, Nov. 7, 1947; s. Edward Adron and Helen Lucille (Morrison) Harrold; m. Mary Ann Padgett, Oct. 21, 1972; children: Teresa Lauren, Derek Christopher. BS, Ind. U., 1969; JD, 1972. Bar: Ind. 1972, US Dist. Ct. (so. dist.)/Ind. 1972, US Ct. Mil. Appeals 1972, US Ct. Appeals (7th cir.) 1982, US Supreme Ct. 1986. Pub. defender Shelby Superior Ct., Shelbyville, Ind., 1976—77; assoc. Adams & Cramer, Shelbyville, Ind., 1976—78; sec. Soshnick, Bate & Harrold, P.C., 1979—85, Bate, Harrold & Bate, P.C., Shelbyville, 1985—96, McNeely, Stephenson, Thopy & Harrold, 1996—; sch. bd. atty. Shelbyville Ctrl. Sch., Ind., 1978—; atty. Shelby County, office of family and children, 1987—96; sch. bd. atty. Blue River Career Programs, 1994—. Capt. U.S. Army, 1972—76, Korea. Named Hon. Mem. Bar Republic of Korea, Ministry of Justice, Seoul, 1975; fellow Ind. Bar Found. Mem.: Shelby County C. of C. (dir., pres. 1996—97), Ind. Pub. Defender Council, Ind. Trial Lawyers Assn., Internat. Legal Soc. Korea, Nat. Sch. Bd. Assn. Council Sch. Atty., Assn. Trial Lawyers Am., Indpls. Bar Assn., Shelby County Bar Assn. (pres. 1990—91), Ind. State Bar Assn. (ho. of dels. 1982—85), ABA, Shelby Rural Elec. Cmty. Fund, Inc. (trustee), Salvation Army (adv. bd. 1982—92), Elks, Lions. Republican. Roman Catholic. Home: 2481 N Richard Dr Shelbyville IN 46176-9487 Office: 30 E Washington St Ste 400 Shelbyville IN 46176-1351

HARROLD, FRANCIS BERNARD, JR., anthropology educator; b. Indpls., May 6, 1948; s. Francis Bernard and Eileen Magella (Brennan) H.; m. Geertruida Catharina de Goede, Aug. 15, 1981; children: John F., James B. BA in Anthropology, Loyola U., Chgo., 1970; MA in Anthropology, U. Chgo., 1974, PhD in Anthropology, 1978. Vis. asst. prof. U. Victoria, B.C., Can., 1978-80; asst. prof. U. Tex., Arlington, 1980-86, assoc. prof., 1986-95, prof., 1995-2000, chair Dept. Sociology and Anthropology, 1995-2000; dean Natural and Social Scis. U. Nebr., Kearney, 2000—. Sci. advisor North Tex. Skeptics, Dallas, 1989-2000. Co-author: The Creationist Movement in Modern America, 1990; co-editor, contbr.: Creationism and Cult Archaeology, 1987, 2d rev. edit., 1995. With USNR, 1971-73. Mem. Am. Anthropol. Assn., Soc. Am. Archaeology, Soc. Préhistorique Française, Sigma Xi, Phi Kappa Phi. Avocations: reading, walking, travel. Office: U Nebr Coll Natural and Social Sci Kearney NE 68849 E-mail: harroldfb@unk.edu.

HARROLD, RONALD THOMAS, research scientist; b. Fulham, London, Eng., Apr. 4, 1933; arrived in U.S., 1963; s. John and Cicely Helen (Eddenden) H.; m. Ann Marie Whitley, Dec. 3, 1955; children: Lesley Ann, Linda Jane. BS, Chelmsford Coll. Tech., Eng., 1962, Twickenham Coll. Tech., 1955. Student apprentice Brit. Thomson-Houston Co., Willesden, London, Eng., 1950-55; lectr. radar tech. Army Sch. Electronics, Arborfield, Berkshire, Eng., 1955-57; devel. engr. English Electric Valve Co., Chelmsford, Essex, Eng., 1957-61; rsch. engr. Sylvania-Thorn Color TV Labs., Enfield, Middlesex, Eng., 1961-63; adv. rsch. scientist Westinghouse Sci. and Tech. Ctr., Pitts., 1963-96, cons., 1996—. Contbr. articles to profl. jours. Fellow IEEE (life); mem. Instn. Elec. Engrs., Oxford Athletic Club. Republican. Episcopalian. Achievements include 26 U.S. patents in field of vapour mist dielectrics, acoustic waveguide monitoring. Home: 4052 Benden Cir Murrysville PA 15668-1336 Office: George Westinghouse Rsch and Tech Park 1310 Beulah Rd Pittsburgh PA 15235-5098

HARROLD, STANLEY, historian, educator; b. Morristown, NJ, Oct. 16, 1946; s. Stanley Cooper and Jeanne Ellen Harrold; m. Judy L. Benson, May 14, 1948; 1 child, Emily. BA, Allegheny Coll., Meadville, Pa., 1968; MA, Kent State U., 1970, PhD, 1975. Prof. of history SC. State U., Orangeburg, SC, 1976—2003. Co-editor so. dissent series U. Press of Fla., Gainesville, Fla., 1997—2003. Author: (history) Subversives: Antislavery Comm. in Washington, D.C., 1828-1865 and other books. Fellow, Nat. Endowment for the Humanities, 1991—92, 1996—97. Mem.: Organization of Am. Historians. Green Party. Home: 515 Willington Dr Orangeburg SC 29118-1850 Office: SC State University 300 College St Orangeburg SC 29117 Personal E-mail: sharrold@scsu.edu. E-mail: sharrold@scsu.edu.

HARROP, DANIEL SMITH, III, psychiatrist; b. Warwick, R.I., June 15, 1954; s. Daniel Smith and Dorothy Jane (Hickey) H. BA, Brown U., 1976, MD, 1979; MBA, Edinburgh Bus. Sch., Scotland, 1997. Diplomate Am. Bd. Med. Examiners, Am. Bd. Psychiatry and Neurology, Am. Bd. Geriatrics, Am. Bd. Forensic Examiners. Resident in psychiatry Brown U., Providence, 1983; med. dir. East Bay Cmty. Mental Health Ctr., Barrington, R.I., 1983-87; asst. unit chief Butler Hosp., Providence, 1988-89, chief gen. treatment unit, 1989-93; clin. asst. prof. psychiatry Brown U., Providence, 1985—; physician advisor Magellan Behavioral Health, Balt., 1991-2000; collaborator lab. for clin. and exptl. psychopathology Harvard Med. Sch., Fall River, Mass., 2000—02; physician advisor Magellan, 2003—. Med. dir. United Behavioral Sys., Warwick, R.I., 1993-96; med. dir. The Corrigan Ctr., Fall River, Mass., 1996-2002; bd. dirs. Health Care Rev., Inc., Providence; cons. in field; chmn. utilization rev. Butler Hosp., Providence, 1985-93; instr. dept. psychiatry Harvard U., 1997-2003; advisor Spectera Health Svcs., Balt., Am. PsychSystems, Bethesda, Md. Pres. parish coun. St. Joseph's Ch., Providence, 1987-91, trustee, 1991—; bd. gov.'s Associated Alumni Brown U., Providence, 1988-92; pres. Assn. Class Officers Brown U., Providence, 1988-92; chair Libertarian Party of R.I., 2000—. Fellow Am. Assn. Integrative Medicine; mem. AMA (life), KC (grand knight 1998, 2002), SAR, Am. Psychiat. Assn., R.I. Med. Soc. (med. edn. com. 1989—), R.I. Psychiat. Soc. (pres. 1989-90), R.I. Group Psychotherapy Soc. (pres. 1989-91), Am. Group Psychotherapy (Assembly 1989-97), Faculty Club of Brown U. (pres. 1994-95), Galilee Beach Club (Narragansett, R.I., pres. 1995-98), Mass. Med. Soc. (med. edn. com. 1999—), R.I. Hist. Soc. (life), Roman Cath. Alumni Assn. Brown U. (pres. 1982-83, 93-97), Soc. Sons. & Daughters The Pilgrims, Sons of the Union Vets. of Civil War, Ancient Order of Hibernians, Masons (worshipful master 2001-03), Internat. Order of Odd Fellows, Sierra Club, Serra Internat., Sigma Xi, Sigma Chi (grand coun. 1981—). Roman Catholic. E-mail: drdharrop@yahoo.com.

HARROP, DIANE GLASER, shop owner, mayor, writer, consultant; b. Lafayette, Ind., June 2, 1953; d. Donald Anthony and Mary Ophelia (Rohner) G.; m. Randolph Allen Harrop, Aug. 7, 1976; children: William Donald, Steven Randolph. BE, U. Kans., 1975. Rschr. U. Kans. Speech Dept., Lawrence, 1973-75; clk., book designer Pruett Pub. Co., Boulder, Colo., 1975; debate coach, English tchr. Olathe (Kans.) High Sch., 1975-76; cash items teller Converse County Bank, Douglas, Wyo., 1976-79; owner, mgr. R-D Pharmacy & Books, Douglas, 1979—2001; mayor City of Douglas, 1989-91, coun. mem., 1991-93; columnist Casper Star Tribune, 1993—; weekly columnist Douglas Budget Newspaper, 1994; exec. dir. Wyo. Healthcare Commn. Appt. Wyo. Econ. Devel. and Stabilization Bd., 1991-97, vice chmn. 1994-96, chmn. 1996-97; grants chmn. Wyo. Cmty. Found. Bd. Creator original jewelry (silverwork 1st prize winner Wyo. State Fair 1978). First woman councilmember City of Douglas, 1987-89; gov's. appointee, 1st chmn. State Adv. Coun. on Innovative Edn., Wyo., 1991; bd. trustees pres. Converse County Hosp., 1998—, aux. charter pres., 1985; sec.-treas. Converse County Joint Powers Bd., 1987; bd. dirs. Nicolaysen Art Mus., 1987; mem. Wyo. Mcpl. League Legis. Com. (chmn. 1988—); mem., exhibitor Firearms Engravers Guild of Am., 1988, 89; moderator Congl. Ch.; Douglas chpt. pres. Wyo. Jaycee Women, 1984-85; mem. P.E.O. Sisterhood Chpt. N, 1983-84, Zonta Internat. (treas. 1982-83); pres. Friends of Wyoming State Fair, 1990—; bd. dirs. Ea. Wyoming Mental Health, 1991, Converse County United Way, 1993—; Wyo. adv. com. Dwight D. Eisenhower Math. and Sci. Grant, 1992; mem. parents adv. coun. Douglas H.S., 1994—; chmn. grants com. Wyo. Cmty. Found., 1996—; vice chmn. bd. trustees Converse County Meml. Hosp.; chmn. Converse County Coalition Against Family Violence and Sexual Assault; participant Leadership Wyo., 2003—. Recipient Celebrate Literacy award Internat. Reading Assn. Wyo., 1988, Outstanding Community Svc. award Douglas C. of C., 1991, Apple for Edn. award Gov. Mike Sullivan, 1992, Kellogg Found. scholarship to Heartland Ctr. for Leadership Devel. Seminars, 1993; named one of Outstanding Young Women in Am., 1983-86. Mem. Mountains and Plains Booksellers (bd. dirs. 1992-94), Douglas C. of C., Am. Booksellers Assn., Nat. Fedn. Ind. Businesses, Kiwanis (Douglas chpt. sec. 1994-95, pres. 1996-97), Kiwanis (pres. 1996-97). Republican. Avocations: hand engraving, silversmithing, reading, writing, teaching.

HARROP, WILLIAM CALDWELL, retired ambassador, foreign service officer; b. Balt., Feb. 19, 1929; s. George A. and Esther (Caldwell) H.; m. Ann G. Delavan, Aug. 22, 1953; children— Mark D., Caldwell, Scott N., George H. AB, Harvard U., 1950; postgrad., Grad. Sch. Journalism U. Mo., 1953-54; fellow, Woodrow Wilson Sch., Princeton U., 1968-69. Fgn. Service officer, 1954-93; vice consul, 1954-55; 2d sec. Rome, 1955-58; internat. relations officer Dept. State, 1958-63; 1st sec. Brussels, 1963-66; consul Lubumbashi, Congo, 1966-68; dir. Office Research for Africa, Dept. State, Washington, 1969; dep. chief mission Am. embassy, Canberra, Australia, 1973-75; U.S. ambassador to Guinea, 1975-77; dep. asst. sec. of state for Africa, 1977-80; ambassador to Kenya and Seychelles, 1980-83; insp. gen. Dept. State and Fgn. Service, 1983-86; ambassador to Zaire, 1987-91, 1992-93; ret., 1994. Chmn. Am. Fgn. Svc. Assn., 1970-73, bd. dirs.; bd. dirs. Assn. for Diplomatic Studies and Tng. Bd. dirs. Population Svcs. Internat. Humane Soc. Washington D.C., Henry L. Stimson Ctr. Served with USMCR, 1951-52. Recipient Dept. State Merit Service award, 1968, Presdl. Disting. Service award, 1985, State Dept. Disting. Service award, 1987. Mem.: Chevy Chase (Md.) Club, Met. Club (Washington), Fly Club (Cambridge, Mass.). Address: 3615 49th St NW Washington DC 20016-3214 E-mail: HarropBill@mac.com.

HARROUN, DOROTHY SUMMER, painter, educator; b. El Paso, Tex., Nov. 29, 1935; d. Daniel Stuert and Eleanor (Flowers) H.. BFA, U. N.Mex., 1957; postgrad., U. Paris Sorbonne, 1957—58; MFA, U. Colo., 1960. Art dir. Wood-Reich Advt. Agy., Boulder, 1960—61; lectr. U. Colo., Boulder, 1961—62; art tchr. Langley-Porter Neuropsychiat. Inst. U. Calif., 1963; lectr. San Francisco State Coll., 1964—65; tchr. Art Ctr. Sch., Albuquerque, 1975—79; tchr. watercolor, drawing U. N.Mex., 1980—81. One-woman shows include The Gondolier Gallery, Boulder, Colo., 1961, 1962, Sta. KAFE-FM Gallery, San Francisco, 1963, 1964, Lovelace-Bataan Hosp., Albuquerque, 1976, 1979, Ea. N.Mex. U., 1981, Rathaus, Kelkheim, Germany, N.Mex. State U., United World Coll., Montezuma, N.Mex., 2002, exhibited in group shows at White Mus., San Antonio, 1960, Hyannis, Mass., Waterbury, Conn., Newport, R.I., 1964—65, Mus. N.Mex., Santa Fe, 1966, Ogunguit (Maine) Art Ctr., 1977, Am. Watercolor Soc. 112th Ann., N.Y.C., 1979, Coos Art Mus., Coos Bay, Oreg., 1980, We. Slope Show, Montrose, Colo., 1981, 1982, Ga. Watercolor Soc. Open, 1983, We. Fedn. Watercolor Socs., 1984, 1985, 1986, 1987, 1988, Sun Carnival Art Show, El Paso, 1984, El Paso Mus. Art, 1987, N.Mex. Watercolors show, Gov.'s Gallery, State Capitol, 1988, State Fair Fine Arts Gallery, Albuquerque, 1988, Ch. Farm House Mus., London, 1988—89, St. John's Coll., Santa Fe, 1991, Gallery of the Rep., 1993, Oil Water, Santa FE 1994, Magnifico Invitational Keynote Show, Albuquerque, 1995, Represented in permanent collections U. N.Mex., U. Colo., Fine Arts Mus., Carlsbad, N.Mex., N.Mex. State Capitol, Santa FE, also pvt. collections, U.S., France, Italy, Germany; author, illustrator Take Time to Play and Listen, 1963, Phun-y Physics, 1975, illustrator Mini Walks on the Mesa, 1989. Pres. fine arts alumni bd. U. N.Mex., 1989—. Fulbright scholar. Mem.: AAUW (state cultural dir.), N.Mex. Watercolor Soc. (v.p. 1984, pres. 1985), Nat. League Am. Pen Women (pres. Albuquerque br. 1982—83), Artist Equity Assn. (pres. Albuquerque chpt. 1977—79). Home: 1365 Thunder Rdg Santa Fe NM 87501-8875

HARROW, NANCY (MRS. JAN KRUKOWSKI), jazz singer, songwriter, editor; b. NYC, Oct. 03; d. Benjamin and Frances (Kirschenbaum) H.; m. Jan Krukowski; children: Damon, Anton. BA, Bennington Coll. From copy editor to editor William Morrow & Co., NYC; editor Am. Jour., NYC, 1972-73, editor-at-large, 1974—. Vocalist Tommy Dorsey Orch., 1958; singer Jazz Gallery, Café Au Gogo, Mars Club, N.Y.C. and Paris, 1961-64, Cookery, Plaza Hotel, Upstairs at Cecil's, NYC, 1975-76, Rachel's, Lush Life, Freddy's, Blues Alley, NYC and Washington, 1984-85; singer WDR Big Band, Cologne, Brussels, Holland, NYU Highlights in Jazz, Mazur Theatre, 1986; singer Jan Wallman's NYC, 1987, 89, Stockholm Jazz Festival, 1988, Michael's Pub, 1990, Judy's Supper Club, The Salon, NYC, 1995-96; The Marble Faun, 1999, The Salon, NYC, Maya the Bee Puppet Show, 200045 Bleecker Theater, N.Y.C. Recording artist (albums) Wild Women Don't Have the Blues, 1961, You Never Know, 1963, Anything Goes, 1979; songwriter: (John Lewis music) As Long As It's About Love, Distant Lover, 1981; recording artist (albums) The John Lewis Album for Nancy Harrow, 1981; composer: (Nancy Harrow music and lyrics) 5 songs for Secrets album, 1992, 12 songs for the Lost Lady album, 1992—93; recording artist (albums) Two's Company: Nancy Harrow with Jack Wilkins, 1984, You're Nearer, 1986, Street of Dreams, 1990; composer: (Raymond Patterson lyrics) A Little Blue, 1990; recording artist (albums) The Beatles and Other Standards, 1990, Two's Company: Nancy Harrow with Jack Wilkins, 1991, Secrets, 1992, Lost Lady, 1994; composer: (Nancy Harrow music and lyrics) 21 songs for Maya the Bee, 2000, 13 songs for The Marble Faun, 1999; recording artist (albums) You're Nearer, 1998, The Marble Faun, 1999, Maya the Bee, 2000; composer: (Nancy Harrow music and lyrics) 11 Songs for Winter Dreams, 2003; recording artist (albums) Winter Dreams, 2003. Mem.: Century Assn. Address: 130 E End Ave New York NY 10028-7553 E-mail: nancyjazz@aol.com.

HARRY, CHARLES THOMAS, economist; b. Anaheim, Calif., Nov. 26, 1973; s. Ronald Wayne Harry and Marianne Elizabeth O'Riley, Frank John Bohac (Stepfather) and Marty Harry(Stepmother); m. Torin Michelle Lee, Sept. 5, 1999. BA in History, BA in Econs., U. Colo., Boulder, 1995, MA in Econs., 2000. Fin. svcs. rep. U. Colo. Fed. Credit Union, Boulder, Colo., 1995—97; internat. trade analyst Australia New Zealand Direct Line, Santa Ana, Calif., 1997—98; market rsch. officer U. Colo. Fed. Credit Union, Boulder, Colo., 1998—2000; nat. security analyst for (econ. consequence mgmt.) Sci. Applications Internat. Co (SAIC), McLean, Va., 2001—. Recipient citation, Def. Threat Reduction Agy., 2002. Mem.: Jaycees (founding mem. Reston, Va. chpt.). Roman Catholic. Achievements include development of Economic Consequence Assessment Model (ECAM) identifies to government decision makers the impact to the economy of a WMD related terrorist event; research in relationship between exchange rate pressure and the level of privately held debt within a country. This research helps to predict when a central bank will defend its currency; development of economic models to estimate the impact to the national and local economies resulting from hostile attacks against the United States. Avocations: travel, spelunking, hiking, photography. Office: Sci Applications Int Corp (SAIC) 1710 SAIC Dr McLean VA 22102 Personal E-mail: charles_harry@hotmail.com.

HARSANYI, JANICE, soprano, educator; b. Arlington, Mass., July 15, 1929; d. Edward and Thelma (Jacobs) Morris; m. Nicholas Harsanyi, Apr. 19, 1952; 1 son, Peter Michael. BMus, Westminster Choir Coll., 1951; postgrad., Phila. Acad. Vocal Arts, 1952-54. Voice tchr. Westminster Choir Coll., Princeton, N.J., 1951-63, chmn. voice dept., 1963-65; lectr. music Princeton Theol. Sem., 1956-63; voice tchr. summer sessions U. Mich., 1965-70; artist-in-residence Interlochen Arts Acad., 1967-70; voice tchr. N.C. Sch. Arts, Winston-Salem, 1971-78; music faculty Salem Coll., 1973-76; condr. voice master classes, choral clinics various colls., 1954—; prof. voice Fla. State U., Tallahassee, 1978—, chmn. dept., 1979-83. Concert singer, 1954—, debut, Phila. Orch., 1958; appearances with, Am., Detroit, Houston, Minn., Nat., Symphony of Air orchs., Bach Aria Group, 1967-68, maj. music festivals, U.S., 1960— ; toured with, Piedmont Chamber Orch., 1971-78, concerts and recitals, in major U.S. cities, also in Belgium, Eng., Ger., Italy, Switzerland and Sweden; rec. artist, Columbia, Decca, CRI records. Mem. Nat. Assn. Tchrs. Singing, Music Tchrs. Nat. Assn., Coll. Music Soc., Riemenschneider Bach Inst., Sigma Alpha Iota, Pi Kappa Lambda. Home: 2116 Trescott Dr Tallahassee FL 32308-0732 Office: Florida State Univ Sch Music Tallahassee FL 32306

HARSHA, PHILIP THOMAS, aerospace engineer; b. N.Y.C., Feb. 22, 1942; s. Palmer and Catherine (Redinger) H.; m. Jean Ann Quinn, Oct. 23, 1965; children: Peter Charles, Evan Michael. BS in Engring. Sci., SUNY, Stony Brook, 1962, MS in Engring. Sci., 1964; PhD in Aerospace Engring., U. Tenn., 1970. Combustion rsch. engr. GE, Cin., 1964-67; lead rsch. engr. Aro, Inc., Arnold Engring. Devel. Ctr., Tenn., 1969-74; rsch. specialist R & D Assoc., Marina Del Rey, Calif., 1974-76; divsn. mgr. Sci. Applications Internat. Corp., Chatsworth, Calif., 1976-85; chief aero. scientist Lockheed Aero. Sys. Group, Burbank, Calif., 1985-88; chief project engr. Rocketdyne divsn. Rockwell Internat., Canoga Park, Calif., 1988-90; dep. program dir. Nat. Aero-Space Plane Program, 1990-95; program mgr. The Boeing Co., Huntington Beach, Calif., 1994—, Boeing Tech. fellow, 2002—. Contbr. articles to profl. jours.

Recipient Disting. Alumnus award U. Tenn. Space Inst., 1984. Mem. AIAA, ASME, N.Y. Acad. Sci., Sigma Xi. Republican. Methodist. Home: 1607 Ocean Ave Seal Beach CA 90740-6548 Office: The Boeing Co 5301 Bolsa Ave Huntington Beach CA 92647-2099

HARSHBARGER, RICHARD B. economics educator; b. Lafayette, Ind., May 6, 1934; s. Albert E. and Olive M. (Shambaugh) M.; m. Jane L. Newcomer, Aug. 24, 1958; children: Lisa, Jon. BS, Manchester Coll., 1956; MA, Ind. U., 1958, PhD, 1964. Fuels economist Tenn. Valley Authority, Chattanooga, 1958; econ. prof. Manchester Coll., North Manchester, Ind., 1960-99. Vis. prof. Pasadena (Calif.) Coll., 1968-69, Eastern Nazarene Coll., Quincy, Mass, 1977-78. Mem. Manchester (Ind.) Park Bd., 1972—76, Manchester Sch. Bd., 1972—76, Town Forum, 1986—, Indsl. Policy Com., North Manchester, 1990—; pres. Shepherd Ctr., 2002—; bd. dirs. Bethany Theol. Sem., Oak Brook, Ill., 1987—92, Camp Mack, Milford, Inc., 1986—92, 2001—; mem. fin. com. Wabash County Found., 1997—. Fellow NSF, 1958-59, grad. fellow Ind. U., 1956-58. Mem. Am. Econ. Assn., Midwest Econ. Assn., Ind. Acad. Social Sci. (dir. 1965-66), Ind. Econ. Forum (pres. 1973-74), Rotary (pres. 1979-80). Democrat. Mem. Ch. of Brethren.

HARSHFIELD, NEIL ALAN, sculptor, educator; b. Washington, Aug. 4, 1962; s. Robert Leslie and Jessie Helena (Day) Harshfield. BA, George Mason U., 1988; MFA, Tulane U., 1995. Tchg. asst. George Mason U., Fairfax, Va., 1989-91, Temple U., Phila., 1992; asst. fabricator Nat Coun. on Edn. for Ceramics Conf., Phila., 1993; tchg. asst. Pilchuck Glass Sch., Stanwood, Wash., 1994; asst. prof., glass shop technician, coord. Tulane U., New Orleans, 1994-98, asst. prof. glass, 2000—01, gallery preparator Woldenberg Art Ctr., 1996—2001; asst. prof. sculpture Loyola U., New Orleans, 1998. Gallery preparator Arthur Roger Gallery, New Orleans, 1999-2001; freelance fabricator, engr., Phila., 1991-93, New Orleans, 1994-2001, Washington, 2001—; adv., cons. Arts Coun. New Orleans, 1996-2001; instr. Urban Arts Tng. Program, New Orleans, 1997. Contbr. articles to profl. publs. Contbr. Arts Against AIDS, New Orleans, 1996, Contemporary Arts Ctr., New Orleans, 1996. Mem. Glass Art Soc., Internat. Sculpture Ctr. (Outstanding Sculpture award 1995). Avocations: gardening, cycling, photography. Home: 5501 Seminary Rd # 910 S Falls Church VA 22041-3905

HARSHMAN, DALE RICHARD, physicist; b. Honolulu, Aug. 13, 1956; s. Richard Eugene and LaVonne Olive (Berg) H.; m. Sandra Joan Vecchione, Feb. 2, 1985; 1 child, Joshua Dale. BSc, Pacific Lutheran U., 1978; MSc, Western Wash. U., 1980; PhD, U. B.C., Vancouver, Can., 1986. Rsch. assoc. U. B.C., 1980-86, postdoctoral fellow, 1986, Bell Labs., Murray Hill, N.J., 1986-88, mem. tech. staff., 1988-97; exec. v.p., dir. sci. rsch. Physikon Rsch. Corp., Lynden, Wash., 1997—. Vis. prof. U. Notre Dame, Ind., 1999—, Ariz. State U., Tempe, 1999—2002, adj. prof., 2002—; cons. U.S. Dept. Energy, Arlington, Va., 1992, Argonne, Ill., 93; spkr. in field. Contbr. numerous articles to profl. jours. Recipient William Cochrane prize for physics, Inst. for Postdoc. Studies, Scottsdale, Ariz., 2002; grantee, U.S. Dept. Energy, 1995—98. Mem.: Am. Phys. Soc. Avocations: robotics, bike riding, poetry, music, fishing. Office: Physikon Rsch Corp PO Box 1014 Lynden WA 98264 E-mail: drh@physikon.net.

HARSHMAN, MARC, writer, poet, consultant; b. Union City, Ind., Oct. 1, 1950; s. William Leonard Harshman and Janice Louise Wells; m. Cheryl Ryan, Aug. 25, 1976; 1 child, Sarah Jayne. BA in Religious Studies, Bethany (W.Va.) Coll., 1973; MA in Religion and the Arts, Yale U., 1975; MA in English, U. Pitts., 1978. Children's author, poet, W.Va., 1973—; instr. composition and creative writing U. Pitts., 1978-79; instr. composition W.Va. N. C.C., Wheeling, 1979-82; cons. writing Moundsville, W.Va., 1983—; tchr. grades 5-6 Marshall County Schs., Moundsville, 1986-97. Profl. storyteller, 1976—. Author: (poetry) Turning Out the Stones, 1983, (children's books) A Little Excitement, 1989, Snow Company, 1990, Uncle James, 1993, Only One, 1993, Moving Days, 1994, The Storm, 1995 (Smithsonian Notable award, Parent's Choice award 1995), All the Way to Morning, 1999, (with Cheryl Ryan) Red Are the Apples, 2001,(poetry) Rose of Sharon, 1999, Roads, 2002; co-author: (with Bonnie Collins) Rocks in My Pockets, 1991; mem. editl. rev. W.Va. English Jour., 1996-98. Recipient Alumni Achievement award in lit. Bethany Coll., 1994, W.Va. Lit. Merit award W.Va. Libr. Assn., 1993; Ezra Jack Keats/Kerlan fellow Kerlan Collection/U. Minn., 1994. Mem. Soc. Children's Book Writers, Poets & Writers, Inc., W.Va. English Lang. Arts Coun. (Lang. Arts Tchr. of Yr. 1995), W.Va. Highlands Conservancy, Union Lit. Inst., Internat. Reading Assn., Wilderness Soc., Amnesty Internat. Avocations: gardening, hiking, music, travel.

HARSHMAN, RAYMOND BRENT, lawyer; b. Athens, Ala., Feb. 16, 1948; s. L. Raymond and B. Katherine (Laubenthal) H.; m. Letha Lee, Nov. 30, 1974; 3 children. BSBA, U. Tenn., 1969; JD, So. Meth. U., 1973. Bar: Tex. 1973, U.S. Ct. Appeals (D.C. and 5th cirs.) 1986, U.S. Ct. Appeals (6th cir.) 1989, Colo. 1992, U.S. Ct. Appeals (11th cir.) 1992. Instr., atty. Abilene (Tex.) Christian U., 1973-74; tax acct./tax atty. Exxon Co., USA, Houston, 1974-76; gas contract rep. Tex. Gas Transmission Corp., Houston, 1976-78; atty. Diamond Shamrock Corp., Amarillo, Tex., 1978-81; sr. atty. Diamond Shamrock Exploration Co., Amarillo, Tex., f1981-86; assoc. counsel Maxus Energy Corp., Dallas, 1986-90, sr. counsel, 1991-99; ind. atty. Dallas, 2000; asst. city atty. Austin Energy, 2001—. Mem. State Bar Tex., Fed. Energy Bar Assn. Mem. Ch. of Christ.

HART, ANN WEAVER, educational administration educator; b. Salt Lake City, Nov. 6, 1948; d. Ted Lionel and Sylvia (Moray) Weaver; m. Randy Bret Hart, Sept. 12, 1968; children: Kimberly, Liza, Emily, Allyson. BS in History, U. Utah, 1970, MA in History, 1981, PhD in Ednl. Adminstrn., 1983. Tchr. pub. schs., Salt Lake City, 1970-73, 80-81; jr. high sch. prin. Provo (Utah) Pub. Schs., 1983-84; prof. ednl. adminstrn. U. Utah, Salt Lake City, 1984—98, assoc. dean Grad. Sch. Edn., 1991-93, dean Grad. Sch., 1993—98; provost, v.p. acad. affairs Claremont Grad. U., Calif., 1998—2002; pres. U. N.H., Durham, 2002—. Cons. various sch. dists., 1983—, regional edn1. labs., 1986—; bd. dirs. Citizens Bank N.H. Author: Principal Succession: Establishing Leadership in Schools, 1993, The Principalship, 1996, Designing and Conducting Research, 1996; editor: Ednl. Adminstrn. Quar., 1990-92; contbr. articles to profl. jours. Grantee U. Utah, State of Utah, U.S. Dept. Edn. Mem. Am Ednl. Rsch. Assn., Am. Coun. on Edn., Phi Beta Kappa, Phi Kappa Phi. Avocations: skiing, backpacking, hiking, kayaking, bicycling. Office: Univ of New Hampshire Pres Office 201 Thompson Hall Durham NH 03824

HART, ARTHUR ALVIN, historian, author; b. Tacoma, Feb. 13, 1921; s. Albert Arthur and Erma Lola (Maltby) H.; m. Novella D. Cochran, Feb. 26, 1944; children: Susanna, Robin, Catherine, Allison. BA, MFA, U. Wash., Seattle, 1948; postgrad., Biarritz Am. U., Hans Hofmann Sch. Fine Arts, U. Calif., Berkeley; HHD (hon.), Coll. Idaho, 1985. Head art dept., chmn. divsn. fine arts Coll. Idaho, 1948-53; instr. art Colby Jr. Coll. Women, New London, N.H., 1953-54; head art dept., dir. adult edn. Bay Path Jr. Coll., Longmeadow, Mass., 1955-69; dir. Idaho Hist. Mus., Boise, 1969-75, Idaho Hist. Soc., 1975-86. Lectr. Am. architecture Boise State U., 1970-86 ; mem. Boise Allied Arts Council, 1970-78, Idaho Historic Preservation Coun., 1971-87, Boise Bicentennial Commn., 1975-76, Idaho Centennial Commn., 1985-90, Idaho Humanities Coun., 1985-86; mem. adv. bd. Snake River Regional Studies Ctr., 1969—, Boise Redevel. Agy., 1986-87, Basque Mus. and Cultural Ctr., 1985—, Idaho Aviation Hall of Fame, 1990—. Author: Steam Trains in Idaho, 1971, Space, Style and Structure: Building in Northwest America, 1974, Fighting Fire on the Frontier, 1976, Historic Boise, 1979, The Boiseans: At Home, 1984, Idaho, Gem of the Mountains, 1985, Basin of Gold, 1986, Life in Old Boise, 1989, Camera Eye on Idaho: Pioneer Photography 1863-1913, 1990, Wings Over Idaho: An Aviation History, 1991, Boise Baseball: The First 125 Years, 1994, The Boise Children's Home, 1996, Barns of the West: A Vanishing Legacy, 1996, The Arid Club, Its Life and Times, 1997, Centennial History of the Western Idaho Fair, 1897-1997, 1997, To Protect and To Serve: Law Enforcement in Boise, Idaho, 1863-2000, 2000, Boise: An Illustrated History, 2000, Chinatown: Boise, Idaho, 1870-1970, 2002; contbg. author: Encyclopedia of American Forest and Conservation History, 1983, Dictionary of American Medical Biography, 1984; weekly columnist (newspaper) Idaho Statesman, 1970-95, Boise Weekly, 1995-97, Idaho Mag., 2002—. Mem. Mayor's Boise 2000 Com. Recipient Idaho Statesman Disting. Citizen award, 1973, Allied Arts Coun. award for hist. writing, 1972, Phoenix award for leadership in conservation Soc. Am. Travel Writers, 1982, Idaho Bar Assn. award, 1985, James C. Howland Urban Enrichment award, 1990, Preservationist award Idaho Hist. Preservation Coun., 1999, Disting. Achievement in the Humanities award Idaho Humanities Coun., 2000. Mem. AIA (hon.), AAUP, Coll. Art Assn., Soc. Archtl. Historians (pres. No. Pacific Coast chpt. 1974-76), Am. Assn. Museums (mem. council 1980-82, pres. Western regional conf. 1979-81)

HART, BRENDA REBECCA, retired gifted and talented educator; b. West Point, Ga., Aug. 29, 1941; d. Howard William Godfrey, Sarah Will Clegg; m. William Samuel Hart, Mar. 26, 1961 (dec. Oct. 1971); 1 child, Keith Samuel. BA in Social Studies, La Grange Coll., 1977, MEd in History, 1979. Tchr. gifted and talented State Dept. Edn., Atlanta, 1998—2003, ret., 2003. Collector data State Dept. Edn., Atlanta, 1985—, advance placement, 1998—. Home: 1702 Rosemont Ave West Point GA 31823

HART, BUSTER CLARENCE, lawyer; b. Promise City, Iowa, Mar. 19, 1923; s. Harry H. and Alfreda (DeBolt) H.; m. Jean F. Hart, July 7, 1933; children: Nannette, Kyle, Charles, Charlotte. AB, U. Iowa, 1947; JD, Harvard U., 1950. Bar: Minn. 1951, U.S. Ct. Mil. Appeals 1956, U.S. Supreme Ct. 1956. Ptnr. Briggs and Morgan, P.C., St. Paul, 1951-76, pres., 1976 83, Hart, Bruner, O'Brien & Thornton and predecessors, Mpls., 1983—. V.p. Downtown St. Paul, 1956—59; bd. dirs. Lakewood Coll. Found., 1974—76; mem. Minn. Citizens Com. for Voyageurs Nat. Park, 1975—; co. chmn. United Fund, bd. dirs., 1958—61, 1981—; mem. midwest regional adv. com. Nat. Park Svc. Lt. col. USAR. Fellow: Am. Bar Found.; mem.: Harvard Law Sch. Assn. (state pres. Minn., nat. v.p.), Am. Coll. Constr. Lawyers (past pres.), Am. Coll. Constrn. Arbitrators, Am. Bd. Trial Advocates (state pres. 1973), Am. Coll. Trial Lawyers, Internat. Assn. Ins. Counsel, Ramsey County Bar Assn., Fed. Bar Assn., Minn. Bar Assn. (chmn.ct. rules com. 1973—77), ABA (chmn. tort and ins. practice sect. 1980—81, Martin J. Andrew Lifetime Achievement award, Tips Andrew Hecker Lifetime Achievement award), ATLA, Minn. Club (bd. dirs. 1980—86), St. Paul Athletic Club, Phi Beta Kappa. Office: Fabyanske Westra & Hart 920 2d Ave S Ste 1100 Minneapolis MN 55402 E-mail: bchart@minnlaw.com.

HART, CECIL WILLIAM JOSEPH, otolaryngologist, surgeon; b. Bath, Somerset, Eng., May 27, 1931; came to U.S., 1957. s. William Theodore Hart and Paulina Olive (Adams) Gilmer; m. Brigid Frances Molloy, June 15, 1957 (dec. Nov. 1984); children: Geoffrey Arthur, Paula Mary, John Adams; m. Doris Crystel Katharina Alm, Mar. 14, 1987; children: Kristen-Linnea Alm, Erik Alm, Britt-Marie Alm. BA, Trinity Coll., Dublin, Ireland, 1952, MB, BCH, BAO, 1955, MA, 1958. Diplomate Am. Bd. Otolaryngology. Intern Dr. Steevens Hosp., Dublin, Ireland, 1956, Little Co. Mary Hosp., Evergreen Park, Ill., 1957, mem. staff, 1958-59; resident in otolaryngology U. Chgo. Hosp. and clinic, 1959-62; instr. U. Chgo. Med. Sch., 1962-64, asst. prof., 1964-65; practice medicine specializing in otolaryngology Chgo., 1958—; mem. staff Northwestern Meml. Hosp., 1972-97, Rehab. Inst. Chgo., 1965-97, Children's Meml. Hosp., 1972-97, Little Co. of Mary Hosp., 1977-94, LaGrange (Ill.) Comty. Meml. Hosp., 1977-94, Loyola U. Med. Ctr., 1997—. Tchg. assoc. Cleft Palate Inst., 1968, dir. otolaryngology, 1969-92; asst. prof. dept. otolaryngology-head and neck surgery Northwestern U. Med. Sch., 1965-75, assoc. prof., 1975-92, prof., 1992-97, prof. emeritus, 1997—; lectr. dept. otorhinolaryngology Loyola U., 1972, prof. otolaryngology, head and neck surgery, 1997-2001; med. adv. bd. So. Hearing and Speech Found., Nat. Inst. of Deafness and Other Communicative Disorders, 1989-93. Producer videos, movie; contbr. numerous articles to profl. jours. and mags.; also guest appearances various radio and TV talk shows. NIH fellow U. Chgo., 1962-63; NIH grantee, 1985-88. Fellow Am. Neurotology Soc. (pres. 1974-75, chmn. editorial review & publ. com. 1978-79, constn. and bylaws com. 1979-97), Am. Acad. Otolaryngology-Head and Neck Surgery (chmn. subcom. on Equilibrium 1980-86, computer com. 1987-90), ACS, Inst. Medicine Chgo., Soc. for Ear, Nose and Throat Advances in Children; mem. AMA, Brit. Med. Assn., Ill. State Med. Soc., Chgo. Med. Soc., Am. Cleft Palate Assn., Am. Council Otolaryngology, Am. Otological Soc., Chgo. Laryngological and Otological Soc. (v.p. 1975-76), Northwestern Clin. Faculty Med. Assn. (vice chmn. 1976-78, pres. 1979-81), Barany Soc., Royal Soc. Medicine, Irish Otolaryngological Soc., So. Hearing and Speech Found (med. adv. bd.), Chgo. Hearing and Balance Assn. (pres.), Sigma Xi. Roman Catholic. Avocations: travel, baroque music, symphony, opera, tennis. E-mail: cwjhart@aol.com.

HART, C(HARLES) W(ILLARD), JR., zoologist, curator; b. Farmville, Va., Jan. 30, 1928; s. Charles Willard and Etta Catharine (Sawyer) H.; m. Margaret Waddell Gordon, Sept. 17, 1957 (div. Jan. 1958); m. Nancy Dabney Gardner, June 9, 1962. BA, Hampden-Sydney (Va.) Coll., 1949, BS, 1950; postgrad., Fla. State U., 1950-52, 53-54; MA, U. Va., 1951. Instr. biology Washington Coll., Chestertown, Md., 1954-55, Randolph Macon Woman's Coll., Lynchburg, Va., 1955-56; med. editor Smith, Kline & French Labs., Phila., 1956-58; editor sci. publs. Acad. Natural Scis., Phila., 1958-70, dir. water pollution studies, 1968-74; asst. to dir. Natural History Mus., Smithsonian Instn., Washington, 1974-79, curator dept. invertebrate zoology, 1979-92, chmn. dept., 1988-91, rsch. scientist, curator, 1992-96, rsch. scientist emeritus, 1996—. Author: A Dictionary of the Non-Scientific Names of Freshwater Crayfishes, 1994; (with Janice Clark) An Interdisciplinary Bibliography of Freshwater Crayfishes from Aristotle Through 1987, 1989; editor: (with P. Holt and R. Hoffmann) The Distributional History of the Biota of the Southern Appalachians, Part I: Invertebrates, 1969, (with S.L.H. Fuller) Pollution Ecology of Freshwater Invertebrates, 1974, Pollution Ecology of Estuarine Invertebrates, 1979, (with Dabney G. Hart) The Ostracod Family Entocytheridae, 1974; contbr. numerous articles to profl. jours. Mem. Phila. Rep. City Com., 1966-68; bd. dirs. Archbold Ctr. for Tropical Rsch., Dominica, 1987-96. Fellow AAAS; mem. Am. Soc. Zoologists (com. on rsch. in systematic biology 1974-78), Crustacean Soc. (treas. 1981-85), Biol. Soc. Washington (editor Procs. Biol. Soc. Washington 1978-80, sec. 1986-88), Assn. Southeastern Biologists (editor ASB Bull. 1961-72, pres. 1970-71), Coun. Biology Editors (treas. 1968-71), Explorers Club, Cosmos Club Washington (mem., chair, program com. 1996-98), Cosmos Club Found. (trustee 1998—), Phi Beta Kappa, Sigma Xi. Episcopalian. Avocations: web page design and maintenance, flying (private pilot, instrument and glider ratings), sailing, jewelry design and fabrication, cartography of bermuda. Home: 6449 Walters Woods Dr Falls Church VA 22044-1424 E-mail: winston@patriot.net.

HART, CHRISTOPHER ALVIN, lawyer; b. Denver, June 18, 1947; s. Judson Duncan and M. Murlee (Shaw) H.; children: Adam Christopher, Brooke Corinne; m. Leeann Moore, 2002; B.S. in Aerospace Engring., Princeton U., 1969, M.S. in Aerospace Engring., 1971; J.D., Harvard U., 1973. Bar: D.C. 1973, U.S. Dist. Ct. D.C. 1973, U.S. Ct. Appeals (D.C. cir.) 1973, U.S. Ct. Appeals (8th cir.) 1981, U.S. Supreme Ct. 1985. Assoc. Peabody, Rivlin & Lambert, Washington, 1973-76, Dickstein, Shapiro & Marin, Washington, 1979-81; gen. atty. Air Transport Assn., Washington, 1976-77; dep. asst. gen. counsel U.S. Dept. Transp., Washington, 1977-79; charter, prin. firm Hart & Chavers, Washington, 1981-90; mem. Nat. Transp. Safety Bd., 1990-93; dep. adminstr. Nat. Highway Traffic Safety Adminstrn., 1993-94; assoc. adminstr. for system safety Fed. Aviation Adminstrn., 1994—. Bd. dirs. Howard U. Hosp. Cancer Ctr., Washington, 1983-88, WPFW (Pacific Found.)-FM, 1984-90, Nat. Sleep Found., 1997—. Recipient Superior Performance award U.S. Dept. Transp., 1979. Mem. D.C. Bar (com. ethics 1983-89, mem. bd. profl. responsibility 1989-94), Washington Bar Assn., Fed. Bar Assn., Fed. Communications Bar Assn., Lawyer-Pilots Bar Assn., Black Princeton Alumni (dir. N.Y.C. 1981-87). Democrat. Episcopalian. Home: 1612 Crittenden St NW Washington DC 20011-4218 Office: Fed Aviation Adminstrn 800 Independence Ave SW Washington DC 20591-0001

HART, CLAIRE-MARIE, educator; b. Lawrence, Mass., Dec. 6, 1942; d. Roderick P. and M. Claire (Sullivan) H. BS in Edn., Bridgewater State Coll., 1964; MA, U. R.I., 1968; MAT, Salem State Coll., 1985. Tchr. English B.M.C. Durfee High Sch., Fall River, Mass., 1964-68, Beverly (Mass.) High Sch., 1968—. Adj. prof. English No. Shore C.C., Danvers, Mass., 1970—, Endicott Coll., Beverly, 1997—; mentor cons. Beverly Sch. Dist., 1996—; cons., presenter in field. Mem. subcom. Beverly Sch. Com., 1998-2000; mem. Local Religious Ch. Orgn., Beverly, 1978—, Dem. City Com., Beverly, 1978—. Recipient Outstanding Educator award, Harvard U., Cambridge, Mass., 2000; NEH grantee, 1986, 88. Mem. NEA, MLA, Nat. Coun. Tchrs. English, Dante Soc. Am., New Eng. Assn. Tchrs. English, Mass. Tchrs. Assn. Roman Catholic. Avocations: reading, antiques, gardening, theatre. Home: 5 Cornell Rd Beverly MA 01915-1611 Office: Beverly High Sch 100 Sohier Rd Beverly MA 01915 E-mail: cmhdante@aol.com.

HART, CLIFFORD HARVEY, lawyer; b. Flint, Mich., Nov. 12, 1935; s. Max S. and Dorothy H. (Fineberg) H.; m. Alice Rosenberg, June 17, 1962; children: Michael F., David E., Steven A. AB, U. Mich., 1957, JD, 1960. Bar: Mich. 1960, U.S. Dist. Ct. (ea. and we. dists.) Mich. 1962; cert. civil trial advocate. Assoc. Stevens & Nelson, Flint, 1960-62; ptnr. White, Newblatt, Nelson & Hart, Flint, 1962-64, Dean, Dean, Segar & Hart, P.C. and predecessor firms, Flint, 1965-97; pvt. practice Law Offices Clifford H. Hart, 1997—. Adj. assoc. prof. Flint Sch. Mgmt., U. Mich., 1972—; lectr. Inst. Continuing Legal Edn., Mich.; lectr. Mich. Jud. Inst. Pres. Vis. Nurse Assn., Flint, 1967; pres. Temple Beth El, 1973-75; trustee United Way Genesee County, 1981—, chmn. bd., 1990-91, sec., 1988-89, chmn. bd. dirs. Genesee County and Lapeer County, 1990-91; chair corp. adv. bd. U. Mich., Flint, 1988-93; mem. faculty Inst. Continuing Legal Edn., Ann Arbor, Mich., 1984—. Fellow: Roscoe Pound Found., Mich. Bar Found., Mich. Bar Found. (life); mem.: ATLA (bd. govs. 1979—, chmn. elections com. 1984—87, lectr., budget com. 1987—2004, chair 1989—91, nat. parliamentarian 1990—91, exec. com. 1990—93, nat. treas. 1991—92, exec. com. 1984—85, chair 1998—2004, exec. com. 1998—2004), ABA, Nat. Bd. Trial Advocacy (cert.), Am. Judicature Soc., Genesee County Bar Assn. (pres. 1975—76), Mich. Trial Lawyers Assn. (pres. 1977—78, lectr.), Mich. State Bar Assn. (rep. assembly 1975—81, chmn. negligence law sect. 1981—82), B'nai B'rith (past pres.). Democrat. Office: 1410 Mott Found Bldg 503 S Saginaw St Flint MI 48502-1807 E-mail: clhart@umich.edu.

HART, CLYDE J., JR., federal agency administrator; BS in Polit. Sci. & History with honors, St. Peter's Coll.; JD, Cath. U. Am.; MS in Pub. Policy, George Washington U.; PhD (hon.), Mass. Maritime Acad. Law clk. U.S. Dist. Ct., Washington, 1975-77; assoc. Akin, Gump, Hauer & Feld, Washington, 1977-80; trial atty. Office Gen. Counsel Interstate Commerce Commn., 1980-93, agy. mgmt. counsel, 1993-94; sr. Dem. counsel U.S. Senate Com. on Commerce, Sci. and Transp., 1994-98; adminstr. Maritime Adminstrn. U.S. Dept. Transp., Washington, 1998-2000, acting dep. adminstr. Fed. Motor Carrier Safety Adminstrn., 2000—. Tchr. No. Va. C.C., U. Md. U. Coll., U. Va. With USAF, 1965-69. Mem. Washington Bar Assn., D.C. Bar Assn. Office: Dept Transp 400 7th St SW Rm 316A Washington DC 20590-0003

HART, DANIEL, orchestra executive; Bassist Peoria (Ill.) Symphony Orch., Colo. Springs (Colo.) Symphony, Baton Rouge Symphony Orch.; exec. dir. Va. Symphony Orch., Norfolk, 1994-98, Columbus (Ohio) Symphony Orch., 1998—. Office: Columbus Symphony Orch 55 E State St Columbus OH 43215-4203

HART, DANIEL ANTHONY, bishop; b. Lawrence, Mass., Aug. 24, 1927; s. John J. and Susan M. (Tierney) H.. BSBA, Boston Coll., 1956; MEd, Boston State Coll., 1972; MDiv, St. John's Sem., Brighton, Mass., 1974. Priest Roman Cath. Ch., 1953. Asst. pastor, Lynnfield, Mass., 1953—54, Wellesley, Mass., 1954—56, Malden, Mass., 1956—64; vice-chancellor Archdiocese of Boston, 1964—70; asst. pastor Peabody, Mass., 1970—76; titular bishop of Tepelta, aux. bishop of Boston, 1976—95; regional bishop S. region, 1976—95; archdiocesan vicar for pastoral devel., 1976—85; bishop of Norwich, 1995—2003; bishop emeritus of Norwich, 2003—. Pres. Boston Senate of Priests, 1972—74; mem. exec. bd. Nat. Fedn. Priests' Couns., 1973—75. Roman Catholic. Address: 213 Broadway Norwich CT 06360-4307 E-mail: bphart@norwichdiocese.org.

HART, EDWARD LEROY, poet, educator; b. Bloomington, Idaho, Dec. 28, 1916; s. Alfred Augustus and Sarah Cecilia (Patterson) H.; m. Eleanor May Coleman, Dec. 15, 1944 (dec. Dec. 1990); children: Edward Richard, Paul LeRoy, Barbara, Patricia; m. Leah Yates Bryson, Apr. 30, 1993 (dec. Aug. 2001); m. Frances Cannon Lee, June 7, 2002. BS, U. Utah, 1939; MA, U. Mich., 1941; DPhil (Rhodes scholar), Oxford (Eng.) U., 1950. Instr. U. Utah, Salt Lake City, 1946; asst. prof. U. Wash., Seattle, 1949-52, Brigham Young U., Provo, Utah, 1952-55, assoc. prof., 1955-59, prof., 1959-82, prof. emeritus, 1982—. Vis. prof. U. Calif., Berkeley, 1959-60, Ariz. State U., summer 1968. Author: Minor Lives, 1971, Instruction and Delight, 1976, Mormom in Motion, 1978; (poems) To Utah, 1979, Poems of Praise, 1980; More Than Nature Needs, 1982, God's Spies, 1983; contbr. articles to profl. jours. Lt. USNR, 1942-46. Am. Philos. Soc. grantee, 1964; First prize in poetry and biography Utah State Arts Coun., 1973, 75; Fulbright-Hays sr. lectr. Pakistan, 1973-74; recipient Charles Redd award Utah Acad., 1976, Coll. Humanities Disting. Faculty award Brigham Young U., 1977, presdl. citation Brigham Young U. Commencement, 1998. Fellow Am. Coun. Learned Socs., Found. Econ. Edn.; mem. Phi Beta Kappa, Phi Kappa Phi. Democrat. Mem. Lds Ch. Home: 1401 Cherry Ln Provo UT 84604-2848 Office: Brigham Young U Dept English Provo UT 84602 *As a young writer in graduate school, I made the shocking discovery one day that I had written some things I did not really believe. I wanted to be a writer, but I made a vow in my journal that I would not do so at the expense of my integrity: that I would never write anything again that I did not believe and accept with all my being. I have kept that promise, and at the same time have tried to be creative and resourceful. I do not believe that my writing has suffered from the attempt to be honest, but if it has, that is a small price to pay for self-respect.*

HART, EDWARD WALTER, physicist; b. Easton, Pa., Jan. 14, 1918; s. Abraham S. and Sara (Rosenstrauch) H.; m. Flori L. Feder, Dec. 11, 1940 (dec. 1976); children: Enid L. Boasberg, Lucinda Hart-Gonzalez; m. Joanne Kreider, Aug. 5, 1978. BS, CCNY, 1938; PhD, U. Calif., Berkeley, 1950. Physicist Theoretics Group U. Calif. Radiation Lab., Berkeley, 1946-51, Corp. R&D, Gen. Electric Co., Schenectady, N.Y., 1951-77; prof. mechanics and materials sci. Cornell U., Ithaca, 1977-88, prof. emeritus, 1988—. Battelle vis. prof. Ohio State U., Columbus, 1975; vis. prof. Tech. U. Braunschweig, West Germany, 1982. Contbr. articles to profl. jours. Pres. Schenectady Civic Ballet Co., 1960-63. With USN, 1940-45. Recipient Meritorious Civilian Svc. award USN, 1945, sr. U.S. Scientist award Alexander von Humboldt Found., 1982. Fellow Am. Phys. Soc.; mem. ASME, AIME, Metall. Soc. Home: 42 Horizon Dr Ithaca NY 14850-9769 Office: Cornell U Bard Hall Ithaca NY 14853

HART, ELIZABETH ANN, foundation administrator; b. Moulton, Ala., Sept. 14, 1942; d. Maburn L. Bertie Hale and Julia Mae Evans; m. Bruce Burleson Hart, Dec. 19, 1964; 1 child, Alexandra Natasha Burleson Hart. Diploma in Nursing, Brigham & Women's Hosp., Boston, 1963; BA in Psychology and English, George Washington U., Washington, 1971; postgrad. in business, Le Tourneau U., Longview, Tex., 1999—. RN, N.Y. Co-therapist Psychiatric Inst., Washington, 1969—72; staff nurse NIMH, Bethesda, Md., 1966—67; instr. biology Vernon Ct. Jr. Coll., Newport, RI, 1965—66; chmn., CEO Susan G. Komen Breast Cancer Found., Dallas, 1994—95; pres., CEO Hart Internat., Dallas, 1995—, Easter Seals Rehab. Svcs., Dallas, 1999—, Easter Seals Greater Dallas, 2002. Instr. biology and gen. sci. Miramar Sch. Girls, Newport, R.I., 1965-66; cons. Nat. Cancer Inst., Bethesda, 1993—, Ctr. Non-Profit Mgmt., Dallas, 1995—, Cancer Cube, 1996—, Dept. Defense, Washington, 1997-99; cons. U.S. Army Breast Cancer Rsch. Program, 1993-97, consumer evaluation subcom., writing group, 1994, exec. com. integration panel, 1994-95, exec. com. liaison subcom., 1995-96; adv. coun. sch. nursing U. Tex., Austin, 1994-99; patient adv. com. NSABP/BCPT, 1995, subcom. clin. ctr. performance evaluation, 1995; bd. dirs. Nat. Cancer Policy Bd., Bethesda, 1997-99; data safety and monitoring com., Internat. Breast MRI Consortium. Exec. prodr. (film) Women's Lives Dialogues on Breast Cancer, 1996; prodr. (video) Building for the Future, 2001. Pres. Women's Guild United Cerebral Palsy, 1985, Presbyn. Women, 1994-99; active Nat. Plan on Breast Cancer, Washington, 1995-2000; v.p. devel. Yellow Rose Found., 1996, v.p. cmty. outreach, 1997, Dallas Action Symphony Orch. League, Friends of Timberlawn. Recipient Vol. of Yr. award United Cerebral Palsy Assn. Met. Dallas, 1983, 101% Vol. award, 1983. Mem. Dallas-Ft. Worth Internat. Soc. Republican. Avocations: music, reading, mountain climbing, painting. Home: 9051 Oak Path Ln Dallas TX 75243 Office: Easter Seals Rehab Svcs 4443 N Josey Ln Carrollton TX 75010 E-mail: hart.elizabeth@worldnet.att.net., ehart@easterseals.com.

HART, ERIC MULLINS, finance company executive; b. Clanton, Ala., May 6, 1925; s. Eric and Myrtle (Mullins) H.; m. Joy Porter, May 16, 1953; children: Anne Porter, Eric Mullins. BS, U. Ala., 1946; grad., Harvard Advanced Mgmt.

Program, 1970. With Internat. Paper Co., 1946-69, asst. to v.p.-treas., 1962-64, comptroller, 1964-69; pres. Red River Paper Mill, Inc., 1964-69; fin. v.p. Lever Bros. Co., 1969-83, dir., 1969-83, Unilever U.S. Inc., 1981-83, Macmillan, Inc., 1975-88; exec. in residence Columbia U. Bus. Sch., 1983-88. Trustee King Sch., Stamford, Conn., 1970-76. Mem. Union League Club (N.Y.C.), Lakewood Golf Club, Fairhope Yacht Club, Sigma Alpha Epsilon. Home: 106 Oak Bend Ct Fairhope AL 36532

HART, FREDERICK MICHAEL, law educator; b. Flushing, N.Y., Dec. 5, 1929; s. Frederick Joseph and Doris (Laurian) H.; m. Joan Marie Monaghan, Feb. 13, 1956; children: Joan Marie, Ellen, Christiane, F. Michael, Margaret, Andrew, Brigid, Patrick. BS, Georgetown U., 1951, JD, 1955; LL.M., N.Y. U., 1956; postgrad., U. Frankfurt, Germany, 1956-57. Lectr., dir. food law program N.Y. U., N.Y.C., 1957-58, asst. prof., 1958-59; prof. law Albany Law Sch., Union U., 1959-61, Boston Coll., 1961-66, Law Sch., U. N.Mex., Albuquerque, 1966—, dean, 1971-79, acting dean, 1985-86; dir. Law Sch., U. N.Mex. (Indian Law Center), 1967-69; vis. prof. U. Calif., Davis, spring 1981. Pres., chmn. bd. trustees Law Sch. Admission Test Council, 1974-76 Author: Forms and Procedures Under the Uniform Commercial Code, 1963, Uniform Commercial Code Reporter-Digest, 1965, Handbook on Truth in Lending, 1969, Commercial Paper Under the U.C.C, 1972, Student Guide to Secured Transactions, 1985, Student Guide to Sales, 1987; editor: Am. Indian Law Newsletter, 1968-70. Served to lt. USAF, 1951-53. Mem. ABA (law sch. accreditation com. 1986-93, skills tng. com. 1995-98, nominating com. 1987), Order of Coif, Phi Delta Phi. Roman Catholic. Home: 1505 Cornell Dr NE Albuquerque NM 87106-3703 Office: U NMex Sch Law 1117 Stanford Dr NE Albuquerque NM 87131-1431

HART, GURNEE FELLOWS, investment counselor; b. Chgo., Apr. 26, 1929; s. Percival Gray and Marguerite May (Fellows) H.; m. Marjorie Walker Leigh, Apr. 23, 1966. BA cum laude, Pomona Coll., 1951; MBA, Stanford U., 1955; vis. scholar, Jesus Coll., Cambridge, Eng., 1994-95. With Willis & Christy, L.A., 1955-65; investment counsel Scudder, Stevens & Clark, Inc., L.A., 1965-67; with Scudder, Stevens & Clark, N.Y.C., 1967—, ptnr., 1972-85, mng. dir., 1985-94, adv. mng. dir., 1991—. Bd. dirs. Lincoln Ctr. for the Performing Arts, Inc., 1981-86, N.Y. Philharmonic, 1974—, vice-chmn., exec. com., 1976-96, trustee, 1988—; chmn. Friends of N.Y. Philharm., 1975-82; bd. dirs., v.p. Berkshire Farm Ctr. and Svcs. for Youth, 1972-83; trustee Pomona Coll., 1982—; bd. dirs., treas. Am. Friends of Cambridge U., 1997-2000; bd. dirs. Cambridge U. Devel. Office in U.S., Inc., 1998-2000; chmn. Cambridge in Am., 2000—; trustee The Cambridge Found., U.K., 2001—. 1st lt. inf. USAR, 1951—53, Korea. Decorated Bronze Star. Mem. St. Andrew's Soc. State of N.Y., Soc. Mayflower Desc., Century Assn., Univ. Club, Knickerbocker Club, Indian Harbor Yacht Club (Greenwich, Conn.), Phi Beta Kappa. Republican. Episcopalian. Home: 133 E 64th St New York NY 10021-7045

HART, HERBERT MICHAEL, military officer; b. St. Louis, Oct. 19, 1928; s. Herbert Malcom and Helen Genevieve (Quigley) Hart; m. Teresa Keating, Oct. 13, 1958 (dec. Sept. 11, 2002); children: Bridget, Erin, Bret, Tracy, Megan, Michael, Patrick. BS in Journalism, Northwestern U., 1951. Commd. 2d lt. USMC, 1951, advanced through grades to col., 1972, infantry platoon, co. and bn. comdg. officer, 1952—53, 1957—60, 1969-70; Arab, Israeli, Persian plans officer U.S. Strike Command, Mid. East and Tampa, Fla., 1967-69; head profl. edn. Dept. Navy, Washington, 1977-78; head hist. br. Marine Corps. Hqrs., Washington, 1973-77, dep. dir. pub. affairs, 1978-80, dir. pub. affairs, 1980-81, ret., 1981; dir. pub. affairs Res. Officers Assn. of U.S., Washington, 1982-94. Cons. office of History U.S. Army Corps Engrs., 1981—; mem. adv. bd. ad hoc com. Nat. Park Svc., 1985—; mem. com. on Cemeteries and Memls. VA, 1987-92; mem. coun. advisors Nat. Park Conservation Assn., 1992—. Author 9 mil. history books; editor ROA Nat. Security Report, 1983-94; mem. editl. bd. Mil. History mag., 1983-95; asst. editor Leatherneck Mag., Washington, 1946-47; editor-in-chief Daily Northwestern, Evanston, Ill., 1949-51. Decorated 2 Purple Heart medals, 2 Legion of Merit medals; recipient Award of Merit Am. Assn. State and Local History, 1976, Cultural Achievement award Sec. of Interior, 1979, Conservation Svc. award Sec. Interior, 1986, named Hon. Ky. Col. by Gov. of Ky. Fellow Co. Mil. Historians; mem. Potomac Westeners (pres. 1974-75, 84-85), Res. Officers Assn. U.S. (life), Marine Corps Res. Assn. (life), Marine Corps Combat Corres. Assn. (life), Marine Corps Hist. Found. (charter, bd. dirs. 1983-87), Assn. U.S. Army, Army. Hist. Found. (charter), Nat. Pk. Svc. Employee and Alumni Assn. (life), VFW (life), Am. Legion (life), Mil. Order Purple Heart (life), Civil War Preservation Trust (charter mem.), Mil. Officers Assn. (life), 1st Marine Divsn. Assn. (life), 3rd Marine Divsn. Assn. (life), Coun. Am. Mil. Past (co-founder 1966, exec. dir. 1971—), Western History Assn. (charter), Nat. Assn. Uniformed Svcs. (life), Coast Def. Study Group, Naval and Maritime Corrs. Circle, State Hist. Soc. S.D. (life), Ft. Adams, R.I. Trust (charter), Ft. Douglas, Utah, Mus. Assn. (life), Civil War Fortifications Study Group (charter), Friends of Ft. Davis, Tex. (life), Battlefield Preservation Coalition (dir. 1991—), Friends of Ft. Ward, Va. (charter), Friends of Manassas Battlefield, Va. (charter), Nat. Trust Hist. Preservation, Theodore Roosevelt Assn., Va. Hist. Soc., Order of Indian Wars (companion), Apollo Soc. (bd. dirs. 1983-87), Am. Civil Def. Assn. (bd. advisors 1991—), Soc. Mil. History (trustee 1978-83), Ft. Phil Kearny/Bozeman Trl. Assn. (life), Ft. DeRussy La. Friends, Ft. Point and Presidio Assn. (life), Mil. Order of Carabao, U.S. Cavalry Assn. (life), K.C., Soc. Profl. Journalists, Theta Xi (life). Republican. Roman Catholic. Avocation: photography. Office: PO Box 1151 Fort Myer VA 22211-0151 Home: 7510 Gambrill Rd Springfield VA 22153-1809

HART, JACK ROBERT, newspaper editor; b. Tacoma, Sept. 7, 1946; s. John Sebald Hart and Alice Agnes Hurlbut; m. Cherie Denise Boston, Dec. 20, 1968 (div. Oct. 1976); children: Joshua John, Aaron Lee, Jesse Robert. BA, U. Wash., 1968; PhD, U. Wis., 1975. Instr. U. Wis. Ctr. Sys., Janesville, 1970-71, Calif. State U., Northridge, 1971-74; assoc. prof. U. Oreg., Eugene, 1974-81, acting dean, 1981; reporter Register-Guard, Eugene, 1980; reporter, editor The Oregonian, Portland, 1981-89, staff devel. dir., 1989-98, mng. editor, 1998—. Site dir. Nat. Writers' Workshop, Portland, 1994-95, 98; columnist Editor & Pub. Mag., N.Y.C., 1987-99; prof. Oreg. State U., Lewis and Clark Coll., U. Oreg., Portland State U., 1996—; spkr. at workshops in field; Ruhl tchg. fellow U. Oreg., 1988; mem. vis. faculty Poynter Inst. for Media Studies, Am. Press Inst. Author: The Information Empire, 1978; contbr. articles to profl. jours.; editor: Pulitzer Prize, Nat. Headliners Award, Ernie Pyle Award, Am. Soc. Newspaper Editors, Nat. Writing Award, Scripps-Howard Nat. Bus. Writing Award, and other nat. and regional writing awards. 2d lt. U.S. Army, 1968-71. Recipient Disting. Tchg. award Am. Soc. Newspaper Editors, 1980, Purple Shield, U. Wash., 1968, Disting. Svc. award U. Wis., 2001. Mem. Soc. Profl. Journalists, Oreg. Fly Fisherman, Phi Beta Kappa. Office: The Oregonian 1320 SW Broadway Portland OR 97201-3499

HART, JAMES WARREN, retired academic administrator, retired football player; b. Evanston, Ill., Apr. 29, 1944; s. George Ezrie and Marjorie Helen (Karsten) H.; m. Mary Elizabeth Mueller, June 17, 1967; children: Bradley James and Suzanne Elizabeth (twins), Kathryn Anne. BS, So. Ill. U., 1967. Quarterback St. Louis Cardinals Profl. Football Team, 1966—83, Washington Redskins Profl. Football Team, 1984; radio sports personality Sta. KMOX, 1975—84, Sta. KXOK, 1985—86; sports analyst Sta. WGN Radio, Chgo., 1985—89; athletics dir. So. Ill. U., Carbondale, 1988—99, assoc. chancellor for external affairs, 1999—2000; head coach So. Ill. Spl. Olympics, 1973—90, Mo. Spl. Olympics, 1976—78; co-owner Dierdorf & Hart's Steak House (2 locations), St. Louis; spl. asst. to vice chancellor for instnl. devel. So. Ill. U., 1999—2002. Co-author: The Jim Hart Story, 1977. Gen. campaign chmn. St. Louis Heart Assn., 1974-88; hon. chmn. St. Louis Sr. Olympics, 1986-88. Named Most Valuable Player in Nat. Football Conf., 1974, Most Valuable Player with St. Louis Cardinals, 1973, 1975, 1978, Man of Yr., St. Louis Dodge Dealers, 1975—76, Miller High Life, 1980; named to So. Ill. U. Sports Hall of Fame, 1978, Mo. Sports Hall of Fame, 1998, Mo. Valley Conf. Hall of Fame, 2001, Chicagoland Sports Hall of Fame, 2003. Mem.: AFTRA, NFL Players Assn. (Brian Piccolo Nat. YMCA award 1980, Byron Whizzer White award 1976, Brian Piccolo Nat. YMCA Humanitarian award 1980), Fellowship Christian Athletes. Republican.

HART, JAMES WHITFIELD, JR., retired corporate public affairs executive, lawyer; b. Greenwood, Fla., Dec. 20, 1935; s. James Whitfield Sr. and Lela (Cox) H.; m. Patricia Ann Landrum, Mar. 11, 1961; children: William Gordon, Melanie Ann. AA, Chipola Jr. Coll., 1956; JD, U. Ala., 1973; MBA, MIT, 1982. Bar: Ala. 1974, Colo. 1976; cert. flight instr. News dir., anchorman Sta. WTVY-TV, Dothan, Ala., 1958-60, Sta. WSFA-TV, Montgomery, Ala., 1960-62; exec. dir. Am. Petroleum Inst., Montgomery, 1962-75; mgr. pub. affairs Gulf Oil Corp., Atlanta, 1975-76, dir. pub. affairs Denver, 1976-81, sr. dir. pub. affairs Pitts., 1981-85; sr. v.p. Blue Cross/Blue Shield, Jacksonville, Fla., 1985-86; sr. v.p., gen. mgr. Hill & Knowlton, Denver, 1986-88; v.p. pub. affairs PanEnergy Corp., Houston, 1988-97; v.p. Duke Energy Corp., 1997-99; ret. Res. dir. pub. affairs Office Sec. Air Force, 1988-95; bd. dirs. Vita-Living, Inc.; chmn. interstate natural gas Am. Pub. Affairs Com., 1994. Mem. adv. bd. City of Sugar Land Airport; former pres. Ala. N.G. Assn.; bd. dirs. Opportunity Fla., Boy Scouts; pres. Chipola Jr. Coll. Found. Brig. gen. USAFR, 1990-95. Decorated Disting. Svc. medal, Legion of Merit, Meritorious Svc. medal, Air Force Commendation medal; recipient Meritorious Svc. award and Disting. Svc. award State of Ala., Outstanding Young Man of Am. award U.S. Jaycees, 1965, Outstanding Pub. Rels. Practitioner award, 1991, Pub. Rels. Practitioner of Yr., 1996. Mem. ABA, Pub. Rels. Soc. Am., Tex. Pub. Rels. Assn. (bd. dirs., chmn. pub. affairs coun. 1996, pres. 1996, Gold Spur award 1999), Coun. Assn. Execs. (former pres.), Am. Petroleum Inst., Am. Gas Assn., Pub. Affairs Coun. (past chmn.), Res. Officers Assn. (life), Air Force Assn. (life), Tex. Coun. Econ. Edn. (bd. dirs.), Tex. Rsch. League (bd. dirs.), Forum Club Houston, Houston Club, Univ. Club Houston, Rotary, Sigma Delta Kappa (former chancellor). Baptist. Home: 7371 Cox Rd Bascom FL 32423-9411 E-mail: jimwhart@digitalexp.com.

HART, JOHN, professional sports team executive; b. Tampa, Fla., July 21, 1948; m. Sandi DeVorak; 1 child, Shannon. Degree in History and Physical Edn., U. Cen. Fla., 1973. Minor league mgr. Montreal Expos, 1969-75, Balt. Orioles, 1975-88, third base coach, 1988; spl. assignment scout, interim mgr. Cleve. Indians, 1989-91, exec. v.p. and gen. mgr., 1991—. Named Major League Baseball Exec. of the Yr., The Sporting News, 1994, 1995. Office: Cleveland Indians Jacobs Field 2401 Ontario St Cleveland OH 44115-4003

HART, JOHN CLIFTON, lawyer; b. Chgo., Apr. 29, 1945; s. Clifton Edwin and Eleanor (Zielinski) H.; m. Dianne Lynn Wenzel, Jan. 18, 1969; children: David Clifton, Steven Philip, Kristin Dianne. BS, Loyola U., 1967; postgrad., Northwestern U., 1967-69; JD, U. N.D., 1972. Bar: Minn. 1973, U.S. Dist. Ct. Minn. 1973, Tex. 1979, U.S. Dist. Ct. (no. dist.) Tex. 1979, U.S. Dist. Ct. (we dist.) Tex. 1981, U.S. Dist. Ct. (ea. dist.) Okla. 1981, U.S. Dist. Ct. (ea. dist.) Tex. 1984, U.S. Dist. Ct. (no. dist.) Okla. 1999, U.S. Ct. Appeals (5th and 8th cirs.) 1980, U.S. Supreme Ct., 1997. Ptnr. Robins, Zelle, Larson & Kaplan, Mpls., 1973-81; v.p. Gollaher & Hart, Dallas, 1981-84; pres. Hart & Engen, Dallas, 1984-87, Hart & Assocs., Dallas, 1987-88; mng. ptnr. S.W. regional office Robins, Kaplan, Miller & Ciresi, 1988-93; ptnr. Cantey & Hanger L.L.P., 1993-98, Brown, Herman, Dean, Wiseman, Liser & Hart, L.L.P., 1998—. Contbr. articles to profl. jours. Maj. USAF, 1969-73. Mem. ABA, State Bar Tex., Tarrant County Bar Assn., Fedn. Ins. and Corporate Counsel, Loss Exec. Assn. Republican. Lutheran. Office: Brown Herman Dean Wiseman Liser & Hart LLP 306 W 7th St Ste 200 Fort Worth TX 76102-4905 E-mail: jhart@brownherman.com.

HART, JOHN EDWARD, lawyer; b. Portland, Oreg., Nov. 21, 1946; s. Wilbur Elmore and Daisy Elizabeth (Bowen) H.; m. Bianca Mannheimer, Mar. 29, 1968 (div. 1985); children: Ashley Rebecca, Rachel Bianca, Eli Jacob; m. Serena Callahan, Nov. 9, 1991; 1 child, Katelyn Elizabeth. Student, Oreg. State U., 1965-66; BS, Portland State U., 1971; JD, Lewis and Clark Coll., 1974. Bar: Oreg. 1974, U.S. Dist. Ct. Oreg. 1974, U.S. Ct. Appeals (9th cir.) 1975. Ptnr. Schwabe, Williamson and Wyatt, Portland, 1973-92, Hoffman, Hart & Wagner, Portland, 1992—. Adj. faculty U. Oreg. Dental Sch., 1987—; legal cons. Oreg. Chpt. Obstetricians, Gynecologists, Portland, 1985—, Am. Cancer Soc. Mammography Project, 1987—. Contbr. articles to profl. jours. Co-chmn. Alameda Sch. Fair, Portland, 1983. With U.S. Army, 1967-68. Mem. ABA, Am. Coll. Trial Lawyers, Am. Bd. Trial Advocates (pres. 1995) Am., Inns of Ct., Oreg. State Bar Assn., Oreg. Assn. Def. Counsel (pres. 1989), Multnomah Athletic Club. Democrat. Presbyterian. Avocations: jogging, weight lifting, outdoor activities. Office: Hoffman Hart & Wagner 1000 SW Broadway Ste 2000 Portland OR 97205-3072

HART, JOHN LEWIS (JOHNNY HART), cartoonist; b. Endicott, N.Y., Feb. 18, 1931; s. Irwin James and Grace Ann (Brown) H.; m. Bobby Jane Hatcher, Apr. 26, 1952; children: Patti Sue, Perri Ann. Ed. pub. schs. Free-lance cartoonist, 1954-58; commerical artist GE, Johnson City, NY, 1957-58; syndicated cartoonist, 1958—. Comic strip. B.C., nationally syndicated, 1958—, (with Brant Parker) The Wizard of Id, 1964—; collections include: Hey B.C., 1958, Hurray for B.C., 1958, Back to B.C., 1959, B.C. Strikes Back, 1961, What's New B.C., 1962, B.C.- Big Wheel, 1963, B.C. is Alive and Well, 1964, The King is a Fink, 1964, Take a Bow, B.C., 1965, The Wonderous Wizard of Id, 1965, B.C. on the Rocks, 1966, The Peasants are Revolting, 1966, B.C. Right On, 1967, B.C. Cave In, 1967, Remember the Golden Rule, 1967, There's A Fly in My Swill, 1967, The Wizard's Back, 1968, B.C., 1972, B.C. Cartoon Book, 1973. Served with USAF, 1950-53, Korea. Recipient Best Humor Strip awards, Nat. Cartoonists Soc., 1967-71; Reuben Award, Nat. Cartoonist Soc., 1969, named Outstanding Cartoonist of Year, 1968; Yellow Kid award, 1970; Internat. Congress Comics for best cartoonist, Lucca, Italy; Best Humor Strip award, French Comics Council, 1971; Public Service Award, NASA, 1972. Mem. Nat. Comics Council, Nat. Cartoonists Soc. Achievements include premiering nationally pub. cartoon in Sat. Eve. Post, 1954. Office: care Creators Syndicate 5777 W Century Blvd Ste 700 Los Angeles CA 90045-5675

HART, JOHN WILLIAM, theology and ecology educator; b. NYC, Oct. 5, 1943; s. Thomas Esmond and Veronica Frances (Merz) H.; m. Jane Helen Morell, Aug. 16, 1975; children: Shanti, Daniel. BA, Marist Coll., 1966; STM, Union Theol. Sem., 1972, MPhil, 1976, PhD, 1978. Dir. Heartland Project, Midwestern Cath. Bishops, 1979-81; prof. religion various acad. instit. in NY, Conn., Tex. and S.D., 1975—83; assoc. prof. religious studies Coll. of Gt. Falls, Mont., 1983-85; prof. theology Carroll Coll., Helena, Mont., 1985—. Vis. asst. prof. religion Howard U., Washington, 1978-79; prof. religion, various insts., 1975-83; project writer Columbia River Pastoral Letter, 1998-2001; dir., founder environtl. studies program Carroll Coll., 1997—; lectr. in field in 24 states in US, Brazil, Can., Italy, Switzerland, Eng., Nepal, 1980—. Author: The Spirit of the Earth: A Theology of the Land, 1984, Ethics and Tech.: Innovation and Transformation in Cmty. Contexts, 1997; ghost author: various ch. documents on theology and ecology; contbr. articles to profl. publ., periodicals, and encys., chpt. t; author: (Ch. documents) What Are They Saying About...Environmental Theology?, 2004. Del. Internat. Indian Treaty Coun., Geneva, 1987, 90, UN Internat. Human Rights Commn., Templeton Oxford Sems. in Sci. and Christianity, 1999-2001, Earth Charter, Italy, 2002; bd. dir. Grassroots Globalization Network affiliate Earth Island Inst., 2001-; assoc. Ctr. for Maximum Potential Bldg. Sys., Austin, Tex., 2002-. Recipient Templeton Sci.-Religion award, 1995; Danforth Found. fellow, 1973-74; NEH grantee, 1985, 86, 2003; AAR/Lilly Tcgh. Scholar in Religion, 1997-98. Mem. Soc. Christian Ethics, Am. Acad. Religion, Mont. Wilderness Assn., Mont. Environ. Info. Ctr., Alternative Energy Resources Orgn., Sierra Club. Democrat. Office: Carroll Coll Theology Dept Helena MT 59625-0001 E-mail: jhart@carroll.edu. *Humanity has been entrusted with a sacred intergenerational responsibility: to care for creation, conserve the common ground of the biotic community in its Earth home.*

HART, JOSEPH H. bishop emeritus; b. Kansas City, Mo., Sept. 26, 1931; Student, St. John Sem., Kansas City, St. Meinrad Sem., Indpls. Priest Roman Cath. Ch., 1956. Consecrated titular bishop of Thimida Regia, aux. bishop Cheyenne, Wyo., 1976; apptd. bishop of Cheyenne, 1978—2001. Office: Bishops Residence Chancery Office PO Box 1468 Cheyenne WY 82003-0426*

HART, JOSEPH THOMAS CAMPBELL, lawyer; b. Orange, N.J., May 23, 1936; s. Maurice I. and Anne G. (Campbell) H. AB, Fordham U., 1958, JD, 1961. Bar: N.Y. 1962, U.S. Dist. Ct. (so. and ea. dists.) N.Y. 1966, U.S. Ct. Appeals (2d cir.) 1974, U.S. Ct. Appeals (5th cir.) 1983. Assoc. Dewey, Ballatine, Bushby, Palmer & Wood, N.Y.C., 1962-65, Fulton, Rowe, Hart & Coon, N.Y.C., 1965-71, ptnr., 1971—. Sec. The G. Unger Vetlesen Found., N.Y.C., 1987, The Ambrose Monell Found., N.Y.C., 1994. Mem. Assn. of the Bar of the City of N.Y. Office: Fulton Rowe Hart & Coon One Rockefeller Plaza New York NY 10020

HART, KAREN ANN, advertising executive; b. Olean, N.Y., July 11, 1943; d. John Eugene and Lillian Lila (Gardner) H. BSN, D'Youville Coll., Buffalo, 1965. RN, Ohio, N.Y., Calif. Staff nurse, head nurse, supr. Montefiore Med. Ctr., Bronx, N.Y., 1965-77; nurse recruiter L.A. New Hosp., 1978-79, Midway Hosp., L.A., 1979-80; dir. nurse recruitment Akron (Ohio) City Hosp., 1980-87; exec. dir. Nat. Assn. Health Care Recruitment, Akron, 1987-96; sr. v.p. health care divsn. Bernard Hodes Group, N.Y.C., 1996—. Contbr. articles to profl. jours. Recipient Women in Comm. award Women Aware Program, 1986. Mem. Nat. Assn. Health Care Recruitment (past officer, Disting. Mem. award 1986, 87), Northeastern Ohio Assn. Health Care Recruitment (past officer), Sigma Theta Tau. Democrat. Roman Catholic. Avocations: traveling, writing, reading, swimming. Home: 201 N Hawkins Ave Akron OH 44313-6425 Office: 220 E 42nd St New York NY 10017 E-mail: khart@ny.hodes.com.

HART, KATHERINE MARIE, environmental scientist; b. Windsor, Ont., Can., Feb. 7, 1956; d. Francis Xavier and Barbara Helen Hart; 1 child, Kevin. BS, U. Mich., 1978; MS, Va. Tech., 1981. Environ. scientist U.S. FDA, Washington, 1980-85; environ. scientist office toxic substances US EPA, Washington, 1985—89, environ. protection specialist design for environ. program, 1994—; sr. project mgr. Jellinek, Schwartz & Connolly, Arlington, Va., 1989-94. Contbr. articles to profl. jours.; author procs. in field. Recipient Spl. Recognition award Inst. for Interconnecting and Packaging Electronic Circuits, 1996 Mem. Phi Kappa Phi, Phi Sigma. Avocations: skiing, camping, hiking, travel. Home: 4302 Bushie Ct Alexandria VA 22312 Office: US EPA 7406 1200 Pennsylvania Ave NW Washington DC 20460 Fax: 202-564-8893. E-mail: hart.kathy@epa.gov.

HART, KENNETH NELSON, lawyer; b. Providence, Jan. 13, 1930; s. Gerald Ellerbeck and Dorothy Naomi (Nelson) H.; m. Carol Lee Hourula, Oct. 1, 1957; children: Lindsey, Lowell, Allison, Stephanie, Abigail, Jessica, Kevin, Rebecca. AB, Colby Coll., 1951; LLB, Boston U., 1957. Bar: Mass. 1957, N.Y. 1961, U.S. Ct. Appeals (2d cir.) 1963, U.S. Ct. Appeals (6th cir.) 1965, U.S. Supreme Ct. 1969, U.S. Ct. Appeals (3d. cir., D.C. cir.) 1981, U.S. Ct. Appeals (8th cir.) 1981. Trial atty. antitrust divsn. Dept. Justice, 1957-61; ptnr. Donovan Leisure Newton & Irvine, N.Y.C., 1961-97, chmn. exec. com., 1986-89, chmn. litigation dept., 1995-97; ptnr. Orrick Herrington & Sutcliffe, N.Y.C., 1998. Mem. bd. overseers Colby Coll., 1991-98. Served with USMC, 1951-53. Fellow Am. Coll. Trial Lawyers. Office: 187 Westcote Dr Wakefield RI 02879-5037 E-mail: knhart@yahoo.com.

HART, KERRY, college administrator, music educator; b. L.A., Oct. 2, 1951; s. Merrill A. and Rita Florence Hart; m. Jacqueline Therese Schaible, Aug. 17, 1974; children: Arin, Brooke, Dustin. BA in Music Edn., Met. State Coll., Denver, 1973; MusM, U. No. Colo., 1977, D Music Edn., 1989. Dir. music Dolores County H.S., Dove Creek, Colo., 1974-76, Guernsey (Wyo.)-Sunrise Schs., 1977=78, Cowley County C.C., Arkansas City, Kans., 1978-81; dir. instrumental music Cortez (Colo.) Pub. Schs., 1981-83; dir. bands, divsn. chmn. Western Nebr. C.C., Scottsbluff, 1983-90; assoc. prof. music, dept. head Adams State Coll., Alamosa, Colo., 1990-2000; v.p. arts and enrichment studies Mohave C.C., Bullhead City, Ariz., 2000—02; dean arts and humanities Laramie County C.C., Cheyenne, Wyo., 2002—. Mem. music edn. task force Colo. Dept. Edn., Denver, 1994-2000; mem. Colo. Adv. Com. for Tchr. Licensing, Denver, 1994; mem. grants rev. bd. Ariz. Commn. on Arts, Phoenix, 2000—; adjudicator various music festivals, Colo., Nebr., Kans., Wyo., S.D., 1978; nat. spkr. various music workshops throughout U.S., 1998—. Author: Using Music To Enhance Teaching Effectiveness in the Elementary Classroom, 1996, Old Songs Made New, 1997; contbr. over 35 articles to profl. jours. Recipient award for excellence for manuscript Assn. Baha'i Studies, Can., 1989; music scholar U. No. Colo., 1976, 77, 85, 87. Mem. Coll. Music Soc., Music Educators Nat. Conf., Colo. Music Educators Assn. (bd. dirs. 1992-2000, chmn. univ. coun. 1992-98), Bullhead City C. of C., Kiwanis. Mem. Baha'i Faith. Avocations: hiking, backpacking, canoeing, camping. Home: 618 Vista Ln Cheyenne WY 82009 Office: Laramie County CC 1400 E College Dr Cheyenne WY 82007 E-mail: hartline@vcn.com.

HART, KITTY CARLISLE, arts administrator; b. New Orleans, Sept. 3, 1917; d. Joseph and Hortence (Holtzman) Conn; m. Moss Hart, Aug. 10, 1946 (dec. 1961); children: Christopher, Cathy. Ed., London Sch. Econs., Royal Acad. Dramatic Arts; DFA (hon.), Coll. New Rochelle; DHL (hon.), Hartwick Coll.; LHD (hon.), Manhattan Coll., Amherst Coll. Chmn. emeritus N.Y. State Council on the Arts. Former panelist: TV show To Tell the Truth; actress on stage and in films including The Marx Brothers A Night at the Opera, 1936; Broadway theatre appearance in On Your Toes, 1983-84; singer, Met. Opera; one woman show on Great Performances My Broadway Memories, 1999; TV moderator and interviewer; author: (autobiography) Kitty, 1988; contbr. book revs. to jours. Assoc. fellow Timothy Dwight Coll. of Yale U., NYU, Skidmore Coll.; bd. dirs. Empire State Coll.; formerly spl. cons. to N.Y. Gov. on women's opportunities; mem. vis. com. for the arts MIT Recipient Nat. medal of Arts from Pres. Bush, 1991. Office: Arts Coun 915 Broadway Fl 8 New York NY 10010-7108

HART, LARRY CALVIN, lawyer; b. Dec. 24, 1942; s. Clifford C. and Evelyn M. (Dupler) Hart; m. Leslie K. Bolek, Apr. 1986. ABA, Oteroo Coll., 1963; BS, Colo. State U., 1967; JD, Loyola U., L.A., 1974. Bar: Calif. 74, U.S. Dist. Ct. (cen. dist.) Calif. 74, U.S. Ct. Appeals (9th cir.) 79, U.S. Dist. Ct. (ea. and no. dists.) Calif. 80. Assoc. Ned Good, L.A., 1974—76, Hagenbaugh & Murphy, L.A., 1976—77; ptnr. Hart & Michaelis, L.A., 1977—84, Brill, Hunt & Hart, L.A., 1984—86, Musick, Peeler & Garrett, L.A., 1987—. Instr. Inst. Safety and Sys. Mgmt. U. So. Calif., L.A., 1982—; hearing officer L.A. Superior Ct., 1982—. Mem.: Calif. Bar Assn., Def. Rsch. Inst., Lawyer Pilots Bar Assn., Aviation Ins. Assn. Calif. (v.p. 1983—84, pres. 1986—87), Assn. So. Calif. Def. Counsel (bd. dirs. 1980—83). Office: Musick Peeler & Garrett 1 Wilshire Blvd Ste 2000 Los Angeles CA 90017-3876 E-mail: L.Hart@mpglaw.com.

HART, LEROY BANKS, financial software executive; b. July 12, 1954; s. Bill and Helen (Lauver) Hart; m. Virginia Sattazahn, June 26, 1976; children: Peter, Timothy, Michael, Evan. BS, Kutztown State U., 1976; postgrad., Pa. State U., 1978—79, St. Joseph's Coll., 1979—81. Acct. Security of Am. Life., Reading, Pa., 1976—78, EDP coord., 1978—80, asst. v.p., contr., 1981—82; exec. v.p. Eastern Software Corp., 1984—88; pres. Hart Fin. Svcs., 1982—84, 1988—, ERA Ulrich Realty Co., 1990—97, Hart Software, Inc., 1990—. Trustee Zion Evang. Congl. Ch., 1978—84, Lakeside Evang. Congl. Ch., 1987—88, Evang. Sch. Theology, 1991—2001, Twin Pines Camp Conf. and Retreat Ctr., 1990—, Mohn's Hill Meml. Evang. Congl. Ch., 1994—. Fellow: Life Office Mgmt. Assn. Home and Office: 5 Buck Run Mohnton PA 19540-1220

HART, LORING EDWARD, academic administrator; b. Bath, Maine, Sept. 22, 1924; s. Joseph Edward and Elizabeth (Hayes) H.; m. Marilyn Louise Cummings, Jan. 7, 1950; children: Ellen Louise, Matthew Cummings. BA, Bowdoin Coll., 1948; MA, U. Miami, 1951; PhD, Harvard U., 1961; degrees (hon.), Bowdoin Coll.; degree (hon.), Norwich U. Teaching fellow Harvard U., 1954-56; instr. English U. Ky., 1956-57; from asst. prof. to prof. Norwich U., Northfield, Vt., 1957-83, head dept. English, 1961-68, dean of faculty, 1968-69, v.p., dean, 1969-72, pres., 1972-82; assoc. dir. devel. campaign Bowdoin Coll., Brunswick, Maine, 1983-86; pres. St. Joseph's Coll., Standish, Maine, 1987-95. With armored inf. AUS, World War II, ETO. Decorated Bronze Star, Combat Inf. badge; recipient Outstanding Civilian Svc. award Air Force, Army. Mem. Phi Beta Kappa, Sigma Nu. Address: PO Box 13 Yarmouth ME 04096-0013 E-mail: blandingat@aol.com.

HART, MELISSA ANNE, congresswoman; b. Pitts., Apr. 4, 1962; d. Donald P. and Albina Simone Hart. BA, Washington and Jefferson Coll., 1984; JD, U. Pitts., 1987. Pa. state senator, 1990-2000; mem. U.S. Congress from 4th Pa. dist., 2001—; mem. fin. svcs. com., judiciary com., sci. com. Chmn. Sen. Fin. Com.; vice chmn. Sen. Urban Affairs & Housing Com.; bd. dirs. C.C. Allegheny County, Pitts. Cancer Inst., SWPA Vets. Home Adv. Coun. Bd. dirs. Vietnam Vets. Leadership Program; bd. trustees U. Pitts. Mem. Pa. Bar Assn., Allegheny County Bar Assn., North Suburban Builders Assn. Republican. Office: 1508 Longworth Ho Office Bldg Washington DC 20515-3804 also: 2525 Rochester Rd Ste 202 Cranberry Township PA 16066*

HART, MICHAEL VINCENT, writer; b. Kiev, Russia, June 5, 1971; arrived in U.S.A., 1988; s. Tatyana Susan Hart. BA, Calif. State U., 1993, MA, 1995; PhD, U. So. Calif., 1999. Tchg. asst. U. So. Calif., L.A., 1998—99; lectr. Calif. State U., Long Beach, Calif., 1999—2000; asst. prof. Centenary Coll., Shreveport, La., 2000—. Author: American Internet Advantage, 2000, 11 poetry books. Mem.: Internat. Studies Assn., Am. Polit. Sci. Assn. Avocations: travel, foreign languages, chess. Office: Centenary College 2911 Centenary Blvd Shreveport LA 71134

HART, MILDRED, retired counselor; b. Ever, Ky., Apr. 7, 1937; d. Dewey Otis and Malta Virginia (Adams) Cooper; m. Joseph Paul Surace, Oct. 26, 1956 (dec. Jan. 1966); children: Marisa Surace Craig, Vincent, Angela, Stephen (dec. 1994); m. James Robert Hart, June 26, 1994. BS in Edn., Ohio State U., 1974, MA in Guidance-Counseling, 1976. Cert. elem. and secondary tchr., secondary prin., supr., Ohio; lic. profl. counselor, Ohio. Sec. H.G. Snyder & Assocs., accts., Columbus, Ohio, 1958-63; tchr. Columbus Pub. Schs., 1974-79, counselor, 1977-99, chmn. student svcs. dept., 1985-99. Adjustor Bancohio Nat. Bank, Columbus, 1985-93. Author: (booklet) College Handbook for Independence High School Students, 1988. Leader Girl Scouts U.S., Columbus, 1969-73. Mem. NEA, Ohio State U. Alumni Assn., Nat. Honor Soc., Pi Lambda Theta (sec. Ctrl. Ohio chpt. 1985-93, 99—, treas. Ctrl. Ohio chpt. 1997-99), Phi Kappa Phi. Democrat. Roman Catholic. Avocations: travel, reading, cooking, antiques. Home: 2328 Sedgwick Dr Columbus OH 43220-5431

HART, PAMELA WALKER, artist, educator, writer; b. Jacksonville, Fla., Dec. 5, 1943; d. Frank Patton Jr. and Beatrice Caroline Cox Walker; m. Donald H. Hart, Feb. 12, 1972. BA in Fashion Merchandising, Fla. State U., 1965; BS in Art Edn. with honors, U. Nebr., 1978; MS in Edn. with honors, Elmira (N.Y.) Coll., 1989. Cert. tchr. art K-12, N.Y., Wis. Dept. mgr. Maas Bros., Tampa, Fla., 1965-67; regional office mgr. Cole of Calif., Atlanta, 1968-70; art tchr. grade K-12 various pub. schs., Rome, N.Y., Madison, Wis., 1979-88. Spkr., presenter Munson Williams Proctor Art Inst., Utica, N.Y., 2001, Rome (N.Y.) Club, 2001. One-woman shows include Gannett Gallery, SUNY, Marcy, 1989, 1992, Mohawk Valley Ctr. for Arts, Little Falls, N.Y., 1995, Library Club, Westernville, N.Y., 2001, Rome Club, N.Y., 2001, exhibited in group shows at The Gallery, Manlius, N.Y., 1998, Art at Hospice Ctr., Syracuse, N.Y., 1998, Edith Barrett Gallery, Utica Coll. of Syracuse U., 2000, Ctrl. N.Y. Cmty. Arts Coun., 2001, exhibited in group shows, Art Assn., Cooperstown, N.Y., 1996, Everson Art Mus., Syracuse, 1997, Gannett Gallery, SUNY, Utica-Rome, 1997, Ctrl. N.Y. Cmty. Arts Coun., Utica, 1999, 2003, So. Vt. Art Ctr., Manchester, 1999, Allied Art Gallery, Richland, Wash., 1999, Nat. Acad. Mus., N.Y.C., 2000, Hiestand Gallery, U. Miami, Oxford, Ohio, 2001, Gallery of Contemporary Art, U. Colo., Colo. Springs, 2001, Van Vechten-Lineberry Art Mus., Taos, N.Mex, 2001, Nat. Arts Club, N.Y.C., 2001, Art Assn. Galleries, Cooperstown, 2001, Fifth Ave. Gallery, Nat. Assn. of Women Artists, N.Y.C., 2003, Represented in permanent collections Lib. Nat. Mus. Women in the Arts, book, Best of Sketching and Drawing, 1999. Election inspector Oneida County Bd. of Electors Town of Western, 1999-2000. With USAF, 1970-74, col. USAFR, 1974-95. Recipient Golden Poet award World of Poetry, 1991, 1st prize SUNY, Marcy, 1995, 99, Spl. Recognition award Rome Art Assn., 1996, 3d prize Mohawk Valley Ctr. for the Arts, 1997, 98, Merit award East Wash. Watercolor Soc., 1999, Adolph and Clara Obrig prize Nat. Acad. Mus., N.Y.C., 2000, Watermedia prize Cooperstown Art Assn., 2001. Mem.: AAUW, Nat. Soc. Arts and Letters, Nat. Assn. Women Artists, Nat. Women's History Mus., Nat. Mus. Women in the Arts, Inst. Noetic Scis., Soc. for Layerists in Multi-Media, Ctrl. N.Y. Watercolor Soc. Office: LookGlas Images PO Box 337 Westernville NY 13486 E-mail: lookglas@americu.net.

HART, PAUL VINCENT, JR., emergency and family medicine physician, inventor; b. Estherville, Iowa, Sept. 28, 1950; s. Paul Vincent and Florence Mary (Gehringer) H.; m. Susan Murphey, Sept. 27, 1989. BS, Iowa State U., 1972; MD, Creighton U., 1976. Diplomate Am. Bd. Emergency Medicine. Resident in gen. surgery U. Minn., Mpls., 1976-77; emergency physician Wheeling (W.Va.) Med. Ctr., 1977-79; pvt. practice family practice and emergency medicine, Kansas City, Kans., 1979-84, Westwood, Kans., 1985—. V.p. Organ Design & Mfg., Westwood, 1989—; cons. Hepatocyte Transformation Lab. Hannover (Germany) U. Med. Sch., 2000—. Mem. AMA, Am. Acad. Family Physicians. Republican. Roman Catholic. Achievements include patents for transformed kidney cells for renal assist device; patents pending for bioartifical kidney; co-patentee liver assist devices. Office: 2813 W 51st St Westwood KS 66205-1748 E-mail: pvhartmd@aol.com.

HART, PEGGY I. small business owner; b. Cut Bank, Mont., Feb. 3, 1941; d. Victor Hugo and Mildred Jimmie Keifer; m. Don Frank Hart, Sept. 8, 1963. BS, Mont. State U., Bozeman, 1963. Co-owner Hart Air Ltd., Long Beach, Calif., 1986—. Mem. NRA, Aircraft Owners and Pilots Assn., Calif. Gun Owners, 99s Internat. Women Pilots, Order Eastern Star, Ladies Oriental Shrine. Republican. Avocation: aviation activities. Office: Hart Air Ltd 2830 E Wardlow Rd Long Beach CA 90807-5318

HART, REGINALD, advocate, writer, adult education educator; b. New Orleans, Apr. 25, 1969; s. Charles Reginald Hart and Gwendolyn Henrietta Fraise. Educator Henrietta Found., Chgo., 1989—. Author: (book) Vagabond Spiritual, 2002. Adv. for the homeless Henrietta Found., Chgo., 2002—. Avocations: advocacy for the homeless, racial unity. Office: Henrietta Press PO Box 806551 Chicago IL 60680

HART, RICHARD BANNER, lawyer; b. Winston-Salem, NC, Apr. 9, 1932; s. Samuel Bruce and Cordia M. (Lamb) H.; m. Jean Elizabeth Shinn, Apr. 28, 1956; 1 dau., Fabra. AB in Polit. Sci, U. N.C., Chapel Hill, 1957, JD, 1959. Bar: N.C. 1959, Tenn. 1970, U.S. Supreme Ct. 1991; CLU. Assoc. counsel Jefferson Standard Life Ins. Co., Greensboro, N.C., 1959-70; with NLT Corp. and Nat. Life and Accident Ins. Co., Nashville, 1970-73, asst. v.p., counsel, 1973-75, sec., counsel, 1975-84; v.p., sec., assoc. gen. counsel Am. Gen. Ins. Cos., Nashville, 1982-88; v.p., sec., gen. counsel Intereal Co., 1984-85; spl. counsel Bowne of Nashville, Inc., 1988-94, Richard B. Hart & Assocs., 1988—; judge City of Belle Meade, Nashville. Lectr. in field; adv. com. U.S. Dist. Ct. (mid. dist.) Tenn. Civil Justice Reform Act 1990. Bd. editors U. N.C. Law Rev., 1958-59. Budget com. Guilford County United Fund, N.C., 1968-69; bd. dirs. Guilford County Mental Health Assn., 1968-69; treas. Nashville Exch. Club Charities, 1987-88; trustee West End United Meth. Ch., 1998-2000; vol. The Talking Libr.; bd. govs. Shakespeare on the Cumberland. With U.S. Army, 1953-55. Mem. Assn. Life Ins. Counsel, Am. Corp. Counsel Assn. (pres., chmn. bd. dirs. Tenn. chpt. 1990-92), Am. Soc. Corp. Secs. (exec. com., pres. S.E. region 1979-81), Tenn. Mcpl. Judges Assn., Nashville Com. Fgn. Rels., English Speaking Union U.S. (bd. dirs. 1998—, pres. Nashville br. 1999-01), Phi Delta Phi, Phi Kappa Sigma (nat. officer, exec. bd. 1971-77), Phi Kappa Sigma Ednl. Fund, Inc. (trustee 1997-00), Exch. Club (Nashville) (bd. dirs. 1984-85), Univ. Club (Nashville). Home: 2815 Kenway Rd Nashville TN 37215-1903

HART, RICHARD WESLEY, religious organization administrator, pastor; b. Greensboro, N.C., Feb. 21, 1933; s. Shelly Monroe and Virginia (Boaz) H.; m. 1954; (div. May 1969); children: Richard Wesley Jr., Larry Earl, Howard Clayton; m. Shirleen Atkins Chance, Aug. 16, 1997. BDiv, Toccoa Falls (Ga.) Coll., 1951; DDiv, Evang. Christian Sem., 1966. Regional dir. Am. Evang. Christian Chs., Fontana, Calif., 1958-66; pres. Evang. Christian Chs., San Bernardino, Calif., 1966-83; founder, dir. Reidsville (N.C.) Urban Ministry, 1983—. Mem. Rep. Nat. Com., Washington, 1991—; establisher AGAD Scholarship Fund, 1992. Mem. Am. Vets. Avocation: coin and old currency collector. Home and Office: 2125 Smith St Reidsville NC 27320-6513 *My aim in life has always been to set specific goals and formulate a plan to reach those goals and to listen to others whose views may differ from mine-but from whose views I may be able to increase my own knowledge.*

HART, ROBERT GORDON, federal agency administrator; b. San Francisco, Dec. 28, 1921; s. Edwin and Ruth Graves (Thompson) H. Student, Am. Inst. Banking, 1939-41. Br. mgr. Bank of Kodiak, Alaska, 1942-46; folk art cons. Indsl. Rsch. Adv. Coun., Honolulu, 1950-51; mgr. So. Highlanders, Inc., N.Y.C., 1946-52; Southwestern rep. Indian Arts and Crafts Bd., Santa Fe, 1954-57; treas. Westbury Music Fair, Inc., 1957; dir. pub. rels. Constructive Rsch. Found., N.Y.C., 1958-59; editor, dir. publs. Bklyn. Mus., 1959-61; gen. mgr. Indian Arts and Crafts Bd., 1961-93; ret. Indian Arts and Crafts Bd., Dept. Interior, Washington, 1993; gen. mgr. Dept. Interior, Washington, 1961-93; pres. The Crafts Report Ednl. Fund, 1990. Art and craft cons. Mus. Internat. Folk Art, Santa Fe, 1954-57; chmn. Fed. Inter-Departmental Agy. for Arts and Crafts, 1963-93; U.S. del. OAS for Reunion Technica des Artesanias. Author: How to Sell Handicrafts, 1953, Alaska, 1959. Bd. dirs. Bur. Occupational Extension Svcs., N.Y.C., N.Y. Elder Crafts-Corp., Year of Am. Craft, 1993; mem. nat. adv. bd. Foxfire Fund, Inc., 1981—; mem. nat. adv. editorial bd. The Crafts Report, 1983-93; pres. The Crafts Report Ednl. Fund., 1990. With AUS, 1943-45. Recipeint N.Y. State Gov.'s award for outstanding svc., 1951; hon. fellow Am. Craft Coun., 1993. Mem. Conseil Internat. des Musées, Am. Assn. Museums, Am. Craftsman's Council, World Crafts Council, Am. Polit. Sci. Assn. Home: 4100 N Charles St Apt 808 Baltimore MD 21218-1025

HART, ROBERT LEE, retired English educator; b. Phila. s. Harry F. and Marion (Smith) H.; m. Valerie J. Shroeder; children: Jeffrey R., Daniel P. BS, West Chester U., 1960; EdM, Temple U., 1970; EdD, Nova Southeastern U., 1993. English instr. U.S. Army Tng. Ctr., San Juan, P.R., 1960-62; English tchr. Clearview H.S., Mullica Hill, N.J., 1962-70; prof. English Gloucester County Coll., Sewell, NJ, 1970—2001; ret., 2001. Cons. in field, 1996—; collaborative learning cons. various confs., workshops, 1993—. Author: Write On!, 1976, Collaborative Learning, 1991, Writing With Computers, 1991. Mem. Rep. Nat. Com., 1995—; sec. Coll. Acad. Assembly, Gloucester County Col, 1996-98. Mem. Nat. Coun. Tchrs. English, Tchg. English in the Two-Yr. Coll., Coll. Composition and Comm. Presbyterian. Avocations: photography, bicycling, walking, swimming, golf. Office: Gloucester County Coll 1400 Tanyard Rd Sewell NJ 08080-4222 E-mail: rhart@gccnj.edu.

HART, ROBERT M. lawyer; b. N.Y.C., Nov. 7, 1944; s. Charles John and Helen Ann (Hammond) H.; m. Dale Elizabeth McConaughy, Nov. 21, 1970; 3 children. BA, Marist Coll., 1966; JD, Duke U., 1969. Bar: N.Y. 1969, U.S. Ct. Appeals (2d cir.) 1970, U.S. Dist. Ct. (so. dist.) N.Y. 1979. Assoc. Donovan Leisure Newton & Irvine, N.Y.C., 1969-71, 74-77, London, 1972-73, ptnr. N.Y.C., 1977-84, 88-94, Dorsey & Whitney, N.Y.C., 1984-88; sr. v.p., gen. counsel, sec. Alleghany Corp., N.Y.C., 1994—; dir., chmn. comp.com. Chgo. Title Corp., 1998-2000. Sr. lectr. law Duke U., Durham, N.C., 1986—. Contbr. articles to profl. jours. Sr. Fellow Duke U., 1983—. Mem. ABA (securities regulation com. 1981—), N.Y. State Bar Assn., Assn. Bar City N.Y. (securities regulation com. 1979-82), Am. Law Inst. Office: Alleghany Corp 375 Park Ave Ste 3201 New York NY 10152-3297

HART, RODERICK P. communications educator, researcher, author; b. Fall River, Mass., Feb. 17, 1945; s. R. P. and Mary Claire (Sullivan) H.; m. Margaret Louise McVey, Aug. 27, 1966; children— Christopher, Kathleen BA, U. Mass., 1966; MA, Pa. State U., 1968, PhD, 1970. From asst. prof. to assoc. prof. Purdue U., West Lafayette, Ind., 1970-79; prof. U. Tex., Austin, 1979-83, Shivers chair comm., prof. govt., 1983—. Author: Public Communication, 1975, 83, The Political Pulpit, 1977, Verbal Style and the Presidency, 1984, The Sound of Leadership, 1987, Modern Rhetorical Criticism, 1990, Seducing America, 1994, Campaign Talk, 2000; mem. editl. bd. Human Comm. Rsch., 1980-86, Quar. Jour. Speech, 1983—. Recipient Disting. Rsch. award, 1993. Fellow Internat. Comm. Assn.; mem. Internat. Soc. Polit. Psychology, Ctr. for Study of Presidency, Nat. Comm. Assn. (chmn. research bd. 1981-84, ann. monograph award 1972, 74, 83, Woolbert Rsch. award 1984, Disting. scholar 1996). Democrat. Avocations: reading, athletics. Home: 1601 W Lynn St Austin TX 78703-3445 Office: U Tex at Austin Dept Comm Studies Jesse H Jones Communication Ctr Austin TX 78712

HART, RONALD WILSON, radiobiologist, educator, toxicologist, researcher, government research executive; b. Syracuse, N.Y., Mar. 23, 1942; s. Wilson and Annabell Hart. BS, Syracuse U., 1967; MS, U. Ill., 1970, PhD, 1971; postgrad. (Nat. Cancer Inst. trainee), Oak Ridge Nat. Lab., 1973. USPHS trainee, 1970-71; asst. prof. dept. radiology Ohio State U., Columbus, 1971-75, dir. radiation biology rsch. divsn., 1971-82, assoc. prof. depts. biology, biophysics, preventive medicine, 1976-78, assoc. prof. pharmacology, medicinal chemistry dept. preventive medicine, 1977-78, dir. chem., biomed. environ. rsch. group dept. preventive medicine, 1977-82, prof. depts. radiology, preventive medicine, pharmacology, medicinal chemistry, vet. pathobiology, 1978-82; dir. Nat. Ctr. for Toxicological Rsch., Jefferson, Ark., 1980-92; Disting. scientist in residence Nat. Ctr. for Toxicol. Rsch., 1992-2000; rsch. prof. Strang Cancer Prevention Rsch. Ctr. Rockefeller U., 2000—. Disting. prof. U. Poona, India, 1978—, Cairo U., 1989—; disting. prof. carcinogenesis Guang Zhou Med. Coll., China, 1988—; adj. prof. U. Ark. for Med. Sci., 1980—, U. Tenn. Health Scis., 1983— ; adj. prof. pharmacology Coll. Pharmacy, U. Ark., 1997—; cons. Oak Ridge Nat. Lab., 1971-75, Brookhaven Nat. Lab., 1975-78, Argonne Nat. Lab., 1975-78, EPA, 1976, 78, Am. Indsl. Health Council, 1978, PPG Industries, 1978, Informatics, 1978-80, FDA, 1980; mem. Nat. Acad. Scis./NRC Bd. on Toxicology and Environ. Health Hazards, 1976-82; mem. interagy. staff group Office Sci. and Tech. Policy Exec Office of Pres., 1982-85, chmn., 1983-85; chmn. bd. dirs. Ark. Sci. and Tech. Authority, 1983-84, mem., 1985-88; bd. dirs. Chem. Overseas Link, First Comml. Bank, 1989-94, Telescan, Inc., 1991-00, Mindography, 2001-02, Microgen, Inc., 2003—; mem. adv. bd. Petrotech, 1991-92, VoiceNet, 1998-99, Waterchef Inc., 2001-03, Micromed Labs., 2002—, Biomed, 2002—, Applied DNA Scis., Inc., 2003—, Fla. A&M U. Rsch. Ctr., 1985—, Waterchef Inc., 2001-02, Micromed Labs., 2002—, Biomed, 2003—; bd. visitors Memphis State U., 1984-90; mem. adv. bd. Miss. State U., 1987-96; chair task force on risk assessment/risk mgmt. HHS, 1985, chmn. com. to coordinate environ., health and related programs, 1985-88, chmn. sci. panel Agent Orange working group, 1986-88, mem. USAF toxicology rev. panel, 1987; chmn. Intergovtl. Task Force on Tech. Transer, 1987-88, DHHS Task Force on Tech. Transfer, 1987-88; mem. Inter Govt. Commn. on Competitiveness, 1987-94; apptd. del. to U.S.-USSR Emerging Leaders Summit, chmn. Sci. and Tech. Commn., 1988; disting. adj. prof. Moscow State U., 1989—, Guanzou (China) Med. U., 1988—, U. Udina, Italy, 1999-2002; chmn. Ark. Sch. for Math. and Sci. Found., 1997-2003. Contbr. chpts. to books, numerous articles to profl. jours. Recipient Hopkins award for grad. research, 1971; recipient Japanese Med. Assn. award, 1978; Karl-August-Forester award W. Ger., 1980, award of merit FDA, 1982, 85, 86, Sr. Exec. Service award, 1982, 84, 85; Superior Service award USPHS, 1983, Gov.'s Award Outstanding Service, State of Ark., 1985, Letter of Commendation, Pres. of U.S., 1985, Commr's Spl. Citation, FDA, 1987, Pres. Rank award for Meritorious Service, 1987, Superior Svc. award outstanding accomplishment Guangzhou Med. Coll., 1988, Bose medal Bose Inst., 1994; Internat. Union Against Cancer; named Syracuse U. Outstanding Alumnus, 1976 Fellow Gerontol. Soc., Am. Coll. Toxicology (past pres.), Risk Anal Soc., Am. Assn. Clin. Chemistry, AAAS (Am. Assn. for the Advancement of Sci.); mem. Radiation Research Soc., Biophys. Soc., Photochem. and Photobiol. Soc., Sr. Execs. Assn., Sigma Xi. Office: 4821 Crestwood Little Rock AR 72207

HART, RUSSELL HOLIDAY, retired lawyer; b. Chgo., May 1, 1928; s. Russell Holliday and Allegra (Prince) H.; m. Mary Gehres, June 16, 1951; children: Holiday Hart McKiernan, Robert Russell, Andrew Richard. AB, DePauw U., 1950; JD, Ind. U., 1956. Bar: Ind. 1956, U.S. Dist. Ct. (no. and so. dists.) Ind. 1956, U.S. Ct. Appeals (7th cir.) 1965, U.S. Supreme Ct. 1973. Assoc. Stuart & Branigin, Lafayette, Ind., 1956-61, ptnr., 1961-99; ret., 1999. Lectr. Ind. Continuing Legal Edn. Forum; tchr. trial lawyers Nat. Inst. for Trial Advocacy. Served with U.S. Army, 1951-53. Fellow: Acad. Law Alumni Ind. U. Sch. Law;, Ind. Bar Found. (sec., v.p. 1985), Internat. Acad. Trial Lawyers, Am. Coll. Trial Lawyers, Am. Bar Found., Internat. Soc. Barristers; mem.: ABA (del.), Nat. Assn. Railroad Trial Counsel (past pres.), Def. Trial Counsel of Ind. (past pres.), Ind. Def. Trial Counsel (diplomate), Tippecanoe County Bar Assn. (past pres.), Ind. Bar Assn. (pres.-elect 1986—87, pres. 1987—88, bd. mgrs., former treas., chmn. trial lawyers sect.). Office: Stuart & Branigin PO Box 1010 Lafayette IN 47902-1010

HART, SARAH V. federal agency administrator; BS in Criminal Justice, U. Del.; JD, Rutgers U. Prosecutor Phila. Dist. Attys. Office; chief counsel Pa. Dept. Corrections, 1995—2001; dir. Nat. Inst. Justice U.S. Dept. Justice, Washington, 2001—. Vice chair legal affairs com. Am. Correctional Assn.; chmn. sentencing and corrections subcom. Federalist Soc.; bd. dirs. Crime Victims Law Inst.; mem. appellate procedural rules com. Pa. Supreme Ct.; trainer in field. Contbr. articles to profl. jours. Office: US Dept Justice Nat Inst Justice 810 7th St NW Washington DC 20531

HART, STUART NEWTON, psychologist, educator; b. Cozad, Nebr., Aug. 13, 1937; s. Newton Mallory and Mary Elizabeth Hughes H.; m. Virginia Sue Walsmith, Aug. 7, 1980; children: Angela Elizabeth Turner, Brannon Walsmith, Damon G., Gavin S. BA, Calif. State U., Long Beach, 1961, MA, 1964; PhD, Ind. State U., 1972. Lic. psychologist; nat. cert. sch. psychologist. Tchr., counselor Long Beach Schs., 1960-64, Vigo County Schs., Terre Haute, Ind., 1964-68, asst. dir. diagnostic counseling and remedial ctr., 1968-69; dir. learning disability unit Riley Childrens Hosp., Indpls., 1972; asst. to assoc. prof. ednl. psychology Ind. U., Purdue U., Indpls., 1973—, dir. Office for the Study of Psychol. Rights of the Child, 1980-2001; prof. counseling, ednl. devel. Purdue U., Indpls. Vice chairperson Ind. Govs., 1988-93; mem. exec. com. Ptnrs. in Politics, 1988-95; chair, pres. Faculty of Sch. Edn., U. Purdue, 1978, 93, 94, 2000-01, prof. emeritus, 2001—; rep. NGO group for CRC, UN Gen. Assembly Spl. Session on Children, 2002. Recipient Sagamore of Wabash award, 2001. Fellow Am. Psychol. Assn.; mem. Internat. Sch. Psychology Assn. (chairperson children's rights com. 1991—, pres. 1991-92). Home: 303 Sassafras Cir Noblesville IN 46060

HART, TERRY JONATHAN, communications executive; b. Pitts., Oct. 27, 1946; s. Jonathan Smith Hart and Lillian Dorothy (Zugates) Hart Pierson; m. Mary Jane McKeever, Aug. 13, 1999; children: Amy, Lori. B of Mech. Engring., Lehigh U., 1968, DEng (hon.), 1988; MS, MIT, 1969; MEE, Rutgers U., 1978. Mem. tech. staff AT&T Bell Labs., Whippany, N.J., 1968-69, 73-78, supr., 1984—, head cellular systems strategic planning, 1989—; astronaut NASA Johnson Space Ctr., Houston, 1978-84, captured solar maximum satellite, 1984, div. mgr. Telstar 4 Satellite Program; pres. Loral Skynet, Bedminster, N.J., 1997—. Patentee in field. Served to lt. col. USAF Air N.G., 1969-90. Recipient N.J. Disting. Service medal, NASA Space Flight medal, Pride of Pa. medal; named N.J. Aviation Hall Fame. Mem. IEEE, Sigma Xi, Tau Beta Pi. Avocations: skiing, golf. Office: Loral Skynet 500 Hills Dr 3rd Fl Bedminster NJ 07921-1538

HART, TIMOTHY RAY, lawyer, dean; b. Portland, Jan. 5, 1942; s. Eldon V. and Wanda J. (Hillyer) H.; m. Mary F. Barlow, Aug. 31, 1964 (div. Dec. 1975); children: Mark, Matthew, Marisa, Martin; m. Annette Bryant, Aug. 8, 1981. AA, San Jose City Coll., 1968; BA, San Jose State U., 1970; MA, Wash. State U., 1973; JD, San Joaquin Coll. Law, Fresno, Calif., 1983. Bar: Calif. 1983, U.S. Dist. Ct. (ea. dist.) Calif. 1983. Police officer City of Santa Clara, Calif., 1965-71; chief of police U. Idaho, Moscow, 1971-73; crime prevention officer City of Albany, Oreg., 1973-75; instr. criminal justice Coll. of Sequoias, Visalia, Calif., 1975-81, dir. paralegal dept., 1982-83, chmn., dir. adminstrn. justice divsn., 1983-88, assoc. dean instrn., 1988—; sole practice law Visalia, 1983—. Apptd. dep. chief police City of Sanger (Calif.), 1995, apptd. chief of police, 2001-02. Parliamentarian Interagy. Youth and Cmty. Svcs., Inc. With USAF, 1960-63. Mem. ABA, ATLA, Calif. Bar Assn., Assn. Criminal Justice Educators, Am. Criminal Justice Assn., Delta Phi. Mennonite. Home: 1012 W Hemlock Ave Visalia CA 93277-7435 Office: Coll Sequoias 915 S Mooney Blvd Visalia CA 93277-2214 E-mail: timothyh@cos.edu., tim95law@juno.com.

HART, WILLIAM C. underwriter, educator, writer; b. Orange, N.J., Jan. 6, 1947; s. William Gerard and Etchen (Alsberg) Hart; m. Wendy Clarkson, Oct. 14, 1978 (div.); m. Charlotte R. Wagner, Oct. 7, 1989. AB, Fla. So. Coll., 1969; diploma, NYU, 1975; postgrad., Dale Carnegie Inst., 1994; profl. garden tng. program, Longwood Garden, Kennett Sq., Pa., 1976. Cert. land title profl. Land Title Inst. Va. Regional underwriter Chgo. Title Ins. Co., Dallas, 1980-83; sr. adv. title officer Lawyers Title Ins. Corp., New Brunswick, NJ, 1983-85; chief title officer Am. Title Ins. Co., Miami, Fla., 1985-92; chief title underwriter emeritus T. A. Title Ins. Co., Media, Pa., 1993—; prin. Title Law Assocs., Phila., 1999—. Lectr. N.J. Land Title Sch., Upsala Coll., East Orange, NJ, 1972, Land Title Sch., Austin, 1982, N.J. Lawyers Title Inst., Summit, 1984—85, Land Title Inst. Va., 1990, 91; instr. Neumann Coll. CLE Cert., 1995—97, NBI, Inc., 2003—. Author: (book) Standard Title Underwriting Practices, 1991, Creditors Rights and Title Insurance, Questionable Title, Remedies & Extra-Hazardous Risks, 1991, Title Insurance Underwriting Principles and Exception Language, 1992, Instructions as the Use of Title Insurance Endorsements, 1992, Title Insurance Underwriting Process, 1994, The Law of Titles in Florida, 1996, The Law of Titles in New York, 1996, The Law Titles in Pennsylvania, 1998; editor: New Jersey Titles Annotated, 1986, Alta Title Counsel, 1989—, Title Law Annotated, 2000—, The Law of Titles, 2002, Title Management Today, 2003—; contbg. editor: book Patton & Palomar on Land Titles, 2003. Mem.: USGA (assoc.), Internat. Platform Assn., Internat. Platform Assn., Pa. Land Title Assn. (mem. forms com. 1989—92, 1994), N.J. Land Title Assn. (chmn. title officers com. 1987—88), Pa. Sheriffs Assn., Fraternal Order Police (assoc.), World Affairs Coun. Phila., Golden Horshoe Golf & Country Club, Ashbourne Country Club, Sigma Phi Epsilon. Republican. Avocations: martial arts (black belt), golf, stamp collecting, gardening. Home: 612 Boyer Rd Cheltenham PA 19012-1610 Office: Title Law Assocs PO Box 56690 Philadelphia PA 19111 E-mail: TitleLaw@comcast.net.

HART, WILLIAM CARL, retired civil engineer; b. Wilsey, Kans., Sept. 14, 1924; s. Kirk Elver and Grace Elizabeth (Yost) H.; m. Ruby Lucille Newbery, June 21, 1944; children: Jeffrey Bruce, David Michael, Patricia Jeanne. BS in Civil Engring., Kans. State U., 1948. Registered profl. engr., Kans. Constrn. surveyor U.S. Bur. Reclamation, Grand Lake, Colo., 1948-51, constrn. inspector, 1951-54, supervisory constrn. engr. Stockton, Kans., 1954-61, Wichita, Kans., 1961-65, Willows, Calif., 1965-70, constrn. office head, 1970-75, Gilroy, Calif., 1975-87; ret., 1987. Head tech. info. exch. team on methodology of constructing large canals USSR, Bur. Reclamation, 1976; cons. World Bank, 1980. Cpl. U.S. Army, 1943-46, ETO. Recipient Meritorious Svc. award Dept. Interior, 1973. Fellow ASCE; mem. NSPE (life), U.S. Com. on Irrigation Drainage and Flood Control (life), Lions Club (sec. 1977—). Presbyterian. Avocations: genealogy, photography, fishing. Home: 1371 Redwood Ln Gilroy CA 95020-4724

HART, WILLIAM LEE, IV, legislative staff member; b. Anchorage, Alaska, Oct. 8, 1971; s. William Lee III and Barbara Lee Hart. BA in History, U. Idaho, 1994. Sales rep. Bill Hart & Assoc., Meridian, Idaho; 1st Congl. Dist. field rep. Craig for Senate, Boise, Idaho, 1996; campaign mgr. Ron Crane for State Treas., Meridian, 1997-98; press sec. U.S. Senator Larry Craig, Washington, 1998-2001, sr. comm. mgr., 2002—; comm. dir. Congressman C.L. Otter, Washington, 2001—02. Mem. Alpha Kappa Lambda (pres., dir. corp. bd. Alpha Phi chpt. 1994—, Alumni of Yr. 1996). Republican. Episcopalian. Home: 415 S Cleveland St Arlington VA 22204 Office: US Senator Larry Craig SH 520 Washington DC 20510

HART, WILLIAM THOMAS, federal judge; b. Joliet, Ill., Feb. 4, 1929; s. William Michael and Geraldine (Archambeault) H.; m. Catherine Motta, Nov. 27, 1954; children: Catherine Hart Fornero, Susan Hart DaMario, Julie Hart Boesen, Sally Hart Collins, Nancy Hart McLaughlin. JD, Loyola U., Chgo., 1951. Bar: Ill. 1951, U.S. Dist. Ct. 1951, U.S. Ct. Appeals (7th cir.) 1954, U.S. Ct. Appeals (D.C. cir.) 1977. Asst. U.S. atty. U.S. Dist. Ct. (no. dist.) Ill., Chgo., 1954-56; assoc. Defrees & Fiske, 1956-59; spl. asst. atty. gen. State of Ill., 1957-58; assoc. then ptnr. Schiff, Hardin & Waite, 1959-82; spl. asst. state's atty. Cook County, Ill., 1960; judge U.S. Dist. Ct. Ill., 1982—; now sr. judge. Mem. exec. com. U.S. Dist. Ct. (no. dist.) Ill., 1988-92; mem. com. on adminstrn. fed. magistrates sys., Jud. Conf. U.S., 1987-92, 7th cir. Jud. Coun., 1990-92; mem. edn. com. Fed. Jud. Ctr., 1994-99; chair No. Dist. Ill. Ct. Hist. Assoc., 1998—. Pres. adv. bd. Mercy Med. Ctr., Aurora, Ill., 1980-81; v.p. Aurora Blood Bank, 1972-77; trustee Rosary H.S., 1981-82, 93-98; bd. dirs. Chgo. Legal Asst. Found., 1974-76. Served with U.S. Army, 1951-53. Decorated Bronze Starl named to Joliet/Will County Hall of Pride, 1992. Mem. 7th Cir. Bar Assn., Law Club, Legal Club, Soc. Trial Lawyers, Union League Club of Aurora, Ill. (hon.), Inn of Ct., Serra Club of Aurora (v.p. 2000). Office: US Dist Ct No Dist Ill US Courthouse Rm 2246 219 S Dearborn St Chicago IL 60604-1702

HARTBERG, WARREN KEITH, biologist, educator; b. Watseka, Ill., Jan. 24, 1941; s. Warren Eugene and Marie Isabelle Hartberg; m. Rebecca Crosby, Feb. 2, 1964; children: Gretchen Mackenzie, Adam, Joanna Meek. AB, Wabash Coll., 1963; MS, U. Notre Dame, 1965, PhD, 1968. Entomologist, geneticist WHO, Dar es Salaam, Tanzania, 1968-70; from asst. prof. to assoc. prof. Ga. So. Coll., Statesboro, 1970-80, coord. Inst. Anthropology & Parasitology,

1971-83, acting head biology, 1979-80, prof., 1980-86; chmn., prof. Baylor U., Waco, Tex., 1986—. Cons.Internat. Ctr. Insect Physiology and Ecology, Mombasa, Kenya, 1970-77. Contbr. articles to profl. jours. Chmn. bd. dirs. In-as-Much Project, Inc., Statesboro, 1975-76; bd. dirs. Bullock County Wildlife Club, Statesboro, 1983-85. Fellow Tex. Acad. Scis.; mem. Am. Mosquito Control Assn., Soc. Vector Ecology, La. Mosquito Control Assn., Tex. Mosquito Control Assn. (bd. dirs. 1991-99, sec., 1991, v.p. 1995-97, pres. 1998), Sigma Xi. Avocations: model railroading, fishing, military history. Home: 13000 Sandalwood Dr Waco TX 76712-3136 Office: Baylor U Biology Dept Waco TX 76798

HART-DULING, JEAN MACAULAY, clinical social worker; b. Bellingham, Wash. d. Murry Donald and Pearl N. (McLeod) Macaulay; m. Richard D. Hart, Feb. 3, 1940 (dec. Mar. 1973); children: Margaret Hart Morrison, Pamela Hart Horton, Patricia L. Hart-Jewell; m. Lawrence Duling, Jan. 20, 1979 (dec. May 1992); children: Lenora Daniel, Larry, Jayne Munch. BA, Wash. State U., 1938; MSW, U. So. Calif., 1961. Lic. clin. social worker, Calif.; accredited counselor, Wash. Social worker Los Angeles County, 1957-58; children's svc. worker Dept. Children's Svcs., L.A., 1958-59; program developer homemakers svcs. project Calif. Dept. Children's Svcs., L.A., 1962-64; developer homemaker cons. position State of Calif., L.A., 1964-66; supr. protective svcs. Dept. Children's Svcs., L.A., 1966-67; dep. regional svc. adminstrn. Dept. Los Angeles County Children's Svcs., 1967-76; adminstr. Melton Home for Developmental Disability, 1985-86; pvt. practice pro bono therapy Calif. and Wash. Therapist various pro bono cases. Mem. Portals Com., L.A., 1974, Travelers Aid Bd., Long Beach, Calif. 1969. Recipient Nat. award work in cmty., spl. award for work with emotionally disturbed Com. for Los Angeles, 1974. Mem. AAUW, NASW, Acad. Cert. Social Workers, Calif. Lic. Clin. Soc. Workers, Wing Point Golf and Country Club (Bainbridge Island, Wash.), Los Angeles County Retirement Assn. Republican. Congregationalist. Avocations: golf, bridge. Office: Apt 212 7300 Quill Dr Downey CA 90242-2016 E-mail: hart4942@aol.com.

HARTE, ANDREW DENNIS, transportation company executive, travel agent; b. Bronx, N.Y., Jan. 23, 1946; s. Bernard and Gertrude (Romm) H. BA, CUNY-Hunter Coll., 1968; MS in Spanish, SUNY, New Paltz, 1975, MS in English, 1979; MA in French, NYU, 1975; MS in Reading, L.I. U., 1979. Cert. tchr., 48 states. Tchr. Hendrick Hudson Sch., Montrose, N.Y., 1968-69, Mahopac Schs., N.Y., 1969-70, Croton-Harmon Schs., N.Y., 1970-83; pres., owner Dominion Limousine Corp., Peekskill, N.Y., 1989—. Mem. local com. N.E. Conf. on Tchg. Fgn. Langs., N.Y.C., 1979-83. Mem. Am. Assn. Tchrs. French (life), Am. Assn. Tchrs. Spanish and Portuguese (life), N.Y. State Assn. Fgn. Lang. Tchrs. (life, bd. dirs. 1983-86), Mensa (life), The Intertel Soc., Phi Delta Kappa (life, editor, historian). Avocations: foreign and domestic travel, language study, philately, reading, current events. Office: Dominion Limousine Corp PO Box 328 Peekskill NY 10566-0328 E-mail: aharte@dominionlimo.com.

HARTE, CHRISTOPHER MCCUTCHEON, investment manager; b. Hanover, NH, Nov. 20, 1947; s. Edward Holmead and Janet (Frey) H.; m. Kay Marie Wagenknecht, Feb. 11, 1984 (dec.); 1 child, William; m. Katherine Stoddard Pope, June 10, 1999. BA, Stanford U., 1969; MBA, U. Tex., 1974. Assoc. McKinsey and Co., Inc., Dallas, 1974-76; dir. rsch. and promotion Austin Am. Statesman, Tex., 1976-79; pvt. practice pub., comm., 1979-83; mem. advanced mgmt. devel. program Miami Herald, Fla., 1983-85; asst. to pres. newspaper div. Knight-Ridder Inc., Miami, Fla., 1985-86; pres., pub. Ctr. Daily Times, State Coll., Pa., 1986-89, Akron Beacon Jour., Ohio, 1989-92; pres. Portland Press-Herald and Maine Sunday Telegram, 1992-94; ptnr. Cerrito Ptnr. Bd. dir. Harte-Hanks, Inc., Geokinetics, Inc., Crown Resources, Mincron Inc. Office: 217 Commercial St Ste 200 Portland ME 04101-4680

HARTELIUS, CHANNING JULIUS, lawyer; b. Gt. Falls, Mont., Oct. 2, 1946; s. Chester Werner and Hildegarde Margaret (Kelm) H.; children: Rhonda, Kerry, Chanin, Courtney. B.A. with honors, U. Mont., 1968, J.D. with honors, George Washington U., 1971. Bar: Va. 1971, Mont. 1971. Asst. atty. gen. Mont., 1971; ptnr. Wuerthner & Hartelius, Gt. Falls, 1972-73, Hartelius & Lewin, Gt. Falls, 1973-78, Hartelius & Assocs., P.C., Gt. Falls, 1978-87, Hartelius, Ferguson, Baker and Kazda, P.C., 1987—; asst. city atty., Gt. Falls, 1972-76; instr. Coll. Gt. Falls, 1980. Participant Leadership Gt. Falls, 1983; bd. dirs. Selective Svc., 1995—. Served to capt. Q.M.C., USAR, 1971-82. Recipient presdl. award of excellence U.S. Jaycees, 1976. Mem. ABA, Am. Trial Lawyers Assn., Mont. Bar Assn., Cascade County Bar Assn. (pres. 1997), Great Falls Jaycees (pres. 1976), Mont. Hist. Soc. Lutheran (pres. Ch. 1996, 97). Clubs: Toastmasters (pres. 1975, 97), Meadow Lark Country. Contbr. articles to legal jours.; author: Understanding Bankruptcy, A Guide, 1981; Montana Handbook on Contract for Deeds, 1982; co-author: Law and the Municipal Ecology, 1971. Home: 825 4th Ave N Great Falls MT 59401-1511 Office: PO Box 1629 Great Falls MT 59403-1629

HARTER, CAROL CLANCEY, university president, English language educator; m. Michael T. Harter, June 24, 1961; children: Michael R., Sean P. BA, SUNY, Binghamton, 1964, MA, 1967, PhD, 1970; LHD, Ohio U., 1989. Instr. SUNY, Binghamton, 1969-70; asst. prof. Ohio U., Athens, 1970-74, ombudsman, 1974-76, v.p., dean students, 1976-82, v.p. for adminstrn., assoc. prof., 1982-89; pres., prof. English SUNY, Geneseo, 1989-95; pres. U. Nev., Las Vegas, 1995—. Co-author: (with James R. Thompson) John Irving, 1986, E.L. Doctorow, 1990; author dozens of presentations and news columns; contbr. articles to profl. jours. Bd. dirs., mem. exec. com. NCAA, 2000—; mem. exec. com. Nev. Devel. Authority, 2001—; bd. dirs. Nev. Test Site Devel. Corp., 2000—; trustee Associated Western Univs., 2001—. Office: U Nev Office Pres 4505 S Maryland Pkwy # 1001 Las Vegas NV 89154-1001 E-mail: harter@ccmail.nevada.edu.

HARTER, DONALD HARRY, neurologist, medical educator; b. Breslau, Germany, May 16, 1933; came to U.S., 1940; naturalized, 1945; s. Harry Morton and Leonor Evelyne (Goldmann) H.; m. Lee Grossman, Dec. 18, 1960 (div. 1976); children: Kathryne, Jennifer, Amy, David; m. Rikki Horne, May 18, 1985 (div. 1986); m. Marjorie Brandt Dahlin, Oct. 12, 1990. AB, U. Pa., 1953; MD, Columbia U., 1957. Diplomate Am. Bd. Psychiatry and Neurology. Intern in medicine Yale-New Haven Med. Center, 1957-58; asst. resident, then resident neurology N.Y. Neurol. Inst., 1958-61; guest investigator Rockefeller U., 1963-66; mem. faculty Columbia Coll. Physicians and Surgeons, 1960-75, prof. neurology and microbiology, 1973-75; vis. fellow Clare Hall, Cambridge, Eng., 1973-74; attending neurologist N.Y. Neurol. Inst., Presbyn. Hosp., 1973-75; Charles L. Mix prof. Northwestern U., 1975-85, Benjamin and Virginia T. Boshes prof. neurology, 1985-87, chmn. dept. neurology, 1975-87, Northwestern Meml. Hosp., Chgo., 1975-87; dir. rsch. scholars program Howard Hughes Med. Inst./NIH, Bethesda, 1989-2000; with dept. neurology George Washington U. Med. Ctr., Washington, 1987—. Vis. sci. officer Howard Hughes Med. Inst., 1986—87, sr. sci. officer, 1987—2000; clin. prof. neurology George Washington U. Sch. Medicine and Health Scis., 1987—2001, prof. emeritus of clin. neurology, 2001—; vis. rsch. fellow dept. of pathology U. Cambridge, England, 2000—01; mem. adv. com. on fellowships Nat. Multiple Sclerosis Soc., 1976—79, chmn., 1977—79, rsch. programs adv. com., 1989—94; mem. Nat. Commn. on Venereal Disease, HEW, 1970—72; mem. med. adv. bd. Am. Parkinson Disease Assn., 1976—90, Myasthenia Gravis Found., 1980—87; mem. sci. adv. coun. Nat. Amyotrophic Lateral Sclerosis Found., 1978—85; mem. bd. sci. counselors Nat. Inst. Dental Rsch. NIH, 1990—95; sr. sci. advisor Amyotrophic Lateral Sclerosis Assn., 1992—; vis. life mem. Claire Hall, Cambridge, England, 2000—01. Mem. editorial bd. Neurology, 1976-82, Annals of Neurology, 1983-89; mem. adv. bd. Archives of Virology, 1975-81. Recipient Joseph Mather Smith prize Columbia U., 1970, Lucy G. Moses award, 1970, 72, Donald W. Mulder award The ALS Assn., 1998; Am. Cancer Soc. scholar, 1973-74; USPHS spl. fellow, 1963-66, Guggenheim fellow, 1973. Fellow: AAAS, Am. Acad. Neurology, Infectious Diseases Soc. Am.; mem.: Am. Soc. Virology, Am. Soc. Microbiology, Deutsche Gesellschaft fur Neurologie (corr.), Am. Neurol. Assn., Am. Soc. Clin. Investigation, Univ. Club Washington, Yale Club N.Y.C., Cosmos Club, Phi Beta Kappa, Sigma Xi. Office: George Washington U Med Ctr Ste 7-404 2150 Pennsylvania Ave NW Washington DC 20037-3201

HARTER, HUGH ANTHONY, foreign language educator; b. Columbus, Ohio, Dec. 13, 1922; s. Anthony Hugh and Georgiana (Hayes) H.; m. Driscilla Escher, Aug. 31, 1959 (div. 1961); m. Frances D. Reichman, Oct. 7, 1970; stepchildren: Ellen Berliner, Andrew Berliner, Nancy Berliner Rudolph. Student, Ohio Wesleyan U., 1940-41, Hamilton Coll., 1943, Ecole du Syndicat de la Haute Couture, Paris, 1947, NYU, 1975, New Sch. Social Research, 1975; BA cum laude, Ohio State U., 1947, PhD, 1959; MA cum laude, Mexico City Coll., U. Ams., 1951. Student teaching asst. Ohio State U., 1946-47, grad. teaching asst., 1951-53; asst. to prof. French Mexico City Coll., U. Ams., 1951; instr., asst. prof. Romance langs. Wesleyan U., Middletown, Conn., 1953-59; assoc. prof. Elmira Coll., 1959-60; Andrew Mellon postdoctoral fellow U. Pitts., 1960-61, spl. lectr., 1963-64, NDEA Insts. fellow, 1962, 63; assoc. prof. Chatham Coll., 1961-64, Loyola U., Chgo., 1964-66; prof. Ohio Westeyan U., Delaware, 1966-84; chmn. dept. Romance langs. Ohio Wesleyan U., Delaware, 1966-80, Robert Hayward prof. modern fgn. langs., 1976-84, dir. Internat. Inst. of Spain, 1984-87, prof. emeritus. Pres. Vitalicio, Fundacion Juan Ruiz, Segovia, Spain, 1971-86, Horizons for Learning, Delaware, Ohio, 1974—, Cursos Americanos e Internacionales, Segovia, 1986-1998; acct. Columbus Coated Fabrics Corp., Columbus, 1941-42; auditor European Post Exchange System, Bad Nauheim, Germany, 1948; co-owner John Anthony Studios, Columbus, 1954-64; v.p., dir. Von Mock Assocs., N.Y.C., 1969-70; spl. lectr. U. Catolica de Santa Maria, Arequipa, Peru, 1969; dir. Acad. Program in Segovia, 1969-1998. Author: Return to Patton's France 1944's Odyssey Retraced, 1999, Gertrudis Gomez de Avellaneda, 1981, Tangier and All That, 1993, reissue, 1997, D'Utah Beach aux Ardennes: Itiéraires 1944-1994, 1996; co-author: (with J. D. Mitchell) Staging a Spanish Classic: El hospital de los locos, 1990; translator, author: The Scavenger, 1962, Femmes/Hommes, 1977, The Butts (Driss Chraïbi), 1983, Mother Comes of Age (Driss Chraïbi), 1983, Mother Spring (Driss Chraïbi), 1989, Past Tense (Driss Chraïbi), 1990, The Distant Friend (Claude Roy), 1990, Shadow of Paradise: Vicente Aleixandre, 1987, Remembrance of a Time Just Past, 1993,,(most recent) Shattered Vision (Rabah Belamri), 1994, Shattered Vision (Rabah Belamri), 1994,; translator, editor: A History of Spanish Literature, 1971; co-editor: (with Willis Barnstone) Riconenete y Cortadillo, 1960, (with R.C. Allen, Jr.) A First Spanish Handbook for Teachers in Elementary Schools, 1961, A Second Spanish Handbook for Teachers in Elementary Schools, 1962; lyricist: More About the Pear Tree, The Death of the Soldier Guard, 1976. Bd. dirs. Centro Segovia, 1971-80; v.p. Delaware (Ohio) Heritage Inc., 1973-75, bd. dirs., 1975-78, pres., 1978-80; pres. Delaware Shakespeare Soc., 1980-81. Served with M.I. 3d Army, Normandy, No. France, then Air Transport Command, U.S. Army, ETO. Recipient medals of St. Calais, Vendome, Blois, Dombasle, Utah Beach, Avranches, Blois, St. Calais, Ouzouer, 1994, medaille d'Honneur of Confedn. Europeene des Anciens Combattants, 1992, 93; named Hon. Citizen City of Segovia, 1976; summer rsch. grantee Andrew Mellon Found., Morocco, 1973; spl. grantee Govt. of Morocco, 1975; spl. langs. grantee Mellon Mediterranean Studies, Algeria and Tunisia, 1977. Mem. AAUP, MLA, Am. Assn. Tchrs. Spanish and Portuguese, Authors' Guild, Coll. Lang. Assn., ASCAP, La Academia de San Quirce (Segovia corr.) Home: 135 Bow St #8 Portsmouth NH 03801 E-mail: hughharter@aol.com.

HARTER, JOHN J. economic analyst; b. Canyon, Tex., Jan. 31, 1926; s. Ralph E. and Grace S. Harter; m. Irene T. Harter, May 25, 1957; children: Tian, Tonia, Lal. BA, U. So. Calif., 1948, MA, 1953; M of Econ., Harvard U., 1963. Lectr. in history U. So. Calif., L.A., 1948-53; fgn. svc. officer, various fgn. assignments Geneva, South Africa, Chile, Thailand, Dept. of State, Washington, 1954-83; oral historian, Washington, 1983—2003; conf. affairs officer Am. Fgn. Svc. Assn., Washington, 1989-96; freelance writer, cons. Washington, 1983—; declassifier Agy. for Internat. Devel., Washington, 1998—. Author: The Language of Trade, 1984. Sec., mem. vestry Am. Ch., Geneva, 1969-70. Mem. Diplomatic and Consular Officers Ret., Am. Fgn. Svc. Assn. Democrat. Episcopalian. Home: 4872 Admiration Dr Virginia Beach VA 23464-3149 E-mail: jjitharter@aol.com.

HARTER, PHILIP J. lawyer, educator; b. Columbus, Ohio, Apr. 14, 1942; s. Joseph M and Edith R. Harter; m. Nancy G. Gammel; 1 child, Alexa. AB, Kenyon Coll., 1960—64; MA in Math., U. Mich., Ann Arbor, 1965—66, JD, 1966—69. Bar: D.C. 1971, Supreme Ct. U.S. 1979. Vis. prof. of law Vt. Law Sch., South Royalton, Vt., 1999—2003; dir. program on democracy and governance; mediator The Mediation Inst., Washington, 1998—2003; Earl F. Nelson prof. law U. Mo., Columbia, 2003—. Author: Negotiating Regulations: A Cure for Malaise, 1981. Recipient Gellhorn award, Federal Bar Assn., 1998, award for Outstanding Contribution to the Pub. Policy of fostering the use of ADR, Soc. of Profls. in Dispute Resolution, 1992, award for Outstanding Achievement for Excellence and Innovation in Alternative Dispute Resolution, Ctr. for Pub. Resources, 1992. Mem.: ABA (chmn. sect. adminstrv. law and regulatory practice 1995—96, chmn. working group on regulatory reform 1995—98). Avocation: bicycling. Address: 201 S Glenwood Ave Columbia MO 65211 Office: U Missouri Hulston Hall Columbia MO 65211 E-mail: harterpj@missouri.edu.

HARTFORD, KATHLEEN LISCHKO, financial services company executive; b. Plainfield, N.J., June 25, 1958; d. James and Margaret (Galella) Lischko; m. John Hartford, Feb. 23, 1984 (div. Feb. 1996). BS in Econs. summa cum laude, Rutgers U., 1980. Asst. economist Fed. Res. Bank of N.Y., 1980-82; sr. v.p. McLoughlin Piven, N.Y.C., 1982-84; sr. v.p. investments Prudential Securities, Danbury, Conn., 1984—. Contbr. articles to Citizens News, 1992—; singer, guitar player Girls on the Side. Mem. Danbury C. of C., Greater Danbury Bus. Network Assn. Roman Catholic. Avocations: music, swimming, hiking, boating, tennis. Office: Prudential Securities Lee Farm Corp Pk 83 Wooster Heights Rd Ste 105 Danbury CT 06810-7538

HARTGEN, VINCENT ANDREW, museum director, educator, artist; b. Reading, Pa., Jan. 10, 1914; s. William J. and Jane (Hadfield) H.; m. Frances Caroline Lubanda, July 6, 1940; children: David Thomas, Stephen Anthony. BFA, U. Pa., 1940, MFA, 1941; DFA (hon.), U. Maine, 1987. Traveling curator Anna Hyatt Huntington Exhbn. of Sculptures, 1937-39; dir. U. Maine Art Gallery; prof., head art dept. U. Maine, 1946-75, John H. Huddilston prof. art, 1962-82, John H. Huddilston prof. emeritus, 1983—2002, curator art collections, 1975-82. Art adviser Cultural Olympics, U. Pa., 1939-41; mem. Gov.'s Commn. Arts and Humanities, 1966-70 Works in collections including, Boston Mus. Fine Arts, Brooks Meml. Mus., Memphis, Howard U. Collection, John and Norma Marin Collection, Mus. Contemporary Arts, Houston, Wichita (Kans.) Art Mus., Butler Inst. ARts, Youngstown, Ohio, Everhart Mus., Scranton, Pa., U. Maine, Art Collection, Wadsworth Atheneum, Hartford, Smith, Colby colls., Reading (Pa.) Mus., Phoenix Art Mus., ITT Collection, Brandeis U., Elvejhem (Wis.) Mus., Kalamazoo Inst. Coll., Walker Art Inst., Mpls., Sheldon Swope Gallery, Terre Haute, Ind., one-man exhibits include Binet Gallery, N.Y.C., Md. Inst., Howard U., Everhart Mus., Claflin U., Coll. of Pacific, U. Idaho, Bermuda Art Assn., Chase Gallery N.Y., Farnsworth Mus., Rockland, Maine, State Dept. Art in the Embassies, Fifty Drawings Cen. Place Gallery, Bangor, Maine Art Gallery, 1992, U. Maine, 1994; also more than 150 throughout mus. and galleries in U.S. Trustee Haystack Mountain Sch. Crafts, Liberty, Maine, 1953-55. Served with U.S. Army, 1942-45. U. Pa. fellow; recipient BAID award, 1935, Soldier Art award, 1945; Audubon Artists award, 1950, Audubon Artists medal for creative aquarelle, 1965, Silver medal Audubon Artists, 1974, Distinguished Faculty award, 1965, Gov.'s Art award State of Maine, 1967, Franklin Mint Bicentiennial Medal Design award, 1972, U. Maine Alumni Black Bear award, 1974; named A Maine State Treasure State of Maine Dept. Edn., 1994. Mem. AAUP, Audubon Artists, Am. Watercolor Soc., Phi Kappa Phi. Home: Orono, Maine. *To have lived, and to have seen such an incredible and beautiful world as this is to easily understand my consummate joy in having been an artist and teacher for such a long life.* Died Nov. 27, 2002.

HARTGER, BARBARA J. marketing professional; b. Grand Rapids, Mich., June 14, 1950; d. Harold Vos Hartger and Marjorie Hartger Bjork. AA, Pine Manor Jr. Coll., 1970; BFA, Sch. of Art Inst. Chgo., 1974. Animator, audio-visual dir, tech. dir. Wernecke Studios, Greyhound Exposition Svcs., Chgo., 1974—79; mem. spl. activities program IBM, Rochester, Minn., 1979—83, mktg. support, IBM Nat. Support Ctr., Office Exzec. Briefing Ctr. Dallas, 1983—89, comm. specialist, mgr. IBM SWG naming program, 1999—2003. Pres. Country Villas Homeowners Assn., Carrollton, Tex., 2002—; pub. info. chmn. United Way of Olmsted County, 1982—83. Recipient Gold award, United Way Am., 1980, Vol. Recognition award, State of Minn., 1983, cert. of appreciation, Dallas County Juvenile Dept., 1988, Appreciation award, Rochester Area C. of C., 1979. Mem.: Leadership Tex. Episcopalian. Avocations: theater, travel, symphony, choral music, skiing. Office: IBM 1505 LBJ Freeway Dallas TX 75234

HARTGROVE-FREILE, JANICE LYNN, psychologist, educator, writer; b. Fresno, Calif., Dec. 4, 1948; d. Albert Rayford Hartgrove and Doris Hartley McAllister, Charlotte Hartgrove (Stepmother); m. Scott Harris Freile, Jan. 26, 1978; children: Betony Star, Cody Sage, Shane Sequoyah. BA, Rice U., 1970; MA, U. of Houston, 1978; postgrad., U. Tex., 1988—97. Prof. of psychology North Harris Coll., Houston, 1983—. Author: (study guide) Language Development Guide for Introduction to Psychology (North Harris Coll. Writing award, 2001). Recipient Environ. Vision award, Tex. Corp. Recycling Coun., 1995, Leadership Excellence award, Nat. Inst. for Staff and Orgnl. Devel., 2001. Mem.: AAUP (chpt. sec. 2002—). Episcopalian. Avocations: environment, travel. Home: 235 Road 3433 Cleveland TX 77327 Office: North Harris Coll 2700 WW Thorne Dr Houston TX 77073 Office Fax: 281-618-5477. E-mail: hartgrov@nhmccd.edu.

HARTH, ERICA, French language and comparative literature educator; b. N.Y.C. BA, Barnard Coll., 1959; MA, Columbia U., 1962, PhD in French, 1968. Instr. French NYU, 1964-66; from instr. to asst. prof. Columbia U., 1967-71; lectr. Tel-Aviv U., Israel, 1971-72; asst. prof. Brandeis U., 1972-75, assoc. prof. French, 1975-85, prof. French and comparative lit., 1985-92; prof. humanities and women's studies Brandies U., 1992—. Author: Cyrano de Bergerac and the Polemics of Modernity, 1970, Ideology and Culture in Seventeenth Century France, 1983, Cartesian Women: Versions and Subversions of Rational Discourse in the Old Regime, 1992, Last Witnesses: Reflections on the Wartime Internment of Japanese Americans, 2001; contbr. articles to profl. jours. NEH fellow, 1970, 89, Am. Coun. Learned Socs. fellow, 1978, 90, Bunting Inst. fellow, 1990. Mem. MLA.

HARTH, ROBERT JAMES, performing arts executive; b. Louisville, June 13, 1956; s. Sidney and Teresa O. H.; 1 child, Jeffrey David Harth Curtis. BA in English, Northwestern U., 1977; DMusic (hon.), Cleve. Inst. Music. Assoc. mgr. Ravinia (Ill.) Festival Assn., 1977-79; v.p., gen. mgr. Los Angeles Philharm. Assn., 1979-89, Hollywood Bowl, 1979-89; pres., chief exec. officer Aspen (Colo.) Music Festival and Sch., Music Assocs. of Aspen, Inc., 1989-2001; exec., artistic dir. Carnegie Hall, 2001—. Hon. trustee Aspen Music Festival and Sch.; trustee Am. Symphony Orch. League, bd. trustees. Mem.: Curtis Inst Music (bd. overseers), European Concert Hall Orgn. Office: Carnegie Hall 881 Seventh Ave New York NY 10019

HARTH, SIDNEY, musician, educator; b. Cleve., Oct. 5, 1929; s. Leonard and Anne (Dunnire) H.; m. Teresa Testa, July 7, 1949; children: Laura, Robert. Mus.B., Cleve. Inst. Music, 1947; studied with, Joseph Knitzer, Mishel Piastro, Georges Enesco. Assoc. prof. U. Louisville, 1953-58; faculty DePaul U., 1959-62; chmn. dept. music, A.W. Mellon disting. prof. Carnegie-Mellon U., Pitts., 1963-73; mem. faculty Aspen (Colo.) Music Festival, 1963-74; exchange artist Les Jeunesses Musicales de France, 1952; with Mrs. Harth nat. tour, 1952; concertmaster Louisville Orch., 1953-58, Chgo. Symphony, 1959-62; condr. Evanston (Ill.) Orch., 1960-62; assoc. condr., concertmaster Los Angeles Philharm., 1973-79; chief guest condr. Jerusalem Symphony, 1975-77; music dir. Puerto Rico Symphony, 1977-79; condr. Can. Nat. Chamber Orch., 1979, 80; concertmaster N.Y. Philharm., 1980-81; orch. dir. Mannes Coll. of Music, 1981-84; prof. SUNY, Stony Brook, 1981-82, Yale U., 1982-99; prin. condr. Natal Symphony Orch., Durban, South Africa, 1994-99. Dir. orchestral activities Hartt Sch. Music, U. Hartford, 1991-93; violin Wieniawski competition laureate, Poland, 1957; orch. dir., vis. prof. U. Houston, 1985; dir. orchestral studies Carnegie-Mellon U., Pitts., 1989-90; faculty, Carnegie-Mellon U., 2000—, dir. Orchestral Sch. Music and condr. orch., Duquesne U., Pitts., 2001—. Ann. internat. tours including Yugoslavia, Poland, Belgium, Austria, Eng., USSR, Poland, Czechoslovakia, Romania, Switzerland, Holland., Vanguard, Iramac, Concert Hall Soc., Stradivari Records; contbr. articles to nat. mags. Recipient Ysaye medal; Wieniawski medal. Home: 135 Westland Dr Pittsburgh PA 15217-2538

HARTH-BEDOYA, MIGUEL, conductor; b. Lima, Peru, 1968; Degree, Curtis Inst. Music, Juilliard Sch. Music dir. Eugene (Oreg.) Symphony Orch.; now music dir. Ft. Worth Symphony Orch.; assoc. dir. L.A. Philharmonic Orch. Music dir., condr. N.Y. Youth Symphony Carnegie Hall; guest condr. N.Y. Philharm., L.A. Philharm., Fla. Orch., Seattle Symphony, Colo. Symphony, Que. Symphony, Auckland Philharm., New Zealand, Puerto Rico Symphony, Buenos Aires Philharmonia, Evansville Philharm. Orch., Ind.; condr. Juilliard Orch. tour, France, 1993, Japan, 95, St. Luke's Orch., 1995; founder, artistic dir. New Opera Co. Peru, Orquestra Filarmonica de Lima; mem. conducting faculty Juilliard Sch. Office: Fort Worth Symphony Orch 330 E 4th St Ste 200 Fort Worth TX 76102-4019

HARTIGAN, KARELISA DOROTHY, classics educator; b. Stillwater, Okla., Mar. 5, 1943; d. Charles Henry and Elsie Florence Voelker; m. Barry Hartigan, Apr. 21, 1966 (div. Feb. 1978); 1 child, Timothy Lawrence; m. Kevin Michael McCarthy, Dec. 22, 1992. BA in Classics, Coll. of Wooster, 1965; AM in Classics, U. Chgo., 1966, PhD in Classics, 1970. Asst. prof. St. Olaf Coll., Northfield, Minn., 1969-73; asst. prof., assoc. prof. Greek studies U. Fla., Gainesville, from 1973, prof., 1991—, co-dir. Ctr. for Greek Studies, 1980—, assoc. dir. honors program, 1989-95. Author: The Poets and the Cities, 1979, Ambiguity and Self-Deception, 1991, Greek Tragedy on the American Stage, 1995, Myths Behind Our Words, 1998, Muse on Madison Avenue, 2001; editor Text and Presentation jour., 1983-94; editor spl. issues Classical and Modern Lit.; Classical Reflections, 1980. Recipient Excellence in Tchg. award Am. Philol. Assn., 1985; Disting. Alumni Prof. award U. Fla., 1987-89, Univ.-Wide Tchg. award, 1990, Tchg. award, 1994, Disting. Prof. award, 2001. Mem. Modern Greek Studies Assn. (sec. 1983-1986), Classical Assn. Mid. West and South (pres. so. sect. 1986-88, nat. pres. 1992-93). Avocations: bicycling, swimming, travel, cooking, dogs. Office: University of Florida Ctr Greek Studies PO Box 117435 Gainesville FL 32611-7435 E-mail: kvhrtgn@classics.ufl.edu.

HARTKE, CHARLES A. state legislator; b. Effingham, Ill., May 7, 1944; m. Kathy Hartke; 2 children. Farmer; mem. from 108th dist. Ill. Ho. of Reps., 1985—. Vice chmn. agr. com.; chmn. counties and twps. com.; mem. appropriations com., elem. and secondary edn. com., transp. and motor vehicles com., children com., econ. devel. and legis. info. system com., pub. safety and infrastructure appropriations coms., vets. affairs com. Home: PO Box 1205 Effingham IL 62401-1205*

HARTKE, STEPHEN PAUL, composer, educator; b. Orange, N.J., July 6, 1952; s. George William Hartke, Jr. and Priscilla Nancy (Redfearn) Elfrey; m. Lisa Louise Stidham, Sept. 12, 1981; 1 child, Alexander Stidham. BA magna cum laude, Yale U., 1973; MA, U. Pa., 1976; PhD, U. Calif., Santa Barbara, 1982. Advt. mgr. Theodore Presser Co., Bryn Mawr, Pa., 1977-78; advt. and art dir. European Am. Music Corp., Clifton, N.J., 1978-79; ednl. dir. Carl Fischer Inc., N.Y.C., 1980; Fulbright prof. composition U. São Paulo, Brazil, 1984-85; prof. composition Sch. Music U. So. Calif., L.A., 1987—. Vis. composer Coll. Creative Studies U. Calif., Santa Barbara, 1981-83, 85-87; composer-in-residence L.A. Chamber Orch., 1988-92. Composer: Caoine, 1980, Sonata-Variations for violin and piano, 1984 (Kennedy Friedheim award 1985), Oh Them Rats Is Mean In My Kitchen, 1985, Pacific Rim for orch., 1988, The King of the Sun, 1988, Symphony Number 2, 1990, Concerto for violin and orch., 1992, Wulfstan at the Millennium, 1995, The Ascent of the Equestrian in a Balloon, 1995, Sons of Noah, 1996, The Horse with the Lavender Eye, 1997, Piano Sonata, 1998, The Rose of the Winds, 1998, Tituli, 1999, Gradus, 1999, Cathedral in the Thrashing Rain, 2000, Concerto for Clarinet and Orchestra, 2001, Beyond Words, 2001; recs. on CRI, New World Records, ECM EMI record labels. Recipient Acad. award AAAL, 1993, Rome prize Am. Acad. in Rome, 1992, Stoeger award Lincoln Ctr. Chamber Music Soc., 1997; Composer-in-Residence grantee Nat. Endowment for Arts (1990, 91), Commn. grantee Koussevitzky Music Found., 1992, Fromm Found. Commn. grantee, 1994, Inst. for Am. Music Commn. grantee; Guggenheim fellow, 1997. Mem. Opera Am., Am. Mus. Ctr. Office: U So Calif Sch Music 308 University Park Los Angeles CA 90089-0001

HARTLE, ROBERT WYMAN, retired foreign language and literature educator; b. Kongmoon, China, Sept. 1, 1921; s. Jacob Everett and Margaret (Wyman) H.; m. Ann Dorothy Mordhorst, Jan. 5, 1980; 1 son, Robert Wyman, Jr.; children by previous marriage: Shirley Ann (Mrs. Jan McDaniel), John Wyman. BA, MA, U. Tex., 1947; AM, Princeton U., 1949, PhD, 1951. Instr. French Princeton U., 1950-53, asst. prof., 1953-60; assoc. prof. modern langs. U. Oreg., 1961-63; asst. prof. Romance langs. Queens Coll. (now CUNY-Queens Coll.), N.Y.C., 1960-61, prof., chmn. dept. Romance and Slavic langs., 1963-65, assoc. dean faculty, 1964-65, dean faculty, 1965-70, prof., 1972-87, prof. emeritus, 1987—, chmn. ad hoc legal affairs com., mem. univ. acad. senate, 1979-81, dir. PhD program in France, 1970-72, mem. senate. Founder, dir. programs of study abroad, 1963-70; vis. prof. Inst. Liberal Arts, Emory U., 1985-93. Author: Index du vocabulaire du théâtre classique: Racine, 8 vols, 1956-64; transl. Tartuffe (Molière), 1963; contbr. articles on the iconography of Alexander the Great, 17th century French art and architecture, Hellenistic Art, 1955—; French translator Papers of Robert Morris, 1973-84; French cons. Papers of Thomas Jefferson, Princeton U. Press, 1986—. Bd. dirs. Am. Ctr. for Students and Artists, Paris, 1970-78. Decorated officer Ordre des Palmes Académiques (France), knight Order of Merit (Italy), officer's cross Order of Merit (Germany). Mem. MLA, AAUP (pres. chpt. 1975-80) Home: 1803 Westminster Way NE Atlanta GA 30307-1134

HARTLESS, KEITH D. music educator; b. Camp LeJune, NC, Nov. 16, 1955; s. Bobby D. and Pearlie E. Hartless; m. Alice B. Buckland; children: Adam, Amanda. MusB Edn., James Madison U., Harrisonburg, Va., 1979. Cert. Music Edn. Va. Dept. Edn., 1979. Dir. of instrumental music Rockingham County Schs., Harrisonburg, Va., 1979—84; dir. of vocal music programs Roanoke (Va.) County Schs., 1984—. Dir. of music Melrose Bapt. Ch., Roanoke, Va., 1991—96; dir. of music Preston Oaks Bapt. Ch., Roanoke, Va., 1998—2000. Dir.: (clinician) Eagle Eyrie Select Chorus, 1995, Christianburg Pub. Schs. All-County Chorus, 1995, Botetourt County Schs. All-County Chorus, 1995, 1997, Henry County Schs. All-County Chorus, 1996. Kick off entertainer United Way, Roanoke, Va., 1995; field judge Va. Commonwealth Games, Roanoke, Va., 1994; block chmn. Am. Cancer Soc., Roanoke, Va., 2000—02, Am. Heart Assn., Roanoke, Va., 2000. Mem.: NEA, Contemporary Accapella Soc. Am., Nat. Assn. of Jazz Educators, Dist. VI Choral Dirs. Assn., Va. Choral Dirs. Assn. (Dist. chmn. 1996—98), Va. Music Educators Assn., Music Educators Nat. Conf., Roanoke County Edn. Assn., Va. Edn. Assn., Am. Choral Dirs. Assn., Internat. Brotherhood of Magicians. Baptist. Avocations: topiary, golf, magic, travel, woodworking. Home: 5430 N Garden Ln Roanoke VA 24019 Office: Northside HS 6810 Northside HSl Rd Roanoke VA 24019 Personal E-mail: khartles@rbnet.com. E-mail: khartless@rcs.k12.va.us.

HARTLEY, ALAN HASELTON, lexicographer, stevedoring administrator; b. Duluth, Minn., Dec. 3, 1946; s. Alfred and Ann Hardy (Haselton) H.; m. Susan Beers Rice, June 21, 1969; two children. BA, Carleton Coll., 1969; MS, U. Wash., 1972. Geologist Exxon Minerals, Ely, Minn., 1969-70, 77; ranger Nat. Park Svc., Isle Royale, Mich., 1973-77; comml. fisherman Sivertson Fisheries, Duluth, Minn., 1974-80; stevedoring supt. Empire Stevedoring, Duluth, 1981-95, Rogers Terminal (Cargill), Duluth, 1995—. Contract lexicographer Oxford English Dictionary, 1995—, New Oxford Am. Dictionary, 2000-01. Mem. editl. staff: Oxford American College Dictionary, 2001. Trustee Longshoremen's Fringe Benefit Funds, Duluth. NSF fellow, 1970-72. Home: 119 W Kent Rd Duluth MN 55812-1152

HARTLEY, BOB, professional hockey coach; b. Hawkesbury, Ont., Can., Sept. 7, 1960; m. Micheline; children: Kristine, Steve. Coach Hawkesbury Hawks, 1987-91; head coach Laval Titans, 1991-93, Cornwall Aces, 1993-94, 1994-95, Colo. Avalanche, 1998—2002; coach Hershey Bears, 1996-98; head coach Atlanta Thrashers, 2003—. Office: The Atlanta Thrashers One CNN Ctr Atlanta GA 30303-2762

HARTLEY, CARL WILLIAM, JR., lawyer; b. Carthage, Mo., Aug. 12, 1946; s. Carl William and Doris Eillene (Wilcox) H.; m. Martha Anderson Gouch (div. 1991); children: Zach, Jordan. BS, U. Fla., 1968, JD with High Honors, 1976. Bar: Fla. 1976, U.S. Dist. Ct. (so. dist.) Fla. 1976, U.S. Dist. Ct. (mid. dist.) Fla. 1980. Sales rep. Scott Paper Co., Miami, Fla., 1971-73; assoc. Grenberg, Traurig et al., Miami, 1976-80; ptnr. Thomas Thomas Hartley & Spraker, Orlando, Fla., 1980-83, Holland & Knight, Orlando, 1983-85, Hartley & Wall, Orlando, 1985—. Editor U. Fla. Law Rev., 1976. Democrat. Methodist. Avocations: fishing, hunting, camping. Office: Hartley & Wall PO Box 2168 Orlando FL 32802-2168 E-mail: cwhsec@hartleywall.com.

HARTLEY, CELIA LOVE, nursing consultant, writer, retired nursing educator, nursing administrator; b. Colfax, Wash., Oct. 25, 1935; d. Thomas Warren and Ella Marie (Kerkman) Love; m. Lawrence Dosser (div.); children: Laurie Denise Draper, Byron Garth Dosser; m. Gordon E. Hartley, Dec. 17, 1972. Diploma, Deaconess Hosp. Sch. Nursing, Spokane, 1956; BSN, U. Wash., 1965, MSN, 1968. RN, Wash., Calif. Staff nurse Deaconess Hosp., Spokane, 1956-62; charge nurse Northgate Gen. Hosp., Seattle, 1963-65; hosp. supr. Stevens Meml. Hosp., Edmonds, Wash., 1965-66; prof. nursing Shoreline C.C., Seattle, 1967-73, dir. nursing edn., asst. div. chmn. health occupations, 1973-92; chair health sci. divsn. Coll. of the Desert, Palm Desert, Calif., 1992-99, prof. emerita, 1999—; nursing curriculum cons. Pres. Coun. on Nursing Edn. in Wash. State, 1992; adv. com. Antioch West and Seattle U., 1979-81, Nursing Edn. Com. Higher Edn. Coordinating Bd., 1990, Western Wash. U. Nursing, 1984, Seattle Pacific U. Nursing, 1992; other coms. various orgns., 1979—; presenter in field. Author: (with Janice Ellis) Nursing in Today's World: Challenges, Issues, and Trends, 1980, 8th rev. edit., 2004, Managing and Coordinating Patient Care, 1991, 3d edit., 2000, Fundamentals of Nursing, 1992; mem. editl. bd. Assoc. Degree Nurse, 1987-91, Jour. Nursing Edn., 1991—; contbr. articles to profl. jours. Mem. ANA, Nat. League of Nursing (bd. dirs. 1981-84, appeal panel Coun. AD Programs 1988-91, 95-98, chmn.-vice chmn. various com.), Wash. Constituent League (v.p. 1986-87, chmn. nominating com. 1984-85, chmn. membership com. 1985-86), Calif. Nursing Strategic Planning Com., Sigma Theta Tau. Methodist. Home: 3234 Mabana Rd Camano Island WA 98282 E-mail: cegohart@aol.com.

HARTLEY, CORINNE, painter, sculptor, educator; b. L.A., July 24, 1924; d. George D. and Marjorie (Fansher) Parr; m. Thomas L. West, Sept. 3, 1944 (div. 1970); children: Thomas West III, Tori West, Trent West; m. Clabe M. Hartley, Aug. 27, 1973 (div. 1997). Attended, Chouinard Art Inst., L.A., 1942-44, Pasadena (Calif.) Sch. Fine Arts, 1952-54. Paste up artist Advt. Agy., L.A., 1944; fashion illustrator May Co., L.A., 1944-45; freelance fashion illustrator Bullock's, L.A., 1946-76. Art tchr. Pasadena Sch. Fine Arts, 1965—69; pvt. art tchr., owner studio, Venice, Calif., 1970—2000, Newport Beach, Calif., 2000—; presenter art workshops; works pub. and distributed by Art in Motion, Prints and Cards, Vancouver, B.C., Canada, 1990—. Gallery representation includes Dassin Gallery, L.A., 1981—, Legacy Gallery, Scottsdale, Ariz., 1989—, G. Stanton Gallery, Dallas, 1990—, Coda Gallery, Palm Desert, Calif., 1993—, Huntsman Gallery, Aspen, Colo., 1995—, Carol Kavanaugh Gallery, Des Moines, 1996—, Jones & Terwilliger Gallery, Carmel, Calif., 1997—, Lee Youngman Gallery, Calistoga, Calif., 1997—, Mountain Trails Gallery, Park City, Utah, 2000, Terbush Gallery, Santa Fe, 1997—. Recipient Purchase award Nat. Orange Show, San Bernardino, Honor award All City Art Festival, Barnsdall Park, L.A., Best of Show award Clumer Mus. Wash., 3d pl. award still life Calif. Art Club, award of excellence Oil Painters Am./Springville Mus., Utah, N.Mex., others. Mem. Calif. Art Club, Oil Painters Am. Republican. Avocation: singing in church choir.

HARTLEY, CRAIG SHERIDAN, mechanical and materials engineer; b. Quantico, Va., Dec. 9, 1937; s. Cleo Stancil and Velva Marie (Grayson) Bowers; m. Cornelia Margaret McMann, June 7, 1958; children: Margaret Ann, Katherine Jeanne, David Brian. BMetE, Rensselaer Poly. Inst., 1958; MS, Ohio State U., 1961, PhD, 1965; MFA, U. Fla., 1980. Registered profl. engr., Ala., Fla., La., N.Y. Project engr. USAF Materials Lab., WPAFB, Ohio, 1959-66; postdoctoral fellow NSF, 1965-66; prof. materials sci. and engring. U. Fla., Gainesville, 1966-80; chair materials sci. and engring. SUNY, Stony Brook, 1980-82; assoc. dean enging. La. State U., Baton Rouge, 1982-86; program dir. NSF, Washington, 1986-87; chair materials sci. and engring. U. Ala., Birmingham, 1987-90; dean engring. Fla. Atlantic U., Boca Raton, 1990-96; program dir. NSF, 1996-97; guest rschr. Nat. Inst. of Stds. and Tech., Gaithersburg, Md., 1997-98; program officer Dept. of Energy, Germantown, Md., 1998-2000; program mgr. AFOSR/NA, Arlington, Va., 2000—. Cons. Materials Cons., Inc., Gainesville, 1975-90, Brookhaven (N.Y.) Nat. Lab., 1980-82, NSF, Washington, 1987—. Contbr. articles to jours. Acta Metallurgica et Materialia, Exptl. Mechanics, Philos. Mag., Jour. Applied Physics. Pres. Gainesville Little Theatre, 1967-69, Fla. Theatre Conf., 1977-79. Capt. USAF, 1959-62. Grantee NSF, 1966-69, 82-85, Office of Naval Rsch., 1967-69, AEC, 1973-79, Nuclear Regulatory Commn., 1976-79, Army Rsch. Office, 1983-86. Fellow AAAS, ASM Internat., mem. ASME, The Metall. Soc. (mining, metals and materials sect., chmn. edn. and profl. affairs com. 1990-92), Soc. Exptl. Mechanics. Unitarian Universalist. E-mail: cmcshart@bellatlantic.net.

HARTLEY, DEAN S., III, operations research specialist; b. Florence, S.C., Dec. 30, 1946; s. Dean S. Hartley, Jr. and Ruth B. Hartley; m. Eileen O. O'Connor, July 27, 1972; children: Theresa E., Elise A. AB in Math. and Fgn. Langs. summa cum laude, Wofford Coll., 1968; PhD in Math., U. Ga., 1973. Mil. ops. rsch., dep. br. head Gen. Purpose Forces Br., CCTC, Washington, 1973—77; ops. rsch. Milliken & Co, Spartanburg, SC, 1977—79, prodn. planning mgr LaGrange, Ga., 1979—84, mktg. mgr., 1984—86; rsch. staff mem. Oak Ridge (Tenn.) Nat. Lab., DOE, 1986—90; sr. rsch. staff mem. Y12 Complex, DOE, Oak Ridge, 1990—2001; prin. Hartley Consulting, Oak Ridge, 2001—. Dir. Mil. Ops. Rsch. Soc., Washington, 1994—99, Inst. for Ops. Rsch. and Mgmt. Sciences, Linthicum, Md., 1995—97, Linthicum, 2001—02; v.p. Inst. for Mgmt. Sciences and Ops. Rsch., Linthicum, Md., 2003—. Author: (scientific book) Predicting Combat Effects; assoc. editor: Mil. Ops. Rsch.; contbr. chapters to books, articles to profl. jours. Chmn. Bell for Gov. Troup County Rep. Party, LaGrange, 1984. Capt. U.S. Army, 1973—77. Decorated Joint Services Commendation medal Dept. Def. Mem.: Mil. Ops. Rsch. Soc., INFORMS Coll. on Simulation, Decision Analysis Soc., Inst. for Mgmt. Scis. and Ops. Rsch., Mil. Applications Soc. (pres. 1993—95), Phi Beta Kappa. Republican. Episcopalian. Achievements include development of Oak Ridge Spreadsheet Battle Model. Avocations: science fiction, martial arts, shooting. Office: Hartley Consulting 106 Windsong Ln Oak Ridge TN 37830 Office Fax: 865-482-3268. E-mail: dshartley3@comcast.net.

HARTLEY, DUNCAN, fundraising executive; b. Sept. 27, 1941; s. Harold Shephard and Catherine Carmichael (Hursley) H.; m. Adrienne Ashley, Aug. 19, 1971. BA, U. Mich., 1964; MA, Wayne State U., Detroit, 1966, PhD. Instr. English dept. Wayne State U., 1969-71; asst. prof. William Paterson Coll., 1971-74; adminstr. ednl. resources, chpt. liaison Young Pres.'s Orgn., N.Y.C., 1974-78; dir. planned giving Carroll Coll., Waukesha, Wis., 1978-80; dir. capital gifts Greater N.Y. Coun. Boy Scouts Am., N.Y.C., 1980-84; dir. individual giving, exec. dir. pres.'s coun. Meml. Sloan-Kettering Cancer Ctr., N.Y.C., 1984-96; assoc. dean of devel. and alumni affairs Sch. Medicine Case Western Res. U., Cleve., 1996—. Co-editor, author: The Sociology of the Arts, 1974. Mem. Princeton Club of N.Y., Audiophile Soc. Presbyterian. Avocation: audio equipment reviewing. Home: 310 E Stonebrooke Ct Chagrin Falls OH 44022-2100 Office: Case Western Res U Sch Medicine 10900 Euclid Ave Cleveland OH 44106-1712

HARTLEY, HAL, film director; b. Islip, N.Y., Nov. 3, 1959; BA with honors in Film, SUNY, Purchase, 1984. Writer, dir.: (feature films) The Unbelievable Truth, 1990, Trust, 1991, Simple Men, 1992, Amateur, 1994, Flirt, 1995 (short films) Dogs, The Cartographer's Girlfriend, (TV films) Surviving Desire, 1989, Theory of Achievement, 1991, Ambition, 1991, Henry Fool, 1997, The Book of Life, 1998, Monster, 2000, Kimono, 2000. Office: Possible Films Inc 39 W 14th St Ste 406 New York NY 10011-7489

HARTLEY, JAMES EDWARD, lawyer; b. Orange, N.J., Nov. 4, 1949; s. George and Carolyn (Stewart) H.; m. Judy Franklin, Mar. 1, 1986; 1 child, Jonathan. BA, U. Calif., Berkeley, 1971, JD, 1974. Bar: Colo. 1974, U.S. Dist. Ct. Colo. 1974, U.S. Ct. Appeals (10th cir.) 1975, U.S. Supreme Ct. 1981, U.S. Ct. Appeals (Fed. cir.) 1993. Assoc. Holland & Hart, Denver, 1974-80, ptnr., 1980—. Adj. prof. Denver U. Law Sch., 1985-86. Co-author: Private Litigation Under Section 7 of the Clayton Act: Law and Policy, 1989, Antitrust Pitfalls in Outpatient Services, 1992, Rule of Reason Monograph, 1999, State Antitrust Practice and Procedure, 1999; asst. editor: ABA Antitrust Law Jour., 1994-98. Mem. ABA (coun. antitrust law sect. 2003—), Nat. Health Lawyers Assn., Colo. Bar Assn., Denver Bar Assn., Order of Coif, Phi Beta Kappa. Home: 2540 Briarwood Dr Boulder CO 80305-6804 Office: Holland & Hart LLP 555 17th St Ste 3200 Denver CO 80202-3950

HARTLEY, JAMES R. musician, writer; b. Wash., Dec. 23, 1948; s. James Aaron Hartley and Ruth Virginia Pope; m. Carol Ann Creed, Apr. 14, 1994 (div. Dec. 18, 2001). AA TV, Radio, Montgomery Coll., 1981. Tech. asst. Montgomery County Pub. Schs., Rockville, Md., 1968—84; musician self-employed, Md., 1980—, 1980—. Newsletter editor / pub. Wash. Baseball Hist. Soc., Germantown, Md., 2001—. Author (pub.): Washington's Expansion Senators (1961-1971), 1998. Recipient award, Phi Theta Kappa, 1981. Mem.: Soc. Am. Baseball Rsch., Washington Baseball Hist. Soc. (newsletter editor, pub. 2001—), Major League Baseball Players Alumni Assn. Democrat. Christian. Achievements include authored and published the first extensive history of the Washington senators expansion baseball team from 1961-71. Avocations: baseball history, golf. Office: Corduroy Press PO Box 2248 Germantown MD 20875 E-mail: natnative7@aol.com.

HARTLEY, KAREN JEANETTE, lawyer, mediator, consultant; b. Oakland, Calif., Aug. 2, 1950; d. Samuel Louis and Jean Iris (Beven) Ostrow; m. Terry Van Hook, Aug. 29, 1970 (div. Mar. 1976); m. William Headley, Jan. 22, 1977 (div. Mar. 1988). BA in Psychology with highest honors, UCLA, 1972; DMin, Sch. of Theology, Claremont, Calif., 1976; JD cum laude, U. San Diego, 1982. Bar: Calif. 1982, U.S. Dist. Ct. (9th cir.), 1983, Hawaii 1991, Oreg. 1996; ordained to ministry, Meth. Ch., 1973. Intern to asst. United Meth. Ch., 1969-71; asst. minister St. Paul's United Meth. Ch., San Bernardino, Calif., 1973-74; assoc. minister Claremont United Meth. Ch., 1974-76; sr. minister Santee (Calif.) United Meth. Ch., 1977-79; clk. Calif. Supreme Ct., San Francisco, 1981; cons. Regional Dept. Edn., San Diego, 1979-81; assoc. atty. Duke, Gerstel, Shearer & Bregante, San Diego, 1983-84, Finley, Kumble, Wagner et al, San Diego, 1984-87; prin. atty., mediator Hartley & Assocs., San Diego, 1987-95, Eugene, Oreg., 1996—99; coord. pub. policy dispute resolution for human svc. agys. Oreg. Dept. Human Svcs., Salem, 1999-2001; prin. atty. Hartley & Assocs., Eugene, 2001—. Mediator San Diego Mediation Ctr., 1990-95; prof. negotiation and mediation, instr. Mediation Clinic U. Oreg. Sch. Law, Eugene, 1996-97; instr. constrn. law Lane C.C., Eugene, 1996-99. Mem. Oreg. Bar Assn., Lan County Bar Assn. Avocations: art, travel. E-mail: karenhartley7@aol.com.

HARTLEY, MICHAEL J. online travel executive; CEO Cheap Tickets, Inc., Honolulu, 1986—. Recipient Hawaii Ernst & Young Entrepreneur of Yr. award, 2000. Office: Cheap Tickets Inc 1440 Kapiolani Blvd Honolulu HI 96814-3612

HARTLEY, PHILIP. L. academic administrator, psychology educator; b. Eureka, Calif., Apr. 13, 1946; s. Duane D. and Katherine M. Hartley; m. Donna R. Hartley, Aug. 1, 1970; 1 child, Stephanie. BA, Humboldt State U., 1969; MA, U. Calif., Riverside, 1971, PhD, 1976. Psychology lectr. Calif. State U., San Bernardino, 1985-90; prof. psychology Chaffey Coll., Alta Loma, Calif., 1973-83, divsn. chair, 1983-92; dean instrn. Mendocino Coll., Ukiah, Calif., 1992-98; v.p. Coll. of the Canyons, Santa Clarita, Calif., 1998—. Contbr. articles to profl. jours. Mem. Rotary. Avocations: scuba diving, photography, wine growing and making. E-mail: philhart@earthlink.net.

HARTLEY, ROGER EDWARD, political science educator; b. Charleston, W.Va., Apr. 26, 1969; s. Roger Lee Hartley and Beverly Ann Hauschilt; m. Melissa Lynn English, Jan. 25, 1997. BS in Pub. Affairs, Ind. U., 1991; MA in Polit. Sci., U. Ga., 1993, PhD in Polit. Sci., 1999. Instr. CUNY-John Jay Coll., N.Y.C., 1997, CUNY-Baruch Coll., N.Y.C., 1997; asst. prof. pub. affairs Roanoke Coll., Salem, Va., 1998-2001; asst. prof. Sch. Pub. Adminstrn. and Policy U. Ariz., Tucson, 2001—. Advisor Truman Meml. Scholarship, Roanoke Coll., Salem, 1999-2000; appointed to bd. legal document preparers Ariz. Supreme Ct. State Bd., 2003—. Author: Alternative Dispute Resolution in Civil Justice Systems, 2002; contbr. articles to profl. jours. Bd. dirs., sec. of bd. Conflict Resolution Ctr., Roanoke, Va., 1999-2001. Mem. Law and Soc. Assn., Am. Polit. Sci. Assn., So. Polit. Sci. Assn., Am. Judicature Soc. Independent. Avocations: running, sports, hiking, herb gardening. Office: U Ariz Sch Pub Adminstrn & Policy McClelland Hall 405 Tucson AZ 85721 Home: 1445 E Waverly St Tucson AZ 85719

HARTLEY, SEAN JOSEPH, composer, lyricist, music educator; s. Joseph Milton and Emmy Lu Hartley; life ptnr. David Hughes. BA, Brandeis U., 1976; MA, Manhattan Sch. Music, 1989. Dir. The Theater Wing, Kaufman Ctr., N.Y.C., 1989—. Lyricist, playwright Cupid And Psyche, Number the Stars; composer: (musical play) Young Moses; playwright, lyricist Joseph and Koza. Democrat. Presbyterian/Buddhist. Avocation: tennis. Office: Kaufman Ctr 129 W 67 St New York NY 10023 Personal E-mail: shartley@ekcc.org.

HARTLINE, DARRELL G. retired healthcare executive; b. Litchfield, Ill., Oct. 16, 1939; s. Robert Carl and Marguerite A. (Wells) H.; m. Jane A. Fesser, June 11, 1961; 1 child, Jeffrey Lynn. BS, So. Ill. U., 1962. Auditor Arthur Andersen & Co., Chgo., 1962-65; chief fin. officer Mercy Hosp., Davenport, Iowa, 1965-70, The Genesee Hosp., Rochester, N.Y., 1970-92, Quorum Health Resources, Inc., Lockhaven Hosp., Nashville, 1992-2001. Mem. various coms. N.Y. State Dept. Health, Albany, 1974-87; cons. N.Y. State Coun. on Health Care Financing, Albany, 1979-83, Health Mgmt. Svcs., Syracuse, N.Y., 1980-84, bd. dirs also. Bd. dirs., treas. Vis. Nurse Svcs., Rochester, N.Y., 1982-87, Rochester Dist. Heating Co-op, 1986-92, Vis. Nurse Found., Rochester, 1987-93; bd. dirs., chmn. Cmty. Care of Rochester, 1987-93; bd. dirs., treas. Piper Aviation Mus., 1995-96. With USAR, 1961. Mem. Hosp. Assn. N.Y. State (various coms.), Rochester Regional Hosp. Assn. (various coms.), Health Care Fin. Mgmt. Assn. (bd. dirs., past officer, William Fullmur award 1974, Robert H. Reeves award 1985, Frederick T. Muncie award 1992, Spl. Chpt. Recognition award 1992) Lutheran. Avocations: target shooting, boating, flying, fishing, hockey. Home: 1407 Cardinal Dr W Lock Haven PA 17745

HARTLINE, THOMAS WILLIAM, aerospace engineer; b. Reading, Pa., Oct. 30, 1958; s. William Thomas and Betty Hartline; m. Mary E Hoban, Sept. 24, 1983; children: Elizabeth Rose, Victoria Lee, Abigail Mae, Thomas Jr. William. BS in Aerospace Engring., US Naval Acad., Annapolis, Md., 1981; MSME, U. of Ala., Huntsville, 1995. Helicopter pilot U.S. Navy HC-6, Norfolk, Va., 1983—85; helicopter flight instr. U.S. Navy HT-18, Pensacola, Fla., 1985—89; helicopter pilot/ safety officer U.S. Navy - USS TARAWA, San Diego, 1989—91; aerospace engr. PRC Inc., Huntsville, Ala., 1991—94; aerospace sys. safety engr. NASA, Marshall Space Flight Ctr., Huntsville, Ala., 1994—2001, mgr., advanced projects assurance dept., 2001—. Comdr. . USNR, 1981—2002. Decorated Navy - Marine Corps Commendation Medal, ; recipient NASA Silver Snoopy award, 1994. Mem.: AIAA, The Am. Legion, Naval Helicopter Assn., U.S. Naval Acad. Alumni Assn. (life; pres. - local huntsville chpt. 1994—96, pres. Huntsville chpt. 1994—96). Avocations: running, scale model building, computers. Home: 112 Crestview Cir Madison AL 35758 Office: NASA Marshall Space Flight Center QS10 Huntsville AL 35812 E-mail: thomas.w.hartline@nasa.gov.

HARTLING, EARLE CHARLES, environmental engineer; b. L.A., May 5, 1956; s. Earle Vaughn and Edna Catherine (Wireman) H.; m. Shirley Lorraine Gjurgevich, Nov. 24, 1990; 1 child, Vaughn Thomas. BS in Biology, Loyola Marymount U., L.A., 1978, MS in Environ. Sci. and Engring., 1981. Cert. qualified environ. profl., IPEP. Project engr. Sanitation Dists. of L.A. County, Whittier, 1981-94, water recycling coord., 1994—. Guest lectr. Environ. Sys. Engring. Program, Calif. State U., Long Beach, 1993-94. Prodr. video: Water for a Dry Land, 1989 (Best Video award Calif. Water Pollution Control Assn. 1989); contbg. chpt.: Using Reclaimed Water to Augment Potable Water Resources, 1998, Wastewater Reclamation and Reuse, 1998; contbr. articles to profl. jours. Founding mem. Recycling and Conservation Task Force, Culver City, Calif., 1989-96 mem. L.A. County Reclaimed Water Adv. Com., 1990—, pres., 2000—; mem. Culver City Emergency Response Team, 2001—, instr., 2002—, tng. and edn. mgr., 2003—; mem. Calif. Water Recycling Task Force, 2002. Mem. WateReuse Assn. (chmn. indsl. reuse subcom. 1997—, trustee Calif. sect. 2002-, Outstanding Svc. award 1995), Water Environ. Fedn., Calif. Water Environment Assn. (chmn. groundwater mgmt. subcom. 1994—), Mensa, Tau Beta Pi, Alpha Sigma Nu. Roman Catholic. Avocations: wood furniture restoration, backpacking, beach volleyball, racquetball. Home: 4314 Jasmine Ave Culver City CA 90232-3427 Office: Sanitation Dist LA County PO Box 4998 Whittier CA 90607-4998 E-mail: ehartling@lacsd.org.

HARTLYN, JONATHAN, political scientist, educator; BA magna cum laude, Clark U., 1974; MPhil, Yale U., 1976, PhD, 1981. Asst. prof. Vanderbilt U., Nashville, 1981-87, assoc. prof., 1987-88, U. N.C., Chapel Hill, 1988-97, prof., 1997—, chair dept. polit. sci., 2000—, dir. Inst. Latin Am. Studies, 1997—2000. Author: The Politics of Coalition Rule in Colombia, 1988, The Struggle for Democratic Politics in the Dominican Republic, 1998; co-author: Latin America in the Twenty-First Century,2003; co-editor: Latin American Political Economy, 1986, The United States and Latin America in the 1990s, 1992, Democracy in Developing Countries: Latin America, 2d edit., 1999; contbr. articles to profl. jours. Tinker Found. fellow, 1985-86. Mem. Am. Polit. Sci. Assn., Latin Am. Studies Assn., Phi Beta Kappa. Office: U NC Dept Polit Sci Cb 3265 Hamilton Hl Chapel Hill NC 27599-3265 E-mail: hartlyn@unc.edu.

HARTMAN, ARLEEN, artist; b. Cleve., Jan. 17, 1954; d. Raymond Joseph and Margaret (Schuman) H. BA, Cleve. State U., 1981; MFA, U. Cin., 1984. Tchr. Deer Elem. Sch., Banchang, Thailand, 1973-74; artist Cleve., 1979—; asst. prof. art Bowling Green State U., Huron, Ohio, 1993-94; instr. Capitol U., Cleve., 1994—. Vis. artist various schs., Ohio, 1970-94; lectr. art CCC/CSU/UC, Cleve. and Cin., 1983-90, 1998-2003, CSU Inst. Gifted & Talented, Cleve., 1987-92, 96—; lectr. Cleve. State U., 1987-89; vis. asst. prof., 1989-92; gallery dir. BGSU-Firelands Coll., Huron, 1993-94; radio host pub. affairs WCSB-FM, Cleve., 1991-92; lectr. in field. One-woman shows include Out Art: A Purgative Event, 1992, Urban Life, 1992, Possession of Women, 1992, Dia de Los Muertos Celebration, 1993, Feminism Spanning the Americas: The Scream Continues, 1994, Women Rage: Men Listen, 1994, Land Sculptures, 1994, World War Four, 1995, Calling the Question, 1995, Turn, 1996. Coord. Celebrating Women's Sexualities, Cleve., 1987, Shadow Project, Cleve., 1985. Avocations: reading, travel, experimental work in creativity. Home: 3503 Virginia Ave Cleveland OH 44109-2465 Studio: 4701 Perkins Ave Cleveland OH 44113

HARTMAN, BRUCE, writer; b. Passaic, N.J., Dec. 7, 1948; s. Paul and Billye Hartman; m. Martha G. Hartman; children: Fred, Tom, Jack. BA, Wesleyan U., 1969. Author: (novels) The Great Leap Forward, 1980, The Unexamined Life, 1986, (screenplays) Judgment, 1993, Accidents Waiting to Happen, 1996; composer: (songs) In My Next Lifetime, Fifteen Minutes of Fame, In a Perfect World, Ask a Country Girl.

HARTMAN, CARL (HOWARD CARL HARTMAN), reporter; b. Morris Twp., N.J., Jan. 9, 1917; s. Dennis and Ruth (Shavelson) H.; m. Josephine M. Troxell, Aug. 25, 1942; 1 dau., Jessica A. Student, George Washington U., 1932-33; AB, Princeton, 1936; MS in Journalism, Columbia, 1942. Engaged in gold mining, Calif., 1936-37; translator, publicity, copy boy, reporter various newspapers, 1937-40; fgn. editor Puerto Rico World-Jour., San Juan, P.R., 1940-41; reporter, rewrite man N.Y.C. News Assn., 1941; Washington corr. Jewish Telegraphic Agy., also Overseas News Agy., 1942-44; city editor Puerto Rico World-Jour., 1944; with AP, 1944—, various assignments internationally, 1944-57, corr., 1957-59, staff mem. Frankfurt, 1959, corr. Berlin, 1959-63, Bonn and European Econ. Affairs, 1963-67, Common Market and NATO, Brussels, 1967-78; European editor N.Y.C., 1978; reporter internat. econ. affairs AP World Svcs., Washington, 1978-96; arts and humanities, 1997—. Alternate Pulitzer travelling fellow, 1942 Mem. Berlin Fgn. Press Assn. (pres. 1960-61), Anglo-Am. Press Assn. Paris (dir. 1951, 56), Overseas Writers Club, Nat. Press Club, Phi Beta Kappa. Home: 1066 Thomas Jefferson St NW Washington DC 20007-3832 Office: Associated Press 2021 K St NW Fl 6 Washington DC 20006-1082

HARTMAN, CARMEN TERESA, language educator; b. Velez, Colombia, Sept. 18, 1954; arrived in US, 1986; d. Roque Julio Ortiz and Librada Nieves; m. William N. Hartman, Feb. 15, 1986; 1 child, Sarah P.;1 child from previous

marriage, Daniel Ortiz. BA, U. La Gran Colombia, 1977; cert. in Applied Linguistics, U. Essex, 1979; MA, SUNY, Albany, 1992, PhD with hons., 2000. Asst. to project mgr. GE, Maracalbo, Venezuela, 1978—85; tchr. pub., pvt. high sch., Albany, Schenectedy, NY, 1986—92; educator, lectr., tchg. asst. SUNY, Albany, 1993—99; labor svc. rep. Dept. Labor, Albany, 1999—2000; educator Union Coll., Schenectady, 2000, Schenectady C.C., 2001—. Tutor Spanish Shenendehowa Sch. Dist., Clifton Park, NY, 1995—. Author: The Trapping Effect of the Signifier Over Subject and Text, 2003. Mem.: MLA, Soc. Hispanistas (spkr.). Avocations: travel, book collecting, reading. Office: Schenectady Couny Cmty Coll Washington Ave Schenectady NY 12305

HARTMAN, CATHY, economist, educator; d. Frank and Velma Ciardullo; m. Michael Hartman. PhD, U. of Colo., 1985—91. Mgmt. intern City of Phoenix, 1972—73; econ. analyst Santa Clara County Planning Dept., San Jose, Calif., 1973—76; econ. cons. Urban Life Consultants, Calgary, Canada, 1976—78; adj. prof. Pitts. State U., 1978—80; assoc. dir. Economics Inst., Boulder, Colo., 1980—83; asst. prof. U. of Calgary, Canada, 1983—89; assoc. prof. UT State U., 1989—92. Mem.: Ladies Golf Assn. Logan Golf and Country Club (pres. 2002—03). Office: Utah State University 3510 Old Main Hill Logan UT 84322-3510

HARTMAN, CHARLES HENRY, not-for-profit developer, education educator, consultant; b. Red Lion, Pa., Feb. 1, 1933; s. Earl Eugene and Jeannette (Kline) Hartman; m. Patricia A. Cooper, Aug. 3, 1956 (div. May 1974); children: Elizabeth Jean, Amy Joan; m. Catherine M. Wheeler, June 7, 1975; children: Eric Michael, Jennifer Leigh, David Wheeler, Scott Andrew; m. Andrea S. Anderson, July 8, 2000. BS, Millersville U., 1954; MA, Mich. State U., 1958, EdD, 1962. Tchr. Hollidaysburg Pub. Schs., Pa., 1956-57; assoc. prof. Ill. State U., Normal, 1959-62; vis. lectr. edn. U. Wis., Madison, 1962-63, Milw., 1963-64; dir. edn. Automotive Safety Found./Hwy. Users Fedn., Washington, 1964-70; dep. adminstr. Nat. Hwy. Traffic Safety Adminstrn., U.S. Dept. Transp., Washington, 1970-73; pres. Motorcycle Safety Found., Irvine, Calif., 1973-84; also pres. Touchstone Mgmt. Svcs., Delta, Pa., 1984-88; exec. v.p. AAHPERD, Reston, Va., 1988-90; exec. dir. Am. Coll. Health Assn., Balt., 1990-98; pres. Nonprofit Orgn. Mgmt. and Consultation, 1998—2002. Cons. Nat. Assn. Women Hwy. Safety Leaders, Md. State Dept. Edn., 1969—70, dir. Nat. Safety Coun., Chgo., 1976—79; vice chmn. traffic conf., 1976—78; presdl. appointee Nat. Hwy. Safety Adv. Commn., Washington, 1977—80; gov.'s appointee Pa. Task Force Alcohol and Hwy. Safety, 1981—82; vice chmn. Alliance Traffic Safety, 1981—83, chmn., 1983—85; mem. policy com. Hwy. Users Fedn.; lectr. bus. adminstrn. Capitol Campus Pa. State U., Middletown, 1987—88; bd. dirs. Lincoln Intermediate Unit # 12, 1987—89, 1991—93; sr. cons. York Nonprofit Mgmt. Devel. Ctr., 1998—2000; office mgr. Law Offices Andrea S. Anderson, 2001—; spkr. in field. Sch. dir. Red Lion (Pa.) Area Schs., 1986—2003, pres. sch. bd., 1988, 1996—2003, v.p., 1989—95; mem. York 2000 Commn.; trustee Nat. Motorcycle Fund; pres. Howard County C. of C., Columbia, Md., 1985—87. With U.S. Army, 1954—56. Named to Hall of Fame, Red Lion Area Sch. Dist., 1993; recipient Traffic Safety Educator of the Yr. award, Wis. Traffic Edn. Assn., 1972, Sec.'s award, U.S. Dept. Transp., 1973. Fellow: Am. Acad. Safety Edn.; mem.: NEA, Pa. Sch. Bds. Assn., Assn. Advancement Automotive Medicine, Am. Driver and Traffic Safety Edn. Assn., Pres. Assn./Am. Mgmt. Assn., Soc. Automotive Engrs., Am. Soc. Assn. Execs. (vice-chmn. evaluation com. 1984—85, chmn. 1985—86), Phi Delta Kappa. Republican. Home: 122 E McKinley Rd Delta PA 17314 Office: 901 Delta Rd Red Lion PA 17356-9179 E-mail: charley@asa-law.com.

HARTMAN, CHERRY, clinical social worker; b. Portland, Oreg, Sept. 26, 1947; d. Dale Clifton and Dorothy Ella (Buterbaugh) H. BA, Lewis & Clark Coll., 1968; MSW, Portland State U., 1975. Caseworker State of Oreg., Grants Pass, 1968-71; dir. counseling Luth. Family Svc., Portland, 1971-80, Phoenix Rising Found., 1980-89; pvt. practice Portland, 1989—2001; dir. social svc. William Temple House, Portland, 2001—. Author: Be-Good-To-Yourself Therapy, 1987, More Be-Good-To-Yourself Therapy, 1993, The Fearless Flyer, 1997, The Well-Heeled Murders, 1998; contbr. articles to profl. jour. Active rev. bd. health maintenance of Oreg.; mem. Continuous Quality Improvement team for legacy Portland Adventist Hosp. Named Woman of Yr., Cascade Voice Newspaper, 1985, Multnomah County Cmty. Hero, 2003. Mem. Lic. Clin. Social Workers Assn. (ednl. review com.) Democrat. Avocations: canoeing, bicycling. Home: 3144 NE 25 Ave Portland OR 97212 Office: William Temple House 2023 NW Hoyt Portland OR 97209

HARTMAN, CHESTER WARREN, public interest organization executive; b. N.Y.C., Apr. 12, 1936; s. Irving Lincoln and Dorothy (Friedman) H.; m. Amy Ellen Fine, Aug. 3, 1985; children: Jeremy, Benjamin. AB, Harvard U., 1957, PhD, 1967. Asst. prof. Harvard U., Cambridge, Mass., 1966-70; sr. rsch. assoc. Nat. Housing Law Project, Berkeley, Calif., 1970-74; fellow Inst. for Policy Studies, Washington, 1981-90, Transnat. Inst., Amsterdam, 1990-96; pres., exec. dir. Poverty and Race Rsch. Action Coun., Washington, 1990—. Mem. adv. bd. FNMA Office Housing Rsch., Washington, 1992—; sec. Nat. Low Income Housing Coalition, Washington, 1994-97; vis. prof. U. N.C., Chapel Hill, 1981, Yale U., New Haven, Columbia U., N.Y.C., U. Calif., Berkeley, Cornell U., Ithaca, N.Y. Author: Housing and Social Policy, 1974, Transformation of San Francisco, 1984, Between Eminence and Notoriety: Four Decades of Radical Urban Planning, 2002, City for Sale: The Transformation of San Francisco, 2002; editor: Critical Perspectives on Housing, 1986, Winning America, 1988, Double Exposure: Poverty and Race in America, 1997, Challenges to Equality: Poverty and Race in America, 2001; cons. editor Ency. Housing, 1991—. Mem. adv. com. Mass. Housing Fin. Agy., Boston, 1969-70; co-chair San Franciscans for Affordable Housing, 1979; bd. dirs. Urban League of Greater Boston, 1968-70. With U.S. Army, 1959-60. Home: 3372 Stuyvesant Pl NW Washington DC 20015-2454 Office: Poverty & Race Rsch Action Coun Ste 200 3000 Connecticut Ave NW Washington DC 20008-2529 E-mail: chartman@prrac.org.

HARTMAN, DAVID G. actuary; b. Evanston, Ill., July 10, 1942; s. Fred E. and Martha Hartman; m. Katherine A. Holmes; children: Timothy, Andrew. Student, Ripon Coll., 1960-62; BBA, U. Mich., 1964, M in Actuarial Sci., 1965. Various positions Kemper Ins. Co., Chgo., 1966-71; mng. dir., sr. v.p., chief actuary Chubb & Son, Warren, N.J., 1971—. Trustee Overlook Hosp., Summit, NJ, 1993—2002; elder New Providence Presbyn. Ch., NJ, 1973—75, 1986—88. Fellow: Casualty Actuarial Soc. (v.p. 1985—86, cert.), Can. Inst. Actuaries; mem.: ASTIN (chair 2003—), Actuarial Stds. Bd. (pres. 1987—88, bd. dirs. 1996—2001, chmn. 1998—99), Internat. Actuarial Assn. (coun. 1996—), Am. Acad. Actuaries (v.p. 1983—85, pres.-elect 1992—93, pres. 1993—94, cert.). Office: Chubb Group of Ins Cos 15 Mountain View Rd Warren NJ 07059-6795

HARTMAN, DEANNA MEARS, retired family counselor, addiction counselor; b. Norfolk, Va., Aug. 11, 1937; d. James Gordon Jr. and Sarah Talmadge (Johnson) Mears; m. David Luther Brinkley Jr. (div.); children: Kim Brinkley Hebebrand, David III, Jeffrey Lawrence Brinkley; m. Shirish Ramachandra Pandya, June 7, 1978 (dec.). AA, U. Akron, 1980; BA, Va. Wesleyan, 1983; MA, Antioch U., 1994. Cert. cognitive behavioral therapist; nat. cert. counselor. Dir. edn. svcs. Va. Coun. on Alcoholism, Drugs, Norfolk, 1985-87, exec. dir., 1990-93; outpatient program specialist Maryview Psychiat. Hosp., Portsmouth, Va., 1988-89; clin. therapist City of Portsmouth, 1988-89; educator, therapist City of Va. Beach, 1984-86, 93-95; mental health counselor Glasgow High Wellness Ctr., Newark, Del., 1995; family counselor, addiction specialist Williamsburg Pl., Farley Ctr., Williamsburg, Va., 1997—. Founder Survivors of Suicide, Virginia Beach, 1982-86, vol. educator AARP Bear, Del., 1995. Contbr. articles to profl. jours., various presentations. Bd. dirs. Hospice of Virginia Beach, 1983-85, Safe Place, 1988-90, Civitan Internat., 1990-92, comty. adv. coun. for curriculum Coll. of Edn., Old Dominion U., Norfolk, 1991-92. Named Rookie of Yr., Civitan Internat., 1991; recipient Disting. Svc. award Va. Alcohol and Drug Abuse Counselors, 1992. Mem. AAUW, Nat. Coun. Sexual Addiction and Compulsivity, Nat. Assn. Alcohol and Drug Abuse Counselors, Am. Christian Counselors Assn., Obsessive Compulsive Disorders Found., Am. Counselors Assn., Nat. Assn. Cognitive Behavioral Therapists, Parents and Friends of Lesbians and Gays. Avocations: reading, bird watching, walking, writing, vol. work. E-mail: deannahartman@aol.com.

HARTMAN, DONALD DEWAYNE, retired secondary education educator, writer; b. Toledo; s. Claude R. and Beulah C. Hartman; m. Royldene Howard, Sept. 25, 1960. BA, U. Ams., Mexico City, 1960; MA, U Montevallo, Ala., 1976, AA, 1983. Tchr. Spanish, Jefferson County Pub. Schs., Birmingham, Ala., 1962-70, asst. prin., 1970-72, coord. fgn. lang., 1972-98; ret., 1998. Author: The Lemurian Connection, 1990; co-author: Hot Chocolate for the Mystical Lover, 2001, Magical Souvenirs, 2002. Sgt. U.S. Army, 1960-64. Republican. Methodist. Avocations: woodworking, painting, writing, travel. Home: 1298 Davis Acres Dr Alpine AL 35014

HARTMAN, EARL KENNETH, writer; b. Chgo., Jan. 31, 1943; s. Ferdinand Frederick and Betty Marie (Sjerslee) H.; m. Linda Lee Griffin, July 10, 1981 (div. June 1988); m. Beatrice Gail Adams, Mar. 11, 1989. BA, Fla. Atlantic U., 1980, B of Edn., 1981. Promotion mgr., spl. issues editor Asheville (N.C.) Citizen-Times, 1966—67; reporter Shelby (N.C.) Daily Star, 1967; copy editor Palm Beach Post-Times, West Palm Beach, Fla., 1968—69; dist. exec. Boy Scouts Am., West Palm Beach, Fla., 1973—76, Albany, Ga., 1983—84; tchr., asst. dir. Unity Sch., Delray Beach, Fla., 1981—83; tchr. Tift County (Ga.) Bd. Edn., 1984—85; sr. reporter Island Reporter, Sanibel Island, Fla., 1985—87; free-lance writer Fort Myers, Fla., 1987—; creator, developer Choice Games Series, 2000—. Mem. Nat. Eagle Scout Assn., Acad. Am. Poets. Avocation: photography. Home and Office: 1210 Westfield Dr Fort Myers FL 33919-2244 E-mail: earlnight2@att.net.

HARTMAN, FREDERICK COOPER, biochemist, researcher; b. Memphis, Aug. 17, 1939; s. Fred Francis and Raymie Constance (Cooper) H.; m. Patricia Jean Ballard, Sept. 7, 1961; children: Patricia Suzanne, Sheila Katherine. BS in Chemistry, Memphis State U., 1960; MS in Biochemistry, U. Tenn., 1962, PhD in Biochemistry, 1964; postgrad., U. Ill., 1964-66. Sr. rsch. biochemist Oak Ridge Nat. Lab., 1966-99, group leader protein chemistry, 1972-99, sect. head molecular and cellular scis., 1975-88, dir. biology divsn., 1988-97; prof. dept. biochemistry U. Tenn., Knoxville, 1999—. Mem. editl. bd. Jour. Biol. Chemistry, BioSci., Jour. Protein Chemistry; contbr. numerous articles to profl. jours. Grantee Dept. Agr., 1978—, NSF, 1980-87, fellow USPHS, 1962-64, NIH, 1963, 65. Fellow AAAS; mem. Am. Chem. Soc. (Pfizer award 1979, nominating com. 1982), Am. Soc. Biol. Chemists (nominating com. 1979, 81), Am. Soc. Plant Physiologists, Protein Soc., Sigma Xi. Home: 103 Dansworth Ln Oak Ridge TN 37830-8754 Office: Biology Div Oak Ridge Nat Lab Oak Nat Lab Oak Oak Ridge TN 37830

HARTMAN, GEOFFREY H. language professional, educator; b. Germany, Aug. 11, 1929; came to U.S., 1946, naturalized, 1946; s. Albert and Agnes (Heumann) H.; m. Renee Gross, Oct. 21, 1956; children: David, Elizabeth. BA, Queens Coll., N.Y.C., 1949, LHD (hon.), 1990; PhD, Yale U., 1953; LHD (hon.), Hebrew Union Coll./Inst. Religion, 2003. Mem. faculty Yale U., 1955-62; assoc. prof. English U. Iowa, Iowa City, 1962-64, prof. English, 1964-65, Cornell U., Ithaca, N.Y., 1965-67; prof. English and comparative lit. Yale U., 1967—, Karl Young Prof., 1974-94, Sterling prof., 1994-97, prof. emeritus, 1997—; disting. vis. scholar George Washington U., 1998-2000; disting. prof. New Sch. U., 2001-03. Vis. lectr. and/or prof. U. Chgo., U. Wash., Hebrew U., Jerusalem, U. Zurich, Switzerland, Princeton U., NYU, Tel Aviv U., U. Konstanz, Germany; Clark lectr. Trinity Coll., Cambridge, 1983; Tamblyn lectr. U. Western Ont., 1983; Wellek lectr. U. Calif., Irvine, 1992, Tanner lectr. U. Utah, 1999; dir. Sch. Theory and Criticism, Dartmouth Coll., 1982-87, also sr. fellow; Haskins lectr. ACLS, 2000. Author: The Unmediated Vision, 1954, Andre Malraux, 1960, Wordsworth's Poetry, 1964 (Christian Gauss award Phi Beta Kappa 1965), Beyond Formalism, 1970, The Fate of Reading, 1975, Akiba's Children, 1978, Criticism in the Wildernes, 1980, Saving the Text, 1981, Easy Pieces, 1985, The Unremarkable Wordsworth, 1987, Minor Prophecies, 1991, The Longest Shadow, 1996, The Fateful Question of Culture, 1997, A Critic's Journey, 1999, Scars of the Spirit, 2002; editor: Hopkins: A Collection of Critical Essays, 1966, Selected Poetry and Prose of William Wordsworth, 1970, Romanticism: Vistas, Instances, Continuities, 1973, Psychoanalysis and the Question of the the Text, 1978, Shakespeare and the Questions of Theory, 1985, Bitburg in Moral and Political Perspective, 1986, Midrash and Literature, 1986, Holocaust Remembrance: The Shapes of Memory, 1993. Trustee English Inst., 1978-85; Revson project dir. Video Archive Holocaust Testimonies, Yale, 1982—. Served with AUS, 1953-55. Decorated chevalier Order of Arts and Letters govt. of France, 1997; recipient Disting. Alumnus award Queens Coll. CUNY, 1971, award Nat. Found. Jewish Culture, 1997, René Wellek prize Am. Assn. Comparative Lit., 1998, Disting. Scholar award Keats-Shelley Assn., 1998; Fulbright fellow U. Dijon, France, 1951-52, study fellow Am. Coun. Learned Socs., 1963, 79, Guggenheim fellow, 1969, 86, fellow Humanities Ctr. Wesleyan U., 1972, NEH, 1975, Inst. Advanced Studies Hebrew U., 1986, Inst. Humanities U. Calif., Irvine, 1989, Woodrow Wilson Internat. Ctr., 1995, Sackler Inst., U. Tel Aviv, 1997, Wissenschafts Coll., Berlin, 1998; assoc. fellow Ctr. Rsch. Philosophy and Lit. U. Warwick, Eng., 1993; Gauss seminarist Princeton U., 1968; Fulbright Disting. lectr., 1986, 87; corr. fellow British Acad. Mem. Modern Lang. Assn. (exec. council 1977-80), Am. Acad. Arts and Scis. Home: 260 Everit St New Haven CT 06511-1309

HARTMAN, GEORGE DAVID, chemist, director; PhD, Ohio State U., 1968—73. Exec. dir. medicinal chemistry Merck Rsch. Labs, West Point, Pa., 1995—. Medicinal researcher (drug discovery) Discover of Aggrastat. With U.S. Army, 1971—72. Roman Catholic. Achievements include patents for for cancer drugs; discovery of drug Aggrastat. Avocations: golf, travel. Office: Merck & Co Inc Sumneytown Pike West Point PA 19446 E-mail: george_hartman@merck.com.

HARTMAN, GEORGE EITEL, architect; b. Ft. Hancock, N.J., May 7, 1936; s. George Eitel and Evelyn (Ritchie) H.; m. Ann Burdick, May 22, 1965 (div. Oct. 2000); children— Sarah, Joshua; m. Jan Cigliano, Jan. 21, 2001. BA, Princeton, 1957, M.F.A., 1960. Registered architect, Md., Washington, Va. Pvt. practice architecture, 1964-65; ptnr. Hartman-Cox Architects, Washington, 1965—; Design critic Cath. U. Am., 1964-69, U. Md.; Kea Disting. prof. architecture N.C. State U., 1973-74, prof. architecture, 1977. Chmn. adv. coun. Princeton U. Sch. Architecture, 1985-87; mem. architecture rev. panel Fgn. Bldg. Office, Dept. State, 1991—, mem. architecture adv. bd. Works include EURAM office bldg, Washington, Waterfront Center, Washington; Brewer residence, Chevy Chase, Md., Conant residence, Potomac, Md., Nat. Humanities Center, Raleigh, N.C., Nat. Permanent Bldg., Washington, 1001 Pennsylvania Ave, Washington; Folger Shakespeare Library, Washington, Immanuel Presbyn. Ch., McLean, Va., Sumner Sch., Washington, H.E.B. hdqrs., San Antonio, Market Square, Washington, Franklin Sq., Washington, Pa. Plaza, Washington, U.S. Embassy, Kuala Lumpur, Malaysia, Chrysler Mus., Norfolk, Va., 555 11th St., Washington. Served to 2d Lt., F.A. AUS, 1957. Recipient Louis Sullivan award for architecture, 1972, 100 Nat., State and Local Design awards, 1967—; fellow Am. Acad. in Rome, 1977-78. Fellow AIA (pres. Washington chpt. 1975, chmn. nat. capitol com. 1976, chmn. nat. com. on design 1977, AIA Nat. Honor award 1970, 71, 81, 83, 89, 94, AIA Firm award 1988); mem. U.S. Commn. Fine Arts, Cosmos Club (pres. 1985). Home: 1657 31st St Washington DC 20007 Office: Hartman Cox Architects 1074 Thomas Jefferson St NW Washington DC 20007-3832

HARTMAN, HERBERT ARTHUR, JR., oncologist; b. Halstead, Kans., Aug. 8, 1947; s. Herbert Arthur and Margrete Laverne (Schroeder) H.; m. Cynthia Craig, Dec. 26, 1971; m. April Craig, Herbert Arthur III. BA in Chemistry, U. Kans., 1969, MD, 1973. Diplomate Am. Bd. Internal Medicine, Am. Bd. Med. Oncology. Resident in internal medicine U. Nebr. Med. Ctr., Omaha, 1973-76, fellow in med. oncology, 1976-78; pvt. practice, Omaha, 1978—; chmn. dept. medicine Immanuel Med. Ctr., Omaha, 1988-90. Clin. assoc. prof. internal medicine U. Nebr. Med. Sch., 1979—. Contbr. articles to med. jours. Pres. Nebr. Cancer Soc., 1991. Fellow Am. Coll. Physicians; mem. AMA, Am. Soc. Internal Medicine, Am. Soc. Clin. Oncology, Nebr. Med. Assn. (bd. dirs. 1989-95), Metro Omaha Med. Soc. (exec. com. 1987—), N.Y. Acad. Scis., Mensa, Omaha C. of C. (bd. dirs. 1998-00). Republican. Episcopalian. Avocations: walking, personal finance, reading. Home: 6211 Chicago St Omaha NE 68132-2727 Office: Oncology Assocs PC Meth Cancer Ctr 8303 Dodge St Ste 225 Omaha NE 68114-4108

HARTMAN, JAMES AUSTIN, retired geologist; b. Lanark, Ill., Jan. 29, 1928; s. Llewelyn John and Gladys Mae (Doyle) H.; m. Zoe Marie Wiley, June 16, 1951 (dec. Dec. 1996); children: Victoria Lynn, Lester James; m. Annette Wiley Lee, June 9, 1997. BS, Beloit (Wis.) Coll., 1951; MS, U. Wis., 1955, PhD, 1957. Cert. petroleum geologist. Geologist Reynolds Jamaica (W.I.) Mines, Jamaica, W.I., 1951-53, Union Carbide Ore Co., Parimaribo, Surinam, 1956-57; various positions Shell Oil Co., New Orleans, 1957-86; cons. New Orleans, 1986-94; ret., 1994. Bd. mgmt. YMCA, Metairie, 1972-74; pres. Jefferson Com. for Better Schs., Metairie, 1961-63, pres. Westgate PTA, Kenner, La., 1964-65. With U.S. Army, 1946-47. Union Carbide Rsch. fellowship U. Wis., 1954-56. Mem. Am. Assn. Petroleum Geologists (hon., sec. 1981-83, Disting. Svc. award 1985), New Orleans Geol. Soc. (hon., 2d v.p. 1975-76, pres.-elect 1984-85, pres. 1985-86, Outstanding Mem. 1977), Gulf Coast Assn. Geol. Socs. (hon., v.p. 1987, pres. 1988), Sigma Xi. Republican. Episcopalian. Achievements include research in heavy minerals in Jamaican Bauxite, titanium mineralogy of Bauxites, petroleum geology. Home: 4512 Newlands St Metairie LA 70006-4138 also: 936 N Stygler Rd Gahanna OH 43230-2029

HARTMAN, JAMES MATTHEW, lawyer; b. Bklyn., May 28, 1928; s. Irving I. and Esther (Kramer) H.; m. Alys Florence Moses, Sept. 18, 1949 (div. Aug. 1963); children— Victoria I., Elizabeth A., Sarah M.; m. 2d Frances June Ouweleen, Feb. 29, 1964. B.A., NYU, 1950; LL.B., Columbia U., 1953. Bar: N.Y. 1954, U.S. Dist. Ct. (so. and ea. dists.) N.Y. 1957, U.S. Dist. Ct. (we. dist.) N.Y. 1964, U.S. Supreme Ct. 1964, U.S. Ct. Claims 1964, U.S. Ct. Appeals (2d cir.) 1969, U.S. Dist. Ct. (no. dist.) N.Y. 1976, D.C. 1980, Fla. 1982, U.S. Ct. Appeals (6th and 11th cirs.) 1982. Assoc. firm Swain & Moore, N.Y.C., 1954-55; sole practice N.Y.C., 1955-60; assoc. Fellner & Rovins, N.Y.C., 1960-61; ptnr. Harris Beach, Wilcox, Rochester, N.Y., 1962— ; adj. assoc. prof. Cornell U. Law Sch., 1973-77; instr. trial advocacy N.E. Region, Nat. Inst. Trial Advocacy, 1976—, nat. instr., 1981; instr. Hofstra Law Sch., 1978-81, Harvard Law Sch., 1979, Emory Law Sch., 1983, also various bar assns.; mem. Monroe County Med. Malpractice Arbitration Panels. Chmn. com. on health care for elderly Monroe County Health Planning Council, 1971-73; mem. health services and legal services coms. Human Resource Task Force; mem. pres.'s adv. bd., bd. regents McQuaid Jesuit High Sch., 1973-75; mem. Rochester Meml. Art Gallery, Rochester Mus. and Sci. Ctr.; bd. dirs. Rochester Eye Inst.; bd. dirs., mem. fin. com., mem. planning and coordinating com. St. Ann's Home for Aged; nat. bd. dirs. Abota Found. Served with AUS, 1946-48. Mem. ABA, Am. Bd. Trial Advocates (past pres. Rochester chpt., mem. nat. bd. dirs.), N.Y. State Bar Assn. (mem. ho. dels. 1973-76, chmn. trial lawyers sect. 1973-74, various other coms.), Monroe County Bar Assn. (past pres.), Am. Bd. Trial Advocates (Rochester chpt. past pres.), N.Y. Bar Found., Am. Bar Found. Clubs: Oak Hill Country, Hunt Hollow Ski. Home: 15 Oakfield Way Pittsford NY 14534-1886

HARTMAN, JEFFREY EDWARD, pastor; b. Nyack, N.Y., June 23, 1959; s. Edward Harold and Constance Ruth (Gibbs) H.; m. Cynthia Lynn Chason, Aug. 14, 1982; children: Joshua Jefferson, Jeremiah Jordan, Julia Lyndsay. BS, Liberty U., 1982; postgrad., Westminster Theol. Sem., 1984-87, Trinity Evang. Div. Sch., 1990; MDiv, Princeton Theol. Sem., 1998; M in Sacred Theology, Yale U., 2000; M in Theology, Harvard U., 2001; student, Westminster Theological Sem., 2001—. Ordained to ministry, 1985. Assoc. pastor Maranatha Bapt. Ch., Gainesville, Ga., 1982-84; pastor Christ Community Ch., Newfield, N.J., 1984—. Baseball head coach Cumberland Christian Sch., Vineland, N.J., 1991-95; chaplain Newcomb Med. Ctr., Vineland, 1987—. Founder, editor, columnist: Newfield Neighbors newspaper, Newfield, N.J., 1988—. Co-founder, bd. dirs. Compassion Crisis Pregnancy Ctr., Clayton, N.J., 1986-90, chmn. bd. dirs. 1990-95. Recipient John Finley McLaren prize in Bibl. theology Princeton Theol. Sem., N.J., 1997. Office: Christ Community Ch 201 Salem Ave Newfield NJ 08344-9074 E-mail: jeffreyhartman@minister.com.
The tragedy of life is not what happens to you but what you miss.

HARTMAN, LAURA BETH PINCUS, management consultant, writer, academic administrator; b. Chgo., Oct. 6, 1963; m. David Pilchard Hartman, Aug. 2, 1997; children: Emma, Rachel. JD, U. of Chgo., 1998; BS in Social Psychology, Tufts U., 1985. Prof. of bus. ethics Depaul U., Chgo., 1990—, assoc. vp for academic affairs, 1999—. Cons. in field. Master: Soc. For Bus. Ethics (pres. 2001—02). Office: DePaul University Executive Offices One E Jackson Blvd Chicago IL 60604 E-mail: lhartman@depaul.edu.

HARTMAN, LEE ANN WALRAFF, educator; b. Milw., Apr. 21, 1945; d. Emil Adolph and Mabelle Carolyn (Goetter) Walraff; m. Patrick James Hartman, Oct. 5, 1968; children: Elizabeth Marie, Suzanne Carolyn. BS, U. Wis., 1967; postgrad., U. R.I., 1972—73, Johns Hopkins U., 1990, Trinity Coll., 1996. Cert. tchr., Wis., Md. Secondary educator Port Wash. Bd. Edn., Wis., 1967-68; instr. ballet YWCA, Wilmington, Del., 1977-78; tutor Md. Study Skills Inst., Columbia, 1984-86; tchr. Howard County Bd. Edn., Columbia, 1985—. Contbr. articles to profl. jours. Bd. dirs. Columbia United Christian Ch., 1980-83; mem. Gifted and Talented Com., Columbia, 1980—, Lang. Arts Com., 1985—, USCG Officers Wives Club, 1970-72, Hosp. Aux. Bay St. Louis, 1970-72; troop leader Girl Scouts U.S., Columbia, 1980-91, Hospice; exec. bd. PTA, 1990-2000. Recipient Life Achievement award, Internat. Biog. Ctr., 1994, Woman of Yr. award, Am. Biog. Inst., 1994, Shirley Mullinex Tchr. of Yr. award, 1997, State of Md. Home/Hosp. Tchr. of Yr. award, 2001—02. Mem.: NAFE, AAUW (exec. bd. 1985—, v.p. Howard County br. 1990—92, pres. Howard County br. 1998—2000, chair membership 2003—), Internat. Platform Assn. (mem. citizen's adv. com. 1995—), Home Hosp. Tchrs. Assn. Md. (chair pub. rels., sec. 1994—98, v.p. 1998—99, pres. 1999—2002), Beaverbrook Homemakers Assn. (pres. 1995—97). Avocations: reading, swimming, skiing, ballet. Home: 5070 Durham Rd W Columbia MD 21044-1445 Office: Howard County Bd Edn Rte 108 Columbia MD 21044

HARTMAN, LENORE ANNE, physical therapist; b. Cleve., May 27, 1938; d. Howard Andrew and Emma Elizabeth (Beck) H. BS in Agriculture, Ohio State U., 1960, MS in Agriculture, 1963; postgrad., Kans. State U., 1963-67; cert. in phys. therapy, U. Kans., 1968. Staff phys. therapist R.J. Delano Sch. for the Handicapped, Kansas City, Mo., 1969-74; chief phys. therapist Children's Mercy Hosp., Kansas City, 1974-78; relief staff Mass Gen. Hosp., Boston, 1969-70; staff phys. therapist Menorah Med. Ctr., Kansas City, 1979-87. Clin. instr. phys. therapy St. Louis U., 1974-78, U. Ky., 1974-78, U. Mo., Columbia, 1973-78, U. Kans. Med. Ctr., Kansas City, 1974-87; mem. med. adv. com. Hospice Care of Mid Am., Kansas City, 1984-87; staff phys. therapist S.W. Gen. Hosp., 1992—; phys. therapy cons. Rocky River Riding Therapeutic Riding Program, 1994-97; chapel organist St. Luke's Hosp., Kansas City, 1978-87. Contbr. articles to profl. jours. Ohio del. Internat. Farm Youth Exch., Brazil, 1962. Mem. Internat. Farm Youth Exch. Assn. (life), Am. Phys. Therapy Assn. (del. to nat. 1975-76), Mo. Phys. Therapy Assn. (chmn. northwest dist. 1974-76), Am. Guild of Organists (chmn. profl. concerns com. Greater Kansas City chpt. 1983), Japan Am. Soc., Ohio State U. Alumni Assn. (life), Ohio Phys. Therapy Assn., Am. Morgan Horse Assn., U.S. Dressage Fedn., North Ohio Dessage Assn., Western Reserve Carriage Assn., Am. Driving Soc., Omicron Delta Epsilon, Phi Delta Gamma. Avocations: sketching, dog obedience training, gardening, dressage. Office: SW Gen Health Ctr Dept Physical Therapy Middleburg Heights OH 44130

HARTMAN, MARILYN D. English and Art education educator; b. Denver, May 2, 1927; d. Leland DeForest Henshaw and Evelyn Wyman Henshaw; m. James Hartman, Oct. 7, 1949 (dec. Dec 1989); children: Charles, Alice, Mary Hale. Student, U. Denver, 1947; BA, U. Colo., 1958; MA, UCLA, 1965, EdD in English Edn., 1972. Calif. life std. tchg. credential English and art, Colo. secondary English and art. Tchr. Denver Pub. Schs., 1959—65; asst. prof. San Fernando Valley State U., Northridge, Calif., 1970—72, San Diego State U. Mem., presenter Am. Ednl. Rsch. Assn., L.A., 1965-72; mem. Nat. Coun. Tchrs. English, L.A., 1965-72; officer Pi Lambda Theta-Alpha Delta chpt., L.A., 1970-72; with Ctr. for the Study Dem. Instns., L.A., 1970-72; tchg. asst., 1964, discussion leader linguistics; tchr. evaluator UCLA, 1970-72, Iliff Sch. Theology, Denver U.; cons. Dept Edn., Riley, 1992-2000, State Dept., 1992-2000, to Pres. Clinton, 1992-2000. Author: Linguistic Approach to Teaching English, 1965, Two Letters and Some Thoughts, 1968, Sound and Meaning of BE Speech, 1969, Teaching a Dialect, 1970, Contrastive Analysis: BE and SE Teaching, 1972, Touch the Windy Finger, 1980, Under the Hand of God, 2000; author: (with Bill Kirton) (short stories) O God, 1970, On Her Own: To Know and Not Know, 2002; author: The Luckiest People, 2002. Chmn. Denver Metro Area Food Drive, 1985, Interfaith Alliance; mem. Dem. Nat. Com., 1992—2002. Mem.: VFW, NOW, AAUW, Women in the Arts, Interfaith Alliance, Nat. Philatelic Soc., Am. Philatelic Assn., Common Cause, Sierra

Club, Franciscan Missions, Natural Resources Def. Coun., Kempe Children's Found., Colo. Fedn. Dem. Women's Clubs, Inc. (officer 2001). Avocations: singing, painting, writing, teaching, counseling.

HARTMAN, MARSHALL J. lawyer; b. Chgo., Mar. 9, 1934; s. Paul and Anna Lily (Rose) H.; m. Patricia Gail Henig, July 30, 1961; children: Ann, Judy, Danny. A.B., U. Chgo., 1954; BHebrew Letters, Coll. Jewish Studies, Chgo., 1954; JD, U. Chgo., 1957. Bar: Ill. 1958, U.S. Dist. Ct. (no. Dist.) Ill., U.S. Ct. Appeals (7th cir), U.S. Supreme Ct. 1962. Youth dir. South Side Hebrew Congregation, Chgo., 1958 61; asst. pub. defender, Cook County, Chgo., 1963-70; probation officer Cook County Juvenile Ct., 1958-60, asst. to presiding judge, 1960-63; nat. dir. defender services Nat. Legal Aid and Defender Assn., 1970-76; vis. assoc. prof. U. Ill., Chgo., 1978— ; exec. dir. Criminal Def. Consortium of Cook County, Chgo., 1976-78; treas., gen. counsel Nat. Defender Inst., Chgo., 1978-89; with Lake County Pub. Defender, Waukegan, Ill. 1989—; chief pub. defender 19th jud. cir. Lake County, Ill. Author: Hartman's Handy Guide, 1968, Constitutional Criminal Procedure Handbook, 1986; contbr. articles to profl. jours. Mem. Am. Jewish Congress. 1st lt. USAR, 1961-62. Recipient Reginald Heber Smith award, Nat. Legal Aid and Defender Assn., 1978; Silver Circle award U. Ill., 1982, 85. Mem. Ill. Pub. Defender Assn. (pres.), Ill. Acad. Criminology (v.p., pres.), ABA (ho. of dels.), Chgo Bar Assn. Democrat. Home: 6554 S Spaulding Ave Chicago IL 60629-3445 Office: Lake County Pub Defender 18 N County St Waukegan IL 60085-4304

HARTMAN, MARY S. historian, educator; b. Mpls., June 25, 1941; married. BA, Swarthmore Coll., 1963; MA, Columbia U., 1964, PhD, 1970. From instr. to asst. prof. Rutgers U., 1968-75; from assoc. prof. to prof. history Douglass Coll., Rutgers U., 1975—; dean Douglas Coll. Rutgers U., 1982-94; dir. Inst. for Women's Leadership Douglass Coll., 1994—; prof. Rutgers U., 1994—. Author: Clio's Consciousness Raised, 1974, Victorian Murderesses, 1978; editor: Talking Leadership: Conversations with Powerful Women, 1999, The Household and the Making of History: A Subversive View of the Western Past, 2003. Office: 162 Ryders Ln New Brunswick NJ 08901-8555

HARTMAN, MATTHEW G. music educator; s. Mark W. and Pamela J. Hartman; m. Toni A. Stefano, June 11, 1970. MusB in Edn., U. Akron, 1995; MusM, Temple U., 1997. Asst. condr. Akron Symphony Chorus, Ohio, 1993—95; apprentice and asst. condr. Mendelssohn Club Phila., 1995—97; dir. vocal music Bethesda-Chevy Chase H.S., Bethesda, Md., 1997—, internat. baccalaureate internat. lectr. in music history, 1997—. Sec. Stonemill Homeowners Assn., Reisterstown, Md., 2001—02. Mem.: Md. Choral Dirs. Assn., Am. Choral Dirs. Assn., Montgomery County Music Educators Assn., Md. Music Educators Assn., Music Educators Nat. Conf., Mortar Bd. (mem. Pierian chpt. 1995), Golden Key, Pi Kappa Lambda. Office: Bethesda-Chevy Chase HS 4301 East-West Hwy Bethesda MD 20814 Personal E-mail: matthew_hartman@fc.mcps.k12.md.us. E-mail: mghartman@aol.com.

HARTMAN, NANCY LEE, physician; b. Philipsburg, Pa., July 29, 1951; Grad., Barbizon Sch. Modeling, 1970; AA in Med. Tech., Harcum Jr. Coll., 1971; BA in Biology and Med. Tech., Lycoming Coll., 1974; MS in Med. Biology, L.I. U., 1977; MD, Am. U. of Caribbean, Plymouth, Montserrat, W.I., 1981. Cert. med. technologist. Med. tech. Lock Haven (Pa.) Hosp., 1971-72, Williamsport (Pa.) Hosp., 1972-73, Renovo (Pa.) Hosp., 1974; microbiology, med. tech. Jersey Shore (Pa.) Hosp., 1974; microbiologist N.Y. Hosp. and Cornell Med. Ctr., N.Y.C., 1974-75, Drekter and Heisler Labs., N.Y.C., 1975, North Shore Labs., Inc., Syosset, N.Y., 1976-78; lab. technician North Shore Hosp., Manhasset, N.Y., 1981-82, Nat. Health Labs., Inc., Bethpage, N.Y., 1982; resident internal medicine program Interfaith Med. Ctr., Bklyn., 1983-84; med. cons. Shapiro & Baines, Mineola, N.Y., 1985-88; resident pathology program Lenox Hill Hosp., N.Y.C., 1986-87; resident clin. pathology Beth Israel Med. Ctr., N.Y.C., 1988-89; resident internal medicine Lenox Hill Hosp., 1990; med. specialist, pres. Advt. Ltd., Glenwood Landing, N.Y., 1990-92. Med. cons. Leader Mfg., Inc., Quebec, Can., 1988-89, Meiselman, Boland, Reilly and Pittoni, Mineola, 1988-92, Law Offices of Sybil Shainwald, N.Y.C., 1989-91, Reichenbaum and Silberstein, Great Neck, N.Y., 1990-92, Audio Visual Med. Mktg., Inc., N.Y.C., 1990-92, Law Office of Peter D. Kolbrener, Westbury, N.Y., 1990-92, Siben & Siben, Bayshore, N.Y., 1990-92, 93-94, Whiteman & Gorray, Uniondale, N.Y., 1990-92, Law Offices of Jed Neil Kirsch, Mineola, 1990-92, Gandin, Schotsky & Rappaport, Melville, N.Y., 1990-92, Doniger, Garland & Engstrand, N.Y.C., 1991-92, Law Offices of Steven Miller, Mineola, 1991-92, Law Offices of Harry Organek, Westbury, 1991-92, Law Offices of Michael Flomenhaft, N.Y.C., 1991-92, Damashek, Godosky & Gentile, N.Y.C., 1991-92, Easton & Clark, Levittown, N.Y., 1991-92, Tomas, Simonhoff, O'Brien, and Adourian, Haddonfield, N.J., 1993-94, Med. Surveillance, Inc., Westchester, Pa., 1993-94; rsch. fellow The Rockefeller U., N.Y.C., 1996, med. cons., 1996—. Author: The Pocket Handbook of Infectious Agents and Their Treatments, 1987; contbr. articles to profl. jours. Mem. Rep. Presdl. Task Force. Recipient Allied Health Professions Traineeship grant, 1975-77. Mem. AMA, Am. Med. Women's Assn., Am. Soc. Clin. Pathologists (registered med. technologist), Internat. Platform Assn., Am. Soc. Microbiology. Avocations: jogging, scuba diving, small plane flying, tennis, golf. Home: PO Box 374 Roslyn NY 11576-0374

HARTMAN, RITA MARIA, psychiatrist; b. N.Y.C., Dec. 21, 1956; MD, Georgetown U., 1982. Diplomate Am. Bd. Psychiatry. and Neurology, Am. Bd. Child Psychiatry. Med. dir. Mohave Mental Health Clin., Bullhead City, Ariz., 1987-91; pvt. practice, L.A., 1992—94, Wilkes-Barre, Pa., 1995-99. Psychiatrist L.A. County Jail, 1999—. Mem.: Am. Acad. Psychiatry and Law, Am. Acad. Child and Adolescent Psychiatry. Office: 450 Bauchet St Los Angeles CA 90012-2907

HARTMAN, ROBERT LEROY, artist, educator; b. Sharon, Pa., Dec. 17, 1926; s. George Otto and Grace Arvada (Radabaugh) H.; m. Charlotte Ann Johnson, Dec. 30, 1951; children: Mark Allen, James Robert. BFA, U. Ariz., 1951, MA, 1952; postgrad., Colo. Springs Fine Arts Center, 1947, 51, Bklyn. Mus. Art Sch., 1953-54. Instr. architecture, allied arts Tex. Tech. Coll., 1955-58; asst. prof. art U. Nev., Reno, 1958-61; mem. faculty dept. art U. Calif., Berkeley, 1961—, prof., 1972-91, prof. emeritus, 1991—, chmn. dept., 1974-76. Mem. Inst. for Creative Arts, U. Calif., 1967-68 One man exhbns. include, Bertha Schafer Gallery, N.Y.C., 1966, 69, 74, Santa Barbara Mus. Art, 1973, Cin. Art Acad., 1975, Hank Baum Gallery, San Francisco, 1973, 75, 78, San Jose Mus. Art, 1983, Bluxome Gallery, San Francisco, 1984, 86, U. Art Mus., Berkeley, 1986, Instituto D'Arte Dosso Dossi, Ferrara, Italy, 1989, Victor Fischer Galleries, San Francisco, 1991, Triangle Gallery, San Francisco, 1992, 93, 95, 97, 99, 2000, 2001, 2002, Augusta State U., 1998, Mary Pauline Gallery, Augusta, Ga., 2001, Oakland Mus., 2002; group exhbns. include Richmond Mus., 1966, Whitney Mus. Biennial, 1973, Oakland Mus., 1976, San Francisco Arts Commn. Gallery, 1985 (award), Earthscape Expo '90 Photo Mus., Osaka, Japan, 1990, In Close Quarters, American Landscape Photography Since 1968, Princeton Art Mus., 1993, Facing Eden: 100 Years of Landscape Art in The Bay Area, San Francisco, 1995, Colorado Springs Fine Arts Ctr., 1998; represented in permanent collections, Nat. Collections Fine Arts, Colorado Springs Fine Arts Center, Corcoran Gallery, San Francisco Art Inst., Roswell Mus., Princeton Art Mus. U. Calif. humanities research fellow, 1980 Office: U Calif Dept Art Berkeley CA 94720-0001

HARTMAN, ROBERT S. retired paper company executive; b. Chgo., Oct. 7, 1914; s. Edward A. and Blanche S. (Straus) H.; m. Betty Regenstein, Oct. 25, 1941; children: Ann, Ruth. Student, Northwestern U., 1933-34. Br. mgr. Draper & Kramer, Inc., 1937-41; pres. Arvey Corp., Chgo., 1957-85. Vice pres., bd. dirs. Chgo. Boys Clubs. Served with AUS, 1943-46. Mem. Chgo. Envelope Mfg. Assn. (pres. 1949-51), Envelope Mfg. Assn. Am. (dir. 1950-54) Clubs: Lake Shore Country (Glencoe, Ill.), Mayacoo Lakes (W. Palm Beach, Fla.). Home: 220 Woodley Rd Winnetka IL 60093-3739

HARTMAN, RONALD G. lawyer; b. Harrisburg, Pa., Aug. 13, 1950; s. Manny and Helene (Levine) H.; m. Leslie Ann Golomb, May 31, 1980; children: Molly, Samuel. BA, U. Pitts., 1972, JD, 1975. Bar: Pa. 1975, U.S. Dist. Ct. (we. dist.) Pa. 1975. Assoc. Baskin & Sears, Pitts., 1975-84; ptnr. Reed Smith LLP, Pitts., 1985—. Bd. dirs. Citizens League Southwestern Pa., Pitts., 1988, Am. Cancer Soc.-Allegheny County chpt., Pitts., exec. com., 1990—; bd. dirs. Jewish Family and Children's Svc. of Pitts., pres. 1995-97; bd. dirs. United Jewish Fedn. Greater Pitts., 1995-97, 98-2000, co-chmn. bus. and profl. divsn., 1989-91, mem. steering com. atty. divsn., 1992—; chair Cardoza Soc., 1999-2001; bd. dirs. Jewish Chronicle, 1997-2000. Mem. ABA, Pa. Bar Assn., Allegheny County Bar Assn. Jewish. Avocations: jogging, reading. Home: 500 Glen Arden Dr Pittsburgh PA 15208-2809 Office: Reed Smith LLP 435 6th Ave Pittsburgh PA 15219-1886

HARTMAN, ROSEMARY JANE, retired special education educator; b. Gainesville, Fla., Aug. 24, 1944; d. John Leslie and Irene (Bowen) Goddard; m. Alan Lynn Gerber, Feb. 1, 1964 (div. 1982); children: Sean Alan, Dawn Julianne Silva, Lance Goddard; m. Perry Hartman, June 27, 1992. BA, Immaculate Heart Coll., 1967; MA, Loyola U., 1974. Cert. resource specialist. Tchr. L.A. Unified Schs., 1968-78; resource specialist Desert Sands Unified Sch. Dist., Palm Desert, 1978-83, Palm Springs Unified Schs., 1983-99, ret., 1999. Co-author: The Twelve Steps of Phobics Anonymous, 1989, One Day At A Time in Phobics Victorious, 1992, The Twelve Steps of Phobics Victorious, 1993; founder Phobics Victorious, 1992. Mem. Am. Assn. Christian Counselors (charter), Nat. Assn. of Christian Recovery, Anxiety Disorders Assn. Am. Office: Phobics Victorious PO Box 695 Palm Springs CA 92263-0695 E-mail: rosemary_jane@earthlink.net.

HARTMAN, RUTH CAMPBELL, educator; b. Galion, Ohio, Aug. 18, 1938; d. Richard Lewis and Florence Evelyn (Ireland) Campbell; m. Richard Louis Hartman, Jan. 14, 1956; children: Jeffery Lee, Marsha Elaine, Jerry Steven. BS, Ohio State U., 1970; MEd, U. LaVerne, 1976, postgrad., 1985—, U. Akron, 1977-85. cert. tchr., Ohio. Tchr. Willard (Ohio) City Schs., 1964-65; educator Mansfield (Ohio) City Schs., 1966—, home tutor, 1971-81, educator, 1977—, faculty advisory com., 1990-2001, young authors coord., 1991-92, co-coord. career edn., 1991-97; owner, dir. Hope Sch., Plymouth, Ohio, 2002—. Cons. Ohio State U., Ashland (Ohio) Coll., Mt. Vernon (Ohio) Nazarene Coll., 1976—. Co-author: Handbook for Student Teachers, 1983; contbr. to Norde News. Dir. of contruction Hope School. Mem NEA, Ohio Edn. Assn., North Cen. Ohio Tchrs. Assn., Mansfield Edn. Assn. Republican. Methodist. Avocations: reading, traveling, tennis, music. Home: RR 1 Plymouth OH 44865-9801 Office: Hope School 4200≧ Opdyke Rd Plymouth OH 44865-

HARTMAN, SALLY P. toxicologist; b. Boston, Feb. 15, 1945; BA, U. Rochester, 1967; MA, Temple U., 1973. Jr. medicinal chemist SmithKline and French Labs., Phila., 1967-72; rsch. assoc. Fels Rsch. Inst. Temple U., Phila., 1972-78; asst. prof. chemistry N.H. Tech. Coll., Laconia, 1983-85; from lab. scientist to supr. toxicology State of N.H. Pub. Health Labs., Concord, 1986—. Office: State of NH Pub Health Labs 6 Hazen Dr Concord NH 03301-6510 E-mail: shartman@dhhs.state.nh.us.

HARTMAN, STEPHEN WHEELER, education educator; b. Oceanside, N.Y., May 1, 1940; s. Raymond William and Marianne Knapp H.; m. Phyllis D. Hartman, Nov. 24, 1978 (div. Apr. 1982); children: Stephanie Regina, Alan Gerard. BA, Hofstra U., 1962; MPA, Wayne State U., 1965; PhD, Syracuse U., 1969. Instr. Wayne State U., Detroit, 1965-66; asst. prof. U. Conn., Storrs, 1967-69, Fla. Atlantic U., Boca Raton, 1969-76; prof. N.Y. Inst. of Tech., Old Westbury, 1977-2000, MBA dir., 1998-2000; fin. dir. Town of Babylon, N.Y., 1988. Telecomms. cons. U.S. Army Res., Albany, N.Y., 1989-91. Co-author: The McGraw-Hill Pocket Guide to Business Finance, 1991, Guide to Business Finance, 1992, Dictionary of Personal Finance, 1992, Dictionary of Business, 2000, Dictionary of Real Estate Terms, 1996, International Business Dictionary, 1999, The Manager's Handbook of Client/Server Computing in Business and Finance, 2003. Candidate for Suffolk County Comptroller, Dem. Party, Suffolk, 1978. Home: 68 Wesleyan Rd Smithtown NY 11787-3013

HARTMAN, SUSAN MARGARET, community mental health nurse; b. Newark, NY, Oct. 6, 1947; d. Francis and Ann Elizabeth (Kelly) Smith; m. Robert Charles Hartman, June 13, 1970; children: Kerry Ann, Charles Robert. BS in Art, Nazareth Coll., 1970; AAS in Nursing with distinction, Monroe C.C., Rochester, N.Y., 1984. RN, N.Y.; cert. HIV/AIDS education, ARC. Tchr. art and gym St. Michael Sch., Newark, 1976-86; RN telemetry Clifton Springs (N.Y.) Hosp. and Clinic, 1984-85; RN psychiatry U. Rochester (N.Y.) Med. Ctr., 1985-87; community mental health nurse Wayne County Mental Health, Lyons, N.Y., 1987—; co-coord. critical incident stress debriefing team Wayne County, Newark, 1993-95. Pres., v.p., sec. East Palmyra (NY) Fire Dept. Aux., 1971—; EMT/firefighter East. Pa. Fire Dept., 1993—; counselor Crisis Pregnancy Ctr., Palmyra, 1991-92; program com. Cornell Coop. Ext., Newark, 1991—; instr. CPR and first aid, 1990—; DSHR nationally cert. counselor TWA 800 disaster; infection control officer, Wayne Behavioral Health Network, 1991—; chmn. staff health com., staff safety com., Wayne Co. Mental Health. Poet: A Whispering Silence, 1997; contbr. articles to profl. jours. Vol. disaster nurse ARC, Newark, 1986—; vol. sch. nurse St. Michael Sch., Newark, 1984—86; active Palmyra Vol. Ambulance, 1998—2000; sec. St. Michael Pastoral Coun., 2000—02, social ministry com., 1999—2002. Recipient cert. appreciation Everybody Rides, Newark, 1990, cert. appreciation Wayne County Svcs. Bd., 1991, 93, cert. appreciation ARC, 1991, 2 cert. for 2 different actions Commn. Svc. Bd., 1991, NUS-CSP Planning award, 1994; named EMS of Yr. East Palmyra Fire Dept., 1996-97. Avocations: raise and train horses, dogs, swimming, drawing and painting, gardening. Home: 4122 N Creek Rd Palmyra NY 14522-9203 E-mail: Pinecrk@RedSuspenders.com.

HARTMAN-ABRAMSON, ILENE, adult education educator; b. Detroit, Nov. 8, 1950; d. Stuart Lester and Freda Vivian (Nash) Hartman; m. Victor Nikolai Abramson, Oct. 24, 1941. BA, U. Mich., 1972; MEd, Wayne State U., 1980, PhD in Higher Edn., 1990. Cert. continuing secondary tchr., Mich. Program developer and instr. William Beaumont Hosp., Royal Oak, Mich., 1972—74; vocat. counselor for emigres Jewish Vocat. Svc. and Cmty. Workshop, Detroit, 1974—81; program developer and cons. Detroit Psychiat. Inst., 1982; instr. for foreign students Oakland C.C., Farmington Hills, Mich., 1983-99. Mem. adv. bd. Mich. Dept. Edn., Detroit, 1981; lectr. Internat. Conf. Tchrs. English to Speakers of Other Langs., 1981; guest presenter Wayne State U., Lawrence Tech. U., 1991, U. Mich. Anxiety Disorders Program, 1993; presenter rsch. presentations Nat. Coalition for Sex Equity in Edn., Ann Arbor, Mich.; presenter at seminar on learning anxiety Interdisciplinary Studies program Wayne State U., 1995; chair profl. stds. and measures com. Mich. Devel. Edn. Consortium, editor newsletter, 1997; mem. rehab. adv. coun. State of Mich.; guest lectr. med. edn./residency tng. initiatives Detroit Med. Ctr. Hutzel Hosp., Providence Hosp., Beaumont Hosp., Detroit Med. Ctr., Harper Hosp.; adj. faculty Wayne State U., 2000; adj. prof. internat. comms. Lawrence Tech. U., 2000—. Mem. editl. bd. Mensa Rsch. Jour.; contbr. articles to prof. jours. Mem. Am. Acad. on Physician and Patient, Am. Mensa (rsch. rev. com.). Jewish. Avocations: self-defense for women, Karate. Office: Lawrence Tech U 21000 W Ten Mile Rd Southfield MI 48075-1058 E-mail: ah2574@wayne.edu., ihabramson@aol.com.

HARTMAN-IRWIN, MARY FRANCES, retired language professional; b. Portland, Oreg., Oct. 18, 1925; d. Curtiss Henry Sabisch and Gladys Frances (Giles) Strand; m. Harry Elmer Hartman, Sept. 6, 1946 (div. June 1970); children: Evelyn Frances, Laura Elyce, Andrea Candace; m. Thomas Floyd Irwin, Apr. 11, 1971. BA, U. Wash., 1964-68; postgrad., Seattle Pacific, 1977-79, Antioch U., Seattle, Wash., 1987, Heritage Inst., 1987. Lang. educator Kennewick (Wash.) Dist. # 17, 1970-88. Guide Summer Study Tours of Europe, 1971-88. Sec. Bahai Faith, 1971-99, libr., 2000, Pasco, Washington, 1985-88; trustee Mid. Columbia coun. Girl Scouts U.S. Fulbright scholar, 1968. Mem. NEA, Wash. Edn. Assn., Kennewick Edn. Assn., Nat. Fgn. Lang. Assn., Wash. Fgn. Lang. Assn., Literacy Coun. (literacy tutor Tillamook Bay C.C.). Avocations: painting, sewing, writing essays and short stories. Home: PO Box 247 Netarts OR 97143-0247 E-mail: maryi@oregoncoast.com.

HARTMANIS, JURIS, computer scientist, educator; b. Riga, Latvia, July 5, 1928; arrived in U.S., 1950, naturalized, 1956; s. Martins and Irma (Liepins) Hartmanis; m. Ellymaria Rehwald, May 16, 1959; children: Reneta, Martin, Audrey. Student, U. Marburg, 1947-49; MA, U. Kansas City, 1951; PhD, Calif. Inst. Tech., 1955; LHD (hon.), U. Dortmund, Germany, 1995; D, DHL, U. Mo., 1999. Instr. Cornell U., Ithaca, NY, 1955-57, prof., 1965—, Walter R. Read prof. engring., 1980—, chmn. dept. computer sci., 1965-71, 77-82, 92-94; Dr. H.C. U. Mo., Kansas City, 1999. Asst. prof. Ohio State U., 1957—58; rsch. mathematician GE R&D Ctr., Schenectady, 1957—65; asst. dir. NSF Computer and Info. Sci. & Engring., Arlington, Va., 1996—99. Author (with R. E. Stearns): (book) Algebraic Structure Theory for Sequential Machines, 1966; author: Feasible computations and Provable Complexity Properties, 1978; editor: SIAM Jour. Computing; assoc. editor: Jour. Computer and Sys. Scis., 1966—, Jour. Math. Sys. Theory, 1966—89; co-editor: Springer-Verlag Lecture Notes in Computer Sci., 1973—. Recipient Turing award, 1992, B. Bolzano Gold medal, Acad. Scis. Czech Republic, 1995, Grand medal, Latvian Acad. of Sci., 2001. Fellow: AAAS, Computing Machinery, Am. Acad. Arts and Scis.; mem.: NAE, Latvian Acad. Sci. (fgn., Grand medal 2001), Assn. N.Y. Acad. Scis., Am. Math. Soc., Sigma Xi. Home: 324 Brookfield Rd Ithaca NY 14850-2008 Office: Cornell Univ Upson Hall Ithaca NY 14853 E-mail: jh@cs.cornell.edu.

HARTMANN, ANN W. financial planner; b. Detroit, Mar. 5, 1941; d. Robert Allan and Eunice Elizabeth (Seitz) Wilson; m. James Cline Hartmann, July 18, 1970 (dec.); m. Richard W. Brockmeyer, Oct. 1, 1994 (div. 1999). BA, Montclair State Coll., 1962; MBA in Fin., Rutgers U., 1975. CLU, ChFC. Tchr. Bloomfield (N.J.) Bd. Edn., 1962-63; administr. Girl Scouts USA, Pa., Mich., 1963-72, YWCA of Am., N.J., Ohio, 1972-77; dir. fin. and field personnel Sycor, Inc., Ann Arbor, Mich., 1977-79; sr. cons. Health Systems Group, Ann Arbor, 1979-80; fin. planner Hartmann & Assocs., Toledo, 1980—. Adj. faculty U. Toledo, 1983-87, Lourdes Coll., Sylvania, Ohio, 1987-98; faculty Cigna/Lincoln Nat. Edn. Events, 1984—; speaker in field. Editor: (newsletter) Money Talks, 1982—. 1st v.p. Girls Clubs Am., N.Y.C., 1985—87; pres. Maumee Valley coun. Girl Scouts U.S.A., Toledo, 1990—97; trustee Spiritual Counselling and Edn. Ctr., 2002—, The Friendly Ctr., 2003—, Zonat Club Toldeo I Found. Bd., 2003—; nat. aquatic sch. staff instr., trainer ARC, Mich., 1974—80, 1974—80. Named Hines award Honoree Nat. Bd. Child Welfare, 1986. Mem.: NASD (arbitrator), Soc. Fin. Svcs. Profls. Found. (pres. 2001—03), Am. Arbitration Assn., Toledo Estate Planning Coun. (bd. dirs. 1992—98), Toledo Assn. Life Underwriters (v.p. 1991—94, pres. elect 1994, pres. 1995), Soc. Fin. Svc. Profls. (pres. Toledo chpt. 1988—90, nat. bd. dirs. 1993—96, nat. nominating com. 1996—97, sec. 1998—99, treas. 1999—2000, pres.-elect 2000—01, pres. 2001—02, 2001—03, immediate past pres. 2002—03), Am. Arbitration Assn. (comml. panel, arbitrator), Zonta Club Toledo (bd. dirs. 1987—88). Republican. Methodist. Avocations: sailing, bridge, needlework. Office: Hartmann & Assocs 6635 W Central Ave Toledo OH 43617-1029

HARTMANN, BRUCE, publishing executive; m. Tami Hartmann; children: Melissa, Jacquelyn, Brian. BA in Journalism, W. Va. U., 1979. With advt. Balt. (Md.) Sun, 1981—87; mgr. Lowell (Mass.) Sun, 1987—90; adv. dir. Knoxville News-Sentinel, 1990—93, asst. gen. mgr., 1993, gen. mgr., v.p., 1993—98; pub., pres. The Knoxville News-Sentinel Scripps Howard Newspapers, Knoxville, Tenn., 1998—. Pres. Hist. Tenn. Theatre Found.; bd. dir. Knoxville (Tenn.) Area Chamber Partnership, Knoxville (Tenn.) Zoo, Knoxville (Tenn.) Sports Cup, United Way, Knoxville, St. Mary's Found., Knoxville. Office: The Knoxville News-Sentinel PO Box 59038 Knoxville TN 37950-9038*

HARTMANN, FREDERICK HOWARD, political science educator emeritus; b. N.Y.C., July 6, 1922; s. Frederick Herman and Grace (MacNamara) H.; m. Regina Lou Kiracofe, Dec. 26, 1943; children: Lynne Merry, Vicky Carol, Peter Howard. AB, U. Calif. at Berkeley, 1943; MA, Princeton, 1948, PhD, 1949; student, Grad. Inst. Internat. Studies, U. Geneva, Switzerland, 1947. Instr. politics Princeton, 1947; from asst. prof. to prof. polit. sci. U. Fla., 1948-66; dir. Inst. Internat. Relations, 1963-66; Alfred Thayer Mahan prof. maritime strategy U.S. Naval War Coll., 1966-88, prof. emeritus, 1988—, spl. acad. advisor, 1966 86. Vis. prof. Wheaton (Mass.) Coll., part-time, 1966-69, Brown U., part-time, 1968-69, U. R.I., part-time, 1970-71, Tex. Tech U., 1974-75; vis. prof. polit. sci. U. Calif., Berkeley, 1979-80, Middle East Tech. U., Ankara, Turkey, 1988. Author: The Relations of Nations, 4th edit., 1973, 5th edit., 1978, 6th edit., 1983, Spanish edit., 1986, The Swiss Press and Swiss Foreign Affairs, 1960, Germany Between East and West, 1965, The New Age of American Foreign Policy, 1970, Naval Renaissance: The U.S. Navy in the 1980s, 1990, (Chinese transl. 1994), America Under Threat, 2002; (with Robert L. Wendzel) To Preserve the Republic, 1985, Defending America's Security, 1988, America's Foreign Policy in a Changing World, 1994; editor: Basic Documents of International Relations, 1951, Readings in International Relations, 1952, World in Crisis, 4th edit., 1973; contbr. to: System for Educating Military Officers in the U.S., 1976, The Conservation of Enemies, 1981. U. Fla. rep. Fla. Bd. Control Com. Acad. Freedom, 1961-62; mem. Fulbright Nat. Selection Com., 1954-56; U.S. del. 4th Conf. Naval War Colls. Am., 1966, 6th Conf., 1970, 10th Conf., 1980, 12th Conf., 1985. Served to lt. (j.g.) USNR, 1943-46; capt. Res. Recipient Meritorious Civilian Service medal Dept. Navy, 1985; Fulbright research prof. U. Bonn, Germany, 1953-54; Rockefeller grantee, 1959; Exxon Corp. grantee, 1973 Mem. AAUP (pres. U. Fla. chpt. 1959-60, mem. nat. council 1963-66), Am. Polit. Sci. Assn., Internat. Studies Assn. (pres. New Eng. div. 1971-72), New Eng. Polit. Sci. Assn. (exec. com. 1982-84), Fla. Blue Key, Pi Sigma Alpha, Delta Phi Epsilon. Home: 8457 Twin Rocks Rd Granite Bay CA 95746-8123

HARTMANN, FREDERICK WILLIAM, newspaper editor; b. Wilmington, Del., Feb. 3, 1928; s. William and Louise (Askani) H.; m. Mary Lucille Nelson, Oct. 16, 1954; children: Michele Mary, Randi Lucille, Frederick Andrew, Eric William, Adam Nelson. BA, U. Del., 1951; postgrad., Am. U., 1952; MS, Columbia U. Grad. Sch. Journalism, 1953. Reporter AP, N.Y.C., 1954; dir. news and sports WDEL Radio, Wilmington, 1954-56; reporter Morning News, News-Jour. Co., Wilmington, 1956-60, asst. city editor, 1961-62, city editor, 1962-64, Morning and Evening Jour., 1964-67, met. editor, 1967-72, asst. to pres., 1972-74, dir. corp. mktg., 1974-75, exec. editor, 1975-80, v.p., 1977-80; mng. editor Fla. Times-Union, Jacksonville, 1980-83; exec. editor Times-Union/Jacksonville Jour., Jacksonville, 1983-88, Times-Union, Jacksonville, 1988-98, ret., 1998. Lectr. U. Del., 1971, 72; Pulitzer prize juror, 1981, 82. Mem. budget com. United Way of Del., 1973, 74; v.p. Brandywine Little League, 1973; bd. dirs. United Cerebral Palsy Assn. of Del., 1970-72. Served with AUS, 1946-48. Mem. Theta Chi. Home: 3852 Mcgirts Blvd Jacksonville FL 32210-4337 E-mail: freditor39@aol.com.

HARTMANN, GEORGE HERMAN, retired manufacturing company executive; b. N.Y.C., Nov. 6, 1927; s. George Dietrich Herman and Margaret Bertha (Winkler) H.; m. Anne Katharine Martin, July 9, 1960; children: Michael George, Steven Herman, Katharine Margaret, Elizabeth Anne. AB, Dartmouth Coll., 1949, MS in Mech. Engring, 1950. With Gen. Electric Co., 1950-70; v.p. mfg. Gen. Signal Corp., 1970-71; exec. v.p., then pres. GE Espanola, 1971-74; pres. Davol Co. (subs. Internat. Paper Co.), 1975-78, corp. v.p. human resources, then v.p. materials, 1979-80; pvt. investor, 1980-81; group v.p. Textron Inc., Providence, 1981-92; ret., 1992. Trustee R.I. Coun. Econ. Edn., 1977, vice chmn. 1983-92; trustee Am. Sch., Bilbao, Spain, 1972-74, chmn., 1973-74; trustee Joint Coun. Econ. Edn., 1986-91, Nat. Security Indsl. Assn., 1988-92, Calvin K. Kazanjian Econs. Found., Inc., 1996—; zoning bd. mem. Lyme, NH; U.S. del. NATO Indsl. Adv. Group, 1989-92; mem. adv. com. Lebanon (N.H.) Airport, 2000—. Served to lt. USNR, 1955-60. Mem. NAM (dir. 1977-80), R.I. C. of C. (dir. 1977-78), Greater Providence C. of C. (dir. 1976-78), N.Y. Yacht Club, Cruising Club Am. (Parkinson Meml. Trophy for Transoceanic Passage 1993, 97), Ocean Cruising Club. Republican.

HARTMANN, HENRIK ANTON, medical educator; b. Sandar, Norway, Mar. 20, 1920; came to U.S., 1950; m. Anastatia Smith, Sept. 17, 1952; children: Lisa, Tony, Jeni, Arne, Signe. MD, Oslo U., 1949. Diplomate Am. Bd. Pathology. Prof. U. Wis., Madison, 1955—. Vis. prof. Ullevaal Hosp., Oslo, 1969-70; vis. scientist Inst. Neurobiology, Gothenburg, Sweden, 1958; cons. VA Hosp., Madison. Contbr. numerous articles to profl. jours. Lt. Norwegian Army, 1944-45. Rsch. grantee NIH. Mem. Internat. Neurochemistry Soc., Am. Neuropathology Assn. Home: 10 S Kenosha Dr Madison WI 53705-4619 Office: U Wis 1300 University Ave Madison WI 53706-1510

HARTMANN, JAMES M. lawyer; b. N.Y.C., Mar. 8, 1946; s. Morton Woodrow and Miriam Rose H.; m. Nancy K. Deming, May 20, 1988. BA, St. Lawrence U., 1967; MA, U. Wis., 1968; JD, Bklyn. Law Sch., 1974. Bar: N.Y. 1975, U.S. Dist. Ct. (so. and ea. dists.) N.Y. 1975, U.S. Ct. Appeals (2d cir.) 1975, U.S. Dist. Ct. (no. and we. dists.) N.Y. 1989, U.S. Supreme Ct. 1991. Gen. atty. U.S. Dept. Justice, N.Y.C., 1975-76, trial atty., 1976-79; pvt. practice N.Y.C., 1979-86, Delhi, N.Y., 1989—; head dept. litig. Frenkel & Hershkowitz, N.Y.C., 1986-89. Spl. dist. atty. Del. County, Delhi; mem. libr. com. Supreme

Ct., Delhi, 1992—. Mem. N.Y. State Bar Assn., N.Y. Trial Lawyers Assn., N.Y. State Criminal Def. Lawyers Assn., Del. County Bar Assn. (mem. grievance com. 1994—), Pi Sigma Alpha. Office: PO Box 206 Rte 10 Delhi NY 13753

HARTMANN, KENNETH, lawyer; b. Chgo., Apr. 2, 1950; s. Orvel Arthur and Anita (Everding) Hartmann; m. Carol Beth Draeger, Aug. 5, 1978; children: Elizabeth Ann, Kristen Carol. BA with high honors, U. Ill., 1971; JD, U. Chgo., 1977. Bar: Ill. 77, U.S. Dist. Ct. (no. dist.) Ill. 77. Assoc. Sonnenschein, Carlin, Nath & Rosenthal, Chgo., 1977—79, Coffield, Ungaretti, Harris & Slavin, Chgo., 1979—81; ptnr. Rudnick & Wolfe, Chgo., 1981—85, 1993—98, Piper Rudnick LLP, Chgo., 1998—. Mem.: Phi Beta Kappa. Republican. Lutheran. E-mail: Kenneth.Hartmann@piperrudnick.com.

HARTMANN, ROBERT ELLIOTT, manufacturing company executive, retired; b. Bklyn., Apr. 10, 1926; s. James and Edna Mae (Schroeder) H.; m. Anne Marie Mongiello, Feb. 15, 1948; children: Barbara Hartmann Kaszor, Donna Hartmann Dow. BS, Miami U., Oxford, Ohio, 1946. CPA, N.Y. Acct. Price, Waterhouse & Co., N.Y.C., 1948-57; mgr. fin. acctg. Air Products & Chems., Allentown, Pa., 1957-58; v.p. Alpha Portland Cement Co. divsn. Alpha Portland Industries, Inc., Easton, Pa., 1958-82. Sec. Slattery Group, Inc. (formely Alpha Portland Industries, Inc.), Easton, 1962-89; sec., treas. Energy and Resource Recovery Corp., until 1982; sec., treas., dir. H.O.H. Corp., until 1982; past pres. Moravian Book Shop, Inc. Bd. dirs. Bethlehem Area Moravians. Served to lt. Supply Corps USNR, World War II. Mem. Inst. Mgmt. Accts. (pres. Lehigh Valley chpt. 1973-74), Financial Execs. Inst. (treas. N.E. Pa. chpt. 1972-74), Am. Inst. C.P.A.s. Mem. Moravian Ch. Home: 285 Bridle Path Rd Bethlehem PA 18017-3867

HARTMANN, ROBERT SANKEY, hospital administrator, communications and fundraising executive; b. June 9, 1948; s. Robert Trowbridge and Roberta (Sankey) H.; m. Ruth Eva Satterwhite, Dec. 2, 1978; children: Daniel Satterthwaite, David Trowbridge. BA in Speech/Drama cum laude, Occidental Coll., 1969, MA in Speech/Drama, 1971; student, Guildhall Sch. Music & Drama, London, 1970; mgmt. devel. course, Harvard Bus. Sch., 1974. Spl. asst. to chmn. Nat. Endowment for Arts, Washington, 1973-78; lobbyist for Daniel J. Edelman Washington, 1978; creative dir., lobbyist Hill and Knowlton, Washington, 1978-81; sr. v.p. Ruder Finn & Rotman, Washington, 1981-84; dir. pub. rels. World Wildlife Fund, Washington, 1984—86; sr. v.p. and dir. pub. rels. Abramson Assocs., Inc., 1986-90; v.p. pub. affairs, mktg. and devel. Nat. Rehab. Hosp., Washington, 1990—. Chmn. bd. dirs. Met. Meth. Nursery Sch., 1989—94. Named Outstanding Young Man Am., 1983. Mem. Pub. Rels. Soc. Am. (Thoth award 1984), Internat. Assn. Bus. Communicators (Gold Quill award 1984), Westmoreland Citizens Assn. (pres. 1992-93), Nat. Press Club, Capitol Hill Club, Silver Owl Club. Home: 5023 Worthington Dr Bethesda MD 20816-2748 Office: Nat Rehab Hosp 102 Irving St NW Washington DC 20010-2949 E-mail: robert.s.hartmann@medstar.net.

HARTMANN, ROBERT TROWBRIDGE, newspaperman, presidential counselor; b. Rapid City, S.D., Apr. 8, 1917; s. Miner Louis and Elizabeth (Trowbridge) H.; m. Roberta Sankey, Jan. 17, 1943; children: Roberta H. Brake, Robert S. AB, Stanford U., 1938. Reporter Los Angeles Times, 1939-41, 45-48, editorial writer, 1948-54, chief Washington bur., 1954-63; chief (Mediterranean and Middle East Bur.), 1963-64; FAO info. adviser Washington, 1964-65; editor Republican Conf. U.S. Ho. Reps., 1966-69; minority sgt.-at-arms U.S. Ho. Reps., 1969-73; chief staff to the Vice Pres., 1973-74; counsellor (with cabinet rank) to Pres. Gerald R. Ford, 1974-77; sr. research fellow Hoover Instn., Stanford U., 1977—; trustee Gerald R. Ford Found., 1981—. Mem. U.S. Ho. of Reps. Mission to Peoples' Republic of China, 1972. Author: Palace Politics, An Inside Account of the Ford Years, 1980. Asst. to permanent chmn. Rep. Nat. Conv., 1968, 72; bd. visitors U.S. Naval Acad., 1977-80. Served from ensign to capt. USN, 1941-45, PTO; ret. Recipient Sigma Delta Chi Distinguished Service award for Washington Corrs., 1957; Better Understanding citation English Speaking Union of U.S., 1958; Overseas Press Club citation, 1961; Freedoms Found. citation, 1963; Distinguished Eagle Scout award Boy Scouts Am., 1975; Reid Found. fellow, 1951 Mem. Navy League, Hammer and Coffin Soc., Delta Chi, Sigma Delta Chi, Delta Sigma Rho. Mem. Ch. of Christ. Clubs: Nat. Press (Washington), Army and Navy (Washington), Capitol Hill (Washington); Mil. Order of the Carabao, Chevaliers du Tastevin; Country Club of St. Croix (V.I.). Home: 5001 Baltimore Ave Bethesda MD 20816-1607 *I'm not sure I have "achieved success" but I have had a very good life so far. The greatest evil in life is a lie, and the greatest blessings are love and laughter.*

HARTMANN, WILLIAM HERMAN, pathologist, educator; b. N.Y.C., Mar. 13, 1931; BA, Syracuse U., 1951; MD, SUNY, 1955. Diplomate Am. Bd. Pathology. Exec. v.p. Am. Bd. Pathology, Tampa, Fla., 1993—. Office: Am Bd Pathology PO Box 25915 Tampa FL 33622-5915

HARTNESS, SANDRA JEAN, venture capitalist; b. Jacksonville, Fla., Aug. 19, 1944; d. Harold H. and Viola M. (House) H. AB, Ga. So. Coll., 1969; postgrad., San Francisco State Coll., 1970-71; MA in Taxation, Golden Gate U., 1997. Rschr. Savannah (Ga.) Planning Commn., 1969, Environ. Analysis Group, San Francisco, 1970-71; dir. Mission Inn, Riverside, Calif., 1971-75; developer Hartness Assocs., Laguna Beach, Calif., 1976—. Ptnr. Western Neuro-Care Ctr., Tustin, Calif., 1983—89; pres. Asset Svcs., Inc., 1981—. V.p., mem. bd. dirs. Evergreen Homes, Inc., 1986-90; bd. govs. Human Rights Campaign, 2001—. Recipient numerous awards for cmty. svc. Democrat.

HARTNETT, JAMES PATRICK, engineering educator; b. Lynn, Mass., Mar. 19, 1924; s. James Patrick and Anna Elizabeth (Ryan) H.; m. Shirley Germaine Carlson, July 14, 1945 (div. 1969); children: James, David, Paul, Carla, Dennis; m. Edith Zubrin, Sept. 10, 1971. BS in Mech. Engring, Ill. Inst. Tech., 1947; MS, MIT, 1948; PhD, U. Calif., Berkeley, 1954. Engr. gas turbine div. Gen. Electric Co., 1948-49; rsch. engr. U. Calif., Berkeley, 1949-54; asst. prof. to prof. mech. engring. U. Minn., 1954-61; Guggenheim fellow, vis. prof. U. Tokyo, Japan, 1960; cons. ICA, Seoul, Korea, 1960; Fulbright lectr., cons. mech. engring. U. Alexandria, Egypt, 1961; H. Fletcher Brown prof. mech. engring., chmn. dept. U. Del., 1961-65; engring. cons., 1954-74; prof., head dept. energy engring. U. Ill., Chgo., 1965-74; dir. Energy Resources Ctr., 1974-98. Sci. exch. visitor, Romania, 1969; vis. prof. Israel Inst. Tech., 1971; cons. Asian Inst. Tech., Bangkok 1977; 1st Dr. Arcot Ramachandran prof. heat transfer Indian Inst. Tech., Madras, 1995-96. Editor: Recent Advances in Heat and Mass Transfer, 1961; co-editor: Internat. Jour. Heat and Mass Transfer, 1960—, (with T.F. Irvine, Jr.) Advances in Heat Transfer, 1963—, Heat Transfer-Japanese Research, Soviet Research, 1971, Fluid Mechanics-Soviet Research, 1971; contbr. articles on heat transfer, fluid mechanics, energy to tech. jours. Mem. organizing com. and sci. coun. Internat. Centre Heat and Mass Transfer, Ankara, Turkey, 1969—; mem., sec. Ill. Energy Resources Commn., 1974-85; mem. sci. coun. Regional Center for Energy, Heat and Mass Transfer for Asia and Pacific, 1976—; sec. Midwest Univs. Energy Consortium, 1980—. Recipient Profl. Achievement award Ill. Inst. Tech. Alumni Assn., 1977; recipient Luikov medal Internat. Ctr. Heat and Mass Transfer, 1981; Japan Soc. for Promotion of Sci. fellow, 1987. Fellow ASME (Meml. award heat transfer divsn. 1969, 40th Anniversary award 1989, AIChE-ASME Max Jakob Meml. award 1989), Indian Nat. Acad. Engring., Japanese Soc. Mech. Engrs. (hon.); mem. Internat. Higher Edn. Acad. of Scis./Moscow (Disting. prof. 1997), Sigma Xi, Tau Beta Pi, Pi Tau Sigma. Address: Univ of Ill 1919 W Taylor St Chicago IL 60612-7246

HARTNETT, JOSH, actor; b. St. Paul, July 21, 1978; s. Daniel and Molly Hartnett(Stepmother). Student, SUNY, Purchase. Actor: (TV series) Cracker, 1997—98; (films) Halloween: H2O, 1998, The Faculty, 1998, The Virgin Suicides, 1999, Here on Earth, 2000, Blow Dry, 2001, Member, 2001, Town & Country, 2001, Pearl Harbor, 2001, O, 2001, Black Hawk Down, 2001, The Same, 2001, 40 Days and 40 Nights, 2002, Hollywood Homicide, 2003; (TV films) Debutante, 1998. Named ShoWest Male Star of Tomorrow, 2002. Office: c/o Jerry Sandrew Pub Rels 6363 Wilshire Blvd Ste 413 Los Angeles CA 90048*

HARTNETT, MARY, lawyer; b. St. Louis, Jan. 17, 1959; d. William Joseph and Kathleen (Hannefin) Hartnett; m. Richard Boyce Norland, Oct. 25, 1980; children: Daniel Richard Hartnett Norland, Kathleen Patricia Hartnett Norland. BA with honors, Grinnell Coll., 1980; postgrad., NYU, 1983; JD magna cum laude, Georgetown U., 1985. Bar: D.C. 1985, U.S. Ct. Appeals (D.C. cir.) 1985, U.S. Dist. Ct. D.C. 1986. Correspondent Middle East Exec. Reports, Bahrain, 1981-82; assoc. Vinson & Elkins, Washington, 1985-86, Coudert Bros. Internat. Law Firm, Washington and Moscow, 1989-96, of counsel Washington, 1996-98; adj. prof. law Georgetown U. Law Ctr., Washington, 1999—, exec. dir., bd. dirs. Women's Law and Pub. Policy Fellowship, 1998—. Mem. civil pro bono panel U.S. Dist. Ct., Washington, 1991-95; mem. Edmund Muskie Fellowship Legal Selection Com., Washington and N.Y.C., 1994. Contbr. more than 30 articles to profl. jours. Vol. atty. D.C. Emergency Domestic Rels. Project, Women's Legal Def. Fund, Washington, 1994-95; patient vol. Hospice of No. Va., Arlington, 1994-95; local coord. Meals on Wheels, Arlington, 1994-95; Dem. candidate for State Rep. from 71st Dist. Iowa, 1980. Root-Tilden scholar, 1980. Mem. ABA, Women's Bar Assn., D.C. Bar Assn. Congregationalist. Avocations: tennis, hiking. Office: Georgetown U Law Ctr Women's Law/Pub Policy Fell 600 New Jersey Ave NW Fl 334 Washington DC 20001-2075

HARTNETT, THOMAS ROBERT, III, lawyer, author; b. Sioux City, Iowa, July 19, 1920; s. Thomas and Florence Mary (Graves) H.; m. Betty Jeanne Dobbins, Mar. 3, 1943; children: Thomas Robert Joseph, Jeanine Elizabeth, Dennis Edward, Glenn Michael. Student, Trinity Coll., 1937-39; LLB, U. So. Calif., 1948. Bar: Tex. 1948, U.S. Dist. Ct. (no. dist.) Tex., 1949, U.S. Ct. Appeasl (5th cir.) 1954, (10th cir.) 1955, (11th cir.) 1983, U.S. Supreme Ct., 1957. Pvt. practice, Dallas, 1948-88; of counsel Hartnett Law Firm, Dallas, 1988—. Author: The Root of the Whys, 1998. With USAAF, 1939-45. Mem. State Bar Tex., Dallas Bar Assn. Republican. Roman Catholic. Home: 5074 Matilda St Apt 224 Dallas TX 75206-4268 Office: 4900 Thanksgiving Tower 1601 Elm St Dallas TX 75201-7254

HARTNETT, WILL FORD, lawyer; b. Austin, Tex., June 3, 1956; s. James Joseph and Emily (High) Hartnett; m. Tammy Lynn Cotton, Dec. 7, 1996; children: Will, Winston. BA, Harvard U., 1978; JD, U. Tex., 1981. Bar: Tex. 1981, U.S. Ct. Appeals (5th cir.) 1985, U.S. Supreme Ct. 1985; cert. in Estate Planning and Probate Law Tex. Bd. Legal Specialization. Assoc. Turner & Hitchins, Dallas, 1981-82; ptnr. The Hartnett Law Firm, Dallas, 1982—. Bd. dirs. Tex. Guaranteed Student Loan Corp., Austin, 1987-90. Co-author: Annual Survey of Wills and Trusts, 1986. Mem. Tex. Ho. of Reps., 1991—; vice chmn. House Jud. Affairs Com., 1995-2002, chmn., 2003—; mem. Tex. Jud. Coun. Fellow: Tex. Bar Found., Am. Coll. Trust and Estate Coun.; mem.: SAR, Dallas Bar Assn., Mensa, St. Nicholas Soc., Harvard Club Dallas (bd. dirs., treas. 1983—95). Republican. Roman Catholic. Home: 4722 Walnut Hill Ln Dallas TX 75229-6354 Office: The Hartnett Law Firm 4900 Thanksgiving Tower Dallas TX 75201 E-mail: will@hartnettlawfirm.com.

HARTNICK, ALAN JAY, lawyer, law educator; b. N.Y.C., Feb. 27, 1930; s. Saul and Sally Hartnick; m. Karen L. Hartnick; children: Jonathan (dec.), Kate, Christopher, Maggie. AB magna cum laude, Syracuse U., 1950; JD cum laude, Harvard U., 1953. Bar: N.Y. 1953. Ptnr. Abelman, Frayne and Schwab, N.Y.C. Adj. prof. Seton Hall U. Sch. Law, Newark, 1976—79, NYU Sch. Law, 1978—2001, Fordham Law Sch., 2003—; vis. lectr. Yale Law Sch., 1979; mem. copyright office adv. com. Libr. Congress, Washington, 1981—84; cons. Register of Copyright, 1989; U.S. del. Com. Govt. Experts on the Printed Wk. World Intellectual Property Orgn., Geneva, 1987. Editor-in-chief Jour. Copyright Soc., 1984-87; contbr. articles to profl. jours. Lt. USNR, 1953-56. Mem. Copyright Soc. USA (pres. 1982-84, hon. trustee 1984—), Mag. Pubs. Assn. (legal affairs com. 1983—), N.Y. State Bar Assn. (com. chair copyright and trademark 1988—), Assn. of the Bar of the City of N.Y. (copyright and literary property com. 1964-67, 78-81, 91-94, 98—, entertainment law com. 1994-97, ad hoc info. superhighway com. 1994-95), Phi Beta Kappa. Home: 168 E 74th St New York NY 10021-3561 Office: Abelman Frayne & Schwab 150 E 42nd St Fl 26 New York NY 10017-5621

HART-NOLAN, ELSIE FAYE, elementary education educator; b. Shelbyville, Ill., Oct. 15, 1920; d. James Ray and Maude May (Allison) Cain; m. Harold Delbert Bible, June 15, 1941 (div. Apr. 1948); children: Gary H., Rex E. (dec.); m. Frederick Christopher Hart, July 28, 1950 (dec. Dec. 1994); children: Susan Hart Eichman, Pamela L.; m. Jerome F. Nolan, May 1, 1999. Elem. teaching cert., Ea. Ill. U., 1942; BS in Edn., No. Ill. U., 1968; postgrad., Rockford Coll., 1972-73. Cert. elem. tchr., Ill. Tchr. Findlay (Ill.) Elem. Sch., 1942-47; tchr. Winnebago County Schs., Rockford, Ill., 1948-52, Rockford Parochial Schs., 1957-63, Rockford Pub. Schs., 1964-82, substitute tchr., 1982—. Author: The On and the Under Dog, 1992; contbr. articles to profl. jours. Vol. tchr. Rockford Parochial schs. Recipient Cert. of Commendation in recognition of meritorious svc. Ill. Supt. Pub. Instrn., 1974; nominated Ill. Retired Tchrs. Hall of Fame. Mem. AAUW (historian Rockford chpt. 1970—), Ill. Ret. Tchrs. Assn., Winnebago/Boone Ret. Tchrs. Assn., Women of the Moose, Holy Family Women's Guild, Rockford Women's Club (sec. 1970, publicity com. 1971, membership com. 1972, ways/means com. 1988-91, bd. dirs. 1993-94, long-range planning com. 1994—, program com. 1994-95, dir. 1995-98), Nat. Women's Hall of Fame. Republican. Roman Catholic. Avocations: dancing, swimming, golf, volunteer teaching, fundraising. Home: 3611 Pinecrest Rd Rockford IL 61107-1307

HARTOV, ALEXANDER, engineering educator; arrived in U.S., 1979; BSEE, Northeastern U., 1984; MS, Dartmouth Coll., 1988, PhD, 1991. Asst. prof. Dartmouth Coll., Hanover, NH, 1996—2002, assoc. prof., 2002—. Address: 53 School St Lebanon NH 03766-1628

HARTRICK, JANICE KAY, lawyer; b. Baytown, Tex., Oct. 15, 1952; BA, Rice U., 1974; JD, U. Houston, 1976. Bar: Tex. 1977, La. 1980. With contracts sect. Texaco Corp., Houston, 1977-78; asst. gen. counsel Cities Exploration Co., Watson Oil Corp., Houston, 1978-79; sr. atty. Coastal Corp., Houston, 1979-87; chief counsel, v.p. Seagull Energy Corp., Houston, 1987-97; gen. counsel, sr. v.p. EEX Corp., Houston, 1997-2000; asst. gen. counsel Apache Corp., 2000—. Coun. Thompson and Knight, LLP, Houston. Contbg. editor Regulation of the Natural Gas Industry, 1980-84. Vice chair adv. bd. Internat. Oil and Gas Ednl. Ctr., Southwestern Legal Found.; trustee Rocky Mountain Mineral Law Found. Mem. ABA (chair oil and gas exploration and prodn.), Tex. Bar Assn., State Bar of Tex. (oil, gas and mineral law sect. chair 1999), La. Bar Assn. Avocation: track. Office: Apache Corp 2000 Post Oak Blvd Ste 100 Houston TX 77056-4400

HARTSBURG, JUDITH CATHERINE, small business owner; b. Terre Haute, Ind., June 16, 1955; d. Ferris Lee and Mary Ann (Tully) Roberson; m. Donald Matthew Seprodi, Aug. 1, 1972 (div. Oct. 1994); children: Antoinette Seprodi, Jacob Seprodi, Brooklyn Seprodi; m. Joseph Wayne Hartsburg, Feb. 14, 1998. AA, Ivy Tech, 1990; grad., Dale Carnegie Course. Lic. property/casualty ins. agt.; notary pub. Sec. Equifax, Oklahoma City, 1975-76; ins. clk. Northside Family Medicine, Del City, Okla., 1976; office mgr. Dick Clark Ins., Terre Haute, 1981, Simrell's, Terre Haute, 1981-85; ADC acctg. clk./typist V Vigo County Welfare, Terre Haute, 1985-86, head ADC acctg., clk./typist IV, 1986-87; purchasing agt. Bruce Fox, Inc., New Albany, Ind., 1987-88; acctg. mgr. Terre Haute Coke and Carbon, 1988-96, acting sec. bd. dirs., 1989; ptnr., owner Thistlehare; office mgr. Terre Haute Truck Ctr., 1996; internet programmer, webmaster Advanced Microelectronics, Inc., Vincennes, Ind., 1997—2001; ptnr., entrepreneur Ceilings, Walls & All, 2000—. Ptnr., owner Thistlehare; bookkeeper Seprodi Constrn., Terre Haute, 1989—; grad. asst. Dale Carnegie Inst.; owner Take-A-Letter. Author: (poetry) Between Darkness and Light, In-Between Days. Coach, bd. dirs. Terre Haute Youth Soccer Assn., 1979—82; player N. Tex. Women's Soccer Assn., Plano, 1977—78. Recipient Dale Carnegie Highest award for Achievement. Mem.: AIPB, NAFE, Profl. Bookkeepers Assn., Am. Notary Assn., Vigo County Taxpayers Assn. Democrat. Roman Catholic. Avocations: gardening, camping, sewing, piano. Home: PO Box 323 Sandborn IN 47578-0323 E-mail: stocksnbears@tds.net., jhartsburg@hotmail.com.

HARTSELL, HORACE ED, college president; m. Joyce Powell; 6 children. BS, U. Fla.; MS, Fla. Atlantic U.; D in Adminstrn. of Higher Edn., Auburn U. Founder East Ark. C.C.; with Broward C.C., Fla. Atlantic U.; pres. Pensacola Jr. Coll., 1990-98, pres. emeritus, 1999—; interim pres. Daytona Beach C.C., 1998-99. Vice-chair, chair Fla. Coun. of Pres.; mem. coun. Pres.'s Legis. com. Founder, mem. Leadership Fla. Named Bus. and Profl. Leader of Yr. Pensacola News Jour., 1983; recipient Disting. Life Svc. award Fla. Assn. of C.C., 1997, Adminstrn. Commn. award, 1997. Mem. Pensacola Area C. of C. (chmn.). Home: Daytona Beach Cmty Coll 301 Gatlin Ln Minor Hill TN 38473 Office: Daytona Beach Cmty Coll PO Box 2811 Daytona Beach FL 32120-2811

HARTSELL, SAMUEL DAVID, insurance agent; b. Aberdeen, Miss., Oct. 15, 1937; s. Walter Eugene and Clara Otis (Jennings) H.; m. Virginia McAden, June 14, 1959; children: Cynthia H. Jones, Susan H. Sexton. BS in Engring., Va. Polytech. Inst. & State U., 1959; MS in Fin. Svcs., The Am. Coll., 1984. CLU, ChFC; accredited estate planner; registered health underwriter. Ins. agt. Principal Mutual Life Ins Co, Birmingham, Ala., 1972-92; sales engr. U.S. Steel Corp., Birmingham, 1959-72. Contbr. articles to profl. jours. Named Man of Distinction, Shades Valley Sun newspaper, 1985. Fellow: Life Underwriter Tng. Coun.; mem.: Am. Soc. CLU's, Nat. Assn. Accredited Estate Planning Couns., Million Dollar Round Table. E-mail: hartdave@bellsouth.net.

HARTSFIELD, HENRY WARREN, JR., electronics executive, retired astronaut; b. Birmingham, Ala., Nov. 21, 1933; s. Henry Warren and Alice Norma (Sorrell) H.; m. Judy Frances Massey, June 30, 1957; children: Judy Lynn, Keely Warren. BS, Auburn U., 1954; postgrad., Duke U., 1954-55, Air Force Inst. Tech., 1960-61; MS, U. Tenn., 1970; DSc (hon.), Auburn U., 1986. Commd. 2d lt. USAF, 1955, advanced through grades to col., 1974, assigned to tour with 53d Tactical Fighter Squadron, 1961-64; instr. USAF Test Pilot Sch., Edwards AFB, Calif., 1965-66; assigned to Manned Orbiting Lab. USAF, 1966-69; astronaut, NASA Lyndon B. Johnson Space Ctr., 1969-97, mem. support crew Apollo 16, Skylabs 2, 3, 4 missions, pilot STS-4; comdr. STS-41D, STS-61A; ret., 1977; civilian astronaut NASA; dep. dir. Flight Crew Ops. Directorate, 1987-89; dir. tech. integration and analysis Office Space Flight, NASA Hqrs., 1989-90; dep. dir. ops. space sta. projects Marshall Space Flight Ctr. NASA, 1990-91; mgr. man-tended capability phase Space Sta. Freedom Program, 1991-94; mgr. Internat. Space Sta. Ind. Assessment at Johnson Space Ctr., 1994-97; ret., 1998; dir. Houston ops. Raytheon Sys. Co., 1998-99; v.p. aerospace engring. svcs. Raytheon Tech. Svcs. Co., 1999—. In space: 483 hours. Decorated Meritorious Service medal, D.S.M. NASA, 1982, 88, Space Flight medal NASA, 1982, 84, 85; recipient Nat. Geog. White Space Trophy, 1973 Mem. Soc. Exptl. Test Pilots, Air Force Assn., Sigma Pi Sigma Office: Raytheon 2224 Bay Area Blvd Houston TX 77058-2008 E-mail: henry_w_hartsfield@raytheon.com., hhartsfield@raytheon.com.

HARTSHORN, ROLAND DEWITT, lawyer; b. Cordele, Ga., May 27, 1921; s. George DuBois and Nola Nancy (Redwine) H.; m. Mildred Stromick, Aug. 15, 1953; children— Marie Anne Hartshorn Kuhn, Elizabeth Lee, Roland David. J.D., Emory U., 1948. Bar: Va. 1956, D.C., 1956, Ga. 1948. Sole practice, Atlanta, 1948-50; sole practice, 1956-70; ptnr. Thomas, Thomas & Hartshorn, Springfield, Va., 1970-75; ptnr. Holst & Hartshorn, Arlington and Falls Church, Va., 1975— . Served to capt. U.S. Army, 1950-56. Mem. Fairfax County Bar Assn. Republican. Presbyterian. Lodges: Lions, Moose. Home: 3103 Sleepy Hollow Rd Falls Church VA 22042-3126 Office: Holst & Hartshorn 6400 Arlington Blvd Falls Church VA 22042-2336

HARTSOCK, JANE MARIE, nurse, educator; b. Rock Island, Ill., Nov. 19, 1948; d. George Vincent and Patricia Anna (Holland) Woeber; m. Donald Lee Hartsock, Jan. 16, 1971; children: Cara Elizabeth, David Vincent. BS in Nursing, Marycrest Coll., 1977; MA, U. Iowa, 1982. Cert. oncology nurse, clin. nurse specialist. Head nurse U.S. Naval Hosp., Great Lakes, Ill., 1970-71; staff nurse Moline (Ill.) Pub. Hosp., 1971-72, instr. Sch. Nursing, 1977-87; nurse bone marrow transplant unit U. Minn., 1987-92; instr. Mpls. C.C., 1988-92, Trinity Sch. Nursing, 1992-94; staff nurse oncology Trinity Med. Ctr., 1992-2000; assoc. prof. Trinity Coll. Nursing, 1994-2000; med.-surg. clin. nurse specialist McKee Med. Ctr., Loveland, Colo., 2001—. Mem. adj. faculty Marycrest Internat. U., 1998. Contbr. chpt. to book. Song leader, Blue Grass Ch., 1977-87. With USN, 1970-72, maj. Nurse Corps USAR, 1990—. Mem. AAUW, ANA, Nurse Educators Assn. (pres. 1984-85), Oncology Nursing Soc., Internat. Platform Assn., Res. Officer Assn., Nat. Assn. Clin. Nurse Specialists, Pioneer Club (Blue Grass, Iowa, sec. 1983-87), Sigma Theta Tau (pres.). Home: 622 Peach Tree Pl Loveland CO 80538 E-mail: jharts7440@aol.com.

HARTSOCK, JOHN C. communications educator and scholar; b. Silver Spring, Md., Jan. 2, 1951; s. John Kaus and Lydia (Fetler) H.; m. Linda D. Hartsock, Jan. 1, 1997; 1 child, Peter J. BA, Prescott (Ariz.) Coll., 1973; MA, U. Md., 1977; PhD, SUNY, Albany, 1996. Asst. prof. Marist Coll., Poughkeepsie, N.Y., 1989-97; assoc. prof. comm. studies SUNY, Cortland, 1997—. Reporter The Capital, Annapolis, Md., 1982-85, Democrat and Chronicle, Rochester, N.Y., 1985, States News Svc., Washington, 1986-87, UPI, Washington, 1987. Author: A History of American Literary Journalism, 2000; contbr. articles to profl. jours. Recipient Mark Twain award, AP, Balt., 1982, 1983, 1984, Fulbright scholar, 1993. Mem.: Assn. for Edn. in Journalism and Mass Comm. (award for best history 2000), Am. Journalism Historians Assn. (Book of the Yr. award 2000), Sigma Delta Chi (award 1984). Avocations: writing, reading, carpentry. Home: 80 S Main St Homer NY 13077-1623 Office: State Univ of New York PO Box 2000 Cortland NY 13045 E-mail: hartsockj@cortland.edu.

HARTSOCK, LINDA SUE, educational and management association executive; b. St. Joseph, Mo., Feb. 20, 1940; d. Waldo Emerson and Martha (Skelkop) H. BS, Ctrl. Meth. Coll., Fayette, Mo., 1962; MEd, Pa. State U., 1965, EdD, 1971. Cert. assn. exec. Am. Soc. Assn. Execs. Tchr. Jr. High Sch. (North Kansas City (Mo.) Public Sch. System), 1962-63; sr. resident Pa. State U., 1963-64, asst. coordinator residence halls, 1964-65, residence hall coordinator, 1965-66, asst. dean women, 1966-68, asst. dean students, 1968-71; researcher Center for Study Higher Edn., 1971, dir. new student programs, 1971-72; nat. dir. program AAUW, 1972-76; exec. dir. Adult Edn. Assn., 1976-80; now ret. chief exec. officer Integrated Options, Inc., assn., edn. and mgmt. svcs., Greenbackville, Va.; designer tng. and ednl. programs for various orgns. and assn. V.p. fin. Com. for Full Finding Edn., 1979; mem. first adv. panel convened future directions of a learning soc. project Coll. Entrance Exam. Bd., 1978, mem. planning group for Course-By-Newspaper exam. project, 1979; bd. dirs. Coalition Adult Edn. Orgns., 1976; mem. White House Conf. on Aging Planning, 1979; mem. nat. adv. bd. Nat. Center Higher Edn. Mgmt. System Project to Develop a Taxonomy for the Field of Adult Edn., 1978; nat. adv. council on adult edn. Futures and Amendments Project, 1977; adv. Collection of Census Data, Nat. Center Ednl. Stats., 1977; mem. public policy com., program com. chmn. Adv. Council Nat. Orgns. to Corp. for Public Broadcasting, 1976; adv. devel. New Mediated Programs, Office Instructional Resources, Miami Dade Community Coll., 1976; mem. innovative awards com. Nat. Univ. Extension Assn., 1977; field reader U.S. Dept. Edn., 1981-83 Mem. editl. bd. Off to Coll. mag. 1972-74; contbr. articles to profl. jours. Mem. Greenbackville Va. Fire Dept. Women's Aux., 2000—; mem. aquatics com. Lower Shore UMCA, Pocomoke City, Md., 2003; mem. aquaitics com. Lower Shore YMCA, 2002—. Recipient Disting. Alumni award Central Meth. Coll., 1978. Mem. Am. Soc. Assn. Execs. (individual membership coun. 1979-81, edn. com. 1985-88, 92-94, univ. affairs commn. 1989-92, awards com. 1991), Washington Women's Forum (budget, program and exec. coms. 1978-82), Alumni Soc. Coll. Edn. Pa. State U. (bd. dirs., chairperson strategic planning com. 1986, Outstanding Alumni award), Aquatics Com.Lower Shore UMCA-Pocomove City, Md.

HARTSOUGH, GAYLA ANNE KRAETSCH, management consultant; b. Lakewood, Ohio, Sept. 16, 1949; d. Vernon W. and Mildred E. (Austin) Kraetsch; m. James N. Heller, Aug. 20, 1972 (div. 1977); m. Jeffrey W. Hartsough, Mar. 12, 1983; 1 child, Jeffrey Hunter Kraetsch Hartsough. BS, Northwestern U., 1971; EdM, Tufts U., 1973; MEd, PhD, U. Va., 1978. Vol. VISTA, Tenn., 1970-71; asst. tchr. Perkins Sch. for the Blind, Watertown, Mass., 1971-72; resource tchr. Fairfax (Va.) County Pub. Schs., 1972-76; asst. dir. ctr. U. Va., Charlottesville, 1976-78; sr. program officer Acad. for Edn. Devel., Washington, 1978-80; mng. cons. Cresap/Towers Perrin, Washington and L.A., 1980-86; pres. KH Consulting Group, L.A., 1986—. Mem. nat. adv. coun. Northwestern U. Sch. Speech, Evanston, Ill., 1992—; cons. in field. Contbr. more than 20 articles to profl. jours. Co-founder L.A. Higher Edn. Roundtable, L.A., 1987-94; mem. nat. adv. coun., co-chair for Sch. of Speech Campaign $1 Billion, Northwestern U.; mem. Coun. 100 Northwestern U., 1999—. Recipient Outstanding Woman of Achievement award Century City C. of C., 1991. Mem. Orgn. Women Execs. (past pres., bd. dirs. L.A. 1986-95).

Home: 15624 Royal Ridge Rd Sherman Oaks CA 91403-4207 Office: KH Consulting Group 1901 Ave Of Stars Ste 1900 Los Angeles CA 90067-6020 Fax: 310-203-5419. E-mail: khcggak@aol.com.

HARTT, GROVER, III, lawyer; b. Dallas, Apr. 12, 1948; s. Grover Jr. and Dorothy June (Wilkins) H. BA with high honors, So. Meth. U., 1970, LLM in Tax, 1986; JD with high honors, Tex. Tech U., 1973. Bar: Tex. 1973, U.S. Dist. Ct. (no. dist.) Tex. 1974, U.S. Dist. Ct. (we. dist.) Tex. 1975, U.S. Ct. Appeals (5th cir.) 1975, U.S. Supreme Ct. 1976, U.S. Dist. Ct. (ea. dist.) Tex. 1999. Law clk. to presiding justice Ct. Criminal Appeals Tex., Austin, 1973-75; atty. Hartt and Hartt, Dallas, 1975-79; atty., advisor Office Spl. Counsel U.S. Dept. Energy, Dallas, 1979-80, dep. chief counsel, 1981-83; trial atty. tax divsn. U.S. Dept. Justice, Dallas, 1983-86, dep. atty.-in-charge tax divsn., 1986-95, asst. chief southwestern region civil trial sect. tax divsn., 1995—. Nat. spkr. on taxation, bankruptcy and litigation. Contbg. author: Collier on Bankruptcy; contbr. articles to profl. jours. Recipient Atty. Gen's award for disting. svc., 1996. Fellow Am. Coll. Bankruptcy; mem. ABA (mem. ct. procedure com. tax sect., chmn. bankruptcy litigation subcom. 1995—, mem. bus. bankruptcy com. bus. law sect., vice chmn. tax and fed. claims subcom. 1996-2000, chmn. 2000—), Tex. Bar Assn., Dallas Bar Assn., Am. Bankruptcy Inst., Coll. of State Bar of Tex., John C. Ford Am. Inn of Ct. (master of the bench 2000—). Office: US Dept Justice Tax Div 717 N Harwood St Ste 400 Dallas TX 75201-6506 E-mail: grover.hartt@usdoj.gov.

HARTUNG, PATRICIA MCENTEE, therapist; b. Syracuse, N.Y. d. James Henry and Frances Julia (Yehle) McEntee; m. Duane James Hartung, July 30, 1960; children: James Joseph, Tamara Ann, John Patrick, Jennifer Lynn. BS, LeMoyne Coll., 1957; MSW, Boston U., 1959. Diplomate Am. Bd. Examiners in Clin. Social Work; lic. social worker, Fla. Social worker Dept. of Pub. Welfare/Child Welfare Div., Bay Shore, N.Y., 1959-60, Dept. Pub. Welfare/Alcohol Rehab. Prog., Omaha, 1961; cons./social worker Carnegie Gardens Nursing Home, Melbourne, Fla., 1970-72; parent educator Brevard Community Coll., Cocoa, Fla., 1968-74; therapist Circles of Care, Rockledge, Fla., 1974-81, program dir. Titusville, 1981-93, therapist, 1981-99; ret., 1999. Adv. com. When Entering New Directions I, Cocoa, 1988—93, 1999—; mem. Family Svc. Planning Team, Titusville, Fla., 1991—93. Mem. NASW, AAUW (Ctrl. Brevard chpt., v.p. membership 1991-93, pres. 1993-95),Acad. Cert. Social Workers. Democrat. Roman Catholic. Avocations: gardening, music, travel.

HARTUNG, ROLF, environmental toxicology educator, researcher, consultant; b. Bremen, Germany, Mar. 1, 1935; came to U.S., 1952, naturalized, 1958. BS in Wildlife Mgmt., U. Mich., 1960, M in Wildlife Mgmt., 1962, PhD in Wildlife Mgmt., 1964. Diplomate Am. Bd. Toxicology. Instr. in wildlife mgmt. U. Mich., Ann Arbor, 1963, lectr. in indsl. health, 1964, asst. prof. indsl. health, 1965—69, assoc. prof. environ. and indsl. health, 1969—73, prof. environ. toxicology, 1973—97, prof. emeritus, 1997—, chmn. toxicology program, 1974—80. Com. or sub-com. mem. Nat. Acad. Scis., 1971-72, 79-97, Mich. Dept. Natural Resources, 1977-97; mem. Mich. Environ. Rev. Bd., 1982-86; mem. hazardous materials com. U.S. Congress Office Tech. Assessment, 1980-83; chmn. com. on environ. effects, transport and fate of sci. adv. bd. EPA, 1982-87, mem. exec. com. of sci. adv. bd., 1982-87. Editor, contbg. author: Environmental Mercury Contamination, 1972; assoc. editor Jour. Toxicology and Indsl. Health, 1984-87, Ency. of Toxicology, 1998; contbr. chpts. to books and articles to profl. jours. Recipient H. M. Wight award U. Mich., 1963; NSF fellow, 1960-64. Mem. Am. Indsl. Hygiene Assn., Mich. Indsl. Hygiene Assn., Soc. Environ. Toxicology and Chemistry, Soc. Toxicology, Wildlife Disease Assn., Wildlife Soc., Sigma Xi, Phi Sigma, Phi Kappa Phi. Home: 3125 Fernwood St Ann Arbor MI 48108-1955 E-mail: rhartung@umich.edu

HARTWELL, LELAND HARRISON, geneticist, educator; b. Los Angeles, Oct. 30, 1939; s. Majorie (Taylor) H.; m. Theresa Naujack. BS, Calif. Inst. Tech., 1961; PhD, MIT, 1964. Postdoctoral fellow Salk Inst., 1964-65; asst. prof. U. Calif., Irvine, 1965-67, assoc. prof., 1967-68, U. Washington, Seattle, 1968-73, prof., 1973—; pres., dir. Fred Hutchison Cancer Rsch. Ctr., Seattle, 1997—. Rsch. prof. Am. Cancer Soc., 1990—. Recipient Eli Lilly award, 1973, NIH Merit award, 1990, GM Sloan award, 1991, Hoffman LaRoche Mattia award, 1991, Gairdner Found. Internat. award, 1992, Simon Shubitz award U. Chgo., 1992, Brandeis U. Rosenstiel award, 1993, Sloan Kettering Cancer Ctr. Katherine Berkan Judd award, 1994, Genetics Soc. of Am. medal, 1994, MGH Warren Triennial prize, 1995, Keith Porter award Am. Soc. Cell Biology, 1995, Carnegie Mellon Dickson award, 1996, Louisa Gross Horwitz prize Columbia U., 1995, Albert Lasker Basic Med. Rsch. award Albert and Mary Lasker Found., 1998, Brinker Internat. award for basic sci. Susan G. Komen Breast Cancer Found., 1998, Disting. Alumni award Calif. Inst. Tech., 1999, City of Medicine award, 1999, medal of honor Am. Cancer Soc., 1999, Léopold Giffuel prize Assn. pour la Recherche sur le Cancer, France, 2000, The Massry prize The Meira and Shaul G. Massry Found., Nobel prize, 2001; Guggenheim fellow, 1983-84; Am. Bus. Cancer Rsch. grantee, 1983—; Am. Cancer Soc. scholar; laureate Passano Found., 1996. Mem. NAS, AAAS, Am. Soc. Microbiology, Am. Soc. Cell Biology, Genetics Soc. Am. (pres. 1990). Office: Fred Hutchinson Cancer Rsch Ctr 1100 Fairview Ave N, PO Box 19024 Seattle WA 98109-4417

HARTWELL, STEPHEN, investment company executive; b. Phila., Apr. 10, 1915; s. Stephen Warren and Elizabeth (Thompson) H.; m. Elizabeth van Laer Speer, Feb. 21, 1946 (div. 1973); children: Stephen Warren II, Robert van Laer; m. Norma Bostick, Dec. 9, 1978. BS in Adminstrv. Engring., Lafayette Coll., 1936. Investment analyst Pa. Co. Banking & Trusts, 1936-41; procurement officer electronic equipment CAA, 1947-48; indsl. specialist AEC, 1948-49, chief progress and stats. sect., prodn. div., 1949-51, chief constr. engring. reports br., 1951-54; exec. v.p. Atomic Devel. Securities Co. (and successor cos.), 1954-68; v.p. Washington Mut. Investors Fund, Inc., 1968-81, pres., 1981-85, chmn., 1985—2001, chmn. emeritus, 2001—. Pres. Washington Investment Advisers Inc., 1992-2001; chmn. emritus Tax Exempt Bond Fund Md., 2001, Tax Exempt Fund Va., 1986-97, chmn. emeritus, 1997—; pres., bd. dirs. Colchester Corp., Woodbridge, Va., 1971—; chmn. WMIF Mgmt. Corp., Washington, 1986— Hartick LLC, 1997—; bd. dirs. Wentz Corp., Wilmington, Del., Johnston Lemon Group Inc.; trustee Ameribanc Investors Group, 1985-95. Mem. Fairfax County (Va.) Planning Commn., 1961-67, chmn., 196466; mem. No. Va. Regional Planning and Econ. Devel. Commn., 1963-64, Fairfax County Rep. Com., 1955-61, 66-70, 79-81; bd. govs. Gunston Hall Sch., Va.; active Mt. Vernon Life Guards, 1992—, chmn., 1998 —; trustee Am. U., 1983-88, trustee emeritus, 1990 ; trustee Woodlawn Found., 1983-89; trustee, treas. Found. for Middle East Peace, 1993—, Fairfax Hosp. Assn., 1986-93; trustee, treas. Inova Health Systems, 1987-96, chmn. investment and pension com., 1997-2002; chmn. Jefferson Hosp., Alexandria, Va., 1986-92; chmn. Virginia Coll. Bldg. Authority, Richmond, Va., 1994-2001; mem. Commonwealth Coun. Richmond, Va., 1998-2002. Maj. AUS, 1941—45. Mem.: NASD (Dist. 10 com. 1968—71), SAR, Nat. Economists Club, Washington Soc. Investment Analysts, Met. Club, Mt. Vernon Country Club, Phi Alpha (pres.), Zeta Psi (trustee Ednl. Found. 1997—, pres. 1999—2000). Home: Riversedge PO Box 33 Mount Vernon VA 22121-0033 Office: AMA Bldg 1101 Vermont Ave NW Fl 12 Washington DC 20005-3583 E-mail: stephcom@msn.com.

HARTWICK, GARY GLENN, entertainment company executive; b. New Orleans, Jan. 8, 1943; s. Glenn Edwin and Viola Rita Hartwick, m. Patricia Jean Brown, 1968 (dec. 1979); m. Nancy Allen Kelly, Feb. 16, 1980; children Timothy T., Jeffrey J. Student, U. Rochester, 1961-69, MBA, 1982; postgrad., U. Denver, 2000—. Sr. engring. programmer Rochester (N.Y.) Applied Sci. Assocs., 1969-71; v.p. software engring. Pi-Rad, Inc., Rochester, 1972-82; mgr. electronics products engring. Scientifia-Atlanta, 1982-87; dir. residental video applications Bellcore, Red Bank, N.J., 1987-93; sr. dir. strategic mktg. DSC Comm., Petaluma, Calif., 1993-94; v.p. tech. and ops. Viacom Inc., N.Y.C., 1994—. Vice chmn. tech. security com. Davic, 1995-98; inst. dir. Nat. Comm. Forum, 1995. Trustee Natural History Mus. of Adirondacks, Tupper Lake, N.Y., 2000—; adviser Paul Smiths (N.Y.) Coll. With USN, USNR, 1961-63. Mem. IEEE, Soc. Motion Picture and TV Engrs. (bd. editors 1989—), Saranac Lake Fish and Game Club, Rochester Yacht Club. Democrat. Episcopalian. Avocations: yacht racing, model railroading, pilot. Home: PO Box 1368 Lake Placid NY 12946 Office: Viacom 1515 Broadway New York NY 10036 E-mail: gary.hartwick@viacom.com.

HARTWICK, THOMAS STANLEY, technical management consultant; b. Vandalia, Ill., Mar. 19, 1934; s. William Arthur and Bernice Elizabeth (Daniels) H.; m. Alberta Elaine Lind, June 10, 1961; children: Glynis Anne, Jeffrey Andrew, Thomas Arthur. BS, U. Ill., 1956; MS, UCLA, 1958; PhD, U. So. Calif., 1969. Mgr. quantum electronics dept. Aerospace Corp., El Segundo, Calif., 1973-75, asst. dir. electonics research lab., 1975-79; mgr. electro-optical devel. lab. Hughes Aircraft Co. subs. Gen. Motors Corp., El Segundo, 1979-82, chief sci. advanced tactical programs, 1982-83; mgr. electro-optics research ctr. TRW Corp., Redondo Beach, Calif., 1983 86, mgr. microelectrics ctr., 1986-90, program mgr., 1990-96. Chmn., bd. dirs. Laser Tech., Inc., Hollywood, Calif., 1990-94; cons. mem. U.S. Dept. Def. Adv. Group on Electronic Devices, Washington, 1977—, group C chmn., 1988-94, main group chmn., 1998—; mem. Japan/U.S. Tech. Assessment Team, Washington, 1984; mem. Army Rsch. Labs. Adv. Bd., 1993-95; bd. dirs. 3D Tech. labs., Inc., IMEC, Inc.; chmn. Nat. Rsch. Coun. FAA Security, 1997-2002, chmn. trans. sec. adminstrn., 2002—; mem. adv. bd. Continuum Ventures, 2000—; chmn. bd. dirs. Cystal Rsch.; mem. tech. adv. bd. Corvis Inc. Contbr. articles to profl. jours.; inventor FAR Infrared Laser, 1975. Mem. Am. Phys. Soc., Optical Soc. Am., (com. mem. 1976-79), Am. Def. Preparedness Assn. (dep. chmn. West Coast seminar 1987-88), mem. Nat. Res. Coun. Comm. Optical Sci and Engring., 1995-99, mem. NAS (nat. assoc. 2002), Nat. Res. Coun. Nat. Materials Adv. Bd. 2000—). Avocations: piano, sports.

HARTWIG, THOMAS LEO, civil engineer, environmental engineer, sports association administrator; b. Pitts., June 16, 1952; s. Leo William and Bertha Barbara (Lukas) H.; m. Cynthia L. Grupp, 1987; children: Adam T. and Megan K. (twins). BSChemE, U. Notre Dame, 1974. Registered profl. engr., Pa., N.Y., Ohio, W.Va. Mgr. infiltration, inflow Killom Assocs., Pitts., 1974-76, ops. engr., 1976-80, mgr. ops. divsn., 1980-81, mgr. ops., assoc., 1981, v.p., 1981-83, v.p., mgr. mcpl. environ. engring., 1983-86, sr. v.p., mgr. mcpl. environ. engring., 1986-96, sr. v.p., gen. mgr., 1996-98, also bd. dirs., exec. v.p., gen. mgr., 1998—; mgr. income Franklin Park Athetlic Assn.; mgr. North Allegheny Basketball Assn.; exec. v.p. Killam Assocs., 2001—; sr. assoc., mngr. We. Pa. office Malcolm Pirnie, Wexford, Pa., 2001—. Commr. Ingomar/Franklin Park Athletic Assn. Mem. NSPE, ASCE, Water Environ. Fedn., Water Environ. Assn. Pa. (program co-chmn. 1983), Engrs. Soc. Western Pa., Profl. Engrs. in Pvt. Practice, Western Pa. Pollution Control Assn. (1st v.p.), Am. Acad. of Environtl. Engr. (diplomate environtl. engring). Democrat. Roman Catholic. Home: 2534 Shellburne Dr Wexford PA 15090-7936 Office: Malcolm Pirnie Inc 7500 Brooktree Dr Ste 300 Wexford PA 15090

HARTY, JAMES D. former manufacturing company executive; b. Bridgeport, Conn., Oct. 5, 1929; s. John S. and Catherine (Lee) H.; m. Margaret O'Connor, June 4, 1955; children: Shaun, Kevin, Maura, Megan. Degree in indsl. engring, U. Bridgeport, 1962. Analyst E.I. DuPont, 1947-51; prodn. control mgr. Sikorsky Aircraft, 1954-62; plant mgr. Stanley Works, 1962-68; corp. mgr. prodn. and inventory control ITT, 1968-70; corp. dir. mfg. projects Singer Co., N.Y.C., 1970-74; pres., chief operating officer Raymond Corp., Greene, N.Y., 1974-84, also dir., now ret.; owner, cons. J.D. Harty Assocs., Hilton Head Island, S.C., 1984-94. Mem. engring. tech. adv. com. and M.B.A. adv. bd. SUNY-Binghamton, mem. found.; mem. Sch. Bd. Found., Hilton Head Island, S.C. 1st lt. U.S. Army, 1951-53, Korea. Recipient Corp. Leadership award MIT, 1987. Mem. Am. Mgmt. Assn. (Internat. Svc. award), Am. Prodn. and Inventory Control Soc. (past internat. v.p. edn. and rsch., Disting. Svc. award), Hilton Head Island Computer Club, Country Club of Hilton Head. Home: 4 Herring Gull Ln Hilton Head Island SC 29926-2655 E-mail: jdharty@adelphia.net.

HARTY, JAMES QUINN, lawyer; b. Phila., Dec. 10, 1925; s. William Lawrence and Marie Sarita (Quinn) H.; m. Ann Elizabeth McGeeney, July 23, 1955; children: Michael, Martha Harty Scheines, Christopher, Patrick, Mark, Paul. AB, LaSalle Coll., 1949; MBA, U. Pa., Phila., 1952, LLB, 1959. Bar: Pa. 1961. Personnel mgr. Corning (N.Y.) Glass Works, 1952-56; lectr. Wharton Sch. U. Pa., Phila., 1956-59; assoc. Reed, Smith, Shaw & McClay, Pitts., 1961-70, ptnr., 1971-95, Plummer DeWalt & Linn, Pitts., 1995—. Research editor: Office Management Handbook, 1958. Mem. Thornburg Zoning Rev. Bd., Thornburg Borough Coun., Pitts., 1968-76. With USN, 1943-46, PTO, CBI. Fulbright lectr. U. Kanazawa, Japan, 1959-60. Mem. Pa. Bar Assn. (chmn. labor sect. 1982), Allegheny Bar Assn., Pitts. Athletic Assn. Clubs: Pitts. (gov. 1986-87), Chartiers Country (Pitts.). Roman Catholic. Avocation: golf. Office: Plummer Harty Owsiany & Archer LLP 57th fl US Steel Tower 600 Grant St Pittsburgh PA 15219-1912 E-mail: jharty@p2law.com.

HARTY, THOMAS H. publishing executive; Advt. dir. Reader's Digest; assoc. pub. TV Guide, N.Y.C., 1998—99, v.p., publisher, 1999—2001; sr. v.p., gen. mgr. Golf Digest Cos., Trumbull, Conn., 2002—. Office: Golf Digest 5520 Park Ave Trumbull CT 06611-3400*

HARTZ, BRIAN DAVID, physical therapist, educator, small business owner; b. Lancaster, Pa., Dec. 15, 1972; s. John F. and Nancy K. Hartz; m. Amy M. Walker, June 9, 2001; 1 child, Zachary W. BSc in Biology, Rider U., 1995; MPT, Hahnemann U., 1998; DPT, Temple U., 2003. Owner/ pres. HARTZ Phys. Therapy, Lititz, Pa., 2000—; adj. prof. Rider U., Lawrenceville, NJ, 1999—2001, Franklin and Marshall Coll., Lancaster, Pa., 2002—. Named Phys. Therapist of the Yr., Lancaster AMBUCS, 2003; recipient AMBUCS Phys. Therapy Scholarship, AMBUCS - Lititz Chpt., 1996—98. Mem.: Pa. Phys. Therapy Assn., Am. Phys. Therapy Assn. Home: 164 Riveredge Dr Leola PA 17540 Office: HARTZ Physical Therapy 100 Highlands Dr Ste 100 Lititz PA 17543

HARTZ, HARRIS L. lawyer; b. Balt., Jan. 20, 1947; s. Alvin Sidney and Muriel (Abrams) H.; m. Deborah Dillingham, July 23, 1977; children— Jacob Cameron, Andrew Samuel. A.B. summa cum laude, Harvard U., 1967, J.D. magna cum laude, 1972. Bar: N. Mex. 1972, U.S. Dist. Ct. N.Mex. 1972, U.S. Ct. Appeals (10th cir.) 1973. Asst. U.S. atty. Dept. Justice, Albuquerque, 1972-75; asst. prof. Coll. Law, U. Ill., Champaign, 1976; atty., exec. dir. Gov.'s Organized Crime Prevention Commn., Albuquerque, 1977-79; assoc. Poole, Tinnin & Martin, P.A., Albuquerque, 1979-82; assoc. Miller, Stratvert, Torgerson & Brandt, Albuquerque, 1982-83, ptnr., dir., 1983-88; judge N. Mex. Ct. Appeals, 1988-99; judge U.S. Court Appeals (10th cir.) Albuquerque, N. Mex., 2001-. Case and devels. editor Harvard Law Rev., 1971-72, editor 1970 71; bd. editors Litigation Mag., 1983-86. Mem. exec. com. Bernalillo County Republican Party, Albuquerque, 1982-83; Rep. nominee for N.Mex. Supreme Ct. elections, 1986, 92, 96; chmn. N.Mex. Racing Commn., 1987-88. Recipient Founders' award Nat. Kidney Found., N.Mex., 1997; nominee Joan Pew award Nat. Assn. State Racing Commrs., 1988. Mem. ABA (mem. adv. com. standing com. law & nat. security 1995-97), Am. Law Inst. (advisor restatement law agy. 1996—), Albuquerque Com. on Fgn. Relations (chmn. 1981-82), Am. Judicature Soc., Rotary Club of Albuquerque (pres. 1996-97), Phi Beta Kappa. Office: 710 US Courthouse 333 Lomas Blvd NW Albuquerque NM 87102*

HARTZ, LUETTA BERTHA, legal secretary; b. Sept. 29, 1947; d. Alfred Bernard Carl and Bertha Martha (Stauffer) Janz; m. James Patrick Hartz, Dec. 31, 1975 (dec. 1995). Student, Madison (Wis.) Bus. Coll., 1965—66. With Employers Ins. of Wausau, Wis., 1966-68; casualty rater Sentry Ins. Co., Stevens Point, Wis., 1968—70, casualty supr., 1970-71, casualty trainer, 1971-72, customer svc. corr., 1972-74, bur. technician, 1974-75, customer svc. and acctg. mgr. Concord, Mass., 1975-79, personal lines property processing mgr., 1979-81, personal lines casualty processing mgr., 1981-83, comml. lines underwriting svcs. mgr., 1983-85, comml. lines ops. mgr., 1985-87; agt. Lewis P. Bither Ins. Agy., Inc., Tewksbury and Tyngsboro, Mass., 1988—90; acct. rep. Brewer & Lord LLC, Acton, Mass., 1990-98, acct. exec., 1998—2001; legal sec. Ruder, Ware & Michler LLSC, Wausau, Wis., 2002—. Campaign treas. Reps., county clk. candidate, Portage County, Wis., 1972. Mem. Nat. Assn. Ins. Women, Mass. Assn. Ins. Women (Middlesex chpt. 1984-96), Maynard Country Club (bd. govs. 1984-86, 96-97). Roman Catholic. Home: 1124 Western Ave Mosinee WI 54455-5202

HARTZ, STEVEN EDWARD MARSHALL, lawyer, educator; b. Cambridge, Mass., July 11, 1948; s. Louis and Stella (Feinberg) H.; m. Janice Lindsay, June 12, 1976. AB magna cum laude, Harvard Coll., 1970; JD, U. Chgo., 1974. Bar: N.Y. 1975, U.S. Dist. Ct. (so. and ea. dists.) N.Y. 1975, U.S. Ct. Appeals (2d cir.) 1975, Fla. 1979, U.S. Dist. Ct. (so. dist.) Fla. 1979, U.S. Tax Ct. 1979, U.S. Ct. Appeals (5th cir.) 1979, U.S. Supreme Ct. 1979, U.S. Ct. Appeals (11th cir.) 1981, U.S. Dist. Ct. (mid. dist.) Fla. 1984. Assoc. Cleary, Gottlieb, Steen & Hamilton, N.Y.C., 1974-79; asst. U.S. atty. U.S. Dept. Justice, Miami, Fla., 1979-82, dep. chief criminal divsn., chief fraud and pub. corruption sect., 1981-82; sole practice Miami, Fla., 1982-90; of counsel Akerman, Senterfitt & Eidson, P.A., Miami, 1980, ptnr., shareholder, 1991— . Lectr. dept. English, U. English, U. Miami, 1984, adj. assoc. prof., 1985-86. Co-author: Housing, A Community Handbook, 1973. Vol. atty. Mobilization for Youth Legal Svcs., N.Y.C., 1978. Recipient Dirs.' award U.S. Dept. Justice, 1981; Fulbright Hays scholar, 1970. Mem. ABA, FBA, Fla. Bar Assn., N.Y. State Bar Assn., Dade County Bar Assn., Assn. Bar City N.Y., Phi Beta Kappa. Office: One Southeast 3rd Ave 28th Fl Miami FL 33131-4943

HARTZELL, ANDREW CORNELIUS, JR., retired lawyer; b. Balt., Nov. 5, 1927; s. Andrew Cornelius and Mary Frances (Milholland) H.; m. Mary Leontine McPhillips, July 31, 1954; children: Andrew Cornelius III, Stephen Carroll, Mary Leontine, James Francis, John Michael, Peter Milholland. BA, Yale U., 1950, LL.B., 1953. Bar. N.Y. 1953, Ohio 1955, U.S. Supreme Ct. Law clk. Fed. Judge Irving R. Kaufman, N.Y.C., 1953-54; assoc. Thompson, Hine & Flory, Cleve., 1954-63, Debevoise, Plimpton, Lyons & Gates, N.Y.C., 1963-65; ptnr. Debevoise & Plimpton and predecessor firms, 1966-96; chmn. litigation dept. Debevoise Plimpton and predecessor firms, 1989-92, of counsel, 1996-98. Author: The Treacherous Snows, 1993; contbr. articles to legal jours. and to Antitrust Advisor, McGraw-Hill Pub. Co., 1971, 78; Note and Comment editor Yale Law Jour, 1952-53. Mem. bd. archtl. rev. Village of Scarsdale, N.Y., 1965-67; mem. Adv. Coun. on Environ. Conservation, 1986-90, chmn., 1987-89; mem. Sch. Facilities Adv. Com., 1988-90; bd. dirs. Friends of Scarsdale Parks, 1991-2000; mem. Scarsdale Bowl com., 2001-02; Bd. Assessment Review, 1998-2003; Rep. candidate for Congress 18th dist. N.Y., 1994. With U.S. Army, 1946-48. Fellow Am. Coll. Trial Lawyers; mem. ABA, Union Internat. des Avocats, Scarsdale Golf Club, Yale Club N.Y., Town and Village Club (Scarsdale), Am. Alpine Club. Roman Catholic. Home: 7 Eastwoods Ln Scarsdale NY 10583-6401 Office: Debevoise & Plimpton 919 Third Ave New York NY 10022-3904

HARTZELL, CHARLES R. research administrator, biochemist, cell biologist; b. Butler, Pa., Aug. 12, 1941; s. Charles R. and Ada Grace (Giles) H.; m. Marguerite K. Getty; children: Scott David, Amy Lynette. BS, Geneva Coll., 1963; PhD, Indiana U., 1967; MDiv, Union Theol. Sem., 2002. Post-doctoral fellow Ind. U., Bloomington, 1967; rsch. fellow Commonwealth Sci. and Industry Rsch. Orgn., Melbourne, Australia, 1967-68; rsch. fellow, asst. rsch. prof. U. Wis., Madison, 1968-71; asst. prof. Pa. State U., University Park, 1971-75, assoc. prof., 1975-78; sr. rsch. scientist Alfred I. DuPont Inst., Wilmington, Del., 1978-80, dir. rsch., 1981-97, Nemours Children's Clinics, Fla., 1987—2001; rsch. mgr. The Nemours Found., Jacksonville, 1987—2001; prof. pediat. Jefferson Med. Coll., Phila., 1989—; dir. Cross Heart Ministries, Inc., Wilmington, 2002—. Contbr. articles to profl. jours. NIH fellow, 1968-70; established investigator Am. Heart Assn., 1970-75. Mem. Am. Soc. Biochemistry and Molecular Biology, Am. Soc. Cell Biology, AAAS. Republican. Presbyterian. Avocations: ballroom dancing, music, carpentry, exercise. Office: Cross-Heart Ministries Inc 34 Colefax Ct Wilmington DE 19804-2950 Fax: 302-636-0190. E-mail: chartzell@juno.com.

HARTZELL, IRENE JANOFSKY, psychologist; d. Leonard S. and Annelies Janofsky; 1 child, Mark Adam. BA, U. Calif., Berkeley, 1963, MA, 1965; PhD, U. Oreg., 1970. Psychologist Lake Washington Sch. Dist., Kirkland, Wash., 1971-72; staff psychologist VA Med. Ctr., Seattle, 1970-71, Long Beach, Calif., 1973-74; dir. parent edn. Children's Hosp., Orange, Calif., 1975-78; clin. psychologist Kaiser Permanente, Woodland Hills, Calif., 1979-94; clin. instr. pediats. U. Calif. Irvine Coll. Medicine, 1975-78. Author: The Study Skills Advantage; contbr. articles to profl. jours. Intern Oreg. Legis., 1974-75. U.S. Vocat. Rehab. Adminstrn. fellow U. Oreg., 1966-67, 69. Mem.: APA.

HARTZELL, JOHN MASON, poet, service technician; b. Hardtner, Kans., Jan. 23, 1945; s. Kenneth and Freda Irene (Hamilton) H. AA in Nursing, Pratt County Jr. Coll., 1965; BA in Sociology, Southwestern Coll., 1973. Svc. technician Automacic Coin Machine Co., Winfield, Kans., 1975—. Contbr. poetry to anthologies and profl. pubis. Recipient numerous awards for poetry, including Nat. Libr. Poetry, Internat. Soc. Poets, Kans. Author's Club. Mem. VFW, Am. Legion. Presbyterian. Avocations: collecting records, horseshoes, poetry. Home: 1434 E 1st Ave Winfield KS 67156-1808

HARTZELL, KARL DREW, retired university dean, historian; b. Chgo., Jan. 17, 1906; s. Morton C. and Bertha V. (Drew) H.; m. Anne Lomas, Sept. 7, 1935; children: Karl Drew, Richard Lomas, Julian Crane; m. Elizabeth Farnum Guibord, Oct. 2, 1993. PhB cum laude, Wesleyan U., 1927; AM, Harvard U., 1928, PhD, 1934. Mem. faculty European history and Western civilization Carleton Coll., 1930-31; mem. faculty European history and western civilization dept. Ga. Sch. Tech., 1935-40; with SUNY, Geneseo, 1940-47; historian N.Y. State War Coun., 1945-46; adminstrv. officer Brookhaven Nat. lab., 1947-52; dean Cornell Coll., Iowa, 1952-56, Bucknell U., 1956-62; acting chief adminstrv. officer SUNY, Stony Brook, 1962-65, adminstrv. officer, 1965-71; libr. Inst. Advanced Studies of World Religions, cons. Author: The Empire State at War: World War II, 1949, Opportunities in Atomic Energy, 1950, A Philosophy for Science Teaching, 1957; editor: The Upperclass Student and His Curriculum, 1955; co-editor: The Study of Religion on the Campus of Today, 1967. Wilbur Fisk scholar, Wesleyan U. Fellow Soc. for Values in Higher Edn. (sr. mem.); mem. Soc. Christian Ethics, Phi Beta Kappa. Republican. Home: Elstead #210 1000 Vicars Landing Way Ponte Vedra Beach FL 32082 Home (Summer): PO Box 166 Shelter Island Heights NY 11965-0166

HARTZLER, GENEVIEVE LUCILLE, physical education educator; b. Hammond, Ind., June 19, 1921; d. Lewis Garvin and Effie May (Orton) H. BS in Edn., Ind. U., 1944; MEd, U. Minn., 1948. Tchr. phys. edn. Griffith (Ind.) Pub. Schs., 1944-45, Northrup Collegiate Sch., Mpls., 1945-47; supr. student tchrs., 1947-79; tchr. phys. edn. Marquette (Mich.) Pub. Schs., 1948-50, Albion (Mich.) Pub. Schs., 1951-56, Jackson (Mich.) Pub. Schs., 1957-79, coord., project dir., tchr., coach, 1979-83. Chair equity workshop Jackson Pub. Schs., 1979-83; chair various convs., 1964-70. Mem. Am. Heart Assn., Jackson, 1977-83; mem., chair Women in Mgmt., Jackson, 1981-83; mem. Bus. and Profl. Women, Jackson, 1980-90. Recipient Honor awards Young Woman's Christian Assn. and Mich. Divsn. Girls and Women's Sports. Mem. AAHPERD, NEA, Mich. Assn. Health, Phys. Edn. and Recreation (Honor award), Mich. Edn. Assn. (Women's Cultural award), Delta Kappa Gamma (Woman of Distinction award). Avocations: golf, swimming, travel, reading. Home: 703 Bay Meadows Cir Lady Lake FL 32159-2285 E-mail: genhar621@webtv.net.

HARTZLER, GEOFFREY OLIVER, retired cardiologist; b. Goshen, Ind., Nov. 6, 1946; s. Robert Willis and Emma Irene (Blosser) H.; m. Lois Anne Kauffman, June 1967 (div. May 1983); children: Abigail, Christine, Amanda; m. Dorothy Eloise Arnn, July 1985. BA, Goshen Coll., 1968; MD with honors, Ind. U., 1972. Diplomate Am. Bd. Internal Medicine, Bd. in Cardiovascular Disease. Intern Mayo Grad. Sch. Medicine, Rochester, Minn., 1972-73, fellow in medicine, 1973-74, fellow in cardiology, 1974-76; assoc. cons. internal medicine and cardiovascular disease Mayo Clinic, Rochester, 1976-77; instr. medicine Mayo Med. Sch. and Grad. Sch. Medicine, Rochester, 1976-79; cons. cardiovascular disease and internal medicine Mayo Clinic and Mayo Found., Rochester, 1977-80; dir. invasive diagnostic electrophysiology Mayo Clinic, Rochester, Minn., 1979-80; cardiologist Cardiovascular Cons., Inc., Kansas City, Mo., 1980-93; clin. prof. medicine U. Mo., Kansas City, 1985-95. Cons. cardiologist Mid-Am. Heart Inst., Kansas City, 1980-95; dir. advanced angioplasty fellowship program St. Luke's Hosp., Kansas City, 1985-92, med. dir. cardiovascular clin. rsch. ctr. Mid-Am. Heart Inst., 1993-95; cons. Advanced Cardiovascular Systems, Inc., Santa Clara, Calif., 1983-95; past mem. editl. or rev. bd. Am. Jour. Cardiology, Jour. Am. Coll. Cardiology, Cath. and CV Diagnosis, others; co-founder Ventritex, Inc., Sunnyvale, Calif., 1985-88, Triax Internat., Inc., Lenexa, Kans., 1989-96; prin., bd. dirs. Kustom Signals, Inc., Lenexa, 1990-96, LMP Steel & Wire Co., Maryville, Mo., 1992—, Hartz Properties, Inc., Prairie Village, Kans., 1993—, Lett Electronics, Inc., Topeka, 1995-98, Intraluminal Therapeutics, Inc., Kansas City, Kans., 1997—. Contbr. articles to profl. jours., chpts. to books; made TV presentations to lay people on aspects of cardiology. Recipient KK Chen award, 1970, E.V. Allen scholarship, 1971, Osler award U. Miami, 1986, 1st Ann. Career Achievement award Cardiol. Rsch. Found., 1994. Fellow Am. Coll. Cardiology, Coun. on Clin.

Cardiology of Am. Heart Assn., Soc. for Cardiac Angiography; mem. AMA, Mo. State Med. Assn., Jackson County Med. Assn., Am. Heart Assn., Alpha Omega Alpha. Avocations: music, motorcycling, reading, traveling, business. Office: 2600 Verona Rd Shawnee Mission KS 66208-1266

HARTZOG, IRA BARNES, aviation executive; b. Hobart, Okla., July 15, 1918; s. Ira Barnes, Sr. and May Bentley (Arnold) H.; m. Ruth Jane Thompson; children: Ira B. III, Clarice Mears, Betty Roth, Nancy Anderson. Cert. airline transport pilot FAA, flight instr. Flt. instr. Coleman (Tex.) Flying Sch., 1941-42; pilot Air Transport Command, worldwide, 1943-46; tng. capt. Pan Am. Airways, Latin Am., 1946-48; pilot Irvin Air Chute, Inc., Buffalo, N.Y., 1949-52; chief divsn. mgr. Butler Corp., Dallas, 1952-55; founder Flt. Proficiency Svc., Inc., Ft. Worth, Tex., 1954-55; divsn. mgr. Butler Co., Chgo., 1955-60. Founder, CEO Hartzog Aviation, Inc., Rockford, Ill., 1960-84, Airmanship, Inc., Ill., Calif. and Ariz., 1978-99; adv. bd. Beech Aircraft Corp., Wichita, 1960-64, So. Ill. Univ., Carbondale, 1980-84. Prodr.: (video tapes) Aviation Safety Tng. Video Tapes (24 titles), 1980-97; contbr. articles to profl. jours. Mem. Quiet Bird Men, 1957-2002, Hump Pilot's Assn., 1958-2002, Retired Officer's Assn., 1959-2002. Decorated Disting. Flying Cross, U.S. Army Air Forces, Air medals, Theater ribbons, others. Mem. Nat. Bus. Aircraft Assn. (disting., bd. dirs. 1962-63). Avocations: reading, travel, video production, writing. Home: 13840 W Elmbrook Dr Sun City West AZ 85375-5427 E-mail: iragoz@aol.com.

HARUTUNIAN, ALBERT T(HEODORE), III, judge; b. San Diego, May 15, 1955; s. Albert Theodore Jr. and Elsie Ruth H.; m. Rebecca Blair, 1999. BA, Claremont McKenna Coll., 1977; JD, U. Calif., Berkeley, 1980. Bar: Calif. 1980, U.S. Dist. Ct. (so. dist.) Calif. 1980, U.S. Ct. Apppeals (9th cir.) 1982, U.S. Supreme Ct. 1984. Law clk. to Hon. Howard B. Turrentine U.S. Dist. Ct., San Diego, 1980-81; assoc. Luce, Forward, Hamilton & Scripps, San Diego, 1982-87, ptnr., 1988-95; judge San Diego Mcpl. Ct., 1995-98, San Diego Superior Ct., 1998—. Spl. counsel standing com. on discipline U.S. Dist. Ct. Calif., San Diego, 1983-85; chmn. San Diego Bar Labor and Employment Sect., 1988-89; chmn. fed. cts. com. Calif. State Bar, 1989-90. Bd. dirs. ARC San Diego chpt., 1992-2002, Crime Victims Fund, 1995-97; bd. govs. Muscular Dystrophy Assn., San Diego, 1985; grad. LEAD Inc., San Diego, 1986; planning com. San Diego United Way, 1986-92. Named one of Outstanding Young Men of Am., 1983; recipient Outstanding Service award 9th Cir. Jud. Conf., 1986. Mem. ABA, Calif. State Bar Ct. (referee 1985-88), Am. Arbitration Assn. (arbitrator 1986-95), Calif. Judges Assn. (mem. criminal law and procedure com. 1997-2000), Boalt Hall Alumni Assn. (bd. dirs. 1994-97), Claremont McKenna Coll. Alumni Assn. (founding dir. San Diego chpt. 1984-2000), Rotary (bd. dirs. San Diego club 1995—). Republican. Avocations: music, golf. Office: San Diego Superior Ct PO Box 122724 San Diego CA 92112-2724

HARVARD, RITA GRACE, real estate agent, volunteer; b. Aurora, Ill., June 28, 1929; d. Walter Scott Fredenhagen and Grace Lucille Towsley-Fredenhagen; m. Anton Castagnoli (div. Mar. 10, 1978); children: Susan G., Jodie A., Thomas A.; m. John Francis Harvard. BA, Monmouth Coll., 1951. Educator 5th grade Dixon (Ill.) Pub. Sch., 1951—53; real estate mgr. Naperville (Ill.) Prince Castles Co., 1972—85; sec.-treas. Naperville Creamery Co., 1985—2000. Part-time vol. asst. tchr. Naperville Pub. Sch. Sys., 1968. Trustee North Ctrl. Coll., 1982—; mem. instnl. rev. bd. Edward Hosp., Naperville, 1992—; active Bd. Fire and Police Commr., City of Naperville, Ill., 1996—; trustee Naperville YMCA, 1996—; active Naperville Century Walk Bd., 1999—; trustee Monmouth Coll., Ill., 1974—81; hon. chmn. annual benefit Naperville United Way, 1988; bd. mem. Grace Meth. Ch. Found., 1993—, Naperville Heritage Soc., 1970—75, 1980—85, Grade Sch. and Jr. High Home and Sch. Assns., 1965—75, DuPage County Hist. Soc., 1975—78, Original Naperville Recycling Ctr., 1970—75, Edward Hosp. Aux., 1955—61. Named Outstanding Woman Leader of DuPage County, YWCA/DuPage, 1995; recipient Disting. Svc. award, Naperville Jaycees, 1993, Gael D. Swing award for meritorious svc., North Ctrl. Coll., 1995, Naperville Family Spirit award, 1997, Crystal award, Citibank Naperville, 1997, Outstanding Alumna award, Naperville Ctrl. H.S., 1998. Mem.: LWV, AAUW (Woman of Yr. award Naperville br. 1988), PEO, Naperville Heritage Soc. (Outstanding Svc. award 1999—2000), Rep. Women's Club, Rotary Club Naperville (chmn. membership devel. 1992—2000, cmty. svc. and membership devel. com. 1998—2002, past pres. 1994—95, Rotarian of Yr. award 1995). Methodist. Home: 439 LeProvence Cir Naperville IL 60540

HARVER, ANDREW ROBERT, psychology educator; b. Youngstown, Ohio, Oct. 29, 1955; s. Andrew and Eleanor Dzuracky H.; m. Nancy Hall Harver, June 30, 1984; children: Philip, Emma. BS, U. Wash., 1979; MS, Ohio U., 1982, PhD, 1984. Postdoct. fellow Dartmouth Med. Sch., 1984-87; rsch. asst. prof. SUNY, Stony Brook, 1987-91; asst. prof. to prof. U. N.C., Charlotte, 1991—, interim assoc. dean the grad. sch., 2001—02, chair dept. health behavior and adminstrn., 2002—. Editl. bd. Chest, 1999—; co-editor: Self-Management of Asthma, 1998; contbr. articles to profl. jours. including Psychophysiology, Biological Psychology, Am. Jour. of Respiratory and Critical Care Medicine. Mem. Am. Thoracic Soc. (program chair BS assembly 1999-2000), Internat. Soc. for the Advancement of Respiratory Psychophysiology (pres. 1999-2000). Avocations: camping, gardening, traveling, antiques. Office: UNC Charlotte 9201 University City Blvd Charlotte NC 28223-0001 E-mail: aharver@carolina.rr.com., arharver@email.uncc.edu.

HARVEY, A. RAYMOND, mathematician, educator; b. Lewiston, Maine, Jan. 12, 1921; s. J. Edward and Eva B. (Langelier) Harvey; 1 child, Heather De Geus. BS, Bates Coll., Lewiston, Maine, 1942; PhD, Harvard U., 1947. Tchg. fellow Harvard U., Cambridge, Mass., 1943—46; from instr. to asst. prof. U. N.H., Durham, 1946—48; rsch. fellow Calif. Inst. Tech., Pasadena, Calif., 1948—49; from asst. prof. to full prof. math. San Diego State U., 1949—92, prof. emeritus, 1992—. Fulbright lectr. U. Baghdad, Iraq, 1958—59; vis. prof. Coll. of the V.I., Charlotta-Amalia, 1963. Mem.: Math. Assn. Am., Am. Math. Soc. Home: 2350 Calle de la Garza La Jolla CA 92037

HARVEY, ALBERT C. lawyer; m. Nancy Rutherford; children: Anne, Elizabeth. BS, U. Tenn., 1961, JD, 1967. Law clk. Tenn. Supreme Ct.; asst. to pub. defender Shelby County, 1969-71; ptnr. Thomason, Hendrix, Harvey, Johnson & Mitchell, Memphis. Instr. med. and dental jurisprudence U. Tenn., Memphis. Bd. editors Tennessee Law Review. Pres. Goodwill Boys Club, 1983-85; active YMCA, Arthritis Found., Citizens Assn. Memphis and Shelby County, Shelby County War Memls.; sr. warden of vestry Calvary Episcopal Ch. Maj. gen. USMCR, comdg. gen. 4th Marine divsn. Recipient Sam A. Myar, Jr. award Tenn. Bd. Law Examiners, 1978. Fellow: Tenn. Bar Found. (pres. 1993—94), Am. Bar Found. (life); mem.: Memphis Area C. of C. (pres. mil. affairs coun.), Am. Inns. of Ct., Memphis Bar Assn. (v.p. 1989, pres. elect 1990, pres. 1991, pres. young lawyers divsn.), Tenn. Bar Assn. (bd. govs., pres. young lawyers conf., pres. 2002—03), Am. Bd. Trial Advocates (adv.), Am. Judicature Soc. (nat. bd. dirs.), ABA (bd. govs., ho. dels. charter mem. and coun. sect. litigation, young lawyers sect., fellow young lawyers divsn., com. on ethics and profl. responsibility, ethics 2000 spl. com.), Ctrl. Garden Area Assn. (pres.), Univ. Club Memphis (pres.), Kiwanis, Phoenix Club (1st v.p.), Navy League, U. Tenn. Nat. Alumni Assn. (pres. Memphis chpt., nat. bd. govs.). Office: 1 Commerce Sq 29th Fl Memphis TN 38103

HARVEY, ALEXANDER, II, federal judge; b. Balt., May 3, 1923; s. Fred B. and Rose (Hopkins) H.; m. Mary E. Williams, Feb. 24, 1951; children: Elizabeth H., Alexander IV. BA, Yale U., 1947; LLB, Columbia U., 1950. Bar: Md. 1950. Assoc. Ober, William, Grimes & Stinson, Balt., 1950-66, ptnr., 1953-66; asst. atty. gen. Md., 1957-58; judge U.S. Dist. Ct. Md., 1966-86, chief judge, 1986-91, sr. judge, 1991—. Mem. Gov.'s Com. To Study Blue Sky Law of Md., 1961; mem. character com. Ct. Appeals Md. for 8th Jud. Cir. Bd. dirs. Balt. Symphony Assn., 1966-68; pres., dir. Balt. Opera Guild, 1960; bd. dirs. Balt. Coun. Social Agys., 1957-63; trustee Ch. Home and Hosp., Balt., 1952-71. 1st lt. AUS, World War II, ETO. Mem. Am., Md., Balt. bar assns., Phi Beta Kappa. Episcopalian (vestry 1967-70). Home: 7300 Brightside Rd Baltimore MD 21212-1011 Office: US Dist Ct 101 W Lombard St Ste 404 Baltimore MD 21201-2605

HARVEY, ANDRE, sculptor; b. Hollywood, Fla., Oct. 9, 1941; s. Edmund H. and Jeanne C. (Bright) H.; m. Roberta R. Rush, Jan. 12, 1964. BA, U. Va., 1963. Sculptor, Rockland, Del., 1971—. Exhbns. include: Images of Am. Exhbn., Moscow, London, Paris, The Internat. Ctr. for Wildlife Art, Gloucester, U.K., Nat. Sculpture Soc., N.Y.C., NSS Port of History Mus., Phila., Nat. Acad. of Design, N.Y.C., Tiffany & Co., N.Y.C., Nat. Audubon Soc., N.Y.C., Hunter Mus., Chattanooga, Brandywine River Mus., Chadds Ford, Pa., Gibbes Art Gallery, Charleston, S.C., Phila. Flower Show, Longwood Gardens, Kennett Square, Pa., Contemporary Sculpture at Chesterwood, Stockbridge, Mass., Palazzo Mediceo, Seravezza, Italy, others; selected pub. collections include: Winterthur (Del.) Mus., The Frederik Meijer Gardens, Grand Rapids, Mich., Brandywine River Mus., Chadds Ford, Pa., Botanic Garden Ctr. & Conservatory, Ft. Worth, Tex., MBNA Am., Wilmington, Del., Nature in Art Trust, Gloucester, U.K., U. Va., Charlottesville, Del. Art Mus., Wilmington, Greenville Mus., S.C., others; specific bronze sculptures include: The Apple Thief, Rain Before Morning, Places in the Sun, First Light, Helen, Chloe and Lucinda, Scent of Honeysuckle, Water's Edge, Morning Glory, Spring Ballet, others. Recipient Joel Meissner award Nat. Sculpture Soc., N.Y.C., 1980, Tallix Foundry award, 1989. Fellow: Nat. Sculpture Soc.; mem.: Artist's Equity, Internat. Sculpture Ctr. Avocation: antique automobilia. Home: PO Box 8 Rockland DE 19732-0008 E-mail: info@andreharvey.com.

HARVEY, AUBREY EATON, III, industrial engineer; b. Charlottesville, Va., Oct. 20, 1944; s. Aubrey Eaton Jr. and Jaquelin Ambler (Nicholas) H.; m. Elizabeth Dillard Pettit, June 6, 1964; children: Eleanor Taylor, Philip Ambler. BS, U. Ark., 1966; MA, U. Va., 1970; PhD, U. Ark., 1974. Asst. prof. indsl. engring. dept. Tex. A&M U., College Station, 1973-74; asst. prof. dept. systems analysis Miami U., Oxford, Ohio, 1974-78; analyst computer svc. Norfolk and Western Railway, Roanoke, Va., 1978-80, systems analyst computer svc., 1980-83; ops. rsch. analyst Norfolk (Va.) Southern Corp., 1983-90, sr. ops. rsch. analyst, 1991; rsch. assoc. Va. Polytech Inst. and State U., Blacksburg, 1991-93, rsch. scientist, 1993-94; sr. ops. rsch. analyst Rsch. Mgmt. Cons., Inc., McLean, Va., 1994-95; adv. knowledge engr. Elec. Data Systems Corp., Herndon, Va., 1995-99, sr. sys. analyst, 1999—2002, sr. sys. engr., 2002—. Cons. Ark. Dept. Labor, Little Rock, 1971-72, Ark. Health Systems Found., Little Rock, 1972-73; adj. faculty Va. Polytech Inst. and State U., 1980-85. Contbr. articles to profl. jours. Pres. U. Va. Law and Grad. Young Reps., Charlottesville, 1969; treas. Va. Young Reps., Richmond, 1970, 71. Recipient Hammer award HUD/REAC SASS System. Mem. Inst. Ops. Rsch. and Mgmt. Scis., Inst. Indsl. Engrs. (divsn. dir. 1983-84), Disting. Svc. award 1985), Sigma Xi, Alpha Pi Mu, Omega Rho. Episcopalian. Achievements include development of a track quality index; developed a consensus measure; developed the immigration and naturalization svc. compensation expert system and attorney scheduling expert system; designed a patent and trademark office patent application imaging system; designed the FAA NAS aeronautical information management enterprise system and FAA Air Traffic Control Sys. Command Ctr. web pages. Home: 11019 Saffold Way Reston VA 20190-3804 E-mail: aubrey.harvey@eds.com.

HARVEY, BIRT, retired pediatrician, educator; b. Teheran, Iran, Nov. 24, 1928; five children. BA, Johns Hopkins U., 1948; MD, N.Y.U., 1952. Pvt. practice, 1958-88; prof. pediat. emeritus Stanford U., Palo Alto, Calif., 1995—. Past sr. fellow Inst. Health, Policy Studies, U. Calif., San Francisco. Mem. Inst. Med. Nat. Acad. Scis. (emeritus), Am. Acad. Pediatrics (past pres.), Am. Pediat. Soc. (emeritus).

HARVEY, CHARLES ALBERT, JR., lawyer; b. Beverly, Mass., Sept. 28, 1949; s. Charles A. and Phyllis B. (O'Rourke) H.; m. Whitney Ann Neville, Sept. 21, 1985; children: John Whitney, Charlotte Baird. AB, Assumption Coll., 1971; JD, U. Maine, 1974. Bar: Maine 1974, Mass. 1974, U.S. Supreme Ct. 1979. Assoc. Verrill & Dana, Portland, Maine, 1974-79, ptnr., 1979-95, Harvey & Frank, Portland, 1995—. Assoc. chief counsel President's Commn. on Accident at Three Mile Island, Washington, 1979; mem. adv. com. on civil rules Maine Supreme Jud. Ct., 1978-91, chmn. adv. com. on cameras in trial cts., 1991-93, cons. on civil rules, 1996—, chmn. adv. com. on civil rules, 1987-91; chmn. adv. com. on local rules U.S. Dist. Ct. Maine, 1985—, mem. civil justice adv. com., 1992-97; chmn. Maine Gov.'s Select Com. on Jud. Appointments, 1987-91; mem. Senator Olympia J. Snowe's adv. com. on appointment of U.S. Dist. Judge, U.S. Atty. and U.S. Marshal, 2001-02; chmn. grievance commn. Maine Bd. Overseers of the Bar, 1996-97. Contbr. articles to profl. jours. Trustee Portland Sympnony Orch., 1980-89, pres., 1987-89, adv. trustee, 1989—; trustee Portland Stage Co., 1984-87, adv. trustee, 1987—; trustee Waynflete Sch., 1990-96; adv. trustee Maine Childrens Mus., 1992-1999, Maine Vol. Lawyers for the Arts, 1994-1999. Fellow Portland Mus. of Art, 1993—. Fellow Am. Coll. Trial Lawyers, Maine Bar Found.; mem. Am. Law Inst. Republican. Office: 2 City Ctr Portland ME 04101-4010

HARVEY, CHRISTINE LYNN, publishing executive; b. Bklyn., Dec. 7, 1962; AS in Liberal Arts, Nassau C.C., 1982; BA in Comm. Arts, Adelphi U., 1985. Cert. EMT, 1983-86. Franchise mgr. N.Y. Daily News, Mineola, 1981-84; copywriter, vido prodr., 1984-85; pub. rels. assoc. King Features Syndicate, N.Y.C., 1986; account exec. Promotional Broadcasting Svc., Babylon, N.Y., 1986-87; sr. account mgr. L.I. Bus. News, Ronkonkoma, N.Y., 1987-91; sr. ptnr. Karen Saeger Assocs., Stony Brook, N.Y., 1990—; editor The Steuben News, Ridgewood, N.Y., 1992—; founder, pub., editor-in-chief New Living, Stony Brook, 1991—; pub. rels. cons. Am. Health Found., Valhalla, NY, 1994—96; radio prodr./dir./host New Living Prodns., Stony Brook, 1997—98. Clin. hypnotherapist, Reiki master, 1999; TV prodr. Outlook Mag., 1985; TV news reporter, field prodr. LI News Tonite, 1984. Avocations: running, swimming, cycling, hiking, golf. Office: New Living 1212 Route 25A Ste 1B Stony Brook NY 11790-1919

HARVEY, COLIN EDWIN, veterinary medicine educator; b. Reading, Berkshire, Eng., May 20, 1944; s. Edwin William Alexander and Marian Harvey; m. Catherine Ellen Rein, May 24, 1969; children— Susan Victoria, Edwin Rein. B.V.Sc., F.R.C.V.S., Bristol U., Eng., 1966; MA (hon.), U. Pa., 1974. Intern, resident U. Pa. Sch. Vet. Medicine, Phila., 1966-69, from asst. prof. to assoc. prof., 1969-80, prof. surgery, 1980-92, prof. surgery, dentistry, 1992—, vice chair dept. clin. studies, 1996—2002; adj. prof. U. Pa. Sch. Dental Medicine, Phila., 1984—. Author: Veterinary Dentistry, 1985, Small Animal Surgery, 1990, Small Animal Dentistry, 1993; others; editor: Vet. Surgery, 1982-87, Jour. Vet. Dentistry, 1994-2000. Organizer, commr. Fairmount Soccer League, Phila., 1982-87. Recipient Simon award Brit. Small Animal Vet. Assn., 1983, Bourgelat award, 1994. Fellow Acad. Vet. Dentistry (charter, sec. 1987-89), Coll. Physicians Phila., Royal Coll. Vet. Surgeons; mem. AVMA, Am. Coll. Vet. Surgery (diplomate), Am. Vet. Dental Coll. (diplomate, charter, pres. 1990-92, sec. 2001—, Emily award 1993), Am. Vet. Dental Soc. (sec. 1985-89, Edn. and Rsch. award 1995), Internat. Vet. Ear, Nose and Throat Assn. (co-organiser), European Vet. Dentist Coll. (diplomate). Avocations: reading, walking, watching. Home: 10 Llanfair Rd Apt 2 Ardmore PA 19003-2325 Office: U Pa Sch Vet Medicine 3900 Delancey St Philadelphia PA 19104-4107 E-mail: ceh@vet.upenn.edu.

HARVEY, CYRIL LESLIE, education educator; b. Bagotville, Demerara, Aug. 5, 1950; arrived in U.S., 1971; s. Cyril Leslie Vernon and Lucille Emelda Harvey. BS in Biology and Econs., U. Miami, Fla., 1979; M. Environment Study, Dalhousie U., Halifax, N.S., Can., 1987; MA in Multiculture Edn., Calif. State U. Dominguez, Carson, 1997; MA in Ednl. Curriculum, Calif. State U. Dominguez, 1997; postgrad., Calif. Coast U., Santa Ana, 2000—. Lic. life sci. tchr. Calif. Tchr. Ministry of Edn., Upper Dem Rio, Guyana, 1969—71, West Dem Rio, Guyana, 1975; fisheries officer Ministry of Agr., Georgetown, Guyana, 1980—83; tchr. L.A. Unified Sch. Dist., 1989—. Mem. student ct. judiciary U. V.I., St. Thomas, 1972—73; mem. tchg./coaching team nat. athletics champions Ministry of Edn., Upper Demerara, 1970—71; mem. sch. improvement coun. Henry Clay Mid. Sch./L.A. Unified Sch. Dist., 2000—01; proof reader Jour. of Caribbean Studies, 1987; participating scientistJoint Shrimp Tagging cruise, Western and Caribbean Fisheries Ctr. Brazil, French Guyana, Suriname and Guyana Food and Agr. Orgn., UN. Contbr. Recipient Grad. Fellow award, Dalhousie U., 1985—87, Cert. of Achievement for Application and Diffusion of Rsch., U.S. Dept. Agr., 1982. Mem.: AAAS, Phi Kappa Phi. Avocations: tennis, cricket, bicycling, chess, running. Home: 12920 S Manhattan Pl Gardena CA 90249-1905

HARVEY, DAVID W. humanities educator; b. Gillingham, Kent, Eng., Oct. 31, 1935; s. Frederick Hercules and Doris Maud Harvey; m. Haydee Salmun, Dec. 23, 1998; 1 child, Delfina Eva. BA, St. Johns Coll., Cambridge, England, 1957, MA, PhD, St. Johns Coll., Cambridge, England, 1962; Doctorate (hon.), Buenos Aires U., Argentina, 1997, Roskilde U., Denmark, 1992, Uppsala U., Sweden, 2000. Lectr. U. Bristol, England, 1961—69; from assoc. prof. to prof. Johns Hopkins U., Balt., 1969—90; prof. Oxford U., England, 1987—93; prof. geography Johns Hopkins U., Balt., 1993—2001; prof. anthropology CUNY, 2001—. Author: (book) Explanation in Geography, Social Justice & the City, The Limits to Capital, The Urbanisation of Capital, Consciousness and the Urban Experience, The Condition of Postmodernity, The Urban Experience, Justice, Nature, and the Geography of Difference, Spaces of Hope, Spaces of Capital. Recipient Patron's medal, Royal Geog. Soc., 1995, Anders Retzius Gold medal, Sweden, 1989; Guggenheim fellow, 1987. Home: 30 East End Avenue Apt 5A New York NY 10028-7053 Office: CUNY Graduate Center 365 Fifth Avenue New York NY 10016 E-mail: dharvey@gc.cuny.edu.

HARVEY, DONALD, artist, educator; b. Walthamston, Eng., June 14, 1930; s. Henry and Annie Dorothy (Sawell) H.; m. Elizabeth Clark, Aug. 9, 1952; children— Shan Mary, David Jonathan. Art tchrs. diploma, Brighton Coll. Art, 1951. Art master Ardwyn Grammar Sch., Wales, 1952-56; mem. faculty dept. art U. Victoria, B.C., Can., 1961-95, now prof. emeritus painting. One man exhbns. include, Albert White Gallery, Toronto, 1968, retrospective, Art Gallery of Victoria, 1968; represented in permanent collections, Nat. Gallery Can., Montreal Mus., Albright-Knox Mus., Seattle Art Mus. Mem. accessions com. Art Gallery of Victoria, 1969-72. Can. Council fellow, 1966 Mem. Royal Can. Acad. of Arts (full academician), Can. Group Painters, Can. Painters and Etchers. Home: 1025 Joan Crescent Victoria BC Canada V8S 3L3

HARVEY, DONALD JOSEPH, history educator; b. N.Y.C., Oct. 4, 1922; s. William Harold and Helen (Chiampou) H.; m. Jacqueline Rozendaal, June 11, 1955; 1 child, Nanette. BA cum laude, Princeton U., 1943; MA, Columbia U., 1948, PhD, 1953; postgrad., U. Paris, 1950-51. Instr. Hunter Coll., CUNY, 1951-56, asst. prof., 1956-60, asso. prof., 1960-67, prof. history, 1967-84, emeritus, 1984—, chmn. dept. history, 1968-71. Reader/cons. univ. presses Yale, Cornell, State U. N.Y.; cons. Rockefeller Found. humanities fellowship program, 1974-78, Nat. Endowment for Humanities, 1977-85, Funk & Wagnall's, 1989-91; cons. on hist. TV series Sta. WGBH-TV, Boston, 1987. Author: (with E.M. Earle) Modern France, 1951, France Since the Revolution, 1968, (with W.O. Shanahan) Nationalism: Essays in Honor of Louis Snyder, 1981; assoc. editor: (with H. Rowen) Reviews in European History, 1973-79; contbr. articles to profl. jours. Served to capt., arty. AUS, 1943-46, ETO. Ford Found. fellow, 1954-55; Fulbright alternate, 1959-60 Mem. Am. Hist. Assn., Soc. for French Hist. Studies, AAUP, Phi Alpha Theta. Home: 666 Main St Apt 404 Winchester MA 01890-1959 Office: 695 Park Ave New York NY 10021-5024

HARVEY, DONALD PHILLIPS, retired naval officer; b. Geddes, S.D., Jan. 24, 1924; s. Ernest Lyle and Beryl (Phillips) H.; m. Deborah Stults, Dec. 13, 1952; children: Craig, Lynn, Reid, Anne. BS, U.S. Naval Acad., 1947; MA, MALD, Fletcher Sch. Law and Diplomacy, 1961. Commd. ensign U.S. Navy, 1947, advanced through grades to rear adm., 1973, service as fleet intelligence officer in Pacific; service in CIA, NSA, Bahrain, DIA; dir. Naval Intelligence, Washington, 1976-78; dir. program requirements TRW, Washington, 1978-89. Cons. ONI, DIA, NSA. Chmn. bd. Inst. Intelligence Edn. Decorated DSM, Legion of Merit, Meritorious Service medal, Joint Commendation medal (2), Navy Commendation medal (2). Mem. U.S. Naval Inst., Nat. Mil. Intelligence Assn. (emeritus bd. dirs.), Assn. Former Intelligence Officers (ex-pres., ex-chmn.). Republican. Episcopalian. Home: 440 Island Circle Sarasota FL 34242-1940 E-mail: ddharvey@comcast.net.

HARVEY, DOUGLASS COATE, retired photographic company executive; b. Batavia, N.Y., Aug. 28, 1917; s. Homer A. and Dells S. Harvey; m. Elizabeth Kellas, June 27, 1942; children: Robert, Anne, Katharine, Douglass Coate Jr. BSME with highest distinction, Purdue U., 1939, DEng (hon.), 1982. With Eastman Kodak Co., Rochester, N.Y., 1939-82, dir. corp. product devel., 1970-73, v.p., gen. mgr. apparatus divsn., 1973-77; exec. v.p., gen. mgr. Eastman Kodak Co. (mgr. U.S. and Canadian photog. divns.), 1977-82; ret., 1982. Commr. Monroe Co. Case Commn. Former trustee Alfred (N.Y.) U.; former exec. bd. Otetiana (N.Y.) coun. Boy Scouts Am.; former chmn. bd. dirs. Rochester and Monroe County YMCA, nat. bd. dirs., 1979-81; ret. chmn. engring. adv. coun. Clarkson U., Potsdam, N.Y.; former bd. mgrs. Meml. Art Gallery; trustee Internat. former Mus. Photography, Adirondack Pk. Inst., Inc., former bd. dirs. George Eastman Ho. Mus. Photography. Named Outstanding Mech. Engr., Purdue U., 1991. Mem. Nat. Acad. Engring., Optical Soc. Am., Photog. Soc. Am., Soc. Photog. Scientists and Engrs., Rochester Engring. Soc., Rochester C. of C., Nat. Security Indsl. Assn. (ret., trustee 1973-78), Rochester Country Club (former mem. bd. stewards), Genesee Valley Club, Lake George Club (Diamond Point, N.Y.), Rotary, Tau Beta Pi, Pi Tau Sigma. Republican. Home: 3155 East Ave Rochester NY 14618-3427 E-mail: dch25@juno.com.

HARVEY, ELIZABETH SCHROER, lawyer; b. Rockford, Ill., June 17, 1960; d. Philip Paul and E. Rebecca (Whisler) Schroer. BA in History and Polit. Sci., U. Iowa, 1982; JD, So. Ill. U., 1986. Bar: Ill. 1986, U.S. Dist. Ct. (no. dist.) Ill. 1990, U.S. Dist. Ct. (cen. and so. dists.) Ill. 1995. Rsch. atty. Ill. Supreme Ct., Springfield, 1986-87; atty. Ill. Pollution Control Bd., Chgo., 1987-95; environ. ptnrs. McKenna, Storer, Rowe, White & Farrug, Chgo., 1995-2001, Swanson, Martin & Bell, Chgo., 2001—. Contbr. articles to profl. publs. Mem. Environ. Law Inst., So. Ill. U. Law Alumni Assn.,U. Iowa Alumni Assn. Office: Swanson Martin & Bell 1 IBM Plz Ste 2900 Chicago IL 60611 E-mail: eharvey@smbtrials.com.

HARVEY, ELTON BARTLETT, III, lawyer; b. Albany, N.Y., Oct. 26, 1946; s. Elton Bartlett Jr. and Marjorie Irene (Johnson) H.; children: Tamilyn, Jocelyn Janel, Josiah Bartlett, James Mullen, Benjamin Dante. BA, U. Conn., 1969; MA, U. New Haven, 1976; JD, Western New Eng. Coll., 1986. Bar: Conn. 1986, U.S. Dist. Ct. Conn. 1986. Title officer Conn. Atty.'s Title Ins. Co., Rocky Hill, Conn., 1980-83; counsel, mgr. Safeco Title Ins. Co., Hartford, Conn., 1983-87, Am. Title Ins. Co., Hartford, 1987-88; prin. Osborne & Harvey, Farmington, 1988-95; ptnr. Harvey Law Assocs., Farmington, 1995—. Mem. ABA, Conn. Bar Assn. Office: Harvey Law Assocs 3 Melrose Dr Farmington CT 06032-2249 E-mail: ebh@harveylaw1.com.

HARVEY, GLENN FRANCIS, association manager; b. Tarentum, Pa., May 10, 1940; s. Howard F. and Evelyn H.; m. Linda M. Herr, Mar. 19, 1960; children: Jeffrey Howard, Lisa Anne. BSEd., Slippery Rock State Coll., 1961; M.Ed., Duquesne U., 1964; MBA, U. Pitts., 1975. Tchr. Fox Chapel Area Schs., Pitts., 1961-67; exec. dir. Instrument Soc. Am., Research Triangle Park, NC, 1967-99; cons., 1999—2003; exec. dir. Am. Ceramic Soc., Westerville, Ohio, 2003—. Mem. Am. Soc. of Assn. Execs., Coun. Engring. and Sci. Soc. Execs. Republican. E-mail: glennharvey@worldnet.att.net.

HARVEY, GLORIA-STROUD, physician assistant; b. Washington, D.C., Apr. 16; d. Robert W. and Ruth Elizabeth (Brown) Stroud; m. Jimmy Lawrence Harvey; children: Dana, Daman, Byron, Justin. BS, U. Md., 1968; physician asst. cert., Howard U., 1977. Physician asst. Weaver Clinic, Ahoskie, N.C., 1977-80, Western State Hosp., Staunton, Va., 1980-84, Walter Reed Army Med. Ctr., Washington, 1984-91, John Amsted Hosp., Butner, N.C., 1991—, U. N.C., Chapel Hill, 1991—. Physician asst. Aroyga, Durham, N.C., 1992—, Maria Parham Hosp., Henderson, N.C. Bd. dirs. Unique Builders, Henderson N.C., 1994-95, Cultural Initiatives, 1995. Mem. Am. Bus. Women's Assn., N.C. State-Employed Physician Assts.' Assn. (chmn. 1994), Triangle Assn. for Physician Assts., N.C. Assn. for Physician Assts. Methodist. Home: 2693 Hidden Spring Ln Oxford NC 27565-6146

HARVEY, GORDON EARL, historian, educator, writer; s. Gordon Lee and Georgia Stewart Harvey; m. Marie Mignon Horn, July 28, 1990; children: Preston Stewart, Hudson Andrews. BS, MA, U. of Ala. at Birmingham, 1994; PhD, Auburn U., 1998. Asst. prof. of history U. of La., Monroe, 1999—. Vis. instr. Auburn U., 1998—99. Author: (historical monograph) A Question of Justice: New South Governors and Education, 1968-1976. Named Tchr. of the Yr., Student Govt. Assn., U. La. at Monroe, 2001, Top Ten Outstanding Prof.,

Alpha Lambda Delta, 2002, Outstanding Prof., Auburn U. Panhellenic Coun., 1999, 1999. Mem.: Phi Kappa Phi (assoc.), Phi Alpha Theta (assoc.; chpt. adviser 2000—03). Office: Univ Louisiana at Monroe 700 University Ave Monroe LA 71201

HARVEY, GREGORY MERRILL, lawyer; b. Morris Twp., N.J., Jan. 6, 1937; s. Merrill Piercy and Dorothy Ceola (Gregory) H.; m. Emily Mitchell Wallace, June 14, 1969. AB, Harvard U., 1959; JD, Harvard Law Sch., 1962. Bar: Pa. 1963. Assoc. Morgan, Lewis & Bockius, Phila., 1962-69, ptnr., 1969-99, Montgomery, McCracken, Walker & Rhoads, Phila., 1999—. Chmn. City of Phila. Bd. Ethics, 1984-91; trustee Fairmount Park Art Assn., Phila., 1981—; co-chmn. 8th Ward Dem. Exec. Com., Phila., 1984—; bd. dirs. Ams. for Dem. Action Southeastern Pa. chpt., 1966-, bd. dirs. Conservation Ctr. Art and Historic Artifacts, Phila., 1995-. Recipient James Madison award Soc. Profl. Journalists, 1986, Judge Learned Hand Human Rels. award Am. Jewish Com., 1991. Fellow Am. Coll. Trial Lawyers; mem. ABA, Pa. Bar Assn., Phila. Bar Assn., Phila. Club, Franklin Inn (Phila.), Merion Cricket Club (Haverford, Pa.), Racquet Club (Phila.), Phi Beta Kappa. Home: 1939 Panama St Philadelphia PA 19103-6609 Office: Montgomery McCracken et al 123 S Broad St Philadelphia PA 19109-1099 E-mail: gharvey@mmwr.com.

HARVEY, JAMES CARDWELL, political science educator, consultant; b. Italy, Tex., July 15, 1925; s. Fred N. and Ola Victoria (Whitt) Harvey; m. Lillian Smith Harvey, July 11, 1974; children: Nakea, Jasmine;1 child from previous marriage, Nancy. BA, So. Meth. U., 1949; MA, U. Tex., Austin, 1952; PhD, U. Tex., 1955; MA, U. Ariz., 1969. Asst. prof. Pan Am. U., U. Tex., El Paso, 1957—64; assoc. prof. Ft. Lewis Coll., 1964—65; assoc. prof., chmn. dept. Western N.Mex. U., 1965—68; prof. Coll. Artesia, 1969—70, Jackson State U., 1970—74, 1975—2001; HUD fellow, 1974—75; prof. pub. adminstrn. Miss. Valley State U., 2001—03; prof. history Judson State U., 2003—. Cons. HUD, 1976, Hinds City Bd. Suprs. Author: Civil Rights During the Kennedy Administration, 1971, Black Civil Rights During the Johnson Administration, 1973; contbr. Mem. resources bd. Jackson Cmty. Housing; bd. dirs. Jackson Urban League, 1981—82. With USNR, 1942—46, PTO. Fulbright scholar to France, 1952—53, HUD fellow, 1974—75. Mem.: Am. Soc. Pub. Adminstrn. Democrat. Episcopalian.

HARVEY, JAMES GERALD, educational counselor, consultant, researcher; b. California, Mo., July 15, 1934; s. William Walter and Exie Marie (Lindley) H. BA Amherst Coll., 1956; MAT (fellow), Harvard U., 1958, MEd, 1962. Asst. to dean grad. sch. edn. Harvard U., Cambridge, Mass., 1962-66, dir. admissions, fin. aid, 1966-69; dir. counseling service U. Calif., Irvine, 1970-72; ednl. cons., Los Angeles, 1972—. Author: (ednl. materials) HARVOCAB Vocabulary Program, 1985—. 1st lt. USAF, 1958-61. Amherst Mayo-Smith grantee, 1956-57; UCLA Adminstrv. fellow, 1969-70. Mem. Am. Ednl. Research Assn., Nat. Council Measurement in Edn. Address: 1845 Glendon Ave Los Angeles CA 90025-4653

HARVEY, JAMES MATHEWS, JR., communications specialist; b. Detroit, Dec. 5, 1964; s. James M. and Leotha (Frazier) Harvey; m. Leesa Ann Hatch, June 10, 2000; 1 child, James (Trey) III. BS, Troy State U., 1987. Media assoc. Ctr. for Environ. Rsch., Troy, Ala., 1987-88; prodr., dir. Coop. Ext. Svc. (became Coop. Ext. Sys. 1995), Auburn, Ala., 1988—99; media coord. Ala. Indsl. Devel. Tng., Montgomery, 1999—2001; pub. comms. specialist Shelby County Ala. Govt., Columbiana, 2001—. Dir. videos including: Nature's Way, 1988, Red Drum: A Struggle for Survival, 1989, Pond Management, 1991; slide series including: Nature's Way, 1988, Beach Mice and Their Habitat, 1989; dir., editor Safety in the Logging Woods series, 1989-95, Forestry in Alabama, 1993, Small Business Resources Series, 1995, Adult Education Principles for Loggers, 1996, Multiple Use Management, 1996; assoc. producer, dir. Extension Today, 1990; assoc. producer satellite programs Principles of Parenting and State of Our Environment, 1991, White-Tailed Deer Management, 1991-92, Residential Landscaping, 1992, Small Business Resources, 1994, Wildlife Damage Management, 1995, Alabama Forest Resources Today, 1996; creator, prodr. Ala. 4-H Congress Video, 1990-99, 4-H Performing Arts Video, 1993-99; prodr., dir. Street Trees and Sewing Update for Entrepreneurs, 1994, Tax Fraud Prevention, 1995, AU Presents, 1998; guest columnist The Messenger, 1993-94. Mem. agrl. adv. com. Pike County H.S., Brundidge, Ala., 1983-95, pres. 1995-2000; bd. dirs. Pike County Agrl. Complex Bd., 1996. Mem. Nat. Assn. County Info. Officers, Troy State U. Journalism Alumni Assn. Baptist. Avocations: music, movies, tennis, model trains. Home: 1332 Waxwing Trl Alabaster AL 35007-9027 Mailing: PO Box 1151 Troy AL 36081-1151 Office: Shelby County Planning 115 County Svcs Dr Pelham AL 35124-6128

HARVEY, JOHN ADRIANCE, psychology and pharmacology educator, researcher, consultant; b. N.Y.C., Oct. 14, 1930; s. John Adriance Harvey and Paula Ann (Truhar) Oestreich; m. Rhoda S. Sadigur, Dec. 20, 1958; children: David Alexander, Andrew Martin, Michael Allen. AB, U. Chgo., 1955, PhD, 1959. Research assoc. U. Chgo., 1959-61, asst. prof., 1961-67, assoc. prof., 1967-68; prof. psychology and pharmacology U. Iowa, Iowa City, 1968-88; prof. pharmacology and physiology, chief div. behavioral neurobiology Drexel U. Coll. Medicine, Phila., 1988—. Guest worker Maudsley Hosp., London, 1966-67; chmn. biopsychology rsch. rev. com. NIH, 1983-85; chmn. behavioral neurobiology rsch. rev. com. NIMH, 1986-90, mem. adv. panel; mem. extramural sci. adv. bd. Nat. Inst. on Drug Abuse, 1990—. Author: Behavioral Analysis of Drug Action, 1971, (with Barry Kosofsky) Cocaine: Effects on the Developing Brain; editor Jour. Pharmacology and Exptl. Therapeutics, 1990-98; contbr. numerous articles to profl. jours. Recipient Rsch. Devel. award, NIMH, 1963—68, Rsch. Scientist award, 1969—74. Fellow APA (pres. divsn. 28 1984-85), Am. Coll. Neuropsychopharmacology; mem. Am. Soc. for Pharmacology and Exptl. Therapeutics (editl. adv. bd.), Soc. for Neurosci. (fin. com.), Soc. for Neurochemistry, European Soc. for Neurochemistry, Pavlovian Soc., Soc. for Biol. Psychiatry, Behavioral Pharmacol. Soc. (pres. 1996-98). Home: 1 Druim Moir Ct Philadelphia PA 19118 Office: Drexel U Coll Medicine Dept Pharmacology/Physiol 245 N 15th St Mail Stop 488 Philadelphia PA 19102 E-mail: john.harvey@drexel.edu.

HARVEY, JOHN COLLINS, physician, educator; b. Youngstown, Ohio, Sept. 11, 1923; s. J. Paul and Mary J. (Collins) H.; m. Adele Dillon, Nov. 26, 1949; children: Elizabeth V.R. (Mrs. Charles Yon), John Collins Jr., William Charles II, Amy L.R. (Mrs. L. F. Reese), Margaret J.B. (Mrs. Gregory Granitto). Grad., Phillips Exeter Acad., 1941; BS, Yale U., 1944; MD, Johns Hopkins U., 1947, MLA, 1968; MAS, Johns Hopkins, 1974; MA, St. Mary's U., 1975, PhD in Theology, 1988; DSc (hon.), Barry U., 1992. Diplomate: Am. Bd. Internal Medicine. Successively house officer, asst. resident, resident Osler Med. Service, Johns Hopkins Hosp., 1947-53, physician, 1953-73; successively instr., asst. prof., asso. prof., prof. medicine Johns Hopkins, 1953-73; prof. medicine Georgetown U., Washington, 1973-89, prof. medicine emeritus, 1989—; sr. rsch. scholar Kennedy Inst. of Ethics, Georgetown U., Washington, 1989—, Ctr. for Clin. Bioethics, Georgetown Med. Ctr., 1993—. Vis. prof. medicine U. Ibadan, Nigeria, 1964; hon. assoc. prof. medicine Guy's Hosp., London, 1973 Co-editor: Catholic Perspectives on Medical Morals, Catholic Studies in Bioethics; Contbr. articles to profl. publs. Mem. various local, state and nat. govt. med. adv. coms.; trustee emeritus Washington Home for Incurables, mem. emeritus med. adv. com. Sacred Congregation for Causes of Saints, Holy See, Vatican City. Col. (ret.) M.C., USAR. A. Blaine Brower Traveling fellow ACP to Guy's Hosp. London, 1956; sr. scholar Kennedy Inst. Ethics, Georgetown U., 1973-89. Fellow ACP (master), APHA; mem. AAAS, AMA, Am. Clin. and Climatol. Assn., Biophys. Soc., Johns Hopkins Soc. Scholars, Tudor and Stuart Club (Balt.), Cosmos Club, Knights of St. Gregory, Knights of Malta, Phi Beta Kappa, Sigma Xi, Alpha Omega Alpha. Republican. Roman Catholic. Home: 12610 Three Sisters Rd Potomac MD 20854-6359 Office: Georgetown U Med Ctr Bldg D Ctr Clin Bioethics Rm 238 4000 Reservoir Rd NW Washington DC 20007-2145 Fax: (202) 687-8955. E-mail: jcviola@aol.com., jcharvey@georgetown.edu.

HARVEY, JOHN GROVER, mathematics educator; b. Waco, Tex., Aug. 10, 1934; s. John Grover and Mary Inez (Davidson) H. AA, Navarro Jr. Coll., Corsicana, Tex., 1953; BS, Baylor U., 1955; MS, Fla. State U., 1957; PhD, Tulane U., 1961. Instr. math. U. Ill., Urbana, 1961-63, asst. prof., 1963-66; assoc. prof. math. U. Wis., Madison, 1966-75, prof., 1975-2001, prof. emeritus, 2001—. Prin. investigator Wis. R & D Ctr. for Cognitive Learning, Madison, 1968-78. Editor: Matching High School Preparation to College Needs: Prognostic and Diagnostic Testing, 1996.; editor, contbg. author: Models for Technology Teacher Education in Mathematics, 1997; contbr. chpts. to books. Mem. Math. Assn. Am. (assoc. editor 1969-74, chmn. com. on testing 1988-93), Am. Ednl. Rsch. Assn., Nat. Coun. Tchrs. of Math., Am. Math. Soc. Episcopalian. Home: 330 Morgan St # 506 New Orleans LA 70114-1070

HARVEY, JOSEPH PAUL, JR., orthopedist, educator; b. Youngstown, Ohio, Feb. 28, 1922; s. Joseph Paul and Mary Justinian (Collins) H.; m. Martha Elizabeth Toole, Apr. 12, 1958; children: Maryalice, Martha Jane, Frances Susan, Helen Lucy, Laura Andre. Student, Dartmouth Coll., 1939-42; MD, Harvard U., 1945. Diplomate: Nat. Bd. Med. Examiners. Intern Peter Bent Brigham Hosp., Boston, 1945-46; resident Univ. Hosp., Cleve., 1951-53, Hosp. Spl. Surgery, N.Y.C., 1953-54; instr. orthopedics Cornell Med. Coll., N.Y.C., 1954-62; mem. faculty Sch. Medicine, U. So. Calif., Los Angeles, 1962-92; prof. orthopedic surgery U. So. Calif., 1966-92, prof. emeritus, 1992—; chmn. sect. orthopedics Keck Sch. Medicine, U. So. Calif., 1964-78. Dir. dept. orthopedics U. So. Calif.-Los Angeles County Med. Center, 1964-79, mem. staff, 1979— Editor-in-chief: Contemporary Orthopedics, 1978-96. Served to capt. AUS, 1946-48. Exchange orthopedic fellow Royal Acad. Hosp., Upsala, Sweden, 1957 Fellow Western Orthop. Assn., Am. Acad. Orthop. Surgery, A.C.S., Am. Soc. Testing Materials; mem. AMA, Calif. Med. Assn., Los Angeles County Med. Assn., Am. Rheumatism Assn., Am. Orthop. Assn., Internat. Soc. Orthopedics and Traumatology. Clubs: Boston Harvard. Home: 432 Arlington Dr Pasadena CA 91105-2850

HARVEY, JUDITH GOOTKIN, elementary school educator, real estate agent; b. Boston, May 29, 1944; d. Myer and Ruth Augusta (Goldstein) Gootkin; m. Robert Gordon Harvey, Aug. 3, 1968; children: Jonathan Michael, Alexander Shaw. BS in Edn., Lesley Coll., Cambridge, Mass., 1966; MS in Edn., Nazareth Coll., Rochester, NY, 1987. Kindergarten tchr. Williams Sch., Chelsea, Mass., 1966-69; owner, tchr. Island Presch., Eleuthera, The Bahamas, 1969-70; substitute tchr. Brighton Cen. Sch., Rochester, NY, 1985-95; agt. Prudential Rochester Realty, Pittsford, NY, 1994—98. Author, dir. : (plays) The Parrot Perch, 1991. Bd. dir. in charge pub. rels. George Eastman Ho. Coun., mem. award steering com. honoring Lauren Bacall, 1990, chmn. gala celebration honoring Audrey Hepburn, 1992, mem. steering com. honoring Ken Burns, 1995; mem. art in bloom steering com. for fashion show Meml. Art Gallery, 1994; co-chmn. Fashionata, Rochester Philharm. Orch., 1990; mem. steering com. of realtors Ambs. to Arts; mem. Parrot Players Acting Group, 1990—; mem. steering com. Reels and Wheels Antique Car Festival, 1995, 1996; bd. dir. Birmingham Bloomfield Newcomers, 2000—03, in charge spl. events, 2000—02; com. mem. Birmingham Antiques Festival, 2000—02; co-chair World of James Bond Gala and the Spring Fashion Show, 2001, Saturday Night Fever...Live It! Gala and Spring Fashion Show, 2002; historian Birmingham Bloomfield Newcomers, 2002—03. Mem.: Multimillion Dollar Prodr.'s Club, Genesee Valley Club, Chatterbox Club. Avocations: acting, directing, gardening, writing, bridge.

HARVEY, KATHERINE ABLER, civic worker; b. May 17, 1946; d. Julius and Elizabeth (Engelman) Abler; m. Julian Whitcomb Harvey, Sept. 7, 1974. Student, La Sorbonne, Paris, 1965-66; AAS, Bennett Coll., 1968. Asst. libr. McDermott, Will & Emery, Chgo., 1969-70; libr. Chapman & Cutler, Chgo., 1970-73, Coudert Freres, Paris, 1973-74. Adv., organizer libr. Lincoln Park Zool. Soc. and Zoo, Chgo., 1977-79, mem. soc.'s women's bd., 1976—; chmn. libr. com., 1977-79, sec., 1979-81, mem. exec. com., 1977-81, mem. Jr. bd. Alliance Francaise de Chgo., 1970-76, treas., mem. exec. com., 1971-73, 75-76, mem. women's bd., 1977-80, 95—; trustee Chgo. Acad. Scis., 1986-88; adv. coun. med. program for performing artists Northwestern Meml. Hosp., 1986-94, mem. exec. com., 1992—, bd. treas., 1992—; pres., bd. dirs. William Ferris Chorale, 1988-89; mem. Fred Harvey Fine Arts Found., 1976-78, Phillips Acad. Alumni Coun., Andover, Mass., 1977-81, mem. acad.'s bicentennial celebration com. class celebration leader, 1978, co-chmn. for Chgo. acad.'s bicentennial campaign, 1977-79, mem. student affairs and admissions com., 1980-81. Mem. aux. bd. Art Inst. Chgo., 1978-88; mem. Know Your Chgo. com. U. Chgo. Extension, 1981-84; mem. guild Chgo. Hist. Soc., 1978—, bd. dirs., 1993—; mem. women's bd. Lyric Opera Chgo., 1979—, chmn. edn. com., 1980, mem. exec. com., 1980-84, 88—, treas. women's bd., 1983-84, 1st v.p. 1988-90; mem. women's bd. Northwestern Meml. Hosp., 1979—, treas., chmn. fin. com., 1981-84, 92-94, mem. exec. com., 1981-88, 92—, devel. com. 1995-97, 2d v.p. 1996-97, 1st v.p. 1997—, founding chair pres. com. 1993—, pres. 1999—, dir. Northwestern Meml. Hosp., 1999—, pres. women's bd. 1999—, 1st v.p. 1997-99; vis. com. Sch. Music Northwestern U., 1995—; bd. dirs. Found. Art Scholarships, 1982-83; bd. dirs. Glen Ellyn (Ill.) Children's Chorus, 1983-90, founding chmn. pres.'s com., 1983—; mem. women's bd. Chgo. City Ballet, 1983-84; bd. dirs. Grant Park Concerts Soc., 1986-92; chmn. pres. com. Chgo. Children's Choir, 1991-93. Mem. Antiquarian Soc. of Art Inst. Chgo. (life), Guild of Chgo. Historical Soc., Arts Club Chgo. (dir. 1996—), Chgo. Symphony Soc. (life), Friday Club (corre. sec. 1981-83), Casino Club (gov. 1982-88, sec. 1984-85, 1987-88, 1st v.p. 1985-86, 2d. v.p. 1986-87), Cliff Dwellers Club. Home: 1209 N Astor St Chicago IL 60610-2314

HARVEY, MARC S(AN), lawyer, historian, law educator; b. NYC, May 4, 1960; s. M. Eugene and Coleen (Jones) H. BA with highest honors, So. Ill. U., 1980; Pre-Law, Wash. U., 1980; JD, Southwestern U., 1983; MBA, Loyola Marymount U., L.A., 1984-86; postgrad., Oxford U., Christ Ch. Coll., 1994—97. Bar: Calif., U.S. Supreme Ct. Counsel U.S. SBA, L.A., 1982-83; counsel enforcement div. U.S. SEC, L.A., 1983-84; counsel State Farm Ins. Co., L.A., 1984-85, 20th Century Ins. Co., Woodland Hills, Calif., 1985-86; pvt. practice Encino, Calif., 1986—. Lectr. in field. Contbr. articles to profl. jours. Judge pro tem Culver Mcpl. Ct.; charter mem., trustee Rep. Presdl. Task Force, Washington, 1981—; mem. Nat. Rep. Senatorial Com., Washington, 1983—, Rep. Congl. Leadership Coun., Washington, 1987—, Rep. Senatorial Inner Cir., Washington, 1988—. Recipient 1st pl. essay award, VFW, 1976. Mem.: SAG, AFTRA, ATLA, ABA, L.A. Trial Lawyers Assn., Calif. Trial Lawyers Assn., Nat. Thespian Soc., Themis Soc., U.S. Supreme Ct. Hist. Soc. Fax: 818-990-5812.

HARVEY, MARK SUMNER, composer, minister, educator, musician; b. Binghamton, N.Y., July 4, 1946; s. Robert Mark and Marjorie Grace (Tolley) H.; m. Kate Matson, Aug. 14, 1983. AB, Syracuse U., 1968; ThM, Boston U., 1971, PhD, 1983. Ordained to ministry United Meth. Ch. as deacon, 1970, as elder, 1975. Intern min. Old West United Meth. Ch., Boston, 1969-71, staff mem., assoc. min., 1971-73; min. with jazz and arts community Emmanuel Ch., Boston, 1974—93; with Harvard-Epworth United Meth. Ch., 1993—. Music faculty mem. MIT, Cambridge, Mass., 1981—; founder, music dir. Aardvark Jazz Orch., 1973—, New Am. Music Ensemble, 1969— Composer chamber, choral, jazz orch. pieces; 6 CD recs. of original compositions; contbr. articles to profl. jours. Pres., founder The Jazz Coalition, inc., Boston, 1971-83; trustee Mass. Cultural Alliance, Boston, 1971-73, 81-87; mem. music adv. panel Mass. Coun. on the Arts and Humanities, Boston, 1971-75, 79-82, Meet the Composer/Reader's Digest Commissioning Program, 1989; mem. arts adv. com. Harvard U. Ctr. for Study of World Religions, 1991-97. Fellow NEH, 1987, The Whiting Found., 1986; recipient Contbn. to Cultural Activity award Mass. Cultural Alliance, 1987, City of Boston, 1980. Fellow Soc. for the Arts, Religion, and Contemporary Culture (chmn. 1991-95, bd. dirs. 1986—); mem. ASCAP, Am. Acad. Religion, Soc. for Am. Music, Duke Ellington Soc., Am. Studies Assn., Theta Chi Beta. Office: PO Box 8721 JFK Sta Boston MA 02114

HARVEY, MORRIS LANE, lawyer; b. Madisonville, Ky., Apr. 22, 1950; s. Morris Lee and Margie Lou (Wallace) H.; m. Mary Topel Harvey; children: Morris Lane Jr., John French, Laura Kathleen. BS, Murray State U., 1972; JD, U. Ky., 1974. Bar: Ill. 1975, U.S. Dist. Ct. (so. dist.) 1979. Assoc. Hanagan & Dousman, Mt. Vernon, Ill., 1975-77; ptnr. Feiger, Quindry, Molt & Harvey and successor firms, Fairfield, Ill., 1977-85; sole practice Fairfield, 1986-97, Mt. Vernon, 1997—. Instr. Frontier C.C., Fairfield, 1977-79; spl. asst. atty. gen. State of Ill., Fairfield, 1977-82; Ill. pres. Woodman of World Life Ins. Soc., 1985-87; mem. nat. fraternal com., 1987-89, nat. legis. com., 1989-93, nat. jud. com., 1993-97. Recipient Outstanding Young Man Am. U.S. Jaycees, 1978, 81, 89. Mem. ABA, Ill. Bar Assn., Assn. Trial Lawyers Am., Ill. Trial Lawyers Assn., Am. Judicature Soc. Home: 5 Webster Hill Est Mount Vernon IL 62864-2346 Office: 2029 Broadway St Mount Vernon IL 62864-2910

HARVEY, NICHOLAS D. N., JR., lawyer; b. Balt., May 7, 1948; m. Margaret K. (Knox) H.; 2 children. BA, Colgate U., 1970; LLM, U. Puget Sound, 1976. Bar: Wash. 1976, N.H. 1980, Vt. 1980. Ptnr. Stebbins, Bradley, Harvey & Miller, P.A., Hanover, NH, 1980—. 1st lt. USAF, 1970-72. Office: Stebbins Bradley Harvey & Miller 41 S Park St Hanover NH 03755-2109 E-mail: nharvey@sbhmlaw.com.

HARVEY, NORMAN RONALD, retired finance company executive; b. Rahway, N.J., Aug. 17, 1933; s. George Henry and Jennie Louise (Proudfoot) H.; m. Gail Molitor, May 26, 1962; 1 dau., Anne. BA in Econs., Cornell U., 1955; MBA in Investments, NYU, 1962. Security analyst Bankers Trust Co., N.Y.C., 1958-61, Anchor Corp., Elizabeth, N.J., 1961-64; dir. research Auerbach, Pollak & Richardson, N.Y.C., 1964-75; chief investment officer E.W. Axe & Co., Inc., Tarrytown, N.Y., 1975-82; sr. v.p., equity funds investment officer Merrill Lynch Asset Mgmt., Princeton, N.J., 1982-99; ret. Served to 1st lt. USAR, 1957-58. Corson Meml. scholar, 1951 Mem. NY Soc. Security Analysts, The Union League NY, Edgcomb Tennis Club,Eagle Rock Yacht Club. Republican. Home: 39 Florence Ln Princeton NJ 08540-2631 also: 27 Woodland Ave Kennebunk ME 04043

HARVEY, PATRICIA JEAN, special education administrator, retired; b. Newman, Calif., Oct. 27, 1931; d. Willard Monroe and Marjorie (Greenlee) Clougher; m. Richard Blake Harvey, Aug. 29, 1965; children: G. Scott Floden, Timothy P. BA, Whittier Coll., 1966, MA, 1971. Resource specialist Monte Vista High Sch. and Whittier (Calif.) High Sch., 1977-98; dept. chair spl. edn. Whittier (Calif.) High Sch., 1982-94; ret., 1998. Author: (tchrs. manual) The Dynamics of California Government and Politics, 1970, 90; co-author: Meeting The Needs of Special High School Students in Regular Education Classrooms, 1988. Active Whittier Fair Housing Com., 1972; pres. Women's Aux. Whittier Coll., 1972-73, sec., 1971-72; historian Docian Soc. Whittier Coll., 1963-64, pres. 1965-66. Democrat. Episcopalian. Home: 424 E Avocado Crest Rd La Habra Heights CA 90631-8128 Office: The Learning Advantage Ctr 13710 Whittier Blvd Ste 206 Whittier CA 90605-4407

HARVEY, PAUL, news commentator, author, columnist; b. Tulsa, Sept. 4, 1918; s. Harry Harrison and Anna Dagmar (Christensen) Aurandt; m. Lynne Cooper, June 4, 1940; 1 child, Paul Harvey. Litt.D. (hon.), Culver-Stockton Coll., 1952, St. Bonaventure U., 1953; LL.D., John Brown U., Ark., 1959, Mont. Sch. Mines, 1961, Trinity Coll. Fla., 1963, Parsons Coll., 1968; H.H.D., Wayland Bapt. Coll., 1960, Union Coll., 1962, Samford U., 1970, Howard Payne U., Tex., 1978, Sterling Coll., 1982; Degree (hon.), Rosary Coll., 1996. Announcer radio sta. KVOO, Tulsa; sta. mgr. Salina, Kans.; spl. events dir. radio sta. KXOK, St. Louis; program dir. radio sta. WKZO, Kalamazoo, 1941-43; dir. news and information OWI, Mich., Ind., 1941-43; news commentator, analyst ABC, 1944—; syndicated columnist Los Angeles Times Syndicate (formerly Gen. Features Corp.), 1954—; TV commentator, 1968. Author: Remember These Things, 1952, Autumn of Liberty, 1954, The Rest of the Story, 1956, You Said It, Paul Harvey, 1969, Our Lives, Our Fortunes, Our Sacred Honor; Album rec. Yesterday's Voices, 1959, Testing Time, 1960, Uncommon Man, 1962. Bd. dirs. John D. and Catherine T. MacArthur Found.; mem. bd. govs. Orchestral Assn. Chgo. Symphony Orch. Recipient citation DAV, 1949, 11 Freedoms Found. awards, 1952-76, radio award Am. Legion, 1952, citation of merit, 1955, 57, Cert. of merit VFW, 1953, Bronze Christopher's award, 1953, award of honor Sumter Guards, 1955, nat. pub. welfare services trophy Colo. Am. Legion, 1957,Great Am. KSEL award, 1962, Spl. ABC award, 1973, Ill. Broadcaster award, 1974, John Peter Zenger Freedom award Eagles, 1975, Am. of Year award Lions Internat., 1975, Outstanding Broadcast Journalism award, 1980, Gen. Omar N. Bradley Spirit of Independence trophy, 1980, Man of Yr. award Chgo. Broadcast Advt. Club, 1981, Golden Radio award Nat. Radio Broadcasters Assn., 1982, Best Speaking Voice award Am. Speech, Lang. and Hearing Assn., 1982, Horatio Alger award, 1983, Outstanding Broadcast Personality award Advt. Club Balt., 1984, Meritorius Svc. award Am. Acad. Family Physicians, 1984, Cert. of Appreciation Humane Soc. of U.S., 1985, Genesis award The Fund for Animals, 1986, Okla. Assn. Broadcasters award, 1987, Henry G. Bennett Disting. Svc. award Okla. State U., 1987, James Herriot award Humane Soc. U.S., 1987, Lowell Thomas award, 1989, Gold medal Internat. Radio & TV Soc., 1989, Others award Salvation Army, 1989, Journalism award Internat. Radio Festival, 1989, Marconi award Network Personality of Yr., 1989, 91, 96, 98, Dante award, 1990, William Booth award Salvation Army, 1990, Journalism award Chgo. Hall of Fame, 1990, Bd. of Dirs. award Nat. Religious Broadcasters, 1991, Great Am. Race Legend's award Interstate, 1991, Good Guy award Am. Legion, 1992, Outstanding Pub. Spkr. award Toastmasters Internat., 1992, Paul White award Radio T.V. News Dirs., 1992, Peabody award 1993, 94, Spirit of Broadcasting award NAB, 1994, Silver award Am. Advertising Fedn., 1994, Hall of Fame award Broadcasting & Cable Mag., 1995, Am. Spirit award USAF, 1996, Lifetime Achievement award Radio Mercury, 1997, Lifetime Achievement award Gold Angel, 1998, Lifetime Achievement award Radio Mercury, 1997; elected to Okla. Hall of Fame, 1955, Nat. Assn. Broadcasters Hall of Fame, 1979; named Top Commentator of Yr. Radio-TV Daily, 1962, Laureate Lincoln Acad. of Ill., 1987 (Ill. highest honor); to Emerson Radio Hall of Fame, 1990, among 20th Century's Most Significant Americans George Mag., 1998. Mem. Washington Radio and Television Corrs. Assn., Aircraft Owners and Pilots Assn. Clubs: Chicago Press. Achievements include having broadcasts and columns reprinted in Congressional Record 102 times. Office: 333 N Michigan Ave Ste 1600 Chicago IL 60601-4005

HARVEY, PETER C. state attorney general; BA in Polit. Sci., Morgan State U., 1979; JD, Columbia U., 1982. Bar: N.Y. 1984, D.C. 1985, N.J. 1989. Asst. U.S. atty. Dist. N.J., 1986—89; spl. asst. to N.J. Atty. Gen., 1989—90; law clk. for Hon. Dickinson R. Debevoise, Dist. Judge; ptnr. Riker, Danzig, Scherer, Hyland and Perretti LLP, Morristown, NJ; 1st asst. atty. gen., dir. divsn. criminal justice State of N.J., 2002—03, atty. gen., 2003—. Mediator U.S. Dist. Ct., NJ, N.J. Supreme Ct.; mem. lawyers' adv. com. U.S. Dist. Ct. for the Dist. N.J., U.S. Ct. of Appeals (3d cir.). Office: Richard J Hughes Justice Complex PO Box 080 Trenton NJ 08625*

HARVEY, RICHARD DUDLEY, marketing consultant; b. Atlanta, Sept. 24, 1923; s. Robert Emmett and June (Dudley) H.; m. Donna Helen Smith, Oct. 12, 1944 (dec. Mar. 1990); 1 child, Louise Dudley; m. Catherine M. McFarland, Nov. 13, 1993. BA, U. Denver, 1947; postgrad., Harvard U., Stanford U. Various positions in sales, sales promotion & mktg. The Coca-Cola Co., St. Louis, Denver, Atlanta, 1948-60, v.p., brand mgr., mktg. mgr., mktg. dir. Atlanta, 1965-70, v.p. orgn. & mktg. devel., 1970-75; sr. v.p. mktg. Olympia (Wash.) Brewing Co., 1975-78; pres. Sound Mktg. Svcs., Inc., Seattle, 1978-93, Harvey Mktg. Corp., Upper Montclair, N.J., 1994—. Vice chmn. bd. Roman Meal Co., Tacoma, Washington, 1990—; dir. Lone Star Brewing Co., San Antonio, 1976-78. Trustee Episcopal Radio-TV Found., Atlanta, 1961-88, vice chmn., 1975-84, emeritus trustee, 1988—; bd. dirs. Oreg. Shakespearean Festival Assn., 1982-86; vol. Nat. Exec. Svc. Corps., N.J., N.Y.C., 1997—; chmn. mktg. com., trustee Seattle Symphony, 1983-88; mem. gov.'s adv. com. bus. devel. and job retention, State of Wash., 1988-92; mem. Montclair HIst. Preservation Commn., 1998-2000; mem. cmty. adv. bd. Montclair State U., 2002—. Served with USAAF, 1942-45. Mem. Am. Mktg. Assn. (pres. Seattle chpt. 1983-84); The Arc of N.J. (bd. dirs. 1997-98, exec. com. 1998-99), Mktg. Comm. Execs. Internat. (pres. Seattle chpt. 1984-85), Inst. Mgmt. Cons. (pres. N.J. chpt. 1995-96), Seattle Tennis Club, Bradford Bath and Tennis Club, Phi Beta Kappa, Omicron Delta Kappa. Home: 23 Heller Dr Montclair NJ 07043-2507 Office: Harvey Mktg Corp PO Box 43-129 Montclair NJ 07043-0129 E-mail: dlckharvey@earthlink.net.

HARVEY, ROBERT MARTIN, artist; b. Lexington, N.C., Sept. 16, 1924; arrived in Spain, 1971; s. Samuel Guy and Maggie Pearl (Welch) H.; m. Flora Pennington, Aug. 14, 1948 (div. 1955); 1 child, Marc Scott. Student, Ringling Art Sch., Sarasota, Fla., 1942-44, Louis Ribak, Taos, N.Mex., 1948, San Francisco Inst. Art, 1957. Dir. Cultural Week, Macharaviaya, Malaga, 1989. One-person exhibitions throughout U.S., Eng., and Spain; group exhibitions include Corcoran Gallery of Art, Washington, Ringling Mus. of Art, Sarasota, City of San Francisco, Nat. Collection of Guinea, Ecuatorial, Africa, The Fine Arts Mus. of the South, Mobile, Ala., Stanford (Calif.) U. Mus., Zamora (Spain) Mus. Art. Ford Found. Purchase, Corcoran Gallery of Art, Washington, 1962; recipient 1st prize, Painting of the Yr., Mead Corp., Art Across Am., 1965, Hon.

Mention, L'Oreal Corp., Madrid, 1985, Painters for 1992, Cadiz, Spain, 1988; named European rep. Galleria Alfredo Vinas, Malaga. Avocations: gardening, cooking. Home and Office: La Huerta del Angel 29791 Macharaviaya Malaga Spain

HARVEY, RONALD GILBERT, research chemist; b. Ottawa, Ont., Can., Sept. 9, 1927; came to U.S., 1948; s. Gilbert and Adeline (LeClair) H.; m. Helene H. Szpara, May 18, 1952; 1 child, Ronald Edward. BS in Biology, UCLA, 1952; MS in Chemistry, U. Chgo., 1956, PhD in Chemistry, 1960. Project leader Sinclair Rsch. Labs., Harvey, Ill., 1956-58; instr. U. Chgo., 1960-63, asst.prof., 1964-68, assoc. prof., 1968-75, prof., 1975-97, prof. emeritus, 1997—; postdoctoral fellow Imperial Coll., London, Eng., 1963-64. Cons. Nat. Cancer Inst., Washington, Farmacon Corp., Oakbrook, Ill., CIDAC, Palo Alto, Calif., 1978-80; OMNI Research Mayaguex, P.R., 1973-74, Nat. Inst. Environ. Health Sci., Washington, Am. Cancer Soc., Atlanta, U.S.-Israel Binational Sci. Found. Author: Polycyclic Aromatic Hydrocarbons Chemistry and Carcinogenesis, 1991, Polycyclic Aromatic Hydrocarbons, 1997; editor: Polycyclic Hydrocarbons and Carcinogenesis; mem. editl. bd. Polycyclic Aromatic Compounds (1990-), Mini Reviews in Organic Chemistry (2003-); contbr. more than 430 articles to profl. jours. Recipient ISPAC award for rsch. in polycyclic hydrocarbon chemistry, 1995. Fellow Royal Chem. Soc., Am. Inst. Chemists; mem. AAAS, Am. Chem. Soc., Am. Assn. Cancer Rsch., Sigma Xi. Achievements include patents for synthesis of alpha-olefins, anti-androgen compounds. Home: 10550 Golf Rd Orland Park IL 60462-7420 Office: U Chgo Ben May Inst 5841 S Maryland Ave Chicago IL 60637-1463 E-mail: rharvey@huggins.bsd.uchicago.edu.

HARVEY, RUFUS WILLIAM, nonprofit organization administrator; b. Los Angeles, Aug. 4, 1947; s. Rufus Watson and Edith May (Osborne) H.; m. Sherliane Claudette Raab, Sept. 1, 1974; children: Rufus Brandon, Wendy Jean, Joshua Paul. BA, UCLA, 1972. Freelance musician, Canyon Country, Calif., 1965—; tax preparer, 1983—; faculty assoc. The Master's Sem., Sun Valley, Calif., 1994-2000; dir. pub. rels. TransWorld Missions, L.A., 1977-79; bookkeeper Glendale, Calif., 1979-84; dir. acctg. Insight for Living, Fullerton, Calif., 1984-88; adminstr. Grace Cmty. Ch., Sun Valley, 1988-2000. Enrolled agent IRS, Washington, 1990—. Controller Grace to You, Valencia, Calif., 1992—. Mem. Christian Mgmt. Assn., Nat. Assn. Enrolled Agents, Nat. Soc. Accts., Inst. of Mgmt. Accts., Assn. of Cert. Fraud Examiners, Calif. Soc. Enrolled Agents, Calif. Soc. of Acct. & Tax Profls. Republican. Protestant. Avocations: musician, trumpet player. Office: Grace To You 28001 Harrison Pky Valencia CA 91355

HARVEY, SIMON, actor, writer; b. Tel Aviv, July 17, 1958; came to U.S., 1959; s. Eric and Esther (Tabori) S. BA, Columbia U., 1980; MFA, U. So. Calif., 1988. Actor television and theatre; freelance writer, 1980—. Actor: (TV appearances) Munster Today, 1989—90, Lifestories, 1990, Knots Landing, 1990, Parker Lewis Can't Lose, 1991, Reasonable Doubts, 1992, Beverly Hills 90210, 1992, Days of Our Lives, 1992, The Young and the Restless, 1992, Friends, 1996, Timecop, 1997, The Drew Carey Show, 1997, Payne, 1999, Port Charles, 2001, The Tick, 2001, Sabrina, the Teenage Witch, 2002, Oliver Beene, 2003; mem. : Free Shakespeare Co., 1980—82; Players Workshop of Second City, 1981—82; Kern Shakespeare Festival, 1987; Utah Shakespeare Festival, 1988; Theater of N.O.T.E., 1990—92; actor: appeared in L.A. Theater prodns.; writer Frontiers Newsmag, 1994; author, performer: (plays) Still Negative... After All These Years, 1998. Mem. SAG (awards nominating com. 1995, 97, 2002), AFTRA, AEA. Office: The Levin Agy 8484 Wilshire Blvd Ste 750 Beverly Hills CA 90211-3219 E-mail: simonharvey@yahoo.com.

HARVEY, VIRGINIA MARIE, nurse, administrator; b. Bronx, N.Y., Dec. 6, 1959; d. John Robert and Adrienne (Bennett) Erd; m. William S. Harvey, Oct. 1, 1983. AAS, Rockland C.C., 1979; BS, Mercy Coll., 1982. RN, N.Y., N.J. Staff nurse Englewood (N.J.) Hosp., 1979-81; charge nurse Rockland Psychiat. Ctr., Orangeburg, N.Y., 1983-86, nurse adminstr., 1986—. Mem. ANA (cert. mental health and psychiat. nurse). Avocations: boating, shopping. Home: 26 Sand St Garnerville NY 10923-1423 Office: Rockland Psychiat Ctr Orangeburg NY 10962

HARVEY, WILLARD ALBERTSON, JR., writer, publisher; b. Huntingdon, Pa., Dec. 20, 1931; s. Willard Albertson and Mary Elsie (LaMotte) H.; m. Jo Anne Feick, Feb. 6, 1954; children: Patricia Jo, Merrily Jo, Willard Louis. BA in Econs., Washington & Jefferson Coll., 1953. Sales clk. G.C. Murphy Co., Pitts., 1948-53; account mgr. Aluminum Co. Am., Pitts., 1953-93; mng. ptnr. NKP CAR, Cin., 1993—2001. Author: Cabooses of the Nickel Plate Road, 1992, Mikes of the Nickel Plate Road, 1995, Passenger Cars of the Nickel Plate Road, 1995, Railroads of the Ohio Valley, I, 1996, II, 1997, III, 1998, IV, 2002, Depots of the Nickel Plate Road, 2001; editor: NKPH & TS Mag. reprints, 1993, 94. Bible tchr. Anderson Hills United Meth. Ch., Cin., 1972—, choir mem., 1973—, chairperson music com., 2000-02, nominating com., 1999-2002, worship com., 2002-2004. Mem. Nickel Plate Hist. & Tech. Soc. (nat. sec., info. dir.), Cin. R.R. Club. Republican. Avocations: photography, model building, travel. E-mail: wil23harv@aol.com.

HARVEY, WILLIAM BRANTLEY, JR., lawyer, former lieutenant governor; b. Walterboro, S.C., Aug. 14, 1930; s. William Brantley and Thelma (Lightsey) H.; m. Helen Coggeshall, Dec. 30, 1952; children: Eileen L., William Brantley, III, Helen C., Margaret D., Warren C. AB in Polit. Sci., The Citadel, 1951, LLD (hon.), 1978; JD magna cum laude, U. S.C., 1955. Bar: S.C. 1955. Since practiced in, Beaufort, S.C.; sr. ptnr. Harvey & Battey; mem. S.C. Ho. of Reps. from Beaufort County, 1958-74, chmn. rules com., mem. constl. revision com.; lt. gov. State of S.C., 1974-78. Bd. dirs., past chmn. Carolina Motor Club (AAA); mem. exec. com. Assoc. Marine Inst., past chmn.; bd. dirs., sec. Beaufort Marine Inst.; past chmn. Beaufort County Transp. Com.; pres. S.C. Bar, 1986—87; mem. S.C. State Bd. for Tech. and Comprehensive Edn.; chmn. AMI Found. Former commr. S.C. Dept. Hwys. and Pub. transp.; former commr., vice chmn. S.C. Parks, Recreation and Tourism Commn.; mem. Coastal Caroline coun. Boy Scouts Am.; pres. Beaufort Indsl. Park, Beaufort County Devel. Corp.; bd. dirs. The Citadel Found., Boys and Girls club of Beaufort; Lowcountry Habitat for Humanity, Mustard Seed Found. Mem. ABA, S.C. Bar Assn., Beaufort County Bar Assn., Rotary, Phi Beta Kappa, Kappa Alpha, Phi Delta Phi, Omicron Delta Kappa. Presbyterian (elder). Home: 501 Pinckney St Beaufort SC 29902-4739 Office: Harvey & Battey Attys PO Box 1107 1001 Craven St Beaufort SC 29902-5577 E-mail: wbharvey@islc.net.

HARVEY, WILLIAM ROBERT, university president; b. Brewton, Ala., Jan. 29, 1941; s. Willie D. C. and Mamie Claudis (Parker) H.; m. Norma Baker, Aug. 13, 1966; children: Kelly Renee, William Christopher, Leslie Denise. BA, Talladega Coll., 1961; EdD, Harvard U., 1972. Asst. govt. affairs to dean Harvard U. Grad. Sch. Edn., 1969-70; adminstrv. asst. to pres. Fisk U., Nashville, 1970-72; v.p. student affairs/dir. planning Tuskegee (Ala.) Inst., 1972-76, v.p. adminstrv. services, 1976-78; pres. Hampton (Va.) U., 1978—; owner Pepsi-Cola Bottling Co., Houghton, Mich., 1986—, also bd. dirs. Dir. 1st Union Nat. Bank, Va., Va., Md., D.C., N.C., S.C., Tenn., Trigon Blue Cross Blue Shield Va., Newport News Shipbuilding, Fannie Mae. Contbr. articles to profl. jours. Bd. dirs. United Way, Peninsula Econ. Devel. Council; vice-chmn. President's nat. adv. council ESEA; mem. Harvard U. Alumni Council; mem. nat. adv. com. Woodrow Wilson Nat. Fellowship Found. Served with U.S. Army, 1962-65. Woodrow Wilson Martin Luther King fellow, 1968-70; Woodrow Wilson Found. intern fellow, 1970-72; Harvard U. Higher Edn. Adminstrv. fellow, 1968-70 Mem. Am. Coun. Edn., Am. Assn. Higher Edn., Nat. Assn. Equal Opportunity in Higher Edn., Va. Assn. Higher Edn., 100 Black Men (charter mem. Newport News chpt.), Nat. Guardsmen (Norfolk chpt.), Peninsula C. of C. (dir.), Coun. Ind. Colls. in Va., Omega Psi Phi, Phi Delta Kappa, Sigma Pi Phi. Baptist. Office: Hampton U Office of Pres Hampton VA 23668 E-mail: presidentsoffice@hamptonu.edu. *It is very important today for people to have the opportunity to do some thinking about ethics and morals. It is my firm belief that decency is as important as degrees and this means not only being good doctors, lawyers, professors, engineers and nurses, but good moral leaders who have a sense of community and service as well.*

HARVEY, O.S.F.S. JOHN F, priest, theologian, educator; b. Phila., Apr. 14, 1918; s. Patrick Joseph Harvey and Margaret Harkins. BA in Philosophy, Cath. U. Am., 1941, MA in Psychology, 1946, STD in Moral Theology, 1951; DHL (hon.), Assumption Coll., 1986, Allentown Coll. of St. Francis de Sales, 1988. Ordained priest Roman Cath. Ch., 1944. Prof. moral theology DeSales Sch. Theology, Washington, 1949—87, pres., 1965—77; assoc. prof. Dunbarton Coll. of Holy Cross, Washington, 1948—73; vis. prof. Theol. Union, Sydney, Australia, 1979; pres. Cluster of Ind. Theol. Schs., Washington, 1980—83; co-founder, dir. Courage, N.Y.C., 1980—. Vis. prof. Diocesan Sem., Melbourne, Australia, 1976, Seton Hall U., South Orange, NJ, 1997—98, South Orange, 2000, St. Joseph's Sem., Dunwoodie, NY, 1982—2002; adj. prof. med. and sexual ethics Allentown, 1987—2001; presenter in field; appeared on numerous TV and radio programs. Author: The Moral Theoloty of the Confessions of St. Augustine, 1951, The Homosexual Person: New Thinking in Pastoral Care, 1987, The Truth About Homosexuality: The Cry of the Faithful, 1996, Polish edit., 1999; editor: Homosexuality: Challenges for Change and Reorientation, issue of Jour. of Pastoral Counseling, 1993; editor: (with Gerard Bradley) New Perspectives Concerning Homosexuality With Special Reference to the Rearing of Children, 2003, Same Sex Attraction, A Parents' Guide, 2003, author various pamphlets; contbr. numerous articles to profl. jours. Recipient award for disting. writing, Linacre Quar., 1984—84, Courage in Faith award, Franciscan U. Steubenville, 1998, St. Stephen Defender of the Faith award, Coalition of Concerned Catholics in the Albany Diocese, 1999, Lifetime Achievement award, Parents and Friends Christian Ministries, 2000, Award for Outstanding Leadership as Dir. of Courage, Cardinal Cooke Found., N.Y.C., 2003. Mem.: Cath. Theol. Soc. Am., Fellowship of Cath. Scholars (Cardinal Wright award for outstanding svc. in ch. 1988), Soc. Cath. Social Scientists. Roman Catholic. Avocations: baseball, football, basketball. Home: DeSales U 2755 Station Ave Center Valley PA 18034 Office: Courage Ch of St John the Bapt 210 W 31st St New York NY 10001 Home Fax: 610-282-2254.

HARVICK, KEVIN, race car driver; b. Bakersfield, Calif., Dec. 8, 1975; m. DeLana Linville, Feb. 28, 2001. Student, Bakersfield Jr. Coll., 1997. Racecar driver Richard Childress Racing, Welcome, NC, 2000—. Named champion, NASCAR Winston West, 1998, Busch Series, 2001, Rookie of the Yr., 2000, Winston Cup Raybestos, 2001. Office: c/o Richard Childress Racing PO Box 1189 Welcome NC 27374-1189

HARVIE, CRAWFORD THOMAS, lawyer; b. N.Y.C., Mar. 28, 1943; s. William Mead and Barbara Adele (Johnson) H.; m. Iris Ruth Alofsin, June 10, 1972; children: Katherine, Edward. AB, Stanford U., 1965; LLB, Yale U., 1968; cert. advanced mgmt. program, Harvard U., 1992. Bar: N.Y. 1969. Assoc. Debevoise & Plimpton, N.Y.C., 1971-75; counsel TRW, Inc., Cleve., 1976-77, sr. counsel, 1978-79, asst. gen. counsel, v.p., 1980-83; v.p. law TRW Automotive, Cleve., 1983-90; v.p., assoc. gen. counsel TRW Inc., 1990-95; sr. v.p., gen. counsel, sec. Goodyear Tire and Rubber Co., Akron, Ohio, 1995—. Trustee Cleve. Inst. of Music, 1989—, Akron Art Mus.; bd. overseers Blossom Music Ctr. Mem. Am. Corp. Counsel Assn., Assn. of Gen. Counsel, Chief Legal Officer Roundtable-U.S. Home: 6537 Thornbrook Cir Hudson OH 44236-3552 Office: Goodyear Tire and Rubber Co 1144 E Market St Akron OH 44316-0001

HARVIEUX, ANNE MARIE, psychotherapist; b. St. Paul, Sept. 5, 1945; d. Walter Wallace and Magdalene C. (Rauer) H. BA, Mt. Mary Coll., Milw., 1970; MSW, U. Wis., Milw., 1979. LCSW Wis. Caseworker Washington County Dept. Social Svc., West Bend, Wis., 1970-72; social worker St. Michael's Hosp., Milw., 1972-74; adminstrv. asst. Family Hosp., Milw., 1974-82; dir. social svc. Beloit (Wis.) Meml. Hosp., 1982-87; dir. counseling svc. Beloit Clinic, 1987-92; dir. social svcs. N.W. Gen. Hosp., Milw., 1992-95; program adminstr. Childrens Hosp. Infant Death Ctr. of Wis., Milw., 1995—. Mem. adv. bd. Credible Care, Janesville, Wis., 1987-92, Parkside Lodge Wis., Beloit, 1989-92. Bd. dirs. Waukesha (Wis.) Mental Health Assn., 1980-82; mem. women's exch., 1990-92, Family Violence Coun., Beloit, 1983-85, Rock County Mental Health Assn., Janesville, Wis., 1986. Beloit Teen Pregnancy Task Force, 1988-91; v.p. First Light Group Home, Beloit, 1984-87; chair Wis. Maternal Child Health Coalition, 2001—. Mem. NASW, Assn. for Social Work Adminstrs. in Health Care (pres. 1995-96). Home: 2744 Sandra Ln Waukesha WI 53188-2024 Office: Childrens Hosp of Wis PO Box 1997 9000 W Wisconsin Ave Milwaukee WI 53226-3518 E-mail: aharvieux@chw.org., anneh@csd.uwm.edu.

HARVILL, MELBA SHERWOOD, retired university librarian; b. Bryson, Tex., Jan. 22, 1933; d. William Henry and Delta Verlin (Brawner) Sherwood; m. L. E. Harvill Jr., Feb. 2, 1968; children: Sherman T., Mark Roling. BA, North Tex. State Coll., 1954; MA, North Tex. State U., 1968, MLS, 1973, PhD, 1984. Tchr. Graham (Tex.) Ind. Sch. Dist., 1966-68; reference libr. Midwestern U., Wichita Falls, 1968—73; dir. librs. Midwestern State U., Wichita Falls, 1973-2000. Presenter in field. Vol. Boy Scouts Am., Wichita Falls, 1969—74, Wichita Falls Sr.-Jr. Forum, 1978—2000, mem. exec. bd. girls club, ways and means com., sec., asst. treas.; chmn. United Way Midwestern State U., 1975—76; mem. talent coordinating com. Wichita Falls Centennial Celebration; vol. Conv. and Vis. Bur., Lone Stars, 1993—; grad. Leadership Wichita Falls, 1990; pres. Southside Girls Club, 1997—98; auditor, budget com. chair Woman's Forum, 1997—99; ednl. programming chair Wichita Falls Arts Coun., 2001—; mem. U. North Tex. Advancement Adv. Coun.; bd. dirs. YWCA Wichita Falls, 1987—94, pres. bd. dirs., 1989—91, 1994—95; bd. dirs. River Bend Nature Works. Recipient Svc. award Sr.-Jr. Forum, Wichita Falls United Way Community Svc. award, 1975, Svc. award YWCA Bd. Dirs., 1991; named Met. BPW Woman of Yr., 1980. Mem. ALA, LWV (program v.p., pres. 1991-92), Tex. Libr. Assn. (mem. planning com., mem. membership com., mem. legis. com., mem. rsch. and grants com., chairperson dist VII, chairperson adminstrn. round table), Tex. Coun. State U. Librs. (sec.-treas. 1990-92), Wichita Falls Rotary North (sec. 1993-96), U. North Tex. Alumni Assn. (bd. dirs. 1992-94, 97-2002), Phi Alpha Theta, Pi Sigma Alpha, Phi Delta Phi, Gamma Theta Upsilon, Alpha Chi, Beta Phi Mu. Democrat. Avocations: spectator sports, swimming, music, reading, travel. Home: 4428 BUS 287J Iowa Park TX 76367 E-mail: mharvill33@aol.com.

HARVILLE, MARTHA LOUISE, special education educator; b. Detroit, Sept. 28, 1958; d. Henry and Emma Jean (Campbell) H.; m. Russell Smith, May 1, 1993; children: David-Akem, Russell Timothy. BA in Edn., Queens Coll., 1981, MS in Edn., 1986; D in Curriculum and Tchg., Columbia U., 2000. Cert. tchr. spl. edn., elem. tchr. N-6, sch. dist. adminstr., N.Y.; lic. asst. prin., N.Y. Caseworker Bur. of Child Welfare, Jamaica, N.Y., 1981-82; tchr. spl. edn. Pub. Sch. 46Q, Bayside Queens, N.Y., 1982-83, Pub. Sch. 213Q, Bayside Queens, N.Y., 1983-85; Pub. Sch. 153, Maspeth, 1986; gen. indsl. arts tchr. Ind. Sch. 227Q/Louis Armstrong East, Elmhurst, N.Y., 1985-89; spl. edn. tchr. Pub. Sch. 153, Bayside Queens, 1986; tchr. technology Ind. Sch. 227Q/Louis Armstrong East, Elmhurst, N.Y., 1990-91, 93-94; staff devel. specialist Cen. Bd. Edn., Bklyn., 1989-90; rsch. asst. Columbia U. Tchr.'s Coll., N.Y.C., 1991—, curriculum instructional specialist of tech., 2003—; rsch. asst., intern Ctr. Adaptive Tech., N.Y.C., 1991—; tech. cons. CSTIP project Tchrs. Coll. Columbia U. IUME Ctr. Computer tchr. Bd. Edn. Dist. 26, Bayside Queens, 1983-85; software evaluator, Bd. Edn., Bklyn., 1988-89; yearbook adv. Ind. Sch. 227Q, 1986-89; adj. lectr. Big Buddy Program at Queens Coll., Flushing, N.Y., 1989-90; owner Harville's. Inventor in field; contbr. articles to profl. jours. Mem. exec. bd. Reach for Cultural Heights, 1992—; mem. Lincoln Ctr. Inst., 1984—; del. Citizen Amb. Program, Spokane, Wash., 1995; dep. gov. Am. Biog. Rsch. Inst., 1995—; coach 1st Lego League. Recipient Svc. award Girl Scouts US., Jamaica, 1980. Mem. Queens Coll. Alumni, Edn. Adminstrn. Orgn. Columbia U., Queens Coll. Grad. Student Assn. (pres. 1988), Kappa Delta Pi. Avocations: theatre, drawing, reading, hobbies.

HARVIN, CHARLES ALEXANDER, III, state legislator, lawyer; b. Sumter, S.C., Feb. 7, 1950; s. Charles Alexander Harvin, Jr. m. Cathy Jane Brand; 1 child, Mary Franklin; Grad. in history and polit. sci. Baptist Coll., Charleston, S.C., 1972, Augusta Law Sch., 1976; hon. degree Sherman Chiropractic Coll., Spartanburg, S.C., 1979, Francis Marion Coll., 1986; LLD (hon.) Charleston So. Univ., 1988. Mem. S.C. Ho. of Reps., 1976—, asst. majority leader, majority whip, 1978-82, majority leader, 1982—, mem. ways and means com., vice chmn. rules com., majority leader Emeritus Ho. of Reps., S.C., 1987—. Pres. Bapt. Coll. Young Dems., 1970-72; officer Charleston County Young Dems., 1971-72; chmn. 6th Congl. Dist. Young Dems., 1975-76; life mem. S.C. Young Dems.; chmn. Clarendon County Dem. Com.; vice chmn. S.C. Dem. Com., 1976-78, also mem. exec. com.; del. Dem. Nat. Conv., 1984; mem. S.C. Gov.'s Agr. Study Com.; U.S. Constn. Bicentennial Commn., 1985— ; trustee S.C. Hall of Fame; vice chmn. alumni bd. Bapt. Coll., 1975-76; bd. visitors Clemson U., 1977-78,.Med. Univ. S.C., 1986-87, Charleston So. Univ., 1988-90. Maj. USNG. Recipient Outstanding Service award Charleston County Young Dems., 1972, S.C. Young Dems., 1977; Disting. Service award S.C. Dem. Com., 1981; appreciation award S.C. Tech. Edn. Colls., 1981; Legislator of Yr. award S.C. Young Dems., 1982, S.C. Student Legislature, 1981, S.C. State Library Bd., 1982, S.C. Assn. for Deaf, 1985; award S.C. Coun. for Exceptional Children, 1982, S.C. Agrl. Cmty., 1982; Outstanding Legislator Service award United Parcel Svc., 1984; Disting. Svc. award Bapt. Coll. of Charleston Alumni Assn., 1984, also numerous other awards and commendations. Mem. ABA, Am. Judicature Soc., S.C. Trial Lawyers Assn., Clarendon County Farm Bur., Clarendon County Hist. Soc. (v.p. 1983-84, pres. 1985-86), S.C. State Employees Assn., NAACP, Huguenot Soc. of S.C., First Families of S.C., Alpha Phi Omega (life). Lodges: Masons, Shriners. Office: South Carolina Ho of Reps PO Box 11867 Columbia SC 29211-1867

HARVIN, DAVID TARLETON, lawyer; b. Houston, Feb. 15, 1945; s. William Charles and Ruth Helen (Beck) H.; m. Sarah Ann Hartman, Apr. 21, 1973; children: Kimberly Kate, William Hartman, John Andrew. BA, Yale U., 1967; JD, U. Tex., 1970. Bar: Tex. 1970, U.S. Dist. Ct. (so. dist.) Tex. 1972, U.S. Dist. Ct. (ea. dist.) Tex. 1977, U.S. Dist. Ct. (no. dist.) Tex. 1979, U.S. Dist. Ct. (we. dist.) Tex. 1988, U.S. Ct. Appeals (5th cir.) 1971, U.S. Supreme Ct. 1977. Law clk. U.S. Ct. Appeals (5th cir.), 1970-71; assoc. Vinson & Elkins L.L.P, Houston, 1971-77, ptnr., 1977—, mgmt. com., 2000—. Trustee Episcopal Theol. Sem. of S.W., 1995-2002, Stehlin Found. for Cancer Rsch., 1986-96, Kinkaid Sch., 1997-2003; vice-chancellor Episcopal Diocese of Tex. Fellow Am. Coll. Trial Lawyers, Tex. Bar Found., Houston Bar Found.; mem. ABA, Houston Country Club, The Downtown Club. Home: 111 Maple Valley Rd Houston TX 77056-1007 Office: Vinson & Elkins LLP 1001 Fannin St Ste 2300 Houston TX 77002-6706

HARVUOT, CATHLEEN MARY, elementary school educator, consultant; b. Cleve., June 16, 1951; d. Richard William and Josephine Mary (Shubiak) Vasicek; m. Clifford Allen Harvuot, July 25, 1987. BS in Elem. Edn., U. Akron, Ohio, 1973; MEd in Supervision of Instruction, Ohio U., 1978. Cert. elem. edn., spl. edn., nursery, and kindergarten tchr., N.Y., sch. adminstr., N.Y., elem. principal, supr., Ohio. Tchr. Cambridge (Ohio) City Schs., 1973-78; tchr. remedial reading East Muskingum Schs., New Concord, Ohio, 1978-81; tchr. 2d and 3d grades Englewood (N.J.) Schs., 1981-82; tchr. 1st grade Haworth (N.J.) Schs., 1982-83; tchr. spl. edn. Leonia (N.J.) Pub. Schs./Anna C. Scott Schs., 1983-85; tchr. 1st grade Ardsley (N.Y.) Unified Free Sch. Dist./Concord Rd. Sch., 1985-89, tchr. 2d grade, 1989-94; asst. prin. North Mianus Sch. Greenwich (Conn.) Pub. Schs., 1994-97; prin. Franklin Ave. Sch., Pearl River (N.Y..) Schs., Pearl River, 1997—2000; ednl. cons. Summit Co. Ednl. Svc. Ctr., Cuyahoga Falls, Ohio, 2000—. Cons. Bd. Coop. Svcs. of Westchester County for Social Studies, N.Y., 1986-90; ind. cons. for DMP math. program, Ardsley, 1987-89; maths. curriculum leader Ardsley Schs., 1988-89. Mem. ASCD, Nat. Coun. Tchrs. of Maths., Internat. Reading Assn. (pres., v.p. Muskingum chpt. 1980-81). Home: 8502 Waterside Dr Sagamore Hills OH 44067

HARWARD, DONALD WEST, retired academic administrator; m. Ann Harward; 2 children. B, Maryville Coll.; M, Am. U.; PhD, U. Md. Prof. U. Del., 1968—82; v.p. acad. affairs Coll. Wooster, Ohio, until 1989; pres. Bates Coll., Lewiston, Maine, 1989—2002, pres. emeritus, 2002—. Chmn. and co- founder LA Excels. Fellow: Assn. of Am. Colleges and Universities (sr.). Office: 256 College St Lewiston ME 04240-6021

HARWELL, BETH H. political organization worker; b. Norristown, Pa., July 24, 1957; married; 2 children. B, David Lipscomb U.; MS, George Peabody Coll.; PhD, Vanderbuilt U. State legislator; mem. Tenn. State Legis., 1988—; chmn. Tenn. Republican Party, 2001—. Republican. Office: 1922 West End Ave Nashville TN 37203 also: 107 War Meml Bldg Nashville TN 37243 Address: 42 Wyn Oak Nashville TN 37205-5001*

HARWELL, DAVID WALKER, retired state supreme court chief justice; b. Florence, S.C., Jan. 8, 1932; s. Baxter Hicks and Lacy (Rankin) H.; married; children: Robert Bryan, William Baxter. LL.B., JD, U. S.C., 1958; HHD (hon.), Frances Marion U., 1987. Bar: S.C. 1958, U.S. Dist. Ct. S.C. 1958, U.S. Ct. Appeals 1964, U.S. Supreme Ct. 1961. Circuit judge 12th Jud. Ct. S.C., 1973-80; justice S.C. Supreme Ct., 1980-91, chief justice, 1991-94; ret., 1994; spl. counsel Nelson, Mullins, Riley and Scarborough. Mem. S.C. Ho. of Reps., 1962-73. Served with USNR, 1952-54. Mem. Am. Bar Assn., Am. Trial Lawyers Assn., S.C. Bar Assn., S.C. Trial Lawyers Assn. (Portrait and Scholarship award 1986). Presbyterian. Office: PO Box 2459 Myrtle Beach SC 29578-2459

HARWELL, EDWIN WHITLEY, judge; b. Ashland, Ala., June 4, 1929; s. William Thomas and Effie Belle (Whitley) H.; m. Olma Lillian Motes, Nov. 27, 1957. Student, Jacksonville State U., 1948-49; BS, JD, U. Ala., 1952. Bar: Ala. bar 1952. Practicing atty., 1954-71; circuit judge, 1971-77; city judge City of Oxford, 1977—; individual practice law, 1977—. Served with AUS, 1952-54. Mem. Ala. Bar Assn., Calhoun County Bar Assn. (past pres.), VFW, Ala. Mcpl. Judges Assn. (past pres.), United Comml. Travelers, Elk, Moose, Anniston Exch. (past pres.). Baptist. Home: 813 Blue Ridge Dr Anniston AL 36207-3328

HARWELL, KENNETH E. chemist, researcher, consultant; b. Bell Springs, Tex., Sept. 11, 1921; s. Samuel Franklin and Hettie Mae (King) H.; m. Joye Murphy, Dec. 19, 1961. BS in Chemistry, Baylor U., 1945; MA in Organic Chemistry, U. Tex., 1947, PhD in Organic Chemistry, 1952. Spl. problems chemist Union Carbide Chems. Co., Texas City, Tex., 1947-48; rsch. scientist Cotton Rsch. Com. of Tex., Austin, 1948-50; rsch. chemist Celanese Corp. of Am., Clarkwood, Tex., 1951; project supr., rsch. chemist, electronics engr. Tex. A&M Rsch. Found., College Station, 1952-54; asst. prof., assoc. mem. grad. faculty Tex. A&M Coll., College Station, 1952-54; sr. rsch. chemist Jefferson Chem. Co., Austin, 1954-58; owner, mgr. Tex. Fine Chems. Co., Austin, 1958-59; dir., mgr., treas. Quality Chems. Corp., Austin, 1960; rsch. chemist, exploratory rsch. sect. petrochems. divsn. Continental Oil Co., Ponca City, Okla., 1961-65; sr. rsch. chemist plastics divsn. Gulf R & D Corp., Merriam, Kans., 1965-72; rsch. chemist R&D dept. Cook Paint and Varnish Co., Kansas City, Mo., 1972-79; owner, mgr. Merriam Chem. Devel. Co., Edwardsville, Kans., 1979-89; cons. Skiatook, Okla., 1989—. R & D cons. Nalle Plastics, Inc., Austin, 1958-59. Author 1 book; contbr. articles to profl. jours.; patentee in field. Mem. AAAS, AIChE, NRA, Am. Chem. Soc., Sigma Xi, Phi Lambda Upsilon. Avocations: photography, writing, travel. Home: PO Box 158 Skiatook OK 74070-0158

HARWELL, WILLIAM EARNEST (ERNIE HARWELL), broadcaster; b. Washington, Ga., Jan. 25, 1918; s. Davis Gray Harwell; m. Lula Tankersley, Aug. 30, 1941; children: William Earnest, Jr., Gray Neville, Julie, Carolyn. AB, Emory U., 1940; LittD (hon.), Adrian Coll., 1985; LHD (hon.), No. Mich. Coll., 1990. Sports dir. Sta. WSB, Atlanta, 1940-43; announcer Atlanta Crackers, 1946-48, Bklyn. Dodgers, 1948-49, N.Y. Giants, 1950-53, Balt. Orioles, 1954-59, Detroit Tigers, 1960—91, 1993—2002; ret., 2002. Announcer All-Star games, World Series, NBC, CBS Radio, pro football Balt. Colts, N.Y. Giants; broadcaster Master's golf tournament, NBC, 1942, 46. Author: Tuned to Baseball, 1985, Diamond Gems, 1991, The Babe Signed My Shoe, 1994, Stories From My Life in Baseball, 2001; composer songs including I Don't Know Any Better, Move over Babe, Only a Fool, One-Room World, One Dream, Sing Every Song. With USMC, 1942-46. Recipient Lowell Thomas Broadcast award, 1985, Alvin Foon award Mich. Jewish Sports Hall of Fame, 1988, 90, Big Mac award Detroit News, 1989, Golden Compass award Campfire Inc., 1989, Life Directions Enrichment award, 1989, Nat. Lifetime Nat. Achievement award March of Dimes, 1991, Joe Louis award, 1991, Ken Hubbs Meml. award, 1991, Stanley Kresge award, 1994, U. Detroit Jesuit Magis award, 1995; named Most Durable Baseball Announcer, Guinness Book Records, 2003; inducted Baseball Hall of Fame, Cooperstown, 1981, Mich. Sports Hall of Fame, Emory U. Hall of Fame, Nat. Sportscasters' and Sportswriters Hall of Fame, Am. Sportscasters Hall of Fame, Catch Hall of Fame, Ga. Broadcasters Hall of Fame, Nat. Radio Hall of Fame, 1998, SAE Leadership Hall of Fame, 2001. Mem. ASCAP, Sigma Alpha Epsilon. Home: 25387 Witherspoon St Farmington Hills MI 48335-1367

HARWICK, BETTY CORINNE BURNS, sociology educator; b. L.A., Jan. 22, 1926; d. Henry Wayne Burns and Dorothy Elizabeth (Menzies) Routhier; m. Burton Thomas Harwick, June 20, 1947; children: Wayne Thomas, Burton Terence, Bonnie Christine, Beverly Anne Carroll. Student, Biola, 1942-45,

Summer Inst. Linguistics, 1945, U. Calif., Berkeley, 1945-52; BA, Calif. State U., Northridge, 1961, MA, 1965; postgrad., MIT, 1991. Prof. sociology Pierce Coll., Woodland Hills, Calif., 1966-95, pres. acad. senate, 1976-77, pres. faculty assn., 1990-91, chmn. dept. for philosophy and sociology, 1990-95, co-creator, faculty advisor interdisciplinary program religious studies, 1988-95. Chmn. for sociology L.A. C.C. Dist., 1993-95; occasional cmty. guest lectr. religious studies and sociology, 1995—. Author: (with others) Introducing Sociology, 1977; author: Workbook for Introducing Sociology, 1978. Faculty rep. Calif. C.C. Assn., 1977-80. Alt. fellow NEH, 1978. Mem. Am. Acad. Religion, Soc. Bibl. Lit., Am. Sociol. Assn. Presbyterian. Home: 19044 Superior St Northridge CA 91324-1845

HARWIT, MARTIN OTTO, astrophysicist, writer, educator, museum director; b. Prague, Czechoslovakia, Mar. 9, 1931; came to U.S., 1946, naturalized, 1953; s. Felix Michael and Regina Hedwig (Perutz) Haurowitz; m. Marianne Mark, Feb. 1, 1957; children: Alexander, Eric, Emily. BA in Physics, Oberlin Coll., 1951; MA in Physics, U. Mich., Ann Arbor, 1953; PhD in Physics, Mass. Inst. Tech., 1960. NATO postdoctoral fellow Cambridge (Eng.) U., 1960-61; NSF fellow Cornell U., Ithaca, N.Y., 1961-62, asst. prof. astronomy, 1962-64, asso. prof., 1964-68, prof., 1968-87, prof. emeritus, 1988—, chmn. dept. astronomy, 1971-76, co-dir. program for history and philosophy of sci. and tech., 1985-87; dir. Nat. Air and Space Mus. Smithsonian Instn., Washington, 1987-95. E.O. Hulburt fellow Naval Rsch. Lab., Washington, 1963-64; Nat. Acad. Sci. exch. visitor Czechoslovak Acad. Sci., Prague, 1969-70; v.p., dir. Spectral Imaging Inc., Concord, Mass., 1971-77; external mem. Max Planck Soc., Inst. Radioastronomy, Bonn., West Germany, 1979— ; cons. NASA.; chair for space history Nat. Air and Space Mus., Smithsonian Instn., 1983; chmn. astrophysics mgmt. ops. working group, NASA, 1985-87; Adriaan Blaauw prof. U. Groningen, The Netherlands, 2002. Author: Astrophysical Concepts, 1973, 3d edit., 1998 (transl. into Chinese 1981), (with N.J.A. Sloan) Hadamard Transform Optics, 1979, Cosmic Discovery-The Search, Scope and Heritage of Astronomy, 1981 (transl. into German and French 1982), (with the mus. staff) Treasures of the National Air and Space Museum, 1995, An Exhibit Denied: Lobbying the History of Enola Gay, 1996 (transl. into Japanese 1997): editor: (with M. G. Hauser) The Extragalactic Infrared Background and its Cosmological Implications, International Astronomical Union Symposium 204, 2001. With U.S. Army, 1955-57. Recipient Alexander von Humboldt Found. sr. U.S. scientist award Max Planck Inst. Radioastronomy, 1976-77; NSF grantee, 1963-68; Research Corp. grantee, 1970-75; NASA grantee, 1965—; Air Force Cambridge (Mass.) Research Labs. grantee, 1969-74. Fellow AAAS (chmn. sect. on astronomy, 2001-02, coun. mem. 2002-03), Am. Phys. Soc. (chmn. div. history of physics 1986-87, chmn. astrophysics div. 1988-89), Royal Astron. Soc.; mem. Soc. for History of Tech., Am. Astron. Soc. Home: 511 H St SW Washington DC 20024-2725

HARWOOD, ELEANOR CASH, librarian; b. Buckfield, Maine, May 29, 1921; d. Leon Eugene and Ruth (Chick) Cash; m. Burton H. Harwood, Jr., June 21, 1944 (div. 1953); children: Ruth (Mrs. Wiliam R. Cline), Eleanor, James Burton. BA, Am. Internat. Coll., 1943; BS, New Haven State Tchrs. Coll., 1955. Libr. Rathbun Meml. Libr., East Haddam, Conn., 1955-56; asst. libr. Kent (Conn.) Sch., 1956-63; cons. Chester (Conn.) Pub. Libr., 1965-71. Author: (with John G. Park) The Independent School Library and the Gifted Child, 1956, The Age of Samuel Johnson, LLD, Remember When, 1987, (essay) Growing Up in Chester, 1993, Moosley Yours, 1996, Chester, Years Ago, 2002. Mem. United Ch. Lt. (j.g.) USNR, 1944-46, WWII. Named Eleanor C. Harwood prize in her honor, Rev. Jacob Meml. Christian Coll., India, libr. named in her honor, 2003; recipient medal, Am. Theater-Victory. Mem. ALA, Conn. Libr. Assn., Chester Hist. Soc. (trustee 1970-72), DAV, Am. Legion, Am. Legion Aux., Soc. Mayflower Descs., Appalachian Mountain Club. Home: 10 Maple St # 255 Chester CT 06412-0255

HARWOOD, JERRY, market research executive; b. Jersey City, June 19, 1926; s. Louis and Dorothy (Cohen) Horowitz; m. Ruthella Zimmerman, June 25, 1950; children: Robin Jill, Dean Brook. BA cum laude, L.I. U., 1949; MA, NYU, 1953. Tech. instr. U.S. Bur. Census, 1950-51; v.p., assoc. research dir. Kenyon & Eckhardt Advt., N.Y.C., 1962-66; sr. v.p., dir. research Needham, Harper & Steers Advt., N.Y.C., 1966-73; sr. v.p., group research dir. Benton & Bowles Advt., N.Y.C., 1975-88; mktg. cons. Short Hills, NJ, 1988—; mem. Census Adv. Com., 1976-83. Adj. assoc. prof. NYU Grad. Sch. Bus., 1984-85 Pres. Temple B'nai Jeshurun, 1980-82, Jewish Family Svc. of MetroWest, 1984-87, N.J. Jewish News, 1992-95; v.p. Mental Health Assn. Essex County, 1992-99; mem. Essex County Child Placement Rev. Bd., 1988—; bd. dirs. Am. Jewish Com., 1996—; trustee Hebrew Immigrant Aid Soc., 1997-98. Mem. Am. Mktg. Assn. (pres. N.Y.C. chpt. 1970-71, nat. v.p. pub. policy and issues 1973, nat. v.p. mktg. rsch. 1981-82, mem. editl. bd. 1992-98, chmn. Marketing Hall of Fame 1995-98), Nat. Assn. Jewish Family and Children Agys. (pres. 1997-99). Home and Office: 22 Athens Rd Short Hills NJ 07078-1312 E-mail: jandrharwood@aol.com. *The individual who respects the rights, opinions and needs of others is the individual who manages his own life most productively and successfully.*

HARWOOD, JULIUS J. metallurgist, educator; b. N.Y.C., Dec. 3, 1918; m. Naomi Beitner, 1983; children: Dane L., Gail A., Caren L., Rochelle. BS, CCNY, 1939; MS, U. Md., 1953; D of Engring. (hon.), Mich. Tech. U., 1986. Materials engr. U.S. Naval Gun Factory, 1940-46; metall. Off Naval Rsch., 1946-60; mgr. metall. sci. lab. Ford Motor Co., Dearborn, Mich., 1960-69, mgr. rsch. planning engring. and rsch. staff, 1969-71, dir. Material Sci. Lab, engring. and rsch. staff, 1971-83; prof. engring. Wayne State U., Detroit, 1984; pres. Ovonic Synthetic Material Co., Troy, Mich., 1984-87, Harwood Cons., Orchard Lake, Mich., 1987—, West Bloomfield, Mich. Adj. prof. Wayne State U., Detroit, 1975. Contbr. articles to profl. jours. Fellow AAAS, Metall. Soc. (pres. 1973), Am. Soc. Metals (John H. Shoemaker award 1977), Engring. Soc. of Detroit (Gold Medal award 1983); mem. Am. Inst. Mining, Metall. and Petroleum Engrs. (pres. 1976, hon.), Am. Ceramic Soc. (Orton lectr. 1978), Nat. Acad. Engrs. Office: 5023 Pheasant Cv West Bloomfield MI 48323-2093

HARWOOD, LARRY D. education educator; s. Marvin D and Velma Williams Harwood; m. Dottie J Almen-Harwood, Nov. 29, 1986; children: Theodore, Elspeth. MA, Trinity Evang. Div. Sch., 1980—84; PhD, Marquette U., 1992—98. Instr., philosophy Marquette U., Milw., 1995—98; philosophy prof. Viterbo U., La Crosse, Wis., 1998—. Contbr. articles to profl. jours. Softball coord. Coulee Region Home Edn. Assn., La Crosse, Wis., 2000—03. Recipient Alex Chiu award, Viterbo U., 2001—02. Mem.: Conf. on Christianity and Lit., Nineteenth Century Studies Assn. Protestant. Avocations: genealogy, gardening, travel, fishing. Office: Viterbo University 815 South 9th St La Crosse WI 54601 E-mail: ldharwood@viterbo.edu.

HARWOOD, ROBERT BERNARD, JR., state supreme court justice; b. Oct. 17, 1939; Student, U. of the South, 1958—59; BS in Commerce and Bus. Adminstrn., U. Ala., 1962, JD, 1963. Spl. asst. atty. gen. State of Ala., 1969—75; dep. city judge City of Tuscaloosa, Ala., 1975—80; cir. judge Tuscaloosa County, 1991—2001; assoc. justice Ala. Supreme Ct., 2001. Lectr. law and trial advocacy U. Ala., 1979—83, 1989—99. Mem. exec. bd. Black Warrior coun. Boy Scouts Am., 1976—, pres., 1993, mem. leadership assn. United Way Tuscaloosa County; mem. Carroll Creek Vol. Fire Dept.; bd. dirs. FOCUS on Sr. Citizens of Tuscaloosa County. Recipient Silver Beaver award, Black Warrior Coun. Boy Scouts Am., 1994. Mem.: Am. Judges Assn., Tuscaloosa County Bar Assn. (pres. 1978—79), Tuscaloosa Inn of Ct. (pres. 1991—92), Ala. Bar Assn., ABA, Tuscaloosa County Cattlemen's Assn., Ala. Cattlemen's Assn., Order of the Coif. Republican. Episcopalian. Office: Ala Supreme Ct 300 Dexter Ave Montgomery AL 36104-3741*

HARWOOD, RONALD, screenwriter, playwright; b. Cape Town, South Africa, Nov. 9, 1934; Student in acting, Royal Acad. Dramatic Art, London, 1952. Author: (plays) Country Matters, 1969, The Good Companions, 1974, The Ordeal of Gilbert Pinfold, 1978, The Dresser, 1980 (Evening Std. award, 1980); author: (with Christopher Hampton) The Night of the Day of the Imprisoned Writer, 1981; author: After the Lions, 1982, Tramway Road, 1984, The Deliberate Death of a Polish Priest, 1985, Interpreters: A Fantasia on English and Russian Themes, 1985, J.J. Farr, 1988, Another Time, 1989, Reflected Glory, 1991, Taking Sides, 2001, (screenplays) The Barber of Stamford Hill (TV), 1962, Private Potter, 1962, A High Wind in Jamaica, 1965, Drop Dead Darling, 1966, La Ragazza con la Pistola (English adaptation), 1968, Diamonds for Breakfast, 1968, Eyewitness, 1970, One Day in the Life of Ivan Denisovich, 1970, Operation Daybreak, 1976, Evita Peron (TV), 1981, The Dresser, 1983, The Doctor and the Devils, 1985, The Deliberate Death of a Polish Priest (TV), 1986, Mandela (TV), 1987, Cin cin, 1991, The Browning Version, 1994, Cry, the Beloved Country, 1995, Garderober (TV), 1997, Taking Sides, 2001, The Pianist, 2002 (Oscar award best adapted screenplay, 2002), Majstor (TV), 2002, The Statement, 2003; prodr.: (films) The Dresser, 1983; script cons. : Cromwell, 1970. Office: c/o Judy Daish Assocs 83 Eastbourne Mews London W2 6LQ England*

HARWOOD, STANLEY, retired judge, lawyer; b. N.Y.C., June 23, 1926; s. Benjamin and Hannah (Schwartz) H.; m. Deborah Weinerman, June 18, 1950 (dec. 1995); children: Richard, Ellen Harwood Jacobs, Michael, Jonathan; m. Cathleen Hamilton, May 25, 1997. AB, Columbia U., 1949, LLB, 1952. Bar: N.Y. 1954, U.S. Dist. Ct. (ea. and so. dists.) N.Y. 1956, U.S. Supreme Ct. 1960. Assoc. Benjamin Harwood, Bklyn., 1953-56; pvt. practice Levittown, N.Y., 1956-65; law clk. to justice N.Y. Supreme Ct., Mineola, 1961-65, justice, 1982-92, appellate divsn., 1987-92; ptnr. Mishkin, Miner, Harwood & Semel, Mineola, 1965-69, Shayne, Dachs, Stanisci & Harwood, Mineola, 1969-81, Bower & Gardner, N.Y.C., 1992-94; counsel Jaspan, Schlesinger & Hoffman, 1994—. Mem. N.Y. State Assembly, 1966-72; chmn. Nassau County Dem. Com., 1973-81; commr. elections Nassau County Bd. Elections, 1976-81; bd. dirs. Nat. Conf. Christians and Jews, 1993-98. With USNR, 1944-46, U.S. Merchant Marines. Mem. N.Y. State Bar Assn., Nassau County Bar Assn. (chmn. cts. com. 1971-73, chmn. pro bono com. 1988-90, bd. dirs. 1997-2000, Nassau-Suffolk Law Svcs. Committment to Justice medal 2002), Mill River Club. Jewish. Home: 2 Bull Calf Ln Centerport NY 11721-1669 Office: Jaspan Schlesinger & Hoffman 300 Garden City Plz Garden City NY 11530-3324 Fax: 516-393-8282. E-mail: sharwood@jshllp.com.

HARWOOD, VIRGINIA ANN, retired nursing educator; b. Lawrenceville, Ohio, Nov. 5, 1925; d. Warren Leslie and Ruth Ann (Wilson) H.; m. Kenneth Dale Juillerat, Dec. 21, 1946 (div. 1972); children: Rozanne Augsburger, Vicki Anderson, Carol Mann, Karen Albaugh. RN, City Hosp. Sch. Nursing, Springfield, Ohio, 1946; BSN, Ind. U., 1968; MS in Edn., Purdue U., 1973, PhD, 1982. Cert. psychiat./mental health nurse, ANA. Staff nurse various hosps., 1946-60; pub. health nursing supr. Whitley County Health Dept., Columbia City, Ind., 1960-65; nursing supr., coordinator staff devel. Ft. Wayne (Ind.) State Hosp., 1965-69; faculty sch. nursing Parkview Hosp., Ft. Wayne, 1969-74; faculty dept. nursing Ball State U., Muncie, Ind., 1974-77; dir. nursing program Thomas More Coll., Ft. Mitchell, Ky., 1977-79; faculty sch. nursing Purdue U., West Lafayette, Ind., 1979-80; dean sch. nursing Ashland (Ohio) Coll., 1980-83; retired, 1983-86; charge nurse admission psychiat. unit VA Med. Ctr., Marion, Ind., 1986-93, ret., 1994—. Active Rep. Nat. Com., 1978—, U.S. Senatorial Club, 1984—, Rep. Pres. Task Force, 1982—; mem. ch. coun. Grace Luth. Ch., Gas City, Ind., 1993-96; bd. dirs. Luth. Ctr., Ball State U., Muncie, Ind., 1994-96; bd. mgrs. Covington Creek Condominium Assn., 1997-2001; vol. Foellinger-Freeman Bot. Conservatory, 1993—. Mem. Am. Nurses Found., Ohio State Nurses Assn. (pres. Mohican dist. 1981-83), Mensa, Intertel, Sigma Theta Tau, U.S. Amateur Ballroom Dancing Assn. (bd. dirs. Ft. Wayne chpt. 1998—, v.p. 2000, pres. 2001), Ft. Wayne Woman's Club. Avocations: travel, reading, dancing, orchid culture. Home: 6611 Quail Ridge Ln Fort Wayne IN 46804-2875

HARYADI, SATISH GOVINDARAM, structural engineer, researcher; b. Bangalore, Karnataka, India, July 18, 1965; came to U.S., 1991; s. Govinda Ram and Janaki G. Haryadi; m. Bhagavathi B. Yedur, Dec. 20, 1992; 1 child, Neehar. BEng, Rashtreeya Vidyalaya Coll. Engring., Bangalore, 1987; MEng, U Visvesvariah Coll. Engring., Bangalore, 1990; PhD, Va. Tech., 1996. Project asst. Indian Inst. Sci., Bangalore, 1987-91; structural engr. Quantum Cons. Inc., Lansing, Mich., 1997-98; sr. structural engr. Altair Engring., Troy, Mich., 1998—. Asst. to editor Madflyer Newsletter, Blacksburg, Va., 1994-96; reviewer, contbr. conf. and jour. papers for profl. socs. Mentor Focus-Hope, Detroit, 1999. Scholar U. Visvesvariah, 1988-90. Mem. AIAA, ASME, Am. Soc. Engring. Edn., Soc. Automotive Engrs., Ctr. Composite Materials and Structures. Avocations: computer building, software development, reading, plants, psychology. Home: 3619 Blue Heron Ln Bloomfield Hills MI 48309 Office: Thyssenkrupp Budd Co PO Box 2601 3155 W Big Beaver Rd Troy MI 48007-2601 E-mail: sharyadi@altair.com.

HARYONO, IGNATIUS WIBISONO, writer; s. Henricus Harjono Martodirjo and Anastasia Kusmaria Soemodirjo; m. Wijakti Karlina Harlim, Dec. 24, 1943. PhD, Rosevelt U., Brussels, 1980; DD, Rosevelt U. Belgium, Brussels, 1981. Philosophy docent Pajajaran State U., Bandung, Indonesia, 1968—73; u. prof. Parahyangan Cath. U., Bandung, 1972—79; prof. State and Cath. U., Bandung, 1972—78; asst. to provincial Order of the Holy Cross, Bandung, 1975—79; asst. to bishop Diocese of Bandung, 1978—80; asst. to chaplain Cath. Ch., L.A., 1990—; requisitions mgr. QuestDiagnostics Inc. Dir. USA Today, Glendale, 1985—90. Author: (book) Was Mary Also Redeemed, 1989, poems in Nat. Libr. of Poetry; contbr. articles to religious publs. Dir. religious edn. Indonesian Cath. Cmty. of Archdiocese, L.A., Calif., 1994—2000; dir., leader Bible Readers Club, 1995. Lt. col. titular chaplaincy Indonesian Army, 1972—79. Recipient Presdl. award, W. Java Cath. Youth Orgn., 1973, 1979, Moderator award, Cathedral Youth Orgn., 1978, 1979, Indonesian Cath. Cmty. award, 2001, award, KKIA Inc., 2001. Master: Iggy LLC (immigrants helper 2000—01, pres., owner). Populist. Roman Catholic. Avocation: travel.

HASAN, AHMED ABUL KASHEM, biomedical researcher, research scientist; b. Faridpur, Bangladesh, Jan. 7, 1955; s. Adeluddin Ahmed (dec.) and Hamida Begum; m. Tahmina Ferdaus, Mar. 2, 1984; children: Jishan Adel, Joshua Adel. HSC, Dhaka (Bangladesh) Coll., 1973; MD Diploma with Honors, Moscow 2nd Med. Inst., 1980; PhD in Internal Medicine, Cardiology, Acad. Med. Scis., Moscow, 1986. splst.-cardiologist, Moscow, 1986; gen. practitioner internal medicine, Moscow, 1980; cardiologist, gen. med. practitioner Bangladesh Med. Coun., 1981. House physician Hosp. Inst. Internal Medicine Acad. Med. Scis., Moscow, 1980-82, staff cardiologist, fellow Hosp. Inst. Clin. Cardiology, 1982-86; cardiology cons. Dhaka, Bangladesh, 1986-87; postdoct., rsch. assoc. dept. biochemistry and thrombosis rsch. Temple U., Phila., 1987-91; rsch. asst., prof. dept. med. biochemistry Temple U. Sch. Medicine, Phila., 1991; rsch. investigator dept. internal medicine U. Mich. Med. Ctr., Ann Arbor, 1991-96, asst. rsch. scientist, asst. prof. dept. internal medicine, 1996—2002; founder, v.p., dir. rsch. Thromgen, Inc., Ann Arbor, 1995—2002; program adminstr. Nat. Heart, Lung and Blood Inst., NIH, Bethesda, Md., 2002—. Spkr. in field. Contbr. numerous articles to sci. and med. jours., chpts. to books including Jour. Biol. Chemistry, Procs. NAS, Blood, Thrombosis & Haemostasis, Am. Jour. Physiology, Biochemistry, Circulation; reviewer Am. Inst. Biol. Scis., Am. Nat. Acad. Scis., Am. Jour. Physiology. Fellow Am. Coll. Cardiology (assoc.); mem. AHA (coun. on clin. cardiology 1986, coun. on thrombosis 1990), AAAS. Home: 18497 Perdido Bay Terr Leesburg VA 20176 Office: NHLBI/NIH 6701 Rockledge Dr RICL II Bethesda MD 20892 E-mail: hasana@nhlbi.nih.gov.

HASAN, NASIR, internist; b. London, July 22, 1962; came to U.S., 1994; s. Nizam Ul and Razia Hasan; m. Samira Hayee, Sept. 26, 1991; children: Muhammed Ali, Safdar Ali. MB, ChB, Liverpool (Eng.) U., 1987. Diplomate Am. Bd. Internal Medicine, Am. Bd. Quality Assurance and Utilization Rev. Physicians. Ho. officer, sr. ho. officer, registrar various hosps., Eng., 1988-94; intern in internal medicine Hahnemann U. Hosp., Phila., 1994-95, resident in internal medicine, 1995-97; hospitalist physician Northeastern Hosp., Phila., 1997—. Recipient Physicians Recognition award AMA, 1999. Mem. ACP, Royal Coll. Physicians (U.K.). Moslem. Avocations: martial arts, tourism. Office: Northeastern Hosp 2301 E Allegheny Ave Philadelphia PA 19134-4497

HASAN, NAUSHERWAN, civil engineer, consultant; b. Sialkot, Pakistan, Feb. 4, 1941; came to U.S., 1973; s. Sheikh M. and Rashida Hasan; m. Sonia Ariff, Jan. 6, 1973; 1 child, Saad. BSCE, Karachi (Pakistan) U., 1962; MSCE, Northwestern U., 1964. Registered profl. engr., N.Y. Asst. engr. on Mangla Dam, Binnie & Ptnrs., Mangla, Pakistan, 1962-63; rsch. asst. Northwestern U., Evanston, Ill., 1963-64; sr. engr. Zafar and Assocs., Karachi, 1966-73; engr. Ebasco Svcs. Inc. (now Raytheon Engrs. and Constructors, N.Y.C., 1964-66, sr. engr., 1973-81, prin. engr., 1981-86, cons. engr., 1986—. Presenter Hydropower Conf., Nice, 1995. Author: High Performance Concrete in Severe Environment, 1993, Watermain Retrofit with Low Shrink Concrete, 1998, San Roque Power Tunnel Steel Liner, 2003. Sec., bd. of trustees Muslim Majlis, S.I., N.Y., 1988-98, 2003—, tchr., 1991-93. Mem. ASCE, ASTM (various subcoms. of C-9 com. 1979—). Republican. Moslem. Achievements include research on concrete longevity. Office: Wash Group Internat 2 Penn Plz New York NY 10121

HASAN, SAIYID ZAFAR, social work educator; b. Allahabad, India, July 5, 1930; came to U.S., 1971, naturalized, 1979; s. Saiyid Akhtar and Alia (Khatoon) H.; m. Nuzhat Ara, Nov. 3, 1961; children: Shirin, Simin, Akbar, Jafar. BA with honors, U. Lucknow, India, 1948, MA, LLB, 1949, diploma in social svc., 1950, MS in Social Work, 1955; D Social Work, Columbia U., 1958. Cert. social worker, Ky. Rsch. asst. U. Lucknow, 1950-51, lectr. social work, 1951-57, reader, 1957-65, prof., head dept., 1965-71; prof. social work U. Ky., Lexington, 1971-98, dean Coll. Social Work, 1979-96. Mem. Coun. Social Work Edn., Washington, 1971-98; mem. adv. council Multidisciplinary Ctr. on Gerontology and Human Devel., Lexington, 1981—. Author: Federal Grants and Public Assistance, 1963, Research in Sociology and Social Work, 1971, Mental Health Professionals Perceive Knowledge and Skill Needs, 1981—, Mental Health-Rural Aging Multidisciplinary Curriculums, 1982; contbr. articles to profl. jours. Active civic and social orgns., India; pres. Tenant Svcs. and Assistance, Inc., Lexington, 1980-82; active United Way of Bluegrass, Lexington, 1983—. UN social welfare scholar, 1954-56. Mem. AAUP, Indian Assn. Trained Social Workers, Coun. Social Work Edn. Home: 735 Brookhill Dr Lexington KY 40502-3312 Office: U Ky Coll Social Work Lexington KY 40506-0001

HASAN, SYED EQBAL, environmental geologist, educator; b. Patna, Bihar, India, Apr. 15, 1939; came to U.S. 1973; s. Syed Mohammad and Heyat (Imam) H.; m. Faruukh Hasan, Jan. 26, 1968; children: Danish, Zeenat, Zeba. BS, Patna U., 1960; MS, Roorkee U., India, 1963; PhD, Purdue U., 1978. Jr. geologist Geol. Survey of India, Lucknow, 1965-70, sr. geologist, 1971-73; vis. asst. prof. Mich. Tech. U., Houghton, 1978, U. Ariz., Tucson, 1978-79; asst. prof., then assoc. prof. geology U. Mo., Kansas City, 1979-97, prof., 1998—, dir. Ctr. for Applied Environ. Rsch., 1996—. Author: (textbook) Geology and Hazardous Waste Management, 1996 (Claire P. Holdrege award Assn. Eng. Geologists 1998). Recipient Educators Environ. Excellence award U.S. EPA's Region VII, 1999. Fellow: Geol. Soc. Am. (Burwell Jr. award com., engring. geology div. 2001—), Geol. Soc. India (life); mem.: Internat. Assn. Engring. Geologists, Assn. Engring. Geologists, Assn. Mo. Geologists, Phi Kappa Phi. Avocations: photography, tennis. Office: Univ of Mo Dept Geosciences Kansas City MO 64110-2499 Fax: (816) 235-5535. E-mail: hasans@umkc.edu.

HASCHAK, PAUL G. librarian, writer; b. Cleveland, Ohio, May 13, 1948; s. George and Sophie Haschak; m. Linda Brayden, Jan. 6, 1942; children: Lorraine Lovel, Teri Hopkins. BA, Cleve. State U., 1976; MLS, La. State U., 1985. Lectr., chem. info. sources Southeastern La. U., 2001—02, libr., 1989—. Bd. of governors Internat. Consortium for the Advancement of Academic Publ., Athabasca, Canada, 2000—. Contbr. articles to profl. jours. E-4 U.S. Army, 1968—70, Fort Knox, KY; Qui Nhon, Vietnam. Mem.: ALA, Am. Chem. Soc., Assn. of Coll. and Rsch. Libraries. Home: 207 Ruland Hammond LA 70401 Office: Southeastern Louisiana University Slu 10896 Hammond LA 70402 Office Fax: 985-549-3995. E-mail: phaschak@selu.edu.

HASE, DAVID JOHN, lawyer; b. Milw., Feb. 27, 1940; s. John Henry and Catherine Charlotte (Leekley) H.; m. Penelope Sue Pritchard, Sept. 2, 1964; children: Jeffrey David, Jennifer Anne, John Paul. AB, Dartmouth Coll., 1962; LLB, U. Wis., 1965. Bar: Wis. 1965, U.S. Dist. Ct. (ea. dist.) Wis. 1965, U.S. Ct. Appeals (7th cir.) 1971, U.S. Ct. Appeals (D.C. cir.) 1975, U.S. Ct. Appeals (9th cir.) 1989, U.S. Supreme Ct. 1975. Assoc. Grootemaat, Cook & Franke, Milw., 1965-67, ptnr., shareholder, 1968-70; shareholder Cook & Franke S.C., Milw., 1970-73; legal counsel to gov. Wis., Madison, 1973-74; dep. atty. gen. State of Wis., Madison, 1974-76; assoc. Foley & Lardner, Milw., 1976-77, ptnr., 1977-94; shareholder Cook & Franke S.C., Milw., 1994—. Mem. Sch. Bd., Mequon, Wis., 1971-94, treas., 1973-75, pres., 1975-94. Mem. ABA. Democrat. Home: 2108 W Raleigh Ct Mequon WI 53092-5416 Office: Cook & Franke SC 660 E Mason St Ste 401 Milwaukee WI 53202-3877 E-mail: hase@cf-law.com.

HASEGAWA, TOMOHIRO, marketing manager; b. San Francisco, Nov. 26, 1962; s. Akira and Miyoko (Okada) H.; 1 child, Audrey Kei Hueymiin. BSEE, MSEE, MIT, 1985. Data clk. Bell Labs., Murray Hill, N.J., 1979-80; computer programmer Ctr. for Space Rsch., MIT, Cambridge, Mass., 1981-82; coop. engring. intern Hewlett Packard Co., Andover, Mass., 1982-85, rsch. and design engr., 1985-92; sales devel. mktg. mgr. Hewlett Packard/Agilent Techs., 1992-2001; mktg. mgr. Imaging Sys. Divsn. Agilent Techs., Japan, 2001—. Coll. recruiter Hewlett Packard Co., Andover, 1987-92. Inventee (with others) pulsed doppler flow mapping apparatus, method and apparatus for elimination of mirroring in signal processing system; contbr. articles to profl. jours. Recipient Raymond Freany Meml. award Town of New Providence (N.J.), 1980; MIT scholar, 1984-85. Mem. Straight Down & Spare Parts Volleyball Clubs, Eta Kappa Nu, Tau Beta Pi. Avocations: travel, music, competative sports. Office: Hewlett Packard Co 3000 Minuteman Rd Andover MA 01810-1099 Home: # 212 733 Turnpike St North Andover MA 01845-6157 E-mail: tomo_hasegawa@agilent.com., tho1845@yahoo.com.

HASEK, DOMINIK, hockey player; b. Pardubice, Czech Republic, Jan. 29, 1965; Goaltender Buffalo Sabres, 1992—. Recipient Vezina Trophy, 1994, 1995, 1996, 1997, 1998, Hart Trophy, 1996—97, 1997—98, Lester B. Pearson, 1997. Office: Buffalo Sabres Marine Midland Arena One Seymour H Knox III Plaza Buffalo NY 14203

HASEK, JANE ELLEN, academic administrator; b. Chgo., Feb. 23, 1940; d. Harold Chester and Margaret Lillian (Kennedy) Blecher; m. Wayne Earl HAsek, Aug. 7, 1960; children: Susan Randall, Mark. B of Liberal Studies, U. Okla., 1978; MS in Higher Edn., Drake U., 1982, MS in Nursing, 2000; D of Ednl. Adminstrn., U. No. Iowa, 1987. Instr. oper. rm. tech. St. Francis Hosp., Waterloo, Iowa, 1970-71; instr. emergency med. tech. Hawkeye Inst. Tech., Waterloo, Iowa, 1971-82; coord. cardiac rehab. program St. Francis Hosp., 1970-72, supr. spl. care units, 1970-74, dir. insvc., 1971-74; ednl. cons. Black Hawk Area Family Practice Residency Program, Waterloo, 1978-81; coord. adult health occupations Hawkeye Inst. Tech., 1974-80; v.p. edn. Allen Meml. Hosp., Waterloo, 1980-95; chancellor Allen Coll., Waterloo, 1989—. Mem. task force Iowa Bd. Nursing, Des Moines; cons. N.E. Iowa Family Practice Residency, Waterloo, 1977-83; mem. gov.'s task force Emergency Med. Svc., Des Moines, 1976-82, Nursing Shortage, 2001. Newsletter editor Tech. Edn. News, 1977, Iowa Bd. Nursing, 1989-90. Bd. dirs. Iowa State Dept. Health, Des Moines, 1989-2002; cmty. advisor Jr. League, Waterloo/Cedar Falls, Iowa, 1994-95; bd. dirs. Kiwanis, Waterloo, 1993-95, pres. 2002-03; pres. sch. bd. Reinbeck (Iowa) Schs., 1981-90. Recipient Gov.'s award Outstanding Vol. Svc., Iowa, 1991; named Alumni of Yr., Lincoln Gen. Hosp. Sch. Nursing, 1989, INA Teresa Christy awardee, 1997. Mem. ANA, Nat. League Nursing, Iowa Nurses Assn. (rsch. bd.), Iowa League Nursing (v.p. 1989-90, pres. 1998-2000), Phi Delta Kappa, Sigma Theta Tau. Independent. Methodist. Avocations: skiing, travel, biking. Office: Allen Coll Nursing 1825 Logan Ave Waterloo IA 50703-1916 E-mail: hasekje@ihs.org.

HASELEY, DENNIS, psychoanalyst, writer; s. Robert and Margaret Haseley; m. Claudia Lament, Oct. 12, 1986; 1 child, Connor. AB, Oberlin Coll., 1972; MSW, NYU, 1982; grad., N.Y. Psychoanalytic Inst., 2000. Mem. faculty Hunter Coll., N.Y.C., 1986—96; asst. clin. prof. NYU Med. Ctr., 2001—; faculty NYU Psychoanalytic Inst., 2001—; pvt. practice in psychoanalysis and psychotherapy N.Y.C. Author: A Story for Bear (Top Ten, Booksense 76, 2002), My Father Doesn't Know About the Woods and Me, The Counterfeiter, The Cave of Snores, Kite Flier (Am. Booksellers Pick of the Lists; Notable Trade Book in the Field of Social Studies, 1986), The Soap Bandit, The Scared One (Parents' Choice Remarkable Book for Lit., 1983), The Old Banjo (Jr. Lit. Guild Selection; Child Study Assn. Children's Books of the Yr., 1983), (TV series) The Pirate Who Tried to Capture the Moon, The Amazing Thinking Machine, Crosby, Getting Him, Horses with Wings, Dr. Gravity, Ghost Catcher, Shadows, The Thieves Market. Ficton fellow, Artists' Fellowships/N.Y. Found. for the Arts, 1994, Leopold Schepp Found. scholar in Social Work, 1981. Mem.: APA, NASW, Internat. Psychoanalytic Assn., Soc. Children's Book Writers and Illustrators, Author's Guild, Psychoanalytic Assn. of NY. Avocation: running. Office: 31 Wash Sq W Penthouse B New York NY 10011

HASELKORN, ROBERT, virology educator; b. Bklyn., Nov. 7, 1934; s. Barney and Mildred (Seplowin) H.; m. Margot Block, June 23, 1957; children: Deborah, David. AB, Princeton U., 1956; PhD, Harvard U., 1959. Asst. prof. biophysics U. Chgo., 1961-64, assoc. prof., 1964-69, prof., chmn. dept., 1969-84, F.L. Pritzker Disting. Service prof. dept. molecular genetics and cell biology, 1984—; dir. Ctr. for Photochemistry and Photobiology, 1987—; pres. Integrated Genomics, Inc., 2000—01. Chmn. bd. dirs. Integrated Genomics, Inc., Chgo., 1997—; cons. virology and rickettsiology study sect. USPHS, 1969-73; mem. sci. adv. bd. Sloan-Kettering Inst., 1978-79; mem. nitrogen fixation panel U.S. Dept. Agr., 1978-79; mem. panel sci. advs. UNIDO Internat. Ctr. for Genetic Engring. and Biotech., 1984-94, 97—; mem. recombinant DNA adv. com. NIH, 1991-95; adj. scientist Woods Hole Oceanographic Instn., 1994—. Editor: Virology, 1973-2000; mem. editl. bd. Molecular Microbiology; contbr. articles to profl. jours. Trustee Marine Biol. Lab., Woods Hole, Mass., 2003—. Recipient USPHS Rsch. Career Devel. award, 1963-69, Interstate Postgrad. Med. Assn. Rsch. award, 1967, Darbaker prize Bot. Soc. Am., 1982, Gregor Mendel medal in biol. scis. Acad. Scis. Czech Republic, 1996, Buzatti-Traverso lectr., CNR, Rome, 1997; Am. Cancer Soc. postdoctoral rsch. fellow ARC Virus Rsch. Unit, Cambridge, Eng., 1959-61, Guggenheim fellow Institut Pasteur, Paris, 1975, Sackler fellow Tel Aviv U., 1987. Fellow AAAS, Am. Acad. Arts and Scis. (chmn., midwest coun., v.p. 1993-99), Am. Acad. Microbiology; mem. NAS, Internat. Soc. Plant Molecular Biology (pres. 1987-89). Home: 5834 S Stony Island Ave Chicago IL 60637-2060 Office: U Chgo 920 E 58th St Chicago IL 60637 E-mail: rh01@uchicago.edu.

HASELMANN, JOHN PHILIP, management consultant; b. Summit, N.J., Feb. 25, 1940; s. John and Elizabeth Haselmann; divorced; children— Terri Lee, Karen Lynn, Guy Philip BSEE, N.J. Inst. Tech., 1961; MBA in Indsl. Mgmt., Ops. Research and Mgmt. Sci., U. Pa., 1963. Asst. dir. Behavior Systems, Phila., 1961-63; prof. econs. Union Coll., 1964-66; mgr. mgmt. sci. div. Western Electric Co., Princeton, NJ, 1970-73; mgr. mktg. sci. div. AT&T Long Lines, Bedminster, NJ, 1974-78; pres., founder, chmn. of bd. Info. Mgmt. Group, Morristown, NJ, 1978-83; pres. Trinet Inc., Morristown, NJ, 1984-85; pres., founder, chmn. of bd. Entity Advt. and Graphics, Inc., Florham Park, NJ, 1986-88, Integrated Mktg. Svcs., Inc., Parsippany, NJ, 1989—; founder and exec. dir. Am. Employers Assn., Washington, 1989—95; co-founder, vice chmn., exec. v.p., bd. dirs. TCI Comm. Mgmt. Corp., Parsippany, NJ, 1991-95; pres., founder, chmn. bd. Computer Tech. Integration, 1995—; founder, exec. dir. Assn. for the Adv. Knowledge-Mgmt., Morristown, NJ, 2001—. Guest lectr. on application of sci. to problems in mtkg. Columbia Grad. Sch. Bus., Sloan Sch. MIT, Wharton Grad. Sch. U. Pa. Author: Computers and Data Processing Applied to a Personnel Processing System as a Management Tool, 1963, How to Improve the Effectiveness of Your Advertising/Marketing/Sales Investment, 1987, How to Lower the Cost of Getting an Order and Increase Revenues through Improved Market Analysis and Sales Management, 1990. Mem. Am. Mgmt. Assn., Am. Soc. Assn. Execs., Am. Soc. Profl. Cons. Republican. Lutheran. Avocations: golf, sailing. Office: PO Box 339 Morristown NJ 07963-0339 E-mail: jhaselmann@rcn.com.

HASELTINE, FLORENCE PAT, obstetrician, gynecologist, research administrator; b. Phila., Aug. 17, 1942; d. William R. and Jean Adele Haseltine; m. Frederick Cahn, Mar. 12, 1964 (div. 1969); m. Alan Chodos, Apr. 18, 1970; children: Anna, Elizabeth. BA in Biophysics, U. Calif., Berkeley, 1964; PhD in Biophysics, MIT, 1969; MD, Albert Einstein Coll. of Medicine, 1972. Diplomate Am. Bd. Ob-Gyn., Am. Bd. Reproductive Endocrinology. Asst. prof. dept. ob-gyn. and pediatrics Yale U., New Haven, 1976—82, assoc. prof. dept. ob-gyn. and pediatrics, 1982—85; dir. Ctr. for Population Research, Nat. Inst. Child Health and Human Devel. NIH, Bethesda, Md., 1985—; founder Haseltine System, Inc., Products for the Disabled, 1995—. Co-author: Woman Doctor, 1976, Magnetic Resonance of the Reproductive System, 1987; co-editor: 25 books on reproductive scis. Bd. dirs. Older Women's League, 1998—, Am. Women in Sci., 1998—. Fellow: AAAS (bd. dirs.); mem.: Soc. Cell Biology, Soc. for Advancement Women's Health Rsch. (founder, bd. dirs.), Soc. Gynecol. Investigation, Inst. of Medicine. Office: NIH/NICHD Ctr Population Rsch 6100 Executive Blvd Rm 8b07 Bethesda MD 20892-0001

HASELTINE, JAMES LEWIS, artist, consultant; b. Portland, Oreg., Nov. 7, 1924; s. William Ambrose and Clara Thusnelda (Scharpf) H.; m. Jane Winsberg, Nov. 14, 1948 (div. 1953); m. Margaret Ann Wilson, Aug. 15, 1955; children: Thomas, Jean, Kay, Suzanne, Angela. Student, Ark. State Coll., 1943-44, Reed Coll., 1946-47, Mus. Art Sch., 1947, 49, Art Inst. Chgo., 1947-48, Bklyn. Mus. Sch., 1950-51. Dir. Salt Lake Art Ctr., Salt Lake City, 1961-67; exec. dir. Wash. State Arts Commn., Olympia, Wash., 1967-80; prof. artist, 1950—. Vis. lectr. art history U. Utah, Salt Lake City, 1964-65; panel mem. Nat. Endowment for the Arts, Washington, 1969-80; various art cons. positions, 1980—. Author: 100 Years of Utah Painting, 1965 (Mormon History Assn. award 1965); paintings and prints represented in permanent collections Portland Art Mus., Oakland Art Mus., Mus. Art U. Oreg., Mus. Fine Arts U. Utah, Tacoma Art Mus., Willamette U., Salem, Oreg. Mem. search com. for pres. Evergreen State Coll., Olympia, 1984; trustee Portland Art Mus., 1953-55. With U.S. Army, 1942-46, ETO. Mem. Western Assn. Art Mus. (pres. 1964-66), Artists Equity Assn. (nat. dir. 1955-58, chmn. Oreg. chpt. 1953-55), Western States Arts Found. (bd. dirs. 1975-77), Brit.-Am. Art Assn. (trustee 1980-84). Home and Office: 3820 Sunset Beach Dr NW Olympia WA 98502-3542

HASELTON, MARY MICHELSON, retired foreign service officer, artist; b. Kansas City, Mo., May 15, 1920; d. Michael A. and Jeannette (MacFarlane) Michelson; m. George Harry Haselton, Sept. 4, 1964 (dec. Jan. 1995). Student, Washburn U., 1939-41, U. Tex., 1947-52; B in Liberal Arts, Harvard U., 2001. Rsch. sec. Mil. Intelligence U.S. Army, Econ. Def. Bd., Washington, 1941-43; statis. analyst Quartermaster U.S. Army Depot, San Antonio, 1943-44; office mgr. physicians San Antonio, 1944-46; sec. to dir. rsch. IMF, Washington, 1946-47; legis. asst. U.S. Senate, Washington, 1954-59; internat. rels. tchr. Simons Rock Coll., Great Barrington, Mass., 1966-72; fgn. svc. officer Dept. State, Washington, 1960-64, 74-79. Sr. assoc. mem. St. Antony's Coll., Oxford (Eng.) U., 1972—. Exhbns. include Tex. Watercolor Soc., Delgado Mus., New Orleans. Bd. dirs., exec. com. Austin Symphony Orch., 1947-53; mem. various coms. Tex. Fine Arts Assn., Austin, 1947-53; U.S. del. to world population conf. UN, Bucharest, Romania, 1974, Mexico City, 1975. Recipient numerous awards for paintings. Avocations: painting, music, philosophy, science, religion. Home: 85 S Main St Hanover NH 03755 E-mail: mhaselton@valley.net.

HASELWOOD, ELDON LAVERNE, retired education educator; b. Barnard, Mo., July 19, 1933; m. Joan Haselwood; children: Ann, Karen, Polly, Amy. BS in Edn., U. Omaha, 1960; MA in Libr. Sci., U. Denver, 1963; PhD, U. Nebr., 1972. Libr. Omaha Pub. Schs., 1960-61, Lewis Cen. Community Schs., Council Bluffs, Iowa, 1961-63; documents libr. U. Omaha, 1963-66; prof. dept. tchr. edn. U. Nebr., Omaha, 1966—, coord. ednl. tech. Coll. Edn., 1993—2002, ret., 2002. Cons. Nat. Park Svc., Omaha, 1978—. Cpl. U.S. Army, 1953-55. Mem. ALA (councilor 1988-91, excellence in teaching award 1987), Am. Assn. Sch. Librs., Mountain Plains Libr. Assn. (rep. 1999—), Nebr. Libr. Assn. (pres. 1981, meritorious svc. award 1983, Mad Hatter award 1998), Nebr. Ednl. Media Assn. (disting. svc. award 1993), Iowa Assn. Ednl. Media, Nebr. Libr. Commn. (commr. 1981-86). Home: 615 S 122nd St Omaha NE 68154-3015

HASEN, BURTON STANLEY, artist; b. N.Y.C., Dec. 19, 1921; s. Herman Harold and Mina (Leibowitz) H. Student, Art Students League, 1940-42, 46, H. Hoffmann Sch. Fine Arts, 1947-48, Acad. dela Grande-Chaumiere, Paris, 1948-50; student (Fulbright grantee), Acad. delle Belle-Arti, 1959-60. Tchr. Sch. Visual Arts, N.Y.C., 1953-2000, Mpls. Sch. Art and Design, 1966 One-man shows include T'Pandje Gallerie, Belgium, 1981, Anita Shapolsky Gallery, 1987, 1992, 94, Gallery 1100-Niagara, Buffalo, 1993, Staller Ctr. for Arts, SUNY, Stony Brook, 1995, Hamilton Coll., Clinton, N.Y., 1996, Hugode Pagano gallery, N.Y.C., 1997, Nat. Jewish Mus., Washington, 1997, Islip Art Mus., N.Y., 2003; group shows include Mus. Modern Art, Paris, 1951, Whitney Mus. Am. Art, N.Y.C., 1964, Corcoran Gallery Art, Washington, 1959, Kresge Art Center, U. So. Ill., 1961, Krannert Art Mus.-U. Ill., Urbana, Am. Acad. Arts and Letters, N.Y.C., 1965, Berlin Acad. Arts, 1956, W.G. Picker Gallery, 1969, Colgate U., Hamilton, N.Y., 1969, Mus. Modern Art, N.Y.C., 1966, Met. Mus. Art, N.Y.C., 1952, Worcester (Mass.) Art Mus., 1968, Walker Art Center, Mpls., 1966, Bklyn. Mus., 1954, Artist Choice Mus., N.Y.C., NAD, N.Y.C., 1985, Anita Shapolsky Gallery, 1989, 90, 92, 2000, Neo Persona Gallery, 1989, 90, Rider Coll., 1992, Albright-Knox Mus., 1992, Islip Art Mus., 1992, Cleve. Inst. Art, 1993, Swiss Cultural Inst., 1993, David Anderson Gallery, Buffalo, 1993, Henry St. Settlement, N.Y.C., 1993, Sordoni Art Gallery, Wilkes-Barre, Pa., 1994, Nat. Acad., 1995, 96, 97, 99, 2000, 01, 03, Alysia Duckler Gallery, Portland, 1996, Pagano Gallery, N.Y.C., 1997, 98, Sheldon Meml. Art Gallery, U. Nebr., Lincoln; represented in permanent collections Walker Art Center, Worcester Art Mus., Hampton Inst., CIBA-GEIGY Co., Bibliotheque Nationale, Paris, N.Y. Pub. Library, Princeton U., Columbia U., Mus. Fine Art, Portland, Maine, N.Y. Crestview Coll., Muhlenberg, Fine Prints Dept., SUNY, Buffalo, 1989, CCNY, Rider U., Lawrenceville, N.J., 1993, Islip Mus., East Islip, N.Y., Hamilton Coll., Clinton, N.Y., Nat. Jewish Mus., Washington, Southeast Mo. State U., Cape Gradeau, Mo., Birmingham, Southern Coll., Ala., Hudgens Ctr. Arts, Duluth, Ga., Savannah Coll. Art and Design, Birmingham Mus. Art, Ala., High Mus., Miami, Fla., Newberger Mus. Art, Purchase, N.Y.; illustrator books, 1959-89, Beyond the Furies, 1985, Franklin Mint, Phila., 1991, Alea Mag., 1993, Newark Mus., 1993, Islip (N.Y.) Mus., 1994; archives include Smithsonian Mus. Am. Art, Centre Georges Pompidou, Musée d'Art Moderne, Paris. Served with AUS, 1942-46. Recipient Emily Lowe Found. Purchase prize, 1955; N.Y. Found. Arts grantee, 1990, Nat. Acad. Design, 2001; Florsheim Grant 1993, 1997; Pollack Krasner fellow 1995-96, 1999-2000, 2003. Mem. Nat. Acad. Design, Fulbright Alumni Assn., N.Y. Artists Equity. E-mail: burthasen@aol.com. *The motivating force of my life has been the desire to paint meaningful paintings that express my innermost feelings. Art for me is the exhilarating experience of discovering new worlds. Each work is a projection of myself into the cosmic universe. This compulsion to paint my fantasy has never faltered or been self-deceptive.*

HASEN, RICHARD LESLIE, law educator; b. Bklyn., Sept. 30, 1964; BA, U. Calif., Berkeley, 1986; JD, UCLA, 1991, PhD, 1992. Asst. prof. law Chgo.-Kent Coll. Law, 1994-97; asst. prof. Loyola Law Sch., L.A., 1997-99, prof. law, William Rains fellow, 1999—. Author: The Supreme Court and Election Law: Judging Equality From Baker v. Carr to Bush v. Gore, 2003; co-author: Election Law-Cases and Materials, 2001. Office: Loyola Law Sch 919 S Albany St Los Angeles CA 90015 Fax: 213-380-3769. E-mail: rick.hasen@lls.edu.

HASENAUER, JUDITH ANNE, lawyer; b. Rochester, NY, Sept. 28, 1946; d. William F. and Arline (Burns) H. AA, Monroe C.C., 1966; AB, U. Rochester, 1969; JD, Golden Gate U., 1973; CLU, Am. Coll., 1974. Bar: Calif. 1974, Conn. 1974, U.S. Dist. Ct. Conn. 1975, N.Y. 1983, D.C. 1983, Fla. 1993. Ptnr. Blazzard, Grodd & Hasenauer P.C., Westport, Conn., 1974—. Chmn. regulatory affairs com. Nat. Assn. for Variable Annuities, 1997—. Contbr. articles to profl. jours. Bd. dirs. Friends of Norwalk C.C., Conn., 1977-83; sec. Fairfield County CLUs, Conn., 1983-85. Office: Blazzard Grodd & Hasenauer PC 1600 S Federal Hwy Ste 500 Pompano Beach FL 33062 E-mail: judith.hasenauer@bghpc.com.

HASENFUS, HAROLD JOSEPH, retired mechanical engineer, naval technical director; b. NY, NY, Apr. 9, 1921; s. Joseph Vincent and Ethel Elizabeth (Galvan) Hasenfus; m. Mary Margaret Boone, Nov. 7, 1945; children: James Joseph, Stephen Francis, Jean Marie, Edward Harold. BSME, CCNY, 1943; MSEE, Va. Tech., 1981, MS in physics, 1986. Cert. Vatican's Cert. of Recognition St. Joan of Arc's Roman Cath. /MD, 1959. Rsch. asst.-Manhattan Project U of Chgo., Chgo., 1944; project engr., Manhattan Project Fercleve Corp., Oak Ridge, Tenn., 1945; ordnance engr. Ballistic Rsch. Lab., Aberdeen Proving Ground, Md., 1946—52; chief Ballistic Rsch. Lab., rocket br., Aberdeen Proving Ground, Md., 1952—60; head,satellite applications div. Naval Weapons Lab., Dahlgren, Va., 1960—61; tech. dir. Naval Space Surveillance Sys., Dahlgren, Va., 1961—86, tech. dir. emeritus, 1986—. Cons. Nat. Def. Indsl. Assoc., 1955—60; cons., satellite detection Naval Space Surveillance Sys., Dahlgren, Va., 1986—88; del., Tripartite Conf. on armaments U.S. Army, Quebec, Canada, 1959; del., Tripartite Conf. on artificial Earth satellites U.S. Navy, 1971. Author: (poem) John Adams' Reward, 2002. Chmn., Cub Scout Com. Boy Scouts of Am., Dahlgren, Va., 1971—86. Decorated Group Achievement Dept. of the Navy ; recipient Tech. Dir. emeritus, Naval Space Surveillance Sys. Mem.: ASME (life), AIAA (sr.), Am Inst. for Aeronautics and Astron. (Dir. 1960—62), Am. Rocket Soc., MD Sect. (Pres. 1959), Com. on Guidance for MD, Am. Math. Soc. (hon.), Res. Officers Assoc. (life), Nat. Def. Indus. Assoc. (life), Am. Assoc. for the Advancement of Sci. (life). Democrat. Roman Catholic. Achievements include development of rocket weapons, oversaw advances in the understanding of rockets as artillery weapons. Avocations: singing, languages, acting, poetry, pen and ink drawing. Home: 311 Ingleside Drive, Fredericksburg VA 22405-2344

HASEN-SINZ, SUSAN KATHERINE, state agency administrator, actress; b. LaGrange Park, Ill., Jan. 30, 1965; d. Hans and June Catherine (Huml) H.; m. Mark Thomas Sinz, Aug. 31, 1991; children: Rachel Katherine, Emily June, Kathleen Ruth. BA in Polit. Sci., Spanish, U. Ill., 1987; postgrad., Loyola U., Chgo. Actress Springfield (Ill.) Theatre Ctr., 1987—; mem. mgmt. staff Ill. Dept. Driver Svcs., Chgo., Gov.'s Office, Ill. Dept. Pub. Aid; dep. chief fin. and adminstrn. Gov.'s Office Ill. Toll Hwy. Authority, Downers Grove, chief of adminstrn., 2002—03; dir. human resources City of Largo, Fla., 2003—. Speaker various youth groups, 1985—; dance instr. YMCA, Springfield, 1987, counselor Miss Ill./USA Pageant, Arlington Heights, Ill., 1987; fellow adminstrv. hearings under Sec. of State Jim Edgar, Springfield, 1987—. Lead actress A Day in Hollywood-A Night in the Ukraine, 1987 (Best of Springfield award), 42d St., Ill., 1991—, Oklahoma, Ill., The Dance Factory, Chgo., A...My Name Is Still Alice, Chgo.; actress Manny, nat. tour A Christmas Carol, 1989, Joseph and the Amazing Technicolor Dreamcoat, Ill.; supporting actress Singin' in the Rain, Ill.; backup singer Kenny Rogers Christmas Tour, Ill.; actress, singer, dancer Jesus Christ Superstar, 1992; singer Miss Ill./USA Pageant, 1987; understudy Puttin On the Ritz, Ill., West Side Story, Ill. Active in drama ministry Hope Ch., Springfield; soloist Christ Ch. of Oak Brook, Ill., 1983—, leader youth group Koinonia, also Sunday sch. tchr., elder; student del. Internat. Strategic Affairs Conf., N.Y.C., 1987—; mem. campaign staff Jim Edgar for Gov. Ill., 1991; judge Miss Teen Ill./U.S.A. Pageant; staff asst. Congressman Harris Fawell's Office; rep. for 13th dist. Ill.; vol., singer Salvation Army (youth adv. com.); committeewoman DuPage County Rep. Ctrl. Com., 1999—; social chair, treas. Oak Brook Rep. Women, 1999—; elder Christ Ch. of Oak Brook, 2000-02; bd. dirs. Oak Brook Civic Assn. Recipient Miss Amity award Miss. I.../U.S.A., 1986; scholarship winner Miss Illini contest; Lincoln fellow Mem.: Internat. Bridge Tunnel and Turnpike Assn. (vice chmn. adminstrn. com.), U. Ill. Alumni Assn. (named one of 100 top srs. at Champaign-Urbana campus 1986, named outstanding student 1986—87), Kappa Alpha Theta Alumni Assn. (pres. standards com. 1986—87, songleader 1986—87, chaplain), Kappa Alpha Theta. Home: 24 Sheffield Ln Oak Brook IL 60523-2355 Office: One Authority Dr Downers Grove IL 60515-1703

HASERICK, JOHN ROGER, retired dermatologist; b. Mpls., Sept. 23, 1915; s. Ernest B. and Addie (Swanson) H.; m. Jane Margaret Fleckenstein, May 10, 1941; children: John Roger, Jane. BA, Macalester Coll., 1937; MD, U. Minn., 1941, MS in Dermatology, 1946. Diplomate: Am. Bd. Dermatology (pres. 1975). Intern Ancker Hosp., St. Paul, 1940-41; resident in medicine Univ. Hosps., Mpls., 1941-42, resident in dermatology, 1945-46; pvt. practice Pinehurst, N.C., 1970-87; head dept. dermatology Cleve. Clinic, 1948-67; prof. Case Western Res. U., Cleve., 1967-70; clin. prof. medicine and dermatology Duke U., Durham, N.C., 1970-85; with Pinehurst Dermatology Clinic, 1970-87; clin. prof. dermatology U. Minn., 1997—. Author: LE Primer, 1972, The Wolves Club, 2002; contbr. 75 articles to med. jours.; author: (CD-ROM) Consultations in Lupus Erythematosus, 2003. Mem. Vols. in Medicine, Martin County Med. Soc., Stuart, Fla., 1997—. Recipient Discovery award Dermatology Found., 1999. Fellow ACP; mem. AMA (Hektoen Silver award 1952), Am. Acad. Dermatology (pres. 1974), Am. Soc. Dermatopathology (pres. 1975, Founder's award 1996), N.C. Med. Assn., Am. Soc. Investigative Dermatology, Am. Dermatol. Assn., Country Club of N.C. (Pinehurst), Wolves Club (Pinehurst, pres. 1983). Achievements include discovering LE factor (antinuclear) in blood of patients wih lupus erythematosus. Home: 52 Middleton Pl Southern Pines NC 28387 E-mail: haserick@juno.com.

HASH, ROBERT BRUCE, medical educator; b. Huntington, W.Va., May 28, 1957; m. Jennie Gail Wood; children: Laura, Melissa. MD, U. Louisville, 1982. Assoc. prof. family medicine Mercer U. Sch. Medicine, Macon, Ga., asst. dean acad. affairs. Office: Mercer U Sch Medicine 1550 College St Macon GA 31207

HASHMI, SAJJAD AHMAD, business educator, university dean; b. India, Dec. 20, 1933; m. Monica Ruggiero; children: Serena, Jason, Shawn, Michelle. BA, U. Karachi, 1953, MA, 1956; PhD in Ins., U. Pa., 1962. Lectr. Ohio State U., Columbus, 1962-64; asst. prof. Roosevelt U., Chgo., 1964-66; prof. Ball State U., Muncie, Ind., 1966-83, chmn. dept. fin., 1973-83; Jones disting. prof., dean Sch. Bus. Emporia (Kans.) State U., 1983—. Cons. and speaker to profl. ins. agts., Indpls., Louisville, Springfield, Ill.; tech. advisor Ind. Arts Commn.; vice chmn. bd. trustees Kans. Ins. Edn. Found.; bd. dirs. Blue Cross and Blue Shield of Kans.; appeared on TV and radio programs, testified before N.Y., Kans. and Ind. legis. coms. Author: Insurance is a Funny Business, 1972, Automobile Insurance, 1973, Contemporary Personal Finance, 1985, Make Every Second Count, 1989, Strategies for The Future, 1990; contbr. articles, revs., monographs to profl. publs. Named Prof. of Yr., Ball State U. Students, 1971, Outstanding Tchr. of Yr., Ball State U., 1970. Mem. Am. Risk and Ins. Assn., Midwest Fin. Assn., Fin. Mgmt. Assn., Emporia C. of C., Emporia Country Club, Rotary, Beta Gamma Sigma, Sigma Iota Epsilon, Alpha Kappa Psi, Gamma Iota Epsilon, Phi Kappa Phi. Home: 2909 Lakeridge Rd Emporia KS 66801-5982 Office: Emporia State U Sch of Bus 1200 Commercial St Emporia KS 66801-5087 E-mail: hashmisa@emporia.edu.

HASKAL, ZIV J. radiologist, medical educator; BA, MD, Boston U., 1986. Cert. Diagnostic Radiology Am. Bd. of Radiology, 1992, Certificate Added Qualifications, Interventional Radiology Am. Bd. of Radiology, 2000. Prof. of radiology & surgery NY Presbyn. Hosp., New York, NY, 1999—; assoc. prof. of radiology Univ. of Pa, Dept of Radiology, Phila., 1992—99. Dir. NY Presbyn. Hosp., New York, NY, fellowship dir.; rsch. lab. dir. Div. of Interventional Radiology/ NY Presbyn. Hosp., New York, NY; dir. Columbia U, New York, NY. Author over 110 sci. articles, books, chapt. Recipient The Best Doctors, NY Mag., Repeated citations, Best Docs, Phila. Mag., Repeated Citations, Sadek Hilal, Faculty Rsch. Award, Columbia U., Radiology, 2000, Top Doctors, Castle Connoly, 2002; grantee Prin. Investigator, Multiple Externally Funded Rsch. Trials, 1992—2002. Fellow: Soc. of Inter. Radiology; mem.: Am. Coll. of Radiology, Am. Roentgen Ray Soc., Radiol. Soc. N.Am., Am. Heart Assn. Achievements include Editorial Board, multiple scientific publications; Chair, multiple national scientific committees; research in National Principal Investigator, research trials. Office: Interventional Radiology MHB4-100 Columbia Presb 177 Fort Washington New York NY 10032

HASKAYNE, RICHARD FRANCIS, petroleum company executive; b. Calgary, Alta., Can., Dec. 18, 1934; s. Robert Stanley and Bertha (Hesketh) H.; m. Lee Mary Murray, 1958 (dec. 1993); m. Lois P. Heard, 1995. B.Comm., U. Alta., 1956; postgrad., U. Western Ont., 1968, LLD, U. Calgary, U. Alta. Chartered acct., Alta. With Riddell, Stead & Co., chartered accts., Calgary, 1956-60; corp. acctg. supr. to v.p. fin. Hudson's Bay Oil & Gas Co., Ltd., Calgary, 1960-73; compt. Canadian Arctic Gas Study Ltd., 1973-75; sr. v.p. to pres. Hudson's Bay Oil & Gas Co. Ltd., Calgary, 1975-81; pres., chief exec. officer Home Oil Co., Ltd., Calgary, 1981-91, also bd. dirs.; chmn. bd. NOVA Corp., Calgary, 1992-98. Pres., CEO Interprovencial Pipe Line Co., 1987—91, Interhome Energy, 1989—91; bd. dirs. Fording Inc., chmn. bd., 2001—03; bd. dirs. EnCana Corp.; chmn. bd. dirs. TransCanada PipeLines; bd. dirs. Weyerhaeuser Co.; chmn. bd. TransAlta Corp., 1996—98, TransCan Pipeline Ltd., 1998—, MacMillan Bloedel Ltd., 1996—99; dir. emeritus CIBC. Chmn. emeritus bd. govs. U. Calgary. Recipient award Officer of the Order of Can., 1997. Fellow Fin. Execs. Inst., Inst. Corp. Dirs.; mem. Calgary Petroleum Club (past pres.), Calgary Golf and Country Club, Earl Grey Golf Club, Ranchmen's Club, U. Calgary Chancellor's Club, The York Club, Libr. Club, Commerce Club, Alta Inst. Chartered Accts., Kappa Sigma Office: 2030 Bankers Hall 855 2d St SW Calgary AB Canada T2P 4J8

HASKEL, JULES J. lawyer; b. Bklyn., Sept. 9, 1929; s. Manny and Sadie Haskel; m. Arlene Teitelbaum, Apr. 19, 1957; children: Lynn S. Haskel Lancaster, Barbara I. Haskel Weiner, Carol Haskel Solomon. BS in Journalism, Medill Sch. Journalism, Northwestern U., 1951; JD, NYU, 1954. Bar: N.Y. 1955, U.S. Dist. Ct. (so. and ea. dists.) N.Y. 1957, U.S. Tax Ct. 1958, U.S. Ct. Appeals (2d cir.) 1981, U.S. Supreme Ct. 1962. Assoc. Grossman & Grossman, N.Y.C., 1954-55; exec. dir. membership campaign ABA, N.Y.C., 1955-56; assoc. Otterbourg, Steindler, Houston & Rosen, N.Y.C., 1956-57, Newman & Bisco, N.Y.C., 1957-59; ptnr. Koopersmith & Haskel, Jamaica, N.Y., 1960-77, Durben & Haskel, Garden City, N.Y., 1977-87, Haskel, Hand & Lancaster, 1988-96, Jaspan Schlessinger Hoffman LLP, 1996—. Mem. surrogate's ct. adv. com. N.Y. State Office of Ct. Adminstrn., 1995—. Mem. law com. UJA-Fedn. Jewish Philanthropies of N.Y., 1978—; bd. dirs. Queens Legal Svcs. Corp., 1970-73. Fellow Am. Coll. Trust and Estates Counsel (fiduciary litig. com. 1994-2002); mem. ABA, N.Y. State Bar Assn. (ho. of dels. 1975-92, chmn. trusts and estates law sect. 1982, v.p. 1984-86, exec. com. 1986-89, chair action unit 4 jud. selection and ct. merger 1990-93), N.Y. State Bar Found. (bd. dirs. 1986-2002), Queens County Bar Assn. (pres. 1973-74, chmn. jud. com. 1978-79, editor bar bull. 1964-66), Jamaica Lawyers Club (pres. 1968-69), Nassau County Bar Assn., NYU Law Alumni Assn. (v.p. 1970-73, 77-81). Jewish. Office: Jaspan Schlessinger Hoffman LLP 300 Garden City Plz Garden City NY 11530-3302

HASKELL, ARTHUR JACOB, retired steamship company executive; b. Newark, Apr. 16, 1926; s. Isidore David and Elena (Greenbaum) H.; m. Amparo Serrano, Dec. 31, 1958 (div.); children: Amparo Rocio, Vincent Isidore, Joaquin Arthur; m. Marge Gibson, June 8, 1986. BS, U.S. Naval Acad., 1947; profl. naval engr., MIT, 1953. Sr. procurement engr. Nat. Bulk Carriers, N.Y.C., 1956-62; asst. plant mgr. Western Gear Corp., Belmont, Calif., 1962-64; project engr. Matson Nav. Co., San Francisco., 1964-70, v.p., 1970-73, sr. v.p., 1973-91, ret., 1991. Mem. marine bd. NRC, 1981-85; bd. mgrs. Am. Bur. Shipping, 1988-92; bd. dirs., budget officer Nat. Liberty Ship Meml. Bd. dirs. San Francisco Marine Exchange, 1975-78, v.p., 1976-77, pres., 1977-78. Served to comd. USN, 1947-56. Mem. Soc. Naval Architects and Marine Engrs. (chmn. No. Calif. sect. 1971-72, v.p. 1973-83, exec. com. 1977-80, 83-96, hon. v.p. for life 1983—, pres. 1989-91), Assn. for Preservation of Presdl. Yacht Potomac (bd. govs. 1984—, co-pres. 1993-99). Home: 287 Sheridan Rd Oakland CA 94618-2717

HASKELL, BARBARA, curator; b. San Diego, Nov. 13, 1946; d. John N. and Barbara (Freeman) H.; m. Leon Botstein; children: Clara Haskell Botstein, Maxim Haskell Botstein. BA, UCLA, 1969. Asst. registrar Pasadena (Calif.) Art Mus., 1969, curatorial asst., 1970, asst. curator, 1970, assoc. curator, 1970-72, curator painting and sculpture, 1972-74, Whitney Mus. Am. Art, N.Y.C., 1975—. Author: Arthur Dove, 1974, Marsden Hartley, 1980, Milton Avery, 1982, Blam! The Explosion of Pop, Minimalism and Performance 1958-64, 1984, Georgia O'Keefe: Works on Paper, 1985, Ralston Crawford, 1985, Charles Demuth, 1987, Red Grooms, 1987, Donald Judd, 1988, Burgoyne Diller, 1990, Agnes Martin, 1992, Joseph Stella, 1994, The Am. Century: Art and Culture 1900-1950, 1999, Edward Steichen, 2000, Elie Nadelman, 2002. Named Woman of Yr., Mademoiselle mag., 1973. Office: Whitney Mus Am Art 945 Madison Ave New York NY 10021-2701 E-mail: barbara_haskell@whitney.org.

HASKELL, BARRY GEOFFRY, computer company researcher; b. Lewiston, Maine, 1941; s. George Raymond and Dorothy H.; m. Ann Kantrow, Sept. 13, 1964; children: Paul Eric, Andrew. AA, Pasadena City Coll., 1962; BSEE, U. Calif., Berkeley, 1964, MSEE, 1965, PhD, 1968. Electronics engr. Lawrence Livermore (Calif.) Lab., 1965; rsch. asst. Electronics Rsch. Lab. U. Calif., Berkeley, 1965-68; mem. tech. staff AT&T Bell Labs., Holmdel, N.J., 1968-76, head radio comm. rsch. dept., 1976-83, visual comm. cons., 1984-86, head visual comm. rsch. dept., 1987-95; head image processing rsch. dept. AT&T Labs., Middletown, N.J., 1996-99; sr. scientist Apple Computer, Inc., Cupertino, Calif., 2002—. Adj. prof. Rutgers U., New Brunswick, N.J., 1976-79, CCNY, 1983-84, Columbia U., N.Y.C., 1987, 93; negotiator Internat. Stds. Orgn., Am. Nat. Stds. Inst., Internat. Telecom. Union - Telecom Sector. Co-author: Image Transmission Tech., 1979, Digital Pictures, 1988, 2d edit., 1995, Digital Video—An Introduction to MPEG-2, 1996; contbr. articles to profl. jours.; patentee in field. Recipient Elec. Engring. Dept. Outstanding Alumnus award U. Calif., Berkeley, 1998; co-recipient Japan's Computer and Comm. prize, 1997, N.J. Inventor Hall of Fame Inventor of Yr., 2000; AT&T fellow, 1998. Fellow IEEE, Phi Beta Kappa; mem. Sigma Xi. Avocations: sailing, skiing, guitar playing. Office: Apple Computer 302-3K5 2 Infinite Loop Cupertino CA 95014

HASKELL, BRENTON ERNEST, health facility administrator; MD with distinction, U. Alta., Edmonton, Can., 1978; MS, Wright State U., 1985. Diplomate Am. Bd. Preventive Medicine. Intern Regina (Can.) Gen. Hosp., 1978—79; resident in aerospace medicine Wright State U., Dayton, Ohio, 1983—85; regional aviation med. officer Civil Aviation Medicine, Toronto, Canada, 1990-97; med. dir. occupl. health program Columbus (Ohio) Health Dept., 1997-2000; asst. med. dir. Allen Meml. Hosp. Occupl. Health, Waterloo, Iowa, 2000—. Office: 1825 Logan Ave Waterloo IA 50703-1916

HASKELL, DONALD MCMILLAN, lawyer; b. Toledo, July 2, 1932; s. Irwin Wales and Grace (Lee) H.; m. Carol Jean Ross, June 19, 1954; children: Deborah Lee, Catherine Jean, David Ross. BA, Coll. of Wooster, 1954; JD, U. Mich., 1957. Bar: Ill. 1957, U.S. Dist. Ct. (no. dist.) Ill. 1958, U.S. Ct. Appeals (7th cir.) 1960, U.S. Supreme Ct. 1963, U.S. Ct. Appeals (10th cir.) 1974, Oreg. 1990. Ptnr. McKenna, Storer, Rowe, White & Haskell and predecessors, Chgo., 1957-75; sr. ptnr. Haskell & Perrin, Chgo., 1975-89, of counsel, 1989-2000. Commr. Clatsop County, Oreg., 1991-94; bd. dirs. N.W. Oreg. Econ. Alliance, 1993-98. Trustee Columbia River Maritime Mus., 1991—; chmn. Clatsop County Rep. Com., 1994-95; mem. Astoria Planning Commn., 1999-2002, chmn., 2001-02. Fellow Am. Bar Found., Ill. Bar Found.; mem. ABA (ho. of dels. 1982-92, bd. govs. 1987-90), Lawyers Club Chgo., Astoria Country Club. Lutheran. Home: 600 W Lexington Ave Astoria OR 97103-5726 Office: Wecoma Ptnrs Ltd PO Box 777 100 16th St Astoria OR 97103-3634

HASKELL, JAMES THOMPSON, cultural organization administrator; b. Bangor, Maine, Apr. 5, 1960; s. Percy Leonard and Marguerite Elaine (Thompson) Haskell; m. Aimee Pollack, Aug. 5, 1984 (div. Apr. 1993); m. Donna Jean Randall, Oct. 30, 1993; 1 child, Jason Roberto. BA, Boston U., 1982; MPA, Suffolk U., 1987. Adminstrv. asst. Perkins Sch. Blind, Watertown, Mass., 1983-85, Southwest Boston Sr. Svc., Roslindale, Mass., 1985-86; asst. grants adminstr. City of Gloucester, Mass., 1986-87, grants adminstr., 1987-89; asst. exec. dir. Gloucester Housing Authority, 1989-94; exec. dir. Salem (Mass.) Harbor Cmty. Devel. Corp., 1994—. Mem. Life Initiative Investment Com., 2001—; mem. commonwealth adv. group Sovereign Bank, 2002—. Sec. Gloucester Human Svcs. Coun., 1992—94; mem. Ipswich (Mass.) Housing Partnership, 1994—2002; treas. Salem Arts Ctr., Inc., 1996—; mem. North Shore Housing Trust, 2000—. Mem.: Met. Planning Orgn. (mem. environ. justice com. 2002—), Mass. Assn. CDCs (vice chair 1995—98, 2000—02, chair 1998—2000), Salem C. of C. (sec. 1994—96). Avocations: hiking, cross country skiing, travel. Office: Salem Harbor Comty Devel 102 Lafayette St Salem MA 01970-3625 E-mail: jim@shcdc.org

HASKELL, JOHN HENRY FARRELL, JR., investment banking company executive; b. N.Y.C., Jan. 24, 1932; s. John Henry Farrell and Paulette (Heger) H.; m. Francine G. Le Roux, June 30, 1955; children: Michael J., Christopher E., Diana F. T. BS, U.S. Mil. Acad., 1953; MBA with distinction, Harvard U., 1958. Assoc. Dillon, Read & Co., N.Y.C., 1958-61, mgr. European office Paris, 1961-66, v.p (now UBS Investment Bank) N.Y.C., 1964-75, mng. dir., 1975-99, sr. advisor, 2000—. Pres., CEO The France Fund, Inc., 1986—89; bd. dirs. Pall Corp., Security Capital Corp.; mem. adv. coun. Overseas Pvt. Investment Corp., 1972—75. Bd. dirs. Belgian-Am. Ednl. Found.; pres. bd. trustees French Inst./Alliance Francaise. Decorated Legion of Honor, Ordre National du Merite France; recipient Presdl. Recognition award For Community Service, 1986. Mem. Coun. Fgn. Rels., French-Am. C. of C. (councillor), Assn. Grads. of U.S. Mil. Acad. (trustee 1984-87), Am. Soc. French Legion of Honor (bd. dirs., v.p.), Links Club, Univ. Club, Meadow Brook Club (Jericho, N.Y.), Bohemian Club (San Francisco), Eagle Springs Golf Club (Wolcott, Colo.). Home: 120 East End Ave New York NY 10028-7552 Office: UBS Investment Bank 299 Park Ave New York NY 10171-0002 E-mail: john.haskell@ubsw.com.

HASKELL, MOLLY, writer; b. Charlotte, N.C., Sept. 29, 1939; d. John Haskell and Mary Clark; m. Andrew Sarris, May 31, 1969. BA, Sweet Briar Coll.; student, U. London, England, Sorbonne, Paris. Pub. rels. assoc. Sperry Rand; writer, editor French Film Office, New York; film critic Village Voice, Viva, New York Magazine, Vogue, 1969-74, 74-80; film reviewer "Special Edition" Pub. TV; film reviewer "All Things Considered" Nat. Pub. Radio; adj. prof. film Columbia U., New York, 1996; writer. Artistic dir. Sarasota French Film Festival. Author: From Reverence to Rape: The Treatment of Women in the Movies, 1973, rev. edit., 1987, Love and Other Infectious Diseases: A Memoir, 1990, Holding My Own in No Man's Land, 1997; (plays) The Last Anniversary, 1990; contbr. articles and essays to jours. Recipient Nat. Bd. Review of Motion Pictures award, 1989, Chevalier de l'Ordre des Artes et des Lettres, 1989, Disting. Alumna award Sweet Briar Coll., 1994. Mem. Nat. Soc. of Film Festival Selection Critics, N.Y. Film Critics Circle, N.Y. Film Festival Selection Com., N.Y. Inst. for the Humanities, The Century Club, Phi Beta Kappa.

HASKELL, MONICA M. art association administrator; b. Milw., July 21, 1952; d. John E. Cannon and Delphine M. Bruckwick; m. Scott Haskell, Dec. 18, 1976 (div. Dec. 1996). BFA, U. Wis., 1975; MA, Troy State U., 1995. Adminstr. Montessori Children's Sch., Key West, Fla., 1995-97; exec. dir. Fla. Keys Coun. of the Arts, Key West, 1997—. Founder First Montessori Charter Sch. on Fla., 1996. Contbg author: Monroe County Environmental Story, 1990. Bd. dirs., chair Monroe County Planning Commn., Fla., 1990-96; exec. dir. Key West Literary Sem., 1988-95; dir. S. Fla. Cultural Consortium, Miami; dir./sec. Fla. Assn. of Local Arts Agys., West Palm Beach; bd. dirs. Bd. of Adjustment, Fla. Keys, 1986, Key West Art in Pub. Places Bd., 1999—; grant rev. panelist Fla. Dept. of State, Divsn. Cultural Affairs, Tallahassee, 1999-2000, Fla. Commn. on Tourism, Gov.'s Com. on Eco.Heritage and Cultural Tourism, 2000, contractors exam. bd., 2001—. Recipient Outstanding Achievement award Fla. Assn. Librs., 1990. Mem. Ams. for the Arts, Fla. Assn. Pub. Art Adminstrs., Key West Women's Club, Key West Art and Hist. Soc. Republican. Office: Fla Keys Coun of Arts PO Box 717 Key West FL 33041-0717

HASKELL, PAUL GERSHON, retired law educator; b. Boston, Mar. 31, 1927; s. David Israel and Leah (Paris) H.; m. Sarah Potter Evarts, Jan. 22, 1955; children: Peter, Thomas, John. AB, Harvard U., 1948, LLB, 1951. Bar: N.Y. 1952. Assoc. Kelley, Drye, Newhall & Maginnes, N.Y.C., 1951-56, White & Case, N.Y.C., 1956-59; asst. gen. counsel The Houston Corp., St. Petersburg, Fla., 1959-60; resident counsel, asst. treas. Ednl. Testing Service, Princeton, N.J., 1960-62; prof. law Georgetown U., Washington, 1962-67, Case Western Res. U., Cleve., 1967-79, U. N.C., Chapel Hill, 1979-83, Graham Kenan prof. law, 1983-91, William R. Kenan prof. law, 1991-98; ret., 1998. Co-author: Preface to Estates In Land and Future Interests, 1966, 2d edit., 1984; author: Preface to the Law of Trusts, 1975, Preface to Wills, Trusts and Adminstration, 1987, 2d edit. 1994, Why Lawyers Behave As They Do, 1998; contbr. articles to profl. jours. Bd. dirs. Cleve. Fair Housing Inc., 1967-70; trustee Harvard Club of Cleve., 1976-79. Served with USN, 1945-46. Mem. ABA (spl. com. to revise standards for legal edn. 1970-73, coun., sect. on legal edn. and admissions to bar 1973-76, standing com. on legal assts. 1976-80). Republican. Home: 1805 Rolling Rd Chapel Hill NC 27514-7505 Office: U NC Sch Of Law Chapel Hill NC 27599-3380 E-mail: phaskell@email.unc.edu.

HASKELL, PETER ABRAHAM, actor; b. Boston, Oct. 15, 1934; s. Norman Abraham and Rose Veronica (Golden) H.; m. Ann Compton, Feb. 27, 1960 (div. 1974); m. Dianne Tolmich, Oct. 26, 1974; children: Audra Rosemary, Jason Abraham. BA, Harvard U., 1962; student, N.Y. Law Sch., 1982-83. Actor (films) Finnegans Wake, 1965, Legend of Earl Durand, 1972, Christina, 1974, Forty Days of Musa Dagh, 1982, Riding the Edge, 1987, Child's Play II, 1990, Child's Play III, 1991, Robot Wars, 1993; (TV series) Bracken's World, NBC, 1968-70, Rich Man Poor Man, Book II, ABC, 1976-77, Ryan's Hope, ABC, 1982-83, Search for Tomorrow, NBC, 1983-85, Rituals, Metromedia, 1985, The Law and Harry McGraw, CBS, 1987-88; (TV films) Love, Hate, Love, 1970, The Eyes of Charles Sand, 1972, Mandrake, 1977, The Cracker Factory, 1979, Christine Cromwell, 1990, Columbo, 1991, Maid for Each Other, 1992, Faces of Deception, 1993, Never Talk to Strangers, 1997; dir. Nightgames, 2000. Wwith U.S. Army, 1954-56. Mem. SAG, AFTRA, Actors Equity. Democrat. Avocations: photography, skiing. Office: care Eric Klass 139 S Beverly Dr Ste 331 Beverly Hills CA 90212-3020

HASKELL, THOMAS LANGDON, history educator; b. Washington, May 26, 1939; s. Anthony Porter and Martha Averill (Bullock) H.; m. Dorothy Ann Wyatt, Aug. 27, 1966; children: Alexander Bullock, Susan Wyatt. BA, Princeton U., 1961; PhD, Stanford U., 1973. From instr. to prof. Rice U., Houston, 1970—, Samuel G. McCann prof. history, 1987—. Vis. mem. Inst. Advanced Study, Princeton, N.J., 1978-79. Author: Emergence of Professional Social Science, 1977, 2d edit. 2001, Objectivity is Not Neutrality, 1998; editor: The Authority of Experts, 1984; co-editor (with Richard Teichgraeber) The Culture of Capitalism, 1993; mem. bd. editors Jour. Am. History, 1983-86, Am. Hist. Rev., 1988-91; contbr. articles to profl. jours. Lt. USN, 1961-65. Guggenheim Found. fellow, 1986-87; fellow NEH, Rockefeller Found., Mellon Found., Am. Coun. Learned Socs. Fellow Ctr. Advanced Study in Behavioral Scis.; mem. Orgn. Am Historians, Am. Hist. Assn. Office: Rice U Dept History Houston TX 77005-1892

HASKELL, WYATT RUSHTON, lawyer; b. Birmingham, Ala., May 15, 1940; s. Preston Hampton and Mary Wyatt (Rushton) H.; m. Susan Porter Nabers, June 1, 1968; children: John Howze, Henry Devereux, Samuel Drayton. AB, Amherst Coll., 1961; LLB, Yale U., 1965. Bar: Ala. 1965. Assoc. Bradley, Arant, Rose & White, Birmingham, 1966-71; staff atty. So. Natural Gas Co., Birmingham, 1971-73; ptnr. Haskell, Slaughter, Young & Rediker, LLC, Birmingham, 1973—. Vis. rsch. asst. U. Muenster, Germany, 1965—66; vis. prof. U. Ala. Law Sch., 1970—73; bd. dirs. Bio Horizons Implant Systems, Inc. Contbr. articles to profl. jours. Bd. dirs. Ala. Shakespeare Fest, Montgomery, Folger Shakespeare Libr., Washington. Thomas Pope fellow Trinity Coll., Oxford. Mem. ABA, Ala. Bar Assn., Birmingham Bar Assn., Mountain Brook Club. Presbyterian. Home: 2964 Cherokee Rd Birmingham AL 35223-2609 Office: Haskell Slaughter et al 1400 Park Place Tower 2001 Park Place North Birmingham AL 35203 E-mail: wrh@hsy.com.

HASKETT, DIANNE LOUISE, former mayor, lawyer, consultant; b. London, Ontario, Canada, Mar. 4, 1955; d. Allan Douglas and Frances Shirley (Crone) H.; m. Jacek Kotowicz; 1 child, Annie. BA, U. Waterloo, On., Can., 1974; LLD, U. Western On., Can., 1977; LLM, London Sch. Economics, Eng., 1979. Lawyer Law Soc. of Upper Can., Canada, 1980—; founding ptnr. Haskett, Menear Assoc., Law Firm, 1980—94; speechwriter, internat. cons., and pub. rels. advisor Washington Contact, 2001—; immigration bus. coord. Law Offices of Lewis and Associates, Springfield, Va.; Senate and Congl. campaign advisor. V.p. London Urban Alliance on race rels. Contbr. articles to profl. jours. City councillor London City Coun., 1991-94; mayor, 1994-2000; founder Open Homes Can., London, Ont., 1992; founding mem. London Citizens Com., 1980-84; v.p. Ark Aid Street Mission Inc., London, On., 1986-88. Recipient Pericles award Am. Hellenic Ednl. Progressive Assn., 1999; Grad. scholar Rotary Internat., 1978-79; Paul Harris fellow Rotary Clubs London, 1998. Mem. Law Soc. of Upper Can. Avocations: journalism, collecting antiques and rare books, reading, speech making. Home: 2970 Kildare Ln Fairfax VA 22031 E-mail: dhaskett@washingtoncontact.com.

HASKIN, DAYTON WILLIAM, English language educator, researcher; b. Ann Arbor, Mich., Sept. 14, 1946; s. Dayton William and June Kathryn Haskin; m. Margaret Ann Thomas, 1990; children: Thomas Henry, Peter William, Helen Marie. BA, U. Detroit, 1968; MA, Northwestern U., 1970; BD with honors, U. London, 1975; PhD, Yale U., 1978. Instr. in English John Carroll U., University Heights, Ohio, 1970-72; prof. Boston Coll., Chestnut Hill, Mass., 1978—. Author: Milton's Burden of Interpretation, 1994; contbr. numerous articles to profl. jours. Guggenheim fellow, 1996—97. Mem. MLA, John Donne Soc. (exec. bd. 1990—, pres. 1994-95), Milton Soc. Am., John Bunyan Soc. (bd. advisors). (pres. 1996-97).

HASKIN, J. MICHAEL, lawyer; b. Kansas City, Mo., Sept. 25, 1949; s. Harley V. and Geraldine E. (Porterfield) H.; m. Pamela J. Lutz, May 22, 1999. BA, Baker U., 1971; JD, U. Mo., 1976. Bar: Kans. 1976, Mo. 1987, U.S. Fed. Tax Ct., U.S. Supreme Ct. Ptnr., atty. Haskin, Hinkle, Slater & Snowbarger, Olathe, Kans., 1976-83, Dietrich, Davis, Dicus, Rowlands, Schmitt & Gorman, Kansas City, Mo., 1984-88; pres., atty. J. Michael Haskin, PA, Olathe, 1989—. Bd. dirs., exec. com., The Assn. K-10 Corridor Devel., Inc., Lawrence, 1993-95. City councilman-at-large City of Olathe, 1989-93, mayor, 1993-95; mem., vice chmn., chmn. Stormwater Mgmt. Adv. Coun., Johnson County, Kans., 1989-95; bd. dirs. Olathe Pub. Libr., 1989-90, 93-95; bd. dirs. Hidden Glen Arts Festival, vice chmn., chmn., 1990—); mem. Mid-Am. Regional Coun. Perimeter Transp. Com., 1995—. Recipient Boss of Yr. award Johnson County Legal Secs. Assn., 1991-92, Cmty. Leadership award Olathe Area C. of C., 1992. Mem. Kans. Bar Assn., Mo. Bar Assn., Olathe Rotary Club (bd. dirs., pres. 1981—, Paul Harris award 1992, Olathe Rotarian of Yr. 1995), Olathe Arts Alliance (pres. 1988), Kaw Valley Philological Soc. Republican. Methodist. Avocations: golfing, sailing. Office: PO Box 413 100 E Park St Ste 203 Olathe KS 66061-3463 E-mail: haskinlawoffice@aol.com.

HASKIN, LARRY ALLEN, academic administrator, geochemist, educator; b. Olathe, Kans., Aug. 17, 1934; s. Harvard Glenn and Mary Virginia (Callaway) H.; m. Mary Anita Gehl, Dec. 21, 1963; children: Dierk Allen, Rachel Lee, Jean Marie. BA, Baker U., 1955; PhD, U. Kans., 1960. Asst. prof. Ga. Inst. Tech., 1959-60; instr. U. Wis., Madison, 1960-61, asst. prof., 1961-65, assoc. prof., 1965-68, prof. chemistry, 1968-73; cons. NASA, 1970-73, Argonne Nat. Lab., 1960-68; chief planetary and earth scis. divsn. NASA-JSC, 1973-76; prof. earth and planetary scis., chemistry Washington U., St. Louis, 1976-90, R.E. Morrow Disting. prof. earth and planetary scis., prof., 1986-2000, chmn. dept. 1976-90. Mem. Mercury rev. panel NAS, 1970-71; mem. U.S. Nat. Com. on Geochemistry, 1975-78; mem. NASA Solar Sys. Exploration Com., 1983-87, mem. mgmt. coun., 1984-86, adv. com. Space and Earth Scis., 1985-88; mem. NRC Com. Planetary and Lunar Exploration, 1985-88, 97-99; mem. NASA Adv. Coun., 1988-90, Lunar and Planetary Rev. Panel, mem. cosmochemistry rev. panel, 1996-98. Recipient Exceptional Sci. Achievement award NASA, 1971; Guggenheim fellow Max Planck Inst. for Nuclear Physics, Heidelberg, Germany, 1966-67 Fellow The Meteoritical Soc., St. Louis Acad. of Sci.; mem. Am. Chem. Soc., Geochem. Soc. (v.p. 1985-87, pres. 1987-89), Am. Geophys. Union, AAAS, Phi Beta Kappa, Sigma Xi. Achievements include research on trace inorganic elements in meteoritic, lunar, martian, and terrestrial matter.

HASKINS, CHARLES GREGORY, JR., lawyer; b. Chgo., Jan. 27, 1951; s. Charles G. and Ellen Barbara (Essman) H.; m. Gail Beaubien Ferbend, June 14, 1987; 1 child, Charles Robert. BA, U. Ill., 1972; JD, John Marshall Law Sch., 1976. Bar: Ill. 1976, U.S. Dist. Ct. (no. dist.) Ill. 1976. Assoc. George J. Cullen, Ltd., Chgo., 1976-82; shareholder George J. Cullen & Assoc., Ltd., Chgo., 1982-89, Cullen, Haskins, Nicholson & Menchetti, Chgo., 1989—. Mem.: ATLA, Workplace Injury Litigation Group (bd. dirs. 1997—2001, sec. 2001—02), Chgo. Bar Assn. (chmn. indsl. commn. com. 1987—88), Ill. Trial Lawyers Assn. (bd. mgrs. 1989—, co-chmn. workers compensation com. 1991—2001, co-editor Case Notebook 1992—, treas. 1997), Ill. Bar Assn., Workers Compensation Lawyers Assn. (bd. dirs. 1986—96, pres. 1989). Democrat. Roman Catholic. Avocations: golf, water skiing, snow skiing. Office: Cullen Haskins Nicholson & Menchetti 35 E Wacker Dr Ste 1760 Chicago IL 60601-2271

HASKINS, JAMES LESLIE, mathematics educator; b. St. Louis, Aug. 10, 1947; s. Delbert George and Betty Ann (Reese) H.; m. Jane T. Barnard; children: Todd M., Nathan E., Elizabeth M. BS in Applied Math. and Computer Sci., Washington U., St. Louis, 1969, MBA, 1983; MAT, Webster U., 1971; postgrad., St. Louis U., 1995—. Tchr. math. Desmet Jesuit H.S., St. Louis, 1969-70, John Burroughs Sch., St. Louis, 1970—. Adj. prof. Washington U., St. Louis, 1982-2000, St. Louis U., 1994-97; traveling team mem. Woodrow Wilson Found., Princeton, N.J., 1991-95; instr. Command and Gen. Staff Officer Course USAR, St. Louis, 1991-94; bd. dirs. Martha Rounds Acad., St. Louis. Author: Algebra, 1990. Bd. dirs. Forsyth Sch., St. Louis, 1986-91, bldgs./grounds com., 1986-92; credit com. chmn. Credit Union, St. Louis, 1989-96. Woodrow Wilson fellow, 1990. Mem. Nat. Coun. Tchrs. of Math., Mo. Coun. Tchrs. Math., Math. Educators Greater St. Louis (exec. bd. 1991—, pres. 1997), Beta Tau Sigma. Democrat. Roman Catholic. Avocations: travel, sports, antiques. Home: 2857 Laclede Station Rd Saint Louis MO 63143-2809 Office: John Burroughs Sch 755 S Price Rd Saint Louis MO 63124-1899 E-mail: jhaskins@jburroughs.org.

HASKVITZ, ALAN PAUL, elementary education educator, consultant; b. Mpls., Sept. 7, 1942; s. Harry and Rose (Portugal) H.; married, Apr. 1, 1970; children: Anna, Maxwell Harry. AA, Chaffey Coll., 1963; MS, Calif. State U., 1965; BE, Meml. Coll., St. John's, Newfoundland, 1972; MA, Calif. State U., L.A., 1970. Cert. secondary tchr., adminstr., Calif.; cert. tchr., Ont., Newfoundland, N.Y.; cert. cmty. coll. instr., Calif.; cert. audio-visual. Tchr. Cornwall (Ont.) Sch. Bd., Can., 1970-78; vice prin. Quest School for the Gifted, Oshawa, Ont., 1978-80; tchr. Corono (Calif.) Sch. Sys., 1980-81, Walnut (Calif.) Sch. Dist., 1987—; cons. Edn. Strategies, Alta Loma, Calif., 1981—. Lectr. U. Calif., 1970—89, Calif. Poly., 1970—89, Western Wash. U., 2000; pres.-elect Nat. Coun. for the Social Scis.; mem. Nat. Critical Thinking Com., Coun. of Chief State Sch. Officers, Nat. Assessment of Ednl. Progress, Nat. Responder Com. on Tchrs. and Schs., Constl. Rights Found., Western States Accreditation Commn., Cal Poly Master Tchr. Com. on Student Tng. Programs; evaluator Nat. Coun. for Accreditation of Tchr. Edn.; spkr. to numerous orgns., meetings and confs.; sr. Olympian weightlifter. Author: Resources for Social Studies Educators; syndicated automobile journalist: The Car Family; contbr. numerous articles to profl. jours.; features in: Futures videos, Project citizen video, Time, Newsweek, CNN, ABC, CBS, NBC, NPR, numerous textbooks. Commr. City of Rancho Cucamonga, 1986—; pres. United Counties Sports, Cornwall, 1980-84; bd. advisors Americans All. Named USA Today All Am. Educator, 2000; named one of 100 Most Influential Educators in Am.; named to Nat. Tchrs. Hall of Fame, 1997; recipient Am.'s Profl. Best Tchr. award, Learning mag., 1989, Heroes in Edn. award, Reader's Digest, George Washington medal, Freedom Found., 1992, Spirit of Edn. award, NBC, 1997, Nat. Bicentennial Tchg. award, Bicentennial Com., 1993, Presdl. award for environ. edn., 1988, Calif. Dept. Water Agencies, Cmty. award, Walnut Valley Water Dist., 1989, Outstanding Citizen award, L.A. County Supr., 1994, Outstanding Tchr. award, Christa McAuliffe award, 1996, Nat. Coun. for Social Studies, 1992, Nation's Best Program, 1994, Nation's Outstanding Mid. Sch. Tchr., 1996, Agr. Tchr. of Yr., Nat. Coun. for Social Studies, 1995, Baylor U., Calif. Agr. in Classroom, Robert Cherry Internat. Tchr. of Yr., 1997, Campbell's Tchrs. in Am. award, Disney Regional Winner, Busch Environ. award, 1996, Nat. Garden award, Leavey award for pvt. enterprise edn., 1998, Freedom Found., Calif. Water Environ. Edn. award, Calif., 1995, Agy. for Water Edn., Calif. History Tchrs. of Yr., Daus. of Am. Colonies, 1999, Crystal Apple award, NBC, 1998, Bell award, Calif. Sch. Bd. Assns., 1987, 1997, numerous awards for sch. programs. Achievements include devel. of Reach Every Child and the Children's Speed Reading Record Holders. Home: 9655 Carrari Ct Alta Loma CA 91737-1653 E-mail: freealan@yahoo.com.

HASLAM, GERALD WILLIAM, writer, educator; b. Bakersfield, Calif., Mar. 18, 1937; s. Fredrick Martin and Lorraine Hope (Johnson) H.; m. Janice Eileen Pettichord, July 1, 1961; children: Frederick W., Alexandra R., Garth C., Simone B., Carlos V. BA, San Francisco State U., 1963, MA, 1965; PhD, Union Grad. Sch., 1980. Instr. English San Francisco State U., San Francisco, 1966-67; asst. prof. English Sonoma State U., Rohnert Park, Calif., 1967-70, assoc. prof. English, 1970-74, prof. English, 1971-97, emeritus prof. English, 1997—; prof. Fromm Inst./U. San Francisco, 2001—. Adj. prof. Union Grad. Sch., Cin., 1984—, The Nat. Faculty, Atlanta, 1984—. Editor various anthologies; author various booklets, monographs, film scripts, (fiction) Okies: Selected Stories, 1973, Masks: A Novel, 1976, The Wages of Sin: Collected Stories, 1980, Hawk Flights: Visions of the West, 1983, Snapshots: Glimpses of the Other California, 1985, The Man Who Cultivated Fire and Other Stories, 1987, That Constant Coyote: California Stories, 1990, Condor Dreams and Other Fictions, 1994, The Great Tejon Club Jubilee, 1996, Manuel and the Madman, 2000, Straight White Male, 2000, (non-fiction) Voices of a Place, 1987, Coming of Age in California, 1990, The Other California, 1990, The Great Central Valley: California's Heartland, 1993, Workin' Man Blues: Country Music in California, 1999, Coming of Age in California, 2d enlarged edit., 2000. With U.S. Army, 1958-60. Creative Writing fellow Calif. Arts Coun., 1989; recipient Benjamin Franklin award, 1993, Bay Area Book Reviewers' Non-fiction award, 1994, Commonwealth Club medal for Calif., 1994, Merit award Assn. State & Local History, 1994, Commendation citation, 2001; Fulbright sr. lectr., 1986-87, Josephine Miles award, 1990, Ralph J. Gleason award, 2000, Carey McWilliams award, 2001, Western States Book Fiction award, 2001, Sequoia - Giant of the Valley award, 2003. Mem. NAACP, Great Valley Ctr. (adv. bd.), Western Lit. Assn. (bd. dirs., past pres., Disting. Achievment award 1999), Calif. Studies Assn. (steering com., founding mem.), Calif. Hist. Assn., Calif. Tchrs. Assn., San Francisco State U. Alumni Assn. (life), Union Inst. Alumni Assn., Multi-Ethnic Lit. of U.S. (founding mem.), Robinson Jeffers Assn. (founding mem.), Sierra Club, The Nature Conservancy, Calif. Trout (founding mem.), Tulare Basin Archeology Group, Defenders of Wildlife, Common Cause, Yosemite Assn. (bd. dirs.). Roman Catholic. Avocations: bicycling, hiking, fishing. Office: Sonoma State U 1801 E Cotati Ave Rohnert Park CA 94928-3609 E-mail: ghaslam@sonic.net.

HASLAM, JAMES A., III, petroleum sales executive; b. Mar. 9, 1954; BA, U of Tenn., Knoxville. CEO Pilot Corp., Knoxville, 1958—. Office: Pilot Corp PO Box 10146 Knoxville TN 37939-0146*

HASLAM, ROBERT THOMAS, III, lawyer; b. Taunton, Mass., May 4, 1946; s. Robert Thomas and Marcella Neale (Compton) H.; m. Mary Ashley Brayton, June 14, 1969; children: Laurel Ashley, Julia Compton. BS Aeronautics and Astronautics, MIT, 1968; JD, Hastings Coll., 1976. Bar: Calif., 1976. Atty., ptnr. Heller, Ehrman, Menlo Park, Calif., 1976—. Capt. USAF 1969-73. Mem. ABA (co-chair litigation, intellectual property sect. 1993—). Avocations: tennis, soccer. Office: Heller Ehrman 275 Middlefield Rd Menlo Park CA 94025-3506 Home: 861 Overlook Ct San Mateo CA 94403-3843

HASLANGER, MARTIN FREDERICK, pharmaceutical company executive, researcher; b. Dayton, Ohio, Mar. 27, 1947; s. John Frederick and M. Isabelle (McEowen) H.; m. Martha Louise Anderson, June 29, 1969; children: Andrea Louise, Jonathan Frederick. BS in Chemistry, Denison U., 1969; PhD in Chemistry, U. Mich., 1974. Postdoctoral fellow (with E.J. Corey) chemistry dept. Harvard U., Cambridge, Mass., 1974-76; rsch. investigator Squibb Inst. Med. Rsch., Princeton, N.J., 1976-80, sr. rsch. investigator, 1980-81, group leader, 1981-85; assoc. dir. Schering-Plough Rsch., Bloomfield, N.J., 1985-88, dir. chem. rsch., 1988-92; dir. chemistry, biochemistry pharm. Lilly Rsch. Labs., Indpls., 1992-94, dir. tech. core, 1994—2001; pres. Sphinx Pharms. divsn. Eli Lilly & Co., Indpls., 1994—2001; pres., CEO Amphora Discovery Corp., Research Triangle Park, NC, 2001—. Contbr. articles to profl. jours., including Jour. Am. Chem. Soc., Jour. Organic Chemistry, Pharacologist, European Jour. Pharmacology, others. Mem. AAAS, Am. Chem. Soc., Am. Heart Assn., N.Y. Acad. Scis., Phi Lambda Upsilon. Achievements include discovery of new drug; design and synthesis of enzyme inhibitors and receptor antagonists, peptide mimetics, optimization of small molecule-large molecule interactions; high through put screening and combinatorial chemistry; 45 patents. Home: 7123 Creekwood Chapel Hill NC 27514

HASLANGER, PHILIP CHARLES, journalist; b. Menominee, Mich., May 11, 1949; s. Harry LeRoy and Agnes Gertrude (Seidl) H.; m. Rosemary Ann Raasch Carta, May 27, 1972 (div.); children: Brian David, Sarah Marie; m. Ellen Jean Reuter, Apr. 9, 1983; children: Michael Kenneth, Julia Jane. BA in Sociology, U. Wis., 1971, MA in Journalism, 1973. With The Capital Times, Madison, Wis., 1973—, mng. editor, 1998—. Author: Stories of Call, 1998. Mem. Nat. Conf. Editl. Writers (bd. dirs. 1993, 94, 97, 2003, officer 1999-2002), New Media Fedn. Avocations: reading, music, hiking, theology. Home: 5409 Vicar Ln Madison WI 53714-3443 Office: The Capital Times 1901 Fish Hatchery Rd Madison WI 53713-1248 E-mail: phaslanger@madison.com.

HASLETT, JARED WOODDELL, physicist, educator; b. Akron, Ohio, Oct. 11, 1930; s. George William and Mildred W. H.; m. Winona Rose Goss, 1954 (div.); children: Jonathan, Joel, Jeanne; m. Diane Margaret Crowley, Sept. 4, 1965; children: Ethan, Benjamin. MS, Ill. Inst. of Tech., 1955. Physicist U. Chgo., 1956-57; educator U. Ill., Chgo., 1959-94. Dir. undergrad. studies dept. physics U. Ill., Chgo.; resident rsch. assoc. Argonne (Ill.) Nat. Labs., 1959—65; rsch. physicist Chgo. Wesley Meml. Hosp., 1966; cons. physicist Michael Reese Hosp., Chgo., 1966—67; cons. on Rudolf Steiner's works to various libraries, 1998—. Author: Works of Rudolf Steiner in English Translation, 1998. Treas. Waldorf Sch. of Chgo., 1975-77; libr. Rudolf Steiner Group Anthroposophical Soc. in Am., 1971-75. Faculty fellowship NSF, 1988, 89. Mem. AAAS (life), Anthroposophical Soc., Bioelectromagnetics Soc., Am. Mensa Ltd.(life), Am. Radio Relay League, Agni Yoga Soc., Moose (life), Sigma Pi Sigma, Sigma Xi (life). Espicopalian. Avocations: chess, tennis, cycling, amateur radio. E-mail: JHaslett@uic.edu.

HASLETT, JIM, professional football coach; b. Pittsburgh, Pa., Dec. 9, 1955; BA in Elem. Edn., Ind. U. of Pa., 1978. Profl. football player Buffalo Bills and NY Nets, 1979-87; asst. football coach U. Buffalo, 1988-89; asst. coach Los Angeles Raiders, 1993-94, Pittsburgh Steelers, 1996-99; head coach New Orleans Saints, 2000—; mem. College Football Hall of Fame, 2001. Office: New Orleans Saints 5800 Airline Dr Metairie LA 70003-3876*

HASNAIN, MEMOONA, medical educator, medical researcher; b. Karachi, Sindh, Pakistan, May 2, 1966; arrived in U.S., 1998; d. Syed Hazur and Shirin Hasnain; m. Ehsan Ullah, Oct. 6, 1988; children: Hassan Nawaz Janjua, Farooq Nawaz Janjua. MD, U. Karachi, 1989; M Health Professions Edn., U. Ill., Chgo., 2000, PhD, 2001. House officer dept. ob-gyn. Dist. Hdqrs. Hosp., Mardan, Pakistan, 1990—91; house officer dept. internal medicine Fauji Found. Med. Ctr., Rawalpindi, Pakistan, 1992—93; med. officer Hearts Internat. Hosp., Internat. Islamic U., Rawalpindi, 1993—94; med. officer dept. ob-gyn. Kamal Hosp., Karachi, Pakistan, 1994—95; med. educator WHO Ctr. Rsch. and Tng. of Health Profls., Coll. Physicians and Surgeons, Pakistan, 1995—98; rsch. asst. med. decision making, dept. med. edn. Coll. Medicine U. Ill., Chgo., 1998—2001, rsch. info. specialist, 2001, instr. dept. med. edn., 2001—, asst. prof. pub. health in family medicine, adj. asst. prof. health policy and adminstrn., 2002—, vis. asst. prof. family medicine, 2001—02, interim dir. rsch., 2002, dir. rsch., 2002—. Contbr. articles to profl. jours. Recipient Chgo. Bar Assn. Pub. Health award, U. Ill. Chgo. Scholarship Assn., 2001, Ray E. Helfer Award for Innovation in Pediatric Edn., Ambulatory Pediatric Assn., 2001; Internat. fellow, Coll. Physicians and Surgeons, Pakistan, 1998—99, AAUW Ednl. Found., 2000—01. Mem.: APHA, Pakistan Med. and Dental Coun., Soc. for Tchrs. Family Medicine, Assn. Med. Edn. in Pakistan (life), Phi Kappa Phi, Delta Omega (Lambda chpt.). Islam. Office: Univ Ill Chgo Dept Family Medicine 1919 W Taylor St Chicago IL 60612 Office Fax: 312-996-2579. E-mail: memoona@uic.edu.

HASNEY, CHRISTOPHER WILLIAM, retired investment company executive, educator; b. Pasadena, Calif., Aug. 4, 1951; s. James Francis and Sherry (H. BS, Santa Clara Coll., 1970, MS, Coll. for Fin. Planning, 1994. Fin. planner, Sierra Vista, Ariz., 1983-86; assoc. v.p. investments Dean Witter Reynolds, Inc., Sierra Vista, Ariz., 1986-96; ret., 1996. Assoc. faculty Cochise Coll., Sierra Vista, 1988-94. Co-author: The American Bridge Series, 1998; contbr. articles to profl. jours. Asst. tech. dir. Sierra Repertory Co., 1984—. Capt. U.S. Army, 1976-84. Mem. Am. Contract Bridge Assn., Rotary (pres. Sierra Vista South 1993-94, Paul Harris fellow 1992). Republican. Avocations: water skiing, Karate, golf, bridge, theater. Home: PO Box 2792 Sierra Vista AZ 85636-2792

HASS, JOSEPH MONROE, automotive executive; b. Syracuse, N.Y., July 28, 1955; s. Joseph Monroe and Susan Faith (Betts) H.; m. Lisa Michelle Palmer, Aug. 14, 1982. BS in Secondary Edn., Tenn. Temple U., 1977. Diesel mechanic Cummins Engines Tenn., Chattanooga, 1978-81, mgr. tng. Nashville, 1981-85; svc. fl. foreman Cummins Cumberland, Nashville, 1985-86, CompuChek technician, 1986-87, fleet systems support engr., 1987-89, tech. advisor, instr., 1989-90, dir. devel., 1990—. Mem. ASTD, Am. Assn. Individual Investors, Citizens Against Govt. Waste, Exptl. Aircraft Assn., Heritage Found. Avocations: music, sailing, carpentry, cycling, reading. Office: Cummins Cumberland 706 Spence Ln Nashville TN 37217-1190 E-mail: joseph.m.hass@cummins.com.

HASS, ROBERT BERNARD, literature educator; b. Bethesda, Md., June 21, 1962; s. Louis Frederick and Rosalyn Gasque Hass; m. Susan Love Love, June 4, 1994; 1 child, Matthew Joseph. BA in English, Pa. State U., 1985, MFA, 1993, PhD in English Lit., 1999; MA in English, U. Fla., 1987. Lectr. Pa. State U., University Park, 1999—2001; asst. prof. Edinboro U. Pa., 2001—. Author: (literary criticism) Going By Contraries: Robert Frost's Conflict With Science, Yeats-Eliot Review, Studies in English Literature; contbr. literary criticism, ; author: (poems) Black Warrior Review, Poetry, Sewanee Review, Poet Lore, Intervention, Sewanee Review, Rafters, Cumberland Poetry Review, Poetry Northwest. Election supr. Mifflin County Bd. Elections, Lewistown, Pa., 1999—2000. Recipient Leonard Steinberg prize, Acad. Am. Poets, 1992, Intro Jours. award, Associated Writing Programs, 1993; fellow, Bread Loaf Writers' Conf., 1993. Mem.: MLA, Am. Lit. Assn., Assn. for the Study Lit. and the Environment, Robert Frost Soc., Phi Kappa Phi. Republican. Roman Catholic. Avocations: fly fishing, hiking, climbing, birding, running. Home: 66 North Pine St Lewistown PA 17044 Office: Edinboro Univ English Dept 236 Centennial Hall Edinboro PA 16444 Personal E-mail: rhass@edinboro.edu. E-mail: rhass@edinboro.edu.

HASS, ROBERT L. writer, educator; b. San Francisco, 1941; Prof. Dept. English U. Calif., Berkeley. Author: (books of poetry) Sun Under Wood: New Poems, 1996, Human Wishes, 1989, Praise, 1979, Field Guide, 1973; co-translator vols. of poetry with Czeslaw Milosz including: Facing the river, 1995; author/editor essays and translation including: The Essential Haiku: Versions of Basho, Buson, and Issa, 1994, Twentieth Century Pleasures: Prose on Poetry, 1984 (Nat. Book Critics Circle award); editor: Best American Poetry, 2001. Bd. dirs. Internat. Rivers Network. Apptd. Poet Laureate of U.S., 1995-97; MacArthur "Genius" fellow; named Educator of the Yr., N.Am. Assn. on Environ. Edn., 1997, chancellor Acad. Am. Poets, 2000. Office: Steven Barclay Agy 321 Pleasant St Petaluma CA 94952-2648 E-mail: bobhass@uclink4.berkeley.edu.

HASSAN, FRED, pharmaceutical executive; b. Pakistan, Nov. 12, 1945; came to U.S., 1970; s. Syed Fida and Zeenat (Hussain) H.; m. Noreen Shah, Mar. 15, 1969. BS in Chem. Engring. with honors, U. London, 1967; MBA, Harvard U., 1972. Chem. engr., sales mgr. Dawood Corp., Lahore, Pakistan, 1967-70; sales rep. Richardson-Vicks, N.Y.C., 1970; project mgr., corp. planning Sandoz Pharms. Corp., East Hanover, NJ, 1972-74, chief ops. officer, 1984-86, CEO, 1987-89; mgr. planning Dorsey Labs. div. Sandoz Pharms. Corp., Lincoln, Nebr., 1974-76, dir. mktg., 1975-80; CEO Sandoz Pakistan, Karachi, 1980-83; sr. v.p. Am. Home Products, Madison, NJ, 1995, exec. v.p., bd. dirs., 1995-97; pres. Wyeth Ayerst Labs., Madison, NJ, 1989-93; CEO Pharmacia Corp., Peapack, NJ, 1997—2003, chmn., 2000—03; pres., CEO Schering-Plough Corp., Kenilworth, NJ, 2003—. Bd. dirs. Avon Products Inc., CIGNA corp. Named CEO of Yr. in global pharmaceutical industry, Financial Times, 1999. Mem. Alliance for Aging Rsch. (bd. dirs. 1987-89, 96—), Pharm. Rsch. & Mfrs. Am. (chmn. bd. dirs.). Office: Schering-Plough Corp 2000 Galloping Hill Rd Kenilworth NJ 07033*

HASSAN, HOSNI MOUSTAFA, microbiologist, biochemist, toxicologist and food scientist, educator; b. Alexandria, Egypt, Sept. 3, 1937; came to U.S., 1961; s. Moustafa Hosni and Sania M. (El-Hariri) H.; children: Jehan, Suzanne, Nora Elizabeth. BSc, Ain Shams U., Cairo, 1959; PhD, U. Calif., Davis, 1967. Asst. prof. Cairo High Polytech. Inst., 1968-70, U. Alexandria, 1970-72; vis. prof. McGill U., Montreal, 1972-74; rsch. asst. prof. U. Maine, Orono, 1974-76; rsch. assoc. biochemistry Duke U. Med. Ctr., Durham, N.C., 1976-79; assoc. prof. McGill U. Med. Sch., Montreal, 1979-80, N.C. State U., Raleigh, 1980-84, prof., 1984-93, prof., head microbiology dept., 1993—, head dept. microbiology, interim head toxicology dept., 1999-2001. Mem. editl. bd. Free Radicals in Biology and Medicine, 1984—; author: (chpts.) Enzymatic Basis of Toxicology, 1980, Biological Role of Copper, 1980, Advances in Genetics, 1989, Stress Responses in Plants, 1990, FEMS Microbiol. Reviews, 1994, Lung Biology Series, Vol. 15, 1997, others; author/co-author over 100 rsch. publs. Fellow NIH, 1967, Fulbright sr. fellow, Paris, 1987-88; NIH-NSF grantee N.C. State U., 1982, 83-93. Fellow Am. Inst. Chemists, Sigma Xi; mem. Am. Soc. Biol. Chemists and Molecular Biology, Am. Soc. for Microbiology (pres.-elect and pres. N.C. chpt. 1993-95). Democrat. Achievements include discovery of the toxicity and mutagenicity of oxygen free radicals and the protective role of the antioxidant enzymes superoxide dismutases and hydroperoxidases; the mechanism of regulation of the synthesis of the enzyme Mn-superoxide dismutase and catelases in bacteria. Home: 2637 Freestone Ln Raleigh NC 27603-3950 Office: NC State U Microbiology Dept PO Box 7615 Raleigh NC 27695-7615 E-mail: hosni_hassan@ncsu.edu.

HASSAN, IBNE, lawyer, diplomat, political scientist; b. Najibabad, India, Jan. 2, 1938; s. Alhaj M. Abdul Aziz and Hasrat Jehan Begum. BA in Pub. Law and Govt., Purdue U., 1963; MA in Internat. Rels., Fordham U., 1964; PhD in Polit. Econ., Columbia U., 1966; PhD in Pub. Adminstrn., NYU, 1968; PhD in Internat. Rels., Oxford (Eng.) U., 1972; LLB, LLM, PhD in Internat. Law, Cambridge (Eng.) U., 1977. CEO Fgn. Devel. Corp., N.Y.C., London, Geneva, 1965-81; dir. gen. Kalos World Order Found., N.Y.C., 1971-81; prin. assessor Found. New World Edn., Geneva, 1972-77; sr. assoc. Tufts U., Medford, 1978-79; permanent rep. to UN Ctr. Devel. Policy, Washington, 1981-85; spl. rep. Inst. Internat. Security Studies, Washington, 1981-85; chief commr. Commn. Mid. Ea. Affairs, Washington, 1981-85; disting. prof. Johns Hopkins U., Washington, 1981-83; regional pres. Internat. Law Chambers, Washington, 1986—. Sr. fellow UN, N.Y.C., 1970-71, spl. advisor, 1983-85, mission assessor, 1994-96, spl. rep., 1998—; dir. Oxford Conf. Internat. Affairs, 1970, Philip Jessup Moot Internat. Law, Cambridge, Eng., 1975; mem. faculty bd. law, Cambridge (Eng.) U., 1974-77; vis. assoc. Geneva U., 1971-72; mem. adv. bd. World Peace News, N.Y.C., 1977-81; sr. fellow, vis. scholar Harvard U., Cambridge, Mass., 1977-78, 86-87; vis. scholar Yale U., New Haven, 1978-79, Columbia U., N.Y.C., 1996-98; vis. fellow Princeton U., 1979-80; regional rep. World Fedn. UN Assns., 1970-71, Internat. Students Movement for the UN, 1970-71; legal assoc. Internat. Law Commn., 1971-72; jud. asst. Internat. Ct. Justice, 1973-74. Contbr. numerous treatises and articles to polit. and legal publs. Internat. scholar Inst. World Affairs, 1964, 65; internat. fellow UN, 1968, 70, Internat. fellow Hague Acad. Internat. Law, 1972, 74, 75, 94, Internat. fellow Internat. Inst. Human Rights, 1975, 76, Internat. fellow Inst. Internat. Law & Rels., 1976, 77, 79, 81, 86, 94, 96, Litigious fellow European Ct. Human Rights, 1972-73; recipient Hyder Meml. Award of Merit, Aligarh U., 1951, Lit. Award of Merit, Majlis-i-Ilmistan, 1958, Internat. Award of Merit, Purdue U., 1962, Purdue Calumet award, 1962, Goldrush Medallion award, 1963, Acad. Excellence award Purdue Hassars, 1963, Student of the Yr. award Internat. Reporter, 1962, Quaid-i-Azan Award of Merit, Oxford U. Pakistan Soc., 1968, Meritorious Achievement award New World Edn. Found., 1972, World Peace award World Peace News, 1977, World Order award Kalos World Order, 1978, Man of Achievement award Internat. Biog. Centre, 1986, Disting. Leadership award Am. Biog. Inst., 1994, Twentieth Century Achievement award, 1995, Twentieth Century Award for Achievement, Internat. Biog. Centre, 2000, Disting. Achievement award WAFUNIF, 2001, Internat. Peace and Security award Internat. Biog. Centre, 2001. Fellow World Lit. Acad., Acad. of Polit. Sci.; mem. Am. Soc. Internat. Law, Global Policy Forum, Internat. Polit. Sci. Assn., Internat. Bar Assn., Internat. Peace Bur., Punjab Bar Coun., Internat. Soc. for Mil. Law, UN Assn. (UK, USA, Pakistan), Internat. Law Assn., Internat. Econ. Soc., Internat. Devel. Coun., Soc. for Internat. Devel., Royal Commonwealth Soc., Royal Inst. Internat. Affairs, Pakistan Inst. Internat. Affairs, Internat. Inst. of Strategic Studies, Fedn. Internationale des Avocats, Carnegie Coun., Am. Polit. Sci. Assn., World Jurist Coun., Rhodes Scholar Assn., Oxford Soc., Oxford Union Soc., Cambridge Soc., Cambridge Union Soc., Harvard Coun. Internat. Rels., Harvard Grad. Soc., World Inst. of Achievements, Oxford Mgmt. Soc., Pi Sigma Alpha. Avocations: gardening, painting, photography, music, riding. Home: DHPCC 20486 UN Plz New York NY 10017-0005 E-mail: ibn-e-hassan@hotmail.com., wafunif@wafunif.org.

HASSAN, SAYED MOHAMMED, analytical chemist; b. Cairo, Oct. 18, 1944; came to U.S., 1988; s. Mohammed Hassan Ali; m. Souad Ali Shaaban, July 12, 1973; children: Wael, Ghada, Hany. B Pharmacy and Pharm. Chemistry, U. Cairo, 1966, M Pharm. Sci., 1973, PhD in Pharm. Sci., 1975. Drug control analyst Nile Co. for Pharms., Cairo, 1966-67, Drug Control and Rsch. Ctr., Cairo, 1967-74; asst. lectr. to prof. and head dept. analytical chemistry Faculty of Pharmacy, Al-Mansoura, Egypt, 1974-88; prin. rsch. chemist DynCorp/U.S. EPA, Athens, Ga., 1988-95; mgr. chem. instrumentation dept. crop and soil scis. Coll. Agrl. and Environ. Scis., U. Ga., Athens, 1996-99; assoc. rsch. scientist, dir. lab. for environ. analysis Dept. Crop & Soil Scis., U. Ga., Athens, 2000—. Cons. Nat. Orgn. Drug Control and Rsch., Cairo, 1976-88, Kahira Co. for Chem. and Pharm. Industries, Cairo, 1987-88. Contbr. articles, revs. to profl. jours. Recipient Abdul Hameed Shoman award Shoman Found., Jordon, 1984. Mem. AAAS, Am. Chem. Soc., N.Y. Acad. Scis., Assn. Ofcl. Analytical Chemists, Egyptian Biochem. Soc., Chem. Soc. Egypt, Pharm. Soc. Egypt, Sigma Xi. Avocations: stamp collecting, fishing, walking, chess, computer programming.

HASSAN, SERGIO ALEJANDRO, physicist, biophysicist, researcher; b. Buenos Aires, Mar. 14, 1968; s. Manuel and Mara (Pavoni) H. MSc in Physics, Inst. Balseiro, Bariloche, Argentina, 1994; DSc, UNICAMP, Sao Paulo, Brazil, 1997. Assoc. Mt. Sinai Med. Ctr., N.Y.C., 1998-2000, sr. post doc., 2000—01, faculty, 2001—. CNEA fellow Argentinian Govt., CAPES fellow Brazilian Govt., FAPESP fellow Sao Paulo State, dept. physiology and biophysics Mt. Sinai Sch. Medicine, 1998-2001. Office: Mount Sinai Med Ctr One Gustave Levy Pl New York NY 10029 Fax: 212-860-3369. E-mail: mago@inka.mssm.edu.

HASSAN, STEPHANIE ANITRA, writing educator, consultant; b. Rochester, N.Y., June 8, 1975; d. Abdul Aleem and Judarah M. Hassan. BA in English, U. at Buffalo, 1998; PhD in Rhetoric and Composition, U. at Albany, 1999—. Writing tutor U. Writing Pl., Amherst, 1996—98; writer, journalist Generation Mag., Amherst, 1997—98; writing tutor U. Writing Ctr., Albany, 2000—01, asst. dir., 2001—02; writing cons. St. Anne Inst., Albany, 2002—; instr. of writing Union Coll., Schenectady, NY, 2002—03, U. of Albany, 2002—. English dept. rep. U. Grad. Student Orgn., Albany, 2001—; elected rep. Grad. English Conf. Com., Albany, 2002—, English Grad. Student Orgn., Albany, 2000—01. Vol. Literacy Volunteers of Am., Buffalo, 1998—2003. Recipient Targeted Academic Tchg. assistantship, U. at Albany, 2000—03, Minority Academic fellowship, 1999—2000. Mem.: MLA, Nat. Assn. of Tchrs. of English. Avocations: creative writing, reading literature and poetry, arts and crafts. Office: U at Albany English Dept 400 Washington Ave Albany NY 12222 Personal E-mail: shasan01@msn.com. E-mail: sh9672@albany.edu.

HASSEL, RUDOLPH CHRISTOPHER, English educator; b. Richmond, Va., Nov. 16, 1939; s. Rudolph Christopher and Helen Elizabeth (Poehler) H.; m. Sedley Louise Hotchkiss, June 16, 1962; children: Bryan Christopher, Paul Sedley. BA, U. Richmond, 1961; MA, U. N.C., 1962; PhD, Emory U., 1968. English instr. Mercer U., Macon, Ga., 1962-65; asst. prof. Vanderbilt U., Nashville, 1968-73, assoc. prof., 1973-85, prof., 1985—. Dir. grad. studies English dept. Vanderbilt U., 1974-81, dir. undergrad. studies, 1991, 99-00; mem. exec. com. Folger Inst., Washington, 1986-95; cons. State of Tenn., Nashville, 1987-93; cons. for various univ. presses and profl. jours. Author: Renaissance Drama and the English Church Year, 1979, Faith and Folly in Shakespeare's Romantic Comedies, 1980, Songs of Death, 1987; contbr. articles to Shakespeare Quar., Shakespeare Jahrbuch, Comparative Drama, Studies in Philology, and others and poems to Vanderbilt Rev. and Arts and Letters. Mem. choir Christ Episcopal Ch., Nashville, 1974-95, outreach vol., 1974—, vestryman, 1980-83; vol. United Way, Vanderbilt U., 1980—, Habitat for Humanity. Woodrow Wilson Found. fellow, 1962; Emory U. fellow, 1965; Folger Libr. fellow, 1976; Am. Philol. Soc. fellow, 1986. Mem. MLA, Internat. Shakespeare Assn., Shakespeare Assn. Am., Malone Soc. New Variorum Editor (Richard 3 vol.), Omicron Delta Kappa. Avocations: biking, hiking, tennis, gardening, woodcrafting. Home: 107 Pembroke Ave Nashville TN 37205-3728 Office: PO Box 129B Nashville TN 37202-0129 E-mail: r.chris.hassel@vanderbilt.edu.

HASSELBALCH, MARILYN JEAN, state official; b. Omaha, Jan. 2, 1930; d. Paul William and Helga Esther (Nodgaard) Campfield; m. Hal Burke Hasselbalch, June 13, 1954 (div. 1973); children: Kurt Campfield, Eric Burke, Peter Nels, Ane Catherine Hasselbalch McBride. BA with high distinction, U. Nebr., 1951. Cert. secondary tchr., Nebr. Pub. sch. tchr., Omaha and Long Beach, Calif., 1951-55; staff asst. U.S. Congressman Charles Thone, Lincoln, Nebr., 1973-78, Gov. of Nebr., Lincoln, 1978-82; exec. asst. Nebr. State Treas., Lincoln, 1983-86; sr. asst. Nebr. Gov. Kay A. Orr, Lincoln, 1987-91; exec. dir. Nebr. Appraiser Licensing Bd., Lincoln, 1991—. Mem. camp bd. dirs. YMCA, Nebr., 1969-70; mem. Nebr. Edn. Policies Commn., 1982; state conv. del. Rep. Party Nebr., 1986, 88; gov.'s rep. Nebr. State Hist. Soc., Lincoln, 1987-89; del. Edn. Commn. on States, Balt., 1988; participant strategic leadership for gubernatorial execs. Duke U., 1988; sec. Mission bd. Christ Luth. Ch., 1993—; treas. Danish Sisterhood #90, 1995—. Named to Outstanding Young Women Am., 1961, Woman of Yr., Rho Epsilon, 2000. Mem.: Assn. Appraiser Regulatory Ofcls. (bd. dirs. 1995—2002, publs. com. 1998—2002), Lancaster County Rep. Women (exec. bd. 1988), Nat. Fedn. Rep. Women, Danish Sisterhood Am., Am. Legion Aux., Phi Beta Kappa, Kappa Tau Alpha, Theta Sigma Phi. Lutheran. Avocations: reading, writing, travel, history, entertaining. Home: 4705 South St Lincoln NE 68506-1257 Office: Real Estate Appraiser Bd Nebr State Office Bldg Lincoln NE 68509

HASSELL, CLINTON ALTON, chemist, educator; b. Seagraves, Tex., Oct. 26, 1945; s. Clinton Andrew (Brit) and Virginia Cotten Hassell; m. Patricia Darnell Berryhill, June 12, 1947; children: Clint Alan, Sharina Michelle. BS, Baylor U., 1969; PhD, Tex. A&M U., 1975. Lectr. Tex. A&M U., College Station, 1976—79, vis. asst. prof., 1979—82; lectr. Baylor U., Waco, 1982—2000, sr. lectr., 2000—. Tour spkr. Am. Chem. Soc., Washington, 1979—2002; lectr. Tex. Engring. Ext. Svc., College Station, 1981—82; area supr. Baylor in Israel Archaeol. Dig, Tel Malhata, Israel, 1990—2000. Author: Test Item File for General Chemistry, 1997, Solutions Manual for General Chemistry, an Integrated Approach, 1996, Selected Solutions Manual for General Chemistry, an Integrated Approach, 1996; : 3d edit., 2002, Chemical Investigations for Changing Times, 1992, 4th edit., 2001, Solving Problems in Chemistry, 1977, 2d abridged edit., 1981, Advanced Problems in Applied Chemistry, 2000; contbr.: Test Item File for General Chemistry, 7th edit., 2002; author: (novel) Chemistry in Whispering Caves, 1998; contbr. articles to profl. jours. Team mem. Marriage Encounter, Waco, Tex., 1983—93; dir. sunday sch. Ctrl. Bapt. Ch., Bryan, Tex., 1980—82; asst. dir. sunday sch. Columbus Ave. Bapt. Ch., Waco, Tex., 1983—88. Mem.: Phi Lambda Upsilon (life; treas. 1974—75), Sigma Pi Sigma (life). Avocation: numismatics. Office: Baylor Univ Box 97348 Waco TX 76798 Office Fax: 254-710-2403. E-mail: alton_hassell@baylor.edu.

HASSELL, DARRIS ANTHONY, Spanish educator; b. Ft. Jackson, SC, Aug. 4, 1969; s. Ray Allen and Laura Betty Ann Hassell. BA in Spanish, Wofford Coll., 1991; MA in Spanish Lit., U. SC, 2001. Workflow clk. SC. Nat. Bank, Columbia, 1991—92; Spanish tchr. Sumter (SC) H.S., 1992—94; adj. instr. of Spanish U. SC, Columbia, 1996—97, Lancaster, 1997—2001, Spanish instr., 2002—; elem. sch. Spanish tchr. V.V. Reid Elem. Sch., Columbia, 1997—2000. Fgn. lang. cons. SC Dept. of Edn., Columbia, 1996; specialized instrn. in Spanish Springs Meml. Hosp., Lancaster, 2002. Musician church music department CD recording; team member Nat. Grass Champions BB Divsn. Ch. steward, musician, sec. Sons of Allen Brown Chapel A.M.E. Ch., Columbia, 1998—2003. Named Man of the Year, Brown Chapel A.M.E. Church, 2002—03. Mem.: Kappa Alpha Psi (assoc.; polemarch 1990—91). Democrat. Methodist. Avocations: volleyball, travel, food, Spanish, conversation. Home: 6410 Easter St Columbia SC 29203-5065 Office: U SC-Lancaster PO Box 889 Lancaster SC 29721 Home Fax: 803-289-4106. Personal E-mail: hassell@gwm.sc.edu.

HASSELL, JEAN TREVERTON, dietetics educator; b. Rochester, PA, Mar. 16, 1929; d. Edson Marion and Dorothy Gertrude (Treverton) Hays; m. Gordon Elmer Hassell, Sept. 8, 1951; children: Karen, Megan. BS cum laude, Syracuse U., 1951; MS, Kent State U., 1974. Clin. dietitian Rochester (Pa.) Gen. Hosp., 1951-52; home economist H.J. Heinz Co., Pitts., 1952-54; clin. & tchg. dietitian St. Vincent de Paul Hosp., Norfolk, Va., 1955-56, Trumbull Meml. Hosp., Warren, Ohio, 1962-88; Kellogg resident in med. dietetics Ohio State U., Columbus, 1980; prof. dietetics Youngstown (Ohio) State U., 1977—, chair dept. human ecology, 2001—. Cons. The Gastroenterology Clinic, Warren, 1974-83; vis. lectr. Pa. State U., Sharon, 1975-79, 80-84. Bd. dirs. Eas. Ohio Area Health Edn. Network, Youngstown, 1991-2001, WIC Program, Youngstown, 1987—, Am. Cancer Soc., 1977-87. Grantee Ross Labs., 1991, Ea. Ohio Area Health Edn. Network, 1993-95, 97—, Ohio Dept. Edn., 1994-95. Mem. Am. Dietetic Assn. (abstract reviewer 2003, site visitor and program reviewer Commn. on Accreditation for Dietetics Edn. 1996-2002, Outstanding Dietetic Educator 2000), Ohio Dietetic Assn. (Outstanding Coordinated Program in Dietetics Edn. for Ohio 2000), Mahoning Valley Dietetic Assn. (pres. 1985-86, sec. 1994-96), Am. Soc. Parenteral and Enteral Nutrition, Phi Kappa Phi, Chi Omega, Kappa Omicron Nu. Republican. Presbyterian. Avocations: tennis, swimming, bridge, cooking. Home: 7401 Mines Rd SE Warren OH 44484-3836 Office: Youngstown State Univ One University Plaza Youngstown OH 44555 E-mail: jhassell@ysu.edu.

HASSELL, LEROY ROUNTREE, SR., state supreme court chief justice; b. Aug. 17, 1955; BA in Govt. and Fgn. Affairs, U. Va., 1977; JD, Harvard U., 1980. Bar: Va. Former ptnr. McGuire, Woods, Battle and Boothe; now justice Supreme Ct. of Va. Former mem. Va. gen. assembly task force to study violence on sch. property. Former mem. adv. bd. Massey Cancer Ctr.; mem. policy com., former chmn. Richmond Sch. Bd., ; former bd. dirs. Richmond Renaissance, Inc., Richmond chpt. ARC, Garfield childs Fund, Carpenter Ctr. for Performing Arts, St. John's Hosp., Legal Aid Ctrl. Va.; vol. Richmond Pub. Schs., Hospice vol.; elected sch. bd. chmn. 4 terms. Recipient Liberty Bell award 1985, 86, Black Achievers award, 1985-86, Outstanding Young Citizen award Richmond Jaycees, 1987, Outstanding Young Virginian award Va. Jaycees, 1987; one of youngest persons to both serve on the Richmond Sch. Bd. and to serve as bd. chmn. Mem. Va. Trial Lawyers Assn., Assn. Trial Lawyers Am., Va. Assn. Def. Attys., Old Dominion Bar Assn., Va. Bar Assn. Office: Supreme Ct of Virginia PO Box 1315 Richmond VA 23218-1315

HASSELMAN, RICHARD B. retired transportation company executive; b. Jersey City, Nov. 28, 1926; s. Benjamin R. and Clara A. (Borchert) H.; m. Mildred E. Schaber, May 29, 1954; children: Richard Dwight, James Christopher. BME, Yale U., 1947; MBA, NYU, 1949. Student engr. N.Y. Central R.R., 1947-49, trainee, 1949-52, brakeman, 1952-53, signalman, freight agt., 1953; transp. insp. Eastern region Syracuse, N.Y., 1953-55; trainmaster Mowhawk divsn. Albany, N.Y., 1955-57; divsn. trainmaster Syracuse divsn., 1957; divsn. supt. Boston & Albany divsn., 1957-59; dist. transp. supt. Western region Cleve., 1959-60; gen. supt. yards and terminals N.Y. Ctrl. Sys., N.Y.C., 1960-63; gen. mgr. Ind. Harbor Belt and Chicago River & Ind. R.R., Hammond, Ind., 1963; gen. mgr. No. Region N.Y. Cen. R.R., Detroit, 1964, gen. mgr. So. Region Indpls., 1964-66, gen. mgr. Western Region Cleve., 1967; asst. v.p. transp. N.Y. Ctrl. Sys., N.Y.C., 1967-68; v.p. transp. Penn. Ctrl., Phila., 1968-76; pres. Ind. Harbor Belt RR, 1968-87; sr. v.p. ops. Consol. Rail Corp., Phila., 1976-89; transp. cons., 1989—. Home and Office: 5289 Ladyfinger Lake Rd Sanibel FL 33957-2436

HASSELMEYER, EILEEN GRACE, medical research administrator; b. Bklyn., May 23, 1924; d. Edwin Allen and Margaret Grace (Cody) H. RN, Bellevue Sch. Nursing, 1946; BS, NYU, 1954, MA, 1956, PhD, 1963. Mem. staff Pediatric Metabolic and Nutritional Rsch. Svc., NYU Children's Med. Svc., Bellevue Hosp., N.Y.C., 1946-56, study coord., 1951-56; rsch. nursing supr. Met. Hosp., N.Y.C., 1951; lectr. pediatric nutrition rsch. U. Tex. Sch. Nursing, 1952-53; nursing dir. nutritional rsch. studies Children's Hosp. of John Seely Hosp. (U. Tex. Med. Br.), Galveston, 1952-53; lectr. and nursing rsch. assoc. nutritional svc. pediat. dept. Hosp. Infantile, Mexico City, 1953; nursing dir. rsch. unit Willowbrook State Sch., S.I., 1953-54; commd. USPHS, 1956, advanced through grades to asst. surgeon gen.-rear adm., 1981; ret. 1989; nurse cons. Divsn. Nursing Resources, Bur. Med. Svcs., USPHS, Washington, 1956-59; prin. investigator Handling and Premature Infant Behavior project, NYU, N.Y.C., 1961-63; sr. nurse cons. Div. Nursing, Bur. State Svcs., USPHS, Washington, 1963; spl. asst. for prematurity Office of Dir., Nat. Inst. Child Health and Human Devel., Bethesda, Md., 1963-66, acting dir. perinatal biology and infant mortality program, extramural programs, 1967-68, dir., 1969-74, asst. to dir. for perinatology, 1974-80; chief pregnancy and infancy br. Ctr. for Rsch. for Mothers and Children, 1974-79, acting chief clin. nutrition and early devel. br., 1979-80; assoc. dir. for sci. rev. Office of Dir., 1979-89; spl. asst. to dir. N.C. for Nursing Rsch., 1986-89; exec. dir. Uniform Svcs. U. Health Sci., Fed. Coll. Nursing Feasability Study Task Force, 1989-92. Annie W. Goodrich vis. prof. Yale U. Sch. Nursing, New Haven, 1968-69; asst. surgeon gen. USPHS, Dept. Health and Human Svcs., 1981-89, chmn. interagy. panel on sudden infant death syndrome, 1974-82, others. Contbr. articles to profl. jours. Recipient NICHD Recognition of Outstanding Performance, 1973, plaque for 25 yrs. dedicated svc., 1987, Chief Nurse Officer's medal USPHS, 1989; USUHS Commendable Svc. medal, 1990; USPHS Surgeon Gen.'s Cert. of Appreciation, 1990; HEW-USPHS Commendation medal, 1975; recipient Perinatal Research Soc. award, 1979; NYU Sch. Edn., Health, Nursing and Arts Professions Creative Leadership award, 1980; Achievement award Nat. Sudden Infant Death Syndrome Found., 1987, Eileen G. Hasselmeyer Disting. Sci. Achievement award Sudden Infant Death Syndrome Alliance, 1990; Outstanding Performance award NCNR, 1987, Meritorious Svc. medal HHS-USPHS,

1989; cert. appreciation NIH-NCNR, 1989; Nat. League for Nursing Commonwealth fellow, 1959-62; NIH fellow, 1962-63; Am. Nurses Found. grantee, 1962-63; State of Conn. Maternal and Infant Program grantee, 1969; Sigma Theta Tau research grantee, 1969-71; Yale U. Sch. Nursing developmental grantee, 1969; disting. alumnae award Bellevue Alumnae Assn., 1997. Mem. Pub. Health Svc. Commd. Officers Assn., Bellevue Alumnae Assn.

HASSELMO, NILS, academic administrator, linguistics educator; b. Kola, Sweden, July 2, 1931; arrived in U.S., 1958; s. A. Wilner and Anna Helena (Backlund) Hasselmo; m. Patricia June Tillberg, Oct. 25, 1958; children: Nils Peter, Michael Erik, Anna Patricia. Fil. mag., Uppsala U., 1956, Fil. lic., 1962, PhD (hon.), 1979; BA, Augustana Coll., Ill., 1957, DHL (hon.), 1995; PhD, Harvard U., 1961; LHD (hon.), North Park Coll. Theol. Sem., 1992. Asst. prof. Swedish Augustana Coll., Rock Island, Ill., 1958—59, 1961—62; from assoc. prof. to prof. Scandinavian langs. and lit. U. Minn., Mpls., 1965—83, 1988—2001, chmn. Scandinavian langs. and lit., 1970—73; dir. U. Minn. Ctr. for N.W. European Langs. and Area Studies, Mpls., 1970—73; assoc. dean U. Minn. Coll. Liberal Arts, Mpls., 1973—78; v.p. for adminstrn. and planning U. Minn., Mpls., 1980—83; sr. v.p. acad. affairs, provost U. Ariz., Tucson, 1983—88, prof. English and linguistics, 1983—88; pres. U. Minn., Mpls., 1988—97, Assn. Am. Univs., Washington, 1998—. Vis. com. dept. Germanic langs. and lit. Harvard U., Cambridge, Mass., 1981—86; trustee Nat. Merit Scholarship Corp., 1992—97. Author: Amerikasvenska, 1974, Swedish America: An Introduction, 1976; editor: Perspectives on Swedish Immigration, 1978. Active Gov.'s Task Force on Technology and Improvement of Employment, Minn., 1982—83; trustee Am. Scandinavian Found., 1992—; bd. dirs. Swedish Coun. Am., 1978—, chmn. bd., 1999—2001; bd. dirs. Walker Art Ctr., 1989—95; bd. overseers Mpls. Coll. Art and Design, 1982—83; bd. dirs. Carnegie Found. for Advancement of Tchg., 2002—. Sgt. Royal Signal Corps Swedish Army, 1951—54. Decorated Royal Order of North Star Sweden; named Swedish-Am. of Yr., Swedish Govt. and Vasa Order Am., 1991; recipient King Carl XVI Gustaf's Bicentennial medal in Gold, Sweden, 1976, Ellis Island medal of honor, 1993; fellow Fulbright-Hays fellow, 1968. Mem.: MLA, Univ. Rsch. Assn. (trustee 1993—97), Nat. Assn. State Univs. and Land Grant Colls. (exec. com. acad. affairs coun. 1986—88, chmn. coun. pres. and chancellors 1992—93, chair bd. 1994—95), Swedish-Am. Hist. Soc. (chmn. bd. 1984—86), Royal Gustavus Adolphus Acad., Vetenskaps-Soc., Linguistic Soc. Am., Soc. for Advancement Scandinavian Study (pres. 1971—73).*

HASSEN, IRFAN WADOOD, physician; b. Sri Lanka, Nov. 22, 1944; came to U.S., 1973; m. Zoe Hassen; children: Imla, Farwah. MB BS, U. Ceylon, 1967. Diplomate Am. Acad. of Disability Analysts. Med. dir. Blair County Prison, Pa., 1976-86; asst. med. dir. County Nursing Home, Altoona, Pa., 1986-89; pvt. practice Frederick, Md., 1989—. Fellow Am. Acad. Family Physicians.

HASSENFELD, ALAN GEOFFREY, consumer products company executive; b. Providence, Nov. 16, 1948; s. Merrill Lloyd and Sylvia (Kay) H. BA, U. Pa., 1970. Asst. to pres. Hasbro Industries, Inc., Pawtucket, R.I., 1969-72, v.p. internat. ops., 1972-78, v.p. mktg. and sales, 1978-80, exec. v.p., 1980-84, pres., 1984-89, chmn., CEO, 1989—2003; chmn. Hasbro, Inc., Pawtucket, RI, 2003—. Bd. dirs. Foster Parents Plan, 1989—, Assn. Gov. Bds. Univs. and Colls.; trustee Miriam Hosp., 1984-93, Brown U., 1990, Bryant Coll., 1992; adv bd. Big Bros. of R.I., 1991; chmn. Right Now! Coalition, 1991—; chmn. Gov.'s Adv. Council on Refugee Resettlement, 1986; bd. overseers U. Pa. Sch. Arts and Scis., 1986—, Harvard U. Sch. Pub. Health, 1997; chmn. bd. overseers Brown U. Med. Sch., 1997; trustee R.I. and Southeastern New Eng. region, NCCJ, 1988, Deerfield Acad., 1996; bd. dirs. Jewish Fedn. R.I., 1989—, Bus. for Social Responsibility, 1994, Founds. Milken Families, 1993; chmn. World Scholar Athlete Games, 2001, bd. trustees U.S. Coun. for Internat. Bus., 2002—; mem. exec. com. Internat. Tennis Hall of Fame, 2000; dir. The Jerusalem Found., 1995—, dean coun. Harvard U., 1995. With AFNG, 1967-73. Mem. R.I. Commodores (adm. 1991-98). Office: Hasbro Inc 1027 Newport Ave Pawtucket RI 02861-2500

HASSERT, BRENT, state legislator; Owner Hassert Landscaping; mem. from 83d dist. Ill. Ho. of Reps., 1993—. Formerly mem. Will County Bd. Commrs.; formerly chmn., exec. Pub. Works and Natural Resources Coms., Will County; formerly commr. Will County Forest Preserve; formerly mem. Ill. Task Force for Solid Waste Legislation. Home: 1413 Sherman Rd Ste 60 Romeoville IL 60446-4092*

HASSETT, JOSEPH MARK, lawyer; b. Buffalo, May 1, 1943; m. Carol A. Melton, June 23, 1984; children: Matthew, Meredith. BA summa cum laude, Canisius Coll., 1964; LL.B. cum laude, Harvard U., 1967; MA with 1st class honors, Univ. Coll. Dublin, 1981, PhD, 1985. Bar: N.Y. 1967, D.C. 1970, U.S. Supreme Ct. 1976. Assoc. Hogan & Hartson, Washington, 1970-74, ptnr., 1974—. Bd. trustees Canisius Coll. Author: Yeats and the Poetics of Hate, 1986; contbr. articles to profl. publs. Mem. ABA, D.C. Bar Assn. Home: 6035 Crimson Ct Mc Lean VA 22101-1818 Office: 555 13th St NW Washington DC 20004-1109

HASSETT, VALERIE JANE, interior designer, architect, educator; b. San Diego, Calif., Dec. 22, 1962; d. Roger John and Cecealia Virginia (Cibrich) H. Student, U. Tenn., 1982-86; BFA in Interior Design, Va. Commonwealth U., Richmond, 1988; MArch, Va. Poly. U., Alexandria, 1993. Registered profl. interior designer, Va., cert. constrn. documents technologist, registered profl. architect, Va., cert. Nat. Coun. of Archtl. Registration Bds. Interior architect Washington Area Transit Authority, 1988-90, 91-92, Prince William County Va. Govt., 1993-96, RTKL, Balt., 1996-97; instr. Mt. Vernon Coll. at Georgetown U., Washington, 1997-99; project mgr., head interior design dept. Sharadan, Behm, Eustice and Assocs. Ltd., Arlington, Va., 1997—; assoc. prof. No. Va. C.C., 2000. Mem. professions fellowship rev. panel AAUW, 2003. Exhibitions include Nat. Bldg. Mus., 1995, 1996. Chmn. women in architecture film festival Nat. Mus. Women in the Arts, 1990, 2000. Mem. AIA (bd. dirs., chair women in architecture com. No. Va. chpt. 1993—), Internat. Interior Design Assn. (past pres. Mid-Atlantic chpt.), Neighborhood Design Ctr. Balt. Avocation: paper making. Office: Sheridan Behm Eustice & Assocs 3440 Fairfax Dr Arlington VA 22201-4431 E-mail: vjhassett@aol.com.

HASSID, SAMI, architect, educator; b. Cairo, Apr. 19, 1912; came to U.S., 1957, naturalized, 1962; s. Joseph S. and Isabelle (Israel) H.; m. Juliette Mizrahi, June 29, 1941; children: Fred, Muriel. Diploma in architecture with distinction, Sch. Engring., Giza, Egypt, 1932; BA in Architecture with honors, U. London, Eng., 1935; M.Arch., U. Cairo, 1943; PhD in Architecture, Harvard U., 1956. Tchr. Alexandria (Egypt) Tech. Sch., 1932-34; successively tchr., lectr., asst. prof. U. Cairo, 1934-56; prof. architectural theory and design U. Ein-Shams, Cairo, 1957; mem. faculty U. Calif., Berkeley, 1957—, prof. architecture, 1964-79, prof. emeritus, 1979—; also assoc. dean U. Calif. (Coll. Environ. Design), 1977-83, faculty asst. to vice-chancellor for campus planning, 1980-85, dir. campus planning office, 1983-84; archtl. practice Cairo, 1932-57, Berkeley, 1957-85; from draftsman to sr. designer office Ali Labib Gabr (architect), Cairo, 1935-47; ptnr. Sami Hassid and Youssef Shafik, Cairo, 1947-57, Hassid and Kelemen, Berkeley, 1963-65. Author: The Sultan's Turrets, 1939, Architectural Construction Details, 1954, Development and Application of a System for Recording Critical Evaluations of Architectural Works, 1964, Architectural Education U.S.A, 1967, (with others) Innovations in Housing Design and Construction Techniques as Applied to Low-Cost Housing, 1969, Surface Materials in Architecture, 1970, Doctoral Studies in Architecture, 1971, Methods for the Development of Shipboard Habitability Design Criteria, 1974, Fire Safety in Buildings, A Course Offering Package, 1976, (with others) The Berkeley Campus Space Plan, 21 publs., 1981-83; Proc. Workshop on Seismic Upgrading of Existing Bldgs., NSF, 1982; prin. works include Hill House; student hostel, Am. U. Cairo, 1952. Commr. Calif. Bd. Archtl. Examiners, 1961-71. Fulbright grantee, 1954-56; recipient First prize Al-Chams Competition, Cairo, 1947, First prize San Francisco AIA Hdqrs. Competition, 1963 Fellow AIA; mem. Bldg. Research Inst., Assn. Collegiate Schs. Architecture. Democrat. Jewish (trustee temple; v.p. East Bay synagogue council 1970-71). Home: Sami Hassid FAIA 2851 Rockridge Dr Pleasant Hill CA 94523

HASSIG, ROSS, anthropologist; b. Clarksburg, W.Va., Dec. 12, 1945; s. Ronald Ross and Janice (Martin) H. BA, So. Ill. U., 1968; JD, Vanderbilt U., 1972, MA, 1974; PhD, Stanford U., 1980. Bar: Tenn. 1973. Asst. prof. Vanderbilt U., Nashville, 1979-83, Columbia U., N.Y.C., 1983-86, assoc. prof., 1986-91, U. Okla., Norman, 1991-93, prof., 1993—. Author: Trade, Tribute and Transportation: The Sixteenth-Century Political Economy of the Valley of Mexico, 1987 (Howard Francis Cline Meml. prize Conf. Latin Am. History 1987), Aztec Warfare: Imperial Expansion and Political Control, 1988, War and Society in Ancient Mesoamerica, 1992, Mexico and the Spanish Conquest, 1994, Time, History, and Belief in Aztec and Colonial Mexico, 2001; co-author: (with J. Richard Andrews) Ruiz de Alarcon, Treatise on the Heathen Superstitions and Customs that Today Live Among the Indians Native to this New Spain 1629; editor Ethnohistory, 1992-97, assoc. editor, 1986-92; mem. bd. editors Anthropological Theory, 1998—, Ancient Mesoamerica, 2001—. With U.S. Army, 1968—70. Fellow Dumbarton Oaks, 1988-89, John Simon Guggenheim Meml. Found., 1997-98, Sainsury Rsch. Unit U. East Anglia, 1999; Weatherhead fellow NEH, 1997-98, Lloyd Lewis/NEH fellow Newberry Libr., 2000-2001; grantee Orgn. Am. States, 1977-78, NSF, 1986, Harry Frank Guggenheim Found., 1989, 90, 1990-91, Wenner-Gren Found. Anthrop. Rsch., 1999, NEH, 2000-2001, Huntington Libr./Brit. Acad. fellow, 2001. Mem. N.Y. Acad. Scis. (co-chair anthropology sect. 1987 88, co-vice-chair 1986). Home: 1131 Robinhood Ln Norman OK 73072

HASSLER, DONALD MACKEY, II, English language educator, writer; b. Akron, Ohio, Jan. 3, 1937; s. Donald Mackey and Frances Elizabeth (Parsons) H.; m. Diana Cain, Oct. 8, 1960 (dec. Sept. 1976); children: Donald, David; m. Sue Smith, Sept. 13, 1977; children: Shelly, Heather. BA (Sloan fellow), Williams Coll., 1959; MA (Woodrow Wilson fellow), Columbia U., 1960, PhD, 1967. Instr. U. Montreal, 1961-65; instr. English Kent (Ohio) State U., 1965-67, asst. prof., 1967-71, assoc. prof., 1971-76, prof., 1977—, acting dean honors and exptl. coll., 1979-81, dir., 1973-83, coord. writing cert. program, 1986-91, chmn. undergrad. studies, 1987-91, dir. Wick Poetry Competition, 1987-91, coord. grad. studies, 1991-94; sec. faculty senate Kent (Ohio State U., 1996—, coord. maj. program, 1998—. Author: Erasmus Darwin, 1974, The Comedian as the Letter D: Erasmus Darwin's Comic Materialism, 1973, Asimov's Golden Age: The Ordering of an Art, 1977, Hal Clement, 1982, Comic Tones in Science Fiction, 1982, Patterns of the Fantastic, 1983, Patterns of the Fantastic II, 1984, Death and the Serpent, 1985, Isaac Asimov, 1991; mng. editor Jour. Extrapolation, 1986-87, co-editor, 1987-89, editor, 1990-2001, exec. editor, 2002—; co-editor (with Sue Hassler) Letters of Arthur Machen and Montgomery Evans, 1923-1947, 1993, (with Clyde Wilcox) Political Science Fiction, 1997; adv. editl. bd. Hellas, 1988—; editl. bd. Paradoxa, 1994—. Co-chmn. Kent Am. Revolution Bicentennial Commn., 1974-77; deacon Presbyn. Ch., 1971-74, elder, 1974-77; sec. Kent State Faculty Senate, 1996—, chancellor's faculty adv. com., 1996—, univ. priorities and budget adv. coun., 1998—; spkr. Smithsonian Yesterday's Tomorrow's exhibit, 2003. Recipient J. Lloyd Eaton award, Eaton Libr. Collection U. Calif., Riverside, 1993. Mem. Sci. Fiction Rsch. Assn. (treas. 1983-84, pres. 1985-86, Thomas D. Clareson award 2001), Kiwanis (bd. dirs. 1974-76), Phi Beta Kappa (pres. 1983-84). Home: 1226 Woodhill Dr Kent OH 44240-2832 E-mail: extrap@kent.edu.

HASSON, JAMES KEITH, JR., lawyer, law educator; b. Knoxville, Tenn., Mar. 3, 1946; s. James Keith and Elaine (Biggers) Hasson; m. Jayne Young, July 27, 1968; 1 child, Keith Samuel. BA, Duke U., 1967; JD, 1970. Bar: Ga. 1971, DC 1971. Assoc. Sutherland, Asbill & Brennan, Atlanta, 1970—76; ptnr., 1976; prof. law Emory U., Atlanta, 1976—94; chmn. bd. dir. House-Hasson Hardware Co., Knoxville, 2000—. Editor: (jour.) Taxation; contbr. articles. Recipient Pres. Disting. Svc. award, 1980. Mem.: Atlanta Bar Assn. (counsel 1977—80), ABA (com. chmn. 1983—85), IRS Commr. (exempt orgn. adv. group), Atlanta Civilian Review Bd., Reinhardt Coll. (bd. trustees 2001—), Met. Atlanta Crime Commn. (chmn. 1986—87, trustee), Foxfire Fund (trustee 1988—2001, chmn. bd. dir.), Leadership Atlanta, Lawyers Club. Presbyn. Home: 3185 Chatham Rd NW Atlanta GA 30305-1101 Office: Sutherland Asbill & Brennan 999 Peachtree St NE Ste 2300 Atlanta GA 30309-3996

HASSON, RAYMOND EDWARD, III, artist, writer; b. Columbus, Ohio, Oct. 13, 1946; s. Raymond Edward Jr. and Elsie Lucille (Offord) H.; m. Judith Ann Shabbott, Oct. 12, 1968; children: Geoffrey Randall, Mathew Francis, Christopher Jon. AA with high honors, Three Rivers Cmty. Tech. Coll., 1995; BA in Fine Art summa cum laude, Ea. Conn. State U., 1997. Enlisted USN, 1965, apptd. chief petty officer, 1978, instr., 1965-90; dist. mgr. IC Systems Inc., Mpls., 1990-92; artist Pumpkin Hill Studio, Ledyard, Conn., 1996—. Command career counselor USS U.S. Grant, Charleston, S.C., 1975-77; navigation instr. U. Va., Charlottesville, 1977-80. Exhibited in group shows at The Nude Show, North Woodstock, Conn., 1995, 33d Ann. Milford (Conn.) Green Fall Show, 1995, The Green Marble Coffee House, Westerly, R.I., 1996, 97, 98, Mystic (Conn.) Art Assn., 1996, 97, 98, Florence Griswold Mus., Old Lyme, conn., 1996, 97, Akus Gallery, Willimantic, Conn., 1997, Pfizer, Inc., Groton, Conn., 1997, Wood-Pawcatuck Watershed Assn., Carolina, R.I., 1997; represented in numerous personal and corp. collections; editor Ledyard Adventure Club newsletter, 1996—; contbr. articles to profl. jours., tech. pubs., newspapers. Recipient Artist-at-Work award Florence Griswald Mus., 1996, 97, 98. Mem. ASTD, Nat. Assn. Fed. Credit Unions (cert. compliance officer), Mystic Art Assn. (artist-at-work coord. 1999, co-chair young-at-art exhibit 1998, 99), Omicron Delta Kappa. Avocations: hiking, woodworking, bird watching. E-mail: honraymond@msn.com.

HASSOUN, HEITHAM TALAL, surgeon, researcher; b. Portland, Oreg., Feb. 8, 1971; s. Talal and Magida Hassoun; m. Danette Marlene Persyn, May 13, 1998; 1 child, Hannah Heitham. BA in Natural Scis., Johns Hopkins U., 1993; MD, Baylor Coll., 1997. Resident U. Tex., San Antonio, 1997—99, trauma rschr. ctr. fellow Houston, 1999—2001, resident, 2001—. Contbr. articles. Recipient Young Investigator award, Am. Mobility Soc., 2000, Basic Sci. Competition award, Am. Coll. Surgery, S. Tex., 2001, 2002. Mem.: Shock Soc., Assn. Acad. Surgery. Office: Univ Tex Houston Med Sch Dept Surgery 6431 Fannin 4-264 Houston TX 77030-1501

HAST, ADELE, editor, historian; b. N.Y.C., Dec. 6, 1931; d. Louis and Kate (Miller) Krongelb; m. Malcolm Howard Hast, Feb. 1, 1953; children: David Jay, Howard Arthur. BA magna cum laude, Bklyn. Coll., 1953; MA, U. Iowa, 1969, PhD, 1979. Rsch. assoc. Atlas Early Am. History Project, Newberry Library, Chgo., 1971-75; assoc. dir. Atlas Great Lakes Indian History Project, 1976-79, Hist. Boundary Data File Project, 1979-81; editor in chief Marquis Who's Who, Inc., Chgo., 1981-86; survey dir. Nat. Opinion Rsch. Ctr., U. Chgo., 1986-89; rsch. fellow Newberry Libr., Chgo., 1989-95, scholar in residence, 1995—; exec. editor St. James Press, Chgo., 1990-92; mng. editor Hist. Ency. of Chgo. Women U. Ill., Chgo., 1991-93, dir., editor Hist. Ency. of Chgo. Women project, 1993-2001, sr. rsch. assoc. Ctr. for Rsch. on Women and Gender, 1999—. Mem. faculty Newberry Libr. Summer Inst. Cartography, 1980. Author: Loyalism in Revolutionary Virginia, 1982, American Leaders Past and Present: The View from Who's Who in America, 1985; compiler: Iowa, Missouri, vol. 4 of Historical Atlas and Chronology of County Boundaries, 1788-1980, 1984; editor: International Directory of Company Histories, vols. 3-5, 1991-92, Women Building Chicago 1790-1990: A Biographical Dictionary, 2001; assoc. editor: Atlas of Great Lakes Indian History, 1987; curator exhibit on Chgo. history Spertus Inst. of Jewish Studies, 2002-03, contbr. articles to profl. jours. Mem. profl. adv. grad. program pub. history Loyola U., 1986—; treas., bd. dirs. Chgo. Map Soc., 1980-81, 93-95; mem. New Trier Twp. H.S. Bd. Caucus, 1972-74; mem. acad. coun. Am. Jewish Hist. Soc., 1985—; pres. Chgo. Jewish Hist. Soc., 1980-81, bd. dirs., 1977—. Recipient Alumna of Yr. award Bklyn. Coll., 1984, Colonial Williamsburg Found. grantee-in-aid, 1975, Brit. Acad. rsch. fellow, 1979; Am. Coun. Learned Socs. grantee-in-aid, 1980; NEH rsch. grantee, 1985, 87, 93-95, 97-98, fellow Women's Archive, 2003—. Fellow Royal Hist. Soc., Phi Beta Kappa, Kappa Delta Pi; mem. Am. Hist. Assn., Orgn. Am. Historians, Chgo. Area Women's History Conf. (sec., treas. 1994—, bd. dirs. 1990—), Caxton Club (coun. 1990-93). Office: Newberry Library 60 W Walton St Chicago IL 60610-3380

HAST, MALCOLM HOWARD, medical educator, biomedical scientist; b. N.Y.C., May 28, 1931; s. Irving William and Rose Lillian (Berlin) H.; m. Adele Krongelb, Feb. 1, 1953; children: David Jay, Howard Arthur. BA, Bklyn. Coll., 1953; postgrad., U. So. Calif., 1955-57; MA, Ohio State U., 1958, PhD (NIH fellow), 1961; CBiol, FIBiol, Gt. Britain, 1991. Instr. U. Iowa, 1961-63; NIH spl. fellow U. Iowa (Coll. Medicine), 1963-65, asst. prof., 1965-69; assoc. prof. otolaryngology-head and neck surgery Northwestern U. Feinberg Sch. Medicine, Chgo., 1969—74; prof. Chgo., 1974—; dir. research otolaryngology Northwestern U. Med. Sch., Chgo., 1969-93, prof. cell and molecular biology (anatomy), 1977—2001; prof. basic and behavioral scis. Northwestern U. Dental Sch., 1989-2001; assoc. med. staff Northwestern Meml. Hosp., 1969-90, health profl., 1990-93; rsch. assoc. zoology Field Mus. Natural History, 1995—; guest scientist Max Planck Inst. für Psychiatrie, 1976; vis. prof. Royal Coll. Surgeons Eng., 1980-86, U. Edinburgh, 1987; assoc. editor Clinical Anatomy, 1995—. Mem. task force on new materials Am. Bd. Otolaryngology, 1969-72; dir. Ill. Soc. Med. Rsch., 1973-77; mem. Internat. Anat. Nomenclature Com., 1983-91; guest scientist Zoologisches Forchungsinstitut und Mus. A. Koenig, 1988; mem. Northwestern U. Feinberg Sch. of Med. Admissions com., 1991-, chmn., 1998-; Brodel meml. lectr. Assn. Med. Illustrators, 1995; mem. Chgo. Clin. Ethics Programs. Prin. investigator, editor Annotated Translation of Vesalius' Fabrica, 1995-; contbr. articles to profl. jours., chpts. to books. Mem. adv. bd. Ctr. Deafness, 1977-80; bd. dirs. Cliff Dwellers Arts Found., 1979-82; trustee Wilmette Libr. Bd., 1982-83, Wilmette Bd. Health, 1999-. Served with U.S. Army, 1953-55. NATO sr. fellow in sci. Oxford U., Eng., 1978; NIH rsch. grantee, 1964-84, 95—, NSF rsch. grantee, 1975-77, NEH grantee, 1995-2002; recipient Gould Internat. award, 1971, Disting. Alumnus award of Honor, Bklyn. Coll., 1977, Alumnus of Yr. award, 1984; Arnott demonstrator Royal Coll. Surgeons Eng., 1985. Fellow AAAS, Linnean Soc. London, Inst. Biology, Am. Speech-Hearing Assn., Royal Soc. Medicine; mem. AMA, AAUP (chpt. pres. 1977-82), Am. Physiol. Soc. (animal care and experimentation com. 1976-82), Am. Assn. Clin. Anatomists, Chgo. Laryngol. and Otol. Soc. (coun. 1988-89), Am. Soc. Mammalogists, Anat. Soc. Gt. Britain and Ireland, Am. Assn. History Medicine, Soc. Med. History Chgo., Amnesty Internat. (coord. Chgo. Health profs. group 1986-87), Am. Assn. Anatomists, Nat. Eagle Scout Assn., Sigma Xi (chpt. pres. 1971-72), Sigma Alpha Eta. Achievements include research on neuromuscular physiology, embryology and comparative anatomy of the larynx, history of medicine. Office: 303 E Chicago Ave Chicago IL 60611-3093

HASTEN, RALPH GERALD, minister, protective services official; b. Mineola, Tex., June 18, 1926; s. Judge Roberts and Rose Chap Hasten; m. Wynona Cauthen Hasten, Aug. 24, 1947; children: Deborah Ann Gagne, David Ward. BA, Southwestern U., 1951; ThM, So. Meth. U., 1954. Pastoral appts., 1951—63; field rep. Presbyn. Min.'s Fund, Ft. Worth, 1963—66, Min.'s Life and Casualty Union, Houston, 1966—69; vocat. rehab. counselor Tex. Rehab. Commn., Houston, 1969—91; dep. sheriff Harris County Sheriff's Dept., Houston, 1991—97, sgt., 1997—. Part-time pastor United Meth. Ch., Houston, 1966—91. Author: (book) Grampoetry for Grandkids of All Ages, 1997, More Grampoetry for Grandkids of All Ages, 2000, JD's Joyful Jailhouse Jawings, 2001. Chaplain CAP, Houston, 1970—72, Goodwill Industries, Inc., Houston, 1978—81. Sgt. USMC, 1944—47. Mem.: Fraternal Order of Police (cert. mem.). Democrat. United Methodist. Avocations: horticulture, writing, hunting, fishing, family-centered activities. Home: 9603 Rockhurst Dr Houston TX 77080 Office: Harris County Sheriff's Dept 1307 Baker St Houston TX 77002

HASTERT, DENNIS (J. DENNIS HASTERT), congressman; b. Aurora, Ill., Jan. 2, 1942; m. Jean Kahl, 1973; children: Joshua, Ethan. BA, Wheaton Coll., 1964; MS, No. Ill. U., 1967. Tchr., coach Yorkville (Ill.) High Sch.; mem. Ill. House Reps., Springfield, 1980-86, U.S. Congress from 14th dist. Ill., 1987—, chief dep. majority whip, 1994-99, speaker of the house, 1999—, mem. commerce com., mem. govt. reform and oversight com. Mem.: Lions (Yorkville). Republican. Office: US Ho of Reps 235 Cannon House Office Bldg Washington DC 20515-1314*

HASTIE, JOHN DOUGLAS, lawyer; b. Guthrie, Okla., Dec. 9, 1939; BA, U. Okla., 1961, LLB, 1964. Bar: Okla. 1964. Atty. Hastie and Kirschner, Oklahoma City, 1974-96, Andrews Davis Legg Bixler Milsten and Price, Oklahoma City, 1996-2001, Phillips McFall McCaffrey McVay & Murrah, P.C., Oklahoma City, 2001—. Adj. prof. U. Okla. Coll. Law, 1982—90, 2000—02; cons., lectr. in field. Contbr. articles to profl. jours. Capt. U.S. Army, 1964-66. Mem. ABA, Okla. Bar Assn., Cleve. County Bar Assn., Assn. of Bar of City of N.Y., Am. Coll. Real Estate Lawyers (gov. 1990-2000, exec. com. 1992-2000, pres. 1999, Frederick S. Lane award 2002), Anglo-Am. Real Property Inst., Am. Law Inst., Am. Coll. Mortgage Attys., Internat. Bar Assn. Home: 914 Living Springs Trail Washington OK 73093 Office: Phillips McFall McCaffrey McVay & Murrah 401 W Main St Ste 444 Norman OK 73069-1319 E-mail: jdhastie@hastielaw.com.

HASTINGS, ALAN, environmental biology educator; b. Riverhead, N.Y., Aug. 27, 1953; s. Julius and Celia Hastings. BA, MS, Cornell U., PhD, 1977. Asst. prof. Wash. State U., Pullman, 1977-79; prof. U. Calif., Davis, 1979—. Editor Jour. Math. Biology, 1975; author: Population Biology: Concepts and Models, 1997. Mem. AAAS, Soc. for Indsl. and Applied Math., Soc. Math. Biology (pres. 1999-2001), Ecol. Soc. Am. (sect. chair 1991-93). Office: U Calif Davis Dept Environ Sci & Policy 1 Shields Ave Davis CA 95616 E-mail: amhastings@ucdavis.edu.

HASTINGS, ALCEE LAMAR, congressman, former federal judge; b. Altomonte Springs, Fla., Sept. 5, 1936; s. Julius C. and Mildred L. H.; 1 child. BA, Fisk U., 1958; postgrad., Howard U. Sch. Law, 1958-60; JD, Fla. A&M U., 1963. Bar: Fla. 1963. Mem. firm Allen and Hastings, Ft. Lauderdale, 1963-66; pvt. practice law Ft. Lauderdale, 1966-77; judge Cir. Ct. Broward County, Fla., 1977-79, U.S. Dist. Ct. (so. dist.) Fla., 1979-89; mem. U.S. Congress from 23d Fla dist., 1993—; mem. rules com., intelligence com. Adj. prof. criminal justice dept. Nova U.; lectr. So. Regional Council on Black Am. Affairs; lectr., cons. Internat. Juvenile Officers Assn., Peace Corps Vols. in Avon Park, Fla., 1966; legal counsel Community Action Migrant Program, Broward County Classroom Tchrs.; mem. Gov.'s Conf. on Criminal Justice, State of Fla.; lectr., cons. to elem. and secondary public and pvt. schs., chs., synagogues, social orgns., civic orgns., colls. and univs. in U.S.; co-propr. Tri-City News Host TV program: Pride, Sta. WPLG; columnist: West Side Gazette. Atty. various civic assns., Broward County and State of Fla.; mem. Bi-Racial Adv. Commn., Broward County Personnel Adv. Commn.; sec. Fla. Council on Aging; chmn. Broward Youth Services Task Force; mem. State of Fla. Edn. Commn., Task Force on Crime, Democratic Exec. Com; candidate for Fla. Ho. of Reps., Fla. Senate, U.S. Senate, Fla. Public Service Commn.; bd. dirs. Urban League of Broward County, Child Advocacy, Inc., The Starting Place, Broward County Sickle Cell Anemia Found., Fla. Voters League, Broward County Council on Human Relations; trustee Mt. Hermon A.M.E. Ch., Ft. Lauderdale, Broward Community Coll., Bethune Cookman Coll. Recipient numerous awards and honors including; Humanitarian award Broward County Young Democrats, 1978; Citizen of Year award Zeta Phi Beta, 1978; Sam Delevoe Human Rights award Community Relations Bd. of Broward County, 1978, Glades Festival of Afro Arts award Zeta Phi Beta, 1981; named Man of Year, Com. Italian Am. Affairs, 1979-80; Judge Alcee Hastings Day proclaimed for City of Daytona Beach in his honor on Dec. 14, 1980. Mem. ABA (standing com. profl. discipline), Nat. Bar Assn. (Chmn.'s award 1981), Am. Trial Lawyers Assn., Fla. Bar Assn., U.S. Dist. Judges Council., A.M.E. Ch. Clubs: Elks, KP. Democrat. Office: US Ho of Reps 2235 Rayburn Ho Office Bldg Washington DC 20515-0923 E-mail: alcee.pubhastings@mail.house.gov.*

HASTINGS, BEVERLY ANN, alcohol/drug abuse services professional; b. Dallas, Aug. 24, 1951; d. Henry Armond and Marjorie Alice McAdams; children: Kody Delaney, Jody Armond. AA, Eastfield Coll., 1998; BA magna cum laude, U. Tex., Dallas, 2002; grad. studies in counseling, Amberton U., 2003. Cert. chem. dependency counselor Tex. Commn. on Alcohol and Drug Abuse, 1994, advanced addictions counselor Tex. Commn. on Alcohol and Drug Abuse, 1994, criminal justice specialist Nat. Assn. Forensic Counselors, 1996, addictions counselor Nat. Assn. Alcohol and Drug Abuse Counselors, 1991, alcohol and drug counselor level III diplomate Tex. Cert. Bd. Alcoholism and Drug Abuse Counselors, 1989. Cmty. svc. rep. ASAP Family Treatment Program, L.A., 1986—93; dist. mgr. Spl. Care Hosp. Mgmt., Dallas, 1994—2001; program dir. and case mgr. intensive outpatient svcs. A New Begining, 2002—. Chair, co-founder Realm (Resources & Edn. Labor Mgmt.), L.A., 1993—94. Mem.: Tex. Assn. Addiction Profls. (bd. dir. 2001—02), Phi Theta Kappa, Psi Chi. Avocations: snorkeling, traveling, movies, reading, water skiing. Home: 9527 Teagarden Rd Dallas TX 75217

HASTINGS, DONALD FRANCIS, actor, writer; b. Bklyn., Apr. 1, 1934; s. Charles Benedict and Hazel May (Kirk) H.; m. Noretta Kennedy, Dec. 29, 1956 (div. Feb. 1980); children: Jennifer, Julie Ann, Matthew; m. Leslie Denniston,

June 7, 1980; 1 dau., Katharine Scott. Student pvt., pub. schs., N.Y. State. Appeared on network radio shows, 1940-53, including Cavalcade of Am; appeared in plays including Life With Father, 1941-43, I Remember Mama, 1944-45, On Whitman Avenue, 1946, Young Man's Fancy, 1947, Summer and Smoke, 1948; various TV shows, from 1947, including Captain Video, 1949-55, Studio One, 1955, Big Story, 1959, Chevrolet on Broadway, 1948, Edge of Night, 1956-60, As The World Turns, 1960—; author: scripts of As The World Turns, 1972-73, Guiding Light, 1974, 77, film Prisoner at Gilbert House, 1976. Mem. AFTRA, Screen Actors Guild, Actors Equity, Writers Guild-East. Roman Catholic. Office: 549 Tripp Rd Millerton NY 12546-4751

HASTINGS, EDWARD WALTON, theater director; b. New Haven, Apr. 14, 1931; s. Edward Walton and Madeline (Cassidy) H. BA, Yale, 1952; postgrad., Royal Acad. Dramatic Art, London, 1953, Columbia U., 1955-56. Bd. dirs. Asian/Am. Theater Co., 1986, Arts Internat., 1987, Eugene O'Neill Found., 1993; guest instr. Shanghai Drama Inst., 1984. Dir. Australian premiere Hot L Baltimore, 1975, Shakespeare's People nat. tour, 1983, Nothing Sacred, Hong Kong, 1992, Come Back Little Sheba, Gogol Theater, Moscow, 1995, Dial M for Murder nat. tour, 1995, Beggars Opera, Santa Fe Opera, 2000, H.M.S. Pinafore, Santa Fe Opera, 2001,, Italian Girl, Santa Fe Opera, 2002, others; exec. dir. Am. Conservatory Theatre, San Francisco, 1965-80, artistic dir., 1986-92; freelance dir., 1980-86. Served with U.S. Army, 1953-55. Mem. Coll. of Fellows of the Am. Theatre. Clubs: Elizabethan (New Haven). Office: Am Conservatory Theatre 30 Grant Ave San Francisco CA 94108-5800

HASTINGS, EDWIN H(AMILTON), lawyer; b. Yonkers, N.Y., Jan. 2, 1917; s. Edwin H. Jr. and Emily (Clark) H.; m. Mabel Hurst, July 12, 1941 (div. June 1957); children: Judy H. Hastings Johnson, Jill S. Hastings Cane; m. Suzanne Saul, July 1, 1957; 1 child, Andrew C. AB, Amherst Coll., 1938; LLB, Columbia U., 1941. Bar: N.Y. 1941, R.I. 1946, U.S. Dist. Ct. R.I. 1947, U.S. Ct. Appeals (1st cir.) 1950, Mass. 1951. Assoc. Larkin, Rathbone & Perry, N.Y.C., 1941-42, Tillinghast, Collins & Tanner, Providence, 1946-53; ptnr. Tillinghast Collins & Graham, Providence, 1953-96, Tillinghast Licht Perkins Smith & Cohen, Providence, 1996—, cons. ptnr. estate planning and adminstrn. Bar examiner State of R.I., 1968-74, chmn. of bd., 1972-74; chmn. com. on future of criminal law R.I. Supreme Ct., 1973-75; bar examiner U.S. Dist. Ct. R.I., 1981-84. 1st lt. U.S. Army, 1942-46, 51-52, Korea. Mem. ABA, R.I. Bar Assn., Lawyers Alliance World Security. Baptist. Avocation: bird watching. Home: 210 Payton Ave Warwick RI 02889-5133 Office: Tillinghast Licht Perkins Smith & Cohen 10 Weybosset St Providence RI 02903-2818 E-mail: ehastings@tlslaw.com.

HASTINGS, HAROLD MORRIS, science educator; b. Dayton, Ohio, Nov. 21, 1946; s. Julius M. and Celia A. (Morse) H.; m. Gretchen E. Saalbach, June 2, 1968; children: Curtis, Matthew. BS, Yale U., 1967; MA, Princeton U., 1969, PhD, 1972. From instr. to assoc. prof. math. Hofstra U., N.Y., 1968-81, prof., 1981—, dept. chmn., 1985-90, 93-96, assoc. dean, 1990-93, chair dept. physics, 1999—. Vis. assoc. prof. SUNY, Binghamton, 1974-75, U. Ga., Athens, 1978-79; prin. Hastings, Saalbach Assocs., Inc., Garden City, N.Y., 1983-96; prin. Prisma Med. Tech., 1999—; mem. working group on supercomputers NASA, Greenbelt, Md., 1985-90. Author: (with D. Edwards) Cech and Steenrod Homotopy Theory, 1974; editor: (with M. Kochen) Advances in Cognitive Sci., 1988, (with G. Sugihara) Fractals: A User's Guide for the Natural Scis., 1993, Fraktale: Ein Leitfaden für Anwender, 1996; contbr. articles to profl. jours. Patentee in field for computerized acoustic fetal monitor, ultrasonic tissue classification; research in non-linear dynamics, excitable media, bio-medicine. Pres., v.p. Garden City Lay Ecumenical Com., N.Y., 1983-93. Grantee NSF, Woodrow Wilson Found., NAS, NIH. Mem. Am. Math. Soc., Am. Phys. Soc., Soc. Math. Biology. Avocations: running, photography, music. Office: Hofstra Univ Dept of Physics CHPHB 102 151 Hofstra Univ Hempstead NY 11549-1510 E-mail: Harold.Hastings@Hofstra.edu.

HASTINGS, JOHN JACOB, writer, lyricist, consultant, activist; b. Walla Walla, Wash., Oct. 7, 1953; s. Frederic William and Margaret Mary (McElliggot) Hastings. AA, Walla Walla C.C., 1976; BFA, Ea. Wash. U., 1979. Mgr. Monroe Cigar Co., Chgo., 1980-83; prof. Harry Truman C.C., Chgo., 1981; farmer Touchet, Wash., 1986-99. Author: Four Score Seven, 1995; (poetry) Playing Possum, 1995, Back on the Stack, 1998, Linda's Lullaby in Heaven, 1998, Penultimate Glory, 1998, Excellent annus, 1998, Eiriecalm, 2000, Moods, Anew, 2001; lyricist: Hilltop Records, Hollywood, Calif., 1997-98. Moderate Nat. Orgn. Dems., 1975-2003; precinct com. mem. Walla Walla (Wash.) County Dem. Ctrl. Com., 1992-99, mem. Dem. Nat. Com., 1998, 2003, Dem. Senatorial Campaign, 1998, 2000, 2001, 2002, 2003, Westchester County Dem. Party, 2000-2003; activist Peace Movement, Walla Walla and Bellingham, Wash., 1977-86; mem. MADD, ACLU. Mem. Nat. Geographic Soc., Nat. Trust for Hist. Preservation, Walla Walla Pioneers Hist. Soc. (faculty mem.), Nat. Assn. Women in Arts (assoc.), Smithsonian Instn., Libr. Congress (assoc.), Ea. Wash. U. Alumni, Nat. Parks and Conservation Assn. Wilson Ctr., Handyman's Club Am., Nature Conservancy, Hastings Art Soc. (pres, C.L.O.), N.Y. Acad. Polit. Sci., N.Y. Acad. Sci. Roman Catholic. Avocations: letter writing, conservationist, tree planter, advocate. Home and Office: 3275 Lexington Ave # 10 Mohegan Lake NY 10547-1652 E-mail: jjhastings1@msn.com.

HASTINGS, JOHN WOODLAND, biologist, educator; b. Salisbury, Md., Mar. 24, 1927; s. Vaughan Archelaus and Kathrine (Stevens) H.; m. Hanna Machlup, June 6, 1953; children: Jennifer, David, Laura, Karen. BA, Swarthmore Coll., 1947; MA, Princeton U., 1950, PhD, 1951; MA, Harvard U., 1966. AEC postdoctoral fellow Johns Hopkins, 1951-53; instr. to asst. prof. biol. scis. Northwestern U., 1953-57; from asst. prof. to prof. biochemistry U. Ill. at Urbana, 1957-66; prof. biology Harvard, 1966-87, Paul C. Mangelsdorf prof. natural scis., 1987—; master Pforzheimer House, 1976-96. Summer rsch. participant Oak Ridge Nat. Lab., 1958; vis. lectr. biochemistry Sheffield (Eng.) U., 1961-62; instr. physiology Marine Biol. Lab., Woods Hole, Mass., 1961-66, dir., 1962-66, dir. marine ecology, 1989-91, mem. corp., 1961, trustee, 1966-74, exec. com., 1968-74; guest prof. Rockefeller U., 1965-66, Inst. Biol. Phys. Chemistry Paris, 1972-73, U. Konstanz, Ger., 1979-80, Nat. Biology Inst., Okazaki, Japan, 1986, U. Munich, 1993; Disting. vis. scientist Calif. Inst. Tech., 2000, Jet Propulsion Lab., 2000--; mem. panel molecular biology NSF, 1963-66, mem. adv. com. biology and medicine, 1968-71; com. postdoctoral fellowships chemistry Nat. Acad. Scis., 1965-67, com. photobiology, 1965-71, com. on phototherapy, 1971-73, com. on low frequency radiation, 1975-77; mem. Commn. Undergrad. Edn. in Biol. Scis., 1965-66; space biology com. NASA, 1966-71; biochemistry tng. com. Nat. Inst. Gen. Med. Scis., 1968-72; a founding mem., mem. internat. adv. bd. Marine Biol. Lab., Eilat, Israel, 1968—; faculty assoc. Calif. Inst. Tech., 2000. Contbr. profl. jours. Served with USNR, 1944-45. Guggenheim fellow, 1965-66, NIH fellow, 1972-73, Yamada Found. fellow, Osaka, Japan, 1986; recipient Alexander von Humboldt prize, 1979, Humboldt fellow, 1993. Fellow AAAS, NAS, Am. Soc. Biol. Chemists, Biophys. Soc., Soc. Am. Microbiologists, Am. Soc. Photobiology (pres. 1999-2001), Soc. Gen. Physiology (pres. 1963-65), Am. Acad. Arts and Scis., Soc. Chemi- and Bio-luminescence (founding pres. 1994-98), Pierian Found. (pres. 1999—), Johns Hopkins Soc. Scholars. Home: 14 Concord Ave Cambridge MA 02138-2356 Office: 16 Divinity Ave Cambridge MA 02138-2020 E-mail: hastings@fas.harvard.edu.

HASTINGS, LAWRENCE VAETH, lawyer, physician, educator; b. Flushing, N.Y., Nov. 23, 1919; m. Doris Lorraine Erickson, Dec. 11, 1971. Student, Columbia U., 1939-40, student Law Sch., 1949-50; student, U. Mich. Engring. Sch., 1942-43, Washington U., 1943-44, U. Vt., 1943; MD, Johns Hopkins U., 1948; JD, U. Miami, 1953. Bar: Fla. 1954, U.S. Supreme Ct. 1960, D.C. 1976; cert. Am. Bd. Legal Medicine. Intern U.S. Marine Hosp., S.I., N.Y., 1948-49; asst. surgeon, sr. asst. surgeon USPHS, 1949-52; asst. resident surgery Bellevue Hosp. Med. Ctr., 1951; med. legal cons., trial atty. Miami, Fla., 1953—; ptnr. Lawrence V. Hastings, P.A.; asst. prof. medicine U. Miami, 1964-70, lectr. law, 1966; past adj. prof. St. Thomas U. Law Sch., Miami, Fla. Contbr. articles to profl. pubs. Bd. dirs. Miami Heart Inst.; past trustee Barry U., Miami; trustee Fla. Internat. U., 1979-82. Served with AUS, 1943-46. Fellow Acad. Fla. Trial Lawyers, Am. Coll. Legal Medicine, Law-Sci. Acad. Found. Am.; mem. ABA, AMA, ATLA, Fla. Bar Assn., Dade County Bar Assn., Am. Acad. Forensic Scis., Fla. Med. Assn., Dade County Med. Assn., Fla. Bar (vice chmn. med. legal com. 1957, vice chmn. trial tactics com. 1963-65, chmn. steering com. trial tactics and basic anatomy seminars), Pitts. Inst. Legal Medicine, Johns Hopkins Med. and Surg. Assn., Pithotomy Club, Assn. Mil. Surgeons, U. Miami Law Alumni Assn. (pres. 1967), Acad. Psychosomatic Medicine, Fairbanks Ranch Country Club (Rancho Santa Fe, Calif.), Alpha Delta Phi, Phi Eta Sigma, Phi Alpha Delta. Clubs: Surf (bd. govs. 1976—, chmn. bd. 1980-82, pres. 1978-80), Com. 100, Indian Creek Country, Miami Beach, River of Jacksonville; N.Y. Athletic, Metropolitan, Princeton (N.Y.C.). Roman Catholic. Achievements include first to institute jury verdict lawsuit of Green vs. Am. Tobacco in 1960 resulting in 1964 Surgeon Gen.'s report that cigarettes are hazardous to health. Address: Palm Beach Towers 44 Cocoanut Row Palm Beach FL 33480

HASTINGS, L(OIS) JANE, architect, architecture educator; b. Seattle, Mar. 3, 1928; d. Harry and Camille (Pugh) H.; m. Norman John Johnston, Nov. 22, 1969. B.Arch., U. Wash., Seattle, 1952, postgrad. in Urban Planning, 1958. Architect Boeing Airplane Co., Seattle, 1951-54; recreational dir. Germany, 1954-56; architect (various firms), Seattle, 1956-59, pvt. practice architecture, 1959-74; instr. archtl. drafting Seattle Community Coll., part-time 1969-80; owner/founder The Hastings Group Architects, Seattle, 1974—; lectr. design Coll. Architecture, U. Wash., 1975; incorporating mem. Architecta (P.S.), Seattle, 1980, pres., from 1980. Mem. adv. bd. U. Wash. YWCA, 1967—69; mem. Mayor's Com. on Archtl. Barriers for Handicapped, 1974—75; chmn. regional public adv. panel on archtl. and engring. services GSA, 1976; mem. citizens adv. com. Seattle Land Use Adminstrn. Task Force, 1979—; AWIU guest of Soviet Women's Con., 1983; spkr. Pacific Rim Forum, Hong Kong, 1987; guest China Internat. Conf. Ctr. for Sci. and Tech. of the China Assn. for Sci. and Tech., 1989; mem. adv. com. Coll. architecture and urban planning U. Wash., 1993; mem. accreditation team U. Oreg. Coll. Architecture, 1991, N.J. Inst. Tech. Sch. Architecture, 1992; juror Home of the Yr. ann. award AIA/Seattle Times, 1996; mem. architect selection com. Wash. State capital carillon project, Pratt Art Ctr. new bldg., 2001. Design juror for nat. and local competitions, including Red Cedar Shingle/AIA awards, 1977, Current Use Honor awards, AIA, 1980, Exhibit of Sch. Architecture award, 1981; Contbr. to: also spl. features newspapers, articles in profl. jours. Sunset mag. Mem. bd. Am. Women for Internat. Understanding, del. to, Egypt, Israel, USSR, 1971, Japan and Korea, 1979, USSR, 1983; mem. Landmarks Preservation Bd. City of Seattle, 1981-83; mem. Design Constrn. Rev. Bd. Seattle Sch. Dist., 1985-87; mem. mus. con. Mus. History and Industry, 1987—; leader People to People del. women architects to China, 1990. Recipient AIA/The Seattle Times Home of Month Am. award, 1968; Exhbn. award Seattle chpt. AIA, 1970; Environ. award Seattle-King County Bd. Realtors, 1970, 77,; AIA/House and Home/The American Home Merit award, 1971, Sp. Honor award Wash. Aggregates and Concrete Assn., 1993, Prize bridge Am. Inst. Steel Contrn., 1993; Honor award Seattle chpt. AIA, 1977, 83; Women Achievement award Past Pres. Assembly, 1983, Washington Women and Trading Cards, 1983; Nat. Endowment for Arts grantee, 1977; others; named to West Seattle High Sch. Hall of Fame, 1989, Woman of Achievement Matrix Table, 1994; named Woman of Distinction, Columbia River Girl Scout Coun., 1994. Fellow AIA (pres. Seattle chpt. 1975, pres. sr. coun. 1980, state exec. bd. 1975, N.W. regional dir. 1982-87, Seattle chpt. found. bd. 1985-87, Bursar Coll. Fellows 1989-90, Coll. of Fellows historian 1994—, internat. rels. com. 1988-92, vice chancellor 1991, chancellor 1992, Seattle chpt. medal 1995, Northwest & Pacific region Medal of Honor 2002, Leslie N. Boney Spirit of Fellowship award 2003), Internat. Union Women Architects (v.p. 1969-79, sec. gen. 1985-89, del. UIA Congress, Montreal 1990), Am. Arbitration Assn. (arbitrator 1981—), Coun. of Design Professions, Assn. Women Contrs., Suppliers and Design Cons., Allied Arts Seattle, Fashion Group, Tau Sigma Delta, Alpha Rho Chi (medal). *It is not the quantity but the quality of space that is important.*

HASTINGS, PAUL J. pharmaceutical executive; BS, U. R.I., 1984. With Hoffman LaRoche, 1984—94; v.p., mktg. and sales and European gen. mgr. Synergen, Inc., 1989—94; v.p. global mktg. Genzyme Corp., 1994—98; pres. Genzyme Therapeutics Europe, 1994—98, Genzyme Therapeutics Worldwide, 1994—98, Chiron BioPharms., 1999—2001; pres., CEO, dir. Axys Pharms.; pres., CEO QLT, Inc., Vancouver, Canada, 2002—. Bd. dirs. ViaCell, Inc., Leading Edge Endowment Fund, Arriva Pharmaceuticals, Inc., B.C. Biotech., St. Paul's Hosp. Office: QLT Inc 887 Great Northern Way Vancouver BC Canada V5T 4T5

HASTINGS, RALPH B. music educator; b. Malone, N.Y., Mar. 8, 1947; s. Samuel Phillip and Alice Gertrude (Geddes) Hastings; m. Donna Gay Leonard, June 24, 1972; children: Lee Bristol, Ruth Emily Hastings DeBellis. AAS in Music, Onondaga C.C., Syracuse, N.Y., 1967; BS in Music Edn., SUNY, Potsdam, 1969, MS in Music Edn., 1973, MM in Music History and Lit., 1995. Cert. K-12 music edn. Organist St. Mark's Episcopal Ch., Malone, NY, 1965, First Bapt. Ch., Malone, NY, 1967—2003; tchr. music N. Bangor/Harison Elem. Sch. Malone Ctrl. Sch., 1969—73, tchr. music St. Joseph's Elem. Sch., 1973—78, tchr. music Malone Mid. Sch., 1978—. Band dir. Malone Mcpl. Band, 1966—76; tchr. music pvt. studio, 1975—91. Composer: (organ composition) prelude on Two Am. Folk Hymns, 1984, Toccata on Kingsfold, 1988, prelude on Praise Him, 1995, prelude on Jesus, Jesus Rest Your Head, 1995, (choral work) The Wandering Wisemen, 1995. Mem.: N.Y. State Sch. Music Assn. (accompanist 1970—), Am. Soc. Composers, Authors and Pubs., Am. Guild Organists (mem. St. Lawrence chpt.), Order of Ea. Star (N.Y. dist. grand lectr. 1978, assoc. grand sentinel 1997, grand musician 1999, chief commr. of appeals 2000, grand musician 2001, N.Y. dist. grand lectr. 2003, Grand Marshall 2004), Pi Kappa Lambda (Am. Acad. of Dist. Students). Avocations: reading, cooking. Home: 175 Perry Rd North Bangor NY 12966

HASTINGS, RICHARD DOC, congressman; b. Spokane, Wash., Feb. 7, 1941; m. Claire Hastings; 3 children. Student, Columbia Basin Coll., 1958—61, Ctrl. Wash. U., 1964. Mem. Wash. State Ho. of Reps., 1979-87; pres. Columbia Basin Paper & Supply, 1983-94; mem. U.S. Congress from 4th Wash. dist., 1995—; mem. rules com., budget com., standards of official conduct com., asst. majority whip. Bd. dirs. Yakima Fed. Savings & Loan; chmn. Franklin County Republican Com., 1974-78 USAR, 1962—68. Republican. Office: US House Reps 1323 Longworth Ho Office Bldg Washington DC 20515-0001*

HASTINGS, WILLIAM CHARLES, retired state supreme court chief justice; b. Newman Grove, Nebr., Jan. 31, 1921; s. William C. and Margaret (Hansen) H.; m. Julie Ann Simonson, Dec. 29, 1946; children— Pamela, Charles, Steven. B.Sc., U. Nebr., 1942, JD, 1948; LHD (hon.), Hastings Coll., 1991. Bar: Nebr. 1948. With FBI, 1942-43; mem. firm Chambers, Holland, Dudgeon & Hastings, Lincoln, 1948-65; judge 3d jud. dist. Nebr., Lincoln, 1965-79, Supreme Ct. Nebr., Lincoln, 1979-88, chief justice, 1988-95; ret., 1995. Bd. dirs. Nat. Conf. Chief Justices, 1989-91. Pres. Child Guidance Ctr., Lincoln, 1962, 63; v.p. Lincoln Community Coun., 1968, 69; vice chmn. Antelope Valley coun. Boy Scouts Am., 1968, 69; pres. 1st Presbyn. Ch. Found., 1968—; mem. Lincoln Parks and Recreation Adv. Bd., Govs. task force correctional dept. medical svcs., 2000; mem. Nebr. Pub. Employees Retirement Bd. Served with AUS, 1943-46. Named to Nebr. Jaycee Hall of Fame, 1998. Mem. ABA, Nebr. Bar Assn. (George H. Turner award 1991, Pioneer award 1992), Am. Jud. Soc., Lincoln Bar Assn., Nebr. Dist. Judges Assn. (past pres.), Nat. Conf. Chief Justices (past bd. dirs.), Am. Judicature Soc. (Herbert Harley award 1997), Phi Delta Phi. Republican. Presbyterian (deacon, elder, trustee). Club: East Hills Country (pres. 1959-60). Home: 1544 S 58th St Lincoln NE 68506-1407

HASTINGS, WILMOT REED, lawyer, writer; b. Salem, Mass., May 29, 1935; s. Abner Horace and Florence (Hylan) H.; m. Joan Amory Loomis, Aug. 30, 1958; children: W. Reed, Jr., Melissa H., Claire A. AB magna cum laude, Harvard U., 1957, LL.B. magna cum laude, 1961; postgrad., U. Paris, 1957-58. Bar: Mass. 1961. Law clk. Chief Justice Raymond S. Wilkins, Boston, 1961-62; assoc. firm Bingham, Dana & Gould, Boston, 1962-68; 1st asst. and dep. atty. gen. Mass., 1968-69; spl. asst. and exec. asst. to undersec. state, 1969-70; gen. counsel HEW, 1970-73; ptnr. Bingham, Dana & Gould (now Bingham McCutchen), Boston and London, 1973-90; writer, 1990—. Home and Office: 45 Ward Ave Northampton MA 01060

HASTY, WILLIAM GRADY, JR., lawyer; b. Canton, Ga., July 7, 1947; s. William Grady and Hazel Bonnie (Wyatt) H.; m. Linda Lacey Nichols, Aug. 9, 1969; children: William Grady III, Lauren Elise, Jeffrey Nichols. AA, Reinhardt Coll., 1967; BS, U. Ga., 1969; JD, Mercer U., 1974. Bar: Ga. 1974, U.S. Dist. Ct. (no. dist.) Ga. 1975, U.S. Ct. Appeals (11th cir.) 1975. Adv. bd. dirs. Wachovia Bank; chmn. bd. dirs. C&D Landfill, Inc. Chmn. Cherokee County Recreation Commn., 1975-85; charter mem. Leadership Cherokee County, 1987, steering com., 1988—; active Leadership Ga.; sec., exec. com., bd. trustees Reinhardt Coll., 1988-92, Cherokee County Hosp. Authority, Northside Hosp., Cherokee; bd. dirs. Northside Hosp., Cherokee. Named Outstanding Citizen Cherokee County Commr., 1986, 87. Mem. VFW, ATLA, Ga. Bar Assn., Canton Bar Assn., Blue Ridge Bar Assn., Trial Lawyers Assn. Ga., Phoenix Soc. Atlanta, Canton Golf Club, Moose Club, Atlanta Track Club, Cherokee County C. of C., Commerce Club Atlanta. Avocations: running, fishing, hunting. Home: 1746 Cumming Hwy Canton GA 30114-8043 Office: William G Hasty Jr PC PO Box 1818 211 E Main St Canton GA 30114-2710

HASUND, SVEIN HARALD, mechanical engineer; b. Oslo, Sept. 25, 1942; came to U.S., 1965; s. Inge and Ingeborg Pauline (Kreftung) H.; child from previous marriage, Monica; m. Pauline Grace MacDonald Beith; children: Ian, Craig. AI in Mech. Engring., Schous Tech. Sch., Oslo, Norway, 1965; BSME, U. Colo., 1967; MSME, Stevens Inst. Tech., 1970. Registered engr.-in-tng., Colo. Estimator, controls engr. Exxon Rsch. & Engring., Florham Pk., N.J., 1967-74, cost schedule supervisor, 1974-77, project control supr., 1977-81; supervising engr. Arco Alaska Inc., Anchorage, 1981-83, project. mgr., 1983-88, dir. engring. and projects, 1988-95; owner SHH Consulting, 1995—. Project dir. Roche Carolina, Inc., 1996. Webelos leader Boy Scouts Am., Anchorage, 1982-83, asst. troop leader, 1984-85; foster parent State of Alaska, Anchorage, 1984-93; bd. dirs., pres. Anchorage Ski Club, 1984-90; bd. dirs. Anchorage Organizing Com., Winter Olympics, 1988-91, tech. com. cons., 1989; bd. dirs., treas. Anchorage Youth Symphony, 1990-91; mem. Mcpl. Budget Adv. Commn., Anchorage, 1988-95. Sgt. C.E., Norwegian Army, 1961-63. Recipient Chmn.'s award C. of C., Anchorage, 1988; Paul Harris fellow Rotary Internat., 1992. Mem. Rotary Internat. (youth exch. officer 1988-95), Project Mgmt. Inst., Tau Beta Pi. Avocations: skiing, tennis, gardening, reading. Home: 2535 Westward Dr Lafayette CO 80026 E-mail: shasund@att.net.

HASWELL, CARLETON RADLEY, banker; b. Milw., May 18, 1939; s. Clayton Lyman and Jane (Radley) H.; m. Almut Haberkamp, Dec. 10, 1966; children— Angela, Robin. BS, Northwestern U., 1961; MBA, NYU, 1967. Chief internat. credit officer Chem. Bank, N.Y.C., 1963-87; dir. Chem. Internat. Inc., N.Y.C., 1981-86, Chem. Internat. Fin., N.Y.C., 1981-84; pres. Carleton Haswell Assocs., 1987—. Dir., United Givers, Wayne, N.J., 1980-83. Served with U.S. Army, 1961-63. Mem.: Isles Yacht Club Fla. Republican. $D Home and Office: Villa 514 2645 W Marion Ave Punta Gorda FL 33950-5979

HATCH, DAVID GLEN, musician, educator; b. Provo, Utah, Dec. 6, 1953; s. Glendon and Arlene Kay Hatch; m. Paula Hatch, Dec. 19, 1985; children: Erika, Denise, Ryan, Jessica, Christopher. MusB, Brigham Young U., 1978; MusM, U. Mo., Kansas City, 1980, DMA cum laude; studied with, Joanne Baker, Paul Pollei, Robert Smith. Soloist, guest artist numerous chamber and symphony orchs. including Carnegie Hall, N.Y.C., Kennedy Ctr., Washington, Bascilica di Mecenzio, Rome, Ch. of the Madeleine, Paris, Music Hall of Composers, Moscow, Crystal Cathedral, Calif.; performer master classes of internat. artists/tchrs. including Leon Fleisher, Nelita True, Karl Schnable, Adele Marcus, Charles Rosen, Gilbert Kalish; tchr. master classes worldwide; adjudicator, lectr., clinician univs., local and state music orgns., piano competitions, music festivals, and state music convs. Musician: (recs.) 18 albums including rec. with Budapest Symphony Orch. (Grammy award nominee for Best Classical Album and Best Instrumental Soloist(s) with Orch., 1999); contbr. Founder, dir. Utah Valley Young Keyboard Competition, Provo, 1992—. Named semi-finalist (twice), Gina Bachauer Internat. Piano Competition, nat. finalist, William C. Byrd Competition; recipient Listener's Choice award for Best Album/Instrumentalist for My Romantic Favorites, Vol. III CD, LDS Booksellers Assn., 1997. Mem.: Music Tchrs. Nat. Assn. (nat. cert. tchr. music), Pi Kappa Lambda. Avocations: travel, sports. Home: 995 N 1520 E Orem UT 84097 Fax: 801-224-0039. E-mail: drhatch1@xmission.com.

HATCH, DENISON HURLBUT, JR., lawyer; b. Greenwich, Conn., Sept. 7, 1949; s. Denison Hurlbut and Louise (Bingham) H.; m. Wendy Ann Swanson, Sept. 4, 1971;children: Denison H. III, Erica Swanson. AB, Cornell U., 1971; JD, Northwestern U., 1980. Bar: Del. 1980, U.S. Dist. Ct. Del. 1980, U.S. Ct. Appeals (3rd cir.) 1983, U.S. Ct. Claims 1984, U.S. Tax Ct. 1984, U.S. Supreme Ct. 1983. Assoc. Morris, Nichols, Arsht & Tunnell, Wilmington, Del., 1980-88, ptnr., 1989—. Mem. ABA (taxation sect.), Del. Bar Assn. (asst. to pres. 1983-84), Richard Rodney Inn of Ct., Wilmington, 1985-87. Republican. Home: PO Box 1347 Wilmington DE 19899-1347 Office: And Tunnell 1201 N Market St Ste 1347 Wilmington DE 19801-1163 E-mail: dhatch@mnat.com.

HATCH, FREDERICK TASKER, chemicals consultant; b. Boston, Aug. 27, 1924; s. Frederick Southard and Beatrice (Tasker) H.; m. Virginia Weeks, Mar. 3, 1946; children: Daniel F., Daphne A., Deborah J., Douglas E. BA, Dartmouth Coll., 1944; MD, Harvard U., 1948; PhD, MIT, 1960. Diplomate Nat. Bd. Med. Examiners. Intern Roosevelt Hosp., N.Y.C., 1948-49; rsch. fellow Columbia U., N.Y.C., 1949-52; established investigator Am. Heart Assn./Mass. Gen. Hosp., Boston, 1960-65; sr. scientist, sect. leader Lawrence Livermore (Calif.) Nat. Lab., 1965-80, asst. assoc. dir., 1980-87, cons., 1987—. Mem. lipid metabolism adv. com. Nat. Heart, Lung and Blood Inst., Bethesda, Md., 1968-73. Assoc. editor Lipids Jour., 1964-73; author chpts. in books; contbr. numerous articles to profl. jours. Sec. Land Conservation Task Force, Meredith, N.H., 1989-90, chmn. Hwy. Task Force, 1994—. Capt. USAR, 1952-55. Fellow Am. Inst. Chemists; mem. Am. Chem. Soc., Am. Soc. Biochemistry and Molecular Biology, Environ. Mutagen Soc., Arteriosclerosis Coun. of Am. Heart Assn. (exec. com. 1971-73). Avocations: tree farmer, skiing, hiking, biotechnology investing. Home and Office: 27 Pease Rd Meredith NH 03253-5506 E-mail: fhatch@cyberportal.net.

HATCH, GEORGE CLINTON, television executive; b. Erie, Pa., Dec. 16, 1919; s. Charles Milton and Blanche (Beecher) Hatch; m. Wilda Gene Glasmann, Dec. 24, 1940; children: Michell Arnow, Diane Glasmann Orr, Jeffrey Beecher, Randall Clinton, Deepika Hatch Avanti. AB, Occidental Coll., 1940; MA in Econs., Claremont Coll., 1941; HHD (hon.), So. Utah U., 1988. Pres. Comms. Investment Corp., Salt Lake City, 1945-95; chmn. Double G Comm. Corp., Salt Lake City, 1956—; dir. Republic Pictures Corp., Los Angeles, 1971-94; pres. Sta. KVEL, Inc., 1978-94. Pres. Standard Corp., Ogden, 1993-98, Hatch Family LLC, 1998—; past mem. Salt Lake adv. bd. First Security Bank Utah; past chmn. Rocky Mountain Pub. Broadcasting Corp.; past chmn. bd. govs. Am. Info. Radio Network; past bd. govs. NBC-TV Affiliates. Past pres. Salt Lake Com. on Fgn. Relations; past mem. Utah Symphony Bd., Salt Lake City; past chmn. and mem. Utah State Bd. Regents, 1964-85. Recipient Svc. to Journalism award U. Utah, 1966, silver medal Salt Lake Advt. Club, 1969, Disting. Svc. award Utah Tech. U., 1984, Disting. Utahan Centennial Yr. award Margaret Thatcher U.K., Utah Festival, 1996. Mem. Nat. Assn. Broadcasters (past pres., radio bd. dirs., ambassador to Inter-Am. mtgs. in Latin Am. 1962), Utah Broadcasters Assn. (past pres., Mgmt. award 1964, Hall of Fame award 1981), Salt Lake City Advt. Club (silver medal 1969), Phi Beta Kappa, Phi Rho Pi (life). Democrat. Avocations: hiking, rock art. Office: Hatch Family LLC 1537 Chandler Dr Salt Lake City UT 84103-4220

HATCH, HAZEN VAN DEN BERG, lawyer; b. Battle Creek, Mich., Jan. 18, 1932; s. Hazen Jesse and Clare Janet (van den Berg) H.; m. Mary Lou Holmes, Dec. 27, 1955; children: Mary, David. BA, Dartmouth Coll., 1953; JD, U. Mich., 1956. Bar: Mich. 1956, U.S. Supreme Ct. 1959. Ptnr. various firms, Marshall, Mich., 1960-81, Hatch & Smith, Kalamazoo, Mich., 1981-93, Butler Durham & Toweson, Kalamazoo, Mich., 1993—. Contbr. articles to profl. jours. Del. Mich. Constitutional Conv., Lansing, 1961-62; trustee Marshall Sch. Bd., 1971-72. Lt. USAR, 1957-60. Recipient citation Mich. State Bar Assn., 1962. Fellow Mich. State Bar Found., Am. Coll. Trial Lawyers; mem. ABA, Kalamazoo County Bar Assn. Republican. Episcopalian. Avocation: golf. Office: Butler Durham & Toweson 202 N Riverview Dr Kalamazoo MI 49004-1310

HATCH, JOHN D. lawyer; b. Atlanta, Aug. 26, 1942; s. Ernest Healey and Charlotte Blanchard (Chazal) H.; m. Pamela Faye Carr, June 13, 1964; children: Wendy H. Duncan, A. Candice Hatch, Teresa H. Caraker. AA, Ctrl. Fla. Jr. Coll., Ocala, 1962; BS, Fla. State U., 1964; JD, Georgetown U., 1971. Bar: Fla. 1971, Conn. 1972, Tex. 1992, U.S. Dist. Ct. Conn. 1973, U.S. Dist. Ct. (no. dist.) Tex. 1992, U.S. Tax Ct. 1979, U.S. Supreme Ct. 1979; gen. securities lic., gen. prin. lic. Lt. USNR, 1964-71; atty. AEtna Life & Casualty, Hartford, Conn., 1971-74,

counsel, 1974-83; v.p. and gen. counsel Continental Corp., N.Y.C., 1983-85; v.p. spl. ops. Comml. Life Ins. Co., Piscataway, N.J., 1985-87; v.p. and gen. counsel Associated Madison Cos., Inc., N.Y.C., 1987-88; sr. v.p. Resource Deployment, Inc., N.Y.C. and Ft. Worth, 1988-91; pres. Ins. Horizons, Inc., Ocala, Fla., 1992—, John D. Hatch, P.C., Ocala, 1992—. Gen. counsel Am. Health & Life Ins. Co., Ft. Worth, 1995—; bd. dirs. Pub. Svc. Mut. Ins. Co., N.Y.C., London and Midland Gen. Ins. Co., London, Ont. Mem. ABA (chmn. TIPS employee benefits com. 1983-84, TIPS fin. svcs. com. 1992-93), Assn. Life Ins. Counsel, Fed. Bar Assn., Internat. Assn. Ins. Law. Republican. Roman Catholic. Avocations: reading, boating, tennis. Home and Office: 840 SE 5th St Ocala FL 34471-2306

HATCH, KENNETH DEROY, gynecologist, oncologist; b. Benkelman, Nebr., 1946; MD, U. Nebr., 1971. Diplomate Am. Bd. Ob-Gyn.; cert. in gynecologic oncology. Intern U. Nebr. Hosp., Omaha, 1971-72; resident in ob-gyn. U. Ala. Med. Ctr., Birmingham, 1974-76, fellow, 1976-78, med. staff, 1994; prof. U. Ariz., 1990-94, chmn. dept. ob-gyn., 1995—. Mem. ACS, AMA, ACOG, SGO (pres. 2003), ASCCP (pres. 1998), Alpha Omega Alpha. Office: U Ariz Coll Medicine 1501 N Campbell Ave Tucson AZ 85724-0001

HATCH, MICHAEL WARD, lawyer; b. Pittsfield, Mass., Nov. 19, 1949; s. Ward Sterling and Elizabeth (Hubbard) H.; m. Lisa Schilling, June 8, 1974; children: Stuart, Andrew, Gillian. AB in Econs., St. Lawrence U., 1971; JD, Yale U., 1974. Bar: Wis. 1974, N.Y. 1980. Ptnr., chmn. real estate group Foley & Lardner, Milw., 1974—. Mem. ABA, N.Y. State Bar Assn., Wis. Bar Assn., Milw. Bar Assn., Am. Coll. Real Estate Lawyers, Urban Land Inst., Nat. Multi Housing Coun., Mortgage Bankers Assn. Wis., Bldg. Owners and Mgrs. Assn., Local Initiatives Support Corp., Milw. Athletic Club, Town Club. Avocations: architecture, historic preservation. Office: Foley & Lardner 777 E Wisconsin Ave Ste 3800 Milwaukee WI 53202-5367

HATCH, MIKE, state attorney general; m. Patti Hatch; 3 children. BS in Polit. Sci. with honors, U. Minn., Duluth, 1970; JD, U. Minn., 1973. Commr. of commerce State of. Minn., 1983—89; pvt. practice law; atty. gen. State of Minn., 1999—. Democrat. Office: Minn Atty Gen's Office 1400 NCL Tower 445 Minnesota St Saint Paul MN 55101*

HATCH, ORRIN GRANT, senator; b. Homestead Park, Pa., Mar. 22, 1934; s. Jesse and Helen (Kamm) H.; m. Elaine Hansen, Aug. 28, 1957; children: Brent, Marcia, Scott, Kimberly, Alysa, Jess. BS, Brigham Young U., 1959; JD, U. Pitts., 1962; LLD (hon.), U. Md., 1981; MS (hon.), Def. Intelligence Coll., 1982; LLD (hon.), Pepperdine U., 1990, So. Utah State U., 1990. Bar: Pa. 1962, Utah 1962. Ptnr. firm Thomson, Rhodes & Grigsby, Pitts., 1962-69, Hatch & Plumb, Salt Lake City, 1976; U.S. senator from Utah, 1977—; past chmn. labor and human resources com. U.S. Senate, chmn. Senate judiciary com., chmn. subcom. on internat. trade, mem. fin. com., senate Rep. policy com., com. on Indian affairs, aging com., mem. select com. on intelligence, 1997—. Author ERA Myths and Realities, 1983; contbr. articles to newspapers and profl. jours. Recipient Outstanding Legislator award Nat. Assn. Rehab. Facilities, Legislator of Yr. award Am. Assn. Univ. Affiliated Programs, Legis. Leadership award Health Profl. Assn., many others. Mem. Am., Nat., Utah, Pa. bar assns., Am. Judicature Soc. Republican. Mem. Lds Ch. Avocations: golf, poetry, piano playing, composer lyrics.

HATCH, ROBERT, medical educator; b. Madrid, Apr. 12, 1957; s. James Royce and Marion Hill Hatch; m. Susan Bell Gochenour, May 26, 1984; children: Richard Sumner, Melissa Rose. AB, BS, U. Calif., Davis, 1979; MD, MPH, UCLA, 1984. Bd. cert. Am. Bd. Family Practice, recert. Physician Nat. Health Svc. Corps, Groveland, Fla., 1988-91; asst. prof. U. Fla., Gainesville, 1991-97, assoc. prof., 1997—. Chmn. med. sch. admissions com. U. Fla., 1995-98; med. dir. U. Fla. Comprehensive Assessment and Remediation Evaluation Svc., 1998—. Author: (book) Fracture Management for Primary Care, 1998; author, developer: (psychometric scale) Spiritual Involvement and Beliefs Scale, 1998; contbr. sci. articles to profl. jours. Vol. physician Equal Access Clinic for the Homeless, Gainesville, 1992—. Mem. Am. Acad. Family Physicians, Soc. Tchrs. of Family Medicine, Physicians for a Nat. Health Program. Avocations: triathlons, herpetology. E-mail: hatch@dean.med.ufl.edu.

HATCH, RONALD RAY, engineer; b. Freedom, Okla., Dec. 28, 1938; s. Richard Verni and Elma Lottie (Carberry) H.; m. Nancy Elene Bates, Dec. 30, 1960; children: Richard, Rebecca, Sondra, Wendy, Randall, Ronald, Jeffrey, Nathan, Abigail, Peter, Robert, Marcy, Melanie. BS in Physics and Math., Seattle Pacific Coll., 1962. Physicist Johns Hopkins Applied Physics Lab., Silver Spring, Md., 1963-65; engr. Boeing Co., Seattle, 1965-70, Magnavox, Torrance, Calif., 1970-93; cons. Wilmington, Calif., 1993—95. Author: Escape from Einstein, 1992; contbr. numerous articles to profl. jours. Mem. Inst. Navigation (marine rep. 1991-93, we. region v.p. 1992-93, chair Satellite Div. 1998-2000, pres. 2001-02, Johannes Kepler award 1994, Col. Thomas Thurlow award 2000). Republican. Baptist. Achievements include 13 patents most concerning Global Positioning System (GPS). Home and Office: 1142 Lakme Ave Wilmington CA 90744-3517

HATCH, ROSS RIEPERT, weapon system engineering executive; b. N.Y.C., Sept. 6, 1934; s. Aylmer Roscoe and Ebba (Riepert) H.; m. Phyllis Anne Hess, July 21, 1961; children: Robert Ross, Michael Aylmer. BS in Engring., U.S. Naval Acad., Annapolis, Md., 1956; MS in Engring. Electronics, U.S. Naval Postgrad. Sch., Monterey, Calif., 1964; MS in Fin. Mgmt., George Washington U., 1972. Commd. ensign USN, 1956, advanced through grades to capt., 1977, ret., 1985, dept. head destroyers, cruisers, ice-breakers, 1956-71; commanding officer guided missile destroyer USS Semmes (DDG-18), Charleston, S.C., 1971-72; commanding officer guided missile cruiser USS Belknap (CG-26), Norfolk, Va., 1979-82; head missile br. Office of Chief Naval Ops., Washington, 1972-76; program mgr. Naval Sea Sys. Command, Washington, 1976-79, dir. combat sys., 1982-85; strike/cruise missile program mgr. Applied Physics Lab.-Johns Hopkins U., Laurel, Md., 1985-96, asst. dept. head power projection dept., 1996-99. Weapon systems cons., combat systems cons., 1999—. Editor procs. Precision Strike Tech. Symposium, 1990-98. Scout master Boy Scouts Am., 1972-75. Recipient Legion of Merit, Sec. of Navy, Arlington, Va., 1985; Hatch Outcrop Antarctica named in his honor U.S. Bd. of Geographic Names, Washington, 1962. Mem. IEEE (life), Am. Soc. Naval Engrs., Precision Strike Assn. (bd. dirs. 1988—), U.S. Naval Inst., Glacier Soc. (advisor, historian 1999—). Republican. Episcopalian. Avocations: photography, studio art glass, computers, travel. Home: 9538 Helenwood Dr Fairfax VA 22032-2006

HATCH, SALLY RUTH, foundation administrator, writer, consultant; b. Grand Rapids, Mich., Apr. 16, 1935; d. George and Evangeline (Boerma) Meyer; m. S. John Byington, Nov. 27, 1964 (div. Dec. 1988); children: Nancy Lee Rhodes, Barbra Ann Byington; m. Robert C. Hatch, Sept. 20, 2003. BA, Western Mich. U., 1957; MA, U. Md., 1962. Cert. tchr. k-8, Md. Grad. asst. U. Md., College Pk., 1959-60; tchr. U. Chgo. Lab. Sch., 1963-64, Grand Rapids, Mich., 1957-59. 64-65, Montgomery County Md. Pub. Schs., Rockville, Md., 1961-63; learning specialist Endeavor Learning Ctr., Rockville, 1987-88; asst. to pres. Women in Military Svc., Arlington, Va., 1988-89; exec. asst. Korean War Vets. Meml. Adv. Bd., Washington, 1989-91; pub. safety cons., civic activist, 1991—2000. Cons. Children Early Edn. Program, Bur. Edn. for Handicapped, Dept. edn., Washington, 1975-80; diagnostician pvt. practice. Author: Marriage Through Divorce and Beyond. Pres. Greater Springfield (Va.) Rep. Women's Clubs, 1980s, v.p., 1980s; dist. dir. Fairfax County Rep. Com., 1988; vol. Fairfax County Pub. Schs. Enrollment Study, 1985, coord. Capitol Hill Cmty. Policing Coun.; mem. MPD's Chief of Police Citizens Adv. Coun.; project dir. Guns into Plowshares Sculpture Project; mem. Ward 6 Crime Task Force; mem. coun. Neighbors Who Care of DC; exec. bd. dirs. MidNortheast Family Strengthening Collaborative. Recipient vol. recognition award Fairfax Pub. Schs., 1985; fellow Metro Urban Concerns Ministry. Mem. LWV (study rep. 1980's), Capitol Hill Restoration Soc. (pub. safety issues chair). Avocations: reading, writing poetry and music, active sports, church activities. Home and Office: 3406 Offutt Rd Randallstown MD 21133-3512 E-mail: sr.by@earthlink.net.

HATCH, STEVEN GRAHAM, foundation administrator; b. Idaho Falls, Idaho, Mar. 27, 1951; s. Charles Steven and Margery Jane (Doxey) H.; m. Rhonda Kay Frasier, Feb. 13, 1982; children: Steven Graham, Kristen Leone, Cameron Michael, Landon Jeremiah, McKell Margery. BA, Brigham Young U., 1976; postgrad. mgmt. devel. program, U. Utah, 1981. Founder, pres. Graham Maughan Enterprises, Provo, Utah, 1975-2000, Internat. Mktg. Co., 1980-2000, Mcht. Acct. Svcs., 1996—; registered rep., br. office supr. World Fin. Group, Orem, Utah, 2001—; devel. dir. Summitview Found., Provo, 2001—. Bd. dirs. Goldbrickers Internat., Inc., Net Solutions Internat. Inc.; co-founder Authorize.net, 1997. Sec.-treas. Zions Estates, Inc., Salt Lake City and Kansas City, Mo.; trustee Villages of Quail Valley, 1984-88; missionary France Mission, Paris, 1970-72, pub. rels. dir., 1972. Recipient Duty to God award, 1970. Mem. Provo Jaycees, Internat. Entrepreneurs Assn., Mormon Booksellers Assn., Samuel Hall Soc. (exec. v.p, 1979), U.S. C. of C., Provo C. of C. (chmn. legis. action com. 1981-82, mem. job svc. employer com.), Rotary (pres. Provo 1995-96, area rep. 1996-97, Paul Harris fellow). Republican. Mem. Lds Ch. Office: World Fin Group 1358 W Bus Park Dr Ste 229 Orem UT 84058

HATCH, WILDA GENE, broadcast company executive; b. Ogden, Utah, Nov. 28, 1917; d. Abraham Lincoln and Edris Alida (Toombs) Glasmann; m. George Clinton Hatch, Dec. 24, 1940; children: Michell Arnow, Diane G. Orr, Jeffrey B., Randall C., Deepika Avanti. BA, Stanford U., 1939; HHD (hon.), Weber State U., 1981. Pres. The Std. Corp., Ogden, 1955-93; v.p. Sta. KUTV, Salt Lake City, 1956-94. Pres. Women's State Legis. Coun., Salt Lake City, 1967-69; active LWV, Salt Lake City, 1965—. Democrat. Avocations: hiking, rock art, fishing. Home: 1537 Chandler Dr Salt Lake City UT 84103-4220

HATCHER, CHARLES ROSS, JR., surgeon, health facility administrator; b. Bainbridge, Ga., June 28, 1930; s. Charles Ross and Vivian Elizabeth (Miller) Hatcher; m. Phyllis Gregory Slappey, July 9, 1988; children from previous marriage: Marian Barnett Thorpe, Charles Hatcher III. BS magna cum laude, U. Ga., 1950; MD cum laude, Med. Coll. Ga., 1954. Intern Johns Hopkins Hosp., Balt., 1954-55; resident surgery Peter Bent Brigham Hosp., Boston, 1955-56, Johns Hopkins Hosp., 1958-62; prof. surgery, chief cardiothoracic surgery Emory U. Sch. Medicine, Atlanta, 1971-90; dir., CEO Emory Clinic, Atlanta, 1976-84; v.p. health affairs, dir. Woodruff Health Scis. Ctr., Emory U., 1984-96; dir. emeritus; chmn., CEO Emory HealthCare, 1995-96. Bd. dirs. Life of the South Corp., Japan Am. Soc. Contbr. Capt. U.S. Army, 1956—58. Mem.: ACS, So. Thoracic Surg. Assn. (pres. 1984), So. Surg. Assn., Am. Cancer Soc., Soc. Thoracic Surgeons (pres. 1986—87), Am. Assn. Thoracic Surgery, Am. Surg. Assn., Am. Coll. Chest Physicians (bd. regents 1977—81, bd. govs. 1974—77), Am. Coll. Cardiology (bd. govs. 1976—80), Johns Hopkins Soc. Scholars, Gov.'s Club Tallahassee, Fla., Bainbridge Country Club, Piedmont Driving Club, Rotary Club (bd. dirs. Atlanta chpt. 1976—80), Capital City Club, Alpha Omega Alpha, Sigma Xi, Phi Beta Kappa. Methodist. Home: 1105 Lullwater Rd NE Atlanta GA 30307-1245 Office: Emory U Woodruff Health Scis Ctr 1365B Clifton Rd NE # 6205 Atlanta GA 30322-1013 E-mail: charles_hatcher@emoryhealthcare.org.

HATCHER, DARIEN, hockey player; b. Sterling Heights, Mich., June 14, 1972; Defense Dallas Stars, 1991—; winner Stanley Cup, 1999, World Cup, Team U.S.A., 1996. Office: Reunion Arena Dr Pepper Star Ctr 211 Cowboys Pky Irving TX 75063 5931

HATCHER, DONALD W. government agency administrator; Commd. USAF, 1975, advanced through grades to chief master sgt.; supt. Air Force Element Def. Lang. Inst. Fgn. Lang. Ctr., Presidio of Monterey, Calif.; command chief master sgt. Air Intelligence Agy., Lackland AFB, Tex. Office: Lackland AFB 102 Hall Blvd Ste 201 San Antonio TX 78243-7009

HATCHER, HERBERT JOHN, biochemist, microbiologist; b. Mpls., Dec. 18, 1926; s. Herbert Edmond and Florence Elizabeth (Larson) H.; m. Beverly J. Johnson, Mar. 28, 1953 (dec. July 1985); children: Dennis Michal, Steven Craig, Roger Dean, Mark Alan, Susan Diane, Laura Jean; m. Louise Fritsche Nelson, May 24, 1986; children: Carlos Howard Nelson, Kent Robert Nelson, Carolyn Louise Tyler. BA, U. Minn., 1953, MS, 1964, PhD, 1965. Bacteriologist VA Hosp., Wilmington, Del., 1956-57; microbiologist Smith, Kline, French, Phila., 1957-60, Clinton (Iowa) Corn Processing, 1966-67; microbiologist, biochemist Econs. Lab. Inc., St. Paul, 1967-84; biochemist EG&G Idaho Inc., Idaho Falls, 1984-90; co-owner B/CG Cons. Svcs., Idaho Falls, 1990—. Chmn. bd. edn. Cross of Christ Luth. Ch., Coon Rapids, Minn., 1974-76; pres. chpt. Aid Assn. Luths., Idaho Falls, 1986; pres.-elect St. Johns Luth. Ch., 1988, pres., 1989. With USNR, 1945-46. Avocations: skiing, hiking, camping, hunting, fishing.

HATCHER, JOE BRANCH, management consultant; b. Ft. Worth, July 28, 1936; s. W. Joe and Jessie Mae Hatcher; m. Irma Gail Collins, Apr. 18, 1957; children: Gregory Layne, Geoffrey Alan, Gailyn. BA, U. Wichita, 1960; MA, U. Kans., 1967, PhD, 1968. Mem. English lit. faculty Baker U., Baldwin City, Kans., 1966-74; asst. to pres. Park Coll., Kansas City, Mo., 1974-75; v.p. Albion (Mich.) Coll., 1976-81; pres. Hendrix Coll., Conway, Ark., 1981-91; vice chmn. 1st Comml. Bank, Little Rock, 1992-95, also bd. dirs., 1992-95; cons. Hatcher & Assocs., Conway, 1995—. Mem.: Conway C. of C. Methodist. Avocation: tennis. Office: 916 Heather Cir Conway AR 72034-9395 Personal E-mail: jhatcher@cyberback.com.

HATCHER, MILTON WRIGHT, psychologist, educator; b. Memphis, Jan. 16, 1944; s. Wright Hill Hatcher and Jessamine Huff; m. Deborah Merritt, Jan. 4, 1974 (div. Aug. 31, 1980); children: Amanda, Lindsay; m. Letha Kae Hatcher, Mar. 22, 1983; 1 child, William. BS, Miss. State U., Starkville, 1967, MS, 1968, PhD, 1974. Dir. treatment, chief psychologist George W. Jackson Mental Health Ctr., Jonesboro, Ark., 1974—79; forensic svc. clinician Lee Mental Health, Ft. Myers, Fla., 1984—87; dir. mental health ctr. Clewiston (Fla.) Mental Health, 1987—88; probation officer 14th Jud. Dist. Ark., Mountain Home, 1988—93; asst. prof. psychology Ark. State U., Mountain Home, 1994—. Mem.: AAUP, APA. Home: PO Box 268 Clarkridge AR 72623 Office: Ark State Univ 1600 College Mountain Home AR 72653

HATCHETT, EDWARD BRYAN, JR., state auditor, lawyer; b. Glasgow, Ky., Aug. 8, 1951; s. Edward Bryan and Leona Katherine (Azbill) H.; m. Judie Etta James, Aug. 3, 1973; children: Catherine Wade, Elizabeth Black, James Edward Bryan. BA, Centre Coll., Danville, Ky., 1973; JD, U. Louisville, 1976; diploma Nat. Grad. Trust Sch., Northwestern U., 1980; diploma Stonier Grad. Sch. Banking, U. Del., 1986; diploma Ky. Mgmt. Inst., Western Ky. U., 1988. Bar: Ky. 1976. Editorial asst. Dept. Agr., Washington, 1971; edn. rsch. asst. Ky. Legis. Rsch. Commn., Frankfort, 1972; law clk. Dept. Law, City of Louisville, 1973-76; pvt. practice Glasgow, 1978-88; v.p., trust officer New Farmers Nat. Bank, Glasgow, 1980-88, sec., 1986-88; asst. gen. counsel Ky. Dept. Fin. Instns., Frankfort, 1977, commr., 1988-94, dir. securities divsn., 1992-94; auditor pub. accts. Commonwealth Ky., 1996—. Chmn. Ky. Fin. Instns. Bd., Frankfort, 1988-94; bd. dirs. Commonwealth Preservation Advs., Inc., Frankfort; pres. Barren County Bar Assn., Glasgow, 1988, Estate Planning Coun. So. Ky., Bowling Green, 1988. Gov.'s appointee Ky. Heritage Coun., Frankfort, 1985-88; pres. Mammoth Cave Area 4-H Found., Glasgow, 1981; lay reader Ch. of the Ascension, 1988—; elected Ky. Auditor of Public Accounts, 1995, re-elected, 1999. Named nat. pub. speaking champion Future Farmers Am., 1970. Mem. N.Am. Securities Adminstrs. Assn., Nat. Assn. State Auditors, Controllers and Treasurers (bond com. 1997—), Nat. State Auditors Assn., Frankfort Rotary Club. Democrat. Episcopalian. Avocations: historical research, golf. Home: 454 Chinook Trail Frankfort KY 40601-1602 Office: 144 Capitol Ave Frankfort KY 40601-2831 E-mail: hatchett@kyauditor.net., ebhatchett@aol.com.

HATEM, GHALEB FAYEZ, ophthalmologist, hospital administrator; b. Al-Sowieda, Syria, Dec. 24, 1947; s. Fayez S. and Hadieh Y. Hatem; m. Layla Jarmakani, Nov. 13, 1987; children: Sami, Dina, Ziena, Sara. PCB, Damascus (Syria) U., 1966, MD, 1972. Diplomate Am. Bd. Ophthalmology. Vice chmn. dept. EENT Oakwood Hosp., Dearborn, Mich., 1991-95, chmn., 1997—. Mem. adv. com. Arab Chaldean Coun., Detroit, 1994—. Recipient Disting. Svc. award, Am. Druze Soc., 1986. Fellow: Vitreous Soc., Arab Am. Med. Assn. (nat. pres. 2002—, Disting. Svc. award 1994), Am. Acad. Neurology, Am. Acad. Ophthalmology. Office: 4655 S Telegraph Rd Dearborn Heights MI 48125-1936

HATFIELD, DEBORAH L. lawyer; b. Kenosha, WI, Apr. 28, 1970; d. James Oscar and Charlotte Ann (Hess) H. AA in Arts & Scis., Univ. Wisconsin-Marathon Ctr., Wansau, WI, 1990, BA Bus. Admin., Univ. Wisconsin-Whitewater, Whitewater, WI, 1992; JD, Univ. Wisconsin, Madison, WI, 1996. Bar, Wisconsin, 1996. Atty. Hatfield Law Office, Elcho, WI, 1996—. Langlade Co. Child Support Agency, Antigo, WI, 1999—. Judge, mock trial, 1997—. 1st vice pres., Lions-Hyland Lakes, Deerbrook, WI, 1997—. Recipient Woman of the yr., AAUW, Wansau, WI, 1992. Mem. Wisconsin Bar Assn., Langlade County Bar Assn. Lutheran. Office: Hatfield Law Office N11226 Antigo St Elcho WI 54428-9613

HATFIELD, ELAINE CATHERINE, psychology educator; b. Detroit, Oct. 22, 1937; d. Charles E. and Eileen (Kalahar) H.; m. Richard L. Rapson, June 15, 1982. BA, U. Mich., 1959; PhD, Stanford U., 1963. Asst. prof. U. Minn., Mpls., 1963-64, assoc. prof., 1964-66; asso. prof. U. Rochester, 1966-68, U. Wis., Madison, 1968-69, prof., 1969-81; now prof. U. Hawaii, Honolulu, chmn. dept. psychology, 1981-83. Author: Equity: Theory and Research, 1978, Mirror, Mirror: The Importance of Looks in Everyday Life, 1986, Psychology of Emotions, 1991, Love, Sex and Intimacy, 1993, Emotional Contagion, 1994, Love and Sex: Cross-cultural Perspectives, 1996, Rosie, 2000; contbr. articles to profl. jours. Recipient Disting. Scientist award Soc. Exptl. Social Psychology, 1993. Fellow APA; mem. Soc. Sci. Study of Sex (pres., Disting. Scientist award 1996, Alfred Kinsey award 1998). Home: 3334 Anoai Pl Honolulu HI 96822-1418 Office: U Hawaii 2430 Campus Rd Honolulu HI 96822-2216 E-mail: elaineh@Hawaii.edu.

HATFIELD, JACK KENTON, lawyer, accountant; b. Medford, Okla., Jan. 26, 1922; s. Loate L. and Cora (Walsh) H.; m. D. Ann Keltner, Dec. 5, 1943 (dec. Sept. 1988); children: Susan Kathryn Hatfield Bechtold, Sally Ann Hatfield Clark; m. K. Dean Walker, Aug. 7, 1997; m. Dores Hamaker, Aug. 9, 2000. BS in BA, Phillips U., Enid, Okla., 1947; BA, Phillips U., 1953; LLB, Oklahoma City U., 1954, JD, 1967. Bar: U.S. Dist. Ct. (we. dist.) Okla. 1954, U.S. Supreme Ct. 1961, U.S. Dist. Ct. (no. dist.) Okla. 1967, U.S. Ct. Appeals (10th cir.) 1968; CPA 1954. Pvt. practice, Enid, Okla., 1954-58; with Dept. Interior, Tulsa, 1958-77; pvt. practice, Tulsa, 1977—. Mem. ABA, Okla. Bar Assn., Tulsa Co. Bar Assn., Am. Inst. CPA's, Okla. Soc. CPA's. Clubs: Petroleum. Avocations: photography, tennis. Home: 4013 E 86th St Tulsa OK 74137-2609 Office: 7060 S Yale Ave Ste 601 Tulsa OK 74136-5739

HATFIELD, JAMES ALLEN, theater arts educator, administrator; b. Marion, Ind., May 1, 1953; s. Frederick Marion and Mary Josephine (Murray) H.; 1 child, Edward Everett. BS, Ball State U., 1974, MA, 1975; PhD, Wayne State U., 1981. Asst. prof. Oakland U., Rochester, Mich., 1978-83; assoc. prof. Jackson (Miss.) State U., 1983-86; assoc. prof., chmn. theater dept. Butler U., Indpls., 1986-90; prof., dir. theater dept. U. Tex., Tyler, 1990—. Bd. dirs. Opera South, 1984-86; mem. Performance evaluation com. Miss. Arts Commn., Jackson, 1983-86; vice-chair Tex. Kennedy Ctr./Am. Coll. Theatre Festival, 1992-95, state chair, 1996-99. Dir., designer: (operas) Lost in the Stars, 1987, The Marriage of Figaro, 1988, The Merry Widow, 1989, The Great Soap Opera, 1990; (plays) My Sister in This House, 1988 (Am. Coll. Theatre Festival nomination), Another Antigone, 1991 (Am. Coll. Theatre Festival N.E. Tex. Cert. of Excellence), The Doctor in Spite of Himself, 1991, Thymus Vulgaris, 1991, Antigone, 1992, Habeas Corpus, 1992, The Norman Conquests, 1992, Getting Married, 1993, Anatol, 1993, Old Times, 1993, La Ronde, 1994, As You Like It, 1994, You Never Can Tell, 1994, Oleanna (Am. Coll. Theatre Festival Critics Choice Cert. of Excellence), 1994, Oleanna, 1995, KC/ACTF Region VI Production, Later Life, 1995 The Heiress, 1995, 3 Courtelines, 1995, Lettice & Lovage, 1995, Best of Friends, 1996, Phaedra, 1996, Octavia, 1996, Mrs. Klein, 1996, A Midsummer Night's Dream, 1997, Love Letters, Ravenscroft, 1998, The School for Wives, 1998, Love Letters, 1998, Mandrake, 1999, Molly Sweeney, 1999, Indiscretions, 1999, Mandrake, 1999, Love, Shakespeare to Coward, 2000, Coriolanus, 2000, Blithe Spirit, 2001, Comic Potential, 2001, Othello, 2003; (mus. theater prodns.) Candide, 1987, Sunday in the P George, 1988, Marry Me a Little, 1989 (Am. Coll. Theatre Festival Nomination), Two by Two, 1993, Candide, 1998, Kismet, 2000, My Fair Lady, 2001, The Sound of Music, 2002, The Fantasticks, 2002, Annie, 2003; (dir., playwright) Rosalis, 2002, She's Shakespeare Loving, 2002. State chmn. Kennedy Ctr./Am. Coll. Theatre Festival, 1996-99; bd. govs. The Assn. for Theatre in Higher Edn., 1997-99. Recipient medal of excellence in lighting Am. Coll. Theatre Festival, 1978, Outstanding Tchg. award U. Tex. Chancellor's Coun., 1993, KC/ACTF Bronze medal for excellence in theatre, 1999, 2000, 01. Mem. Am. Fedn. Musicians, Assn. for Theatre in Higher Edn. (governing coun.), Speech Communication Assn., Assn. Communication Adminstrn., Soc. Stage Dirs. and Choreographers, Tex. Ednl. Theatre Assn., Am. Alliance for Theatre and Edn., South West Theatre Assn. Avocations: photography, graphic design, sailing. Office: U Tex Dept Theater PO Box 8152 Tyler TX 75711-8152

HATFIELD, JERRY LEE, plant physiologist, biometeorologist; b. Wamego, Kans., May 1, 1949; s. Virgil H. and Elsie L. (Fischer) H.; m. Patricia JoAnne Reigle, Sept. 1, 1968; children: Mark E., Andrew J. BS, Kans. State U., 1971; MS, U. Ky., 1972; PhD, Iowa State U., 1975. Biometeorologist U. Calif., Davis, 1975-83; plant physiologist USDA-Agrl. Rsch. Svc., Lubbock, Tex., 1983-89; lab. dir. Nat. Soil Tilth Lab., USDA-Agr. Rsch. Svc., Ames, Iowa, 1989—. Editor: Biometeorology and Integrated Pest Management, 1982, Limitations to Plant Root Growth, vol. 19, Advances in Soil Science, 1992, Soil Biology: Impacts on Soil Quality, Advances in Soil Science, 1993, Crops Residue Management, Advances in Soil Science, 1994, Utilization of Manure as a Soil Resource, Advances in Soil Science, 1998, Innovative Weed and Soil Management, Advances in Soil Science, Nitrogen in the Environment, 2001; contbr. over 295 articles to profl. jours. Recipient Arthur S. Flemming award for outstanding svc. to fed. govt., 1997, Disting. Svc. award in agr., Kans. State U., 2002. Fellow Soil Sci. Soc. Am., Am. Soc. Agronomy (editor jour. 1989-95, editor-in-chief 1996-2002, Agronomic Svc. award 1999), Crop Sci. Soc. Am.; mem. Am. Geophys. Union, Am. Meteorol. Soc. (chair agrl./forest com. 1980-81, agrl. and forest meteorology com. 1999—), Indian Agrometeorol. Soc. (hon.), Soil and Water Conservation Soc. (program chair 1997-98, Pres. Leadership award 1998), Phi Kappa Phi. Republican. Avocations: golfing, reading, photography, landscaping. Office: USDA Agrl Rsch Svc Nat Soil Tilth Lab 2150 Pammel Dr Ames IA 50011-0001 E-mail: hatfield@nstl.gov.

HATFIELD, JULIE STOCKWELL, journalist, newspaper editor; b. Detroit, Mar. 22, 1940; d. William Hume and Ruth Reed (Palmer) Stockwell; m. Philip Mitchell Hatfield, Aug. 1, 1964 (div. 1979); children— Christian Andrew, Juliana, Jason David; m. Timothy Leland, Nov. 23, 1984; stepchildren— Christian Bourso, London Chamberlain BA, U. Mich, 1962. Staff reporter Women's Wear Daily, NYC, 1962-64; freelance feature writer Bath Brunswick Times, Wis. State Jour., 1964-68, Quincy Patriot Ledger, Mass., 1968-77; freelance music critic, fashion editor Boston Herald, 1977-79; fashion editor Boston Globe, 1979-95, living/arts writer, 1995-96, soc. columnist, 1996-2001, travel writer, 2001; freelance travel writer, 2001—; fashion editor The Newbury St. and Back Bay Guide, Boston. Author: (with others) Guide to the Thrift Shops of New England, 1982 Recipient Lulu award Men's Fashion Assn., 1985, Atrium award for Outstanding Writing on Fashion U. Ga., 1987, 92; Nat. Endowment Arts grantee, 1973. Mem.: Soc. of Am. travel writers. Episcopalian. Avocation: piano. E-mail: juliestockwell@peoplepc.com.

HATFIELD, MARK ODOM, former senator; b. Dallas, Oreg., July 12, 1922; s. Charles Dolen and Dovie (Odom) H.; m. Antoinette Kuzmanich, July 8, 1958; children: Mark, Elizabeth, Theresa, Charles. AB, Willamette U., 1943; AM, Stanford U., 1948. Instr. Willamette U., 1949, dean students, assoc. prof. polit. sci., 1950-56; mem. Oreg. Ho. of Reps., 1951-55, Oreg. Senate, 1955-57; sec. State of Oreg., 1957-59, gov., 1959-67; U.S. senator from Oreg., 1967-97. Chmn. appropriations com., energy and natural resources com., rules and adminstrn. com., joint printing com., joint libr. com., select com. Indian Affairs, Republican Policy Com.; chmn. Appropriations subcom. on transp. & related agencies. Author: Not Quite So Simple, 1967, Conflict and Conscience, 1971, Between A Rock and A Hard Place, 1976; co-author: Amnesty: The Unsettled Question of Vietnam, 1976, Freeze! How You Can Help Prevent Nuclear War, 1982, The Causes of World Hunger, 1982; co-author: What About the Russians, 1984, Vice Presidents of the United States 1789-1993, 1997. Lt. (j.g.) USN, 1943-45, PTO. Recipient over 100 hon. degrees Republican. Baptist. Office: PO Box 8639 Portland OR 97207-8639

HATFIELD, SUSAN WILLIAMS, school psychologist; b. Sioux City, Iowa, June 12, 1932; d. Keith Eugene Strange and Victorine Jessie (Williams) Strange Bridenbaugh; m. Robert Eugene Hatfield, Aug. 16, 1958 (div. Sept. 1973); children: Heidi Hatfield Fagerquist, Rex Hatfield. Student, Smith Coll., 1950-52; BA, U. N.Mex., 1955, MA, 1958; postgrad., U. Minn., 1974; EdD, U. S.D., 1976. Cert. sch. psychologist, Iowa. Camp swimming counselor Sioux Trails for Girl Scout Camp, Sioux City, 1951; grad. asst. in psychology U. N.Mex., Albuquerque, 1955-56; dist. dir. Sioux Trails Girl Scout Coun., Sioux City, 1958; part owner, mgr. Hatfield Apt. Bldg., Sioux City, 1958-68; psychologist Goodwill Industries, Sioux City, 1961-62; census taker, office worker U.S. Census Bur., Sioux City, 1970; life ins. agt. Bob Hatfield Ins. Co., Sioux City, 1970-73; psychologist Dr. Richard Satterfield, Sioux City, 1973-76; rsch. asst. U. S.D., Vermillion, 1974-76; pvt. practice Sioux City, 1976—; sch. psychologist Western Hills Area Edn. Agy., Sioux City, 1976-99; ret., 1999. Cons. to lawyer, Sioux City, 1982; cons., psychologist Goodwill Industries, Sioux City, 1990-94, Vocat. Rehab. Dept., Sioux City, 1993—; workshop presenter U. N.Mex., Albuquerque, 1980; participant/dir. rsch. projects in reading, written lang., math. for sch. children; grad. Sioux City Police Dept. Citizens Acad. IX, 1999. Contbr. papers to profl. jours. Mem. Jr. League, Sioux City, 1959-66, Found. Bd. for Family Planning, 1988—, Planned Parenthood of Greater Iowa, 1968—, St. Luke's Hosp. Aux., 1996—, PEO, Sioux City, 1955-73; bd. dirs. Sioux Trails Girl Scout Coun., Sioux City, 1959-62; vol., case aide for returnees from mental health instns. ARC, Sioux City, 1961-66; bd. dirs., v.p., regional rep. pres. Planned Parenthood, Sioux City, 1968-74, 84-97; bd. dirs., pres. Siouxland Drug Abuse Coun., Sioux City, 1974; Sunday sch. tchr. 1st Congl. Ch., Sioux City, 1964-68; leader Brownie troop, Girl Scout troop, Cub Scout troop, 1966-70; mem., chairperson Iowans for Med. Control of Abortion, Sioux City, 1968-73; mem., workshop presenter Women's Polit. Caucus, Sioux City, 1973-80; com. mem. for youth seminar Morningside Coll., Sioux City, 1973; mem., precinct chairperson, del. Dem. Party, Sioux City, 1980-94, vol. Mercy Hosp., Sioux City, 2001. Recipient Award of Honor We. Hills Area Edn. Agy., 1999. Mem. NOW, Nat. Assn. for Sch. Psychologists, Portfolio Club. Democrat. Unitarian Universalist. Avocations: swimming, reading, traveling, fine arts, cross country skiing, belly dancing. Home and Office: 17 Congress Ave Sioux City IA 51104-4053 E-mail: suehat17@aol.com.

HATGIL, PAUL PETER, artist, sculptor, educator; b. Manchester, N.H., Feb. 18, 1921; s. Peter and Katina (Karkadou) H.; m. Katherine Haritos. BS, Mass. Coll. of Art, 1950; MFA, Columbia U., 1951. Instr. art U. Tex., Austin, 1951-54, asst. prof., 1954-56, assoc. prof., 1956-67, prof., 1967-85, prof. emeritus, 1985—, design curator Archer M. Huntington Gallery Mus., 1965-68. Vis. instr. Columbia U. (summer) 1958; designed and installed Tex. Pavilion Exhbn., N.Y. World's Fair; coord. for Gov. John Connolly's Exhbn. of Art and Conf. on the Arts; aux. edn. officer Dist. 8 U.S. Coast Guard, 1965-74. Author: Establishing Residency in Greece. 1988, (autobiography) Apostolos, The Immigrant's Son, 1990; (book) Contemporary Encaustic Painting, 1994; contbr. numerous articles and papers to profl. jours. One-Woman shows include Baylor U. Gallery, Bass Concert Hall, U. Tex.; exhbns. include: 42 annual faculty exhbns. U. Tex., Austin, 2d, 3d, 4th Internat. Invitational Exhbn. of Ceramic Art Smithsonian Mus., Washington, 2d, 3d and 7th Nat. Decorative Arts Exhbns., Wichita, Kans., Internat. Invitational Exhbn. of Ceramic Art Iowa State U., Ceder Rapids, Flatbed Print Gallery, 1985-2003, St. Stephen's Emeriti Exhbn., Tex., Austin (Tex.) Mus. Fine Arts; pvt. collections including St. Paul's Luth. Ch., U. Tex. Bus. Administrn. Bldg., Huston Tillotson Coll., Seguin Luth. Coll., U. Tex. Faculty Club, U. Tex. Coll. Fine Arts, Woodlands Corp., Houston, Zapata Corp., Houston, Warren Cravens Corp., Houston, U.S. Mil. Ins. Corp., Harry Litwin Industries, Wichita, Kans., Coopers & Lybrand Corp., Houston, Cesar Design Inc., Cleve., Abilne (Tex.) 1st Nat. Bank, Tchr. Retirement Sys., Austin, FAA, Panama C.Z., Austin (Tex.) Mus. Art, Fox Collection, Austin, Tex., Voutsinas Collection, Elgin, Tex., Iatrou Collection, Austin, Tex.; videos collections include Ceramic History 1951-1976, Baylor U. Archives, Art in Texas - 1951-2000, Baylor U.; work featured in Encaustic Painting, 2000. With USAAF, 1943-45, PTO. Recipient Estelle Grey Meml. prize in art, Margaret Flowers prize in art, White Mus., San Antonio, Wolff and Marx prize in art, Dallas Mus. of Fine Arts; purchase prizes Dallas Mus. of Art, Laguna Gloria Mus. Austin; grantee U. Tex. Mem. Am. Hellenic Ednl. and Progressive Assn. (pres. Stephen F. Austin chpt. 312, dist. gov., 1999-2002, nat. ednl. found. bd. mem.). Home: 2203 Onion Creek Pky Unit 7 Austin TX 78747-1648

HATHAWAY, CARL EMIL, investment management company executive; b. Boston, Aug. 12, 1933; s. Carl Barbour and Tekla (Neumaier) H.; m. Gail Humphries Oglee, Dec. 6, 1958 (div. Oct. 23, 1996); children: Brian Kent, Carl Nichols, Andrew Oglee; m. Martha Livingston, Jan. 1, 1999. BA, Harvard U., 1955; MBA, Cornell U., 1959. With Morgan Guaranty Trust Co. N.Y., 1959-81, sr. v.p. pension investments, vice chmn. trust and investments dept., 1969-81; pres. Hathaway & Assocs. Ltd. (instl. investment mgmt.), Rowayton, Conn., 1981—, Hathaway Ptnrs., Inc., Rowayton, Conn., 1994—. Bd. dirs. Pacer Tech., Fountainhead Water. Served to lt. (j.g.) USNR, 1955-57. Mem.: Links (N.Y.C.), Blind Brook (Purchase, N.Y.), Harvard (Fairfield County, Conn.), Eastward Ho Country (Chatham, Mass.), Shorehaven Golf Club (Norwalk, Conn.). Home: 526 Flax Hill Rd Norwalk CT 06854-2317 Office: Hathaway & Assocs Ltd Rowayton Ave Norwalk CT 06853

HATHAWAY, CHARLES E. academic administrator; BS in Physics, Tex. A&M U., 1958; PhD in Physics, U. Okla., 1965. Mem. faculty dept. physics Kans. State U., Little Rock, 1965-81, dept. head, 1971-81; dean Coll. Sci. and Engring. U. Tex., San Antonio, 1981-86; v.p. acad. affairs Wright State U., 1986-93; chancellor U. Ark., Little Rock, 1993—2002, Donaghey Disting. prof., chancellor emeritus, 2003—. Founder, sr. editor Met. Univs.: An Internat. Forum. Fellow Woodrow Wilson fellow, U. Okla. Mem.: Am. Assn. State Colls. and Univs. (bd. dirs.), Ark. Sci. and Tech. Authority. Office: U Ark Little Rock Office of Chancellor Emeritus 2801 S University Ave Little Rock AR 72204-1000 E-mail: cehathaway@ualr.edu.

HATHAWAY, DAVID ROGER, physician, medical educator, scientist; b. Lafayette, Ind., Jan. 8, 1948; s. Ralph Roger Hathaway and Marjorie Alice Friend; m. Elaine Mary Green, Aug. 3, 1974; children: Julia E., Alison S. AB, Ind. U., 1970, MD, 1975. Diplomate Am. Bd. Internal Medicine, Cardiovascular Diseases. Clin. asst. NHLBI/NIH, Bethesda, Md., 1977-79; intern Ind. U. Med. Ctr., Indpls., 1975-76, resident, 1976-77, chief resident, 1979-80, from asst. prof. to assoc. prof., 1980-86, prof., 1986-95, chief cardiovascular divsn., 1990-95, dir. Krannert Inst. Cardiology, 1990-95; exec. dir. cardiovasc. rsch. Bristol-Myers Squibb Pharm. Rsch. Inst., Princeton, N.J., 1995-96, v.p. Cardiovascular Drug Discovery, 1996—. Lt. comdr. USPHS, 1977-79. Fellow Am. Coll. Cardiology; mem. Am. Fedn. for Clin. Rsch. (pres. 1987-88), Am. Soc. for Clin. Investigation, Assn. Am. Physicians (sec. 1991-96, councillor 1996—), Assn. Univ. Cardiologists, Phi Beta Kappa, Alpha Omega Alpha. Achievements include patents for composition and method for delivery of drugs, method for preventing restenosis following reconfiguration of body vessels, hemostatic puncture closure device, method and apparatus for intravascular drug delivery.

HATHAWAY, FRED WILLIAM, lawyer; b. Lewiston, Maine, Sept. 18, 1956; s. William Dodd and Mary Lee (Bird) H.; m. Lee Broadfoot, June 11, 1988; children: William Broadfoot, Benjamin Dodd. BA, Harvard U., 1979; JD, U. Maine, 1985. Bar: Maine 1985, D.C. 1986, U.S. Patent Office 1986, Virginia 1999. Assoc. Robbins & Laramie, Washington, 1985-90, Venable, Baetjer, Howard & Civiletti, LLP, Washington, 1990-95, Burns, Doane, Swecker & Mathis, LLP, Alexandria, Va., 1995—; ptnr., adj. prof. Georgetown U. Law Ctr., 1998—. Mem. ABA (chair various coms., sub.-coms). Episcopalian. Avocations: rowing, golf, carpentry. Office: Burns Doane Swecker & Mathis LLP 1737 King St Ste 500 Alexandria VA 22314-2727 E-mail: fredh@burnsdoane.com.

HATHAWAY, GARY RAY, lawyer; b. Liberal, Kans., July 5, 1942; s. Addison E. And Helen M. (Nix) H.; m. Sonja J. Brewer, Aug. 6, 1977. BA, Southwestern Coll., Winfield, Kans., 1964; JD, Washburn U., 1969. Bar: Kans. 1969, U.S. Dist. Ct. Kans. 1969, U.S. Ct. Appeals (10th cir.) 1979, U.S. Supreme Ct. 1978. County atty. Grant County, Ulysses, Kans., 1971-72, 80-84; ptnr. Hathaway, Kimball and Campbell, Ulysses, Kans., 1972-2000; pvt. practice Ulysses, Kans., 2000—. City atty. City of Ulysses, 1972-76. Mem. N.Am. Elk Breeders Assn., Am. Legion, Elks, Kiwanis, Phi Alpha Delta. Republican. Home: 218 N Wilson St Ulysses KS 67880-1950 Office: Law Office PO Box 27 Ulysses KS 67880-0527

HATHAWAY, LYNN MCDONALD, education advocate, administrator; b. N.Y.C., Mar. 28, 1939; d. William Douglas IV and Dorothy Edna (Homan) McDonald; m. Earl Burton Hathaway II, July 7, 1962; children: Earl Burton III, Amanda McDonald. BA, Bryn Mawr Coll., 1960. Editl. asst. Mademoiselle mag., N.Y.C., 1960-61; adminstrv. asst. Peace Corps office Nat. Coun. Chs., N.Y.C., 1961-62; vice chmn. cmty. rsch. N.Y. Jr. League, 1969-70; editor, chmn. N.Y. Entertains cookbook, 1973-74; edn. chair London Svc. League, 1979-80; pres., dir. London Svc. League, Jr. League, 1980-82; ind. writer, editor London, 1983. Bd. dirs. Friends of Ferguson Libr., Stamford, Conn., 1988, mem., rec. sec., v.p., pres., 1988-95, trustee, 1996-01, sec. bd. trustees, 2000—, citizen adv., 2001—, continuing chair student life com.; trustee, mem. exec. com., chair student life com. Conn. State U. Sys., 1991—, sec. bd. trustees, 1999—. Mem. Bryn Mawr Alumnae Assn. (pres. London 1983-86, internat. councillor 1988-90). Episcopalian. Home: 50 Old North Stamford Rd Stamford CT 06905-3961 Fax: 203-359-2511. E-mail: lynnhath@aol.com.

HATHAWAY, REBECCA GAYLE, health facility administrator; b. Decatur, Ill., Apr. 6, 1950; d. Jack R. and Mildred E. (Mecum) Hathaway. Diploma, St. Lukes Hosp. Sch. Nursing, St. Louis, 1971; BSN, St. Louis U., 1974, MSN, 1976. Cardiovascular clin. nurse specialist UCLA Med. Ctr., asst. dir. nursing, assoc. dir. nursing, 1976-91; v.p. City Hope Nat. Med. Ctr., 1991-95; asst. adminstr. ops. Scripps Meml., Encinitas, Calif., 1995-97; adminstr. Scripps Meml. Hosp., Encinitas, 1997—2001, Kaiser Med. Ctrs., Fremont and Hayward, Calif., 2002—. Editorial bd. J.B. Lippencott, Dimensions in Critical Care Nursing, 1982-89, Aspen Systems, Critical Care Quarterly, 1981—; nat. adv. com. Nursing Profl. Seminar Consultants, Inc., Albuquerque, 1980-88; lectr., cons. in field. Contbr. numerous articles to profl. jours. Recipient Mgmt. and Profl. Staff Incentive award UCLA Med. Ctr., 1989, UCLA Med. Ctr. Spl. Performance award, 1984, Rufus D. Putney Meml. award, 1971, Excellence award Am. Acad. Nurse Practitioners, State of Calif., 1995, Total Excellence in Mgmt. award San Diego Bus. Jour., 1997, Tribute to Women in Industry award YWCA, 1998. Mem. AACN, Am. Orgn. Nurse Execs., Am. Coll. Healthcare Execs., Assn. Calif. Nurse Leaders (Leadership award 2001), Sigma Theta Tau. E-mail: rebecca.g.hathaway@kp.org.

HATHAWAY, RICHARD DEAN, retired language educator; b. Chillicothe Ohio, Aug. 8, 1927; s. Dale and Edith (Hart) H.; m. Viola Hale, Apr. 16, 1978; children by previous marriage: Linda Hathaway Ellis, Bruce. AB summa cum laude, Oberlin Coll., 1949; AM, Harvard U., 1952; PhD, Western Res. U., 1964. Instr. English Oberlin Jr. H.S., 1949-50; chief interviewer U.S. Bur. of Census, Boston, 1952-53; exec. sec. New Eng. Fellowship of Reconciliation, Boston, 1953-55; instr. in English, Rensselaer Poly. Inst., Troy, N.Y., 1957-62; from asst. prof. to assoc. prof. SUNY, New Paltz, 1962-69, prof., 1970—2001; ret., 2001. Assoc. prof. Millsaps Coll., Jackson, Miss., 1965-66. Author: Sylvester Judd's New England, 1981, The Henry James Scholar's Guide to Web Sites, 1997; (computer software) Text: A Program About Literature, 1990; contbr. articles to profl. jours. Chair legis. com. SCLC Poor People's Campaign, 1968. Served with USNR, 1945-46. Mem. MLA. Mem. Religious Soc. of Friends. Home: 11 Crescent Ln New Paltz NY 12561-2809

HATHAWAY, ROBERT MORSE, historian; b. Richmond, Va., Dec. 23, 1947; s. Robert Morse and Lelia Gardner Hathaway; m. Susan Finch Hathaway, Aug. 8, 1970; children: Amy McGuire, Kristin Hathaway-Hansen, Kelly. BA, Wake Forest U., 1969, MA, 1972; PhD, U. N.C., 1976. Instr. dept. history U. N.C., Chapel Hill, 1976—77; asst. prof. history Wilson Coll., Chambersburg, Pa., 1977—79, Middlebury (Vt.) Coll., 1979—81, Barnard Coll., N.Y.C., 1981—82; staff historian CIA, Washington, 1982—86; assoc. professorial lectr. dept. history George Washington U., Washington, 1983—90; profl. staff fgn. affairs com. U.S. Ho. Reps., Washington, 1986—99; dir. Asia program Woodrow Wilson Internat. Ctr. for Scholars, Washington, 1999—. Editl. bd. Diplomatic History, 1990—93; dir. Congl. Study Group on Japan, Washington, 2001—. Author: Ambiguous Partnership: Britain and America, 1944-1947 (1980-81 Truman Book award, 1982), Great Britain and the United States: Special Relations Since World War II, 1990; co-author: Richard Helms as Director of Central Intelligence, 1966-1973, 1993. With U.S. Army, 1969—71. Congl. fellow, Am. Polit. Sci. Assn., 1985—86. Mem.: Asia Soc., Soc. for Historians Am. Fgn. Rels., Coun. on Fgn. Rels. Avocations: tennis, poker, backgammon. Home: 12103 Snow Shoe Ct Herndon VA 20170 Office: Woodrow Wilson Center 1300 Pennsylvania Ave NW Washington DC 20004-3027 E-mail: hathawar@wwic.si.edu.

HATHAWAY, RUTH ANN, chemist; b. Sidney, Ohio, Dec. 6, 1956; d. Earl Eugene and Mary Helen (Smith) Schmidt; m. Bruce Alan Hathaway, May 16, 1981. BS in Sci., Huntington Coll., 1979; postgrad., Purdue U., 1979-80. Instr. Harvey Mudd Coll., Claremont, Calif., 1981-82; head chemist So. Indsl. Products, Cape Girardeau, Mo., 1983-86; cons. Cape Girardeau, 1987-89; alterationist Patricks Cleaner, Cape Girardeau, 1988-89; lab. dir. Delta-Y Electric Co., Sedgewickville, Mo., 1989-91; quality control/quality assurance dir. Environ. Analysis South, Cape Girardeau, 1991-95; cons. Hathaway Cons., Cape Girardeau, 1995—. Editor: Safety Considerations in Microscale Lab, 1991; contbr. articles to profl. jours. Mem. exec. bd. dirs. NAACP, Cape Girardeau, 1986—; chmn. disaster com. ARC, Cape Girardeau, 1986-91; dir. S.E. Mo. Regional Sci. Fair, 1992-2002. Mem. Am. Chem. Soc. (divsn. environ. chem. health and safety 1989-98, local sect. nat. chemistry week coord., 1988-99), Am. Inst. Chemists, S.E. Mo. Local Emergency Planning Com. (chmn. 1987-98). Republican. Home and Office: 1810 Georgia St Cape Girardeau MO 63701-3816 E-mail: hathaway_consulting@hotmail.com.

HATHCOCK, JOHN EDWARD, vocalist; b. Memphis, Sept. 6, 1955; BA in Psychology, Memphis State U., (now U. Memphis), 1986; studied with Dr. David Williams, U. Memphis, 1992-97; studied with Ethel Maxwell, 1982-98; AAS in Graphic Art Tech. summa cum laude, S.W. Tenn. C.C., 2001; MA in Music summa cum laude, postgrad., Am. World U., Iowa City, Iowa, 2002—. Cert. Internet Webmaster 2003. Singer, performer, composer opera and sacred classical music; vocal coach, 1999—. Pres. Position Prodns., 1988-90; pres., founder Soaring Spirit Music, 1996—. Author: Seasons of Wonder, 1995; author poems; patentee in field; exec. prodr., vocal performer Grace: The Eternal Song. Mem. Bellevue Choir, 1991-92, Memphis Vocal Arts Ensemble, 1993, The Heritage Found. Recipient Mr. Wheelchair Am. award, 1990, Man of Yr. award, Happi Internat. Talent, 1990, Trailblazer award, City of Memphis, 1990. Mem.: Internat. Soc. Poets, Beethoven Club (dir. pub. rels. 1993), Phi Theta Kappa (Nat. Dean's List 1999—2000, 2000—01). Baptist. Fax: 901-683-6805.

HATHEWAY, ALSON EARLE, mechanical engineer; b. Long Beach, Calif., Nov. 15, 1935; s. Earle Miller and Carla (Barnhart) H.; m. Robin Lewis, Aug. 24, 1968; children: Jason Teale, Teale. BSME, U. Calif., Berkeley, 1959. Registered profl. engr., Calif. Engr. Boeing Aerospace Co., Seattle, 1959-60, Ford Aerospace Co., Newport Beach, Calif., 1960-66; mgr. Xerox Corp., Pasadena, Calif., 1966-72, Hughes Aircraft Co., Culver City, Calif., 1972-76, Gould Inc., El Monte, Calif., 1976-79; pres. Alson E. Hatheway Inc., Pasadena, 1979—. Instr. U. La Verne, Calif., 1989—, indsl. seminars in optomechanics, 1986—. Editor: Procs. Structural Mechanics of Optical Systems II, 1987, Procs. Precision Instrument Design, 1989, Procs. Optomechanical and Precision Instrument Design, 1995, 97, 99, 2001, 02, Procs. Actuator Technology and Applications, 1996, 98; contbr. articles to profl. jours. Fellow Soc. Photo-Optical Instrumentation Engr. (instr. 1987—, conf. chmn. 1987, 89, 91, 94, 96, 97, 98, 99, 2001, 02, 03, program chmn. 1990, 91, 96); mem. AIAA (sr., chmn. San Gabriel Valley sect. 1992-93), ASME, Am. Soc. Precision Engrs., Calif. Soc. Profl. Engr. (treas. 1965-66), Optical Soc. So. Calif. (pres. 1986-87), Opto-Mech. Engring. and Precision Instrument Design Tech. Group (chmn. 1992—), Assn. Old Crows. Achievements include patents on optical scanner, precision transducer, micrometer tip cushion, and optical calibration target; findings on Optical Analog and optomechanical constraint equations; development of Angstrom and Rubicon actuators and Hector calibration standards. Home: 419 S Meridith Ave Pasadena CA 91106-3512 Office: 595 E Colorado Blvd Ste 400 Pasadena CA 91101-2018

HATHEWAY, JOHN HARRIS, advertising agency executive; b. Waterbury, Conn., Aug. 9, 1926; s. Fred Whipple and Louise (Wood) H.; m. Patricia Mary Flaherty, Sept. 24, 1955; children: John Harris, Geoffrey Mills, Sara Wood. AB, Dartmouth Coll., 1948; MBA, Amos Tuck, 1950. With Young and Rubicam Inc., N.Y.C., 1950-89, sr. v.p., mgmt. supr., 1968-74, sr. v.p., group dir., 1974-83, exec. v.p., group dir., 1983-87, exec. v.p., western regional dir., 1987-89, also dir. Bd. overseers Hanover Inn, N.H., 1968-78, 94—. Mem. editl. bd. Dartmouth Life, 1991—. Mem. Council of Alumni Dartmouth, 1968-90, mem. alumni awards com., 1982-86, chmn., 1986-90, chmn. pub affairs adv. com., 1990—; pres. Dartmouth Class 1948, 1994-98; assembly of overseers Dartmouth-Hitchcock Med. Ctr., 1996—; mem. Dean's Council, Dartmouth Med. Sch. 2001-; bd. dirs. Chappaqua Summer Sch. Program, Horace Greeley Ednl. Fund, 1978-85, Upper Valley Hostel, 1999—; dir. Friends of Hopkins and Hood, 1990—; mem. Diocesan Mission Com.; mem. com. Parents' Fund, U. Vt., 1981-86. Served with AUS, 1945-46. Recipient Alumni award Dartmouth Coll., 1980 Mem. Dartmouth Coll. of N.Y. Alumni Assn. (pres. 1965-66, bd. dirs. 1958-64, 67-70, 72-87), Waccabuc Country Club, Manchester (Vt.) Country Club, Hanover Country Club, Dartmouth Club Upper Valley (dir. 1994—), Phi Beta Kappa. Episcopalian (vestryman, warden). Home: 10 Buell St Hanover NH 03755-2416 Office: Young and Rubicam Inc 285 Madison Ave New York NY 10017-6486

HATHORNE, GAYLE GENE, musician, family historian; b. Concordia, Kans., Sept. 3, 1953; d. Richard and R. Virginia (Huscher) Hathorne; 1 child, Amanda Kimberly. BMusic, Manhattan Sch. Music, N.Y.C., 1976; Artist's Diploma, Karajan Akademie, Berlin Philharm. Orch., 1980. Backstage hornplayer Bayreuth (Germany) Festival, 1977; 3d/1st solo hornist Stadt. Orch., Solingen, Germany, 1980-88; genealogy instr. Blue Ridge C.C., 1999—2002; membership mgr., office mgr. N.Y. Geneal. and Biog. Soc., 2002—. Substitute tchr. music and German, Henderson County Pub. Schs., 1988-98; pvt. horn tchr., Hendersonville, 1989— Sr. editor Tarheel Tattler, 1994-96, River Ramblings, 1994-96; editor Kuykendall Gazette, 1996-97; performer on CDs/cassettes; extra in film 28 Days, 1999. Nat. Fedn. Music Clubs nat. scholar, 1971. Mem. DAR (state pub. rels. N.C. Soc. 1997-99, organizing regent Abraham Kuykendall chpt. 1996), Children of Am. Revolution (organizing sr. pres. French Broad River Soc. 1992, state libr. 1996-98). Democrat. Avocations: genealogical research, photography, travel, writing, listening to opera. E-mail: ghathorne@nygbs.org.

HATLEN, BURTON NORVAL, English educator; b. Santa Barbara, Calif., Apr. 9, 1936; s. Julius Herbert and Lillie (Torvend) H.; m. Barbara Karlson, Sept. 20, 1961 (div. Nov. 1982); children: Julia, Inger; m. Virginia Nees, Nov. 10, 1983. BA, U. Calif., Berkeley, 1958; MA, Columbia U., 1959; Harvard U. 1961; PhD, U. Calif., Davis, 1972. Asst. prof. English King Coll., Bristol, Tenn., 1961-62; instr. U. Cin., 1962-65; asst. prof. U. Maine, Orono, 1967-72, assoc. prof., 1972-81, prof., 1981—, chmn. dept. English, 1985-88; interim dean Coll. Arts and Humanities, 1996-97. Dir. Nat. Poetry Found. Author: George Oppen: Man and Poet, 1981, (poems) I Wanted To Tell You, 1988. Mem.: MLA. Democrat. Office: U of Maine Dept Of English Orono ME 04469-0001

HATLER, PATRICIA RUTH, lawyer; b. Las Vegas, Nev., Aug. 4, 1954; d. Houston Eugene and Laurie (Danforth) Hatler; m. Howard A. Coffin II; children: Sloan H. D. Coffin, Laurie H. M. Coffin. BS, Duke U., 1976; JD, U. Va., 1980. Bar: Pa. 1980, Ohio 2002. Assoc. Dechert, Price & Rhoads, Phila., 1980-83; assoc. counsel Independence Blue Cross, Phila., 1983-86, sr. v.p., gen. counsel, corp. sec., 1987-99; exec. v.p., gen. counsel, corp. sec. Nationwide, Columbus, 1999—. Home: 17 N Parkview Ave Bexley OH 43209-1427 Office: Nationwide One Nationwide Plaza Columbus OH 43215 E-mail: hatlerp@nationwide.com.

HATTEBERG, LARRY MERLE, photojournalist; b. Winfield, Kans., June 30, 1944; s. Merle Lawrence and Mary Dorothy (Early) H.; m. Judy Beth Keller, June 6, 1965; children: Sherry Renee, Susan Michelle. Student, Kans. State Tchrs. Coll., 1962-63, Emporia-Wichita State U., 1963-66. Photographer Sta. KAKE-TV, Wichita, Kans., 1963, photojournalist, 1966-67, chief photographer, 1967-81, assoc. news dir., 1981-87, exec. news dir., 1987-88, co-anchor 5 p.m. newscast, 1988-92; co-anchor Evening News broadcasts KAKE-TV, Wichita, Kans., 1992—. Co-chmn. faculty Nat. Press Photographers TV Workshop, U. Okla., 1975—. Author: Larry Hatteberg's Kansas People,1991; developed Hatteberg's People series for TV, 1974. Served with USAR, 1966-72. Regional semi-finalist NASA Journalist-in-Spece Program; recipient Brotherhood award Kans. region NCCJ, 1995, regional lifetime Emmy award TV segment Hatteberg's People, Regional Emmy, 2000. Life mem. Nat. Press Photographers Assn. (Nat. TV News Photographer of Yr. award 1975, 77, Joseph Sprague award 1983, Joseph Costa award 1991). Office: 1500 N West St Wichita KS 67203-1323

HATTEN, ROBERT RANDOLPH, lawyer; b. Charlottesville, Va., Jan. 27, 1948; s. John Quackenbush and Mary Lou (Payne) Hatten; m. Anne Meredith Sherman, Aug. 14, 1970 (div. Jan. 1981); children: Catharine Cary, Anne Meredith; m. Sandra Sue McMullen, Oct. 26, 2002. BA, Hampden-Sydney Coll., 1969; JD, Washington & Lee U., 1972. Bar: Va. 1972, U.S. Dist. Ct. (ea. dist.) Va. 1973, U.S. Ct. Appeals (4th cir.) 1973, U.S. Supreme Ct. 1982. Law clk. U.S. Dist. Ct. (ea. dist.) Va., Norfolk, 1972-73; assoc. Patten & Wornom, Newport News, Va., 1973-75; ptnr. Patten, Wornom & Watkins, Newport News, 1976—. Bd. dirs. Asbestos Health Claimants Com., Johns Manville Bankruptcy Region, N.Y.C., 1983-89; mem. MDL Steering Com., 1991—. Contbr. articles to profl. jours. Bd. dirs. Peninsula Big Bros. Assn. Hampton Va., 1974-79; chmn. Newport News League of Downtown Churches, 1978; bd. trustees Lexington (Ky.) Theol. Sem., 1992-2001, Hampden-Sydney Coll., 1994-2000. Mem. ATLA (mem. key congl. liaison, spl.), Am. Bd. Trial Advocates, Va. Trial Lawyers Assn. (bd. govs. 1985-91, spl. award for courageous advocacy 1987), Newport News Bar Assn. Clubs: James River Country (Newport News). Democrat. Avocations: golf, boating. Office: Patten Wornom Hatten & Diamonstein LC 12350 Jefferson Ave Ste 360 Newport News VA 23602-6955 Home: 5466 Colraine Pt Gloucester VA 23061-4570

HATTEN, WILLIAM SEWARD, manufacturing company executive; b. Chgo., Apr. 7, 1917; s. William Seward and Margaret (Ahearn) H.; m. Marjorie Popp, Dec. 29, 1939; 1 dau., Patricia Marie (Mrs. Dudley D. Pendleton III). BA, Lawrence Coll., 1939; MBA, Northwestern U., 1944; PhD, Kennedy-Western U., 2000. Indsl. engr. Sears, Roebuck & Co., 1940-43; mgr. control div. Chgo. Ordnance Dist., 1943-45; owner Eskimo Ice Cream Co., Tucson, 1945-50; gen. mgr. Utica Knitting Co., N.Y., 1950-54; cons. Worden & Risberg, Phila., 1954-64; pres., chief exec. officer, dir. Clayton Mark & Co., Evanston, Ill., 1964-67; chmn. bd. Ken-Ray Brass Products, Inc., Vermont, Ill., 1964-67; pres., chief exec. officer, dir. Harper-Wyman Co., Hinsdale, Ill., 1967-69; exec. v.p. Warner Electric Brake & Clutch Co., Beloit, Wis., 1969-72; group v.p. engines and generators, dir. Kohler Co., Wis., 1973-80; pres. Hatten & Assocs., Lakeland, Fla., 1980—. Mem. Am. Ordance Assn., Northwestern U. Grad. Bus. Alumni Assn., Lone Palm Golf Club (Lakeland, Fla.), Lakeland Yacht and Country Club (Lakeland, Fla.), Union League (Chgo.), Phi Delta Theta. Episcopalian. Office: Hatten & Assocs 410 Cheverly Dr E Lakeland FL 33813-1207

HATTER, RICHARD WAYNE, foundation administrator, artist; b. Mangum, Okla., June 30, 1953; s. Travis Wayne and Catherine Elzora (Rozell) H. BS, Okla. State U., 1975; MPA, U. Colo., Colorado Springs, 1980. Grants mgr. dept. radiation therapy and nuclear medicine Thomas Jefferson U., Phila., 1984-86; dir. sponsored projects-rsch. Office for Instl. Advancement, Phila. Coll. Pharmacy and Sci., 1986-88; dir. devel. Courant Inst. Math. Scis., Office Univ. Devel., NYU, N.Y.C., 1988-90, dir. corp. and found. rels., 1988-90, dir. devel. faculty arts and sci., 1990-94, sr. dir., asst. dean for devel., faculty arts and scis., 1994-96; v.p. for devel. Am. Acad. in Rome, 1996-97; dir. devel. and pub. rels. John Simon Guggenheim Meml. Found., N.Y.C., 1997—. Solo art show Phila. Art Alliance, 1988. Mem. Planned Giving Group of Greater N.Y. Recipient cert. of recognition Sigma Xi, 1988. Mem.: Assn. Fund Raising Profls. Home: 310 E 23d St Apt 9G New York NY 10010-4706 Office: John Simon Guggenheim Meml Found 90 Park Ave New York NY 10016-1301 E-mail: rh@gf.org.

HATTERSLEY-SMITH, GEOFFREY FRANCIS, retired government research scientist; b. London, Apr. 22, 1923; s. Wilfred Percy Ashby and Ethel Mary (Willcocks) H.-S.; m. Maria Kefallinou, May 12, 1955; children: Kara Mary, Fiona Anastasia Student, Winchester Coll., Eng., 1937-41; BA, Oxford U., Eng., 1948, MA, 1951, DPhil, 1956. Base leader Falkland Islands Dependencies Survey, 1948-50; def. sci. staff officer Def. Rsch. Bd., Ottawa, Ont., Can., 1951-73; prin. sci. officer Brit. Antarctic Survey, Cambridge, Eng., 1973-91. Sec. Antarctic place names com. Fgn. and Commonwealth Office,

London, 1975-91. Author: North of Latitude Eighty, 1974, Present Arctic Ice Cover, 1974, The History of Place Names in the Falkland Islands Dependencies, 1980, The History of Place Names in the British Antarctic Territory, 1991, Geographical Names in the Ellesmere Island National Park Reserve, 1998; editor: The Norwegian with Scott, 1984. Sub-lt. Royal Navy, 1942-46. Fellow Royal Soc. Can. (Acad. Scis.), Royal Geog. Soc. (Founder's Gold medal 1966), Arctic Inst. N. Am. (gov. 1963-66), Arctic Circle Club (pres. 1967-69), Arctic Club (pres. 1976), Antarctic Club (London) (com. mem. 1983-85). Avocations: polar history; gardening. Home: The Crossways Kent Cranbrook TN17 2AG England

HATTERVIG, KAREN ANN, lawyer; b. Mitchell, S.D., Oct. 13, 1948; d. Gordon E. and Emma Sophia Larson; m. Jack A. Hattervig, Dec. 20, 1967 (div. Aug. 1973); children: Kimberly A., Thorpe-Jeffrey M. AA, BS, U. S.D., 1977, JD, 1981. Bar: S.D. 1981, U.S. Dist. Ct. (so. dist.) 1981, U.S. Ct. Appeals (8th cir.) 1981. Assoc. Strange, Strange & Palmer, Sioux Falls, S.D., 1981-82; supervising atty. East River Legal Svcs., Sioux Falls, S.D., 1982—. Active Minnehaha County Family Violence Task Force, Sioux Falls, 1982—, chair, 1994-99; chair S.D. Advocacy Network for Women, Sioux Falls, 1995—; active Wheels to Work Com., Sioux Falls, 1997—; treas. S.D. Coalition for Children, Sioux Falls, 1992-2001; chair Cmty. Outreach, Inc., Sioux Falls, 1994-2001. Named Friend of Social Work NASW. Mem.. SD State Bar Assn. (chair family law com. 2002—). Democrat. Lutheran. Office: East River Legal Svcs 335 N Main Ave Ste 300 Sioux Falls SD 57104-6038 E-mail: e02@erlservices.com.

HATTERVIG, ROBIN LYNN, dentist; b. Desmet, S.D., Apr. 4, 1958; s. Gene Willis and Harriet Ione (Larson) H.; m. Mirinda Marie Noonan, May 7, 1988; children: Erik Hunter, Auden Archer, Tate Fisher. BS, U. S.D., 1980; DDS, U. Nebr., 1984. Pvt. practice, Howard, S.D., 1984—. Mem. Howard Sch. Bd., 1997—, pres., 2000-03; bd. dirs. East River Healthcare, 1991-97, pres., 1992-94; trustee Bethany Luth. Ch., 1988-93, v.p., 1995-96, pres., 1997-98. Fellow Acad. Gen. Dentistry (pres. S.D. chpt. 1996-99), Internat. Coll. Dentists; mem. ADA, S.D. Dental Assn. (trustee 2000-03), S.D. Dental Found., Pierre Fauchard Acad. (pres. S.D. chpt. 1998—), Am. Numismatic Assn., Howard Cmty. Club, Howard Svc. Club (pres. 1994), Phi Beta Kappa, Omicron Kappa Upsilon. Republican. Lutheran. Avocations: coin collecting, woodworking. Home: 302 E Howard Ave Howard SD 57349-9021 Office: 112 N Main St Box 339 Howard SD 57349 E-mail: rhattervig@alliancecom.net.

HATTERY, ROBERT RALPH, radiologist, educator; b. Phoenix, Dec. 15, 1939; s. Robert Ralph and Goldie M. (Secor) H.; m. D. Diane Sittler, June 18, 1961; children: Angela, Michael. BA, Ind. U., 1961, MD, 1964; cert. in diagnostic radiology, Mayo Grad. Sch. Medicine, 1971. Diplomate Am. Bd. Radiology. Intern Parkland Meml. Hosp.-Southwestern Med. Sch., Dallas, 1964-65; fellow Mayo Clinic, Rochester, Minn., 1967-70, cons., 1970-81, chmn. dept. diagnostic radiology, 1981-86; instr. radiology Mayo Med. Sch., 1973-75, asst. prof. radiology, 1975-78, assoc. prof. radiology, 1978-82, prof. radiology, 1982—. Chair Mayo Group Practice Bd., 1991-93; chmn. bd. govs Mayo Clinic, Rochester, 1994-98; trustee Mayo Found., 1992-2002; trustee Am. Bd. Radiology. Author numerous jour. articles and abstracts, book chpts. Capt. USAF, 1965-67, Willford Hall Hosp., San Antonio. Fellow Am. Coll. Radiology; mem. Radiol. Soc. N.Am. (bd. dirs. 1999—), Am. Roentgen Ray Soc., Soc. Computed Body Tomography (pres. 1982-83), Soc. Genitourinary Radiography (pres. 1986-88), Am. Bd. Radiology (exec. dir.). Office: American Bd Radiology 5441 E Williams Blvd Tucson AZ 85711 E-mail: rhattery@theabr.org.

HATTIN, DONALD EDWARD, geologist, educator; b. Cohasset, Mass., Nov. 16, 1928; s. Edward Arthur and Una Vestella (Whipple) H.; m. Marjorie Elizabeth Macy, July 15, 1950; children: Sandra Jane, Ronald Scott, Donna Jean. BS, U. Mass., 1950; MS, U. Kans., 1952, PhD (Shell fellow), 1954. Asst. instr. geology U. Kans., 1950-52, instr., 1953-54; asst. prof. geology Ind. U., Bloomington, 1954-60, assoc. prof., 1960-67, prof., 1967-95, prof. emeritus, 1995—; asst. geologist Kans. Geol. Survey, 1952, research assoc., 1959-68, 70-74, 77-82, 86-87. Vis. prof. Ernst-Moritz-Arndt U., Greifswald, German Dem. Republic, 1985; geologist Ind. Geol. Survey, 1957-58; cons. in field; mem. N.Am. Commn. on Stratigraphic Nomenclature, 1987-90, 91-94; vis. disting. prof. U. Kans., 1991. Author: Stratigraphy of the Wreford Limestone, 1957, Stratigraphy of the Carlile Shale, 1962, Stratigraphy of the Graneros Shale in Central Kansas, 1965, Stratigraphic and Depositional Environment of Greenhorn Limestone of Kansas, 1975, Upper Cretaceous Stratigraphy and Depositional Environments of Western Kansas, 1978, Stratigraphy and Depositional Environment of Smoky Hill Chalk, Niobrara Chalk, Western Kansas, 1982, W. Ferdinand Macy, 1852-1901: Painter of New England Landscapes, 2003. Capt. reserves USAF, 1950—59, lt. USAF, 1955—57. Recipient Erasmus Haworth Disting. Alumni honors in geology U. Kans., 1976, Alumni Disting. Tchg. award Coll. Arts and Scis. Ind. U., 1988, Disting. Tchg. and Mentoring award Grad. Sch. Ind. U., 1995; NSF grantee, 1975-77, 88-90, Am. Chem. Soc. grantee, 1978-80, 84-86; NSF fellow, 1969. Fellow: Geol. Soc. Am. (grantee 1975); mem.: Paleontol. Soc., Soc. Econ. Paleontologists Mineralogists, Am. Assn. Petroleum Geologists (Outstanding Educator award Ea. sect. 1993). Office: Ind U Dept Geol Scis Bloomington IN 47405

HATTON, BARBARA R. academic administrator; b. La Grange, Ga., June 4, 1941; d. William H. and Katye (Tucker) H.; 1 child, Kera M. Washington. BS, Howard U., 1962; MA, The Atlanta U., 1966; MEA, Stanford U., 1971, PhD, 1976. Assoc. dir. Stanford (Calif.) U., 1970-72, asst. prof. edn. adminstrn. and policy studies, 1976-79; chair Dept. Adminstrn. & Supervision, acting assoc. dean The Atlanta U., 1979-80; dean, prof. Tuskegee U., Ala., 1984-88; dep. dir. The Ford Found., N.Y., 1988; scholar-in-residence So. Edn. Found., Atlanta, 1992—; pres. S.C. State U., Orangeburg, 1993—, Knoxville Coll., 1997—. Mem. adv. com. Tchr. Edn. Project Assn. Am. Colls.; mem. review panel Fifth Yr. Non-Trad. Edn. Programs Ala. Dept. Edn.; mem. futures task force Am. Assn. Colls. for Tchr. Edn.; noms. com. New Deans Orientation Com. Trainer New Dean's Inst. Am. Assn. of Colls. of Tchr. Edn.; commn. on ednl. quality So. Regional Edn. Bd.; mem. Math. Standardization Com. Atlanta Pub. Schs.; reader Jour. Ga. Ednl. Rsch. Assn.; chmn. subcommittee on provisional certification and reciprocity, exec. com. Bd. Regents and State Bd. of Edn., State of Ga. Mem. S.C. Humanities Coun., Orangeburg C. of C.; bd. dirs. Assn. Presbyn. Colls. and Univs., Tenn. Rsch. Valley, Knoxville Symphony; active Met. Drug Com., Coll. Bds. Equity 2000 Project. Fellow NDEA, EPDA; recipient The Rose award U. S.C., 1993, Drum Major for Justice awards, 1993. Mem. Am. Ednl. Rsch. Assn., Am. Assn. Sch. Adminstrs., Exec. Women's Assn., Rotary Knoxville, Alpha Kappa Alpha Sorority Inc., Phi Chi Hon. Soc., Phi Delta Kappa Hon. Soc. Office: Knoxville Coll 901 College St Knoxville TN 37921-4724

HATTON, BRENDA SHIRLEY (LINDA WELLINGTON), writer, poet, songwriter, nurse; b. Winchester, Ky., Apr. 28, 1945; d. Benjamin Marion and Minnie (Rice) Huff; m. Wallace Glenn Hatton, Feb. 8, 1964; children: Carolyn, Sherry Lynn, Connie Gail and Ronnie Dale (twins). Student, Ea. Ky. U., 1995; cert., Ctrl. Ky. Tech. Coll., 1999. Cert. nurse aide, Ky., 1999. Active Mountain Glory Gospel. Contbr. poems to books;, singer (stage name Linda Wellington) ; singer: (gospel album) There Stands Jesus, 1997, A Celebration Party, 2003; singer: (with Mountain Glory Gospel) Old Time Convention, 2000, Gatlinburg Project vol. 6, 2001; mem.: His Music Group; singer: (albums) A Celebration Party, 2003. Mem. Ky. Mountain Creative Coalition. Mem. So. Gospel Music Assn., Broadcast Music Inc., Internat. Platform Assn. Ch. Of God. Avocations: fishing, camping, singing, meeting people, discovering new places. Home: 2007 Bethel Rd Lancaster KY 40444-9737 E-mail: indiared@hotmail.com.

HAU, LENE, physicist, optics scientist; BS in Math. and Physics, U. Aarhus, Denmark, 1984, MS, 1986, PhD in Physics, 1991. Mem. sci. staff Rowland Inst., 1991; Gordon McKay prof. applied physics and prof. physics Harvard U., Cambridge, Mass., 1999—. MacArthur fellow, 2001. Office: Harvard U Dept Physics 17 Oxford St Lyman 229 Cambridge MA 02138

HAU, LENE VESTERGAARD, physicist, educator; arrived in U.S., 1989; BS in Math. and Physics, U. Aarhus, Denmark, 1984; MS in Physics, U. Aarhus, 1986, PhD in Physics, 1991. Gordon McKay prof. applied physics, prof. physics Harvard U., Cambridge, Mass., 1999—. Recipient J.C. Jacobsen 200 Yr. Anniversary award, Carlsberg Found., Denmark, 1989, MacArthur Genius award, MacArthur Found., 2001—03, Aereshaandvaerker, Haandvaerkerforeneingen i Koebenhavn and Her Majesty Queen Margrethe II of Denmark, 2001, NKT prize, Danish Phys. Soc., 2001, Ole Roemer medal, Pres. U. Copenhagen, 2001, prize, TopDanmark Fonden, 2000, Samuel Friedman Rescue award, Friedman Found., 2001; scholar, Carlsberg Found., 1985. Mem.: Royal Danish Acad. Scis. Achievements include first to slow light to the speed of a bicycle and subsequently to a complete stop. Office: Harvard Univ Dept Physics Oxford St Cambridge MA 02138 E-mail: hau@physics.harvard.edu.

HAUB, MARK D. exercise physiologist; b. Kansas City, Mo., Sept. 15, 1969; s. Theodore David Haub and Peggy Sue Boten; m. Michelle R. Straub, Feb 18, 1995. BA, Ft. Hays State U., 1992; MS, U. Kans., 1996, PhD, 1998. Rsch. fellow Donald W. Reynolds Ctr. on Aging, Little Rock, 1998—2000; asst. prof. Kans. State U., Manhattan, 2000—. Dir. Human Metabolism Lab., Manhattan, 2001—. Recipient Student Rsch. award, Gatorade Sports Sci. Inst., 1997. Mem.: Am. Diabetes Assn. (assoc.), Am. Soc. Nutritional Scis. (assoc.), N. Am. Assn. for Study of Obesity (assoc.), Am. Coll. Sports Medicine (assoc. Outstanding Student Rsch. award 1994, 1996). Episcopalian. Avocation: exercise. Office: Dept of Human Nutrition 127 Justin Hall Manhattan KS 66506 Office Fax: 785-532-3132.

HAUBEN, JAY ROBERT, computer technician, writer, editor; b. N.Y.C., May 9, 1941; s. Sidney and Beatrice H. Hauben; m. Ronda Hauben, Aug. 23, 1964; 1 child, Micheal. BS, CUNY, 1963; MA, Harvard U., 1964. Curriculum developer Harvard Project Physics, Cambridge, Mass., 1964-66, Elem. Sci. Study, Watertown, Mass., 1967-69; physics tchr. Stillman Coll., Tuscaloosa, Ala., 1966-67; rubber worker Am. Biltrite, Cambridge, Mass., 1972-79; sci. instrnl. technician Henry Ford C.C., Dearborn, Mich., 1979-94, sci. tchr., 1980-94; computer technician Columbia U., N.Y.C., 1994—. Presenter internet history workshop Assn. Internet Rschrs., 2002; spkr. in field. Author: (book) Electrical Gadget Suggestion Book, 1968, John Kemeny Biography in Computer Pioneers, 1995, Wiener, Licklider and the Computer as Communication Device in Echoes and Reflections, 1998; editor: Amateur Computerist, 1991—; contbr. articles to newspapers, ency. entries. Watch dog Dearborn Bd. Edn., 1987—89; participant Usenet discussions, 1991—. Scholar, N.Y. State Regents, 1959—63; Woodrow Wilson fellow, 1963—64. Home: 244 W 72d St Apt 15D New York NY 10023 E-mail: hauben@columbia.edu.

HAUBEN, MANFRED, physician; b. N.Y.C., Apr. 9, 1959; s. Richard and Zora (Soumerai) H. BA in Chemistry, NYU, 1980; MD, N.Y. Med. Coll., 1984, MPH, 1990, DTMH, 1989. Diplomate Nat. Bd. Med. Examiners, Am. Bd. Preventive Medicine, Am. Bd. Clin. Pharmacology. Resident dept. pathology Columbia Presbyn. Med. Ctr., N.Y.C., 1985-86; resident in cmty. and preventive medicine Our Lady Med. Ctr., N.Y.C., 1987-89, fellow clin. preventive medicine and chief resident, 1989-90; assoc. med. dir. Sterling-Winthrop, Inc., N.Y.C., 1990-94; assoc. med. dir. safety evaluation and epidemiology Pfizer, Inc., 1994-00, med. dir., team leader safety evaluation and epidemiology, 2000-01; med. dir. Med. Safety Evaluation, 2001—. Adj. clin. asst. prof. cmty. and preventive medicine N.Y. Med. Coll., 1993—, adj. asst. prof. pharmacology, 2000—; clin. asst. prof. dept. medicine NYU Sch. Medicine, 2000—, adj. clin. prof. pharmacology, 2000—. Contbr. articles to profl. jours. Mem.: AMA (Physician Recognition award), Am. Soc. Clin. Pharmacology and Therapeutics, Biophys. Soc., Drug Info. Assn., Am. Acad. Pharm. Physicians, Am. Coll. Clin. Pharmacology, Internat. Soc. Pharmacoepidemiology, Am. Phys. Soc., Alpha Omega Alpha.

HAUBEN, RONDA JOAN, researcher, writer, scholar; b. Harrisburg, Pa., Jan. 10, 1944; d. Max Stern and Anne Michaela Stern; m. Jay Robert Hauben, Aug. 23, 1964;1 child, Michael. BA, Queens Coll., 1963; MA, Tufts U., 1969. Instr. humanities Stillman Coll., Tuscaloosa, Ala., 1966-67; instr. drama Wheelock Coll., Boston, Mass., 1969-70; tchr. computing UAW-Ford Edn. Program, Dearborn, Mich., 1984-87; tchr. internet and unix classes ACIS at Columbia U., N.Y.C., 1996; rschr. and writer, ind. scholar, N.Y.C., 1994—. Spkr. in field, book reviewer. Co-author: Netizens: On the History and Impact of Usenet and the Internet, 1997; contbr. Ency. of Computers and Computer History, 1997, Circleid and Telepolis; editor: (newsletter) Amateur Computerist, 1988—. Woodrow Wilson Found. tchg. fellow, 1966-67; Tufts U. scholar. Home: 244 W 72d St Apt 15D New York NY 10023 E-mail: ronda@panix.com.

HAUBER, FREDERICK AUGUST, ophthalmologist; b. Pitts., July 3, 1948; s. Michael H. and Cecilia (Azinger) H.; m. Cathy Lu Rosellini, Aug. 3, 1981; children: Elizabeth Alexandra, Natalia Fredericka. BS in Microbiology cum laude, U. Pitts., 1970; MD, U. Tenn., 1974. Intern U. South Fla., Tampa, 1975, resident in ophthalmology, 1982; pvt. practice Pasco Eye Inst., New Port Richey, Fla., 1983—. Asst. clin. prof. U. South Fla., Tampa, 1984—; rechr., spkr. in field, 1990—; cons. Optimed, Inc. Contbr. articles to profl. jours. Advisor health care cost containment com., Tarpon Springs, Fla., 1988; founder Pasco County Diabetes Assn.; mem. bd. counsellors U. Tampa. Fellow ACS, Am. Acad. Ophthalmology; mem. Southeastern U.S. Debate Soc. Achievements include patent for achromatic intraocular lens; first to insert glaucoma pressure regulator; development of binary optical intraocular lens, color vision eye chart system. Office: Pasco Eye Inst 5347 Main St New Port Richey FL 34652-2506

HAUBER, PATRICIA ANNE, educator; b. Phila., Feb. 16, 1953; d. Frederick Joseph and Dorothy Marie (Delaney) Hauber AA, Montgomery County Community, Blue Bell, Pa., 1973; BS, Bloomsburg U., 1975; MEd, Lehigh U., 1985, elem. prin. cert., secondary prin. cert., 1990. Tchr. North Penn Sch. Dist., Lansdale, Pa., 1975—85; sci. coord., tchr. St. Jude Sch., Chalfont, Pa., 1985—2001. Instr., trainer ARC, CPR programs, Lansdale, Pa., 1979-90. Mem. AAAS, ASCD, AAUW, Nat. Coun. Tchrs. Math., Nat. Sci. Tchrs. Assn., Math. Assn. Am., Assn. Women in Math., Pa. Sci. Tchrs. Assn., Pa. Assn. for Supervision and Curriculum Devel., Pa. Coun. Tchrs. of Math., Phi Delta Kappa. Democrat. Roman Catholic. Avocations: antiques, crafts. Home: 391 Huckleberry Ln Harleysville PA 19438-2334

HAUBERG, ROBERT ENGELBRECHT, JR., lawyer; b. Jackson, Miss., Oct. 26, 1943; s. Robert Engelbrecht and Robbie Mae (Bowen) H.; m. Claudia Carithers; children: Greta, Patrick, Michael. BA, U. Miss., 1965; MA, Yale U., 1967, JD, 1970. Bar: N.Y. 1971, U.S. Dist. Ct. (so. dist.) N.Y. 1971, U.S. Ct. Appeals (2d cir.) 1971, D.C. 1974, U.S. Dist. Ct. D.C. 1974, U.S. Ct. Appeals (D.C. cir.) 1974, U.S. Supreme Ct. 1974, U.S. Ct. Appeals (5th cir.) 1988, U.S. Dist. Ct. (no. dist.) Tex. 1989, U.S. Dist. Ct. (so. dist.) Miss. 1989, Miss. 1991, U.S. Dist. Ct. (no. dist.) Miss. 1991. Assoc. Donovan, Leisure, Newton & Irvine, N.Y.C., 1970-73; asst. U.S. atty. U.S. Dept. Justice, Washington, 1973-76, trial atty., 1976-79, asst. chief, 1979-86, sr. trial atty., 1986-90, sr. litigation counsel Dallas Bank Fraud Task Force, 1990-91; ptnr. Watkins, Ludlam, Winter & Stennis, P.A., Jackson, Miss., 1991-98; shareholder Baker, Donelson, Bearman & Caldwell, Jackson/Washington, Miss., 1998—. Contbr. numerous articles to profl. jours. Mem. ABA (mem. anti-trust, criminal justice, litigation sects.), D.C. Bar Assn., Miss. Bar, Internat. Bar Assn., Yale Law Sch. Assn. (D.C. pres. 1986-87, exec. com. 1987-88, 93-97), Beta Theta Pi. Episcopalian. Avocations: sports, music. Home: 3946 Old Canton Rd Jackson MS 39216-3617

HAUBOLD, SAMUEL ALLEN, lawyer; b. Watertown, S.D., July 29, 1938; s. Gustuv Herman and Leone Marjorie (York) H.; m. Caroline V. Thompson. Sept. 27, 1969; 1 child, Caroline A. BS in Engring., Northwestern U.; JD, Harvard U. Bar: Ill. 1966, N.Y. 1990, U.S. Dist. Ct. (no. dist.) Ill. 1966, U.S. Ct. Appeals (7th cir.) 1970, U.S. Ct. Appeals (9th cir.) 1979, U.S. Supreme Ct. 1974. Assoc. Kirkland & Ellis, Chgo., 1966, ptnr., 1972—; resident ptnr. Kirkland & Ellis Internat., London, 1994—. Served to lt. USN, 1960-63. Mem. ABA, Ill. Bar Assn., Internat. Bar Assn., Mid-Am. Club, Saddle and Cycle Club (Chgo.), The Hurlingham Club (London), City of London Club. Presbyterian. Home: 40 S Eaton Pl London SW1W 9JJ England Office: Kirkland & Ellis Internat Old Broad St London EC2N 1HQ England

HAUBRICH, ROBERT RICE, biology educator; b. Claremont, N.H., May 4, 1923; s. Frederick William and Marion Norma (Rice) H. BS in Forestry, Mich. State U., 1949, MS in Zoology, 1952; PhD in Biology, U. Fla., 1957. Asst. prof. biology East Carolina U., Greenville, N.C., 1957-61, Oberlin (Ohio) Coll., 1961-62, Denison U., Granville, Ohio, 1962-64, assoc. prof. biology, 1964-67, prof. biology, 1968-88, chair dept. biology, 1968-69, alumni chair, 1983-89, prof. emeritus, 1988—. Assoc. dir. Earlham Coll. Biol. Sta., Syracuse, Ind., 1967-72; mem. marine sci. edn. consortium Duke Marine Lab., Beaufort, N.C., 1983-88; libr. reader Marine Biol. Lab., Woods Hole, Mass., 1965—. Contbr. articles to profl. publs. Sgt. USAF, 1943-46. Fellow AAAS, Ohio Acad. Sci.; mem. Internat. Soc. History, Philosophy and Social Studies. Avocations: swimming, hiking. Home and Office: Denison U Dept Biology Granville OH 43023

HAUCH, VALERIE CATHERINE, historian, educator; b. Washington, May 20, 1949; d. Charles Christian and Ruthadele Bertha (LaTourrette) H.; life ptnr Jacquelyn Farrow. BA in History, Kalamazoo Coll., 1971; MA in Medieval Studies, Western Mich. U., 1977; grad. cert. C.C. Teaching, U. St. Thomas, St. Paul, 1995. Social sci. analyst congl. rsch. svc. Libr. Congress, Washington, 1971-72; ind. contractor Minn. Hist. Soc., St. Paul, 1987-88, adminstrv. asst., 1990—; cmty. edn. tchr. Mpls. Pub. Schs., 1990—; instr. Fla. Com. Coll., 2003. Instr. Minn. Sch. Bus., 1999—, Fla. C.C., Jacksonville, 2003—. Mem. Am. Hist. Assn., Am. Assn. Mus., Phi Beta Kappa. Home: 3540 33rd Ave S Minneapolis MN 55406-2725

HAUCK, BARBARA JEAN, fund raising executive, writer, artist; b. Princeton, N.J., Mar. 11, 1948; d. Lester Winfield Hauck and Jean Catherine Dawson Rodda; stepdau. Paul Mott Rodda; m. Robert Francis Fogarty (div. Feb. 1984); children: Corey Michael, Matthew Robert; m. Richard David Claffey, Aug. 12, 1989; stepchildren: Kelly, Shannon Claffey Hughes; 1 adopted child, Martina Vidovic. BS in Art, Skidmore Coll., 1985; MA in Speech and Comm. Studies, Edinboro U., 1996. Graphic designer various cos., Lancaster and Erie, Pa., 1980-88, printing saleswoman Erie, 1988-93; publicist and dir. mktg. Bay City Promotions, Erie, 1992-95; freelance advt. and promotions, Erie, 1992-97; grad. asst. Edinboro (Pa.) U., 1994-96; exec. dir. Warner Theatre Preservation Trust, Erie, 1996—. Dir. devel. Arts Coun. Erie Endowment, 2000—; mem. adv. bd. Highland Festival, Edinboro, 2000-01. One-woman shows, 1983, 90, 91; exhibited in group shows, 1980—; contbr. articles and poems to various publs. Vol. tchr. Neighborhood Art House, Erie, 1996-2000; fundraiser Jane Earll for State Senate, Erie, 1996, Mike Dunlavey for Judge, Erie, 1999; coord. phone bank Tom Ridge for Gov., Erie, 1998; mem. exec. com. Erie Rep. Com., 1998-99. Recipient Golden Roosters award Erie Advt. Club, 1997; hon. Paul Harris fellow Rotary Club, Erie, 1997. Mem. Assn. Fund Raising Profls. (chmn. legis. and govt. affairs), Women's Roundtable. Roman Catholic. Avocations: painting, weaving, skiing, hiking, reading. Office: Warner Theatre Preservation Trust 811 State St PO Box 1645 Erie PA 16507-9645

HAUCK, FREDERICK HAMILTON, retired naval officer, astronaut, business executive; b. Long Beach, Calif., Apr. 11, 1941; s. Philip and Virginia (Hustvedt) H.; m. Dolly Bowman, Aug. 27, 1962 (div.); children: Whitney Irene, Stephen Christopher; m. Susan Cameron Bruce, June 27, 1993. BS in Physics, Tufts U., 1962; MS in Nuclear Engring., MIT, 1966. Commd. ensign USN, 1962, advanced through grades to capt., 1983; pilot Attack Squadron 35, USS Coral Sea, 1968-70; instr. pilot Attack Squadron 42, Oceana, Va., 1970-71; test pilot Naval Air Test Ctr., Patuxent River, Md., 1971-74; ops. officer Carrier Air Wing 14, Miramar, Calif., USS Enterprise, 1974-76; exec. officer Attack Squadron 145, Wash., 1976-78; astronaut NASA, Houston, 1978-89; space shuttle pilot shuttle transp. system mission 7, 1983; space shuttle comdr. STS-51A, 1984; assoc. adminstr. for external rels. NASA, 1986; space shuttle comdr. STS 26, 1988; dir. Navy Space Systems (OP-943), Washington, 1989-90, ret., 1990; pres., CEO AXA Space (formerly Internat. Tech. Underwriters), Bethesda, Md., 1990-. Comml. space transp. adv. com. Dept. Transp., 1990-98, chmn. COMSTAC task group on Soviet entry into world space markets; mem. comml. programs adv. com. NASA, 1991-92, mission rev. group on spacecraft salvage and repair, 1992; mem. panel on space launch industry U.S. Congress Office Tech. Assessment, 1994-95; chmn. NASA External Ind. Readiness rev. group for Second Hubble space Telescope Servicing Mission, 1995-97; mem. Nat. Rsch. Coun. Aeronautics & Space Engring. Bd., 1996—, internat. space sta. meteoroid/debris risk mgmt. com., 1995-97, chair space shuttle meteoroid/debris risk mgmt. com., 1997—; chair bd. overseers Schs. Arts and Scis., Tufts U. Co-author: An Analysis of the Salvage/Repair Market for Commercial Communications Satellites, 1993; contbg. author: The Greatest Adventure, 1995. Trustee Tufts U.; bd. govs. St. Albans Sch., 1989-95. Decorated Def. D.S.M. (2), Def. Superior Svc. medal, Legion of Merit, DFC, Air medal (9), Navy Commendation Medal with Gold Star and Combat V, NASA D.S.M, NASA medal for Outstanding Leadership, NASA Space Flight medal (3), Presdl. Cost Saving Commendation; named to U.S. Astronaut Hall of Fame, 2001; recipient AIAA Haley Space Flight award, Disting. Svc. award, Tufts U. Alumni Assn., 2000. Fellow: AIAA, Soc. Exptl. Test Pilots; mem.: Nat. Assoc. Nat. Academies, Early and Pioneer Naval Aviators Assn., Am. Astron. Soc. (bd. govs. 1997—2000), Assn. Space Explorers (v.p. 1991—93, bd. govs. 2000), Winter Harbor Yacht Club (Maine). Office: AXA Space 4800 Montgomery Ln 11th Fl Bethesda MD 20814-3429 E-mail: hauck@axaspace.com.

HAUCK, MADELINE (AGNES HAUCK), special and adult basic education educator; b. Flushing, N.Y. d. Frances and Loretta (Bethel) DeCarmine; m. Walter Hauck; children: Walter, Frank, Laura. BS in Elem. Edn., U. Bridgeport, Conn., 1969; MA in Spl. Edn., Fairfield (Conn.) U., 1978. Cert. spl. and adult edn. tchr., Conn.; cert. substitute tchr., Conn. Tchr. spl. edn. Kennedy Ctr., Inc., Bridgeport, 1972-94. Tchr. adult basic edn. Bridgeport Bd. of Edn., 1972-94. Charter mem., v.p. Jr. Woman's Club, Fairfield, 1965; pres. Welcome Alumni Club, Fairfield, 1971; mem. Fairfield Woman's Club, 1976—, program chmn., 1987; dir.-at-large Fairfield Ch. housing for elderly, 1982—, nominating com., 1997, 98, decorating com., 1997, 98, 99, 2000. Recipient Recognition award Conn. State Fedn. of Coun. for Exceptional Children, 1992. Mem. Jaycees (Tchr. of Yr. 1979), Conn. Assn. Pub. Schs. Adult Educators. Roman Catholic. Avocations: gymnastics, theater, nutrition, swimming, book discussion. Home: 104 Roberton Xing Fairfield CT 06432-1162

HAUCK, MARGUERITE HALL, broadcasting executive; b. Bayside, N.Y., June 30, 1948; d. Carlyle Washington and Anzonette Marguerite (Asmussen) Hall; m. Harry Lennon, 1996. Student, Syracuse U., 1966-67; BA summa cum laude, Queens Coll., CUNY, 1974. Assoc. producer Animatic Prodns., Ltd., N.Y.C., 1968-72; mktg. analyst BBDO, Inc., N.Y.C., 1974-75, CBS, Inc., N.Y.C., 1975-76; dir. mktg. and research FM nat. sales, Radio div. CBS Radio, N.Y.C., 1976-85; dir. mktg. and research Christal Radio Sales div. Katz Communications, 1985-87; pres. Lennon Hall Antiques, Inc., 1986-94; v.p. research and mktg. Christal Radio Sales divsn., Katz Media, 1987-97; v.p., dir. sales mktg. KATZ Radio Group subs. of CLEAR Channel Media, N.Y.C., 1997—. Author: The 321 Billion Dollar Market, 1981, The Mid-Day Myth Exploded, 1982; columnist, TV-Radio Age mag., 1982, 89. Bd. dirs. Queens Coll. Student Services Corp., 1973-74. Recipient Queens Coll. Disting. Service award, 1974 Office: KATZ Radio Group 125 W 55th St New York NY 10019-5369

HAUCK, MICHAEL GEORG, real estate company executive; b. Frankfurt, Germany, Apr. 22, 1927; s. Alexander and Anne Marie (Oswalt) Hauck; m. Doraline Gräfin Grote, Dec. 28, 1970; children: Alix Puhl, Gregor H. Hon. chmn. Hauck & Aufhauser, Frankfurt, 1956-93. Bd. dirs. Michelin Reifenwerke, Karlsruhe, Germany. Contbr. articles to profl. jours. Bd. dirs. FDH Goethe Haus, Frankfurt, 1962-93, Frankfurt C. of C., 1965-89. With German Army, 1944-45. Recipient Bundesverdienstkreuz 1 Klasse, Pres. Germany, 1992, Pres. Frankfurt Stock Exch., 1986-89. Mem. Rotary. Office: MG Hauck GmbH & Co KG Lindenning 17 60431 Frankfurt Germany

HAUDA, WILLIAM EDWARD, II, emergency physician; b. Madison, Wis. BS in Zoology with honors, U. Wis., 1987, MD, 1992. Diplomate Am. Bd. Emergency Medicine, Am. Bd. Forensic Medicine; cert. forensic examiner. Intern in emergency medicine Johns Hopkins Hosp., Balt., 1992-93, resident in emergency medicine, 1993-95; fellow in ped. emergency medicine Inova Fairfax Hosp., Falls Church, Va., 1995-97; emergency physician Emergency Physicians No. Va., Falls Church, 1995—; operational med. dir. Fairfax County Police Dept., 2000—; dir., instr. pediat. advanced life support course Inova Fairfax Hosp., 1997—. Med. examiner Va. Commonwealth Dept. Health, 1996—. Contbr. chpts. to books. Mem. AMA, Am. Coll. Emergency Medicine, Am. Coll. Forensic Examiners, Nat. Assn. EMS Physicians, Va. Homicide Investigators Assn., Soc. Acad. Emergency Medicine. Office: Inova Fairfax Hosp Dept Emergency Medicine 3300 Gallows Rd Falls Church VA 22042-3300

HAUDENSCHILD, CHRISTIAN CHARLES, pathologist, educator; b. St. Gallen, Switzerland, May 3, 1939; arrived in U.S., 1972; s. Charles Haudenschild. MD, U. Basel, 1968. Diplomate Am. Bd. Pathology. Rsch. fellow, assoc. F. Hoffman-LaRoche Exptl. Medicine, Basel, Switzerland, 1968-72; rsch. assoc. Children's Hosp. Med. Ctr., Boston, 1973-74; rsch. assoc. in surgery and pathology Harvard U. Med. Sch., Boston, 1974-76, clin. instr. pathology, 1976-80; resident in pathology Boston City Hosp., 1974-76; from asst. prof. to assoc. prof. Boston U. Sch. Medicine, 1976—82, prof., 1982-92; assoc. pathologist Mallory Inst. Pathology, Boston, 1977-92; assoc. vis. physician Boston City Hosp., 1977-92; rsch. prof. pathology George Washington U. Sch. Medicine, Washington, 1992-95, prof. pathology and medicine, 1996—. Cons. Boston VA Hosp., 1978—92; asst. vis. pathologist Univ. Hosp., Boston, 1986—92; hon. cons. prof. U. Studi, Siena, Italy, 1985; adj. prof. Boston U. Sch. Medicine, 1992—, Georgetown U., Washington, 1992—95; disting. vis. scientist Armed Forces Inst. Pathology, Washington, 1992—; disting. vis. prof. U. Utrecth, Netherlands, 1993—; head exptl. pathology dept. Holland Lab. ARC, Rockville, Md., 1992—. Contbr. articles to profl. jours., chapters to books. Grantee Rsch., HEW, NIH, Nat. Heart, Lung and Blood Inst., Am. Heart Assn., 1978—. Mem.: AMA, Wash. Acad. Medicine, Internat. Acad. Pathology, Am. Assn. Pathologists, Am. Soc. Cell Biology, Swiss Med. Soc., Am. Heart Assn. (fellow coun. arteriosclerosis). Achievements include patents in field. Office: Holland Lab ARC 15601 Crabbs Branch Way Rockville MD 20855-2736 E-mail: haudenschilde@usa.redcross.org.

HAUER, JAMES ALBERT, lawyer; b. Fond du Lac, Wis., Apr. 3, 1924; s. Albert A. and Hazel M. (Corcoran) H.; children: Stephen, John, Paul, Christopher, Patrick. BCE, Marquette U., 1948, LLB, 1949; bank mgmt. cert., Columbia U., 1957, U. Wis., 1959. Bar: Wis., U.S. Dist. Ct. (ea. dist.), U.S. Ct. Appeals (9th cir.), U.S. Dist. Ct. (fed. dist.) 1958. Patent counsel Ira Milton Jones, Milw., 1949; chief counsel Wauwatosa Realty, Milw., 1950-57; v.p. Wauwatosa (Wis.) State Bank, 1957-67; pres. Milw. We. Bank, 1967-69, Prem Constrn. Co., Milw., 1969-73; pvt. practice Elm Grove, Wis., 1973-86, Sun City, Ariz., 1986—. Pres., bd. dirs. Sunshine Svc., Sun City, Meals on Wheels, Sun City. With USMCR, 1942-45. Mem. Wis. Bar Assn., Ariz. Patent Law Assn. (charter). Office: 9915 W Royal Oak Rd #1098 Sun City AZ 85351-3161

HAUF, JOHN GEORGE, real estate broker; b. N.Y.C., July 19, 1939; s. George John and Rose Cecelia Hauf; children: Jason, Susan. BSBA, Fordham U., 1961; MBA in Econs., NYU, 1966. Cert. real estate broker, appraiser. Mktg. assoc. SCM Corp., N.Y.C., 1964—66; rsch. assoc. Daniel Yankelovich, Inc., Phila., 1966—69; mktg. dir. Dun & Bradstreet, Inc., N.Y.C., 1969—77, Rural Transport, New Brunswick, NY, 1977—80; real estate broker Edward S. Gordon Co., N.Y.C., 1980—85, Richar Ellis & Co., N.Y.C., 1985—91, Coldwell Banker, Washington Cross, Pa., 1991—. Mem. com. Real Estate Bd. of Bucks County, Doylestown, Pa., 1995—; mem. hwy. com. Upper Makefield Twp., Washington Crossing, 2000—; pres. Upper Makefield Hist. Soc., Washington Crossing; mem. trail com. Upper Makefield Twp., Washington Crossing, 2001—; mem. Friends of Delaware Canal, New Hope, Pa., 1997—. Mem.: Upper Makefield Businessman's Assn., Phi Theta Kappa. Avocations: historical preservation activities, sailing, painting, skiing, reading. Home: PO Box 63 Washington Crossing PA 18977 Office: Coldwell Banker 1118 General Washington Blvd Washington Crossing PA 18977

HAUFE, BONNIE CAMPBELL, foundation affiliate; b. S.I., N.Y., Aug. 18, 1961; d. Ernest Paul and Catherine (Gilman) H. BA in Bus. Mgmt., Mary Baldwin Coll., 1984. Asst. in hospitality svcs. Colonial Williamsburg (Va.) Found., Inc., 1988—. Entrepreneur BC Haufe Enterprises, Williamsburg, 2002—. Mem. Williamsburg Cmty. Chapel Bible Study., Citizens Against Govt. Waste. Jesse Ball Dupont scholar, 1982; named ABI Woman of Yr., 1993. Mem. Meml. Soc. Tidewater (bd. dirs. 1996-99), World Future Soc. (readers panel), Environ. Def. Fund. Avocations: environmental issues, creative writing. Home: PO Box 1826 Williamsburg VA 23187-1826

HAUFT, AMY GILBERT, artist; b. Cin., Apr. 9, 1957; d. Neil Edward and Eleanor (Snyder) H. BFA, U. Calif., Santa Cruz, 1980; postgrad., Skowhegan Sch. Painting, Maine, 1981; MFA, Art Inst. Chgo., 1983. Prof. Tyler Sch. Art, Phila., 1989—; vis. lectr. Princeton (N.J.) U., 1989; mem. vis. faculty Calif. Inst. Arts, Valencia, 1988. One-Woman shows include P.S.I. Mus., L.I., 1987, New Mus., N.Y.C., 1989, Contemporary Arts Forum, Santa Barbara, Calif., 1990, Ctr. for Arts Wesleyan U., Middletown, Conn., 1990, Berland/Hall Gallery, N.Y.C., 1991, Andrea Rosen Gallery, N.Y.C., 1993, Quint/Krichman Gallery, San Diego, 1993, Pub. Art Fund, N.Y.C., 1993-94, Lipton Owens Co., N.Y.C., 1994, Galeria Wschodnia, Lodz, Poland, 1997, Derek Eller Gallery, N.Y.C., 1998, Beaver Coll. Art Gallery, Phila., 1998, Am. Acad. Rome, 1999, Cooper Union, N.Y.C., 1999, Art Container Project, N.Y.C., 2001; exhibited in group shows at Mus. Contemporary Art, Chgo., 1987, ArtPark, Lewiston, N.Y., 1988, Bklyn. Mus., 1990, Internat. Artists Mus., Lodz, Poland, 1993, John Michael Kohler Arts Ctr., Sheboygan, Wis., 1995, Neuberger Mus., SUNY Purchase, 1995, Katonah (N.Y.) Mus., 1996, Gallery Joe, Phila., 2001. Grantee Flintridge Found., 1989, Artmatters, Inc., 1989, 88, ArtPark, 1988, N.Y. State Coun. Arts, 1987, Pub. Art Fund, 1993; Civitella Ranieri Found. fellow, 1995, N.Y. Found. fellow, 1995-96, Howard Found. fellow, 1995-96, Artslink grantee, 1997, Phila. Exhbns. Initiative, Pew Charitable Trust, 1998, Saint-Gaudens Meml. fellow, 1998-99, N.Y. Found. fellow, 2000-01. Studio: 1155 Manhattan Ave Brooklyn NY 11222-6102

HAUG, EDWARD JOSEPH, JR., retired mechanical engineering educator, simulation research engineer; b. Bonne Terre, Mo., Sept. 15, 1940; s. Edward Joseph and Thelma (Harrison) H.; m. Carol Jean Todd, July 1, 1979; 1 child, Kirk Anthony. BSME, U. Mo., Rolla, 1962; MS in Applied Mechanics, Kans. State U., 1964, PhD in Applied Mechanics, 1966. Rsch. engr. Army Armaments Command, Rock Island, Ill., 1969; chief sys. analysis Army Weapons Command, Rock Island, Ill., 1970, chief sys. rsch., 1971-72, chief concepts and tech., 1973-76; prof. U. Iowa, Iowa City, 1976—2003, Carver Disting. prof., 1990—2003, dir. Ctr. for Computer Aided Design, 1983-95; dir. Nat. Advanced Driving Simulator and Simulation Ctr., 1992-98. Author 9 books on computer aided design and dynamics; editor 5 books; contbr. numerous papers to profl. jours. Capt. U.S. Army, 1966-68. Recipient Innovative Info. Tech. award Computerworld/Smithsonian Instn., 1989, Colwell Merit award Soc. Automotive Engrs., 1989. Fellow ASME (Design Automation award 1991, Machine Design award 1992), Am. Acad. Mechanics. Achievements include patents for Constant Recoil Automatic Cannon, and for Real-Time Simulation System. Home: 2440 County Rd 500 Bayfield CO 81122-8729 E-mail: haug@nads-sc.uiowa.edu.

HAUGAARD, NIELS, pharmacologist, educator; b. Copenhagen, Feb. 25, 1920; came to U.S., 1940, naturalized, 1952; s. Gotfred C. and Karen L. (Pedersen) H.; m. Ella Elizabeth Shwartzman, June 22, 1947 (dec. Feb. 1980); children: David Gregory, Lisa Karen; m. Dorothy Tosi, 1983; children: Gregory, Kimberly, Pamela. Student, U. Copenhagen, 1938-40; AB with honors, Swarthmore Coll., 1942; PhD in Biochemistry, U. Pa., 1949. Instr. U. Pa., Phila., 1949-52, asst. prof. rsch. medicine, 1952-54, asst. prof. pharmacology, 1954-60, assoc. prof., 1960-65, prof., 1965-87, emeritus prof., 1987—, mem. Med. Coun., 1972-75, chmn. Grievance Commn., 1986; mem. cardiovascular scis. study sect. NIH, 1978-82. Sect. editor Chem. Abstracts, 1960-65; mem. editl. bd. Circulation Rsch., 1964-69, Molecular and Cellular Biochemistry, 1986-96; contbr. articles to profl. jours. Mem. Bristol Twp. (Pa.) Sch. Bd., 1957-60. Guggenheim Found. fellow, 1952; Commonwealth Found. fellow, 1965 Mem. ACLU, Am. Soc. Biol. Chemists, Am. Soc. Pharmacology and Exptl. Therapeutics (editorial bd. jour. 1965-68). Achievements include rsch. on mechanism of hormone action, oxygen toxicity, mitochondrial metabolism, bladder function and metabolism, role of lipoic acid in acetyl choline formation. Office: Urology Rsch Lab Hosp Univ Pa Ravdin Courtyard Bldg Philadelphia PA 19104

HAUGAN, GERTRUDE M. clinical psychologist; b. New Richland, Minn. d. Henry Albert and Ella Pauline (Gardson) H. BA, George Washington U., 1952, MA, 1956; PhD, U. Md., 1970. Lic. psychologist, D.C., Md. Research psychologist New Eng. Med. Ctr., Boston, 1959-62; intern clin. psychology Hall Psychiat. Inst., Columbia, S.C., 1968-69; fellow in pediatrics Sch. Medicine Johns Hopkins U., Balt., 1970-71; clin. psychologist adloescent program Devel. Services Ctr., Washington, 1971-72, chief children's unit, 1972-85; chief Devel Services Ctr., Washington, 1986-94. Cons. in psychology Ea. Shore State Hosp., Cambridge, Md., 1969-71, in child psychology Ctr. for Spl. Edn., Annapolis, Md., 1972-76; instr. in child psychology Montgomery Coll., Rockville, Md., 1977-78. Contbr. articles to profl. jours. Mem. profl. adv. council Easter Seal Soc. for Disabled Children and Adults, Washinton, 1987. Mem. APA, D.C. Psychol. Assn., Am. Assn. on Mental Retardation, Phi Beta Kappa. Home: 4720 S Chelsea Ln Bethesda MD 20814-3720

HAUGEN, DAVID LEE, surgeon; b. Portland, Oreg., Dec. 14, 1935; MD, U. Oreg./Health Scis. U., 1962. Diplomate Am. Bd. Surgery. Intern Santa Clara County Hosp., San Jose, Calif., 1962-63; resident U. Oreg. Hosp. - Clinics, 1965-70, Karolinska Hosp., Stockholm, 1968-69; staff Sutter Roseville Comm. Hosp., Calif., 1970—; sr. staff Mercy San Juan Hosp., Carmichael, Calif., 1970—; courtesy staff Sutter Hosp., 1970—. Mem. Am. Coll. Surgeons, Calif. Med. Assn. Office: Ste # 275 Two Medical Plaza Dr Roseville CA 95661

HAUGEN, MARGARET ELLEN, daycare administrator; b. Butte, Mont., June 14, 1948; d. W. Stewart and Margaret Anne (Murphy) Zeigler; children: Cherie Anne, Alek Hemmel Spach. Student, Scranton Coll., 1983—84. Dental asst. Dr.Stephen Jones, Butte, 1967—69; religious edn. tchr. St. Patrick's Ch., Butte, 1963—70; daycare provider, 1970—. Vol. tutor Lit. Program, Butte. Named to Wall of Tolerance, Nat. Campaign for Tolerance, 2002. Home: 608 Welcome Way #2 Darby MT 59829

HAUGEN, TROY MARLIN, music educator; b. Hawley, Minn., Feb. 9, 1974; s. Marlin and Carol Haugen. BA in Music Edn., Concordia Coll., 1996; student, Minn. State U., 2000—. Band dir. Waubun-Ogema-White Earth Cmty. Schs., Waubun, Minn., 1996—98, Frazee H.S., Frazee, Minn., 1998—2002, dean of students, 2000—. Mem.: Minn.. Assoc. Sec. Sch. Prins., Nat. Assoc. Sec. Sch. Prins., Minn. Music Educators Assn. Office: Frazee Vergas Public Schools Highway 87 Frazee MN 56544 Office Fax: 218-334-4696. E-mail: thaugen@frazee.k12.mn.us.

HAUGH, CLARENCE GENE, agricultural engineering educator; b. Spring Mills, Pa., Oct. 11, 1936; s. Clarence Glenn and Estella Jane (Baney) H.; m. Patricia Anne Breon, June 16, 1962; children: Amy Elizabeth Dodds, Jennifer Lea Ulsh, Mitchell Breon. BS in Agrl. Engring., Pa. State U., 1958; MS in Agrl. Engring., U. Ill., 1959; PhD, Purdue U., 1964. Registered profl. engr., Fla. Asst. prof. U. Fla., Gainesville, 1964-65, Purdue U., Lafayette, Ind., 1965-68, assoc. prof., 1968-72, prof., 1972-79, Va. Poly. Inst. & State U., Blacksburg, 1979—, dept. head, 1979-86, ret., prof. emeritus. Mem. Nat. Engring. Accreditation Commn., 1985-90; trustee Chippokes Plantation, Surry, Va., 1980-91; cons. King Faisall U., Hofhuf, Saudi Arabia, 1984-86. Patentee in field; contbr. over 50 articles to profl. jours. Asst. scoutmaster Boy Scouts Am., Blacksburg, 1985-91; deacon, elder, trustee Covenant Presbyn. Ch., Lafayette, 1968-76; adminstrv. bd. Blacksburg Meth. Ch., 1979-82. Served as 1st lt. USAF, 1958-64. Fellow Am. Soc. Agrl. Engrs. (bd. dirs. 1989-91, chmn. 12 tech. coms., Young Rschr. award 1976); mem. Am. Soc. Engring. Edn. (chmn. agrl. engring. sect. 1982-83), Inst. Food Technologists, Soc. Rheology, Internat. Soc. Agromaterials Sci. and Engring. (sci. bd. 1992—), Arnold Air Soc., Rotary, Masons, Shriners, Sigma Xi, Tau Beta Pi, Alpha Epsilon, Gamma Sigma Delta, Phi Tau Sigma, Alpha Zeta, Phi Beta Delta. Lodges: Rotary, Masons, Shriners. Republican. Methodist. Avocations: sailing, backpacking, collecting antiques. Home: 406 Murphy St Blacksburg VA 24060-2539 Office: Va Poly Inst & State U Dept Biol Sys Engring 314 Seitz Hall Blacksburg VA 24061 E-mail: haugh@vt.edu.

HAUGH, DAN ANTHONY, mechanical engineer; b. Lawrence, Kans., Feb. 16, 1953; s. Oscar Martin and Rita (Rosso) H.; m. Jay McLaughlin, Mar. 19, 1983; children: Alden Elizabeth, Emily Marston. BSME, U. Kans., 1978. Engr. R & D Boeing, Wichita, Kans., 1978-80, specialist engr. propulsion dept., 1980-83; midwest engring. mgr. PSI Bearings, Inc., Wichita, Kans., 1983-85; midwest sales mgr. Jamaica Bearings Co., Inc., Lawrence, 1983-91, dir. engring. New Hyde Pk., NY, 1991—2003. Bd. dirs. Aeros, Inc., Lawrence, 1986—. Bd. dirs. West Hills Home Assn., Lawrence, 1989-94. Mem. ASME, Internat. Gas Turbine Inst., Profl. Aviation Maintenance Assn., Robot Inst. Am., Sch. Engring. Soc., U. Kans. Alumni Assn., Exptl. Aircraft Assn., B-17 Hist. Soc. Home: 1512 University Dr Lawrence KS 66044-3148

HAUGH, LARRY DOUGLAS, statistics educator; b. Gary, Ind., June 11, 1944; s. William Edward and Mary Patricia (McFarland) H.; m. Jane Anne Booher, Aug. 21, 1966; children: Wendi Allyn, Joshua Douglas, Jeremy Alan. BA summa cum laude, Wabash Coll., 1966; MA in Math., U. Wis., 1967, MS in Stats., 1970, PhD in Stats., 1972. Asst. prof. stats. U. Fla., Gainesville, 1972-75; faculty assoc. IBM, Burlington, Vt., 1978-81; statistician Shell Research, Amsterdam, The Netherlands, 1981-82; prof. U. Vt., Burlington, 1975—; dir. statistics program, 1990—. Lectr. in field, 1981—, U. Tenn., 1985-92; cons. in field. Assoc. editor Technometrics, 1981—86; co-editor: book; mem. editl. bd. Quality Progress, 1992—; contbr. over 170 articles, procs. and abstracts to profl. jour., chapters to books; assoc. editor Jour. Am. Statistics Assn., 1996—2001; editor: Quality Engring., 1996—. Recipient several rsch. grants including NIH, Nat. Inst. Occupl. Safety & Health, Nat. Inst. Disability & Rehab. Rsch., Fulbright-Hays, 1970-71; O'Donoghue Sports Injury award Am. Ortho. Soc. for Sports Medicine, 1999; fellow Woodrow Wilson, 1966, NDEA, 1969-70; NSF trainee, 1966-67. Mem. Am. Statis. Assn. (chair com. on presentation awards 1980-81, chair quality and productivity sect. 1993, Presentation award 1977), Am. Soc. for Quality (sr.), Internat. Biometric Soc., Internat. Statis. Inst., Royal Statis. Soc. (chartered statistician). Office: U Vt 16 Colchester Ave Burlington VT 05401-1455 E-mail: haugh@emba.uvm.edu.

HAUGHEY, JAMES MCCREA, lawyer, artist; b. Courtland, Kans., July 8, 1914; s. Leo Eugene and Elizabeth (Stephens) H.; m. Katherine Hurd, Sept. 8, 1938; children: Katherine (Mrs. Lester B. Loo), Bruce Stephens, John Caldwell. Student, Deep Springs Coll., 1930-31; LLB, U. Kans., 1939. Bar: Kans. 1939, Mont. 1943. Landman Carter Oil Co., 1939-43; practice in Billings, Mont., 1943-98; ptnr. Crowley, Haughey, Hanson, Toole & Dietrich, 1950-86, counsel, 1986-98; ret. dir. Mont.-Dakota Resources Group Inc., 1998. One-man shows include, U. Kans., U. Mont., Mont. State U., Concordia Coll., Nebr., C.M. Russell Mus., Great Falls, Mont., Boise Mus. Art, Mont. State Mus., Helena, Sandzen Gallery, Bethany Coll., Lindsborg, Kans., Yellowstone Art Mus., Billings, Mont., also numerous group shows. Pres. Rocky Mountain Mineral Law Found., 1957-58, trustee, 1955— ; pres. Mont. Inst. Arts Found., 1965-67; pres. Yellowstone Art Center Found., 1969-71, trustee, 1964-81; mem. Mont. Ho. of Reps., 1960-64, Mont. Senate, 1966-70, senate minority leader, 1969-70. Recipient Gov.'s award for Arts, 1981 Fellow Mont. Inst. Arts (Permanent Collection award 1960), Am. Artists Profl. League; mem. ABA, Am. Coll. Real Estate Lawyers, Yellowstone County Bar Assn. (pres. 1960-61), U. Kans. Law Soc. (bd. govs. 1989-92), Am. Watercolor Soc. (Midwest v.p. 1978-82), N.W. Watercolor Soc. (life), Midwest Watercolor Soc., Kans. Watercolor Soc. (hon.), Mont. Watercolor Soc. (hon.), Phi Delta Theta, Phi Delta Phi. Republican. Episcopalian. Home: 2351 Solomon Ave Apt 276 Billings MT 59102-2889 Office: Crowley Haughey Hanson Toole & Dietrich TransWestern Pla II 490 N 31st St Billings MT 59101-1256 E-mail: jhaughey@crowleylaw.com, jimhoy4@attbi.com.

HAUGHT, JACK GREGG, lawyer; b. Indpls., Dec. 18, 1958; s. Jack Laidley and Marilyn Louise (Richardson) H.; m. Sarah Edith Lynn, Sept. 28, 1991; children: Elizabeth, Jack. AB, Ind. U., 1980; JD, U. Mich., 1983. Bar: Ohio 1983, D.C. 1986, U.S. Dist. Ct. (so. dist.) Ohio 1984, U.S. Ct. Appeals (6th cir.) 1983. Assoc. Topper, Alloway, Goodman, DeLeone & Duffey, Columbus, Ohio, 1983-85, Benesch, Friedlander, Coplan & Aronoff, Columbus, 1986-89, ptnr., 1993—; assoc. Dickstein, Shapiro & Morin, Washington, 1989-90; dep. atty. gen. Atty. Gen. Office, Columbus, Ohio, 1991-93. Contbg. editor The Developing Labor Law, 2d edit., 1987. Sr. advisor to Ohio campaign Clinton/Gore 1992 Campaign, Columbus, 1992; polit. dir. Ohio primary election Dukakis for Pres., Boston, 1988; chair Ohio Elections Commn., Columbus, 1993-94; mem. Presdl. Rank Rev. Bd., Washington, 1993; del. Dem. Nat. Conv., Atlanta, 1988, N.Y. 1980. Democrat. Office: Benesch Friedlander Coplan & Aronoff 88 E Broad St Ste 900 Columbus OH 43215-3553 Home: 2436 Bexley Park Rd Columbus OH 43209-2120 Fax: 614-223-9330. E-mail: jghaught@bfca.com.

HAUGHT, JAMES ALBERT, JR., journalist, newspaper editor, author; b. Reader, W.Va., Feb. 20, 1932; s. James Albert and Beulah (Fish) H.; m. Nancy Carolyn Brady, Apr. 22, 1958; children: Joel, Jacob, Jeb, Cassie. Student, Morris Harvey Coll., 1950-52; part-time, W.Va. State Coll., 1960-63. Apprentice printer Charleston Daily Mail, 1951-53; reporter Charleston Gazette, 1953—, varied positions as night and weekend city editor, music and film critic, govt., schs., suburban, religion and investigative reporter, 1970-82, assoc. editor, 1983-92, editor, 1992—. Author: Holy Horrors, 1990, Science in a Nanosecond, 1990, The Art of Lovemaking, 1992, Holy Hatred, 1994, 2000 Years of Disbelief, 1996; sr. editor (part-time): Free Inquiry mag., 1996—. Recipient award Headliners Club, 1971, 1st Ann. Consumer Writing prize Nat. Press Club, 1973, Nat. Hwy. Safety Writing award Uniroyal Tire Co., 1975, First Amendment award Sigma Delta Chi, 1977, Merit award ABA, 1977, Consumer Writing prize Nat. Press Club, 1979, 83, Spl. award Religion Newswriters Assn., 1980, Health Journalism award Am. Chiropractic Assn., 1981, 83, First Amendment award People for Am. Way, 1986, Nat. award for edn. reporting Edn. Writers Assn., 1989, Hugh M. Hefner First Amendment award Playboy Found., 1989, Benjamin Fine award for edn. reporting Nat. Assn. Secondary Sch. Prins., 1990, Clarion award Women in Comms., 2000, 02, Nat. Headliners award, 2001, Green Eyeshade award, 2003. Democrat. Unitarian Universalist. Home: 15 Killen Hollow Dr Cross Lanes WV 25313-3513 Office: Charleston Gazette 1001 Virginia St E Charleston WV 25301-2895 E-mail: haught@wvinter.net., haught@wvgazette.com.

HAUGHT, SHARON KAY, lawyer; b. East Chicago, Ind., Jan. 31, 1959; d. Edwin Frank and Shirlee Mae Lebryk; m. Jeffrey Paul Haught, Aug. 17, 1991; children: Don Roger, Stephanie Marie. BS, Ball State U., 1981; JD, U. Dayton, 1984. Bar: Ohio 1984. Assoc. atty. Bank One Dayton (Ohio) NA, 1983-85; assoc. counsel Rubbermaid Inc., Wooster, Ohio, 1985-2000. Sec. St. Mary of the Immaculate Conception Sch.-Sch. Support Orgn., 2001-02; den leader Boy Scouts Am., 1999-2003, cubmaster, 2001-02, asst. cubmaster, 2002-03; girl scout leader Girl Scouts USA, 2001-03. Mem. ABA, Ohio Bar Assn. Republican. Roman Catholic. Avocations: music, art, photography, writing, computers. Home: 1589 Brentwood Dr Wooster OH 44691

HAUGHT, WILLIAM DIXON, lawyer, writer; b. Kansas City, Kans., June 12, 1939; s. Walter Dixon and Florence Louise (Rhoads) H.; m. Julia Jane Headstream, July 22, 1967; 1 dau., Stephanie Jane. BS, U. Kans., 1961; LL.B., U. Kans., 1964; LL.M., Georgetown U., 1968. Bar: Kans. 1964, Ark. 1971. Assoc. Stanley, Schroeder, Weeks, Thomas & Lysaught, Kansas City, Kans., 1968-70; ptnr. Wright, Lindsey & Jennings, Little Rock, 1970-91; pvt. practice Little Rock, 1991-95; ptnr. Haught & Wade, 1996—. Author: Arkansas Probate System, 1977, 6th ed. 1999, (with others) Probate and Estate Administration: The Law in Arkansas, 1983. Served to capt. USAR, 1964-68, Korea, Washington. Mem. ABA (coun. chmn. coms.), Am. Coll. Trust and Estate Counsel (regent, editor studies program, chmn. editl. bd., state chair), Internat. Acad. Estate and Trust Law, Am. Law Inst., Am. Counsel Assn., Ark. Bar Assn. (chmn. probate law sect., chmn. econs. of law practice com., chmn. agrl. law com., chmn. juris law reform com.), Ctrl. Ark. Estate Coun., Pulaski County Bar Assn., Ark. Bar Found., Country Club of Little Rock. Presbyterian. Office: Haught & Wade 111 Center St Ste 1320 Little Rock AR 72201-4405 E-mail: wdh@haughtwade.com.

HAUGHTON, VICTOR MELLET, physician, educator; b. Willimantic, Conn., July 7, 1939; s. Victor Mellet Haughton Jr. and Marian Branch; m. Kirsti Helen Staib, Feb. 3, 1940; children: Signe haughton, Karianne Spoo, Paul Victor. MD, Yale U., 1967. Diplomate Am. Bd. Radiology. Intern New Eng. Med. Ctr., Boston, 1967-68; resident Peter Bent Brigham Hosp., Boston, 1970-74; prof. radiology Med. Coll. of Wis., Milw., 1980-98, U. Wis., Madison, 1998—. Cons. pharm. cos. and med. device mfgs. Author: Cranial Computed Tomography: A Comprehensive Text, 1985, Cranial and Spinal Magnetic Resonance Imaging, 1987, Computed Tomography, 1984, others; inventor catheter placement system providing retraction of the sharp upon disengagement of the catheter from the handle; patentee in field; contbr. chpts. to books and articles to profl. jours. Lt. comdr. USPHS, 1968-70. Grantee NIH, 1984. Mem. Am. Soc. Neuroradiology (treas. 1999-2001, v.p. 2002—), Radiol. Soc. N.Am. Office: U Wis Hosps 600 Highland Ave Madison WI 53792

HAUGLAND, JERRY LEE, accounting educator; b. Sutherland, Nebr., Aug. 26, 1941; s. Jacob Reinertsen and Louise Anna (Burklund) H.; m. Susan Warrell, July 24, 1982; children: Charles, Michael. BSBA, U. Nebr., 1962, MA, 1966; PhD, Okla. State U., 1975. Cert. mgmt. acct. Instr. S.E. Mo. State U., Cape Girardeau, 1966-73, asst. prof., 1973-75, assoc. prof., 1975-79, prof., 1979—, coord. MBA program, 1976-86. Bd. dirs. Haugland Ranch Inc., Sutherland, 1984—; acctg. program cons. Northeastern State U., Tahlequah, Okla., 1989. Book reviewer Scott, Foresman and Co., 1993, Prentice Hall, 1993, John Wiley and Co., 1993, South-Western, 1995, Richard D. Irwin, 1997; contbr. articles to profl. jours. Treas. Optimist Club, Cape Girardeau, 1975, 76. Recipient Outstanding Svc. award Alpha Kappa Psi, 1978, Outstanding Svc. award Beta Gamma Sigma, 1997. Mem. Am. Acctg. Assn. (state chairperson 1977, membership com. 1981), Mo. Assn. Acctg. Edn. (bd. dirs. 1976-78, v.p. 1979, pres. 1980), Beta Alpha Psi. Office: SE Mo State Univ One University Pla Cape Girardeau MO 63701

HAUGLAND, SUSAN WARRELL, education educator, consultant; b. Portland, Oreg., Aug. 29, 1950; d. George William and Commery Wallace (Coleman) Warrell; children from previous marriage: Charles, Michael. BS in Child Devel., Oreg. State U., 1972; PhD in Psychology, Saybrook Inst., 1976. Cert. family and consumer scis. Dir., head tchr. Lafayette Co-op Nursery Sch., Detroit, 1973-75; handicapped svcs. coord. OutWayne County Head Start, Wayne, Mich., 1975-76; asst. prof. child devel. Va. Poly. Inst. and State U., Blacksburg, 1976-79; prof. emeritus child devel. S.E. Mo. State U., Cape Girardeau, 1979-99, prof. emeritus, 1999—; pres. K.I.D.S. & Computers, Inc., Cape Girardeau, 1999—; prof. early childhood edn. The Met. State Coll. of Denver, 2000—. Dir. Ctr. for Child Studies, Cape Girardeau, 1979-99, Kids Interacting with Devel. Software, Cape Girardeau, 1985—; chair Human-Environ. Studies, Cape Girardeau, 1990-93; judge Developmental Software Awards, 1991—, Child Mag. Awards, 1992-99. Author: Helping Young Children Grow, 1980, Developmental Evaluations of Software for Young Children, 1990, Young Children and Technology: A World of Discovery, 1997, Haugland Developmental Software Scale, 1997, Haugland/Gertzog Developmental Scale for Web Sites, 1998; dept. editor Early Childhood Education Jour., 1992—; contbr. numerous articles to profl. jours. Grantee numerous orgns.; recipient Gov.'s award for Teaching Excellence, 1996. Mem. Assn. for Childhood Edn. Internat., Nat. Assn. for Edn. Young Children, Nat. Assn. for Early Childhood Tchr. Educators, Tech. and Young Children Caucus, Omicron Nu. Democrat. Methodist. Avocations: reading, travel, cooking, bicycling. E-mail: susanhaugland@hotmail.com.

HAUHART, ROBERT CHARLES, lawyer, educator; b. St. Louis, Dec. 17, 1950; s. Shields and Naomi (Allen) H. BS, So. Ill. U., 1972; MA, Washington U., St. Louis, 1973; JD, U. Balt., 1981; PhD, U. Va., 1982. Bar: Md. 1982, Pa. 1984, U.S. Dist. Ct. (mid. dist.) Pa. 1984, U.S. Ct. Appeals (3d cir.) 1984, U.S. Dist. Ct. (no. dist.) N.Y. 1987, U.S. Ct. Appeals (2d cir.) 1987, N.Y. 1988, D.C. 1989, U.S. Dist. Ct. D.C. 1989, U.S. Ct. Appeals (4th and D.C. cirs.) 1989. Sole practice, Balt., 1982-84; assoc. Rieders, Travis Law Firm, Williamsport, Pa., 1985-86; atty. Lewisburg (Pa.) Prison Project, 1984-86, Prisoners Legal Services N.Y., 1986-88, D.C. Pub. Defender Service, 1988—2001. Adj. prof. SUNY, Plattsburgh, 1987-88, George Washington U., Washington, 1992; vis. assoc. prof. Towson (Md.) State U., 1980-84; vis. prof. U. Maine, 2002—, U. N.Mex., 2003—. Author: Paralegal Manual for Prisoner Advocacy, 1985, Prisoners' Civil Actions in Federal Court, 1986, Due Process Administration Reviews, 1986, Rule 37 F.R.C.P. Motions to Compel, 1987. Mem. ABA, Am. Sociol. Assn., Balt. City Bar Assn. (dir. speaker's bur. 1982-83). Home: 25 Placitas Trails Rd Placitas NM 87043 Office: U NMex Social Sci Bldg Rm 1103 Albuquerque NM 87131-1166 Home and Office: 1111 Pigeon Hill Rd Steuben ME 04680 Business E-Mail: vze2dtmm@verizon.net.

HAULE, JAMES MARK, literature educator; b. Detroit, Mich., Nov. 26, 1945; s. Robert Paul and Eileen Monica Haule; m. Margaret Ann Cyzeska, Nov. 29, 1968; children: Patricia Eileen Jones, Katherine Colette Graham. PhD, Wayne State U., Detroit, 1974. Prof. English U. Tex. - Pan Am., Edinburg, Tex.,

1978—. Co-editor (criticism) Virginia Woolf: Editing & Interpreting the Modernist Text; editor: (edition) The Shakespeare Head Press Edition of Virginia Woolf's THE WAVES. Office: Univ Tex - Pan Am 1201 W University Dr Edinburg TX 78539-2999

HAUMSCHILD, MARK JAMES, pharmacist; b. West Bend, Wis., Apr. 6, 1951; s. James Harlow and Helen Marie (Bohn) H.; m. Mary Jo Snider, Oct. 15, 1976; 1 child, Ryan James. BA in Chemistry, Fla. Atlantic U., 1973; BS in Pharmacy, U. Fla., 1976; MS in Mgmt., U. South Fla., 1982; PharmD, Mercer U., 1984. Cert. nuc. pharmacist; cert. nutritional support pharmacist; cert. geriatric pharmacist. Continuing edn. instr. St. Petersburg (Fla.) Jr. Coll., 1977-81; staff pharmacist Morton F. Plant Hosp., Clearwater, Fla., 1976-78, nuclear pharmacy coordinator, 1978-83, clin. pharmacist, 1984-86, resident, 1984-85; ctr. mgr. Foster Infusioncare, St. Petersburg, 1986-88; gen. mgr. Healthinfusion Inc., St. Petersburg, 1988-95; pres. Pharm D. Cons., Largo, Fla., 1984—; regional dir. ops.-Fla. UPC Health Network, Clearwater, Fla., 1995-98; scientific mgr. Aventis, Inc., Largo, 1998—. Adj. instr. Coll. Pharmacy, U. Fla., Gainesville, 1980-86. Fellow Am. Soc. Cons. Pharmacists; mem. Am. Soc. Hosp. Pharmacists, S.W. Soc. Hosp. Pharmacists, Am. Pharm. Assn. (cert. in nuclear pharmacy), Soc. Nuclear Pharmacy, Am. Coll. Hosp. Adminstrs., S.W. Fla. Soc. Hosp. Pharmacists (cert. nuclear pharmacist), Beta Gamma Sigma, Phi Kappa Phi. Republican. Avocations: golf, walking, reading, snowboarding. Home: 12494 104th Ter Largo FL 33778-3407 Office: Aventis Inc 12494 104th Terrace N Largo FL 33778-3407

HAUN, JOHN DANIEL, petroleum geologist, educator; b. Old Hickory, Tenn., Mar. 7, 1921; s. Charles C. and Lydia (Rhodes) H.; m. Lois Culbertson, June 30, 1942. AB, Berea Coll., 1948; MA, U. Wyo., 1949, PhD, 1953. Registered profl. engr., Colo. Geologist Stanolind, Amoco, Vernal, Utah, 1951-52; v.p. Petroleum Research Corp., Denver, 1952-57; mem. faculty dept. geology Colo. Sch. Mines, Golden, 1955-80, prof., 1963-80, part time, 1980-85, emeritus prof., 1983—; cons. Barlow & Haun, Inc., Evergreen, Colo., 1957-90. Cons. Potential Gas Agy., 1966-78, mem. com., 1978—; mem. adv. com. Colo. Water Pollution Control Commn., 1969-70; mem. adv. council Kans. Geol. Survey, 1971-76; del. Internat. Geol. Congress, Sydney, Australia, 1976; U.S. rep. Internat. Com. on Petroleum Res. Classification UN, N.Y.C., 1976-77; mem. oil shale adv. com. Office of Tech. Assessment, Washington, 1976-79, mem. U.S. natural gas availability adv. panel, 1983; mem. Colo. Oil and Gas Conservation Commn., 1977-87, vice-chmn., 1983-85, chmn. 1985-87; mem. energy resources com. Interstate Oil and Gas Compact Commn., 1978—; mem. exec. adv. com. Nat. Petroleum Coun., 1968-70, 79-89, mem. com. on unconventional gas sources, 1978-80; com. on Arctic oil and gas resources, 1980-81; mem. U.S. Nat. Com. on Geology Dept. Interior and NAS, 1982-89, chmn., 1985-87; mem. com undiscovered oil and gas resources, 19881-91, com. status and rsch. objectives in solid-earth scis.: critical assessment, 1988-92, Nat. Rsch. Coun.; del. Internat. Geol. Congress, Paris, 1980, Moscow, 1984; mem. Colo. Oil and Gas legis. com., 1993-94. Editor: The Mountain Geologist, 1963-65, Future Energy Outlook, 1969, Methods of Estimating the Volume of Undiscovered Oil and Gas Resources, 1975; asst. editor: Geologic Atlas of the Rocky Mountain Region, 1972; co-editor: Subsurface Geology in Petroleum Exploration, 1958, Symposium on Cretaceous Rocks of Colorado and Adjacent Areas, 1959, Guide to the Geology of Colorado, 1960; contbr. articles to profl. jours. Served with USCG, 1942-46. Recipient Disting. Svc. award Am. Assn. Petroleum Geologists, 1973, Mines medal Colo. Sch. Mines, 1995, Fellow Geol. Soc. Am., AAAS; mem. Am. Assn. Petroleum Geologists (editor 1967-71, pres. 1979-80, hon. mem. 1984, Sidney Powers Meml. award 1995, Disting. Educator award 2000), Am. Inst. Profl. Geologists (hon. mem., v.p. 1974, pres. 1976, exec. com. 1981-82, Ben H. Parker Meml. award 1983), Am. Geol. Inst. (governing bd. 1976, 79-82, sec.-treas. 1977-78, v.p. 1980-81, pres. 1981-82, Ian Campbell medal 1988, William B. Heroy Jr. award 1996), Rocky Mountain Assn. Geologists (sec. 1961, 1st v.p. 1964, pres. 1968, hon. mem. 1974), Soc. Econ. Paleontologists and Mineralogists, Am. Petroleum Inst. (com. exploration 1971-73, 78-88), Nat. Assn. Geology Tchrs., Wyo. Geol. Assn. (hon. life), Colo. Sci. Soc. (hon. life), Sigma Xi, Sigma Gamma Epsilon, Phi Kappa Phi. Home: 1238 Kerr Gulch Rd Evergreen CO 80439-6397

HAUNSCHILD, ROBERT L. bank executive; b. 1949; CFO PNC Bank Corp, Pitts., 1994—2002, PNC Fin. Svcs. Group, Inc., Pitts., 2000—02; sr. v.p., CFO, contr. PNC Bank Corp., Pitts., 2001—02. Office: PNC Financial Services Group Inc 249 5th Ave Pittsburgh PA 15222-2709*

HAUPENTHAL, LAURA ANN, clinical psychologist; b. Rochester, N.Y., May 22, 1951; d. Carl Vincent and Helen (Hadden) H.; m. Alvin LaFrance Beers Jr., June 1, 1985. BS, No. Ariz. U., 1976, MA, 1977; EdD, U. No. Colo., 1979. Lic. psychologist, Colo., Calif. Lectr. Arapahoe Community Coll., Littleton, Colo., 1980; asst. prof. stress mgmt. U. No. Colo., Greeley, 1980; clin. psychologist Am. Med. Ctr., Denver, 1980-82, Anaheim (Calif.) Psychol. Assocs., 1986-87, Garden Park Med. Clinic, Inc., Anaheim, 1986-89, CIGNA Healthplans, Fountain Valley, Calif., 1986-88; psychol. cons. Irvine (Calif.) Internal Medicine Assocs., 1987-89; clin. psychologist Van Steenhouse and Assocs., Aurora, Colo., 1989-90, Colo. Family Ctr., Littleton, 1980-85, 90-93; pvt. practice clin. psychology Denver, 1993—. Day camp counselor Rochester (N.Y.) Parks and Recreation, 1969; vol. counselor Marc Sch. for Handicapped, Mesa, Ariz., 1973, Cath. Social Svcs., Flagstaff, Ariz., 1976; counselor, house parent Our House, Inc., Greeley, 1977-78, Contbr. articles to profl. publs. Mem. Am. Acad. Behavioral Medicine (diplomate), Nat. Register Health Svc. Providers in Psychology, Am. Psychol. Assn., Colo. Psychol. Assn., Colo. Women Psychologists, Assn. Applied Psychophysiology and Biofeedback, Orange County Psychol. Assn., Am. Soc. of Psychiat. Oncology/AIDS. Avocations: skiing, yoga. Office: 6500 S Quebec St Ste 300 Englewood CO 80111-4674

HAUPT, ADRIENNE LYNN, nurse administrator; b. St. Louis, Ill., 1948; d. Dewey Kirk and Glenda Stafford; 1 child, Daniel. BS in Nursing, U. Md. Walter Reed Army Inst. of Nursing, 1970; MSEd, U. So. Calif., 1982; postgrad., Southwest Tex. State U., 1982. Commd. 1st Lt. U.S. Army, 1970, advanced through grades to Lt. Col.; staff nurse, pediatrics U.S. Army Hosp., Ft. Knox, Ky., 1970-72; community health nurse William Beaumont Army Med. Ctr., El Paso, Tex., 1972-73, Tripler Army Med. Ctr., Hawaii, 1973-75; chief comty. health nurse U.S. Army Hosp., Ft., Meade, Md., 1975—78, asst. chief, community health nurse Ft. Hood, Tex., 1978-81, chief, community health nurse Seoul, Korea, 1981-83; asst. chief, community health nurse Walter Reed Army Med. Ctr., Washington, 1983-87; chief nurse Joint Task Force, Bravo Comayagua, Honduras, 1984; chief community health nurse U.S. Army Hosp., Ft. Hood, Tex., 1987-89; ret., 1989. Decorated Legion of Merit medal, Meritorious Svc. medal. Mem. Am. Nurses Assn. (cert. nurse adminstr. and community health nurse), Am. Pub. Health Assn. Avocations: walking, reading, needle work. Home: 5412 E Shaw Butte Dr Scottsdale AZ 85254-4780

HAUPT, RANDY LARRY, electrical engineering educator; b. Johnstown, Pa., Aug. 11, 1956; s. Howard and Anna Mae Haupt; m. Sue E. Slagle, Feb. 17, 1979; children: Bonny Ann, Amy Jean. BSEE, USAF Acad., 1978; MS in Engring. Mgmt., Western New Eng. Coll., 1981; MSEE, Northeastern U., 1983; PhD in Electrical Engring., U. Mich., 1987. Registered profl. engr., Colo. Commd. 2d lt. USAF, 1974, advanced through grades to lt. col., 1990, project engr. OTH-B Radar electronic systems divsn., 1978-80, rsch. engr. in microwave antennas Rome Air Devel. Ctr., 1980-84; instr., then asst. prof. elec. engring. USAF Acad., Colo., 1987-91; dir. rsch. dept. elec. engring. USAF, Colo., 1990-91, chief comm. div. dept. elec. engring., 1991—; assoc. prof. USAF Acad., Colo., 1991-94, prof., 1994-97, dept. for ops. dept. elec. engring., 1995-97; prof., chair dept. elec. engring. U. Nev., Reno, 1997—. Vis. rsch. engr. Los Alamos Nat. Lab., 1992; presenter numerous papers and tech. reports in field. Author: (with others) Practical Genetic Algorithms, 1998; contbr. numerous articles to engring. jours. Nordic ski team coach USAF Acad., 1992-93. Recipient USAF Rsch. and Devel. award, 1983, 87, Frank J. Seiler award for rsch. excellence, 1990, 92, Founder's Gold medal, 1993, 6 Rome Air Devel. Ctr. Sci. Achievement awards; named Outstanding Mil. Educator in Electrical Engring., 1992, USAF Mil. Engr. of Yr., 1993, Fed. Engr. of Yr., Nat. Soc. Profl. Engrs., 1993; rsch. grantee Rome Air Devel. Ctr., 1988-90, Frank J. Seiler Rsch. Lab., 1990—, Cray Rsch., Inc., 1991-92, Phillips Lab., 1992—. Mem. IEEE (sr., student br. counselor 1988-90, reviewer Transactions on Antennas and Propagation 1984—), Am. Soc. for Engring. Edn. (reviewer), Applied Computational Electromagnetics Soc., Tau Beta Pi. Achievements include research in electromagnetics, scattering, antennas, electro-optics, numerical methods, chaos theory, radar, systems engineering, communications systems. Office: U Nev Dept Elec Engring 260 Reno NV 89557-0001

HAUPT, ROGER A. advertising executive; CEO Leo Burnett Co., Inc., Chgo., 1999-2000, BCom3, 2000—. Office: BCom3 Group 35 W Wacker Dr Chicago IL 60601

HAUPT, SHERI LYNN, pharmacist; b. Neptune, NJ, Sept. 1, 1968; d. Robert Stephen and Roberta Jean (Burton) Fisher; m. Robert Jacob Haupt, Apr. 30, 1994. BS, L.I. U., 1993. Staff pharmacist Walgreen's Pharmacy, Neptune City, NJ, 1993; pharmacist, pharmacy mgr. Thrift Drug/Eckerd, Havre de Grace, Md., 1993—2002; pharmacy mgr. Happy Harry's, Perryville, Md., 2002—. Republican. Lutheran. Avocations: cycling, music, needlepoint, puzzles. Home: 1716 Gillingham Dr Bel Air MD 21015-2014

HAUPTMAN, HERBERT AARON, mathematician, educator, researcher; b. N.Y.C., Feb. 14, 1917; s. Israel and Leah (Rosenfeld) Hauptman; m. Edith Citrynell, Nov. 10, 1940; children: Barbara, Carol Hauptman Fullerton. BS in Math., CCNY, 1937; MA, Columbia U., 1939; PhD, U. Md., 1955, PhD (hon.), 1985, CCNY, 1986, U. Parma, Italy, 1989, D'Youville Coll., 1989, Bar-Ilan U., Israel, 1990, Columbia U., 1990, Tech. U., Lodz, Poland, 1992, Queen's U., Kingston, Ont., Can., 1994, Niagara U., 1996, U. Toledo, 1999, Medaille Coll., 2002. Statistician U.S. Census Bur., Washington, 1940—42; civilian instr. electronics and radar U.S. Army Air Force, Boca Raton, Fla., 1942—43; physicist, mathematician Naval Rsch. Lab., Washington, 1947—70; mathematician Hauptman-Woodward Med. Rsch. Inst., 1970—72, exec. v.p., rsch. dir., 1972—85, pres., rsch. dir., 1985—87, pres., 1988—, also bd. dirs.; prof. biophys. scis. SUNY, Buffalo, 1970—, prof. computer scis., 1992—, disting. prof. structural biology, 2001—. Chmn. N.Y. State Inst. on Superconductivity, 1988—98; mem. sci. adv. bd. Biocryst, 1989—; math. instr. U. Md., 1958—70; chmn. Intercongress Symposium Direct Methods in Crystallography, Buffalo, 1976; pres. Assn. Ind. Rsch. Insts., 1979—80; mem. U.S. Nat. Com. for Crystallography, 1979—81, 1982—85, 1988—89; mem. sci. adv. bd. Biophan, 2001—. Author (with J. Karle): Solution of the Phase Problem, 1953; author: Crystal Structure Determination: The Role of the Cosine Seminvariants, 1972; editor: Direct Methods in Crystallography, Proceedings of the 1976 Intercongress Symposium, 1978; contbr. chpts. to books, articles to profl. jours. Trustee Buffalo Gen. Hosp., 1990—96; chmn. comm. com. Philos. Soc. Washington, 1966—67, corr. sec., 1967—69. Lt. (j.g.) USNR, 1943—46. Named Western N.Y. Man of Yr., Buffalo C. of C., 1986, YMCA Dinner, 1986, 90th Nobel Ann. Dinner, 1991; named to Nobel Hall Mus. Sci. and Industry, 1986, Townsend Harris Hall of Fame, 1989, U. Md. Alumni Hall of Fame, guest of honor Roswell Park Meml. Inst., 1985, YMCA Luncheon, others, invited guest Am. Nobel Convocation, 1987, 1988, Weizmann Nat. Dinner, 1998, others; recipient Belden prize (Gold medal) in Math., 1935, RESA award in Pure Scis., 1959, Citizen of Yr. award, Buffalo Evenings News, 1986, Schoelkopf award, Am. Chem. Soc., 1986, Gold Plate award, Am. Acad. Achievement, 1986, Nat. Libr. Medicine medal, 1987, Law Sch. award, Maimonides Chabad House, 1986, others, (with J. Karle) Patterson award, 1984, Nobel Prize in Chemistry, 1985; fellow sr. fellow for travel, lectures and rsch. in Italy, NATO, 1973; grantee NSF, 1972—92, NIH, 1992—. Fellow: Jewish Acad. Arts and Scis. (medal 1986), Washington Acad. Scis.; mem.: NAS, AAAS, Math. Assn. Am., Am. Crystallographic Assn. (mem. Fankuchen award com. 1988), Am. Phys. Soc., Am. Math. Soc., Saturn Club (guest of honor 1985), Cosmos Club, Sigma Xi (sec. Buffalo chpt. 1971—72), Phi Beta Kappa. Avocation: stained glass art, swimming, hiking . Office: Hauptman Woodward Med Rsch 73 High St Buffalo NY 14203-1196 E-mail: hauptman@hwi.buffalo.edu.

HAUPTMAN, LAURENCE MARC, history educator; b. New Paltz, New York, May 18, 1945; s. David and Frieda (Landesman) H.; m. Ruth (Jacobs), May 23, 1970; children: Beth, Eric. BA, N.Y. Univ., 1966, MA, 1968, PhD, 1971. From instr. to assoc. prof. State Univ. of N.Y., New Paltz, NY, 1971-82, prof., 1982-99, disting. prof. History, 1999—. Hist. cons. for Am. Indian nations including Cayuga Nation, Mashantucket Pequot Tribal Nation of Conn., Oneida Nation of Wis., Seneca Nation of Indians, N.Y.; expert witness Senate select com. on Indian Affairs, U.S. Congress, 1990, House subcom. on interior and insular affairs, 1990, Cayuga Indian land claims, 2000; Alexander Flick lectr. in N.Y. history N.Y. State History conf., 1998. Author: The Iroquois and the New Deal, 1981, The Iroquois Struggle for Survival, 1986 (Notable Book of Yr. Choice mag.), Formulating Am. Indian Policy in N.Y. State, 1988, The Iroquois Indians in the Civil War: From Battlefield to Reservation, 1993, Tribes & Tribulations, 1995, Between Two Fires: Am. Indians in the Civil War, 1995 (Notable Book of Yr., Choice mag.), Conspiracy of Interests: The Iroquois Dispossession and the Rise of N.Y. State, 1999 (John Ben Snow Book prize), Chief Daniel Bread and the Oneida Nation of Indians of Wisconsin, 2002; editor: Neighbors and Intruders, 1978, The Oneida Indian Experience: Two Perspectives, 1988, The Pequots in Southern New England, 1990, A Seneca Indian Sgt. in the Civil War, 1995, The Oneida Indian Journey: from N.Y. to Wisconsin, 1999. Recipient: Peter Doctor Meml. Award, Peter Doctor Fellowship Found. of Iroquois Indians, 1987, 98, NYS-UUP Award for Excellence in Teaching, 1991, Excellence in Rsch. Award N.Y. State Bd. of Regents, 1992, book prize State Hist. Soc. Wis., 1999. Mem.; Am. Hist. Assn., Orgn. Am. Historians, Western History Assn., Am. Soc. for Ethnohistory, N.Y. State Hist. Assn. Avocations: golf, travel. Home: 2 Sarafian Rd New Paltz NY 12561-3816

HAUPTMAN, MICHAEL, broadcasting company executive; b. Bklyn., Jan. 6, 1933; s. Hyman A. and Toba L. (Hershman) H.; m. Betty Holzman, Nov. 28, 1957; children: James, William. BA, U. Vt., 1954. Program dir. Sta. WSTC, Stamford, Conn., 1960-61; prodn. mgr. Sta. WABC, N.Y.C., 1961-62, advt., promotion mgr., 1962-63; with Sta. WINS, N.Y.C., 1963-67, Sta. KYW-TV, Phila., 1967-68; mgr. mktg. services Westinghouse Broadcasting Co., N.Y.C., 1968-69; dir. retail mktg. ABC owned radio stas., N.Y.C., 1969-72, dir. planning, 1972-73; v.p. ABC Radio, 1973-76, sr. v.p., 1976-81; v.p.-in-charge ABC Radio Enterprises, Inc., 1981-83; v.p. ABC Video Enterprises Inc., 1983-85; pres. Nat. Communications Corp., Cos Cob, Conn., 1985-89, 90—; pres. Physicians Radio Network div. Primark Corp., v.p. Health Info. Internat., 1989-90; pres. Group H Radio, Inc., 1992—. Address: 13 Carriage Rd Cos Cob CT 06807-1301 E-mail: carriage13@aol.com.

HAUPTMANN, RANDAL MARK, biotechnologist; b. Hot Springs, SD, July 6, 1956; s. Ivan Joy and Phyllis Maxine (Pierce) H.; m. Beverly Kay Suko, May 22, 1975; 1 child, Erich William. BS, S.D. State U., 1979; MS, U. Ill., 1982, PhD, 1984. Postdoctoral rschr. Monsanto Corp. Rsch., St. Louis, 1984-86; vis. rsch. scientist U. Fla., Gainesville, 1986-88; asst. prof. No. Ill. U., DeKalb, 1988-90, dir. plant molecular biology ctr., 1989-90; sr. rsch. scientist Amoco Life Sci. Techs., Naperville, Ill., 1990-94; dir. advanced tech. Seminis Vegetable Seeds, Woodland, Calif., 1994-98; gen. mgr. Ball Helix, West Chicago, Ill., 1998—2003. Author: (with others) Methods in Molecular Biology, 1990; contbr. articles to profl. jours. Mem. Internat. Assn. Plant Tissue Culture, Internat. Soc. Plant Molecular Biology, Am. Soc. Plant Physiologists, Tissue Culture Assn. (Virginia Evans award 1982), Sigma Xi, Gamma Sigma Delta. Democrat.

HAUSCHILD, DOUGLAS CAREY, optometrist; b. Manchester, Conn., Oct. 3, 1955; s. Vernon Francis and Barbara Gwendolyn (Rose) H.; 1 child, Chelsea Anna. BA in Biology magna cum laude, Wesleyan U., 1977; OD, New Eng. Coll. Optometry, 1981. Clinician Boston Eye Clinic, 1978-81; assoc. Drs. Todd, Todd & Hauschild, Hendersonville, N.C., 1981-84; owner, optometrist Weaverville (N.C.) Eye Assocs., 1984—, Asheville (N.C.) Eye Care Assocs., 1985—. Clinician Walter Reed Army Med. Ctr., 1980, West Roxbury VA Med. Ctr., 1981, NEWENCO Pediatric/Geriatric Sply. Clinic, 1981; nominee Buncombe County Bd. of Health. Contbr. health articles to newsletters; singer New Day Singers, 2000-02. Mem. Henderson County Bd. Health, 1983—85; instr. phys. edn. Evangel. Chapel Christian Acad., Asheville, 1985—86; mem., soloist Bent Creek Bapt. Ch. Choir; leader Bent Creek Bapt. Ch. Care Group, 1987—91; choir mem., soloist, cantor St. Eugene's Roman Cath. Ch., 1992—; mem. St. Eugene's Pastoral Coun., 1995—98, chair, 1997—98; bd. dirs. New Day Singers, 2000—02; actor Asheville Cmty. Theatre, 1988—; mem., soloist Asheville Choral Soc. and New Day Singers, 2000—; soloist Midday Musicals, 2002—. Mem. Am. Optometric Assn., So. Coun. Optometrists, N.C. State Optometric Soc., Mtn. Dist. Optometric Soc., Am. Pub. Health Assn., Lions (past pres.), KC (grand knight 2000-02), Elks, Beta Sigma Kappa, Delta Tau Delta. Republican. Avocations: photography, animal husbandry, gardening, theater, numismatics. Office: Weaverville Eye Assocs PO Box 1620 Weaverville NC 28787-1620 Fax: 828-645-7279. E-mail: eyecheckup@aol.com.

HAUSE, EDITH COLLINS, college administrator; b. Rock Hill, SC, Dec. 11, 1933; d. Ernest O. and Violet (Smith) Collins; m. James Luke Hause, Sept. 3, 1955; children: Stephen Mark, Felicia Gaye Hause Friesen. BA, Columbia Coll., SC, 1956; postgrad., U. NC, Greensboro, 1967, U. SC, 1971—75. Tchr. Richland Dist. II, Columbia, 1971—74; dir. alumnae affairs Columbia Coll., 1974—82, v.p. alumnae affairs, 1989—99, ret., 1999. Named Outstanding Tchr. of Yr., Richland Dist. II, 1974; recipient Disting. Svc. award, Columbia Coll. Alumae Assn., 2003, Columbia Coll. Medallion, 2003. Mem.: Nat. Soc. Fund Raising Execs., Coun. for Advancement and Support Edn., Columbia Network for Female Execs., SC Advocates for Women on Bds. and Commrs. (bd. dirs.), SC Assn. Alumni Dirs. (pres. 1996—98). Republican. Methodist. Home: 92 Mariners Pointe Rd Prosperity SC 29127-7674

HAUSEL, WILLIAM DAN, economic geologist, martial artist, public speaker, writer, artist; b. Salt Lake City, July 24, 1949; s. Maynard Romain and Dorthy (Clark) H.; children: Jessica Siddhartha, Eric Jason. BS in Geology, U. Utah, 1972, MS in Geology, 1974. Astronomy lectr. Hansen Planetarium, Salt Lake City, 1968-72; rsch. asst. U. Utah, 1972-74; tchg. asst. U. N.Mex., Albuquerque, 1974-75; project geologist Warnock Cons., Albuquerque, 1975; geologist U.S. Geol. Survey, Casper, Wyo., 1976-77; staff geologist Geol. Survey of Wyo., Laramie, 1977-81, dep. dir., 1981-91, sr. econ. geologist, 1991—. Assoc. curator mineralogy Wyo. State Mus., Cheyenne, 1983-90; cons. Western Gold Exploration and Mining, Anchorage, 1988, 89, Chevron Resources, Georgetown, Mont., 1990, Fowler Resources, Phillipsburg, Mont., 1992, Bald Mountain Mining, U.S., 1993, A and E Diamond Exploration, Calif., 1993, Echo Bay Exploration, Diamond Exploration, U.S., 1994, Western rchon, 2003; instr. diamond exploration methods, U. Wyo., 1988, 94, Wyo. Geol. Assn., 1993, N.Am. Exploration, 1994, MK Gold, 1996, Rocky Mountain Prospectors, 2001, 02, 03; state rep. JUKO-KAI Internat., Wyo., 1994; U.S. dir. open divsn., Shorin-Ryu Karate 1996, open divsn. head, Shorin-Ryu Karate and Kobudo (Juko-kai Internat.), 1997—; instr. martial arts dept. phys. edn., U. Wyo., 1993—, Campus Shorin-Ryu Karate and Kobudo Club, 1977—. Author: Partial Pressures of Some Lunar Lavas, 1972, Petrogenesis of Some Representative Lavas, Southwestern Utah, 1975, Exploration for Diamondiferous Kimberlite, 1979, Gold Districts of Wyoming, 1980, Ore Deposits of Wyoming, 1982, Geology of Southeastern Wyoming, 1984, Minerals and Rocks of Wyoming, 1986, The Geology of Wyoming's Precious Metal Lode and Placer Deposits, 1989, Economic Geology of the South Pass Greenstone Belt, 1991, Economic Geology of the Cooper Hill Mining District, 1992, Mining History and Geology of Wyoming's Metal and Gemstone Districts, 1993, Geology, Mining Districts and Ghost Towns of the Medicine Bow Mountains, 1993, Diamonds, Kimberlite and Lamproite in the United States, 1994, Pacific Coast Diamonds-An Unconventional Source Terrane, 1995, Economic Geology of the Seminoe Mountains Greenstone Belt, 1994, The Great Diamond Hoax of 1872, 1995, Geology and Gold Mineralization of the Rattlesnake Hills, Granite Mountains, Wyoming, 1996, Copper, Lead, Zinc, Molybdenum and Associated Metal Deposits of Wyoming, 1997, Diamonds and Mantle Source Rocks in the U.S., with Special Emphasis on the Wyoming Craton, 1998, Water Training Techniques for Martial Artists, 1998, Diamond Fever, 1999, Gemstones and Other Unique Minerals and Rocks of Wyoming, 2000, Diamond Deposits - Origin, Exploration and History of Discovery, 2002, numerous others; permanent art collections exhibited at Grand Bazaar, Wyo., Artisans Gallery, Wyo.; sketches have appeared on covers of Diamond Deposit, 2002, Searching for Gold in Wyoming, 2002; contbr. more than 450 articles to sci. and profl. jours. and contbr. to 8 books. Grantee NASA, 1981, Office of Surface Mining, 1979, U. Wyo., 1981-92, U.S. Geol. Survey Coop. Geol. Mapping Initiative, 1985-88, 98, 2001, 02, 03, Union Pacific Resources, 1991-94, State of Wyoming Diamond Rsch. grantee, 1998-2000; recipient Pres.'s Cert. Excellence Am. Assn. Petroleum Geologists, 1992, Outstanding Contributions award Wyo. Geol Assn., 1992, Prospector's Best Friend award Rocky Mountain Prospector's and Treasure Hunter's Assn., 1998, Grandmaster Instr. of the Yr. award World Karate Assn., 1998, Open Shorin-Ryu Instr. of the Yr. award JKI, 1998, Internat. Instr. of Yr. award, 2001, Grand Master of the Yr., 2002, Headfounder of the Yr., 2002; named Laramie Lyceum Disting. Lectr., 1994, Disting. Lectr. Dept. Geology and Geophysics, U. Wyo., 1998; named to Kevin Bell's Karate Hall of Fame, 1998, World Karate Union Hall of Fame, 2000, Millennium Hall of Fame, 1998, N.Am. Black Belt Hall of Fame, 2001, Nat. Rockhound and Lapidary Hall of Fame, 2001, World Martial Arts Hall of Fame, 2002, Universal Martial Arts Hall of Fame, 2002. Mem. Wyo. Geo. Assn., Wyo. Profl. Geologists, U. Utah Geology Club (pres. 1969-71), Laramie Bushido Dojo Karate (pres. 1985-88), U. Wyo. Campus Shotokan Karate Club (instr. 1988-93), Shorin-Ryu Karate and Kobudo Club (U. Wyo. Campus headmaster 1993—), Juko-Kai Internat., Seiyo-no Shorin-Ryu Karate Kobudo Kai Assn. Avocations: Karate, Ju Jitsu, martial arts, sketching. Home: 4238 Grays Gable Rd Laramie WY 82072-6911 Office: Wyo State Geol Survey U Wyo PO Box 3008 Laramie WY 82071-3008 also: Shorin Ryn Karate & Kobudo Club Univ Wyo PO Box 3625 Laramie WY 82071-3625 Fax: 307-766-2605. E-mail: dhausel@uwyo.edu.

HAUSELT, DENISE ANN, lawyer; BS, Cornell U., 1979, JD, 1983. Bar: N.Y. 1984, Ill. 1984, U.S. Dist. Ct. (we. dist.) N.Y. 1984, U.S. Bankruptcy Ct. 1984. Summer assoc. Wildman, Harrold, Allen & Dixon, Chgo., 1982; assoc. Nixon Peabody LLP, Rochester, N.Y., 1983-86; asst. counsel Corning (N.Y.) Inc., 1986-93, divsn. counsel, 1993-99, asst. gen. counsel, 1999-2000, asst. gen. counsel, asst. sec., 2000—01, corp. sec., 2001—. Bd. dirs. 171 Cedar Arts Ctr., The Rockwell Mus. Mem. adv. coun. Cornell Law Sch.; sec. Rockwell Mus., and Corning Inc. Found., Corning Mus. of Glass. Recipient Am. Jurisprudence Constl. Law prize, Cornell U., 1981. Mem.: ABA, Cornell Law Assn., Am. Corp. Counsel Assn. Republican. Avocations: sailing, skiing. Office: Corning Inc Riverfront Plz Mp Hq E2 Corning NY 14831-0001

HAUSER, ANDREW MAX, cardiologist; b. Detroit, May 31, 1947; s. Alex and Helen (Schwartz) H.; m. Jane Johnson, June 18, 1979; children: Elizabeth, Emily, Jessica. MD, U. Mich., 1972. Diplomate Am. Bd. Internal Medicine, Am. Bd. Cardiovasc. Disease. Dir. cardiology noninvasive lab. William Beaumont Hosp., Royal Oak, Mich., 1978—; cardiologist Northpointe Heart Ctr., Berkley, Mich., 1986—. Pres. Am. Heart Assn. Mich., 1987—88, Am. Heart Assn. Detroit Metro Bd., 2000—02. Contbr. chpts. to books, articles to profl. jours. Pres. Detroit Heart Club, 1986. Comm. Vol. of Yr., Am. Heart Assn. Mich. Fellow ACP, Am. Coll. Cardiology; mem. AMA., Am. Soc. Echocardiography (trustee 2002—), Mich. Soc. Echocardiography (founding pres. 1981-82, pres. 1997), Photo Guild (Photograph of Yr. 1996) Avocations: photography, sailing. Office: Northpointe Heart Ctr 27901 Woodward Ave Berkley MI 48072-0919

HAUSER, BERNICE WORMAN, director; m. A. Daniel Hauser; children: Mitchell Alan, Lisa Ann. BA cum laude, Hunter Coll., 1953, MS, 1956; MS in Adminstrn. and Supervision, CUNY, 1978. Tchr. Yonkers Pub. Schs., N.Y.C., 1953-54, N.Y. Pub. Schs., N.Y.C., 1954-60; primary sci. tchr., cons. Pub./Parochial/Ind. Schs., N.Y.C., 1960-72; tchr., primary sci. chair Walden Sch., N.Y.C., 1972-80, coord. student tchrs., 1980-88, curriculum cons., prin. sci. chair, 1988-91; asst. to headministress Horace Mann Sch., N.Y.C., 1991-93, dir. inter-campus acitivities, 1993—. Cons. Scholastic Publs., N.Y.C., 1980—; bd. dirs. CUNY Pub.-Pvt. Schs. Partnership Coun. Author: How to Help Your Child at Home with Science, 1991, The Cat in the Hat Comes Back, 1997, You're the Apple of My Eye, 1998, (adoption issues) Am. Baby, 1984; primary corres. articles Tchr. Clearinghouse for Sci., 1987—; editor: Horace Mann Bull., 1993—; contbr. articles to Ind. Sch., Bull. of Sci. Tech & Soc., Parents League Bull., others. Mem. parks coun. Ctrl. Park Conservancy, 1970—; mem. Citizens Com. For Better N.Y., N.Y.C., 1980—; cons., speaker and writer Adoptive Parents Com., N.Y.C., 1975—; trustee, v.p., nominating chair Louis Wise Svcs. for Children, N.Y.C., 1976—. Recipient Impact II award Exxon, 1987, Jeremy Rifkin award NASTS, 1991; honoree United Jewish Appeal for Disting. Vol. Svc. to Louise Wise Svcs., 1998. Fellow Phi Delta Kappa; mem. AAUW, ASCD, Nat. Sci. Tchrs. Assn. (presenter 1985—), Nat. Assn. Ind. Schs., Nat. Assn. Sci. Tech. and Soc., Assn. Tchr. Ind. Schs. (program chairperson), N.Y. Assn. Ind. Schs. (liaison), Hunter Coll. High Sch. Alumni Assn. (past pres), Phi

Beta Kappa, Epsilon Pi Tau, Cum Laude Soc. Avocations: indoor gardening, theater, opera, reading, writing. Office: Horace Mann Sch 231 W 246th St Bronx NY 10471-3430 E-mail: Bernice_Hauser@horacemann.org.

HAUSER, CHARLES NEWLAND MCCORKLE, newspaper consultant; b. Newton, N.C., Feb. 3, 1929; s. John Nathaniel and Charlotte (McCorkle) H.; m. Jane Anne Edwards, Dec. 29, 1956; children: David McCorkle, Susan Jane. AB, U. N.C., 1954; postgrad., Harvard U., 1968. Ordained elder United Presbyn. Ch. U.S.A., 1977. Washington corr. Charlotte (N.C.) Observer, 1961-62, Carolinas editor, 1962-65; fgn. corr. UPI, London, 1958-59, Paris, 1959-60; mng. editor Greensboro (N.C.) Daily News, 1965-66; exec. editor Greensboro News & Record, 1967-68; v.p., gen. mgr. Virginian-Pilot & Ledger Star, Norfolk, Va., 1969-73; v.p., exec. editor Providence Jour. and Evening Bull., 1973-89; cons., 1990—. Lectr. Am. Press Inst., Reston, Va., 1969-89, U. R.I., 1987-90, U. N.C., 1991-92, 2001, Duke U., 1995—; bd. dirs. Sun Coast Media Group, Venice, Fla.; adj. assoc. prof. Brown U., Providence, 1981-82. Bd. trustees Writers Ctr., Chautauqua Inst., N.Y. Retired colonel USAR. Decorated Bronze Star medal, Purple Heart. Mem. Am. Soc. Newspaper Editors, Alpha Tau Omega. Clubs: Nat. Press (Washington). Home and Office: 1031 Fearrington Post Pittsboro NC 27312-5503 E-mail: writer888@earthlink.net.

HAUSER, CHRISTOPHER GEORGE, lawyer; b. Syracuse, N.Y., May 15, 1954; s. W. Dieter and Nancy (Keating) H. BA, Washington & Jefferson Coll., 1976; JD, Dickinson Sch. Law, 1979. Bar: Pa. 1979, U.S. Dist. Ct. (we. dist.) Pa. 1981, N.Y. 1987, U.S. Supreme Ct. 1992. Legal asst. Pa. Dept. of Justice, Harrisburg, 1978-79; assoc. McDowell, McDowell, Wick & Daly, Bradford, 1979-83; ptnr. McDowell, Wick, Daly, Gallup, & Hauser, and predecessor firm McDowell, McDowell, Wick & Daly, Bradford, 1983—; broker, owner Re/Max Alpine Sales, Ellicottville, N.Y., 1991-93. Pres./owner Alpine Sales and Rental Mgmt., Inc., Ellicottville, N.Y., 1987-94; chmn. adv. bd. Office Econ. Cmty. Devel., Bradford, 1988—. Chmn. campaign Bradford Area United Way, 1984, v.p., 1987—89, pres., 1990—92; chmn. Downtown Bradford Revitalization Corp., 1986—, Bradford Parking Authority, 1986—94, 1999—; pres. Allegheny Highlands coun. Boy Scouts Am., Falconer, NY, 1986—88; dir. Bradford Econ. Devel. Corp., 1987 , Exch. Club 1989—91; sec., treas. Bradford Redevel. Authority, 1992—96, chmn., 1992—96, 1996—; active Bradford Area Citizens Adv. Com., 1992; dir. N.W. divsn. Pa. Economy League, 1997—2002; dir., sec. Bradford Area Alliance, 1997—98, solicitor, 1998—; bd. dirs. Rt. 219 Assn., 1996—98; v.p. Continental One, 1998—, pres., 2000—; dist. justice McKean County, Pa., 2000—; dir. Bradford Regional Med. Ctr., 2000—. Recipient Outstanding Svc. award Bradford Area United Way, 1985, Silver Beaver award Allehany Highlands coun. Boy Scouts Am., 1990, Founder's award Order Arrow Boy Scouts Am., 1991, Cmty. Svc. award City of Bradford Office Econ. and Cmty. Devel., 1995; named Bus. Person of Yr. Bradford C. of C., 1986, One of Outstanding Young Men Am. U.S. Jaycees, 1983. Mem. N.Y. Bar Assn., Pa. Bar Assn., McKean County Bar Assn. (v.p. 1992-93, pres. 1994-96), Bradford Area Jaycees (pres. 1983-85), Pennhills Club (sec. 1985-90, 99-2000, pres. 1990-92, 2000—02, chmn. exec. com. 2002—), Bradford Club. Republican. Episcopalian. Home: 110 Congress St Bradford PA 16701-2228 Office: McDowell Wick Daly Gallup & Hauser PO Box 361 78 Main St Bradford PA 16701-2026 E-mail: cghauser@charter.net., mwdlaw@charter.net.

HAUSER, ELLOYD, finance company executive; Founder and CEO United Check Clearing Corp., 1984—98; pres., CEO Solutran Customized Payment Solutions (formerly United Check Clearing Corp), 1998—2001; chmn. Solutran, 1998—. Office: Solutran 3600 Holly Ln N Ste 60 Plymouth MN 55447-1286

HAUSER, GABRIEL JACOB, pediatrician; b. Tel Aviv, Dec. 1, 1953; s. Heinrich and Edith Hauser; m. Tova, June 20, 1978; children: Nir, Guy, Hagar. MD, Tel Aviv U.; MBA, Georgetown U., 2000. Diplomate Am. Bd. Pediats. Intern Tel Aviv Med. Ctr., 1977-78, resident in pediats., 1982-86; fellow critical care Children's Nat. Med. Ctr., Washington, 1986-89; chief pediat. critical care Georgetown U. Hosp., Washington, 1989—, dir. pediat. ICU, 1989—, med dir. pediat. inpatient svcs., 2000—. Assoc. prof. pediats. Georgetown U., Washington, 1992-2000, prof., 2000—, scholar Ctr. for Clin. Ethics, 1992—, assoc. prof. physiology, 1994-2000, prof., 2000—, vice-chmn. dept. pediat., 2002— Capt., field physician Israeli Army, 1978-82. Fellow Am. Acad. Pediats., Coll. Critical Care Medicine, Am. Coll. Chest Physicians; mem. AMA, Shock Soc., Soc. Exptl. Biology and Medicine, Washington Critical Care Soc. (pres. 1996-97), Soc. Critical Care (mem. chpt. com. 1995—). Jewish. Avocations: tennis, guitar, skiing. Office: Georgetown U Hosp 3800 Reservoir Rd NW Washington DC 20007-2113 E-mail: hauserg@georgetown.edu.

HAUSER, GUSTAVE M. cable television and electronic communications company executive; b. Cleve., Sept. 3, 1929; s. Abraham and Stella H.; m. Rita Abrams, June 10, 1956; children: Glenvil A., Patricia A. AB, Western Res. U., 1950; JD, Harvard U., 1953; LLM, NYU, 1957; diploma in law, U. Paris, 1958. Bar: Ohio 1953, N.Y. 1957. Instr. Harvard U. Law Sch., Cambridge, Mass., 1955-56; counsel internat. affairs Office Sec. Def., Washington, 1958-60; v.p. Gen. Telephone & Electronics Internat., N.Y.C., 1960-71; exec. v.p. Western Union Internat., N.Y.C., 1971-73; pres., CEO Warner Cable Corp., N.Y.C., 1973-75, chmn., chief exec. officer, 1975-79, Warner Amex Cable Communications, Inc., N.Y.C., 1979-83; chmn., CEO Hauser Comm., Inc., N.Y.C., 1983—. Chmn, bd. dirs. Orion Network Sys., Inc., Washington, 1996-98. Author: A Guide to Doing Business in the European Common Market, 1960. Chmn., bd. dirs. Hauser Found., Inc., 1989—; trustee Steep Rock Land Trust, 1992—; trustee, vice-chmn. The Mus. TV and Radio, 1992—; exec. com. Harvard U., com. on univ. resources, 1997—; bd. dirs. The Cable Ctr., 1997—. Served with AUS, 1953-55. Named to, Cable Hall of Fame, 2003. Mem. Nat. Cable TV Assn. (dir. 1976-84, exec. com. 1978-84, vice chmn. 1983-84). Office: Hauser Comm 712 5th Ave New York NY 10019-4108

HAUSER, HARRY RAYMOND, lawyer; b. N.Y.C., July 12, 1931; s. Milton I. and Lillian (Perlman) H.; m. Deborah Marlowe, Aug. 6, 1954; children: Mark Jeffrey, Joshua Brook, Bradford John, Matthew Milton. AB, Brown U., 1953; JD, Columbia U., 1959. Bar: N.Y. 1959, Mass. 1963, Wash. 1972. Practice in, N.Y.C., 1959-61, Boston, 1962—2002; atty. Sperry Rand Corp., 1959-61, Hotel Corp. Am., N.Y.C., 1961-62, v.p., sec., gen. counsel, 1962-70; mem. firm Gadsby & Hannah, 1971—2002. Life trustee Temple Israel, Boston; pres. emeritus, dir. N. Bennett St. Sch. Mem. ABA, N.Y. State Bar Assn., Mass. Bar Assn., D.C. Bar Assn., Internat. Bar Assn. Home: 1175 Chestnut St #2 Newton Upper Falls MA 02464-1336

HAUSER, HELEN ANN, lawyer, consultant; b. Miami, Fla., July 23, 1948; d. Philip Jay and Ruth (Saltman) Fruitstone; m. Mark Jay Hauser; children: Robert Jeffrey, Cheryl Elaine, Lauren Yvonne. BA in English, Duke U., 1970; MA in English, U. Fla., 1972, PhD, 1975; JD, U. Miami, 1982. Bar: Fla. 1982, U.S. Dist. Ct. (so. dist.) Fla. 1982, U.S. Ct. Appeals (11th cir.) 1986, U.S. Supreme Ct. 1987, U.S. Dist. Ct. (mid. dist.) Fla. 1994. Instr. various colls., 1973-79; clk. to presiding justice Fla. 3d Ct. of Appeals, 1982-84; ptnr. Pines & Hauser, Miami, 1984-89; assoc. Law Offices of David P. Dittmar, Miami, 1989-91; ptnr. Dittmar & Hauser, P.A., Miami, 1991—. Vol. Guardian ad Litem Program, Juvenile Ct., Miami, 1985—; bd. dirs. Alhambra Orch. Angier B. Duke scholar Duke U., 1966-70; Harvey T. Reid fellow U. Miami Law Sch., 1979-82. Mem. Dade County Bar Assn., South Miami-Kendall Bar Assn., Fla. Assn. Women Lawyers. Avocations: playing violin, viola. Office: Dittmar & Hauser 3250 Mary St Ste 400 Miami FL 33133-5232 E-mail: hhauserjd@aol.com.

HAUSER, JOHN REID, electrical engineering educator; b. Advance, N.C., Sept. 19, 1938; s. Reid R. and Lillian (Sheek) H.; m. Ann Covington, June 15, 1962; children: John R. Jr., James W., Daniel R. BS, N.C. State U., 1960; MS, Duke U., 1962, PhD, 1964. Mem. tech. staff Bell Telephone Labs., Winston-Salem, N.C., 1960-62; rsch. engr. Rsch. Triangle Inst., Rsch. Triangle Pk., N.C., 1963-66; asst. prof. N.C. State U., Raleigh, 1966-68, assoc. prof., 1968-73, Disting. prof., 1983—, prof., 1973—. Dir. Solid State Electronics Lab., N.C. State U., 1984—. Author: Fundamentals of Silicon Internal Devel. Tech., vol. II, 1968; contbr. over 150 articles to profl. jours. Recipient R.J. Reynolds Indsl. award for excellence N.C. State U., 1982, Univ. Rsch. award, Semiconductor Ind. Assn., 2002. Fellow IEEE (Outstanding Engr. in N.C. award, 1978); mem. Am. Phys. Soc., Am. Soc. for Engring. Edn. Home: 6800 Phillips Ct Raleigh NC 27607-4924 Office: NC State U Dept Elec Engring Raleigh NC 27695-3001

HAUSER, JOHN RICHARD, marketing and management science educator; b. Scranton, Pa., Apr. 19, 1949; s. Jesse Ransberry and Muriel Florence (Myers) H.; m. Marija Danüte Eiva Hauser, June 9, 1979; children: Marius John, Aleksas Jonas, Rolandas Aras. SB in Elec. Engring., SM in Elec. Engring. and Civil Engring., MIT, 1973, ScD in Ops. Rsch., 1975. Asst. prof. mktg. and transp. Northwestern U., Evanston, Ill., 1975-80; assoc. prof. mgmt. sci. MIT, Cambridge, Mass., 1980-84, prof. mgmt. sci., 1984-89, Kirin prof. mktg., 1989—, head mktg. group, 1988—2003, co-dir. Internat. Ctr. Rsch. on Mgmt. of Tech., 1993-2000, rsch. dir. Ctr. for Innovation in Product Devel., 1997-2000; Marvin Bower fellow Harvard U., Cambridge, Mass., 1987-88; prin. Applied Mktg. Sci., Waltham, Mass., 1989—. Vis. lectr. European Inst. Bus. Adminstrn., Fontainbleau, France, 1985; trustee Mktg. Sci. Inst., Cambridge, Mass., 2003—; spkr., lectr. in field; expert witness in field; cons. in field. Author: Applying Marketing Management: Four Simulations, 1986, (with others) Essentials of New Product Management, 1986, Design and Marketing of New Products, 2nd edit., 1993, Enterprise: An Integrating Management Exercise, 1989; editor-in-chief Mktg. Sci., 1989-94; contbr. articles to profl. jours. NSF fellow, 1971-74; grantee in field; recipient Parlin award, 2001. Mem. Am. Mktg. Assn. (1st Pl. Thesis Supervision award 1981, Paul D. Converse award 1996, MSI award 1996, Parlin award 2001), European Mktg. Acad., Inst. Mgmt. Sci. (1st Pl. Best Paper award 1982, 83, 93), Product Devel. and Mgmt. Assn., Tau Beta Pi, Eta Kappa Nu, Sigma Xi. Episcopalian. Avocations: sailing, skiing, basketball. Office: MIT E56-314 38 Memorial Dr Cambridge MA 02142-1347 E-mail: jhauser@mit.edu.

HAUSER, JOYCE ROBERTA, marketing professional; b. N.Y.C. d. Abraham and Helen (Lesser) Frankel; divorced; children: Mitchell, Mark, Ellen BA, SUNY, 1976; PhD, Union Inst. and U., 1987. Editor Art in Flowers, 1956-58; pres. Joyce Advt., 1958-65; ptnr. Hauser & Assocs., Pub. Rels., 1966-75; dir. broadcasting Bildersee Pub. Rels., 1973-75; pres. Hauser & Assocs., Inc., Pub. Rels., 1975-78; COO, pres. Hauser-Roberts, Inc., Pub. Rels./Mktg., N.Y.C., 1978—85; pres. Mktg. Concepts & Communications Inc., N.Y.C., 1985-92; moderator show Perceptions Sta. WEVD, 1975-77, Speaking of Health Sta. WNBC, 1977-89, 97 Health Line, Sta. WYNY, 1980-83, Conversations with Joyce Hauser, Sta. WNBC, 1975-86, What's on Your Mind, Sta. WYNY, 1983-84, Talk-Net, 1983-90; entertainment critic Sta. NBC, 1986-92. Instr. Baruch Coll., CCNY, 1980 85; assoc. prof. NYU, 1987—, prof. edn., 1992—, developer pub. rels. specialization. Sr. editor Art & Leisure News Svc., 1988—, editor-in-chief N.Y. State Comms. Annual, 1999—; contbg. editor Alive, 1976-77; author: Good Divorces, Bad Divorces: A Case for Divorce Mediation, 1995; contbr. 70 articles to profl. jours., chpts. to books. Mem. Citywide Health Adv. Coun. on Sch. Health, 1970-88, treas., 1980-92; mem. adv. bd. degree programs NYU Sch. Continuing Edn.; mediator/arbitrator Victim Svcs. Agy., 1986-87, Inst. Mediation and Conflict Resolution, 1985-86. Named one of 10 Top Successful Women, Cancer Soc., 1976, Tchr. of Yr., Zeta Beta Tau, 1989-90, one of 20 Top Women in Pub. Rels., 1981, Prof. of Yr. Sch. of Edn., 1999, Prof. of Yr., NYU Sch. Edn., 1999-2000; recipient Professionalism award Sta. WNBC, 1980; John E. Wilson fellow, 1996-97. Mem. AFTRA, Pub. Rels. Soc. Am., Nat. Assn. Communicators, Nat. Assn. Scholars, N.Y. State Communicators (treas., v.p. 1996, pres. 1997), N.Y. State Comms. Assn. (editor annual 1998), Acad. Family Mediators, Soc. Profl. Dispute Resolutions, Drama Desk, Outer Critics Cir., N.Y. Press Club. Home: 115 E 82nd St New York NY 10028-0831

HAUSER, MICHAEL GEORGE, astrophysicist; b. Chgo., Dec. 3, 1939; s. Julius and Sylvia Ann (Gross) Hauser; m. Miriam Freedman, Sept. 11, 1960 (div. May 1977); children: Karen Celia(dec.), Gerald Paul; m. Deanna Grove, May 8, 1981; stepchildren: Lisa Dawn Greening, Amy Lynne Canby, Elizabeth Ann Grove. B.Engring. Physics with distinction, Cornell U., 1962; PhD in Physics (NSF fellow), Calif. Inst. Tech., 1967. Instr. Princeton U., 1967-70, asst. prof. physics, 1970-72; sr. rsch. fellow in physics Calif. Inst. Tech., 1972-74; head infrared astronomy group lab. for high energy astrophysics Goddard Space Flight Center, Greenbelt, Md., 1974-77, head sect. infrared astrophysics Lab. for Extraterrestrial Physics, 1977-85, head infrared astrophysics br. Lab. Extraterrestrial Physics, 1985-87, head infrared astrophysics br. Lab. Astronomy and Solar Physics, 1987, chief Lab. Astronomy and Solar Physics, 1988-95; dep. dir. Space Telescope Sci. Inst., Balt., 1995—. Mem. joint sci. working group Infrared Astron. Satellite, 1977-84; prin. investigator Diffuse Infrared Background Experiment, Cosmic Background Explorer, 1977-97; mem. NASA Space Sci. Adv. Com., 1994-97. Vice pres. PTA, Kensington (Md.) Jr. High, 1977-78, mem. exec. bd., 1978-79. Named Hon. Woodrow Wilson fellow, 1962; recipient Exceptional Sci. Achievement medal, NASA, 1984, 1991, John C. Lindsay award, Goddard Space Flight Ctr., 1986, Award of Merit, 1995, Meritorious Exec. award, Exec. Svc., 1994, AURA Sci. award, Assn. Univs. for Rsch. in Astronomy, 1998. Fellow Am. Phys. Soc., AAAS; mem. Am. Astron. Soc., Internat. Astron. Union (v.p. commn. 21, 1991-94), Sigma Xi. Achievements include rsch. in elem. particle physics, astronomy, and cosmology. Office: Space Telescope Sci Inst 3700 San Martin Dr Baltimore MD 21218-2464 E-mail: hauser@stsci.edu.

HAUSER, RAY LOUIS, research engineer, entrepreneur; b. Litchfield, Ill., Apr. 16, 1927; s. A. Vernon and Grace (Gregg) H.; m. Consuelo Wright Minnich, Sept. 2, 1951; children: Beth, Cynthia, Dewi, Chris. BS, U. Ill., 1950; M in Engring., Yale U., 1952; PhD, U. Colo., 1957. Registered profl. engr., Colo., safety engr., Calif. Sr. project engr. Conn. Hard Rubber Co., New Haven, 1950-52; rsch. staff U. Colo., Boulder, 1954-57; material tech. staff Martin Co., Denver, 1957-61; owner, mgr. Hauser Labs., Boulder, 1961-89; materials/process cons., expert witness Ray Hauser Expertise, Boulder, 2000—. Bd. dirs. Surface Solutions Inc.; vis. lectr. U. Colo., Boulder, 1957-63. Pres. Boulder Civic Opera, 1971-72. Sgt. U.S. Army, 1952-54. Recipient U. Colo. medal, 1995, Gold medal Colo. Engring. Coun., 1999. Fellow AAAS; mem. AIChE, Soc. Plastics Engrs. (bd. dirs. 1959-62), Assn. Cons. Chemists and Chem. Engrs. (bd. dirs. 1986), Am. Assn. Lab. Accreditation (bd. dirs. 1986-91), Rotary (bd. dirs. 1975-77). Home and Office: 5758 Rustic Knolls Dr Boulder CO 80301-3029 E-mail: ray@rayhauser.com.

HAUSER, RICHARD ALAN, Federal Agency Administrator, Lawyer; b. Litchfield, Ill., Feb. 26, 1943; s. Melvin Henry and Helen Maxine (Roberts) H.; m. Carol E. Clampett, Jan. 2, 1965 (div. 1974); children: Jennifer Macey, Sarah Hampton; m. Karen Rollow Allen, July 26, 1977; children: Kristin Anne, Erica Christine, Alissa Marie. BS, U. Pa., 1965; JD cum laude, U. Miami, 1968. Bar: Fla., D.C. Law clk. U.S. Dist. Ct. Fla., Miami, 1968-70; asst. U.S. atty. Dept. Justice, Miami, 1970-71, atty. adviser Dept. Atty. Gen.'s Office Washington, 1971-73, asst. dir. Office of Policy Planning, 1974-75; assoc. counsel White House, Washington, 1973-74, dep. counsel to pres., 1981-86; pvt. practice Washington, 1975-81; ptnr. Baker & Hostetler, Washington, 1986—; gen. counsel U.S. Dept. H.U.D., Washington, 2001—. Chmn. Pennsylvania Ave. Devel. Corp., 1988-96; mem. Internat. Ctr. Settlement of Investment Disputes, 1986-94; chmn. bd. dirs. The Luther Inst., Washington; bd. dirs. Lutheran Brotherhood Mutual Funds. Bd. dirs. Washington Hosp. Ctr., 2000—. Recipient Spl. Asst. U.S. Atty. award for Superior Performance, Dept. Justice Mem. Fla. Bar Assn., D.C. Bar Assn., Va. Bar Assn., Chevy Chase Club, Met. Club (bd. govs.), Econ. Club. Office: US Dept HUD Gen Counsel 451 7th St SW Washington DC 20410-9000

HAUSER, RITA ELEANORE ABRAMS, lawyer; b. N.Y.C., July 12, 1934; d. Nathan and Frieda (Litt) Abrams; m. Gustave M. Hauser, June 10, 1956; children: Glenvil Aubrey, Ana Patricia. AB magna cum laude, CUNY Hunter Coll., 1954; D in Polit. Economy with highest honors, U. Strasbourg, France, 1955; Licence en Droit, U. Paris, 1958; student, Harvard U., 1955-56; LLB with honors, NYU, 1959; LLD (hon.), Seton Hall U., 1969, Finch Coll., 1969, U. Miami, Fla., 1971, Colgate U., 1995. Bar: D.C. 1959, N.Y. 1961, U.S. Supreme Ct. 1967. Atty. U.S. Dept. Justice, 1959-61; pvt. practice N.Y.C., 1961-67; ptnr. Moldover, Hauser, Strauss & Volin, 1968-72; sr. ptnr. Stroock & Stroock & Lavan, N.Y.C., 1972-92, of counsel, 1992—; pres. The Hauser Found., N.Y.C., 1990—; presdl. apptd. mem. Pres.'s Fgn. Intelligence Bd. and Intelligence Oversight Bd., 2001. Handmaker lectr., Louis Brandeis Lecture Series, U. Ky. Law Sch.; lectr. internat. law Naval War Coll. and Army War Coll.; lectr. St. Anthony's Coll., Oxford (England) U., 2002; Mitchell lectr. in law SUNY, Buffalo; USIA lectr. constl. law Egypt, India, Australia, New Zealand; bd. dirs. The Eisenhower World Affairs Inst.; U.S. chmn. Internat. Ctr. for Peace in Middle East, 1984-92; bd. dirs. Internat. Peace Acad., chair 1993—; U.S. pub. del. to Vienna follow-up meeting of Conf. on Security and Cooperation in Europe, 1986-88; mem. adv. panel in internat. law U.S. Dept. State, 1986-92, Am. Soc. Internat. Law Award to honor Women in Internat. Law; mem. Pacific Coun. on Internat. Policy, 1998-2000; bd. dirs. The Rand Corp. Contbr. articles to profl. jours. U.S. rep. to UN commn. on Human Rights, 1969-72; mem. U.S. del. to Gen. Assembly UN, 1969; vice chmn. U.S. Adv. Com. on Internat. and Cultural Affairs, 1973-77; mem. N.Y.C. Bd. Higher Edn., 1974-76, Stanton Panel on internat. info., edn., cultural rels. to reorganize USIA and Voice of Am., 1974-75, Mid. East Study Gruop Brookings Inst., 1975, 87-88, U.S. del. World Conf. Internat. Women's Yr., Mexico City, 1975; co-chair Com. for Re-election Pres., 1972, Presdl. Debates project LVW, 1976, Coalition for Regan/Bush; adv. bd. Nat. News Coun., 1977-79; bd. dirs. Bd for Internat. Broadcasting, 1977-80, Catalyst, Internat. Peace Acad., The Aspen Inst., The RAND Corp., U.S. Coun. Germany; trustee, exec com. N.Y. Philharm. Soc.; trustee Lincoln Ctr. Performing Arts; adv. bd. Ctr. For Law and Nat. Security, U. Va. Law Sch., 1978-84; vis. com. Ctr. Internat. Affairs Harvard U., 1975-81, John F. Kennedy Sch. Govt., Harvard U., 1992—, chair adv. bd. Hauser Ctr. for Non-Profit Orgns. at Harvard U.; dean's bd. advisor's Harvard Law Sch., 1996—, vice-chair, nat. co-chair univ. fund-raising campaign, 1997-2000, vice chmn. com. on univ. resources, 2002-; bd. advisors Mid. East Inst., Harvard U.; bd of visitors Georgetown Sch. Fgn. Svc., 1989-94; chmn. adv. panel Internat. Parlimentatry Group for Human Rights in Soviet Union, 1984-86; mem. Lawyers Com. for Human Rights, 1995—; mem. spl. refugee adv. panel Dept. State, 1981; bd. fellows Claremont U. Ctr. & Grad. Sch., 1990-94; former trustee Internat. Legal Ctr., Legal Aid Soc. N.Y., Freedom House; mem. Lawyer's Comm. Human Rights, 1996—. Fulbright grant U. Strasbourg, 1955; Intellectual Exch. fellow Japan Soc.; recipient Jane Addams Internat. Women's Leadership award, 1996, Women in Internat. Law award Am. Soc. Internat. Law, 1995, Fulbright award for Fulbright Alumni, 1997, Servant of Justice award, Legal Aid Soc. N.Y., 2000. Fellow ABA (life, mem. standing coms. on law and nat. security 1979-85, standing com. on world order under law 1969-78, standing com. on jud. selection, tenure, compensation 1977-79, coun. sect. on ind. rights and responsibilities 1970-73, advisor bd. jour. 1973-78); mem. Am. Soc. Internat. Law (v.p. 1988—, mem. exec. com. 1971-76), Am. Fgn. Law Assn. (bd. dirs.), Am. Arbitration Assn. (past bd. dirs.), Ams. Soc. (bd. dirs. 1988—), Coun. Fgn. Rels. (bd. dirs.), Internat. Inst. for Strategic Studies (London, bd. dirs. 1994—), Internat. Adv. Bd., Jaffee Ctr. for Strategic Studies, Tel Aviv Univ. (1999—), Am. Coun. on Germany, The Atlantic Coun. U.S., Friends of the Hauge Acad. Internat. Law (bd. dirs.), Assn. of Bar of City of N.Y., Catalyst (bd. dirs. 1989-96). Republican. Office: Stroock & Stroock & Lavan 180 Maiden Ln Fl 17 New York NY 10038-4937 also: The Hauser Found Office of Pres 712 5th Ave New York NY 10019-4108

HAUSER, SARAH B. artist; b. San Francisco, 1956; d. John Norman and Florence DeBonis Hauser; life ptnr. Jeffrey Warren Lerer. BFA, NYU, 1983; student, Art Students League, 1990—93, Cooper Union, 1996—, Manhattan Graphics, 1996—, Lower East Side Print Shop, 1996—, Koho Sch. Sumi-E, 2000—. Artist-tchr. Arts Connection, NYC, 1996—, Dieu Donne Papermill, NYC, 1996—2000; asst. instr. Japan Soc., N.Y.C., 2001. Exhibitions include Barrett Art Ctr., Poughkeepsie, NY, 1999, Woman Made Gallery, Chgo., 1999, Bedford Gallery, Dean Lesher Ctr. Arts, NYC, 1999, Feminist Expo, Balt., 2000, Purdue U. Galleries, 2000, Bklyn. Botanic Garden, 2000, Sumei Multidisciplinary Arts Ctr., NJ, 2000, Nomo Gallery, Kampala, Uganda, 2000, Woman Made Gallery, Chgo., 2000, Open Space Gallery, Allentown, Pa., 2000, New Leaf Editions, Vancouver, Can., 2000, Hiram Blauvelt Mus., Oradell, NJ, 2000, Ga. Coll. and State U., 2000, Veliko Turnovo Mcpl. Art Gallery, Bulgaria, 2000, Beit Gavriel Cultural Ctr., Israel, 2000, Contemporary Mus. of Balt., 2000—02, Yad Lebanim Gallery, Israel, 2001, Fulton St. Gallery, NYC, 2001, La. State, Baton Rouge, 2001, LSU Union Art Gallery, 2001, Bklyn. Botanic Garden, 2001, Canton Artists Guild, Conn., 2001, Conn. Graphic Arts Ctr., 2001, Fredericksburg Ctr. Creative Arts, Va., 2001, Woman Made Gallery, Chgo., 2001, Woodward Gallery, NYC, 2001, Kirkland Arts Ctr., 2001 (Grand Prize for "Mona Is", 2001), Gallery of Que. Printmaking Coun., 2001—02, Purdue U. Galleries, 2001, Bklyn. Botanic Garden, 2002, Woodward Gallery, NYC, 2002, No. Nat., Rhinelander, Wis., 2002, Nat. Small Works Exhibit-Washington Printmakers Gallery, 2002, AI&G 11 Ann. Nat. Exhbn., 2002, PrintAlliance Sept. 11 Meml. Portfolio, 2002, Perkins Ctr. Arts, NJ, 2002, Montreal Internat. Miniature Prints Biennial, 2002, Delta Nat. Small Prints Exhbn., 2002, Toy Theater Exhbn., NYC, 2003, Boston Printmakers, 2003, Internat. Print Ctr. of NY, 2003, Iowa State U., 2003, Holter Mus., 2003, Long Beach Arts, 2003, Hudson Opera House, 2003, Woodward Gallery, 2003, Kirkland Arts Ctr., 2003, Printmaking Biennial, 2003, No. Nat., Rhinelander, Wis., 2003, Nat. Small Works Exhibit-Wash. Printmakers Gallery, 2003, one-woman shows include John Jay Gallery, 2002, exhibited in group shows at Spring Studio, NYC, 1994—96, Noho Gallery, 2000, Bedford Gallery, Dean Lescher Ctr. Arts, 2002, Represented in permanent collections Woodward Gallery, U. Oregon, Nat. Assn. Women Artists, Vivian and Gordon Gilkey Ctr. of Portland Art Mus., Spencer Mus. (U. Kans.), KIWA (Japan), Iowa U. Print Soc., NY Pub. Libr., prin. works include .Spiffy, 1998 (Esther K. Gayner Meml. award, 2001), Lady & 4 Dogs in Central Park, 1999, Chinese Crested with Red Sweater, 1999, 3 Dogs in a Truck, 1999, Mona Is, 2001 (Grand Prize Kirkland Arts Ctr. Printmaking Biennial, 2001), Little Jazz, 2001 (Medal of Honor, Elizabeth Morse Genius Found. printmaking award, 2003), La Vision du Bouledogue I, 2001 (Elizabeth Fenn Meml. award, 2001), Panchito, 2002 (1st prize graphics, 2002, Hortense Ferne Meml. award Printmaking, 2002, 4th prize printmaking, 2003), Guadalupe Montaña I, 2003 (Silver award, Dialogue Magazine, 2003), Coos Bay Mus. (3d prize), pub. art project, Art Unleashed, Lancaster, Pa., 2002, work included in books and periodicals, 2000—, website, www.sarahhauser.womanmade.net, 2001. Recipient 3rd prize Ann. Print Exhbn., Charlevoix Art Gallery, 1999. Mem.: Nat. Assn. Women Artists, New York Artist's Cir., Baren Artist's Cir., Sumi-e Soc. Am., Lower East Side Printshop (keyholder), Woodward Gallery. Office: Sarah Hauser PO Box 2234 New York NY 10009 E-mail: cucamongie@aol.com.

HAUSER, STEPHEN L. medical educator; SB, MIT, 1971; MD, Harvard Medical School, 1975. Postdoctoral fellow in immunology Harvard Med. Sch., 1980—83; postdoctoral fellow Institut Pasteur, Paris, 1983—86; chair, Robert A. Fishman dist. prof. neurology U. Calif., San Francisco, 1987—. Editor Harrison's Principle of Internal Medicine. Fellow American Academy of Arts and Sciences, American Associations of Physicians. Mem.: Institute of Medicine, 1999-. Office: U Calif San Francisco Dept Neurology PO Box 114 San Francisco CA 94143-0001

HAUSER, WILLIAM BARRY, history educator, historian; b. Washington, May 2, 1939; s. Philip Morris and Zelda Barnett (Abrams) H.; children: Benjamin Lester, Aaron Davidson, Zachary Barnett. SB in Math., U. Chgo., 1960; MA in East Asian Studies, Yale U., 1962, PhD in History, 1969. Lectr., asst. prof. U. Mich., Ann Arbor, 1967-69, 70-74; asst. prof. history U. Rochester, N.Y., 1974-77, assoc. prof. history, 1977-83, prof. history, 1983—, chmn. dept. history, 1979-85. Author: Economic Institutional Change in Tokugawa Japan, 1974, (with Jeffrey P. Mass) The Bakufu in Japanese History, 1985; contbr. articles and revs. to profl. publs. Fellow Fulbright-Hays fellow, U.S. Dept. State, Osaka, Japan, 1964—66, NEH fellow, 1972—73, 1982—83, Mellen Faculty fellow, U. Rochester, 1977, Japan Found. fellow, 1976, 1982. Mem. Assn. for Asian Studies (chmn. adv. com. Bibliography of Asian Studies 1984-96). Avocations: cooking, gardening. Home: 425 Westminster Rd Rochester NY 14607-3231 Office: U Rochester Dept History Rochester NY 14627-0070 E-mail: wbha@mail.rochester.edu.

HAUSERMAN, JACQUITA KNIGHT, management consultant; b. Donalsonville, Ga., Apr. 23, 1942; d. Lendon Bernard and Ressie Mae (Robinson) Knight; m. Mark Kenny Hauserman, July 8, 1978 (div. Mar. 1998). BS in Math., U. Montevallo, Ala., 1964; MA in Tchg. Math., Emory U., 1973; MBA in Fin., Ga. State U., 1978. Fin. analyst Cleve. Electric Illuminating Co., 1982-83, gen. supr. employment svc., 1983-85, sr. corp. planning advisor, 1985-86, dir. customer svc., 1986-88, v.p. adminstrn., 1988-90; v.p. customer svc. & cmty. affairs Centerior Energy Corp., Independence, Ohio, 1990-93, v.p. customer support, 1993-95, v.p. bus. svcs., 1995-97; v.p., chief devel. officer Summa Health Sys., Akron, Ohio, 1999-2000; prin. Arcadia Consulting, Pepper Pike, Ohio, 2000—. Bd. dirs. Cascade Devel. Corp., Am. Stone Industries; ind. cons. Trustee John Carroll U., U. Heights, Ohio. Home and Office: 8440 Danbury Blvd #204 Naples FL 34120 E-mail: jkh2clev@aol.com.

HAUSFELD, JAMES FRANK, executive director; b. Chgo., July 22, 1955; s. James J. and Geraldine M. (Nesladek) H.; m. Loretta Brown, Sept. 16, 2000; 1 child, Laura Beth. BA in Comm., Columbia Coll., 1976. Producer, cameraman Chgo. Bulls Basketball Team, 1976-77; media specialist Bell and Howell, Chgo., 1977-79; producer, dir. New Trier Technology Coop., Winnetka, Ill., 1979-94, exec. dir., 1994—, adminstr. in charge devel. high speed data and video network, mem. adv. coun., 1995—. Mem. State of Ill. Instnl. Tech. Adv. Coun., 1994—; mem. ind. video competition jury Chgo. Internat. Film Festival, 1979-86; freelance editor, cameraman On Location, Ltd., Chgo., 1983-90; freelance video editor, videographer Bougainville Prodns., 1991—. Producer, editor, dir.: (videotapes) North Suburban Spl. Edn. Dist.-One Child at a Time, 1984, The Pursuit of Excellence-Illinois Style, 1985, Social Service: A Committment to Caring, 1987, To Enrich Their Lives, 1989, Nazi Concentration Camps: an Eyewitness Account, 1990, Peer Helping: A Code of Friendship, 1992, Education and the Common Denominator: The Teacher, 1995, Abriendo Puertas: The Winnetka Schools Foreign Language Program, 1996, New Trier Technology Cooperative 1997 Institute Day: Thinking in the Future Tense, 1997, The Grade 3 Virtual Museum Project, 1999, Dancin' Through the Decades, 2001; editor (videotapes) Perspectives on China, 1987, The Other Side of Summer: The Wrecking of Old Comiskey Park, 1993, Wrigley Field: Beyond the Ivy, 2001. Mem. Internat. TV Assn. Clubs: Argyle-Magnolia Glenwood Block (capt. 1985-89), Montrose Elite (Chgo.); BMG Music Service (Indpls.). Roman Catholic. Avocations: softball, darts, collecting music, attending Chgo. White Sox games. Home: 1431 W Argyle St Chicago IL 60640-3502 Office: New Trier Tech Coop 385 Winnetka Ave Winnetka IL 60093-4238 E-mail: hausfelj@nttc.org.

HAUSHALTER, HARRY, lawyer; b. Tel Aviv, July 7, 1945; s. Leo and Ruth H.; m. Theresa Ann Lukowicz. BA magna cum laude, Rutgers U., 1967, JD, 1970. Bar: N.J. 1970, U.S. Dist. Ct. 1970, U.S. Ct. Appeals (3rd cir.) 1982, U.S. Supreme Ct. 1982. Tax atty. Arthur Anderson & Co., Newark, 1970-71; dep. atty. gen. N.J. Atty. Gen.'s Office, Trenton, 1972-90; atty. Conley & Haushalter, Princeton, N.J., 1990-98; pvt. practice Hamilton, N.J., 1998—. Author: Matthew Bender/N.J. Taxes, 1982. Trustee Rutgers Ctr. for Govt. Svcs., 1994—; mem. Supreme Ct. Com. on N.J. Jud. Tax Ct., 1982-2002. Mem. Phi Beta Kappa. Office: Harry Haushalter Atty-at-Law 2119 Route 33 Ste A Hamilton NJ 08690-1740

HAUSLER, WILLIAM JOHN, JR., microbiologist, educator, public health laboratory administrator; b. Kansas City, Kans., Aug. 31, 1926; s. William John and Clifton (McCambridge) H.; m. Mary Lois Rice, Apr. 19, 1949 (dec. 1999); children: Cheryl Kaye Johnson, Kenneth Randall, Eric Rice, Mark Clifton; m. Jeanne Seeberger, May 26, 2001. AB in Microbiology, U. Kans., 1951, MA in Microbiology, 1953, PhD in Microbiology, Math., 1958. Diplomate Am. Bd. Med. Microbiology (chmn. 1979-82, Profl. Recognition award 1995). Asst. instr. U. Kans., Lawrence, 1951-56, rsch. asst., 1956-58; assoc. bacteriologist Iowa State Hygienic Lab., Iowa City, 1958-59, asst. dir., prin. bacteriologist, 1959-65, dir., 1965-95; dir. emeritus, 1995—; asst. prof. U. Iowa Coll. Medicine, Iowa City, 1959-66, assoc. prof., 1966-90, prof., 1990—; assoc. prof. U. Iowa Coll. Dentistry, 1966-90, prof., 1990—. Cons. to Iran WHO, 1969, U.S. EPA, 1970-72, CDC, 1965—, People's Republic China WHO, 1990, WHO Western Pacific Region, 1991, UNDP India, 1992; cons. to industry; mem. mil. infectious diseases rsch. program Am. Inst. Biol. Scis., 2002. Editor: Standard Methods for the Examination of Dairy Products, 1972, Manual Clinical Microbiology, 3d edit., 1980, 4th edit., 1985, 5th edit., 1991, Compendium of Methods for the Microbiological Examination of Foods, 1980, 2d edit., 1984, Diagnostic Procedures for Bacterial Mycotic and Parasitic Infections, 1981, Laboratory Diagnosis of Infections Diseases: Principles and Practice, 1988; co-editor: Topley & Wilson's Microbiology and Microbial Infections, 9th edit., 1997; mem. editl. bd. various profl. jours.; contbr. articles to profl. jours. Councilman City Govt., University Heights, Iowa, 1966-69; commr. Iowa Air Pollution Control Commn., 1967-74; mem. exec. com. Iowa Dept. Environ. Quality, 1974-80, Nat. Com. for Clin. Lab. Standards, bd. dirs., 1987-93. Lt. comdr. USNR, 1944-67. Recipient Henry Albert Meml. award Iowa Pub. Health Assn., 1974. Fellow APHA, Am. Acad. Microbiology (chmn. 1983-89, Profl. Recognition award 1995); mem. Am. Soc. Microbiology, Assn. State and Territorial Pub. Health Lab. Dirs. (pres. 1984-85, Lifetime Achievement award 1998), Sigma Phi Epsilon, Rotary (Paul Harris fellow). Avocations: photography, woodworking, wilderness backpacking. Home: 11 The Woods NE Iowa City IA 52240-7986 Office: U Iowa Hygienic Lab Oakdale Hall Iowa City IA 52242 E-mail: iahausler@yahoo.com.

HAUSMAN, ARTHUR HERBERT, electronics company executive; b. Chgo., Nov. 24, 1923; s. Samuel Louis and Sarah (Elin) H.; m. Helen Mandelowitz, May 19, 1946; children: Susan Lois, Kenneth Louis, Catherine Ellen. BS in Elec. Engring. U. Tex., 1944; S.M., Harvard U., 1948. Electronics engr. Engring. Research Assos., St. Paul, 1946-47; supervisory electronics scientist U.S. Dept. Def., Washington, 1948-60; now advisor, v.p., dir. research Ampex Corp., Redwood City, Calif., 1960-63, v.p. ops., 1963-65, group v.p., 1965-67, exec. v.p., 1967-71, exec. v.p., pres., chief exec. officer, 1971-83, chmn. bd., 1981-87, chmn. bd. emeritus, 1987—. Chmn. tech. adv. com. computer peripherals Dept. Commerce, 1973-75; mem. Pres.'s Export Coun.; chmn. Subcom. on Export Adminstrn., 1984-88; bd. dirs. Drexler Tech. Inc., Vista Rsch. Inc., Calif.-Amplifier, Inc. Trustee United Bay Area Crusade.; mem. vis. com. dept. math. MIT; Bd. dirs. Bay Area Council. Served with USNR, 1944-54. Recipient Meritorious Civilian Service award Dept. Def. Mem. IEEE, Army Ordnance Assn. (dir. chpt. 1969-71), Am. Electronics Assn. (dir.) Clubs: Commonwealth of Calif.; Cosmos.

HAUSMAN, CARL DANE, writer, journalism and media educator; b. San Antonio, July 17, 1953; s. Carl Dane and Joyce Bell (Ingraham) H.; m. Susan V. Rezen, Aug. 1, 1980 (div. Sept. 2, 1991); m. Sherry Peng, Dec. 23, 1995. BA, U. State of NY, Albany, 1986; MA, Antioch U., 1988; PhD, Union Grad. Sch., 1990; post doctoral fellowship, N.Y.U., 1991. Anchor, reporter WENY AM/FM/TV, Elmira, N.Y., 1975-77; broadcast journalist Syracuse (N.Y.) U., 1977-80; freelance journalist and author Worcester, Mass., 1980-90; Mellon fellow, vis. instr. N.Y.U., 1990-92; sr. fellow Inst. for Global Ethics, Camden, Maine, 1992-93; pres. Ctr. for Media in the Pub. Interest, Carlisle, Pa., 1993—2000; assoc. prof. journalism Rowan U., 1997—. Cons. editor HarperCollins Pubs., N.Y.C., 1991-93; mng. editor Insights, Inst. for Global Ethics, Camden, 1993-2002. Author: The Decision Making Process in Journalism, 1991, Crisis of Conscience, 1992, Crafting the News, 1993; co-author Modern Video Production, 1993, Lies We Live By, 2000; editor Bus. Ethics Newsline, 1998—. Campaign mgr. Oswego (N.Y.) County Rep. Com., 1975; dir. Camden (Maine) Conf., 1992. Mem. Soc. Profl. Journalists, Radio TV News Dirs. Assn., Authors' Guild. Republican. Lutheran. Avocations: golf, running, weight lifting. Home: 600 Quincy Ct Glassboro NJ 08028-3009

HAUSMAN, GARY J. social sciences educator; b. Elizabeth, N.J., Jan. 29, 1957; s. Eugene A. Hausman and Marian C. Schipper. BA, U. Chgo., 1979; MA, U. Va., 1982; PhD, U. Mich., 1996. Fellow Dharam Hinduja Indic Rsch. Ctr. Columbia U., N.Y.C., 1996—97; adj. asst. prof. anthropology dept. U. N.C., Chapel Hill, 2002—. Mem. steering group Roja Muthiah Rsch. Libr., London, 2000—01. Contbr. articles to profl. jours. Fellow Jr. Rsch., Am. Inst. Indian Studies, 1990-1991, Sr. Rsch., 1997-1998, Charlotte W. Newcombe Doctoral Dissertation, Woodrow Wilson Found., 1994-1995, History, Wellcome Trust, 1999-2000; grantee Spl. Recognition, NSF, 1982. Mem.: Tamilnadu History Congress, Soc. Values Higher Edn., Soc. Social History Medicine, Soc. Social Studies Sci., Soc. Med. Anthropology, Internat. Assn. Study Traditional Asian Medicine, History Sci. Soc., Brit. Soc. History Sci., Assn. Asian Studies, Am. Hist. Assn., Am. Anthrop. Assn., Am. Acad. Religion. Office: U NC Dept Anthropology 301 Alumni Bldg CB# 3115 Chapel Hill NC 27599-3115

HAUSMAN, HARRIET SECELEY, administrator; b. Chgo., Apr. 8, 1924; d. Samuel and Lena Rubin; m. Martin C. Hausman, June 30, 1946 (dec. Apr. 1988); children: Daniel, Barbara. Student, U. Ill., 1941—42, Northwestern U., 1943—45; BS, Rosary Coll., 1972. Asst. tchr. Winfield (Ill.) Sch., 1945; psych testing Hines Vet. Hosp., Maywood, Ill., 1972-74; social worker Cook County Hosp., Chgo., 1973; pres. Power Parts Co., Chgo., 1947-87, CEO, 1987-92. Author: Reflections, A History of River Forest, 1975. Trustee River Forest (Ill.) Twp., 1978-90; bd. dirs. ACLU, 1988—, v.p.; bd. dirs. Jewish Childrens Bur., pres. 1970-92, v.p., 1992—; v.p., bd. dirs. Bldg. Better Futures (BBF), 1992-96, v.p. BBF Scholarship Bd., 1997-; vice chmn. scholarship com., 1998-. Named Woman Entrepreneur of Yr., 1992, U.S. Transp. Cmty. Svc. award Oak Park and River Forest, 1980, 96, 90, 92, 96, 99. Democrat. Jewish. Avocations: symphony, opera, drama, gardening, travel.

HAUSMAN, HOWARD, electronics executive; b. N.Y.C., July 4, 1945; s. Edward A. and Bella H.; m. Gloria Lynn; children: Lawrence Stuart, Bradley Russel. BSEE, Poly. Inst. N.Y., 1967, MSEE, 1971. Computer programmer Harry Kahn Assocs., Great Neck, N.Y., 1965-67; engr. Airborne Instruments Lab., Deer Park, N.Y., 1967-72; dept. head Miteq Inc., Hauppauge, N.Y., 1972-81; pres. Syncom Industries Inc., Bohemia, N.Y., 1981—; chief scientist Microphase Systems Inc., Hauppage, N.Y., 1992—; v.p. engring. Miteq Inc., Hauppage, 1996—; pres. Syncom Industries, Bohemia, 1999—. Mem. tech. cons. com., v.p. local adv. counsel 1st supervisory dist. Bd. Coop. Ednl. Services, Suffolk County, N.Y., 1986—; cons. Arista Devices, Inc., Ronkonkoma, N.Y., 1974-81; prof. Hofstra U., Hempstead, N.Y., 1996; adj. prof. Polytech. U., Farmingdale, N.Y., 1978—. Contbr. articles to profl. jours. Mem. IEEE (sr.), AIAA (sr.), AAAS, Nat. Contracts Mgmt. Assn., N.Y. Acad. Scis., Am. Inst. Aeronautics and Astronautics (sr.). Home: 105 Hidden Ponds Cir Smithtown NY 11787-5229 Office: Syncom Industries Inc 80 Orville Dr Bohemia NY 11716-2534 E-mail: hhausman@miteg.com. *As we acquire more knowledge we realize how little we know. It is a very humbling experience that tends to limit our creativity. It is important that we realize the subliminal negative feedback effects inherent in our learning experience and consciously focus our energies on piercing the envelope of the psychologically comfortable known universe.*

HAUSMAN, JERRY ALLEN, economics educator, consultant; b. Weirton, W.Va., May 5, 1946; s. Harold H. and Rose (Hausman); m. Margaretta Stone, Dec. 21, 1968; children: Nicholas, Claire. AB, Brown U., 1968; B.Phil., Oxford U., 1972, D.Phil., 1973. Mem. faculty MIT, Cambridge, 1973—, prof. econs., 1979—. Contbr. articles to profl. jours. Marshall scholar, 1970-72; recipient Frisch medal Econometrics Soc., 1980; John Bates Clark award Am. Econs. Assn., 1985. Office: MIT Dept Econs 77 Massachusetts Ave Dept Econs Cambridge MA 02139-4307

HAUSMAN, JILL SUSAN, cantor, vocalist, lyricist, poet, composer; d. Alan Louis Hausman and Roslyn Diamond Wolf; m. Harold John Hawkins, Apr. 4, 1975; children: Theodore Jeffrey Hawkins, Aaron David Hawkins. AB, Smith Coll., 1974. Environ. analyst U.S. Army Corps Engrs., N.Y.C., 1974; biologist Interstate Sanitation Commn., N.Y.C., 1975—78, Fred C. Hart Assocs., N.Y.C., 1978; cantor, rabbinic work Boro Pk. Progressive Synagogue, Bklyn., 1994—. Actor: Ft. Salem Theater; singer: Amato Opera, N.Y. Choral Soc. Summer Sings; singer, lyricist (classical CD) Lieder in Our Language, 2001, poet (song cycle of 5 poems) Animals Like Me (Gerald Busby), 2002; composer: (music) Misheberach, Ahavatolah, Ahava Raba, Ashreinu. Singer S.E.R.V.E. the Handicapped. Democrat. Avocations: cooking, biking, reading. Home: 12 W 96th St New York NY 10025 Office: Boro Park Progressive Synagogue 1515 46th St Brooklyn NY 11219

HAUSMAN, KEITH LYNN, hospital administrator, physical therapist; b. Cleve., Nov. 20, 1949; s. Harold Herbert and Betty (Reed) H.; 1 child, Sierra Dawn. BS, Loma Linda U., 1972, MA in Pub. Health, 1975. Lic. real estate broker; cert. instrument multiengine flight instr., air transport pilot. Acting adminstr. Thomas Rehab. Hosp., Asheville, N.C., 1976-77; pres. Marion County Hosp., Jefferson, Tex., 1977-81, Jellico (Tenn.) Community Hosp., 1981-91, health care cons., 1991—; pres. Premier Rehab., Inc., 1994—, Premier Vending, Inc., 2000—, Premier Vending Wholesale, Inc., 2002—. Bd. dirs. Pvt. Indsl. Coun. SDA4, Tenn., 1989-2000. Fellow Am. Coll. Health Care Execs., mem. Tenn. Hosp. Assn. (bd. dirs. 1991, pres. Mid-East dist. 1991), Campbell County C. of C. (bd. dirs. 1989-92). Republican. Seventh-Day Adventist. Home: PO Box 541 Jellico TN 37762-0541 E-mail: flyboy@2geton.net.

HAUSMAN, KEITH WAYNE, secondary school educator; b. Bethlehem, Pa., Mar. 11, 1967; s. Elwood Wayne Hausman Jr. and Gloria Jean Hausman. BS in Elem. Edn. and English, Kutztown (Pa.) U., 1990, MA in English, cum laude, 1997. Cert. tchr. English, Comm. and Elem. Edn. Pa. Day-to-day substitute tchr. Salisbury Twp. Sch. Dist., Allentown, Pa., 1990—99; English tchr. Anson H.S., Wadesboro, NC, 2000—02; English instr. Lehigh Carbon Cmty. Coll., Schnecksville, Pa., 2002—. Co-advisor Beta Club, Wadesboro, NC, 2000—02. Mem.: N.C. Assn. Educators. Republican. Gnostic. Avocations: baking, candy-making, writing poetry, Old English music. Home: 528 E Federal St Allentown PA 18103

HAUSMAN, STEVEN JACK, health science administrator; b. Phila., May 20, 1945; s. Leo and Bella Hausman. BA, U. Pa., 1967, MS, 1968, PhD, 1972. Postdoctoral fellow Inst. for Cancer Rsch., Phila., 1972-75; staff fellow Nat. Inst. on Aging, Balt., 1975-77; spl. asst. to assoc. dir. Nat. Inst. Arthritis, Metabolism and Digestive Diseases, Bethesda, Md., 1977-78, dir. ctrs. program, 1978-86; dep. dir. extramural program Nat. Inst. Arthritis and Musculoskeletal and Skin Diseases, Bethesda, 1986-90, dep. dir., 1990—, dir. extramural program, 1997—2002. Mem. AAAS, Am. Assn. Immunologists, Soc. In Vitro Biology, Am. Chem. Soc., Am. Soc. for Cell Biology. Office: NIAMS-NIH 31 Center Dr Msc2350 Bldg 31 Bethesda MD 20892-0001

HAUSMAN, WARREN HOWARD, educator; s. Herbert Frank Hausman and Elizabeth Fylgia Lorenson; m. Joan Linda Rascoe; children: Jeffrey W., Gregory J. BA in Econs., Yale U., 1961; PhD, MIT, 1966. Asst./assoc. prof. Johnson Sch. Mgmt., Cornell Univ., Ithaca, NY, 1965—70; assoc. prof Sloan Sch. Mgmt., M.I.T., Cambridge, Mass., 1970—73; assoc. prof. U. Rochester, NY, 1973—77; prof. Stanford (Calif.) U., 1977—, chair, dept. indsl. engring. and engring. mgmt., 1982—92. Cons. Hausman Consulting, Stanford, 1967—; pres.-elect Ops. Rsch. Soc. Am., Linthicum, Md., 1994—94; founder and dir. Supply Chain Seminars, Stanford, 1994—; co-founder Supply Chain Online, Stanford, 2001—; bd. dirs. SupplyChainge, Inc., Portland, Oreg. Co-author: (book) Quantitative Analysis for Management (multiple edits.), 1969—97; contbr. articles to profl. jours. Mem.: Inst. for Ops. Rsch. and the Mgmt. Scis. (bd. mem. 1994—97). Office: Stanford Univ Mgmt Sci & Engring Dept Stanford CA 94305-4026 Office Fax: 650-843-1725. E-mail: hausman@stanford.edu.

HAUSMAN, WILLIAM RAY, fund raising and management consultant; b. Bradford, Pa., Apr. 22, 1941; s. Raymond Harvey and Eleanor Janet (Freeman) H.; m. Rosalyn Schmidt, Aug. 16, 1963; children: Valerie Noelle, Stephanie Carol. AB, Wheaton Coll., 1963; MA, Trinity Evang. Div. Sch., 1966, DD (hon), 1981; postgrad., North Park Theol. Sem., 1968-69; EdM, Harvard U., 1977. Ordained to ministry Evang. Covenant Ch., 1971. Minister Christian edn. Glen Ellyn (Ill.) Covenant Ch., 1966-69; from registrar, dir. admissions to assoc. dean Trinity Evang. Div. Sch., Deerfield, Ill., 1969-80; pres. North Park Coll. and Theol. Sem., Chgo., 1980-86; from cons. to group mgr. Donald A. Campbell & Co., Inc., Chgo., 1986-94, v.p. ea. regional mgr., 1994—, sr. v.p., 1995—. Bd. dirs. Rockport Chamber Music Festival. Mem. Assn. Fundraising Profls. (cert.), Lehigh County Hist. Soc., Coun. Advancement and Support Edn., New Eng. Hist. Geneal. Soc. Office: Campbell & Co Eastern Regional Office 85 Eastern Ave Ste 305 Gloucester MA 01930-1869 E-mail: wrh@campbellcompany.com.

HAUSNER, JOHN HERMAN, judge; b. Detroit, Oct. 31, 1932; s. John E. and Anna (Mudrak) H.; m. Alice R. Kieltyka, Aug. 22, 1959. Ph.B. cum laude, U. Detroit, 1954, MA, 1957, JD summa cum laude, 1966. Bar: Mich. 1967, U.S. Ct. Appeals (6th cir.) 1968, U.S. Supreme Ct. 1971, U.S. Tax Ct. 1976, U.S. Ct. Claims 1976, U.S. Ct. Mil. Appeals 1976. Tchr. Detroit Pub. Schs., 1954, 56-59; tchg. fellow U. Cin., 1959-61; instr. U. Detroit, 1961-74, assoc. prof. 1967-69; asst. U.S. atty. Detroit, 1969-73; chief asst. U.S. atty. ea. dist. Mich., 1973-76; judge 3rd Jud. Cir. Mich., Wayne County, 1976-94; ret. 3d Jud. Cir. Mich., Wayne County, 1994, 1994. Lectr. Law Sch.; faculty adviser Nat. Jud. Coll., 1978-79. Author: Sebastian, The Essence of My Soul, 1982; contbr. articles to Detroit Advertiser. Served with U.S. Army, 1954—56. Mem. Fed. Bar Assn. (mem. exec. bd. Detroit chpt. 1976-82), State Bar Mich., Mich. Retired Judges Assn., Blue Key, Alpha Sigma Mu. Republican. Home: 22433 Louise St Saint Clair Shores MI 48081-2034 also: 8420 E Desert Palm Tucson AZ 85730-4723

HAUSNER, KARL, health products executive; b. Schwansdorf, Bavaria, Aug. 28, 1929; arrived in U.S., 1952; s. Josef and Florentine Hausner; m. Hermine Schwab, Mar. 16, 1956. BS, Agrl. Coll., Landsberg, Bavaria, 1952. Rsch. engr. Internat. Harvester Co., Chgo., 1953—59; founder, owner Siemens Med. U.S.A., Hinsdale, Ill., 1959—64, divsn. mgr. Union, NJ, 1964—69; pres., owner Elmed Inc., Addison, Ill., 1969—. Lectr. Inst. German-Am. Rels., Pitts., 1999—, Soc. German-Am. Studies, Cin., 1999—; active Pvt. Land Owners Wis., Sauk City, 1990—. Slave labor camp, 1945—46, Czechoslovakia. Achievements include design of various med. devices; patents pending for farm implement carrier. Home: 28 Concord Dr Oak Brook IL 60523 Office: Elmed Inc 60 W Fay Ave Addison IL 60101 Business E-Mail: medical@elmed.com.

HAUSTEIN, JANIS M. musician, music educator; d. Bertrand Matthew Haustein and Gladys Evangeline Youngren-Haustein. MS in Chemistry, Marquette U., 1970; MA in Theology, MA in Music, Notre Dame U., 1989; DMA, Am. Conservatory of Music, 1997. Cert. tchr. Grad. rsch. asst. Marquette U., Milw., 1969—70; instrumental tchr. Totino Grace H.S., Fridley, Minn., 1978—80; cmty. svc. worker Sch. Sisters of Notre Dame, Mankato, Minn., 1980—82; music dir., liturgist Christ the King Parish, Mpls., 1982—87; grad. asst. music dept. Notre Dame U., South Bend, Ind., 1987—89; music dir., organist All St. Episcopal Ch., Western Springs, Ill., 8919, Christ Mediator Evang. Luth. Ch. Am., Chgo., 1996—; mem. faculty Am. Conservatory of Music, Chgo., 1994—98. Chmn. fine arts com. Sch. Sisters of Notre Dame, 1991—96, chmn. organ restoration com., 1992—95; dir. summer choral festival South Suburban Musicians, Midlothian, Ill., 1990; coord., dir. anniversary and internat. liturgical music events; presenter organ dedication concerts. Contbr. articles to profl. publs.; author, dir. : (video) Johnson Organ Op 499, 1993. Mem. women's concern com. Coll. of St. Catherine, 1984—86; state del. Dem. Party, Mpls., 1982. Fellow: Organ Hist. Soc.; mem.: Am. Guild Organists (sec. bd. dirs.), Music Tchrs. Nat. Assn., Mu Phi Epsilon. Avocations: gardening, hiking, biking, Swedish folk painting, reading. Home: 7821 W 89th St Hickory Hills IL 60457

HAUTZINGER, JAMES EDWARD, lawyer; b. Apr. 15, 1936; s. Julius M. and Iva (Beach) H.; m. Susan Jean O'Brien, June 20, 1959; children: Peter Grattan, Sarah Jean, Andrew Beach; m. Leslie Ann Walker, Apr. 21, 1979; m. Anne Phillips, Oct. 28, 2000). BA, Grinnell Coll., 1958; JD, U. Chgo., 1961. Bar: Colo. 1961, U.S. Dist. Ct. Colo. 1961, U.S. Supreme Ct. 1973, U.S. Ct. Appeals (10th cir.) 1961, U.S. Ct. Appeals (5th cir.) 1981, U.S. Ct. Appeals (9th cir.) 1980. Assoc. Sherman & Howard, Denver, 1961-67; ptnr., 1967-98; counsel, 1999—. Exec. com. Coll. Labor and Employment Lawyers, 1998—; legal counsel People for Haskell campaign, 1972-78, Hart for Senate campaign, 1980; alt. del. Dem. Nat. Conv., 1968; vis. com. U. Chgo. Law Sch., 1978-80. Mng. editor Chgo. Law Rev., 1960. Mem. ABA, Colo. Bar Assn. (labor law com.), Denver Bar Assn., Indsl. Rels. Rsch. Assn., Denver Athletic Club, Phi Beta Kappa, Order of Coif. Office: Sherman & Howard 633 17th St Ste 3000 Denver CO 80202-3665 E-mail: jhautzin@sah.com.

HAUVER, CONSTANCE LONGSHORE, lawyer; b. Abington, Pa., Oct. 9, 1938; d. Malcolm Rettew and Margaret Evans (Lyon) L.; m. Arthur R. Hauver, 1962 (div. Mar. 1979); 1 child, Sian; m. Giles Toll, 1990. BA with high honors, Swarthmore Coll., 1960; MA, UCLA, 1962; JD magna cum laude, U. Denver, 1967. Bar: Colo. 1968, U.S. Dist. Ct. Colo. 1968, U.S. Tax Ct. 1970. Libr. Friends Com. on Nat. Legis., Washington, 1960-61; lectr. U. Hawaii, Honolulu, 1963-64; assoc. Sherman & Howard, Denver, 1968-73, ptnr., 1973-91; vol. naturalist Lookout Mountain Nature Ctr., 1998—. Mem. grievance com. Colo. Supreme Ct., 1981-86. Co-contbr. legal articles. Trustee Rocky Mountain Women's Inst., Denver, 1987-90, Swedish Med. Ctr. Found., Denver, 1978-85; bd. dirs. Women's Forum Colo. Inc., Denver, 1988-89, Girls Count, Denver, 1995-2000, pres., 1996-97. Named New Vol. Naturalist of Yr., Lookout Mountain Nature Ctr., 1998, Vol. Naturalist of Yr., 2001; recipient Athena award, Alliance Profl. Women, 1987. Fellow Am. Coll. Probate Counsel; mem. Colo. Bar Assn. (chair probate and trust law sect. 1982-83), Denver Bar Assn. (del. to ABA Ho. of Dels. 1986-88), Rocky Mountain Estate Planning Coun. (pres. 1980-81). Democrat. Mem. Soc. Of Friends. Avocations: mountain climbing, kayaking, skiing, reading.

HAVA, MILOS, retired pharmacologist, medical educator; b. Prague, Czech Republic, Oct. 15, 1927; arrived in U.S., 1968, naturalized, 1983; s. Emanuel and Eta Hava; m. Maria M. Hava, Sept. 5, 1951. MD, Charles U., Prague, 1952, PhD in Pharmacology, 1955. Cert. Ednl. Coun. for Fgn. Med. Grads., 1974. Asst. prof. pharmacology Charles U., 1952—55; sr. rsch. worker Czech Acad. Sci., 1955—58; dir. dept. pharmacology Rsch. Inst. Natural Products, Prague, 1958—68; assoc. prof. pharmacology U. Kans., Kansas City, 1968—73; prof. pharmacology U. Ill., Peoria, 1973—75; asst. med. dir. Marion Labs., Kansas City, 1975—79; dir. clin. rsch. Carter-Wallace, Cranbury, NJ, 1979—82, Wyeth, Phila., 1982—94; ret. Adj. prof. diagnostic imaging Temple U. Med. Sch., Phila., 1983—. Co-author: The Vinca Alkaloids, 1973; contbr. articles to profl. jours. Mem.: Am. Soc. Pharmacology and Exptl. Therapy. Avocations: reading, music, tennis, swimming, tai chi. Home: 126 South St Philadelphia PA 19147

HAVAS, HELGA FRANCIS, microbiologist, immunologist; b. Vienna, Nov. 26, 1915; came to U.S., 1940; m. Peter Havas, 1939; children: Eva Catherin, Stephen Walter. MA, Columbia U., 1943; PhD, Lehigh U., 1950. Rsch. chemist Cornell U., Ithaca, N.Y., 1945-46; rsch. fellow Lehigh U., Bethlehem, Pa., 1947-50; rsch. assoc. Inst. Cancer Rsch., Phila., 1950-63; assoc. prof. dept. microbiology Temple U. Sch. Medicine, Phila., 1963-72, prof. dept. microbiology, 1972-84, prof. emeritus, 1984—. Internat. Student Svc. fellow Lyon (France) U., 1938-39: Abbott Labs fellow Columbia U., N.Y.C., 1940-41; Katherine Comstock Thorne fellow Lehigh U., 1947-50; spl. fellow USPHS, Temple U. Sch. Medicine, Phila., 1964-66; recipient Career Devel. award USPHS-NIH, 1967-71. Mem. Am. Assn. for Cancer Rsch., Am. Soc. Microbiology, Am. Assn. Immunologists, Sigma Xi. Home: 1515 The Fairway Jenkintown PA 19046-1435 Office: Temple U Sch Medicine Dept Microbio Immunology 3400 N Broad St Philadelphia PA 19140-5104 E-mail: HHavas2416@aol.com.

HAVAS, PETER, physicist, educator; b. Budapest, Hungary, Mar. 29, 1916; came to U.S., 1941, naturalized, 1948; s. George G. and Irene (Harmos) H.; m. Helga Francis Höllering; children: Eva Catherine, Stephen Walter. Student, U. Vienna, Austria, 1937-38; Absolutorium, Technische Hochschule, Vienna, 1938; PhD, Columbia U., 1944. Rsch. fellow Institut de Physique Atomique, Lyon, France, 1938-41; lectr. in physics Columbia U., N.Y.C., 1941-45; instr. physics Cornell U., 1945-46; asst. prof. physics Lehigh U., Bethlehem, Pa., 1946-49; assoc. prof., 1949-54; prof., 1954-65; prof. physics Temple U., Phila., 1965-81; prof. emeritus, 1981—. Mem. Inst. for Advanced Study, Princeton, N.J., 1953-54, Bohr Inst., Copenhagen, 1954, Argonne Nat. Lab., 1958; vis. prof. U. Göttingen, Germany, 1973; adj. prof. physics U. Pa., 1982-88, Utah State U., 1987-90. Mem. editl. bd. Acta Phys. Austriaca, 1968-76, Jour. Math. Physics, 1975-77, KINAM (mex.) 1979—; mem. editl. adv. bd. The Collected Papers of Albert Einstein, 1989-91. Guggenheim fellow, 1953-54. Fellow AAAS, Am. Phys. Soc., Soc. Gen. Relativity and Gravitation (internat. com. 1980-89), Acad. Scis. at Phila. (bd. dirs. 1983—). Achievements include rsch. on classical and quantum theories of radiation, theory of relativity, especially equations of motion, found. problems, math. physics, history and philosophy of physics. Office: Temple U Dept Physics Philadelphia PA 19122

HAVEKOST, DANIEL JOHN, architect; b. Fremont, Nebr., May 12, 1936; s. Alvin Deidrich and Magdalen (Osterman) H.; m. Patricia Jo Haney, June 6, 1959 (div. June 1983); children: Christopher, Karen; m. Sandra Schwendemann, Aug. 29, 1993 (div. Nov. 1999). Lic. architect, Colo., Calif., Tex., N.D.; cert. Nat. Council Archtl. Registration Bds. Designer Papachristou & Assoc., Denver, 1959-61; architect Anshen & Allen, San Francisco, 1961-62; assoc. Hornbein & White, Denver, 1962-63; ptnr. Papachristou & Havekost, Denver, 1963-64; prin. Havekost & Assocs., Denver, 1964-71; pres. HWH Assocs., Inc., Denver, 1971-91, Havekost & Lee Architects P.C., Denver, 1991-95, Havekost & Assocs., P.C., 1996—. Vis. lectr. U. Colo., Denver, 1969, 72, 82; sec., treas. Encore Devel. Corp., Denver, 1984-91. Prin. works include Havekost Residence (Western Mountain Region AIA award 1971), Reverend's Ridge (Western Mountain Region AIA award 1973), Grant Street Mansion (Colo. Soc. Archs. AIA award 1979), Encore Redevel. (AIA award 1985,86), Antlers Redevelopment, Vail, Colo., 2002. Bd. dirs. Denver Cmty. Design Ctr., 1968-72, Hist. Paramount Found., Denver, 1980-94, Hist. Denver, 1978-82;

panel mem. Gen. Svcs. Adminstrn., Denver, 1978-79, mem. plan enforcement rev. and variation com., Denver, 1970-76. Served with USNR, 1954-62. Recipient Archtl. Excellence awards WOOD Inc., 1968-82, Honor award for Adaptive Re-use, Historic Denver, 1975, WOOD Design award Nat. Cattlemen's Hdqrs., 1982. Fellow AIA (pres. Denver chpt. 1978-81, chmn. Colo. chpt. govt. affairs com. 1984-91, pres. Colo. chpt. 1981-83, Colo. hist. preservation officer 1982—, recipient Fisher Traveling award of Colo. AIA Ednl. Fund 1988, excellence archtl. design award 1960). Avocations: skiing, tennis, drawing. Office: Havekost & Assocs PC 1121 Grant St Denver CO 80203-2301

HAVEL, RICHARD JOSEPH, physician, educator; b. Seattle, Feb. 20, 1925; s. Joseph and Anna (Fritz) Havel; m. Virginia Johnson, June 25, 1947; children: Christopher, Timothy, Peter, Julianne. BA, Reed Coll., 1946; MS, MD, U. Oreg., 1949. Intern Cornell U. Med. Coll., N.Y.C., 1949—50, resident in medicine, 1950—53; clin. assoc. Nat. Heart Inst., NIH, 1953—54, research assoc., 1954—56; faculty Sch. Medicine, U. Calif., San Francisco, 1956—, prof. medicine, 1964—; assoc. dir. Cardiovascular Research Inst., 1961—73, dir., 1973—92. Chief metabolism sect., dept. medicine, 1967—97; dir. Arteriosclerosis Specialized Ctr. Rsch., 1971—96; mem. bd. sci. counselors Nat. Heart, Lung and Blood Inst., 1976—80; chmn. food and nutrition bd. NRC, 1987—90; pres. Lipid Rsch., Inc., 1999—. Editor: Jour. Lipid Rsch., 1972—75; mem. editl. bd.: Jour. Biol. Chemistry, 1981—85, Jour. Arteriosclerosis, 1980—; contbr. chapters to books, articles to profl. jours. Established investigator Am. Heart Assn., 1956—61, chmn. coun. on arteriosclerosis, 1977—79; with USPHS, 1951—53. Recipient Disting. Achievement award, Am. Heart Assn., 1993, Bristol-Myers award for nutrition rsch., 1989, gold medal, Charles U., Prague, Czech Republic, 1996. Fellow: AAAS (Theobald Smith award 1960); mem.: NAS, Western Soc. Clin. Investigation (Mayo Soley award 1997), Am. Inst. Nutritional Sci., Am. Soc. for Clin. Investigation, Assn. Am. Physicians, Am. Soc. Clin. Nutrition (McCollum award 1993), Am. Acad. Arts and Scis., Inst. Medicine NAS, Alpha Omega Alpha, Phi Beta Kappa. Office: U Calif San Francisco Cardiovascular Rsch In San Francisco CA 94143-0130

HAVEL, RICHARD W. lawyer; b. Fairmont, Minn., Sept. 20, 1946; s. Thomas Earl and Elizabeth (Shiltz) H.; m. Arlene Havel, July 6, 1968; children: Stephanie, Derek. BA, Notre Dame U., 1968; JD, UCLA, 1971. Bar: Calif., U.S. Dist. Ct. (no., ea., cen. and so. dists.) Calif., U.S. Ct. Appeals (9th cir.). Atty. Shutan & Trost, L.A., 1971-80, Sidley & Austin, L.A., 1980—. Instr. law U. Loyola, 1975-80; bd. govs. Fin. Lawyers Conf., 1991-94, 95-98, officer, 1998-2001; spkr., panelist Bankruptcy Litigation Inst., 1989-95, ALI-ADA, 1989, 90, 91; chmn. L.A. City Indsl. Devel. Authority, 1993-98, bd. dirs., 1998-2000. Contbr. articles to profl. jours. Trustee Jonsson/UCLA Cancer Ctr., 1998—. Fellow Am. Coll. Bankruptcy, 1997; mem. ABA, Calif. Bar Assn., L.A. County Bar Assn. (comml. law & bankruptcy sect. bankruptcy subcom. 1986-89, exec. com. 1987-90, lawyer assistance com. 1985—), UCLA Law Alumni Assn. (trustee 1996—). Office: Sidley & Austin 555 W 5th St 40th Fl Los Angeles CA 90013-1010 E-mail: RHavel@Sidley.com.

HAVEL, VACLAV, former president of Czech Republic, playwright; b. Prague, Czechoslovakia, Oct. 5, 1936; s. Václav M. and Božena (Vavrečková) H.; m. Olga Splíchalová, July 9, 1964 (dec. Jan. 1996); m. Dagmar Veškrnová, Jan. 4, 1997. Student, Czech Tech. Coll., Prague, 1955-57, Acad. Mus. Arts, 1966; hon. degree, York U., Toronto, 1982; D honoris causa, U. Toulouse, France, 1982, U. Lyon, 1984, U. Columbia, N.Y.C., 1990, Hebrew U., Jerusalem, 1990, U. of F. Palacky, Charles U., U. of J.A. Komensky, Czechoslovakia, 1990, LeHigh U., Bethlehem, Pa., 1991, U. Brusel, 1991, Harvard U., 1995, U. New South Wales, Australia, 1995, Vilnius U., Lithuania, 1996, Trinity Coll., Dublin, 1996, Bar-Ilan U., Ramat Gan, Israel, 1997, Taras Shevchenko Nat. U., Kiev, Ukraine, 1997, U. Jordan, Amman, 1997, U. Glasgow (U.K.), 1998, U. Oxford (U.K.), 1998, U. Pretoria (South Africa), 1998, U. St. Thomas, Minn., 1999, U. Manitoba, Winnipeg, Can., 1999, Mich. U., 2000, Bikent U., Ankara, Turkey, 2000, Janacek Acad. Music & Performing Arts, Brno, Czech Republic, 2001. Technician chem. lab., 1951-55; scenery technician ABC Theatre, Prague, 1959-60; dramatic adviser, asst. producer, author Theatre on Railings, Prague, 1960-68; mem. Club Engaged Non-Party Mems., 1968; chmn. Club Ind. Writers, 1968; imprisoned 4 times, spent nearly 5 years in prison, 1977-89; pres. Czechoslovakia, Prague, 1989-92; now pres. Czech Republic, Prague, 1993—2003. Author: Antikódy, 1964, Letters to Olga, 1983, O lidskou identitu, 1984, Disturbing the Peace, 1986 (Polit. Book of Yr. Friedrich-Elbert-Found. 1990), Do ruznych stran, 1989, Speeches, 1990, Open Letters: Selected Writings 1965-90, Summer Meditations, 1991, Dear Citizens, 1992, Václav Havel 92 & 93, 1994, 95, 96, Art of the Impossible, 1997, Toward a Civil Society, 1994, (with others) The Power of Powerless, 1986, Václav Havel or Living in Truth, 1986, others, (plays) The Garden Party, 1963, The Memorandum, 1965 (Off Broadway award The Village Voice 1968), The Increased Difficulty of Concentration, 1968 (Off Broadway award The Village Voice 1970), The Beggar's Opera, 1972, Audience, 1975, Private View, 1975, The Mountain Hotel, 1976, Protest, 1979, The Mistake, 1983, Largo Desolato, 1984, Temptation, 1985, Redevelopment, 1987, Tomorrow!, 1988; contbr. articles to profl. jours. With Czechoslovakian Army, 1957-59. Recipient Austrian State prize for European lit., 1969, Jan Palach prize, 1981, Erasmus prize, 1986, Prize of Liberty, 1989, Olof Palme prize, 1989, Simon Bolivar prize UNESCO, 1990, Charlemagne prize, Sonning prize, Averell Harriman Democracy award, B'nai Brith prize, Freedom award, Raoul Wallenberg Human Rights award, 1991, Order of White Eagle, Indira Gandhi prize, Phila. Liberty medal, Jackson H. Ralston prize, 1994, Dutch Freedom Fighters medal Geuzenpenning Found., Netherlands, 1995, Catalonia Internat. prize Catalonian Inst. Mediterranean Studies, Barcelona, Spain, 1995, Future of Hope award, Hiroshima, Japan, 1995, European Statesman award Inst. for East-West Studies, N.Y.C., 1997, Le Prix Special Europe award Internat. Assn. Theatrical Critics, France, 1997, J. William Fulbright prize Washington, 1997, Peace and Democracy award Burma, 1997, Compostela Group prize, Spain, 1998, First Decade award Gazeta Wyborcza, Poland, 1999, Open Society prize, Hungary, 1999, St. Adalbert prize St. Adalbert Found., Slovakia, 1999, Evelyn F. Burkey award Authors Guild Am., 2000, Olympic Gate award Internat. Olympic Com., 2000, Civil prize Found. Staatsbrugerlicher Stiftung, 2000, Wild Geese award Wild Geese Prague, 2000, others. Achievements include leading the Czechoslovak Velvet Revolution. E-mail: president@hrad.cz.

HAVELUND, KLAUS, computer scientist; b. Copenhagen, Oct. 17, 1955; s. Hjalmar and Else Havelund; 1 child, Iza Bahn. HD in Bus. and Orgn. Theory, Copenhagen Bus. Sch., Denmark, 1986; MS in Computer Sci., U. Copenhagen, 1986, PhD in Computer Sci., 1994. Rschr. Danish Datamatics Ctr. (DDC), Lyngby, Denmark, 1984—88, CRI, Birkeroed, Denmark, 1988—91, Ecole Normale Superievre, Paris, 1991—94, Ecole Polytechnique and U. Paris 6, Paris, 1994—96, U. Aalborg, Aalborg, Denmark, 1996—97, Kestrel Tech., NASA Ames Rsch. Ctr., Moffett Field, Calif., 1997—, Recom Tech., NASA Ames, 1997—2001. Author: (textbook) The RAISE Specification Language, 1992. Human Capital Mobility scholar, European Union, 1994—96. Achievements include development of first prototype of the Java PathFinder tool, a software tool for debugging software using model checking; RAISE methodology for developing software. Office: NASA Ames Rsch Ctr Ms 269-2 Moffett Field CA 94035-1000 Office Fax: 650-604-3594. Personal E-mail: khavelund@yahoo.com. E-mail: havelund@email.arc.nasa.gov.

HAVENS, CANDACE JEAN, planning consultant; b. Rochester, Minn., Sept. 13, 1952; d. Fred Z. and Barbara Jean (Stephenson) H.; m. Bruce Curtis Mercier, Feb. 22, 1975 (div. Apr. 1982); 1 child, Rachel; m. James Arthur Renning, Oct. 26, 1986; children: Kelsey, Sarah. Student, U. Calif., San Diego, Darmouth Coll., 1970-72, Am. U., Beirut, 1973-74; BA in Sociology, U. Calif., Riverside, 1977; MPA, Harvard U., 1994. Project coord. social svc. orgn. Grass Roots II, San Luis Obispo, Calif., 1976-77; planner City San Luis Obispo, 1977-86, city parking, spl. projects mgr., 1986-88; spl. asst. to city adminstr. City of San Luis Obispo, 1989, planning cons., mediator, 1991—; mgmt. rsch. specialist Bank of Boston, 1995-96; owner Office Suites, San Luis Obispo, Calif., 1997-2000, ADR Collaborative, 1997—. Past pres. Nat. Charity League, Riverside; mem. San Luis Obispo Med. Aux., 1986-93, San Luis Obispo Arts Coun., 1986—; pres. bd. dirs. San Luis Obispo Children's Mus., 1990-91, CFO, 1993; mediator in Newton (Mass.) Cts., 1996, San Luis Obispo, 1997; pres. Underwood Elem. PTO, 2000-2001; chmn. traffic coun., City of Newton, 2002—. Mem.: AAUW, Newton Transp. Task Force, Inst. Transp. Engrs., Mass. Assn. Mediation Profls. and Practitioners, Am. Planning Assn., Am. Inst. Cert. Planners, Assn. Conflict Resolution, Toastmasters (sec. 1986—87, v.p. 1987—88, pres. 1989—90, treas. 1991—92). Avocations: photography, running, arts, cooking, travel, languages. Office: 25 Hunnewell Ave Newton MA 02458-2214

HAVENS, CAROLYN CLARICE, librarian; b. Nashville, Sept. 11, 1953; d. Charles Buford and Iris Mae (Anderson) H.; m. Hilton Harris Huey, June 9, 1990; children: Heather Louise, Quentin Harris. AA, Sue Bennett Coll., 1973; BA in English, U. West Fla., 1974; MLS, U. Ky., 1981. Tchr. Escambia High Sch., Pensacola, Fla., 1974-75; salesperson Univ. Mall, Pensacola, 1975-77; libr. tech. U. Ky., Lexington, 1978-82; libr. Auburn (Ala.) U., 1982—. Contbr. articles to profl. jours. and newspapers; editorial bd.: A Dynamic Tradition, 1991. Bd. dirs. Nat. Kidney Found. Ala., Opelika, 1986-89; active Conscientious Alliance for Peace, Auburn, 1989—. Clergy and Laity Concerned, Atlanta, 1991—. Mem. ALA, Southeastern Libr. Assn., Ala. Libr. Assn., North Am. Serials Interest Group, Ala. Assn. Coll. and Rsch. Librs., Studio 218. Democrat. Methodist. Avocations: painting, writing, photography. Office: Auburn U Ralph Draughon Libr Auburn AL 36849-5606

HAVENS, CHARLES W., III, retired lawyer; b. Balt., Mar. 22, 1936; m. Lucille Bowman; children— Charles W. IV, Jessica Madaline AB, Franklin and Marshall Coll., 1958; LL.B., U. Va., 1961. Bar: D.C. 1961, Va. 1961, U.S. Supreme Ct. Assoc. Covington & Burling, Washington, 1961-66; spl. asst. to gen. counsel Dept. Def., Washington, 1966-67, spl. asst. to asst. sec. def., 1967-70; gen. counsel then pres. Reins. Assn. Am., Washington, 1970-81; ptnr. LeBoeuf, Lamb, Leiby & MacRae, Washington, 1981—2000; ret., 2000. Contbr. articles to profl. jours. Mem. AIDA Reins. and Ins. Arbitration Soc. (founding, bd. dirs.), Met. Club, John's Island Club. Clubs: Metropolitan (Washington). Avocation: golf. Home: # 396 1000 Beach Rd Vero Beach FL 32963 Office: LeBoeuf Lamb Greene MacRae 1875 Connecticut Ave NW Washington DC 20009-5728 Home (Summer): 4045 Mansion Dr NW Washington DC 20007

HAVENS, HARRY STEWART, former federal assistant comptroller general, government consultant; b. Little Rock, Dec. 18, 1935; s. Ralph Murray and Catherine Clara (Clark) H.; m. Frances Jones, June 12, 1960. BA in Econs. magna cum laude, Duke U., 1957; BA in Philosophy, Politics, Econs., Oxford U., England, 1959, MA, 1963. Economist U.S. Budget Bur., Washington, 1964-66, budget examiner, 1966-70, chief housing br., 1970-72, dep. dir. human resources divsn., 1972-74; chief income maintenance br. U.S. Office Mgmt. and Budget, Washington, 1972-74; dir. program analysis divsn. U.S. GAO, Washington, 1974-80, asst. comptroller gen., 1980-93, pvt. practice cons. Washington, 1993—. Cons. Orgn. Econ. Coop. & Devel., Paris, 1993—, U.S. GAO, 1993-96, Supreme Soviet of Russian Fedn., 1992-93, State Duma of Russian Fedn., 1994; hon. councillor Atlantic Coun. U.S., 1995—. Contbr. articles to profl. jours.; contbr. book chpts. Rhodes scholar, 1957. Home and Office: 4515 Neptune Dr Alexandria VA 22309-3129 E-mail: havensh@aol.com.

HAVENS, KEITH CORNELL, artist; b. Mpls., Sept. 27, 1921; s. Lee Willard and Ruth Marguerite (Mallett) Havens; m. Marian Gail Niggeler, Mar. 11, 1944; 1 child, Shelley Ross. Cert., Mpls. Sch. Art, 1949. Instr. drawing, painting and design, dir. studio classes, instr. night sch. classes Mpls. Sch. Art, 1949-58; assoc. prof. art Spl. Sch. Assoc. Arts, St. Paul, 1959-73. Co-founder, instr. Minnetonka Ctr. Art and Edn., Wayzata, Crystal Bay, Minn., 1950—70; dir. Twin Cities Theater Galleries, Mpls., St. Paul, 1952—72; arch.'s cons., designer spl. equipment Mpls. Sch. Art, 1956—58; instr. watercolor painting St. Paul Sch. Art, 1958—59; judge Lutsen Art Fair, 1975, Mpls. Photo Club, 1975; co-founder, logo designer Superior Hiking Trail, 1985. Author: (book) Fantanimals, 1980; North Meml. Hops., Robbinsdale, Minn., 1962, 1963, one-man shows include Duluth Art Inst., 1994, numerous others. Recipient 1st award, Women's Club Art Show, 1952, 1st award-watercolor, Minn. State Fair Art Exhibit, 1953. Achievements include finder, polisher of the world's largest Thomsonite gem-stone, 1985; design of sculptured "Wordy Bird" exhib. superior waters gallery, spring, summer, 2003; One Man Exhibit, "Energy of Life" (ink drawings) grand Marais Publ. Libr., 2003. Avocations: gardening, photography, model building, painting, jewelry.

HAVENS, LESTON LAYCOCK, psychiatrist, educator; b. Bklyn., July 31, 1924; s. Valentine Britton and Nellie Falk (Laycock) H.; m. Susan Elizabeth Miller, May 19, 1973; 1 child, Emily E.; children by previous marriage: Christopher W., Jeffry B. (dec.), Jennifer F., Sarah B. BA, Williams Coll., 1947; MD, Cornell U., 1952; MA (hon.), Harvard U., 1987; LHD, Mass. Sch. Profl. Psychology, 1993. Intern N.Y. Hosp., 1952-53, asst. resident internal medicine, 1953-54; resident, chief of svc. Mass. Mental Health Ctr., Boston Psychopathic Hosp., 1954-58, staff visit and asst. clin. dir., 1958-62, prin. investigator studies in visual word perception, 1960-66, program dir. psychiat. rehab. internship program, 1962-68, program dir. med. student teaching, 1964-81; asst. prof. psychiatry Harvard Med. Sch., Boston, 1963-64, assoc. clin. prof. psychiatry, 1965-71, psychoanalyst, 1967—, prof. psychiatry, 1971—. Cargnegie vis. prof. humanities MIT, 1968; H. B. Williams traveling prof. Australian and New Zealand Coll. of Psychiatrists, 1975; chief psychiat. cons. Mass. Rehab. Commn., 1959-65; mental health adminstr. Region VI, Mass. Dept. Mental Health, 1968-69; dir. residency tng. Cambridge Hosp., 1987-96, co-dir. edn., 1996—. Author: Approaches to the Mind, 1973, Participant Observation, 1977, Making Contact, 1986, A Safe Place: Laying the Groundwork of Psychotherapy, 1989, Coming to Life, 1993, Learning To Be Human, 1994, The Real Life Guide to Psychotherapy Practice, 2000; contbr. articles to profl. jours. Served to 2d lt. AUS, 1944-46. Recipient H.C. Solomon award, 1977, Benjamin Rush award APA, 1995. Mem. Am. Psychiat. Assn., Soc. Biol. Psychiatry (A.E. Bennett award 1958), Mass. Soc. for Rsch. in Psychiatry (McCurdy prize 1962), Phi Beta Kappa, Alpha Omega Alpha. Home: 151 Brattle St Cambridge MA 02138-2243 Office: Cambridge Hosp 1493 Cambridge St Cambridge MA 02139-1099

HAVENS, MURRAY CLARK, political scientist, educator; b. Council Grove, Kans., Aug. 21, 1932; s. Ralph Murray and Catherine Clara (Clark) H.; m. Agnes Marie Scharpf, July 5, 1958 (dec. 1969); children: Colin Scott, Theresa Agnes; m. Carolyn Trost, May 5, 1997. BA, U. Ala., 1953; MA (Woodrow Wilson fellow 1953-54), Johns Hopkins U., 1954, PhD, 1958. Postdoctoral fellow Brookings Instn., Washington, 1958-59; asst. prof. polit. sci. Duke U., 1959-61; from asst. prof. to prof. U. Tex., Austin, 1961-73; vis. lectr. U. Sydney (Australia), 1966; prof. polit. sci. Tex. Tech U., Lubbock, 1973-98, chmn. dept., 1975-83, prof. emeritus, 1999—. Author: City Versus Farm?, 1957, The Challenges to Democracy, 1965, The Politics of Assassination, 1970, Assassination and Terrorism, 1975, Texas Politics Today, 1995; book rev. editor Jour. Politics, 1971-83; contbr. numerous articles to profl. jours. Served with AUS, 1954-56. Mem. Am. Polit. Sci. Assn., So. Polit. Sci. Assn., Southwestern Polit. Sci. Assn. (pres. 1983-84), AAUP, Phi Beta Kappa. Home: 8636 Sawyer Brown Rd Nashville TN 37221

HAVENS, PAMELA ANN, college official; b. Plattsburgh, N.Y., Nov. 30, 1956; d. Thomas L. and MaryAnn (Zalen) Romeo; m. Stephen L. Havens, Aug. 9, 1986; children: Stephanie Leigh, Skylar Lucas. BA, Eisenhower Coll., 1978; MA summa cum laude, SUNY, Plattsburgh, 1987; AAS summa cum laude, Cayuga C.C., 1999. VISTA vol. Retired Sr. Vol. Program, Plattsburgh, 1978-79; copywriter, newsperson Stas. WEAV-AM/WGFB-FM, Plattsburgh, 1979-83; traffic clk. Sta. WCFE-TV, Plattsburgh, 1983-84, pub. info. coord., 1984-85; coll. rels. officer Clinton Cmty. Coll., Plattsburgh, 1985-89; dir. publs. and comm. Cayuga C.C., Auburn, N.Y., 1989-2001; dir. stewardship Hamilton Coll., Clinton, N.Y., 2001—. Mem. adv. bd., vice-chair St. Mary's Sch. PTA, Clinton, NY, 2002—. Mem. adv. com. Cayuga C.C. Presch. Ctr., 1999-2001. Named Young Careerist Alternate Bus. and Profl. Women's Club, 1986; recipient award ACC/CCC Alumni Assn., 2000. Mem.: CASE, AAUW, Nat. Coun. Mktg. and Pub. Rels. (Pro Devel. award 1999, Disting. Svc. award 2000), Eisenhower Coll. Aumni Assn. (bd. dirs. 1990—97, chmn. bd. 1992—95), Phi Theta Kappa. Avocations: fiction and poetry writing, doll and bear collecting, olympic pin collecting, tap dancing. Office: Hamilton Coll 198 College Hill Rd Clinton NY 13323 E-mail: phavens@hamilton.edu.

HAVENS, TIMOTHY JOHN, physicist; b. Bismark, N.D., Feb. 1, 1956; s. Harold Lloyd and Luanne Virginia (Cowan) H.; m. Janine Louise Ley, June 19, 1981; children: Garrett Wade, Stanley McKay, Luke Timothy. BS, Eckerd Coll., 1980; PhD, Coll. of William and Mary, 1985. Asst. prof. physics Francis Marion U., Florence, S.C., 1985-90; summer rsch. fellow Med. U. S.C., Charleston, 1986; sr. engr. GE Med. Systems, Florence, S.C., 1990—. Contbr. articles to Phys. Rev. Letters, IEEE Trans. on Mag., Jour. of Applied Sci.; patentee in field. Grantee NSF, 1990, Fed. Edn. for Scon. Security Act. Mem. Am. Phys. Soc., S.C. Acad. Sci. Home: 1208 Madison Ave Florence SC 29501-4254 Office: GE Med Systems PO Box 100539 Florence SC 29501-0539 E-mail: timothy.havens@med.ge.com., sc_havens@yahoo.com.

HAVER, JURGEN F. marketing consultant; b. Joliet, Ill., July 16, 1932; s. Elmer William and Hermina (Peters) H.; m. Judith Costello, May 19, 2001; children: Jason, Kyra, Peter, Brigit. BA, Wartburg Coll., 1956. Feature writer Daily Peoples Press, Owatonna, Minn., 1959-60; editor Lyon County Independent, Marshall, Minn., 1960-62; asst. advt. dir. Burpee Seed Co., Phila., 1962-66; advt. mgr. for Organic Gardening, Theater Crafts and Quinto Rodale Press, Emmaus, Pa., 1966-67; promotion of electronics mag. staff Kiver Pubs., Chgo., 1968-69; advt. dir. Henry Regnery Co., Chgo., 1969-70; pub. rels. dir. Hess's Dept. Stores, Allentown, Pa., 1970-76; cons. Haver Mktg., Taos, N.Mex., 1976—; spl. cons. Gov. N.Mex., 1995—2002; mng. editor Parenting with Spirit mag., 2000—03. Co-founder U. N.Mex. Inst. for Entrepreneurial Success; faculty mktg. Moravian Coll., U. Pa. Sch. Dentistry, Pa. State U. Author: Personalized Guide to Marketing Strategy, 1982; contbr. articles to trade mags. and profl. jours. Mem. Internat. Bus. Writers (past pres.), Am. Mktg. Assn. (past pres.). Address: PO Box 70 Moriarty NM 87035- E-mail: jurgenh@nmia.com.

HAVER-ALLEN, ANN, communications director; d. Vivian Faye Haver; m. William Allen, June 21, 1986; children: Jason Allen, Summer Allen. Journalism degree, Thomas Edison State Coll., Trenton, N.J. Reporter Angleton Times, Tex., 1985—86; mng. editor Princeton Packet Group, NJ, 1986—90, Engel Pub. Ptnrs., West Trenton, NJ, 1990—92; dir. engring. comm. Princeton U., NJ, 1992—. Free-lance editor NCI Comm. Inc., Princeton, NJ, 1995—2000; competition judge Internat. Assn. of Bus. Communicators, Morristown, NJ, 2001—; accolades program chair Coun. for the Advancement and Support of Edn., Washington, 2002—; screening judge The Assn. of Ednl. Pubs., Logan Twp., NJ, 2003—. Dir.(editor): (mag.) EQuad News (IRIS Award of Excellence from the IABC, 2002, APEX Award for Publ. Excellence, 2002); editor: (journal) Multimedia in the classroom (APEX Award for Publ. Excellence, Best Rewrites, 2000); photographer Flagler College (Best of Show, Middlesex County Fair, 2001), Mission Tumacacori (Best of Show, Middlesex County Fair, 2000). Comm. Red Heart Coastal Mvskoke Clan, Robertsdale, Ala., 2001—03. Recipient Edtl. Excellence, Princeton Packet, 1986—89, First Pl. (4), second Pl. (2), third Pl. (1) hon. mention (6), N.J. Press Assn., 1987, 1988, 1989, Blue Ribbon of Excellence, Nat. Newspaper Assn., 1988, First Pl., photography, Middlesex County Fair, 1999, 2001, Award of Distinction, The Communicator Awards, 2002. Mem.: Nat. Assn. for Female Execs., Internat. Assn. of Bus. Communicators, Women in Comm., Ednl. Press Assn. of Am., Coun. for the Advancement and Support of Edn., Red Heart Coastal Mvskoke Clan. Office Fax: 609-258-6744. Personal E-mail: allen@princeton.edu.

HAVERLY, DOUGLAS LINDSAY, librarian, historian; b. Stamford, N.Y., Apr. 16, 1925; s. De Forest Ward and Amy Elizabeth (Lindsay) H. Student, Albany Bus. Coll., 1948, Alfred U., 1948-49, Russell Sage Coll., 1950-52. With N.Y. State Libr., Albany, 1949-77; with Bur. Testing N.Y. State Dept. Edn., Albany, 1978-82; ret., 1982. Pres., curator Donald C. Ringwald Marine Navigation Ltd., Albany, 1987—. With USN, 1943-54. Mem. Steamship Hist. Soc. (budget dir. 1973-76, bd. dirs. 1977-80, organizer Hudson Valley chpt. 1974, chmn. 1975-78, libr. 1990-93), Hudson River Maritime Ctr., Sons and Daus. of Pioneer Rivermen, Palatines to Am. (historian N.Y. chpt. 1991-95), Herkimer (N.Y.) Hist. Soc., Schoharie County Hist. Soc. (life), Clan Lindsay Assn. USA Inc. (charter), N.Y. Hist. Soc., Ulster County Geneal. Soc., Van Aken/Auken Newsletter. Avocation: genealogy. Home and Office: DC Ringwald Marine Nav Ltd 23 Wedgewood Dr Loudonville NY 12211-1940

HAVERSTOCK, LYNDA M. lieutenant governor; m. Harley Olsen; 4 children. MEd, PhD in Clin. Psychology, U. Saskatchewan. Pvt. practice clin. psychologist; lt. gov., 2000—. Instr. Sask. U., N.B. U., Canada; past radio talk show host. Author: (handbook) Fighting the Farm Crisis, (book) Safety and Health in Agriculture; contbr. articles. Recipient Triple E award. Office: Govt House 4607 Dewdney Ave Regina SK S4P 3V7 Canada Office Fax: 306-787-7716. E-mail: lgo@ltgov.sk.ca.

HAVEY, J. MICHAEL, psychologist, educator; b. Madison, Ind., July 24, 1953; s. Merle Freeman and Dorothy Elizabeth (Waldon) H.; m. Kathy Jo Kratz, Oct. 22, 1977; children: Elizabeth Anne, Sarah Catherine. AB magna cum laude, Hanover (Ind.) Coll., 1975; MS in Edn., Ind. U., 1980; EdD, Ball State U., 1985. Lic. sch. psychologist, Ill., Ind.; lic. psychologist, Ind. Tchr. Southwestern H.S., Hanover, 1975-81; counselor Southeastern Career Ctr., Versailles, Ind., 1981-82; sch. psychologist Greater Lafayette (Ind.) Area Spl. Svcs., 1985-88; prof. psychology Ea. Ill. U., Charleston, 1988—. Spl. edn. due process hearing officer Ill. State Bd. Edn., 1992-98. Contbr. articles to profl. jours. Chmn. work area on missions Wesley United Meth. Ch., Charleston, 1992—95, mem. adminstrv. coun., 1992—95; mem. sch. bd. Charleston Cmty. Sch. Dist., 1995—2003, sec., 1999—2001, v.p., 2001—03. Mem. Nat. Assn. Sch. Psychologists, Ill. Sch. Psychologists Assn. (contbg. editor 1991-99, governing bd. 1991-93, pres.-elect 1999-2000, pres. 2000-01, past pres. 2001-02), Internat. Sch. Psychologists Assn. Avocations: reading, biking. Home: 2813 Kimwood Dr Charleston IL 61920-4314 Office: Eastern Illinois Univ Dept Psychology Charleston IL 61920 E-mail: jmhavey@eiu.edu.

HAVICK, JOHN J. political science educator; b. Omaha, Apr. 29, 1940; s. J.C. and Alice M. H.; m. Barbara Wagner, June 26, 1965; children: Ann, Steve. BA, Coe Coll., 1962; MA, U. Iowa, 1966, PhD, 1975. Instr. Luther Coll., Decorah, Iowa, 1968-70; vis. instr. Iowa State U., Ames, 1974; from asst. to assoc. prof. polit. sci. Ga. Inst. Tech., Atlanta, 1975—. Govt. programs cons. Job Tng., Rome, Ga., 1984-85. Author: American Democracy in Transition: A Communications Revolution, 1991; editor, contbr.: Communications Policy and the Political Process, 1983; contbr. articles to profl. jours. Fellow NIMH, 1977, NEH, 1981. Mem. Am. Polit. Sci. Assn. Home: 536 Lynn Valley Way Stone Mountain GA 30087-4861

HAVIGHURST, CLARK CANFIELD, law educator; b. Evanston, Ill., May 25, 1933; s. Harold Canfield and Marion Clay (Perryman) H.; m. Karen Waldron, Aug. 28, 1965; children: Craig Perryman, Marjorie Clark. BA, Princeton U., 1955; JD, Northwestern U., 1958. Bar: Ill. 1958, N.Y. 1961. Assoc. Debevoise Plimpton Lyons & Gates, N.Y.C., 1958, 61-64; assoc. prof. law Duke U., Durham, NC, 1964-68, prof., 1968-86, 2002—, William Neal Reynolds prof., 1986—2002, emeritus, 2002—; interim dean Duke U. Sch. Law, 1999. Dir. Program on Legal Issues in Health Care Duke U., 1969-88; adj. scholar Am Enterprise Inst. Pub. Policy Rsch., 1976—; resident cons. FTC, Washington, 1978, Epstein, Becker & Green, Washington, 1989-90; scholar in residence Inst. Medicine of NAS, Washington, 1972-73, RAND Corp., Santa Monica, 1999. Author: Deferred Compensation for Key Employees, 1964, Regulating Health Facilities Construction, 1974, Deregulating the Health Care Industry, 1982, Health Care Law and Policy, 1988, 2d edit., 1998, Health Care Choices: Private Contracts as Instruments of Health Reform, 1995; editor Law and Contemporary Problems jour., 1965-70. With U.S. Army, 1958-60. Mem. Inst. Medicine of Nat. Acad. Sci., Order of Coif Office: Duke U Sch Law PO Box 90360 Durham NC 27708-0360 E-mail: hav@law.duke.edu.

HAVILAND, BANCROFT DAWLEY, lawyer; b. Yonkers, N.Y., May 13, 1925; s. Harold Bancroft and Dorothy (Dawley) H.; m. Dorothy MacFarland, Oct. 30, 1945; children: Lucy, William, Thomas, Amy. BA in Polit. Sci., U. Pa., 1947, LLB, 1949. Bar: N.Y. 1951, Pa. 1952. Gowen teaching fellow U. Pa. Law Sch., Phila., 1949-50; assoc. Donovan, Leisure, Newton & Irvine, Phila., 1950-51, Schnader, Harrison, Segal & Lewis, Phila., 1951-61, ptnr., 1961-90, ret., 1991. Trustee Westtown (Pa.) Friends' Sch., 1960-94, Media-Providence (Pa.) Friends' Sch., 1960-95; chmn. Westtown Sch. Com., 1988-93; commr. Rose Tree Soccer Club, Media, 1971-98, Aston Twp., Pa., 1954-61; justice of peace Middletown Twp., Pa., 1963-65. Lt. (j.g.) USN, 1943-45, PTO. Mem. ABA, Pa. Bar Assn., Phila. Bar Assn., Am. Judicature Soc., Order of Coif

Lodges: Lions. Democrat. Mem. Soc. Of Friends. Avocations: woodworking, reading, gardening. Home: 21 Kendal Dr Kennett Square PA 19348 Office: Schnader Harrison Segal & Lewis 1600 Market St Ste 3600 Philadelphia PA 19103-7287

HAVILAND, DAVID SANDS, architectural educator, researcher, administrator; b. Rome, N.Y., Apr. 26, 1942; s. William Erwin and Barbara Hannon (Huguenin) H.; m. Kathleen Anne Kelly, July 8, 1973; children: Kelly Sands, Wallace Sands. BS, Rensselaer Poly. Inst., 1964, BArch, 1965, MArch, 1967. Rsch. asst., instr. Rensselaer Poly. Inst., Troy, N.Y., 1965-67, asst. prof. architecture, 1967-70, assoc. prof., 1970-79, prof., 1979—, dean Sch. of Architecture, 1980-90, v.p., student life, 1994-2000, v.p. Inst. Advancement, 2000—. Vis. prof. constrn. mgmt. and engring. U. Reading, Eng., 1990-96. Editor: The Architect's Handbook fo Profl. Practice, 12th edit., 1994; contbr. articles to profl. jours. V.p. Rensselaer Newman Found.; pres. Howard and Bush Found. Recipient James L. Haecker award for disting. rsch. leadership, 1996, also numerous rsch. grants. Mem. AIA (Inst. award 1989), N.Y. State Assn. Architects. Home: 63 Pinewoods Ave Troy NY 12180-4701 Office: Rensselaer Polytech Inst Inst Advancement Troy Bldg 110 8th St Troy NY 12180-3590

HAVILAND, JAMES WEST, physician, educator; b. Glens Falls, N.Y., July 18, 1911; s. Morrison LeRoy and Mabel Eva (West) Haviland; m. Mary Katherine Burden, Aug. 30, 1997; children from previous marriage: James Marshall, Elizabeth Bullard, Donald Sherman, Martha Adams Clauser. AB, Union Coll., Schenectady, 1932; MD, Johns Hopkins, 1936. Intern medicine Johns Hopkins Hosp., 1936—37, intern, asst. resident, chief outpatient dept. pediatrics, 1937—38, asst. resident medicine, 1939—40, New Haven Hosp., 1938—39; instr. medicine Yale Med. Sch., 1938—39; chief services crippled children Wash. Dept. Social Security, also Dept. Health, 1940—42; lectr. medicine U. Wash. Sch. Nursing, 1946—60; practice medicine Seattle, 1946—86; clin. asst. prof., to clin. prof. U. Wash. Sch. Medicine, 1947—77, emeritus prof., 1977—, asst. dean, 1949—53, 1954—59, acting dean, 1953—54, assoc. dean, 1972—76. Trustee N.W. Kidney Ctr. Served to lt. comdr. med. corps USNR, 1942—46. Fellow: Am. Geog. Soc. N.Y.; mem.: ACP (pres. 1970), AMA (coun. med. edn. 1966—76, chmn. 1974—76), AAAS, Inst. Medicine NAS, Am. Assn. History of Medicine, Am. Clin. and Climatol. Assn. (pres. 1981—82), North Pacific Soc. Internal Medicine, Pacific Interurban Clin. Club, King County Med. Soc. (pres. 1962), Seattle Acad. Internal Medicine (pres. 1952—53), Wash. State Med. Assn. (sec.-treas, 1948—51), Alpha Omega Alpha, Sigma Xi, Phi Beta Kappa, Kappa Alpha. Home: 8208 SE 30th St Mercer Island WA 98040-3011*

HAVILAND, KAY LYNN (KADE HAVILAND), English literature educator; b. Deer Lodge, Mont., July 16, 1952; d. Jackson C. and Juanita Maxine (Voelkel) Price; children: Jesse Jean, Kelsey Ann, Molly Claire. MA in Guidance and Counseling, Adams State Coll., 1994. Cert. addictions counselor, counseling psychologist Arapahoe House Denver Outpatient Clinic, Denver, 1996—. Asst. therapist, CORE obesity project, Weight Choice Program dept. pediatrics U. Colo., 1998—2001, asst. therapist State of Colo. Alcohol Drug Abuse Division; treatment trainer Denver Health Hosp., 2001—. Author, editor; (mag.) Human Interest, 1987 8 (1st place award 1989); contbr. articles to profl. jours. Mem. ACA, Colo. Counselors Assn. Avocations: calligraphy, cross-country skiing, reading.

HAVIR, BRYAN THOMAS, urban planner; b. Allentown, Pa., Feb. 9, 1963; s. Donald John and Ruth Mary (Schmoyer) H. BA in Polit. Sci., History, Pa. State U., 1985, MPA, 1990; cert. in Environ. Studies, Delaware Valley Coll., 1994; postgrad., U. Pa., 1994—, Temple Ambler U., 2003—. Planning intern City of Allentown, 1984-85; legal rschr. Pa. State U., University Park, 1985; enforcement officer zoning and code South Whitehall Twp., Allentown, 1985-86; asst. site planner Montgomery County Planning Commn., Norristown, Pa., 1986-87; asst. planner Mercer County Planning Bd., Trenton, N.J., 1987-88; planning dir., zoning code enforcement officer Warwick Twp., Jamison, Pa., 1988-90; coord. cmty. devel. Evesham Twp., Marlton, N.J., 1991-97; dir. cmty. planning Heritage Conservancy, Doylestown, Pa., 1997-98; asst. twp. mgr. Cheltenham Twp., Elkins Park, Pa., 1998—. Sec. to bd. dirs. McCandless Opticians, Inc. Asst. scoutmaster Boy Scouts Am., Allentown, 1980—; mem. Lehigh County Hist. Soc.; bd. dirs. Bucks County Agrl. Land Preservation Bd., 1990; active Preservation N.J.; mem. exec. bd. Old York Rd. Hist. Soc., 2001—; mem. Tookany Creek Watershed Steering Com., 2000—. Mem. Am. Planning Assn., Am. Soc. Pub. Adminstrn., Urban Land Inst., Ams. for Dem. Action, Pa. State U. Alumni Assn., Keystone Soc., Acad. Polit. Sci., Am. Inst. Cert. Planners, N.J. Bd. Profl. Planners, N.J. Assn. Planning and Zoning Adminstrs., Nat. Trust for Hist. Preservation, Pa. Land Trust Alliance, Nat. Eagle Scout Assn., Ranconcas Conservancy Watershed Assn., Heritage Conservancy. Democrat. Lutheran. Avocations: history, fgn. affairs, boating, auto racing, hockey. Home: 404 Old Farm Rd Wyncote PA 19095-2034 Office: Cheltenham Twp Adminstrn Bldg 8230 Old York Rd Elkins Park PA 19027-1589 Fax: 215-887-1561.

HAVIS, ALLAN STUART, playwright, theatre educator; b. N.Y.C., Sept. 26, 1951; s. Mickey and Esther H. Havis; m. Julia Fulton; 1 child, Simone Michelle. BA, CCNY, 1973; MA, Hunter Coll., 1976; MFA, Yale U., 1980. Film animation tchr. Guggenheim Mus., N.Y.C., 1974-76; playwriting tchr. Dramatist Guild, N.Y.C., 1985-87, Ulster County C.C., Stoneridge, N.Y., 1985-88; prof. theatre, head playwriting program U. Calif.-San Diego, La Jolla, 1988—. Author: (novel) Albert the Astronomer, 1979, (plays) Morocco, 1986 (HBO award), Lilith, 1991, The Gift, 1998, (anthology) Plays by Allan Havis, 1989, A Daring Bridge, 1997, Ladies of Fisher Cove, 1997, Sainte Simone, 1997, (play) A Vow of Silence, 1996, (anthology) Plays by Allan Havis, 1997; editor, contbr.: American Political Plays of 1990's, 2000—. Dramaturg Young Playwrights Festival, N.Y.C., 1984, juror, 1993; juror N.J. Arts Coun., Trenton, 1987; panelist Theatre Communications Group, N.Y.C., 1987; juror McKnight Playwriting Fellowship, 1995. Playwriting fellow Nat. Endowment for the Arts, 1986, Rockefeller Found., 1987, Guggenheim Found., 1987-88; recipient New American Plays award Kennedy Ctr./Am. Express, Washington, 1988, Dramatists Guild/CBS award, 1995, HBO award, 1996. Democrat. Jewish. Avocations: tennis, motorcycles, Karate (black belt), swimming, horseback riding. Office: Dept of Theatre Univ Calif-San Diego La Jolla CA 92093 E-mail: ahavis@ucsd.edu.

HAVLICEK, FRANKLIN J. communications executive; b. N.Y.C., July 18, 1947; s. Raymond Joseph and Rosalia Maria (Zona) H.; m. Louise Sferrazza, Dec. 21, 1980. BA, Columbia U., 1968, JD, 1973, MA, 1977, MPhil, 1980; cert., Internat. Inst. Human Rights, Strasbourg, France, 1972. Bar: N.Y. 1974, U.S. Dist. Ct. (so. and ea. dists.) N.Y. 1974, U.S. Ct. Appeals (2d cir.) 1975, U.S. Supreme Ct. 1979, D.C. 1990. Atty. Battle & Fowler, N.Y.C., 1973-78; spl. advisor to Mayor of N.Y.C., 1978-82; ptnr. Seham, Klein, Zelman, N.Y.C., 1982-84; dir. labor rels. NBC, N.Y.C., 1984-88; v.p. personnel, indsl. rels. and environ. svcs. Washington Post, 1988-97; pres. stratagem adv. svcs. Washington, 1997-98; with Internat. Monetary Fund, Washington, 1998—. Adj. prof. internat. & pub. affairs Columbia U., N.Y.C., 1978-88, Sch. Pub., Affairs & Sch. Internat. Svc., Am. U., Washington, 1999—. Editor: Collective Bargaining, 1979, Presidential Selection, 1982, Election Communications, 1984; contbr. numerous articles on law, govt., communications to mags., newspapers. Exec. com. N.Y. Gov.'s Task Force in Schs. and Bus., 1986-88; counsel Vietnam Vets. Meml. Commn., 1982-85, State Commn. on Dioxin, 1983-85; candidate for U.S. Senate in N.Y., 1986; mem. U.S. U.S.S.R. Emerging Leaders Summit, 1988, 90; bd. dirs. World Affairs Coun., 1991-97, Washington Performing Arts Soc., 1995-97, Internat. Peace Acad., 1989-90, World Media Colloquium UNESCO, 1989; U.S. Tech. expert ILO, 1990; cons. to UN High Commr. for Human Rights in Bosnia, 1992; study grant on media and communications European Cmty., 1994; cons. Cath. Relief Svcs., Kosovo, 1999. With U.S. Army, 1968-70. Ford Found. fellow, 1977; study grantee on media and comms. European Cmty., 1994. Mem. ABA, Assn. of Bar of City of N.Y., Am. Polit. Sci. Assn., Am. Acad. Polit. Sci., N.Y. Acad. Scis. Clubs: City N.Y. (trustee 1985-87). Roman Catholic. Avocations: tennis, running, climbing, films, architectural restoration. Home: 6024 Western Ave Chevy Chase MD 20815-3344 Office: Internat Monetary Fund 700 19th St NW Washington DC 20431 E-mail: fhavlicek@imf.org., fhavlicek@aol.com.

HAVLICEK, JOSEPH PAUL, educator; b. West Lafayette, Ind., Apr. 7, 1964; s. Joseph Jr. and Betty Jo Prater H. BSEE, Va. Tech., 1986, MSEE, 1988; PhD in Elec. & Computer Engring., U. Tex., Austin, 1996. Software developer Mgmt. Systems Labs., Blacksburg, Va., 1984-87, IBM/Ralph Kirkley Assocs., Austin, Tex., 1993; elec. engr. Naval Rsch. Lab., Washington, 1989-97; asst. prof. elec. and computer engring. U. Okla., Norman, 1997—2002, assoc. prof. elec. and computer engring., 2002—. Co-author: (chpt.) Handbook of Image and Video Processing, 2000; contbr. articles to profl. jours. Mem. IEEE, AAUP, Eta Kappa Nu, Tau Beta Pi, Phi Kappa Phi. Avocations: music, biking, hiking, backpacking. Home: 2912 Glasgow Dr Norman OK 73072 Office: Sch Elec & Computer Engring 202 W Boyd Rm 219 Norman OK 73019-1023 E-mail: joebob@ou.edu.

HAVLICEK, MICHAEL, medical association administrator; Pres.,CEO ALS (Lou Gehrig's Disease) Assn. Office: ALS Lou Gehrigs Disease Assn 27001 Agoura Rd Ste 150 Agoura Hills CA 91301-5104

HAVLIN, JOHN LEROY, soil scientist, educator; b. Chgo., May 8, 1950; s. Joseph Leroy and Dorothy Jean (Williams) H.; 1 child, Jonathon Cary. MS, Colo. State U., 1980, PhD, 1983. Asst. prof. U. Nebr., Scottbluff, 1983-85, Kans. State U., Manhattan, 1985-90, prof. dept. agronomy, 1990-96; prof. N.C. State U., Raleigh, 1996—. Author: Soil Fertility and Fertilizers; contbr. articles, chapters to books. Named Researcher of Yr., Nat. Fertilizer Solutuions Assn., 1989; recipient Werner L. Nelson Rsch. award, 1991, R.E. Wagner award, 2003; fellow Tchr. fellow, Nat. Assn. Coll. Tchrs. of Agr., 1994. Fellow: Soil Sci. Soc. Am. (Edn. award 2002), Am. Soc. Agronomy; mem.: Soil and Water Conservation Soc., Phi Kappa Phi, Sigma Xi, Gamma Sigma Delta (Outstanding Tchr. award 1992). Republican. Presbyterian. Achievements include research in advancement of dryland soil and crop managment technologies to improve productivity and profitability; crop rotation and tillage effects on soil organic matter and productivity; dryland fertilizer managment and precision farming. Home: 8709 Bluff Pointe Ct Raleigh NC 27615-4195 Office: NC State U Dept Soil Sci Raleigh NC 27695-0001 E-mail: havlin@ncsu.edu.

HAVNER, KERRY SHUFORD, civil engineering and solid mechanics educator; b. Huntington, W.Va., Feb. 20, 1934; s. Alfred Sidney and Jessie May (Fowler) H.; m. Roberta Lee Rider, Aug. 28, 1954; children: Karen Elese Smith, Clark Alan, Kris Sidney. BSCE, Okla. State U., 1955, MS, 1956, PhD, 1959. Registered prof. engr., Okla. Stress analyst Douglas Aircraft Co., Tulsa, 1956; from instr. to asst. prof. civil engring. Okla. State U., Stillwater, 1957-62; sr. stress and vibration engr. Garrett Corp., Phoenix, 1962-63; sect. chief solid mechs. rsch. missile/space systems divsn. McDonnell-Douglas Corp., Santa Monica, Calif., 1963-68; lectr. civil engring. U. So. Calif., L.A., 1965-68; from assoc. prof. to prof. civil engring. N.C. State U., Raleigh, 1968-82, prof. civil engring. and materials sci., 1982-99, prof. emeritus, 1999—. Sr. vis. dept. applied math. and theoretical physics U. Cambridge, 1981, 89. Author: Finite Plastic Deformation of Crystalline Solids, 1992; contbg. author: Mechanics of Solids, The Rodney Hill 60th Anniversary Volume, 1982; contbr. articles to Jour. Applied Math. and Physics, Jour. of Mechs. and Physics of Solids, Acta Mechanica, Procs. and Phil. Trans. Royal Soc., others; hon. sci. adv. bd. Mechs. of Materials; editl. adv. bd. Internat. Jour. Plasticity. 2d lt. U.S. Army, 1961, 1st lt. USAR, 1962. Rsch. grantee NSF, 1971, 74, 76, 78, 81, 83, 87, 91, 94; vis. fellow Clare Hall, 1981; recipient Melvin R. Lohmann medal Okla. State U., 1994. Fellow ASCE (sec. engring. mechs. divsn. 1983-85, chmn. 1987-88, chmn. engring. mechs. adv. bd. 1990-91, chmn. TAC-CERF awards com. 1991-94; assoc. editor Jour. Engring. Mechs. 1981-83), Am. Acad. Mechanics (assoc. editor Mechanics, 1991-97); mem. ASME, Soc. Engring. Sci., Soc. Indsl. and Applied Math., Sigma Xi. Democrat. Methodist. Achievements include research in theories and analyses of anisotropic hardening and finite deformation in crystalline materials, particularly metals. Home: 3331 Thomas Rd Raleigh NC 27607-6743 Office: NC State U PO Box 7908 Raleigh NC 27695-7908 E-mail: havner@eos.ncsu.edu.

HAVRILCSAK, GREGORY MICHAEL, history educator; b. Uniontown, Pa., Feb. 18, 1951; s. Michael and Geneveve Anne (Satterfield) H.; m. Laura Ann Hart; 1 child, Karen Elizabeth. BA, U. Mich., Flint, 1978; MA, Oakland U., 1989; postgrad., U. Va., 1995. Instr. history St. Mary's Sch., Swartz Creek, Mich., 1978-79, Riverside Mil. Acad., Gainesville, Ga., 1979-85, Notre Dame High Sch., Harper Woods, Mich., 1985-88, East Detroit Cmty. Schs., Eastpointe, Mich., 1986-91, Notre Dame High Sch., Harper Woods, Mich., 1991—, chmn. dept. social sci., 1996, debate and forensics coach, 1998—. Dir. social studies learning ctr. correctional edn. divsn. L'Anse-Creuse Cmty. Schs., Mt. Clemens, Mich., 1986-89; adj. instr. history Monroe (Mich.) County C.C., 1988-94, Oakland C.C., Auburn Hills, Mich., 1989-2000; adj. lectr. in history Coll. Arts and Scis., U. Mich., Flint, 2000—; Monticello-Stratford Hall Plantation Summer Seminar for Tchrs., 1995; with Inst. on the Tchg. of Advanced Placement European History, St. Johnsbury Acad., Vt., 1992, Internat. Symposium on the War of 1812 on the Great Lakes, U. Windsor, 1988; radio host Havrilcsak's History, WSDS AM 1480, 1998-99. Vol. Big Bros./Big Sisters, Macomb County, Mich., 1987—89; pres. Ventura Condominium Homeowners Assn., 1999—2001. With USN, 1969—71. Named Outstanding Young Men of Am., U.S. Jaycees, 1980. Mem. Mich. Hist. Soc., Oakland U. Alumni Assn., U. Mich. Alumni Assn., Orgn. Am. Historians, Mich. C.C. History Assn., Ctr. Tchg. Mich. History, Phi Alpha Theta. Avocations: photography, travel. Home: 15744 Charles R Ave Eastpointe MI 48021 Office: Notre Dame High Sch 20254 Kelly Rd Harper Woods MI 48225-1287 E-mail: greghav@umflint.edu.

HAWASH, MICHAEL ANDREW, lawyer; b. Middlesbrough, Eng., Mar. 30, 1966; came to U.S., 1981; s. Ralph Hawash and Linda (Burnip) Kuschel. BA in History, U. Tex., 1990, BA in Govt., 1991; JD, U. Houston, 1994. Bar: Tex. 1994, U.S. Dist. Ct. (so., no., ea., and we. dists.) Tex. 1995, U.S. Ct. Appeals (5th cir.) 1996, U.S. Dist. Ct. (ea. dist.) La. 1996. Assoc. Meyer Orlando & Evans PC, Houston, 1993-2000, Verner Liipfert Bernhard McPherson and Hand, Chartered, Houston, 2000-01; spl. counsel Adams & Reese, Houston, 2001—. Mem. ABA, Fed. Bar Assn., Maritime Law Assn., State Bar Tex., Houston Young Lawyers Assn., Houston Bar Assn., Computer Game Developers Assn., Phi Delta Phi, Phi Kappa Psi. Home: 1840 Kipling Houston TX 77098 Office: Adams & Reese LLP 4400 One Houston Ctr 1221 McKinney Houston TX 77010 E-mail: hawashma@arlaw.com.

HAWE, DAVID LEE, manufacturing consultant, venture capitalist; b. Columbus, Ohio, Feb. 19, 1938; s. William Doyle and Carolyn Mary (Hassig) H.; m. Margret J. Hoover, Apr. 15, 1962; children: Darrin Lee, Kelly Lynn. Lic. real estate broker, Calif. Project mgr. ground antenna systems W.D.L. Labs., Philco Corp., 1960-65; credit mgr. for Western U.S. Am. Hosp. Supply Corp., Burbank, Calif., 1965-74; owner, mgr. Hoover Profl. Equipment Co., Contract Health Equipment Co., Guasti, Calif., 1974-75; pres. Baslor Care Svcs.; owner convalescent homes Santa Ana, Calif., 1975-80; pres. Application Assocs., 1980-2000; CEO Xiron Inc., 1985-2000; owner Tripro Assocs. Bd. dirs., chmn. bd. dirs. Xiron, Inc.; bd. dir. Medisco Co., Casa Pacifica, Broadway Assocs., C-Squard Inc., Xiron Corp., C and C Group, Application Assocs. Inc. Bd. dirs. Santa Ana Cmty. Convalescent Hosp., 1974-79, pres. 1975-79. With USN, 1954-56. Mem. Am. Vacuum Soc. Republican. Roman Catholic. Home: 18082 Hallsworth Cir Villa Park CA 92861-4503

HAWES, BESS LOMAX, retired anthropologist; m. Baldwin Hawes; children: Corey, Naomi, Nicholas. BA, Bryn Mawr U., 1941; MA, U. Calif., 1970; PhD (hon.), Kenyon Coll., 1994, U. N.C., 1995. With music divsn. N.Y. Pub. Libr.; prof. anthropology Calif. State U., Northridge, 1963—74, Smithsonian Instn., 1974—76; dir. Folk Arts Program Nat. Endowment for Arts, 1977—92; ret., 1992. Recipient Nat. Medal of Arts, Pres. Clinton, 1993.

HAWES, GRACE MAXCY, retired archival specialist, writer; b. Cumberland, Wis., Feb. 4, 1926; d. Clarence David and Mabel Hannah (Erickson) Maxcy; student U. Wis., 1944-46; BA, San Jose State U., 1963, MA, 1971: m. John G. Hawes, Aug. 28, 1948 (dec.); children: Elizabeth, John D., Mark (dec.), Amy; m. E. Zumbrunnen, 1993. Library asst. NASA, Langley, Va., 1948-49; archival specialist Hoover Archives, Stanford U., 1976-80, adminstrv. asst., 1980-82; archival specialist Hoover Inst., 1982-89, rsch. archivist, 1989-93, 97—. Author: The Marshall Plan for China: Economic Cooperation Administration, 1948-1949, 1977. Home: PO Box 129 822 N Lake Dr Shell Lake WI 54871-9336 Address: 925 Ponselle Ln Capitola CA 95010

HAWES, LOUISE E, writer, education educator; b. Boulder, Colo., June 21, 1943; d. Maurice and Isabel Hawes; m. Stephen Jacobson, Dec. 26, 1965 (div. 1980); children: Marc Jacobson, Robin Jacobson. BA, Swarthmore Coll.; MFA, Vt. Coll. Writer, advt. dir. Stanley Kaplan, NYC, 1980—93; faculty mem. Vt. Coll., Writing Program, Montpelier, 1997—. Spkr., guest lectr., writer in residence various colleges and conferences, 1992—. Author: (novels) Waiting for Christopher, 2002, Rosey in the Present Tense, 1999—2000. Recipient Years Best Young Adult Books, NYC Pub. Libr., 2003, Young Adult Choice, Internat. Reading Assn., 1998, Best Books, Young Adult Libr. Services Assn., 2002. Mem.: Writers and Illustrators, Soc. of Children's Books, Authors Guild. Achievements include founding faculty of nation's first MFA program in writing for children at Vt. College. Avocations: sculpting, reading, drawing. E-mail: mail@louisehawes.com.

HAWES, NANCY ELIZABETH, mathematics educator; b. Phila., Oct. 28, 1944; d. Charles E. and Margaret M. (Cassel) H. BS in Edn., Millersville (Pa.) State Coll., 1966; MAT, Purdue U., 1970; M.Div., Ea. Bapt. Theol. Sem., Phila., 1979. Ordained deacon A.M.E. Zion Ch., 1978, elder, 1980. Tchr. math. Penncrest High Sch./Rose Tree Media (Pa.) Sch. Dist., 1966-68; asst. pastor Wesley A.M.E. Zion Ch., Phila., 1975-82; pastor St. John A.M.E. Zion Ch., Bethlehem, Pa., 1982-88, Mt. Tabor A.M.E. Zion Ch., Avondale, Pa., 1988-90; assoc. pastor Wesley A.M.E. Zion Ch., Phila., 1990—; tchr. math. Upper Merion Area Sch. Dist., King of Prussia, Pa., 1968—. Sponsor, Upper Merion Area High Sch. Math. Team, 1987—. Mem. Nat. Coun. Tchrs. Math., Math. Assn. Am., Pa. Coun. Tchrs. Math., Assn. Tchrs. Math. of Phila. and Vicinity. A.M.E. Zion Ch. Office: Upper Merion Area High Sch 435 Crossfield Rd King Of Prussia PA 19406-2363

HAWES, SUE, lawyer; b. Washington, Mar. 30, 1937; d. Alexander Boyd and Elizabeth (Armstrong) H.; m. James E. Brodhead, June 21, 1963; children: William James Pusey Brodhead, Daniel Alexander Hawes Brodhead. BA, Sarah Lawrence Coll., 1959, MA, 1963; JD, Whittier (Calif.) Sch. of Law, 1983. Bar: Calif. 1988, U.S. Dist. Ct. (ctrl. dist.) Calif. 1990. Dancer and choreographer, N.Y.C., Washington, Latin Am., Europe, 1959-62; instr., dir. dance program dept. theatre and phys. edn. Smith Coll., Northampton, Mass., 1963-65; instr. dept. dance UCLA, 1973-75; freelance script supr. L.A., 1976-80; prin. Law Office of Sue Hawes, L.A., 1988-96. Articles editor Whittier Law Rev., 1982-83. Bd. dirs. Nuc. Age Peace Found., 2003—; active Santa Barbara Symphony League; mem. Santa Barbara Women's Polit. Com.. Mem. State Bar Calif., Actors' Equity Assn. Democrat. Avocations: music, gardening, politics.

HAWES, WILLIAM KENNETH, communication educator, author; b. Grand Rapids, Mich., Mar. 6, 1931; s. William Kenneth and Cora Elizabeth (Tibble) H.; m. Ella Margaret Plant, Aug. 13, 1961 (dec. 1998); children: William III, Robert Ernest. AB, Eastern Mich. U., 1955; AM, U. Mich., 1956, PhD, 1960. Tchg. asst. U. Mich., Ann Arbor, 1956-57; instr. English and speech Eastern Mich. U., Ypsilanti, 1956-60; asst. prof., mgr. KTCU Tex. Christian U., Ft. Worth, 1960-64; vis. assoc. prof., mgr. WUNC U. N.C., Chapel Hill, 1964-65; assoc. prof., mgr. KUHF U. Houston, 1965-76, prof., 1976—. Admissions bd. Biomed. Program, Sch. Allied Health Scis., U. Tex. Health Sci. Ctr., Houston, 1974-93; lectr. J. William Fulbright, Taiwan, 2001; resident Rockefeller Found., Bellagio, Italy, 2003. Author: The Performer in Mass Media, 1978, American Television Drama, 1986, Television Performing, 1991, 2d edit., 2003, Ante La Cámara, 1993, Chinese edit., 1999, Public Television: America's First Station, 1996, Live Television Drama, 1946-1951, 2001, Filmed Television Drama, 1952-1958, 2002; contbg. author: Understanding Radio, 1967, 85, La Radio: Une Carrière, 1970, Understanding Television, 1978, Television Station Management and Operations, 1989; editor: Pornography Cinema Community Standards, 1975, 82, 93; prodr., creator TV series including Video Workshop, 1967—; film guest Fed. Republic of Germany, 1981. Active Houston Pub. TV, Mus. Fine Arts-Houston, Fulbright Found. Recipient Avery Hopwood award U. Mich., 1957; grantee U. Houston and/or NEH, 1981, 83, 86, 87, 91, 2003; named to U. Houston London Program, 1984, 94; Rockwell award, 1996. Mem.: ACLU, Mus. of Fine Arts Houston, Am. Film Inst. Home: Parc V-902 3600 Montrose Blvd Houston TX 77006-4658 Office: U Houston Sch of Comm Houston TX 77204-4072 Fax: 713-743-2604. E-mail: whawes@mail.uh.edu.

HAWK, CAROLE LYNN, retired insurance company executive, research analyst; b. Springfield, Ill., June 17, 1947; d. Warren Wesley and Mary June (Moore) Weiser; m. Charles Edward Hawk, Aug. 2, 1963; 1 child, Cynthia Jean Hawk-Lindzy. Student, Lincoln Land C.C., Springfield, 1970-75, Ind. U., South Bend, 1982-83. Cert. data processor, computer programmer, systems profl., assoc. in customer svc.; assoc. Ins. Regulatory Compliance. Systems analyst Office Ill. Sec. of State, Springfield, 1969-78; software specialist Clark Equipment Co., Buchanan, Mich., 1978-84; GC0S6 software analyst Contel Corp., Wentzville, Mo., 1984-87; tech. rsch. analyst The Horace Mann Cos., Springfield, 1988—2002; ret., 2002. Mem., vol. interpreter Dana-Thomas House Found.; adult literacy tutor; active Friends of the Fox Theatre, St. Louis; vol. usher Sangamon State Auditorium U. of Ill., Springfield; pres. Smedley Home Town Meml. chpt., 2000—. Fellow Life Mgmt. Assn.; mem. Assn. Info. Tech. Profls. (sec. Capital chpt. 1993-94, exec. pres. 1995, pres. 1996, exec. v.p. 2001), Ctrl. Ill. Life Mgmt. Inst. (co. rep. 1995-2000), Toastmasters (sec. Horace Mann chpt. 1992, pres. 1993, gov. area 1 1994-95, gov. dist. C 1995-97, v.p. edn. 1997-98, v.p. pub. rels. 1998-99, v.p. edn. 1999-2000, pres. 2002—).

HAWK, DAWN DAVAH, secondary education educator; b. Dodge, Nebr., Apr. 14, 1945; d. Fred John and Marcella Martha (Kunes) Lerch; m. Floyd Russell Hawk, June 14, 1969. BAE, Wayne State Coll., 1967. Cert. tchr., Nebr., Iowa, Ariz. English tchr. Tekamah (Nebr.) Pub. Sch., 1967-69, West Lyon Community Schs., Inwood, Iowa, 1970-74, Norfolk (Nebr.) Cath. Schs., 1974-85; English tchr., libr. Beemer (Nebr.) Pub. Schs., 1969-70; English and reading tchr. San Manuel (Ariz.) Sch. Dist., 1986—. Chair dept. adaptive edn. San Manuel H.S., 1992—2003; tutor in field. Active Catalina Luth. Ch., Tucson. Recipient Cooper Found. award for excellence in teaching U. Nebr., 1983. Fan award to study at Gilder/Lehrman Inst. Am. History, Radcliffe Inst. for Advanced Study at Harvard, 2002; NEH edn. grantee, 1987, 89, 91, 95; Ariz. Reading Assn. grad. scholar, 1995; Michael Jordan Fundamentals grantee, 2002. Mem. NEA, Nat. Coun. Tchrs. English, Internat. Reading Assn., Ea. Pinal Lit. Coun., Ariz. English Tchrs. Assn., Tucson Area Reading Coun. (bd. advisors), San Manuel Tchrs. Assn. Avocations: reading, writing poetry, travelling, visiting museums, golf. Home: 3950 E Hawser St 5 Tucson AZ 85739-9537 Office: San Manuel HS PO Box 406 San Manuel AZ 85631-0406 E-mail: azhawks@att.net.

HAWK, FLOYD RUSSELL, secondary school educator; b. Fresno, Calif., Oct. 7, 1945; s. Floyd Edward and Velma Irene (Lyon) H.; m. Dawn Davah Lerch, June 14, 1969. BA in Bus., Wayne State Coll., 1971. Cert. tchr. Ariz. Tchr. W. Lyon Pub. Schs., Inwood, Iowa, 1970-74, Norfolk (Nebr.) Cath. Schs., 1974-76, Madison (Nebr.) Pub. Schs., 1977-85, Young (Ariz.) Pub. Schs., 1985-86, San Manuel (Ariz.) High Sch., 1986—. State rep. Nat. Coaches Assn., Madison, Nebr., 1980-82; bd. dirs. Pinal County Adult Literacy, San Manuel. Mem. adv. bd. Multiple Sclerosis Soc.; commd. deacon Catalina Luth. NEH grantee, 1995. Mem. NEA, Ariz. Edn. Assn., Ariz. Bus. Edn. Assn., Ariz. Hist. Soc., Optimist Club (pres. 1972, lt. gov. 1973). Lutheran. Avocations: baseball, reading, teaching, church work. Office: San Manuel HS PO Box 406 San Manuel AZ 85631-0406

HAWK, GEORGE WAYNE, retired electronics company executive; b. Warren, Ohio, Feb. 21, 1928; s. Oscar Wilmer and Morda Irene (Klingensmith) H.; m. Charline Hines Bond, Feb. 12, 1955; children: George Wayne, David James, John Robert. BS in Aero. Engring, Purdue U., 1951; MSME, U. So. Calif., 1955; postgrad., U. Tenn. Registered profl. engr., Ind. Asst. R & D officer gas dynamics facility Arnold Engring. Devel. Ctr., Tullahoma, Tenn., 1951-53; project engr. Hughes R & D Lab., Culver City, Calif., 1953-56; sr. rsch. engr. Goodyear Aircraft Corp., Akron, Ohio, 1956-57; with Moog Inc., East Aurora, N.Y., 1957-81, v.p. aerospace divsn., 1968-69, exec. v.p., dir., gen. mgr. controls divsn., 1969-76, exec. v.p., dir. pres. controls group, 1976-81; pres. G.W. Hawk Inc., 1981-86; pres., CEO Acme Electric Corp., 1986-91, chmn. bd. dirs., CEO, 1992-94; chmn. bd. dirs. Comptek Rsch. Inc., 1983-87, M.H.P. Machines, Inc., Buffalo, 1983-92. Chmn. bd. dirs. B.I.S. Ptnrs.; bd. dirs. Comptek Rsch., Inc., Western N.Y. Tech. Devel. Corp., past chmn. Contbr. articles profl. jours.; patentee in field. Past chair and vice chair bd. dirs. Buffalo Philharm. Orch., lifetime dir.; past pres. Greater Niagara Frontier coun. Boy Scouts Am.; past chmn. bd., pres. Greater Buffalo Devel. Found.; trustee, treas. Buffalo Gen.

Hosp. Found.; pres. Niagara Aerospace Mus.; bd. dirs. Niagara Luth. Home Found.; past bd. dirs. Fluid Power Ednl. Found.; bd. regents emeritus Canisius Coll. With U.S. Army, 1946—48, 1st lt. USAF, 1951—53. Inducted into Niagara Frontier Aviation Hall of Fame. Fellow AIAA (assoc.); mem. Air Force Assn. (pres. Larry D. Bell chpt. 1978), Navy League, Am. Def. Preparedness Assn., Nat. Fluid Power Assn. (past chmn. bd.), Nat. Conf. on Fluid Power (past conf. dir.) Buffalo C. of C. (past vice chmn.). Avocations: private pilot (twin engine-instrument), skiing, golf, fishing. Home: 1634 Hubbard Rd East Aurora NY 14052-3011 E-mail: hawkwabunk@msn.com.

HAWK, KATHLEEN PATRICIA, broadcast consultant; b. Butler, Pa., Feb. 12, 1945; d. Allen Clarence and Betty Ruth (Wilson) Pollock; m. Robert Ferdinand Hawk, Dec. 31, 1966; 1 child, Allen Robert. BSc, Parsons Coll., Fairfield, Iowa, 1966. Ind. internat. radiofrequency/microwave cons./personal wireless telecom./facilities siting cons., wireless facility siting cons., Butler, Pa., 1990—. Invited reviewer U.S. Congress, Office of Tech. Assessment, Wireless Technologies and the Nat. Info. Infrastructure, 1995; participant numerous seminars, confs., telecomms. adv. com.; mem. elec. sensitivity network. Author: Case Study in the Heartland, 1996; freelance writer Pitts. Post Gazette; contbr. articles to profl. jours. Worthy advisor Rainbow Girls, 1961; mem. Nat. Coalition of Citizens and Pub. Ofcls. for Local Control; founding mem., bd. dirs. Cellular Phone Task Force; bd. dirs. Delbert Parkinson Christian Cancer Coalition. Mem. Bioelectromagnetics Soc., Associated Bioelectromagnetics Technologists, Butler Natural Living Group, 1000 Club, Butler Country Club, 38 Year Card Club, Am. Legion Aux., Am. Golf Hall of Fame. Republican. Achievements include research on human and animal health in close proximity to telecomms. facilities. Avocations: gourmet cooking, crafts, sports, pub. speaking, politics. Home and Office: 122 Thornwood Dr Butler PA 16001-3442 E-mail: kathyhawk@webtv.net.

HAWK, L. DANIEL, minister, religious studies educator; b. Upper Sandusky, Ohio, June 24, 1955; s. Lewis D. and Barbara L. Hawk; m. Linda Marie Smith; children: Daniel John, Andrew Elias. BA, Otterbein Coll., 1977; MDiv, Asbury Theol. Sem., Wilmore, Ky., 1980; PhD, Emory U., 1990. Elder East Ohio Conf. of the United Meth. Ch., 1983. Instr. religion Emory U., Atlanta, 1987—89; asst. prof. religion Centenary Coll. La., Shreveport, 1990—95; prof. old testament and Hebrew Ashland (Ohio) Theol. Sem., 1995—; assoc. pastor Ridgewood United Meth. Ch., Parma, Ohio. Vis. prof. Old Testament S.Am. Theol. Sem., Colon, Argentina, 2000, Russia United Meth. Theol. Seminary, Moscow, 2002. John Wesley fellow, Found. for Theol. Edn., 1990—93. Mem.: Wesleyan Theol. Soc., John Wesley Fellowship, Inst. Bibl. Rsch., Cath. Bibl. Assn., Soc. Bibl. Lit. Office: Ashland Theol Seminary 910 Center St Ashland OH 44805

HAWK, MARSHA K. health facility administrator; b. Tacoma, May 9, 1948; d. Neal Jay and Alice Eleanor McKechnie; m. Robert Marion Hawk, Sept. 22, 1980 (div. Aug. 13, 1982); 1 child, Brandon Neal. BA, Western Wash. U., 1971; student, Chapman U., Tacoma, 1986—88. Habilitative tng. specialist Rainier Sch., Buckley, Wash., 1986—88, sheltered workshop advisor, 1988—89, habil. plan adminstr., 1989—90; devel. disabilities specialist Western State Hosp., Tacoma, 1990—98, traumatic brain injury specialist, 1994—98, dir. Brain Injury Resource Ctr., 1998—. Pres. Wash. State Traumatic Brain Injury Adv. Bd., 2002; presenter 1st ann. Am. Indian Vet. Conf., Bellingham, Wash., 2002. Mem. New Wings Coalition for Day Program, Seattle, 2002. Mem.: Brain Injury Assn. Wash. (bd.dirs. 2002), Saguna Yoga (instr. 1997—2002), Quiet Thunder Chi Gong Club (pres. 2001—02). Avocations: cross country skiing, camping, travel. Office: Western State Hosp Brain Injury Resource Ctr 9601 Steilacoom Blvd SW Tacoma WA 98498-7213 Fax: 253-756-2879. Business E-Mail: hawkmak@dshs.wa.gov.

HAWK, PAULETTA BROWNING, student elementary school educator; b. Gilbert, W.Va., Aug. 10, 1952; d. Walter Browning and Gracie (Johnson) Tyner; children: Clifford Thompson III, Angie Thompson. AA, Cen. Fla. Community Coll., Ocala, 1988; BS in Elem. Edn., U. Cen. Fla., 1991; MEd in Curriculum and Instrn., Nat. Louis U., 1996. Med. receptionist Bluefield (W.Va.) Clinic, 1975-76; ins. clk. Bristol (Tenn.) Meml. Hosp., 1976-78; med. sec. Inter-Mountain Pathology Assn., Bristol, Tenn., 1978-80; substitute tchr. Citrus County Sch. Bd., Inverness, Fla., 1980-81, guidance sec., 1981-85, acct. I (on profl. leave of absence), 1990-91; office mgr. Victor Nothnagel, O.D., Inverness, 1985-87; tchr. Inverness Primary, 1991—99, Banyan Elem., Sunrise, Fla., 1999—2002; tchr. Brooksville (Fla.) Elem., 2002—. Vol. Nat. Arthritis Found., 1988-89, Inverness Primary Sch., Citrus County Sch. Bd., 1989. Mem. Phi Theta Kappa. Democrat. Baptist. Avocations: reading, swimming, cycling, gardening, clay modeling. Home: 415 Tulip Ln Inverness FL 34452

HAWK, PHILLIP MICHAEL, service corporation executive; b. Oklahoma City, June 14, 1939; s H. M. and Rosetta (Cross) H.; m. Nancy Batton, Aug. 13, 1966; children— Tabatha Lynn, Phillip Michael BBA, U. Okla., 1961. Pub. rels. exec. Coca Cola Co., Dallas, 1961-63; salesman svc. Reynolds Metals Co., Dallas, 1963-65; corp. dir. mktg. Cole Pubs. Co., Dallas, 1965-71; sr. v.p. Club Corp. of Am., Dallas, 1972-90; pres. Interclub Corp., Blackwell, Tex., 1990-93, CEO club acquisiton and devel., 1993—; CEO Clubnet, Kingwood, Tex., 1996—2001. Bd. dirs. Club Corp. Mex. Exec. v.p. United Golf Group, N.Y.C., 1998-2000; v.p. Acquisitions Renaissance Golf Group, LLC, 2001-. Republican. Avocation: golf. Office: Renaissance Golf Group 938 Kingwood Dr # 1221 Kingwood TX 77339

HAWK, STEPHEN L. music educator, musician; s. William Dean and Betty J. Hawk; m. Mechelle A. Tassart, Jan. 6, 1984; children: Christopher S., Austin M., Kyle W. BA in Music Edn., Western Ill. U., 1986; MusM, U. Tex., 1988, MusD Arts, 1992. Cert. tchr. Ill. Tchg. asst. U. Tex., Austin, 1986—89; prof. music Slippery Rock U. of Pa., 1989—. Prin. trumpet Civic Light Opera Orch., Pitts., 1994—, Pitts. Broadway Orch., Pitts., 1994—; first trumpet Manchester Craftsmen's Guild Big Band, Pitts., 1998—. Co-producer: CD recording The Hawk's Out (Outstanding Big Band Rec., Cadence Mag., N.Y.C., 1998); musician: (performed on the Oprah Winfrey Show) Nancy Wilson Christmas; musician: (featured soloist) Pitts. Ballet Orch.; musician: (featured soloist/one of two americans) (solo trumpet recitals) International Trumpet Festival/Moscow, Russia. Mem. session trustees Ctr. Presbyn. Ch., Slippery Rock, 1994—2002. Scholar, Western Ill. U. Music Dept. Faculty, 1982—86. Mem.: Coll. Band Directors Nat. Assn., Internat. Trumpet Guild, Internat. Assn. of Jazz Educators (past pres. Pa. unit 1996—98). Office: Slippery Rock U of Pa 219 Swope Music Hall Slippery Rock PA 16057 Office Fax: 724-738-4469. E-mail: stephen.hawk@sru.edu.

HAWKE, BERNARD RAY, planetary scientist; b. Louisville, Oct. 22, 1946; s. Arvil Abner and Elizabeth Ellen (Brown) H. BS in Geology, U. Ky., 1970, MS, 1974, Brown U., 1977, PhD in Planetary Geology, 1978. Geologist U.S. Geol. Survey, 1967-68; researcher U. Ky., 1972-74, Brown U., 1974-78; planetary scientist Hawaii Inst. Geophysics, U. Hawaii, Honolulu, 1978—; dir. NASA Pacific Regional Planetary Data Ctr., 1981—; prin. investigator NASA grants. Assoc. dir. Hawaii Space Grant Coll. Author papers in field. Served with USAR, 1970-72. Decorated Bronze Star Mem. Geochem. Soc., Meteoritical Soc., Am. Geophys. Union, Am. Chem. Soc., Geol. Soc. Am., Sigma Xi, Sigma Gamma Epsilon, Alpha Tau Omega. Republican. Office: U Hawaii SOEST Hawaiian Inst Geophysics Honolulu HI 96822

HAWKE, JOHN DANIEL, JR., United States Comptroller of the Currency; b. N.Y.C., June 26, 1933; s. John Daniel and Olga (Buchbinder) H.; m. Marie Reddan, June 15, 1962 (dec. Mar. 1991); children: Daniel, Caitlin, Anne, Patrick BA, Yale U., 1954; LL.B., Columbia U., 1960. Bar: D.C. 1961, U.S. Supreme Ct. 1968. Law clk. to judge U.S. Ct. Appeals (D.C. cir.), Washington, 1960-61; counsel Select Subcom. on Edn., U.S. Ho. of Reps., Washington, 1961-62; assoc. Arnold & Porter, Washington, 1962-66, ptnr., 1967-75, 78-95; gen. counsel bd. govs. Fed. Res. System, Washington, 1975-78; under sec. for domestic fin. Dept. of Treasury, Washington, 1995-98, comptroller of the currency, 1998—; dir. Fed. Deposit Ins. Corp., Washington, 1998—. Adj. prof. law Georgetown U., Washington, 1971-87; lectr. law Columbia U., N.Y.C., 1979; bd. advisers Morin Ctr. for Banking Law Studies, Boston U. Sch. Law, 1982—, lectr., 1984-88; mem. Shadow Fin. Regulatory Com., 1986-95; lectr. in field. Author: Commentaries on Banking Regulation, 1985; chmn. editorial adv. bd. Banking Policy Report, 1982-95; contbr. numerous articles to profl. jours., chpt. to book. Mem. Fed. City Coun., 1990-95; trustee Found. for Nat. Capital Region, 1992-98; trustee Washington Opera, 1992-96; mem. Pres.'s Com. on the Arts and Humanities, 1996-2001. 2d lt. USAF, 1955-57. Mem. Fed. Bar Assn. (banking law com., chmn. 1976-78), Cosmos Club, Exchequer Club, Econ. Club, Yale Club, Vineyard Haven Yacht Club. Home: 3800 Harrison St NW Washington DC 20015-1926 Office: Comptroller of the Currency 250 E St SW Washington DC 20219-0001

HAWKE, PAUL HENRY, historian; b. Canton, Ohio, Mar. 9, 1958; s. Richard Carl and Sara (Hemming) H.; m. Gaynel O. Allen, May 2, 1987; children: Cailean Stewart, Angela Jeanette. BA in History, Geography, Hist. Preservation, Mary Washington Coll., 1982; postgrad., Temple U., 1983, U. Ark., 1984-85; MA in History and Heritage Preservation, Ga. State U., 1993. Park tech. Petersburg (Va.) Nat. Battlefield, 1978-81; intern Fredericksburg (Va.) and Spotsylvania Nat. Mil. Park, 1981-82; park ranger Independence Nat. Hist. Park, Phila., 1982-83; park historian Pea Ridge (Ark.) Nat. Mil. Park, 1983-85; historian Southeast Regional Office, Atlanta, 1985-95. S.E. coord. Am. Battlefield Protectio Program, Atlanta, 1991-95, Civil War sites adv. commn. staff, 1991-93; coord. Nat. Historic Landmarks Program, Atlanta, 1986-95; chief interpretation and resources mgmt. Shiloh (Tenn.) Nat. Mil. Park, 1995-2000; chief Am. Battlefield Protection Program, Washington, 2000—. Co-author: Civil War Battlefield Guide, 1991; editor The Parapet: Newsletter of the Civil War, 1992-2000; asst. editor, author: Jour. of Civil War Fort Study Group, 1994. Water safety chmn. Am. Nat. Red Cross, Benton County, Ark., 1984-85, water safety instr., Canton, Ohio, 1975-80, Fredericksburg, Va., 1980-82, small craft safey inst., Benton County, Ark., 1984-85, Canton, 1975-80. Named Ky. Col., Gov. of Ky., 1992. Mem. Civil War Fortification Study Group (sec., treas.), Coast Def. Study Group, Assn. of Nat. Park Rangers, Assn. for Preservation of Civil War Sites, Nat. Trust for Hist. Preservation, Civil War Trust, Soc. of Mil. Historians. Avocations: swimming, travel, movies, military history, sports. Home: 6314 Morning Dew Ct Clarksville MD 21029-1150 Office: Nat Park Svc 1849 C St NW 2255 Washington DC 20240 E-mail: paul_hawke@nps.gov.

HAWKE, ROBERT DOUGLAS, retired state legislator; b. Gardner, Mass., July 20, 1932; s. Arthur Eugene Hawke and Gladys Emma (Waite) Sorton; m. Nancy Marie Morchetti, July 20, 1958; children: Linda, Cynthia, Heather, Dean, Mark. BA, Northeastern U., 1954; LLB, Boston U., 1956; MA, Fitchburg State U., 1970. Cert. tchr., Mass. Tchr. Murdock High Sch., Winchendon, Mass., 1956-66, Gardner (Mass.) High Sch., 1966-90; mem. Mass. Ho. of Reps., Boston, 1990-97. Trustee Heywood Hosp., Gardner, 1981—, Gardner Mus., 1980-83, Baldwinville Nursing Home, templeton, Mass.; mem. So. Gardner Hist. Soc., 1984—; adv. bd. Mt. Wachusett C.C., Gardner, 1968-81; chmn. Gardner Rep. Com., Rep. City Com., 1966-76; area campaign coord. Reagan Com., North Ctrl. Mass., 1980-84; councillor at large to Gardner City Coun., 2001—; pres. Consortium of New Eng. Cmty. Art Mus., 1999-2002.. Named Citizen of Yr. Grange of Gardner, 1993, So. Gardner Hist. Soc., 1993, Legislator of Yr. award Worcester County League of Sportmen's Clubs, 1996. Mem. Nat. Rep. Legis. Assn., Nat. Conf. State Legislators, Polish Am. Citizens Club, Account Exec. for Greater Gardner C. of C., Eagles, councillor at large, City Coun., Gardner 2001-. Republican. Baptist. Avocations: reading, tennis, softball. Home: 162 Pearl St Gardner MA 01440-2357

HAWKE, ROBERT FRANCIS, dentist; b. Pasadena, Calif., Oct. 26, 1946; s. George Herbert and Mildred Estelle (Wood) H.; m. Emily Sue Wilkins, Aug. 17, 1973; 1 child, Kristen. BA, U. Ariz., 1969; DDS, Baylor U., Dallas, 1973. Assoc. B.J. Barber, Tucson, 1976-78; ptnr. Barber-Hawke, P.C., Tucson, 1978-87; pvt. practice Tucson, 1987—. Bd. dirs., pres. Delta Dental Ariz., Phoenix, 1985-91. Mem. Tucson Bus. Alliance, 1981—, pres., 1983, 94, Comty. Auto Immune Deficiency Syndrome Adv. Coun., Tucson, 1987-90, Auto Immune Deficiency Syndrome Edn. Project, Tucson, 1988-90. Maj. U.S. Army. Fellow Am. Coll. Dentists, Internat. Coll. Dentists; mem. ADA (alt. del. 1988-92, del. 1994-2000, 14th dist. chmn. polit. action com. 1995-98), Ariz. State Dental Assn. (trustee 1988, v.p. 1991, pres.-elect 1992-93, pres. 1993-94, past pres. 1994-95, mem. legal liaison com. 1993-94, chmn. coun. on constitution and bylaws 1996-97, chmn. coun. on budget planning 1992-93, chmn. coun. on ins. 1998-2003, Svc. award 2002), So. Ariz. Dental Soc. (bd. dirs. 1983-89, pres. 1987-88), Pierre Fauchard Acad., Give Kids a Smile Day (So. Ariz. chmn. 2003—), Rotary (Paul Harris fellow), Beta Beta Beta. Republican. Evangelical. Avocations: golf, jogging, tennis, racquetball, reading. Home: 6745 E Tivani Dr Tucson AZ 85715-3348 Office: 1575 N Swan Rd Ste 200 Tucson AZ 85712-4068 E-mail: hawkerobertf@qwest.net., robertfhawke@comcast.net.

HAWKE, ROGER JEWETT, lawyer; b. N.Y.C., July 2, 1935; s. John Daniel and Olga (Buchbinder) H.; m. Rose Marie Ferri, Aug. 15, 1964; children— Christopher, Allison, John BA cum laude, Amherst Coll., 1956; LL.B., Columbia U., 1959. Bar: N.Y. 1960, U.S. Supreme Ct. 1976. Assoc. Donovan, Leisure, Newton & Irvine, N.Y.C., 1960, 62-65; asst. U.S. atty. U.S. Atty.'s Office, So. Dist. N.Y., N.Y.C., 1965-69; assoc. Brown, Wood, Ivey, Mitchell & Petty LLP, N.Y.C., 1969-71, ptnr., 1971—2001, Sidley Austin Brown & Wood LLP, N.Y.C., 2001—. Arbitrator Nat. Assn. Securities Dealers. Acting village justice Village of Lloyd Harbor, N.Y., 1977-83, trustee, 1983-99; police commr., 1983-99, dep. mayor, 1983-99. With U.S. Army, 1961-62. Fellow: Am. Coll. Trial Lawyers; mem.: ABA, Am. Law Inst., N.Y. Law Inst. (exec. com.), Assn. of Bar of City of N.Y., Lloyd Neck Bath (pres. 1981). Office: Sidley Austin Brown & Wood LLP 787 Seventh Ave New York NY 10019

HAWKER, KENO, mayor, trucking company executive; BA, Wis. State U.; MBA, U. Wis. Owner & pres. Hawker Trucks & Materials, Inc.; mem. coun. City of Mesa, Ariz., 1986—94, 1998—2000, vice mayor, 1990—92, mayor, 2000—. Mem. U.S. Conf. Mayors, Ariz. League of Cities and Towns Bd., Williams Gateway Authority, Regional Public Transportation Authority, Ariz. Mcpl. Water Users Assn., Nat. League of Cities Transp. Task Force, Nat. League of Cities Transp. Infrastructure and Svcs. Steering Com., Maricopa Assn. Govt.'s Regional Coun., Maricopa Assn. Govt.'s, Mesa Chamber of Commerce; chair Regional Coun. Transp. Subcom. Mem.: Maricopa Assn. Govts. (treas.), Mesa HoHoKams, Mesa Baseline Rotary. Avocations: biking, hiking, climbing, rappelling, travel. Office: Mesa City Plaza 20 E Main St Mesa AZ 85201 Address: Hawker Trucks and Materials Inc 315 S Morris Mesa AZ 85210 E-mail: mayor_hawker@ci.mesa.az.us.*

HAWKES, CAROL ANN, academic administrator; b. N.Y.C. d. Howard N. and Lavinia M. (Lally) H. BA, Barnard Coll., 1943; MA, Columbia U., 1944, PhD, 1949. Dir. acad. English liberal arts div. Katharine Gibbs Sch., N.Y.C., 1950-57; prof. English, chmn. dept. English and comparative lit. Finch Coll., N.Y.C., 1957-75; v.p. for ednl. affairs, dean of coll. Hartwick Coll., Oneonta, N.Y., 1975-80; pres. Endicott Coll., Beverly, Mass., 1980-87; assoc. v.p. for acad. affairs Western Conn. State U., Danbury, 1987—. Trustee Norwich U., Hartwick Coll. Author: Master's Degree Programs and the Liberal Arts College, 1968. Harvard Sch. Dental Medicine fellow. Mem. MLA, LWV, Modern Humanities Rsch. Assn., Am. Assn. Higher Edn., Princeton Club (N.Y.C.), Columbia U. Club New Eng., Phi Beta Kappa. Office: Western Conn State U Academic Affairs Danbury CT 06810 E-mail: hawkesc@wcsu.edu.

HAWKES, MARY NEWGEON, minister, educator, retired; b. Thessaloniki, Greece, June 27, 1934; arrived in U.S., 1937; d. William Emory and Jessie Newgeon Hawkes. AB in Music, Doane Coll., 1956; MA in Religious Edn., Hartford Sem., 1958; EdD in Religious Edn., Columbia U. Tchrs. Coll./Union Theol. Sem., 1983. Ordained to ministry United Ch. of Christ, 1980. Dir. Christian edn. United Chs. of Christ, Middletown and Hartford, Conn., 1958—67; ecumenical ch. worker German Protestant Ch., Hamburg/Berlin, 1967—69; dir. Christian edn. United Chs. of Christ, Conn., N.Y., Mich., 1969—76, interim min. Conn., N.Y., Vt., 1986—88, 1994—98, pastor North Bennington, Vt., 1988—94; sec. edn. programs United Ch. Bd., Homeland Min., N.Y.C., 1981—85; pastor 1st Congl. Ch., Deer River United Cmty. Ch., Carthage, NY, 1998—2002. V.p., pres. Village Ecumenical Min, Carthage, NY, 1999—2002; resource person United Ch. of Christ N.Y. Women, 1999—2002. Mem. editl. bd.: hymnal Sing of Life and Faith, 1963—67, content editor: religious songbook Sing to God, 1981—84, co-author, editor: Festivals of Christmas, 1981—83. Mem. family life com. Bennington (Vt.) Pub. Schs.; bd. dirs. Adult Day Care Program, Bennington, 1990—93; editor newsletter Adam Hawkes Family Assn., Saugus, Mass., 2002—; v.p. Greater Hartford Coun. Chs., 1963—66. Recipient Doane Builder award, Doane Coll., 1981. Mem.: AAUW, Alban Inst., Ptnrs. in Edn. United Ch. of Christ, Children's Def. Fund, N.H. Peace Found., Amnesty Internat., Habitat for Humanity, So. Poverty Law Ctr., Common Cause. Democrat. United Ch. Of Christ. Avocations: music, travel. Home: 107 Morningside Commons Brattleboro VT 05301-3633

HAWKEY, G. MICHAEL, lawyer, real estate investor and developer; b. Apr. 17, 1941; m. Frances Tripp, Feb. 27, 1971; children: Samuel, Eliza, MacKenzie. AB, Princeton U., 1963; postgrad., Columbia Bus. Sch., 1964; LLB, Cornell U., 1967. Bar: Mass. 1967. Atty. Sullivan & Worcester LLP, Boston. Founder Sun Valley Properties, Pocatello, Idaho, Mettowee Valley Properties, Pawlet, Vt.; lectr. Mass. Restaurant Assn. Author: The Union-Management Controversy Over Subcontracting and Plant Relocation, 1963. Bd. dirs. Pacific. Internat. Inst., Lewiston, Idaho, 1992—97, St. Lukes Cancer Rsch. Found., Cork, Ireland, 1994—97; N.Am. bd. Michael Smurfit Grad. Sch. Bus., Univ. Coll., Dublin, 1994—98; trustee Maruzen Hawthorne Coll., Antrim, NH, 1991—92; bd. govs. Wianno Club, 1982—98; bd. dirs. Greyhawk Village Assn., Sun Valley, Idaho, 2001—. Mem. Internat. Coun. Shopping Ctrs., Mass. Real Estate Fin. Assn. (bd. dirs. 1989-92), Sr. Execs. Club of Mass. Real Estate Fin. Assn., Mass. Conveyancers Assn., The Country Club (Brookline, Mass.), Wianno Club Home: 26 Arlington Rd Wellesley MA 02481-6129 Office: Sullivan & Worcester LLP 1 Post Office Sq Ste 2300 Boston MA 02109-2129

HAWKINS, ASHTON, museum executive, lawyer; b. N.Y.C., May 11, 1937; s. Ashton W. and Kyra S. Hawkins. Grad., Phillips Exeter Acad., 1955; BA cum laude, Harvard U., 1959, JD, 1962. Bar: N.Y. 1963, U.S. Supreme Ct. 1968. Assoc. Cadwalader, Wickersham & Taft, N.Y.C., 1962-65; asst. atty. gen. State of N.Y., 1965-68; asst. sec. Met. Mus. Art, N.Y.C., 1968, sec., 1969-74, sec., counsel, 1974-77, v.p., sec., counsel, 1977-87, exec. v.p. and counsel to the trustees, 1987—. Chmn. bd. Dia Ctr. for the Arts, 1985-96; co-founder Mus. Law Conf., 1973; bd. advisers Libr. Am., 1996—. Trustee, sec. George Pompidou Art and Culture Found., 1980; bd. dirs. N.Y. Landmark Preservation Found., 1986—, World Monuments Fund, (bd. trustees World Monuments Fund 1996—); v.p. Duke Ellington Meml. Fund, 1986—; dir. Mcpl. Art Soc., 1988—; trustee Wolfsonian Instn., 1995—. Mem. Assn. Bar City N.Y., Coun. on Fgn. Rels., Century Club, Knickerbocker Club. Office: Gersten Savage & Kaplowitz 9th Flr 101 E 52nd St New York NY 10022

HAWKINS, BRETT WILLIAM, political science educator; b. Buffalo, Sept. 15, 1937; s. Ralph C. and Irma A. (Rowley) H.; m. Linda L. Knuth, Oct. 31, 1974; 1 child, Brett William. AB, U. Rochester, 1959; MA, Vanderbilt U., 1962, PhD, 1964. Instr. polit. sci. Vanderbilt U., 1963; instr. in polit. sci. Washington and Lee U., 1963-64, asst. prof., 1964-65, U. Ga., Athens, 1965-68, assoc. prof., 1968-70, U. Wis., Milw., 1970-71, prof., 1971-99, ret, 2000. Author: Nashville Metro, 1964, The Ethnic Factor in American Politics, 1970, Politics in the Metropolis, 2d edit, 1971, Politics and Urban Policies, 1971, The Politics of Raising State and Local Revenue, 1978, Professional Associations and Municipal Innovation, 1981; contbr. articles to profl. jours., chpts. in edited vols. Mem. Phi Beta Kappa, Iota of N.Y. Home: 5318 N Kent Ave Whitefish Bay WI -5109 E-mail: bretthwk@yahoo.com.

HAWKINS, BRIAN L. academic administrator, educator; b. Lafayette, Ind, Aug. 5, 1948; s. Robert H. and Majorie Joan (Bradley) H.; m. Lisa Ellen Herrick, Dec. 30, 1970; children: Timothy, Steven. BA, Mich. State U., 1970, MA, 1972; PhD, Purdue U., 1975. Asst. prof. U. Tex., San Antonio, 1975-76, asst. dean of bus., 1976-81; assoc. v.p. acad. affairs Drexel U., Phila., 1981-86, assoc. v.p. computing and telecommunications, 1984-86; v.p. Brown U., Providence, 1986—, spl. asst. to pres., assoc. provost acad. planning, 1990-92, v.p. acad. planning and adminstrn., 1992-96, sr. v.p. acad. planning and adminstrv. affairs, 1997-98; pres., CEO EDUCAUSE, 1998—. Trustee EDUCOM, Washington, 1986-90, chmn. bd., 1989-90; Trustee, Univ. of Richmond, 1999-2003, Dir., Forum for the Future of Higher Ed., 1999-present. Author: Managerial Comm., 1981; editor: Managing & Organizing Info. Resources on Campus, 1990, The Mirage of Continuity: Reconfiguring Academic Info. Resources in the 21st Century, 1998; Tech. Everywhere, 2002. Bd. dir. CAUSE, 1992-96.

HAWKINS, CARMEN DOLORAS, lawyer; b. L.A., Sept. 17, 1955; d. Lenell Herman Hawkins and Doloras Mondy. BA, U. Calif., Santa Cruz, 1977; JD, Georgetown U., 1981. Bar: Washington 1981, Calif. 1982, U.S. Dist. Ct. (cen. dist. Calif.) 1982, U.S. Ct. Appeals (9th cir.) 1982. Assoc. Law Offices of Thomas G. Neusom, L.A., 1982-83; pvt. practice law L.A., 1984-88; atty. L.A. Community Coll., 1984-85; gen. counsel L.A. Trade Tech. Coll. Found., 1986-88; of counsel Wilson, Becks & Pyfrom, L.A., 1986-88; dep. city atty. L.A., 1988—. Bd. dirs. Calif. Dems. for New Leadership, Los Angeles, 1985-88; mem. New Frontier Dem. Club, Los Angeles, 1984-88, New Dem. Channel, Los Angeles, 1984-88; commr. City of Los Angeles Commn. on Bicentennial of U.S. Constitution, 1976, 87-89. Recipient Community Service award Los Angeles City Council, 1985, Community Service award Calif. State Senator Diane Watson, 1985, Community Service award Black Women Lawyers, 1986, Community Service award Los Angeles Councilman David Cunningham, 1986. Mem. ABA, Calif. Bar Assn. (com. on ethnic minorities 1988-92), L.A. County Bar Assn., L.A. County Barristers Assn. (exec. com. 1986-91), NAACP, Black Women Lawyers of L. A. (parliamentarian 1985-86), John M. Langston Bar Assn., Jack & Jill of Am., Los Angeles Chapter. Democrat. African Methodist Episcopalian. Avocations: bicycling, tennis. E-mail: chawkin@atty.lacity.org.

HAWKINS, CYNTHIA, artist, educator; b. N.Y.C., Jan. 29, 1950; d. Robert D. Hawkins and Elease Coger; m. Steven J. Chaiken, Feb. 5, 1977 (div. Aug. 1985); m. John Edward Owen, Aug. 24, 1985; children: Ianna, Zachary. BA, Queens Coll., 1977; MFA, Md. Inst. Coll. Art, 1992. Tchg. asst. Md. Inst. Coll. of Art, Balt., 1990-92; adj. instr. Rockland C.C., Suffern, N.Y., 1993-96, Parsons Sch. Design, N.Y.C., 1996, The Coll. at New Paltz, SUNY, 1996-98, Ramapo Coll. of N.J., 1998-99; dir. galleries Cedar Crest Coll., Allentown, Pa., 2000—03; curator Rush Art Gallery, 2003—; ind. curator Lore Regenstein Gallery, 2003—. Mentor Empire State Coll., Nyack, N.Y., 1994; artist-in-residence The Studio Mus. Harlem, N.Y., 1987-88, Va. Ctr. for Creative Arts, Sweet Briar, Va., 1995-96; vis. artist Round House Press, Hartwick Coll., Oneonta, N.Y., 1994; curator Rockland Ctr. for Arts, art dept. Rockland C.C., Nyack, 1994-95, The Rotunda, 1994-95; vis. lectr. Forman Gallery, Hartwick Coll., Oneonta, 1994, Rockland C.C., Suffern, 1994-95; presenter in field. One-woman shows include, Paul Klapper Libr., Queens Coll., N.Y., 1974, Just Above Midtown/Downtown Gallery, N.Y.C., 1981, Frances Wolfson Art Ctr., Miami (Fla.)-Dade C.C., 1986, Cinque Gallery, N.Y.C., 1989, Essex (Md.) C.C., 1991, Queens Coll. Art Ctr., Benjamin S. Rosenthal Libr., Queens Coll., CUNY, Trinity Luth. Ch., New Milford, Conn., 1993, exhibited in group shows, Queens Coll. Gallery, N.Y.C., 1973, Emily Lowe Gallery, Hempstead, N.Y., 1979, Jamie Szoke Gallery, N.Y.C., 1984, Grace Borgenicht Gallery, N.Y.C., 1986, Aljira Gallery, Newark, 1989, Dome Gallery, N.Y.C., 1990, Decker Gallery, Balt., 1991, Kromah Gallery, Balt., 1992, Arts Alliance Haverstraw, N.Y., 1993, Nabisco Gallery, East Hanover, N.J., 1994, Artist Space, N.Y.C., 1993, Bronx Mus. Arts, 1994, U. Notre Dame at Balt., 1995, No. Westchester Ctr. for Arts, Mt. Kisco, N.Y., 1996, Hopper House, Nyack, 1996, Rush Art Gallery, N.Y., 1999, Foxglove Gallery, Stroudsburg, Pa., 2002, Represented in permanent collections, The Bronx Mus. of Arts, N.Y.C., Trinity Luth. Ch., New Milford, Dept. of State, Washington, The Printmaking Workshop, Chevron Corp., Calif., Cameron and Colby, N.Y.C., C.D. Walsh Assocs., Conn., Brooks Sausage Co., Kenosha, Wis., The Habitat Co., Chgo., Brown Mgmt., Balt.; art works featured in pubs. including N.Y. Times, Village Voice, 25 Years of African American Women Artist, Home Mag. Mem. com. Art in Pub. Places, Rockland County, 1999—2001. Recipient 2d pl. award for mixed media Atlanta Life Ins. Co. exhbn. and competition, 1984; fellow Va. Ctr. for Creative Arts, 1996, The Studio Mus. in Harlem, 1987-88, Patricia Robert Harris fellow U.S. Dept. Edn., 1990-92. Democrat. Episcopalian. E-mail: chawkins@cedarcrest.edu.

HAWKINS, DALE CICERO, aviator, educator, engineer; b. Topeka, June 17, 1958; s. Dale R. Coleman and Linda C. (Parks) Meiergerd; m. Patricia Bermudez, Nov. 20, 1982; 1 child, Athena C. AS in Electronic Engring. Tech. with honors, Cleve. Inst. Electronics, 1987, BS in Electronic Engring. Tech. summa cum laude, 1993, MS in Engring. and Tech. Mgmt. summa cum laude, 1998; doctoral candidate, Northcentral U. Cert. quality engr., regulatory affairs cert.; cert. comml. pilot, flight instr. Electronic engring. technician Litton G & CS, L.A., 1979—82; sr. electronics technician Cedars-Sinai Med. Ctr., L.A., 1982—85; svc. engr. Litton AMS, San Diego, 1985—86; elect. engr. tech.

IMED Corp. R & D, San Diego, 1987—93, regulatory affairs engr., 1993—98; mgr. regulatory affairs Laborie Med. Technologies, Williston, Vt., 1998—2000; flight instr. Daniel Webster Coll., Nashua, NH, 2001—02; CMD post controller, safety & tng. mgr. Vt. Air N.G., 2001—02; exec. dir. SFR Valuations, LA, 2003—. Participant Space Life Scis. mission Space Sta. Freedom, NASA; project mgr. Internat. Space Sta. Infusion Pump Project, 1995-98; adj. prof. engring. and tech. mgmt. So. Calif. U. for Profl. Studies, 1999-2000. Co-author: The Art of Hsin Hsing Yee Ti Kenpo Kung Fu, 1991; contbr. articles to profl. jours. Active UN Assn., 1979—, bd. dirs., 1994-98; sr. officer USCG Aux., 1980—2001, aviator, flotilla comdr., 1994-95; USCG liaison U.S. Naval Sea Cadet Corps., NAS Miramar, 1985-98; officer USAF Aux., 2000—. With USN, 1976-79. Numerous US Navy, Coast Guard, and Air Force citations and svc. awards; named Outstanding Citizen Exch. Club, 1989. Mem. IEEE, Nat. Assn. Flight Instrs., Am. Soc. for Quality, Airline Pilots Assn., Alpha Beta Kappa. Achievements include contributions to patents for improved switching power supply and medical device interunit interface connector system; research in H2 generation of reversed biased capacitors, and in lead-acid battery life prolongation. Home and Office: 20401 Soledad Canyon Rd #225 Canyon Country CA 91351

HAWKINS, DAVID RAMON, psychiatrist, writer, researcher, religious studies educator; b. Milw., June 3, 1927; s. Ramon Nelson and Alice-Mary (McCutcheon) H.; m. Susan Humphrey; children: Barbara Catherine, Sarah Humphrey. BS, Marquette U., 1950; MD, Med. Coll. Wis., Milw., 1953; PhD, Columbia Pacific U., 1995. Med. dir. North Nassau Mental Health Ctr., Manhasset, N.Y., 1956-80; dir. rsch. Brunswick Hosp., L.I., N.Y., 1968-79; pres. Acad. Orthomolecular Psychiatry, N.Y.C., 1970-80; dir. Inst. Spiritual Rsch., Sedona, Ariz., 1979-88, The Rsch. Inst., Sedona, 1988—. Chmn. Inst. Advanced Theoretical Rsch., 1993—; guest on TV news and interview shows including McNeal-Lehrer, Barbara Walters, Today; chief of staff Mingus Mountain RTC, 1995; cons. psychiatrist MJL Hosp., Cottonwood, Ariz., 1995; cons. USN, HEW, Congress; lectr. in field. Author (with Linus Pauling): Orthomolecular Psychiatry, 1973; author: Power vs. Force, 1995, The Eye of the I, 2001, I, 2002; contbr. articles to profl. jours. With U.S. Navy, 1945-46, PTO. Decorated knight Sovereign Order St. John of Jerusalem (Denmark); Tae Ryoung Sun Kak Tosun (Korea); Rsch. grantee N.Y. State Dept. Mental Hygiene, annually, N.Y. State Legis., 1967-87; recipient Mosby Book award, 1953. Mem. AMA, APA, Ariz. Med. Soc., Ariz. Psychiat. Soc., Alpha Omega Alpha. Avocations: inventing, designing, architecture. Office: Rsch Inst 151 Keller Ln Sedona AZ 86336-9748 *Our lives are created more by our vision of the future then they are by the details of our past.*

HAWKINS, DAVID ROLLO, SR., psychiatrist, educator; b. Springfield, Mass., Sept. 22, 1923; s. James Alexander and Janet (Rollo) H.; m. Elizabeth G. Wilson, June 8, 1946; children: David Rollo Jr., Robert Wilson, John Bruce, William Alexander. BA, Amherst Coll., 1945; MD, U. Rochester, N.Y., 1946. Intern Strong Meml. Hosp., Rochester, 1946-48; Commonwealth Fund fellow in psychiatry and medicine U. Rochester, 1950-52; instr. psychiatry U. N.C. Sch. Medicine, 1952-53, asst. prof., 1953-57, asso. prof. psychiatry, 1957-62, prof., 1962-67; prof., chmn. dept. psychiatry U. Va. Sch. Medicine, 1967-77, Alumni prof. psychiatry, 1967-79, asso. dean, 1969-70; psychiatrist-in-chief U. Va. Hosp., 1967-77; prof. psychiatry Pritzker Sch. Medicine, U. Chgo., 1979-90, U. Ill., 1990—, clin. prof. psychiatry U. N.C., Chapel Hill, 1992—. Dir. liaison and consultation svcs. dept. psychiatry Michael Reese Hosp., Chgo., 1979-87, chmn., 1987-92; assoc. attending physician N.C. Meml. Hosp., Chapel Hill, 1952-62, attending physician, 1962-67; cons. Watts Hosp., Durham, 1952-67, VA Hosp., Fayetteville, N.C., 1956-67, Eastern State Hosp., Williamsburg, Va., 1971—, VA Hosp., Salem. Va., 1969-79, mem. deans com., 1971-77; spl. rsch. fellow Inst. Psychiatry, U. London, 1963-64, Fogarty internat. rsch. fellow, 1976-77, U.S.-USSR and Romania health exch. fellow, 1978. Rev. editor Psychosomatic Medicine, 1958-70; assoc. editor Psychiatry, 1970-92. Mem. small grants com. NIMH, 1958-62; mem. nursing rsch. study sect. NIH, 1965-67; mem. Gov.'s Commn. Mental, Indigent and Geriatric Patients, 1968-72; mem. rsch. evaluation com. Va. Dept. Mental Hygiene and Hosps., 1970-73; mem. behavioral sci. test com. Nat. Bd. Med. Examiners, 1970-73. Served as capt. M.C., AUS, 1948-50. Fellow Am. Coll. Psychoanalysts (charter bd. regents 1979-81, treas. 1989-91, pres.-elect 1992, pres. 1994), Am. Psychiat. Assn.; mem. AAUP, Am. Psychosomatic Soc. (mem. coun. 1959), AMA, Group for Advancement Psychiatry (bd. dirs. 1987-89), Assn. Am. Med. Colls. (coun. acad. socs. 1973-78), Am. Psychoanalytic Assn., Am. Coll. Psychiatrists, AAAS, Va. Psychoanalytic Soc., Washington Psychoanalytic Soc., Chgo. Psychoanalytic Soc., N.C. Psychoanalytic Soc., Ill. Psychiat. Soc. (coun. 1981-82, pres.-elect 1987, pres. 1988-90), Soc. Neurosci., Am. Assn. Chmn. Depts. Psychiatry (sec.-treas. 1971-73, pres. 1974-75), Sleep Rsch. Soc., Nat. Bd. Med. Examiners (exam. com. 1983-87), Phi Beta Kappa, Sigma Xi, Alpha Omega Alpha. Address: 405 Deming Rd Chapel Hill NC 27514-3207

HAWKINS, DEBORAH CRAUN, community health nurse, family practice nurse practitioner; b. Atlanta, Feb. 13, 1941; d. Adolph F. and Suzanne (Catchings) Spear; m. Hugh M. Hawkins, Jr.; children: Kimberley Ann, Susan Elizabeth. BSN, U. Va., 1962, MSN, 1981; post-master's cert., Va. Commonwealth U., 1999. Cert. nursing adminstrn. advanced, family nurse practitioner. Pub. health nurse supr. Va. Dept. Health, Charlottesville, 1975-85, pub. health nurse mgr. Culpeper, 1985-96; pvt. practice nurse practitioner, 1999—. With Nurse Corp USN, 1961—63, with Nurse Corp USNR, 1989—2001, comdr., ret. USNR. Mem.: Va. Coun. Nurse Practitioners, Va. Pub. Health Assn., Va. Nurses Assn., Am. Acad. Nurse Practitioners, Sigma Theta Tau. Home: 2312 Banbury St Charlottesville VA 22901-1823 E-mail: debhawk@aol.com.

HAWKINS, DONALD THOMSON, information scientist, consultant; b. Oakland, Calif., Aug. 13, 1942; s. Donald S. and Ruth T. (Thomson) H.; m. Patricia L. Pallister Hawkins, Apr. 25, 1967; 1 child, Michael. BS, U. Calif. Berkeley, 1964, MS, 1966, PhD, 1970. Info. scientist Bell Labs., Murray Hill, N.J., 1971-77, supv., 1977-86; tech. staff AT&T, Basking Ridge, N.J., 1986-96; pres. InfoResources, Stirling, NJ, 1996—98; dir. Intranet Content Info. Today, Inc., 1998—. Editor-in-chief Info. Sci. & Tech. Abstracts, 1998—; mem. editl. bd. Online, 1980-96; contbr. articles to profl. jours. Recipient Excellence in Writing award UMI, 1994. E-mail: d.t.hawkins@att.net.

HAWKINS, EDWARD J. retired lawyer; b. Fall River, Mass., June 24, 1927; s. Edward Jackson and Harriet (Sherman) H.; m. Janet Schwerdt; children: Daniel, George, Robert, Harriet. Grad., Phillips Acad., Andover, Mass., 1945; AB summa cum laude, Princeton U., 1950; LLB magna cum laude, Harvard U., 1953. Bar: Ohio 1954, D.C. 1990. Assoc., ptnr. Squire, Sanders & Dempsey, Cleve., 1953-78, ptnr. Cleve. and Washington, 1982-96, counsel, 1997-99; ret., 2000. Chief tax counsel U.S. Senate Fin. Com., Washington, 1979-80, minority tax counsel, 1981; gen. chmn. Cleve. Tax Inst., 1969. Contbr. articles to profl. jours. With U.S. Army, 1945-46. Mem. ABA (vice chmn. govt. rels. tax sect. 1987-89), D.C. Bar Assn., Phillips Acad. Alumni Assn. (alumni coun. 1967-70), Quadrangle Club. Democrat. Home: 7404 Park Terrace Dr Alexandria VA 22307-2039 E-mail: ejhawkins2@aol.com.

HAWKINS, ELINOR DIXON (MRS. CARROLL WOODARD HAWKINS), retired librarian; b. Masontown, W.Va., Sept. 25, 1927; d. Thomas Fitchie and Susan (Reed) Dixon; m. Carroll Woodard Hawkins, June 24, 1951; 1 child, John Carroll. AB, Fairmont State Coll., 1949; BS in Libr. Sci., U. N.C., 1950. Children's libr. Enoch Pratt Free Libr., Balt., 1950-51; head circulation dept. Greensboro (N.C.) Pub. Libr., 1951-56; libr. Craven-Pamlico Libr. Svc., New Bern, N.C., 1958-62; dir. Craven-Pamlico-Carteret Regional Libr., New Bern, N.C., 1962-92. Storyteller children's TV program Tele-Story Time, 1952-58, 63—; bd. dirs. Triangle Bank of New Bern. Mem. New Bern Hist. Soc., 1973—, Tryon Palace Commn., 1974—; mem. adv. bd. Salvation Army. Mem. N.C. Assn. Retarded Children, Pilot Club (pres. 1957-58, v.p. 1962-63). Baptist. Home: PO Box 57 Cove City NC 28523-0057

HAWKINS, ELLIS DELANO, manufacturing executive, insurance executive, gaming executive; b. Princeton, Ark., Feb. 13, 1941; s. Eddie and Anne Beadie (Smith) H.; m. Vera Mae Smith, Aug. 19, 1969 (div. Sept. 1979); children: Angela, Stacey, Rhonald. AA, Shorter Jr. Coll., 1958; BBA, Calif. Coast U., 1981, MBA, 1983. Cert. in statis. process control; lic. ins. agt., Ill. Operator drill press Choctaw Inc., Poyen, Ark., 1962-65; supr. Chrysler Corp., Detroit, 1965-76, Alcan Aluminum, Terre Haute, Ind., 1976-86; Borg-Warner, Chgo., 1986-91, ins. exec., 1991—; pres., chief exec. officer Jes-El-Ed Inc., Chgo., 1980—, also bd. dirs. Bd. dirs., sec. Idlewild Civic Investment, Inc.; prodn. mgr., photographer St. James Trumpet, 1989; mem. bd. rsch. advisors ABS Inc., 1993; spkr. in field. Scoutmaster Boy Scouts Am. Troop 53, Malvern, Ark., 1962; solicitor United Found., Detroit, 1971; life mem. NAACP. With USN, 1958-62. Recipient Commendation Letter Tribune Star, 1986, Appreciation Letter, M.L. King Convocation Com., 1986. Mem. Am. Legion (chmn. Spl. Olympics 1982-89, Plaque 1985, Cert. of Appreciation 1989), Idlefellows Social Club. Democrat. Avocations: golf, bowling, writing, photography. *Personal philosophy: To care and be concerned for others. Be willing to help someone by sharing yourself including information and or assistance. You have to believe and give thanks.*

HAWKINS, EMMA B. humanities educator; b. Ardmore, Okla., July 28, 1946; d. Bernard C. and Occie E. (Morris) H. BA, Okla. Bapt. U., 1968; MDiv, Southwestern Bapt. Theol. Sem., 1976; MA, U. North Tex., 1990, PhD in English (Medieval), 1995. Instr. U. North Tex., Denton, 1990-95; lectr. Lamar U., Beaumont, 1995-97, asst. prof., 1997—2002, assoc. prof., 2003—. Chair program and arrangements South Cen. Conf. on Christianity and Lit., 1999, mem. exec. bd., 1999—; presenter numerous papers at profl. confs. Bus. mgr. Lamar Jour. Humanities; contbr. chpt. to book, articles to profl. jours. Recipient Go the Extra Mile award, 1997. Mem. MLA (sec. Old and Mid. English sect. South Ctrl. chpt. 1997, chair Old and Mid Eng. sect. chpt. 1998), Tex. Medieval Assn., Conf. on Coll. Tchrs. English, South Ctrl. Conf. Christianity and Lit. (chair various sessions, James Sims award 2000), Phi Kappa Phi, Sigma Tau Delta. Office: Lamar U PO Box 10023 Beaumont TX 77710-0023

HAWKINS, FALCON BLACK, JR., federal judge; b. Charleston, S.C., Mar. 16, 1927; s. Falcon Black Sr. and Mae Elizabeth (Infinger) H.; m. Jean Elizabeth Timmerman, May 28, 1949; children: Richard Keith, Daryl Gene, Mary Elizabeth Hawkins Eddy, Steely Odell II. BS, The Citadel, 1958; LLB, U. S.C., 1963, JD, 1970. Bar: S.C. bar 1963. Leadingman electronics Charleston (S.C.) Naval Shipyard, 1948-60; salesman ACH Brokers, Columbia, S.C., 1960-63; from assoc. to sr. ptnr. firm Hollings & Hawkins and successor firms, Charleston, 1963-79; U.S. dist. judge Dist. of S.C., Charleston, 1979—, chief judge, 1990-93, sr. status, 1993—. Served with Mcht. Marines, 1944-45, with AUS, 1945-46. Mem. Jud. Conf. 4th Jud. Circuit, ABA, S.C. Bar Assn., Charleston County Bar Assn., Am. Trial Lawyers Assn., S.C. Trial Lawyers Assn., Carolina Yacht Club, Hibernian Soc. Charleston, Masons. Democrat. Presbyterian. Office: Hollings Jud Ctr PO Box 835 Charleston SC 29402-0835 Fax: 843-579-1499.

HAWKINS, FRANCES PAM, finance educator; b. Woodland, Ala., Dec. 2, 1945; d. Lowell M. and Bernice E. Mcmanus; children: Scott Cummings, Veronica Lovvorn. AS in Bus., Southern Union C.C., 1989; BS in Bus. Edn., Auburn U., 1990, MEd, 1992. Ptnr. C & S Pharmacy, Roanoke, Ala., 1974—90; bus. office tech. instr. West Ga. Tech. Coll., Lagrange, Ga., 1991—. Bus. tech., divsn. chair West Ga. Tech. Coll., Lagrange, 1999—, bus. office tech. adv. com. mem., 1992—, chairperson libr. com., 2001—; mem. tech. in edn. com. Ga. Dept. Edn., Atlanta, 2001—. Team leader March of Dimes, LaGrange, 1998—. Mem.: Ga. Bus. Edn. Assn., So. Bus. Edn. Assn., Nat. Bus. Edn. Assn. (com. mem. 2001), Auburn Alumni Assn., Phi Beta Lambda (sec. 1997—2001, nat. bd. dirs. future bus. leaders Am. 2001—, local advisor 1992—, state advisor 1999—, pres. Ga. Found. Inc. 1998—). Methodist. Office: West Ga Tech Coll 303 Fort Dr Lagrange GA 30240 Office Fax: 706-845-4339. Business E-Mail: phawkins@westgatech.edu.

HAWKINS, FRANCIS GLENN, banker, lawyer; b. Jamesville, Mo., May 31, 1917; s. Ottas G. and Mary (Uhrig) H.; m. Virginia Mavis Saker, Jan. 18, 1947; children: Glenn Joseph, Russell Brian. AB, S.W. Mo. U., 1938; MA, Okla. State U., 1941; JD, U. Tulsa, 1955. Reporter Monahans (Tex.) Express, 1938-39; trainee Montgomery Ward, Springfield, Mo., 1941-42; rsch. asst. Fed. Res. Bank, Kansas City, 1945-46; with Bank of Okla., Tulsa, 1946-82, sr. v.p., sr. trust officer, sr. v.p. charge bank ops., 1970-73, sr. v.p. charge adminstrv. svcs., 1973-77, sr. v.p., sr. trust officer, trust divsn., 1977-81, sr. v.p. and trust counsel, 1981-82; trust counsel, 1982-91; with Robinson, Boese, Orbitson & Lewis; pvt. practice, 1982-90. Trustee Tulsa Jr. Coll. Found., 1978-90. Capt. USAAF, 1942-45, ETO; lt. col. USAFR, ret. Decorated Air medal with oak leaf cluster, Bronze Star medal. Mem. Am. Inst. Banking (life, past chpt. pres.), Tulsa Estate Planning Forum (past pres.), Okla. Bankers Assn. (past pres. trust div.), Okla., Tulsa County bar assns., Tulsa C. of C., Pi Gamma Mu, Phi Alpha Delta. Home and Office: 5035 E 66th St S Tulsa OK 74136-3316

HAWKINS, FRANK NELSON, JR., investor relations consultant, writer; b. Macon, Ga., Sept. 2, 1940; s. Frank N. and Lottie (Norton) H.; m. Inge Lehmitz, Apr. 22, 1967; children: Liv Marion Taylor, Daphne Virginia. BA, Cornell U., 1962. Corr. AP, New Delhi, 1969-70, Jakarta, Indonesia, 1970-71, chief bur. Manila, 1971-73, chief Middle East svcs. Beirut, 1973-75; bus. mgr., adminstrv. dir. AP-Dow Jones, London, 1975-80; dir. corp. rels. Knight-Ridder, Inc., Miami, Fla., 1980-83, v.p. corp. rels. and planning, 1983-94; pres. Access Asia Group, Hong Kong, 1994-95; CEO Hawk Assocs., Inc., 1995—. Author: Ritter's Gold, 1980. Bd. dirs. Keys Marine Conservatory. Capt. U.S. Army, 1963-67. Mem. Assn. Former Intelligence Officers, Zool. Soc. Fla. (pres. 1992-93), Nat. Investors Rels. Inst., Fla. Keys Electric Corp. (bd. dirs.), Upper Keys Rotary Club (pres. 2002-03), The Nature Conservancy, The Islamorada Fishing Club (bd. dirs.). Office: Hawk Assocs Inc 204 Ocean Dr Tavernier FL 33070-2342

HAWKINS, GREGORY J. consumer products company executive; BSBA, Oreg. State U. With J.C. Penney, GTE, Mitel Corp.; v.p. sales Ingram Micro., Inc., v.p. major accounts div. consumer markets, sr. v.p. global sales; CEO, chmn. of bd. buy.com, 1999—. Office: Carebuy com 85 Enterprise Aliso Viejo CA 92656-2614

HAWKINS, IDA FAYE, elementary school educator; b. Ft. Worth, Dec. 28, 1928; d. Christopher Columbus and Nanie Idella (Hughes) Hall; m. Gene Hamilton Hawkins, Dec. 22, 1952; children: Gene Agner, Jane Hall. Student, Midwestern U., 1946-48; BS, North Tex. State U., 1951; postgrad., Lamar U., 1968-70; MS, McNeese State U., 1973. Tchr. DeQueen Elem. Sch., Port Arthur, Tex., 1950-54, Tyrrell Elem. Sch., Port Arthur, Tex., 1955-56, Roy Hatton Elem. Sch., Bridge City, Tex., 1967-68, Oak Forest Elem. sch., Vidor, Tex., 1968-91, ret., 1991. Elementary school educator; b. Ft. Worth, Dec. 28, 1928; d. Christopher Columbus and Nannie Idella (Hughes) Hall; m. Gene Hamilton Hawkins, Dec. 22, 1952; children: Gene Agner, Jane Hall. Student Midwestern U., 1946-48; BS, N. Tex. State U., 1951; student Lamar U., 1968-70; MS, McNeese State U., 1973. Tchr. DeQueen Elem. Sch., Port Arthur, Tex., 1950-54, Tyrrell Elem. Sch., Port Arthur, 1955-56, Roy Hatton Elem. Sch., Bridge City, Tex., 1967-68, Oak Forest Elem. Sch., Vidor, Tex., 1968-91, ret. 2d v.p. Travis Elem. PTA, 1965-66, 1st v.p., 1966-67; corr. sec. Port Arthur City coun. PTA, 1966-67; Sunday sch. tchr. Presbyn. Ch., 1951-53, 60-66. Named Tchr. of Yr., Oak Forest Elem., 1984-85. Mem. NEA, Tex. State Tchrs. Assn. 2d v.p. Travis Elem. PTA, 1965-66, 1st v.p., 1966-67; corr. sec. Port Arthur City Coun. PTA, 1966-67; Sunday sch. tchr. Presbyn. Ch., 1951-53, 60-66. Named Tchr. of Yr., Oak Forest Elem., 1984-85. Mem. NEA, Tex. State Tchrs. Assn. Home: 6315 Central City Blvd #611 Galveston TX 77551-3806

HAWKINS, JACQUELYN, elementary and secondary education educator; b. Russell Springs, Ky., Apr. 30, 1943; d. J.T. Hawkins and Maudie Bell Crew. BS, Andrews U., 1969; MEd, Xavier U., 1976. Cert. elem. tchr., Ohio, reading tchr. elem. and high sch., Ohio. Tchr. Cin. Pub. Schs., 1969-99, Cummins Sch., Cin., 1971-81, Windsor Sch., Cin., 1982-83, 1983-89, acting contact tchr. chpt. 1 reading program, 1989-93, reading recovery tchr., 1993-99; ret., 1999; child care worker, 2002—. Rep. Cin. Coun. Educators, 1986-89, 91-92, 92-93, mem. book com.; mem. sch. improvement program Windsor Sch., 1982-84; mem. Sch. Improvement Program Cin. Chairperson United Way at Windsor Sch. Cin., 1986-89, 90-92, United Negro Coll. Fund Cin., 1986-89, ARC, Windsor Sch., Cin., 1986-89, 90-92; rep. Fine Arts Fund Cin., 1986-88; co-leader 4-H Club, Cin., 1987-88; leader Girl Scouts U.S., Cin., 1988-93; tutor Tabernacle Bapt. Ch., 1989; co-chairperson Windsor ARC, 1991-92. Recipient Cert. Achievement Cummins Sch. Cin., 1978 Democrat. Avocations: travel, reading, needlework.

HAWKINS, JAMES VICTOR, former state official; b. Coeur d'Alene, Idaho, Sept. 28, 1936; s. William Stark and Agnes M. (Ramstedt) H.; m. Gail Ruth Guernsey, June 19, 1959; children— John William, Nancy Clare. BS, U. Idaho, 1959, D of Adminstrv. Sci., 1996; postgrad., Am. Savs. and Loan Inst., 1960-67, Pacific Coast Banking Sch., 1970—. Mgmt. trainee Gen. Telephone Co. of N.W., Coeur d'Alene, 1959-60; asst. mgr. First Fed. Savs. & Loan Assn., Coeur d'Alene, 1960-67; v.p., gen. mgr. Idaho S.W. Devel. Co., Boise, 1967-68; v.p., trust officer First Security Bank of Idaho, N.A., Boise, 1968-72; pres. Statewide Stores Inc., Boise, 1972-82; spl. projects adminstr. Lucky Stores Inc., 1982-84; pvt. practice fin. cons. Boise, 1984-87; dir. dept. commerce State of Idaho, Boise, 1987-96, ret., 1996; mng. ptnr. Hwy. 12 Ventures, 2000—. Bd. dirs. Blue Cross of Idaho, Early Childhood Devel., State of Idaho, Summit Securities, Old Standard Life, Old West Annuity and Life. Bd. dirs., chmn. adv. bd. Coll. Bus. and Econs. U. Idaho; bd. dirs. Idaho Total Quality Inst., Boise United Fund, Boise Art Assn.; pres. U. Idaho Found.; exec. bd. Coun. State Community Affairs Agys.; bd. dirs., pres. Nat. Assn. State Devel. Agys.; mem. Indsl. Devel. Rsch. Coun.; exec. com. Coun. State and Community Devel. Agys.; chmn. Idaho R.R. Adv. Coun. Named Outstanding Young Idahoan Idaho Jr. C. of C., 1967. Mem. Am. Inst. Banking, Boise C. of C., U. Idaho Alumni Assn. (mem. exec. bd.), Elks, Coeur d'Alene, Rotary, Crane Creek Country Club, Hayden Lake Country Club, Phi Gamma Delta. Episcopalian. Home: 2349 N Broadview Pl Boise ID 83702-1290 E-mail: jim@highway12ventures.com.

HAWKINS, JANICE EDITH, medical/surgical clinical nurse specialist; b. Greer, S.C., Sept. 12, 1950; d. Theron Gibson and Christine Edith (Bright) H. Diploma, Greenville (S.C.) Gen. Hosp. Sch. Nursing, 1971; BSN, Med. U. of S.C., 1974; MN, Emory U., 1977. RN, Ga.; CS; cert. specialist, nutrition support nurse. Staff nurse Emory U. Hosp., Atlanta, 1974-76; instr., staff nurse Med. U. of S.C., Charleston, 1978-79; instr. nursing edn., staff nurse Wilford Hall Med. Ctr. Lackland AFB, San Antonio, 1979-83; clin. nurse specialist med.-surg./nutrition support VA Med. Ctr., Decatur, Ga., 1983—2002; clin. nurse specialist in oncology Grady Health Sys., 2003—. Affiliate faculty BCLS Am. Heart Assn., 1989-97; BCLS instrn., trainer, 1997—; presenter in field. Contbr. chpts. to books and articles to profl. jours. Chair Ga. Nurses Polit. Action Com., 1996-2000. Col. USAFR, 2000. Fellow Aerospace Med. Assn. (assoc.); mem. ANA (chair coun. clin. nurse specialists 1989-91, chair coun. nurses in advanced practice 1991-92, task force to delineate the substructure of the Congress Nursing Practice 1990-91), Nurses Orgn. Vets. Affairs (pres. Atlanta chpt. 2000-02), Am. Soc. Parenteral and Enteral Nutrition (nurses com., stds. com. 1988-90, 96-97, nominating com. 1992), Assn. Mil. Surgeons of the U.S., Res. Officers Assn., Ga. Soc. Parenteral and Enteral Nutrition (bd. dirs. 1992-94), Am. Nurses Credentialing Ctr., Med.-Surg. Clin. Nurse Specialists (content expert panel 2001—), Ga. Nurses Assn. (cabinet on govtl. affairs 1989-93, chairperson 1995-96, 5th dist. honoree 1989), Sigma Theta Tau. Home: 1750 Clairmont Rd # 21 Decatur GA 30033-4030 E-mail: janicehawkins@hotmail.com.

HAWKINS, JASPER STILLWELL, JR., architect; b. Orange, N.J., Nov. 10, 1932; s. Jasper Stillwell and Bernice (Ake) H.; m. Patricia A. Mordigan, Mar. 22, 1980; children: William Raymond, John Stillwell, Karen Ann, Jasper Stillwell III. B.Arch., U. So. Calif., 1955. Registered architect, Calif., Ariz., N.Mex. Founder, prin. Hawkins & Lindsey & Assocs., L.A., 1958-90, Hawkins Lindsey Wilson Assocs., L.A. and Phoenix, 1978-85; pres. Fletcher-Thompson Assocs., 1981-84; prin. Jasper Stillwell Hawkins, F.A.I.A., architect, Phoenix, 1990—. Bd. visitors Nat. Fire Acad., 1978-80; bd. dirs. Nat. Inst. Bldg. Scis., 1976-85, chmn. bd. dirs., 1981-83, consultative council, 1978— ; mem. com. protection of archives and records centers GSA, 1975-77; mem. archtl. adv. panel Calif. State Bldg. Standards Commn., 1964-70; mem. U.S. del. to UN Econ. Commn. for Europe Working Party on Bldg., 1978-84; mem. U.S. presdl. del. to Honduran Presdl. Elections, 1985; mem. com. standards and evaluation Nat. Conf. States on Bldg. Codes and Standards, 1971-74; mem. Am. Arbitration Assn., 1992-2002; trustee Underwriter's Labs., 1984-2002, mem. nat. coun. Archtl. Registration Bds., 1971—; participant and speaker numerous confs. Contbr. articles to profl. jours.; maj. works include Valley Music Theatre, L.A., Houston Music Theatre, Sundome Theatre and R.H. Johnson Ctr., Sun City West, Ariz., Bell Recreation Ctr., Sun City, U. Calif. at Irvine Student Housing, Oxnard (Calif.) Fin. Ctr., condominium devels., Lakes Club, Sun City. Mem. Nev. Gov.'s Commn. Fire Safety Codes, 1980-81, Pres. Reagan's Commn. on Housing, 1981-82, City of Phoenix ACDC Task Force, 1985-86, ACDC Aesthetics Commn., 1986-89, City of Phoenix Camelback East Village Planning Com., 1983-89; mem. fire rsch. panel Nat. Bur. Stds., 1978-81; chmn. NAS fire assessment rev. com., 1987-88, com. on analytical methods for designing bldgs. for fire safety, 1977-78; chmn. bldg. seismic safety coun. ind. rev. panel San Francisco War Meml. Opera House, 1995. Recipient design awards from Ariz. Rock Products Assn., Theater Assn. Am., Nat. Food Facilities, House and Home Mag., Practical Builders Mag., Am. Builders Mag., Nat. Inst. of Bldg. Sci. Inst. award, 1995, others. Fellow AIA (mem. codes and stds. com. 1970—, chmn. 1970-73, nat. liaison commn. with Assoc. Gen. Contractors 1969-70, chmn. nat. fire safety task force 1972-74, chmn. Calif. coun. AIA state code com. 1964-68, chmn. nat. conf. industrialized constrn. 1969-70, nat. com. bldg. industry coordination 1969-70, nat. rep. to Internat. Conf. Bldg. Ofcls. 1969, state Calif. AIA codes com. 1960-70, chmn. 1965-70, nat. AIA codes and stds. com. 1970-80, chmn. 1970-74, nat. crisis adv. com. 1988-89), 1976—; mem. ASCE (task force bldg. codes 1971-74), ASTM, Nat. Fire Protection Assn. (com. bldg. heights and areas 1965-72, chmn. 1968-72, fire prevention code com. 1974-76, bd. dirs. 1985-93, chmn. nat. model codes coordinating com. 1983-86, stds. coun. 1996—, bldg. code task force 2000—), Nat. Fire Acad. (bd. regents 1980-83), Nat. Bur. Stds. Fire (rsch. adv. com. 1979-82), Nat. Acad. Forensic Engrs., Ariz. C. of C. (policy com. 1983-84), Ariz. Biltmore Village Estates Homeowners Assn. (pres. 1981-83), Phoenix C. of C. (chmn. Water task force 1982-83). Office: 1158 E Missouri Ave Ste 220 Phoenix AZ 85014-2720

HAWKINS, JOELLEN MARGARET BECK, nursing educator; b. Harvey, N.D., Dec. 15, 1941; d. Charles Joel and Gertrude Adelaide (Waits) Beck; m. Charles Albert Watson, June 27, 1964 (div. 1978); children: John Charles, Andrew Bruce; m. David Gene Hawkins, Oct. 4, 1978. Student, Oberlin Coll., 1959-61; diploma, Chgo. Wesley Meml. Hosp., Sch. of Nursing, 1964; BSN, Northwestern U., Chgo., 1964; MS, Boston Coll., 1969, PhD, 1977. Cert. women's health nurse practitioner. Staff nurse Sheboygan (Wis.) Meml. Hosp., 1964-65; instr., staff Boston Lying in Hosp., 1965-66, 68-69; staff nurse Brookline (Mass.) Vis. Nurse Assn., 1968, Guy's Hosp., London, 1968; campus nurse Roger Williams Coll., Bristol, R.I., 1969-70; instr. Salve Regina Coll., Newport, R.I., 1970-74; faculty Roger Williams Coll., Bristol, 1974-75; prof. U. Conn., Storrs, 1978-83; asst., assoc. prof. William F. Connell Sch. Nursing Boston Coll., Chestnut Hill, Mass., 1975-78, prof., 1983—. Women's health nurse practitioner Crittenton Hastings House, 1984-2000, U. Conn. Student Health Women's Clinic, 1978-83, Sidney Borum Health Ctr., 2000—, Pine St. Inn Women's Clinic, 2000—. Author: Maternal-Newborn Nursing: Pretest Self-Assessment and Review, 1978, Clinical Experience in Collegiate Nursing Education: Selection of Clinical Agencies, 1981, Health Care of Women: Gynecological Assessment, 1982, Women and the Menopause, 1983, Linking Nursing Education and Practice: Collaborative Experiences in Maternal Child Health, 1987, Dictionary of American Nursing Biography, 1988, Nursing and the American Health Care Delivery System, 4th edit., 1993, Nurse-Social Worker Collaboration in Managed Care: A Model of Community Case Management, 1998, The Advanced Practice Nurse: Current Issues, 5th edit., 2000, Guidelines for Nurse Practitioners in Gynecologic Settings, 8th edit., 2003; editor: Linking Nursing Education and Practice, 1987 (Book of Yr. award Am. Jour. Nursing, 1988), Clin. Excellence for Nurse Practitioners: The Internat. Jour. of NPACE, 1996—, Diversity in Health Care Research: Strategies for Multisite, Multidisciplinary, and Multicultural Projects, 2003; contbr. articles to profl. jours., chapters to books. Recipient Disting. Alumni award North H.S., 1989, Miriam Manisoff award Planned Parenthood Fedn. Am., 1997, Disting. Alumna award Chgo. Wesley Meml. Hosp. Sch. Nursing, 1999; named Nurse Practitioner of Yr. Am. Acad. of Nurse Practitioners, 1995. Fellow Am. Acad. Nursing; mem. ANA, Mass. RNs Assn. (Disting. Nurse Rschr. award 1984, Lucy Lincoln Drown Nursing History award 1994), Internat. Coun. Women's Health, Nat. Acad. Practice, Am. Assn. for History Nursing (nominating chmn. 1989), Assn. Women's Health Obstetric and Neonatal Nurses, Sigma Theta Tau (Elizabeth Russell Belford Founder's award for excellence in

edn. 1993). Democrat. Unitarian Universalist. Avocation: nursing history. Home: 151 Stanton Ave Auburndale MA 02466-3005 Office: Boston Coll William F Connell Sch Nursing 140 Commonwealth Ave Chestnut Hill MA 02467

HAWKINS, JOSEPH ELMER, JR., retired acoustic physiologist, medical educator; b. Waco, Tex., Mar. 4, 1914; s. Joseph Elmer and Maude Burke (Schlenker) H.; m. Jane Elizabeth Daddow, Aug. 24, 1939 (dec. Sept. 2002); children: Richard Spencer Daddow, Peter Douglas Huntington, James Marion Davis, William Alexander Parmley, Priscilla Ann (Mrs. Philip A. Leach). Student, Altes Realgymnasium, Munich, 1929-30; AB, Baylor U., 1933; postgrad., Brown U., 1933-34; BA in Physiology, U. Oxford, 1937, MA, 1966, DSc in Clin. Medicine, 1979; PhD in Med. Sci., Harvard U., 1941. Tchg. fellow in physiology Harvard Med. Sch., 1937-41, instr., 1941-45; asst. investigator Nat. Def. Rsch. Com.-Office Sci. Rsch. & Devel., Harvard U., 1941-43; spl. rsch. assoc. Harvard Psycho-Acoustic Lab., Cambridge, Mass., 1943-45; asst. prof. physiology Bowman Gray Sch. Medicine, Wake Forest Coll., Winston-Salem, N.C., 1945-46; rsch. assoc. neurophysiology Merck Inst. for Therapeutic Rsch., Rahway, N.J., 1946-56; assoc. prof. otolaryngology NYU Sch. Medicine, 1956-63; prof. physiol. acoustics U. Mich., Ann Arbor, 1963-84, prof. otolaryngology emeritus, 1984—, chmn. grad. program in physiol. acoustics, 1969-81. Disting. vis. prof. biology Baylor U., Waco, Tex., 1985-93; mem. NIH sensory diseases study sect., 1958-61, communicative disorders rsch. tng. com., 1965-69, communicative scis. study sect., 1975-79; mem. Nat. Libr. Medicine Communicative Disorders Task Force, 1977-79; lectr. Armed Forces Inst. Pathology, 1969-74; cons. various pharm. cos. Contbr. to: Ency. Brit., 1974, 86, 99, Ency. Neuroscience, 1987, 99, 2003; editor: (with M. Lawrence and W.P. Work) Otophysiology, 1973, (with S.A. Lerner and G.T. Matz) Aminoglycoside Ototoxicity, 1981; contbr. sci. articles to profl. jours. Mem. Bd. Edn., Cranford, NJ, 1958—61. Rhodes scholar Tex. and Worcester Coll., U. Oxford, 1934-37; USPHS spl. fellow Öronkliniken, Sahlgrenska Sjukhuset U. Göteborg, Sweden, 1961-63; NAS exch. lectr. to Yugoslavia and Bulgaria, 1977; Chercheur étranger de l'INSERM, Lab. d'Audiologie Expérimentale, U. Bordeaux II, 1978; recipient Disting. Achievement award Baylor U., 1982, City of Pleven, Bulgaria medal, 1982, U. Bordeaux medal, 1983, Humboldt Rsch. award for sr. U.S. scientists U. Würzburg, 1991, Hon. Citizen award, Bordeaux, 1991, Disting. Alumnus award Baylor U., 1996. Fellow AAAS, Acoustical Soc. Am.; mem. Am. Physiol. Soc., Assn. for Rsch. in Otolaryngology (award of merit 1985), Collegium Oto-rhino-laryngologicum Amicitiae Sacrum, Bárány Soc., European Workshop for Inner Ear Biology, Am. Assn. for History of Medicine, Am. Otol. Soc. (assoc.), Prosper Menière Soc. (hon., Gold medal for basic sci. 1998), Pacific Coast Oto-ophthalmol. Soc. (hon.), Connétablie de Guyenne (Bordeaux, assoc.), Phi Beta Kappa, Sigma Xi. Anglican. Democrat. Achievements include research in ototoxic, noise-induced, and presbyacusic hearing loss. Avocations: Germanic and Romance languages and literature, gardening. Home: Glacier Hills Apt 258 1200 Earhart Rd Ann Arbor MI 48105 Office: U Mich Med Sch Kresge Hearing Rsch Inst Ann Arbor MI 48109-0506 E-mail: josehawk@umich.edu.

HAWKINS, KEVIN ANDREW, music educator; b. Springfield, Mo., June 2, 1962; s. Billy Wayne and Joyce Anne Hawkins; m. Judith Karol Miller, June 27, 1987; children: Klayton, Kyndal. BS in Music Edn., SW Mo. State U., 1985; MusM, Southwestern Bapt. Theol. Sem., 1988; student, S.W. Bapt. Theol. Sem., 1996—. Ordained to gospel ministry 1994. Min. of music and youth First Bapt. Ch., Clever, Mo., 1982—85; min. of music Travis Bapt. Ch., Corpus Christi, Tex., 1988—91, First Bapt. Ch., Picayune, Miss., 1991—96; dir. of choral activities Glendale H.S., Springfield, Mo., 1997—. Mem.: Music Educator's Nat. Conf., Am. Choral Dirs. Assn., Mo. Music Educators Assn., Mo. Choral Dirs. Assn. Republican. Baptist. Avocations: travel, woodworking. Home: 1052 E High Point St Springfield MO 65810 Office: Glendale HS 2727 Ingram Mill Rd Springfield MO 65804 Home Fax: 417-888-2533; Office Fax: 417-823-8995. Personal E-mail: k4hawkins@juno.com.

HAWKINS, LAWRENCE CHARLES, management consultant, educator; b. Greenville County, S.C., Mar. 20, 1919; s. Wayman and Etta (Brockman) H.; m. Earline Thompson, Apr. 29, 1943; children: Lawrence Charles Jr., Wendell Earl. BA, U. Cin., 1941, BEd, 1942, MEd, 1951, EdD, 1970; AA (hon.), Wilmington Coll., 1979; LittD (hon.), Cin. Tech. and C.C.; LHD (hon.), Mt. St. Joseph Coll. Cert. sch. supt., Ohio. Elem./secondary tchr. Cin. Pub. Schs., 1945-52, sch. prin./dir., 1952-67, asst. supt., 1967-69; dean U. Cin., 1969-75, v.p., 1975-77, sr. v.p., 1977-83; vis. asst. prof. Eastern Mich. U., Ypsilanti, summers 1955-60; mem. Cincinnatus Assn., 1971-87. Vice chair Student Loan Funding Corp., 1982-98; mem. cmty. rels. panel Cin. Mayors, 1979—, others; cons. U.S. Dept. Justice, Dept. Edn.; bd. dirs. We. and So. Fin. Group. Bd. dirs. exec. com. Ohio Citizens Coun. Health and Welfare, 1966-73; vice chair Ohio Valley Regional Med. Program, 1972-77, bd. trustees Cmty. Chest and Coun. Cin. Area Inc., 1970-72; bd. dirs. Wilmington (Ohio) Coll., 1980-90, Bethesda Hosp., Cin., 1980-90; trustee Children's Home of Cin., 1978-90, Coll. Mt. St. Joseph, 1989-93; pres., CEO Omni-Man, Inc., 1981-96; bd. dirs. Nat. Underground R.R. Freedom Ctr., 1994-98; owner The L.C.H. Resource; vice chmn. Greater Cin. TV Ednl. Found., WCET-TV, 1983; co-chmn. Cin. area NCCJ 1980-87; nat. bd. dirs. Inroads, 1982-87; bd. trustees Knowledge Wroks Found., 1999—. Served to lt. USAAF, 1943-45 (an original Tuskegee Airman). Recipient award of Merit, Cin. Area United Appeal, 1955, 73, cert. Pres.'s Coun. on Youth Opportunity, 1968, City Cin., 1968, Disting. Svc. citation Greater Cin. NCCJ, 1988; named Great Living Cincinnatian, Greater Cin. C. of C., 1989. Mem. NEA (life), ASCD, Am. Assn. Sch. Adminstrs. (conv.), Nat. Congress Parents and Tchrs. (hon. life; chmn. com.), Phi Delta Kappa, Kappa Delta Pi, Kappa Alpha Psi, Sigma Pi Phi. Home: 3544 Sherbrooke Dr Cincinnati OH 45241-3831

HAWKINS, LORETTA ANN, retired secondary school educator, playwright; b. Winston-Salem, N.C., Jan. 1, 1942; d. John Henry and Laurine (Hines) Sanders; m. Joseph Hawkins, Dec. 10, 1962; children: Robin, Dionne, Sherri. BS in Edn., Chgo. State U., 1965; MA in Lit., Governor's State U., 1977, MA in African Cultures, 1978; MLA in Humanities, U. Chgo., 1998. Cert. tchr., Ill. Tchr. Chgo. Bd. Edn., 1968—2002; lectr. Chgo. City Colls., 1987-89; tchr. English, Gage Park H.S., Chgo., 1988—2002; ret., 2002. Mem. steering com. Mellon Seminar U. Chgo., 1990; tchr. adv. com. Goodman Theatre, Chgo., 1992, mem. cmty. adv. coun., 1996—; spkr. in field; creator 5-4-3-2-1- Essay Writing Method, 1997. Author: (reading workbook) Contemporary Black Heroes, 1992, (plays) Of Quiet Birds, 1993 (James H. Wilson award 1993), Above the Line, 1994, Good Morning, Miss Alex; contbr. poetry, articles to profl. publs.; featured WYCC-TV-Educate, 1996. Mem. Chgo. Tchg. Connections Network, DePaul U. Ctr. Urban Edn., 2001; mem. Chgo. Pub. Schs. Mentoring and Induction of New Tchrs. Program. Fellow Santa Fe Pacific Found., 1988, Lloyd Fry Found. 1989, Andrew W. Mellon Found., 1991, Ill. Arts Coun., 1993; grantee Cmty. Arts Assistance Program Award, Chgo. Dept. Cultural Affairs; recipient Feminist Writers 3d pl. award NOW, 1993, Zora Neale Hurston-Bessie Head Fiction award Black Writer's Conf., 1993, Suave Tchr. Plus award, 2002; numerous others. Mem. AAUW, Nat. Coun. Tchrs. English (spkr. conv.), Am. Fedn. Tchrs., Women's Theatre Alliance, Dramatists Guild of Am., Internat. Women's Writing Guild. Achievements include invention of 5-4-3-2-1 essay writing method. Avocations: films, coins, reading, walking. Home: 8928 S Oglesby Ave Chicago IL 60617-3047

HAWKINS, MARY E. ophthalmologist; b. Flushing, N.Y., Jan. 22, 1950; d. Donald B. and Margaret H. (Smith) H.; m. John H. McAteer, May 24, 1980; children: Rebecca, Jessica. BS, Queen's Coll., 1972; MD, N.Y. Med. Coll., 1975. Diplomate Am. Bd. Ophthalmology. Intern Maimonides Med. Ctr., Bklyn., 1975-76; resident in ophthalmology Brookdale Med. Ctr., Bklyn., 1976-79; fellow in plastic ophthalmology N.Y. Med. Coll., Valhalla, 1979-80; pvt. practice ophthalmology David Soll Assocs., Phila., 1980-81; pvt. practice White Plains, N.Y., 1981—. Assoc. attending physician N.Y. Eye and Ear Infirmary, N.Y.C., 1981—. Mem. AMA, Am. Acad. Ophthalmology, N.Y. State Ophthalmology Soc., N.Y. State Med. Soc. Republican. Office: 75 Linda Ave White Plains NY 10605-1617

HAWKINS, MICHAEL DALY, federal judge; b. Winslow, Ariz., Feb. 12, 1945; s. William Bert and Patricia Agnes (Daly) H.; m. Phyllis A. Lewis, June 4, 1966; children: Aaron, Adam. BA, Ariz. State U., 1967, JD cum laude, 1970; LLM, U. Va., 1998. Bar: Ariz. 1970, U.S. Ct. Mil. Appeals 1971, U.S. Supreme Ct. 1974. Pvt. practice law, 1973—77; U.S. atty. Dept. Justice, Phoenix, 1977—80; pvt. practice law, 1980—84; judge U.S. Ct. Appeals (9th cir.), Phoenix, 1994—. Mem. Appellate Cts. Jud. Nominating Commn., 1985—89. Staff editor: Ariz. State U. Law Jour., 1968—70. Mem. Ariz. Lottery Commn., 1980—83, Commn. on Uniform State Laws, 1988—93. Capt. USMC, 1970—73. Recipient Alumni Achievement award, Ariz. State U., 1995. Mem.: ABA, Nat. Assn. Former U.S. Attys. (pres. 1989—90), Adminstrv. Conf. U.S. (pub. mem. 1985—94), Phoenix Trial Lawyers Assn., Ariz. Trial Lawyers Assn. (bd. dirs. 1976—77, state sec. 1976—77), State Bar of Ariz. (James Walsh Outstanding Jurist Award 2003), Maricopa County Bar Assn. (bd. dirs. 1975—77, 1981—89, pres. 1987—88).

HAWKINS, MONICA SPANN, environmental health scientist; b. Washington, Oct. 18, 1968; d. Melvin Leon and Gloria (Taylor). S. BS, 1991; MPH, George Washington U., 1997; postgrad., George Mason U., 1998—; BS, Howard U., 1991. Cultural diversity coord. Nat. Wildlife Fedn., Washington, 1991-92, membership action coord., 1992-94; analyst ICF Inc., Fairfax, Va., 1994; environ. health scientist EPA, Washington, 1995. Asst. coach Silver Spring (Md.) Track Club, summer 2000, 01, dir. pub. rels., summer 2001—. Avocations: travel, skiing, reading, exercising. Office: EPA 7509 C 1200 Pennsylvania Ave NW Washington DC 20460 E-mail: hawkins.monica@epa.gov.

HAWKINS, PAMELA LEIGH HUFFMAN, biochemist; b. Washington, Oct. 7, 1950; d. Lauria Carl and Maryalice (Flinner) Huffman; m. James Lee Hawkins, Mar. 7, 1981 (div. Aug. 1993). BS in Biochemistry, Va. Polytech. Inst. & State U., Va., 1972; MS in Biochemistry, Pa. State U., Pa., 1975. Sci. info. specialist Inform., Inc., Rockville, Md., 1972; asst. rsch. scientist Union Carbide Corp., Tarrytown, NY, 1975; assoc. rsch. scientist Am. Hosp. Supply Corp., Gibbstown, NJ, 1976-78, rsch. scientist Miami, Fla., 1978-85; R & D scientist Baxter Healthcare Corp., Miami, Fla., 1985-95, sr. rsch. scientist, 1993-95; prin. scientist Sigma Diagnostics, St. Louis, 1995—2002; sr. scientist Biotech. Rsch. and Devel., Sigma-Aldrich, 2002—. Contbr. articles to profl. jour. Recipient Baxter Diagnostics Tech. award for Thromboplastin-IS, 1990, Baxter Internat. Tech. award, 1991. Mem. Mortar Bd., Phi Sigma, Gamma Sigma Delta, Phi Lambda Upsilon. Lutheran. Achievements include US and European patent for fresh blood (unfixed) hematology control, 3 US and 1 European patents for improved extraction methods for preparing thromboplastin reagents, patent for thromboplastins for recombinent tissue factor, US patent for thromboplastin reagents based on recombinent technology, production of thromboplastin IS, Innovin, Two US patents-US Pat. No. 6,528,273, 2003, Methods for Quality Control of Prothiombin Thromboplastin Time (PT) and Activated Partial Thromboplastin Time (APTT) Assays using coagulation controls-for coagulation controls for prothrombin time and activated partial thromboplastin time, various others. Office: Sigma Diagnostics 545 S Ewing Ave Saint Louis MO 63103-2991

HAWKINS, PEGGY ANNE, veterinarian; b. Omaha, Dec. 9, 1956; d. Robert Leon and Karen Lynne Hawkins. BS, Iowa State U., 1982, DVM, 1991, MS, 1992. Vol., h.s. tchr. U.S. Peace Corps, Lesotho, 1982-85; lab. technician Iowa State U., Ames, 1986-87, tchg. asst., 1990-92; veterinarian, swine practitioner White Oak Mills/ProGenetics, Elizabethtown, Pa., 1992-94; tech. svcs. veterinarian Pfizer, Animal Health Group, Lee's Summit, Mo., 1994-96, product devel. vet. advisor N.Y.C., 1996—2001, vet. med. mgr., 2001—02; health svcs. vet. Monsanto Choice Genetics, St. Louis, 2002—. Vol. tchr. Jr. Achievement, N.Y.C. Pub. Schs., 1999. Recipient Swine Proficiency award Purina Mills, Inc., 1991; Iowa State U. scholar. Mem.: AVMA, Iowa Vet. Med. Assn., Am. Assn. Swine Veterinarians (Found. fellow 1998—). Avocations: travel, photography, hiking. Office: Monsanto Co 800 Lindbergh Blvd Saint Louis MO 63167

HAWKINS, RICHARD ALBERT, medical educator, administrator; b. Greenwich, Conn., Mar. 27, 1940; s. Albert Rice and Florence Marie Elizabeth (Hansen) H.; m. Enriqueta Elias, May 9, 1964; children: Richard Alfred, Paul Andrés. BSc magna cum laude, San Diego State U., 1963; PhD, Harvard U., 1969; LHD (hon.), U. Phoenix, 1994. Rsch. fellow Metabolic Rsch. Lab. Radcliffe Infirmary, Oxford (Eng.) U., 1969-71; staff fellow in neurochemistry St. Elizabeth Hosp., Washington, 1971-72, NIMH/NIAAA sr. staff fellow in neurochemistry, 1972-74; chief phys. sci. br. FDA, Rockville, Md., 1974-76; assoc. prof. neurosurgery and physiology NYU Med. Ctr., N.Y.C., 1976-77; prof. anesthesia and physiology Pa. State U., Hershey (Pa.) Med. Ctr., 1977-88; prof., chmn. physiology and biophysics Herman M. Finch U. Health Scis./Chgo. Med. Sch., North Chicago, Ill., 1988-93, prof., 1988—, exec. v.p. acad. affairs, chief academic officer North Chicago, Ill., 1993-98, provost, 1998, pres., CEO, 1999—2003, Scholl Coll. Podiatric Medicine, 2001—03. Hon. prof. U. Valencia, Spain, 1989—. Contbr. numerous articles to profl. jours. Recipient Meritorious Rsch. award Morris Parker Found., 1992. Fellow Am. Heart Assn.; mem. Am. Physiol. Soc., Am. Soc. Neurochemistry, Biochem. Soc., Soc. for Neurosci., Alpha Omega Alpha. Home: 950 N Michigan Ave Chicago IL 60611 Office: Finch U Health Scis Chgo Med Sch 3333 Green Bay Rd North Chicago IL 60064-3037 Fax: 847-775-6510.

HAWKINS, RICHARD MICHAEL, lawyer; b. Nevada City, Calif., July 23, 1949; s. Robert Augustus and Virginia June (Hawke) H.; m. Linda Lee Chapman, Sept. 27, 1975; child, Alexandra Michelle. BS in Math., U. Calif., Davis, 1971; JD, U. Calif., San Francisco, 1974; LLM in Taxation, U. Pacific, 1983. Bar: Calif. 1974, U.S. Dist. Ct. (ea. dist.) Calif. 1974, U.S. Dist. Ct. (no. dist.) Calif. 1982, U.S. Ct. Claims 1982, U.S. Tax Ct. 1982, U.S. Ct. Appeals (9th cir.) 1982, U.S. Supreme Ct. 1982. From assoc. to ptnr. Larue & Francis, Nevada City, 1974-76; ptnr. Larue, Roach & Hawkins, Nevada City, 1977-78; of counsel Berliner & Ellers, Nevada City; ptnr. Berliner, Spiller & Hawkins, Nevada City, 1981; sole practice Grass Valley, Calif., 1981—. Bd. dirs. 49er Fire Dist., Nevada City, 1977-81, 89-98, asst. fire chief, 1981-83, fire chief, 1983-89. Mem. ABA, Calif. State Bar (cert. specialist in estate planning, trust and probate law 1990), Nevada County Bar Assn. (v.p. 1976), Order of Coif, Phi Kappa Phi. Republican. Roman Catholic. Avocations: running, showing Morgan horses. Home: 14762 Banner Quaker Hill Rd Nevada City CA 95959-8813 Office: 10563 Brunswick Rd Ste 2 Grass Valley CA 95945-7801 Fax: (530) 272-7861. E-mail: rhawk53@aol.com.

HAWKINS, ROBERT B. think tank executive; PhD, U Wash. Chmn. Adv. Commn. on Intergovt. Rels., Washington, 1982-93; dir. Am. pub. policy program Woodrow Wilson Internat. Ctr. for Scholars, Washington; pres., CEO Inst. for Contemporary Studies, Oakland, Calif. Tv co-host, That's Politics, 1987-91; radio California Political Review; Books American Federalism: A New Partnership for the Republic, Self-government by District: Myth and Reality. Office: Inst Contemporary Studies Latham Sq 1611 Telegraph Ave Ste 406 Oakland CA 94612-2140

HAWKINS, ROBERT GARVIN, management educator; b. Gower, Mo., Feb. 3, 1936; s. Floyd G. and Grace (Long) H.; m. Estelle Turcic, June 9, 1962; children: Paul R., Kenneth J. AB, William Jewell Coll., 1958; PhD, NYU, 1966. Cons. computer systems Equitable Life, N.Y.C., 1958-61; from instr. to prof. NYU, 1964-80, vice dean, prof., 1980-84; dean Sch. Mgmt. Rensselaer Poly. Inst., Troy, N.Y., 1984-92; dean Ivan Allen Coll. Ga. Inst. Tech., Atlanta, 1993-98. Bd. dirs. James Investment Rsch., Inc., Alpha, Ohio, Petricca Industries, Inc., Pittsfield, Mass.; cons. in field. Co-author: Gold and World Power, 1965, U.S. in International Markets, 1976; editor: Economic Effects of MNCs, 1977; contbr. articles to profl. jours. Bd. dirs. Family and Children Svcs., Montclair, NJ, 1976—81, Troy Music Hall Assn., 1985—92, Japan-Am. Soc. of Ga., 1993—99. Sgt. Air NG, 1957—64. Named Outstanding Alumni, William Jewell Coll., 1979; grantee in field. Mem. Am. Econ. Assn., Am. Fin. Assn. (exec. sec. 1977-83), Acad. Internat. Bus. (pres. 1983-84, fellow 1981). Home: PO Box 194 Spencertown NY 12165

HAWKINS, SIDNEY TAYLOR, mathematician, educator; s. Jos Dewitt and Odalie Elizabeth Hawkins; children: Sharon Celestine, Latafta Spivey. BS in Math., Grambling State U., 1973; MS in Math., La. Tech. U., 1975, Tulane U., 1995; PhD in Math., La. State U., 1999. Asst. chemist D.H.& J Industries, Monroe, La., 1976—78; instr. math. Grambling (La.) State U., 1979—81; asst. prof. math. Dillard U., New Orleans, 1981—88, Xavier U., New Orleans, 1988—95, La. State U., Baton Rouge, 1997—99; assoc. prof. math. Alcorn (Miss.) State U., 1999—. Asst. prof. of math. Dillard U., New Orleans, 1981—88, Xavier U. of New Orleans, New Orleans, 1988—95, La. State U., Baton rouge, La., Usa, 1997—99; assoc. prof. of math. Alcorn State U., Alcorn, Miss., Usa. Recipient Gov.'s Award, Gov. of La., 1988, Mayor's Award, Mayor's Office, 1988. Mem.: Nat. Assn. Math. (life), Pi Mu Epsilon (life). Home: 10151 Curran Blvd New Orleans LA 70127 Office: Alcorn State Univ 1000 ASU Dr #30 Alcorn MS 39096 Office Fax: 601-877-3989. E-mail: shawkins@loman.alcorn.edu.

HAWKINS, TRAVIS MONTGOMERY, SR., horticulturist, landscape consultant; b. Tullahoma, Tenn., Nov. 17, 1959; s. James Henry Jr. and Willo Anne (Hitt) H.; children: Travis Montgomery Jr., Evan Michael; m. Susan Lynn McFadden; stepchildren: Amanda N. Shadeck, Ryan C. Shadeck, Alexis D. Shadeck. BS in Agr., U. Tenn., 1981. Landscape maintenance foreman Laurel Landscaping Co., Corbin, Ky., 1981-83; landscape designer William Cannon Landscaping Co., Tullahoma, 1983; gen. mgr., designer Oakside Nursery, Shelbyville, Tenn., 1983-85; grounds, motor pool and forestry ops. supr. U. of the South, Sewanee, Tenn., 1985—. Instr. Motlow State C.C., Tullahoma, 1983-84; grounds and maintenance cons. St. Andrew's Sewanee Sch., 1987-91. Youth counselor Cowan (Tenn.) Fellowship Ch., 1988-90, governing coun., 1990-91; mem. Franklin Counties Bd. Zoning Appeals, 1987—; mem. Franklin Counties Planning Commn., 1997-2001; grad. Leadership Franklin County Class of 1998. Mem. Nat. Inst. Parks and Grounds Mgmt. (bd. dirs. 1999-2001), Profl. Grounds Mgmt. Soc., Tree City U.S.A. Bd. (charter, chmn. 1990-91), Franklin County C. of C. (amb., vol. 1997-2000), Monteagle Rotary Club (Paul Harris fellow 1988, treas. 1988-90, pres. 1990-91). Baptist. Avocations: volleyball, tennis, gardening. Home: 121 Brandi Cir Winchester TN 37398-1472 Office: U of the South Alabama Ave Sewanee TN 37383-0001 E-mail: travis.m.hawkins@sewanee.edu.

HAWKINS, WILLIAM E. N. newspaper editor; b. N.Y.C., Dec. 4, 1943; s. Frank Nelson and Lottie (Norton) H.; m. Diane Taylor, Apr. 1, 1967; children: William E.N. Jr., Geoffrey W.T. BA, Cornell U., 1966. Reporter Patriot-News, Harrisburg, Pa., 1968-73, Balt. Evening Sun, 1973-78, city editor, 1978-83, asst. mng. editor, 1983-88; exec. editor The Herald-Sun, Durham, N.C., 1988—; v.p. The Durham Herald Co., 1994—. Vis. media fellow Duke U., 2002. Mem. bicentennial adv. com. U. N.C., 1992-93. 1st lt. U.S. Army, 1966-68, Vietnam. Decorated Bronze Star. Mem. Am. Soc. Newspaper Editors, AP Mng. Editors, N.C. Press Assn. (pres. 2001-2002, bd. dirs. 1992-96), N.C. Press Found., Soc. Profl. Journalists, Americal Divsn. Vets. Assn. Presbyterian. Avocation: skiing. Home: 7 Hartley Pl Durham NC 27707-2437 Office: The Herald-Sun 2828 Pickett Rd Durham NC 27705-5613

HAWKINS, WILLIS MOORE, aerospace and astronautical consultant; b. Kansas City, Mo., Dec. 1, 1913; s. Willis M. Hawkins and Elizabeth (Daniels) Hawkins Walter; m. Anita Stanfill, June 22, 1940 (dec. Dec. 1982); children: Nancy Gay, Willis M. III, James Walter. BS in Aero. Engring., U. Mich., 1937, ED (hon.), 1965; DSc (hon.), Ill. Coll., 1966. Registered profl. engr., Calif. Engring. trainee Grumman Corp., Bethpage, N.Y., 1936; sr. layout engr. Lockheed Corp., Burbank, Calif., 1937-49, chief, preliminary design, 1949-53; asst. gen. mgr., dir. engring. Lockheed Missiles & Space Div., Sunnyvale, Calif., 1953-61; gen. mgr., corp. v.p. Lockheed Space Div., Sunnyvale, 1961; corp. v.p. sci. and engring. Lockheed Corp., Burbank, 1962-63; asst. sec. R & D U.S. Army, 1963-66; sr. v.p. sci. and engring. Lockheed Corp., Burbank, 1966-74, corp. dir., 1972-80, sr. adv. Calabasas, Calif., 1974-76, sr. v.p. aircraft, 1979-80, sr. advisor, 1980-95; pres. Lockheed Calif. Co., 1976-79. Bd. dirs. George C. Marshall Inst., Washington. Chmn. aero. and space engring. bd. NRC, 1960, aero. panel Naval Studies Bd., 1989—92, Army star study bd. Army Sci. & Tech. Com., Washington, 1988—91; Army strategic tech. com., 1989—91; mem. NASA Rsch. Coun., 1978—85; trustee Leelanau Ctr. for Edn., Glen Arbor, Mich., 1987. Recipient Disting Civilian Svc. medal with oak leaf cluster, U.S. Army, 1965—66, Disting. Pub. Svc. medal, NASA, 1975, Nat. Medal of Sci., Pres. of U.S., 1988. Fellow: AIAA (hon.); mem.: NAE (various coms., founders lectr.), Nat. Aero. Assn. (Wright Bros. lectr. 1982, bd. dirs.), Royal Aero. Soc., Tau Beta Pi. Republican. Avocation: flying.

HAWKINSON, BRIAN PATRICK, professional association executive; b. El Paso, Tex., Mar. 3, 1956; s. Norman A. and Shirley M. Hawkinson; m. Deborah A. Duncan, Sept. 2, 1978; children: Erin C., Michael P. BBA, James Madison U., 1978; MBA, Va. Tech., 1995. Materials contr. Aminoil USA Inc., Denver, 1982-84; prodn. acct. Phillips Petroleum Co., Sidney, Mont., 1984-85; assoc. dir. N.E. region United Way of Am., Alexandria, Va., 1985-92, dir. nat. corp. rels., 1992-94; loan officer N.Am. Mortgage Co., Vienna, Va., 1994-96; dir. ctr. for pub. affairs mgmt. Pub. Affairs Coun., Washington, 1996—; exec. dir. Found. for Pub. Affairs, Washington, 2002—. Editor: Public Affairs Management Reports, 2001— (APEX award 2002); contbg. editor: Assessing, Managing and Maximizing Public Affairs Performance, 1997 (APEX award, 1998), ImPACT, 1996— (Best in the Bus. 1996). Vestry St. Luke's Episcopal Ch., Alexandria, 1995-97; bd. dirs. Waynewood Recreation Assn., Alexandria, 1997-2000. Capt. U.S. Army, 1978-82. Office: Public Affairs Coun 2033 K St NW Ste 700 Washington DC 20006-1019

HAWKS, BARRETT KINGSBURY, lawyer; b. Barnesville, Ga., July 13, 1938; s. Paul K. and Nettie Glenn (Barrett) H.; m. S. Kathleen Pafford, Apr. 3, 1965 BBA, Emory U., 1960, LL.B., 1963; LL.M., Harvard U., 1964. Bar: Ga. Clk. Supreme Ct. Ga., 1963; Assoc. Gambrell, Russell, Moye & Richardson (now Smith, Gambrell & Russell), Atlanta, 1961-65; assoc. Sutherland, Asbill & Brennan, Atlanta, 1965-70, ptnr., 1970-82, 93—, Paul, Hastings, Janofsky & Walker, 1982-93. Served to lt. comdr. USNR. Mem. ABA (mem. coun. group pub. utility, transp. and comms. law sect.), State Bar Ga. (bd. govs. 1981-88), Atlanta Bar Assn., D.C. Bar Assn., Emory Law Sch. Alumni Assn. (pres. 1996-97), Emory Law Sch. Coun. (chmn., 1997-98), Capital City Club, Highlands Country Club. Presbyterian. Home: 3835 Club Dr Atlanta GA 30319-1109 Office: Sutherland Asbill & Brennan 999 Peachtree St NE Ste 2300 Atlanta GA 30309-3996

HAWKS, HOWARD L. energy executive; B in Acctg., U. Nebr., Lincoln; MBA, U. Nebr., Omaha. With GM, InterNorth, 1966—86; co-founder, CEO Tenaska, Inc., Omaha, 1987—. Bd. dirs. Creighton U. Bd. dirs. Joslyn Art Mus., Omaha Henry Doorly Zoo, Knights of Ak-Sar-Ben. Named to Hall of Fame, Omaha C. of C., 2002; recipient Disting. Alumnus award, U. Nebr. at Omaha Coll. Bus., 1999. Office: Tenaska Energy Inc 1044 N 115th St Ste 400 Omaha NE 68154-4446*

HAWKS, JAMES WADE, county highway superintendent, county surveyor; b. Lexington, Nebr., Mar. 20, 1957; s. Glenn Emmett and C. Jo Anne (Warren) H.; m. Janelle Sue Kloepping, May 14, 1977; children: James Matthew Hawks, Nathaniel Thomas Hawks. AA, Mid Plains C.C., North Platte, Nebr., 1992; BS in Adminstrn., U. Nebr., Kearney, 1996; MBA, U. Nebr., 2002. Cert. govt. fin. mgr. Nebr. Safety Coun. Adv. Bd. Dawson county surveyors dept. Dawson County surveyor's/Engrs. Office, Lexington, 1980-87; engring. office mgr. Tagge Engring. Cons., North Platte, 1987-88; county surveyor, county hwy. supt. Lincoln county, North Platte, 1988—. Mem. adv. bd. Southeast C.C., Milford; bd. dirs. Nebraskaland, Inc. Chmn. Lincoln County Sheriff's Merit Commn., North Platte, 1990-98; pres. Nebraskaland Days, Inc., 1999, 2000, bd. dirs., 2000, pres., 2000-01, 2002, ch-chair. Mem. Profl. Surveyors Assn. of Nebr. (pres., chmn. exam workshop 1990—, bd. dirs. 1993—, v.p. 1995-97), Nat. Assn. of County Engrs., Nebr. Assn. of County Engrs., Surveyors and Hwy. Supts. (sec.-treas. 1994, v.p. 1995, pres. 1996), Nebr. Assn. County Ofcls. Bd. Dirs., North Platte Sunrise Rotary, Sigma Beta Delta, Phi Theta Kappa. Republican. Lutheran. Avocations: hunting, fishing, reading, working. Home: 1601 Sunset Dr North Platte NE 69101-6418 Office: Lincoln County Surveyor 2010 Rodeo Rd North Platte NE 69101-2603

HAWKS, SHELLEY DRAKE, educator; b. Oklahoma City, Nov. 22, 1960; d. John Whitfield and Carole J. (Gungoll) Drake; m. James D. Hawks III, Sept. 16, 1989; children: Samuel Drake, John Auer. BA, Dartmouth Coll., 1983; AM, Harvard U., 1986; postgrad., Brown U., 2001—. Exhbn. coord. Chinese contemporary oil paintings GHK Co., N.Y.C., 1986—87; dept. asst. Asiatic dept. Mus. Fine Arts, Boston, 1988—90; adj. faculty RISD, Providence, 1999—2001. Vol. Afghans for Civil Soc., Concord, Mass., 2003. Unitarian-Universalist.

HAWKS, WILLIAM T. federal agency administrator; b. Oxford, Miss., Nov. 22, 1944; m. Diane Allen. BS in Agrl. Econ., Miss. State U., 1968, M in Agrl. Econ., 1970. Farmer, mng. ptnr. Hawks Farming, Miss., 1970—; senator Miss.

State Sen., 1994—99, mem. agrl. & environ. com.; undersec. mktg. and regulatory programs USDA, Washington, 2001—. Vice chmn. fees, salaries, adminstrn., and labor coms.; mem. coms. agrl., environtl. protection, conservation, water resources, fin., investigate state offices, ports and marine resources, wildlife and fisheries. Mem. DeSoto Coun., DeSoteo County SWCD, Delta Coun. With USAR, 1968—70, with Army Nat. Guard, 1970—72, with Air Nat. Guard, 1972—80. Mem. DeSoto County Farm Bur., Delta Wildlife Fedn., Miss. Corn Growers. Methodist. Office: USDA 1400 Independence Ave SW Washington DC 20250

HAWLEY, ANNE, museum director; b. Iowa City, Iowa, Nov. 3, 1943; d. Marshall Newton and Leone Ardith (Wilson) Hawley; m. Bruce Ivor McPherson, Sept. 4, 1977; 1 child, Katherine Black. BA, U. Iowa, 1966; MA, George Washington U., 1969; LHD (hon.), Lesley Coll, 1987; LHD (hon.), Williams Coll., 1989, Babson Coll., 1990, sr. exec. prog., Kennedy Sch. Govt, Harvard Univ., Intern in edn., Washington, 1967-69; research assoc. Nat. Urban League, Washington, 1969-71, Ford Found. Study Leadership in Pub. Edn., Washington, 1971-73; exec. dir. Cultural Edn. Collaborative, Boston, 1974-77, Mass. Council Arts/Humanities, Boston, 1977-89; mus. dir. Isabella Stewart Gardner Mus., Boston, 1989—; resident Nat. Hist. Soc. 1993—; adv. com. Nat. Trust of Historic Preservation, 1993—; vis. com. Fitchburg Art Mus., 1992-94. Bd. dirs. New Eng. Found. for Arts, 1978-89, Nat. Assembly/State Arts Agencies, Washington, 1981-83, Greater Boston Arts Fund, 1984-89, Boston Archtl. Found., 1986-89, Nat. Art Stabilization Fund, 1990-95, Boston Fenway Program, 1990-93. Trustee Inst. Contemporary Art, Boston, 1990—, Old Sturbridge Village, 1991-94; vis. comm. Sch. Mus. Fine Arts, Boston, 1989—, adv. bd. Mass. Coll. Art, 1979-81. Fulbright scholar, 1986; recipient Design Travel Grant, Women's Travel Club, Boston, Mass., 1982, Polaroid travel grant, 1987, Fund for Mutual Understanding travel grant to USSR, 1988, Art award Mass. Coll. Art, 1987, Lyman Ziegler award Commonwealth of Mass., 1988. Mem. Nat. Endowment for Arts (mus. panel 1978-81, task force on trng. and devel. of artists and art edu., 1978, dance panel 1982-84, design panel 1978-81, 88—, Pres. Clinton's transition team for arts and humanities, 1992-93), Boston Soc. Architecture (hon. mem. 1989); Radcliffe Alumnae Career Svcs. (adv. comm. 1974). Office: Isabella Stewart Gardner Mus 2 Palace Rd Boston MA 02115-5807

HAWLEY, ELLIS WAYNE, historian, educator; b. Cambridge, Kans., June 2, 1929; s. Pearl Washington and Gladys Laura (Logsdon) H.; m. Sofia Koltun, Sept. 2, 1953; children— Arnold Jay, Agnes Fay. BA, U. Wichita, 1950; MA, U. Kans., 1951; PhD (research fellow), U. Wis., 1959. Instr. to prof. history North Tex. State U., 1957-68; prof. history Ohio State U., 1968-69, U. Iowa, 1969-94, prof. emeritus, 1994—, chmn. dept. history, 1986-89. Hist. cons. Pub. Papers of the Presidents: Hoover, 1974-78. Author: The New Deal and the Problem of Monopoly, 1966, The Great War and the Search for a Modern Order, 1979, (with others) Herbert Hoover and the Crisis of American Capitalism, 1973, Herbert Hoover as Secretary of Commerce, 1981, Federal Social Policy, 1988, Herbert Hoover and the Historians, 1989; contbr. articles to profl. jours., essays to books Investigator Project to Study Hist. in Iowa Pub. Schs., Iowa City, 1978-79; cons. Quad Cities hist. project Putnam Mus., Davenport, 1978-79. Served to 1st lt. inf. AUS, 1951-53 North Tex. State U. Faculty Devel. grantee, 1967-68, U. Iowa, 1975-76. Mem. Am. Hist. Assn., Orgn. Am. Historians, So. Hist. Assn., AAUP (mem. exec. coun. Iowa chapt. 1982-84), Iowa Hist. Soc. Democrat. Home: 2524 E Washington St Iowa City IA 52245-3724 E-mail: e-hawley@worldnet.att.net.

HAWLEY, FRANK JORDAN, JR., venture capital executive; b. Roanoke Rapids, N.C., Oct. 3, 1927; s. Frank Jordan and Mary (Miller) H.; m. Alethea Wood, Sept. 12, 1959; children: Frank J. III, Mark R., Andrew D., Stuart W., Alethea S. BS in Physics, U. N.C., 1949; MBA, Harvard U., 1955. Rsch. analyst Eaton & Howard, Inc., Boston, 1955-59; banking assoc. Lazard Freres, N.Y.C., 1959-64; portfolio mgr. Stein, Roe & Farnham, N.Y.C., 1964-69; exec. v.p. Laidlaw Coggeshall, Inc., N.Y.C., 1969-74; gen. ptnr. Foster Mgmt. Co., N.Y.C., 1974-82; mng. ptnr. Saugatuck Capital Co., Stamford, Conn., 1982—. Chmn. bd. Data Circuit Sys., Inc., San Jose, Calif. Chmn. bd. Waterloo Rest. Ventures, Inc., Vancouver, Oreg.; bd. mem. Floor & Decor, Inc., Atlanta, Ga.; vice pres., treas. New Canaan (Conn.) YMCA, 1981-85; trustee Chocorua Chapel Assn., Squam Lake, N.H.; bd. visitors U. N.C., Chapel Hill, 1990-94; trustee Kenan Inst. Pvt. Enterprise of U. N.C. Lt. (j.g.) USN, 1950-53, Korea. Mem. Links Club, Harvard Club (N.Y.C.), New Canaan Country Club, Mill Reef Club (Antigua), Bald Peak Club (N.H.), Phi Beta Kappa. Republican. Episcopalian. Avocations: tennis, fly fishing, hunting. Home: 613 Silvermine Rd New Canaan CT 06840-4325 Office: Saugatuck Capital Co 1 Canterbury Grn Stamford CT 06901-2032

HAWLEY, HAROLD PATRICK, educational consultant; b. Paducah, Ky., Jan. 8, 1945; s. Mathew Mark and Mae (Herndon) H.; m. Ann Dunbar, 1971 (dec. 1982); Lucrecia Thomas, Aug. 27, 1983; children: Cherise, Charlotte. AA, Paducah Jr. Coll., 1965; BA, U. Ky., 1968; MS, Ind. U., New Albany, 1974; EdD, Ind. U., Bloomington, 1977; postgrad., Mary Baldwin Coll., 1988, Ala. A&M U., 1996. Liaison to adjutant gen. 5th army U.S. Army, Ft. Carson, 1970, Bien Hoa, Vietnam, 1969-70; English tchr. Southwestern Consol. Schs., Hanover, Ind., 1971-73; asst. prin. Whitewater Consol. Sch., Lyons, Ind., 1978-80; assoc. prof., dir. secondary edn. Birmingham (Ala.)-So. Coll., 1980-86, chmn. freshman seminar, 1984-86; 1988-95 Ga. Dept. Edn., Atlanta, 1988-95; evaluator So. Assn. Schs. and Colls., 1988—; ednl. cons. Ga. Dept. Edn., Atlanta, 1988-95; chmn. Effective Sch. Rsch. Program, 1991; asst. prof. elem. edn. program Ala. A&M U., 2000—01, asst. prof. secondary edn. and multicultural edn., 2001—, advisor svc. frat., 2003; dir. Harlem Renaissance Project, Lee H.S., 2003. Adj. prof. Ind. U., Bloomington, 1975-80, Samford U., 1980-84, Auburn U., 1987, U. Ala., Gadsen, 1984-85, Brenau U., Gainesville, Ga., 1988-96, Reinhardt Coll./Brenau Coll. Collaboration, 1995—, Ala. A&M U., 1999, univ. supr., 1996—; cons. Intervarsity Beach Project, 1982—, Ford Ednl. Found., Parker H.S., Birmingham, Ala., 1981-85, Christian Acad., Cornerstone, Baton Rouge, 1983-84, FCA, 1983, Happy Valley Elem., Fairview Elem. Schoolwide Project, 1995, Walker County Curriculum Specialist, 1995-96, Nicholas Soc., 1997—; tech. advisor Polk County Schoolwide Projects, 1995; ednl. cons. Ga. Dept. Edn., Atlanta, 1988-95; coord. 9th Dist. Schs. of Excellence, Ga., 1988-92; ednl. cons. Effective Schs. Rsch./Authentic Ins.; team leader sch. improvement teams Ga. Dept. Edn., Calhoun, 1995; numerous ESEA Instrnl. Confs., Ga., 1993-94; presenter ESEA Instrnl. Conf., Statesboro, 1994, Carrolton, Ga., 1995; dir. 1st State Remedial Edn. Conf., Lafayette, Ga., 1994; dir. 1st statewide instrnl. conf. ESEA, 1995-96, Lone Oak Edn. Svcs., 1998; participant Inst. for Comm. Seminars, Birmingham So. Coll., 1983-86; tech. advisor Floyd County Schoolwide Project, 1995—, Dade County Schoolwide Project, 1996; student tchr. supr. Covenant Coll., Chattanooga, 1996—; dir. Title I Northwest Ga. Instrnl. Conf., 1996; ednl. cons. Attention Deficit Disorder/HD, 1995—; dir. Lone Oak Edn. Svcs. 1999—; rsch. asst. North Ala. Tchr. Exch., Normal, Ala., 2000—; featured presenter, Mutt Intell. 2003, ALA convention of English Tchrs., 2003; presenter in field. Author: (with Don Manlove) Classroom Climate Teacher-Student Relations, Expectancy Effects, 1976; rsch. asst. (with Floyd Coppedge) Binford Middle School Project, Bloomington, Ind., 1976, Individual Instrn. Project, 1975, Lebanon High Sch. Project, 1975-76, Katherine Hamilton Rsch. Project, New Albany, Ind., 1974 (with Carol Lewis). Bd. dirs. Boys Club of Am., Paducah, Ky., 1963-65; tech. adv. Polk County Consolidated Schs., 1995-96, Dade County Consolidated Schs., 1995. Basketball scholar, 1965, attention deficit rsch. scholar univ. supr., Ala. A&M U., 1997—; Spenser grantee, 1981, Mellon grantee, 1985; grad fellow Okla. State Sch. Supt.,1975-77, Nat. Study Sch. Evaluation fellow Ind. U., 1977. Mem. Ga. Com. Leaders Assn., Internat. Platform Assn., Phi Delta Kappa. Avocations: jogging, basketball, camping. Home: 117 Darlington Rd NE Huntsville AL 35801-1513

HAWLEY, JOSEPH B. property management executive, educator; b. Red Bank, N.J., May 1, 1963; s. Bart J. and Genevieve M. Hawley. BA, Kean Coll. N.J., 1986; MA, Rutgers U., 1989, PhD, 1998. V.p. Bay Haven Property Mgmt., Atlantic Highlands, N.J., 1985—. Chmn. Atlantic Highlands Dem. Exec. Com., 1990-92, 96—; mem. Atlantic Highlands Planning Bd., N.J. Dem. State Com., Trenton, 1994—, Henry Hudson Regional Bd. Edn., Highlands, N.J., 1986; pres. Kean U. Class of 1986, 1985-86, Kean U. Student Orgn., Inc., 1984-85; founding mem. Kean U. Peace Edn. Resource Ctr., trustee, 1986-90. Mem. Atlantic Highlands Bd. Edn. Mem. Kiwanis (pres. Phila. chpt. 1989-90), Phi Alpha Theta. Roman Catholic. Avocations: long distance running, weightlifting. Home: 25 Ocean Blvd Atlantic Highlands NJ 07716 Office: Bay Haven Property Mgmt 25 Ocean Blvd Atlantic Highlands NJ 07716

HAWLEY, NANCI ELIZABETH, association administrator; b. Detroit, Mar. 18, 1942; d. Arthur Theodore and Elizabeth Agnes (Fylling) Smisek; m. Joseph Michael Hawley, Aug. 28, 1958; children: Michael, Ronald, Patrick (dec.), Julie Anne. Pres. Tempo 21 Nursing Svcs., Inc., Covina, Calif., 1973-75; v.p. Profl. Nurses Bur., Inc., L.A., 1975-83; owner, CEO Hawley & Assocs., Covina, 1983-87; exec. v.p. Glendora (Calif.) C. of C., 1984-85; dir. membership West Covina (Calif.) C. of C., 1985-87; exec. dir. San Dimas (Calif.) C. of C., 1987-88; mgr. pub. rels. Soc. for Advancement of Material and Process Engrs., Covina, 1988-92; small bus. rep. South Coast Air Quality Mgmt. Dist., 1992-94; bus. counselor Commerce and Trade Agy., Small Bus. Devel. Ctr., 1994; exec. v.p. Ontario (Calif.) C. of C., 1994-97; CEO, RMH Elec. Contractors, Colorado Springs, Colo., 1997-98; exec. v.p. Teen Resources, Inc., Colorado Springs, 1998; registrar Am. Birding Assn., Colorado Springs, 1999—. V.p. Sangabriel valley chpt. Women in Mgmt. Recipient Youth Motivation award Foothill Edn. Com., Glendora, 1987. Mem. NAFE, Colo. Assn. Nonprofit Orgns., Pub. Rels. Soc. Am., Soc. Nat. Assn. Publs., Am. Soc. Assn. Execs., Nat. Assn. Member ship Dirs., Profl. Communicators Assn. So. Calif., Profl. Conf. Mgrs. Assn., West End Bus. Assn. (pres. 1997-99), Western Assn. Chamber Execs. (Spl. merit award for mag. pub. 1995), Profl. Conv. Mgrs. Assn., Kiwanis (sec. 1989-90, pres. West Covina 1990-91, Kiwanian of Yr. 1989), Rotary. Avocations: reading, walking, painting, gardening, birdwatching. Office: PO Box 6599 Colorado Springs CO 80934-6599 E-mail: nanmick58@aol.com.

HAWLEY, PHILIP METSCHAN, retired retail executive, consultant; b. Portland, Oreg., July 29, 1925; s. Willard P. and Dorothy (Metschan) H.; m. Mary Catherine Follen, May 31, 1947; children: Diane (Mrs. Robert Bruce Johnson), Willard, Philip Metschan Jr., John, Victor, Edward, Erin (Mrs. Kevin Przybocki), George. BS, U. Calif., Berkeley, 1946; grad. advanced mgmt. program, Harvard U., 1967. With Carter Hawley Hale Stores, Inc., L.A., 1958-93, pres., 1972-83, chief exec. officer, 1977-93, chmn., 1983-93. Bd. dirs. Weyerhaeuser Co. Trustee Calif. Inst. Tech., U. Notre Dame; chmn. L.A. Energy Conservation Com., 1973-74. Decorated hon. comdr. Order Brit. Empire, knight comdr. Star Solidarity Republic Italy; recipient Award of Merit L.A. Jr. C. of C., 1974, Coro Pub. Affairs award, 1978, Medallion award Coll. William and Mary, 1983, Award of Excellence Sch. Bus. Adminstrn. U. So. Calif., 1987, Bus. Statesman of Yr. award Harvard Bus. Sch., 1989, 15th ann. Whitney M. Young Jr. award L.S. Urban League, 1988; named Calif. Industrialist of Yr. Calif. Mus. Sci. and Industry, 1975. Mem. Calif. Retailers Assn. (chmn. 1993-95, dir.), Beach Club, Calif. Club, L.A. Country Club, Bohemian Club, Pacific-Union Club, Newport Harbor Yacht Club, Multnomah Club, Links Club, Phi Beta Kappa, Beta Alpha Psi, Beta Gamma Sigma. Office: 800 W 6th St Ste 920 Los Angeles CA 90017

HAWLEY, PHILLIP EUGENE, investment banker; b. Tecumseh, Mich., Dec. 9, 1940; s. Paul P. and Vadah Arlene (Lawhead) H.; m. Linda Darlene Miller, Feb. 14, 1957; children: Pierre Lee, Paul Marvin, Danny Parke, David Eugene, Martin Edward. Student in mgmt., Yale U., 1959-63; BSBA, Northwestern Coll., Tulsa, 1980. With Credit Bur. Ft. Myers (Fla.), Inc., 1956—; chmn. bd. dirs., regional mgr. Credit Bur. Internat. Corp., Ft. Myers, 1993—; pvt. investigator Transworld Investigators, Inc., 1964, now v.p.; mgr., founder real estate co. Gold Coast Devel. Corp., 1965, pres., Phillip Hawley Investment Banking Co. Bd. dirs. Caribbean Industries Internat. Corp., Future Investment Corp. Author: Law and It's Alternative to Chaos, 1958, The Happiest Man in the World, 1970, The Best Buys in Fort Myers, 1982. Named Outstanding Individual, Fla. Fedn. Young Reps., 1971; recipient Presdl. Sports award, 1979. Mem. Am. Collectors Assn. (scholar degree Collection Bus. Acad. 1994, fellow degree 1996), Fla. Collectors Assn. (Outstanding Spkr. 1967), Assn. Credit Burs. Am., Med.-Dental Hosp. Burs. Am., Fla. Assn. Mortgage Brokers, Fla. Assn. Pvt. Investigators, Am. Numismatic Assn., Gideons Internat., Collier-Lee Wrestling Assn. (co-founder, bd. dirs. 1974—). Mem. Nazarene Ch. Home: 6535 Winkler Rd Fort Myers FL 33919-8167 Office: Internat Collection Svc Inc 255 Tamiami Trl S Nokomis FL 34275-3136

HAWLEY, RAYMOND GLEN, pathologist; b. Cambridge, Kans., Jan. 13, 1939; s. Pearl Washington and Gladys Laura (Logsdon) H.; m. Phyllis Ann Williams, Aug. 25, 1963; children: Bradford, Anthony, Douglas. BS, Kans. State U., 1961; MD, U. Kans., 1965. Intern Wesley Med. Ctr., Wichita, 1965-66; pathology resident Riverside Meth. Hosp., Columbus, Ohio, 1966-70; pathologist St. Joseph Hosp., Concordia, Kans., 1973-75, St. Joseph Med. Ctr., Wichita, 1975—82, Via Christi Regional Med. Ctr., Wichita, 1983—2000; with Coffeyville (Kans.) Regional Med. Ctr., 2000—. Maj. U.S. Army, 1970-73. Fellow Am. Coll. Pathologists; mem. AMA, Am. Soc. Clin. Pathologists, Kans. Soc. Pathology (sec.-treas. 1989-99). Home: 512 Spruce St Coffeyville KS 67337-4834 E-mail: rhawley@cox.net.

HAWLEY, ROBERT CROSS, lawyer; b. Douglas, Wyo., Aug. 7, 1920; s. Robert Daniel and Elsie Corienne (Cross) H.; m. Mary Elizabeth Hawley McClellan, Mar. 3, 1944; children— Robert Cross, Mary Virginia, Laurie McClellan. BA with honors, U. Colo., 1943; LLB, Harvard U., 1949, JD, 1989. Bar: Wyo. 1950, Colo. 1950, U.S. Dist. Ct. Colo. 1950, U.S. Dist. Ct. Wyo. 1954, U.S. Ct. Appeals (10th cir.) 1955, Tex. 1960, U.S. Ct. Appeals (5th cir.) 1960, U.S. Supreme Ct. 1960, U.S. Dist. Ct. (so. dist.) Tex. 1961, U.S. Ct. Appeals (D.C. cir.) 1961, U.S. Ct. Appeals (8th cir.) 1979, U.S. Ct. Appeals (11th cir.) 1981, U.S. Dist. Ct. (we. dist.) Tex. 1987. Assoc. Bannister Weller & Friedrich, Denver, 1949-50; sr. atty. Continental Oil Co., Denver, 1952-58, counsel, Houston, 1959-62; ptnr., v.p. Ireland, Stapleton & Pryor, Denver, 1962-81; ptnr. Dechert Price & Rhoads, Denver, 1981-83, Hawley & Vanderwerf, Denver, 1983-94; sole practice, Denver, 1994—; pres. Highland Minerals, Denver; bd. dirs. Bank of Denver; speaker oil and gas insts. Contbr. articles to Oil & Gas Pubs. Bd. dirs. Am. Cancer Soc., Denver, 1967-87, treas., 1981-82; chmn. U. Colo. Devel. Found., 1960-61; bd. dirs. Rocky Mountain Arthritis Found., 1987—, sec., 1993-94, vice chmn. Colo., 1994—; mem. adv. bd. ARC, 1988—; chmn. 1st Annual Retarded Children Campaign, 1963; dir. East Seal Chpt., 1966-68; bd. dirs. Craig Hosp., 1964-68. Lt. col. U.S. Army, Korean War. Recipient Alumni Recognition award U. Colo., Boulder, 1958, Meritorious Service award Monticello Coll., Godfrey, Ill., 1967, Humanitarian award Arthritis Found., 1992, Honored Lawyer award Law Club, 1993; Sigma Alpha Epsilon scholar, 1941-43. Mem. Denver Assn. Oil and Gas Title Lawyers (pres. 1983-84), Denver Petroleum Club (pres. 1978-79), Harvard Law Sch. Assn. Colo. (pres. 1980-81), Associated Alumni U. Colo. (pres. and bd. dirs. 1956-57), Law Club, Denver (pres. 1958-59), ABA, Colo. Bar Assn. (bd. govs. 1999—), Denver Bar Assn., Tex. Bar Assn., Wyo. Bar Assn., Fed. Energy Bar Assn. (legal and lands com.), Interstate Oil and Gas Compact Comm., Harvard Alumni Assn., Rocky Mountain Oil and Gas Assn., Rocky Mountain Petroleum Pioneers (pres. 1991-92), Wyo. Pioneer Assn., Chevaliers du Tastevin, Denver Country Club, Petroleum Club, Gyro Club, Univ. Club Denver, Garden of the Gods Club (Colo. Springs), Colo. Arlberg Club, Mile High Club, U. Colo. Alumni Club (Living Legend award). Republican. Episcopalian. Author, co-author: Landman's Handbook, Law of Federal Oil and Gas Leases, Problems of Surface Damages, Federal Oil and Gas Leases--The Sole Party in Interest Debacle. Address: Unit 71 2552 E Alameda Ave Denver CO 80209-3322

HAWN, GOLDIE, actress; b. Washington, Nov. 21, 1945; d. Edward Rutledge and Laura (Steinhoff) H.; m. Gus Trinkonis, May 16, 1969 (div.); m. Bill Hudson (div.); children: Oliver, Kate Garry, Wyatt Russell. Student, Am. U. Profl. dancer, 1965; profl. acting debut in Good Morning, World, 1967-68; mem. company TV series Laugh-In, 1968-70; films include: The One and Only Genuine Original Family Band, 1968, Cactus Flower, 1969 (Acad. award best supporting actress 1969), There's A Girl In My Soup, 1970, $, 1971, Butterflies Are Free, 1971, The Sugarland Express, 1974, The Girl from Petrovka, 1974, Shampoo, 1975, The Duchess and the Dirtwater Fox, 1976, Travels with Anita, 1978, Foul Play, 1978, Seems Like Old Times, 1980, Lovers and Liars, 1981, Best Friends, 1982, Swingshift, 1984, Overboard, 1987, Bird on a Wire, 1989, Deceived, 1991, Housesitter, 1992, Death Becomes Her, 1992, Crisscross, 1992, The First Wives Club, 1996, Everyone Says I Love You, 1996; exec. producer and star films Private Benjamin, 1980, Protocol, 1984, Wildcats, 1986, My Blue Heaven (co-exec. prodr. only), 1990, Something to Talk About, 1995 (exec. prodr. only), The Out of Towners, 1999, Town and Country, 1999, The Banger Sisters, 2002; host TV spl. Pure Goldie, 1970, Goldie Hawn Special, 1978, Goldie and Liza Together, 1980, Goldie and Kids: Listen to Us!, 1982. Office: care ICM Ed Limato & S Dontanville 8942 Wilshire Blvd Beverly Hills CA 90211-1934

HAWORTH, CHARLES RAY, lawyer; b. Little Rock, June 23, 1943; s. Clarence Frederick and Vinita Leona (Bowers) H.; m. Nancy Anne Patterson, Aug. 16, 1970; 1 child, Alan. BA, U. Tex., 1965, JD, 1967. Bar: Tex. 1967, U.S. Dist. Ct. (no. dist.) Tex. 1968, U.S. Dist. Ct. (we. and so. dists.) Tex. 1988, U.S. Dist. Ct. (ea. dist.) Tex. 1989, U.S. Ct. Appeals (5th cir.) 1968, U.S. Ct. Appeals (11th cir.) 1982, U.S. Supreme Ct. 1971; bd. cert. civil trial law Tex. Bd. Legal Specialization. Law clk. U.S. Ct. Appeals (5th cir.), Houston, 1967-68; assoc. Coke & Coke, Dallas, 1968-71; prof. law Washington U. Sch. Law, St. Louis, 1971-79; ptnr. Johnson & Gibbs, Dallas, 1979-85, Andrews & Kurth, Dallas, 1985-92; mng. ptnr. Scott, Douglass, Luton & McConnico, L.L.P., Dallas, 1992-95; ptnr. Owens, Clary & Aiken, L.L.P., Dallas, 1995—. Vis. prof. U. Va. Sch. Law, Charlottesville, 1975-76, U. Tex. Sch. Law, Austin, 1977; cons. Dept. Justice, Washington, 1978. Editor: Congress and the Courts, 1977; contbr. numerous articles to profl. jours. Bd. dirs. Dallas Opera, 1991-2000. Grantee Dept. of Justice, 1978. Mem.: Dallas Bar Assn. (chair bus. litigation sect. 2002), Tex. Bar Assn., Tower Club. Republican. Avocation: fishing. Office: Owens Clary & Aiken LLP 700 N Pearl St Ste 1600 Dallas TX 75201

HAWORTH, DALE KEITH, art history educator, gallery director; b. Denver, Sept. 8, 1924; s. Murle Calvin and Hildur Elizabeth (Lindquist) H.; m. Ruth Anne Cushing, July 25, 1948 (div. 1980); children: Brooke Karen, Leah Anne, Nicholas Cushing; m. Karen Friedmann Beall, Dec. 31, 1983. BS in Edn., Washington U., 1950, MA, 1951; PhD, U. Iowa, 1960. Instr. art history Washington U., St. Louis, 1951-53, fellow in charge of exhbns., 1954-56; instr. art history Beloit (Wis.) Coll., 1953-54, U. Iowa, Iowa City, 1957-60; prof. art history Carleton Coll., Northfield, Minn., 1960—77, 1979—96, dir. exhbns., 1979-96; acting chief, prints and photographs div. Libr. Congress, Washington, 1977-79; now prof. emeritus Carleton Coll., Northfield, Minn. Vis. prof. art history U. Pa., Phila., 1961, 63, U. Minn., Mpls., 1970-71, 73-74; vis. prof. humanities Internat. Christian U., Tokyo, 1990; vis. scholar art history Doshisha U., Kyoto, Japan, 1983, 94; cons. Kress Found., Ohio, 1964; mem. com. for developing advanced placement exam. in history of art Coll. Bd., 1991-93; reader, table leader art history Ednl. Testing Svc., 1990-93. Contbr. articles to profl. jours. V.p. Northfield Arts Guild, 1964-66, pres. Northfield Parents Council, 1970. Served as staff sgt. USAC, 1943-46, PTO. Fulbright scholar, 1956-57, 1962; research grantee HEW, 1967-68; vis. scholarship U.S. Friendship Commn., 1983. Mem. Archeol. Inst. Am., Sch. Am. Rsch., Coll. Art Assn. Avocation: drawing. E-mail: kouveli@aol.com.

HAWORTH, DANIEL THOMAS, chemistry educator; b. Fond du Lac, Wis., June 27, 1928; s. Arthur Valentine and Mary Lena (Wattawa) H.; m. Mary Hormuth, Dec. 27, 1952; children: Daniel G., M. Judith, Steven T. BS, U. Wis., Oshkosh, 1950; MS, Marquette U., 1952; PhD, St. Louis U., 1959. Nuclear chemist Bur. of Ships, Washington, 1952-53; rsch. chemist Allis-Chalmer Mfg. Co., Milw., 1958-60; instr. chemistry Marquette U., Milw., 1955, from asst. prof. to assoc. prof., 1960-68, prof., 1968—. Vis. prof. chemistry U. Wis.-Milw., 2001—02. Contbr. numerous articles to profl. jours.; patentee in field. Served as cpl. U.S. Army, 1953-55. Recipient Pere Marquette award for tchg. excellence Marquette U., 1971, Nicolos Salgo Outstanding Tchr. award, 1971. Mem. Am. Chem. Soc. (emeritus), N.Y. Acad. Scis., Wis. Acad. Arts/Scis./Letters, Sigma Xi (emeritus). Roman Catholic. Avocation: philately. Home: 3483 N Frederick Ave Milwaukee WI 53211-2902 Office: Marquette Univ Dept Chemistry PO Box 1881 Milwaukee WI 53201-1881 E-mail: daniel.haworth@marquette.edu.

HAWORTH, GERRARD WENDELL, office furniture manufacturing company executive; b. Alliance, Nebr., Oct. 9, 1911; s. Elmer R. and Lulu (Jones) H.; m. Dorcas A. Snyder, June 22, 1938 (dec.); children: Lois, Richard, Joan, Mary, Julie; m. 2d Edna Mae Van Tatenhove, Feb. 3, 1979. AB, Western Mich. U., 1937; MA, U. Mich., 1940. Tchr. Holland High Sch., Mich., 1937-48; founding chmn. Haworth Inc., Holland, Mich., 1948—. Office: Haworth Inc 1 Haworth Ctr Holland MI 49423-9576

HAWORTH, JAMES CHILTON, pediatrics educator; b. Gosforth, Eng., May 29, 1923; emigrated to Can., 1957, naturalized, 1972; s. Walter Norman and Violet Chilton (Dobbie) H.; m. Eleanor Marian Bowser, Oct. 18, 1951; children— Elizabeth Marian, Peter Norman James, Margaret Jean, Anne Ruth. M.B., Ch.B, U. Birmingham, Eng., 1945, MD, 1960. House physician Birmingham Gen. and Children's Hosps., 1946-47; fellow Cin. Children's Hosp., 1949-50; house physician Hosp. for Sick Children, London, 1951; pediatric registrar Alder Hey Children's Hosp., Liverpool, Eng., 1951-52; sr. registrar Sheffield Children's Hosp., 1953-57; pediatrician Winnipeg (Man., Can.) Clinic, 1957-65; asst. prof. dept. pediatrics U. Man., Winnipeg, 1965-67, assoc. prof., 1967-70, prof., 1970-94, head dept. pediatrics, 1979-85, senate mem., 1985-90, prof. human genetics, 1987-94, prof. emeritus, 1994—, sr. scholar dept. biochemistry and med. genetics, 1999—. Mem. active staff Health Scis. Centre-Children's, 1957-93; cons. staff St. Boniface Hosp., 1974-93; hon. staff Health Sci. Ctr., 1993—. Contbr. numerous articles to profl. jours. Bd. dirs. Man. Med. Svc. found., 1988—, exec. dir., 1995—. Served with Royal Naval Vol. Res., 1947-49. Fellow Royal Coll. Physicians (Can., London), Can. Coll. Med. Geneticists (hon.); mem. Can. Soc. Clin. Investigation, Am. Acad. Pediat., Am. Pediatric Soc., Soc. Pediatric Rsch., Can. Pediatric Soc. Home: 301 Victoria Crescent Winnipeg MB Canada R2M 1X8 Office: Childrens Hosp Dept Pediatrics 678 William Ave Winnipeg MB Canada R3E 0W1

HAWORTH, LAWRENCE LINDLEY, philosophy educator; b. Chgo., Dec. 14, 1926; s. Lawrence Lindley and Ruth Ethyl (Johnson) H.; children: Lawrence Lindley III, Ruth Ellis. BA with highest distinction, Rollins Coll., 1949; MA, U. Ill., 1950, PhD (Univ. fellow), 1952. Asst. prof. U. Ala., 1952-54, asst. dean, 1953-54; asst. prof. Purdue U., 1954-59, assoc. prof., 1959-65; prof. philosophy U. Waterloo, Ont., Can., 1965-96, disting. prof. emeritus, 1996—, dir. Ctr. for Soc., Tech. and Values, 1984-86, chmn. dept. philosophy, asso. dean grad. studies, assoc. dean computing and rsch., 1967-70, 88-89. Author: The Good City, 1963, Decadence and Objectivity, 1977, Autonomy, 1986, Value Assumptions in Risk Assessment, 1991, A Textured Life: Empowerment and Adults with Developmental Disabilities, 1999; contbr. articles to profl. jours. Served with AUS, 1945-46. Purdue U. rsch. fellow, 1956, 59, 64; U. Waterloo rsch. fellow, 1967, 68, 69, 70; Can. Coun. leave fellow, 1971-72; Can. Coun. rsch. grantee, 1973-75, 81-83, 85-87, Social Sci. and Humanities Rsch. Coun. leave fellow, 1985-86, rsch. grantee 1981-84, 85-87, 91—. Fellow Royal Soc. Can.; mem. Canadian Philos. Assn., Phi Beta Kappa. Office: U Waterloo Dept Philosophy Waterloo ON Canada N2L 3G1

HAWORTH, MICHAEL ELLIOTT, JR., aerospace company executive; b. Pitts., Dec. 18, 1928; s. Michael E. and Margarett (Thomas) H.; m. Elizabeth Jean Evans, Dec. 20, 1949; children: Michael Elliott III, Jean Evans. Student, U. Ala., 1946-50; BS, Samford U., 1958. Gen. mgr. Haworth Engrng. & Mfg. Co., Birmingham, Ala., 1954-56; chief contract negotiator U.S. Army Ordnance, Birmingham, 1956-61; dir. procurement Kennedy Space Center NASA, 1961-67; v.p., sec. Hayes Internat. Corp., Birmingham, 1967-86, pres., chief exec. officer, 1986-88, also bd. dirs.; pvt. investor, 1989-99. Life mem. Bapt. Med. Ctr.-Montclair Aux. With Q.M. Corps, U.S. Army, 1952-54. Mem. Am. Def. Indsl. Assn. (life, chpt. pres. 1969-71, 82-85), Nat. Aerospace Svcs. Assn. (dir. 1971-74, chmn. 1972-73), Coun. Def. and Space Industry Assns. (vice chmn. 1973-74, chmn. 1974-75), Nat. Contract Mgmt. Assn. (bd. dirs. Birmingham area chpt. 1976-78, lifetime cert. profl. contracts mgr.), Birmingham Urban League (dir. 1971-75), Phi Gamma Delta, Country Club of Birmingham, The Club. Home: 4805 Mill Springs Cir Birmingham AL 35223-1682 E-mail: melliotth@charter.net.

HAWORTH, RANDAL DIGBY, plastic surgeon; b. L.A., Sept. 19, 1961; s. William and Annalise Haworth. BA in Biology, U. Calif., Santa Cruz, 1982, BA in Chemistry, 1992; MD, U. So. Calif., L.A., 1988. Diplomate bd. cert. Am. Bd. Plastic Surgeons. Resident gen. surgery Cornell N.Y. Hosp., 1988—93; fellow plastic surgery UCLA Med. Ctr., 1993—95; pvt. practice Beverly Hills, Calif., 1995—. Contbr. Bd. dirs. Sheba Med. Ctr.; Mem. Pres.'s Cir. The Thaleans, Cedars Sinai Med. Ctr., 1999—; Mem. L.A. Mus. Art, Mus. Contempory Art,

L.A. Named one of Best Surgeons in Am., Rsch. Coun. Am. Mem.: Am. Soc. Plastic Surgeons, Alpha Omega Alpha. Avocations: art, music, skiing. Office: Ste 105 436 N Bedford Dr Beverly Hills CA 90210

HAWORTH, RICHARD THOMAS, geophysicist, senior public service executive; b. Wirksworth, Eng., May 24, 1944; s. Bertram and Eleanor (Buxton) H.; m. Wilma Haworth, Sept. 13, 1969; children: Neil, Mark. BSC with honors in Physics with Geology and Math, Durham U., 1965; PhD in Geophysics, Cambridge U., 1968. Rsch. mgr., rsch. sci. Bedford Inst. Oceanography-Geological Survey of Can. (Atlantic), Dartmouth, Canada, 1968—83; chief geophysicist Brit. Geological Survey, 1983-90; dir. gen. sedimentary and marine geosci. br. Geological Survey of Can., Ottawa, 1990-2000; program leader Knowledge Generation and Info. Mgmt., 2000—; asst. dep. minister Dept. Natural Resources, Can., 2000—. Faculty advisor, external examiner Nottingham, Leeds, Newcastle, London, Liverpool, Oxford, Dalhousie, McGill (Can.); mem. program com. Internat. Assn. Geodesy, 1989; numerous overseas projects on all continents with recent focus on Africa, S.E. Asia; mem. Law of the Sea World Summit on Sustainable Devel., UN. Contbr. over 100 articles to profl. jours., symposia; reviewer pubs. in field. Derbyshire County Exhibition scholar, Shell postgraduate scholar in geophysics. Fellow Geol. Assn. Can. (program chmn. 1980), Geol. Soc. London (chartered geologist, mem. coun. 1985-88, v.p. 1986-88, adv. editor jour. 1985-2000), Geol. Soc. Am.; mem. Am. Geophys. Union. Avocations: choral singing, tennis. Office: Natural Resources Can 580 Booth St Ottawa ON Canada K1A 0E4 E-mail: haworth@nrcan.gc.ca.

HAWRYLUK, RICHARD JANUSZ, physicist; b. Mansfield, Eng., June 7, 1950; came to U.S., 1952; s. Michal and Jozefa H.; m. Mary Katherine McMahon, Feb. 7, 1976; children: David, Kevin. BS, MS, MIT, 1972, PhD, 1974. Dep. dir. Princeton Plasma Physics Lab., 1974—. Cons. Lincoln Lab., Lexington, Mass., 1970-74, 79. Contbr. over 100 articles to profl. jours. and conf. proceedings. Recipient Disting. Assoc. award Dept. of Energy, 1995, Kaul Found. prize for excellence in plasma physics rsch. and technology, 1996. Fellow Am. Phys. Soc. (Excellence in Plasma Physics award 1988). Achievements include research on heating and confinement of Tokamak plasmas and electron beam lithography. Office: Princeton Plasma Physic Lab PO Box 451 Princeton NJ 08544-0451 E-mail: rhawryluk@pppl.gov.

HAWS, HALE LOUIS, medical consultant; b. Anaheim, Calif., June 15, 1923; s. Lloyd Albert and Nancy Jean (Hale) H.; m. JoAn Penn Haws; children: Kathleen Seghieri, Jay B., Jerald L. BA, Pepperdine Coll., 1947; MD, UCLA, 1958. Diplomate Med. Bd. Calif., Am. Bd. Preventive Medicine, Bd. Life Ins. Medicine. Intern Gorgas Hosp., Canal Zone, 1958-59; pvt. practice L.A., 1959-60; plant med. dir. Chrysler Corp., Commerce, Calif., 1960-71; physician, surgeon Narcotic Control, Dept. Corrections, L.A., 1961-75; v.p. med. svcs. Pacific Mut. Life Ins. Co., Newport Beach, Calif., 1962-81; consulting med. dir. Calif., 1981—. Dir. Best Life Assurance Co. of Calif., Irvine, 1981-97; med. adv. bd. Equifax Svcs., Inc., Atlanta, 1977-81; spkr. in field. Mem. Church of Christ. Recipient Cert. of Appreciation, Selective Svc. Sys., 1975; scholar Kaiser Family Found., 1957. Fellow Am. Coll. Preventive Medicine, Am. Coll. Angiology, Am. Coll. Occupl. and Environ. Medicine, Am. Geriatrics Soc.; mem. Am. Acad. Ins. Medicine, Am. Coun. Life Ins., Calif. Scholastic Soc. (life), Pepperdine Alumni Assn. (dir. 1968-70). Avocations: art collecting, classic/antique autos, continuing medical education, reading, gardening. Home: 5268 Royal Canyon Ln Paradise CA 95969-6683 E-mail: hale@dcsi.net.

HAWS, ROBERT JOHN, lawyer; b. Highland Park, Ill., Aug. 1, 1947; s. Robert William and Ardyth E. (Meintzer) H.; m. Theresa M. Giaimo, Oct. 9, 1982; children: Benjamin Robert, Theodore Matthew. BA, Rutgers Coll., 1969; JD, Seton Hall U., 1976. Bar: N.J. 1976, U.S. Dist. Ct. N.J. 1976, U.S. Supreme Ct. 1986; cert. civil trial atty. Dep. atty. gen. State of N.J., Trenton, 1977-83; pvt. practice, Milltown, N.J. Mem. ABA, ATLA, N.J. Trial Lawyers Assn., N.J. State Bar Assn., Middlesex County Bar Assn. Democrat. Roman Catholic. Avocation: skiing, travel, mountain biking. Home: 275 Edlys Ln North Brunswick NJ 08902-3057 Office: 86 Washington Ave Milltown NJ 08850

HAWTHORNE, DOUGLAS D. medical association administrator; b. N.J. two children. BBA, M in Health Care Adminstrn., Trinity U., San Antonio. Intern San Antonio Hosp.; with Presbyn. Health Care Sys., 1970—97, pres., CEO, 1983—97, Tex. Health Resources, Arlington, 1997—. Bd. dirs. United Way; mem. exec. com. Dallas Red Cross; active Circle Ten. Boy Scouts Am. Recipient Leonard A. Duce award for outstanding contbn. to the field of health care adminstrn., 1977; named Healthcare Leader of the 21st Century for State of Tex., Hosps. mag.; named to The Dallas Dozen Up-and-Comers to Watch, Dallas Times Herald, 1986.

HAWTHORNE, LEROY, JR., humanities educator, musician; b. Monroe, La., Feb. 2, 1957; s. Leroy Hawthorne, Sr. and Betty Williams Hawthorne; m. Gurtie Mae Osborne, May 16, 1982; children: Crystal Gayle, Leroy Hawthorne, III, Christopher James, Tyler Cherelle. BS in Music Edn., Grambling (La.) State U., 1980, MA in Libr. Sci. in Humanities, 1991. Cert. tchr. Bd. of Edn., Colo., 1984. Residence hall couselor Grambling State U., Grambling, La., 1980—82; substitute tchr. Caddo Parish Sch. Bd., Shreveport, La., 1982—83; orch. tchr. Morehouse Parish Sch. Bd., Bastrop, La., 1984—86; field admissions rep. La. Bus. Coll., Monroe, La., 1988—89; instr. of humanities and guitar Grambling (La.) State U., 1991—. Musical dir. Jennifer Holliday Rec. Artist, LA, 1992, musician, 92. Prodr.: (compact disc audio recording) Grambling State University; musician: Dorsaey Summerfield & The Polyphonics, Army Nat. Guard. Musician Pilgrim Rest Bapt. Ch., Ruston, La., 1991—2002. With Nat. Guard U.S. Army, 1979—84. Decorated Oustanding Svc. Adjuctant General's award Army Nat. Guard; recipient Oustanding Svc. Musician Appreciation award, Pilgrim Rest Bapt. Ch., 1996, 1999, 2001, Oustanding Musicianship award, The Links, Inc., 2002, Oustanding Svc. Musician Appreciation award, Pilgrim Rest Bapt. Ch., 2002. Democrat. Baptist. Home: P O Box 543 Grambling LA 71245 Office: Grambling State University 403 Main Street Grambling LA 71245

HAWTHORNE, MARION FREDERICK, chemistry educator; b. Ft. Scott, Kans., Aug. 24, 1928; s. Fred Elmer and Colleen (Webb) Hawthorne; m. Beverly Dawn Rempe, Oct. 30, 1951 (div. 1976); m. Diana Baker Razzaia, Aug. 14, 1977. BA, Pomona Coll., 1949; PhD (AEC fellow), U. Calif. at Los Angeles, 1953; DSc (hon.), Pomona Coll., 1974; PhD (hon.), Uppsala U., 1992. Rsch. assoc. Iowa State Coll., 1953-54; rsch. chemist Rohm & Haas Co., Huntsville, Ala., 1954-56, group leader, 1956-60, lab. head Phila., 1961; prof. chemistry U. Calif., Riverside, 1962-68, UCLA, 1968—, U. Calif., 1998—. Vis. lectr. Harvard U., 1960, vis. prof., 68; vis. lectr. Queen Mary Coll., U. London, 1963; vis. prof. U. Tex., Austin, 1974; mem. sci. adv. bd. USAF, 1980—86, NRC Bd. Army Sci. and Tech., 1986—90; disting. vis. prof. Ohio State U., 1990; mem. dir.'s external adv. bd. divsn. M Los Alamos Nat. Lab., N.Mex., 1991—94; lectr. in field. Editor-in-chief: Inorganic Chemistry, 1969—2000, assoc. editor:, 1966—69. Decorated Meritorious Svc. medal USAF; named Sr. Scientist Alexander von Humboldt Found., Inst. Inorganic Chemistry U. Munich, 1990—96, Centenary lectr., Royal Soc. Chemistry, London, 1998; recipient Chancellors Rsch. award, 1968, Herbert Newby McCoy award, 1972, Am. Chem. Soc. award Inorganic Chemistry, 1973, Glenn T. Seaborg medal, 1997, Tolman Medal award, 1986, Nebr. sect. Am. Chem. Soc. award, 1979, Disting. Svc. Advancement of Inorganic Chemistry award, Am. Chem. Soc., 1988, Disting. Achievements in Boron Sci. award, 1988, Bailar medal, 1991, Polyhedron medal and prize, 1993, Chem. Pioneer award, Am. Inst. Chemists, 1994, Willard Gibbs medal, Am. Chem. Soc., 1994, Internat. award in Polyhedral Borane Chemistry, Internat. Com. on Boron Chemistry, 1996, Basolo medal, Am. Chem. Soc., 2001, King Faisal Internat. Sci. prize, 2003; fellow Sloan Found., 1963—65, Japan Soc. Promotion Sci., 1986, Disting. Vis. scholar, Chinese U. Hong Kong, 2001. Fellow: AAAS; mem.: Internat. Soc. Neutron Capture Therapy for Cancer (mem. exec. com. 1992—2000, pres. 1996—98), Am. Acad. Arts and Scis., U.S. Nat. Acad. Scis. (award in chem. scis. 1997), Göttingen Acad. Scis. (corr.), Aircraft Owners and Pilots Assn. (named Col. Confederate Air Force 1984), Cosmos Club, Sigma Nu, Alpha Chi Sigma, Sigma Xi (Monie A. Ferst award 2003). Home: 3415 Green Vista Dr Encino CA 91436-4011 E-mail: mfh@chem.ucla.edu.

HAWTHORNE, MARK R. investigator, educator; b. San Francisco, Nov. 21, 1951; s. Richard E. and Barbara L. Hawthorne; m. Sheila Y. Laughridge, Sept. 18, 1977; children: Andrew J., Ashley D. AA, San Francisco C.C., 1977; BA, Golden Gate U., 1981, MPA, 1998. Sr. dep. sheriff San Francisco Sheriff's Office, 1972-78; police sgt./inspector San Francisco Police Dept., 1978-84, crime scene investigator, 1984—, coord. mentor program, 1996—. Instr. City Coll., San Francisco, 1986—, San Francisco Police Regional Tng. Acad., 1990—; guest lectr. U. San Francisco Law Sch., 1997-98; chair blood com. San Francisco Police Dept., 1996—. Author: First Unit Responder, 1998. Sgt. U.S. Army Nat. Guard, 1970-76. Fellow Internat. Assn. for Identification (cert. sr. crime scene analyst, cert. latent print examiner, past pres. Calif. divsn. 1995-96), Fingerprint Soc. Eng.; mem. Calif. Assn. Criminal Justice Educators, Pi Alpha Alpha. Home: 1314 Plymouth Ave San Francisco CA 94112-1241 Office: San Francisco Police Dept 850 Bryant St Rm 577-16 San Francisco CA 94103-4603

HAWTHORNE, MINNIE, elementary school educator; b. Jackson, Miss., Feb. 15, 1949; d. Tommie Lee and Rosetta (Tolbert) Harris; m. Cedric Hawthorne; 1 child, Cedric. BS, Jackson State U., 1970; MS, Ind. U., 1971. Tchr. Hinds C.C., Utica, Miss., 1974-80, Chgo. Bus. Coll., 1988-93; cadre tchr. Chgo. Pub. Schs., 1994-96; tchr. Yazoo County Schs., Yazoo City, Miss., 2000—. Co-sponsor, sponsor Phi Beta Lamba, Utica, 1974-80. Mem. Yazoo County Fair and Civic League, Yazoo City, 1996-97. Mem. Pi Omega Pi. Avocations: playing piano, community volunteering for americorps, vista. Home: 217 E 3d St Yazoo City MS 39194

HAWTHORNE, NAN LOUISE, Internet resources consultant, web designer, writer, editor; b. Hawthorne, Nev., Jan. 3, 1952; d. Louis Frederick Haas Jr. and Merle Forrest (Ohlhausen) Ritter; m. James Denver Tedford, Dec. 20, 1981. BS, No. Mich. U., 1981. Mng. dir. CyberVPM.com, Seattle, 1997—; content devel. eSight Careers Network, 1999—; mng. dir. nanhawthorne.com. Author: Loving the Goddess Within, 1990, Building Better Relationships with Volunteers, 1997, Managing Volunteers in Record Time, 1997, Recognizing Volunteers Right From the Start, 1998; contbr. articles to profl. jours. Mem. Assn. Vol. Adminstrs. (tech. com. 1998—), Soc. Profl. Journalists. Office: PO Box 1229 22833 Bothell-Everett Hwy 102 Bothell WA 98021-9366 E-mail: hawthorne@nanhawthorne.com.

HAWTHORNE, VICTOR MORRISON, epidemiologist, educator; b. Glasgow, Scotland, June 19, 1921; came to U.S., 1978; s. John Morrison and Isabel Stuart (Crowe) H.; m. Jean Christie Mackenzie, Aug. 19, 1948; children: Hilary June, Wendy Victoria, Joan Rosalind. MD ChB, U. Glasgow, 1951, MD, 1962, DSc (hon.), 1996; diploma, Scottish Coun. for Health Edn., 1976. Sr. lectr. dept. epidemiology U. Glasgow, 1967-78, sr. research fellow dept. community medicine, 1978-91; cons. physician Nat. Health Service, Glasgow Health Bd., 1966-78; coordinator Scottish MMR services Nat. Health Service Scotland, 1970-78; prof. epidemiology U. Mich., Ann Arbor, 1978-91, chmn. dept., 1978-86, prof. dept. family practice, 1982-91, prof. epidemiology emeritus, 1991—95. Chmn. epidemiology study sect. NIH, Bethesda, Md., 1979-83, active, 1979-93; chmn. kidney disease adv. com. Mich. Dept. Pub. Health, Lansing, 1979-95, mem. chronic disease adv. com., 1979; chmn. Continuing Med. Edn./Pub. Health Consortium Mich., 1987—2002; hon. dir. Bayer Rsch. unit Royal Coll. Physicians of Edinburgh, 1987-93, hon. cons. Royal Coll. Physicians of Edinburgh Diabetes Register, 1989-01, U. Mich. Complementary & Cardiovascular Rsch. Ctr., 1999-. Author: First Aid For Medical Students, 1978, Tuberculosis, Respiratory and Cardiovascular Risks of Dying in the West of Scotland, 1985; contbr. articles to profl. jours. Capt. Brit. Army IORA, 1941—46. Recipient Bronze medal U. Helsinki, 1985; Victor Hawthorne: Young Investigator Rsch. Award Program established in his honor Mich. Dept. Pub. Health, 1986. Fellow Royal Coll. Physicians and Surgeons of Glasgow, Royal Coll. Physicians of Edinburgh, Faculty of Pub. Health Medicine, Soc. Antiquaries of Scotland, Am. Coll. Epidemiology. Mem. Ch. of Scotland Avocations: sketching, gardening. Office: Univ Mich Sch Pub Health Dept Epidemiology 109 Observatory St Ann Arbor MI 48109-2029

HAWVER, CAROLYN DUNN, pharmaceutical production executive; b. Tarrytown, N.Y., Nov. 2, 1954; d. Robert Thomas and Carolyn Pamelia (McMichael) Dunn; m. Kenneth Flint Hawver, July 8, 1994; children: Andrew Eakins, Christian Eakins, Charles Eakins. BS in Chemistry and Math., Meredith Coll., Raleigh, N.C., 1976; MS, N.C. State U., Raleigh, N.C., 1984. Rsch. chemist Colgate-Palmolive, Piscataway, N.J., 1984-88, group leader, 1989-91, tech. mgr. N.Y.C., 1992-93, focused factory mgr. Jeffersonville, Ind., 1994-96; dir. Novartis Pharmaceuticals, Suffern, N.Y., 1997—. Office: Novartis Pharmaceuticals 25 Old Mill Rd Suffern NY 10901-4106 Home: 1006 Laurel Ridge Dr Mcdonough GA 30252-8421 Fax: 914-368-6934. E-mail: carolyn.hawver@pharma.novartis.com., hawver@earthlink.net.

HAWVER, DENNIS A. psychological consultant; s. Carl Fullerton and Frances Jewell H.; m. Anne M. Augustyn, 1961 (div. Oct. 1974); children: Timothy, Laura, Derek; m. Judith M. Anderson, Jan. 28, 1977. BA, U. Akron, 1964, MA, 1965; PhD, Temple U., Phila., 1964-70. Dir. rsch. Temple U., Phila., 1964-70, instr. Grad. Sch., 1968-70, internal cons., 1964-70; mng. ptnr. Cardall Assocs., Princeton, N.J., 1970-72; nat. program dir. The RHR Inst., N.Y.C., 1972-80; pres. The Hawver Group, N.Y.C. and Princeton, 1980—. Pres. The Hawver Group, N.Y.C. and Princeton, 1980— ; pres. Princeton chpt. Inst. Mgmt. Cons. Author: How to Improve Your Negotiating Skills, 1983; contbr. to bus. and profl. jours.; developer rsch. and tng. programs; internat. cons. in exec. identification and devel. and bus. negotiations. Chmn. Leadership Devel. Com. of Princeton C. of C. Mem. APA, Soc. Indsl. and Organizational Psychology, Internat. Assn. Applied Psychology, Inst. Mgmt. Cons. (CMC), Soc. Assessment Sys. Practitioners, Internat. Pers. Mgmt. Assn. Assessment Coun. Office: The Hawver Group 21 Park Place W Cranbury NJ 08512-3224 E-mail: hawvergrp@aol.com.

HAX, ARNOLDO CUBILLOS, management educator, industrial engineer; b. Santiago, Chile, Aug. 9, 1936; came to U.S., 1961; s. Egon and Adela (Cubillos) H.; m. Neva Mimica, Jan. 28, 1962; children: Andrew, Neva. Degree in Indsl. Engring. with highest honors, Cath. U. Chile, Santiago, 1960; MS in Insdl. Engring., U. Mich., 1963; PhD in Ops. Rsch., U. Calif., Berkeley, 1967. Asst. prof. math. Sch. Engring., Cath. U. Chile, 1960-61, dir., assoc. prof. Ops. Rsch., 1963-65; asst. specialist Ops. Rsch. Ctr. U. Calif., Berkeley, 1965-67; mgmt. cons. ops. rsch. Arthur D. Little, Inc., Cambridge, Mass., 1976-70; lectr. Bus. Sch. Harvard U., Boston, 1970-72; assoc. prof. Sloan Sch. Mgmt., MIT, Cambridge, 1972-76, prof., 1976—, Alfred P. Sloan prof., 1985—, dep. dean, 1987-90; Thomas Henry Carroll Ford Found. vis. prof. bus. Harvard Bus. Sch., 1993-94. Indsl. engr. Chilean Inst. Steel, Santiago, 1960-61; lectr. linear programming Centro Interam. de Ensenanza de Estadistica, Santiago, 1963-65; cons. ops. rsch. and stats. CADE, Santiago, 1963-65; cons. stategic planning processes Digital Equipment Corp., Motorola, GM, Citibank, Westinghouse Electric, others in U.S., Europe, Mex., S.Am., Can.; Ford Found. vis. prof. bus. sch. Harvard U., 1993-94. Co-author: (with D. Candea) Production and Inventory Management, 1984 (Inst. Indsl. Engrs.-Joint Pubs. Book of Yr. award 1985), (with N. Majluf) The Strategy Concept and Process: A Pragmatic Approach, 1991, 2d edit., 1996, Strategic Management: An Integrative Perspective, 1984, (with D. Wilde) The Delta Project: Discovering New Sources of Profitability in a Networked Economy, 2001; author: (with others) Manuale di Gestione della Produzione, 1975, Studies in Management Science, Vol. 1, Logistics, 1975, Modern Trends in Logistics Research, 1976, Applied Mathematical Programming, 1977, Conflicting Objectives in Decisions, 1977, Handbook of Operations Research, 1978, Studies in Operations Management, 1978 (also editor), Disaggregation: Problem in Manufacturing and Service Organizations, 1979, Applications of Management Science, Vol. 1, 1981, The Management Handbook, 1981, Implementation of Stategic Planning, 1982, Production Handbook, 1987; editor: Readings in Strategic Management, 1984, Planning Strategies That Work, 1987; strategic mgmt. editor Interface jour., 1981—; former editor Ops. Rsch. jour., Naval Rsch. Logistics Quar.; contbr. numerous articles to profl. jours. and publs. Thomas Henry Carroll Ford Found. vis. prof. bus. Harvard U. Bus. Sch., Cambridge. Mem. Inst. Mgmt. Scis., Ops. Rsch. Soc., Am. Inst. Indsl. Engrs., AAAS, Am. Inst. Decision Scis., Vineyard Haven Yacht and Tennis Club, Alpha Pi Mu. Home: 242 Otis St Newton MA 02465-2525 Office: MIT Sloan Sch Mgmt 50 Memorial Dr Cambridge MA 02142-1347

HAXO, FRANCIS THEODORE, marine biologist; b. Grand Forks, N.D., Mar. 9, 1921; s. Henry Emile and Florence (Shull) H.; m. Judith Morgan McLaughlin, Apr. 15, 1961; children: John Frederick, Barbara, Philip, Francis Theodore, Aileen. BA, U. N.D., 1941; PhD, Stanford U., 1947. Teaching, research asst. Stanford U., 1941-44, acting instr., 1943; research asst. Calif. Inst. Tech., 1946; research asso. Hopkins Marine Sta., Pacific Grove, Calif., 1946-47; from instr. to asst. prof. plant physiology Johns Hopkins U., 1947-52; mem. faculty U. Calif. Scripps Inst. Oceanography, La Jolla, 1952-88, prof. biology, 1963-88; prof. emeritus, 1988—; chmn. marine biology dept. U. Calif. Scripps Inst. Oceanography, 1960-65, chmn. marine biology research div., 1960-77; instr. marine botany Marine Biol. Lab., Woods Hole, Mass., 1949-52, 70. Vis. faculty botany U. Calif. at Berkeley, 1957, U. Wash. Marine Lab., Friday Harbor, 1963 Abraham Rosenberg fellow Stanford, 1945. Fellow AAAS, San Diego Zool. Soc.; mem. Am. Soc. Photobiology, Phycological Soc. Am., Western Soc. Naturalists, Internat. Phycological Soc., Phi Beta Kappa, Sigma Xi. Achievements include spl. rsch. photosynthesis, plant pigments, physiology of algae. Home: 6381 Castejon Dr La Jolla CA 92037-6933

HAXTON, DAVID, filmmaker, photographer; b. Indpls., Jan. 6, 1943; s. John Laird and Dorothy Margaret (Peters) H.; m. Kay Elizabeth Keller, Feb. 8, 1969. BA, U. South Fla., 1965; MFA, U. Mich., 1967. Prof. computer graphics William Paterson Coll., Wayne, N.J., 1974-95, U. Ctrl. Fla., Orlando, 1995—. One-man shows include: Sonnabend Gallery, N.Y.C., 1979, 80, 81, 83, Paris, 1978, Mus. Modern Art, N.Y.C., 1978, Rosa Esman Gallery, N.Y.C., 1986, U. Ctrl. Fla., 1998, Ikon Galerie, 2001; group shows include: Whitney Mus. Am. Art, N.Y.C., 1979, 81, 83, Rosa Esman Gallery, N.Y.C., 1986, Anne Plumb Gallery, N.Y.C., 1987, Ringling Art Mus., Sarasota, Fla., 1987, Digital Film Exhbn., Ikon Galerie, Germany, 2001, True Fictions, Ludwig Forum, Aachen, Germany, 2002, Orlando Mus. Art, 2003; represented in permanent collections, Mus. Modern Art, N.Y.C., Whitney Mus. Am. Art, N.Y.C., Denver Art Mus., Australian Mus. Art. Recipient awards for computer animation direction Gold Plaque award Chgo. Internat. Film Festival, 1988, 89, Art Dream award Siggraph Film and Video Show, 1988, Nat. Computer Graphics Assn. 2d award, 1989, Siggraph Animation Screening award, 1990, NCGA Video Show 3rd award, 1991, 1st pl. award Alias Desing Competition, 1991, Siggraph Electronic Theater award, 1992, Pri Ars Electronica award, 1993, UN Cabinet D'Amateurs Cinematheque Francaise, Films, 1995, Siggraph Animation Screening Rm. award, 1997, Siggrapa Animation Theatre, 1999, 2000, Siggraph Art Show, 2001; N.Y. Coun. on Arts grantee, 1977-78, Nat. Endowment for Arts grantee, 1978-79; Individual Artist fellow, 1979-80; Nat. Computer Graphics Assn. faculty student, 1992, 2d prize award, 1991. Office: U Ctrl Fla Dept Art Orlando FL 32789

HAY, BETTY JO, civic worker; b. McAlester, Okla., June 6, 1931; d. Duncan and Kathryn Myrtle (Albert) Peacock; m. Jess Thomas Hay, Aug. 3, 1951; children: Deborah Hay Spradley, Patricia Lynn Daibert. BA, So. Meth. U., 1952. Bd. dirs. White House Preservation Fund, 1980-87, Nat. Parents as Tchrs., 1991-94; bd. dirs. Nat. Mental Health Assn., 1978-87, pres., 1986, mem. fin. com. and child adolescent com., 1978-79, mem. resource devel. com., 1980-83; v.p. fundraising Mental Health Assn. Tex., 1980, bd. dirs., 1974-90, pres., 1983-894; bd. dirs. Mental Health Assn., Dallas County, 1972-88, pres., 1981-82; bd. dirs. United Way Met. Dallas, 1983-94, treas., 1989; bd. dirs. Assn. Higher Edn. North Tex., 1980-82, vice chmn., 1981-83, chmn., 1984-85; mem. adv. bd. Sch. Social Work, U. Tex., Arlington, 1983-94; mem. Nat. Commn. on Children, 1989-92, Woman's divsn. Dallas Coun. on World Affairs, March of Dimes Aux., 1982—; bd. dirs. Baylor Coll. Dentistry, 1987-94, mem. exec. com., 1989, vice chmn., 1992; mem. Tex. Commn. on Children and Youth, 1994-95; pres. Tex. Mental Health Found., 1982—; active other charitable orgns. Address: 7236 Lupton Cir Dallas TX 75225-1737

HAY, DENNIS LEE, lawyer; b. L.A., Feb. 18, 1958; s. Frank Henry, Jr. and Kyoko (Sukuya) H.; m. Kerry Lynne Hatfield, Aug. 11, 1984; children: Michelle, Jason, Katherine. BS in Fin., San Jose State U., 1984; JD, U. Honolulu, 1988. Bar: Calif. 1989. Law clk. Legal Aid Soc. of Alameda Co., Hayward, Calif., 1985-87, Cohn, Becker & Jacquint, Hayward, Calif., 1987, Souza, Coats, McInnis, Mehlhaff & Hay, Tracy, Calif., 1987-89, assoc. counsel atty., 1989-92; ptnr. Mehlhaff & Hay, Tracy, Calif., 1992—; judge pro tem San Joaquin Superior Cts. Prof. law U. Honolulu Law Sch., Modesto, Calif. Mem. Calif. Bar Assn., San Joaquin County Bar Assn. (chairperson bus. litig. sect. com. 1997-98, judicial liaison com. 2002-2003). Republican. Presbyterian. Avocations: drag racing, horse back riding, raquetball. Office: Mehlhaff & Hay PO Box 1129 23950 S Chrisman Rd Tracy CA 95378-1129

HAY, ELIZABETH DEXTER, embryology researcher, educator; b. St. Augustine, Fla., Apr. 2, 1927; d. Isaac Morris and Lucille Elizabeth (Lynn) H. AB, Smith Coll., 1948; MA (hon.), Harvard U., 1964; ScD (hon.), Smith Coll., 1973, Trinity Coll., 1989; MD, Johns Hopkins U., 1952, LHD (hon.), 1990. Intern in internal medicine Johns Hopkins Hosp., Balt., 1952-53; instr. anatomy Johns Hopkins U. Med. Sch., Balt., 1953-56, asst. prof., 1956-57, Cornell U. Med. Sch., N.Y.C., 1957-60, Harvard Med. Sch., Boston, 1960-64, Louise Foote Pfeiffer assoc. prof., 1964-69, Louise Foote Pfeiffer prof. embryology, 1969—, chmn. dept. anatomy and cellular biology, 1975-93; prof. dept. cell biology, 1993—. Cons. cell biology sect. NIH, 1965-69; mem. adv. coun. Nat. Inst. Gen. Med. Sci., NIH, 1978-81; mem. sci. adv. bd. Whitney Marine Lab., U. Fla., 1982-86; mem. adv. coun. Johns Hopkins Sch. Medicine, 1982-96; chairperson bd. sci. counselors Nat. Inst. Dental Rsch., NIH, 1984-86; mem. bd. sci. counselors Nat. Inst. Environ. Health Sci., NIH, 1990-93. Author: Regeneration, 1966; (with J.P. Revel) Fine Structure of the Developing Avian Cornea, 1969; editor: Cell Biology of Extracellular Matrix, 1981, 2d edit., 1991; editor-in-chief Developmental Biology Jour., 1971-75; contbr. articles to profl. jours. Mem. Scientists Task Force of Congressman Barney Frank, Massach, 1982-92. Recipient Disting. Achievement award N.Y. Hosp.-Cornell Med. Ctrl. Alumni Coun., 1985, award for vision rsch. Alcon, 1988, Excellence in Sci. award Fedn. Am. Socs. Exptl. Biology. Mem. Soc. Devel. Biology (pres. 1973-74, E.G. Conklin award 1997), Am. Soc. Cell Biology (pres. 1976-77, legis. alert com. 1982—, E.B. Wilson award 1989, chair 40th anniversary 2000), Am. Assn. Anatomists (pres. 1981-82, legis. alert com. 1982—, Centennial award 1987, Henry Gray award 1992), Am. Acad. Arts and Scis., Johns Hopkins Soc. Scholars, Nat. Acad. Sci., Inst. Medicine, Internat. Soc. Devel. Biologists (exec. bd. 1977, keynote spkr. 1st Australian EMT conf. 2003), Boston Mycol. Club. Home: 14 Aberdeen Rd Weston MA 02493-1733 Office: Harvard Med Sch Dept Cell Biology 220 Longwood Ave Boston MA 02115-5701

HAY, GEORGE AUSTIN, actor, artist, musician, director; b. Johnstown, Pa., Dec. 25, 1915; s. George and Mary Louise (Austin) H. BS, U. Pitts., 1938; postgrad., U. Rochester, 1939; MLitt, U. Pitts., 1948; MA, Columbia U., 1948. Dir. Jr. League hosp. shows, N.Y.C., 1948-53. *As a kind of legacy from his physician and surgeon father, Austin Hay has enjoyed a regimen of lifelong healthfulness. In his impressionable youth, he became markedly inspired by knowing two young local figures: an obscure endlessly exuberant, surprisingly skilled, astonishingly agile, indefatigable teacher in his own home town--by the name of Gene Kelly; and a lanky assistant to a prestidigitator in a neighboring small town--unknown Princeton student, James Stewart. To a youngster, all this exemplified magical adventureland. Manifestly from such extraordinary early influences, a career in theater and movies followed. Through ensuing halcyon times, friendships continued with notables in the field, among them, "the most trusted man in America," television's Walter Cronkite, in whose home and yacht, on Martha's Vineyard, Austin Hay has been welcomed. In a lively saga of effort to broaden horizons and enhance the quality of life, he performs in a variety of disciplines, is productive in different fields of creative endeavor. Being born on Christmas day, he helps nurture in a joyous way a continuing ethic of integrity, and healthful living.* Producer, dir. off-Broadway prodns., 1953-55; motion picture casting dir. for Dept. Def. films, Astoria Studios, N.Y., 1955-70, motion picture producer-dir., U.S. Dept. Transp., Washington, 1973—, Office Presdl. Personnel, The White House, 1993—; group exhbns. of paintings and sculpture include, Lincoln Ctr., N.Y.C., 1965, Parrish Art Mus., Southampton, N.Y., 1969, Carnegie Inst., 1972, Duncan Galleries, N.Y.C., 1973, Bicentennial Exhbn. Am. Painters, Paris, 1976, Chevy Chase Gallery, 1979, Watergate Gallery, 1981, Le Salon des Nations a Paris, 1983; rep. permanent collections, Met. Mus. Art, N.Y.C., Library Congress, also, pvt. collections; bibliog. reference to works pub. in History of Internat. Art, 1982; author, illustrator: Seven Hops to Australia, 1945, The Moving Image, A Career in Pictures, 1990; Dir.: Bicentennial documentary Highways of History, 1976; dir.: film World Painting in Museum of Modern Art, 1972; Composer: Rhapsody in E Flat for piano and strings, 1950; writer: TV program Nat. Council Chs., 1965; Broadway appearances include: What Every Woman Knows, 1954; original Broadway run of Inherit the Wind, 1955-57; created role of Prof. Fiveash in

premiere of The Acrobats, White Barn Theater, Westport, Conn., 1961; feature films include: Murder, Inc., 1960, Pretty Boy Floyd, 1960, The Landlord, 1970, Child's Play, 1971, Chekhov's The Bet, 1978, Being There, 1980, No Way Out, 1986, Her Alibi, 1988, Air Force One, 1997, Guarding Tess, 1994, Contact, 1997 The Contender, 2000, Head of State, 2003; TV appearances include Am. Heritage, 1961, Americans-A Portrait in Verses, 1962, Naked City, 1962, U.S. Steel Hour, 1963, Another World, 1965, Edge of Night, 1968, As the World Turns, 1969, Love Is a Many-Splendored Thing, 1972, The Adams Chronicles, 1976, A Woman Named Jackie, 1991; piano soloist in concerts and recitals, 1937; performer Cruise Ship, Europe, 1938; author, illustrator: The Arts Scene; contbr. articles to periodicals. App. time adv. panel, pres.'s coun. Col. William and Mary; mem. World Affairs Coun., Am. Archit. Found.; bd. govs. Home of Pres. James Monroe; trustee Home of Pres. James Monroe; mus. donor turn-of-century doctor's office from estate of surgeon father; With AUS, 1942—46; PTO; bd. dirs. Washington Film Coun. Recipient Loyal Svc. award Jr. League, 1953, St. Bartholomew's Silver Leadership award, 1966, Gold medal Accademia Italia, 1980, Smithsonian Instn. Pictorial award, 1982; Fed. Govt. Honor award in recognition 45 yrs. dedicated svc., 2000; subject of biog. work: Austin Hay, Adventures of a Christmas Child, 1970. Mem. NATAS, AFTRA, SAG, Am. Artists Profl. League, Allied Artists Am., Internat. Bach Soc., Beethoven Soc. (bd. dirs.), Nat. Soc. Arts and Letters (bd. dirs.), Music Libr. Assn., Nat. Symphony Orch. Assn., Actors Equity Assn., Nat. Trust Hist. Preservation, SAR, Nat. Parks and Conservation Assn., Shakespeare Oxford Soc., St. Andrew's Soc., Victorian Soc. (bd. dirs.), Cambria County Hist. Soc., Am. Philatelic Soc., Am. Mus. Moving Image, Jimmy Stewart Mus. (Indiana, Pa.), English Speaking Union (bd. dirs.), Nat. Arts Club (N.Y.C.), Players Club (N.Y.C.), Nat. Travel Club, Columbia U. Club, Nat. Press Club, Arts Club of Washington, Cosmos Club, Classic Car Club Am., Nat. Naval Med. Command, Sigma Chi, Phi Mu Alpha.

HAY, GEORGE ALAN, law and economics educator; b. N.Y.C., Feb. 4, 1942; s. George N. and Marjorie H. (Prote) H. BS, Le Moyne Coll., 1963; MA, Northwestern U., 1967, PhD, 1969. From asst. to assoc. prof. econs. Yale U., New Haven, 1967-74; dir. econs. antitrust div. U.S. Dept. Justice, Washington, 1973-79; prof. law and econs. Cornell U., Ithaca, N.Y., 1979-92, Edward Cornell prof. law, prof. econs., 1992—. Vis. prof. law U. Sydney, 1992, vis. fellow Balliol Coll., Oxford, 2001. Contbr. articles on antitrust to profl. jours. Fulbright scholar Oxford U., 1984-85. Mem. ABA, Am. Econ. Assn., Assn. Am. Law Schs. (chmn. antitrust sect. 1985-87). Office: Cornell Law Sch 214 Myron Taylor Hall Ithaca NY 14853-4901

HAY, HOWARD CLINTON, lawyer; b. Portland, Maine, Apr. 16, 1944; s. Willis and Ruth (Clark) H.; m. Carol Anne Newsome, Dec. 21, 1968; children: Mark, David, Scott. AB (with distinction), Duke U., 1966; JD magna cum laude, U. Mich., 1969. Bar: U.S. Supreme Ct. 1977, Calif. 1970. Law clerk U.S. Ct. Appeals, Boston, 1970; atty. NLRB; ptnr. Paul, Hastings, Janofsky & Walker, Costa Mesa, Calif., 1971—. Program chmn. Certificate in Employee Rels. Law; instr. U. S.C. Grad. Sch. Bus. Editor Mich. Law Review; contbr. articles to profl. jours. Mem. State Bar Calif. (exec. com. labor and employment sect.), Calif. Bar Assn. Office: Paul Hastings Janofsky & Walker 695 Town Center Dr Fl 17 Costa Mesa CA 92626-1924 E-mail: howardhay@paulhastings.com.

HAY, JESS THOMAS, retired finance company executive; b. Forney, Tex., Jan. 22, 1931; s. George and Myrtle Hay; m. Betty Jo Peacock, 1951; children: Deborah Hay Spradley, Patricia Hay Daibert. BBA, So. Meth. U., 1953, JD magna cum laude, 1955. Bar: Tex. Assoc. Locke, Purnell, Boren, Laney & Neely, 1955 61, partner, 1961-65; pres., chief exec. officer Lomas Fin. Corp., Dallas, 1965-69, chmn. bd., chief exec. officer, 1969-94; chmn. bd., chief exec. officer, trustee Lomas & Nettleton Mortgage Investors, 1969-92; chmn., CEO Capstead Mortgage Corp. (formerly Lomas Mortgage Corp.), 1985-91. Chmn. HCB Enterprises Inc; bd. dirs. Trinity Industries, Inc., Exxon Corp., Viad Corp., SBC Comm. Inc. Former mem. Dem. Nat. Com., also former nat. fin. chmn.; former chmn. bd. regents U. Tex. Sys.; former mem. Dallas Citizens Coun., Dallas Assembly; mem. Greater Dallas Planning Coun.; mem. WWII Meml. Adv. Bd.; bd. dirs. Tex. Rsch. League, North Tex. Food Bank, Child Care Partnership Dallas, Dallas County Hist. Found.; chmn. bd. Tex. Found. for Higher Edn.; trustee Southwestern Med. Found. Recipient Disting. Service award Assn. Governing Bds. of Univs. and Colls., 1987. Mem. ABA, Dallas Bar Assn., Tex. Bar Assn., Am. Judicature Soc., Newcomen Soc. N.Am., U.S. C. of C. Methodist. Home: 7236 Lupton Cir Dallas TX 75225-1737 Office: 5956 Sherry Ln Ste 1413 Dallas TX 75225

HAY, JOHN LEONARD, lawyer; b. Lawrence, Mass., Oct. 6, 1940; s. Charles Cable and Henrietta Dudley (Wise) H.; m. Ruth Murphy, Mar. 16, 1997; 1 child, Ian. AB with distinction, Stanford U., 1961; JD, U. Colo., 1964. Bar: Colo. 1964, Ariz. 1965, D.C. 1971. Assoc. Lewis and Roca, Phoenix, 1964-69, ptnr., 1969-82, Fannin, Terry & Hay, Phoenix, 1982-87, Allen, Kimerer & LaVelle, Phoenix, 1987-94, Gust Rosenfeld, Phoenix, 1994—; judge pro tem Ariz. Ct. Appeals, 1999—. Bd. dirs. Ariz. Life and Disability Ins. Guaranty Fund, 1984-95, chmn., 1993-95. Co-author: Arizona Corporate Practice, 1996, Representing Franchisees, 1996. Mem. Dem. Precinct Com., 1966-78, Ariz. State Dem. Com., 1968-78; chmn. Dem. Legis. Dist., 1971-74; mem. Maricopa County Dem. Cen. Com., 1971-74; bd. dirs. ACLU, 1973-78; bd. dirs. Community Legal Svcs., 1983-89, pres., 1987-88; bd. dirs. Ariz. Club, 1994-96. Mem. ABA, Ariz. Bar Assn., Maricopa County Bar Assn. (bd. dirs. 1972-85), Assn. Life Ins. Counsel, Ariz. Licensors and Franchisors Assn. (bd. dirs. 1985—, pres. 1988-89), Ariz. Civil Liberties Union (bd. dirs. 1967-84, 95-2002, pres. 1973-77, 97-2000, Disting. Citizen award 1979), Phoenix C. of C. (chmn. arts and culture task force 1997-99). Home: 201 E Hayward Ave Phoenix AZ 85020-4037 Office: Gust Rosenfeld 201 E Washington St Ste 800 Phoenix AZ 85004- E-mail: jhay@gustlaw.com., johnlhay@cox.net.

HAY, LEWIS, III, utilities company executive; b. 1955; BS in Elec. Engring., Lehigh U., 1977; M in Indsl. Adminstrn., Carnegie-Mellon U., 1982. Gen. foreman U.S. Steel Corp., Pitts., 1977-80; v.p., mng. ptnr. strategy practice Strategic Planning Assocs., Washington, 1982-91; exec. v.p., CFO U.S. Foodsvc. Inc., Columbia, Md., 1991-99; CFO FPL Group, Inc., Juno Beach, Fla., 1999—2000; pres. FPL Energy, 2000—01. Office: FPL Group Inc PO Box 14000 North Palm Beach FL 33408

HAY, RICHARD LE ROY, geology educator; b. Goshen, Ind., Apr. 29, 1926; s. Edward Le Roy and Angela H.; m. Barbara J. Herbert, Dec. 13, 1956; 1 child, Randall E.; m. Lynn Simonds, July 14, 1973. BS, Northwestern U., 1946, MS, 1948; PhD, Princeton U., 1952. Asst. prof. geology La. State U., Baton Rouge, 1955-57; asst. prof. to prof. geology and geophysics U. Calif., Berkeley, 1957-83; Ralph E. Grim prof. geology U. Ill., Urbana-Champaign, 1983-97. Geologist U.S. Geol. Survey, intermittently 1948-84; adj. prof. U. Ariz., 1999—. Author: Geology of the Olduvai Gorge, 1976. Recipient Arnold Guyot award, Nat. Geog. Soc., 1978, Leakey prize, L.S.B. Leakey Found., 2001. Fellow AAAS, Geol. Soc. Am. (Kirk Bryan award 1978, Rip Rapp award 2000), Mineral. Soc. Am., Calif. Acad. Sci. Home: 4320 N Alvernon Way Tucson AZ 85718-6180

HAY, ROBERT DEAN, retired management educator; b. LaPorte, Ind., Nov. 17, 1921; s. Carl Roy and Almetta (Diedrich) H.; m. Margaret B. Appelman, 1944; children— Sue Ann, Carol Lynn, Taj Margaret. BS, U. Okla., 1949, MBA, 1950; PhD, Ohio State U., 1954. Mem. faculty U. Ark., Fayetteville, 1949-90, mem. emeritus, 1990—, prof. mgmt., 1959-86, Univ. prof., 1986-90. Author: (with F. Broyles) Athletic Administration, 1979, (with Ed Gray and Paul Smith) Business and Society, 1989, Strategic Management in Non-Profit Organizations, 1990; also 10 other books. Served with USAAF, 1942-47. Mem. Am. Bus. Communications Assn., Acad. Mgmt., Case Rsch. Assn., other profl. orgns. Office: U Ark Dept Mgmt Fayetteville AR 72701

HAY, SAMUEL ARTHUR, theater educator, playwright; b. Barnwell, S.C., Mar. 26, 1937; s. Thomas Jr. and Maebelle Glover H.; m. Delores Ricks Glover, June 1, 1986 (div. Aug. 1988). BA, Bethune-Cookman Coll., 1959; MA, Johns Hopkins U., 1967; PhD, Cornell U., 1971. Asst. prof. English and African Am. studies U. Md., Catonsville, 1971-74; dir. Africana studies and rsch. ctr. Purdue U., West Lafayette, Ind., 1974-78; prof. theatre arts and Afro-Am. studies Washington U., St. Louis, 1978-79, chair Afro-Am. studies, 1979-79; prof., chair dept. comm. and theatre arts Morgan State U., Balt., 1979-88; prof. theatre arts, exec. dir. theatre N.C. A&T State U., Greensboro, 1993—2002; vis. prof. Lafayette Coll., Easton, Pa., 2002—. Vis. prof. Afro Am. studies U. Calif., Berkeley, 1987-88; archivist The Ed Bullins Collection, Greensboro, N.C., 1988-2000; artistic dir. Cottage Theatre, Riviera Beach, Fla., 1988-93; mng. dir. The Bullins Meml. Theatre, Emeryville, Calif., 1987-88; instr. English and drama Roosevelt H.S., West Palm Beach, Fla., 1971-74; convener Nat. Symposium on Ed Bullins N.C. A&T State U., Greensboro, 1997, Nat. Symposium on Paul Robeson N.C. A&T State U., Greensboro, 1988, Nat. Symposium on Alice Childress N.C. A&T State U., Greensboro, 1996, Nat. Symposium on August Wilson N.C. A&T State U., Greensboro, 1995. Author: (books) Focus on Literature, 6 vols., 1978, African American Theatre: A Historical and Critical Analysis, 1994, Ed Bullins: A Literary Biography, 1997 (CHOICE award 1998), (plays) Cream and Brown Sugar, 1997 (Am. Coll. Theatre Festival Region IV winner 1997), David Richmond, 1999 (Best Play of 1999 Kennedy Ctr./Am. Coll. Theatre Festival 1999). Cons. N.C. Shakespeare Fest., High Point, 1994-99, Nat. Black Theatre Fest., Winston-Salem, N.C., 1998—, Simon & Schuster Lang. Arts, Nassau, Bahamas, 1992-94. Recipient Harvard U. Found. medallion Harvard U., 1995, Dist. scholar N.C. A&T State U., 1995, Achievement award Arena Players Balt., 1987, Best Play Nat. Theatre of Detroit, 1985. Fellow Nat. Conf. African Am. Theatre, Inc. (founder, pres 1980-90); mem. Nat. Asns. Sch. Theatre (bd. dirs. 2000—), Nat. Symposium on African Am. Theatre (founder, pres. 1993—), Assn. Theatre in Higher Edn., Black Theatre Network. Democrat. Episcopalian. Avocations: tennis, walking, traveling. Home: PO Box 1183 Easton PA 18042-1183 Office: Lafayette Coll Dept Govt & Law Easton PA 18042 Fax: 610-330-5397. E-mail: samhay3@aol.com.

HAY, SUSAN STAHR HELLER, museum curator; b. Mpls., Oct. 12, 1938; d. John Lewis and Suzanne Wallace (Finley) Heller; m. Edwin J. Anderson (div.); 1 child, Fletcher Scott Anderson; m. Edward Merrill Hay, July 20, 1984. BA in French Linguistics, Cornell U., 1960; MA in French Lit., Brown U., 1963; MA in Am. Civilization, U. Pa., 1981. From curatorial asst. to mus. curator Nat. Hist. Park, Phila., 1976-78; editor W. B. Saunders Co., Phila., 1978-79; asst. mng. editor Am. Quar., 1979-80; teaching fellow U. Pa., Phila., 1980-81; curatorial asst. costume and textiles Phila Mus. Art, 1981-82, asst. curator costume and textiles, 1982-85; curator costume and textiles Mus. Art R.I. Sch. Design, Providence, 1985—. Lectr. and presenter papers in field. Contbr. articles to profl. jours. Past v.p., trustee Coggeshall Farm Mus., Bristol, R.I.; past trustee Smith's Castle Historic Site, Wickford, R.I. Cooper-Woods Meml. Travel Study grant English Speaking Union, 1978. Mem. Am. Assn. Mus., Costume Soc. Am. Textile Soc. Am., Ctr. Internat. d'Etudes des Textiles Anciens., Tex. Soc. Am. Office: RI Sch Design Mus Art 224 Benefit St Providence RI 02903-2723

HAY, THOMAS FRANKLIN, music educator; b. Humboldt, Tenn., Nov. 17, 1943; s. Homer Franklin Hay and Mildred Hay Shivers; m. Lisa Lewis Hay, Sept. 7, 1980; children: Jason, Lea. BS, U. Tenn., Martin, 1966; postgrad., La. Tech. U., Ruston, 1972. Cert. profl. U.S. Profl. Tennis Assn. Band dir. Weakly County Bd. Edn., Martin, Tenn., 1966—68, City of Humboldt, Tenn., 1968—73; sales mgr. Princeton Industries, Ind., 1973—79, tennis profl. Jackson Country Club, Tenn., 1979—84; dir. tennis West Tenn. Jr. Devel., 1984—92; dir. bands Chester County Bd. Edn., Henderson, Tenn., 1992—. Choir dir., clinician, adjudicator; spkr. in field. Author: (weekly newspaper article) Tennis Instructor, 1981—92; host, writer: (PBS TV series) All About Tennis with Tom Hay, 1980—; contbr. articles to profl. jours. and mags. Tennis tchr. City of Jackson City Pks., 1989; Sunday sch. tchr. City of Jackson, Tenn., 2001—. Named Outstanding Tchr., Govs. Sch. for Artists, 1998, 2000; named to Honor Role of Tenn. Artists, Tenn. Arts Acad., 2001; recipient Tenn. Ednl. award for Tennis Pro of Yr., 1984, So. Tennis Ednl. award for Pro of Yr., 1984. Mem.: Tenn. Band Masters Assn., Music Educators Nat. Conf., West Tenn. Sch. Band and Orch. Assn., West Tenn. Sch. Bd. Assn. (state rep. 1971—73, jazz rep. 1998—2002), Phi Beta Mu. Methodist. Achievements include intiation of West Tenn. Jr. Devel. Tennis Program; represented Tenn. in Sr. Tennis Cup, 1984. Avocations: tennis, swimming, reading, spending time with family. Office: Chester County HS Band 552 E Main Henderson TN 38340

HAYAKAWA, KAN-ICHI, retired food science educator; b. Shibukawa, Gumma, Japan, Aug. 12, 1931; came to U.S., 1961, naturalized, 1974; s. Chyogoro and Kin (Hayakawa) H.; m. Setsuko Maekawa, Feb. 18, 1967. BS, Tokyo U. Fisheries, 1955; PhD, Rutgers U., 1964. Rsch. fellow Canners' Assn. Japan, 1955-60; asst. prof. food sci. Rutgers U., New Brunswick, N.J., 1964-70, assoc. prof. food sci., 1970-77, prof. food engring., 1977-82, Disting. prof. food engring., 1982-99, prof. emeritus, 1999—, ret., 1999. OAS vis. prof. U. Campinas, Brazil, summers 1972, 73, 94; cons. to food processing cos.; organizer, chmn., participant NSF sponsored U.S.-Japan Coop. Conf., Tokyo, 1979; lectr. Industry R&D Inst. and Nat. Taiwan U., 1982, Wuxi Inst. Light Industry, China, 1986, Tokyo U. of Fisheries, 1992. Co-editor: Heat Sterilization of Food, 1983. Contbr. articles to books, profl. jours. and encys.; developer new math methods for predicting safety of food processes; found theoretical and exptl. theorems on heat and mass transfer in biol. material with or without strain--stress formation. Rsch. grantee USPHS, 1966-73, Nabisco Found., 1975-76, NSF, 1981-82, travel grantee NSF, 1972, Rutgers Rsch. Found., 1977, rsch. grantee Advanced Food Tech. Ctr., 1985-89, John von Neumann Nat. Supercomputer Ctr., 1989-90, Pitts. Nat. Supercomputer Ctrs., NSF, 1990-97, Cray Rsch. Inc., 1993-95, U.S. Army Natick R&D Ctr., 1992-94, USDA, 1994-98. Fellow Inst. Food Technologists; mem. ASHRAE (life, chmn. tech. com. on thermophys. property values of food 1981-85, mem. com. 1981-96), Sigma Xi.

HAYAKAWA, TORU, neurosurgeon; b. Osaka, Japan, Sept. 24, 1934; s. Tetsuo and Shizu Hayakawa; m. Naoko Oda, May 30, 1969; children: Takashi, Makoto. MD, Osaka U., 1959, PhD, 1964. Intern Osaka (Japan) U. Med. Sch., 1959-60, resident, 1960-64; surgeon Sakai City Hosp., 1964-65, resident, 1965-67; asst. Osaka U. Med. Sch., 1967-77; assoc. dept. neurology U. Minn., Mpls., 1973-75; sr. neurosurgeon Ctr. for Adult Diseases, Osaka, 1977-80; asst. prof. Osaka U. Med. Sch., 1981-89, assoc. prof., 1989-90, prof., chmn. dept. neurosurgery, 1990—98; dir. Kansai Rosai Hosp., 1998—. Mem. Japanese Neurosurg. Soc. (mem. neurosurg. bd.). Home: 1-2-10-704 Mikage Yamate Higachinada Kobe 658 Japan Office: Kansai Rosai Hosp. 3-1-69 Inabaso Amagasa ki 660-8511 Japan

HAYASE, PAUL HIROMI, lawyer; b. Warren, Ohio, Mar. 20, 1955; s. Charles Koji and Michiko (Watanabe) H.; m. Aug. 12, 1978. BA, Yale Univ., 1976; JD, Univ. Pa., 1980. Bar: Calif. 1980, U.S. Dist. Ct. (cen. dist.) Calif. 1980, U.S. Ct. Appeals (9th cir.) 1980. Assoc. MacDonald, Halsted & Laybourne, L.A., 1980-85; sr. v.p., gen. counsel Knapp Communications Corp., L.A., 1985—. V.p., bd. dirs. Japanese Evang. Missionary Soc., L.A., 1981-85. Internat. scholar Svc. Employees Internat., Washington, 1973-77; Centennial scholar Japanese C. of C., L.A., 1973. Mem. Japanese-Am. Bar Assn., L.A. County Bar Assn., L.A. Jr. C. of C. Democrat. Baptist. Office: Knapp Communications Corp 5900 Wilshire Blvd Los Angeles CA 90036-5013

HAYASHI, ALAN T, mathematics educator; b. Honolulu, Mar. 10, 1954; s. Harold T. and Sally S. Hayashi; married. BSc, AB, U. Calif., Riverside, 1975; postgrad., Ohio State U., 1983-84. Cert. secondary tchr., single subject tchg. and comty. coll. instr. credentials, Calif. Tchr., coach boys track and girls basketball Jurupa Jr. High Sch., Jurupa Unified Sch. Dist., Riverside, Calif., 1976-79; tchr. math., coach acad. decathlon and knowledge bowl Channel Islands High Sch., Oxnard (Calif.) Union High Sch. Dist., 1979-91; instr. Oxnard Coll., Ventura County C.C. Dist., 1989—, dept. chmn., 1995, 98, 2001—03. Casino dealer Harrah's Hotel & Casino, Stateline, Nev., 1980-81; teaching asst., instr. Ohio State U., Columbus, 1983-84; mathematician Pacific Missile Test Ctr., U.S. Dept. Def., Point Mugu, Calif., 1990; textbook reviewer Calif. Dept. Edn., 1981, 89; statistician Channel Islands High Sch. football team, 1980-92; asst. dir. summer inst. Calif. State Math. Project/Tri-County Math Project, 1996, co-dir., 1997-2001; mem. faculty U. Calif.-Santa Barbara Extension, 1999; co-dir. Calif. Profl. Devel. Initiative Algebra Inst., 2000-03. Contbg. author: Prentice-Hall Interactive Math Program, 1998. Newsletter editor Internat. Rels. Coun. Riverside, 1975-77. Recipient Chpt. Outstanding Tchr. award Calif. Mini-Corp., 1991-92, Tandy Tech. scholar nat. semi-finalist, 1990-91; named Tchr. of Yr., Calif. Scholastic Fedn. chpt., 1989, Channel Islands H.S. Tchr. of Yr., 1983, Oxnard Coll. Acad. Senate Treas., 1994, 97; NSF fellow, 1981, 82, Calif. Math Project/Tri-County Math Project fellow, 1994, sr. fellow, 1995, TCMP Leadership Network fellow, 1995-99. Mem. NEA, Math. Assn. Am., Nat. Coun. Tchrs. Math., U. Calif.-Riverside Alumni Assn., Calif. Fedn. Tchrs., Ventura County Math. Coun. (bd. dirs. 1998—, v.p. 1999-2003), Nat. Coun. Suprs. Math., Claif. Math. Coun. Office: Oxnard Coll 4000 S Rose Ave Oxnard CA 93033-6699

HAYASHI, KIM, music educator; b. Patterson, NJ, May 15, 1950; s. Mitsuru Hayashi and Mary Louise Hiyashi. MusB in Piano and Music Edn, U. Wash., 1978; MusM, U. Oreg., 1981, U. Ariz., 1987, D Mus Arts, 1995. Pvt. studio piano tchr. Seattle, Eugene, Oreg. and Tucson, 1972—; asst. undergrad. advisor Sch. Music U. Wash., Seattle, 1977—79; grad. tchg. asst. U. Oreg., Eugene, 1979—81, U. Ariz., Tucson, 1986—88; solo and chamber music performer, 1980—; dir. chamber music in pub. schs. Az. Friends of Chamber Music, Tucson, 1995—. Adj. faculty mem. Sch. Music U. Oreg., Eugene, 1982—86; adj. faculty dept. fine arts Pima Coll., Tucson, 1996—; preconcert lectr. Ariz. Friends of Chamber Music, 1999—; clinician Nev. State Music Tchrs. Assn., Las Vegas, 1997, Rosie's Music House, Phoenix, 2003. Chmn. Yamaha Corp. piano donation Berger Performing Arts Ctr., Ariz. State Schs. for Deaf and Blind, 1993—97. Named Theodore Presser Music Edn. scholar, U. Wash., 1971; Rotary fellow for study abroad, Staatliche Hochschule Musik, Freiburg, Germany, 1981—82, rsch. grantee, Grad. Coll. U. Ariz., 1988. Mem.: Phi Eta Sigma, Music Tchrs. Nat. Assn., Tucson Music Tchrs. Assn. (organizing chmn. command performances 1995, mem. command performancers com. 1995—2002), Ariz. State Music Tchrs. Assn. (adjudicator 1994—, chmn. James R. Anthony Honors Recital Auditions 1995—99, chmn. fundraising for James R. Anthony Honors Recital 1995—2002), Phi Beta Kappa. Office: 2925 E Adams St Tucson AZ 85716

HAYASHI, TETSUMARO, retired literature educator, writer, editor; b. Sakaide City, Japan, Mar. 22, 1929; arrived in U.S., 1954, naturalized, 1969; s. Tetsuro and Shieko (Honjyo) Hayashi; m. Akiko Sakuratani, Apr. 14, 1960; 1 child, Richard Hideki. BA, Okayama (Japan) U., 1953; MA, U. Fla., 1957; MALS, Kent State U., 1959, PhD, 1968. Assoc. dir. Culver-Stockton Coll. Libr., Canton, Mo., 1959-63; instr. English Kent (Ohio) State U., 1965-68; from asst. prof. to assoc. prof. Ball State U., Muncie, Ind., 1968—77, prof., 1977-93; dir. Steinbeck Rsch. Inst., 1981-93; vis. grad. prof. Kwassui Women's Coll., Japan, 1993-96; v.p., grad. prof. English Yasuda Women's U., Hiroshima, Japan, 1996-2001, dir. grad. studies in English, 1997-99; ret., 2001. Sr. editl. cons. Steinbeck Yearbook, 2001—03. Author: (book) Sketches of American Culture, 1960, John Steinbeck: A Concise Bibliography, 1967, Arthur Miller Criticism, 1969, Robert Greene Criticism, 1971, Shakespeare's Sonnets: A Record of 20th Century Criticism, 1972, Index to Arthur Miller: Criticism, 1976; editor: A Looking Glass for London and England (Thomas Lodge, Robert Greene), An Elizabethan Text, 1970, Steinbeck's Literary Dimension, 1973, Steinbeck's Literary Dimension, Series II, 1991, A Study Guide to Steinbeck: A Handbook of His Major Works, 1974, 1979, 1993, 24 others; editor: (with Richard Astro) Steinbeck: The Man and His Work, 1971, John Steinbeck: A Dictionary of His Fictional Characters, 1976; founder, editor-in-chief: Steinbeck Quar., 1968—93, Steinbeck Monograph Series, 1970—93; contbr. articles to profl. jours. Executor Pruis Award Fund and Burkhardt Award Fund, Ball State U. Found., Muncie, 1978—. Named Disting. English Alumnus, Kent State U., 2002; grantee, Am. Philos. Soc., 1975, 1981, Am. Coun. Learned Socs., 1976, Bernard Boyd Meml. Found., 1986, Lyndon B. Johnson Found., 1987, others; Rotary Internat. Jr. fellow, U. Fla., 1957, Folger Sr. fellow, 1972. Mem.: MLA, Shakespeare Assn. Am., Am. Lit. Assn. Home: 4300 W Kings Row Muncie IN 47304-2436

HAYASI, NISIKI, physicist, applied mathematician, business executive, inventor; b. Niigata City, Japan, Mar. 12, 1929; came to U.S., 1963; s. Matsuki and Fuku (Fukushima) H.; m. Chikako Nomura, Nov. 21, 1952; children: Fujio, Kay Keiko Makishi. AB, First Coll., Tokyo, 1949; SB, SM, U. Tokyo, 1952, PhD, 1962. Tech. ofcl., rsch. fellow Transp. Tech. Rsch. Inst., Japanese Ministry Transp., Tokyo, 1952-61; rsch. fellow Nat. Aero. Lab., Sci. and Tech. Agy., Tokyo, 1961-62, aerothermodynamics br. mgr. Nat. Aerospace Lab., 1962-64; postdoctoral assoc. NASA Ames Rsch. Ctr., Moffett Field, Calif., 1964-65; program mgr., staff scientist Lockheed Corp., Marietta, Ga., 1965-70; mgr. advanced tech. Langston divsn. Harris Corp., Cherry Hill, N.J., 1971-74; sr. mng. dir. Fgn. Ops. divsn. SPS Techs., Inc., Jenkintown, Pa., 1975; exec. dir. Tech. Transfer Cons., Cherry Hill, N.J., 1975-88; pres. Culti Corp., Cherry Hill, 1977—; dir. Japanese Lang. Svcs., Cherry Hill, 1989—. Vis. asst. prof. U. Cin., 1963-64; postdoctoral scholar U. Pa., 1971-73; exec. con. Tomoku Co., Ltd. Tokyo., 1974-78; NAS-NRC postdoctoral rsch. assoc. 1964, 65. Contbr. numerous articles to profl. jours.; patentee in U.S., France, Netherlands, Germany, Japan. Pres. Japanese Sch. Greater Phila. PTA, 1973-74, Burlington Atari User Devotees, 1986-87, Japanese Assn. of Greater Phila., 1991. Japanese Govt. overseas fellow, 1963. Fellow: AIAA (assoc.); mem.: Nat. Mgmt. Assn., Am. Translators Assn., PC World Online Adv. Coun., Sigma Gamma Tau. Achievements include pioneering work on computer aided design for aircraft wings during 1965-70. Office: Culti Corp 1230 Millhaven Drive Copley OH 44321 E-mail: doc_hayasi@geocities.co.jp.

HAYBACH, PATTY JEAN, writer, medical/surgical nurse; d. David A. and Anita Haybach. Diploma in nursing, Ann May Sch. Nursing, Neptune, N.J., 1974; BS, Coll. N.J., 1982; MS, U. Colo., Denver, 1993. CCRN, AACN, 1975. Critical care staff nurse Jersey Shore Med. Ctr., Neptune, 1974—76, Paul Kimball Hosp., Lakewood, NJ, 1977—80; pvt. duty nurse Stouffer's Nurses Registry, Belmar, NJ, 1980—82; asst. dir. ACLS program Medix Ambulance Svc., Tustin, Calif., 1986—87, dir. ACLS program, 1987—88; home care nurse Parkview Home Care, Pueblo, Colo., 1989—91; writer Pinellas Park, Fla., 1993—. Author: (book) Meniere's Disease: What You Need to Know, 1998, BPPV: What You Need To Know, 2000; co-author (book update) Balancing Act, 2001; author: (continuing education course) Hearing and Balance: At Risk From Drugs. Mem.: Sigma Theta Tau.

HAYCOCK, CHRISTINE ELIZABETH, retired medical educator, health educator; b. Mt. Vernon, N.Y., Jan. 7, 1924; d. John B. and Madeline (Sears) H.; m. Sam Moskowitz, July 6, 1958 (dec. Apr. 1997). SB, U. Chgo., 1948; MD, SUNY, Bklyn., 1952, MA in Polit. Sci., Rutgers U., 1981. RN, N.J.; diplomate Am. Bd. Surgery. Intern Walter Reed Army Med. Ctr., Washington, 1952-53; resident in surgery St. Barnabas Med. Ctr., Newark, 1954-58, St. John's Episcopal Hosp., Bklyn., 1958-59; pvt. practice Newark, 1959-68; asst. prof. surgery, N.J. Med. Sch. U. Med. and Dentistry N.J.-N.J. Med. Sch., Newark, 1968-75; assoc. prof. surgery, N.J. Med. Sch. UMDNJ, Newark, 1975-89, prof. clin. surgery, 1989-92; prof. emeritus, 1992—. Chief GYN Svc., VA Hosp., East Orange, N.J. Trauma Soc.; pres. Med. Amature Radio Coun., 1981, bd. dirs. (Coun. award 1978); mem. editl. bd. Jour. N.J. Med. Soc., 1979-95, The Physician and Sports Medicine, 1975-98, The Main Event, 1987; adv. com. N.J. Phys. Conditioning of the Police Tng. Commn., 1984-96. Editor: Trauma and Pregnancy, 1985, Sports Medicine for the Athletic Female, 1980; contbr. articles to profl. jours. Chmn. bd. Essex County chpt. Am. Cancer Soc., West Orange, N.J., 1978-79, bd. mgrs., Livingston, N.J., 1962—, hon. life mem., 1992. With U.S. Army, 1947-86, col. Res. ret. Recipient Outstanding Alumnae award Bloomfield Coll., 1971, Res. Forces Achievement award, 1974, Distinguished Lecturer award Downstate Med. Ctr., 1976, Dr. Frank L. Babbott Meml. award SUNY Alumni Assn., 1982, Pres. Honor citation, N.J. Assn. Phys. Edn. and Health Tchrs., 1982, Commendation medal, 1982, Meritorious Svc. medal, 1986, Presdl. Citation, N.J. Assn. for Health, Phys. Edn. and Recreation, 1984, Med. Bd. Svc. award Newark City Hosp., 1986, Bertha Van Hoosen award Am. Med. Women's Assn., 1997; grantee Abbott Labs, 1981-82. Fellow ACS (hon. life, N.J. com. on trauma 1970-91), Am. Coll. Sports Medicine (trustee 1978-80), Photog. Soc. Am. (chmn. video/motion picture divsn. 1993-95; Silver medal jour. award 2000, 02); mem. AMA, Am. Med. Women's Assn. (bd. dirs. 1976-86, pres. 1980, hosp. assn. com. 1985—, Silver Medallion award 1980), Zonta Internat., Assn. Women Surgeons (treas. 1989-91, chair found. com. 1991-95, sec. 1995-99, Disting. Surgeon award 1990), N.J. Women's Assn. (pres. 1976, treas. 1989-92, Woman of Yr. 1987), Amateur Radio Relay League. Republican. Avocations: photography, dog training and showing, sports, collecting elephants, amateur radio. Home: 361 Roseville Ave Newark NJ 07107-1721

HAYCOCK, DEAN ALLEN, writer, consultant; b. Atlantic City, Mar. 20, 1952; s. Don Allan Haycock and Florence Moratelli; m. Marie Elizabeth Culver. PhD, Brown U., 1986. Rsch. assoc. Rockefeller U., N.Y.C., 1985—87; sr. rsch.

investigator Sterling Winthrop Pharm. Rsch. Divsn., Rensselaer, NY, 1987—93; freelance sci. and med. writer Salem, NY, 1993—2002. Cons. The Am. Inst. for Rsch., Washington, 1995—2001, ACT, Inc., Iowa City, 2001—02, Integrated Strategic Info. Services, Inc., CALIF., 1994—95. Mem.: Nat. Writers Union, Am. Assn. of Med. Writers, Nat. Assn. of Sci. Writers. Independent. Office: Burton Press PO Box 310 Salem NY 12865-0310 Business E-Mail: haycock@nasw.org.

HAYCOCK, KENNETH ROY, educator, consultant, administrator; b. Hamilton, Ont., Can., Feb. 15, 1948; s. Bruce Frederick T. and Doris Marion P. (Downham) H.; m. Sheila Tripp, Jan. 28, 1990. BA, U. Western Ont., 1968, diploma in edn., 1969; specialist cert., U. Toronto, Can., 1971; MEd, U. Ottawa, Can., 1973; AMLS, U. Mich., 1974; EdD, Brigham Young U., 1991. Tchr., dept. head Glebe Collegiate Inst., Ottawa, 1969-70, Col. By Secondary Sch., Ottawa, 1970-72; cons. Wellington County Bd. Edn., Guelph, Ont., 1972-76; coord. libr. svcs., supr. instrn. Vancouver (B.C.) Sch. Bd., Canada, 1976-84, acting mgr., elem./secondary edn., 1984-85, dir. instrn., head program svcs., 1985-89, 91-92; prin. Waverley Elem. Sch., 1989-91; prof. Sch. Libr., Archival and Info. Studies U. B.C., Vancouver, 1992—, dir., 1992—2002. Instr. univs. and colls.; pres. Ken Haycock and Assocs., Inc. Editor Tchr. Libr.; author various books; contbr. articles to profl. and scholarly jours. Trustee Guelph Pub. Libr., 1975-76; trustee West Vancouver Sch. Bd., 1993-99, chair, 1994-97, councilor Dist. of West Vancouver, 1999-2002; trustee West Vancouver Pub. Libr., 1999-2001. Recipient award Beta Phi Mu, 1976, Queen Elizabeth Silver Jubilee medal, 1977. Fellow: Can. Coll. Tchrs.; mem.: ASCD (urban curriculum leaders 1985—92, internat. panel 1990—94), ALA (coun. 1995—99, exec. bd. 1999—2003, Herbert and Virginia White Advocacy award 2001), Coun. for Can. Learning Resources (pres. 1995—98), Internat. Assn. Sch. Librarianship (dir. N.Am. 1993—95, exec. dir. 1995—2000, Ken Haycock Leadership Devel. award named in his honor 2001), B.C. Libr. Assn. (Ken Haycock Student Conf. award named in his honor 1999), Assn. for Libr. and Info. Sci. Edn. (sec. coun. dean and dirs. 1993—96), Ont. Libr. Assn., Can. Libr. Assn. (life; pres. 1977—78, Outstanding Svc. award 1991), B.C. Sch. Libr. Assn. (Ken Haycock Profl. Devel. award named in his honor 1984, Disting. Svc. award 1989), Can. Sch. Libr. Assn. (pres. 1974—75, Margaret B. Scott award of merit 1979, rsch. award 1984, Disting. Sch. Adminstr. award 1989, rsch. award 1995), Am. Assn. Sch. Librs. (pres. 1997—98, Baker and Taylor Disting. Svc. award 1996), Internat. Fedn. Libr. Assns. and Instns. (sect. on Edn. and Tng. 1997—, chair 1999—2001), Phi Delta Kappa (Young Leader in Edn. award). Home: 5118 Meadfeild Rd West Vancouver BC Canada V7W 3G2 Office: U BC Sch Libr Arch & Info 854C-1956 Main Mall Vancouver BC Canada V6T 1Z1 E-mail: ken.haycock@ubc.ca.

HAYDEN, ALBERT A. retired historian, educator; b. Cape Girardeau County, Mo., Sept. 18, 1923; s. Howard Ebren and Clara Anna (Rust) H.; m. Priscilla Anne Hayden, Sept. 11, 1954 (dec. Sept. 2000); children: Keith A., Anne M. BA in History with honors, U. Ill., 1950; MA, Bucknell U., 1952; PhD, U. Wis., 1959. Instr. to prof. history Wittenberg U., Springfield, Ohio, 1959-94, ret., 1994. Vis. assoc. prof. history Kent (Ohio) State U., 1964. Mng. editor: Studies in Brit. History and Culture, 1976-94; author: New South Wales Immigration Policy, 1971; contbr. numerous articles to profl. jours. With USAAF, 1943-46. Recipient Disting. Svc. award Ohio Acad. History, 1994; Fulbright grantee, 1954-55. Mem. Am. Hist. Assn., Midwest Conf. on Brit. Studies, N.Am. Conf. Brit. Studies, Ohio Acad. History (exec. coun. 1982-85). Home: 1329 Eastgate Rd Springfield OH 45503-2423

HAYDEN, ANTHONY, secondary and elementary educator; b. N.Y.C., Sept. 12, 1929; s. Frank Case Hayden and Helena Marsh (Maschmedt) H.; m. Margret Boy, Apr. 17, 1957; children: Aaron, Andreas, Anthony, James, Sean. Student, Yale U., 1946-47; BS, Columbia U., 1954, MA, 1963. Various jobs, 1946—82; tchr. Harvey Sch., Hawthorne, N.Y., 1956-57, Allen Stevenson Sch., N.Y.C., 1957-69, Brunswick Sch., Greenwich, Conn., 1969-82; substitute tchr. Greenwich Bd. Edn., 1982—, Stamford (Conn.) Bd. Edn., 1982—. Mem. Greenwich Citizens for Nuc. Weapons Freeze, 1972—, Greenwich Dem. Town Com., 1960—. Justice of the Peace, Town of Greenwich, 1985—. Avocations: contra dancing, gardening, reading. Home: 76 Shore Rd Old Greenwich CT 06870-2216 E-mail: ahaydensr@earthlink.net.

HAYDEN, DOLORES, author, architect, educator; b. N.Y.C., Mar. 15, 1945; d. J. Francis and Katharine (McCabe) H.; m. Peter Horsey Marris, May 18, 1975; 1 child, Laura Hayden Marris. BA, Mt. Holyoke Coll., 1966; diploma in English studies, Cambridge (Eng.) U., 1967; LHD (hon.), Mt. Holyoke Coll., 1987; MArch, Harvard U., 1972; MA (hon.), Yale U., 1991. Registered architect. Lectr. U. Calif., Berkeley, 1973; assoc. prof. MIT, Cambridge, 1973-79; prof. UCLA, 1979-91, Yale U., New Haven, 1991—. Author: Seven American Utopias, 1976, The Grand Domestic Revolution, 1981, Redesigning the American Dream, 1984 (notable book award ALA, 1984, award for outstanding publ. in urban planning Assn. Collegiate Schs. of Planning 1986), rev. edit., 2002, The Power of Place: Urban Landscapes as Public History, 1995 (Assn. Am. Pubs. award), Playing House, 1998, Line Dance, 2001, Building Suburbia, 2003; also articles (Best Feature Article award Jour. Am. Planning Assn. 1994). Guggenheim fellow, 1981, Rockefeller Humanities fellow, 1980, ACLS/Ford fellow, 1989, Nat. Endowment for the Humanities fellow; recipient Radcliffe Grad. Soc. medal, 1991, Preservation award L.A. Conservancy, 1986, Vesta award Woman's Bldg., L.A., 1985, Design Rsch. award Nat. Endowment for the Arts, Feminist scholarship in the arts. Mem. Am. Studies Assn., Orgn. Am. Historians, Am. Planning Assn. (Diana Donald award 1987, various awards L.A. and Calif. chpts.), Urban History Assn. (dir. 1991-93). Avocations: travel, poetry. Office: Yale Univ Sch Architecture PO Box 208242 180 York St New Haven CT 06520-8242 E-mail: dolores.hayden@yale.edu.

HAYDEN, HARROLD HARRISON, information company executive; b. Cin., Jan. 16, 1942; s. Harold Richard and Blanche Marie (Sargent) H. BA, Millikin U., Decatur, Ill., 1964; MA, DePaul U., Chgo., 1970. Dir. mktg. tng. Automatic Electric, Northlake, Ill., 1968-70; dir. Universal Tng. Co., Wilmette, Ill., 1970-80; pres. Performance Achievement Group, Chgo., 1980-85; v.p. Lead Mgmt. Service, Chgo., 1985-90, Qualified Lead Systems, Chicago Heights, Ill., 1990—; pres. Intramark, Chicago Heights, Ill., 1992-94, chmn., 1995-97, 2000—; pres. Pace Airline Svcs. USA, Chgo., 1994—97, 2000—01, v.p. Synergistic Networks, 2001—. Exec dir. Internat. Meetings Inst., 1997-2000. Author: (multimedia package) Successful Telephone Selling, 1979, Santa Fe Railroad Data, 1975, Best Ill. award, 1975; editor Secrets of Successful Telemarketing, 1985. Mem. Ohlmstead Hist. Soc., Riverside, Ill., 1985; bd. dirs. 44th Ward Bus. Com., Chgo,. 1985-86; exec. mgr. British Consortium, 1989-91; bd. dirs. North Park Village, 1993-96; bd. dirs. Ill. Acad. Criminology, 1996-2000, pres., 2002-2003; vols. v.p. Am. Police Ctr. and Mus., 1996—. Recipient award Best Condo Bldg., Northside Real Estate Bd., Chgo., 1985. Mem. Am. Mgmt. Assn. (spkr. 1979-85), Pine Point Ski Club, Simply Singles (CEO). Avocations: sailing, skiing. Office: Intramark One World Trade Ctr 1540 Merchandise Mart Chicago IL 60654 E-mail: hhh55@aol.com.

HAYDEN, JOHN CARLETON, priest, history educator; b. Bowling Green, Ky., Dec. 30, 1933; s. Otis Roosevelt and Gladys (Gatewood) H.; m. Jacqueline Green, Apr. 8, 1972; children: Jonathan Christopher Janani, Johanna Christina Jamila. BA, Wayne State U., 1955; MA, U. Detroit, 1962; LTh with honors, Coll. Emmanuel and St. Chad, Saskatoon, Sask., Can., 1963, MDiv, 1991; PhD, Howard U., 1972. Ordained deacon Episc. Ch., 1963, priest, 1964. Tchr. St. Mary's Sch. for Indian Girls, Springfield, S.D., 1955-56, Detroit Pub. Schs., 1956-59; instr. St. Chad's Secondary Sch., Regina, Sask., 1962-64; Anglican chaplain U. Sask., Regina, 1963-67, instr. history, 1965-68; asst. prof. history Howard U., Washington, 1972-78, scholar in ch. history, 1978-79; chmn. dept. history Morgan State U., Balt., 1979-86; prof. history Frostburg (Md.) State U., 1986-87; assoc. dean Sch. Theology, U. of South, Sewanee, Tenn., 1987-92; lectr. ch. history Howard U., 1992—; priest-in-charge St. Michael and All Angels Ch., Adelphi, Md., 1992-94; instr. history Montgomery C.C., 1992-94; Episcopal/Anglican chaplain Howard U., Washington, 1994—2002, lectr. history, 1994—. Reader Gen. Ordination Exams., 1990-92, Evangelical Edn. Soc., 1987-99, dir.; assoc. priest All Sts. Chapel, Sewanee, 1987-92; priest assoc. sisterhood St. John the Divine, Toronto, 1978—; rector Holy Comforter Ch., Washington, 1982-86; coord., cons. steering com. Afro-Anglican Conf., 1992-95; confrater St. Gregory's Abbey, 1954—; assoc. Sisters of St. Mary, Sewanee Province, 1992—. Contbr. articles to profl. jours. Bd. dirs. Washington Urban League, 1983-87; life mem. NAACP, Nat. Urban League; pres. Sask. Assn. for Retarded Children, Regina, 1966-68; sec. bd. dirs. St. Mary's Episcopal Ctr., 1988-92; bd. dirs. Nat. Coun. Chs., 1988-95; mem. program com. Kanuga Conf. Ctr., 1989-94, mem. diversity com. bd. advisors, 1994-2000, bd. dirs., 2000—; mem. bd. advisors St. Andrew's/Sewanee Sch., 1990-99; convenor, steering com. Episc. Coun. on Global Mission. 1989-90; trustee Washington Episcopal Sch., 1992—. Recipient rsch. award Am. Philos. Soc., 1976, Absalom Jones award Washington Nat. Cathedral, 1987, Univ. svc. award Grambling (La.) State U., 1990, Disting. Svc. award Kanuga Conf. Ctr., 1991; Angus Dunn fellow Washington Diocese, 1973, 74, 78, 95, 96, 98, 99, 2000, 01, 03, rsch. grantee Spencer Found., 1975; Robert B. Moton scholar, 1978; Coolidge fellow Columbia U. Assn. for Religion and Intellectual Life, summer 1998. Mem. Union Black Episcopalians (life, trainer, parliamentarian). Democrat. Avocations: reading, meditation, travel. Office: Howard U Sch of Divinity 2400 Shepherd St NE Washington DC 20017 E-mail: FatherCarl30@aol.com.

HAYDEN, JOHN OLIN, English literature educator, writer; b. Los Angeles, Dec. 18, 1932; s. John Ellsworth and Norah Elizabeth (Bussens) H.; m. Mary Kathleen Garland, Dec. 18, 1965; children— Michael, John, Mark, Ann BA, U. Calif.-Santa Barbara, 1958; MA, Columbia U., 1959, PhD, 1965. Asst. prof. U. Colo., Boulder, 1964-66; assoc. prof. English lit. U. Calif.-Davis, 1966-75, prof. English lit., 1975-94, prof. emeritus, 1994—. Author: Romantic Reviewers, 1969, Polestar of the Ancients, 1979, William Wordsworth and the Mind of Man, 1993, Why the Great Books are Great, 1998; editor: Sir Walter Scott, 1970, Wordsworth: The Poems, 1977, Wordsworth: The Prose, 1988, Wordsworth: Selected Poetry, 1994. Served with USAF, 1951-55 E. J. Noble Found. fellow Columbia U., N.Y.C., 1959-61; fellow NEH, 1971, Am. Council Learned Socs., 1984 Democrat. Roman Catholic. Avocation: numismatics. Home: 25199 Carlsbad Ave Davis CA 95616-9434 Office: U Calif English Dept Davis CA 95616 E-mail: johayden@ucdavis.edu.

HAYDEN, JOHN W. real estate company executive; BA, Northwe. U.; MBA, Miami U. With Midland Co., 1981, v.p., 1987-96, sr. exec. v.p. Am. Home Groups, 1987=96, pres. Am. Modern Ins. Group, 1994-98, sr. exec. v.p., 1996-98, pres., CEO, 1998—, also bd. dirs. Office: Midland Co 7000 Midland Blvd Amelia OH 45102-2608

HAYDEN, JOSEPH PAGE, JR., company executive; b. Cin., Oct. 8, 1929; s. Joseph Page and Amy Dorothy (Weber) H.; m. Lois Taylor, Dec. 29, 1951; children: Joseph Page III, William Taylor, John Weber, Thomas Richard. BS in Bus, Miami U., Oxford, Ohio, 1951; student, U. Cin. Law Sch., 1952; DL (hon.), Miami U., 1986. With mobile home div. Midland-Guardian Co., Cin., 1952-61, v.p., 1954-60; pres., chief exec. officer, dir. Midland Co., Cin., 1961-80, chmn. bd., CEO, dir., 1980-98, chmn. exec. com., bd. dirs., 1998—. Former bd. mem. Firsat Corp. (now U.S. Bank); former Cin. mem. bus. adv. com. Miami U., Oxford, Ohio; former mem. pres.'s council Xavier U., Cin.; former trustee Miami U. Found. Mem. Bankers Club, Met. Club (Cin., Ohio), Comml. Club (Ohio), Boca Bay Pass Club (Fla.), Lemon Bay Golf (Fla.), Useppa Island Club (Fla.), Sigma Chi. Clubs: Queen City, Hyde Park Golf and Country, Boca Grande (Fla.). Office: 7000 Midland Blvd Amelia OH 45102-2608

HAYDEN, LINDA C. librarian, educator; b. Hazard, Ky. d. Walter H. and Nancy Catherine (Gott) Combs. BA, Coll. of William and Mary, 1966; MA in Teaching, Spalding U., 1976, postgrad., 1987; MSLS, U. Ky., 2002. Cert. elem. and early childhood edn. tchr., Ky., cert. public mgr., Governmental Svc. Ctr., Ky. Tchr. York County Pub. Schs., Poquoson, Va., 1966-67; asst. coord. children's svcs. Louisville Free Pub. Libr., 1969-74; tchr. Ursuline Spl. Edn. Ctr., Louisville, 1975-79; tchr., owner Multi-Handicapped Tutoring, Louisville, 1979-80; tchr. J-Town Presch., Inc., Jeffersontown, Ky., 1983-84; therapist Pine Tree Villa Nursing Home, Louisville, 1982-84; asst. prin., tchr. Brown's Lane Acad., Louisville, 1984-86; tchr. Jefferson County Pub. Schs., Louisville, 1986-94; access svcs. libr., reference adn interlibr. loan libr., acad. libr., asst. prof. Ky. State U., 1994—. Part-time pub. rels. and outreach asst. Ky. Commn. on Cmty. Volunteerism and Svc., 1998-99. Vol. tutor ESL with refugees, 1990-91. Mem.: ALA, Leadership Edn. Alumni Assn., Internat. Soc. for Tech. in Edn., Amnesty Internat., Pi Lambda Theta. Democrat. Avocations: music, sports, outdoors, cooking, computers.

HAYDEN, LISA C. interpreter, translator, language educator, writer; d. Thomas and Doris Hayden; m. Park Espenschade, July 0, 1999. BA, U. of Pa., 1981—85, MA, 1985—89. Comm. specialist Hannaford Bros. Co., Scarborough, Maine, 1990—92; resident dir. Am. Coun. of Teachers of Russian, Moscow, 1992—93; program dir. United Way Internat., Moscow, 1993—94; dir., moscow project office IREX, Internat. Partnerships Project, Moscow, 1995—96; dir. Inst. Internat. Edn., 1996—98; freelance writer Scarborough, Maine, 1998—; russian interpreter & translator Maine Med. Ctr., Portland, 1999—; russian tchr. & translator The Lang. Exch., Portland, 1999—. Cons. Eurasia Found., Christian Children's Fund, Moscow, 1994—95. Co-chair, treas. The Archangel Com., Portland, Maine, 1988—92; vol. Soup Kitchen, Children's Shelter, Moscow, 1993—94. Tchg. fellowship, U. of Pa., 1985—87. Avocations: gardening, cooking, travel, reading. Office: PO Box 6635 Scarborough ME 04070-6635 Personal E-mail: lisahesp@maine.rr.com.

HAYDEN, MICHAEL V. career officer, federal agency administrator; m. Jeanine Carrier; children: Margaret, Michael, Liam. BA in History, grad. Res. Officer Tng. Corps, Duquesne U., 1967, MA in Am. History, 1969; postgrad., Acad. Instr. Sch., Maxwell AFB, Ala., 1975, Squadron Officer Sch., 1976, Air Command and Staff Coll., 1978, Def. Intelligence Agy., Bolling AFB, D.C., 1980, Armed Forces Coll., Norfolk, Va., 1983, Air War Coll., Maxwell AFB, Ala., 1983. Commd. 2d lt. USAF, 1967, advanced through grades to maj. gen., 1996, analyst, briefer Hdqrs. Strategic Air Command, 1970-72, chief intelligence divsn. Hdqrs. 8th Air Force Andersen AFB, Guam, 1972-75; acad. instr., cadet comdt. Res. Officer Tng. Corps St. Michael's Coll., Winooski, Vt., 1975-79; chief intelligence 51st Tactical Fighter Wing USAF, Osan Air Base, South Korea, 1980-82; air attache U.S. Embassy, Sofia, Bulgaria, 1984-86; politico-mil. affairs officer Strategy Divsn. USAF, Washington, 1986-89; dir. for def. policy and arms control NSC, Washington, 1989-91; chief Sec.'s Staff Group Office Sec. Air Force USAF, Washington, 1991-93, dir. intelligence directorate Hdqrs. U.S. European Command Stuttgart, Germany, 1993-95, spl. asst. to comdr. Hdqrs. Air Intelligence Agy. Kelly AFB, Tex., 1995, comdr. Air Intelligence Agy., dir. Joint Command Control, 1996-97; dep. chief of staff UN Command, U.S. Forces Korea, 1997—99; dir. NSA/chief CSS USAF, Ft. Meade, Md., 1999—. Decorated Air Force Achievement medal, Def. Superior Svc. medal with oak leaf cluster, Legion of Merit, Bronze Star, Meritorious Svc. medal with two oak leaf clusters, Air Force Commendation medal. Office: USAF 9800 Savage Rd Fort George G Meade MD 20755-6000*

HAYDEN, PAUL ALLAN, speech pathology educator, consultant, researcher; b. Williston, N.D., Jan. 29, 1949; s. George L. Hayden and Ortense M. Bernier; m. Elaine Margret Stauder, Aug. 19, 1975; children: Dan, Jessica. BA in Speech Pathology summa cum laude, Moorhead (Minn.) State U., 1971, MS in Speech Pathology, 1972; PhD in Speech Pathology, Purdue U., 1975. Cert. speech pathologist. Prof. communicative disorders dept. U. Wis., River Falls, 1975—. Dept. chmn., 1988—; cons. area hosps. and nursing homes, Wis., 1980—. Faculty rep. Young Coll. Reps., River Falls, 1996—. Mem. Am. Speech Lang. and Hearing Assn. (presenter confs.), Wis. Speech Lang. and Hearing Assn., Phi Eta Sigma, Phi Kappa Phi. Office: Dept Communicative Disorders U Wis-River Falls River Falls WI 54022 Fax: (715) 425-3800. E-mail: paul.a.hayden@uwrf.edu.

HAYDEN, RAYMOND PAUL, lawyer; b. Rochester, N.Y., Jan. 15, 1939; s. John Joseph and Orpha (Lindsay) H.; m. Suzanne Saloy, Sept. 1, 1962; children: Thomas Gerard, Christopher Matthew. BS in Marine Transit, SUNY Maritime Coll., 1960; LLB, Syracuse U., 1963. Bar: N.Y. 1963, U.S. Ct. Appeals (2d cir.) 1963, U.S. Dist. Ct. (ea. and so. dists.) N.Y. 1964, U.S. Supreme Ct. 1967. Assoc. Haight Gardner Poor & Havens, N.Y.C., 1963-70; asst. gen. counsel Commonwealth Oil Co., N.Y.C., 1970-71; ptnr. Hill Rivkins & Hayden LLP, N.Y.C., 1971—. Mem. Coll. Coun., SUNY Maritime Coll., 1977-98, chmn., 1983-98; mem. adv. coun. Tulane U. Admiralty Law Inst. Served as lt. (j.g.) USNR, 1960-70. Mem. ABA (chmn. standing com. on admiralty and maritime law 1982-86), Maritime Law Assn. U.S. (chmn. com. on admissions 1974-82, exec. com. 1988-91, membership sec. 1996-98, 2nd v.p. 1998-2000, 1st v.p. 2000-02, pres. 2002—), India House Club (bd. dirs. 2002—), Brookville Country Club (N.Y.). Office: Hill Rivkins & Hayden LLP 45 Broadway New York NY 10006-3739 E-mail: rhayden@hillrivkins.com.

HAYDEN, VERN CLARENCE, financial planner; b. Endicott, N.Y., Jan. 24, 1937; s. Clarence Butch and Ruth (Storm) H. BA, Wheaton Coll., 1959; postgrad., NYU, 1960, U. Oreg., 1963, Am. U., 1966, U. So. Calif., 1967. Cert. Fin. Planner. Pvt. practice, San Rafael, Calif., 1970-83. Cons. Am. Express, Firemens Fund, San Rafael, 1979, 80; workshop speaker IBM, Pitney Bowes, Champion Internat., Texaco, 1980—. Author: Money Use It or Lose It, 1980, The Process of Financial Counseling, 1981, How to Build Using Seminars, 1988, The Hayden Investment Matrix, 1990, Getting An Investment Game Plan, 2002, Getting An Investment Game Plan...Creating It, Working It, Winning it, 2003; contbg. editor, weekly columnist TheStreet.com.; contbr. articles to profl. jours.; regular guest on CNBC's Money Club; contbg. editor, weekly columnist TheStreet.com. Bd. regents Coll. Fin. Planning, Denver; chmn. Nat. Endowment for Fin. Edn.; bd. dirs., bd. stds. for cert. fin. planners; chmn. legacy and planned giving So. Conn. Am. Cancer Soc. With USAF, 1962-68. Mem. Internat. Assn. Fin. Planning (pres. 1975, founding pres. Westchester/Rockland, N.Y. 1987, pres. 1989), Inst. Cert. Fin. Planners (bd. govs., bd. standards and practices), IBCFP. Republican. Avocations: handball, racquetball, reading, travel, writing. Office: 830 Post Rd E Westport CT 06880-5222 E-mail: Hayden4t9@aol.com.

HAYDEN, WILLIAM ROBERT, lawyer; b. Chgo., May 22, 1947; s. Robert George and Dorothy (Honan) H.; m. Carol Ann Brock, Aug. 12, 1978; 1 child, Nathaniel. BA, Kans. State U., 1969; JD with honors, George Washington U., 1972. Bar: D.C. 73, U.S. Dist. Ct. D.C. 75, U.S. Ct. Appeals (D.C. cir.) 75, Ariz. 78, U.S. Dist. Ct. Ariz. 78, U.S. Ct. Appeals (9th cir.) 79, U.S. Ct. Appeals (10th cir.) 97, U.S. Ct. Appeals (11th cir.) 01, Colo. (U.S. Dist. Ct.) 2002. Mem. gen. counsel's staff NLRB, Washington, 1973-75; assoc. O'Donoghue and O'Donoghue, Washington, 1975-78, Snell and Wilmer, Phoenix, 1978-82, ptnr., 1982—. Contbg. editor: Developing Labor Law, 1974, Employment Discrimination Law, 1989. Mem. ABA (labor and employment law sect.), Nat. Panel, Am. Arbitration Assn. (employment dispute resolution), Ariz. Bar Assn. (exec. com., past chmn. labor and employment law sect. 1984-89, employment civil jury instructions com.), Maricopa County Bar Assn., D.C. Bar Assn., Ariz. C. of C. (employee rels. subcom.). Avocations: tennis, softball, skiing. Office: Snell & Wilmer 1 Arizona Ctr Phoenix AZ 85004 E-mail: bhayden@swlaw.com.

HAYDOCK, WALTER JAMES, banker; b. Chgo., Dec. 14, 1947; s. Joseph Albert and Lillian V. (Adeszko) H.; m. Bonnie Jean Thompson, Aug. 22, 1970; children: Nicole Lynn, Matthew Michael. Student, Harvard Bus. Coll., 1969-71, Daily Coll., 1971-73; BS in Acctg., DePaul U., 1976. Computer operator, jr. programmer Pepper Constrn. Co., Chgo., 1972-73; input analyst Continental Bank, Chgo., 1973-76, data control supr., 1976-79, corp. fixed asset adminstr., 1979-83, properties sys. analyst, 1983-87, props. sr. sys. supr., 1987-91; unit chief conversions Fed. Deposit Ins. Corp., Chgo., 1992-93, info. security specialist, 1993-96; info. security officer U. Ill., Chgo., 1996—2001, info. sys. admin., 2001—. Pres. Wal-Bon., Inc.; distbr. Lic. Disney Character Mdse. Mem. Southwest Suburban Bd. Realtors. Home: 13525 Marissa Ct Homer Glen IL 60449 Office: 914 S Wood St M/C 807 Chicago IL 60612-7338 E-mail: whaydock@uic.edu.

HAYDON, JOSEPH A. (JODIE), state representative; b. Bardstown, Ky., Mar. 1, 1945; m. Carolyn Haydon; children: Allison, Amy. BA, Bellarmine Univ., 1967. State Rep. House of Rep., Dist. 50, Ky., 1996—; v.p. Nally and Hayden LLC, 1970—; contractor. Chair Nazareth Village Bd., 1999—2002; mem. Wilson and Muir Bank Bd., 1988—2002, Bardstown City Council, 1988—92; Chair Flaget Meml. Hosp. Bd., 1982—88. Nat. Guard, 1968—69, Vietnam. Mem.: Fin. comm., St. Joseph Ch., Planning and Zoning Comm., Pine Mt. Settlement Sch. (past chair 1990), Nelson County Planning Comm., Nelson County Chamber of Commerce, Nelson County Chamber of Commerce, Nelson County Bellarmine Coll. Alumni (pres.), Knights of Columbus Coun. 1290 (past Grand Knight 1995), Kentuckians for Better Transport. Bd., Bellarmine Univ. Alumni, (past pres. 1997), Bardstown Transport. Planning Comm., Bardstown Chamber of Commerce, Optimist Club. Democrat. Catholic. Office: Capitol Capitol Annex Rm 457B Frankfort KY 40601 also: District 106 Hillcrest Barstown KY 40004*

HAYDUK, JOHN MATTHEW, English and journalism educator; b. Gary, Ind., Oct. 2, 1953; s. Michael and Dorothy Hayduk; m. Patricia Ann Cook, Nov. 5, 1977. BS in Edn., Ind. U., Gary, 1988, MS in Edn., 1996. Lic. tchr., Ind. Electrician U.S. Steel, Gary, 1974-85; tchr. Sch. City East Chgo., Ind., 1989-91, Duneland Sch. Corp., Chesterton, Ind., 1991—. Named Most Influential Tchr., 5% Club, 1993, 95, 96, 98, 99, 2002, 03. Mem. NEA, Ind. State Tchrs. Assn., Duneland Tchrs. Assn., Ind. U. Alumni Assn., Ind. U. N.W. Alumni Assn., Columbia Scholastic Press Advisers Assn., Nat. Parks Conservation Assn., Kappa Delta Pi. Roman Catholic. Avocations: classic automobiles, reading, astronomy, music. Home: 2009 Chamblee Dr Valparaiso IN 46383-3801 Office: Chesterton HS 2125 S 11th St Chesterton IN 46304-8934 E-mail: john.hayduk@duneland.k12.in.us.

HAYEK, CAROLYN JEAN, retired judge; b. Portland, Oreg., Aug. 17, 1948; d. Robert A. and Marion L. (DeKoning) H.; m. Steven M. Rosen, July 21, 1974; children: Jonathan David, Laura Elizabeth. BA in Psychology, Carleton Coll., 1970; JD, U. Chgo., 1973; webmaster cert., Lake Washington Tech. Coll., 2000. Bar: Wash. 1973. Assoc. Jones, Grey & Bayley, Seattle, 1973-77; pvt. practice Federal Way, Wash., 1977-82; judge Federal Way Dist. Ct., 1982-95; ret., 1995. Task force Alternatives for Wash., 1973-75; mem. Wash. State Ecol. Commn., 1975-77; columnist Tacoma News Tribune Hometown Sect., 1995-96; bus. law instr. Lake Washington Tech. Coll., 2000-2001; exec. dir. People's Meml. Assn., Seattle, 2002—. Bd. dirs. 1st Unitarian Ch., Seattle, 1986-89, vice-chair 1987-88, pres. 1988-89; ch. adminstr. Northlake Unitarian Universalist Ch.; treas. Eastshore Unitarian Universalist Ch. Women's Perspective, 2001-2002; den leader Mt. Rainier coun. Boy Scouts Am., 1987-88, scouting coord., 1988-89; bd. dirs. Twin Lakes Elem. Sch. PTA; v.p. Friends of the Libr. Kirkland, 2000—; mem. Kirkland Planning Commn., 2002—. Recipient Women Helping Women award Federal Way Soroptimist, 1991, Martin Luther King Day Humanitarian award King County, 1993, Recognition cert. City of Federal Way Diversity Commn., 1995. Mem. AAUW (co-pres. Kirkland-Redmond br. 1999-2000, co-v.p. Lake Washington br. 2001-2003, pres. Federal Way br. 1978-80, 90-92, chair state level cmf. com. 1986-87, diversity com. 1991-98, state bd. mem. 1995-97, dir. ESL project), ABA, Wash. Women Lawyers, Wash. State Bar Assn., King County Dist. Ct. Judges Assn. (treas., exec. com. 1990-93, com. chair, chair and rules com. 1990-94), Elected Wash. Women (dir. 1983-87), Nat. Assn. Women Judges (nat. bd. dirs., dist. bd. dirs. 1984-86, chmn. rules com. 1988-89, chmn. bylaws com. 1990-91), Fed. Way Women's Network (bd. dirs. 1984-91, 95-97, pres. 1985, program co-chair 1989-91, co-editor newsletter), Greater Fed. Way C. of C. (dir. 1978-82, sec. 1980-81, v.p. 1981-82), Sunrise Rotary (com. svc. chair, bd. dirs., membership com., Federal Way chpt. 1991-96, youth exch. officer 1994-95), Washington Women United (bd. dirs. 1995-97), Unitarian Universalist Women's Assn. (chair bylaws com. 1996), Eliot Inst. (bd. dirs. 1996-2000, vice-chair 1998-99, bd. chair 1999-2000, webmaster 1999-2002), Plaza on State Owners Assn. (bd. dirs. 1997-2000, pres. 1997-99, sec. 1999-2000, webmaster 2000—). E-mail: cjh@kirklandplaza.com.

HAYEK, JOHN WILLIAM, lawyer; b. Iowa City, Jan. 25, 1941; s. Will J. and Marjorie B. (Kurtz) H.; m. Patricia M. Hess, Dec. 21, 1968; children: Grace, Matthew, Andrew. BA, Harvard U., 1963, JD, 1966. Bar: Iowa 1966, U.S. Dist. Ct. (so. dist.) Iowa 1967, U.S. Dist. Ct. (no. dist.) Iowa 1968, U.S. Ct. Appeals (8th cir.) 1973. Ptnr. Hayek, Hayek, Brown & Moreland, L.L.P., Iowa City, 1966—. 1st asst. county atty. Johnson County, Iowa City, 1967-70; spl. counsel City of Iowa City, 1970-90, city atty., 1974-81; mem. 6th Jud. Dist. Nominating Commn., 1978-83. Fellow Iowa Acad. Trial Lawyers; mem. Iowa Bar Assn., Johnson County Bar Assn. (pres. 1982-83), Assn. Trial Lawyers Iowa, Nat. Bd. Trial Advocacy, Iowa Def. Counsel Assn. Mason Ladd Inn of Ct. (emeritus master of the bench). Unitarian Universalist. Home: 531 Kimball Rd Iowa City IA 52245-5830 Office: Hayek Hayek Brown & Moreland LLP 120 1/2 E Washington St Iowa City IA 52240-3924

HAYEK, SALMA, actress; b. Coatzacoalcos, Veracruz, Mexico, Sept. 2, 1968; d. Sami Hayek Domingues and Diana H. Television work includes: Un Nuevo amanecer, 1988, Teresa, 1989, The Sinbad Show, 1993, Roadracers, 1994, El Vuelo del aguila, 1996, The Hunchback, 1997, In the Time of the Butterflies (also exec. prod.), 2001; Television appearances: Dream On, 1992, Nurses, 1992, Action, 1999. Films include Mi Vida Loca, 1993, Four Rooms, 1995, Desperado, 1995, Fair Game, 1995, From Dusk Til Dawn, 1996, Fled, 1996, Fools Rush In, 1997, Follow Me Home, 1997, Breaking Up, 1997, Sister Diastole, 1997, The Velocity of Gary, 1998, The Faculty, 1998, 54, 1998, Dogma, 1999, Wild Wild West, 1999, No One Writes to the Colonel, 1999, Shiny New Enemies, 2000, Frida, 2000, Timecode, 2000, Chain of Fools, 2000, Living It Up, 2000, Traffic, 2000, Hotel, 2001, Frida (also prod.), 2002, Spy Kids 3-D: Game Over, 2003, Once Upon a Time in Mexico, 2003; dir, exec. prod.: The Maldonado Miracle, 2003.

HAYERS, PAUL HUGH, lawyer; b. Wichita Falls, Tex., Dec. 2, 1942; s. Carl Edward and Emogene (Wagoner) H.; m. Jannis Baker, Aug. 16, 1964; children: Stephanie Laura, Christopher Mark. BBA, So. Meth. U., 1964; JD, Georgetown U., 1967. Bar: Tex. 1967, U.S. Dist. Ct. (no. dist.) Tex. 1968, U.S. Ct. Appeals (5th cir.) 1975, U.S. Ct. Appeals (11th cir.) 1981. Ptnr. McKelvey & Hayers, Electra, Tex., 1967-84, mng. owner, 1984—. Commr. City of Electra, 1972-75, 80-86, mayor pro-tem, 1974, 75, 85, city atty., 1976-80, 86—; chmn. Wichita County Tax Appraisal Dist., Wichita Falls, Tex., 1980-87; bd. dirs. Tex. Assn. Appraisal Dists., 1985-86; chmn. Wichita County Child Welfare Bd., 1979-84. Mem. State Bar Tex., Wichita County Bar Assn., Electra C. of C., Rotary (pres. 1984), Lions (pres. 1971-72). Democrat. Methodist. Home: PO Box 391 Electra TX 76360-0391

HAYES, ALICE BOURKE, academic administrator, biologist, educator; b. Chgo., Dec. 31, 1937; d. William Joseph and Mary Alice (Cawley) Bourke; m. John J. Hayes, Sept. 2, 1961 (dec. July 1981). BS, Mundelein Coll., Chgo., 1959; MS, U. Ill., 1960; PhD, Northwestern U., 1972; DSc (honoris causa), Loyola U., Chgo., 1994; HHD (honoris causa), Fontbonne Coll., 1994; LHD (honoris causa), Mount St. Mary Coll., 1998; DSc (hon.), St. Louis U., 2002. Rschr. Mcpl. Tb San., Chgo., 1960-62; faculty Loyola U., Chgo., 1962-87, chmn. dept., 1968-77, dean natural scis. div., 1977-80, assoc. acad. v.p., 1980-87, v.p. acad. affairs, 1987-89; provost, exec. v.p. St. Louis U., 1989-95; pres. U. San Diego, 1995—2003, pres. emerita, 2003—. Mem. space biology program NASA, 1980—86; mem. adv. panel NSF, 1977—81, Parmly Hearing Inst., 1986—89; del. Bot. Del. to South Africa, 1984, to People's Republic of China, 1988, to USSR, 1990; reviewer Coll. Bd. and Mellon Found. Nat. Hispanic Scholar Awards, 1985—86; bd. dirs. Pulitzer Pub. Co., Loyola U. Chgo., San Diego Found., Jack-in-the-Box, ConAgra. Co-author books; contbr. articles to profl. publs. Campaign mem. Mental Health Assn. Ill., Chgo., 1973-89; trustee Chgo.-No. Ill. divsn. Nat. Multiple Sclerosis Soc., 1981-89, bd. dirs., 1980-88, com. chmn., sec. to bd. dirs., vice chmn. bd. dirs.; trustee Regina Dominican Acad., 1984-89, Civitas Dei Found., 1987-92, Rockhurst Coll., Loyola U., Chgo., San Diego Found.; trustee St. Ignatius Coll. Prep. Sch., bd. dirs., 1984-89, sec., vice chmn.; bd. dirs. Urban League Met. St. Louis, St. Louis Sci. Ctr., 1991-95, Cath. Charities St. Louis, 1992-95, St. Louis County Hist. Soc., 1992-95, Cath. Charities San Diego, 1996—, San Diego Hist. Soc., 1996—. Old Globe Theater, 1996—, also trustee. Named to Teachers' Hall of Fame Blue Key Soc.; fellow in botany U. Ill., 1959-60; fellow in botany NSF, 1969-71; grantee Am. Orchid Soc., 1967; grantee HEW, 1969, 76; grantee NSF, 1975; grantee NASA, 1980-85. Mem. AAAS, AAUP (corp. rep. 1980-85), Am. Assn. for Higher Edn., Am. Assn. Univ. Adminstrs. (mem. program com. nat meeting 1988), Am. Soc. Gravitational and Space Biology, Assn. Midwest Coll. Biology Teachers, Am. Soc. Plant Physiology, Bot. Soc. Am., Am. Inst. Biol. Scis. Acad., Chgo. Network, Soc. Ill. Microbiologists (edn. com. 1969-70, Pasteur award com. 1975, pub. rels. com. 1974, chair speakers' bur. 1974-79), Chgo. Assn. Tech. Socs. (acad. liaison 1982-85, awards com. 1984-89), Am. Coun. on Edn. (corp. rep. higher edn. panel), Ctr. Rsch. Librs. (nominating com. 1986), North Ctrl. Assn. Colls. and Schs. (cons., evaluator Commn. on Higher Edn. 1984-95, commr.-at-large 1998-94), Mo. Women's Forum Club, Sigma Xi, Delta Sigma Rho, Sigma Delta Epsilon, Phi Beta Kappa, Alpha Sigma Nu. Roman Catholic. Home: 6801 N Loron Chicago IL 60646

HAYES, ALLENE VALERIE FARMER, government executive; b. Sept. 23, 1958; d. Thomas Jonathan and Allena V. (Joyner) Farmer; m. Thomas Gary Hayes; children: Tommia Chanel, Alle Victoria. Student, Richmond Coll., London, 1980; BA, Clark U., 1980; cert., U. Oxford, England, 1981; MLS, U. Md., 1986. Libr. asst. NUS Corp., Gaithersburg, Md., 1981-82; cataloger Libr. of Congress, Washington, 1982-84, copyright specialist, 1984-85; congl. fellow Ho. of Reps. Com. on D.C., Washington, 1985—. English tutor, writer Natural Motion, Washington, 1983-84; intern, archivist Howard U., Washington, 1985; intern Libr. Congress Intern Program, 1991-92. Compiler: Single Mother's Resource Directory, 1984; compiler, editor: Policy Research, 1985; author booklet: D.C. Statehood Issue, 1986. Mem. U. Md. Coll. Park Black Women's Coun., 1984; vol. Congl. Black Caucus Found., Washington, 1985 (fellow 1985). Recipient Fgn. Study award Am. Inst. for Fgn. Study, 1981. Mem. NAACP, ALA, Libr. of Congress Profls. Assn., Daniel A.P. Murray Afro-Am. Culture Assn. of Libr. of Congress (mem. exec. bd., newsletter editor, pres. 1994—), D.A.P. Murray African Am. Culture Assn. (pres. 1994-96), Delta Sigma Theta (tutor 1986). Avocations: travel, writing, dance, drama, tennis. Home: 2405 17th St NE Washington DC 20018-2051 Office: Libr of Congress 101 Independence Ave SE Washington DC 20540-0002

HAYES, ANDREW WALLACE, II, consumer products company executive; b. Corning, Ark., Aug. 21, 1939; s. Andrew Wallace and Helen (Latimer) H.; m. Sandra Smith, Dec. 28, 1963; children: Andrew Wallace III, Helen Cathleen, Benjamin Bailey. AB, Emory U., 1961; MS, Auburn U., 1964, PhD, 1967. Diplomate Am. Bd. Toxicology, Am. Bd. Forensic Medicine, Am. Bd. Forensic Examiners; cert. nutrition specialist. NIH postdoctoral fellow, rsch. assoc. div. toxicology Vanderbilt U. Sch. Med., Nashville, 1966-68; asst. prof. dept. microbiology U. Ala., Tuscaloosa, 1968-71, assoc. prof. dept. microbiology, 1971-75, prof. depts. microbiology and biochemistry, 1975; assoc. prof. dept. pharmacology and toxicology U. Miss. Med. Ctr., Jackson, 1975-76, prof. dept. pharmacology and toxicology, 1976-80, program dir. NIEHS tng. program in environ. toxicology, 1977-80; dir. toxicology rsch. Rohm and Haas Co., Spring House, Pa., 1980-84, dir. regulatory affairs, agrl. chemicals (worldwide) Phila., 1984; corp. toxicologist RJR Nabisco Inc., Winston-Salem, N.C., 1984; corp. toxicologist, dir. biochem. and biobehavioral rsch., Bowman Gray Tech. Ctr. R.J. Reynolds Tobacco Co., Winston-Salem, N.C., 1984-86, corp. toxicologist, group dir. biochem. and biobehavioral rsch., 1986-87, corp. toxicologist, v.p. biochem. and biobehavioral rsch., 1987-92; prof. Bowman Gray Sch. Medicine Wake Forest U., Winston-Salem, 1992; v.p. corp. product integrity The Gillette Co., Boston, 1993—2002; IUTOX faculty risk assessment summer sch., 1990, 92, 94, 96, 98, 2000, 02; prin. Gradient Corp., Cambridge, Mass., 2002—03. Vis. sr. scientist biochemistry dept. Cen. Vet. Lab., New Haw, Weybridge, Surrey; Eng., 1977; vis. scientist Harvard U. Sch. Pub. Health, Boston, 2002—; disting. lectr. U. Calif., 1979; vis. prof. dept. vet. pub. health Tex. A&M U., 1979-91; rsch. prof. dept. physiology and biophysics Sch. Dentistry, Temple U., 1981-84, Phila. Coll. Pharmacy and Sci., 1982-84, dept. medicine and toxicology program Duke U., 1986 2001, dept. pharmacology and toxicology Med. Coll. Va., 1987—, Sch. Vet. Med., Va. Poly. Inst., 1988—, Sch. Pub. Health U. Mass, Amherst, 1994—; dept. pharmacology and toxicology Sch. Medicine, U. Louisville, 1997—; mem. faculty Wayne State U., 1987; collaborator Interlab. Collaborative Study for Aflatoxin B1, FDA, 1977, Aflatoxin Check Sample Survey, Internat. Agy. Rsch. on Cancer, 1978; mem. Target Organ Toxicity Conf. Steering Com., 1978-88, Panel on Equivalent Safety Concept of Maritime Hazardous Materials, Nat. Materials Adv. Bd., NAS, 1979 82, Safe Drinking Water Com., Bd. Toxicology and Environ. Health Hazards, NAS, 1979-81, Environ. Health Scis. Rev. Com. NIEHS, 1981-85, sci. program com. Internat. Congress Toxicology, 1982-83, Testing Task Group, CMA, 1981-84, Chem. Systems Lab. Toxin Def. Group Rev. Panel, U.S. Army, 1982, TDB/CIS User Assessment Panel Life Scis. Rsch. Office, FASEB, Bethesda, Md., 1982; alt. del. Internat. Union Toxicology, 1982-83; advisor U.S. Army Med. Command, 1982-84; del. Internat. Union Toxicology, 1984-86; cons. Walter Reed Army Inst. Rsch., 1984-86; mem. selection com. Immunotoxicology Found., 1986, Commn. on Comm., Internat. Union Toxicology, 1986-89, program com. Toxicology Forum, 1986-87, toxicology adv. bd. Raven Press, N.Y.C., 1982-96; mem. external adv. bd. La. Inst. Toxicology, 1996—; bd. dirs. Toxicology Edn. Found., 1997-2001, pres., 1998-2000; mem. sci. adv. bd. Inst. In Vitro Scis., 1997-2002; mem. commn. strategic devel. INTOX, 1997; bd. dirs. Ctrs. for Alternatives to Animal Testing, 1995—. Author: Mycotoxin Teratogenicity, 1981; editor: Toxicology of the Eye, Ear and Other Special Senses, 1985, Extrapolation of Dosimetric Relationships for Inhaled Particles and Gases, 1989, Prinicples and Methods of Toxicology, 4th edit., 2001, Human and Experimental Toxicology, 1993—, Jour. Toxicology, Cutaneous and Ocular Toxicology, 2001—; co-author: Loomis's Essentials of Toxicology, 4th edit., 1996; co-editor: Target Organ Toxicity Series, 1989—; founding editor Comments of Toxicology, 1986—; assoc. editor Regulatory Toxicology and Pharmacology, 1986—, Toxicology and Applied Pharmacology, 1980, editor, 1981-86, mem. editl. bd., 1978-80; mem. editl. bd. Archives Environ. Contamination and Toxicology, 1987-2000, Environ. Toxin Series, 1987-95, Toxicology, 1978-83, Jour. Toxicology and Environ. Health, 1979—, Food and Chem. Toxicology, 1987—; mem. editl. coun. Toxicon, 1980-90; contbr. articles to profl. jours., chpts. to books. Mem. adv. coun. Auburn U., 1987—97; mem. dept. environ. health Harvard Sch. Pub. Health, 1997—; mem. nat. coun. Fla. Coll., 1980—97; bd. dirs. Join Hands--The Health and Safety Alliance, 1995—2001; trustee Am. Assn. for Accreditation of Lab. Animal Care, Chgo., 1984—89. Named Exec. of Yr. Winston-Salem chpt. Profl. Secs. Internat., 1989-90; recipient cert. of merit, EPA, 1981, Rsch. Career Devel. award NIH, 1973-78. Fellow Acad. Toxicological Scis. (bd. dirs. 1993-2001), Inst. Biology; mem. Inst. Toxicology (mem. external adv. bd. 1996—); mem. Soc. Toxicology (co-chmn. tech. com. 1978, chmn. 1978-79, pres. Mid-Atlantic chpt. 1983-84, v.p. mech. sect., 1981-82, 82-83, animals in rsch. com. 1996-99, chmn. 1998-99, bd. dirs. toxicology edn. found. 1996—, pres. 1998-2000), The Cosmetic, Toiletry, and Fragrance Assn. (mem. sci. adv. exec. com. 1999-2002), Am. Soc. Pharmacology and Exptl. Therapeutics (chmn. com. on environ. pharmacology 1981-82, coun. sect. toxicology), Am. Chem. Soc. (com. on chemistry and pub. affairs task force on TSCA Interagy. Testing Com.'s Preliminary List of Chem. Substances, 1977-80), Am. Soc. for Nutritional Scis., Am. Soc. for Microbiology (environ. microbiology com. 1975-76), Internat. Union Pharmacology (sect. on toxicology), Internat. Soc. Regulatory Toxicology and Pharmacology, Sigma Xi. Mem. Ch. of Christ. Avocation: fishing. Office: Harvard Sch Public Health Harvard Univ Boston MA 02142 E-mail: awallacehayes@comcast.net.

HAYES, ANN CARSON, computer services executive; b. Hamlin, Tex., Apr. 25, 1941; d. Fred Elbert and Nona Faye (Riddle) Carson; m. James Russell Brown, May 7, 1959 (div. July 1973); children: James Allen, Daniel Russell, Robert Anthony, Debra Faye Brown; m. Robert Lee Hayes, Nov. 15, 1975. AAS, Howard Coll., Tex., 1972; student, Regents Coll., N.Y.C., 1986. Lic. ins. agt., Nat. Assn. for Self-Employed. Freelance artist, Big Spring, Tex., 1956-76; real estate agt. Century 21, Littleton, Colo., 1976-78, Huntsville, Ala., 1978-79; art dir. Hayes and Co., Splendora, Tex., 1979—; CEO Hayes Enterprises, New Caney, Tex., 2000—. Executor Hayes Tax Svc., New Caney, 1992. Mem. NAFE. Democrat. Episcopalian. Avocations: sculpting, glass etching. Home and Office: 20152 Split Oak Dr New Caney TX 77357-3565

HAYES, ARTHUR HULL, JR., physician, clinical pharmacology educator, medical school dean, business executive, consultant; b. Highland Park, Mich., July 18, 1933; s. Arthur Hull and Florence Margaret (Gruber) Hayes; m. Barbara Anne Carey, July 16, 1960; children: Arthur Hull III, Elizabeth, Katherine. AB magna cum laude, U. Santa Clara, 1955, D (hon.) in Pub. Svc., 1980; MA, Oxford U., 1957; postgrad., Georgetown U., 1957—60; MD, Cornell U., 1964; LLD (hon.), St. John's U., 1983; DSc (hon.), N.Y. Med. Coll., 1983. Diplomate Am. Bd. Clin. Pharmacology. Intern in medicine N.Y. Hosp., N.Y.C., 1964—65, resident in cardiology, 1967—68; assoc. prof. pharmacology, asst. prof. medicine, assoc. dean Cornell U. Med. Coll., N.Y.C., 1968—72; prof. pharmacology and medicine, chief div. clin. pharmacology Pa. State Coll. Medicine, Hershey (Pa.) Med. Center, 1972—81; U.S. commr. food and drugs, asst. surgeon gen. USPHS, Rockville, Md., 1981—83; provost, dean N.Y. Med. Coll., 1983—86, prof. medicine, pharmacology and community and preventive medicine, 1983—99; pres., CEO EM Pharms., Inc., Hawthorne, NY, 1986—91; pres. MediSci. Assocs., Inc., New Rochelle, NY, 1991—. Trustee U.S. Pharmacopeial Conv., 1980—81, 1985—, pres., 1985—90; bd. dirs. Cadbury-Schweppes, Stamford, Conn., Synergen, Inc., Denver, Myriad Genetics, Inc., Salt Lake City, Food and Drug Law Inst., Washington; chmn. Coun. Family Health, N.Y.C., Medic Alert Found., Inc., Turlock, Calif., 1991—93; prin. Ctr. Excellence in Govt. Contbr. articles to profl. jours.; editl. bd. Rational Drug Therapy, Clin. Pharmacology and Therapeutics, Med. Advt. News, Jour. Clin. Pharmacology, Today's Therapeutic Trends, Pharmaceutical Medicine, Prescriber's Newsletter, World Pharm. Report. Permanent deacon Roman Cath. Ch.; bd. dirs. Peace Found., N.Y.C.; bd. regents Santa Clara (Calif.) U.; mem. bd. overseers L.I. U. Coll. Pharmacy. Capt. med. corps U.S. Army, 1965—67. Decorated Knight of Holy Sepulchre (comdr.); recipient Foch medal, Govt. France, 1953, Nobili medal, U. Santa Clara, 1955, Good Physician award, Cornell Med. Coll., 1964, Faculty Devel. award, Pharm. Mfrs. Assn. Found., 1968, Bronze medallion seal award, DHHS, 1982, Disting. Pub. Svc. award, 1983, Founders Day award, Lebanon Valley Coll., 1983, Henry Elliot Disting. Svc. Clin. Pharmacology award; fellow Danforth, 1955, NIH, 1960—62; scholar Rhodes, 1955. Fellow: ACP, Am. Acad. Pharm. Physicians, Acad. Pharm. Scis., Am. Coll. Chest Physicians, Royal Soc. Medicine, N.Y. Acad. Medicine, Am. Soc. Clin. Pharmacology and Therapy (Henry Elliot Disting. Svc. Clin. Pharacology award 1993), Am. Coll. Cardiology, Coll. Physicians Phila.; mem.: AMA, Assn. Am. Med. Colls. (coun. of deans., con. acad. socs.), Med. Soc. State of N.Y., Harvey Soc., N.Y. Acad. Scis., Am. Pharm. Assn. (hon.), Am. Fedn. Clin. Rsch., Am. Soc. Clin. Pharmacology and Therapeutics (pres. 1980—81), Am. Soc. Pharmacology and Exptl. Therapeutics, Knights of Malta, KC, Alpha Omega Alpha, Sigma Xi, Phi Beta Kappa, Alpha Omega Alpha. Roman Catholic. Office: MediScience Associates 71 Elk Ave New Rochelle NY 10804-4212

HAYES, BERNARD M. military officer, researcher; s. Robert and Hallie Hayes. BSc, NC Agrl. and Tech. State U., 1979—84. Officer US Army, Fayetteville, NC, 1984—88, maj., us army reserves Washington, 1984—, officer Little Rock, 1988—92, 1992—94, 1994—96; rsch. analyst Northrop Grumman, Falls Ch., Va., 1996—. Co-founder The Greater Manassas Mentoring Network, Va., 1997—2000; mem. Christians Involved Together With Youth, Manassas, Va., 1995—2001; pres. Outreach Com. First AME Ch., Manassas, Va., 1999—2003; nominating com. chair Prince William County ARC, Manassas, Va., 1996—2000. Decorated Meritorious Svc. medal US Army, Master Parachutist Badge. Mem.: Women in Def. African Meth. Episcopal. Avocations: photography, running. Personal E-mail: bhayes5786@aol.com.

HAYES, BONAVENTURE FRANCIS, priest; b. Buffalo, Nov. 8, 1941; s. Carl Milford and Louise Christine (Kolb) H. BA in Philosophy, St. Bonaventure U., 1964; MA in Semitics, Licentiate in Sacred Theology, Cath. U. Am., 1972; MLS, SUNY, Buffalo, 1988. Joined Franciscan Order, Roman Cath. Ch., 1961, ordained priest, 1967. Lectr. Christ The King Sem., Allegany, N.Y., 1968-70, from asst. prof. to assoc. prof., libr. dir. East Aurora, N.Y., 1976—; archivist Holy Name Province, Franciscan Order, N.Y.C., 1988—. Various adv. bds. 1982—. Contbr. articles to profl. jours. Mem. Am. Theol. Libr. Assn., Western N.Y. Cath. Libr. Assn. (pres. 1989-91), Cath. Bibl. Assn., Soc. Bibl. Lit., Cath. Libr. Assn. (nat. exec. bd. 1991-97, v.p., 1997-99, pres. 1999-2001), Beta Phi Mu. Republican. Home and Office: Christ the King Sem Libr 711 Knox Rd East Aurora NY 14052-9444 E-mail: bhayes@cks.edu.

HAYES, BRENDA SUE NELSON, artist; b. Rockford, Ill., May 26, 1941; d. Reuben Hartvick and Mary Jane (Pinkston) Nelson; m. John Michael Hayes, Jan. 26, 1964; 1 child, Amy Anne. BFA in Graphic Design, U. Ill., 1964. Exec. officer JMH Corp., Indpls., 1971—. Exhibited at Art Source, Bethesda, Md., The Corp. Collection, Kansas City, Mo., The Hang Up Gallery, Sarasota, Fla., Dean Johnson Gallery, Indpls., Ind., Art Phase I, Chgo., JMH Gallery, Indpls., Swan Coach House Gallery, Atlanta, Arnot Art Mus., Elmira, N.Y., Indpls. Mus. Art, Pindar Gallery, Soho, N.Y., Franklin (Ind.) Coll.; represented in permanent collections at Holy Family Hosp., Des Plaines, Ill., Lilly Endowment, Dow Venture Ctr. Internat. Hdqs., Wishard Hosp., Indpls., Deloitte Touche, Inc., USA Group, Indpls., Am. Trans. Airlines, Indpls., Indpls. Art Ctr., IBM, AT&T, U.S. Sprint, NWS Corp., Chgo., Meth. Hosp., Indpls., Eli Lilly Corp., Indpls. and Chgo., Hewlett-Packard, Trammell Crow, Dow Consumer Products, Melvin Simon & Assocs., Dow Elanco Corp. Hdqs., Ikon Inc., Support Net, Bank One, All Steel, L.A., Verizon/Celular One, NBD Bank Processing Ctr. Lobby, Indpls., Mckinney Processing Bank Ctr., Indpls., Cellular One Regional Offices, Nat. City Plaza, Riley Children's Hosp., Indpls., 250 pvt. collections. Bd. dirs. Contemporary Art Soc. for Indpls. Mus. Art, 1993—, sec., 1992-94; charter mem. Nat. Mus. Women in Arts, Habitat for Humanity, Wall of Tolerence, Ctr. for Tolerance, Birmingham, Ala. Lydia Bates scholar U. Ill., 1961-63, Ill. Found. of Study scholar, 1963-64, resident schoar, 1960-64; recipient Panhellenic award for Study U. Ill., 1963-64, Gallery Exhbn. awards. Mem.: Nat. Mus. Women in the Arts (charter), Gamma Alpha Chi (Outstanding Woman in Journalism 1964). Home: 157 E 71st St Indianapolis IN 46220-1011 Studio: 921 E 66th St Indianapolis IN 46220-1137

HAYES, BURGAIN GARFIELD, lawyer; b. Ft. Ord, Calif., May 20, 1948; children: Christine, Katherine, Burgain IV, Mary Margaret. BA, Am. U. Sch. Internat. Studies, 1969; JD, U. Tex., 1975. Bar: Tex. 1975, U.S. Dist. Ct. (we. dist.) Tex. 1976, U.S. Ct. Appeals (5th cir.) 1981, U.S. Dist. Ct. (so. dist.) Tex. 1983, U.S. Dist. Ct. (ea. dist.) Tex. 1984, U.S. Dist. Ct. (no. dist.) Tex. 1985, U.S. Dist. Ct. (we. dist.) Okla. 1986, U.S. Dist. Ct. (no. dist.) Okla. 1986, U.S. Ct. Appeals (10th cir.) 1986, U.S. Supreme Ct. 1985. Trial prosecutor, chief civil sect. County Atty.'s Office, Austin, Tex., 1974-77; assoc. Clark, Thomas, Winters and Shapiro, Austin, 1977-82; ptnr. Clark, Thomas & Winters, Austin, 1982—. Editor: Tex. Internat. Law Jour., 1973-74. Served to 1st lt. U.S. Army, 1969-72. Mem. ABA (product liability adv. coun.), Fed. Bar Assn., Internat. Assn. Def. Counsel, Tex. State Bar Assn., Tex. Assn. Def. Counsel, Def. Rsch. Inst. Avocations: fishing, sports. Home: 2802 Deercreek Cir Austin TX 78703 Office: Clark Thomas & Winters 700 Lavaca St Austin TX 78701-3109 E-mail: bgh@ctw.com.

HAYES, BYRON JACKSON, JR., retired lawyer; b. L.A., July 9, 1934; s. Byron Jackson and Caroline Violet (Scott) H.; m. DeAnne Saliba, June 30, 1962; children: Kenneth Byron, Patricia DeAnne. Student, Pomona Coll., 1952-56; BA magna cum laude, Harvard U., LLB cum laude, 1959. Bar: Calif. 1960, U.S. Supreme Ct. 1963. Assoc. McCutchen, Black, Verleger & Shea, L.A., 1960-68, ptnr., 1968-89, Baker & Hostetler, 1990-97; ret., 1998. Trustee L.A. Urban Found., 1996—, CFO, 1998-2000, v.p., CFO, 2000—; trustee L.A. Ch. Ext. Soc. United Meth. Ch., 1967-77, pres., 1974-77, chancellor ann. conf. Pacific and S.W., 1979-86, dir. 1010 devel. corp., 1993—, v.p., 1995—; dir., pres. Pacific and S.W. United Meth. Found., 1978-84; dir., v.p. Padua Hills, Inc., 1999—; pres. Pamona Coll. Torchbearers, 2001-03. Named Layperson of yr. Pacific and S.W. Ann. Conf., United Meth. Ch., 1981; recipient Bishop's award, 1992, 2000. Mem. ABA, Am. Coll. Mortgage Attys. (regent 1984-93, pres. 1993-94), Calif. Bar Assn., Los Angeles County Bar Assn. (chmn. real property sect. 1982-83), Toluca Lake Property Owners Assn. (sec. 1990-94), Toluca Lake C. of C. (dir. 2001—), Pomona Coll. Alumni Assn. (pres. 1984-85), Pomona Coll. Torchbearers (pres. 2001-2003), Lakeside Golf Club.

HAYES, CAROL JEANNE, physical education educator; b. Cambridge, Mass., Apr. 18, 1942; d. Joseph Raymond and Gertrude Marie (Poitras) Boudreau; m. James Anthony Hayes, Oct. 24, 1964 (wid. Mar. 1978); children: James Anthony, Sharon Marie. BSEd, Boston State Coll., 1963, MEd, 1978, postgrad., 1980, Boston State Coll./Salem State, 1986—. Cert. CPR and first aid provider. Phys. edn./health instr. Wilmington (Mass.) Pub. Schs., 1963-65, 72—; part-time phys. edn. tchr. Concord (Mass.) Pub. Schs., 1968-69. Trainer Spl. Olympics participants, Wilmington, 1983-86; Little League mgr., LExington, 1974-76; bike safety com. Wilmington Police Dept., 1983-85; coord. After Sch. Tournaments, North Intermediate Sch., Wilmington, 1986-91; mem. adv. coun. Woburn St. Sch., 1992—, mem. crisis team, 1993—; peer mediation trainer, 1997—. Author: (curriculum) Elementary/Adaptive/Kindergarten, 1986. Badge counselor Boy Scouts Am., Lexington, 1978-84; vol./minister of comfort St. Brigid, 1978—, care eucharistic minister, 1993—; mem. Lexington Hist. Soc.; coord. Heart Week Activities for Intermediate Students, 1990—; others. Mem. AAHPERD, NEA, MAHPERD, MTA, Wilmington Tchrs. Assn. (exec. bd. 1972, bargaining team 1992, greivance com. 1991, pres. 1995—), Mass. Tchrs. Assn., Mass./AHPERD. Roman Catholic. Avocations: travel, reading, golf, swimming. Home: 9 Farmcrest Ave Lexington MA 02421-7112 Office: Wilmington Pub Schs Wilmington MA 01887

HAYES, CHARLES AUSTIN, economic development executive, consultant; b. Norlina, N.C., Nov. 4, 1946; s. Clarence Holt and Eleanor Mitchell (Spain) H.; m. Janet McDougald Perkinson, Mar. 7, 1998; 1 child, Elizabeth Warren; stepchildren: Grant Levi Perkinson, Anna Stewart Perkinson. BSBA, East Carolina U., 1972, MA in Edn., 1974. Cert. econ. developer. Instr. in bus. Isothermal Community Coll., Forest City, N.C., 1972-73, Wilson (N.C.) Tech. Coll., 1973-74; county mgr., indsl. developer Warren County, Warrenton, N.C., 1974-78; prin. Warrenton Ins. & Real Estate, 1978-86; pres. Moore County Econ. Devel. Corp., Pinehurst, N.C., 1986-96; pres., CEO Rsch. Triangle Regional Partnership, N.C., 1996—. Author: Managing Financial and Marketing Rural Economic Development. Mem. friends of children com. Bapt. Children's Home, 1986-96; ex officio dir. Pinehurst Area Conv. and Vis. Bur., 1988-96; chair Internat. Visitors Coun., Raleigh, NC, 2002. With U.S. Army, 1968-69, Vietnam. Recipient Disting. Svc. award, Warren County, N.C., 1977. Mem. Internat. Devel. Rsch. Coun., N.C. Indsl. Assn. (pres. 1978-79), Am. Econ. Devel. Coun., So. Indsl. Devel Coun., Sandhills C. of C. (ex officio), Pinehurst Country Club, Rotary (Sandhills, N.C.) (bd. dirs. 1989-96. Avocations: golf, reading, traveling. Office: Research Triangle Regional Partnership PO Box 80756 Raleigh NC 27623-0756 E-mail: chayes@researchtriangle.org.

HAYES, CLAUDE QUINTEN CHRISTOPHER, research scientist, inventor; b. N.Y.C., Nov. 15, 1945; s. Claude and Celestine (Stanley) H.; m. Solvi Wold, 2002. BA in Chemistry and Geol. Sci., Columbia U., 1971, postgrad., 1972-73, N.Y. Law Sch., 1973-75; JD, Thomas Jefferson Law Sch., 1978. Cert. community coll. tchr. earth scis., phys. sci., law, Calif. Tech. writer Burroughs Corp., San Diego, 1978-79; instr. phys. scis. Nat. U., San Diego, 1980-81; instr. bus. law, earth scis. Miramar Coll., 1978-82; sr. systems analyst Gen. Dynamics Convair, 1979-80, advanced mfg. technologist, sr. engr., 1980-81; pvt. practice sci. and tech. cons. Calif., 1979—; instr. phys. sci., phys. geography, bus. law San Diego Community Coll. Dist., 1976-82, 85-90; U.S. Dept. Def. contractor Def. Nuclear Agy., Strategic Def. Initiative Agy., USAF, Def. Advance Rsch. Projects Agy., 1986—, U.S. Army, 1991—, USN, 1995-2000. Adj. prof. phys. chemistry San Diego State U., 1986-87; bus. and computer sci. def. rsch. contractor to Maxwell Labs., Honeywell Inc., Naval Ocean Sys. Ctr.; tech. cons. Pizza Hut, Inc., Carts of Colo., Smiths Industries; guest lectr. in endothermics applied to protective devices and clothing. Contbr. articles to profl. jours.; patentee in field. Mem. Am. Chem. Soc., N.Y. Acad. Sci., Am. Inst. Aero. and Astronautics, Princeton Columbia Barnard Club. Avocations: travel, technical, ancient history, art, people. Home and Office: 3737 3rd Ave Apt 308 San Diego CA 92103-4133

HAYES, COLLEEN BALLARD, writer, photographer; b. Kansas City, Mo. d. Charles Richard and Mary Frances (Ballard) Hayes. BA in English, U. Kans., 1972. Assoc. editor, reporter Johnson County (Kans.) Sun newspapers, Kans., 1967-68; editor, writer press releases and pub. rels. Met. Plan Agy., 1968-70; writer speeches, Freedom of Info. and other letters for Pres. U.S., U.S. Senators, U.S. State Reps., midwest govs., EPA, 1972-82. Contbr. articles and photography to Elle Mag., Travel-Holiday, Country Inns Mag., Archtl. Digest publs., Confederate Veteran Mag., The Boston Globe, The Phila. Inquirer, Chgo. Tribune, L.A. Times, The Balt. Sun, more than 70 others; contbr. photography to Odyssey, San Francisco Examiner, The Denver Post, Christian Science Monitor, The Detroit News, The Orlando Sentinel, St. Petersburg Times, St. Louis Post Dispatch, The Kansas City Star, San Jose Mercury News, N.Y. Daily News, The Plain Dealer, Chicago Sun-Times, Des Moines Register, Richmond (Va.) Times-Dispatch, Women's Sports and Fitness, The Calgary Herald, others in U.S. and Can.; co-author: Anthology Am. Holidays; contbr. numerous nat. and regional poetry anthologies, to Nat. Scholastic Mag. (recipient writing award), Mo. Hist. Rev., others; lead in drama prodns. at regional theaters and Topeka Civic Theater; commentator on WIBW-TV, performed role of Medea on KTWU Pub. TV, guest interview KCUR-FM, others. Named to Hon. Order Ky. Cols.; recipient 1st Prize Bethany Coll. Creative Writing award, others, Key to City of St. Joseph, Mo., City and Regional Tennis awards, numerous others. Mem. Jackson County Hist. Soc., Quantrill Hist. Soc., Pony Express Hist. Soc., St. Andrew Scottish Soc., Woodside Racquet Club. Avocations: history, international and adventure travel, lap swimming, tennis, golf. E-mail: bcolin77@hotmail.com., bballard7@yahoo.com.

HAYES, CONSTANCE J. pediatric cardiologist; b. Cortland, N.Y., July 16, 1937; d. John Burns and Anna Marie (McGuire) H.; m. Edward William Lewison, Nov. 8, 1980. RN, BS, Coll. St. Rose, 1959; MD, Loyola U., Chgo., 1965. Diplomate Am. Bd. Pediatrics, Am. Bd. Pediatric Cardiology, Nat. Bd. Med. Examiners. Resident in pediat. St. Vincent's Hosp., N.Y.C., 1965-68; fellow in pediat. cardiology Columbia U., N.Y.C., 1968-71, assoc. pediat. coll. p. & s., 1971-72, asst. prof. clin. pediat., 1972-80, assoc. clin. prof. pediat., 1980-99, prof. clin. pediat., 1999—. Contbr. articles to profl. jours. Fellow Am. Acad. Pediatrics, Am. Coll. Cardiology; mem. Am. Heart Assn., N.Y. Heart Assn., Pediatric Cardiology Soc. Greater N.Y. (pres. 1987-88). Office: Columbia Presbyn Med Ctr 3959 Broadway New York NY 10032-1551

HAYES, CYNTHIA ANN (C.A. HAYES), administrative assistant, writer; b. L.A., Sept. 11, 1954; d. Lafayette and Verna (O'Gee) H.; 1 child, LaLaunie Charisse. Student, U. Calif., L.A., 1972-75. Clerk underwriting unit Great Am. Insurance Co., L.A., 1978-79; administrv. asst. Bill Dodd Real Estate Co., L.A., 1979-80, L.A. Dept. Water and Power, 1980—; v.p. Images By Haze, Laguna Niguel, Calif., 1990-91. Author: The My Family Collection, 1985, That Lovely Piece of Art, 1997, The Death of Lillie Maroe, 1998, The Night Aunt Ives Went to Sleep, 1999. Donor The Brotherhood Crusade, The Donor's Welfare Plan. Mem. U. Calif. L.A., The Duvall Found. Democrat. Baptist. Avocations: sewing, creating graphic designs, sailing, cycling, attending concerts and theater. Mailing: PO Box 922152 Sylmar CA 91392-2152

HAYES, DAVID JOHN ARTHUR, JR., legal association executive; b. Chgo., July 30, 1929; s. David J.A. and Lucille (Johnson) H.; m. Anne Huston, Feb. 20, 1963; children— David J.A. III, Cary AB, Harvard U., 1952, JD, 1961. Bar: Ill. Trust officer, asst. sec. First Nat. Bank of Evanston, Ill., 1961-63; gen. counsel Ill. State Bar Assn., Chgo., 1963-66; asst. dir. ABA, Chgo., 1966-68, div. dir., 1968-69, asst. exec. dir., 1969-87, v.p., 1987-88, assoc. exec. v.p., 1989-90, sr. assoc. exec. v.p., 1990, exec. dir., 1990-94, exec. dir. emeritus, 1994—; exec. dir. Naval Res. Lawyers Assn., 1971-75; asst. sec. gen. Internat. Bar Assn., 1978-80, 90—, Inter-ABA, 1984—. Contbr. articles to profl. jours. Capt. JAGC, USNR Fellow Am. Bar Found. (life); mem. Ill. State Bar Assn. (ho. of dels. 1972-76), Nat. Orgn. Bar Counsel (pres. 1967), Chgo. Bar Assn., Michigan Shores Club. Home: 908 Pontiac Rd Wilmette IL 60091-1349 Office: ABA 750 N Lake Shore Dr Chicago IL 60611-4403 E-mail: djahayes@aol.com.

HAYES, DAVID MICHAEL, lawyer; b. Syracuse, N.Y., Dec. 2, 1943; s. James P. and Lillie Anna (Wood) H.; m. Elizabeth S. Tracy, Aug. 26, 1972; children: Timothy T., AnnElizabeth S. AB, Syracuse U., 1965; LLB, U. Va., 1968. Bar: Va. 1968, N.Y. 1969. Assoc. Hiscock & Barclay, Syracuse, 1968-72; asst. gen. counsel Agway Inc., Syracuse, 1972-81, gen. counsel, sec., 1981-87, v.p., gen. counsel, sec., 1987-92, sr. v.p., gen. counsel, sec., 1992-2001; of counsel Bond, Schoeneck & King, Syracuse, 2001—. Adj. prof. law Syracuse U. Coll. Law, 1995—; former chmn. Nat. Coun. of Farmer Coops. Legal Tax and Acctg. Com. Bd. dirs., former pres. Boys and Girls Club of Syracuse. With Army N.G., 1968-74. Mem.: ABA, Va. State Bar, N.Y. State Bar Assn. (ho. of dels. 1995—99, 2002—, exec. com. of antitrust sect. 2001—), Onondaga County Bar Assn. (pres. 1998), N.Y. Bar Found., Skaneateles Country Club, Century Club. Democrat. Office: BS&K One Lincoln Ctr Syracuse NY 13202-1355 Fax: 315-281-8100. E-mail: dhayes@bsk.com.

HAYES, DAVID RYAN, mathematics educator; b. Raleigh, N.C., July 14, 1937; s. Woodrow Rufus and Eleanor Ruth (Crocker) H.; m. Carla Ann Bradshaw, Sept. 2, 1961 (div. 1980); children: Robert, Christopher, Jonathan. AB, Duke U., 1959, PhD, 1963. Asst. prof. U. Tenn., Knoxville, 1963-65, assoc. prof., 1965-67, U. Mass., Amherst, 1967-72, prof., 1972—2002, Emeritus prof., 2002—. Visiting prof. Oxford (Eng.) U., 1974-75, Harvard U., Cambridge, Mass., 1981, U. Calif., San Diego, 1983, Imperial Coll. of Sci. and Tech., London, 1989. Contbr. numerous articles to profl. jours. NSF postdoctoral fellow Harvard U., 1966-67. Mem. Am. Math. Soc., Math. Assn. Am. Democrat. Office: U Mass Dept Math And Stats Amherst MA 01003

HAYES, DAVID VINCENT, sculptor; b. Hartford, Conn., Mar. 15, 1931; s. David Vincent and Adelaide (Brown) H.; m. Julia Moriarty, June 22, 1957; children: David Matthew, Brian James, Mary Judith, John Mark. AB, U. Notre Dame, 1953; MFA, Ind. U., 1955. Vis. lectr. visual and environ. studies Harvard U., 1972-73; regent U. Hartford, 1992-94. One man shows include Ind. U., 1955, Wesleyan U., Middletown, Conn., 1958, Mus. Modern Art, 1959, Willard Gallery, N.Y.C., 1961-64, 66, 69, 71, U. Notre Dame-Ind. U., 1963, Root Art Center, Clinton, N.Y., 1963, Galerie David Anderson, Paris, France, 1966, Columbus (Ohio) Mus., 1974, Martha Jackson Gallery, N.Y.C., 1974, Everson Mus., Syracuse, N.Y., 1975, DeCordova Mus., Lincoln, Mass., 1977, Springfield (Mass.) Mus., 1978, SUNY, Albany, 1978, Dartmouth Coll., 1979, Amherst Coll., 1979, Nassau County (N.Y.) Mus., 1979, Saratoga Performing Arts Center, Sarasota Springs, N.Y., 1980, Old State House, Hartford, 1981, Shippee Gallery, N.Y.C., 1984, 86, Elaine Benson Gallery, Bridgehampton, N.Y., 1993, Anderson Gallery, Buffalo, 1994, Prudential Ctr., Boston, 1996, U. New Haven, 1997, Orlando City Hall, Boca Raton Mus., 1998, Colgate U., Hamilton, N.Y., 1999, Sasaki Assocs., Watertown, Mass., 2000, Fordham U., New York, 2000, Denise Bibro Gallery, New York, 2000, Sculpture 2000, New London, Conn., Lyric Theatre, Stuart, Fla., 2001; numerous group shows, 1959—; represented in permanent collections Mus. Modern Art, Guggenheim Mus., Carnegie Inst., Hirshhorn Mus., Washington, U. Notre Dame, Mus. Fine Arts, Houston, Wadsworth Atheneum, Hartford, Addison Gallery Am. Art, Andover, Mass., Currier Gallery Art, Manchester, N.H., Williams Coll., Dartmouth Coll., Harvard U., Colgate U., Hartwood Acres, Pitts., Hartford Pub. Library, Snite Mus., Notre Dame, Ind., Western Mich. U., Kalamazoo, U. Hartford, Hamilton Coll., Clinton, N.Y., others. Regent, U. Hartford, Conn., 1992-96. Recipient Logan medal Art Inst. Chgo., 1960; Fulbright research grantee, 1961; Guggenheim fellow, 1961; grantee Nat. Inst. Arts and Letters, 1965. Mem. Sculptors Guild N.Y. (bd. dirs. 1994-2000). E-mail: dvhayes@snet.net.

HAYES, DEBRA TROXELL, family nurse practitioner; b. Highland, Ill., Oct. 11, 1952; d. Robert E. and Marilyn M. (Schwend) Troxell; m. Jay F. Hayes, May 31, 1985; children: Amy Myers, Eric Myers. Diploma, Graham Hosp. Sch. Nursing, 1973; BSN, Sangamon State U., Springfield, Ill., 1985; MS, U. Ill., Chgo., 1995. RN, Ill.; cert. family nurse practitioner. Staff and relief charge nurse, head nurse Mason Dist. Hosp., Havana, Ill., 1973-77; staff and relief charge nurse, day charge nurse Graham Hosp., Canton, Ill., 1979-85; nurse coord. problem pregnancy program Cath. Social Svcs., Peoria, Ill., 1985-86; nurse clinician Oncology Hematology Assocs., Peoria, 1986-95; FNP Coleman Clinic, Ltd., Canton, Ill., 1995—. McFarland scholar Mason Dist. Hosp., 1970, Illinois Farm Bur. Nurse Practitioner scholar, 1993-94. Mem. ANA, Ill. Nurses Assn., Ill. Nurse Practitioner Coun. Home: 9526 W Lake Lancelot Dr Mapleton IL 61547-9430 E-mail: debhayesfnp95@hotmail.com.

HAYES, DENNIS EDWARD, geophysicist, educator; b. St. Joseph, Mo., Oct. 3, 1938; s. William Franklin and Gertrude Margaret (Lorson) H.; m. Leslie Eve Price, May 17, 1978; children—Jennifer, Katharine, Elizabeth, Élan. BSE. summa cum laude, Kans. U., 1961; PhD, Columbia U., 1966. Research asso. Columbia U., 1966-71, sr. research asso., 1971-74, asso. prof., 1974-77, prof. geophysics, 1977—, chmn. dept. geol. scis., 1989—94, 1997—2002; chmn. exec. com. Arts and Scis. faculty, 1994-96; assoc. dir. Lamont-Doherty Geol. Obs., 1978—2002; deputy dir. edn. Lamont-Doherty Obs. Columbia U., 1998—2002. Mem. ocean scis. bd. and polar rsch. bd. NAS; mem. adv. panel to earth scis. divsn. NSF, polar programs divsn., ocean scis. divsn.; vis. prof. Stanford U., 1981, vis. prof., Ecole Normal Superior (ENS), Paris, 2002; mem. IOC Commn. on Non-living Resources, Joint Oceanographic Insts. for Deep Earth Sampling Planning Commn., 1977-87; mem. Univ. Nat. Oceanog. Lab. Sys. coun., 1991—. Editor books including Antarctic Oceanology II, 1972, Marine Geophysics of S.E. Asia, I and II, 1978, 83, Marine Geology/Geophysics of the Circum-Antarctic, 1991; contbr. numerous articles to profl. jours. Recipient Haworth Disting. Alumni Honors in Geology Kans. U., 1977; NSF fellow, 1961-65; John Simon Guggenheim fellow, 1980-81 Fellow Am. Geophys. Union, Geol. Soc. Am.; mem. Soc. Exploration Geophysicists, Am. Assn. Petroleum Geologists, Tau Beta Pi. Home: 6 Century Rd Palisades NY 10964-1503 Office: Lamont-Doherty Geol Obs Palisades NY 10964 E-mail: deph@ldeo.columbia.edu. *I believe maintaining one's personal integrity may be the single most important ingredient in a successful and satisfying career.*

HAYES, DONALD PAUL, JR., elementary and secondary education educator; b. Boston, Aug. 30, 1947; s. Donald P. and Grace E. (Moore) H.; m. Deborah J. Moore, July 15, 1978 (div. 2001); children: Erin Eliza, Heather Alice, Jill Melina. AB, Salem State Coll., 1969; MEd with high distinction, Rivier Coll., 1992. Cert. tchr., prin., Mass. Tchr. Lowell (Mass.) Pub. Schs., 1969—. Author, coord., developer Micro-Soc. Pub. Strand Curriculum, 1981-95; author: Locke Family Genealogy Supplement I, 1979, Historic Andover, 1971, Guide to Andover History, 1976, Locke Family Genealogy Supplement II, 2002; mem. adv. bd. Equity, Choice, 1986-94, New Schools, New Communities, 1994-96; co-author: The Micro-Society School, 1992, Piscataqua Pioneers, 2000, Locke General Supplement II, 2002; editor Locke Sickle and Sword, 1972—. Sec. Locke Family Assn., Rye, N.H., 1971—; asst. dir. Samuel Parris Archaeol. Excavation, 1970-73; active Andover (Mass.) Hist. Commn., 1974-78; pres. Andover Hist. Soc., 1976-78, 1st Parish Unitarian Universalist Ch., Chelmsford, Mass., 1992-93; 1st sgt. Danvers Alarm List Co., Danvers, Mass., 2000—. Recipient Award of Appreciation, Airflow Club of Ami, 1998, Locke Family Assn., 1980, 97, Andover Hist. Soc., 1978, Town of Andover, 1976, 78. Mem. Airflow Club Am. (v.p. 1994-98, nat. dir. 2001—), Piscataqua Pioneers (chaplain 1995-96, v.p. 1996-2002, sec. 2002—, 1st sgt. Danvers Alarm List Co. 2000—), New England Hist. Geneal. Soc., Soc. Automotive Historians, Sons Union Vets. Civil War, SAR. Mem. Unitarian Universalist Ch. Avocations: antique cars, historical research. Home: 90 Swan St U202 Lowell MA 01852 Office: Lowell High Sch 50 Father Morissette Blvd Lowell MA 01852-1050 E-mail: donald.hayes@comcast.net.

HAYES, DORIS ANN, elementary education educator, consultant; b. Chgo., Dec. 19, 1943; d. Frank Bertrum and Irene Marie Rzechula H. BA, Northeastern Ill. U., 1965; cert. in photography, Triton Jr. Coll., River Grove, Ill., 1984; postgrad., George Williams Coll., 1968; MA in edn., Viterbo U., 2001. Cert. elem. tchr., Ill., Wi. Elem. tchr. phys. edn., libr. Webster Elem. Sch., 1965-94; elem. libr. Trevor (Wis.) Grade Sch., 1996-98, Wilmont (Wis.) Grade Sch., 1998-99; Spanish tchr. Salem (Wis.) Grade Sch., 1999—; dist. gifted and talented coord. Salem J2 Sch. Dist., Salem, Wis., 2000—. Cons., spkr., presenter in field. Author numerous poems; contbr. articles to local newspapers and mags. Active Burlington (Wis.) Area Arts Coun., 1998—, Redbird Studios Writers Group, Milw., 1997-98. Writers Grant Burlington Area Arts Coun., 1999; Fulbright Meml. Fund scholar Japan-U.S. Edni. Commn., 2000. Mem. Am. Fedn. Tchrs., Wis. Edn. Assn., Wis. Fgn. Lang. Assn., Whitewater Talented & Gifted Assn., Wis. Talented & Gifted Assn., Ill. Assn. Gifted Students, Assn. Exptl. Edn., Friends Fulbright Meml. Fund. Avocations: photography, camping, swimming, writing, art. Home: 8065 Sage St Burlington WI 53105 Office: Salem Grade Sch 8828 Antioch Rd Salem WI 53168 E-mail: hayesdor@salem.k12.wi.us.

HAYES, EDWIN JUNIUS, JR., business executive; b. Brockton, Mass., July 20, 1932; s. Edwin Junius and Edith Franklin (Miller) H.; m. Brenda Storrs, Apr. 19, 1958; children: Bradford, Jonathan, Christopher. AB, Dartmouth Coll., 1954, MBA, 1955; cert., U. Manchester (Eng.) Inst. Sci. and Tech., 1972. Various mgmt. positions Gen. Mills, 1955-67; product group mgr. Quaker Oats Co., Chgo., 1967-69; dir. mktg. Quaker Oats Ltd. (U.K.), London, 1969-72, v.p. internat., mng. dir., 1972-76; v.p. internat. William Underwood Co., Boston, 1976-77, exec. v.p., 1977-79; pres., chief exec. officer M. Grumbacher, Inc., N.Y.C., 1979-85; prin. and dir. Center for Concept Development Inc., N.Y.C., 1985-88, 92-01; pres., chief executive officer Diethelm and Keller (USA) Ltd., 1988-92, Delta Tech. Coatings, Inc., 1988-92. Dir. Norfra Shipping Co. Advisor Nat. Art Edn. Assn. Mem. Nat. Maritime Mus. Greenwich (Eng.), Delta Upsilon.

HAYES, ERIC JAMES, consulting company executive; b. Airdrie, Scotland, Aug. 28, 1941; s. David and Ellen (O'Donnell) H.; m. Eva Mary Smith, Apr. 4, 1970; children: Anthony David, Stephen James. BSc, Strathclyde U., 1963; MSc, McMaster U., 1965; PhD, U. Ill., 1970. Chartered engr. Industry analyst Rowe & Pitman, London, 1973-75; mgr. Inco Europe, London, 1975-97; dir. Abacus Consultancy, Chelmsford, U.K., 1997—. Chmn. World Bur. of Metal Statistics, Ware, U.K., 1995-97. Editor: World Stainless Steel, 1982-95; contbr. articles to profl. jours. Home: 6 Linroping Ave Canvey Island SS8 8NE England Office: Abacus Consultancy 59 New Street Chelmsford CM1 1NE England

HAYES, ERNEST M. podiatrist; b. New Orleans, Jan. 21, 1946; s. Ernest M. and Emma Hayes; m. Bonnie Ruth Beigle, Oct. 16, 1970. BA, Calif. State U., Sacramento, 1969; BS, Calif. Coll. Podiat. Medicine, San Francisco, 1971, DPM, 1973. Diplomate Am. Coun. Cert. Podiatric Physicians and Surgeons, 1989-. Resident in surg. podiatry Beach Cmty. Hosp., Buena Pk., Calif., 1973-74, dir. residency program, 1974-75; pvt. practice Anaheim, Calif., 1974-80, Yreka, Calif., 1980-95, Machias, Lubec and Calais, Maine, 1995—. Courtesy staff Down East Cmty. Hosp., 1997—; sr. clin. instr. So. Calif. Podiatric Med. Ctr., LA, 1975—78; vice chmn. podiatry dept. Good Samaritan Hosp., Anaheim, Calif., 1978—79; mem. med. staff Mercey Med. Ctr., Mt. Shasta, Calif.; CEO Siskiyou Foot Group, Yreka, 1980—95; pres. Down East Podiatry, Machias, Maine, 1995—. Bd. dir. Little Bogus Ranches Home Owners Assn., 1981—83, pres., 1983—84. Fellow: Nat. Coll. Foot Surgeons; mem.: Am. Assn. Podiatric Physicians and Surgeons, 1989, Kiwanis. Baptist. Home: PO Box 538 Lubec ME 04652-0538

HAYES, GAIL BOYER, writer, editor; b. Palo Alto, Calif., July 31, 1943; d. Paul Delos and Eliza Whicker Boyer; m. Denis Allen Hayes, Jun 14, 1971; 1 child, Lisa Antoinette. BA, UCLA, 1966; JD, Hasting Coll. of Law, 1976. Sr. editor Careers Today mag., Del Mar, 1968-69; co-host, asst. prodr. KCET-TV, L.A., 1969-70; speechwriter, editor Coun. on Environtl. Quality, Washington, 1970-71; program dir. Evirontl. Law Inst., Washington, 1976-79; atty. Holland & Hart, Denver, 1981-82, Hopkins, Mitchell & Carley, San Jose, Calif., 1982—84; writer Seattle, 1993—. Author: (book) Solar Access Law, 1979, Pulmonary Hypertension, 1998, 2001, (book revs.) St. Louis Post Dispatch, 1970—91, mag. and newspaper articles, short stories. Vol., bd. dirs. Pulmonary Hypertension Assn. Mem. Bar: D.C. Bar Assn., Bar of the State of Colo., State Bar of Calif., Order of Coif. E-mail: boyerhayes@attbi.com.

HAYES, GERALD JOSEPH, lawyer; b. Bronx, N.Y., July 24, 1950; s. James Joseph and Gladys (Guest) H.; m. Diane Elizabeth Willoughby, July 21, 1984; children: Erin Jane, Thomas Joseph, Cara Elizabeth. BA, U. Mass., 1972; JD, U. Miami, 1978. Bar: N.Y. 1979, U.S. Dist. Ct. (so. dist.) N.Y. 1979. Assoc. Baker & McKenzie, N.Y.C., 1978-85, ptnr., 1985—, mng. ptnr., 1995, 97, 99—, mem. policy com., 1997—, nominating com., 2002—. Mem. Bus. Coun. for UN, 1990-95. Nat. alumni adv. bd. U. Miami Sch. Law, 1992—. Mem. ABA (atomic energy com. pub. utility law sect. 1983, vice chair internat. tort and ins. law com., tort and ins. practice sect. 1997—), Assn. Bar City N.Y. (com. on nuclear tech. and law 1979-82, 85-88, com. on ins. law 1983-84), Nat. Assn. Ins. Commrs. (adv. com. on internat. law 1989-90), Nat. Risk Retention Assn. Office: Baker & McKenzie 805 3rd Ave New York NY 10022-7513

HAYES, GORDON GLENN, civil engineer; b. Galveston, Tex., Jan. 2, 1936; s. Jack Lewis and Eunice Karen (Victery) H. BS in Physics, Tex. A&M U., 1969. Registered profl. engr., Alaska, Tex. Rsch. technician Shell Devel. Co., Houston, 1962-68; rsch. assoc. Tex. Trans. Inst., College Station, 1969-71, asst. rsch. physicist, 1971-74, assoc. rsch. physicist, 1974-80; traffic safety specialist Alaska Dept. Transp. & Pub. Facilities, Juneau, 1981-83, state traffic engr., 1983-85, traffic safety standards engr., 1985-90; owner Alaska Roadsafe Cons., Juneau, 1990-92, Hayes Highway Consulting, Carson City, Nev., 1992-93, Livingston, Tex., 1993—. Author of numerous pubs. in the hwy. safety field; producer of numerous documentary films in the hwy. safety field. Petty officer USN, 1953-57. Mem. ASCE, Nat. Com. on Uniform Traffic Control Devices (signs tech. com.) Inst. Transp. Engrs. Avocations: fishing, boating, camping. Home: 209 Crystal Creek Dr Livingston TX 77351-9730

HAYES, ISAAC, rhythm and blues singer, composer; b. Covington, Tenn., Aug. 20, 1942; Formerly singer rhythm and blues recs., Stax Records; albums recorded included Black Moses, Hot Buttered Soul, Enterprise: His Greatest Hits, Hotbed, Isaac Hayes Movement, ... To Be Continued, U-Turn, 1986, Love Attack, 1988, Greatest Hit Singles, (with Dionne Warwick) A Man and A Woman, Don't Let Go, And Once Again, Lifetime Thing, Back to Back (with Barry White), Branded, Raw and Refined; (with Donald Dunn and Al Jackson Jr.) Present; composer: musical score film Shaft (Grammy and Oscar awards); appeared on TV show Rockford Files; film appearances include: Escape from New York, Counterforce, I'm Gonna Git You Sucka!, Guilty As Charged, Robin Hood: Men in Tights, Out of Sync, It Could Happen To You; from 1962, wrote songs with David Porter. Office: Avenue Mgmt 276 5th Ave #507 New York NY 10001

HAYES, J. MICHAEL, lawyer; b. St. Louis, Dec. 10, 1946; s. Frank J. and Louise J. (Lough) H.; m. Vicky J. Verbocy, May 27, 1972; children: Thomas K., James M. BS summa cum laude, SUNY, Brockport, 1973; JD, SUNY, Buffalo, 1976. Bar: N.Y. 1977, U.S. Dist. Ct. (we. dist.) N.Y. 1977. Assoc. Smith, Murphy & Schoepperle, Buffalo, 1977-79, Tenney, Smith & Scott, Buffalo, 1979-82, Terry D. Smith, Buffalo, 1982-86; ptnr. Smith, Keller, Hayes & Miner, Buffalo, 1986-94; pvt. practice, Buffalo, 1994—. Office: 69 Delaware Ave Rm 1111 Buffalo NY 14202-3805 E-mail: jmh@jmichaelhayes.com.

HAYES, JACK IRBY, historian, educator; b. Danville, Va., Aug. 13, 1944; s. Jack Irby and Minnie Lee (Conner) H.; m. Bernadine Joy Arnn, June 5, 1966; children: Emily Wilson, Julia Arnn. BS in History, Hampden-Sydney Coll., 1966; MA in History, Va. Poly. Inst. and State U., 1968; PhD in History, U. S.C., 1972; BS in Bus., Averett Coll., 1987. Dir. continuing edn. U. S.C., Columbia, 1972-74; asst. prof. history Averett Coll., Danville, 1974-77, assoc. prof., 1977-82, prof., 1982-90, W.C. Daniel prof. history and polit. sci., 1990—, chmn. dept. history, 1976—. Adj. prof. grad. sch. Va. Poly. Inst. and State U., Blacksburg, 1977-79; archival cons. Dibrell Bros., Inc., Danville, 1990-91. Author: A History of Averett College, 1984, Dan Daniel and the Persistence of Conservatism in Virginia, 1997, South Carolina and the New Deal, 2001. Jud. ethics adv. com. Commonwealth Va., 1999—; bd. dirs. The Womack Found., 1982-90, Danville Mus. of Fine Arts and History, 1992-98; pres. Hughes Meml. Home, 1999—; mem. Danville Dem. Com., 1984—; elder, trustee First Presbyn. Ch., Danville; mem., past pres. Citizens Bd., Danville Corps., Salvation Army. Grantee Va. Found. for Humanities and Pub. Policy, Charlottesville, 1976-87, Commn. on Bicentennial of U.S. Constn., Washington, 1989, 90; Westmoreland Davis Meml. Found. fellow, 1967-68, Seminar for Hist. Adminstrs. fellow, Colonial Williamsburg, Va., 1967, Louis P. Jones fellow, U. S.C., 1998; named one of Outstanding Young Men of Am., 1977. Mem. So. Hist. Assn., Assn. for Preservation of Va. Antiquities (life), Kiwanis (lt. gov. div. 2 capital dist. 1991-92, pres. Danville club 1989), So. Assn. Colls. and Schs. (mem. re-accreditation com. 1986-99), German Club Danville. Avocations: running, tennis. Home: 245 Linden Dr Danville VA 24541-3523 Office: Averett Coll 420 W Main St Danville VA 24541-3612

HAYES, JACQUELINE CREMENT, real estate broker; b. Chgo., Aug. 12, 1941; d. John and Lottie (Czech) Crement; m. Larry G. Hayes, Mar. 4, 1972 (div. Dec. 1978). BA in Mgmt., DePaul U., 1977. Lic. real estate broker, Ill. Bldg. mgr. LaSalle Bank Bldg., Chgo., 1978-80; v.p., gen. mgr. The Hayman Co., Chgo., 1981-83; pres. Jacqueline Hayes & Assoc., Chgo., 1983—; ptnr. The Retail Group, Chgo., 1986-93. Panelist retail planning seminar Dept. Planning, City of Chgo., 1988, steering com. River North urban design plan, 1987—89, pedestrian count, 1989, Streeterville urban design plan, 1990—95, Downtown Framework Plan, 1990—95, Ctrl. Area Plan, 1999—2002; mem. mentorship program Woman of Destiny, 1992—93; mem. Retail Task Force, City of Chgo. on Ctrl. Area Plan, 1999—. Docent Chgo. Archtl. Found.; mem. Burnham Park Planning Bd., Chgo., bd. dirs., mem. exec. com., v.p., chmn. planning, zoning and urban design, chmn. civic affairs, chosen mem. of last decade, 1999; leader task force on homelessness; spokesperson Greater North Michigan Ave. Assn., Chgo., 1986—; mem. adv. coun. Friends of Downtown, 1987—89; liaison to real estate com. Streeterville Orgn. of Active Residents, 1998—; sponsor Looking Glass Theatre Co., 2000; liaison retail com. Ctrl. Michigan Ave. Assn.; founder, pres. Help Ease Local Poverty; bd. dirs. Cactus Theatre, 1990—92; bd. dirs., mem. franchising task force, chmn. nominating com., chair beautification com. Lawson House YMCA, 1993—. Named Broker of Yr. Chgo. Sun-Times, 1986, one of Top Businesswomen Crain's Chgo. Bus., 1990-91, Woman of Destiny, 1990-92, one of 100 Women Who Make a Difference Today's Chgo. Woman, 1995; recipient Cert. of Leadership, YWCA of Met. Chgo., 1997. Mem. NAFE, Internat. Coun. Shopping Ctrs., Comml. Real Estate Orgn. (bd. dirs., v.p., chmn. membership 1986-89), Am. Biol. Inst. (rsch. bd. advisors, Disting. Leadership award), Chgo. Real Estate Exec. Women (bd. dirs., sec., mentorship program 1988—), Chgo. Assn. Commerce and Industry (mem. govt. affairs com., mem. taxation com., mem. midwest aviation coalition), Urban Land Inst., River North Assn., Met. Planning coun. (mem. bus. leaders for transp. com.), Women in Planning and Devel., Women in Retail Leasing (founder 1993), Lambda Alpha (bd. dirs., sec. 1994, v.p. edn. 1995, v.p. programs 1996, pres. 1997, mem. of Yr. 1995). Office: Jacqueline Hayes & Assocs 155 N Harbor Dr Ste 301 Chicago IL 60601-7386 E-mail: jhayes-associates@attglobal.net.

HAYES, JAMES ANTHONY, city planner, business owner; b. Dubuque, Iowa, Jan. 28, 1970; s. John Hutchinson and Helen Cecelia H.; m. Susan Elizabeth Sheetz, Mar. 9, 1996; 1 child, John Jacob. BS in Planning, Iowa State U., 1992; M in City Planning, Ga. Inst. Tech., 1995. Cert. planner Am. Inst. Cert. Planners. Assoc. planner City of Prior Lake (Minn.), 1993; grad. rsch. asst. Ga. Inst. Tech., Atlanta, 1993-94; planning intern Ctrl. Atlanta Progress, 1994-95; planner I Adams County, Commerce City, Colo., 1995-96, planner II, 1996-97, planning mgr., 1997—. Owner Hayes Enterprises, Denver, 1996—, Hayes Real Estate, LLC, 2002—; mgr.-mem. Hayes-Sheetz, LLC, 1999—; spkr. in field. Recipient Student Planning award Am. Inst. Cert. Planners, 1996. Mem. Am. Planning Assn., Golden Key. Avocations: computers, home remodeling, basketball, golf. Office: Adams County 4955 E 74th Ave Commerce City CO 80022-1535

HAYES, JAMES DONALD, pharmaceutical research scientist; b. Quitman, Ga., Jan. 15, 1969; s. Donald Rodney Hayes and Linda Joyner Parker. BS in Chemistry, BS in Biology, Valdosta State U., 1994; PhD in Chemistry, U. South Fla., 2000. Sr. analytical scientist Bausch & Lomb, Tampa, Fla., 2000—. Mem.: Am. Chem. Soc., Am. Soc. for Mass Spectrometry, Am. Assn. Pharm. Scientist. Home: 17918 Haven View Ln Lutz FL 33558 Office: Bausch & Lomb 8500 Hidden River Pkwy Tampa FL 33637-1014 Office Fax: 813-975-7745. Personal E-mail: donnie_hayes@bausch.com. E-mail: donnie_hayes@bausch.com.

HAYES, JANET GRAY, retired business manager, former mayor; b. Rushville, Ind., July 12, 1926; d. John Paul and Lucile (Gray) Frazee; m. Kenneth Hayes, Mar. 20, 1950; children: Lindy, John, Katherine, Megan. AB, Ind. U., 1948; MA magna cum laude, U. Chgo., 1950. Psychiat. caseworker Jewish Family Svc. Agy., Chgo., 1950-52; vol. Denver Crippled Children's Service, 1954-55, Adult and Child Guidance Clinic, San Jose, Calif., 1958-59; mem. San Jose City Coun., 1971-75, vice mayor, 1973-75, mayor, 1975-82; co-chmn. com. urban econs. U.S. Conf. Mayors, 1976-78, co-chmn. task force on aging, mem. sci. and teck task force, 1976-80, bd. trustees, 1977-82; bd. dirs. League Calif. Cities, 1976-82, mem. property tax reform task force, 1976-82; chmn. State of Calif. Urban Devel. Adv. Com., 1976-77; mem. Calif. Commn. Fair Jud. Practices, 1976-82; client-community relations dir. Q. Tech., Santa Clara, Calif., 1983-85; bus. mgr. Kenneth Hayes MD, Inc., 1985-88; CEO Hayes House, Book Distbr., 1998—. Mem. Dem. Nat. Campaign Com., 1976; mem. Calif. Dem. Commn. Nat. Platform and Policy, 1976; del. Dem. Nat. Conv., 1980; bd. dirs. South San Francisco Bay Dischargers Authority; chmn. Santa Clara County Sanitation Dist.; mem. San Jose/Santa Clara Treatment Plant Adv. Bd.; chmn. Santa Clara Valley Employment and Tng. Bd. (CETA), League to Save Lake Tahoe adv. bd., 2000—; past mem. EPA Aircraft/Airport Noise Task Group; bd. dirs. Calif. Center Rsch. and Edn. in Govt, Alexian Bros. Hosp., 1983-92; bd. dirs., chmn. adv. council Public Tech. Inc.; mem. bd. League to Save Lake Tahoe, 1984-2000; pres. bd. trustees San Jose Mus. Art, 1987-89, founder, adv. bd. Calif. Bus. Bank, 1982-85. AAUW Edn. Found. grantee. Mem. Assn. Bay Area Govts. (exec. com. 1971-74, regional housing subcom. 1973-74), LWC (pres. San Francisco Bay Area chpt. 1968-70, pres. local chpt. 1966-67), Mortar Bd., Phi Beta Kappa, Kappa Alpha Theta. E-mail: janetgrayhayes@sbcglobal.net.

HAYES, JOHN DANIEL, lawyer; b. Chgo., Jan. 8, 1931; s. Peter Stephen and Genevieve Mary (Dunn) H.; LL.B., DePaul U., 1959. Bar: Ill. 1959; assoc. Philip H. Corboy, Chgo., 1959-63; prin. John D. Hayes & Assos., Ltd., Chgo. from 1963; now ptnr. Hayes & Power, Chgo.; mem. Ill. Med. Injury Ins. Reparations Commn., 1976— ; mem. adj. faculty Chgo.-Kent Coll. Law 1977— ; mem. chief judge's com. case flow mgmt. Circuit Ct., 1979— Contbg. author texts Ill. evidence, product liability law and med. malpractice

Fellow Am. Coll. Trial Lawyers (Ill. com.), Internat. Acad. Trial Lawyers; mem. ABA, Ill. Bar Assn. (chmn. med. legal relations com. 1979—), Chgo. Bar Assn. (pres.; former mem. bd. mgrs., past chmn. several coms.), Cook County Bar Assn., Am. Judicature Soc., Soc. Trial Lawyers, Ill. Trial Lawyers Assn. (pres. 1973-74), Assn. Trial Lawyers Am. (state committeeman 1973-75, bd. govs. 1977—), Inner Circle Advocates, Am. Bd. Trial Advocates, Am. Bd. Profl. Liability Attys., Ill. Inst. Continuing Legal Edn. (lectr. 1967—). Office: Hayes & Power 310 S Michigan Ave Chicago IL 60604-4207

HAYES, JOHN FRANCIS, lawyer; b. Salina, Kans., Dec. 11, 1919; s. John Francis and Helen (Dye) H.; m. Elizabeth Ann Ireton, Aug. 10, 1950; children: Carl Ireton, Ann Chandler. AB, Washburn Coll., 1941; LL.B., 1946. Bar: Kans. 1946, Mo. 1987. Pvt. practice, Hutchinson, Kans., 1946—; dir. Gilliland & Hayes, P.A. (and predecessors), 1946—. Mem. Commn. Uniform State Laws, 1975—; bd. dirs. Cen. Bank and Trust Co., Hutchinson, Cen. Fin. Corp., Waddell & Reed Funds. Mem. Kans. Ho. of Reps., 1953-55, 67-79, majority leader, 1975-77. Served as capt. AUS, 1942-46. Fellow Am. Bar Found., Am. Coll. Trial Lawyers; mem. Hutchinson C. of C. (pres. 1961), Kans. Assn. Def. Counsel (pres. 1972-73), Internat. Assn. Def. Counsel. Republican. Home: 31 Pawnee Dr Hutchinson KS 67502 Office: 20 W 2nd Ave Fl 2 Hutchinson KS 67501 also: 1211 Penntower Bldg 3100 Broadway St Kansas City MO 64111-2406 also: Epic Ctr 301 N Main Ste 1300 Wichita KS 67202

HAYES, JOHN FREEMAN, architect; b. Media, Pa., June 16, 1926; s. James Alfred and Katharine Stoddard (Williams) H.; m. Anne Gitt Fox, Apr. 5, 1952; children— John Fox, Thomas Freeman, Anne Clarke. Grad., Haverford Sch., 1944; B.Arch., U. Pa., 1950. With various cos., 1954-60; partner Hayes & Hough (Architects), Phila., 1960-95; sr. cons. Blackney Hayes Architects, Phila., 1995—. Pres., The Carpenters Co. of the City and County of Phila., 1993. Served with USNR, 1944-46; served with USAF, 1951-53. Fellow Am. Inst. Architects. Clubs: Martins Dam, Phila. Curling. Episcopalian. Office: Blackney Hayes Architects 105 S 12th St Philadelphia PA 19107-4809

HAYES, JOHN PATRICK, electrical engineering and computer science educator, consultant; b. Newbridge, Ireland, Mar. 3, 1944; s. Patrick Joseph and Christine (Duggan) H.; m. Joan Benson, June 7, 1969; children: Thomas, Michael. BE in Elec. Engring., Nat. U. Ireland, Dublin, 1965; MS in Elec. Engring., U. Ill., 1967, PhD in Elec. Engring., 1970. Systems engr. Royal Dutch Shell Co., The Hague, The Netherlands, 1970-72; asst. prof. elec. engring. and computer sci. U. So. Calif., L.A., 1972-77, assoc. prof., 1977-82; prof. U. Mich., Ann Arbor, 1982—2002, Shannon prof. engring. sci., 2002—. Cons. in field. Author: Computer Architecture and Organization, 1978, 3d edit., 1998, Digital System Design and Microprocessors, 1984, Hierarchical Modeling for VLSI Circuit Testing, 1990, Layout Minimization for CMOS Cells, 1992, Introduction to Digital Logic Design, 1993; contbr. articles to profl. jours. Fellow: IEEE (assoc. editor jour. 1989—94), Assn. Computing Machinery (assoc. editor jour. 1978—81); mem.: Sigma Xi. Office: U Mich Dept Elec Engring & Computer Sci Ann Arbor MI 48109 E-mail: jhayes@eecs.umich.edu.

HAYES, JOHN PATRICK, retired manufacturing company executive; b. Manistee, Mich., May 9, 1921; s. John David and Daisy (Davis) H.; m. Margaret Barbara Butler, Apr. 12, 1947; children— John Patrick, Timothy Michael. BS, U. Detroit, 1947. With Nat. Gypsum Co., 1947-90, group v.p., 1970-75, pres., 1975-90, chmn. bd., chief exec. officer, 1983-90, also bd. dirs. Served to 1st lt. AUS, 1942-45.

HAYES, JOYCE MERRIWEATHER, secondary education educator; b. Bay City, Tex., Aug. 29, 1943; d. Calvin and Alonia (Harris) Merriweather. BS, Wiley Coll., Tex., 1967; postgrad., U. N.Y., Stony Brook, 1968; MS in Guidence Counseling, Ea. Mich. U., 1974; postgrad., Mercy Coll., 1991-92, Ea. Mich. U., 1991-92; MEd, U. Detroit, 1992. English tchr. Terrance Manor Mid. Sch., Augusta, Ga., 1968-69, Longfellow Jr. H.S., Flint, Mich., 1969-81, No. H.S., Flint, 1981—2002, chmn. English dept., 1992—2002; edn. cons. Ventures Edn. Systems Corp., N.Y.C., 2000—. English and speech tchr. Jordan Coll., Flint, 1989-91; adult edn. tchr. Mott Adult H.S., Flint, 1978-80, on-state content stds. com.; presenter workshops in field.; motivational spkr. Composer 3 gospel songs. Vol. Second Ward City Coun., Flint, 1989, Cmty. Coun., Flint, 1992-93, Cmty. Wide Assn. Coun., Flint, 1993; intercessory prayer warrior, 1995—; area dir. Home Ministry new mem. class tchr., Grace Emmanuel Bapt. Ch., co-coord. spl. svc. for Nat. Coun. Tchr. of Eng. Conv. Detroit, 1997. Named Saginaw Valley Tchr. of Yr., 2001, No. Alumni Tchr. of Yr., 2001. Mem. NEA, Nat. Coun. Tchrs. English (chair workshops 1992-93, mem. nominating com. 1994), Mich. Edn. Assn., United Tchrs. of Flint (in-svc. com., Flares-English tchrs.), Phi Delta Kappa (Xinos advisor, del. to conf. 1999, past pres., textbook selection com.). Home: 621 Thomson St Flint MI 48503-1942 Office: Ventures Edn Sys Corp 245 Fifth Ave Ste 802 New York NY 10016 E-mail: silverfoxhayes@aol.com.

HAYES, KEVIN GREGORY, university administrator; b. Jamestown, N.Y., May 14, 1941; s. Francis Joseph and Mary Blanche (Driscoll) H.; m. Marilyn Jane Dougherty, Dec. 7, 1968; children: Tracy Lynn, Brendan Paul. AA in Humanities, Jamestown C.C., 1966; BA in English, Allegheny Coll., 1968; MA in Journalism, Pa. State U., 1974; EdD, Okla. State U., 1995. Broadcaster James Broadcasting Co., Jamestown, 1959-63, 65-66; program dir. Regional Broadcasters, Meadville, Pa., 1966-69; asst. radio-TV editor Pa. State U., University Park, 1969-71, assoc. publs. editor, 1971-75, publs. editor, 1975-80, asst. dir. agrl. comm., 1980-83, interm dir., 1983-84; info. specialist, chief of party Swaziland Cropping Systems Rsch. and Extension Tng. Project, 1984-87; asst. dir. agrl. comms. Pa. State U., University Park, 1987-88; prof., head agrl. com., Divsn. Agrl. Scis. and Natural Resources, Okla. State U., Stillwater, 1988-94, prof., distance edn. coord., 1994-99, asst. dean grad. coll., 1997-98, prof., dir. agrl. comm. svcs., 1999—2002; prof., instrnl. tech. in devel. specialist U.S. Agy. for Internat. Devel., Washington, 2002—. Author: On Coming Home, 1979, Distance Learning Policies in Postsecondary Education, 1995. With U.S. Army, 1963-65. Recipient Pioneer ACE award Agrl. Communicators in Edn., 1976. Mem. KC (grand knight 1990-92, dist. dep. 1992-97, state advocate 1997-99, state treas. 1999-2001, state sec. 2001-2002), Phi Kappa Phi (pres. chpt. 24, 1999-2000), Kappa Tau Alpha, Epsilon Sigma Phi. Roman Catholic. Avocations: creative writing, photography, woodworking, gardening. Home: 20709 Parkside Cir Potomac Falls VA 20165-1515 Office: US Agy Internat Devel Rm 3 09-096 1300 Pennsylvania Ave NW Washington DC 20523-3901 E-mail: khayes@usaid.gov.

HAYES, LARRY B. lawyer; b. Atlanta, Oct. 4, 1939; s. Luther F. and Ruby (Thomas) H.; m. Rebecca Thomason, Feb. 7, 1959; children: Laura Alison, Lawrence Bruce. BS in Pharmacy, U. Fla., 1962; JD, St. Mary's U., 1977. Bar: Tex. 1978, U.S. Dist. Ct. (no. dist.) Tex. 1979, U.S. Ct. Appeals (5th cir.) 1979; cert. personal injury trial law, Tex. Trial counsel Windle Turley PC, Dallas, 1978-82; ptnr. Ware & Hayes, Dallas, 1982-83; sr. trial atty. Green, Hayes & Ryan, Dallas, 1983-86; ptnr. Cantey & Hanger, Ft. Worth, 1986—. Mem. Tex. Bar Assn., Tex. Assn. Def. Counsel, Def. Rsch. Inst., Tarrant County Bar Assn., Tarrant County Civil Trial Lawyers Assn., Ridglea Country Club, Phi Delta Phi. Home: 910 Houston St Apt 802 Fort Worth TX 76102-6228 Office: Cantey & Hanger Burnett Plaza 801 Cherry St Ste 2100 Fort Worth TX 76102-6898

HAYES, LEWIS MIFFLIN, JR., lawyer; b. Mpls., May 5, 1941; s. Lewis Mifflin and Helen Camille (Vail) H.; m. Patricia Louise Schwab, June 3, 1967; m. Roberta Jane Hobson, Dec. 29, 1977; m. Diana Amorosino, Mar. 31, 1983; m. Debra Hines, Nov. 12, 1993; children: Rhoda Margaret, Lewis Mifflin, III, Robert Nelson. AB cum laude in Polit. Sci., Kenyon Coll., Gambier, Ohio, 1963; LLB with distinction, Duke U., 1966. Bar: N.Y. 1967, N.J. 1974, U.S. Sup. Ct. 1974, U.S. Tax Ct. 1978, U.S. Dist. Ct. (so. and ea. dist.) N.Y. 1968, U.S. Dist. Ct. N.J. 1974, U.S. Ct. Apls. (2d cir.). Assoc. Mudge Rose Guthrie & Alexander, N.Y.C., 1966-73, Gifford, Woody, Carter & Hays, N.Y.C., 1973-76; ptnr. Hayes and Jenkins, N.Y.C. and Elizabeth, N.J., 1976-80; pvt. practice Elizabeth, 1980-88, N.Y.C., 1980—, Summit, N.J., 1988-92, Scotch Plains, N.J., 1992—. Trustee The Vail-Deare Sch., 1979-83. With U.S. Navy, 1966-68. Mem. N.J. State Bar Assn. Presbyterian. Clubs: Seaside Park (N.J.) Yacht. Home: 310 Pearl Pl Scotch Plains NJ 07076-1328 Office: 1810 Front St Scotch Plains NJ 07076-1103

HAYES, M. M.M. publishing executive; b. Chgo., Nov. 30, 1945; d. William C. and Minnie Marie (Prunty) Mitchell; m. James E. Hayes, July 12, 1969; children: James J., Will. BA, U. Ill., 1967; MFA in Writing, Vt. Coll., 1991. Promotion & continuity writer CBS, Chgo.; pub. rels. rep. J. Walter Thompson Advt. Agy., Chgo.; prof. Columbia Coll. Mo., Crystal Lake, Ill. Editor and pub.: book StoryQuarterly, 1994—2003. Mem.: Heartland Literary Soc. (bd. dirs.), Poetry Ctr. Chgo. (bd. dirs.). Avocations: travel, photography, hiking, swimming, tango. Home and Office: 431 Sheridan Rd Kenilworth IL 60043 Office Fax: 240-218-5388. E-mail: minniemarie@earthlink.net., storyquarterly@yahoo.com.

HAYES, MARY ESHBAUGH, editor, writer; b. Rochester, N.Y., Sept. 27, 1928; d. William Paul and Eleanor Maude (Seivert) Eshbaugh; m. James Leon Hayes, Apr. 18, 1953; children: Pauli, Eli, Lauri Le June, Clayton, Merri Jess Bates. BA in English and Journalism, Syracuse U., 1950. With Livingston County Republican, Geneseo, N.Y., summers, 1947-50, mng. editor, 1949-50; reporter Aurora Advocate, Colo., 1950-52; reporter-photographer Aspen Times, Colo., 1952-53, columnist, 1956—, reporter, 1972-77, assoc. editor, 1977-89, editor-in-chief, 1989-92, contbg. editor, 1992—. Tchr. Colo. Mountain Coll., 1979, Aspen corr. Reuters, 1997—. Author, editor: The Story of Aspen, 1996; contbg. editor: Destinations Mag., 1994-97, Aspen Mag., 1996—; editor: Aspen Pot Pourri, 1968, rev. edit., 2002. Recipient Living Landmark award, Aspen Hist. Soc., 2002. Mem. Nat. Fedn. Press Women (1st prizes in writing and editing 1976-80, 1st prize Aspen Potpourri rev. 1990, 2002, 1st prize Story of Aspen 1996, 1st prize in adv. photography 1998), Colo. Press Women's Assn. (writing award, 1974, 75, 78-85, sweepstakes award for writing 1977, 78, 84, 85, 91-2003, 2d place award 1976, 79, 82, 83, 94, 95, Woman of Achivement 1986). Home: PO Box 497 Aspen CO 81612-0497 Office: Box E Aspen CO 81612

HAYES, MARY DIANNE WIXTED, lawyer; b. Danbury, Conn., Jan. 4, 1942; d. Francis Joseph and Mary (Zwyner) Wixted; m. Paul P. Hayes, Jr., June 18, 1966. BA in Economics, Regis Coll., Weston, MA, 1961—64; JD, Suffolk U. Law Sch., Boston, 1968, LLM, 1968—70; MEd in Religious Edn., Boston Coll., Chestnut Hill, MA, 1989, MA in Theology, 1990—97; STL, Weston SJ Sch. of Theology, Cambridge, MA, 1997—2002. Bar: Mass. 1970, U.S. Dist. Ct. (Mass.) 1971, U. S. Supreme Ct. 1973, U.S. Ct. Appeals (1st cir.) 1979. Ptnr. Hayes and Hayes, Quincy, Mass., 1970—; volunteer atty. Irish Pastoral Centre, 1998—. Town meeting mem. Town of Milton, Milton, Mass., 1977—93; mem. Secular Franciscan Order, Boston, 1985—. Mem.: Am. Immigration Lawyers Assn., Mass. Conveyancers Assn. Inc., Mass. Assn. Women Lawyers (pres. 1993—94), Mass. Bar Assn. (chair probate law sect. coun. 1995—97), S. Shore Regis Club, Weston, Mass. (pres. 1973—75). Roman Catholic. Office: Hayes and Hayes 31 Newcomb Street Quincy MA 02169-4507 Office Fax: 617-770-0191. Business E-Mail: Wixtedhaye@aol.com.

HAYES, MARY PHYLLIS, retired savings and loan association executive; b. New Castle, Ind., Apr. 30, 1921; d. Clarence Edward and Edna Gertrude (Burgess) Scott; m. John Clifford Hayes, Jan. 1, 1942 (div. Oct. 1952); 1 child, R. Scott. Student, Ball State U., 1957-64, Ind. U. East, Richmond, 1963; diploma, Inst. Fin. Edn., 1956, 72, 76. Teller Henry County Savs. and Loan, New Castle, 1939-41, loan officer, teller, 1950-62, asst. sec., treas., 1962-69, sec., treas., 1969-73, corp. sec., 1973-84; v.p., sec. Ameriana Savs. Bank (formerly Henry County Savs. and Loan), New Castle, 1984-91; exec. sec. Am. Nat. Bank, Nashville, 1943-44. Corp. sec. Ameriana Fin. Svcs., 1984-91. Treas. Henry County Chpt. Am. Heart Assn., New Castle, 1965-67, 76-87, vol. Indpls. chpt. 1980—; membership sec. Henry County Hist. Soc., New Castle, 1975-90; sec. Henry County chpt. ARC, New Castle, 1976-91; elected mem. Found. Inst. Fin. Edn., 1991—; mem. Internat. Platform Assn., 1974—, Woman's Club 1992—; vol. Ind. Basketball Hall of Fame, 1993—. Mem. Inst. Fin. Edn. (sec.-treas. East Ctrl. Ind. chpt. 1973-91), Ind. League Savs. Insts. (25 Yrs. award 1975, 40 Yrs. Cert. award 1988), Internat. Platform Assn., Henry County Cmty. Found., Ind. Hist. Soc., Heritage Found., Henry County Hist. Soc. (mem. sec.), Altrusa (past officer, bd. dirs. New Castle chpt.), PEO-CG (past chaplain, sec., past pres. 1994-95, v.p. 2001-03), Woman's Club (treas. 2000-01), Ind. Hist. Soc., New Castle Henry County C. of C., Guyer Opera House Guild, Art Ctr. of Henry County, Psi Iota Xi (past sec.-treas.). Mem. Christian Ch. Avocations: music, traveling, history, swimming.

HAYES, MAXINE DELORES, physician, pediatrician; b. Nov. 29, 1946; children: Leon Williams, Kevin Williams. AB in Biology, Spelman Coll., 1969; MD, SUNY Buffalo, 1973; MPH, Harvard U., 1977; DSc (hon.), Spelman Coll., 2000. Intern pediat. Vanderbilt Hosp., Nashville, 1973-75; resident Children's Hosp., Boston, 1975-76; dir. Divsn. Parent-Child Health Svcs., Olympia, Wash., 1988-90, asst. sec., 1990-93, Cmty. and Family Health, Olympia, 1993-2000, acting health officer, 1998-2000; state health officer Wash. State Dept. Health, 2000. Pres. Assn. Maternal and Child Health Programs, Washington, 1995-97; nat. program dir. Robert Wood Johnson Child Health Initiative, 1994-97. Recipient Outstanding Contbns. in Field of Pub. Health award Wash. State Pub. Health Assn., 1994, Guardian of Women's Health award Aradia Women's Health Ctr., 1996, Stockton Kimball award for medicine SUNY, Buffalo, 2000, Dr. Nathan Davis award AMA, 2002, Richard P. Nelson Lecture Series award Iowa Pub. Health Assn., 2002, Lifetime Achievement award Wash. Health Found., 2003. Fellow Am. Acad. Pediatrics; mem. APHA. Avocations: opera, art, science. Office: Wash State Dept Health PO Box 47890 Olympia WA 98504-7890 E-mail: maxine.hayes@doh.wa.gov.

HAYES, NORMAN ROBERT, JR., lawyer; b. Schenectady, N.Y., Apr. 12, 1948; s. Norman Robert Sr. and Ethel May (Blair) H.; m. Alice S. Margitan, Oct. 14, 1972; children: Robert, Charles. BS, Clarkson U., 1970; JD, Union U., 1973. Bar: N.Y. 1974, U.S. Dist. Ct. (no. dist.) N.Y. 1974, U.S. Supreme Ct. 1978. Ptnr. Wemple, Daly, Casey, Hayes, Watkins & Harter, Schenectady, 1973-86; pvt. practice Clifton Park, N.Y., 1986-96; ptnr. Gordon, Siegel, Mastro, Mullaney, Gordon & Galvin, Clifton Park, N.Y., 1996—. Pres. Hayes Indsl. Inc., 1998—; chmn. Saratoga Econ. Devel. Corp., Saratoga Springs, NY; bd. dirs. Provantage Funding Corp., Ebeling Assocs.; adv. bd. dirs. Chase Manhattan Bank. Pres. County Knolls South Civic Assn., Clifton Park, 1975-76, Saratoga Closing Svcs., 2002. Served to capt. U.S. Army, 1973-74. Mem. ABA, N.Y. State Bar Assn., Schenectady County Bar Assn., Lake George Club (dir., treas. 2002). Republican. Office: 3380 State Route 9L Lake George NY 12845-5511 E-mail: bob6@capital.net.

HAYES, PATRICIA ANN, health facility administrator; b. Binghamton, N.Y., Jan. 14, 1944; d. Robert L. and Gertrude (Congdon) H. BA in English, Coll. of St. Rose, 1968; PhD in Philosophy, Georgetown U., 1974. Tchr. Cardinal McCloskey High Sch., Albany, N.Y., 1966-68; teaching asst. Georgetown U., Washington, 1968-71; instr. philosophy Coll. of St. Rose, Albany, 1973-75, instr. bus., spring 1981, adminstrv. intern to acad. v.p., 1973-74, dir. admissions, 1974-78, dir. adminstrn. and planning, 1978-81, v.p. adminstrn. and fin., treas., 1981-84; pres. St. Edward's U., Austin, Tex., 1984-98; exec. v.p., COO Seton Healthcare Network, Austin, 1998—2001, 2003—, interim pres., CEO, 2001—02. Trustee RGK Found.; bd. dirs. Topfer Family Found.; exec. bd. Austin Idea Network. Roman Catholic. Office: Seton Med Ctr 1201 W 38th St Austin TX 78705-1006

HAYES, PAULA FREDA, governmental official; b. Apr. 5, 1950; d. Ario Louis and Elena Marguerite (Gentile) Freda; m. Robert J. Hayes, Sept. 6, 1975; children: Brendan Michael, Lauren Ann. BA magna cum laude, R.I. Coll., 1972; MPA, Syracuse U., 1973. Criminal justice planner City of Syracuse, NY, 1973-75, asst. crime control coord., 1975-77; supervisory grants specialist Nat. Endowment Arts, Washington, 1977-78; criminal justice program analyst Dept. Justice, Washington, 1978-79, program mgr. arson discretionary grant program, 1979-80, sr. mgmt. analyst, 1980-81; dir. legis. and analysis divsn. Office of Insp. Gen., Dept. Agr., Washington, 1982-89, asst. insp. gen. for policy devel. and resources mgmt., 1989—2003, asst. insp. gen. for planning and spl. projects, 2003—. Roman Catholic. Office: USDA Office Insp Gen 1400 Independence Ave SW Rm 5E Washington DC 20250-0002

HAYES, PHILIP HAROLD, lawyer; b. Battle Creek, Mich., Sept. 1, 1940; s. Robert Harold and Maurine (Page) H.; m. Robin Hayes, May 20, 1995; 1 child, Rian; children from previous marriage: Elizabeth, Courtney. AB, Ind. U., 1963, JD, 1967. Bar: Ind. 1967, U.S. Dist. Ct. (so. dist.) Ind. 1967, D.C. 1977, U.S. Ct. Appeals (7th cir.) 1992. Dep. prosecutor Vanderburgh County, Evansville, Ind., 1967-68; ptnr. Cox & Hayes, Evansville, 1969-72; senator State of Ind., Evansville, 1971-74; pvt. practice Evansville, 1973-74, 77-79, 1980—; U.S. congressman U.S. Ho. of Reps., Washington, 1975-77; ptnr. Hayes & Young, Evansville, 1980-90, Hayes & Tornatta, Evansville, 1990-92. Legal counsel Airport Authority Dist., Evansville, 1980-84, Redevel. Commn., Evansville, 1984-88, Health and Hosp. Corp., Evansville, 1984-88, Vanderburgh County Atty., 2001-02. Editor, moderator pub. affairs TV program, 1977-78. Mem. ATLA, Evansville Bar Assn., D.C. Bar Assn., Ind. Bar Assn. Home: 218 Glenview Dr Evansville IN 47710-3737 Office: 400 Court St Evansville IN 47708 E-mail: phaylaw@aol.com.

HAYES, RANDY ALAN, family therapist; b. Johnston City, Ill., Jan. 12, 1950; s. Clarence Lee Jr. and Mable Marie (McClain) H.; m. Donna Faye Carriker, Oct. 9, 1971; 1 child, Colin. BA, So. Ill. U., 1972; postgrad., U. Dubuque Theol. Sem., 1973-74; MS, No. Ill. U., 1975; post grad., Columbia Pacific U., 1996. Cert. rational emotive therapy, family life educator; cert. substance abuse counselor; ordained as deacon United Meth. Ch., 1973; lic. local pastor United Meth. Ch.; lic. clin. profl. counselor; nat. cert. counselor; clin. cert. mental health counselor. Day sch. dir. Village of Progress, Oregon, Ill., 1974-76; team coord. Children's Devel. Ctr., Rockford, Ill., 1976-78; career counselor Highland C.C. CETA, Freeport, Ill., 1978-79; family therapist, clin. dir. Stephenson County Assn. for Prevention of Child Abuse, Freeport, 1979-92; dir. quality assurance Sinnissippi Ctrs., Inc., 1992—; pastor Brookville-Elkhorn United Meth. Chs., Polo, Ill., 1996-98, Zion United Meth. Ch., Mendota, Ill., 1996-98. Pre-marriage cons. Rochelle (Ill.) United Meth. Ch., 1985—91; mem. adminstrv. bd. Polo United Meth. Ch., 1975—90; cons. quality assurance, 1998; guest faculty mem. Family Info. Svcs., 2001—; lectr. Joint Commn. Resources, 2000—. Pub.: Handbook of Quality Training and Implementation, 2001, Behavior Health Mgmt., 2000—; contbr. Vol. Ogle County Hospice Assn., Oregon, 1990; campaign coord. Am. Cancer Assn., Polo, 1987-93; bd. dirs. Ogle County Mental Health Assn., Oregon, 1974-76; den leader Polo Cub Scouts, 1988-91; violinist Sauk Valley Coll. String Orch., 1992-96. Mem.: Ill. Counselors Assn., Ill. Coun. Family Rels. (bd. dirs. 1990—2000, pres. 1993, immediate past pres. 1994), Nat. Coun. Family Rels. Avocations: collecting asian art, crafting fiber and textile art, writing poetry. Home: 401 N Congress Ave Polo IL 61064-1306 Office: 125 S 4th St Oregon IL 61061-1609

HAYES, RICHARD DONALD, architect; b. Evanston, Ill., Dec. 6, 1954; s. Joseph P. and Florence A. (Balmes) H.; m. Bessie Athene Gallanis, May 27, 1995. BArch with honors, Ill. Inst. Tech., 1981. Registered arch., Ill. Arch. Thomas Jon Rosengren, Inc., Evanston, 1981-83; project arch. Holabird & Root, Chgo., 1983-94; project mgr. VOA Assocs., Inc., Chgo., 1994-95; sr. project mgr. A. Epstein and Sons Internat., Inc., Chgo., 1995—2001; dir. architecture David Woodhouse Architects, 2002—. Project mgr. Ill. Bell Telephone Co. switching station, 1988 (story in Progressive Architecture 1990), Ameritech Svcs. data ctr., 1991-93, Amoco Corp. plz. redevel., 1992-94, ABN-AMRO Svcs. data ctr. expansion, 1994-95, Rose Hulman Inst. Tech. student union addition, 1994-95, Hyatt Regency 800-room hotel, 1996-97, Morton Arboretum new vis. ctr., 2002-. Adv. bd. Nat. Vietnam Vets. Art Mus., Chgo., 1996-99. Mem. AIA (real estate com. 1988-92), Assn. for Project Mgrs., U.S. Sailing Assn., Chgo. Yacht Club, BMW Car Club Am. Home: 979 Cherry St Winnetka IL 60093-2412 Office: David Woodhouse Architects 811 W Evergreen Ave Chicago IL 60622

HAYES, ROBERT (ROBIN HAYES), congressman; b. Concord, N.C., Aug. 14, 1945; m. Barbara; children: Winslow, Bob. BA in History, Duke U., 1967. Businessman, Concord, 1967—; mem. U.S. Congress from 8th N.C. dist., 1999—; mem. agr. com., armes svcs. com., transp. and infrastructure com.; vice chair. Congress. Sportsmen's Caucus. Current owner, operator of Mt. Pleasant Hosiery Mill; other bus. ventures include Arctic So. Turbines, Mack Sales of Birmingham, Colville Environ. Svcs., Palmer Mt. Farms (hwy. contractor) and Central Motor Lines. Elected mem. Concord Bd. Aldermen, 1978; elected 1992 to N.C. Ho. Reps., where he served as majority whip. Under former Gov. Jim Martin, served on the Wildlife Resources Commn., Coun. on Drug Abuse and as chmn. Cabarrus County Drug Task Force, Prison Fellowship in N.C. Nominated 1996 as Rep. candidate for gov. of N.C. Mem. 1st Presbyn. Ch. Concord. Chosen as Legislator of Yr. by Nat. Rep. Legislator's Assn., 1996. Republican. Office: 130 Cannon Ho Office Bldg Washington DC 20515-0001*

HAYES, ROBERT BANKS, II, assistant principal; b. Greensboro, North Carolina, Oct. 30, 1933; s. Golas Lee and Vivan Frances (Crenshaw) Hayes; 1 child, Bryant M. Colson. BS, No. Carolina A. and T. St., Greensboro, N.C., 1955; EdM, Univ. N.C., Chapel Hill, N.C., 1970. Asst. prin. Greensboro City Sch., Proximity, Greensboro, NC, 1967—71, Greensboro City Sch., Smith H.S., Greensboro, NC, 1970—73, Greensboro City Sch., Page H.S., Greensboro, NC, 1993—94; adj. prof. of edn. N.C. A. and T. St. U., Greensboro, NC, 1995—2000; asst. prin. Guilford County Sch., Dudley H.S., Greensboro, NC, 2001, Guilford County Sch., N.W. H.S., Greensboro, NC, 2002, Guilford County Sch., Andrews H.S., High Point, NC, 2003. Tchr. Eng. and French Yadkin H.S., Boonville, NC, 1960—62, Lincoln Heights, Wilkesboro, NC, 1962—66, Wilkes Central, Wilkesboro, NC, 1965—66. Airman first class USAF, 1956—60, San Antonio, Tex. Recipient Asst. Prin. of the Yr., N.C. Assn. of Edn., 1984, 1988. Mem.: N.C. Assn. of Edn., Nat. Greene Sertoma Club. Democrat. Baptist. Home: 1722 Pichard St Greensboro NC 27401-3916

HAYES, ROBERT BRUCE, former college president, educator; b. Clarksburg, W.Va., Nov. 15, 1925; s. Bruce and Ruby (Hitt) H.; m. Ruth Harrison, July 19, 1947 (dec.); children: Steven, Ruthann, Mark; m. Kathleen Peters. Student, Fairmont (W.Va.) State Coll.; BA, Asbury Coll., Wilmore, Ky., 1950; MEd, U. Kans., 1956, EdD, 1960. Tchr., prin. elem. and secondary schs., Kans., 1951-57; chmn. dept. edn. and psychology Asbury Coll., Wilmore, Ky., 1957-59; dir. tchr. edn. Taylor U., Upland, Ind., 1959-65; dean Coll. Edn. Marshall U., Huntington, W.Va., 1965-74, pres., 1974-83; prof. edni. adminstrn. Coll. Edn., Marshall U., 1983-90; exec. v.p. Warner So. Coll., Lake Wales, Fla., 1991-92; interim dean coll. bus. Marshall U., Huntington, W.Va., 1992-93, coord. accreditation, 1993-95, pres. emeritus, 1992-95, provost, 1996-97, 99; interim v.p. Cmty. & Tech. Coll., 1995-97. Mem. W.Va. Adv. Com. Tchr. Edn., 1965-74; dir. Twentieth St. Bank Editor, contbr.: 1966 Yearbook of Assn. Student Teaching. Bd. dirs. Cabell Wayne United Way, 1981; chmn. bd. Green Acres, 1983; commr. Cabell County (W.Va.), 1983-88. Served with USMCR, 1944-46. Recipient Green Acres award for contbn. to mentally retarded, 1972, Golden Knight award Nat. Mgmt. Assn., 1981 Mem. Huntington Area C. of C. (dir. 1974-83), Phi Delta Kappa, Kiwanis. Methodist. Home: 347 Bradley Foster Dr Huntington WV 25701-9451 Office: Marshall U Sch of Medicine Huntington WV 25755-0001

HAYES, ROBERT BRUCE, radiological engineer; b. Provo, Utah, May 16, 1968; s. Almon Kay Hayes and Dayanna Varney; m. Jenifer Hayes, Sept. 11, 1993; children: Malachi Robert, Nathaniel Luke, Stephen David, James Phillip. BS in Math. and Physics, U. Utah, 1994, MS in Physics, 1997, PhD in Nuclear Engring., 1999. Engr.-in-tng. Lab. instr. in nuclear enging program U. Utah, Salt Lake City, 1998, rsch. assoc., 1999—. Head EPR Rsch. Lab. U. Utah, Ctr. Applied Dosimetry, 1997-99, adj. prof. math. and physics Coll. of S.W., 2000—, program chmn. Am. Nuc. Soc. Radiation Protection Shielding Divsn., 2003-. Contbr. articles to prof. jours.; publ. referee for multiple jours. in field; inventor in field. With USN, 1987-89. Mem. Health Physics Soc., N.Am. Nuc. Soc., Gideons. Republican. Avocations: creation science, bible reading, research, exercise, reading. Office: Westinghouse TRU Solutions Radiological Tech PO Box 2078 MS 452 06 Carlsbad NM 88221-5608 E-mail: Robert.Hayes@Wipp.ws.

HAYES, ROBERT E. lawyer; b. Denver, Nov. 12, 1950; BA, U. S.D., 1973, JD with honors, 1976. Bar: S.D. 1976, U.S.Ct. Appeals (8th cir.), 1977, U.S. Supreme Ct. 1980, U.S. Ct. Claims 1988, U.S. Ct. Appeals (D.C. cir.) 1989. Law clk. to Hon. Fred J. Nichol U.S. Dist. Ct. S.D., 1976-77; assoc. Davenport, Evans, Hurwitz & Smith, Sioux Falls, SD, 1977—79, ptnr., 1980—. Editor-in-chief U. S.D. Law Rev., 1975-76. Mem. ABA, State Bar S.D. (chmn. debtor-creditor com. 1983-86, 1991-94, 1996-99, pres. 2002-03, Minnehaha County Bar Assn., Phi Beta Kappa. Address: Davenport Evans Hurwitz & Smith LLP 206 W 14th St PO Box 1030 Sioux Falls SD 57101-1030*

HAYES, ROBERT EMMET, retired insurance company executive; b. Los Angeles, Nov. 21, 1920; s. Robert and Marion Verbeck (Weatherwax) H.; m. Alice McCarthy, June 26, 1943; children: Kathleen Byers, Joanne, Marianne Frank, Robert Emmet Jr., Janet Gheer, Philip. AB, Loyola U., Los Angeles, 1941. Group ins. rep. Aetna Life Ins. Co., N.Y., Conn., Calif., Oreg., 1941-46; co-pilot Matson Nav. Co., San Francisco, 1946-47; employee benefit cons. Cosgrove & Co., Los Angeles, 1947-57; v.p. Marsh & McLennan, Inc., Los Angeles, 1957-62, Equitable Life Assurance Soc., N.Y.C., 1962-67; sr. v.p., group nat. accounts Met. Life Ins. Co., N.Y.C., from 1967; now ret. Served with USN, 1941-45. Home: 18670 Polvera Dr San Diego CA 92128-1122

HAYES, ROBERT FRANCIS, lawyer; b. Boston, Jan. 1, 1941; s. Robert Francis and Miriam Frances (Comfrey) H.; m. Nancy Hite Roach, Apr. 26, 1969; children: Robert Francis III, Katherine M., Rebecca C. AB, Harvard U., 1962, JD, 1965. Bar: Mass. 1965. With Ropes & Gray, Boston, 1966—. Trustee Thayer Acad., Braintree, Mass., 1985-96; dir. Jordan Hosp., Inc., Plymouth, Mass., 1984—; trustee, dir. Duxbury (Mass.) Beach Reservation, Inc., 1986—. Office: Ropes & Gray One International Pl Boston MA 02110 E-mail: RHayes@Ropesgray.com.

HAYES, ROBERT HERRICK, technology management educator; b. Wakeeney, Kans., July 17, 1936; s. Daniel Frank and Ruth Dee (Herrick) H.; m. Priscilla Jane Alden, Aug. 25, 1963; children: Melissa, Jonathan, Michelle. BA, Wesleyan U., 1958; MS, Stanford U., 1962, PhD, 1966; AM (hon.), Harvard U., 1973. Prof. Harvard U., Boston, 1966-91, Caldwell prof. bus. adminstrn., 1991-2000, sr. assoc. dean, 1992-98, emeritus, 2000—. Bd. dirs. Helix Tech. Corp., Mansfield, Mass., Applera Corp., Norwalk, Conn. Co-author: Restoring our Competitive Edge, 1984 (Assn. Am. Pubs. award 1984), Dynamic Manufacturing, 1988, Manufacturing Renaissance, 1995, Strategic Operations, 1996. Trustee Wesleyan U., Middletown, Conn., 1985-88. Recipient McKinsey award 1980, 81, 82, Outstanding Alumnus award Wesleyan U., 1983. Avocations: sailing, reading, travelling. Office: Harvard Bus Sch Soldiers Fld Boston MA 02163-1317 E-mail: rhayes@hbs.edu.

HAYES, ROBERT MAYO, university dean, library and information science educator; b. N.Y.C., Dec. 3, 1926; s. Dudley Lyman and Myra Wilhelmina (Lane) H.; m. Alice Peters, Sept. 2, 1952; 1 son, Robert Dendrou. BA, UCLA, 1947, MA, 1949, PhD, 1952. Mathematician Nat. Bur. Standards, Washington and Los Angeles, 1949-52; mem. tech. staff Hughes Aircraft Co., 1952-54; head applications group Nat. Cash Register Co., 1954-55; head bus. systems group Magnavox Co., 1955- 60; pres. Advanced Information Systems, Inc., Los Angeles, 1960-64; v.p., sci. dir. Electrada Corp., Los Angeles, 1960-64; lectr. dept. math. UCLA, 1952-64, prof. library and info. sci., 1964-91, dean, 1974-89, dean emeritus, 1989—, dir. Inst. Libr. Rsch., 1965-70; prof. emeritus, 1991—. Vis. lectr. Am. Univ., 1959, U. Wash., 1960-62; Windsor lectr. U. Ill., 1970; vis. prof. U. NSW, 1979, 93, Tskuba U., 1987, Nankai U., 1987, Loughborough U., 1989, Keio U., Japan, 1994, Khazar U., Azerbaijan, 1995; mem. adv. com. White House conf. Libr. and Info. Svcs., 1979; v.p. Becker & Hayes, Inc., 1969-73, 93-96; cons. On Line Computer Libr. Ctr., 1990-94. Author: Strategic Management for Academic Libraries, 1993, Models for Library Management, Decision-Making and Planning, 2001; co-author: Introduction to Information Storage and Retrieval:Tools, Elements, Theory, 1963, Handbook of Data Processing for Libraries, 2d edit., 1974, Strategic Management for Public Libraries, 1996; U.S. regional editor: Problems in Info. Storage and Retrieval, 1959—63; editor: Info. Scis. Series, 1963—75; mem. editl. bd.: Libr. Info. Sci. Rsch., 1978—. Recipient Profl. Achievement award, UCLA Alumni Assn., Beta Phi Mu award, ALA, 1st Tezak award, U. Zagreb, 1990. Mem. ALA (pres. info. sci. and automation div. 1969), Am. Soc. Info. Sci. (pres. 1962-63, nat. lectr. 1968, Award of Merit 1993), Am. Math. Soc., Assn. for Computing Machinery (assoc. editor jour. 1959-69, nat. lectr. 1969), Cosmos Club, Phi Beta Kappa, Sigma Xi. Home: 3943 Woodfield Dr Sherman Oaks CA 91403-4239 Office: UCLA 405 Hilgard Ave Los Angeles CA 90095-9000

HAYES, SAMUEL LINTON, III, business educator; b. Phila., Feb. 23, 1935; s. Samuel L. and Ann Walsh (Barclay) H.; m. Barbara Frances Lloyd, Dec. 21, 1963; children: Elizabeth Ann, Susan Lloyd, Judith Linton. AB, Swarthmore Coll., 1957; MBA with distinction, Harvard U., 1961, DBA, 1966. Asst. prof. bus. adminstrn. Columbia U., N.Y.C., 1965-68, assoc. prof., 1968-70; vis. assoc. prof. Harvard U., Cambridge, Mass., 1970-72, prof., 1972-75, Jacob Schiff prof. investment banking, 1975—98, Jacob Schiff prof. emeritus, 1999—, chmn. faculty Research and Mgmt. Ctr., 1979-81, prof. emeritus, 2000. Cons. in field; bd. dirs. Tiffany & Co., Eaton Vance Mut. Funds, Telect, Inc. Mem. editorial bd. Harvard Bus. Rev., 1976-84, Harvard Bus. Sch. Press, 1986-89; contbr. articles to profl. jours. Mem. Mass. Fin. Adv. Bd., 1976-87, chmn., 1978-87; trustee Swarthmore Coll., 1983-94, 96—, New Eng. Conservatory, 1989—; hon. dir. Nat. Scoliosis Found. With USN, 1957-59. Mem.: Am. Guild Organists, Fin. Mgmt. Assn., Dedham Country and Polo Club, Harvard Club (N.Y.C.). Office: Harvard U Sch Bus Cumnock Hall 300 Soldiers Field Rd Boston MA 02163 E-mail: shayes@hbs.edu.

HAYES, SHIRLEY ANN, special education educator; b. Lindsay, Calif., June 15, 1955; d. Clarence Berwine and Betty Francis (Matthews) Fox; m. Darren Wayne Hayes, Feb. 11, 1990; children: Norman Tony Whited Jr., Samuel Hayes, James Hayes. AA, Porterville Jr. Coll., Calif., 1982; BA, Calif. State U., Bakersfield, 1984; specialist credential, Fresno (Calif.) Pacific Coll., 1985. Resource specialist cert. Tchg. asst. Porterville Devel. Ctr., 1977-84, tchr. of severely handicapped, 1984—. Sec. PTA, West Putnam Sch., Porterville, 1992. Mem. Ednl. Svc. Profl. Orgn. (chair 1990), Calif. State Employees Assn. (bargaining unit rep. 1990—). Avocations: artist, cooking, antique car restoration. Home: PO Box 8624 Porterville CA 93258-8624 Office: Porterville Devel Ctr PO Box 2000 Porterville CA 93258-2000

HAYES, STEPHEN KURTZ, writer; b. Wilmington, Del., Sept. 9, 1949; s. Ira Maurice and Carolyn (Kurtz) H.; m. Rumiko Urata, Apr. 14, 1980; children: Reina Emily, Marissa Christine. BA, Miami U., Oxford, Ohio, 1971. Ordained Tendai sect Japanese Esoteric Buddhist priest, 1991. Adj. prof. master bus. mgmt. program McGregor Sch., Antioch U. Author: The Ninja and Their Secret Fighting Art, 1981, Ninjutsu: Art of the Invisible Warrior, 1984, The Mystic Arts of the Ninja, 1985; Ninja: Spirit of the Shadow Warrior, Vol. I, 1980, Warrior Ways of Enlightment, Vol. II, 1981, Warrior Path of Togakure, Vol. III, 1983, Legacy of the Night Warrior, Vol. IV, 1984, Wisdom from the Ninja Village of the Cold Moon, 1984, Ninja Realms of Power, 1986, Tulku, 1985, Ancient Art of Ninja Warfare, 1988, Lore of the Shinobi Warrior, 1989, Action Meditation, 1992, Enlightened Self-Protection, 1992, How to Own the World, 2000. Bd. mem. Tibetan Cultural Ctr.; founder Stephen K. Hayes' Quest Ctr. for Martial Arts Tng., 1996. Named to Black Belt Hall of Fame, Black Belt. mag., 1985. Mem. Tibetan Med. Inst. (life), Togakure Ryu Ninjutsu (10th degree black belt), To-Shin Do (founder, 1997). Home: PO Box 326 Bellbrook OH 45305-0326 Office: PO Box 291947 Dayton OH 45429-0947 E-mail: daytonquest@skhquest.com.

HAYES, STEPHEN MATTHEW, librarian; b. Detroit, Sept. 30, 1950; s. Matthew Cleary and Evelyn Mary (Warren) H. BS in Psychology, Mich. State U., 1972; MLS, Western Mich. U., 1974; MS in Adminstrn., U. Notre Dame, 1979. Cons. Western Mich. U., Kalamazoo, 1974; libr. U. Notre Dame, Ind., 1974-76, ref. and pub. documents libr., 1976-94; libr. Bus. Svcs. Libr., 1994—. Adv. bd. Ebsco's Bus. Sch., 2003—. Author/contbr.: What is Written Remains: Historical Essays on the Libraries of Notre Dame, 1994; editor: Environmental Concerns, 1975; contbr.: Depository Library Use of Technology: A Practitioner's Perspective, 1993. Apptd. mem. Depository Libr. Coun. to Pub. Printer, 1994—97. Recipient Rev. Paul J. Foik award, 1998. Mem. AAUP, ALA (govt. documents roundtable 1978—, chair 1987-88, chair pubs. com. 1989-91, coord. com. on access to info. 1989-90, 93-95, exec. bd. dirs. 1988-91, awards com. 1991-93, chair Godort orgn. com. 1991-93, Godort legis. com., 1999-2002, bus. ref. and svc. sect. 1994—, bus. & adult ref. roundtable 1995—, edn. com. 1996-98, resolution com. 1997-99, task force or restrictions on access to govt. info. 2002-03), Assn. Pub. Data Users (census com., steering com. 1987-96), Indigo (fed. rec. commn. chair 1992-93). Roman Catholic. Avocations: horseback riding, quilting, gardening. Home: PO Box 6032 South Bend IN 46660-6032 Office: U Notre Dame L012 Mendoza Coll Of Business Notre Dame IN 46556-5646 E-mail: stephen.m.hayes.2@nd.edu.

HAYES, SYLVIA RICHMOND, music educator; b. Lawrenceburg, Tenn.; d. Edward David and Blanche Audrey (Sells) Richmond; m. Gene Edwin Hayes; B.S., George Peabody Coll. Tchrs., M.Mus. Edn., 1968; postgrad. Tenn. State U.; postgrad. in data processing Columbia State Community Coll. Band dir., tchr. English, high sch., Loretto, Tenn.; dir. band, tchr. music Coffman Sch., Lawrenceburg, 1972—89, Leoma (Tenn.) Sch., 1989-94; tech. coord. Lawrence County Sch. Sys., 1994— . Choir and music dir., sec. Immanuel Baptist Ch. Mem. Bus. and Profl. Women's Club (Career Woman of Yr. 1972), Lawrence County Edn. Assn. (treas. bd. dirs., sec. 1988-98, pres. 1998-99), Midele Edn. Assn. (Tenn.), Tenn. Edn. Assn., NEA, Middle Band and Orch. Assn., Music Educators Nat. Conf. Democrat. Club: Lioness (pres. 1977-78). Office: Lawrence County Bd Edn 700 Mahr Ave Lawrenceburg TN 38464

HAYES, TIMOTHY GEORGE, lawyer, consultant; b. New London, Conn., June 27, 1954; s. George Melen and Lauretta C. (Bresnahan) Hayes; m. Barbara Joan White, Jan. 27, 1983; children: Laura Katherine, Kevin Michael. BS, Fla. State U., 1976, MS, 1977; JD, Stetson Coll. Law, 1982. Bar: Fla. 1982, U.S. Dist. Ct. (mid. dist.) Fla. 1983. Legis. aide Fla. State Rep. George H. Sheldon, Tallahassee, 1978-79; assoc. Alice K. Nelson, P.A., Tampa, Fla., 1982-83; ptnr. Cotterill, Gonzalez & Hayes, Lutz, Fla., 1983-84, Cotterill, Gonzalez, Hayes & Grantham, Lutz, 1984-88; sr. ptnr. Hayes & McClelland, Lutz, 1988-90, Hayes, Winick & Albrechta, Lutz, 1990-91, Hayes & Albrechta, P.A., Lutz, 1991-93, Hayes & Assocs., Lutz, 1993—. Bd. dirs. Tampa Bay Commuter Rail Authority, Tampa, 1990—97, Pasco County Econ. Devel. Coun., New Port Richey, Fla., 1990—92, Pasco Food Bank, chmn. bd., 2003; bd. dirs. Sunshine Youth Soccer Assn., 1997—99; bd. dirs., coach Ctrl. Pasco United Soccer Assn., 1995—2003, pres., 1996—98; mem. Tampa-Orlando High-Speed Transp. Study Task Force, 1992—94; mem. adv. bd. Pasco-Hernando C.C., 1994—95; bd. dirs., v.p. Heritage Park Found.; citizens adv. com. Pasco County Parks and Recreation, 1999—, Pasco County Natural Gas Pipeline, 2000; pres. United Soccer Assn., 2000—02; v.p. Hillsborough County Young Dems., Tampa, 1978, pres., 1979. Named Outstanding Young Man in Am., Jaycees, 1980, Citizen of Yr., Ctrl. Pasco C. of C., 2002; recipient Sam Walton Bus. Leader award, 1998. Mem.: ABA (real property, probate and trust law sect.), Fla. Bar Assn. (environ. and land use law sect., real property, probate and trust law sect.), Land O' Lakes C. of C. (v.p. 1988—89, pres. 1991—92, chmn. bd. 1992—93, bd. dirs.). Roman Catholic. Avocations: soccer, bicycling, camping, gardening. Office: Hayes & Assocs 21859 State Road 54 Ste 200 Lutz FL 33549-6986

HAYES, TROY ALLYN, forensic scientist; b. Ketchikan, Alaska, July 15, 1973; s. Allyn and Diane Hayes; children: Talisa, Shoghi, Moriah. BS, Oreg. State U., 1995, MS, 1996; postgrad., U. of Calif., San Diego, 1998—2002. EIT Oreg. Engr. Lawrence Livermore Nat. Lab., Livermore, Calif., 1995; rsch. assoc. Oreg. State U., Corvallis, 1996—2001; rsch. asst. U. of Calif., San Diego, 1998—2001; sr. forensic scientist Inst. of Risk and Safety Analyses, Woodland Hills, Calif., 2001—. Author: (book chpt.) Properties of Amorphous Silicon and Its Alloys; contbr. articles, reports, and papers to profl. publs. and confs. Recipient Rsch. grant, Sigma Xi, 2000—01. Mem.: Minerals, Metals and Materials Soc., Materials Rsch. Soc. Home: 5274 Campo Rd Woodland Hills CA 91364 Office: Inst Risk and Safety Analyses 5324 Canoga Ave Woodland Hills CA 91364 Personal E-mail: tttshayes@netscape.net.

HAYES, WILBUR FRANK, retired biology educator; b. Rhinelander, Wis., Nov. 10, 1936; s. Wilbur Mead and Evelyn (Stritesky) H.; m. Dawn Olivia Waldorf, July 21, 1979 (div. Feb. 1991); stepchildren: Lynn, Robert, Dana, Richard, Gary, Kevin. BA, Colby Coll., 1959; MS, Lehigh U., 1961, PhD, 1965. Postdoctoral fellow Yale U., New Haven, 1965-67; asst. prof. biology Wilkes Coll., Wilkes-Barre, Pa., 1967-71, assoc. prof., 1971-99, assoc. prof. emeritus, 2000—. Vis. prof. Northeastern U., Boston, 1987-88. Contbr. articles to profl. jours. Chmn. bd. dirs. Northea. Pa. chpt. Am. Heart Assn., Wilkes-Barre, 1986-87. Mem. Soc. for Integrative and Comparative Biology, Pa. Acad. Sci., Microscopy Soc. Am., Sigma Xi (pres. Wilkes Coll. chpt. 1976-77, sec.-treas. 1984-87, 88-91). Republican. Congregationalist. Avocations: downhill skiing, photography, travel, colonial american history. Home: 47 Stanley St Wilkes Barre PA 18702-2308 Office: Wilkes U Dept Biology Wilkes Barre PA 18766

HAYES, WILLIAM MEREDITH, pilot, retired career officer; b. San Antonio, Mar. 28, 1947; s. Oscar Junior and Mary Kathrn (Leuthart) Hayes; m. Beverly Jeanne Lowe, May 20, 1972; children: Loren Elaine, Colin Meredith. BA, Western Ky. U., 1971. Cert. naval aviator, airline transport pilot FAA. Commd. ensign USCG, 1973, advanced through grades to capt., 1994; asst. ops. officer USCG Base, Honolulu, 1973-74; pub. affairs officer USCG Air Sta., Mobile, Ala., 1975-78; tng. officer USCG Group/Air Sta., Corpus Christi, Tex., 1978-81; head Falcon jet tng. USCG Aviation Tng. Ctr., Mobile, 1981-87; air ops. officer USCG Air Sta., Miami, Fla., 1987-92, exec. officer Elizabeth City, N.C., 1992-94; commdg. officer USCG Activities, San Diego, 1994-97; chief office of ops. 8th C.G. Dist., New Orleans, 1997; pilot Humana, Inc., Louisville, Ky., 1997—. Bd. dirs. USO, San Diego, Armed Svcs. YMCA, San Diego; mem. mil. adv. coun. C. of C., San Diego, 1994—. Contbr. articles to profl. jours. Recipient Humanitarian Svc. medal USCG, Corpus Christi, 1978, Commendation medal USCG, Miami, 1992, Achievement medal USCG, Elizabeth City, 1994, Meritorious Svc. medal, 1997. Mem. SCV, Amateur Radio Relay League, Sons of the Am. Revolution, Delta Tau Delta (life, chpt. v.p. 1969-70). Avocations: fishing, amateur radio, golf. Home: 2420 Napoleon Blvd Louisville KY 40205-2011 Office: Humana 1180 Standiford Ct Louisville KY 40213-2019

HAYES GLADSON, LAURA JOANNA, psychologist; b. Winnebeau, N.C., Mar. 26, 1943; d. Victor Wilson and Pansy Lorraine (Springsteen) Hayes; m. Jerry Allen Gladson, June 20, 1965 (div. Mar. 1992, remarried Dec. 27, 1997); children: Joanna Kaye, Paula Rae. BA, So. Coll., 1965; MEd, U. Tenn., Chattanooga, 1977; EdD, Vanderbilt U., 1985. Lic. psychologist, Ga. Psychol. intern Lakeshore Mental Health Inst., Knoxville, Tenn., 1985-86; counselor, psychologist Tara Heights Enterprises, Atlanta, 1986—; psychologist, owner Assoc. Psychol. Svcs., Inc., Ringgold, Ga., 1990—. Bd. dirs. Theraplay, Inc., Ringgold; founder Abused Children in Therapy, Inc., 1997. Mem. APA, Christian Assn. for Psychol. Studies, Ga. Psychol. Assn. Democrat. Home: 327 Homestead Cir Kennesaw GA 30144-1335 Office: Assoc Psychol Svcs Box 700 479 Cotter St Ringgold GA 30736-5149

HAYES JR. RICHARD J. engineering company executive; b. Evanston, Ill., Jan. 8, 1964; s. Richard J and Mary L Hayes; m. Danette G Kauffman, Aug. 25, 1990; children: David A Cansler, Makayla M Cansler, Kelly Ms Hayes. BA, U. of Kans., 1982—86; Grad. CGSOC, US Army Command and Gen. Staff Coll., 1998—2002. Cert. hazardous materials manager, Inst. of Hazardous Materials Mgmt., 2000. Constrn. mgr. Hall Kimbrell, Lawrence, Kans., 1987—89; officer, US Army 1-127 FA Kans. Army N.G., Ottawa, Kans., 1987—89; project mgr. Fluor Daniel, Chgo., 1989—93; officer, US Army 2-122 FA Ill. Army N.G., Chgo., 1989—2002; v.p. RMS Inc., Mnpls., 1993—97, Profl. Svc. Industries, Inc., Hillside, Ill., 1997—; lt. col. -comdr. 2-122 F.A. Ill. Army N.G., Chgo., 2002—. Bd. mem. Ill. Assn. of Environ. Professionals, Chgo., 2002—. Co-author: Asbestos Control and Replacement Guidelines for the Electric Industry. Home: 1140 Gail Dr Buffalo Grove IL 60089 Office: Professional Service Industries Inc 4415 W Harrison St Ste 510 Hillside IL 60162 Home Fax: 801-729-9532; Office Fax: 708-236-0721. Personal E-mail: rihayes@yahoo.com. E-mail: richard.hayes@psiusa.com.

HAYFLICK, LEONARD, microbiologist, cell biologist, gerontologist, educator, writer; b. Phila., May 20, 1928; s. Nathan Albert and Edna (Silbert) H.; m. Ruth Louise Heckler, Oct. 3, 1954; children: Joel, Deborah, Susan, Rachel, Anne. BA in Microbiology and Chemistry, U. Pa., 1951, MS in Med. Microbiology, 1953, PhD in Med. Microbiology and Chemistry, 1956. McLaughlin rsch. fellow in infection and immunity, dept. microbiology U. Tex. Med. Br., Galveston, Tex., 1956-58; assoc. mem. Wistar Inst. Anatomy and Biology, Phila., 1958-68; asst. prof. rshc. medicine U. Pa., Phila., 1966-68; prof. med. microbiology Stanford (Calif.) U. Sch. Medicine, 1968-76, senator-at-large, Basic Med. Scis., 1970-73, chmn. gen. rsch. support grant com., 1972-74; sr. research cell biologist Children's Hosp., Oakland, Calif., 1976-81; prof. zoology, prof. microbiology and immunology U. Fla., Gainesville, 1981-87, dir. Ctr. for Gerontol. Studies, Coll. Liberal Arts and Scis., 1981-87; prof. anatomy U. Calif. Sch. Medicine, San Francisco, 1988—. Mem. subcom. on mycoplasmataceae Internat. Com. Bacteriol. Nomenclature, 1965-78; mem. steering com. cell and devel. biology film program MIT, 1970-73; chmn. Calif. State Com. Health White Ho. Conf. Aging, 1971-72, Calif. state rep., 1972; Nat. Cancer Planning Com. Nat. Cancer Inst., NIH, 1972; chmn., adult devel. and aging rsch. and tng. com. Nat. Inst. Child Health and Human Devel., NIH, 1972-73; non-resident fellow Inst. Higher Studies, Santa Barbara, Calif., 1973—; mem. Argonne Nat. Lab. rev. com. biol. and med. rsch. div. Argonne Nat. Lab., 1973-76; mem. rsch. adv. com. Tchrs. Ins. and Annuity Assn. Am.-Coll. Retirement Equities Funds, N.Y.C., 1974-80; founding mem. Nat. Adv. Coun. on Aging, Nat. Inst. on Aging, NIH, Bethesda, Md., 1975; cons. Office of Dir. Nat. Cancer Inst., Bethesda, 1963-74; vis. scientist Ctr. for Aging Weizmann Inst. Sci., Rehovoth, Israel, 1980, 86; mem. adv. bd. Internat. Exchange Ctr. Gerontology, Fla. Univ. System, Tampa, 1982-86; mem. jury for Sandoz prize in gerontology and geriatrics, 1985-89; bd. dirs. Ctr. for Climacteric Studies, Inc., Gainesville, 1985-88; expert cons. various coms. U.S. Congress, vis. prof. Oita Med. U., Japan, 1991-95, U. Parma, Italy, 1991, Kurume U. Med. Sch., Japan; lectr. in field. Author: How and Why We Age, 1996; editor: Biology of the Mycoplasmas, 1969, Handbook of the Biology of Aging, 1977; sr. editor Biol. Scis. Microfiche Collection Info. on Gerontology and Geriatric Medicine Univ. Microfilms Internat., Ann Arbor, Mich., 1984-98; editor-in-chief Exptl. Gerontology, 1984-98; asst. editor In Vitro jour. Tissue Culture Assn., 1969-75; editor biol. scis. sect. Jour. Gerontology, 1975-80; assoc. editor Cancer Rsch., 1972-80; mem. editorial bd. Jour. Bacteriology, 1964-72, Jour. Virology, 1967-70, Infection and Immunity jour., 1968-78, Exec. Health Report, 1970—, Mechanisms of Aging and Devel., 1972—, Gerontology and Geriatrics Edn., 1980—, A Revista Portuguesa de Medicina Geriatrica, 1987—; mem. adv. com. Bergey's Manual of Determinative Bacteriology, 1965-78; bd. dirs., mem. editorial bd. Bollettino Dell Instituto Sieroterapico Milanese, Archivo de Microbiologia ed Immunologia, Milan, Italy, 1968—; contbr. numerous articles in field to profl. jours. Staff sgt. U.S. Army, 1946-48. Recipient Samuel Roberts Noble Found. Rsch. Recognition award, 1984; co-recipient Sandoz prize Internat. Assn. Gerontology, 1991, Biomed. Scis. & Aging award U. So. Calif., 1974, Rsch. Recognition award Samuel Roberts Noble Found., 1984; Karl-Forster lectr. Acad. Sci. and Lit., Mainz, Germany, 1983, Hoffman-LaRoche lectr. Waksman Inst. Microbiology Rutgers U., 1984, Wadworth Meml. Fund lectr. Rush-Presbyn.-St. Luke's Med. Ctr., Chgo., 1984, hon. lectr. Rosenfield Program Pub. Affairs Grinnell Coll., 1989, invited speaker Sandoz lectrs. in Gerontology, Basle, Switzerland, 1986, 92, numerous other lectureships U.S.A., Can. and Europe, 1970—, Career Devel. award Nat. Cancer Inst., NIH, 1962-70, Lifetime Achievement award Soc. In Vitro Biology, 1996, Van Wezel prize Euro. Soc. Animal Cell Technology, 1999, Lord Cohen of Birkinhead medal Brit. Soc. Rsch. on Aging, 1999. Fellow AAAS, Gerontol Soc. Am. (program and awards com. 1972-77, chmn., exec. com. biol. scis. sect. 1972-74, com. on internat. rels. 1980-82, pub. policy com. 1980-82, pres. 1982-83, ann. Robert W. Kleemeier award 1972, Brookdale award 1980); mem. Am. Soc. for Microbiology, Tissue Culture Assn. (hon., trustee 1966-68, program com. 1970, mem. coun. 1972-74, v.p. 1974-76, pres. Calif. chpt. 1971-73), Soc. for Exptl. Biology and Medicine (councillor 1984-88), Assn. for Advancement of Aging Rsch. (adv. coun. 1970-71), Am. Aging Assn., Am. Cancer Soc. (virology and cell biology study sect. 1974-76), Internat. Assn. Microbiol. Standardization (sec. cell culture com. 1963-73, chmn. 1985—, mem. coun. 1987-89), Internat. Orgn. for Mycoplasmology (Presdl. award 1984), Am. Gerontol. Soc. (v.p., coun. 1972-74, 81-83, program com. 1977-79, bd. dirs. 1981-83), Am. Fedn. Aging Rsch. (bd. dirs., exec. com., rsch. adv. com. 1981—, chmn. study sect. 1987—, v.p. 1988—, Leadership award 1983), Fedn. Am. Socs. for Exptl. Biology, Aging Prevention Rsch. Found. (sci. adv. bd. dirs.), Am. Assn. for Cancer Rsch., Am. Soc. Pathologists, Calif. Found. for Biomed. Rsch., Am. Longevity Assn. (sci. adv. bd. dirs. 1981—), Western Gerontology Assn. (coun. 1972-74, bd. dirs. 81-83), Internat. Assn. Gerontology (mem. Am. exec. com. 1972-75, treas., exec. com. 1985-89, co-recipient Sandoz award gerontology 1991), Found. on Gerontology (sci. adv. bd. 1985—), Soc. Medicine and Natural Sci., Ukrainian Acad. Med. Scis. (fgn., academician 1991), French Biol. Soc. (fgn.), Euro. Soc. Animal Cell Tech. (Van Wezel prize), Brit. Soc. Rsch. on Aging (Lord Cohen of Burkinhead medal). Office: U Calif 36991 Greencroft Close PO Box 89 The Sea Ranch CA 95497-0089

HAYGARTH, JOHN CHARLES, industrial scientist; b. Keighley, West Yorkshire, England, Sept. 4, 1940; s. Thomas Geoffrey and Sarah Elizabeth Haygarth; m. Linda De Esta Anberg, Sept. 27, 1975 (div. June 23, 2000); 1 child, Kara Ann. PhD, U. Leeds, 1965. Rsch. geophysicist UCLA, 1965—70; rsch. scientist Dupont, Wilmington, Del., 1968—69; sr rsch. scientist Teledyne Wah Chang, Albany, Oreg., 1970—79, chief process engr., 1979—80, prin. rsch. scientist, 1980—84, dir. R&D, 1984—96, sr rsch. fellow, 1996—2000; market devel. mgr. Westinghouse Western Zirconium, Ogden, Utah, 2000—02; tech. cons. Ogden, 2002—. Bd. dirs. Oreg. Metals Initiative, Portland, Oreg., 1985—2000, Linfield Rsch. Inst., McMinnville, Oreg., 1985—2000, nuc. engring. dept. Oreg. State U., Corvallis, 1986—. Contbr. articles to profl. jours. Mem.: AAAS, Metals, Minerals and Materials Soc., Am. Chem. Soc. Achievements include Patent For Composite Shot-An Alloy That May Be Used As A Non-Toxic Substitute For Lead For Shotgun Shot With Improved Ballistic Performance Compared To Lead. Home: PO Box 13435 Ogden UT 84412 Personal E-mail: jchaygarth@relia.net.

HAYGOOD, JOHN WARREN, retired lawyer; b. Richmond, Tex., Sept. 16, 1924; s. Claude Culberson and Jessie (Scott) H.; m. Mary Forea McGill, Aug. 25, 1946 (div. 1979); children: Scott McGill, Reid Alexander (dec.), Holly Mary. BA, Centenary Coll., 1947; JD, Tulane U., 1950. Bar: La. 1950, U.S. Dist. Ct. (we. dist.) La. 1952, U.S. Ct. Mil. Appeals 1956, U.S. Supreme Ct. 1959, U.S. Ct. Appeals (5th cir.) 1960, U.S. Dist. Ct. (ea. dist.) La. 1966, U.S. Dist. Ct. (mid. dist.) La. 1966, U.S. Dist. Ct. (so. dist.) Miss. 1968. Pvt. practice, Shreveport, La., 1950; assoc. Brown & Fleniken, Shreveport, 1952-53; atty. Ark. Fuel Oil Corp., Shreveport, 1953-58; ptnr. Stagg, Cady, Haygood & Beard, Shreveport, 1958-65, Jones, Walker, Waechter, Poitevent, Carrere & Denegre, New Orleans, 1965-87; ret., 1987. Instr. trial practice Tulane U. Law Sch., 1974 Named Outstanding Class Agt. Tulane Alumni Fund, 1980. Mem.: La. Bar Assn., P-51 Mustang Pilots Assn., P-40 Warhawk Pilot Assn., Phi Delta Phi, Kappa Alpha Order, Omicron Delta Kappa. Home: 1300 Aris Ave Metairie LA 70005-1714

HAYGOOD, ROBERT COLLINS, industrial psychologist, educator, consultant; b. Jacksonville, Fla., Oct. 17, 1926; s. James Douglas and Margaret (Collins) H.; m. Danielle Hagerty Haygood, Aug. 23, 1963; children: Daniel Paul, Charles Douglas, Harold Bennett. BS, U. Ill., 1949; MS, U. Utah, 1959, PhD, 1963. Lic. psychologist, Ariz. Sr. rsch. engr. N.Am. Aviation-Autonetics, Anaheim, Calif., 1959-64; from asst. to assoc. prof. Kans. State U., Manhattan, 1964-69; prof. Ariz. State U., Tempe, 1970-97, prof. emeritus, 1997—. Vis. lectr. Calif. State Coll., Long Beach, 1969-70; cons. Advanced Risk Control Sys. Internat., Scottsdale, Ariz., 1994-97, VA, Kansas City, 1965-69; cons. various hosps., Phoenix, 1971-74. Mem. editl. staff, manuscript reviewer Jour. Exptl. Psychology, 1965-72; contbr. articles to profl. jours. Chmn. Ariz. State Bd. Psychol. Examiners, Phoenix, 1974-75; dist. leader Arizonans for McGovern, Phoenix, 1972. Staff sgr. USAF, 1953-57. Sr. rsch. assoc. Nat. Rsch. Coun., NASA, 1977-78; predoctoral rsch. fellow USPHS, U. Utah, 1958-59. Mem. Am. Psychol. Soc., Southwestern Psychol. Assn. (bd. dirs. 1973), Human Factors and Ergonomics Soc. (chpt. pres., sec.-treas. 1979—). Avocations: jazz, dance band arranging, international travel. Home: 6616 E Calle Redondo Scottsdale AZ 85251 Office: Ariz State U Dept Psychology Tempe AZ 85287 E-mail: danibobhaygood@cox.net.

HAYHURST, JAMES FREDERICK PALMER, career and business consultant, inspirational speaker, author; b. Toronto, May 24, 1941; s. W. Palmer and Jean E. (Hunnisett) H.; children: Cindy, Jim, Barbara. H.BA, U. Western Ont., 1963. Brand man Procter & Gamble, Toronto, 1963-66, exec. v.p., 1975-82; pres. Hedwyn Communications Inc., Toronto, 1983-86; chmn. Saatchi & Saatchi Compton Hayhurst, Toronto, 1983-86; owner Wyldwyn Holdings Ltd., Toronto, 1986—; pres. The Hayhurst Career Ctr., Toronto, 1988—, The Right Mountain Crew, 1994—. Author: The Right Mountain, 1996. Chmn. Outward Bound Can., 1985-87; founding co-chmn. Trails Youth Initiatives. Mem. Toronto Golf Club, Olde Fla. Golf Club (Naples), Caledon Mountain Trout Club. Office: The Right Mountain Inc 378 Fairlawn Ave Toronto ON Canada M5M 1T8 *True success is the attainment of purpose without compromising your core values.*

HAYKEN, GERALD DREUX, orthopedic surgeon; b. N.Y.C., Oct. 11, 1949; s. Morris Jay and Dorothy Margaret (McNally) H.; m. Tonette Theresa Farinacci, Aug. 13, 1972; children: Gregory Steven, Valerie Marie. BA in

Biology, Hofstra U., 1971; MD, Temple U., 1976. Diplomate Am. Bd. Orthopaedic Surgery. Intern, resident U. Pa. Hosp., Phila., 1976-81; orthop. surgeon Burlington County Orthopaedic Specialists PA, Mt. Laurel, NJ, 1981—. Med. advisor Liberty Mutual Ins. Co., Boston, 1994—; treas. So. Jersey Bone and Joint Surgery Inc., Mt. Laurel, 1994-95; bd. dirs. Orthop. Network, Inc. Contbr. articles to profl. jours. Vol. Leather's Playground, Medford, N.J., 1995. Fellow Am. Acad. Orthop. Surgeons, mem. N.J. Orthop. Soc., Phila. Orthop. Soc., Union League Phila. Avocations: skiing, scuba diving, sailing. Office: Burlington County Orthopaedic Specialists PA 204 Ark Rd Mount Laurel NJ 08054-3100

HAYMAN, HARRY, association executive, electrical engineer; b. Lewistown, Pa., Mar. 20, 1917; s. Sidney and Nettie (Hirsch) H.; m. Edith Harriet Levitz, Mar. 18, 1946; children: Gail A., Beth (Mrs. Stanley Truman), Sidney F., Stuart A. BS, NYU, 1938; postgrad., George Washington U., 1947-50. Engr. FCC, Washington, 1940-54; pres., gen. mgr. radio sta. WPGC, Morningside, Md., 1954-55; project mgr. U.S. Navy and FAA, Washington, 1956-60; program mgr NASA project Apollo, Washington, 1960-71; chmn. IEEE Computer Soc., Washington, 1965, exec. sec. N.Y.C., 1971-82, dir. confs. and tutorials Silver Spring, Md., 1982-89, coord. robotics and automation divsn., 1988—. Vice pres. Nat. Childrens Center, 1960; pres. Henryton State Hosp. Assn., 1970, 74; Bd. dirs. D.C. Assn. Retarded Children, 1956-70, pres. Washington chpt., 1953-55; pres. Gt. Oaks Aux., 1975-78. Served with USNR, 1944-46. Recipient Apollo Achievement award 1969. Mem. IEEE (treas. Computer Soc. Internat. Conf. 1970, treas. Internat. Conf. on Computer Comm. 1972, spl. asst. to chmn. Conf. on Computer Comm. 1974, coord., treas. Internat. Conf. on Robotics and Automation 1980-96). Home: 3037C Exeter Dr Boca Raton FL 33434 Office: 1201 Elm Grove Cir Silver Spring MD 20905-7020 E-mail: h.hayman@ieee.org.

HAYMAN, MARTIN ARTHUR, psychiatrist, educator; b. N.Y.C., Dec. 5, 1929; s. Louis and Cecelia (Klatzkin) H.; m. Traude E. Sighartner, June 9, 1957; children: Douglas, Kenneth. BA cum laude, NYU, 1951, MD, 1955. Diplomate Am. Bd. Psychiatry and Neurology, Nat. Bd. Med. Examiners. Intern Meadowbrook Hosp., East Meadow, N.Y., 1955-56; pvt. practice Nassau County, N.Y., 1959-73; sr. physician VA Med. Ctr., Northport, N.Y., 1973; resident in psychiatry SUNY Med. Ctr., Stony Brook, 1974-77, asst. prof. clin. psychiatry, 1977—. Dir. psychiatry South Brookhaven Health Ctr., Patchogue, N.Y., 1977-91; attending physician Brookhaven Meml. Hosp. Med. Ctr., Patchogue, 1977-91. Reviewer jour.; contbr. articles to profl. jours. Mem. ad hoc com. Helping Older People Emotionally, Suffolk County, 1981-82. Capt. M.C., USAF, 1956-58. Fellow Acad. Psychosomatic Medicine; mem. AMA (Physician's Recognition awards 1970—), Am. Psychiat. Assn., Med. Soc. N.Y., Suffolk County Med. Soc., Phi Beta Kappa, Beta Lambda Sigma (vice chancellor 1951). Home and Office: PO Box 626 20 Redwood Dr Great River NY 11739-0626 E-mail: mhayman@pol.net.

HAYMAN, RICHARD WARREN JOSEPH, conductor; b. Cambridge, Mass., Mar. 27, 1920; s. Fred Albert and Gladys Marie (Learned) Hayman; m. Maryellen Daly, June 25, 1960; children: Suzanne Marie, Olivia Kathryn. D Hum. (hon.), Detroit Coll. Bus., 1980. Freelance composer, arranger 20th Century Fox, Warner Bros., MGM, Universal Film Studios; music arranger, dir. Vaughn Monroe Orch. records and TV show, N.Y.C., 1945-50; chief arranger Arthur Fiedler and Boston Pops Orchestra, 1950-95, mus. dir. Mercury Record Corp., N.Y.C., 1950-65, Time-Mainstream Records, N.Y.C., 1960-70; prin. pops condr. Detroit Symphony Orchs.; prin. pops condr. McDonnell Douglas chair St. Louis, 1976—, prin. pops condr. Birmingham (Ala.), Hartford (Conn.), Calgary (Can.), Grand Rapids (Mich.) Symphony Orch., London (Ont., Can.) Orch. Composer: No Strings Attached, Dansero, Skipping Along, Carriage Trade, Serenade to a Lost Love, Olivia, Suzanne, Freddie the Football. Recipient Best Instrumental Record award, Sta. WERE, Cleve., 1963, McDonnell Douglas award, 2000, Star dedicated, Hollywood Blvd. Walk of Fame. Mem.: ASCAP, NARAS (Best TV Comml. Jingle award 1960), Am. Fed. Musicians. Roman Catholic. Office: Richard Hayman Prodns 784 US Highway 1 Ste 22B North Palm Beach FL 33408-4411 Mailing: St Louis Symphony Orch 718 N Grand Blvd Saint Louis MO 63103-1011*

HAYMES, JERRY LYNN, entertainment industry executive; b. Verron, Tex., Aug. 30, 1940; s. Arthur L. and Georgia H.; m. Brenda Dee, Aug. 1, 1962 (div. June 1981); children: Tracy, Darren. BS, Abilene Christian Univ., 1975; AS, Kilgore Coll., 1988; MusD, London Conservatory of Music, London, 1963. Drummer/singer Norman Petty Studio, Clovis, N.Mex., 1955-57, Sun Records, Memphis, 1957; performer, 1960—; CEO, various radio stations, Longview, Tex., 1977, Umpire Entertainment, Longview, Tex., 1980—. Bd. dirs. Country Music Assn., Nashville, 1960's, Internat. Talent Buyer Assn., 1970's; adv. bd., bd. dirs. Texas County Music Assn., 1995—. Record promotor It's A Heart Ache, 1978 (Gold Record 1978); songwriter What Then?, 1956 (Gospel music award 1967), So Fine, 1959 (Triple Gold Record 1981); drummer Party Doll, 1957 (Gold Record 1957). Pres. S.W. Conf. Baseball Umpire Assn., Tex., 1968—98; adv. Vernon Reg. Jr. Coll. Fine Arts Dept., 1997—. With U.S. Army, 1960—62, with U.S. Army, 1967, Vietnam. Named to Tex. Music Hall of Fame; recipient Sun Legends Group Rock-a-Billy Artist award, Rock-n-Roll Hall of Fame, 1996, Top Ten Record Artist/Musician for Past 45 Years award, Billboard Mag., 1999. Mem. Sons of Confederate Vet., Am. Fed. of Musicians, Baseball Umpire Assn. (pres. 1979-84). Avocations: collecting music memorbilia, sports officiating. Office: Umpire Entertainment 1507 Scenic Dr Longview TX 75604-2319 Office Fax: 903-234-2944.

HAYMOND, PAULA J. psychologist, diagnostician, hypnotherapist; b. Warsaw, Ind., Sept. 29, 1949; d. George Milton and Phyllis (Freeman) H. BA, Butler U., 1971, MS, 1973; EdD, Ind. U., 1982. Lic. psychometrist, Ind.; lic. psychologist, Tex. Sr. asst. psychology dept. Butler U., Indpls., 1970-71; behavioral clinician I psychology dept. Ind. Boys Sch., Plainfield, 1973-75, behavioral clinician II diagnostic unit, 1975-78, Ind. Girls Sch., Indpls., 1978-80; human factors cons. Lund Cons. Inc., N.Y.C., 1981-82; adminstr. DePelchin Children Ctr./Bayou Pl., Houston, 1982-85; diagnostician Larry Ppollock PhD & Assoc., Houston, 1985-88; ptnr. Montrose Psychotherapy P.C., Houston, 1988—; vol. CEO Noah's House, Houston, 1998—. Biofeedback therapist Teresa A. Atkinson RPT, Houston, 1989-91; psychology supr. Larry Pollock PhD & Assocs., Houston, 1990-91; instr. Wharton County Jr. Coll. Police Acad., 1990-99; presenter S.W. Women's Conf., Houston, 1990, 5th Internat. Congress on Ericksonian Approaches to Hypnosis and Psychotherapy, 1992; seminar instr. Inst. Group and Family Psychotherapy, Moscow, Russia, 1994. Presenter U. Tex. Dental Sch., Houston, 1990, 91. Recipient Symbol of Excellence award, Goodwill Industries, 1999, Rehab. Profl. of Yr. award, Tex. Rehab. Assn., 2001. Mem. APA, AACD, Am. Soc. Clin. Hypnosis, Nat. Bd. Crt. Clin. Hypnotherapists, Biofeedback Soc. Tex., Exec. and Profl. Assn. Houston (bd. dirs., comty. affairs com. 1993-96, bd. trustees 1996-98), Delta Delta Delta, Kappa Kappa Kappa. Avocations: dressage, show jumping. Office: Montrose Psychotherapy PC 812 Hawthorne St Houston TX 77006-3902

HAYNER, HERMAN HENRY, lawyer; b. Fairfield, Wash., Sept. 25, 1916; s. Charles H. and Lillie (Reifenberger) H.; m. Jeannette Hafner, Oct. 24, 1942; children: Stephen, James K., Judith A. BA, Wash. State U., 1938; JD with honors, U. Oreg., 1946. Bar: Wash. 1946, Oreg. 1946, U.S. Dist. Ct. Wash. 1947, U.S. Ct. Appeals (9th cir.) 1947. Asst. U.S. atty. U.S. Dept. Justice, Portland, Oreg., 1946-47; atty. City of Walla Walla, Wash., 1949-53; ptnr. Minnick-Hayner, Walla Walla, 1949—. Mem. Wash. State exec. bd. U.S. West, Seattle, 1988-95. Regent Wash. State U., Pullman, 1965-78; dir. YMCA, Walla Walla, 1956-67. Lt. col. Infantry, 1942-46. Decorated Bronze Star medal and Four Battle Stars; recipient Disting. Svc. award Jr. C. of C., 1951, Wash. State U. Alumni award, 1988. Fellow ABA, Am. Coll. Trust & Estate Counsel; mem. Wash. State Bar Assn., Walla Walla County Bar Assn. (pres. 1954-55), Walla Walla C. of C. (merit award 1977, dir. 1973-88), Rotary (pres. 1956-57), Walla Walla Country Club (pres. 1956-57). Republican. Presbyterian. Avocations: golf, photography. Home: PO Box 454 Walla Walla WA 99362 Office: Minnick-Hayner PO Box 1757 Walla Walla WA 99362 E-mail: chayner@aol.com.

HAYNES, CALEB VANCE, JR., geology and archaeology educator; b. Spokane, Wash., Feb. 29, 1928; m. Elizabeth Hamilton, Jan. 11, 1954 (div. 1991); 1 child, Elizabeth Anne. Student, Johns Hopkins U., 1947-49; degree in geol. engring., Colo. Sch. Mines, 1956; PhD, U. Ariz., 1965. Mining geology cons., 1958-60; sr. project engr. Am. Inst. Research, Golden, Colo., 1956-60; sr. engr. Martin Co., Denver, 1960-62; geologist Nev. State Mus. Tule Springs Expedition, 1962-63; research asst. U. Ariz., Tucson, 1963-64, asst. prof. geology, 1965-68, prof. geosci., anthropology, 1974-99, Regents prof., 1991-99, Regents prof. emeritus, 1999; assoc. prof. So. Meth. U., Dallas, 1968-73, prof., 1973-74. Served with USAF, 1951—54. Guggenheim fellow 1980-81, Smithsonian sr. post doctoral fellow, 1987 ; grantee NSF, Nat. Geographic Soc., others. Fellow: AAAS, Geol. Soc. Am. (Archaeol. Geology award 1984); mem.: Soc. Am. Archaeology (Fryxell award 1978), Am. Quaternary Assn. (pres. 1976—78, Disting. Career award 2002), Nat. Acad. Sci., Sigma Xi. Office: U Ariz Dept Anthropology Tucson AZ 85721-0001

HAYNES, CHERYL LYNN, secondary school educator; b. Ohio; BS, Ohio U., 1973—77; MS, Ohio State U., 1977—81. Family and consumer sci. tchr. Lancaster City Schools, Ohio, 1977—.

HAYNES, DOUGLAS MARTIN, physician, educator; b. N.Y.C., Jan. 25, 1922; s. Daniel Hagood and Courtenay (Collins) H.; m. Elizabeth B. Johnson, June 17, 1961; children: Douglas Marshall, Lewis Daniel. BA, BS, So. Meth. U., 1943; MD, Southwestern Med. Coll., 1946; MA, Louisville Presby. Theol. Sem., 1989, ThM, 1994. Diplomate Am. Bd. Obstetrics and Gynecology (assoc. examiner). Intern in pathology Parkland Meml. Hosp., Dallas, 1946-47, resident obstetrics and gynecology, 1949-52; asst. prof. obstetrics and gynecology U. Tex. Southwestern Med Sch., 1952-55; assoc. prof. obstetrics and gynecology U. Louisville Sch. Medicine, 1955-57, prof., 1957-87, prof. emeritus, 1987—, chmn. dept., 1957-69; interim dean U. Louisville Sch. Medicine (Sch. of Medicine), 1969-70, dean, 1970-72. Author: Medical Complications During Pregnancy, 1969; Contbr. articles to med. jours. Served to capt., M. C. AUS, 1947-49. Fellow Am. Gynec. and Obstet. Soc.; mem. Am. Coll. Obstetricians and Gynecologists, A.C.S., Central Assn. Obstetricians and Gynecologists (v.p. 1977-78), So. Med. Assn., Phi Beta Kappa, Phi Chi, Delta Chi, Alpha Omega Alpha, Phi Kappa Phi. Democrat. Episcopalian. Home: 5204 Tomahawk Rd Louisville KY 40207-1643

HAYNES, GARY ALLEN, photographer, journalist, newspaper editor; b. Beloit, Kansas, Jan. 25, 1936; s. Blair W. and Evelyn H. (Allen) F.; children by previous marriage: Stephanie L., Philip A., Emily L.; m. Audrey M. (Edwards); stepchildren: Jane Kelly, Katie Kelly. BS in journalism, Kans. State U., 1957. Staff photographer Salina (Kans.) Jour., Salina, Kans., 1957; photographer UPI, Detroit, 1958, mgr. picture bur. Phila., 1959-62, Atlanta, 1962-63, spl. projects photographer N.Y.C., 1964, mgr. picture bur. L.A., 1964-68; photographer Internat. Olympic Photo Pool, Tokyo, 1964; mgr. divsn. news pictures UPI, Chgo., 1968-70, asst. to mng. editor newspictures N.Y.C., 1970-71; nat. picture editor N.Y. Times, N.Y.C., 1971-74; photo editor San Francisco Examiner, San Francisco, 1974; dir. graphic arts Phila. Inquirer, Phila., 1974-95, asst. mng. editor; with Photography weekly column, syndicated by Knight Newspapers (later Knight Ridder), 1976-87; cons. N.Y. Times, N.Y.C., 1996—. Photographer NASA Photo Pool, 1962-63; spkr., del., USA.USSR Photo Summit, Moscow, 1990, Washington, 1991. Contbg. photographer: (book) Four Days-The Historical Record of Death of President Kennedy, 1963, A Week at Kansas State, 1988; picture editor: Assignment Am., 1972, A Day In the Life of Calif., 1989; judge, W.R. Hearst photojournalism competition, San Francisco, 1986-88; lectr., photography and photo editing, Am. Press Inst., Reston, Va., 1987-96, The New Sch., 1991, Internat. Ctr. Photography, NY., 1990, U. Arts, Phila., 1989-91, Kans. State U., Manhattan, 1989-99, 2000, Kans. State U., photo workshop, Salina, Kans.2002, Temple U., Phila., 1992. Capt., Adj. Gen. Corps, U.S. Army, 1957-58. Recipient, first pl. award, Look mag., Sports Photo Contest, 1962, first and Best of Show awards, The White House News Photographers Assn., 1962, Photo awards World Press Photo, first and third pl. gen. news, 1963, Sweepstakes award, Atlanta Press Assn., Sweepstakes first and third pl. awards Gen. News, 1964, Judges Spl. award for newspaper picture editing, 1979, best use of photos in newspaper zoned edit NPPA/Pictures of Yr. Competition, Silver medal mag. photo editing, Soc. Newspaper Design, 1988, Pictures of Yr. eighteenth Ann. Competition first pl. spot news, first pl. feature, first pl. gen. news. Mem., Nat. Press Photographer's Assn., Sigma Delta Phi. Home: 1473 N Ill Rte 2 Oregon IL 61061 E-mail: verity@rochelle.net.

HAYNES, GEORGE CLEVE, lawyer, author; b. St. Louis, Jan. 15, 1946; s. George Cave and Helen Marie (Cleve) H. B.A., So. Ill. U., Edwardsville, 1969; J.D., Ill. Inst. Tech., 1974. Bar: Wash. 1977, U.S. Dist. Ct. (we. dist.) Wash. 1977, U.S. Ct. Appeals (9th cir.) 1978, U.S. Supreme Ct. 1982. judge pro tem Seattle Mcpl. Ct., 1977-84, King County Superior Ct., 1980; instr. Edmonds Community Coll., Wash., 1983-84; gen. counsel Alternative Intervention Resources King County, Seattle, 1984—; literary agt., Harold Matson Co., N.Y. Mem. Wash. State Bar Assn., Sherlock Holmes Soc. of London, La Soc. Dante Alighieri. Club: Diogenes. Office: Harold Matson Co 276 5th Ave New York NY 10001-4509

HAYNES, GREGORY KENT, engineer; b. Ft. Dix, N.J., Nov. 14, 1956; s. Robert Edmund and Marion Louise (Smith) H. BS in Chemistry summa cum laude, Morgan State U., 1982, postgrad., 1989-91; BS in Biochemistry, U. Md., 1983, BSEE, 1983, postgrad., 1988—89, U. Md., Baltimore County, 1991—94; MS in Chemistry, Wash. State U., 1985. Engring. asst. TVA, Muscle Shoals, Ala., 1974, 75; lab. asst. Towson (Md.) State U., 1977-78; assoc. engr. Bendix Field, Columbia, Md., 1987-88; prof. chemistry Morgan State U., 1994—. Mem. Timonium Presbyn. Ch. Mem. Charlotte Hall Mil. Acad. Alumni Assn., Balt. Poly. Inst. Alumni Assn., U. Md. Alumni Assn. Engr., Sigma Pi Sigma, Pi Mu Epsilon, Phi Lambda Upsilon. Avocations: computer, writing, television, group meetings, prayer. Home: 3232 Tioga Pky Baltimore MD 21215-7925

HAYNES, JOHN MABIN, retired utilities executive; b. Albany, N.Y., Apr. 22, 1928; s. John Mabin and Gladys Elizabeth (Phillips) H.; m. Marion Enola Hamilton, Apr. 7, 1956; children: John David, Douglas Hamilton, Robert Paul. BS, Utica Coll., Syracuse U., 1952. Accountant Price Waterhouse & Co., N.Y.C., Syracuse, N.Y., 1953-61; successively auditor, adminstrv. asst., asst. treas., treas., treas. and v.p., sr. v.p. Niagara Mohawk Power Corp., Syracuse, 1961-88; past pres., chmn., dir. N.Y. Bus. Devel. Corp., Syracuse. Past dir., pres. N M Uranium, Inc.; past dir., treas. Canadian Niagara Power Co. Ltd.; past treas. Moreau Mfg. Co., St. Lawrence Power Co.; past treas. Empire State Power Resources, Inc.; past dir. and treas. Beebee Island Corp.; past bd. dirs. treas. Opinac Investments Ltd., Opinac Energy Ltd., Opinac Holdings Ltd.; past mng. dir. Niagara Mohawk Fin. N.V. Mem. Westhill Cen. Sch. Bd. Edn., 1968-73, pres., 1969-71; treas. Henderson County Humane Soc., 1989-90. With AUS, 1945-47. Mem. Nat. Assn. Accountants (past dir.), Am. Gas Assn. (fin. com.), Fin. Execs. Inst. Clubs: Bond of Syracuse (past dir.), Masons. Home: 3108 Cove Loop Rd Hendersonville NC 28739-8870 E-mail: jackhaynes@mchsi.com.

HAYNES, KAREN SUE, academic administrator, educator; b. Jersey City, July 6, 1946; d. Edward J. and Adelaide M. (Hineson) Czarnecki; m. James S. Mickelson; children: Kingsley Eliot Mickelson, Kimberly Elizabeth Mickelson, David Mickelson. BA, Goucher Coll., 1968; MSW, McGill U., 1970; PhD, U. Tex., 1977. Cons. Inst. Nat. Planning, Cairo, 1977-78; asst. prof. Ind. U., Indpls., 1978-81, assoc. prof., 1981-85; prof. social work U. Houston, 1985-95, dean, 1985-95; pres. U. Houston-Victoria, Tex., 1995—. Founding presdl. sponsor Tex. Network Women Higher Edn.; formula adv. com. Tex. Coord. Bd. Higher Edn. Author: (book) Sage Publications, 1984, Longman, 1986, 1996, Springer, 1989, Allyn and Bacon, 2000, 2003; contbr. articles to profl. jours. Mem.: Leadership Houston, Leadership Tex., Leadership Am., Nat. Alliance Info. and Referral (pres. 1983—87), Internat. Assn. Schs. Social Work, Coun. Social Work Edn., Am. Coun. Edn. Network (mem. exec. bd. dirs.), Am. Assn. State Colls. and Univs. (sec., treas., mem. exec. bd. dirs. 2003—), NASW. Avocation: poetry. Office: U Houston-Victoria 3007 N Ben Wilson St Victoria TX 77901-5731

HAYNES, MARCIA MARGARET, insurance agent; b. Bay City, Mich., June 28, 1931; d. Frederick O. and Margaret M. (Oakes) Rouse; m. N. Fred Haynes, July 20, 1957;children: Carol M. Krashen, David F. Haynes, Julie A. Beaty. BA, Denison U., Granville, Ohio, 1953. With advt.-sales dept. Birmingham (Mich.) Eccentric, 1953-55; tchr. Port Huron (Mich.) Area Schs., 1955-58; student tchr. coord. Mich. State U., Port Huron, Mich., 1967-70; insurance agent Northwestern Mut. Life Ins. Co., Port Huron, Mich., 1981—. Leader, Girl Scout U.S., Port Huron, 1956-57; treas. and bus. mgr., Port Huron Little Theater, Port Huron, 1959-1961; sec., v.p., and pres., Mus. of Arts and History, 1968-69, 74-80; sec., v.p. bd. dirs., Port Huron Hosp. Aux., 1960-70; trustee, Hist. Soc. of Mich., Ann Arbor, 1975-81; coord. of preservation Round Island Lighthouse, Straits Mackinac, Mich., 1972-76; chmn. Horizons, Port Huron Bicentennial Com., Port Huron, 1976; active in Rep. State Bicentennial Com, Lansing, Mich. 1976; trustee, St. Clair County C.C., Port Huron, 1981-2005, vice chmn., 1985-95; bd. dirs., Stuart House Mus., Mackinac Island, Mich., 1978, Internat. Symphony, Port Huron and Sarnia, Ont., Can., 1983-86; sec., treas., Blue Water Area Tourism Bur., Port Huron, 1985-87; adv. bd., Cmty. Found. of St. Clair County, Port Huron, 1986-91, 94-2001; vestry Grace Episcopal Ch., 1990-93; bd. dirs. Am. Heart Assn. St. Clair County, 1994-99; v.p. fin. Blue Water coun. Boy Scouts Am., 1995-99; exec. com. Port Huron/Marysville C. of C., 1997-99. Mem. Nat. Life Underwriters, Port Huron Estate Planning Coun. (pres. 1985-86), Mich. Mus. Assn. (bd. dirs. 1984-86), Rotary, Port Huron Golf Club.

HAYNES, MOSES ALFRED, physician; b. Guyana, Nov. 17, 1921; came to U.S., 1947, naturalized, 1955; s. Milton Alphonso and Charlotte Mildred (Alleyne) Haynes; m. Hazel Louise Edgecombe, July 1, 1951; 1 child, Theresa Sue Aldrich. BS, Columbia U., 1951; MD, SUNY, 1954; MPH, Harvard U., 1963. Intern St. John's Episcopal Hosp., Bklyn., 1954-55; physician USPHS Indian Hosp., Cheyenne Agy., S.D., 1955-59; asst. prof. community medicine U. Vt., 1959-64; assoc. prof. Sch. Pub. Health, Johns Hopkins, 1966-69; prof. preventive and social medicine and pub. health UCLA, 1969-77; assoc. dean Drew Postgrad. Med. Sch., Los Angeles, 1969-77, chmn. dept. cmty. medicine, 1969-74, acting dean, 1975-76, dean, pres., 1979-86; dir. Drew/Meharry/Morehouse Consortium Cancer Ctr., 1986-90. Pres. SECON Inc., 1977-79; vis. prof. Med. Coll., Trivandrum, Kerala, India, 1964-66; mem. cancer support rev. com. Nat. Cancer Inst. Chmn. health task force Urban Coalition, 1968—69; mem. Pres.'s Com. Health Edn., 1972; exec. dir. Nat. Med. Assn. Found., 1968—69; mem. bd. sci. counselors, divsn. cancer prevention and control Nat. Cancer Inst., 1989—93, chmn., 1991—93; mem. adv. com. Nat. Ctr. Health Stats., 1974—76; bd. dirs. Ptnrs. for Prevention, 1991—92; chmn. bd. dirs. Charles Drew U. Medicine and Sci., 2001—; mem. adv. bd. Fogarty Internat. Ctr., 1992—93; mem. U.S. Preventive Svcs. Task Force, 1985—86. With USPHS, 1955—59. Fellow Am. Coll. Preventive Medicine, (pres. 1983-85); fellow AAAS; mem. Inst. Medicine of Nat. Acad. Sci. (internat. health bd., com. human rights 1986-89), Inst. Medicine (council 1983-86), Alpha Omega Alpha. Home: 29249 Firthridge Rd Palos Verdes Peninsula CA 90275-4713 E-mail: mahaynes@cox.net. *Being is more important than doing.*

HAYNES, PAUL R. lawyer; b. Danbury, Conn., Dec. 15, 1950; s. Richard Osborn and Doris Louise (Rowe) H.; m. Karen Marie Traboldt, Nov. 3, 1979; children: Matthew, Joshua, Laura. BA, SUNY, Oneonta, 1972; JD, Albany U., 1976. Bar: N.Y. 1977, U.S. Dist. Ct. (so., ea. and no. dists.) N.Y. 1979, U.S. Ct. Appeals (2d cir.) 1979, U.S. Supreme Ct. 1980. Law clk. Hon. Allan Dixon Rensselaer County Family Ct., Troy, N.Y., 1975-76; assoc. Reed & Reed, Esqs., Poughkeepsie, N.Y., 1977-80, pvt. practice Wappingers Falls, N.Y., 1980—. Mem. tel-law com. United Way of Dutchess County, Poughkeepsie, N.Y., 1977; mem. Cmty. Ambulance Svc., Wappingers Falls, N.Y., 1986—; cubmaster Pack 40 Dutchess County Coun., Boy Scouts Am., Wappingers Falls, 1991-94; asst. scoutmaster Troop 40, Hudson Valley Coun., Hopewell Junction, N.Y., 1996—. Mem. ABA, ATLA, N.Y. State Bar Assn., Dutchess County Bar Assn., Rotary (sec. 1985-87, pres. 1987-88, Paul Harris fellow 1987), Greater So. Dutchess C. of C. (county issues com. 1980—), Wappingers Falls Bus. and Profl. Assn. (charter), Pi Gamma Mu. Republican. Office: 161 W Main St Wappingers Falls NY 12590-1568

HAYNES, PETER LANCASTER, retired utility executive; b. Ellsworth, Maine, July 8, 1939; s. Charles A. and Hazel G. (Giles) H.; m. Judith A. Bates, Aug. 26, 1961; children: Jeffrey, Timothy, Christopher. BS, U. Maine, 1961; MBA, Cornell U., 1963. Registered profl. engr., Vt. V.p. switched svcs. New Eng. Telephone, Boston, 1978-83, v.p. mktg., 1983-85; pres., CEO Nynex Enterprises, N.Y.C., 1985-90, Quality Logistics Mgmt., Inc., Bedford, N.Y., 1991-92, Consumers Water Co., Portland, Maine, 1992-99. Pres. Portland Symphony; chmn. Maine Med. Ctr.; bd. govs. Boys and Girls Club Am., Atlanta. Mem.: Cornell Club N.Y. Home: 98 Starboard Reach Yarmouth ME 04096-6158 E-mail: plhaynes@aol.com.

HAYNES, R. MICHAEL, lawyer; b. Safford, Ariz., Oct. 3, 1940; s. Rodman and Angeline (Fragale) H.; m. Anne Marie de Almeida, Aug. 15, 1972; 1 child, Michelle Chloe. BA, Rutgers U., 1963, JD with honors, 1968. Bar: N.Y. 1969, N.J. 1977, D.C. 1992, U.S. Dist. Ct. (so. and ea. dists.) N.Y. 1973, U.S. Ct. Appeals (2d cir.) 1973, U.S. Supreme Ct. 1973, U.S. Dist. Ct. N.J. 1977, U.S. Dist. Ct. D.C. 1992. Assoc. Cooper, Ostrin, DeVargo & Ackerman, N.Y.C., 1968-69; asst. dist. atty., dep. chief rackets bur. N.Y. County Dist. Atty.'s Office, N.Y.C., 1969-74; exec. asst. dist. atty. spl. narcotics Prosecutor's Office, N.Y.C., 1974-76; asst. U.S. atty. Dist. N.J., Newark, 1976-79; minority counsel Com. on Small Bus., U.S. Senate, Washington, 1979-81, chief counsel, 1981-86; gen. counsel Nat. Assn. Small Bus. Investment Cos., Washington, 1986-90; founding ptnr. Law Offices R. Michael Haynes, Washington, 1990—2000; prin. Semmes, Bowen & Semmes, P.C., Washington, 2000—. Adj. prof. L.I. U., 1975-76; instr. N.Y. State Commn. Investigation, 1974-75, Atty. Gen.'s Adv. Inst., Dept. Justice, 1978-79; counsel White House Conf. on Small Bus., 1980 Advisor Washington Internat. Sch. Mock Trial Team, 1991-95. Recipient Atty. Gen.'s Spl. Achievement award, 1977 Mem. ABA (chmn. SBIC subcom. small bus. com. 1986-89), Fed. Bar Assn. (chmn. small bus. com. fin. insts. and economy sect. 1988-89), U.S. C. of C. (small bus. coun. 1987-89), SEC Govt. Bus. Forum on Capital Formation (exec. com. 1988-89). Republican. Office: 3509 Idaho Ave NW Washington DC 20016-3151 E-mail: rmhaynes@lawyer.com. *The law holds everyone equally accountable, but requires of a lawyer a higher duty to honor the principles that the law prescribes while at the same time serving the people whom it governs. To that end, a lawyer must insure that the law itself remains just and fair and that those who make and enforce the law do so with integrity.*

HAYNES, RALPH LEWIS, internist, pulmonary diseases, consultant; b. Germany, Dec. 23, 1942; m. Patricia Ritchie Haynes; children: Lesley Erin, Joseph Russell, Mathew Lewis, Walter Christopher, Christine Emma, Carol Elizabeth. BSc, W.Va. U., 1966; MD, Emory U., Atlanta, 1970. Diplomate Am. Bd. Internal Medicine and Pulmonary Diseases. Commd. lt. U.S. Army, 1966, advanced through grades to maj. gen., 1997; clin. assoc. prof. Emory U., Atlanta, 1985-93, clin. prof. medicine, 1993—; dep. dir. med. support, J4, The Joint Staff The Pentagon, Washington, 2000 . Dir. respiratory svcs. St. Joseph Hosp., Atlanta, 1977—; dean's adv. com. Emory U., 1988-. Contbr. chpts. to books. Bd. dirs. ATlanta Chamber Players, 1982-90, St. Joseph's Health Sys., Atlanta, 1982—. Named to Honorable Order of Ky. Cols., Order of Mil. Med. Merit. Fellow ACP, Am. Coll. Chest Physicians; mem. Mil. Order Temple of Jerusalem, Atlanta Med. Assn. (v.p., pres., sec., treas.), Atlanta Rotary (bd. dirs. 1996-98). Episcopalian. Avocations: military history, european history, asthma. Home: 250 Riverwood Ct Atlanta GA 30328 Office: 5505 Peachtree Dunwoody Rd NE Atlanta GA 30342-1705 E-mail: haynesrl@js.pentagon.mil., haynesralph@yahoo.com.

HAYNES, RICHARD WALTER, research scientist; b. Washington, July 7, 1945; s. Walter Edward Haynes, Mary Haynes; m. Paula Gilly; children: Amy, Jeremy. BS, Va. Tech., Blacksburg, VA, 1967; MS, Blacksburg, Va, 1968; PhD, N.C. State U., 1975. Rschr. Pacific N.W. Rsch. Sta., Portland, Oreg., 1975—83, project leader, 1983—91, program mgr., 1991—. Mem.: Soc. Am. Foresters (Forest Sci. award 2001). Avocation: canoeing. Office: US Forest Svc Box 3890 Portland OR 97208 Office Fax: 503-808-2033. Business E-Mail: rhaynes@fs.fed.us.

HAYNES, THOMAS MORRIS, philosophy educator; b. Waukesha, Wis., Oct. 24, 1918; s. George Albert and Lois (Morris) H.; m. Jane Louise Riggs, Sept. 12, 1942; children: Christopher Thomas, Jonathan Marshall, Carolyn Martha. AB, Butler U., 1941; PhD, U. Ill., 1949. Indsl. engr. RCA, Indpls., 1942-44; research and devel. engr. P.R. Mallory, Indpls., 1944-46; U. Ill. postdoctoral fellow Faculty Law U. Paris, 1949-50; instr. philosophy U. Ill., 1950-51; research asst. U. Ill. (Coll. of Law), 1950-51; instr. philosophy Lehigh U., 1952-54, asst. prof., 1954-61, asso. prof., 1961-69, prof., 1969-83, prof. emeritus, adj. prof., 1983-91. Founder, pres. World-Sense, Inc.; dir. World-Sense Dialogue. Mem. AAUP, Am. Philos. Assn., N.Y. Acad. Scis., Environ.

Def. Fund, World Wildlife Fund, Natural Resources Def. Coun., The Wilderness Soc., Nat. Wildlife Fedn. (assoc.), The Nature Conservancy, Worldwatch Libr., Union Concerned Scientists (sponsor), Amnesty Internat., Woodrow Wilson Internat. Ctr. for Scholars (assoc.), Phi Beta Kappa, Phi Kappa Phi. Home: 175 W North St Apt 427A Nazareth PA 18064-1439

HAYNES, ULRIC ST. CLAIR, JR., dean; b. Bklyn., June 8, 1931; s. Ulric St. Clair and Ellaline (Gay) H.; m. Yolande Toussaint, Sept. 20, 1969; children: Alexandra, Gregory. BA, Amherst Coll., 1952; JD, Yale U., 1956; LLB (hon.), Ind. U., 1981, John Jay Coll., 1981, Fisk U., 1982, Ala. State Coll., 1982; JD, Butler U., 1988; LLB (hon.), Mercy Coll., 1994. Exec. asst. N.Y. State Dept. Commerce, Albany, 1956-57; adminstrv. officer UN European Office, Geneva, 1959-60; asst. to rep. Ford Found., Lagos, Nigeria, Tunis, Tunisia, 1960-63; asst. officer in charge Moroccan affairs Dept. State, Washington, 1963, officer in charge Southwest Africa and High Commn. Ters. Affairs, 1963-64; mem. NSC staff White House, 1965-66; pres. Mgmt. Formation Inc., N.Y.C., 1966-70; sr. v.p., ptnr. Spencer Stuart and Assocs. Mgmt. Consultants, N.Y.C., 1970-72; v.p. for mgmt. devel. Cummins Engine Co., Columbus, Ind., 1972-74, v.p. for Mid-East and Africa, 1974-77; ambassador to Algeria Am. Embassy, Algiers, 1977-81; v.p. internat. bus. planning Cummins Engine Co., 1981-83; acting pres. SUNY/Coll. at Old Westbury, 1985-86; pres. AFS Intercultural Programs, N.Y.C., 1986-88; cons. N.Y.C., 1989-91; exec. dean Hofstra U. Sch. Bus., Hempstead, N.Y., 1991-96; exec. dean internat. rels. Hofstra U., Hempstead, NY, 1996—2003. Bd. dirs. Pall Corp., ReliaStar Life Ins. Co. N.Y., INNCOM Internat., Inc. Contbr. articles to profl. publs. Mem. selection com. Henry Luce Found. Asian Scholars Program; mem. Middle East adv. com. Human Rights Watch; trustee Deep Springs Coll., 1999—. Root-Tilden scholar; John Hay Whitney scholar; Leopold Schepp Found. scholar. Mem. Coun. Fgn. Rels., Coun. Am. Ambs., Yale Club of N.Y.C., The Pilgrims of the U.S., Am. Acad. Diplomacy. Democrat. Episcopalian. Home: 2403 Timothy Ln Kissimmee FL 34743 Personal E-mail: uhaynesjr@yahoo.com.

HAYNES, WILLIAM FORBY, JR., retired internist, cardiologist, educator; b. Newark, June 6, 1926; s. William Forby and Grace (Brien) H.; m. Constance Simpson, July 2, 1960; children: William, Suzanne, David; m. Aline Linehan James, Aug. 25, 1984. BS, U.S. Mcht. Marine Acad., 1946; AB, Princeton U., 1950; MD, Columbia U., 1954; MA in Theology, La Salle U., 2001. Diplomate Am. Bd. Internal Medicine (subcert. in cardiovasc. diseases), Nat. Bd. Med. Examiners. Intern St. Luke's Med. Ctr., N.Y.C., 1954-55; ship's med. officer U.S. Navy, 1955—57; resident St. Luke's Med. Ctr., N.Y.C., 1957-59; fellow in cardiology N.Y. Heart Assn., N.Y.C., 1959-60; pvt. practice specializing in internal medicine/cardiology Princeton, N.J., 1960-97; ret., 1997. Asst. clin. prof. medicine Robert Wood Johnson Med. Sch., 1972—; sr. attending internal medicine Princeton Med. Ctr., 1960-89, ret., hon. staff, 1997—; lectr. on spirituality and med. practice, 1982—; mem. adv. coun. Ctr. for Study of Religion, Princeton U., 2000—. Author: (book) A Physician's Witness to the Power of Shared Prayer, 1990, Minding the Whole Person: Cultivating a Healthy Lifestyle from Youth Through the Senior Years, 1994; contbr. articles. Ensign USNR, 1944-45, PTO; lt. M.C., 1955-57. Recipient Archbishop Theodore McCarrick award for Distig. Svc., 1997, 250th Anniversary award Princeton Swimming and Diving Team, 2000, LaSalle Grad. Religion Achievement award, 2001. Fellow: ACP, Am. Coll. Chest Physicians, Am. Coll. Cardiology, Theta Alpha Kappa; mem.: U.S. Masters Swimming Assn. (top ten), Princeton U. Friends of Swimming (pres. 1975—87), Forums Inst. Pub. Policy, Princeton Officers Soc. (v.p.), Princeton U. Alumni Coun. Athletics, Third Order of St. Francis, Mercer County Heart Assn. (trustee 1964—76, v.p. 1970, Cardiologist of Yr. 1995), Old Guard at Princeton (v.p.), Nassau Club, Univ. Cottage Club Princeton. Episcopalian. Co-inventor GI String for detecting intestinal bleeding, 1960. Home and Office: 6 Skyfield Dr Princeton NJ 08540-7403 E-mail: wfhaynes@comcast.net.

HAYNES, WILLIAM J(AMES), II, lawyer; b. Waco, Tex., Mar. 30, 1958; s. William James and Caroline H.; m. Margaret Frances Campbell, 1982; 3 children. BA, Davidson Coll., 1980; JD, Harvard U., 1983; LLD (hon.), Stetson U., 1999. Bar: N.C. 1983, Ga. 1989, D.C. 1990. Law clk. to Hon. James B. McMillan U.S. Dist. Ct. N.C., Charlotte, 1983-84; assoc. Sutherland, Asbill & Brennan, Washington, 1989; spl. asst. to gen. counsel Dept. Def., Washington, 1989-90; gen. counsel Dept. Army, Washington, 1990-93; ptnr. Jenner & Block, Washington, 1993-96; v.p., assoc. gen. counsel Gen. Dynamics Corp., Falls Church, Va., 1996-98; gen. counsel Gen. Dynamics Marine Group, 1997-98; ptnr. Jenner & Block, Washington, 1999—2001; gen. counsel Dept. of Defense, 2001—. Capt. U.S. Army, 1984-88. Mem. ABA, N.C. Bar Assn., D.C. Bar Assn., Ga. Bar Assn. Presbyterian. Avocation: tennis. Office: General Counsel of Dept Def 1600 Defense Pentagon Washington DC 20301

HAYNIE, BETTY JO GILLMORE, personal property appraiser, antiques dealer; b. Jackson, Ala., July 3, 1937; d. Joe McVey and Mary Elizabeth (Bolen) Gillmore; m. William T. Haynie Jr., Aug. 21, 1960; children: Virginia Elizabeth, Mary Allison. BA, U. Ala., 1959, MA, 1960, postgrad., U. So. Miss., U. Ala., Birmingham; grad. Paris program, Parsons Sch. Design, 1992; grad., Winter Inst., Winterthur, Del., 1994. Tchr. Demopolis (Ala.) Elem. Sch., 1960-61; instr. in history U. Livingston, Ala., 1961-64; tchr. history for jr. high Brooke Hill Sch. for Girls, Birmingham, Ala., 1965; instr. in history Jefferson State Jr. Coll., Birmingham, 1965-67; tchr. history and govt. Mt. Brook High Sch., Birmingham, 1970-71; instr. history U. Ala., Birmingham, 1971-72, Jefferson Davis Jr. Coll., Gulfport, Miss., 1978-81, Faulkner Jr. Coll., Fairhope, Ala., 1983-86; instr. spl. courses U. South Ala., Mobile, 1988—2003, instr. Elderhostel programs, 1990—99. Owner Crown and Colony Antiques, Fairhope, Ala., 1982—92, Antiques and Fine Art, Fairhope, Ala., 1997—; co-owner Gillmore Plantation, Jackson, Ala., Ala., 1987—, and other properties. Contbr. articles to historical mags. Mem.: DAR, Internat. Soc. Appraisers, Clarke County Hist. Soc., Nat. Trust for Hist. Preservation. Presbyterian. Avocations: tennis, creative writing, traveling. Home: PO Box 485 Montrose AL 36559-0485

HAYNIE, THOMAS POWELL, III, physician; b. Hearne, Tex., Aug. 9, 1932; s. Thomas Powell Jr and Sue Cummings Haynie; m. Bette Flossel, Mar. 10, 1956 (dec. Apr. 2002); children: David Powell, Amy Cummings, Sue Cummings, Garner Powell. Student, U. South, Sewanee, Tenn., 1949-51, U. Tex., Austin, 1951-52; MD, Baylor U., 1956. Diplomate Am Bd Internal Med, Am Bd Med Oncology, Am Bd Nuclear Med. Intern, then resident in internal medicine U. Mich. Med. Center, Ann Arbor, 1956-60, instr., 1960-62; asst. prof. medicine, dir. nuclear med. service U. Tex. Med. Br., Galveston, 1962-65; assoc. prof. medicine U. Tex.-M.D. Anderson Cancer Ctr., Houston, 1965-75; prof. U. Tex.-M.D. Anderson Hosp. and Tumor Inst., Houston, 1975-95, James E. Anderson prof. nuclear medicine, 1988-95, prof. emeritus of nuclear medicine, 1995—, chief sect. nuclear medicine, 1967-84, chmn. dept. nuclear medicine, 1984-93, head dept. internal medicine, 1977-84. Adj prof radiology Baylor Col Med, Houston, 1996—; pres Am Col Nuclear Med, 1993—94; consult in field. Contbr. articles in field, chapters to books; editor: Jour Nuclear Med, 1985—89. Mem.: AMA, ACP, AAAS, Am. Coll. Radiology, Tex. Assn. Physicians Nuclear Medicine, Tex. Med. Assn., Soc. Nuclear Medicine, Assn. Univ. Radiologists, Am. Thyroid Assn., Radiol. Soc. N.Am., Am. Coll. Nuclear Medicine, Am. Coll. Nuclear Physicians, Order St. Lazarus of Jerusalem, Sigma Xi, Phi Gamma Delta. Episcopalian. Office: 1515 Holcombe Blvd Houston TX 77030-4009 E-mail: thaynie@mdanderson.org.

HAYNIE, TONY WAYNE, lawyer; b. Houston, Sept. 26, 1955; BA, U. Okla., 1978; postgrad., Boston U., Heidelberg Br., Fed. Republic Germany, 1980-81; JD, U. Tulsa, 1984; MBA, Okla. State U., 1993. Bar: Okla. 1985, U.S. Dist. Okla. 1985, U.S. Ct. Appeals (10th cir.) 1987, U.S. Ct. Appeals (5th cir.) 1992, U.S. Ct. Appeals (7th and D.C. cirs.) 1998, U.S. Supreme Ct. 1990. Assoc. Conner & Winters, Tulsa, 1984-90, ptnr., 1991-92, shareholder, dir., 1992—; pres., CEO The Colonneh Co., Tulsa, 1991—. Arbitrator N.Y. Stock Exch., 1991—93; trustee Transvoc, Inc., 1995—2000, pres. bd. trustees, 1998—99; adj. prof. Coll. Law U. Tulsa, 2002—. Adv. bd. mem. Tulsa Area United Way, 1998-99. 1st lt. U.S. Army, 1978—82. Mem. ABA (sect. bus. law and litig., chair subcom. on expert witness on trial evidence com. of litig. sect. 1991-94), Am. Inns of Ct. (master Hudson-Hall-Wheaton chpt. 1996—), Okla. Bar Assn., Okla. Bar Found., Tulsa County Bar Assn., Tulsa County Bar Found., Phi Delta Phi. Democrat. Methodist. Office: Conner & Winters 3700 1st Place Tower 15 E 5th St Tulsa OK 74103-4391 E-mail: thaynie@cwlaw.com.

HAYNSWORTH, ROBERT FRANCIS, JR., anesthesiologist; b. El Paso, Tex., Aug. 11, 1954; MD, U. Tex., Houston, 1981. Cert. in anesthesiology, specialty in pain mgmt. Flex intern Tex. Tech. U. Health Sci. Ctr., Lubbock, 1981-82, resident in anesthesiology, 1982-84, chief resident in anesthesiology, 1983-84; fellow in pain mgmt. U. Tex. S.W. Med. Sch., Dallas, 1984—85; attending anesthesiologist Baylor U., Tex., 1992—2002, attending physician, 1992—2002; clin. dir. Baylor Pain Mgmt. Ctr., 1992—. Office: 530 Clara Barton Blvd Ste 215 Garland TX 75042-5740

HAYO, GEORGE EDWARD, management consultant; b. L.A., Nov. 2, 1934; s. George Edward Hayo Sr. and Esther Marie (Goodman) Arthur; m. Nixie Joanne Hunt, Aug. 4, 1956; children: Michael Edward, Kenneth Marvin, Michelle Virginia. BS in Applied Math., Calif. State U., 1960; MBA in Mgmt., U. Denver, 1968. Cert. mgmt. cons. Mathematician U.S. Naval Civil Engring. Lab., Port Hueneme, Calif., 1961-63; corp. systems planner No. Natural Gas Co., Omaha, 1963-66; asst. to pres. C.A. Norgren Co., Littleton, Colo., 1966-68; sr. staff cons. Emerson Electric, St. Louis, 1968-71; dir. adminstrn. Fisher Radio, N.Y.C., 1971-72; v.p., dir. The Emerson Cons., N.Y.C., 1973-87; pres. The Hayo Cons., Albuquerque, 1988—. Arbitrator Am. Arbitration Assn., N.Y., 1985—. Contbr. articles to profl. jours. Mem. Inst. Mgmt. Cons., Am. Inst. Plant Engrs., Am. Prodn. and Inventory Control Soc. Avocations: running, sailing, golf. Home and Office: The Hayo Cons 536 Stagecoach Rd SE Albuquerque NM 87123-4123 E-mail: hayocon@aol.com.

HAYON, ELIE M. chemist, educator; b. Cairo, May 15, 1932; came to U.S., 1965; s. Mayer E. and Regina (Cohen); m. Nina Mokady, 1982; 1 child, Rona B.Sc., U. Strathclyde, Glasgow, Scotland, 1954; PhD, Durham U., Newcastle-upon Tyne, Eng., 1957. Brit. Empire Cancer Research fellow Kings Coll., Newcastle-upon Tyne, 1957-58, Brookhaven Nat. Lab., Upton, N.Y., 1958-60, Cambridge (Eng.) U., 1960-62, Centre Nuclear Studies, Saclay, France, 1963-65; head phys. chemistry Natick (Mass.) Labs., 1966-75, Gen. Foods Corp., Tarrytown, N.Y., 1976-78; dean grad. studies and research, prof. chemistry Queens Coll., City U.N.Y., 1978—. Contbr. articles to profl. jours. Mem. numerous profl. assns. in U.S. and U.K. Home: 240 E 82nd St New York NY 10028-2703 Office: 6 Einstein St Ra ananna Israel E-mail: hayon32@zahav.net.il.

HAY-ROE, VICTOR, plastic surgeon; b. Edmonton, Alta., Can., Dec. 23, 1930; s. Edmund Archer and Ruth Mildred (Maddison) Hay-Roe; m. Elizabeth Mae Davison, May 8, 1953 (div. 1978); children: Glenn Cameron, Elizabeth Diane, Scott Richard; m. Lynn Siu, Apr. 19, 1980. BSc, U. Alta., 1953, MD, 1955. Resident in surgery Queen's Hosp., Honolulu, 1956-59; resident in plastic surgery U. Pitts. Sch. Medicine, 1963-66; chief of plastic surgery Honolulu Med. Group, Inc., 1967—. Clin. assoc. prof. plastic surgery, U. Hawaii, Honolulu, 1973—; trip leader, Interplast plastic surgery team to Samoa, 1978, Jamaica, 1988, 90. Mem. Hawaii Plastic Surgery Soc. (pres. 1986-88), Northwest Soc. Plastic Surgeons, Am. Soc. Plastic Surgeons. Republican. Avocations: chess, needlepoint, cross-stitch, tennis, philately. Home: 2277 Halekoa Dr Honolulu HI 96821-1056 Office: Honolulu Med Group Inc 550 S Beretania St Honolulu HI 96813-2405

HAYS, E. EARL, youth organization administrator; b. Uniontown, Kans. s. Earl Loren and Avis Marie (Mccollum) H.; m. Betty Ann Frigo, Nov. 21, 1966. BA, Whittier Coll., 1962; MA, Ottawa U., 1993; PhD, Pacific Western U., 1993. Dir. pub. rels., fin., dist. exec. Boy Scouts Am. L.A. Area Coun., 1962-71; asst. dir. exploring Boy Scouts Am. Nat. Coun., North Brunswick, N.J., 1971-73; dir. fin. svcs. Boy Scouts Am. Golden Empire Coun., Sacramento, 1973-75; dir. field svc. Boy Scouts Am. Santa Clara County, San Jose, Calif., 1975-77; scout exec., CEO Boy Scouts Am. Clinton Valley Coun., Pontiac, Mich., 1977-82, Boy Scouts Am. Grand Canyon Coun., Phoenix, 1982—. Bd. dirs. Pontiac Oakland Symphony, 1980-82; pres. United Way Exec. Dirs. Assn., Phoenix, 1984-85. Fellowship honor Boy Scouts Am., 1991, James E. West fellow, 1994. Mem. Ottawa U. Alumni Assn. (bd. dirs. 1995-98), Nat. Eagle Scout Assn. (life, Disting. Eagle Scout 1998), Rotary (pres. Pontiac 1982, bd. dirs., sec.) Phoenix 100 Club (Paul H. Harris fellow). Democrat. Lutheran. Avocations: travel, music, reading, scuba, golf. Office: Grand Canyon Coun 2969 N Greenfield Rd Phoenix AZ 85016-7715

HAYS, HOWARD H. (TIM HAYS), editor, publisher; b. Chgo., June 2, 1917; s. Howard H. and Margaret (Mauger) H.; m. Helen Cunningham, May 27, 1947 (div. Dec. 1988); children: William, Thomas; m. Susie Gudermuth, Sept. 1992. BA, Stanford U., 1939; LLB, Harvard U., 1942. Bar: Calif. 1946. Spl. agt. FBI, 1942-45; reporter San Bernardino (Calif.) Sun, 1945-46; asst. editor Riverside (Calif.) Daily Press, 1946-49, editor, 1949-65, editor, co-pub., 1965-83, editor, pub., chief exec. officer, 1983-88, editor, chmn., chief exec. officer, 1989-92, chmn. bd., 1992-97, chmn. emeritus, 1997—. Mem. Pulitzer Prize Bd., 1976-86; mem. AP Bd., 1980-89, vice chmn. 1988-89. Mem. nat. com. Wash. U. Sch. of Art, 1992—2003; bd. visitors John S. Knight Fellowships for Profl. Journalists, Stanford U., 1983—98. Recipient Dist. award Calif. Jr. C. of C., 1951; named Pub. of Year Calif. Press Assn., 1968 Mem.: New Directions for News (bd. dirs. 1982—86), Am. Press Inst. (bd. dirs. 1973—, chmn. 1978—83), Internat. Press. Inst. (chmn. Am. Com. 1971—72, mem. exec. bd. 1977—83), Am. Soc. Newspaper Editors (dir. 1969—76, pres. 1974—75), Calif. Bar Assn., Tower Grove Pk. (bd. dirs. 1999—, vice chmn. 2000—), Stanford Alumni Assn. (dir. 1970—74). Home: 3724 Utah Pl Saint Louis MO 63116-4831

HAYS, JAMES FRED, geologist, educator; b. Little Rock, July 10, 1933; s. Orren Lee and Virginia (Russell) H.; m. Diane Lee Huntoon, Dec. 22, 1956; 1 dau., Lee Anne. AB, Columbia U., 1954; MS (NSF fellow), Calif. Inst. Tech., 1961; PhD, Harvard U., 1966. Geologist U.S. Geol. Survey, 1961; guest investigator Geophys. Lab., Carnegie Instn. of Washington, 1965; Soc. Fellows jr. fellow Harvard U., 1963-66, asst. prof. geology, 1966-69, assoc. prof., 1969-72, prof., 1972-84, chmn. dept. geol. scis., 1981-82; dir. div. earth scis. NSF, 1982-87, sr. sci. advisor, 1987-91, dir. earth scis. div., 1991-95. Cons. NASA Astronaut Tng. Program, 1969-73; mem. NASA Lunar Sample Analysis Planning Team, 1973-76, chmn. Lunar and Planetary Rev. Panel, 1978-81; prin. investigator Apollo Lunar Sample Program; vis. prof. chemistry and geology Ariz. State U., 1978-79; adminstrs. bd. Harvard and Radcliffe Colls., 1976-78; mem. Harvard Ctr. for Earth and Planetary Physics, 1970-84, sci. adv. bd. Mt. St. Helens Nat. Volcanic Monument, 1983-87, adv. com. on mining and minerals rsch. Dept. Interior, 1983-85, Working Group for U.S.-Peoples' Republic of China Agreement for Cooperation in Earth Scis., 1982-87, Space Grant Rev. Panel NASA, 1992-95; NRC com. on Rsch. Opportunities and Priorities for EPA, 1995-97; exec. sec. Pres.'s Com. on Nat. Medal Sci., 1987-91; vis. scholar U. Ariz., 1997—. Assoc. editor: Nature of the Solid Earth, 1970, Jour. Geophys. Research, 1978-80, 83-85. Served to capt. USNR, 1954-59. Recipient Presdl. Rank award U.S. Govt., 1994; NSF grantee, 1974-82, NASA grantee, 1971-82 Fellow AAAS (councilor 1989-92), Geol. Soc. Am. (councilor 1988-91), Mineral. Soc. Am.; mem. Am. Geophys. Union, Geol. Soc. Washington, Potomac Geophys. Soc., Am Ornithologists Union, Naval Res. Assn., Harvard Club (N.Y.C. and Washington), Cosmos Club, Phi Beta Kappa, Sigma Xi. Rsch. and publs. on exptl. petrology and geochemistry. Home: 3381 W Foxes Den Dr Tucson AZ 85745-5107

HAYS, LOUISE STOVALL, retail fashion executive; b. Crenshaw, Miss., Aug. 30, 1916; d. Ernest Sydney and Anne Mary (Ray) Stovall; m. James Marion Klaer, June 30, 1938 (dec. Jan. 1962); m. Samuel Jackson Hays, Apr. 29, 1965 (dec. March 14, 2001); stepchildren: Elizabeth Razee, Samuel Jackson III, Carruthers Donelson. Grad., Memphis Sch. of Commrce; student, U. Memphis. Sec. Goldsmith's, Memphis, 1938, exec. sec., 1939, fashion coord., 1941-47, fashion dir., 1947-50, dir. fashion promotions and spl. events, 1950-74. Cons. Mademoiselle mag., 1964. Bd. dirs. Am. Heart Assn., 1960s, Memphis Arts Coun., 1964, Brooks Mus. Art, Memphis, 1989; chmn. Memphis Heart Gala, 1978. Named Vol. of Yr., Brooks Mus. League, 1987, Memphis Brooks Mus., 1989. Republican. Episcopalian. Avocations: art, poetry writing, travel. Home: 1701 Village Ridge Pl Collierville TN 38017-8700

HAYS, MARGUERITE THOMPSON, nuclear medicine physician, educator; b. Bloomington, Ind., Apr. 15, 1930; d. Stith and Louise (Faust) Thompson; m. David G. Hays, Feb. 4, 1950 (div. 1975); children: Dorothy Adele, Warren Stith Thompson, Thomas Glenn. AB cum laude, Radcliffe Coll., 1951; postgrad., Harvard U. Med. Sch., 1954; MD, UCLA, 1957; Sc.D. (hon.), Ind. U., 1979. Diplomate Am. Bd. Internal Medicine, Am. Bd. Nuclear Medicine. Intern UCLA Sch. Medicine, 1957-58, resident, 1958-59, 61-62, USPHS postdoctoral trainee, 1959-61, USPHS postdoctoral fellow, 1963-64, asst. prof. medicine, 1964-68, SUNY-Buffalo, 1968-70, asst. prof. biophys. sci., 1968-74, assoc. prof. medicine, 1970-76, clin. assoc. prof. nuclear medicine, 1973-77; asst. chief nuclear medicine VA Med. Ctr., Wadsworth, Calif., 1967-68; chief nuclear medicine Buffalo VA Med. Ctr., 1968-74, assoc. chief of staff for rsch., 1971-74; dir. med. rsch. svc. VA Central Office, Washington, 1974-79, asst. chief med. dir. for R&D, 1979-81; chief of staff Martinez VA Med. Ctr., Calif., 1981-83; prof. radiology Sch. Medicine U. Calif., Davis, 1981-93, prof. medicine and surgery, 1983-91, assoc. dean, 1981; clin. prof. diagnostic radiology and nuclear medicine Stanford U. Sch. Medicine, 1990—; assoc. chief of staff for rsch. Palo Alto VA Med. Ctr., Palo Alto, 1983-97, staff physician, 1997-99, cons., 1999—. Vis. rsch. scientist Euratom, Italy, 1962-63; chmn. radiopharm. adv. com. FDA, 1974-77; co-chmn. biomedicine com. Pres.'s Fed. Coun. on Sci., Engring. and Tech., 1979-81; mem. rsch. restructuring adv. com. Va. R&D Office, 1995-96, chair task group to restructure R&D Career Devel. Program, 1996-97; chmn. coop. studies evaluation com., Med. Rsch. Svc., VA, 1990-93; mem. sci. rev. and evaluation bd. Health Svcs. Rsch. and Devel. Svc., VA, 1988-91, chmn. career devel. com., 1991-99, chmn. career devel. com. Rehab. Rsch. and Devel. Svc., 1997—. Rsch. grantee VA, 1968-2003. NIH grantee, 1964-71; recipient Exceptional Svc. award Sec. Vets. Affairs, 2000. Fellow ACP; mem. Soc. Nuclear Medicine (chmn. publs. com., trustee, v.p. 1983-84), Am. Thyroid Assn. (bd. dirs. 1993-96), Endocrine Soc., Western Assn. Physicians. Home: 270 Campesino Ave Palo Alto CA 94306-2912 Office: 3801 Miranda Ave Palo Alto CA 94304-1207 E-mail: ritahays19@yahoo.com.

HAYS, MELISSA PADGETT, lawyer; b. West Islip, NY, June 18, 1968; d. Olin Wright Jr. and Ellen (Medlin) Padgett; m. Robert Bond Hays, III, Mar. 21, 1998. BA, Emory U., 1990; JD, U. Ga., 1994. Bar: Ga. 1994, U.S. Dist. Ct. (so. dist.) Ga. 1994, Supreme Ct. of Ga., 1994, Tenn. 1998, Supreme Ct. of Tenn. 1998. Assoc. Harrison & Shapiro, Augusta, Ga., 1994-95, Garrett & Gilliard, P.C., Augusta, 1995-97; pvt. practice, Augusta, 1997-98; atty., litigation counsel Unum Provident Corp., Chattanooga, 1998—2002, asst. v.p., counsel, 2003—. Alumni mem. Leadership Augusta, 1997—; mem. Jr. League Chattanooga, 2000—. Mem. ABA, State Bar Ga., Tenn. Bar Assn., Southeastern Tenn. Lawyers Assn. for Women (pres. 2003). Office: Unum Provident Corp Law Dept 1 Fountain Sq Chattanooga TN 37402-1307

HAYS, OTIS EARL, JR., writer; BA, U. Ark., 1938; grad. study journalism, Northwestern U., 1945-46. Prof. journalism Henderson State Coll., 1946-48, U. Tulsa, 1948-51; fgn. svc. officer USIA, Washington, 1966-75; freelance author Pierce City, Mo., 1975—. Intelligence officer U.S. Army, 1941-45, 51-66. Home and Office: RR 3 Box 464 Pierce City MO 65723-9608

HAYS, PATRICK GREGORY, health care executive; b. Kansas City, Kans., Sept. 9, 1942; s. Vance Samuel and Mary Ellen (Crabbe) H.; m. Penelope Ann Hall, July 3, 1976; children: Julia L., Jennifer M., Emily J., Drew D. BS in Bus. Adminstrn, U. Tulsa, 1964; M.H.A., U. Minn., 1971; postgrad., U. Mich. Grad. Sch. Bus. Adminstrn., 1977. Mfg. analyst N.Am. Rockwell Corp., Tulsa, 1964-66; asst. adminstr., adminstr. for ops. Henry Ford Hosp., Detroit, 1971-75; exec. v.p. Meth. Med. Ctr. of Ill., Peoria, 1975-77; adminstr. Kaiser Found. Hosp., Los Angeles, 1977-80; pres. Sutter Community Hosps. and Sutter Health, Sacramento, 1980-95; pres., CEO Blue Cross Blue Shield Assn., Chgo., 1995—2000; faculty, School of Policy, Planning and Devel. U. So. Calif., Los Angeles. Bd. dirs. VHA, Inc., 1995-2001; trustee Cen. Area Teaching Hosps., Inc., L.A., 1977-79; mem. exec. com. St. Jude Children's Rsch. Hosp. Midwest Affilate, Peoria, 1975-77; past chmn. adv. bd. grad. program in health svcs. adminstrn. U. So. Calif., Sacramento; bd.dirs. Hosp.Coun. No.Calif., 1986, The Healthcare Forum, 1987-89; bd. dirs., exec. com. Found. Health Inc., HMO, 1987-90; chmn. bd. Option Care Inc., 1986-90, Calif. Assn. Hosp. and Health Systems, 1991; regent Am. Coll. Healthcare Execs., 1989-95, founding pres. Sacramento Regional Purchasing Coun.; mem. adv. bd. the Governance Inst.; bd. dir. U.S. Bank of Calif., 1993-95, mem. civil justice reform act com., U.S. Dist. Ct., Ea. Calif.; adj. faculty Ariz. State U.; bd. dirs. Trinity Health, Novi, Mich., chmn. orgn. integrity and audit com. Contbr. articles on health services to publs. Mem. Pvt. Industry Coun., Sacramento Employment and Tng. Agy., 1984-85; bd. dirs. Consumer Credit Counselors Sacramento, 1984-87, Sacramento Area United Way, campaign chair, 1992-93; bd. dirs. Comstock Club, 1986-89; pres. Sacramento Camellia Festival Assn., 1987-88; chmn. Whitney M. Young Jr. Award, 1987; pres. Sacramento Regional Purchasing Coun., 1989-90. With U.S. Army, 1966-69. Decorated Army Commendation medal, cert. of appreciation Dept. Army; recipient Commendation resolution Calif. Senate, 1979, Whitney M. Young award Sacramento Urban League, 1983; named Chief Exec. Officer of Yr., Soc. for Healthcare Planning and Mktg. of Am. Hosp. Assn., 1991; USPHS fellow, 1969-71, Calif. Assn. Hosps. and Health Systems Walker fellow, 1989. Fellow Am. Coll. Healthcare Execs. (Calif. regent, Gold medal for career excellence 2003); mem. Calif. Assn. Hosps. and Health Systems (chmn. bd. dirs. 1991), Sacramento-Sierra Hosp. Assn. (exec. com., bd. dirs., pres. 1984), Royal Soc. Health (U.K.), Am. Mgmt. Assn. (Pres. Club), Hollywood C. of C. (revitalization com. 1979), Sacramento C. of C. (bd. dirs. 1982-85, 87-88), Vol. Hosps. Pacific (bd. dirs.), Rotary (bd. dirs. Sacramento 1987-89), Kappa Sigma (treas.). Presbyterian. *Personal philosophy: Most people want to excel at what they do. Management's job, at its essence, is to remove the barriers to their success.*

HAYS, RICHARD SECREST, minister; b. Warren, Ohio, Feb. 1, 1951; s. Robert Collins and Sarah Lewis (Secrest) H.; m. Paula Jeanne Barron, Dec. 27, 1975; children: Elizabeth Anne, Andrew Paul. AB, Lafayette Coll., Easton, Pa., 1973; postgrad., U. Edinburgh, Scotland, 1973-74; MDiv, Pitts. Theol. Sem., 1976. Ordained to ministry Presbyn. Ch. (USA), 1976. Student asst. to chaplain Lafayette Coll., Easton, 1971-73, Edgewood Presbyn. Ch., Pitts., 1975-76; pastor Rockford (Ohio) Presbyn. Ch., 1976-87, First Presbyn. Ch., Waverly, Ohio, 1987—. Exec. sec. Rockford C. of C., 1985-87; jour. clk. Maumee Valley Presbytery, Findlay, Ohio, 1986-87; gen. assy. commr. Presbyn. Ch. (USA), Hartford, 1982, Albuquerque, 1996, Charlotte, 1998; moderator Scioto Valley Presbytery, 1998-99; chair Coalition for Appalachian Ministry, 2000-2002; jour. clk. Scioto Valley Presbytery, 2001—. Recipient David Fowler Atkins prize Lafayette Coll., 1973, Comty. Svc. award Pike County Rotary Club, 2001. Mem. Pike County C. of C. Democrat. Office: First Presbyn Ch 211 Schmitt Dr Waverly OH 45690-1280 *When the burdens of ministry get heavy, I remember the words of a trusted mentor, "What the people need is someone to love them". That reminds me that if God loves me and I love the people, then the people will grow to love God.*

HAYS, ROBERT GLENN, journalism educator; b. Carmi, Ill., May 23, 1935; s. Lewis Earl and Margaret Elizabeth (White) H.; m. Mary Elizabeth Corley, Dec. 21, 1957; children: Alan Gregory, David Robert. BS in Journalism, So. Ill. U., 1961, MS in Journalism, 1972, PhD, 1976. Reporter Granite City (Ill.) Press-Record, 1961-63; pub. rels. writer So. Ill. U., Carbondale, 1963-66; alumni publs. editor, 1966-71; rschr., asst. scientist Ill. Bd. Natural Resources/Conservation, 1971-73; primary campaign mgr. Paul Simon for Congress, Ill., 1974; asst. prof. journalism Sam Houston State U., Huntsville, Tex., 1974-75; assoc. prof. journalism U. Ill., Urbana, 1975-86, 87-99; prof. emeritus, 2000; chair mass comm. dept. S.E. Mo. U., Cape Girardeau, 1986-87. Mem. lit. rev. panel Jour. Applied Comms., 1990—, manuscript rev. bd., 1992—; editor rsch. sect. ACE Quar., 1978-80; assoc. editor Jour. Correctional Edn., 1969-70. Co-author: G-2: Intelligence for Patton, 1971, new edit., 1999; author: Country Editor, 1974, State Science in Illinois, 1980, A Race at Bay, 1997; editor: Early Stories From the Land, 1995; contbr. articles to profl. jours. Mem. steering com. Champaign County (Ill.) ACLU, 1992-95; dep. registrar Champaign County Clk. Office, 1988-91. With U.S. Army, 1955-57. Mem. NOW, Internat. Assn. Agrl. Communicators in Edn. (vice chair tchg. divsn. 1991-93, Rsch. Excellence award 1993, Tchg. Excellence award 1994), Assn. Edn. in Journalism and Mass Comm., Investigative Reporters and Editors, Rsch. Soc. Am. Periodicals, Ill. Press Assn., Soc. Profl. Journalists. Democrat. Home: 2314 Glenoak Dr Champaign IL 61821-6220 E-mail: r-hays1@uiuc.edu.

HAYS, ROBERT WILLIAM, communications consultant, educator, writer; b. Atlanta, Oct. 17, 1925; s. Calvin Samuel and Elizabeth (Green) H.; m. Rebecca Copeland, June 15, 1950; children: Michael, David, William. Student, Duke U., 1943-44; AB summa cum laude, Presbyn. Coll. S.C., 1947; MEd, Emory U., 1957. Comml. mgr. Sta. WSFT-AM, Thomaston, Ga., 1947-48, Sta. WLBC

Clinton, S.C., 1948; co-owner Clinton Plastic Co., 1948-49; instr. English So. Tech. Inst. (now So. Polytechnic State U.), Chamblee, Ga., 1950-51; supr. of tng. course devel. Lockheed Aircraft Corp., Marietta, Ga., 1951-52; asst. prof. So. Tech. Inst. (now So. Polytechnic State U.), Chamblee, Ga., 1952-57, head English dept. Marietta, 1953-73, assoc. prof., 1958-60, prof., 1960-85, prof. emeritus, 1985—. Cons. in communications, Marietta, 1965—, Mid. East, 1968-70. Author: Pacific Parodies, 1947, Principles of Technical Writing, 1965, Practically Speaking in Business, Industry and Government, 1969, Guide to Technical Writing, 1970, (with others) Getting Your Message Across, 1981; author poetry; contbr. numerous articles to profl. jours. Adv. bd. Salvation Army, Marietta, 1996—; program dir., Marietta History Mus./Kiwanis Culture Capsule, 1999. Lt. (j.g.) USNR, 1943-46. Hixson fellow Kiwanis, 1996; recipient Arthur Williston award, 1967, Internat. Tech. Communications Conf. Honor, 1980, 83, Cmty. Svc. award King Ctr., 1994, 95. Fellow: Soc. for Tech. Comm. (life Disting. award 1993); mem.: Ga. Poetry Soc., Kiwanis (program dir. 1999). Home: 3360 Trickum Rd Marietta GA 30066-4683 E-mail: haysR@aol.com.

HAYS, RONALD JACKSON, career officer; b. Urania, La., Aug. 19, 1928; s. George Henry and Fannie Elizabeth (McCartney) H.; m. Jane M. Hughes, Jan. 29, 1951; children: Dennis, Michael, Jacquelyn. Student, Northwestern U., 1945-46; BS, U.S. Naval Acad., 1950. Commd. ensign U.S. Navy, 1950, advanced through grades to adm., 1983; destroyer officer Atlantic Fleet, 1950-51; attack pilot Pacific Fleet, 1953-56; exptl. test pilot Patuxent River, Md., 1956-59; exec. officer Attack Squadron 106, 1961-63; tng. officer Carrier Air Wing 4, 1963-65; comdr. All Weather Attack Squadron, Atlantic Fleet, 1965-67; air warfare officer 7th Fleet Staff, 1967-68; tactical aircraft plans officer Office Chief Naval Ops., 1969-71; comdg. officer Naval Sta., Roosevelt Roads, P.R., 1971-72; dir. Navy Planning and Programming, 1973-74; comdr. Carrier Group 4, Norfolk, Va., 1974-75; dir. Office of Program Appraisal, Sec. of Navy, Washington, 1975-78; adc. and chief staff, comdr. in chief U.S. Atlantic Fleet, Norfolk, Va., 1978-80; comdr. in chief U.S. Naval Force Europe, London, 1980-83; vice chief naval ops. Dept. Navy, Washington, 1983-85; comdr. in chief U.S. Pacific Command, Camp H.M. Smith, Hawaii, 1985-88; pres., chief exec. officer Pacific Internat. Ctr. for High Tech. Rsch., Honolulu, Hawaii, 1988-92; tech. cons., 1992—. Decorated D.S.M. with 3 gold stars, Silver Star with 2 gold stars, D.F.C. with silver star and gold star, Legion of Merit, Bronze Star with combat V, Air Medal with numeral 14 and gold numeral 3, Navy Commendation medal with gold star and combat V. Baptist. Home and Office: 869 Kamoi Pl Honolulu HI 96825-1318 E-mail: rjhayshawaii@msn.com.

HAYS, RUTH, lawyer; b. Fukuoka, Japan, Sept. 20, 1950; d. George Howard and Helen Jincy (Mathis) H. AB, Grinnell Coll., 1972; JD, Washington U., 1978. Bar: Mo. 1978. Law clk. U.S. Ct. Appeals (8th cir.), St. Louis, 1978-80; assoc. Husch & Eppenberger, LLC, St. Louis, 1980-87, ptnr., 1987—. Articles editor Urban Law Annual, 1977-78. Bd. dirs. Childhaven, St. Louis, 1982-93, pres. 1987-88. Olin fellow Monticello Coll. Found., St. Louis, 1975-78; recipient Spl. Svc. award Legal Svs. Ea. Mo., 1993. Mem. ABA, Mo. Bar Assn., Bar Assn. Met. St. Louis, Employee Benefits Assn. (pres. 1995), Order of Coif, Phi Beta Kappa. Office: Husch & Eppenberger LLC 190 Carondelet Plz Ste 600 Saint Louis MO 63105

HAYS, STEELE, retired state supreme court judge; b. Little Rock, Mar. 25, 1925; s. L. Brooks and Marion (Prather) H.; m. Peggy Wall, July 12, 1980; children from previous marriage: Andrew Steele, Melissa Louise, Sarah Anne. BA, U. Ark., 1948; JD, George Washington U., 1951. Bar: Ark. 1951. Adminstrv. asst. to Congressman Brooks Hays, 1951 53; practice in Little Rock, 1953-79; mem. firm Spitzberg, Mitchell & Hays, 1953-79; circuit judge 6th Jud. Circuit Ark., Little Rock, 1969-70; judge Ark. Ct. Appeals, 1979-81; assoc. justice Ark. Supreme Ct., 1981-95; ret., 1995. Chmn. Bd. Law Examiners, 1968-70 Mem. Ark. com. U.S. Civil Rights Commn.; del. Presbyn. Ch. Consultation on Ch. Union, 1968-70; trustee Presbyn. Found.; chancellor Episcopal Diocese of Ark. Mem. Ark. Bar Assn. (past sec.-treas.), Sigma Chi, Delta Theta Phi. Home: 12 Deerwood Dr Conway AR 72034-6113

HAYS, THOMAS CHANDLER, holding company executive; b. Chgo., Apr. 21, 1935; s. Marion C. and Carolyn (Reid) H.; m. Mary Ann Jergens, June 8, 1958; children: Thomas, Michael, Paul, Jennifer. BS, Calif. Inst. Tech., 1957, MS, 1958; MBA with high distinction, Harvard U., 1963. Ops. rsch. analyst Lockheed Corp., L.A., 1963-64, Andrew Jergens Co. (formerly Am. Brands, then Fortune Brands 1997—), Cin., 1964-70, v.p. product mgmt., 1970-76, v.p. mktg., 1976-78; exec. v.p. Andrew Jergens Co. (formerly subs. Am. Brands, then Fortune Brands 1997—), Cin., 1978; pres., CEO Andrew Jergens Co. (formerly subs. Am. Brands), Cin., 1979-80; v.p. mktg. Am. Tobacco Co. (former subs. Am. Brands, then Fortune Brands 1997—), 1980-81, exec. v.p., 1981-85, pres., 1985-87, pres., COO, 1985-86, CEO, 1986-87, chmn., 1987-88, also bd. dirs.; chmn. Fortune Brands Internat. Corp., 1988-90; v.p. Fortune Brands, Inc. (formerly Am. Brands, Inc.), Old Greenwich, Conn., 1984-85; v.p. tobacco, 1985-87; pres., COO Fortune Brands, Inc. (formerly Am. Brands, Inc.), Old Greenwich, Conn., 1988-94, chmn., CEO, 1995—, also bd. dirs., 1981—, chmn. exec. com., 1996—. Bd. dirs. ACNielsen, Gallaher Ltd. Trustee Andrew Jergens Found., The Devereux Found.; bd. dirs. Fairfield County Cmty. Found. 1st lt. USAF, 1958-62. Baker scholar Harvard U., 1963. Mem. Southwestern Area Commerce and Industry Assn. (bd. dirs.), Amb. Roundtable, Bus. Roundtable, Conf. Bd. and Econ. Club, Cin. Country Club, Darien Country Club, Bel Air Bay Club, Tokeneke Club, brd. trustees, Deveraux Found. Address: Fortune Brands 300 Tower Pkwy Lincolnshire IL 60069-3640

HAYS, THOMAS CLYDE, lawyer; b. Franklin, Ind., Mar. 3, 1951; s. Clyde Gilbert and Anna Marie (Hill) H.; m. Mary Linda Lux, June 19, 1976; children: Thomas Clyde Jr., Lindsay Marie. AB, Ind. U., 1973; JD, Woodrow Wilson Coll. of Law, 1977. Bar: Ga. 1977, U.S. Dist. Ct. (no. dist.) Ga. 1977, Ind., 1979, U.S. Dist. Ct. (so. dist.) Ind. 1979. Assoc. Spence, Garrett & Spence, Alpharetta, Ga., 1977-78, Reeves and Collier, Atlanta, 1978-79, Kitley and Schreckengast, Beech Grove, Ind., 1979-82; ptnr. Schreckengast and Hays, Indpls., 1982-85, Lewis & Wagner, Indpls., 1985—. Mng. ptnr., pres. Briar Ln. Homeowners Assn., 1984. Mem. ABA, Ind. State Bar Assn., Ga. State Bar Assn., Indpls. Bar Assn. (litigation sect.), Def. Trial Counsel of Ind., Nat. Inst. for Trial Advocacy (diplomate, advanced sem. 1987), Def. Rsch. Inst., Am. Bd. Trial Advocates, Carmel Dad's Club, Optimist Club (pres. Southdside club 1984-85). Republican. Roman Catholic. Avocations: golf, bicycling. Home: 11214 Westminster Ct Carmel IN 46033-3702 Office: Lewis & Wagner 500 Place 501 Indiana Ave Ste 200 Indianapolis IN 46202-6146 E-mail: thays@lewiswagner.com.

HAYS, THOMAS S. medical educator, medical researcher; b. Winter Haven, Fla., Dec. 20, 1954; married. BS in Zoology, U. N.C., 1976, PhD in Cell Biology, 1985. Rsch. asst. dept. zoology U. N.C., Chapel Hill, 1975—76; rsch. asst. dept. biol. scis. Duke U., Durham, NC, 1976—79; asst. instr. quantitative and analytical microscopy Marine Biol. Lab., Woods Hole, Mass., 1981—83; asst. instr. optical microscopy U. Calif., Santa Cruz, 1982; postdoctoral fellow dept. molecular, cellular and devel. biology U. Colo., Boulder, 1985—89; asst. prof. dept. genetics and cell biology U. Minn., St. Paul, 1989—95, assoc. prof. dept. genetics and cell biology, 1995—. External reviewer NSF, 1989—. Reviewer: Jour. Cell Biology, Jour. Biol. Chemistry, Molecular Biology of the Cell, Molecular Cell Biology, Proceedings Nat. Acad. Sci. USA, Cell Motility and the Cytoskeleton, Jour. Cell Sci., Genetics; contbr. articles to profl. jours. Recipient Basil O'Connor Scholar award, March of Dimes, 1993, Establishe Investigator award, Am. Heart Found., 1996; fellow H.V. Wilson, U. N.C., 1983, R.J. Reynolds, 1983, Postdoctoral, NIH, 1985—88; grantee Tng., 1991—95, 1995—, Rsch. Tng., NSF, 1991—95, March of Dimes, 1995—; scholar Founders, Marine Biol. Lab., 1980. Mem.: Genetics Soc. Am., Am. Soc. Cell Biology. Office: U Minn Dept Genetics Cell Biology & Devel 6-160 Jackson Hall 321 Church St SE Minneapolis MN 55455

HAYS, WILLIAM GRADY, JR., corporate financial and bank consultant; b. Covington, Ga., July 9, 1927; s. William Grady and Ella Maude (Wofford) H.; m. Emily Ann Holcombe, Aug. 1, 1954; children: Woodfrin Grady, Steven Gregory, William Danfield. BS, U. Ga., 1949; M.Litt., U. Pitts., 1950. Pres. First So. Corp., Atlanta, 1955-57; v.p. Comml. Trust Co., 1957-59; pres., CEO Comml. Acceptance Corp., 1959-74; fin. cons. William G. Hays & Assocs., Inc., 1974—; cons., CEO N.Am. Acceptance Corp., 1974—; cons. Kaleidoscope, Inc., 1979—, Speir Ins. Agy., Inc., 1982—; CEO United Am. Fin. Corp., Knoxville, Tenn., 1983—. Cons. Banque Nationale De Paris, Nat. Westminister Bank, PLC, United Bank of Kuwait, PLC, Security Pacific Nat. Bank, First Nat. Bank of Boston; trustee Beacon Fin. Group, Inc., 1986; cons. Micro Mart, Inc., 1987; examiner World Bazzar Franchise Corp., 1992; spl. master Hannover Corp. Am., 1991; spl. agt. Diversified Growth Corp., 1989; trustee Internat. Trading Inc., 1993, Aledo Fin. Svcs., Inc., 1985, Flexel, Inc., RDM Sports Inc. Contbr. articles to profl. jours. Mem. Kappa Delta Pi. Clubs: Cherokee Town and Country, Univ. Yacht. Republican. Presbyterian. Home: 2755 Normandy Dr NW Atlanta GA 30305-2822 Office: 1100 Spring St NW Ste 450 Atlanta GA 30309-2847

HAYTAIAN, GARABED (CHUCK HAYTAIAN), state legislator; b. N.Y.C., Jan. 28, 1938; s. David and Zakia (Vaniskhian) H.; m. Joan Harriett Mardenly, 1961; children: David Ned, Debra Lucy Snyder, Darrell Charles. BS, U. Ala., 1961. Elec. engr. Am. Machine & Foundry, 1961-62, Grumman Aircraft Engr. Corp., 1962-66; pres. Mardenly Cleaners & Sons, Inc., 1966-82; mktg. dir. east coast L. Robert Kimball & Assoc., 1982-86; exec. cons. Group Tech. Inc., 1986-90; bus. adminstr. Hovanian Armenian Sch., 1990; mktg. dir. Superior Graphics, Inc., 1990—; freeholder Warren County, N.J., 1976-81; assemblyman dist. 23 N.J. State Assembly, 1982—; chmn. N.J. State Rep. Party, 1995—2001. Minority whip N.J. State Assembly, 1984-85, asst. minority leader, 1985-86, majority leader, 1986-89, minority leader, 1990-92, spkr., 1992— Recipient disting. svc. award Sussex County Edn. Assn., 1990, disting. citizen award Boy Scouts Am., 1988, ten year svc. award Am. Cancer Soc., 1984; named freshman assemblyman of yr. Nat. Assn. Counties, 1982, legis. of yr., 1983. Bd. dirs. Warren County C.C., 1988—; trustee Centenary Coll., 1988—. Mem. Hackettstown C. of C., Tall Cedars Lebanon, Masons. Republican.

HAYTER, JOHN ELDON, music educator; b. Warsaw, Mo., Apr. 14, 1929; s. Clay Glen Hayter and Alta Grace Gregory. BS in Edn., Ctrl. Mo. State U., Warrensburg, 1952; MA, Sangamon State U., Springfield, Ill., 1974. Cert. tchr. Mo. Tchr. Logan Elem. Sch., Clinton, Mo., 1947—48; bandmaster USN Fleet Sonar Sch., Key West, Fla., 1954—56; tchr. Dept. Def. Dependent Sch., Anmara, Turkey, 1962—64, Wiesbaden, Germany, 1964—65; condr. Jacksonville Symphony Orch., Ill., 1968—70; tchr., orch. condr. Sch. Dist. 117, Jacksonville, Ill., 1955—90. Orch. chmn. Ill. Music Educators Assn. Dist. IV, Jacksonville, Ill., 1965—89. Author: Sri Lanka-A Late 20th Century Adventure, 1996. Election judge Dem. Party, Jacksonville, Ill., 1990—. With USN, 1952—56. Mem.: Ansar Shrine Chanters (choral dir. 1984—), Ansar Masonic Shrine, Shawnee Lodge AF&AM. Democrat. Methodist. Avocations: travel, photography, cooking, gardening, sailing. Home: 3 Millwood Manor Jacksonville IL 62650

HAYTHE, WINSTON MCDONALD, lawyer, educator, consultant, real estate investor; b. Reidsville, NC, Oct. 10, 1940; s. McDonald Swann and Henrietta Elizabeth (East) H.; m. Glenann Leigh Rogers, Aug. 17, 1963 (div. 1977); children: Sheila Elaine, Kevin McDonald, Rhonda Leigh. BS, S.W. Mo. State U., 1963; JD, Coll. William and Mary, 1967; postgrad., U. Va., 1968—69; grad., Command and Gen. Staff Sch., Ft. Leavenworth, Kans., 1982, U.S. Def. U., 1984; LLM, U.S. Army JAG Sch., 1976. Bar: Va. 1967, D.C. 1969. Assoc. Rhyne & Rhyne, Washington, 1969-72; sr. trial atty. AEC, Washington, 1972-73; asst. gen counsel, sr. atty. Consumer Produce Safety Commn., Washington, 1973-82; staff dir. legal office EPA, Washington, 1982-83, sr. atty. for enforcement policy, 1985-91, sr. atty. Nat. Enforcement Tng. Inst., 1991-94, asst. dir., 1994-96, sr. legal counsel, 1996-2001; sr. counsel Office of Criminal Enforcement, Forensics and Tng., 2001—. Legis. fellow U.S. Senate, Washington, 1983-85; adv. com. paralegal studies U. Md., 1980-95, chmn., 1992-95; adj. prof. law, 1978-94; law faculty U.S. Army Judge Adv. Gen.'s Sch., Charlottesville, Va., 1969-94, Nat. Advocacy Ctr. U.S. Dept. Justice, Columbia, S.C., 1999—; cons. Barrister Ent., Washington, 1978—; elected mem. undergrad. programs adv. coun. U. Md., 1993-95; guest lectr. George Washington U. Sch. Law, 1999-2002, adj. prof. law, 2002-. Trustee Georgetown Presbyn. Ch., 1995-98, v.p. trustees, 1996, pres. trustees, 1997-98, elder, mem. session, 2000-03, clk. of session, 2003—. Col. JAGC, USAR, 1967-94, ret. Fellow: Found. Fed. Bar Assn. (life); mem.: Found. of the Fed. Bar (sustaining life), The Social List of Washington, Fed. Bar Assn. (fed. career svcs. divsn. 1974—90, nat. coun. 1998—), DC Bar Assn., Va. State Bar Assn., Coll. William and Mary Law Sch. Assn. (bd. dirs. 1988—95), Cosmos Club, Knights Templar, Kappa Mu Epsilon. Presbyterian. Avocations: playing organ, piano, theater, concerts, reading. Home: 2141 P St NW Apt 402 Washington DC 20037-1031 Office: EPA (MC-2235A) 1200 Pennsylvania Ave NW Washington DC 20460-0001 E-mail: whaythe@hotmail.com.

HAYTON, BERNARD QUENTIN, JR., library media specialist; b. Effingham, Ill., July 8, 1942; s. Bernard Q. and Sarah Elizabeth (Mann) H.; m. Susan K. Harmeson, Aug. 19, 1967; children: Raymond Todd, Katherine Ann. BS in Edn., Ill. State U., 1967; MS in Edn. Media, Ind. U., 1970. Cert. libr. media specialist, Ill., Mont. Media dir. Rich Cen. High Sch., Olympia Fields, Ill., 1967-70; audio-visual dir. Niles North High Sch., Skokie, Ill., 1970-71; audio-visual specialist New Trier High Sch., Winnetka, Ill., 1971-75; libr. Busby (Mont.) Sch., 1975-76; dir. libr. and media Morris (Ill.) Community High Sch., 1976-98; retired, 1998. Media instr. Northeastern Ill. U., Chgo., 1970-75; chmn. Festival of Christmas Crafts, Morris, 1980-94; mem. ednl. adv. com. Chgo. Tribune, 1991-97. Scoutmaster Boy Scouts Am., 1963; mem. Presbyn. Ch., 1988. Mem. SAR. Avocations: crafts, avid reading, traveling, camping. Home: 1248 Park Blvd Morris IL 60450-1247 E-mail: BHaytonJr@aol.com.

HAYUNGA, MARY ANN, women's health nurse; b. Bklyn., May 1, 1948; d. John and Theresa (Grombliniak) Mendelewski; m. Eugene Hayunga, Dec. 11, 1971; children: Christina, Joseph, Michael, Robert. Diploma, Bklyn. Meth. Hosp., 1967; BS, Empire State Coll., 1977; MPH, Johns Hopkins U., 1984. Classroom and clin. instr. Albany (N.Y.) Vocat. Sch., 1975-76; childbirth educator CEA, Kensington, Md., 1980-83; supr. pediatric and surg. specialities Kaiser Permanente, Kensington, 1987-89; clin. instr., adj. prof. maternal/child health and med.-surg. nursing Montgomery Coll., 1992—; mem. nursing faculty Kaplan Ednl. Svcs., N.Y.C., 1997—. With (Nurse Corps) U.S. Army Res., 1974—. Mem. APHA, Polish Legion Am. Vets. Home: 10603 Wheatley St Kensington MD 20895-2623

HAYUTIN, DAVID LIONEL, lawyer; b. Phoenix, Apr. 19, 1930; s. Henry and Eva (Gaines) H.; m. Lee June Rodgers, June 15, 1951 AB, U. So. Calif., Los Angeles, 1952, JD, 1958. Bar: Calif. 1958. Assoc. Pillsbury Winthrop LLP and predecessor firms, Los Angeles, 1958-67, ptnr., 1967—. Author: Distributing Foreign Products in the United States, 1988, revised edit., 2000; assoc. editor So. Calif. Law Rev.; contbr. legal articles to profl. jours. Served to lt. (j.g.) USN, 1952-55. Mem. ABA, Internat. Bar Assn., Calif. Bar Assn., Maritime Law Assn., Mountaingate Country Club. Republican. Avocations: opera, golf. Office: Pillsbury Winthrop LLP 725 S Figueroa St Los Angeles CA 90017-5524 E-mail: dhayutin@pillsburywinthrop.com.

HAYWARD, ALLEN WILLIAM, government lawyer; b. Olympia, Wash., Jan. 5, 1951; s. Donald Jackson and Barbara Jean H.; m. Sharon Theresa Eberle, July 8, 1991. B of Polit. Sci., Willamette U., 1974; JD, Seattle U., 1977. Spkr's atty. Wash. State Ho. of Reps., Olympia, 1979—. Parliamentarian Wash. State Rep. Party, Seattle, 1982-86. County chair Thurston County Reps., Olympia, 1980-82. Mem. Wash. State Bar Assn. Office: Wash State Ho of Reps PO Box 40600 Olympia WA 98504 E-mail: Hayward_al@leg.wa.gov.

HAYWARD, EDWARD JOSEPH, lawyer; b. Springfield, Mo., Dec. 4, 1943; s. Joseph Hunter and Rosemary Hayward; m. Ellinor Duffey, Aug. 30, 1968; children: Jeffrey, Stephen, Susan. Student, U. d'Aix Marseille, Aix-en-Provence, France, 1963-64; AB, Stanford U., 1965; JD magna cum laude, Harvard U., 1971. Bar: N.Y. 1972, Minn. 1980. Assoc. Cleary, Gottlieb, Steen & Hamilton, N.Y.C. and Brussels, 1971-74, Oppenheimer Wolff & Donnelly, LLP, Brussels, 1975-79, ptnr. Mpls., 1978—. Pres. Twin Cities Fgn. Trade Zone Inc., Mpls., 1983-84. Chmn. legis. com. Minn. World Trade Assn., Mpls., 1984-87. Served to capt. U.S. Army, 1965-68. Mem.: ABA, Minn. Bar Assn. (councillor internat. law sect. 1983—, sec. 1986—88, vice chmn. 1988—89, chmn. 1989—90), Dist. Export Coun. (chmn. 1996—), German-Am. C. of C. (bd. dirs. 1994—99, 2000—), French-Am. C. of C. (bd. dirs. 1983—, pres. 1985—87, 1996—2001, nat. sec. 1988—). Republican. Presbyterian. Avocations: languages, sports. Home: 6625 W Shore Dr Minneapolis MN 55435-1528 Office: Oppenheimer Wolff & Donnelly LLP 45 S 7th St Ste 3300 Minneapolis MN 55402-1609

HAYWARD, ELIZABETH, lawyer, artist; b. Quincy, Mass., Aug. 27, 1964; d. William and Patricia Hayward. BS, Salem (Mass.) State Coll., 1986; JD, New Eng. Sch. Law, Boston, 1993. Bar: Mass. 1994. Legis. aide Mass. Ho. of Reps., Boston, 1987-88, rsch. asst., 1988-89; staff counsel Mass. Office Inspector Gen., Boston, 1993-96, asst. gen. counsel, 1996-97, dep. gen. counsel, 1997—. Vol. Youth Enrichment Svcs., Boston, 1999—. Recipient Am. Jurisprudence award in consti. law Lawyer's Coop. Pub., Boston, 1992. Mem. ABA, Assn. Inspectors Gen. (bd. dirs. 1996—), S-Kimos Ski Club. Democrat. Roman Catholic. Avocations: oil and acrylic painting, snowboarding, golf. Office: Office Inspector Gen 1 Ashburton Pl Boston MA 02108-1518

HAYWARD, FREDRIC MARK, social reformer; b. N.Y.C., July 10, 1946; s. Irving Michael and Mildred (Feingold) Hayward; m. Ingeborg Beck, Aug. 18, 1971 (div. 1974); 1 child, Jack. BA, Brandeis U., Waltham, Mass., 1967; MA, Fletcher Sch. Law & Diplomacy, Medford, Mass., 1968, MALD, 1969. Exec. dir. Men's Rights, Inc., Boston, 1977—. Bd. dirs., J Banta, Inc.; vis. lectr. Tufts U., Medford, Mass., 1979; lectr. in field; conductor workshops in field; mem. adv. bd. Ctr. for Men's Studies, 1988-93; host, prodr. The SacraMENshow; founder Nat. Coalition Just Draft; co-founder Free Men Boston; co-founder, v.p. Children's Rights Coun. Sacramento, SAFE (Stop Abuse for Everyone); co-founder, treas. The Fathers' Symposium, 1996—. Author 3 published anthologies; contbg. editor: The Liberator, Forest Lake, Minn., 1988-89; contbg. writer Spectator, Berkeley, Calif., 1988-2001; contbr. articles to profl. jours. Farrell Fellowship on Men, 1989; Fletcher Sch. Law and Diplomacy fellow, 1967-69; recipient award of Excellence Nat. Coalition of Free Men, 1993, award Western Access Video Excellence, 1995. Mem. Nat. Congress for Men (bd. dirs. 1981-90), Am. Fedn. TV and Radio Artists, Men. Internat. (bd. dirs. 1982-86). Office: Mr Inc PO Box 163180 Sacramento CA 95816-9180

HAYWARD, JEAN, artist, musician, interior designer, performance artist; b. L.A., Calif., Apr. 4, 1917; d. Herbert Hastings Eastwood and Irma Isabul Arundell; m. Bob Hayward (dec.); m. George R. Collins (dec. Sept. 26, 1939); children: Julia Ann, Stephen, George, Mark. BA, U.C.L.A., L.A., 1938. Mime story telling with orchestras, all around the world; designer clothing line of denim for Bullock's Willshire; architecture and design houses, Santa Barbara. Contbr. articles to profl. jour.;, performer symphony soloist. Vol. Jr. League, Santa Barbara, Calif., 1946—70. Mem.: Buman Wood Golf Club. Republican. Episc. Avocation: horseback riding. Home: 300 Hot Springs Rd Santa Barbara CA 93108

HAYWARD, OLGA LORETTA HINES (MRS. SAMUEL ELLSWORTH HAYWARD), retired librarian; b. Alexandria, La. d. Samuel James and Lillie (George) Hines; m. Samuel E. Hayward, July 12, 1945; children: Anne Elizabeth, Olga Patricia (Mrs. William Ryer). AB, Dillard U., 1941; BSLS, Atlanta U., 1944; MALS, U. Mich., 1959; MA in History, La. State U., 1977. Tchr. Marksville (La.) H.S., 1941-42; head libr. Grambling (La.) Coll., 1944-46; br. libr. br. nine New Orleans Pub. Libr. System, 1947-48; reference libr. So. U. Baton Rouge, 1948-73, libr. bus. and social scis. libr., 1973-84, libr. collection devel. consent decree program, 1984-86, chairwoman dept. reference, 1986-88, ret., 1988. Author: Graduate Theses of Southern University, 1959-71, A Bibliography of Literature By and About Whitney Moore Young Jr., 1929-71, 1972, The Influence of Humanism on Sixteenth Century English Courtesy Texts, 1977; also other bibliographies. Bd. dirs. La. Diocese Episcopal Cmty. Svcs., 1972-78; mem. banquet com. Baton Rouge chpt. Nat. Conf. Christians and Jews, 1981-2000, Nat. Conf. for cmty. and Justice, 2001-02. Recipient recognition, La. LIbr. Assn., 2003. Mem. life, La. Libr. Assn. (chair-elect subject specialists divsn. 1986-87, chairwoman subject specialists sect. 1987-88, Lucy B. Foote award subject specialists sect. 1990), Spl. Librs. Assn. (pres. La. chpt. 1978-79, Roll of Honor award 1995). Episcopalian. Home: 1632 Harding Blvd Baton Rouge LA 70807-5442 Office: 1632 Harding Bvd Baton Rouge LA 70807-5442

HAYWARD, THOMAS ZANDER, JR., lawyer; b. Oct. 21, 1940; s. Thomas Z. and Wilhelmina (White) H.; m. Sally Madden, June 20, 1964; children: Thomas Z., Wallace M., Robert M. BA, Northwestern U., 1962, JD, 1965; MBA, U. Chgo., 1970. Bar: Ill. 1966, Ohio 1966, U.S. Dist. Ct. (no. dist.) Ill. 1966, U.S. Supreme Ct. 1970. Assoc. Defrees & Fiske, Chgo., 1965-69, ptnr., 1969-81, Boodell, Sears, Giambalvo & Crowley, Chgo., 1981-87, Bell, Boyd, Lloyd, Chgo., 1987—. Mem. mgmt. and exec. coms. Bell, Boyd, Lloyd. Trustee Northwestern U., 1980-84, 97—, vice-chmn., 2000—; bd. dirs. Ill. Continuing Legal Edn., 1987-92, Chgo. area Found. for Legal Svcs., 1983—. Recipient Northwestern U. Alumni Svc. award, 1973. Mem. ABA (ho. of dels. 1984—, fed. jud. com. 1993-97, bd. govs., exec. com. 1998-2001, chmn. fin. com., chair 2003—), Ill. State Bar Assn., Chgo. Bar Assn. (pres. 1983-84, dir., v.p. 1998—), Chgo. Bar Found. (bd. dirs., v.p. 2003—), Chgo. Club, Casino Club, Barrington Hills Country Club (pres. 1985-87). Republican. Presbyterian. Home: 8 W County Line Rd Barrington IL 60010-2613 Office: Bell Boyd & Lloyd 3 1st Nat Plz 70 W Madison St Ste 3300 Chicago IL 60602-4284

HAYWARD-WILLIAMS, CAROLYN ROSE, management and technology consultant; b. Phila., Oct. 10, 1963; d. William L. and Elizabeth F. (Fogg) Hayward; m. Terence Gary Williams, Feb. 17, 1996; 1 child, Elizabeth Rose Williams. B in Engring., Vanderbilt U., 1987; MS, Johns Hopkins U., 1991; MBA, U. Md., 1993. Student engr. Gen. Motors, Ypsilanti, summers 1985-86; sr. systems engr. Westinghouse Electric, Balt., 1987—91; assoc. Booz-Allen & Hamilton, Balt., 1992, prin. London, 1993—. Presenter numerous tech. and bus. analyses, presentations in field. Mem. IEEE. Avocations: skiing, horseback riding, travel, reading. Office: Booz Allen & Hamilton 7 Savoy Ct Strand London WC2R OJP England E-mail: hayward_carolyn@bah.com.

HAYWOOD, ANNE MOWBRAY, pediatrics, virology, and biochemistry educator; b. Balt., Feb. 5, 1935; d. Richard Mansfield and Margaret (Mowbray) H. BA in Chemistry, Bryn Mawr Coll., 1955; MD, Harvard U., 1959. Cert. Am. Bd. Pediat. Intern U. Calif. Med. Ctr., San Francisco, 1959-60; fellow biochemistry dept. Columbia U., N.Y.C., 1961-62; fellow divsn. biology Calif. Inst. Tech., Pasadena, 1960-61, 62-64; asst. prof. microbiology, microbiology dept. Northwestern U. Med. Sch., Chgo., 1964-66, Yale U. Med. Sch., New Haven, 1966-73; resident in pediat. U. Wash., Seattle, 1974-75, pediat. infectious disease fellow, 1975-76, Vanderbilt U., Nashville, 1976-77; assoc. prof. pediat. and microbiology U. Rochester, N.Y., 1977—. Vis. asst. prof. Rockefeller U., N.Y.C., 1971-72; vis. scientist biophysics unit Agrl. Rsch. Coun., Cambridge, Eng., 1972-74, Inst. for Immunology and Virology, U. Zürich, Switzerland, 1987; vis. assoc. prof. dept. zoology U. Calif., Davis, 1986; vis. assoc. prof. McArdle Lab. for Cancer Rsch., U. Wis., 1999-2000. Co-author: Practice of Pediatrics, 1977, Infections in Children, 1982, Liposome Letters, 1983, Practice of Pediatrics, 1987, Molecular Mechanisms of Membrane Fusion, 1988, Membrane Fusion, 1991, Encyclopedia of Human Biology, 1991, 2d edit., 1997, Cell and Model Membrane Interactions, 1991. Fogarty Internat. Ctr. Sr. fellow NIH, 1987, European Molecular Biology Orgn. fellow, 1973-74, NIH Spl. fellow, 1971-73, Am. Cancer Soc. Postdoctoral fellow, 1960-62; Harvard Med. Sch. scholar, 1955-59, Harriet Judd Sartain scholar, 1955-59, N.Y. Alumnae scholar Bryn Mawr Coll., 1951-55. Mem. Biophys. Soc., Am. Soc. for Molecular Biology. Democrat. Office: U Rochester Med Ctr PO Box 777 Rochester NY 14642-8777 E-mail: ahyw@mail.rochester.edu.

HAYWOOD, B(ETTY) J(EAN), anesthesiologist; b. Boston, June 1, 1942; d. Oliver Garfield and Helen Elizabeth (Salisbury) H.; m. Lynn Brandt Moon, Aug. 29, 1969 (div. Aug. 1986); children: Kaylin, Kris Lee, Kelly, Kasy R. BSc, Tufts U., 1964; MD, U. Colo., 1968; MBA, Oklahoma City U., 1993; Grad., Air War Coll., 1997. Intern Wilford Hall AFB, San Antonio, 1968-69; resident in pediatrics U. Ariz., Tucson, 1971-72, resident in anesthesiology, 1972-74; dir. anesthesia dept. Pima County Hosp., Tucson, 1975-76; staff anesthesiologist South Community Hosp., Oklahoma City, 1977—, Moore (Okla.) Mcpl. Hosp., 1981-94, chief of anesthesia, 1990-94; staff anesthesiologist St. Anthony Hosp., Oklahoma City, 1982—; instr. dept. anesthesia U. Okla. Health Sci. Ctr., Oklahoma City, 1999—; col. USAF, active duty for Op. Enduring Freedom Wilford Hall Med. Ctr., Lackland AFB, Tex., 2001—02. Chief of ethics com.

S.W. Med. Ctr., 1996. Bd. dirs. N.Am. South Devon Assn., Lynnville, Iowa, 1978—86; mem. med. com. Planned Parenthood Okla., 1992—; col. USAFR, 1968—. Mem. AMA, NAFE (co-dir. Oklahoma City chpt. 1996—), World South Devon Assn. (U.S. rep. 1985, 88), Tufts U. Alumni Assn. (rep.), Chi Omega (treas. 1963-64). Republican. Presbyterian. Avocations: skiing, sailing. Home: 6501 Hunting Hill Ln Oklahoma City OK 73116-3523 E-mail: Beej1942@aol.com.

HAYWOOD, BRUCE, retired academic administrator; b. York, Eng., Sept. 30, 1925; came to U.S., 1951, naturalized, 1957; s. Joseph Edgar and Eva (Street) H.; m. Isona Gretchen Shelley, June 21, 1947; children— Anne Margaret, Elizabeth Shelley. Student, U. Leeds, Eng., 1947-48; BA, McGill U., 1950, MA, 1951; PhD, Harvard, 1956. Mem. faculty Kenyon Coll., 1954, prof. German lit., 1960-63, dean coll., 1963-67, provost, 1967-80; pres. Monmouth (Ill.) Coll., 1980-94; ret., 1994. Author: The Veil of Imagery, 1959. Served with Brit. Army, 1943-47. Mem. Am. Assn. Tchrs. of German. Home: 1885 Cornelia Rd Galesburg IL 61401-1423

HAYWOOD, H(ERBERT) CARL(TON), psychologist, educator; b. Taylor County, Ga., July 2, 1931; s. Howard Chapman and Rosebud (Smith) H.; m. Nancy Patricia Roberts, Oct. 5, 1951 (div. Mar. 1971); children: Carlton, Terence, Elizabeth, Kristin; m. Dona June Wooldridge Tapp, Sept. 6, 1993 (div. Mar. 2000). AB, San Diego State Coll., 1956, MA, 1957; PhD, U. Ill., 1961. Mem. faculty George Peabody Coll. (merged with Vanderbilt U. 1979), Nashville, 1962-93; Alexander Heard disting. svc. prof., 1993-94; prof. psychology George Peabody Coll. (merged with Vanderbilt U. 1979), Nashville, 1969-93, prof. spl. edn., 1975-79, prof. emeritus, 1994—, dir. mental retardation research tng. program, 1968-70; dir. Inst. Mental Retardation and Intellectual Devel., 1970-73, Office Research Adminstrn., 1974-76, John F. Kennedy Center Research Edn. and Human Devel., 1971-83; prof. neurology Vanderbilt U. Sch. Medicine, 1971-93; prof. psychology and edn., dean grad. sch. edn. & psychology Touro Coll., N.Y.C., 1993-2000. Vis. prof. U. Toronto, 1965-66; sr. fellow Vanderbilt Inst. Pub. Policy Studies, 1983-88; chmn. Nat Mental Retardation Research Center Dirs., 1979-82; adv. bd. Ill. Inst. Developmental Disabilities, Chgo., 1970-78, Eunice Kennedy Shriver Center Mental Retardation, Waltham, Mass., 1973-80, Tenn. Dept. Mental Health, 1964-92, mem. nat. child health and human devel. council NIH, 1983-88; cons. President's Com. on Mental Retardation, 1968-73; mem. sci. rev. com., health research facilities br., div. edn. and research facilities NIH, 1967-71 Author (with Brooks and Burns): Bright Start: Cognitive Curriculum for Young Children, 1992; editor: Brain Damage in School Age Children, 1968, Social Cultural Aspects of Mental Retardation, 1970; editor: (with Begab and Garber) Prevention of Retarded Development in Psychosocially Disadvantaged Children; editor: (with J.R. Newbrough) Living Environments for Developmentally Retarded Persons, 1981; editor: (with D. Tzuriel) Interactive Assessment, 1992; editor: (with S. Friedman) Developmental Follow-Up: Domains, Concepts, and Methods, 1994; editor: Am. Jour. Mental Deficiency, 1969—79, Jour. Cognitive Edn. and Psychology, 1999—; mem. editl. bd.: Jour. Abnormal Child Psychology, 1973—89, Contemporary Psychology, 1982—85, Acta Paedologica, 1983—87, Jour. Mental Deficiency Rsch., 1984—2001, Internat. Rev. Rsch. in Mental Retardation, 1982—97; contbr. articles. Bd. trustees Am. U. Rome, 2000—. With USN, 1950-54. Fellow Am. Assn. Mental Retardation (v.p. psychology 1975-77, 1st v.p. 1978-79, pres. 1980-81), APA (pres. Div. 33 1978-79, mem. Coun. of Reps. 1980-82); mem. Internat. Assn. Cognitive Edn. (pres. 1988-92), Soc. Rsch. in Child Devel., Inst. Medicine, Am. Psychol. Soc. Democrat. Episcopalian. *Dominant values include enthusiasm for scholarship, equal parts of dedication to science for its own sake and concern for social progress, and the conviction that self-concern and self-seeking constitute the most dangerous threat to the collective goals of humanity. The future lies in education designed to stretch minds and develop processes of critical thought rather than to impart job-oriented skills.*

HAYWOOD, L. JULIAN, physician, educator; b. Reidsville, N.C., Apr. 13, 1927; s. Thomas Woodly and Louise Viola (Hayley) H.; m. Virginia Elizabeth Paige, Dec. 3, 1953; 1 child, Julian Anthony. BS, Hampton Inst., 1948; MD, Howard U., 1952. Intern St. Mary's Hosp., Rochester, N.Y., 1952-53; resident L.A. County Hosp., 1956-58; fellow cardiology White Meml. Hosp., 1959-61; traveling fellow U. Oxford, Eng., 1963; instr. medicine Loma Linda (Calif.) U., 1960-61, asst. prof., 1961-73, assoc. clin. prof., 1973-82, clin. prof., 1982—; asst. prof. medicine U. So. Calif., 1963-67, assoc. prof., 1967-76, prof., 1976—. Past dir. comprehensive sickle cell ctr. LA County/U. So. Calif. Med. Ctr., dir. ECG Dept., 1996—, past dir. coronary care unit, physicians tng. program (Regional Med. Programs), 1970-75; cons. Los Angeles County Coroner, Indsl. Accident Bd. Calif., Health Care Tech. Divsn., USPHS, Nat. Heart and Lung Inst.; past mem. cardiology adv. com. divsn. heart and vascular diseases; bd. dirs., pres. Sickle Cell Diseases Found.; mem. Armed Forces Epidemiol. Bd., 1996—; pres. U. So. Calif. Salerni Collegium, 1997-98; bd. dirs. Charles Drew U. Medicine and Scis., 1999—. Contbr. articles profl. jours.; Mem. editorial bds.: Jour. Nat. Med. Assn. Past pres., hon. mem., bd. dirs. Am. Heart Assn. Greater L.A., 1989—. With M.C. USNR, 1954-56. Recipient award of merit Los Angeles County Heart Assn., 1968, 69, 73, 75, Disting. Alumnus award Howard U., 1982, Louis B. Russel award Am. Heart Assn., 1988, Merit award, 1991, Heart of Gold award Am. Heart Assn./Greater L.A. Affiliate, 1989, Dedicated Svc. award, 1991, 93, award of Achievement in Rsch., 1994, 20th Anniversary Founder's award Assn. Black Cardiologists, 1994, Disting. Svc. award Howard U. Sch. Medicine, 1996; J.B. Johnson Meml. lectr., 1975, 88; honoree Internal Medicine sect. Nat. Med. Assn., 1988; named Alumnus of Yr.-at-Large, Hampton U., 1993. Fellow ACP, AAAS, L.A. Acad. Medicine, Am. Coll. Cardiology (Disting. Svc. award 2001, Cert. of Appreciation 2003), Am. Heart Assn. (coun. on clin. cardiology, coun. on atherosclerosis, exec. com. coun. on epidemiology, long range planning com., dir., past sec., v.p. Greater L.A. affiliate, pres.); mem. AMA, AAUP, Am. Fedn. Clin. Rsch., Western Soc. Clin. Investigation, Assn. Advancement Med. Instrumentation, Nat. Med. Assn. (Charles Drew Med. Soc.), N.Y. Acad. Scis., Hampton Inst. Alumni Assn. (past pres. L.A. chpt.), Med. Faculty Assn. U. So. Calif. Sch. Medicine (past pres.), Assn. Physicians L.A. County Hosp. (pres. 1991—), Western Assn. Physicians, Fedn. Am. Scientists, Assn. Black Cardiologists (Walter Booker Innovation award 1990), Assn. Acad. Minority Physicians (councilor, pres.-elect 1992-93, pres. 1993-94), Alpha Omega Alpha, Am. Coll. Physicians (Laureate award So. Calif. Region I 1997). Home: 3551 Lowry Rd Los Angeles CA 90027-1433 Office: LAC&USC Med Ctr Box 305 1200 N State St Los Angeles CA 90033-1029 Office Fax: 323-226-7458. E-mail: jhaywood@hsc.usc.edu.

HAYWOOD, THEODORE JOSEPH, physician, educator; b. Monroe, N.C., Feb. 13, 1929; s. Jesse Beman and Mary (McDonald) H.; m. Nancy Hume Ferguson, Dec. 21, 1959; children: Elizabeth Linscott, Keene McDonald, Mark Shepard. BS, The Citadel, 1948; MD, Vanderbilt U., 1952. Diplomate: Am. Bd. Pediatrics, Am. Bd. Allergy and Immunology. Pvt. practice allergy, Houston, 1958—; mem. staff Tex. Children's Hosp., 1958—, mem. active staff Pediatrics, 1963—; mem. faculty Baylor U. Coll. Medicine, 1958—, clin. assoc. prof. pediatrics and allergy, 1977—. Assoc. mem. U. Tex. McDonald Obs., 2000—. Served with M.C. AUS, 1955-57. Fellow Am. Coll. Allergists, Am. Acad. Allergy and Immunology, Am. Acad. Pediatrics; mem. Sigma Xi. Clubs: River Oaks Country (Houston). Republican. Episcopalian. Home: 2923 Ferndale Pl Houston TX 77098-1117 Office: McGovern Allergy & Asthma Clinic 4710 Bellaire Blvd Ste 200 Bellaire TX 77401-4505 E-mail: mac@mcgovernallergy.com.

HAYWORTH, J(OHN) D(AVID), JR., congressman, former sportscaster; b. High Point, N.C., July 12, 1958; s. John David and Gladys Ethel (Hall) H.; m. Mary Denise Yancey, Feb. 25, 1989; children: Nicole Irene, Hannah Lynne, John Micah. BA in Speech and Polit. Sci., N.C. State U., 1980. Sports anchor, reporter Sta. WPTF-TV, Raleigh, N.C., 1980-81, Sta. WLWT-TV, Cin., 1986-87; sports anchor Sta. WYFF-TV (formerly Sta. WFBC-TV), Greenville, S.C., 1981-86, Sta. KTSP-TV, Phoenix, 1987-94; mem. U.S. Congress from 5th Ariz. dist., Washington, 1995—; mem. ways and means com., mem. resources com., asst. whip. Radio commentator; play-by-play broadcaster. Dist. committeeman Ariz. Rep. Com., Scottsdale, 1988-89; bd. dirs. Am. Humanics Found., Ariz. State U., Tempe, 1991-92; chmn. Scout-A-Rama, Theodore Roosevelt coun. Boy Scouts Am., 1991-92. Recipient honor roll award Atlantic Coast Conf., 1977, Young Am. award Unharrie coun. Boy Scouts Am., 1979, Friend of Edn. award Sch. Dist. Greenville County, 1985, Sch. Bell/Friend of Edn. award S.C. Dept. Edn., 1985. Mem. Rotary (bd. dirs. Phoenix 1989-90). Republican. Baptist. Avocations: reading, distance running, bible study, public speaking, television trivia. Office: US House Reps 2434 Rayburn Ho Office Bldg Washington DC 20515-0306*

HAZAN, MARCELLA MADDALENA, writer, educator, consultant; b. Cesenatico, Italy, Apr. 15, 1924; d. Giuseppe and Maria (Leonelli) Polini; m. Victor Hazan, Feb. 24, 1955; 1 child, Giuliano. Dr. in Natural Scis., U. Ferrara, 1952, Dr. in Biology, 1954. Rschr. Guggenheim Inst., 1955-58; prof. math. and biology Italian State schs., 1963-66; founder Sch. of Italian Cooking, N.Y.C., 1969-94, Marcella Hazan Sch. of Classic Italian Cooking, Bologna, Italy, 1976-94, Master Classes in Classic Italian Cooking, Venice, Italy, 1986-98. Pres. Hazan Classic Enterprises, Inc., 1978-99. Author: The Classic Italian Cookbook, 1973, More Classic Italian Cooking, 1978, Marcella's Italian Kitchen, 1986, Essentials of Classic Italian Cooking, 1992, Marcella Cucina, 1997. Roman Catholic. Address: 1212 Gulf Of Mexico Dr # 109 Longboat Key FL 34228 Fax: (941) 387-0183.

HAZARD, CHRISTOPHER WEDVIK, international business executive; b. N.Y.C., Aug. 9, 1943; s. Herbert Ray and Ellen Clausine (Wedvik) H.; m. Sally Grace Woodruff, Sept. 1, 1966; children: Mark Alexander, Julie Lynne. BA, Ohio State U., 1965; MPA, U. Colo., 1973; postgrad., U. Pa., The Wharton Sch. Officer USAF, 1965-86; near east region dir. ops. Def. Security Assistance Agy., Washington, 1982-86; exec dir. internat. mktg. United Def. Ltd. Partnership, Arlington, Va., 1986—. Pres. M. Vernon Citizens Assn., Alexandria, Va., 1984-85, mem., 1982—; mem. Colonial Williamsburg Found., Neighborhood Friends of Mt. Vernon. Recipient Def. Superior Svc., Sec. of Def., 1986, Joint Svc. Achievement, Dept. of Def., 1984; decorated Air Force Meritorious Svc. medal. Mem.: Soc. Am. Period Furniture Makers. Avocations: international affairs, historic preservation, gardening, woodworking.

HAZARD, GEOFFREY CORNELL, JR., law educator; b. Cleve., Sept. 18, 1929; s. Geoffrey Cornell and Virginia (Perry) H.; m. Elizabeth O'Hara; children: James G., Katherine W., Robin P., Geoffrey Cornell III. BA, Swarthmore Coll., 1953, LLD (hon.), 1988; LLB, Columbia U., 1954; LLD (hon.), Gonzaga U., 1985, U. San Diego, 1985, Ill. Inst. Tech., 1990, Republica Italiana, 1998. Bar: Oreg. 1954, Calif. 1960, Conn. 1982, Pa. 1994. Assoc. Hart, Spencer, McCulloch, Rockwood & Davies, Portland, Oreg., 1954-57; exec. sec. Oreg. Legis. Interim Com. Jud. Adminstrn., 1957-58; assoc. prof. law, then prof. U. Calif., Berkeley, 1958-64; prof. law U. Chgo., 1964-71, Yale U., 1971-94, prof. mgmt., 1979-83, acting dean Sch. Orgn. and Mgmt., 1980-81, Sterling prof. law, 1986-94; trustee prof. U. Pa., Phila., 1994—. Mem. Adminstrv. Conf. U.S., 1971-78; jud. conf. U.S. com. on rules practice and procedure, 1994-2000. Author: (Law text) Research in Civil Procedure, 1963, Ethics in the Practice of Law, 1978; author: (with D.W. Louisell, C. Tait, W. Fletcher) Pleading and Procedure, 1972; author: 8th rev. edit., 1999; author: (with M. Taruffo) (Law text) American Civil Procedure, 1994; author: (with S. Koniak and R. Cramton) Law and Ethics of Lawyering 3d edit., 1999; author: (with W.W. Hodes) Law of Lawyering 3d edit., 2000; author: (with F. James and J. Leubsdorf) Civil Procedure 5th rev.edit., 2001; editor: Law in a Changing America, 1968; editor: (with D. Rhode) Legal Profession: Responsibility and Regulation, 1985; co-editor (with D. Rhode): Professional Responsibility and Regulation, 2002; contbr. Served with USAF, 1948-49. Fellow Am. Bar Found. (exec. dir. 1964-70, rsch. award 1986), Am. Acad. Arts and Scis.; mem. ABA (cons. code jud. conduct 1970-72, reporter stds. jud. adminstrn. 1971-77, reporter model rules of profl. conduct 1978-83), Am. Law Inst. (reporter restatement of judgments 1973-81, dir. 1984-99), Nat. Legal Aid and Defender Assn., Am. Judicature Soc., Selden Soc., Pa. Bar Assn., Calif. State Bar, Phi Beta Kappa. Episcopalian. Avocations: tennis, history, golf. E-mail: ghazard@law.upenn.edu.

HAZARD, JOHN W., JR., secondary school educator; b. Zanesville, Ohio, June 4, 1945; BA, Denison U., 1967; MA, Ohio U., 1968; postgrad., U. Va., 1971—72, Wayne State U., 1973—78. English instr. U. Memphis, 1968—71; English tchr. Cranbrook Schs., Bloomfield Hills, Mich., 1972—. Cmty. svc. developer and coord. Cranbrook Schs., Bloomfield Hills, Mich., 1987—. Contbr. poetry. Mem.: Acad. Am. Poets. Avocation: guitar, photography.

HAZARD, ROBERT CULVER, JR., hotel executive; b. Balt., Oct. 23, 1934; s. Robert Culver and Catherine B. H.; m. Mary Victoria Cranor, Jan. 2, 1981; children by previous marriage: Alicia W., Letitia A., Robert Culver, III, Thomas E.J., Anne. BA cum laude, Woodrow Wilson Sch., Princeton U., 1956; postgrad., Johns Hopkins U., U. Denver. Mktg. rep. IBM Corp., Denver, 1959-68; with Am. Express Co., 1968-74, v.p. exec. accounts, 1973-74; CEO Best Western Internat., 1974-80; CEO, retired chmn. Choice Hotels Internat., Silver Spring, Md., 1980-96; chmn. Creative Hotel Assocs., Phoenix, 1996—. Capt. USAF, 1956-59. Recipient Man of Yr. award Motel Brokers Assn. Am., 1976, Silver Plate award Hospitality mag., 1979, Albert E. Koehl award HSMA, 1992, Cecil B. Day Hospitality award AAHOA, 1993, Silver Plate award Lodging Hospitality Mag., 1995. Mem.: Am. Hotel and Lodging Assn. Office: Creative Hotel Assocs LLC 6230 N 51st Pl Paradise Valley AZ 85253 E-mail: roberthazard@msn.com.

HAZEKAMP, PHYLLIS WANDA ALBERTS, retired library director; b. Chgo. d. John Edward and Mary Ann (Demski) Wojciechowski. BA, De Paul U., 1947; MSLS, La. State U., 1959; postgrad., Santa Clara U., U. Chgo. Cert. tchr., Calif., Ariz. Libr. Agrl. Experiment Sta., U. Calif., Riverside, 1959-61; tech. libr. Lockheed Tech. Libr., Palo Alto, Calif., 1962-63; asst. law libr. Santa Clara (Calif.) U. Law Sch., 1963-72; libr. dir. Carmelite Seminary, San Jose, Calif., 1973-78; reference libr. San Jose State U., 1978-79; libr. dir. SAI Engrs., Santa Clara, 1980-81, Palmer Coll. Chiropractic, San Jose, 1981-90, Camp Verde (Ariz.) Cmty. Libr., 1990-98; ret., 1998. Mem. Cultural Commn., Santa Clara, 1968-72; pres. Santa Clara Art Assn., 1973-74; cons. various librs.; lectr. in field. Bd. dirs. Camp Verde Art Commn., 1994—; spkr. Ho. of Ruth, 2000—; pres. Montezuma Chapel Ladies Guild, 1999—2001, 2003—, book rev. chmn., 2003—; bd. dirs. Beaver Creek Adult Ctr., 2000—02; vol. various orgns. Avocations: writing articles, painting, teaching, giving talks to groups.

HAZEL, JAMES R. C., JR., small business owner, volunteer; b. Sturgis, Ky., Oct. 11, 1940; s. James R.C. Hazel Sr. and Lucille Vivian (Brumfield) Palmer; m. Donna Jean Wideman, July 8, 1960; children: Juliee Teresa Hazel Norman (dec.), James R.C. III. AA, Kellogg Cmty. Coll., 1990; grad., E.K. Williams Profl. Mgmt. Sch. With family auto svc. sta., 1952-64, mgr., 1964; pres., owner Jim Hazel's CITCO and Auto Parts Store, Battle Creek, Mich. Mem. adv. bd. Auto Wares, Inc.; bd. dirs. Battle Creek Cmty. Found. Active S.W. Mich. coun. Boy Scouts Am., 1970—, vice chmn., 1987-93; bd. dirs. Sherman Lake Y Ctr., 1990—, v.p., 1996; chmn. Battle Creek Cmty. Leadership Acad., 1985—; bd. dirs. Art Ctr. Battle Creek, 1985-88; chairperson small bus. div. fund drive United Arts Coun., 1987; mem. adv. bd. United Way; sponsor Youth to Sweden Hockey Tournament, 1979; charter mem. Y-Ctr., co-chmn. capital campaign, 1990; charter mem. Binder Park Zoo; sponsor, patron various civic orgns.; mem. adv. com. youth initiates program W.K. Kellogg Found., 1989. Named Dealer of Yr., Pure Oil Co., 1967, Super Citizen, City of Battle Creek, 1989, Scene Mag. Man of Yr., 1997; recipient Silver Beaver award Boy Scouts Am., 1983, George award Battle Creek Enquirer, 1988; Carnation Cmty. Svc. award Battle Creek Vol. Bur., 1985, Vol. of Yr. award, 1998; Small Bus. of Yr. award 1992, 1st Ann. Pride award Harper Creek Schs., 1992, Book of Golden Deeds award Exch. Club, 1994, Disting. Citzen award Calhoun Area Vocat. Ctr., 1989, Calhoun County Intermediate Sch., 1994; named to Vol. Hall of Fame, 1999. Mem. Mich. Svc. Sta. Dealers Assn. (bd. dirs. 1980-90, vice chairperson polit. action com.), Mich. Auto Parts Assn. (bd. dirs. 1989—), Battle Creek C. of C. (charter, vice chmn. 1986-89, chmn. Leadership Acad., Small Bus. of Yr. award 1992), Ducks Unltd., Rotary (bd. dirs. Battle Creek chpt. 1992—, Red Rose award 1998, Paul Harris fellow 1999), Optimists (life, sec., treas. Harper Creek Club 1979, Achievement in Edn. award 1989), Masons (Mason of Yr. 2001), Shriners. Avocations: photography, backpacking, reading, travel. Home: 6695 E Dr N Battle Creek MI 49014-8558 Office: Jim Hazel's Citgo 14301 Beadle Lake Rd Battle Creek MI 49014-8213

HAZEL, JOSEPH PATRICK, retired law educator; b. 1933; STL, Gregorian U., Rome, 1960; MEd, U. Loyola, Chgo., 1968; JD, U. Tex., 1971. Bar: Tex. 1971. Briefing atty. Ct. Criminal Appeals, Austin, Tex., 1971-72; assoc. Gibbins & Spivy, Austin, 1872-76; pntr. Spivey, Hazel & Grigg, Austin, 1976-78; of counsel Spivey, Grigg, Kelly & Knisely, Austin, 1978-87; Tiny Gooch prof. trial practice U. Tex., Austin, 1984—. Lectr. U. Tex., 1975-78, adj. prof., 1978-84. Editor The Advocate. Mem. State Bar Tex., Barristers, Order of Coif. Office: U Tex Sch Law 727 E Dean Keeton Austin TX 78705-3224

HAZEL, MARY BELLE, university administrator; b. Orange, N.J., May 30, 1932; d. Morris M. Sr. and Robena (Brinkley) Thomas; m. James H. Hazel, Sept. 28, 1958 (div. Sept. 1976); children: Sharon Marie Hazel-Griggs, James Thomas. BS in Bus. Adminstrn., Seton Hall U., South Orange, N.J., 1992, MA in Edn. cum laude, 1998. Publs. asst. advt. and pub. rels. dept. Foster Wheeler Corp., N.Y.C., 1969-87; ind. contractor, 1987-92; adminstrv coord. dean's office UMDNJ Sch. Health Related Professions, Newark, 1992—. Elder Elmwood United Presbyn. Ch. Mem. AAUW, NAFE, Smithsonian Nat. Assn., Soc. Allied Health Professions N.J., Spinal Cord Injured-Family Support Group-Kessler Inst. Rehab.

HAZEL, STEWART JEROME, physician; b. Lanesboro, Minn., Sept. 30, 1953; s. Roy Orin and Fern Theodosia (Harrison) H.; m. Mary Ellen Schlosser, July 13, 1974; 1 child, Ian. Student, St. John's U., 1971-73; BS, U. Minn., 1976, DVM, 1977, MD, 1984; MS, Colo. State U., Ft. Collins, 1981. Bd. cert. Am. Bd. Ophthalmology. Pvt. practice Eye Physicians and Surgeons, Edina, Minn., 1989-90, Mankato (Minn.) Clin., 1990-91; ophthalmologist Duluth (Minn.) Clin., 1991—. Leader Cub Scouts of Am., 1992-94, pack consel mem., 1994-95; Lt. Col. Air Force, 1995—. Fellow Am. Acad. Ophthalmology; mem. Minn. Med. Assn., Lake Superior Med. Soc. Avocations: skiing, swimming. Office: Duluth Clin 400 E 3rd St Duluth MN 55805-1951

HAZELIP, HERBERT HAROLD, academic administrator; b. Bowling Green, Ky., Aug. 3, 1930; s. Herbert and Maggie Marie (Ferguson) H.; m. Helen Frances Royalty, Mar. 23, 1956; children: Patrick Harold, Jeffrey Alan. AA, Freed-Hardeman Coll., Henderson, Tenn., 1948; BA, David Lipscomb Coll., Nashville, 1950; MDiv, So. Bapt. Theol. Sem., 1958; PhD, U. Iowa, 1967. Ordained to ministry Ch. of Christ, 1947. Min. Cen. Ch. Christ, Owensboro, Ky., 1950-53, Taylor Blvd. Ch. Christ, Louisville, 1954-64, Cen. Ch. Christ, Cedar Rapids, Iowa, 1964-67, Highland St. Ch. Christ, Memphis, 1967-86; dean, prof. Harding U. Grad. Sch. Religion, Memphis, 1967-86; pres. Lipscomb U., Nashville, 1986-97, chancellor, 1997—. Author: Discipleship, 1977, A Devotional Guide to Bible Lands, 1979, Anchors in Troubled Waters, 1981, Lord, Help Me When I'm Hurting, 1984, Happiness in the Home, 1985, Questions People Ask Ministers Most, 1986, Jesus: Our Mentor and Model, 1987, Becoming Persons of Integrity, 1988, Anchors for the Asking, 1989. Mem. Rotary. Avocations: travel, reading. Office: David Lipscomb U 3901 Granny White Pike Nashville TN 37204-3903 E-mail: harold.hazelip@lipscomb.edu.

HAZELL, PATRICK JAMES, musician, producer; b. Burlington, Iowa, Sept. 23, 1945; s. Arthur Franklin and Wilma Dot (Reed) Hazell; m. Pamela Ann Cummings, Oct. 28, 1967; children: William Plock, Jonathan M., David J., Aira M. BLS, U. Iowa, 1991. Owner Blue Rhythm Recordings, Washington, Iowa, 1961—. Composer, prodr. over 30 albums including Patrick Hazell, 1980, Vicksburg, 1990, Sound Tracks, 1997, Blue Blood, 1997. Mem. NARAS, Arts Midwest, Broadcast Musicians Inc., Iowa Arts Coun., Iowa Blues Hall of Fame (inducted 2000). Mem. Libertarian Party. Avocations: swimming, travel, reading, prarie gardening, photography. Home and Office: 220 E 17th St Washington IA 52353 E-mail: pat@patrickhazell.com.

HAZELL, ROBERT JOHN DAVIDGE, policy institute director, government educator; b. Apr. 30, 1948; s. Peter Hazell and Elizabeth Complin Fowler; m. Alison Sophia Mordaunt, 1981; 2 children. MA with honors, Wadham Coll., Oxford. Bar, 1973. Barrister, England, 1973-75; with immigration dept., policy planning unit, gaming bd., race rels., broadcasting, prison and police depts. Home Office, 1975-89; dir. Nuffield Found., London, 1989-95; dir. constn. unit Sch. Pub. Policy Univ. Coll. London, 1995—, prof. govt. and the Constn., 1998—. Author Conspiracy and Civil Liberties, 1974; editor The Bar on Trial, 1978, Constitutional Futures, 1999, The State and the Nations: The First Year of Devolution in the UK, 2000; contbr. to profl. jours. Recipient Haldane medal RIPA, 1978; CS Travelling fellow, 1986-87. Avocations: opera, canoeing. Office: Sch Pub Pol U Coll London Constn Unit 29 Tavistock Sq London WC1H 9QU England

HAZELRIGG, GEORGE ARTHUR, JR., systems engineer, educator; b. Summit, N.J., Oct. 28, 1939; s. George Arthur Hazelrigg and Dorothy Hetty (Howell) Orr; m. Lauretta Blanche Powell, Aug. 31, 1968; children: George A. III, Geoffrey A. BS, N.J. Inst. Tech., 1961, MS, 1963; MA, Princeton U., 1966, MSE, 1968, PhD, 1969. Engr. Curtiss-Wright, Wood Ridge, N.J., 1961-63, Jet Propulsion Lab, Pasadena, Calif., 1966-67; staff sci. Gen. Dynamics, San Diego, 1968-71; rsch. staff Princeton U., 1971-75; dir., systems engr. Econ, Inc., Princeton, 1976-82; sr. advisor for tech. integration NSF, Arlington, Va., 1982—; prof. of systems engring. (sabbatical) Inst. for Advanced Engring., Seoul, 1993. Dir. ECON, Inc., Princeton, 1974-84; cons. Princeton Synergetics, Inc., 1986—. Author: Systems Engineering: An Approach to Information-Based Design, 1996; editor: Opportunities for Academic Research in a Low Gravity Environment, 1986; assoc. editor Jour. Spacecraft and Rockets, 1977-82. Named Disting. Alumnus, N.J. Inst. Tech., Newark, 1989. Mem. AIAA, ASME, IEEE (sr.), Am. Soc. for Engring. Edn., Tau Beta Pi. Avocation: commercial pilot. Home: 8427 Idylwood Rd Vienna VA 22182-5309 Office: NSF 4201 Wilson Blvd Arlington VA 22230-0001 E-mail: ghazelri@nsf.gov.

HAZELRIGG, MEREDITH KENT, education consultant; b. Allegan, Mich., Mar. 28, 1942; s. Burke Browning and Genevieve (Sakal) H.; m. Niimi Junko, Dec. 23, 1980; children: Niimi Ken. BA, Mich. State U., 1965, MA, 1967; PhD, Newport U., 1994. With Mich. Dept. Social Services, Lansing, 1964-68; tchr. Lansing Pub. Schs., 1965-67; faculty dept. English Lansing Community Coll., 1966-69; lang. skills program dir. Malcolm X Communication Skills Acad., Lansing, 1970-71; owner Red Carpet Bus. Service, Lansing, 1972-77; dir., owner KLS, Sayama-shi, Japan, 1979—. Prof. English dept. Kanagawa U., Yokohama, Japan, 1987—; writer, advt. dir. West Side News, Lansing, 1970-71; adj. prof. U. Md., Tokyo, 1979-83; dir. Far East divsn. Allegan Edn. Found., 1979—; assoc. prof. dept. humanities Rissho U., Saitama and Tokyo, 1992—. Author: (with Antico) Insight through Fiction, 1970; (with Snowden and Atkin) NihONSENSE, 1987, Sound and Sense for International Communication, 1987, Uncle Ebeneezer's Book for Creative Children, 1988, Explaining NihON-SENSE, 1988, Bing, Bang, Boom! (in Japanese), 1989, Understanding NihON-SENSE, 1990, English Guide to Pronunciation for Japanese, 1990, Cross-Cultural Encounters, 1992, Overcoming Miscommunication in English, 1994, (with Hayakawa) Some 250 Japanese Senryu and Then Some, 1997; columnist Allegan County Photo Jour., Allegan News-Gazette, 1972-76. Rsch. dir. Allegan Potato Prodrs. Assn., 1972—78; commr., sec., chmn. Allegan City Planning Commn., 1972—78; Japan asst. dist. commr. Boy Scouts Am.; bd. dirs. Lansing Community Art Gallery, 1966—68, Capital Art Gallery, 1970—72; bd. dirs. Boar's Head Players, 1967—70; bd. dirs. Allegan Area Cmty. Ctr. Recipient Itoen 1st prize for poetry, 1996, Kikkoman Grand prize for cooking, 1985. Mem.: Allegan City Hist. Soc., Am. Platform Assn., Japan Civil Liberties Union, Tokyo English Lit. Soc., Japan Assn. Translators, Soc. Writers, Editors and Translators, Japan Assn. of Practical English, The Phonetic Soc. Japan, Fgn. Corrs. Club., Kiwanis, Lions Club Internat. Avocations: ceramics, graphic arts, gardening, gourmet cooking, oenology. Home: PO Box 155/348 Cutler St Allegan MI 49010 Office: AEF Far East Divsn 468-1 Mizuno Sayama-shi Saitama-Ken 350-1317 Japan E-mail: aeffed@accn.org.

HAZELTINE, BARRETT, electrical engineer, educator; b. Paris, Nov. 7, 1931; came to U.S., 1932; s. L. Alan and Elizabeth (Barrett) H.; m. Mary Frances Fenn, Aug. 25, 1956; children: Michael B., Alice W., Patricia F. BSE, Princeton U., 1953, MSE, 1956; PhD, U. Mich., 1962; ScD (hon.), SUNY, Stony Brook, 1988. Registered profl. engr., R.I. Asst. prof. engring. Brown U., 1959-66, assoc. prof., 1966-72, prof., 1972—; asst. to dean Brown U. (The Coll.), 1962-63, asst. dean, 1968-74, assoc. dean, 1974-93; Robert Foster Cherry chair for disting. teaching Baylor U., 1991-92; prof. U. Botswana, 1993. Lectr., vis. prof. U. Zambia, Lusaka, 1970-71; -76-77; vis. prof. U. Malawi-Poly., Blantyre, 1980-81, 83-84, 88-89, Africa U. Mutare, Zimbabwe, 1996-97, 2000; asst. to mgr. rsch. labs., space and info. sys. divsn. Raytheon Co., 1964-65, cons., 1965-67; cons. R.I. Utilities Commn., 1977-80, others. Author: Introduction to Electronic Circuits and Applications, 1980, Appropriate Tech-

nology: Tools, Choice and Implications, 1998, Field Guide to Appropriate Technology, 2003; editor: The Weaver, 1982—90. Trustee Stevens Inst. Tech. Recipient award for excellence in instrn. Western Electric, 1968; grantee NSF, Dept. Edn.; grantee Met. Life Ins. Ednl. Found.; Fulbright fellow 1988-89, 93. Mem. IEEE (sr., chmn. Providence sect. 1971-72), Providence Engring. Soc. (pres. 1977-78), Am. Soc. Engring. Edn., Sigma Xi, Tau Beta Pi. Congregationalist (deacon). Clubs: Providence Art, Providence Review. Achievements include patents for color recognition system. Home: 60 Barnes St Providence RI 02906-1502 Office: Brown U Div Engring Providence RI 02912-0001 E-mail: Barrett_Hazeltine@brown.edu.

HAZELTINE, GERALD LESTER, food products executive; b. Beloit, Wis., Apr. 10, 1924; s. Frank Raymond and Ella (Bush) H.; m. Luella Agnes Heath, Aug. 15, 1953. Grad. high sch., Rockton, Ill., 1941. Farm hand, Wis., Ill., 1938-42; steelworker Carnegie Ill. Steel Corp., Gary, Ind., 1942-48; r.r. sect. hand Chgo. Northwestern R.R., Clarance, Iowa, 1948-49; machine operator Quaker Oats Co., Cedar Rapids, Iowa, 1950-81; owner, operator Hazeltine Honey Co., Toddville, Iowa, 1949—. Beekeeping cons., Linn County, Iowa, 1970—. With U.S. Army, 1942-45. Decorated Bronze stars, Victory medal. Jehovah'S Witness. Avocations: reading, writing, gardening. Home and Office: 8300 Tower Terrace Rd Toddville IA 52341-9617

HAZELTINE, JOYCE, former state official; b. Pierre, S.D. m. Dave Hazeltine; children: Derek, Tara, Kirk. Student, Huron (S.D.) Coll., No. State Coll., Aberdeen, S.D., Black Hills State Coll., Spearfish, S.D. Former asst. chief clk. S.D. Ho. of Reps.; former sec. S.D. State Senate; sec. of state State of S.D., Pierre, 1987—2003. Adminstrv. asst. Pres. Ford Campaign, S.D.; Rep. county chmn. Hughes County S.D.; state co-chair Phil Gramm for Pres., 1996. Mem. Nat. Assn. Secs. of State (exec. bd., pres.), Women Execs. in State Govts. (bd. dirs.). Republican. E-mail: joyceh@sos.state.sd.us.*

HAZELTON, JUANITA LOUISE, librarian; b. Glendale, Calif., June 12, 1942; d. James Chester and Eddith Pearl (Henson) McCrain; m. Merrill Edward Hazelton, Apr. 27, 1968; children: Larry Scott, James Edward. BA in Arts and Letters, U. Oreg., 1964; MLS, U. Tex., 1970; tchg. cert., Tex. Woman's U., 1984. Cert. county libr., 1997. Librarian Dallas Pub. Libr., 1966-69; libr. asst. Austin Coll., Sherman, Tex., 1974-75; tchr., librarian Gunter (Tex.) Ind. Sch. Dist., 1984-94; librarian Plano (Tex.) Pub. Libr., 1994-95; libr. dir. Van Alstyne (Tex.) Pub. Libr., 1995—. Tech. com. Gunter Ind. Sch. Dist., 1994; campus devel. com. Van Alstyne Ind. Sch. Dist., 1997, campus devel. com., 1998—; A-V com., ad hoc planning com. N.E. Tex. Libr. Sys., Garland, Tex., 1997-98. Contbg. author: Telling Our Stories-Texas Family Secrets, 1997 (Gold Star award 1997); Bookshelf columnist Van Alstyne Leader, 1995—. Den leader, adv. coun. Cub Scouts, Gunter, 1984-88; club leader, adv. coun. 4-H, Gunter, 1988-95. Recipient Libr. of Yr., N.E. Tex. Libr. Sys., 1996; named Bus. Citizen of Yr. Van Alstyne C. of C., 1998, named to Tall Texans, 2003. Mem. Tex. Libr. Assn. (treas. dist. 5, 2000-01), TALL Tex., Toastmasters Internat., Van Alstyne Genealog. Assn., Tex. Storytelling Assn. Republican. Mem. Ch. of Christ. Avocations: collecting kachinas and folk tales, amateur storytelling, computers, genealogy, writing poetry and family history. Office: Van Alstyne Pub Libr PO Box 629 117 N Waco Van Alstyne TX 75495 E-mail: jhazelton@vanalstynepl.lib.tx.us.

HAZELTON, PENNY ANN, law librarian, educator; b. Yakima, Wash., Sept. 24, 1947; d. Fred Robert and Margaret (McLeod) Pease; m. Norris J. Hazelton, Sept. 12, 1971; 1 child, Victoria MacLeod. BA cum laude, Linfield Coll., 1969; JD, Lewis and Clark Law Sch., 1975; M in Law Librarianship, U. Wash., 1976. Bar: Wash. 1976, U.S. Supreme Ct. 1982. Assoc. law libr., assoc. prof. U. Maine, 1976-78, law libr., assoc. prof., 1978-81; asst. libr. for rsch. svcs. U.S. Supreme Ct., Washington, 1981-85, law libr., 1985, U. Wash., Seattle, 1985—, prof. law, assoc. dean libr. and computing svcs., 1985—. Tchr. legal rsch., law librarianship, Indian law; cons. Maine Adv. Com. on County Law Librs., Nat. U. Sch. Law, San Diego, 1985-88, Lawyers Cooperative Pub., 1993-94, Marquette u. Sch. Law, 2002. Author: Computer Assisted Legal Research: The Basics, 1993; author: (with others) Washington Legal Researcher's Deskbook, 3d edit., 2002; contbr. articles; gen. editor Specialized Legal Rsch. (Aspen). Recipient Disting. Alumni award U. Wash., 1992. Mem. ABA (sect. legal edn. and admissions to bar, chair com. on librs. 1993-94, vice chair 1992-93, 94-95, com. on law sch. facilities 1998—), Am. Assn. Law Schs. (com. law librs. 1991-94), Law Librs. New Eng. (sec. 1977-79, pres. 1979-81), Am. Assn. Law Librs. (program chmn. ann. meeting 1984, exec. bd. 1984-87, v.p. 1989-90, pres. 1990-91, program co-chair Insts. 1983, 95), Law Librs. Soc. Washington (exec. bd. 1983-84, v.p., pres. elect 1984-85), Law Librs. Puget Sound, Wash. State Bar Assn. (chair editl. adv. bd.), Wash. Adv. Coun. on Librs., Westpac. Office: U Wash Marian Gould Gallagher Law Libr 1100 NE Campus Pkwy Seattle WA 98105-6605

HAZEN, ELIZABETH FRANCES, retired special education educator; b. Lamar, Colo., May 27, 1925; d. Otis Garfield and Cora B. (Baker) McDowell; children: H. Ray, Bobby D., Anita K. Iezza, Gloria G. Gill. AA, Lamar Jr. Coll., 1946; BS in Edn., Southwestern Okla. U., 1967, MS in Edn., 1969; postgrad., Ea. Ky. U., 1983. Cert. speech-hearing therapist, reading specialist, learning and behavior disorders, Ky. Elem. tchr. Granada (Colo.) Sch., 1946-51, South Ctrl. Elem. Sch., Lamar, Colo., 1951-52; lead tchr. Tom Thumb Pre-Sch., Ellsworth AFB, S.D., 1961-62; math. and sci. tchr. Elk City (Okla.) Elem. Sch., 1966-67; beginning speech tchr. Sayer Jr. Coll., Okla., 1967-68; speech and hearing therapist Burns Flat (Okla.) Schs., 1967-69, Maconaquah Sch. Corp., Bunker Hill, Ind., 1969-72; reading specialist Myers Mid. Sch., Louisville, Ky., 1972-76; tchr. Core Westport Jr. H.S., Louisville, 1977-79, chmn. Core dept., 1978-79; learning disabled resource tchr. Jeffersontown H.S., Louisville, 1979-80, Waggoner Mid. Sch., Louisville, 1980-81, Westport Mid. Sch., Louisville, 1981-94; ret., 1994. Chmn. exceptional children's edn. dept. Westport Mid. Sch., Louisville, 1983-91; speech and hearing therapist Burns Flat (Okla.) Bd. Edn., 1967-69. Bd. dirs. Westport Middle Schs. PTA/Student Assn., 1989-90. Named Outstanding Tchr. of Disadvantaged, State of Okla., 1969. Mem. NEA (ret.), Ky. Mid. Sch. Assn., Ky. Edn. Assn. (ret.), Ky. Ret. Tchrs. Assn., Jefferson County Tchrs. Assn. Home: 1207 McVey Rd Sedalia MO 65301-8869

HAZEN, PAUL MANDEVILLE, banker; b. Lansing, Mich., 1941; married. BA, U. Ariz., 1963; MBA, U. Calif., Berkeley, 1964. Asst. mgr Security Pacific Bank, 1964-66; v.p. Union Bank, 1966-70; chmn. Wells Fargo Realty Advisors, 1970-76, with, 1979—2001, exec. v.p., mgr. Real Estate Industries Group, 1979-80, mem. exec. office Real Estate Industry Group, 1980, vice-chmn. Real Estate Industries Group, 1980-84, pres., chief oper. officer Real Estate Industries Group, 1984—, also dir. Real Estate Industries Group, 1984—; pres., treas. Wells Fargo Mortgage & Equity Trust, San Francisco, 1977-84; with Wells Fargo & Co., San Francisco, 1978—2001, from exec. v.p. to vice-chmn., pres., chief operating officer, 1981—95, chmn, CEO, 1995-2000, chmn. bd. dirs., Accel Kohlberg Kravis, Roberts and Co., Menlo Park, Calif., 2001—. Trustee Wells Fargo Mortgage & Equity Trust; bd. dirs. Pacific Telesis Group. Office: Accel Kohlberg Kravis Roberts and Co 2500 Sand Hill Rd Ste 100 Menlo Park CA 94205*

HAZEN, ROBERT MILLER, research scientist, writer; b. Rockville Centre, NY, Nov. 1, 1948; s. Dan Francis and Dorothy Ellen (Chapin) H.; m. Margaret Hindle, Aug. 9, 1969; children: Benjamin Hindle, Elizabeth Brooke. BS, SM, MIT, 1971; PhD, Harvard U., 1975. NATO fellow U. Cambridge, England, 1975—76; rsch. sci. Geophys. Lab., Carnegie Instn., Washington, 1976—; Robinson prof. earth sci. George Mason U., 1990—. Author: Comparative Crystal Chemistry, 1982, Music Men, 1987, The Breakthrough, 1988, Science Matters, 1990, Keppers of the Flame, 1991, New Alchemist, 1993, Why Aren't Black Holes Black?, 1997, The Diamond Makers, 1999, The Sciences, 2000; contbr. articles to profl. jours.; musician (trumpeter): Washington Chamber Symphony, Nat. Gallery Orchestra, also recordings. Recipient Deems Tayor award, ASCAP, 1989, Wood Sci. Writing prize, 1998. Fellow: AAAS, Mineral Soc. Am. (editor, coun., Mineral Soc. Am. award 1982, Disting. Lectr.); mem.: Internat. Guild Trumpeters, History of Sci. Soc., Am. Chem. Soc. (Ipatief prize 1985), Am. Geophys. Union, Phi Lambda Upsilon, Sigma Xi. Avocations: doubles volleyball, ballroom dancing, Am. art. Office: Geophys Lab 5251 Broad Branch Rd NW Washington DC 20015-1305 E-mail: hazen@gl.ciw.edu.

HAZEN, TERRY CLYDE, microbial ecologist, educator; b. Pontiac, Mich., Feb. 7, 1951; s. Leo Robert and Phyllis Virginia (Hawley) H.; m. Gayle Kanne Reinecke, June 12, 1972; children: Tracy Heather, Brooks Trevor. BS with honors, Mich. State U., 1973, MS, 1974; PhD, Wake Forest U., 1978. Rsch. assoc. Wake Forest U., Winston-Salem, N.C., 1978-79; asst. prof. biology U. P.R., Rio Piedras, 1979-82, assoc. prof., 1982-85, prof., 1985-88, acting chmn. dept., 1984-85, chmn. grad. studies, 1980-84; scientist E.I. DuPont de Neumours Co., Westinghouse Savannah River Lab, Aiken, S.C., 1987-89; sr. scientist Westinghouse Savannah River Co., 1989-93, fellow scientist, 1993-98, sect. mgr. environ. tech., 1994-98; staff scientist Lawrence Berkeley (Calif.) Nat. Lab., 1998—, head ecology dept., 1998—, lead environ. remediation, tehc. program, 1998—, head Ctr. Environ. Biotech., 1998—. Cons. micro-computer applications in lab.; tchr., cons. in water quality. Contbr. over 150 articles to profl. jours. Head coach Pee Wee Football of P.R., 1983; mem. bd. visitors Wake Forest U. Winner 1st prize Sci. Writing, Puerto Rican Culture Soc., 1983. Mem. AAAS, AM. Soc. Microbiology, Sigma Xi (rsch. award 1977). Republican. Home: 2983 Rustle Ct Fairfield CA 94533-2980 Office: Lawrence Berkeley Nat Lab 1 Cyclotron Rd Ms 70A 3317 Berkeley CA 94720-0001

HAZEN, WILLIAM A. secondary school educator; b. Grand Forks, N.D., Jan. 16, 1938; s. Gordon Bradford Hazen and Catherine Ellen Vassau; m. Frances Dee Pound, Dec. 21, 1964 (div. June 8, 1982); 1 child, Stephen James; m. Rachael A. Smith, Jan. 2, 1987. BA in History, U. Wash., 1960; MA in Edn., Chapman U., 1975; JD, San Joaquin Coll. Law, 1986. Bar: Calif. 1986; life diploma edn. Calif., 1971. Tchr. Hanford (Calif.) H.S., 1964—87; lawyer Law Offices of Steve Barnes, Hanford, 1987—89; tchr. Kings County Supt. Schs., Hanford, 1989—2002. Mem. state coun. edn. Calif. Tchrs. Assn., 1970—73, polit. edn. cons., 1972—74; chmn. resolutions com. Spkr. of Ho. Dels., Calif. Coun. for the Social Studies, 1971—72. Active State Dem. Ctrl. Com., 1975, 1977, 1979, Kings County Dem. Ctrl. Com., 1974—79, sec., 1974—75, vice chmn., 1975—76, chmn., 1977—78; pres. Ken Knudson Meml. Scholarship Fund, 1980—. Capt. U.S. Army, 1960—68. Mem.: Hanford Bonsai Soc., Taoist Temple Preservation Soc. Democrat. Avocations: travel, sailing, reading. Home: 235 W Amber Way Hanford CA 93230

HAZENFIELD, HUGH NORMAN, surgeon; b. Indpls., May 6, 1942; s. Harold Henry and Pearle Esther (Attig) H.; m. Barbara Lynn Shellabarger; Aug. 15, 1964; children: Anthony Michael, Andrew Bradley. BA, U. Chgo., 1964, MD, 1968. Diplomate Am. Bd. Otolaryngology. Chmn. divsn. otolaryngology Cook County Hosp., 1975-79, assoc. med. dir., 1978-79; chmn. divsn. otolaryngology Head and Neck Surgery Michael Reese Hosp., Chgo., 1979-89, assoc. v.p. profl. affairs, 1987-89; chmn. dept. surgery Wahiawa Gen. Hosp., 1989—92, Kapiolani Med. Ctr. for Women and Children, 1989—, St. Francis Med. Ctr. West, 1990—, Kapiolani Med. Ctr. at Pali Momi, 1993—. Attending surgeon Children's Meml. Hosp., Chgo., 1976-89; cons. Larabida Hosp., Chgo., 1984-89. Contbr. articles to med. jours. Bd. dirs. St. Mary's Sch., Evanston, Ill., 1981-84, Lincoln Opera, Chgo., Wahiawa Hosp., 1989—, Wahiawa Hosp. Assn., 1991—, chmn., 1995-97; bd. dirs. Hawaii Opera Theatre, 1997—, v.p., 2001—. Served with USN, 1969-71. Fellow Am. Acad. Otolaryngology, ACS, Chgo. Laryngological and Otological Soc., Hawaii Soc. Otolaryngology—Head and Neck Surgery. Avocations: computer science, sailing, classical music. Office: 302 California Ave #716 Wahiawa HI 96786 also: 98-1079 Moanalua Rd Ste 660 Aiea HI 96701-4714

HAZEWINKEL, VAN, manufacturing executive; b. L.A., Oct. 2, 1943; s. Ben J. and Betty J. (Bishop) H.; m. Linda Bennett, Sept. 11, 1965; children: Van, Karey. BS, Calif. State U., Long Beach, 1967. With Daily Indsl. Tools Inc., Costa Mesa, Calif., 1959—, v.p., 1966-78, pres., 1978—. Founding mem. bd. dirs. Greater Irvine (Calif.) Indsl. League, 1970-73. Mem. Soc. Mfg. Engrs. Office: 3197 Airport Loop Dr Ste D Costa Mesa CA 92626-3424

HAZIYU, WALLACE MULEYA, secondary school educator; b. Southern Province, Zambia, Sept. 3, 1961; s. Donald Haziyu Simakala and Sarah Mukakopolo Munkombwe. BA in Edn., U. of Zambia, 1998. Cert. Tchr. 1989. Secondary sch. tchr. Ministry of Edn., Lusaka, Zambia, 1984—93; staff devel. fellow U. of Zambia, Lusaka, 1999—. Sch. cert. examiner Examinations Coun. of Zambia, Lusaka, 1989—. Editor: Zambia Assn. Math. Edn., 1992—2000. Mem.: Am. Math. Soc. Avocation: chess. Home: 1004 West Nevada St Urbana IL 61801-3767 Office: Univ of Ill Urbana-Champaign 1409 West Green St Urbana IL 61801-2943 also: Dept Math Box 32379 Lusaka Zambia Office Fax: 260-1-253952. Personal E-mail: haziyu@uiuc.edu.

HAZLEHURST, ROBERT PURVIANCE, JR., lawyer; b. Spartanburg, S.C., Jan. 7, 1919; s. Robert Purviance and Lottie Lee (Nicholls) H.; m. Mary Kierulff, Feb. 20, 1947 (dec. July 1971); children: Ellen Hazlehurst Courtney, Charlotte Hazlehurst Leonesio, Anne Hazlehurst Goldberg; m. Dorothy Wilson Deemer, Jan. 7, 1972. AB, Princeton U., 1940; LL.B., Yale U., 1947. Bar: N.J. 1947. Since practiced in Newark and Morristown; ptnr. Pitney, Hardin, Kipp & Szuch, 1952-89. Bd. dirs. Princeton Fund, 1966-71, chmn. ann. giving campaign, 1967-68 Sec., trustee Greater Newark Hosp. Devel. Fund; trustee Kent Pl. Sch., Summit, N.J., 1960-70; trustee, v.p. Silver Hill Found., New Canaan, Conn., 1973-85; trustee United Hosps. Newark, 1958-73, pres., 1970-73. Served to capt. USAAF, 1942-45. Mem.: Short Hills (N.J.), Nassau (N.J.). Home: 38 Sinclair Ter Short Hills NJ 07078-1714

HAZLETON, RICHARD A. chemicals executive; b. 1941; Pres., ceo Dow Corning Corp, Midland, Mich., 1965—, chmn., CEO. Office: Dow Corning Corp PO Box 994 Midland MI 48686-0001

HAZLETT, GEORGE ALVIN, minister, mediator; b. Youngstown, Ohio, June 18, 1939; s. George R. and Ruth A. Hazlett; m. Myrna A. Hazlett; children: Karen McLaughlin, Paul, Dale. ThD, Internat. Bible Sem., 1983. Ordained minister Nazarene Course of Study; cert. private mediator. Minister Church of the Nazarene, 1963—2001; mediator Akron Better Bus. Bureau, Akron, Ohio, 2000—. Participant 7-Building Programs Church of the Nazarene, 1963—2001; radio broadcaster for 26 yrs.; TV ministry, 4 yrs. Author: (weekly newspaper column) "Think About It", in Farm and Dairy News. City chaplain City Coun., Marietta, Ohio, Salem, Ohio. Office: 1084 Camelia Dr Hartville OH 44632

HAZLETT, MARK A. lawyer; b. N.Y.C., Aug. 18, 1948; BA, Stanford U., 1970, JD, 1973. Bar: Hawaii 1973. Ptnr. Cades, Schutte, Fleming & Wright, Honolulu. Mem. adv. com. to Commr. of Fin. Insts., 1984-86; adj. prof. of law U. Hawaii Law Sch., 1995—. Co-editor: Hawaii Commercial Real Estate Manual, 1988; co-editor, co-author: Hawaii Real Estate Financing Manual, 1990, Hawaii Real Estate Law Manual, 1997. Mem. ABA, Hawaii State Bar Assn. (dir. fin. svcs. divsn. 1982-83, chmn. real property and fin. svcs. sect. 1984, bd. dirs. 1982-98). Office: Cades Schutte Fleming & Wright PO Box 939 1000 Bishop St Honolulu HI 96808

HAZZARD, MARY ELIZABETH, nurse, educator; b. Evansville, Ind., Mar. 2, 1941; d. John Waven and Lucille Elizabeth (Theobold) H.; 1 child, Mary Lucille. BSN, Nazareth Coll., 1963; AM, NYU, 1965, PhD, 1970; family nurse practitioner, U. Tenn., 1997. Cert. min.; cert. family nurse practitioner. Staff nurse Caldwell County War Meml. Hosp., Princeton, Ky., 1962, staff nurse supr., 1963, 65; asst. nurse St. Joseph's Hosp., Louisville, 1962-63; teaching fellow NYU, 1966, instr., 1966-68; nursing sister-in-charge Meru (Kenya) Dist. Hosp., 1966; asst. prof. U. Va. Sch. Nursing, Charlottesville, 1968-70, assoc. prof., 1970-74, dir. learning resources, 1971-74; assoc. prof. Sangamon State U., Springfield, Ill., 1974-79; prof. Western Ky. U., Bowling Green, 1979-99; prof. emeritus, 1998; prof. Nat. U., LaJolla, Calif., 1998—. Head dept. nursing Western Ky. U., Bowling Green, 1979-96; adj. assoc. prof. U. Ky., Lexington, 1983-94; curriculum cons. MacMurray Coll., Jacksonville, Ill., 1978, U. Louisville, 1981; pres. So. Coun. on Collegiate Edn. in Nursing, 1993-95; nurse practitioner Cmty. Health Care Plus, Brownsville, 1997-98, St. Vincent DePaul Med. Clin. Homeless, San Diego, 1998—. Author: Review of Med-Surg Nursing, 1976, Nursing Outline Series: Critical Care Nursing, 1978; also articles; mem. edit. rev. bd. Health Care for Women Internat., 1984—. Pres. So. Coun. on Collegiate Edn. in Nursing, 1993-95. Fellow Am. Acad. Nursing; mem. ANA, Ky. Nurses Assn. (pres. 1986-87), Ky. Assn. Baccalaureate and Higher Degree Programs (sec. 1986-87), Ky. Cols., Sigma Theta Tau, Pi Lambda Theta. Democrat. Roman Catholic. Office: Nat U 11255 N Torrey Pines Rd La Jolla CA 92037-1011 E-mail: mhazzard@nu.edu.

HAZZARD, SHIRLEY, author; b. Sydney, Australia, Jan. 30, 1931; d. Reginald and Catherine (Stein) H.; m. Francis Steegmuller, Dec. 22, 1963 (dec. Oct. 1994). Ed., Queenwood Sch., Sydney, to 1946. With Combined Services Intelligence, Hong Kong, 1947-48, U.K. High Commr.'s Office, Wellington, N.Z., 1949-50, UN (Gen. Service Category), N.Y.C., 1952-61. Boyer lectr., Australia, 1984, 88. Author: Cliffs of Fall and Other Stories, 1963; (novels) The Evening of the Holiday, 1966, People in Glass Houses, 1967, The Bay of Noon, 1970, The Transit of Venus, 1980, History Defeat of an Ideal: A Study of the Self-Destruction of the United Nations, 1973, History Countenance of Truth, 1990; (novel) The Great Fire, 2003; (memoir) Greene on Capri, 2000. Trustee N.Y. Soc. Library. Named Hon. Citizen of Capri, 2000; recipient 1st prize, O. Henry Short Story awards, 1976, Lit. award, Nat. Inst. Arts and Letters, 1966, Nat. Book Critics Circle award for Fiction, 1981, Clifton Fadiman medal for Lit., 2001, Guggenheim fellowship, 1974. Fellow Royal Soc. Lit.; mem. AAAL, Nat. Arts and Scis., Century Club (N.Y.C.). Address: 200 E 66th St Apt C1705 New York NY 10021-9187

HAZZARD, WILLIAM RUSSELL, geriatrician, educator; b. Ann Arbor, Mich., Sept. 5, 1936; s. Albert Sidney and Florence Bernice (Woolsey) Hazzard; m. Ellen Bennett Friedman, June 10, 1961; children: Susan Lovejoy Roque, Russell Holden, Rebecca Cornell Oliver, Daniel Bennett. AB, Cornell U., 1958, MD, 1962. Diplomate Am. Bd. Internal Medicine, Am. Bd. Geriatrics. Resident in internal medicine U. Wash. Sch. Med. and Affiliated Hosps., Seattle, 1966—67, fellow in endocrinology and metabolism, 1965—66, 1967—69; from instr. to prof. medicine U. Wash., Seattle, 1969—82, dir. Northwest Lipid Rsch. Clinic, 1972—78; investigator Howard Hughes Med. Inst., U. Wash., Seattle, 1972—80; chief divsn. gerontology and geriatric medicine, 1978—82; prof. medicine, assoc. dir. dept. medicine Johns Hopkins Med. Instns., Balt., 1982—86, dir. ctr. on aging, 1983—86; prof., chmn. dept. internal med. Bowman Gray Sch. Medicine of Wake Forest U., Winston-Salem, NC, 1986—98; dir. J. Paul Sticht Ctr. on Aging of Wake Forest U., Winston-Salem, NC, 1987—97; sr. adv. J. Paul Ctr. On Aging of Wake Forest U., 1998—; prof. medicine U. Wash., Seattle, 1999—; dir. geriatrics and extended care VA Puget Sound Health Care Sys., 1999—. Vis. lectr., hon. sr. registrar Oxford (Eng.) U., 1977—78, St. Thomas Sch. Medicine, London, 1977—78; dir. sect. gerontology and geriatric medicine VA Puget Sound Health Care Sys., Seattle, Tacoma, Wash., 1999—. Editor: Principles of Geriatric Medicine and Gerontology, 1984, 1989, 1993, 1999, 2003; contbr. over 200 articles to jours. in field. Lt. USNR, 1963—65. Recipient, Nat. Heart, Lung, and Blood Inst., 1971-1982. Fellow: ACP; mem.: Coun. on Aging (nat. advisor), Nat. Inst. on Aging (aging rev. com. 1990—94, Geriatric Medicine Acad. award 1980), Am. Clin. and Climatol. Assn., Assn. Am. Physicians, Am. Soc. Clin. Investigation (mem. emeritus), Am. Fedn. Biomed. Rsch. (mem. emeritus), Am. Heart Assn. (Coun.on Arterosclerosis), Gerontol. Soc. Am. (chmn. clin. med. sect. 1984), Am. Geriatrics Soc. (bd. dirs. 1988—, pres. 1993), Inst. Medicine of NAS. Avocations: gardening, conservation and nature study, music, athletics. Home: 3515 E Conover Ct Seattle WA 98122-6426 Office: VA Puget Sound Health Care Sys Geriatric Extended Care 1660 S Columbian Way Seattle WA 98108-1532 E-mail: william.hazzard@med.va.gov.

H'DOUBLER, FRANCIS TODD, JR., surgeon; b. Springfield, Mo., June 18, 1925; s. Francis Todd and Alice Louise (Bemis) H'D; m. Joan Louise Huber, Dec. 20, 1951 (dec. Dec. 1983); children: Julie H'Doubler Thomas and Sarah H'Doubler Muegge (twins), Kurt, Scott; m. Marie Ruth Duckworth, Jan. 18, 1986 Student, Washington U., St. Louis, 1943, Miami U., Oxford, Ohio, 1943-44; BS, U. Wis., 1946, MD, 1948. Intern Milw. Hosp., 1948-49; resident in surgery U.S. Naval Hosp., Oakland, Calif., 1950-51; practice medicine specializing in alternative medicine Springfield, Mo., 1952—; mem. courtesy staff St. John's Hosp., Springfield, L.E. Cox Hosp., Springfield. Bd. dirs. Union Planters Bank. Active Singing Doctors; chmn. fundraising drive YMCA, 1960-61, Sch. Bond and Tax Levy Com., 1958, Greene County Rep. Com., 1974-75; past bd. trustees Shriners Hosps., past chmn. spinal cord injury com., past chmn. rsch. com., past chmn. long range planning com., emeritus mem. rsch. com.; mem. Commn. to Reapportion Mo. Senate, 1971, Rep. State Fin. Com., 1972-75, steering com. Wilson's Creekl Battlefield Nat. Park, 1951-61, pres.'s adv. coun. Sch. Ozarks, Point Lookout, Mo., 1975-89; trustee Cottey Coll., Nevada, Mo., past bd. chmn.; bd. trustees Forest Inst. With USNR, 1943-46, 49-51. Decorated Bronze Star with V, Purple Heart with oak leaf cluster; recipient Disting. Service award Mo. Jaycees, 1959; Humanitarian award S.W. Mo. Drug Travelers Assn., 1971; named Young Man of Yr., City of Springfield, 1959 Fellow Am. Coll. Nuclear Medicine (founder's group); mem. AMA, Greene County Med. Assn., Mo. Med. Soc., Southwestern Surg. Congress, Mo. Surg. Assn., Soc. Nuclear Medicine, Am. Thyroid Assn., Springfield Jr. C. of C. (past pres.), Springfield C. of C., DAV, VFW, SAR, Am. Legion, Green Gang (co-founder), Sigma Nu (Outstanding Alumnus nat. award 1980), Nu Sigma Nu. Clubs: Hickory Hills Country. Lodges: Mason (33 deg.), Shriners (imperial potentate 1980-81), Red Cross of Constantine, Order DeMolay Legion Honor (hon.), Royal Order Scotland. Presbyterian.

HE, BIN, biomedical engineer, educator; b. Zhejiang, China, Aug. 14, 1957; s. Liangjin Zhu and Suqing He; m. Wenjing Ye, July 30, 1986; children: Eric J., Jefferey. BS, Zhejiang U., 1982; PhD, Tokyo Inst. Tech., 1988; postdoctoral study, Harvard U./MIT, 1989-91. Rsch. scientist Harvard U./MIT, Cambridge, Mass., 1991-94; dir. biomed. functional imaging and computation lab. U. Ill., Chgo., 1994—, prof., 2003—. Vis. prof. Zhejiang U., 2001—. Guest editor IEEE Transactions on Info. Tech. in Biomedicine, 1998-2001, Critical Revs. in Biomed. Engring., 1998-2002, Electromagnetics, 2000-01, Methods of Info. in Medicine, 1998-2000, IEEE Engring. in Medicine and Biology Mag., 1997-98; assoc. editor Medical Physics, IEEE Transactions on Info. Tech. in Biomedicine, 1999-, IEEE Transactions on Biomed. Engring., 2002—; gen. chair 3d Internat. Workshop on Biosignal Interpretation, 5th Internat. Conf. on Bioelectromanetism; reviewer NSF, Arlington, Va., 1998—, Med. Rsch. Coun. Can., Ottawa, 1998—, NIH, Bethesda, Md., 2000 —; editor book series on bioelectric engring., 2001—; contbr. articles to profl. jours. Bd. dirs. Am. Zhu Kezhen Edn. Found., Calif., 1998-2001; pres. Japan Zhejiang U. Alumni Assn., Tokyo, 1988-89; exec. com. Higher Inst. Biomed. Engring., Hangzhou, China, 1998. Recipient Biomed. Engring. Rsch. award Whitaker Found., 1992, Young Investigator 2d Pl. award N.Am. Soc. Pacing and Clin. Electrophysiology, 1992, Rsch. Fellowship award Am. Heart Assn., 1990, Tejima prize, 1989, NSF Career award, 1999, univ. scholar award U. Ill., 1999, Established Investigator award AHA, 2001, U. Ill. Chgo. Coll. Engring. Faculty Rsch. award 2002. Mem. IEEE (sr., local arrangement chair internat. sci. meeting on electromagnetics in medicine 1996-97, theme co-chair internat. conf. engring. in medicine and biology 1997-98, vice-chmn. EMB Chgo. chpt. 1997-98, tech. program chair Asia-Pacific conf. on Biomed. Engring. 2000, chmn. EMBS regional conf. com., 2002-03, ADCOM mem., 2002-04), Biomed. Engring. Soc., Internat. Soc. Bioelectromagnetism (v.p. 2000-02, pres. 2002—). Achievements include development of laplacian electrocardiography and three dimensional electrocardiography tomographic imaging technology, as well as development of electrophysiological neuroimaging. Office: U Ill MC-063 851 S Morgan St Chicago IL 60607-7042 Fax: 312-996-5921. E-mail: bhe@uic.edu.

HE, HONGYU, mathematician, educator; b. Pengzhou, China; s. Decai He and Defang Yue. MS, Ohio State U., 1993; PhD, MIT, 1998. Mentor Rsch. Sci. Inst., Washington, 1996-98; asst. prof. Cornell U., Ithaca, N.Y., 1998-99, Ga. State U., Atlanta, 1999—. Cons. Lesley Coll., Cambridge, Mass., 1996. Recipient Gold medal Internat. Math. Olympiad Com., Canberra, Australia, 1988. Mem. AAAS, Am. Math. Soc., Sigma Xi. Office: Ga State U Dept Math and Stat 30 Pryor St Atlanta GA 30303 Fax: (404) 651-2246. E-mail: livingstone@alum.mit.edu.

HE, JIANG, medical scientist; b. Dazhu, Sichuan, China, June 21, 1970; s. Zhongli He and Zhongshu Leng; m. Yafang Huang, Oct. 23, 1970. PhD, Peking U., Beijing, China, 1994—97. Rsch. asst. prof. Chinese Acad. Forestry, Beijing, 1997—99; rsch. assoc. Cath. U. Louvain, Brussels, 2000—01; sr. rsch. assoc. U. Mass. Med. Sch., Worcester, 2001—. Patentee in field; contbr. articles. Mem.: AAAS, Am. Assn. Pharm. Scientists, Am. Chem. Soc., Sigma Xi. Office: Divsn Nuclear Medicine U Mass Med Sch 55 Lake Ave N Worcester MA 01655

HE, TIAN-XIAO, mathematician, educator; b. Anqing, People's Republic of China, Apr. 27, 1954; arrived in U.S., 1985; s. Meng-Qing and Xing-Sheng He; m. Yulan Zhu; 1 child, Henry Huan. MS, Hefei U. Tech., People's Republic of China, 1981; PhD, Dalian U. Tech., Peoples Republic of China, 1987, Tex.

A&M U., 1991. Lectr. Huaibel (People's Republic of China) Tchr.'s Coll., 1975-78; asst. prof. Hefei U. Tech., 1982-85, assoc. prof., 1986—91; rsch. assoc. Tex. A&M U., College Station, 1985-88, asst. lectr., 1989-91; asst. prof. Ill. Wesleyan U., Bloomington, Ill., 1991-95, assoc. prof., 1995—99, prof., 2000—. Author: Some Topics on Multidimensional Numerical Integration, The Theory of Advanced Mathematics, The Skill for Solving Mathematical Problem of Qualifying Examination of Graduate Students, Multivariate Interpolation, Dimensionality Reducing Expansion of Multivariate Integration; editor Jour. Math. Rsch. and Exposition; editor: Wavelet Analysis and Multiresolution Methods, Analysis, Combinatorics and Computing; contbr. over 60 articles to profl. jours. Recipient Disting. Leadership award ABI, 1990, Disting. Rsch. award Tex. A&M U., 1991, Student Senate Prof. of the Yr., 1994. Office: Illinois Wesleyan U Dept Of Math Bloomington IL 61702

HE, TIANYUAN, molecular biologist; b. Bengbu, Anhui, China, Apr. 6, 1955; came to U.S., 1998; s. Mintong He and Xiuqing Chen; m. Mei Wang, Sept. 13, 1983; 1 child, Biwei. B, Bengbu Med. Coll., 1983; M, Nanjing (China) Med. U., 1994; PhD, Shanghai Second Med. U., 1997. Asst. tchr. dept. biochemistry Benbgu Med. Coll., 1982-90, lectr., 1990-91; lectr. dept. biochemistry Shanghai Second Med. U., 1997-98; rsch. fellow dept. dermatology U. Mich., Ann Arbor, 1998—. Author: Medical Biochemistry, 1995; contbr. articles to profl. jours. Mem. AAAS, Soc. for Investigative Dermatology, Chinese Soc. Molecular Biochemistry. Office: U Mich Ann Arbor MI 48109 Home: 3283 Braeburn Cir Ann Arbor MI 48108-2615 E-mail: tyhe@umich.edu.

HE, XIAOHONG, finance educator; b. Beijing, May 15, 1953; came to the U.S., 1984; d. DongChang He and Zhuobao Li; m. Ping Su, June 29, 1949; 1 child, Xiaowei Su. MA in Internat. Bus., U. Tex., Dallas, 1986, MS in Fin., 1989, PhD in Internat. Mgmt., 1991. Engr., rschr. China's Nat. Acad. Agr. Mechanization Bldg., Beijing 1977-84; rsch. assoc. Hass Bus. Sch. U. Calif., Berkeley, 1984-85; mgmt. cons. Greyhound Lines & China Auto Import Co. Dallas, 1985-89; v.p. China Auto Import Co., Dallas, 1989-91; dir. Far East Econ. Devel. Greyhound Lines, Dallas, 1989-91; dir. Internat. Bus. ExchangeProg. Quinnipiac U., Hamden, Conn., 1991-93, prof., chair internat. bus. and mktg. dept., 1997—2000, dir. Internat. Bus. Rsch., 1993-94, chair internat. bus., 2001—. Contbr. articles to profl. jours., chpts. to books. Recipient Outstanding R&D Award, China's Machine Building Min., 2d Prize, 1983, 3rd Prize 1979-81, Citation of Excellence award ANBAR Electronic Intelligence, U.K., 1998, Literati Club award for excellence, MCB Univ. Press, U.K., 1999, Excellence in Tchg. award Quinnipiac U., 2003. Mem. Internat. Mgmt. Devel. Assn., Nat. Assn. Global Bus., Acad. Mgmt., Assn. Internat. Trade and Fin., Acad. Internat. Bus. (Best Paper award N.E. chpt. 1992), Soc. Global Bus. Edn. Office: Quinnipiac U Sch Bus 275 Mount Carmel Ave Hamden CT 06518-1961 E-mail: Xiaohong.He@quinnipiac.edu.

HE, XIN, computer scientist, educator; b. Beijing, Apr. 8, 1953; came to U.S., 1980; MS in Math., Ohio State U., 1981, MS in Computer Sci., 1984, PhD, 1987. Asst. prof. SUNY, Buffalo, 1987—93, assoc. prof., 1993—2002, prof., 2002—. Recipient Rsch. Initiation award NSF, 1990; grantee NSF, 1993, 2000. Mem. IEEE, Assn. Computing Machinery. Office: SUNY at Buffalo Dept Computer Sci & Engring 201 Bell Hall Buffalo NY 14260-2000

HE, YI, neurosurgeon, researcher; b. Chengdu, Sichuan, China, Oct. 11, 1963; m. Jing Xu; 1 child, Xinyi. MD, Third Mil. Med. U. in China, Chongqing, 1984; PhD, Nat. U. Singapore, 1998. Cert. medicine. Resident in neurosurgery Chengdu Gen. Hosp., 1984—87, specialist in neurosurgery, 1990—94; fellow Baylor Col. Med., 1998—2001; prin. investigator Coll. Medicine Baylor U., Houston, 2001—. Rsch. scholar Nat. U. Singapore, 1994—98. Recipient Internat. Rsch. Grant awards, Parkinson's Disease Found., 2001. Mem.: Soc. Neurosci.

HEACKER, THELMA WEAKS, retired elementary school educator; b. Lakeland, Fla., Nov. 27, 1927; d. Andrew Lee and Stella Dicy (Hodges) Weaks; m. Howard V. Heacker, Aug. 21, 1947; children: Victor, Patricia, Paula, Jonathan, Johannah; m. V.L. Brown, Mar. 31, 1991. BA, Carson-Newman Coll., Jefferson City, Tenn., 1949; MA, Tenn. Technol. U., 1980; postgrad., U. Tenn. Cert. elem. and secondary tchr., Tenn.; cert. secondary tchr., Ga. Elem. tchr. Hamblen County Pub. Schs., Morristown, Tenn., 1949; secondary tchr. Morgan County-Coalfield High Sch., Coalfield, Tenn., 1986-87, Roane County-O. Springs High Sch., Oliver Springs, Tenn., 1949-71; elem. tchr. Morgan County-Petros-Joyner Sch., Oliver Springs, 1975-93. Vol. Keystone Elder Day Care, 2000—. Named Tchr. of Yr., 1986. Mem. NEA, Tenn. Edn. Assn., Ea. Tenn. Edn. Assn., Morgan County Edn. Assn., RCTA, HCTA Home: 102 Ulena Ln Oak Ridge TN 37830-5237 Office: Petros Joyner Elem Sch Petros-Joyner Rd Oliver Springs TN 37840-9700

HEACOCK, DONALD DEE, social worker; b. Anthony, Kans., Feb. 21, 1934; s. C.W. and Thelma Olive (Hilton) H.; m. Margaret Newberry, Sept. 4, 1953; children: Teresa Ellen, Mark Dee. AB, Washburn U., 1956; BD cum laude, United Sem., 1959; MSW, Barry Coll., 1971; ThD, Slidell Bapt. Sem., 1999. Ordained priest Episcopal Ch., 1965; diplomate in clin. social work. Parish minister St. John's Ch., Clinton, Mich., 1961-66; chaplain Margarita, Canal Zone, 1966-69; tchr. Christ Ch. Acad. Secondary Sch., Colon, Panama, 1966-69; counselor South Fla. Neighborhood Youth Corp., Miami, 1969-70; chief social svc., instr. pediat. comprehensive health care U. Miami, 1971-72; asst. dir. Alpha House, Dade County, Fla., 1972-73; field supr. Barry Coll., 1972-73; marriage and family therapist Psychiat. Assocs., Shreveport, La., 1973-75; pvt. practice social work Shreveport, 1975—. Dir. Holy Cross Child Placement Agy., Inc., 1984; lectr. sociology Centenary Coll., 1981-88. With USAF, 1959-61. Mem. Am. Assn. Marriage and Family Therapy, Nat. Assn. Social Workers, Acad. Cert. Social Work, Masons, Phi Kappa Mu, Phi Gamma Mu. Home: 748 Thora Blvd Shreveport LA 71106-1824 Office: Ste 357 910 Pierremont Rd Shreveport LA 71106-2063 E-mail: Domahea@aol.com.

HEAD, BEN THOMAS, lawyer; b. Oklahoma City, Nov. 1, 1920; s. Ben Thomas Head and Virginia (Broados) Pine; m. Mary C. Johnston, June 17, 1949 (div. June 1983); children: Marcy, Paul, Eric; m. June Leftwich, Mar. 22, 1986. BBA, U. Okla., 1942, LLB, 1948, JD, 1970. Bar: Okla., Tex. Pres., chmn., chief exec. officer RepublicBank, Austin, Tex., 1978-84; sr. lectr. banking U. Tex., Austin, 1984-88; U.S. trustee U.S. Dist. Ct. (so. and we. dists.) Tex., Houston, 1988-93. Pres., CEO United Va. Bank (now SunTrust), Newport News, Va., 1975-78; chmn. City Savs., San Angelo, Tex., 1986-87. V.p. Oklahoma City C. of C., 1973, chmn. Austin C. of C., 1983; pres. progress com. Newport News., Va., 1978; bd. dirs., chmn. fin. com. Austin Presbyn. Sem., 1982-90; bd. dirs. fin. com. Tex. Presbyn. Found., 1988—; trustee, vice chmn. bd., Hampton U., 1980—. Col. U.S. Army, 1942-46, India. Named Exec. of Yr. Austin C. of C., 1983. Mem. Rotary. Avocations: golf, walking. Home: 3234 Tarryhollow Dr Austin TX 78703-1639 Office: 816 Congress Ave Ste 1200 Austin TX 78701-2442

HEAD, ELIZABETH, lawyer; b. Rochester, Minn., Dec. 17, 1930; d. Walter Elias and Ruth Winnogene (Evesmith) Bonner; m. C.J. Head, Dec. 30, 1950; 1 child, Alison Elizabeth. BA, U. Chgo., 1949, JD, 1952. Bar: Ill. 1952, Calif. 1955, N.Y. 1958, U.S. Supreme Ct. 1963, D.C. 1978. Atty. Nat. Labor Rels. Bd., Washington, 1953-54; assoc. Johnston & Johnston, San Francisco, 1954-56; atty. Aminoil Inc., San Francisco, 1956-57; teaching assoc. Law Sch. Columbia U., N.Y., 1957-58; assoc. Skadden Arps, N.Y., 1958-60; atty. The Coca-Cola Corp., N.Y., 1961-65; assoc. Kaye Scholer, N.Y., 1965-72, ptnr., 1973-82; mem. Hall & Estill, Tulsa, 1983-87; vis. fellow antitrust analysis Fed. Energy Regulatory Commn., Washington, 1987-89; gen. counsel Columbia U., N.Y.C., 1989-97. Arbitrator, mediator, 1998—. Trustee Mary Baldwin Coll., Staunton, Va., 1983-87. Mem. ABA (standing com. on dispute resolution 1983-90), Assn. of Bar of City of N.Y. (non-profit orgns. com. 1989-90, chair 1992-95, health law com. 1997-2000), Century Assn., Order of Coif, Phi Beta Kappa. Avocations: travel, music, art, theatre. Office: 303 E 57th St # 47F New York NY 10022-2947

HEAD, HAYDEN WILSON, JR., judge; Student, Washington and Lee U., 1962-64; BA, U. Tex., 1967, LLB, 1968. Bar: Tex. Assoc. Head & Kendrick, Corpus Christi, Tex., 1968-69, 1972-76, ptnr., 1976-81; judge U.S. Dist. Ct. (so. dist.) Tex., Corpus Christi, 1981—. Chmn. 5th Cir. Com. on Criminal Pattern Jury Instr., 1986—; mem. jud. conf. U.S. Com. on Security and Facilities, 2002—. Lt. JAGC, USNR, 1969-72 Fellow: Tex. Bar Found.; mem.: State Bar Tex., Am. Inn of Ct. (pres. 2001—). Office: US Dist Ct 1133 N Shoreline Blvd Corpus Christi TX 78401

HEAD, IVAN LEIGH, law educator; b. Calgary, Alta., Can., July 28, 1930; s. Arthur Cecil and Birdie Hazel (Crockett) H.; m. Barbara Spence Eagle, June 23, 1952; children: Laurence Allan, Bryan Cameron, Catherine Spence, Cynthia Leigh; m. Ann Marie Price, Dec. 1, 1979. BA, U. Alta., 1951, LLB, 1952; LLM, Harvard U., 1960; LLD (hon.), U. Alta., 1987, U. West Indies, 1987, U. Western Ont., 1988, U. Ottawa, 1988, U. Calgary, 1989, Beijing U., 1990, St. Francis Xavier U., 1990, U. Man., 1991, U. Notre Dame, 1991, Carleton U., 1996. Bar: Alta. 1953; Queen's Counsel, Can. Practiced in, Calgary, 1953-59; partner Helman, Barron & Head, 1955-59; fgn. service officer Dept. External Affairs, Ottawa, Kuala Lumpur, 1960-63; prof. law U. Alta., 1963-67; assoc. counsel to Minister of Justice, Govt. of Can., 1967-68, spl. asst. to prime minister of Can., 1968-78; pres. Internat. Devel. Rsch. Centre, Ottawa, 1978-91; prof. law, dir. Liu Centre for the study of global issues U. B.C., Vancouver, Canada, 1991—99, prof. emeritus, 2000—. Sr. fellow Salzburg Seminar; bd. dirs. Acad. Ednl. Devel., Can. World Youth. Author: International Law, National Tribunals and the Rights of Aliens, 1971, On a Hinge of History, 1991, The Canadian Way, 1995; editor: This Fire Proof House, 1967, Conversation with Canadians, 1972; contbr. articles to profl. jours. Trustee Internat. Food Policy Rsch. Inst., 1979-88; mem. Ind. Commn. on Internat. Humanitarian Issues, 1983-87. Decorated officer Order of Can.; officer Grand Cross, Order of The Sun (Peru); Chief Justice's medallist U. Alta. Law Sch.; Frank Knox Meml. fellow Harvard Law Sch., 1959-60; named to Sports Wall of Fame U. Alta. Mem. Internat. Law Assn., Can. Council Internat. Law, Can. Inst. Internat. Affairs, Am. Soc. Internat. Law, Law Soc. Alta., Inter-Am. Dialogue. Anglican. Home: 2343 Bellevue Ave West Vancouver BC Canada V7V 1C9 Office: U BC Faculty of Law Vancouver BC Canada V6T 1Z1 E-mail: ivanhead@shaw.ca.

HEAD, JAMES PHILIP, lawyer; b. Cin., Nov. 7, 1969; s. James Franklin and Phyllis Finkelmeier Head; m. Tanya Lynn Iberg, June 14, 1997; 1 child, Chrstianna Caitlin. BA in Econs., U. Md., 1992; JD, George Washington U., 1995; LLM in Tax, Georgetown U., 2000. Bar: Md. 1995, D.C. 1996, Va. 1996. Atty. Cohen & Troxell, P.C., McLean, Va., 1996—97, Sherman, Meehan, Curtin & Ain, Washington, 1997—2000, Williams Mullen, McLean, 2000—. Mem.: ABA, Md. Bar Assn., D.C. Bar Assn., Va. Bar Assn., U. Club Washington, Phi Beta Kappa. Office: Williams Mullen 8270 Greensboro Dr Ste 700 Mc Lean VA 22102

HEAD, JAMES W., III, geological sciences educator; b. Richmond, Va., Aug. 4, 1941; BS, Washington and Lee U., 1964, DSc, 1995; PhD, Brown U., 1969. With NASA/Bellcomm, Inc., Washington, 1968—72; interim dir. Lunar Sci. Inst., Houston, 1973—74; asst. prof. Brown U., Providence, 1973—74, assoc. prof., 1974—80, prof. geol. scis., 1980—95, Louis and Elizabeth Scherck disting. prof., 1995—. Vis. assoc. Calif. Inst. Tech., Pasadena, 1990-91; prof. Universidad Complutense, Madrid, 1997. Contbr. chpts. to books, more than 300 articles to profl. jours. Recipient medal for exceptional sci. achievement NASA, also pub. svc. medal; award Alpha Circle of Omicron Delta Kappa, 1990. Fellow AAAS, Am. Geophys. Union, Geol. Soc. Am. (G.K. Gilbert award 2002), Meteoritical Soc.; mem. Am. Astron. Soc., European Geophys. Union. Office: Brown U Box 1846 Dept Geo-Scis Providence RI 02912 E-mail: James_Head_III@brown.edu.

HEAD, JONATHAN FREDERICK, cell biologist; b. Syracuse, N.Y., Nov. 23, 1949; s. Arthur Everard and Lillian Myrtle (Hendra) H.; m. Priscilla Catherine Tambone, July 28, 1984; 1 child, Catherine Elizabeth. BS in Zoology, Syracuse U., 1971; MA in Biology, Bklyn. Coll., 1977; PhD in Biology, Fordham U., 1985. Rsch. asst. Naylor Dana Inst. Disease Prevention/Am. Health Found., Valhalla, N.Y., 1974-78, Cornell U. Med. Coll., N.Y.C., 1978, Mt. Sinai Sch. Medicine, N.Y.C., 1978-84, rsch. assoc., 1984-86, rsch. asst. prof., 1986-87; dir. tumor cell biology Ctr. Clin. Scis./Internat. Clin. Labs., Nashville, 1986-89; pres. Mastology Rsch. Inst., Baton Rouge, 1989—; dir. R&D Med. Thermal Diagnostics, Baton Rouge, 1995—2001, Innovative Drug Techs., Edmond, Okla., 1999—. High Complexity Clin. Lab. dir. Am. Bd. Bioanalysis, 1988—; med. lab. dir. Clin. Chemistry, State of Tenn., 1988—; clin. lab. scientist/specialist, State of La., 1995—; adj. assoc. prof. Tulane U. Sch. Medicine, New Orleans, 1989—; adj. prof. Delta State U., Cleveland, Miss., 1992—; researcher and lectr. in field of cancer. Contbr. articles, abstracts and chpts. to sci. publs. Mem. State of La. Adoption Cmty. Adv. Bd., 1992-95. Mem. AAAS, Am. Assn. Cancer Rsch., Am. Soc. Clin. Oncology, Am. Acad. Thermology, Internat. Soc. Biol. Therapy Cancer, European Soc. Med. Oncology, N.Y. Acad. Scis. Methodist. Home: 6144 Hagerstown Dr Baton Rouge LA 70817-3917 Office: Mastology Rsch Inst 17050 Med Ctr Dr 4th Fl Baton Rouge LA 70816

HEAD, LOUIS ROLLIN, surgeon; b. Madison, Wis., Apr. 8, 1924; s. Jerome R. and Jean (Milne) H.; m. Emily Johnson, Sept. 15, 1951; children: Emily, Julia, Marjorie, Mary, Anne, Louis, Frederic. AB, Amherst Coll., 1945; MD, Johns Hopkins U., 1952. Diplomate Am. Bd. Surgery, Am. Bd. Thoracic Surgery. Intern Northwestern U. Hosp., Chgo., 1952-53; resident in gen. surgery U. Chgo., 1953-57; fellow in thoracic surgery Northwestern U., 1957-58; fellow in cardiac surgery St. Vincent's Charity Hosp., Cleve., 1958-60; assoc. in surgery Northwestern U. Med. Sch., Chgo., 1960-88; field rep. The Joint Commn. on Accreditation of Healthcare Orgns., Oakbrook Terrace, Ill., 1990-95, assoc. dir. standards interpretation, 1995-97; pvt. practice Evanston, Ill., 1997—. Author: (paperback, ebook) Dancing In The Dark, and the Nature, of Escape and Evasion in Croatia During the Second World War, 2002, 2d edit., 2003. 2d lt. USAF, 1942—45, Italy. Rsch. grantee John Hartford Found., N.Y., 1963-71. Fellow Am. Assn. Cardiac and Thoracic Surgery, Ill. Thoracic Surg. Soc., Chgo. Surg. Soc.; mem. Air Force Escape and Evasion Soc. (life). Republican. Anglican. Achievements include development of implantable artificial lung. Avocations: tennis, fishing. Home: Apt 2-South 1107 Lake St Evanston IL 60201-4147 Office: 524 W Diversey Pkwy Chicago IL 60614-1610 E-mail: DrLRHead@earthlink.net.

HEAD, PATRICK JAMES, lawyer; b. Randolph, Nebr., July 13, 1932; s. Clarence Martin and Ellen Cecelia (Magirl) H.; m. Eleanor Hickey, Nov. 24, 1960; children: Adrienne, Ellen, Damian, Maria, Brendan, Martin, Sarah, Daniel, Brian. AB summa cum laude, Georgetown U., 1953, LL.B., 1956, LL.M. in Internat. Law, 1957. Bar: D.C. 1956, Ill. 1966. Assoc. John L. Ingolsby (and predecessor firm), Washington, 1956-64; gen. counsel internat. ops. Sears, Roebuck & Co., Oakbrook, Ill., 1964-70, counsel midwest ter. Skokie, Ill., 1970-72; v.p. Montgomery Ward & Co., Inc., Washington, 1972-76, v.p., gen. counsel, sec. Chgo., 1976-81; v.p., gen. counsel FMC Corp., Chgo., 1981-96; ptnr. Altheimer E. Gray, Chgo., 1997—2001, Williams Montgomery and John, Chgo., 2001—. Bd. visitors Northwestern Law, 1988-91. Mem. Chgo. Crime Commn.; bd. regents Georgetown U., Washington, 1981-87; bd. visitors Georgetown Law Sch., 1992—. Mem. ABA, D.C. Bar Assn., Chgo. Bar Assn., Am. Law Inst. Clubs: Met. (Washington); Chgo, Internat. Democrat. Roman Catholic. Office: Williams Montgomery & John Ltd 20 N Wacker Dr 21st Fl Chicago IL 60606-7407

HEAD, WILLIAM IVERSON, SR., retired chemical company executive; b. Tallapposa, Ga., Apr. 4, 1925; s. Iverson and Ruth Britain (Hubbard) H.; m. Mary Helen Ware, June 12, 1947; children: William Iverson, Connie Suzanne Head Toohey, Alan David. BS, Ga. Inst. Tech., 1949; D of Textile Engring. (hon.), World U., 1983; PhD in Indsl. Mgmt., Columbia Pacific U., 1988. Textile engr. Tenn. Eastman Co., Kingsport, 1949-56, quality control-mfg. sr. textile engr., 1957-67, dept. supt., 1968-74; supt. acetate yarn dept., bus. team, chem. divsn. Eastman Kodak Co., Kingsport, 1975-85. Info. officer U.S. Naval Acad., 1983-97; adv. bd., rsch. assoc. Point One Adv. Group, Inc., 1988—. Capt. USNR, 1943-83. Mem.: VFW, Internat. Soc. Philos. Enquiry (pers. cons. 1978—79, v.p. 1979—80, sr. rsch. fellow and internat. pres. 1980—85, diplomate, trustee 1986—, chmn. bd. trustees 1987—2002, Whiting Meml. award 1993), Wisdom Soc. (Award of Honor 2000), Mil. Officers Assn. Am., Sons of Confederate Vets., Sons of Revolution, Res. Officers Assn. (pres. Tenn. dept. 1981—82, nat. councilman 1991—98, nat. coun. steering com. 1993—97), Assn. Naval Aviation, Internat. Platform Assn., Prometheus Soc., Naval Res. Assn., Mil. Order World Wars, Internat. Legion of Intelligence, Mensa (pres. Upper East Tenn. 1976—79). Unitarian Universalist. Achievements include patents for textured yarn technology in U.S., Great Britain, Federal Republic of Germany, Japan and France. Home: 4035 Lakewood Dr Kingsport TN 37663-3374

HEAD, WILLIAM PACE, historian, educator; b. Miami, Oct. 15, 1949; s. Downer Pace and Ella Marguerite (Crittenden) H.; m. Randee Lynne Geiger, June 6, 1975; children: Matthew Brian, Evan Zachery. AS Bus., Miami-Dade C.C., 1969; PhD History, Fla. State U., 1980, BA History, 1971; MA History, U. Miami, 1974. Asst. prof. history U. Ala., Huntsville, 1981-84; historian USAF, Robins AFB, Ga., 1984—, chief Office of History WR-ALC, 1996—. Adj. prof. history Fla. State U., Tallahassee, 1980-81, Macon (Ga.) State Coll., 1985—, Mercer U., 1985-92, Ga. Mil. Coll., 1986-94; site dir. Ala. Heritage Festival, Ala. Humanities Coun., Huntsville, 1981; hist. advisor WMAZ-TV Robins at Fifty, 1991, Ga. Pub. TV, The State of War: Ga. in WWII, Atlanta, 1994. Author: America's China Sojourn, 1983, Reworking the Workhorse: The C-141B, 1984 (Best in AF 1985), Yenan, 1985, Every Inch a Soldier, 1995 (Best in AF 1996), War From Above the Cloud, 2002; co-author, editor: Plotting a True Course: Reflections on Strategic Attack Theory and Doctrine, the Post-World War II Experience, 2003; co-author: Time Capsule: A History of Robins AFB, 1936-96, 1997; editor Tet Offensive, 1996, Looking Back at the Vietnam War, 1993, Eagle in the Desert, 1996, Weaving A New Tapestry: Asia In The Post Cold War World, 1999, War From Above the Clouds: B-52 Operations During the Second Indo China War, 2002; mem. editl. bd. Asia, Jour. Third World Studies, 1985-98. Mem. Houston County Dem. Com. Coun., Warner Robins, Ga., 1990—; active little league baseball and basketball, Warner Robins City League, 1992—; hist. judge, Ga. Hist. Day/Ga. Humanities Coun., Atlanta, 1988—. Recipient Spl. Commendation award Ala. State Senate, Huntsville, 1986, Air Force Spl. Achievements award, 1994; Fla. State U. grad. fellow, 1977. Mem. Assn. Third World Studies (nom. com. chmn. 1989-98, exec. coun. post 1 1999-2002, pres. 2003), Ga. Assn. Historians (pubs. com. 1984-99), Assn. Asian Studies (program chmn. 2003), Soc. Mil. History, Soc. Hist. Fed. Govt., Phi Kappa Phi. Democrat. Methodist. Avocations: golf, travel, tennis, sports. Home: 111 Chantilly Dr Warner Robins GA 31088-6329 Office: USAF-Warner Robins ALC 955 Robins Pky Robins AFB GA 31098-2423 E-mail: pamccall@webtv.net.

HEAD, WILLIS STANFORD, music educator, performer; b. Memphis, June 21, 1953; s. Willis Lockhart and Mildred (Garrard) H. B in Music Edn., Ark. State U., 1975, M in Music Edn., 1980. Percussion instr. Dixie Music Camp, Jonesboro, Ark., 1972-81; timpanist Tupelo (Miss.) Symphony Orch., 1973-74, N.E. Ark. Symphony, Jonesboro, 1974-81; band dir. Mammoth Spring (Ark.) High Sch., 1975-77; percussionist Memphis Symphony and Little Symphony, 1981—. "Artists in Schs.", Memphis, 1985—; bd. dirs. Lindenwood Percussion Studio, Memphis, 1980—. Lectr. Mid-South Bible Coll., Memphis, 1982—; percussion instr. Shelby State Community Coll. Memphis, 1984—; percussion cons. Harding Acad., Memphis, 1985—, Osceola (Ark.) High Sch., 1986—, Millington (Tenn.) High Sch., 1987—; timpanist Jackson (Tenn.) Symphony Orch. Mem. Percussive Arts Soc. (sec. treas. 1977-78), Nat. Assn. Recording Arts and Scis., Phi Mu Alpha Sinfonia Frat., Kappa Delta Pi. Home: 652 S Prescott St Memphis TN 38111-4325 Office: Lindenwood Percussion Studio 2400 Union Ave Memphis TN 38112-4318

HEADLEE, RAYMOND, psychoanalyst, educator; b. Shelby County, Ind., July 27, 1917; s. Ortis Verl and Mary Mae (Wright) H.; m. Eleanor Case Benton, Aug. 24, 1941; children: Sue, Mark, Ann. AB in Psychology, Ind. U., 1939, A.M. in Exptl. Psychology, 1941, MD, 1944; grad., Chgo. Inst. Psychoanalysis, 1959. Diplomate: Am. Bd. Psychiatry and Neurology (examiner 1964—). Intern St. Elizabeth's Hosp., Washington, 1944-45, resident in psychiatry, 1945-46, Milw. Psychiat. Hosp., 1947-48, pres. staff, 1965-70; practice medicine specializing in psychiatry and psychoanalysis Elm Grove, Wis., 1949—; clin. asst. prof. psychiatry Med. Coll. Wis., 1958-59, clin. asso. prof., 1959-62, clin. prof., 1962-2000, chmn. dept. psychiatry, 1963-70; prof. psychology Marquette U., 1966-76; Bd. dirs. Elm Brook (Wis.) Meml. Hosp., 1969-71; ret., 2000. Author: (with Bonnie Corey) Psychiatry in Nursing, 1949, I Think, Therefore I Know, 1996; contbr. numerous articles to profl. jours. 1st lt. Ft. Knox Armored Med. Rsch. Lab., AUS, 1945, to col. USPHS. Fellow Am. Psychiat. Assn. (life), Am. Coll. Psychiatry (emeritus); mem. State Med. Soc. Wis. (editorial dir. 1971-77), Wis. Psychiat. Assn. (pres. 1971-72), Milw. Club. E-mail: 1amplg@mymailstation.com. *My life story represents a gradual and often difficult transition from the puritan ethic, which got me into this book, to a lighter style of living. This is what the Germans call Lebenskünstler.*

HEADRICK, JOHN DAVID, music educator; b. Augusta, Ga., Dec. 9, 1975; s. Mickey L. and Brenda K. Headrick. MusB, U. S.C., 1999. Band dir. Pelion (S.C.) Mid. Sch., 1999—. Mem.: Nat. Assn. Music Educators. Home: 605 Catawba Circle Columbia SC 29201

HEADRICK, THOMAS EDWARD, lawyer, educator; b. East Orange, N.J., June 28, 1933; s. Lewis Barnard and Marian Elizabeth Headrick; m. Mary Margaret Shontz, June 27, 1957; children— Trevor, Todd. BA, Franklin and Marshall Coll., 1955; B.Litt., Oxford (Eng.) U., 1958; LL.B., Yale U., 1960; PhD, Stanford U., 1975. Bar: Conn. 1960, Calif. 1962. Asst. dir. Ansonia (Conn.) Redevel. Agy., 1959-60; law clk. to justice Wash. State Supreme Ct., Olympia, 1960-61; assoc. firm Pillsbury, Madison & Sutro, San Francisco, 1961-64; mgmt. cons. Emerson Cons., London, 1964-66, Baxter, McDonald & Co., Berkeley, Calif., 1966-67; asst. dean Stanford U. Law Sch., 1967-70; v.p. acad. affairs Lawrence U., 1970-76; dean law sch. U. at Buffalo, 1976-85, prof. law, 1976—, interim dean arts and letters faculty, 1990, disting. svc. prof., 1993—, provost, 1995-99, sr. counselor to pres., 1999, interim dean architecture and planning, 1999. Cons. Nat. Endowment for Humanities, NSF; legal commentator Sta. WKBW-TV, 1978-80 Author: The Town Clerk in English Local Government, 1962; co-editor Law and Policy, 1988-92. Mem. Phi Beta Kappa. Office: University at Buffalo 411 O'Brian Hall Buffalo NY 14260-1100 E-mail: headrick@buffalo.edu.

HEADY, EUGENE JOSEPH, lawyer; b. Poughkeepsie, N.Y., Jan. 25, 1958; s. William and Margaret Patricia Heady; children: Anthony Ray, Emily Rene, Katie Shanell. BS in Engring., U. Hartford, 1981; JD cum laude, Tex. Tech. U., 1996. Bar: Tex. 1996, Ga. 1997, Colo. 1997, Fla. 1998, Supreme Ct. Ga. 1997, U.S. Dist. t. (no. dist.) Ga. 1997, U.S. Ct. Appeals Ga. 1997, U.S. Dist. Ct. (no. dist.) Tex. 2001. V.p. Heady Electric Co., Inc., Poughkeepsie, N.Y., 1980-83; project mgr. ANECO, Inc., West Palm Beach, Fla., 1987-93; assoc. Smith, Currie & Hancock LLP, Atlanta, 1996—. Editor-in-chief: Tex. Tech Law Rev. vol. 27, 1995-96; student editor: Tex. County Ct. Bench Manual, 1996, Bench Book for the Tex. Jud., 1996; editor: Tex. Tech Legal Rsch. Bd., 1995-96; co-author: Ga. Suppl. to Fifty State Construction Lien and Bond Law, 1996, 97, 98, 2001, 02, 03, Ga. chpt. Fifty State Construction Lien and Bond Law, 2000; author: chpts. in Alternative Clauses to Standard Construction Contracts, 1998, 99, 2000; contbr. numerous articles to profl. jours. Mem. ABA (forum on the constrn. industry, vice-chmn. region IV sect. of pub. contract law), Scribes-The Am. Soc. Writers on Legal Subjects. Avocations: writing, reading. Home: 2412 Waterscape Trl Snellville GA 30078-7740 Office: Smith Currie & Hancock LLP 2600 Harris Tower 233 Peachtree St NE Ste 2600 Atlanta GA 30303-1530 Fax: 404-688-0671. E-mail: gjheady@smithcurrie.com.

HEADY, FERREL, retired political science educator; b. Ferrelview, Mo., Feb. 14, 1916; s. Chester Ferrel and Loren (Wightman) H.; m. Charlotte Audrey McDougall, Feb. 12, 1942; children— Judith Lillian, Richard Ferrel, Margaret Loren, Thomas McDougall. AB, Washington U., St. Louis, 1937, A.M., 1938, PhD, 1940; hon. degrees, Park Coll., 1973, John F. Kennedy U., 1974, U. N.Mex., 1993. Jr. adminstrv. technician, also adminstrv. asst. Office Dir. Personnel, Dept. Agr., 1941-42; vis. lectr. polit. sci. U. Kansas City, 1946; faculty U. Mich., 1946-67, prof. polit. sci., 1957-67; dir. Inst. Pub. Adminstrn., 1960-67; acad. v.p. U. N.Mex., Albuquerque, 1967-68, pres., 1968-75, prof. pub. adminstrn. and polit. sci., 1975-81, prof. emeritus, 1981—. Asst. to commr. Com. Orgn. Exec. Br. of Govt., 1947-49; dir., chief adviser Inst. Pub. Adminstrn., U. Philippines, 1953-54; mem. U.S. del. Internat. Congress Adminstrn. Scis., Spain, 1956, 80, Germany, 1959, Austria, 1962, Poland, 1964, Mexico, 1974; exec. bd. Inter-Univ. Case Program, 1956-67; sr. specialist in residence East-West Center, U. Hawaii, 1965; mem. Conf. on Pub. Service, 1965-70; chmn. bd. Assoc. Western Univs., 1970-71; commr. Western Interstate Commn. Higher Edn., 1972-77; mem. commns. on bus. professions and water

resources, mem. exec. com. Nat. Assn. State Univs. and Land Grant Colls., 1968-75 Author: Administrative Procedure Legislation in the States, 1952, (with Robert H. Pealy) The Michigan Department of Administration, 1956, (with Sybil L. Stokes) Comparative Public Administration: A Selective Annotated Bibliography, 1960, Papers in Comparative Public Administration, 1962, State Constitutions: The Structure of Administration, 1961, Public Administration: A Comparative Perspective, 1966, rev. edit., 1979, 6th edit., 2001, One Time Around, 1999; contbr. profl. jours. Chmn. state affairs com. Ann Arbor Citizens Coun., Mich., 1949-52; mem. exec. com. Mich. Meml.-Phoenix Project and Inst. Social Rsch., 1960-66; mem. Gov. Mich. Constl. Revision Study Commn., 1960-62; schs. and univs. adv. bd. Citizens Com. for Hoover Report, 1949-52, 54-58; cons. to Ford Found., 1962; chmn. Coun. on Grad. Edn. in Pub. Adminstrn., 1966; mem., vice chmn. N.Mex. Gov.'s Com. on Reorgn. of State Govt., 1967-70; mem. N.Mex. Am. Revolution Bicentennial Commn., 1970-73, N.Mex. Gov.'s Com. on Tech. Excellence, 1969-75, Nat. Acad. Pub. Adminstrn.; mem., vice chmn. N.Mex. Constl. Revision Commn., 1994-95. Served to lt. USNR, 1942-46. Recipient Faculty Disting. Achievement award U. Mich., 1964, N.Mex. Disting. Pub. service award, 1973, award of distinction U. N.Mex. Alumni Assn., 1975, Outstanding Grad. Tchr. award U. N.Mex., 1981-82, Fulbright sr. lectureship, Colombia, 1992, Waldo award for career contbns. to lit. and leadership of pub. adminstrn., 1994. Mem. Am. Polit. Sci. Assn., Am. Soc. Pub. Adminstrn. (pres. 1969 70), AAUP (chmn. com. 'I' 1957-61), Am. Council Edn. (mem. comm. on fed. relations 1969-72), Phi Beta Kappa, Phi Beta Kappa. Presbyterian. Home: 2901 Cutler Ave NE Albuquerque NM 87106-1714

HEAGARTY, MARGARET CAROLINE, pediatric physician; b. Charleston, W.Va., Sept. 8, 1934; d. John Patrick and Margaret Caroline (Walsh) H. BA, Seton Hill Coll., 1957; BS, W.Va. Sch. Medicine, 1959; MD, U. Pa., 1961; DSc honoris causa, Iona Coll., 1989. Diplomate: Am. Bd. Pediatrics. Intern Phila. Gen. Hosp., 1961—62; resident in pediatrics St. Christopher's Hosp. for Children, Phila., 1962—64; dir. pediatric ambulatory care services N.Y. Hosp.-Cornell Med. Ctr., N.Y.C., 1969—78; dir. pediatrics Harlem Hosp. Ctr. Columbia U., N.Y.C., 1978—2000, prof. pediatrics coll. physicians & surgeons, 1987—2000, prof. emerita coll. physicians and surgeons, 2000—. Cons. Dept. HEW Promotion of Child Health, Washington; mem. Com. Community Oriented Primary Care Inst. Medicine, Washington; mem. Robert Wood Johnson Found. Program for Prepaid Managed Health Care, 1984; mem. governing council Inst. Medicine, Nat. Acad. Scis., 1986 Author: Changing the Medical Car System-Report of an Experiment, 1974, Medical Sociology: A Systems Approach, 1975, Child Health: Basics for Primary Care, 1980. Grantee Commonwealth Found., 1981, Robert Wood Johnson Found., 1983, Ctr. for Disease Control, 1985, Health Rsch. and Svc. Adminstrn., 1988, Nat. Inst. Allergy/Infectious Disease, 1988. Fellow Inst. Medicine (steering group for nat. forum on future of children and their families 1987—); mem. Ambulatory Pediatric Assn. (pres. 1976-77), Soc. Pediatric Research, Am. Pediatric Soc., Am. Acad. Pediatrics (com. on hosp. care 1988—), Assn. Pediatric Program Dirs., Nat. Bd. Med. Examiners. Home: 2520 Kingsland Ave Bronx NY 10469-6108 E-mail: mheagarty@aol.com.

HEAGGANS, RAPHAEL CHESARE, education educator; b. Kings Mountain, N.C. s. Joseph Theodore and Dorothy Seigle H. BA, Winston-Salem State U., 1994; MA, Winthrop U., 1997; EdD, W.Va. U., 2003. Cert. English tchr. Nat. Coun. Tchrs. English. Lang. arts tchr. Troutman (N.C.) Mid. Sch., 1997-98; instr. English Winston-Salem (N.C.) State U., 1998-2000; coll. instr. edn. W.Va. U., Morgantown, 2000—03. Grad. asst. W.Va. U., Morgantown, 2000-03. Editor (newsletter) Bobcat Tales, 1997. DuBois fellow, 2001-2003, doctoral fellow Wash. State U. Mem. Alpha Phi Alpha. Democrat. Avocations: exercise, reading, writing, traveling.

HEAL, GEOFFREY MARTIN, economics and business educator; b. Bangor, Wales, Apr. 9, 1944; s. Thomas John and Gwen Margaret (Owen) H.; m. Felicity Chandler, 1967 (div. 1979); m. Ann Marie Biafore, 2000; children: Bridget, Marie, Natasha. BA first class, Cambridge U., 1966, PhD, 1969. Dir. studies Christs Coll., Cambridge U., 1967-73; prof. econs. Sussex U., Brighton, Eng., 1973-81, head dept. econs., 1976-81; mng. editor Rev. Econ. Studies, London, 1973-78; dir. Economists Adv. Group, London, 1975-80; prof. Essex U., Colchester, Eng., 1981-83; exec. dir. Fin. Telecommunications, London, 1984-89; prof. Grad. Sch. Bus., Columbia U., N.Y.C., 1983—, sr. vice dean Grad. Sch. Bus., 1991-94; Fulbright prof. U. Siena, Italy, 1997; Paul Garret prof. pub. policy and corp. responsibility Columbia U., N.Y.C., 1995—, prof. Sch. Internat. and Pub. Affairs, 2002—. Cons. U.K. Dept. Energy, London, 1973-76, U.S. Dept. Energy, Washington, 1976-78, OPEC Sec. Gen., Vienna, Austria, 1979-81, OECD, Paris, 1994, Global Environ. Facility, World Bank, 1994, Internat. Brotherhood of Teamsters, 1995-2000, United Mineworkers of Am., 1990-98; mem. Pew Oceans Commn.; dir. Beijer Inst., Royal Swedish Acad. Scis, 2001—; chair Nat. Rsch. Coun. Com. on Valuing Svcs. of Aquatic Ecosystems, 2002-2003. Author: The Theory of Economic Planning, 1973, Public Policy and the Tax System, 1976, Economic Theory and Exhaustible Resources, 1979, Linear Algebra and Linear Economics, 1980, The Evolving International Economy, 1987, Oil in the International Economy, 1991, The Economics of Exhaustible Resources, 1993, Sustainability: Dynamics and Uncertainty, 1998, Valuing the Future, 1998, Topological Methods in Social Choice, 1998, The Economics of Increasing Returns, 1999, Environmental Markets, 2000, Nature and the Marketplace, 2000. Grantee NSF, NOAA, Sloan Found. Fellow: Royal Soc. Arts, Econometric Soc.; mem.: Union of Concerned Scientists (dir.). Home: 800 W End Ave # 13E New York NY 10025-5467 Office: Columbia Univ Bus Sch Uris Hall New York NY 10027 E-mail: gmh1@columbia.edu.

HEALD, BRUCE DAY, English and music educator, historian; b. Boston, June 5, 1935; s. Henry M. and Muriel D. (Day) H. m. Helen Peaslee, May 21, 1960; children: William Forristall III, Craig, Eric Bentley, Allyson Kaye. AA, Boston U., 1956; BS in Music Edn., Lowell State U., 1959; MA, Columbia Pacific U., 1984, PhD, 1985. Supr. music Ashland-Meredith Union 2, Meredith, N.H., 1959-64; dir. music, lectr. fine arts Belknap Coll., Center Harbor, N.H., 1963-65; dir. bands Plattsburgh (N.Y.) City Schs., 1969-70; supr. music Inter-Lakes Sch. Dist., Meredith, 1965-69, dir. music edn., 1970-77; dir. instrumental music Kennebunk (Maine) High Sch., 1977-79; prodn. mgr. Annalee Mobilitee Dolls, Meredith, 1979-81; lectr. English and journalism Moultonborough Acad., 1981-86; dir. music Congl. Ch., Laconia, N.H., 1985-86; chair English dept. Holy Trinity Sch., Laconia, 1987—2000; mentor Columbia Pacific U., 1986—; instr. music N.H. Coll., Manchester, 1988—; historian Weirstimes Pub. Co., 1992—2001. Lectr. English lit. Plymouth State Coll., 1995-97, lectr. U.S. history, 1998—. Author: Follow the Mount, 1968, 70, 93, 97, Postmaster of the Lake, 1971, Mail Service on the Lake, 1980, Steamboats in Motion, 1984, New Hampshire Learnin' Days, 1987, Boats 'n Ports I and II, 1989, Landmarks and Legacy, 1990, The Boston See Party, 1991, Reminisce the Valley, 1992, Shadows in the Window, 1995, Images of America: Meredith, 1996, Images of America: The Lakes Region of New Hampshire, 1996, vol. I and II, 1998, Images of America: The Upper Merrimack to Winnipesaukee by Rail, 1997, Images of America: Boats and Ports in Lake Winnipesaukee, vol. I and II, 1998, Images of America: The White Mountains Region by Rail, 1999, Image of America: Plymouth State College, 1999, Images of America: Stereoptic Memories of the White Mountains, 2000, Images of America: Lakes and Ponds of the Granite State, 2000, Images of Rail: The Boston and Maine in the 19th Century, 2001, Images of Rail: The Boston and Maine in the 20th Century, 2001, Images of the Civil War: N.H. in the Civil War, 2001, Images of America: Around Squam Lake, 2002, History & Guide: The Franconia Gateway, 2002, Images of Rail: Boston and Maine Locomotives, 2002, The Adventures to the Great American Railroads, 2003, Images of America: Main Streets in New Hampshire, 2003; composer: Kennebunk Concert March, The Hills of Old N.H., Moultonboro Concert March, Cascades, Trilogy. Commr. Parks and Playgrounds, Meredith, 1966-69; selectman Town of Meredith, 1971-76; pres. Lake Winnipesaukee Hist. Soc. Served with USMC, 1954-62. Mem. Masons. Republican. Home: PO Box 1052 Meredith NH 03253-1052 E-mail: doctor@fcgnetworks.net.

HEALD, DARREL VERNER, retired Canadian federal judge; b. Regina, Sask., Can., Aug. 27, 1919; s. Herbert Verner and Lottie (Knudson) H.; m. Doris Rose Hessey, June 30, 1951; children: Lynn, Brian. BA, U. Sask., 1938, LL.B., 1940. Bar: Called to Sask. bar 1941. Ptnr. firm Noonan, Embury, Heald, Molisky and Gritzfeld, Regina, until 1964; atty. gen. and provincial sec. Province Sask., 1964-71; MLA for Lumsden dist. Sask. Legislative Assembly, Regina, 1964-71; judge trial divsn. Fed. Ct. Can., Ottawa, Ont., 1971-75; judge Fed. Ct. Appeal, Ottawa, 1975-94. Served with RCAF, 1941-45. Home: 44 Aleutian Rd Ottawa ON Canada K2H 7C8

HEALD, JASON A. composer, music educator; b. Soap Lake, Wash., Feb. 8, 1958; BS, Lewis and Clark Coll., 1979; MMus, U. Portland, 1989; PhD, U. Oreg., 1998. Adj. prof. Linfield Coll., McMinnville, Oreg., 1986—96, Western Oreg. U., Monmouth, 1994—98; prof. Umpqua C.C., Roseburg, Oreg., 1998—. Composer: (composition) Passwords, 1998, Aaron's Exodus, 2000, Tennyson Songs, 2000, Requiem, 2001, String Quartet #4, 2002. Office: Umpqua CC PO Box 967 Roseburg OR 97470 Office Fax: 541-440-4637. Business E-Mail: healdj@umpqua.cc.or.us.

HEALD, MORRELL, humanities educator, educator; b. Oak Park, Ill., July 16, 1922; s. Howard Leslie and Helen (Morrell) H.; m. Barbara Legg, June 25, 1949; children: David M., Seth G., Sarah H. AB, Yale U., 1946, A.M., 1947, PhD, 1951. Instr. history Yale, 1950-53; mem. faculty Case Inst. Tech., 1953-68, assoc. prof. history, 1958-68, chmn. dept. humanities and social studies, 1959-62; prof. Am. studies Case Western Res. U., 1968-87, Samuel B. and Virginia C. Knight prof. humanities, 1982-88, prof. emeritus, 1988—, chmn. div. spl. interdisciplinary studies, 1971-78, 79-82. Vis. prof. Am. history Indian Inst. Tech., Kanpur, 1966-67; dir. Armington Research Program on Values in Children, 1978-80, chmn. adv. com., 1978-82 Author: The Social Responsibilities of Business: Company and Community, 1900-1960, 1970, Japanese edit., 1974, 2d edit., 1988, Transatlantic Vistas: American Journalists in Europe, 1900-1940, 1987; (with Lawrence S. Kaplan) Culture and Diplomacy: The American Experience, 1977; co-editor: The Aims and Organization of Liberal Studies, 1966. Vice pres. Cleveland Heights Your Schools Com., 1962, pres., 1965; Pres. of the First Ward Democratic Club, Cleveland Heights, 1962; mem. Cleve. Heights Landmarks Commn., 1987-01. Served with AUS, 1943-45, ETO. Mem. Soc. for History of Am. Fgn. Rels., Western Res. Hist. Soc. (publs. com. 1981-89), Phi Beta Kappa. Episcopalian. Home: 10450 Lottsford Rd #4215 Mitchellville MD 20721

HEALD, PAUL JUSTIN, law educator, writer; b. Evanston, Ill., Apr. 19, 1959; s. James Eudean Heald and Anita Kosir Phyllis; m. Jill Allison Crandall, Aug. 24, 1984; children: Andrea Merlin, Lewis Arthur, Margaret Ruth. AB, U. of Ill., 1980, AM, 1982; JD, U. of Chgo., 1988. Asst prof. of English Fla. A & M U., Tallahassee, 1983—85; from asst. to assoc. prof. of law U. of Ga., Athens, 1989—99, Allen Post prof. of law, 1999—. Author: (novels) No Regrets, (nonfiction) Literature and Legal Problem Solving; contbr. articles to profl. jours. (D. Francis Bustin prize, 1988). Chair Athens Area Emergency Food Bank, Athens, 1995—96. Recipient NEH Summer fellowship, NEH, 1984. Mem.: AALS (corr.). Office: U Ga Sch Law Herty Dr Athens GA 30602 Office Fax: 706-542-7404. E-mail: heald@uga.edu.

HEALEY, BARTH, editor, philatelist; b. N.Y.C., Sept. 22, 1939; s. Raymond B. and Ellen F. Healey; m. Lee Gelfer, Feb. 11, 1966 (dec. May 2003); children: Matthew, Adam. BA in Math., Coll. the Holy Cross, 1960; cert. in conflict and dispute resolution, NYU, 2001. Tchr. Christ the King H.S., Roma, Lesotho, 1961-63; regional dir. Cath. Relief Svcs., Dhaka, Bangladesh, 1965-67; corr. AP-Dow Jones, Rome, 1969-78; staff editor Petroleum Intelligence Weekly, N.Y.C., 1978-80; sr. staff editor The N.Y. Times, N.Y.C., 1980—. Fulbright lecturer in journalism, Anglo-American Coll. and Skvorecky Literary Acad., Prague, 2003; Editor Am. Philatelic Congress, 1995-98; co-editor: Changemakers (Ashoka Fellowship), 1998-2000; contbr. articles to profl. jours. and mags. Pres. Park Civic Assn., Port Washington, N.Y., 1985-97. Avocations: stamp collecting, reading, mathematical puzzles. Office: The NY Times Newsroom 229 W 43rd St New York NY 10036-3959 E-mail: healey@nytimes.com.

HEALEY, DAVID LEE, investment company executive; b. Pomona, Calif., Dec. 13, 1950; s. Robert Lincoln Sr. and Bernice (Mayes) H.; children: Paul Marcus, Elaina Rose. BS, U. Tulsa, 1978, postgrad. in law, 1979-80; cert., N.Y. Inst. Fin., 1980. Sales mgr. Magnavox, Tulsa, 1978-80; dir. tng. First State Fin., Tulsa, 1980-81; asst. v.p. Prudential-Bache Securities, Tulsa, 1981-86, E.F. Hutton, Tulsa, 1986-91, UBS PaineWebber, Inc., Tulsa, 1991—. Sales cons., Tulsa, 1981—. Judge Miss Teen USA pageant, 1984; chair endowment fund adv. com. Tulsa YWCA. Sgt. USAF, 1974-78. Mem. Internat. Assn. Fin. Planners (bd. dirs. 1984), Toastmasters Internat. (speakers bur.). Republican. Baptist. Avocations: computer programming, antique car restoration, public speaking. E-mail: david.healy!pwj.com. Home: RR 1 Box 120 Cleveland OK 74020-9729 Office: UBS 2431 E 61st St 8th Fl Tulsa OK 74136-1211

HEALEY, DEBORAH LYNN, education administrator; b. Columbus, Ohio, Sept. 15, 1952; d. James Henry and Marjorie Jean Healey; 1 child, Jesse Healey Winterowd. BA in German/Religion, Queen's U., 1974; MA in Linguistics, U. Oreg., 1976, PhD in Edn., 1993. Instr. Lane C.C., Eugene, Oreg., 1976-77; instr., materials developer Rogue C.C., Ashland, Oreg., 1977-79; instr. Chemeketa C.C., Salem, Oreg., 1979-80; instr., computer ops. English Lang. Inst. Oreg. State U., Corvallis, 1979-85, 88-93; instr., computer ops. Yemen-Am. Lang. Inst., Sana'a, Yemen, 1985-88; programmer, cons. Internat. Soc. for Tech. in Edn., Eugene, 1989-91; coord. instr. English Lang. Inst. Oreg. State U., Corvallis, 1993-95, tech. coord., 1995-99, dir., 1999—; acad. specialist U.S. Dept. State, Thailand, 2000, Brazil, 1995, Qatar, Oman, 2002. Macintosh support Computer-Enhanced Lang. Instrn. Archive, 1993—; computer cons. in field. Author: (book) Something To Do On Tuesday, 1995; co-author: (chpts.) A Handbook for Language Program Administrators, 1997, CALL Environments Research, Practice and Critical Issues, 1999; editor, author Computer-Assisted English Lang. Learning Jour., 1990-98; co-editor (ann. publ.) CALL Interest Sect. Software List, 1990—; co-author (software) The House, At The Zoo, 1993. Recipient D. Scott Enright TESOL Interest Sect. Svc. award, 2001. Mem. TESOL (interest sect. chair 1992-92), Oreg. TESOL (newsletter editor 1981-84), Nat. Assn. Fgn. Student Advisors-Assn. Internat. Educators, Am. Ednl. Rsch. Assn., Computer Assn. Lang. Instrn. Consortium. Avocations: language learning, traveling, music, reading. Office: ELI Oreg State Univ 301 Snell Hall Corvallis OR 97331-8515

HEALEY, EDWARD HOPKINS, retired architect; b. Dubuque, Iowa, Jan. 3, 1925; s. George Beach and Marian (Hopkins) H.; m. Alice Letitia Dawson, Sept. 11, 1954; children: Susan Healey Toussaint, Carolyn Healey Olson, Ellen Hopkins Healey. BS in Architecture, U. Ill., 1950; cert., Ecoles D'Art Americaines, Fountainbleau, France, 1950. Registered architect, Iowa, Ill., Wis., Minn. Ptnr. Brown & Healey, Architects, Cedar Rapids, Iowa, 1953-60, Brown, Healey & Bock, Architects and Engrs., Cedar Rapids, 1960-81; pres. Brown, Healey & Bock, Architects, Planners, Interior Designers, Cedar Rapids, 1981-90, Brown, Healey, Stone & Sauer, Architects, Planners, Interior Designers, Cedar Rapids, 1990-95; ret., 1995. Del. The White House Conf. on Libraries and Info. Svcs., Washington, 1979, 91; pres. profl. adv. bd. dept. architecture Iowa State U., Ames, 1981-82; pres. East Cen. Regional Library Bd., Cedar Rapids, 1981-84; mem. Iowa Library Commn., Des Moines, 1987-90, chmn., 1987-89; bd. dirs. Iowa Cultural Affairs Adv. Coun., Des Moines, 1987-89; trustee Linn County Hist. Mus., 1990—, pres., 1995-96; trustee Brucemore, 1983-89 mem. Johnson County Hist. Preservation Commn., 2003. Fellow AIA (Iowa medal of Honor 1996, pres. Iowa chpt. 1965-66); mem. ALA, Nat. Coun. Archtl. Registration Bds. (bd. dirs. 1975-77), Literary Club (sec. 1980-86, pres. 1987-88). Avocations: sailing, swimming. Home: 3717 Cottage Reserve Rd NE Solon IA 52333

HEALEY, FRANK HENRY, retired research executive; b. Worcester, Mass., Oct. 5, 1924; s. Frank H. and Elizabeth (MacGillivray) H.; m. Loretta Marguerite Finnigan, June 5, 1948; children: Steven Allan, Elaine Elizabeth, Frank Henry. AB, Clark U., 1947, PhD, 1949. Asst. prof. chemistry Lehigh U., Bethlehem, Pa., 1949-56; with Lever Bros. Co., Edgewater, N.J., 1956-88, v.p. research and devel., 1964-73, research v.p., 1973-78, v.p. research and engring., 1978-80, research v.p., dir., 1968-88; pres. Lever Research Inc., Edgewater, 1982-88. Served to lt. (j.g.) USN, 1943-46. Mem. Indsl. Rsch. Inst. (pres. 1977-78, bd. dirs. 1972-79), Assn. Rsch. Dirs., Am. Chem. Soc., Dirs. Indsl. Rsch., Am. Oil Chemists Soc., Soap and Detergent Assn. (steering com. tech. and materials divsn.), Ridgewood Country Club (sec. 1981-82, bd. dirs. 1990-94), Hobbyists Unlimited (v.p. 1994-95, pres. 1996). Home: 255 W Ridgewood Ave Ridgewood NJ 07450-3629

HEALEY, JOHN JOSEPH, engineering executive, civil engineer; b. Jersey City, N.J., Feb. 5, 1941; s. William T. and Ellen Therese Healey; m. Dorothy Anne Graebe, Oct. 26, 1963; children: William, Mary, Sean, Mark. BCE, Manhattan Coll., 1962; MS, U. Ill., 1963; PhD, Rutgers U., 1970. Profl. engr., N.Y., N.J. Rsch. engr. David Taylor Model Basin, Carderock, Md., 1963—65; lectr. Richmond Coll., Staten Island, NY, 1968—69, CUNY, Staten Island, 1968—69; sr. rsch. engr. Am. Iron & Steel Inst., N.Y.C., 1969—71; assoc. Ammann & Whitney, N.Y.C., 1971—78; sr. cons. Ebasco Svcs. Inc., N.Y.C., 1978—85; pres. Ebasco Infrastructure Divsn., N.Y.C., 1985—93; pres., CEO Raytheon Infrastructure Svcs., N.Y.C., 1993—95; chmn., pres., CEO Greenhorne & O'Mara, Inc., Greenbelt, Md., 1995—. Contbr. articles. Mem.: ASCE, Cons. Engrs. Coun., Design Profls. Coalition, Soc. Am. Mil. Engrs., Constrn. Industry Roundtable. Independent. Roman Catholic. Avocations: boating, golf. Home: 1400 Oyster Cove Dr Grasonville MD 21638 Office: Greenhorne & O'Mara Inc 9001 Edmonston Rd Greenbelt MD 20770 Office Fax: 301-220-2483. E-mail: Jhealey@G-and-O.com.

HEALEY, KERRY MURPHY, lieutenant governor; b. Omaha, Apr. 30, 1960; d. Edward Morris and Shirley (Cumming) M.; m. Sean Michael Healey, Dec. 28, 1985; children: Alexander Edward, Averill Adair. AB in Govt., Harvard Coll., 1982; PhD in Law and Polit. Sci., Trinity Coll., Dublin, Ireland, 1991. Proctor freshman dean's office, vis. reseacher Law Sch. Harvard U., Cambridge, Mass., 1985—86; legal policy analyst ABT Assocs., Inc., Cambridge, 1986—87; pub. policy cons. Bklyn. and Boston, 1990—99; mem. Mass. Rep. State Com., 1999—; chmn. Mass. Republican Party, 2001—02; lt. gov. State of Mass., 2003—. Del. UN NGO assembly, 1994-95. Author: State and Local Experience with Drug Paraphernalia Laws, 1987, Victim and Witness Intimidation: New Developments and Emerging Responses, 1995; co-author: Compendium of Federal Justice Statistics, 1989, Handbook of Drug Control in the United States, 1990, Prosecutorial Response to Heavy Drug Case Loads, 1993. Bd. dirs., Mass. Women's Polit. Caucus, 1999-2001; bd. dirs., North Shore C.C. Found., Danvers, Mass., 1999-2002, Friends of Beverly (Mass.) Hosp., 1999-2001; co-chair North Shore United Way Campaign, Beverly, 2001, bd. dirs. YWCA, N.Y.C., 1992-95, mem. YWCA World Svc. Coun., 1992—. Grad. fellow Rotary Internat., 1983-84; rsch. grantee Mark DeWolfe Howe Fund of Harvard Law Sch., 1986. Mem. Harvard Club N.Y.C. (mem. schs. com. 1987-95), N.Y. Jr. League (rep. N.Y.C. ednl. priorities panel 1992-95), Cosmopolitan Club (N.Y.C.), Union Club (Boston). Office: State House Office of the Governor Room 360 Boston MA 02133

HEALEY, LYNNE KOVER, editor, writer, broadcaster, educator; b. L.I., N.Y. d. R. Bascom and M Fuchs, div.; children: Christine Josepha, Lauren Teresa. BA in Comm., Rutgers U., 1983; MA in English, Drew U., 1987. Editor A.M. Best Co., Oldwick, N.J., 1985-91; communications cons. MetLife Ins. Co., 1992—2002; freelance writer, editor, 2002—. Adj. prof. English Middlesex County Coll., Edison, NJ, DeVry U., North Brunswick, NJ, Raritan Valley C. C., No. Branch, NJ. Bd. dirs. Women's Crisis Svcs. Mem. Meeting Planners Internat. (bd. dirs. N.J. chpt., co-chairperson com. for Give Kids the World project), Rutgers U. Alumni Assn. (exec. com.), Alpha Sigma Lambda (grad. sch. scholar 1986, bd. dirs. Rutgers chpt.). Avocations: photography, golf, dancing, swimming, skiing.

HEALEY, ROBERT WILLIAM, school system administrator; b. Charleston, Ill., Sept. 29, 1947; s. William Albert and Ruth M. (Wiedenhoeft) H.; m. Sharon Barbara Grande, Aug. 7, 1982; children: William Robert, Steven Anthony. BS in Elem. Edn., Ea. Ill. U., 1970, MS in Ednl. Adminstrn., 1972; EdD in Curriculum and Supervision, No. Ill. U., 1977. Cert. elem. teaching K-9, gen. adminstrv. K-12, Ill. Prin. Glidden Elem. Sch., De Kalb, Ill., 1972-74, Lincoln Elem. Sch., De Kalb, 1974-83, Littlejohn Elem. Sch., De Kalb, 1983-84, Littlejohn and Cortland Elem. Schs., De Kalb, 1984-85; prin., dist. coord. testing and evaluation Jefferson Elem. Sch., De Kalb, 1986-96; dir. personnel DeKalb Sch. Dist., 1996—98, dir. HR, 1999—2001, asst. to supt., 2001—03; interim prin. Brooks Elem. Sch., DeKalb, 2002. Dir. Title I Elem. and Secondary Edn. Act., Pre-Sch. Base Line Program, 1972-74; dir. gifted edn. Bd. Edn. Negotiating Team, 1974-81, coordinator dist. testing and evaluation, 1981-84, coordinator spl. edn., 1984-86; mem. adv. bd. Evanston (Ill.) Educators Computer Software, 1983—; dir. testing DeKalb Sch. Dist. 428, 1986—; treas. No. Ill. Commn. for Gifted Edn., Oakbrook, 1980-82; mem. various elem. sch. planning and program councils, De Kalb, 1973-2003; coordinator numerous sch. programs, De Kalb, 1973-2003; leader numerous workshops DeKalb, 1976-85; sec. De Kalb Sch. Bd. Study com. on sch. lunch programs, 1976-77; cons. Scholastic Testing Service, 1980-83; chmn. dist. reading com., De Kalb, 1986—; mem. bd. edn. collective bargaining team, 2001—. Coordinator 10 yr. study of student achievement in DeKalb Schs., 1980-83; author numerous presentations, 1975-84; co-author: DeKalb School District Parent Handbook, 1986; contbr. articles to profl. jours; inventor multi-purpose table and stage. Chmn. Task Force I DeKalb Sch. Dist., 1973-75; treas. No. Ill. Planning Commn., 1980-82; active Supts. Task Force on Spl. Edn., DeKalb, 1976-79, Mayor's Commn. DeKalb Planning Commn. for Yr. of Child, DeKalb, 1979, Dist. Computer Com., DeKalb, 1980-83, Dist. Revenue and Donations Com., 1980-83, Ill. PTA. Recipient Disting. Program award Nat. Assn. for Tchr. Educators, Chgo., 1978; named Citizen of Day, Sta. WLBK, De Kalb, 1983; Reading is Fundamental grantee Lincoln Sch., 1980-83, Ill. Ctr., 1980-83, Ill. Arts Coun., Littlejohn Sch., 1984, Jefferson Sch., 1986; named master, Ill. Adminstrs. Acad., 1995. Mem. NEA (life), ASCD, NAESP (Nat. Disting. Prin. award representing Ill. 1995), Ill. Prins. Assn. (Prin. of Yr. award 1995, Herman Graves award 1998), Ill. Assn. for Supervsion and Curriculum Devel., Soc. Am. Inventors, Ill. Coun. Gifted Edn. Avocations: swimming, computer, home. Office: De Kalb Cmty Unit Sch Dist 901 S 4th St Dekalb IL 60115-4411

HEALEY, THOMAS J. former government official, brokerage house executive; b. Balt., Sept. 14, 1942; m. Margaret Sachs Healey; children— Megan, Jeremiah AB, Georgetown U., 1964; MBA, Harvard U., 1966. Chartered fin. analyst, real estate counselor. Mgr. project fin. group Dean Witter, 1975-82; mng. dir., mgr. corp. fin. Dean Witter Reynolds Capital Markets, 1982-83; asst. sec. domestic fin. Dept. of Treasury, Washington, 1983-85; v.p. real estate Goldman Sachs & Co, N.Y.C., 1985-88, mng. dir. pension svcs. group, 1988-99, mng. dir. instl. sales and mktg., 1999-2000, adv. dir., 2001—. Fellow, adj. lectr. John F. Kennedy Sch. Govt. Harvard U., 2001—. Home: Van Bureun Rd New Vernon NJ 07976 Office: Goldman Sachs & Co 32 Old Slip Fl 18 New York NY 10005-3504 also: 85 Broad St New York NY 10004 E-mail: tom.healey@gs.com.

HEALY, ALICE FENVESSY, psychology educator, researcher; b. Chgo., June 26, 1946; d. Stanley John and Doris (Goodman) Fenvessy; m. James Bruce Healy, May 9, 1970; 1 child, Charlotte Alexandra. AB summa cum laude, Vassar Coll., 1968; PhD, Rockefeller U., 1973. Asst. prof. psychology Yale U., New Haven, 1973-78, assoc. prof. psychology, 1978-81, U. Colo., Boulder, 1981-84, prof. psychology, 1984—. Rsch. assoc. Haskins Labs., New Haven, 1976—80; com. mem. NIMH, Washington, 1979—81; co-investigator rsch. contract USAF U. Colo., 1985—86, prin. investigator rsch. contract U.S. Army Rsch. Inst., 1986—; prin. investigator rsch. contract Naval Tng. Sys. Ctr., 1993—94; rsch. grant prin. investigator U.S. Army Rsch. Office U. Colo., 1995—2002; rsch. grant prin. investigator NASA, 1999—. Co-author: Cognitive Processes, 2d edit., 1986; editor: Memory and Cognition, 1986—89; co-editor (with S. M. Kosslyn and R. M. Shiffrin): (Essays in Honor of William K. Estes) From Learning Processes to Cognitive Processes Vol I, 1992; co-editor: (with S.M. Kosslyn and R.M. Shiffrin) From Learning Theory to Connectionist Theory: Essays in Honor of William K. Estes, Vol. II, 1992; co-editor: (with L.E. Bourne Jr.) Learning and Memory of Knowledge and Skills: Durability and Specificity, 1995, Foreign Language Learning: Psycholinguistic Studies on Training and Retention, 1998; editor: Jour. Exptl. Psychology, 1982—84; co-editor (with R. W. Proctor): Experimental Psychology, 2003; contbr., articles to profl. jours. and chpts. to books. Recipient Sabbatical award, James McKeen Cattell Fund, 1987—88; grantee, NSF, 1977—86, 2003—, Spencer Found. Rsch. grant, 1978—80. Fellow: AAAS (nominating com. 1988—91, chair nominating com. 1991, chair-elect psychology sect. 1994, chair psychology sect. 1995—96, retiring chair psychology sect. 1996—97), APA (exec. com. divsn. 3 1989—92, chair membership com. 1992—93, exec. com. divsn. 3 2001—), Soc. Exptl. Psychologists (pres.-elect 2003—); mem.: Soc. for Applied Rsch. in Memory and Cognition, Cognitive Sci. Soc., Rocky Mountain Psychology Assn. (pres.-elect 1993—94, pres. 1994—95, past pres. 1995—96), Soc. Math. Psychology, Psychonomic Soc. (governing bd. 1987—92, publs. com. 1989—93), Univ.

Club, Sigma Xi, Phi Beta Kappa. Avocation: French pastries. Home: 840 Cypress Dr Boulder CO 80303-2820 Office: U Colo Dept Psychology PO Box 345 UCB Boulder CO 80309-0345 E-mail: ahealy@psych.colorado.edu.

HEALY, BERNADINE P. physician, educator, federal agency administrator, organization executive; b. N.Y.C., Aug. 2, 1944; d. Michael J. and Violet (McGrath) Healy; m. Floyd Loop, Aug. 17, 1985; children: Bartlett Anne Bulkley, Marie McGrath Loop. AB summa cum laude, Vassar Coll., 1965; MD cum laude, Harvard Med. Sch., 1970. Diplomate Am. Bd. Med. Examiners, Am. Bd. Cardiology, Am. Bd. Internal Medicine, lic. physician Md., Ohio. Intern in medicine Johns Hopkins Hosp., Balt., 1970—71, asst. resident, 1971—72; staff fellow sect. pathology Nat. Heart, Blood & Lung Inst., NIH, Bethesda, Md., 1972—74; fellow cardiovascular div. dept. medicine Johns Hopkins U. Sch. Medicine, Balt., 1974—76, fellow dept. pathology, 1975—76, asst. prof. medicine and pathology, 1976—81, assoc. prof. medicine, 1977—82, asst. dean postdoctoral programs and faculty devel., 1979—84, assoc. prof. pathology, 1981—84, prof. medicine, 1982—84, dean Coll. Med. and Pub. Health, 1995—, prof. internal medicine, physiology, 1995—; active staff medicine and pathology Johns Hopkins Hosp., 1976—, dir. CCU, 1976—84; pres. ARC, 1999—2001; advisor on weapons of mass destruction & bioterrorism White House, DC, 2001—. Dep. dir. Office Sci. and Tech. Policy Exec. Office of Pres., White House, Washington, 1984—85; chmn. Rsch. Inst. The Cleve. Clinic Found., 1985—91, sr. health and sci. policy advisor, 1994—95; dean Med. Sch. Ohio State U., 1995—97; dir. NIH, Bethesda, Md., 1991—93; vice-chmn. Pres.' Coun. Advisers on Sci. and Tech., 1990—91; mem. Spl. Med. Adv. Group, Dept. Vet.'s Affairs, 1990—91, chmn. adv. panel for Basic Rsch. for 1990s, Office Tech. Assessment, 1990—91, mem. NHLBI Task Force on Atherosclerosis, 1990; mem. Vis. Com. Bd. Overseers Harvard Med. Sch. and Sch. of Dental Medicine, Boston, 1986—91; councillor Harvard Med. Alumni Assn., 1987—90; mem. Nat. Adv. Bd. Johns Hopkins Ctr. for Hosp. Fin. and Mgmt., 1987—91, Bd. Overseers Harvard Coll., 1989—; chmn. Office of Tech. Assessment Panel New Devels. in Biotech., U.S. Congress, 1986—87; mem. U.S.-Brazil Panel on Sci. and Tech., 1987; mem. White House Sci. Coun., 1988—89; cons. Nat. Heart, Lung and Blood Inst., NIH, 1976—91; mem. adv. com. to dir. NIH, 1986—91; chmn. steering com. Post-CABG Clin. Triai, 1987—91; bd. dirs. Medtronic, INc., Mpls., Nat. City Corp., Cleve., Nova Pharms., Balt.; mem. adv. bd. Bayer Fund for Cardiovasc. Rsch., N.Y.C., 1987—89; trustee Edison BioTech. Ctr., Cleve., 1990—; chmn. Ohio Coun. on Rsch. and Econ. Devel., 1989—91. Editl. cons. numerous jours.:, abstract reviewer:, editl. bd.: Jour. Cardiovasc. Medicine, 1980—91, Am. Jour. Cardiology, 1981—82, Circulation, 1981—, Jour. Am. Coll. Cardiology, 1982—84, Am. Jour. Medicine, 1986—91; contbr. articles to profl. jours. Recipient Nat. Bd. Ann. award for Medicine, Med. Coll. Pa., 1983; fellow Eloise Ellery fellow, 1965—66, Stetler Rsch. fellow, 1976—77; scholar Matthew Vassar scholar, 1962—65, Harvard Nat. scholar, 1965—70. Mem.: ACP, Inst. Medicine NAS, Am. Bd. Internatl Medicine (bd. dirs. 1983—87, bd. govs. 1986—), Am. Soc. Clin. Investigation, Assn. for Women in Sci., Am. Med. Women's Assn., Internat. Acad. Pathology, Assn. Am. Med. Colls., Am. Coll. Cardiology (bd. govs. 1979—82), Am. Heart Assn. (fellow coun. on clin. cardiology, coun. on circulation, dir. 1983—84, pres. 1988—89, award 1983—84, 1990), Am. Fedn. Clin. Rsch. (pres. 1983—84), Johns Hopkins U. Soc. Scholars, Alpha Omega Alpha, Phi Beta Kappa.

HEALY, CLETUS S. J. priest; b. Newton, Iowa, Oct. 26, 1917; s. John and Anna (Dwyer) H. AB, St. Louis U., 1942, lic. in philosophy, 1945; lic. in theology, St. Mary's, Kans., 1951. Tchr. Marquette Univ. H.S., Milw., 1953-68; journalist Twin Cir., Milw., 1968-74; tel. sales Cath. Sales, Milw., 1974-81; mgr. Cath. Books & Gifts, Milw., 1981—. Editor, pub.: Christian Social Principles - Communism, 1957; columnist Vatican Voices, 1974-79; editor Vatican Voices, 1979-2002. Home: 10100 W Bluemound Rd Wauwatosa WI 53226 Office: Cath Books and Gifts 7346 W Greenfield Ave Milwaukee WI 53214

HEALY, DANIEL THOMAS, secondary education educator; b. Wenona, Ill., May 25, 1930; s. Timothy John and Helen Ann (Duller) H.; m. Beverly Ann Imm, Oct. 1, 1966; 1 child, Owen Jay. AA, Fresno (Calif.) City Coll., 1972; BS, Calif. State U., Fresno, 1974; MA, Azusa (Calif.) Pacific U., 1980. Farmer, Wenona, 1948—58; mgr. Garfield Grain Elevator, Wenona, 1958—66; supt. Cargill Inc., San Joaquin, Calif., 1966—69; educator Redlands (Calif.) Unified Sch. Dist., 1974—92, Orangewood H.S., Redlands, 1992—. Advisor Future Farmers of Am., Redlands High Sch., 1974-88; leader Osage Livewires 4-H Club, Wenona, 1950-55. Performer on nat. TV, movies including Hero and Hot Shots II, appearances as Pres. Bush celebrity look-alike, 1990—. Sgt. U.S. Army, 1953-54. Fellow Am. Legion (life mem.), Elks (life). Roman Catholic. Office: Orangewood High Sch 515 Texas St Redlands CA 92374-3071

HEALY, GEORGE WILLIAM, III, lawyer, mediator; b. New Orleans, Mar. 8, 1930; s. George William and Margaret Alford H.; m. Sharon Saunders, Oct. 26, 1974; children: George W. IV, John Carmichael, Floyd Alford, Hyde Dunbar, Mary Margaret. BA, Tulane U., 1950, JD, 1955. Bar: La. 1955, U.S. Supreme Ct. 1969. Assoc. Phelps, Dunbar, Marks, Claverie & Sims, New Orleans, 1955-58; ptnr. Phelps Dunbar LLP, 1958-95; of counsel Phelps Dunbar, 1996—. Mem. U.S. del. Comité Maritime Internat., Tokyo, 1969, Lisbon, 1985, Paris, 1990, Sydney, 1994, titulary mem. Mem. planning com. Tulane U. Admiralty Law Inst., dir. World Trade Ctr., 1993—; dir. New Orleans Pro Bono Project, 1995-97, La. Orgn. for Jud. Excellence, 1997—. Fellow Am. Bar Found., Am. Coll. Trial Lawyers, Maritime Law Assn. U.S. (mem. exec. com. 1984-87, 2d v.p. 1988-90, 1st v.p. 1990-92, pres. 1992-94), La. Bar Found.; mem. ABA (ho. dels. 1993-95, 97-2000), New Orleans Bar Assn. (pres. 1992), Def. Rsch. Inst., La. Assn. Def. Counsel, New Orleans Assn. Def. Counsel, Com. Maritime Internat. Am. Found. (dir. 1990—), New Orleans Bar Assn. Inn of Ct. (master), Boston Club., La. Club, Stratford Club, Plimsoll Club, Recess Club (pres. 1978), Pinfeathers Hunting Club, New Orleans Lawn Tennis Club, Propeller Club, Mariners Club. Republican. Episcopalian. Home: 6020 Camp St New Orleans LA 70118-5902 Office: Canal Place 365 Canal St Ste 2000 New Orleans LA 70130-6534 Fax: 504-568-9130. E-mail: healyg@phelps.com.

HEALY, GERALD BURKE, otolaryngologist; b. Boston, Mar. 31, 1942; s. Gerald E. and Margaret C. (Burke) H.; m. Anne Herron, June 3, 1991; children: Elisabeth, Laurie. AB cum laude, Boston Coll., 1963; MD, Boston U., 1967; MBA (hon.), Harvard U., 1990. Diplomate Am. Bd. Otolaryngology, Am. Bd. Laser Surgery, Nat. Bd. Med. Examiners; lic. physician, Mass., Pa. Surg. intern Univ. Hosp., Boston, 1967-68, resident in surgery, 1968-69, resident in otolaryngology, 1969-72; instr. otolaryngology Boston U. Sch. Medicine, 1974-75, asst. prof., 1975-77, assoc. prof., 1977-83, prof., 1983—; assoc. dir. otolaryngology Boston VA Hosp., 1975-76; assoc. otolaryngologist-in-chief The Children's Hosp., Boston, 1976-79, otolaryngologist-in-chief, 1979—; exec. v.p. Am. Bd. of Otolaryngology, Houston. Instr. otolaryngology Tufts U. Sch. Medicine, 1975-88; assoc. prof. otolaryngology Harvard Med. Sch., 1979-88, prof. otology and laryngology, 1988—; chief otolaryngology Valley Forge Army Med. Ctr., Phoenixville, Pa., 1972-73, William Beaumont Army Med. Ctr., El Paso, 1973-74; assoc. dir. otolaryngology Boston City Hosp., 1975-76; bd. dirs. Am. Bd. Otolaryngology, 1986—; mem. com. on certification Am. Bd. Med. Specialistis, 1988—. Reviewer Jour. Pediatrics, 1976—, Pediatrics, 1977—, New Eng. Jour. Medicine, 1979—, Annals of Otology, Rhinology and Laryngology, 1982-88, The Laryngoscope, 1986-88; mem. editorial bd. Internat. Jour. Pediatric Otolaryngology, 1979—, The Laryngoscope, 1988—, Annals of Otology, Rhinology and Laryngology, 1988—. Maj. U.S. Army, 1972-74. Fellow ACS, Am. Coll. Chest Physicians, Am. Acad. Pediatrics; mem. Am. Bd. Emergency Medicine (bd. dirs. 1988—), Am. Soc. Pediatric Otolaryn. (pres. 1987), Am. Laryngol. Assn. (exec. coun. 1985—), Am. Broncho-Esophagological Assn. (exec. coun. 1983—, pres. 1990-91), Am. Acad. Otolaryngology-Head and Neck Surgery (chmn. outcomes com. 1991), Am. Acad. Facial Plastic and Reconstructive Surgery, Soc. Univ. Otolargyngologists, Mass. Med. Soc., New Eng. Otolaryn. Soc., Pediatric Otolaryn. Study Group. Office: Childrens Hosp 300 Longwood Ave Boston MA 02115-5737

HEALY, JAMES CASEY, lawyer; b. Washington, Feb. 19, 1956; s. Joseph Francis Jr. and Patricia Ann (Casey) H.; m. Kelly Anne Quinn, Nov. 4, 1995; 1 child, Caitlin Quinn. BS, Spring Hill Coll., 1978; JD, Emory U., 1982. Bar: Ga. 1983, Conn. 1983, U.S. Dist. Ct. Conn. 1984, U.S. Tax Ct. 1984, U.S. Supreme Ct. 1987. Assoc. Gregory and Adams PC, Wilton, Conn., 1982-87, ptnr., 1988-89, mng. ptnr., 1990-94, v.p., 1995—. Spl. counsel Wilton Police Commn., 1986-98; mem. Parks and Recreation Commn., 1991-2002, sec., 1991-93, 2002-, chmn., 1997-2002; corporator Ridgefield Bank, 1997—; sec. Fire Commn., 2002—. Bd. dirs. Mark Lavin Meml. Offshore Med. and Safety Found., Empire, Mich., 1987—97; bd. dirs. Village Market, Inc., 1988—90; chmn. leadership giving program United Way, 1991; bd. mgrs. Wilton Children's Ctr., 1996—98; athletic fields subcom.of building com. Wilton H.S., 1998—99; steering com. Wilton Family Recreation and Activity Ctr., 2000; bd. trustees Wilton Hist. Soc., 2001—; bd. dirs. Wilton Teen Ctr., 2001—. Mem. State Bar Ga., State Bar Conn. (exec. com., planning and zoning sect. 1992-94, 98—), Am. Planning Assn., Stamford/Norwalk Regional Bar Assn. (law office mgmt. com. 1994-96, co-chmn. land use com. 1996—, real estate broker's contract com. 1997-98), Real Estate Fin. Assn., Wilton C. of C. (bd. dirs. 1994-96). Republican. Roman Catholic. Office: Gregory and Adams 190 Old Ridgefield Rd Wilton CT 06897-4023 E-mail: jhealy@gregoryandadams.com.

HEALY, JANE ELIZABETH, newspaper editor; b. Washington, May 9, 1949; d. Paul Francis and Connie (Maas) H.; children: Randall, Kevin. BS, U. Md., 1971. Copy clk. N.Y. Daily News, Washington, 1971-73; met. reporter Orlando (Fla.) Sentinel, 1973-81, editorial writer, 1981-83, chief editorial writer, 1983-85, assoc. editor, 1985-92, mng. editor, 1993—2001, editl. page editor, 2001—. Recipient Pulitzer Prize, Columbia U., 1988, Sigma Delta Chi Disting. Service award, 1988. Mem. Am. Soc. Newspaper Editors. Office: Orlando Sentinel 633 N Orange Ave Orlando FL 32801-1349

HEALY, JOANNE P. accounting educator; b. Corning, N.Y., Sept. 8, 1949; d. Clayton Arthur and Beverly Jean Palmer; m. Darwin G. Burress; children: Samuel A., Clayton J., Joseph A. BA in Math., SUNY, Geneseo, 1971; PhD, SUNY, Buffalo, 1994; MBA, Rochester Inst. Tech., 1980. CPA, Colo.; CMA; CFP. Payroll supr. Voplex Corp., Pittsford, N.Y., 1972-74; acct. Davenport Machine Tool divsn. Dover Corp., Rochester, N.Y., 1974-78; staff acct. Bonadio, Insero & Co., Rochester, 1979-80; asst. prof. SUNY, Geneseo, 1982-87, 91-93, tchg. asst. Buffalo, 1987-91; assoc. prof. Kent (Ohio) State U., 1993—. Contbr. articles to profl. jours. Mem. AICPA, Am. Acctg. Assn., Inst. Mgmt. Accts. (dir. manuscripts 1984-85, 94-98, v.p. adminstrn. and fin. 1996-98), Ohio Soc. CPAs. Avocations: sewing, fishing. Office: 18236 Alois Ln Lake Milton OH 44429 E-mail: jhealy@bsa3.kent.edu.

HEALY, JOHN JOSEPH, financial analyst, economist; b. Long Island City, N.Y., Jan. 24, 1945; s. John Joseph and Margaret Esther (Kelly) Healy. BA, St. John's U., 1966, MBA in Econs., 1968. Market rsch. analyst Sinclair Oil Corp., N.Y.C., 1968—69; econ. analyst GM Corp., N.Y.C., 1969—75, staff economist, 1975—91, sr. staff economist, 1991—94, sr. fin. analyst, stock transfer liaison, 1994—. Home: 30-12 44th St Long Island City NY 11103-2402 E-mail: john.healy@gm.com.

HEALY, JOSEPH FRANCIS, JR., lawyer, retired air transportation executive; b. NYC, Aug. 11, 1930; s. Joseph Francis and Agnes (Kett) H.; m. Patricia A. Casey, Apr. 23, 1955; children: James C., Timothy, Kevin, Cathleen M., Mary, Terence. BS, Fordham U., 1952; JD, Georgetown U., 1959. Bar: D.C. 1959. With gen. traffic dept. Eastman-Kodak Co., Rochester, N.Y., 1954-55; air transp. examiner CAB, Washington, 1955-59; practiced in Washington, 1959-70, 80-81; asst. gen. counsel Air Transport Assn. Am., 1966-70; v.p. legal Eastern Air Lines, Inc., N.Y.C. and Miami, Fla., 1970-80; ptnr. Ford, Farquhar, Kornblut & O'Neill, Washington, 1980-81; v.p. legal affairs Piedmont Aviation, Inc., Winston Salem, N.C., 1981-84, sr. v.p., gen counsel, 1984-89, ret., 1989; sr. v.p., gen. counsel Trans World Airlines Inc., Mt. Kisco, N.Y., 1993-94. Mem. bd. visitors Sch. Law Wake Forest U., 1988-96. 1st lt. USAF, 1952-54. Mem.: Nat. Aero. Assn., Internat. Aviation Club (Washington), Phi Delta Phi, Beta Gamma Sigma. Home: 104 Overlink Ct Lynchburg VA 24503-3200

HEALY, JOSEPH ROBERT, lawyer; b. Troy, N.Y., Apr. 15, 1939; s. Thomas Francis and Isabel Kathryn (Eagle) H.; m. Sylvia Anne Tuccillo, May 14, 1976; 1 child, Daniel Joseph. BA in Sociology, Siena Coll., 1961; JD, Albany Law Sch., 1965. Bar: N.Y. 1973, U.S. Dist. Ct. (no. dist.) N.Y. 1973. Claims examiner Social Security Adminstrn., Glens Falls, N.Y., 1961-62; personnel examiner N.Y. State Dept. Civil Svc., Albany, 1962-69, sr. legal examiner, 1969-71, atty., 1971-75, sr. atty., 1975-82; assoc. atty., 1982-87; dir. civil svc. security ops., 1987-88; adminstrv. counsel internal controls, 1988-92; dir. investigations, 1992—. Author newsletter N.Y. State Orgn. Mgmt. Condifential Employees News Network. Active Woodland Hills Homeowners Assn., Clifton Park, N.Y. Republican. Roman Catholic. Home: 5 George Dr Clifton Park NY 12065-1811 E-mail: JHealy71@Hotmail.com.

HEALY, JUDITH ANN, school social worker; b. Nov. 4, 1942; d. Howard and Elenora (Hutchison) Crothers; children: Eric David (dec.), Mark Daniel. AAS, Moraine Valley Community Coll., Palos Hills, Ill., 1979; BS, Nat. Coll. Edn., 1980; postgrad., George Williams Coll., 1983-86; MSW, Loyola U., Chgo., 1987. Cert. sch. social worker, Ill.; lic. clin. social worker. Counselor Community Resources for Youth, Palos Park, Ill., 1977-79; case mgr., weekend coord. Proviso Assn. for Retarded Citizens, Hillside, Ill., 1979-87; sch. social worker Arbor Park Sch. Dist. 145, Oak Forest, Ill., 1987—; therapist Midwest Resources, 1994—99. Social worker cons. Village Inn, Intermediate Care Facility for Developmentally Disabled Adults, Dixon, Ill., 1987-89. Vol. Cmty. Response, Oak Park, Ill., 1991-96, ARC; case worker Armed Forces Svcs. Great Lakes Naval Base; maj. Civil Air Patrol, aerospace officer, dep. comdr. cadets; youth leader Morgan Park Bapt. Ch., Chgo., 1976-81, Christian edn. chair, 1995—; mem. cabinet Am. Bapt. Chs. Metro Chgo., 2000—. Named Sr. of Yr., Lewis Composite Squadron, 2001. Mem. NASW, Ill. Assn. Sch. Social Workers, Assn. Individual Devel. Home: 8148 W 111th St # 2A Palos Hills IL 60465-3234

HEALY, MARGARET MARY, retail marketing executive; b. Bklyn., Dec. 31, 1938; d. Nicholas Joseph and Margaret Marie (Ferry) H.; m. Robert L. Parker, 1979 (div. 1988); 1 child, Nicole Parker. BA, Manhattanville Coll., 1961; cert., NYU, 1967, Columbia U., 1971. Account exec. Geer, DuBois & Co., Inc., N.Y.C., 1965-71; dir. mktg. comm. Dry Dock Savs. Bank, N.Y.C., 1971-72; oper. v.p. Bloomingdales, N.Y.C., 1972-79; owner, pres. Healy & Pratts, Inc., N.Y.C., 1979-88; mgr. corp. pub. rels. J.C. Penney Co., Dallas, 1988-92; owner, pres. PH Network, Dallas, 1992—; co-owner, mng. dir. Network Assocs. Internat., Dallas, 1997-98. Mem. bd. advisors North Fork Bancorp, Melville, N.Y., 1997-99. Co-author: Salute to Italy Celebrity Cookbook, 1984, Salute to America Celebrity Cookbook, 1986. Bd. dirs. Dallas Children's Theater, 1989—. Recipient Cmty. Svc. award VFW, 1978. Roman Catholic. Avocations: Mexican culture, travel, reading Irish literature. Home and Office: PH Network 132 Tullamore Rd Garden City NY 11530-1139 E-mail: phnetwork@earthlink.net.

HEALY, MARY (MRS. PETER LIND HAYES), singer, actress; b. New Orleans, Apr. 14, 1918; d. John Joseph and Viola (Armbruster) H.; m. Peter Lind Hayes, Dec. 19, 1940 (dec. Apr. 1998); children: Peter Michael, Cathy Lind. Student parochial schs., New Orleans; hon. degree, St. Bonaventure U. With 20th Century Fox, Hollywood, Calif. Author: Twenty-five Minutes from Broadway, 1961; pictures and others, 1937-40; Broadway prodns. Around the World, 1943-46; (with husband) TV series Inside U.S.A, 1949, Peter and Mary Show, Star of the Family, 1952, Peter Lind Hayes Radio show, CBS, 1954-57; Broadway prodn. Who Was That Lady, 1957-58, Peter Lind Hayes show, ABC-TV, 1958-59, Peter and Mary, ABC-Radio, 1959—, Peter and Mary in Las Vegas; TV-film; Star (with husband) WOR radio show, 6 yrs; TV film series Fin. Planning for Women; (with husband) Film The 5000 Fingers of Dr. T, 1953; Appeared in: (with husband) Film Peter Loves Mary, 1960, When Television Was Live, 1975; films: You Ruined My Life, 1986, Looking To Get Out with Jon Voight, 1985. Mem. Pelham Country Club. Roman Catholic. Home: Canyon Gate 8641 Robinson Ridge Dr Las Vegas NV 89117-5807

HEALY, MICHAEL PATRICK, lawyer; b. Sioux Falls, SD, Apr. 27, 1962; s. Patrick Joseph and Carolyn Cathrine (Billion) H.; m. Sarah E. Recker, Dec. 30, 1989 (div. Nov. 19, 1992); m. Sonya R. Dollar, Sept. 27, 1997. Bar: Mo. 1987, Kans. 1989, So. Dakota, 2003, US Dist. Ct. (we. dist.) Mo. 1987, US Ct. Appeals (8th cir.), US Ct. Appeals (10th cir.), US Dist. Ct. Kans. 1989, US Supreme Ct. 1995. Assoc. Stites McIntosh Knepper & Hopkins, Kans. City, Mo., 1987-94; ptnr. McIntosh Knepper Hobson & Healy, Kans. City, Mo., 1994-2000; gen. coun. D.M.I., Inc., Sioux Falls, SD, 1994—; mem. The Healy Law Firm, LLC, 2000—. V.p., gen. counsel J.L. Healy Constrn. Co., Sioux Falls, 1993-95. Mem. Am. Trial Lawyers Assn., Mo. Assn. Trial Lawyers, Mo. Bar Assn. Democrat. Methodist. Office: The Healy Law Firm LLC 1201 Walnut St #2200 Kansas City MO 64106-2506 E-mail: mphealy@sbcglobal.net.

HEALY, NICHOLAS JOSEPH, lawyer, educator; b. N.Y.C., Jan. 4, 1910; s. Nicholas Joseph and Frances Cecilia (McCarthy) H.; m. Margaret Marie Ferry, Mar. 29, 1937; children: Nicholas, Margaret Healy Parker, Rosemary Healy Bell, Mary Louise Healy White, Donall, Kathleen Healy Hamon. AB, Holy Cross Coll., 1931; JD, Harvard U., 1934. Bar: N.Y. 1935, U.S. Supreme Ct. 1949. Pvt. practice, N.Y.C., 1935—42; mem. Healy & Baillie (and predecessor firms), 1948—. Spl. asst. to atty. gen. U.S., 1945-48; tchr. admiralty law NYU Sch. Law, 1947-86, adj. prof., 1960—; Niels F. Johnsen vis. prof. maritime law Tulane Maritime Law Ctr., 1986; vis. prof. maritime law Shanghai Maritime Inst. (now Shanghai Maritime U.), 1981, 86, 88. Contbr. chpts. to Ann. Survey Am. Law, 1948-87; author: (with Sprague) Cases on Admiralty, 1950; (with Currie) Cases and Materials on Admiralty, 1965; (with Sharpe) Cases and Materials on Admiralty, 1974, 3rd edit., 1998; (with Sweeney) The Law of Marine Collision, 1998; editor: Jour. Maritime Law and Commerce, 1980-90, mem. editl. bd., 1969-79, 91—; assoc. editor: American Maritime Cases; mem. scientific bd. Il Dirittimo Marittimo; contbr. to Ency. Brit. Chmn. USCG Adv. Panel on Rules of the Road, 1966-72; mem. permanent adv. bd. Tulane Admiralty Law Inst. Lt. (s.g.) USNR, 1942-45. Fellow Am. Coll. Trial Lawyers; mem. ABA (ho. of dels. 1964-66), N.Y. State Bar Assn., Assn. of Bar of City of N.Y., N.Y. County Lawyers Assn., Maritime Law Assn. U.S. (pres. 1964-66), Assn. Average Adjusters U.S. (chmn. 1959-60), Com. Maritime Internat. (exec. coun. 1972-79, v.p. 1985-91, hon. v.p. 1991—), Ibero-Am. Inst. Maritime Law (hon.). Home: 132 Tullamore Rd Garden City NY 11530-1139 Office: Healy & Baillie 29 Broadway Fl 27 New York NY 10006-3201 Fax: 212-425-0131. E-mail: nhealy@healy.com.

HEALY, PATRICIA COLLEEN, social worker; b. Denver, Aug. 24, 1935; d. Cecil John and Gracia Maude (Walker) Schulte; m. John Patrick Healy III, Aug. 3, 1957 (div. Jan. 1972); 1 child, Sean Patrick. BA, Sacred Heart Coll., Wichita, 1957; MSW, U. Kans., 1983; postgrad., Wichita State U., 1974, 75, 89, Emporia (Kans.) State U., 1990, U. Kans., 1998. Lic. specialist clin. social worker, Kans.; cert. in spinal cord injury medicine. Proofreader Wichita Pub. Co., 1953; clk. typist Nat. Sales, Inc., Wichita, 1954-58, Dept. of Army, Ft. Leavenworth, Kans., 1958-60, Air Force, McConnell AFB, Kans., 1962-63; clk., typist VA Regional Office, Wichita, 1963-66; self-employed typist Wichita, 1966-70; ward clk., typist VA Regional Office and VA Med. Ctr., Wichita, 1970-73; vets. benefits counselor VARO, Wichita, 1973-83; social worker VA Med. Ctr., Wichita, 1983-2000; ret.; pvt. practice, 2000—. Author filmstrip, columns, book revs., feature stories and poetry. Former mem. Ctrl. Plains AAA Coun. on Aging; bd. dirs. Ind. Living Ctr. South Ctrl. Kans., 1990-96, Sedgwick Co. Dept. Aging Cmty. Svc. Adv. Bd.; mem. Clin. Social Work Fedn., 2003; vol. Sr. Svcs. Mem.: Kans. Authors Club. Roman Catholic. Avocations: writing, reading, photography, music, knitting and sewing.

HEALY, PATRICK JAMES, civil engineer; b. Clinton, Mass., Aug. 20, 1965; s. James P. and Florence I. (Radock) H.; m. Rebecca E. Dono, Aug. 31, 1996. AS in Arch., Wentworth Inst. Tech., 1985, BS in Civil Engring., 1987. Registered profl. engr., Mass.; cert. profl. in erosion aad sediment control. Staff engr. Thompson-Liston Assocs., Inc., Boylston, Mass., 1987-89, project mgr., 1990-96, sr. project mgr., 1996—. Bd. dirs. MALSCE, Inc. Mem. properties com. YMCA Greater Worcester, Mass., 1992—; bd. dirs. Hillside Restoration Project; selectman Town of Boylston, 1993-2002. Recipient Young Alumni award Wentworth Alumni Assn., Inc., Boston, 1997. Mem. ASCE, Mass. Assn. Land Surveyors and Civil Engrs. (chpt. pres. 1998-99), Boston Soc. Civil Engrs., Wentworth Alumni Assn. (bd. dirs. 1992-96), KC. Republican. Roman Catholic. Avocations: skiing, travel. Home: PO Box 693 Boylston MA 01505-0693 Office: Thompson-Liston Assocs Inc PO Box 570 51 Main St Boylston MA 01505-1950 E-mail: civil.engineer@juno.com.

HEALY, STEVEN MICHAEL, accountant, city official; b. Chgo., July 20, 1949; s. Daniel Francis and Angelina (Massino) H. BA, U. Ill., Chgo., 1971; MBA, Dominican U., 1984. Br. mgr. Assocs. Capital Co., Chgo., 1971-74; credit analyst Motorola, Inc., Schaumburg, Ill., 1974-76; office mgr. Triple "S" Steel Corp., Franklin Park, Ill., 1976-79; accounts payable supr. Zenith Electronics, Chgo., 1979-84; supr. acctg. Village of Oak Park, Ill., 1984-86; bus. analyst Cablevision of Chgo., Oak Park, 1986-87; dir. fin. Village of Maywood, Ill., 1988-91; dir. fin., treas. City of DeKalb, Ill., 1991-93; dir. fin. Village of Cahokia, Ill., 1993—. Mem. Friends of Oak Park Libr., Friends of the Conservatory, Oak Park Village Players Group, Cahokia Econ. Devel. Commn.; bd. dirs. Oak Park Employees Credit Union; treas. Cahokia Assn. for the Tricentennial; pres. sch. bd. Cahokia Unit Sch. Dist. 187; bd. dirs. Cahokia C. of C., 2000—. Mem.: Ill. Govt. Fin. Officers Assn., Nat. Govt. Fin. Officers Assn., Dominican U. MBA Alumni Assn. (founder, soc. com. 1984—), U. Ill. Alumni Assn., Village Oak Park Chess Club, Cath. Alumni Club, Kiwanis (Cahokia club), Kishwaukee Sunrise Rotary, Maywood Rotary, Rotary Club of St. Clair Valley (chair, sec.), Oak Park Area Jaycees. Avocations: participation sports, reading, travel, writing, chess. Home: 2013 Oak Tree Ln Cahokia IL 62206-1408 Office: 103 Main St Cahokia IL 62206-1019

HEALY, THERESA ANN, former ambassador; b. Bklyn., July 14, 1932; d. Anthony and Mary Catherine (Kennedy) H. BA, St. John's U., 1954, LLD (hon.), 1985. Tchr. elem. and secondary schs., N.Y.C., 1951-55; with U.S. Fgn. Svc., 1955-94, amb. to Sierra Leone, 1980-83; with Ctr. for Internat. Affairs, U. South Fla., Tampa, 1983-84; faculty Nat. Def. U., Washington, 1984-86; with pers. and mgmt. policy bur. U.S. Dept. State, 1986-92; with Office of Freedom of Info., 1992-94; ret., 1994. Cons. Dept. State, 1996—, Office of Freedom Info., 1997—; arbitrator NASD-Dispute Resolution, 1999—. Mem. Am. Fgn. Svc. Assn., Diplomatic and Consular Officers Ret. Roman Catholic. Home: 6800 Fleetwood Rd Apt 1002 Mc Lean VA 22101-3610 E-mail: healyta@aol.com.

HEANEY, ANTHONY PATRICK, research scientist; b. Omagh, Ireland, June 13, 1963; s. Patrick John Heaney and Catherine Coyle; m. Brigid Connolly, July 0, 1994; children: Thomas, Cormac, Blathnaid. BSc, Queens U., 1980—87; MD, Queen's U., 1980—87, PhD, 1992—95. Diplomate Royal Coll. of Physicians, 1991, Diplomate of Specialist training European Med. Colleges, 1995. Hon. lectr. Manchester U., Manchester, England, 1995—97; asst. prof. of medicine David Geffen Sch. of Medicine at UCLA, Los Angeles; med. dir., neuroendocrine tumor ctr. Cedars-Sinai Med. Ctr., Los Angeles, 2002—. Contbr. articles to profl. jours. Med. advisor So. Calif. Carcinoid Fighters Orgn. Recipient Fulbright scholarship, Fulbright Commn., 1998, Merck Sr. Fellows award, The Endocrine Soc., 1999, Chancellors award for postdoctoral rsch., UCLA, 2000, Internat. Scholar award, Pfizer, 2001; Sir Samuel Leonard Simpson fellowship, Royal Coll. of Physicians of London, 1997. Mem.: The Endocrine Soc., The Royal Coll. of Physicians of Glasgow (corr.). Achievements include discovery of estrogen regulates the novel transforming gene, PTTG; the human pituitary corticotroph cell expresses the steroid receptor, PPAR-gamma. Avocation: tennis. Office: Cedars-Sinai Med CtrB-126 8700 Beverly Blvd Los Angeles CA 90048 Office Fax: 310-423-0440. E-mail: heaneya@cshs.org.

HEANEY, GERALD WILLIAM, federal judge; b. Goodhue, Minn., Jan. 29, 1918; s. William J. and Johanna (Ryan) H.; m. Eleanor R. Schmitt, Dec. 1, 1945; children: William M., Carol J. Student, St. Thomas Coll., 1935—37; BSL, U. Minn., 1939, LLB, 1941. Bar: Minn. 1941. Lawyer securities div. Dept. of Commerce Minn., 1941—42; mem. firm Lewis. Hammer, Heaney, Weyl & Halverson, Duluth, 1946—66; judge U.S. Ct. Appeals (8th cir.), 1966—88, sr. judge, 1988—. Bd. regents U. Minn., 1964—65; Mem. Dem. Nat. Com. from Minn., 1955. Capt. AUS, 1942—46. Mem.: ABA, Am. Judicature Soc., Minn. Bar Assn. Roman Catholic. Office: US Ct Appeals 8th Cir US Courthouse & Federal Bldg 315 W 1st St Duluth MN 55802-1605 also: US Ct Appeals 8th Cir 111 S 10th St Rm 24-32 St Louis MO 63102*

HEANEY, MARK, internist, oncologist, hematologist; b. Hagerstown, Md., Nov. 3, 1958; MD, PhD, U. Va., 1986. Diplomate Am. Bd. Internal Medicine, Am. Bd. Oncology, Am. Bd. Hematology. Intern SUNY, Stony Brook, 1987-88, resident in internal medicine, 1988-90; fellow in med. oncology/hematology Meml. Sloan-Kettering Cancer Ctr., N.Y.C., 1990-93, asst. attending physician,

1996—. Instr. Cornell U. Med. Coll., N.Y.C., 1993-96, asst. prof., 1996—. Catherine and Frederick R. Adler chair jr. faculty, 1996-2001. Office: Meml Sloan-Kettering Cancer Ctr Box 489 1275 York Ave New York NY 10021-6094 E-mail: m-heaney@ski.mskcc.org.

HEANEY, SEAMUS JUSTIN, poet, educator; b. Mossbawn, County Derry, No. Ireland, Apr. 13, 1939; s. Patrick and Margaret H.; m. Marie Devlin, 1965; children: Michael, Christopher, Catherine. BA, Queen's U., Belfast, 1961; postgrad., St. Joseph's Coll., Belfast, 1961-62; PhD (hon.), Queen's U., Belfast. Tchr. St. Thomas's Secondary Sch., Belfast, No. Ireland, 1962-63; lectr. St. Joseph's Coll. Edn., Belfast, 1963-66, Queen's U., Belfast, 1966-72; free-lance writer, 1972-75; lectr. Carysfort Coll., 1975-81; Boylston visiting prof. rhetoric and oratory Harvard U., 1982—96, Ralph Waldo Emerson poet-in-residence, 1996—; prof. poetry Oxford U., 1989-94. Author: Eleven Poems, 1965, Door into the Dark, 1969, Death of a Naturalist, 1966 (Somerset Maugham award 1967, Cholmondeley award 1968), Wintering Out, 1972, North, 1975 (W.H. Smith award, Duff Copper prize), Stations, 1975, Bog Poems, 1975, Field Work, 1979, Poems: 1965-75, 1980, Preoccupations: Selected Prose 1968-78, 1980, Sweeney Astray: A Version from the Irish, 1984, Station Island, 1984, The Haw Lantern, 1987 (Whitbead award), The Government of the Tongue, 1988, The Place of Writing, 1990, New Selected Poems, 1966-78, 1990, (play) The Cure at Troy (A Version of Sophocles' Philoctetes), 1991, Seeing Things, 1991, (Oxford lectures) The Redress of Poetry, 1995, The Spirit Level, 1996; ed. poetry anthologies., Beowulf, A New Verse Translation, 1999, Electric Light, 2001, Finders Keepers: Selected Prose, 2002. Recipient Eric Gregory award, 1966, Faber Meml. prize, 1968, Irish Acad. Letters award, 1971, Denis Devlin Meml. award, 1973, Am.-Irish Found. award, 1975, E.M.Forster award Nat. Inst. Arts and Letters, 1975, Bennett Award, 1982, Premio Mondello (Internat. Poetry prize) Mondello Found., Palermo, Sicily, 1993, Nobel Prize for Literature, 1995. Mem. Royal Dublin Soc. (hon. life), Am. Acad. Arts and Letters (fgn. hon.), Am. Acad. Arts and Scis. (hon. life), Irish Acad. Letters. Office: Harvard U Dept English Cambridge MA 02138

HEANUE, ANNE ALLEN, retired librarian; b. Ft. Oglethorpe, Ga., Feb. 7, 1940; d. James Edward and Mary (Dennean) Allen; m. Kevin E. Heanue, July 20, 1963; children: Mary, Brian, Patricia. BA cum laude, Dunbarton Coll., 1962; MA, Georgetown U., 1966; MS in Libr. Sci., Cath. U. Am., 1976. Libr. Deloitte Haskins and Sells, Washington, 1977-79; asst. to dir. Am. Libr. Assn., Washington, 1979-81, asst. dir., 1981-84, assoc. dir., 1984-98; ret., 1998. Bd. dirs. Alexandria (Va.) LWV, 1967-78; chmn. Alexandria Spl. Edn. adv. com., 1978-79; mem. Alexandria Gypsy Moth Control Commn., 1991-96; vol. White House, 1999—; trustee Freedom to Read Found., 2003—; mem. cancer care com. Inova Alexandria Hosp. Found., 2003—. Recipient Fed. Librs. Round Table Achievement award, 1988. Mem. ALA, Hist. Soc. Washington, D.C., Va. Hist. Soc., Rappahannock Hist. Soc., D.C. Libr. Assn. (bd. dirs. 1994-97), Beta Phi Mu, Pi Gamma Mu. bd. trustees, Freedom to Read Found., 2003-; mem. cancer care Com., Inova Aledandria Hosp. Found., 2003-. Roman Catholic. Avocations: reading, travel, theater.

HEAP, JAMES CLARENCE, retired mechanical engineer; b. Trinidad, Colo. s. James and Elsie Mae (Brobst) H.; m. Alma Mae Swartzendruber. Registered profl. engr., Wis. Sr. mech. engr. Cook Electric Research Lab, Morton Grove, Ill., 1955-56; assoc. mech. engr. Argonne (Ill.) Nat. Lab., 1956-66; sr. project engr. Union Tank Car Co., East Chicago, Ind., 1966-71; sr. engr. Thrall Car Mfg. Co., Chicago Heights, 1971-77; research design engr. Graver Energy Systems, Inc., East Chicago, Ind., 1977-79; mech. cons. design engr. Pollak & Skan, Inc., Chgo., 1979-83, ret., 1983. Cons. mech. design and stress analysis, 1965-83. Author: Formulas for Circular Plates Subjected to Symmetrical Loads and Temperatures, 1966; contbr. tech. papers to profl. jour.; patentee in field. Served with USAF, 1946-47. Mem. ASME, Christian Businessmen's Com. U.S., The Gideon's Internat. Home: 1406 Ashton Ct Goshen IN 46526-4679 *Personal philosophy: To assist and encourage others as ascertained through the perseverance by the fortitude and guidance of my "Savior Jesus Christ".*

HEAP, SYLVIA STUBER, educator; b. Clifton Springs, N.Y., Sept. 25, 1929; d. Stanley Irving and Helen (Hill) Stuber; m. Walker Ratcliffe Heap, June 9, 1951; children: Heidi Anne, Cynthia Joan, Walker Ratcliffe III. BA cum laude, Bates Coll., 1950; postgrad., U. Conn. Sch. Social Work, 1952-54, Boston U. Sch. Social Work, 1953-54, SUNY, Brockport, 1979, SUNY, Potsdam, 1980; MS in Adult Edn., Syracuse U., 1989. Dir. Y-Teens YWCA, Holyoke, Mass., 1950-51; social group worker West Haven (Conn.) Cmty. House, 1951-54; program dir. YWCA, Ann Arbor, 1954-55, part-time, 1955-59; mem. adv. bd. divsn. continuing edn. Jefferson C.C., 1965—, chmn. adv. bd., 1968-98. Pres. Jefferson County Med. Soc. Aux., 1971-72; bd. dirs. St. Lawrence Valley Ednl. TV, 1973-83, sec., 1976-80, treas., 1980-82; v.p., 1982-83, dir. Chem. People Project, 1983; bd. dirs. Watertown Lyric Theatre, 1973-83, bd. dirs. N.Y. State Med. Soc. Aux., 1974-85, 2d v.p. bd., 1979-80; fitness instr. Jefferson Community Coll., Watertown, 1977-86; chmn. health projects N.Y. State Med. Soc. Aux., 1981-85. Named Citizen of Yr., Greater Watertown C. of C., 1975, Friend of C.C., N.Y. State Bd. Trustees, 1988. Mem. AAUW, Bates Key, Alliance with the Jefferson County Med. Soc., Phi Beta Kappa. Unitarian Universalist (UN office envoy 1978—, St. Lawrence dist. envoy 1992—).

HEAPHY, JANIS BESLER, newspaper executive; b. Kalamazoo, Oct. 10, 1951; d. Elvin Julius and Margaret Louise (Throndike) Olson; m. Douglas R. Dern, Aug. 15, 1980 (div. Nov. 1985); m. Robert Thomas Heaphy, Feb. 11, 1989; 1 child, Tanner. BS, Miami U., 1973, MEd, 1976. Tchr. Edgewood Jr. H.S., Seven Mile, Ohio, 1973—75; acct. exec. L.A. Times, 1976—79, sr. acct. exec., 1986—87, ea. mag. mgr., 1987—89, nat. advt. mgr., 1989—92, retail advt. mgr. then sr. v.p.. advt./mktg., 1992—97; acct. exec. L.A. Mag., 1979—82; mgr. L.A. Omni Mag., 1982—86; pub. Sacramento Bee, 1997—. Co-editor: Secrets of the Master Sellers, 1987. Mem.: Advt. Club L.A. Avocations: home decorating, reading, swimming, music. Office: Sacramento Bee PO Box 15779 2100 Q St Sacramento CA 95852*

HEAPHY, JOHN MERRILL, lawyer; b. Escanaba, Mich., Apr. 27, 1927; s. John Merrill and Catherine R. (Feeney) H.; m. Martha Jean Knowles, Nov. 16, 1951; children— John Merrill III, Catherine Jean Heaphy DeThorne, Barbara H. Murphy. BA, U. Mich., 1950, JD, Wayne State U., 1953. Bar: Mich. 1954. Atty. office of gen. counsel HEW, Washington, 1954-57; ptnr. Vandeveer & Garzia, P.C. and predecessor firms, Detroit, 1958-86, pres. firm, 1986-92; ret. Served with USNR, 1945-46. Fellow Am. Coll. Trial Lawyers; mem. ABA, Internat. Assn. Def. Counsel, Mich. Bar Assn., Delta Theta Phi, Alpha Sigma Phi. Republican. Home: 14650 N Desert Rock Dr Tucson AZ 85737-7135 E-mail: JHHeaphy@aol.com.

HEAPS, MARVIN DALE, retired food services company executive; b. Boone, Iowa, June 26, 1932; s. Donald and Mary Isabel (Robson) H.; m. Martha Coleman Davis, July 4, 1957; children— Mitchell, Matthew, Martha. BA in Econs, Whitworth Coll., 1953; postgrad., George Washington U., 1957; MBA (Achievement scholar), U. Pa., 1959. Asso. McKinsey & Co. (mgmt. cons.), Washington, Geneva and N.Y.C., 1960-66; dir. service systems engring. Automatic Retailers of Am., Phila., 1967, v.p., 1968; sr. v.p. ARA Svcs., Inc., Phila., 1969-71; pres. ARA Food Svcs. Co., 1971-75; exec. v.p. ops. ARA Svcs., Inc., 1975-77, pres., chief operational officer, 1977-81; pres./chief exec. officer Marvin D. Heaps Assos., Inc., 1981—. Bd. dirs. Adult Communities Total Svc., chmn., 1997—; cons. to Office Edn., HEW; mem. food svc. industry adv. com. Exec. Office Pres., 1969—. Active Whitworth Coll.; chmn. Salvation Army. Lt. USN, 1955-59. Mem. Conf. Bd., Am. Mgmt. Assn., Assn. Internat. Devel., Nat. Automatic Mdse. Assn. (dir.), Wharton MBA Alumni Club. Republican. Presbyterian (elder). Home and Office: 1079 Kennett Way West Chester PA 19380 E-mail: dale0626@aol.com.

HEARD, ALEXANDER, retired educator and chancellor; b. Savannah, Ga., Mar. 14, 1917; s. Richard Willis and Virginia Lord (Nisbet) H.; m. Laura Jean Keller, June 17, 1949; children: Stephen Keller, Christopher Cadek, Francis Muir, Cornelia Lord. AB, U. N.C., 1938, LL.D., 1968; MA, Columbia U., 1948, PhD, 1951, LL.D., 1965; 25 other hon. degrees. U.S. Govt. service in depts. Interior, War and State, 1939-43; research asso. bur. pub. adminstrn. U. Ala., 1946-49; research asso. Inst. Research in Social Sci., U. N.C., 1950-51, research prof., 1952-58; asso. prof. polit. sci. U. N.C., 1950-51, prof. polit. sci., 1952-63, dean Grad. Sch., 1958-63; prof. polit. sci. Vanderbilt U., 1963-85, chancellor, 1963-82. Author: (asst. to V.O. Key, Jr.) Southern Politics in State and Nation, 1949, (with Donald S. Strong) Southern Primaries and Elections, 1950, A Two-Party South?, 1952, The Costs of Democracy, 1960, rev. edit., 1962, The Lost Years in Graduate Education, 1963, Made in America: Improving the Nomination and Election of Presidents, 1991, Speaking of the University: Two Decades at Vanderbilt, 1995, editor and contbr.: State Legislatures in American Politics, 1966; editor, contbr. (with Michael Nelson) Presidential Selection, 1987. Chmn. Pres.'s Commn. on Campaign Costs, 1961-62; spl. adviser to Pres. U.S. on campus affairs, 1970; Dir. Citizens' Research Found., 1958-71, pres., 1968-71; mem. U.S. Adv. Commn. Intergovtl. Relations, 1967-69, Trustee Ford Found., 1967-87, chmn., 1972-87; trustee Robert A. Taft Inst. Govt., 1973-76, Ctr. for Study of Presidency, 1988-91; chmn. Task Force on So. Rural Devel., 1974-77; public trustee Nutrition Found., 1976-82; mem. council Rockefeller U., 1977-82; mem. Commn. on U.S. Policy Toward So. Africa, Fgn. Policy Study Found., 1979-85. Lt. USNR, 1943-46. Mem. Internat. Polit. Sci. Assn., Am. Polit. Sci. Assn. (v.p. 1962-63), So. Polit. Sci. Assn. (pres. 1961-62), Assn. Am. Univs. (dir. council fed. relations 1969-70, v.p. 1973-74, pres. 1974-75), Council on Fgn. Rels., Belle Meade Country Club (Nashville), (N.Y.C.), Sigma Alpha Epsilon. Episcopalian. Home: 2100 Golf Club Ln Nashville TN 37215-1224 Office: Vanderbilt U 401 Kirkland Hall Nashville TN 37240

HEARD, WILLIAM ROBERT, retired insurance company executive; b. Indpls., Apr. 25, 1925; s. French and Estelle (Austin) H.; attended Ind. U.; m. Virginia Ann Patrick, Feb. 6, 1951; children: Cynthia Ann, William Robert, II. With Grain Dealers Mut. Ins. Co., 1948, exec. v.p., Indpls., 1978-79, pres., CEO, dir., 1979-90, chmn. bd., 1990-94; pres., CEO, dir. Companion Ins. Co., 1979-90, chmn. bd., 1990-94; dir., chmn. bd., fin. com., 1990-94; ret., 1994; past chmn. Alliance Am. Insurers; chmn., exec. com. IRM; pres., dir. Grain Dealers Mut. Agy., Inc., chmn. bd., 1990-94, 15 N. Broadway Corp. Served with USNR, 1942-46. Mem. Assn. Mill and Elevator Ins. Cos. (chmn., bd. dirs.), Ins. Inst. Ind. (bd. dirs., exec. com.), Ind. BBB (bd. dirs., exec. com., vice chmn.), Excess of Loss Assn. (vice chmn., bd. dirs.), Sales and Mktg. Execs. Indpls. (past pres.), Sales and Mktg. Execs. Internat. (past bd. dirs.), Fla. 1752 Club (past pres.), Property and Casualty Ins. Council, Ind. Insurors Assn. (bd. dirs.), Hoosierland Rating Bur. (bd. dirs.), Ind. Mill and Elevator Rating Bur. (bd. dirs.), Ins. Claims Svc. (bd. dirs.), Property Loss Rsch. Bur. (bd. dirs., chmn.), Mill and Elevator Rating Bur. (bd. dirs.), Mill and Elevator Fire Prevention Bur. (bd. dirs.), Econ. Club of Indpls., VFW, Am. Legion, Hon. Order Ky. Cols., Pearl Harbor Survivors Assn. (hon.), Indpls. Skyline Club, Pi Sigma Epsilon. Office: Grain Dealers Mut Ins 1752 N Meridian St Indianapolis IN 46202-1404

HEARD, WILLIAM T. automotive executive; b. Columbus, Ga., Sept. 8, 1934; s. William Tillman Sr. Heard; m. Sara Bolin; children: Bill III, Edward. BA, Auburn U., 1956. With Muscogee Motor Co.; prin. Bill Heard Chevrolet (formerly Muscogee Motor Co.); CEO Bill Heard Enterprises Inc. (formerly Bill Heard Chevrolet). Pres. Boys Club, Jr. Achievement, United Way Columbus, Coll. Coll. Found.; treas., chmn. fin. com. Columbus Mus.; chmn. Columbus Olympic Fund Raising Found.; mem. 1st Presbyn. Ch. of Columbus, past chmn. bd. deacons. Named Disting. Alumnus of Auburn U. Coll. Bus., 1994. Mem. Rotary, C. of C. (pres.). Office: Bill Heard Enterprises Inc PO Box 6749 Columbus GA 31917-6749*

HEAREY, ELIZABETH BERLE, lawyer; b. East Orange, N.J., Mar. 3, 1947; d. Charles Henry and Winifred (McCubbin) Berle; m. Charles DeLisle Hearey Jr., June 13, 1970; children: Raymond DeLisle, Katherine Berle, Sarah Elizabeth. BA with honors, Wellesley Coll., 1969; JD, U. Calif., San Francisco, 1974. Bar: Calif. 1974, U.S. Dist. Ct. (no. dist.) Calif. 1974. Dep. county counsel Contra Costa County, Martinez, Calif., 1975-86; assoc. Williams & Woods, Martinez, 1992-95, Atkinson, Andelson, Loya, Ruud & Romo, Pleasanton, Calif., 1995—. Mem. Contra Costa County Bar Assn., Phi Beta Kappa. Office: Atkinson Andelson Loya Ruud & Romo 5776 Stoneridge Mall Rd Pleasanton CA 94588-2832 E-mail: ebh@aalrr.com.

HEARIN, ROBERT MATLOCK, JR., lawyer; b. Tuscaloosa, Ala., Jan. 15, 1946; s. Robert M. Hearin and Annie Laurie Swaim; m. Zetta M. Bryant, Mar. 25, 1972; children: Andrew, Timothy. BA, U. Miss., 1968; JD, Tulane U., 1971. Bar: La. 1971, Calif. 1976, Tex. 1993. Mng. atty. New Orleans Legal Assistance Corp., 1972-75; sole practice law New Orleans, 1976-95; mng. atty. Hearin & Warriner, LLC, New Orleans, 1995—. Baseball coach Carrollton Booster Club, Inc., New Orleans, 1991, 92, 95, 97. 1st lt. U.S. Army, 1971-72. Mem.: L.A. Bar Found. (charter mem.). Presbyterian. Avocations: travel, sports, cooking. Office: Hearin & Warriner LLC 830 Union St Ste 400 New Orleans LA 70112-1405 E-mail: rmhjr@neworleanslaw.com.

HEARLE, DOUGLAS GEOFFREY, public relations consultant; b. N.Y.C., Apr. 7, 1933; s. Douglas G. and Regina Irene (Booth) H.; m. Mary Elizabeth Hogan, July 13, 1957; children: Douglas, Christopher, Matthew. BA, Iona Coll., 1954, MBA, 1970. Reporter-editor N.Y. Jour.-Am., N.Y.C., 1954-63; pub. relations mgr. Borden Inc., N.Y.C., 1963-66; account exec. Hill & Knowlton, N.Y.C., 1966-70, v.p., 1970-73, sr. v.p., 1973-80, exec. v.p., 1980-86, vice chmn., 1989-90, also bd. dirs.; founder, pres. Douglas G. Hearle & Co., N.Y.C., 1993—. Pres. John W. Hill Found., N.Y.C., 1980-86; founder, pres. Douglas G. Hearle & Assoc., Inc., N.Y.C., 1986-89; pres., CEO Carl Byoir & Assocs., N.Y.C., 1990-92; adj. prof. Iona Coll., 1982-84, Coll. New Rochelle, 1996—, Fordham U., 1998-99; disting. lectr. Ball State U., 1981, U. Tex., 1984. V.p. Bd. Edn., Pelham, N.Y., 1972-78; v.p. N.Y. Newspaper Reporters Assn., 1961-63; mem. exec. coun. Boy Scouts Am., 1967-69; vice chmn. bd. trustees Coll. New Rochelle, 1989-95; bd. dirs. The Roper Ctr., U. Conn., 1990—; pres. Danny Fund, Pelham, N.Y., 2003-. Recipient Disting. Service award Asean P.R. Congress, Jakarta, Indonesia, 1981; recipient Citizen of Yr. award Pelham Men's Club, 1978, Five Most Respected award by PR Week, 1988, All Star award Inside PR Mag., 1992. Mem. Silurians, N.Y. Newspaper Reporters Assn., Asia Soc., Internat. C. of C., Pelham Country Club, Sky Club of N.Y. Republican. Roman Catholic. Home: 20 Maple Ave Pelham NY 10803-2220 Office: PO Box 480 Pelham NY 10803-0480

HEARLE, EDWARD F.R. retired management consultant; b. Pasadena, Calif., Apr. 21, 1931; s. John R. and Kathleen W. (Brathwaite) H.; m. Patricia Ann Woodbridge, Dec. 23, 1958; children: Kevin C., Keith W., Jeffrey R. AB, Occidental Coll., 1952; MPA, UCLA, 1954. Cert. mgmt. cons. Inst. Mgmt. Consulting. Asst. to city adminstr. City of Covina, Calif., 1956-59; analyst The Rand Corp., Santa Monica, Calif., 1959-65; sr. dir. Griffenhagen Kroeger, San Francisco, 1965-66; office dir. U.S. Govt., Washington, 1966-67, sr. v.p. Booz Allen & Hamilton, Washington, 1967-92; ret. Cons. UN, N.Y., 1964-70. Co-author: A Data Processing System for State and Local Governments, 1963. Pres. Westminter Presbyn. Retirement Corp., Lakeridge, Va., 1985-92; dir. The Gathering, 2003, Jacksonville Symphony Assn., 1998, Jacksonville Cmty. Coun., Inc., 1998; bd. dirs. Trinity Internat. Found., 1998, chair, 2000. With U.S. Army, 1954-56. Home: 1331 N 1st St 1002 Jacksonville Beach FL 32250

HEARN, BEVERLY JEAN, secondary education educator, librarian; b. Lexington, Tenn., Sept. 10, 1953; d. James Lawrence and Marie (Sparks) Kee; m. Larry Joseph Hearn, June 15, 1973; children: Matthew Joseph, David Andrew. BA, Union U., 1974; MLS, George Peabody Coll. for Tchrs., 1975; EdD, Memphis State U., 1991. Acqusitions librarian Union U., Jackson, Tenn., 1975-80, reference librarian, 1980-86; tchr. Madison County Bd. Edn., Jackson, 1986—. Instr. Memphis State U., 1990-95, Jackson State C.C., 1992-97; freelance cataloger, 1978-86. Mem. TESOL, NEA, Internat. Reading Assn., Assn. for Curriculum Devel. Democrat. Baptist. Home: 558 Wallace Rd Jackson TN 38305-2839

HEARN, DAVID, advertising executive; In mgmt. pos. Procter & Gamble, Del Monte, Smiths Crisps, Pepsico, United Biscuits; CEO, mng. dir. Goodman Fielder Ltd., Australia, 1995—2001; chmn., CEO Bates Worldwide, N.Y.C., 2002—; exec. dir. Cordiant Comm. Group Plc, 2002—03. Office: Bates Worldwide 498 Seventh Ave New York NY 10018*

HEARN, GEORGE HENRY, lawyer, steamship corporate executive; b. Bklyn., July 4, 1927; s. Henry G. and Grace A. (Flaherty) H.; m. Cecelia Anne Philbin, June 28, 1952; children: Annemarie Jude, Margaret Mary, George Henry. BA, St. Francis Coll., 1950; student, Fordham U., 1948; LLB, St. John's U., 1954. Bar: N.Y. 1955, U.S. Supreme Ct. 1960, D.C. 1965. Jr. ptnr. Haight, Gardner, Poor and Havens (specializing admiralty matters), N.Y.C., 1954-61; mem. CAB, 1961-64; commr. Fed. Maritime Commn., 1964-75, maritime adminstr. Govt. Sultanate of Oman, 1975-80; counsel to firm Hill, Rivkins, Carey, Loesberg & O'Brien (specializing in maritime and transp. law), N.Y.C., 1977-82; exec. v.p. Waterman Steamship Corp., N.Y.C., 1982—. Lectr. transp. Georgetown U., Am. U., Tulane U., St. Francis Coll. Contbr. articles to profl. jours. Pres. Fleet Week Found., 1990—; dist. commr. Boy Scouts Am., 1958—, mem. N.Y.C. coun., 1958—61; chmn. Kings County spkrs. com. 1960 presdl. election of John F. Kennedy; vice-chmn. com. nationalists and intergroup rels. N.Y. State Dem. Com., 1960—. Served USNR, WWII, PTO. Recipient Disting. Svc. award U.S. Jr. C. of C., 1958; named Man of Yr., N.Y. Freight Forwarders and Brokers Assn., 1968, Cathedral Club of Bklyn., 1974. Mem. D.C. Bar Assn., Fed. Bar Assn., Maritime Adminstrv. Bar Assn., Maritime Law Assn., Soc. Maritime Arbitrators, U.S. Maritime Assn. Port of N.Y. and N.J. (pres., Man of Yr. 2000), India House (bd. govs.), Adminstrv. Conv. U.S., St. Patrick's Soc. Bklyn. (past pres.), Am. Com. Italian Migration (rec. sec. Bklyn. divsn.), KC. Home: 250 Lido Blvd Point Lookout NY 11569 Office: 1 Whitehall St New York NY 10004-2109 also: 1000 16th St NW Washington DC 20036-5705 E-mail: hearngh@intship.com.

HEARN, JOYCE CAMP, retired state legislator, educator, consultant; b. Cedartown, Ga. d. J.C. and Carolyn (Carter) Camp; m. Thomas Harry Hearn; children: Theresa Hearn Potts Bailey, Kimberly Ann Johnson, Carolyn Lee Becker. Student, U. Ga.; BA, Ohio State U., 1957; postgrad., U. S.C. Former h.s. tchr.; dist. mgr. U.S. Census, 2d Congl. Dist., 1970; mem. S.C. Ho. of Reps., 1975-89. Asst. minority leader, 1976-78, 86-89; chmn., commn. alcohol beverage control, 1989-91; pres., cons. Hearn & Assocs., Columbia, S.C., 1995—. Mem. Richland County Planning Commn., 1974-76; bd. dirs. Meml. Youth Ctr. and Stage South; chmn. Sexual Assault Awareness Week; vice chmn. Dist. Rep. Com., 1968; Rep. chmn. 2d Congl. Dist., 1969; Rep. chmn. Richland County, 1972; del., platform com. Rep. Nat. Conv., 1980, 84; moderator Kathwood Bapt. Ch., 1979-80, former asst. Sunday Sch. tchr.; bd. dirs. Small Bus. Devel. Ctr., S.C., Columbia Coll. Bd. Vis., Columbia Urban League, Fedn. of Blind; trustee Columbia Mus. Art; apptd. to Alcohol Beverage Control Bd., 1989, apptd. chmn. commn., 1990-92, commr., 1991-94; bd. dirs. Lupus Found., 1990—; chair nat. adv. com. Occupl. Safety and Health, 1980-88. Recipient Outstanding Citizen award Columbia Rape Coalition, 1977, Disting. Svc. award Claims Mgmt. Assn., S.C., 1977, Nat. Fedn. Blind S.C., 1978, Columbia Urban League, 1983, MADD, 1985, Outstanding Legislator of Yr. award Alcohol and Drug Abuse Assn., 1980, Retarded Citizens Assn., 1982, S.C. Rehab. Assn., 1984, S.C. Assn. of Deaf, 1987, Legislator of Yr., Fedn. of Blind, 1988, Disting. Legislator, DAV, 1989; honoree Easter Seals, 1989; numerous other awards. Mem. Nat. Order of Women Legislators (v.p., pres.), Order of the Palmetto, S.C. Women's Club, Columbia Women's Club (bd. dirs.), Larkspur Garden Club.

HEARN, SHARON SKLAMBA, lawyer; b. New Orleans, Aug. 15, 1956; d. Carl John and Marjorie C. (Wimberly) Sklamba; m. Curtis R. Hearn. BA magna cum laude, Loyola U., New Orleans, 1977; JD cum laude, Tulane U., 1980. Bar: La. 1980, Tex. 1982; cert. tax specialist. Law clk. to presiding judge U.S. Ct. Appeals Fed. Cir., Washington, 1980-81; assoc. Johnson & Swanson, Dallas, 1981-84, The Kullman Firm, New Orleans, 1984—. Recipient Am. Legion award, 1970. Mem. ABA, La. State Bar Assn., Tex. State Bar Assn., Dallas Women Lawyers Assn. Democrat. Roman Catholic. Home: 106 Bordeaux St Metairie LA 70005-4231 Office: The Kullman Firm 1600 Energy Ctr 1100 Poydras St New Orleans LA 70163-1101

HEARN, THOMAS K., JR., university president; b. Opp, Ala., July 5, 1937; s. Thomas H. Hearn; m. Laura Walter; children: Thomas K., William Neely, Lindsay. BA summa cum laude, Birmingham-So. Coll., 1959; BD, Baptist Theol. Sem., 1963; PhD (NDEA fellow), Vanderbilt U., 1965. Instr. Birmingham-So. Coll., 1964—65; asst. prof. Coll. William and Mary, 1965—68; assoc. prof., 1968—74; prof. philosophy U. Ala., Birmingham, 1974—83, chmn. dept. philosophy, 1974—76; dean U. Ala. Sch. Humanities, Birmingham, 1976—78; v.p. U. Ala. Univ. Coll., Birmingham, 1978—83; pres. Wake Forest U., Winston-Salem, NC, 1983—. Contbr. articles to profl. jours. Recipient Thomas Jefferson Teaching award, 1970; fellow, Council Philos. Studies, 1968, Coop. Program in Humanities, 1969—70; grantee, Nat. Found. Humanities, 1967, Faculty Summer grant, Coll. William and Mary, 1970, 1972—73. Mem.: AAUP, Newcomen Soc. N.Am., David Hume Soc., Am. Philos. Assn., Soc. Philosophy Religion (pres. 1974—75), So. Soc. Philosophy, Psychology (exec. council 1974—77, Jr. award), Phi Kappa Phi, Omicron Delta Kappa, Phi Beta Kappa. Home: 1000 Kearns Ave Winston Salem NC 27106-5824 Office: Wake Forest U Office of Pres PO Box 7226 Winston Salem NC 27109 E-mail: tkh@wfu.edu.

HEARN, WILLIAM CHARLES, music educator, music minister; b. Gainesville, Fla., Jan. 27, 1943; s. Joseph Charles and Willis Belle Hearn; m. Elizabeth Roberta Hearn, June 4, 1966; children: Toni Lyn, Timothy Lyn. BA in Music, Northeastern State U., Tahlequah, Okla., 1966. Tchr. vocal music Alice Robertson Jr. HS, Muskogee, Okla., 1966—82, Muskogee HS, 1982—. Min. music Calvary Bapt. Ch., Muskogee, 1963—74, Ctrl. Bapt. Ch., Muskogee, 1974—92, Oldham Meml. Bapt. Ch., Muskogee, 1992—. Named Tchr. of Yr., Muskogee Pub. Schs., 1995; named to Music Hall of Fame, Northeastern State U., 2000. Mem.: NEA, Music Educator's Nat. Conf., Nat. Assn. Jazz Educators, Am. Choral Dirs. Assn., Okla. Music Dirs. Assn., Muskogee Edn. Assn., Okla. Choral Dirs. Assn., Okla. Edn. Assn. Avocations: gardening, woodworking, furniture building. Home: 2902 Gibson St Muskogee OK 74403 Office: Muskogee HS 3200 E Shawnee Rd Muskogee AL 77403 Office Fax: 918-684-3751. E-mail: bchmusic@hotmail.com.

HEARNE, GEORGE ARCHER, academic administrator; b. Tampa, Fla., Oct. 31, 1934; s. William Duncan and Marguerite Estelle (Archer) H.; m. Jean May Helmstadter, June 9, 1956; children: Diana Leslie, George Harrison. BA, Bethany Coll., 1955; MDiv, Yale U., 1958; MA, Ill. State U., 1968; HHD (hon.), Culver-Stockton Coll., 1986; LLD, Bethany Coll., 1997. Min. Arlington Christian Ch., Jacksonville, Fla., 1958-59; dir. admissions Eureka (Ill.) Coll., 1960-70, v.p. student devel., 1970-73, dean admissions and student devel., 1973-77, dean admissions and coll. rels., 1977-82, v.p. coll. rels., 1982-84, exec. v.p., 1984-85, pres., 1985—. Bd. dirs. Christian Ch., Ill., Wis. and Ind., 1985—, Higher Edn. divsn. Christian Ch., St. Louis, 1985—; pres. Eureka Bd. Edn., 1967-76; active various cmty. drives. Mem. Assoc. Colls. Ill. (bd. dirs. 1985—), Fedn. Ill. Ind. Colls. and Univs. (bd. dirs. 1985—, exec. com. 2000—), Coun. for Advancement and Support of Edn., Coun. Ind. Colls., Coun. of Pres. (higher edn. div.). Lodges: Rotary. Avocations: reading, music, antiques, golf. Office: Eureka Coll 300 E College Ave Eureka IL 61530-1562 E-mail: ghearne@eureka.edu.

HEARNE, MARY, retired legal secretary, artist; b. Dallas County, Ark., Aug. 2, 1934; d. Henry Evans Hearne and Olive Glover Abbott. Student, U. Ark., Little Rock, 1975-80. Dance instr. Arthur Murray Dance Studio, Orlando, Fla., 1958-61; sec., ct. reporter Little Rock AFB, 1967-81; legal sec. Friday, Eldridge & Clark, Little Rock, 1982-92; ret., 1992. Represented by The Collector Art Gallery, Design Ctr., Washington. One-woman shows at Ark. State Capitol Bldg., Little Rock, 1980, Ark. Arts Ctr., Little Rock, 1980, Ark Terr. Restoration, Little Rock, 1982, Ozark Folk Ctr., Mountain View, Ark., 1985, Gov.'s Conf. Rm., 1986, Plantation Agr. Mus., Scott, Ark., 1994; exhibited at group shows at Ark. Arts Ctr., Little Rock, 1979, Gallery 4, St. George, Utah, 1984, Gallery 2, Charlottesville, Va., 1984, The Collector Art Gallery, Hot Springs, Ark., 1994, The Collector Art Gallery, Washington, 1996, Statehouse Conf. Ctr., 1999, H. Lee Moffitt Cancer Ctr. and Rsch. Inst., Tampa, Fla., 1999; represented in permanent collection of Naval Nuclear Guided Missile Cruiser; 4 paintings selected for Ark. Sesquicentennial commemorative mugs, 1986; 3 paintings selected for 1-year display at office of Senator David Pryor, Washington, 1994-95, included in White House collection. Recipient Ambassador of Goodwill cert., 1980. Mem. N.Y. Artists Equity Assn., Nat. Mus. Women in the Arts (registered). Avocations: horseback riding, gardening, hiking. Home: 424 Burnside Dr Little Rock AR 72205-2235

HEARON, SHELBY, writer, lecturer, educator; b. Marion, Ky., Mar. 18, 1931; d. Charles Boogher and Evelyn Shelby (Roberts) Reed; m. William Halpern, Aug. 19, 1995; children from previous marriage: Anne Rambo, Reed. BA, U. Tex., 1953. Disting. vis. prof. U. Ill., Chgo., 1993, Colgate U., 1993, U. Miami,

Fla., 1994, U. Mass., Amherst, 1994-96, Middlebury Coll., 1996-98. Author: Armadillo in the Grass, 1968, The Second Dune, 1973, Hannah's House, 1975, Now and Another Time, 1976, A Prince of a Fellow, 1978, Painted Dresses, 1981, Afternoon of a Faun, 1983, Group Therapy, 1984, A Small Town, 1985, Five Hundred Scorpions, 1987, Owing Jolene, 1989, Hug Dancing, 1991, Life Estates, 1994, Footprints, 1996, Ella in Bloom, 2001; contbr. articles, short fiction and book revs. to various publs. Pres. Tex. Inst. Letters, 1980; chair lit. panel Tex. Commn. on Arts, 1980; mem. lit. panel N.Y. Coun. on Arts, 1985. Recipient Syndication prize, NEA/PEN, 1984—85, 1985, 1987, 1988, Lit. award, Am. Acad. Arts and Letters, 1990; fellow, Guggenheim, 1982, Nat. Endowment Arts, 1983; grantee, Ingram Merrill, 1987. Mem.: PEN, Associated Writing Programs, Tex. Inst. Letters (Fiction award 1973, 1978), Poets and Writers Inc., Authors Guild. Democrat. Presbyterian. Home: 246 S Union St Burlington VT 05401-4514

HEARREAN, KRISTOPHER JAMES, mechanical engineer; b. Bedford, Tex., Oct. 18, 1975; s. Jerry Porras and Elizabeth Heath. AA Gen. Studies, Spokane Falls C.C., Spokane, Wash., 1996; BS in Mech. Engring., Wash. State U., Pullman, 2000; MS in Mech. Engring., U. Calif., Davis, 2002. Engr. in tng., Wash., 2000. Mech. engring. intern Lockheed Martin Hanford, Richland, Wash., 1999; mem. tech. staff Sandia Nat. Lab., Livermore, Calif., 2000—. Acad. scholar, Nat. Acad. Nuc. Tng., 1999. Mem.: ASME (assoc.).

HEARST, GARRISON (GERALD GARRISON HEARST), professional football player; b. Lincolnton, Ga., Jan. 4, 1971; Student, Ga. State U. Running back Phoenix Cardinals, 1993, Arizona Cardinals, Phoenix, 1994—95, Cin. Bengals, 1996, San Francisco 49ers, 1997—. Named running back, The Sporting News Coll. All-Am. 1st team, 1992; recipient Doak Walker award, 1992. Office: c/o San Francisco 49ers 4949 Centennial Blvd Santa Clara CA 95054-1229

HEARST, JOHN EUGENE, chemistry educator, researcher, consultant; b. Vienna, July 2, 1935; came to U.S., 1938; s. Alphonse Bernard and Lily (Roger) H.; m. Jean Carolyn Bankson, Aug. 30, 1958; children: David Paul, Leslie Jean. B.E., Yale U., 1957; PhD, Calif. Inst. Tech., 1961; D.Sc. (hon.), Lehigh U., 1992. Postdoctoral rschr. Dartmouth Coll., Hanover, N.H., 1961-62; prof. chemistry U. Calif., Berkeley, 1962-95, prof. emeritus, 1996—, Miller rsch. prof., 1970-71; founder, dir. HRI Rsch. Inc., 1978—; sr. rsch. scientist Lawrence Berkeley Lab., 1980-99, faculty chemist, 2000—, dir. divsn. chem. biodynamics, 1986-89; founder, sr. cons. Advanced Genetics Rsch., Inc., Oakland, Calif., 1981-84; founder, dir. Steritech Inc., Concord, Calif., 1992-96; founder, dir., v.p. new sci. opportunities Cerus Corp., Concord, 1992—. Disting. lectr. Purdue U., 1986; Merck Centennial lectr. Lehigh U., 1992, Robert A. Welch Found. lectr., 1992-93; adv. bd. Pharm. and Chem. Scis. Graduate Program Univ. of the Pacific, 2000—; cons. Codon, Inc., 1993-97. Author: Contemporary Chemistry, 1976. editor: General Chemistry, 1974; exec. editor Nucleic Acids Rsch., 1990-93; inventor, patentee in field. Bd. dirs. U. No. Calif., 1993-95, dir. Disability Policy and Planning Inst., Berkeley, 2000—. Recipient Sci. Profl. Devel. award NSF, 1977-78, The Berkeley citation, 1999, Mortimer Bortin award for outstanding rsch. in bone marrow transplant, 2000; John Simon Guggenheim fellow, 1968-69, European Molecular Orgn. sr. fellow, 1973-74. Mem. AAAS, Am. Chem. Soc., Biophys. Soc., Am. Soc. Biol. Chemists, Am. Soc. for Photobiology (coun., pres. elect 1990-91, pres. 1991-92, Rsch. award 1994), Am. Phys. Soc. Home: 101 Southampton Ave Berkeley CA 94707-2036 Office: Cerus Corp 2411 Stanwell Dr Concord CA 94520-4824

HEARST, WILLIAM RANDOLPH, III, newspaper publisher; b. Washington, June 18, 1949; s. William Randolph and Austine (McDonnell) H.; m. Margaret Kerr Crawford, Sept. 23, 1990; children: William, Adelaide, Caroline. AB, Harvard U., 1972. Reporter, asst. city editor San Francisco Examiner, 1972-76, publisher, 1984-96; editor Outside Mag., 1976-78; asst. mng. editor Los Angeles Herald Examiner, 1978-80; mgr. devel. Hearst Corp., 1980-82; v.p. Hearst Cable Communications Div., 1982-84; now ptnr. Perkins, Coffield & Buyers, Menlo Park, Calif. Bd. dirs. Sun Microsystems; trustee Carnegie Inst. Washington. Office: Excite At Home Corp 450 Broadway St Redwood City CA 94063

HEART, SANDY See HORNER, SANDRA

HEART, TRACY, therapist, counselor, human resources specialist; b. La Jolla, Calif., Mar. 25, 1961; d. Palmer and Sandra Lee (Sweeney) Osborn. BA in Psychology, Lewis & Clark Coll., 1983, MA in Counseling Psychology, 1992; profl. cert. human resources mgt., Portland State U., 2000. Practicum and contract therapist Luth. Family Svcs., Portland, Oreg., 1991-92; triage, intake therapist Network/CERES Behavioral Health, Portland, 1993-97; counselor pvt. practice, Tigard, Oreg., 1995—2001; human resource specialist Providence Health Sys., 2000—.

HEARTT, CHARLOTTE BEEBE, university official; b. N.Y.C., Nov. 12, 1933; d. Stacey Kile and Charlotte Beebe; m. William Hollis Peirce, 1954 (div. 1960); children: Daniel Converse, William Kile; m. Stephen Heartt, 1962 (div. 1968); children: Thomas Beebe, Sarah Lincoln. BA, Wellesley Coll., 1954. Intern Office of V.p. Richard Nixon, Washington, 1953; asst. Computing Numerical Analysis Lab. U. Wis., Madison, 1954-56; dir. fund raising Boston Arts Festival, 1961; asst. to dean coll. rels. Radcliffe Coll., Cambridge, Mass., 1961-62; sec. to chmn. dept. city planning Harvard U., Cambridge, 1962; Fulbright program adviser, study abroad adviser Brandeis U., 1966-71, dir. office internat. programs, 1971-76, dir. found. and corp. rels., 1976-79; dir. corp. rels., asst. dir. devel. Smith Coll., Northampton, Mass., 1979-81, dir. devel., 1981-95, dir. prin. gifts, 1995-98; ind. cons., 1999—. Mem. Commonwealth Task Force on the Open Univ., 1973; bd. dirs. Coun. on Internat. Ednl. Exch., 1973-77, mem. exec. com., 1975-77; bd. dirs. Boston Area Seminar for Internat. Students, 1973-76; mem. adv. com. New England Colls. Fund, 1981-95; trustee Berkshire Sch., 1989-98, trustee emerita, 1999—; bd. dirs. Hampshire Cmty. United Way, 1996-2000; mem. devel. com. Belmont Day Sch., Belmont, Mass., 2000—, Boston (Mass.) Leadership Gift Cons. Wellesley Coll., 2002—. Mem. Sect. on U.S. Study Abroad (nat. sec., regional rep. 1972-74), Nat. Assn. Fgn. Student Affairs (nat. commr. liaison), Nat. Assn. Women Deans, Adminstrs. and Counselors (internat. students and programs com. 1974-76), Nat. Soc. Fund Raisers, Coun. for Advancement and Support Edn. Home: 11 Carver Rd Wellesley MA 02481-5351 E-mail: heartt@attbi.com.

HEATH, BERTHANN JONES, education administrator; b. Dallas, May 4, 1938; d. James Lafayette and Allie Mae (Hudson) Jones; m. John Willie Heath, Jr., July 14, 1963 (div. 1975); 1 child, John William, III. BS cum laude, Pepperdine U., 1959; MS, UCLA, 1960. Nat. cert. family and consumer scientist. Tchr., dept. chair LA Unified Sch. Dist., Calif., 1960-69, dist. resource tchr., 1972-75; counselor LA HS, Calif., 1968-72; regional supr., home econ. edn. Calif. State Dept. Edn., 1975-85; program mgr., sch.-to-career transition San Diego City Sch., Calif., 1985-2000; cons., 2000—; owner Berthann's Enterprises, 2000—. Trustee Consumer Credit Counselors of San Diego and Imperial Counties, Calif., 1986-2000; mem. adv. com. Calif. State Dept. Edn. Home Econs. and Health Careers, Sacramento, 1985-98; mem. articulation team SDUSD and San Diego C.C.s, 1987-2000. Author, contbr. to curriculum guides, pamphlets and leaflets. V.p. San Diego chpt. The Links, Inc., 1995-97; presenter TV-8 Looks at Learning and Inside San Diego, 1985-95. Recipient Appreciation/Commendation award Calif. Dept. Edn., 1987, Nat. Gourmet Cook award Nat. Assembly, Links, Inc., 1996, Fin. Literacy Program Svc. award Consumer Credit Counselors of San Diego and Imperial Counties, 1996, Am. Assn. Family and Consumer Scis. Nat. Leader of Yr. award, 1998; named Woman of Distinction, Women, Inc., 1999. Mem. Am. Vocat. Assn. (bylaws chair family and consumer scis. edn. divsn. 1993-97), Nat. Assn. Local Suprs. of Family and Consumer Scis. (pres. 1992-93), Am. Vocat. Assn. (mem. policy and planning com. 1991-97), Calif. Assn. Family and Consumer Scis. (mem. San Diego chpt., chair secondary edn. 1985-95, state chair edn. com. 1989-90, ex-officio mem. articulation com. 1989-96), So. Calif. Biotech. Consortium (charter 1994-96), Links, Inc., Alpha Rho Tau, Delta Sigma Theta, Kappa Omicron Nu, Phi Delta Kappa. Avocations: food design and recipe experimentation, writing, elder care research and development. Office: Berthann's Enterprises PO Box 452934 Los Angeles CA 90045

HEATH, CEDRIC ALEXANDER, nurse, health services administrator, real estate agent, insurance agent, financial analyst; b. St Elizabeth, Jamaica, West Indies, Sept. 3, 1941; came to U.S., 1968; s. Nathaniel David and Ina Ernestine (Williams) H. BS in Nursing summa cum laude, Long Island U., 1973; MPA in Health Svcs. Adminstrn., NYU, 1978, DPA in Health Policy and Mgmt., 1989. Registered nurse, N.Y.; lic. realtor, insurance agent, financial analyst. From hosp. attendant to Head nurse N.Y. State Hosps., 1969-74; from nurse adminstr. to clinic adminstr. N.Y. State Health Facilities, 1975-80; treatment team leader Manhattan Psychiat. Ctr., N.Y.C., 1980-85; chief of svc. Kirby Forensic Psychiat. Ctr., N.Y.C., 1985-91, Bronx (N.Y.) Psychiat. Ctr., 1991—. Real estate agent Bloomsville Realty Corp., Bronx, N.Y., 1995-97, CJ Realty Works, Inc., Bronx, 1997—; ins. agent Nat. Benefit Life Ins. Co., N.Y.C., 1997—; personal fin. analyst Primerica Fin. Svcs., White Plains, N.Y., 1997—. Named Gentleman of Distinction, BYKOTA Club of N.Y., 1990; recipient Anne E. Port award 1973. Mem. Am. Soc. Pub. Adminstrn., Soc. Optimates, Bronx-Manhattan Bd. Realtors. Home: 3708 Pratt Ave Bronx NY 10466-5929 Office: Bronx Psychiat Ctr 1500 Waters Pl Bronx NY 10461-2723

HEATH, CHARLES DICKINSON, lawyer, telephone company executive; b. Waterloo, Iowa, June 28, 1941; s. George Clinton and Dorothy (Dickinson) H.; m. Carilyn Frances Cain, June 3, 1972. BBA, U. Iowa, 1962, JD, 1966; MBA, U. Ariz., 1963. Bar: Iowa 1966, Pa. 1969, Ind. 1970, U.S. Supreme Ct. 1971, Wis. 1973, Ariz. 1975, Mich. 1979, Fla. 1979, Calif. 1989. Asst. gen. counsel Kohler Co., Wis., 1973-79; securities and tax counsel Kellogg Co., Battle Creek, Mich., 1979-81; assoc. gen. counsel Universal Telephone Inc., Milw., 1981-89, also corp. sec., 1987-89; atty. CenturyTel, Inc., LaCrosse, Wis., 1989—.

HEATH, DOUGLAS EDWIN, geography educator; b. Beverly, Mass., Dec. 3, 1948; s. Arnold Currier and Gladwyn Lorraine (Blackwell) H.; m Ellen Rosemary Morris, June 5, 1971; 1 child, Laura Ellen. BS in Geology, Bucknell U., 1971; MA in Geography, Syracuse U., 1974, PhD in Geography, 1978. Prof. Northampton C.C., Bethlehem, Pa., 1977—. Contbr. articles to profl. jours, including; Jour. Geography, Profl. Geographer, Jour. of the Water Pollution Control Fedn. Mem. Assn. Am. Geographers, Nat. Coun. for Geographic Edn. (Disting. Tchg. Achievement 1983), Nat. Assn. Geosci. Tchrs, Sierra Club, Nat Resources Def. Coun., Omicron Delta Kappa. Democrat. Unitarian Universalist. Avocations: backpacking, photography. Home: 516 Sherwood Rd Ho Ho Kus NJ 07423-1513 Office: Northampton CC 3835 Green Pond Rd Bethlehem PA 18020-7568 E-mail: dheath@northampton.edu.

HEATH, DWIGHT BRALEY, anthropologist, educator; b. Hartford, Conn., Nov. 19, 1930; s. Percy Leonard and Luise (Hosp) H.; 1 child, David Braley (dec.). AB in Social Rels., Harvard U., 1952; PhD in Anthropology, Yale U., 1959. Mem. faculty Brown U., 1959—, prof. anthropology, 1970—. Dir. Ctr. for Latin Am. Studies, 1984-87, 88-89; vis. prof., U.S. and abroad, cons. in field. Author: A Journal of the Pilgrims at Plymouth, 1963, 86, Land Reform and Social Revolution in Bolivia, 1969, Historical Dictionary of Bolivia, 1972, Contemporary Cultures and Societies of Latin America, 1965, 74, 3d edit., 2002, Cross-Cultural Approaches to the Study of Alcohol, 1976, Alcohol Use and World Cultures, 1980, Cultural Factors in Alcohol Research and Treatment of Drinking Problems, 1981, International Handbook on Alcohol and Cultures, 1995, Drinking Occasions, 2000; contbr. articles to profl. jours. With AUS, 1952-54. Grantee Nat. Acad. Scis., 1974, Am. Philos. Soc., 1972, Social Sci. Research Council, 1958, Doherty Found., 1956-57, Nat. Inst. Alcohol Abuse and Alcoholism, 1976-81. Mem. AAAS, Am. Anthrop. Assn., Am. Ethnol. Soc., Am. Soc. Ethnohistory, Royal Anthrop. Inst., L.Am. Studies Assn. Office: Brown U Dept Anthropology PO Box 1921 Providence RI 02912-1921

HEATH, FRANK BRADFORD, retired dentist; b. Houston, Dec. 11, 1938; s. Robert Bradford and Maudie H. (Sweeney) H.; m. Heide J.M. Schmidt, Aug. 20, 1965; children: Dirk Alan, Shannon Erika, Kent Bradford. BA, Sam Houston State U., 1961; DDS, U. Tex., Houston, 1965. Pvt. practice, Houston, 1967-2000; ret., 2000. Capt. U.S. Army, 1965-67. Fellow Acad. Gen. Dentistry, Acad. Dentistry Internat.; mem. ADA, Tex. Dental Assn., Houston Dist. Dental Soc., Delta Tau Delta, Xi Psi Phi. Republican. Methodist. Home: 12904 W Shadow Lake Ln Cypress TX 77429-5907 E-mail: fbheath@houston.rr.com.

HEATH, GARY BRIAN, manufacturing firm executive, engineer; b. Pueblo, Colo., Nov. 5, 1954; s. William Sidney Heath and Eleanor Aileen (Mortimer) Svedman, Donald Svedman (Stepfather). BSME, U. So. Colo., 1979; MBA, U. Phoenix, 1984. Engr. ADR Ultrasound Corp., Tempe, Ariz., 1979-81; sr. engr. Technicare Ultrasound, Englewood, Colo., 1981-83; engring. mgr. COBE Labs., Inc., Lakewood, Colo., 1983-89; dir. mfg. Gambro BCT, Inc., Lakewood, 1989-96, v.p. mfg., 1996-2000, chief operating officer, 2000—. Mem.: Soc Plastic Engrs, Soc Mfg Engrs. Achievements include patents for fluid flow transfer device, pressure diaphragm for fluid flow device. Avocations: skiing, fishing, reading, weight training. Home: 7 Mule Deer Trail Littleton CO 80127 Office: Gambro BCT Inc 10811 W Collins Ave Lakewood CO 80215-4409 E-mail: gary.heath@gambrobct.com.

HEATH, GEORGE ROSS, oceanographer; b. Adelaide, Australia, Mar. 10, 1939; s. Frederick John and Eleanora (Blackmore) H.; m. Lorna Margaret Sommerville, Oct. 5, 1972; children: Amanda Jo, Alisa Jeanne. BSc, Adelaide U., 1960, BSc with honors, 1961; PhD, U. Calif., San Diego, 1968. Geologist S. Australian Geol. Survey, Adelaide, 1961-63; asst. prof. oceanography Oreg. State U., Corvallis, 1969-72, assoc. prof., 1972-75, prof., dean, 1978-84; assoc. prof. oceanography U. R.I., Narragansett, 1974-77, prof., 1977-78; dean U. Wash., Seattle, 1984-96, prof., 1984—, dean emeritus, 1996—; pres., exec. dir. Monterey Bay Aquarium Rsch. Inst., Moss Landing, Calif., 1996-97. Mem. bd. oceans and atmosphere Nat. Assn. State Univs. and Land Grant Colls., 1982-96, co-chmn. exec. com., 1992-93; chmn. legis. com. Commn. on Food, Environment and Renewable Resources, 1994-96; chmn. bd. ocean sci. and policy NRC, 1984-85, mem. bd. radioactive waste mgmt., 1982-90; bd. govs. Joint Oceanographic Instns., Inc., 1978-96, chmn., 1982-84; v.p. sci. com. on oceanic rsch. of Internat. Coun. of Sci. Unions, 1984-90; chmn. performance assessment peer rev. panel Waste Isolation Pilot Plant, 1987-98; bd. dirs. Monterey Bay Aquarium Rsch. Inst; found. com. Coll. Marine Sci. and Fisheries, Sultan Qaboos U., Muscat, Sultanate of Oman, 1994—; adv. panel Odyssey, 1990—, bd. govs., 1999-2000; environ. analyst Sta. KIRO-TV, Seattle, 1993; bd. govs. Consortium for Oceanographic Rsch. & Edn., 1994-98, chmn., 1996-98; bd. govs. Seattle Aquarium Soc., 1998—; mem. Nat. Sea Grant rev. panel, 2001—. Contbr. articles to profl. jours. Recipient Fulbright award, 1963. Fellow AAAS, Geol. Soc. Am., Am. Geophys. Union; mem. Oceanography Soc. Home: 12513 237th Way NE Redmond WA 98053 Office: U Wash Sch Oceanography PO Box 357940 Seattle WA 98195-7940 E-mail: rheath@u.washington.edu.

HEATH, HUNTER, III, endocrinologist, researcher; b. Dallas, June 8, 1942; s. Hunter Jr. and Velma M. (Brandon) H.; m. Glenna A. Witt, July 25, 1965; 1 child, Ethan Ford. BA in Chemistry, Tex. Tech Coll., 1964; MD, Washington U., 1968. Intern, then resident in medicine U. Wis. Hosps., Madison, 1968-70; fellow in endocrinology and metabolism Walter Reed Army Med. Ctr., Washington, 1970-72; chief endocrinology sect. Letterman Army Med. Ctr., San Francisco, 1972-74; rsch. fellow in biochemistry and metabolism Mayo Grad. Sch. Medicine, Rochester, Minn., 1974-76, from asst. prof. to prof. medicine, cons./rschr. endocrinol., 1976-91, head endocrine rsch. unit, 1984-88, assoc. dir., dir. clin. rsch. ctr., 1986-88, dir. for rsch. Scottsdale, Ariz., 1988-90; prof. medicine, chief divsn. endocrinology, metabolism and diabetes U. Utah, Salt Lake City, 1991-96; med. dir. endocrinology Eli Lilly and Co., Indpls., 1996—, sr. med. dir. endocrinology, 2003—. Mem. adv. com. NIH, Bethesda, Md., 1985-88; pres., bd. dirs. Advances in Mineral Metabolism, Inc., Rochester, 1986-89, treas. 1994-96; mem. select panel of physicians FAA, Washington, 1986-87. Bd. dirs. Utah affiliate Am. Diabetes Assn., 1992-93; bd. dirs. Utah affiliate Arthritis Found., 1993-96, Ind. affiliate, 1996-98; mem. Sch. Dist. Task Force on Lang. Arts Edn., Rochester, 1984. Maj. U.S. Army, 1970—74. Fellow ACP (editl. bd. 1985-88); mem. Am. Soc. for Bone Mineral Rsch. (councillor 1985-88), Endocrine Soc. (publs. com. 1985-88, 2001-). Avocations: sport aviation, writing, music. Office: Eli Lilly and Co Lilly Corporate Ctr Indianapolis IN 46285-0001

HEATH, JAMES EDWARD, physiology educator, retired; b. Evansville, Ind., May 3, 1935; s. Max Levy and Mae Blossom (McNutt) H.; m. Maxine Shoemaker, Apr. 2, 1955; children: Cynthia Maxine, Pamela Diane, Jessica Scott. BA, UCLA, 1957, MA, 1958, PhD, 1962. Asst. prof. physiology U. Ill., Urbana, 1964-67, assoc. prof. physiology, 1967-72, prof. physiology, 1972-75, 75-95, head dept. physiology, 1976-82, prof. emeritus, 1995—; prof., dept. chmn. U. Fla., Gainesville, 1974-75. Cons. evaluator North Ctrl. Assn., 1978-95; vis. scholar U. Tex., Austin, 1996—. Editor Physiology Zoology, 1975-92, Jour. Thermal Biology, 1975—; mem. editl. bd. Ann. Rev. Physiology, 1980-85; contbr. over 100 articles to profl. jours. NSF, NIH grantee; Fulbright fellow, 1986-87. Fellow AAAS; mem. Am. Physiol. Soc., Ecol. Soc. Am. (editl. bd. 1972-76), Soc. Ichthyology and Herpetology, SAR, SCV, Descs. of War 1812. Avocations: sailing, guitar, model railroading. Home: 104 Hummingbird Cir Buchanan Dam TX 78609-4457 Office: U Ill Dept Physiology 405 S Goodwin Ave Urbana IL 61801-3702 E-mail: jheath@tstar.net.

HEATH, JEFFREY A. executive recruiter; b. Kent, Washington, Sept. 30, 1950; s. Harold Herbert and Charlotte (Mitchell) H.; m. Karen Sue Bradley, Sept. 12, 1982. BS in Psychology, Manhattan Coll., 1975; MBA in Finance, Pace U., 1978. With Lafayette Radio Corp., Syosset, NY, 1972-77; sales mgr. U.S. JVC Corp., Elmwood Park, N.J., 1977-79, nat. corp. adminstr., 1979-81; pres. Mgmt. Recruiters Internat., N.Y.C., 1981-98; CEO The Landstone Group, 1998—. Bd. dirs. New Castle Conservation Bd., Chappaqua, N.Y., 1984-90. Mem. Psi Chi. Republican. Home: 9 Crystal Spring Rd Chappaqua NY 10514-1412 Office: 295 Madison Ave Fl 36 New York NY 10017-6304 E-mail: jah@landstonegroup.com.

HEATH, JEROME BRUCE, information systems educator; b. East Chicago, Ind., Nov. 12, 1939; s. King Ralph and Doris Lois (Young) H.; m. Joan M. Wall, Aug. 20, 1960 Idiv. Aut. 1990); children: Linda, Deej, Lisa, Dean; m. Valerie May Meyers, Jan. 6, 1991. BA, Monmouth Coll., 1962; MBA, U. Minn., 1985; PhD, U. Hawaii, 1997. Environ. engr. Waldorf Paper, St. Paul, 1970-76; chem. engr. Combustion Equip., Fridley, Minn., 1976-80; project engr. EKA, Raissio, Appleton, Wis., 1980-83; computer coord. Nat. Coll., St. Paul, 1988-90; mem. faculty Metro State U., St. Paul, 1990-93, Hawaii Pacific U., Honolulu, 1993-97, North Seattle C.C., 1997-98; mem. staff Dept. Social and Health Svcs., Info. Sys. Svcs. Divsn. State of Wash., Olympia, Wash., 1999—2001; assoc. prof. mgmt. info. sys. Met. State U., 2001—. Computer trainer Access, Honolulu, 1993-97; reviewer Idea Group Pub., Hershey, Pa., 1997—. Author textbook: Structured Program Design, 1993; contbr. article, poem and chpt. to profl. publs. Vice chair Lino Lakes (Minn.) Planning and Zoning Bd., 1978-80. Honeywell fellow, 1984. E-mail: jerry.heath@metrostate.edu.

HEATH, JINGER L. cosmetics executive; b. 1952; Homemaker, 1973-81; part-time interior decorator, cons., 1981; chmn. bd. Beauticontrol Cosmetics Inc., Carrollton, Tex., 1981—. Office: Beauticontrol Cosmetics Inc 2121 Midway Rd Carrollton TX 75006-5039

HEATH, JOSEPH JOHN, lawyer; b. Watertown, N.Y., Mar. 19, 1946; s. Robert Edward and Lucille Frances (Gerringer) H.; 1 child, Travis Jackson. B.A., Syracuse U., 1968; J.D., SUNY-Buffalo, 1974. Bar: N.Y. 1975, U.S. Dist. Ct. (no. dist.) N.Y. 1976. Trial atty. Attica Bros. Legal Def., Buffalo, 1975-76; ptnr. Heath, Rosenthal & Weissman, Syracuse, 1976—; adj. prof. SUNY-Oswego, 1982-83; clin. prof. Syracuse U., 1982; sec. bd. dirs. G.C. Hanford Co., Syracuse, 1986, Allflex Mfg. Co., Syracuse, 1986. Mem. Onondaga County Child Abuse Citizen's Adv. Coun., Onondaga County Dist. Atty.'s Adv. Coun; bd. dirs. Hiscock Legal Aid Soc., 1984. Served with USN, 1968-70. Mem. Nat. Lawyers Guild, Onondaga County Bar Assn., N.Y. State Bar assn., N.Y. State Defenders Assn. Democrat. Roman Catholic. Office: 716 E Washington St Ste 104 Syracuse NY 13210-1550

HEATH, JOSEPHINE WARD, foundation administrator; b. San Jose, Calif., Sept. 5, 1937; d. James Hugh and Adella Ward; m. Stratton Rollins Heath Jr.; children: Stratton, Kristin Heath-Colon, Joel. BS, Ea. Oreg. State U., 1959; MS, U. Wis., 1960. Commr. Boulder (Colo.) County, 1982-90; tchg. fellow John F. Kennedy Sch. of Govt., Harvard U., Cambridge, Mass., 1991; spl. asst. to the dir. White Ho. Office of Nat. Svc., Washington, 1993; pres. Jurismonitor, Boulder, 1993-95; tchr., project liberty John F. Kennedy Sch. Govt., Harvard U., Cambridge, 1994-98; pres. The Cmty. Found., Boulder, 1995—. Tchr. Bad Kreuznach, Germany, 1966-67, El Paso, Tex., 1963-64, Appleton, Wis., 1961-62; regional dir. ACTION, Denver, 1977-79. Editor: Alternative Work Patterns, 1977. Candidate U.S. Senate, Colo., 1992, 1990; commr. Met. Baseball Stadium Dist., Maj. League Colo. Rockies, 1991—; county commr. Boulder County, 1982-90; co-founder Women's Found. of Colo., 1987; trainer for elected offcls. in Ctrl. Europe, 1994-98. Named to Colo. Women's Hall of Fame, 2000. Mem. Internat. Women's Forum (bd. dirs. 1986-89), Women's Forum of Colo. (pres. 1991). Democrat. Avocations: skiing, hiking, sports. Home: 2455 Vassar Dr Boulder CO 80305-5728 Office: The Cmty Found 1123 Spruce St Boulder CO 80302-4001 E-mail: JosieHeath@aol.com.

HEATH, MARK E. lawyer; b. Smyrna, Tenn., Mar. 18, 1961; s. David William and Reba Mae Heath; m. Pamela Shane Embry, May 12, 1984; 1 child, Mary Margaret. BA (cum laude), Western Ky. U., 1983; JD, U. of Ky., 1986. Atty.: Ky. 1986, DC 1989, W.Va. 1990, Admitted: U.S. Ct. of Appeals for the Sixth Circuit 1990, U.S. Ct. of Appeals for the Fourth Circuit 1996, U.S. Supreme Ct. 1997. Capt., atty. U.S. Army Judge Adv. General's Corps, Ft. McPherson, Ga., 1987—89; ptnr. Heenan, Althen & Roles, LLP, Charleston, W.Va., 1989—2002; counsel Spilman, Thomas & Battle, PLLC, Charleston, W.Va., 2003—. Program chmn. Energy & Mineral Law Found. 23rd Ann. Ky. Mineral Law Conf., Lexington, Ky., 1998; trustee Energy & Mineral Law Found. Ky. Mineral Law Conf., Lexington, Ky., 1999—; program chmn. Energy & Mineral Law Found. Ky. 26th Ann. Mineral Law Conf., Lexington, Ky., 2001; co-chairman, program com. Energy & Mineral Law Found. 27th Ann. Mineral Law Conf., Lexington, Ky., 2002. Contbr. articles to profl. jours. Chmn., trustees Elizabeth Meml. United Meth. Ch., Charleston, W.Va., 1995. Capt. U.S. Army, 1987—89. Decorated Commandant's List U.S. Army Judge Adv. General's Corps, Army Commendation mdal Ft. McPherson, Ga. Mem.: ABA. Methodist. Avocations: travel, history. Home: 1958 Parkwood Rd Charleston WV 25314 Office: Spilman Thomas & Battle PLLC 300 Kanawha Blvd E Charleston WV 25301 Office Fax: 304-340-3801. E-mail: mheath@spilmanlaw.com.

HEATH, PAUL A. psychologist; b. Oct. 17, 1936; Student, Okla. Bapt. U., 1955-56; B Secondary Edn., U. Ctrl. Okla., 1959, M Tchg., 1961; EdD, U. Okla., 1970, postgrad., 1972-74. Lic. psychologist, Okla. Secondary tchr., jr. high sch. counselor Western Heights Sch. Dist., Oklahoma City, 1959-62; vocat. rehab. counselor Okla. Divsn. Vocat. Rehab., 1962-65; agy. and sheltered workshop dir. United Cerebral Palsy of Greater Okla., Inc., Oklahoma City, 1965-67; counseling psychologist, officer-in-charge VA Adminstrn. Regional Office, Oklahoma City, 1968—2000; pvt. practice Oklahoma City, 2000—. Contracting counseling psychologist Okla. Psychol. and Edn. Ctr., Inc., Muskogee, 1966-68; vocat. expert witness Bur. Hearing and Appeals, Oklahoma City, 1966-68; part-time grad. tchr. U. Ctrl. Okla., Edmond; mem. Bd. Mental Health and Substance Abuse Svcs., 1998-99. Sunday sch. tchr., Oklahoma City, 1958-65; bd. dirs. Found. for Disabled Adults, Oklahoma City, 1973-74, United Cerebral Palsy of Greater Oklahoma City, 1974-85; bd. dirs., chair bldg. com. Rainbow Hills Ctr. for Ind. Living, 1984-85; bd. dirs., treas. Group Home Cerebral Palsy of Greater Oklahoma City, 1984-86; rep. Muskogee VA Regional Office at Fed. Exec. Bd., Oklahoma City, 1995-2000; bd. dirs., treas., v.p., pres. Oklahoma City Murrah Bldg. Survivors Assn., 1995-2002; mem. final jury com. Oklahoma City Meml. Found., 1997; mem. Oklahoma Bd. of Edn., 1983-87, v.p., 1987. Recipient Employee of Yr. award Air Force Assn., 1996, Pub. Svc. award Okla. Fed. Exec. Bd., 1997, award Exec. Office of Pres. of U.S., 1999. Home: 1320 SW 69th St Oklahoma City OK 73159-3218 Office: 1601 SW 89th St Ste 500 Oklahoma City OK 73159

HEATH, RICHARD EDDY, lawyer; b. N.J., Nov. 15, 1930; s. W. Eddy and Dorothy (Brown) H.; m. Beth M., June 17, 1955; children: Ellen Louise, David Montgomery, Karen Elizabeth, Deborah Anne. BA cum laude, Swarthmore Coll., 1952; LLB cum laude, Harvard U., 1955. Bar: N.Y., Fla. Teaching fellowship Harvard Law Sch., Cambridge, Mass., 1955-56; assoc. Hodgson and Russ, Buffalo, N.Y., 1956-61, ptnr., 1961—. Bd. dirs. Cliffstar Corp., Dunkirk, N.Y. Trustee Children's Hosp., Buffalo, 1975-98; trustee U. at Buffalo Found., 1966-89, sec., 1976—. Recipient Walter P. Cooke award U. Buffalo, 1978.

HEATH, RICHARD MURRAY, retired hospital administrator; b. Amanda, Ohio, Sept. 24, 1927; s. Cecil E. and Mary Eva (Murray) H.; m. Charlene Wilson, June 4, 1948; children: Jenifer Sue, Janet Lynn. BS in Edn, Wilmington (Ohio) Coll., 1949; MS in Social Adminstrn, Case Western Res. U., 1953; MS in Hosp. Adminstrn, Northwestern U., 1958. Adminstr. Orient (Ohio) State Hosp., 1956-61; asst. supt. Colo. State Hosp., 1961-72; dir. instl. services N.Y. State Dept. Mental Hygiene, 1972-77; dir. Mohawk Valley Psychiat. Centers, 1977-93; ret., 1993. Project dir. NIMH grants; survey cons. Joint Commn. Accreditation of Hosps. Author articles in field. Served with USNR, World War II. Recipient Kleber award N.Y. State Assn. for Blind, 1976 Mem. NASW (charter), Assn. Mental Health Adminstrs. (pres. 1970, gov. region II 1986-89, Peipenbrink award 1992), Am. Coll. Healthcare Execs., Masons, Scottish Rite (32 degree).

HEATH, RICHARD RAYMOND, investment company executive, retired; b. La Junta, Colo., June 22, 1929; s. Perry Stanford and Genevieve Anabelle (Whitney) H.; m. Arlene Newbrow, Nov. 3, 1961. BA in Econs., U. Colo., 1951, LLB, 1954. Bar: Colo. 1954, Calif. 1957, Ark. 1973. Mem. firm Neyhart & Grodin, San Francisco, 1957-66; dep. Peace Corps dir. Ivory Coast, 1966-68; dir., 1968-69; Peace Corps dir. Mali, 1969-72; dir. Ark. Dept. Fin. and Adminstrn.; also chief fiscal officer, commr. revenues State of Ark., mem. gov.'s cabinet, 1972-77; dir. San Francisco Internat. Airport, 1977-81; v.p., dir. mktg. AIS, Inc., 1981-84; exec. v.p., CFO United Bank, San Francisco, 1984-85; chmn., CEO Nat. Bus. Resources Inc., 1985-87; ptnr. Hakman & Co., Investment Bankers, 1987-2000; chmn., CEO Podarok Internat., Inc., 1993-96; chmn., pres. Heath Mgmt. Svcs., 1994-2000; chmn. Laser Design Internat., LLC, 1996—. Chmn., CEO 1st Calif. Bus. and Indsl. Devel. Corp., United Bus. Ventures; bd. dirs. V-Ray Imaging, Inc.; vice chmn. Multi-State Tax Commn., 1973-74, chmn., 1976-77, mem. exec. com., 1974-77; del. Conf. State Bar Dels. Bd. dirs., treas. San Francisco Midsummer Mozart Festival, 1986-92, chmn., 1999-2000; mem. nat. bd. dirs. Coalition for a Dem. Majority, 1973-76; chmn. bd. dirs. FORUM; mem. conservative caucus nat. Tax Limitation Com., 1980—; mem. rep. presdl. task force Rep. nat. Com., 1980-91. Mem. State Bar Calif., San Francisco Bar Assn. (past chmn. indsl. accident com.), San Francisco Lawyers Club, Am., Calif. trial lawyers assns., San Francisco Planning and Urban Renewal Assn., Nat. Parks Assn., Calif. Applicants Attys. Assn. (v.p.) Clubs: Little Rock Racquet, Little Rock Athletic, San Francisco Tennis (gov.), Rotary Internat., World Trade. Home: One Treetops Lane #902 Little Rock AR 72202-1660

HEATH, ROGER CHARLES, state senator, writer; b. Franklin, N.H., Jan. 21, 1943; s. Everett M. and Madeline (White) Heath; m. Martha Weeks. BS, No. Ariz. U., 1966. Tchr. pub. schs., N.H., Ariz., N.Y., 1966-69; mgr. E.M. Heath Stores, Inc., NH, 1969-73, now dir., treas., 1969-73; mem. N.H. Ho. of Reps., 1979-84, N.H. Senate, 1984-92, chmn. ways and means com., 1985-87, asst. majority whip, 1988-92; asst. dir. Gov.'s Office Energy and Cmty. Svc., Concord, 1992-97, tchr., 1997—; tchr. English electives Winisquam Regional H.S., 2001—. Author: The Policital Spectrum, The Language of Politics, 1978; contbr. articles to nat. mags. Vice chmn. NH Pub. Radio Adv. Bd., 1981—84; commr. Ednl. Commn. of States, 1985—87, Atlantic States Marine Fisheries Commn.; chmn. Christa McAuliffe Planetarium Commn., 1989—92; chmn. natural resources com. NH Rep. Platform Com., 1983; del. eastern regional conf. Coun. of State Govts., 1985, 1985; mem. Coun. of State Govts. Environ. Task Force. Mem. Nat. Coun. State Legislatures, Am. Legis. Exch. Coun. (membership coord., chmn. nat. task force on edn. 1985-92), Nat. Conf. State Legislatures (internat. trade com.), Internat. Assn. for Energy Econs., Gun Owners N.H. (bd. dirs., v.p. 1980-84), Mead Wilderness Base High Adventure Program (adv. com.), Winnipesaukee Sportsmen's Club (bd. dirs. 1980-87), Masons. Avocations: early home restoration, fishing, hunting, taurine.

HEATH, ROSS BRADLEY, consulting company executive; b. Geneva, Ill., June 26, 1959; s. Donald Jeremiah Heath and Louise Zalithea H. BA in English, Augustana Coll., 1982; MS in Tech. Mgmt., U. Md., 1996. Program mgr. performance engring. Getronics (formerly J.G. Van Dyke & Assocs.), Alexandria, Va., 1992-2000; cons. network architect EDS, Washington, 2001—. Mem. City of Alexandria Commn. on Aging, 1989-92; master of ceremonies Annual Lighting of Nat. Christmas Tree, Ellipse, Washington, 1999. Grantee Andrew Mellon Found., 1979; recipient award of Merit City of Alexandria Commn. on Aging, 1993, Cert. of Recognition City of Alexandria, 1993. Mem. Toastmasters (pres. 1998-99, Schweitzer award 1998, Toastmaster of Yr. 1998-99). Avocations: public speaking, writing. E-mail: ross.heath@mindspring.com.

HEATH, THOMAS CLARK, lawyer; b. Sarasota, Fla., Feb. 6, 1948; s. Roy Fulmer and Ruby (Clark) Heath; m. Anne Frances Wilson, Sept. 6, 1980; 1 child, Benjamin. BSBA, U. Fla., 1970, JD, 1973. Bar: Fla. 1973, U.S. Dist. Ct. (so. dist.) Fla. 1976, U.S. Ct. Appeals (11th cir.) 1976. Assoc. Howell, Kirby, Montgomery et al, Ft. Lauderdale, Fla., 1973-75, Carey, Dwyer, Cole, Selwood & Bernard, Ft. Lauderdale, Fla., 1975-81; ptnr. Hainline, Billing, Cochran & Heath, Ft. Lauderdale, Fla., 1981-85, Billing, Cochran, Heath, Lyles & Mauro, Ft. Lauderdale, Fla., 1985—, West Palm Beach, Fla., 1985—. Fellow Am. Bd. Trial Advocacy (charter); mem. Am. Assn. Hosp. Attys., Assn. Trial Lawyers Am., Trial Attys. Am., Fla. Defense Lawyers Assn. Avocations: fishing, hunting. Office: Billing Cochran Heath Lyles & Mauro 888 SE 3rd Ave Ste 301 Fort Lauderdale FL 33316-1159

HEATHCOCK, CLAYTON HOWELL, chemistry educator, researcher; b. San Antonio, Tex., July 21, 1936; s. Clayton H. and Frances E. (Lay) H.; m. Mabel Ruth Sims, Sept. 6, 1957 (div. 1972); children: Cheryl Lynn, Barbara Sue, Steven Wayne, Rebecca Ann; m. Cheri R. Hadley, Nov. 28, 1980. BSc, Abilene Christian Coll., Tex., 1958; PhD, U. Colo., 1963. Supr. chem. analysis group Champion Paper and Fiber Co., Pasadena, Tex., 1958-60; asst. prof. chemistry U. Calif.-Berkeley, 1964-70, assoc. prof., 1970-75, prof., 1975—, chmn., 1986-89, dean Coll. of Chemistry, 1999—. Chmn. Medicinal Chemistry Study Sect., NIH, Washington, 1981-83; mem. sci. adv. coun. Abbott Labs., 1986-97. Author: Introduction to Organic Chemistry, 1976; editor-in chief Organic Syntheses, 1985-86, Jour. Organic Chemistry, 1989-99; contbr. numerous articles to profl. jours. Recipient Alexander von Humboldt U.S. Scientist, 1978, Allan R. Day award, 1989, Prelog medal, 1991, Centenary medal Royal Soc. Chemistry, 1995. Mem. AAAS, Am. Acad. Arts and Scis., Am. Chem. Soc. (chmn. divsn. organic chemistry 1985, Ernest Guenther award 1986, award for creative work in synthetic organic chemistry 1990, A.C. Cope scholar 1990, H.C. Brown medal 2002), Nat. Acad. Scis. (H.C. Brown award 2002), Royal Soc. Chemistry (Centenary medal 1995), Am. Soc. Pharmacology. Home: 5235 Alhambra Valley Rd Martinez CA 94553-9765 Office: U Calif Dept Chemistry Berkeley CA 94720-1460 E-mail: heathcock@cchem.berkeley.edu.

HEATHCOTTE, BARRY W. mechanical engineer, consultant; b. Evansville, Ind., July 10, 1937; s. James Junior and P. Loretta Heathcotte; m. Barnita L. Perry; children: Roger W., Karen R., Elaine M. AS in Bus., U. Evansville, 1973. Cert. mfg. engr. Drafter Alcoa, Newburgh, Ind., 1964—66; graphic design group leader Babcock & Wilcox Co., Mt. Vernon, Ind., 1966—79; contract mgr. Internat. Steel Co., Evansville, 1979—80; chief dep. auditor Vanderburgh County, Evansville, 1980—82; engring. liaison M & E Engring., Evansville, 1982—84, C. Gott & Assocs., Evansville, 1984—86; cons. Geometrics Consulting, Evansville, 1982- . Co-founder, chmn. adv. com. Evansville Elite Soccer Club. Mem.: ASME (codes and stds. com. 1980—), Soc. Mfg. Engrs. (sr.). Roman Catholic. Office: Geometrics Consulting 1500 Conlin Ave Evansville IN 47714 Fax: 419-793-5363. E-mail: barheath@evansville.net.

HEATHCOTTE, TOBY FESLER, writer, retired educator; d. Howard Dale Fesler and Beulah Mae Crosley; children: Brandon, Brock. MAT, Ind. U., 1968. Lic. tchr. h.s. and coll. Tchr speech, drama, English Phoenix Union H.S. Dist., 1969—94; writing tchr. Maricopa C.C. Dist., Glendale, Ariz., 1996—2000. Writer, prodr. plays Ariz. State U., Tempe, 1989—93. Author: Program Building: A Practical Guide for High School Speech and Drama Teachers, 2003 (San Diego Book Award, 1994); author: (with Betty Joy) Seeds for Fertile Minds: Eight Curriculum Integration Tools, 1995; author: (fiction) Alison's Legacy, 2000. Contest chair Ariz. Authors Assn., Phoenix, 2000—. Mem.: Inst. Noetic Scis. Unity Ch. Avocations: writing, theater. Home: 6145 W Echo Ln Glendale AZ 85302

HEATLEY, DANY, hockey player; b. Freibourg, Germany, Jan. 21, 1981; Right wing Atlanta Thrashers, 2001—; named WCHA's rookie of the yr., 1999—2000. Office: Atlanta Hockey Club Inc 1 CNN Ctr 13 S Atlanta GA 30303

HEATON, CHARLES HUDDLESTON, retired church musician; b. Centralia, Ill., Nov. 1928; s. Wilbur Estel Heaton and Nina Huddleston; m. Jane Pugh, Apr. 17, 1954 (dec. Sept. 1999); children: Rebecca Lynn Turner, Charles Jr., Matthew Aaron. BMus, DePauw U., 1950; M of Sacred Music, Union Theol. Sem., N.Y.C., 1952, D of Sacred Music, 1957. Min. of music 2d Presbyn. Ch., St. Louis, 1956-72; organ tchr. So. Ill. U., Carbondale, 1962-64; dir. music Temple Israel, St. Louis, 1959-70; lectr. music Pitts. Theol. Sem., 1973-76; organist, dir. East Liberty Presbyn. Ch., Pitts., 1972-93; ret. Interim organist, choirmaster Calvary Episc. Ch., Pitts., 1996—97; organist in residence Trinity Cathedral, Pitts., 1993—96, 1997—2002; cons. organ design various chs. and schs. Author: How to Build a Church Choir, 1958, Worship Services of Sacred Music, 1962. Fellow Am. Guild Organists (nat. councillor 1967-70, regional chmn. 1970-72); mem. Organ Hist. Soc. Avocations: reading, walking. Home: 5932 Elgin St Pittsburgh PA 15206-1644 E-mail: charles.h.heaton@gte.net.

HEATON, CHARLES LLOYD, dermatologist, educator; b. Bryan, Tex., May 8, 1935; s. Homer Lloyd and Bessie Blanton (Sharp) H. BS, Tex. A&M U., 1957; MD, Baylor U., 1961; MA (hon.), U. Pa., 1973. Diplomate Am. Bd. Dermatology. Intern Jefferson Davis Hosp., Houston, 1961-62; resident Baylor U., 1962-65; sr. attending physician Phila. Gen. Hosp., 1965-69, chief of svc., 1970-77; mem. dept. dermatology U. Pa. Sch. Medicine, 1966-78; assoc. prof. dermatology U. Pa., 1973-78, U. Cin., 1978-85, prof., 1985—, interim dir. dept. dermatology, 1998. Author: Audiovisual Course in Venereal Disease, 1972, (with D.M. Pillsbury) Manual of Dermatology, 1980; contbr. 35 articles to profl. jours., 12 chpts. to books. Served to lt. comdr. USPHS, 1965-67. Named Ohio Dermatologist of Yr., 2000. Fellow ACP, AAD, Coll. Physicians of Phila.; mem. AMA, Soc. Investigative Dermatology, Am. Venereal Disease Assn., Am. Dermatol. Assn., Royal Soc. Medicine (London), Cin. Dermatol. Soc., Alpha Omega Alpha. Home: 5534 E Galbraith Rd Apt 25 Cincinnati OH 45236-2840 Office: U Cin Coll Coll Medicine Dept Dermatology 231 Bethesda Ave Cincinnati OH 45229-2827 E-mail: charles.heaton@uc.edu.

HEATON, JON C. lawyer; b. Brigham City, Utah, Aug. 31, 1942; s. Harley Lowry and Anne Jane (Lundburg) H.; m. Penny Bourquin, Dec. 30, 1961; children: John Patrick, Timothy A., J. Scott, Jennifer, L., Annelise. BS in Bus. with honors, U. Colo., 1964; JD, Vanderbilt U., 1972. Bar: Utah 1972, U.S. Dist. Ct. Utah 1972. Assoc. Butler, McHugh, Butler, Tune & Watts, Nashville, 1972, Prince, Yeates & Geldzahler, Salt Lake City, 1972-76, ptnr., 1976-80, sr. ptnr., 1980—. Bd. dirs., officer Koflach USA, Salt Lake City, 1988-92, Marker Bindings, Salt Lake City, 1983-96; atty. Park City (Utah) Ski Resort, 1975—, U.S. Ski Team, Park City, 1978-84, Whitmores Inc., Pentalon Corp.; judge pro tem 3d Cir. Cts., Salt Lake City, 1980—; mem. archtl. bd. State Utah. With USAF, 1964-69; brig. gen. Utah Air N.G. Mem. ABA, Utah State Bar, Salt Lake County Bar Assn., N.G. Assn. U.S., Order of Coif, Pi Kappa Alpha. Republican. Avocations: tennis, boating, wilderness areas, skiing, flying. Office: 175 E 4th S Ste 900 Salt Lake City UT 84111-2357 E-mail: jch@pyglaw.com.

HEATON, LARRY CADWALDER, securities company executive; b. St. Louis, Aug. 19, 1934; s. John Raymond and Martha Elizabeth (Simpson) H.; m. Dorothy Mueller, Dec. 10, 1933; children: Tannice Jo, Larry C. II, Kent M., Eric S., Elmo D.J., David J. II. Student, So. Ill. U., 1959; BSBA, U. Tampa, 1962; postgrad., Chgo. Kent Coll. Law, 1962-65. Registered investment advisor. Adjuster N.Y. Ctrl. R.R., Chgo., 1962-65; salesman/sales mgr. SCM Inc., Chgo., 1965-68; agt., gen. agt. Thomas Jefferson Life Ins., Champaign, Ill., 1969-75; gen. agt. Ctrl. Nat. Life Ins., Jacksonville, Ill., 1975-80; pres., co-founder Nurses Guaranteed Retirement Life Ins., Jacksonville, Fla., 1980-85; gen. agt., mgr. Nat. Old Line Ins., Little Rock, 1985-95; pres., owner Larry C. Heaton & Assocs., Jacksonville, Fla., 1996—. Chmn. PFL Agts. Adv. Bd., Little Rock, 1992. Co-author state manual: Illinois Young Republicans, 1965 (Nat. Young Republican award). Adminstrv. asst., speech writer Ill. Young Republicans, 1962-68; precinct capt. Cook County Rep. Orgn., Oak Park, Ill., 1965-68; mem. Rep. Presdl. Task Force, Washington, 1982—; mem. House/Senate Adv. Bd., Washington, 1985—. Sgt. U.S. Army, 1953-56. Active vestry, jr. warden/vestry San Jose Episcopal Ch., 1999-2002, sr. warden/vestry, 2002-2003. Recipient Bronze plaque Nat. Assn. Life Underwriters, 1973, Nat. Performance award Nat. Assn. Life Underwriters, 1973, Nat. Quality award Nat. Assn. Life Underwriters, 1974, Million Dollar Round Table award Nat. Assn. Life Underwriters, 1970-85. Mem. Inst. CFPs, Internat. Assn. Fin. Planning, Certified Estate Planner, Certified Charitable Tax Deductible Adv., NCF, Masons (32d degree). Republican. Episcopalian. Avocations: family, golf, painting, sailing.

HEATON, PATRICIA, actress; b. Cleve., Mar. 4, 1959; d. Chuck and Pat Heaton; m. David Hunt, 1992; 4 children BA in Theater, Ohio State U., 1980. Actress playing Debra Barone on Everybody Loves Raymond CBS-TV, 1996—. Appearances include (TV series) Room for Two, 1992-93, Someone Like Me, 1994, Women of the House, 1995, Everybody Loves Raymond, 1996— (Best Actress in Quality Comedy Viewers for Quality TV award 1998, Outstanding Lead Actress in Comedy Series Emmy award, 2000 and 2001); (TV episodes) Alien Nation, 1989, thirtysomething, 1990, (TV movie) Shattered Dreams: The Charlotte Fedders Story, 1990, (films) Beethoven, 1992, Memoirs of an Invisible Man, 1992, The New Age, 1994, Space Jam, 1996, (stage) The Johnstown Vindicator, 1987, Don't Get God Started, 1987-88, Miracle in the Woods, 1997, author (book): Motherhood and Hollywood, 2003. Hon. chairperson Feminists for Life. Recipient Emmy Award, 2000, 2001. Office: Internat Creative Mgmt 8942 Wilshire Blvd Beverly Hills CA 90211-1934

HEATWOLE, JOHN LAWRENCE, historian, sculptor; b. Washington, Mar. 24, 1948; s. John Lawrence and Lily Marie (Preston) H.; m. Kathleen Stoffel, June 1968 (div. Aug. 1970); 1 child, David Frederick; m. Miriam Dale, Dec. 18, 1971. Rschr. Libr. of Congress, Washington, 1968-74; head woodcarver Va. Craftsmen, Inc., Harrisonburg, 1974-76; sculptor Bridgewater, Va., 1976—. Cons. various Shenendoah Valley Pub. TV Prodns., 1975—, Nat. Pub. TV's Silent Witnesses—America's Historic Trees, 1999, Va. Mil. Inst. film Field of Lost Shoes—The Battle of New Market, 2000, Warm Springs Turnpike Hist. Wayside, Rockingham County, Va., 2001; hist. cons. Mus. of the Shenandoah Valley, Winchester, Va., 2003, PBS film Valley of Fire, 2002; advisor Bridgewater (Va.) Bicentennial Com., 1976—81, Mus. Am. Frontier Culture, Staunton, Va., 1985—86, Soc. Port Republic Preservationists, 2000—; lectr. Nat. Park Svc., 1980—; historian Roanoke Pub. TV's Jackson in the Shenendoah, 1997; dir. Blue Ridge Uplands Symposium, 2002, Shenandoah Valley Civil War Findings Seminar, 2002; curator and presenter Early Am. Frontier Exhit, W. Va. Dept. Humanities, Lost River, W.Va., 2002; cons. McCormick Civil War Inst., Winchester, 2003; presenter Civil War Assocs. Symposium, James Madison U., Harrisonburg, W.Va., 2003, Civil War Edn. Assn. Symposium, Winchester, Va., 2003. Author: (books) Shenandoah Voices, 1995 (Shenandoah Valley Folklore Soc. award 1995), The Burning—Sheridan's Devastation of the Shenandoah Valley, 1998 (Davis award for preservation of So. history 1999), Remember Me Is All I Ask—Chrisman's Boy Company, 2000, Preface- Unionists and the Civil War Experience, 2003, Introduction - Pennsylvania Bucktails, 2003; contbr. artwork to Fine Woodworking Mag. Internat., 1989; contbr. articles to woodworking mag.; one-person shows include U.S. Senate Rotunda, Washington, 1991; exhibited in group shows Del. Art Mus., 1985-89. Bicentennial rep. Libr. of Congress, Washington, 1974; chmn. Rockingham County Bicentennial Commn., 1975-78; commr. Shenandoah Valley Battlefields Nat. Hist. Commn., New Market, Va., 1997-2000; historian, trustee Shenandoah Valley Battlefields Found., New Market, 2001—. Recipient Sculpture award, Pendragon Gallery, 1985, Peservation award, Shenandoah Valley Folk Arts Revival Soc., 1996, President's award for preservation Shenandoah Valley History, Shenandoah U., Winchester, Va., 2002. Mem. Shenandoah Valley Civil War Roundtable (pres. 1980-89), Ft. Harrison, Inc. (bd. dirs. 1985-87), Harrisonburg-Rockingham Hist. Soc. (curator 1975-78), Greenbrier Hist. Soc. Home: 202 W Bank St Bridgewater VA 22812 E-mail: jlheatwole@aol.com.

HEATWOLE, MARK M. lawyer; b. Pitts., Jan. 28, 1948; s. Marion Grove and Phyllis Adelle (Leiter) H.; m. Sarah Ann Collier, Dec. 30, 1970; children: Mary Phyllis, Elizabeth Collier, Anna Bell. BA, Washington and Lee U., 1969, JD, 1972. Bar: Ill. 1972, U.S. Dist. Ct. (no. dist.) Ill. 1972, U.S. Ct. Appeals (7th cir.) 1977, U.S. Supreme Ct. 1980, U.S. Tax Ct. 1987. Assoc. Chadwell & Kayser, Ltd., Chgo., 1972-79, ptnr., v.p., 1979-89; ptnr. Winston & Strawn, Chgo., 1990—. Treas. Lyric Opera Chgo. Guild, 1980—81, v.p., 1980—81, chmn. fundraising, 1986; vice-chmn. Gorton Cmty. Ctr., 1986; chmn. bd. Gorton Cmty. Ctr. Found., 1986—89; trustee Barat Coll., 1982—85, The Admiral, Chgo., 1988—2001, Allendale Assn., 1991—2000; mem. Art Inst. of Chgo. Old Masters Soc., 1999—; Mem. 1st ward Rep. com. on candidates Lake Forest (Ill.) Caucus, 1985—88, chmn., 1987—88, vice-chmn., 1989—90, chmn., 1990—91; mem. session Lake Forest Presbyn. Ch., 1978—84, chmn. ch. and society com., 1980; bd. dirs. Lyric Opera Chgo. Guild, 1976—, Lake Forest Symphony, 1987—91, Rehab. Inst. Chgo. Enterprises, 1991—2001, Gorton Community Ctr., 1982—88. Mem.: ABA (continuing legal edn. com. 1978—79, mem. antitrust com. young lawyers sect. 1978—81, com. on civil practice and procedure antitrust sect. 1980, bus. law sect. 1986—, patent trademark and copyright sect. 1990—), Chgo. Bar Assn. (chmn profl. responsibility com. young lawyers sect. 1977—78, mem. exec. com. 1978—79, bd. dirs.), Lawyers Club, Winter Club, Econ. Club Chgo., Shoreacres Club (bd. govs. 1996—, pres. 2002—). Republican. Office: Winston & Strawn 35 W Wacker Dr Ste 4200 Chicago IL 60601-1695 E-mail: mheatwol@winston.com.

HEBDA, LAWRENCE JOHN, data processing executive, consultant; b. East Chicago, Ind., Apr. 9, 1954; s. Walter Martin and Barbara (Matczynski) H.; m. Cynthia Ruta Aizkalns, June 17, 1978. BS, Purdue U., 1976; MBA, U. Iowa, 1983. Cert. data processor. Programmer Inland Steel Co., East Chicago, 1976-77; data analyst Deere & Co., Moline, Ill., 1977-82, systems analyst, 1982-83, project mgr., 1983-84, dealer systems cons., 1984-85, corp. planning analyst, 1985-87, systems edn. adminstr., 1987-88, telecommunications analyst, 1988; info. systems sr. cons. Hewitt Assocs., Lincolnshire, Ill., 1988-93, MIS bus. mgr., 1994-97, mgr. software distbn./oper. sys., 1997-2000, mgr. client/server application support, 2000—02, application project mgr., 2002—. Instr. computer sci. dept. Coll. Lake County Ill., 1996—, mem. computer info. systems adv. bd., 1999—. Mem. Nat. Rep. Congl. Com., 1982-85; charter mem. Rep. Presdl. Task Force, 1980; chmn. pastoral coun. Roman Cath. Ch., 1994-95. Recipient Cert. Recognition, Nat. Rep. Congl. Com., 1982-85, Presdl. Achievement award Rep. Nat. Com., 1984. Mem. Data Processing Mgmt. Assn., Am. Legion, Internat. Platform Assn., DAV Comdr.'s Club, King's Men Religious Orgn. (v.p. 1985, pres. 1986-87), Toastmasters Internat. (assoc. area gov. 1983-84), K.C. (3d degree coun. 8022, 2001, Dep. Grand Knight 2002-03, fin. sec., 2003-). Roman Catholic. Home: 675 Sussex Cir Vernon Hills IL 60061-2123 Office: Hewitt Assocs 100 Half Day Rd Lincolnshire IL 60069-3242

HEBEL, DORIS A. astrologer; b. Chgo., Jan. 1, 1935; d. Erich and Anna Dorothea (Hircy) H.; m. Leon L. Bram, Apr. 29, 1961 (div. Dec. 1973); 2 children. Libr. Campbell-Mithun, Chgo., 1958-61, Kenyon & Eckhardt, Chgo., 1961-64; pres. Astro-Technic Forecasting, Chgo., 1965—. Author: Contemporary Lectures, 1975, Celestial Psychology, 1985; contbr. various articles in astrological jours. and magazines. Mem. Am. Fedn. Astrologers (life), Nat. Coun. for Geocosmic Rsch. (life, nat. bd. dirs. 1975-80), Nat. Astrol. Soc., Assn. for Astrol. Networking, Internat. Soc. for Astrol. Rsch. Avocations: reading, singing, walking, metaphysical subjects, arts. Home and Office: 150 W Maple St Apt 1518 Chicago IL 60610-5433

HEBELER, HENRY KOESTER, retired aerospace and electronics executive; b. St. Louis, Aug. 12, 1933; s. Henry and Viola O. (Koester) H.; m. Mirriam Robb, Aug. 12, 1978; children by previous marriage: Linda Ruth, Laura Ann. BS in Aero. Engring., MS, MIT, 1956, MBA, 1970. Gen. mgr. rsch./engring. Boeing Aerospace Co., Seattle, 1970-72, pres., 1980-85; v.p. bus. devel. The Boeing Co., Seattle, 1973-74, exec. coun. and corp. v.p. planning, 1988-89; pres. Boeing Engring. & Constrn. Co., Seattle, 1975-79, Boeing Electronics Co., Seattle, 1985-87. Bd. dirs. Microelectronics and Computer Tech. Corp.; mem. fusion panel Ho. of Reps., 1979-81, energy rsch. adv. bd. Dept. Energy, 1980-81, task force on internat. industry Def. Sci. Bd., 1982-84, adv. com. nat. strategic materials and minerals program U.S. Dept. Interior, 1986—. Author: Your Winning Retirement Plan, 2001. Bd. govs. Sloan Sch., MIT, 1980-84; bd. visitors Def. Systems Mgmt. Coll., Ft. Belvoir, Va. Recipient Mead prize for aero. engrs., 1956; Kuljian humanities award, 1954; Sperry Gyroscope fellow, 1956; Sloan fellow M.I.T., 1970 Mem. AIAA, Nat. Aeros. Assn., Assn. of U.S. Army, Armed Forces Comm. and Electronics Assn. (bd. dirs.), Aviation Hall of Fame, Ala. Space and Rocket Ctr. (sci. and adv. com. 1980-85), Nat. Space (bd. govs. 1980-85), Meridian Valley Country Club. Achievements include patents in field. Home and Office: 24600 140th Ave SE Kent WA 98042-5160

HEBENSTREIT, JAMES BRYANT, agricultural products executive, bank and venture capital executive; b. Long Beach, Calif., Mar. 8, 1946; s. William Joseph and Jean (Stark) H.; m. Marilyn Bartlett, Aug. 23, 1986. AB, Harvard U., 1968, MBA, 1973. Pres. Terra-Light div. Butler Mfg. Co., Boston, 1980-82, Capital for Bus., Inc. (SB/C, venture capital affiliate Commerce Bancshares), St. Louis and Kansas City, Mo., 1982-87; sr. v.p. fin., CFO Commerce Bancshares, Inc., Kansas City, 1985-87, bd. dirs., 1987—; pres. Bartlett and Co., Kansas City, 1992—. Lt. USNR, 1968-71. Home: 1016 W 58th St Kansas City MO 64113-1133 Office: Bartlett & Co 4800 Main St Kansas City MO 64112-2510

HEBENSTREIT, JEAN ESTILL STARK, religion educator, practitioner; d. Charles Dickey and Blanche (Hervey) Stark; m. William J. Hebenstreit, Sept. 4, 1942; children: James B., Mark W. Student Conservatory of Music, U. Mo. at Kansas City, 1933-34; AB, U. Kans., 1936. Authorized C.S. practitioner, Kansas City, 1955—; bd. dirs. 3d Ch., Kansas City, 1952-55, chmn. bd., 1955, reader, 1959-62; authorized C.S. tchr. C.S.B., 1964—; chmn. bd. dirs. First Ch. of Christ Scientist, Boston, 1977-83. Mem. Christian Sci. Bd. of Lectureship, Christian Sci. Bd. Edn.; bd. trustees The Christian Sci. Pub. Soc., bd. dirs. First Ch. Christ.Scientist, 1977-83, chmn., 1981-82. Contbr. articles to C.S. lit. Pres. Mother Ch., The First Ch. of Christ, Scientist, 1999, bd. dirs., 1977-83, chmn., 1981-82. Mem. Art of Assembly Parliamentarians (charter, 1st pres.), Pi Epsilon Delta, Alpha Chi Omega (past pres.), Carriage Club. Home: 310 W 49th St Ste A-2 Kansas City MO 64112-2425 Office: 310 W 49th St Apt A-3 Kansas City MO 64112-2425

HEBERLEIN, ALICE LATOURRETTE, healthcare educator, physical education educator, coach; b. L.A., Mar. 7, 1963; d. Louis and Jean Marie LaTourette; m. Dave Heberlein, Mar. 20, 1993. BA, Idaho State U., 1985, MA, 1987. Tchr., coach Pocatello (Idaho) H.S., 1985—93; head women's volleyball coach Idaho State U., Pocatello, 1993—95; tchr., coach Pocatello H.S., 1995—99, Century H.S., Pocatello, 1999—, chair health dept., 2001—, chair phys. edn. dept., 2003—. Mem. nursing adv. bd. Vo-Tech H.S., Pocatello, 1995—2001; bd. dirs. Idaho Tennis Assn., Boise, 1998—99. Named Coach of Yr., Idaho H.S. Activity Assn., 1990—91, Jour. Coach of Yr., Idaho State Jour., 1999, Region 5 Coach of Yr., 1986—87, 1989—90, 1991—2000, Region 4-5-6 Coach of Yr., 2001. Mem.: Pocatello Edn. Assn. Achievements include coaching volleyball teams, 1989, H.S. state champions, 1990, 4th pl. State of Idaho, 2000, 2d pl. State of Idaho, 2001. Avocations: cross country skiing, hiking, tennis, snow shoeing, skate skiing. Home: 2934 Silverwood Pl Pocatello ID 83201 Office: Century HS 7801 Diamondback Dr Pocatello ID 83204

HEBERLING, TIMOTHY ALAN, information scientist; b. Portsmouth, Va., Sept. 3, 1955; s. Donald Anthony and Phyllis Elaine (McMillan) H.; m. Judith Ann Tohill, June 13, 1992; children: Ellen, Ben, Hanna. Student, James Madison U., 1973-74; BS in Computer Sci., Va. Tech., 1986. Commd. 2nd lt. USAF, 1986, advanced through grades to capt., 1990, law enforcement specialist, 1975-79, entry controller Chievres, Belgium, 1979-82, security police flight chief Enid, Okla., 1982-83; comms.-computer officer Air Force Hdqts., Washington, 1987-91; info. systems officer Def. Info. Systems, Reston, Va., 1991-94; sr. systems adminstr. The White House, Washington, 1994-96; ret. USAF, 1995; sr. info. systems engr. Mitretek Systems, McLean, Va., 1996-97; tech. mgr. AOL Internet Svcs., Sterling, Va., 1997—. Cons. WebVisor, Leesburg, Va., 1996—. Blood drive coord. Def. Info. System Agy., Reston, 1991-94, United Way vol. Decorated various Air Force medals. Mem. Air Force Security Police Assn. Home: 19553 Herndon Ct Leesburg VA 20175-6759 Office: Am Online Internet Svcs 22080 Pacific Blvd Sterling VA 20166-9304 E-mail: wwwvisor@aol.com.

HEBERT, BLISS EDMUND, opera director; b. Faust, N.Y., Nov. 30, 1930; s. Wilfrid Joseph and Merle Addasah (Bliss) H. BA, Syracuse U., 1951, M.Mus., 1952; piano pupil of, Robert Goldsand, Simone Barrere, Lelia Gousseau. Gen. mgr. Washington Opera Soc., 1960-63; guest dir. Juilliard Sch., 1975-76; mem. faculty Boston U., 1952-53, U. Wash., 1969. Stage dir., Met. Opera, N.Y.C., 1973-75, N.Y. City Opera, 1963-75, Santa Fe Opera, 1957—; dir. opera companies of, San Francisco, 1963, Houston, 1964, Seattle Opera, 1967, Toronto, 1972, San Diego, 1970, Vancouver, B.C., 1969, Ft. Worth, 1966, Washington, 1959, Cin., 1968, Portland, Oreg., 1969, Caramoor Festival, Katonah, N.Y., 1966, La Gune Festival, 1968—, New Orleans, 1970, Balt., 1972, Tulsa, 1975, Miami, Fla., 1975, Charlotte, N.C., 1975, Dallas, 1977, Shreveport, La., 1977, Chgo., 1983, Montreal, 1984, Boston, 1984, Cleve., 1988, Opera Northern Ireland, 1988, Virginia Opera, 1991, Opera Mexico City, 1993, Austin Opera, 1993, Florentine Opera, Milw., 1994; rec. artist, Columbia records; as stage dir. for Igor Stravinsky's major operas under his conducting. Served AUS, 1954-56. Mem. Lambda Chi Alpha, Phi Mu Alpha. Office: care John S Miller 801 W 181st St Apt 20 New York NY 10033-4518

HEBERT, CAROL ANN, software engineer; b. Mass., Aug. 30, 1958; d. Rene E. Hebert and Beverly J. Millgate; 1 child, James Michael. AS with high honors, Holyoke (Mass.) C.C., 1981; BSCS summa cum laude, U. Ctrl. Fla., 1987. Engr. software NCR, Lake Mary, Fla., 1988-92; staff software engr. IBM Corp., Beaverton, Oreg., 1993—. Co-inventor, patentee Power Failure Detection and Shutdown Timer, 1994. Mem. Phi Kappa Phi, Sigma Rho, Golden Key Honor Soc. Avocations: forestry, horseback riding, environmental/humane activism, hiking, guitar. Office: IBM Corp 15450 SW Koll Pkwy Beaverton OR 97006-6063

HEBERT, CHRISTINE ANNE, elementary education educator; b. Waltham, Mass., Aug. 31, 1953; d. Alfred Lionel and Virginia Eugenia (Nogas) Mellor; m. Dennis Armand Hebert, Dec. 18, 1976; 1 child, Kirsten Erica. BS in Early Childhood Edn., Wheelock Coll., Boston, 1975; MS in Spl. Edn., Coll. William and Mary, Williamsburg, Va., 1985; postgrad., Old Dominion U., 1996-99. Cert. elem. tchr., learning disabled, emotional disturbances. Title I aide Fryeburg (Maine) Pub. Schs., 1975-76; title I tutor Conway (N.H.) Pub. Schs., 1976-77; presch. tchr. Elmendorf AFB, Anchorage, 1978-80; counselor, caregiver Intermission/Parent Resource Ctr., Anchorage, 1980-81; residential counselor Group Home for MR Adults, Bridton, Maine, 1983-84; tchr. learning disabled Norfolk (Va.) Pub. Schs., 1985-90, tchr. elem., 1990—, lead tchr. sci., 1992—, tchr. magnet sch. math. and sci., 1995—, sci. tchr. specialist, 1998-99, elem. tchr., 1999—. Tutor Learning Resource Ctr., Virginia Beach, Va., 1986-89; inclusion tchr., 1993-95, 2000—; mem. NASA Tchr. Enhancement Inst., summers 1994, 97; nat. instrnl. leader Activities for Integration of Math. and Sci., 1997-2000. Recipient Norfolk Sch. Bell award, 1994-95; faculty scholar Coll. William and Mary, 1984-85; AT&T fellow Va. Sci. Mus., 1997. Mem. ASCD, Internat. Reading Assn., Nat. Coun. for Tchrs. English, Optimists (pres. Bayside chpt. 1996-97), Kappa Delta Pi. E-mail: chebe@cox.net.

HEBERT, KATHLEEN, information technology executive; Cons. Boston Cons. Group, Boston; from intern to corp. v.p. Microsoft, Redmond, Wash., 1988—2001, corp. v.p., 2001—. Office: One Microsoft Way Redmond WA 98052-6399

HEBERT, LYNN DAVID, science and computer educator, writer; b. Rutland, Vt., Aug. 6, 1940; s. Lynn Robert Hebert and Helen Elizabeth Jasmin. AB in Philosophy and Classics, St. Michael's Coll., Winooski, Vt., 1963; EdM in Sci. Edn., SUNY, Buffalo, 1976, EdD in Sci. Edn., 1986. Cert. secondary tchr. sci. and computers Vt. Adj. prof. biol. and phys. sci. Coll. St. Joseph, Rutland, Vt., 1993—; adj. prof. computer programming Castleton (Vt.) State Coll., 1999—; adj. prof. sci. and computers C.C. Vt., Rutland, 1993—; sci. and computer tchr. and coord. Fair Haven (Vt.) Union H.S., 1983—93; sci. tchr., dept. head Park Sch. Buffalo, Amherst, NY, 1969—80. Author: (novel) Bigfoot Autumn, 2001; contbr. poetry and stories to anthologies. With USNR, 1964—66. Avocations: hiking, camping. Office: Coll St Joseph 71 Clement Rd Rutland VT 05701-3899 Personal E-mail: ldhebert@vermontel.net.

HEBERT, MARGARET BURNS, social worker; b. Houston, June 24, 1947; d. Albert Leroy Jr. and Margaret Stewart (Forristall) Burns; m. James Byron Hebert, Apr. 18, 1970; children: Margaret, Miia, Mary Grace, Madeleine. BA, Tulane U., 1969; MA, U. S.W. La., 1972; MSW, La. State U., 1977. Welfare technician Vermilion Parish Div. of Family Svcs., Abbeville, La., 1974; foster care caseworker Lafayette (La.) Office of Community Svcs., 1974-75, Vermilion Parish Office of Community Svcs., Abbeville, 1977-78, social work supr., 1978-82; sch. social worker Vermilion Parish Sch. Bd., Abbeville, 1982-85, 95—; sch. counselor Mt. Carmel Elem. Sch., Abbeville, 1985-88; pvt. practice Abbeville, 1998—2002. Regional del. Dem. Caucus, Thibodeaux, La., 1972; foster parent Lafayette Area Office of Family Svcs., 1980-82; bd. dirs. Vermilion Parish Milk Fund, Abbeville, 1975-78, Acadiana Symphony Assn., Lafayette, 1989; bd. dirs. Family Tree, Lafayette, 1999—; mem. Abbey Players Community Theatre; facilitator Family Life Community, 1979-89. Democrat. Roman Catholic. Mem. NASW (bd. dirs. La. chpt. 1984-86), Assn. for Social Work Vendorship (bd. dirs. 1988-89), La. Social Svc. Suprs. Assn. (founder Lafayette chpt. 1980-82), La. Sch. Social Work Network (chair La. chpt. 1985, Lafayette region rep. 1999—), Confrerie de l'Omelette Geante (bd. dirs. 1995-99, chevalier 1997—, treas. 2003—). Avocations: needlework, sewing. Home and Office: 108 N Louisiana St Abbeville LA 70510-5117 E-mail: meghebert@aol.com.

HEBERT, MARIANNE, librarian; b. Milford, Conn., Mar. 30, 1956; d. Donald Gerard and Bernice Coulombe Hebert. BFA, U. Conn., 1980; M.Liberal Studies, Wesleyan U., Middletown, Conn., 1989; MLS, U. Ill., 1991. Head tech. svcs. SUNY-Purchase Libr., NY, 1991—98, Ea. Conn. State U., Willimantic, 1998—2001; automation coord. SUNY-Potsdam Libr., 2001—. Recipient Chancellor's Award for Excellence in Librarianship, SUNY, 1998. Mem.: N.Y. Tech. Svcs. Librs. (treas. 1996—97, sec. 1997—98), New Eng. Libr. Assn. (chair acad. sect. 1998—2000), Beta Phi Mu. Office: SUNY-Potsdam 44 Pierrepont Ave Potsdam NY 13676

HEBERT, MARY OLIVIA, retired librarian; b. Nov. 11, 1921; d. Arthur Frederick and Clara Marie (Golden) Meyer; m. N. Hal Hebert, Sept. 9, 1943 (dec. Mar. 1969); children: Olivia, Stephen (dec. 1989), Christina, Deborah (dec. 1999), Beth, John, James. Secretarial positions in advt., 1942-43; v.p. Hebert Advt. Co., 1955-66; adminstrv. asst. comms. Blue Cross, St. Louis, 1966-69, libr., 1969-91; ret., 1991. Part-time archivist Cathedral Basilica of St. Louis, 1999. Mem. Spl. Librs. Assn. (pres. St. Louis Metro chpt. 1984), St. Louis Med. Librs., St. Louis Regional Libr. Network (coun. 1986-89). Roman Catholic.

HEBERT, ROBERT D. academic administrator; b. Abbeville, La., Nov. 14, 1938; married. BA, U. Southwestern La., 1959; MA, Fla. State U., 1961, PhD, 1966. Asst. prof. history Miss. State U., 1962-69, assoc. prof. history, 1969-76; prof. McNeese State U., 1976—, v.p. acad. affairs, 1980-87, pres., 1987—. Office: McNeese State U Office Pres Lake Charles LA 70609-0001

HEBERT, THOMAS JOSEPH, university educator; b. New Roads, La., May 3, 1964; s. Avit Joseph Hebert and Penelope Rose Bergeron; m. Janine Francis Bodin, Oct. 10, 1990; children: Emily Renee, Nicholas Joseph. BS, U. La., 1987, MS, 1989; PhD, Tulane U., 1996. Asst. prof. in psychology So. U. at New Orleans, 1996—. Adj. prof. U. La., Lafayette, 1989-90, Loyola U., New Orleans, 1995-96, Tulane U., 1995-96; psychol. assoc. Normal Life, Inc., Lafayette, 1988-89. Contbr. articles to profl. jours. Mem. Saint Pius Men's Club. Mem. AAAS, AAUP, Soc. for Neurosci. Democrat. Roman Catholic. Avocations: playing guitar, sports. Home: 1370 Mithra St New Orleans LA 70122-2014 Office: So U at New Orleans 6400 Press Dr New Orleans LA 70126-1009

HECHE, ANNE, actress; b. Aurora, Ohio, May 25, 1969; d. Donald Heche. Appearances include (film) An Ambush of Ghosts, 1993, The Adventures of Huck Finn, 1993, A Simple Twist of Fate, 1994, Milk Money, 1994, I'll Do Anything, 1994, The Wild Side, 1995, Pie in the Sky, 1995, Walking and Talking, 1996, The Juror, 1996, Volcano, 1997, Donnie Brasco, 1997, Wag the Dog, 1997, I Know What You Did Last Summer, 1997, Return to Paradise, 1998, Six Days Seven Nights, 1998, Psycho, 1998, The Third Miracle, 1999, Auggue Rose, 2000, Prozac Nation, 2001, John Q., 2002, Timepiece, 2003; (TV movies) O Pioneers!, 1992, Girls in Prison, 1994, If These Walls Could Talk, 1996, Wild Side, 1996, One Kill, 2000, (TV series) Another World, 1988-92, Murphy Brown, 1991-92, Ally McBeal, 2001 (TV spls.) Soap Opera Digest, 1989, The 16th Ann. Daytime Emmy Awards, 1989, (stage) Getting Away with Murder, 1991-92. Recipient Emmy award Another World.

HECHLER, KEN, former state official, former congressman, political science educator, writer; b. Roslyn, N.Y., Sept. 20, 1914; s. Charles Henry and Catherine Elizabeth (Hauhart) H. *Grandfather George Hechler emigrated from Germany in 1854, enlisted with Union infantry at Parkersburg, West Virginia, wounded at Antietam and discharged at Wheeling, West Virginia. Great Uncle John Hechler captured at Chickamauga, died in Andersonville Prison. Father University of Missouri graduate, managed Clarence H. Mackay's 600 acre farm estate on Long Island, elected to numerous Republican county offices and President of Board of Education, secretary-treasurer of New York Guernsey Breeders' Association, bank president. Mother was a school teacher in St. Louis County, elected to numerous Republican county offices on Long Island, noted raiser and exhibitor of Chrysanthemums.* BA, Swarthmore Coll., 1935; AM, Columbia U., 1936, PhD, 1940; LittD (hon.), U. Charleston, 1988; HHD (hon.), W. Va. Inst. Tech., 1988, LLD (hon.), 2001. Lectr. govt. Barnard Coll., Columbia Coll., N.Y.C., 1937-41; rsch. asst. to Judge Samuel I. Rosenman, 1939-50; rsch. asst. on Pres. Roosevelt's pub. papers, 1939-50; sect. chief Bur. Census, 1940; pers. technician Office Emergency Mgmt., 1941; adminstrv. analyst Bur. of Budget, 1941-42, 46-47; spl. asst. to Pres. Harry S. Truman, 1949-53; rsch. dir. Stevenson-Kefauver campaign, 1956; adminstrv. aide Senator Carroll of Colo., 1957; mem. 86th-94th Congresses from 4th W.Va. dist., 1959-77; sec. of state State of W.Va., 1985-2001. Sci. and tech. com. 86th to 94th Congresses from 4th W.Va. Dist., chmn. Energy (Fossil Fuels) Subcom.; mem. Joint Com. on Orgn. of Congress, 1965-66, NASA Oversight Subcom. (U.S. Congress); asst. prof. politics Princeton U., 1947-49; prof. polit. sci. Marshall U., Huntington, W.Va., 1957, 82-84, 2001-2002; sci. cons. U.S. House Com. on Sci. and Tech., 1978-80; radio, TV commentator Sta. WHTN, Huntington, 1957-58, Sta. WWHY, 1978; adj. prof. polit. sci. U. Charleston (W.Va.), 1981; keynote spkr. Harry Truman lecture ser. USAF Acad., 1995; lectr. Harry S. Truman Libr., George C. Marshall Found., Washington & Lee U. Law Sch., 1996, Harry S. Truman Coll. of Chgo., 1997, Southern Ilinois Univ., 1998, Mid. Ga. Coll., Appalachian State U., Ill. Wesleyan, Ill. State U., 1999, U. Va., 2000., Central Mich. U. 2000, Yale U. Law Sch., 2001, Duquesne U. Sch. Law, 2002, U. No. Fla., 2003, U. Mich., Flint, 2003, Ea. Mich. U., 2003; panelist, Truman Symposium, Key West, Fla., 2003; disting. vis. scholar, W. Va. State Coll., Inst., W. Va., 2001; adj. prof. polit. sci. Marshall U., 2001—. *Only Congressman to march with Martin Luther King in Selma, Alabama. First Congressman sponsoring legislation to limit coal dust and provide strict safety standards in Federal Coal Mine Health and Safety Act of 1969. Fought against corruption in coal union, risked life to campaign for Jock Yablonski, insurgent candidate later murdered. Crusaded against strip mining and mountain top removal of coal. Helped mobilize secretaries of state and attorneys general in 33 states to limit campaign spending. Led campaign to more fairly appraise and tax West Virginia natural resources owned by out-of-state corporations. Cracked down on West Virginia political corruption.* Author: Insurgency: Personalities and Politics of the Taft Era, 1940, The Bridge at Remagen, 1957, rev. edit.,tech. advisor of motion picture based on book, 1969, 1998, West Virginia Memories of President Kennedy, 1965, Toward the Endless Frontier, 1980, The Endless Space Frontier, 1982, Working with Truman, 1982, 3d edit., 2001; weekly columnist Cabell Record, Hampshire Rev., Elk River and Little Kananha News, W.Va. Hillbilly, 1990-2000. Bd. dirs. W.Va. Humanities Coun., 1982-84; del. Dem. Nat. Conv., 1964, 68, 72, 80, 84; mem. W.Va. State Dem. Exec. Com., 1998-99. Served to maj. AUS, 1942-46; served to col. Res. Adm. Nebr. Navy, 1995. Decorated Bronze Star; named W.Va. Son of Yr., W.Va. State Soc. of D.C., 1969, W.Va. Speaker of Yr., W.Va. U., 1970, Grand Marshall, Annual Martin Luther King Parade, Huntington, 2003, Mountaineer of the Yr., Graffiti Mag., 2003; recipient Conservation award Nat. Audubon Soc., 1973, Mother Jones award W.Va. Environ. Coun., 1995, Civil and Human Rights award Martin Luther King Commn. W.Va., 2001; subject of biography by Dr. Charles H. Moffat, Ken Hechler: Maverick Public Servant, 1987; Smithsonian Instn. lectr. on 50th Anniversary of Pres. Truman, 1985; Harry S Truman award for Pub. Svc., 2002; Marshall Univ. student senate, Prof. of the Year, 2002. Mem. Am. Polit. Sci. Assn. (assoc. dir. 1953-56), Civitan, Am. Legion, VFW, DAV, Judson Welliver Soc. of Presdl. Speech-Writers, Elks, Hon. mem. Golden Key Internat. hon. soc., 2002. Democrat. Episcopalian. Walked 530 miles with Granny D on behalf of campaign reform. Home: 101B Greenbrier St Charleston WV 25311-2130

HECHLER, PAULINE URBANO KING, fundraiser; b. L.A., Mar. 21, 1948; d. Paul DeWitt Urbano and Mary-Louise (Strong) Rhodes; m. George Rangeley King, Jan. 25, 1969 (div. Oct. 1996); children: Anne de Rosset King, Phoebe King Fox, David Rangeley King; m. Gene A. Hechler, June 22, 2001. BA in English Lit., U. Wash., 1971. Project dir. Ariz. Cmty. Found., Phoenix, 1988-94; fundraising cons. Phoenix, 1994-95; dir. devel. Ballet Ariz., Phoenix, 1995-96; v.p. Scottsdale (Ariz.) Healthcare Found., 1996—2002; dir. devel. St. Gregory Coll. Preparatory Sch., 2003—. Bd. trustees All Saints' Episcopal Day Sch., Phoenix, 1986-89; mem. founding bd. Maricopa County Ct. Apptd. Spl. Advocates, Phoenix, 1983-84; chmn. task force on children & families Ariz. Supreme Ct., Phoenix, 1987-89; chmn. override and bond election Phoenix Union H.S., 1994-95; bd. dirs. Nat. Spirit of Women Found., 1998-2002. Recipient State Bar Ariz. award of Appreciation, Phoenix, 1990. Mem. Assn. Fundraising Profls. (bd. dirs.). Independent. Episcopalian. Avocations: hiking, gardening, children's issues. Office: St Gregory Coll Prep Sch 3231 N Craycroft Rd Tucson AZ 85712

HECHT, ALAN DANNENBERG, insurance executive; b. Balt., Aug. 31, 1918; s. Lee I. and Miriam (Dannenberg) H.; m. Margaret R. Moses, June 27, 1943 (dec. Nov. 1, 1984); children: Stephen Lee, Nancy H., Elizabeth Ann; m. Marcia Levin Oberfeld, Dec. 8, 1985. BS, Johns Hopkins U., 1940, M Liberal Arts, 1976. CLU, 1951. Solicitor Travelers Ins. Co., 1945-60; partner Hecht-Schoenfeld Ins. Agy., 1960-62; merged and formed Wolman-Hecht-Schoenfeld, Inc., 1962, v.p., 1962-64, Wolman-Hecht, Inc., 1964-91, pres., 1971-92, chmn., 1992; v.p. Tongne Brooks & Co., Inc. (merged with Wolman-Hecht, Inc.), 1992-95; founder, pres. Alan D. Hecht & Co., Inc., 1966—; gen. agt. Sunamerica Life Ins. Co. Am. and other cos., Balt., 1960—; assoc. Ins., Inc., Balt., 1995—. Pres. Balt. Estate Planning Coun., 1978-79; tchr. CLU econs. and fin. Johns Hopkins U., 1954-81; mem. faculty dept. econs. Mount St. Mary's Coll., Emmitsburg, Md., 1981-84; past bd. graders Am. Coll. Life Underwriters. Pres. Balt. Jewish Council, 1971-73; life and qualifying mem. Million Dollar Round Table, 1985, mem. resolutions com., 1976; bd. dirs. Balt. chpt. Am. Jewish Com., pres., 1958-60, former mem. nat. exec. com.; trustee Sinai Hosp. of Balt., 1959-68. Served to 1st lt. AUS, 1941-45. Recipient Nat. Quality award Nat. Assn. Life Underwriters; Nat. Sales Achievement award; Szold award Temple Oheb Shalom Brotherhood, 1980; George S. Robertson award Balt. Life Underwriters Assn., 1981 Mem. Soc. Fin. Svc. Profls. (CLU, ChFC, dir. 1957—, nat. sec. 1962-63, pres. 1964-65, Helen Hottenbacher award Balt. chpt. 1991), Omicron Delta Kappa, Pi Delta Epsilon. Jewish (pres. congregation 1968-70, past dir.). Home and Office: 111 Hamlet Hill Rd Apt 312 Baltimore MD 21210-1521 E-mail: heclev@aol.com. *With some background in economics, I believe that we can improve our life and environment only by greater productivity. Each person should accept responsibility for finishing assigned tasks at every level, no matter how menial or unimportant that task may seem. I would add that courtesy and respect for others should be a top priority for the successful growth and future of our great country.*

HECHT, ANTHONY EVAN, poet; b. N.Y.C., Jan. 16, 1923; s. Melvyn Hahlo and Dorothea (Holzman) H.; m. Patricia Harris, Feb. 27, 1954 (div. 1961); children: Jason, Adam; m. Helen D'Alessandro, June 12, 1971; 1 child, Evan Alexander. BA, Bard Coll., 1944, DLitt (hon.), 1970; MA, Columbia U., 1950; LHD (hon.), Georgetown U., 1981, Towson State U., 1983, U. Rochester, 1987, St. John Fisher Coll., 1989. Tchr. Kenyon Coll., 1947, State U. Iowa, 1948, NYU, 1949, Smith Coll., 1956-59; assoc. prof. English, Bard Coll., 1961; faculty U. Rochester, 1967; John H. Deane prof. poetry and rhetoric, 1968; Hurst prof. Washington U., fall 1971; vis. prof. Harvard U., 1973, Yale U., 1977; faculty Salzburg Seminar in Am. Studies, 1977; univ. prof. Georgetown U., 1985-93. Cons. in poetry Libr. of Congress, 1982-84; trustee Am. Acad. in Rome, 1983—; Andrew Mellon lectr. fine arts Nat. Gallery Art, 1992; Rockefeller Found. resident Villa Serbelloni, Bellagio, Italy, 1993; Bogliasco Found. resident Centro Studi Ligure per le Arte e le Lettere, 1997, 99. Author: A Summoning of Stones, 1954, The Seven Deadly Sins, 1958, A Bestiary, 1960, The Hard Hours, 1968 (Brit. Poetry Book Soc. choice, 1967, Miles Poetry award Wayne U., Pulitzer prize, 1968, Russell Loines award Nat. Inst. Arts and Letters), Millions of Strange Shadows, 1977, The Venetian Vespers, 1979, Obbligati: Essays in Criticism, 1986, The Transparent Man, 1990, Collected Earlier Poems, 1990, The Hidden Law: The Poetry of W.H. Auden, 1993, On the Laws of the Poetic Art, 1995, The Presumptions of Death, 1995, Flight Among the Tombs, 1996, A Gehenna Florilegium, 1998, The Darkness and the Light, 2001, Melodies Unheard: Essays, 2003, Poems (in Russian translation), 2003; contbr. intro.; co-author, co-editor: Jiggery Pokery, 1967; ; translator (with Helen Bacon): Seven Against Thebes (Aeschylus), 1973; editor: The Essential Herbert, 1987; co-author: Anthony Hecht in Conversation with Philip Hoy, 1999. Recipient Prix de Rome, 1950, Brandeis U. Creative Arts award, 1965; Guggenheim fellow, 1954, 59; Hudson Rev. fellow, 1958; Ford Found. fellow, 1960; Rockefeller Found. fellow, 1967; Fulbright prof. Brazil, 1971; recipient Bolligen prize, 1983, English Speaking Union award, 1981, Charles Kellogg award Bard Coll., 1982, Eugenio Montale award for Poetry, 1983, Harriet Monroe award, 1987, Ruth B. Lilly award, 1988, Aiken Taylor award The Sewanee Rev., 1989, Dorothy Tanning award for poetry, 1997, Robert Frost medal, 2000, Horace Mann Disting. Alumnus award 2000; NEA grantee, 1989. Fellow Acad. Am. Poets (hon., chancellor 1971-95); mem. Am. Acad. Arts and Letters, Am. Acad. Arts and Scis., Century Assn., Phi Beta Kappa. Home: 4256 Nebraska Ave NW Washington DC 20016-2130 Fax: 202-244-0469.

HECHT, DONALD STUART, lawyer; b. N.Y.C., Mar. 20, 1941; s. Murray Hecht and Jeanne (Morris) Friedman; m. Laura Ruth Dodes, Sept. 9, 1967; children: Brian, Daniel. BA, Hofstra Coll., 1962; JD, Bklyn. Law Sch., 1969. Bar: N.Y. 1970, U.S. Dist. Ct. (so. and ea. dists.) N.Y. 1975. Assoc. Sitomer, Sitomer & Porges, N.Y.C., 1970-73, Silver, Saperstein, Barnet & Soloman, N.Y.C., 1973-81; ptnr. Weber & Scharf, Massapequa, N.Y., 1981-82; sole practice Port Washington, N.Y., 1982-90; pvt. practice Manhasset, N.Y., 1991-96; small claims arbitrator Dist. Ct. Nassau County, 1988—; pvt. practice Garden City, N.Y., 1996-98; pvt. prac. Jericho, NY, 1998—. Cons., lectr. Bd. Cooperative Ednl. Svcs., Nassau County, N.Y. 1985—. Contbg. author, editor: Guardianship Practice in New York State, 1997; law columnist: Able Newspaper for the Disabled. Bd. dirs. United Cerebral Palsy Assn. Nassau County, 1982-87, 2002—, Epilepsy Found. of Long Island, 1983-99, v.p. 1987-96; bd. appeals Village of Port Washington North, 1984-85, trustee, 1985-87, dep. mayor, 1986-87; mem. Nassau County Dem. Com., 1984-87. 1st lt. USAF 1962-66. Mem. ABA, New York State Bar Assn., Bar Assn. Nassau County, Nat. Acad. Elder Law Attys., Am. Judges Assn., Lions (bd. dirs. 1982-83, asst. sec. 1983-84, Disting. Svc. award 1983, Lion of Yr. 1984), Iota Theta. Avocations: hiking, cooking, gardening. Home: 37 Seaview Ln Port Washington NY 11050-1737 Office: 350 Jericho Tpke Jericho NY 11753-1317 E-mail: dschecht@ix.netcom.com.

HECHT, FREDERICK, physician, researcher, writer, educator, consultant; b. Balt., July 11, 1930; s. Malcolm and Lucile Burger (Levy) H.; m. Irene Winchester Duckworth, Aug. 29, 1953 (div. 1977); children: Frederick Malcolm, Matthew Winchester, Maude Bancroft, Tobias Ochs; m. Barbara Kaiser McCaw, May 29, 1977; children: Kerrie Kristine, Brian Stuart. Student, U. Paris, 1950-51; BA, Dartmouth Coll., 1952; student, Boston U., 1955-56; MD, U. Rochester, N.Y., 1960. Lic. physician, Oreg., Ariz., Nev., Kans.; diplomate Am. Bd. Pediatrics, Am. Bd. Med. Genetics. Intern Strong Meml. Hosp., Rochester, N.Y., 1960-61, resident, 1961-62, U. Wash. Hosp., Seattle, 1962-64, asst. in pediat., med. genetics, 1962-64, instr. pediatrics, med. genetics, 1962-65; asst. in pediat. U. Rochester, 1960-62; prof. pediat. U. Oreg., Portland, 1965-78; founder, pres., dir. S.W. Biomed. Rsch. Inst., Scottsdale, Ariz., 1978-89; founder, pres. Hecht Assocs. Inc., Jacksonville, Fla., 1989—; prof. zoology Ariz. State U., Tempe, 1978-89; prof. ob-gyn. U. Nev., Reno and Las Vegas, 1983-89; dir. molecular medicine Children's Mercy Hosp., Kansas City, Mo., 1990-91; prof. medicine U. Mo., Kansas City, 1990-91; founder, dir. div. molecular medicine Children's Mercy Hosp., Kansas City, Mo., 1990-91. Vis. prof. cytogenetics and molecular genetics Adelaide Children's Hosp., North Adelaide, South Australia, 1992; prof. medicine Lab. de Génetique Moleculaire des Cancers Humains, l'Université de Nice, France, 1992-95; bd. dirs. Youth Law Ctr., San Francisco; prof. med. U. Mo., Kansas City, 1990-91. Author: Fragile Sites on Human Chromosomes, 1985; editor: Trends and Teaching in Medical Genetics, 1977; co-editor in chief: Webster's New World Medical Dictionary, 2000; mem. editl. bd. Am. Jour. Human Genetics, Cancer Genetics and Cytogenetics; chief editor MedTerms.com, 2000--; assoc. chief editor MedicineNet.com, 1997—; contbr. over 600 articles to profl. jours. Sgt. M.I. Corps, U.S. Army, 1952-55. NIH grantee, 1968-89, USPHS grantee, 1968-89; recipient Pediatric Rsch. award Ross Labs., 1970; Royal Soc. Medicine traveling fellow, London, 1971-73. Mem. Am. Pediatric Soc., Am. Soc. Human Genetics (bd. dirs.), Am. Acad. Pediatrics (charter mem. genetics sect. 1990), Soc. Pediatric Rsch., Western Soc. Pediatric Rsch. (bd. dirs.), Nat. Found. Jewish Genetic Diseases. Jewish. Avocations: writing, publishing nonfiction, fiction and poetry, gardening. Office: Hecht Assocs Inc 4134 McGirts Blvd Jacksonville FL 32210-4362 Fax: 904-384-5136. E-mail: TBHecht@AOL.com.

HECHT, HAROLD ARTHUR, orchidologist, chiropractor; b. St. Louis, Mo., Apr. 30, 1921; s. William Frederick and Myrtle Regina (Hugo) H.; m. Barbara Evelyne Ross, Nov. 19, 1942. D Chiropractic Medicine, Logan Coll. Sole practice, St. Louis, 1942-95; orchidologist, 1950—. Judge Orchid Digest Corp., 1959; internat. lectr., photographer in field radiotelephone engr., 1942. Contbr. articles to profl. jours. Mem. World Orchid Cong. (founding com. 1954), Mid-Am. Orchid Cong. (founder, pres. 1959, judge 1968), Am. Orchid Soc. (grand jurist, judge 1968), Mark Twain Orchid Soc. (pres. 1966, 90), Mo. Orchid Soc. (pres. 1959), European Orchid Congress (USA com. 1967). Republican. Avocations: philatelist, numismatist, amateur radio operator, antiquary, linguist.

HECHT, IRENE, artist, educator; b. N.Y.C., Dec. 1, 1949; d. Seymour and Rhoda (Ginsberg) H. BA, Case Western Res. U., Cleve., 1971. Artist Portraits, Inc., N.Y.C., 1976—, Grand Cen. Galleries, N.Y.C., 1985—; tchr. Del. Mus. Sch. Art, Wilmington, 1984-87. Portraits include Louis Nizer, 1982, Arthur Krim, 1983, Charles Scribner IV, 1984, Isaac Stern, 1988, Martin Bookspan, 1989, Zubin Mehta, 1990, Kathleen Battle, 1995, Nobel Laureate Eugene Wigner, 1991, Bill Bradley, 1998, Emanuel Ax, 1999, Itzak Perlman, 1999, Robert M. Morganthau, 2003, others; represented in permanent collection Nat. Arts Club, Princeton U., Lotos Club. Mem. Nat. Arts Club, Artists Fellowship, Lotos Club.

HECHT, IRENE MARGRET, lawyer; b. Edmonton, Alta., Can., Dec. 2, 1956; came to U.S., 1964; d. Erich Ernst and Auguste (Schindler) H. BA in Speech Comm. magna cum laude, U. Wash., 1977, JD with honors, 1980. Bar: Wash., 1980. Assoc. Keller Rohrback, Seattle, 1980-85; ptnr. Keller Rohrback LLP, Seattle, 1986—. Mem. Internat. Assn. Def. Counsel, Rainier Club. Avocations: hiking, climbing, travel. Office: Keller Rohrback LLP 1201 3rd Ave Ste 3200 Seattle WA 98101-3052 E-mail: ihecht@kellerrohrback.com.

HECHT, MARIE BERGENFELD, retired educator, author; b. N.Y.C., Oct. 21, 1918; d. Frank Falle and Marie (Trommer) Bergenfeld; BA, Goucher Coll., 1939; MA, New Sch. for Social Research, 1971; m. Morton Hecht, Jr., Dec. 17, 1937 (div.); children: Ann (Mrs. David Bloomfield), Margaret, Laurence, Andrew. Tchr. Am. history Mineola High Sch., Garden City Park, N.Y., 1960-80. Mem. Am. Hist. Assn., Orgn. Am. Historians. Author (with Herbert S. Parmet): Aaron Burr: Portrait of an Ambitious Man, 1967; Never Again: A President Runs for a Third Term, 1968; John Quincy Adams: A Personal History of An Independent Man, 1972; The Women, Yes, 1973; Beyond the Presidency: The Residues of Power, 1976; Odd Destiny: The Life of Alexander Hamilton, 1982, The Church on the Hill, 1987. Address: 5 Hewlett Pl Great Neck NY 11024-1605

HECHT, MARION B. mental health counselor, mental health therapist; b. Bklyn., Nov. 21, 1966; d. Herman and Selma Sonnenblick; m. Ronald J. Hecht; 1 child, Henry. MA, Goddard Coll., Plainfield, Vt., 1991; postgrad., Goddard Coll., 1998, Hofstra U., U. Minn., U. Iowa, Montclair State U. Lic. profl. counselor, N.J., D.C.; registered art therapist Am. Art Therapy Assn.; cert. guidance counselor, tchr. of handicapped, N.J. Dept.Edn.; cert. cognitive

behavioral therapist Nat. Assn. Cognitive Behavioral Therapists. Mental health specialist, gerontologist Bay Ridge Ctr. for Older Adults, Bklyn., 1989-90; art therapist, mental health therapist Rockaway Mental Health Svcs., Far Rockaway, N.Y., 1990-91, Coney Island Hosp., 1991—93; pvt. practice No. N.J. Counseling Svcs., 1996—; tchr. home instrn., spl. edn. Montclair & South Orange (N.J.) Pub. Schs., 1997-2000. Mem.: NJ Counseling Assn., NJ Mental Health Counselors Assn. Avocations: sports, reading, computer, drawing. Office: 15 Village Plaza South Orange NJ 07079 Office Fax: 973-597-1357. E-mail: rhecht2258@aol.com.

HECHT, MARJORIE MAZEL, editor; b. Cambridge, Mass., Dec. 21, 1942; d. Mark and Theresa (Shuman) Mazel; m. Laurence Michael Hecht, July 2, 1972 BA cum laude, Smith Coll., 1964; postgrad., London Sch. Econs., 1964-65; MSW, Columbia U., 1967. Dir. Forest Neighborhood Service Ctr., N.Y.C., 1967-70, Wiltwyck Sch. for Boys, Bronx Center, N.Y., 1970-73; mng. editor Fusion Mag., Washington, 1977-87, 21st Century Sci. & Technol. Mag., Washington, 1987—; sci editor Exec. Intelligence Rev., Washington, 1997—. Co-author: Beam Defense: An Alternative to Nuclear Destruction, 1983 (Aviation and Space Writers award 1983); editor: Colonize Space! Open the Age of Reason, 1985, The Holes in the Ozone Scare: The Scientific Evidence That the Sky Isn't Falling, 1992. Press rep. LaRouche Campaign, N.Y.C., 1984 Democrat. Jewish. Avocation: astronomy. Office: 21st Century Sci & Technol Mag PO Box 16285 Washington DC 20041-6285 E-mail: tcs@mediasoft.net.

HECHT, NATHAN LINCOLN, state supreme court justice; b. Clovis, N.Mex., Aug. 15, 1949; s. Harold Lee and Mary Loretta (Byerly) H. BA, Yale U., 1971; JD cum laude, So. Meth. U., 1974. Bar: Tex. 1974, D.C. 1975, U.S. Dist. Ct. D.C. 1975, U.S. Dist. Ct. (no. and we. dists.) Tex. 1976, U.S. Ct. Appeals (D.C. cir.) 1975, U.S. Ct. Appeals (5th cir.) 1976, U.S. Supreme Ct. 1979. Law clk. to judge U.S. Ct. Appeals (D.C. cir.), 1974-75; assoc. Locke, Purnell, Boren, Laney & Neely, Dallas, 1976-80, ptnr., 1981; dist. judge 95th Dist. Ct., Dallas, 1981-86; justice Tex. 5th Dist. Ct. Appeals, 1986-89, Texas Supreme Ct., Austin, 1989—. Contbr. articles to profl. jours. Bd. visitors So. Meth. U., Dallas, 1984-87; trustee Children's Med. Found., Dallas, 1983-89; bd. dirs. Children's Med. Ctr. North, Dallas, 1985-89; elder Valley View Christian Ch., Dallas, 1981—. Lt. USNR, 1971-79. Named Outstanding Young Lawyer of Dallas, Dallas Assn. of Young Lawyers, 1984. Fellow Tex. Bar Found., Am. Bar Found.; mem. ABA, Dallas Bar Assn., D.C. Bar Assn., Am. Law Inst. Republican. Avocations: piano, organ, jogging, bicycling. Office: Tex Supreme Ct PO Box 12248 201 West 14th Room 104 Austin TX 78711*

HECHT, PATRICIA LAYTON, elementary school educator, writer, consultant; b. Toms River, N.J., Apr. 19, 1935; d. Harry J. and Elsie Graham (Pile) Layton; m. Kenneth Parker Keller, Apr. 14, 1956 (div. 1969); children: Alexandra Niles Keller Calabrese, Corinne Graham Keller, Jennifer Layton Keller; m. Sylvester J. Hecht, May 16, 1970 (div. 1975). BS, Douglass Coll., 1956; MA in History, Rutgers U., 1960; postgrad., U. Alaska, 1957, Monmouth Coll., 1981. Cert. elem. tchr., N.J. 1st grade tchr. Ladd On-Base Schs., Fairbanks, Ala., 1956-57; English, history tchr. Elizabeth (N.J.) Schs., 1957; 1st grade tchr. Middletown (N.J.) Twp. Schs., 1958, 1st, 2d grade tchr., 1958-60, 8th grade history tchr., 1960-61; pvt. tutor Middletown, 1961-64; editor The Monmouth Unitarian, Lincroft, N.J., 1969-70; 2d grade tchr. Elberon Sch., Long Branch, N.J., 1972-87, 1st grade tchr., 1987-91, 1st grade tchr. computer sci. tech., 1991-94; ret., 1994. Critic reader Scott Foresman Co., Glenview, Ill., 1990-91; curriculum writing Long Branch Schs., 1972—. Author: Math Made Easy For Grade One, 1991, The Little Vowel Books, 1991, Nicholas Niles Was Born Today, 1991, Mainly Lame-Brain Listening Games, 1991; author (play) Lincoln, 1990; researcher, author McHugh Genealogy, 1966, My Mother's Family: A Niles-Pile Genealogy, 1970. Recipient Golden Apple Tchr. award Cable TV Network, 1989, N.J. Tchr. of Month award, 1989. Mem. NEA, Long Branch Sch. Employees Assn. (rep. 1990-91, 92-93, editor LBSEA Beacon 1992-93), N.J. Edn. Assn., Nat. Trust for Hist. Preservation. Avocations: american history, video photography, travel, swimming, dancing. Home: 390 Ocean Ave Apt 2A Long Branch NJ 07740-5757

HECHT, RUDOLPH C. physician, educator; b. Hamburg, Germany, Apr. 16, 1927; arrived in U.S., 1954; s. Otto and Rose (Caro) Hecht; m. Ilse Hecht, May 22, 1958; children: David H., Martin O., Thomas C., Anita. BSc, Nat. U. Mex., 1947, MD, 1954. Diplomate Am. Bd. Family Medicine, lic. Tex., 1957, Wis., 1973, diplomate State Bd. Med. Examiners. Pvt. practice, LaFeria, Tex., 1957—73; prof. U. Wis., Madison, 1973—82, Med. Coll. Wis., Milw., 1985—88; pvt. practice Wis., 1988—99. Author: Autobiography: The Early Years, 2000. Internat. Travel fellow, Pan Am. Health Orgn., 1977. Home: 141 N Hancock St Madison WI 53703-2311

HECHT, WILLIAM DAVID, accountant; b. N.Y.C., Nov. 7, 1941; s. Adolph J. and Lillian (Shore) H.; m. Francine Rosen, Aug. 22, 1964; children: Peter, Dana, Allison. BS in Acctg., Queens Coll., 1962; JD, Bklyn. Law Sch., 1971; LLM in Taxation, NYU, 1974. Bar: N.Y. 1972. Ptnr., mem. mgmt. com. Weiser LLP, N.Y.C., 1964—. Mem. faculty Found. Acctg. Edn., N.Y.C.; lectr. in field. Contbr. articles to CPA Jour. Mem. ABA, AICPA, N.Y. State Soc. CPAs, N.J. State Soc. CPAs, N.Y. State Bar Assn. Republican. Jewish. Avocations: skiing, basketball. Home: 8 Tutor Pl East Brunswick NJ 08816-3658 Office: Weiser, LLP 399 Thornall St Edison NJ 08837-2236 E-mail: whecht@mrweiser.com.

HECHT, WILLIAM F. electric power industry executive; b. 1943; BSEE, Lehigh U., 1964, MSEE, 1970. Engr. Pa. Power & Light Co., Allentown, 1964-68, project engr., 1968-72, sr. project engr., 1972-75, mgr. distbn. planning, 1975-76, exec. dir. corp. energy planning coun., 1976-78, mgr. systems planning, 1978-84, v.p. systems power, 1984-87, v.p. mktg., 1987-90, exec. v.p., 1990-93, CEO, chmn., pres., 1993—. Office: PP&L Utilities 2 N 9th St Allentown PA 18101-1139

HECHTER, MICHAEL NORMAN, sociologist; b. LA, Nov. 15, 1943; s. Oscar Milton and Gertrude (Horowitz) H.; children: Joshua, Eliana. AB, Columbia U., 1966, PhD, 1972. From asst. prof. to prof. U. Wash., Seattle, 1970-84; prof. sociology, dir. research group for instnl. analysis U. Ariz., Tucson, 1984—99; prof. sociology U. Wash., Seattle, 1999—. Univ. lectr., fellow New Coll., Oxford (Eng.) U., 1994-96; vis. prof. U. Bergen, Norway, 1984. Author: Internal Colonialism, 1975, Principles of Group Solidarity, 1987, Containing Nationalism, 2000; editor: The Microfoundations of Macrosociology, 1983, Social Institutions, 1989, The Origin of Values, 1993, Social Norms, 2001, Theories of Social Order, 2003. Fellow Russell Sage Found., 1988-89, Ctr. Advanced Study Behavioral Scis., 1990-91, Udall Ctr. for Studies in Pub. Policy. Mem.: Soc. for Comparative Rsch., Internat. Sociol. Assn., Sociol. Rsch. Assn., Am. Sociol. Assn. Office: U Wash Dept Sociology Seattle WA 98195 E-mail: hechter@u.washington.edu.

HECHTMAN, HOWARD, financial analyst; b. N.Y.C., Sept. 1947; s. Charles and Pauline (Barmatz) H.; m. Marsha Louise Garwin, Dec. 19, 1976 (div. 1984). BS, Bklyn. Poly. U., 1968, MS in Physics, Adelphi U., 1970, MBA in Mgmt. with distinction, 1972; Cert. in Labor Rels., Cornell U., 1999, Advanced Cert. in Labor Rels., 2000. Grad. teaching asst. physics Computer Ctr. Adelphi U., Garden City, N.Y., 1970-72; from asst. to assoc. analyst N.Y.C. Transit Authority, 1973—. Capt. N.Y. State Guard. Named Patron of Arts Soc. for Theater Arts Resources, 1989-90; recipient Cert. of Merit Rep. Nat. Com., 1990. Mem. Soc. Am. Mil. Engrs., Civil Svc. Tech. Guild (del. 1994-2003), Poly U. Alumni Assn. (alumni bd. dirs. 1978—, life dir. 1996—). Office: NYC Transit Authority MOW Finance Rm 1261 370 Jay St Brooklyn NY 11201-3817 E-mail: colgeeprime@yahoo.com.

HECK, ALBERT FRANK, retired neurologist; b. Balt., Oct. 9, 1932; s. Albert Franklin and Dorothy Mary Heck; divorced; children: Albert William, Karl Andrew, Robert Conrad, Paul Christopher. AB, Johns Hopkins U., 1954; MD, U. Md., 1958. Diplomate: Am. Bd. Psychiatry and Neurology. Intern Mercy Hosp., 1958-59; NIH fellow in neurology U. Md., Balt., 1959-62, faculty, instr. to prof., 1964-77; prof., chmn. dept. neurology U. Tenn. Center for Health Scis., Memphis, 1977-82, dir. neurosci. program, 1978-82; prof. neurology W. Va. U., 1982-2000, ret., 2000—. Vis. prof. Medezinische Hochschule Hannover, W. Ger., 1973-74 Contbr. writings to profl. pubs. Served with M.C. U.S. Army, 1962-64. Recipient jr. investigator award NIH, 1965, U.S. sr. scientist award, 1973; Humboldt Found. prize Fed. Republic Germany, 1973-74 Fellow Am. Acad. Neurology, ACP, Stroke Council Am. Heart Assn.; mem. Am. Neurol. Assn., Internat. Coll. Angiology, Alpha Omega Alpha. Achievements include research in field. Home: 10906 Baronet Rd Owings Mills MD 21117

HECK, DEBRA UPCHURCH, information technology, procurement professional; b. Valparaiso, Fla., Nov. 4, 1956; d. Robert P. and Sallaine S. (Sledge) Upchurch; m. Robert J. Heck, May 31, 1980; children: Andrew W., Jennifer A. BS in Math., Purdue U., 1978, MS in Mgmt., 1980. Analyst mgmt. sci. Monsanto Corp. Mgmt. Sci., St. Louis, 1980-81; sys. analyst Monsanto Agr. Group, St. Louis, 1981-82, sr. sys. analyst, 1982-84; sr. analyst mgmt. sci. Monsanto Polymer Products Group, St. Louis, 1984-86; total quality fundamentals instr. Monsanto Co., St. Louis, 1985-86; project mgr. Monsanto Chem. Co., St. Louis, 1986-88; group leader Monsanto Corp. MIS, St. Louis, 1988-92, sr. group leader, 1992-95; info. tech. dir. Monsanto Bus. Svcs.-Fin., St. Louis, 1995-96; from info. tech. dir. to exec. dir. global procurement Pfizer Monsanto Bus. Svcs.-Fin. & Procurement, St. Louis, 1996—2003, exec. dir. global procurement Pfizer, 2003—. Trustee, chair fall gathering, doubles, social com. Ethical Soc., St. Louis, 1982—; mem. sci. adv. com., PTO bd. Parkway Sch. Dist., St. Louis, 1992—; vol. St. Louis Assn. for Retarded Citizens, 1978-85. Recipient Leader award, YWCA Monsanto Corp., 1999. Mem. Nat. Assn. Purchasing Mgmt., Human Resource Sys. Profls., Leadership Am. Alumni (award 1994). Avocations: travel, sports, friends, family. Office: Pharmacia Corp 575 Maryville Ctr Saint Louis MO 63141

HECK, HENRY D'ARCY, retired toxicologist, consultant; b. Bryn Mawr, Pa., Apr. 18, 1939; s. Harold Joseph and Lydia Suzanne (Holt) H.; m. Mercedes Casanova, Dec. 21, 1984; children: Katherine (Mrs. Daniel Troy), Julia, John Schmitz, Lara (Mrs. Daniel King). AB, Princeton U., 1962; PhD, Northwestern U., 1966. Asst. prof. chemistry U. Calif., Berkeley, 1968-72; chemist Stanford Rsch. Inst., Menlo Park, Calif., 1972-77; scientist Chem. Ind. Inst. Toxicology, Research Triangle Park, N.C., 1977-85, sr. scientist, 1985-99. Adj. assoc. prof. U. N.C., Chapel Hill, 1983-99, Duke U., Durham, N.C., 1987-99 Assoc. editor: Fundamental and Applied Toxicology, 1986-1991, editor-in-chief, 1991-97. Fellow NSF, NIH, EMBO, 1963-68; mem. AAAS, Am. Chem. Soc., N.C. Soc. Toxicology (pres. 1995-96), Soc. Toxicology (Frank Blood award 1983, Inhalation Toxicol. Paper of Yr. award 1987, 93). Home: 101 Halcyon Cv Washington NC 27889-7901 E-mail: hechen@cox.net.

HECK, JONATHAN F. athletic trainer, photographer; b. Vineland, N.J., Sept. 6, 1965; s. Walter Alfred Heck and Louise Girone. BS, William Paterson U., 1989; M in Exercise and Sports Sci., U. Fla., 1991. Coord. athletic tng. Richard Stockton Coll. N.J., Pomona, 1991—. Editor Current Concepts Sports Medicine, 1993-96; assoc. editor Sports Medicine Update, 1997; article reviewer: American Society for Testing and Materials: Safety in American Football; contbr. articles to profl. jours. Mem. Nat. Athletic Trainers Assn. (cert. athletic trainer), Athletic Trainers Soc. N.J. Home: 2505 Oleander Ct Mays Landing NJ 08330 Office: Richard Stockton Coll NJ Jim Leeds Rd Pomona NJ 08240 Office Fax: 609-748-5510. E-mail: JonHeck@aol.com., Iaprod87@stockton.edu.

HECK, KARL THOMAS, community development planner; b. Syracuse, N.Y., Apr. 19, 1965; s. Carl Joseph and Jean Martha (Burdick) H.; m. Stephanie Lenore Delczeg, June 5, 1993. BA, Le Moyne Coll., 1986; MS, U. Toronto, 1990. Sales rep. Gestetner Corp., Syracuse, N.Y., 1986-87; employment and grants coord. Delaware County, Sidney, N.Y., 1990-91; adminstrv. coord. Tompkins County Planning, Ithaca, N.Y., 1991-93, cmty./econ. devel. coord., 1994-99; dep. dir. Cortland Housing Authority, NY, 1999—2003; cmty. devel. specialist Greene County Planning and Econ. Devel., Cairo, NY, 2003—. Staff liaison Tompkins County Adv. Bd. on Tourism, Ithaca, 1995-99. Chess columnist Syracuse Herald-Am., 1994—. Recipient Paper award Ont. Indsl. Devel. Authority, 1990. Mem. N.Y. State Chess Assn. (dir., treas. 1997—). Avocations: chess, reading. Home: 30 Ferguson Rd Dryden NY 13053-9716 Office: Greene County Planning and Econ Devel 909 Green County Office Bldg Cairo NY 12413 E-mail: sldkth@clarityconnect.com.

HECK, MELODY ANN, library director; b. Kewanee, Ill., July 8, 1957; d. Edwin and Helen M. Nelson; m. Michael Robert Heck, Feb. 25, 1984; children: David M., Holly Ann Elizabeth. Cert. libr. tech. asst., Black Hawk Coll., 1996. Staff librarian Galva (Ill.) Pub. Libr., 1975-84, asst. dir., 1984-96, libr. dir., 1996—. Mem. ALA, Ill. Libr. Assn. Avocations: reading, needlework. Office: Galva Pub Libr Dist 120 NW 3rd Ave Galva IL 61434-1326

HECK, RICHARD T. tree farmer; b. Madison, Ind., Sept. 16, 1924; s. Richard Charles and Virginia (Tevis) H.; m. Ruth Irwin Heck, June 27, 1948; children: Richard Gregory, Rebecca Jeanne. Student, Admiral Farragut Naval Acad., Pine Beach, N.J., 1942-43, Hanover Coll, 1947-48. Tree farmer, Hanover, Ind., 1943—. Vol. firefighter, 1946—; mem. arson investigation team Jefferson County, Ind., 1983-90, Hanover Twp. Vol. Fire Co., 1956—; trustee Hanover Coll., 1991-2000. With USN, 1944-54, WWII, Korea. Named to Hon. Order of Ky. Cols., 1971, Sagamore of Wabash, 1973; named Ind. Outstanding Tree Farmer, Ind. Tree Farm Commn., 1983, Nat. Outstanding Tree Farmer Am. Forest Found., 1984, Good Steward award Nat. Arbor Day Found., 1984, North Ctrl. Region Outstanding Tree Farmer, 1984, Ind. Conservationist of Yr., Ind. Dept. Natural Resources, 1985, Forest Conservationist of the Yr. Ind. Wildlife Fedn., 1987. Mem. Soc. Am. Foresters (hon.), Nat. Forestry Assn. (life), Ind. Foresty and Woodland Owners Assn. (bd. dirs. 1984-95, Ind. state tree farm com. 1984—), NRA (life), Ind. Vol. Firemans Assn. (life), Nat. Muzzle Loading Rifle Assn. (life), Internat. Assn. Arson Investigators, Inc., Nat. Eagle Scout Assn., Soc. Ind. Pioneers, Am. Legion, Wahpanipe Muzzle Loading Rifle Club, Connor Prairie Rifles Club, Masons, Elks. Republican. Presbyterian. Avocations: hunting, fishing, hiking, collecting indian artifacts, competitive muzzle loading shooting. Address: 110 Clemmons St Hanover IN 47243-9659

HECK, RONALD MARSHALL, chemical engineer; b. Balt., Sept. 23, 1943; s. Joshua H. and Rita Mercedes (Young) H.; m. Barbara Thompson, June 16, 1990; children: Ron, Kimberly, Teresa. BS in Chem. Engring. cum laude, U. Md., 1965, PhD in Chem. Engring., 1969. Rsch. chem. engr. Celanese Chem. Co., Corpus Christi, Tex., 1969-72; sr. rsch. chem. engr. Engelhard Industries, Menlo Park, NJ, 1972-77, sect. head, 1977-84, engring. mgr. Union, N.J., 1984-87; group leader Engelhard Corp., Menlo Park, 1987-94; sr. devel. assoc. Engelhard Industries, Menlo Park, 1994—2003; cons. RMH Cons., 2003—. Contbr. articles to profl. jours.; patentee in field. Mem. Kingwood (N.J.) Twp. Sch. Bd., 1975, pres. 1978. Mem. Am. Inst. Chem. Engrs., Air and Waste Mgmt. Assn., Soc. Automotive Engrs., Am. Men and Women in Sci., Tau Beta Pi. Home: 269 Kingwood Station Rd Frenchtown NJ 08825-3615

HECK, ROSE, state legislator; m. Raymond Heck; children: Nancy, Laury, Rosemary, Suzan. Attended, Seton Hall U. Assemblywoman dist. 38 N.J. State Assembly. Joint edn. com. N.J. State Assembly, regulated profl. com., past chair sr. citizens & social svc. com., environ com., chair joint adv. coun. women; mng. editor Hasbrouck Heights Publ. Co. Recipient alumna award Acad. Sacred Heart; named citizen of yr. Hasbrouck Heights Men's Assn. Mem. N.J. Press Assn., Hasbrouck C. of C., Lodi C. of C. Home: 2 Mercer St Ste 5A Lodi NJ 07644-1601*

HECK, THOMAS F. librarian, performing arts educator; b. Washington, July 10, 1943; s. Harold Joseph and Suzanne Holt H.; m. Anne Elizabeth Goodrich, June 2, 1968; children: Larissa, John. French bac, 1 ere Partie, Paris, 1961; BA in Liberal Arts/Music History, U. Notre Dame, 1965; PhD, Yale U., 1970; MLS, U. So. Calif., 1977. Asst. prof., libr. Wis. Conservatory Music, Milw., 1977-78; head music and dance libr. Ohio State U., Columbus, 1978-2000; asst. prof. music history Chapman U., Orange, Calif., 1975-76; asst. prof. dept. fine arts John Carroll U., Cleve., 1974-75; asst. prof. music history Case Western Res. U., Cleve., 1971-74. Author: Commedia dell'arte: A Guide to the Primary and Secondary Literature, 1988, Mauro Giuliani: Virtuoso Guitarist and Composer, 1995, Picturing Performance: The Iconography of the Performing Arts in Concept and Practice, 1999; editor: The Music Information Explosion and its Implications, 1992; rev. editor Fontes Artis Musicae, 1988-92; gen. editor: Coll. Music Soc. Reports, 1992-95. 1st lt. U.S. Army, 1970-71. Fellow, Nederland Inst. Advanced Study, Wassenaar, 1994—95, Fulbright fellow, 1968—69, 1995—96. Mem. Authors Guild, Am. Musicological Soc., Am. Soc. Theatre Rsch., Music Libr. Assn., Coll. Music Soc. (life), Internat. Assn. Music Librs., Internat. Fedn. Theatre Rsch., Guitar Found. Am. (founder, archivist 1978-94). Avocations: foreign languages and culture, foreign travel, photography, audio-visual media, bicycling. E-mail: insights@aya.yale.edu.

HECKATHORN, DOUGLAS D. sociologist, educator, epidemiologist; b. Wichita, Kans., May 15, 1948; s. Donald L. Heckathorn and Frances E. Haney; m. Susan N. LoBello, Oct. 4, 1949. PhD, U. Kans., 1974. Prof. sociology Cornell U. Sr. editor: Rationality and Society; contbr. articles to Harvard Jour. Law and Pub. Policy (Lon Fuller Prize in Jurisprudence, 1989). Office: Cornell University 344 Uris Hall Ithaca NY 14853 Office Fax: 607-255-8473. E-mail: douglas.heckathorn@cornell.edu.

HECKEL, JOHN LOUIS (JACK HECKEL), aerospace company executive; b. Columbus, Ohio, July 12, 1931; s. Russel Criblez and Ruth Selma (Heid) H.; m. Jacqueline Ann Alexander, Nov. 21, 1959 (div. 1993); children: Heidi, Holly, John; m. Linda Holleran, Aug. 1, 1994. BS, U. Ill., 1954; PhD with honors, Nat. U. San Diego, 1984. Divsn. mgr. Aerojet Divsn., Azusa, Calif., 1956-70, Seattle and Washington, 1956-70; pres. Aerojet-Space Gen. Co., El Monte, Calif., 1970-72, Aerojet Liquid Rocket Co., Sacramento, 1972-77; group v.p. Aerojet Sacramento Cos., 1977-81; pres. Aerojet Gen., La Jolla, Calif., 1981-85, chmn., CEO, 1985-87; pres., COO GenCorp., Akron, 1987-94, also bd. dirs. Bd. dirs. WD-40 Corp. Bd. dirs. San Diego Econ. Devel. Corp., 1983-86, Akron Regional Devel. Bd., Akron Gen. Hosp., Summit County United Way; pres. Summit Edn. Partnership Found., Akron. Recipient Disting. Alumni award U. Ill. Ann. Alumni Conv., 1979 Fellow AIAA (assoc.); mem. Aerospace Industries Assn. Am. (gov. 1981), Navy League U.S., Am. Def. Preparedness Assn., San Diego C. of C. (bd. dirs.)

HECKEL, RICHARD WAYNE, metallurgical engineering educator; b. Pitts., Jan. 25, 1934; s. Ralph Clyde and Esther Vera (Zoerb) H.; m. Peggy Ann Simmons, Jan. 3, 1959 (dec. Apr. 1998); children: Scott Alan, Laura Ann Rowe. BS in Metall. Engring., Carnegie Mellon, 1955, MS, 1958, PhD, 1959. Sr. research metallurgist E.I. duPont de Nemours & Co., Wilmington, Del., 1959-63; prof. metall. engring. Drexel U., Phila., 1963-71; head dept. materials sci. and engring. Carnegie Mellon, Pitts., 1971-76; prof. materials sci. and engring. Mich. Tech. U., Houghton, 1976—96, prof. emeritus, 1996—; tech. dir., owner Engring. Trends, Houghton, 2000—. Commr. at large Engring. Workforce Commn., 1997—, with Engring. Trends (e-commerce). Contbr. articles to profl. jours. Served as 1st lt. Ordnance Corps, U.S. Army, 1959-60. Recipient Lindback Teaching award Drexel U., 1968; Research award Mich. Tech. U., 1985 Fellow ASM Internat. (life; Bradley Stoughton Young Tchr. of Metallurgy award 1969, Phila. Ednl. Achievement award 1967); mem. The Metals, Minerals and Materials Soc., Am. Welding Soc. (Adams Meml. mem. 1966), Am. Soc. Engring. Edn., Sigma Xi, Omicron Delta Kappa, Tau Beta Pi, Phi Kappa Phi, Alpha Sigma Mu. Address: Engring Trends 1281 Hickory Ln Houghton MI 49931-1609 E-mail: engtrend@up.net.

HECKELMANN, CHARLES NEWMAN (CHARLES LAWTON), author, publishing consultant, b. Bklyn., Oct. 24, 1913; s. Edward and Sophia (Hodum) H.; m. Anna M. Auer, Apr. 17, 1937; children: Lorraine Heckelmann Kane, Thomas Edward. BA maxima cum laude, U. Notre Dame, 1934. Sports feature writer Bklyn. Eagle, 1934-37; editor-in-chief Cupples & Leon, N.Y.C., 1937-41, Popular Library, N.Y.C., 1941-58, v.p., 1953-58; pres., editor-in-chief Monarch Books, Inc., N.Y.C., 1958-65; mng. editor, rights dir. David McKay, N.Y.C., 1965-68; sr. editor Cowles Book Co., N.Y.C., 1968-71; sr. editor, rights dir. Hawthorn Books, N.Y.C., 1971-72, editor-in-chief, 1972-75, v.p., 1972-75; book editor Nat. Enquirer, 1975-78. Author: Vengeance Trail, 1944, Lawless Range, 1945, Six-Gun Outcast, 1946, Deputy Marshal, 1947, Guns of Arizona, 1949, Let The Guns Roar, 1950, Two-Bit Rancher, 1950, Outlaw Valley, 1950, Danger Rides the Range, 1950, Fighting Ramrod, 1951, Hell In His Holsters, 1952, The Rawhider, 1952, Hard Man With A Gun, 1954, Bullet Law, 1955, Trumpets in the Dawn, 1958, The Big Valley, 1966, The Glory Riders, 1967, Writing Fiction for Profit, 1968, Stranger from Durango, 1971, Return to Arapahoe, 1980, Wagons to Wind River, 1982; books and stories adapted for motion pictures Deputy Marshal, 1949; Stranger from Santa Fe, 1947, Frontier Feud, 1948; author (pen name Charles Lawton): Clarkville's Battery, 1937, Ros. Hackney, Halfback, 1937, The Winning Forward Pass, 1940, Home Run Hennessey, 1941, Touchdown to Victory, 1942, Jungle Menace, 1937. Life mem. Nat. Cowboy Hall of Fame and Western Heritage Ctr. Mem. Cath. Writers Guild of Am. (pres. 1949-52), Western Writers of Am. (v.p. 1955-57, pres. 1964-65), Torch Club of Boca Raton (bd. dirs.). *Life, as I view it, is a series of milestones that periodically challenge our faith and will to succeed. It does not really matter if we don't pass each test. What is important, however, is to maintain a firm commitment to push ahead toward our goal.*

HECKEMEYER, ANTHONY JOSEPH, circuit court judge; b. Cape Girardeau, Mo., Jan. 20, 1939; s. Paul Q. and Frances E. (Goetz) H.; m. Elizabeth Faye Littleton, Feb. 13, 1964; children: Anthony Joseph, Matthew Paul, Mary Elizabeth, Andrew William, Sarah Kathryn. BS, U. Mo., 1962, JD, 1972; grad., Nat. Judicial Coll., 1980, Juvenile Coll., 1984. Bar: Mo. Mem. Mo. Ho. Reps., Jefferson City, 1964-72; sole practice Sikeston, Mo., 1972-81; presiding cir. judge State of Mo., Scott and Mississippi Counties, 1981—. Chmn. alcohol and substance abuse com. Nat. Council of Juvenile and Family Ct. Judges, Reno, 1987-88, presenter at U. Reno; majority party whip, chmn., vice chmn. agr. com., higher edn. com. as a miscellaneous resolution com. Named Outstanding Conservation Legislator Sears, 1968, Found. Mo. Wildlife Fedn., 1968, Man of Yr., Sikeston C. of C., 1989. Mem. Mo. Trial Judges Assn. (pres. 1995). Office: Presiding Cir Judge PO Box 256 Benton MO 63736-0256

HECKER, ERWIN, retired obstetrician/gynecologist; b. Balt., July 15, 1923; MD, Tulane U., 1947. Diplomate Am. Bd. Ob-Gyn. Intern, resident ob-gyn Garfield Meml. Hosp., Washington, 1947-49; resident ob-gyn Sinai Hosp., Balt., 1949-50, 52-54; ob-gyn Balt., 1954—; ret., 1997. Past ob-gyn Sinai Hosp., Balt., Greater Balt. Med. Ctr. Lt. (s.g.) U.S. Navy, 1950-52. Fellow Am. Coll. Ob-Gyn; mem. Md. Ob-Gyn Soc. Home: 107 River Oaks Circle Baltimore MD 21208-1367 E-mail: ehecker md1@comcast.net.

HECKER, GERALD ARTHUR, ophthalmologist, historian; b. Montreal, Que., Can., Feb. 11, 1937; BA, NYU, N.Y.C., 1959; BS, U. Geneva, 1961, MD, 1965. Diplomate Am. Bd. Ophthalmology. Resident in ophthalmology N.Y. Polyclinic Med. Sch., N.Y.C., 1968-71; fellow oculoplastic surgery Manhattan Eye and Ear Hosp., N.Y.C., 1971-72, attending surgeon, 1972—; pvt. practice, 1972—. Asst. prof. Mt. Sinai Med. Sch., N.Y.C., 1985—. Capt. U.S. Army, 1966-68. Decorated Bronze Star. Mem. N.Y. Acad. Medicine, Am. Acad. Ophthalmology.

HECKER, LAWRENCE HARRIS, industrial hygienist; b. Detroit, July 14, 1944; s. Joseph and Rose Vivian (Harris) H.; m. Phyllis Rosalind Cohen, June 29, 1966; children: Charles Aaron, David Alan. BA in Geography and Chemistry, Wayne State U., 1965, MS in Indsl. Hygiene, 1967; MS in Air Pollution, U. Mich., 1969, PhD of Indsl. Health, 1972. Cert. indsl. hygienist Am. Bd. Indsl. Hygiene. Asst. prof. indsl. and environ. health U. Mich., Ann Arbor, 1972-78; mgr., dir. corp. indsl. hygiene Abbott Labs., North Chgo., Ill., 1978-94, dir. corp. health and safety regulatory affairs, 1994—. Cons. Ann Arbor, 1970-78, Northbrook, Ill., 1996—; chief chemist, ind. hygienist Environ. Health Labs. Franklin, Mich., 1966-68; lab. technician Wayne State U., Detroit, 1964-66. Contbr. numerous articles to profl. jours. Mem.: AAAS, ASTM, APHA, AAAS, Nat. Assn. Mfrs. (chmn. safety com. 1992—, vice chair occupl. safety and health com. 2002—, occupl. safety and health com., ergonomics com.), Bus. Coun. on Indoor Air (bd. dirs.), Pharm. Safety Group, Pharm. Rsch. and Mfrs. Assn., Remote Sensing of Atmosphere, Orgns. Resource Councillors (respirator com., chmn. respiratory study task force, risk assessment task force, permissible exposure limti adv. com. task force, TB task force, chmn. latex rubber task force, PVC task force, ergonomics task force), Halogenated Solvents Industry Alliance, Ethylene Oxide Industry Coun. (bd. dirs. 1980—, vice chmn. bd. and exec. com. 1982—95, phthalate ester panel), Am. Chemistry Coun. (occupl. safety and health com., OSHA legis. group, Ethylene Glycol panel, bd. dirs. 2001), Internat. Stds. Orgn. (chmn. tech. com. 194 biol. evaln. med. devices 2001—, U.S. del. Geneva, convener tech. com. 194, working group 11, working groups 1, 12, 14, 15, liaison ISO tech. com. 210 and 172 joint working group 4, ISD TC210 working group 4, liaison global harmonization task force study group 1), Assn. Advancement Med. Tech. (product safety working group, PVC working group, toxicology task group, proposition 65

working group, latex working group, chair med. device utilization study group), Assn. Advancement of Med. Insturmentation, Air Pollution Control Assn., Am. Indsl. Hygiene Assn. (bd. dirs. 1983—86), Am. Conf. Govtl. Indsl. Hygienists, Am. Chem. Soc., Advanced Am. Acad. Indsl. Hygiene, Sigma Xi. Home and Office: 3823 Russett Ct Northbrook IL 60062-4263 Office: Abbott Labs 200 Abbott Park Rd Bldg Ap52-s Abbott Park IL 60064-6212 E-mail: Heckerl@aol.com., L.Hecker@abbott.com.

HECKER, MICHAEL HANNS LOUIS, retired electrical engineer, speech scientist; b. Hamburg, Germany, Mar. 30, 1936; came to U.S., 1948; s. Hanns Ewald Hecker and Wilhelmine (Corinth) Klopfer; m. Elizabeth Ann Bowen, Sept. 3, 1960 (div.); 1 child, Serena Suzanne; m. Dorothy Louise Dunlap, Mar. 12, 1971. BSEE with honors, Northeastern U., 1959; MSEE, MIT, 1961; PhD in Speech & Hearing Scis., Stanford U., 1974. Sr. rsch. engr. Bolt Beranek and Newman Inc., Cambridge, Mass., 1964-67, SRI Internat., Menlo Park, Calif., 1967-95. Cons. forensic acoustics, Los Altos, Calif., 1967-98; retained by White House during Watergate investigation to examine presdl. tapes; sci. cons. Nat. Commn. Rev. Fed. & State Laws Relating to Wiretapping & Electronic Surveillance, 1974-76. Author: Speaker Recognition, 1971; co-editor: Speech Evaluation in Psychiatry/Medicine, 1981; contbr. articles to profl. jours., chpts. to med. books. 1st lt. U.S. Army, 1962-64. NIH grantee, 1982-88. Mem. Eta Kappa Nu, Tau Beta Pi, Sigma Xi. Achievements include studies of speech changes related to emotional states, psychological stress, and neurologic disorders; developed methods of speech analysis to assess behavioral risk for coronary heart disease. E-mail: midohecker@earthlink.net.

HECKERT, PAUL CHARLES, sociologist, educator; b. May 30, 1929; s. Paul Kester and Clara Belle (Plessinger) H.; m. Sara Mae Raezer, Sept. 6, 1952; children: Paul Andrew, Druann Maria, Daniel Alex, Nathanael Alan, Diane Manette. AB, Catawba Coll., 1951; B.D., Lancaster Theol. Sem., 1954; MS, Cornell, 1959, PhD., 1964. Ordained minister United Ch. of Christ, 1954. Missionary United Ch. of Christ, Honduras, 1954-60; clergyman of various Methodist chs. N.Y., 1960-64; assoc. prof. sociology, also chmn. dept. Catawba (N.C.) Coll., 1964-68, prof., 1968-72; also chmn. joint dept. sociology with Livingstone Coll. Salisbury, N.C.; chmn. dept. sociology Frostburg (Md.) State U., 1972-87, prof., 1987-94. Participant Prison Visitation and Support Visitor, 1995—; del. Rowan Coop. Christian Ministry, 1968-72; Spanish and sociology vol. tchr. fed. prison; mem. leadership devel. com. Pa. West Conf., United Ch. of Christ, 1973-78. Bd. dirs. Salisbury Rowan Cmty. Svc. Coun., 1971-72. Served with AUS, 1948-50. Ford fellow, summer 1968, NASA/ASEE summer faculty fellow, 1969, 77, AEC summer faculty fellow, 1973. Contbr. book revs. to profl. jours. Recipient Vol. of Yr. award, Fed. Correctional Instn., 2001; grantee, NEH, 1975, 1979, 1983, 1986. Mem. AAAS, Am. Sociol. Assn., Rural Sociol. Soc., Alleghany County Ret. Tchrs. Assn. (mem. chmn. 1997, pres.-elect 1998, pres. 1999), Phi Kappa Phi, Alpha Kappa Delta, Sigma Delta Pi, Delta Tau Kappa. Home: 13 N Woodlawn Ave Cumberland MD 21502-7254

HECKLER, FREDERICK ROGER, plastic surgeon; b. N.Y.C., Mar. 7, 1942; s. Frances George; children: Jeremy, Michael, Adrienne, Lauren. Student, Tufts U., 1959-62, MD, 1966. Diplomate Nat. Bd. Med. Examiners, Am. Bd. Surgery, Am. Bd. Plastic Surgery with qualification in surgery of the hand. Intern in surgery U. Chgo. Med. Ctr., 1966-67; resident in gen. surgery Tufts New Eng. Med. Ctr., Boston, 1967-69; fellow in surgery Malmo (Sweden) Gen. Hosp., 1969-70; resident in plastic surgery Wilford Hall USAF Med. Ctr., San Antonio, 1973-75; fellow in hand surgery Denver Gen. Hosp., 1976-77; chief surgery USAF Hosp., Taiwan, 1976-77; asst. prof. surgery U. Miss. Med. Ctr., Jackson, 1977-79, chief divsn. plastic surgery, 1979-82; dir. divsn. plastic surgery Allegheny Gen. Hosp., Pitts., 1982—; clin. assoc. prof. plastic surgery U. Pitts. Sch. Medicine, 1982—. Active med. staff Miss. Cripple Children's Treatment and Tng. Ctr., Miss., 1981-82; dir. cleft palate clinic Allegheny Gen. Hosp., Pitts., 1982-88; attending physician St. Margaret Meml. Hosp., Pitts., 1984-89, Montefiore Hosp., Pitts., 1986-89, Divine Providence Hosp., Pitts., 1991—, North Hills Passavant Hosp., Pitts., 1993; cons. med. staff Harmarville Rehab. Ctr., Inc., Pitts., 1985; cons. in plastic surgery VA Hosp., Pitts., 1993—, Miss. Meth. Rehab. Ctr., Jackson, 1977-82, VA Hosp., Jackson, 1977-82; dir. burn unit U. Miss. Med. Ctr., Jackson, 1979-82, co-dir. hand surgery svc., 1979-82; mem. med. staff Miss. Crippled Children's Treatment and Tng. Ctr., Jackson, 1981-82; presenter in field. Contbr. numerous articles to profl. publs., chpts. to books; assoc. editor Jour. Plastic and Reconstructive Surgery. Lt. col. USAF, 1972-76. Mem. AMA, ACS, Am. Soc. Plastic and Reconstructive Surgeons, Am. Assn. Plastic Surgeons, Assn. Mil. Plastic Surgeons, Soc. Air Force Clin. Surgeons, Am. Burn Assn., Internat. Soc. for Burn Injuries, Am. Cleft Palate Assn., Plastic Surgery Rsch. Coun., Am. Soc. for Surgery of Hand, Am. Assn. Hand Surgery, Royal Soc. Medicine, Assn. Acad. Chmn. of Plastic Surgery, Lipolysis Soc. N.Am., Allegheny County Med. Soc., Pa. Med. Soc., Ohio Valley Plastic Surg. Soc., Pitts. Surg. Soc. Office: Allegheny Gen Hosp 320 E North Ave Pittsburgh PA 15212-4756

HECKLER, WALTER TIM, association executive; b. Kimberley, Republic South Africa, Jan. 30, 1942; s. Walter Martin and Mavis Joyce (Cardinal) H.; m. Renée Anne Tamborello, Dec. 16, 1984; children: Cindy, Mark, Timothy, David, Chelsea, Mia. BS in Biology, Lamar U., Beaumont, Tex., 1963. Chief rsch. technician M.D. Anderson Cancer Inst., Houston, 1963-69; rsch. asst. Salk Inst. Biol. Studies, La Jolla, Calif., 1969-70; dir. tennis Westwood Country Club, Houston, 1970-75; gen. mgr. Chancellors Racquet Club, Houston, 1975-82; chief exec. officer U.S. Pro Tennis Assn., Houston, 1982—. Named to USPTA Internat. Tennis Tchr. Hall of Fame, 2000, recipient Tennis Ednl. Merit award, 2002. Mem. Am. Soc. Assn. Execs., U.S. Profl. Tennis Assn. (pres. 1980-82), Profl. Assn. Diving Instrs. Avocations: tennis, diving, boating, skiing. Office: US Profl Tennis Assn World Hdqrs 1 USPTA Centre 3535 Briarpark Dr Houston TX 77042-5245

HECKLINGER, RICHARD E. ambassador; b. Syracuse, N.Y. m. Carol Pratt. Grad., St. Lawrence U.; JD, Harvard U.; grad. in advanced internat. studies, Johns Hopkins U. Joined Fgn. Svc., Dept. State, Washington, 1967—, prin. dep. asst. sec. for econ. and bus. affairs, sr. advisor and exec. asst. to under sec. for econ. affairs; dep. chief mission U.S. Mission to OECD; dep. asst. sec. for European and Can. affairs Dept. State, sr. insp. Office Insp. Gen., advisor to under sec. for polit. affairs, dir. Internat. Energy Policy Office; acting dep. asst. sec. for internat. affairs Dept. Energy, Washington; amb. to Thailand, Am. Embassy, Bangkok. Office: APO AP 96546 Am Ambassador To Thailand Washington DC 20521-0001

HECKMAN, CAROL A. biology educator; b. East Stroudsburg, Pa., Oct. 18, 1944; d. Wilbur Thomas and Doris (Betts) H. BA, Beloit (Wis.) Coll., 1966; PhD, U. Mass., Amherst, 1972. Rsch. assoc. Yale U. Sch. Medicine, New Haven, 1973-75; staff mem. Oak Ridge (Tenn.) Nat. Lab., 1975-82; adj. assoc. prof. U. Tenn.-Oak Ridge Biomed. Grad. Sch., 1980-82; assoc. prof. Bowling Green (Ohio) State U., 1982-86, prof. biology, 1986—. Cons. NSF, Washington, 1977-80, NIH, Rockville, Md., 1996-98; dir. EM facility Bowling Green State U., 1982—; NSF trainee, Amherst, 1967-70; vis. prof. Univ. Coll. London. Contbr. articles to profl. jours., chpts. to books. Internat. Cancer Rsch. Tech. fellow Internat. Union Against Cancer, 1980, Heritage Found. fellow, 1982, guest rsch. fellow, Uppsala, Sweden, 1989-90; grantee NSF, 1981-84, 90-92, NIH, 1987-88, 98-2001, Dept. of Def., 2000-02. Mem. AAAS, Am. Soc. Cell Biology, Microscopy Soc. Am., N.W. Ohio Microscopy (sec.-treas. 1986-90, pres. 1990-94), Soc. In Vitro Biology, Mid-Am. Drug Devel. (pres. 1999), Ohio Acad. Sci., Sigma Xi. Episcopalian. Achievements include research evaluation and development of in vitro anticarcinogens. Home: 861 Ferndale Ct Bowling Green OH 43402-1609 Office: Bowling Green State U Dept Biol Scis Bowling Green OH 43403-0001

HECKMAN, GARY WALTER, military career officer; b. Des Moines; m. Sally Mitchell; children: Wendy, Ryan, Benjamin. BA in Edn., U. No. Iowa, 1972; MPA, Troy State U., 1981; grad., Air Command and Staff Coll., 1981, Armed Forces Staff Coll., 1984, Air War Coll., 1989; M in Nat. Security and Strategic Studies, Naval War Coll., 1992. Commd. 2d lt. USAF, 1973, advanced through grades to brig. gen., 1997, C130 transport and AC-130 gunship aircrew and staff, 1974-79, with hdqs., 1979-80, 92-94, plans officer 1st spl. ops. wing, 1980-83, with hdqs. European Commandhdqrs., 1984-87, with hdqs. Air Force spl. ops., 1987-89, dep. dir. programming and policy Mil. Airlift Command, 1989-91, commdr. 16th Spl. Ops. Group Hurlburt Field, 1994-96; dir. resources (J8), chief of staff J7/J8 US Spec Ops Cmd., 1996—. Decorated Legion of Merit with one oak leaf cluster, Def. Meritorious Svc. medal, Meritorious Svc. medal with three oak leaf clusters, Air medal, Joint Svc. Commendation medal, Air Force Commendation medal, Air Force Achievement medal.

HECKMAN, HENRY TREVENNEN SHICK, steel company executive; b. Reading, Pa., Mar. 27, 1918; s. H. Raymond and Charlotte E. Shick H.; AB, Lehigh U., 1939; m. Helen Clausen Wright, Nov. 28, 1946; children: Sharon Anita (dec.), Charlotte Marie. Advt. prodn. mgr. Republic Steel Corp., Cleve., 1940-42, editor Enduro Era, 1946-51, account exec., 1953-54, asst. dir. advt., 1957-65, dir. advt., 1965-82; partner Applegate & Heckman, Washington, 1955-56; advt. mgr. Harris Corp., 1956-57. Permanent chmn. Joint Com. for Audit Comparability, 1968-93; chmn. Media Comparability Coun., 1969-83; chmn. indsl. advertisers com. Greater Cleve. Growth Assn., 1973-76; chmn. publs. com. Lehigh U., 1971-76; pres.'s adv. coun. Ashland Coll., 1966-76; advt. adv. council Kent State U., 1976-81; exec. com. Cleve. chpt. ARC, 1968-74; mem. Republican Fin. Exec. Com., 1966-87; coord. adv. coun. pub. svcs. campaign Employer Support for Guard and Res., 1973-83, 90-93. Comdr. USNR, 1942-46, 51-53; Korea. Named to Advt. Effectiveness Hall of Fame, 1967; named Advt. Man of Yr., 1969; recipient G.D. Crain, Jr. award, 1973; Disting. Alumnus award Lehigh U., 1979; elected to Cleve. Graphic Arts Council Hall of Distinction, 1981. Mem. Indsl. Marketers Cleve. (past pres., Golden Mousetrap award 1968), Bus. Mktg. Assn. (pres. 1968-69, Best Seller award 1966, Hall of Fame, 1973), Assn. Nat. Advertisers (chmn. shows and exhibits com. 1966-74, dir. 1969-72), Am. Iron and Steel Inst. (com. chmn. 1961-69), Steel Svc. Ctr. Inst. (advt. adv. com. 1965-77), New Eng. Soc., Western Res. Soc., SAR (pres. 1979, Archibald Willard award 1996), Ohio Soc. SAR (Hub Scott award 1995), Mil. Order World Wars (comdr. 1980), Early Settlers, Cleve. Advt. Club (pres. 1961-62, Hall of Fame 1980), Ctr. for Mktg. Comm. (chmn. bd. 1965), Pi Delta Epsilon. Clubs: Cheshire Cheese (pres. 1982), Cleve. Grays (trustee 1980-82), Cleve. Skating. Home: 6000 Nob Hill Dr Apt 401 Chagrin Falls OH 44022-3358

HECKMAN, JAMES JOSEPH, economist, econometrician, educator; b. Chgo., Apr. 19, 1944; s. John Jacob and Bernice Irene (Medley) H.; m. Lynne Pettler, 1979; children: Jonathan Jacob, Alma Rachel. AB in Math. summa cum laude (Woodrow Wilson fellow), Colo. Coll., 1965, LLD (hon.), 2001; MA in Econs., Princeton U., 1968, PhD in Econs. (Harold Willis Dodds fellow), 1971; MA (hon.), Yale U., 1989; LLD (hon.), Colo. Coll., 2001; D (hon.), U. Chile, 2002, UNAM, Mex. From lectr. to assoc. prof. Columbia U., 1970-74; assoc. prof. econs. U. Chgo., 1973-76, prof., 1976—, Henry Schultz prof. of econ., 1985-95, Henry Schultz Disting. Svc. prof., 1995—, prof. econs. Harris Sch. Pub. Policy, 1990—, dir. Ctr. for Program Evaluation Harris Sch. Pub. Policy, 1991—, dir. Econs. Rsch. Ctr. Dept. Econs., 1997—; A. Whitney Griswold prof. econs. Yale U., New Haven, 1988-90, Sterling prof., 1990, prof., dept. stats., 1990; dir. Ctr. for Program Evaluation Harris Sch. Pub. Policy U. Chgo., 1991—, dir. Econs. Rsch. Ctr. Dept. Econs., 1997—. Rsch. assoc. Nat. Bur. Econs. Rsch., 1970-77, sr. rsch. assoc., 1977-85, 87—; Irving Fisher prof. econs. Yale U., 1984; treas. Chgo. Econ. Rsch. Assocs.; rsch. assoc. Econs. Rsch. Ctr.-NORC, 1985—; cons. in field; cons. Chgo. Urban League, 1978-86; mem. status Black Ams. com. NRC; lectr. in field.; hon. prof. U. Tucuman, Argentina, 1998, Hangzhou U. Sci. and Tech., Wuhan, China, 2001. Author: (with Alan KRueger) Inequality in America, 2003; editor Jour. Polit. Economy, 1981-87; assoc. editor Jour. Econometrics, 1977-83, Jour. Labor Econs., 1983—, Econs. Revs., 1987—, Rev. of Econs. and Statistics, 1994—, Jour. Econ. Perspectives, 1989-96, Labor Econs., 1992—; author (with B. Singer and G. Tsiang) Lecture Notes on Longitudinal Analysis, 1994; editor: (with B. Singer), Longitudinal Analysis of Labor Market Data, 1985; (with E. Leamer) Handbook of Econometrics, Vol. 5, vol. 6, Incentives in Govt. Bureaucracies: A Study of Performance Standards And Their Effects, The Economic Approach to Program Evaluation; Am. editor Rev. Econ. Studies, 1982-85; contbr. articles to profl. jours. Founding faculty and curriculum com. U. Chgo. Harris Sch. Pub. Policy. Recipient Louis Benezet Alumni prize Colo. Coll., 1985, Nobel Prize in Econs., 2000, Paul Harris award Internat. Rotary Assn., 2002; J.S. Guggenheim Found. fellow, 1978-79, Social Sci. Rsch. Coun. fellow, 1977-78, Ctr. for Advanced Study in Behavioral Scis. fellow, 1978-79. Fellow Am. Bar Found. (sr., rsch. affiliate 1989-91, sr. rsch. fellow 1991—), Econometric Soc. (mem. coun. 2001—), Am. Acad. Arts and Scis., Am. Statis. Assn.; mem. Nat. Acad. Scis. Am. Econ. Assn. (exec. com. 2000—, John Bates Clerk prize 1983), Midwest Econs. Assn. (pres.-elect 1996-97, pres. 1997-98), Am. Statis. Assn., Indsl. Rels. Rsch. Assn., Econ. Sci. Assn. (founder), Phi Beta Kappa. Home: 4807 S Greenwood Ave Chicago IL 60615-1913 Office: U Chgo Dept Econs 1126 E 59th St Chicago IL 60637-1580 E-mail: jjh@uchicago.edu.

HECKMAN, JEROME HAROLD, lawyer; b. Washington, June 7, 1927; s. Morris and Pauline (German) H.; m. Margot Resh, June 16, 1948 (div. Oct. 1977); children: Eric Stephen, Carey Eugene; m. Ilona Ely Grenadier, Jan. 2, 1986. BSS, Georgetown U., 1948, LLB, 1953, JD, 1967. Bar: D.C. 1953, U.S. Supreme Ct. 1965. Assoc. Dow, Lohnes & Albertson, Washington, 1954-59, ptnr., 1959-62; sr. ptnr. Keller and Heckman, Washington, 1962—. Gen. counsel Soc. of Plastics Industry Inc., N.Y.C., Washington, 1954—, Broadcasting Publs. Inc. Mag., Washington (co. sold to L.A. Times), 1968-87, Disposables Assn. Inc. (now named Internat. Nonwovens and Disposables Assn.), 1958-67. Contbr. articles to profl. jours. Chmn. regional Rep. com., Md., 1966-72; pres. Plastics Acad., 1995-97. Named to Hall of Fame of Plastics Industry, 1987; recipient Spes Hominum award, Nat. Sanitation Found., 1987, William Bradbury award, Soc. Plastics, 2000, Paul R. Dean Disting. Alumni award Georgetown U. Law Ctr., 2001; Dirs. Citation, Ctr. Food Safety and Applied Nutrition, 2000, FDA. Mem. ABA, Bar Assn. D.C., George Town Club, Woodmont Country Club, Phi Delta Phi. Avocations: golf, tennis. Office: Keller & Heckman 1001 G St NW Ste 500 Washington DC 20001-4545

HECKMAN, LUCY T. librarian; b. Queens, N.Y., June 9, 1954; d. Charles and Ruth Heckman. BA in English, St. John's U., Jamaica, N.Y., 1976, MLS in Libr. Info. Sci., 1977; MBA, Adelphi U., 1981. Catalog libr. St. John's U. Libr., Jamaica, 1977—82, reference libr., 1982—2001, head reference, 2002—. Author: Franchising in Business, 1989, The New York Stock Exchange, 1992, Nasdaq, 2001. Mem.: ALA (sec. bus. ref. and svcs. sect. 1998—2000), Beta Phi Mu. Avocations: photography, antiques. Home: 100-50 223 St Queens Village NY 11429

HECKT, MELVIN DEAN, lawyer; b. Dysart, Iowa, Apr. 21, 1924; s. Wesley T. and Ada Merle(Lawyer) H.; m. Dorothy M. Simons, Sept. 4, 1948; children— Janice, Paul, Mary, Barbara, William, Thomas. B.A. in Econs., State U. Iowa, 1948, J.D., 1950. Bar: Minn., 1950, Iowa 1950, U.S. Dist. Ct. (Minn.), U.S. Supreme Ct. Assoc. Snyder, Gale, Hoke, Richards, Janes (name changed to Bassford, Heckt, Lockhart & Mullin), Mpls., 1950-55, ptnr., 1955—94, prtnr. Luther, Heckt & Cameron, 1994-. Served with USMC, 1943-45. Decorated Bronze Star. Mem. Iowa Bar Assn., Minn. Bar Assn., Am. Legion, VFW, dir. Marine Corps Heritage Found., U.S. Marine Raider Assn. (past pres.). Republican. Lutheran. Contbr. articles to profl. jours. Address: 601 Carlson Pkwy Ste 750 Minnetonka MN 55305-5241

HECTOR, BRUCE JOHN, lawyer; b. Newark, Feb. 18, 1950; s. Henry Francis and Doris Mary (Campbell) H.; m. Carol Ann Seely, Aug. 10, 1974. BA in English, Coll. of the Holy Cross, 1971; JD, NYU, 1974. Bar: N.J. 1974, U.S. Dist. Ct. N.J. 1974, N.Y. 1976, U.S. Dist. Ct. (ea. and so. dists.) N.Y. 1976, U.S. Ct. Appeals (4th cir.) 1977, U.S. Ct. Appeals (3d cir.) 1981. Assoc. Podvey & Sachs, Newark, 1974-75, Hill, Rivkins et al, N.Y.C., 1975-81; atty. Becton Dickinson & Co., Franklin Lakes, N.J., 1981-87, sr. atty., 1987-91, assoc. gen. counsel, 1992—. Lectr. in field. Contbr. articles to profl. publs. Leader explorer law post Boy Scouts Am., Glen Rock, N.J., 1985-88; chmn. devel. com. Village Sch. for Children, 2002—. Mem.: N.J. Corp. Counsel Assn. (bd. dirs. 1995—97, v.p., sec. 1997—99, pres. elect 1999—2001, pres. 2002—, v.p.), N.J. State Bar Assn., Am. Corp. Counsel Assn., Maritime Law Assn. U.S. (proctor in admiralty 1981—). Democrat. Episcopalian. Avocation: jazz guitar. Home: 170 Gramercy Pl Glen Rock NJ 07452-2310 Office: Becton Dickinson & Co 1 Becton Dr Franklin Lakes NJ 07417-1880 Fax: (201) 848-9228.

HECTOR, LOUIS JULIUS, lawyer; b. Fort Lauderdale, Fla., Dec. 11, 1915; s. Harry Howard and Grace Elizabeth (Kellerstrass) H.; m. Dorothy Anne Dooley, Aug. 12, 1950 (dec. 1973); children: Denis Howard, Dorothy Anne, William Frederic, Louis Julius; m. Nancy Bean Hilles, Dec. 11, 1976. BA, Williams Coll., 1938; postgrad., Christ Church Oxford (Eng.) U., 1939; LLB, Yale U., 1942. Atty. Dept. Justice, Washington, 1942-43; asst. to under sec. Dept. State, 1944; pvt. practice Miami, 1946-47; pres. Hector Supply Co., Miami, 1948-56; mem. CAB, 1957-59; sr. ptnr. Steel, Hector & Davis, Miami, 1959—. Trustee emeritus U. Miami, Rockefeller U., Nat. Humanities Ctr., 1985-91; dir. emeritus Chamber Music Soc. Lincoln Ctr., 1987—; chmn. Lucille P. Markey Charitable Trust, 1983-97 . Served with OSS. Mem. Am. Acad. Arts and Scis. Home: One Grove Isle Dr # 809 Miami FL 33133-6530 Office: 200 S Biscayne Blvd Miami FL 33131-2310

HEDAHL, GORDEN ORLIN, theatre educator, university dean; b. Minot, N.D., Jan. 2, 1946; s. Chester Owen and Delores May (Johnson) H.; m. Kathleen Josephine Sawin, Sept. 2, 1967 (div.); children: Marc Oscar, Melissa Ann; m. Jean Louise Loudon, Dec. 31, 1983. BS, U. N.D., 1968, MA, 1972; PhD, U. Minn., 1980. Postdoctoral fellow Purdue U., West Lafayette, Ind., 1981-82; prof. theater U. Wis., Whitewater, 1970-92, chair dept. theatre and dance, 1986-89, assoc. dean Coll. Arts, 1989-90, acting assoc. vice chancellor, 1991-92, dean Coll. Arts. and Scis. River Falls, 1998—; dean Coll. Liberal Arts U. Alaska, Fairbanks, 1993-98; acad. planner U. Wis. System, 1990-91. Author: (plays) Tall Tales and True, 1976, The Brothers Grimm, 1977, Land of the Rising Sun, 1979, Trolls and Other Fjord Folk, 1983, Andersen's Storybook, 1986, The Magic of Oz, 1987, African Folk Tales, 1989, Tell Me a Story, 1992; assoc. editor: Guide to Curriculum Planning in Classroom Drama and Theatre, 1989. Recipient Roseman Excellence in Teaching award U. Wis., Whitewater, U. Wis. Mem. Am. Coun. of Colls. of Arts and Scis., Am. Alliance for Theatre and Edn., Internat. Coun. of Fine Arts Deans, Theatre in Higher Edn., Rotary. Lutheran. Office: U Wis Coll Arts and Scis 410 S 3d St River Falls WI 54022-5001 E-mail: gorden.o.hedahl@uwrf.edu.

HEDBERG, JOHN CHARLES, investor; b. St. Paul, Minn., June 27, 1933; s. William Rueben and Esther Mathilda (Jenson) H.; m. Sarah Cornelia McLouth, Sept. 10, 1954 (div. Sept. 1981); children: John, Theodore, Lisa, Benjamin; m. Carrie Ann Walker, Sept. 19, 1986; children: Patrick, Holly, Emily. BS with distinction, U. Minn., 1955, JD, 1960. Sec.-treas. Chateau Co-Op Restaurant, 1951-54; acctg. intern Gen. Mills, Kankakee, Ill., 1955-56; law clk. Judge Laurens L. Henderson, Phoenix, 1960-61; law ptnr. Cox & Hedberg, Phoenix, 1961-71; pvt. practice Phoenix, 1971-73; ptnr. Hedberg & Kirschbaum, Phoenix, 1973-78; legal counsel Sea Ray Boats, Phoenix, 1970-78, v.p., legal counsel, 1978-87; dir. Sea Ray Credit Corp., 1980-87, Sea Ray Boats, Inc., 1982-89, pres., 1988-89, Sea Ray Boats Europe BV, 1988-89. Bd. dirs. Healthwaves Corp., Phoenix; trustee Ray Employees' Stock Ownership Trust and Ray Employees Retirement Plan, 1979-89; advocate before Ariz. and appellate cts., U.S. Dist. Ct., Ariz., 9th Cir. Fed. Ct. Appeals. Chmn. U. Minn. Rep. Club, Mpls., 1954-55; chancellor's assoc. U. Tenn., Knoxville, 1987-89; treas./dir. Esperanza, 1989—. Mem. Beta Gamma Sigma. Avocations: tennis, reading. Home: 12636 S Honah Lee Ct Phoenix AZ 85044-3510

HEDBERG, PAUL CLIFFORD, broadcast executive; b. Cokato, Minn., May 28, 1939; s. Clifford L. and Florence (Erenberg) Hedberg; m. Juliet Ann Schubert, Dec. 30, 1962; children: Mark, Ann. Student, Hamline U., 1959-60, U. Minn., 1960-62. Program dir. Sta. KRIB, Mason City, Iowa, 1957-58, Sta. WMIN, Mpls., 1959; staff announcer Time-Life broadcast Sta. WTCN-AM-TV, Mpls., 1959-61, Crowell Collier Sta. KDWB, St. Paul, 1961-62; founder, pres. Sta. KBEW, Minn., 1963-81; founder, owner Sta. KQAD and KLQL-FM, Luverne, Minn., 1971-88; co-founder Sta. KMRS-AM, KKOK-FM, Morris, Minn., 1956-94, pres., 1974-94; founder, pres. Courtney Clifford Inc., Mpls., 1977-79; founder, owner Market Quoters Inc., Blue Earth, Iowa, 1974-96; pres. Complete Commodity Options Inc., Blue Earth, 1977-91; pres., owner Sta. KEEZ-FM, Mankato, Minn., 1977-92; founder, pres. Sta. KUOO-FM, Spirit Lake, Iowa, 1984-99; owner Sta. KRIB and KLSS-FM, Mason City, 1984-97; owner, pres. Sta. KAYL-AM-FM, Storm Lake, Iowa, 1990-99; pres. KLGA AM-FM, Algona, Iowa, 1993-99; CEO Hedberg Broadcasting Group, Blue Earth, 1976-99; pres. KSOU AM-FM, Sioux Center, Iowa, 1996-99. Pres. Blue Earth Indsl. Svcs. Corp., 1970—76, bd. dirs., Minn. Good Rds., v.p., 1976—79, pres., 1979—81; bd. dirs. Spirit Lake Industries; mem. affiliates bd. NBC Radio Network, 1990—95, chmn., 1991—95; pres., CEO Arnolds Park (Iowa) Amusement Pk., 1990—95; founder Sta. KUQQ-FM, Spirit Lake-Milford, 1996—99, Sta. KIHK-FM, Rock Valley, Iowa, 1997—99; founder, developer Bridgewater Devel., Spirit Lake, 1999. Mem. Iowa Gt. Lakes Airport Commn., 1986—92; bd. dirs. Pavek Mus. Wonderful Wireless, St. Louis Park, Minn., 1987—. Named to, Mus. Broadcasting Hall of Fame, 2002; recipient Disting. Svc. award, Blue Earth Jaycees, 1971. Mem.: Iowa Broadcasters Assn. (Broadcaster of the Yr. 1998), Minn. AP Broadcasters (pres. 1966, bd. dirs. 1976—78), Minn. Assn. Broadcasters (radio bd. dirs. 1975—86, v.p. 1980—81, pres. 1983—84), Nat. Assn. Broadcasters (bd. dirs. 1985—89, 1993—95), Blue Earth C. of C. (pres. 1967, Leadership Recognition award 1967), Iowa Lakes C. of C. (bd. dirs. 1985—86), Shriners, Masons, Gredeh L. C. (founder 1995—). Lutheran. Home: 4400 Gulf Shore Blvd N Naples FL 34103-2216 Office: Bridgewater Devel Office PO Box 157 Spirit Lake IA 51360-0157

HEDBRING, CHARLES, computer consultant, writer; b. Wadsworth, Ohio, July 26, 1945; s. Olle S. and Margaret (Dickers) H. BA, Northwestern U., Evanston, Ill., 1969; MS, SUNY, Geneseo, 1974; EdS, Vanderbilt U., 1975; EdD, Columbia U., 1982. Nat. and internat. cons. Rsch. grantee N.Y.C. Bd. Edn., 1983-87; award Assn. of Gifted and Talented, 1979, Computer Software award Nat. Assn. Schs., 1990. Avocations: computers, sports, piano, guitar, motorcycles. Home and Office: 310 Riverside Dr Apt 1712 New York NY 10025-4127 E-mail: steppec@aol.com.

HEDDELL, GORDON S. federal agency administrator; b. St. Louis, Aug. 13, 1943; BA in Polit. Sci., U. Mo.; MA, U. Ill. (formerly Sangamon State U.). Asst. spl. agt. in charge U.S. Secret Svc., Phila., deputy asst. dir. office tng., spl. agt. in charge v.p. protective divsn., 1995—98, asst. dir. office inspection, 1998—2000; inspector gen. U.S. Dept. Labor, Washington, 2000—. With U.S. Army. Former Woodrow Wilson Pub. Svc. fellow. Office: US Dept Labor 200 Constitution Ave NW Washington DC 20210

HEDDEN, DEBRA GORDON, music educator; b. Clinton, Iowa, Apr. 5, 1951; d. Otto Edward and Edna Firm (Griffin) Bruhn; m. Steven K. Hedden, Aug. 16, 2002. BA in Music Edn., U. Iowa, 1973; MA in Music Edn., U. No. Iowa, 1985, EdD in Curriculum and Instrn., 1997. Cert. music tchr. Elem. music tchr. Lincoln Community Schs., Mechanicsville, Iowa, 1973-76; elem. music tchr., German tchr. Hudson (Iowa) Community Schs., 1976-93; assoc. prof. music edn., chair music edn. U. No. Iowa, 1993—. Mem. North Ctrl. Accreditation Team, 1980—; clinician, presenter at various convs., 1977—; mem. musician's del. to China and Kazakhstan, 1992; condr. Iowa Opus Concert, 1996, various choral festivals; master tchr. Heartland Choral Festivals, Des Moines, 1996, 98; presenter Internat. Music Edn. Symposium, Tasmania, 1999. Contbr. to Teaching Examples: Ideas for Music Educators, 1994, Strategies for Teaching K-4 General Music, 1996; contbr. articles to profl. publs., including Tchg. Music, Contbns. to Music Edn., Music Edn. Rsch., Music Educators Jour. and Gen. Music Today. Grantee Iowa Dept. Edn., 1985, 87. Mem. Iowa Music Educators (bd. dirs., exec. sec. 1984—), Am. Choral Dirs. Assn., Phi Delta Kappa, Pi Kappa Lambda. Democrat. Avocations: sewing, painting. Office: U No Iowa 42 6BPAC Cedar Falls IA 50614-0802

HEDDEN, GREGORY DEXTER, environmental science educator, consultant; b. Louisville, Sept. 13, 1919; s. Thomas Clark and Gladys (Dexter) H.; m. Genevieve Groves, Sept. 9, 1950; children— Thomas Dexter, James Jeffrey BS in Chemistry and Meteorology, U. Chgo., 1942, cert. in meteorology, 1943, SM, 1950, PhD in Phys.-Organic Chemistry, 1951. Asst. to dir. Inst. Air Weapons, U. Chgo., 1951-54; rsch. chemist DuPont Co., Wilmington, Del., 1954-59; tech. dir. Trionics, Madison, Wis., 1959-62; pres. Madison Rsch., 1962-65; dir. Wis. Tech. Svcs., 1966-69; prof. environ. scis., distance edn. for indsl. users, dir. sea grant adv. svcs. U. Wis., Madison, 1969-83. Contbr. articles to profl. jours.; patentee in field. Capt. USAAF, 1942-46. Recipient New Product award Indsl. Research, 1963, award of honor Underwater Mining Inst., 1981, spl. award Gov. of Wis., 1983, Disting. Service award U. Wis. Sea Grant Inst., 1983; U.S. Rubber Co. fellow U. Chgo., 1950. Fellow AAAS, Am. Inst. Chemists; mem. Am. Chem. Soc., Wis. Acad. Sci., Arts and Letters, Tech. Transfer Soc., Kiwanis, Sigma Xi. Republican. Home: 4410 Travis Ter Madison WI 53711-1402 E-mail: gdhedden@facstaff.wisc.edu.

HEDDEN, KENNETH FORSYTHE, chemical engineer; b. Glendale, Calif., Aug. 13, 1941; s. Marion William and Pauline (Forsythe) H.; m. Ann Ellen Young, Jan. 26, 1963 (div. 1990); children: Randolph, Stephen, William; m. Suzanne A. Whitlock, Feb. 10, 1990. BS, U. Calif., Berkeley, 1963; PhD, U. Calif., Davis, 1968; M in Pub. Adminstrn., U. Ga., 1980. Registered profl. engr., sanitarian, specialist microbiologist. Research fellow Tufts U. Med. Sch., Boston, 1968-70; research assoc. Purdue U., Lafayette, Ind., 1970-72; lab. supr. Anheuser-Busch, Inc., Lafayette, 1972-75; sanitary engr. U.S. Army Environ. Hygiene Agy., Aberdeen (Md.) Proving Ground, 1975-78, EPA, Athens, Ga., 1978-83, chem. engr. Environ. Monitoring Systems Lab. Las Vegas, Nev., 1983-88; environ. engr. Warner Robins Air Logistics Ctr., Robins AFB, Ga., 1988-94, environ. chemist, 1994—. Contbr. articles to profl. jours. Col. USAR. Mem. Conf. Fed. Environ. Engrs., Sigma Xi, Alpha Chi Sigma. Republican. Baptist. Avocations: gardening, bowling, stamp collecting, woodworking, black powderguns. Home: 1736 Hwy 49 Fort Valley GA 31030-6802 Office: WR-ALC/MADLC 420 Richard Ray Blvd Robins AFB GA 31098-1640 E-mail: eaglestationinc@hotmail.com.

HEDERSTROM, MATT, engineer; b. Rota, Spain, Feb. 2, 1973; s. Paul and Judy Hederstrom; m. Lena Hederstrom, July 5, 1997; 1 child, Sasha. MS, Va. Tech., Blacksburg, 1997. Flight controls engr. Lockheed Martin Skunk Works, Palmdale, Calif., 1997—2000; dir. of product mgmt. ANPC, Hood River, Oreg., 2000—. Recipient Disting. Engring. Project Achievement award, Engineers' Coun., 1999, 2000, Chmn.'s award, Brit. Aerospace, 2000. Mem.: AIAA. Office: ANPC 11 Third St Hood River OR 97031 Office Fax: 541-386-2124. E-mail: mhederstrom@anpc.com.

HEDGE, ARTHUR JOSEPH, JR., corporate executive; b. Hudson County, N.J., Sept. 19, 1936; s. Arthur Joseph and Mary Cecelia (Kieran) H.; m. Julie Norton Dahm, Apr. 15, 1961; children: Arthur Joseph III, Peter Michael, Gregory Carlton. BS, St. Peter's Coll., Jersey City, 1960; MS, MIT, 1973. Several mktg. postions Data Processing divsn. IBM, N.Y.C., 1960-68, sr. mktg. mgr. Data Processing divsn. Chgo., 1968-70, br. mgr. Data Processing divsn. N.Y.C., 1970-73, dir. mktg. practices Data Processing divsn. White Plains, N.Y., 1973-74, regional mgr. Data Processing divsn. Chgo., 1974-77, v.p. mgmt. svcs. Data Processing divsn. White Plains, 1977-80, v.p. Real Estate and Constrn. divsn., 1980-85, pres. Real Estate and Constrn. divsn., 1985-87, IBM v.p. and pres. Real Estate and Constrn. divsn., 1987-88, IBM v.p. Corp. Real Estate and Constrn. divsn. Stamford, Conn., 1988-90, v.p. environ. affairs, 1990-93; pres., CEO, bd. dirs. Kroll Environ. Enterprises Inc. subs. Kroll Assocs., Stamford, 1993-97; chmn. Jannon Holdings, LLC, Stamford, 1997-2001, ABR Group, LLC, Westport, Conn., 2003—. Mem. adv. bd. Wharton Real Estate Ctr., Phila., 1988-94. Mem. vis. com. Harvard U. Grad. Sch. Design, Cambridge, 1985-91, Chgo. Crime Commn., 1974-77, Urban Gateways Exec. Com., Chgo., 1974-77, Conn. Bus. and Industry Assn. Exec. Com., Hartford, 1989-92, trustee, 1988-92; chmn. Bd. Regents Fairfield (Conn.) Coll. Prep. Sch., 1978-84; chmn. bd. dirs. White Plains Hosp. Ctr., 1985-92, trustee, bd. dirs., 1978—; chmn. bd. trustees Am. Festival Theatre, Stratford, Conn., 1988-93; trustee Coun. for Arts, White Plains, 1982-89, The Presbyn. Hosp. N.Y.C., 1993—; bd. dirs. N.Y. and Presbyn. Hosps., Inc., 1996—; vice chmn. HealthStar Network, 1996-97, 99, chmn., 1998. Alfred P.Sloan fellow MIT, 1972-73. Mem. Westchester County Assn. (vice-chmn. 1989-92, trustee bd. dirs. 1986-96), Southwestern Area Commerce and Industry Assn. of Conn. (bd. dirs. 1992-2001), Conn. Golf Club (bd. dirs. 1980-85). Roman Catholic. Avocations: golf, reading, the arts. Office: ABR Group LLC 320 Post Rd West Westport CT 06889

HEDGE, THOMAS LYLE, JR., rehabilitation services professional; b. Radford, Va. s. Thomas Lyle Hedge, Sr. and Mary Frances (Askew) Hedge; m. Lyd Annette Canavan, Oct. 1, 1978; children: Erin, Eric, Emily, Evan. BA, U. Calif., Riverside, 1972; MD, U. So. Calif., 1976. Asst. med. dir. Northridge (Calif.) Hosp. Ctr. for Rehab., 1980—84, assoc. med. dir., 1984—88, med. dir., 1988—. Past pres. Calif. Soc. Phys. Medicine & Rehab., 2000—01; adv. bd. Guillain Barre Syndrome Found. Internat., Pa., 2001—. Named Physician of Yr., Calif. Gov. Commn. for Employment of Disabled, 1990; recipient Individual Outstanding Svc., Nat. Assn. Rehab. Facility, 1986. Office: Ctr for Rehab Northridge Hosp Med Ctr 18300 Roscoe Blvd Northridge CA 91328-4167

HEDGES, DONALD WALTON, lawyer; b. Kansas City, Mo., May 24, 1921; s. Byron C. and Irma (McCleary) H.; m. Mary Elizabeth Mancill, Jan. 29, 1944 (div.); children: Judith Elizabeth, Donna Louise, Byron C. II, Steven M.; m. Diane Scheid, Jan. 15, 1965; children: Scott Andrew, Hillary Carson. Student, Principia Coll., 1939-40; BS, U. Pa., 1943, LLB, 1947; D. Bus. Sci. (hon.), Webber Coll., 1947. Bar: Pa. 1949, U.S. Ct. Appeals (3d cir.) 1979, U.S. Dist. Ct. (ea. dist.) Pa. 1949. Law clk. to Chief Justice Horace Stern Pa. Supreme Ct., 1948-49; mem. firm Mancill, Cooney, Semans & Hedges, 1949-64; ptnr. Wolf, Block, Schorr & Solis Cohen, Phila., 1965-82, Obermayer, Rebmann, Maxwell & Hippel, Wayne, Pa., 1986-88; pvt. practice law, Wayne, Pa., 1948—. Dir. Servotronics, Inc. Former trustee Atwater Kent Mus. Lt. (j.g.) Air Force USNR, 1943—46. Decorated Distinguished Flying Cross, Air medal. Mem. ABA, Pa. Bar Assn., Phila. Bar Assn., Juristic Soc. Phila., Beta Theta Pi. Clubs: Union League (Phila.); Sharswood Law (U. Pa.), Merion Cricket. Episcopalian. Home: 538 Whitford Hills Rd Exton PA 19341-2050

HEDGES, EDITH RITTENHOUSE, nutrition and family and consumer sciences educator; b. Oakland, Calif., Mar. 15, 1937; d. Lloyd Lee and Florence Muriel (McCurdy) Rittenhouse; m. Frank Hill Hedges III, Dec. 16, 1967. BS in Nutrition/Dietetics, U. Nev., Reno, 1960; MS in Nutrition Rsch., U. Wis., 1962; postgrad., Purdue U., 1971-75, U. Ill., 1975-78. Rsch. asst., cmty. nutritionist U. Wis., Madison, 1960-62; nutritionist Nat. Sch. Lunch program USDA Regional Office, N.Y.C., 1962-64; nutritionist, home economist Am. Friends Svc. Com., Mex., 1964-66; instr. English pub. secondary sch., Tonatico, Mex., 1965-66; from instr. to asst. prof. Eastern Ill. U., Charleston, 1966-93, prof. emeritus, 1993—. Cons. nutritionist Coles County Mental Health Dept., 1982-85, 97. Mem. Coles County Arts Coun., Charleston, 1990—; vol. Ptnrs. in Adult Literacy, Ill. Recipient Rehab. Achievement award Mercy Hosp. Rehab. Ctr., Urbana, Ill., 1987; named Woman of Achievement Women's Studies Coun., Eastern Ill. U., 1994, Outstanding Vol. Docent, Tarble Art Ctr., 1984, 85, 86. Mem. LWV (Coles County pres. 2002—), Ea. Ill. U. Annuitants Assn.(editor newsletter 1995—), Zonta (chair various coms.), Handweavers Guild Am. (prs. local guild 1983-85), Coalition of Citizens with Disabilities in Ill. Mem. Soc. Of Friends. Avocations: photography, watercolors, camping, birdwatching. Home: 21324 E County Road 400N Charleston IL 61920-9077

HEDGES, HARRY GEORGE, computer scientist, educator; b. Lansing, Mich., Oct. 7, 1923; s. Charles William and Elsie (Frost) H.; m. Mary J. Corbishley, June 14, 1944 (dec.); children: Susan, Martha; m. Kamla J. King, July 24, 1988. BS, Mich. State U., 1949, PhD, 1960; MS, U. Mich., 1954. Electronics engr. USAF Wright Air Devel. Center, Dayton, Ohio, 1949-51; research asso. U. Mich., 1951-54; instr. Mich. State U., East Lansing, 1954-60, asst. prof., 1960-63, asso. prof., 1963-69, prof., chmn. dept. computer sci., 1969-84, prof. emeritus, 1988—; sr. staff assoc. NSF, 1984-88, head Office Cross-Disciplinary Activities, 1988-92, program dir. undergrad. edn., 1992, program dir. exptl. & integrative activities, 1993—. Dir. Nat. Electronics Conf., Inc., 1968-75 Tech. editor: Analysis of Discrete Physical Systems, 1967; mem. Computer Sci. Bd, 1973-84; chmn., 1974-75. Chmn. Selective Service Bd. 264, Lansing, 1970-76. Served with AUS, 1943-46, PTO. NSF sci. faculty fellow, 1960 Mem. Am. Soc. Engring. Edn. (chmn. N.Central sect. 1968-69), IEEE (dir. 1967-69, treas. 1969, vice chmn. 1973, chmn. 1974, Southeastern Mich. sect.). Home: 4331 Embassy Park Dr NW Washington DC 20016-3607 E mail: hedgeshk@starpower.net.

HEDGES, KAMLA KING, library director; b. Covington, Va. d. John Wilton and Rhoda Alice (Loughrie) K.; m. Harry George Hedges, July 24, 1988. AB, Coll. of William and Mary, 1968; MLS, Vanderbilt U., 1969. Law and legis. reference libr. Conn. State Libr., Hartford, 1969-74; dep. law libr. Steptoe and Johnson, Washington, 1974-78; law libr. Wilkinson, Cragun and Barker, Washington, 1978-83; corp. libr. The Bur. of Nat. Affairs, Inc., Washington, 1983-94, dir. libr. rels., 1995—. Compiler: (directories) BNA's Directory of State and Federal Courts, Judges, Clerks, 1995, BNA's State Administrative Codes and Registers, 1995; contbr. chpt. to law manual. Bd. dirs. Friends of the Law Libr. of Congress, 2000—. Mem. Am. Assn. Law Librs. (exec. bd. dirs. 1984-87), Spl. Libr. Assn. Episcopalian. Home: 4331 Embassy Park Dr NW Washington DC 20016-3607 Office: Bur Nat Affairs Inc 1231 25th St NW Washington DC 20037-1197

HEDGES, MARK STEPHEN, clinical psychologist; b. Chgo., Feb. 15, 1950; s. Norman T. and Doris Mae (Walters) H.; m. Janice Finnie, Aug. 16, 1975; children: Anna, Miriam. BS, Purdue U., 1972; MA, U. S.D., 1974, PhD, 1977. Psychology intern Western Mo. Mental Health Ctr., Kansas City, 1975-76; psychologist, dir. psychol. svcs. Northeastern Mental Health Ctr., Aberdeen, SD, 1977—. Chmn. Northeastern Area Local Interagy. Team; mem. citizens rev. panel S.D. Dept. Social Svcs. Mem. APA, S.D. Assn. Sch. Psychologists, Phi Beta Kappa, Psi Chi, Phi Kappa Phi. Methodist. Office: Northeastern Mental Health Ctr 703 3rd Ave SE Aberdeen SD 57401-4508

HEDGES, PATRICK ARMAND, information technology and communications and computer systems security specialist; b. Ft. Bragg, NC, June 2, 1948; adopted s. Harold Harrel and Marcelle Marie Julienne (Zeyen) H.; m. Penelope Ann Huff, Aug. 20, 1968 (div. Feb. 1981); children: Johnn Patrick, Sean Armand, Cristina Marie. *Patrick Hedges father was in the United States Army of the 562nd Ambulance Company, 425th, Battoon, during WWII, when he and his wife were introduced in Belgium. His mother was born in Houffalize, Belgium. During the war she worked in the Hospital Baviere as a registered nurse, in Liege, and fought as a member of the Belgium underground army as an information courier. She was also an adjutant of a resistance group to the occupying Germans during the war and she saw 40 of her group lost during her five years in the Belgian resistance. She has five medals and a number of citations that she received for her allegiance during WWII, including the Cross of War. She received her US citizenship on June 27, 1957.* AA, St. Leo Coll., Ft. Monroe, Va., 1985, Air Command and Staff Coll., Langley AFB, Va., 1990, Air War Coll., Kelly AFB, Tex., 1993. Computer programmer Applied Tech. Lab., Ft. Eustis, Va., 1978-81, computer sys. analyst, 1983—84; dep. dir. intelligence support Hdqrs. Tactical Air Command, Langley AFB, 1984—85, tech. advisor intelligence support, 1985—86; chief sys. application, computer sys. analyst 1912 Computer Sys. Group, Langley AFB, Va., 1986—91; chief air force computer security Air Force Info. Warfare Ctr., San Antonio, 1991-94; chief info. protection tech. support Air Force Comm. Agy., Scott AFB, Ill., 1994—2001, chief comm. Air Force security program, 2001—. Contbr. articles to profl. jours. With U.S. Army, 1968-77, Vietnam. Decorated Bronze Star, Vietnam Cross of Gallantry Unit, Meritorious Svc. medal, Army Commendation medal with oak leaf, Vietnam Svc. medal with three campaign stars. Avocations: collecting books, coins and stamps, woodworking. Home: 2412 Antiquity Ln Belleville IL 62221

HEDGES, RICHARD HOUSTON, lawyer, epidemiologist; b. Louisville, July 16, 1952; s. Houston and Frances Ruth (Zemo) H.; m. Donna Jean Hough. BA, U. Ky., 1974; MA, Ea. Ky. U., 1975, MPA, 1983; PhD, U. Ky., 1986; JD, Capital U. Law, 1994. Bar: Ohio 1995. Rehab. specialist Commonwealth of Ky., Somerset, 1976-81, chief health planner Frankfort, 1981-82; asst. prof. U. Ky., Lexington, 1985-87; rsch. assoc. dept. med. behavioral sci. U. Ky. Coll. Medicine, Lexington, 1982-85; program adminstr. Rollman Psychiat. Inst., Cin., 1987-88; asst. prof. Ohio U., 1988-92, assoc. prof., 1992—; assoc. Garry Hunter, LPA, Athens, Ohio, 1997-98; ptnr. Thomas & Hedges LLC, 1998-99; pvt. practice, Athens, 1999—; magistrate Village of Coolville, Ohio, 2001—, Village of Chauncey. Asst. city atty. City of Nelsonville, Ohio, 1997—2001, city pros., 1997—2001; dir. divsn. on aging Ohio U. Health Promotion and Rsch., 1990—92, MHA grad. program coord., 1995—96; bd. dirs. Washington County Mental Health and Addiction Recovery Svcs., 1998—99; exec. dir. pro tem Health Recovery Svcs., 1998; solicitor Village of Chauncey, 2000. Author: Bioethics, Healthcare and the Law, 1999; contbr. articles to profl. jours. Mem. Athens County Domestic Violence Task Force, Athens County Victim's Assistance Adv. Fellow NIMH, 1984-86. Mem.: ATLA, ABA, Athens County Bar Assn., Washington County Bar Assn. (trustee at large 2000—02), Ohio Bar Assn., Am. Health Lawyers Assn., Healthcare Fin. Mgmt. Assn., Soc. Ohio Healthcare Attys., Ohio Acad. Trial Lawyers, Phi Delta Phi, Pi Sigma Alpha. Episcopalian. Avocations: backpacking, volleyball, bicycling, sailing. Home: 275 Mooreland Rd Belpre OH 45714-9702 Office: 8 N Court St Ste 507 Athens OH 45701-2450 also: Ohio U Sch Health Sci E346 Grover Ctr Athens OH 45701 Fax: 740-592-3724.

HEDIEN, COLETTE JOHNSTON, lawyer; b. Chgo., 1939; d. George A. and Catherine (Bugan) Johnston; m. Wayne E. Hedien; 3 children. BS with honors, U. Wis., 1960; JD, DePaul U., 1981. Bar: Ill. 1981. Tchr. Sch. Dist. 39, Wilmette, Ill., 1960-63, Tustin (Calif.) Pub. Schs., 1964-66; extern law clk. to judge Chgo., 1980, U.S. Atty.'s Office, Chgo., 1980; pvt. practice Northbrook, Ill., 1981—. Atty. Chgo. Vol. Legal Svcs.; mem. Chgo. Appellate Law Com., 1982-83, chmn., 1987-88; chmn. Northbrook Planning Commn., 1984-89; founder Am. Women of Surrey (Eng.), 1975-77; founding dir. U. Irvine Friends of Libr., 1965-66; guidance vol. Glenbrook High Sch., 1984-89; trustee Village of Northbrook, 1989—; mem. Women's Bd. Field Mus. Bd. dirs. Ill. Project for Spl. Needs Children, 1998—. NSF scholar, 1962. Mem. ABA (com. on real property), Ill. Bar Assn., Chgo. Bar Assn., North Shore Panhellenic Assn. (rep. 1989—), Phi Kappa Phi, Kappa Alpha Theta (bd. dirs.).

HEDIEN, WAYNE EVANS, retired insurance company executive; b. Evanston, Ill., Feb. 15, 1934; s. George L. and Edith P. (Chalstrom) H.; m. Colette Johnston, Aug. 24, 1963; 3 children. BSME, Northwestern U., 1956, MBA, 1957. Engr. Cook Electric Co., Skokie, Ill., 1957-64; bus. mgr. Preston Sci., Inc., Anaheim, Calif., 1964-66; security analyst Allstate Ins. Co., Northbrook, Ill., 1966-70, portfolio mgr., 1970-73, asst. treas., 1973-78, v.p., treas., 1978-80, sr. v.p., treas., 1980-83, exec. v.p., chief fin. officer, 1983-85, vice chmn., chief fin. officer, 1986, pres., 1986-89, chmn., 1989-94, The Allstate Corp., 1993-94, also bd. dirs.; retired, 1994. Mem. adv. coun. Kellogg Grad. Sch. Mgmt., Northwestern U.; bd. dirs. The PMI Group, Inc., Field Mus. Natural History, Morgan Stanley Dean Witter Funds. Mem. Comml. Club Chgo. Office: WEH Assocs 5750 Old Orchard Rd Ste 530 Skokie IL 60077-1081

HEDIN, EDNA JENKS, musician, educator; b. Ft. Worth, Nov. 15, 1924; d. Edward Lee and Tressie (Jackson) Jenks; A.A., Central Coll. Women, Conway, Ark., 1945; B.Music, Okla. Baptist U., 1948; M.Ed., Tex. Tech. U., 1972; m. Alvin Morris Hedin, Apr. 1, 1947; children— John Alvin, Edward Morris, James Lee. Grad. asst. Central Coll. Women, Conway, 1946-47; pvt. tchr. piano, mus. dir. kindergarten Shawnee, Okla., 1948-49; dir. jr. high choir Crooked Oak Sch., Oklahoma City, 1950-51; tchr. music Norfolk Consol. Sch., Cushing, Okla., 1951-55; Artesia (N.Mex.) pub. schs., 1955— ; adj. instr. N.Mex. State U., Carlsbad; organist First Bapt. Ch., 1955— ; tchr. piano and organ; piano soloist and accompanist; judge pianists and ch. choirs. Mem. Nat. Guild Piano Tchrs., Music Tchrs. Nat. Assn. (nat. cert. mem.), Phi Kappa Phi, Sigma Alpha Iota, Kappa Delta Pi, Delta Kappa Gamma. Republican. Baptist. Home: 1 Cajun Ct Roswell NM 88201 3408 Office: Chapel at New Mex Mil Inst Roswell NM 88201 E-mail: studioone@zlanet.com.

HEDKE, RICHARD ALVIN, retired gifted education educator; b. Evanston, Ill., Aug. 27, 1940; s. Alvin C. and Leona Amanda (Kieper) H.; m. Carol Ann Bormet, July 21, 1962; children: Deborah, Kristen. BS in Elem. Edn., Concordia U., 1968, MA in Curriculum and Instrn., 1975; postgrad., No. Ill. U., 1980—2002, Nat. Lewis U., 1980—2002, Gov.'s State U., 1980—2002. Cert. K-9 tchr., Ill. Classroom tchr., athletic dir. Immanuel Luth. Sch., Kingston, N.Y., 1962-65, St. Paul Luth. Sch., Addison, Ill., 1965-67, St. Peter Luth. Sch., Schaumburg, 1967-74; classroom tchr. Schaumburg Twp. Dist. 54 Schs., 1974—79, 1997—2002, tchr. gifted students, 1979-97. Vis. summer sch. instr. High Sch. Dist. 214, Ill., 1983-86, gifted students math. and sci. Dist. 20, 1987; mem. grad. adv. com. Concordia U., 1984-85; dir. future studies summer program High Sch. Dist. 214; presenter various confs. including Nuts 'N Bolts Confs. No. Ill. Planning Commn. for Gifted Edn., 1979-87, Ill. State Gifted Conf., 1980; adj. faculty Aurora U., 1990, 91, 92, 93. Author gifted students curriculum Dist. 54, 1979-98. Mem. long-range planning action com. Project Horizon, 1987-90; mem. sch. leadership team, 1999—. Mem. NEA, Nat. Assn. Gifted Children (mem. future studies subcom., visual and performing arts subcom., presenter Mid-Winter Conf. 1986), Nat. Coun. Tchrs. Math. (presenter various meetings), Ill. Coun. Tchrs. Math. (presenter various meetings, named Outstanding Math. Educator), Ill. Coun. Gifted, Ill. Sci. Tchrs. Assn., Ill. Edn. Assn., Schaumburg Edn. Assn., World Future Soc. Avocations: photography, community theater acting and singing, travel. Home: 36 Brookstone Dr Fredericksburg VA 22405-2794

HEDLEY, ROBERT PEVERIL, retired petroleum and chemical company executive; b. Orange, N.J., Aug. 23, 1937; s. David H. and Helen (Peveril) H.; m. Barbara A. King, July 25, 1959; children: Jon P., Susan A., Kenneth G. AB, Dartmouth Coll., 1959; MBA, Amos Tuck Sch., 1960. Mem. exec. tng. program Colgate-Palmolive Co., N.Y.C., 1960-63; fin. analyst Texasgulf, Inc., N.Y.C., 1963-65, asst. treas. N.Y.C. and Stamford, Conn., 1965-81, treas. Stamford, 1981, v.p., treas., 1981-94. V.p., treas. Elf Aquitaine, Inc., 1983-94. Mem.: Sky Club. Republican. Home: 56 Rilling Ridge New Canaan CT 06840-4314

HEDLEY-WHYTE, E(LIZABETH) TESSA, neuropathologist; b. London, Jan. 17, 1937; came to U.S., 1960; d. George Stanley and Elizabeth Margery (Hacking) Waller; m. John Hedley-Whyte, Sept. 19, 1959. MB, BS, Durham (U.K.) U., 1960; MD, U. Newcastle Upon Tyne (U.K.), 1976; AM (hon.), Harvard U., 1992. Diplomate Am. Bd. Pathology, Examiner neuropathology. Resident in pathology Children's, New Eng. Deaconess and Peter Bent Brigham Hosps., Boston, 1960-65; fellow Cerebral Palsy Found., 1965-66; asst. neuropathologist Children's Hosp., 1966-68, neuropathologist, 1968-77; pathologist New Eng. Deaconess Hosp., 1977-81; asst. prof., assoc. prof., prof. pathology Harvard Med. Sch., Boston, 1968—; assoc. neuropathologist Mass. Gen. Hosp., Boston, 1981-83, neuropathologist, 1983—, dir. neuropathology tng., 1983—, dir. pathology residency tng., 1985-96; cons. neuropathologist Children's Hosp. and Beth Israel Hosp., Boston, 1977—. Cons. NIH, 1976-81; mem. residency rev. com. for pathology Accreditation Coun. on Grad. Med. Edn., 1996-2001. Mem. editl. bd. Jour. Neuropathology and Exptl. Neurology, 2000—, Human Pathology, 2000—; N.Am. editor Neurobiology and Applied Neurobiology, 1991-99; contbr. articles to profl. jours. Wellcome Trust fellow, 1984-85. Mem. Nat. Insts. for Nervous and Communicative Disorders and Stroke (chair program project com. 1979-81), Am. Assn. Neuropathologists (pres. elect 1994-95, pres. 1995-96, v.p., chair coms. 1976-90), Diagnostic Slide Session (moderator 1995—), New Eng. Soc. Pathologists (sec., treas., pres. 1980-86), Boston Soc. Neurology and Psychiatry (pres. 1994-95). Avocations: gardening, skiing, needlework. Office: Mass Gen Hosp 14 Fruit St Boston MA 02114-2620

HEDLEY-WHYTE, JOHN, anesthesiologist, educator; b. Newcastle-upon-Tyne, Eng., Nov. 25, 1933; arrived in U.S., 1960, naturalized, 1965; s. Angus and Nancy (Nettleton) H.-W.; m. Elizabeth Tessa Waller, Sept. 19, 1959. Student, Harrow Sch., 1947-52; BA (Rothschild scholar Clare Coll.), Cambridge U., 1955, MB, 1958, MA, 1959, MD, 1972; AM (hon.), Harvard U., 1967. House surgeon St. Bartholomew's Hosp., London, 1958-59; resident in anesthesia Mass. Gen. Hosp., 1960-62, hon. anesthetist, 1977—; clin. asst. anesthesia Harvard U., 1961-63, instr., 1963-65, clin. assoc., 1965-67, assoc. prof., 1967-69, prof., 1969-76, 1st David S. Sheridan prof. anaesthesia and respiratory therapy, 1976—; prof. dept. health policy and mgmt. Harvard U. Sch. Pub. Health, 1988-2000, mem. leadership coun., 2003—, leadership coun., 2003—; chmn. faculty seminar in health and medicine Harvard U., 1975-76; anesthetist-in-chief Beth Israel Hosp., Boston, 1967-88, chmn. com. on rsch., 1976-82. Cons. in field; mem. tech. adv. bd. on med. devices tech. Am. Nat. Standards Inst., 1973-83; U.S. del. Internat. Electrotech. Commn., 1989-91, 92—; leader U.S. del. Internat. Orgn. Standardization, Geneva, 1973-89, chmn. com. TC 121, SC 3 on anaesthetic and respiratory equipment, 1978—. Author: Respiratory Care, 1965, Applied Physiology of Respiratory Care, 1976, Continuous Anesthesia Vapor Monitoring, 1990, Operating room and Intensive Care Alarms and Information Transfer, 1992; contbr. articles to profl. jours. Recipient Hichens prize St. Bartholomew's Hosp., London, 1957. Fellow ACP (life), German Soc. Anaesthesia and Intensive Care Medicine (hon., life), ASTM (hon., chmn. com. F29 1983-89, Merit award 1994, user vice chmn. 2000—), Royal Coll. Anaesthetists (hon., life); mem. Am. Physiol. Soc., Abernethian Soc. (past pres.), Am. Soc. Anesthesiologists (chmn. com. mech. equipment 1977-82, chmn. com. on equipment and standards 1982-84), Mass. Soc. Anesthesiologists (pres. 1973-74), Am. Soc. Pharmacology and Exptl. Therapeutics, Roxbury Soc. Med. Improvement (libr. 1970-88, sec.-treas. 1988—), Mass. Med. Soc. (coun. 1975-78), Fairhaven Preservation Assn. (chmn. 1990—), Boodle's Club, The Country Club, Somerset Club, Harvard Club of Boston, Vicarage Club. Democrat. Episcopalian. Achievements include discovery that human blood has a constant relative solubility for oxygen. Office: VA Med Ctr 1400 VFW Pkwy Boston MA 02132-4927

HEDLUND, BARBARA SMITH, musician, educator, music publisher; b. Orlando, Fla., Apr. 11, 1951; d. John Gerald and Marie Elizabeth (Shaulis) Smith; m. Ronald W. Hedlund, Nov. 12, 1974; 1 child, Alexander. BM magna cum laude, Phila. Music Acad., 1983. Prin. cellist N.J. Symphony, Newark, 1978-83, NEPA Philharm., Scranton/Wilkes Barre, Pa., 1978-84; prin. and quartet cellist Westfield (N.J.) Symphony, 1983-84; substitute cellist N.Y. Philharm., 1980-83; prin. cellist Ill. Symphony, Springfield, 1984-91, Champaign-Urbana (Ill.) Symphony, Ill., 1984—, Opera Ill., Peoria, 1988—; prof. music Ill. Wesleyan U., Bloomington, 1986-94; prin. cellist Danville (Ill.) Symphony, 1995—. Mem. cello faculty Wilkes (Pa.) Coll.; vis. prof. cello U. Ill., Urbana, 1985-90; arts adminstr. Wesleyan Faculty Recital Series, 1986-94, Ill. Chamber Orch., 1985-91, Virtuoso Obbligato Aria Collection, 1994—, Orch. Leitung and Kammermusik Coord. Klassisches Music Festival, 1991-97; co-dir. Springfield Summer Strings, 1995; personnel mgr. Opera Ill. Orch., 1988—; founder 1st Choice Music Svcs., 2003. Soloist with orchs. include Opera Theater of St. Louis, N.W. Symphony, Chgo., Wesleyan Civic Orch., Purdue U. Symphony, Ill. Sympnony, CU Symphony, Danville Symphony; solo recitals include appearances at Met. Opera Gala, Charleston, Ill., Smith Music Hall, U. Ill.-Urbana, Nat. Soc. Arts & Letters, Springfield, Tarbel Arts Ctr., Charleston, Sandwich (Ill.) Opera House, Springer Cultural Ctr., Champaign, Ill., Esterhazy Palace, Eisenstadt, Austria, 1992, 95, 1997, Aspen Music Festival, 1982, 91; appeared in 16 Broadway shows including Fiddler on the Roof, Porgy and Bess, Shenandoah, Annie, Cats, Oklahoma, Beatlemania, My Fair Lady, Peter Pan and others; recordings include popular sound tracks, albums, live performances, radio and TV commmls.; pub. Cellobration Publications, 1994—; assoc. prodr. and solo cellist video documentary PBS The Song and the Slogan about Carl Sandburg, 2003; contbr. articles to profl. jours.; tours include Music of Andrew Lloyd Webber, Phantom of the Opera, Shirley Bassey Orch. Adoption search buddy Adoptees Liberty Movement, Ill., N.Y., N.J., 1981—; founder and adminstr. Baroque Artists of Champaign-Urbana, 1996-99; bd. dirs. Champaign-Urbana Symphony, 1986-94; parent vol. Coop. Nursery Sch., Urbana, 1986-87, Yankee Ridge Elem. Sch., 1992-94; vol. Urbana Nursing Home, 1966-99; adminstr. Ill. Coun. of Orchs. (named Baroque Artists Chamber Ensemble of Yr. 1999). Recipient Meritorious Svc. award Ill. Coun. Orchs., 1999. Mem. Am. Fedn. Musicians, Chgo. Cello Soc., Internet Cello Soc., String Soc. Artists (founder, co-dir., 1985—). Home and Office: Music Pub Prodn Offices 505 Eliot Dr Urbana IL 61801-6727 E-mail: vcello1@aol.com.

HEDLUND, CHARLES JOHN, oil company executive, conservationist; b. Appleton, Minn., Nov. 3, 1917; s. William Martin and Sophia Stickney Hedlund; m. Helen Marie Thorstenson, Aug. 30, 1940; children: Susan Louise, Patricia Jo, Ann Elizabeth, Christopher Charles. B Chem. Engring., B Bus. Adminstrn., U. Minn., 1940; LLD (hon.), Am. U., Cairo, 1993. Refinery engr. Std. Oil Co. La., Baton Rouge, 1940-46; with coord. and econs. dept. Std. Oil Co. (N.J.) (now Exxon), N.Y.C., 1947-52; dir. program Petroleum Adminstrn. for Def., Washington, 1952-53; mgr. coord. and econ. dept. Std. Oil Co. (N.J.), N.Y., 1954-59; exec. v.p. Esso Std. Italia, Genoa, Italy, 1960-61; pres. Svenska Esso AB, Stockholm, Sweden, 1962-66; v.p. mktg. Esso Europe, London, 1967; v.p. Exxon, pres. Esso Mid. East, N.Y., 1968-80. Mem. exec. com. Arabian Am. Oil Co., Dhahran, Saudi Arabia, 1968-80; chmn. petroleum working group NATO, Paris, 1952-53. Chmn. Anglo Am. Sch.-Stockholm, 1962-66; trustee The Nature Conservancy, 1978-87(chmn. 1984-85), N.Y. adv. bd. Salvation Army, 1970-80, Am. Mus. Natural History, 1979-89, Conservation Internat., 1987— (founding chmn. 1987-95), Am. U. Cairo, 1976— (chmn. 1980-92). Named to Order of Arts and Scis. 1st Class, Govt. Egypt, 1993. Mem. Baltrusol Golf Club (N.J.), Country Club Fla., Ocean Club Fla. (trustee 1997-99), The Little Club, Century Assn. (N.Y.), Lansdowne Club (London), Tau Beta Pi, Beta

Gamma Sigma, Phi Lambda Upsilon. Republican. Episcopalian. Avocations: conservation, education, golf, tennis. Home: 58 Country Rd S Village Of Golf FL 33436-5612 Office: Conservation Internat 1919 M St NW Washington DC 20036

HEDLUND, JAMES H. traffic safety consultant; b. Ithaca, N.Y., July 24, 1941; s. Glenn H. and Helen H. H.; m. Betta E., June 27, 1964; children: John H., Peter W. BA, Cornell U., 1963; PhD, U. Mich., 1968. Asst. prof. math. U. Mass., Amherst, 1968-74, Smith Coll., Northampton, Mass., 1974-76; math. statistician Nat. Hwy. Traffic Safety Adminstrn., Washington, 1976-82, chief math. analysis, 1982-87, dir. driver rsch., 1987-89, dir. alcohol programs, 1990-95, assoc. adminstr., 1995-97; prin. Hwy. Safety North, Ithaca, N.Y., 1998—. Mem. adv. bd. Century Coun., 1997—. Mem. editl. bd.: Accident Analysis and Prevention, 1990—. Recipient Govt. Leadership award Nat. Commn. Against Drunk Driving, 1997. Mem.: Math. Assn. Am., Am. Math. Soc. Lutheran. Avocation: music. Home: 110 Homestead Rd Ithaca NY 14850

HEDLUND, PAUL JAMES, lawyer; b. Abington, Pa., June 26, 1946; s. Frank Xavier and Eva Ruth (Hoffman) H.; m. Marta Louise Brewer, Dec. 7, 1985; children: Annemarie Kirsten, Brooke Ashley, Tess Kara. BSME, U. Mich., 1968; JD, UCLA, 1973. Bar: Calif. 1973, D.C. 1994, U.S. Dist. Ct. (ctrl. dist.) Calif. 1977, U.S. Dist. Ct. (ea. dist.) Calif. 1991, U.S. Dist. Ct. (no. dist.) N.Y. 1994, U.S. Patent and Trademark Office 1978, U.S. Ct. Appeals (9th cir.) 1994, U.S. Supreme Ct. 1997. Staff engr. So. Calif. Edison, L.A., 1968-70; ptnr. Hedlund & Samuels, L.A., 1974-88, Kananack, Murgatroyd Baum & Hedlund (and predecessor firms), L.A., 1988-92; shareholder Baum, Hedlund, Aristei, Guilford & Schiavo, L.A., 1993—. Mem. discovery and trial teams MDL 817 aircrash at Sioux City Iowa United Airlines, Chgo., 1989; mem. plaintiffs' steering com. Alaska Airlines crash off Pt. Mugu, Calif., 2000; mem. plaintiffs' exec. com. Sept. 11, 2001 Tort Litigation; lectr. in field. Recipient Safety award, Nat. Air Disaster Found., 2002. Mem.: LA County Bar Assn., Consumer Attys. of LA, DC Bar Assn., State Bar Calif. Office: Baum Hedlund Aristei Guilford & Schiavo 12100 Wilshire Blvd Ste 950 Los Angeles CA 90025-7107 E-mail: phedlund@baumhedlundlaw.com.

HEDLUND, RICHARD PAUL, historian, educator, retired historian; b. Haver, Mont., Oct. 19, 1937; s. Wilmer Paul and Beth Kliest Hedlund; m. Betty Jane Terrill McEwan, June 26, 1967; stepchildren: Diana Lynn McEwan, Janet Lee McEwan Hovekamp. BA, U. Ky., 1960, MA, 1964; PhD U. Ky., 1976. Prof. history U. Ky., Ashland, 1965—98; ret., 1998. Vis. prof. Princeton (NJ) U., 1985, 87, 89; writer Ashland Daily Ind., 1989. Contbr. Basketball coach Ashland C.C., 1966—67; mem. Ky. Bicentennial Commn., 1976—81; bd. dirs. Ashland Highlands Mus., 1990—98. Mem.: Friends Ky. Pub. Archives (bd. dirs.), So. Hist. Soc., Diplomatic History Soc., Civil War Roundtable, Henry Clay Soc., Orgn. Am. Historians, So. Accreditation Assn., Sigma Delta Chi, Phi Alpha Theta. Democrat. Avocations: reading, writing, basketball, travel. Home: 3432 Belvoir Dr Lexington KY 40502

HEDLUND, RONALD, baritone; b. Mpls., May 12, 1934; s. Cyril and Mildred H.; m. Barbara Smith, Nov. 12, 1974; children: Eric, Alexander. BA, Hamline U.; MusM, Ind. U. Mem. faculty dept. music U. Ill., 1970-74, 83—; bass soloist, instr. classical music seminar Eisenstadt and Vienna, Austria. Singing voice cons. Carle Clinic Speech Ctr., Urbana, 1994—. Appeared throughout U.S. including opera cos. of San Francisco, Chgo., Houston, Miami, Seattle, Dallas, Ft. Worth, Phila., Washington, Omaha, Santa Fe, Lake George, Boston, N.Y.C. Opera, Met. Opera Nat. Co., New Orleans, Spoleto Festival, Edinburgh Festival, Vancouver Opera, Conn. Opera, Aspen Festival, R.I. Opera, Chgo. Opera Theater, Opera Theatre St. Louis, Utah Opera, Peoria Civic Opera, Ill. Opera Theatre; soloist with numerous orchs., recitals throughout U.S. Served with USNR, 1958-63. Office: 1st Choice Music Svcs 505 Eliot Dr Urbana IL 61801-6727

HEDLUND, RONALD DAVID, academic administrator, researcher, educator; b. Joliet, Ill., June 16, 1941; s. Henry Gustav and Betty Marie (Nelson) H.; m. Ellen Louise Parrish, Aug. 22, 1964; children: Karen Marie, David Peter. BA, Augustana Coll., 1963; MA, U. Iowa, 1964, PhD, 1967. Asst. prof. U. Wis., Milw., 1967-73, assoc. prof., 1973-77, dir. social sci. rsch. facility, 1978-80, prof., 1977-89, assoc. dean of rsch. Grad. Sch., 1980-89; vice provost of rsch., prof. U. R.I., Kingston, 1989-96, acting dean grad. sch., 1995-96; vice provost rsch. and grad. edn., prof. Northeastern U., Boston, 1996—. Co-chair rsch. network R.I. Partnership Sci. & Tech., Providence, 1990-93; bd. dirs. Econ. Innovation Ctr., Newport, R.I.; mem. R.I. legis. commn. on creating high-tech jobs and Univ. Contbr. numerous articles to profl. jours. Mem. Kingston Fire Dist. Study Com., 1990. NSF grantee, 1967, 77, 84, 95, Ford Found. grantee, 1985. Mem. Am. Polit. Sci. Assn., Internat. Polit. Sci. Assn., Nat. Coun. Univ. Rsch. Adminstrs., Midwest Polit. Sci. Assn. (exec. coun. 1987-90), Soc. of Rsch. Adminstrs., Southern Polit. Sci. Assn., Western Polit. Sci. Assn. Lutheran. Avocation: gardening. Office: Northeastern U 112 Hayden Hall Huntington Ave Boston MA 02115

HEDMAN, JANICE LEE, business executive; b. Elmhurst, Ill., Feb. 7, 1938; d. George Marion Hickman and Vera Beryl (Olsen) Sample; m. Daryl F. Hedman, Aug. 29, 1971 (div. Aug. 1983); children: Kevin G., Gregory Scott, Danny L., Shelly L. Wolanski-Bannon. Student, U. Puget Sound, 1970, Tacoma (Wash.) Community Coll., 1980. Head teller Puget Sound Nat. Bank, Tacoma, 1970-75; real estate agt. Shorewood Realty, Gig Harbor, Wash., 1975-80; mktg. rep. Western Fin. Planning, Inc., Tacoma, 1981-83; co-owner Schatz Avant Garde, Gig Harbor, 1984-86; asst. mgr. Classic Restaurant, Gig Harbor, 1984; co-owner Hedman Enterprises, Gig Harbor, 1976-93, owner, property mgr., 1993—; v.p. adminstrn. Teardrop Am., Inc., Wenatchee, Wash., 1986-90; pres. Teardrop N.W. Inc., Wenatchee, 1988-90; co-owner J&R Mktg., Wenatchee, 1989-90; mktg. specialist John L. Scott, Inc., Tacoma, 1991—2002; sr. mktg. rep. R & D, Excel Telecom., Gig Harbor, 1996-98, owner, mgr., 1993—; co-owner He-mi-co Instruments, 1999—; owner Hedman Enterprises, 1993—; retired. Asst., Women's Task Force, Tacoma, 1980-81; asst. in fund raising events Am. Cancer Soc., 1992-95. Mem. Epsilon Sigma Alpha (pres. 1980-81, v.p. 1981-82).

HEDREN, PAUL LESLIE, national park administrator, historian; b. New Ulm, Minn., Nov. 12, 1949; s. Thomas Harry and Muriel Mary (Kunz) H.; m. Janeen Margaret Wolcott, June 19, 1974 (div. 1997); children: Ethne Olivia, Whitney Elizabeth. BA, St. Cloud State Coll., 1972. Park ranger, historian Ft. Laramie (Wyo.) Nat. Hist. Site, 1971-76; historian Big Hole Nat. Battlefield, Wisdom, Mont., 1976-78; chief ranger, historian Golden Spike Nat. Hist. Site, Brigham City, Utah, 1978-84; supt. Fort Union Trading Post Nat. Hist. Site, Williston, N.D., 1984-97, Niobrara Nat. Scenic River/Mo. Nat. Recreational River, O'Neill, Nebr., 1997—. Author: First Scalp for Custer, 1980, With Crook in the Black Hills, 1985, Fort Laramie in 1876, 1988 (Best Book of 1988 Wyo. State Hist. Soc.); editor: Campaigning with King, 1991 (Merit award State Hist. Soc. Wis. 1991), The Great Sioux War 1876-77, 1991, Traveler's Guide to the Great Sioux War, 1996, We Trailed the Sioux, 2003; contbr. articles to profl. jours. Bd. dirs. Conv. and Vis. Bur., Williston, 1984-96, pres., 1994-96. Mem. Co. Mil. Historians, Western History Assn. (mem. coun. 1990-93). Avocations: writing, lecturing on Am. western history. Office: Nat Park Svc PO Box 591 Oneill NE 68763-0591

HEDRICH, CLEDA POLLARD, real estate broker, writer; b. Richmond, Va., July 3, 1940; d. Herschel Newton and Frances Morton Pollard; m. Norman Hedrich, Mar. 27, 1967; children: Norman Lee, Bradley Charles. BA, U. of N.C., 1960—62. Real Estate Broker State of Fla., 1974. Exec. asst. to the pres. London & Cheshire Ins. Co., London, 1962—63; exec. asst. Eurofinance, Paris, 1963—64; psychiat. asst. Emory U. (Grady Hosp.), Atlanta, Ga., 1965—66; elem. tchr. City of Chgo. Sch. Sys., Chgo., 1967—67; book editor MacMillan Pub. Co., N.Y.C., 1967—69; editor Internat. Jour. of Psychiatry, Internat. Jour. of Child Psychotherapy, Internat. Jour. of Psychoanalytical Psychotherapy, N.Y.C., 1970—72; real estate broker/owner Pollard & Hedrich Realty Inc., Bonita Springs, Fla., 1976—; vice pres./owner Hickory Homes, Inc., Bonita Springs, 1976—. Author: (novels) A Pl. to Go Someday, (mystery novel) Threat of a Stranger, (novels) Where Paths Meet, (screenplays) (juvenile novel) Threat of a Stranger. Personal E-mail: cleda@hedrichgroup.com.

HEDRICK, ERIC TODD, musician, educator; b. Petersburg, W.Va., Dec. 12, 1964; s. Gary Alan Hedrick and Carla Bergdall Brown; m. Lelia Meade Alexander, Mar. 6, 1993; children: Eddie, Julie. BS, Musicians Inst., Hollywood, Calif., 1991. Freelance musician, Harrisonburg, Va., 1984—; freelance rec. artist, 1985—; pvt. practice instr., 1991—; freelance music transcriber, 1991—. R-Conservative. Lutheran. Avocations: woodworking, British cars and motorcycles. Home and Studio: 1721 Evergreen Dr Harrisonburg VA 22801 Personal E-mail: eandl@shentel.net.

HEDRICK, FLOYD DUDLEY, retired government official, writer; b. Lynchburg, Va., Jan. 19, 1927; s. Silas Dudley and Alice (Stowe) H.; m. Rachel Conelia Childress, May 27, 1950; children: Susan Kaye, Alice Rae. Grad., Va. Comml. Coll., 1948, Advanced Mgmt. Program, Harvard, 1971; PhD, U. Ctrl. Calif., 1981. Purchasing agt., supt. stores Trailways, Inc., 1947-65; v.p. purchasing Macke Co., Washington, 1966-72; pres. subs. Atlantic Supply Co., Hyattsville, Md., 1967-72; chief procurement and supply divsn. Library of Congress, Washington, 1973-97; mem. Inter-Agy. Procurement Policy Com., 1973-89, Inter-Agy. Metrecation Com., 1976-93. Pres. Lynchburg chpt. Fed. and State Credit Unions, 1956-57 Author: Purchasing Management in the Smaller Company, 1971, Purchasing for Owners of Small Plants, 1976, 79; assoc. editor: Purchasing Handbook, 1973, 81. Served with USNR, 1944-46, 50-52. Mem. Am. Mgmt. Assn. (purchasing planning coun. 1969-92, editor Mgmt. Handbook 1981, named to Wall of Fame 1982), Nat. Assn. Purchasing Mgmt. (v.p. 1972-73, chmn. orgn. and planning com., Disting. Svc. award 1976, J. Shipman gold medal 1986), Purchasing Mgmt. Assn. Washington (pres. 1969-70), Isaak Walton League (v.p. Lynchburg 1957), Masons (32d degree). Clubs: Mason (32 deg.). Home: Annandale, Va. Died July 9, 2003.

HEDRICK, GEARY DEAN, small business owner; b. Wytheville, Va., Feb. 9, 1940; s. James Luther and Alma June (Webb) H.; m. Priscilla Ann Moore, Dec. 27, 1958; children: Geary Dean Jr., Darla Ann, Darren Keith. BA in Econs., Wofford Coll., 1975. Enlisted U.S. Army, 1960, advanced through ranks to sgt. major, 1978, ret., 1982; pres. Hedrick Gen. Maintenance/Contracting, Inc., Gurnee, Ill., 1982—. Del. Civic Ctr. Found. Libertyville, Inc., 1986—. Decorated Purple Heart, Bronze Star, DSM, Air medal; Cross of Gallantry with palm Rep. of Vietnam. Mem.: Lions (pres. 1987-88, various offices 1984—). Avocations: hunting, fishing, swimming, weightlifting, football. Home and Office: 37055 Mulberry Ln Gurnee IL 60031-1057

HEDRICK, JOAN DORAN, writer, university educator; b. Balt., May 1, 1944; d. Paul Thomas and Jane (Connorton) Doran; m. Travis K. Hedrick, Aug. 26, 1967; children: Jessica, Rachel. AB, Vassar Coll., 1966; PhD, Brown U., 1974. Instr. Wesleyan U., Middletown, Conn., 1972-74, asst. prof. English, 1974-80; prof. history Trinity Coll., Hartford, Conn., 1994—, also dir. women's studies program, 1987-98. Vis. asst. prof. Trinity Coll., Hartford, 1980-81, vis. assoc. prof., 1981-82. Author: Solitary Comrade: Jack London and His Work, 1982, Harriet Beecher Stowe: A Life, 1994 (Pulitzer Prize for biography 1995); editor: The Oxford Harriet Beecher Stowe Reader, 1999. Mem. MLA, Am. Studies Assn., Orgn. Am. Historians, Soc. Am. Historians. Office: Trinity College Dept of History 300 Summit St Dept Of Hartford CT 06106-3186*

HEDRICK, JOHN O. transportation executive; b. Sellersville, Pa., Sept. 16, 1944; s. John O. and Ruth Moyer H.; m. Patricia Marie Lott, Jan. 13, 1968; children: Sharon Kathleen Hedrick Busby, Michael Bryan. BS, NYU, 1966; MA, U. Ga., 1986. Lic. pvt. pilot. Various mgmt. positions So. Railway Co., Atlanta, 1966-74; pres. Pullman Palace Dining Co., Atlanta, 1974-77; realtor Doster Realty Co., Monroe, Ga., 1977-81; exec. dir. Catskill Rail Com., Stamford, N.Y., 1981-85; prin. cons. PTSI Transp., Bryn Mawr, Pa., 1985-90; gen. mgr. Western Md. Scenic R.R., Cumberland, Md., 1990-92, Railway Engring. Assocs., Balt., 1992-93; cons., project mgr. PTSI Transp., Bryn Mawr, Pa., 1992-93; gen. mgr., exec. dir. W.Va. State Rail Authority, Moorefield, 1993-99; dir. capital and bus. devel. (facilities coord.) VIA Met. Transit, San Antonio, 1999—. Mem. adv. com. W.Va. Infrastructure and Jobs Devel. Coun., Charleston, 1995-99. Contbr. articles to profl. jours. Mem. Urban Land Inst., Am. Real Estate and Urban Econs. Assn., Internat. Right of Way Assn., Am. Assn. Railroads Supts., The Lexington Group, Phi Kappa Phi, Beta Gamma Sigma. Home: 13107 Hunters Fox St San Antonio TX 78230-2023 Office: 800 W Myrtle St San Antonio TX 78212-4233 Fax: 210-362-2592. E-mail: johedrick@juno.com.

HEDRICK, LARRY WILLIS, retired airport executive; b. Newton, Kans., Dec. 23, 1939; s. A.C. and Goldie (Kerns) H.; m. Nancy Cashin, July 21, 1962; children: Christina, Kathleen, Thomas. BL, U. LaSalle, Chgo., 1973. Lic. airport mgr., Mass, pilot and instrument technician. Airport mgr., dir. civil def. Newton City-County Airport, 1966-73; airport mgr. Barnes Mcpl. Airport, Mass., 1973-77, Niagara Falls Internat. Airport, 1977-81, Greater Buffalo (N.Y.) Internat. Airport, 1981-87; appointed airport adminstr. Pt. Columbus Internat. Airport, Columbus, Ohio, 1987-91; appointed exec. dir. Columbus Airport Authority, 1991-2000; ret., 2001. Founding bd. mem. Airline Passengers of Am., 1987; guest speaker various univs. and airport confs. Bd. dirs. Greater Columbus Conv. and Visitors Bur., 1992; past squadron commdr. CAP Kans. Wing. With USN, 1958-62. Mem. Am. Assn. Airport Execs. (accredited 1973, nat. sec. 1982, treas. bd. dirs. 1983, 1st v.p. 1985, 2d v.p. 1984, nat. pres. 1986-87, Disting. Svc. award 1994), Nat. Fire Protection Assn. (airport industry's only rep.), Mass. Airport Mgmt. Assn. (pres. 1975-76).

HEDRICK, LOIS JEAN, retired investment company executive, state official; b. Topeka, Kans., Jan. 25, 1927; d. Arthur Lenard and Nellie Cecelia (Johnson) Lungstrum; m. Clayton Newton Hedrick, Apr. 26, 1949; 1 dau., Carol Beth. Cert., Strickler's Bus. Coll., 1947; student, Washburn U., Topeka, 1980-83. Staff sec. Kans. State Senate, Topeka, 1946-65; co-owner Hedrick's Market, Topeka, 1953-67; exec. sec. to sr. legal counsel Security Benefit Life Ins. Co., Topeka, 1963-71; asst. corp. sec. Security Mgmt. Co., Topeka, 1971-92, Security Distbrs. Inc., SBL Planning Inc., SBL Fund, Security Action Fund, Security Equity Fund, Security Investment Fund, Security Ultra Fund, Security Bond Fund, Security Cash Fund, Security OmniFund, Security Tax-Exempt Fund, Security Benefit Group Ins., Security Mgmt. Co.; mem. Kans. Adv. Coun. on Aging, 1990-93; mgmt. cons. United Way of Greater Topeka, 1981-89, mem. pub. rels. staff, 1982—. Rep. precinct woman, organizer, chmn. Topeka and Shawnee County Crime Blockers, 1976—; vol. fundraiser Am. Heart Assn., Stormont-Vail Hosp. Expansion, 1976-77; chmn. Plant a Tree for Century III, 1976; chmn. Greater Topeka Edn. Com., 1981—; organizing staff sec., fundraiser Christian Rural Overseas Program, 1951, staff sec. USAF Supply Depot, 1951-53; vol. community and various hosps.; dir. Topeka Women's Bowling Assn., 2000—. Named Woman of Yr. Am. Bus. Women's Assn., 1970, Sec. of Yr. Profl. Secs., Internat., 1975. Mem. Greater Topeka C. of C. (chmn. edn. com. 1981—, ambassador chmn. high sch. honors banquet 1982—), Adminstrv. Mgmt. Soc. (dir., pres. 1976—). Republican. Home: 1556 SW 24th St Topeka KS 66611-1329

HEDRICK, PEGGY SHEPHERD, lawyer; b. Lake City, Iowa, Dec. 30, 1936; d. Clayton Conner and Clyttie Lucinda (Leake) Shepherd; m. Charles Webster Hedrick Sr., Dec. 8, 1955; children: Charles Jr., J. Lucinda Kennaley, Lois Kathryn. BA in Sociology and German, Pitzer Coll., 1972; JD, U. LaVerne Coll. Law, 1980, Yeshiva U., 1981. Bar: Mo. 1981, U.S. Dist. Ct. (so. dist.) Mo. 1981, U.S. Ct. Appeals (8th cir.) 1981. Pvt. practice, Springfield, Mo., 1981; staff atty. Legal Aid Southwest Mo., Springfield, Mo.; pvt. practice Springfield, Mo., 1984—. Election monitor, Bosnia-Herzegovina, 1998, Bosnia-Herzegovina, 2001, Kosovo, 01. Contbr. articles and photographs to profl. jours; team mem. Archeol. projects in Egypt, 1970-75, 84, sponsored by Smithsonian Inst. Bd. dir. Mayor's Commn. Human Rights, Dogwood Coun. Girl Scouts Am., Rape Crisis, Greene County League Women Voters; candidate Cir. Ct. Judge, 1988. Nominated Danforth Found. scholar, Pitzer Coll. Democrat. Southern Baptist. Office: PO Box 11027 Springfield MO 65808-1027 E-mail: peggy@peggyhedrick.com.

HEDRICK, WALLY BILL, artist; b. Pasadena, Calif., 1928; s. Walter Thomas and Velma Laurel (Thurman) H. Student, Otis Art Inst., Los Angeles, 1947, Calif. Coll. Arts and Crafts, 1954; B.F.A., Calif. Sch. Fine Arts, 1955; MA, San Francisco State U., 1958. Instr. San Francisco State U., 1958-59, Calif. Sch. Fine Arts, 1960-64, Art Inst. San Francisco, 1964-70, San Francisco Acad. Art, 1971, San Jose State U., 1972-73, Indian Valley Coll., 1974—. Instr. summer session Art. Inst. San Francisco, 1978; instr. U. Calif., Davis, 1984, 86. One-man shows include Pasadena (Calif.) Arts Ctr., 1950, M.H. de Young Meml. Mus., San Francisco, 1955, Calif. Sch. Fine Arts, San Francisco, 1956, Oakland (Calif.) Mus., 1958, Isaacs Gallery, Toronto, Can., 1961, New Mission Gallery, San Francisco, 1963, San Francisco Art Inst., 1967, Sonoma Satte Coll., Calif., 1968, 63 Bluxome St., San Francisco, 1975, Gallery Paule Anglim, San Francisco, 1982, 84, 89, 90, Emanuel Walter Gallery, 1985, Atholl McBean Gallery, 1985, Natsoulas-Novelozo Gallery, Davis, Calif., 1989, Mills Coll. Art Gallery, 1994, Gallery Paule Anglim, 1994, Calif. Mus. of Art, 1999, Linc Real Art Gallery, San Francisco, Calif., 2002, Sonoma State U. Art Gallery, Rohnert Pk., Calif., 2002; group exhibitions include Gallery Paule Anglim, San Francisco, 1992, ACGI Gallery, Berkeley, Calif., 1993, The Crocker Mus., Sacramento, 1994, The Oakland Mus., Calif., 1994, San Francisco Art Inst., 1994, Richmond Art Ctr., Calif., 1995, San Francisco Women Artists Gallery, 1995, Whitney Mus. Am. Art, N.Y.C., 1995, Walker Art Ctr., Mpls., 1996, M.H. de Young Meml. Mus., 1996, numerous others; represented in permanent collections, Aldrich Mus. Contemporary Art, Ridgefield, Conn., Mus. Modern Art, N.Y.C., Smithsonian Instn., San Francisco Mus. Modern Art, City and County San Francisco, L.A. County Mus. Art, Laguna (Calif.) Mus., Mus. Contemporary Art, Ridgefield, Conn., Oakland Mus., Calif. State U. Sonoma, U. Calif. San Francisco. San Francisco Art Commn., San Francisco Art Inst., San Francisco Internat. Airport, Univ. Art Mus., Berkeley, Calif., Mills Coll., Oakland; represented by Gallery Paule Anglim. Served with AUS, 1950-52. Recipient Adeline Kent award, 1985, Golden Bear award Calif. State Fair, 1990, merit award, 1991, award of excellence, 1996; grantee Nat. Endowment Arts, 1962, 82, 93, Marin Arts Coun.-Bucks Found., individual artist grantee San Francisco Found., 1985-86, Adolph and Esther Gottlieb Found. grantee, 1997, Pollack-Krasner Found. grantee, 1999. Office: PO Box 94 Bodega CA 94922-0094

HEDRICK, WILLIAM DAVID, secondary school educator, musician, educator; b. Greenfield, Tenn., Aug. 30, 1944; s. John Charles and Christine Lenore Hedrick. BS, Campbellsville (Ky.) U., 1966; M in Music Edn., Ea. Ky. U., 1969; EdD, U. Sarasota, Fla., 1981. Cert. Ky. Tchr. Internship Program Ky. Dept. Edn., 1995, tchr. music K-12 Ky. Dept. of Edn. Assoc. musical dir./cast mem. Stephen Foster - The Musical, Bardstown, Ky., 1972—; chmn., dir. vocal music Shelby County H.S., Shelbyville, 1976—82, 1989—; instr. voice and keyboard St. Catherine Coll., Springfield, Ky., 1985—89. Singer: Lexington Singers, Inc., Shelby County Cmty Theater; music arranger, composer Ky. Opera Assn. Amb. of goodwill Commonwealth of Ky., 1980, min. of music/organist First Bapt. Ch., Shelbyville, 1992—98; choirmaster, organist First Presbyn. Ch., Ashland, Ky., 1983—86. Named one of Outstanding Young Men of Am., 1979. Mem.: NEA (assoc.), Music Tchrs. Nat. Assn., Ky. Music Educators Assn. (dist. choral chmn. 1990—93), Shelby County Edn. Assn. (assoc.), Am. Choral Dirs. Assn. (assoc.), Ky. Choral Dirs. Assn. (assoc.), Music Educators Nat. Conf. (assoc.), Ky. Cols., Commonwealth of Ky. (hon.). Republican. Baptist. Achievements include patents for digital automated piano tuner. Avocation: computer music/digital technology. Office: Shelby County HS 1701 Frankfort Rd Shelbyville KY 40066-0069 Personal E-mail: dochedrick@aol.com. E-mail: dhedrick@shelby.k12.ky.us.

HEDRICK, WYATT SMITH, pharmacist; b. Roswell, N.Mex., Sept. 28, 1951; s. Wyatt Smith and Roberta Walker (Stuart) H. BS in Pharmacy, U. N.Mex., 1974; MS in Hosp. Pharmacy, U. Houston, 1978. Registered pharmacist, N.Mex., Tex. Pharmacy intern St. Mary's Hosp., Roswell, N.Mex., 1973, Ea. N.Mex. Med. Ctr., Roswell, 1973-74, U-SAVE Drug, Roswell, 1974-75; pharmacy resident U. Tex. Med. Br. Hosps., Galveston, 1977-78; staff pharmacist Meml. Gen. Hosp., Las Cruces, N.Mex., 1978, Las Palmas Med Ctr., El Paso, Tex., 1978—. Mem. Am. Soc. Health-Sys. Pharmacists, Tex. Soc. Health-Sys. Pharmacists, El Paso Area Soc. Health-Sys. Pharmacists. Avocations: reading, traveling, physical fitness. Home: 1028 Quinault Dr El Paso TX 79912-1223 E-mail: whedr34182@aol.com.

HEDSTROM, MITCHELL WARREN, banker; b. Buffalo, Apr. 14, 1951; s. Eric Leonard and Eloise (Herrick) H.; m. Zoe C. Dyson, Apr. 28, 1990. BS, Northeastern U., Boston, 1975; MS, MIT, 1977. Acct. officer Citibank, N.A., N.Y.C., 1978-80, sr. acct. officer, 1980-82, asst. v.p., 1982-84, v.p., 1984—, restructuring com., 1989-95, chmn. bank adv. com. for Panama, Sudan and Senegal, 1993-95; sr. risk mgr. pvt. banking group Citibank Switzerland, Geneva, 1996-97; group portfolio mgr., sr. risk mgt., pvt. banking group Citibank, N.A., N.Y.C., 1998—2003, sr. v.p., chief trust officer, 2004—. Mem. Coun. on Fgn. Rels., Coral Beach and Tennis Club. Episcopalian. Office: Citibank NA 153 East 53rd Street 23d Floor New York NY 10022-4699

HEEBNER, ALBERT GILBERT, economist, educator, bank executive; b. Phila., Mar. 7, 1927; s. Albert and Julia (Zwada) Heebner; m. Dorothy Mae Kiler, Aug. 16, 1952. AB, U. Denver, 1948; AM, U. Pa., 1950, PhD, 1967. Instr. econs. Coll. Wooster, Ohio, 1950-52; with Phila. Nat. Bank subs. CoreStates Fin. Corp, 1952-87, economist, 1960-87, asst. v.p., 1961-64, v.p., 1964-70, sr. v.p., 1970-73, exec. v.p., 1973-83; exec. v.p., chief economist CoreStates Fin. Corp., Phila., 1983-87; Disting. prof. econs. Eastern Coll., St. Davids, Pa., 1987-97, disting. prof. econs. emeritus, 2000—. Lectr. fin. Wharton Sch., U. Pa., 1968—69; spl. asst. to chmn. Coun. Econ. Advisers, Washington, 1971—72; vis. prof. econs. Swarthmore (Pa.) Coll., 1976; adj. prof. Ea. Coll., St. Davids, 1982; mem. Inflation Policy Task Force adv. com. to Pres.-elect Reagan, 1980; mem. investment adv. bd. to City of Phila. Bd. Pensions, 1980—85; bd. dirs. Nat. Bur. Econ. Rsch., 1983—85; bd. dirs., vice-chmn. Global Interdependence Ctr., 1992—. Author: (book) Negotiable Certificates of Deposit: The Development of a Money Market Instrument, 1969; contbr. articles to profl. jours. Trustee Eastern U., 2001—. With USNR, 1945—46. Named to Wall of Fame, N.E. HS, Phila., 1996; recipient Alumni Cmty. Svc. award, 1995. Fellow: Nat. Assn. Bus. Econs. (contbr. Econ. Policy Survey, pres. 1975—76); mem.: Phila. Coun. Bus. Economists, Fgn. Policy Rsch. Inst., World Affairs Coun. Phila., Union League Phila., Conf. Bus. Econs. (chmn. 1987—88), Am. Econ. Assn., Sunday Breakfast Club. Baptist. Home: 1515 The Fairway 471 W Rydal PA 19046-1491 E-mail: agheebner@aol.com. *I have always striven for excellence in everything that I undertake-reaching for the highest standards of which I am capable, not just meeting requirements. While I like to think that I have earned my way, I am deeply indebted to key people who encouraged me, mentored me, and steered me to opportunities. Thus, I do not see my career as a solo venture.*

HEEBNER, AMY L. educator, writer, artist; b. Cin. BFA, Calif. Inst. Arts, Valencia, 1975; MA, NYU, 1978; EdD, Columbia U., 1990; student, Dolmetscherschule, Zürich, 1992-93. Adj. prof. St. Francis Coll., Bklyn., 1980-83; asst. to dept. chair Columbia U. Tchrs. Coll., N.Y.C., 1983-84; instr. Columbia U., N.Y.C., 1984-89, rsch. fellow, 1985-87, Ford Found., N.Y.C., 1988; sr. rsch. assoc. Tchrs. Coll., Columbia U., Berkeley, Calif., N.Y.C., 1989-91; adj. mem. faculty City U., Zurich, 1993-94; pres., prin. rschr., artist Zinnia Rsch. & Design Inc., N.Y.C., 1996—. Cons. N.Y.C. Bd. Edn., 1987-88, Directorate of Vocat. and Adult Edn. of the Netherlands, N.Y.C., 1989, Ctrl. Netherlands Poly., N.Y.C., 1990, CAD-Tech Internat. AG, Rumlang, Switzerland, 1992, others; asst. prof. Minn. State Colls. and Univs., 1994-95; bd. dirs. Banfill-Locke Ctr. for the Arts, Fridley, Minn.; vis. scholar Columbia U. Tchrs. Coll., 1998-99; founding mem. Victory Theater, N.Y.C., 1976-80; artist, tchr. Empire State Youth Theater Inst., Albany, NY, 1978; drama specialist Hewitt Sch., N.Y.C., 1980-83. Contbr. chpt. to Computers in English and Language Arts, 1989, Education Through Occupations in American High Schools, vol. 1, 1995; author articles and rsch. reports and presentations on visual literacy, visual sociology, and other topics, screenplays, including Missing Data; actress An Evening of American Folk Theater, LA, 1975, The Zero Show, LA, 1975; actress, co-writer The Ecstasy of St. Zero, The Ecstacy of St. Zero (Retold); actress Luminous Bodies, Paradise Regained; actress Double Gothic, Prisoners of the Invisible Kingdom, Moonchildren; dir. The Trial of Joan of Arc at Rouen, 1431, 1983-84. Recipient 1st prize in drawing, photography, graphics Banfill-Locke Ctr. for the Arts, 1997; Columbia U. Tchrs. Coll. scholar, 1983-84; Frances Blood Meml. scholar Calif. Inst. of Arts, 1973-74.

HEEBNER, JOHN E. optical engineer, researcher; b. Orange, NJ, Dec. 30, 1974; s. Harry Wills Heebner and Lily Masias. BE, Stevens Inst. Tech., 1996; MS in Engring., U. Rochester, 1997; PhD optics, Univ. Rochester, 2003. Rschr. Allied Signal Inc., Morristown, NJ, 1994, Instruments SA, Edison, NJ, 1996, U. Rochester, NY, 1996—2003, Lawrence Livermore Nat. Labs., 2003. NSF

fellow, 1997, Soc. Am. Mil. Engr. fellow, 1994, NASA Space Grant fellow, 1994. Mem. Optical Soc. Am., Am. Phys. Soc., SPIE Avocations: Tae Kwon Do, softball, racquetball, squash, skiing. E-mail: heebner@optics.rochester.edu.

HEED, PETER W. state attorney general; b. West Chester, Pa., Apr. 2, 1950; s. Walter R. and Elizabeth Allen Heed; m. Patricia Longo, Oct. 3, 1983; children: Travis, Ethan. BA, Dartmouth Coll., 1972; JD, Cornell U., 1975. Bar: N.H. 1975, U.S. Dist. Ct. N.H. 1975, U.S. Ct. Appeals (1st cir.) 1976. Asst. atty. gen. State of NH, Concord, 1975-80; assoc. Cristiano and Krumphold, Keene, NH, 1980-82; sr. ptnr. Green, McMahon & Heed, Keene, NH, 1982—2001; county atty. Cheshire County, NH, 2001—03; atty. gen. State of NH, 2003—. Instr., paralegal studies, Keene State Coll., 1980-84; bd. govs. N.H. Health & Welfare Coun., Keene, 1985-90. Co-author: Canoe Racing: The Competitor's Guide, 1992; dir./prodr. (video) The General Clinton Regatta, 1989. Moderator, Town of Westmoreland, N.H., 1998—; mem. zoning bd. adjustment, Town of Roxbury, N.H., 1989-90; bd. govs., v.p. Norris Cotton Cancer Ctr., Dartmouth-Hitchand Hosp., Lebanon, N.H., 1993—; mem. U.S. Marathon Canoe and Kayak Team, 1982-83. Mem. ATLA (sustaining mem. 1987-2000), N.H. Trial Lawyers Assn. (bd. dirs. 1987-93). Republican. Avocations: canoe and kayak racing (7 times Nat. Marathon and Downriver Canoe Champion, World Masters Marathon Canoe Champion, Nike World Masters Games, 1998), nordic ski racing, marathon running, U.S. history. Office: PO Box 612 Keene NH 03431-0612 also: Atty Gen 33 Capitol St Concord NH 03301

HEEFNER, WILLIAM FREDERICK, lawyer; b. Perkasie, Pa., July 8, 1922; s. Russell Edgar and Lydia Victoria (Spielman) H. BA, Ursinus Coll., 1942, LLD, 1975; LLB, Temple U., 1949. Bar: Pa. 1951. Assoc. Curtin & Heefner, Morrisville, Pa., 1951-66, sr. partner, 1966-93, of counsel, 1993—. Bd. dirs. William Penn Savings & Loan Assn., Morrisville; founder, dir. 1st County Bank, Doylestown, Pa., 1995—. Bd. dirs. Bedminster Twp. Planning Commn., 1961-94, sec., 1961-90; treas. Bucks County Dem. Com., 1966-90; treas. Bucks County Dem. Com., 1966-90, bd. dirs., 1969—; v.p., treas., chmn. fin. com. Ursinus Coll., 1976-90, pres. bd. dirs., 1990-97; pres., trustee Mercer Mus. and Spruance Libr., 1974-90, 91—; pres. Fonthill Trust and Mus.; bd. dirs. Bucks County Conservancy (now Heritage Conservancy), 1976—, Pa. Hist. and Mus. Commn., 1989-95, Bucks County Hist. Soc., 1990—. 1st lt. inf. AUS, 1942-46. Decorated Purple Heart; recipient Henry Chapman Mercer awd. for contrib. to Bucks Co. heritage, 1998. Fellow Am. Bar Found.; mem. ABA, Pa. Bar Assn. (mem. ho. dels. 1971-79, mem. bd. govs. 1976-79, chmn. law office econs. and mgmt. com. 1972-73), Bucks County Bar Assn. (pres. 1965-66), Met. Club. (N.Y.C.), Symposium Club, Rotary Internat. (Paul Harris fellow 1996), Phi Alpha Delta. Lutheran. Home: 555 Old Bethlehem Rd Perkasie PA 18944-3825 Office: Curtin and Heefner 250 N Pennsylvania Ave Morrisville PA 19067-1104

HEEGER, ALAN JAY, physicist, educator; b. Sioux City, Iowa, Jan. 22, 1936; s. Peter J. and Alice (Minkin) Heeger; m. Ruthann Chudacoff, Aug. 11, 1957; children: Peter S., David J. BA, U. Nebr., 1957; PhD, U. Calif., Berkeley, 1961; degree (hon.), U. Mons, Belgium, 1993; DTech (hon.), Linköping (Sweden) U., 1996; PhD (hon.), Abo Akademie, Turku, Finland, 1998; DHL (hon.), U. Mass., 1999; DSc (hon.), U. Nebr., 1999, So. China U. Tech., Japan Adv. Inst. Sci. & Tech., Bar Ilan U., Israel. Asst. prof. U. Pa., Phila., 1962—64, assoc. prof., 1964—66, prof. physics, 1966—82, U. Calif., Santa Barbara, 1982—, dir. Inst. for Polymers and Organic Solids, 1983—2000; pres. UNIAX Corp., Santa Barbara, 1990—94, chief tech. officer, 1999—2002. Dir. Lab. for Rsch. on Structure of Matter, U. Pa., 1974—81; acting vice provost for rsch. U. Pa., 1981—82; Morris Loeb lectr. Harvard U., 1973. Editor-in-chief Synthetic Metals jour., 1983—2000, contbr. sci. articles to profl. jours. Recipient John Scott medal, City of Phila., 1989, Oliver P. Buckley prize, 1983, Pres. medal for disting. achievement, U. Pa., 2000, Balzan prize for sci. of new materials, Balzan Found., Italy and Switzerland, 1995, Nobel prize in Chemistry, 2000; fellow, Alfred P. Sloan, Guggenheim; grantee, Govt. Fellow: Am. Physics Soc. (Buckley prize for solid state physics 1983); mem.: NAE, NAS, Korean Acad. Scis. (fgn.). Achievements include patents in field. Office: U Calif Dept Physics Santa Barbara CA 93103 E-mail: ajh@physics.ucsb.edu.

HEEGER, GERALD ARTHUR, university president; b. Akron, Iowa, Jan. 15, 1943; s. Peter J. and Alice (Minkin) H.; m. Geraldine Ruth Gyarfas, June 16, 1968; children— Brian, Robin. BA, U. Calif.-Berkeley, 1965; MA, U. Chgo., 1968, PhD, 1971. Dir. South Asia Studies program U. Va., Charlottesville, 1971-72; chmn. dept. polit. studies Adelphi U., Garden City, N.Y., 1976-79, dean, univ. coll., 1980-83, provost, 1983-87, exec. v.p., 1985-87; dean The New Sch., 1987-90; dean Sch. Continuing Edn. NYU, N.Y.C., 1991-99; pres. U. of Maryland University Coll., College Park, Md., 1999—. Recipient Cert. of Appreciation Assn. for Vol. Adminstrn. 1981, Sesquicentennial Associateship Inst. for Advanced Studies, 1973; Fulbright-Hayes grantee, 1973 Mem. Am. Polit. Sci. Assn., Assn. for Asian Studies Office: U MD U Coll 3501 Univ Blvd E Adelphi MD 20783

HEELAN, PATRICK AIDAN, philosophy educator; b. Dublin, Mar. 17, 1926; s. Matthew Henry and Pauline (Beirens) H. Student, Belvedere Coll., 1938-42; BA, Univ. Coll., Dublin, 1947, MA, 1948; PhD, St. Louis U., 1952; STL, Jesuit Theol. Faculty, Dublin, 1959; student, Princeton U., 1960-62; PhD, U. Louvain, 1964. Ordained priest Soc. Jesus, Roman Catholic Ch., 1958; lectr. math. physics Univ. Coll., Dublin, 1964-65; research asso. Dublin Inst. Advanced Studies, 1952-54, 64-65; asst. prof. philosophy Fordham U., 1965-67, asso. prof., 1967-70; prof. philosophy, chmn. dept. SUNY at Stony Brook, 1970-74, acting v.p. liberal studies, 1975-77, v.p. liberal studies, 1977-79, prof. philosophy, 1979-92, dean humanities and fine arts, 1990-92; exec. v.p. Georgetown U., Washington, 1992-95, William Gaston prof. philosophy, 1995—; external appraiser philosophy and arts and scis. programs U. Western Ont., Lowell U., John Carroll U., San Diego State U. Acad. adv. coun. Inst. for Advanced Cath. Studies. Author: Quantum Mechanics and Objectivity, 1965, Space-Perception and Philosophy of Science, 1983; festschrift: Hermeneutic Philosophy of Science, Van Gogh's Eyes and God: Essays in Honor of Patrick A Heelan, S.J., 2002. Fulbright fellow, 1960-62; NSF sr. fellow, 1983 Mem. AAAS, Am. Cath. Philos. Assn. (coun. 1973-75), Ctr. for Integrative Edn. (coun. 1972-74), Am. Philos. Assn. (program com. Ea. sect. 1975, nominating com. 1988), Philosophy Sci. Assn., Brit. Soc. Philosophy Sci., Soc. Phenomenology and Existential Philosophy, N.Y. Acad. Scis., Internat. Orgn. for Hermeneutics and Sci., Phi Beta Kappa, Sigma Xi. Address: 3612 O St NW Washington DC 20007-2615 Office: Georgetown Univ Philosophy Dept 234 New N Washington DC 20057-0001 E-mail: heelanp@georgetown.edu.

HEEN, WALTER MEHEULA, retired judge, former political party executive; b. Honolulu, Apr. 17, 1928; s. Norma K. Tada; 1 child, Cameron K. BA in Econs., U. Hawaii, 1953; JD, Georgetown U., 1955. Bar: Hawaii 1955, U.S. Dist. Ct. Hawaii 1955. Dep. corp. counsel, Honolulu, 1957-58; territorial ho. of reps., 1958-59; mem. State Ho. Reps., 1959-64; state senator, 1966-68; mem. Honolulu City Coun., 1969-72, chair, 1972-74; state dist. ct. judge, 1972-74; state cir. ct. judge, 1974-78; U.S. atty. U.S. Dist. Hawaii, 1978-80, U.S. dist. ct. judge, 1981; assoc. judge State Intermediate Ct. Appeals, 1982-94; ret., 1994. Past pres. Honolulu Hawaiian Civic Club; precinct club pres. Dem. Party, 1956-72, former chmn.; chmn. Hawaii Dem. Party, 1998-2001; vice chmn. Oahu Dem. County Com., 1956-62, chmn., 1962-64; del. State Dem. Party Conv., 1956-70; com. mem. Andy Anderson for Gov., 2002. Recipient Lei Hulu Mamo award, 1992; named Outstanding Young Man of the Yr., 1962. Mem. Native Hawaiian Bar Assn. (dir. 1994—). Avocations: photography, fishing, surfing, golf, family activities. Address: 350 Ward Ave Ste 106 Honolulu HI 96814 Office: 404 Ward Ave Ste 201 Honolulu HI 96814-3300

HEER, DAVID MACALPINE, sociology educator; b. Chapel Hill, N.C., Apr. 15, 1930; s. Clarence and Jean Douglas (MacAlpine) H.; m. Nancy Whittier, June 29, 1957 (div. 1980); m. Kaye S. Heymann, Dec. 11, 1980 (dec. April 2000); children: Douglas (dec.), Laura, Catherine. AB magna cum laude, Harvard U., 1950, MA, 1954, PhD, 1958. Statistician population div. U.S. Bur. Census, Washington, 1957-61; lectr., asst. research sociologist U. Calif., Berkeley, 1961-64; asst. prof. demography Harvard U. Sch. Public Health, Boston, 1964-68, assoc. prof., 1968-72; dir. Population Rsch. Lab., U. So. Calif., L.A., 1995—2000, prof. sociology, 1972—2000, dir. sociology emeritus, 2000—; sr. fellow Ctr. Comparative Immigration Studies, U. Calif. San Diego, 2000—. Mem. population research study sect. NIH, 1971-73 Author: After Nuclear Attack: A Demographic Inquiry, 1965, Society and Population, 1968, (with Pini Herman) A Human Mosaic: An Atlas of Ethnicity in Los Angeles County, 1980-86, 1990, Undocumented Mexicans in the United States, 1990, Immigration in America's Future: Social Science Findings and the Policy Debate, 1996; editor: Readings on Population, 1968, Social Statistics and the City, 1968. Mem. Population Assn. Am. (dir. 1970-73), Internat. Union Sci. Study Population. Home: 3890 Nobel Dr Unit 1002 San Diego CA 92122-5782

HEER, NICHOLAS LAWSON, Arabist and Islamist educator; b. Chapel Hill, N.C., Feb. 8, 1928; s. Clarence and Jean Douglas (MacAlpine) H. BA, Yale U., 1949; PhD, Princeton U., 1955. Transl. analyst Arabian Am. Oil Co., Saudi Arabia, 1955-57; asst. prof. Stanford U., Calif., 1959-62; vis. lectr. Yale U., New Haven, 1962-63; asst. prof. Harvard U., Cambridge, Mass., 1963-65; assoc. prof. U. Wash., Seattle, 1965-76, prof. Near Eastern langs. and civilization, 1976-90, prof. emeritus, 1990—; chmn. dept. Near Eastern langs. and civilization U. Wash, 1982-87. Middle East curator Hoover Instn., Stanford, Calif., 1958-62 Editor: Tirmidhi: Bayan al-Farq, 1958, Jami: Al-Durrah al-Fakhirah, 1981, Islamic Law and Jurisprudence: Studies in Honor of Farhat J. Ziadeh, 1990; translator: Jami: The Precious Pearl, 1979, (with Kenneth Honerkamp) Three Early Sufi Texts, 2003. Mem. Am. Oriental Soc., Middle East Studies Assn., Am. Assn. Tchrs. of Arabic (treas. 1964-76, pres. 1981, dir. 1982-84) Home: 1821 10th Ave E Seattle WA 98102-4214 Office: U Wash Dept Near Ea Langs & Civ PO Box 353120 Seattle WA 98195-3120 E-mail: heer@eskimo.com., heer@u.washington.edu.

HEERENS, ROBERT EDWARD, physician; b. Evanston, Ill., July 2, 1915; s. Joseph and Karen (Larsen) H.; m. Martha Virginia Lysne, Aug. 21, 1943; children: Kisti Lyn, Martha Jill, Nancy Ann, Robin Jan, Sara Bryce. AB, Kalamazoo Coll., 1938; postgrad., U. Ala. Med. Sch., 1939, 41; MD, Northwestern U., 1944. Diplomate Am. Bd. Family Practice. Intern U.S. Naval Hosp., Great Lakes, Ill., 1943-44, resident, 1946-47; gen. practice medicine Rockford, Ill., 1947—; pres. med. staff Swedish-Am. Hosp.; mem. staffs St. Anthony, Rockford hosps.; clin. assoc. prof. family medicine Rockford Sch. Medicine, also dir. ind. studies, mem. exec. com.; mem. admissions com. U. Ill. Coll. Medicine, 1970—, promotions com., 1973-75, mem. Senate Med. Ctr., 1975-77, also mem. acad. council, mem. adv. com. on family practice. Bd. dirs. Rockford Community Chest, 1954-60, Vis. Nurse Assn.; pres. Winnebago Tb Assn., 1960-61, Winnebago County Bd. Health, 1961-69; mem. Rockford Community Devel. Com.; mem. Community Action Com., 1969-71; pres. Northwestern Area Agy. on Aging, 1991-93. Served with M.C., USN, 1942-47. Recipient Disting. Svc. award Pub. Health Winnebago County Health Dept., 1997, Unique Achievement award Gov. of Ill., 1992, Betty Henry award for Cmty. Svc., 2000, Sr. of Yr. award Lifescape Cmty. Svcs., 2000. Mem. AMA, Am. Acad. Family Physicians (Ill. del. to congress of dels. 1959-71, mem. pub. relations com. 1967-74, chmn. pub. relations com. 1971-74, bd. dirs. 1970-73, exec. com. 1972-73, v.p. 1974), Ill. Acad. Gen. Practice (pres. 1958), Ill. Acad. Family Physicians (Pres.'s award 2000), Ill. Med. Soc. (chmn. pub. relations com. 1961-62, Pub. Svc. award 1994), Winnebago County Med. Soc. (v.p. 1965, pres. 1966), Rockford C. of C. (pres. 1962, chmn. edn. com.), Phi Beta Phi Home: 5664 Spring Brook Rd Rockford IL 61114-5553

HEESCHEN, DAVID SUTPHIN, astronomer, educator; b. Davenport, Iowa, Mar. 12, 1926; s. Richard George and Emily (Sutphin) H.; m. Eloise St. Clair, June 11, 1950; children: Lisa Clair, David William, Richard Mark. BS, U. Ill., 1949, MS, 1951; PhD, Harvard U., 1954; ScD (hon.), W.Va. Inst. Tech., 1974, New Mex. Inst. Tech., 1989. Instr. Wesleyan U., Middletown, Conn., 1954-55; lectr., rsch. assoc. Harvard U., 1955-56; scientist Nat. Radio Astronomy Obs., 1956-77, sr. scientist, 1977-92; emeritus, 1992—; dir. Nat. Radio Astronomy Obs., 1962-78; rsch. prof. astronomy U. Va., 1980-92; Karl Jansky lectr., 1993. Cons. NASA, 1960-61, 68-72, Univs. Space Rsch. Assn., 1996-99, Nat. Radio Astronomy Obs., 1997-99. Contbr. sci. jours. Bd. dirs. Fla. Keys Land and Sea Trust, 2000—. G.R. Agassiz fellow Harvard Obs., 1953-54; Recipient Disting. Public Svc. award NSF, 1980, Alexander von Humboldt Sr. Scientist award 1985 Fellow AAAS; mem. NAS, Am. Acad. Arts and Sci., Am. Philos. Soc., Am. Astron. Soc. (v.p. 1969-71, pres. 1980-82), Internat. Astron. Union (v.p. 1976-82), Internat Sci. Radio Union. E-mail: dheeschen@earthlink.net.

HEESE, WILLIAM JOHN, music publishing company executive; b. N.Y.C., June 4, 1936; s. William Theodore and Anna Marie (Bissinger) H.; m. Charlotte Anne Schlosser, Feb. 11, 1961; children: William, Philip, Peter. Student, Bronx C.C., 1971, Sch. for Visual Arts, 1972. Clk. Music Dealers Svc., Inc., N.Y.C., 1953-60; salesman Hansen Publs., N.Y.C., Miami Beach, Fla., 1960-61; mgr. sales Shapiro, Bernstein & Co., Inc., N.Y.C., 1961-69, M.C.A. Music (divsn. Music Corp. Am.), N.Y.C., 1970—71; gen. mgr. Sam Fox Music, N.Y.C., 1971—74; v.p. sol. projects Carl Fischer, Inc., N.Y.C., 1974—. Dir. Scott Tower Housing Co., Inc., 1970-80, pres., v.p., sec.; dir. Our Lady of Angels Ch., 1978-82, mem. parish coun., Our Lady of Fatima Parish, 1983-; dir. Vets. Little League, mgr., coach, 1976-88; dir. East Coast Conf. Baseball League, 1989-91, mgr., coach sr. divsn., 1989-90; mgr., coach Unltd. Age Baseball Team, Westchester Baseball Assn., 1991-93. With Army N.G., 1959-65. Mem.: Retail Print Music Dealers Assn., Music Pubs. Assn. (sec. 1982—84, dir. 1980—84, 1984—92, 1996—2000, treas. 1985—87), KC. Republican. Home: 1 Fountain Ln Scarsdale NY 10583-4654 E mail: billh@carlfischer.com.

HEESSEL, ELEANOR LUCILLE LEA, retired state agency administrator; b. Diller, Nebr., Nov. 6, 1916; d. Edward Richard and Gertrude (Loock) Henrichs; m. Stanley Guy Lea, Mar. 6, 1936; children: Dianna Evenson, Cylesta Peters, Jeffrey, Chad; m. William H. Heessel, May 28, 1997. Student, Fairbury State Coll. Owner Modern Furniture Store, Fairbury, Nebr., 1945-80; dist. mgr. Field Enterprises, Chgo., 1966-80; libr. resource person Fairbury Pub. Libr., 1982-85; job coord. Blue River Area Agy. on Aging, Lincoln, Nebr., 1985-87. Bd. mem. Operation ABLE, Lincoln, 1987-92, Nat. Grandparent Program, Beatrice, Nebr., 1985-87. Pres., dist. v.p. United Meth. Women; Sunday Sch. supt. Meth. Ch., Fairbury; v.p. sch. bd. Fairbury Pub. Sch. Bd., 1956-62; bd. mem. Girl Scouts U.S.A., 1950-56. Mem. Toastmasters (v.p. pub. rels. Lincoln 1992-94). Republican. Avocations: reading, skiing, group study. Home: 7641 Tahiti Ln #104 Lake Worth FL 33467

HEESTAND, DIANE ELISSA, education educator, medical educator; b. Boston, Oct. 9, 1945; d. Glenn Wilson and Elizabeth (Martin) Heestand. BA, Allegheny Coll., 1967; MA, U. Wyo., 1968; edn. specialist, Ind. U., 1971, EdD, 1979. Asst. prof. communication Clarion (Pa.) State Coll., 1971; asst. prof. learning resources Indiana U. of Pa., 1971-72; asst. prof. communication U. Nebr. Med. Ctr., Omaha, 1972-74; assoc. prof. learning resources Tidewater Community Coll., Virginia Beach, Va., 1975-78; ednl. cons. U. Ala. Sch. Medicine, Birmingham, 1978-81; dir. learning resources, assoc. prof. med. edn. Mercer U. Sch. Medicine, Macon, Ga., 1981-88; asst. dean ednl. devel. and resources Ohio U. Coll. Osteopathic Medicine, 1989-90; assoc. prof. clin. med. edn., dir. biomed. communications U. So. Calif. Sch. Medicine, L.A., 1990-95, acting chair dept. med. edn., 1992-95; prof., dir. office ednl. devel. U. Ark. for Med. Scis., Little Rock, 1995—. Cons. Lincoln (Pa.) U., summer, 1975; vis. fellow Project Hope/China, Millwood, Va., summer, 1986. Author (teleplay) Yes, 1968 (award World Law Fund 1968); producer, dir. (slide tape) Finding a Way, 1980 (1st Pl. award HESCA 1981, Susan Eastman award 1981). Rsch. sect. chair So. Group on Ednl. Affairs, 1998-2000. Grantee Porter Found., 1984, Ark. Dept. Higher Edn., 1996-97, UAMS Spl. Devel., 1997-99; Family and Preventive Medicine fellow HRSA, 2003—. Mem. Health Scis. Comm. Assn. (bd. dirs. 1982-86, pres.-elect 1987-88, pres. 1988-89, Spl. Svc. award 1990), Assn. Ednl. Comm. and Tech. (pres. media design and prodn. div. 1985-86), Assn. Biomed. Comm. Dirs. (bd. dirs. 1993-95), Soc. of Dirs. of Rsch. in Med. Edn. (steering com. 2000—, chair-elect 2002, chair 2003), Generalists in Med. Edn. (steering com. 1998-2001, chmn. 1999-2000). Democrat. Presbyterian. Avocations: tennis, gardening, golf.

HEFFELFINGER, KARL WILLIAM, retired draftsman; b. Patterson, N.J., Aug. 29, 1938; s. William Alvin and Mary Elizabeth (Beisel) Heffelfinger; m. Joan Ann Skutches; children: Eileen Peters, Kim Horvath, Michael Peters. Grad. H.S., Allentown, Pa., 1956. Constrn. carpenter various contractors, Allentown, Pa., 1962—72; draftsman, designer PPL, Inc., Allentown, 1972—95. Author: (Book) 10 December, 2000, Satan at the Helm, 2001, (book) Spriggs, 2002, (Book) Headlong to Hell, 2003. ET3 USN, 1957—61. Mem.: Navy League U.S., Am. Legion. Avocations: cooking, photography. Home: 432 Kuehner Ave Slatington PA 18080 E-mail: kwh432@aol.com.

HEFFELFINGER, THOMAS BACKER, lawyer; b. Mpls., Feb. 13, 1948; BA in History, Stanford U., 1970; JD, U. Minn., 1975. Bar: Minn. 1976, U.S. Dist. Ct. Minn. 1977, U.S. Ct. Appeals (8th cir.) 1983. Law clk. Office of the Hennepin County Atty., 1974-76, asst. atty. juvenile divsn., 1976, asst. atty. criminal divsn. trial sect., 1977-82, asst. atty. major offender unit, 1978-81, supr. burglary unit, 1981-82; asst. U.S. atty. criminal divsn. Dist. Minn., U.S. Dept. Justice, 1982-88, atty. white collar crime sect., 1982-85, supr. narcotics and firemans sect., 1985-86; ptnr. Opperman Heins & Paquin, 1988-91; U.S. atty. Dist. Minn., U.S. Dept. Justice, 1991-93; ptnr. Bowman and Brooke, 1993—2000, Best & Flanagan, 2000—01; U.S. atty. U.S. Dept. Justice, Minn., 2001—. Contbr. articles to profl. jours. Candidate Hennepin County Atty., 1986; bd. dirs. Mpls. Chpt. ARC, 1987—; mem. Hennepin County Task Force on Youth and Drugs, 1987-88, Minn. Ho. of Reps. Rep. Caucus Drug Task Force, 1989-90, Minn. Commn. on Violent Crime, 1991; chmn. Minn. Commn. on Jud. Selection, 1990-91; lectr. in field. Mem. Fed. Bar Assn., Minn. Bar Assn., Hennepin County Bar Assn. Office: 600 US Courthouse 300 S 4th St Minneapolis MN 55415*

HEFFERAN, COLIEN JOAN, economist; b. Mpls., May 13, 1949; d. Bernard and Rosemary Arnsdorf; m. Hollis Spurgeon Summers, Oct. 14, 1987; 1 child, Margaret Vimont Summers. BS, U. Ariz., 1971; MS, U. Ill., 1974, PhD, 1976. Asst. prof. Pa. State U., University Park, 1975-79; econ., rsch. leader Agrl. Rsch. Svc., USDA, Hyattsville, Md., 1979-88; adminstr. Coop. State Rsch., Edn. and Ext. Svc., 1988—. Adj. prof. U. Md., University Park, 1982-88; chmn. Ctr. for Family, Washington, 1985-87; vis. fellow Australian Nat. U., Canberra, NSW, 1989-91. Mem. editl. bd. Jours.-Family Econ. Issues, 1987—. Recipient Outstanding Citizen award U. Ariz., 1985, Outstanding Alumni award U. Ill., 1986, Presdl. Rank award as Disting. Fed. Exec., 2000. Mem. Am. Econ. Assn., Am. Coun. on Consumer Interests. Democrat. Roman Catholic. E-mail: chefferan@reeusda.gov.

HEFFERNAN, JAMES ANTHONY WALSH, language and literature educator; b. Boston, Apr. 22, 1939; s. Roy Joseph and Kathleen (Walsh) H.; m. Nancy Coffey, June 27, 1964; children: Virginia, Andrew. AB cum laude, Georgetown U., 1960; PhD, Princeton U., 1964. Instr. English U. Va., 1963-65; asst. prof. English Dartmouth Coll., Hanover, N.H., 1965-70, assoc. prof., 1970-76, prof., 1976—, chmn. dept. English, 1978-81, Frederick Sessions Beebe prof. in art of writing, 1997—. Cons. Mt. Holyoke, 1986, PMLA, 1986-87, Johns Hopkins U., 1987, NYU, 1987, 89, U. Press New Eng., 1987, U. Press Chgo., 1988, NEH, 1988, 90, Rutgers U., 1988, U. Md., 1988, Vanderbilt U., 1989, Barnard Coll., 1992; dir. summer seminar English romantic lit. and visual arts NEH/Dartmouth Coll., Hanover, 1987, 89; spkr. various seminars; lectures on James Joyce's Ulysses videotaped for The Teaching Co., 2001. Author: Wordsworth's Theory of Poetry: The Transforming Imagination, 1969, The Re-Creation of Landscape: A Study of Wordsworth, Coleridge, Constable and Turner, 1985, Museum of Words: The Poetics of Ekphrasis from Homer to Ashbery, 1993; co-author: Writing: A College Handbook, 5th edit., 2000, Writing: A Concise College Handbook, 1st edit., 1996; editor: Space, Time, Image, Sign: Essays on Literature and the Visual Arts, 1987, Representing the French Revolution: Literature, Historiography and Art, 1992; contbr. articles to profl. jours. Trustee Vermont Acad., 1992-2001. Woodrow Wilson fellow, 1960-61, Franklin Murphy, Jr. fellow, 1961-62, R.K. Root fellow, 1962-63, Dartmouth Coll., 1968-69, NEH fellow, 1991; grantee Dartmouth Coll., 1971, 74, 87, NEH, 1984, 87, 89. Mem. MLA (evaluator essays, presenter, del. various convs.), Assn. Literary Scholars and Critics (coun. 1996-99). Office: English Dept Dartmouth College Hanover NH 03755 E-mail: jamesheff@dartmouth.edu.

HEFFERNAN, JAMES VINCENT, lawyer; b. Washington, Oct. 6, 1926; s. Vincent Jerome and Hazel Belle (Wiltfong) Heffernan; m. Virginia May Adams, June 26, 1954; children: David V., Douglas J., Alan P., Margaret L., Thomas A. AB, Cornell U., 1949, JD with distinction, 1952. Bar: D.C. 1953, Md. 1959, U.S. Ct. Claims 1955, U.S. Tax Ct. 1953, U.S. Supreme Ct. 1958. Assoc. Sutherland, Asbill & Brennan, Washington, 1952-59, ptnr., 1959—. Adj. prof. Georgetown U., Washington, 1978—79. Contbr. articles to profl. jours. With USN, 1945—46. Mem.: ABA, Bar Assn. D.C., Fed. Bar Assn., Kenwood Golf and Country Club, Met. Club (Washington), KC, Order Coif, Phi Alpha Delta. Democrat. Roman Catholic. Home: 5216 Falmouth Rd Bethesda MD 20816-2913 Office: Sutherland Asbill & Brennan LLP 1275 Pennsylvania Ave NW Washington DC 20004-2415 E-mail: james.heffernan@sablaw.com., jvh3@cornell.edu.

HEFFERNAN, JOHN WILLIAM, retired journalist; b. Stockbridge, Hants., Eng., Oct. 21, 1910; came to U.S., 1946; s. John and Alice Ann (Edwards) H.; m. Edith Curry, Dec. 10, 1948 (dec. Aug. 1990); 1 stepchild, Anthony Edward; m. Martha Powell Hensley, Apr. 25, 1992. Student, Clarks Coll., Eng., 1924-26. Sub-editor Central News, London, 1929-34, Press Assn., London, 1934-36, sports reporter, 1936-39; fgn. corr. Reuters, N.Y.C., 1946; fgn. corr. at UN, N.Y.C., 1946-57; chief corr. Reuters, Washington, 1957-76; ret., 1976. Bd. dirs. Gasparilla Island Bridge Auth., 1995—97. Co-author: Frontlines, 2001. Pres. Gasparilla Island Conservation and Improvement Assn., Boca Grande, Fla., 1994; bd. dirs. Gasparilla Island Bridge Com., 1996-97. With Brit. Army, 1941-46, promoted maj. 1945. Decorated Comdr. Order of Brit. Empire, 1969. Mem. Nat. Press Club (pres. 1969), UN Corr. Assn. (pres. 1956), Overseas Press Club. Avocations: golf, swimming. Home: PO Box 687 Boca Grande FL 33921-0687

HEFFERNAN, NATHAN STEWART, retired state supreme court chief justice; b. Frederic, Wis., Aug. 6, 1920; s. Jesse Eugene and Pearl Eva (Kaump) H.; m. Dorothy Hillemann, Apr. 27, 1946; children: Katie (Mrs. Howard Thomas), Michael, Thomas. BA, U. Wis., 1942, LLB, 1948; postgrad. in bus., Harvard U. Sch. Bus. Adminstrn., 1943-44; LLD (hon.), Lakeland Coll., 1995; LLD, U. Wis., 1999. Bar: Wis. 1948, U.S. Dist. Ct. (we. dist.) Wis. 1948, U.S. Dist. Ct. (ea. dist.) Wis. 1950, U.S. Ct. Appeals (7th cir.) 1960, U.S. Supreme Ct. 1960. Assoc. firm Schubring, Ryan, Peterson & Sutherland, Madison, Wis., 1948-49; practice in Sheboygan, Wis., 1949-59; partner firm Buchen & Heffernan, 1951-59; counsel Wis. League Municipalities, 1949; research asst. to gov. Wis., 1949; asst. dist. atty. Sheboygan County, 1951-53; city atty. City of Sheboygan, 1953-59; dep. atty. gen. State of Wis., 1959-62; U.S. atty. Western Dist. Wis., 1962-64; justice Wis. Supreme Ct., 1964—, chief justice, 1983-95. Lectr. mcpl. corps., 1961-64, appellate procedure and practice U. Wis. Law Sch., 1971-83; faculty Appellate Judges Seminar, Inst. Jud. Adminstrn., NYU, 1972-87; former mem. Nat. Council State Ct. Reps., chmn., 1976-77; ex-officio dir. Nat. Ctr. State Cts., 1976-77, mem. adv. bd. appellate justice project; former mem. Wis. Jud. Planning Com.; chmn. Wis. Appellate Practice and Procedure Com., 1975-76; mem. exec. com. Wis. Jud. Conf., 1978—, chmn., 1983; pres. City Attys. Assn., 1958-59; chair Citizens Panel on Election Reform; co-chair Equal Justice Coalition. Wis. chmn. NCCJ, 1966-67; past exec. bd. Four Lakes Coun., Boy Scouts Am.; gen. chmn. Wis. Dem. Conv., 1960, 61; mem. Wis. Found.; bd. dirs. Inst. Jud. Adminstrn.; visitors U. Wis. Law Sch., 1970-83, chmn., 1973-76; past mem. corp. bd. Meth. Hosp.; former curator Wis. Hist. Soc., curator emeritus, 1990; trustee Wis. Meml. Union, Wis. State Libr., William Freeman Vilas Trust Estate; v.p. U. Wis. Meml. Union Bldg. Assn.; former deacon Conglist. Ch. Lt. (s.g.) USNR, 1942-46, ETO, PTO. Recipient Disting. Svc. award NCCJ, 1968, Ann. Disting. Svc. award Wis. Mediation Assn., 1995, Lifetime Achievement award Milw. Bar Assn., 1995, Disting. Svc. award Dem. Party Sheboygan County, 1995; Disting. Jud. fellow Marquette U. Law Sch., 1996. Fellow Am. Bar Found. (life), Inst. for Jud. Adminstrn. (hon., bd. dirs., mem. faculty seminar), Wis. Bar Assn. (chmn. Wis. bar com. study on legal edn. 1995-96, hon. chmn. Equal Justice Coalition 1997—, Goldberg award for disting. svc.), Wis. Bar Found.; mem. ABA (past mem. spl. com. on adminstrn. criminal justice, mem. com. fed.-state delineation of jurisdiction, jud. adminstrn. com. on appellate ct., com. appellate time standards), Am. Law Inst. (life, adv. com. on complex litigation), Dane County Bar Assn., Sheboygan County Bar Assn., Am. Judicature Soc. (dir. 1977-80, chmn. program com. 1979-81), Wis. Law Alumni Assn. (bd. dirs., Disting. Alumni Svc. award 1989), Nat. Conf. Chief Justices (bd. dirs.), Nat. Assn. Ct. Mgmt., Wis. Rivers Alliance (bd. dirs.), Order of Coif, Iron Cross, U. Club (Madison, Wis.), Phi Kappa Phi, Phi Delta Phi. Clubs: Madison Lit. (pres. 1979-80); Harvard (Milw.); Harvard Bus. Sch. (Wis.). Home: 17 Thorstein Veblen Pl Madison WI 53705

HEFFERNAN, PATRICIA CONNER, management consultant; b. N.Y.C., Oct. 11, 1946; d. Arthur S. and Catherine (Center) Conner; m. John Joseph Heffernan, Sept. 13, 1969 (dec. June 1996). BA, U. Va., 1968; MBA, Suffolk U., 1980. Cert. mgmt. cons. Office mgr. Wobbly Barn, Killington, Vt., 1968-72; bus. mgr. Woodstock Country Sch., Vt., 1972-74; assoc. dean Vt. Law Sch., Royalton, Vt., 1974-83; mgmt. cons. Heffernan & Assocs., Killington, 1982-87; mgmt. cons., v.p. Sandage Inc., Burlington, Vt., 1987-92; mgmt. cons., ptnr. Mktg. Ptnrs., Inc., Burlington, 1992—. Vt. del. White House Conf. on Small Bus.; mem. region 1 adv. coun. SBA. Mem. Vt. Gov.'s Commn. on Women; bd. dirs. Rutland Regional Med. Ctr., 1986-91, New Eng. Bus. for Social Responsibility, 1990-93; trustee, pres. Killington Mountain Sch., 1978-85; mem. Killington Planning Commn., 1975-87, Killington Zoning Bd., 1979-84, Vt. Epilepsy Assn., 1977—, Vt. Telecom. Commn., Vt. Econ. Devel. Adv. Coun.; mem. Vt. steering com. for ACE Nat. Identification Program for Women in Higher Edn., 1978-83. Named Outstanding Leader, Vt. YWCA, 1985, Woman of Yr., Vt. Bus. and Profl. Women Found., 1986, Woman in Bus. Adv., SBA, 1993. Mem. Inst. Mgmt. Cons. (v.p. New Eng. region, nat. bd. dirs. 1991-93), Nat. Assn. Women Bus. Owners, Vt. Bus. Assn. for Social Responsibility (bd. dirs., pres. 1991—), Womwn Bus. Owners Vt. (founder, bd. dirs. 1983—, pres. 1984-86). Office: Mktg Ptnrs Inc 176 Battery St Burlington VT 05401-5296 E-mail: pheffernan@marketing-partners.com.

HEFFERNAN, PETER JOHN, state official; b. Hartford, Conn., Feb. 19, 1945; s. Kenneth F. and Vivian (Lacourse) H. m. Rosemary Margaret Eagan, May 29, 1971; children: Peter John, Matthew Paul. BA, Providence Coll., 1967; MBA, George Washington U., 1971. Adminstrv. resident Waltham (Mass.) Hosp., 1970-71, asst. dir., 1971-74, v.p. adminstrn. and gen. svcs., 1974-78, exec. v.p., 1978-86; pres., chief exec. officer Cardinal Cushing Gen. Hosp., Brockton, Mass., 1986-87; regional v.p. Weatherby Health Care, Norwell, Mass., 1987-90; regional adminstr. health svcs. divsn. Mass. Dept. Correction, Jamaica Plain, 1990—; sr. surveyor Nat. Commn. on Correctional Health Care, 1999—. Co-preceptor health care adminstrn. George Washington U., 1977; mem. faculty evening div. Stonehill Coll., 1990—. Mem. instructional conf. coun. New Eng. Hosp. Assembly Inc., 1976; bd. dirs. Waltham Boys Club, 1977, Hosp. Svcs. of New Eng., 1980-83. USPHS trainee, 1967-70. Fellow Am. Coll. Hosp. Adminstrs.; mem. Health Care Mgmt. Assn. Mass., ACHE Regents Adv. Council, 1991—, Lions. Roman Catholic. Home: 352 Mayflower Cir Hanover MA 02339-2119 Office: Mass Dept Correction Health Svcs Divsn PO Box 426 Bridgewater MA 02324

HEFFINGTON, JACK GRISHAM, lawyer, banker, insurance company executive, horse breeder; b. Lawrenceburg, Tenn., Mar. 8, 1944; s. Charles Alexander and Kathlyn (Grisham) Heffington; m. Nancy Caroline Heffington, Sept. 29, 1979; children: Jacquelyn Elliott, Caroline Sutherland. BS, Memphis State U., 1967; JD, U. Ark., 1971. Bar: Tenn. 1971, Ala. 1972. Ptnr. Heffington Law Firm, Murfreesboro, Tenn., 1972—; owner Tan Oak Farms, Murfreesboro. Pres., chmn. Mid. Tenn. Mortgage Co., Murfreesboro, 1973—, Keg Life Ins. Co. of S.C., Columbia, 1977—; pres. South Tex. Bankers Life Ins. Co., Birmingham, Ala., 1983—; dir., gen. counsel First Nat. Bank Rutherford County, 1979—83; vice chmn. World Svc. Life Ins. Co. Am., Winchester, Tenn., 1993—. Mem.: ABA, Tenn. Bar Assn., Ala. Bar Assn., Sigma Delta Chi. Mem. Ch. Of Christ. Home: PO Box 64 Christiana TN 37037-0064 Office: Heffington Law Firm 111 N Maple St Murfreesboro TN 37130

HEFFLER, KAREN FRANKEL, ophthalmology educator; b. Wilmington, Del., Aug. 4, 1960; d. David Matthew and Lois Sheila (Ableman) Frankel; m. Curt Lewis Heffler, June 28, 1981; children: Lauren, Daniel, Rachel. BA summa cum laude, U. Pa., 1982, MD, 1986. Diplomate Am. Bd. Ophthalmology. Intern in internal medicine Bryn Mawr (Pa.) Hosp., 1986-87; resident in ophthalmology Scheie Eye. Inst., U. Pa., Phila., 1987-90, fellow in cornea and external disease, asst. chief svc., 1990-91; asst. prof. MCP-Hahnemann U., Phila., 1991—, dir. cornea and refractive surgery, 1995—; instr. Wills Eye Hosp., Phila., 1999-2000. Cons. Laurel Rehab. Svc., 1995—. Contbr. articles to med. jours. Mem. AMA (physician's recognition award 1993—), Am. Acad. Ophthalmology, Internat. Soc. Refractive Surgery, Pa. Acad. Ophthalmology, Pa. Med. Soc., Women in Ophthalmology, St. George Med. Cancer Soc. (pres. 1983-84), Alpha Omega Alpha, Phi Beta Kappa. Office: Univ Eye Specialists 219 N Broad St Philadelphia PA 19107 also: 40 Monument Bala Cynwyd PA 19004

HEFFLINGER, LEROY ARTHUR, agricultural manager; b. Omaha, Feb. 14, 1935; s. Leroy William and Myrtle Irene (Lampe) H.; m. Carole June Wickman, Dec. 23, 1956; children: Dean Alan, Andrew Karl, Roger Glenn, Dale Gorden. BS in Fin., U. Colo., 1957. Mgr. Hefflinger Ranches, Inc., Toppenish, Wash., 1963-97, pres., 1973—. Bd. dirs. Hop Adminstrv. Com., Portland, Oreg., 1980-86; trustee Agr. and Forestry Edn. Found., Spokane, Wash., 1988-94, vice chmn., 1993-94; mem. adv. bd. Central Valley Bank, Toppenish, Wash., 1995—. Vestryman, bd. dirs. St. Michael's Ch., Yakima, Wash., 1969-74; mem. capital campaign com. Heritage Coll., Toppenish, 1990-91; bd. dirs. Am. Hop Mus., 1997—. Capt. USAF, 1958-63. Named Vol. of Yr., Am. Hop Mus., 1999; named Chevalier, Order of the Hop, 1992. Mem. Hop Growers Am. (past pres. 1982-95, bd. dirs.), Hop Growers Wash. (past treas. 1978-83, bd. dirs.), Beta Theta Pi. Republican. Episcopalian. Avocations: travel, golf, photography, antique guns. Office: Hefflinger Ranches Inc 6001 Englewood Ave Yakima WA 98908-2339

HEFFNER, DANIEL JASON, film producer; b. N.Y.C., Mar. 30, 1956; s. Richard Douglas and Elaine Peggy (Segal) H.; m. Beth Klein, May 26, 1991; children: Jeremy Aaron, Zachary David. BS in Comm., Ithaca Coll., 1978. Prodn. exec. Columbia Pictures, L.A., 1982-85; prodn. exec., prodr. Walt Disney Pictures, L.A., 1985-88; v.p. prodn. Buena Vista Pictures Distbn. divsn. Walt Disney Co., L.A., 1988-91; prodr. Serendipity Prodns., Inc., 1991—. Asst. dir. (film) The Big Chill, 1982; co-prodr. (film) Cocktail, 1988; exec. prodr. (film) The Good Mother, 1988; co-exec. prodr. (film) Holy Matrimony, 1993; asst. dir., 2d unit dir. (film) The Seventh Veil, 1999; line prodr., 1st asst. dir. (film) Highway 395, 1999, (film) Sheer Bliss, 2000, (film) Flying Virus, 2001; co-prodr. (film) George of the Jungle 2, 2002, co-prodr. (film) "Saw", 2003. Mem.: Dirs. Guild Am. Democrat. Jewish. Home: 4119 Woodman Ave Sherman Oaks CA 91423-4331 Fax: 818-789-0213. E-mail: danheffner@earthlink.net.

HEFFNER, RICHARD DOUGLAS, historian, educator, communications consultant, television producer; b. N.Y.C., Aug. 5, 1925; s. Albert Simon and Cely (Bender) H.; m. Anne de la Vergne, Dec. 14, 1946; m. Elaine Segal, July 30, 1950; children: Daniel Jason, Charles Andrew. AB, Columbia U., 1946, MA (Mitchell fellow), 1947. Teaching asst. history U. Calif. at Berkeley, 1947-48; instr. Am. history Rutgers U., 1948-50, univ. prof. communications, pub. policy, 1964—; lectr. history Columbia, 1950-52; prof. history Sarah Lawrence Coll., 1952-53; dir. pub. affairs WNBC-TV, N.Y.C., 1955-57; dir. programs Met. Ednl. TV Assn., N.Y.C., 1957-59; editorial cons. CBS, Inc.; mem. editorial bd., dir. spl. projects CBS-TV Network, 1959-61; v.p., gen. mgr. ednl. TV Channel 13 WNET, N.Y.C., 1961-63; pres. Richard Heffner Assocs., Inc., N.Y.C., 1964—. Mem. program adv. bd. Teleprompter Corp.; dir. commn. on campaign costs 20th Century Fund, 1968-69; dir. study of TV's environ. messages Ford Found., 1970-72; chmn. bd. classification and rating adminstrn. Motion Picture Assn. Am., 1974-94. Producer-moderator The Open Mind, NBC-TV, 1956—59, Channel 13, N.Y.C., 1973—, moderator-host Nat. Ednl. TV series People and Politics, 1964, exec. editor-host WPIX-TV From the Editor's Desk, 1981—86; author: A Documentary History of the United States, 1952, A Documentary History of the United States, 6th edit., 1999, 7th 50th Anniv. edit., 2002, Conversations with Elie Wiesel, 2001, A Conversational History of Modern America, 2003; editor: Alexis de Tocqueville's Democracy in America, 1956. Mem. exec. com. and vice chmn. bd. N.Y.C. Police Found.; chmn. judiciary com. on cameras in the cts. N.Y. State, 1987-89. Sr. fellow Freedom Forum Media Studies Ctr., N.Y.C., 1994-95. Mem. AAAS, Acad. Motion Picture Arts and Scis., Am. Hist. Assn., Nat. Assn. Ednl. Broadcasters, Phi Beta Kappa. Clubs: Century. Home: 90 Riverside Dr New York NY 10024-5306 Office: 320 Park Ave New York NY 10022-6815 E-mail: richarddheffner@aol.com., openmindtv@aol.com.

HEFFRON, HOWARD A. lawyer; b. N.Y.C., Oct. 3, 1927; s. Jack and Sophie (Malkin) H.; m. Stella Meller, July 4, 1946; children: James, Robert, Nancy. AB, Columbia U., 1948; LL.B., Harvard U., 1951. Bar: N.Y. State 1953, D.C. 1953. Practiced in, N.Y.C. and Washington, 1953-58, 61-66, 69-77, 79—; asst. U.S. atty. So. Dist. N.Y., 1953-57; 1st asst. tax div. and asst. dep. atty. gen. Dept. Justice, Washington, 1958-61; chief counsel Fed. Hwy. Adminstrn., Dept. Transp., Washington, 1967-69; apptd. by Pres. and confirmed by Senate as dir. Office Rail Pub. Counsel, Washington, 1977-79; prof. law U. Wash., Seattle, 1965-67. Cons. Pres.'s Commn. on Law Enforcement and Adminstrn. of Justice, Washington, 1965-66, Nat. Commn. on Product Safety, Washington, 1969-70 Author: Federal Consumer Safety Legislation, 1970. With U.S. Army, 1946-47.

HEFFRON, MICHAEL EDWARD, software engineer, computer scientist; b. Battle Creek, Mich., Dec. 18, 1949; s. Michael Richard and Maxine Beverly (Piper) Heffron; m. Judith M. Dole, June 22, 2002; children from previous marriage: Karen, Jennifer. BS in Computer Sci., Ariz. State U., 1986; MS in Computer Sci., Colo. Tech. U., 1998, D in Computer Sci., 2001. Engring. asst. Motorola, Inc., Scottsdale, Ariz., 1977-81; calibration lab. supr. ADR Ultrasound, Tempe, Ariz., 1982-83; engring. aide Motorola, Inc., Scottsdale, 1983-86; v.p. CyberSoft, Inc., Tempe, Ariz., 1986-90; engr. Injection Rsch. Specialists, Inc., Colorado Springs, Colo., 1990-91; software devel. mgr. Injection Rsch. Specialists Co. div. Pacer Industries, Colorado Springs, 1991-92; sr. systems engr. Computer Data Systems Inc., Rockville, Md., 1992-93; software engr. Coergon, Inc., Boulder, Colo., 1993-95, Loral Comm. Systems (purchased by Lockheed Martin 1996), Colorado Springs, Colo., 1995-96, Lockheed Martin, Colorado Springs, 1996-97; sr. software engr. L-3 Comms. Corp. (formerly Lockheed Martin Wideband Sys.), Colo. Springs, 1997-99, prin. software engr., 1999—. Patentee in field. Served with USAF, 1970-77. Mem. IEEE, Assn. Computing Machinery, Soc. Reliability Engrs. Office: L-3 Comms Corp 1150 Academy Park Loop Ste 240 Colorado Springs CO 80910-3716

HEFFRON, WARREN A. medical educator, physician; b. St. Louis, Nov. 7, 1936; s. Willard Page H. and Alma Alberta Revington; m. Rosalee Bowdish, June 10, 1961; children: Kimberly, Wanda, Kara, Arthur. AB, U. Mo., 1958, MD, 1962. Diplomate Am. Bd. Family Practice (pres. 1998—). Rotating intern U. Calif., Orange, 1962-63; physician Hosp. Castaner (P.R.), 1966-68; resident internal medicine U. N. Mex., Albuquerque, 1968-71, asst. prof., chief divsn., 1971-76; assoc. prof., asst. chair Family Cmty. and Emergency Medicine, Albuquerque, 1976-82; prof., chmn. Family Committee and Emergency Medicine, Albuquerque, 1982-93; chief med. staff U. N. Mex. Hosp., Albuquerque, 1993—. Bd. dirs. Am. Acad. Family Physicians, Am. Bd. Family Practice, dir. family Med. Residency Program, Albuquerque, 1971-82; vis. prof., cons. Dept. Cmty. Health, Punjab, India, Christian Med. Coll., Punjab U., Ludihiana; prof. Dept. Family and Cmty. Medicine, Albuquerque, 1993—; various internat. vis. professorships. Contbr. numerous articles to profl. jours. Mem. free clinic Albuquerque Rescue Mission. Lt. comdr. USPHS, 1964-66. Recipient Recognition award Am. Med. Assn. Physicians, 1971, 74, 77, 80, 83, 86, 89, 92, 95, 98, N. Mex. Family Physician of the Yr. award, 1990. Mem. N. Mex. Am. Acad. Family Physicians (pres. 1985, N. Mex. Family Dr. of Yr. award, chpt. svc. award 1988), Am. Bd. Family Practice (pres. 1998-99), N. Mex. Med. Soc. (pres. 1996-97, Robbins award Cmty. Svc. 1981), Soc. Tchrs. of Family Medicine (bd. dirs., treas. 1997, Smilkstein award for internat. family medicine edn. 1998), Christian Med. and Dental Soc. (bd. dirs. 1998-2003, pres. 2003, residence rev. com. for family practice 1999-2003), World Orgn. Family Drs. (v.p. for the Ams. 2000). Methodist. Home: 2406 Ada Pl NE Albuquerque NM 87106-2550 E-mail: wheffron@salud.unm.edu.

HEFLEY, JOEL M. congressman; b. Ardmore, Okla., Apr. 18, 1935; s. J. Maurice and Etta A. (Anderson) H.; m. Lynn Christian, Aug. 25, 1961; children: Jana, Lori, Juli. BA, Okla. Baptist U., 1957; MS, Okla. State U., 1962. Exec. dir. Community Planning and Research, Colorado Springs, Colo., 1966-86; mem. Colo. State Ho. of Reps., 1977-78, Colo. State Senate, 1979-86, U.S. Congress from 5th Colo. dist., 1987—; mem. armed svcs. com.; mem. natural resources com.; mem. small bus.-SBA com.; mem. nat. security com.; chmn. stds. of offcl. conduct com. Mem.: Rotary, Colorado Springs Country. Republican. Baptist. Office: Ho of Reps 2372 Rayburn Ho Office Bldg Washington DC 20515-0605*

HEFLIN, HOWELL THOMAS, former senator, lawyer, former state supreme court chief justice; b. Poulan, GA, June 19, 1921; s. Marvin Rutledge and Louise D. (Strudwick) H.; m. Elizabeth Ann Carmichael, Feb. 23, 1952; 1 son, Howell Thomas. AB, Birmingham So. Coll., 1942; JD, U. Ala., 1948, LLD (hon.), U. No. Ala., Samford U., Tuskegee U., Del. Law Sch., Widener Coll., Troy State U., Ala. Christian Coll., Tuskegee U., Livingston U., Ala. A&M U., Ala. State U., Stillman Coll.; DHH (hon.), Birmingham So. Coll., 1980; DHL (hon.), Talledega Coll.; DSc (hon.), Auburn U. Bar: Ala. 1948. Practiced in, Tuscumbia; sr. ptnr. firm Heflin, Rosser and Munsey; chief justice Supreme Ct. Ala., 1971-77; chmn. Nat. Conf. Chief Justices, 1976-77; mem. U.S. Senate from Ala., Washington, 1979-97; mem. judiciary com., agr. com.; Ala. A&M U. Bd. dirs. Meth. Pub. House, 1952-64; lectr. U. Ala., 1946-48, U. North Ala., 1948-52; Tazewell Taylor vis. prof. law Coll. William and Mary, 1977. Mem. Ala. Edn. Commn., 1957-58; chmn. Colbert County A.R.C., 1950; Ala. field dir. Crusade for Children, 1948; pres. Ala. Com. Better Schs., 1958-59; chmn. Tuscumbia Bd. Edn., 1954-64, Ala. Tenure Commn., 1959-64; pres. U. Ala. Law Sch. Found., 1964-66; co-chmn. NCCJ, Tri-Cities area, 1949-70; chmn. Brotherhood Week; bd. dirs., v.p. Nat. Center for State Cts., 1975-77; trustee Birmingham So. Coll.; hon. pres. Troy State U. Served to maj. USMC, 1942-46. Decorated Silver Star, Purple Heart; recipient Ala. Citizen of Yr. award Ala. Cable TV Assn., 1973, 82; Outstanding Alumnus award U. Ala. and Birmingham So. Coll., 1973; Herbert Lincoln Harley award Am. Judicature Soc., 1973; Justice award, 1981; Ala. Citizen of Year award Ala. Broadcasters Assn., 1975; mem. Ala. Acad. Honor; named Outstanding Appellate Judge in U.S., ATLA, 1976; recipient Highest award Am. Judges Assn., 1975, Thomas Jefferson award Ala. Press Assn., 1979; Inst. Human Relations award, 1980; Silver Chalice award Am. Council on Alcoholism, 1980; Disting. Am. award Nat. Football Found. and Hall of Fame; Warren E. Burger award Inst. Ct. Mgmt.; Leadership award Am. Security Council, 1985-96; Disting. Svc. award Nat. Ctr. State Cts.; Leadership award Southeastern Soc. Am. Forresters, 1986, Taxpayers Hall of Fame, 1987, Patriotic Civilian award U.S. Army, 1987, Henry Jackson Senatorial Leadership award, 1987, Golden Plow award Am. Farm Bur., Outstanding Svc. to Sci. award Nat. Bio-med. Rsch. Assn., 1992, Werner Von Braun award Nat. Sci. Coun., 1992; named Progressive Farmer's 1993 Man of Year in Agr., Disting. Svc. award Nat. Rural Electric Coop. Assn, Helen Keller, Outstanding Public Svs. award Am. Found. for Blind, 1996, Nat. Public Svs. award, Am. Heart Assn., 1996, John B. Medarie award, Am. Def. Assn., 1996, Charles Dickens Soc. Lit. award, 1996, Disting. Svc. award NASA, 1996, appreciation award U.S. Army Space and Strategic Def. Commands, 1996, Nat. Achievement award Nat. Contact Mgmt. Assn., 1998, Human Rels. award Ala. Edn. Assn., 1998, Thomas Jefferson award Am. Bd. Trial Advs., 1998, Dr. Martin Luther King Merit Svc. award Etowah County Patriot Hall of Honor, Ala Agriculture Hall of Honor, John Marshall award ABA. Fellow Internat. Acad. of Law and Scis., Internat. Acad. Trial Lawyers, Internat. Soc. Barristers, Am. Coll. Trial Lawyers; mem. Ala. Bar Assn. (pres. 1965-66), Colbert County Bar Assn. (past pres.), Ala. Bar Found. (past pres.), Am. Judicature Soc. (v.p. 1977-79), Ala. Law Sch. Alumni Assn. (past pres.), Ala. Trial Lawyers Assn. (pres.), Nat. Assn. Biomedical Rsch. Assn. (Outstanding Pub. Svc. award, Nat. Veterans award), VFW, Am. Legion, 40 and 8, DAV, Third Marine Div. Assn., Order of Coif, Omicron Delta Kappa, Phi Delta Phi, Tau Kappa Alpha, Lambda Chi Alpha. Democrat. Methodist. Office: PO Box 228 Tuscumbia AL 35674-0228

HEFLIN, MARTIN GANIER, foreign service officer, international political economist; b. Oklahoma City, July 5, 1932; s. Martin Henry and Eugenia Marie (Gabel) H.; m. Sydney Daffin Lewis, Nov. 24, 1954; children— Martin Hays, Stephanie Anne Heflin Pace BA, U. Okla., 1954, MA, 1957; postgrad., U. Redlands, 1955, U. Tex., 1958-59. Vice consul U.S. Consulate, Ponta Delgada, Portugal, 1960-62, U.S. Consulate Gen., São Paulo, Brazil, 1962-64; 2d sec. U.S. Embassy, Tokyo, Japan, 1964-68; prin. officer U.S. Consulate, Sapporo, Japan, 1968-71; fgn. affairs officer U.S. Dept State, Washington, 1971-74; consul, econ. and commerce U.S. Consulate Gen., São Paulo, 1974-76; dir. U.S. Trade Ctr. U.S. Dept. Commerce, São Paulo, 1976-78; counselor econ. and comml. affairs U.S. Embassy, New Delhi, India, 1979-83; minister-counselor, sr. Fgn. Service; prin. officer U.S. Consultate Gen., Monterrey, Mexico, 1983-87; sr. fellow Ctr. for Study of Fgn. Affairs, Fgn. Service Inst., Dept. State, 1987-89; mng. dir. The Naiad Corp., 1990—. Served to 1st lt. USAF, 1954-56. Mem. Am. Fgn. Service Assn., Am. Legion, Phi Delta Theta Roman Catholic. Avocations: golf, photography. Home: 4411 NW 12th Pl Gainesville FL 32605-5500 E-mail: nikkihef@aol.com.

HEFLIN, RUTH JANELLE, English language educator; b. Pratt, Kans., June 19, 1963; d. Charles Albert and Mary Rosella (Mallonee) H.; m. James Paul Cooper, Oct. 27, 1989; 1 child, Harland J.P.C. Cooper. BA, Kans. State U., 1985, MA, 1988; PhD, Okla. State U., 1997. Tchg. asst. Kans. State U., Manhattan, 1986-88, adj. instr., 1988-89, U. Kans., Lawrence, 1989-90, William Jewell Coll., Liberty, Mo., 1990-91, Kansas City (Kans.) C.C., 1990-92, U. Mo., Kansas City, 1990-92; tchg. assoc. Okla. State U., Stillwater, 1992-97, lectr., 1997-98; assoc. prof. Kansas City Kansas C.C., 1998—. Co-dir. Intercultural Ctr, 2001-02; faculty writing cons. Writing Across the Curriculum Project, 2001—; fiction editor Touchstone Mag., Manhattan, 1986-87; photo journalist for ROTC, U.S. Army, Fort Riley, Kans., 1986; presenter in field. Author: I Remain Alive: The Sioux Literary Renaissance, 2000. Pres. Student Assn. of Grad. Students in English, Manhattan, 1987-88; co-chair rsch. com. Kansas City (Kans.) C.C., 1991-92; voting mem. Adj. Instrn. Com., Kansas City, 1991-92; chair Annual English Conf., 1999, Lit. and Fine Arts Festival, 2000; hon. programs coun. Intercultural Coun., 1998—, Critical Thinking Ctr., 2001—, KNEA, 2001—, Faculty Senate, 2002—, SAAC, 2003—; honors coun. and intercultural coun. chair Cmty. Adv. Bd., 1998—; co-chair planning com. Am. Indian Heritage Month Celebration, 1999-2002. Recipient First Place for Fiction, Coll. Woman Mag., 1985; Steve Kraisinger scholar 4-H, Pratt, Kans., 1981-82; Second Century scholar Kans. State U., Manhattan, 1981-82. Mem. MLA, Assn. for Study of Am. Indian Lits., Soc. for Cinematic Study, English Grad. Student Assn. (chair professionalism com. 1995, chair hosting com. 1996). Avocations: swimming, bicycling, soccer, collecting paperweights and horse statues. Office: Kansas City Kans Cmty Coll Humanities and Fine Arts Divsn Kansas City KS 66112 E-mail: hefruth@toto.net.

HEFNER, CHRISTIE ANN, multi-media entertainment executive; b. Chgo., Nov. 8, 1952; d. Hugh Marston and Mildred Marie (Williams) H. BA summa cum laude in English and Am. Lit., Brandeis U., 1974. Freelance journalist, Boston, 1974-75; spl. asst. to chmn. Playboy Enterprises, Inc., Chgo., 1975-78, v.p., 1978-82, bd. dirs., 1979—, vice chmn., 1986-88, pres., 1982-88, COO, 1984-88, chmn., CEO, 1988—. Bd. dirs. Playboy Found.-Playboy Enterprises, Inc., Ill. chpt. ACLU, Mag. Pubs. Assn. Bd. dirs. Nat. Coalition on Crime and Delinquency, Creative Coalition, Rush-Presbyn.-St. Lukes Med. Ctr., MarketWatch.com, Inc., Canyon Ranch Bus. Com. for the Arts, NCTA Diversity Com. Recipient Agness Underwood award, L.A. chpt. Women in Comm., 1984, Founders award, Midwest Women's Ctr., 1986, Human Rights award, Am. Jewish Com., 1987, Harry Kalven Freedom of Expression award, ACLU, Ill., 1987, Spirit of Life award, City of Hope, 1988, Eleanor Roosevelt award, Internat. Platform Assn., 1990, Will Rogers Meml. award, Beverly Hills C. of C. and Civic Assn., 1993, Champion of Freedom award, ADL, 2000, Bettie B. Port Humanitarian award, Mt. Sinai, 2001, John Wayne Cancer Ctr. award, 2001, Christopher Reeve 1st Amendment award, Creative Coalition, 2001, Vanguard award, NCTA, 2002. Mem. Nat. Cable and Telecomm. Assn. (Vanguard award 2002, Interlochen's Path of Inspiration award 2003), Mus. of TV and Radio Media Ctr., Brandeis Nat. Women's Com. (life), Com. of 200, Young Pres. Orgn., Chgo. Network, Voters for Choice, Sierra Club, Emilys List, Sierra Club, Phi Beta Kappa. Democrat. Office: Playboy Enterprises Inc 680 N Lake Shore Dr Chicago IL 60611-4455

HEFNER, HUGH MARSTON, editor-in-chief; b. Chgo., Apr. 9, 1926; s. Glenn L. and Grace (Swanson) H.; m. Mildred M. Williams, June 25, 1949 (div.); children: Christie A., David P.; m. Kimberley Conrad, July 1, 1989 (div.); children: Marston G., Cooper B. BS, U. Ill., 1949. Subscription promotion writer Esquire mag., 1951; promotion mgr. Pubs. Devel. Corp., 1952; circulation mgr. Children's Activities mag., 1953; chmn. bd. HMH Pub. Co. Inc. (now Playboy Enterprises, Inc.), 1953-88; editor-in-chief Playboy mag., from 1953; pres. Playboy Clubs Internat., Inc., 1959-86; editor, pub. VIP mag., 1963-75, Oui mag., 1972-81. Occasional film appearances include History of the World, Part I, 1981, The Comeback Trail, 1982, Beverly Hills Cop II, 1987. Served with AUS, 1944-46. Recipient 1st Amendment Freedom award B'nai B'rith Anti-Defamation League, L.A., 1980, Internat. Pub. award Internat. Press Directory in London, 1997; ; named Man of Yr. Mag. Industry Newlsetter, 1967; named to Pub. Hall of Fame, 1989; honored with Hugh M. Hefner chair in study of Am. film U. So. Calif. Sch. Cinema/TV, 1996, Henry Johnson Fisher award, 2002. Mem.: N.Y. Friars Club (hon.). Office: Playboy Enterprises Inc Ste 302 9302 Wilshire Blvd Beverly Hills CA 90212

HEFNER, JUDITH ANN, priest, counselor; b. Buffalo, Mar. 12, 1947; d. Francis C. and Mary Rix (Hornsby) Hefner. BA, SUNY, Albany, 1969; MSW, U. Md., 1971; MDiv, Va. Theol. Sem., 1996. Ordained priest Episcopal Ch., 1997; cert. Acad. Cert. Social Workers, rehab. counselor, social worker. Social worker Balt. City Dept. Social Svc., 1970-77; svc. coord. Deaf Referral Svc., Inc., Balt., 1977-79; asst. project dir. Pub. Svc. Deaf Liaison Project, Balt., 1979-80; sch. social worker Balt. City Pub. Schs., 1980-82; social worker Children's Rehab. Ctr., Buffalo, 1984-85, Gowanda (N.Y.) Psychiat. Ctr., 1985; rehab. counselor Community Vocat. Rehab. Ctr., Niagara Falls, N.Y., 1985-93; peer counselor Niagara Frontier Ctr. for Ind. Living, 1997-99; counselor N.W. Cmty. Mental Health Ctr., 1999—. Contbr. Pres. Self-Help for Hard of Hearing People, Buffalo, 1984—86; warden Ephphatha Ch. of the Deaf, Buffalo, 1985—90; v.p. Niagara Frontier Ctr. for Ind. Living, 1990—93; vicar St. Matthew's Episcopal Ch., Buffalo, 1999—. Avocation: knitting, sewing. Home: 1307 Ransom Rd Grand Island NY 14072-1481

HEFTER, LAURENCE ROY, lawyer; b. N.Y.C., Oct. 13, 1935; s. Charles S. and Rose (Postal) H.; m. Jacqulyn Maureen Miller, June 13, 1957; children: Jeffrey Scott, Sue-Anne. B.M.E., Rensselaer Poly. Inst., 1957, MS in Mech. Engring., 1960; JD with honors, George Washington U., 1964. Bar: Va. 1964, N.Y. 1967, D.C. 1973. Instr. Rensselaer Poly. Inst., Troy, N.Y., 1957-59; patent engr. Gen. Electric Co., Washington, 1959-63; sr. patent atty. Atlantic Research Corp., Alexandria, Va., 1963-66; assoc. firm Davis, Hoxie, Faithfull & Hapgood, N.Y.C., 1966-69; mem. firm Ryder, McAulay & Hefter, N.Y.C., 1970-73, Finnegan, Henderson, Farabow, Garrett & Dunner, LLP, Washington, 1973—. Professorial lectr. trademark law George Washington U., 1981-90; mem. adv. com. U.S. Patent and Trademark Office, 1988-92, Trademark Rev. Commn., 1986-89. Bd. govs. Brand Names Ednl. Found., 2001—. Named in Best Lawyers in Am., Best Lawyers in Washington. Mem. ABA (chmn. patent office affairs com. patent, trademark and copyright sect. 1976-80, unfair competition com. 1980-81, governing com. franchise forum 1994-97), N.Y. State Bar Assn., D.C. Bar Assn., Va. Bar Assn. (dir. patent, trademark and copyright sect. 1976-78), Internat. Bar Assn. (chmn. trademark com. 1986-90), Am. Patent Law Assn. (chmn. trademark com. 1979-81, dir. 1981-84), U.S. Trademark Assn. (dir. 1982-84), Order of Coif, Alpha Epsilon Pi. Home: 6904 Loch Lomond Dr Bethesda MD 20817-4756 Office: 1300 I St NW Washington DC 20005-3314

HEFTLER, THOMAS E. lawyer; b. Jersey City, 1943; AB, Princeton U., 1965; JD cum laude, NYU, 1968. Bar: N.Y. 1968. Mem. Stroock & Stroock & Lavan LLP, N.Y.C. Office: Stroock & Stroock & Lavan LLP 180 Maiden Ln New York NY 10038-4925

HEFTMANN, ERICH, biochemist; b. Vienna, Mar. 9, 1918; came to U.S., 1939; s. Salomon and Rosa (Seifert) H.; m. Lily Rubin (div. 1966); children: Rex, Lisa, Erica; m. Brigitte Hedwig Sander, Mar. 14, 1968; children: Karen, David. BS, NYU, 1942; PhD, U. Rochester, 1947. Cert. Clin. Chemist. Biochemist USPHS, Boston, 1947-48, NIH, Bethesda, Md., 1948-63, USDA, Pasadena, Calif., 1963-70, Berkeley, Calif., 19790-83; editor Jour. of Chromatography, Amsterdam, The Netherlands, 1983—. Author (books) Biochemistry Steroids, 1960, Steroid Biochemistry, 1970, Chromatography of Steroids, 1976; editor (books) Chromatography, 1961, 67, 75, 83, 92, Modern Methods of Steroid Analysis, 1973. Recipient Humboldt Prize German Govt., 1975. Fellow AAAS; mem. Am. Chem. Soc., Am. Soc. of Biol. Chemists. Home: PO Box 928 Orinda CA 94563

HEGARTY, CAROL IRENE, painter, writer; b. Western Springs, Ill. d. James Harold and Margaret Virginia (French) Hegarty. Student, Principia Coll., Elsah, Ill., 1975-77; BFA, Sch. Art Inst. Chgo., 1980, MFA, 1982. Profl. artist, Aurora, Ill., 1982—; founding mem. Fox River Ctr. Visual Art, Aurora, 1983—87; staff writer Beacon News, Aurora, 1994-96. Adj. prof. art history Waubonsee CC,

Sugar Grove, Ill., 1985—86, adj. prof. art, 1997—; freelance writer, 1994—; adj. prof. art Sch. Art Inst. Chgo., 1997—99, Joliet (Ill.) Jr. Coll., Joliet, 2000—01; vis. assoc. prof. art No. Ill. U., Dekalb, 2000—02; adj. art faculty N. Ctrl. Coll., Naperville, Ill., 2000—01, Kishwaukee CC, Malta, Ill., 2001—. One-woman shows include Prairie Ctr Arts, Schaumburg, Ill., 1994, Campbell Ho. Gallery, Geneva, Ill., 1995, Aurora U., 1999, exhibited in group shows at Artemisia Gallery, Chgo., 1979, Art Inst. Chgo. Rental and Sales Gallery, 1979, 1982, Norris Gallery, St. Charles, Ill., 1986, 1991—95, 1997—2000, Gallery 2, Chgo., Space Gallery, 1991, Campbell Ho. Gallery, 1996—98, Aurora U., 1998, 2000, Aurora Pub. Art Commn., 1998; columnist: ArtWorks, Beacon News, 1996—. Bd. dirs. Fox Valley Arts Coun., 1998—2000, Campbell Ho. Gallery Kane County Events, Geneva, 1998—. Recipient awards for art; George D. and Isabella A. Brown Travelling fellow, 1980, Ox-Bow resident, Saugatuck, Mich., 1997. Home: 1594 Elder Dr Aurora IL 60506-1221 E-mail: chegarty@earthlink.net., carol@carolhegarty.com.

HEGARTY, CHRISTOPHER JOSEPH, management and financial consultant; b. Jersey City; s. Michael John and Catherine Mary (Morrissey) H.; children: Mahren, Cahlil, Michael. PhD in Mgmt. Edn., Creative Devel. Inst., 1977, DD, Am. Inst. Theology, 1998. Investors exec., zone mgr. Investors Diversified Svcs., Mpls., 1960-65; pres. Hegarty & Co., N.Y.C., 1965-67; founder, sr. v.p. Competitive Capital Corp., San Francisco, 1967-69; founder, pres. Charter St. Corp., San Francisco, 1969-71; pres. C.J. Hegarty & Co., Payson, Ariz., 1971—. Chmn. bd. dirs. Advanced Resources Mgmt.; faculty for continuing edn. U. So. Calif.; cons. SRI Internat.; founder, regent Coll. Fin. Planning; prin. Inst. Exceptional Performance, 1989; chmn. emeritus bd. govs. Nat. Ctr. for Fin. Edn.; spl. adv. Alternative Medicine.com., 1991—. Author: How To Manage Your Boss, 1980, Financial Planning for Chief Executives, 1983, Consistently Exceptional Leadership, 1989, Fiscal Fitness for Organizations, 1992, 7 Secrets of Exceptional Leadership, 1997, The Future Belongs to the Omnicompetent, 1997; co-author: Peak Performance for Executives and Professionals, 1983, Out of Harm's Way, 2001, Tyranny of the Familiar, 2002; contbg. editor Fin. Planning mag., 1973-77; mem. editl. bd. Health Consciousness mag., 1989, Alternative Medicine Mag., 1995; spl. advisor Future Medicine Pub., 1992—. Adv. bd. Small Bus. Coun. Am., 1982—; advisor Calif. Gov.'s Task Force for Emergencies, 1981-83; advisor Nat. Foun. Alternative Medicine, 2002; maj. Nat. Chaplains Corps, 1999; bishop Original Ch. of Apostles of Christ, 2002; chmn., bd. govs. Digest Fin. Planning, 1983—; pres., CEO Internat. Ctr. Life Improvement, 1987. Recipient Judge U.S. C. of C. Blue Chip Enterprise award, 1991, Top Preview Spkr. of Yr. award Internat. Platform Assn., 1972, Spl. award Sci. Found., 1977, Leadership and Comm. award Toastmasters Internat., 1978-79, Innovative Mktg. award Sales and Mktg. Assn., 1979, Outstanding Spkr. award Am. Soc. Tng. and Devel., 1980, Spkr. of Decade award Internat. Comm. Congress, 1980, Legion of Honor award Nat. Chaplains Assn., 1981, Leadership award UN, 1981, Excellence award Am. Film Guild; named Spkr. of Yr., Young Pres.'s Orgn., 1982. Mem. Nat. Spkrs. Assn. (founding dir., Continuare Professos Articulatus Excellence award 1977, named to Spkrs. Hall of Fame 1998), Am. Inst. Mgmt. (pres. coun. 1981—), Sales and Mktg. Execs. Internat., Internat. Assn. Fin. Planners (founder, nat. adv. bd., Spokesman of Yr. 1974), Commonwealth Club. Office: CJ Hegarty & Co 1116 S Elk Ridge Dr Ste A Payson AZ 85541 Home: 1116 S Elk Ridge Dr Payson AZ 85541 E-mail: leaders@cutting-edge.com.

HEGARTY, GEORGE JOHN, university rector, English educator; b. Cape May, N.J., July 20, 1948; s. John Joseph and Gloria Anna (Bonelli) H.; m. Joy Elizabeth Schiller, June 9, 1979. Student, U. Fribourg, Switzerland, 1968-69; BA in English, LaSalle U., Phila., 1970; Cert., Coll. de la Pocatiere, Que., Can., 1970; postgrad., U. Dakar, Senegal, 1970, Case Western Res. U., 1973-74, U. N.H., 1976; MA in English, Drake U., 1977; cert., U. Iowa, 1977; DA, Drake U., 1978; Cert., UCLA, 1979, U. Pa., 1981. Tchr. English, Peace Corps vol. College d'Enseignment General de Sedhiou, Senegal, 1970-71; tchr. English Belmore Boys' and Westfields High Schs., Sydney, Australia, 1972-73; teaching fellow in English Drake U., Des Moines, 1974-76; mem. faculty English Des Moines Area Community Coll., 1976-80; assoc. prof. Am. lit. U. Yaounde, Cameroon, 1980-83; prof. Am. lit. and civilization Nat. U. Cote D'Ivoire, Abidjan, 1986-88; dir. ctr. for internat. programs and svcs. Drake U., Des Moines, 1983-91; prof. grad. program intercultural mgmt. Sch. for Internat. Tng., The Experiment in Internat. Living, Brattleboro, Vt., 1991-93; provost, prof. English Teikyo Loretto Heights U., Denver, 1992-94; pres., prof. English, Teikyo Westmar U., Le Mars, Iowa, 1994-95; program dir. Am. degree program Taylor's Coll., Malaysia, 1996-97; v.p. academic affairs, prof. English Teikyo Loretto Heights U., Denver, 1997—2001; rector Webster U., Thailand, 2002—. Acad. specialist USIA, 1983-84; workshop organizer/speaker Am. Field Svcs., 1986; cons. Coun. Internat. Ednl. Exch., 1986; evaluator Assn. des Univ. Partiellment Entierément de Langue Francais, 1987, Iowa Humanities Bd., 1990-91, USAID's Ctr. for Univ. Coop. and Devel., 1991; Fulbright lectr., rschr. Am. Lit U., 2003—; cons. in field. Book reviewer African Book Pub. Record, Oxford, Eng., 1981—, African Studies Rev., 1990—; host, creator TV show Global Perspectives, 1989-91; exhibitor of African art, 1989—; contbr. articles to profl. jours. Commr. Des Moines Sister City Commn., 1984-87, 91; bd. dirs. Iowa Sister State Com., 1988-91; pres. Chautauqua Park Nat. Hist. Dist. Neighborhood Assn., 1991; bd. dirs. Melton Found., 1994-95. Drake U. fellow, 1971-72, 74-76; Nat. Endowment for Humanities grantee, 1981; Fulbright grantee, USIA, 1980-83, 86-88. Mem. Am. Assn. Pres. Ind. Colls. and Univs., NAFSA: Assn. Internat. Educators (sectional chmn. region VI 1986-87, Vt. rep. 1992), Assn. Internat. Edn. Adminstrs., Inst. Internat. Edn. Avocations: collecting tribal art, travel, swimming, writing. Office: 2040 Antananariuo Pl Dulles VA 20189-2040 E-mail: ghegarty@aol.com.

HEGARTY, MARY FRANCES, lawyer; b. Chgo., Dec. 19, 1950; d. James E. and Frances M. (King) H. BA, DePaul U., 1972, JD, 1975. Bar: Ill. 1975, U.S. Dist. Ct. (no. dist.) Ill. 1976, U.S. Supreme Ct. 1980. Ptnr. Lannon & Hegarty, Park Ridge, Ill., 1975-80; pvt. practice Park Ridge, 1980—. Dir. Legal Assistance Found. Chgo., 1983—. Mem. revenue study com. Chgo. City Coun. Fin. Com., 1983; mem. Sole Source Rev. Panel, City of Chgo., 1984; pres. Hist. Pullman Found., Inc., 1984-85; apptd. Park Ridge Zoning Bd., 1993-94; pres. Park Ridge C. of C., 2002--. Mem. Ill. State Bar Assn. (real estate coun. 1980-84), Chgo. Bar Assn., Women's Bar Assn. Ill. (pres. 1983-84), N.W .Suburban Bar Assn., Women's Bar Found. (v.p. 2003), Park Ridge Women Entrepreneurs, Chgo. Athletic Assn. (pres. 1992-93), Park Ridge C. of C. (pres. 2002--). Democrat. Roman Catholic. Office: 301 W Touhy Ave Park Ridge IL 60068-4204

HEGARTY, THOMAS JOSEPH, academic administrator, history educator; b. Boston, Dec. 6, 1935; s. Thomas John and Abigail Barbara (Dunlap) H.; m. Louisa Ivanova, May, 1959; children: Alton Dunlap, Allison McAndrew. AB, Harvard U., 1957, A.M., 1958, PhD, 1965; cert., Inst. Ednl. Mgmt. Harvard U., 1973. Asst. prof. history and history of ideas Brandeis U., Waltham, Mass., 1962-67; assoc. prof. history, chmn. Soviet and East European studies program Boston U., 1967-71; assoc. prof. history, dean grad. studies Boston State Coll., 1971-78; prof. history, v.p. provost SUNY-Potsdam, 1978-82; v.p. acad. affairs Butler U., Indpls., 1982-88, prof. history, 1982-89; sr. cons. Am. Assn. State Colls. and Univs., 1988-89; provost, prof. history U. Tampa, Fla., 1989—. Assoc. Russian Research Ctr., Harvard U., 1968-72; summer 2000 fellow U.S. Holocaust Meml. Mus., 2000. Mem. Tampa Bay Coun. on Fgn. Rels., 1989—; bd. dirs. Internat. Ctr., Indpls., 1983-85, Park-Tudor Sch., 1983-88; mem. 1000 Friends of Fla., 1990—. Fellow Ford Found., 1957-61, Holocaust Ednl. Found., 1999,Inst. for Study of Conflict, Ideology and Policy U. Boston. Mem. Indpls. Coun. World Affairs (bd. dirs. 1988), Indpls. Com. on Fgn. Rels., Am. Assn. State Colls. and Univs., Resource Ctr. for Planned Change, Greater Tampa C. of C., Greater Tampa World Affairs Coun. (pres. 1992—), Japan-Am. Soc. Cen. Fla. Inc. (bd. dirs. 1990, chair edn. coun. 1993), Greater Tampa Internat. Trade Coun., Rotary, Harvard Club of West Cen. Fla., Lit. Club of Indpls., Tampa Club (mem. com. 1990—), Fla. Humanities Coun. (bd. dirs. 1986—), Phi Beta Kappa (Alpha of Harvard U. 1956), Phi Kappa Phi, Phi Alpha Theta. Office: U Tampa Box B Tampa FL 33606-1490 E-mail: thegarty@ut.edu.

HEGEDUS, L. LOUIS, chemical engineer, research and development executive; b. Budapest, Hungary, Apr. 13, 1941; arrived in U.S., 1968; s. Lajos and Anna Hegedus; m. Eva Judith Brem, Mar. 28, 1968; children: Caroline Nora, Monica Michelle. MSChemE, Tech. U., Budapest, 1964, D honoris causa, 1991; PhD, U. Calif., Berkeley, 1972. Rsch. engr. Rsch. Inst. Organic Chem. Industry, Budapest, 1964-65; group leader Daimler-Benz AG, Manheim, Germany, 1965-68; supr. catalysis rsch. Gen. Motors Rsch. Labs., Warren, Mich., 1972-80; dir. inorganic rsch. W.R. Grace Co., Columbia, Md., 1980-84, v.p. rsch. dept., 1984-94, v.p. corp. tech. divsn., 1994-96; v.p. R&D ATOFINA Chems. Inc., King of Prussia, Pa., 1996-2001, sr. v.p. R&D, 2001—. Allan P. Colburn lectr. U. Del., 1976; Union Carbide lectr. SUNY, Buffalo, 1983; B.F. Dodge lectr. Yale U., 1988; J.A. Gerster lectr. U. Del., 1988, Regents lectr. UCLA, 1991, Mason lectr. Stanford U., 1991, disting. faculty lectr. U. Tex., Austin, 1992, Ashton Cary lectr. Ga. Inst. Tech., 1993, Hugh Hulburt Meml. lectr. Northwestern U., 1993, Warren K. Lewis lectr. MIT, 1994; Disting. Landegger lectr. Sch. of Fgn. Svc. Georgetown U., 1995; R.L. Pigford Meml. lectr. U. Del., 1998; mem. adv. bd. chem. thermal bioengrig. divsn. NSF, 1985; mem. adv. bd. dept. chem. engring. Princeton U., 1980-92, U. Calif., Berkeley, 1988-95, U. Wis., Madison, 1987-95, Lawrence Berkeley Lab. Ctr. for Advanced Materials Surface Sci. Program, 1989-93; mem. governing bd. Coun. Chem. Rsch., 1987-90, 92-95, chmn., 1993-94; mem. bd. on chem. sci. and tech., NRC, 1991-95, chmn. com. critical techs., 1992; mem. Commn. on Phys. Scis., Math. and Applications, 1995-98. Author: Catalyst Poisoning, 1984; editor 3 books on catalysis; mem. editl. bd. Inds. and Engring. Chem. Rsch., 1992-95, Hungarian Jour. Chemistry, 1992—, Catalysis Letters, 1993—, Topics in Catalysis, 1994—; contbr. articles to profl. jours. Fellow Am. Inst. Chem. Engrs. (editl. bd. jour. 1978-83, 85-88, R.H. Wilhelm award 1988, Profl. Progress award 1980, Chem. Engr. of Yr. award Detroit 1978, Catalysis and Reaction Engring. Divsn. award 2000); mem. NAE (chmn. chem. engring. sect. 2000), Am. Chem. Soc. (Chemtech Leo Friend award 1981, editl. bd. Indsl. and Engring. Chemistry Rsch., 1992-95), Md. Acad. Scis. (sci. coun. 1987-91), Hungarian Nat. Acad. Engring. (hon.). Avocation: flying. Home: 1104 Beech Rd Bryn Mawr PA 19010 Office: ATOFINA Chems Inc 900 First Ave King Of Prussia PA 19406 E-mail: louis.hegedus@atofina.com.

HEGEDUS, STEPHEN JOHN, mathematician, educator, researcher; b. Wordsley, West Midlands, United Kingdom, Sept. 2, 1973; arrived in U.S., 2000; s. Ferenc and Vera Hegedus; m. Nathalie Adamo, June 19, 1999; 1 child, Dylan Emmanuel. BSc in Math. and Econs., U. Southampton, Eng., 1994, PhD in Math. Edn., 1998. Lectr., rsch. fellow U. Oxford, England, 1998—2000; asst. prof. U. Mass., North Dartmouth, 2000—. Ednl. cons. U.K. Govt., London, 1998—2000; presenter in field. Author: (book) What is Mathematics, (poetry book) Just Passing Through, 1994; contbr. articles to profl. jours. Scholar, Econs. and Social Rsch. Coun., 1995—98. Mem.: Math. Assn. Am. Office: Univ Mass Dartmouth 285 Old Westport Rd North Dartmouth MA 02747 Personal E-mail: shegedus@umassd.edu. E-mail: shegedus@umassd.edu.

HEGEL, CAROLYN MARIE, farmer, farm bureau executive; b. Lagro, Ind., Apr. 19, 1940; d. Ralph H. and Mary Lucile (Rudig) Lynn; m. Tom Lee Hegel, June 3, 1962. Student pub. schs., Columbia City, Ind. Bookkeeper Huntington County Farm Bur. Co-op, Inc., Ind., 1959-67, office mgr., 1967-70; twp. woman leader Wabash County (Ind.) Farm Bur., Inc., 1970-73, county woman leader, 1973-76; dist. woman leader Ind. Farm Bur., Inc., Indpls., 1976-80, 2d v.p., bd. dirs., 1980—, chmn. women's com., 1980—, exec. com., 1988—. Farmer Andrews, Ind., 1962—; dir. Farm Bur. Ins. Co., Indpls., 1980—, exec. com., 1988—, audit com., 2000—, chmn. audit com., 2003—; bd. dirs. Countryway Ins. Co.; spkr. in field, bd. mem. Country Ins., 2002—. Women in the Field columnist Hoosier Farmer mag., 1980—. Mem. rural task force Gt. Lakes States Econ. Devel. Commn., 1987—88; mem. Ind. Farm Bur. Svc. Co., 1980—; active Leadership Am. Program, 1988; Sunday sch. tchr., bd. dirs. children's activities Bethel United Meth. Ch., 1965—; pres. Bethel United Meth. Women, Lagro, 1975—81; bd. dirs. Ind. Farm Bur. Found., Indpls., 1980—, Ind. Inst. Agr., Food and Nutrition, Indpls., 1982—, Ind. 4-H Found., Lafayette, 1983—86; mem. Ind. Rural Health Adv. Coun., 1993—96, Hoosier Homestead Award Cert. Com., Indpls., 1980—; organizer farm divsn. Wabash County Am. Cancer Soc. Fund Dr., 1974; bd. dirs. N.E. Ind. Kidney Found., 1984—, Nat. Kidney Found. of Ind., 1985—89. Named Big Sister of Yr., Wabash County, Ind., 2003; named one of Outstanding Farm Woman of Yr., Country Woman Mag., 1987; recipient State 4-H Home Econs. award, Ind. 4-H, 1960. Mem.: Am. Farm Bur. Fedn. (midwest rep. to women's com. 1986—93), Producers Mktg. Assn. (bd. dirs. 1980—94), Ind. Agrl. Mktg. Assn. (bd. dirs. 1980—94), Women in Comm., Inc. Republican. Home: 3330 N 650 E Andrews IN 46702-9616 Office: Ind Farm Bur Inc PO Box 1290 225 S East St Indianapolis IN 46202-4058 E-mail: chegel@infarmbureau.com.

HEGENDERFER, JONITA SUSAN, public relations executive; b. Chgo., Mar. 18, 1944; d. Clifford Lincoln and Cornelia Anna (Larson) Hazzard; m. Gary William Hegenderfer, Mar. 12, 1971 (dec. 1978). BA, Purdue U., 1965; postgrad., Calif. State U., Long Beach, 1966-67, Northwestern U., 1969-70. Tchr. English, Long Beach (Calif.) Schs., 1965-68; editl. asst. Playboy Mag., Chgo., 1968-70; comms. specialist AMA, Chgo., 1970-72; v.p. Home Data, Hinsdale, Ill., 1972-75; mktg. mgr. Olympic Savs. & Loan, Berwyn, Ill., 1975-79; sr. v.p. Golin/Harris Comms., Chgo., 1979-89; pres. JSH & A, Chgo., 1989—. Bd. dirs. Chgo. Internat. Film Festival, 1989, 90. Author: Slim Guide to Spas, 1984, (video) PR Guide for Chicago LSCs, 1991; editor: Financial Information National Directory, 1972; contbr. articles to profl. jours. Co-chmn. pub. rels. com. Am. Cancer Soc., Chgo., 1984; mem. com. March of Dimes, Chgo., 1986; mem. pub. rels. com. Girl Scouts Chgo., 1989-90, bd. dirs., 1994-95; bd. dirs. Greater DuPage Women's Bus. Coun., 1992-93, Girl Scouts U.S. DuPage County, 1994—; vol. ctr. adv. com. United Way, Chgo., 1990-93; mem. cmty. svc. com. Publicity Club Chgo., 1990—. Recipient 5 Golden Trumpet awards Publicity Club Chgo., 1983, 96, 94, Silver Trumpet awards, 1984, 86, 88, Spectra awards Internat. Assn. Bus. Communicators, 1984, 85, 87, Gold Quill aard, 1985, Bronze Anvil award Pub. Rels. Soc. Am., 1985, award Nat. Creativity in Pub. Rels. award, 1995; named Influential Woman in Bus., 1998. Mem. Am. Mktg. Assn., Publicity Club Chgo., Pub. Rels. Soc. Am., Chgo. Women in Pub., Nat. Assn. Women Bus. Owners, DuPage Area Assn. Bus. Tech. (bd. dirs. 1997), Coun. on Fgn. Rels., Met. Women's Forum, Cinema Chgo. (bd. dirs. 1988-89). Avocations: travel, photography. Office: JSH & A Comms IS 450 Summit #320 Oakbrook Terrace IL 60181 E-mail: jonni@jsha.com.

HEGER, HERBERT KRUEGER, education educator; b. Cin., June 15, 1937; s. J. Herbert and Leona (Krueger) H.; m. Thyra Cleek. AS, Ohio Mechanics Inst., 1956; BS, Miami U., 1962, MEd, 1965; PhD, Ohio State U., 1969. Tchr. Marshall Jr. High Sch., Pomona, Calif., 1962-63; tchr. math. Mt. Healthy High Sch., Ohio, 1963-66; grad. asst., grad. assoc. Miami U.-Ohio State U., 1966-69; dir. Environ. Studies Center Central State U., Wilberforce, Ohio, 1968-69; asst. prof. U. Ky., 1969-75; assoc. dir. Louisville Urban Edn. Center, 1971-75; vis. prof. Sch. Profl. Studies, Pepperdine U., 1975-78; dir. student teaching U. Tex., San Antonio, 1975-77, coordinator curriculum and instrn., 1977-78; assoc. prof. edn. Whitworth Coll., Spokane, Wash., 1978-82, chmn. dept., 1978-79, dean Grad. Sch., 1979-82; prof. edn. U. Tex., El Paso, 1982-99, prof. emeritus, 1999—. Cons. in field Contbr. articles to profl. jours. Mem. Am. Ednl. Rsch. Assn., Nat. Soc. Study Edn., Phi Delta Kappa. Republican. Mem. Christian Ch. (Disciples Of Christ). Home: 2495 Tiffany Dr Las Cruces NM 88011-2008

HEGER, JAMES JOSEPH, internist, cardiologist; b. Pitts., 1946; m. Anne Keller; children: Monica, Stephanie, Brian, Julie. BS, LaSalle Coll., 1968; MD, Georgetown U., 1972. Diplomate Am. Bd. Internal Medicine, Am. Bd. Cardiovascular Disease. Intern St. Vincents Hosp., N.Y.C., 1972-73, resident, 1973-75, 75-76; fellow in cardiology Ind. U. Sch. Medicine, Indpls., 1976-78; staff Ind. U. Hosp., Indpls.; assoc. prof. medicine Ind. U. Sch. Medicine, 1978-88; staff Parkview Hosp., Ft. Wayne, Ind., Luth. Hosp., Ft. Wayne, Ind.; clin. prof. medicine Ind. U. Sch. Medicine, 1988—. Fellow ACP, Am. Coll. Cardiology (Ind. chpt. gov.-pres. 1991-94), Coun. on Clin. Cardiology; mem. Am. Heart Assn. Home: 3235 N Washington Rd Fort Wayne IN 46802-4902

HEGGEN, ARTHUR WILLIAM, insurance company executive; b. Eureka, Calif., Aug. 9, 1945; s. Arlo Murray and Edna Marie (Nelson) H.; m. Betty Louise Roddy, Nov. 21, 1970; children: Cherilyn, Christopher. BS in Indsl Adminstrn., Acctg., Iowa State U., 1967. CPA, Iowa, Fla.; CPCU, FLMI, AIAF. Audit staff mgr. Ernst & Whinney, Des Moines, 1971-84; sr. v.p., treas. Am. Bankers Ins. Group, Inc., Miami, Fla., 1984-96; exec. v.p. Am. Bankers Ins. Co., Miami, Fla., 1996-99, Assurant Group, Miami, 1999—. Bd. dirs. YMCA of Greater Miami; pres. Iowa Ptnrs. of the Yucatan, Des Moines, 1984; pres., treas. Des Moines Hearing Speech Ctr., 1976-82. Capt. USMC, 1967-70, Vietnam. Fellow Life Mgmt. Inst.; mem. AICPA, Soc. CPCU, Fla. Inst. CPAs, Ins. Acct. & Sys. Assn. Office: Assurant Group 11222 Quail Roost Dr Miami FL 33157-6543 also: Assurant Group 260 Interstate North Cir SE Atlanta GA 30339-2210

HEGGENESS, JULIE FAY, foundation administrator, lawyer; b. Long Beach, Calif., Nov. 9, 1959; d. Clark Richard Heggeness, June Lorraine Heggeness; 1 child, Thaddeus. BFA, U. So. Calif., 1982; JD, Western State U., 1998. Cert. specialist planned giving. Dir. Long Beach Meml. Med. Ctr., Long Beach, 1995—99, Meml. Med. Ctr. Found., Long Beach, 1999—. 1st v.p. Camp Fire U.S., Long Beach, 1999—2001; Leadership Long Beach Class of 2003 estate planning and trust coun., bd. mem. at large; mem. Nat. Coun. Planned Giving. Mem.: Long Beach (Calif.) Bar Assn., Assistance League Long Beach, Cameo Profl. Aux. Republican. Roman Catholic. Avocations: golf, gardening, skiing. Office: Meml Med Ctr Found 2801 Atlantic Ave Long Beach CA 90806 Office Fax: 562-933-3652. Personal E-mail: jheggeness@memorialcare.org.

HEGINBOTHAM, JAN STURZA, sculptor; b. Queens, N.Y., Dec. 8, 1954; d. Herman and Evelyn (Cantor) Sturza; m. Donald Wesley Heginbotham, 1975. BA in Art Edn., U. Md., 1975; pvt. study, Boris Blai, Phila., 1976-78; MFA, Am. U., 1992. Tchr., lectr. sculpture workshops Mid-Atlantic and NE region colls. and univs., 1985—; life-drawing workshop coord. Arlington (Va.) Art Ctr., 1986-90, 93; sculpture teaching asst. Am. U., 1990-92, vis. artist, 1998. Solo exhbns. include Cannon Rotunda, U.S. Congress, Washington, 1985, Holy Family Coll., Phila., 1985, Staunton (Va.) Fine Art Assn., 1989, McCrillis Gardens Gallery, Bethesda, Md., 1990, Am. U., Washington, 1992, Art Inst. Gallery, Salisbury, Md., 1999, Exquisite Designs Gallery, Reston, Va., 2001; group shows include Perry House Gallery, Alexandria, Va., 1997, Lexington Art Ctr., Ky., 1997, U. Va., Charlottesville, 1999, Raab Gallery, Phila., 1999, Brookside Gardens Cons., Wheaton, Md., 1999, 2000, Nat. Small Sculpture, Hattiesburg, Miss., 2000, Nathan B. Rosen Mus., Boca Raton, Fla., 2002, Craig Flinner Contemporary, Balt., 2001—. Washington County Mus. of Fine Art, Hagerstown, Md., 2003. Active pub. commn. Montgomery County Pub. Schs., Rockville, Md., 1988, funded commn. proposals Md. Nat. Capital Pk. and Planning Commn., Silver Spring, 1987, 91, Montgomery Pub. Schs., 1985. Recipient Orion Nova award Allied Artists of Am., 1982, Mems. and Assocs. award Allied Artists of Am., 1986, Mayor of Washington award, 1981, award for metal sculpture, Washington County Mus. of Fine Arts/Md. Metals, Inc., Hagerstown, 2003; merit scholar Scottsdale (Ariz.) Artist's Sch., 1987, Graduate Sculptors award Am. Univ., 1992; fellow Am. U., 1990-92. Mem. Washington Sculptors Group. Avocations: reading, yoga, walking. E-mail: the_sculptor@hotmail.com.

HEGLER, ELLEN MARIE, business executive, retired educator; b. Dryden, Oreg., Dec. 16, 1916; d. George Westley Van Buskirk and Marie Frances Mineo; children: Brian Neils, Rollin Grant, Gary Mark. BA in English cum laude, So. Oreg. Coll., 1959, MA in English, 1963; postgrad., UCLA, 1969-70. Cert. secondary tchr., Calif., Oreg. Prodr., announcer Radio Program KYSC, Yreka, Calif., 1947 48; v.p., sec. Carl Hegler Logging Inc., Ashland, 1951-59; social worker Jackson County Pub. Welfare Commn., 1959-60; English tchr. Sr. H.S., Medford, Oreg., 1961-62; fashion editor May Co., L.A., 1963-64; asst. prof. English So. Oreg. Coll., Ashland, 1964-70, Calif. State U., L.A., 1971-72; owner Hegler Enterprises Ltd., Ashland, Medford, 1976—. Contbr. articles to profl. publs. Sec. Ashland Meml. Hosp. com., 1956-58; pub. rels. dir. Sch. Bond Issues, Ashland, 1958; sec., exec. bd. Ashland Hosp. Found., 1981-83; one of founders Nat. Literary Hon. Fraternity, 1958. Avocation: writing. Office: Hegler Enterprises PO Box 165 Ashland OR 97520-0006

HEGSTROM, WILLIAM JEAN, mathematics educator; b. Macomb, Ill., Oct. 21, 1923; s. Carl William and Thelma (Canavit) H. Student Western Ill. U., 1941-42; B.Sc., Rutgers U., 1949, Ed.M. 1952; MA in Teaching, Purdue U., 1964; postgrad. U. Fla., 1961, Fla. Atlantic U., 1965-68; EdD, U. Miami, 1971; m. Grace Ann Paladino, May 3, 1944; children: Elizabeth Louise, William Jean II, Jean (Mrs. Carl Zimbro). Tchr. jr. h.s., South Plainfield, N.J., 1949-52, high sch., Bernardsville, N.J. 1952-54, Oak St. Sch., Bernard's Twp., N.J., 1954-55, high sch., Summit, N.J., 1955-58, jr. h.s., Delray Beach, Fla, 1958-65; chmn. math. dept. John I. Leonard H.S., Lake Worth, Fla., 1965-68, dir. Palm Beach County rsch. project, 1966-68; adj. prof. Fla. Atlantic U., 1965-69, assoc. prof., 1969-70; counselor coord. John Leonard Adult Ctr., Lake Worth, 1965-68; supr. rsch. and evaluation Palm Beach County Sch. Bd., West Palm Beach, Fla., 1970-74; adj. prof. Palm Beach Jr. Coll., 1981-88, Palm Beach Atlantic Coll., 1984-86, asst. prof., 1986-87; Palm Beach Atlantic Coll., 1984-87; cons. math. prof. Palm Beach County Sch. Bd., 1985-87, ret., 1987. With USAAF, 1942-46. Mem. NEA, Nat. Assn. Investors Corp., Am. Assn. Individual Investors, Phi Delta Kappa. Contbr. articles to profl. jours. Home: 225 NE 22nd St Delray Beach FL 33444-4221

HEGWOOD, BARBARA H. b. Jackson, Miss., Jan. 11, 1938; d. Frank Perry and Emily Batton Hemphill; m. Wayne H. Hegwood, July 29, 1961 (div. Nov. 1981); children: Emily E. Meadows, Peggy Hemphill, Wayne H. Jr. BBA, U. Miss., 1960. Asst. to pres. Carter Jewelers, Inc., Jackson, 1976-84; dir. devel. Miss. Children's Home Soc., Jackson, 1986—. Bd. mem. North Mid Town Cmty. Devel. Corp., Jackson, 1996—. Mem. Assn. Fundraising Profls., Exec. Women Internat. (rep.), Delta Delta Delta. Office: Miss Childrens Home Soc 1900 North West St Jackson MS 39202 E-mail: bhegwood@mchsfsa.org.

HEGYELI, RUTH INGEBORG ELISABETH JOHNSSON, pathologist, government official; b. Aug. 14, 1931; came to U.S., 1963; d. John Alfred and Elsa Ingeborg (Sjogren) Johnsson; m. Andrew Francis Hegyeli, July 2, 1966 (dec. June 1982). BA in Scis., U. Toronto, 1958, MD, 1962. Intern Toronto Gen. Hosp., 1962-63; sr. rsch. pathologist Battelle Meml. Inst., Columbus, Ohio, 1967-69; med. officer Nat. Heart and Lung Inst., 1969-73; chief program devel. and evaluation Nat. Heart, Lung and Blood Inst., Bethesda, Md., 1973-76, acting dir. office program planning, 1975-76, asst. dir. internat. rels., 1976-86, assoc. dir. internat. rels., 1986—. Mem. sci. adv. bd. Giovanni Lorenzini Found., Inc., N.Y.C., Milan, 1982—. Coord. editor: Jour. Soviet Rsch. in Cardiovasc. Diseases, 1979-86; editor: Christopher Columbus Commemorative Book on Discovering New Worlds in Medicine, 1992, Internat. Position Paper: Women's Health and Menopause, A Comprehensive Approach, 2002, also 10 sci. books; contbr. poetry to nat. anthologies. Bd. dirs. Soc. Geriatric Cardiology, chmn. internat. com.; nat. adv. bd. Nat. Mus. Women in Arts. Named Hon. Mem. Eagle Tribe of Haida Indians, Queen Charlotte Islands, B.C., Can., 1961, inductee, Internat. Poetry Hall of Fame, 1997; recipient German Friendship award, German Ministry Rsch. and Tech., 1988, Nicolaus Copernicus medal, Academica Medica, 1988, Superior Svc. award, HEW, 1975, DHHS, 1991. Fellow Acad. Medicine, Toronto; mem. Am. Soc. Artificial Internal Organs, N.Y. Acad. Scis., Acad. Am. Poets, World Literary Acad., Fed. Exec. Alumni Assn. (bd. dirs.). Republican. Avocations: poetry, fiction writing, non-fiction writing, art, music. Home: 24301 Hanson Rd Gaithersburg MD 20882-3501 E-mail: hegyelir@nih.gov.

HEGYVARY, SUE THOMAS, nursing school dean, editor, nursing educator; b. Dry Ridge, Ky., Nov. 28, 1943; BSN, U. Ky., 1965; MN, Emory U., 1966; PhD in Sociology, Vanderbilt U., 1974. Asst. prof. nursing and sociology Rush U. Med. Coll., 1974, assoc. prof. med. nursing, chair dept., 1974-77, asst. prof. sociology, 1977-80; prof. nursing, assoc. v.p., assoc. dean Coll. Nursing Rush Presbyn. St. Luke's Med. Ctr., 1977—86; assoc. prof. sociology Rush U. Med. Coll., 1980—86; dean, prof. Sch. Nursing U. Wash., Seattle, 1986—98, adj. prof. Sch. Pub. Health and Cmty. Med. Mem. health care adv. com. Rep. Jennifer Dunn, 1993-96; vis. com. Bd. 50 Emory U. Sch. Nursing, Atlanta, 1990-92; mem. adv. panel outcomes rsch. Nat. Ctr. Nursing Rsch. NIH, 1990-91; external mem. Five Yr. Review com. Coll. Nursing U. Ky., 1989-90; mem. govtl. affairs com. Am. Assn. Colls. Nursing, 1988-92; chair planning com. Wash. State Conf. Nursing Shortage, 1989; mem. Wash. State Commn. Nursing, 1989; mem. adv. com. Child Devel. & Mental Retardation Ctr. U. Wash., 1986—; mem. task force nursing shortage Seattle Area Hosp. Coun., 1987-88; vis. prof., ann. lectr. Sch. Nursing U. Va., Charlottesville, 1988; vis. prof. U. Oulu, Finland, 1985; site visitor accreditation schs. nursing Nat. League Nursing, 1977-80; cons. VA Hosp., Miami, Fla., 1968-69, Vanderbilt U., Nashville, 1971-72, Area Health Edn. Sys., Rockford, Ill., 1975, Western Interstate Commn. Higher Edn., Denver, 1975, Andrews U., Berrian Springs, Mich., 1976, dept. nursing studies Nat. Hosp. Inst., Utrecht, The Netherlands, 1976-80, Haukeland Sykehaus, Bergen, Norway, 1976-77, Sch. Nursing Mar-

quette U., Milw., 1977, Wayne State U., Detroit, 1978, Cath. U. Leuven, Belgium, 1980, Walter Reed Army Med. Ctr., Washington, 1979-83, Dalhousie U. Sch. Nursing, Halifax, N.S., 1981, U. Minn., Mpls., 1988, U. Mo., Columbia, 1992. Editl. adv. bd. Nursing Policy Forum, 1995-96; editl. cons. Nursing Care Guide Pfizer Corp., 1993; editl. bd. Jour. Nursing & Health, 1993—, Nursing Adminstrn. Quarterly, 1988—; mem. manucscript review panel Jour. Nursing Quality Assurance, 1986—, Nursing Outlook, 1983—, Jour. Rsch. Nursing & Health, 1981—, Nursing Rsch., 1979-89; contbr. chpts. to books and articles to profl. jours. Mem. ANA, Am. Acad. Nursing, Sigma Theta Tau. Office: U Wash Sch Nursing BNHS PO Box 357266 Seattle WA 98195-7266

HEIBERG, ROBERT ALAN, lawyer; b. St. Cloud, Minn., June 29, 1943; s. Rasmus Adolph and Irene (Shaffer) H.; m. Sharon Ann Olson, Aug. 2, 1969; children— Eric Robert, Mark Alan, Maren Ann BA summa cum laude, U. Minn., 1965, JD summa cum laude, 1968. Bar: Minn. 1968. Law clk. to assoc. justice Minn. Supreme Ct., 1968-69; assoc. Dorsey & Whitney, Mpls., 1969-73, ptnr., 1974—; instr. Law Sch., U. Minn., 1968-72, instr. legal assts. program, 1972-77. Articles editor Minn. Law Rev., 1967-68 Mem. adv. com. U. Minn. Legal Assts. Program, 1977-84, bd. visitors Law Sch., 1991-96. Mem. ABA (sect. real property, probate and trust law), Minn. Bar Assn. (chmn. com. on legal assts. 1979), Hennepin County Bar Assn., Am. Rose Soc. (accredited judge 1996), Order of Coif, Phi Beta Kappa Republican. Lutheran. Home: 4510 Wooddale Ave Minneapolis MN 55424-1137 Office: Dorsey & Whitney 50 S 6th St Ste 1500 Minneapolis MN 55402-1498 E-mail: heiberg.robert@dorseylaw.com.

HEICHEL, GARY HAROLD, crop sciences educator; b. Park Falls, Wis., Nov. 9, 1940; s. Harold H. and Bernice I. (Comp) H.; m. Iris Fehl Martin, Apr. 24, 1988. BS, Iowa State U., 1962; MS, Cornell U., 1964, PhD, 1968; D of Natural Scis. (hon.), Swiss Fed. Inst. Tech., Zurich, 1998. Asst. plant physiologist Conn. Agrl. Expt. Stat., New Haven, 1968-73, assoc. plant physiologist, 1973-76, plant physiologist, 1976, USDA Agrl. Rsch. Svc., St. Paul, 1976-90, acting rsch. leader, 1988-90; head agronomy dept. U. Ill., Urbana, 1990-95, interim head plant pathology dept., 1994-95, head crop scis. dept., 1995—. Adj. prof. agronomy U. Minn., 1976-90; program mgr. USDA Competitive Rsch Grants Office, 1981. Contbr. chpts. to books, articles to profl. jours. Pres., mem. adminstrv. bd. Cheshire, Conn. United Meth. Ch., 1973-76, v.p. Cheshire Land Trust, 1975-76. Named Civil Servant of Yr., Twin Cities Fed. Exec. Bd., St. Paul, 1984; Paul Harris fellow Rotary Internat., 2002. Fellow AAAS (chair sect. 0 1997-98), Crop Sci. Soc. Am. (pres. 1991-92, award 1987), Am. Soc. Agronomy (exec. com. 1990-92, pres. north ctrl. sect. 1991-93, pres. 1997-98, Svc. award 2001), Am. Soc. Plant Physiologists (trustee 1988-90), Urbana Rotary (bd. dirs. 1997-99). Avocations: classical music, reading, hiking, gardening. Office: U Ill Dept Crop Scis 1102 S Goodwin Ave AW-101 Urbana IL 61801-4730 E-mail: gheichel@uiuc.edu.

HEID, MICHAEL PATRICK, surgeon; b. Miami, Fla. s. Patrick Joseph and Yvonne (Gregory) H. BS in Biology, BA in Psychology, U. South Fla., 1987; D of Osteo. Medicine, Nova Southeastern Coll. Osteopathic Medicine, 1993. Resident in gen. surgery Sun Coast Hosp., Largo, Fla., 1994-98; fellow in surg. critical care Ryder Trauma Ctr., U. Miami, 1998-99; gen. surgeon Surg. Assocs., Clearwater, Fla., 1999—. With USCG, 1979-91. Mem. AMA, Am. Osteo. Assn., Am. Coll. Osteo. Surgeons, Soc. Critical Care Medicine. Democrat. Roman Catholic. Avocations: running, cycling. Office: Surg Assocs 1305 S Fort Harrison Ave Ste H Clearwater FL 33756-3301 Fax: 727-443-6604.

HEIDE, JOHN WESLEY, engineering executive; b. Chgo., Sept. 14, 1946; s. Frederick Bernard Heiner-Heide and Eleanor Francis (Tuttle) Heide; m. Patricia Ann Lynn, Aug. 5, 1967 (div. Jan. 1973); m. Carol G. Gutierrez, Sept. 27, 1999; children: John Wesley, Joseph Edward, Adela B., Monica, Nicholas B., Johanna M. AA, Phoenix Jr. Coll., 1972; BS, Ariz. State U., 1975. Quality assurance engr. Tex. Instruments, Dallas, 1969-70, ITT Courier, Tempe, Ariz., 1975-79; sr. project engr. GTE Comms., El Paso, 1979-83, Telxon Corp., Houston, 1983-87; engring. mgr. United Techs., Niles, Mich., 1987-91, Automotive Industries, Midland, Tex., 1991-94; divsn. quality assurance mgr. Pec Golden Triangle Plastics, El Paso, Tex., 1994-95; indsl. engring. mgr. Elcom, Inc., El Paso, Tex., 1995-97; quality assurance mgr. United for Excellence Inc., El Paso, 1997-99; TQM mgr. Dayco Inc., El Paso, 1999—. Instr. engring. Houston C.C., 1984—85. Author: Reflections, 1990, Scan-It, 1991, A Step Beyond the Fog, 1992, How Cheap Is Cheap, 1993, None but the Brave Walk Alone, 1994, Beyond the Scope, 2001, Tootsie Roll Man, 2002. Candidate for mayor, El Paso, 1980, 82, 84; candidate for State Rep., Berrien Springs, Mich., 1990. With USMC, 1965-69, Vietnam. Mem. NSPE, Soc. Plastics Engrs. (pres.), Inst. Indsl. Engring. (v.p. 1982-83), Soc. Mfg. Engrs. (v.p.), Am. Soc. Quality Control (v.p.). Republican. Lutheran. Avocations: European travel, genealogy, stamp and coin collecting. Home: 9920 Minuteman El Paso TX 79924-1647 Office: 425-B Pan American Dr El Paso TX 79007

HEIDE, KATHLEEN MARGARET, criminology educator, psychotherapist; b. Englewood, N.J., May 25, 1954; d. Victory Hillary and Eleanor (Mulhearn) H. BA in Psychology, Vassar Coll., 1976; MA in Criminal Justice, SUNY, Albany, 1978, PhD in Criminal Justice, 1982. Lic. mental health counselor, Fla.; diplomate Nat. Bd. for Clin. Hypnotherapists; cert. practitioner level So. Inst. Neurolinguistic Programming; lic. psychotherapist Ctr. for Mental Health. Asst. prof. criminology U. South Fla., Tampa, 1981-87, assoc. prof., 1987-94, prof., 1994—. Paper presenter in field to profl. assns. Author: Why Kids Kill Parents: Child Abuse and Adolescent Homicide, 1992, Young Killers: The Challenge of Juvenile Homicide, 1999; mem. editl. bd. Homicide Studies, 1996—; assoc. editor Internat. Jour. Offender Therapy and Comparative Criminology, 1995—. Bd. dirs. Hillsborough County Sexual Abuse Treatment Ctr., Tampa, 1983-87, Hillsborough County Crisis Ctr., 1983-87, Hillsborough Constituency for Children, 1994—. Recipient tchg. award Golden Key, 1993, award So. Sunshine Video Festival, 1995. Mem. APA, Am. Soc. Criminology, Acad. Criminal Justice Scis., Homicide Rsch. Working Group, Tampa Bay Assn. for Women Psychotherapists (pres. 1997-98). Avocations: swimming, boating. Office: U So Fla Dept Criminology 4202 E Fowler Ave Tampa FL 33620-8100 E-mail: kathleenheide@aol.com.

HEIDEL, RICHARD MARK, music educator; s. John Richard and Bertie Bell Heidel; m. Kelly Kay Conklin, Dec. 29, 1971. EdD in Music Edn., U. of Ill., Urbana-Champaign, Illinois, 1995—97; MusM, Tex. Tech U., Lubbock, Texas, 1986—89, MusB Edn., 1982—86. Professional Teaching Certificate Tex. Edn. Agy./Tex., 1986. Dir. of bands Muleshoe H.S., Muleshoe, Tex., 1986—90, Levelland H.S., Levelland, Tex., 1990—93, Monterey H.S., Lubbock, Tex., 1993—95; tchg. asst. U. of Ill., Urbana-Champaign, Ill., 1995—97; dir. of bands Shippensburg U. of Pa, Shippensburg, Pa., 1997—2000, U. of Wis., Eau Claire, Wis., 2000—. Cons. Gettysburg H.S., Gettysburg, Pa., 1998—, Cibola H.S., Rio Rancho, N.Mex., 1997—, Bolingbrook H.S., Bolingbrook, Ill., 1999—2001. Author: (four articles published) Journal of the National Band Association, (journal article) Teaching Music; musician: (performance) Wisconsin Music Educators Association State Conference; contbr. presentation. Mem. Tech Band Alumni Assn., Lubbock, Tex., 1991—93. Recipient Membership, Outstanding Young Men of Am., 1989, Tchr. of the Yr., Muleshoe H.S., 1990, A. A. Harding Award, U. of Ill., 1997, Hon. Membership, Phi Mu Alpha Sinfonia, 2002, Membership, Who's Who Among America's Teachers, 2002. Mem.: Wis. Sch. Music Assn., Wis. Music Educators Assn., Music Educators Nat. Conf., Coll. Band Directors Nat. Conf., Nat. Band Assn. R-Consevative. Protestant. Avocations: civil war history, civil war history, overseas travel, snow skiing. Home: 3323 Midway Street Eau Claire WI 54703 Office: University of Wisconsin-Eau Claire 105 Garfield Avenue Eau Claire WI 54702-4004 Home Fax: 715-836-3952; Office Fax: 715-836-3952. Personal E-mail: heidelrm@uwec.edu. E-mail: heidelrm@uwec.edu.

HEIDELBERG, PAUL, writer; b. Austin, Tex., Dec. 23, 1948; s. James Martin and Alice Huebinger Heidelberg. BFA, San Francisco Art Inst., 1975. Author: (novels) Oceans Apart, 1988, Cook's Return, 1991, (Internet publ.) Paris, Prague and Salzburg: A Remembrance, 1999, poems; contbr. to jours. and mags. With USAF, 1966—70. Mem. Poetry Soc. Am., Hemingway Collection, J.F. Kennedy Libr. Avocations: hiking, bicycling. Home and Office: 715 B NE 17th Ave Fort Lauderdale FL 33304 E-mail: paulheidelberg@yahoo.com.

HEIDELBERGER, KATHLEEN PATRICIA, physician; b. Bklyn., Apr. 13, 1939; d. William Cyprian and Margaret Bernadette (Hughes) H.; m. Charles William Davenport, Oct. 8, 1977. BS cum laude, Coll. Misericordia, 1961; MD cum laude, Woman's Med. Coll. Pa., 1965. Intern Mary Hitchcock Hosp., Hanover, N.H., 1965-66, resident in pathology, 1966-70; mem. faculty U. Mich., Ann Arbor, 1970—, assoc. prof. pathology, 1976-79, prof., 1979—2002; ret., 2002. Mem. Am. Soc. Clin. Pathologists, U.S.-Can. Acad. Pathology, Soc. for Pediatric Pathology, Coll. Am. Pathologists.

HEIDEMANN, ROBERT ALBERT, chemical engineering educator, researcher; b. St. Louis, Aug. 31, 1936; emigrated to Can., 1968; s. William Joseph and Gladys Emilie (Digman) H.; m. Linda Bea Szold, June 9, 1968; children: David, Douglas. B.Sc. in Chem. Engring., Washington U., St. Louis, 1958; Sc.D., Washington U., 1966. Asst. prof. chem. engring. Drexel Inst. Tech., Phila., 1963-68; assoc. prof. U. Calgary (Alta.), 1968-77, prof., 1977—2002, head dept. chem. and petroleum engring., 1981-92, prof. emeritus, 2002—. Vis. prof. Tech. U. Denmark, 1986-87; cons., 1982— Co-author: (with A.A. Jeje and M.F. Mohtadi) Properties of Fluids and Solids, 1984; contbr. articles to profl. jours. Fellow Chem. Inst. Can.; mem. Canadian Soc. Chem. Engrs., Am. Inst. Chem. Engrs., Am. Chem. Soc., Am. Soc. Engring. Edn., Assn. Profl. Engrs., Geologists and Geophysicists of Alta., Tau Beta Pi Home: 63 Discovery Ridge Pt SW Calgary AB Canada T3H 4R1 Office: U Calgary 2500 University Dr NW Calgary AB Canada T2N 1N4 E-mail: heideman@ucalgary.ca.

HEIDEN, CHARLES KENNETH, retired military officer; b. Detroit, July 7, 1925; s. Carl William and Elsie Mae (Langley) H.; m. Nancy Earle Gray, June 7, 1949; 1 son, Charles Gray. BS, U.S. Mil. Acad., 1949; MS in Mech. Engring, U. Mich., 1957; grad. mgmt. execs. program, U. Pitts., 1971. Registered profl. engr., Ky. Enlisted U.S. Army, 1943, commd. 2d lt., 1949, advanced through grades to maj. gen., 1977; services in Panama, France, Korea and Vietnam; dep. dir. ops. Nat. Mil. Command Center, Joint Chiefs of Staff, 1973-74; dir. enlisted personnel U.S. Mil. Personnel Center, Washington, 1974-76; comdr. U.S. Army Mil. Personnel Center, 1977-80; comdg. gen. U.S. Army Tng. Ctr., Ft. Dix, N.J., 1980-81; pres., dir. Montel Metals Inc., 1981-83, Cedar Lake Lodge Inc., La Grange, Ky., 1985-86, chmn. bd. dirs., 1982—98, chmn. emeritus, 1998—; cons. Computer Simulation, 1987-98; chmn. bd. dirs. Cedar Lake, Inc., La Grange, 1994-98, chmn. emeritus, 1998—. Bd. dirs. Park Glen Heights Assn., Annandale, Va., 1974-76, Seven Counties Svcs., 2000—; pres. Our Saviour Luth. Ch., Arlington, Va., 1974-76; mem. code enforcement bd. City Jeffersontown, Ky., 1998-2000. Decorated D.S.M., D.F.C., Legion of Merit with 3 oak leaf clusters, Air medal with 10 oak leaf clusters, Joint Services Commendation medal, Army Commendation medal with 2 oak leaf clusters, Meritorious Service medal with oak leaf cluster; Cross of Gallantry with silver star Vietnam; recipient Pace award Office Sec. Army, 1963 Mem. Armed Forces Relief and Benefit Assn. (dir. 1977-81), West Point Alumni Assn., Forest Garden Assn. (chmn. and pres. 2001—), Am. Legion, U.S. Army War Coll. Alumni Assn. Home: 10500 Forest Garden Ln Louisville KY 40223-6166

HEIDENRY, JOHN M. editor; b. St. Louis, May 15, 1939; s. John Joseph Heidenry and Margaret Adele Morrison; m. Patricia Ann Reynolds, May 30, 1964; children: Mary, John Shakespeare, James Joyce, Margaret. BA, St. Louis U., 1961; Dr. Arts, Inst. for Advanced Study of Human Sexuality, San Francisco, 1999. Reporter St. Louis Rev., 1961—63; mng. editor Herder and Herder, N.Y.C., 1963—73; editor, founder St. Louis Lit. Supplement, 1976—77; editor-in-chief St. Louis Mag., 1977—82; editor Forum Mag., N.Y.C., 1982—89; exec. editor The Week Mag., N.Y.C., 2000—. Author: Theirs Was the Kingdom, 1993, What Wild Ecstasy, 1997. Democrat. Episcopalian. Home: 33-51 80th St Jackson Heights NY 11372 Office: The Week 1040 Sixth Ave New York NY 10018

HEIDER, ANNE HARRINGTON, music educator; BA, Wellesley Coll., 1963; MA, NYU, 1965; DMA, Stanford U., 1981. Assoc. prof., resident choral condr. Roosevelt U.; artistic dir. Bella Voce Profl. Chamber Choir. Recipient Tempo All-Prof. Team, Humanities award, 1993. Office: Roosevelt U Coll Performing Arts 430 S Michigan Ave Chicago IL 60605

HEIDER, JON VINTON, retired lawyer, corporate executive; b. Moline, Ill., Mar. 1, 1934; s. Raymond and Doris (Hinch) H.; m. Barbara L. Bond, Dec. 27, 1960 (div.); children: Loren P., John C., Lindsay L.; m. Mary R. Murray, Jan. 27, 1984. AB, U. Wis., 1956; JD, Harvard U., 1961; grad., Advanced Mgmt. Program, 1974. Bar: Pa. 1962, U.S. Dist. Ct. (ea. dist.) Pa. 1962, U.S. Ct. Appeals (3d cir.) 1962, U.S. Supreme Ct. 1991. Assoc. Morgan Lewis & Bockius, Phila., 1961-66; counsel Catalytic, Inc., Phila., 1966-68, Houdry Process & Chem. Co., Phila., 1968-70; counsel chems. group Air Products & Chems., Inc., Valley Forge, Pa., 1970-75, asst. gen. counsel, 1975-76, assoc. gen. counsel, 1976-78, gen. counsel Allentown, Pa., 1978-80; v.p. corp. affairs, sr. adminstrv. officer-Europe, Air Products Europe, Inc., London, 1980-83; v.p. corp. devel. Air Products & Chems., Inc., 1983-84; v.p., gen. counsel BF Goodrich Co., Akron, Ohio, 1984-88, sr. v.p., gen. counsel, 1988-94, exec. v.p., gen. counsel, 1994-98; ret., 1998. Trustee U. Akron, Bluecoats, Inc.; mem. distbn. com. Charles E. and Mabel M. Ritchie Meml. Found. Lt. USNR, 1956-58. Mem. Assn. Gen. Counsel, Blossom Music Ctr. Bd. Overseers, Sisler McFawn Found. (chmn. distbn. com.), Portage Country Club, Rolling Rock Club, Key Biscayne Yacht Club. E-mail: JHeider-Fl@msn.com.

HEIDISH, LOUISE ORIDGE-SCHWALLIE, transportation specialist, marketing professional; b. Cin., May 21, 1938; d. Leslie Jacob and Louise (Oridge) Schwallie; m. William Edward Heidish, Sept. 2, 1961; children: Sara Louise Heidish-Hurst, Amy Jean. BA in History, Denison U., 1960; MA in History, Miami U., Oxford, Ohio, 1962; MS in Urban Studies, Ala. A&M U., 1994. Secondary tchr. Fox Chapel Sch. Dist., Pitts., 1962-69; part-time instr. U. Ala., Huntsville, 1976-78; substitute history tchr. City of Huntsville Schs., 1977-79; dir. comm. svcs. Heidish Enterprises, Huntsville, 1979-83; transp. specialist City of Huntsville, 1981—. Regional 5 state coord. AAUW and NEH, Huntsville, 1981-83. Author: Biography: Alexander Long 1816-86, 1962, Marketing Ride Sharing, 1994; co-editor: Glimpses into Antebellum Homes, Huntsville, AL, 1999. Mem., project chair, bd. dirs. Huntsville Symphony Orch. Guild, 1974—; sec. Huntsville-Madison County Sr. Ctr., 1981, v.p., 1982, pres., 1983; v.p. Huntsville High Sch. PTA, 1985—86, pres., 1986—88; com. chmn. Panoply of the Arts Festival, Huntsville, 1985—87; mem. adv. bd. women's studies U. Ala., Huntsville, 1998—; mem. adv. bd. capital campaign Fantasy Playhouse, 1998—; publicity chair Huntesville-Madison County Libr. Benefit, 1999; 1st v.p. Huntsville Symphony Orch. Guild, 2001—02, pres., 2002—; mem. benefit com. Greater Huntsvile Humane Soc. Dog Ball, 2001; mem. Huntsville-Madison Co. Leadership Class, 2002—; bd. dirs. search com. Huntsville Symphony Orch. Assn., 2000—03. Mem.: AAUW (local pres. 1979—81, state v.p. 1981—83, regional coord. 1981—83, Outstanding Local Svc. award 1999), S.E. Assn. for Commuter Transp. (regional conf. chair 1995, chpt. treas. 1996, 1997, nat. conf. com. 2000), Pub. Rels. Coun. No. Ala. (newsletter editor 1993, conf. treas. 1994, coun. treas. 1995, coun. sec. 1996, v.p. profl. devel. 1997, v.p. membership 1998, 1999, v.p. projects 2000, pres. 2001, bd. dirs. 1993—, v.p. 1997—2000, pres. 2001), Kappa Kappa Gamma (regional officer 1958—, alumnae officer, local pres., Outstanding Kappa Kappa Gamma Svc. award 4 state region 1997). Presbyterian. Avocations: community arts volunteering, reading, swimming. Office: Pub Transp City Huntsville 500B Church St SW Huntsville AL 35801-4908

HEIDLER, JEANNE TWIGGS, adult education educator; b. Atlanta, Jan. 20, 1956; d. Joseph L. and Sarah Daniel Twiggs; m. David Stephen Heidler, June 13, 1981. PhD, Auburn U., Ala., 1988. Prof. history USAF Acad., Colo., 1993—. Bd. dirs., adv. to internat. org. World History Assn., Phila., 1995—98; editl. bd. Ala. Rev., Montgomery, Ala., 1998—2001. Co-author: (book) Old Hickory's War: Andrew Jackson and the Quest for Empire, The War of 1812, Manifest Destiny, (jour. article) Alabama Review; co-editor: (book) Encyclopedia of the War of 1812, Encyclopedia of the American Civil War (Soc. for Mil. History Disting. Book award, 2001, Dartmouth medal Honorable Mention, 2001, Independent Publ. Assn. Best Reference Work, 2001); contbr. book. Mem.: Soc. for Mil. History (Disting. Book award 2003), So. Hist. Assn., Phi Alpha Theta. Avocations: gardening, hiking. Home: 187 Dolomite Dr Colorado Springs CO 80919 Office: Dept of History Fairchild Dr United States Air Force Academy CO 80840 Personal E-mail: jtheidler@msn.com.

HEIDRICH, ROBERT WESLEY, lawyer; b. Chgo., Aug. 1, 1927; s. Carl G. and Harriet B. (Butzlaff) H.; m. Lennice L. Hubenbecker, June 19, 1948; children: John G., Robert G., Kimberly L. Student, U. Wis., 1944-45, 47-48; JD, DePaul U., 1951. Bar: Ill. 1951, Calif. 1974, Tenn. 1980. Atty. Brunswick Corp., Chgo., 1953-60, 65-69; v.p. Brunswick AG (Switzerland), 1960-61; dir. Brunswick Internat. Fin. AG (Switzerland), 1962-65; sec., corp. counsel Nat. Can Corp., Chgo., 1969-73; v.p., sec., gen. counsel, dir. Rohr Industries, Inc., Chula Vista, Calif., 1973-79; corp. v.p., gen. counsel Holiday Inn Hotels, Memphis, 1979-85; counsel Kaiser Steel Corp., LaVerne, Calif., 1985-87, San Diego Real Estate Devel., 1987—. Chmn. Riverside-Brookfield CMty. Caucus, 1972; bd. dirs., Am. Internat. Sch. Zurich, 1964-65; chmn. Jr. Achievement, Chgo., 1970-75. Served with U.S. Army, 1945-47. Mem. Frederick Law Olmstead Soc. (founding pres. 1967-69). Home: 5157 Long Branch Ave Apt 4 San Diego CA 92107-2032 Office: San Diego Devel PO Box 70075 San Diego CA 92167

HEIDSIECK, ARNOLD, literature educator; b. Leipzig, Germany, Feb. 20, 1937; PhD, Free U. Berlin, Germany, 1966. Asst. prof. NYU, NYC, 1966—73; prof. U. of So. Calif., German, Comparative Lit., Los Angeles, Calif., 1975—. Author: The Intellectual Contexts of Kafka's Fiction. Home: 11 23rd Ave Venice CA 90291 Office: U So Calif Thh 402 Los Angeles CA 90089-0351 Personal E-mail: heidsiec@usc.edu.

HEIGAARD, WILLIAM STEVEN, state senator; b. Gardar, N.D., May 18, 1938; s. Oliver and Gaufey (Erickson) H.; m. Paula Geston, 1960; children: Jody, Rebecca, Sara. BA, U. N.D., 1961, JD, 1967. Bar: N.D. 1967. Asst. atty. gen., Bismarck, N.D., 1970-75; mem. N.D. Ho. of Reps., 1980-81, N.D. State Senate, 1981-92, majority leader, 1987-92; chmn. N.D. State Dem. Party, 2000—01. 1st lt. U.S. Army, 1962-64. Mem. Am. Legion, Eagles, Elks, Phi Delta Phi. Democrat. Lutheran. Office: 1116 N 14th St Bismarck ND 58501-4201 also: ND Democratic Party 1902 E Divide Ave Bismarck ND 58501-2301

HEIGH, RUSSELL IRWIN, gastroenterologist; b. Bklyn., Mar. 17, 1956; BS summa cum laude, L.I. U., 1979; MD, SUNY, Syracuse, 1983. Diplomate Am. Bd. Internal Medicine, Am. Bd. Gastroenterology, Am. Coll. Physician Executives. Intern in internal medicine George Washington U. Med. Ctr., Washington, 1983-84, resident in internal medicine, 1984-86, fellow in gastroenterology, 1986-88; sr. assoc. cons. in gastroenterology Mayo Clinic Rochester, MN, 1988, Mayo Clinic Scottsdale, AZ, 1988-90, cons. in gastroenterology, 1991—. Pres., chmn. of bd. Mayo Health Plan Ariz., Scottsdale, 1997—; mem. bd. govs. Mayo Clinic Scottsdale, 1995—2002, chair managed care activities, 1998—2000, vice-chair bd. govs., 2000—01; mem. Group Practice Bd. Mayo Found., Rochester, Minn., 1997—2002; asst. prof. medicine Mayo Found., 1992. Contbr. articles to profl. jours. Charter mem., bd. trustees Ariz. chpt. Crohn's and Colitis Found. Am., Phoenix, 1995-98; charter mem., bd. dirs. Ariz. chpt. Am. Liver Found., 1991-93. Named Top Doc in Gastroenterology, Phoenix Mag., 1995, Phoenix, 1998, Phoenix Mag., 2002, Col., Hon. Order Ky. Cols. Fellow ACP, Am. Coll. Gastroenterology (bog. 2002—); del. Am. Med. Group Assn.; mem. Am. Gastroenterology Assn., Am. Coll. Physician Execs. Avocations: biking, fishing, kayaking. Office: Mayo Clinic Scottsdale 13400 E Shea Blvd Scottsdale AZ 85259-5499 E-mail: heigh.russell@mayo.edu.

HEIGHAM, JAMES CRICHTON, lawyer; b. Sheffield, Eng., Feb. 9, 1930; came to U.S., 1940; s. Clement and Vida (Crichton) H.; m. Katherine Little, Feb. 24, 1962; children: Thomas K. Blake, Susan Blake, Christopher J. AB, Harvard U., 1951, LLB, 1954. Bar: Mass. 1954, U.S. Supreme Ct. 1970. Assoc. Choate, Hall & Stewart, Boston, 1957-59, 62-65, ptnr., 1966-97; asst. U.S. atty. Dept. of Justice, Boston, 1960-61; ret. ptnr. Choate, Hall & Stewart, Boston, 1997—. Spl. asst. atty. gen. Commonwealth of Mass., Boston, 1968. Chmn. Planning Bd., Belmont, Mass., 1980-94, Capital Budget Com., 1980-94, chmn. fin. com., 1997—. 1st lt. USMC, 1954-57, lt. col. USMC ret. Mem. ABA, Mass. Bar Assn., Boston Bar Assn. Home: 62 Orchard St Belmont MA 02478-3510 Office: Choate Hall & Stewart 53 State St Exchange Pl Boston MA 02109 Fax: 617 248-4000.

HEIKEN, JAY PAUL, physician; b. N.Y.C., Aug. 31, 1952; s. Martin and Sylvia (Fisher) H.; m. Barbara Ellen Rayburn, Dec. 11, 1976 (div. 1982); m. Francine J. Rosen, Apr. 29, 1990; 1 child, Lauren M. BA, Williams Coll., 1974; MD, Columbia U., 1978. Intern Emory U. Hosp., Atlanta, 1978-79; resident in radiology Columbia-Presbyn. Med. Ctr., N.Y.C., 1979-82; fellow abdominal radiology Mallinckrodt Inst. Radiology, St. Louis, 1982-83; asst. prof. Washington U. Sch. Medicine, St. Louis, 1983-87, assoc. prof., 1988-93, prof., 1993—. Dir. abdominal imaging and co-dir. body computed tomography Mallinckrodt Inst. Radiology, St. Louis; mem. Washington U. Cancer Ctr. Author, editor: Manual of Clinical Magnetic Resonance Imaging, 1986, 2d edit., 1991, Computed Body Tomography with MRI Correlation, 3d edit., 1998; contbr. articles to profl. jours. Mem. AMA, Radiol. Soc. N.Am., Am. Roentgen Ray Soc., Am. Coll. Radiology, Greater St. Louis Soc. Radiologists, Soc. Computed Body Tomography and Magnetic Resonance, Internat. Soc. Magnetic Resonance in Medicine, Soc. Gastrointestinal Radiologists, Assn. Univ. Radiologists, Internat. Cancer Imaging Soc. Avocations: skiing, tennis, softball, wine tasting. Home: 1801 Aston Way Chesterfield MO 63005-4579 Office: Mallinckrodt Inst Radiology 510 S Kingshighway Blvd Saint Louis MO 63110-1076 E-mail: heikenj@mir.wustl.edu.

HEIKES, KEITH, science administrator; b. 1957; With Ralston Purina, Chilicothe, Mo., 1978—81, Kabsu, Inc., Manhattan, Kans., 1981—90, Noba Inc., Tiffin, Ohio, 1990—, now COO; v.p. internat. programs 21st Century Genetics; with Coop. Resources Internat., Shawano, Wis. Office: Coop Resources Internat 100 Mbc Dr Shawano WI 54166-6095

HEIL, KATHLEEN ANN, librarian; b. Easton, Pa., Sept. 22, 1949; d. Peter J. and Emily Elizabeth (Miller) H.; m. John Edward Zampier, Aug. 21, 1971; children: Kirsten Lynn, Heather Ann. BS, Millersville State U., 1971; MLS, U. Md., 1987. Librarian Caroline County Sch. System, Denton, Md., 1971-73; library asst. Meml. Hosp., Easton, Md., 1973-76; grants adminstr. Talbot County Public Library, Easton, 1976-80; cons. U. Md. Ctr. on Aging, College Park, 1979-84; grant adminstr. Somerset County Pub. Library, Princess Anne, Md., 1980-82; librarian U. Md., Solomons, Md., 1983—. Sec. Talbot County Interagency Council, Easton, Md., 1977-79, sec. U. Md. Sys. Libarary Dirs., 1996-97. Contbr. articles to profl. jours. Pres. Calvert H.S. Band Boosters, Prince Frederick, Md., 1990-91; sec. South Middle Sch. Music Supporters, Lusby, Md., 1988-89, 92-93; lay leader Olivet United Methodist Ch., Lusby, 1984-91, 98—; leader-disciple Olivet-Solomons Charge, Lusby, 1996—. Recipient Curve Bar Girl Scounts, Easton, Penn., 1967. Mem. Internat. Assn. of Aquatic and Marine Sci. Librs. and Info. Ctrs. (treas. 1996-98). Avocations: gardening, costume design, choir. Home: 12963 Ottawa Dr Lusby MD 20657-3255 Office: U Md Ctr for Environ Sci Chesapeake Biol Lab 1 William St Solomons MD 20688

HEIL, MARY RUTH, former counselor; b. Westerville, Ohio, June 8, 1921; d. George Walter and Bertha Ellen (Shrodes) H. BS in Edn., Ohio State U., 1944; MEd, Wayne State U., 1956; cert. advanced study, Western Carolina U., 1987; cert. theol. edn., U. South, 1987. Cert. counselor, tchr., Ohio, Ky., Mich., Fla., N.C. Tchr. 7th grade Cheshire (Ohio) Sch., 1942-43; tchr. biology, English Ohio Soldiers' and Sailors' Orphans' Home, Xenia, 1943-47; tchr. 7th grade Lakeview High Sch., Winter Garden, Fla., 1947-48; tchr. English, journalism Pine Mountain (Ky.) Settlement Sch., 1948-49; field and established camp dir. Columbus (Ohio) and Franklin County Girl Scouts, 1949-50; tchr. Mary Lyon Jr. High Sch., Royal Oak, Mich., 1950-56, 57-62, Coston Secondary Modern Girls' Sch., Greenford, Middlesex, Eng., 1956-57; tchr. English West Henderson High Sch., Hendersonville, N.C., 1962-65, guidance counselor, 1965-86. Chmn. Mayor's Com. Employment of Handicapped, Hendersonville, 1972-74; v.p. Mountain Ramparts Health Planning Bd., Asheville, N.C., 1972-76, Western Carolina Health Systems Agy. Bd., Morganton, N.C., 1976-82; bd. dirs., sec., com. chmn., Henderson County Dispute Settlement Bd., 1989-95; exec. com., bd. dirs. Western Carolina Presbyn. Retirement Com., 1987-94; active Henderson County Coun. Women, Hendersonville, 1994-96, treas.; mem.-at-large Pisgah coun. Girl Scouts U.S., 1994-98, chair fund devel. com., 1995-98, exec. com., 1997-98; bd. dirs. Henderson County Coun. on Aging, 1998-2001, chair nominating com., 1999. Named Woman of Achievement, Hendersonville Bus. and Profl. Women's Club, 1978, Civitan Citizen of Yr., Civitan Club, Hendersonville, 1986; named to Order Ky. Cols., 1988; recipient

award, Galludent U., Washington, 1986, Thanks Badge, Pisgah Coun., Girl Scouts U.S., 1998, state degree of Style, Dignity, Title and Honor of Dame, Baron of Shalford, Eng., 2000, cert., Rt. Hon. Thomas de Shalford, 2000. Mem. NEA, ACA, Royal Oak Edn. Assn. (pres. 1954-56), N.C. Assn. Educators (pres. dist. 1970-72), Henderson County Mental Health Assn. (bd. dirs. 1965-74), Alpha Delta Kappa (N.C. 1st v.p. 1978-80, state pres. 1980-82, S.E. region grand v.p. 1987 89), Kappa Delta Pi. Democrat. Episcopalian. Avocations: golf, bowling, raising irish setters, classical music. Home: 726 Academy Rd Hendersonville NC 28792-9428

HEIL, MICHAEL LLOYD, military officer, academic administrator; BS in Engring. Scis., USAF Acad., Colo., 1975; MS in Flight Structures, Columbia U., 1976; PhD in Solid Mechanics, Air Force Inst. Tech., 1986; MS in Nat. Resource Strategy, Indsl. Coll. of Armed Forces, 1994. Registered profl. engr., Colo. Commd. 2d lt. USAF, 1975, advanced through grades to col., 1995; structural engr. F-15 Sys. Program Office, Wright-Patterson AFB, 1976—79; asst. prof. engring. mechanics, exec. officer Dept. Engring. Mechanics, USAF Acad., 1979—83; chief C-17 Structures Divsn., C-17 Sys. Program Office, Wright-Patterson AFB, Ohio, 1986—88; advanced cruise missile variant program mgr. Advanced Cruise Missile Sys. Program Office, Wright-Patterson AFB, Ohio, 1988—89; dep. dir. Astronautical Scis. Divsn., Astronautics Lab., Edwards AFB, Calif., 1989—90, Propulsion Directorate, Phillips Lab., Edwards AFB, Calif., 1990—93; asst. dir. countermeasures Ballistic Missile Def. Orgn., The Pentagon, Washington, 1994—95; comdr. Air Force Phillips Lab., Kirtland AFB, N.Mex., 1995—97; insp. gen. Hqrs. Air Force Material Command, Wright-Patterson AFB, 1997—98; comdr. Arnold Engring. Devel. Ctr., Arnold AFB, Tenn., 1998—2001; comdt. Air Force Inst. Tech., Wright-Patterson AFB, 2001—03; dir. propusion directorate Air Force Rsch. Lab., Wright-Patterson AFB, 2003—. Decorated Legion of Merit with two oak leaf clusters, Air Force Commendation medal. Office: Air Force Rsch Lab Office of Pub Affairs Dayton OH 45433-7765 Home: 2247 Princess Dr Beavercreek OH 45434

HEIL, PAUL SAMUEL, radio program producer; b. Reading, Pa., June 8, 1947; s. David Paul and Virginia May (Gaul) H.; m. Shelia Kay Troyer, Dec. 19, 1982; children: Jason David, Andrew Troy. BA in English, Elizabethtown Coll., 1969. News dir. Sta. WGAL Radio, Lancaster, Pa., 1969-77; news anchor Sta. WSBA Radio, York, Pa., 1977; news dir. Sta. WGAL-TV, Lancaster, 1977-79; owner, exec. producer The Gospel Greats, Lancaster, 1979—; owner Springside Mktg., Lancaster, 1986—. Producer, host weekly 2 hour nationally syndicated Gospel Greats program, 1980—. Monthly columnist Christian Music News, 1986-87, Singing News Mag., 1987-94. Recipient Silver Mike award So. Gospel Music Assn., 1983-84, Fan award Singing News, 1986-98, Marvin Norcross award, 1991; named Favorite Gospel Disk Jockey So. Gospel Music News, 1984, People's Choice Favorite Disk Jockey Gospel Music News, 1985, 86, 87. Mem. So. Gospel Music Guild (founder 1986, pres. 1990-99), Gospel Music Assn. (v.p. 1991-92), So. Gospel Music Assn. (adv. bd. 1995—). Republican. Mennonite. Home: 1519 Springside Dr Lancaster PA 17603-6356 Office: Heil Enterprises 921 Nissley Rd Lancaster PA 17601-1456 E-mail: paul@heilenterprises.com.

HEIL, TERRY W. defense electronic company executive; b. Fairfield, Iowa; BS, Parsons Coll., 1960; MS, U. Ariz., Tucson, 1963; PhD, U. Ariz., 1966. With Singer Co., Stamford, Conn., 1966—, v.p. reconaissance services, 1975-78, v.p., programs mgr., 1978-82, v.p., pres. Singer div. products, 1982-83, v.p., pres. HRB Singer div., 1983-84, group v.p., 1984-86, exec. v.p., 1987—88; sr. v.p., group exec., inf. systems group E-Systems Inc., 1988—90, sr. v.p., 1990—94; sr. v.p., intelligence & comm. systems div. Raytheon E-Systems, 1994—96; v.p. Raytheon Co., 1996—, sr. v.p., intelligence programs for the command control and info. systems div., 1997—2002, v.p., business integration, 2002—. Office: Raytheon Co 1200 S Jupiter Rd Garland TX 75042*

HEILBORN, GEORGE HEINZ, investor; b. Cologne, Germany, Feb. 27, 1935; arrived in U.S., 1941; s. Walter and Christine (Spiegel) H.; m. Phyllis Dorothy Ehrhardt, Sept. 30, 1972; children: Stephanie, Allison. BA, Northwestern U., 1956; AM, Harvard U., 1958. With Thompson Ramo Wooldridge Products Co., El Segundo, Calif., 1958-60; project mgr. Electronics div. Gen. Mills, Mpls., 1960-61, Philco Corp., Willow Grove, Pa., 1961-63; pres., chmn. Info. Processing Systems, Inc., Hackensack, N.J., 1963-92; pres. G.H. Heilborn & Co., Inc., 1992—. Mem. bd. vis. Coll. Arts and Scis., Northwestern U., 1992—, alumni regent, 1997—; mem. grad. sch. alumni coun. Harvard U., 1993-2000, chmn., 1996-98; trustee Family Counseling Svc., Ridgewood, N.J., 1992-95; mem. fin. and investment com. Children's Aid and Family Counseling, N.J., 1996—. Mem. Computer Dealers and Lessors Assn. (founding mem. 1971, pres. 1980-82, chmn. 1982-84), Equipment Leasing Assn. Am., U.S.-USSR Trade and Econ. Coun., N.Y. Acad. Scis., Harvard Club of N.Y. Home: 385 Knollwood Rd Ridgewood NJ 07450-4814 Office: G H Heilborn & Co Inc One University Plz Hackensack NJ 07601

HEILBRON, DAVID M(ICHAEL), lawyer; b. San Francisco, Nov. 25, 1936; s. Louis H. and Delphine A. (Rosenblatt) H.; m. Nancy Ann Olsen, June 21, 1960; children: Lauren Ada, Sarah Ann, Ellen Selma. BS summa cum laude, U. Calif., Berkeley, 1958; AB first class, Oxford U., Eng., 1960; LL.B. magna cum laude, Harvard U., 1962. Bar: Calif. 1962, U.S. Dist. Ct. (no. dist.) Calif. 1963, U.S Ct. Appeals (9th cir.) 1963, U.S. Ct. Appeals (D.C. cir.) 1972, U.S. Ct. Appeals (8th cir.), 1985, U.S. Ct. Appeals (1st cir.) 1987, U.S. Ct. Appeals (10th cir.) 1988, U.S. Ct. Appeals (7th cir.) 1988, U.S. Ct. appeals (11th cir.) 1988, U.S. Dist. Ct. Nev. 1982, U.S. Dist. Ct. (cen. dist.) Calif. 1983, U.S. Supreme Ct. 1988, U.S. Ct. Appeals (3rd cir.) 1992, (6th cir.), 1995, U.S. Ct. Appeals (2d cir.) 1998, U.S. Ct. Appeals (5th cir.) 1998. Assoc. McCutchen, Doyle, Brown & Enersen, San Francisco, 1962-69, ptnr., 1969—, mng. ptnr., 1985-88. Vis. lectr. appellate advocacy U. Calif., Berkeley, 1981-82, 82-83. Bd. trustees Golden Gate U., 1993-97, vice chair, 1995-97; bd. dirs. San Francisco Jewish Cmty. Ctr., 1974—, Legal Aid Soc., 1974-78, Legal Assistance to Elderly, San Francisco, 1980, San Francisco Renaissance, 1982—; pres. San Francisco Sr. Ctr., 1972-75; co-chmn. San Francisco Lawyers' Com. for Urban Affairs, 1976. Rhodes scholar. Fellow Am. Bar Found.; mem. ABA, Am. Coll. Trial Lawyers, Am. Arbitration Assn. (bd. dirs. 1986-98, 2002–, adv. coun. No. Calif. chpt. 1982—, chmn. 1987, jud. coun. 1986-88, exec. bd. 1994-98, instr. and panelist arbitrator tng. programs), Am. Acad. Appellate Lawyers, State Bar Calif. (chmn. com. cts. 1982-83, bd. govs. 1983-85, mem. commn. on discovery 1984-86, pres. 1985-86), Calif. Acad. Appellate Lawyers, Coll. Comml. Arbitrators, Bar Assn. San Francisco (chmn. conf. dels. 1975-76, pres. 1980). Clubs: Calif. Tennis. Democrat. Office: McCutchen Doyle Brown & Enersen 3 Embarcadero Ctr San Francisco CA 94111-4003

HEILBRON, JOHN L. historian, educator; b. San Francisco, Mar. 17, 1934; s. Louis Henry and Delphine A. (Rosenblatt) Heilbron; m. Patricia Ann Lucerno, Mar. 25, 1959 (dec. Dec. 1993); m. Alison Margaret Browning, May 28, 1995. AB, U. Calif., Berkeley, 1955, MA, 1958, PhD, 1964; Laurea in Philosophy (hon.), U. Bologna, 1988; PhD (hon.), U. Pavia, 2000, U. Uppsala, 2000. Asst. dir. Sources History Quantum Physics, Berkeley, Copenhagen, 1961-64; asst. prof. history, philosophy sci. U. Pa., Phila., 1964-67; from asst. prof. to assoc. prof. history U. Calif., Berkeley, 1967—73, prof., 1973-94, Class of 1936 prof. history and history sci., 1985-94, prof. emeritus, 1994, dir. Office History Sci. and Tech., 1973-94, editor Hist. Studies Phys. Scis., 1980—, vice chancellor, 1991-94, chair acad. senate, 1988-90; Andrew Dickson White prof. at large Cornell U., 1984-90. Sr. rsch. fellow Worcester Coll., Oxford, 1997—, Oxford Mus. History Sci., 1997—; vis. prof. Yale U., 2002—. Author: (book) Elements of Early Modern Physics, 1981, H. G. J. Moseley, The Life and Letters of an English Physicist, 1887-1915, 1974, Historical Studies in the Theory of Atomic Structure, 1981, Physics at the Royal Society During Newton's Presidency, 1983, The Dilemmas of an Upright Man: Max Planck as Spokesman for German Science, 1986, Weighing Imponderables and Other Quantitative Science Around 1800, 1993, Geometry Civilized: History, Culture, Technique, 1998, The Sun in the Church: Cathedrals as Solar Observatories, 1999, The Dilemmas of an Upright Man: Max Planck as Spokesman for German Science, 2000, Ernest Rutherford and the Explosion of the Atoms, 2003; author: (with P. Forman and S. Weart) Physics circa 1900: Personnel, Funding and Productivity of the Academic Establishment, 1975; author: (with W. Shumaker) John Dee on Astronomy, 1978, Electricity in the 17th and 18th Centuries: A Study of Early Modern Physics, 1979, 1999; author: (with R. W. Seidel and B. R. Wheaton) Lawrnece and His Laboratory: Nuclear Science in Berkeley, 1931-61, 1981; author: (with B. R. Wheaton) Literature on the History of Physics in the 20th Century, 1981, An Inventory of Published Letters to and from Physicists, 1982; author: (with E. Crawford and R. Ullrich) The Nobel Population: 1901-1937: A Census of Nominees and Nominators for the Prizes in Physics and Chemistry, 1987; author: (with Seidel) A History of the Lawrence Berkeley Laboratory, Vol. 1: Lawrence and His Laboratory, 1990; author: Ernest Rutherford, 2003; editor: (book) Benjamin Franklin's Briefe von der Elektrizität, 1983, The Oxford Companion to the History of Modern Science, 2003; editor: (with T. Frängsmyr and R. Rider) The Quantifying Spirit in the 18th Century, 1990. Mem.: Royal Swedish Acad. Scis. (fgn.), Am. Philos. Soc., Am. Acad. Arts and Scis., Brit. Soc. History Sci., History Sci. Soc. (Sarton medal, Pfizer prize), Internat. Acad. History Sci. (pres. 2001—, Koyré medal). Home: April House Shilton near Burford OX18 4AB England Office: Oxford Mus History of Sci Broad St Oxford OX1 3A2 England E-mail: john.heilbron@dial.appleinter.net.

HEILBRONER, ROBERT LOUIS, economist, writer; b. N.Y.C., Mar. 24, 1919; s. Louis and Helen (Weiller) H.; m. Joan Knapp (div.); children: Peter, David; m. Shirley E. T. Davis. BA, Harvard U., 1940; PhD, New Sch. Social Rsch., 1963; LLD, LaSalle Coll., Ripon Coll., L.I. U., Wagner Coll., SUNY, Purchase, New Sch. for Social Rsch. Norman Thomas prof. emeritus New Sch. for Social Research, 1972—. Lectr. univ., bus. and labor groups. Author: Future as History, 1960, Great Ascent, 1963, Limits of American Capitalism, 1966, Between Capitalism and Socialism, 1970, The Making of Economic Society, rev. edit., 1989, (with James Galbraith) The Economic Problem, rev. edit., 1990, The Worldly Philosophers, rev. edit., 1999, Between Capitalism and Socialism, 1970, An Inquiry into the Human Prospect, rev. edit., 1980, Business Civilization in Decline, 1976, Beyond Boom and Crash, 1978, Marxism: For and Against, 1980, (with Lester Thurow) Five Economic Challenges, rev. edit., 1987, Economics Explained, rev. edit., 1987, The Nature and Logic of Capitalism, 1985, The Essential Adam Smith, 1986, Behind the Veil of Economics, 1988, 21st Century Capitalism, 1993, Visions of the Future, 1995, (with William Millberg) The Crisis of Vision in Modern Economic Thought, 1996, Teachings from the Worldly Philosophy, 1996, also many articles and brochures in field. Chmn. bd. Town Sch., N.Y.C., 1963-73, Council Econ. Priorities, 1973-79. Served to 1st lt. U.S. Army, World War II Decorated Bronze Star; recipient 1st prize Gerald Loeb award for disting. bus. and fin. journalism U. Mo. Sch. Journalism, 1979, UCLA Grad. Sch. Mgmt., 1984, 87; Guggenheim fellow, 1983; named first scholar of yr., N.Y. Coun. for Humanities, 1994. Fellow AAAS; mem. Am. Econ. Assn. (exec. com. 1972, v.p. 1983-84), Assn. for an Evolutionary Economy (Vedlen Commons award 1993), N.Y. Coun. for the Humanities (Scholar of Yr. 1994), Phi Beta Kappa. Office: New School Univ Graduate Faculty, Dept Economics 65 Fifth Ave New York NY 10003

HEILBRUN, JAMES, economist, educator; b. N.Y.C., Dec. 13, 1924; s. Maurice L. and Hortense (Unger) H.; m. Carolyn Gold, Feb. 20, 1945; children: Emily, Margaret, Robert. BS, Harvard Coll., 1945; MA, Harvard U., 1947; PH.D., Columbia U., 1961. Asst. economist Prentice Hall Inc., N.Y.C., 1947-50; econ. analyst Chase Manhattan Bank, N.Y.C., 1951-55; instr. Columbia U., N.Y.C., 1961-65, asst. prof. econs., 1965-70; assoc prof. econs. Fordham U., Bronx, 1970-74, prof., 1974-97, prof. emeritus, 1997—. Research dir. Harlem Devel. Project, Columbia U., 1967-68 Author: Real Estate Taxes and Urban Housing, 1966, Urban Economics and Public Policy, 1973, 3d edit., 1987, (with Charles M. Gray) Economics of Art and Culture, 1993, 2d edit., 2001. Served with USN, 1944-46. Fellow Com. on Urban Econs., 1960-61; fellow Ford Found., 1969-70; UCLA resident scholar, 1978. Mem. Am. Econ. Assn. Home: 151 Central Park W New York NY 10023-1514 E-mail: jheilbrun@wordnet.att.net.

HEILEMAN, JOHN PHILLIP, endocrinologist; b. Phoenix, Feb. 2, 1930; s. Leonidas McHaffie and Rose Madelaine (Murphy) H.; m. Ann Frances O'Hara, Nov. 4, 1961; children: Jeanne Marie, James Andrew, Denise Ann, Matthew John. BS, Ariz. State U., 1951; MD, Loyola U., Chgo., 1955; postgrad., USN Sch. Aviation Medicine, Pensacola, Fla., 1956. Diplomate Am. Bd. Internal Medicine, subspecialty in endocrinology, Intern U.S. Naval Hosp., Gt. Lakes, Ill., 1955-56, resident in internal medicine Cook County Hosp., Gt. Lakes, 1958-60, Vet. Rsch. Hosp., Gt. Lakes, 1960-61; fellow in endocrinology, 1961-62; practice medicine specializing in internal medicine and endocrinology, 1962—; pres. Endocrinology Assocs. P.A., Phoenix, 1971-97. Pres. Ariz. chpt. Am. Diabetes Assn., 1975-77; bd. dirs., Ariz. Kidney Found., 2002—. Lt. comdr., flight surgeon USNR, 1955-58. Fellow ACP, Am. Coll. Clin. Endocrinologists; mem. Ariz. Med. Assn. (sec. 1967-69), Maricopa County Med. Soc., Ariz. Soc. Internal Medicine, Ariz. Country Club. Republican. Roman Catholic. Avocations: tennis, skiing.

HEILENDAY, FRANK TOD, science educator; b. Jersey City, Dec. 31, 1927; s. Frank Walter and Helma Heilenday; m. Joan Heilenday. BS, MIT, 1945, M, 1949, postgrad., 1965—66. Chief office of ops. analysis Hdqs. 8th Air Force, Westover Air Force Base, Mass., 1959—65; chief applied rsch. SAC, Offutt Air Force Base, 1966—84; adj. prof. George Wash. U., Washington, 1986—93; cons. RAND Corp., Santa Monica, Calif., 1992—95; ret. Toyon Rsch., 2003. Cons. Sandia Nat. Lab., Albuquerque, 1988—93, Toyon Rsch., Santa Barbara, 1984—88. Author: (textbook) Principles of Air Defense and Air Vehicle Penetration. Mem.: Rotary. Home: 720 Sherman St NW Olympia WA 98502 Personal E-mail: todjoan@yahoo.com.

HEILICSER, BERNARD JAY, emergency physician; b. Bklyn., Jan. 19, 1947; s. Murray and Esther (Dubrow) H.; m. Marcia Cherry, June 2, 1976; children: Micah, Seth, Jacob. BA, SUNY, Binghamton, 1968; MS, Hahnemann Med. Coll., Phila., 1971; DO, Coll. Osteo. Medicine/Surgery, Des Moines, 1976. Diplomate Am. Bd. Emergency Medicine. Instr. anatomy and physiology U. Pa. and Hahnemann Med. Coll., Phila., 1971-73; staff physician Va. Inst. Tech., Blacksburg, 1977-78; asst. prof. emergency medicine Chgo. Coll. Osteo. Medicine, 1979; emergency physician St. Margaret Hosp., Hammond, Ind., 1979-83, Michael Reese Med. Ctr., Chgo., 1989-91, Ingalls Hosp., Harvey, Ill., 1983—; project med. dir. South Cook County Emergency Med. Svc., Harvey, 1984—. Mem. faculty Chgo. Osteo. Med. Ctr., 1987-99; faculty trauma nurse specialist St. James Hosp., Chicago Heights, Ill., 1980—; preceptor nurse practitioners Purdue U., Hammond, 1981-90; fellow MacLean Ctr. Clin. Med. Ethics, U. Chgo., 1993-94; chmn. ethics com., hosp. med. ethicist Ingalls Hosp., Harvey, Ill., 1994—; cons. The Nat. Bd. Osteo. Med. Examiners, Harvey, 1994-95, ethics com. Am. Coll. Osteo. Emergency Physicians, 1997—; chmn. disaster com. Ill. Region 7 Emergency Med. Svcs./Trauma, 1997—; chair Ill. Region VII EMS Adv. Coun., 2001—; mem. adj. faculty Coll. Health Professions, Govs. State U., 1999—; mem. exec. coun. Ill. Mobile Emergency Response Team, 1999—; med. advisor Combined Agy. Response Team, 1999—. Vol. fireman Flossmoor (Ill.) Fire Dept., 1985—, Matteson (Ill.) Fire Dept., 1980-90; chmn. Ill. Regional 7 EMS Adv. Coun. Fellow Am. Coll. Emergency Physicians; mem. Am. Osteo. Assn., Nat. Assn. Emergency Med. Svcs. Physicians, Am. Coll. Osteo. Emergency Physicians, Nat. Assn. Emergency Med. Technicians, Sigma Sigma Phi. Jewish. Avocations: running, basketball. Office: Ingalls Hosp One Ingalls Dr Harvey IL 60426

HEILIGENSTEIN, CHRISTIAN ENRIC, lawyer; b. St. Louis, Dec. 7, 1929; s. Christian A. and Louisa M. (Dixon) H.; children: Christie; m. Liselotte Warbanoff, Feb. 6, 1981. BS in Law, U.Ill., 1953, JD, 1955. Bar: Ill. 1956, U.S. Dist. Ct. (so. dist.) Ill. 1956, U.S. Ct. Appeals (7th cir.) 1956, U.S. Dist. Ct. (cen. dist.) Ill. 1960, U.S. Supreme Ct. 1978. Assoc. Listeman & Bandy, East St. Louis, Ill., 1955-61; sole practice Belleville, Ill., 1962-84; ptnr., pres. Heiligenstein & Badgley, Belleville, 1984-98; pres. C.E. Heiligenstein, P.C., Belleville, 1998—. Bd. dirs. Union Planters Corp., Union Planters Bank NA, 1998-2000, audit com. 1999-2000, Magna Bank and Magna Group, Inc., 1984-98; chair audit com. Magna Group, Inc., 1994-98. Bd. visitors U. Ill. Coll. of Law, 2000. Recipient Alumni of Month award U. Ill. Law Sch., 1982; C.E. Heiligenstein Chair in Law named in his honor U. Ill., 1999. Mem. Ill. State Bar Assn., Internat. Acad. Trial Lawyers (bd. dirs. 1991-97), St. Clair County Bar Assn., St. Louis Bar Assn., Inner Circle Advs., Am. Bd. Trial Advs. (nat. bd. dirs. 1992, pres. St. Louis, So. Ill. region 1993), Am. Assn. Profl. Liabilities Attys. (Nat. bd. dirs., 1990-99), ATLA (bd. govs. 1985-87), Ill. Trial Lawyers Assn. (bd. mgrs. 1975-88, pres. 1989), Beach Club (bd. dirs. 1996, v.p. 1998), Old Guard Soc. of Palm Beach. Democrat. Home: 5200 Turner Hall Rd Belleville IL 62220-5628 E-mail: l.warbanoj@aol.com.

HEILIGMAN, DEBORAH, writer; b. Allentown, Pa., Apr. 24, 1958; d. Nathan H. and Helen (Rockmaker) Heiligman; m. Jonathan David Weiner, May 29, 1982; children: Aaron Weiner, Benjamin Weiner. AB in Religious Studies, Brown U., 1980. Asst./assoc. editor Moment Mag., Boston, 1980—81; editor Scholastic Mag., N.Y.C., 1981—85; freelance writer/author, 1985—. Author: Into the Night, 1990, Barbara McClintock: Alone in Her Field, 1994, Mary Leakey: In Search of Human Beginnings, 1995, On the Move, 1996 (Best Book of the Yr. by Bank St. Book Com., 1997), From Caterpillar to Butterfly, 1996, Mike Swan, Sink or Swim, 1998, The New York Public Library Guide to Research, 1998, The Story of the Titanic, 1998, Too Perfect, 1999, The Mysterious Ocean Highway: Benjamin Franklin and the Gulf Stream, 2000, Honeybees, 2002 (NSTA/CBC Outstanding Sci. Trade Book for Children, 2002), Babies: All You Need to Know, 2002 (One of Five Best Books of the Yr. by BabyZone.com, 2002), Earthquakes, 2003. Interviewer Brownn Alumni. Mem.: Authors Guild, Soc. Children's Book Writers and Illustrators. Home: 3040 Yorkshire Rd Doylestown PA 18901

HEILMAN, DAVID MICHAEL, scientist, military officer; s. Donald and Linda Heilman; m. Beth Ann Ellefson, Jan. 9, 1999; children: Alyssa, Joshua. BS, Wheeling Jesuit Coll., 1990; MS, Ohio U., 1994. Chemist Mylan Pharmaceuticals, Inc, Morgantown, W.Va., 1994—99; scientist Trimeris, Inc., Durham, NC, 1999—. Comdr. 459th Engr. Co., USAR, Clarksburg, W.Va., 1997—2000; asst. brigade engr. 105th Engr. Bn., 30th eSB, NCARNG, Raeford, NC, 2001—. Steering com. Friends of Hillsborough, NC, 2001. Capt. USAR, 1986—. Decorated Army Commendation medal U.S. Army. Mem.: N.C. N.G. Assn., N.G. Assn. of the US, Army Engr. Assn., Am. Chem. Soc., Am. Assn. Pharm. Scientists, Res. Officers Assn. (life). Achievements include patents pending for Novel Formulation for Subcutaneous Injection of Peptides.

HEILMAN, E. BRUCE, academic administrator; b. La Grange, Ky., July 16, 1926; s. Earl Bernard and Nellie (Sanders) H.; m. Betty June Dobbins, Aug. 27, 1948; children: Bobbie Lynn, Nancy Jo, Terry Lee, Sandra June, Timothy Bruce. BS, Vanderbilt U., 1950, MA, 1951; PhD, Peabody Coll., 1961; postgrad., U. Tenn., U. Omaha, U. Ky.; LLD (hon.), Wake Forest U., 1967, Ky. Wesleyan Coll., 1980, James Madison U., 1986, U. Richmond, 1986; DHum. (hon.), Campbell Coll., 1971; LLD; LHD (hon.), Bridgewater Coll., 1991; DHL, DPS, Campbellsville Coll., 1995. Instr. bus. Peabody Coll., Vanderbilt U., 1950—51, bursar, 1957—60, adminstrv. v.p., 1963—66; instr. accounting Belmont Coll., Nashville, 1951—52; auditor Albert Maloney Co., Nashville, 1951—52; asst. prof. accounting, bus. mgr. Ky. Wesleyan Coll., 1952—54; treas. Georgetown (Ky.) Coll., 1954—57, Georgetown (Ky.) Coll. (Louisville Housing Project), 1954—57; coordinator higher edn. and spl. schs. Tenn., 1960—61; v.p., dean Ky. So. Coll., Louisville, 1961—63; prof. ednl. adminstrn. Peabody Coll. Vanderbilt U., Nashville, 1963—66; pres. Meredith Coll., Raleigh, 1966—71, U. Richmond, Va., 1971—86, chancellor, 1966—2002, chancellor, interim chief exec. officer, 1987—88, chancellor emeritus, 2002—. Bd. dirs. Cooperating Raleigh Colls., 1967-71; cons. indsl. studies in edn. and adminstrn., 1954—; dir., cons. long range planning confs. Fund Advancement Edn., 1960—; cons. acad. Ednl. Study Task, 1964-65; mem. Wake County-Raleigh City Sh. Merger Study Com., 1969; adv. com. N.C. Dept. Pub. Instrn., 1970; bd. dirs. Fidelity Bankers Life Ins. Co., A.H. Robins Co., Richmond, Ctrl. Fidelity Bank, Fidelity Fed. Savs. Bank, Bapt. Theol. Sem., Richmond; mem. adv. bd. Sta. WLEE Radio-TV; chmn. Cardinal Savs. and Loan Assn., Fast Fox, Inc., Office Am., Richmond, Direct Med. Inc., Cordell Med., Va. Escrow & Title co. The Phoenix Corp.; trustee, chmn. bd. advisors, mem. exec. com., devel. coms. Campbellsville (Ky.) Coll; instnl. cons. adv. bd. Paine Webber, Inc. Author: (with others) Sixty College Study, 1954; also booklets and articles. Chmn. blood com. for edn. ARC, 1971; mem. Nashville Urban Renewal Coordinating Com., 1965-66; ann. giving chmn. for N.C. Peabody Coll. Vanderbilt, U., 1970-72; mem. Friends of HOME, 1974—; chmn. trustee orientation com. N.C. Bapt. Conv., 1961; mem. edn. commn. So. Bapt. Conv.; mem. bd. advisors Bapt. Hosp. Sch. Nursing, Nashville, 1956-60, 64—; mem. com. Met. Gen. Hosp. Sch. Nursing, 1965-68; mem. Federated Arts Coun. Richmond, 1975—, Robert Lee coun. Boy Scouts Am., 1975—; mem. devel. adv. bd. Va. Ctr. Performing Arts, 1980; bd. dirs. Bill Wilkerson Speech and Hearing Ctr., Nashville, 1963-64, Bapt. Theology Sem., Richmond, 1964, N.C. Symphony, United Fund Wake County, 1968-71, N.C. Mental Health Assn., 1969-71, Wake County Mental Health Assn., 1969-71, Va. Thanksgiving Festival, 1972, Richmond Pub. Libr., Richmond chpt. NCCJ, Ba. Inst. Sci. Rsch., 1971—, Leadership Metro Richmond, 1980—, Maymont Found., 1996—, Metro Bank, 1996—, chmn. of bd., 1997—; hon. dir. Richmond Ballet, 1971; bd. govs. United Givers Fund Richmond, 1971; trustee Inst. Mediterranean Studies, 1972—, E.R. Patterson Ednl. Found., 1972—, U. Richmond, 1973-86; bd. govs. Marine Corps. Assn., 1990; pres. Marine Mil. Acad., 1964, exec. v.p. bd., 1979—, chmn. bd. trustees, 1994, chmn. bd. trustees, 1994—, bd. dirs. USMC Def. Bat., Chairman, Marine Corps. U. bd. of trustees, Quantico, Va., Nat. Def. Univ. Found., So. Sem. Found., Bapt. Theol. Sem., Richmond, Va.; mem. adv. bd., chmn. devel. com., bd. dirs. Marine Hist. Found.. Served with USMCR, 1944-47. Served with U.S. Army, 1944—47. Recipient award Owensboro (Ky.) Jr. C. of C., 1953; Agrl. and Industry Service award U. Nashville, 1961; Outstanding Civic and Ednl. award Raleigh, 1970; Distinguished Salesman award Richmond, 1972, Disting. Alumni award Campbellsville Coll. and Peabody Coll. Vanderbilt U., Distinguished Citizen of Oldham County (Ky.) award, Va. Assn. Future Farmers Am. award, 1976, Disting. Citizen award Meredith Coll., 1977; named Ky. Col., 1969; Paul Harris Rotary fellow, 1970; Reverse Exchange Eisenhower fellow to Peoples Rep. of China, 1987; named Hon. Pres. Sino-Am. Cultural Soc., 1988. Mem. Internat. Assn. Univ. Pres.'s (N. Am. council 1976—), Nat. Fedn. Bus. Officers, Nat. Fedn. Bus. Officers Cons. Service, So. Assn. Colls. Women (pres. 1969), Nat. Soc. Lit. and the Arts, So. Univ. Conf., Sino Am. Soc. (hon. pres.), Am. Council Edn., Tenn. Edn. Assn., Ky. Ednl. Buyers Assn., Am. Assn. Pres.'s Ind. Colls. and Univs., Ky. Assn. Acad. Deans, Peabody Alumni Assn. Vanderbilt U. (exec. com), Nat., So. assns. coll. and univ. bus. officers, Assn. Governing Bds. Univs. and Colls., Coll. and Univ. Personnel Assn., Internat. Platform Assn., Nashville, Raleigh, Richmond, Va. chambers commerce, Nat. Assn. Ind. Colls. and Univs., Navy League U.S., Marine Corps League, Council Ind. Colls. in Va. (pres. 1974-76), Va. Found. Ind. Colls., Assn. Va. Colls., Assn. So. Bapt. Colls. and Schs. (pres. 1976), N.C. Found. Ch.-Related Colls., Assn. Am. Colls., So. Assn. Colls. and Schs. (trustee 1977), Phi Beta Kappa, Pi Omega Pi, Kappa Phi Kappa, Kappa Delta Pi, Delta Pi Epsilon, Omicron Delta Kappa, Beta Gamma Sigma, Lambda Chi Alpha (Achiever award 1993), Va. Bapt. Hist. Soc., English-Speaking Union, Newcomen Soc. N. Am. Democrat. Baptist (deacon). Clubs: Rotary (Raleigh) (bd. advisers Raleigh 1966-71), Execs. (Raleigh) (v.p., dir. 1971), City (Raleigh); Downtown (Richmond); The Club, Forum. Home: 4700 Cary Street Rd Richmond VA 23226-1703 Office: Chancellor's Office University of Richmond Richmond VA 23173*

HEILMAN, JOHN EDWARD, engineering consultant; b. Chgo., Mar. 20, 1936; s. Frederick John and Kathryn Grace (Schnider) H.; m. Virginia Lois Anderson, Jan. 28, 1956; children: Wayne John, Warren Wesley. BS in Food Engring., Ill. Inst. Tech., 1961. Engr. grocery products divsn. Armour & Co., Chgo., 1959-61, lab. technician, 1958, foreman, 1958-59; process engr. Ctrl. Soya Co., Inc., Ft. Wayne, Ind., 1962-65, supt. Chgo., 1965-68; sr. process engr. Continental Grain Co., Chgo., 1968-75, dir. engring. process divsn. N.Y.C., 1975-77, asst. v.p. process divsn., 1977-79, v.p. world oilseeds group, 1979-91; prin. Heilman Consulting Group, 1991—. Mem. Nat. Fire Protection Assn. (sectional com. solvent extraction, sectional com. agrl. dusts), Am. Oil Chemists Soc. (pres. 1998-99). Republican. Methodist. Home and Office: 6135 Moorfield Ave Colorado Springs CO 80919-4802 E-mail: jheilman@att.net.

HEILMAN, MARLIN STEPHEN, medical products executive; b. Tarentum, Pa., Dec. 25, 1933; s. Glenn Harold and Hilda Barnes; m. Drusilla Carswell, Aug. 18, 1956; children: Philip, Glenda, Carl Barnes, Stephen James, Karen. BA, U. Pa., 1955, MD, 1959. Pvt. practice, Pitts., 1963—65; cons. Westinghouse R & D, Pitts., 1965—67; pres. Medrad, Inc., Pitts., 1968—80, Intec Systems, Inc., Pitts., 1980—84; chmn., CEO Medrad/Intec, Inc., Pitts., 1984—86; chmn. bd. dirs., CEO Vascor, Inc., Pitts., 1986—, Lifecor, Inc., Pitts., 1986—. Founder Medrad, Intec, Medrad/Intec, Vascor & Lifecor; bd. dirs. Western Pa. Allegheny Health Sys., Medrad, Inc., Zoll Med. Corp.; chmn. Alle-iski Med. Ctr. Contbr. articles to profl. jours. Bd. dirs. Ben Franklin Partnership Pa. Capt. USAF, 1961—63. Named Entrepreneur of Yr., Arthur Young/Venture Mag., 1987; named to Nat. Inventors Hall of Fame, 2002; recipient Michel Mirowski Excellence in Cardiology award, 1992; grantee, NIH, 1965, 1968. Address: Vascor Inc 566 Alpha Dr Pittsburgh PA 15238-2912

HEILMAN, PAMELA DAVIS, lawyer; b. Buffalo, July 2, 1948; d. George Henry and Natalie (Maier) Davis; m. Robert D. Heilman, June 27, 1970. AB, Vassar Coll., 1970; JD, SUNY, Buffalo, 1975. Bar: N.Y. 1976, Fla. 1980. Assoc. Hodgson, Russ, Andrews, Woods & Goodyear, Buffalo, 1975-84, ptnr., 1984—. Bd. dirs. United Way Buffalo, 1985-97, vice chmn., 1989-92, chair, 1993-97, gen. campaign chair, 1992; bd. dirs. D'Youville Coll., Buffalo, 2001—, WNY Internat. Trade Coun., Inc., Buffalo, 2001—, Fin. Instns., Inc., Warsaw, 2002—. Mem. ABA, N.Y. State Bar Assn. (vice chmn., exec. com., sect. on internat. law and practice 1988-90), Fla. Bar Assn., Erie County Bar Assn. Office: Hodgson Russ Andrews Woods & Goodyear LLP One M&T Plz Buffalo NY 14211-1638 E-mail: pheilman@hodgsonruss.com.

HEILMAN, WILLIAM JOSEPH, research scientist, consultant; b. Pitts., Aug. 31, 1930; s. William Joseph Heilman Sr., Marcella Marie Heilman; m. Charlotte Marie Andrews; children: Terry Lynn, Christine Marie, Eric William. BS, U. Pitts., 1952; MS, SUNY Syracuse, 1956; PhD, Tex. Tech. U., 1962. Contbr. Recipient R&D 100 award, R&D Mag., 2001. Mem.: Soc. Automotive Engrs., Soc. Tribologist Lubrication Engrs., Am. Chem. Soc. (S.W. Regional Indsl. Innovation award 2002). Achievements include invention of Polyalphaolefin Synthetic Lubricants; Gel candles; patents for more than 100 in field. Home: 14826 LaQuinta Ln Houston TX 77079 Office: Shell Global Solutions Inc 3333 Highway 6 South Houston TX 77082

HEILMANN, CHRISTIAN FLEMMING, corporate executive; b. Apr. 26, 1936; s. Poul Bent and Hedvig Buchwald (Moller) H.; m. Marilyn Mildred Harter, July 9, 1959 (div. 1973); children: Christian Philip, Nicholas John, Claire Marie; m. 2d, Judith Lucy Tucker, Sept. 15, 1973; children: Per Flemming, Niels Henrik. MA, Cambridge (Eng.) U., 1957. Mng. dir., CEO Metal Box South Africa Ltd., Johannesburg, 1970-77; trustee Nat. Devel. and Mgmt. Found., South Africa, 1970-75; v.p. Continental Can Co., Stamford, Conn., 1977-78; pres. Continental Group Europe, Brussels, Belgium, 1978-80, Continental Diversified Industries, Stamford, Conn., 1980-81; exec. v.p., chief administrative officer Continental Group, Inc., Stamford, Conn., 1982-84; dir., pres, CEO Am. Can Can, Inc. (name changed to Onex Packaging Inc. 1986), Rexdale, Ont., 1984-89; N.Y. rep. Danes Worldwide, 1996; chmn., CEO Brockway Standard, Inc., Atlanta, 1989-94; dir., bd. dirs. Whitlock Packaging Co., Okla., 1998—. Mem. adv. coun. U. Toronto Bus. Sch., 1985-92; bd. dirs. Porter Chadburn, Inc., Omaha, Porter Chadburn PLC, London, O'Shaughnessy Funds, Inc. U.S. rep. Nat. Olympic Com. Denmark, 1994—96; attache Danish Sports Orgn. for the Disabled 1996 Paralympic Games in Atlanta; mem. Cornell U. Coun., 1996—2000, 2002—; trustee Am. Scandinavian Found., Paul Smith's Coll., St. Regis, NY, 1999—; bd. dirs. Cambridge in Am., 1996—2002, Jacob Riis Settlement House, N.Y.C., 1996—, v.p., 1999; elected Wilkins fellow Downing Coll., Cambridge U., 2000. Decorated Knight Order of Dannebrog (Denmark); recipient Ellis Island medal of honor, 2002. Mem. Danish-Am. Soc. (bd. dirs. 1990-2003, pres. 1996-2000), Danish Am. C. of C. (bd. dirs. 1995-2003), Greenwich Country Club.

HEIM, ALBERTA JANE, publishing executive, writer; b. Davenport, Iowa, Jan. 23, 1947; d. Albert George Wieser and Marjorie May Myers; children: John Heim II, Jeffrey. BA, DePauw U., 1969. Pub. Touchstone Adventures, Paw Paw, Ill., 1996—; dir. organic edn. ctr. Oreg. Tilth, Inc., Salem, 1997—2000; pres. Ill. Tilth Organic Inst., Steward, 2001—. Vis. lectr. Coll. DuPage, Glen Ellyn, Ill., 1977; vis. spkr. Orgn. Govt. in Mgmt., Baton Rouge, 1982. Author: (book) The Directory of Working Women, 1982, What To Do When the Stock Market Falls, 1996, Car Living, 1999, Car Living Your Way, 2001. Vol. Menlo Orgn., Beaverton, Oreg., 1993—94, Rockford Area Literacy Coun., Ill., 2001—. Named Career Woman of the Month, Cosmopolitan Mag., 1982; recipient Outstanding Working Women's Exceptional Achievement award, The Woman's Adv., 1981; grantee Edn. Grant for Organic Edn. Ctr., Newman's Own Found., 1998, 1999. Mem.: Amnesty Internat. Office: Touchstone Adventures PO Box 177 Paw Paw IL 61353 Personal E-mail: ajarcher@earthlink.net.

HEIM, DIXIE SHARP, family practice nurse practitioner; b. Kansas City, Kans., Feb. 28, 1938; d. Glen Richard and Freda Helen (Milburn) Stanley; m. Theodore Eugene Sharp, Aug. 12, 1960 (dec. Apr., 1972); children: Diane Yvonne Price, Andrew Kirk, Bryan Scot; m. Roy Bernard Heim, June 14, 1979. Diploma nursing, St. Luke's Hosp. Sch. Nursing, Kansas City, Mo., 1959; family practice nurse clinician, Wichita State U., 1974. Cert. advanced registered nurse practitioner, Kans. Nurse surg. ICU Staff Kaiser Found. Hosp., San Francisco, 1959-61; oper. rm. supr. St. Luke's Hosp., Kansas City, Mo., 1962-63; emergency rm., oper. rm. supr. Lawrence (Kans.) Meml. Hosp., 1963-72; nurse clinician various doctors, Lawrence, 1973-81; nursing supr. spl. projects St. Francis Hosp. and Med. Ctr., Topeka, 1981-94; primary health care giver Health Care Access, Lawrence, 1992-94; nurse practitioner Dr. Glen Bair, Topeka, 1990-94; advanced registered nurse practitioner Dr. Jerry H. Feagan, Topeka, 1994, McLouth (Kans.) Med. Clinic, 1994—, Jefferson County Meml. Hosp., Winchester, Kans., 1995-96; family practice nurse practitioner Robert E. Jacoby II, M.D., Mathew Bohm M.D., Topeka, Kans., 1995-2000. Preceptor nurse practitioner program U. Kans., 1993-2001, registered nurse program Washburn U., 1996-2001; primary health care provider Jefferson County Law Enforcement Ctr., Oskaloosa, Kans., 1995-96. V.p. Am. Bus. Women. Assn. Lawrence chpt., 1969, sec. 1968; vol. Children's Hour, Lawrence, 1965-72, Comty. Resource for Career edn., 1975-76; adv. bd. E. Ctrl. Kans. Econs. Opportunity Corp., Lawrence, 1993-95; mem. Rep. Women Douglas County, Lawrence, 1994-2001. Recipient Nursing the Heart of Health Care award Kaiser Permanente, 1994. Mem. ANA, Am. Acad. Nurse Practitioners (cert.), Kans. State Nurses Assn. (v.p. 1958, chairperson fund raising campaign 1994, bd. dirs. 1996). Home: 540 Arizona St Lawrence KS 66049-2100 Office: Flannery & McBratney MDs PA 3550 S 4th St # 10000 Leavenworth KS 66048 E-mail: DKtrDixie@aol.com.

HEIM, KATHRYN MARIE, psychiatric nurse, author; b. Milw., Sept. 29, 1952; d. Lester Sheldon Wilcox and Laura Dora (Corpie) Wilcox Sears; m. Vincent Robert Gouthro, June 30, 1970 (div. 1976); 1 child, Robert Vincent; m. George John Heim, Sept. 17, 1977 (div. 1988). AS in Nursing, Milw. Area Tech. Coll., 1983; BS in Nursing, NYU, 1986; MS in Mgmt., Cardinal Stritch Coll., 1988; PhD in Human Behavior, Newport U., 1997. Cert. psychiatric and mental health nurse, AMA. Staff geriatric nurse Clement Manor, Greenfield, Wis., 1983; nurse, health educator Milw. Boys Club, 1983-84; nurse mgr. Milw. County Mental Health Complex, 1984—2002, mem. gero-psychiat. inpatient adv. com., 1986-87, mem. joint practice com., guest rels. com., 1999-2001; hospitality com., 1999-2000; RN Psychiat. Acute Care Day Hosp., 1992—2002, cmty. support RN case mgr., 2002, Milw. County Dept. Aging, 2002—. Cons. Positive Perspectives, 1999-2000; rschr. on loneliness as it relates to mental health, 1989-92. Mem. wellness task force Milw. County Mental Health Complex, 1988-89, chairperson sensory deficit com. Geropsychiatry, 1989-90; active Boy Scouts Am., Milw., 1978-80. Mem. ANA (cert. gerontol. nurse), NAFE (network dir. Milw. chpt. 1982-92), Wis. Nurses Assn., NYU Alumni Assn., Cardinal Stritch Alumni Assn. (class rep. 1986-88), Milw. Area Tech. Coll. Alumni Assn. Avocations: yoga, jogging, reading, writing. Home: 226 N 63rd St Milwaukee WI 53213-4137 Office: Milwaukee County Dept ging 235 W Galena St Milwaukee WI 53212 E-mail: kheim@wi.rr.com.

HEIM, MARCY LYNN SCHULTZ, foundation executive; b. Theresa, Wis., Nov. 15, 1957; d. Robert Julius and Irene Laura (Wecker) Schultz; m. Kenneth J. Heim; stepchildren: Carly, Elliott; children: Robert James, David Joseph. BS in Natural Scis. with distinction, U. Wis., 1979. Exec. asst. Wis. Phys. Therapy Svcs., Madison, 1975-80; dir. pub. rels. Wis. DHI Coop., Madison, 1980-83; sr. dir. devel. U. Wis. Found., Madison, 1983—. Lead singer Marcy & The Highlights, 1980—; pres. Marcy Heim Diversified Svcs., 1995—. Vol. United Way of Dane County, 1987, Salvation Army, 1990—; treas. Van Hise Elem. PTO, 1994-95; grad. Leadership Greater Madison, 1997; bd. dirs. Middleton H.S. Choral Boosters, 2001-03, co-chair musical breakfast fundraising event, 2001-03; mem. Jr. League of Madison, 2002—. Recipient Outstandng Svc. award, Wis. Agrl.Rsch. Sta., 2003. Mem. Nat. Agr. Alumni and Devel. Assn. (bd. dirs. 1994-2002, edn. com. 1992-93, chair edn. com. 1994-96, pres.-elect 1996-97, pres. 1998-2000, Nat. Profl. Achievement award 1997, Disting. Svc. award 2002), Nat. Agr. Mktg. Assn., Pub. Rels. Soc. Am., Assn. Women Bus. Coalition (bd. dirs. 1988-91), Women in Comm. Inc. (bd. dirs. 1988-91, pres. Madison chpt. 1990-91), Daus. of Demeter (bd. dirs. 1995-2000, pres.-elect 1996, pres. 1997), Kiwanis (chair/co-chair agr. conservation and environ. com. Downtown Madison chpt. 1991-2002, bd. dirs. 1996-2000, found. bd. dirs. 2000-02), Assn. Fundraising Profls. (cert. fundraising exec.; Outstanding Fund Raising Execs. award 1997), Middleton Kiwanis Club, Alpha Zeta. Republican. Lutheran. Avocations: singing, dancing, aerobics. Home: 471 Presidential Ln Madison WI 53711-1153 Office: U Wis Found PO Box 8860 Madison WI 53708-8860 E-mail: marcy.heim@uwfoundation.wisc.edu.

HEIM, TONYA SUE, nurse, small business owner; b. Huntingburg, Ind., Nov. 9, 1948; d. Harold William and Marjorie Elouise (Buse) Rothert; m. James Frederick Heim, Sept. 6, 1969; children: Brian Christopher, Andrea Christine. Diploma, Deaconness Sch. Nursing, Evansville, Ind., 1969; BS in Mgmt., Oakland City U., 2001; student, U So. Ind., 2001—. RN Ind., cert. HIV/AIDS instr., infection control, Healthcare Corp. Compliance Assn. Oper. rm. staff nurse St. Joseph's Hosp., Huntingburg, 1969-71, emergency rm. staff nurse, 1969-71, staff nurse obstetrics dept., 1971-73, supr. obstetrics dept., 1973-85, dir. obstetrics oper. rm., 1985-88, dir. nursing, 1988-89, dir. obstetrics, oper. rm., infection control sterilizing, 1989-95, dir. surg. svcs., 1995-99, dir. corp. compliance, 1999—2003, dir. quality svcs./corp. compliance officer, 2003—; owner, operator Holland (Ind.) Toning and Tanning Ctr., 1987—. Co-owner Heim Hardware, 1989—. Instr., trainer ARC So. Ind., 1970-92; chmn. health profl. adv. com., mem. exec. com. So. Ind./Ill. chpt. March of Dimes, 1978-92; v.p., chmn. program com., bd. dirs. So. Hills Counseling Ctr., Jasper, Ind., 1988-94—; event coord. Hoosiers fo Safety Belts, Dale, Ind., 1987; troop co-leader Girl Scouts Am., Holland, 1986-88; active Southridge Band Boosters, Huntingburg, 1986-91; mem. AIDS coun. S.W. Dubois County Sch. Corp., 1988—; mem. adv. coun. Prenatal Substance Use Prevention Program, 1989-93; mem. HIV prevention cmty. planning com., Ind. State Dept. Health, 1994-95; chmn. schs. com., chmn. Midwest AIDS Tng. and Edn. Ctr. com., founding co-chmn. Dubois County AIDS Cmty. Action Group, Huntingburg, 1991—; mem. S.W. Dubois County Sch. Bd., 1992—, pres., 1995-97; active March of Dimes, 1978-90; mem. legis. com. Ind. State Sch. Bd. Assn., 1996-97, chmn. legis. com., 2000-01, mem. awards com. 2001—;, chmn. awards com. 2002; mem. perinatal adv. bd. S.W. Ind., 1997—. Mem. ANA (bd. dirs.), NAACOG, Ind. Coun. Nurse Mgrs., Assn. for Practitioners in Infection Control (Amelia K. Sloan lectureship Ind. 1992, pres.-elect 2002, pres. 2003), Assn. Oper. Rm. Nurses, Huntingburg C. of C., Beta Sigma Phi (v.p.). Republican. Lutheran. Avocation: reading. Home: PO Box 88 403 S 2nd Ave Holland IN 47541-0506 Office: St Josephs Hosp 1900 Medical Arts Dr Huntingburg IN 47542-9190 E-mail: theim@psci.net.

HEIMAN, GROVER GEORGE, JR., editor, writer; b. Galveston, Tex., July 26, 1920; s. Grover George and Rose Mary (Ulch) H.; m. Virginia D. Williamson, Feb. 14, 1942 (dec.); children: Virginia, Grover, Deborah, Richard. Student, Lee Coll., 1937-40, U. Tex., 1940-41; BS in Commerce cum laude, U. So. Calif., 1959. With USAAF, 1941-45; News reporter Corsicana (Tex.) Daily Sun, 1945-47; commd. 2d lt. USAAC, 1942; advanced through grades to col. USAF, 1963; spl. asst. to USAF Chief of Staff, Pentagon, Washington, 1959-63; chief of info. Allied Air Forces So. Europe, Naples, Italy, 1963-66; chief mags. and books divsn. Dept. Def., Pentagon, 1966-68; ret., 1968; mng. editor Armed Forces Mgmt. mag., Washington, 1968-70; assoc. editor Nation's Business mag., Washington, 1970-76, industry editor, 1976-78, mng. editor, 1978-80, editor, 1980-82, editor emeritus, 1982-99. Chmn. Naples Dependent Schs. bd., 1964-65. Author: (with Rutherford Montgomery) Jet Navigator, 1959, Jet Tanker, 1961, Jet Pioneers, 1963, (with Virginia Myers) Careers For Women In Uniform, 1971, Aerial Photography, 1973. Decorated DFC, Legion of Merit. Mem. Nat. Press Club, Beta Gamma Sigma. Roman Catholic.

HEIMAN, MARK LOUIS, research scientist; b. Ft. Belvior, Va., Oct. 9, 1952; s. Sol Heiman, Lois Ann Heiman; m. Sharon Kay Spears; children: Justin, Mary. PhD, La. State U. Med. Ctr., 1978. Rsch. asst. prof. medicine Tulane U. Sch. Medicine, New Orleans, 1982—86; sr. scientist Eli Lilly and Co., Idpls., 1987—90, rsch. scientist, 1990—95, sr. rsch. scientist, 1995—2000, rsch. advisor, 2000—. Dir. obesity rsch. Eli Lilly and Co., 2000—01. Mem.: Am. Obesity Assn., N.Am. Assn. for Study of Obesity, Endocrine Soc. Jewish. Avocation: Motorcycles. Home: 7523 Brookview Cir Indianapolis IN 46250 Office: Eli Lilly and Co Lilly Corporate Ctr Indianapolis IN 46285 Office Fax: 317 276 9574. Personal E-mail: p2itary@aol.com. Business E-Mail: heiman_mark_L@Lilly.com.

HEIMAN, MARVIN STEWART, finance company executive; b. Chgo., Sept. 16, 1945; s. Samuel J. and Mildred (Miller) H.; m. Adrienne Joy Nathan, Aug. 7, 1966; children: Scott, Michelle, Adam. Student, Roosevelt U., 1963-67. Pres. Curtom Record Co., Chgo., 1969-80, Gold Coast Entertainment, Chgo., 1980-82; ptnr. Profl. Real Estate Securities Co., Lincolnwood, Ill., 1982-86; pres., chmn. bd. Sussex Fin. Group, Inc., Skokie, Ill., 1986—; ptnr. Spago Restaurant, Chgo., 1997—. Bd. dirs. Skokie Bank, Drovers Bank, Chgo., Met. Health Care; ptnr. Cole Taylor Banks, Chgo., 1984—, bank examining com., 1986—, ptnr. Chgo. White Sox Am. League Baseball Club, 1981—, Gore/Bronson Bancorp, 1988, Sun Life of Can., 1993. Mem. Rep. Nat. Com., 1980—, Simon Wiesenthal Ctr., 1988. Recipient Men of Achievement award Cambridge, Eng., Nat. Quality award Nat. Assn. Life Underwriters, 1992. Mem. Internat. Assn. Fin. Planners, Chgo. Assn. Life Underwriters, Real Estate Securities Syndication Assn. Am., Nat. Assn. Securities Dealers (registered rep.), Am. Jewish Com. (Humanitarian award 1978), Internat. Platform Assn., Million Dollar Round Table, Pres.'s Club (Am. funds com. 1992). Avocations: baseball, tennis, music. Office: Sussex Fin Group Inc 707 Lake Cook Rd Deerfield IL 60015-5613

HEIMANN, BEVERLY ANN, business educator, consultant; b. Canton, Ohio, June 20, 1955; d. Arthur Leonard and Marian Patricia Orkis; m. David Eugene Heimann, July 30, 1977 (div. Aug. 1989); children: D. Ryan, Desirae. BA, Walsh Coll., Canton, Ohio, 1977; MBA, Kent State U., 1982, PhD, 1992. Personnel analyst Ford Motor Co., Canton, Ohio, 1977—82; asst. prof. Walsh Coll., Canton, Ohio, 1982—85; instr. Kent State U., Canton, Ohio, 1987—90; prof. Ashland U., Ashland, Ohio, 1991—. Cons. Westfield Groups, Westfield, Ohio, 1999—, Richland County, Ohio, 2001, City of Massillon, Ohio, 2002. Contbr. articles to profl. jours. Facilitator Massillon YWCA, Massillon, Ohio, 1997; Perry local team process Perry Local Schs., Massillon, Ohio, 1991—94. Mem.: Acad. Mgmt., Beta Gamma Sigma, Delta Mu Delta (hon.). Avocations: cooking, walking, reading. Office: Ashland U 211 Andrews Hall Ashland OH 44805 Business E-Mail: bheimann@ashland.edu.

HEIMANN, JOHN GAINES, investment banker; b. N.Y.C., Apr. 1, 1929; s. Sidney M. and Dorothy V.B. (Gainesburg) H.; m. Margaret E. Fechheimer, Dec. 2, 1956 (div.); children: Joshua Gaines, Eliza Faith; m. Maria Cristina Anzola, Oct. 17, 1989. BA in Econs., Syracuse (N.Y.) U., 1950; LLD (hon.), St. Michael's Coll., 1979. V.p. Smith, Barney & Co., N.Y.C., 1955-66; sr. v.p., dir. E.M. Warburg, Pincus & Co., Inc., N.Y.C., 1967-75; N.Y. State supt. banks, 1975-76; N.Y. State commr. housing and community renewal, 1976-77; compt. of the currency, 1977-81; co-chmn. exec. com. Warburg, Paribas, Becker, N.Y.C., 1981-82; dep. chmn. A.G. Becker Paribas Inc., Paribas Internat., 1982-84; vice chmn. Merrill Lynch Capital Markets, N.Y.C., 1984-91; chmn. Europe/Middle East Merrill Lynch, London, 1988-90; chmn. global fin. instns. group office of chmn. Merrill Lynch & Co. Inc., N.Y.C., 1991-99; chmn. Fin. Stability Inst. of the Bank for Internat. Settlements, N.Y.C., 1999-2001; sr. advisor Fin. Stability Inst. Bank for Internat. Settlements, 2001; sr. advisor Merrill Lynch & Co., Inc., 2001—03. Chmn. Merrill Lynch Internat. Bank; chmn. Fin. Svcs. Coun.; mem. exec. com. Inst. Internat. Fin.; chmn. Fed. Fin. Instns. Exam. Coun., 1979-81, Comml. Reinvestment Task Force, 1978-81, 20th Century Task Force on Internat. Debt Crisis; lectr. Harvard U., Yale U., Columbia U., U. Calif., NYU; mem. adv. bd. sch. mgmt. Fishman-Davidson Ctr. for Study of Svc. Sector; chmn. Brit-N.Am. com.; trustee Nat. PolicyAssn.; vice chmn., chmn. securities subcom. Am. Banking and Securities Assn. of London; chmn. N.Y. State Supt.'s Adv. Com. on Transnat. Banking Instns., 1981; co-chmn. Derivatives Policy Group; mem. Fed. Res. Bank of N.Y.'s Internat. Capital Markets Adv. Com.; mem. adv. com. on fin. svcs. Dept. U.S. Treasury; mem. Prep for Prep; mem. governing coun. Ctr. for Study of Fin. Instns. Bd. dirs., treas. Group of Thirty; bd. dirs. Am. Ditchley Found., Citizens Com. for N.Y.C.; mem. N.Y.C. Housing Partnership, Citizens Com. for Affordable Housing; trustee Hampshire Coll., mem. strategic com. France Tresor; mem. Citizens Com. for N.Y. C., bd. dirs., Inst. Internat. Fin.; mem. adv. coun. Ctr. for Econ. Policy Rsch.; mem. Coun. Fgn. Rels. Named Housing Man of Yr. Nat. Housing Conf., 1976; recipient Bank Adminstrn. Key for Disting. Svc., 1980, Alexander Hamilton award Treasury Dept., 1981, Brotherhood award NCCJ, 1986, Pacesetter award Nat. Assn. Bank Women, Inc., 1986. Mem. Nat. Policy Assn. (vice chmn.), Fgn. Rels. Coun. Democrat. Office: Warburg Pincus 466 Lexington Ave Fl 11 New York NY 10017

HEIMANN, JOSHUA GAINES, commercial banker; b. N.Y.C., Mar. 1, 1959; s. John Gaines and Margaret Edith (Fechheimer) H.; m. Karen Olin, July 26, 1987; children: Alexandria Rand, Carson Olin. Rachel Eliza. BA, Hampshire Coll., 1982; MBA, NYU, 1988. Mgmt. assoc. Rep. Nat. Bank of N.Y., N.Y.C., 1982-85, asst. treas., 1985-86, asst. v.p., 1986-88, v.p., 1988-92; v.p. and regional ops. officer Republic Nat. Bank of N.Y., Buenos Aires, 1992—95. Trustee Citizens Budget Commn. Mem. Young Mortgage Bankers Assn. Democrat. Avocations: horseback riding, hiking, mountain biking, collecting jazz.

HEIMANN-HAST, SYBIL DOROTHEA, language arts and literature educator; b. Shanghai, May 8, 1924; came to U.S., 1941; d. Paul Heinrich and Elisabeth (Halle) Heimann; m. David G. Hast, Jan. 11, 1948 (div. 1959); children: Thomas David Hast, Dorothea Elizabeth Hast-Scott. BA in French, Smith Coll., 1946; MA in French Lang. and Lit., U. Pitts., 1963; MA in German Lang. and Lit., UCLA, 1966; diploma in Spanish, U. Barcelona, Spain, 1972. Cert. German, French and Spanish tchr., Calif. Assoc. in German lang. UCLA, 1966-70; asst. prof. German Calif. State U., L.A., 1970-71; lectr. German Mt. St. Mary's Coll., Brentwood, Calif., 1974-75; instr. French and German, diction coach Calif. Inst. of Arts, Valencia, 1977-78; coach lang. and diction UCLA Opera Theater, 1973-93, ret., 1993, lectr. dept. music, 1973-93; interviewer, researcher oral history program UCLA, 1986-93; dir., founder ISTMO, Santa Monica, Calif., 1975—. Cons. interpreter/translator L.A. Music Ctr., U.S. Supreme Ct., L.A., J. Paul Getty Mus., Malibu, Calif., Warner New Media, Panorama Internat. Prodn., Sony Records, 1986—; voice-over artist; founder, artistic dir. Westside Opera Workshop, 1986-94. Author of poems. Mem. KCET Founder Soc. UCLA grantee, 1990-91. Mem. AAUP, MLA, SAG, AFTRA, KCET Founder Soc., Sunset Succulent Soc. (v.p., bd. dirs., reporter, annual show chmn.), German Am. C. of C., L.A. Avocations: performing arts, literature, history, plants, designing and knitting sweaters. Home and Office: River's Edge 111 Dekoven Dr Apt 606 Middletown CT 06457-3463

HEIMBERG, MURRAY, pharmacologist, biochemist, physician, educator; b. Bklyn., Jan. 5, 1925; s. Gustav and Fannie (Geller) H.; children by previous marriage: Richard G., Steven A.; m. Anna Frances Langlois Knox, July 12, 1964; stepchildren: Larry M. Knox, David S. Knox. BS, Cornell U., Ithaca, N.Y., 1948, MNS, 1949; PhD in Biochemistry (NIH fellow), Duke, 1952; MD, Vanderbilt U., 1959. NIH Postdoctoral fellow in biochemistry Med. Sch. Washington U., St. Louis, 1952-54; research asso. physiology Med. Sch. Vanderbilt U., 1954-59, asst. prof. to prof. pharmacology, and asst. prof. medicine, 1959-74; prof., chmn. dept. pharmacology, prof. medicine U. Mo., 1974-81; prof. and chmn. dept. pharmacology, prof. medicine, endocrinology and metabolism U. Tenn., Health Sci. Ctr., Memphis, 1981-96; Van Vleet prof. pharmacology U. Tenn., Memphis, 1986-96, Disting. prof. pharmacology and medicine, 1996-99, disting. prof. pharmacology and medicine emeritus, 2000—. Cons. NSF, NIH; cons., established investigator Am. Heart Assn.; attending physician U. Tenn. Hosps. and Memphis VA Hosp.; dir. lipid metabolism clinic U. Tenn. Med. Group. Contbr. articles to profl. jours. Served with inf., AUS, 1943-45, ETO. Decorated Purple Heart, Bronze Star; recipient Lederle Med. Faculty award; research grantee. Fellow AAAS, Am. Coll. Clin. Pharmacology, Am. Heart Assn.; mem. Am. Soc. Biol. Chemistry and Molecular Biology, Am. Soc. Pharmacology and Exptl. Therapeutics, Endocrine Soc., Am. Diabetes Assn., So. Soc. Clin. Investigation. Home: 105 Devon Way Memphis TN 38111-7711 E-mail: mheimberg@utmem.edu., mheimber@midsouth.rr.com.

HEIMBOLD, CHARLES ANDREAS, JR., ambassador; b. Newark, May 27, 1933; s. Charles Andreas and Mary Joseph (Corrigan) Heimbold; m. Monka Astrid Barkvall, Sept. 22, 1962; children: Joanna, Eric, Leif, Peter. BA cum Laude, Villanova U., 1954; LLB cum laude, U. Pa., 1960; LLM, NYU, 1966; postgrad., Hague Acad. Internat. Law, 1959. Bar: N.Y. 1962. Assoc. Milbank, Tweed, Hadley & Mc Cloy, 1960-63; staff atty. Bristol-Myers Squibb Co., N.Y.C., 1963-70, dir. corp. devel., 1970-73, v.p. planning and devel., 1981-84, sr. planning and devel., 1981-84, pres., health care group, 1984-88, pres., health care group and sr. v.p. planning and devel., 1988-89, dir., 1989, exec. v.p., 1989-92, pres., 1992-94, pres., CEO, 1994-95, chmn., CEO, 1995-2001, chmn. bd. dirs., 2001; U.S. amb. to Sweden, 2001—. Trustee U. Pa., mem. bd. overseers Law Sch. With USN, 1954—57. Mem.: Assn. Bar City of N.Y., Causeway Club, Riverside Yacht Club. Home: Pilot Rock Ln Riverside CT 06878-2409 Office: Bristol Myers Squibb Co 345 Park Ave Fl 3 New York NY 10154-0004

HEIMBURGER, IRVIN LEROY, retired surgeon; b. Tsinan, China, Sept. 28, 1931; came to U.S., 1934; s. LeRoy Francis and Margaret Coleman (Smith) H.; m. Marcia Jean Enlow, June 30, 1963; children: Angela R., Jeffrey L., Christian I., Jenny E. BA, Drury Coll., 1953; MD, Vanderbilt U., 1957. Diplomate Am. Bd. Surgery, Am. Bd. Thoracic Surgery. Intern Vanderbilt U. Hosp., Nashville, 1957-58; resident in surgery Ind. U. Hosp., Indpls., 1958-63; thoracic fellow Leeds (Eng.) U. Hosp., 1963-64; from instr. to clin. assoc. prof. Ind. U. Med. Ctr., Indpls., 1964-80; med. staff St. Mary Med. Ctr., Evansville, Ind., 1966—, Deaconess Hosp., Evansville, Ind., 1966—. Contbr. articles to profl. jours. Pres. Vanderburgh County Med. Soc., Evansville, Ind., 1977-78. Fellow ACS (pres. Ind. chpt. 1977-78); mem. Cen. Surg. Assn., Internat. Cardiovascular Soc., Soc. Thoracic Surgeons, Midwest Surg. Soc., Am. Philat. Soc. Home: 7700 Newburgh Rd Evansville IN 47715-4530

HEIMERDINGER, JOHN FREDERICK, association executive; b. N.Y.C., June 3, 1932; s. Frederick M. and Jane R. (Rosenthal) H.; AB magna cum laude, Princeton U., 1954; MSSW, Columbia U., 1956; m. Suzanne Schrier, June 20, 1954 (dec. Aug. 1987); m. Marilyn Zurow Wilkes, Apr. 2, 1989; children: Charles F., Daniel J., Linda R. With Ladenburg, Thalmann & Co., N.Y.C., 1956-73, adminstrv. mgr., 1958-64, gen. ptnr., 1964-72, sr. exec. v.p., vice chmn. bd., 1972-73; assoc. exec. dir. Jewish Guild for Blind, N.Y.C., 1973-77, pres., chief exec. officer, 1977-97; dir. On-Line Systems Inc., 1968-73, Cooperstown Corp. Md.; adj. assoc. prof. Columbia U. Sch. Social Work, ret. 2001; mem. panel arbitrators Nat. Assn. Security Dealers, The N.Y. Stock Exchg. Mem. Byram Hills Sch. Bd., 1965-70, v.p., 1969, 70; active Armonk Ind. Fire Co., 1958—, chief dept., 1979-81; dist. fire commr., Town of North Castle, 1981—; mem. adv. coun. Sch. Social Work, Columbia U., 1975-88, vice chmn., 1979-83, chmn., 1983-88; trustee No. Westchester Hosp., 1982-94; dir. Westechester Medical Ctr., 1998—; dir. chmn. bd. Vis. Nurse Svc. Hudson Valley; mem. nat. com. A Campaign for Columbia; mem. spl. gifts com. A Campaign for Princeton, N.Y.C. Recipient medal Alumni Fedn. of Columbia U., 1980. Mem. NASW, Nat. Assn. Emergency Med. Technicians, Internat. Assn. Fire Chiefs, Am. Mgmt. Assn., Am. Arbitration Assn., Phi Beta Kappa. Democrat. Jewish. Clubs: Sunningdale Country. E-mail: joheim@aol.com. Home: 13 Thornwood Rd Armonk NY 10504-2807 Office: Cooperstown Corp 707 Westchester Ave White Plains NY 10604

HEIMFELD, SHELLY, hematologist, researcher, immunologist, researcher; b. May 11, 1955; PhD, U. Calif., 1983. Rsch. scientist, co-principal investigator SyStemix, Palo Alto, Calif., 1988—90; vis. scientist dept. of immunology DNAX Rsch. Inst., 1990—91; rsch. scientist, dir. biol. rsch. CellPro, Bothell, Wash., 1991—95, dir. discovery and intellectual property, 1995—98; staff scientist, dir. facility cellular therapy Fred Hutchinson Cancer Rsch. Ctr., Seattle, 1998—2001, assoc. mem., dir. facility cellular therapy, 2001—; dir., facility cellular therapy Seattle Cancer Care Alliance, 2001—; dir., c-gmp cell processing facility Fred Hutchinson Cancer Rsch. Ctr., 2001—. Mem.: AAAS, Internat. Cytokine Soc., European Hematology Assn., Am. Soc. Blood and Bone Marrow Transplantation, Am. Soc. Gene Therapy, NY Acad. Scis. Achievements include patents for 1992 Patent # 5, 087, 570; Homogeneous Mammalian Hematopoietic Stem Cell Composition; Methods and Devices for Culturing Human Hematopoietic Cells and Their Precursors; Apparatus and Method for Particle Separation in a Closed Field. Office: Fred Hutchinson Cancer Rsch Ctr 1100 Fairview Ave N D5-390 PO 19024 Seattle WA 98109 Office Fax: 206-667-4937. Personal E-mail: sheimfel@fhcrc.org. E-mail: sheimfel@fhcrc.org.

HEIMLICH, HENRY J. physician, surgeon, educator; b. Wilmington, Del., Feb. 3, 1920; s. Philip and Mary (Epstein) Heimlich; m. Jane Murray, June 3, 1951; children: Philip, Janet, Elisabeth. BA, Cornell U., 1941, MD, 1943; DSc (hon.), Wilmington Coll., 1981, Adelphi U., 1982, Rider Coll., 1983, Alfred U., 1993. Diplomate Am. Bd. Surgery, Am. Bd. Thoracic Surgery. Intern Boston City Hosp., 1944; resident VA Hosp., Bronx, 1946—47, Mt. Sinai Hosp., N.Y.C., 1947—48, Bellevue Hosp., N.Y.C., 1948—49, Triboro Hosp., Jamaica, NY, 1949—50; attending surgeon divsn. surgery Montefiore Hosp., N.Y.C., 1950—69; dir. surgery Jewish Hosp., Cin., 1969—77; prof. advanced clin. scis. Xavier U., Cin., 1977—89; assoc. clin. prof. surgery U. Cin. Coll. Medicine, 1969—78. Pres. Heimlich Inst.; mem. Pres.'s Commn. on Heart Disease, Cancer and Stroke, 1965; pres. Nat. Cancer Found., 1963—68, bd. dirs., 1960—70; founder Heimlich Inst. Found. Author: Postoperative Care in Thoracic Surgery, 1962; author: (with M.O. Cantor, C.H. Lupton) Surgery of the Stomach, Duodenum and Diaphragm, Questions and Answers, 1965; contbr. chapters to books, articles to profl. jours.; prodr.(film): Esophageal Replacement with a Reversed Gastric Tube (Medaglione Di Bronzo Minerva, 1961), Reversed Gastric Tube Esophagoplasty Using Stapling Technique, How to Save a Choking Victim: The Heimlich Maneuver, 1976, 1982, How to Save a Drowning Victim: The Heimlich Maneuver, 1981, Stress Relief: The Heimlich Method, 1983, (video): Dr. Heimlich's Home First Aid Video, 1989 (Vira award, 1989); editl. bd. films Reporte's Medicos, 1962. Cmty. Devel. Found., 1967—70; Save the Chidlren FEdn., 1967—68; United Cancer Coun., 1967—70. Served to lt. (s.g.) USNR, 1944—46. Recipient Lasker award for Pub. Svc., Lasker Found., 1984, China-Burma-India Vets. Assn. Americanism award, 1988, 1st Heimlich Humanitarian award, Spirit of Am. Festival, 1994, Heimlich Inst. established in perpetuity by Deaconness Assns., Inc. Fellow: ACS (chpt. pres. 1964), Am. Coll. Gastroenterology, Am. Coll. Chest Physicians; mem.: AMA (cons. to jour.), Ctrl. Surg. Assn., Collegium INternat. Chirurgiae Digestive, Pan Am. Med. Assn., Am. Gastroent. Assn., Soc. Surgery Alimentary Tract, N.Y. Soc. Thoracic Surgery, Cin. Soc. Thoracic Surgery, Soc. Thoracic Surgeons (founding mem.). Achievements include development of Heimlich Operation (reversed gastric tube esophagoplasty) for replacement of esophagus; invention of Heimlich chest drain valve, Heimlich Micro-Trach (HMT) for COPD, emphysema and cystic fibrosis; development of Heimlich Maneuver to save lives of victims of food choking and drowning and prevents and overcomes asthma attacks (listed in Random House, Oxford Am. and Webster dictionaries); Computers for Peace, a program to maintain peace throughout world and A Caring World. Office: Heimlich Inst Found Inc 311 Straight St Cincinnati OH 45219-1018 E-mail: heimlich@iglou.com. *I have never been satisfied with existing methods and seek to simplify and improve them. After devising an operation for replacement of the esophagus, I became aware that with one such discovery I could help more people in a few weeks than in my entire lifetime as a surgeon in the operating room. The Heimlich Maneuver, which saves thousands of choking and drowning victims as well as asthmatics annually, confirmed this realization. My ultimate goal is to avoid needless death and promote well-being for the largest number of people by establishing a philosophy that will eliminate war and promote a caring world. Seeking to find a cure for cancer, AIDS, and Lyme disease through malariotherapy.*

HEIN, DAVID, humanities educator; b. Balt., Oct. 2, 1954; s. Charles L. and Ruth Zeller (Giese) Hein. BA, U. Va., 1976, PhD, 1982; MA, U. Chgo., 1977. English master Blue Ridge Sch., St. George, Va., 1982-83; asst. prof. religion Hood Coll., Frederick, Md., 1983-89, assoc. prof., 1989-94, prof., 1994—, chair dept. religion and philosophy, 1988—, interim co-dean, 2000—01. Mem. archives adv. com. Episcopal Diocese Md., Balt., 1995—; Ferris lectr. Emmanuel Episcopal Ch., Balt., 2002. Author: (book) Noble Powell and the Episcopal Establishment in the Twentieth Century, 2001; co-author: Essays on Lincoln's Faith and Politics, 1983, The Episcopalians, 2003; editor: A Student's View of the College of St. James, 1988, Readings in Anglican Spirituality, 1991; mem. editl. bd. Md. Hist. Mag., 1991—95, Anglican and Episcopal History, 1991—; contbr. articles to profl. jours. Trustee St. Paul's Sch., Brooklandville, Md., 1996—. Canon Lawton Meml. scholar, St. Deiniol's Residential Libr., 2001. Mem.: Colonnade Club. Episcopalian. Home: 305 Grove Blvd Frederick MD 21701-4812 Office: Hood Coll 401 Rosemont Ave Frederick MD 21701-8575 E-mail: hein@hood.edu.

HEIN, HERMAN AUGUST, physician; b. Olin, Iowa, July 30, 1936; s. Herman Fredrick and Marie Meta (Reyelts) H.; m. Carol Rae Bergquist, Aug. 31, 1958; children: Tracey, Paul. BA, Wartburg Coll., 1959; MD, U. Iowa, 1963. Diplomate Am. Bd. Pediats. and Neonatal/Perinatal Medicine. Instr. Univ. of Tex. Coll. of Medicine, Dallas, 1964-65; pediatrician, pvt. practice Dubuque, Iowa, 1966-73; dir. Iowa Statewide Perinatal Care Program, Iowa City, 1973—; asst. prof. Univ. of Iowa Coll. of Medicine, Iowa City, 1973-76, assoc. prof., 1976-81, prof., 1981—. Spl. cons. Iowa Dept. Pub. Health, Des Moines, 1990—. Med. cons. SIDS Alliance, Des Moines, 1996—; apptd. to Nat. Commn. to Prevent Infant Mortality, Washington, 1987-93. Recipient Nat. Unsung Hero award Newsweek Mag., 1988. Fellow Am. Acad. Pediat., Am. Pediat. Soc.; mem. Iowa Med. Soc. Independent. Lutheran. Avocations: golf, cooking. Office: Dept Pediatrics 200 Hawkins Dr Iowa City IA 52242-1009

HEIN, JENNIFER LOOMIS, information technology consultant; b. Santa Monica, Calif., Feb. 16, 1962; d. James N. and Priscilla June (MacKenzie) Loomis; 1 child, MacKenzie James. BS in Bus. Administrn., Calif. State U., Northridge, 1993; MBA, Calif. Lutheran U., 2001. Contr. The Friedman Group, Culver City, Calif., 1990-94; asst. v.p. corp. expansion and devel. Pacific Rim Assurance Co., Woodland Hills, Calif., 1995-96; dir. fin. analysis Sterling Software, Woodland Hills, Calif., 1996-99; dir. fin. reporting, planning and analysis Cardiac Rhythm Mgmt. divsn. St. Jude Med., 1999-2000; sr. project mgr. Info. Tech. Group, Inc., Encino, Calif., 2000—. Mem. Am. Mensa. Presbyterian. Avocations: travel, hiking, reading, painting, skiing. Home: 3159 Foxtail Ct Thousand Oaks CA 91362-4902 Office: 16000 Ventura Blvd Ste 600 Encino CA 91436-2753 E-mail: jennifer_hein@bigfoot.com., jhein@itgusa.com.

HEIN, KAREN KRAMER, pediatrician, epidemiologist; b. N.Y.C., Feb. 2, 1944; d. Irving W. and Ruth (Eisenberg) Kramer: m. Ralph Dell, Aug. 28, 1983; children: Ethan, Molly. BA, U. Wis., 1966; B of Med. Sci., Dartmouth Med. Sch., 1968; MD, Columbia U., 1970. Intern Bronx Mcpl. Hosp., Bronx Mcpl. Hosp. Ctr., 1970, resident, 1971-73; dir. adolescent AIDS program Montefiore Med. Ctr., N.Y.C., 1987-94; prof. pediat. Albert Einstein Coll. Medicine, NYC, 1991—, prof. epidemiology and social medicine, 1993—, clin. prof. pediat., epidemiology and social medicine N.Y.C., 1995—; exec. officer Inst. Medicine NRC, Washington, 1995—; pres. William T. Grant Found., N.Y.C., 1998—2003. Cons. N.Y.C. Dept. Health, 1980-85, N.Y.C. Bd. Edn., 1987-93; bd. dirs. Dartmouth Med. Sch., Hanover, NH. Author: AIDS: Trading Fears for Facts Consumer Reports Books, 1989; contbr. articles to profl. jours. Named Outstanding Physician, Dept. Health and Human Svcs., 1989, Adminstrs. Citation award, 1993. Fellow Am. Bd. Pediatrics; mem. Am. Pediatric Soc., Soc. for Pediatric Rsch., Am. Acad. Pediatrics, Soc. for Adolescent Medicine (pres. 1992-93). Address: Box 607 Jacksonville VT 05342

HEIN, TODD JONATHAN, accountant; b. Encino, Calif., May 11, 1960; s. Walter Adolph Jr. and Valerie Wynann (Phipps) H.; 1 child, MacKenzie James. BA in Econs., UCLA, 1982; cert. in fin. planning, U. So. Calif., 1987; MS in Taxation, Golden Gate U., 2001. CPA, Calif., CFP, CLU. Account analyst Exec. Life Ins. Co., L.A., 1983; acct. Satriano & Young, L.A., 1983-85; personal acct. Barron Hilton; pres. Hilton Hotels Corp., Beverly Hills, Calif., 1985-86; acct. Gursey, Schneider & Co., L.A., 1987-88; agent Nat. Life of Vt., L.A., 1988-89; spl. agt. Northwestern Mut. Life, Woodland Hills, Calif., 1989-96; sr. acct. Gursey, Schneider & Co., LLP, L.A., 1996-98; sr. staff accountant Engel, Kalvin, McMillan & Kipper, LLP, L.A., 1998-99; tax mgr. Sher, Sherr, Gelb & Co., Sherman Oaks, Calif., 1999—. Mem. AICPA, Calif. Soc. CPAs, Inst. Cert. Fin. Planners,Sierra Club. Avocations: hiking, reading, astronomy, travel, rock climbing. Office: Sher Sherr Gelb & Co 15060 Ventura Blvd Ste 300 Sherman Oaks CA 91403-2426

HEINDEL, NED DUANE, chemistry educator; b. Red Lion, Pa., Sept. 4, 1937; s. Penrose Horace and Dorothy May (Strayer) H.; m. Linda Clarella Heefner, Aug. 26, 1959. BS, Lebanon Valley Coll., Annville, Pa., 1959; D.Sc. (hon.), Lebanon Valley Coll., 1985; MS, U. Del., 1961, PhD, 1963; postdoctoral studies, Princeton U., 1964; DSc (hon.), Albright Coll., 1993. Instr. chemistry U. Del., 1962-63; asst. prof. chemistry Ohio U., Ironton, 1964-65, Marshall U., Huntington, W. Va., 1964-66; asst. prof. to assoc. prof. chemistry Lehigh U., Bethlehem, Pa., 1966-73, H.S. Bunn prof., 1973—, dir. Ctr. Health Scis., 1980-88; prof. nuclear medicine Hahnemann Med. U., Phila., 1971—. Cons. Pa. State Police Crime Lab., Bethlehem, 1975-88; cons. safety program J.T. Baker Chem. Co., Phillipsburg, N.J., 1978-83; regional lectr. Mid. Atlantic region Sigma Xi. Author: Iron, Armor and Adolescents, 1982; editor: Chemistry of Radiopharmaceuticals, 1978; contbr. numerous articles to profl. jours. Trustee Keystone Jr. Coll., LaPlume, Pa., 1975-90, Ctr. for History of Chemistry, Phila., 1982—, Nat. Found. for History of Chemistry, Phila., 1988—. Recipient Alumni Assn. award Lebanon Valley Coll., 1971; fellow NSF, 1963-64; recipient numerous rsch. grants. Mem. Am. Chem. Soc. (councilor, bd. dirs., pres. 1994, Harry and Carol Mosher award 1995), Royal Soc., Soc. Nuclear Medicine, Am. Assn. Pharm. Scientists, Sigma Xi. Republican. Methodist. Home: 200 Hexenkopf Rd Easton PA 18042-9570 Office: Dept Chem Lehigh U Bethlehem PA 18015

HEINDL, CLIFFORD JOSEPH, physicist, researcher; b. Chgo., Feb. 4, 1926; s. Anton Thomas and Louise (Fiala) H. BS, Northwestern U., 1947, MS, 1948; AM, Columbia U., 1950, PhD, 1959. Sr. physicist Bendix Aviation Corp., Detroit, 1953-54; student rschr. Oak Ridge Nat. Lab., 1954-55; asst. sect. chief Babcock & Wilcox Co., Lynchburg, Va., 1956-58; research group supr. Jet Propulsion Lab., Pasadena, Calif., 1959-65, mgr. research and space sci., 1965—. Served with AUS, 1944-46. Mem. AIAA, Am. Nuclear Soc., Health Physics Soc., Planetary Soc., Am. Phys. Soc. Home: 179 Mockingbird Ln South Pasadena CA 91030-2047 Office: 4800 Oak Grove Dr Pasadena CA 91109-8001

HEINDL, JASON EUGENE, research scientist; BA, Amherst Coll., Amherst, MA, 1993—97. Grad. student Harvard Med. Sch., Boston, Mass., 2002—; rsch. assoc. U. of Calif., Berkeley, Berkeley, Calif., 2001—02, Howard Hughes Med. Inst., Ann Arbor, Mich., 2000—01; peace corps vol. US Peace Corps, Ghana, 1997—2000. Mem.: Am. Chem. Soc., AAAS, NY Acad. of Sciences, Sigma Xi. Lutheran.

HEINDL, MARY LYNN, magazine editor; b. Ridgway, Pa., Aug. 10, 1937; d. Linus Michael and Hildur Johanna Josephine (Johnson) H. BA in English, U. Pitts., 1966. Office mgr. Std. Svc., Inc., Pitts., 1956-63, J.C. Keaney & Sons, Inc., Pitts., 1964-67; exec. dir. Pitts. chpt. AIA, Pitts., 1967-74; asst. exec. dir. Builders Assn. of Metro Pitts., 1975-81; coord. practice devel. Peat Marwick Mitchell, Pitts., 1982; adminstr. CADD tng. Val-Mark Cos., Pitts., 1982-83; mgr. inpex Expositions, Pitts., 1984-85; exec. dir. Western Pa. Restaurant Assn., Pitts., 1985-87; editor Dynamic Bus. SMC Bus. Couns., Pitts., 1987—. Named Western Pa. Media Advocate of Yr. U.S. SBA, 1992; recipient Seldon Hale award Nat. Assn. of Home Builders, 1976, Apex award, 2000, 03. Mem.: AIA (hon.), Altrusa Internat. (pres. 1978). Republican. Lutheran. Avocations: music, gardening, swimming, literature. Home: 651 Shady Dr E Pittsburgh PA 15228-2300 Office: SMC Bus Couns 1382 Beulah Rd Bldg 801 Pittsburgh PA 15235-5068

HEINDL, PHARES MATTHEWS, lawyer; b. Meridian, Miss., Dec. 14, 1949; s. Paul A. and Leila (Matthews) H.; m. Linda Ann Williamson, Sept. 21, 1985; children: Lori Elizabeth, Jesse Phares, Jared Matthews. BSChemE, Miss. State U., 1972; JD, U. Fla., 1981. Bar: Fla. 1981, Calif. 1982, U.S. Dist. Ct. (cen. dist.) Calif. 1983, U.S. Dist. Ct. (mid. dist.) Fla. 1983; cert. civil trial lawyer Fla. Bar. Assoc. Lafollette, Johnson et al, L.A., 1982-83, Sam E. Murrell & Sons, Orlando, Fla., 1983-84; pvt. practice Orlando, Fla., 1984-93, Altamonte Springs, Fla., 1993—. Bd. cert. civil trial lawyer. Precinct coord. Freedom Coun., Orlando, 1986; pres. Friends of the Wekiva River, 1999-2001. Mem. Fla. Bar Assn., Calif. Bar Assn., Seminole County Bar Assn. (pres. civil trial sect. 1998), ATLA, Christian Legal Soc. (past pres. Ctrl. Fla.), Fla. Acad. Trial Lawyers, Workers Compensation Rules Com. Republican. Avocation: kayak racing. Home: 2415 River Tree Cir Sanford FL 32771-8334 Office: 222 S Westmonte Dr Ste 208 Altamonte Springs FL 32714-4269

HEINE, LEONARD M., JR., investment executive; b. N.Y.C., Nov. 14, 1924; s. Leonard Max and Elise (Frey) H.; m. Sandra Fleming, Oct. 14, 1966; children; Michael Kenneth, Nancy Ellen, Thomas Charles, Christopher Altman. BS in Econs., U. Pa., 1948. Salesman Lehman Bros., N.Y.C., 1952-58; sales mgr. Rothschild, N.Y.C., 1958-62; gen. ptnr. R.J. Buck & Co., N.Y.C., 1962-70; pres., founder, chmn. Mgmt. Asset Corp., Westport, Conn., 1970-90; investment mgr., chmn., pres. LMH Fund Ltd., 1983—; pres. Heine Mgmt. Group, Inc., 1983—. Chmn., pub. Weston (Conn.) Voice. Treas. Weston Pub. Libr., 1980-81; trustee Preservation Found., Palm Beach, Fla.; bd. dirs. Fairfield Home Elderly; nat. commr. Anti-Defamation League; bd. dirs. Intracoastal Health Sys., West Palm Beach, Fla.; trustee Albert Einstein Coll. Medicine's Soc. Founders. With U.S. Army, 1943-46. Decorated Purple Heart. Mem. Am. Soc. Profl. Cons., Birchwood Country Club (Westport), U. Pa. Club (N.Y.C.), Palm Beach Country Club (Fla.). Republican.

HEINE, STEVEN ROBERT, telecommunications industry executive, poet, writer; b. Salem, Oreg., Dec. 16, 1953; s. Walter Roman and Marie Ellen Heine; m. Catherine Ann Heine, June 8, 1985; 1 child, Angela Marie. BS in History and Polit. Sci., Portland State U., Oreg., 1976. Telecom. mgr. State of Oreg., Salem, 1992—. Cons. in field; cartoonist various cmty. pubs., 1978—80. Author: 9 books of poetry; contbr. ; actor: (films) The Hunted, Good Cops/Bad Cops. Dir. Oreg. Lit. Coun., Salem, 1983—86; poetry dir. Oreg. State Fair, Salem, 1986—, Marion County Fair, Salem, 1990—2001. Named Author of the Mo., Salem Libr., 1990, featured author, English Tchrs. in Israel mag., 1998; recipient Honor for Heroism, 1971. Mem.: Oreg. State Poetry Assn. (bd. dirs. 1990). Office: PO Box 7574 Salem OR 97303

HEINECKE, DEBORAH ANN, pediatrics nurse; b. Marcos, Tex., Sept. 8, 1954; d. Casimir J. and Mary L. (Trunk) Bosak; m. James A. Heinecke, June 19, 1976. Diploma, Mercy Hosp. Sch. of Nursing, Pitts., 1972-74; BSN, Duquesne U., 1986, MSN in Nursing Adminstrn., 1994; MS in Human Resource Mgmt., LaRoche Coll., 1994. RN, Pa.; cert. neonatal intensive care nurse. Staff nurse Mercy Hosp., Pitts., 1974-80; staff nurse, asst. nurse mgr. neonatal ICU Magee Women's Hosp., Pitts., 1981-87; nurse coord. Pediatric Nursing Specialists, Pitts., 1988-89; staff nurse neo-natal ICU Magee-Women's Hosp., Pitts., 1989-91; case coord. ventilator assisted children/home program Children's Hosp. of Pitts., Pitts., 1991-98; case mgr. Highmark Blue Cross/Blue Shield, Pitts., 1998-99; case coord. Ventilator Assisted Children/Home Program, Pitts., 1999—. Mem. Nat. Assn. Neonatal Nurses, Three Rivers Assn. Neonatal Nurses (former sec.), Sigma Theta Tau (former chair mentoring Epsilon Phi chpt.). Home: 243 Meredith St Pittsburgh PA 15210-3946 E-mail: dheinecke@yahoo.com.

HEINEKEN, FREDERICK GEORGE, biochemical engineer; b. Chgo., Oct. 22, 1939; s. Frederick W.G. Heineken and Marie Helene Faber Heineken; divorced; 1 child, Christopher P. BS, Northwestern U., 1962; PhD, U. Minn., 1966. Sr. biochem. engr. Monsanto, St. Louis, 1966-71; postdoctoral fellow U. Colo., Denver, 1972-74, rsch. assoc., instr., 1974-76; sr. project engr. Cobe Labs., Lakewood, Colo., 1977-79, dept. head, 1979-81, therapy scientist, 1981-84; cons. Heineken & Assocs., Potomac, Md., 1985—; program dir. NSF, Washington, 1985—. Trustee 1st Universalist Ch., Denver, 1980-83, vice-moderator, 1984. Recipient Young Investigator award, NIH, 1974. Mem. AIChE, AAAS, Am. Chem. Soc. (councilor 1990—), Assn. for Advancement of Med. Instrumentation, Am. Soc. for Artificial Organs, St. Louis Ski Club (pres. 1971) Home: 7908 Turncrest Dr Potomac MD 20854-2772 Office: NSF Engring 4201 Wilson Blvd Arlington VA 22230-0001 E-mail: fheineken@nsf.gov.

HEINEL, ROBERT STEVEN, social services administrator; b. Detroit, Feb. 10, 1943; s. Steve J. and Hazel M. (Cupples) H. BA, Wayne State U., 1971; MSW, Mich. State U., 1985. Cert. social worker, Mich. Program dir. regional office U.S. Dept. Vets. Affairs, Detroit, 1972-77; vets. counselor Grand Traverse County, Traverse City, Mich., 1979-87; instr. Mich. State U., East Lansing, 1988-90; dir. vets. affairs Livingston County, Howell, Mich., 1991—. Newspaper columnist Veterans Corner, 1994-2002; editor Nacvso News, 1999-2000. Mem. Consortium on Aging, Livingston County, 1991—. With U.S. Army, 1965-68. Mem. NASW, Am. Legion, Vietnam Vets. Am., Nat. Assn. County Vets. Svc. Officers, Phi Kappa Phi, Phi Alpha. Avocations: motorcycle touring, swimming, writing. Office: Livingston County Vets Affairs 2300 E Grand River Ave Ste 109 Howell MI 48843-7585 E-mail: bob@co.livingston.mi.us.

HEINEMAN, ANDREW DAVID, retired lawyer; b. N.Y.C., Nov. 5, 1928; s. Bernard and Lucy (Morgenthau) H. BA, Williams Coll., 1950; LLB, Yale U., 1953. Bar: N.Y. 1953. Assoc. Proskauer Rose Goetz & Mendelsohn, N.Y.C., 1953—63; ptnr. Proskauer Rose LLP, N.Y.C., 1963—2002; ret., 2002. Pres., chmn. bd. dirs. Ernest and Mary Hayward Weir Found., N.Y.C., 1969-87, trustee Mt. Sinai Hosp. Med. Sch. and Med. Ctr., 1976—, Williams Coll., 1980-95, Abelard Found., 1976-96; Asphalt Green, 1992-96; bd. dirs. Jewish Home and Hosp. for Aged, 1967—, vice chmn. bd. dirs., 1992, chmn. bd. dirs. 1993-97; exec. asst. Citizens for Kennedy and Johnson, N.Y.C., 1960; mem. N.Y. Gov.'s Commn. on Minorities in Med. Schs., 1982. Mem. Yale Law Sch. Assn. N.Y. (pres. 1970-73), Yale Law Sch. Alumni Assn. (v.p. 1973-76, exec. com.), Audubon Soc., North Country Bird Club, Linnaean Soc. (life), Fedn. N.Y. State Bird Clubs, Brit. Naval Photog. Club. Office: Proskauer Rose LLP 1585 Broadway New York NY 10036-8299

HEINEMAN, BEN WALTER, corporation executive; b. Wausau, Wis., Feb. 10, 1914; s. Walter Ben and Elsie Brunswick (Deutsch) H.; m. Natalie Goldstein, Apr. 17, 1935; children: Martha Heineman Pieper, Ben Walter. Student, U. Mich., 1930-33; LLB, Northwestern U., 1936; LLD (hon.), Lawrence Coll., 1959; LL.D. (hon.), Lake Forest Coll., 1966, Northwestern U., 1967; LHD, DePaul U., 1986. Bar: Ill. 1936. Pvt. practice law and govt. svc., Chgo., Washington, Algiers, 1936-56; chmn. bd. dirs. Four Wheel Drive Auto Co., 1954-57; chmn. C. & N.W. Ry. Co., 1956-72; founder, former chmn., CEO Northwest Industries, Inc., 1968-85. Dir., chmn. exec. com., bd. dirs. 1st Nat. Bank, Chgo.; chmn. orgn. com. First Chgo. Corp., 1965-86; Chmn. White House Conf. to Fulfill These Rights, 1966, Pres.'s Task Force on Govt. Orgn., 1966-67, Pres.'s Commn. Income Maintenance Programs, 1967-69 Life trustee U. Chgo.; chmn. Ill. Bd. Higher Edn., 1962-69; trustee, mem. investment com. Savs. and Profit Sharing Fund Sears Roebuck Employees, 1966-71; trustee, mem. exec. com., chmn. audit com. Rockefeller Found., 1972-78; life dir. Lyric Opera, Chgo.; life trustee Orchestral Assn.; sustaining fellow Art Inst. Chgo., 20th century acquisition com.; dir. emeritus The Corning (N.Y.) Glass Mus. Fellow ABA, AAAS, Am. Bar Found. (life); mem. Am. Law Inst. (life), Ill. Bar Assn., Chgo. Bar Assn., Ephraim Club (Wis.), Yacht Club, Mid-Am. Club, Chgo. Club, Wayfarers Club, Std. Club (life), Quadrangle Club, Comml. Club (life), Carlton Club, Order of Coif, Phi Delta Phi (hon.). Office: 180 E Pearson St Apt 4304 Chicago IL 60611-2171 E-mail: BWH@hmansi.net.

HEINEMAN, BENJAMIN WALTER, JR., lawyer; b. Chgo., Jan. 25, 1944; s. Benjamin Walter and Natalie (Goldstein) H.; m. Jeanne Cristine Russell, June 7, 1975; children: Zachary R., Matthew R. BA magna cum laude, Harvard U., 1965; B.Letters, Balliol Coll., Oxford U., Eng., 1967; JD, Yale U., 1971. Bar: D.C. 1973, U.S. Supreme Ct. 1973. Reporter Chgo. Sun Times, 1968; law clk. Assoc. Justice Potter Stewart U.S. Supreme Ct., 1971-72; staff atty. Center for Law and Social Policy, 1973-75; with Williams Connolly and Califano, Washington, 1975-76; exec. asst. to sec. HEW, Washington, 1977-78, asst. sec. for planning and evaluation, 1978-79; partner Califano, Ross & Heineman, Washington, 1979-82, Sidley & Austin, Washington, 1982-87; sr. v.p., gen. counsel, sec. Gen. Electric Co., Fairfield, Conn., 1987—. Author: The Politics of the Powerless: A Study of the Campaign Against Racial Discrimination, 1972, Memorandum for the President: A Strategic Approach to Domestic Affairs in the 1980's, 1981; editor-in-chief: Yale Law Jour., 1970-71. Rhodes scholar, 1965-67 Mem. Phi Beta Kappa. Office: General Electric Co 3135 Easton Tpke Fairfield CT 06431-0001

HEINEMAN, DAVID, lieutenant governor; b. Falls City, Nebr., May 12, 1948; s. Jean Trevers and Irene Larkin H.; m. Sally Ganem, 1977. BS, U.S. Mil. Acad., 1970. Sales rep. Procter & Gamble, 1976-77; campaign mgr. Daub for Congress, 1977-78; dep. dir. Policy Rsch. Office, Nebr., 1979; dir. Nebr. State Rep. Exec. Com., 1979-81; chief of staff to Congressman Daub, 1983-88; office mgr. for Congressman Bereuter, 1990-94; city councilman City of Fremont, Nebr., 1990-94; state treas. State of Nebr., 1994—2000, Lt. Gov., 2001—. Decorated Army Commendation medal; recipient Outstanding Rep. Vol. award Douglas County Rep. Party, 1976, Outstanding Young Am. award Jaycees, 1980. Mem. Nat. Assn. State Treas. (pres. 1999-2000), Nat. Electronic Commerce Coordinating Coun. (exec. com. 1998-2000). Republican. Office: PO Box 94863 Lincoln NE 68509 E-mail: dave.heineman@email.state.ne.us.*

HEINEMAN, HEINZ, chemist; b. Berlin, Aug. 21, 1913; came to U.S., 1938; s. Felix and Edith (Boehm) H.; m. Elaine Patricia Silverman, Feb. 12, 1948 (dec. Dec. 1993); children: Susan Carol, Peter Michael; m. Barbara A. Tenenbaum, Apr. 23, 1995. PhD, U. Basel, Switzerland, 1938. Sect. chief Houdry Process Corp., Marcus Hook, Pa., 1948-57; dir. chem. and engring. rsch. M.W. Kellogg Co., N.Y.C., 1958-69; rsch. mgr. Mobil R & D Co., Princeton, N.J., 1969-78; disting. scientist Lawrence Berkeley Lab., U. Calif., Berkeley, 1978—. Cons. Mobil R & D Co., Catalytica Assocs. Founding editor Catalysis Revs., 1968—; contbr. articles to profl. jours. Mem. Adult Sch. Bd., Princeton, 1968-72, Flood Control Commn., Princeton, 1970-75, Gov.'s Coun. for Rsch., N.J., 1976-78. Recipient Disting. Scientist award U.S. Dept. Energy, 1976, H.H. Lowry award, 1993. Mem. NAE, AIChE (Disting. Lectr. award), Am. Chem. Soc. (pres. ret. chemists group Washington sect. 2001, Indsl. and Engrng. Chemistry award 1972), Washington Chem. Soc. (mgr. 2002), Internat. Congress Catalysis (pres. 1960-64), Catalysis Soc. N.Am. (E.J. Houdry award 1974), Spanish Acad. Sci. (hon.), Catalysis Club Phila. Avocations: music, photography. Home: 4600 Connecticut Ave NW Apt 206 Washington DC 20008-5702 Office: Lawrence Berkeley Lab 901 D St NW Ste 950 Washington DC 20024 E-mail: Hheinemann@LBL.gov.

HEINEMAN, PAUL LOWE, consulting civil engineer; b. Omaha, Oct. 24, 1924; s. Paul George and Annie L. (Lowe) H.; m. Gloria Nixon; children by previous marriage: Karen E., John F., Ellen F. Student, U. Omaha, 1942-43; BSC.E., Iowa State U., 1945, MS, 1948. Registered profl. engr. Mo., Calif., N.Y., Kans., 25 other states and Republic of Colombia. Instr. Iowa State U., 1946-48; designer, project mgr. Howard, Needles, Tammen & Bergendoff (Cons. Engrs.), Kansas City, Mo., 1948-64, ptnr., 1965-86; exec. v.p. Howard, Needles, Tammen & Bergendoff Internat., Inc., Kansas City, 1967-84, pres., v.p. subs., 1983-86. Bd. dirs., sec.-treas. emeritus The Road Info. Program. Served with C.E. Corp USNR, 1945-46. Fellow ASCE, Am. Cons. Engrs. Coun., Inst. Traffic Engrs.; mem. NSPE, Am. Ry. Engring. Assn., Am. Concrete Inst., Am. Arbitration Assn., Engrs. Club (Kansas City). Presbyterian (elder 1958—). Home and Office: 2 J St Lake Lotawana MO 64086-9749

HEINEMAN, WILLIAM A. political scientist, educator; b. Buffalo, Feb. 23, 1965; s. Duane T. and Sarah Stack H.; m. Linda M. Heineman, July 8, 1989; children: Joanna B., Katharine L. BA in History, U. Rochester, 1987; M in Pub. Policy, Harvard U., 1989. Intelligence analyst CIA, Washington, 1989-95; instr., asst. prof., chair history and govt. dept. No. Essex C.C., Haverhill, Mass., 1996—. Mem.: Am. Polit. Sci. Assn. Office: No Essex Cmty Coll Elliott Way Haverhill MA 01830 E-mail: wheineman@necc.mass.edu.

HEINEMANN, HEINZ, chemist, educator, researcher, consultant; b. Berlin, Aug. 21, 1913; came to U.S., 1938; s. Felix and Edith (Boehm) H.; m. Elaine Patricia Silverman, Feb. 12, 1948 (dec. Dec. 1993); children: Susan Carol, Peter Michael; m. Barbara A. Tenenbaum, Apr. 23, 1995. Diploma, U. Berlin, 1935; PhD, U. Basel, Switzerland, 1937. Rsch. chemist Danciger Oil & Refineries, Pampa, Tex., 1940-41, Attapulgus Clay Co., Phila., 1941-48; sect. chief Houdry Process Corp., Marcus Hook, Pa., 1948-57; dir. chem. & engring. rsch. M.W. Kellogg Co., N.Y.C., 1957-69; mgr. catalysis rsch. Mobil R & D Corp., Princeton, N.J., 1969-78; disting. scientist Lawrence Berkeley Lab., U. Calif., 1978—; lectr. in chem. engring. U. Calif., Berkeley, 1979-90. Pres. Internat. Congress on Catalysis, 1956-60; cons. numerous chem. and petroleum cos., 1978—. Editor Catalysis Revs. jour., 1966-86; author 130 publs. on catalysis and fuel chemistry; contbr. 6 chpts. to books, numerous articles to publs. Mem. Flood Control Commn. Princeton Twp., 1970-75, Gov's Adv. Coun. Rsch., Trenton, N.J., 1976-78; dir. Princeton Art Assn. Recipient Phila. Catalysis Soc. award, 1976, Disting. Scientist award U.S. Dept. Energy, 1978, Homer H. Lowry award U.S. Dept Energy, 1994; Advances in Catalysis Chemistry II symposium held in his honor, Salt Lake City, 1982. Fellow AAAS; mem. Am. Chem. Soc. (Indsl. and Engring. Chem. award 1972, numerous offices),

Catalysis Soc. N.Am. (Applied Catalysis award 1975), Nat. Acad. Engring., Internat. Congress Catalysis (pres. 1956-60), Ret. Chemists Group (pres. 2001). Achievements include over 50 patents in field; invention of and participation in commercialization of 16 industrial processes. Home: 4600 Connecticut Ave NW Apt 206 Washington DC 20008-5702 Office: Lawrence Berkeley Lab 905 D St SW Washington DC 20024-2115 E-mail: hheinemann@lbl.gov.

HEINEMANN, STEPHEN F. molecular neurobiologist educator; BS, Calif. Inst. Tech., 1962; PhD, Harvard U., 1967; postgrad., MIT, Stanford U. Prof. molecular neurobiology lab. Salk Inst., 1989—, dir. molecular neurobiology lab., 1989-95, chmn. of the faculty, 1992-93. Adj. prof. U. Calif. Med. Sch., San Diego. Section editor: Jour. Neurosci. Molecular Neurosci.; mem. assoc. editl. bd. Current Opinion in Neurobiology, Proceedings of the Royal Soc. series B, Hippocampus, Cellular and Molecular Neurobiology, Receptors and Channels, Neuron, 1987-91, Jour. Neurosci., 1987-91. Recipient Disting. Achievement in Neurosci. Rsch. award Bristol-Myers Squibb, 1995; named Schmidt. Lectr. U. Pa., Feigen Lectr. Stanford U., Cooper Lectr., Flynn Lectr. Yale U. Mem. NAS (vice-chair com. IBRO), Inst. Medicine, Max-Planck Inst. (external mem.), Soc. Neurosci. (councilor 1992, Grass lectr.). Achievements include research in structure and function of brain receptors and their role in neurological disease and mental illness. Office: The Salk Inst PO Box 85800 San Diego CA 92186-5800

HEINEN, JAMES ALBIN, electrical engineering educator; b. Milw., June 23, 1943; s. Albin Jacob and Viola (DeBuhr) H. BEE, Marquette U., 1964, MS, 1967, PhD, 1969. Registered profl. engr., Wis. Data analyst Med. Sch. Marquette U., Milw., 1963, teaching asst. elec. engring. dept., 1964-65, 65-66, research asst., 1966, NASA trainee, 1966-69, asst. prof., 1969—71, research assoc. Provost's Office, 1970, asst. prof. and grad. adminstr., 1971-73, assoc. prof., chmn. elec. engring. dept., 1973-76, assoc. prof., 1976-80, prof. elec. engring. and computer sci., 1980-87, prof., dir. grad. studies elec. and computer engring., 1987-95, prof. elec. and computer engring., 1995—99, rsch. prof., 1999—2000, prof. emeritus, 2000—, dir. signal processing rsch. ctr., 1990-99, co-dir. ctr. intelligent systs., controls, and signal processing, 1999—. Cons. in field Contbr. numerous articles and revs. on elec. engring. and computer sci. to profl. jours. Recipient Outstanding Engring. Tchr. award Marquette U., 1979, Teaching Excellence award Marquette U., 1985. Mem. IEEE (various coms., tech. reviewer Trans. Automatic Control 1969—, Trans. Circuits and Systems Soc. 1980—, Signal Processing Soc. 1980—, sr. mem., Meml. award Milw. sect. 1981, assoc. editor Trans. Circuits and Systems 1983-85, assoc. editor Trans. Indsl. Electronics 1996-2000), Am. Soc. Engring. Edn., Sigma Xi, Tau Beta Pi, Eta Kappa Nu (Most Oustanding Elec. Engring. Tchr. in U.S. award 1974), Pi Mu Epsilon, Alpha Sigma Nu. Home: 8200 W Menomonee River Pky Wauwatosa WI 53213-2537 Office: Marquette U Haggerty Hall Rm 211 PO Box 1881 Milwaukee WI 53201-1881 E-mail: james.heinen@marquette.edu.

HEINEN, JOHN TIMOTHY, environmental engineer; b. Oshkosh, Wis., Sept. 30, 1966; s. Larry John and Marie Jane Heinen, John Paul Fink and Judith Loretta Bloedow; m. Leslie Dawn Gahagan (div. Jan. 2, 1997); children: Timothy J., Zoë N. BS in Indsl. Tech. summa cum laude, U. Wis., Platteville, 1989. Cert. hazardous waste mgmt. Lion Tech., Inc., 2000, storm water pollution prevention mgmt. Fedn. of Environ. Techs., 2001. R&D engr. Intermet Foundries, Inc., Lynchburg, Va., 1990—93; indsl. engr. Richland Ctr. Fdy. Co., Richland Center, Wis., 1993—95, indsl. systems engr., 1995—2000, environ. dir., 2000—. Chmn. Richland County Local Emergency Planning Com., Richland Center, 1999—. Contbr. articles. Mem.: AASS, Ocean Arks, Internat., Am. Fdy. Soc. (environ. com., sec. 1996—99), Gt. Lakes Pollution Prevention Roundtable, Fedn. of Environ. Techs., Am. Chem. Soc., Nature Conservancy, Smithsonian Instn., Nat. Geog. Soc., Am. Black Holocaust Mus., Sierra Club, Epsilon Pi Tau, Phi Kappa Phi. Avocation: studies in: cosmology, philosophy, cultural anthropology, complex systems, natural & artificial intelligence and ecology. Home: 215 South Park St Richland Center WI 53581 Office: Richland Center Foundry Company 1000 Foundry Dr Richland Center WI 53581 Office Fax: 608-647-6126. Personal E-mail: atla201@yahoo.com. Business E-Mail: jheinen@rcfoundry.com.

HEINER, DOUGLAS CRAGUN, pediatrician, educator, immunologist, allergist; b. Salt Lake City, July 27, 1925; s. Spencer and Eva Lillian (Cragun) H.; m. Joy Luana Wiest, Jan. 8, 1946; children: Susan, Craig, Joseph, Marianne, James, David, Andrew, Carolee, Pauli. BS, Idaho State U., 1946; MD, U. Pa., 1950; PhD, McGill U., 1969. Intern Hosp. U. Pa., Phila., 1950-51; resident, fellow Children's Med. Ctr., Boston, 1953-56; asst. prof. pediatrics U. Ark. Med. Ctr., Little Rock, 1956-60; assoc. prof. pediatrics U. Utah Med. Ctr., Salt Lake City, 1960-66; fellow in immunology McGill U., Montreal, 1966-69; prof. of pediatrics Harbor-UCLA Med. Ctr., Torrance, 1969-94; disting. prof. of pediatrics UCLA Sch. Medicine, 1985-94, prof. emeritus, 1994—; med. specialist Russia Latter-day Saints Missions, 1997-99. Author: Allergies to Milk, 1980; mem. editl. bd. Jour. Allergy and Clin. Immunology, 1975-79, Allergy, 1981-88, Jour. Clin. Immunology, 1981-87, Pediat. Asthma, Allergy and Immunology, 1986-94; contbr. over 150 original articles to profl. jours. and chpts. to books. Scoutmaster Boy Scouts Am., Salt Lake City, 1963; com. chmn. Rancho Palos Verdes, 1979-81; high coun. mem. LDS Ch., Rancho Palos Verdes, 1983-86. with U.S. Army, 1952-53, Korea. Recipient Disting. Alumnus award Idaho State U., 1987. Fellow: Am. Coll. Allergy, Asthma and Immunology (Disting. fellow 1996), Am. Acad. Allergy and Immunology (food allergy com. 1981—94), Am. Pediatric Soc.; mem.: Am. Acad. Pediatrics, Clin Immunology Soc., Am. Assn. Immunologists, Western Soc. for Pediatric Rsch. (Ross award 1961), Soc. for Pediatric Rsch. Republican. Avocations: gardening, tennis, fishing. E-mail: dheiner@mobileblue.com.

HEINEY, JOHN WEITZEL, former utility executive; b. Lancaster, Pa., Nov. 9, 1913; s. George and Gertrude G. (Weitzel) H.; m. Betty M. Horn, Apr. 12, 1941. BS in Bus. Adminstrn, Lehigh U., 1935. With various subsidiaries Am. Water Works Co., 1935-41, 46-60; pres., chief exec. officer, dir. Indiana Gas Co., Inc., Indpls., 1960-73, chmn. bd., chief exec. officer, 1973-78, chmn. bd., 1978-84; pres., dir. Ohio River Pipe Line Corp., 1964-73, chmn. bd., 1973-78; pres., chmn. Gen. Assurance Services, Ltd., 1975-84. Bd. dirs. United Fund Greater Indpls., 1960-77; bd. dirs. Community Hosp. Indpls., 1968-73, 75-81, chmn., 1972-73; bd. dirs., chmn. Community Hosps. Found., 1983-89. Served to lt. col., inf. AUS, 1941-46. Decorated Bronze Star medal; named Sagamore of Wabash, Gov. of Ind., 1997. Mem. Am. Gas Assn. (past chmn. spl. com. on consumer affairs, 1st vice chmn. 1968, chmn. 1969, dir. Disting. Svcs. award com. 1975), Ind. Gas Assn. (past pres. and dir.), Inst. Gas Tech. (trustee 1965, chmn. bd. trustees 1968), Internat. Gas Union (mem. council and bur. 1973-75), Ind. C. of C. (dir. 1973-80), Newcomen Soc. N.Am., Beta Theta Pi. Clubs: Meridian Hills Country.

HEINEY, PAUL A. chemist, educator; s. Donald W. and Ann Borgman Heiney. BA, U. Calif., Santa Barbara, Calif., 1977; PhD, MIT, 1982. Prof. of physics U. of Pa., Phila., 1982—. Contbr. articles to profl. jours. Fellow: Am. Phys. Soc.; mem.: AAAS, AAUP, Am. Crystallographic Assn., Internat. Liquid Crystal Soc., Am. Chem. Soc. Office: Dept Physics U Pennsylvania 209 S 33rd St Philadelphia PA 19104 E-mail: heiney@physics.upenn.edu.

HEINEY, SUE PORTER, psychosocial oncology nurse; b. Pickens, S.C., Mar. 23, 1950; d. Garvin Edward and Effie Elizabeth (Anderson) Porter; m. Michael Vincent Heiney, May 21, 1949; children: Elizabeth Porter, Amanda Jean. BSN, U. S.C., 1979, MN, 1981, PhD, 1998. Charge nurse Roper Hosp., Charleston, S.C., 1971-72, Greenville (S.C.) Gen. Hosp., 1972-73, Bapt. Med. Ctr., Columbia, S.C., 1973-75, head nurse, 1975-79; staff nurse Richland Meml. Hosp., Columbia, 1979-81, clin. nurse specialist, 1981-83, Children's Hosp. Ctr. for Cancer, Columbia, 1983-93; mgr. psychol. oncology S.C. Cancer Ctr., Palmetto Health, Columbia, 1993—. Past mem. editorial bd. Oncology Nursing Forum; mem. editorial bd. Children's Health Care, Jour. Psychosocial Oncology. Named Outstanding Alumnus, U. S.C. Coll. Nursing, 1990; recipient Excellence in Practice award S.C. Hosp. Assn., 1992, 93, Joan Ashley Fifick Meml. lectureship, 1997. Fellow Am. Acad. of Nursing; Mem. ANA, Assn. Pediatric Oncology Nurses (sec. 1987-88, pres.-elect 1988-9, pres. 1989-91, past pres. 1991-92), Am. Cancer Soc. (nat. nursing adv. com. 1989-92, Lane W. Adams award 1991), Oncology Nursing Soc. (Mara Mohensen Flaherty Meml. lectr. 1995, nat. rsch. com. 1993-98), Sigma Theta Tau (Media award 1989, Founders award 1991). Baptist. Avocations: hiking, reading. Home: 108 Greengate Dr Columbia SC 29223-5806 E-mail: sue.heiney@palmettohealth.org.

HEINICKE, RALPH MARTIN, consultant; b. Hickory, N.C., Sept. 3, 1914; s. Martin John and Lydia Sophia (Kurth) H.; m. Sarah Anne Hall, July 31, 1944; 1 child, Mark. BS, Cornell U., 1936; PhD, U. Minn., St. Paul, 1950. Agr. chemist Shell Oil Co., N.Y.C., 1939-43; tech. advisor Jintan-Dolph, Osaka, Japan, 1962-86; assoc. faculty U. Hawaii, Honolulu, 1950-66; chemist Pineapple Rsch. Inst., Honolulu, 1950-55; dir. rsch. Dole Co., Honolulu, 1955-72; v.p. Biol. Control Systems, Honolulu, 1981-86; pres. Biotech. Resources Inc., Clarksville, Ind., 1990-94; cons. Morinda, Inc. Cons. various drug cos., 1972—; cons. on the xeronine-sys. Inventor, patentee on xeronine; inventor, patentee on nerve toxin insecticide. Master sgt. U.S. Army, 1942-45, CBI. Democrat. Avocations: music, writing, philosophy, new theory of physics. E-mail: rhein1@email.msn.com.

HEININGER, S(AMUEL) ALLEN, retired chemical company executive; b. New Britain, Conn., June 13, 1925; s. Alfred D. and Erma Geraldine (Kline) H.; m. Barbara Ashenfelter Griffith, June 16, 1948 (dec. Oct. 6 1994); children: Janet, Kathryn, Kenneth, Keith; m. Margot Moran Danis, Nov. 27, 1998. AB, Oberlin Coll., 1948; MS, Carnegie Inst. Tech., 1951; D.Sc., 1952. Research chemist Monsanto Chem. Co., Dayton, Ohio, 1952-56, group leader, 1956-58, project mgr. devel. dept. Organic Chems. div. St. Louis, 1958-59, mgr. fine chems. intermediates and market exploration sect., 1959-65, dir. comml. devel., 1965-67, dir. food and fine chems., 1967-71, dir. corp. plans and devel., 1971-74; gen. mgr. plasticizers div. Monsanto Indsl. Chems. Co., St. Louis, 1974-76; dir. corp. research lab. Monsanto Chem. Co., St. Louis, 1977, v.p. research and devel., 1977-79, v.p. corp. plans and bus. devel., 1980-86, v.p. resource planning, 1986-90; retired, 1990. Contbr. articles to profl. jours.; U.S., fgn. patentee in field. Alderman City of Warson Woods, Mo., 1961—65, police commr., 1967—71; trustee St. Louis Sci. Ctr., 1997—, Repertory Theatre, 1998—2000; bd. dirs. Gen. Protestant Children's Home, 1999—, Episcopal City Mission, 1998—2001, Chem. Heritage Found., 2003—. Served to lt. USNR, 1943—46. Mem. Am. Chem. Soc. (pres.-elect 1990, pres. 1991), Indsl. Rsch. Inst. (pres. 1987-88), Soc. Chem. Industry, N.Y. Acad. Scis., U.S./Mex. Found. (bd. dirs.), Old Warson Country Club, Frontenac Racquet Club, Univ. Club (St. Louis), St. Andrews Club (Delray Beach). Republican. Episcopalian.

HEINKE, REX S. lawyer; b. Harrisburg, Ill., June 9, 1950; s. William Richard and Versa Lee Heinke; m. Margaret Ann Nagle, May 6, 1978; children: William Rex, Meghan Bradley. BA, U. Witwatersrand, Johannesburg, Republic of South Africa, 1971; JD, U. Columbia, 1975. Bar: Calif. 1975. Ptnr. Gibson, Dunn & Crutcher, L.A., 1983-99, Greines, Martin, Stein & Richland, Beverly Hills, Calif., 1999—2001, Akin, Gump, Strauss, Hauer & Feld, L.A., 2001—. Office: 2029 Century Park E Ste 2400 Los Angeles CA 90067 E-mail: rheinke@akingump.com.

HEINKE, WARREN E. social services administrator; b. Salem, Oreg., Jan. 26, 1943; s. Edward Carl and Charlotte Marie (Jensen) H.; m. Mariel Margaret Seefeldt, July 21, 1973; children: Erik Jens, David William, Jill Margrethe. BA in Polit. Sci. with honors, U. Oreg., 1965; MA in Polit. Sci., cert. in Russian area studies, U. Wis., 1968, MSSW, 1970. Lic. clin. social worker, Ill. Social worker II, III Wis. Divsn. Cmty. Svcs., Fond du Lac, 1970-79, supr. II Wisconsin Rapids, 1979-82; regional v.p. Children's Home & Aid Soc. Ill., Rockford, 1982—. Mem. 7th St. Area Devel. Coun., Rockford, 1995-97. Mem. NASW (statewide nominations and leadership identification com. 1997-99, dist. program com. 1994-95, Social Worker of Yr. 2002), Foster Family Based Treatment Assn. (chmn. Ill. chpt. 1996-99, vice chmn. 1995-96, 2001-03, nat. conf. presenter St. Louis, 1996, Toronto, 1997, Mpls., 1999, Cin. 2000, co-chair nat. conf., Chgo. 2002), Child Welfare League Am. (regional conf. presenter Sioux Falls, S.D., 1975, Indpls. 1976). Democrat. Lutheran. Avocations: gardening, piano, playing the bassoon, playing the accordion, reading. Home: 2203 Oxford St Rockford IL 61103-4162 Office: Childrens Home & Aid Soc 910 2d Ave Rockford IL 61104

HEINLE, RICHARD ALAN, lawyer; b. New Kensington, Pa., May 13, 1959; s. Robert Alan and Barbara Jane (Klimeck) H.; m. Sharon Eileen Farrell, Oct. 20, 1990; children: Kelly, Kyra, Casey. AB with highest honors, U. Chgo., 1981; JD cum laude, Georgetown U., 1984. Bar: Ill. 1984, Fla. 1994. Assoc. Arnstein & Lehr, Chgo., 1984-89, Foley & Lardner, Chgo., 1989-93, ptnr. Orlando, Fla., 1994—2003; with Pohl & Short, P.A., Winter Park, Fla., 2003—. Counsel Better Bus. Bur. Ctrl. Fla., Orlando, 1996-2003, bd. dirs., 2003-. Bd. dirs. Better Bus. Bur. Ctrl. Fla., 2003—. Mem.: Fla. C. of C. (bd. dirs. 1999—2000), Mfrs. Assn. Ctrl. Fla. (bd. dirs. 1995—), Phi Beta Kappa. Roman Catholic. Avocations: golf, running. Home: 8100 Vineland Oaks Blvd Orlando FL 32835-8215 Office: Pohl & Short PA 280 W Canton Ste 410 Winter Park FL 32789 E-mail: rheinle@alumni.uchicago.edu.

HEINLEN, DANIEL LEE, alumni organization administrator; b. Columbus, Ohio, Nov. 16, 1937; s. Calvin Xenophon and Charlotte Elizabeth (Lanman) H.; m. Roberta Bishop, Mar. 20, 1966 (div. 1975); m. Gelene Vogel Kozlowski, June 17, 1978; children: Stephanie Heinlen, Kate Kozlowski Isler, Amy. BS in Social Work, Ohio State U., 1960. Youth program dir., extension dir. YMCA, Pitts., 1960-65; field dir. Alumni Assn., Ohio State U., Columbus, 1965-67, assoc. dir., 1967-73, dir. alumni affairs, 1973-92; pres., CEO Ohio State U. Alumni Assn., Inc., Columbus, 1992—; sec. Alumni Assn. Bd., Columbus, 1973—; pub. mag. Alumni Assn., Ohio State U., 1973—. Ex-officio trustee Ohio State U. Found.; presdl. search com. Ohio State U., 1990, 97, 2002; trustee Coun. for Advancement and Support of Higher Edn., Washington, 1986-88, 90-94, chmn., 1992-93; chmn. 75th anniversary Colloquium, Columbus, 1988, chmn. ann. assembly alumni track, 1988, chmn. ann. assembly, 1990; chmn. Mgmt. Inst. for Alumni Assn. Execs., Chgo., 1996, pres., 1994-96, bd. dirs., 1988-96; founding bd. Coun. Alumni Assn. Execs. 1989-96, pres. 1992-93; chmn. Univ. ProNet, Inc., Palo Alto, Calif., 1996-99, chmn. alumni dirs. Big Ten, 1973, 84, 93; mem. Ohio State U. Pres.'s Coun., 1991-98; bd. dirs. River Road Hotel Corp.; founding chmn. Self-Governing Alumni Forum, 2000—; chmn. task force on alumni advocacy Inter Univ. Coun., 2002. Author chpts. in books. Exec. com. NW Ordinance U.S. Constn. Bicentennial Commn., Ohio, 1986-88; bd. dir. Non-profit Mailers Fedn., Wash., 1985-88; mem. OSU Com. on Student Fin. Aids, Columbus, 1973-99, exec. com. Acad. Disting. Tchg., 1995—, Newcomen Soc. N.Am., 1975-90, 93—. Recipient Ohio State U. Coll. of Social Work Disting. Svc. award, 1996; named Hon. Trustee Easter Seal Rehab. Ctr. of Ctrl. Ohio, Columbus, 1988-92; D.L. Heinlen award for univ. advocacy named in his honor Ohio Sate U. Alumni Assn., Inc., 1995. Mem. Rotary (bd. dirs. Columbus Club 1986, v.p. 1987-89, pres. 1989-90), Univ. Club (bd. dirs., 2nd v.p. 1985-88, 94-95, 1st v.p. 1996), Faculty Club (mem. bd. control 1978-80, pres.-elect 1999, pres. 2000-01), Kit Kat (exec. com. 1999-2002, sec. 2001—), Golden Key Nat. Honor Soc. (hon. mem.), Sphinx Coun. Avocations: tennis, sporting clays. Home: 2981 E Powell Rd Lewis Center OH 43035-9517 Office: Ohio State U Alumni Assn Inc 2200 Olentangy River Rd Columbus OH 43210-1035 E-mail: heinlen.4@osu.edu.

HEINRICH, RANDALL WAYNE, lawyer; b. Houston, Nov. 29, 1958; s. Albert Joseph Sr. and Beverly June Earles; m. Linda Carol Cheek, June 6, 1993; children: Angela Leigh, Conrad Randall. BA, Baylor U., 1980, postgrad., 1981, Rice U., 1981-82; JD, U. Tex., 1985. Bar: Tex. 1985. Assoc. Baker & Botts, Houston, 1985-87, Chamberlain, Hrdlicka, White, Williams & Martin, Houston, 1987-91, Norton & Blair, Houston, 1991-92; mem. Gillis Paris & Heinrich, Houston, 1992—; mng. dir. Baytree Investors, Houston, 1993-97. Mem. dirs.' circle Houston Grand Opera, 1991, The Arts Symposium, 1991, Center Stage, Alley Theater, Houston, 1992-93, Houston Entrepreneurs' Forum, 1990-91; bd. dirs. The Cadre, 1991-92; pres. Exchange Club of Bayou City, 1992-93. Mem. ABA (YLD securities law com. 1993-95, vice chmn. 1994-95), NASD Pool Securities Arbitrators, Am. Arbitration Assn. (mem. nat. panel neutrals), Houston Bar Assn., Forum Club Houston, Phi Delta Theta. Baptist. Home: 4318 Saint Michaels Ct Sugar Land TX 77479-2986 Office: Gillis Paris & Heinrich 8 Greenway Plz Ste 818 Houston TX 77046

HEINRICH, TIMOTHY JOHN, lawyer; b. Houston, Nov. 30, 1961; s. Albert J. and Beverly J. Heinrich; m. Tammy K. Morgan, Aug. 10, 1985; children: John, Allison, Michelle, Philip. BA, Washington U., St. Louis, 1984; JD, U. Tex., 1987. Bar: Tex. 1987. Assoc. Hiller Kornfeld Axelrad & Falik, Houston, 1987-90; assoc., shareholder Boyar & Miller, Houston, 1990—. Lay leader Terrace United Meth. Ch., Houston, 1994-97. Mem. Kiwanis (lt. gov. Houston 1997-98). Office: Boyar & Miller 4265 San Felipe St Ste 1200 Houston TX 77027-2917

HEINS, ESTHER, botanical artist, painter; b. Bklyn, Nov. 10, 1908; d. Israel and Margaret (Brown) Berow; m. Harold Heins; Sept. 8, 1929 (dec. 1987); children: Marilyn Heins, Judith Leet. BS in Edn., Mass. Coll. Art, 1929. Freelance artist, Boston, 1930-60; bot. artist, illustrator plant introductions Arnold Arboretum, Boston, 1960—. Contbr. bot. illustrations to profl. jour.; one-woman shows include Graham Arader Gallery, NYC, Harvard Radcliffe Hilles Libr., Arnold Arboretum, Boston Pub. Libr., Schlesinger Libr., Cambridge, Mass.; group shows include Hunt Inst. for Bot. Documentation, Pitts., Arnold Arboretum, Munich, Germany, Smithsonian, Washington, Oakland, Calif., others; represented in permanent collections at Mus. Fine Arts, Boston, Hunt Inst. for Bot. Documentation, Schlesinger Libr., Radcliffe Coll., Arnold Arboretum, Boston Pub. Libr., Fogg Mus., Cambridge, and numerous others in pvt. collections; illustrator, contbr. essay: (book) Flowering Trees and Shrubs: The Botanical Paintings of Esther Heins, 1987; illustrator many covers Jour. AMA., the most recent 2002. Mem. Guild of Natural Sci. Illustrators. Avocations: attending concerts of boston symphony, gardening. Home: 8 Mitchell Rd Marblehead MA 01945-1130

HEINS, JOHN, publishing executive; Staff writer Forbes Mag., N.Y.C., L.A.; asst. to CEO Gruner & Jahr Internat., Paris; Pres., CEO Parents Mag., N.Y.C., 1994-2000, Gruner & Jahr USA Pub., N.Y.C., 1994-2000; v.p. sales and internat. ops. Netscape Comm., 2000—.*

HEINS, MARILYN, college dean, pediatrics educator, writer; b. Sept. 7, 1930; d. Harold and Esther (Berow) H. m. Milton P. Lipson, 1958; children: Rachel, Jonathan. AB, Radcliffe Coll., 1951; MD, Columbia U., 1955. Diplomate Am. Bd. Pediats. Intern N.Y. Hosp., N.Y.C., 1955-56; resident in pediats. Babies Hosp., N.Y.C., 1956-58; asst. pediatrician Children's Hosp. Mich., Detroit, 1959-78; dir. pediats. Detroit Receiving Hosp., 1965-71; asst., assoc. dean student affairs Wayne State U. Med. Sch., Detroit, 1971-79; assoc. dean acad. affairs U. Ariz. Med. Coll., Tucson, 1979-83, vice dean, 1983-88, prof. pediats., 1985-88. Author: (with Anne M. Seiden) Child Care/Parent Care, 1987, ParenTips, 1999; mem. editl. bd. Jour. AMA, 1981-91; contbr. articles to profl. jours. Bd. dirs. Planned Parenthood So. Ariz., 1983, pres., 1988-89, Ariz. Ctr. for Clin. Mgmt., 1991—, Nat. Bd. Med. Examiners, 1983-88; mem. adv. bd. So. Ariz. Women's Fund, 1992—, Ariz. State Hosp., 1985-88. Recipient Alumni Faculty Svc. award Wayne State U., 1972, Recognition award, 1977, Women on the Move Achievement award YWCA Tucson, 1983, Tucson Women of Vision award Weizmann Inst., 1997, pres.'s disting. svc. award Ariz. Med. Assn., 1997. Home: 6530 N Longfellow Dr Tucson AZ 85718-2416 E-mail: marilynheins@earthlink.net.

HEINS, SISTER MARY FRANCES, educator, nun; b. Galveston, Tex., Nov. 12, 1927; d. George and Rosella (Eckenfels) H. BA, Dominican Coll., 1954; MEd, Lamar U., 1973. Joined Dominican Sisters, Roman Cath. Ch., 1946. Tchr. parochial schs., Tex. and Calif., 1948-68; tchr., head sci. dept., asst. prin. Kelly H.S., Beaumont, Tex., 1968-80; co-prin., then prin. St. Pius X H.S., Houston, 1980-84; tchr., head sci. dept. O'Connell Jr. H.S., Galveston, 1984-86; prin. O'Connell H.S., Galveston, 1989-97; tchr., adminstrv. asst., computer coord., sci. fair coord. Galveston Cath. Sch., 1986-89, tchr. sci., 1997—2003; tchr. theology O'Connell HS, Galveston, Tex., 2003—. Mem. Goals for Beaumont Edn. task force Beaumont C. of C., 1979-80. Mem. interfaith com. Galveston Hist. Found., 1990; mem. ch. involvement com. City-wide Conf. on Youth Violence; participant Galveston Historical Foundations Annual Home Tours, Annual Home and Garden Show benefitting the Animal Shelter. Recipient Outstanding Tchr. award Beaumont A&M Club, 1971, O'Connell Booster of Yr. award, 1995-96; named One of Top 50 Tchrs. in the City, 1998; grantee NSF. Mem. Nat. Cath. Edn. Assn., Nat. Assn. Tchrs. Math., Lamar U. Alumni Assn., World Future Soc., Sci. Tchrs. Assn. Tex. (Outstanding Tchr. 1980), Galveston C. of C. (mem. edn. com. 1990-91), Galveston Garden Club (rec. sec. 2000-04), Delta Kappa Gamma (pres. Eta chpt. 1978-80, Omicron chpt. 1988-90, rec. sec. 1998-2000, historian 2002—, Chpt. Achievement award 1990, 97). Democrat. Roman Catholic. Avocations: needlepoint, word puzzles, reading, collecting owls, collecting apples. Home: 4420 Ave L Galveston TX 77550 Office: O'Connell HS 1320 Tremont Galveston TX 77550 E-mail: smfheins@aol.com.

HEINTZ, CAROLINEA CABANISS, retired home economics educator; b. Roanoke, Va., Jan. 19, 1920; d. Luther Bertie and Emblyn Bird (Jennings) Cabaniss; m. Howard Elmer Smith, Dec. 19, 1942 (div. Aug. 1975); children: Emblyn Davis, Cynthia Shannon, Cheryl Peterson, Melyssa Sexton; m. Raymond Walter Heintz, May 21, 1977; 1 stepchild, James. BS in Home Econ. Edn., U. Ala., Tuscaloosa, 1941; vocat. home econ. degree, Montevallo Coll., 1941. Cert. vocat. home econs. tchr. Swimming instr. Camp Mudjekeewis, Centerlovel, Maine, summer 1940; home econs. tchr. Roanoke Pub. Schs., 1941-43; dietitian U. Va., Charlottesville, 1943; nutrition edn. specialist Liberty Health Ctr. Svcs., Liberty Center, Ohio, 1974-80; home economist Dayton Hudson Dept. Store, Toledo, 1980-84; splty . food instr., continuing edn. U. Toledo, 1984-85. Pres., mem. Greater Toledo Nutrition Coun., 1966-98; bd. dirs. Sunset House Aux., pres. 1999-2001. Co-editor ch. cookbook Loaves and Fishes and Other Dishes, 2000. Spkr. United Way, Toledo, 1965-90; founder, pres. Mobile Meals Toledo, Inc., 1968-71, mem. adv. bd., 1988-95, 2001-03, bd. dirs., chmn. pub. rels., 1997-99, nominating com., 2000-03, Spirit of Mobile Meals award, 1998; affiliate mem. Arts Commn., Toledo, 1976-77; chmn. Saphire Ball, Toledo Symphony Orch., Toledo Opera, 1978; adminstrv. coord. Feed Your Neighbor program Met. Chs. United, Toledo, 1979-86; deacon Collingwood Presbyn. Ch., 1969-71, elder, 1972-74, 77-79, 97-99, 2001-03, trustee, 1984-86, elder, clk. of session, 1991-94, stewardship chmn., 1996-97, del. to Maumee Valley Presbytery, 1991-99; mem. steering com. Interfaith Hospitality Network, 1992-94, bd. dirs., 1993-94; alt. del. Gen. Assembly Presbyn. Ch. U.S.A., 1993, del.-commr., 1994. Recipient Woman of Toledo award St. Vincent Hosp. and Med. Ctr. Guild, 1967, 80, Outstanding Community Svc. award United Way, 1987, Henry Morse vol. award, Greater Toledo award United Way, 1998, runner-up Nat. Vol. of the Year award Project Meal Found., Reynolds Metal Co., 1998. Mem. AAUW (bd. dirs. 1974-76, 94-96, 97-98, chmn. mem. gourmet group 1966-99, 2001, 03, edn. found. chmn. 1994-96, book sale chmn. 1998, nominating com. chmn.), Ohio Med. Aux. (1st v.p. 1973-74), Aux. Acad. Medicine (pres. 1967-68, chmn. edn. gourmet group 1966-99, 2001-03, Health Care award 1974), Indian Trails Garden Club (pres. 1997-98), Sigma Kappa (various alumni offices). Republican. Avocations: volunteering, gourmet cooking, traveling, entertaining, bridge. Home: # 108 4030 Indian Rd Toledo OH 43606-2225

HEINTZ, JOHN EDWARD, lawyer; b. Bronxville, N.Y., Dec. 12, 1948; s. Howard Theodore and Ruth Janet (Brodhead) Heintz; m. Lynn Ann Ohman, June 21, 1980; children: Eric John, Jennifer Ann. BA, Cornell U., 1970; MPA, Princeton U., 1974; JD, NYU, 1977. Assoc. Covington & Burling, Washington, 1977-86; shareholder Popham, Haik, Schnobrich & Kaufman, Ltd., Washington, 1986-91; ptnr. Howrey, Simon, Arnold & White, LLP, Washington, 1991-2000, Gilbert Heintz & Randolph LLP, Washington, 2000—. Contbr. articles to profl. jours. Democrat. Avocations: sailing, swimming. Office: Gilbert Heintz & Randolph LLP Ste 700 1100 New York Ave NW Washington DC 20005-3987 E-mail: heintzj@ghrdc.com.

HEINTZ, JOSEPH E. financial services company executive; CFO, KPMG LLP (formerly Peat Marwick Mitchell & Co.), N.Y.C., 1992—. Bd. dirs. Thru Point Inc. Office: KPMG LLP 345 Park Ave New York NY 10154

HEINTZ, MARY ETHEL, business owner; b. N.Y.C., Aug. 27, 1943; Owner, bookkeeper, paralegal, tax preparer, med. billing Services, Etc., Englewood, Fla., 1983—. Coord. Police Athletic League, Englewood, 1992-93. Mem. Englewood C. of C. Home and Office: 935 N Boundary Rd Englewood FL 34223-2312

HEINTZ, PAUL CAPRON, lawyer; b. Urbana, Ill., June 4, 1940; s. Leo H. and Allyn Capron H.; m. Jane Develin, June 8, 1963; children: Helen C., Sandra DeH., Robert B.D., Edward S.A. AB, Kenyon Coll., 1962; LLB, U. Pa., 1965.

Bar: Pa. 1965, U.S. Dist. Ct. (ea. dist.) Pa. 1965. Assoc. Obermayer, Rebmann, Maxwell & Hippel LLP, Phila., 1965-74, ptnr., 1974—. Author: Remick's Pennsylvania Orphans' Court Practice (7 vols.), 1982—, Dunlap-Hanna Forms (14 vols.), 1984—; author newspaper column Aviation, 1969-82. Bd. dirs. Aviation Coun. Pa., 1980—; chmn. bd. Phila. divsn. Am. Cancer Soc., 1985-87; trustee Franklin Inst., Phila., 1982—; pres. Lower Merion Bd. Sch. Dirs., Montgomery County, Pa., 1983-86; bd. dirs. Nat. Constitution Ctr., 1994—; bd. dirs. Com. of 70, 1997—. Recipient Disting. Svc. award Am. Cancer Soc., 1983, Aviation Achievement award Aviation Coun. Pa., 1984, Disting. Estate Planner award Phila. Estate Planning Coun., 1996, Disting. Aviation Svc. award Pa. Bur. Aviation, 2001. Mem. ABA, Am. Coll. Trust and Estate Counsel (Pa. state chair 2002—), Pa. Bar Assn. (chmn. aviation law sect. 1975-80, ho. dels. 1980-90), Phila. Bar Assn. (bd. govs. 1979, 89-92, 93-94, chmn. probate law sect. 1979, asst. treas. 1993-94), Phila. Bar Edn. Ctr. (treas. 1992-94), Phila. Estate Planning Coun. (bd. dirs. 1997-2000), Haverford Civic Assn. (bd. dirs. 1972-2002), Aircraft Owners and Pilots Assn. (bd. dirs. 1974—, chmn. 2002--), Merion Cricket Club, Union League (bd. dirs. 1992-96, v.p. 1993-96). Republican. Episcopalian. Avocations: flying, sailing, swimming, tennis. Home: 269 Booth Ln Haverford PA 19041-1716 Office: Obermayer Rebmann Maxwell & Hippel LLP 1617 JFK Blvd Ste 1900 Philadelphia PA 19103-1821 E-mail: paul.heintz@obermayer.com.

HEINTZELMAN, CAROL ANN, social work educator; b. Allentown, Pa., Sept. 24, 1942; d. Allen George and Emma Amanda (Strauss) H. BA, Muhlenberg Coll., 1965; MSW, Howard U., 1970; D of Social Work, Cath. U., 1980. Lic. social worker, Pa. Group worker Luth. Social Svcs., Bklyn., 1966-68; supr. Dept. of Pub. Welfare, Winchester, Va., 1970-71; instr. social welfare and sociology Shepherd Coll., Shepherdstown, Pa., 1971-75; asst. prof. of social work Elizabethtown (Pa.) Coll., 1976—78; prof. social work Millersville (Pa.) U., 1978—. Bd. dirs. Luthercare, Lititz, Pa., 1979-85, 86-93, 95-01. Mem. AAUW, NASW, Coun. on Social Work Edn., Pa. Assn. of Undergrad. Social Work Educators, Pa. Soc. of Teaching Scholars, Delta Kappa Gamma. Democrat. Lutheran. Avocations: travel, theatre, music, reading. Home: 11 Townsend Ct Lancaster PA 17603-6796 Office: Millersville U Millersville PA 17551 E-mail: carol.heintzelman@millersville.edu.

HEINY, JAMES RAY, lawyer; b. Albert Lea, Minn., Oct. 7, 1928; s. Albin James and Lola Marguerite (Keig) H.; m. Wava Jeanine Isaacson, Sept. 2, 1951 (dec. 1980); children: Jon Carl, Jane Ellen Heiny Smith, Ann Elizabeth Heiny Hohenshell, Thomas James; m. Norma Lou West, July 24, 1982. BA, Grinnell Coll., 1950; JD, U. Iowa, 1953. Bar: Iowa 1953. Assoc. Westfall, Laird & Burington, Mason City, Iowa, 1955-58; ptnr. Laird, Heiny, McManigal, Winga, Duffy & Stambaugh, Mason City, 1958—. Pres. Luth. Social Svcs. Iowa FODN, 1987—2001; bd. dirs. YMCA, Mason City, 1972—75; pres. Good Shepherd Geriatric Ctr., Inc., Mason City, 1960—72. With U.S. Army, 1953—55. Mem. ABA, Iowa State Bar Assn. (bd. govs. 1986-91), Cerro Gordo County Bar Assn. (pres. 1976). Republican. Avocations: amateur radio, bird watching, sports. Home: 2040 Hunters Ridge Dr Mason City IA 50401-7500 Office: Laird Heiny McManigal Winga Duffy & Stambaugh 300 Wells Fargo Bank Bldg Mason City IA 50401 E-mail: jamesrh4@MCHSI.com., laird@netconx.net.

HEINZ, RONEY ALLEN, civil engineering consultant; b. Shawano, Wis., Dec. 29, 1946; s. Orville Willard and Elva Ida (Allen) H.; m. Judy Evonne Olney, Oct. 30, 1965. BSCE, Mont. State U., 1973. Surveyor U.S. Army Corps Engrs., Seattle, 1966-73; civil engr. Hoffman, Fiske, & Wyatt, Lewiston, Idaho, 1973-74, Tippetts-Abbott-McCarthy-Stratton, Seattle, 1977-79; asst. editor Civil Engring. Mag. ASCE, N.Y.C., 1974-77; constrn. mgr. Boeing Co., Seattle, 1979-83; owner, gen. mgr. Armwavers Ltd., South Bend, Wash., 1983—; pres. Great Walls Internat. Inc., 1993-95, 99—, Heinz Internat., Inc., 1995—, Interocean Mgmt. Svcs., Inc., Panama, 1998—2002. Mem. dams and tunnels del. to China, People to People Internat., Spokane, 1987; mem. U.S. com. on Large Dams. Asst. editor Commemorative Book Internat. Congress on Large Dams, 1987; contbr. articles to profl. publs., including Civil Engring. Mag., Excavator Mag., Internat. Assn. for Bridge and Structural Engring., Japan Concrete Inst., others. Internat. dir. Canaan Christians Fund, Aberdeen, 1993—; bd. dirs. Seaman's Ctr., Aberdeen, Wash., 1990—; chmn. Com. on Sustainable Devel. of Wash.-Africa Network, 2000-02. Recipient First Quality award Asphalt Paving Assn. Wash., 1991. Mem. ASCE (sec. met. sect. 1975-76, assoc. mem. forum), ASTM (Student award 1973)., U.S. Soc. on Dams. Republican. Lutheran. Achievements include management of first commercial installation worldwide of sediment control by water jets, of development of first private harbor and container terminal in Panama in Manzanillo Bay, Colon. Home and Office: Armwavers Ltd PO Box 5 South Bend WA 98586-0782 E-mail: armwaversltd@worldnet.att.net., roney@heinz-intl.com.

HEINZ, SUSAN GOLDIN, educational association administrator; b. Little Compton, R.I. d. S. Goldin and M.F. Fuller; m. Winfield B. Heinz, Dec. 20, 1963, divorced. BA magna cum laude with highest honors, Brown U., 1953; MA in Internat. Rels., Harvard U., 1956; MA/Film History, Crit., UCLA, 1972; postgrad., Am. U. of Beirut, Beirut, Lebanon, 1959. Internat. economist U.S. Govt., Washington, 1956-63; edn. coordinator Jr. Arts Ctr., L.A., 1968-73; film cons., lectr. L.A., 1973-78; pres., v.p. L.A. Mcpl. Arts Commn., 1973-78; exec. dir. Palos Verdes Art Ctr., Rancho Palos Verdes, Calif., 1974-78; dir., corp. programs The Asia Soc., N.Y.C., 1978-87, dir. corp. programs and corp. membership dept., 1987-95, v.p. contemporary affairs and corp. program divsn., 1995-97; cons. on Asia, N.Y.C., 1997—. Exec. com. L.A. Sister City Program. Crosby fellow for grad. sch.; Am. Film Inst. scholar, 1972-73; Smithsonian Instn. grantee. Mem. Cosmopolitan Club, Phi Beta Kappa, Phi Sigma Alpha. Avocations: reading, travel.

HEINZ, TERESA F. foundation administrator; b. Mozambique; m. John Heinz (dec.); m. John Kerry. BA in Romance Langs., Lit., U. Witwatersrand, Johannesburg, South Africa; grad., U. Geneva, 1963; PhD (hon.), Beloit Coll., Wis., Bank ST. Coll. Edn., N.Y., Drexel U., Pa., Med. Coll. Pa. Cons. UN Trusteeship, N.Y.C.; chmn. Heinz Family Found., Pitts., Howard Heinz Endowment; trustee Vira I. Heinz Endowment. Endowed creation of professorship environ. mgmt. Harvard Bus. Sch., chair environ. policy John F. Kennedy Sch. Govt.; vice chair Environ. Def.; past mem. external adv. bd. Inst. Biospheric Studies, Yale U.; mem. adv. bd. Earth Comm. Office; founder Second Nature; co-founder, bd. dirs. Alliance to End Childhood Lead Poisoning; bd. dirs. Carnegie Corp., Family Comm.; trustee Brookings Inst.; former bd. dirs., trustee Phillips Exeter Acad., St. Paul's Sch., Georgetown U.; co-founder Nat. Coun. Families TV. Founding mem., co-chair Congl. Wives Soviet Jewry; trustee governing bd. Yale Art Gallery; mem. trustees coun. Nat. Gallery Art; bd. dirs. Carnegie Inst., Pitts. Avocation: art collecting. Office: Heinz Family Offices Ste 619 1201 Pennsylvania Ave NW Washington DC 20004-2401

HEINZ, ULRICH WALTER, theoretical physics educator; b. Ludwigshafen/Rhein, Fed. Republic Germany, Apr. 25, 1955; s. Walter Jakob and Ortrud (Goepelt) H.; divorced; children: Jutta Franziska, Richard Stefan, Juergen Andreas; m. Christiane Heinz-Neidhart, Sept. 17, 1994; children: Matthias Claus, Michael Neidhart. Dipl.-Phys., J. W. Goethe U., Frankfurt, Fed. Republic of Germany, 1978, Dr. phil. nat., 1980, Habilitation, 1984. Rsch. asst. J. W. Goethe U., Frankfurt, Fed. Republic of Germany, 1978-80, rsch. assoc., 1982-84; postdoctoral fellow Yale U., New Haven, 1980-82; vis. asst. prof. Vanderbilt U., Nashville, 1983-84; asst. physicist Brookhaven Nat. Lab., Upton, N.Y., 1984-86, assoc. physicist, 1986-87; prof. U. Regensburg, Fed. Republic Germany, 1987-2000; staff mem. CERN, Geneva, Switzerland, 1998-2000; prof. Ohio State U., Columbus, 2000—. Cons. Oak Ridge (Tenn.) Nat. Lab., 1983-84; guest scientist Brookhaven Nat. Lab., Upton, N.Y., 1987—; PAC mem. CERN, Geneva, 1988-91, 98-2002. Contbr. over 200 scientific articles to profl. jours. Vertrauensdozent Studienstiftung des Deutschen Volkes, Bonn, Fed. Republic of Germany, 1991-2000. NATO Foreign Exchange fellow, 1981, DFG Habilitation fellow, 1981; BMFT Rsch. grantee, 1988-2000, GSI Rsch. grantee, 1991-2000; recipient Hess Prize, 1988. Fellow Am. Phys. Soc.; mem. AAAS, German Phys. Assn. Office: Ohio State U Dept Physics 174 W 18th Ave Columbus OH 43210 E-mail: heinz@mps.ohio-state.edu.

HEINZ, WILLIAM DENBY, lawyer; b. Carlinville, Ill., Nov. 26, 1947; s. William Henry and Margaret (Denby) H.; children: Kimberly, Rebecca, Elizabeth; m. Catherine Lamb Heinz. BS, Millikin U., 1969; JD, U. Ill., 1973. Bar: Ill. 1973, U.S. Dist. Ct. (no. dist.) Ill. 1974, U.S. Ct. Appeals (3d cir.) 1982, U.S. Ct. Appeals (5th cir.) 1973, U.S. Ct. Appeals (7th cir.) 1976, U.S. Supreme Ct. 1979. Law clk. to judge U.S. Ct. Appeals (5th cir.), Tuscaloosa, Ala., 1973-74; assoc. Jenner & Block, Chgo., 1974-80, ptnr., 1980—; mem. faculty NITA, 1981—. Adj. prof. Northwestern U. Sch. Law, 1995—; mem. bd. dir. The North Am. Co. for Life and Health Ins., 2002—; bd. visitors U. Ill. Coll. Law, 1990-93, pres.'s coun. U. Ill.; bd. dirs., chair Legal Aid Bur., Chgo.; bd. dirs. exec. com. Met. Family Svcs. Chgo. Recipient Disting. Grad. award U. Ill. Coll. Law, 1995. Fellow Am. Coll. Trial Lawyers; mem. ABA, Ill. Bar Assn. (civil practice and procedure sect. coun., com. on liaison with Ill. ARDC, task force on multi-disciplinary practice), Chgo. Bar Assn. (jud. evaluation com. 1990-93), ARDC Ill. Profl. Responsibility Inst., Cribbett Soc., U. Ill. Coll. Law, Legal Club (bd. dirs. 1998-2000), Westmoreland Country Club. Home: 437 Sheridan Rd Kenilworth IL 60043-1220 Office: Jenner & Block 1 E Ibm Plz Fl 46 Chicago IL 60611-3586 E-mail: wheinz@jenner.com.

HEINZE, JOHN EDWARD, microbiologist, industrial researcher/developer; b. Tulsa, Nov. 3, 1947; s. Edward J. and Koreta (Merkle) H.; m. Rebecca Jo Williams, Jan. 30, 1971; 1 child, Steven Edward. BS, Okla. Baptist U., Shawnee, 1970; PhD, U. Ill., Urbana, 1975. Rsch. biologist NIH, Bethesda, Md., 1975-77; sr. microbiologist Armour-Dial, Inc., Scottsdale, Ariz., 1977-80, group leader, 1980-83; rsch. mgr. The Dial Corp., Scottsdale, Ariz., 1983-89; rsch. assoc. Vista Chem. Co., Austin, Tex., 1989-92, rsch. mgr., 1992-95; cons. Washington, 1995—. Chmn. tech. com. Coun. for LAB/LAS Environ. Rsch., 1993-95, tech. dir., 1995—; speaker in field. Author: (book article) The Bacterial Spore, Vol. 2, 1984; contbr. articles to profl. jours. Capt. USAR, 1970-80. Recipient Award of Merit Chemistry and Engring. News mag., 1970; Waksman fellow Am. Soc. for Microbiology Found., 1972-75. Mem. Am. Soc. for Microbiology (pres. Ariz. br. 1983-84, newsletter editor 1987-89), Soap and Detergent Assn. (chmn. subcom. 1991-95). Achievements include development of first antibacterial liquid hand soap for consumer use; use of microorganisms to clean up 60,000 tons of benzene-contaminated sludge. Office: John Adams Assocs 529 14th St NW Ste 655 Washington DC 20045-1601

HEINZEN, BERNARD GEORGE, lawyer; b. Hendricks, Minn., Sept. 18, 1930; s. Bernard Martin and Thelma Harrington (Bowers) H.; m. Maryann Mullen, Aug. 25, 1978; children from previous marriage: John Masters, Robert Kenneth (dec.), James Warren, William Martin. BA, Carleton Coll., 1953; LLB, NYU, 1956. Bar: Minn. 1956, U.S. Supreme Ct. 1969, Pa. 1978. Atty., legal adviser U.S. Dept. State, Washington, 1956-58; assoc. Dorsey & Whitney, Mpls., 1960-65, ptnr., 1966-76; spl. asst. atty. gen. State of Minn., St. Paul, 1967-70; gen. counsel Consol. Rail Corp., Phila., 1976-77; counsel Harvey, Pennington, Herting & Renneisen, Ltd., Phila., 1977-83; pres. Bernard G. Heinzen, Ltd., Phila., 1978—; ptnr. Stassen, Kostos & Mason, Phila., 1983-85; pres., bd. dirs. Rittenhouse Town Watch, Inc., Phila., 1993—; gen. counsel Logan Capital Mgmt., Inc., Phila., 1995—. Dir. Chamber Orch. of Phila., 1995—; adviser U.S. del. to Geneva Conf. on Law of Sea, 1958. Contbr. Stanford Law Rev., 1959; assoc. editor NYU Law Rev., 1955-56. Mem. Citizens Com. on Pub. Edn., Mpls., 1964-76; exec. com. state cen. com. Minn. Rep. Party, 1967-71; vestryman The Ch. of the Holy Trinity, Phila., 1998—. 1st lt. U.S. Army, 1957-60. Mem. ABA, Phila. Bar Assn., Minn. Bar Assn. (chmn. com. on ins. 1970-73), Am. Judicature Soc. (life), Racquet Club Phila., Union League Phila., Phi Beta Kappa. Republican. Episcopalian. Home: 1901 Walnut St Philadelphia PA 19103-4640 Office: 1 Liberty Pl 1650 Market St Ste 5200 Philadelphia PA 19103-7305

HEINZERLING, LARRY EDWARD, communications executive; b. Elyria, Ohio, Aug. 28, 1945; s. Lynn Louis and Agnes Corinne (Dengate) H.; m. Sharyn Lee Jorgensen, Jan. 11, 1969 (div. 1985); children: Jesse, Kristen, Benjamin; m. Sieglinde Wolf, Aug. 1, 1985 (dec. Mar. 1998); stepchildren: Andreas Klohnen, Eva Klohnen; m. Ann Kathleen Cooper, May 12, 2001; 1 stepchild: Tom Keller. BA in Polit. Sci., Journalism, Ohio Wesleyan U., 1967; MA in Internat. Journalism, Ohio State U., 1969. Reporter AP, Columbus, Ohio, 1969-71, corr. Lagos, Nigeria, 1971-74, bur. chief Johannesburg, South Africa, 1974-78, mng. dir. Frankfurt, Germany, 1978-83, dir. world services N.Y.C., 1983-87; dep. dir. AP World Svc., N.Y.C., 1987-2000, also spl. asst. to AP pres., dep. internat. editor, 2000—. News coverage includes: coverage West Africa including Sahel drought, 1971-74, coverage Soweto riots, Mozambique independence, Angola, Rhodesia (now Zimbabwe); co-editor: Fundamental Analysis Worldwide: Investing and Managing Money in International Capital Markets, 1996. Trustee Ohio Wesleyan U., 1993-96, Bancroft, Inc., 1993-97, Bancroft Schs. and Cmtys., 1997-2002. Recipient Headliners award Headliners Club, Atlantic City, 1977, AP reportorial Performance award Mng. Editors, N.Y.C., 1977; nominated for Pulitzer Prize, 1976. Mem. Phi Delta Theta. Roman Catholic. Avocations: foreign affairs, history, philosophy, science. Office: AP 50 Rockefeller Plz New York NY 10020-1605 E-mail: lheinzerling@ap.org.

HEIPLE, JAMES DEE, state supreme court justice; b. Peoria, Ill., Sept. 13, 1933; s. Rae Crane and Harriet (Birkett) H.; B.S., Bradley U., 1955; J.D., U. Louisville, 1957; Certificate in Internat. Law, City of London Coll., 1967; grad. Nat. Jud. Coll., 1971; LLM U. Va., 1988; m. Virginia Kerswill, July 28, 1956 (dec. Apr. 16, 1995); children: Jeremy Hans, Jonathan James, Rachel Duffield. Bar: Ill. 1957, Ky. 1958, U.S. Supreme Ct. 1962; partner Heiple and Heiple, Pekin, Ill., 1957-70; circuit judge Ill., 10th Circuit 1970-80; justice Ill. Appellate Ct., 1980-90; justice Ill. Supreme Ct., 1990—, ret., 2000. V.p., dir. Washington State Bank (Ill.), 1959-66; dir. Gridley State Bank (Ill.), 1958-59; village atty., Tremont, Ill., 1961-66, Mackinaw, Ill., 1961-66; asst. pub. defender Tazewell County, 1967-70., jud. clerk Ill. Appellate Ct., 1968-70. Chmn. Tazewell County Heart Fund, 1960. Pub. Adminstr. Tazewell County, Ill., 1959-61; sec. Tazewell County Republican Central Com. 1966-70; mem. Pekin Sch. Bd., 1970; mem. Ill. Supreme Ct. Com. on Profl. Responsibility, 1978-86. Recipient certificate Freedoms Found., 1975, George Washington honor medal, 1976, Bradley Centurion award Bradley U., 1995; named Disting. Alumnus, U. Louisville, 1992. Fellow ABA (life), Ill. Bar Found. (life), Ky. Bar Found. (life); mem. Ky., Ill. (chmn. legal edn. com. 1972-74, chmn. jud. sect. 1976-77, chmn. Bench and Bar Council 1984-85), Tazewell County Bar Assn. (pres. 1967-68), Ill. Judges Assn. (pres. 1978-79), Ky., Ill., Pa. hist. socs., S.A.R., War of 1812, Sons of Union Vets., Delta Theta Phi, Sigma Nu, Pi Kappa Delta. Methodist. Clubs: Filson; Union League (Chgo.), Country (Peoria). Lodge: Masons (33 degree). Office: 207 Main St Ste 500 Peoria IL 61602-1362

HEIRMAN, DONALD NESTOR, training engineering company executive, consultant; b. Mishawaka, Ind., Aug. 16, 1940; s. Chester J. and Agnes M. Heirman; m. Lois M. Heirman. BSEE, Purdue U., 1962, MSEE, 1963. Mem. tech. staff, then disting. mem. tech. staff AT&T Bell Labs., Holmdel, N.J., 1963-83; mem. tech. staff Am. Bell, Holmdel, 1983-84; supr. AT&T Info. Systems, Holmdel, 1984-88; mgr. global product compliance lab. AT&T Bell Labs., Holmdel, 1989-1996, Lucent Technologies Inc., 1996-97; adj. prof., sr. rsch. scientist, assoc. dir. wireless EMC Ctr. for Study of Wireless EMC, U. Okla., 1997—. Cons. in field, 1998—; course dir. Ctr. for Profl. Advancment, East Brunswick, N.J., 1988—; mem. exec. and tech. mgmt. coms. U.S. Nat. Com. IEC, 1995—; U.S. tech. expert subcoms. (SC) A and I, Internat. Spl. Com. on Radio Interference (CISPR), 1986—; sec. SC A, 1998-2000, chair, 2000-02; chmn. SC A, WG1, 1998-2002; chmn. Am. Nat. Stds. Inst. Accredited Stds. Com. C63, vice chair, 2002—, chair Subcom. 1, 1986—; pres. Nat. Coop. for Lab. Accreditation, 1999-2001. Author of tech. papers on electromagnetic compatibility (EMC), 1973—. Cmdr. USNR, 1963-85, ret. Named Disting. Mem. Tech. Staff, AT&T Bell Labs., 1982. Fellow IEEE (stds. bd. 1990—, vice chmn. 1998-99, chmn. 2000-2001, bd. govs. 2001—, Centennial medal 1984, Disting. Svc. award 1993, Charles Proteus Steinmetz award 1996-97, Millennium medal 2000); mem. IEEE Electromagnetic Compatibility Soc. (bd. 1981-93, 97-99, pres. 1980-81, chmn. stds. com. 1982-2000, v.p. for stds. 1997—, Laurence G. Cumming award 1986, Stoddart award 1995). Office: Don Heirman Consultants 143 Jumping Brook Rd Lincroft NJ 07738-1442

HEISE, CLARENCE BUDDY, secondary school educator, real estate developer; b. Upland, Calif., Nov. 1, 1953; s. Clarence Elmer Heise and Ardys Mary Byer; m. Bonnie Lee Heise, Dec. 15, 1979 (div. Dec. 2000); children: Justin, Jacob. BS, Fresno Pacific Coll., 1977. Tchr. grades K-12 Laton (Calif.) Unified Sch. Dist., 1977—79; tchr. grades 6-8 Cutler Orosi (Calif.) Unified, 1979—84, band dir. grades 6-8, 1986—90; band dir. grades 9-12 Visalia (Calif.) Unified Sch. Dist., 1984—86; band dir. grades 6-12 Kings Canyon Unified Sch. Dist., Reedley, Calif., 1990—. Founder: Muskrat Ramblers (Youth Jazz Band), featured tubaist: Baroque Strings. Mem.: Fresno Madera Calif. Music Educators Assn. (band rep. 1996—2002, Jazz Instr. of the Yr. 2002), Calif. Band Dirs. Assn. (transp. dir. 1999—2002, band rep. 1979—), Calif. Music Educators Assn. (Outstanding Jazz Educator 2002), Am. Sch. Band Dirs. Assn. Mennonite. Avocations: fishing, travel. Home: 1404 S Klein Ave Reedley CA 93654-3722 Office: Reedley HS 675 W Manning Reedley CA 93654

HEISE, DOROTHY HILBERT, librarian, government official; b. Erie, Pa., June 17, 1945; d. George William and Annette Genevieve (Forrester) Hilbert; m. Charles W. Heise, June 29, 1968 BSLS., Edinboro State U., Pa., 1968; postgrad., Catholic U., 1971-72; MLS, U. Md., 1987. Cert. sch. librarian, N.J., Va., Md. Librarian Toms River Intermediate Sch., N.J., 1968-70; librarian Prince George's County Schs., Md., 1970-72, Congl. Sch., Falls Church, Va., 1972-75, Consumer Product Safety Commn., Washington, 1976-77; tech. info. specialist Raytheon Service Co., Crystal City, Va., 1977-79, U.S. Dept. Agr., Washington, 1979—, head Econ. Research Service Reference Ctr., 1981—85; rsch. libr. Nat. Agr. Libr., 1985—. Recipient award for contbn. to Econ. Research Service Reference Ctr., U.S. Dept. Agr., 1985, award for contbn. to sci.gov website, 2001, award for contbn. to InvasiveSpecies.gov, 2001, award for NAL's Kids' Sci. website, 2001. Mem. ALA, Gamma Sigma Sigma. Lutheran. Avocations: needlecrafts; painting. Home: 8569 Tyrolean Way Springfield VA 22153-2241 Office: Nat Agrl Libr 1400 Independence Ave SW Washington DC 20250-7201

HEISE, MARILYN BEARDSLEY, public relations company executive; b. Cedar Rapids, Iowa, Feb. 26, 1935; d. Lee Roy and Angeline Myrtle Beardsley; m. John W. Heise, July 9, 1960; children: William Earnshaw, Steven James, Kathryn Kay Benninghoff. BA, Drake U., 1957. Prodn. mgr. Vend Mag., 1958—59; account exec. The Beveridge Orgn., Chgo., 1959—62; editor, pub. The Working Craftsman mag., Northbrook, Ill., 1971-78; columnist Chgo. Sun-Times, 1973-78; pres. Craft Books, Inc., Northbrook, 1978-84; v.p. Sheila King Pub. Rels., Chgo., 1984-87, Aaron D. Cushman, Inc., Chgo., 1987-88; pres. Creative Cons. Assocs., Inc., Glencoe, Ill., 1989—91, Heartfelt Charity Cards, 1991—. Mem. adv. panel Nat. Crafts Project, Ft. Collins, Colo., 1977; mem. adv. panel and com. Nat. Endowment for Arts, Washington, 1977; mem. editl. adv. bd. The Crafts Report, Seattle, 1978-86. Recipient achievement award Women in Mgmt., 1978. Mem. Pub. Rels. Soc. Am. (accredited). Office: Heartfelt 540 W Frontage Rd Ste 1060 Northfield IL 60093-1299

HEISEN, JOANN HEFFERNAN, health care company executive; b. Washington, Md., Jan. 25, 1950; d. Milton F. and Jeanne (Berger) Heffernan; children: Douglas, Gregory, Cynthia, Courtney. BA, Syracuse U., 1972. Comml. lending officer Chase Manhattan Bank, N.Y.C., 1972-77; CFO Kenmill Textile Corp., N.Y.C., 1977-82; v.p. corp. affairs Primerica Corp., Greenwich, Conn., 1982-89; asst. treas. Johnson & Johnson, New Brunswick, N.J., 1989-90, v.p., mem. corp. staff, 1990-91, treas., corp. officer, 1991-94, contr., 1994-96, CIO, mem. exec. com., 1997—, v.p., CIO. Bd. trustees Princeton Med. Ctr. Bd. dirs. Women's Rsch. and Edn. Inst., Washington, 1990—. Recipient Women Achiever award YWCA N.Y., 1983, TWIN award Nat. YMCA, 1987, Dist. Alumni award Syracuse U., 1990. Mem. Fin. Women's Assn. (pres. 1980-81), Econ. Club N.Y. Office: Johnson & Johnson One Johnson & Johnson Pla New Brunswick NJ 08933

HEISER, ARNOLD MELVIN, astronomer; b. Bklyn., Feb. 9, 1933; s. Hyman Samuel and Sadie (Kretchmer) H.; m. Vivian Carol Jacobs, June 6, 1964; children: Naomi Elizabeth, David Alan. AB, Ind. U., 1954, MA, 1956; PhD, U. Chgo., 1961. Rsch. asst. Ind. U., 1954-56; rsch. fellow U. Chgo., 1956-61; asst. prof. physics and astronomy Vanderbilt U., Nashville, 1961-66, assoc. prof., 1966-99, prof. emeritus, 1999—. Dir. A.J. Dyer Obs., 1972-86; H. Shapley vis. prof. Am. Astron. Soc., 1969—. Subscriptions editor Comms. of the Internat. Amateur-Profl. Photoelectric Photometry, 1993-99; contbr. articles to profl. jours. Mem. Am. Astron. Soc., Internat. Astron. Union, Tenn. Acad. Sci., Sigma Xi. Home: 6132 Gardendale Dr Nashville TN 37215-5602 E-mail: a.heiser@vanderbilt.edu.

HEISER, CHARLES BIXLER, JR., botany educator; b. Cynthiana, Ind., Oct. 5, 1920; s. Charles Bixler and Inez (Metcalf) H.; m. Dorothy Gaebler, Aug. 19, 1944; children— Lynn Marie, Cynthia Ann, Charles Bixler III. AB, Washington U., St. Louis, 1943, MA, 1944; PhD, U. Calif. at Berkeley, 1947. Instr. Washington U., St. Louis, 1944-45; assoc. botany U. Calif. at Davis, 1946-47; mem. faculty Ind. U., Bloomington, 1947—, prof. botany, 1957—, Disting. prof., 1979-86, disting. prof. emeritus, 1986—. Author: Nightshades, The Paradoxical Plants, 1969, Seed to Civilization, The Story of Man's Food, 1973, The Sunflower, 1976, The Gourd Book, 1979, Of Plants and People, 1985, Weeds in my Garden, 2003. Guggenheim fellow, 1953; NSF Sr. Postdoctoral fellow, 1962; recipient Pustovoit award Internat. Sunflower Assn., 1985, Raven Outreach award, 2002. Mem. Am. Soc. Plant Taxonomists (pres. 1967, Asa Gray award 1988, Raven Outreach award 2002), Bot. Soc. Am. (Merit award 1972, pres. 1980), Soc. Study Evolution (pres. 1974), Soc. Econ. Botany (pres. 1978, Disting. Econ. Botanist 1984), Nat. Acad. Scis., Phi Beta Kappa, Sigma Xi. Achievements include research and numerous publications on systematics flowering plants, natural and artificial hybridization, origin cultivated plants. Home: 605 Bell Trace Ct Bloomington IN 47408-4410 E-mail: cbheiser@bio.indiana.edu.

HEISER, JAMES S. manufacturing company executive; b. 1956; BA in Econs., U. Va.; JD, Stanford U. Asst. gen. counsel, v.p. Ducommun Inc., Long Beach, Calif., 1985—96, gen. counsel, treas., CFO, 1996—. Office: Ducommum Inc 111 W Ocean Blvd Ste 900 Long Beach CA 90802

HEISER, NANCY E. freelance/self-employed writer, coach; b. Paterson, N.J., Sept. 24, 1953; d. William Henry Heiser and Joan Marie Muller; m. Jeffrey Louis Cohen, Aug. 12, 1979; children: Daniel Cohen, Jillian Cohen. BA, Colby Coll., 1975; MS in Libr. Sci., Columbia U., 1977. Reference libr. Hobart and William Smith Colls., Geneva, NY, 1977—79, L.I. U., Bklyn., 1979—80; reference specialist Congl. Rsch. Svc. Libr. of Congress, Washington, 1980—84; freelance writer Brunswick, Maine, 1984—; varsity tennis coach Brunswick H.S., 2001—. Corporator Mid Coast Hosp., Brunswick, 1996—; editl. cons., Brunswick, 1992—; founder Zipline Press, 2001—. Author, pub.: Seat-of-the-Pants Suppers, 2001; contbr. short stories and essays to various publs., articles. Mem.: Maine Media Women (grantee 2000), Maine Writers and Pubs. Alliance (bd. sec. 1999—2000, bd. dirs. 1999—2001). Avocations: tennis, choral singing, piano. Office: Zipline Press PO Box 622 Brunswick ME 04011

HEISER, ROLLAND VALENTINE, former army officer, foundation executive; b. Columbus, Ohio, Apr. 25, 1925; s. Rudolph and Helen Cecile H.; m. Gwenne Kathleen Duquemin, Feb. 26, 1949; children: Helen Heiser Sanford, Charlene Heiser Wolff. BS, U.S. Mil. Acad., 1947; MS in Internat. Affairs, George Washington U., 1965. Commd. 2nd lt. U.S. Army, 1947; advanced through grades to lt. gen., 1976; army planner, 1973-74; comdr. 1st Armored divsn., 1974-75; chief of staff U.S. Army, Europe, 1975-76; chief of staff U.S. European Comd., 1976-78; ret., 1978; pres. New Coll. Found., Sarasota, Fla., 1979—2003. Mem. Fla. Bd. Govs. Gov., bd. govs. State U. Sys. Fla.; trustee emeritus New Coll. Found. Decorated D.S.M. with oak leaf cluster, Def. Superior Svc. medal, Legion of Merit (3), Bronze Star, others. Mem. Sarasota Devel. Com. 100, Retired Officers Assn., Greater Sarasota C. of C., Ret. Officers Sarasota (past pres., dir.), Masons. Republican. Episcopalian. Home: 4104 Las Palmas Way Sarasota FL 34238-4532

HEISER, WALTER CHARLES, librarian, priest, educator; b. Milw., Mar. 16, 1922; s. Walter Matthew and Lauretta Katherine (Kopmeier) H. AB, St. Louis U., 1945, AM, 1947, STL, 1955; MSLS, Cath. U. Am., 1959. Joined S.J., Roman Cath. Ch., 1940, ordained priest, 1953. Latin tchr. St. Louis U. High Sch., 1947-50; divinity libr. Saint Louis U., St. Louis, 1955—; mem. faculty dogmatic and systematic theology St. Louis U. Div. Sch., 1966-92; ret. Cons. catalog Cath. supplement Wilson Sr. High Sch. Libr., 1968-77. Rev. editor Theology Digest, 1963—. Mem. Cath. Libr. Assn. Home: 3601 Lindell Blvd Saint Louis MO 63108-3301 Office: 3650 Lindell Blvd Saint Louis MO 63108-3302

HEISERMAN, ROBERT GIFFORD, lawyer; b. El Paso, July 5, 1946; s. Robert Gifford and Nancy Mildred (Wardlow) H.; m. Nancy Fay Price, Oct. 20, 1973; 1 child, Laura. BA, U. Oreg., 1968; JD, U. Denver, 1971. Bar: Ct. Colo. 1972, US Dist. Ct. Colo. 1972, US Dist. Ct. N.Mex. 1972, US D

1972, US Dist. Ct. (so. dist.) Ala. 1974, US Ct. Appeals (10th cir.) 1975, US Supreme Ct. 1976. Legis. draftsman N.Mex. Legislature, Santa Fe, 1972-73; pvt. practice Santa Fe, 1973, Denver, 1974—. Adj. prof. immigration and nationality law and profl. responsibility courses U. Denver, 1981—. Active Emergency Med. Svc. Coun., Denver, 1981—84. Mem. ABA, Am. Immigration Lawyers Assn. (nat. bd. gov., chmn. profl. ethics and grievances com. 1982-89, 98-2000, founder Colo. chpt., treas. Colo. chpt. 1978-81), Colo. Bar Assn., Denver Bar Assn., DC Bar Assn. Democrat. Methodist. Office: 1675 Broadway Ste 2280 Denver CO 80202-4675 Home: Ste 2280 1675 Broadway Denver CO 80202-4675 E-mail: info@heiserman.com.

HEISEY, RAYMOND K. civil engineer; b. Harrisburg, Pa., Nov. 9, 1956; s. Raymond K. and Lucy M. (Simonetti) Heisey; m. Rachael C. Guerra, Apr. 26, 1985; 1 child, Amanda. BSCE, Lehigh U., 1978. Registered profl. engr., Mo., roof cons. From project engr., engring. mgr. to corp. accts. mgr. Butler Mfg. Co., Kans. City, Mo., 1979—2000, corp. accts. mgr., 2000—02, regional sales mgr., 2002—. Mem.: ASCE, Roof Cons. Inst. Achievements include patents in field. Office: Butler Mfg Co 1540 Genessee St Kansas City MO 64102

HEISHMAN, RICCI LYNN, information technology educator; b. Front Royal, Va., Sept. 18, 1959; s. Edgar Wade and Mabel Lee H.; m. Miriam Grace Miller, Aug. 10, 1991. AS in Engring., No. Va. C.C., 1988; BS in Computer Engring., U. Cin., 1991; MS in Info. Sys., Am. U., 1997. Nuclear engring. technologist U.S. Navy, 1977-83; sr. assoc. engr. IBM, Manassas, Va., 1984-93, Loral, Manassas, 1993-95, Lockheed Martin, Manassas, 1995-97; asst. prof. No. Va. C.C., Manassas, 1997-2001, assoc. prof., 2001—. Chair industry and pub. rels. Va. Inst. Excellence in Semicondr. Tng., 1997-2000. Bd. dirs. property owners of Shenandoah Farms, 1993-95. With U.S. Navy, 1977-83 Recipient Navy Achievement medal; NSF grantee, 1999. Mem. IEEE, Assn. for Computing Machinery, Mensa. Avocation: writing fiction. Home: 1111 Old Linden Rd Linden VA 22642-5268 Office: No Va Cmty Coll 6901 Sudley Rd Manassas VA 20109-2399 E-mail: rheishman@nv.cc.va.us.

HEISLER, ELWOOD DOUGLAS, hotel executive; b. Wilmington, Del., June 29, 1935; s. Elwood Dean and Laura Matilda (Hutchison) H. BA, Mich. State U., 1957; postgrad., Johns Hopkins U., 1979—. Asst. mgr. Kents Restaurants, Atlantic City, 1957; innkeeper Treadway Inns Corp., NY and Mass., 1960—68, Holiday Inns, Inc., Lansing and Troy, Mich., 1969—77; gen. mgr. Quality Inns, Inc., Towson, Md., 1977—89, Quality Suites Hotel, Mt. Laurel, NJ, 1989—94, Accor Hotels, Windsor Locks, Conn., 1994—98, Best Western Inn on River, Niagara Falls, NY, 1999, Milner Hotel, Boston, 1999—2001, Wellesley (Mass.) Travel Inn, 2001—02, Wellesley Inn On-the-Square, 2002—. Author manual for resort ops., 1965, The Rising Sun of the Japanese Hotel Industry, 1980. Sec. Md. adv. coun. Future Bus. Leaders Am.; bd. dirs. Gunpowder Youth Camps, Inc.; mem. Balt. Coun. on Fgn. Affairs; v.p. Ea. Shore Soc. Balt. 1st lt. U.S. Army, 1957-59. Named Top Ten Innkeeper, Holiday Inns Internat., 1975, Md. Bus. Person of Yr., Future Bus. Leaders Am., 1981, Bus. Person of Yr. nat. chpt. 1981; recipient award of merit Baltimore County C. of C., 1982, Outstanding Svc. award Md. Future Bus. Leaders Am., 1984, Balt. Mayor's citation, 1984; Paul Harris fellow Rotary Found., 1983. Mem. Am. Hotel and Motel Assn., N.J. Hotel and Motel Assn., Hotel Sales Mgmt. Assn., Baltimore County C. of C. (v.p.), St. George Soc. N.Y., Advt. Club. Balt. (bd. govs.), SAR, Soc. Sons of St. George Phila., German Soc. Md., German Soc. Pa., Amicale Soc. Francaise Balt., Welsh Soc. Phila., St. David's Soc. N.Y., St. Andrew's Soc. Conn., St. Davids Soc. Conn., Mass. Lodging Assn., German Soc. N.Y.C., Rittenhouse Family Assn., Supreme Ct. Hist. Soc., Hist. Soc. Del., Md. Hist. Soc., Nantucket Hist. Assn., Burlington County Hist. Soc., Md. Ret. Officers Assn., Balt. Yacht Club, Lideerkranz Club, Williams Club (N.Y.C.). Republican. Congregationalist. E-mail: edouglasheisler@yahoo.com.

HEISLER, KENNETH AVERY, surgeon; b. N.Y.C., Nov. 19, 1949; m. Kristen Kenny Heisler; children: Matina E., Kenneth A. Jr. BA, Columbia U., 1971, MD, 1975. Intern Columbia-Presbyn. Med. Ctr., N.Y.C., 1975-76, resident, 1976-80; attending surgeon Falmouth (Mass.) Hosp., 1980—, chief staff, 1989-91. Dir. Med. Profl. Mutual Ins. Co. Trustee Cape Cod Healthcare, 1996-99; dir. Ctr. for Health Care Negotiation. Surg. fellow Columbia U., N.Y.C., 1975-80. Fellow Am. Coll. Surgeons, mem. AMA, Am. Soc. Gen. Surgeons (charter), Mass. Med. Soc. (trustee), Am. Soc. of Gen. Surgeons, Barnstable Dist. Med. Soc. (Cape Cod, Martha's Vineyard, Nantucket Counties pres., 1989-96), Boy Scouts of Am.(exec. bd., Cape Cod and Island Coun.). Office: 78 Main St Falmouth MA 02540-2667

HEISLER, NORMA BOODMAN, psychotherapist; b. N.Y.C., Nov. 11, 1933; d. David Louis and Belle (Hochstein) Boodman; m. Arthur Heisler, Aug. 9, 1952 (dec. 1997); children: Mariam, Daniel. Cert. art, Pratt Inst., 1956; BA in Psychology, Bklyn. Coll., 1972; MSW, NYU, 1977; postgrad., N.Y. Sch. for Study of Psychoanalytic Psychotherapy, 1979-83, Karen Horney Inst. Study Psychoanalysis, 1984-86, Erickson Inst., 1992-93; PhD, Nat. Inst. Expressive Therapy, 1996. Cert. clin. social worker, art therapist, Am. Acad. Bereavement. Personnel asst. R.H. Miller, N.Y.C., 1952-56; freelance comml. artist Wolf Studios and Lowenstein Studios, 1957-69; tchr. Yeshivab Onel Moshe, N.Y.C., 1971-72; family counselor, art therapist Lillian Sklar Filler Day Care Ctr., N.Y.C., 1973-76; therapy intern L.I. Coll. Hosp., N.Y.C., 1976-77; tchr. adult edn. Kingsborough C.C., N.Y.C., 1978-79; psychotherapist N.Y. Psychotherapy and Counseling Ctr., 1978-89; part-time pvt. practice, 1981-92; field instr., supr. social work C.I.H., 1989-92; pvt. practice, 1992—. Instr. hypnotherapy for Dental Practice, 2001. One-woman shows include Jewish Cmty. House, N.Y.C., 1960, Montserrat Gallery, 1998—2003, Javits Art Expo, 2002—03, Monserrat-Salon, 2003—, exhibited in group shows at Caravan Art Gallery, 1953, 1954, 1955, Duncan Gallery, 1958, Bklyn. Mus., 1956, 1957 (award), Art U.S.A., 1958, Kottler Gallery, 1958, Directions Gallery, 1959, Boston Art Festival, 1960, Pa. Acad. Fine Arts, Phila., 1961, St. Louis U., 1962, Ruth Sherman Gallery, 1965, Ahda Artzt Gallery, 1969, N.Y. World's Fair, Ahda Artz Group, 1970, 1971, Gallery Show, 1998, Montserrat Gallery, 1998—, Gallery Alexia, 1999, Stephen Gang Gallery, Art Expo Javits Ctr., 2002, 2003, Javits, 2003. Recipient Latham award for Brotherhood, 1954, 1955, 1956, 1957, 1959, Grumbacher award of Merit, 1960, Art awards. Fellow: Soc. Clin. Social Workers; mem.: N.Y. Artists Equity Assn., Am. Orthopsychiat. Assn., Soc. Advancement of Psychoanalytic Devel. Psychology, Nat. Expressive Therapy Assn., NASW. Jewish. Home: 2373 E 7th St Brooklyn NY 11223-5434 Fax: 718-934-5467.

HEISLER, QUENTIN GEORGE, JR., lawyer; b. Jefferson City, Mo., June 30, 1943; s. Quentin George and Helen (Reynolds) H.; m. Susan Davis, Jan. 24, 1970; children: Sarah, Thomas, Margaret. AB magna cum laude, Harvard U., 1965, JD, 1968. Bar: Ill. 1968, U.S. Dist. Ct. (no. dist.) Ill. 1969, Fla. 1977. Assoc. McDermott, Will & Emery, Chgo., 1968-69, 70-75, ptnr., 1975—; legal counsel Office Minority Bus. Enterprise, Dept. Commerce, Washington, 1969-70. Co-author: Working With Family Businesses, 1995; gen. editor: Trust Administration in Illinois, 1979. Chmn. Winnetka Caucus, Ill., 1983; mem. Winnetka Bd. Edn., 1985-89; trustee Shedd Aquarium, Hadlley Sch. for the Blind, 1988-2002; bd govs. Winnetka Cmty. House, 1998-99. Fellow Am. Coll. Trust and Estates Counsel; mem. Chgo. Coun. Estate Planning, Univ. Club, Harvard Club (bd. dirs. Chgo. chpt. 1984-95, pres. bd. 1989-91), Skokie Country Club (Glencoe, Ill.), Racquet Club (Chgo.). Office: McDermott Will & Emery 227 W Monroe St Ste 3100 Chicago IL 60606-5096

HEISLER, STANLEY DEAN, lawyer; b. The Dalles, Oreg., Jan. 11, 1946; s. Donald Eugene and Roberta (Van Valkenburgh) Heisler. BA, Willamette U., 1968, JD, 1972. Bar: Oreg. 1972, U.S. Ct. Claims 1972, U.S. Tax Ct. 1972, U.S. Ct. Appeals (9th cir.) 1972, D.C. 1973, U.S. Ct. Appeals (fed. cir.) 1973, U.S. Ct. Mil. Appeals 1973, N.Y. 1985, U.S. Supreme Ct. 1985. Assoc. Heisler & Van Valkenburgh, The Dalles, 1973-74; ptnr. Heisler, Van Valkenburgh & Coats, The Dalles, 1975-81, Heisler & Heisler, The Dalles, 1982-84, Cohen & Shalleck, N.Y.C., 1985-88, Phillips, Nizer, Benjamin, Krim & Ballon, N.Y.C., 1988-91, Squadron, Ellenoff, Plesent, Sheinfeld & Sorkin, N.Y.C., 1991-94; mng. ptnr. Shays & Kemper, LLP, N.Y.C., 1994-98, Shays, Rothman, & Heisler, LLP, N.Y.C., 1999-2000, Shays, Heisler & Rosenthal, LLP, N.Y.C., 2000-01; pvt. practice Stanley D. Heisler, PC, N.Y.C., 2001—. Speechwriter Sec. of State Tom McCall, Salem, 1965, Gov. Tom McCall, Salem, 1966—68; speechwriter, legis. asst. U.S. Senator Bob Packwood, Washington, 1969—73; vice chmn. Pres.'s Air Quality Adv. Bd., Washington, 1973—76. Mem.: SAR, ABA, Assn. of Bar of City of N.Y., N.Y. State Bar Assn., St. Georges Soc., Sons of the Revolution, Edmund Rice (1638) Assn., Soc. of the Descs. Washington's Army at Valley Forge, Soc. Mayflower Descs. (bd. dirs. N.Y. chpt. 2001—), Soc. for the Promotion of Hellenic Studies, New Eng. Soc. in City of N.Y., Soc. Colonial Wars (mem. coun. N.Y. State chpt. 2003—), Princeton Club, Univ. Club (N.Y.C. and Portland, Oreg.), Arlington Club. Republican. Episcopalian. Home: 400 E 77th St Apt 8J New York NY 10021-2342 Office: Stanley D Heisler PC 276 5th Ave New York NY 10001-4509 E-mail: s.heisler@worldnet.att.net.

HEISLEY, MICHAEL E., SR., manufacturing executive; b. Washington; m. Agnes Heisley; 5 children. BA, Georgetown U., 1960. Formerly with Robertson-Ceco Corp., Toms Foods, Inc., WorldPort Comm. Inc., Pettibone Corp.; chmn., CEO Heico Cos. LLC, St. Charles, Ill., 1979—; owner Memphis Grizzlies (formerly Vancouver Grizzlies), 2000—. Chmn. Davis Wire Corp., Toms Foods, Inc. Mem. St. Patrick's Cath. Ch. Mem. Turnaround Mgmt. Assn., Union League Club, Chgo. Club. Office: Heico Cos LLC 70 W Madison St Ste 5600 Chicago IL 60602*

HEISNER, JOHN RICHARD, lawyer; b. Dinuba, Calif., May 11, 1947; s. Robert Irving and Elinor May (Van Duyne) H.; children— John Richard, Sara Lynn Rodriguez; m. Margo Elizabeth Sanchez, Apr. 17, 1982; stepchildren— John L. Cook, James P. Cook. B.S., U. Oreg., 1969; J.D., U. San Diego, 1972. Bar: Calif. 1973, U.S. Dist. Ct. (ea. dist.) Calif. 1980, U.S. Dist. Ct. (so. dist.) Calif. 1982, U.S. Dist. Ct. (cen. dist.) Calif. 1987, U.S. Dist. Ct. (no. dist.) Calif. 2002. Dep. dist. atty. County of San Diego, San Diego, 1981-86; asst. dist. atty. County of Tulare, Visalia, Calif., 1979-80; sr. ptnr. Heisner, Yoshimoto and Cline, Visalia, 1980-81; spl. asst. U.S. atty. So. Dist. Calif., San Diego, 1982-86; civil litigator Morgan, Lewis & Bockius, San Diego, 1986-87; Mulvaney & Kahan, 1987-93; Lorenz Alhadeff Cannon & Rose, 1993-1998, shareholder Sullivan Hill Lewin Rez & Engel, 1998-. Campaign chmn. Robert Van Auken for Judge, Visalia, 1981; campaign organizer Charles R. Hayes for Judge, San Diego, 1982; examiner Eagle Scout rev. bd. San Diego council Boy Scouts Am., 1982—; adj. prof. U. San Diego Sch. of Law, 1993—; Leo McCarthy for Lt. Gov., 1986. Named Citizen of Week, Oceanside Blade Tribune, Calif., 1974. Mem. ABA, Calif. Bar Assn., Calif. Dist. Attys. Assn., Tulare County Bar Assn., San Diego County Bar Assn. Democrat. Lodges: Blackmer Masonic Lodge #442, Scottish Rite-Albert Pike Award, Al Bahr Shrine, York Rite, Knights Templar (Albert Pike award). Home: Unit 321 1099 1st St Coronado CA 92118-1370

HEISS, DAVID JAMES, editor; b. Siagon, Vietnam, Oct. 1972; BA in English, U. Redlands, 1995. Editor, writer, paginator Redlands (Calif) Daily Facts, 1999—. Contbg. author: Coming of Dawn, 1993. Instr., coach volleyball Redlands YMCA, 1998—. Mem. Redlands Hort. and Improvement Soc. (newsletter editor 2000—), Town and Gown, Sigma Kappa Alpha (alumni assn. officer 2001--). Office: Redlands Daily Facts 700 Brookside Redlands CA 92373

HEISS, HARRY GLEN, archivist; b. Fort Smith, Ark., Jan. 3, 1953; s. Fred William and Mary Kathryn (Hall) H. BA, U. Ark., 1975, MA, 1984; archives cert., Western Wash. U., 1979. Archives intern Oreg. State Archives, Salem, 1979; asst. archivist Smithsonian Instn. Archives, Washington, 1980-85; archivist Nat. Air and Space Mus., Washington, 1985-87, Jefferson Nat. Expansion Meml., Nat. Pk. Svc., St. Louis, 1988-91, Libr. Congress, Washington, 1991-2000, Shenandoah Nat. Park, Nat. Pk. Svc., Luray, Va., 2000—02, Bur. Pub. Debt, U.S. Dept. Treasury, Washington, 2002—. Mem. Soc. Am. Archivists, Mid-Atlantic Archives Conf., D.C. Archivists. Democrat. Avocations: family history, bicycle touring, camping. Home: 2001 N Adams St Apt 225 Arlington VA 22201-3752 Office: Bur Pub Debt US Treasury 999 E St NW Rm 500B Washington DC 20239-0001 E-mail: Harry.Heiss@bpd.treas.gov.

HEISS, RICHARD WALTER, former bank executive, consultant, lawyer; b. Monroe, Mich., July 8, 1930; s. Walter and Lillian (Harpst) H.; m. Nancy J. Blum, June 21, 1952; children: Kurt Frederick, Karl Richard. BA, Mich. State U., 1952; LLB, Detroit Coll., 1963, LLD (hon.), 1982; LLM, Wayne State U., 1969; cert., Stanford U. Exec. Program, 1979. Bar: Mich. 1963, U.S. Dist. Ct. (federal dist.) Mich. 1963. Asst. trust officer Mfrs. Nat. Bank of Detroit, 1960-62, trust officer, 1962-66; v.p., trust officer Mfrs. Nat. Bank Detroit, 1966-68, v.p., sr. trust officer, 1968-75, 1st v.p., sr. trust officer, 1975-77, sr. v.p., 1977-89, exec. v.p., 1989-92; vice chair Detroit Coll. Law Found., 1995—2000, chair, 2001—. Pres., CEO, Mfrs. Nat. Trust Co. Fla., 1984-88, chmn. bd., 1988-92; lectr. Inst. Continuing Legal Edn., Procknow Grad. Sch. Banking, U. Wis., Southwestern Grad. Sch. Bank, Am. Bankers Assn., Banking Sch. South; chmn. mem. exec. com. Trust Mgmt. Seminar, 1980; expert witness fiduciary law, 1993-2003. Mem. Legal-Fin. Network, Cmty. Found. S.E. Mich.; bd. dirs. Hist. Trinity, Inc., 1992—; trustee Detroit Coll. Law at Mich. State U., 1972—, pres., 1983-94; pres. Mich. State U. Bus. Sch. Alumni Bd., 1983; mem. allocation and evaluation com. United Way S.E. Mich., 1989-92. 1st lt. AUS, 1952-57. Fellow State Bar Mich. Found.; mem. Mich. Bar Assn., Am. Bankers Assn. (pres. 1981, exec. com. trust divsn., pvt. banking com. 1984-89, investment adv. com. 1984-89), Mich. Bankers Assn. (chmn. trust divsn. exec. com. 1975), Detroit Golf Club (bd. dirs., pres. 1983), Mich. Srs. Golf Assn. (bd. govs. 1994-), Club at Seabrook Island, Delta Chi, Sigma Nu Phi. Republican. Lutheran. Home and Office: 30684 Sudbury Ct Farmington Hills MI 48331-1368

HEISSENBUTTEL, ROBERT HOLMES, physician; b. Grove City, Pa., May 20, 1937; s. Ernest G. and Jean Elizabeth (McCormick) Heissenbuttel; m. Sharon Lee Breen, July 4, 1964; children: William Holmes, Beth Ann. BA, Thiel Coll., 1959; MD, Columbia Coll. Physicians and, Surgeons, 1963. Diplomate Am. Bd. Internal Medicine, subspeciality in cardiovascular disease. Intern Columbia-Presbyn. Med. Ctr., N.Y.C., 1963-64, resident in internal medicine, 1964-65, fellow in cardiology, 1967-69, asst. physician, 1969-74, asst. attending physician, 1974-80, assoc. attending physician, 1980-98, attending physician, 1998—; instr. to assoc. prof. clin. medicine Columbia U., N.Y.C., 1969-98, clin. prof. medicine, 1998—. Contbr. articles to profl. jours. With med. corps USNR, 1965-67. Fellow Am. Coll. Physicians; mem. Am. Heart Assn. Clin. Cardiology, Med. Soc. County of N.Y., Med. Soc. State of N.Y., Alpha Omega Alpha. Avocations: tennis, platform tennis. Office: 161 Fort Washington Ave New York NY 10032-3713

HEISTAD, DONALD DEAN, cardiologist; b. Chgo., Apr. 2, 1940; m. Sandra J.; children: Wendy, Dean. BS, U. Ill., 1959; MD, U. Chgo., 1963. Asst. prof. medicine U. Iowa Coll. Medicine, Iowa City, 1970-73, assoc. prof. medicine, 1973-76, prof. medicine, 1976—, prof. pharmacology, 1987—, prof. cardiology, dir. cardiovascular divsn., 1995—, Zahn prof. cardiology, 1999—. Bd. dirs. Iowa Ctr. on Aging. Editor: Cerebral Blood Flow: Effects of Nerves, 1982; assoc. editor: Hypertension, 1989-93, Circulation Rsch., 1980-85, consulting editor; editor-in-chief: Arteriosclerosis, Thrombosis, and Vascular Biology, 1999—; contbr. more than 400 papers to profl. jours. and chpts to books. Pres. U. Iowa Faculty Senate, Iowa City, 1980-81; vice-chair coun. on circulation Am. Heart Assn., 1994-96, chair, 1996-98. Capt. U.S. Army, 1967-70. Recipient Irving S. Wright award Stroke Coun., 1976, Harry Goldblatt award Coun. for High Blood Pressure Rsch., 1980, Merit award, 1987, Disting. Lecture award Coun. on Thrombosis, George E. Brown Meml. Lectr., Am. Heart Assn., 1999, Rsch. Achievement award, 2001; Disting. Alumni award U. Chgo., 1991, Novartis award Coun. High Blood Pressure Rsch., 1997; Landis award, Microcirculation Soc., 2001. Fellow Coun. for High Blood Pressure Rsch., Am. Soc. for Clin. Investigation, Assn. Am. Physicians, Assn. Univ. Cardiologists (sec.-treas. 1998-2001, pres. 2002-03), Am. Physiol. Soc. (chair cardiovascular sect. 1995-96, Wiggers award 1999); mem. Internat. Soc. and Fedn. Cardiologists. Democrat. Office: U Iowa Coll Medicine Dept Medicine Iowa City IA 52242 E-mail: donald-heistad@uiowa.edu.

HEISTAND, ANITA MAY, writer; b. Chardon, Kans., Apr. 26, 1934; d. Alvin Corwin and Vera May (Hachenberg) Brown; m. Kenneth Wesley Heistand, Oct. 19, 1951; children: Kenneth Bruce, Rebecca Dell, Janette Elaine. Author articles to Kans. Mag., Reader's Digest, Harris' Farmers' Almanac, Ozark Mountaineer, Kansas City Star; writings included in anthologies: Christmas in the Ozarks, 1993, Legacy of Love, 1995, God's Vitamin C for the Christmas Spirit, 1996, Southeast Kansas, Land of Discovery, 1995. Mem. Kans. Authors Club (pres. dist. 3 1995-99), Joplin Writers Guild (past pres.), Pittsburg Christian Writers (past pres.). Republican. Baptist. Home: 10250 SE 100th St Galena KS 66739-1580

HEISTEIN, ROBERT KENNETH, obstetrician and gynecologist; b. Newark, Oct. 14, 1940; s. Samuel M. and Elizabeth M. (Jellinek) H.; m. Vallery Gubner, Aug. 26, 1967; children: Jonathan, Erica, Michael. BA, U. Vt., 1962, MD, 1966. Diplomate Am. Bd. Ob-gyn. Intern Newark Beth Israel Med. Ctr., 1966-67, resident in ob-gyn., 1967-70, attending staff, 1972—; asst. chief dept. ob-gyn. Patuxent River Naval Hosp., Md., 1970-72; pvt. practice medicine specializing in ob-gyn., Millburn, N.J., 1972—. Mem. staffs St. Barnabas Med. Ctr., Livingston, N.J., Overlook Hosp., Summit, N.J. Served with USNR, 1970-72. Fellow ACS, Am. Coll. Ob-Gyn., Internat. Coll. Surgeons, Am. Fertility Soc., N.J. Acad. Medicine, Am. Soc. Abdominal Surgeons; mem. N.J. Med. Soc., Am. Assn. Gynecol. Laparoscopists. Office: 235 Millburn Ave Millburn NJ 07041-1711

HEITKAMP, HEIDI, former state attorney general; b. Breckenridge, Minn. m. Darwin Lange; children: Althea Lange, Nathan Lange. BA, U. N.D., 1977; JD, Lewis and Clark Coll., 1980. Intern asst. Environ. Study Conf., Washington, 1976; legis. intern N.D. Legis. Coun., Bismarck, 1977; exec. dir. Northwestern Environ. Def. Ctr., Portland, 1978—79; rsch. asst. Nat. Resources Law Inst., Portland, 1979; atty. enforcement divsn. EPA, Washington, 1980—81; asst. atty. gen. Office of N.D. State Tax Commr., Bismarck, 1981—85, adminstrv. counsel, 1985—86, tax commr., 1986—92; atty. gen. State of N.D., Bismarck, 1993—2001. Del. Am. Coun. Young Polit. Leaders UK Internat. Def. Conf., 1988; trustee Fedn. Tax Adminstrs., 1991; presdl. appointee trade and environment policy adv. com. Office of Trade Reps., 1996. N.D. State Crusade chmn. Am. Cancer Soc., 1988—89. Named One of 20 Young Lawyers Making a Difference, ABA Barrister mag., 1990; recipient Young Achiever award, Nat. Coun. Women, 1987; fellow Toll fellow, Coun. State Govts., 1986. Mem.: Nat. Assn. Atty. Gens. Democrat. Office: 21 Captain Leach Dr Mandan ND 58554

HEITLER, GEORGE, lawyer; b. N.Y.C., Sept. 3, 1915; s. John J. and Celia (Zeichner) H.; m. Florence A. Posner, Apr. 21, 1940; children: James B., Richard S. BS, Columbia U., 1936, JD, 1938. Bar: N.Y. 1938, Ill. 1962. Asso. firm Cutler, Wilson & McMahon, N.Y.C., 1938-40; spl. asst. to David L. Podell; counsel to Hays, Podell & Schulman, N.Y.C., 1940; asso. atty. firm Coughlan & Russell; also mng. agt. and asst. sec. Central Manhattan Properties, Inc., N.Y.C., 1940-43; chief clk., legal adviser rents and claims bd. 4th Service Command, U.S. Army, 1943-45; engaged as bus. exec., also house counsel various comml. orgns., 1946-57; asst. sec., staff counsel Blue Cross Assn., N.Y.C., 1957-60, corporate sec., staff counsel, 1960-61; v.p., sec. Chgo., 1961-71; sr. v.p., corporate sec., gen. counsel, 1971-81; sr. v.p., legal counsel Nat. Blue Shield Assn., 1978-81; counsel to Kaye, Scholer, Fierman, Hays & Handler, N.Y.C., 1981-85. Spl. adviser Dept. Labor, also speaker and panelist. Author articles. Mem. Am., Chgo. bar assns., Assn. Bar City N.Y. Home: 700 John Ringling Blvd Sarasota FL 34236-1555 E-mail: fgheitfl@aol.com.

HEITMAN, GREGORY ERWIN, state agency administrator; b. Lewiston, Idaho, June 7, 1947; s. Elmer William and Carmelita Rose Ann (Kinzer) H.; m. Phyllis Ann Pryor, Sept. 25, 1982. BS in Math., U. Idaho, 1969, MBA, 1971; student, Wash. State U., 1965-67. Student communications dir. Assoc. Students U. Idaho, Moscow, 1970-72, advisor, apt. mgr. dept. housing, 1971-72; traffic fatality analyst Idaho Dept. Transp., Boise, 1973-74; ops. mgr. Region IV Health & Welfare State of Idaho, Boise, 1974-78, supr. computer svcs., div. environ. in health and welfare, 1978-85; coord. field svcs., program dir. Idaho Bur. Vital Records and Health Stats., Boise, 1985—; acting dir. Idaho Ctr. for Health Stats., Boise, 1988-89, spl. asst. program and policy devel., 1989—. Mem. med. records adv. com. Boise State U., 1987—, cons., lectr. 1987—. Active various charitable orgns.; precinct committeeman Dem. of Latah County, 1972; election day coord. Ada County, 1986; vol. Am. Cancer Soc., 1990, Easter Seals, 1992, Arthritis Found., 1996. Mem. Idaho Pub. Health Assn., Assn. Vital Records and Health Statistics, Idaho Pub. Employees Assn., Assn. Govt. Employees. Roman Catholic. Avocations: bowling, card collecting. Home: 1762 E Summerridge Dr Meridian ID 83642-5586 Office: Idaho Vital Stats PO Box 83720 Boise ID 83720-3720

HEITMAN, SUSAN MARIE, artist; b. Detroit, Aug. 16, 1954; d. William and Lillian (Slager) Kobos; m. Roger Melvin Heitman, Sept. 18, 1976; 1 child, Brenda Jean. BFA, Ea. Mich. U., Ypsilanti, 1988, MA, 1995. Artist, Plymouth, Mich., 1995—. Exhibited in group shows at Ann Arbor (Mich.) Art Ctr., 1995-97, Detroit Artists Mkt., 1995-97, Ann Arbor Women Painters, 1995-99, The New Regionalism, 1996-98, Jackson Area Show, 1997 (Merit award), State of Arts, Saginaw Twp., Mich., 1997, Ctrl. Mich. U. Art Gallery, Mt. Pleasant, 1997, Suomi Internat. Collection Art/Design, Hancock, Mich., 1997, First Internat. Open WomanMade Gallery, Chgo., 1998, National Women Made Gallery, Chgo., 1998, Bonifas Fine Arts Ctr., Escanaba, Mich., 1998, Beyond the Surface Nat., Paint Creek Ctr. for the Arts, Rochester, Mich., 1999, Sisson Gallery, Dearborn, Mich., 1999, Nat. Women in Art Exhibit, Wallace Smith Gallery, Oakland C.C., Farm Hills, Mich., 1999, LaPetite VII Nat. Alder Gallery Coburg, Wash., 1999-2000, Documenta 2000, Mus. Contemporary Art, Pontiac, Mich., Grand Rapids Mus. Art, Sextet, Buckham Gallery, Flint, 2001, Mich. All-Media Art Competition, Shiawassee Arts Coun., Owasso, 2003. Coord. crafts Northville (Mich.) Christian Assembly, 1997, tchr. crafts, 1995-96. Recipient Exceptional Merit award Ella Sharp Mus., Jackson, Mich., 1997; grad. fellow Ea. Mich. U., 1994-95, 1987 Symposium of Arts & Sci., East Mich. U., Bestof Show Ella Sharp Mus., Jackson, Mich., 2001, Hon. Mention Scarab Club, Detroit, 2001, Left Bank Gallery, Pauline Angel Donor's award, Flint, 2001, The Art Ctr. Merit award, Mt. Clemens, Mich., 2002, Second Place award Shiawassee Arts Coun., 2003. Mem. Detroit Artists Mkt., Ann Arbor Art Assn., Ann Arbor Women Painters (co-chairperson 1995—, co-chairperson exhibits 1997, 98—, chair exhibits 1998-99, Merit award 1996), Paint Creek Ctr. Arts. Mem. Assembly of God. Avocations: gardening, travel, gourmet cooking, reading, Web surfing. Home: 5303 Napier Rd Plymouth MI 48170-5033 E-mail: smheitman@hotmail.com.

HEITMANN, GEORGE JOSEPH, business educator, consultant; b. N.Y.C., Nov. 27, 1933; s. Frederick Charles and Henrietta (Boesl) H.; m. Marian Kingsley, Sept. 3, 1960; children: James, Noel, Peter. AB, Syracuse U., 1956; MA, Princeton U., 1960, PhD, 1963. Prof. mgmt. sci. Pa. State U., University Park, 1958—94, chmn. dept., 1978—87, dir. internat. programs Coll. Bus. Adminstrn., 1989—94, prof. emeritus, 1994—; chmn. dept. acctg., bus. and econs., dean internat. programs Muhlenberg Coll., Allentown, Pa., 1994—. Econ. advisor Ministry of Planning and Devel., Govt. of Libya, Tripoli, 1964-66; cons. energy policy staff Exec. Office of Pres., Washington, 1968-70; vis. prof. Universität zu Köln, Cologne, Fed. Republic of Germany, 1974; vis. prof. Ruhr Universität, Bochum, Fed. Republic of Germany, 1970, 74, 77, W.Va. U., Morgantown, 1975, Shanghai Inst. Mech. Engring., Peoples Republic of China, 1985, U. Maastricht, 2002; cons. Helsinki Inst. Bus. Econs., Finland, 1980; Pa. State U. resident advisor U. West Indies, Kingston, Jamaica, 1987-89. Contbr. articles to profl. jours. Served as 1st lt. U.S. Army, 1957. Mem. Am. Econ. Assn., Decision Scis. Inst., Phi Beta Kappa. Home: 930 S 24th St Allentown PA 18103-3706 Office: Muhlenberg Coll Ettinger Bldg Allentown PA 18104-5586 E-mail: heitmann@muhlenberg.edu.

HEITNER, JOHN A. (JACK HEITNER), English language educator, writer; b. Bklyn., May 7, 1931; s. Samuel and Constance (Stannage) H.; m. Susanne James, 1956 (div. 1985); children: Randall, Steven, Wendi. BA cum laude, Hofstra U., 1959; MA, Cornell U., 1960; PhD, U. Rochester, 1968. Instr. SUNY, Albany, 1962-65; assoc. prof. Ctrl. Conn. State U., New Britain, 1965—. Lectr. Am. lit. N.W. U., Lanzhou, China, summer 1990, Chingdao (China) U., summer 1990; presenter in field. Author: The Search for the Real Self, 1978, At the Edge of Consciousness, 1987, rev. edit., 1996; contbr. articles and poems to profl. jours. Chmn. Caucus of Local Party Presdl. Nominations, New Britain, 1976; del. Dem. Congl. Caucus, New Britain, 1976, Dem. State Caucus, Southington, Conn., 1972; founder, coord. Ctrl. Literary Soc., 1983—, Humanistic Edn Support Group, 1973. 1st lt. USMC, 1951-54. N.Y. State Coll. tchg. fellow N.Y. State Regents, 1959-61. Mem. AAUP, Melville Soc., Hawthorne Soc., Mar Twain Circle, John Gardner Soc. (paper presenter 2000), Kappa Delta Pi. Me Eckankar Ch. Avocations: world travel, rock climbing, hiking, mount climbing. Office: Ctrl Conn State U Stanley St New Britain CT 06053

HEITNER, KENNETH HOWARD, lawyer; b. Jersey City, Apr. 1, 194 Charles Fred and Molly (Vogelman) H.; m. Anne Barbara Siegel, June 14, 1 children: Douglas, Andrew, Elizabeth. BA, Rutgers U., 1969; JD, NYU, 1975 LLM, 1977. Bar: N.Y. 1974, U.S. Dist. Ct. (so. and ea. dists.) N.Y. 1975

Tax Ct. 1976. Assoc. Weil, Gotshal & Manges, N.Y.C., 1973-81, ptnr., 1981—. With U.S. Army, 1969-75. Mem. ABA, N.Y. State Bar Assn. (exec. com. on bankruptcy, corps., net oper. losses, reorgns.), Tax Club, Assn. Bar City N.Y., Fairview Country Club (Greenwich, Conn., bd. govs. 1983-90). Office: Weil Gotshal & Manges LLP 767 5th Ave Fl Concl New York NY 10153-0119 E-mail: Kenneth.Heitner@Weil.com.

HEITSCH, JAMES LAWRENCE, mathematician, educator; b. Ypsilanti, Mich., July 15, 1946; s. Robert Dawson and Josephine Louise (Davidson) H.; m. Lynn Bowser, Sept. 9, 1967; children: Christine, Laura. BS, U. Ill., 1967; MS, U. Chgo., 1968, PhD, 1971. Lectr. U. Calif., Berkeley, 1971-73; asst. prof. U. Ill., Chgo., 1973-79, assoc. prof., 1979-85, prof., 1985—. Vis. prof. U. Lyon, France, 1989, U. Paris, 1997-98; vis. assoc. prof. Pont. U. Catolica, Rio de Janeiro, 1975-76, U. Lille, France, 1981; mem. Math. Sci. Rsch. Inst., Berkeley, 1984-85, Inst. Advanced Study, Princeton, N.J., 1982. Contbr. articles to profl. jours. Japan Soc. for Promotion of Sci. fellow, Sapporo, Japan, 1986-87; NSF Rsch. grantee, 1972-91, 94-96. Mem. Am. Math. Soc. (chair com. on acad. freedom, tenure and employment security 2000-01). Roman Catholic. Home: 1011 Dempster St Evanston IL 60201-4210

HEITSCH, LEONA MASON, artist, writer; b. Pontiac, Mich., Jan. 6, 1931; d. Russell Leonard and Margaret M. (Arnold) Mason; m. Charles Weyand Heitsch, July 5, 1952; children: Russell, Carric, Grace, Charles, Irene. BA in chemistry, U. Mich., 1952. Ednl. asst. Spl. Sch. Dist., St. Louis County, Mo., 1969-81. Commentator Sta. KUMR, Rolla, Mo., 1996—. Author: (pvt. printing) Echoes of the Ridge, 1985, Get Him to St. Louis, 1983; contbg. author: (poem anthology) Seasons of the Ozarks, 1998, Missourians Write About Reading, 2002, Apples, Apples Everywhere; contbr. poetry, articles to various publs. Sec., activist Mo. Assn. Children with Learning Disabilities, St. Louis, 1973-75; fundraising, writing Friends of Foster-Dolbeer Farm, Walled Lake, Mich., 1996—; contbg. poet Wis. Breastfeeding Coalition, Lac du Flambeau, 1996—; activist Poets Against the War, 2003. Recipient honorable mention Mo. Writers Week award for poetry, 1992, 94, grand prize Artists Embassy Internat., San Francisco, 1997, Editors Challenge award Internat. Soc. Authors and Artists, Abilene, Tex., 1997, included in Memories and Memoirs, Anthology of Mo. authors, 2000; featured in Grandmother Earth IX, 2003, Grist, Mo. State Poetry Soc., 2003. Mem. St. Louis Poetry Soc., Rolla Area Writers Guild. Home and Office: Ridge Orchards HC 1 Box 66 Bourbon MO 65441-9305

HEITZ, EDWARD FRED, freight traffic consultant; b. Chgo., May 18, 1930; s. Fredo and Hildur (Olson) H.; m. Gaymae Woodrow Heitz, Apr. 28, 1960; children: Merry, Ted. Student, Northwestern U., Chgo., 1950-55. Registered I.C.C. practitioner. Supr. transp. rsch. Internat. Minerals and Chem. Corp., Chgo., 1946-58; asst. freight traffic mgr.-rate rsch. C.& N.W.Ry., Chgo., 1958-64; traffic mgr. U.S. Dept. Agriculture, Washington, 1964-78; agriculture transp. analyst Fed. R.R. Adminstrn., Washington, 1978-82; freight traffic cons. Falls Church, Va., 1982-96; ret., 1996. Participant with Am. Arbitration Assn. in program applying arbitration techniques to settlement of class action insur. claims for first time, 1998-2000. Commr. Boy Scouts Am., Fairfax County, Va., 1974-77; chmn. Community Action Agy. County of Fairfax, 1975-77; v.p. Coun. of Fairfax PTAs, 1975; deacon Arlington Ch. of Christ, Falls Ch. Ch. of Christ; mem. Fairfax Com. of 100. *In my techinical work, I found that a problem properly defined is a problem solved, or on the way to a rational solution. The same approach to social and civic problems has brought good benefits with one addition: Define what's important.*

HEITZ, JAMES W. anesthesiologist, internist; b. Balt., Oct. 22, 1963; s. James Wade and Barbara Jean (Johnson) H. BA, Vassar Coll., 1985; MD, U. Md., 1989. Diplomate Am. Bd. Internal Medicine, Am. Bd. Anesthesiology, Nat. Bd. Med. Examiners. Intern then resident in internal medicine Pa. Hosp., Phila., 1989-92, auxiliary staff physician Albert Einstein Med. Ctr., Phila., 1991—; staff physician, divsn. emergency svcs. Pa. Hosp., 1992-93; anesthesiology resident U. Pa., Phila., 1993-96; staff anesthesiologist St. Agnes Med. Ctr., Phila., 1996—. Contbr. to Com. for ReCertification, Am. Bd. Internal Medicine, Phila., 1995-99; asst. instr. dept. surgery Temple U. Sch. Podiatric Medicine, 1998—. Mem. ACP, AMA, Am. Soc. Anesthesiologists, am. Bd. Internal Medicine. Office: St Agnes Med Ctr Dept Anesthesiology 1900 S Broad St Philadelphia PA 19145-2304

HEITZENRODER, DAVID AUGUST, financial services professional, investment advisor, investment banker; b. Pitts., Oct. 24, 1939; s. Frederick A. and Mildred L. (Wickline) H.; m. Judith Munson, Sept. 18, 1971 (div. Mar. 1976); m. Barbara Hunter Behrend, Mar. 10, 1979; 1 child, Christine R. BSBA, Pa. State U., 1964. CPA, Pa.; accredited estate planner; life underwriting tng. coun. fellow. Staff acct. Price Waterhouse, Pitts., 1964-66; assoc. dir. devel. U. Pitts., 1966-69; v.p., sec., treas. Innovative Sys., Inc., Pitts., 1970-75; sr. auditor Consol. Natural Gas, Pitts., 1975-77; v.p. mktg. The Credit Bur., Inc., Pitts., 1977-78; nat. account coord. Automatic Data Processing, Pitts., 1978-81; mgr. corp. gen. accounts H.H. Robertson Co., Pitts., 1981-83; v.p. comml. lending Union Nat. Bank, Pitts., 1983-86; assoc. Gateway Fin. Group, Pitts., 1986-90; mng. ptnr. Rosewood Capital Ptnrs., Pitts., 1990—; prin. Rosewood Investment Advisors, Pitts., 2001—. Bd. advisory Launcyte, Inc., 2000—. Author, lectr. in field. Mem. Family Firm Inst., Pitts., 1990—, chmn., 1993-94. With USN, 1957-60. Mem. Fin. Planning Assn., Inst. Cert. Investment Mgmt. Cons., Pa. Inst. CPAs (exec. com. 1987-89, Disting. Svc. award 1992), Soc. Carbide Tool Engrs., Nat. Tooling Machining Assn., Soc. Mfg. Engrs., Assn. for Corp. Growth (bd. dirs. 1994—, pres. 1998-99), Estate Planning Coun., Univ. Club, Pitts. Golf Club. Republican. Presbyterian. Avocations: gardening, music, squash, tennis. Home: 604 Pitcairn Pl Pittsburgh PA 15232-1433 Office: Rosewood Capital Ptnrs/Rosewood Investment Advisors 239 4th Ave Ste 1012 Pittsburgh PA 15222-1715

HEITZMAN, FRANK EDWARD, architect; b. Litchfield, Ill., Aug. 24, 1946; s. Carroll Kramer and Mary Patricia (Hanafin) H.; m. Sandra Frensko, June 14, 1969; children: Christopher, Nicholas, Alexandra. BArch, U. Ill., 1970, MArch, 1975. Assoc. Skidmore, Owings & Merrill, Chgo., 1971—83; owner Heitzman Architects, Oak Park, Ill., 1983—85, 1987—; ptnr. Heitzman & Thorpe Architects, Oak Park, 1986—87; pres. Urban Resource Group Inc., Oak Park, 1989—. Instr. Triton Coll., River Grove, Ill., 1983—. head dept. architecture and interior design, 1999—; adj. faculty interior design So. Ill. U., 1987—, mem. interior design program adv. com., 1987—; adj. faculty mem. U. Ill. Sch. Architecture, 1989—; chmn. Oak Park (Ill.) Hist. Preservation Commn., 1990-96; juror NCIDQ nat. interiors qualification exam, 1991; chair Oak Park Universal Access Commn., 1997—; ADA for Ill. steering com., 1997—; bd. dirs. chair restoration com. Pleasant Home Found., 1999—. Mem. Oak Park Landmarks Commn., 1979-86; mem. Mayor's Adv. Commn. Bldg. Code Amendments, Chgo., 1983-86; chmn. accessibility code task force State Ill., Chgo., 1986, intern devel. coord., 1994—; mem. Oak Park Accessibility Policy Task Force, 1994; bd. dirs. Historic Pleasant Home Found., 1998—, chair restoration com., 1999—. Triton Coll. grantee 1985; recipient Disting. Service award Landmarks Preservation Coun., 1986, Faculty of Yr. award Ill. C.C. Trustees Assn., 2000. Mem. AIA (bd. dirs. Chgo. chpt. 1984—, bd. dirs. Ill. Coun. 1984-88, pres. Chgo. chpt. 1988-89, Excellence in Edn. award 2002), AIA Found. (sec. Chgo. chpt. 1989—, pres. Chgo. chpt. 1990-91), Nat. Coun. Archtl. Registration Bds. (juror 1979, 86), Am. Soc. Interior Designers, Met. Planning Coun., Landmarks Preservation Coun. Ill. (easement monitor 1983—, mem. adv. bd. Ill. statewide program com. 1987—), Chgo. Archtl. Assistance Ctr. (bd. dirs. 1989 —), Bright New City Ed., Oak Park-River Forest C. of C. Democrat. Roman Catholic. Home: 213 S Euclid Ave Oak Park IL 60302-3205 Office: Heitzman Architects 111 N Marion St Oak Park IL 60301-1004 E-mail: hietzman@attbi.com.

HEIVILIN, DONNA MAE, government executive; b. Clear Lake, Iowa, May 12, 1937; d. Nels Oliver Ouverson and Nellie Bernice (Humphrey) Ouverson-Loats; m. Thomas Stuart Heivilin, Dec. 26, 1961 (div. Dec. 1971); children: Vincent Stuart, James Edward. Student, Iowa State U., 1956-57; BA, U. Minn., 1959; MPA, George Washington U., 1974, DPA, 1988. Assoc. dir. Navy issues, nat. security and internat. affairs U.S. Gen. Acctg. Office, Washington, 1985-88, dir. logistics issues, nat. security and internat. affairs, 1988-93, dir. def. mgmt., NASA issues, 1993-95, vice chair job process reengring. team, 1995-96, dir. planning & reporting, nat. security & internat. affairs, 1996-99, dir. quality and risk mgmt., 1999-2000, dir. applied rsch. and methods, 2000—. Pres. Nat. Coun. Assn.'s Policy Scis., Washington, 1980-83. Profiler editor Pub. Budget and Fin. Jour, 1985-98. Mem. Exec. Women in Govt. (pres. 1996-97), Am. Assn. Budget and Programming Analysts (bd. dirs 1980-83, 98-99), Coun. Logistics Mgrs., Soc. Logistics Engrs., World Future Soc., The Profl. Futurists Assn., The Internat. Alliance for Women (bd. dirs. 1997—, treas. 1998, 1st v.p. 1999, pres. 2000-2001), McLean Mavins, Phi Kappa Phi. Avocations: recreational walking, plays, shakespeare, country music. Home: 5330 36th St N Arlington VA 22207-1816 Office: GAO 441 G St NW Rm 6105 Washington DC 20548-0001 E-mail: donna.heivilin@verizon.net., heivilind@gao.gov.

HEIZER, IDA ANN, retired real estate broker; b. Oxford, Colo., Mar. 14, 1919; d. Albert Henry and Ella (Engbrook) Ordener; m. Donald Heizer, Apr. 7, 1947; children: Robert John. Diploma, Brown's Bus. Coll., 1939; student Otero Jr. Coll., 1946-47, U. So. Colo., 1962; grad. Realtors Inst., Nat. Assn. Real Estate Bds., 1972. Cert. closer real estate, cert. residential specialist. Clk., Montgomery Ward Co., LaJunta, Colo., 1935-37; bookkeeper Colo. Bank & Trust Co., LaJunta, 1937-38; cashier/bookkeeper Fox Theatre, LaJunta, 1939-40; clk. Civil Service, LaJunta, 1940-45; steno/abstractor Deaf Smith Abstract Office, Hereford, Tex., 1948-50; sec. Otero County Agt. Office, Rocky Ford, Colo., 1953-55; real estate broker Pueblo Realty & Service Co., Inc., Colo., 1958-86; ret., 1988. Mem. Pueblo Bd. Realtors, Nat. Assn. Real Estate Appraisers, Nat. Assn. Realtors, Colo. Assn. Realtors, Women's Council Realtors, Daus. of the Republic Tex., Beta Sigma Phi. Home and Office: 331 Van Buren St Pueblo CO 81004-1807

HEJTMANEK, DANTON CHARLES, lawyer; b. Topeka, July 22, 1951; s. Robert Keith and Bernice Louise (Krause) H.; m. Julie Hejtmanek; 1 child, Brian J. BBA in Acctg., Washburn U., 1973, JD, 1975. Bar: Kans. 1976, U.S. Dist. Ct. Kans. 1976, U.S. Tax Ct. 1976. Ptnr. Schroer, Rice, Bryan & Lykins, P.A., Topeka, 1975-86, Bryan, Lykins, Hejtmanek & Fincher P.A., Topeka, 1986—. Mem. ABA (rep. young lawyers Kans. and Nebr.), ATLA, Kans. Bar Assn. (pres. young lawyers 1985), Kans. Trial Lawyers Assn., Sertoma (pres. 1983, internat. pres. 1998-99). Republican. Presbyterian. Avocations: snow skiing, travel. Home: 2800 SW Burlingame Rd Topeka KS 66611-1316 Office: Bryan Lykins Hejtmanek & Fincher PA 222 SW 7th St Topeka KS 66603-3734

HEKMATPANAH, JAVAD, neurosurgery educator; b. Isfahan, Iran, Mar. 25, 1934; came to U.S., 1957; m. Lyra Van Wien, Aug. 15, 1959; children: Daria, Kevin, Cameron. MD, U. Tehran, Iran, 1956. Diplomate Am. Bd. Neurol. Surgery, Am. Bd. Psychiatry and Neurology. Intern in psychiatry Chehrazi Hosp., Tehran, 1955-57; intern Mt. Sinai Hosp., Chgo., 1957-58; resident in neurology U. Wis., Madison, 1958-61; resident in neurosurgery U. Chgo. Hosp., 1961-64, instr., chief resident, 1963-64, asst. to assoc. prof. neurosurgery, 1964-75, prof. neurosurgery, 1975—. Mem. AMA, ACS, Am. Acad. Neurology, Am. Assn. Neurol. Surgeons, Soc. Neurol. Surgeons, Ctrl. Neurosurg. Soc. (pres. 1974-75), Chgo. Med. Soc., Chgo. Neurol. Soc. (pres. 1979-80), Rsch. Soc. Neurol. Surgeons, Sigma Xi. Office: U Chgo Sch Medicine Div Neurol Surgery 5841 S Maryland Ave Chicago IL 60637-1463

HELANDER, BRUCE PAUL, artist; b. Great Bend, Kans., Jan. 27, 1947; s. Amos Louis and Carmen Marie (Seoane) H.; children: Klee, Camila. BFA, R.I. Sch. Design, 1969, MFA, 1972. With R.I. Sch. Design, Providence, 1970-79, dir. extension programs, 1977-78, provost, 1978-79; pub., editor Art Express mag., N.Y.C. and Providence, 1980-82; dir., pres. Helander Gallery, Palm Beach, Fla., 1982-95, N.Y.C., 1989-94, with Hollywood Film Inst., L.A., 1995; collage commns. for Miami New Times, City Link Mag., Palm Beach Times Mag., Red Herring Mag., 1998; art critic South Fla. Times. Set designer Irving Berlin, Puttin' on the Ritz, Pope Theatre, Manalapan, Fla.; art critic Marques of Distinction, London, Palm Beach mag, Clematis mag., Palm Beach Times. One-man shows O.K. Harris Gallery, Birmingham, Mich., 1991, Lorenzo Rodriguez Gallery, Chgo., Martine Caulier Gallery, Paris, Peder Bonnier Gallery, N.Y.C., 1994, Marisa del Re Gallery, N.Y.C., 1995, 97, C.G. Rein Gallery, Mpls. and Scottsdale, 1998, Mus. of Art, Ft. Lauderdale, Fla., Virtual Gallery, Los Gatos, Calif., 1998, Regency Fine Art, Atlanta, 1998, Geo. Contemporary Fine Arts Gallery, San Diego, 1998, Addi Gallery, Maui, Hawaii, 1998, Timothy Yarger Fine Art, L.A., 1999, Coral Springs Mus. Art, 1999, Venezuela Nat. Mus., 1999, Galleria di Palazzo Fuseri, Venice, Italy, 2001, Burton Marinkovich Gallery, Washington, Bernice Steinbaum Gallery, Miami, Waddington-Tribby Fine Art, 2002, Boca Raton, Fla., Norton Mus. Art, West Palm Beach, Fla., 2003; permanent collections include The Whitney Mus., Boston Mus. Fine Arts, Guggenheim Mus., San Jose Mus., Vassar Coll. Mus., Kemper Mus. Fine Arts, Met. Mus. Art, Phila. Mus. Art, Chgo. Art Inst., Norton Mus., Smithsonian Instn., Albany Mus., Montreal Mus. Art, Phila. Mus. Art, Butler Art Inst., Youngstown, Ohio, L.A. County Mus. Art, Albright-Knox Mus. Buffalo, Bklyn. Mus., San Francisco Mus. of Modern Art, The White House, Washington, Abergs Mus., Stockholm, Mus. Modern Art, N.Y.C., United Nations, N.Y.C., The Vatican Mus., Rome, many more; collage commns. for New Yorker Mag., Nations Bank, Miami, Fla., Washington Opera, Children's Miracle Network, West Palm Beach, Montgomery Armory Art Ctr., West Palm Beach, Absolut Vodka, Sweden, Ballet Fla., Boston Film Festival, Palm Beach Film Festival; set designs Fla. State Repertory Theatre; neck tie designs Nicole Miller, Inc. Bd. dirs. Fla. Repertory Theatre, Palm Beach, 1989-92, Armory Sch., West Palm Beach, 1986-88, 96—; provost, v.p. acad. affairs R.I. Sch. Design, Providence, 1978-81; commr. Archtl. Rev. Bd. Town of Palm Beach; artistic bd. Palm Beach County Sch. of the Arts Found., 1995—. Fellow NEA, 1975, South Fla. Cultural Consortium. Mem.: 308 Club (pres. West Palm Beach chpt. 1984—94). E-mail: helander@bellsouth.net.

HELANDER, ROBERT CHARLES, lawyer; b. Chgo., Oct. 30, 1932; s. William Eugene and Grace Pauline H.; m. Betty Jane Vinson, Apr. 8, 1961; children— Diana Chaffin, Alexander Christian, Nicholas Charles. BA, Amherst Coll., 1953; JD, Harvard U., 1956, P.MD, 1971. Bar: D.C. 1956, Ill. 1956, N.Y. 1979, U.S. Supreme Ct. 1960. Practice law, Chgo., 1956-62; Amherst fellow in Middle East, 1960-61; mem. firm Helander, Farmanfarmaian & Ghany, Tehran, Iran, 1962-65; assoc. gen. counsel Internat. Basic Economy Corp., Lima, Peru, 1965-68, v.p., 1968-71; v.p. devel. and adminstrn., gen. counsel IBEC, N.Y.C., 1971-73, group v.p. and pres., 1973-76; ptnr. firm Jones, Day, Reavis & Pogue (Surrey & Morse), N.Y.C., 1976-93; ptnr. Kaye, Scholer, Fierman, Hays & Handler, LLP, N.Y.C., 1993—2001; mng. ptnr. InterConsult, LLP, 2002—. Pres. Accion Internat., 1978-88; chmn. Pan Am. Soc., 1979-88, Am. Fund for Ind. Univs., 1987— , Fund for Multinat. Mgmt. Edn., 1981-91; bd. dirs. Internat. Law Inst., 1975, Ams. Soc., 1982—, Univ. Andes Found., 1983—, Near East Found., 1977—, Bolivarian Soc., 1980—, IESA Found., 1991—, chmn. Internat. Coun. Escuela Superior Adminstrn. de Negocios, 1999—, pres. Am. Foreign Law Assn., 2001-. Named Comendador, Orden del Sol (Peru). Fellow Am. Bar Found. (life); mem. ABA (chmn. inter-Am. law com. sect. internat. law and practice 1978-83, editor-in-chief Inter-Am. Legal Materials 1983 91, del to Inter Am. Bar Assn.), Assn. of Bar of City of N.Y. (inter-Am. affairs com.), Inter-Am Bar Assn. (pres.), Am. Fgn. Law Assn. (pres. 2001—), Coun. Fgn. Rels., Carnegie Coun., Century Club. Republican. Episcopalian. Home: 3 Mountainview Dr Mountainside NJ 07092-2510 Office: PO Box 1337 Mountainside NJ 07092 E-mail: rch@interconsultllp.com.

HELBERG, SHIRLEY ADELAIDE HOLDEN, artist, educator; b. Solvay, NY; d. Isaac Edgar and Gladys Evelyn (Tucker) Holden; m. Burton Edvard Helberg; children: Keir Holm, Kristin Vaughan, Kecia Tucker Lau, Kandace Holden Mead, Kraig Brownlee. BE, Johns Hopkins U., 1969; MFA, Md. Inst. Art, 1975. Tchr. Norris Dam Govt. Sch., Tenn., 1945—46, various schs., N.J., Pa., N.Y., Bergenfield, Manchester (Pa.) Pub. Schs., 1965-84, Balt. City Schs., 1988-96; demonstration tchr. Balt. City Schs., O'Donnell Heights Sch., 1992. One-woman shows include U. Va. Charlottesville, 1974, Cayuga Mus. Art and History, Auburn, N.Y., 1974, Hist. Soc. York Mus., Pa., 1977, York Coll., 1984, Country Club York; represented in permanent collections Pres. Richard Nixon; author: (poetry) Chosen Few, 1998; author, illustrator: The Kitty Cat Who Wanted to Fly, 1999, The Jumping Frog of Calaveras County, 1999. Bd. dirs. York (Pa.) Arts Coun., 1964—66. Named Outstanding Tchr. Northeastern Sch. Dist. Bd. Edn. Mem. NEA, DAR, AAUW, Daus. of Union Vets., Nat. League Am. Pen Women (Pa. State art chmn. 1972-74, pres. orgn. 1974-76, nat. scholarship chair 1976-98, registrar 1986-88, 5th v.p. 1988-90, Disting. Svc. award 1978, 80, 82, 84, 86, 88, 90, 92, Disting. Achievement award 1988, 94), Pa. State Edn. Assn., Internat. Platform Assn., Harrisburg Art Assn., York Art Assn., Pa. Watercolor Soc., Johns Hopkins Faculty Club. Republican. Methodist. Home: 5433 Pigeon Hill Rd Spring Grove PA 17362-8854 also: 727 S Ann St Baltimore MD 21231-3402 Home: 727 S Ann St Baltimore MD 21231

HELBURN, ISADORE B. retired arbitrator, mediator, educator; b. Cin., Aug. 14, 1938; s. I.B. and Jeanette (Greenburg) H.; m. Judith Dee Horwitz, Aug. 21, 1960; children: Graham D., Robin L. Holt. BS with honors, U. Wis., 1960, MS, 1962, PhD, 1966. Mem. faculty U. Tex., Austin, 1968-97, prof. indsl. relations Grad. Sch. Bus., 1979-92, ret., 1992—. Contract prof. Area Estudios de Postgrado, U. Carabobo, Valencia, Venezuela, summer 1974; mem. arbitration panels Fed. Mediation and Conciliation Service, 1972—, Am. Arbitration Assn., 1974—, Nat. Mediation Bd., 1983—. Author: (with others) Total Group Productivity Motivation in Business, 1961, Progress Sharing at American Motors, 1964, Manpower, Employment and Income, A Statistical Profile of Texas, 1969, Public Employer-Employee Relations in Texas: Contemporary and Emerging Developments, 1971, (with others) Local Option Recognition and Bargaining: The Texas Fire Fighter and Police Experience, 1976; contbr. articles to profl. jours. and chpts. to books. Served to capt. U.S. Army, 1966-68. Recipient Jack G. Taylor Teaching Excellence award U. Tex., Austin, 1970. Mem. Nat. Acad. Arbitrators, Indsl. Rels. Rsch. Assn. Jewish.

HELD, DIRK TOMDIECK, classics educator; b. N.Y.C., Mar. 24, 1939; s. Oskar Eduard Heinrich and Ethel Crofton (Hunt) H.; m. Elizabeth Candace Allen, June 16, 1962; children: Elizabeth Ives Held Jensen, Kristin Allen. AB, Brown U., 1960, PhD, 1972. Instr. St. Mark's Sch., Southborough, Mass., 1960-62, Emory U., Atlanta, 1967-71; from asst. prof. to prof. Conn. Coll., New London, 1971—, Elizabeth Kruidenier prof. classics, 2001—, assoc. dean faculty, 1993-95, spl. asst. to provost, 1995-98. Vis. scholar Cambridge (Eng.) U., 1978. Asst. editor Helios, 1975-79; contbr. articles to profl. jours. Pres., bd. trustees Pine Point Sch., Stonington, Conn., 1976-82, North Stonington (Conn.) Citizens Land Alliance, 1991-92; mem. mgn. com. Am. Sch. Classical Studies of Athens, 1980—. NEH fellow, 1974. Mem. Am. Philol. Assn. (com. for the classical tradition 1998-2001), Am. Philos. Assn., Soc. Ancient Greek Philosophy, Ariston Club (sec. 1998—). Avocations: ice hockey, opera, travel. Home: 142 Hangman Hill Rd North Stonington CT 06359-1308 Office: Conn Coll BX 5456 270 Mohegan Ave New London CT 06320-4125 E-mail: dthel@conncoll.edu.

HELD, GEORGE, English educator; b. White Plains, N.Y., Jan. 28, 1935; s. Carlysle and Janet Beulah (Maugans) H.; m. Jean Stuart Reinecke, June 20, 1958 (div. Aug. 1967); m. Cheryl Lynn Filsinger, May 15, 2002. BA, Brown U., 1958; MA, U. Hawaii, 1962; PhD, Rutgers U., 1967. Instr. English Kamehameha Sch., Honolulu, 1958-64; tchg. asst. Rutgers U., New Brunswick, N.J., 1965-66; from asst. prof. to assoc. prof. English Queens Coll., Flushing, N.Y., 1967—. Bd. mem., co-editor South Fork Natural History Soc. newsletter, 1988—; co-editor The Ledge Poetry Jour., 1991—. Fulbright lectr., 1973-76. Mem. Assn. Literary Scholars & Critics. Avocations: writing poetry, gardening, bird watching. Home: 285 W 4th St New York NY 10014-2222

HELD, GEORGE ANTHONY, architect; b. Paterson, N.J., Sept. 4, 1949; s. George William and Carmella (De Negri) H.; m. Patricia Anne Corrado, Sept. 5, 1976; children: Nicole, Ryan. BS in Archtl. Tech., N.Y. Inst. Tech., 1972, BArch, 1977. Registered profl. arch., N.J., N.Y., R.I., Md.; registered planner N.J. Architect intern Gerard J. Oakley, AIA, Teaneck, N.J., 1972-76; ptnr. Aybar Partership, Ridgefield, N.J., 1976-88; owner George A. Held, AIA & Assocs., Clifton, N.J., 1988—. Mem. Clifton Econ. Devel. Assistance Commn., 1994, vice chmn., 1998-2002, chmn. Clifton Zoning Task Force, 2001; mem. Clifton Beautification Com., 1997. Mem. AIA, N.J. Soc. Architects (dir. 1984-86), Architects League N.J. (dir. 1982-86, sec. 1986-88, Dirs. award 1985, 88, Vegliante award 1986, Firm award 1999). Roman Catholic. Home: 47 Westview Rd Wayne NJ 07470-6253 Office: George A Held AIA & Assocs 587 Getty Ave Clifton NJ 07011-2151 E-mail: gaheldaia@aol.com.

HELD, JOE ROGER, veterinarian, epidemiologist; b. L.A., June 23, 1931; s. Edward Samuel and Carmen Antoinette (Planas) H.; m. Carolyn Ann Friderich, May 26, 1956; children: Lisa Held Doseff, Robert Joseph, Leslie Held Barnett, Teresa Held Johnson. AA, Pasadena City Coll., 1950; BS, U. Calif., Davis, 1953, DVM, 1955; MPH, Tulane U., 1959. Lic. veterinarian, Calif. Pvt. practice, Pasadena, Calif., 1957-58; various positions USPHS, 1959-72; dir. div. rsch. svcs. NIH, Bethesda, Md., 1972-84; asst. surgeon gen. USPHS, Bethesda, 1975-84; dir. Pan Am. Zoonoses Ctr., Buenos Aires, 1984-87; coord. vet. pub. health Pan Am./WHO, Washington, 1987-89; v.p. primate ops. Charles River Labs., Arlington, Va., 1989-91, dir. Washington office, 1991; dir. Lab. Animal Health Svcs. of Microbiol. Assocs., Rockville, Md., 1992-96, ret., 1996. Cons., Arlington, 1991—; chmn. AID Rinderpest Biosafety Commn., Washington, 1991; mem. USDA, APHIS panel on sci. and tech., Washington, 1987-91; mem. Pew Health Profl. Com. adv. panel on vet. medicine, Durham, N.C., 1991. Contbr. over 70 publs. to scientific jours. Rear adm. USPHS, 1955-84. Recipient Outstanding Svc. medal Uniformed Svcs., Univ. Health Sci., Bethesda, 1985. Mem. AAAS, Am. Vet. Med. Assn. (alt. del. 1981-84, Charles River prize 1984, XII Internat. Vet. Congress prize 1989), Am. Vet. Epidemiology Soc. (pres. 1990-93, K.F. Meyer award 1982), Assn. Mil. Surgeons of U.S. (chmn. vet. med. sect. 1977, McCallam award 1990), Am. Assn. for Lab. Animal Sci., Am. Assn. for World Health, NIH Alumni Assn. (pres. 1991-93), Am. Coll. Lab. Animal Medicine (hon.). Home: 1300 Crystal Dr Apt 505 Arlington VA 22202-3234 E-mail: joeheld@msn.com.

HELD, LILA M. art appraiser; b. Cleve., Oct. 5, 1925; d. Mark and Edythe H. (Dobrin) Bloomberg; m. Jacob Herzfeld, Oct. 20, 1946 (div. 1964); children: Garson, Michael; m. Merle Donald Held, Feb. 19, 1966 (dec. 1997); children: Joanne, Barbara. Student, Coll. William and Mary, 1945-46, Ohio State U., 1943-44, Case Western Res. U., 1944-45, postgrad., 1962-66; student, Akron U., 1960-61; BS in Art Edn., Kent State U., 1961-62; M in Valuation Sci., Lindenwood Coll., 1989. Instr. art Canton (Ohio) YMCA, 1965, Beachwood (Ohio) Bd. Recreation, 1967-68; substitute tchr. art, art history Cleveland Heights, Ohio, 1967-68; freelance artist, writer, researcher, 1940—; art cons., appraiser Art Consultants Assocs., Englewood, Colo., 1985—. Curatorial aid Denver Art Mus., 1985-89; fine arts appraiser, Cleve., 1989—. Works exhibited in museums and galleries in Cleve., Akron, Richmond, Va., St. Louis; speaker in field; judge at numerous art shows. Mem. Cleve. Artists Found.; mem. Akron (Ohio) Art Mus., Butler Inst. of Am. Art, Cleve. Mus. Natural History, Western Res. Hist. Soc., Toledo Mus. of Art; sec. Coun. of Cleve. Ctr. of Contemporary Art; active Continuing Edn. Assn. Case-Western Res. U., Allen Meml. Art Mus. Mem. Am. Soc. Appraisers (sr. mem., cert. in fine arts), Cleve. Mus. Art, Cleve. Ctr. for Contemporary Art (vol.), Contemporary Art Soc. of Cleve. Mus. of Art (bd. dirs.), Nat. Coun. Jewish Women, Ohio Contemporary Glass Alliance, Art Alliance for Contemporary Glass, Temple Mus., Mus. of Am Folk Art, Allbright-Knox Mus. (Buffalo, N.Y.). Avocations: reading, travel, theatre, music, literature. Home and Office: 16695 Chillocothe Rd Chagrin Falls OH 44023 E-mail: artvalue@msn.com.

HELD, NANCY B. perinatal nurse, lactation consultant; b. Winchester, Mass., Sept. 4, 1957; d. Ann and Laurence Babine; m. Lew Held, May 22, 1976; children: David, Jessica. BSN, NYU, 1979; MS, U. Calif., San Francisco, 1992. Cert. Internat. Bd. Lactation Cons. Examiners. Labor/delivery nurse Pascack Valley Hosp., Westwood, N.J., 1979-83; obstetrics educator Drs. Pinski, Wiener & Grasso, Westwood, N.J., 1982-85; ob/gyn office nurse Drs. Power Hagbom Holter & Clark, San Francisco, 1986-87; asst. to dir. maternity svcs. Women's Health Assn., Greenbrae, Calif., 1987-89; perinatal edn. and lactation ctr. clin. coord. Calif. Pacific Med. Ctr., San Francisco, 1989-99; owner North Bay Lamaze, 1988-96; co-owner Health Designs, San Rafael, 1997-98; exec. dir. Day One LLC, San Francisco, 1999—. Speaker and cons. in field. Recipient Founders Day award, NYU. Fellow Am. Coll. Childbirth Educators; mem. Assn. Women's Health Obstetric and Neonatal Nursing (spkr. nat. con. 1993, nat. rsch. utilization team 1993), Am. Soc. Psychoprophylaxis (chpt. co-pres.), Nurses Assn. of Am. Coll. Ob/Gyn, Internat. Childbirth Educators Assn., Internat. Lactation Cons. Assn., Sigma Theta Tau. E-mail: nheld@dayonecenter.com.

HELD, ROYER BURNELL, economics educator; b. Hinton, Iowa, Oct. 30, 1921; s. Albert Herbert and Neva Lucille (Royer) H.; m. Edith Marie Ladue, Apr. 9, 1949; children: Royer Ladue, Marcia Lee Held Poland, Eunice Lucille Held Ockerman, Karl Eliot, Karen Ann Held Hales. BS, Iowa State U., 1947, MS, 1950, PhD, 1953. Asst. prof. agrl. and policy, pub. affairs ext. Mich. State U., East Lansing, 1953-54; assoc. prof. Pa. State U., State College, 1954-56; natural resource economist Resources for the Future, Washington, 1956-65; div. chief Bur. Outdoor Recreation, Dept. Interior, Washington, 1965-67; prof., head

dept. recreation resources and landscape architecture Colo. State U., Ft. Collins, 1967-87, prof. emeritus, 1987—. Co-Author: The Federal Lands, 1957, Land for the Future, 1960, Soil Conservation in Perspective, 1965, Rural Land Uses and Planning, 1984. Served to 1st lt. U.S. Army, 1943-46, ETO. Mem. Nat. Recreation and Parks Assn., Am. Planning Assn., Soil Conservation Soc. Am. Democrat. Unitarian Universalist. Avocations: civic activities, gardening, bird watching, reading, writing. Home: 4760 Venturi Ln Fort Collins CO 80525-3748

HELDER, JAN PLEASANT, JR., lawyer; b. Marysville, Calif., Jan. 18, 1963; s. Jan Pleasant Sr. and Roleane Phylis (Harrison) H.; m. Barbara Irene Loring, July 14, 1990; children: Russell Wright, Zachary Allen, David Grant. BA in Econs., Calif. State U., Sacramento, 1986; JD, Georgetown U., 1989. Bar: Mo. 1989, U.S. Dist. Ct. (we. dist.) Mo. 1989, Kans. 1990, U.S. Dist. Ct. Kans. 1990, U.S. Ct. Appeals (10th cir.) 1994, U.S. Tax Ct. 1994. Exec. asst. to pres. Sacramento Trade Exch., 1983-84; legis. asst. Calif. Postsecondary Edn. Commn., Sacramento, 1985-86; assoc. Spencer, Fane, Britt & Browne, Kansas City, Mo., 1989-94, Sonnenschein Nath & Rosenthal, Kansas City, Mo., 1994-96, ptnr., 1996-2000, Stueve Helder Siegel LLP, 2001—. Judge pro tem City of Prairie Village (Kans.) Mcpl. Ct.; bd. dirs. Edn., Inc., bd. sec., 1994-95; bd. dirs. Young Audiences, vice pres., 1997-98, vice chmn., 1999-2001, sec., 2001-02. Bd. editor Bus. Torts Reporter, 1996—. Chair Calif. State Student Assn., Sacramento and Long Beach, 1984-85; mem. Leadership Mo., Jefferson City, 1992; mem. Centurions Leadership Program, 1993-95, mem. steering com., 1994-95; bd. dirs. Ivanhoe Neighborhood Coun., 2003—. Pursuit of Worthwhile Endeavors scholar Calif. State U., Sacramento, 1982. Mem. ABA (vice-chair bus. torts subcom., bus. and corp. litigation com., bus. sect. 1993-95, task force on Litigation Reform, chair bus. torts subcom. 1995—, co-chair, Task Force on Year 2000 Legislation, 1999—), co-chair, Task Force on Litigation Reform and Rule Revision, 1999—, ATLA, Nat. Inst. Trial Advocacy (western regional 1993), Kans. Assn. Trial Lawyers, Mo. Bar Assn., Kans. Bar Assn., Kansas City Met. Bar Assn., Johnson County Bar Assn., Greater Kansas City C. of C. (chair subcom. on labor and jud. 1990-91, fed. affairs com. 1989—), Ross T. Roberts Inn Ct. (barrister 1991-92), Am. Law Inst. Republican. Presbyterian. Avocations: jazz and classical and choral music, golf, tennis, running, politics. Home: 2216 W 63rd St Shawnee Mission KS 66208-1903 E-mail: helder@shslitigation.com.

HELDMAN, JAMES GARDNER, lawyer; b. Cin., Mar. 7, 1949; s. James Norvin and Jane Marie (Gardner) H.; m. Wendy Maureen Saunders, Sept. 3, 1978; children: Dustin A., Courtney B. AB cum laude, Harvard U., 1971; JD with honors, George Washington U., 1974. Bar: D.C. 1975, U.S. Dist. Ct. (D.C. dist.) 1975, U.S. Ct. Appeals (D.C. cir.) 1975, U.S. Supreme Ct. 1980, Ohio 1981. Assoc. Perazich & Kolker, Washington, 1974-79, Wyman, Bautzer, Kuchel & Silbert, Washington, 1979-81, Strauss & Troy, Cin., 1981-83, ptnr., 1984—. Mem. ABA, Ohio State Bar Assn., Cin. Bar Assn. Avocations: tennis, platform tennis, biking. Office: Strauss & Troy The Fed Res Bldg 150 E Fourth St Cincinnati OH 45202-4018

HELDMAN, PAUL W. lawyer, grocery store company executive; BS, Boston U., 1973; JD, U. Cin., 1977. Bar: Ohio 1977. Assoc. Beckman, Lavercombe & Well, 1977-82; atty. The Kroger Co., Cin., 1982-86; sr. atty. Kroger Co., Cin., 1986-87, sr. counsel, 1987-89, v.p., gen. counsel, 1989-92; v.p., sec., gen. counsel The Kroger Co., 1992-97, sr. v.p., sec., gen. counsel, 1997—. Office: The Kroger Co 1014 Vine St Ste 1000 Cincinnati OH 45202-1100

HELDRICH, PHILIP JOSEPH, English educator, academic administrator, writer; b. Chgo., Nov. 6, 1965; BA, U. Calif., San Diego, 1988; MA, Kans. State U., 1993; PhD, Okla. State U., 1997. Assoc. prof. English Emporia (Kans.) State U., 1997—. Dir. Bluestem Press, 1998—. Author: (poems) Good Friday, 2000; contbr. poems, short stories, and articles to profl. and lit. jours.; fiction editor Cimmaron Rev., 1994—, Midland Rev., 1995-96; editor-in-chief Midland Rev., 1995-96; editor Flint Hills Rev., 1998—. Clinton Keeler fellow, Okla. State U., 1997; recipient Paul Klemp Renaissance Studies award, Okla. State U., 1996, Janemarie Luecke Meml. prize in poetry, 1996, Edward Jones Milton Textual Studies award, 1995, Janemarie Luecke Meml. prize in feminist studies, 1995, 2d place award in fiction Okla. State Univ., 1995, 1st place award in fiction, Kans. State U., 1993, 1st prize Coun. on Nat. Lits. award in fiction, 1998, honorable mention award in fiction Karamu mag., 1997, Herman Swafford Fiction award Potpourri Mag., 1999, X.J. Kennedy Poetry prize, 1999, Fla. Rev. Editors prize in nonfiction, 2001. Mem. MLA, Am. Culture Assn. (regional chair), Southwest Popular and Am. Culture Assns. (v.p. 1998-2000, pres. 2000—, program chair, 2003—, regional chair ann. conf.). Office: Emporia State U Dept English 1200 Commercial St Emporia KS 66801-5087 E-mail: heldricp@emporia.edu.

HELENBROOK, BRIAN TODD, education educator; b. Buffalo, Nov. 4, 1969; s. Robert George and Marilyn Frances Helenbrook; m. Julie Ann Herel, Nov. 7, 1997; children: Charles Francis, Samuel Robert. BS, U. of Notre Dame, 1987—91; PhD, Princeton U., 1992—97. Rsch. assoc. Stanford U., Stanford, Calif., 1998—2001; asst. prof. Clarkson U., Potsdam, NY, 2001—. Office: Clarkson University MAE Dept Box 5725 Potsdam NY 13699-5725

HELENIAK, DAVID WILLIAM, lawyer, educator; b. St. Paul, June 27, 1945; s. George L. and Elizabeth (Child) H.; m. Kathryn Moore, Jan. 14, 1967; children: Claire Elizabeth Moore, Charlotte Margaret Moore. AB, U. Mich., 1967; MSc in Econ., London Sch. of Econ., 1969; JD, Columbia U., 1974. Bar: N.Y. 1975. From assoc. to sr. ptnr. Shearman & Sterling, N.Y.C., 1974—2001, sr. ptnr., 2001—; exec. asst. to dep. sec. U.S. Dept. of the Treasury, Washington, 1977-78, asst. gen. counsel, 1978-79. Instr. in econs. U. Wis., Eau Claire, 1969-71; dir. N.Y.C. Partnership, 2001-, N.Y.C. Ballet, 2001-; mem. Coun. Fgn. Rels. Pres. The MacDowell Colony Inc., 1987-93. Mem. Lawrence Beach Club, Century Assn. Office: 599 Lexington Ave Fl C2 New York NY 10022-6030

HELFAND, ARTHUR E. podiatrist; b. Phila., Jan. 12, 1935; s. Nathan H. and Esther H.; m. Myra Werner, May 23, 1976; children— Jennifer Bess, Lewis Aaron. D.Podiatric Medicine, Temple U., 1957. Diplomate Am. Bd. Podiatric Orthopedics, Am. Bd. Podiatric Pub. Health, Am. Bd.Podiatrics and Primary Podiatric Medicine (bd. dirs. 1992-95). Pvt. practice, Phila., 1957—2002; active staff James B. Giuffre Med. Ctr., Phila., 1958-89, coord. dept. podiatry, 1959-68, co-chief, 1968-78, chief, 1978-89, dir. podiatric edn., 1968-89; dir. clin. rsch. Pa. Coll. Podiatric Medicine, Phila., 1963-64, prof. podiatry, coord. clinics, 1964-70, prof. podiatry, chmn. dept. community health and aging, 1970-98, prof. podiatric medicine, podiatric orthopedics, 1998—2002; prof. Sch. Podiatric Medicine Temple U., Phila., 1998—2002, prof. emeritus, 2002—. Mem. staff Thomas Jefferson U. Hosp., Phila., 1973-2002, now hon. staff; cons. podiatry dept. surgery Phila. VA Hosp., 1973-82, 89-93; adj. prof. depts. orthopedic surgery and medicine Jefferson Med. Coll., Phila., 1976-2002, adj. prof. orthopedic surgery, podiatry, vis. assoc. prof. cmty. health and preventive medicine, 1977-79; cons. staff Wills Eye Hosp., 1980-2002; affiliate staff Joslin Ctr. for Diabetes, Boston, 1993-96, Joslin Ctr. for Diabetes at Wills and Jefferson, 1993-96; hon. staff Temple U. Hosp.; cons. staff Temple U. Children's Hosp.; cons. Dept. Vets. Affairs, Podiatric Svc., Washington; cons. in field. Mem. editl bd. Rehab. Today, 1990-93; contbr. chpts. to books and over 312 articles to profl. jours.; editor five textbooks. Bd. dirs. Pa. Diabetes Acad., 1988-2002, treas., 1991-93, 95-97, chmn. 1993-95. Recipient Lifetime Achievement award Podiatry Mgmt., 1991. Fellow ACP, Am. Pub. Health Assn., Pa. Pub. Health Assn., Royal Soc. Health; mem. AMA, AAUP, Am. Geriatrics Soc., Am. Coll. Foot Orthopedists, Am. Soc. Podiatric Medicine (pres. 1994-95), Am. Podiatry Assn. (pres. 1982-83), Pa. Podiatry Assn., Phila. County Podiatry Soc., Am. Soc. Podiatric Dermatology, Am. Assn. Hosp. Podiatrists, Del. Valley Geriatrics Soc. (bd. dirs. 1989—, pres. 1999-2000), Gerontol. Soc., Temple U. Alumni Assn., Internat. Acad. Preventive Medicine, Am. Assn. Diabetes Educators, Am. Assn. Colls. Podiatric Medicine.

HELFAND, EUGENE, chemist; b. Bklyn., Jan. 8, 1934; s. Saul and Helen Helfand; m. Sondra Ruth Yoskowitz, Nov. 17, 1957; children: Robin Hope, Dawn Alisa, Russ Daniel. BS summa cum laude, Poly. Inst. Bklyn., 1955; MS, Yale U., 1957, PhD, 1958. Mem. tech. staff AT&T Bell Labs., Murray Hill, N.J., 1958-60, supr. chem. computations group, 1960-83, disting. mem. tech. staff, 1983-96; cons. Lucent Techs., Bell Labs., Murray Hill, 1996-98. Adj. prof. Yeshiva U., N.Y.C., 1960-62, Poly. Inst. Bklyn., 1963-64; mem. panel on polymer sci. and engring. NRC, 1979-81. Contbr. articles to profl. jours. Guggenheim Meml. Found. fellow Stanford U., 1969-70. Fellow Am. Phys. Soc. (chmn. divsn. high polymer physics 1987-88, prize 1989); mem. Am. Chem. Soc., Soc. of Rheology, Soc. Info. Display, Sigma Xi, Phi Lambda Upsilon. Achievements include research in theory of polymers, colloids and liquid crystal displays. Office: Lucent Techs Bell Labs PO Box 636 New Providence NJ 07974-0636

HELFAND, MARCY CAREN, lawyer; b. Chgo., Sept. 2, 1954; d. Irwin and Pauline H.; children: Eric and Alexis Weisbrod. BS with high hons., So. Meth. U., 1976, JD cum laude, 1979. Bar: Tex. 1979, U.S. Dist. Ct. (no. dist.) Tex.; cert. comml. real estate law, Tex. Bd. of Legal Specialization. Assoc. Freytag, Marshall, et al, Dallas, 1979-83, Jones, Day, Reavis & Pogue, Dallas, 1983-84; Of Counsel Morgan & Weisbrod, Dallas, 1984-94; pvt. practice Dallas, 1994—. Precinct chair Dallas Dem. Orgn., 1979—. Mem. ABA (chair remedies, miscellaneous clauses real property, probate and trust section 1993-95, chair lit. com. 2001-2003), Dallas Assn. Young Lawyers (chair continuing legal edn. com. 1983), Dallas Bar Assn., Coll. State Bar of Tex., Order of Coif. Home: 7191 Kendallwood Dr Dallas TX 75240-5510 Office: 5580 Lbj Fwy Ste 270 Dallas TX 75240-6293 E-mail: mhelfand@swbell.net.

HELFER, MICHAEL STEVENS, lawyer, business executive; b. N.Y.C., Aug. 2, 1945; s. Robert Stevens and Teresa (Kahan) H.; m. Ricki Rhodarmer Helfer; children: Lisa, David, Matthew. BA summa cum laude, Claremont Men's Coll., 1967; JD magna cum laude, Harvard U., 1970. Bar: D.C. 1971. Law clk. to chief judge U.S. Ct. Appeals D.C., 1970-71; asst. counsel subcom. on constl. amendments Senate Judiciary Com., 1971-73; assoc. Wilmer, Cutler & Pickering, Washington, 1973-78, ptnr., 1978-2000, mgmt. com., 1990-98, chmn., 1995-98; exec. v.p. for corp. strategy Nationwide Ins./Fin. Svcs., Columbus, Ohio, 2000—03; pres. Nationwide Strategic Investments, 2002—03; gen. counsel Citigroup, Inc., N.Y.C., 2003—. Bd. dirs. Lawyers for Children Am., 1997-, Wexner Ctr. for Arts, 2002. Mem. Am. Law Inst. Democrat. Home: 1049 Park Ave Apt 6C New York NY 10128 E-mail: helferm@citigroup.com.

HELFER, RICKI TIGERT, banking consultant; b. N.C., Feb. 4, 1945; m. Michael S. Helfer; 1 child, Matthew. BA with honors, Vanderbilt U.; MA, U. N.C.; JD with honors, U. Chgo. Law. clk. to Hon. John Minor Wisdom U.S. Ct. Appeals; counsel to Jud. Com. U.S. Senate, Washington, 1978-79; assoc., ptnr. Leva, Hawes, Symington, Martin and Oppenheimer, 1979-83; sr. counsel internat. fin. Treasury Dept., Washington; chief internat. lawyer Fed. Reserve Bd., 1985-92; ptnr. Gibson, Dunn & Crutcher, Washington, 1992-94; chmn. FDIC, Washington, 1994-97; nonresident sr. fellow The Brookings Inst., Washington, 1998-99; prof. law, dir. fin. instns. program Washington Coll. Law, Am. U., Washington, 2000—; cons. Am. Cmty. Bankers, Washington, 2000—. Bd. govs., chmn. audit com. Phila. Stock Exch., 1997-99; cons. internat. banking and fin. regulation. Bd. dirs. Girl Scouts U.S., 1995-99, Life Pt. Hosps., Inc., 1999—; mem. vis. com. U. Chgo. Law Sch., 1989-92, 94-97. Mem. ABA (former chair internat. banking and fin. com.), Am. Law Inst., Coun. Fgn. Rels., Washington Fgn. Law Soc. (past pres.). Office: Am Cmty Bankers #400 900 19th St NW Washington DC 20006-2110

HELFERS, ERIC C. financial analyst; BS, Coll. Charleston, Charleston, SC, 1966; MS, U. So. Calif., Los Angeles, CA, 1973. Military officer U.S. Army, Washington, 1966—86; sr. engr. cost BAE Sys., Washington, 1986—, lead engr. satellite comms. projects. Adj. grad. Inst. Johns Hopkins, U. Md., U. Coll., 1989—. Fellow: INFORMS (Ops. Rsch.). Achievements include development of Algorithms for Targeting Strikes in a LOC, Army Ops RES Symposium 1973; Kinetic Energy Weapons, ORSA Symposium, 1991. Avocation: gardening. Office: BAE Systems 7619 Lake Glen Dr Glenn Dale MD 20769-2004 E-mail: eric.helfers@baesystems.com.

HELFERT, ERICH ANTON, management consultant, writer, educator; b. Aussig/Elbe, Sudetenland, May 29, 1931; came to U.S., 1950; s. Julius and Anna Maria (Wilde) H.; m. Anne Langley, Jan. 1, 1983; children: Claire L., Amanda L. BS, U. Nev., 1954; MBA with distinction, Harvard U., 1956, DBA, 1958. Newspaper reporter, corr., Neuburg, Germany, 1948—52; rsch. asst. Harvard U., 1956-57; asst. prof. bus. policy San Francisco State U., 1958-59; asst. prof. fin. and control Grad. Sch. Bus. Adminstrn. Harvard U., 1959-65; internal cons., then asst. to pres., dir. corp. planning Crown Zellerbach Corp., San Francisco, 1965-78, asst. to chmn., dir. corp. planning, 1978-82, v.p. corp. planning, 1982-85; mgmt. cons. San Francisco, 1985—. Co-founding dir., chmn. Modernsoft, Inc.; mem. Dean's adv. coun. San Francisco State Bus. Sch., sch. fin. Golden Gate U.; bd. dirs., past chmn. and pres. Harvard U. Bus. Sch. No. Calif.; trustee Saybrook Inst. Author: Techniques of Financial Analysis, 1963, 11th edit., 2003, Valuation, 1966, Valley of the Shadow, 1997, (with others) Case Book on Finance, 1963, Controllership, 1965; contbr. articles to profl. jours. Exch. student fellow U.S. Inst. Internat. Edn., 1950, Ford Found. doctoral fellow, 1956. Mem. Assn. Corp. Growth (past pres., bd. dirs. San Francisco chpt.), Inst. Mgmt. Cons., Commonwealth Club, Phi Kappa Phi. Roman Catholic. Home: 111 St Matthews Ave No 307 San Mateo CA 94401-4519 E-mail: heleassod@rcn.com.

HELFGOTT, ROY B. economist, educator; b. Bklyn., Oct. 27, 1925; s. Moses N. and Dorothy A. (Levine) H.; m. Gloria Wolff, July 4, 1948; 1 son, Daniel Andrew. BS in Social Sci, City Coll., N.Y., 1948; MA, Columbia U., 1949; PhD, New Sch., 1957. Rsch. dir. N.Y. coat bd. Internat. Ladies Garment Workers Union, N.Y.C., 1949-57; indsl. rels. analyst Wage Stblzn. Bd., N.Y.C., 1952; economist N.Y. Met. Regional Study, 1957-58; asst. prof. econs. Pa. State U., University Park, 1958-60; rsch. dir. Indsl. Rels. Counselors, N.Y.C., 1960-66, 67-68; adj. assoc. prof. Baruch Coll., 1961-68; indsl. devel. officer UN, N.Y.C., 1966-67; head UN mission, Lower Mekong Basin, 1967; disting. prof. econs. N.J. Inst. Tech., Newark, 1968-93, disting. prof. econs. emeritus, 1993—. Cons. Orgn. Resources Counselors, Inc., N.Y.C., 1968—; pres. Indsl. Rels. Counselors, Inc., N.Y.C. Author: Computerized Manufacturing and Human Resources, 1988, Labor Economics, 1974, 2d edit., 1980; co-author: Industrial Planning, 1969, Management, Automation and People, 1964, Made in New York, 1959; co-editor: Industrial Relations to Human Resources and Beyond, 2003; editor IR Concepts, 1993—. Served with AUS, 1944-46, ETO. Decorated Bronze Star with Oak Leaf Cluster, Combat Inf. badge; fellow Inter-Univ. Inst. Social Gerontology, Berkeley, Calif., 1959; sr. Fulbright rsch. scholar U.K., 1955-56. Mem. Am. Econ. Assn., Indsl. Rels. Rsch. Assn., Met. Econ. Assn. (pres. 1978-79), Phi Beta Kappa.

HELFRICH, PAUL A. orchestra executive; BA in Music, MA in Arts Adminstrn., Ind. U. Asst. mgr., dir. mktg. Kalamazoo (Mich.) Symphony Orch. Soc.; exec. dir. Erie (Pa.) Philharm., 1993-96, W.Va. Symphony Orch., Charleston, 1996—. Office: W Va Symphony Orch PO Box 2292 Charleston WV 25328-2292

HELGASON, SIGURDUR, mathematician, educator; b. Akureyri, Iceland, Sept. 30, 1927; came to U.S., 1952; s. Helgi and Kara (Briem) Skulason; m. Artie Gianopulos, June 9, 1957; children: Thor Helgi, Anna Loa. Student, U. Iceland, 1946, D honoris causa, 1986; MS, U. Copenhagen, 1952, D honoris causa, 1988; PhD, Princeton U., 1954; D honoris causa, Uppsala U., 1996. C.L.E. Moore instr. MIT, Cambridge, 1954-56, asst. prof. math., 1960-61, assoc. prof. math., 1961-65, prof. math., 1965—; lectr. Princeton (N.J.) U., 1956-57; Louis Block asst. prof. math. U. Chgo., 1957-59; asst. prof. Columbia U., 1959-60. Vis. mem. Inst. Advanced Study, Princeton, 1964-66, 74-75, 83-84, 98, Mittag-Leffler Inst., 1970-71, 95. Author: Differential Geometry and Symmetric Spaces, 1962, Differential Geometry, Lie Groups and Symmetric Spaces, 1978, Groups and Geometric Analysis, 1984, Geometric Analysis on Symmetric Spaces, 1994, Radon Transform, 1999; editor Progress in Math., 1980-86, Perspectives in Math. Academic Press, Cambridge, 1985—; contbr. articles to profl. jours. Decorated Major Knight's Cross of Icelandic Falcon, 1991; recipient Jessen diploma Danish Math. Soc., 1982, Gold medal U. Copenhagen, 1951; Guggenheim fellow, 1964-65. Mem. Am. Acad. Arts and Scis., Royal Danish Acad. Scis. and Letters, Icelandic Acad. Scis., Am. Math. Soc. (Steele prize 1988). Avocations: music, photography. Office: MIT 77 Massachusetts Ave Dept Math Cambridge MA 02139-4307

HELGELAND, BRIAN THOMAS, film director, writer, producer; b. Providence, Jan. 17, 1961; m. Nancy Helgeland. Grad., Marymount U., LA; BA U. Mass., 1983. Writer (screenplays) A Nightmare on Elm Street 4: The Dream Master, 1988, 976-EVIL, 1988, Lethal Weapon 4, 1998, Highway to Hell, 1992, Assassins, 1995, Conspiracy Theory, 1997, The Postman, 1997, Blood Work, 2002, Mystic Rivers (also dir.), 2003, The Order, 2003; writer, co-prodr. L.A. Confidential (N.Y. Film Critics Circle award 1997, Boston Soc. of Film Critics award 1997, Broadcast Film Critics Assn. award, 1997, Acad. award 1998, Fla. film Critics award 1998, Writers Guild of Am. award 1988); dir., prodr., writer. A Knight's Tale, 2001; dir. Tales from the Crypt, 1989, Payback, 1999; dir, writer: Sin Eater, 2003. Office: Creative Artists Agency 9830 Wilshire Blvd Beverly Hills CA 90212*

HELGENBERGER, MARG, actress; b. Nov. 16, 1958; m. Alan Roseberg; 1 child, Hugh. BS, Northwestern U., 1982. Appeared in TV series Ryan's Hope, 1984-86, The Shell Game, 1987, China Beach, 1988-91 (Emmy award; named Primetime Programming Individual Outstanding Supporting Actress in Drama Series, 1990, 91), CSI:Crime Scene Investigation, 2000-; co-host of New Year's Rockin' Eve, 1988, Home, 1989, (TV movies) Blind Vengence, 1990, Death Dreams, 1991, In Sickness and In Health, 1992, Through the Eyes of a Killer, 1992, When Love Kills: The Seduction of John Hearn, 1993, Stephen King's The Tommyknockers, 1993, Where Are My Children?, 1994, Lie Down with Lions, 1994, Partners, 1994, Perfect Murder, Perfect Town: Jon Benet and the City of Boulder, 2000; appeared in films Always, 1989, After Midnight, 1989, Crooked Hearts, 1991, Desperate Motive, 1993, The Cowboy Way, 1994, Bad Boys, 1995, Species, 1995, Erin Brockovich, 2000.

HELGERSON, JOHN LEONARD, federal agency administrator; b. Madison, S.D., Feb. 8, 1944; B, St. Olaf Coll., 1966; M, Duke U., 1968, PhD, 1970. With CIA, 1971—, deputy dir. intelligence, 1989—93, chmn. nat. intelligence coun., 2001—02; dep. dir. Nat. Imaging and Mapping Agy., 2000—01; inspector gen. CIA, 2002—. Office: CIA Office of Inspector General Washington DC 20505

HELGERSON, JOHN WALTER, lawyer; b. Cleve., Aug. 27, 1938; s. Floyd G. and Evelyn Ann (Wilder) H.; m. Dorothy Elizabeth Hart, Dec. 5, 1984, children from previous marriage: Heidi Wilder, Holly Ward. A.B., Wittenberg U., 1960; J.D., Yale U., 1963. Bar: Ohio 1963. Assoc., Porter Wright Morris & Arthur, Columbus, Ohio, 1963-93, ret. 1993, ptnr., 1968— ; ret. 1993; bd. dirs. Bry-Air, Inc., Sunbury, Ohio; mng. dir. Windsong Ltd., Grenada; chmn. lawyers div. United Way, 1979. Served to capt. USAR, 1963-70. Mem. Blue Key, Phi Gamma Delta, Pi Sigma Alpha, Pi Delta Epsilon, Tau Pi Phi, Capital Club, Grenada Yacht Club. Republican. Unitarian. Avocations: sailing, scuba diving, travel, deep sea fishing. Home: PO Box 26 Saint George's Grenada

HELGERSON, RICHARD, English literature educator; b. Pasadena, Calif., Aug. 22, 1940; s. Donald Theodore and Viola Dolores (Huss) H.; m. Marie-Christine David, June 8, 1967; 1 child, Jessica. BA, U. Calif., Riverside, 1963; MA, Johns Hopkins U., 1964, PhD, 1970. Prof. English Coll. Notre-Dame d'Afrique, Atakpamé, Togo, 1964-66; asst. prof. English U. Calif., Santa Barbara, 1970-76, assoc. prof., 1976-82, chair dept. English, 1989-93, prof. English, 1982—. Vis. prof. Calif. Inst. Tech., Pasadena, 1987-88; chair Huntington (Calif.) Libr. Rsch. Rev., 1986-87; faculty rsch. lectr. U. Calif., Santa Barbara, 1998. Author: The Elizabethan Prodigals, 1976, Self-Crowned Laureates, 1983, Forms of Nationhood, 1992 (James Russell Lowell prize MLA, Brit. Coun. prize in humanities), Adulterous Alliances, 2000; contbr. numerous articles to profl. jours. Fellow Woodrow Wilson Found., 1963-64, NEH, 1979-80, Huntington Libr., 1984-85, Guggenheim Found., 1985-86, Folger-NEH, 1993-94, NEH, 1998-99, U. Calif. Pres.'s fellow, 1998-99, Borchard Found. fellow, 2003. Mem. MLA (exec. com. English renaissance div. 1988-92), N.Am. Conf. on Brit. Studies, Renaissance Soc. Am., Spenser Soc. Am. (pres. 1988), Shakespeare Assn. Am., Western Humanities Conf. (exec. com. 1988-91). Democrat. Home: 334 E Arrellaga St Santa Barbara CA 93101-1106 Office: U Calif Dept English Santa Barbara CA 93106

HELGERSON, STEVEN DALE, epidemiologist, educator; b. Centralia, Wash., Oct. 31, 1946; s. Stanford Donald and Blanche Irene (Dean) H.; m. Linda Elizabeth Ortmeyer, Nov. 22, 1967; 1 child, Brandon Elizabeth. BS with honors, U. Puget Sound, 1968; MA in Biomed. History, U. Wash., 1971, MD, 1973, MPH, 1980. Diplomate Nat. Bd. Med. Examiners; cert. pub. health and preventive medicine Am. Bd. Preventive Medicine. Psychiatry resident U. Wash. Affiliated Hosps., 1973-74; preventive medicine resident U. Wash. Sch. Pub. Health and Cmty. Medicine, 1976-80; clin. instr. pub. health Sch. Medicine Oreg. Health Scis. U., 1980-82; clin. asst. prof. U. Wash.-Sch. Pub. Health and Cmty. Medicine, Portland, Oreg., 1983-84, clin. assoc. prof. epidemiology Seattle, 1990; asst. clin. prof. epidemiology and pub. health Yale U. Sch. Medicine, 1985, assoc. clin. prof. epidemiology, 1986; lectr. U. Ariz. Sch. Medicine, Tucson, 1987-89; pvt. practice Epidemiology for Action, 1997—; assoc. clin. prof. epidemiology U. Wash. Sch. Pub. Health & Cmty. Medicine, Seattle, 1999—; assoc. prof. cmty. medicine U. N.D., Grand Forks, 2000—. Contbr. chpts. to books and articles to profl. jours. Capt. USPHS, 1974-96. Fellow Am. Coll. Preventive Medicine; mem. AMA, APHA, Am. Assn. for the History of Medicine, Commd. Officers Assn., Phi Kappa Phi, Phi Sigma. Office: Epidemiology for Action 601 Belmont Ave E F-11 Seattle WA 98102

HELGESON, DUANE MARCELLUS, retired librarian; b. Rothsay, Minn., July 2, 1930; s. Oscar Herbert and Selma Olivia (Sateren) H. BS, U. Minn., 1952. Libr. Chance-Vought Co., Dallas, 1956-59, Sys. Devel. Corp., Santa Monica, Calif., 1959-62, Lockheed Aircraft, Burbank, Calif., 1962-63, C.F. Braun Co., Alhambra, Calif., 1963-74; chief libr. Ralph M. Parsons Co., Pasadena, Calif., 1974-79; pres. Mark-Allen/Brokers-in-Info., L.A., 1976-80; phys. sci. libr. Calif. Inst. Tech., Pasadena, 1980-84; corp. libr. Montgomery Watson, Pasadena, 1985-94; ret., 1994. Mem. adv. bd. L.A. Trade Tech. Coll., 1974-79, U. So. Calif. Libr. Sch., 1974-79. Editor: (with Joe Ann Clifton) Computers in Library and Information Ctrs., 1973. With USAF, 1952-54. Mem. Spl. Librs. Assn. (chmn. nominating com. 1974). Home: 2706 Ivan Hill Ter Los Angeles CA 90039-2717

HELGESON, JAMES G. education educator; b. Great Falls, Mont., June 6, 1947; s. Alden W. and Victoria M. Helgeson; m. Kathryn L. Peacock, July 3, 1976; children: Erik W., Erika S. BA, Ea. Wash. U., 1965—69, MBA, 1976—80; PhD, U. of Oreg., 1980—84. Prof. of mktg. Gonzaga U., Spokane, 1984—. Contbr. various jour. articles, academic publications. 1st lt. U.S. Army, 1970—72, Vietnam. Recipient Scholar of the Yr., Gonzaga U., 1995; scholar Jepson Rsch. Sholarship, Various. Mem.: Am. Mktg. Assn. Republican. Avocations: bicycling, running, home maintainence. Home: 828 W Montgomery Spokane WA 99205 Office: Gonzaga University School of Business Administration Spokane WA 99258 E-mail: helgeson@gonzaga.edu.

HELGESON, JOHN PAUL, plant physiologist, researcher; b. Barberton, Ohio, July 25, 1935; s. Earl Adrian and Marguerite (Dutcher) H.; m. Sarah Frances Slater, June 10, 1957; children: Daniel, Susan, James. AB, Oberlin Coll., 1957; PhD, U. Wis., 1964. NSF postdoctoral fellow dept. chemistry U. Ill., Urbana, 1964-66; from asst. to prof. botany and plant pathology U. Wis., Madison, 1996—2002, prof. emeritus, 2003—. Plant physiologist USDA Argl. Rsch. Svc. plant disease resistance unit, Madison, 1966-90, rsch. leader, 1990-2003; program dir. USDA, Washington, 1982-83; vis. scientist Lab. of Cell Biology, Versailles, France, 1985-86. Lt. USAF, 1957-60. Mem. Bot. Soc. Am., Am. Phytopathol. Soc., Internat. Soc. Plant Molecular Biologists, Am. Soc. Plant Physiologists. Achievements include development of tissue culture procedures for studying interactions of plants and fungi, of somatic hybridizations to obtain new disease resistances in plants. E-mail: jph@plantpath.wisc.edu.

HELINSKI, DONALD RAYMOND, biologist, educator; b. Balt., July 7, 1933; s. George L. and Marie M. (Naparstek) H.; m. Patricia G. Doherty, Mar. 4, 1962; children: Matthew T., Maureen G. BS, U. Md., 1954; PhD in Biochemistry, Western Res. U., 1960; postdoctoral fellow, Stanford U., 1960-62. Asst. prof. Princeton (N.J.) U., 1962-65; mem. faculty U. Calif., San Diego, 1965—, prof. biology, 1970—, chmn. dept., 1979-81, dir. Ctr. for Molecular Genetics, 1984-95, assoc. dean Natural Scis., 1994-97. Mem. com. guidelines for recombinant DNA research NIH, 1975-78 Author papers in field. Mem. Am.

Soc. Biol. Chemists, Am. Soc. Microbiology, AAAS, Am. Acad. of Arts and Scis., Am. Acad. Microbiology, Nat. Acad. Scis., European Molecular Biology Orgn. (assoc.). Office: Bonner Hall 9500 Gilman Dr La Jolla CA 92093-0322 E-mail: dhelinski@ucsd.edu.

HELL, JOHANNES WILHELM, neuroscientist, researcher; b. Selb, Bayern/Oberfranken, Germany, Aug. 20, 1960; s. Johann Baptist and Theresia Hell; m. Mary Catherine Louise Horne, Aug. 1, 1993. Diploma in biochemistry, Eberhard-Karls-U., Tuebingen, Germany, 1987; PhD, Maximilians U., Munich, Germany, 1991. Rsch. assoc. U. of Wash., Seattle, 1991—95; asst. prof. U. of Wis., Madison, 1995—2001; assoc. prof. U. of Iowa, Iowa City, 2001—. Achievements include discovery of localized signaling by cAMP in cells and a macromolecular signaling complex (beta2 adrenergic receptor, Gs, adenylyl cyclase, PKA, PP2A, calcium channel Cav1.2). Office: U of Iowa 51 Newton Rd Iowa City IA 52242-1109 Office Fax: 319-335-7965.

HELLAND, GEORGE ARCHIBALD, JR., management consultant, manufacturing executive, former government official; b. San Antonio, Nov. 28, 1937; s. George Archibald and Ruth (Gorman) H.; m. Josephine Howell, June 9, 1962 (div. 1989); children: Jane Elizabeth, Thomas Gorman; m. Antonia Scott Day, Nov. 24, 1990. BS in Mech. Engring., U. Tex., 1959; MBA with distinction, Harvard U., 1961. Registered profl. engr., Tex. With Cameron Iron Works, Inc., Houston, 1961-77, asst. sales mgr., 1963, dist. sales mgr., 1964, dist. sales mgr., U.K., Africa, 1965, product mgr., 1966, plant mgr., Leeds, Eng., 1967, mgr. oil tool products, 1968, v.p., 1969-75, exec. v.p., 1975-77; with Weatherford Internat., Inc., Houston, 1977-79, v.p., 1977, pres., CEO, dir., 1978-79; pres. McEvoy Oilfield Equipment Co. (name changed to Sii McEvoy div. Smith Internat., Inc. 1980), Houston, 1979-85, McCall Industries, Inc., Houston, 1986-87, bd. dirs.; gen. mgmt. cons., 1987-90; dep. asst. sec. of energy for export assistance U.S. Dept. Energy, Washington, 1990-93; v.p. Dreser Industries, Inc., Houston, 1993-97. Sr. assoc. Cambridge Energy Rsch. Assocs., 1997—; pres. Lockwood Corp., Gering, Nebr., 1986-87; chmn. bd. dirs. SIE Internat., Inc., Ft. Worth, Gas Turbine Efficience Holdings Corp., 2002—; prin. Innova Ptnrs., 1988-90; bd. dirs. NSGroup, Newport, Ky., Hunting PLC, London; chmn. bd. dirs. Tohhein Corp., Ft. Wayne, Ind.; chmn. bd. dirs. Gas Turbine Efficiency, Inc., Houston. Bd. dirs. Jr. Achievement Internat., Briarwood Sch., Houston; trustee S.W. Rsch. Inst., Eurasia Found., Washington; mem. exec. com. Jr. Achievement of S.E. Tex. Recipient Five Outstanding Young Texans award Tex. Jr. C. of C., 1972; named Outstanding Young Houstonian Houston Jr. C. of C., 1972; Disting. Grad. Sch. Engring. U. Tex., 1977. Mem. ASME, Am. Inst. Mining, Metall. and Petroleum Engrs., Am. Petroleum Inst. (bd. dirs.), Inst. Gas Engrs. (U.K.), Tex. Soc. Profl. Engrs., Am. Wellhead Equipment Assn. (pres. 1967), Petroleum Equipment Suppliers Assn. (pres. 1976-77), Houston C. of C., Tau Beta Pi, Phi Eta Sigma, Pi Tau Sigma, Sigma Nu, Friars Soc. Presbyterian. Home and Office: 2622 W Lane Dr Houston TX 77027-4914 E-mail: ghelland@worldnet.att.net.

HELLAND, MARK DUANE, small business owner; b. Eldora, Iowa, May 19, 1949; s. Duane J. and Mary Carolyn (Bloomberg) H.; m. Lois Ann Lebakken, Aug. 15, 1970; children: Alissa, Jonathan. BA, Luther Coll., 1971; JD, U. Minn., 1974; postgrad., Harvard U., 1985, 88. Bar: Minn. 1974, Wis. 1980. Assoc. Berg Law Offices, Stewartville, Minn., 1974-77; v.p. Legal Systems, Inc., Eau Claire, Wis., 1977-78; sr. editor Lawyers Coop. Pub. Co., Rochester, N.Y., 1978-80; exec. dir. Profl. Edn. Systems, Inc., Eau Claire, 1980-81, chief exec. officer, 1981-88, pub., 1988-91, Wiley Law Publs., Colorado Springs, Colo., 1991-93; pres. PESI, Eau Claire, 1993, PESI Law Publ., LLC, Eau Claire, 2001—. Author: Minnesota Probate System, 1980, Wisconsin Rules of the Road, 1985. Mem. Greater Eau Claire C. of C. Office: PESI 200 Spring St Eau Claire WI 54703-3225 E-mail: mhelland@pesi.com.

HELLAND, SHERMAN M. writer; b. Racine, Wis., Nov. 16, 1913; s. Severin and Marie Kutinka (Fyhrie) H.; m. Rose Martha Steuck, Aug. 12, 1939; children: Mary, Sandra, Karen, Harold. Mgr. retail meats C&W Haummersen, Racine, Wis., 1933-35; sales area developer George A. Hormel Co., Austin, Minn., 1936-51; mgr. bus. analysis U.S. Govt., Richmond, Va., 1951-53; sales mgr., beef grader Donner Packing Co., Milw., 1953-54; supr. chain store meat Godfrey Co., Waukesha, Wis., 1954-55, purchaser, merchandiser select beef and lamb, 1956-57, with, 1958-76. Cons. agr., livestock, breeding feeding, merchandising retail meat, 1991—. Author: Hoofs, Amen, 1978, E. Coli Kills--Wake Up or Die, 1997. Pres. Old Jr. Club of Milw. County, 1980. With USN, 1945. Mem. Am. Legion (chpt. pres. 1981-82). Republican. Lutheran. Avocations: flying, hunting, golf, fishing, philosophy. Home and Office: 5020 S 55th St Apt 303 Greenfield WI 53220-5370

HELLBUSCH, LESLIE CARL, neurosurgeon; b. Columbus, Nebr., Nov. 25, 1945; s. Carl Ludwig and Dora Lily Hellbusch; m. Joan Marie Swanson, May 28, 1988; children: Jeffrey, Laurie, Nicholas, Sarah. BS, U. Nebr., 1968; MD, Northwestern U., 1972. Diplomate Am. Bd. Neurol. Surgery, Am Bd. Pediat. Neurosurgery. Intern Evanston (Ill.) Hosp., 1972-73; resident in neurosurgery Baylor Coll. Medicine, Houston, 1973-77; pvt. practice neurosurgery Omaha, 1977—; chmn. neurosurgery Meth. Hosp., Omaha, 1981-85, 90-91; vice-sect. chief sect. neurosurgery U. Nebr. Med. ctr., Omaha, 1994—, clin. assoc. prof. surgery, 1987-98, clin. prof. surgery, 1998—. Tng. dir. resident physicians Meth. Hosp., Children's Hosp., 1994—; presenter in field. Contbr. articles to profl. jours. Trustee Children's Hosp., Omaha, 1990-95; bd. dirs. Heartland Equine Therapeutic Riding Acad., 1989-92, v.p., 1990-91, pres. 1992. Mem. AMA, Am. Assn. Neurol. Surgeons, Nebr. Med. Assn. (alt. del. 1980-90, del. 1991-98, clin. affairs com. 1996-98), Met. Omaha Med. Soc., Iowa-Midwest Neurosurg. Soc., Omaha-Midwest Med. Soc., Nebr. Acad. Neurologists and Neurosurgeons, Rocky Mountain Neurosurg. Soc., Phi Beta Kappa, Phi Eta Sigma, Theta Nu. Avocations: jogging, skiing, coaching soccer. Home: 109 S 92d St Omaha NE 68114 Office: Midwest Neurosurgery PC Ste 305 8005 Farnam Dr Omaha NE 68114 Fax: (402) 298-9253.

HELLEINER, GERALD KARL, economics educator; b. St. Pölten, Austria, Oct. 9, 1936; s. Karl Ferdinand and Grethe (Deutsch) H.; m. Georgia Stirrett, Aug. 16, 1958; children— Jane Leslie, Eric Noel, Peter David. BA, U. Toronto, 1958; PhD, Yale U., 1962; LLD (hon.), Dalhousie U., 1988; DLitt (hon.), U. W.I. Asst. prof. Yale U., 1961—65; assoc., then prof. U. Toronto, 1965—98, prof. emeritus, disting. rsch. fellow Monk Ctr. Internat. Studies, 1998—. Dir. Econ. Rsch. Bur., Dar es Salaam, Tanzania, 1966-68; vis. fellow Inst. Devel. Studies, 1971-72, 75, Queen Elizabeth House, Oxford, 1979. Dir. Econ. Rsch. Bur., Dar es Salaam, Tanzania, 1966-68; vis. fellow Inst. Devel. Studies, Sussex, 1971-72, 75, Queen Elizabeth House, Oxford, 1979. Rsch. coord. Group of 24, 1990-98; bd. dirs., chmn. bd. trustees Internat. Food Policy Rsch. Inst., 1988-94; bd. dirs. North-South Inst., 1976-92, chmn., 1990-92; bd. dirs. Internat. Devel. Rsch. Ctr., 1985-91, Econ and Social Rsch. Found., 1995-2000, African Capacity Bldg. Found., 1997-2003; chmn. Internat. Lawyers and Economists Against Poverty, 2003—. Guggenheim fellow, 1971-72 Fellow Royal Soc. Can.; mem. Can. Econs. Assn., Can. Assn. Study Internat. Devel., Am. Econs. Assn., Can. African Studies Assn., Order of Can. (officer). Office: 150 Saint George St Toronto ON Canada M5S 3G7 E-mail: ghellein@chass.utoronto.ca.

HELLENBRAND, SAMUEL HENRY, lawyer, diversified industry executive; b. NYC, Nov. 11, 1916; s. Louis H. and Fannie (Cohen) H.; children: Kathy Noreen, Linda Caryn. LL.B., Bklyn. Law Sch. St. Lawrence U., 1941, LL.M., 1942. Bar: NY 1942. With NY Ctrl. R.R., NY, 1942-68, atty., asst. to gen. atty., tax atty., 1947-52, gen. tax atty., 1952-56, dir. taxes fin. dept., 1956-63, v.p. planning and devel., 1963-64, v.p. real estate, 1964-68; v.p. indsl. devel. and real estate Penn Ctrl. Co., 1968-70, v.p. real estate and taxes, 1970-71; pres. Pa. Co., Pa., 1970-71; v.p. exec. asst. to pres., dir. real estate affairs ITT, 1971-81; chmn. fin. com., vice-chmn. AMTRAK, 1982-90. Mem. ABA, Assn. Bar City NY Home: 177 E 75th St New York NY 10021-3230

HELLENBRAND, WILLIAM E. physician, cardiologist; MD, Downstate Med. Ctr., Bklyn., 1970. Cert. Pediatric Cardiology Am. Acad. of Pediat., 1977. Dir. of pediatric catheterization lab. Yale New Haven Hosp., New Haven, 1976—99, Children's Hosp. of N.Y.- Presbyn., N.Y., NY, 1999—. Maj. U.S. Army, 1973—75, Washington. Office: Columbia Univ Sch of Medicine 3959 Broadway 2 North New York NY 10032 Office Fax: 212-342-5704. E-mail: wh148@columbia.edu.

HELLENGA, ROBERT R. language educator, writer; b. Milw., Aug. 5, 1941; s. Theodore Edward Hellenga and Marjorie Johnson; m. Virginia K. Hellenga, Aug. 31, 1963; children: Rachel, Heather, Caltrine. BA, U. Mich., 1963; PhD, Princeton U., 1968. Tchr. English Knox Coll., Galesburg, Ill., 1968—. Co-dir. Seminar in Humanities Newberry Libr., Chgo., 1973—74; dir. Florence programs Associated Colls. of Midwest, Florence, Italy, 1982—83. Author: The Sixteen Pleasures, 1994 (Soc. of Midland Authors, 1994), The Fall for Sparrow, 1998, Blues Lessons, 2001. Recipient Award, Ill. Arts Coun., 1981—2001; fellow, NEA, 1981—82. Avocations: blues guitar, Italian cooking. Home: 343 Prairie St Galesburg IL 61401 Office: Knox Coll Classics Dept 2 E South St Galesburg IL 61401-4999

HELLER, ABRAHAM, psychiatrist, educator; b. Claremont, N.H., Mar. 17, 1917; s. David and Rose Heller; m. Lora S. Levy, June 16, 1957; 1 child, Judith Rose. BA, Brandeis U., 1953; MD, Boston U., 1957. Diplomate Am. Bd. Med. Examiners, Am. Bd. Psychiatry and Neurology. Resident in psychiatry U. Colo., Denver, 1958-61; chief in-patient psychiatry Denver Gen. Hosp., 1961-65, asst. dir. psychiat. services, 1965-70, assoc. dir. psychiat. services, 1970-73, dir., community mental health services, 1970-72; chief psychiatry, dir. community mental health ctr. Newport (R.I.) Hosp., 1973 77; clin. assoc. prof. psychiatry Brown U., Providence, 1973-77; prof. psychiatry, community health Wright State U., Dayton, Ohio, 1977-91, vice chmn. dept., 1980-91, prof. emeritus, 1991—. Fellow Am. Psychiat. Assn. (disting. sr.), Am. Orthopsychiat. Assn., Am. Assn. for Social Psychiatry. Jewish. Home: 1400 Runnymede Rd Dayton OH 45419-2924 Office: Wright State U Sch Medicine Dept Psychiatry PO Box 927 Dayton OH 45401-0927 E-mail: abraham.heller@wright.edu.

HELLER, ADAM, chemist, researcher; b. Cluj, Romania, June 25, 1933; came to U.S., 1962; s. Ephraim and Blanche (Nissel) H.; m. Ilana Grossbard, July 26, 1956; children: Ephraim, Jonathan. MSc, Hebrew U., 1957, PhD, 1961; D honoris causa, Uppsala U., Sweden, 1991. Postdoctoral rsch. assoc. U. Calif., Berkeley, 1962-63; mem. tech. staff Bell Labs., Murray Hill, N.J., 1963-64, 75-77, GTE Labs., Bayside, N.Y., 1964-70, mgr. exploratory rsch. Waltham, Mass., 1970-75; head electronic materials rsch. dept. AT&T Bell Labs., Murray Hill, 1977-88; prof. chem. engring. U. Tex., Austin, 1988—; co-founder, chief sci. advisor TheraSense, Inc., Alameda, Calif., 1996—. Lectr. in field; adv. bd. Nat. Renewable Energy Lab., Golden, Colo., 1987-93, Basic Energy Scis. Dept. Energy, 1993-96; adj. prof. Brandeis U., Waltham, 1972-75, CUNY, 1968-88; lectr. UCLA, 1984, Weizmann Inst., Israel, U. Guelph, Ont., Can., 1984, Tel-Aviv U., 1987; guest prof. Coll. de France; co-founder, chief sci. advisor TheraSense Inc., 1996—. Editor: Semiconductor Liquid Junction Solar Cells, 1977, Inorganic Resists, 1982; contbr. articles to profl. jours., patentee in field. Recipient Faraday medal Royal Chem. Soc. (London), 1996, Spiers medal, 2000. Fellow AAAS, Electrochem. Soc. (Battery Divsn. award 1978, Grahame award Phys. Electrochemistry divsn. 1987, Vittorio De Nora-Diamond Shamrock award 1988, De Nora Gold medal 1988), Am. Chem. Soc. (Chemistry of Materials award 1994); mem. U.S. Nat. Acad. Engring. Jewish. Achievements include glucose microsensors for the management of diabetes; electrochem. biosensors; lithium batteries; liquid lasers; electrochemical solar cells; biofuel cells. E-mail: heller@che.utexas.edu.

HELLER, AIMEE KIM, writer; b. Miami Beach, Fla., Feb. 17, 1971; d. David A. and Beverly Z. Heller; m. Craig M. Zimmerman, 2001. BS in Mass Comm., Boston U., 1991. Creative dir. Ziccardi Ptnrs. Frierson Mee, N.Y.C., 1999—2003; pres. Decibel Inc., N.Y.C., 2000—. Creator www.handturkey.com. Author and illustrator: (book and short film) A Story About Flowers, 1993, (book and short film) A Story About Two Turkeys, 1993, Katie's Bath, 1994, The Penguin Who Went Casual, 1995, Edward, 1997, Midland, 2003. Avocation: meandering.

HELLER, AL, marketing consultant, business journalist; BA in Comms., Queens Coll., 1972; MBA in Mktg., Fordham U., 1977. Mng. editor Disclosure Record, Floral Park, N.Y., 1973-76; asst. pub. rels. dir. Fordham U., N.Y.C., 1977-81; contbg. writer and editor Venture, N.Y.C., 1982-84; assoc. editor Chain Store Age Supermarkets, N.Y.C., 1982-83; sr. editor Discount Store News, N.Y.C., 1983-86; exec. editor Drug Store News and Drug Store News for the Pharmacist, N.Y.C., 1986-93; editor-in-chief Supermarket HQ Quar., N.Y.C., 1990-93, Nonfoods Mdsg., N.Y.C., 1993-96. Pres. Al Heller Editl. Svcs., 1996—; screening judge Jesse Neal awards Am. Bus. Media, N.Y.C., 1993—95. Author: Selling into Home Depot, 1997, Category Management in the Mass Market: Best Practices, 1998, Ernst & Young Retail Information Technology Report, 1999, 2d edit., 2000; co-author: The Passive Solar Dome Greenhouse Book, 1979, Tipping the Food Scale retail report, 2003; contbr. Ernst & Young Global Internet Retailing Report, 2000, 2d edit., 2001, Tipping the Food Scale: Consumer-Approved Food & Beverage Approaches fot the Drug Store, 2002. With USCG Res., 1969-75. Mem. Soc. Profl. Journalists, Nat. Writers Union. Avocations: writing, sports, photography, reading. Office: Al Heller Editl Svcs 28 Warren Dr Syosset NY 11791-6328

HELLER, ARTHUR, advertising agency executive; b. Bklyn., Mar. 14, 1930; s. Max and Tecla (Jacobs) H.; m. Phyllis Olarsch, Dec. 25, 1954; children: Todd, Tracy. BA, Bklyn. Coll., 1951, MA, 1952. Speech and speech correction tchr. N.Y.C. Bd. Edn., 1951-55; v.p., assoc. media dir., media analysis and planning Benton & Bowles, Inc., 1955-66; with Ted Bates & Co., N.Y.C., 1966—, v.p., media dir., 1966-69, v.p., assoc. dir. media-program dept., 1969-71, sr. v.p., 1971—, also account dir., 1974-78; sr. v.p., dir. media-programming-mktg. services Griffin Bacal Inc., N.Y.C., 1978-82, exec. v.p., 1982-97, also bd. dirs.; pres. Heller Mktg. & Comms. Former dir. media programming worldwide, former gen. mgr. Griffin Bacal Can. Served with AUS, 1952-54. Mem. Actors Equity Assn.

HELLER, BARBARA R. former dean, nursing educator; BS, Boston U., 1962; MS, Adelphi U., 1966; EdM, Columbia U., 1971, EdD, 1973; postgrad., U. Md., 1986-90. RN Md., Mass., N.Y., Pa., Va. Chmn. dept. nursing SUNY, Farmingdale; asst. dean acad. programs, Coll. Nursing Villanova U.; prof. and chair dept. edn., adminstrn. and health policy, Sch. Nursing U. Md., Balt., dean Sch. Nursing, 1990—2002, prof., 2002—. Dir. rsch. and edn. nursing dept., Clin. Ctr., NIH, 1983-84; congl. fellow in health policy and edn. Hon. Constance A. Morella, U.S. House of Reps., 1989-90; vice chair, mem. bd. dirs. Computer Based Patient Record Inst., 1992-94, So. Coun. on Collegiate Edn. for Nurses, So. Regional Edn. Bd., chmn. task force on telecomms., numerous others; cons. in field. Co-editor: (book) Information Management in Nursing and Health Care, 1995; contbr. chpts. to books, articles to profl. jours. Mem. bd. dirs. Paul's Place, Open Gates; chair adv. bd. Gov's. Wellmobile. Recipient Innovative Health Program award Md. Found. for Nursing, 1995, Outstanding Educator of Am. award, Alumni award for Nursing Excellence Boston U., Alumni award for Nursing Practice Tchr's. Coll. Columbia U.; numerous grants. Fellow Am. Acad. Nursing; mem. ANA, Am. Assn. Colls. Nursing, Am. Soc. Med. Informatics Assn., Am. Assn. Higher Edn., Nat. League Nursing, Md. Nurses Assn., Md. Assn. Higher Edn., Gerontological Soc., Nurses in Washington Roundtable, Women's Pol. Caucus Md., Exec. Women's Network Balt., Sigma Theta Tau, Phi Kappa Phi. Office: Univ of MD Sch Nursing 655 W Lombard St Rm 725 Baltimore MD 21201-1506

HELLER, (DOUGLAS) BRIAN, human services administrator; b. N.Y.C., Jan. 16, 1937; s. Alexander Samuel Heller and Beatrice (Halm) Piening; m. Sandra Newell Durré, May 27, 1959 (div. June 1970); m. Rita Jo McClure Cunningham, Dec. 21, 1980; children: Peter David, Alison Elise Auerbach, Julia Elizabeth Gray, Noël Elizabeth Huntsinger. BA, Syracuse U., 1961; MA, U. Chgo., 1964, PhD, 1975. Exec. dir. Roosevelt Health Plan, Chgo., 1975-77; pres. Heller Assocs., Chgo., 1977-84; v.p., exec. dir. Maxicare Health Plans, Chgo., 1984-87; v.p. Travelers Health Network, Chgo., 1987-89; pres., CEO Cmty. Corrections Sys., Inc., Nashville, Ind., 1989-92; exec. dir. Meth. Delivery Sys., Indpls., 1992-94; CEO, Susquehanna Regional PHO, Binghamton, NY, 1994-2000; pres., CEO Mercy Health System Physician Hosp. Orgn., Toledo, 2000—02; pres. Managed Liability Assocs., Washington, 2002—. Cons. Office Health Maintenance Orgns. Dept. HEW, Rockville, Md., 1965—75; part-time asst. prof. U. Ill., Chgo., 1973—75; cons. Ameritech Ind., Indpls., 1993—94; prin. Managed Liability Assocs., LLC, 1999—; pub. Managed Health Liability, 1999—2000; adj. instr. Roundtable Group, Washington, 2003—. Chmn. allocation panel Broome County United Way, Binghamton, 1996—2000; pres. bd. dirs. Mental Health Assn. So. Tier, 1995—2000, Art Mission, 1999—2000; bd. dirs. Brown County C. of C., Nashville, Ind., 1991—94, Brown County Cmty. Corrections, Nashville, 1993—94, Ind. Pub. Health Found., Indpls., 1994—96. NIMH fellow, 1963—64, APHA fellow, 1970, Travel fellow, NIH, 1972. Mem.: Masons (32 degree). Avocations: painting, ukulele playing and collecting. Office: Managed Liability Assocs 50 F St NW Ste 600 Washington DC 20001 E-mail: bheller@aol.com.

HELLER, DEAN, state official; b. Castro Valley, Calif., May 10, 1960; m. Lynne Brombach, children: Hilary, Harrison, Andrew, Emmy. BS with honors, USC. Former mem. Ways & Means & Carson City Rep. Cent. Committee; former Rep. Assembly Caucus; former Nev. St. Assembly; former sr. cons. Bank of Amer.; former stockbroker, broker, trader Pac Stock Exchange; chief dep. Office of State Treas.; sec. of state State of Nev., Carson City, 1994—97, 1998—. Active Boy Scouts Am.; bd. dirs. Western Nev. Cmty. Coll. Found. Mem.: N.Am. Securities Adminstrs. Assn., Natl. Assn. Sec. of State. Republican. Home: 110 Plantation Dr Carson City NV 89703-5410 Office: Sec State 101 N Carson St Ste 3 Carson City NV 89701-4786*

HELLER, DOROTHY, artist; b. N.Y.C., June 15, 1926; d. Samuel and Rebecca (Cohn) H. Studied with Hans Hofman, N.Y.C., 1942. One-woman shows include Tibor de Nagy Gallery, N.Y.C., 1953, Galerie Facchetti, Paris, 1955, Pondexter Gallery, N.Y.C., 1956, 57, East Hampton Gallery, N.Y.C., 1963, Betty Parsons Gallery, N.Y.C., 1972, 76, 78, U. Pa., 1976, Cathedral St. John the Divine, N.Y.C., 1976; exhibited in group shows Denver Art Mus., 1953, Whitney Mus. Ann., 1957, Mus. Modern Art Traveling Show, 1963, Betty Parsons Gallery, 1972-81, U. Calif. Art Mus., 1974, Met. Mus. Art, N.Y.C., 1979, Otis Art Inst., 1979, Bklyn. Coll. Art Gallery, 1990; represented in permanent collections Met. Mus. Art, N.Y.C., U. Calif. Art Mus., Berkeley, Cornell U., Johnson Mus., Ithaca, N.Y., Wadsworth Atheneum, Hartford, Conn., Smithsonian Instn. Archives, Washington, Zimmerli Mus., New Brunswick, N.J., Alexandria (La.) Mus., Auburn (Ala.) U., Whitney Comm., N.Y.C., Chase Manhattan Bank, N.Y.C., numerous others. Recipient Internat. Woman of Yr. award, 1976.

HELLER, FRANCIS H(OWARD), law and political science educator emeritus; b. Vienna, Aug. 24, 1917; came to U.S., 1938, naturalized, 1943; s. Charles A. and Lily (Grunwald) H.; m. Donna Munn, Sept. 3, 1949 (dec. Dec. 1990); 1 child, Denis Wayne. Student, U. Vienna, 1935-37; JD, MA, U. Va., 1941, PhD, 1948; DHL (hon.), Benedictine Coll., 1988. Asst. prof. govt. Coll. William and Mary, 1947; asst. prof. polit. sci. U. Kans., Lawrence, 1948-51, assoc. prof., 1951-56, prof., 1956-72, Roy A. Roberts prof. law and polit. sci., 1972-88, prof. emeritus, 1988—, assoc. dean Coll. Liberal Arts and Scis., 1957-66, assoc. dean of faculties, 1966-67, dean, 1967-70, vice chancellor for acad. affairs, 1970-72. Vis. prof. Inst. Advanced Studies, Vienna, 1965, U. Vienna Law Sch., 1985, 97, Trinity U., Tex., 1992. Author: Introduction to American Constitutional Law, 1952, The Presidency: A Modern Perspective, 1960, The Korean War: A 25-Year Perspective, 1977, The Truman White House, 1980, Economics and the Truman Administration, 1982, USA: Verfassung und Politik, 1987, NATO: The Founding of the Alliance and the Integration of Europe, 1992, The Kansas State Constitution: A Reference Guide, 1992, The United States and the Integration of Europe, 1996. Mem. Kans. Commn. on Constl. Revision, 1957-61, Lawrence City Planning Commn., 1957-63, ednl. adv. commn. U.S. Army Command and Gen. Staff Coll., 1969-72; bd. dirs. Harry S. Truman Libr. Inst., 1958-96, v.p., 1962-96; bd. dirs. Benedictine Coll., chmn., 1971 79; mem. nat. adv. coun. Ctr. for Study of Presidency, 1991-97. Pvt. to 1st lt. arty. AUS, 1942-47, capt. 1951-52, maj. USAR, ret. Decorated Silver Star, Bronze Star with cluster; recipient Career Teaching award Chancellor's Club, 1986, Silver Angel award Kans. Cath. Conf., 1987, Disting. Svc. citation U. Kans., 1998. Mem. Am. Polit. Sci. Assn. (exec. council 1958-60), Order of Coif, Phi Beta Kappa, Pi Sigma Alpha (mem. nat. council 1958-60) Home: 3419 Seminole Dr Lawrence KS 66047-1622 Office: U Kans Sch Law Green Hall 1535 W 15th St Lawrence KS 66045-7577 E-mail: fheller@ku.edu.

HELLER, FREDERICK, retired mining company executive; b. Detroit, May 6, 1932; s. Robert and Lois (Mouch) Heller; m. Catherine C. Flynn, Mar. 26, 1955; m. Rosamund Clifford, July 10, 1964; children: Thomas M., John G., Cynthia R. BA, Harvard U., 1954. With Hanna Mining Co., Cleve., 1957-87, v.p. sales, 1973-76, sr. v.p. sales and transp., 1976-81, sr. v.p. mktg., 1981-84; sr. v.p. sales and mktg. M.A. Hanna Co., Cleve., 1984-87; dir. exec. com. Tucson Bot. Gardens, 2002—. Trustee, exec. com. Cleve. Inst. Art, 1977-82; trustee, fin. com. McGregor Home, 1978-86. 1st lt. U.S. Army, 1954-56. Mem. Tucson Country Club. Home: 4825 N Camino Sumo Tucson AZ 85718-7403

HELLER, GEORGE GLEN, retired computer scientist, educator; m. Iby Violette Heller, Sept. 16, 1954; children: Neil Coleman children: Karen Anne des Jardins, Leslie Joyce Siegel, Steven Keith. BS in Bus. Adminstrn., Temple U., 1951; BS in Elec. Engring., Humanities and Engring., MIT, 1959. Programmer IBM, Kingston, NY, 1959—60, cons. HONE application planning, network security, installation productivity Palo Alto, Calif., 1983—90, programming rsch. Bethesda, Md., 1960—1061, prin. investigator, info. retrieval rsch., 1961—64, PL/I lang. tech. Poughkeepsie, NY, 1964—65, edn. rsch. adminstr., 1965—71, software developer, 1959—90. Dir.(large scale computer education program): (in secondary schools) Breakthrough in High School Computer Education (Numerous Publications in US and overseas.); author: (computer education exhibits) Musical Composition and Sketching in a Junior High School (at World Computer Edn. Congress, Amsterdam the Netherlands and ACM Nat. Meeting in NYC, 1970), (introduce computers to preschool) Proposal presented at the Education Panel of International Federation of Information Processing (IFIP) Congress in New York City 1965; chairman, education committee (computer science curricula) ACM Computer Science Curricula for Colleges and Universities published in Communications of ACM 1964 1nd 1965; author (organizer): (computers to help handicapped) Computer education programs for blind and otherwise handicapped persons at ACM and IBM; author: (invited speaker) (presentation at rio symposium) The Role of Professional Computer Societies in Computer Education -for Developing Countries 1972; author: (and invited us participant) (computer education in secindary schools) An Outline Guide for Teachers, August 1970, Published by International Federation for Information Processing (IFIP) sponsored by United Nations Office of Economic Development and Cooperation (OECD) translated to many languages; editor: (ednl. pubs.) Hands on Network Environ., 1972—76, 38 vols. demo guides, Installation Productivity Options Pubs., 1977—82. Spkr., holocaust survivor B'nai B'rith, Philadelphia, Pa., 1947—51, Temple Beth Jacob, Redwood City, Calif., 2000—03. Recipient Leadership Award, United Jewish Appeal, 1975, 1976. Mem.: IEEE (life), NY Acad. Scis., Assn. Computing Machinery (chmn. edn. com. 1961—64, mem. nat. coun. 1966—68, dir. edn. 1971—72, editor ednl. pubs. edit. bd. 1962—63). Achievements include Elected to Pi Gamma Mu, National Social Science Honor Society 1950; Member, Awards and Prizes Committee, American Federation of Information Processing Societies 1963; Member, Planning Committee International Federation of Information Processing Congress, NYC 1965; Elected Active Member, New York Academy of Sciences, 1971; Recipient of the George B. Morgan award of the MIT Educational Council, 1983; first to A1 list of publications describing work appears on pages 26-34 of Report of the Conference on Computer Oriented Mathematics and the Secondary School published by NCTM.

HELLER, GEORGE NORMAN, music educator; b. Ypsilanti, Mich., Dec. 19, 1941; s. Julius G. and Norma (Smith) H.; m. Judy A. Watkins, Mar. 14, 1987; children: Scott B. Thompson, Jennifer L., David P. BMus, U. Mich., 1963, MMus, 1969, PhD, 1973. Organist/choirmaster St. Andrews Ch., Dexter, Mich., 1961-63; tchr. music Summerfield Schs., Petersburg, Mich., 1963-64, Haslett (Mich.) Pub. Schs., 1964-66, Farmington (Mich.) H.S., 1969-71; teaching fellow U. Mich., Ann Arbor, 1971-73; instr. Eastern Mich. U., 1972—73; prof. music edn. U. Kans., Lawrence, 1973—2002, prof. emeritus, 2002—. With U.S. Army, 1966-68. Named to Kans. Music Educators Assn. Hall of Fame, 2003. Mem. Music Educators Nat. Conf., Coll. Music Soc., Soc. for Am. Music, Kans. Music Educators Assn. (named to Hall of Fame 2003), Soc. for Ethnomusicology, Music Libr. Assn.

HELLER, HANES AYRES, lawyer; b. New Orleans, Mar. 10, 1940; s. John Roderick and Susie Mae (Ayres) H.; m. Patricia R. Hawkins, Oct. 19, 1996; children: Hanes Ayres, Lee McGavock. BA, Yale U., 1962; LLB, Harvard U., 1965. Assoc. firm Dewey, Ballantine, Bushby, Palmer & Wood, N.Y.C., 1965-68; atty. CPC Internat. (now Bestfoods), Englewood Cliffs, N.J., 1968-76,

divsn. counsel Best Foods divsn., 1976-78, assoc. gen. counsel, 1978-80, gen. cousnel N.Am. divsn., 1980-82, v.p., gen. counsel, 1982-84; asst. gen. counsel CPC Internat., 1982-87, dep. gen. counsel, 1987-95, v.p. legal affairs, 1995-97, v.p., gen. counsel, sec., 1997—. Mem. ABA, N.Y. State Bar Assn., Assn. Bar City N.Y., Assn. Gen. Consnel. Home: 3 Lenape Dr Montville NJ 07045-9722 Office: Best Foods Internat Plz Englewood Cliffs NJ 07632

HELLER, H(EINZ) ROBERT, financial executive; b. Cologne, Germany, Jan. 8, 1940; s. Heinrich and Karoline (Hermann) H.; m. Emily Mitchell, Dec. 5, 1970; children: Kimberly, Christopher. MA in Econs., U. Minn., 1962; PhD, U. Calif., Berkeley, 1965. Instr. U. Calif., Berkeley, 1965; assoc. prof. econs. UCLA, 1965-71; prof. U. Hawaii, Honolulu, 1971-74; chief fin. studies divsn. Internat. Monetary Fund, Washington, 1974-78; sr. v.p., dir. internat. econ. rsch. Bank of Am., San Francisco, 1978-86; mem., bd. govs. Fed. Res. System, Washington, 1986-89; exec. v.p. VISA Internat., San Francisco, 1989-91; pres., CEO VISA, U.S.A., San Francisco, 1991-93; exec. v.p. Fair, Isaac and Co., San Rafael, Calif., 1994-2001. Bd. dirs. Fair, Isaac and Co., Plus Sys. Inc., Interlink, Merchant Bank Svcs. Corp., Bay Area Coun., San Francisco, Sonic Automotive, BMW of N.Am., Inc., mem. adv. bd.; vice-chmn. Fed. Fin. Instns. Examination Coun., 1988-89; mem. Nat. Adv. Coun. Internat. Monetary and Fin. Policies, 1987-89, U.S. Coun. Internat. Bus., N.Y.C., 1979—; trustee World Affairs Coun., 1990-96; mem. adv. bd. Nat. Ctr. Fin. Svcs., U.Calif., Berkeley, 1984-90, Ctr. Fin. Sys. Rsch., Ariz. State U., Tempe, 1989, Inst. Internat. Edn., San Francisco, 1989; mem. Bay Area Internat. Forum, 1989, Bay Area Coun., 1992; dir. Am. Inst. Contemporary German Studies, Johns Hopkins U., Washington, 1989; dir. Wharton Fin. Instns. Ctr., U. Pa., 1989—. Author: International Trade, 1968, rev. edit. 1973, International Monetary Economics, 1974, The Economic System, 1972, Japanese Investment in the U.S., 1974; mem. editorial bd. Jour. Money, Credit and Banking, 1975-83, Internat. Trade Jour., 1985-88. Dir. Marin Gen. Hosp., 2001— Mem. Bankers Club of San Francisco, Royal Econ. Soc., Am. Econ. Assn., Western Econo. Assn. (exec. bd. 1977-81), San Francisco Yacht Club, Tiburon Peninsula Club. Avocations: sailing, skiing.

HELLER, JACK ISAAC, lawyer; b. Passaic, N.J., July 12, 1932; m. Naomi Heller AB, U. Chgo., 1952; LLB, Columbia U., 1958. Teaching fellow, research asst. internat. program in taxation Harvard Law Sch., 1958-61; tax economist Latin Am. Bur., U.S. AID, 1962-65; with Office Gen. Counsel, AID, 1965-66; legal adviser AID, Brazil, 1966-67, asst. dir., 1967-68; dir. Office of Devel. Programs, Latin Am. Bur., AID, 1969-72; atty., mgr. spl. projects Office Gen. Counsel, Gen. Electric Co., 1972-74; pvt. practice Washington, 1974—; ptnr. Heller & Rosenblatt, Washington, 1991—. Co-dir. programs in Latin Am. U. Ill. Coll. Law, 1975-80, spl. programs in China, 1982-86; pres. 1998-2000, dir. Pan Am. Devel. Found. Author: Tax Incentives for Industry in Less Developed Countries, 1963. Served with AUS, 1953-55. Home: 3431 Porter St NW Washington DC 20016-3125 Office: Heller & Rosenblatt 1101 15th St NW Washington DC 20005-5002 E-mail: hellerji@erols.com.

HELLER, JANET RUTH, English language, writing and literature educator; b. Milw., July 8, 1949; d. William Charles and Joan Ruth (Pereles) H.; m. Michael Alexander Krischer, June 13, 1982. Student, Oberlin Coll., 1967-70; BA, U. Wis., 1971, MA, 1973; PhD, U. Chgo., 1987. Coord. writing program U. Chgo., 1976-81, lectr. creative writing, 1981-82; instr. English No. Ill. U., DeKalb, 1982-88; asst. prof. English Nazareth Coll., Kalamazoo, 1989-90, Grand Valley State U., Allendale, Mich., 1990-97, Albion Coll., 1998, 2001—02; asst. prof. women's studies and English Western Mich. U., 1999—. Author: Coleridge, Lamb, Hazlitt, and the Reader of Drama, 1990; editor: Primavera Jour., 1974-82; contbr. articles to profl. jours.; commd. poem and display by Friends of Poetry, Kalamazoo, 1990-91. Recipient award Friends of Poetry, 1989. Mem. MLA (reg. del. 1985-87), Midwest MLA, Mich. Coll. English Assn. (campus rep. 1990—, sec.), Nat. Coun. Tchrs. English, N.Am. Soc. Study of Romanticism, Soc. Study of Midwestern Lit. (bd. dirs. 1999—, pres. 2003). Democrat. Jewish. Avocations: hiking, birdwatching, canoeing, biking, gardening. E-mail: janet.heller@wmich.edu.

HELLER, JEFFREY M. data systems executive; m. Carol; children: Scott, Debbie. BBA, U. Tex. Joined Electronic Data Sys. Corp., 1968, sys. engr., 1969-70, participant N.Y. Stock Exch. study, 1970, various mgmt. positions, 1970-72, mgr. regional data ctr., 1972-73, regional mgr. health care bus. Ea. U.S., 1973-74, corp. v.p., 1974-79, head Tech. Svcs. group, 1979-87, sr. v.p., 1987-96, pres., COO, 1996—2000, vice chmn., 1996—2002, also bd. dirs., pres., COO, 2003—. Bd. dirs. Mutual of Omaha, Trammell Crow Co. Mem. Longhorn found., U. Tex. Chancellor's Coun.; trustee Southwestern Med. Found.; bd. dirs. Zale Lipshy U. Med. Ctr.; chmn. U. Tex. Engring. Found. Adv. Coun. Capt. USMC, 1960-66. Mem. Dallas Symphony Assn. (bd. dirs.). Office: Electronic Data Systems Corp 5400 Legacy Dr Plano TX 75024-3199*

HELLER, JENNIFER LYNN, developmental studies specialist, consultant; b. Ann Arbor, Oct. 16, 1971; d. George Norman Heller and Eleanor Allberry, Judy Heller (Stepmother); life ptnr. Michael S. Wolverton. BA in Religious Studies, BS in Edn., U. of Kans., 1996, BA in Am. Studies, MEd in Tchg. and Leadership, U. of Kans., 1998. Secondary English edn. Kans., Mo., 1997. English tchr. North Kans. City Sch. Dist., Mo., 1997—99; adj. assoc. prof. English Johnson County C.C., Overland Pk., Kans., 1998—; devel. studies specialist Donnelly Coll., Kans. City, 2002—. Writing consulting, 1997—. Peer reviewer Jour. of Religion and Popular Culture; author: Jour. of Religion and Popular Culture, (book) Choosing Their Own Course: Independent Study and Self-Directed Learning in theSecondary Language Arts Classroom. Precinct chair Dem. Party, Lawrence, Kans., 2001—02. Mem.: Nat. Assn. for Devel. Edn., MLA, Am. Acad. of Religion. Office: Donnelly Coll 608 N 18th St Kansas City KS 66102 E-mail: jheller@donnelly.edu.

HELLER, JOHN GAYLORD, orthopaedic surgery educator; b. Cleve., Aug. 24, 1957; s. Frederick Heller and Catherine Flynn Heller Doig; m. Katherine Powell, Aug. 10, 1985; children: Laura Flynn, Hannah Carrington. AB in Biochemistry, Harvard U., Boston, 1979; MD, Johns Hopkins U., 1983. Diplomate Am. Bd. Orthopaedic Surgery. Surgical intern Case Western U, 1983-84; orthopaedic resident U. Hosps. Cleveland, 1984-88; fellow in spine surgery U. Calif., San Diego, 1989; prof. orthopaedic surgery Emory U. Sch. Medicine, Atlanta, 1999—, asst. prof., 1989-94, assoc. prof., 1994-99, dir. spine fellowship Emory Spine Ctr., 1999—. Contbr. more than 75 articles and revs. to med. jours., chpts. to books. Kashiwagi-Suzuki orthopaedic travelling fellow Japanese Orthopaedic Assn., Tokyo, 1996; recipient Mario Boni award European Cervical Spine Rsch. Soc., 2000. Mem. Cervical Spine Rsch. Soc. (chmn. clin. outcomes rsch. com. 1995-2000, resident rsch. award 1989, Volvo award for low back pain rsch. 2002). Avocations: tennis, wine collecting. Office: Emory Spine Ctr 2165 N Decatur Rd Decatur GA 30033-5307 Fax: 404-778-7117. E-mail: john_heller@emoryhealthcare.org.

HELLER, JOHN L., II, construction executive; b. Galesburg, Ill., Jan. 23, 1953; s. John L. and Wilma (Medows) H.; m. Brenda June Baxter, Nov. 17, 1972 (div. 1995); children: Holly Renee, Kelly Susanne; m. Shirley D. Parrish, Sept. 27, 1997. Sales rep. H&K Electric Supply, Inc., Chillicothe, Mo., 1971-73, Schwan Sales Enterprises, Inc., Chillicothe, 1973-79, sales mgr. Aurora, Mo., 1979-81, nat. promotions mgr. Marshall, Minn., 1981-86; pres. ABar Assocs., Inc., Marshall, 1986-89, ADCO Sales Advt. and Cons. Firm, Marshall, 1989-90; sales mgr. food svc. div. Cookies Food Products, Inc., Wall Lake, Iowa, 1989-90; regional sales mgr. Tony's Food Svc. divsn. Schwan's Sales Enterprises Inc., Blue Springs, Mo., 1990-93; regional dir. Zartic, Inc., Blue Springs, 1993-95, Redi-Foods, Inc., Blue Springs, Mo., 1995-97, CMS, Ltd., Blue Springs, 1997—. Mem. Blue Springs C. of C. Republican. Baptist. Avocations: hunting, fishing, boating, golf. Home: 2331 NE Springbrook St Blue Springs MO 64014-1403 Office: CMS Ltd 2331 NE Springbrook Blue Springs MO 64014 E-mail: jlhbsmo@aol.com.

HELLER, JOHN RODERICK, III, lawyer, business executive; b. Harrisburg, Pa., Aug. 14, 1937; s. John Roderick and Susie May (Ayres) H.; children: Elizabeth, Carolynn, John. AB summa cum laude, Princeton U., 1959; AM in History, Harvard U., 1960, JD magna cum laude, 1963. Bar: D.C. 1964. Assoc. Wilmer, Cutler & Pickering, Washington, 1963-65, 68-71, ptnr., 1971-82, of counsel, 1982-85; spl. asst. to dir. for India, AID, New Delhi, 1966-67, regional legal adviser for Pakistan, 1967-68; pres. Bristol Compressors, Inc., Va., 1982-85; pres., dir. NHP, Inc., 1985-97, also bd. dirs.; chmn. Carnton Capital Assocs., Washington, 1997—. Bd. dirs. Auto-Trol Tech. Corp., Fed. City Coun., York Internat. Corp., The Phillips Collection; chmn. Civil War Trust, WETA, Nat. Capital Recapitalization Corp.; prof. law George Washington U., 1976—81. Author: The Confederacy Is On Her Way Up the Spout: Letters to South Carolina 1861-64, 1992, An Upcountry Chronicle, 1998. Recipient Meritorious Honor award U.S. Dept. State, 1967. Mem. ABA, Soc. of Cincinnati, Cosmos Club, Met. Club (Washington). Presbyterian. Office: Carnton Capital Assocs 2445 M St NW Ste 460 Washington DC 20037-1435

HELLER, JULES, artist, writer, educator; b. N.Y.C., Nov. 16, 1919; s. Jacob Kenneth and Goldie (Lassar) H.; m. Gloria Spiegel, June 11, 1947; children: Nancy Gale, Jill Kay. AB, Ariz. State Coll., 1939; AM, Columbia U., 1940; PhD, U. So. Calif., 1948; DLitt, York U., 1985. Spl. art instr. 8th St. Sch., Tempe, Ariz., 1938-39; dir. art and music Union Neighborhood House, Auburn, N.Y., 1940-41; prof. fine arts, head dept. U. So. Calif., 1946-61; vis. asso. prof. fine arts Pa. State U., summers 1955, 57; dir. Pa. State U. (Sch. Arts), 1961-63; founding dean Pa. State U. (Coll. Arts and Architecture), 1963-68; founding dean Faculty Fine Arts York U., Toronto, 1968-73; prof. fine arts Faculty of Fine Arts, York U., 1973-76; dean Coll. Fine Arts, Ariz. State U., Tempe, 1976-85, prof. art, 1985-90; prof. emeritus, dean emeritus, 1990—. Vis. prof. Silpakorn U., Bangkok, Thailand, 1974, Coll. Fine Arts, Colombo, Sri Lanka, 1974, U. Nacional de Tucumán, Argentina, 1990, U. Nacional de Cuyo, Mendoza, Argentina, 1990; lectr., art juror; Cons. Open Studio, 1975-76; mem. vis. com. on fine arts Fisk U., Nashville, 1974; co-curator Leopoldo Méndez exhbn. Ariz. State U., Tempe, 1999. Printmaker; exhibited one man shows, Gallery Pascal, Toronto, U. Alaska, Fairbanks, Alaskaland Bear Gallery, Visual Arts Center, Anchorage, Ariz. State U., Tempe, Lisa Sette Gallery, 1990, Centro Cultural de Tucumán, San Miguel de Tucumán, 1990; retrospective exhbn. Ariz. State U., Tempe, 1999, Town Hall, Paradise Valley, Ariz., 1999-2000; exhibited numerous group shows including Canadian Printmaker's Showcase, Pollack Gallery, Toronto, Mazelow Gallery, Toronto, Santa Monica Art Gallery, L.A. County Mus., Phila. Print Club, Seattle Art Mus., Landau Gallery, Kennedy & Co. Gallery, Bklyn. Mus., Cin. Art Mus., Dallas Mus. Fine Arts, Butler Art Inst., Oakland Art Mus., Pa. Acad. Fine Arts, Santa Barbara Mus. Art, San Diego Gallery Fine Arts, Martha Jackson Gallery, N.Y.C., Yuma Fine Arts Assn., Ariz., Toronto Dominion Centre, Amerika Haus, Hannover, Fed. Rep. Germany, U. Md., Smith-Andersen Galleries, Palo Alto, Calif., Grunewald Ctr. Graphic Arts, L.A., Steel Pavilion, Phoenix, 2003, Univ. So. Fla., Tampa, Sheldon Meml. Gallery, Lincoln, Nebr., Santa Cruz (Calif.) Mus., Drake U., Iowa, Bradley U., Ill., Del Bello Gallery, Toronto, Honolulu Acad. Fine Arts, New Orleans Mus. Art, Steel Pavilion, Phoenix, 2003; represented in permanent collections, Nat. Mus. Am. Art Smithsonian Instn., Washington, Long Beach Mus. Art, Library of Congress, York U., Allan R. Hite Inst. of U. Louisville, Ariz. State U., Tamarind Inst., U. N.Mex., Zimmerli Mus. Rutgers U., N.J., Can. Council Visual Arts Bank, also pvt. collections; author: Problems in Art Judgment, 1946, Printmaking Today, 1958, revised, 1972, Papermaking, 1978, 79; co-editor: North American Women Artists of the Twentieth Century, 1995, Codex Méndez, 1999; contbg. artist: Prints by California Artists, 1954, Estampas de la Revolución Mexicana, 1948; illustrator: Canciónes de Mexico, 1948; author numerous articles. Adv. bd. Continental affairs com. Americas Soc., 1983-86. With USAAF, 1941-45. Can. Coun. grantee; Landsdowne scholar U. Victoria; Fulbright scholar, Argentina, 1990. Mem. Coll. Art Assn. (Disting. Teaching of Art award 1995), Authors Guild, Internat. Assn. Hand Papermakers (steering com. 1986—), Nat. Found. Advancement in the Arts (visual arts panelist 1986-90, panel chmn. 1989, 90), Internat. Assn. Paper Historians, Internat. Coun. Fine Arts Deans (pres. 1968-69), So. Graphics Coun. (printmaker emeritus award 1999). E-mail: jules.heller@asu.edu.

HELLER, LOIS JANE, physiologist, educator, researcher; b. Detroit, Jan. 4, 1942; d. John and Lona Elizabeth (Stockmeyer) Skagerberg; m. Robert Eugene Heller, May 21, 1966; children: John Robert, Suzanne Elizabeth. BA, Albion Coll., 1964; MS, U. Mich., 1966; PhD, U. Ill., Chgo., 1970. Instr. med ctr. U. Ill., Chgo., 1969-70, asst. prof., 1970-71, U. Minn., Duluth, 1972-77, assoc. prof., 1977-89, prof., 1989—. Author: Cardiovascular Physiology, 5th edit., 2003; contbr. numerous articles to profl. jours. Mem. Am. Physiol. Soc., Am. Heart Assn., Soc. Exptl. Biology and Medicine, Internat. Soc. Heart Rsch., Sigma Xi. Avocation: birding. Home: 9129 Congdon Blvd Duluth MN 55804-0005 Office: Univ Minn Sch of Medicine Duluth MN 55812

HELLER, MARK, communications executive; b. Sheboygan, Wis., Apr. 26, 1955; s. Clarence Milton Jr. and Ruth (Richter) H.; m. Denise J. Braunel, May 6, 2000. AS in Elec. Engring., Kenosha Tech. Inst., 1975. Chief engr. Sta. WGLB-AM & FM, Port Washington, Wis., 1972-74, Sta. WLIP-AM FM, Kenosha, 1974-77; dir. engring. Stas. KFXM and KDUO-FM, San Bernardino, Calif., 1978-80, Stas. WVON and WGCI-FM, Chgo., 1979-82; network coordinator Chgo. Bulls Basketball Team, 1980-82; pres. Sta. WTRW, Two Rivers, Wis., 1982—, Mishicot (Wis.) Broadcasting Corp., 1988-92; gen. ptnr. Heller Broadcasting Group, Verona, Wis., 1988-91, Wis. Gt. Lakes Broadcasting, Port Washington, 1991-94; owner Sta. WGLB-AM & FM, Pt. Wash., Wis., 1993-94. Author: Sixty Successful Safety and Service Ad Campaigns, 1987, 88; producer (album, cassette) Harold Schultz Orch. Echoes of the Romy Gosz Era, 1988. Mem. Soc. Broadcast Engrs. (chmn. 1982), Lions (sec. 1990-92, zone chmn. 1992-93, chair Wis. State Conv. Conr. 1992-93, pres. 1993-94). Lutheran. Avocations: sky-diving, flying. Home and Office: Sta WTRW 1414 16th St Two Rivers WI 54241-3031 E-mail: wtrw@lsol.net.

HELLER, MARY BERNITA, psychotherapist; b. Roland, Iowa, Feb. 11, 1934; d. Casper and Blanche (Hanson) Stenberg; m. John R. Heller, June 7, 1958; children: Kristen, Jonathan, Kathryn. BA, St. Olaf Coll., 1956; MSW, Fordham U., 1970. Cert. social worker, N.Y.; bd. cert. diplomate in social work. Psychiatric social worker Beloit Children's Home, Ames, Iowa, 1957-58; caseworker Luth. Community Svcs., N.Y.C., 1958-59, Soc. Seamen's Children, Staten Island, N.Y., 1971-75; psychiatric social worker Staten Island Mental Health, 1971-75; psychotherapist Mid-Hudson Cons. Ctr., Wappinger Falls, N.Y., 1976-94; pvt. practice Poughkeepsie, N.Y., 1977—; psychotherapist Windsor Counseling Group, New Windsor, N.Y., 1989—. Supr. Luth. Community Svcs., N.Y.C., 1987-96. Bd. dirs. Children;s Home of Poughkeepsie, 1983-88, Seafarers and Internat. House, N.Y.C., 1990-96, v.p., 2002—; mem. candidacy com. Met. N.Y. Synod, N.Y.C., 1986-94, v.p., 1992-2002; mem. coun. Hudson Valley Philharm., Poughkeepsie, 1983-88. Fellow Am. Orthopsychiat. Assn.; mem. NASW, Acad. Cert. Social Workers. Democrat. Lutheran. Avocations: alpine skiing, plants. Home: 24 Thornwood Dr Poughkeepsie NY 12603-4633 Office: 55 Wilbur Blvd Poughkeepsie NY 12603-3424

HELLER, PAUL MICHAEL, film company executive, producer; b. N.Y.C., Sept. 25, 1927; s. Alex Gordon and Anna (Rappaport) H.; children: Michael Peter, Charles Paul. Student, Drexel Inst. Tech., 1944-45; BA, Hunter Coll., 1950. Freelance scenic designer, N.Y.C., 1952-61; film producer, 1961—; instr. NYU, N.Y.C., 1964-66; prodn. exec. Warner Bros., 1970-71; pres. Paul Heller Prodns. Inc., Beverly Hills, Calif., 1973—. Producer over 30 films including David and Lisa, 1962, Enter the Dragon, 1973, First Monday in October, 1981, Withnail and I, 1987, My Left Foot, 1989, The Lunatic, 1990, The Annihilation of Fish, 1999; mus. multi-media prodr. The Skirball Cultural Center Museum, 1997, The Hong Kong Museum of History, 2000. Founding mem. Com. 100, Am. Film Inst. Served with U.S. Army. Recipient spl. award Nat. Assn. Mental Health. Mem. Dirs. Guild Am., Screen Actors Guild, Actors Equity Assn., Acad. Motion Picture Arts and Scis., Brit. Acad. Film and TV Arts (bd. dirs.), Hearst Castle Preservation San Simeon (bd. dirs.), Lotos Club (N.Y.C.). Home and Office: 1666 N Beverly Dr Beverly Hills CA 90210-2316 E-mail: pheller@earthlink.net.

HELLER, PEGGY OSNA, psychotherapist, poetry therapist; b. Bklyn., Nov. 21, 1936; d. Charles S. and Miriam (Mendelson) Freundlich; m. Eugene Paul Heller, Aug. 3, 1957 (div. 1986); children: Elise Karen, Meredith Leslie. BA, Bklyn. Coll., 1958; MSW, Cath. U. Am., 1983; PhD, Pacific Western U., 1995. Diplomate Acad. Cert. Social Workers (lic. clin. social worker); registered clin. poetry therapist. Speech correction tchr. N.Y.C. Bd. Edn., 1958-60; program dir., instr., writer test courses Stanley H. Kaplan Ednl. Ctrs., N.Y.C., Washington, 1959-81; clin. social worker D.C. Therapy Group, Washington, 1983-85; bibliotherapist Psychiat. Inst. Washington, 1985-87; pvt. practice, poetry therapist, psychotherapist Potomac, Md., 1985—. Lectr. Create Ctr. for Therapy, Growth and Tng., Bethesda, Md., 1984-92, Cath. U. Am., Washington, 1984-89, Lesley Coll., Cambridge, Mass., 1992, Fla. Internat. U., Miami, 1992; poetry therapy cons. Mt. Vernon Hosp., Alexandria, Va., 1987-90, Dominion Hosp., Falls Church, Va., 1990-92, Psychiat. Inst., Washington, 1992-95; dir. Nat. Ctr. Poetry Therapy Edn., 1993—, Poetry Therapy Tng. Inst., 1995;co-dir. Wordsworth Ctr. Growth & Healing, 1997—. Mem. editl. staff Jour. Poetry Therapy, 1986—, Jour. Arts in Psychotherapy, 1988—; contbr. articles to profl. jours. Former program dir. Beverly Farms PTA, Potomac, Md., Hoover Cmty. Sch., Potomac; founder Last Friday Playreading Club, Potomac, 1983—. Mem. NASW, Am. Group Psychotherapy Assn., Nat. Assn. Poetry Therapy (pres. 1991-93, Disting. Svc. award 1993), Nat. Assn. Poetry Therapy Found. (v.p. 1993-96, pres. 1996-97), Nat. Fedn. Biblio/Poetry Therapy (treas. 1987-97), Bibliotherapy Round Table (treas. 1984—), Greater Washington Soc. Clin. Social Work, Mensa. Avocations: theatre, walking, swimming. Home and Office: 7715 Whiterim Ter Potomac MD 20854-1775 E-mail: PegOHeller@aol.com.

HELLER, PHILIP, lawyer; b. N.Y.C., Aug. 12, 1952; s. Irving and Dolores (Soloff) Heller; married; children: Howard Philip, John Philip, Madison Irene. Attended, Harvard Coll.; BA summa cum laude, Boston U., 1976, JD, 1979. Bar: Mass 1979, NY 1980, US Ct Appeals (1st, 2d & 9th cirs) 1980, US Supreme Ct 1983, Calif 1984, US Dist Ct (all dists) Calif, US Dist Ct (ea & so dists) NY, US Dist Ct Mass. Law clk. to judge Cooper U.S. Dist. Ct. (so. dist.) N.Y., N.Y.C., 1979; ptnr. Fagelbaum & Heller LLP, L.A. Mem.: ABA (litigation sect), Los Angeles County Bar Asn, Calif Bar Asn. Office: Fagelbaum & Heller LLP 2049 Century Park E Ste 2050 Los Angeles CA 90067-3168 Fax: 310-286-7086. E-mail: ph@philipheller.com.

HELLER, RICHARD H. writer, editor, book critic, publisher; b. Yonkers, N.Y., Oct. 16, 1924; s. Otto and Mary (Cohen) H.; m. Sonja Mentikov; 1 son, Matthew. AB cum laude, Syracuse U., 1948. Editor, also editorial dir. Sterling Group, N.Y.C., 1954-62; editor Dell Pub. Co.; also editorial dir. Dell Mags., N.Y.C., 1962-68; v.p., editor-in-chief Pyramid Books, N.Y.C., 1968-72; pres., editor, pub. Heller & Son, Inc., New Rochelle, N.Y., 1972-82; columnist and book critic Gannett Westchester Newspapers, 1976-81; dir. mktg. Macmillan Pub. Co., 1979-80. Author: Who's Who in TV, 1967, The Adventure Book, 1976; Editor: The President Speaks, 1964, The Life and Death of Robert F. Kennedy, 1968. Served in USMC, 1941-43. Mem. Am. Soc. Mag. Editors, Nat. Book Critics Circle, Sigma Delta Chi, Sigma Alpha Mu. Clubs: Dutch Treat.

HELLER, ROBERT MARTIN, lawyer; b. N.Y.C., Feb. 12, 1942; s. Philip B. and Mildred B. (Friedman) H.; m. Amy S. Wexler, July 11, 1965; children: David B., Pamela L. BA, Columbia U., 1963, LLB, 1966. Bar: N.Y. 1967, D.C. 1992, U.S. Dist. Ct. (so. and ea. dists.) N.Y. 1970, U.S. Ct. Appeals (2d cir.) 1967, U.S. Supreme Ct. 1976. Law clk. to judge U.S. Ct. Appeals (2d cir.), N.Y.C., 1966-67; atty. adviser to commr. FTC, Washington, 1967-69; asst. to mayor for housing, city planning, transp. and model cities, sec. to cabinet City of N.Y., 1971-73; ptnr. Kramer Levin Naftalis & Frankel LLP, N.Y.C., 1974—, mng. ptnr., 1991-94. Adj. prof. architecture Columbia U., 1975—77; bd. visitors Columbia Law Sch., 1992—2000. Bd. govs. Hebrew Union Coll./Jewish Inst. Religion, 1996—; pres. bd. dirs. 1056 Fifth Ave. Corp., 1994-96; vice chair Union Am. Hebrew Congregations, 1999—; trustee Rabbi Marc H. Tanenbaum Found. James Kent scholar; Harlan Fiske Stone scholar. Mem. ABA, N.Y. State Bar Assn., Assn. of Bar of City of N.Y. (com. on antitrust and trade regulation 1996-99), Phi Beta Kappa. Avocations: aerobic walking, photography. Home: 1056 5th Ave New York NY 10028-0112 Office: Kramer Levin Naftalis & Frankel LLP 919 3rd Ave New York NY 10022-3902

HELLER, RONALD GARY, manufacturing company executive, lawyer; b. N.Y.C., May 29, 1946; s. Max and Lucy (Weinwurm) H.; m. Joyce R. Mueller, May 29, 1969; children— Caren, Amy, Beth BA, CCNY, 1967; postgrad., U. Wis. Law Sch., 1967-68; JD, Fordham U., 1972. Bar: N.Y. Assoc. Cahill Gordon & Reindel, N.Y.C., 1972-77; asst. sec. Cluett, Peabody & Co. Inc., N.Y.C., 1977-81, sec., 1981-86, v.p., sec., gen. counsel, 1986-87; asst. gen. counsel Ingersoll-Rand Co., Woodcliff Lake, N.J., 1988-2000, sec., 1991—, v.p., dep. gen. counsel, 2000—. Served with USAR, 1969-75 Mem. Am. Soc. Corp. Secs.

HELLER, RONALD IAN, lawyer; b. Cleve., Sept. 4, 1956; s. Grant L. and Audrey P. (Lecht) Heller; m. Shirley Ann Stringer, Mar. 23, 1986 (dec. 2001); 1 child, David Grant. AB with high honors, U. Mich., 1976, MBA, 1979, JD, 1980. Bar: Hawaii 1980, U.S. Ct. Claims 1982, U.S. Tax Ct. 1981, U.S. Ct. Appeals (9th cir.) 1981, U.S. Supreme Ct. 1992; Trust Ter. Pacific Islands 1982, Rep. Marshall Islands 1982; CPA, Hawaii. Assoc. Hoddick, Reinwald, O'Connor & Marrack, Honolulu, 1980-84; ptnr. Reinwald, O'Connor & Marrack, Honolulu, 1984-87; stockholder, bd. dirs. Torkildson, Katz, Fonseca, Moore & Hetherington, Honolulu, 1988—. Adj. prof. U. Hawaii Sch. Law, 1981; arbitrator ct.-annexed arbitration program First Cir. Ct., State of Hawaii; author, instr. Hawaii Taxes. Bd. dirs. Hawaii Women Lawyers Found., Honolulu, 1984-86, Hawaii Performing Arts Co., Honolulu, 1984-93; panel of arbitrators Am. Arbitration Assn., 1987-99; actor, stage mgr. Honolulu Cmty. Theatre, 1983-87, Hawaii Performing Arts Co., Honolulu, 1982-87. Named NFIB Hawaii outstanding sm. bus. vol. 1998. Fellow Am. Coll. Tax Counsel; mem. AICPAs (coun. 1994-96, 2002-2003), ABA, Hawaii State Bar Assn. (chair tax sect. 1997-98, chair state and local tax com. 1994-95), Hawaii Soc. CPAs (chmn. tax com. 1985-86, legis. com. 1987-88, bd. dirs. 1988-2003, pres. 1994-95), Hawaii Women Lawyers. Office: Torkildson Katz Fonseca Moore & Hetherington 700 Bishop St Ste 1500 Honolulu HI 96813-4187 E-mail: rheller@torkildson.com.

HELLER, RUTH M. writer; b. Winnipeg, Man., Can., Apr. 2, 1923; d. Henry and Leah Rosenblat; m. Richard Philip Gross; m. Henry David Heller, Dec. 21, 1951 (dec. Dec. 21, 1951); children: Paul Garson, Philip. BA in Fine Arts, U. Calif., Berkeley, 1946. Cert. med. sec. Calif. Sec. to chief pathologist Mt. Zion Hosp., San Francisco, 1947—51; author, illustrator children's books San Francisco and N.Y.C., 1981—. Cons., presenter reading and libr. confs., schs. Author, illustrator: children's books Behind the Mask, 1995 (Kans. State Reading Circle 1996-97 title, PLA Top Titles for Adult New Readers, 1995), Up, Up and Away, 1991 (Bank St. Coll. Child Study 1991 Children's Books of Yr.), Merry-Go-Round, 1990 (IRA Children's Choices for 1991), Many Luscious Lollipops, 1989, Kites Sail High, 1988, A Cache of Jewels, 1987, Color, 1995 (Kans. State Reading Circle 1996-97 title, Ohio Tchrs.' and Pupils' Reading Circle 1996-97 selection, Am. Bookseller Spring 1995 Pick of the Lists, Parenting Mag. 1995 Reading Magic award, IRA Children's Choices for 1996), Plants That Never Ever Bloom, 1984, The Reason for a Flower, 1983, Animals Born Alive and Well, 1982, Chickens Aren't the Only Ones, 1981 (Reading Rainbow Feature Title). Recipient Children's Sci. Book award, N.Y. Acad. Sci., 1983; fellow Yaddo fellow, 1980. Mem.: Soc. Childrens Book Writers and Illustrators, Soc. Illustrators San Francisco, Soc. Illustrators N.Y., Authors League Am., Authors Guild. Democrat. Jewish. Avocations: reading, cooking, travel, walking.

HELLER, STEPHEN REID, lawyer; b. Norfolk, Va., Jan. 25, 1956; s. Selwyn Bernard and Dorothy Leah H.; m. Karen Heller, June 13, 1982; children: Ilana Ruth, Naomi Ann. Degree in psychology, U. South Fla., 1978; JD, So. Meth. U., 1982. Bar: Tex. 1983, U.S. Ct. Appeals (5th cir.) 1983, U.S. Supreme Ct. 1988. Assoc., pvt. firm, Dallas, 1982-84; assoc. gen. counsel Safeco Title Co., Dallas, 1984-86; from assoc. to shareholder Stigall and Maxfield, Dallas, 1986-89; shareholder Hutchison, Boyle, Brooks and Fisher, Dallas, 1989-93; pvt. practice Dallas, 1993—. Bd. dirs. various internat. cos. Co-founder Dallas Virtual Jewish Cmty. web-page, 1994—, Bridwell Judaica lectr. series, 1994—; dir., v.p. Am. Jewish Com., 1990—2000; pres. Dallas Jewish Hist. Soc., 1992—96; founder Classic Jewish Text Seminars, 1989—; founding dir. Tex. Zionist Movement, Dallas, 1999—, Three Stars Cinema, 2000—, Beyt & Midrash of North Tex., 1999—; trustee So. Meth. U. Libr. Sys., 1999—. Mem. Dallas Bar Assn., Internat. Law Soc. Avocations: weight lifting, hiking. Office: 2651 N Harwood St Ste 200 Dallas TX 75201-1583

HELLER, STEVEN ANTHONY, management consultant; b. Budapest, Hungary, Sept. 1, 1938; came to U.S., 1939; s. Gedeon and Elizabeth (Spitzer) H; m. Peggy Grace Fulton, June 30, 1968; children: Thomas Charles, Emily Elizabeth, George Fulton. BS in Econs., U. Pa., 1961, MBA, 1977. Media planner, buyer Benton & Bowles, Inc., N.Y.C., 1962—64; account exec. Compton Advt. Inc., N.Y.C., 1964—67; brand mgr. Bristol Myers Co., Inc., N.Y.C., 1967—71; dir. mktg. I.U. Internat., Phila., 1971—75; v.p. mktg., communications Meritor, Inc., 1975—78; v.p. mktg. services, planning Block

Drug Co., Inc., Jersey City, 1978—82; v.p. mktg. Gen. Brands, Inc., N.Y.C., 1982—84; ptnr. Cardinal Properties, Greenwich, Conn., 1984—94; exec. v.p. Martin H. Bauman Assoc., N.Y.C., 1995—. Served with AUS, 1957-58. Mem.: Phila. Racquet, Beacon Hill (Summit, N.J.). Home: 95 Druid Hill Rd Summit NJ 07901-3226 Office: Martin H Bauman Assoc 375 Park Ave New York NY 10152-0002

HELLER, TERRY L(YNN), English literature educator, writer; b. Geneseo, Ill., Feb. 3, 1947; s. Rollin G. and Betty (Ragan) H.; m. Linda Mary Marchand, June 7, 1969; 1 child, Gabriel A. AB, North Cen. Coll., 1969; AM, U. Chgo., 1970, PhD, 1973. Vis. asst. prof. U. Mo., St. Louis, 1973-74; Fulbright lectr. U. Turin, Italy, 1974-75; prof. English Coe Coll., Cedar Rapids, Iowa, 1975—. Author: The Delights of Terror, 1987, The Turn of the Screw, 1989; author short stories; editor: The Country of the Pointed Firs and Other Fiction by Sarah Orne Jewett, 1996, Internet Sarah Orne Jewett Text Project, 1998—. NEH summer fellow, 1995, 1977, Danforth Found. fellow, 1980—, Andrew Mellon Found. fellow U. Kans., 1982, ACM Newberry fellow, 1998. Mem. AAUP, Modern Lang. Assn., Midwest Modern Lang. Assn., Sci. Fiction Rsch. Assn. Office: Coe Coll Dept of English 1220 1st Ave NE Cedar Rapids IA 52402-5008

HELLER, THOMAS GERALD, lawyer; b. Grand Rapids, Mich., Aug. 31, 1967; s. Ludwig Herbert and Virginia Ann (Pierce) Heller; m. Michele Ann Ashamalla, Apr. 20, 1996; children: Ava Rose, Nathan Carl. AB in English Lit., U. Mich., Ann Arbor, 1989; JD, UCLA, 1992. Bar: Calif. 1992, Mich. 1994. Assoc. Kirkland and Ellis, L.A., 1992—97; dep. atty. gen. Calif. Dept. Justice, L.A., 1997—. Mem.: Phi Beta Kappa, Order of Coif. Office: Calif Dept Justice 300 S Spring St Los Angeles CA 90013

HELLERMAN, LEO, retired computer scientist and mathematician; b. Bklyn., Feb. 8, 1924; s. Azriel and Rebecca (Hellerman) H.; children: David Seth, Lisa Beatrice Kopchik, Daniel Asa. BEE, CCNY, 1946; PhD, Yale U., 1958. 1950patent examiner U.S. Patent Office, Washington, 1948; engr. IBM, Poughkeepsie, NY, 1956—73, Böblingen, Germany, 1974, Kingston, NY, 1975—87; ret., 1987. Lectr. Fachtagung Struktur und Betrieb von Rechensystemen, Braunschweig, Fed. Republic Germany, 1974. Contbr. articles to profl. jours. Mem. Am. Math. Soc., Math. Assn. Am., Sigma Xi. Achievements include patent for logic performing device; development of first algebraic symbol manipulation program, of first statistical design of electronic circuits; a theory of computational work, of moment free methods for processing discrete distributions. Home: 12 Feller Rd Rhinebeck NY 12572-2306 E-mail: catseye@ulster.net.

HELLERSTEIN, ALVIN KENNETH, judge; b. N.Y.C., Dec. 28, 1933; s. Max and Rose (Lichtenstein) H.; m. Mildred Markow, June 29, 1936; children— Dina, Judith, Joseph AB, Columbia U., 1954, LL.B., 1956. Bar: N.Y. 1956, U.S. Ct. Appeals (2d cir.) 1960, U.S. Supreme Ct. 1964, U.S. Ct. Appeals (D.C. cir.) 1978, U.S. Ct. Appeals (3d and 9th cirs.) 1980, U.S. Ct. Appeals (10th cir.) 1981, U.S. Ct. Appeals (1st cir.) 1985, U.S. Ct. Appeals (8th cir.) 1996. Ptnr. Stroock & Stroock & Lavan, N.Y.C., 1969-98, retired, 1998—, judge U.S. Ct. Dist. Ct. (so. dist.) N.Y., 1998—. Lectr. Am. Law Inst., Practicing Law Inst. Contbr. articles to profl. jours. Past chmn. Bd. Jewish Fdn. Served to capt. JAGC, U.S. Army, 1957-60 Fellow Am. Bar Found. (life); mem. ABA, Assn. Bar City N.Y. (past chmn. com. on judiciary 1992-95, past exec. com., past chmn. com. on fed. cts.), Fed. Bar Coun., Internat. Assn. Jewish Lawyers and Jurists, N.Y. State Bar Assn. Democrat.

HELLERSTEIN, DAVID JOEL, psychiatrist, writer; b. Cleve., Dec. 30, 1953; s. Herman Kopel and Mary Leah (Feil) H.; m. Lisa Perry, Oct. 16, 1983; children: Sarah Nicole, Benjamin, Jason Samuel. AB, Harvard U., 1976; MD, Stanford U., 1980. Intern, then resident psychiatry N.Y. Hosp. Cornell Med. Ctr., 1980-84; fellow pub. psychiatry Columbia Presbyn. Med. Ctr.-N.Y. State Psychiat. Inst., N.Y.C., 1984-85; attending psychiatrist Beth Israel Med. Ctr., N.Y.C., 1985-2000; instr. psychiatry Mt. Sinai Med. Ctr., N.Y.C., 1985-88, asst. prof. psychiatry, 1988-93; physician in charge psychiat. outpatient svcs. Beth Israel Med. Ctr., N.Y.C., 1989-96, chief outpatient psychiatry divsn., 1996-2000; asst. prof. psychiatry Albert Einstein Coll. Medicine, N.Y.C., 1993-96, assoc. prof. psychiatry, 1996-2000, dir. mood disorders rsch. unit, 1994-2000; clin. dir. N.Y. State Psychiatric Inst., 2000—; assoc. prof. clin. psychiatry Columbia U. Coll. of Physicians and Surgeons, NYC, 2000—; dir. mood disorders rsch. unit St. Luke's Roosevelt Hosp. Ctr., 2001—. Author: (novel) Loving Touches, 1987, (essay collection) Battles of Life and Death, 1986, (non-fiction) A Family of Doctors, 1994, (novel) Stone Babies, 2000; contbr. articles to profl. jours.; contbg. editor N.Am. Rev., 1981—, Sci. Digest, 1986-87, 7 Days mag., 1988-90, M.D. Mag., 1990-95. MacDowell Colony fellow, 1984, 86, 88. Fellow APA; mem. PEN, Am. Psychiat. Assn. (editor N.Y. County Dist. newsletter, 1989-2001; chmn. publs. com. N.Y. County chpt. 1989-2001, pres.-elect 1997-98, pres. 1998-99), Author's Guild. Democrat. Jewish. E-mail: djh102@columbia.edu.

HELLERSTEIN, NINA SALANT, French literature and language educator; b. N.Y.C., Mar. 29, 1946; d. Allan and Martha (Cantor) Salant; m. Walter Hellerstein, Aug. 31, 1970; children: Michael, Margaret. BA, Brown U., 1968; MA, U. Chgo., 1969, PhD, 1974. Adj. asst. prof. Baruch Coll. CUNY, N.Y.C., 1974-75; vis. asst. prof. Vassar Coll., Poughkeepsie, N.Y., 1975-76; instr. Rosary Coll., River Forest, Ill., 1976-78, Roosevelt U., Chgo., 1976-78; asst. prof. U. Ga., Athens, 1978-83, assoc. prof. French literature and language, 1983-92, prof., 1992—, acting head dept. Romance langs., 1992—93, dir. Avignon, 2002. Author: Mythe et Structure Dans Les 'Cing Grandes Odes', 1990; mem. editorial bd. South Atlantic Rev., 1990-93, 97—; contbr. articles to profl. jours. Grantee Ford Found., 1968-72, U. Ga., 1982, 91, 97. Mem. MLA, MADD, Am. Assn. Tchrs. French, Paul Claudel Soc. (v.p. 1978-79, sec.-treas. 1979-80, 2000—, pres. 1981-82), Handgun Control, Inc., Societe Paul Claudel, Assn. des Amis de la Fondation St. John Perse. Jewish. Avocations: travel, cooking, reading. Office: U Ga Dept Romance Langs Athens GA 30602

HELLERSTEIN, WALTER, lawyer; b. N.Y.C., June 21, 1946; s. Jerome Robert and Pauline Alice H.; m. Nina Laurie Salant, Aug. 31, 1970; children; Michael, Margaret. AB, Harvard U., 1967; JD, U. Chgo., 1970. Bar: D.C. 1970, Ill. 1976, N.Y. 1989. Law clk. U.S. Ct. Appeals (2d cir.), N.Y.C., 1967-71; atty. Air Force Gen. Counsel's Office, Washington, 1971-73; assoc. Covington & Burling, Washington, 1973-75; asst. prof. law U. Chgo., 1976-78; assoc. prof. law U. Ga., Athens, 1978-84, prof. law, 1984-98, Francis Shackelford prof. taxation, 1999—; of counsel Morrison & Foerster, N.Y.C., 1986-96; ptnr. Sutherland, Asbill & Brennan, Atlanta, 1996-98; counsel KPMG, 1999—. Cons. Orgn. Econ. Coop. and Devel., 1999—, UN, 2000—; mem. sci. com. Centro Europeo di Studi Tributarie sall'Electronic Commerce, 1999—. Co-author: State and Local Taxation of Natural Resources, 1986, State Taxation, vols. 1 & 2, 3d edit., 1998, State and Local Taxation, 7th edit., 2001, Electronic Commerce and Multijurisdictional Taxation, 2001; editl. adv. bd. Nat. Tax Jour., 1983—, Multistate Tax Analyst, 1986—, chmn. editl. adv. bd. State Tax Notes, 1991—, Jour. Taxation, 1993—; contbr. articles to profl. jours. Recipient Multistate Tax Commn. 25th Ann. award for outstanding contbn. 1992. Fellow Am. Coll. Tax Counsel; mem. ABA, Nat. Tax Assn. (dir. 1981-83), Ill. State Bar Assn., D.C. Bar Assn., N.Y. State Bar Assn., Am. Law Inst., Order of Coif, Phi Beta Kappa. Home: 239 Westview Dr Athens GA 30606-4731 Office: U Ga Law Sch Athens GA 30602-6012 E-mail: wallyh@uga.edu .

HELLHAKE-HALL, GERRI ANN, critical care nurse, cardiology nurse; b. Lincoln, Ill., Aug. 29, 1960; d. Ronald Bruce and Bonnie Jean (Eager) Hellhake. LPN, John Wood C.C., Quincy, Ill., 1981; ADN, Southea. C.C., Keokuk, Iowa, 1987; BSN, Hannibal-LaGrange Coll., Hannibal, Mo., 1994; MSN, So. Ill. U., Edwardsville, 1997. CCRN, cert. family nurse practitioner, PALS, TNCC, ENPC, ACLS instr. Staff nurse cardiology Quincy Physician's and Surgeon's Clinic, 1988-91; staff nurse ICU St. Mary Hosp., Quincy, 1991-92; staff nurse critical care Blessing Hosp., Quincy, 1987-88, staff nurse renal dialysis, 1991-93, staff nurse cardiology dept., 1993-98; nurse emergency dept. Hannibal Regional Hosp., 1996-98, Proctor Hosp., Peoria, 1999—; family nurse practitioner Renal Care Assocs., East Peoria, Ill., 1999—2002, HeartCare Midwest, 2002—. Mem. AACN, Emergency Nurse Assn., Alpha Chi, Sigma Theta Tau. Home: 1201 Springfield Rd East Peoria IL 61611 Office: HeadCare Midwest 5401 N Knoxville Ste 204 Peoria IL 61614

HELLIE, RICHARD, Russian history educator, researcher; b. Waterloo, Iowa, May 8, 1937; s. Ole Ingeman and Mary Elizabeth (Larsen) H.; children: Benjamin, Michael; m. Shujie Yu, Feb. 26, 1998. BA, U. Chgo., 1958, MA, 1960, PhD, 1965; postgrad., U. Moscow, 1963-64. Asst. prof. Rutgers U., 1965-66; asst. prof. Russian history U. Chgo., 1966-71, assoc. prof., 1971-80, prof., 1980-2001, dir. Ctr. for East European, Russian and Eurasian Studies, 1997—, Thomas E. Donnelley prof., 2001—. Author: Muscovite Society, 1967, Enserfment and Military Change in Muscovy, 1971 (Am. Hist. Assn. Adams prize 1972), Slavery in Russia 1450-1725, 1982 (Laing prize U. Chgo. Press 1985, Russian translation with new post-Soviet foreword Kholopstvo v Rossii, 1450-1725, 1998), 1982, The Russian Law Code (Ulozhenie) of 1649, 1988, The Economy and Material Culture of Russia 1600-1725, 1999; editor: The Plow, the Hammer and the Knout: An Economic History of Eighteenth Century Russia, 1985, Ivan the Terrible: A Quarcentenary Celebration of His Death, 1987, The Frontier in Russian History, 1993, The Soviet Global Impact 1945-1991, 2003; editor quar. jour. Russian History;, 1988 contbr. numerous articles to profl. jours. Fgn. area tng. fellow Ford Found., 1962-65, Guggenheim fellow, 1973-74, fellow NEH, 1978-79; grantee NEH, 1982-83, summer, 1988, NSF, 1988-90, Bradley Found., 1988-91. Mem. PEN, Nat. Hist. Soc., Am. Soc. Legal History (program com. for ann. meetings 1976), Am. Assn. Advancement Slavic Studies (editorial bd. Slavic Rev. 1979-81), Econ. History Assn., Assn. for Comparative Econ. Studies, Nat. Assn. Scholars, Jean Bodin Soc. for Comparative Instl. History, Chgo. Consortium Slavic and East European Studies (pres. 1990-92), Nat. Hist. Soc. (founding, bd. govs. 1999-2002). Home: 5807 S Dorchester Ave Apt 13E Chicago IL 60637-1729 Office: U Chgo Dept History 1126 E 59th St # 78 Chicago IL 60637-1580 E-mail: hell@midway.uchicago.edu.

HELLING, RICKY ALLEN, professional baseball player; b. Devils Lake, N.D., Dec. 15, 1970; Student, Stanford U. Pitcher, Tex., 1994-95, 1994-95, Fla. Marlins, 1996-97, Tex. Rangers, Arlington, 1997—2001, Arizona Diamondbacks, 2002—. Named Am. Assn. Pitcher of the Yr. for Oklahoma City, 1996. Office: Arizona Diamondbacks PO Box 2095 Phoenix AZ 85001 Fax: 817-273-5206.

HELLIWELL, THOMAS MCCAFFREE, physicist, educator; b. Minneapolis, Minn., June 8, 1936; s. George Plummer and Eleanor (McCaffree) H.; m. Bernadette Egan Busenberg, Aug. 9, 1997. BA, Pomona Coll., 1958; PhD, Calif. Inst. Tech., 1963. Asst. prof. physics Harvey Mudd Coll., Claremont, Calif., 1962-67, assoc. prof., 1967-73, prof., 1973—, chmn. dept. physics, 1981-89, chair of faculty, 1990-93, Burton Bettingen prof. physics, 1990—. Author: Introduction to Special Relativity, 1966; author papers in field of cosmology, gen. relativity and quantum theory. Sci. faculty fellow NSF, 1968. Mem.: AAAS, Am. Phys. Soc., Am. Assn. Physics Tchrs. Avocations: music, hiking. Office: Harvey Mudd Coll Dept Physics 301 E 12th St Claremont CA 91711-5901

HELLMAN, ARTHUR DAVID, law educator, consultant; b. NYC, Dec. 9, 1942; s. Charles and Florence (Cohen) H. BA magna cum laude, Harvard U., 1963; JD, Yale U., 1966. Bar: Minn. 1967, U.S. Ct. Appeals (3d cir.) 1976, U.S. Ct. Appeals (9th cir.) 1979, U.S. Supreme Ct. 1980, Pa., 1985. Law clk. to assoc. justice Minn. Supreme Ct., 1966-67; asst. prof. William Mitchell Coll. Law, St. Paul, 1967-70, U. Conn. Sch. Law, West Hartford, 1970-72; vis. asst. prof. U. Ill. Coll. Law, Champaign, 1972-73; dep. exec. dir. Commn. on Revision Fed. Ct. Appellate System, Washington, 1973-75; assoc. prof. U. Pitts. Sch. Law, 1975-80, prof., 1980—. Supervising staff atty. U.S. Ct. Appeals 9th cir., San Francisco, 1977-79, evaluation com., 1999-2001; vis. assoc. prof. U. Pa. Sch. Law, Phila., 1979; faculty Practicing Law Inst. Program on Fed. Appellate Practice, N.Y.C., 1984, Fed. Jud. Ctr. Nat. Workshop for Judges of U.S. Cts. of Appeals, 1993; planner Nat. Conf. Empirical Rsch. in Judicial Adminstrn., Tempe, Ariz., 1988; gen. editor U.S. Ct. Appeals 9th Cir. Project Improvements in Judicial Adminstrn., 1987-91; prin. investigator intercir. conflicts study Fed. Jud. Ctr., 1990; lectr., cons. and expert witness in field. Author: Laws Against Marijuana-The Price We Pay, 1975, Restructuring Justice-The Innovations of the Ninth Circuit and the Future of the Federal Courts, 1990; editor: Major Cases in First Amendment Law: Freedom of Speech, the Press, and Assembly, 1984; bus. editor: Yale U. Law Jour. Mem. liaison task panel on psychoactive drug use/misuse Pres.'s Commn. on Mental Health, 1977-78; conferee Pound Conf., 1976, The Future and the Courts Conf., 1990; conferee Nat. Conf. on State-Fed. Jud. Relationships, 1992; adv. bd. Western Legal History, 2001—. Recipient Chancellor's Disting. Rsch. award, U. Pitts., 2002; U. Pitts. Sch. Law disting. faculty scholar, 2001—. Fellow Am. Bar Found.; mem. ABA (subcom. on stds. of com. appellate staff attys., jud. adminstrn. divsn., future of cts. com. 1992—, conferee Nat. Conf. on State-Fed. Jud. Rels. 1992, conferee summit on civil justice improvements 1990), Pa. Bar Assn. (discovery rules com. 1995—), Am. Law Inst., Supreme Ct. Hist. Soc., Am. Judicature Soc. (drafting com. project on jud. election campaigns, bd. dirs. 1985-89, justice reform com. 1992-95, chair civil justice reform subcom. 1993-95, chair civil justice reform com. 1995-97, invited witness, hearings of the Subcommittee on Cts., the Internet and Intellectual Property of the US House Judiciary Com. on: Final Report of the Commn. on Structural Alternatives for the Fed. Cts. of Appeals (1999); Fed. Judicial Discipline (2001); unpublished judicial opinions (2002); The Federal Judiciary: Is There a Need for Additional Judges? (2003). Office: U Pitts Law Sch Pittsburgh PA 15260

HELLMAN, F(REDERICK) WARREN, investment advisor; b. N.Y.C., July 25, 1934; s. Marco F. and Ruth (Koshl) H.; m. Patricia Christina Sander, Oct. 5, 1955; children: Frances, Patricia H., Marco Warren, Judith. BA, U. Calif., Berkeley, 1955; MBA, Harvard U., 1959. With Lehman Bros., N.Y.C., 1959-84, ptnr., 1963-84; exec. mng. dir. Lehman Bros., Inc., N.Y.C., 1970-73, pres., 1973-75; ptnr. Hellman Ferri Investment Assocs., 1981-89, Matrix Ptnrs., 1981—; chmn. Hellman & Friedman LLC, San Francisco. Bd. dirs. DN & E Walter, Levi Strauss & Co., Nasdag Stock Mkt. Inc., Sugar Bowl Corp.; chmn. Hellman & Friedman, LLC; hon. trustee The Brookings Inst.; chmn. Voice of Dance. Former chmn. The San Francisco Found. Mem. Bond Club, Piping Rock Club, Century Country Club, Pacific Union Club. Office: Hellman & Friedman LLC 1 Maritime Plz Fl 12 San Francisco CA 94111-3404

HELLMAN, PETER STUART, technical manufacturing executive; b. Cleve., Oct. 16, 1949; s. Arthur Cerf and Joan (Alburn) H.; m. Alyson Dulin Ware, Sept. 18, 1976; children: Whitney Ware, Garrettson Stuart. BA, Hobart Coll., 1972; MBA, Case Western Res. U., 1984. V.p. Irving Trust Co., N.Y.C., 1972-79; fin. planning assoc. Std. Oil Co., Cleve., 1979-82, mgr. fin. planning, 1982-84, dir. ops. analysis, 1984-85, asst. treas., 1985-86, treas., 1986-87, gen. mgr. crude oil supply and trading, 1987-89, v.p., treas. TRW Inc., Cleve., 1989-91, exec. v.p., CFO, 1991-94, asst. pres., 1994-95, pres., COO, bd. dirs., 1995-99; exec. v.p., CFO, chief adminstrv. officer Nordson Corp., Westlake, Ohio, 2000—. Bd. dirs. Nordson Corp., QWest Comm. Internat. Inc. Mem. vis. com. Case Western Res. U. Weatherhead Sch. Mgmt.; trustee Case Western Res. U., Chagrin River Land Conservancy, Western Reserve Acad., Lorin County CC Found., Cleve. Clinic Foun. Urol. Inst. Office: Nordson Corp 28601 Clemens Rd Westlake OH 44145-1119

HELLMAN, RICHARD, endocrinologist; b. N.Y.C., Jan. 19, 1943; s. Gabriel Michael and Rose Hellman; m. Julie Lynn Hellman, Aug. 17, 1997; children: Leslie Gayle. BA in Math., NYU, 1962; MD, Chgo. Med. Sch., 1966. Diplomate Am. Bd. Internal Medicine, Am. Bd. Endocrinology and Metabolism, Nat. Bd. Med. Examiners. Intern in straight medicine U. Kans., Kansas City, 1966-67, resident in internal medicine, 1967-68, 71-72, fellow in endocrinology and metabolism, 1972-73; asst. prof. medicine U. Mo., Kansas City Sch. Medicine, 1973-75, assoc. prof. medicine, 1975-81, clin. assoc. prof. medicine, 1981-95, clin. prof. medicine, 1998—; pvt. practice physician North Kansas City, Mo., 1981—. Chair adv. bd. Mo. Diabetes Control program CDC, ATlanta, 1981-86; med. dir. Midwest Diabetes Care Ctr., Kansas City, 1981-86, Diabetes Treatment Ctr., Trinity Luth. Hosp., Kansas City, Mo., 1986-94; med. dir., founder, Heart of Am. Diabetes Rsch. Foundation, North Kans. City, 1991—; mem. Physicians Consortium for Performance Improvement, 2000—. Contbr. articles to profl. jours. Active Mo. Inst. Quality Health Care Mo. Patient Care Review Found., 1999—; mem. Mayor's Minority Health Improvement Task Force, Kansas City, 2001. Mem. AMA (accreditation program 1998-99, work group, cons. on applications of med. informatics and performance measures 2001), Am. Assn. Clin. Endocrinologists (bd. dirs. 1999—, chair continuing med. edn. 2000-2001, chair legis. and regulatory com. 2000-, strategic planning com. 2000-2001), Am. Coll. Endocrinology (bd. dirs. 2001—), Met. Med. Soc. Greater Kansas City (sec. 1999, bd. dirs. 1999-2000, pres. 2000-01, Meritorious Svc. award 2002), Nat. Diabetes Alliance (mem. tech. expert panel). Office: Ste 210 2750 Clay Edwards Dr North Kansas City MO 64116 Office Fax: 816-421-1654.

HELLMAN, SAMUEL, radiologist, physician, educator; b. N.Y.C., July 23, 1934; s. Henry Sidney and Anna (Egar) Hellman; m. Marcia Sherman, June 30, 1957; children: Jeffrey, Richard, Deborah Susan. BS magna cum laude, Allegheny Coll., 1955, DSc (hon.), 1984; MD cum laude, SUNY, Syracuse, 1959, DSc (hon.), 1993; MS (hon.), Harvard U., 1968. Med. intern Beth Israel Hosp., Boston, 1959—60; asst. resident radiology Yale Sch. Medicine and Grace-New Haven Hosp., 1960—62, postdoctoral fellow radiotherapy and cancer research, 1962—64; postdoctoral fellow Inst. Cancer Research and Royal Marsden Hosp., London, 1965—66; asst. prof. radiology Yale Sch. Medicine, 1966—68; assoc. prof. radiology Harvard Med. Sch., 1968—70; dir. Joint Center for Radiation Therapy, 1968—83, assoc. prof., chmn. dept. radiation therapy, 1971, prof., chmn. dept., 1971—83, also Alvan T. and Viola D. Fuller-Am. Cancer Soc. prof.; physician-in-chief Meml. Sloan Kettering Cancer Ctr., 1983—88, Benno Schmidt chair in clin. oncology, 1983—88; dean div. biol. sci. and Pritzker Sch. Medicine, v.p. for Med. Ctr. U. Chgo., 1988—93, Pritzker Prof., 1988—93, Pritzker Disting. Svc. Prof., 1993—. Chmn. bd. sci. counselors divsn. cancer treatment Nat. Cancer Inst., 1980—84; bd. govs. Argonne Nat. Lab., 1990—93; trustee Brookings Inst., 1992—; bd. dirs. Varian Med. Systems Inc., Insightec; mem. sci. adv. bd. Ludwig Inst. for Cancer Rsch. Contbr. numerous articles to med. jours. Trustee Allegheny Coll., 1979—98, chmn. bd. trustees, 1987—93. Recipient Rosenthal award for cancer rsch., 1980, medal, City of Paris, 1986, award for Outstanding Contbns. to Cancer Care, Assn. Cmty. Cancer Ctrs., 1993. Fellow: AAAS; mem.: N.Y. Acad. Scis., Soc. Chmn. Acad. Radiology Depts., Inst. Medicine NAS, Assn. Am. Physicians, Am. Cancer Soc., Am. Soc. Hematology, Am. Assn. Cancer Rsch., Am. Soc. Clin. Oncology (pres. 1986, David A. Karnovsky lectr. 1994), Assn. Univ. Radiologists, Am. Coll. Radiology (gold medal 2003), Am. Soc. Therapeutic Radiologists (pres. 1983, Gold medal 1991), Am. Radium Soc., Alpha Omega Alpha, Sigma Xi, Phi Beta Kappa. Home: 4950 S Chicago Beach Dr Chicago IL 60615-3207 Office: U Chgo Divsn Biol Scis 5841 S Maryland Ave Chicago IL 60637-1463 E-mail: s-hellman@uchicago.edu.

HELLMANN, DAVID BRUCE, medical educator; b. Louisville, Mar. 2, 1951; BA magna cum laude, Yale U., 1973; MD, Johns Hopkins U., 1977. Diplomate Am. Bd. Internal Medicine, Am. Bd. Rheumatology, lic. physician Md. Intern, resident Johns Hopkins Hosp., Balt., 1977-80; fellow in rheumatology/clin. immunology U. Calif., San Francisco, 1980-82, asst. clin. prof. medicine, 1982-86; chief Moffitt Arthritis Clinics, San Francisco, 1984-86; acting chief divsn. rheumatology/clin. immunology U. Calif., San Francisco, 1985—86; dep. dir. dept. medicine Johns Hopkins U., Balt., 1986-94, exec. vice chmn. dept. medicine, 1995-2000, med. dir. Faculty Practice Ctr., 1991-93, dir. Osler Med. Housestaff Tng. Program, 1992-2000, Mary Betty Stevens Prof. Medicine, 1996—; chmn. dept. medicine Johns Hopkins Bayview Med. Ctr., 2000—; acting dir. dept. medicine Johns Hopkins Hosp., Balt., 1994-95. Assoc. physician-in-chief Johns Hopkins Hosp., Balt., 1986-94, acting physician-in-chief, 1994-95; lectr. in field. Assoc. editor Medicine, 1993—; co-author: Rheumatology Committee, MKSAP II, 1995—; reviewer Jour. Rheumatology, Arthritis and Rheumatism, Western Jour. Medicine, Medicine, Jour. Clin. Investigation, Jour. of AMA; contbr. articles to profl. jours. Chmn. profl. edn. com. Md. chpt. Arthritis Found., 1991, 92, 93, 94. Recipient Kaiser Award for excellence in teaching U. Calif.-San Francisco, 1986, Cert. of Distinction in Teaching, 2d Yr. Med. Sch. Class, 1986, Profl. Edn. award Md. chpt. Arthritis Found., 1991, Disting. Svc. award for profl. edn., 1993, Faculty Teaching award Osler Med. Housestaff, 1992, Johns Hopkins Minority Faculty Assn. award, 1993; Henry Strong Denison scholar, 1975. Fellow ACP (gov. 1998-2002), Am. Coll. Rheumatology; mem. Am. Bd. Internal Medicine (dir. 2000—), Assn. Program Dirs. Internal Medicine, Internat. Network for Study of the Systemic Vasculitides, Alpha Omega Alpha. Office: Johns Hopkins Bayview Med Ctr A-I-W 4940 Eastern Ave Baltimore MD 21224

HELLMER, LYNNE BEBERMAN, education educator; b. Nome, Alaska, Sept. 26, 1947; d. Max and Elizabeth Forrer (Chapman) Beberman; m. William T. Fillman, Nov. 8, 2003; children: Joshua Max, Lucas Andrew. BS, Eastern Illinois U., 1970; MEd, U. Ill., 1997. Tchr. Effingham (Ill.) Schs., 1970-72; personnel officer U. Ill., Urbana, 1972-81, tng. dir., 1981-93, dir. human resource devel., 1993-2000; sr. dir. systemwide profl. devel. Calif. State U., 2000—. Pres. Univ. Clearinghouse, Champaign, 1992—; founder Biennial Conf. for Working Women, 1984-2000. Bd. dirs. Coll. and Univ. Pers. Assn. Found., 1998-2000. Recipient Nat. Achievement award for creativity Coll. and Univ. Pers. Assn., 1985-86, Outstanding Svc. and Leadership award Coll. and Univ. Pers. Assn. Midwest, 1991, Optimas award Workforce mag., 1996; named Most Valuable Cmty. Leader, Ill., Student Soc. for Pers., 1989. Mem. Coll. and Univ. Pers. Assn. (sec., treas. Midwest region 1988-89; editor Midwest News 1988-92, chair 1993-94, Creative Achievement and Publ. award 1998). Avocation: musician. Office: Office of the Chancellor Calif State U 401 Golden Shore St Fl 4 Long Beach CA 90802-4275 E-mail: lhellmer@calstate.edu.

HELLMERS, NORMAN DONALD, retired historic site director; b. New Orleans, Feb. 3, 1944; s. Leonard H. and Meta J.C. (Wegener) H.; m. Patricia I. O'Brien, May 29, 1966; children: Jennifer I., Jeffrey N. BA, Concordia U., River Forest, Ill., 1966; postgrad., U. Iowa, 1966-67, La. State U., 1968. Writer, photographer Nebr. Game and Pks. Commn., Lincoln, 1969-71; ranger nat. pks. various locations, 1972-73; dist. naturalist Shenandoah Nat. Pk., Luray, Va., 1973-76; chief interpretation Grand Portage (Minn.) Nat. Monument, 1976-81; supt. Lincoln Boyhood Nat. Meml., Lincoln City, Ind., 1981-90, Lincoln Home Nat. Hist. Site, Springfield, Ill., 1990—2003; ret., 2003. Lutheran. Avocations: photography, genealogy.

HELLMUTH, GEORGE WILLIAM, architect; b. Detroit, Nov. 21, 1942; s. George Francis and Mildred Lee (Henning) H.; m. Camille Byrns Carmody, Feb. 20, 1965 (div. 2003); children: George, Holly, Julie, Emily. BA in Architecture, Yale U., 1964; MBA, Eastern N.Mex. U., 1969; BArch, CCNY, 1979. Sr. prin. Hellmuth, Obata & Kassabaum, Washington, 1971—. Capt. USAF, 1965-69. Mem. AIA, Sky Club (N.Y.C.). Roman Catholic. Office: Hellmuth Obata & Kassabaum PC 3223 Grace St NW Washington DC 20007-3614 Home: 2721 N Ohio St Arlington VA 22207 E-mail: george.hellmuth@hok.com.

HELLMUTH, WILLIAM FREDERICK, JR., economics educator; b. Washington, Jan. 8, 1920; s. William Frederick and Sybel (Grant) H.; m. Jean A. Dieffenbach, Feb. 14, 1943; children: James (dec.), Suzanne, William L., Peter G. BA, Yale U., 1940, PhD, 1948. Instr. econs. Yale U., 1945-48; mem. faculty Oberlin Coll., 1948-68, prof. econs., 1958-68; dean Oberlin Coll. (Coll. Arts and Scis.), 1960-67; dep. asst. sec. treasury for tax policy, 1968-69; v.p. arts, prof. econs. McMaster U., Hamilton, Ont., Can., 1969-73, also bd. govs., 1969-73; prof. econs. Va. Commonwealth U., 1973-87, chmn. dept. econs., 1973-82; emeritus prof., 1987—. Economist Fed. Res. Bd., 1954-56; prof. U. Wis., 1959, Univ. Coll., Dar es Salaam, Tanzania, 1965, 66 Mem. Nat. Com. Taxation with Representation; mem. Oberlin City Coun., 1957-63, 67-68; pres. 1st Unitarian Ch., Richmond, 1976-78; mem. welfare adv. bd. City of Richmond, 1976-83; staff dir. Capital City Govt. Commn., 1980-81; treas. adv. bd. Richmond Cmty. H.S., 1986-92; bd. dirs. Common Cause Va., 1988-96, Shepherd's Ctr. of Richmond, 1985-91, 94-96, Va. Interfaith Ctr. for Pub. Policy, 1987-96, Va. State Dem. Com., 1994-96. Maj. F.A., AUS, WWII. mem. finance comm., Eskaton, 2001-. Decorated Air medal, Bronze Star. Mem. SAR, Nat. Tax Assn., Beta Gamma Sigma, Phi Beta Kappa. Home: 3939 Walnut Ave # 187 Carmichael CA 95608-7309 E-mail: bjhcool@sbcglobal.net.

HELLON, MICHAEL THOMAS, tax consultant, political party official; b. Camden, N.J., June 24, 1942; s. James Bernard and Dena Louise (Blackburn) H.; m. (div.); 2 children. BS, Ariz. State U., 1972. Ins. investigator Equifax, Phoenix, 1968-69; exec. v.p. Phoenix Met. C. of C., 1969-76; exec. Londen Ins. Group, 1976-78; pres. Hellon and Assocs., Inc., 1978—. Small claims hearing officer Pima County Justice Ct., 1990—; mem. Pima County Bd. Adjustments, 1993-2000, Pima County Merit Commn., 2000—; nat. def. exec. res. U.S. Dept. of Commerce, 1986-97; bd. dirs. Equity Benefit Life Ins. Co., Modern Income Life Ins. Co. of Mo., First Equity Security Life Ins. Co., Tucson Classics. Mem.

Ariz. Occupl. Safety and Health Adv. Coun., 1972-76, mem. Speaker's Select Com. Auto Emissions, 1976; Phoenix Urban League, 1972-73, Area Manpower Planning coun., 1971-72, Phoenix Civic Plaza Dedication Com., 1972, Phoenix Air Quality Maintenance Taks Force, 1976; pres. Vis. Nurse Svc., 1978-79; Rep. precinct capt., 1973—; state campaign dir. Arizonans for Reagan Com., 1980; alt. del. Rep. Nat. Conv., 1980, 84, 88; mem. staff Reagan-Bush Nat. Conv., 1984; campaign mgr. for various candidates, 1972-82; mem. exec. com. Ariz. Rep. Party, 1989-90, chmn., 1997-99; mem. Rep. Nat. Com., 1992—, mem. exec. com., 1997—; bd. dirs. ATMA Tng. Found., 1981-84. Served with USAF, 1964-68. Decorated Bronze Star medal, Purple Heart; Recipient George Washington Honor medal Freedom's Found., 1964; commendation Fed. Bar Assn., 1973. Mem. U.S. C. of C. (pub. affairs com. western divsn. 1974-76), Inst. of Property Taxation, Internat. Assn. Assessing Officers, U.S. Dept. Commerce Exec. Res., Ariz. C. of C. Mgrs. Assn. (bd. m em. 1974-76), Tucson C. of C., Trunk 'N Tusk Club, Catalina Soccer Club (bd. dirs. 1984-88). Home: 1261 W Hopbush Way Tucson AZ 85704-2647 Address: 6700 N Oracle Rd #110 Tucson AZ 85704

HELLRUNG, STEPHEN ANDREW, lawyer; b. St. Louis, July 7, 1947; s. J. W. and Alice T. Hellrung; m. Margaret M. Frailey; children: Margaret, Carolyn, Joseph, Leigh. AB, U. Notre Dame, 1969, JD, 1972. Bar: Mo. 1972, U.S. Dist. Ct. (ea. dist.) Mo. 1972, Ill. 1978, N.Y. 1983, Minn. 1998, N.C. 2000. Assoc. Rassieur, Long, Yawitz & Schneider, 1972—78; asst. gen. counsel A.E. Staley, Decatur, Ill., 1978—82; sr. v.p., sec., gen. counsel Bausch & Lomb, Inc., Rochester, NY, 1983—97; sr. v.p., gen. counsel, sec. Pillsbury Co., Mpls., 1997—98, Lowe's Cos., Inc., 1999—. Office: Lowes Companies Inc 1605 Curtis Bridge Rd Wilkesboro NC 28697

HELLUMS, JESSE DAVID, chemical engineering educator and researcher; b. Stamford, Tex., Aug. 19, 1929; s. John V. and Fannie May (Beauchamp) H.; m. Marilyn Biel, July 13, 1957; children— Mark William, Jay David. BS, U. Tex., 1950, MS, 1957; PhD, U. Mich., 1960. Registered profl. engr., Tex. Process engr. Mobil Oil Co., Beaumont, Tex., 1950-54; mem. faculty Rice U., Houston, 1960—, prof. chem. engring., 1968—, dir. biomed. engring. lab., 1968-80, chmn. dept., 1969-75, dean engring., 1980-88; A.J. Hartsook prof., 1987—, A.J. Hartsook prof. emeritus, 1998—. Adj. prof. Baylor U. Coll. Medicine, 1966—, U. Tex. Med. Sch., 1977—; NSF sci. faculty fellow Cambridge (Eng.) U., 1967-68; vis. prof. Imperial Coll., London, 1973-74, U. Tsukuba, Japan, 1995; vis. scholar U. Calif., San Diego, 1988; spl. vis. prof. Tokyo Inst. Tech., 1989, 98; eminent scientist Inst. Phys. & Chem. Rsch., Japan, 1997. Author papers in field. 1st lt. USAF, 1954. Recipient Rsch. award NIH, 1986, Rsch. award Biomed. Engring. Soc., 1993. Fellow AIChE; mem. AAAS, AAUP, Nat. Acad. Engring., Am. Heart Coun. Thrombosis, Am. Inst. Med. Biol. Engrs. (founding fellow), Am. Chem. Soc., Am. Soc. Artificial Internal Organs, Microcirculation Soc., Soc. Rheology, Internat. Soc. Oxygen Transport to Tissue, Biomed. Engring. Soc. (sr. mem.). Home: 2202 Albans Rd Houston TX 77005-1520 Office: Rice Univ Biomed Eng Lab PO Box 1892 Houston TX 77251-1892 E-mail: jhellums@rice.edu.

HELLY, WALTER SIGMUND, engineering educator; b. Vienna, Aug. 22, 1930; came to U.S., 1938, naturalized, 1944; s. Edward and Elizabeth (Bloch) H.; m. Dorothy Oxman, Mar. 4, 1956; 1 dau., Miranda. BA, Cornell U., 1950; MS, U. Ill., 1954; PhD, Mass. Inst. Tech., 1959. With Sylvania Electric Co., Waltham, Mass., 1954-56; sr. engr. Melpar Co., Boston, 1956-59; mem. tech. staff Bell Telephone Labs., N.Y.C., 1959-62; sr. engr. Port of N.Y. Authority, 1962-65; prof. ops. research Poly. Inst. N.Y., 1966—. Cons. on traffic flow. Author: Urban Systems Models, 1975; Book rev. editor: Jour. Ops. Research, 1970— ; Contbr. articles to profl. jours. Mem. Ops. Research Soc. Am. (past chmn. transp. sci. sect.) Home: 91 Central Park W New York NY 10023-4600 Office: 333 Jay St Brooklyn NY 11201-2907 E-mail: whelly@nyc.rr.com.

HELLYER, CONSTANCE ANNE (CONNIE ANNE CONWAY), writer, musician; b. Puyallup, Wash., Apr. 22, 1937; d. David Tirrell and Constance (Hopkins) H.; m. Peter A. Corning, Dec. 30, 1963 (div. 1977); children: Anne Arundel, Stephanie Deak Cunningham; m. Don W. Conway, Oct. 12, 1980. BA with honors, Mills Coll., 1959. Grader, rschr. Harvard U., Cambridge, Mass., 1959-60; rschr. Newsweek mag., N.Y.C., 1960-63; author's asst. Theodore H. White and others, N.Y.C., 1964-69; freelance writer, editor Colo., Calif., 1970-75; writer, editor Stanford (Calif.) U. Med. Ctr., 1975-79; comm. dir. No. Calif. Cancer Program, Palo Alto, 1979-82, Stanford Law Sch., Palo Alto, 1982-97; mgr., vocalist, pianist String of Pearls Band, 1991—, co-leader China tours, 1999, 2001, 2002. Founding editor (newsletters) Insight, 1978-80, Synergy, 1980-82, Stanford Law Alum, 1992-95; editor (mag.) Stanford Lawyer, 1982-98; contbr. articles to profl. jours. and mags. Recipient silver medal Coun. for Advancement and Support Edn., 1985, 89, award of distinction dist. VII, 1994. Mem. No. Calif. Sci. Writers Assn. (co-founder, bd. dirs. 1979-93), Nat. Assn. Sci. Writers, Phi Beta Kappa. Democrat. Home: PO Box 828 Cannon Beach OR 97110

HELLYER, TIMOTHY MICHAEL, protective services officer; b. Chgo., Nov. 30, 1954; s. William Al and Dotha Helen (Buckman) H.; m. Nancy Ruth O'Donnell, Nov. 29, 1986; children: Jennifer Lynn, Allyson Jean. Student, So. Ill. U., 1985-86. Cert. firefighter III; cert. paramedic. Firefighter/paramedic Palatine (Ill.) Fire Dept., 1980—. Instr. CPR, Chgo. Heart Assn., 1976—; pres. N.W. Assn. Provider Emergency Med. Svcs. Sys., 1989-92; mem. No. Ill. Critical Stress Debriefing Team. Deacon Palatine Presbyn. Ch., 1989-92; mem. comm. coun. Sch. Dist. 300, 1993—, mem. Year Round Sch. com., 1998-99; mem. improvement team Westfield Cmty. Sch., 1993—. Named Firefighter of the Yr., Jaycees of Palatine, 1987. Mem. Prehosp. Care Providers Ill. (bd. dirs. 1990), St. Francis Hook and Ladder Soc., Ill. Profl. Firefighters Assn., Smithsonian Instn., Nat. Trust Historic Preservation, Nat. Geographic Soc., U.S. Naval Inst., Nat. Space Soc. Republican. Presbyterian. Avocations: collecting disney memorabilia, gardening, model railroading. Home: 1600 Kensington Dr Algonquin IL 60102-5104 Office: Palatine Fire Dept 39 E Colfax St Palatine IL 60067-5297 E-mail: hellyer4@aol.com.

HELM, DEWITT FREDERICK, JR., consultant, professional association administrator; b. Charlotte, NC, Apr. 24, 1933; s. DeWitt Frederick Sr. and Blanche Buchanan (DeBusk) H.; divorced; children: DeWitt Frederick III, Mary McNair Helm Bishop; m. Anne M. Valle, Mar. 1, 2002. BS in History, Davidson (N.C.) Coll., 1956. Mgr. advt. Vick Chem. Co., N.Y.C., 1956-63; mgr. consumer products Pfizer, Inc., N.Y.C., 1963-66; mgr. consumer product acquisition and devel. A.H. Robins Co., Richmond, Va., 1966-69; exec. v.p. Miller Morton Co., Richmond, 1969-72, pres., 1972-81, Miller Morton of Can. Ltd., 1969-81; sr. v.p. Jack Morton Prodns. Inc., Washington, 1981-84; exec. v.p. Assn. Nat. Advertisers, Inc., N.Y.C., 1984, pres., 1984-93, also bd. dirs.; mng. ptnr. DH Assocs., Palm City, Fla., 1994-97, The Advt. Partnership LLC, N.Y.C., 1996—. Deacon, elder Presbyn. Ch., United Meth. Ch., 1990; trustee Christ Ch., NYC, 2000-03; bd. dirs. Nat. Tobacco Festival, Richmond, 1977-81, Traffic Audit Bur., NYC, 1984-93. With U.S. Army, 1956-58. Mem. Consumer Healthcare Products Assn. (bd. dirs., exec. com. 1972-80, chmn. 1973-75), Coun. Better Bus. Burs. (bd. dirs. 1989-93), Am. Advt. Mus. (founding dir., nat. bd. 1987—), Smithsonian Instn.'s Ctr. for Advt. History (adv. bd. 1989—), Advt. Coun. (bd. dirs., treas. 1984-93, life bd. dirs. 2002—), Advt. Rsch. Found. (bd. dirs. 1984-93), World Fedn. Advertisers (bd. dirs., mgmt. com. 1984-93), Media-Advt. Partnership for Drug-Free Am. (mgmt. bd.), Wintergreen (Va.) Club, Sky Club, Met. Club (N.Y.C.), Harbour Ridge Club (Fla.). E-mail: taphelm@aol.com.

HELM, DONALD CAIRNEY, hydrogeologist, engineer, educator; b. Yokohama, Japan, Mar. 26, 1937; s. Nathan Teal and Rebecca Forsyth (Cairney) H.; m. Usha Monica Sundari Muliyil, Dec. 1961 (div. 1982); m. Karen Emily Reed, Sept. 3, 1982; 1 child, Rebecca Bernice Vera. *Grandparents Verling Winchell Helm (1875-1907) and Martha Teal Helm (1873-1952) moved from Indiana to Japan as newlyweds in the late 19th century to help establish the Japanese YMCA. Father Nathan, uncle Winchell, and aunt Kathryn Helm Turner were born in Japan, whereas aunt Margaret Helm Starn was born in the U.S. The Rev. Dr. Nathan Helm (1904-84) returned to Japan in 1927 with Rebecca (1904-95) his Scottish-American bride whom he met at Wooster College. He taught Latin and Greek at Mriji Gakuin in Tokyo. Siblings Charles William Helm (1931-) of Perth, Australia and Martha Christian Helm Miller (1928-89) of Dallas and Jakarta were also born in Japan.* AB in Math. cum laude, Amherst Coll., 1959; MDiv in Theology, Hartford Sem. Found., 1962; postgrad., Colo. Sch. Mines, 1962-63, 64-65; MS in Geol. Engring., U. Calif.-Berkeley, 1970, PhD in Civil Engring., 1974. Registered profl. engr., Australia, U.S.A. Vol. in rural devel. Mitraniketan Project, Kerala State, India, 1963-64; hydraulic engr. U.S. Geol. Survey, Portland, Oregon, 1965-68, Berkeley, Calif., 1968-69, research hydrologist Sacramento, 1969-78, Las Vegas, Nev., 1991-93, Carson City, Nev., 1993-96; ret., 1999; research physicist Lawrence Livermore Nat. Lab., U. Calif., 1978-84, ret. 1990, group leader, geohydrology and environ. studies group, 1981-84; prin. research scientist Geomechanics Div. Commonwealth Sci. and Indsl. Research Orgn. (CSIRO), Melbourne, Australia, 1984-92, ret. 1992, hydraulics group leader, 1984-86, chmn. selection com. for hiring research scientists, 1986, rep. to Research Officers Assn., 1986-87, mem. ex-officio divisional staff cons. com., 1986-87; rsch. hydrogeologist Nev. Bur. Mines and Geology U. Nev., Reno, Las Vegas, 1989-98, vis. rsch. scientist Nev. Bur. Mines and Geology Reno, 1989-92; chief Las Vegas Office, 1989-93; prof. geology U. Nev., Reno, 1992-98, adj. prof., 1998—; Samuel P. Massie prof. civil engring. Morgan State U., Balt., 1996—. Instr. U.S. Geol. Survey Advanced Groundwater Sch., Denver, 1972-78, UNESCO Internat. Workshop on Land Subsidence, Mexico City, 1979, Pacific Sch. Religion, Berkeley, Calif., 1982, courses on subsidence for various mining cos., Western Australia, 1985, for U.S. Geol. Survey rsch. hydrologists, Tucson, 1987; advisor, mem. nat. steering com. Geothermal Subsidence Rsch. Program, U.S. Dept. Energy, 1976-84; vis. sr. rsch. scientist State Elec. Commn. Victoria, Australia, 1982-83, U.S. Bur. Reclamation, Phoenix, 1984; mem. subcom. on math. modeling of subsidence NSW Dept. Mineral Resources, 1984-86; internat. exch. scientist from Australia to Inst. Soil and Rock Mechanics, Acad. Sinica (Chinese Acad. Sci.), Wuhan, 1988, to dept. civil engring. U. Colo., Boulder, 1990; mem. grad. faculty joint CSIRO-James Cook U. program in rock engring., 1989-90, dept. geol. scis. U. Nev., Reno, 1990-98, hydrology/hydrogeology program, 1991-95, hydrol. scis. program, 1995-98, dept. civil engring., 1994-98, dept. geosci. U. Nev., Las Vegas, 1992-93; coord. multi-agy. rsch. project on subsidence of the Las Vegas Valley, 1989-91; mem. nat. liaison com. between ASCE, Geol. Soc. Am. and Assn. Engring. Geologists, 1997-2000; adj. prof. Royal Melbourne Inst. Tech., 1997—, U. Nev., Reno, 1998—, Va. Poly. Inst. and State U., 1999—. Contbr. articles to sci. jours., chpts. to books. Co-chmn. New Eng. Student Christian Movement, 1958-59; mem. high sch. com. Am. Friends Service Com., Salem Oreg., 1966-68; bd. dirs. Ctr. Theology and Natural Scis., Grad. Theol. Union, Berkeley, Calif., 1981-84, Montessori Sch. Council, Melbourne, 1986-87; mem. Md. Tributary Team for Protecting the Chesapeake Bay, 1997-2000, Balt. Mayor's Transition Team (water and waste-water com.), 2000. Recipient Bennett-Tyler award in systematic theology, 1962, Award for Best Paper of Yr. Disciplines of Environ. and Engring. Geology from Assn. Engring. Geologists, 1994, Cert. of Appreciation Chinese (Taiwanese) Inst. of Civil and Hydraulic Engring. Com. of Geotech. Engring., 1992, U. Jos, Nigeria, 1998, Fed. U. Tech., Minna, Nigeria, Ahmadu Bello U., Nigeria, 1998; Innaugural occupant of U.S. Dept. Energy's Samuel P. Massie Chair of Excellence in Environ. Disciplines, Morgan State U., 1996—. Fellow Geol. Soc. Am., Inst. Engrs. Australia (Coll. Civil Engrs.); mem. NSPE, ASTM (com. solid waste disposal), AAUP, AAAS, ASCE, ASME, Am. Geophys. Union, Am. Water Resources Assn., Assn. Engring. Geologists, Assn. Geoscientists for Internat. Devel., Nat. Water Well Assn., N.Y. Acad. Scis., Internat. Soil Mechanics and Found. Engring., Internat. Assn. Engring. Geology, Internat. Soc. Rock Mechanics, Nev. Water Resources Assn., Md. Soc. Profl. Engrs. (pres. Balt. chpt., Md. bd. dirs., state v.p.), SAR (mem. bd. mgrs. John Eager Howard chpt.), Berkeley City Club, Outlook Club, Balt. Engrs. Club (bd. dirs.). Mem. Soc. Of Friends. Home: 1413 Bolton St Baltimore MD 21217-4202 Office: Morgan State U Dept Civil Engring Baltimore MD 21251-0001

HELM, JOHN LESLIE, retired mechanical engineer, company executive; b. Red Wing, Apr. 10, 1921; s. Leslie Cornell and Dora (Mcguigan) H.; m. Nancy Ellen Molle, May 15, 1954; children: John Leslie, Juli-Ann, Catherine Marie. BSME, Columbia, 1943, MS, 1944; postgrad. in nuclear engring., U. Conn., 1956-57. Registered profl. engr., NY. Asst. in mech. engring. Columbia U., 1943-44; process engr. Metals Disintegrating Co. unit of Manhattan Project, Elizabeth, NJ, 1944-45; project engr. Aero Manuscripts Inc., 1945-46; staff engr. ctrl. engring. dept. Gen. Foods Corp., White Plains, NY, 1946-52; with Gen. Dynamics Corp., Groton, Conn., 1952-74; supervisory engr. USS Nautilus Propulsion Plant; dep. project mgr., chief engr. S5W Skipjack Submarine Nuc. Propulsion Project; project mgr., chief engr. S5G Narwal Submarine Nuc. Propulsion Project; spl. tech. asst. Office of Pres. Electric Boat divsn. Gen. Dynamics Corp., 1965-72; gen. mgr. Gen. Dynamics Energy Sys., 1972-74; founder, pres., CEO Proto-Power Mgmt. Corp., Groton, 1974-82; also dir.; pres., CEO Proto-Power corp. subs. of Kolmorgen Corp., 1982-89; dir. Electronic Assocs., Inc., West Long Branch, NJ, 1983-89; founder, pres., CEO Transplex Inc., 1990—2003; ret., 2003. Mem. Groton Bd. Edn., 1967-77, chmn., 1976-77; mem. State of Conn. Nuclear Adv. Coun., 1996—. Recipient citation for work on Manhattan Project, War Dept., 1945. Mem. ASME, Shonnecosset Yacht Club, Off Soundings Club, NY Yacht Club, Theta Tau. Republican. Home: 116 Tyler Ave Groton CT 06340-5923

HELM, LEWIS MARSHALL, public affairs executive; b. Riverdale, Md., Sept. 9, 1931; s. William P. and Selma S. (Snyder) Helm; m. Alice L. Kupferman, Sept. 12, 1953. AA in Comms., Am. U., 1957, MS in Pub. Rels., 1979; grad., U.S. Army War Coll., 1977. Newspaper reporter Wichita (Kans.) Eagle, 1950-51, Washington Times-Herald, 1951-54; press asst. Republican Nat. Com., 1954-55; dir. pub. rels. Plumbing Fixture Mfrs. Assn., Washington, 1956-59, Home Mfrs. Assn., 1961-63; pub. rels. cons., 1959-60, 64-68; info. dir. Citizens for Nixon, 1968; asst. to sec. U.S. Dept. Interior, Washington, 1969, dep. asst. sec. mineral resources, 1969-72; asst. sec. for pub. affairs HEW, Washington, 1973-76; pres. Capital Counselors, Inc., Washington, 1976-86; govt. rels. and mktg. cons., 1987—; commr. Washington Suburban Sanitary Commn., 1991-95, vice-chair, 1992-93, chair, 1993-94. Instr. econs. Cath. U. Am., 1974; assoc. lecturing prof. polit., sci. George Washington U., 1980; commentator Sta. WAMU-FM, Washington, 1995—2002; adj. prof. Montgomery Coll., 1996—97; adj. instr. Coll. Journalism U. Md., 1998—; adj. instr. MBA program and Police Leadership Program Johns Hopkins U., 1999—. Co-author: Informing the People: A Public Affairs Handbook, 1981. Exec. dir. Sr. Army res. Comdrs. Assn., 1987—; mem. Soc. of the Cin. in the State of Va.; mem. adv. bd. Vietnam Vets. Inst., 1993—96; bd. dirs. Mid-Atlantic region Audubon Naturalist Soc., 1995—97. Brig. gen. USAR, 1984—88. Decorated Legion of Merit with Oak Leaf Cluster; named Hall of Fame, Sr. Army Res. Comdrs. Assn.; recipient Meritorious Svc. medal, Dept. Interior, USPHS, Dept. Army, Spl. Citation for Disting. Svc., Sec. HEW.

HELMAN, ALFRED BLAIR, retired college president, education consultant; b. Windber, Pa., Dec. 25, 1920; s. Henry E. and Luie (Pritt) H.; m. Patricia Ann Kennedy, June 22, 1947; children: Harriet Ann Helman Hill, Patricia Dawn Helman Magaro. AB magna cum laude, McPherson Coll., 1946, DD, 1956; MA, U. Kans., 1947, postgrad., 1948-51; LLD, Juniata Coll., 1976; LHD, Bridgewater Coll., 1977, Ind. U., 1981, Manchester Coll., 1986. Ordained to ministry Ch. of Brethren, 1942; pastor Newton, Kans., 1944-46, Ottawa, Kans., 1946-54, First Ch. of Brethren, Wichita, Kans., 1954-56; faculty Ottawa U., 1947- 48, 51-54, chmn. div. social scis., 1952-54; faculty U. Kans., 1951-54, Friends U., 1955-56; pres. Manchester (Ind.) Coll., 1956-86, pres. emeritus, 1986—. Chmn. com. on higher edn. Ch. of Brethren, 1965-67, 76-78, nat. moderator, 1975-76, mem. rev. and evaluation com., 1983-85, mem. denominational structure rev. com., 1989-91, mem. pension bd. restructure com., 1986-87; trustee McPherson Coll., 1951-56, chmn., 1955-56; trustee Kans. Found. Pvt. Colls. and Univs., 1955-56; pres. Ind. Conf. Higher Edn., 1960-61; mem. policy bd. dept. higher edn. Nat. Coun. Chs. of Christ Am., 1960-71; mem. pres.'s adv. com. Nat. Assn. Intercollegiate Athletics, 1966-70; mem. exec. com. Ind. Coun. Chs., 1960-62, bd. dirs., 1992-94; bd. dirs. Independent Colls. and Univs. of Ind., 1977-83, 84-86, chmn., 1978-79, 85-86; chmn., interim pres. Coun. Protestant Colls. and Univs., 1967, bd. dirs., 1961-69; bd. dirs. Ctrl. States Coll. Assn., 1965-77, chmn., 1968; pres. Assoc. Colls. of Ind., 1970-72, bd. dirs., 1956-86; mem. commn. on religion in higher edn. Assn. Am. Colls., 1968-71; bd. dirs. CTB, Inc., 1977-92. Author articles on religion and higher edn. Mem. IAUP-UN Commn. on Arms Control Edn., 1991—2002. Named Sagamore of Wabash, Gov. of Ind., 1980, Ky. Col., Gov. of Ky., 1964; recipient Outstanding Local Citizen award, 1972, Sparks-Jones award Associated Colls. Ind., 1977, Legion of Honor award Kiwanis Club North Manchester, 1976, Alumni Honor award, Manchester Coll., 1981, Citation of Merit, McPherson Coll., 2001, Citation for Responsible Philanthropy, Manchester Coll., 2003; elected to Ind. Acad., 1987. Mem. Soc. Historians of Am. Fgn. Rels., Internat. Assn. Univ. Presidents (mem. steering com. N.Am. coun. 1982-84), Ind. Assn. Ch.-Related and Ind. Colls. (pres. 1966-67), Am. Assn. Higher Edn., Am. Acad. Polit. and Social Sci., Nat. Assn. Ind. Colls. and Univs. (bd. dirs. 1983-84), Ind. Acad. Social Scis., Ind. Hist. Assn., Ft. Wayne Rotary (Paul Harris fellow), Quest Club (mem. bd. govs. 1988-90, 92-94, 97-99), Phi Beta Kappa, Phi Alpha Theta, Pi Sigma Alpha, Pi Kappa Delta, Tau Kappa Alpha (hon.).

HELMAN, DONALD LEE, physician, military officer; b. Alexandria, Va., Nov. 23, 1970; s. Donald Lee and Linda Price Helman; m. Jennifer Highley; children: Richard Robert, John Ryne. BS, The Fla. State U., 1988—92; M.D., Uniformed Svc. U. of the Health Sciences, 1993—97. Cert. Pulmonary Disease Am. Bd. of Internal Medicine, 2002, Internal Medicine Am. Bd. of Internal Medicine, 2000, Diplomate, U.S. Med. Licensing Examination USMLE, 1998. Fellow, pulmonary & critical care medicine Walter Reed Army Med. Ctr., Washington, 2000—, resident, internal medicine, 1997—2000. Instr. of medicine Uniformed Svc. U. of the Health Sciences, 2000. Capt. U.S. Army, 1993, Walter Reed Army Med. Ctr. Decorated Army Achievement medal, Army Commendation Medal, Nat. Defence Svc. Medal U.S. Army. Mem.: ACP (assoc.), Soc. of Critical Care Medicine (assoc.), Am. Thoracic Soc. (assoc.), Am. Coll. of Chest Physicians (assoc.), Kappa Sigma Frat. (life), Alpha Omega Alpha Honor Med. Soc. (life). R-Liberal. Baptist. Achievements include research in yielding publication & presentations in the field of Interstitial Lung Disease. Office: Walter Reed Army Med Ctr 6900 Georgia Ave NW Washington DC 20307 Office Fax: 202-782-9032.

HELMAN, GERALD BERNARD, government official; b. Detroit, Nov. 4, 1932; s. Leo and Ann (Glassman) H.; m. Dolores Hammel, May, 1953; children: Ruth Leea, Deborah Gayle, David Robert. AB, U. Mich., 1953, LLB, 1956. Bar: Mich. 1956. Rsch. asst. U. Mich., 1955; intelligence rsch. specialist Dept. State, 1957, econ. consular officer, 1958, polit. officer Vienna, Austria, 1960-62, econ. officer Barbados, 1962-63, fgn. affairs officer Washington, 1963-68; polit. mil. affairs officer, counselor U.S. Mission to NATO, Brussels, Belgium, 1968-73, dep. dir. NATO-Atlantic polit. mil. affairs Washington, 1974-76, dir. UN polit. affairs, 1976-77; dep. asst. sec. Bur. Internat. Orgn. Affairs, 1977-79; U.S. ambassador to UN Orgns. in Europe, 1979-81; dep. and sr. advisor to undersec. for polit. affairs Dept. State, Washington, 1982-91, cons. on Internat. and Telecomm. matters, 1991-92; v.p. Ellipso, Inc., 1992—. Woodrow Wilson fellow Princeton U., 1973 Jewish. Home: 2900 Maplewood Pl Alexandria VA 22302-2424 E-mail: ghelman@ellipso.com.

HELMAN, ROBERT ALAN, lawyer; b. Chgo., Jan. 27, 1934; s. Nathan W. and Esther (Weiss) H.; m. Janet R. Williams, Sept. 13, 1958; children: Marcus E., Adam J., Sarah E. Student, U. Ill., 1951-53; BSL, Northwestern U., 1954, LLB, 1956. Bar: Ill. 1956. Asso. firm Isham, Lincoln & Beale, Chgo., 1956-64, ptnr., 1965-66; ptnr. firm Mayer, Brown, Rowe & Maw, Chgo., 1967—. Bd. dirs. No. Trust Corp., The No. Trust Co., Dreyer's Grand Ice Cream Co., TCPL GP Inc. Co-author: Commentaries on 1970 Illinois Constitution, 1971; assoc. editor Northwestern U. Law Rev., 1955-56; contbr. articles to legal jours. Chmn. Citizens' Com. on Juvenile Ct., Cook County, 1969-81; pres. Legal Assistance Found., Chgo., 1973-76; chmn. vis. com. Northwestern U. Law Sch., 1989-92; bd. dirs. United Charities Chgo., 1967-73; hon. trustee Brookings Instn., Aspen Inst., 1986-92, Mus. of Contemporary Art. Mem. ABA, Chgo. Bar Assn., Am. Law Inst., Chgo. Coun. Lawyers, Legal Club Chgo., Law Club Chgo., Comml. Club, Chgo. Club, Mid-Day Club, Econ. Club, Order of Coif. Home: 4950 S Chicago Beach Dr Chicago IL 60615-3207 Office: Mayer Brown Rowe & Maw 190 S La Salle St Ste 3100 Chicago IL 60603-3441

HELMAN, STEPHEN JODY, lawyer; b. Houston, Dec. 14, 1949; m. Gail Stevenson, 1974; children: Kimberley Brooke, Courtney Elizabeth, Caitlin Rebecca. BA in Spanish and Religion, So. Meth. U., 1971; postgrad., Perkins Sch. Theology, 1971-73; JD with honors, U. Tex., 1978. Bar: Tex., 1978; cert. estate planning and probate law, 1987. Assoc. Graves, Dougherty, Hearon & Moody, Austin, Tex., 1978-85, ptnr., shareholder, 1985-93; ptnr. Osborne, Lowe, Helman & Smith, L.L.P., Austin, Tex., 1993-2000, Osborne & Helman, L.L.P., Austin, Tex., 2001—. Exam commr. in estate planning and probate law, Tex. Bd. Legal Specialization, 1990-94. Contbr. articles to profl. jours. Fellow Am. Coll. Trust and Estate Counsel (mem. profl. standards com. 1990-93); mem. ABA (mem. real property, probate, and trust law sects.), Coll. of the State Bar of Tex., State Bar Tex. (mem. real property, probate and trust law sects.), Travis County Bar Assn. (mem. probate and estate planning sect., pres. 1991-92, dir. 1989-92, ex-officio dir. 1992-93), Order of Coif. Avocations: nature photography, hiking. Office: Osborne & Helman LLP 301 Congress Ave Ste 1910 Austin TX 78701-4041 E-mail: sjhelman@osbornehelman.com.

HELMER, DAVID ALAN, lawyer; b. Colorado Springs, May 19, 1946; s. Horton James and Alice Ruth (Cooley) H.; m. Jean Marie Lamping, May 23, 1987. BA, U. Colo., 1968, JD, 1973. Bar: Colo. 1973, U.S. Dist. Ct. Colo. 1973, U.S. Ct. Appeals (10th cir.) 1993, U.S. Ct. Claims 1990, U.S. Supreme Ct. 1991. Assoc. Neil C. King, Boulder, Colo., 1973-76; mgr. labor rels., mine regulations Climax Molybdenum Co., Inc. divsn. AMAX, Inc., Climax, Colo., 1976-83; prin. Law Offices David A. Helmer, Frisco, Colo., 1983—. Sec., bd. dirs. Z Comm. Corp., Frisco, 1983-90; cmty. bd. dirs. Wells Fargo Bank, N.A., Frisco, 1996—. Editor U. Colo. Law Rev., 1972-73; contbr. articles to legal jours. Bd. dirs. Summit County Coun. Arts and Humanities, Dillon, Colo., 1980-85; advisor Advocates for Victims of Assault, Frisco, 1984—; legal counsel Summit County United Way, 1983-95, v.p., bd. dirs., 1983-88; bd. dirs., legal counsel Summit county Alcohol and Drug Task Force, Inc., Summit Prevention Alliance, 1984—, Pumpkin Bowl Inc./Chldren's Hosp. Burn Ctr., 1989—; chmn. Summit County Reps., 1982-89; chmn. 5th Jud. Dist. (Colo.) Rep. Com., 1982-89; chmn. resolutions com. Colo. Rep. Conv., 1984, del. Rep. Nat. Com., 1984; chmn. reaccreditation com. Colo. Mountain Coll., Breckenridge, 1983, mem. steering com., 1997-99; founder, bd. dirs. Dillon Bus. Assn., 1983-87, Frisco Arts Coun., 1989—; atty. N.W. Colo. Legal Svcs. Project, Summit County, 1983—; mcpl. judge Town of Dillon, 1982—, Town of Silverthorne, Colo., 1982—; bd. dirs. Snake River Water Dist., 1998—, chmn., 2002—. Master Sgt. USAR, 1968-74. Mem. ABA, Colo. Bar Assn., (bd. govs. 1991-93, mem. exec. com. 1995-97), Continental Divide Bar Assn. (prs. 1991-95, v.p. 1995-97), Summit County Bar Assn. (pres. 1990-99), Dillon Corinthian Yacht Club (commodore local club 1987-88, 95-97, vice commodore 1994, club champion 1989-91, 94, 95, 97, 98, 2002, winner Colo. Cup, Colo. State Sailing Championships 1991, Dist. Champion 2000, Champion Dillon Open Regatta 2001), Phi Gamma Delta. Lutheran. Home: PO Box 300 352 Snake River Dr Dillon CO 80435-0300 Office: PO Box 868 611 Main St Frisco CO 80443-0868 E-mail: dave@helmerlaw.com.

HELMER, M(ARTHA) CHRISTIE, lawyer; b. Portland, Oreg., Oct. 8, 1949; d. Marvin Curtis and Inez Bahl (Corwin) H.; m. Joe D. Bailey, June 23, 1979; children: Tim Bailey, Bill Bailey, Kim Easton. BA in English magna cum laude, Wash. State U., 1970; JD cum laude, Lewis & Clark Coll., 1974; LLM in Internat. Law, Columbia U., 1998. Bar: Oreg. 1974. Assoc. Miller Nash, Portland, 1974-81, ptnr., 1981—. Adj. prof. Lewis & Clark Law Sch., 1999—; guest lectr. Xiamen U. Law, China, 1995; mem. Oreg. Bd. Bar Examiners, Portland, 1978-81; del. 9th Cir. Jud. Conf., 1984-87, mem. exec. com., 1987-90. Author: Arrest of Ships, 1985, Has China Adopted the UCC?, 1999. Mem.: ABA (internat. and litig. sections), Internat. Bar Assn., Maritime Law Assn., Oreg. Bar Assn. (bd. govs. 1981—84, treas. 1983—84), World Affairs Coun. (bd. dirs., exec. com., sec.), Multnomah Athletic Club, Phi Beta Kappa. Avocations: antiques, travel, fashion. Office: Miller Nash 111 SW 5th Ave Ste 3500 Portland OR 97204-3699 E-mail: helmer@millernash.com.

HELMETAG, DIANA, music educator; b. Bryn Mawr, Pa., 1965; d. Charles and Ruth Helmetag; m. Steven Glanzmann, 1993. BS in Music Edn. cum laude, Duquesne U., 1987; MusM, Pa. State U., 1990. Instr. Sch. Music Pa. State U., University Park, 1988, 90, lectr. Delaware County campus Media, 1991-95; music tchr. Radnor (Pa.) Twp. Sch. Dist., 1993-94, 95, 96; piano accompanist Villanova (Pa.) Voices Villanova U., 1995-99; instr. Delaware County C.C., Media, 1996; orch. dir. Upper Merion Area Sch. Dist., King of Prussia, Pa., 1996—, subject area leader, 1997—2001, pit orch. dir., 1997, 1998, 2001—; choir dir. and children's orch. dir. Strings Internat. Music Festival Bryn Mawr (Pa.) Coll., 2001—. Pianist, violinist Mu Phi Epsilon recitals, Phila., 1991, 92, 94; orch. dir. Schuylkill Valley Area Orch. Festival, Wayne, Pa., 1996—; founding mem. Montgomery County Honors String Orch. Festival, Plymouth Meeting, Pa., 1999—; music dir. King of Prussia Players, 2000. Orch. dir.,

pianist, violinist Narberth (Pa.) Cmty. Theatre, 1997—. Recipient grad. assistantship Pa. State U., 1987-90. Mem. Am. String Tchrs. Assn. with Nat. Sch. Orch. Assn., Music Educators Nat. Conf., Music Tchrs. Nat. Assn., Coll. Music Soc., Pa. Music Educators Assn. (host. dist. 11 orch. festival 1998, orch. dir. and presiding chair in-svc. conf. 2001, host all-state orch. festival 2002), Phi Kappa Phi, Pi Kappa Lambda. Office: Upper Merion Area Sch Dist 435 Crossfield Rd King Of Prussia PA 19406 E-mail: dhelmetag@umasd.org.

HELMHOLZ, R(ICHARD) H(ENRY), law educator; b. Pasadena, Calif., July 1, 1940; s. Lindsay and Alice (Bean) H.; m. Marilyn P. Helmholz. AB, Princeton U., 1962; JD, Harvard U., 1965; PhD, U. Calif., Berkeley, 1970; LLD, Trinity Coll., Dublin, 1992. Bar: Mo. 1965. Prof. law and hist. Washington U., St. Louis, 1970-81; prof. law U. Chgo., 1981—. Maitland lectr. Cambridge U., 1987; Goodhart prof. Cambridge U., 2000-01. Author: Marriage Litigation, 1975, Select Cases on Defamation, 1985, Canon Law and the Law of England, 1987, Roman Canon Law in Reformation England, 1990, Spirit of Classical Canon Law, 1996, The Ius Commune in England: Four Studies, 2001. Guggenheim fellow, 1986; recipient Von Humboldt rsch. prize, 1992. Fellow Brit. Acad. (corr.), Am. Acad. Arts and Scis., Am. Law Inst., Medieval Acad. Am.; mem. ABA, Am. Soc. Legal History (pres. 1992-94), Selden Soc. (v.p. 1984-87), Univ. Club, Reform Club. Home: 5757 S Kimbark Ave Chicago IL 60637-1614 Office: U Chgo Law Sch 1111 E 60th St Chicago IL 60637-2776 E-mail: dick_helmholz@law.uchicago.edu.

HELMICK, RAYMOND GLEN, priest, educator; b. Arlington, Mass., Sept. 7, 1931; s. Raymond Glen and Alice Cecilia (Clancy) H. BA, Boston Coll., 1956, MA in philosphy, 1957; lic. philosphy, Weston Coll., 1957; lic. theol., Hochschule St. Georgen, Frankfurt, 1964. Joined Jesuit Order, 1949, ordained priest Roman Cath. Ch., 1963. Assoc. dir. Ctr. for Human Rights & Responsibilities, London, 1973-79, Inst. Soc. Rsch., London, 1973-79; found., co-dir. Ctr. of Concern for Human Dignity, London, 1979-81; sr. assoc. Conflict Analysis Ctr., Washington, 1982—; prof. of conflict resolution Boston Coll., 1984—; sr. assoc. Ctr. Strategic & Internat. Studies, Washington, 2000—. Exec. comm. US Interreligious Comm. for Peace in the Middle East, Seattle, 1987—, adv. bd. Organ. for Human Rights in Iraq, Boston, 1992—; bd. dirs. Refugee Immigrant Ministry, Boston. Author: (with Richard Hauser) A Social Option, 1975, La Question Libanaise Selon Raymond Edde, 1990; editor: (with Rodney Petersen) Forgiveness and Reconciliation: Religion, Public Policy and Conflict Transformation, 2001; video documentaries (with John Michalczyk) Out of the Ashes Northern Ireland's Fragile Peace, 1998, Prelude to Kosovo: War and Peace in Bosnia and Croatia, 1999, South Africa: Beyond a Miracle, 2000, Unexpected Openings: Northern Ireland's Prisoners, 2001, Different Drummers: Daring to Make Peace in the Middle East, 2003. Mediation No. Irish conflict, 1972-81, 92—, Kurdish conflict, 1973-81, 87—, Lebanese conflict, 1982—, Israeli-Palestinian conflict, 1986—, Balkan conflict, 1995—. Democrat. Roman Catholic. Office: Boston Coll Chestnut Hill MA 02467 E-mail: helmick@bc.edu.

HELMICK, WALT, state legislator; b. Bergoo, W.Va., Apr. 25, 1944; m. Rita Fay Hedrick; 4 children. BA, W.Va. Inst. Tech., 1992. Tchr.; bus. owner, operator; senator W.Va. State Senate, Charleston, 1989—. Commr. Pocahontas County; mem. Pocahontas County Bd. Edn.; past mem. W.Va. State Dem. Exec. Com.; mem. agr., banking and ins., energy, industry and mining, fin. and coms. W.Va. State Senate. Mem. bd. trustees Pocahontas County Hosp.; chair Pocahontas County Bd. Health; past pres. Marlinton Little League Football, Marlinton Little League Baseball; mem. Region IV Coun., North Ctrl. Cmty. Action; bd. dirs. Pocahontas County Parks and Recreation. Mem. Masons. Democrat. Presbyterian. Office: WVa State Senate Bldg 1900 Kanawha Blvd E Rm 465M Charleston WV 25305-0009 Fax: 304-357-7930.

HELMKE, PAUL (WALTER PAUL HELMKE JR.), mayor, lawyer; b. Bloomington, Ind., Nov. 24, 1948; s. Walter P. and Rowene Mary (Crabill) H.; m. Deborah Jane Andrews, Aug. 23, 1969; children: Laura Andrews, Kathryn Elizabeth. BA with highest honors, Ind. U., 1970; JD, Yale U., 1973. Bar: Ind. 1973, Fla. 1982. Lawyer Helmke Beams Boyer Wagner, Ft. Wayne, Ind., 1973-87, 2003—; mayor City Ft. Wayne, 1988-2000; atty. Barnes & Thornburg, Ft. Wayne, 2000—02. Asst. county atty. Allen County, Ft. Wayne, 1974-87; pres. Nat. Rep. Mayors and Local Ofcls. Orgn., 1993; pres. U.S. Conf. of Mayors, 1997-98. Chmn. Allen-Wells chpt. ARC, Ft. Wayne, 1985-87; candidate for Rep. nomination 4th U.S. Congl. Dist.-Ind., 1980; Rep. nominee for U.S. Senate, Ind., 1998; bd. dirs. Nat. League of Cities, 1995-97, chair pub. safety and crime prevention com., 1995; candidate for Rep. nomination 3d U.S. Congl. Dist. Ind., 2002. Recipient J.C. Gallagher prize Law Sch. Yale U., New Haven, Conn., 1972 Mem. Ind. Assn. Cities and Towns (pres. 1996-97). Republican. Lutheran. Home: 1215 Korte Ln Fort Wayne IN 46807-2920 Office: Helmke Beams Boyer & Wagner 202 W Berry St Ste 300 Fort Wayne IN 46802-2216 Personal E-mail: paulhelmke@aol.com. Business E-Mail: paulhelmke@hbbwlaw.com.

HELMLY, JAMES R. military officer; b. Savannah, Ga. married; two children: Lisa, Melanie. BS, SUNY; grad., Army Command Gen. Staff Coll., Armed Forces Staff Coll., Army War Coll. Enlisted U.S. Army, commd. 2d lt., advanced through grades to Lt. gen., early commd. svc. includes platoon leader 101st airborne divsn., U.S. Army, Ft. Campbell, Ky., and Vietnam; co. comdr. Ft. Benning, Ga.; res. assignments include regimental ops. officer; logistics supply and maintenance officer assignments; comdr. 352d maintenance bn.; dep. chief of staff for tn., dep. chief of staff personnel 449th area support group, Forest Park, Ga.; dep. chief U.S. Army Res., Office to Chief Army Res., Washingtin, 1995—99; comdr. join task force conducting Oper. Provide Refuge, Fort Dix, NJ, 1999—99; military asst., manpower and reserve affairs Office of the Asst., Sec. of the Army, Washington, 1999—2001; commdg. gen. U.S. Army Res.,78th Div., Edison, NJ, 2001—02; comdr. U.S. Army Res. Command, Ft. McPherson, Ga., 2002—; chief U.S. Army Res., 2002—. Office: Office of Chief Army Res 2400 Army Pentagon Washington DC 20310-2400*

HELMREICH, JONATHAN ERNST, history educator; b. Brunswick, Maine, Dec. 21, 1936; s. Ernst Christian and Louise Bertha (Roberts) H.; m. Martha Anne Schaff, Aug. 22, 1959 (div. 1978); children— Anne Linden, Dana Louise, Douglas Ernst Folger; m. Nancy L. Ross, Feb. 21, 1979. BA magna cum laude, Amherst Coll., 1958; MA, Princeton, 1959, PhD, 1961; postgrad. (Fulbright grantee), Free U. of Brussels, 1961-62. Teaching asst. Princeton, 1961; asst. prof. Allegheny Coll., Meadville, Pa., 1962-66, asso. prof., 1966-72, dean of instrn., 1966-81, prof., 1972-98, prof. emeritus, coll. historian, 1998—. Author: Belgium and Europe: A Study in Small Power Diplomacy, 1976, Gathering Rare Ores: The Diplomacy of Uranium Acquisition, 1943-54, 86, U.S. Relations with Belgium and the Congo, 1940-60, 98, Eternal Hope: The Life of Timothy Alden, Jr., 2001, (with others) Rebirth: A History of Europe since World War II, 1st ed. 1992, 2nd ed. 2000; contbr. articles to profl. publs. Mem. Pa. Trial Judge Nominating Commn. for Crawford County, 1973-75; Pres., bd. dirs. United Housing Corp. of Meadville, Fairview Housing Corp. of Meadville; bd. mem. United Way at Western Crawford County, 1996-99. Mem. Am. Hist. Assn., Crawford County Hist. Soc., Phi Beta Kappa, Pi Gamma Mu, Phi Alpha Theta. Clubs: Rotarian. Democrat. Methodist. Home: 370 Jefferson St Meadville PA 16335-1457 E-mail: jhelmrei@allegheny.edu.

HELMRICH, JOEL MARC, lawyer; b. Bklyn., Apr. 15, 1953; s. William and Edna (Steigman) H.; m. Barbara Ellen Richter, Sept. 2, 1984; children: Joshua David, Rachel Marysa. BS, Cornell U., 1975, MBA, 1976; JD, Syracuse U., 1979. Bar: Pa. 1979, U.S. Dist. Ct. (we. dist.) Pa. 1979, U.S. Ct. Appeals (3d cir.) 1997. Assoc. Tucker Arensberg, PC, Pitts., 1979-86; shareholder Tucker Arensberg, Pitts., 1986-99; ptnr. Meyer, Unkovic & Scott LLP, Pitts., 1999—. Mem. Pa. Bar Assn., Allegheny County Bar Assn., Comml. Law League Am., Am. Bankruptcy Inst., Cornell Club. Avocations: golf, tennis. Office: Meyer Unkovic & Scott LLP 1300 Oliver Bldg Pittsburgh PA 15222-2304 E-mail: jmh@muslaw.com.

HELMS, BOBBY GILLESPIE, music educator, consultant; b. Cordele, Ga., Feb. 4, 1972; s. Marvin Eugene and Dorothy Ruth Helms. BS in Music Edn., Ga. Southwestern State U., Americus, 1994. Choral, band and drama dir. Seminole County Mid. Sch., Donalsonvile, Ga., 1995—97; choral and drama dir. Crisp County Mid. Sch., Cordele, Ga., 1997—. Youth dir. First Presbyn. Ch., Donalsonville, Ga., 1994—96; music dir. Swamp Garvy, Colquitt, Ga., 1995—96; performer Kennedy Ctr. Performing Arts, Washington, 1996, Olympics, Atlanta, 1996; min. of music Springfield Bapt. Ch., Jakin, Ga., 1996—98, Warwick (Ga.) United Meth. Ch., 2001—; dir. Crisp Area Theatrical Stars, Cordele, Ga., 2000—; exec. dir. Miss Cordele/Miss Heart of Ga. Scholarship Pageant; mem. Colquitt/Miller County Arts Coun., 1995—96. Actor: (musical) Dames at Sea, 1993, Pippin, 1992. Recipient Outstanding Graduating Music Maj., Ga. Southwestern State U., 1995, Scholarship, 1990-1994, Directors Award, 1994. Mem.: Nat. Music Educators Conf., Ga. Music Educators. Home: 1393 Musselwhite Rd Cordele GA 31015 Office: Crisp County Middle Sch 1116 24th Ave E Cordele GA 31015 Office Fax: 229-276-3466. Personal E-mail: bgillhelms@musician.org.

HELMS, BYRON ELDON, academic administrator; b. Pitts., June 2, 1951; s. John Donald and Evelyn Marie (Wilson) H.; m. Gale Ann Barbarine Helms, Jan. 23, 1976 (div. Mar. 13. 1978); m. Shari Elisa Besterman Helms, Sept. 16, 1978; children: Brandon, Thomas, Nicholas. Ba in English, Duquesne U., Pitts., 1974. Field underwriter N.Y. Life Ins., Pitts., 1974; asst. legal adminstr. Eckert, Seamans, Cherin & Mellott, Pitts., 1974-77; legal adminstr. Hayward, Cooper, Straub & Cramer, Toledo, 1977-78; adminstr., Cell Biology and Physiology U. Pitts. Sch. Medicine, 1978-95; dir. ORS pre-award contracts U. Ill. at Chicago, Chgo., 1995—. P-30 adminstr. Nat. Inst. Child Health and Human Devel., Washington, 1978-94; dir., treas., bd. govs. Faculty Club U. Pitts., 1985-94; charter mem., officer Duquesne U. Arts and Sci. Alumni Assn., Pitts., 1992-94; dir., bd. mgmt. South Hills YMCA, Pitts., 1994-97; tax acct. H&R Block, 1995—. Editor: University of Pittsburgh Financial System Overview, 1986. Longhouse officer YMCA Indian Guide Program. Pitts., 1987-93; mgmt. officer YMCA Trailblazer Program, Pitts., 1991-96; unit coord. United Way, Pitts., 1978-94; mgr., coach Mt. Lebanon (Pa.) Baseball Assn., 1989-94. Recipient Honor award, 1993 Sy Lerner Meml. award, 1994, South Hills YMCA, Pitts., Cmty. Svc. award United Way, Pitts., 1994, Chancellor's Acd. Profl. award for Excellence, U. Ill. Chgo., 2002. Mem. Soc. Rsch. Adminstrs., Nat. Coun. Univ. Rsch. Adminstrs. (treas. Region IV, 2001-03), Am. Mgmt. Assn., Islam Grotto Mystic Order of Veiled Prophets of Enchanted Realm, Grand Lodge of Pa., Crafton Lodge. Republican. Lutheran. Avocations: manage and coach baseball, soccer, football, basketball. Home: 912 Royal Blackheath Ct Naperville IL 60563-2304 Office: Univ of Illinois at Chicago ORS Pre-award Contracts 1737 W Polk St Chicago IL 60612-7227 E-mail: bhelms@uic.edu.

HELMS, CHARLES MILTON, medical educator, consultant; b. Cambridge, Mass., May 5, 1942; s. James Thoburn and Alice Francis (Cooke) H.; m. Lelia Meredith Biggs, June 26, 1966; children: Emily (dcc.), Wesley, Bethany, Timothy. AB, Cornell U., 1964; PhD, U. Rochester, 1969, MD, 1971. Resident Mass. Gen. Hosp., Boston, 1971-73; rsch. assoc. NIH, Bethesda, 1973-76; prof. U. Iowa, Iowa City, 1976—; chief of staff, dir. clin. outcomes and resource mgmt. U. Iowa Hosps. and Clinics, Iowa City, 2003—. Fellow Robert Wood Johnson Health Policy Fellowship Program, Washington, 1985-86; nat. vaccine adv. com. U.S. HHS, 1992-96, 2002—; adv. com. immunization practices Ctr. Disease Control and Prevention, 1997-01. Contbr. articles to profl. jours. and chpts. to books. Bd. dirs. Goodwill Industries Internat., Inc., 1987 93, 94-98, chmn., 1995-97. Med. officer USPHS, 1973-76. Fellow ACP (Laureate award 1997), Infectious Diseases Soc. Am. (chmn. pub. policy com. 1993-97). Methodist. Office: U Iowa Coll Medicine 200 Hawkins Dr Iowa City IA 52242-1009

HELMS, DAVID ALONZO, lawyer, real estate broker; b. Evanston, Ill., July 5, 1934; s. Hugh Judson and Edna (Peterson-Holmes) H.; div.; children— Donald Anthony, Cybil Estelle. BBA, Northwestern U., 1956; JD, U. Calif.-Berkeley, 1969. Bar: N.Y. 1972, Calif. 1973, Ill., 1974; lic. real estate broker. With Matson Navigation Co., San Francisco, 1958-66, mgr. mktg. rsch., passenger ops., 1963-66; assoc. law firm Paul, Weiss, Rifkind, Wharton & Garrison, Esqs., N.Y.C., 1969-72; spl. asst. to mayor of Berkeley, Calif., 1972-73; dep. sec. state, spl. asst. to gov. Calif., 1973-75; exec. sec. Civil Rights Bar Assn., San Francisco, 1975-80; asst. dean, mem. faculty Chgo.-Kent Coll. Law, Ill. Inst. Tech., Chgo., 1979-81; atty., regional coun. FAA, Des Plaines, Ill., 1982-84; vol. atty. Howard Area and Cabrini-Green Law Clinics, Chgo. Vol. Legal Svcs. Found., 1981— ; sole practice law, David A. Helms & Assocs., Evanston and Chgo., 1981— ; legal advisor to nat. pres. op. Push, 1986. Author: Rehabilitation as a Housing Policy, 1980, The Quality of Life; editor: Civil Rights Law Jour., Vol. I & II, 1974-78. Recipient Image award NAACP, 1974, Disting. Svc. award Chgo. Vol. Legal Asst. Found., 1986, Community Svc. award Op. Push, Chgo., 1986-87. Bd. dirs. Pub. Advocates, San Francisco, 1977-79, Elizabeth B. Hill Meml. Scholarship Fund, Evanston, 1986—. Mem. ABA, Chgo. Coun. Lawyers, Cook County Bar Assn., Chgo. Bar Assn. Baptist (mem. legal com., law clinic 1984—), Civil Rights Bar Assn., Ill. State Bar Assn., Nat. Bar Assn. Democrat. Baptist. Avocations: bicycling, jogging, exercising, antiques, photography.

HELMS, J. LYNN, former government agency administrator; b. DeQueen, Ark., Mar. 1, 1925; s. Frank and Mamie (Johnson) H.; m. Lorraine Bisgard, Mar. 16, 1947; children: Loralyn, Jon, Carole, Zack. Dir. mktg. and sales N. Am. Aviation Co., Columbus, Ohio, 1956-62; group v.p. Bendix Corp., Ann Arbor, Mich., 1962-70; pres. Norden div. United Technologies Corp., Norwalk, Conn., 1970-74, Piper Aircraft Corp., Lock Haven, Pa., 1974-81, chmn. bd., 1978-81; adminstr. FAA, Washington, 1981-83. Dir. Birchminster Industries. Served to lt. col. USMC, 1944-55. Decorated Air medal with oak leaf cluster. Fellow AIAA; mem. Soc. Exptl. Test Pilots.

HELMS, JACK ELWIN, JR., mechanical engineer, educator; b. Hot Springs, Ark., Apr. 16, 1948; s. Jack Elwin and Doris Meryle Helms; m. Mary Elizabeth Rogers, July 5, 1974; children: Daniel Brooks, Emily Beth. BS, Henderson State Coll., 1970; BSc in Mech. Engring., U. of Ark., 1973, MS in Mech. Engring., 1974; PhD, La. State U., 1998. Registered profl. engr., Ark. Bd. of Registration for Profl. Engrs. and Land Surveyors, 1978, La. State Bd. of Reg Profl. Engrs. and Land Surveyors, 1991. Mech. engr. Ethyl Corp., Baton Rouge, 1974—76; product engr. Franklin Electric, Jacksonville, Ark., 1976—77; project engr. Ethyl Corp., Magnolia, Ark., 1977—90, mech. devel. advisor Baton Rouge, 1990—92; advisor transp. Ethyl Corp./Albemarle Corp., Baton Rouge, 1992—. Adj. asst. prof. La. State U., Baton Rouge, 1999—. Contbr. articles to profl. jours. 1st lt. US Army, 1970—72, Viet Nam. Recipient First award, James F. Lincoln Arc Welding Found., 1974; fellow grant, Am. Welding Soc., 1995—98. Mem.: ASME (chmn. 1999—2000), Pi Tau Sigma. Avocation: reading. Home: 17846 General Forrest Avenue Baton Rouge LA 70817 Office: Louisiana State University Room 2506 CEBA Building Baton Rouge LA 70803 Office Fax: 225-578-5924. E-mail: jhelms1@lsu.edu.

HELMS, JANET ELTESER, psychology educator, consultant, researcher; b. Kansas City, Mo., May 19, 1947; d. Brown Jerry and Elteser (Barnes) H. BA in Psychology, U. Mo., Kansas City, 1968, MA in Psychology, 1971; PhD in Psychology, Iowa State U., 1975. Lic. psychologist, Md., D.C. Intern Student Counseling Svc. Iowa State U., Ames, 1973—74, staff psychologist Student Counseling Ctr., 1974—75; asst. prof. dept. edn. Wash. State U., Pullman, 1975—77; asst. prof. psychology dept. So. Ill. U., Carbondale, 1977—81, assoc. prof. psychology, 1981, acting dir. counseling psychology program, 1979—80; asst. prof. psychology U. Md., College Park, 1981—83, assoc. prof. psychology, 1983—91, prof. psychology, 1991—99, co-dir. counseling psychology program, 1997—99; prof. counseling psychology, dir. Race-Culture Inst. Boston Coll., Chestnut Hill, Mass., 2000—. Adj. faculty Student Counseling Ctr. So. Ill. U., Carbondale, 1979—81; part-time therapist Women's Med. Ctr., Washington, 1982—85; affiliate Counseling Ctr. U. Md., College Park, 1984—99; pvt. practice, Washington, 1985—94; presenter in field. Author: Practioners Guide, 1982, (manual) Training Manual for Diagnosing Racial Identity, 1991, A Practitioner's Guide to the Edwards Personal Preference Schedule, Black and White Racial Identity: Theory, Research, and Practice, A Training Manual for Diagnosing Racial Identity in Social Interactions, A Race is a Nice Thing to Have: A Guide to Being a White Person or Understanding the White Persons in Your Life, 1992; editor: Black and White racial Identity, 1990; mem. editorial bd. Jour. Counseling Psychology, 1981—; contbr. chpts. to books and articles to profl. jours. Recipient Janet E. Helms award Columbia U., 1991. Fellow APA (sec. div. 17 1987-90,); mem. Assn. Black Psychologists, African Am. Writers' Guild of D.C. Avocation: writing. Office: Dept Psychology U Md College Park MD 20742-0001

HELMS, JESSE, retired senator; b. Monroe, NC, Oct. 18, 1921; s. Jesse Alexander and Ethel Mae (Helms) H.; m. Dorothy Jane Coble, Oct. 31, 1942; children: Jane (Mrs. Charles R. Knox), Nancy (Mrs. John C. Stuart), Charles. Student, Wingate (N.C.) Jr. Coll., Wake Forest Coll. City editor Raleigh (N.C.) Times, 1941-42; news and program dir. Sta. WRAL, Raleigh, 1948-51; adminstrv. asst. to U.S. senators Willis Smith and Alton Lennon, 1951-53; exec. dir. N.C. Bankers Assn., 1953-60; exec. v.p., vice chmn. Capitol Broadcasting Co., Raleigh, 1960-72; U.S. senator from N.C., 1973—2002; sr. mem. Com. on Fgn. Relations; mem. Rules & Adminstrn. Com., Republican Policy Com. Chmn. bd. Specialized Agrl. Publs., Inc., Raleigh, 1964 72; mem. Raleigh City Council, 1957-61. Bd. dirs. N.C. Cerebral Palsy Hosp., Durham, United Cerebral Palsy N.C., Wake County Cerebral Palsy and Rehab. Center, Raleigh, Camp Willow Run, Littleton, N.C.; former trustee Campbell Coll., Wingate Coll., Meredith Coll., John F. Kennedy Coll. Served with USNR, 1942-45, World War II. Recipient Freedoms Found. award for best TV editorial, 1962, for newspaper article, 1973, So. Bapt. Nat. award for Service to mankind, 1972; Gold medal VFW; Conservative Congressional award, 1976; Liberty award Am. Econ. Council, 1978; Disting. Public Service award Public Service Research Council, 1978; Watchdog of Treasury award; Guardian of Small Bus. award; named Man of Yr. Women for Constl. Govt., 1978; Legislator of Yr. award Nat. Rifle Assn., 1978, Taxpayer's Best Friend award Nat. Taxpayer's Union, 1993; other awards. Mem.: Masons (33d degree), Raleigh Execs. Club (past pres.), Rotary (past pres. Raleigh). Republican. Baptist (Deacon).

HELMS, MICHAEL L. priest; b. LaCrosse, Kans., July 4, 1949; s. Martin William Helms and Ellen LaVone Casey. BA, Cardinal Stritch U., 1990; MDiv, Sacred Heart Sch. Theology, 1990. Lic. auto mechanic Grumbein Motors, Dighton, Kans., 1969—77; lic. truck driver Farmers Co-op, Dighton, 1977—85; assoc. pastor St. Patrick Ch., Great Bend, Kans., 1990—92, St. Mary Ch., Garden City, Kans., 1992—93, pastor Marienthal, Kans., 1993—97, St. John the Bapt. Ch., Spearville, Kans., 1997—99, St. Anthony of Padua Ch., Lakin, Kans., 1999—. Mem.: KC (Knight of Yr. 1985, Grand Knight 1984—85). Democrat. Roman Catholic. Avocations: hiking, fishing, swimming, camping, horseback riding. Office: St Anthony of Padua Cath Ch 600 Soderberg St Lakin KS 67860-0983 Home: 600 Soderberg St Lakin KS 67860-0983 Fax: 620-355-6406.

HELMS, REBECCA J. finance educator; d. Merle Allen and Eleanor Lois Helms. BA, U. Evansville, 1980; MS, Ind. State U., 1985. Assoc. prof. acctg. and bus. adminstrn. Ivy Tech State Coll., Madison, Ind., 1996—. Mem. faculty senate Ivy Tech. State Coll., Madison, Ind., 2001—. Treas. Ohio, Ind. Northern Ky. Regional Theater, Aurora, Ind., 2000—03; com. mem. Dearborn County C. of C., Lawrenceburg, Ind., 1997—99. Mem.: Am. Assn. U. Prof., Am. Assn. U. Women, Nat. Bus. Edn. Assn. Office: Ivy Tech State Coll 590 Ivy Tech Dr Madison IN 47250 Business E-Mail: rhelms@ivytech.edu.

HELMS, ROBERT BRAKE, economist, research director; b. Mobile, Ala., Jan. 12, 1940; s. Osburn Charles and Julia May (Moore) H.; m. Sharon Gay Schliebe, Aug. 8, 1964; children: Elissa Lynelle, Jullanne Nanette BS in Agrl. Adminstrn., Auburn U., 1962; MA in Econs., UCLA, 1966, PhD in Econs., 1973. Asst. prof. Loyola Coll., Balt., 1971-74; dir. health policy studies Am. Enterprise Inst., Washington, 1974-81, resident scholar, dir. health policy studies, 1990; dep. asst. sec. planning and evaluation/health HHS, Washington, 1981-84, acting asst. sec. planning and evaluation, 1984-86, asst. sec. for planning and evaluation, 1986-89; exec. dir. Am. Pharm. Inst., 1989-90. Chmn. Sec.'s Task Force on Hosp. Deregulation, Washington, 1981-83, Sec.'s Task Force on Drug Reimbursement, Washington, 1983-85; mem. White House Working Group on Health Policy and Econs., Washington, 1984-85; mem. steering com. Health Policy Agenda Am. People, Chgo., 1984-88; mem. working party on social policy OECD, Paris, 1984-89. Author: Natural Gas Regulation, 1974; editor: Drug Development and Marketing, 1975, The International Supply of Medicines, 1980, Drugs and Health, 1981, American Health Policy: Critical Issues for Reform, 1993, Health Care Policy and Politics: Lessons From Four Countries, 1993, Health Care Reform: Competition and Controls, 1993, Competitive Strategies in the Pharmaceutical Industry, 1996, Medicare in the Twenty-first Century: Seeking Fair and Efficient Reform, 1999. Served to capt. U.S. Army, 1962-64 Republican. Lutheran. Avocations: tennis, travel, internet. Home: 1404 Foggy Glen Ct Silver Spring MD 20906-2092 Office: Am Enterprise Inst 1150 17th St NW Washington DC 20036-4603 E-mail: rhelms@aei.org.

HELMS, WILLIAM COLLIER, III, lawyer; b. Atlanta, July 11, 1945; s. William Collier and Helen (Meharg) H.; m. Anne Moultrie Ball, July 1, 1967; children: William C. IV, Moultrie B., R. Carter. BA, Emory U., 1967, JD, 1970. Bar: S.C. 1970, U.S. Dist. Ct. S.C. 1971, U.S. Ct. Appeals (4th cir.) 1979. Atty. Barnwell, Whaley, Patterson & Helms, Charleston, S.C., 1970—. Mem. ABA, S.C. Defense Trial Attys. Assn. (exec. com. 1984-87), Am. Bd. Trial Advocates, Internat. Assn. Defense Coun., Rotary. Office: Barnwell Whaley Patterson & Helms 885 Island Park Dr Charleston SC 29492 also: PO Drawer H Charleston SC 29402

HELMS GUBA, LISA MARIE, nursing administrator; b. Sioux City, Iowa, Nov. 24, 1962; d. Dean Edward and Betty Lou Victora (Guenther) H. BA in Nursing, Carroll Coll., Helena, Mont., 1986; postgrad., Calif. State U., Sacramento, 1990-92; MSN, Incarnate Word Coll., 1996. Cert. pediatric nurse. Enlisted U.S. Army, 1981, advanced through grades to maj., 1999, nurse, 1986-90, Calif. Nat. Guard, San Francisco, 1990-92, Rio Linda (Calif.) Union Sch. Dist., 1990-92; enlisted USAF, 1992; mem. A.F. Nurse Corps Wilford Hall Med Ctr., Lackland AFB, Tex., 1992-96; asst. nurse mgr. and critical care aeromed. transp. team nurse dir. Malcolm Grow Hosp., Andrews AFB, Md., 1996-2000; dir. Nurse Triage Ctr., 2001—03; nursing exec. Internal Medicine and Women's Health, Dover AFB, 2003—. Deployed to Guantanamo Bay, Cuba, July to Oct. 1994 for Operation Sea Signal, Operation Safe Haven; provider med. care to Haitian/Cuban migrants. Vol. Big sister/Big brother program United Way. Mem. AACN, Emergency Nurses Assn., Nat. Assn. Flight Nurses. Roman Catholic. E-mail: lisaguba@sprintmail.com.

HELMSING, FREDERICK GEORGE, lawyer; b. Mobile, Ala., Dec. 30, 1940; s. Joseph Herman and Mary Gertrude (Zimlich) H.; m. Margaret Sue Oswalt, Mar. 22, 1969; children: Frederick George, Joseph Guy, Margaret Sue. BS in Acctg., Spring Hill Coll., 1963; JD, U. Ala., 1965; LLM in Taxation, NYU, 1967. Bar: Ala. 1965, Fla. 1989. Assoc. Gallalee, Denniston & Edington, Mobile, 1966-76; ptnr. Helmsing, Leach, Herlong, Newman & Rouse, Mobile, 1976—. Instr. U. South Ala., Mobile, 1969-78; instr. law U. Ala., Mobile, 1982 Dem. chmn. 1st Congl. Dist. Campaign, 1976. Fellow: Am. Coll. Trial Lawyers, mem.: ABA (mem. civil and criminal tax penalties com.), Mobile Area C. of C. (mem. taxation and world trade coms.), Mobile Bar Assn., Mobile County Bar Assn. (treas. 1969), Ala. State Bar Assn. (chmn. tax sect. 1979—80), Athelstan Country Club, Mobile County Club. Roman Catholic. Home: 240 Ridgelawn Dr E Mobile AL 36608-2417 Office: Helmsing Leach Herlong Newman & Rouse 200 LaClede Bldg 150 Government St Mobile AL 36602-3114

HELMSTETTER, CHARLES EDWARD, microbiologist; b. Newark, Oct. 18, 1933; s. Charles Edward and Elsa Simpson (Taylorson) H.; m. Wendy Lee; children— Charles Edward, Michael Frederick, Lee Grisetti. BA, Johns Hopkins U., 1955; MS, U. Mich., 1956, U. Chgo., 1957, PhD, 1961. Scientist NIH, Bethesda, Md., 1961-63; USPHS fellow U. Copenhagen, 1963-64; scientist Roswell Park Meml. Inst., Buffalo, 1964-89, dir. dept. exptl. biology, 1974-89; prof. biol. scis. Fla. Inst. Tech., Melbourne, 1989—. Contbr. articles to sci. jours.; mem. editorial bd.: Jour. Bacteriology, 1970-76, 80-86. Recipient Selman A Waksman award Theobald Smith Soc., 1970; yearly NIH grantee, 1965— Mem. AAAS, Am. Soc. Microbiology, Am. Soc. Biol. Chemists, Sigma Xi. Home: 854 Hawksbill Island Dr Melbourne FL 32937-3850 Office: Fla Inst Tech Dept of Biol Scis Melbourne FL 32901 E-mail: chelmste@fit.edu.

HELMS-VANSTONE, MARY WALLACE, anthropology educator; b. Allentown, Pa., Apr. 15, 1938; d. Samuel Leidich and Mary (Wallace) Helms; divorced. BA, Pa. State U., State College, 1960; MA, U. Mich., 1962, PhD, 1967. Instr. Wayne State U., Detroit, 1965-67; asst. prof. Syracuse (N.Y.) U., 1967-68; lectr. Northwestern U., Evanston and Chgo., Ill., 1969-79; prof. U. N.C., Greensboro, 1979—, head dept. anthropology, 1979-85. Author: Asang: A Miskito Community, 1971, Middle America, 1975, Ancient Panama, 1979, Ulysses' Sail, 1988, Craft and the Kingly Ideal, 1993, Creations of the Rainbow

Serpent, 1995, Access to Origins, 1998, The Curassow's Crest, 2000; contbr. articles to profl. jours. Fellow: Am. Anthrop. Assn.; mem.: Medieval Acad. Am., So. Anthrop. Soc. (pres. 1980—81, procs. editor 1982—94), Am. Ethnological Soc., Am. Soc. Ethnohistory (pres. 1976). Avocations: travel, painting, musical activities, crafts. Office: Univ NC Dept Anthropology PO Box 26170 Greensboro NC 27402-6170

HELMUTH, LES N. fund raising executive, non-profit consultant; b. Mattoon, Ill., July 19, 1955; s. Noah B. and Edna L. (Miller) H.; m. Sylvia Jean Clymer, Dec. 16, 1978; children: Aubrey Diane, Mary Caitlin. BA in Music, Ea. Mennonite U., 1978. Dir. alumni and ch. rels. Ea. Mennonite U., 1978-83; dir. devel. Spokane (Wash.) Symphony Orch., 1983-85, Ea. Mennonite H.S., Harrisonburg, Va., 1985—. V.p. Devel. Systems Internat., Inc., Frederick, Md., 1997—2002; pres. Helmuth Consulting, 2002—. Bd. dirs. Rotary, Harrisonburg, 1993-96, Highland Retreat Camp, Bergton, Va., 1993-99. Mem. Assn. Fundraising Profls. (cert., pres. 1998, nat. bd. dirs.), Va. Fundraising Inst. (bd. dirs. 1999—), Harrisonburg-Rockingham County C. of C., Nat. Com. on Planned Giving, Va. Ind. Schs. Devel. Coun. Mennonite. Avocations: music, golf, tennis, travel. Home: 3158 Rawley Pike Harrisonburg VA 22801-4706 Office: Ea Mennonite HS 801 Parkwood Dr Harrisonburg VA 22802-2416

HELMUTH, NED D. certified financial planner; b. Kokomo, Ind., Mar. 24, 1928; s. Dewey J. and Mildred C. (Norton) H.; m. Arlene J. Schwartz, Oct. 5, 1952 (div. 1971); children: Pamela M. Jones, Michael J., Gretchen L.; m. S. Patricia Broadhurst Tautfest, Jan. 4, 1973; 1 child, Carol E. Green. BS in Mktg., Ind. U., 1952; MS in Fin. Services, Am. Coll., 1981. Cert. fin. planner; chartered fin. cons.; chartered life underwriter. Agt. Equitable Life Assurance Soc., Houston, 1952-53, Lafayette, Ind., 1953-58, Nat. Life Ins. Co., Lafayette, 1958—; prin. Ned D Helmuth Fin. Svcs., Lafayette. Nat. trustee Life Underwriters Tng. Council, Washington, 1975-78. Author: The Client Approach-A Quality Method of Selling, 1963, There's No Fun Like Work, 1989. Bd. dirs. South Side Cmty. Ctr., Lafayette, 1955-57, Lafayette Urban MInistry, 1975-78, Big Bros./Big Sisters, Lafayette, 1981-83, Million Dollar Round Table Internat. Found., 1990-93; life mem. Million Dollar Round Table; mem. adv. bd. Salvation Army, Lafayette, 1985-88; trustee Family Svcs., Inc., Lafayette, 1991-93, vol. Network Ind. U. Found. Cpl. U.S. Army, 1946-48, Korea. Named Underwriter of Yr. Lafayette Ind. Assn. Life Underwriters, 1972, Hoosier Underwriter of Yr. Ind. State Assn. Life Underwriters, 1972. Mem.: Hoosier Hills Estate Plnning Coun., Fin. Planning Assn., Am. Soc. CLUs (bd. dirs., v.p. 1965—68), Nat. Assn. Ins. and Fin. Advisors, Rotary Club, Phi Gamma Delta. Avocations: jogging, old Porsches. Home: 612 Winslow Farm Dr Bloomington IN 47401-4590 Office: Ned D Helmuth Fin Svcs 14 N 2d St Ste 200B Lafayette IN 47901-1204 also: 7037 S Tamiami Trl Ste A Sarasota FL 34231-5552 also: 4325 E 3rd St Bloomington IN 47401-5551

HELOISE, columnist, lecturer, broadcaster, author; b. Waco, Tex., Apr. 15, 1951; d. Marshal H. and Heloise K. (Bowles) Cruse; m. David L. Evans, Feb. 13, 1981. BS in Math. and Bus, S.W. Tex. State U., 1974. Owner, pres. Heloise, Inc. Asst. to columnist mother, Heloise, 1974-77, upon her death took over internationally syndicated column, 1977; author: Hints from Heloise, 1980, Help from Heloise, 1981, Heloise's Beauty Book, 1985, All-New Hints from Heloise, 1989, Heloise: Hints for a Healthy Planet, 1990, Heloise from A to Z, 1992, Household Hints for Singles, 1993, Hints for All Occasions, 1995, In The Kitchen With Heloise, 2000, Heloise Conquers Stinks & Stains, 2002; featured on Ask Heloise, Talk Am. Radio Network; contbg. editor Good Housekeeping mag., 1983, Speaker for the House; co-founder, 1st co-pilot Mile Pie in the Sky Balloon Club. Mem. Good Neighbor Coun. Tex.-Mex.; sponsor Nat. Smile Week. Recipient Mental Health Mission award Nat. Mental Health Assn., 1990, The Carnegians Good Human Rels. award, 1994. Mem. AFTRA, SAG, Women in Comm. (Headliner 1994), Tex. Press Women, Internat. Women's Forum, Women in Radio and TV, Confrerie de la Chaine des Rotisseurs (bailli San Antonio chpt.), Ordre Mondial des Gourmets De'Gustateurd de U.S.A., Death Valley Yacht and Racket Club, Zonta. Home: PO Box 795000 San Antonio TX 78279-5000

HELPERT-NUNEZ, RUTH ANNE, clinical social worker, psychotherapist; b. Rosebud, Tex., Jan. 7, 1956; d. Otto Henry and Lorene Margaret (Hoelscher) Helpert; m. J.W. Will Nunez. BS with high honors in Social Work, U. Tex., Austin, 1978, MS in Social Work, 1981. Lic. master social worker-advanced clin. practitioner; lic. marriage and family therapist, Tex. Student intern Child Protective Svcs. Tex. Dept. Human Svcs., Austin, 1978, child protective svcs. specialist Killeen and Belton, 1979-80; grad. student intern Austin Child Guidance Ctr., 1981; caseworker Heart of Tex. Region Mental Health Mental Retardation, Waco, Tex., 1981-83; child protective svcs. specialist Tex. Dept. Human Svcs., Austin, 1983-84; caseworker DayGlo Family Treatment program Austin-Travis County Mental Health Mental Retardation Ctr., 1984-88; therapist, clin. social worker Anthony W. Arden, Ph.D & Assocs., Bryan, Tex., 1989-90, Thomas Edwards, Ph.D., P.C., Bryan, 1990-95; therapist/clin. social worker Brazos Valley Cmty. Action Agy.-Family Health Svcs.: Psychology Svcs., Bryan, 1996-98; contract svcs. provider Bryan, 1998—; therapist. clin. social worker Los Hermanos Ranch, Bryan, 1998-99; pvt. practice psychotherapy Bryan, 1999—. Clin. vol. Scotty's House Child Advocacy Ctr., 1992—; field instr. U. Houston Grad. Sch. Social Work, 1995-96. Bd. dirs. Toy Libr., College Station, Tex., 1989; mem. spkrs. bur. Child Advocacy Resource and Edn. Coalition, 1989-92, v.p., 1991. Mem.: NASW (diplomate in clin. social work, qualified clin. social worker, chmn. Brazos Valley unit 1990—94, bd. dirs. Tex. chpt. 1990—94, exec. com. 1993—94, chmn. profl. stds. com. 1993—94, Lifetime Achievement award Brazos Valley unit 1999), Acad. Cert. Social Workers, Phi Kappa Phi, Phi Theta Kappa. Democrat. Avocations: handbuilding pottery, gardening, renaissance music, playing recorder. Home: 10004 Edge Cut Off Rd Hearne TX 77859-9322 Office: 3608 E 29th St Ste 205 Bryan TX 77802-3814

HELPHAND, BEN J. actuary, consultant; b. Columbus, Nebr., Feb. 2, 1915; s. David and Bess (Krupinsky) H.; m. Bessie H. Stine, Sept. 16, 1937; 1 child, Cathy Dee. Student, U. Nebr., 1932-35; BA, U. Iowa, 1936, MA, 1937. Actuarial asst. Pacific Mut. Life Ins. Co., Newport Beach, Calif., 1937-42, v.p., actuary, 1947-80; corp. actuary Best Life Assurance Co., Irvine, Calif., 1980-87. Actuary Dept. Ins. State S.C., Columbia, 1946-47 Served to maj. USAAF, 1942-46. Fellow Soc. Actuaries (bd. govs.); mem. actuarial clubs Pacific States (past pres.), Los Angeles (past pres.), Am. Acad. Actuaries, Sigma Xi. Home: 1321 Keel Dr Corona Del Mar CA 92625-1238

HELPINGSTINE, DANIEL WALLACE, organization official, freelance writer; b. Hammond, Ind., Apr. 16, 1953; s. Wallace William and Jean (Janerski) H.; m. Delia Lynn Szendrey, Sept. 10, 1977; 1 child, Leah Jo. BA in Polit. Sci., Ind. U., Gary, 1977, B Gen. Studies in Labor Studies, 1982. Gen. laborer Inland Steel Co., East Chicago, Ind., 1978-82; bus. and labor corr., stringer The Times, Hammond, 1982-84; employee specialist Ind. Employment Security Divsn., Hammond, 1984-89; area supr. Lake County Assn. for Retarded, Gary, 1989-90; program mgr. job readiness and placement Chgo. Lighthouse, 1990—. Contbr. articles to newspaper, short stories to lit. publs. Recipient 1st place awards and cert. for novel and short stories Mississippi Valley Writers Conf., 1981, 92, 85, 86, 96, 98, 99. Office: Chgo Lighthouse 1850 W Roosevelt Rd Chicago IL 60608 E-mail: wallynn@aol.com.

HELPPIE, CHARLES EVERETT, III, financial consultant; b. Highland Park, Mich., Feb. 1, 1952; s. Charles Everett and Patricia Elizabeth (Cote) H.; m. Vali Renée Terhune, July 29, 1972. Student, Ea. Mich. U., 1970-73. Sales rep., sales mgr. Mich. Autosonics, Inc., Ann Arbor, 1972-74; mgr. World Wide Movers, Inc., Ypsilanti, Mich., 1973; sales rep. Godfrey Moving & Storage Co., Ann Arbor, 1974-78; account exec. Merrill Lynch Pierce Fenner & Smith, Detroit, 1978-83, E. F. Hutton, Ann Arbor, 1983-87; asst. br. mgr. Shearson Lehman Hutton, Ann Arbor, 1987-90; fin. cons. Shearson Lehman Bros., Detroit, 1991-92; investment exec. Paine Webber, Inc., Farmington Hills, Mich., 1992-99, br. office ins. coord., 1993—, accounts v.p., 1999-2000, v.p. investments, divisional life ins. cons. Birmingham, Mich., 2000—. Artist and engr. auto. models including MPC World Champion, 1977 (1st Pl. 1977). Campaign worker Dem. Com., Ypsilanti, 1965-71; organizer Anti-War Workshops, Ypsilanti, 1968-70; pres., organizer Fin. Svcs. Softball League, Detroit, 1979-83; mem. Colonial Leadership Coun., Boston. Mem. Am. Funds Group (All-Am. Team), Nameless Nat. Luminaries (founder, chartered), Detroit Tigers Fantasy Camp (chartered), Key and Kite Club, Aim Summit Club (chmns. coun. 1992—), Franklin Group of Funds, Paine Webber Premium Producers Guild, Paine Webber Preservation Planning Inst. (cons. forum "Top 75" mem. managed and retirement accounts svcs.), Paine Webber Pacesetter Club. Avocations: model car building and collecting, automobile and auto racing photography, baseball. Office: Paine Webber Inc 210 S Old Woodward Ave Ste 250 Birmingham MI 48009-6114

HELPRIN, MARK, author; b. N.Y.C., June 28, 1947; s. Morris A. and Eleanor (Lynn) H.; m. Lisa Kennedy, June 28, 1980; children: Alexandra Morris, Olivia Kennedy. AB, Harvard U., 1969, AM, 1972; postgrad., Magdalen Coll., Oxford (Eng.) U., 1976-77. Sr. fellow Claremont Inst. Study of Statesmanship and Polit. Philosophy. Author: A Dove of the East and Other Stories, 1975, Refiner's Fire, 1977, Ellis Island and Other Stories, 1981, Winter's Tale, 1983, Swan Lake, 1989, A Soldier of the Great War, 1991, Memoir from Antproof Case, 1995, A City in Winter, 1996, The Veil of Snows, 1997; contbg. editor The Wall Street Jour. Mem. Coun. on Fgn. Rels.; adviser in def. and fgn. rels. Rep. presdl. nominee Robert Dole. Served with Israeli Army and Air Force, 1972-73. Recipient Prix de Rome, Am. Acad. and Inst. Arts and Letters, 1982, Nat. Jewish Book award, 1982. Fellow Am. Acad. in Rome.

HELQUIST, PAUL M. chemistry educator, researcher; b. Duluth, Minn., Mar. 5, 1947; s. Paul O. and Marie E. (Parent) H.; m. Christie M. Wick, June 11, 1970; children: Sandra Ann, Kristina Ann. BSc, U. Minn., Duluth, 1969; MSc, PhD, Cornell U., 1971; PhD honoris causa, U. Uppsala, Sweden, 1988. Postdoctoral fellow Harvard U., Cambridge, Mass., 1973-74; asst. prof. SUNY, Stony Brook, 1974-80, assoc. prof., 1980-84, prof., 1984-86, U. Notre Dame, Ind., 1986—, chmn. dept. chemistry and biochemistry, 1988-93. Mem. exam. bd. Ednl. Testing Svc., Princeton, N.J., 1989-98; cons. Proctor and Gamble Pharms., 1990—, Circagen, 1999-2002; head Walther Cancer Rsch. Ctr. Drug Devel., 1998—; dir. NSF workshops for coll. organic chemistry tchrs., 1999—. Author: Synthetic Organic Chemistry: Modern Methods and Strategy, 1989. Recipient Catacosinos Cancer Rsch. award, 1979, Walther Cancer Inst. award, 2001; grantee NIH, 1977—, NSF, 1979—; Am.-Scandinavian Found. fellow, 1982. Mem. Am. Chem. Soc. (instr. 1981—, Exceptional Achievement award 1991). Avocations: foreign languages, classical music, model building, amateur astronomy. Office: U Notre Dame Dept Chemistry & Biochemistry Notre Dame IN 46556 E-mail: helquist.1@nd.edu.

HELSABECK, ERIC H. emergency physician; b. Winston-Salem, N.C. s. Charles Robert and Ruth Haigler H.; m. Judy Ann Hinkleman; children: Keith, Graham. BS, U. N.C., 1971, MD, 1975. Intern Wilson Meml. Hosp., Johnson City, N.Y., 1975-76, resident in family practice, 1977-78; pvt. practice Bath, N.Y., 1978-82; staff emergency physician Randolph Hosp., Asheboro, N.C., 1983—. Mem.: Am. Coll. Emergency Physicians. Home: 1607 Brevard Dr Asheboro NC 27205-4105

HELSBY, KEITH R. brokerage house executive; BA in bus. adminstrn., Gettysburg Coll., 1966. Audit divsn. Deloitte Haskins and Sells; dir. internal audits N.Y. Stock Exch., mem. mgmt. com., v.p. fin., 1989—95, sr. v.p. and CFO, 1995—. Office: NY Stock Exch Attn: Ray Pellecchia 11 Wall St New York NY 10005*

HELSER, MARILYN A. business educator; b. Lima, Ohio, Oct. 4, 1941; d. Marion Jacob and Helen Elizabeth (Wolfe) Driver; m. George E. Helser, Nov. 25, 1966; children: George Kurtis, Jeffrey Jacob, Gregory Lewis, Sara Elizabeth. BS, Bluffton (Ohio) Coll., 1963; MSE, U. Dayton, 1993. Tchr. Toledo City Schs., 1963-66, Lima City Schs., 1966-68; prof. Lima Tech. Coll., 1972—. Author: (handbook) Document Production, 1991, Medical Document Production, 1993, Keyboarding/Formatting, 1993; (study guide and video) Business English I, 1995. Mem. sch. bd. Allen E. Local Sch., Lafayette, Ohio, 1987—. Mem. Profl. Secs. Internat., Nat. Bus. Edn. Assn., Ohio Sch. Bd. Assn., Ohio Bus. Tchrs. Assn., Lima Tech. Coll. Faculty Assn. (sec. 1992-93). Home: 10720 Lafayette Rd Harrod OH 45850-9435 Office: Lima Tech Coll 4240 Campus Dr Lima OH 45804-3576

HELSLEY, ALEXIA JONES, archivist; b. Louisville, Ky., Sept. 9, 1945; d. George Alexander and Evelyn (Masden) J.; m. Terry Lynn Helsley, Oct. 11, 1969; children: Cassandra Keiser Paschal, Jacob Henry. BA in History, Furman U., 1967; MA in History, U. S.C., 1974; cert., Modern Archives Inst., Washington, 1978, S.C. Exec. Inst., Columbia, 1995. Archival asst. S.C. Dept. Archives and History, Columbia, 1968-69, archivist I, 1969-72, asst. reference archivist, 1972-76, supr. reference and rsch., 1976-88, dir. pub. programs divsn., 1988-96, dir. edn., 1996-99; dir. spl. projects, editor Biograph. Directory S.C. House of Reps., 1999—. Historian Am. Lodging Resources, Inc.; rsch. fellow Inst. So. Studies, U. S.C., 2001-02; adj. faculty Midlands Tech. Coll., 2001-02, U. S.C., Aiken, 2002— Author: Harbison: an Historical Sketch, 1986, First Baptist Church of Irmo: Historical Overview, 1992, Researching Family History: A Workbook, 1992, 96, The 1840 Revolutionary Pensioners of Henderson County, North Carolina, 1996, Unsung Heroines of the Carolina Frontier, 1997, Silent Cities: Cemeteries and Classrooms, 1997, South Carolina's African American Confederate Pensioners, 1923-1925, 1998, South Carolinians in the War for American Independence, 2000; co-author: The Many Faces of Slavery, 1999, S.C. Court Records, 1993, The Changing Face of S.C. Politics, 1993, African American Genealogical Research, 1997; contbr. articles to profl. jours. Chair social and recreation com. Harbison Cmty. Assn., Columbia, S.C., 1984-89; trustee S.C. Hall of Fame, Myrtle Beach, 1988-96; vice-chair Columbia Quincentennial Commn. S.C., 1989-93; pres. Richland Sertoma, Columbia, 1998-99; bd. vis. Presbyn. Coll., 2001-2003. Recipient Willie Parker Peace History Book award, 1997, Lifetime Achievement award, SC Archival Assn., 2002; named to Hon. Order of Ky. Cols., Richland Sertoman of Yr., 2000. Mem.: S.C. Coun. for Social Studies, S.C. Hist. Assn., Soc. Am. Archivists (chair reference, access, outreach sect. 1981—83), Joseph McDowell Nat. Soc. DAR, Pace Soc. Am. (trustee), Henderson County Geneal. and Hist. Soc. (v.p. 1998—2003, charter). Baptist. Home: 1 Northpine Ct Columbia SC 29212-2911 Office: SC Dept Archives History 8301 Parklane Rd Columbia SC 29223-4905 E-mail: helsley@scdah.state.sc.us., alexiahelsley@yahoo.com.

HELSON, HENRY BERGE, publisher, retired mathematics educator; b. Lawrence, Kan., June 2, 1927; s. Harry and Lida G. (Anderson) H.; m. Ravenna W. Mathews, June 12, 1954; children— David M., Ravenna A., Harold E. AB, Harvard U., 1947, PhD, 1950. Lectr. U. Uppsala, Sweden, 1950-51; instr., then asst. prof. math. Yale, 1951-55; mem. faculty U. Calif. at Berkeley, 1955—, prof. math.; retired, 1993. Vis. prof. Swedish univs., spring 1962, U. Paris, Orsay, France, 1966-67, U. Sci. and Tech., Kumasi, Ghana, spring 1969, U. du Languedoc, Montpellier, France, 1971-72, Marseille, France, fall 1976; vis. prof. Indian Statis. Inst., Calcutta, spring 1980; lectr. St. Mary's Coll. of Calif., 2001-02. Author: Invariant Subspaces, 1964, Harmonic Analysis, 1983, The Spectral Theorem, 1986, Linear Algebra, 1990, Honors Calculus, 1992, Calculus and Probability, 1998. Mem. Soc. Friends; treas. Friends Com. on Legis. Calif., 1989-95. Fellow Sheldon Traveling fellow, Warsaw and Wroclaw, Poland, 1947—48. Home: 15 The Crescent Berkeley CA 94708-1701 E-mail: helson@math.berkeley.edu.

HELSPER, JAMES THOMAS, surgical oncologist, researcher, educator; b. Mpls., Mar. 29, 1924; s. Salvius John and Gretchen Louise (Gleissner) H.; m. Mildred Ann Belinsky, June 11, 1951 (div. Aug. 1972); children: James Thomas Jr., Richard Scott, Paige Carla; m. Carolyn Marie Harrison, Dec. 26, 1975; 1 child, Brian Harrison Helsper. BS, St. Vincent Coll., 1945; MD, Jefferson Med. Coll., 1947; postgrad., U. Pa., 1949-50. Lic. physician, Calif., N.Y., N.J., Fla., Mass. Intern Med. Ctr., Jersey City, N.J., 1947-48, residency, 1948-49; resident in surgery U.S. Naval Hosp., Portsmouth, Va., 1951-52; chief resident in surgery Queens Gen. Hosp., N.Y., 1952-53; asst. resident in surgery Meml. Ctr. for Cancer and Allied Diseases, N.Y.C., 1953-54, spl. fellow head and neck svc., 1954, sr. resident in surgery, 1955-57; surg. staff Huntington Meml. Hosp., Pasadena, Calif., Kenneth Norris Jr. Cancer Hosp.; attending surgeon L.A. County U. So. Calif. Med. Ctr.; assoc. clin. prof. surgery U. So. Calif. Sch. Medicine, L.A., prof. surgery, 1996—; head melanoma site team U. So. Calif. Comprehensive Cancer Ctr., L.A., mem. head and neck site team; asst. clin. prof. surgery Loma Linda (Calif.) U. Sch. Medicine; chmn. tumor bd. L.A. County Gen. Hosp., 1963, 70, 81-82; cancer liaison fellow Am. Coll. Surgeons L.A. County/USC Med. Ctr., Norris Cancer Hosp. Head melanoma site team U. So. Calif. Comprehensive Cancer Ctr., L.A., head and neck site team. Capt. USNR. Mem.: L.A. Surg. Soc., L.A. County Med. Assn. (mem. com. on cancer, jr. sect. pres. 1966), Soc. Head and Neck Surgeons (pres. 1988—89), Soc. Surg. Oncology (James Ewing Soc.), Internat. Union Against Cancer (mem. sci. com.), Pasadena Med. Soc., L.A. Acad. Medicine, N.Y. Acad. Medicine, Calif. Med. Assn. (mem. com. on cancer), Am. Soc. Clin. Oncology, Am. Radium Soc., Am. Fedn. Clin. Oncologic Socs., Am. Cancer Soc. (Calif. divsn., L.A. county unit chmn. profl. edn. com. 1965—67, v.p. for program 1967—69, mem. bd. dirs. 1967—, pres. elect 1969—70, mem. pub. info. com. 1969—71, pres. 1970—71, chmn. nom. com. 1971—72, mem. profl. edn. com. 1971—76, Calif. divsn. chmn. profl. edn. com. 1974—75, mem. Macomber Legacy Com. 1975—82, v.p. for program 1984—, pres. elect 1985—86, pres. 1986—87, mem. rsch. com. 1987—88, named Man of Yr. 1991), ACS, AMA, Econ. Round Table L.A., Quiet Birdmen. Avocations: flying, photography, sailing. Office: 1441 Eastlake Ave Los Angeles CA 90089-0112

HELSTAD, ORRIN L. lawyer, legal educator; b. Ettrick, Wis., Feb. 9, 1922; s. Albert J. and Martha H. (Gimse) H.; m. Charlotte Dart Ankeney, June 26, 1954. Student, U. Wis., La Crosse, 1940-42; BS, U. Wis., Madison, 1948, LL.B., 1950. Bar: Wis. 1950. Research assoc. Wis. Legis. Council, 1950-61; assoc. prof. law U. Wis., Madison, 1961-65, prof., 1965-85; assoc. dean U. Wis. (Sch. Law), 1972-75, acting dean, 1975-76, dean, 1976-83, dean emeritus, 1985—, prof. emeritus, 1985—. Mem. consumer advisory council Wis. Dept. Agr., 1970-72; vice chmn. Wis. Supreme Ct. com. on the State bar, 1977; mem. Fed. Jud. Nominating Commn. Western Dist. Wis., 1979-83 Contbr. articles to law revs.; co-author, editor: Wisconsin Uniform Comml. Code Handbook, 1965, 1971. Recipient Disting. Svc. award Wis. Law Alumni Assn., 1991. Fellow Am. Bar Found.; mem. State Bar Wis., ABA (council sect. on local govt. law 1975-79), Wis. Bar Assn., Dane County Bar Assn., Am. Judicature Soc. Unitarian Universalist. Home: 8 Sebring Ct Madison WI 53719-3521

HELSTEDT, GLADYS MARDELL, vocational education educator; b. Forest City, Iowa, May 7, 1926; d. Gordon Ingeman and Pearl Gertrude (Hauan) Field; m. Lowell Lars Helstedt, Aug. 26, 1950; children: Mardell Lynn, David Lowell, Marilee Pearl, Marcia Kay. AA, Waldorf Coll., 1945; BS, Mankato State U., 1969. Bus. tchr. Crystal Lake (Iowa) H.S., Crystal Lake, Iowa, 1945-47; parish sec. St. Paul's Lutheran Ch., Mpls., 1949-51; bus. tchr. Sioux Valley High Sch., Lake Park, Iowa, 1969-70, Radcliffe (Iowa) High Sch., 1970-76; activity dir. Marinuka Manor Care Ctr., Galesville, Wis., 1976-79; bus. tchr. Galesville High Sch., 1979-80; asst. dir. Ret. Sr. Vol. Program, Whitehall, Wis., 1981-83; coord., instr. Western Wis. Tech. Inst., La Crosse, 1984, sr. instr. Tex. State Tech. Coll., Sweetwater, 1985-92; ret., 1992. Dir. music Salem Luth. Ch., Roscoe, Tex., 1985-90. Mem. Philos. Edn. Orgn. (pres. 1982-84), Tex. State Tech. Coll. Women (sec. 1991-92), Bus. Profls. Am. (advisor 1986-92). Avocations: plants, dolls, music, travel, knitting. Home: 570 Quant Ave N Lakeland MN 55043-9545

HELSTERN, LINDA LIZUT, language educator, poet; b. Phila., Aug. 21, 1948; d. Otto Henry and Harriet Lucile (Stillwell) Lizut; m. Richard Andrew Helstern, Aug. 21, 1977; 1 child, Amina Katherine. BA, Hamline U., 1970; MA, U. N.Mex., 1995; PhD, So. Ill. U., 2001. Libr. asst. N.Mex. State Libr., Santa Fe, 1970-71; tchg. asst. dept. English U. N.Mex., Albuquerque, 1971-72; advt./pub. rels. profl. The Barbers, Hairstyling for Men, Mpls., 1972-73; receptionist Leo J. Shapiro & Assoc., Chgo., 1973; devel. asst. Am. Diabetes Assn., Chgo., 1974-75; youth coord. Nat. Multiple Sclerosis Soc., Chgo., 1975-76; comm. mgr. Trans Union Sys. Corp., Chgo., 1976-77; project mgr. Shawnee Design Studio, Carbondale, Ill., 1977-79; project developer coal miner's respiratory disease program Shawnee Health Svc. and Devel. Corp., Carbondale, 1979-81; corp. devel. asst. Coal Rsch. Ctr. So. Ill. U., Carbondale, 1982-86, pub. info. specialist Coll. Engring., 1986-91, asst. to dean for external affairs Coll. Engring., 1991—2002; lectr. English U. Tex. Pan Am., 2002—03, asst. prof. English, 2003—. Adj. instr. English, So. Ill. U., Carbondale, 1998-99, adj. instr. women's studies, SIUC, 2002. Author: (song cycle) Unity Chamber Concert Series, 1993; rschr. TV documentary for Sta. KRWG-TV, 1977; writer, editor: (slide film) Governor Task Force on the Future of Illinois, 1979; author numerous poems. Pres. Jackson County LWV, Carbondale, 1983-87; dir. Girl Scout Day Camp, Carbondale, 1991. Competitive residency fellow Vallecitos Retreat/Witter Bynner Found., 1994. Mem. MLA, Western Lit. Assn., Assn. for Study of Am. Indian Lit., Soc. for Study of Multi-Ethnic Lit. of US, Assn. for Study of Lit. and Environ., Hemingway Soc., Phi Kappa Phi. Home: 289 Egret Lake Rd Carbondale IL 62901-8232 Office: Dept English Univ Tex-Pan American Edinburg TX 78539 E-mail: helsternl@panam.edu.

HELSTROM, CARL WILHELM, electrical engineering educator; b. Easton, Pa., Feb. 22, 1925; s. Carl Wilhelm H.; m. Barbro Elisabet Dahlbom, Oct. 13, 1956; children: Lars Vilhelm, Nils Stefan. BS in Engring Physics, Lehigh U., 1947; MS in Physics, Calif. Inst. Tech., 1949, PhD in Physics, 1951. Adv. mathematician Westinghouse Rsch. Labs, Pitts., 1951-66; prof. U. Calif.-San Diego, La Jolla, 1966-91, prof. emeritus, 1991—. Author: Statistical Theory of Signal Detection, 1968, Quantum Detection and Estimation Theory, 1976, Probability and Stochastic Processes for Engineers, 1991, Elements of Signal Detection and Estimation, 1995. With USNR, 1944—46. Recipient Quantum Comm. award, 1996. Fellow IEEE (editor Trans. on Info. Theory jour. 1967-71, Centennial medal 1984, Third Millennium medal 2000), Optical Soc. Am.; mem. Phi Beta Kappa.

HELTMAN, ROBERT FAIRCHILD, distribution executive; b. Lakewood, Ohio, May 11, 1934; s. Fairchild Long and Sarah Agnes (Fleck) H.; m. Melody Elaine Valentine, Feb. 14, 1992; children: Ken, Kathy, Daniel, Kim, Karen, David, Kerri, Summer. BS, Oberlin Coll., 1956. Mktg. & exec. staffing mgr. GE Co., 1960-88; pres. Leading Edge Products & Svcs. Co., Hendersonville, N.C., 1987—. Contbr. articles to mags. Treas., pres. Homeowner's Assn., Palatine, Ill.; chmn. bd. dirs. Erie (Pa.) City and County Librs.; pres. Adv. Coun. on Vocat. Edn. Pa.; chmn., bd. dirs. Hendersonville County Food Co-op; bd. dirs. Something Special Enterprises & Career Opportunities, Inc. Mem. Masons. Republican. Lutheran. Achievements include invention of Ultimate Hiking Staff; BBOBB Heltman Hollowing Tool; Heirloom Genealogical Baby Cradle. Avocations: hiking, woodworking, reading, gardening, photography. Office: Leading Edge Products & Svcs Co PO Box 545 Hendersonville NC 28793-0545 E-mail: bobh@leadingedgepands.com.

HELTNE, PAUL GREGORY, research scholar; b. Lake Mills, Iowa, July 4, 1941; s. Palmer Tilford and Grace Katherine (Hanson) H.; children— Lisa, Christian. BA, Luther Coll., Decorah, Iowa, 1962; PhD, U. Chgo., 1970. Asst. prof. Johns Hopkins U., Balt., 1970-82; dir. Chgo. Acad. Scis., 1982-91, pres., 1991—99, pres. emeritus, 1999—; co-dir. Nature Polis and Ethics Project, 1994—2002; sr. rsch. scholar Ctr. for Humans and Nature, 2003—. Cons. WHO, Am. Petroleum Inst. Author, editor: Neotropical Primates: Status and Conservation, 1976, Lion-Tailed Macaque, 1985, Science Learning in the Informal Setting, 1988, Understanding Chimpanzees, 1989, Chimpanzee Cultures, 1994. Trustee Balt. Zool. Soc., 1972-82. Mem. Am. Assn. Mus. (edn. task force, accreditation site visitor), Assn. Sci. Mus. Dirs. (sec.-treas. 1986-96), Internat. Primatology Soc., Soc. Integrative and Comparative Biology, Soc. for Study Evolution, Systematic Zoology Soc. Office: Ctr for Humans and Nature 2430 N Cannon Dr Chicago IL 60614

HELTON, ARTHUR CLEVELAND, advocate, lawyer, scholar, writer; b. St. Louis, Jan. 24, 1949; s. Arthur Cleveland Sr. and Marjorie Jane (Russell) H.; m. Jacqueline Dean Gilbert, May 14, 1982. AB, Columbia Coll., 1971; JD, NYU, 1976. Bar: N.Y. 1977, U.S. Dist. Ct. (so. and ea. dists.) N.Y. 1977, U.S. Ct. Appeals (2d cir.) 1978, U.S. Ct. Appeals (1st cir.) 1980, U.S. Ct. Appeals (4th and 9th cir.) 1988, U.S. Ct. Appeals (5th, 7th and 11th cir.) 1989, U.S. Ct. Appeals (3d cir.) 1994, U.S. Supreme Ct. 1980. Assoc. appellate counsel Legal Aid Soc., N.Y.C., 1976-79; assoc. Mailman & Rutheizer, N.Y.C., 1979-82; dir. refugee project Lawyers Com. Human Rights, N.Y.C., 1982-94; dir. migration programs, forced migration projects Open Soc. Inst., N.Y.C., 1994-99; vis. prof. internat. rels. Ctrl. European U., 1997-2000; course co-dir. Summer U. Ctrl. European U., 1999-2000. Adj. prof. law NYU, 1986-99; sr. fellow Coun. Fgn. Rels., 1999-2003; dir. Peace and Conflict Studies, Coun. Fgn. Rels., 2001-2003; chair U.S.A. br. Internat. Social Svcs., 2000; adj. faculty Columbia Law Sch., 2001-2003; pres. Strategic Humanitarian Action and Rsch., 2002—. Author: The Price of Indifference: Refugees and Humanitarian Action in the New Century, 2002; (with others) Forced Displacement and Human Security in the Former Soviet Union: Law and Policy, 2000; The Rights of Aliens and Refugees: The Basic ACLU Guide to Alien and Refugees Rights, 1990; editor:

Transnational Pubs., Inc.; series editor Free Movement, Forced Displacement and Human Security; contbr. articles to profl. jours. Recipient Pub. Svc. award Law Alumni Assn. NYU, 1987, Immigration and Refugee Policy award, Ctr. for Migration Studies, 2000, award for Distinction in Internat. Law and Affairs N.Y. State Bar Assn., 2002; individual grantee The German Marshall Fund, The Ford Found. Fellow Am. Bar Found.; mem. Coun. Fgn. Rels., ABA (co-chmn. immigration and nationality law com. sect. internat. law and practice 1997-2002, coord. com. on immigration law 1997-2000, adv. com. immigration pro bono devel. and bar activation project 2000-02, counselor 2002-2003, commn. on immigration policy, practice and pro bono 2002-2003, goal VIII officer 2003—), Internat. Bar Assn., Assn. Bar N.Y.C. (chmn. com. on immigration and nationality law 1982-85, legal assistance com. 1985-88, civil rights com. 1988-91, internat. human rights com. 1991-94, internat. law com. 1995-98, adminstrv. law com. 1999-2002), Pub. internatl. imm., naturalization, and customs. Home: 245 7th Ave Apt 10B New York NY 10001-7301 Office: Coun Fgn Rels 58 E 68th St New York NY 10021-5953 E-mail: ArthurHelton@msn.com., ahelton@cfr.org.

HELTON, LUCILLE HENRY HANRATTIE, academic administrator; b. Ft. Worth, Mar. 2, 1942; d. P.D. and Virginia (Clark) Henry; m. Wayne Hanrattie, June 26, 1965 (div. Apr. 1986); children: Clark, Chris; m. William M. Helton, Jr., Mar. 19, 1988. BA, So. Meth. U., 1964; MEd, U. Pitts., 1968; cert. in adminstrn., William Paterson Coll., 1984; cert. in mid-mgmt., Tex. Christian U., 1987. Cert. elem. tchr. N.J., Pa., Tex. Nat. field sec. Kappa Kappa Gamma Sorority, Columbus, Ohio, 1964-65; elem. tchr. Pitts. Bd. Edn., 1965-69; co-dir, chmn. dept. maths. Assn. Children with Learning Disabilities Sch., Pitts., 1969-72; tchr. elem., secondary, gifted and remedial and home instrn. programs West Milford (N.J.) Bd. Edn., 1976-84; prin., exec. dir. Hill Sch., Ft. Worth, 1984-2001, exec. dir. Learning Ctr. North Tex., 2001—. Mem. exec. bd. Tex. Assn. Non-pub. Schs. Mem. ASCD, Tex. Ind. Sch. Consortium, Learning Disabilities Assn. Am., Leadership Tex., Coalition for Spl. Needs Students, Orton Dyslexia Soc., Forum Ft. Worth. Democrat. Methodist. Avocations: reading, biking, traveling, nature. Office: The Learning Ctr 1701 River Run Ste 710 Fort Worth TX 76107

HELTON, MAX EDWARD, minister, consultant, religious organization executive; b. Conasauga, Tenn., Nov. 24, 1940; s. Herman Marshall and Nellie Gladys (Haddock) H.; m. Jean Bateman, June 8, 1962; children: Elaine, Melanie, Crista, Becky. BA, Tenn. Temple U., 1963; DD (hon.), Hyles-Anderson Coll., 1973. Ordained minister Bapt. Ch., 1963. Sr. pastor Koolau Bapt. Ch., Kaneohe, Hawaii, 1964-71; exec. v.p. Hyles-Anderson Coll., Crown Point, Ind., 1971-77; sr. pastor Grace Bible Ch., White Plains, N.Y., 1977-83, West Park Bapt. Ch., Bakersfield, Calif., 1983-86; pastor outreach program Grace Bapt. Ch., Glendora, Calif., 1986—88. Founder, pres. Motor Racing Outreach, Harrisburg, N.C., 1988-2002; founder, CEO Internat. Motorsport Svcs., 2002--. Author: Thirty Qualities of Leadership, 1975, Beyond the Checkered Flag, 1996; co-author: From the Heart of Racing, 2001; contbr. articles to profl. jours.; keynote speaker Commonwealth Youth Day, Cayman Brac, B.W.I., 1964. Dep. sheriff Lake County (Ind.) Sheriff Dept., Crown Point, 1974-77; mem. adv. bd. legis. N.Y., Albany, 1980-82, sch. bd. Bakersfield Christian Sch. Dist., 1985-86; bd. dirs. N.C. Racing Hall of Fame Mus., Sports Outreach Am. Recipient Bill France Excellence award, 1992, Mike Rich award, 1993. Mem. Internat. Sports Coalition, Conservative Bapt. Assn. (cons. 1983—, chmn. fellowship com. 1985-87), Nat. Assn. for Stock Car Auto Racing, Championship Auto Racing Teams. Republican. Avocations: motor sports, basketball. Office: Internat Motorsport Svcs PO Box 681117 Charlotte NC 28216 E-mail: maxhelton@aol.com. *Of all the investments in the world, none are as valuable as people. Only people will last forever.*

HELTON, MIKE, professional sports team executive; b. Bristol, Tenn. With radio stations, Bristol, Tenn.; from dir. mktg. to gen. mgr. Daytona Internat. Speedway; pres. Talladega Superspeedway; pub. rels. dir. Atlanta Motor Speedway, 1980—85, gen. mgr., 1985—86; dir. competition NASCAR, Daytona Beach, Fla., 1994—98, sr. v.p., 1998—2000, COO, 1999—2000, pres., 2000—. Bd. dirs. NASCAR. Office: NASCAR 1801 W International Speedway Blvd Daytona Beach FL 32115

HELTON, THOMAS CHARLES, mental health services professional; b. Prattville, Ala., July 10, 1950; s. Thomas Eugene and Lillian Nadine Helton; m. Christopher Edward Helton; 1 child, Nancy Rae Groden. BA in social work, U. of North Ala., 1989. Admin. USN/Mil. Occupl. Code, 1969; admin. asst. Patrol Squadron Thirty-One, Moffett Field, Calif., 1971—74; chief adminstr., Trident Submarine program Naval Tech. Tng. Ctr., Millington, Tenn., 1974—76; counselor, counseling and assistance ctr. Naval Sta., Memphis, 1976—80, drug and alcohol counselor Guantanamo Bay, Cuba, 1980—84; travel agt. Exquisite World Travels, San Diego, 1984—85; counselor, chem. dependency unit Helen Keller Hosp., Sheffield, Ala., 1987—91; sr. counselor Three Springs, Inc., Trenton, Ala., 1991—95; tchr. Magnolia Acad., Columbia, Tenn., 1995—98; mental health profl. Trilogy Inc., Chgo., 2001—. Chmn. Vietnam POW-MIA Movement, Moffett Field, Calif., 1969—71. With USN, 1969—83. Decorated Naval Def. medal, Navy Achievement medal, Civil Action Vietnam medal, Outstanding Young Man of Am., Desert Storm medal. Avocations: camping, writing. Home: 403 Leath Dr NE Fort Payne AL 35967

HELTON, THOMAS OSWALD, lawyer; b. Pulaski, Tenn., June 1, 1940; s. Thomas O. and Alameda (Beeler) H.; m. Barbara Sue Brown, May 29, 1965; 1 child, Joshua M. BS, U. Tenn., Knoxville, 1963; LLB, Vanderbilt U., 1966. Bar: Tenn. 1966, Ga. 1976, U.S. Ct. Appeals (6th and 11th cirs.), U.S. Dist. Ct. (ea. and mid. dists.) Tenn., U.S. Dist. Ct. (no. dist.) Ga., U.S. Supreme Ct. Law clk. to Hon. Frank Gray, Jr. U.S. Dist. Ct. Middle Dist. Tenn., Nashville, 1966-67; law clk. to Hon. Paul C. Weick U.S. Ct. Appeals for 6th Cir., Cin., 1967-68; assoc., mem. Stophel, Caldwell & Heggie, P.C., Chattanooga, 1968-86; mem. firm Caldwell, Heggie & Helton, P.C., Chattanooga, 1986-93; mem. Baker, Donelson, Bearman & Caldwell, Chattanooga, 1993—. Mem. fundraising and allocation United Way, Chattanooga, 1972-88; bd. dirs. Family and Children Services, Inc., Chattanooga, 1980-87; trustee Tenn. River Gorge Trust, 1997-2001. Fellow Tenn. Bar Found., Chatanooga Bar Found., Chattanooga Bar Assn.; mem. Tenn. Bar Assn. (bd. govs. 1985-93), Chattanooga Bar Assn. (bd. govs. 1976-78, sec.-treas. 1978-79, pres.-elect 1979-80, pres. 1980-81), Ga. Bar Assn., Greater Chattanooga Area C. of C. Episcopalian. Home: 200 Fairy Trl Lookout Mountain TN 37350-1614 Office: Baker Donelson Bearman & Caldwell PC 633 Chestnut St Ste 1800 Chattanooga TN 37450-1800

HELTON, TODD, professional baseball player; b. Knoxville, Tenn., Aug. 20, 1973; m. Kristi Helton, Jan. 29. Student, U. Tenn. With Colo. Rockies Maj. League Baseball, 1995—, first baseman, 1999—. Named Runner-up Rookie of Yr., 1999, Profl. Athlete of Yr. Tenn. Sports Hall of Fame, 1998. Office: Colo Rockies 2001 Blake St Denver CO 80205-2008

HELVESTON, EUGENE MCGILLIS, pediatric ophthalmologist, educator; b. Detroit, Dec. 28, 1934; d. Eugene McGillis and Ann (Fay) H.; m. Barbara Hiss, June 15, 1959; children: Martha Hiss, Lisa Hiss. BA, U. Mich., 1956, MD, 1960. Intern St. Joseph Hosp., Ann Arbor, Mich., 1960-61; resident Ind. U. Hosps., Indpls., 1961-66; dir. pediatric opthalmology Ind. U. Sch. Medicine, Indpls., 1967—, asst. prof., 1967-72, assoc. prof., 1972-76, prof., 1976—, chmn., 1981-83, dir. sect. pediatric ophthalmology, 1967—. Fellow in opthalmology Wilmer Inst., Balt., 1966-67 Author: Pediatric Ophthalmology Practice, 1973, Atlas of Strabismus Surgery, 4th edit., 1993, Strabismus: A Decision Making Approach, 1994; chief editor; Am. Orthoptic Jour., 1976-82; contbr. articles to profl. jours. Mem. med. adv. bd. Project Orbis, 1989—. Kellogg scholar, 1959; grantee Heed scholar Heed Found., Chgo., 1966; recipient Outstanding Heed Fellow award, 1975 Fellow ACS, Am. Acad. Ophthalmology, Am. Orthoptic Coun. (pres. 1976-80), Am. Assn. Pediat. Ophthalmology and Strabismus (pres. 1990), Internat. Strabismus Assn. (sec.-treas.). Office: Ind U Sch Medicine 702 Rotary Cir Indianapolis IN 46202-5133

HELVEY, WILLIAM CHARLES, JR., communications specialist; b. Springfield, Mo., Sept. 4, 1942; s. William C. Sr. and Alice (Essary) H.; m. Julia Faye Howard, June 16, 1962; children: Howard, Harold. BS in Art Edn., S.W. Mo. State U., 1965; MA in Art, U. Mo., 1970. Tchr. art Marshfield (Mo.) H.S., 1965-67; med. illustrator, program emphasis mgr. Mo. Regional Med. Program, Columbia, 1968-80; dir. instrl. media Ctrl. Meth. Coll., Fayette, Mo.; comm. cons., Columbia, 1981-83; state comm. sys. specialist Univ. Ext., Lincoln U., Jefferson City, Mo., 1983—. Freelance artist, photographer, presenter in field. One-man shows (50) in art and photography; group shows (over 100) in arts, including Arts Ctr. of the Ozarks, Boone County Hist. Mus., Columbia, Mo., Arrow Rock State Hist. Site, Rozier Gallery, Jefferson City, Mo., Columbia Art League, U.S. Social Security Adminstrn., Nat. 4-H Ctr., Silver Springs, Md.; contbr. numerous articles to profl. jours. Project leader Boone County 4-H Clubs, Columbia, 1977—. Recipient Unsung Hero award U.S. Dept. Agr., 1988, Mo. Specialist award Mo. State Extension, 1990, 93, numerous awards in art, photography, film and video prodn. Mem. Aircraft Owners and Pilots Assn., Columbia Art League (chmn. Boone County art show, 1975—, Lifetime Achievement award in art), St. Louis Artists' Guild, St. Charles Artists' Guild. Avocations: nature, aviation. Home: 908 Shepard Ct Columbia MO 65201-6135 E-mail: bhelvey@aol.com.

HELWEG, OTTO JENNINGS, civil engineer, educator; b. Kalamazoo, Feb. 1, 1936; s. Otto John and Laura Virginia (Jennings) H.; m. Virginia Mae Caldwell, June 28, 1964; children: Otto John II, Mark Web, Steven Jennings. MDiv, Fuller Theol. Sem., Pasadena, Calif., 1966; MS, UCLA, 1967; PhD, Colo. State U., 1975; MS, Memphis State U., 1992; MBA, U. Memphis, 1994. Registered profl. engr., Calif., Colo., Tenn., Tex. Assoc. prof. civil engring. U. Calif., Davis, 1975-83; vis. prof. Tex. A&M U., College Station, 1983-88; prof., dept. chairperson Memphis State U., 1988-92; prof., 1992—96; dean Coll. Engring. and Arch. ND State U., Fargo, 1996—. Cons. U.N.D.P., Ludiana, India, 1980. Author: Improving Well and Pump Efficiency, 1983, Water Resources Planning and Management, 1983, Microcomputer Applications, 1991; contbr. over 100 articles to profl. publs. Capt. USNR, 1958-62. Recipient Nat. Sci. award Nat. Water Well Assn., Worthington, Ohio, 1983. Fellow: ASCE (editor jour. Irrigation and Drainage Engineering 1989-92, Hoover medal 1997); mem. many profl. socs. Home: 3101 26th Ave S Fargo ND 58103-5079 Office: ND State U Coll Engring and Arch Fargo ND 58105 E-mail: ottoj@helweg.com.

HELWICK, CHRISTINE, lawyer; b. Orange, Calif., Jan. 6, 1947; d. Edward Everett and Ruth Evelyn (Seymour) Hailwood; children: Ted C., Dana J. BA, Stanford U., 1968; MA, Northwestern U., 1969; JD, U. Calif., San Francisco, 1973. Bar: Calif., U.S. Supreme Ct. U. S. Ct. Appeals (9th cir.), U.S. Dist. Ct. (no., ctrl., so. and ea. dist.) Calif. Tchr. history New Trier Twp. High Sch., Winnetka, Ill., 1968-69; sec. to the producer Flip Wilson Show, Burbank, Calif., 1970; assoc. Crosby, Heafey, Roach & May, Oakland, Calif., 1973-78; asst. counsel litigation U. Calif., Oakland, 1978-84, mng. univ. counsel, 1984-94, counsel Berkeley campus, 1989-94; gen. counsel Calif. State U. Sys., 1994—. Lectr. in field. Mem. instnl. rev. bd. Devel. Studies Ctr., Oakland, 1990—; mem. Alameda County Fee Arbitration Panel. Mem. Nat. Assn. Coll. and Univ. Attys. (bd. dirs. 1995-98, 2000—, pres. 2002-03), Nat. Assn. Coll. and Univ. Bus. Officers (bd. dirs. 2002—), State Bar Calif. (exec. com. 1980-83, Leadership Calif. 1998), dirs. 1977), Alameda County Bar Found. (adv. trustee 1988-90, bd. dirs. 1991), Order of Coif. Episcopalian. Office: Calif State U 401 Golden Shore 4th Fl Long Beach CA 90802-4275

HELWIG, ARTHUR WOODS, chemical company executive; b. St. Louis, Feb. 1, 1929; s. Gunther Albert and Emma (Schumacher) H.; m. Evelyn Morgan, July 10, 1954; children: Paul, Katherine, Elizabeth, Mary. BS ChemE, U. Mo.-Rolla, 1950, ChemE (hon.), 1966; MS ChemE, U. Ill., 1952. Process engr. Ethyl Corp., Baton Rouge, 1952-53, econs. engr., 1953-56, supr., 1956-59, gen. supt., 1959-64, dir. planning Baton Rouge and Richmond, Va., 1964-74, v.p. planning Richmond, 1974-94; ret. Bd. dirs. Solite Corp., Richmond, Albemarle Corp. Trustee Sci. Mus. Va., Richmond, 1987-99, chmn., 1992, pres. Found., 1984-87. Mem. Va. Inst. Marine Sci. (marine scis. devel. coun. 1994-99), Met. Richmond C. of C. (bd. dirs. 1986), Engrs. Club Richmond (v.p. 1987—, pres. 1988-89). Methodist. Home: 8911 Highfield Rd Richmond VA 23229-7756 E-mail: helwig@msn.com.

HELZ, GEORGE RUDOLPH, chemistry educator, research center director; b. Silver Spring, Md., Mar. 4, 1942; married, 1970; 1 child. AB, Princeton U., 1964; PhD in Geochemistry, Pa. State U., 1971. From asst. prof. to assoc. prof. U. Md., College Park, 1970-84, prof. chemistry, 1984—; dir. Md. Water Resources Rsch. Ctr., 1990—2001. Mem. disinfectants chem. subcom. NAS-NRC, 1978; vis. prof. Stanford U., 1983-84, Cox vis. prof., 1998-99; sr. vis. fellow Manchester (Eng.) U., 1989-90. AAAS Environ. fellow, 1988. Mem. Am. Chem. Soc. (chmn. geochem. divsn. 1985), Am. Geophys. Union, Geochem. Soc. (treas. 1975-78), Geol. Soc. Am., Geol. Soc. Washington (pres. 1996). Achievements include research in aqueous geochemistry; geochemistry of mineral deposits; environmental chemistry; fate of pollutants in estuaries. Office: 3101 Chemistry Bldg 091 College Park MD 20742-0001

HELZER, JAMES DENNIS, retired hospital executive; b. Fresno, Calif., Apr. 27, 1938; s. Alexander and Katherine (Scheidt) H.; m. Joan Elaine Alinder, Feb. 25, 1967; children: Amy, Rebecca. BS, Fresno State Coll., 1960; M.Hosp. Adminstrn., U. Iowa, 1965. Adminstrv. asst. Twilight Haven, Fresno, Calif., 1960-61, adminstr. resident, 1964-65; asst. adminstr. U. Calif. Hosps. and Clinics, San Francisco, 1965-68, Fresno Community Hosp., 1968-71, exec. adminstr., 1971-82, pres., chief exec. officer, 1982-91, Community Hosps. Cen. Calif., 1982-91, cons., 1991-95; adminstr. Veterans Home of Calif., Yountville, Calif., 1995-99; ret., 1999. Served with U.S. Army, 1961-63. Fellow Am. Coll. Hosp. Adminstrs.; mem. Am., Calif. hosp. assns. Clubs: Rotary. Presbyterian. Home: 1164 Secret Lake Loop Lincoln CA 95648-8404

HELZER, JOHN EARL, academic administrator, educator, psychiatrist; b. Rapid City, S.D., Nov. 21, 1941; s. John Josiah and Phyllis Gertrude (Fry) H.; m. Brigitte Ann Marie Kibler, Dec. 16, 1972; children: John Josiah, Paul Emile. Student, Chadron (Nebr.) State Coll., U. Nebr., 1959-63; MD, U. Utah, 1987. Diplomate Am. Bd. Psychiatry and Neurology; lic. psychiatrist Mo., Vt. Rotating intern Sch. of Medicine Barnes and Allied Hosps., Washington U., St. Louis, 1967-68; resident in psychiatry Sch. of Medicine Barnes, Renard and Affiliated Hosps., Washington U., St. Louis, 1968-71, chief resident in psychiatry Sch. of Medicine, 1971-72; asst., trainee in psychiatry NIMH, 1968-71; psychiat. cons. Ga. Regional State Psychiat. Hosp., Augusta, 1973-74; asst. psychiatrist Barnes and Affiliated Hosps., St. Louis, 1974-81, assoc. psychiatrist, 1981-83, psychiatrist, 1981-83; physician utilization rev. com. Barnes Hosp., St. Louis, 1976-80; chief psychiatry Med. Ctr. Hosp. of Vt., Burlington, 1989—; part-time asst. prof. psychiatry Med. Coll. Ga., Augusta, 1972-74; instr. Sch. Medicine Washington U., St. Louis, 1974-76, from asst. prof. to assoc. prof., 1976-83, prof., 1983-89; prof., chmn. dept. Coll. Medicine U. Vt., Burlington, 1989—. Orginator, dir. psychiat. nurse practitioner tng. program Washington U. Sch. of Medicine, 1976-79, dir. psychiat. residency tng. program, 1979-85, dir. Barnes Hosp. Psychiat. Consultation Svc./Washington U. Sch. Medicine, 1977-79, dir. Barnes Hosp. Psychiat. Inpatient Svc./Washington U. Sch. Medicine, 1981-89; psychiat. cons. Pastoral Counseling Ctrs. of Augusta, 1972-74, Luth. Ch. Bd. for Fgn. Missions, 1974-79; cons. psychiatrist Malcolm Bliss Med. Health Ctr., St. Louis, 1974-89; vice-chmn. substance abuse com. Diagnostic and Statistical Manual-IV, 1988—, cons. to post-traumatic stress disorder com., 1988—, cons. to schizophrenia com., 1988—. Reviewer Archives of Gen. Psychiatry, Am. Jour. Psychiatry, Jour. of Studies on Alcohol, Jour. Clin. Psychiatry; contbr. articles to Jour. Nervous & Mental Disorders, Jour. Affective Disorders, Jour. Clin. Psychiatry, Am. Jour. Psychiatry, Jour. Psychiat. Rsch., and numerous others. Maj. M.C., U.S. Army, 1972-74. U. Nebr. Regents scholar, 1959; recipient Physics Achievement award Chem. Rubber Co., 1961-62, Rsch. Scientist Devel. award, 1986-91. Fellow Am. Psychopathol. Assn. (chmn. membership com. 1984—, councilor 1983-84); mem. AAAS, Am. Assn. Dirs. Psychiat. Residency Tng., Am. Acad. Psychiatrists in Alcoholism and Addictions (founder), Assn. European Psychiatrists, Am. Acad. Clin. Psychiatrists, Nat. Alliance for Mentally Ill (assoc.), Psychiat. Rsch. Soc., Royal Coll. Psychiatrists (London affiliate), Eastern Mo. Psychiat. Soc., Rsch. Soc. on Alcoholism, Blue Key, Alpha Phi Sigma, Pi Kappa Delta. Home: 2240 Orch Rd # 2 Charlotte VT 05445 Office: U Vt Dept Psychiatry Coll Of Medicine Burlington VT 05405-0001

HEMADEH, OSSAMA SHARIF, surgeon; b. Al-Kut, Iraq, June 20, 1955; came to U.S., 1982; MD, Damascus (Syria) U., 1979. Diplomate Am. Bd. Surgery. Intern Damascus U., 1978-79; resident surgery McLaren Gen. Hosp.-Mich. State U., East Lansing, 1985-91; surgeon VA Med. Ctr., Bay Pines, Fla., 1991—. Clin. instr. U. So. Fla. Coll. Medicine, 1991-94, clin. asst. prof. 1994—, Cancer liaison physician, 2001-. Mem. ACS, Mass. Med. Soc., Soc. Am. Gastrointestinal Endoscopic Surgeons, Pharmacy and Therapeutic Soc. Home: Unit 505E One Key Capri Treasure Island FL 33706

HEMAN, ROBERT JEROME, JR., printing company executive, association executive; b. Lowell, Mass., Nov. 15, 1926; s. Robert Jerome and Ethyl Bein (Pentz) H.; m. Constance Anne Bodwell, Sept. 18, 1954; children: Roberta, Dawn, Kevin. Student, Suffolk U., 1947-48, Suffolk Law Sch., 1948-50, Worcester Poly. Inst., 1957. Supr., quality control and quality assurance David Clark Co., Worcester, 1956-60; mgr., quality control and quality assurance Harrington & Richardson, Inc., Worcester, 1960-64; dir., quality control and quality assurance Gardner and Am. Optical Corp., Southbridge, Mass., 1964-75; gen. mgr. Acme Blue Print Co., Inc., Worcester, 1975-85, pres. and owner, 1985—; cons. to pres. Acme Blue Print Co., 1992—. Pres. bd. trustees Worcester Pub. Libr., 1987-95; corporator Worcester Art Mus.; mem. Worcester City Beautification Com., 1991-98, Target Worcester, 1991-98. With USN, 1943-46, PTO. Mem. DAV (life), VFW (life), Elks (life, Elk of Yr. 1985-86, chpt. pres., state pres., editor Mass. Elks News 1982-86, sec. Mass. Elk Assn. 1985-98, Grand Lodge activities com., spl. rep.), Am. Legion (life). Roman Catholic. Avocations: stamp collecting, coin collecting, travel. Home: 143 Lovell St Worcester MA 01603-2554 Office: Acme Blue Print Co 102 1/2 Grove St Worcester MA 01605-2629

HEMANN, RAYMOND GLENN, research company executive; b. Cleve., Jan. 24, 1933; s. Walter Harold and Marsha Mae (Colbert) H.; m. Lucile Tinnin Turnage, Feb. 1, 1958; children: James Edward, Carolyn Frances; m. Pamela Schaap Lehr, Dec. 18, 1987. BS, Fla. State U., 1957; postgrad., U.S. Naval Postgrad. Sch., 1963-64, U. Calif., Los Angeles, 1960-62; MS in Systems Engring., Calif. State U., Fullerton, 1970; MA in Econs., Calif. State U., 1972; cert. in tech. mgmt., Calif. Inst. Tech., 1990. Comml., glider and pvt. pilot. Aero. engring. aide U.S. Navy, David Taylor Model Basin, Carderock, Md., 1956; analyst Fairchild Aerial Surveys, Tallahassee, 1957; research analyst Fla. Rd. Dept., Tallahassee, 1957-59; chief Autonetics divsn. N.Am. Aviation, Inc., Anaheim, Calif., 1959-69; v.p., dir. R.E. Manns Co., Wilmington, Calif., 1969-70; mgr. Avionics Design and Analysis Dept. Lockheed-Calif. Co., Burbank, 1970-72, mgr. Advanced Concepts divsn., 1976-82; gen. mgr. Western divsn. Arinc Research Corp., Santa Ana, 1972-76; dir. Future Requirements Rockwell Internat., 1982-85, dir. Threat Analysis, Corp. Offices, 1985-89; pres., CEO Advanced Systems Rsch., Inc., 1989—. Adj. sr. fellow Ctr. Strategic and Internat. Studies, Washington, 1987—; bd. dirs., mem. exec. com. Fla. State U. Rsch. Found., 1995-2003; bd. dirs. Assn. Mgmt. Svc. Inc., Numedeon, Inc., Am. Heart Assn., Pasadena Civic Auditorium Found. Inc., 2000-02; chmn. adv. coun. Coll. Engring. Fla. State U./Fla. A&M U., 1995—; cons. to dir. Ctrl. Intelligence, Nat. Intelligence Coun., Nat. Air Intelligence Ctr., Inst. Def. Analyses, Battelle Meml. Inst., Ctr. Strategic and Internat. Studies; sec., bd. dirs. Calif State U., Fullerton, Econs. Found.; mem. naval studies bd. panels, 1985—, chmn. indsl. panel Nat. Labs. Infrastructure Study, Office Sec. Def., 1995; chmn. indsl. panel Future Dirs. Mil. Aeronautics Study, 1996; asst. prof. ops. analysis dept. U.S. Naval Postgrad. Sch., Monterey, Calif., 1963-64, Monterey Peninsula Coll., 1963; instr. ops. analysis Calif. State U., Fullerton, 1964-67, instr. quantitative methods, 1969-72; program developer, instr. systems engring. indsl. rels. ctr. Calif. Inst. Tech., 1992-96; lectr. Brazilian Navy, 1980, U. Calif., Santa Barbara, 1980, Yale U., 1985, Princeton U., 1986, U.S. Naval Postgrad. Sch., 1986, Ministry of Def., Taiwan, Republic of China, 1990; Calif. Inst. Tech. Assocs., 1992—; mem. exec. forum Calif. Inst. Tech., 1991—. Contbr articles to profl. jours. and new media. Chmn. comdr.'s adv. bd. CAP, Calif. Wing; reader Recording for the Blind, 1989—; bd. dirs. Pasadena Civic Auditorium Found., 2000-02, Boy Scouts Am., 2971-79; bd. dirs., sec.-treas. Jr. All-Am. Football; trustee Art Ctr. Coll. Design, Pasadena, Calif., 2003—. Syde P. Deeb scholar, 1956; recipient honor awards Nat. Assn. Remotely Piloted Vehicles, 1975, 76; named to Hon. Order Ky. Cols., 1985. Fellow AAAS, AIAA (assoc.); mem. IEEE (life), Ops. Rsch. Soc. Am., Air Force Assn., US Marines Meml. Club (life), N.Y. Acad. Scis., Assn. Old Crows., L.A. World Affairs Coun., Phi Kappa Tau (past pres.). Episcopalian. Office: Advanced Sys Rsch Inc 33 S Catalina Ave Ste 202 Pasadena CA 91106-2426

HEMBERGER, GLEN JAMES, university band director, music educator; b. Boulder, Colo., Jan. 18, 1962; s. James Frank and Jacqueline Ann (Kent) H.; m. Linda Dawn Thomas, June 3, 1989. BME, U. Colo., 1985, MMus, 1989; DMA, U. North Tex., 2001. Dir. bands Thornton (Colo.) Sr. High Sch., 1985-87; grad. asst. U. Colo. Bands, Boulder, 1987-89; assoc. dir. bands, mem. music edn. faculty U. R.I., Kingston, 1989-92; assoc. dir. bands Okla. State U., Stillwater, 1992-97; doctoral conducting assoc. U. North Tex., 1997-99; dir. bands Southeastern La. U., 1999—. Clinician R.I. Music Educators' State Conv., 1992, La. Music Educators State Conv., 2000, 2002, summer music camp U. Wis., 1993, 99, Chinese Armed Police Band, Beijing, 1996, 97, Melbourne, Brisbane & Sydney, Australia, 1997, Nat. Taiwan U. Wind Orch., Taipei and Hong Kong, 1996, Beijing Band Dirs. Assn., 1996, 97; guest condr. high schs., honor bands, clinics, 1984—, USCG Band, Okla. Mozart Internat. Music Festival, 1995, 96, Norwegian Band Championships, Hamar, 1999, Trondheim, 2000; founder So. New Eng. H.S. Honor Band, 1991; CD prodr. Drake U. Wind Symphony, 2001; condr., Assn. for Music in Internat. Schs. Internat. Honor Band, The Hague, Netherlands, 2003. Contbr. articles to profl. jours.; presenter in field. Mem. Olympic All-Am. Marching Band, L.A., 1984. Mem. Coll. Band Dirs. Nat. Assn. (mem. jour. staff, nat. athletic band adv. coun., clinician nat. conv. 1995, 97), Internat. Assn. Jazz Educators, Music Educators Nat. Conf., World Assn. for Symphonic Bands and Ensembles, Okla. Music Educators Assn. (clinician state conv. 1995, jazz ensemble performance 1997), Phi Mu Alpha Sinfonia, Kappa Kappa Psi, Tau Beta Sigma, Pi Kappa Lambda, Phi Beta Mu. Home: 3011 Willow Ln Madisonville LA 70447-9125 Office: Southeastern La Univ PO Box 10815 Hammond LA 70402-0815

HEMBREE, HUGH LAWSON, III, diversified holding company executive; b. Ft. Smith, Ark., Nov. 16, 1931; s. Raymond N. and Gladys (Newman) H.; m. Sara Janelle Young, Sept. 1, 1956; children— Hugh Lawson IV, Raymond Scott. BS in Bus. Adminstrn, U. Ark., 1953, JD, 1958. In middle mgmt. Ark.-Best Freight Inc., Fort Smith, 1958-61, dir. finance, 1961-65, v.p., 1965-67; pres., dir. Ark.-Best Corp., Fort Smith, 1967-73, chmn. bd., chief exec. officer, 1973-88; owner, chmn. bd. Mng. ptnr. Sugar Hill Interests; bd. dirs. Okla. Gas and Electric, Oklahoma City. Sec. Fort Smith/Sebastian County Joint Planning Commn., 1959-72; Ark. past chmn. Radio Free Europe Program; past chmn. devel. council, mem. dean's adv. com. Sch. Bus., U. Ark., past chmn. exec. com. univ. devel. assn.; past mem. Sebastian County Regional Park Commn.; past mem. Democratic Central Com. Ark.; past pres. Westark area council Boy Scouts Am., 1985 88, asst. treas. Nat. Exec. Bd. Boy Scouts Am., 1985-88, treas., 1988-92, chair pension investments retirement trust; past area pres., mem. exec. com. South Central region; past Chmn. Ark.-Okla. Livestock and Ednl. Found.; chmn. fund raising program U. Ark., 1973-74; past trustee John Brown U., Siloam Springs, Ark., U. Ark. Found., Hendrix Coll., Conway, Ark.; trustee U. Ark., chmn. bd. trustees Razorback Found.; mem. Philmont Scout Ranch Com. Served to capt. USAF, 1953-55. Recipient Silver Antelope award Boy Scouts Am., 1967, Silver Beaver award, 1969, Silver Buffalo award, 1990, Distinguished Svc. Awd., UA Med. Svcs., 1998, Comm. Svc. Awd., Sam Walton Coll. of Bus., Univ. of Ark., 1998, Svc. Awd. from Razorback Found., 1998; Ark. Leadership and Community Svc. award, 1970, 75, Citation of Disting. Alumnus, U. Ark., 1977, Outstanidng Svc. Alumnus, U. Ark. Coll. of Bus., 1998; named Ark. Outstanding Young Man of Yr., Ark. Jaycees, 1967; James E. West fellow Boy Scouts, Baden Powell fellow Boy Scouts. Mem. World Pres's. Orgn., World Bus. Orgn., Nat. Assn. of Devel. Orgns. (chmn. adv. com. 1969-72), Ark. C. of C. (1st v.p. 1970-73, pres. 1973, 86-87, dir. 1972-74), Ft. Smith C. of C. (pres. 1970-73, 86), Nat. Young Presidents Orgn., World Presidents Orgn., Ark. Alumni Assn. (dir., mem. bldg. com., vice chmn. bd. trustee), Am. Trucking Assn., Nat. Assn. Mfrs. (dir. 1976, regional v.p. 1973-75, regional dir. 1976-77), Ark. Arts Center, Scabbard and Blade, Ark. Bus. Coun., Kissing Camels Golf Club (Colorado Springs), El Paso Club (Colorado Springs), Sigma Alpha Epsilon, Beta Gamma Sigma, Phi Eta Sigma, Delta Theta Phi, Alpha Kappa Psi. Episcopalian (vestryman). Clubs: Masonss (32 deg.), Shriners, Ft. Smith Hardscrabble Country and Town, Garden of the Gods (Colorado Springs), Kissing Camels Golf (Colorado Springs). Home: PO Box 10233 Fort Smith AR 72917 0233 Office. Sugar Hill Farms Inc PO Box 10233 Fort Smith AR 72917-0233

HEMBREE, JAMES D. retired chemical company executive; b. Morris, Okla., Feb. 27, 1929; s. James D. and Mary Eleanor H.; m. Joyce Pickrell, Aug. 25, 1951; children: Victoria Lee Krivacs, Alex James, Kent Douglas. BSCh.E., Okla. State U., 1951; MSCh.E., U. Mich., 1952. Dir. mktg. inorganic chems. Dow Chem U.S.A., Midland, Mich., 1968-78, gen. mgr. designed products dept., 1976-78, v.p., 1978-80, group v.p., 1980-83; pres., chief exec. officer Dow Chem. Can., Sarnia, Ont., 1983-86; ret., 1986. Home and Office: 4620 Jupiter Dr Salt Lake City UT 84124-3900 E-mail: jimhmbr@aol.com.

HEMENWAY, DAVID, public health educator; b. N.Y.C., Mar. 14, 1945; s. Henry Harold and Marjorie Sophie (Wilson) H.; 1 child, Brett Turner. BA, Harvard Coll., 1966; MA, U. Mich., 1967; PhD, Harvard U., 1974. Mgmt. intern Office of Sec. Defense, Arlington, Va., 1967-68; Washington corres. Consumers Union, Washington, 1969; asst. prof. Boston U., 1973-75; prof. Harvard Sch. Pub. Health, Boston, 1975—. Dir. Harvard Injury Control Rsch. Ctr., Boston, 1997—, Harvard Youth Violence Prevention Ctr., Boston, 2000—; chmn. injury prevention coun. Nat. Assn. for Pub. Health Policy, South Burlington, Va., 1988-98. Author: Industrywide Voluntary Product Standards, 1975, Monitoring and Compliance, 1985, Prices and Choices, 1993, Guns and the Constitution, 1995. Injury Rsch. fellow Pew Found., 1986, sr. Soros fellow, 1998-2000; Robert Wood Johnson investigator, 1998-2001. Mem. APHA, Am. Econ. Assn., Nat. Assn. Injury Control Rsch. Ctrs. (pres.). Avocations: modeling, tennis. Home: 28 Adams St Brookline MA 02446-6768 Office: Harvard Sch Pub Health 677 Huntington Ave Boston MA 02115-6096 E-mail: hemenway@hsph.harvard.edu.

HEMENWAY, ROBERT E. academic administrator, language educator; b. Sioux City, Iowa, Aug. 10, 1941; s. Myrle Emery and Katharine Leone (Cook) H.; m. Marilyn Wickstrom, June 16, 1962 (div. 1970); children: Gina, Jeremy; m. Mattie Fenter, May 12, 1972 (div. 1980); children: Robin, Karintha, Matthew, Langston; m. Leah Renee Hattemer, Dec. 19, 1981; children: Zachary, Arna. BA, U. Nebr., Omaha, 1963; PhD, Kent (Ohio) State U., 1966. Asst. prof. English U. Ky., Lexington, 1966-68, assoc. prof. Am. studies U. Wyo., Laramie, 1968-73; prof. U. Ky., Lexington, 1973-86; dean arts and scis. U. Okla., Norman, 1986-89; chancellor U. Ky., Lexington, 1989-95, U. Kans., Lawrence, 1995—. Dean Gov.'s Scholar's Program, Ky., 1984-86. Author: Zora Neale Hurston, 1977 (Best Biography of 1977 award Soc. Midland Authors 1978, Rembert Patrick prize Fla. Hist. Soc. 1978). Mem. Gov.'s Task Force on Literacy, Okla., 1987-89; bd. dirs. Okla. H.S. Sci. and Math., Oklahoma City, 1985-86, Coun. Colls. Arts and Scis., 1987-89. NEH fellow, 1974-75. Mem. MLA, Am. Studies Assn. (nat. coun.), South Atlantic Assn. Depts. English (pres. 1984-85). Lutheran. Avocation: duplicate bridge. Office: Univ Kansas Office of the Chancellor 230 Strong Hall Lawrence KS 66045-7501

HEMENWAY, STEPHEN JAMES, record producer, author; b. San Gabriel, Calif., Aug. 26, 1955; s. Glenn Stephen and Patricia Ann (Reese) H.; (div. 1983); children: April Lynn, Stacie Michelle, Ashley Renee; m. Terri Lynn McAlister, Apr. 19, 1997. AS, Chaffey Coll., Alta Loma, Calif., 1981. Prod. Brass Star Records, Chino Hills, Calif., 1984—; publisher Brass Star Music, Chino Hills, Calif., 1988—. Music arranger Brass Star Records, Chino Hills, 1984—; promoter Games and Entertainment Unlimited, Chino Hills, 1987—; songwriter/publisher Broadcast Music, Inc., 1988-95; pres., music arranger Brass Star Records; chmn., CEO Slouch & Friends, Inc., 1996—. Actor, artist, prodr. Plays, Music, 1968—; music arranger A Chino Hills Christmas, Regina; prodr. Don't Let Your Dreams Slip Away, 1996, Imaginations Mine, 2002; author: (children's series) The Slouch in the Couch, 1998, Never Jump on a Grump, 2003. Dep. sheriff, L.A. County, 1978. Republican. Roman Catholic. Avocations: music, 16-mm. film collecting, football, fishing, camping. Office: PMB-309 4195 Chino Hills Pkwy Chino Hills CA 91709-2618 E-mail: stephenj@slouch.org.

HEMINGWAY, DAVID C. elementary school principal; b. Wilkes Barre, Pa., May 29, 1941; s. Vreeland Edward and Susan Rose H.; m. Patricia W. Hemingway, May 28, 1966; 1 child, David C., Jr. BS, West Chester U., 1964; MEd, U. Del., 1969, postgrad., 1978-82. Elem. tchr. Coatesville (Pa.) Area Sch. Dist., 1964-69, acting elem. prin., 1969-70, elem. prin., 1970-97, Downingtown (Pa.) Area Sch. Dist., 1997—. Treas. bd. dirs. Keystone Fed. Credit Union, Downingtown, 1978—; site vis. U.S. Dept. Edn., Washington, 1997, blue ribbon reviewer Pa. Dept. Edn., Harrisburg, 1996, 98, 2000; tesa coord. Coatesville Area Sch. Dist., 1993—. Co-chair Pub. Employee Divsn., United Charities, Coatesville, 1976; co-founder Coatesville Area Wrestling Boosters, 1984. Named Prin. of Yr., Am. Family Inst., Downington, 1994, Outstanding Adminstr., Coatesville Area Adminstrs., 1985, Outstanding Svc. awards Coatesville Home and Sch./PTA, 1966, 74, 94; recipient Blue Ribbon Prin. award U.S. Dept. of Edn., Washington, 1993-94. Mem. ASCD, NEA, Pa. Elem. Prins., Nat. Elem. Prin. Assn., Pa. Sch. Bd.'s Assn., Phi Delta Kappa. Avocations: antiques, wood carving, sports. Office: Lionville Elem Sch 526 W Uwchlan Ave Downingtown PA 19335-1729 E-mail: dhemingway@dasd.org.

HEMINGWAY, DONALD WILLIAM, military officer, lawyer, educator; b. Salt Lake City, Utah, Mar. 13, 1919; s. William Joseph and Flora Christina (McDonald) Hemingway; m. Donna Laws; children: William David, Delwin Ray, Michael Francis, Mary Dawn, Floralee, Jan Marie. BA in Music, Brigham Young U., Provo, Utah, 1942; JD, USC, 1948; post-grad studies political thought, Sch. Econs., London, 1959—60; student, Air War Coll., Maxwell AFB, Ala., 1976. Bar: Nev. 1949, Utah 1952. Commd. officer USAF, 1959, advanced through grades to lt. col., judge adv., hdqs. 3d air force, USAF, London, Air Defense Command USAF, Colo. Springs, Wright Patterson AFB, Dayton; ret. USAF, 1979; sole practice Salt Lake City, 1976—88. Author: (Book) Follow Me (Scriptural Story of Jesus), 1998, (WWII Dairy) Private Hemingway Goes to War, 2000, (Book) Ancient America Rediscovered, 2000, (novels) (Hist.) Joseph Smith: A Prophet, 2002. Tchr. Brigham Young U., Hawaii, 1988—91, 1993—95; instr. family history, genealogy LDS Ch., 1991—92; missionary LDS, Canada, 1939—41. Recipient Pro Bono Svc. award, Utah State Bar, 1986. Republican. Lds. Avocation: genealogy. Home: 141 2d Ave #304 Salt Lake City UT 84103 E-mail: don.donna@juno.com.

HEMINGWAY, GEORGE FRANCIS, investment company executive, lawyer; b. Budapest, Hungary, Oct. 17, 1947; children: George II, L. Alexander. BFA, NYU, 1972, JD, 1976. Bar: Calif. 1976. Atty. McKenna & Fitting, L.A., 1976—81; sr. litigator Marshall, Bratter, etc., L.A., 1981—83; CEO The Hemingway Group, L.A., 1983—, Ctrl. European Franchise Group, Ltd., Jersey, England, 1992—. Gov. Wilshire Bar Assn., L.A., 1981—84; vis. prof. Budapest U. Econ. Scis., 2000—. Editor: Introduction to Venturing, 2001. Pres. Hemingway Found., Budapest, 1992—. Roman Catholic. Avocations: basketball, reading, travel. Office: The Hemingway Group PO Box 360949 Los Angeles CA 90036

HEMINGWAY, RICHARD WILLIAM, law educator; b. Detroit, Nov. 24, 1927; s. William Oswald and Iva Catherine (Wildfang) H.; m. Vera Cecilia Eck, Sept. 12, 1947; children: Margaret Catherine, Carol Elizabeth, Richard Albert. BS in Bus, U. Colo., 1950; JD magna cum laude (J. Woodall Rogers Sr. Gold medal 1955), So. Meth. U., 1955; LL.M. (William S. Cook fellow 1968), U. Mich., 1969. Bar: Tex. 1955, Okla. 1981. Assoc. Fulbright, Crooker, Freeman, Bates & Jaworski, Houston, 1955-60; lectr. Bates Sch. Law, U. Houston, 1960; assoc. prof. law Baylor U. Law Sch., Waco, Tex., 1960-65; vis. assoc. prof. So. Meth. U. Law Sch., 1965-68; prof. law Tex. Tech U. Law Sch., Lubbock, 1968-71, Paul W. Horn prof., 1972-81, acting dean, 1974-75, dean ad interim, 1980-81; prof. law U. Okla., Norman, 1981-83, Eugene Kuntz prof. oil, gas and natural resources law, 1983-92, Eugne Kuntz prof. emeritus oil, gas & natural resources law, 1992—. Author: The Law of Oil and Gas, 1971, 2d edit., 1983, lawyer's edit., 1983, 3d edit., 1991, West's Texas Forms (Mines and Minerals), 1977, 2d edit., 1991; contbg. editor various law reports, cases and materials. Served with USAAF, 1945-47. Mem. Tex. Bar Assn., Scribes, Order of Coif (faculty), Beta Gamma Sigma. Lutheran. Home: Apt 1024 5000 Old Shepard Pl Plano TX 75093

HEMKE, FREDERICK L. music educator, university administrator; b. July 11, 1935; s. Fred L. and May H. (Rowell) H.; m. Junita Borg, Dec. 26, 1959; children: Elizabeth Hemke Shapiro, Frederic John Borg. Premiere prix, Cons. Nat. de Musique, Paris, 1956; BS in Music Edn., U. Wis., Milw., 1958; MusM in Music Edn., Eastman Sch. of Music, Rochester, N.Y., 1962; DMA in Musical Arts, U. Wis., 1975. Chmn. dept. preparatory wind and percussion Sch. of Music Northwestern U., Evanston, Ill., 1962-75, chmn. dept. music performance and studies, 1962-94, prof. of music (saxophone), 1963—, sr. assoc. dean, 1994—2003, Louis and Elsie Snydacker Eckstein prof. music, 2003—. Faculty athletics rep. Northwestern U., Big 10 Conf., NCAA 1982-2003; cons. La Voz Corp., Sun Valley, Calif., Frederick Hemke Saxophone Reeds, So. Music Co., San Antonio, Hemke Saxophone Series, The Selmer Co., Elkhart, Ind. Instrumental soloist (recordings) The American Saxophone, Music for Tenor Saxophone, Allan Pettersson, Symphony No. 15 (with Stockholm Philharmonic); Quintet for String Quartet & Saxo-Warren Benson, Concerto-Ross Lee Finney; author: The Early History of the Saxophone, Hemke Saxophone Series, So. Music Co. Recipient Excellence in Teaching award Northwestern U. Alumni Assn., Music Alumni Achievement award, U. Wis., Milw.; grantee: Nat. Endowment for the Arts. Mem. Ill. Music Educators Assn., Pi Kappa Lambda, Kappa Kappa Psi, Phi Mu Alpha Sinfonia (past province gov.) Office: Northwestern U Sch of Music 1965 S Campus Dr Evanston IL 60208-0874

HEMLOCK, ROBERTA LEIGH, veterinary technician; b. Chgo., Aug. 24, 1946; d. John Nolan and Gertrude Mathilda (Lahti) Hemlock. AA, Chgo. City Coll., 1966; BFA, Art Inst. Chgo., 1970; AAS, Bel-Rea Inst., Denver, 2001. Intelligence analyst State Dept., England, 1972—73; pres. Hemlock, Hemlock & Others, Chgo., 1973—80; design dir. Hemlock, Hemlock & Others, Chgo., 1973—80; prof. Colo. Inst. of Art, Denver, 1980—93; vp. ops. & design Design Prodns., Inc., Denver, 1993—94; v.p. ops. & editor Syber Media Group, Denver, 1994—96; pvt. practice tech. grantwriter Denver, 1996—2000; vet. technician Huron Animal Hosp., Denver, 2001—03; vet. technician/surgery Erie (Colo.) Animal Hosp., 2003—. Cons. AAUW, 2001—, IAUW, 2001—; mem. adv. bd. CCD of Denver, 2001—. Mem.: NAVTA, Colo. Assn. Cert. Vet. Technicians (cert., state pub. rels. dir. 2001—), Denver Botanic Gardens. Avocations: photography, conceptual writer, publisher. Home: 10648 Huron St # 412 Northglenn CO 80234-4022

HEMMER, PAUL EDWARD, musician, composer, broadcasting executive; b. Dubuque, Iowa, Oct. 12, 1944; s. Andrew Charles and Elizabeth Marie (Goerdt) H.; m. Janet T. Demmer, Feb. 7, 1970; children: Michelle, Steven. BS in Music Edn., U. Wis., Platteville, 1966. Program dir. Sta. WDBQ-AM, Dubuque, Iowa, 1967-93; leader Paul Hemmer Orch., Dubuque, 1967-96; pres. Hemmer Broadcasting, Dubuque, Iowa, 1994—2000; v.p. Radio DBQ, Inc., Dubuque, 2000—. Composer: (musical comedies) Get the Lead Out, 1976, Joe Sent Me!, 1978, Key City Komedy Company, 1981, Steamboat Comin', 1991, Here's to Dubuque, 1998, Sketches from a Drawing Room, 1996; appeared in film Field of Dreams, 1989. Named Citizen of Yr., Dubuque Telegraph-Herald, 1976, Disting. alumni, U. Wis, Platteville, 1999. Mem. Internat. Radio Broadcasters Idea Bank, Rotary. Roman Catholic. Home: 2375 Simpson St Dubuque IA 52003-7720 Office: Radio DBQ 8th Bluff Dubuque IA 52001 E-mail: dbqpaul@mchsi.com.

HEMMERDINGER, H. DALE, real estate executive; b. Washington, Oct. 31, 1944; s. Monroe Elliott Hemmerdinger and Carol Phyllis (Weil) Haussamen; m. Elizabeth Gould, June 25, 1969; children: Damon John, Katherine Molly. BA, NYU, 1967, postgrad., 1967-68. Cert. real estate broker, N.Y. Pres., chief exec. officer The Hemmerdinger Corp., N.Y.C., 1968—, Atco Properties & Mgmt., Inc., N.Y.C., 1968—. Bd. dirs. Realty Found. of N.Y., N.Y.C.; trustee mem. ex-com. fin. com. NYU, 1994—; mem. citizens budget commn., N.Y.C., 1995—; spkr., author articles on real estate and economy Bank Credit Analyst and Grant's Interest Rate Observer publs. Commr. conciliation and appeals bd. City of N.Y., 1978-84; mem. Dem. County Com., N.Y.C., 1978—, N.Y. State Senate Adv. Com., 1980-93, N.Y. State Fin. Control Bd., 1990—; mem. N.Y. State Senate Adv. Coun. on State Productivity, 1990-94; gov. Citizens Housing and Planning Coun., N.Y.C., 1982—; mem. exec. com. Assn. for Better N.Y., N.Y.C., 1984—; trustee, mem. exec. com. Nightingale Bamford Sch., N.Y.C., 1985-93; trustee, vice chmn., mem. exec. com. Police Found., 1986—; trustee NYU, 1993—. Mem. Real Estate Bd. N.Y., Manhattan C. of C., Queens C. of C., Harmonie Club (pres. 1985-86), Sky Club, Univ. Club, Commanderie de Bordeaux, N.Y. Yacht Club. Avocations: sailing, sculling. Office: Atco Properties & Mgmt Inc 555 5th Ave Fl 16L New York NY 10017-2416

HEMMERICH, STEFAN, biomedical scientist, biotechnologist; b. Freiburg, Germany, May 1, 1958; arrived in U.S., 1990; s. Marianne Hemmerich; 1 child, Ophir. PhD, Weizmann Inst. Sci., Rehovot, Israel, 1990. Postdoctoral scientist Rockefeller U., N.Y.C., 1990, U. Calif., San Francisco, 1990-93; rsch. scientist Syntex Inc., Palo Alto, Calif., 1993-95, Roche Bioscience, Palo Alto, Calif., 1995-2000; acting pres., chief sci. officer Thios Biotechnology, Oakland, Calif., 2000—02; head tech. devel. Thios Pharms. Inc., Emeryville, Calif., 2002—. Mem. fellowship review bd. Am. Heart Assn., Dallas, 1994-99. Contbr. articles to profl. jours. Mem. AAAS, Inflammation Rsch. Assn. Office: Thios Pharms Inc 5980 Horton St Ste 400 Oakland CA 94608 E-mail: stefan@thiospharm.com.

HEMMILA, LINDA-KAY, graphics designer; b. Berkeley, Calif., Apr. 7, 1975; d. Dorothy Dolan. AA in Journalism, Contra Costa Coll., 1998; BA in Mass. Commn., U. Calif., Berkeley, 2000. Designer, copy editor Knight-Ridder Newspapers, Richmond, Calif., 1997—98; graphic artist Alameda Newspaper Group, Pleasanton, Calif., 1998; pub. asst. McGraw-Hill Pub., Berkeley, 1999; pub. specialist Pubs.'s Group West, Berkeley, 2000—. Freelance writer Berkeley Daily Planet, 1999. Mem.: Soc. Profl. Journalists. Avocations: guitar, writing, reading. E-mail: lhemmila@alum.calberkeley.org.

HEMMING, BRUCE CLARK, microbiologist; b. Pocatello, Idaho; s. Parley Lynn and Vernetta (Clark) H.; m. Caroline McDaniel, Apr. 20, 1973; children: Eric M., Heidi, Heather, Crystal Lynn, Keri Lynn. BS in Microbiology, Brigham Young U., Provo, Utah, 1974, MS in Biochemistry, 1977; PhD in Plant Pathology, Mont. State U., Bozeman, 1982. Staff rsch. assoc. dept. chemistry Brigham Young U., 1977-78; sr. rsch. biologist molecular biology Monsanto Co., St. Louis, 1982-84, rsch. specialist plant molecular biology, 1984-89, project leader biocontrol crop protection, 1989, sr. rsch. specialist crop protection, 1989-91; pres. Microbe Inotech Labs., Inc., 1991—; exec. prodr. ITP of St. Louis, LLC, 1999—. Chmn. regional com. USDA, Washington, 1986-89, mem. tech. subcom. on biocontrol expt. sta. com. on policy, 1987-89; panel mem. Nat. Rsch. Coun. Briefing, Washington, 1987; disting. guest lectr. Coll. Sci. Utah State U., Logan, 1989. Author: Methods in Enzymology, 1979; co-editor: Iron Chelation in Plants and Soil Microorganisms, 1993; mem. editorial bd. Biology of Metals, Springer-Verlag, 1988-91. Troop committeeman Boy Scouts Am., Manchester, Mo., 1985. Mem. AAAS, Am. Phytopath. Soc., Am. Chem. Soc., Am. Soc. Microbiology, Nat. Registry of Environ. Profls. Achievements include development of first microbial recombinant marker system tested in U.S. environment. Office: Microbe Inotech Labs Inc 12133 Bridgeton Square Dr Bridgeton MO 63044-2616 also: ITP of St Louis LLC 804 Paquerette Ct Ballwin MO 63021-7033 E-mail: info@microbeinotech.com.

HEMMING, VAL G. university dean; b. Rexburg, Idaho, July 9, 1937; m. Alice Bell Hemming; children: Heidi, Julie, Jill, Patrick. BA in Entomology, U. Utah, 1962; MD, U. Utah Coll. Medicine, 1966. Diplomate Am. Bd. Pediatrics, Nat. Bd. Med. Examiners. Commd. 2d lt. USAF, 1965, advanced through grades to col.; pediatric intern U. Utah Affiliated Hosps., 1966—67; resident physician in pediatrics Wilford Hall USAF Med. Ctr., Lackland AFB, Tex., 1968—70; staff pediatrician USAF Hosp., Wiesbaden, Germany, 1970—74; chmn., dir. pediatric residency tng. David Grant USAF Med. ctr., Travis AFB, Calif., 1976—80; assoc. prof. dept. pediatrics Uniformed Svcs. U. Health Scis., Bethesda, Md., 1980—84, prof. dept. pediatrics, 1984—87, prof., chmn. dept. pediatrics, 1987—95, from interim dean to dean F. Edward Hebert Sch. Medicine, 1995—2002, prof. emeritus in pediats., 2002—; splty. cons. in pediatrics to Air Force Surgeon Gen., 1983—90; ret., 1990. Cons. in pediatrics to the asst. sec. for health affairs Dept. of Def., 1988-91; adv. coun. Nat. Inst. of Child Health and Human Devel. Contbr. numerous articles to profl. jours. Mem. Am. Acad. Pediatrics, Am. Pediatric Soc., Infectious Disease Soc. of Am., Western Soc. for Pediatric Rsch., Pediatric Infectious Disease Soc., Lancefield Soc., Internat. AIDS Soc., Am. Soc. for Microbiology. Office: Uniformed Svcs U of Health Scis 4301 Jones Bridge Rd Bethesda MD 20814-4712

HEMMING, WALTER WILLIAM, business financial consultant; b. Vineland, NJ, Oct. 2, 1939; s. Percy A. and Marguerite E. (Smith) H.; m. Shirley L. Derocher, June 10, 1961; children: Cynthia, Catherine, Walter Jr. BS, Syracuse U., 1961. CPA, NY, NH. Prin. Arthur Young & Co., Stamford, Conn., 1961-72; contr. Coca-Cola Bottling Co. NY, Hackensack, NJ, 1972-78; exec. v.p., chief oper. officer KW Inc., Manchester, NH, 1978-81; exec. v.p. fin. and adminstrn., chief fin. officer Coca-Cola Bottling Co. NY, Greenwich, Conn., 1981-86, Coca-Cola Bottling Plants of Maine, South Portland, 1987-88; gen. ptnr. Pleasant Ave. Assoc., 1988—2001, H&H Assoc., 1989-99; v.p. bus devel. Coca-Cola Bottling Co. No. New Eng., Bedford, NH, 1989; prin. Hemming Assoc., 1989—; treas. Island Approaches, Sunset, Maine, 1991—; also bd. dir., Island Approaches, Sunset, Maine. Mem. fin. rev. com. Coca-Cola Bottlers Assn., Atlanta, 1985-89; treas. NH Soft Drink Assn., Manchester, 1979-81; mem. exec. com., loan com., chmn. audit com. Centerpoint Bank, 1990-96, chmn. exec. com., 1995-96; bd. dir. Cmty. Bankshares, Inc., mem. audit com., 1996-97; bd. dir. Centrix Bank & Trust, mem. exec. com., audit com., loan com., chmn. audit com., 1999-2000, chmn. exec. com., 2001-2003. Treas. Clinton (Conn.) United Meth. Ch., 1969-72, Jesse Lee Meth. Ch., Ridgefield, Conn., 1974-77; treas. Hollis (NH) Congl. Ch., 1981, 92-95, asst. treas., 1982-92, deacon, 1988-92, trustee, 1997-2002. Mem. AICPA, NH Soc. CPAs, NY Soc. CPAs. Republican. Avocations: fishing, gardening. Home: PO Box 610 Brookline NH 03033-0610 Office: Hemming Assocs 74 Northeastern Blvd Unit 11 Nashua NH 03062-3192

HEMMINGER, ALLEN EDWARD, retired insurance consultant; b. Oak Harbor, Ohio, Jan. 22, 1933; s. George Fredrick and Hulda Carolyn (Piehl) H.; m. Dora Jane Blanton, May 11, 1957; children: Gay Lynn, Teresa Ann. BSME, Ind. Inst. Tech., 1955. Cons. Indsl. Risk Insurers, Detroit, 1955-89. Mem. Unicycling Soc. Am. (bd. dirs. 1978-81), Internat. Unicycling Fedn. (sec.-treas. 1982-93), The Wheelmen, Internat. Jugglers Assn., The Mus. Box Soc. Internat. Home: 28692 Bayberry Park Dr Livonia MI 48154-3872

HEMMINGER, PAMELA LYNN, lawyer; b. Chgo., June 29, 1949; d. Paul Willis and Lenore Adelaide (Hennig) H.; m. Robert Alan Miller, May 14, 1979; children: Kimberly Anne, Jeffrey Ryan, Eric Douglas. BA, Pomona Coll., 1971; JD, Pepperdine U., 1976. Tchr. Etiwanda (Calif.) Sch. dist., 1971-74; law clerk Gibson Dunn & Crutcher, Newport Beach, Calif., 1974-76, assoc. L.A., 1976-84, ptnr., 1985—. Contbg. author Sexual Harassment, 1992, Employment Discrimination Law, 3d edit. and supplements, 1996; contbr. articles to profl. jours. Mem. Comparable Worth Task Force Calif., Sacramento, 1984, Pepperdine U. Sch. of Law Bd. Visitors, 1990—, Calif. Law Revision Commn., 1998-99; mem., bd. dirs. Dispute Resolution Svcs., 1998—. Named alumnus of yr. Pepperdine Sch. Law, 1996; listed in Best Lawyers in Am., 1998-. Mem. L.A. County Bar Assn. (chair, labor and employment sect. 1996-97), Calif. C. of C. (employment rels. com. 1984—). Republican. Lutheran. Office: Gibson Dunn & Crutcher Ste 4921 333 S Grand Ave Los Angeles CA 90071-3197

HEMMINGHAUS, ROGER ROY, energy company executive, chemical engineer; b. St. Louis, Aug. 27, 1936; s. Roy Geroge and Henrietta E.M. (Knacht) H.; children: Sheryl Ann, Susan Lynn, Sally Ann; m. Dorothy O'Kelly, Aug. 18, 1979; children: R. Patrick, Kelley Elizabeth, Roger Christian. Student, Purdue U., 1954-56; BS in Chem. Engring., Auburn U., 1958; grad. cert., Bettis Reactor Engring., Pitts., 1959; postgrad., La. State U., 1963-66. Various tech. and mgmt. positions Exxon Co. U.S.A., Baton Rouge, 1962-66, Benicia, Calif., 1967-70, Houston, 1970-76; refinery gen. mgr. C.F. Industries, East Chicago, Ind., 1976-77; pres. Petro United Inc., Houston, 1977-80; v.p. planning United Gas Pipe Line, Houston, 1980-82, United Energy Resources, Houston, 1982-84; v.p. corp. planning and devel. Diamond Shamrock Corp. (name changed to Maxus Energy Corp., 1987), Dallas, 1984-85, past exec. v.p.; pres. Diamond Shamrock Refining & Mktg., San Antonio, 1985-99; chmn., dir., former CEO UltraMar Diamond Shamrock, Inc., San Antonio, until 1999; chmn., fed. res. agt. Fed. Res. Bank of Dallas, 1999-2000; dir. Luby's Inc., San Antonio, Tex., 2001—. Dir. InterFirst Bank, San Antonio Adviser Jr. Achievement, Baton Rouge, 1956-66; pres. congregation Lutheran Ch., Baton Rouge, 1965, Moraga, Calif., 1969; chmn. indsl. div. United Crusade, Solano County, Calif., 1970; assoc. gen. chmn. United Way, Tex. Gulf Coast, 1983-84. Served to lt. USN, 1958-62. Mem. Am. Chem. Soc., Am. Inst. Chem. Engrs., Naval Architects and Marine Engrs., Am. Petroleum Inst., San Antonio C. of C. (dir.), Tau Beta Pi, Phi Lambda Upsilon, Phi Kappa Phi, Kappa Alpha Clubs: Fair Oaks Country; Plaza, Petroleum (San Antonio). Office: 2211 NE Loop 410 San Antonio TX 78217-4673

HEMMINGS, FRED, state senator; b. Honolulu, Jan. 9, 1946; Owner Sports Enterprises, Inc., 1970—; rep. Hawaii Ho. of Reps., 1984—90; senator Hawaii State Senate, 2000—. Bd. dirs. Denver Broncos-NFL; floor leader Hawaii Ho. of Reps., 1989-90; mem. ways and means, water, land, energy and environ., transp., mil. affairs, govt. ops. and Hawaiian affairs coms. Hawaii State Senate; minority leader Hawaii State Senate. Author: The Soul of Surfing is Hawaiian, 1997, Surfing, Hawaii's Gift to the World, 1997; co-author: Illustrated Surfing Encyclopedia (in Japanese), 1979; weekly columnist Honolulu Star Bull., 1966; test pilot first artificial wave machine, 1969; talent (commls.) United Airlines, 1966, Kellogg's Cereal, 1967, Eastman Kodak Co., 1970; prodr./host KITV Hawaii Sports Scene, 1972; commentator ABC Wide World of Sports, 1970-75, 78, NBC Sports World, 1979-83; talk show host KGU Radio, 1991-92. Oahu County chmn. Rep. Party Hawaii, 1975-76; founder, prodr. Triple Crown of Surfing, 1983-88; dir. Children's Adv., 1991; trustee Outrigger Duke Kahanamoku Found., 1990-91; mem. Gov.'s Millenium Commn., Hawaii, 2000 Named Athlete of Yr., Honolulu Quarterback Club, 1964; with Goodwill Tours with Duke Kahanamoku, Hawaii, 1966-67, vets. divsn. Nat. Super Stars Competition, 1976; recipient Duke Kahanamoku Sportsman award, 1969, Top Ten Businessmen's award Honolulu Jr. C. of C., 1969, Top Legislator award Small Bus. Hawaii, 1985-90, 2001-2002; mem. championship teams Molokai to Oahu Canoe Race, 1967, 68, 75, Masters 1984; jr. divsn. Makaha Internat. Surfing Champion, 1962, 63, sr. divsn., 1964, 66; champion Peruvian Internat. Surfing, Peru, 1964, World Surfing, P.R., 1968; named to Internat. Surfing Hall of Fame, 1991, Punahou Sch. Athletic Hall of Fame, 1994, Hawaii-Sports Hall of Fame, 1999, Waterman of Yr., Surf Ind. and Manufacturer Assn., 2002. Mem. Assn. Surfing Profls. (life dir.), U.S. Surfing Fedn. (hon. dir.-life 1987), Internat. Profl. Surfing (founder, pres. 1976-83). Avocation: sports. Office: Hawaii State Senate Hawaii State Capitol Rm 208 415 S Beretania St Honolulu HI 96813 Fax: 808 587-7240. E-mail: senhemmings@Capitol.hawaii.gov.*

HEMMINGS, HUGH CARROLL, JR., anesthesiologist, pharmacologist, educator; b. Chapel Hill, N.C., Feb. 4, 1956; s. Hugh Carroll and Dorothy Annette (Bodiford) H.; m. Catherine Radford, Dec. 20, 1980 (div. Feb. 1992); m. Katherine Ann Albert, Apr. 1, 1993; 1 child, Emma. BS, Yale U., 1978, PhD, 1986, MD, 1987. Diplomate Am. Bd. Anesthesiology. Intern medicine Hosp. St. Raphael, New Haven, 1987-88; resident anesthesiology Mass. Gen. Hosp., Boston, 1989-91; fellow cardiac anesthesia N.Y. Hosp., N.Y.C., 1991; asst. prof. Cornell U. Med. Coll., N.Y.C, 1991-96, assoc. prof., 1996—2000, prof., 2000—, vice chari rsch. in anesthesiology, 1995—. Author 20 chpts. in books; contbr. over 70 articles to profl. jours. Mem. Soc. Neurosci., Am. Soc. Anesthesiology, Phi Beta Kappa. Presbyterian. Office: Cornell U Med Coll Box 50 LC 203 525 E 68th St New York NY 10021-4870

HEMMINGS, MADELEINE BLANCHET, management consultant, media consultant, not-for-profit fundraiser; b. Bryn Mawr, Pa., Aug. 14, 1942; d. Wilfred Loyola and Feroline (Sissenere) Blanchet; m. Richard B. Hemmings, Mar. 14, 1970; 1 child, Laurie Cornwall Hemmings Stull. Cert. in lang. and linguistics, U. Friboung, Switzerland, 1961; BS in Indsl. and Labor Rels., Cornell U., 1976. Owner Hallmark Pers. of Pa., Harrisburg, Pa., 1964-70; assoc. dir. human resources Cornell U., Ithaca, NY, 1972-77; policy dir. employee benefits NAM, Washington, 1977-79; policy dir. edn., employment and tng. C of C. of U.S., Washington, 1979-83; v.p. policy Nat. Alliance Bus., Washington 1983-85; pres. W.Va. Roundtable, Charleston, 1985—96; exec. dir. Nat. Assn State Dirs. Vocat. Tech. Edn., Washington, 1987-96; mng. dir. Nat. Telelearning Network, Inc., Washington, 1996-98; pres. Hemmings Assocs., Inc. 1998—2002; grants coord. Wayne-Finger Lakes Bd. of Coop. Edn. Svcs. Newark, NY, 2002—. Select adv. com. to asst. sec. edn., 1989—93; pres. adv com. Fed. Office Vocat. Edn. Performance Stds., 1992—95; ant. adv. bd. Ctr Edn. and Work, U. Wis., 1992—96, Nat. Ctr. Rsch. Vocat. Edn., Berkeley Calif., 1993—96. Author: (book) The New Job Training Partnership Act, 1982 Economic Development Plan, State of West Virginia, 1987, Education for a Working America, 1994, (newsletter) The Techocrat, 1988—95. Exec. dir. Nat Vocat. Tech. Edn. Found., 1987—96; campaign mgr. Connie Cook for Congress, Ithaca, 1984; sponsor U.S. Pony Club, Olney, Md., 1987—96. Mem.

Greater Washington Soc. Assn. Execs. (chief exec. coun. 1989—98), U.S. C. of C. (edn. com. 1987—96), Cornell Pres.' Club. Avocations: thoroughbred breeding and racing, combined training, oil painting. Home: 111 Lea Dr Newark NY 14513 Office: Wayne-Finger Lakes BOCES 131 Drumlin Ct Newark NY 14513 Fax: 301-570-9104. E-mail: mhemmings@wflboces.org.

HEMMINGS, PETER WILLIAM, deceased orchestra and opera administrator; b. London, Apr. 10, 1934; s. William and Rosalind H. ((Jones)) Hemmings; m. Jane Frances Kearnes, May 19, 1962; children: William, Lucy, Emma, Rupert, Sophie. Grad., Gonville and Caius Coll., Cambridge, England, 1957; LLD (hon.), Strathclyude U., Glasgow, 1978; DFA, Calif. State U., 2000. Clk. Harold Holt Ltd., London, 1958-59; planning mgr. Sadlers Wells Opera, London, 1959-65; gen. adminstr. Scottish Opera, Glasgow, 1962-77; gen. mgr. Australian Opera, Sydney, 1977-79; gen. dir. L.A. Music Ctr. Opera, 1984-2000; gen. mgr. New Opera Co., London, 1956-65; dir. Royal Acad. Music. Gen. cons. Compton Verney Opera Project. Lt. Brit. Signal Corps, 1952—54. Decorated Order Brit. Empire. Fellow: Royal Scottish Acad. Music; mem.: Royal Opera House Covent Garden (bd. dirs. from 1999), Opera Am. (bd. dirs.), Royal Acad. Music (hon.), Am. Friends of Sadlers Wells (pres. 1994—99), Garrick Club (London). Anglican. Died Jan. 2001.

HEMNES, THOMAS MICHAEL SHERIDAN, lawyer; b. Chgo., Nov. 10, 1948; s. Paul Gene and Dorothy Marion (Carl) H.; m. Carole Elizabeth Powers Dec. 20, 1970; children: Anna Ryan, Abigail Powers, Jonathan James. AB, Harvard U., 1970, JD, 1974. Bar: Mass. 1976, U.S. Dist. Ct. Mass., 1976, U.S. Dist. Ct. (no. dist.) N.Y. 1985. Law clk. U.S. Ct. Appeals (3d cir.), Phila., 1974-75; assoc. Foley, Hoag & Eliot, Boston, 1975-81, ptnr., 1981—; lectr. Northeastern U. Co-compilor: The Legal Word Book, 1978, rev. edit., 1982; contbr. articles on copyright, trademark, law firm mgmt. and other topics; editor, officer Harvard Law Rev., 1973-74. Corporator Handel & Hayden Soc., Boston, 1980-85, The Trademark Reporter, 1985—. Mem. ABA, Mass. Bar Assn., Boston Bar Assn., Boston Patent Law Assn., U.S. Trademark Assn. (assoc.). Home: 49 Hammond Rd Belmont MA 02478-2249 Office: Foley Hoag & Eliot One Post Office Sq Boston MA 02109

HEMP, RALPH CLYDE, retired reinsurance company executive, consultant, arbitrator, umpire; b. Fresno, Calif., Sept. 9, 1936; s. Ralph Edward and Mabel Alice (Knox) H.; m. Mary Ann Corley, Aug. 25, 1962; children— Ralph Kenneth, Laura Elizabeth BA, San Diego State U., 1961; JD, Western States U., Santa Ana, Calif., 1971. Office mgr. Crawford & Co., L.A., 1961-67; regional claims mgr. Olympic Ins. Co., L.A., 1968—76; sr. v.p. Leatherby Ins. Co., Fullerton, Calif., 1976—86; pres. North Am. Co., Greenwich, Conn., 1986—; chmn. Mt. Eagle Cos., Whitefish, Mont. Republican. Avocations: hunting; fishing; golf; skiing. Home and Office: Mt Eagle Cos PO Box 1971 Whitefish MT 59937-1971

HEMPE, A. HENRY, lawyer, state agency official; b. Milw., Mar. 16, 1938; s. Arnold Herman and Marcia Fleer Hempe; m. Cornelia Macy Gordon, June 26, 1965; children: Andrew, Amy. BS, U. Wis., 1962, JD, 1965. Bar: Wis. 1965, U.S. Dist. Ct. (we. dist.) Wis. 1966. Asst. dist. atty. Rock County, Janesville, Wis., 1965-67, county corp. counsel, 1967-72; ptnr. Hempe & Daniel, Janesville, 1972-76; shareholder, pres. Hempe, Hunsader & Schulz, S.C., Janesville, 1975-86; dep. sec. Wis. Dept. Employment Rels., Madison, 1987-88; commr. Wis. Employment Rels. Commn., Madison, 1987—, chair, commr., 1989-97. Author: Labor-Management Relations in the Public Sector, 2000. Mem., pres., v.p. Beloit (Wis.) Sch. Bd., 1980-86. bd. dirs. Sinnissippi Coun. Boy Scouts Am., Janesville, 1985-90, Rock County Humane Soc., Janesville, 1978-83, Assn. Labor Rels Agys. USA and Can., Washington, 1991-94; chair Human Rels. Commn., Beloit, 1972-76, Bd. Rev., Beloit. With USMCR, 1960-66, also res. Mem.: Wis. Bar Assn. Republican. Avocations: fishing, hunting, softball, jogging, dog training. Home: 5413 Trempealeau Trail Madison WI 53705 Office: Wis Employment Rels Commn 18 S Thornton Madison WI 53703

HEMPEL, JOHN P. mathematics educator; b. Salt Lake City, Oct. 14, 1935; s. Edgar W. and Emma B. (Johnson) H.; m. Edith Froese-Gertzen, Sept. 1, 1965; 1 child, Kristian J. BS, U. Utah, 1957; MS, U. Wis., 1959, PhD, 1962. Asst. prof. Fla. State U., 1962-63, Rice U., Houston, 1964-69, assoc. prof., 1969-76, prof., 1976—. With Inst. Advanced Study, 1971-72; vis. assoc. prof. U. Utah, 1976; vis. prof. U. Mich. 1980-81, U. B.C., 1987-88. Postdoctoral fellow Inst. Advance Study, 1963-64. Mem. Math. Sci. Rsch. Inst. Office: Rice University Dept Math PO Box 1982 6100 South Main Houston TX 77251 E-mail: hempel@math.rice.edu.

HEMPERLY, REBECCA SUE, publishing manager; b. Reading, Pa., June 17, 1966; d. Kenneth Jay and Ann Rebecca (Riehl) H. BA, Wheaton Coll., 1988; MA, Emerson Coll., 1992. Editl. asst. Coll.-Hill Press/Little, Brown, Boston, 1988-90, Little, Brown and Co., Boston, 1990, contracts coord., 1990-92, asst. mgr. contracts, 1992-96, mgr. contracts, 1996-98; paralegal WGBH Ednl. Found., Boston, 1998-99, pub. contracts cons., 1998-99, v.p. client svcs., 2000; client svcs. mgr. Database Pub. Group, Cambridge, Mass., 1999-2000; contracts mgr. Candlewick Press, Cambridge, 2000—. Del. 1st Amendment Congress, 1997; spkr. rights and permissions Assn. Am. Pub., Washington, 1996; mem. diversity task force Little, Brown and Co., Boston, 1993-98. Contbr. essays: The Book Group Book, 3d edit., 2000, Teaching Contemporary Theory to Undergraduates, 1995. Team capt. AIDS walk-a-thon Little, Brown and Co./AIDS Action Com., Boston, 1995-97; phone coord. GLOW, Watertown, Mass., 1989-98; mem. Rails to Trails Conservancy, 1995—. Mem. Women in Publishing, Nat. Writers' Union, Bookbuilders of Boston, Phi Beta Kappa (scholar 1988). Avocations: gardening, cycling, Karate, photography.

HEMPFLING, LINDA LEE, nurse; b. Indpls., July 28, 1947; d. Paul Roy and Myrtle Pearl (Ward) H. Diploma, Meth. Hosp. Ind. Sch. Nursing, 1968; postgrad., St. Joseph's Coll. Cert. medical audit specialist, 2000. Charge nurse Meth. Hosp., Indpls., 1968; staff nurse operating rm. Silver Cross Hosp., Joliet, Ill., 1969; charge nurse operating rm. Huntington (N.Y.) Hosp., 1969-73; night supr. oper. rm., post anesthesia care unit Hermann Hosp., Houston, 1973-76, unit mgr., purchasing coord. oper. rms., 1976-83; RN med. auditor, quality improvement and tng. coord. Nat. Healthcare Rev., Inc., Houston, 1984—98; RN med. auditor Integra Solutions, 1999—. Future Nurses Am. scholar, 1965, Nat. Merit scholar, 1965. Mem.: Tex. Assn. Med. Audit Specialists, Assn. PeriOperative Registered Nurses. Office: 9401 SW Freeway # 631B Houston TX 77074

HEMPHILL, JAMES S. investment management executive, financial advisor; b. Richmond, Va., Sept. 13, 1956; s. John Mickle and Marie Jeanne (de Kiewiet) H.; m. Amy Guise, Oct. 16, 1993; children: John Reagan, Katharine Guise, Alexander Dallett. BA with high honors, Swarthmore Coll., 1978. CFP, CLU, ChFC, CIMA. Legal asst. Schnader, Harrison, Phila., 1978; stockbroker, 2d v.p. Shearson/Am. Express, Media, Pa., 1978-84; asst. v.p. Merrill Lynch, Media, 1984-90; pres. TGS Fin. Advisors, Media, 1990—. Bd. dirs. Suburban Music Sch., Media, 1993-2000, chmn. capital campaign, 1995-96, v.p., 1996-97, pres., 1997-99; rsch. dir. Joachim for Congress, Havertown, Pa., 1982; founder Third Thursday Wine Club, Media, 1993—; commr. Media Sports League, 1985-86; mem. vestry Holy Trinity Episc. Ch., 2001—. Mem. Fin. Planning Assn., Investment Mgmt. Cons. Assn. Republican. Avocations: travel, wine appreciation. Office: TGS Financial Advisors 103 Chesley Dr Media PA 19063-1757

HEMPHILL, MARGARET AYARS, priest, artist; b. San Francisco, Oct. 8, 1931; d. David Preston and Margaret Taylor Ayars; m. James Drain Hemphill, Jan. 2, 1951; children: Greg, Kimberleigh, Ayars, Scofield, Chapin, Ashley. Student, Northwestern U., 1949-51; BA, Mundeline-Loyola U., 1980; M Div., Seabury Western Theol. Sem., Evanston, Ill., 1986, DMin, 2003. Assoc. priest St. James the Less, Northfield, Ill., 1997-99; pastoral affiliate Kenilworth (Ill.) Union, 1995-99; asst. rector St. Thomas Ch., Hanover, NH, 2001. One-woman shows include: All Chgo. U. Club, 1998, Tavern Club, 1973, Clausen Gallery, 1980; group-shows include: Winnetka Women's Club, Evanston Women's Club, North Shore Art League, Tavern Club, Evanston Art League. Episcopalian. Achievements include 1st ordained woman clergy to deliver sermon St. Andrews Ch., Zurich, Switzerland, 1987. Office: St Thomas Episcopal Ch 9 W Wheelock St Hanover NH 03755-1710 E-mail: jdhemp@aol.com.

HEMPHILL, MEREDITH, JR., retired lawyer; b. Spring Lake, N.J., Oct. 12, 1931; s. Meredith and Katharine Hemphill; m. Beverly Bell, Feb. 6, 1960; children: Mary, M. Scott, Geoffrey G., Mark A. BChemE, Rensselaer Poly. Inst., 1953; JD, U. Mich., 1959. Bar: N.Y. 1960, Pa. 1976. Assoc. Cravath, Swaine & Moore, N.Y.C., 1959-67; atty., gen. atty. Bethlehem (Pa.) Steel Corp., 1967-73, asst. gen. counsel, 1973-79, asst. v.p., asst. gen. counsel, asst. sec., 1979-85, asst. gen. counsel, asst. sec., 1985-87, dep. gen. counsel, asst. sec., 1987-96; ret., 1996. With USMCR, 1953-55. Mem. ABA, Pa. Bar Assn., Northampton County Bar Assn., Saucon Valley Country Club. Republican. Home: 238 E Market St Bethlehem PA 18018-6232

HEMPHILL, PAUL JAMES, author; b. Birmingham, Ala., Feb. 18, 1936; s. Paul James Hemphill and Velma Rebecca Nelson; m. Susan Olive, Sept. 1961 (div. Oct. 1975); children: Lisa, David, Molly; m. Susan Farran Percy, Nov. 6, 1976; 1 child, Martha. BA, Auburn U., 1959. Sports writer News, Birmingham, Ala., 1959-61; sports info. dir. Fla. State U., Tallahassee, 1962; sports editor Chronicle, Augusta, Ga., 1963, Times, Tampa, Fla., 1964; gen. columnist Atlanta Journal, 1965-69; editor Atlanta Magazine, 1981; writer-in-residence Brenau Coll., Gainesville, Ga., 1986-92; faculty Emory U., Atlanta, 2000—. Author: The Nashville Sound, 1970, Mayor: Notes on the Sixties,, 1972, (with Ivan Allen Jr.), The Good Old Boys, 1974, Long Gone, 1979, Too Old to Cry, 1981, The Sixkiller Chronicles, 1985, Me and the Boy, 1986, King of the Road, 1989, Leaving Birmingham, 1993, The Heart of the Game, 1996, Wheels, 1997, The Ballad of Little River, 2000, Nobody's Hero, 2002. With USAF, 1959-62. Nieman fellow Harvard U., 1969. Avocations: camping, hiking, fishing.

HEMPLEMAN, WARWICK, small business owner; b. Durham, N.C., Apr. 23, 1959; arrived in Germany, 1988; s. David William and Barbara Florence (Hampe) H.; m. Dagmar P.E. Ross, June 8, 1989 (div. 2001). BA magna cum laude, Adelphi U., 1980. Salesman Gingiss Formalwear, Atlanta, 1977, 79; warehouse worker Feature Sys., N.Y.C., 1980-81; prodn. asst. Giraldi Prodns., N.Y.C., 1981-82; self-employed prodn. asst. and prodn. coord. N.Y.C., 1981-86; self-employed grip/technician, 1985—; owner, founder Applied Film Theory, Munich and Cologne, Germany, 1992—. Cons. mem. Arbeitsgruppe Kran Sicherheit, Berlin, 1999-2002; lectr., instr. Industrie und Handelskammer, Cologne, 1998—; jury mem. CINEC awards, Munich, 1998—. Mem. Internat. Assn. Theatrical and Stage Employees (local 52), Bundesverband von Beleuchter, trustee, 2003-. Office: Applied Film Theory Emil-Hoffmann-Str 55 50996 Cologne Germany

HEMPSTONE, SMITH, JR., diplomat, journalist; b. Washington, Feb. 1, 1929; s. Smith and Elizabeth (Noyes) H.; m. Kathaleen Fishback, Jan. 30, 1954; 1 dau. Student, George Washington U., 1946-47; BA with honors, U. of South, 1950, LittD (hon.), 1969; Nieman fellow, Harvard U., 1964-65. Rewrite man AP, Charlotte, N.C., 1952; with Nat. Geog. mag., Washington, 1954; reporter Louisville Times, 1953, Evening Star, Washington, 1955-56; fgn. corr. Africa, Asia, Europe and Latin Am. for Chgo. Daily News, 1960-66, Washington Evening Star, 1966-69, assoc. editor, 1970-75; exec. editor Washington Times, 1982-84, editor-in-chief, 1984-85; nationally syndicated newspaper columnist, 1970-89; ambassador to Kenya, 1989-93; diplomat in residence U. of the South, Sewanee, Tenn., 1993, Va. Mil. Inst., Lexington, 1994. Fellow Inst. Current World Affairs, 1956-60 Author: Africa, Angry Young Giant, 1961, Rebels, Mercenaries and Dividends-The Katanga Story, 1962, Rogue Ambassador, 1997; (novel) A Tract of Time, 1966, In the Midst of Lions, 1968; editorial bd.: Nieman Reports, 1965-73. Alumni trustee U. South, 1974-78; bd. govs. Inst. Current World Affairs, 1974-78. Recipient Fgn. Corr. award Sigma Delta Chi and Overseas Press Club. Mem. Chevy Chase Club (Md.), Met. Club (Washington). Episcopalian. Home and Office: 7611 Fairfax Rd Bethesda MD 20814-1313

HEMRY, JEROME ELDON, lawyer; b. Kirksville, Mo., July 22, 1905; s. U.S.G. and Rose M. (Plumb) H.; m. Martha L. Langston, Aug. 1, 1934; children: Jerome Louis, Kenneth Marshall. AB, Oklahoma City U., 1926; JD, U. Okla., 1928; LL.M., Harvard U., 1929. Bar: Okla. 1928. Partner Hemry & Hemry, Oklahoma City, 1931-82, of counsel, 1983—; prof. law Central Okla. Sch. Law, 1931-41; dean, prof. law Langston U., 1948-49; dir., counsel Am. Gen. Life Ins. Co. Okla., 1959-79. Pres., gen. counsel Gen. Constrn. Corp., 1941-45; legislative counsel Okla. Chain Store Assn., 1941-44; Mem. Bd. Conf. Claimant's Okla. Ann. Conf.; treas. Oklahoma City S. Dist. Contbr. articles legal jours. Bd. dirs. Family and Children's Service, 1939-56. Mem. Okla. Assn. Mcpl. Attys. (pres. 1956-57), Am., Okla. bar assns., Order of Coif, Phi Delta Phi, Lambda Chi Alpha. Methodist (pres., counsel trustees). Clubs: Lions (Oklahoma City), Men's Dinner (Oklahoma City). Home: 2255 NW 55th St Oklahoma City OK 73112-7716 Office: 531 Couch Dr Oklahoma City OK 73102-2251

HEMRY, LARRY HAROLD, former federal agency official, writer, inventor; b. Seattle, Jan. 4, 1941; s. Harold Bernard and Florence Usborne (Achilles) H.; m. Nancy Kay Ballantyne, July 10, 1964 (div. Apr. 1976); children: Rachel Dalayne, Aaron Harold, Andrew LeRoy. BA, Seattle Pacific Coll., 1963; postgrad., Western Evang. Sem., Portland, Oreg., 1969, 70. Ordained to ministry Free Meth. Ch., 1968. Clergyman Free Meth. Ch., Vancouver, B.C., Can., 1963-64, Mt. Vernon, Wash., 1968-69, Colton (Oreg.) Community Ch., 1969-71; edit clk. Moody Bible Inst., Chgo., 1964-66; pres., founder Bethel Enterprises, Colton, 1969-71; immigration insp. U.S. Immigration and Naturalization Svc., Sumas, Wash., 1972-96. Author, historian: Some Northwest Pioneer Families, 1969, The Hemry Family History Book, 1985; author: An Earnest Plea to Earnest Christians, 1969; contbr. articles to profl. publs.; patentee mech. nut cracker. Chmn. com. to establish and endow the James A. Hemry meml. scholarship fund Seattle Pacific U., 1975. Fellow Seattle Pacific U. (Centurians Club); mem. The Nature Conservancy, The Sierra Club, The Audubon Soc. Avocations: camping, nature study, woodcarving. Home: PO Box 532 Sumas WA 98295-0532

HEMSING, JOSEPHINE CLAUDIA, public relations professional for performing arts; b. Paris, June 5, 1953; d. Albert E. and Esther (Davidson) H.; m. Daniel F. Cameron, Sept. 22, 1990. Student, Sorbonne U. de Paris, 1972-73; BA, Sarah Lawrence Coll., 1974; postgrad., CUNY, 1982-93. Dep. dir. distbn. ASCAP, N.Y.C., 1975-81; assoc. dramaturg and festival coordinator Städtische Bühnen Freiburg, Fed. Republic Germany, 1981-82; publicity asst. Audrey Michaels Pub. Relations, N.Y.C., 1983; publicity assoc. N.Y. Philharmonic, N.Y.C., 1984-85; publicist The Carson Office, N.Y.C., 1985-89; founder, dir. Hemsing Assocs., Inc., N.Y.C., 1989—. Mem. prodn. staff for New Russian Chamber Orch., N.Y.C., 1976-79, Encompass Music Theatre, N.Y.C., 1978-79, Wallgraben Theater on Tour, U.S.A., 1980, Rodger Hess Prodns., N.Y.C., 1982, John Hart Assoc., N.Y.C., 1982, Peter Witt Players Prodns., N.Y.C., 1982-83, numerous Broadway and off-Broadway shows including How I Got That Story, 1982, Twice Around the Park, 1983, Diary of a Madman, 1989; NBC-TV documentary Missiles Go Home, 1981; numerous published translations. Democrat. Home: 401 E 80th St Apt 29K New York NY 10021-0654 Office: 401 E 80th St Apt 14H New York NY 10021-0650 also: Hemsing Int c/o A Forgeron 21 rue Chevert 75007 Paris France E-mail: hemsing@ix.netcom.com.

HENAGER, CHARLES HENRY, civil engineer; b. Spokane, Wash., July 11, 1927; s. William Franklin and Mary Agnes (Henry) H.; m. Dorothy Ruth Parker, May 6, 1950; children: Charles Henry, Jr., Donald E., Roberta R. BS in Civil Engring., Wash. State U., 1950. Registered profl. engr., Wash. Instrumentman Wash. State Dept. Hwys., Yakima, 1950-52; engr. Gen. Electric Co., Richland, Wash., 1952-62; shift supr., reactor GE, Richland, Wash., 1962-63, sr. engr., 1963-65; sr. devel. engr. Battelle Pacific N.W. Labs., Richland, 1965-68, sr. rsch. engr., 1968-90, ret., 1990. Contbr. articles to profl. jours.; patentee in field. Mem. Village at Canyon Lakes Assn., bd. dirs., mem. archtl. control, 1996—98, v.p., 1998, 2000—03. With USN, 1945—46. Fellow: Am. Concrete Inst. (tech. activities com. 1987—89, Del Bloem award 1986); mem.: ASTM (subcom. 1980—92), ASCE (pres. Columbia sect. 1961—62), Kennewick Swim Club (pres. 1962—63), Phi Kappa Phi, Tau Beta Pi, Sigma Tau. Republican. Methodist. Avocations: calligraphy, genealogy. Home: 3413 S Huntington Loop Kennewick WA 99337-2572

HENARD, ELIZABETH ANN, controller; b. Providence, Oct. 9, 1947; d. Anthony Joseph and Grace Johanna (Lokay) Zorbach; m. Patrick Edward Mann, Dec. 18, 1970 (div. July 1972); m. John Bruce Henard Jr., Oct. 19, 1974; children: Scott Michael, Christopher Andrew. Student, Jacksonville (Fla.) U., 1966. Sec. So. Bell Tel. & Tel., Jacksonville, 1964-69; office mgr. Gunther F. Reis Assocs., Tampa, Fla., 1969-71; exec. sec. Ernst & Ernst, Tampa, 1971-72; exec. sec. to pres. Lamalie Assocs., Tampa, 1972-74; exec. sec. Arthur Young & Co., Chgo., 1975; adminstrv. asst. Irving J. Markin, Chgo., 1975; contr., v.p., corp. sec. Henard Assocs., Inc., Dallas, 1983-92; realtor Coldwell Banker Residential Real Estate, Tampa, 1999—. Mem. Dallas Investors Group (treas. 1986-91), Tampa Palms Country Club. Republican. Roman Catholic. Avocations: photography, crafts, golf, reading. Home: 5014 Wesley Dr Tampa FL 33647-1375 E-mail: eahenard@aol.com.

HENAULT, R. R. military officer; b. Winnipeg, Manitoba, Can., 1949; Grad., Ecole Superieure de Guerre, Paris, Nat. Def. Coll. Kingston; BA, U. Manitoba. Enrolled Can. Forces, 1968, advanced through grades to lt. gen., 1968—2001, gen., chief def. staff, 2001—. Office: NDH Dept Nat Defence Maj-Gen George R Pearkes Bldg 101 Colonel by Dr Ottawa ON Canada K1A 0K2

HENBEST, ROBERT LEROY, retired bank and insurance company executive; b. Elmira, N.Y., Aug. 25, 1923; s. Edmund James and Helen Mae (Yost) H.; m. Grace Edith Rowley; children: Judith H. Bayer, Jacqueline Lee, William H., R. Theodore E. Student, Lycoming Coll., 1943, Elmira Coll., 1950, 52, U. Conn., 1951, U. Hartford, 1953; cert., Wharton Bus. Sch., 1955. Ins. mgr. Henbest Ins. Svc., Elmira, 1941-42, 45-47; pres. Henbest & Morrisey, Inc., Elmira, 1945-89; bank dir. Elmira Savs. Bank, 1987-89; ret., 1989. Chmn. Chemung County Safety Orgn.; worked for United Fund; mem. Nat. Soaring Mus., Nat. Warplane Mus., Clemens Ctr. Performing Arts, Arnot Art Gallery, North Presbyn. Ch., trustee; vol. Ret. Sr. Vol. Program, Medicare/Medicaid Assistance Program, claims counselor Courier Arnot-Agden Med. Ctr. 6; treas. Thursday Morning Musicalles; vol. Chemung County Health Dept.; Blood Bank vol. ARC. Maj. USAF, 1943-45, WWII, USAF Res., 1945-66, ret. 1966. Decorated DFC, Air Medal with four oak leaf clusters, Presdl. citation with oak leaf cluster, lead bombardier Euro/Mediterranean Theatre Ribbon, with four battle stars. Mem. VFW (life), Chemung County Ins. Agts. Assn. (pres. 1958), Am. Legion, Curtis Wright Air Force Assn., Profl. Ins. Agts. Assn., Ind. Agts. Assn., Chemung C. of C., 15th Air Force Assn., 451st Bomb Group Assn., Masons, Nat. Warplane Mus. (falcon), Torch Internat. Republican. Home: 12 Roricks Glen Pky Elmira NY 14905-1966 Office: WH Ins Agy Inc 112 Baldwin St Elmira NY 14901-3025

HENBEST, WILLIAM HARRISON, insurance agent; b. Elmira, N.Y., Nov. 14, 1955; s. Robert Leroy and Grace Edith (Rowley) H.; m. Cynthia Jean Rohde, Apr. 26, 1980; children: Danielle Christine, Sarah Kathleen, William Harrison II. BBA, Rochester Inst. Tech., 1978. Fin. analyst A&P, Horseheads, N.Y., 1979 80; multi line underwriter Gen. Accident Ins., Syracuse, N.Y., 1980-82; v.p. Henbest & Morrisey Inc., Elmira, 1982-88; pres. Henbest & Morrisey, Inc., Elmira, 1988-97; pres., CEO W.H. Ins. Agy., Inc., Elmira, 1997—. Sec., treas. Chemung County Agts. Assn., Elmira, 1982—; pres. Agt.'s Adv. Coun. CGU Ins., 1993-2000, Syracuse, N.Y. Com. mem. United Way, Elmira, 1986. Mem. Ind. Ins. Agts. Assn., Chemung County C. of C. (chmn.'s coun., past bd. dirs.), Rotary, Sigma Pi. Republican. Avocations: reading, travel, golf. Home: 82 Demarest Pky Elmira NY 14905-2012 Office: W H Ins Agy Inc 112 Baldwin St Elmira NY 14901-3025 E-mail: bhenbest@stny.rr.com.

HENCH, PHILIP KAHLER, physician; b. Rochester, Minn., Sept. 19, 1930; s. Philip Showalter and Mary Genevieve (Kahler) H.; m. Barbara Joan Kent, July 10, 1954; children: Philip Gordon, John Kahler, Amanda Kent. BA, Lafayette Coll., 1952, MD, U. Pitts., 1958; MSc in Medicine, U. Minn., 1965. Intern U. Colo. Med. Ctr., 1958-59; fellow in medicine and rheumatology Mayo Graduate Sch., Rochester, Minn., 1959-63; with Inst. for Arthritis and Metabolic Diseases, NIH, Bethesda, Md., 1963-64; asst. div. rheumatology Scripps Clinic and Rsch. Found., La Jolla, Calif., 1965-66, assoc., 1966-70, assoc. mem., 1970-74, mem., head, 1974-82, sr. cons., 1982—, adj. asst. mem. dept. neuropharmacology, mem. dept. acad. affairs; asst. clin. prof. U. Calif. Sch. Medicine, San Diego. Cons. to pharm. cos.; mem. People to People Mission to China on study of Aging, 1982; leader People to People Mission to Cuba, 2001. Contbr. articles on rheumatic diseases, pain and sleep disorders to profl. jours.; mem. editl. com. Rheumatism Revs., 1974-84; editl. reviewer Arthritis and Rheumatism, Jour. Rheumatology, 1985—; bd. spl. cons. Patient Care, 1987—. Mem. bd. advisors San Diego Opera; mem. U. Calif. San Diego Police Dept. Sr. Vol. Program. Recipient Arthritis Found. award (6), San Diego chpt., 1971-80; Philip S. Hench scholar Mayo Grad. Sch. Medicine, 1965. Fellow ACP, Am. Coll. Rheumatology (chmn. nonarticular rheumatism study group 1975-82, com. on preventive and rehab. medicine 1984-85, com. on rheumatologic practice 1975-77); mem. AMA, Nat. Soc. Clin. Rheumatologists (pres. 1997-99), Am. Pain Soc., Calif. Med. Assn., Internat. Assn. for Study Pain, La Jolla Acad. Medicine (pres. 1994-96), Arthritis Found (bd. govs. San Diego chpt., Best Doctors in Am. award 1992-93, 94-95, 96-97), San Diego Hist. Soc., San Diego Mus. Fine Arts, San Diego Opera (bd. advisors), La Jolla Chamber Music Soc., La Jolla Profl. Men's Soc., Club of La Jolla. Republican. Avocations: music, swimming, hiking, biking, skiing. Home and Office: 7856 La Jolla Vista Dr La Jolla CA 92037-3530 Fax: 858-453-0113. E-mail: bhench@san.rr.com.

HENCK, CHARLES SEYMOUR, lawyer; b. Knoxville, Apr. 28, 1947; s. F. Seymour and Martha M. Henck; m. Christine Gorenflo Henck, June 16, 1973; children: Stephanie, Alison. BA, Emory Coll., 1969, JD, 1975; LLM, Georgetown U., 1979. Bar: Ga. 1975, U.S. Tax Ct. 1979, D.C. 1979. Atty. Office of Chief Counsel IRS, Washington, 1975-79; assoc. Ballard Spahr Andrews & Ingersoll, Washington, 1980-84, ptnr., 1984—. Fellow Am. Coll. Bond Counsel; mem. ABA, Nat. Assn. Bond Lawyers (bd. dirs. 1992-94). Office: Ballard Spahr Andrews & Ingersoll LLP 601 13th St NW Ste 1000S Washington DC 20005-3807 E-mail: henck@ballardspahr.com.

HENDEE, SUSAN SYKES, culinary and technology educator, consultant; b. Caracas, Venezuela, Aug. 26, 1951; d. Harry John and Mary Elizabeth (Howard) Sykes. PhD, NYU, 2002. Cert. culinary educator. Assoc. prof. N.Y. Inst. Tech., Central Islip, 1995—2002, prof. culinary arts and hospitality, 2002—. Foods cons. CULACON, Islip, 1980—2001. Capt. U.S. Svc. Command, 2000—01. Mem.: Accrediting Commn. (vice chair), Am. Culinary Fedn. Avocations: food, travel, birdwatching. Home: 61 Maple St Islip NY 11751-4605 Office: NY Inst Tech Culinary Arts Ctr 300 Carleton Ave Central Islip NY 11722 Office Fax: 631-348-3247. E-mail: shendee@nyit.edu.

HENDEE, WILLIAM RICHARD, medical physics educator, university official, radiologist; b. Owosso, Mich., Jan. 1, 1938; s. C.L. and Alvina M. H.; m. Jeannie Wesley, June 16, 1960; children: Mikal, Shonn, Eric, Gareth and Gregory (twins), Lara and Karel (twins). BS, Millsaps Coll., Jackson, Miss., 1959; PhD, U. Tex., 1962; DSc (hon.), Millsaps Coll., Jackson, Miss., 1988. Diplomate Am. Bd. Radiology, Am. Bd. Health Physics. AEC fellow Nat. Reactor Testing Sta., Idaho Falls, Idaho, 1960; asst. prof., then assoc. prof. physics Millsaps Coll., 1962-65, chmn. dept., 1964-65; instr. Miss. State U. (extension), 1963; asst. prof., then assoc. prof. radiology (med. physics) U. Colo. Med. Center, 1965-73, prof., 1974-85, chmn. dept., 1978-85; mem. staff VA Hosp., Denver, 1970-85, Mercy Hosp., 1971-85, Denver Gen. Hosp., 1971-85, Beth Israel Hosp., 1974-85; v.p. sci. and tech. AMA, Chgo., 1985-1991; prof. radiology, biophysics, radiation oncology, bioethics Med. Coll. Wis., Milw., 1991—, clin. prof. radiology and biophysics, 1985-91, sr. assoc. dean, v.p., 1991—, dean grad. sch., 1995—. Prof. bioengring. Marquette U., 1993—; vis. lectr. Oak Ridge Assoc. Univs., 1964; adj. prof. radiology Northwestern U. Sch. Medicine, 1986-91. Contbr. articles to profl. jours. Served with USMC, 1957-62. Recipient Disting. Alumnus award Millsaps Coll., 1967, Disting. Svc. award Nat. Wildlife Fedn., 1990, Wright Langham Meml. award U. Ky., 1991; Gilbert X-ray fellow, 1960-62, summer fellow NSF, AEC; campus assoc. Danforth Found. Fellow Am. Coll. Radiology, Am. Inst. Med. and Biol. Engring. (pres. 1998-99); mem. AAAS, Health Physics Soc. (chmn. coms., Elda E. Anderson award 1972), Am. Assn. Physicists in Medicine (pres. 1976-77, Robert S. Landauer Meml. award 1977, William D. Coolidge award 1989), Nat. Wildlife Fedn. (Disting. Svc. award 1990), Soc. Biomed. Engring., (sr. mem.), Soc. Nuclear Medicine (pres. 1980-81, Benedict Cassen Meml. award 1984), Am. Acad. Home Care Physicians (Disting. Svc. award 1991), Omicron Delta Kappa, Theta Nu Sigma. Office: Med Coll Wis 8701 W Watertown Plank Rd Milwaukee WI 53226-3548

HENDEL, ELISA BETH, special education educator, writer; b. Phila., Pa., Mar. 28, 1959; d. Israel E. and Eleanor B. Brownstein; m. Steven Michael Hendel, Nov. 19, 1983; children: Samantha Rae, Robyn Brooke, Melanie Ilyse. BS, Pa. State U., State College, 1981; MEd, Arcadia U., Glenside, Pa., 1983. Lic. tchr. deaf and hearing impaired Pa. and N.J., reading specialist Pa. Dept. of Edn., spl. edn. tchr. N.J. Dept. of Edn. Tchr., interpreter of hearing impaired Montgomery County (Pa.) Intermediate Unit, 1981—83; tchr. hearing impaired Newark Pub. Schs., 1983—85, Somerville H.S., Berkley Heights, NJ, 1985—86; tchr., interpreter hearing impaired Bergen County Spl. Svcs., Paramus, NJ; writer Hen House Press, Inc., Paramus, 2002—, pub., 2002—. Vol., bd. dirs. Found. for Diabetes Rsch., Livingston, NJ, 1998—; online support team mem. Juvenile Diabetes Rsch. Found.-Internat., 2003—; pub. spkr. support for newly diagnosed with type 1 diabetes Juvenile Diabetes Rsch. Found., 2001—. Author, editor, publisher: book A Child in Your Care has Diabetes. A Collection of Information., Web site designer: Hen House Press, Inc.; contbr. articles to mags. Recipient Juvenile Diabetes Rsch. Found. Walk to Cure Diabetes, 2001. Achievements include development of educational plans for students with diabetes. Office: Hen House Press Inc Ste 212 12 Route 17 N Paramus NJ 07652 Home Fax: 201-291-9177; Office Fax: 201-291-9177. Personal E-mail: henhousepress@aol.com. E-mail: henhousepress@aol.com.

HENDEL, MAURICE WILLIAM, lawyer, consultant; b. Holyoke, Mass., Feb. 24, 1909; s. Richard and Helen (Katz) H.; m. Evelyn F. Berger, Dec. 30, 1934; children— Richard C., Eugene L. Ph.B., Brown U., 1930; J.D., Harvard U., 1933. Bar: R.I. 1933, U.S. Dist. Ct. R.I. 1935. Counsel to Sec. of State of R.I., Providence, 1949-79, editor Pub. Laws, 1949-79; cons. to constl. convs. State of R.I., 1954, 62, 68-69, 86; cons. home rule charters cities and towns, 1960—, mem., sec. Statute Consolidation Commn., 1953-56; parliamentarian R.I. Senate, 1949-79. Mem. editorial bd. R.I. Bar Jour. Mem. Dem. City Com., Providence, 1940-60, Dem. Town Com., Lincoln, R.I., 1961-86. Mem. R.I. Bar Assn., Pawtucket Bar Assn. Jewish. Clubs: Kirkbrae Country (Lincoln); Faculty of Brown U. (Providence). Lodge: Masons (past master, high priest). Office: McMahon Hendel McMahon 200 Main St Pawtucket RI 02860-4119 Address: 4 Morgan Ct Lincoln RI 02865-4647

HENDEL, ROBERT CHARLES, medical educator; b. New Haven, Conn., Apr. 16, 1955; s. Stanley and Rowena Hendel; m. Judy K. Hendel, June 19, 1988; children: Jason, Adam. BA, Northwestern U., 1977; MD, George Washington U., 1983. Diplomate Am. Bd. Internal Medicine, Am. Bd. Cardiovascular Disease. Asst. prof. U. Mass. Med. Ctr., Worcester, 1989-90; assoc. prof. Northwestern U., Chgo., 1990-99, Rush-Presbyn.-St. Luke's Med. Ctr., Chgo., 1999—. Mem. Am. Soc. of Nuclear Cardiology (bd. dirs., pres.-elect), Am. Coll. Cardiology, Am. Heart Assn., Soc. of Nuclear Medicine (cardiovascular coun. pres. 1999). Home: 1 Kingswood Ct Deerfield IL 60015-1911 Office: 1725 W Harrison St Chicago IL 60612-3828 E-mail: rhendel@rush.edu.

HENDERSHOT, CAROL MILLER, physical therapist; b. Lancaster, Pa., July 24, 1959; d. Richard Horace and Joan Marie (Nonnenmocher) Miller; m. Richard A. Hendershot, Dec. 29, 1989; 1 child, Scott Michael. BS in Phys. Therapy, Quinnipiac Coll., 1981. Staff phys. therapist Easter Seal Rehab. Ctr., Lancaster, 1981-85, phys. therapy dept. head, 1986-89; staff phys. therapist Community Hosp. of Lancaster, 1985-86, Guilds' Sch. & Neuromuscular Ctr., 1990—. Dir. publicity and pub. rels. Lancaster Dist. United Meth. Women, 1988—89; chmn. ch. and soc. com. Covenant United Meth. Ch., 1987, 1988, mem. chancel choir, 1981—89, mem. adminstrv. bd., 1975—88; trustee Audubon Pk. United Meth. Ch., 1990—93, mem. chancel choir, 1990—92, mem. staff parish rels. com., 1993—94, mem. Jubilee Bell Choir, 1990—, mem. worship com., 1996—, chair worship com., 2003—, dir. Bethlehem and Joy Bells Handbell Choirs, 1994—96, dir. Jubilee Handbell Choir, 1996—. Mem.: Lancaster County Vis. Nurse Assn. (prof. adv. com. 1987—89), Neuro-Devel. Treatment Assn., Beta Beta Beta. Democrat. Methodist. Avocations: sewing, music, cooking, needlework, gardening, stamping. Home: 6007 W Hopi Ct Spokane WA 99208-9046

HENDERSHOTT LOVE, ARLES JUNE, television community relations director; b. Rockford, Ill., Oct. 22, 1956; d. Eugene Bourden and Rose Marie (Erickson) Hendershott; m. Joseph William Love, Sept. 20, 1986. BS with high honors, Ill. State U., 1979; postgrad., U. Mo., Columbia, 1992. Reporter Sta. WTVO-TV, Rockford, 1979-82, news prodr., 1982-83; news assignment editor Sta. WIFR-TV, Rockford, 1983-86, news dir., 1986-97; dir. cmty. rels. Benedek Broadcasting Corp./WIFR-TV, 1997—. Speaker Rockford Pub. Schs., 1980-83, 97—. Producer news story Pee Wee Explosion, 1985 (AP award 1986). Bd. dirs. Rockford Airshow, 1994-95; mem. com. YWCA, Rockford, 1987, Westminister Presbyn. Ch., Rockford, also tchr. Sunday Sch., 1983-2000; bd. dirs. No. Ill. chpt. March of Dimes, 1980-84, NW Ill. chpt. Spl. Olympics, Rockford, 1986—, Discovery Ctr. Mus., Rockford, 1987-90, N.W. Ill. Alzheimer & Related Disorder Assn., 1991, Rockford CrimeStoppers, 1992—; active YWCA Leader Luncheon Coun., 1992-93, leader Lunch Coun., 1994-95; bd. dirs. YWCA Rockford, 1997-99, Am. Lung Assn. Winnebago County, 1997—, Rockford Boys and Girls Club, 1997—; pres. bd. dirs. Am. Hearth Assn. Winnebago County 1999—, bd. dirs. 1997—. Recipient Leadership award Ken-Rock Cmty. Ctr., Rockford, 1980, Presdl. award of honor Rockford Jaycees, 1986, Dist. award Zonta Pub. Rels. Campaign, 1990, Leader Luncheon award YWCA, 1991, Recognize the Abilities Cmty. Svc. award, 1999, Congl. Cert. for Cmty. Svc., 1999, Midwest Affiliate Am. Heart Assn. Spl. Heart award, 1999, Crimestopper of Yr. award Rockford, 1996, 2000, Disting. Svc. award Am. Heart Assn., 2000, award of merit Ill. Pub. Health Assn., 2000, Kiwanis Touch Aufe award, 2003. Mem. AAUW (bd. dirs. 1982-84), NAFE, Radio-TV News Dirs. Assn. (TV state coord. for Ill. 1989-96), Ill. News Broadcasters Assn., Soc. Profl. Journalists, Am. Mgmt. Assn., Archeology Inst. Am., Rockford C. of C. (pres. club 1993—, public policy com. 1997—, amb. 1997—), Univ. Chgo. Oriental Inst., Ill. Assoc. Press (exec. com. 1989—, pres.-elect 1990, pres. 1991), Lens & Shutter Club (pres. 1983-85, others), Zonta. Avocations: traveling, photography. Office: Sta WIFR-TV 2523 S Meridian Rd Rockford IL 61102 E-mail: arles@wifr.com.

HENDERSON, ALAN SCOTT, humanities educator; b. West Palm Beach, Fla., Sept. 1, 1962; s. Clifton Russell Henderson Jr. and Mary Estelle Arnette; life ptnr. Richard Edmon Prior. BA, Fla. State U., 1984; M, Johns Hopkins U., 1985; tchr. cert., U. Va., 1986; PhD, SUNY, Buffalo, 1996. Social studies tchr. Chesapeake (Va.) City Schs., 1986—89; jr. coll. English tchr. Yamagata (Japan) Women's Jr. Coll., 1989—90; intern coord. Harry S. Truman Scholarship Found., Washington, 1990—91; asst. prof. Furman U., Greenville, SC, 1998—. Adj. prof. Furman U., Greenville, S.C., 1996-98; application evaluator Harry S. Truman Scholarship Found., Washington, 1992—; polit. cons. Parents and Taxpayers for Better Greenville Schs., 1996. Author: Housing and the Democratic Ideal: The Life and Thought of Charles Abrams, 2000; editor: Power and the Public Interest, 2002; contbr. articles to profl. jours. Bd. dirs. Greenville Concert Band, 1996—; founding bd. dirs. Friends of the Berea Libr., Greenville, 1997—; campaign cons. S.C. Demo. Com., Greenville, 1996—; ednl. cons. Greenville County Sch. Sys., 1998—. Recipient fellowship Nat. Endowment for Humanities, 1988, Harry S. Truman scholarship, 1982-86, Order of Chevalier Internat. Order of DeMolay, 1982, John Phillip Sousa award John Phillip Sousa Assn., 1980. Mem. ASCD, Japanese Assn. Lang. Tchrs. (program chair 1989-90), Orgn. Am. Historians, Urban History Assn., Soc. Am. City and Regional Planning Assn., Kappa Delta Pi, Nat. Golden Key, Phi Beta Kappa, Phi Kappa Phi, Pi Sigma Alpha, Phi Mu Alpha, Pi Gamma Mu, Omicron Delta Kappa, Omicron Delta Epsilon, Phi Alpha Theta. Democrat. Mem. Soc. Of Friends. Avocations: trumpet playing, travel, wine-making. Home: 8 Aiken Cir Greenville SC 29617 Office: Furman U 3300 Poinsett Hwy Greenville SC 29613 Fax: 864-294-3341. E-mail: scott.henderson@furman.edu.

HENDERSON, ALBERT KOSSACK, publishing company executive, dairy executive, consultant; b. Phila., July 9, 1938; s. Harry Brinton, Jr. and Beatrice (Conford) H.; m. Tamara Ann McCormick, Feb. 14, 1968; children— Christopher Findley, Theodore Leon. Mus.B., Ithaca Coll., 1960; postgrad., N.Y. U. Editorial asst. Hearst Headline, 1960-62; asst. sales mgr. Royal McBee, 1960-64; editor Johnson Reprint Corp., 1964-69; gen. mgr., v.p., treas. Brit. Book Centre, Inc., N.Y.C., 1969-77; dir. Pergamon Press, Inc., v.p., treas., 1971-77; exec. v.p., dir. Newman Grove Creamery Co., Nebr., 1977-81; dir. publs. Am. Solar Energy Soc., N.Y.C., 1981-83; pres. Henderson Assoc. Cons., Bridgeport, Conn., 1980—, Chess Combination, Inc., Bridgeport, 1984—; editor Pub. Rsch. Quar., 1994-2000. Exec. sec. Com. for Preservation Academic and Sci. Info. Resources. Co-chairperson adv. panel for sci. publs. Found. for Internat. Sci. Coop., 1990-92. Mem. Am. Soc. Info. Sci., Soc. Scholarly Publs., Coun. Sci. Editors. Home: Box 2423 Noble Sta Bridgeport CT 06608-0423 E-mail: 70244.1532@compuserve.com.

HENDERSON, ALMA, educator; b. Milw., Mar. 19, 1920; d. Gotthieb and Matilda (Zielke) Siewert; m. George Henderson, Sept. 28, 1946 (dec. May 1997); adopted many African and Chinese young people. Grad., Flight Sch., 1945; BA, Tocoa Falls Coll., 1946; MA, U. Ga., 1973. Missionary tchr. N.Am. Bapt., Cameroon, West Africa, 1947-70; tchr. Athens (Ga.) Christian Sch., 1973-83, U. Ga., Athens, 1983-99. Baptist. Avocations: african and chinese culture, foreign student affairs, theological studies. Home: 7 Sleepy Holw Athens GA 30601-5543

HENDERSON, ARNOLD GLENN, architect, educator; b. Shawnee, Okla., Nov. 10, 1934; s. Henry Glenn and Pearlalee H.; m. Beatriz Eugenia Chavez Escandon; children: Eric Neal, Alex Jon. B.Arch., BS in Archtl. Engring, U. Okla., 1961; MS in Architecture, Columbia U., 1964. Asst. prof. architecture U. Ill., Urbana, 1964-68; assoc. prof. U. Okla., 1968-73, prof., 1973—, disting. lectr., 1984, 88; pvt. practice architecture Norman, Okla., 1975—. Author: Document for an Anonymous Indian, 1974, The Surgeon General's Collection, 1976, (with others) Architecture in Oklahoma, 1978, (with others) The Point Riders Great Plains Poetry Anthology, 1982; co-editor: (with others) Point Riders Press, 1974—; painting exhbns. in Ind., Ill., Okla., La., Wyo., Ark., Kans., Ala., Colo., Tex. and London; author of poetry. Chmn. Norman Housing Authority, 1972-77; mem. Hist. Preservation and Landmark Commn., Guthrie, Okla., 1979-81. Served with U.S. Army, 1953-55. Grantee NSF, Nat. Endowment Arts, AIA, Okla. Arts Coun., Okla. Humanities Com., Graham Found. for Advanced Studies in the Fine Arts. Fellow AIA (award of excellence 1976); mem. Vernacular Architecture Forum, Nat. Trust Hist. Preservation, Okla. Hist. Soc. (Shirk Meml. award 1991), Soc. Archl. Historians, Sigma Tau. Democrat. Roman Catholic. Home: 1208 Barkley Ave Norman OK 73071-4812 Office: U Okla Coll Arch Norman OK 73019-0001 E-mail: ahenderson@ou.edu.

HENDERSON, ARVIS BURL, data processing executive, biochemist; b. Abilene, Tex., Oct. 24, 1943; s. Arvis Vernon and Aubra Lee (Patton) H.; m. Mary Ann Pickett, Mar. 17, 1966 (div. Sept. 1983); 1 child, Michelle Rene; m. Jo Nell Hartsell, July 2, 1985 (dec. May 1996); m. Sally Wolfson, May 25, 2001. AA, San Angelo Coll., 1961; BA, U. Tex., 1966; MAE, Ed. Math. U., 1969; PhD, U. Tex. Health Sci. Ctr., 1976. Postdoctoral fellow U. Tex., Austin, 1976-80; dir. rsch. lab. Instrumentation Specialities Co., Lincoln, Nebr., 1980-81; asst. prof. pediatrics U. Tex. Health Sci. Ctr., Houston, 1981-84; dir. sci. computing S.W. Found. for Biomed. Rsch., San Antonio, 1984-91; assoc. v.p. info. tech. U. Tex., San Antonio, 1991-96, vice provost for computing and info. tech. Arlington, 1996-2000; chief info. officer Howard U., 2000—02, Dept. Health and Family Svcs., State of Wis., Madison, 2002—. Mem. strategic leadership coun. U. Tex., 1997-2000; co-prin. investigator Students' Work Consortium, 1997-99; mem. State Wis. Tech. Leadership Coun., 2002—. Contbr. articles on biomed. research to profl. jours., chpts. to books. Chmn. Alamo Area Quality Workforce Planning Com., 1990-92; active Class XII Gov. Exec. Devel. Program, 1993; reader North Tex. Taping and Radio for the Blind, 1999-2000, bd. dirs., 1999-2003. Recipient Research Service award NIH, 1976-79; fellow U. Tex., 1976-80, Clayton Found. Biochemistry Inst., 1980. Mem. NIH spl. study sect. 9, Data Processing Mgmt. Assn., Assn. Systems Mgmt., Assn. for Computing Machinery. Republican. Episcopalian. Avocation: photography. Home: 6534 Doral Cir Madison WI 53719 Office: Dept Health and Family Svcs 1 W Wilson St Madison WI 53707 E-mail: hendeab@dhfs.state.wi.us., abhphd@charter.net.

HENDERSON, BRUCE WINGROVE, insurance executive; b. Balt., Feb. 20, 1946; s. Wilmer Paul and Margaret Virginia Henderson; m. Karen Todd, Sept. 14, 1968; 1 child, Katie Anne. BA in History, U. Balt., 1968. Sr. acct. exec. Conn. Gen. Life Ins. Co., Hartford, 1970-89; v.p. Marsh Advantage Am., Indpls., 1989—. Author: (trademark for employee benefits plan design) Health Age/Actual Age Plan, 1994. Vol. Dayspring Ctr., Indpls., 1995. With USN, 1969-70. Mem. Soc. of Mary, Nat. Ind. Health Underwriters Assn., Ind. Astron. Soc., Am. Legion, Nat. History Honor Soc., U. Balt. (parliamentarian), Am. Assn. for True Life in God (bd. mem.), Civitas Dei (past program chmn.). Republican. Roman Catholic. Avocations: golf, telescope viewing. Home: 9009 Cloud Bay Ct Indianapolis IN 46236-9172

HENDERSON, CATHERINE LYNN, retired secondary education educator, writer; b. Charleston, W.Va., Oct. 19, 1946; d. Raymond Anis Frame and Alma Madalene Green; m. W. Elliott Henderson, Apr. 12, 1978 (dec. 1985). BA in English, Morris Harvey Coll., 1968; MA in Journalism, Marshall U., 1976. Tchr. Kanawha County Bd. Edn., Charleston, W.Va., 1968—2001; ret., 2001. Stringer Offcl. Detective Group. Author: Fairs, Festivals & Funnin' in West Virginia, 1996; co-author: Essential Strategies for School Security, 2001; contbr. to Wonderful W.Va. Mag., Charleston City Mag. Mem. Nat. Writers Assn., Mystery Writers of Am., Am. Crime Writers League, Sisters in Crime, Soc. of Profl. Journalists. E-mail: murdermostfoul@charter.net.

HENDERSON, CHARLES BROOKE, research company executive; b. Washington, Mar. 13, 1929; s. Robert Neel and Dorothy (Brooke) H.; m. Elizabeth Ann Carter, June 6, 1954; children: Katherine, Roger, Sally. BS, Purdue U., 1950; SM in Chem. Engring, MIT, 1952. With Atlantic Research Corp., Alexandria, Va., 1954-88, dir. research and tech., 1971-76, v.p., 1976-80, sr. v.p., 1980-88, also dir. Chmn. bd. dirs. Arctech Inc., 1988-92. Patentee in field. Active Boy Scouts Am., 1965-69, Girl Scouts U.S.A., 1969-71; treas. Loudoun Symphony, 1993-97, bd. dirs., 1993-2001; bd. dirs. Loudoun Arts Coun., 1997-99. Named Nat. Capital Outstanding Young Engr., 1961, One of Maj. Innovators, Tech. Mag., 1981. Fellow: AIAA (assoc.); mem.: Sigma Xi.

HENDERSON, CONNIE CHORLTON, city planner, artist and writer; b. Cedar Rapids, Iowa, July 16, 1944; d. Robert Brown and Lorraine Madeline (Marquardt) Chorlton; m. Dwight Franklin Henderson, Dec. 24, 1966; 1 child, Patricia. BA, Anderson U., 1966; MA in Edn., St. Francis Coll., Ft. Wayne, Ind., 1972; MPA, U. Tex. San Antonio, 1987. Art coord. Ft. Wayne Cmty. Schs., 1966-67; art tchr. East Allen County Schs., New Haven, Ind., 1968-71, 74-79; instr. Manchester Coll., N. Manchester, Ind., 1971-72; rsch. assoc. Tremar Real Estate Rsch., San Antonio, 1983-84; planning asst. (vol.) City of San Antonio, Tex., 1985-88, planner I, 1988-89, project mgmt. specialist, 1990, conservation edn. coord., 1990-91; planner II San Antonio Water Sys., 1991-96, 2003—, water edn. coord., 1996-97, spl. events. coord., 1998—2002; youth edn. specialist, 2003—. Docent (vol.) San Antonio Mus. Assn.; rsch. mgr. N. San Antonio C. of C., 1988. Artist: numerous paintings and fiber sculptures in juried and invitational shows, 1966-80; poetess: (2d prize Iowa Poetry Day Assn., 1961). Bd. dirs. Tex. Soc. to Prevent Blindness, San Antonio, 1981-83; v.p. U. Tex. at San Antonio Women's Club, 1981-82, pres. 1983-84; mem. San Antonio Conservation Soc., 1985—, mem. Assistance League of San Antonio, 1988—, liason Thrift House, San Antonio, 1995-96; co-pres. River Gardens Family and Friends, 1993-94, sec., 1995-96. Mem. Am. Planning Assn. (cert. planner, asst. dir. San Antonio sect. 1990, dir., 1991-93, Am. Water Works Assn., Univ. of Tex. at San Antonio Alumni Assn. Avocations: travel, reading, landscape design, swimming, mus. visits. Bus. Home: 2410 Shadow Cliff St San Antonio TX 78232-4010 Office: San Antonio Water System PO Box 2449 San Antonio TX 78298-2449 E-mail: chenderson@saws.org.

HENDERSON, DAN W. psychiatric therapist, educator; b. Huntington, W.Va., Oct. 18, 1948; s. VanBuren and Laura Treavel (Mounts) H. BA in Elem. Edn., Marshall U., 1981, MA in Spl. Edn., 1982, MA in Counseling, 1985; PhD in Spiritual Psychology, Christian Bible Coll./Seminary, 2000. Cert. tchr., Calif., Ky., W.Va. cert. counselor, Calif., Ky., W.Va.; lic. profl. counselor nationally cert. counselor and psychologist. Grad. asst. Marshall U., Huntington, 1981-85; tchr. Cabell County Schs., Huntington, 1981-85; program dir. N.E.W. Inc., Hamlin, W.Va., 1986-89; psychiat. therapist Appalachian Regional Hosp., South Williamson, Ky., 1995—; mem. faculty depts. psychology and sociology W.Va. C.C., 1995—; pvt. practice, N.Y.C. Wrestling coach Cammack Jr. High Sch., Huntington, 1983-85; track coach West Jr. High Sch., Huntington, 1983-85; radio announcer, 1987-89; guest spkr. TV and radio, 1996—; condr. seminars and workshops, 1996—; conv. spkr. state conf., 1998—; facilitator, therapist Coalition Against Domestic Violence, 1998—; therapist pediatric weight mgmt. program, 2001—; facilitator anti-smoking cmty. program, 2001— Author: I the Antichrist, 2001. Facilitator Men's Batterers Group, 1998—. Sgt. USAF, 1967-71, Vietnam. Recipient cert. of appreciation ARC, 1993; grad. fellow Marshall U., 1981. Mem. ACA, N.Am. Masters in Psychology, Am. Mental Health Counselors Assn., Lic. Profl. Counelors Assn. (bd. dirs. 2000—),, W.Va. Coling Assn. (bd. dirs. 1998—), Rotary. Democrat. Avocations: writing, photography, travel. Home and Office: 420 8th Ave W Huntington WV 25701-2516

HENDERSON, DANIEL JOSEPH, economist; b. Sacramento, Calif., Feb. 16, 1976; s. Fred Joseph and Susan Marie Henderson; m. Nina Suh Schroeter. Associate of Arts in Mathematics, Sacramento City College, Sacramento, CA, 1994—96; BA in Econs., U. Calif., Davis, 1998; MA in Econs., U. Calif., Riverside, 2000, PhD in Econs., 2003. Tchg. asst. U. Calif., Riverside, 1998—, assoc. in econs., 2001—03; asst. prof. econs. SUNY, Binghamton, 2003—. Named Outstanding Vol. of Yr., Goodwill Industries Inc. of Sacramento Valley, 1997. Mem.: Delta Sigma Pi (life; pres. Nu Rho chpt. 1997—98, Pres.'s award 1997—98). Office: Dept of Economics SUNY Binghamton NY 13902

HENDERSON, DONALD AINSLIE, public health educator; b. Lakewood, Ohio, Sept. 7, 1928; s. David Alexander and Grace Eleanor (McMillan) Henderson; m. Nana Irene Bragg, Sept. 1, 1951; children: Leigh Ainslie, David Alexander, Douglas Bruce. BA, Oberlin (Ohio) Coll., 1950, DS (hon.), 1978; MD, U. Rochester, 1954, DS (hon.), 1977; MPH, Johns Hopkins U., 1960; LLD (hon.), Marietta (Ohio) Coll., 1978; DS (hon.), U. Ill., 1979, U. Md., 1980; MD (hon.), U. Geneva, 1977; LHD (hon.), SUNY, 1981, Johns Hopkins U., 1994, Towson State U., 1994; DS (hon.), Yale U., 1986, Albany Med. Coll., 1989, Lafayette Coll., 1991, U. Mo., 1992, U. Minn., 2003. Diplomate Am. Bd. Preventive Medicine. Intern, then resident Mary Imogene Bassett Hosp., Cooperstown, N.Y., 1954-55, 57-59; chief epidemic intelligence service Center Disease Control, USPHS, Atlanta, 1955-57, chief surveillance sect., 1960-66; chief med. officer smallpox eradication WHO, Geneva, 1966-77; dean Johns Hopkins U. Sch. Hygiene and Pub. Health, 1977-90; assoc. dir. Office Sci. and Tech. Policy, Exec. Office Pres. of U.S., Washington, 1991-93; dep. asst. sec. HHS, Washington, 1993-94; sr. sci. advisor Dept. Health and Human Svcs., HHS, 1994-95; prof. Johns Hopkins U. Sch. Pub. Health, Balt., 1977—; founding dir. Hopkins Ctr. Civilian Biodefense Studies, 1998—; dir., fellow. Office of Pub. Health Emergency Preparedness, Office of Sec. Dept. Health and Human Svcs., 2001—03. Contbr. articles to profl. jours. Named Burroughs Wellcome Vis. Prof., 1996; recipient Ernest Jung prize, 1976, Govt. India-Indian Soc. Malaria and Other Communicable Diseases award, 1975, Rosenhaus Internat. award for excellence, 1975, George MacDonald medal, London Sch. Hygiene and Tropical Medicine, Royal Soc. Tropical Medicine and Hygiene, 1976, Health medal, Govt. Afghanistan, 1976, Spl. Albert Lasker Pub. Health Svc. award, WHO, 1976, Health for All medal, 1990, Joseph C. Wilson award in internat. affairs, 1978, James D. Bruce Meml. award, 1978, Outstanding Alumnus award, Delta Omega, 1980, Disting. Alumnus award, Johns Hopkins U., 1982, Internat. Merit award, Gairdner Found., 1983, Albert Schweitzer Internat. prize for medicine, 1985, Nat. Medal Sci., 1986, Richard T. Hewitt award, Royal Soc. Medicine, 1986, Edward Jenner medal, 1996, Charles Dana Found. award for pioneering achievemnt in health, 1986, Japan prize in preventative medicine, 1988, Health medal 1st Grade, People's Republic China, 1988, Medal of Abnegation Uruguay, 1988, Honor award, Pan Am. Health Orgn., 1990, Abraham Lilienfeld award, Am. Coll, Epidemology, 1991, Award of Excellence, Ronald McDonald Children's Charities, 1992, Surgeon Gen.'s medallion, USPHS, 1992, City of Medicine award, 1993, Walter Reed medal, Am. Soc. Tropical Medicine and Hygiene, 1993, Merit award, Nat. Coun. Internat. Health, 1993, Gold medal, Albert B. Sabin Found., 1994, Oswaldo Cruz Gold medal of merit, Govt. of Brazil, 1995, Soc. citation, Infectious Diseases Soc. Am., 1996, L. Frank Calderone prize, Columbia U. Sch. Public Health, 1999, Takeru Higuchi Meml. award, U. Kans., 1999, Presdl. Medal Freedom, 2002, Joseph Smadel Medal, Infectious Diseases Soc. Am., 2002; fellow Paul Harris fellow, Rotary Internat., 1993. Fellow: Nat. Acad. Arts and Scis., N.Y. Acad. Medicine (hon. John Stearns award 1995, Annapolis Ctr. Sci. award 2000, Silvia and Hebert Berger award 2001), Royal Coll. Physicians (hon.), London Sch. Tropical Medicine and Hygiene (hon.), Am. Acad. Pediat. (hon.); mem.: APHA, Indian Soc. Malaria and Other Communicable Diseases, Royal Soc. Tropical Medicine and Hygiene, Royal Coll. Physicians Edinburgh (Eng.), Internat. Epidemiol. Assn., Inst. Medicine NAS (Pub. Welfare medal 1978). Home: 3802 Greenway Baltimore MD 21218-1825 Office: Hopkins Ctr Civilian Biodef Strategies 111 Market Pl Ste 830 Baltimore MD 21202-4076 E-mail: dahzero@aol.com.

HENDERSON, DONALD BERNARD, JR., lawyer; b. Birmingham, Ala., June 27, 1949; s. Donald B. and Pauline V. (Szulinski) H.; m. Ruth Ann Jeffers, Sept. 12, 1981. BS, U. Ala., 1971, JD, 1974; LLM in Taxation, NYU, 1976. Bar: Ala. 1974, N.Y. 1983. Ptnr. Sirote & Permutt, Birmingham, 1976—83; sr. assoc. Mound, Cotton, Wollan and Greengrass, NYC, 1983—85; ptnr. Kroll & Tract, N.Y.C., 1985-88, LeBoeuf, Lamb, Greene & MacRae, L.L.P., N.Y.C., 1988—. Lectr. Birmingham chpt. Am. Coll., Bryn Mawr, Pa., 1977-82; bd. dirs. Jackson Nat. Life Ins. Co. N.Y., SunLife Assurance Co. N.Y., Zurich Life Ins. Co. N.Y.; counsel Bronxville Planning Bd., 1994-2001. Contbr. articles to profl. jours. Pres. Lenox Hill Dem. Club, N.Y.C., 1989-90; mem. Ala. State Dem. Com., 1978-83, N.Y.C. Cmty. Bd. Number 8, 1987-88, Republican Club of Bronxville; mem., vice-chair Bronxville Planning Bd., 2001—. Mem. ABA, N.Y. Bar Assn., Ala. Bar Assn. (sec. tax sect. 1982-83). Home: 108 Midland Ave Bronxville NY 10708-3206 Office: LeBouf Lamb Greene & MacRae LLP 125 E 55th St New York NY 10022-3502 E-mail: dhenderson@llgm.com.

HENDERSON, DOUGLAS BOYD, lawyer; b. Pitts., Sept. 21, 1935; s. Arthur G. and Mildred E. (Rickenbach) H.; m. Olivia Lauer, July 6, 1957; children: Scotland Weaver, Keith Arthur, Heather Alice Atkinson BS in Indsl. Engring., Pa. State U., 1957; JD with honors, George Washington U., 1963. Bar: Va. 1962, D.C. 1963. Mfs. agt. firm Arthur G. Henderson & Assos., Pitts., 1957-59; patent agt. Swift & Co., Washington, 1959-62; law clk. to Hon. Donald E. Lane U.S. Ct. Claims, Washington, 1962-63; assoc. Irons, Birch, Swindler & McKie, 1963—65; founding ptnr. Finnegan, Henderson, Farabow, Garrett and Dunner LLP, 1965—. Adv. coun. U.S. Ct. Fed. Claims, 1982—; legal adv. bd. Martindale-Hubbell/LEXIS, 1996—. Author: Third Party Practice in the United States Court of Claims or Two's Company, Three's A Crowd, 1976; contbr. articles to profl. jours. Bd. advisors George Washington U. Law Sch., 1991-97. Fellow: Am. Bar Found. (life); mem.: ABA (ho. of dels. 1999—), Am. Arbitration Assn., U.S. Ct. Fed. Claims Bar Assn. (bd. dirs. 1987—90, founder), Supreme Ct. Hist. Soc., Capital Soc., Intellectual Property Owners Assn., Internat. Trademark Assn., Am. Intellectual Property Law Assn., U.S. C. of C. (chmn. patent, trademark and copyright coun. 1980—82), ITC Trial Lawyers Assn. (founder), Bar Assn. D.C. (chmn. Ct. Claims com. 1973—74, chmn. patent, trademark and copyright law sect. 1974—75, bd. dirs. 1975—76, trustee rsch. found. 1980—81, chmn. Ct. Appeals for Fed. Cir. Com. 1982—83), Fed. Cir. Bar Assn. (bd. dirs. 1985—86, mem. jud. selection com. 1990—, bd. dirs. 1996—99, founder 1985), D.C. Bar Assn., Va. State Bar, Va. Bar Assn., Internat. Bar Assn., Tournament Players Club at Avenel, Univ. Club, Burning Tree Club, Club at Franklin Sq. (bd. govs. 1990—95), Congl. Country Club, Delta Theta Phi, Phi Gamma Delta. Home: 10 Beman Woods Ct Potomac MD 20854-5481 Office: Finnegan Henderson Farabow Garrett & Dunner LLP 1300 I St NW Washington DC 20005-3315

HENDERSON, DWIGHT FRANKLIN, dean, educator; b. Austin, Tex., Aug. 14, 1937; s. Ottis Franklin and Leona (Bady) H.; m. Connie Chorlton, Dec. 24, 1966; 1 dau., Patricia Ross. BA, U. Tex., 1959, MA, 1961, PhD, 1966. Assoc. prof. Ind. U., Ft. Wayne, 1966-68, chmn. dept. history, 1968-71, assoc. prof. history, 1971-80, chmn. arts and scis., 1971-76, dean arts and letters, 1976-80, acting chancellor, 1978-79; prof. history, dean Coll. Social and Behavioral Scis. U. Tex., San Antonio, 1980-2000, acting v.p. acad. affairs, 1986-87, interim dean Coll. Engring., 2000-2001; dir. Learning Cmtys. Jour., 2003—; Fulbright lectr. East China Normal U., Shanghai, 2002; dir. Freshman Initiative, 2003—. Author: Private Journals of Georgiana Gholson Walker, 1963, Courts for a New Nation, 1971, Congress, Courts, and Criminals, 1985 Bd. dirs. Ft. Wayne Philharm. Orch., 1973-74, Pub. Transp. Corp., Ft. Wayne, 1975-77, Vis. Nurse Assn., San Antonio, 1989-94, 95-96, Vis. Nurse Assn. Hospice South Tex., 1996—, Employment Network, 1990-96. With AUS, 1962-64. Tex. Soc Colonial Dames fellow, 1964-65, 65-66; Ind. U. fellow, 1968, 70, 72, Fulbright U.S.-German Internat. Edn. Adminstrs. Program, 1993. Mem.: Tex. Assn Deans of Liberal Arts and Scis. (bd. dirs. 1992—98, v.p. 1994, pres. 1995—97)

So. Hist. Assn., Assn. Am. Historians, Phi Alpha Theta, Delta Sigma Rho. Home: 2410 Shadow Cliff St San Antonio TX 78232-4010 Office: U Tex Dept History 6900 N Loop 1604 W San Antonio TX 78249 E-mail: dhenderson@utsa.edu.

HENDERSON, ERNEST, III, health care executive; b. Boston, Oct. 25, 1924; s. Ernest and Mary G. (Stephens) H.; m. Mary Louise Campbell, Dec. 31, 1953; children: Ernest Flagg IV, Roberta Campbell. S.B., Harvard, 1944, MBA, 1949; L.H.D. (hon.), Bard Coll., 1976; DPS, Northeastern U., 1992. With Sheraton Corp. Am., 1946-69, dir., 1953-69, treas., 1956-63, pres., 1963-69, chief exec. officer, 1967-69; pres. Henderson Houses Am., Inc. (and affiliates), 1969-89, chmn., 1989—; pres. Fidelity Products Corp., 1985-89. Bd. dirs. Boston Biotech. Corp. Mem. permanent com. Harvard Class, 1946; permanent sec. Harvard U. Bus. Sch. Class, 1949; Mass. Republican jr. nat. committeeman, 1956-57; mem. Wellesley Town Meeting, 1970-89; grand marshal Wellesley Vets. Day Parade, 1978; vice chmn. emeritii bd. trustees Northeastern U.; trustee Henderson Found., George B. Henderson Found., Cape Cod Symphony, Bard Coll.; trustee, treas. Boston Biomed. Rsch. Inst.; bd. dirs. Wellesley Cmty. Ctr. Inc., Robin Moore Entertainment, Inc.; vice chmn. Better Homes Fund. Lt. (j.g.) USNR, World War II. Named hon. Big Chief Many Tepees and blood brother Creek Indian Nation. Mem. Chief Exec.'s Orgn, Marlowe-Shakespeare Soc. (dir.), Mensa. Clubs: Harvard Business School Assn. (Boston) (past pres.), Travelers Century Club; Circumnavigators. Home: 171 Edmunds Rd Wellesley Hills MA 02481-1331 Office: Henderson Houses Am Inc PO Box 420 Sudbury MA 01776-0420

HENDERSON, FREDA LAVERNE, elementary education educator; b. Parker County, Tex., June 18, 1939; d. Johnnie C. and Golda Arlene (Porter) Holbrooks; m. Ronald S. Henderson, Apr. 12, 1958; children: Ronald Kevin, Kelly Doyle, Chetley Brian, Terry Dean. AA, Am. Inst. Art, 1960; BEd, U. Colo., 1991; MEd, Lesley Coll., 1997. Pvt. tchr. art, Calhan, Colo., 1981-86; elem. tchr. art Ellicott Schs., Colo., 1987-90, tchr. chpt. I, 1991-96, classroom tchr., 1996—. Sec. Ellicott Sch. PTA; chmn. High Sch. Booster Club, 1979-80; active vol. activities, 1964-79. Named Walmart Tchr. of Yr., 2002. Home: 1975 Buck Rd Calhan CO 80808-8515 Office: Ellicott Schs # 22 399 S Ellicott Hwy Calhan CO 80808-8963 E-mail: fredahenderson@hotmail.com.

HENDERSON, GEORGE, educational sociologist, educator; b. Hurtsboro, Ala., June 18, 1932; s. Kidd Large and Lula Mae (Crawford) H.; m. Barbara Ann Beard, Aug. 9, 1952; children: George, Michele, Faith, Lea, Joy, Lisa, Dawn. Student, Mich. State U., 1950-52; BA, Wayne State U., 1957, MA, 1959, PhD in Ednl. Sociology, 1965. Caseworker Ch. Youth Service, Detroit, 1957-59; social economist Detroit Housing Commn., 1960-61; dir. cmty. svcs. Detroit Urban League, 1961-63; program dir. Mayor's Com. for Detroit Youth, 1963-64; asst. dir. delinquency control tng. center Wayne State U., 1964-65; asst. dir. intercultural rels. Detroit Pub. Schs., 1965-66, asst. to supt., 1966-67; assoc. prof. sociology and edn. U. Okla., 1967-69, Sylvan N. Goldman prof. human rels., 1969—, prof. edn., assoc. prof. sociology, 1969—, David Ross Boyd prof. human rels., 1985—, Regents' prof. human rels., 1989—, Kerr-McGee Presdl. prof., 2001—; dean U. Okla. Coll. Liberal Studies, 1996-2000; dir. human rels. U. Okla., 2000—. Chmn. dept. human rels. U. Okla., 1969-95; vis. prof. sociology Langston U., 1969-70; disting. vis. prof. U.S. Air Force Acad., 1980-81; cons. in field. Author: Foundations of American Education, 1970, Teachers Should Care, 1970, America's Other Children, 1971, To Live in Freedom, 1972, Education for Peace, 1973, Human Relations, 1974, Human Relations in the Military, 1975, A Religious Foundation of Human Relations, 1977, Introduction to American Education, 1978, Understanding and Counseling Ethnic Minorities, 1979, Police Human Relations, 1981, Transcultural Health Care, 1981, Physician-Patient Communication, 1981, The Human Rights of Professional Helpers, 1983, The State of Black Oklahoma, 1984, Psychosocial Aspects of Disability, 1984, Mending Broken Children, 1984, College Survival for Student Athletes, 1985, International Business and Cultures, 1987, Understanding Indigeneous and Foreign Cultures, 1989, Values in Health Care, 1991, Social Work Interventions, 1994, Cultural Diversity in the Workplace, 1994, Migrants, Immigrants and Slaves, 1995, Human Relations Issues in Management, 1996, Our Souls to Keep, 1999, Rethinking Ethnicity and Health Care, 1999, Ethnicity and Substance Abuse, 2002. Recipient Outstanding Achievement award Human Rels. Assn., 1975, Human Rels. award Met. Human Rels. Commn. Nashville, 1979, Okla. Dept. of Mental Health award, 1996, Okla. Found. for Excellence medal for outstanding coll./univ. tchr., 2000; named to Okla. Higher Edn. Hall Fame, 2003, Okla. Hall Fame, 2003. Mem. AAUP, ACD, Am. Sociol. Assn., Nat. Assn. Human Rights Works, Assn. Black Sociologists, Inter-Univ. Seminar on Armed Forces and Soc., Internat. Soc. Law Enforcement and Criminal Justice Instrs., Am. Assn. High Edn. (Black Caucus award for Ednl. Svc. 1993), Golden Key, Omicron Delta Kappa, Delta Tau Kappa, Phi Kappa Phi, Kappa Alpha Psi. Democrat. Baptist. Home: 2616 Osborne Dr Norman OK 73069-5031 Office: 601 Elm Ave Norman OK 73019-3100

HENDERSON, GEORGE ERVIN, lawyer; b. Pampa, Tex., June 7, 1947; s. Ervin L. and Elizabeth (Yoe) H.; m. Linda L. Dalrymple, Aug. 22, 1970; children: Andrew, Elizabeth. BA, Tex. Christian U., 1969; JD, Yale U., 1972. Bar: Tex. 1972, U.S. Dist. Ct. (so. dist.) Tex. 1974, U.S. Dist. Ct. (we. dist.) 1978. Assoc. Fulbright & Jaworski, Houston and Austin, 1972-79, ptnr. Austin, 1983—, Sneed & Vine, Austin, 1979-82. Adj. instr. law U. Tex., Austin, 1983-85. Contbr. articles to profl. jours. Mem. S. Tex. Youth Soccer Assn. Rules Com., 1993—, Greater Austin Soccer Coalition, 1995-98; elder Univ. Presbyn. Ch., Austin, Tex., 2001—. Capt. USAR, 1972-78. Mem. ABA, State Bar of Tex. (chmn. corp. banking and bus. law sect. 1983, mem. coun. corp. banking and bus. law sect. 1985-88), Tex. Assn. Bank Counsel (pres. 1985-86), Travis County Bar Assn. (bankruptcy law sect., chmn. 1988-89, vice-chmn. 1997-98), Tex. Law Found., San Antonio Bankruptcy Bar Assn., Uniform Comml. Code Com., Austin Yacht Club, Capital Soccer Club (pres. 1993-95). Office: Fulbright & Jaworski 600 Congress Ave Ste 2400 Austin TX 78701-3271

HENDERSON, GEORGE MILLER, foundation executive, former banker; b. Indpls., Aug. 19, 1915; s. Ben Wymond and Verlinda (Miller) H.; m. Janice Himmelwright, Sept. 2, 1952; children: Donna, Bonnie, Heather, Randall, Darcy. Student, Harvard U., 1960. With S H. Kress & Co., 1933-36; fire control supr. U.S. Forest Svc., Zig Zag, Oreg., 1936-42; asst. mgr. fgn. trade dept. Portland C. of C., 1946-47; with 1st Nat. Bank Oreg., Portland, 1947-80, v.p., 1953-62, sr. v.p., 1962-71, exec. v.p., 1971-80; pres. Oreg. Ind. Coll. Found., 1980-94. Chmn. Portland Aviation Commn., 1950-51, Oreg. Pks. Commn., 1956-86, Columbia Basin Export-Import Conf., 1961-62; pres. Rose Festival Assn., 1953-54, Family Counseling Svc., 1959-60, Pacific Internat. Livestock Exposition, 1965-67; chmn. woorld brotherhood banquet NCCJ, 1963; bd. dirs. Ind. Coll. Funds Am., 1980-94, Nature Conservancy, 1987-90. Mem. Oreg. Bankers Assn. (pres. 1962), Assn. Res. City Bankers, Pacific Northwestern Ski Assn. (pres. 1947-48), Pacific N.W. Trade Assn. (pres. 1964-65), Arlington Club, Multnomah Club, Cascade Club. Home: 7255 SW Benz Park Dr Portland OR 97225-3207

HENDERSON, HARRIET, librarian; b. Pampa, Tex., Nov. 19, 1949; d. Ervin Leon and Hannah Elizabeth (Yoe) H. AB, Baker U., 1971; MLS, U. Tex., 1973. Sch. libr. Pub. Sch. Sys., Pampa, 1971-72; city libr. City of Tyler, Tex., 1973-80, City of Newport News, Va., 1980-84, dir. librs. and info. svcs., 1984-90; dir. Louisville Free Pub. Libr., 1990-97, Montgomery County (Md.) Pub. Librs., 1997—. Del. White House Conf. Librs. and Info. Svcs., 1991; mem. Leadership Louisville, 1991—97, Alliant Health Sys. Adult Oper. Bd., 1991—97; mem. adv. com. dept. edn. Spalding U., 1991—95; mem. Md. Adv. Coun. on Librs., 2001—; diaconate Hiddenwood Presbyn. Ch., Newport News, 1983—85; bd. dirs. Tex. Libr. Sys. Act adv. bd., 1979—80, Peninsula Women's Network, Newport News, 1983—85. Recipient Tribute to Women in Bus. and Industry, Peninsula YWCA, Newport News, 1984. Mem.: ALA (councillor 2001—), Pub. Libr. Assn. (v.p. 1998, pres. 1999), Va. Libr. Assn. (chmn. legis. com. 1981—84, v.p. 1985, pres. 1986), Ky. Libr. Assn. (chair pub. libr. sect. 1995, Outstanding Pub. Libr. Svc. award 1997). Office: Montgomery County Pub Librs Office of Dir 99 Maryland Ave Rockville MD 20850-2330

HENDERSON, HAZEL, writer, lecturer; b. Bristol, Somerset, U.K., Mar. 27, 1933; came to U.S., 1957, naturalized, 1962; d. Kenneth and Dorothy May (Jesseman) Mustard; m. Carter Henderson (div. 1981); 1 child, Alexandra Leslie Camille Henderson Cassidy. Baccalaureate, Clifton Sch., Bristol, U.K., 1950; ScD (hon.), Worcester (Mass.) Poly. Inst., 1975; ScD (hon.), Soka U., 2000, U. San Francisco, 2001. Freelance writer, various locations, 1967—. Vis. regent's lectr. U. Calif., Santa Barbara, 1979; Horace Allbright chair dept. forestry, U. Calif., Berkeley, 1982; adviser, cons., lectr. for founds., non-profit agys., govt. agys. and corps. in over 30 countries; dir. Worldwatch Inst., 1975-2001; advisor Calvert Social Investment Funds.; ptnr. Calvert-Henderson Quality of Life Indicators; guest on over 300 radio and TV programs including Today Show, AM Am., Bill Moyer's Jour.; producer Sunrise Semester series, CBS, 1977, 78, informative series, PBS, 1984; ; mem. commn. on globalization.presenter seminars. Author: Creating Alternative Futures: The End of Economics, 1978, 2d edit., 1996, The Politics of the Solar Age: Alternatives to Economics, 1981, 2d edit., 1988, Paradigms in Progress, 1991, 2d edit., 1995, Building a Win-Win World, 1996, Beyond Globalization, 1999; editor: The United Natiuons: Policy and Financing Alternatives, 1996; syndicated columnist L.A. Times-Mirror Syndicate; contbr. articles to C.S. Monitor, U.S. News and World Report, Time, N.Y. Times, InterPress Svc.; contbr. to anthologies; editorial bd. Futures U.K., Foresight U.K., Futures Rsch. Quar., Future Survey, Resurgence. Adv. coun. U.S. Congress Office Tech. Assessment, Washington, 1974-80; adv. Com. on Future Fla. State Legislature, Tallahassee, 1984-86; mem. Commn. on Globalization, World Commn. on Global Consiousness; internat. adv. bd. Forum 2000, Prague. Named Citizen of Yr. N.Y. Med. Soc., 1967; awardee UN Environ. Program; co-winner Global Citizen award, 1996. Fellow World Bus. Acad., World Futures Study Fedn., Findhorn Found., Global Edn. Assn., Club of Budapest (hon.). Avocations: cycling, gardening, swimming. Office: PO Box 5190 Saint Augustine FL 32085-5190

HENDERSON, HORACE EDWARD, World War II historian, peace advocate; b. Henderson, NC, July 30, 1917; s. T. Brantley and Maude (Duke) H.; m. Vera S. Schubert; children by previous marriage: Terri Kelley, Elizabeth Smith. Student, Coll. William and Mary, 1934-37, Yale U., 1941-42. Owner Henderson Real Estate & Ins., Williamsburg, Va., 1947-52; coordinator Nat. Automobile Dealers Assn., Washington, 1954-56; dir. gen. World Peace Through Law Center, Geneva, 1964-69; chmn. bd. Henderson Real Estate, McLean, Va., 1964-66; exec. dir. World Assn. Judges, 1968-69; pres. Community Methods, Inc., 1969-76; chmn. Congl. Speaker Reform Com., Washington, 1976; exec. v.p. Am. Lawmakers Assn., Washington, 1977; pres. Williamsburg Vacations, Inc., 1983-84. Chmn., pres. Nat. Assn. for Free Trade, San Francisco, 1986-87; mem. adv. bd. Mut. Security Agy., 1952-53; mem. Pres.'s Conf. on Indsl. Safety, 1952-53; exec. com. U.S. Com. for UN, 1954; dir. Nat. Citizens Com. for Hoover Report, 1954; indsl. adv. com. Fed. Civil Def. Adminstrn., 1952-53; cons. to dir. ICA, 1956; dir. spl. liaison, spl. asst. dep. under sec. state, Washington, 1958, dep. asst. sec. state internat. orgn. affairs, 1959-60; dir. Exile Orgns. Free Europe Com., 1962; U.S. del. to ILO, UNESCO, FAO, WHO, ECOSOC, UN. Author: The Greatest Blunders of World War II, 2002, The Scots of Virginia--America's Greatest Patriots, 2001, The Final Word on War and Peace, 2003. Chmn. Va. Rep. party, 1962-64, Americans for Asian Security and Freedom, 1961; campaign dir. Am. Nationalities for Nixon-Lodge, 1960, Rep. candidate for Congress, 1956, for lt. gov. Va., 1957; permanent chmn. Va. Rep. Conv., 1957; asst. nat. dir. Rockefeller for Pres. campaign, 1964, Scranton for Pres. Campaign, 1964; ind. Candidate for U.S. Senator, 1972; mem. Williamsburg (Va.) City Coun., 1948-50; chmn. Com. Against Recognition Red Hungary, 1963; World vice chmn. Operation Brotherhood, 1954-55; owner Powhatan Hist. Corp., Williamsburg, Va., 1957; chmn. World Campaign Conv. for Peaceful Settlement Internat. Disputes, 1975-95, Assn. for Devel. Edn., Washington, 1978-80, World Peace Treaty Campaign, 1997-2003; pres. Internat. Domestic Devel. Corp., 1975; trustee Valley Forge Found., 1952-55, Jr. C. of C, War Meml. Hdqrs.; elder, deacon Presbyn. Ch. Capt., C.E. AUS, 1942-46. Recipient spl. citizenship award Am. Heritage Found., 1953; named outstanding Jaycee of World, 1954 Mem. Jaycees (internat. v.p. 1951), Jr. C. of C. (nat. pres. 1952-53), U.S. C. of C. (dir. 1954), Yale Club, St. Andrew's Soc., Sigma Alpha Epsilon. Visited 47 countries organizing young men's civic groups, 1953-54. Home: 1100 Gough St Apt 15F San Francisco CA 94109-6645 E-mail: DukeHen@cs.com. *As my father always told me, "Life is not getting what you want, but making the best of what you get."*

HENDERSON, ISAAC CRAIG, oncologist, researcher; b. Paullina, Iowa, Aug. 10, 1941; s. Isaac C. and Ora E. (Tjossem) H.; m. Mary Turner Henderson, June 11, 1966; children: Isaac Craig, Amy Hudson. AB, Grinnell (Iowa) Coll., 1963; MD, Columbia U., 1970. Cert. internal medicine, 1977, med. oncology, 1979. Intern Presbyn. Hosp., N.Y.C., 1970-71; resident, 1971-72; rsch. assoc. NIH, 1972-74; instr. medicine Harvard U. Med. Sch., Boston, 1975-76; asst. prof., 1976-84; assoc. prof., 1984-92; dir. Breast Evaln. Ctr. Dana Farber Cancer Inst., 1980-92; dir. clin. cancer program U. Calif., San Francisco, 1992-95; chmn., CEO Sequus Pharm., Inc., Menlo Park, Calif., 1995—99; sr. med. advisor and mem. bd. of dir. Alza Corp., Mountain View, Calif., 1999—2002; CEO Access Oncology, NY, 2001—. Adj. prof., U. Calif., San Francisco, 1995—. Contbr. articles to profl. jours. Served with USPHS, 1972-74. Fulbright Rsch. scholar, 1964-65; Merck, Sharp & Dohme Internat. fellow, 1966; recipient Columbia Presbyn. Med. soc. rsch. prize, 1970. Fellow ACP; mem. Am. Soc. Clin. Oncology, Am. Assn. Cancer Rsch., Soc. Friends. Achievements include research on clin. protocols evaluating new treatment of breast cancer. Office: Access Oncology 1373 Bay St San Francisco CA 94123-2201 E-mail: ichenderson@hotmail.com

HENDERSON, JAMES ALAN, former engine company executive; b. South Bend, Ind., July 26, 1934; s. John William and Norma (Wilson) Henderson; m. Mary Evelyn Kriner, June 20, 1959; children: James Alan, John Stuart, Jeffrey Todd, Amy Brenton. AB, Princeton U., 1956; Baker scholar, Harvard U., 1961-63. With Scott Foresman & Co., Chgo., 1962; chmn., CEO Cummins Engine Co., Inc., Columbus, 1995; staff mem. Am. Rsch. & Devel. Corp., Boston, 1963; faculty Harvard Bus. Sch., 1963; asst. to chmn. Cummins Engine Co., Inc., Columbus, Ind., 1964-65, v.p. mgmt. devel., 1965-69, v.p. personnel, 1969-70, v.p. ops., 1970-71, exec. v.p., 1971-75, exec. v.p., COO, 1975-77, pres., 1977-94, pres., CEO, 1994-95; chmn., CEO, 1995-99. Bd. dirs. Cummins Engine Found., Inland Steel Ind., Chgo., Ameritech, Chgo., Rohm and Haas Co., Phila., Landmark Comm., Norfolk; mem. policy com. The Bus. Roundtable, Washington. Author: Creative Collective Bargaining, 1965. Chmn. exec. com., trustee Princeton U., 1986—92; pres. bd. trustees Culver Ednl. Found. Presbyterian. Home: 301 Washington St Columbus IN 47201 Office: Cummins Engine Co Inc 500 Jackson St Columbus IN 47201

HENDERSON, JAMES HAROLD, entrepreneur, business executive, financial planner; b. Knoxville, Tenn., June 18, 1948; s. Harold Alpheus and Joanna Elizabeth (McCammon) Henderson. BS in Mgmt. and Econs., U. North Ala., 1971; MS in Systems Mgmt., U. So. Calif., Los Angeles, 1981. Cert. fin. planner, registered investment advisor. Commd. U.S. Army, 1971, advanced through grades to capt., 1975, resigned, 1979; owner Worldwide Merchantile and Co., Clarksville, Tenn., Oscoda, Mich. and Cowley, Wyo., 1979—, Cowley, 1979—; freelance fin. planner, Clarksville, Tenn. and Oscoda, Mich., 1979-92; investment advisor James H. Henderson and Co., Oscoda, Mich., 1987-92. Counselor Christian Fin. Concepts, Inc., 1985—89. Asst. army attache to India USAR, 1991—99; def. and army attache to Nepal, 1994; def. and army attache to Ethiopia, Eritrea, Djibwti, 1998. Lt. col., ret. USAR, 1971—99. Mem.: Civil Air Patrol (squadron commdr. 2001—), Officer's Christian Fellowship (area cord. 1984—90), Inst. Cert. Fin. Planners (cert.), Nat. Eagle Scout Assn. Avocations: aviation, water sports, fly fishing, cross-country skiing, travel. Home and Office: PO Box 742 Cowley WY 82420-0742

HENDERSON, JAMES DAVID, history educator; b. Shreveport, La., Apr. 17, 1942; s. James and Barbara (Pardue) H.; m. Linda Roddy, Dec. 17, 1967; children: James, Elizabeth, Jessica, Thomas, Joseph. BA in History, Centenary Coll., 1964; MA in History, U. Ariz., 1965; PhD in History, Tex. Christian U., 1972. Assoc. prof. history Grambling (La.) State U., 1972-86; prof. internat. studies Coastal Carolina U., Conway, 1986—. Author: Meals by Fred Harvey, 1969, Ten Notable Women, 1978, When Colombia Bled, 1985, Conservative Thought, 1988, Reference Guide to Latin American History, 2000, Modernization in Colombia, 2001. Clk. Horry Friends Monthly Meeting. Woodrow Wilson fellow, 197-71, NEH fellow, 1976-77; grantee for 1st Colombia Fulbright Group Study U.S. Dept. Edn., 1985, 10 Coll. Consortium, 1988-91; Fulbright tchg./rsch. in Colombia, 1993-94, 2000. Mem. Assn. N.Am. Colombianists, Am. Hist. Assn., South Eastern Coun. Latin Am. Studies (pres. 1990-91), Latin Am. Studies Assn., Com. on Gran Colombian History (pres. 1989-91). Office: Coastal Carolina U PO Box 1953 Conway SC 29528-6054

HENDERSON, JAMES FORNEY, lawyer; b. Bloomington, Ill., Oct. 10, 1921; s. Ernest James and Helen Darlene (Forney) H.; m. Shirley May Lawson, June 10, 1943 (div. Oct. 1979); children: James Dale, Helen Diane, Lynda Joanne; m. Sonja Ramona Hayward, Nov. 8, 1979. BS, Northwestern U., 1943, JD, 1948. Bar: Ill. 1948, Ariz. 1949, U.S. Dist. Ct. Ariz. 1950, U.S. Ct. Appeals (9th cir.) 1954. Assoc., ptnr. Gust, Rosenfeld & Henderson, Phoenix, 1950-92; ptnr. Scult, French, Zwillinger & Smock, Phoenix, 1992-95, Morrison & Hecker, Phoenix, 1995—2002; of counsel Jennings, Strouss & Salmon, P.L.C., 2002—. Counsel mem. Libel Def. Resource Ctr., N.Y.C., 1989—. Bd. dirs. Samaritan Health Svcs., 1974-92. Lt. USN, 1943-46. Recipient Disting. Svc. award Ariz. Press Club 1986, First Amendment Rights award Sigma Delta Chi 1980-81. Mem. ABA, Def. Rsch. Inst., Ill. Bar Assn., Ariz. Bar Assn., Ariz. Assn. Def. Counsel. Office: Jennings Strouss & Salmon PLC 201 E Washington St 11th fl Collier Ctr Phoenix AZ 85004-2385 E-mail: jhenderson@jsslaw.com.

HENDERSON, JAMES RONALD, industrial real estate developer; b. Columbus, Nebr., Dec. 2, 1947; s. Bill and Roeburta (Hamrick) H.; m. Jamey Lee Blevins, June 30, 1972 (div. Mar. 1993); children: Benjamin James, Katrin Lee, Joseph Marion. BSBA, Okla. State U., 1970. Commd. 2d lt. USAR, 1970, advanced through grades to maj., 1987, ret., 1992; appraiser Dorchester Cos., Tulsa, 1970-72; devel. mgr. Wolf Point Properties, Tulsa, 1972-82; v.p. Mager Mortgage Co., Tulsa, 1972-78; mktg. dir. Tulsa Port of Catoosa, Okla., 1987-89; pres. J. Ronald Henderson Real Estate, Tulsa, 1978—, Henderson Exploration Co., Tulsa, 1982—. Mng. dir. Wolf Point Indsl. Pky. Owners Assn., Tulsa, 1984—. Organizer, incorporator Tulsa Charity Fight Night, Inc., 1993; organizer N.E. Okla. Econ. Devel. Assn., 1988. Maj. USAR ret. Mem. Nat. Assn. Indsl. and Office Pks. (pres. Tulsa chpt. 1990), Propeller Club Port of Catoosa (pres. 1987). Southern Baptist. Avocations: backpacking, history, geology. Office: Henderson Cos 1643 E 15th St Tulsa OK 74120-6044

HENDERSON, JANET LYNN, city commissioner, real estate broker; b. Chgo., Sept. 14, 1943; d. Howard Charles and Lucille Laura (Lambrecht) Harris; m. Todd Dierks Nelson, Jan. 30, 1965 (div. May 1997); children: Erik Nelson, Brooks Nelson, Jessica Nelson, Jillian Nelson; m. Phil M. Henderson, Dec. 26, 1997. BS in Bus. Adminstrn., Elmhurst Coll., 1966. Lic. real estate broker. Career counselor Employee Svcs., Inc., Chgo., 1966-67; acctg. mgr. Ins. Mgmt., Inc., Milw., 1967-70, Hosp. Coun. Greater Milw., 1970-84; broker assoc. Klein & Heuchan, Inc., Clearwater, Fla., 1994-99. Mem. leadership tng. coun. Nat. League Cities, Washington, 1999—2002; mem. internat. com. Fla. League Cities, Tallahassee, 1999—2002. Pres. Dunedin Youth Guild, 1993—; city commr. City of Dunedin, Fla., 1997—2002, vice mayor, 2002; chair Relay for Life, 2003; bd. dirs. Childrens Svc. Soc., 1983—86, Ruth Eckerd Hall Found., Clearwater, Fla., 1998—2003, chair spl. events com.; bd. dirs. Pinellas Planning Coun., Clearwater, Fla., 1998—2002, Watson Ctr., 1999—, Pinellas County Cmty. Found., Bowman Meml. Scholarship Fund Com., 2003—, Leading Ladies, Dunedin. Ill. State scholar, 1962. Mem.: Dunedin Hist. Soc., Friends Libr., Rotary. Republican. Office: Bay Ride Inc PO Box 3563 Clearwater FL 33767 E-mail: jlh1464@aol.com.

HENDERSON, JANICE ELIZABETH, law librarian; b. N.Y.C., Dec. 22, 1952; d. James and Adeline M. (Fitzgerald) H. BA in Psychology, Hunter Coll., 1974; MS in Spl. Edn., CUNY, 1979; MS in Library Sci., Pratt Inst., 1980; JD, Bklyn. Law Sch., 1986. Law librarian Morgan, Lewis & Bockius, N.Y.C., 1977-83; reference librarian Weil, Gotshal & Manges, N.Y.C., 1983-85; law librarian Tenzer, Greenblatt et al, N.Y.C., 1985-86, Robinson, Silverman et al, N.Y.C., 1986-88, Kirkland & Ellis, N.Y.C., 1991-93; assoc. law libr. prof. CUNY Law Sch., N.Y.C., 1989-91; dir. libr. svcs. Epstein, Becker & Green, PC, 1993-98; dir. profl. devel. and libr. svcs. Baker & McKenzie, N.Y.C., 1998—2002; cons. law librarianship N.Y.C., 2003—. Assoc. adj. prof. Sch. Libr. and Info. Sci., St. John's U., N.Y.C., 1990-93; spkr. in field. Book reviewer Legal Info. Alert newsletter, 1984-86. Mem. Am. Assn. Law Librs., Law Libr. Assn. Greater N.Y. (advt. mgr. 1986-89, bd. dirs. 1989-90, mem. continuing legal edn. com. 1990-92, co-chair 1992-94, v.p. 1995-96, pres. 1996-97, past pres. 1997-98), Practicing Law Inst. (mng. the law libr. 1997-98, program chair 1999-2000, program co-chair 2001—). Democrat. Roman Catholic. Home: PO Box 23060 Brooklyn NY 11202-3060 E-mail: janiceehenderson@att.net.

HENDERSON, JANICE ELIZABETH WILSON, respiratory therapist; b. Winter Garden, Fla., Sept. 28, 1958; d. Thomas Andrew and Emily Ann (Black) Wilson; m. Gerald David Henderson, Feb. 14, 1979; children: Erin Lindsey, Jill Rebecca. AS, Daytona Beach C.C., 1986; student, Calif. Coll. Cert. ACLS, respiratory therapy technician, respiratory therapist, pulmonary function technician. Sec. Fish Meml. Hosp. (name now Bert Fish Med. Ctr.), New Smyrna Beach, Fla., 1981—82, respiratory therapist technician, 1982—, respiratory therapist, 1988—, pulmonary function technician, 1996—, coord. pulmonary rehab., 1994—97, coord. continuous quality improvement, 1994—, cardiopulmonary supr., 1997—2001, mem. mgmt. info. team, 1997—, cardiopulmonary mgr., 2001—. Sec. PTA, Oak Hill, Fla., 1995-96; pres. sch. improvement team W.F. Burns Oak Hill Elem. Sch., 1997-98. Mem. Am. Assn. for Respiratory Care, Fla. Soc. Respiratory Care. Democrat. Baptist. Avocations: boating, reading, music. Home: 163 Flamingo Rd Edgewater FL 32141-7206

HENDERSON, JEFFREY J. dean, educator; b. Montclair, N.J., June 21, 1946, s. Frank I. and Amy J. Henderson; m. Patricia J. Johnson, June 21, 1996. PhD, Harvard U., 1972; BA, Kenyon Coll., Gambier, Ohio, 1968, LHD (hon.). Asst. prof. Yale U., New Haven, 1972—78; assoc. prof. U. of Mich., Ann Arbor, 1978—82; prof. U. of So. Calif., L.A., 1982—91, Boston U., 1991—, dean of arts and scis., 2002—. Editor Loeb Classical Libr., Cambridge, Mass., 1998—. Author: (book) The Maculate Muse; translator: Aristophanes: Plays, 4 vols. (Goodwin Award of Merit, Am. Philol Assn., 2001); editor: (collection of essays) Aristophanes: Essays in Interpretation. Recipient sr. faculty fellowship, NEH, 1991—92; fellow, John Simon Guggenheim Found., 1997—98, Danforth Found., 1968—72, Woodrow Wilson Found., 1968—72. Mem.: Am. Philol Assn., Algonquin Club of Boston. Democrat. Avocations: softball, tennis, chess. Office: Boston U 725 Commonwealth Ave Boston MA 02215 E-mail: jhenders@bu.edu.

HENDERSON, JOHN DREWS, architect; b. St. Louis, July 30, 1933; s. Russell Dewey and Hazel Agnes (Drews) H.; m. Barbara Lee Beckman, June 25, 1955; children: Susan Lee, John Beckman. BArch, U. Ill., 1956. Registered architect, Calif. With Delawie, Macy & Henderson, San Diego, Calif., 1966-77, Macy, Henderson & Cole, AIA, San Diego, 1977-86; pres. John D. Henderson, FAIA, 1986—. Mem. San Diego Hist. Sites Bd., 1972-78, Gaslamp Quarter Task Force, 1976-78, Gaslamp Quarter Coun., 1984-86; mem. City Mgr.'s Com. for Seismic Retrofit for Older Bldgs., 1986-92; bd. dirs. Hist. Am. Bldgs. Survey Found., 1984-86; Calif. Hist. Bldgs. Code Safety Bd., 1976-96; apptd. by Gov. of Calif. to State Hist. Resources Commn., 1990-02, reapptd., 1994-98, 98-02, chmn. 1992-93, 2000-01, chmn. Calif. Heritage Fund com. 1993—2001; Calif. advisor Nat. Trust Hist. Preservation, 1975-78; bd. dirs. Gaslamp Quarter Found., 1984-86. Lt. USNR, 1956-59. Recipient Hist. Preservation awards from City San Diego, San Diego Hist. Soc., San Diego chpt. and Calif. Coun. AIA, La Jolla Women's Club, Am. Assn. State and Local History, Am. Inst. Planners, Save Our Heritage Orgn., Rancho Santa Fe Assn., Calif. Preservation Found., Ctrl. City Assn., Gaslmp Quarter Assn. Fellow AIA (officer, dir. local chpt. 1969-73, chpt. pres. 1972, editor guidebooks 1970, 76, state bd. dirs. 1971-73, nat. hist. resources com. 1974-76, 78—, emeritus 2002, regional rep. 1976-78, mem. guidebook com., 2002); mem. San Diego Archtl. Found. (bd. dirs. 1984-86, 89-91), San Diego Hist. Soc. (officer, bd. dirs. 1975, pres. 1975), San Diego (Calif.) Geneal. Soc., San Diego History Campaign (exec. com. 1981-86), San Diego Host Golf Club. Republican. Presbyterian. Home and Office: John D Henderson FAIA-E 4879 Academy St San Diego CA 92109-3460 E-mail: jhende@tns.net.

HENDERSON, JOHNNY, mathematician, educator; b. Santa Monica, Calif., Mar. 26, 1951; s. Ernest Elijah and Madora Allene Henderson; m. Darlene Baxter; 1 child, Kathryn Strunk. PhD, U. Nebr., 1981. Asst. prof. math. U. Mo., Rolla, 1981—84; alumni prof. math. Auburn U., Auburn, Ala., 1984—2000, Scharnagel prof. math., 2000—02; disting. prof. math. Baylor U., Waco, Tex., 2002—. Author: Boundary Value Problems for Functional Differential Equations, 1995; actor: (over 200 articles to profl. jours.); mem. editl. bd. Jour. Math. Analysis and Applications, Comms. on Applied Nonlinear Analysis, Internat. Jour. Applied Math., Math. Scis. Rsch. Jour., others. Vol. Wesley Terr. Retirement Ctr., Auburn, 1984—2002, Meadowlands Terr. Retirement Ctr.,

Waco, 2002—. Recipient Outstanding Achievement award, Ark. Coll., 1993, Ark. Trio Achievement award, Ark. Assn. Student Assistance Programs, 1994, Alumni Achievement award, U. Nebr., 1995, Outstanding Tchg. award, Lamdba Sigma Soc., 2002; fellow, Tamkang U, Taiwan, 1999; Raybould fellow, U. Queensland, Australia, 1997, U. New South Wales fellow, 2003. Mem.: Internat. Soc. Difference Equations, Internat. Fedn. Nonlinear Analysts, Math. Assn. Am. (Disting Tchg. award 2001), Am. Math. Soc., Sigma Xi. Office: Baylor University Dept Math Waco TX 76798

HENDERSON, JULIAN CROWDER, retired pathologist; b. Lawrenceburg, Tenn., Jan. 19, 1938; s. Manning Augustus and Katherine (Kent) H.; m. Merle Frances Masters, Dec. 26, 1961; children: Gregory Stephen, Mary Elizabeth, Katherine Merle. BS, U. North Ala., 1957; MD, Tulane U., 1961. Cert. anatomic and clin. pathology Am. Bd. Pathology. Intern U. Miami (Fla.), 1961-62; resident Tulane U., Charity Hosp., New Orleans, 1962-66; instr. Tulane Med. Sch., New Orleans, 1962-66; assoc. clin. prof. pathology U. Miss. Med. Sch.; pvt. practice anatomic and clin. pathology Jackson, Miss., 1968—2001; ret., 2001. Assoc. dir. lab. Meth. Med. Ctr., Jackson, 1968—, Woman's Hosp., Jackson, 1975—; cons. pathologist Meth. Rehab. Hosp., Jackson, 1975—. Capt. USAF, 1966-68. Fellow Am. Coll. Pathology, Am. Soc. Clin. Pathologists (councilor 1973-77); mem. AMA, Miss. State Med. Assn. (ho. of dels. 1973—, trustee 1992-95, vice chmn. bd. trustees 1995-97, chmn. 1997—), Ctrl. Med. Soc. (pres. 1990-91), Miss. Assn. Pathologists (pres. 1983-84). Republican. Episcopalian. Avocations: travel, hunting, fishing. Home: 2153 Eastover Dr Jackson MS 39211-6720

HENDERSON, KAREN LECRAFT, federal judge; b. 1944; BA, Duke U., 1966; JD, U. N.C., 1969. Ptnr. Wright & Henderson, Chapel Hill, NC, 1969—70, Sinkler, Gibbs & Simons, P.A., Columbia, SC, 1983—86; asst. atty. gen. Columbia, 1973—78; sr. asst. atty. gen., dir. of spl. litigation sect., 1978—82; deputy atty. gen., dir. of criminal div., 1982; judge U.S. Dist. Ct. S.C., Columbia, 1986—90, U.S. Ct. Appeals (D.C. cir.), Washington, 1990—. Apptd. Dist. Ct. Adv. Com. Mem.: ABA (litigation sect. and urban, state and local government law sect.), S.C. Bar (government law sect., trial and appellate practice sect., fed. judges assn.), N.C. Bar Assn. Office: US Ct Appeals 333 Constitution Ave NW Washington DC 20001-2802*

HENDERSON, L(EONA) HARRIETTE, retired social work administrator, consultant; b. Phila., Mar. 8, 1934; d. Luther and Leona (Wilson) Highsmith; m. Charles Leon Henderson, 1958; children: Victor Parks, Craig Lamarr. BA, Fisk U., 1955; MS in Edn., Temple U., 1958; MSW, Adelphi U., 1973. Lic. social worker, N.Y. From caseworker dep. commr. Human Resources Adminstrn./Dept. Social Services, N.Y.C., 1961—86, dep. commr. family svcs., 1986—89; ret., 1989. Social work cons. region 2 Head Start, N.Y.C., 1990—. Trustee Fisk U., Nashville, 1984-87, recruiter, 1984—; music dir. children's choir Good Shepherd Ch., West Hempstead, N.Y., 1970—; alto Carr-Hill Singers, 1983—. Recipient pub. svc. award Fund for City N.Y., 1985, recognition Human Resources Adminstrn.-Women's Advisors, 1989. Mem. Managerial Assn. N.Y.C., Social Work Mgrs. Nat. Network (Exemplar award 1988), NAACP (Social Svc. award 1987), Delta Sigma Theta. Home: Apt 1613 3600 Conshohocken Ave Philadelphia PA 19131-5330

HENDERSON, MADELINE MARY (BERRY HENDERSON), chemist, researcher, consultant; b. Merrimac, Mass., Sept. 3, 1922; d. Burton B. and Irene R. (Murphy) Berry; m. Richard S. Henderson, Nov. 5, 1957; children: Anne M., Matthew R., Katherine M., Laura J. AB in Chemistry, Emmanuel Coll., Boston, 1944; MPA, Am. U., Washington, 1977. Chemist E.I. DuPont, Gibbstown, N.J., 1944-45, MIT, Cambridge, Mass., 1946-52; info. specialist Battelle Meml. Inst., Columbus, Ohio, 1953-55; rsch. assoc. NSF, Washington, 1956-62; computer specialist Nat. Bur. Standards, Washington, 1964-79; cons. Bethesda, 1980—. Chmn. Gordon Rsch. Conf. on Sci. Info. Problems, 1972. Author, co-author, editor books on info. sci.; co-author, author papers, articles on info. sci., standards, and libr. automation. Dept. of Commerce Sci.-Tech. fellow, 1971-72; Am. U. Key Exec. scholar, 1975-77. Fellow AAAS (sec. sect. info. scis. 1978-85); mem. Am. Chem. Soc., Am. Soc. Info. Sci. & Tech. (mem. publs. com. 1983-87, chmn. pub. affairs com. 1987-89, Watson Davis award 1989), Pi Alpha Alpha (nat. honor soc. pub. adminstr.). Office: 30072 Cross Woods Dr Mechanicsville MD 20659-6122

HENDERSON, MARY LOUISE, civic worker; b. Windsor, Ont., Can., Apr. 24, 1928; came to U.S., 1932; d. Kenneth Charles and Florence McGie (Morton) Campbell; m. Ernest Flagg Henderson III, Dec. 31, 1953; children: Ernest Flagg IV, Roberta C. BA, Bard Coll., 1950. V.p. Ruse & Urban, Inc., advt., Detroit, 1950-53. V.p., bd. dirs. Henderson House Am., Sudbury, Mass., 1969—. Pres. Wellesley (Mass.) Friendly Aid Assn., 1970-75, Newton (Mass.) Wellesley Hosp. Aid, 1980-82, 88-89; co-founder, exec. com. mem. Wellesley Community Ctr., 1972—, pres., 1983-85; bd. dirs., mem. exec. com. Norumbega Coun. Boy Scouts Am., 1974-95, pres., 1989-91; mem. exec. com. Knox Coun. Boy Scouts Am., 1995—; trustee Newton-Wellesley Hosp., 1982—, mem. exec. com., 1990-96; bd. dirs., mem. exec. com. Greater Boston adv. bd. Salvation Army, 1985—; mem. nat. adv. bd. Officers Tng. Sch. Salvation Army, 1994—; bd. dirs. Newton-Wellesley Vis. Nurse Assn., 1974—; corporator Boston Bio-Med. Inst., 1990—; mem. corp. Ptnrs. Healthcare Sys., 1999—, also others. Mem. Mensa, Am. Needlepoint Guild (founder, pres. Mass. chpt. 1974-77, bd. dirs. 1974—, nat. historian 1989-97). Republican. Episcopalian. Avocations: travel, reading, needlepoint. Home: 171 Edmunds Rd Wellesley MA 02481-1331

HENDERSON, MAUREEN MCGRATH, medical educator; b. Tynemouth, Eng., May 11, 1926; arrived in U.S., 1960; d. Leo E. and Helen McGrath Henderson. MB BS, U. Durham, Eng., 1949, DPH, 1956. Prof. preventive medicine U. Md. Med. Sch., 1968—75, chmn. dept. social and preventive medicine, 1971—75; assoc. epidemiology Johns Hopkins U. Sch. Hygiene and Pub. Health, 1960—75; prof. epidemiology and medicine U. Wash. Med. Sch., 1975—96, prof. emeritus epidemiology and medicine, 1996—, asst. v.p. and assoc. v.p. health scis., 1975—81, head cancer prevention rsch. program Fred Hutchinson Cancer Rsch. Ctr., 1983—94; mem. Nat. Inst. Environ. Health Scis. Adv. Coun., 1994—97. Chmn. epidemiology and disease control study sect. Nih, 1969—82; chmn. clin. trial rev. com. Nat. Heart Lung and Blood Inst., 1975—79; mem. Nat. Cancer Adv. Bd., 1979—84; mem. bd. Robert Wood Johnson Health Policy Fellowship, 1989—93; bd. radiation effects rsch. NRC, 1991—97. Decorated Order of Brit. Empire; recipient John Snow award, Am. Pub. Health Assn., 1990; scholar Luke-Armstrong, 1956—57, John and Mary Markle, Acad. Medicine, 1963—68. Mem.: Nat. Rsch. Coun. (mem. com. rsch. priorities for airborne particulate matters 1998—2000, mem. report rev. com. 1996—), Am. Epidemiol. Soc. (pres. 1990—91), Internat. Coun. Cancer Rsch. (sci. adv. bd. 1989—92), Soc. Epidemiol. Rsch. (chmn. 1969—70), Assn. Tchrs. Preventive Medicine (pres. 1972—73), Am. Coll. Epidemiology, Inst. Medicine. Home: 5309 NE 85th St Seattle WA 98115-3915

HENDERSON, MAXINE OLIVE BOOK (MRS. WILLIAM HENDERSON III), foundation executive; b. Rush, Colo., Apr. 22, 1924; d. Jesse Frank and Olive (Booth) Book; m. William Henderson III, Apr. 10, 1948 (dec. May 1983); children: William IV, Meredith. BA, U. Colo., 1945. Personnel adminstr. GE Co., Schenectady, N.Y.C., 1945-54; asst. dir. placement Katherine Gibbs Sch., N.Y.C., 1967-70; v.p., dir. William Henderson Cons., Inc., N.Y.C., 1969-83, pres., dir., 1983-86; dir. recruitment Girl Scouts U.S.A., N.Y.C., 1973-78, dir. human resources, 1978-82, dir. career devel., 1982-91, adminstr. human resources, 1991-93; pres., adminstr. World Found., 1993-2000. Pres. Goddard-Riverside-Trinity Sch. Thrift Shop, N.Y.C., 1964-65, Trinity Sch. Mothers' Orgn., N.Y.C., 1965-66, Trinity Sch. Parents Assn.; treas. Brearley Sch. Parents Assn., N.Y.C., 1966-67; mem. L.I. Mus., Smithtown Arts Coun., Met. Mus. Art, N.Y.C. Mem. North Suffolk Garden Club, Nissequogue Beach Club. Episcopalian. Home: 606 W 116th St New York NY 10027-7011

HENDERSON, MELFORD J. epidemiologist, molecular biologist, chemist; b. Birmingham, Ala., Dec. 28, 1950; s. Robert Burton and Rena Henderson; 1 child, Erica. Student, NYU Dental Sch., 1977-79; BS, Bishop Coll., Dallas, 1972; MA, Johns Hopkins U., 1976; MPH, Yale U., 1984. Ordained minister. Research assoc. Bishop Coll., 1972-73; rsch. assoc. Sch. of Pharmacy U. Md., Balt., 1976-77; microbiologist Torigian Labs., Queens, N.Y., 1979-81; pub. health analyst internat. program cardiovascular diseases NIH, Bethesda, Md., 1984; epidemiologist/analyst Task Force on Black and Minority Health, Bethesda, Md., 1985—. Epidemiologist D.C. Govt., D.C. Health Dept., 1985-88, U.S. Govt., Agy. for Health Care Policy and Rsch., 1990; epidemiologist, sr. rsch. assoc. Prospect Assocs., 1989; epidemiologist, program ofcl. U.S. Dept. HHS; program ofcl. Mayor's Health Policy Coun. D.C. Govt. Author 7 scholarly sci. publs. Recipient numerous awards in chemistry and pub. health; NIH fellow, 1973-76, USPHS fellow, 1982-84, rsch. fellow Assn. Black Cardiologists, 1984-85. Mem. APHA, Md. Pub. Health Assn., Blacks in Govt., Soc. for Epidemiol. Rsch., Assn. Black Cardiologists, Beta Kappa Chi.

HENDERSON, MILTON ARNOLD, professional society administrator; b. Chattanooga, June 22, 1922; s. Milton Arnold and Margaret (Rawlings) H.; m. Joyce Crowder (dec. Nov. 13, 1977); children: George, Linda, Philip.; m. Betty Ann Harnage, Aug. 20, 1982. BS, Northwestern U., 1948. Asst. sales mgr. Coca-Cola Bottling Co., Savannah and Macon, Ga., 1948-54; with Gideons Internat., Chgo., 1954-63, field rep., 1954-55, promotion mgr., 1955-56, with Nashville, 1964—, exec. dir., 1956-87, exec. dir. emeritus, 1987—. Editor The Gideon Mag., Gideon Info. Bull., Gideon News Brief, 1956-87; author: Sowers of the Word, a 95-Year History of The Gideons International, 1899-1994, 1995. 1st lt. USAAF, 1942-46; capt. USAF, 1951-52. Recipient Community Leader of Am. award, 1969, Personalities of the South award, 1975, Disting. Alumnus award Howe Mil. Sch., Ind., 1985. Mem. Am. Mgmt. Assn., Nashville City Club. Republican. Presbyterian. Home: 2524 Stones River Ct Nashville TN 37214-1425 Office: 2900 Lebanon Rd Nashville TN 37214-2509

HENDERSON, NANCY GRACE, marketing and technical documentation executive; b. Berkeley, Calif., Oct. 23, 1947; d. John Harry and Lorraine Ruth H. BA, U. Calif., Santa Barbara, 1969; MBA, U. Houston, 1985; teaching credential, UCLA, 1971; MLA, Naropa U., 2002. Chartered fin. analyst. Tchr. Keppel Union Sch. Dist., Littlerock, Calif., 1969-72, Internat. Sch. Prague, Czechoslovakia, 1972-74, Sunland Luth. Sch., Freeport, Bahamas, 1974-75; tchr., dept. head Internat. Sch. Assn., Bangkok, Thailand, 1975-79; exec. search Diversified Human Resources Group, Houston, Tex., 1979-82; data processing analyst Am. Gen. Corp., Houston, 1982-83, personnel and benefits dept., 1983-85, investment analyst, 1985-86, equity security analyst/quantitative portfolio analyst, 1986-87; dir. mktg. and communications Vestek Systems Inc., San Francisco, 1987-90, dir. technical publs., 1990—. Tchr. English as Second Language program Houston Metro. Ministries, 1980-81. Pres., bd. dirs. Home Owners Assn., Walnut Creek, Calif., 1988-90; tchr. English to refugees Houston Metro Ministries, 1982, exec. dir. Internat. Child Abuse Prevention Found., 1989; ch. choir, session, fundraising and com. chmn. Presbyn. Ch.; active Crisis Hotline, 1978-79, 92-93; dir. project Working in Networks for Good Shelter, 1993-95. Named a Notable Woman of Tex., 1984-85. Mem. Assn. for Investment Mgmt. and Rsch., Toastmasters (pres. Houston chpt. 1983, v.p. 1982-83). Avocations: tennis, skiing, hiking, photography, writing short stories and essays. Office: Thomson Vestek 425 Market St Fl 6 San Francisco CA 94105

HENDERSON, PAUL BARGAS, JR., economic development consultant; b. McKees Rocks, Pa., Nov. 20, 1928; s. Paul Bargas and Viola Mae (Mullins) Henderson; m. Betty D. Langewisch, Aug. 25, 1951; children: Keith, Karen, Laura. BS in Mech. and Indsl. Engring., Washington U., St. Louis, 1948, MS in Bus. Adminstrn., 1950; PhD in Indsl. Econs., MIT, 1960. Asst. for mgmt. U.S. Navy Bur. Ordnance, Washington, 1950-58; mgr. sys. tech. Westinghouse Electric Corp., Pitts., 1960-67; program mgr. United Aircraft Corp., Hartford, Conn., 1967-68; dir. data services Allis-Chalmers Corp., Milw., 1968-74; v.p. Fed. Res. Bank N.Y., N.Y.C., 1974-77, sr. v.p., 1977-82, sr. adviser, 1982-84; bank ops. cons. N.Y.C., 1984—2001; econ. devel. cons. in Russia, chmn., CEO Sierra Caucasus Corp., 1990-2001; exec. dir. United Meth. Econ. Devel. Initiative in Kazakstan, 1996—98; asst. prof. econs. Sierra Nevada Coll., Incline Village, Nev., 1997-2001. Bd. dirs. Direct Svcs., Inc. Author: (with E.M. Heigler) Library Automation, 1970, Electronic Funds Transfers and Payments: The Public Policy Issues, 1987; inventor in field. Bd. dirs., treas. Cameron Sta. Cmty. Assn. Office: 336 Cameron Station Blvd Alexandria VA 22304-8623 *There is a recurring necessity to induce change as the basis for comparative advantage; neglect makes it a matter of survival. There is also a constant and greater necessity to sustain existing operations; quality and efficiency depend on repetition. Anticipated change is thus compatible with stable management. Change for survival, and managers capable of inducing it, must be transitory for both are incompatible with sustained organizational success.*

HENDERSON, RALPH HALE, physician; b. N.Y.C., Mar. 5, 1937; s. Ralph Ernest and Clifford West (Sellers) H.; m. Ilze Sarma, May 21, 1966. AB, Harvard U., 1959, MD, 1963, MPH, 1970, M.Pub. Policy, 1972. Intern, then resident in internal medicine Boston City Hosp., 1963-65; joined USPHS, 1965, capt., 1973-81, asst. surgeon gen., 1981-90, svc. in, 1965-69. Asst. chief venereal disease br., state and cmty. svcs. divsn. Ctrs. Disease Control, Atlanta, 1972-73; dir. venereal disease control divsn. Bur. State Svcs., 1973-76; program mgr. expanded program on immunization WHO, Geneva, 1977-78, dir. expanded program immunization, 1979-89, asst. dir. gen., 1990-98, spl. advisor to dir. gen., 1998-99; Lilly lectr. Royal Coll. Physicians, 1989; lectr. disting. lecture series Baylor Coll. Medicine, 1995. Contbr. to med. publs. Trustee Dermatology Found., 1975-77. Recipient Commendation medal USPHS, 1969, Meritorius Svc. medal, 1984, Disting. Svc. medal, 1990, Donald MacKay Meml. medal Royal Soc. Tropical Medicine and Hygiene, 1990, Internat. Child Survival award U.S. Com. UNICEF and the Task Force for Child Survival and Devel., 1992, Ann. Pub. Health Forum award London Sch. of Hygiene and Tropical Medicine, 1994. Mem. Am. Coll. Preventive Medicine. Home: 1098 Mcconnell Dr Decatur GA 30033-3402

HENDERSON, RICHARD MARTIN, retired chemical engineer; b. Winston-Salem, N.C., Dec. 12, 1934; s. Billy Martin and Marion Lucille (Dunn) H.; m. Patricia Lucille Green, Dec. 27, 1958 (div. 1978); children: Marian Patricia, Richard Martin; m. Janice Lee Ferris, Apr. 3, 1981. BBA, Wake Forest U., 1957. Cert. quality engr. Jr. chem. engr. R.J. Reynolds Tobacco Co., Winston-Salem, 1957-58, asst. chem. engr., 1958-65, product devel. group leader, 1965-66, devel. sect. head, 1966-80, div. mgr., 1981-98; ret., 1998. Pres. Y Men's Club of Winston-Salem, 1989, Moravian Music Found., Winston-Salem, 1983; trustee Moravian Theol. Sem.; active United Way of Forsyth County, 1958—, Winston-Salem Arts Coun., 1958—. With Signal Corps, U.S. Army, 1960-61. Recipient Merit award, Moravian Music Found., 1984; Ky. Col. Mem. Am. Soc. for Quality Control (founding dir./sr. mem.), Forsyth Country Club. Republican. Moravian. Achievements include patents for the method of and apparatus for automatically analyzing the degradation of processed leaf tobacco, for the method and apparatus for automatically determining the stem content of baled tobacco, for the method and apparatus for automatically determining the basis weight and moisture content of paper and paper-like substance, for the method and apparatus for automatically sampling a material and transporting it from one location to another remote location. Home: 717 Mitch Dr Winston Salem NC 27104-5127 Office: RJ Reynolds Tobacco Co 401 N Main St Winston Salem NC 27101-3804

HENDERSON, R(ICHARD) WINN, physician; b. Gainesville, Fla., Oct. 3, 1948; s. William P. and Lillian June (Rudd) H.; m. Maureen Skudlarek, 1972 (div. 1985); 1 child, Heather Ann; m. Wanda Joyce Crittenden, Apr. 13, 1997. AB, Lagrange Coll., 1968; MD, U. Ala., 1972. Diplomate Am. Bd. Family Practitioners, Am. Bd. Emergency Medicine. Intern in family practice St. Elizabeth's Med. Ctr., Dayton, 1972-73; resident in aerospace medicine Brooks AFB, 1973; clin. instr. emergency dept. UTMRCH, Knoxville, Tenn., 1976-78; staff emergency physician, dir. emergency physicians Morristown (Tenn.) Hamblen Hosp., 1978-82; staff emergency physician, chmn. emergency dept. St. Mary's Med. Ctr., Knoxville, 1983-84; staff emergency physician Meth. Med. Ctr., Oak Ridge, Tenn., 1984-85; dir. East Tenn. Med./Acute Care Clinic, 1985-90; counselor, rschr. in addiction medicine Kennedy Ctr., Morgantown, W.Va., 1990-92; dir., sr. physician The Recovery Group, Knoxville, 1992—2001. Examiner FAA, 1982-90; internat. radio talk show host Share Your Mission, 1998—, emergency med. adv., 1980. Author: The Cure of Addiction, 1991, Doctor's Don't Lie, 1993, The 12 Steps (Explained and Revised), 1995, Forever Lovers, 1997, The Four Questions, 1998; Share Your Mission, vol. 1, 2000, vol. 2, 2001, vol. 3, 2002, The Sacrifice Diet, 2002; patentee method for cryogenically treating psoriasis with liquid nitrogen. Founder The Destiny House, 1998. Maj. USAF, 1973-76. Mem. Am. Assn. Christian Counselors (charter). Avocations: sculpting, painting. Office: 138 Heavenly View Sylva NC 28779 E-mail: drhenderson7@mchsi.com.

HENDERSON, RICKEY HENLEY, professional baseball player; b. Chgo., Dec. 25, 1958; With minor league baseball clubs, 1976—79; with Oakland Athletics, 1979—84, N.Y. Yankees, 1985—89, Oakland Athletics, 1989—93, Toronto Blue Jays, 1993—94, Oakland Athletics, 1994—95, San Diego Padres, 1996—98, New York Mets, 1998—2000, Seattle Mariners, 2000—. Named Most Valuable Player, Am. League, 1990, Am. Championship Series, 1989; named to All-Star Team, Am. League, 1980, 1982—88, Sporting News Am. League, 1981, 1985, 1990, Silver Slugger Team, 1981, 1985, 1990; recipient Golden Glove award, Am. League, 1981, All-Star Team, 1990—91, Silver Shoe award, Sporting News, 1982, Golden Shoe award, 1983. Achievements include holding a major league record for stolen bases in one season (130), 1982; for most stolen bases in career, player World Series 1989, 90, 93. Office: Seattle Mariners Safeco Field PO Box 4100 Seattle WA 98104

HENDERSON, RITA ELIZABETH, literary agent, journalist; b. Bitburg, German, Mar. 7, 1964; came to U.S., 1964; d. Walter Wanzley and Lola Bell (Boles) H.; adopted children: Christopher Allan Jackson, Kayla Elizabeth Octavia Davis. AAS, Camden County Coll., Blackwood, N.J., 1984; BS, Glassboro (N.J.) State Coll., 1987. Owner Henderson Lit. Representation, Sicklerville, N.J., 1994—; real estate agt. Weichert Realtors, Medford, N.J., 1998—. Author: The Boyz II Men Success Story: Defying the Odds, 1995; entertainment writer The N.Y. Amsterdam News, 1991-95, The Phila. Tribune, 1993-95. Democrat. Roman Catholic. Avocations: music, archery, antique collecting, baseball, computers. Office: Weichert Realtors 107 Taunton Blvd Medford NJ 08055-3400

HENDERSON, ROBB ALAN, minister; b. Wilkes Barre, Pa., Mar. 21, 1956; s. Robert Alan and Mary (Gallup) H.; m. Norma Jean Davis, Nov. 26, 1994; children: Jason Allyn, Gareth Kent. BA in Theology, King's Coll., Wilkes Barre, 1981; MDiv, Lancaster Theol. Sem., 1985; D Ministry, Bethany Theol. Sem., 1990. Ordained to ministry United Meth. Ch. as deacon, 1986, as elder, 1988; ordained into So. Episc. Ch., 1997. Pastor Luzerne (Pa.) United Meth. Ch., 1985-88, Carverton United Meth. Ch., Wyoming, Pa., 1988—93, St. Paul's United Meth. Ch., Scranton, Pa., 1993-94, So. Episcopal Ch. of Wyoming Valley, 2000—. Owner R&R Bus Line, Luzerne, 1990—; chmn. interreligious and ecumenical affairs com. Coun. of Chs., 1989—; bd. dirs. Wyoming Valley Coun. of Chs.; safety dir., dispatcher First Class Coach Co., St. Petersburg, Fla. Chaplain Mt. Zion Vol. Fire Dept., Mt. Zion, Harding, Pa. Mem. Masons (chaplain Kingston lodge 1989), Irem Temple. Home and Office: 230 Harland St Exeter PA 18643 E-mail: marauder-robb@juno.com.

HENDERSON, ROBERT EARL, mechanical engineer, educator, consultant; b. Olean, N.Y., Nov. 1, 1935; s. Kenneth Peter and Marion (Nichols) H.; m. E. Annalee Rosenwie, Aug. 10, 1957 (dec. July 1994); children: Gregory Dwight, Michael Edwin, Lori Elizabeth; m. Mary J. Ball, Dec. 28, 1996. BS, Pa. State U., 1958, MS, 1962; PhD, Cambridge (Eng.) U., 1973. Aerodynamicist McDonnel Applied Rsch. Lab., Pa. State U., 1959-73, assoc. prof. mech. engring., 1973-79, prof., 1979-91, prof. emeritus, 1991—. Cons., 1991-95; chief sci. Noesis, Inc., 1995—; assoc. dir. Garfield Thomas Water Tunnel, 1980-82, head dept. fluid dynamics and turbomachinery, 1983-89, asst. dir. applied sci. div., 1990-91. Contbr. articles to profl. jours. Recipient Disting. Performance award Applied Rsch. Lab., Pa. State U., 1981. Fellow ASME, AIAA (assoc.); mem. Sigma Xi, Pi Mu Epsilon. Home: 400 N Fairfax Dr Ste 800 Arlington VA 22207 Office: 4100 N Fairfax Dr Ste 800 Arlington VA 22203

HENDERSON, ROBERTA MARIE, librarian, educator; b. Mosinee, Wis., July 27, 1929; d. Roy H. and Marie Helena (Dittman) H. BS, Cen. State Tchrs. Coll., Stevens Point, Wis., 1951; MS, U. Wis., 1958; MA, No. Mich. U., 1975; Cert. of Adv. Studies, U. Denver, 1980. Librarian Wiesbaden (Ger.) Am. High Sch., 1954-55, Ashland (Wis.) High Sch., 1955-56; tchr./librarian Clark AFB, Philippines, 1956-57; librarian Prescott (Ariz.) Jr. High Sch., 1958-59, Frankfurt (Ger.) Am. High Sch., 1959-63; tchr./librarian Zama Am. High Sch., Camp Zama, Japan, 1963-66; librarian Ankara (Turkey) Am. High Sch., 1966-68; tutor Nkozi Tchr. Tng. Coll., Mpigi, Uganda, 1968-70; ref. librarian/prof. No. Mich. U., Marquette, 1971-93; retired, 1993; cons. No. Mich. U. and Pub. Librs., 1993—. Coord. faculty workshops No. Mich. U., 1986-88; cons. Escanaba (Mich.) Pub. Libr., 1987, 90, 92. Author slide/tape: Locating Materials in Periodicals and Documents, 1977, Library Materials for Literature Students, 1979. Mem. libr. com. Marquette County Hist. Soc., 1981—; mem. Upper Peninsula Environ. Coalition, Houghton, 1985—; host Marquette-Japan Sister Coalition City Program, 1988. Title II-B fellow, U. Denver, 1979-80; Human Resources Dept., No. Mich. U. grantee, 1986, 87; recipient Disting Faculty award No. Mich. U., 1988. Mem. ALA, AAUP, Libr. Instrn. Roundtable, Phi Kappa Phi (chpt. treas. 1987-91). Avocations: interior decoration, gardening, hiking, cats. Home: 515 E Ridge St Marquette MI 49855-4216

HENDERSON, ROBYN LEE, health association manager; b. Hastings, Nebr., Apr. 3, 1960; d. Darrel Franklin and Bonnalynne Beulah Henderson. BS, Nebr. Wesleyan U., 1982; MHS, Johns Hopkins U., 1996. Aide to spkr. Nebr. Legis., Lincoln, 1981-82; program instr. Close Up Found., Arlington, Va., 1982-84; legis. aide Sen. Jim Exon, Washington, 1984-91; legis. rep. Am. Thoracic Soc., Washington, 1991-94; rsch. assoc. Nat. Health Policy Forum, Washington, 1994-96; govt. policy analyst Nat. Rural Electric Coop. Assn., Arlington, Va., 1996-98; v.p. program svcs. Nat. Rural Health Assn., Kansas City, 1998—2003; with U. Nebr. Pub. Policy Ctr., Lincoln, 2003—. Chair govt. rels. Affinity Group Nat. Health Coun., Washington, 1993-94, Rural Renaissance Network, Washington, 1996-98. Mem. Friends of the Kennedy Ctr., Washington, 1991—98. Recipient Young Alumna Loyalty award Nebr. Wesleyan U., 1980; named Outstanding Young Women of Am., 1984, 87. Mem. APHA, Am. Soc. Assn. Execs., Nat. Rural Health Assn., Kansas City Soc. Assn. Execs., Phi Alpha Theta. Avocations: reading, history, golf, music.

HENDERSON, ROGENE FAULKNER, toxicologist, researcher; b. Breckenridge, Tex., July 13, 1933; d. Philander Molden and Lenoma (Rogers) F.; m. Thomas Richard Henderson II, May 30, 1957; children: Thomas Richard III, Edith Jeanette, Laura Lee. BSBA, Tex. Christian U., 1955; PhD, U. Tex., 1960. Diplomate Am. Bd. Toxicology. Research assoc. U. Ark. Sch. Med., Little Rock, 1960-67; from scientist to sr. scientist and group supr. chemistry and toxicology Lovelace Inhalation Toxicology Research Inst., Albuquerque, 1967—; deputy dir. Nat. Environ. Respiratory Ctr. Lovelace Respiratory Rsch. Inst., Albuquerque, 1998—. Mem. adv. com. Burroughs Wellcome Toxicology Scholar award, 1987-89, NIH toxicology study sect., 1982-86, Nat. Inst. Environ. Health Scis. adv. coun., 1992-95, EPA scientific adv. bd. environ. health commn., 1991-95; mem. bd. sci. counselors EPA, 2002—; mem. Com to Assess the Sci. Base for Tobacco Harm Reduction, adv. group Am. Cancer Soc.on Cancer and the Environment, 1999—, Health Effects Inst. Rsch. Com., 1997—, USEPA Bd. of Sci. Counselors, 2001— Assoc. editor Toxicology Applied Pharmacology, 1989-95, Jour. Exposure Analysis and Environ. Epidemiology, 1991-95; contbr. articles to profl. jours. Named Woman on the Move YWCA, Albuquerque, 1985; grantee NIH, 1958-60, 1960-62, 1986—. Mem. AAAS, NAS (bd. on environ. studies and toxicology 1998—), Am. Chem. Soc. (chmn. ctrl. N.Mex. sect. 1981), Soc. Toxicology (pres. Mountain-West Regional chpt. 1985-86, pres. inhalation specialty sect. 1989—), N.Y. Acad. Scis., Nat. Acad. Scis. (com. toxicology 1985-98, chair 1992-98, com. epidemiology of air pollution 1983-85, com. biol. markers 1986—, com. on risk assessment methodology 1989-92, bd. environ. studies and toxicology 1998—), Nat. Acad. (nat. assoc.). Presbyterian. Home: 5609 Don Felipe Ct SW Albuquerque NM 87105-6765 Office: Lovelace Respiratory Rsch Inst 2425 Ridgecrest Ave SE Albuquerque NM 87108 E-mail: rhenders@lrri.org.

HENDERSON, SABRINA NICOLE, journalist; b. Denver, Feb. 26, 1978; d. Philip Andrew Henderson and Kathleen Susan Port. Bachelors, Point Park Coll., 1998; MA in Polit. Sci., U. Colo., 2002. Editor, publ. Gray Matters Mag., Pitts. and Denver, 1997-99; contbg. writer Pitts. Newsweekly, 1998; editor Earth Obs. Mag., Denver, 1999; mng. editor The Cherry Creek Times Newspaper, Denver, 1999—2002; editor Golden Transcript, Denver, 2002—. Dir. publs. Mentoring Partnership Southwestern Pa., Pitts., 1997-98, Youth Places/Youth Leads, Pitts., 1997-98; writer, photographer Pitts. Coun. Public Edn., 1997-98. Recipient Nat. Collegiate Comm. Arts award, 1997, 98. Mem. Colo. Press Assn. (assoc.), Soc. Profl. Journalists (Point Park chpt. pres. 1997-98). Independent. Avocations: photography, composing, music. Home: 3200 W 26th Ave Denver CO 80211-4033 Office: Sentinel & Transcript Newspapers 1000 10th St Golden CO 80401

HENDERSON, STANLEY DALE, lawyer, educator; b. Monona, Iowa, June 17, 1935; s. Leon Gilbert and Iva Elizabeth H.; m. DeArliss Garretson, June 15, 1957; children: Lesli Kara, Heidi Elizabeth, Holly Ann. AB, Coe Coll., 1957; postgrad. (Woodrow Wilson fellow), Cornell U., 1957-58; postgrad., U. Chgo. Law Sch., 1958-59; JD, U. Colo., 1961. Bar: Colo. 1961, Va. 1973. Law clk. U.S. Dist. Ct., Denver, 1961-62; mem. firm Williams and Zook, Boulder, Colo., 1962-64; mem. faculty U. Wyo. Coll. Law, 1964-69; prof. law U. Va. Law Sch., Charlottesville, 1970, F.D.G. Ribble prof. law, 1976—. Vis. prof. law Ind. U., 1974, Harvard Law Sch., 1978-79, Pepperdine U., 1992-93. Author: (with Dawson and Harvey) Labor Law, (with Meltzer) Contracts; contbr. articles to profl. jours. Mem. Va. State Bar, Am. Law Inst., Am. Arbitration Assn., Order of Coif, Phi Beta Kappa, Phi Kappa Phi. Democrat. Presbyterian. Home: 1615 King Mountain Rd Charlottesville VA 22901-3003 Office: U Va Sch Law Charlottesville VA 22901 Fax: 434-924-7536. E-mail: sdh6k@virginia.edu.

HENDERSON, STEPHEN PAUL, lawyer; b. Oakland, Calif., July 14, 1949; s. Carl Edward and Esther Minnie (Miller) Henderson; m. Josephine Ann Bartlett; children: Catherine Anne, Lauren Elizabeth. BA, Wash. State U., 1971; JD, U. Oreg., 1974. Bar: Oreg. 1974, U.S. Ct. Mil. Appeals 1978, U.S. Tax Ct. 1979, U.S. Ct. Appeals (9th cir.) 1979, U.S. Ct. Appeals (6th cir.) 1990, U.S. Supreme Ct. 1979. Atty. GE Credit Corp., Providence, 1979-81, dept. counsel GE, Schenectady, N.Y., 1981-83, operation counsel Atlanta, 1983-86, divsn. counsel, 1987-89, GE Aircraft Engines, Cin., 1990-97; gen. counsel GE Engine Svcs., Inc., Cin., 1998—. Editor U. Oreg. Law Rev., 1972-73. 2d lt. inf. U.S. Army, 1971, capt. JAGC U.S. Army, 1974—79. Nat. Merit scholar, 1967. Mem.: ABA, Phi Eta Sigma, Fed. Bar Assn., Corp. Counsel Assn. of Atlanta Bar Assn., Cin. Bar Assn., Ohio Bar Assn., Oreg. Bar Assn., Phi Kappa Phi, Phi Beta Kappa. Republican. Episcopalian. Office: GE 1 Neumann Way F125 Cincinnati OH 45215-1915

HENDERSON, THOMAS HENRY, JR., lawyer, legal association executive; b. Birmingham, Ala., Feb. 4, 1939; s. Thomas Henry and Edna (Green) H.; m. Elaine Dauphin (div. 1983); children: Ashley, Michelle; m. Paulette Maehara, June 1988. BSBA, Auburn U., 1961; JD, U. Ala., 1966; LLM, Nat. Law Ctr., George Washington U., 1987. Bar: D.C. 1970, Ala. 1966. Trial atty. organized crime and racketeering sect. U.S. Dept. Justice, Washington, 1966-70, dep. sect. chief mgmt. labor sect., 1970-73; dep. chief counsel, subcom. on adminstrn. practice and procedure U.S. Senate, Washington, 1973-74; dep. sect. chief mgmt. and labor sect. Dept. Justice, Washington, 1974-76, chief pub. integrity sect., 1976-80, sr. counsel criminal div., 1980-83; bar counsel D.C. Ct. Appeals, Washington, 1983 87; CEO, ATLA, Washington, 1988—. Columnist Bar Counsels Page, Washington Lawyer mag., bi-monthly, 1983-87. Pres. Christmas in April, Washington, 1986-87. Mem. Am. Soc. Assn. Execs. (bd. dirs. 1994-97, vice chair 1997-98), Omicron Delta Kappa. Avocations: golf, skiing, fitness, outdoor adventure. Home: 6698 Glenbrook Rd Chevy Chase MD 20815-6515 Office: ATLA 1050 31st St NW Washington DC 20007-4409

HENDERSON, VICTOR WARREN, behavioral and geriatric neurologist, researcher, educator; b. Little Rock, Aug. 20, 1951; s. Philip S. and N. Jean (Edsel) H.; m. Barbara Ann Curtiss, May 24, 1975; children: Gregory, Geoffrey, Stephanie, Nicole. BS, U. Ga., 1972; MD, Johns Hopkins U., 1976; MS, U. Wash., 1996. Diplomate Am. Bd. Psychiatry and Neurology. Intern Duke U., Durham, NC, 1976—77; resident Washington U., St. Louis, 1977—80; fellow Boston U., 1980—81; asst. prof. neurology U. So. Calif., L.A., 1981—86, assoc. prof. neurology, gerontology & psychology, 1986—93, prof. neurology, gerontology & psychology, 1993—2001, chief divsn. cognitive neurosci. & neurogerontology, 1989—2001, dir. lab. memory & memory disorders, 1997—, Kenneth and Bette Volk prof. neurology, 1999—2001; prof. geriatrics, neurology, pharmacology and epidemiology U. Ark. Med. Scis., Little Rock, 2001—, vice chair dept. geriatrics, 2001—. Dir. NIH Alzheimer's Disease Rsch. Ctr. Clin. Core, 1985—2001; dir. neurobehavior Clinic/Bowles Ctr. for Alzheimer's and Related Diseases, 1988—2001; chmn. neurology svc. L.A. County, U. So. Calif. Med. Ctr., 1992—97; vis. scientist MIT, 1988—89; vis. prof. U. Melbourne, 2002; co-dir. State of Calif. Alzheimer's Disease Rsch. Ctr. U. So. Calif., 1999—2001; dir. Dementia Ctr. of Ark., 2001; co-dir. NIH Alzheimer's Disease Ctr., 2001—03; Kearney vis. prof. Mental Health Rsch. Inst. Victoria, Australia, 2002; dir. Rural Aging and Memory Study, 2001—; prof. fellow dept. psychiatry U. Melbourne, 2003 . Author: (with others) Principles of Neurologic Diagnosis, 1985, Hormone Therapy and the Brain, 2000; mem. editl. bd. profl. jours.; contbr. articles to profl. jours. Grantee, Alzheimer's Assn., Calif. Dept. Health Svcs., Adminstrn. on Aging, NIH, French Found., 1984—; scholar Nat. Merit, 1968. Fellow: Am. Acad. Neurology; mem.: Soc. for Behavioral and Cognitive Neurology, N.Am. Menopause Soc. (trustee 2002—), Alzheimer's Assn. (Rsch. award L.A. chpt. 1998), French Found. Alzheimer Rsch., Nat. Aphasia Assn., World Fedn. Neurology, Internat. Menopause Soc., Internat. Neuropsychol. Soc., Soc. for Behavioral and Cogntive Neurology, Gerontol. Soc. Am., Acad. Aphasia, Soc. for Neurosci., Am. Neurol. Assn. Office: U Ark Med Scis Ctr on Aging # 810 4301 W Markham St Little Rock AR 72205

HENDERSON, WILLIAM CHARLES, editor; b. Phila., Apr. 5, 1941; s. Francis Louis and Dorothy Price (Galloway) H. BA, Hamilton Coll., 1963; postgrad., Harvard U., 1963, U. Pa., 1965-66. Assoc. editor Doubleday & Co., N.Y.C., 1972-73; pub. Pushcart Press, Wainscott, N.Y., 1972—; sr. editor Coward, McCann & Geohagan, Inc., N.Y.C., 1973-75; cons. editor Harper & Row Inc., 1976—. Guest lectr. Harvard U., summer 1974, Sarah Lawrence Coll., U. Rochester, summers 1978, 87; lectr. Columbia U., 1978-80, Princeton U., 1984, 86, 87, Johns Hopkins U., 1989, Radcliffe Pub. Course, 1989; mem. nat. adv. bd. Ctr. for the Book Library of Congress, 1979; pres. Pushcart Found.; fiction judge Nat. Book Award, 2001. Author: His Son: A Child of the Fifties, 1981, The Kid That Could, 1990, Her Father, 1995, Tower, 2000; editor, pub.: The Publish It Yourself Handbook, 1973, The Pushcart Prize: Best of the Small Presses, 1976—; editor: Rotten Reviews, 1986, Minutes of the Lead Pencil Club, 1996. Recipient Author award N.J. English Tchrs. Assn., 1972; Newsboy award Horatio Alger Soc., 1973, Carey-Thomas award, 1978, Poor Richard award, 2001. Mem. P.E.N., The Lead Pencil Club (founder). Home and Office: Pushcart Press PO Box 380 Wainscott NY 11975-0380

HENDERSON, WILLIAM DAVID, mechanical engineer; b. El Paso, Tex., May 1, 1950; s. Weldon Oliver and Betty Joyce (Woodson) H.; m. Karen Sue George, July 22, 1972; children: Carrie Ann, Heather Marie. BSME, U. Tex., El Paso, 1974. Registered profl. engr., Tex., 1980. Engr. trainee Otis Engring. Corp., Corpus Christi, Tex., 1974-75, design engr. Dallas, 1975-81, design mgr., 1981-88, staff engr., 1988-91; engring. projects mgr. Baker Oil Tools, Houston, 1991-97; mgr. design engring. OSCA, Houston, TX., 1997-99; tech. profl. leader sand control team Halliburton Energy Svcs., Carrollton, Tex., 1999—. Mem.: ASME. Republican. Baptist. Achievements include 13 patents in methods and apparatus for downhole tools for oil and gas wells. Home: 1207 Vaughan Ln Tioga TX 76271-2933 Office: Halliburton Energy Svcs 2601 E Belt Line Rd Carrollton TX 75006-5401

HENDERSON, WILLIAM EUGENE, education educator; b. Miami, Fla., Sept. 9, 1947; s. William Bartow and Evelyn Mildred (Stansell) H. BA in Polit. Sci., Acctg., U. South Fla., 1967; MS in Guidance, Counseling, Barry U., 1971, EdS in Sch. Psychology, 1976, MBA in Mgmt., Fin., 1981; postgrad., Fla. State U., Northwestern U., U. Miami. Cert. tchr., prin., sch. psychologist, Fla. From tchr. to subject area coord. Miami-Dade County Pub. Schs., Miami, 1968—83, asst. prin., 1983-89, assoc. intern prin., 1989-2001; exec. dir. Miami Shores/Barry U. Charter Sch., 2001—03. Adj. prof. Nova U., Ft. Lauderdale, Fla., 1983-90, Barry U., Miami Shores, Fla., 1987—; assessment cons. Fla. Dept. Edn., Tallahassee, 1979-83, Ednl. Testing Svc., Princeton, N.J., 1981-82. Author: S.O.S. Sourcebook, 1985; author curriculum materials; editor, curriculum reviewer Harcourt Brace Jovanovich, Orlando, Fla., 1985-86. Named Outstanding Econs. Educator Fla. Coun. Econ. Edn., 1981, 82, 93, Outstanding Secondary Social Studies Tchr. Dade County Coun. Social Studies, 1982. Mem. Nat. Coun. Social Studies, Coun. Exceptional Children (chair region II, sec. asst. prin. 1998-2001, Oustanding Exceptional Student Edn. Adminstr. 1988), So. Assn. Schs. and Colls. (chair, facilitator 2001—), Assn. for Supervision and Curriculum Devel., dir. Fla. Consortium of Charter Schs., Phi Delta Kappa, Kappa Delta Pi, Phi Alpha Theta.

HENDERSON, WILLIAM J. association executive; b. Paris, Ill., July 24, 1925; s. William M. and Lena (Johnson) H.; m. Mary Ann Ferguson, July 15, 1950 (dec. Oct. 1985); children: Beth Grafton, Mark W.; m. Virginia Skram, Dec. 24, 1986; children: John Skran, Peggy Skran, Salli Skran. BA, Aurora U., 1950; postgrad., U. Ill., 1951. Adminstrv. asst. Assoc. Industries, Rock Island, Ill., 1951-54; pers. dir. George Evans Corp., Moline, Ill., 1954-58; dir. econ. edn. & pub. rels. Assoc. Industries of Mo., 1958-62; exec. v.p. Assoc. Credit Bureau of Midwest, 1962-72, v.p., 1972-78; pres. Internat. Credit Assn., St. Louis, 1978-91; ret., 1991; pres., CEO Henderson Enterprises, 1991. With USN, 1943-46. Recipient Freedom Found. award Valley Forge, 1956. Mem. U.S. Chamber Am. Soc. Assocs. Execs. (v.p., bd. dirs. 1981-84, mem. exec. com.), Ind. Soc. Assn. Execs. (past pres. 1971-72), Mo. Soc. Assn. Execs., St. Louis Meeting Planners (bd. dirs. 1983—), St. Louis Assn. Execs. (v.p. 1984-85, pres. 1985—), U.S. C. of C. (com. of 100), Running and Fitness Assn. (dir. 1987—), Aurora U. Alumni Assn. (chmn. Gateway chpt.), Masons, Shriners. Home and Office: 14172 Woods Mill Cove Dr Chesterfield MO 63017-3436 E-mail: pianobh@aol.com.

HENDERSON, WILLIAM J. former postmaster general; b. June 16, 1947; 2 children. Grad., U. N.C. With U.S. Postal Svc., postmaster, divsn. gen. mgr., v.p. employee rels., chief mktg. officer, sr. v.p., chief operating officer, 1994-98, postmaster gen., CEO, 1998—2001. Mem. bd. dirs. comScore Networks, Inc., 2001—, Acxiom Corp., 2001—, Quad/Graphics Inc., 2001—. With U.S. Army. Recipient Roger W. Jones award for Exec. Leadership Am. U., 1998, John Wanamaker award U.S. Postal Svc., 1997 Office: comScore Networks Inc 500 W Madison St # 2980 Chicago IL 60661

HENDIN, DAVID BRUCE, literary agent, writer, consultant, numismatist; b. St. Louis, Dec. 16, 1945; s. Aaron and Lillian (Karsh) H.; m. Jeannie Luciano, Oct. 4, 1985; children: Sarah Tsvia, Benjamin Judah, Alexander Jacob. BS in Biology Edn, U. Mo., 1967, MA in Journalism, 1970. Sr. v.p., editorial dir., pub. United Media Inc., N.Y.C., 1970-93; clin. prof. off campus U. Mo. Sch. Journalism, 1971-86; pres. Pharos Books, 1992-3, DH Literary, Inc., Nyack, N.Y., 1993—. Adj. lectr. Columbia U. Sch. Journalism, 1974-76; numismatist Joint Sepphoris Excavation, 1985-88. Author: Everything You Need to Know About Abortion, 1971, The Doctor's Save-Your-Heart Diet, 1972, Death As a Fact of Life, 1973, 1984, Save Your Child's Life, 1973, 86, The Life Givers, 1975, Guide to Ancient Jewish Coins, 1975, The World Almanac Whole Health Guide, 1977, The Genetic Connection, 1978, Collecting Coins, 1979, Guide to Biblical Coins, 1987, 96, 2000; mem. editl. bd. Israel Numismatic Jour., 1992-96, Publs. Bd. Union of Am. Hebrew Congregations, 1993. Bd. dirs. Holyland Conservation Fund, 1973-83; v.p. Council Advancement Sci. Writing, 1975-84; trustee Scripps-Howard Found., 1978-87, Kinsey Inst., 1985-92, Mus. Cartoon Art, 1986 92; chmn. numis. com. The Jewish Mus., 1980-85; mem. adv. com. Sch. Journalims, U. Fla., 1991-97. Recipient award merit Am. Assn. Blood Banks, 1972, Claude Bernard Sci. Journalism award, 1972, cert. commendation Am. Acad. Family Physicians, 1973, Med. Journalism award AMA, 1973, Blakeslee award Am. Heart Assn., 1973, Book of Yr. award Am. Med. Writers Assn., 1977, Best Column award Numismatic Literary Guild, 1993, 2000, Ben Odesser Judaic Literary award 1997, Pres. award Am. Numismatic Assn., 2003. Fellow Am. Numismatic Soc.; mem. Coun. for Advancement Sci. Writing, Am.-Israel Numismatic Assn. (v.p. 1979-85), Kappa Tau Alpha, Sigma Alpha Mu. Office: PO Box 990 Nyack NY 10960 0990

HENDIN, HERBERT, psychiatrist, researcher; b. NYC, Oct. 10, 1926; s. Louis and Pauline Hendin; m. Josephine Gattuso, June 7, 1968; children: Neil, Erik. BA, Columbia U., 1945; MD, NYU, 1949; degree in psychoanalytic medicine, Columbia U., 1959. Cert. N.Y., lic. psychiatry Am. Bd. of Neurology and Psychiatry. From asst. to assoc. prof. of psychiatry Columbia U., N.Y.C., 1960—78; dir. Posttraumatic Stress Disorder (PTSD) rsch. and treatment program VA Hosp., Montrose, NY, 1978—83; dir. Ctr. for Psychosocial Studies N.Y. Med. Coll., Valhalla, NY, 1983—87. Chair search com. for chief of psychiatry VA Hosp., Montrose, NY, 1981—82; mem. editl. bd. Suicide and Life-Threatening Behavior, N.Y.C., 1996—. Author: (book) Suicide and Scandinavia: A Psychoanalytic Study of Culture and Character, 1964; co-author: Psychoanalysis and Social Rsch.: The Psychoanalytic Study of the Non-Patient, 1966; author: Black Suicide, 1966, The Age of Sensation, 1975; co-author: (monograph) Adolescent Marijuana Abusers and their Families, 1981, (book) Wounds of War: The Psycho-logical Aftermath of Combat in Vietnam, 1984, Living High: Daily Marijuana Use in Adults, 1987; author: Suicide in Am., 1995, Seduced by Death: Doctors, Patients, and Assisted-Suicide, 1998; co-author (book) The Clin. Sci. of Suicide Prevention, 2001, The Case Against Assisted Suicide: For the Right to End of Life Care, 2002. Pres. 1045 Pk. Ave Coop., N.Y.C., 1988—96, Columbia U. Tennis Ctr., N.Y.C., 1970—97. Lt. USPHS, 1949—50. Recipient Disting. Rschr. award, Gralnick Found., 1962, Original Rsch. award, Assn. for Psychoanalytic Medicine, 1963, Yearly Lectureship award, Chgo. Inst. for Psychoanalysis, 1966, Louis Dublin award, Am. Assn. of Suicidology, 1982, Langer award, Psychohistory Rev., 1984, Scholar in Residence award, Rockerfeller Found., 1994. Fellow: Am.-Scandinavian Found. (hon.); mem.: Intern. Assoc. Suicide Prevent., Intern. Acad. for Suicide Rsch., Am. Found. for Suicide Prevention (pres. 1987—88, dir. nat. suicide data bank project 1988, exec. dir. 1988—97, med. dir. 1998—), Am. Assn. of Suicidology (Louis Dublin award 1982), Assn. for Psychoanalytic Medicine (dir. 1978—81, Original Rsch. award 1963), Am. Psychoanalytic Assn., Am. Psychiat. Assn., US Pub. Health Svc. (Lt. 1949—50), Coop. (pres., 1045 Pk. Ave., NYC 1988—96), Columbia U. Tennis Ctr. (pres., NYC 1970—97). Avocations: tennis, American and Greek civilization history, painting and art history, opera, Shakespeare's plays. Office: AFSP 22d Fl 120 Wall St New York NY 10005 also: Ste 3C 1045 Pk Ave New York NY 10028 Office Fax: 212-363-6237. E-mail: hhendin@afsp.org.

HENDIN, JOSEPHINE GATTUSO, language educator, writer; d. Charles Salvatore Gattuso and Florence Lorenza Gisondi; m. Herbert Hendin, June 7, 1968; children: Neil, Erik. BA, CCNY, 1960—64; MA, Columbia U., 1964—65, PhD, 1964—68. Asst. prof. Yale U., New Haven, 1968—69; adj. prof. New Sch. Social Rsch., New York, 1969—79; prof. NYU, 1979—, tiro a segno prof. italian am. studies, 2001—. Author: The Right Thing to Do (Am. Book award, 1989), Vulverable People: A View of American Fiction Since 1945, 1978 (Notable Book Yr., 1978); contbr., articles to profl. jours. Dir., expository writing program NYU, 1983, chair, English dept., 1995—99. Recipient Elena Lucrezia Cornaro Award, Nat. Order Sons and Daughters Columbus, 1983-1984, Am. Book Award, Before Columbus Found., 1989; fellow Woodrow Wilson Fellowship, Woodrow Wilson Found., 1964-1966, Vera B. David Fellowship, Columbia U., 1965-1966, President's Fellowship, 1967-1968, John Simon Guggenheim Fellowship, John Simon Guggenheim Found., 1975-1976. Mem.: MLA, Nat. Book Critics Cir., Am. Italian Hist. Assn. (mem. exec. bd. 2001), Nat. Italian Am. Found. Avocations: speedwalking, travel, reading. Office: NYU English Dept 19 University Pl New York NY 10003 Personal E-mail: josephine.hendin@nyu.edu.

HENDL, WALTER, conductor, pianist, composer; b. West New York, N.J., Jan. 12, 1917; s. William and Ella (Wittig) H.; m. Barbara Heisley; 1 dau by previous marriage, Susan. Pvt. study piano with, David Saperton; with, Clarence Adler, 1934-37; pvt. study conducting with, Fritz Reiner; faculty, Sarah Lawrence Coll., 1939-41, Curtis Inst. Music, 1937-41; MusD (hon.), Cin. Coll. Music, 1954; LHD (hon.), Edinboro U. Pa., 1990. Dir. Eastman Sch. Music, Rochester, N.Y., 1964 72; prof. conducting D'Angelo Sch. Music Mercy Hurst Coll., Erie, Pa., 1990-94. Active as condr. and pianist, Berkshire Music Center, 1941-42, asst. condr., pianist, N.Y. Philharmonic 1945-49, mus. dir., Dallas Symphony, 1949-58, Chautauqua (N.Y.) Symphony Orch., 1953-74, asso. condr., Chgo. Symphony Orch., 1958-64, mus. dir., Ravinia (Ill.) Festival, 1959-63; orchestral dir., Erie (Pa.) Philharm., 1976-89, condr. emeritus, 1989—; guest condr. in Europe, USSR, S. Am., Japan, Asia; also recs.; composer: Broadway prodn. Dark of the Moon, 1945, A Village Where They Ring No Bells, Loneliness (recipient Alice M. Ditson award, Columbia 1953).

HENDLER, MICHAEL G. lawyer; b. Balt., May 16, 1942; s. Nathan and Mrs. Hendler; m. Royce Hendler; children: Andrea G., Eileen B. Fox. BA, U. Md., College Park, 1963; JD, U. Md., Balt., 1965. Bar: Md. 1965. Staff atty. Legal Aid Bur., Balt., 1965-66; assoc. Adelberg, Adelberg & Rudow, Balt., 1967-74; ptnr., mem. Adelberg, Rudow, Dorf & Hendler, LLC, Balt., 1974—. Pres. Box 414 Assn., Inc., Balt., 197678; patrol dir. Nat. Ski Patrol, 1983-85. Named to Best Lawyers in Am., 2001—. Fellow Am. Acad. Matrimonial Lawyers (pres. Md. chpt. 1999-2001, v.p. Md. chpt. 1997-99, bd. govs. 1998—), Md. State Bar Assn. (chair family law sect. 1985-86). Office: Adelberg Rudow et al 2 Hopkins Plz Ste 600 Baltimore MD 21201-2908 E-mail: mhendler@adelbergrudow.com.

HENDLER, NELSON HOWARD, physician, medical clinic director; b. N.Y.C., Aug. 15, 1944; s. Albert and Winifred (Siff) H.; m. Lee Meyerhoff, Oct. 20, 1974; children: Samuel, Alexander, Lindsay, Josepha. BA, Princeton U., 1966; MD, U. Md., 1972, MS, 1974. Diplomate Am. Bd. Psychiatry and Neurology. Resident in psychiatry Johns Hopkins Hosp., Balt., 1975; asst. prof. neurosurgery sch. medicine Johns Hopkins U., 1975—; owner, clin. dir. Mensana Clinic, Stevenson, Md., 1978—; assoc. prof. physiology sch. dental surgery U. Md., 1986—. Pres. Reflex Sympathetic Dystrophy Syndrome of Am., 1995-97; bd. dirs. Lightning Strike Elec. Injury Survivors. Author: Diagnosis and Non-Surgical Management of Chronic Pain, 1981; (with others) Coping with Chronic Pain, 1979; editor Diagnosis and Treatment of Chronic Pain, 1982; contbr. 51 articles and 31 chpts. to books and profl. jours.; co-patentee direct current motor protector, 1972. Bd. dirs. Md. Mental Health Assn., Balt., 1976-78, Balt. Zool. Soc., 1978-85; bd. dirs. Am. Orgn. Rehab. through Tng., 1983—, pres. Balt. chpt.; bd. dirs. Am. Technion Soc., 1980-92, pres. Balt. chpt. Recipient Janet Travell award for outstanding contbr. to pain medicine Am. Acad. Pain Mgmt.; Falk fellow Am. Psychiat. Assn., 1975. Fellow Acad. Psychosomatic Medicine, Am. Psychiatric Assn.; mem. Am. Inst. Stress (v.p. 1978-89), Internat. Soc. for Study of Pain, Am. Acad. Pain Mgmt. (bd. dirs. 2002—), Am. Pain Found. (bd. dirs. 1997-2001), Israeli Pain Soc. (hon.), Princeton U. Alumni Assn. Md. (bd. dirs., pres.), Princeton Club N.Y.C., Safari Internat. Club, Loch Raven Skeet and Trap Club. Republican. Jewish. Avocations: bird hunting, skeet and trap shooting, fishing, record big game hunter. Office: Mensana Clinic 1718 Greenspring Valley Rd Stevenson MD 21153-0642

HENDLER, SHELDON SAUL, internist, educator, biochemist, writer; b. Bklyn., May 12, 1936; s. Alexander and Rose (Baskin) H.; m. Joyce Marilyn Hendler, Nov. 8, 1959; children: Ross Alexander, Seth Daniel (dec.). AB, Columbia U., 1957, PhD in Biochemistry, 1969; MD, U. Calif., San Diego, 1980. Postdoctoral fellow Salk Inst. and U. Calif. San Diego, 1969-72; asst. rsch. biologist U. Calif., San Diego, 1973-74, instr. medicine, 1983-87, from asst. prof. to assoc. prof., 1987-2001, clin. prof., 2001—; pres., chmn. dept. biochemistry Univ. Autonoma Baja Calif., Tijuana, Mex., 1974-76; intern U. Calif., Irvine, 1980-81; resident in internal medicine Scripps Mercy Hosp., San Diego, 1981-83, chief med. resident, 1983-84, attending physician, 1983-84; internist Hendler & Hendler Group, La Jolla, Calif., 1984—; CEO, pres., chief sci. officer Vyrex Corp., La Jolla, 1991-2000, also chmn. bd. dirs. Mem. pharmacy nutrition adv. bd. AARP, 1988-98; chmn. bd. sci. advisors Viaderm Pharma, Inc., 1989-93; mem. sci. adv. coun. Archer Daniels Midland, Decatur, Ill., 2000—. Author: The Complete Guide to Anti-Aging Nutrients, 1985, paperback edit., 1986, The Oxygen Breakthrough, 1989, paperback edit., 1990, The Doctors' Vitamin and Mineral Encyclopedia, 1990, paperback edit., 1991, The Purification Prescription, 1991; med. reviewer: The Healing Herbs, 1991; author, editor: Physicians' Desk Reference for Nutritional Supplements, 2001—; editor-in-chief Jour. Med. Food, 1997—; contbr. articles to profl. jours. Dir. San Diego Cmty. Rsch. Group AIDS Rsch., 1989-91; mem. sci. and nutrition subcommittee U.S. Olympic Com., 1990-91; pres. Seth Daniel Hendler Sci. Found., La Jolla, 1994—. Fellow Am. Inst. Chemists; mem. AAAS, ACP, Am. Fedn. Music, Authors League Am., Authors Guild, Soc. Natural Pharmacy (charter), Oxygen Soc., Internat. Soc. Free Radical Rsch., Internat. Soc. Antiviral Rsch., Am. Soc. Biochemistry and Molecular Biology, Am. Chem. Soc., Internat. AIDS Soc., Internat. Assn. Biomedical Gerontology, Am. Aging Assn., Calif. Med. Assn., Calif. Inst. Chemists, N.Y. Acad. Scis., San Diego Med. Soc., Sigma Xi. Avocations: musician, composer, writing poetry. Office: 2159 Avenida de la Playa La Jolla CA 92037 E-mail: shendler@san.rr.com.

HENDLEY, COIT TAYLOR, III, chemistry educator; b. Washington, Apr. 29, 1952; s. Coit Taylor Jr. and Barbara (Davidson) H.; m. Mary Wilson, July 8, 1985; children: Coit Taylor IV, Kevin Patrick. BA in Chemistry, Cornell U., 1975; MA in Sci. Edn., U. Md., 1990. Cert. advanced tchg., Md. Sci. tchr. South River H.S., Davidsonville, Md., 1976-77, Old Mill (Md.) H.S., Davidsonville, Md., 1978-87, Eleanor Roosevelt H.S., Greenbelt, Md., 1987-92, 97—, Frederick Douglass H.S., Upper Marlboro, Md., 1993-97. Mem. U. Md. Balt. County Engring. Adv. Bd., 1996—, Eleanor Roosevelt H.S. Tech. Acad. Faculty Adv. Bd., 1997—, Eleanor Roosevelt H.S. Sci. and Tech. Faculty Adv. Bd., 1997—. Recipient Leo Schubert Meml. award Chem. Soc. Washington, 1997, Md. Presdl. awar for excellence in math. and sci. tchg., 1998, Radioshack Nat. Tchr. award, 2000; Growth Initiatives for Tchrs. fellow GTE, 1996-97. Mem. NEA, Am. Chem. Soc. (educators divsn.), Am. Assn. Physics Tchrs., Nat. Sci. Tchrs. Assn., Md. Assn. Sci. Tchrs., Prince Georgs County Tchrs. Assn. Office: Eleanor Roosevelt HS 7601 Hanover Pkwy Greenbelt MD 20770-2099

HENDLEY, DAN LUNSFORD, retired finance executive; b. Nashville, Apr. 26, 1938; s. Frank E. and Mattie (Lunsford) H.; m. Patricia Fariss, June 18, 1960; children: Dan Lunsford, Laura Kathleen. BA, Vanderbilt U., 1960; grad., Stonier Grad. Sch. Banking, Rutgers U., 1969; postgrad., Program Mgmt. Devel., Harvard, 1972. With Fed. Res. Bank Atlanta, 1962-73, v.p., officer in charge Birmingham br., 1969-73; v.p., exec. v.p. AmSouth Bancorp, 1973-77; exec. v.p. First Nat. Bank Birmingham, 1976-77, pres., 1977-79, chmn. bd., chief exec. officer, 1979-83; pres., chief operating officer Am South Bank, N.A., 1983-90, also dir.; v.p. bus. affairs Samford U., Birmingham, Ala., 1991-94; ret., 1994. Trustee Children's Hosp., Samford U. With Tenn. Air N.G., 1961-67. Mem. Kiwanis, Mountain Brook Club, Shoal Creek Club, The Club. Baptist. Home: 3258 Dell Rd Birmingham AL 35223-1318

HENDLEY, EDITH DI PASQUALE, physiology and neuroscience educator; b. N.Y.C., Sept. 5, 1927; d. Michael and Rose (Parillo) Di Pasquale; m. Daniel Dees Hendley, Apr. 21, 1952; children: Jane Alice, Joyce Louise, Paul Daniel. AB, Hunter Coll. City N.Y., 1948; MS, Ohio State U., 1950; PhD, U. Ill., Chgo., 1954. Instr. U. Chgo., 1954-56; asst. lectr. U. Sheffield, Eng., 1956-57; instr., rsch. assoc. Johns Hopkins U. Sch. Medicine, Balt., 1963-72; sr. investigator Friends Med. Sci. Rsch. Ctr., Balt., 1972-73; from assoc. prof. to prof. U. Vt. Coll. Medicine, Burlington, 1973-94; prof. emeritus, 1994—. Co-author: 6 books; contbr. articles to profl. jours. Rsch. grantee NIH, 1974-95, NSF, 1986-98, Vt. affiliate Am. Heart Assn., 1982-3,The Sugar Assn. Inc., 1984-85. Mem. AAAS, Am. Physiol. Soc., Am. Soc. Pharmacology and Exptl. Therapeutics, Soc. for Neurosci. (exec. com., treas. Vt. chpt. 1978-84), Assn. for Women in Sci. (treas. 1972-74, exec. com., long-range planning com. 1974-76). Avocations: music, opera, theatre, cinema. Home: 10 Highland Ter South Burlington VT 05403-7601 Office: U Vt Coll Medicine Dept Molecular Phys Bi Burlington VT 05405-0001

HENDON, RICKY, state legislator; b. Cleveland, Dec. 8, 1953; Formerly alderman City of Chgo.; mem. Ill. Senate from 5th dist., 1992—. Home: 538 N Western Ave Chicago IL 60612-1422*

HENDRA, BARBARA JANE, public relations executive; b. Watertown, N.Y. d. Frederick R. and Irene J. H. BA, Vassar Coll., 1960. Publicity dir. Fawcett World Library, N.Y.C., 1961-69; v.p., dir. publicity and pub. relation Pocket Books-Simon & Schuster, N.Y.C., 1969-77; corp. dir. publicity and pub. relations Putnam Pub. Group, N.Y.C., 1977-79; pres. Barbara J. Hendra Assocs., Inc., N.Y.C., 1979-91, The Hendra Agy. Inc, Bklyn., 1991—. Adj. prof. NYU, 1981. Contbg. author: Trade Book Marketing, 1983, The Encyclopedia of Publishing, 1995. Mem. Pubs. Publicity Assn. (bd. dirs. 1977-81, pres. 1979-81), Publicity Club N.Y., Soc. Profl. Journalists, Women's Media Group, Book Critics Cir., Vassar Club, Regency Whist Club. Home: 140 Sterling Pl Brooklyn NY 11217-3307 Office: The Hendra Agy Inc 142 Sterling Pl Brooklyn NY 11217-3307

HENDREN, DEBRA MAE, critical care nurse; b. Belle Fourche, S.D., Apr. 27, 1959; d. Clyde Leslie and Kathryn Ann (Daughters); m. Anthony Ray Martinez, May 21, 1983 (div.); m. Cecil B. Hendren, Nov. 21, 1992. AD, Casper Coll., 1987, cert. EMT, 1990; BSN, U. Phoenix, 1997, MSN, 1999. Cert. RN Colo., Wyo., Utah, critical care nurse. Nurse Wyo. Med. Ctr., Casper, North Suburban Med. Ctr. (formerly Humana Hosp. Mountain View), Thornton, Colo., Swedish Med. Ctr., Englewood, Colo., charge nurse ICU, 1993-96; asst.

nurse mgr. North Suburban Med. Ctr., Thornton, Colo., 1996-97, dir. ICU/CCU, 1997-99, dir. ICU/CCU and med. telemetry, 1997-99; healthcare mgmt. cons. West Hudson, Inc., 1999-2000; dir. ICU/CCU Rocky Mountain Med. Ctr., Salt Lake City, 2000-01; ICU clin. instr. Westminster Coll., Salt Lake City, 2000—; dir. cardiopulmonary svcs. St. Mark's Hosp., Salt Lake City, 2001—. Clin. specialist AristoMed, Salt Lake City, 2000—02; adj. faculty Utah campus U. Phoenix, 2003—. Mem.: AACN, Colo. Nurses Assn., Wyo. Nurses Assn., Sigma Theta Tau. Home: 978 W 400 S Layton UT 84041-5239 E-mail: cbhend@att.global.net.

HENDREN, JIMM LARRY, federal judge; b. 1940; BA, U. Ark., 1964, LLB, 1965. With Little & Enfield, 1968-69; pvt. practice Bentonville, Ark., 1970-77, 79-92; chancellor, probate judge Ark. 16th Chancery Dist., 1977-78; U.S. dist. judge We. Dist. Ark., 1992-96, chief judge, 1997—. Served to lt. comdr. JAGC, USN, 1965-70, USNR, 1970-83. Mem. ABA, Ark. Bar Assn. Office: US Dist Ct PO Box 3487 Fayetteville AR 72702-3487

HENDREN, MERLYN CHURCHILL, investment company executive; b. Gooding, Idaho, Oct. 16, 1926; d. Herbert Winston and Annie Averett Churchill; m. Robert Lee Hendren, June 14, 1947; children: Robert Lee, Anne Aleen. Student, U. Idaho, 1944-47; BA with honors, Coll. of Idaho, 1986. With Hendren's Furniture Co., Boise, 1947-69; co-owner, v.p. Hendren's Inc., Boise, 1969-87, pres., 1987—. Bd. dirs. Idaho Law Found., 1978-84; chmn. Coll. of Idaho Symposium, 1977-78, mem. adv. bd., 1981—; bd. dirs. S.W. Idaho Pvt. Industry Coun., 1984-87; pres. Boise Coun. on Aging, 1959-60, mem. adv. bd., 1986—; mem. Gov.'s Commn. on Aging, 1960; Idaho del. to White House Conf. on Aging, 1961; trustee St. Luke's Regional Hosp., 1981-92; mem. adv. bd. dirs. Boise Philharm. Assn., Inc., 1981—, Ballet Idaho; bd. dirs. Children's Home Soc. Idaho, 1988; founding pres. Idaho Congl. Award Program, 1993—; sustaining mem. Boise Jr. League. Mem. Boise C. of C. (bd. dirs. 1984-87), Gamma Phi Beta. Episcopalian. Home: 3504 Hillcrest Dr Boise ID 83705-4503 Office: PO Box 9077 Boise ID 83707-3077 E-mail: rhendren@albertson.edu.

HENDREN, ROBERT LEE, JR., academic administrator; b. Reno, Oct. 10, 1925; s. Robert Lee and Aleen (Hill) H.; m. Merlyn Churchill, June 14, 1947; children: Robert Lee IV, Anne Aleen. BA magna cum laude, LLD (hon.), Coll. Idaho; postgrad., Army Univ. Ctr., Oahu, Hawaii. Owner, pres. Hendren's Inc., 1947—; pres. Albertson Coll. Idaho, Caldwell, 1987—. Bd. dirs. 1st Interstate Bank Idaho. Trustee Boise (Idaho) Ind. Sch. Dist., chmn. bd. trustees, 1960, chmn. bd. trustees Coll. Idaho, 1980-84; bd. dirs. Mountain View coun. Boy Scouts Am., Boise Retail Merchants, Boise Valley Indsl. Found., Boise Redevel. Agy., Ada County Marriage Counseling, Ada County Planning and Zoning Com.; chmn. bd. Blue Cross Idaho. Recipient Silver and Gold award U. Idaho, Nat. award Sigma Chi. Mem. Boise C. of C. (pres., bd. dirs.), Idaho Sch. Trustees Assn., Masons, KT, Shriners, Rotary (Paul Harris fellow). Home: 3504 Hillcrest Dr Boise ID 83705-4503 Office: Albertson Coll Idaho 2112 Cleveland Blvd Caldwell ID 83605-4432

HENDRICK, BENARD CALVIN, VII, lawyer; b. Odessa, Tex., Oct. 7, 1964; s. Benard Calvin VI and Marita Hendrick; m. Amy Camille Weatherby, Nov. 17, 1990; children: Benard Calvin VIII, Kaitlin Camille. BBA summa cum laude, Angelo State U., San Angelo, Tex., 1987; JD, U. Tex., 1990. Bar: Tex. 1990, U.S. Dist. Ct. (ea., we. and no. dists.) Tex. 1991, U.S. Ct. Appeals (5th cir.) 1995. Assoc. Shafer, Davis, Ashley, O'Leary & Stoker, Odessa, 1990-92, ptnr., 1992—. Bd. dirs. Permian Basin Rehab. Ctr., Odessa, 1992-97, Crystal Ball Found., Odessa, 1993-96, Parker House Ranching Mus., 2002—, Black River-A Ctr. for Learning, 1998—, Jim Parker Little League Baseball, 2000—; elder First Christian Ch., Odessa, 1995-98, 2000—. Fellow Tex. Bar Found.; mem. Tex. Assn. Def. Counsel (young lawyers com. 1998-2000), State Bar Tex., Ector County Bar Assn. (pres. 1998-99), Ector County Young Lawyers Assn. (pres. 1995), Def. Rsch. Inst. Republican. Mem. Christian Ch. Avocations: hunting, fishing, tae kwon do (1st degree). Home: 2301 La Due Ln Odessa TX 79762 Office: Shafer Davis Ashley O'Leary & Stoker 700 N Grant Ave Ste 201 Odessa TX 79761-4576

HENDRICK, GEORGE, retired English language educator; b. Stephenville, Tex., Mar. 30, 1929; s. Hoyt and Bessie Lea (Sears) H.; m. Willene Lowery, Jan. 21, 1955; 1 dau., Sarah. BA, Tex. Christian U., 1948, MA, 1950; PhD, U. Tex., 1954. Mem. English faculty S.W. Tex. State U., 1954-56, U. Colo., 1956-60; prof. Am. studies J.W. Goethe U., Frankfurt, Germany, 1960-65; prof. U. Ill., Chgo., 1965-67, Urbana, 1967-99, spl. curator Univ. Libr., 1994-97. Author: Katherine Anne Porter, 1965, Henry Salt: Humanitarian Reformer and Man of Letters, 1977, Remembrances of Concord and the Thoreaus, 1977, (with Fritz Oehlschlaeger) Toward the Making of Thoreau's Modern Reputation, 1980, (with Willene Hendrick) On the Frontier: Dr. Hiram Rutherford, 1981, Thoreau Amongst Friends and Philistines, 1982, (with Margaret Sandburg) Ever the Winds of Chance, 1983, the Selected Letters of Mark Van Doren, 1987; (with Willene Hendrick) Katherine Anne Porter, rev. edit., 1988, Fables, Foibles, and Foobles, 1988, (with Willene Hendrick) The Savour of Salt: A Henry Salt Anthology, 1989, To Reach Eternity: The Letters of James Jones, 1989, (with Willene Hendrick) Ham Jones, Antebellum Southern Humorist: An Anthology, 1990, (with Willene Hendrick and Fritz Oehlschlaeger) Salt's Life of Thoreau, 1993, More Rootabagas, 1993, (with Willene Hendrick) Billy Sunday and Other Poems, 1993 (with Nancy Romero) Literary Treasures of the University Library, 1995, (with Willene Hendrick) Selected Poems of Carl Sandburg, 1996, (with Nancy Romero and Maarten van de Guchte) Alvin Langdon Coburn and H.G. Wells: The Photographer and the Novelist, 1997, (with Willene Hendrick) Incidents in the Life of A Slave Girl and A True Tale of Slavery, 1999, (with Barbara Jones and Jean Geil) Learning About Lincoln at the University of Illinois at Urbana-Champaign, 1999, (with Willene Hendrick) Two Slave Rebellions at Sea: The Heroic Slave by Frederick Douglass and Benito Cereno by Herman Melville, 2000, (with Howe and Sackrider) James Jones and the Handy Writers' Colony, 2001, (with Howe and Sackrider) Writings from the Handy Colony, 2001, (with Willene Hendrick) The Creole Mutiny: A Tale of Revolt Aboard A Slave Ship, 2003. Grantee Am. Coun. Learned Socs., Ford Found., NEH. Mem. MLA, James Jones Soc. (pres. 1991-92). Home: 502 W Main St Apt 122 Urbana IL 61801-2537

HENDRICK, HAL WILMANS, human factors educator; b. Dallas, Mar. 11, 1933; s. Harold Eugene and Audrey Sarah (Wilmans) H.; m. Mary Francis Boyle; children: Hal L., David A., John A. (dec.), Jennifer G. BA, Ohio Wesleyan U., 1955; MS, Purdue U., 1961, PhD, 1966. Cert. profl. ergonomist; bd. cert. forensic examiner. Asst. prof. U. So. Calif., L.A., assoc. prof., 1979-86; exec. dir. Inst. of Safety and Systems Mgmt., U. So. Calif., L.A., 1986-87; prof., dean Coll. of System Sci., U. Denver, 1987-90; prof. U. So. Calif., 1986-95, prof. emeritus, 1995—; prin. Hendrick and Assocs., 1996—. Pres. Bd. Cert. in Profl. Ergonomics, 1992-94. Author: Behavioral Research and Analysis, 1980, 2d edit., 1989, 3rd edit., 1990, Macroergonomics: An Introduction to Work System Design, 2001, Good Ergomonics is Good Economics, 1996; editor 10 books; contbr. articles to profl. jours. Lt. col. USAF, 1956-76. Fellow APA, Am. Psychol. Soc., Human Factors Ergonomics Soc. (pres. L.A. chpt. 1986-87, pres. Rocky Mountain chpt. 1989-90, 95-96); mem. Internat. Ergonomics Assn. (pres. Geneva 1990-94, immediate past pres. 1994-97, sec. gen. 1987-89, exec. com. 1984—, U.S. rep. 1981-87), Ergonomics Soc. (U.K.), Soc. for Indsl. and Orgnl. Psychology. Democrat. Avocations: travel, camping, hiking, reading, fishing. Home and Office: 7100 E Crestline Ave Greenwood Village CO 80111-1600 E-mail: hhendrick@aol.com.

HENDRICK, HOWARD H. state government administrator; b. Oklahoma City, Dec. 22, 1954; s. Robert Alexander and Geneva (Woodlee) H.; m. Tracy Elizabeth Williams, July 1, 1977; children: Chelsey Elizabeth, Cally Victoria, Christiana Juliet, Hudson Hamlin. BS in Acctg., So. Nazarene U., 1977; JD, MBA, U. Okla., 1980; LHD, So. Nazarene U., 1999. Bar: Okla. 1980, U.S. Ct. Claims 1981, U.S. Tax Ct. 1981, U.S. Dist. Ct. (we. dist.) Okla. 1981, U.S. Dist. Ct. (no. dist.) Okla. 1984, U.S. Supreme Ct. 1984; CPA, Okla. Clk., intern, assoc. Speck, Philbin, Fleig, Trudgeon & Lutz, P.C., Oklahoma City, 1977-81; pvt. practice, Bethany, Okla., 1981-84; ptnr. Thom & Hendrick, P.C., Oklahoma City, 1984-93, of counsel, 1994-98; mem. Okla. Senate, 1986-98; pvt. practice, Howard H. Hendrick, P.C., Oklahoma City, 1994-98; exec. dir. Okla. Dept. Human Svcs., 1998—; Gov. Keating's cabinet sec. Health and Human Svcs., 2002—03; Gov. Henry's cabinet sec. Human Svcs., 2003—. Adj. prof. So. Navarene U., Bethany, 1979-87; gov.'s legis. appointee Early Childhood Intervention Interagy. Coord. Coun., Oklahoma City, 1987-98; pres. pro tempore's appointee Okla. State Pension Commn., 1988-94, Okla. legislator Justice Pub. Safety & Consumer Affairs Com. So. Legislators Conf., 1988; chmn. Okla. Rep. Party Platform Com., 1988; health care com. Nat. Conf. of State Legislatures, 1993-98; health care task force Am. Legis. Exch. Coun., 1991-98. Mem. Nat. Children's Alliance, 2003—; chmn. adv. bd. Children's Convalescent Ctr., Inc., Bethany, 1986; mem. adv. bd. Mercy Hospice, 1992—98; bd. dirs. United Way of Greater Okla. City, 1999—; asst. minority floor leader Okla. State Senate, 1989—92, minority floor leader, 1993—94; mem. Christian life bd. Bethany First Nazarene Ch., 1986—, chmn., 1986—89; bd. dirs. Nazarene Theol. Sem., 1997—. Mem. ABA, Okla. Bar Assn., Okla. Soc. CPAs, Bethany C. of C. (Bethany Hall of Fame 1994), Kiwanis (internat. pres. collegiate Kiwanis Internat. 1976-77, pres. Bethany chpt. 1981), Order of the Coif, Phi Alpha Delta, Phi Beta Lambda (named Nat. Mr. Future Bus. Exec. 1977). Republican. Avocations: playing basketball, golf, reading. Office: 7209 NW 31st St Bethany OK 73008-3821

HENDRICK, IRVING GUILFORD, education educator; b. L.A., Aug. 30, 1936; s. Guilford and Ingeborg Johanna (Eid) H.; m. Sandra Lee Scheer, Aug. 16, 1958 (dec. Aug. 1994); children: Julie Lynn, Maralene Ayn, Stephanie Lee; m. Linda DeSoucey Scott, 1996; stepchildren: Denise Levesque, Eve Scott. AB, Whittier Coll., 1958, MA, 1960; EdD with honors, UCLA, 1964. Asst. prof. edn. U. Mich., Flint, 1964-65, U. Calif., Riverside, 1965-69, assoc. prof. edn., 1969-75, prof. edn., 1975—, chair dept. edn., 1970-75, assoc. dean Sch. of Edn., 1975-83, dean Sch. of Edn., 1987-98, asst. vice chancellor of devel., 1998—, dean emeritus. Mem. com. on planning & budget U. Calif. Sys., 1985-87, vice-chair com. on planning & budget, 1986-87, chair subcom. on pvt. devel. activities, 1986-87, chair, 1987-88; mem. subject A com. U. Calif.-Riverside, 1966-68, vice-chair con. on ednl. policy, 1972-73, mem. com. on courses, 1969-71, chair, 1972-73, mem. com. on coms., 1973-74, mem. acad. planning com., 1973-75, chair acad. planning com., 1974-75, mem. budget com. resources sect., 1984-87, chair budget com. resources sect. 1984-87, mem. adv. com., 1974-75, 85-87, mem. highlander awards com., 1967-71, search com. for dean of grad. divsn., 1974, chair com. on faculty devel., 1977-78, learning handicapped credential programs, 1984—, chair exec. vice chancellor search com., 1985, acad. program planning rev. bd. sub-com. on organized rsch., 1986, pres.'s com. on profl. edn., 1988-89, pres.'s budget adv. com., 1987, chair adv. com. on instrnl. tech., 1994—; chancellor's rep. citizen's adv. com. Univ. Area Comty. Plan, Riverside, 1982-83; profl. day spkr. Internat. Sch. Theology, 1985; adv. com. assembly com. on econ. devel. and new techs. State of Calif., 1983-85; proposal reviewer intermediate sch. coll. readiness program Calif. State U., 1986; chair campaign com. to re-elect Dale Holmes County Supt. of Schs., Riverside County, 1990; cons. Riverside County Commn. on Future of Edn., 1993; mem. com. accreditation Calif. Commn. on Tchr. Credentialing, 1995-90, chair, co-chair, 1995-97; presenter papers at numerous profl. meetings. Author: Academic Revolution in California, 1968, Development of a School Integration Plan in Riverside, California: A Hisotry and Perspective, 1968, Public Policy Toward the Education of Non-white Minority Group Children in California, 1848-1970, 1975, The Education of Non-Whites in California, 1848-1970, 1977, California Educations, 1980; co-editor: (with Reginald L. Jones) Student Dissent in the Schools, 1972; contbr. articles to profl. jours.; contbr. book revs. to profl. jours. including History of Edn. Quar., Pacific Hist. Rev., Calif. History, So. Calif. Quar., Jour. Ednl. Adminstrn. and History. Mem. Am. Ednl. Rsch. Assn. (divsn. F editl. com. 1981-82, co-chair divsn. F program ann. program com. 1983-85, chair nominating com. divsn. F 1977, 79, sec. divsn. F 1976-78), Am. Hist. Assn. (Pacific Coast br.), Calif. Coun. on Edn. of Tchrs. (bd. dirs. 1989-93, chair programs com. fall 1991 conf.), Coun. for Exceptional Children (com. on history of individual differences 1985, cons. on oral history project, guest reviewer of manuscripts), History of Edn. Soc. (program com. 1986, nominating com. 1981-82), Nat. Soc. for Study of Edn. (com. on expansion of soc. activities 1972), Pacific Coast History of Edn. Soc. (program chair 1985), So. Assn. of Schs. and Colls. (sr. coll. commn., on-site visitation com. Walden U. 1980), Western Assn. Schs. and Colls. (sr. coll. commn., on-site visitation com. mem. various univs.), Phi Delta Kappa (historian, mem. exec. com. Riverside chpt. 1976-78). Democrat. Lutheran. Achievements include research in history of education, specifically the history of teacher education and education of minority groups, as well as extension of public school's mission to include responsibility for education and training of learning disabled and mentally retarded children. Office: U Calif Sch Edn Riverside CA 92521-0001 E-mail: irving.hendrick@ucr.edu.

HENDRICK, RICKY, race car driver; Race car driver Hendrick Motorsports, Harrisburg, NC. Named Champion, NASCAR Craftsman Truck Series, 2000. Office: c/o Hendrick Motorsports PO Box 9 4400 Papa Joe Hendrick Blvd Harrisburg NC 28075

HENDRICK, ZELWANDA, drama and psychology educator; b. Rusk, Tex., Nov. 28, 1925; d. Lloyd Irvin and Viola Alice (McGuire) Hendrick; A.A., Lon Morris Coll., 1945; B.S., N. Tex. U., 1947; M.A., So. Meth. U., 1958. Tchr. theatre arts Overton (Tex.) High Sch., 1947-49, Nacogdoches (Tex.) High Sch., 1949-50, Boude Storey Sch., Dallas, 1950-53, Kimball High Sch., Dallas, 1953-62; tchr. theatre arts H. Grady Spruce High Sch., Dallas, 1962-78, chmn. fine arts dept., 1963-77, ret., 1978; drama and psychology tchr. Alexander Sch., 1978— ; substitute tchr. Highland Park High Sch., Dallas, 1980— ; part-time tchr. John Robert Powers Finishing Sch., 1951— ; teaching fellow N. Tex. U., 1964-65; ptnr. Adventure II Miniature Horse Ranch, Rusk, Tex., 1985—; co-dir. Adventure II Miniature Horse Show, Lufkin, Tex., 1987—. Active, Tyler (Tex.) Civic Symphony, 1949-50, Tyler Civic Theatre, 1949-50, Dallas Theatre Center, 1960-61; guest dir. Cherokee Civic Theatre, Rusk, 1983, pres. 2002—; mem. adv. com. Smithsonian Instn., 1975; co-sponsor U.S. Inst. Tech. Theatre; del. Democratic Dist. Conv., 1980; candidate Tex. State Legislature, 1980; chmn. Dallas County Transp. Bd., 1982— ; life mem. First United Meth. Ch., Rusk. Mem. Internat. Thespians (state dir.), Tex. Speech Assn. (sec. 1973—), Am. Assn. Ednl. Theatre, Am. Miniature Horse Registry, Friends of the Railroad, Dallas Ednl. Drama Assn. (governing bd.), Tex. Tchrs. Assn., Nat. Forensic League, AAUW, Classroom Tchrs. Dallas, Internat. Platform Assn., Ednl. Arts Assn., Tex. Congress Parent Tchr. Assn. (hon. life), DAR, Daus. Republic of Tex., N. Texas Collie Club, Nat. Assn. Royalty Owners, Tex. Ind. Producers and Royalty Owners Assn., Tex. Farm Bur., Am. Miniature Horse Assn., Paws of E. Tex., Delta Kappa Gamma. Club: Order Eastern Star. Contbr. to A Guide to Student Teaching in Music, 1968-70. Home: 204 E 4th St Rusk TX 75785-1308 Office: Adventure II Miniature Horse Ranch Hwy 84 W Rusk TX

HENDRICKS, DONALD DUANE, retired school librarian; b. Flint, Mich., Nov. 3, 1931; s. Edgar F. and Marion (Scoble) Hendricks; m. Mary Jean Elrich, Feb. 17, 1951; children: Phillip, Scott, Randall. AB, U. Mich., AMLS, 1955; PhD, U. Ill., 1966. With Detroit Pub. Libr., 1955-57; head libr. Owosso Pub. Libr., Mich., 1957-60, Millikin U., 1960-63; dir. librs. Sam Houston State Univ., 1966-70; dir. S. Ctrl. Regional Med. Libr. Program, Dallas, 1970-78, U. Tex. Health Sci. Ctr. Libr., 1971-78, Earl K. Long Libr., U. New Orleans, 1978, dean libr. svcs., 1981-89, reference libr., 1989-92; mgr. St. Tammany Parish Libr. Sys., Mandeville, 1993-96; libr. Delgado CC, Slidell, La., 1996—. Cons. in field. Co-author: (book) Resources of Texas Libraries, 1968, Centralizaed Processing and Regional Library Development - The Midwestern Regional Library System, 1970, The Louisiana State Library Processing Center: An Evaluation, 1971, Medical Libraries, Needs and Services, 1972; author: Centralized Processing and Regional Library Development, 1970; contbr. articles to profl. jours. Grantee, U.S. Office of Edn., 1965. Mem.: ALA, Bibliog. Soc. Am., Bibliog. Soc. (London), Grolier Club (N.Y.C.). Home: 61324 Brittany Dr Lacombe LA 70445-2818 Office: Delgado CC 320 Howze Beach Rd Slidell LA 70458-8515

HENDRICKS, EDWARD DAVID, education director, consultant, speaker, trainer; b. Bridgeport, Conn., July 29, 1946; s. James Lyons and Dorothy (James) H.; m. Elizabeth Mary Jessop, Sept. 14, 1968; children: Maureen, David. BS, BA, U. N.C., Charlotte, 1975; MA, SUNY, Albany, 1976. Cert. assn. exec. Contracts adminstr. Eutectic Corp., Flushing, N.Y., 1969-70, Interroyal Corp., N.Y.C., 1970-71, regional sales mgr., 1971-72; dir. tech. assistance project Conn. Justice Commn., Hartford, 1976-78; dir. Fairfield County Criminal Justice Planning Commn., Stratford, Conn., 1978-79; dir. adminstrn. ACME, Inc., N.Y.C., 1979-81, v.p., 1981-88, pres., 1988-96, Inst. of Mgmt. Cons., N.Y.C., 1990-92, Coun. Consulting Orgns., N.Y.C., 1989-92, Found. for Excel in Cons. and Mgmt., N.Y.C., 1989-92, Edward D. Hendricks & Assocs., 1995—; dir. ctr. corp. edn. Sacred Heart U., 1999—, dir. Leadership Studies Program, 2000—; ptnr. Ignite Spirit LLC, 2001—. Bd. dirs. Profl. Svcs. Coun., Washington, N. Am. Mgmt. Coun., N.Y.C.; steering com. UNDP/ILO Ea. Europe Project, Geneva, 1990-95; keynote speaker Escort Internat. Conf., Sofia, Bulgaria, 1990; dir. Ctr. for Corp. Edn.; dir. leadership studies program Sacred Heart U., 1998—. Author: Student Rights and Responsibilities, 1973, An Insider's Guide To Consulting Success, 1997, Successful Business Networking, 1998, Back on the Right Track, 1999; contbg. author: A History of Consulting, 1987, The Role of Associations, 1990. Campaign coord. James Martin for Congress, Charlotte, 1975; internat. adv. com. mem. U.S. Dept. Commerce, 1994—; treas. Big Bros./Sisters of Fairfield County, Bridgeport, Conn., 1976-78; bd. dirs. United Way of Fairfield County, 1978; permanent deacon Roman Cath. Ch. With USCG, 1965-69. Elected Student Body Pres. U.N.C., Charlotte, 1975; recipient Hon. Mention award NSF, 1972, Acad. Fellowship SUNY, Albany, 1975-76. Fellow Am. Soc. Assn. Execs. (dir. 1991-96); mem. Tri-State Profl. Spkrs. Assn. (treas. 1995-96), N.Y. Soc. Assn. Execs. (pres., bd. dirs. 1986-92, Outstanding Assn. Exec. 1995), Disabled Am. Vets., Mensa, Inst. Mgmt. Cons. (bd. dirs. N.Y. chpt. 1996—). Avocations: speaking, counselling, various sports. Office: 354 Anton St Bridgeport CT 06606-2119 *Luck is not solely a matter of chance. Luck is what happens when opportunity collides with persisitence plus preperation. If you continue learning and continue striving, opportunity will find you.*

HENDRICKS, FLORA ANN, small business owner, social worker, special education educator; b. Cape Girardeau, Mo., Apr. 3, 1955; d. James Philbert and Bessie Geraldine (Mason) Joyce; m. Norman Harold Hendricks, Oct. 5, 1985; stepchildren: Theresa Lynn Ramirez, David Lane Hendricks. BS in Edn., S.E. Mo. State U., 1978; student, U. Mo., 1994. Lifetime cert. tchr., Mo. Warehouse and prodn. line worker Procter and Gamble Corp., Jackson, Mo., summer 1973-78; tchr. spl. edn. I and II Poplar Bluff Regional Ctr., Mo., 1979-83; social svc. worker Jefferson County divsn. Family Svc., Hillsboro, Mo., 1983; case mgr. I, II, III St. Louis Regional Ctr., 1983-94. Office vol. Webster Hills United Meth. Ch., 2002—, office vol. digital art storytelling team, 2002—03; office vol. United Meth. Ch. Mem. NAFE. Democrat. Methodist. Avocations: camping, personal computer. Home: 6339 Treeridge Trl Saint Louis MO 63129-4640

HENDRICKS, GILBERT L., III, neuroendocrine immune physiologist, researcher; b. Richmond, Va., 1959; s. Gilbert L. Jr. and Ina Mae Hendricks. BS in Biology, Pa. State U., 1981, BS in Microbiology, 1984, MS in Physiology, 1989, PhD in Physiology, 1994. Surg. technician Lewistown (Pa.) Hosp., 1982-85; grad. rsch. asst. Pa. State U., University Park, 1987-94; postdoctoral rsch. scientist Biotech. Inst., University Park, 1995-96; instr., rsch. assoc. Pa. State U., University Park, 1998—. Advisor to MS candidates Pa. State U., 1993-94, instr. U.S.-AID Egypt project, 1994, advisor to PhD candidates, 2000—. Contbr. articles to profl. jours. Mem. SAR, Sons of Confederate Vets., Gamma Sigma Delta. Methodist. Achievements include development of assay to measure hormone production by leukocytes; determined corticotropin releasing factor (CRF) stimulates adrenocorticotropic hormone by chicken leukocytes, identified macrophage as primary leukocyte responsible for immune adrenocorticotropic hormone production.

HENDRICKS, J(AMES) EDWIN, historian, educator, consultant, author; b. Pickens, S.C., Oct. 19, 1935; s. J.E. and Cassie (Looper) H.; m. Sue James, June 28, 1958; children— James, Christopher, Lee BA, Furman U., 1957; MA, U. Va., 1959, PhD, 1961. Vis. prof. history U. Va., Charlottesville, summer 1961; asst. prof. history Wake Forest U., Winston-Salem, N.C., 1961-66, assoc. prof., 1966-75, prof., 1975—, chmn. dept. history, 1995-99, dir. Hist. Preservation Program, 1973—. Vis. prof. history U. Tex.-El Paso, summer 1965; preservation cons.; vis. dir. Mus. Albermarle, Elizabeth City, N.C., summer 1975; dir. Preservation Field Sch., summers 1983-86, 88-90, 92-95. Author: (with others) Liquor and Anti-Liquor in Virginia, 1619-1919, 1967; Charles Thomson and the Making of a Nation, 1729-1824, 1979; editor, contbg. author: Forsyth, The History of a County on the March, 1976; author: Wake Forest University School of Law; One Hundred Years of Legal Education, 1994, Seeking Liberty and Justice: A History of the North Carolina Bar Association, 1999. Pres. Hist. Winston, 1979—; chmn. Winston-Salem/Forsyth County Hist. Dists. Commn., 1978-79; pres. Wachovia Hist. Soc., 1983-87. Served with U.S. Army, 1958-59. Recipient R.J. Reynolds rsch. leave, 1973, 87, 01; Am. Philos. Soc. rsch. grantee, 1969, 70. Mem. N.C. Lit. and Hist. Assn. (pres. 1980-81), Hist. Soc. N.C., So. Hist. Assn., Nat. Trust Hist. Preservation, others Lodges: Kiwanis (pres. 1987-88), Torch (pres. Winston-Salem 1987-88). Democrat. Baptist. Office: Wake Forest U Dept History PO Box 7806 Winston Salem NC 27109-7806 E-mail: hendrije@wfu.edu.

HENDRICKS, JAMES POWELL, artist; b. Little Rock, Aug. 7, 1938; s. Leland Fuller and Christia Beatrice (Powell) H.; m. Betty Jean Fleming, Nov. 6, 1960 (div. 1977); children: Elizabeth Jane, Valerie Lee; m. Marcia Reed-Hendricks, 1978 (div.); m. Leslie Jill Cernak, 1999. BA, U. Ark., 1962; M.F.A., U. Iowa, 1964. Instr. art State U. Iowa, 1962-64, Mt. Holyoke Coll., 1964-65; mem. faculty U. Mass., Amherst, 1965—, prof. art, 1977—, dir. undergrad. programs in art, 1968-71, dir. grad. programs art, 1974-77. Vis. artist Seoul Inst. of the Arts, Korea, 1986, Portland Sch. Arts, Maine, 1985, San Diego State U., 1986, Internat. Artist Colony, Ctr. Contemporary Visual Arts, Prilep, Macedonia, 1994. One-man exhbn., Nat. Air and Space Mus., Smithsonian Instn., fall 1969, Hudson River Mus., Yonkers, N.Y., 1970, U. Mass., Amherst, 1971-78, French and Co. Gallery, N.Y.C., 1972, Warren Benedek Gallery, N.Y.C., 1974, Helen Shlien Gallery, Boston, 1980, 82, 84, Smith Coll., Northampton, Mass., 1983, 84, SUNY-Oswego, 1983, Deerfield Acad., Mass., 1984, Portland Sch. Art, 1985, Space Art Gallery, Seoul, 1986, Mus. Fine Arts, Springfield, Mass., 1986, Slater-Price Fine Arts Gallery, N.Y.C., 1989, 90, Ark. Arts Ctr., Little Rock, 1993, Anderson Gallery, 1993, Art Gallery at Macedonia, Skopje, 1994, Westwood Gallery, Inc., N.Y.C., 1996, 2001, 2002, Hart Gallery, Northampton, Mass., 1996; group exhbns. include, Nat. Gallery Art, 1970, Nat. Air and Space Mus., 1976, 4th Internat. Biennial, Medellín, Colombia, 1981, Assemblage/Collage Exhbn. Seoul Inst. of Arts, Korea, in conjunction with World Olympics Arts Festival, 1988, Joy Moos Gallery, Miami, Fla., 1991, Ark. Arts Ctr., Little Rock, 1993, Vesti-dane Gallery, Scottsdale, Ariz., 1997; comms. include: Nat. Gallery Art, NASA, cover for Time mag., 1971, 2 album covers for Neuma Records, Fall 1991; cover commn. for The Mass. Rev., Vol. XXXVII, No. 4, Winter, 1997. Named Ark. Traveler, 1971 Office: U Mass Art Dept Amherst MA 01003

HENDRICKS, JOHN S. broadcast executive; b. 1952; Gov. rels. dir. U. Ala., Huntsville, 1972—73; corp. rels. dir. U. Md., College Park, 1973—78; chmn., CEO The Disney Channel Discovery Comm., Inc., Bethesda, Md., 1982—. Mem.: Am. Assn. Univ. Cons. Office: Discovery Comm Inc 7700 Wisconsin Ave Fl 5 Bethesda MD 20814-3557

HENDRICKS, KENNETH, wholesale distribution executive; b. Sept. 8, 1941; CEO, chmn. ABC Supply, Beloit, Wis., 1982—. Office: ABC Supply One ABC Pkwy Beloit WI 53511-4466*

HENDRICKS, LEONARD D. emergency medicine physician, consultant; b. Chgo., Feb. 29, 1952; s. Leonard D. and Edith V. (Elliott) H.; m. Gail Williams, Aug. 26, 1989. BS in Engring., U. Ill., 1974; MD, U. Wis., 1979. Diplomate Am. Bd. Emergency Medicine, Am. Bd. Forensic Examiners, Am. Bd. Forensic Medicine, Am. Bd. Psychol. Specialties, Am. Acad. Experts in Traumatic Stress subsplty. cert. in forensic traumatology, Am. Bd. Quality Assurance and Utilization Review Physicians with subsplty. cert. in risk mgmt., Am. Bd. Managed Care Medicine. Med. dir. Cuyahoga County Corrections Facility; emergency physician Meridia Huron Hosp., East Cleveland, Ohio; asst. dir. emergency medicine Kaiser Permanente Hosp., Parma, Ohio; emergency physician Western Res. Care System, Youngstown, Ohio; dir. emergency medicine St. Joseph Riverside Hosp., Warren, Ohio; med. dir. emergency medicine Allen Meml. Hosp., Oberlin, Ohio; pres., CEO Avatar Healthcare Svcs.; med dir. urgent care/emergency dept. Peoples Hosp., Mansfield, Ohio; med. dir. emergency dept. Lodi Cmty. Hosp. Cons. Friedman, Domiano and Smith Law Firm, Cleve., Newman & Boyer Law Firm, Chgo., Jaffe & Hough Law Firm, Phila.; regional physician mgr. Birman & Assocs.; instr. emergency medicine Case Western Res. U., Cleve., Northeastern Ohio U., Rootstown; instr. ACLS, Am. Heart Assn.; instr. advanced trauma life support ACS; instr.

pediatric ALS, neonatal resuscitation, Am. Acad. Pediatrics. Fellow Am. Bd. Forensic Examiners, Am. Coll. Medicine, Am. Coll. Emergency Physicians, Am. Acad. Experts in Traumatic Stress, mem. Am. Coll. Physician Execs., Soc. Acad. Emergency Medicine.

HENDRICKS, LEONARD LOYED, industrial engineer, public hearing officer; b. Raleigh, N.C., Nov. 8, 1944; s. Loyed Franklin and Flora Katherine H.; m. Jackie Jean Hinsley, Aug. 21, 1971; children: Todd, Amy. BS, N.C. State U., 1968. Indsl. engr. Almay Cosmetics, Inc., Apex, N.C., 1970-73, Square D Co., Knightdale, N.C., 1973-79. With U.S. Army, 1968-70. Mem.: State Employees Assn. N.C. (membership chmn. 1984—86, scholarship chmn. 1992—2002). Avocations: spectator sports, traveling, investing. Home: 716 King St Cary NC 27513 Office: NC Dept Transp PO Box 25201 1 S Wilmington St Raleigh NC 27611 E-mail: LHendri732@aol.com., lhendricks@dot.state.nc.us.

HENDRICKS, NATHAN VANMETER, III, lawyer; b. Decatur, Ga., Dec. 16, 1943; s. Nathan VanMeter and Ella L. (Ward) H.; m. kathryn A. Barnes, Aug. 19, 1972; children: Nathan VanMeter, Seaton Grantland. BA, Washington and Lee U., 1966, LLB, 1969. Bar: Ga., 1970. Practiced in Swift, Currie, McGhee and Hiers, Atlanta, 1969—, assoc., 1969-70, Henning, Chambers and Mabry, Atlanta, 1970-71, Redfern, Butler and Morgan, Atlanta, 1971-73, ptnr., 1973-77, Cobb, Hyre, Hendricks & Ferguson, Atlanta, 1978-91; pvt. practice Atlanta, 1991—. Contbr. numerous articles to profl. jours. and publs. Chmn. Younger Lawyers Com. Campaign for mayor, Atlanta, 1972, re-election campaign for chmn. of Fulton County Bd. Commnrs., 1986; active host com. 1988 Dem. Nat. Conv.; mem. High Mus. of Art, group leader ann. fund-raising campaign, 1973-75, chmn. young careers group, 1972-73, sec. young men's round table, 1974-75; active ann. fund-raising campaign Atlanta Symphony Orch. Assn., 1977-78, Atlanta Arts Alliance, 1977-79, Atlanta Botanical Garden, 1986-88; bd. dirs. Atlanta Hunter-Jumper Classic, 1978-79, pres., 1979; bd. dirs. Save America's Vital Environment, sec. 1971-74; bd. dirs. Merrie-Woode Found., v.p., 1978-79, chmn., pres., 1981-93, exec. com. Give Wildlife a Chance fund, Ga. Dept. Natural Resources, 1988. Mem. Am., Atlanta (mem. real estate sect. 1972—, com. 1978) bar assns., State Bar of Ga. (mem. real estate sect. 1972—), Lawyers Club Atlanta, Washington and Lee U. Alumni Assn. (dri. 1972-82, pres. Atlanta chpt. 1973-75, Law Sch. Class agt. 1999—),, Ansley Golf Club, Piedmont Driving Club, Wildcat Cliffs Country, The Nine O'Clocks Club, N.C. Soc. of the Cin., Beta Theta Pi, Phi Delta Phi. Home: 230 The Prado NE Atlanta GA 30309-3336 Office: 6085 Lake Forrest Dr NW Ste 200 Atlanta GA 30328-3846

HENDRICKS, RANDAL ARLAN, lawyer; b. Nov. 18, 1945; s. Clinton H. and Edith T. (Anderson) H.; m. Suann Rose, June 1, 1965 (div. 1976); children: Kristin Lee, Daehne Lynn; m. Jill Edith Duke, Mar. 22, 1982; 1 child, Bret Larson-Hendricks. Student, U. Mo., Kansas City, 1963-65; BS with honors, U. Houston, 1968, JD with honors, 1970. Bar: Tex. 1970, U.S. Dist. Ct. (so. dist.) Tex. 1970, U.S. Tax Ct. 1985. Assoc. Baker & Botts, Houston, 1970-71; pvt. practice Houston, 1971—; sr. v.p., mng. dir. Baseball, SFX Sports Group, Inc., 1999-2001, chmn., pres., CEO, 2001—, SFX Baseball Group LLC. Ptnr. Hendricks Sports Mgmt., Houston, 1977-81; pres. Hendricks Mgmt. Co., Inc., Houston, 1981-99; expert witness U.S. Senate Subcom. on Antitrust and Monopoly, 1972; mem. pub. adv. com. Houston/Harris County Sports Facility, 1995-96. Author: Inside the Strike Zone, 1994. Dir. profl. div. Excellence Campaign, U. Houston, 1971; bd. dirs. Cypress Creek Christian Ch., Spring, Tex., 1979-85. Mem. Houston Bar Assn., Assn. Reps. Profl. Athletes (bd. dirs. 1978-88, mem. at large 1978-79, treas. 1979-80, v.p. 1980-81, pres. 1981-82, chmn. ethics com. 1978-80, chmn. baseball com. 1981-88), Sports Lawyers Assn. (bd. dirs. 1992-2000), Order of Barons (chancellor 1969-70), Phi Kappa Phi, Phi Delta Phi. Home: 20802 Highet Pl Tomball TX 77375-7042 Office: 400 Randal Way Ste 106 Spring TX 77388-8908 E-mail: randy.hendricks@SFX.com.

HENDRICKS, SCOTT, corporate budget specialist; b. Ft. Worth, Tex., July 18, 1953; s. Mary Hellen Cook; m. Sharon L. Mattix, Apr. 23, 1994; children: Keri M. Snowden, Robert H. BBA, Tex. Wesleyan U., 1975; MA Orgnl. Mgmt., U. Phoenix, Ariz., 1999. Specialist Gen. Dynamics, Ft. Worth, 1977—88, dept. mgr., 1988—94; staff budget specialist Lockheed Martin Aeronautics Co., Ft. Worth, 1994—. Mayor pro-tem City Of Joshua, Joshua, Tex., 1999—2002. Mem.: Acad. of Mgmt., Nat. Mgmt. Assn., Lions Club Internat. (2d v.p. 2000—01). R-Conservative. Home: 112 Wood Oak Dr Joshua TX 76058 Office: Lockheed Martin PO Box 748 Mz6445 Fort Worth TX 76101 Home Fax: 817-295-8522. Personal E-mail: csmi@usapathway.com.

HENDRICKS, STANLEY MARSHALL, II, executive recruiter, consultant; b. Richmond, Ky., Nov. 15, 1952; s. Stanley Marshall and Margaret Cathleen (Cox) H.; m. Sara Jane Sargent, Aug. 9, 1975; children: Stanley M. III, Elizabeth Jean. BS, Ind. State U., 1976; post baccalaureate degree, Ind. U. Northwest, 1984. Cert. personnel cons. Assoc. A.R. Massena & Assocs., Merrillville, Ind., 1976-77; co-founder, owner Nat. Recruiting Svc., Dyer, Ind., 1977—. Mem. coun. Ind. State U., Terre Haute, 1983-88; pres. Ind. State U. Alumni Coun.; elder, trustee Immanuel Presbyn. Ch., Schererville, Ind., 1978—; bd. dirs., sec. Dollars for Scholars. Mem. Assn. Iron and Steel Engrs., Nat. Assn. Pers. Cons., Fabricating Mfrs. Assn., Iron and Steel Soc., Ind. Soc. Chgo., Am. Tube Assn., Internat. Tube Assn., Ind. State U. Alumni Assn. (v.p., coun. pres.), Order of Omega (hon.), Ky. Cols. (hon.), Rotary (pres., bd. dirs., Paul Harris fellow, asst. dist. gov.), Sycamore Club N.W. Ind. (bd. dirs. 1984-88), Tri-Town Optimist Club (charter). Avocations: flying, woodworking, scuba diving, swimming. Home: 301 Blickview Dr Schererville IN 46375-2372 E-mail: stanhen@jorsm.com.

HENDRICKS, STEVEN RON, music educator; b. Murray, Utah, July 26, 1963; s. Robert Lewis and Beth Adelle (Lawrence) Hendricks; m. Tammie Lynn Hoth, June 8, 1984; children: Tarah, Taylor, Rebecca, Natalie. BMus, Utah State U., 1987; MMus, Brigham Young U., 1990. Cert. tchr. sec. edn. Utah. Band dir. Carbon H.S., Price, Utah, 1987—89, Davis H.S., Kaysville, Utah, 1990—. Dir. Davis Master Chorale, Kaysville, 1996—2001; mem. Mormon Tabernacle Choir, Salt Lake City, 2001—. Recipient Everday Hero in Cmty., O.C. Tanner Co., 2002. Mem.: Utah Music Educators (region festival mgr. 1995—98, UMEA band bd. 1993—97, Superior Accomplishment award 1999), Nat. Band Assn. Mem. Lds Ch. Avocations: singing, golf, strength training. Home: 1333 N 2350 E Layton UT 84040 Office: Davis High School 325 S Main Kaysville UT 84037

HENDRICKSON, BRUCE CARL, life insurance company executive; b. Holdrege, Nebr., Apr. 4, 1930; s. Carl R. and Ruth E. (Bosserman) H.; m. Carol Schepman, June 12, 1952; children: Julie, Mark Bruce. BA, U. Nebr., 1952. C.L.U., chartered fin. cons. Sr. agt. Prin. Life Ins. Co., Holdrege, 1950— . Bd. govs. Central Nebr. Tech. Community Coll.; mem. Nebr. Edn. Commn. of States, Nat. Hwy. Safety Advisors Com.; elder First Presbyterian Ch., Holdrege; pres. Holdrege City Council, 1979-86; pres. Phelps County Community Found.; trustee U. Nebr. Found.; moderator Cen. Nebr. Presbytery, Presbyn. Ch. USA, 1986-88, Gen. Assembly Coun., 1998—; dir. Nebr. Art Collection Found., 1996-2002; mem. pres. club U. Nebr., mem. chancellors club. Served with USNR, 1953-56. Bruce Hendrickson Week declared by Gov. of Nebr., 1975; recipient Distinguished Alumni Achievement award U. Nebr., 1977, Disting. Svc. award Nebr. State Assn. Life Underwriters, 1998. Mem. Nat. Assn. Life Underwriters (pres. 1975-76), Assn. Advanced Life Underwriting, Am. Soc. C.L.U.s., Life Underwriters Polit. Action Com. (chmn. 1989), Life Underwriters Tng. Coun. (trustee 1979-82), Million Dollar Round Table, Phi Kappa Psi. Clubs: Rotary (pres. 1960-61), Holdrege Country (Holdrege); Am. Legion, Elks. Republican. Office: Prin Fin Group PO Box 765 Holdrege NE 68949-0765

HENDRICKSON, CHRIS THOMPSON, civil and environmental engineering educator, researcher; b. Oakland, Calif., Mar. 31, 1950; s. Harold Thompson and E. Jean (Loomis) H.; m. Kathleen Devine, May 28, 1977; children: Andrew, Thomas, Peter. BS, MS, Stanford U., 1973; PhB, Oxford U., 1975; PhD, MIT, 1978. Asst. prof. Carnegie-Mellon U., Pitts., 1978-83, assoc. prof., 1983-87, prof., 1987—; assoc. dean Carnegie Inst. Tech., 1991-96, Duquesne Light Co. prof. engring., 1996—, head dept., 1996—. Author: (with others) Transportation Investment and Pricing Principles, 1984, Project Management for Construction, 1989, Knowledge-based Process Planning for Construction and Manufacturing, 1989, Computer Integrated Building Design, 1993; editor Jour. Transp. Engring.; contbr. articles to profl. publs. Bd. mem. St. Edmund's Acad., Pitts. Recipient C.E. Ladd Rsch. award Carnegie Inst. Tech., 1979; Rhodes scholar, 1973. Mem.: ASCE (com. chmn. 1983—, chmn. urban transp. divsn. 1989—90, dept. heads exec. com. 2000—02, Huber Rsch. award 1989, Masters Transp. Engring. award 1994, Fenves Systems award 2002, Turner Lecture award 2002), Transp. Rsch. Bd. (com. chmn. 1989—96), Am. Econ. Assn., Tau Beta Pi, Phi Beta Kappa. Home: 6933 Rosewood St Pittsburgh PA 15208-2638 Office: Carnegie Mellon U Pittsburgh PA 15213-3890

HENDRICKSON, CONSTANCE C. social worker; b. N.Y.C., Aug. 12, 1926; d. Samuel Udelson and Frances (Planinsek) Cooper; divorced; children: Christopher, Kenneth, Nicholas, Philip, Kirsten. BA, U. Md., 1969, MSW, 1971; DSW, Cath. U. of Am., Washington, 1985. Lic. clin. social worker. Pvt. practice. Office: Ste 201 3000 Connecticut Ave NW Washington DC 20008-2529 E-mail: chendr3000@aol.com.

HENDRICKSON, CONSTANCE MARIE MCRIGHT, chemist, consultant; b. Baton Rouge, June 7, 1949; d. Clifton Eugene and Evelyn Marie (Watson) McRight; m. William Harwell Hendrickson, Dec. 28, 1971; children: Charles Douglas (dec.), David Gillis, Emily Elizabeth Marie. BA, La. Tech. U., 1971; PhD, La. State U., 1975; MEd, U. North Tex., 1984. Cert. profl. chemist. NIH rsch. fellow Johns Hopkins U., Balt., 1975-78; clin. chemistry fellow Sch. Medicine U. Ala., Birmingham, 1978-79; temporary asst. prof. Tex. Wesleyan Coll., Ft. Worth, 1981-82; chief chemist Rockwood Systems Corp., Dallas, 1981-82; dir., owner Ar'Kon Cons., Dallas, 1982—; dir. environ. tech. program Brookhaven Coll., Dallas, 1994-97. Chair Nat. Certification Commn. for Chemists and Chem. Engrs., 1992-94. Fellow Am. Inst. Chemists (chair nat. cert. commn. for chemists and chem. engrs., pres. elect 1996-97, pres. 1998-99, chmn. bd. 2000-01); mem. Am. Chem Soc. (local chair 1987-88, treas. chem. mktg. and econs. divsn. 1990-99), N.Y. Acad. Scis., Nat. Panel Consumer Arbitrators (sr.). Democrat. Achievements include invention of high expansion foams; printing washout solvent; centrifugal purification. Avocations: fossil hunting, folk music, fiddling, zither. Home: 802 S Jefferson St Irving TX 75060-5355 Office: PO Box 171087 Irving TX 75017-1087 also: 1213 Stewart Dr Irving TX 75061-7354 E-mail: chendrickson@soapbuster.com.

HENDRICKSON, DANIEL C. association administrator; b. Upland, Calif. m. July Hendrickson; 1 child, Paul. BS in Math., Calif. State Poly. U., 1967; MBA, Calif. State U., Fullerton. With Autonetics; minuteman chief systems engr. Boeing Corp.; with Air Force Assn., 1981—2001, nat. sec., 2001—. Mem. exec. com., nat. officer Aerospace Edn. Found., mem. pub. awareness and devels. com. Co-author: A Brief History of Minuteman Guidance and Control. Recipient 2 Presdl. citations; fellow Jimmy Doolittle, Aerospace Edn. Found. Office: c/o AFA Nat Hqrs 1501 Lee Hwy Arlington VA 22209-1198

HENDRICKSON, ELIZABETH ANN, retired secondary education educator; b. Bismarck, N.D., Oct. 21, 1936; d. William Earl and Hilda E. (Sauter) Hinkel; m. Roger G. Hendrickson, Apr. 18, 1960; 1 child, Wade William. BA, Jamestown Coll., 1958; postgrad., U. Calif., Davis, 1962, Calif. State U., Sacramento, 1964, U. San Diego, 1985-88, Ottawa U., 1986-88. Cert. tchr., Calif. Tchr. Napoleon (N.D.) High Sch., 1958-59, Kulm (N.D.) High Sch., 1959-61, Del Paso Jr. High Sch., Sacramento, 1961, Mills Jr. High Sch., Rancho Cordova, Calif., 1961-97; ret., 1997. Mem. sch. attendance rev. bd. Folsom-Cordova Unified Sch. Dist. Mem.: AAUW, NEA, Sacramento Area Gifted Assn., Folsom Cordova Ret. Tchrs. Assn. (sec., mem. steering com., mem. newsletter com.), Calif. Ret. Tchrs. Assn., Calif. Tchrs. Assn., Calif. Assn. for Gifted, N.G. Aux., Sgt. Maj. Assn. of Calif. Aux. Enlisted Assns., Soroptimists (news editor Rancho Cordova 1985). Democrat. Lutheran. Home: 2032 Kellogg Way Rancho Cordova CA 95670-2435

HENDRICKSON, GORDON OLAF, archivist; b. Spring Lake, Wis., Dec. 27, 1946; s. Olaf Stene and Margaret Edith Hendrickson; m. Barbara Flasch Hendrickson, June 8, 1974; children: Anders O.F., Rosina B.F., Karl F.F. BS, Wis. State U., 1968; MA, Colo. State U., 1972; PhD, U. of Wyo., 1975. Project archivist Wyo. State Hist. Soc., Cheyenne, 1975—76; asst. prof. U. of Wyo., 1975—76, project dir., 1976—77, Immigration History Rsch. Ctr., St. Paul, 1977—79; assoc. dir. Western Hist. Manuscript Coll. K.C., Kansas City, Mo., 1980—87; state archivist State of Iowa, Des Moines, 1987—. Consulting historian Atty. Gen., Cheyenne, 1987—2001. Editor: (book) Peopling the High Plains, 1977, Living Wyoming's Past, 1983. Leader Boy Scouts Am., Des Moines, 1990—. With U.S. Army, 1969—71. Mem.: Nat. Assn. Govt. Archives and Recs. Adminstrs. (coun. mem. 1994—96), Coun. State Hist. Records Coord. (coun. mem. 1990—94, chair 1992—93, coun. mem. 2003—), Am. Assoc. State and Local History (coun. mem. 1986—88), Midwest Archives Conf., Soc. Am. Archivists. Office: State Archives of Iowa 600 East Locust Des Moines IA 50319

HENDRICKSON, JEROME ORLAND, trade association executive, lawyer; b. Eau Claire, Wis., July 25, 1918; s. Harold and Clara (Halvorson) H.; m. Helen Phoebe Harty, Dec. 27, 1948 (dec. Oct. 1988); children: Jaime Ann, Jerome Orland. Student, Wis. State Coll., 1936-39; JD, U. Wis., 1942. Bar: Wis. 1942, U.S. Supreme Ct. 1955. Sole practice, Eau Claire, Wis., 1946; sales & advt. mgr. Eau Claire Coca-Cola Bottling Co., Inc., 1947-48; exec. sec. Eau Claire Cmty. Chest, 1948-49; in charge dist. Office Am. PEtroleum Inst., Kansas City, Mo., 1950-53, Chgo., 1953-55; exec. dir. Nat. Assn. Plumbing-Heating-Cooling Contractors, 1955-64; sec. Joint Apprentice Text, Inc., 1955-64; exec. v.p. Cast Iron Soil Pipe Inst., Washington, 1964-74; pres. Valve Mfrs. Assn., McLean, Va., 1975-80; exec. v.p. Plumbing and Pipe Industry Coun., Inc., 1981-90. Ret. treas. Wis. Cmty. Chest, 1948-49; treas. All-Industry Plumbing & Heating Modernization Com., 1956-57; co-sec. Joint Industry Program Com., 1958-64. Lt. USNR, 1943-46. Mem. ABA, Wis. Bar Assn., Am. Soc. Assn. Execs., Washington Soc. Assn. Execs., Wis. State Soc. Washington (pres. 1966-68), Nat. Conf. Plumbing-Heating-Cooling Industry (chmn. 1967-69), NAM, U. Wis. Alumni Assn., U. Wis. Law Sch. Alumni Assn. Washington (pres. 1970-74), C. of C. of U.S., Mason (32 degree, Shriner), Washington Golf & Country Club, Internat. Club (Washington), Gamma Eta Gamma (pres. Upsilon chpt. 1941-42). Episcopalian. Home and Office: 1200 Partridge Ln Charlottesville VA 22901-1787

HENDRICKSON, KENT HERMAN, university administrator; b. Radcliffe, Iowa, Mar. 4, 1939; s. Herman Oliver and Minnie Ida (Dubberke) H.; m. Rosemary Lee Bergeson, Sept. 12, 1960 (div. 1981); children: Justin K., Susan K.; m. Ellen J. Waite, Mar. 26, 1994 (div. Dec. 1995). BS in History, Iowa State U., 1961; MALS, U. Mich., 1964. Assoc. dir. for tech. svcs. U. Nebr. Librs., Lincoln, 1964-70, dean of librs., 1985-95, assoc. vice chancellor info. svcs., 1995—; mgr. west coast operations Richard Abel Co., Beaverton, Oreg., 1970-74; v.p. corp. opers. Blackwell N.Am. Inc., Beaverton, Oreg., 1975-79, v.p., 1980-81; assoc. univ. libr. U. Ariz. Libr., Tucson, 1981-85, acting asst. univ libr. for pub. svcs., 1982-84, dir. ctrl. svcs., 1984-85. Mem. Nebr. Conf. on Libr. and Info. Svcs., 1991, mem. adv. com. on integrated postsecondary edn. data system Nat. Ctr. for Edn. Statistics, 1990-93; mem. rsch. librs. adv. com. Online Computer Libr. Ctr. Inc., 1990-96, chair, 1992-93. Contbr. articles to profl. jours.; mem. editorial bd. U. Nebr. Press, 1990-95. Trustee AMIGOS, 1984-85; mem. info. systems and comm. com. U. Nebr.-Lincoln, 1988—, mem. acad. planning com., 1988-93, mem. adv. com. to Sheldon Art Gallery, 1985—, mem. adv. com. to computing resource ctr., 1987—, mem. campus wide campaign for health and human svcs., 1986-87, vice chair, 1986, chair, 1987; bd. dirs. Great Plains Network, 1998—, MidNet, 1995—, The Quilt, 2003—; mem. Edn. Coun. NE Info. Tech. Commn., 1998—; mem. Coun. of Big 12 Chief Info. Officers, 2002—. Mem. Assn. Rsch. Librs. (stats. com. 1989-92, chair 1991-92, mem. mgmt. com. 1992-96, chair 1993-96, chair office mgmt. svcs. adv. com. 1993-96, mem. collection devel. com. 1986-88, bd. dirs. 1993-96), Assn. Coll. and Rsch. Librs. (mem. exec. com. univ. librs. sect. 1992-95, chair pre-conf. planning com. 1992, chair univ. librs. stds. rev. com. 1986-89, chair acad. librs. stats. com. 1986-89), OCLC Users Coun. (mem. fin. com. 1991-92, pres. Users Coun. 1993-94), U. Nebr. Coun. on Librs., Nebr. State Libr. Commn. (mem. strategic planning task force 1987-88). Office: U Nebr-Lincoln University Libraries Lincoln NE 68588-4096 E-mail: khendrickson1@unl.edu.

HENDRICKSON, LOUISE, retired association executive, retired social worker; b. Lansdowne, Pa., Sept. 14, 1916; d. Norman and Gertrude (Powers) H. AA, Long Beach Jr. Coll., 1936; BA, U. Calif., Berkeley, 1938, gen. secondary tchr.'s cert., 1939; MS in Social Work, Columbia U., 1952. Cert. secondary tchr., Calif.; registered social worker, Calif. Dir. young adult program YWCA, Oakland, Calif., 1944-48, dir. group work and informal edn. svcs. Bklyn., 1948-53, exec. dir. Spokane, Wash., 1953-58; field cons. Nat. Bd. YWCA, Chgo., 1958-63, assoc. exec. community divsn. N.Y.C., 1963-66, exec. community divsn., 1966-71, dir. orgn. devel., 1971-74, dep. exec. dir., 1974-82, ret., 1982. Contbr. articles to profl. jours. Pres. Cmty. Welfare Coun., Spokane, 1956-57; mem. majority coun. Emily's List, Washington; mem. Common Cause, LWV. Mem. NASW (charter 1958-62).

HENDRICKSON, ROBERT FREDERICK, pharmaceutical company executive; b. Cambridge, Mass., Jan. 5, 1933; s. Charles H. and Ruth E. Hendrickson; m. Virginia H. Emery, Apr. 27, 1963; children: Karen, Susan, Douglas. AB in Econs. magna cum laude, Harvard U., 1954, MBA, 1958. Engaged in prodn. planning, internat. div. Internat. Latex Corp., Dover, Del., 1958-61; mgr. prodn. planning and control Merck Sharp & Dohme, West Point, Pa., 1961-66, dir. long-range planning, 1966-68, exec. sec. new products com., 1968-69, dir. prodn. planning and control, 1969-71, dir. ops., 1971-72, v.p. ops., 1972-80; sr. v.p. Merck & Co., Inc., Rahway, N.J., 1981-85, sr. v.p. mfg. and tech., 1985-90, ret., 1990; mfg. cons., 1990—. Bd. dirs. Cytogen, Inc.; trustee Carrier Found., 1992—. Bd. dirs. Lenape Valley Mental Health Found., 1972-80, pres., 1976-77; trustee N.J. State Safety Coun., 1980-90, New Eng. Hist. Geneal. Soc., 1999—. With AUS, 1954-56. Mem. North Pa. C. of C. (bd. dirs. 1974-77), Pharm. Mfg. Assn. (chmn. prodn. and engring. sect. 1980-81), NOW Legal Def. and Edn. Fund (bd. dirs. 1987-93), N.J. State C. of C. (bd. dirs. 1985-90), N.J. Coun. for the Humanities (trustee 1992-96). Presbyterian. Home and Office: 204 Gallup Rd Princeton NJ 08540-7306

HENDRICKSON, ROMAN MICHAEL, physician; b. St. Paul, Jan. 4, 1951; s. M.B. and Elizabeth Anne (Dauer) H.; m. Regina Hendrickson (div. 1997); children: Jennifer Michelle, Eric Matthew, Roman Michael Jr.; m. Joan Elaine Hendrickson, June 22, 1997. BA in Modern European History, U. Minn., 1971; BS in Clin. Chemistry, U. South Fla., 1973, MD, 1976. Diplomate Am. Bd. Family Practice, Nat. Bd. Med. Examiners. Clin. chemist spl. chemistry Mease Hosp., Dunedin, Fla., 1973; pvt. practice Ormond Family Practice, Ormond Beach, Fla., 1979-97; chief med. officer, dir. geriatric svcs. Ft. Peck Svc. Unit/Indian Health Svc., Poplar, Mont., 1997—2003; med. dir. Ruby Valley Clinic, Sheridan, Mont., 2003—. Med. dir. Ormond Beach Health Care Ctr., 1980-97, Fla. VA Nursing Home, Daytona Beach, 1993-97, Ctrl. Fla. Home Health Care, Daytona Beach, 1993-97; CEO Quality Care Physicians, Inc., Daytona Beach, 1995-97; adv. panel mem. Key Pharm., 1994-96. Contbr. articles to profl. jours. Fellow: Am. Acad. Family Physicians; mem.: Fla. Acad. Family Physicians (pres. 1992—93), Am. Geriatric Soc., Am. Med. Dirs. Assn. (pres. 1990—92, pres. Mont. chpt. 1999—2001). Republican. Roman Catholic. Avocations: numismatics, skiing (snow and water), fishing, camping, travel. Office: Ruby Valley Hosp PO Box 366 210 Crofoot St Sheridan MT 59749 E-mail: romanhend@hotmail.com.

HENDRICKSON, THOMAS ATHERTON, lawyer; b. Indpls., May 12, 1927; s. Robert Augustus and Eleanor Riggs (Atherton) H.; m. Sandra Bly Shepard, Feb. 6, 1960; children: Thomas Shepard, Heidi Bly, Melanie Parke. BA, Yale U., 1949; LLB, Ind. U., 1952. Bar: Ind. 1952; cert. level II tax assessor-appraiser Ind. Former ptnr. Hendrickson, Travis, Pantzer & Miller. Mem. Indpls. Hist. Preservation Commn., 1982-83; mem. Marion County/Indpls. Hist. Soc., pres., 1984-85; mem. adv. bd. Fund for Landmark Indpls. Properties, 1984-85, Cath. Sem. Found. Indpls., Inc., 1985-94; former Marion County lay rep. planning com. Central Ind. Library Services Authority, recipient Outstanding Service award; former council pres. Indpls. Great Books. Served to lt. (s.g.) USNR, 1945-56. Fellow Ind. Bar Found.; mem. ABA (sec. on taxation, com. on state and local taxation), Ind. State Bar Assn. (taxation sect., ho. of dels. 1971-75, 79-89, asst. editor ABA Property Tax Deskbook 1995-98, author How to Challenge an Indiana Realty Assessment in Interstate Tax Insights 1992), Indpls. Bar Assn. (taxation sect.), Inst. Profls. in Taxation, Nat. Bus. Ins. (spkr. 2001—), Lawyers' Club. Office: 7979 Lantern Rd Indianapolis IN 46256-1827 E-mail: thendrickson6@comcast.net.

HENDRICKSON, WILLIAM GEORGE, business executive; b. Plainview, Minn., May 31, 1918; s. Clarence and Hildegarde (Heaser) H.; m. Virginia M. Price, Sept. 1, 1942; children: Robert, Thomas, Donald, Julie Ann. BS, St. Mary's Coll., Winona, Minn., 1939; MS, U. Detroit, 1941; PhD, U. Wis., 1946; D Humanities, St. Mary's U., Winona, Minn., 1991. Scientist Wis. Alumni Research Found., Madison, 1946-54, dir. devel., 1954-61; v.p. Ayerst Labs. div. Am. Home Products Corp., N.Y.C., 1961-67, exec. v.p., 1967-69; group v.p. Am. Home Products Corp., N.Y.C., 1969-80. Chmn. emeritus bd. St. Jude Med., Inc., St. Paul; bd. dirs. emeritus Rsch. Corp. Techs., Tucson. Mem. Am. Chem. Soc., N.Y. Acad. Scis., Country Club N.C., Royal Poinciana Golf Club, Sigma Xi. Republican. Roman Catholic.

HENDRIE, ELAINE, public relations executive; b. Bklyn. d. David and Pearl Kostell; m. Joseph Mallam Hendrie; children: Susan, Barbara. Asst. acct. exec. Benjamin Sonnenberg Pub. Rels., N.Y.C., 1953-57; pub. rels. cons., writer, editor, dir. pub. rels. and media Religious Heritage of Am., Washington, 1973-75; nat. media coord. NOW, Washington, 1978; media dir. Am. Speech-Lang.-Hearing Assn., Washington, 1979-80; pub. info. officer, head media and mktg. Dept. Navy, Washington, 1980-81; pres. Hendrie & Pendzick, 1982-92, Elaine Hendrie Pub. Rels., 1992—. Prodr., interviewer radio program, sta. WRIV, WALK AM/FM, L.I., N.J., Westchester County, N.Y., Conn., 1974-77; exec. dir. Women in New Directions, Inc., Suffolk County, N.Y., 1974-77, cons., 1981—; resource person for media Nat. Commn. on Observance of Internat. Women's Yr., 1977; cons. Multi-Media Prodns. Inc., N.Y.C., 1978—; adv. bd. Women's Edn. and Counseling Ctr., SUNY, Farmingdale. Mem. Bellport-Brookhaven Hist. Soc. (trustee 1999—). Home: 50 Bellport Ln Bellport NY 11713-2736

HENDRIE, JOSEPH MALLAM, physicist, nuclear engineer, government official; b. Janesville, Wis., Mar. 18, 1925; s. Joseph Munier and Margaret Prudence (Hocking) H.; m. Elaine Kostell, July 9, 1949; children: Susan Debra, Barbara Ellen. BS, Case Inst. Tech., 1950; PhD, Columbia U., 1957. Registered profl. engr., N.Y., Calif. Asst. physicist Brookhaven Nat. Lab., Upton, N.Y., 1955-57, assoc. physicist, 1957-60, physicist, 1960-71, sr. physicist, 1971-97, chmn. steering com., project chief engr. high flux beam reactor design and constrn., 1958-65, acting head exptl. reactor physics div., 1965-66, project mgr. pulsed fast reactor project, 1967-70, assoc. head engring. div., dept. applied sci., 1967-71, head, 1971-72, chmn. dept. applied sci., 1975-77, spl. asst. to dir., 1981-96; dir. Entergy Ops., Inc., 1987-95. Dir. Houston Industries, Inc., Houston Lighting & Power Co., 1985-96; dep. dir. licensing for tech. rev. U.S. AEC, 1972-74; chmn. U.S. Nuclear Regulatory Commn., Washington, 1977-79, 81, commr., 1980, mem. adv. com. on enforcement policy, 1984-85; lectr. nuclear power plant safety MIT, Ga. Inst. Tech., Northwestern U., summers 1970-77; cons. radiation safety com. Columbia U., 1964-72; mem. adv. com. reactor safeguards AEC, 1966-72, chmn., 1970; U.S. mem. sr. adv. group on reactor safety standards IAEA, 1974-78; mem. nat. rsch. coun. com. Internat. Cooperation in Magnetic Fusion, 1983-85; cons. AEC, Nuclear Regulatory Commn., 1974-75, GAO, 1975-77, Electric Power Rsch. Inst., 1982, various nuclear utilities, 1981—. Mem. editorial adv. bd. Nuclear Tech, 1967-77. Served with AUS, 1943-45. Recipient E.O. Lawrence award, 1970, George C. Laurence Pioneering award Am. Nuclear Soc., 1998; decorated comdr. Order of Leopold II (Belgium), 1982 Fellow Am. Nuclear Soc. (dir. 1976-77, v.p. 1983-84, pres. 1984-85), ASME; mem. IEEE, Nat. Acad. Engring., Am. Phys. Soc., ASTM (com. on rsch. and tech. planning 1985-90), Am. Concrete Inst., Inst. Nuclear Power Operation (adv. coun. 1984-90), Nat. Soc. Profl. Engrs., Sigma Xi, Tau Beta Pi. Achievements include research and publications on physics nuclear reactors, nuclear power plant safety, engineering design reactors, electrical power transmission, chem. physics nitrogen dissociation process, structure oxygen molecule. Office: Brookhaven Nat Lab Upton NY 11973

HENDRIKSEN, NEIL EVAN, music educator; b. Salt Lake City, Sept. 27, 1955; s. Oscar James and Dorothy Hendriksen; m. Marie Updegraff, Oct. 20, 1977; children: Jacob Thomas, Daren Bradford, Nathan Edward, Douglas Neil, Lauren Clarice. MusB, U. Utah, 1985. Cert. Secondary Tchr. State of Utah, 1985. Dir. choral activities Woods Cross H.S., Woods Cross, Utah, 1986—; adj. faculty mem. U. Utah, Salt Lake City, 1989—. Clinician, adjudicator Heritage Festivals, Salt Lake City, 1990—, Utah H.S. Activities Assn., Midvale, 1987—;

trombonist, bass trombonist Ballet West/Utah Chamber Orch., Salt Lake City, 1989—; aux. trombonist Utah Symphony Orch., Salt Lake City, 1982—89; trombonist, bass trombonist Pioneer Theatre Co. Orch., Salt Lake City, 1983—89. Musician: numerous symphonic studio performances; singer: numerous soundtracks and studio recordings; musician: numerous studio, movies, advertising and tv appearances; singer: numerous live vocal solo and ensemble performances. Zone commr. Boy Scouts Am., Salt Lake City, 1990—97. Recipient Golden Apple Award, Utah PTA, 1996, Secondary Tchr. of Yr., Davis Sch. Dist., 1996, Tchr. of Yr., Woods Cross H.S., 1996. Mem.: Davis Educators Assn. (assoc.), Utah Educators Assn. (assoc.), NEA (assoc.), Utah Music Educators Assn. (assoc.; vice president.choral 2000—02), Am. Choral Dirs. Assn. (life; utah repertoire/standards chair h.s. 1987—96). Avocations: hiking, target shooting, knife collecting, sight-seeing/travel, camping. Office: Woods Cross High School 600 West 2200 South Woods Cross UT 84087

HENDRIX, BONNIE ELIZABETH LUELLEN, retired elementary school educator; b. Corry, Pa., July 21, 1942; d. Francis Wilson and Frances (Welch) Luellen. BEd, Anderson Coll., 1965; MEd, Berry Coll., 1986. 1st grade tchr. Madison County Bd. Edn., Anderson, Ind.; kindergarten tchr. Walker County Bd. Edn., LaFayette, Ga., 1994—, spl. instrn. asst., 1998—2002, spl. edn. tchr., 1999—2002, tchr. exceptional children, 1999—2000; tchr. Tiny Treasures Day Care Ctr., 2003—; presenter at confs. Mentor tchr. Continuous Quality Instructions Sys; pvt. practice piano tchr. Active community and ch. orgns. Mem. NEA, ASCD, PAGE, Ga. Assn. Edn., Walker Assn. Edn. Home: 76 Old Trion Rd La Fayette GA 30728-3714

HENDRIX, CHARLES C. marriage and family therapist, educator; b. Mo. PhD, Kans. State U., 1989. Lic. marital and family therapist Okla. Assoc. prof. Okla. State U., Stillwater, 1989—. Mem.: Am. Assn. Marriage and Family Therapy. Office: Okla State U 333H Human Environ Scis Stillwater OK 74078 Office Fax: 405-744-2800. E-mail: charlie@okstate.edu.

HENDRIX, JOHN SHANNON, architecture educator; b. Ithaca, N.Y., Apr. 27, 1959; s. John David and Margaret Shannon Hendrix. BFA, Art Inst., 1983; MA, Rhode Island of Design, 1984; MArch, Univ of Ill, 1993; PhD in Architecture, Cornell U., 2001. Adj. prof. Roger Williams U., Rome, 1998—2000, vis. asst. prof. art and archtl. history Bristol, RI, 2000—. Author: The Relation Between Architectural Forms and Philosophical Structures in the Work of Francesco Borromini in Seventeenth-Century Rome, Architectural Forms and Philosophical Structures, History and Culture in Italy. Home: 212 Hope St Bristol RI 02809 Office: Roger Williams Univ One Old Ferry Rd Bristol RI 02809 Office Fax: 401-254-3501. E-mail: jhendrix@rwu.edu.

HENDRIX, JOHN WALTER, lieutenant general United States Army; BS in Elec. Engring., Ga. Tech. U., 1966; student infantry advanced course, U.S. Army Infantry Sch., Ft. Benning, Ga., 1969-70; student fixed wing aviator course, U.S. Army Aviation Sch., Ft. Stewart, Ga., 1970-71; MA in History, Mid. Tenn. State U., 1974; student, U.S. Army Command & Staff Coll, Ft. Leavenworth, Kans., 1977-78, U.S. Army War Coll., Carlisle Barracks, Pa., 1983-84. Commd. 1st. lt. U.S. Army, 1966, advanced through grades to lt. gen., 1997; instr. Mt. Ranger Camp, Company D U.S. Army Infantry Sch., Fort Benning, Ga., 1966-67; comm. officer to comdr. 1st Battalion, 101st Airborne Divsn. U.S. Army, Vietnam, 1967-68; air officer ops. to S-1 (pers.) 1st Battalion 101st Airborne Divsn. U.S. Army, Vietnam, 1968-69, commander Co. D. 1st Battalion, 1969; evaluation officer CSA Evaluation Directorate U.S. Army, Ft. Hood, Tex., 1971-72; asst. prof. mil. sci. Mid. Tenn. State U., Murfreesboro, 1972-74; S-3 (ops.), 2d brigade, 5th infantry divsn. (mechanized) U.S. Army, Ft. Polk, La., 1978-79; comdr. 2d battalion, 13th infantry, 8th infantry divsn. U.S. Army Europe, Germany, 1980-83, comdr. 2d brigade, 8th infantry divsn., 1987-89; asst. divsn. comdr. 1st armored divsn. U.S. Army Europe and 7th Army Desert Shield/ Desert Storm, Saudi Arabia, 1990-91; exec. to Supreme Allied Comdr. Europe Supreme hdqtrs. Allied Powers Europe, Brussels, 1991-92; commanding gen. U.S. Army Infantry Ctr. Ft. Benning then 3d Infantry Divsn. (mechanized, Fort Stewart, Ga., 1996-97; commanding gen. V Corps U.S. Army Europe and Seventh Army, Europe, 1997-99; commanding gen. U.S. Army Forces Command, McPherson, Ga., 1999—. Decorated Defense Disting. Svc. medal, Disting. Svc. medal with oak leaf cluster, Silver Star with oak leaf cluster, Legion of Merit with 3 oak leaf clusters, Bronze Star medal with V device with 3 oak leaf clusters, Defense Meritorious Svc. medal, Meritorious Svc. medal with 4 oak leaf clusters, Air Medals, Army Commendation medal with 5 oak leaf clusters. Office: FORS COM/CG 1777 Hardee Ave SW Fort Mcpherson GA 30330-1062

HENDRIX, JON RICHARD, biology educator; b. Passaic, N.J., May 4, 1938; s. William Louis and Velma Lucile (Coleman) H.; m. Janis Ruth Rouhselange, Nov. 24, 1962; children— Margaret Susan, Joann Ruth, Amy Therese BS, Ind. State U., 1960, MS, 1963; Ed.D., Ball State U., 1974. Sci. supr. Sch. Town of Highland, Ind., 1960-71; instr. Ind. U., Gary, 1968-69; assoc. prof. biology Ball State U., Muncie, 1972-80, prof., 1980-98, prof. emeritus, 1998—. Cons. Ind. Dept. Pub. Instrn., 1967-71, Ctr. for Values and Meaning, 1971— ; mem. Ind. Sci. Edn. Adv. Bd., Dept. Pub. Instrn., 1967-71 Author: The Wonder of Somehow, 1974, The Wonder of Someplace, 1974, The Wonder of Sometime, 1974, Becomings: A Parent Guidebook for In-Home Experiences with Nine to Eleven Year Olds, 1974, Becomings: A Clergy Guidebook for Experiences with Nine to Eleven Year Olds and Their Parents, 1974; contbr. articles to profl. jours. Recipient Outstanding Young Educator award Highland Jr. C. of C., 1968, Outstanding Faculty award in edn. Ind. U. N.W. Campus, 1970, Outstanding Teaching Faculty award Ball State U., 1982, Ball State U. fellowship, 1971-73, Hon. Mem. award Nat. Assn. Biology Tchrs., 1992, Outstanding Undergrad. Sci. Tchr. in Nation, Soc. of Coll. Sci. Tchrs./Kendall Mgmt., 1997; named Ind. Prof. of Yr., Coun. for Advancement and Support of Edn./Carneige, 1997. Fellow Ind. Acad. Sci.; mem. Nat. Sci. Suprs. Assn. (dir. 1969-71), Ind. Sci. Suprs. Assn. (pres. 1968-69), AAUP, Assn. Suprs. and Curriculum Devel., Nat. Biology Tchrs. Assn. (bd. dirs. 1986, 91—), Nat. Sci. Tchrs. Assn. (life), Nat. Soc. Coll. Sci. Tchrs. (undergrad. tchg. award 1997), Central Assn. Coll. Biology Tchrs., Hoosier Assn. Sci. Tchrs. Inc. (bd. dirs. 1968-71, Disting. Svc. award 1997), Ind. Assn. Tchr. Educators, Ind. Assn. Suprs. and Curriculum Devel., Ind. Biology Tchrs. Assn., Kappa Delta Pi, Phi Delta Kappa, Sigma Xi. Home: 8400 W Eucalyptus Ave Muncie IN 47304-9365 E-mail: jonh49@comcast.net.

HENDRIX, LYNN PARKER, lawyer; b. McCook, Nebr., Apr. 24, 1951; s. Jack Hall and Betty Lee (Parker) H.; m. Theresa Louise Zabawa, June 19, 1976; children: Paige Ashley, Parker Jerome, Pierce Reid. BSEE, U. Nebr., 1973, JD with distinction, 1978. Bar: Nebr. 1978, U.S. Dist. Ct. Nebr. 1978, Colo. 1979, U.S. Dist. Ct. Colo. 1979, U.S. Ct. Appeals (10th cir.) 1993, Wyo. 1993, Mont. 1995, N.Y., 2000, U.S. Patent Office, 1994. Surveyor Nebr. Dept. Roads, McCook, 1973; constrn. adminstr. Commonwealth Electric Co., Lincoln, Nebr., 1974, cons. engr., 1975; instr. U. Nebr., Lincoln, 1974-75; law clk. Nebr. Atty.-Gen., Lincoln, 1976-77; assoc. Holme Robert & Owen, LLP, Denver, 1978-83; ptnr. Holme Robert & Owen, Denver, 1984—. Editor-in-chief Nebr. Law Rev., 1977-78, exec. editor, 1976-77; contbr. articles to profl. jours. Sec., bd. dirs. Girls Club Denver, 1984-90, Girls Inc. of Metro Denver, 1992-94; trustee Rocky Mountain Minn. Law Found. Named Adm., Nebr. Navy. Mem. ABA, Colo. Bar Assn., Mont. Bar Assn., Nebr. Bar Assn., Wyo. Bar Assn., N.Y. Bar Assn., S.E. Law Club (pres. 1990-91), Meridian Golf Club, Tau Beta Pi, Sigma Tau (pres.), Eta Kappa Nu. Home: 8125 S Glencoe Ct Littleton CO 80122-3876 Office: Holme Roberts & Owen LLP 1700 Lincoln St Ste 4100 Denver CO 80203-4541

HENDRIX, ROBERT A. otolaryngologist; b. Louisville, Sept. 16, 1951; BS in Math. with honors, Purdue U., 1973, postgrad., 1973-74; MD, U. Ky., 1978. Diplomate Am. Bd. Otolaryngology. Intern in surgery Bystate Med. Ctr., Springfield, Mass., 1978-79; resident in otolaryngology Ohio State U., Columbus, 1980-83; from asst. prof. to assoc. prof. U. Pa., 1983-92, dir. med. edn., 1985-92, acting chmn. dept. otorhinolaryngology, 1990-91, program dir. residency otolaryngology, 1990-91; chief otolaryngology svc. Phila. VA Med. Ctr., 1989-92, med. dir. Speech & Hearing Ctr., 1990-92; pvt. practice Charlotte, N.C., 1992-98; otolaryngologist Nash Gen. Hosp., Rocky Mount, N.C., 1999—, Heritage Hosp., Tarboro, N.C., 2000—. Grantee Am. Cancer Soc., 1988-89. Fellow ACS, Am. Soc. Head and Neck Surgery, Am. Acad. Facial Plastic and Reconstructive Surgery, Am. Acad. Otolaryngology-Head and Neck Surgery, Triological Soc.; mem. Am. Broncho-Esophagological Assn., N.C. Med. Soc., Alpha Epsilon Delta. Office: Carolina Otolaryngology 804 English Rd Ste 200 Rocky Mount NC 27804 also: 215 Smith Church Rd Roanoke Rapids NC 27870 Fax: 252-937-4103. E-mail: tiermensch@aol.com.

HENDRIX, RONALD WAYNE, physician, radiologist; b. St. Louis, June 4, 1943; s. Arthur W. and Lida (Martin) H.; m. Miriam Jensen, June 14, 1969. AB, Wash. U., St. Louis, 1965, MD, 1969. Diplomate Am. Bd. Nuclear Medicine, Am. Bd. Radiology. Intern Wash. U., Barnes Hosp., St. Louis, 1969-70; resident U. Chgo., 1970-73, fellow in nuclear medicine, 1973-74; staff radiologist Symmes Hosp., Arlington, Mass., 1976-77; asst. prof. radiology Northwestern U. Med. Sch., Chgo., 1977-84, assoc. prof. radiology, 1984—; attending physician Northwestern Meml. Hosp., Chgo., 1977—, chief, musculoskeletal radiology, 1977—. Dir. radiology Rehab. Inst. of Chgo., 1986—. Contbr. articles to profl. jours.; contbg. author to several books. Pres. LaSalle St. Ch., 1982—84. Lt. comdr. USN, 1974—76. Mem. Radiol. Soc. of N.Am., Am. Roentgen Ray Soc., Assn. of U. Radiologists, Am. Coll. Radiology, Internat. Skeletal Soc. Office: Northwestern Meml Hosp 710 N Fairbanks Ct Chicago IL 60611-3013 Address: 676 N St Clair Ste 800 Chicago IL 60611

HENDRIX, STEPHEN C. financial executive; b. Phila., Feb. 24, 1941; s. Houston W. and Helen Hendrix; children: Kimberly, Jeffrey, Julie. BA, Tex. Christian U., 1964; M in Internat. Svc., Am. U., 1966; MBA, Ohio State U., 1972. Jr. officer U.S. Dept. State, AID, Washington, 1967-68; mgr. mktg. adminstrn. Amecom divsn. Litton Industries, College Park, Md., 1968-70; mgr. fin. and planning internat. divsn. Anchor Hocking Corp., Lancaster, Ohio, 1970-73; bank rels. mgr. E.I. Dupont de Nemours & Co., Wilmington, Del., 1973-78; corp. treas. mgr. SmithKline Beckman Corp., Phila., 1978-79, asst. treas. domestic, 1979-82, asst. treas. internat., 1982-87, v.p., asst. treas. internat., 1987-89; v.p., treas. SmithKline Beecham Corp. (formerly SmithKline Beckman Corp.), Phila., 1989-91; treas. Armstrong World Industries, Lancaster, Pa., 1993-96; cons. AstraZeneca, Wayne, Pa., 1997-99, LifeSensors Inc., Wayne, 2000—. Contbr. articles to profl. jours. Mem. Assn. for Investment Mgmt. and Rsch., Fin. Execs. Inst., Nat. Assn. Corp. Treas. Home and Office: 1910 Swedesford Rd Malvern PA 19355-8729 E-mail: stevehendrix@yahoo.com.

HENDRIX, SUSAN CLELIA DERRICK, civic worker; b. McClellanville, S.C., Jan. 19, 1920; d. Theodore Elbridge and Susan Regina (Bauknight) Derrick; m. Henry Gardner Hendrix, June 5, 1943; children: Susan Hendrix Redmond, Marilyn Hendrix Shedlock. BA, Columbia Coll., 1941; MA, Furman U., 1961; EdD (hon.), Columbia Coll., 1985. Cert. tchr., S.C. Tchr. Whitmire Pub. Schs., 1941-43, Greenville (S.C.) Pub. Schs., 1944-46, 58-63, dir. Reading Clinic, 1965-68; counselor Greenville County Sch. Dist., 1965-68, dir. pub. rels., 1968-83; grad. instr. Furman U., 1967-69. Cons. Nat. Seminar on Desegration, 1973. Author (with James P. Mahaffey): Teaching Secondary Reading, 1966, Communicating with the Community, 1979, History of Robert Morris Class, 1995; editor: Communique, 1968—83, Celebrating Our Legacy--Oral Interviews, 2001; mem. United Meth. Gen. Conf. editl. and revision com.: Book of Discipline, 1996, 2000; contbr. articles. Trustee Columbia Coll., 1958—70, chmn., 1968—70, Greenville County Rehab. Bd., 1974—76; vice chmn. bd. Jr. Achievement, Greenville, 1978—79; mem. S.C. Commn. on Women, Columbia, 1979—88, chmn., 1982—88; pres. United Meth. Women Buncombe St. Ch., Greenville, 1956—57; mem. adminstrv. bd. Buncombe St. Ch., 1968—, trustee, 1980—88, endowment fund bd. trustees, 1994—, chmn., 2001—, co-chair ch. bldg. com., 1999, lay del. to S.C. Ann. Conf., 1986—, mem. commn. on Archives and History, 2001—; mem. United Meth. Ch. Southeastern Jurisdictional Coun. on Ministries, 1980—88, Southeastern Jurisdictional Commn. on Archives and History, 1984—88; chmn. S.C. Conf. Coun. on Ministries United Meth. Ch., 1980—88, del. gen. conf., 1980, 1984, 1988, 1992; mem. S.C. Conf. Commn. Com., 1995—97; chmn. S.C. Conf. Budgeting Task Force, 1996—97; mem. S.C. Conf. Ann. Fund Com. Camps and Retreats, 1998—2001; mem. strategic planning com. Columbia Coll., 1996—97, class agt., 2000—, mem. com. of 150, 2003; mem. Bd. Global Ministries United Meth. Ch., 1972—80, chmn. fin. com., 1976—80; mem. gen. ch. commn. study of ministry United Meth. Ch., 1984—92, mem. gen. ch. coun. ministries, 1988—96, mem. gen. conf. agys. staff and site location com., 1988—96, rschr. missions project West Africa, 1986, chmn. gen. ch. com. legis., 1992—96, chmn. gen. ch. com. on inter-agy. legis., 1992—96, gen. ch. mission agy. site location com., 1993—96, gen. ch. structure com., 1992—96; mem. S.C. Conf. Africa U. Task Force, 2000—01; charter mem. Nat. Mus. Women in Arts, 1978—. Recipient medallion, Columbia Coll., 1980, Alumnae Disting. Svc. award, 1983, Disting. Achievement award, Women's History Week, Greenville, 1984, S.C. Woman of Achievement award, 1988, Clelia D. Hendrix endowment Archives and History at Buncombe St., United Meth. Ch., 2000; established Clelia D. Hendrix Endowed Scholarship, Columbia Coll., 1988. Mem. S.C. PTA (life), Columbia Coll. Alumnae Assn. (life), Dem. Women, S.C. Women in Govt. (bd. dirs. 1985-87), Alpha Delta Kappa (pres. 1970-72, 90-91). Home and Office: 309 Arundel Rd Greenville SC 29615-1303 E-mail: cleliahendrix@aol.com.

HENDRIXSON, LEWIS HOLSTON, retired federal agency administrator; b. Phila., Jan. 13, 1927; s. Lewis H. and Edna (Wagner) H.; m. Sarah George, May 14, 1955 (div. Oct. 1973); children: Karen, Sarah Chapman; m. Eloise Gorton, Aug. 3, 1974. BA, U. Pa., 1950. Cert. intelligence analyst, linguist Nat. Security Agy. Radio/TV repairman Adams TV, Ardmore, Pa., 1950-52; analyst, linguist, data flow mgr., br. chief Nat. Security Agy., Ft. Meade, Md., 1952-87 (ret.). Mem. Radio Amateur Civilian Emergency Svc., 1993—. Mem. Anne Arundel Radio Club (v.p., bd. dirs. 1990-98), Md. Mobileers, Delta Phi Alpha. Republican. Episcopalian. Avocations: amateur radio, music, writing, languages. Home: 1685 Freemont Ct Crofton MD 21114-2312

HENDRIXSON, PETER S. lawyer; b. Wilmington, Del., Apr. 9, 1947; s. Philip Roe and Betty Jane (Schillo) H.; m. Carolyn Hodge Ford, June 14, 1969; children: Julie Elise, Bradley Scott. BA, Northwestern U., 1969; JD magna cum laude, Harvard U., 1972. Bar: Minn. 1973, U.S. Dist. Ct. Minn. 1973, U.S. Supreme Ct. 1978. Law clerk U.S. Ct. Appeals, Boston, 1972-73; assoc., ptnr. trial dept. Dorsey & Whitney, Mpls., 1973—, chair trial dept., 1989-93, chair trial and adminstrv. group, 1994—, mng. ptnr., 2000—. Editor, officer Harvard Law Review, 1970-72. Treas. Fraser for Mayor Com., Mpls., 1983-95; bd. govs. Children's Theatre, Mpls., 1987-92; various positions Mayflower Congl. Ch.; bd. dirs. La Creche Early Childhood Ctrs., Mpls., 1990-98, Children's Home Soc., St. Paul, 1990—, Guthrie Theater, 1995-00. Mem. Minn State Bar (chair anti-trust law sect. 1992-93), Phi Beta Kappa. Democrat. Congregationalist. Office: Dorsey & Whitney LLP 50 S 6th St Ste 1500 Minneapolis MN 55402

HENDRON, MICHAEL G. management consultant; children: Kaden, Bronte, Corbett. BA in polit. sci., Brigham Young U., 1995; MBA, U. Va., 2000. Devel. intern U.S. C. of C., Wash., 1995; bus. devel. coord. Kanematsu USA, Sunnyvale, Calif., 1995—98; supply chain analyst United Technologies Corp., Hartford, Conn., 1999; sr. strategy cons. Alliance Consulting Group, San Jose, Calif., 2000—01; founder Arcwise Consulting, Walnut Creek, Calif., 2001—02. Program co-director ACCESS Big Sibling Program, Provo, Utah, 1993—94; missionary svc. LDS Ch., Japan, 1990—92. Mem.: Golden Key, Phi Kappa Phi.

HENDRY, ANDREW DELANEY, lawyer, consumer products company executive; b. N.Y.C., Aug. 9, 1947; s. Andrew Joseph and Virginia (Delaney) H.; 1 child, Robert. AB in Econs., Georgetown U., 1969; JD, NYU, 1972. Bar: N.Y. 1973. Va. 1981, Mich. 1984, Pa. 1987. Assoc. Battle and Fowler, N.Y.C., 1972-79; sr. corp. and fin. atty. Reynolds Metals Co., Richmond, Va., 1979-82; sr. staff counsel Burroughs Corp., Detroit, 1982-83, assoc. gen. coun., 1983-86, dep. gen. counsel, 1986-87; v.p. legal affairs Unisys Corp, Blue Bell, Pa., 1987-88, v.p., gen. counsel, 1988-91; sr. v.p., gen. counsel, sec. Colgate-Palmolive Co., N.Y.C., 1991—. Mem. adv. bd. Georgetown U. Law Ctr. Corp. Counsel Inst., 1999—; bd. editors The M&A Lawyer, 1996—, The Met. Corp. Counsel, 1993—; adv. bd. Georgetown Coll., 2002. Dir., chmn., corp. adv. bd. Nat. Legal Aid and Def., Washington, 1992—99; dir. Lawyers Alliance for N.Y., 2000—; trustee The O'Neal School, 2001—; mem. Georgetown Coll. Adv. Bd., 2002—. With JAGC USAF, 1973. Fellow: Am. Bar Found.; mem.: ABA (com. on corp. laws, standing com. on substance abuse), Ctrl. European and Eurasian Law Inst. (dir. 2002, 2002), N.Y. State Bar Assn. (steering com. on commerce and industry 1997—), Am. Corp. Counsel Assn. (pres. Mich. chpt. 1985, chmn. nat. pro bono com. 1985—88, bd. dirs. emeritus N.Y. chpt.), Am. Law Inst., N.Y. Athletic Club. Office: Colgate-Palmolive Co 300 Park Ave New York NY 10022-7499

HENDRY, ARCHIBALD WAGSTAFF, physics educator; b. Darvel, Ayrshire, Scotland, Nov. 18, 1936; came to U.S., 1962; s. William and Maggie (Noble) H.; m. Jeanette Marie Brown, June 20, 1964 (dec.); children: Diana Marie, Andrew William, Gordon Austin. BSc, Glasgow (Scotland) U., 1958, PhD, 1962. Rsch. assoc. U. Calif., San Diego, 1962-64; sr. sci. officer Rutherford Lab. Oxford (Eng.) U., 1964-67; rsch. asst. prof. U. Ill., Urbana, 1967-69; asst. prof. Ind. U., Bloomington, 1969-72, assoc. prof., 1972-76, prof. physics, 1976—2001, assoc. dean for budget, 1985-88, prof. emeritus, 2002—. Contbr. articles to sci. jours. Rsch. grantee Dept. Energy, 1970-95; recipient Pres.' award for excellence in tchg., 1993. Mem. AAUP, Am. Assn. Physics Tchrs., Sigma Xi (past treas. local chpt.). Office: Ind U Physics Dept Bloomington IN 47405 E-mail: hendry@indiana.edu.

HENDRY, JOHN, state supreme court justice; b. Omaha, Aug. 23, 1948; BS, U. Nebr., 1970, JD, 1974. Pvt. practice, Licoln, 1974-1995; county ct. judge 3d Jud. Dist., 1995-98; chief justice Nebr. Supreme Ct., 1998—. Office: Rm 2214 State Capitol Lincoln NE 68509*

HENDRY, ROBERT RYON, lawyer; b. Jacksonville, Fla., Apr. 23, 1936; s. Warren Candler and Evalyn Marguerite (Ryon) H.; children by previous marriage: Lorraine Evalyn, Lynette Comstock, Krista Ryon; m. Janet LaCoste. BA in Polit. Sci., U. Fla., 1958, JD, 1963. Bar: Fla. 1963; bd. cert. in internat. law. Assoc. Harrell, Caro, Middlebrooks & Whiltshire, Pensacola, Fla., 1963-66, Hewlliwell, Melrose & DeWolf, Orlando, Fla., 1966-67, ptnr., 1967-69; ptnr., pres. Hoffman, Hendry, Parker & Smith and predecessor Hoffman, Hendry & Parker, Orlando, 1969-77, Hoffman, Hendry & Stoner and predecessor, Orlando, 1977-82, Hendry, Stoner, Sims & Sawicki, Orlando, 1982-88, Hendry, Stoner, Townsend Sawicki & Brown, 1988-92, Hendry, Stoner, Sawicki & Brown, 1992—, Hendry, Stoner, DeLancett & Brown, 2002. Author: U.S. Real Estate and the Foreign Investor, 1983; contbr. articles to profl. jours. Mem. Dist. Export Coun., 1977-91, vice chmn., 1981, chair, 1995—, mem. nat. steering com., 1997—; bd. dirs. World Trade Ctr. and predecessor, Orlando, 1979-89, pres., 1980-82, 84; chmn. Fla. Gov.'s Conf. on World Trade, 1983; chmn. Fla. coun. on internat. edn., 1993-96; mem. internat. fin. and mktg. adv. bd. U. Miami Sch. Bus., Fla., 1979-90, Commn. on Internat. Edn., 1986-88; bd. dirs. Econ. Devel. Commn. of Mid-Fla., 2001—, Metro Orlando Econ. Devel. Commn., 2000—; mem. Metro Orlando Internat. Bus. Coun., 1994-96, Metro Orlando Internat. Affairs Commn., 1995—, Fla. Econ. Summit, 1996-00; mem. internat. trade and econ. devel. bd. and audit com. Enterprise, Fla., 1997-2000; chmn. Fla. Trade Grant Review Panel, 1998-01; mem. adv. com. Enterprise Fla. Internat. Bus. Devel., 2000—; bd. dirs. Gulf of Mexico States Partnership, Inc., 2001—, Golden Rule Found., 2000—, Gulf of Mex. Partnership, Inc., 2000—; co-chair Gulf of Mex. Accord Com. on Legal Infrastructure, 2002—; bd. advisors Fla. Free Trade Area of the Ams., 2001; founding mem. Scottish Exec., 2002—, Orlando Area Com. on Fgn. Affairs, 2002; mem. internat. programs adv. com. U. Fla. Levin Coll. of Law, 2000—. Lt. U.S. Army, 1958-60, capt. Army N.G., 1960-70. Mem. Fla. Coun. Internat. Devel. (bd. dirs. 1972-85, chmn. 1977-79, adv. bd. 1985-95, chmn. emeritus, 1991—, vice chair 1995-96, chair 1996-98), Fla. Bar (bd. cert. internat. lawyer 1999—, vice chmn. internat. law com. 1974-75, chmn. com. 1976-77, mem. exec. coun. internat. law sect. 1982—, original internat. law certification com. 1998—, chmn. 2001—), Fla. Assn. Voluntary Agys. for Caribbean Action (bd. dirs. 1987—, pres. 1989-91, past pres. 1991—), Orange County Bar Assn. (treas. 1971-74), Soc. Internat. Bus. Fellows, Brit.-Am. C. of C. (bd. dirs. 2000—, sec. 1984-85), Swiss Am. C. of C. (sec. Fla. chpt. 1996—), German Am. Bus. Chamber of Fla. Office: Hendry Stoner DeLancett & Brown 200 E Robinson St Ste 500 Orlando FL 32801-1956

HENEGAN, JOHN C(LARK), lawyer; b. Mobile, Ala., Oct. 14, 1950; s. Virgil Baker and Marie (Fife) Gunter; m. Morella Lloyd Kuykendall, Aug. 5, 1972; children: Clark, Jim. BA in English and Philosophy, U. Miss., 1972, JD with honors, 1976. Bar: Miss. 1976, U.S. Dist. Ct. (no. dist.) Miss. 1976, N.Y. 1978, U.S. Dist. Ct. (so. dist.) N.Y. 1979, U.S. Ct. Appeals (5th and 11th cirs.) 1982, U.S. Ct. Appeals (2nd cir.) 1984, U.S. Dist. Ct. (so. dist.) Miss. 1984, U.S. Ct. Appeals (fed. cir.) 1995, U.S. Supreme Ct. 1995. Law clk. to judge U.S. Ct. Appeals (5th cir.), 1976-77; atty. Dewey, Ballantine, Bushby, Palmer & Wood, N.Y.C. and Washington, 1977-81; exec. asst., chief of staff to Gov. William Winter Jackson, Miss., 1981-84; atty. Butler, Snow, O'Mara, Stevens & Cannada, PLLC, Jackson, 1984—. Lectr. U. Miss. Ctr. for Continuing Legal Edn., 1985, 87, Miss. Jud. Coll., Oxford, 1982; mem. lawyers adv. com. U.S. Ct. Appeals for 5th Cir. Jud. Conf., 1991-93. Editor-in-chief Miss. Law Jour., 1976; editor Miss. Lawyer, 1985; contbr. articles to legal jours. Bd. dirs. Mississippians for Ednl. Broadcasting, Jackson, 1983-90, North Jackson Youth Baseball, Inc., 1991-97, Ctr. and Ctrl. S.W. Miss. Legal Svcs., 1997—, Hinds Co. Bar Assn., 2002—; co-pres. Chastain Mid. Sch. Parent Tchrs. Students Assn., 1995-96; mem. Miss. Ethics Commn., Jackson, 1984-87; del. Hinds County Dem. Conv., 1988; mem. Miss. Dem. Fin. Coun., 1988, Hinds County Dem. Exec. Com., 1989-92; Sunday sch. supt. Covenant Presbyn. Ch., 1989-90, elder, 1996-2002, deacon, 1991-96, moderator of diaconate, 1993-94. Recipient Cmty. Svc. award Hinds County Bar Assn., 1998. Mem. ABA, FBA, Miss. Bar Assn. (chmn. Law Day U.S.A. 1983), Miss. Def. Lawyers Assn., Miss. Law Jour. Alumni Assn. (bd. dirs. 1985—), 5th Cir. Bar Assn., Jackson C. of C., Am. Inns of Ct. (barrister Charles Clark chpt. 1991-93), Phi Kappa Phi, Phi Delta Phi, Omicron Delta Kappa. Avocations: reading, running. Home: 2441 Eastover Dr Jackson MS 39211-6727 Office: 210 E Capitol St Fl 17 Jackson MS 39201-2306 E-mail: john.henegan@butlersnow.com.

HENES, DONNA, celebration artist, ritualist, writer; b. Cleve., Sept. 19, 1945; d. Nathan and Adelaide (Ross) Trugman. Student, Ohio State U., 1963-66; BS, CCNY, 1971, MS in Art Edn., 1972. Prodr. series pub. participatory celebratory events in parks, museums and univs., 100 cities in 9 countries, 1970—. Designer Olympic Medalist Tickertape Parade, N.Y.C., 1984; ednl. cons. New Wilderness Foundation, N.Y.C., 1985; judge Jane Addams Peace Assn. Children's Book Award, N.Y.C., 1983-89; ritual cons. Mama Donna's Tea Garden. Author, designer: Dressing Our Wounds in Warm Clothes, 1982, Noting the Process of Noting the Process, 1977, Celestially Auspicious Occasions, 1996, Moon Watcher's Companion, 2002; author, performer (CD) Reverence to Her: Part I Mythology, the Matriarchy & Me, 1998; pub., editor quar. Always in Season: Living in Sync with the Cycles; author (with others): Peace: Piece by Piece; editor: Celebration News, 1986-92; internationally syndicated columnist; contbr. numerous articles to profl. jours. Co-founder, pres. STAND (Stand Together Affirmative Neighborhood Devel.), N.Y.C.; composer Chants for Peace/Chance for Peace, Sta. WNYC, first peace message in space, 1982. Fellow Nat. Endowment for Arts, 1982, interarts, 1983, N.Y. Found. for Arts, 1986, 90; grantee N.Y. State Coun. on Arts, N.Y.C. State Bicentennial Commn., Com. for Visual Arts, Money for Women, Beard's Fund, Jerome Found., Ctr. for the Media Arts; recipient Citation award Mayor of N.Y.C. David Dinkins. Mem. Internat. Ctr. for Celebration (bd. dirs., co-founder). Avocations: dancing, travel, reading, walking, swimming. E-mail: cityshaman@aol.com.

HENES, SAMUEL ERNST, lawyer; b. Oberlin, Ohio, Jan. 28, 1937; s. Ernst Louis and Martha Hannah (Artz) H. AB with honors, Cornell U., 1959; LL.B., Harvard U., 1962. Bar: Ohio, 1962. Assoc. Arter & Hadden, Cleve., 1962-70, ptnr., 1971-89. Trustee Musart Soc., Cleve., 1980—, pres. 1985-94; trustee Young Audiences Greater Cleve., Inc., 1982-85, George P. Bickford Found., 1981-90; hon. trustee So. Lorain County Hist. Soc., Wellington, Ohio, 1988—. Served to 1st lt. U.S. Army, 1963-65 Mem. ABA, Cleve. Bar Assn., Ohio State Bar Assn. Clubs: Rowfant (Cleve.) (sec. 1985-89). Republican. Methodist. Avocations: book collecting, amateur harpsichordist, swimming, travel. Home: 13605 Shaker Blvd Apt 2B Cleveland OH 44120-1503

HENG, GERALD C. W. lawyer; b. London, Mar. 6, 1941; arrived in U.S., 1964; s. Chong-Kwai and York-Choo (Eng); m. Eileen B-Y Tang; 1 child, Sharmaine. BS with honors, Harvard U., 1967; LLM in Taxation, Boston U., 1985; LLB, London U., 1973; JD, Suffolk U., 1983. Tchr. Malay and English langs. Ministry of Edn., Malaysia and Singapore, 1959-60; adminstr. hosp. and health Ministry of Health, Malaysia and Singapore, 1960-64; Fulbright fellow, scholar Inst. Internat. Edn., N.Y.C., 1964-69; atty. Heng Assocs., London,

1973-83, ptnr. Brookline, Mass., 1983—. Contbr. articles to newspapers including Boston Globe, Singapore Mirror, Boston Mag. and community newspapers. Mem. ABA, ATLA, Asian-Am. Lawyers Assn., Internat. Assn. Asian Ams. (pres. Boston chpt. 1981—), Boston Bar Assn. (specialist on internat. trade and human rights 1987—, gen. law practice and coms.), Mass. Acad. Trial Attys. Home and Office: 19 Lillian Rd Framingham MA 01701-4820 E-mail: gcwebheng@gis.net.

HENG, SIANG GEK, communications executive; b. Singapore, Dec. 4, 1960; came to U.S., 1984. m. G.J. Sturgis, 1991. BSEE with honors, Nat. U. Singapore, 1983; MSEE in Computer Engring., U. So. Calif., 1985; MS in Engring. Mgmt., Nat. Technol. U., 1993. Cisco cert. design assoc., cert. network assoc. Rsch. engr. Nat. Univ. Singapore, 1983-84; sys. mgr. LinCom Corp., L.A., 1985-87; fin. planner N.Y. Life Ins. Co., L.A., 1987-88; mem. tech. staff AT&T Bell Laboratories, Holmdel, N.J., 1988-96; sr. mem. tech. staff AT&T, N.J., 1996-2000, prin. tech. staff mem., 2000—. Freelance computer and comm. cons., N.J., 1987-94. Contbr. articles to profl. jours.; patentee in field. Avocations: music, kickboxing, swimming, reading, weightlifting. Office: AT&T Rm A2-2F34 200 S Laurel Ave Middletown NJ 07748-1998

HENGST, HERBERT RANDALL, retired educator; b. Grand Rapids, Mich., May 22, 1924; s. Marion Cecil and L. Elnora H.; m. Georgina Jane, Apr. 1, 1950; children H. Randall II, Julie Ann. AB, Albion Coll., 1948; MS in Edn., Bowling Green State U., 1949; PhD, Mich. State U., 1960. Tchr. Lake Orion (Mich.) H.S., 1949-51; prin. Ortonville (Mich.) H.S., 1951-53, Barnum Jr. H.S., Birmingham, Mich., 1953-58; instr., asst. prof. Mich. State U., East Lansing, 1958-61; dir. higher edn. Mich. Edn. Assn., Lansing, 1961-64; from assoc. prof. to prof. emeritus U. Okla., Norman, 1964—88, prof. emeritus, 1988—, dir. ctr. studies higher edn., 1971-88, interim dean edn., 1973-74. Cons. Ministry Edn. Riyadh, Saudi Arabia, 1972-79, Arab Bur. Edn. Gulf States, Riyadh, 1979-87; vis. prof. King Saud U., Riyadh, 1974-75; lectr. in field. Co-author: Contemporary Educational Administration, 1982; co-author, editor: The Geo Lynn Cross Chrestomathy, 1998; editor: Planning & Utilization of Instructional Space, 1960, An Institutional Profile, 1972. Pastor Emanuel, Meth. Charge Gunnisonville, Lansing, 1958-60; co-founder Okla. Inst. Viable Future, Norman, 1975—; bd. dirs., tchr., conf. del. McFarlin Meth. Ch., 1998-99. Recipient Disting. Flying Cross, USAF, 1945; scholar vis. scholar, Harvard U., 1986. Mem. Canterbury Choral Soc. (life), Omicron Delta Kappa. Democrat. Avocations: reading, gardening, writing poetry, singing. Home: 2643 S Pickard Norman OK 73072

HENGSTLER, GARY ARDELL, publisher, editor, lawyer; b. Wapakoneta, Ohio, Mar. 23, 1947; s. Luther C. and N. Delphine (Sims) H.; m. Linda K. Spreen, Mar. 8, 1969 (div. Aug. 1986); children: Dylan A., Joel S.; m. Laura M. Williams, Dec. 15, 1986. BS, Ball State U., 1969; JD, Cleve. State U., 1983. Bar: Ohio 1984, U.S. Dist. Ct. (no. dist.) Ohio 1984. Assoc. Blaszak, Schilling, Coey & Bennett, Elyria, Ohio, 1984-85; editor The Tex. Lawyer, Austin, 1985-86; news editor ABA Jour., Chgo., 1986-89, editor, pub., 1989-2000; dir. Donald W. Reynolds Nat. Ctr. Cts. & Media, Reno, 2000—. Home: 5055 Carnoustie Dr Reno NV 89502-9724 Office: Donald W Reynolds Nat Ctr Cts & Media U Nev Jud Coll Bldg 358 Reno NV 89557-0001 Fax: 775 327 2160. E-mail: hengstler@judges.org.

HENICK, NITA HALPERN, retired social worker; b. N.Y.C., Mar. 4, 1925; d. Robert A. and Fanny (Wenick) Halpern; m. William Henick, Sept. 11, 1948; children: Daniel M., Arthur R., Susan L. BA, Queens Coll., CUNY, 1945; student, U. Pa., 1946—48; postgrad., CUNY, 1985. Lic. social worker, N.Y.; cert. social worker. From social worker to social work supr. Coler Meml. Hosp., Roosevelt Island, NY, 1967-90, ret. Co-chair N.Y.C. PACE, 1988-89; bd. dirs. Health Svc. Agy., N.Y.C., 1977-90, chmn. task force on long term care, 1988-90; mem. women's rights groups and environ. conservation groups. Fellow Brookdale Inst. on Aging, N.Y.C., 1985; recipient recognition awards N.Y.C. PACE, 1989. Mem. NASW (pres. N.Y.C. chpt. 1988-90, Recognition award 1990), Acad. Cert. Social Workers (N.Y.C. Coun. citation 1990) Democrat. Jewish. Avocations: traveling, reading, walking, lobbying. Home: 21 10 33 Rd Long Island City NY 11106

HENIG, ROBIN MARANTZ, journalist; b. Bklyn., Oct. 3, 1953; d. Sidney S. and Clare (Stern) Marantz; m. Jeffrey R. Henig, June 17, 1973; children: Jessica, Samantha. BA, Cornell U., Ithaca, N.Y., 1973; MSJ, Northwestern U., Evanston, Ill., 1974. Asst. editor, writer The New Physician Mag., Chgo., 1975-77; asst. mng. editor The Blue Sheet, Washington, 1977-78; features and news editor Bio Science Mag., Washington, 1978-80; freelance writer, 1980—. Author: How A Woman Ages, 1985, The Myth of Senility, 1988, Being Adopted, 1993, A Dancing Matrix, 1994, The People's Health, 1997, The Monk in the Garden, 2000, Pandora's Baby, 2004. Alicia Patterson Found. fellow, 2001; finalist Nat. Book Critics Cir. award, 2001. Mem. Am. Soc. Journalists and Authors (pres. D.C. chpt. 1992-94, June Roth award for Med. Writing 1993, 94, Author of the Yr. 1994), Nat. Assn. Sci. Writers (bd. dirs. 1999—), The Authors Guild. Avocations: reading, tap dancing.

HENIG, SUZANNE, retired educator, writer, editor; b. N.Y.C., Jan. 12, 1936; d. Samuel G. and Gicia (Gottesdiener) Henig. BA, NYU, 1957, MA, 1961, PhD, 1968. V.p. Am. Heritage Soc., Washington, 1975-80; editor Va. Woolf Quar., San Diego, 1976-79; pres. India Expo, San Diego, 1976-81; mng. dir. Aeolian Press, San Diego, 1976—. Pres. Genesis Prodns. of Hollywood, San Diego, 1990-96. Editor Internat. Jour. Medicine, 1996; contbr. articles to profl. jours. V.p. N.Y. Young Reps., N.Y.C., 1953-54. Recipient Thomas Wolfe award for poetry NYU, 1957; grantee ACLS, Leopold Schepp Found., Am. Philos. Soc. Address: 5303 La Jolla Hermosa La Jolla CA 92037

HENIGSON, ANN PEARL, freelance writer, songwriter, lyricist; b. N.Y.C., Jan. 20, 1946; d. Leo and Lillian Shires; m. David Henigson, Oct. 23, 1988 (dec. July 1993); stepchildren: Helaine, Kenneth, Keith. Student, U. Miami, Fla., 1964-68, Miami-Dade Jr. Coll. Author: (song/poem) American Flag, 1986, pub. in Congressional Record, 1990, Dreamin' Reality, 1986, Parents, 1986, Miss Liberty, 1986, Eternal Love, 1986, (Looking at You) Face of Love, 1986, Book Without a Cover, 1986, 8 Days of Hanukkah, 1986, Songwriter, 1986, Hanukkah Sing Along, 1988, Oh Baby, Oh Baby, 1991, Hold Me Tight, 1995, Democracy, Democracy, (Freedom, Freedom) 1995, and numerous others; (cartoons/drawings) Ducks/Birds, 1988. Activist, lobbyist; candidate bd. govs. State of Fla., (non-attorney) 1993; 1st female usherette Temple Israel of Greater Miami High Holy Day Svcs.; mem. Civic League Miami Beach, 1976-89; patron Temple Emanu-El Cultural Series, 1989-90; mem. Friends of Bass Mus., 1991; del. nat. Dem. party, 1970s. Mem. ASCAP, Soc. Profl. Journalists, Quill and Scroll, Toastmasters Internat. (named competent toastmaster), Tiger Bay Club, 1974-91, Sigma Delta Chi. Avocations: football, baseball, stamp collecting, travel, designing jewelry.

HENINGER, GEORGE ROBERT, psychiatry educator, researcher; b. L.A., Nov. 15, 1934; s. Owen P. and Rachel (Cannon) H.; m. Julie Hawkes, June 27, 1957; children: Steven, Catharine, Karen, Brian. BS, U. Utah, 1957, MD, 1960. Diplomate Am. Bd. Psychiatry and Neurology. Intern Boston City Hosp., 1960-61; resident in psychiatry Mass. Mental Health Ctr., 1961-63, chief resident, 1963-64; clin. assoc., clin. neuropharmacology rsch. ctr. St. Elizabeth's Hosp. NIMH, Washington, 1964-65, program specialist, office of dir. Bethesda, Md., 1965-66; asst. prof. psychiatry, assoc. chief rsch. ward Yale U., New Haven, 1966-71, assoc. prof., 1971-76, chief rsch. ward, 1971-78, prof. clin. psychiatry, 1976-78, prof. psychiatry, dir. Abraham Ribicoff Rsch. Facilities, 1978-93, assoc. chmn. rsch. dept. psychiatry, 1988-93, dir. lab. clin. and molecular neurobiology, 1993—. Cons. NIMH, 1975-86, 88-94, NIH, 1987, McGill U., 1989, VA, 1990-94, Nat. Rsch. Coun. Can., 1991-93, Nat. Inst. Aging, 1992-93, Wellcome Trust, 1992-94, Pfizer Inc., Merck, Sharp & Dohme, Inc., The Upjohn Co., Hoffman La Roche, Inc., Burroughs Wellcome Co., Bristol-Meyers Co., Squibb Corp., Kali DuPhar, Inc.; bd. sci. advisors, Neurogen Corp. REviewer manuscripts Archives Gen. Psychiatry, Am. Jour. Psychiatry, Psychiatry Rsch., Biol. Psychiatry, Jour. Affective Disorders, Jour. Clin. Psychopharmacology, Life Scis., Neurochemistry Internat., Psychiatry, Schizophrenia Bull., Psychoneuroendocrinology, Jour. AMA. Sr. asst. surgeon USPHS, 1964-66. Recipient Rsch. Sci. Devel. award Type II, NIMH, 1971, 1st prize Anna Monika Found., 1995; grantee NIMH, 1971, 74, 77, 82, 85, 89, 91. Fellow Am. Coll. Neuropsychopharmacology, Am. Psychiat. Assn.; mem. AAAS, Am. Psychopath. Assn., Soc. Neurosci., Soc. Biol. Psychiatry, Psychiat. Rsch. Soc., N.Y. Acad. Scis., Conn. Psychiat. Soc., Sigma Xi, Phi Kappa Phi, Alpha Omega Alpha. Avocation: running. Office: Yale U 34 Park St New Haven CT 06511

HENINGER, SIMEON KAHN, JR., English language educator; b. Monroe, La., Oct. 27, 1922; s. Simeon Kahn and Elsye (Lieber) H.; m. Irene Callen, July 16, 1957; children— Dale Callen, Kathryn Leigh, Philip Ward, Polly Elizabeth, Simeon Kahn III; m. Dorothy Cooper Langston, May 30, 1971 BS, Tulane U., 1944, BA, 1947, MA, 1949; B.Litt. (Fulbright scholar), Oxford (Eng.) U., 1952; PhD, Johns Hopkins U., 1955. Instr. Duke U., Durham, N.C., 1955-57, asst. prof., 1957-62, assoc. prof., 1962-65, prof., 1965-67; prof. English U. Wis.-Madison, 1967-71; chmn. dept. U. Wis., Madison, 1968-70; prof. English U. B.C., Vancouver, Can., 1971-82; disting. prof. English and comparative lit. U. N.C., Chapel Hill, 1982—. Author: A Handbook of Renaissance Meteorology, 1960, Touches of Sweet Harmony, 1974, The Cosmographical Glass, 1977, Sidney and Spenser: The Poet as Maker, 1989, Proportion Poetical: The Subtext of form in the English Renaissance, 1994; editor: Thomas Watson, The Hekatompathia, 1964, Edmund Spenser, Poetry, 1970, Edmund Spenser, Shepheardes Calender, 1979, Kalendar of Sheepehards, 1979, Framing Fact and Fiction: Perspective in Early Modern England, 1992; asst. editor Modern Language Notes, 1953-55; mem. editorial bd. Duquesne Studies in Lang. and Lit., 1976-93, Renaissance and Reformation, 1976-93, Spenser Studies, 1977-93, Studies in English Lit., 1978-93, John Donne Jour., 1982-93, Huntington Libr. Quar., 1982-86, Spenser Newsletter, 1986-92, Studies in Philology, 1987-93, ANQ: A Quarterly Jour., 1988-93; contbr. articles to profl. jours. Exec. sec.-treas. Southeastern Renaissance Conf., 1958-67; mem. Nat. Shakespeare Anniversary Com., 1963-64; mem. ctrl. exec. com. Folger Inst. Renaissance and 18th Century Studies, 1982-92. Capt. USAAF, 1943-46. Folger Library fellow, 1961, Guggenheim fellow, 1962-63, Southeastern Inst. Medieval and Renaissance Studies fellow, 1967, Huntington Library fellow, 1970-71, 81, Killam Sr. fellow, 1975-76, Folger Inst. fellow, 1984, Ariz. Ctr. for Medieval and Renaissance Studies fellow, 1990. Mem. MLA, ACLU, Renaissance Soc. Am. (adv. coun. 1958-68, 75-80), Spenser Soc. (adv. coun. 1977-80, 86-90, pres. 1988-89), Milton Soc. (adv. coun. 1980-83), Medieval Acad. Am., Phi Beta Kappa Home: 750 Weaver Dairy Rd #247 Chapel Hill NC 27514-1493 E-mail: timdothening@mindspring.com.

HENINGTON, C. DAYLE, retired economist; b. Bartlett, Tex., Mar. 2, 1931; s. Clarence William and Ora (Robbins) H.; m. Julianne, Mar. 12, 1983. BA in Econs., U. Nebr., 194. Enlisted USAF, 1951, commd. 1st lt., 1952, advanced through grades to maj., 1971, ret., 1971; adminstrv. asst. Congressman W.R. Poage, Washington, 1971-77; sr. v.p. Chgo. Mercantile Exch., 1977-92; cons. San Antonio, Tex., 1992—. Democrat. Unitarian Universalist. Home: 10955 Wurzbach Rd Apt 104 San Antonio TX 78230-2537

HENINGTON, DAVID MEAD, library director; b. El Dorado, Ark., Aug. 16, 1929; s. Bud Henry and Lucile Check (Scranton) H.; m. Barbara Jean Gibson, June 2, 1956; children— Mark David, Gibson Mead, Paul Billins. BA, U. Houston, 1951; MS in L.S., Columbia U., 1956. Young adult libr. Bklyn. Pub. Libr., 1956-58; head lit. and history dept. Dallas Pub. Libr., 1958, asst. dir., 1962-67; dir. Waco (Tex.) Pub. Libr., 1958-62, Houston Pub. Libr., 1967-95. Served with USAF, 1951-55. Council on Library Resources fellow, 1970-71; recipient Liberty Bell award Houston Bar Assn., 1976 Mem. ALA, AIA (hon. mem. Tex. chpt.), Am. Mgmt. Assn., Tex. Libr. Assn. (Libr. of Yr. 1976, Disting. Svc. award 1993), Philos. Soc. Methodist. Home: 6225 San Felipe St Houston TX 77057-2809 E-mail: dmhenington@evl.com.

HENISCH, HEINZ KURT, retired physics educator; b. Neudek, Czechoslovakia, Apr. 21, 1922; came to U.S., 1963; s. Leo and Fanny (Soicher) H.; m. Bridget Ann Wilsher, Feb. 6, 1960. BSc, U. Reading, Eng., 1942, PhD, 1949, DSc, 1979. Lectr. U. Reading, 1948-63; prof. physics Pa. State U., University Park, 1963-93, prof. history of photography, 1979-93, prof. emeritus, 1993—. Author 14 books in fields; founder, editor Materials Rsch. Bull., 1966-94, History of Photography, 1977-90; contbr. over 165 articles to profl. jours. Fellow Inst. for Arts and Humanistic Studies, Am. Phys. Soc., Royal Photography Soc., Am. Photographic History Soc. Avocations: writing, piano. Home: 346 Hillcrest Ave State College PA 16803-3416

HENKE, DAN, law educator; b. San Antonio, Feb. 18, 1924; BS, Georgetown U., 1943, JD, 1951; LLM, U. Wash., 1956. Bar: Tex. 1951, D.C. 1951, Calif. 1962, U.S. Supreme Ct. 1959. Bus. economist, office bus. econs. Dept. Commerce, Washington, 1948-51; practice law San Antonio, 1951-55; asst. to law libr. U. Wash., Seattle, 1955-56; head N.J. Bur. Law and Legis. Reference, Trenton, 1956-59; lectr. law U. Calif., Berkeley, 1959-64, prof., 1965-70, law libr., 1959-70; prof. law, dir. legal info. ctr. Calif. Hastings Coll. Law, San Francisco, 1970-91, emeritus prof. law, 1991—. Cons. Am. Bar Found., 1965-66, Fed. Jud. Ctr., 1976. Author: (with Mortimer D. Schwartz) Anglo American Law Collections, 1971, California Legal Research Handbook, 1971, California Law Guide, 1976, (with Betty W. Taylor) Law in the Digital Age: The Challenge of Research in Legal Information Centers, 1996; contbr. articles to legal jours. Mem. ABA, ALA, State Bar Calif. (chmn. com. on computers and the law 1975-76), Am. Judicature Soc., Am. Assn. Law Librs. (Disting. Svc. award 1996), Am. Soc. Info. Sci., Assn. Am. Law Schs., Order of Coif, Beta Phi Mu. Office: 200 Mcallister St Ste 407 San Francisco CA 94102-4707 E-mail: dfhenke@aol.com.

HENKE, JANICE CARINE, educational software developer and marketer; b. Hunter, N.D., Jan. 28, 1938; d. John Leonard and Adeline (Hagen) Hanson; children: Toni L., Tom L., Tracy L. BS, U. Minn., 1965; postgrad., misc. schs., 1969—. Cert. elem. tchr., Minn., Iowa. Tchr. dance, 1953-56; tchr. kindergarten Des Moines Pub. Schs., 1964-65; tchr. elem. Ind. Sch. Dist. 284, Wayzata, Minn., 1969-93; pvt. bus. history Wayzata, 1978—; marketer, promoter health enhancement Jeri Jacobus Cosmetics Aloe Pro, Am. Choice Nutrition, Multiway, KM Matol, Wayzata, 1978—; developer ednl. software, marketer of software Computer Aided Teaching Concepts, Excelsior, Minn., 1983—; Edn. Minn. authorized rep. with Midwest Benefit Advisers, Excelsior, 1993—. Developer, author drug edn. curriculum, Wayzata, 1970-71; mem. programs com. Health and Wellness, Wayzata, 1988-93; chmn. Wayzata Edn. Assn. Ins. Com., 1991-93; mem. Staff Devel. Adv. Bd., Wayzata, 1988-93; coach Odyssey of the Mind, 1989-93. Author, developer computer software; contbr. articles to newspapers. Fundraiser Ind. Reps. Wayzata, 1976-79; mem. pub. rels. com. Lake Minnetonka (Minn.) Dist. Ind. Reps., 1979-81, fundraising chmn., 1981-82; chmn. Wayzata Ind. Reps., 1981-82; sec. PTO, Wayzata, 1981-82. Mem. NEA, Minn. Edn. Assn., Wayzata Edn. Assn. (bd. mem., ins. chairperson). Lutheran. Avocations: swimming, skiing, traveling, reading, learning. Office: Henke Services Inc 20380 Excelsior Blvd Excelsior MN 55331-8733 E-mail: jhenke8464@hotmail.com.

HENKE, MICHAEL JOHN, lawyer, educator; b. Evansville, Ind., Aug. 3, 1940; s. Emerson Overbeck and Beatrice (Arney) H.; m. Leni Edith Anderson, Mar. 20, 1966; children: Blake, Paige, Britt. BA summa cum laude, Baylor U., 1962, LLB, 1965; LLM, NYU, 1966. Bar: Tex. 1965, D.C. 1967. Assoc. Covington & Burling, Washington, 1966-73, Vinson & Elkins, Washington, 1974-76, ptnr., 1976—. Adj. prof. U. Va. Law Sch., 1988-94, 96—; chmn. pro bono adv. com. Legal Aid Soc., D.C., 1990-96, trustee, 1992—, chmn. ways & means com., 1997-2000, v.p., 2000—02, pres., 2002—; Washington adv. coun. Baylor Washington Program, 1989-92; sesquicentennial coun. of 150 Baylor U., 1993-95. Author: (with others) Petroleum Regulation Handbook, 1980, Natural Gas Yearbook, 1995; mem. editl. bd. Nat. Gas Mag., 1992-97, Best Lawyers in America, 1989—, Best Lawyers in Washington, 1997, Worlds Leading Competition and Antitrust Lawyers, 1997—, World's Leading Litigation Lawyers, 1997—; contbr. articles to profl. jours. Founder, chmn. Old Presbyn. Meeting House Day Care Ctr., Alexandria, Va., 1970-74; trustee Alexandria Country Day Sch., 2000-03. Kenneson fellow. Mem. ABA (chmn. energy antitrust subcom. litigation sect. 1987-88, vice chmn. energy litigation com. 1988-89, chmn. 1989-92, chmn. ann. fall meeting 1993, divsn. dir. 1993-95, co-chmn. audiotaping and videotaping com. 1995-96, co-chmn. ins. coverage litigation com. 1996-98, coun. 1998-2001, co-chair task force on judiciary 2001—, Pres.'s Commn. on 21st Century Judiciary 2002-03), D.C. Bar Assn., Tex. Bar Assn., Coll. State Bar Tex., Baylor U. Alumni Assn. (bd. dirs. 1994-98), Am. Civil Trial Bar Roundtable, Met. Club, Belle Haven Country Club, Farmington Country Club (Charlottesville). Democrat. Avocations: skiing, flyfishing, tennis, backpacking. Home: 310 Charles Alexander Ct Alexandria VA 22301-1500 Office: Vinson & Elkins 1455 Pennsylvania Ave NW Fl 7 Washington DC 20004-1013 E-mail: mhenke@velaw.com.

HENKE, ROBERT JOHN, lawyer, mediator, consultant, engineer; b. Chgo., Oct. 13, 1934; s. Raymond Anthony and May Dorothy (Driscoll) H.; m. Mary Gabrielle Handrigan, June 18, 1960; children: Robert Joseph, Ann Marie. BSEE, U. Ill., 1956; MBA, U. Chgo., 1964; JD, No. Ill. U., 1979; postgrad., John Marshall Law Sch. Bar: Ill. 1980, Wis. 1980, U.S. Dist. Ct. (no. dist.) Ill. 1980, U.S. Dist. Ct. (we. and ea. dists.) Wis. 1980, U.S. Supreme Ct. 1984; registered profl. engr., Ill, Wis. Sr. elec. engr. Commonwealth Edison Co., Chgo., 1956-80; elec. engr. Peterson Builders, Sturgeon Bay, Wis., 1982-83; sr. elec., cost estimating engr. Sargent & Lundy Engrs., Chgo., 1985-94; instr. econs. and criminal law NE Wis. Tech. Inst., 1981-82; asst. dist. atty. Door County, Wis., 1981, ct. commr., 1981-82, sole practice, 1981-84, Lake County, Ill., 1984-94; pvt. practice cons., mediator Fish Creek, Wis., 1995-99; cons. Pittsboro, N.C., 1999—. Dir. Scand. Door County, 1981-82. Vice chmn. Door County Bd. Adjustment, 1983-84; atty. coach Wis. Bar Found. H.S. Moot Ct. Competition, Door County, 1984; vol. lawyers program, Lake County, Ill., 1985-95; sec., counsel, bd. dirs. Woodland Hills Condominium Assn., Gurnee, Ill., 1993-94. Served with USAR, 1958-63. Recipient award for pro bono work, 1994. Mem. ABA, IEEE, Wis. Bar Assn., Door Kewaunee Bar Assn. (pres. 1983-84), Chgo. Bar Assn., Am. Assn. Cost Engrs. Roman Catholic.

HENKE, SHAUNA NICOLE, police dispatcher, small business owner; b. San Bernardino, Calif., Oct. 25, 1966; d. Gary Duane and Pamela Denyne (Duke) H. BA, U. San Francisco, 1988. Cert. police officer std. and tng. dispatcher, Calif.; internat. telecommunicator instr. tng. cert. Assn. Pub. Safety Comm. Ofcls. Pub. rels. dir. Sta. KUSF Radio, San Francisco, 1986; theater and recreational asst. Hamilton Field Recreation, Novato, Calif., 1986-89; morning asst., newswriter Sta. KTID Radio, San Rafael, Calif., 1987-88; dispatcher Warren Security, San Rafael, Calif., 1988-89; pub. safety dispatcher Twin Cities Police Dept., Larkspur/Corte Madera, Calif., 1989-94; family svc. worker Head Start, Bogalusa, La., 1994-95; police dispatcher Mandeville (La.) Police Dept., 1995-96, Bogalusa (La.) Police Dept., 1996—; EMS Dispatcher Lifeline EMS, Bogalusa, 1998-2000. Co-owner Eastern Designs. Mem. St. Matthew's Episcopal Churchwomen, Washington Parish. Mem.: Assn. Pub. Safety Ofcls. Internat., Caledonian Soc. of New Orleans. Office: Bogalusa Police Dept 214 Arkansas Ave Bogalusa LA 70427-3810 E-mail: nick0166@yahoo.com.

HENKEL, ARTHUR JOHN, investment banker; b. Bklyn., Aug. 27, 1945; s. Arthur John and Catherine Rita (Burns) H.; m. Coralee S. Olicker, Sept. 27, 1981; children: Andrea Rae, Austin Olicker, Reid Baras, Kyra Leigh. USPHS trainee U. Chgo. Hosps., Clinics, 1969-71, adminstrv. asst. fiscal affairs, 1971; cons. Booz, Allen Hamilton, Inc., N.Y.C., 1972-74; dir. ambulatory ops. New Eng. Med. Ctr. Hosp., Boston, 1974-75, dir. ambulatory care, 1975-77; assoc. mcpl. fin. dept. Kidder, Peabody and Co., Inc., N.Y.C., 1977-78, asst. v.p., 1978-79, v.p., 1979-80, mng. officer health fin. group, 1980-87, dir., 1984-87, mng. dir., 1986-87; v.p. mcpl. fin. dept. Goldman, Sachs & Co., N.Y.C., 1987-95; v.p. Shattuck Hammond Ptnrs., Inc., N.Y.C., 1995-96, mng. dir., 1996-98, Bear, Stearns & Co., Inc., N.Y.C., 1998—. Instr. cmty. health Tufts Sch. Medicine; exec. com. alumni coun. U. Chgo. Program Hosp. Adminstrn., 1972-76; spl. teaching cons. fin. evaluation hosp. capital projects HEW, 1973. Chmn. investments com. Better Boys Found./ NFL Players Assn. awards banquet, 1979, 80—. Recipient Mary Bachmeyer award U. Chgo., 1971, citation Commonwealth Mass., 1976.

HENKEL, DAVID SEABURY, retired lawyer; b. Chatham, Va., Sept. 6, 1913; s. David Socrates and Elizabeth Wood (Vaughan) H.; m. Charlotte Eliot; m. 2d Helen Snow, July 30, 1954; children— Charlotte, David Seabury, Jr. B.A., U. Richmond, 1933; LL.B., U. Va., 1936. Bar: Va. 1935, N.Y. 1937, U.S. Ct. Appeals (2d cir.) 1964, U.S. Dist. Ct. (ea. dist.) N.Y. 1964, U.S. Supreme Ct. 1964. Ptnr., Sullivan & Cromwell, N.Y.C., from 1936, now ret.; dir. USLIFE Corp., The Gen. Tire & Rubber Co. Served to 1st lt. U.S. Army, 1944-46. Mem. ABA, Assn. Bar City N.Y., N.Y. County Lawyers Assn., N.Y. State Bar Assn., Am. Law Inst. Office: 250 Park Ave New York NY 10177-0001

HENKEL, HERBERT LUDWIG, manufacturing executive; b. Austria, 1948; BS in Aerospace Engring. and Applied, MS in Mech. Engring., Poly. U.; MBA, Pace U. Mem. tech. staff Bell Labs.; design engr. Grumman Aerospace; v.p. sales and mktg. Chgo. Pneumatic Tool Co., Hilti, Inc.; pres., COO Southern Fastening Sys. and Unifast Industries, Inc.; pres. Greenlee Textron, Rockford, Ill., 1987-93; pres. indsl. products segments Textron, Inc., 1993-98, exec. v.p., 1998-99, COO, 1998-2000, pres., 1999-2000; also chmn.; CEO Ingersoll-Rand, Woodcliff Lake, N.J., 2000—; chmn., pres., 2000—. Bd. dirs. Pitney-Bowes, C.R. Bard Corp. Office: Ingersoll-Rand 200 Chestnut Ridge Rd Woodcliff Lake NJ 07677

HENKEL, KATHRYN GUNDY, lawyer; b. West Columbia, Tex., Oct. 16, 1952; d. Louis Ory Jr. and Patricia Dolores (Fields) Gundy. BA cum laude, Rice U., 1973; JD cum laude, Harvard U., 1976. Bar: Tex. 1976, U.S. Dist. Ct. (no. dist.) Tex. 1982, U.S. Ct. Appeals (5th cir.) 1994, U.S. Tax Ct. 1981, U.S. Supreme Ct. 1983; bd. cert. estate planning and probate law, Tex. Bd. Legal Specialization. Ptnr. Hughes & Luce, L.L.P., Dallas, 1982—. Author: Estate Planning and Wealth Preservation: Strategies and Solutions, 1997; mem. editl. bd. Estate Planning Mag. Mem. adv. coun. Cmtys. Found. Tex. Inc., 1982—; mem. planned giving adv. com. Children's Med. Ctr., Dallas; bd. dirs., chmn. bd. advisors to found. com. Dallas Opera. Fellow Am. Coll. Trust and Estate Counsel; mem. ABA (vice chair sect. real property, probate and trusts com. on generation-skipping transfers 1992-95, chair sect. of taxation com. on estate and gift taxes 1993-95, coun. dir. sect. taxation 1996-99, co-chair sect. real property, probate and trust law estate planning study com. on law reform), State Bar Tex. (chair sect. taxation 1992-93), Dallas Bar Assn. (past chair sect. taxation), Tex. Bar Found. Roman Catholic. Avocations: reading, travel. Office: Hughes & Luce LLP 1717 Main St Ste 2800 Dallas TX 75201-4685 E-mail: henkelk@hughesluce.com.

HENKELMAN, WALLACE JAMES, critical care nurse, educator; b. Merrill, Wis., Oct. 13, 1946; s. Clarence Henry and Janice Paula Henkelman; m. Anne Marie Halligan, June 5, 1982. MSN, BSN, U. of Tex., San Antonio, TX; BS Zoology, U. of Wis., Madison, WI. Ccrn, AACN, 1985. Nursing instr. C.C. of So. Nev., Las Vegas, Nev., 2001—; intensive care staff nurse Reliable Health Care Services, Las Vegas, Nev., 2003—; clin. nurse specialist Sunrise Hosp., Las Vegas, Nev., 1994—2001. Contbr. articles to nursing jours. Vol. lobbyist Mont. Nurses Assn., Gt. Falls, Mont. 1st. lt. U.S. Army, 1969—84. Decorated Bronze Star for Valor US Army. Mem.: AACN (licentiate), ANA, Am. Assn. of Pain Mgmt. Nurses (licentiate), Nev. Nurses Assn. (licentiate), Nat. Honor Soc., Phi Beta Kappa, Sigma Theta Tau (licentiate). Democrat. Avocations: travel, fishing, hiking. Home: 72 Desert Rain Ct Henderson NV 89074 Personal E-mail: wallyhenk@aol.com.

HENKEN, BERNARD SAMUEL, clinical psychologist, speech pathologist; b. Everett, Mass., May 30, 1919; s. Issac Edward and Sarah B. (Shatzman) H.; m. Charlotte Popovsky, Dec. 20, 1953; children: Karen Beth, Donna Michele. Student, Boston Coll., 1938-41; BS, Harvard U., 1947; MS, Purdue U., 1950; D. Sci. in Psychology, Calvin Coolidge Coll., 1955. Lic. psychologist, cert. sch. psychologist, cert. rehab. counselor, lic. speech pathologist, Mass.; diplomate Am. Assn. Clin. Counselors. Psychologist Carney Hosp., Boston, 1950-51; dir. speech pathology, psychologist Audiology Ctr., Lynn, Mass., 1951-56; psychologist, chief clin. counseling svcs. Brusch Med. Ctr., Cambridge, Mass., 1956-80; speech pathologist Mass. Gen. Hosp., Boston, 1951-52; speech pathologist, sch. psychologist Everett Pub. Schs., 1955-85; psychologist Rescue Inc., 1959-71, v.p., 1972-74; psychologist, clin. counselor North Shore Children's Hosp., Salem, Mass., 1966-74; psychologist Medford (Mass.) Pediatric Assocs., 1974-94. Prof. psychology Calvin Coolidge Coll., Boston, 1958-69; lectr. psychology Lawrence Meml. Hosp., Medford, Mass., 1975-77, univ. extension courses Harvard U., 1960-68; psychologist Alfano Med. Inst., Melrose, Mass., 1956-64; guest lectr. Duke U. Med. Ctr., 1965, 72; co-chair symposium on clin. counseling and medicine Tufts U., 1974. Contbr. articles to profl. jours.; creator Henken Operator Safety Evaluation Technique; editor Clin. Counseling Bulletin, 1970-84. Cpl. M.C., U.S. Army, 1942-45, PTO. Recipient Lifetime Achievement award Mass. Sch. Psychology, 2001. Mem. APA (charter mem. divsn. of psychotherapy), Am. Coll. Counselors (cert. forensic psychol-

ogy), Nat. Assn. Sch. Psychologist Assn. (nat. cert. in sch. psychology), Am. Coll. Counselors, Mass. Speech and Hearing Assn. (treas. 1957-59), Am. Assn. Clin. Counselors (pres. 1959-63), Mass. Sch. Psychologists Assn. (pres. 1972-74). Republican. Jewish. Avocations: sports, music. Home and Office: 118 Waverly Ave Melrose MA 02176-4217

HENKIN, LEON ALBERT, mathematician, educator; b. Bklyn., Apr. 19, 1921; s. Ascher and Rose (Goldberg) H.; m. Ginette Potvin, Sept. 8, 1950; children: Paul Jacques, Julian David. AB, Columbia U., 1941; MA, Princeton U., 1942, PhD, 1947; DS (hon.), U. Ill., Chgo., 1995. Mathematician, Manhattan Dist. Project, 1942-46; Henry B. Fine instr., Frank Jewett postdoctoral fellow Princeton, 1947-49; from asst. prof. to asso. prof. math. U. So. Calif., 1949-53; faculty U. Calif.-Berkeley, 1953-91, prof. math., 1958-91, prof. emeritus, 1991—, chmn. dept., 1966-68, 83-85. Vis. prof. Dartmouth Coll., 1960-61; Fulbright rsch. scholar, Amsterdam, The Netherlands, 1954-55, Technion, Haifa, Israel, spring 1979; Guggenheim fellow, mem. Inst. Advanced Study, Princeton, 1961-62; vis. fellow All Souls Coll., Oxford (Eng.) U., 1968-69; vis. scholar U. Colo., 1975, U. de Paris VII, 1987; Disting. vis. prof. Mills Coll., 1990-95. Author: La Structure Algebrique des theories Mathématique, 1955, (with others) Retracing Elementary Mathematics, 1962, Cylindric Algebras, Part I, 1971, Part II, 1985, Cylindric Set Algebras, 1981 also articles. Mem. U.S. Commn. on Math. Instrn., 1978-83, chmn., 1981-82. Fellow AAAS (coun. del. for math. sect.); mem. Nat. Coun. Tchrs. Math., Assn. Symbolic Logic (pres. 1962-64), Am. Math. Soc. (coun. 1962-64), Math. Assn. Am. (Chauvenet prize 1964, Yueh-Gin Gung and Dr. Charles Y. Hu award 1990), Can. Math. Soc., Assn. for Women in Math., Nat. Assn. Math., ACLU (bd. dirs. Berkeley chpt. 1964-66), Phi Beta Kappa (vis. lectr. 1993-94), Sigma Xi. Home: 9 Maybeck Twin Dr Berkeley CA 94708-2037 Address: Univ of CA-Berkeley Dept Of Mathematics Berkeley CA 94720-3840 E-mail: henkin@math.berkeley.edu.

HENKIN, LOUIS, lawyer, law educator; b. Russia, Nov. 11, 1917; came to U.S., 1923, naturalized, 1930; s. Yoseph Elia and Frieda Rebecca (Kreindel) H.; m. Alice Barbara Hartman, June 19, 1960; children: Joshua, David, Daniel. AB, Yeshiva Coll., 1937; DHL, Yeshiva U., 1963; LLB, Harvard U., 1940; LLD, Columbia U., 1995; JD (hon.), Bklyn. Law Sch., 1997; LLD, Jewish Theol. Sem., 2003. Bar: N.Y. 1941, U.S. Supreme Ct. 1947. Law clk. to Judge Learned Hand, 1940-41; law clk. to Justice Frankfurter, 1946-47; cons. legal dept. UN, 1947-48; with State Dept., 1945-46, 48-57; U.S. rep. UN Com. Refugees and Stateless Persons, 1950; adviser U.S. del. UN Econ. and Social Coun., 1950, UN Gen. Assembly, 1950-53, Geneva Conf. on Korea, 1954; assoc. dir. Legis. Drafting Rsch. Fund, lectr. law Columbia U., 1956-57; prof. law U. Pa., 1958-62; prof. internat. law and diplomacy, prof. law Columbia U., 1962, mem. Inst. War and Peace Studies, 1962—, Hamilton Fish prof. internat. law and diplomacy, 1963-78, Harlan Fiske Stone prof. constl. law, 1978-79, univ. prof., 1979-88, univ. prof. emeritus and spl. svc. prof., 1988—; co-dir. Ctr. for Study of Human Rights, 1978-86, chmn. of directorate, 1986—. U.S. mem. Permanent Ct. Arbitration, 1963-69; adviser U.S. Del. UN Conf. on Law of the Sea, 1972-80; adv. panel on internat. law Dept. State, 1975-80, 93—; human rights com. U.S. Commn. for UNESCO, 1977-80, Internat. Covenant Civil and Polit. Rights, 1999-2002; Carnegie lectr. Hague Acad. Internat. Law, 1965; Frankel lectr. U. Houston, 1969; Gottesman lectr. Yeshiva U., 1975; Lockhart lectr. U. Minn. Law Sch., 1976; Francis Biddle lectr. Harvard Law Sch., 1978; lectr. Columbia U., 1979; Sherrill lectr. Yale U. Law Sch., 1981; Jefferson lectr. U. Pa. Law Sch., 1983; Irvine lectr. Cornell U., 1986; disting. lectr. Coll. Physicians and Surgeons, Columbia U., 1988; Solf lectr. Judge Adv. Gen.'s Sch., 1988; Cooley lectr. U. Mich. Law Sch., 1988; White lectr. La. State U., 1989; prin. lectr. The Hague Acad. Internat. Law, 1989; Blaine Sloane lectr. Pace U. Law Sch., 1991; Gerber lectr. U. Md. Law Sch., 1991; Nathanson lectr. law sch. U. San Diego, 1994; Sibley lectr. U. Ga. Law Sch., 1994; Brandeis lectr. Israel Acad. Scis. and Humanities, 1994; Phi Kappa Phi lectr., James Madison U., 1996, Doris and A. Leo Levin lectr. Bar Ilan U., Israel, 1996; cons. to govt., pres. U.S. Inst. Human Rights, 1970-93, Robert L. Levine lectr. Fordham Law Sch.; chief reporter Am. Law Inst., Restatement of the Law (3d), Fgn. Rels. Law of the U.S., 1979-87; bd. dirs. Lawyers Com. Human Rights, Immigration and Refugee Svcs. Am., v.p., 1994—; pres. Am. Soc. Internat. Law, 1992-94; vis. prof. law U. Pa., 1957-58; mem. human rights com. UN, 2000-02. Author: Arms Control and Inspection in American Law, 1958, The Berlin Crisis and the United Nations, 1959, Disarmament: The Lawyer's Interests, 1964, Law for the Sea's Mineral Resources, 1968, Foreign Affairs and the Constitution, 1972, 2nd edit., 1996, The Rights of Man Today, 1978, How Nations Behave: Law and Foreign Policy, 2nd edit., 1979; (with others) Human Rights in Contemporary China, 1986, Right v. Might: International Law and the Use of Force, 1989, 2nd edit., 1991, The Age of Rights, 1990, Constitutionalism, Democracy and Foreign Affairs, 1990, International Law: Politics and Values, 1995; editor: Arms Control: Issues for the Public, 1961, (with others) Transnational Law in a Changing Society, 1972, World Politics and the Jewish Condition, 1972, The International Bill of Rights: The International Covenant of Civil and Political Rights, 1981; (with others) International Law: Cases and Materials, 3d edit., 1993, 4th edit., 2001, Constitutionalism and Rights: The Influence of the United States Constitution Abroad, 1989, Foreign Affairs and the U.S. Constitution, 1990, Human Rights: Cases and Materials, 1999; bd. editors: Am. Jour. Internat. Law, 1967—, co-editor-in-chief, 1978-84; bd editors Ocean Devel. and Internat. Law Jour., 1973—, Jerusalem Jour. Internat. Relations, 1976—; contbr. articles to profl. jours. Served with AUS, 1941-45. Decorated Silver Star; recipient Law Alumni medal of excellence Columbia U. Sch. Law, 1982, Friedmann Meml. award Columbia Soc. Internat. law, 1986, Hudson medal Am. Soc. Internat. Law, 1995, Leadership in Human Rights award Columbia Human Rights Law Rev., 1995, Human Rights award Lawyers Com. for Human Rights, 1995, Outstanding Rsch. in Law and Govt. award Fellows of Am. Bar Found., 1997, Stefan Riesenfeld award U. Calif., 2003; Guggenheim fellow, 1979-80; Festschrift (Liber Amicorum): Politics, Values and Functions, Internat. Law in the 21st Century, Essays on Internat. Law in his honor, 1997, Louis Henkin Professorship in Human and Constitutional Rights established in his honor Columbia Law Sch., 1999. Fellow Am. Acad. Arts and Scis.; mem. Coun. Fgn. Rels., Am. Soc. Internat. Law (v.p. 1975-76, 88-90, pres. 1992-94, hon. v.p. 1994—, Goler T. Butcher medal for outstanding contbn. to internat. human rights law 2001), Internat. Law Assn. (v.p. Am. br., 1973—), Am. Soc. Polit. and Legal Philosophy (pres. 1985-87), Inst. de Droit Internat., Am. Polit. Sci. Assn., Internat. Assn. Constl. Law (v.p. 1982-95, hon. pres. 1995—), U.S. Assn. Constl. Law (hon. pres. 1997—), Am. Philos. Soc. (Henry M. Phillips prize in jurisprudence 2000). Home: 460 Riverside Dr New York NY 10027-6801 E-mail: henkin@law.columbia.edu.

HENKIN, ROBERT IRWIN, neurobiologist, internal medicine, nutrition and neurology educator, scientific products company executive, taste and smell disease physician; b. L.A., Oct. 5, 1930; s. William and Ida Mildred (Scher) H.; m. Marsha Lynn Jacobs, May 15, 1964 (div. Jan. 1982); children: Amanda Joan, Michael Jonathan, David Gorman, Joshua Adam, Elizabeth Madeline, Hannah Deborah. AB cum laude, U. So. Calif., 1951; MA, UCLA, 1953, PhD, 1956, MD, 1959. Intern in medicine U. Calif. Hosp., L.A., 1959-60; resident in medicine Jackson Meml. Hosp., U. Miami (Fla.), 1960-61; commd. officer USPHS, 1961, advanced through grades to sr. surgeon, resigned, 1975; rsch. assoc. Nat. Inst. Mental Health, NIH, Bethesda, Md., 1961-63, sr. investigator, 1963-69; chief sect. on neuroendocrinology Nat. Heart and Lung Inst., NIH, Bethesda, Md., 1969-75; dir. Ctr. Molecular Nutrition and Sensory Disorders Georgetown U. Med. Ctr., Washington, 1975-85, assoc. prof. pediatrics and neurology, 1975-82, dir. Taste and Smell Clinic, 1985—, prof., 1982—. Pres., CEO Sialon Corp., Washington, 1987—; cons. Campbell Soup Co., 1969-74, USDA/NIH, 1975—, Hooker Chem. Co., Buffalo, 1976-77, Washington Conf. for Zinc, 1985—, Florasynth, N.Y.C., 1986-91, Squibb Pharm. Co., N.Y.C., 1986-87. Author: Zinc, 1975; contbr. articles to profl. jours.; patentee saliva, taste diagnostics, wound healing protein, drugs to treat taste/smell disorders. Recipient Vicennial medal Georgetown U., 1984; Atwater Kent fellow UCLA, 1957, Giovanni di Chiro Sci. award, 1998; grantee Dept. Def., USDA, NIH and various NIH insts., 1969—. Fellow Am. Coll. Nutrition; mem. Biophys. Soc. (charter), Am. Physiol. Soc., Am. Soc. of Nutrition, Am. Soc. Clin. Nutrition, Am. Fedn. Med. Rsch., Am. Soc. Clin. Investigation, Composers Guild Am., Cosmos Club, Phi Beta Kappa, Sigma Xi (nat. lectr. 1984-87, Giovanni di Chiro Sci. award 1998). Avocations: tennis, running, skiing. Home: 6601 Broxburn Dr Bethesda MD 20817-4709 Office: Ctr Mol Nutrn/Sensory Disorders Taste and Smell Clin 5125 MacArthur Blvd NW Ste 20 Washington DC 20016-3300 Fax: 202-364-9727. E-mail: doc@tasteandsmell.com.

HENKLE, JAMES L. industrial designer; b. Cedar Rapids, Iowa, Mar. 13, 1927; s. Elmer E. and Helen Cecile (Black) H.; m. Dorothy Eleanor Shirley, Sept. 7, 1957; 1 child, Gregory Lee. BA, U. Nebr., 1949; Cert. in Indsl. Design, Pratt Inst., 1951. Designer Dave Chapman Indsl. Design, Chgo., 1952-53; tchr. design U. Okla., Norman, 1953-90; furniture designer Norman. Chmn. gallery com. Firehouse Art Ctr., Norman, 1990—. With USN, 1944-45. Recipient Purchase award Ark. Art Ctr., 1975. Democrat. Home and Office: 2719 Hollywood Ave Norman OK 73072-6731

HENLE, JAMES MARSTON, mathematician, educator; s. Peter and Theda Ostrander Henle; m. Portia Cera Casambre, Oct. 14, 1969; 1 child, Frederick Valentin. AB, Dartmouth Coll., 1968; PhD, MIT, 1976. Vis. instr. U. of the Philippines Coll. in Baguio, Baguio City, 1968—70; math. tchr. Burgundy Farm Country Day Sch., Alexandria, Va., 1971—73; prof. math. and logic Smith Coll., Northampton, Mass., 1976—. Author: (text) Infinitesimal Calculus, 1979, An Outline of Set Theory, 1988, Sweet Reason, 1995. Vol. Peace Corps, Philippines, 1968—70. Fellow, Fulbright, 1980. Avocations: music, clarinet.

HENLE, PETER, retired economic consultant, arbitrator; b. N.Y.C., Feb. 12, 1919; s. James and Marjorie (Jacobson) H.; m. Theda W. Ostrander, Aug. 25, 1941; children: Michael G., James M., Paul J. BA, Swarthmore Coll., 1940; MA, Am. U., 1947. Mem. rsch. staff, asst. dir. rsch. Am. Fed. Labor, Washington, 1946-55; asst. dir. rsch. AFL-CIO, Washington, 1955-61; chief economist Bur. Labor Stats., U.S. Dept. Labor, Washington, 1961-71; dep. asst. sec. U.S. Dept. Labor planning, evaluation research, 1977-79; sr. specialist Labor Congl. Research Service, Library of Congress, Washington, 1972-77; econ. cons., arbitrator Arlington, Va., 1979-92. Contbr. articles to profl. jours. Chmn. Arlington County (Va.) Manpower Planning Council, 1975-77; trustee Arlington County Employees Retirement System, 1985-89. With AUS, 1941-42; with USAAF, 1942-45. Recipient Disting. Achievement award U.S. Dept. Labor, 1968; Brookings Instn. fed. exec. fellow, 1971-72 Mem. Nat. Acad. Arbitrators, Indsl. Rels. Rsch. Assn. Address: Collington Retirement 11450 Lottsford Rd Mitchellville MD 20721

HENLEY, ARTHUR, author, editor, television consultant; b. Rockaway Beach, N.Y., Sept. 9, 1921; s. Nathan Siegel and Theresa (Hohauser) H.; m. Janet Radskin, June 3, 1950; children: Eric, Kenneth. Engr. Assoc., Pratt Inst., 1944; BA, CCNY, 1969. Tech. writer Fairchild Camera Co., 1944-45; TV program cons., 1960—; mem. faculty NYU, 1969-70. Mental health cons., Nat. Assn. Mental Health Keynoter, coll. lectr. Radio writer, producer shows Bob & Ray, Make Up Your Mind, 13 by Henley; others; also writer advt. jingles; TV producer Kate Smith Show, Make Up Your Mind, Broadway Open House; TV writer, producer, also indsl. films, others; mag. contbr. Ladies Home Jour., McCalls, Family Health, Public Affairs Com., N.Y. Times, Sat. Eve Post, others, 1961—; author: The Mathematics of Humor, 1948, Demon In My View, 1966, Make Up Your Mind, 1967, Yes Power, 1969, The Right to Lie, 1970, Schizophrenia, 1971, revised edit. 1987, What Other Child-Care Books Don't Tell You, 1972, The Complete Alibi Handbook, 1972, The Difficult Child, 1973, How to Be a Perfect Liar, 1978, Don't Be Afraid of Cataracts, 1978, Don't be Afraid of Cataracts, rev. edit., 1983, Phobias The Crippling Fears, 1987, paperback edit., 1988, Lily & Joel: A Novel of Life, Love and Audio Tapes, 1992, Talking Book and Braille edit., 1994; contbr. to anthologies How to Write for Pleasure and Profit, You and Your Mind, Treasury of Tips for Writers, How to Write Television Comedy, Tools of the Writer's Trade; editor: Interdisciplinary Communications Program, Smithsonian Inst., 1975. Cons. med. editor: Globe Communications, 1976-79; columnist Brides Mag, 1970. Recipient Russell Sage Found. award., TV-Radio Mirror Gold medals (2).; work included in U. Wyo. Am. Heritage Ctr. Mem. Am. Soc. Journalists and Authors, Nat. Assn. Sci. Writers, PEN, AFTRA. Clubs: Nat. Press. Home: 73-37 Austin St Forest Hills NY 11375-6219 Office: A H Prodns 101 W 23rd St # 2462 New York NY 10011-2490 *If I have learned anything from living it is that a static life is no life at all while a life of change without direction is only half a life.*

HENLEY, DEBORAH, newspaper editor; City editor New York Newsday, N.Y.C.; exec. editor The News Journal, New Castle, Deleware, currently. Office: The News Journal 950 W Basin Rd New Castle DE 19720-1006*

HENLEY, DON, singer, drummer, songwriter; b. Linden, Tex., July 22, 1947; m. Sharon Summerall, May 20, 1995. Drummer with band Eagles, L.A.; performer: (albums) The Eagle, 1972, Desperado, 1973, On the Border, 1974, One These Nights, 1975, Hotel California, 1976, The Long Run, 1979, Hell Freezes Over, 1994; performer: (solo, singer, composer) I Can't Stand Still, 1982, Building the Perfect Beast, 1985 (Grammy award for song The Boys of Summer), The End of Innocence, 1989, Actual Miles: Henley's Greatest Hits, 1995, Inside Job, 2000, (songs) Dirty Laundry, 1982, Long Way Home, I Will Not Go Quietly, New York Minute, If Dirt Were Dollars, Little Tin God, The Heart of the Matter. Mem. Active So. Poverty Law Ctr., Walden Woods Project. Named to Songwriters' Hall of Fame, 2000. Office: c/o Warner Bros. Records Inc. 3300 Warner Blvd. Burbank CA 91505*

HENLEY, DOUGLAS E. medical association administrator; m. Mary Henley. MD, U.N.C. Sch. Medicine, Chapel Hill. Diplomate Am. Bd. Family Practice. Pvt. practice, Hope Mills, NC; exec. v.p. Am. Acad. Family Physicians. Mem. editl. bd. Family Practice News, Jour. Family Practice. Mem. N.C. Cervical Cancer Task Force, U.S. Congress' Office of Tech. Assessment Adv. Panel; bd. dirs. Am. Acad. Family Physicians Found. Office: Am Acad Family Physicians PO Box 11210 Shawnee Mission KS 66207-1210

HENLEY, ERIC, physician, educator; b. N.Y.C., Sept. 5, 1951; s. Arthur and Janet (Radskin) H.; m. Susan Wendy Henley; children: Lily Star, Grace Thea. BA, Hamilton Coll., 1972; MD, Georgetown U., 1976; MPH, Harvard U., 1988. Diplomate Am. Bd. Family Practice. Resident in family practice U. Conn., Farmington, 1976-79; family physician Cascade Health Care, Portland, Oreg., 1979-80, Family Practice Group, Cambridge, Mass., 1980-82, rural U.S., 1982-84; comdr. pub. health svc. Indian Health Svc., Kearns Canyon, Ariz., 1984-87, capt. pub. health svc. Albuquerque, 1989-95; assoc. prof. family medicine U. Ill. Coll. Medicine, Rockford, 1996—. Head dept. family and cmty. medicine U. Ill. Coll. Medicine, Rockford, 2000—; med. cons. Winnebago County Health Dept., 2001—. Co-Author: Clinical Medicine of Native Americans, 1998; co-editor Practice Alert Jour. of Family Practice; contbr. articles to profl. jours. Med. dir. South Beloit (Ill.) Sch. Dist., 1999—. Grantee, Indian Health Svc., 1989—91, March of Dimes, 2002—. Fellow Am. Acad. Family Practice; mem. APHA, AAFP, Soc. Tchrs. Family Medicine, Alpha Omega Alpha. Office: U Ill Coll Medicine 1601 Parkview Ave Rockford IL 61107-1822

HENLEY, ERNEST JUSTUS, chemical engineering educator, consultant; b. Sept. 30, 1926; BS, U. Del., 1950; D Engring. Sci., Columbia U., 1953. Asst. prof. nuclear and chem. engring. Columbia U., N.Y.C., 1953-59; prof. chemistry and chem. engring. Stevens Inst. Tech., Hoboken, N.J., 1959-64; chief of party AID Mission, Rio de Janeiro, Brazil, 1964-66; prof. chem. engring. U. Houston, 1964—. Founder, bd. dirs. Maxxim Med., St. Petersburg, Fla.; bd. dirs. Circon Corp., St. Petersburg, Fla., Serve Houston (Tex.), Main St. Theater, Houston, Procedyne Corp., New Brunswick, N.J.; tech. cons.; founding dir. RAI Rsch., 1953-82, Henley Healthcare, 1984-2000. Pres. The Henley Found. Office: U Houston Dept Chem Engring Houston TX 77204-0001 E-mail: henleyej@aol.com.

HENLEY, ERNEST MARK, physics educator, university dean emeritus; b. Frankfurt, Germany, June 10, 1924; came to U.S., 1939, naturalized, 1944; s. Fred S. and Josy (Dreyfuss) H.; m. Elaine Dimitman, Aug. 21, 1948; children: M. Bradford, Karen M. B.E.E., CCNY, 1944; PhD, U. Calif. at Berkeley, 1952. Physicist Lawrence Radiation Lab., 1950-51; research assoc. physics dept. Stanford U., 1951-52; lectr. physics Columbia U., 1952-54; mem. faculty U. Wash., Seattle, 1954—, prof. physics, 1961-95; prof. emeritus, 1995—; chmn. dept. U. Wash., 1973-76, dean Coll. Arts and Scis., 1979-87, dir. Inst. for Nuclear Theory, 1990-91; assoc. dir. Inst. for Nuclear Theory U. Wash., 1991—. Rschr., author numerous publs. on symmetries, nuclear reactions, weak interactions and high energy particle interactions; chmn. Nuclear Sci. Adv. Com., 1986-89. Author: (with W. Thirring) Elementary Quantum Field Theory, 1962, (with H. Frauenfelder) Subatomic Physics, 1974, 2nd edit. 1991, Nuclear and Particle Physics, 1975; mng. editor Jour. Modern Physics, 1992—. Bd. dirs. Pacific Sci. Ctr., 1984-87, Wash. Tech. Ctr., 1983-87; trustee Associated Univs., Inc., 1989—, chmn. bd., 1993-96. Recipient sr. Alexander von Humboldt award, 1984, T.W. Bonner prize Am. Physics Soc., 1989, Townsend Harris medal CCNY, 1989; F.B. Jewett fellow, 1952-53, NSF sr. fellow, 1958-59, Guggenheim fellow, 1967-68, NATO sr. fellow, 1976-77. Fellow AAAS (chmn. physics sect. 1989-90), Am. Phys. Soc. (chmn. div. nuclear physics 1979-80, pres. 1992, sec. treas. N.W. sect. 1999—), Am. Acad. Arts and Scis.; mem. NAS (chmn. physics sect. 1998-2001), Sigma Xi. Office: Univ Wash Physics Dept PO Box 351560 Seattle WA 98195-1560 E-mail: henley@phys.washington.edu.

HENLEY, JOSEPH OLIVER, manufacturing company executive; b. Sikeston, Mo., June 25, 1949; s. Fred Louis and Bernice (Chilton) H. m. Jane Ann Rhodes, Aug. 21, 1971 BSBA, U. Mo., 1972; MBA, Mich. State U., 1973. Ops. analyst Midland-Ross, Inc., Cleve., 1974, prodn. control mgr., 1974-75; engring. systems mgr. Cameron-Waldron div., Somerset, N.J., 1989-95, prodn. control mgr., 1976-77; prodn. planning and mfg. systems mgr. ICM div. Massey Ferguson, Inc., Akron, Ohio, 1977-78; sr. audit specialist mfg. United Techs. Corp., Hartford, Conn., 1978-82; mfg. control systems mgr. UT Diesel Systems div., Hartford, Conn., 1983-84, materials mgr., 1983-84, internal cons., 1984-86; inventory mgr. Pratt & Whitney Aircraft div., Hartford, Conn., 1986-89, mgr. sychronous mfg., 1989-95; dir. mfg. Case Corp., Racine, Wis., 1996-2000; mfg. exec. cons., 2000—. With Army N.G., 1970-72 Mem. Nat. Assn. Purchasing Mgmt., Am. Prodn. and Inventory Control Soc., Assn. for Mfg. Excellence (N.E. region bd. dirs.), Beta Gamma Sigma, Sigma Iota Epsilon, Omicron Delta Epsilon. Presbyterian. Home: 2400 SW Winterfield Ct Lees Summit MO 64081 Office: 2400 SW Winterfield Ct Lees Summit MO 64081

HENLEY, PATRICIA JOAN, principal; b. Harrison, Ark., Dec. 30, 1944; d. Durward Milford and Nola V. (Foresee) Ellis; m. Robert Lee Henley; children: Robert, Kevin, Laura. BA, Wichita State U., 1968; MS, Pittsburg (Kans.) State U., 1973, EdS, 1976; PhD, Kans. State U., 1980. Tchr. Wichita (Kans.) Pub. Schs., 1968-70; tchr. Oswego (Kans.) Pub. Schs., 1970-73; elem. prin. Aurora (Mo.) Schs., 1973-77; grad. teaching asst. Kans. State U., Manhattan, 1977-78; asst. supt. Turner Unified Sch. Dist. #202, Kansas City, Kans., 1978-82; supt. Platte County Schs., Platte City, Mo., 1982-89; dep. supt. Kansas City (Mo.) Schs., 1989-91; elem. prin. Ft. Osage Schs., Independence, Mo., 1991—. Instr. grad. courses U. Mo. Kansas City; assessor, supt. mem. Mo. Dept. Elem. and Secondary Edn. Spl. Edn. Panel. Recipient Outstanding Leadership award Jackson County Inter-Agy. Coun., 1995, Heroes in Edn. award Reader's Digest, 1995; named Bus. Woman Yr. Townsend Publs., 1989. Mem. Nat. Assn. Elem. Sch. Prins. (Nat. Disting. prin. 1994), Mo. Assn. Elem. Sch. Prins., Kansas City Suburban Assn. Elem. Sch. Prins., Rotary. Office: Cler-Mont Cmty Sch 19009 Susquehanna Rdg Independence MO 64056-3103

HENLEY, PAUL THOMAS, music educator, researcher; b. Aberdeen, SD, Dec. 2, 1966; s. Gerald Dennis and Nadene Audrey Henley; m. DeAnn Francis Lybeck, Aug. 4, 1990; children: Victoria Ann, Micah Gerald, Katrina Louise. MusB, U. of SD, 1985—89; MA in edn., fine arts and humanities, Chadron State Coll., 1990—95; PhD in music edn., La. State U. and A&M Coll., 1996—99. Dir. of bands Belle Fourche Ind. Sch. Dist., SD, 1989—91, Chadron City Schools, Nebr., 1991—94, Wahlert H.S., Dubuque, Iowa, 1994—96; asst. prof. music U. of Montana-Western, 1999—2000; asst. prof. of music SW Mo. State U., 2000—03; tchg. and learning specialist Tex. State Tchrs. Assn., 2003—. Chair Mo. Soc. of Music Tchr. Edn., 2000—; membership coord. MayDay Group, 2001—; advisor Student Mo. NEA, 2002—03. Author: (book reviews) Choral Journal; mem. editl. com. Missouri Journal of Research in Music Education, 2002—; contbr. articles. Mem. PTA; evangelism com. Messiah Luth. Ch., Springfield, Mo., 2002. U. fellowship, La. State U. and A&M Coll., 1996—99, Funding for Results award, SW Mo. State U., 2001, Music Educators Scholarship Found., 1990, scholar, Blue Cross/Blue Shield of Nebr., 1992. Mem.: MayDay Group (membership coord. 2001—02), NEA, Am. Choral Directors Assn., Music Educators Nat. Conf., Pi Kappa Lambda. Evangelical Lutheran Church Of America. Office: Tex State Tchrs Assn 316 W 12th St Austin TX 78701 Office Fax: 417-836-6726. E-mail: paulhenley@smsu.edu.

HENLEY, RICHARD JAMES, health facility administrator; b. Wroclaw, Poland, May 31, 1956; came to U.S., 1959; s. Henry and Lidia (Alper) Horczak. BA and MA summa cum laude, CCNY, 1978. Asst. to v.p. fin. Mt. Sinai Med. Ctr., N.Y.C., 1978-80, dir. fin. planning, 1980-81, assoc. dir. fin., 1982-84, dir. fin. profl. svcs., 1984-85; v.p. fin., treas. Vassar Bros. Med. Ctr., Poughkeepsie, NY, 1985-92, sr. v.p. for adminstrn., treas., 1992-97, exec. v.p., treas., 1997—; exec. v.p., COO, CFO Health Quest, Poughkeepsie, 1999—. Treas. VBH Corp., Poughkeepsie, 1986-99, Found. for Vassar Bros. Med. Ctr., 1986-2003, VBH Ins. Co., Ltd., 1988-, pres., 1991—, Riverside Diversified Svc., Inc., 1986-92, pres., 1992—, Riverside Mgmt. Svc., Inc., 1986-92, pres., 1992—, Alamo Amulance Svc., 1986-92, pres., 1992-; pres. Hudson Valley Home Care, Inc.; pres. HealthServe, LLC; bus. adv. coun. SUNY, New Paltz, 1999—. Contbr. articles to profl. jours. Treas. Bardavon 1869 Opera House, Poughkeepsie, 1986-91, Family Svcs. Dutchess County, Poughkeepsie, 1987-88, Samuel F. B. Morse Hist. Site, 1998-99; pres. Hudson Terr. Owners' Corp., Poughkeepsie, 1987-88; bd. dirs. Dutchess County Econ. Devel. Corp., 1999—, chmn., 2003—. Fellow Healthcare Fin. Mgmt. Assn. (nat. dir. 1994-96, nat. sec. 1996-97, nat. treas. 1997-98, nat. chmn. elect 1998-99, nat. chmn. 1999-2000, cost effectiveness award 1979-80, William G. Follmer Merit award 1986, Robert H. Reeves Merit award 1989, Fredric T. Muncie Mert award 1991, Medal of Honor award 1994, Stephen A. Ryan Meml. award 2003), Am. Heart Assn. (bd. dirs.), Am. Coll. Health Exec. (regent Hudson Valley Adirondack 2002—). Office: Health Quest 45 Reade Pl Poughkeepsie NY 12601-3947 E-mail: rhenley@health-quest.org.

HENLEY, ROBERT LEE, school system administrator; b. Aug. 7, 1934; m. Patricia J. Ellis; 3 children. BA, Washington U., St. Louis, 1957, MEd, 1958; EdD, U. Mo., 1967. Tchr., counselor, pers. office, bus. mgr., asst. supt. Mehlville Sch. Dist., St. Louis, 1958-75; supt. schs. Independence (Mo.) Pub. Schs., 1975-93; asst. prof. U. Mo., Kansas City, 1991—. Cons. in field; instr. various colls. & univs., St. Louis and Columbia, 1975—. Trustee Andrew Drumm Inst., Independence, 1980—; bd. dirs. Am. Cancer Soc., Independence, 1978—; adv. com. Kansas City Arts Ptnrs. Program, 1990—. Recipient Community Leader award Comprehensive Mental health Svcs., Jackson County, Mo., 1983, Disting. Svc. award Mo. chpt. Am. Assn. on Mental Deficiency, 1983, Outstanding Educator award State of Mo., 1985, Innovation in Edn. award Nat. Ctr. for Ednl. Computing, 1985-86, Exec. Educator 100 award Exec. Educator Mag., 1987, Sch. Adminstr. award Kennedy Ctr./Alliance for Arts Edn., Washington, 1988, Disting. Svc. award Am. Assn. Sch. Adminstrs., 1993; named Mo. Supt. of Yr., 1992. Mem. Am. Assn. Sch. Adminstrs., Mo. Assn. Sch. Adminstrs. (exec. com. 1988—, Robert L. Pearce award 1991, Disting. Svc. award 1993), Jackson County Sch. Adminstrs. Assn. (pres. 1981), Mid-Am. Assn. Sch. Supts., Met. Sch. Study Group (pres. 1985-86), Independence C. of C.

HENLEY, TERRY LEW, computer company executive; b. Seymour, Ind., Nov. 10, 1940; s. Ray C. and Barbara Marie (Cockerham) H.; children: Barron Keith, Troy Grayson, Walker Reed; m. Jennifer L. Baldwin, Sept., 1991. BS, Tri-State U., 1961; MBA, Loyola U., 1980, D of Psychology, 1982. R & D engr. Halogens Rsch. Lab. Dow Chem. Co., Midland, Mich., 1961-63, lead process engr., polymer plant Bay City, Mich., 1964, supt. bromide-bromate plants Midland, 1964-68; nat. sales mgr. Ryan Industries, Louisville, 1968-70; internat. sales mgr. Chemineer, Inc., Dayton, Ohio, 1970-77; cons. mktg. Xenia, Ohio, 1977-78; pres. Med-Systems Mgmt., Inc., Dayton, 1978-99, Medconnect Ltd., 1994—, Statis. Outcome Rsch. Corp., 1994-99; chmn. United Telemgmt. Inc., Dayton, 1991—; dir. HealthServe, LLC, 2000—03; pres. Cost Recovery Corp., 2003—. Author: Chemical Engineering, 1976; contbr. articles to profl. jours.; patentee in field. Chmn. Presdl. Bus. Commn. Mem. ASTM (com.), AIChE, Internat. Assn. Fire Chiefs, Am. Hosp. Assn., Computer Based Patient Record Inst., Internat. Graphoanalysis Soc., Radiology Bus. Mgmt. Assn., Am. Nat. Std. Inst. (X12 health ins. com.), Am. Med. Peer Rev. Assn., Am. Mgmt. Assn., Med. Group Mgmt. Assn., Ohio Handwriting Analysts Assn., Ohio Ambulance Assn., Internat. Assn. Fire Chiefs, Ohio Fire Chiefs Assn. Inc., Ohio Firefighters Assn., Healthcare Fin. Mgmt. Assn., Assn. Electronic Healthcare Transactions, Data Interchange Stds. Assn., Inc., U. S. C. of C. (telecomm

infrastructure rsch. task force, health and benefits policy com., Civic award 1990), Am. Med. Info. Assn., Freedom in Medicine Found. Home: 278 N Childrens Home Rd Troy OH 45373-8653 Office: HealthServe LLC 7812 Mcewen Rd Dayton OH 45459-3910

HENN, FRITZ ALBERT, psychiatrist; b. Alden, Pa., Mar. 26, 1941; s. Fredrich and Luise (Kimm) H.; m. Suella Weiland, Aug. 1, 1964; children: Sarah, Stephen. BA, Wesleyan U., Middleton, Conn., 1963; PhD, Johns Hospkins U., 1967; MD, U. Va., 1971. Dir. rsch. tng. U. Iowa Hosps. and Clinics, Iowa City, 1975; asst. prof. U. Iowa, Coll. of Medicine, Iowa City, 1974-78, assoc. prof., 1978-81, prof. dept. psychiat., 1981; prof., chmn. SUNY, Stony Brook, 1982-94; dir. L.I. Rsch. Inst., Stony Brook, 1982-83, Inst. of Mental Health Rsch., Stony Brook, 1983—; prof. psychiatry U. Heidelberg, Germany, 1994; dir. Ctrl. Inst. for Mental Health, Germany, 1994. Pres. Winter Conf. on Brain Rsch., 1990-92. Mem. editorial bd. Jour. Neurochemistry, 1980-90, Archives Gen. Psychiatry, 1983—. Cons. Project Dawn Justice Dept., 1973-74. Fellow Life Ins. Medicine Rsch. Fund, 1968-71, Falk fellow Am. Psychiat. Assn., 1972-74. Mem. AMA, Am. Coll. Psychiatrists, Am. Coll. Neuropsychopharmacology, Soc. for Neurol. Sci., Psychiat. Rsch. Soc. (pres. 1992), Am. Soc. Neurochemistry, Sigma Xi, Alpha Omega Alpha. Office: Mental Health Inst PO 12 21 20 68072 Mannheim Germany Fax: 49-621-1703760. E-mail: henn@as200.ZI-MANNHEIM.de.

HENNAGAN, MONIQUE, Olympic athlete; b. Columbia, S.C., May 26, 1976; Degree in psychology, U. N.C., 1998. Co-winner 4X400 meter relay U.S.A. Track and Field Team, Sydney, 2000; part time human resources supr., recruiter for hub ops. UPS. Recipient 400 meter champion, USA Indoor, 2003, Bronze medalist 4x400 meter, World Indoor, 2nd pl. at Adidas Boston Indoor Games, US Indoor 400m, 2002. Office: USA Track and Field Team One RCA Dome Ste 140 Indianapolis IN 46225

HENNAH, VIVIAN LISA, school system administrator; b. New Haven, Conn. d. George Albert and Bernaddette Keen; m. Allen Harold Stanley, Nov. 20, 1996; children: Harold Beid, Stanley Rudloph;1 child, Allen Jr. Pub. sch., New Haven. Writer Gifted and Talented, New Haven, 1975—78. Contbr. poet: poetry book Young Words and Vision, Whisper, Giggles Laugh, Patterns of Life, 2003, Best Poets and Poems of 2003. Home: 151 Cedar St New Haven CT 06519

HENNEBERGER, WALTER CARL, retired physicist; b. Bradley, Ill., Jan. 17, 1930; s. Peter and Gertrude Henneberger; m. Gerlinde Emma Gleissner, Aug. 17, 1967; children: Bernard, Petra Utke. BS, Purdue U., 1952, MS, 1956; Dr. Rer. Nat., Georg Aug. U., Göttingen, Germany, 1959. Asst. prof. of physics Fordham U., N.Y.C.; post-doctoral scholar Dublin Inst. for Advanced Studies, 1962—63; asst. prof. of physics So. Ill. U., Carbondale, 1963—67, assoc. prof. of physics, 1967—72, prof. of physics, 1972—95, prof. of physics, emeritus, 1995—. Chair dept. of physics So. Ill. U., 1974—76. Pfc. U.S. Army, 1954—55. Mem.: K of C. Roman Catholic. Avocation: clock repair and restoration. Office: Dept Physics So Ill U Mailcode 4401 Carbondale IL 62901-4401 Home Fax: 618-453-1056. Personal E-mail: walth@siu.edu.

HENNEKE, EDWARD GEORGE, lawyer; b. Flint, Mich., Jan. 28, 1940; s. Edward G. and Anna I. (Kielhorn) H.; m. Donna M. Wardosky, Jan. 24, 1970; children: Dawn, Shelley, Charlene; stepchildren: Scott, Tracy, Kurt Fraim. AA, Flint Jr. Coll., 1960; BS, U. Mich., Flint, 1962, JD, U. Mich., Ann Arbor, 1965. Bar: Mich. 1965, U.S. Dist. Ct. (ea. dist.) Mich. 1967, U.S. Ct. Appeals (6th cir.) 1974, U.S. Supreme Ct. 1971. Asst. pros. atty. Genesee County Pros. Atty., Flint, 1965-67; assoc. Ransom, Fazenbaker & Ransom, Flint, 1967-74; prin. ptnr. Keil, Ransom & Henneke, Flint, 1975-88, Henneke, McKone Fraim & Dawes, P.C. (and predecessor firm), Flint, 1988—. Flushing city atty., 1999—. Mem. planning com. Flushing Twp., 1986-92; bd. appeals, 1993—. Named Outstanding Alumnus, Flint U. Mich., 1971. Mem. ABA, Genesee County Bar Assn. (dir. 1978-81, pres. 1981-82). Avocations: hunting, golf, skiing. Office: Henneke McKone Fraim & Dawes PC 2222 S Linden Rd Ste G Flint MI 48532-5413 E-mail: ehenneke@hmfdlaw.com.

HENNELL, ROBERT WILLIAM, III, secondary school educator; b. Mount Vernon, Ohio, Sept. 9, 1952; s. Robert William Hennell, Jr. and Emily Gloria (Catrino) Hennell; m. Elizabeth Ellen Jameson, July 7, 1984; children: Joseph Robert, Jaclyn Grace. MusB magna cum laude in music edn., Bowling Green (Ohio) State U., 1974, MusM in Conducting, 1977. Cert. tchr. Ohio, 1974, music educator Music Educator's Nat. Conf., 1991. Dir. of bands Antwerp (Ohio) Local Schs., 1974—75; grad. asst. Bowling Green (Ohio) State U., 1975—77; dir. of bands Antwerp (Ohio) Local Schs., 1977—80; project coord. - LPGA pro-am golf tournament The J.M. Smucker Co., Orrville, Ohio, 1991—92; asst. golf coach Orrville (Ohio) HS, 2001—; dir. of bands Orrville (Ohio) City Schs., 1980—. Cons. Capital U. Complete Band Dir. Workshop, Columbus, Ohio, 1990; guest condr. Firelands Conf. Honor Band, Greenwich, Ohio, 2000. Condr. Orrville (Ohio) Cmty. Band, 1981—90; mem. Orrville Exch. Club, Ohio, 1982—, chmn. youth of month project, 1989—90; civilian participant US Army War Coll., Carlisle Barracks, Pa., 1991; coach Orrville (Ohio) Youth Baseball League, 1993—96. Recipient Golden Apple Achiever award, Ashland Oil Co., 1995. Mem.: Am. Sch. Band Dirs. Assn. (state chair 1986—88, state band clinic chair 1987, all-state band chair 1987), Ohio Music Edn. Assn. (adjudicated event chair 1984—86, band affairs chair 1989—91, dist. pres. 1991—93, adjudicator 1980—99), Music Educator's Nat. Conf. (profl. certification steering com. 1993—94), Ohio HS Golf Coach's Assn., Phi Kappa Phi, Phi Beta Mu. Avocations: reading, book collecting, travel, golf, baseball. Home: 1331 Independence Drive Orrville OH 44667 Office: Orrville City Schools 841 North Ella Street Orrville OH 44667

HENNELLY, EDMUND PAUL, lawyer, oil company executive; b. N.Y.C., Apr. 2, 1923; s. Edmund Patrick and Alice (Laccorn) H.; m. Josephine Kline; children: Patricia A. Anglin, Pamela J. Farley. BCE, Manhattan Coll., 1944; JD, Fordham U., 1950. Bar: N.Y. 1950. Instr. Manhattan Coll., 1947-50; litigation assoc. Cravath, Swaine & Moore, 1950-51, sr. litigation assoc., 1953-54; asst. gen. counsel CIA, Washington, 1951-52; assoc. counsel Time, Inc., N.Y.C., 1954-56; asst. legis. cons. Mobil Oil Corp., N.Y.C., 1956-60, legis. cons., 1960-61, mgr. domestic govt. rels. dept., 1961-67, mgr. govt. rels. dept., 1967-73, gen. mgr. govt. rels. dept., 1974-78, gen. mgr. pub. affairs dept., 1978-86; pres., CEO C. Remainder Corp., N.Y.C., 1986—. Bd. dirs. South Cay Trust. Contbr. articles on engring. and law to profl. jours. Trustee, vice chmn. Daytop Village Found.; mem. adv. com. N.Y. State Legis. Com. on Higher Edn., Nassau County (N.Y.) Energy Commn., L.I. Citizens' Com. for Mass Transit, N.Y. State Def. Coun.; mem. White House Conf. on Natural Beauty, 1963; bd. dirs. Nat. Coun. on Aging; exec. com. Pub. Affairs Rsch. Coun. of Conf. Bd.; mem. Nassau County Econ. Devel. Planning Coun.; commr. nat. com. Commn. for UNESCO, 1982-85, head U.S. del. with personal rank of amb. 22d Gen. Conf., 1983, mem. internat. adv. panel, 1989—; mem. Pres.' Intelligence Transition Team, 1980-81; cons. Pres.'s Intelligence Oversight Bd.; trustee Austen Riggs Ctr., Pub. Affairs Found. Lt., USNR, 1943-46, PTO, ETO. Decorated Knight of Malta, Knight of Holy Sepulchre. Mem. ABA, Fed. Bar Assn., Assn. Bar City of N.Y., Acad. Polit. and Social Scis., Am. Good Govt. Soc. (trustee), Tax Coun. (bd. dirs.), Pub. Affairs Coun. (bd. dirs.), Freedom House (trustee), Am. Mgmt. Assn., Pi Sigma Epsilon, Delta Theta Phi, Army-Navy Club, Meadows Country Club, Sarasota Yacht Club, Island Hills Country Club, Explorers Club, Knights of Malta, Knights Holy Sepulchre. Clubs: Army-Navy, Explorers. Lodges: K.M., Knights Holy Sepulcher. Home: 84 Sequams Ln E West Islip NY 11795-4508 also: 3941 Hamilton Club Cir Sarasota FL 34242-1109 Office: C Remainder Corp 21 Argyle Sq Babylon NY 11702-2712

HENNEMAN, STEPHEN CHARLES, psychotherapist; b. Chgo., June 17, 1949; s. Charles Philip Jr. and Marion Louise (Eichberger) Henneman; m. Patricia Anne York, Feb. 14, 1975 (div. Sept. 1980); 1 child, Charles Philip III; m. Marion Jean McDermand, Oct. 4, 1980; stepchildren: Ervin F. Jr. Schrock, Lisa Ann Schrock, Thomas M. Schrock. BA in Journalism, Colo. State U., 1971; MA in Counseling, U. N.D., 1987. Lic. profl. counselor. Commd. 2d lt. USAF, 1971, advanced through grades to maj., 1984; missile launch officer 570th Strategic Missile Squadron, Davis Monthan AFB, Ariz., 1972-76; info. officer 321st Strategic Missile Wing, Grand Forks AFB, N.D., 1976-79; missile combat crew flight comdr. 446th Strategic Missile Squadron, Grand Forks AFB, 1980-82; missile combat crew comdr. evaluator 321st Strategic Missile Wing, Grand Forks AFB, 1982, wing nuclear surety officer, 1982-83, chief weapon safety branch, 1983-85; asst. ops. officer 320th Strategic Missile Squadron, F E Warren AFB, Wyo., 1985-86; dep. wing inspector 90th Strategic Missile Wing, F E Warren AFB, 1986-88; ops. officer 319th Strategic Missile Squadron, F E Warren AFB, 1988-89; dep. chief war res. materiel div. Hdqrs. U.S. Air Forces in Europe, Ramstein Air Base, Fed. Republic Germany, 1989-92; vol. and outreach coord. Safe House/Sexual Assault Svcs., Inc., Cheyenne, Wyo., 1992-93; quality control investigator Dept. Employment State of Wyoming, Cheyenne, 1993-95; counselor Wyo. State Penitentiary, Rawlins, 1995-96, counseling team leader, 1996-97; residential counselor Aurora (Colo.) Cmty. Mental Health Ctr., 1997-99, mental health clinician, 1999-2001, profl. counselor, 2001—. Advocate, counselor Safehouse/Sexual Assault Svcs., Inc., Cheyenne, 1985-89; sec., bd. dirs. Carbon County Citizens Organized to See Violence Ended, 1996-97. Mem. ACA, Am. Mental Health Counselors Assn., Colo. Counselors Assn. Avocations: photography, popular music recordings collecting, reading. E-mail: schenneman@comcast.net.

HENNEMEYER, ROBERT THOMAS, diplomat; b. Chgo., Dec. 1, 1925; s. Rudolph Johannes and Mary Matilda (Petersen) H.; m. Joan Therese Renaud, Dec. 28, 1954; children— Christian, Paul, Robin Ph.B., U. Chgo., 1947, MA, 1950; student, Chgo. Tchrs. Coll., African area studies Oxford U., Eng., 1960-61, U. Md., 1965-67. Tchr. high schs., Chgo., 1948-50; instr. Woodrow Wilson Jr. Coll., Chgo., 1951; commd. fgn. service officer U.S. Dept. State, 1952; cultural officer Bremen, Fed. Republic Germany, 1952-53; officer-in-charge Bremerhaven, Fed. Republic Germany, 1953-54; asst. U.S. officer Allied Gen. Secretariat, Bonn, Fed. Republic Germany, 1954-56, spl. asst. to ambassador, 1954-56; econ. officer Consulate Gen., Munich, 1956-58; internat. relations officer Dept. State, 1958-60; consul, dep. chief mission Dar es Salaam Tanganyika, 1961-64; faculty adviser U.S. Naval Acad., Annapolis, 1964-66; personnel officer Dept. State, Washington, 1966-68; chief polit. sec. Am. embassy Oslo, Norway, 1968-71; consul gen. Dusseldorf, Fed. Republic Germany, 1971-75; dep. asst. sec. Bur. of Security and Consular Affairs Dept. State, 1976-78; consul gen. Munich, 1978-80; sr. insp. and exec. dir. Dept. State, 1980-83, exec. asst. to Under Sec., 1983-84; U.S. ambassador Banjul, The Gambia, 1984-86; fgn. affairs advisor U.S. Cath. Conf., Washington, 1986-88, dir. office internat. justice and peace, 1988-90; pvt. cons., 1990—. Served with AUS, 1943-46 Mem. DACOR, Fgn. Service Assn., Alpha Delta Phi Address: 1701 Clower Creek Dr Sarasota FL 34231-8928

HENNEN, THOMAS WALDO, lawyer; b. Tacoma, Nov. 28, 1945; s. Waldo Gerhart and Ruth Elzora (George) H. AA, Highline Coll., 1966; BS in Mech. Engring., Wash. State U., 1969; JD, U. Maine, 1973. Bar: Wash. 1973, Calif. 2001, U.S. Ct. Claims 1975, U.S. Patent Office 1975, U.S. Ct. Customs and Patent Appeals 1975. Design engr. Boeing Aircraft Co., Seattle, 1969-70; patent atty. Office Naval Rsch., Arlington, Va., 1975, Naval Sea Sys. Command, Washington, 1978-79; patent staff asst. for tech. and administrv. ops. Office Naval Rsch., Arlington, Va., 1979-82; patent atty. Naval Weapons Ctr., China Lake, Calif., 1975-78; dpe. patent counsel Ridgecrest, Calif., 1982-86; counsel info., space and def. sys. Boeing, Kent, Wash., 1986-97, counsel info. and comm. sys. Seattle, 1998; counsel Boeing Space and Comm. Group, Seal Beach, Calif., 1999—2002; counsel integrated def. sys. Boeing Air Force Systems, 2003—. Coach Civitan Soccer Club, Arlington, Va., 1981-82. Mem. ASME, Wash. State Patent Law Assn., Am. Corp. Counsel Assn., NRA (life). Office: Boeing Integrated Def Systems 2515 MC 110-SB50 Seal Beach CA 90740-1515 E-mail: thennen@socal.rr.com.

HENNES, ROBERT TAFT, former management consultant, investment executive; b. Jamestown, N.Y., Mar. 8, 1930; s. Theodore Preston and Lucille (Kane) H.; m. Frances Walker Pratt, May 9, 1953 (div. 1962); children: Robert Taft, Duncan Pratt, Margaret Nickerson, Theodore Preston II; m. Grace Margaret Bruton, Oct. 9, 1971. AB, Harvard U., 1951; MBA, U. Pa., 1952. With Lummus Co., N.Y.C., 1952-62; exec. v.p., dir. Conahay & Lyon, Inc. (advt.), N.Y.C., 1962-70; sr. v.p. Cole & Assos., Boston, 1970-72; chmn., dir. Hennes & Cox Inc., N.Y.C., 1972-77; sr. dir. Spencer Stuart & Assos., N.Y.C., 1977-88. Dir. Oldwyck Industries, Inc., N.Y.C. Mem. Kennett Square Golf and Country Club, Harvard Club of N.Y. Home: PO Box 728 Kennett Square PA 19348-0728

HENNESSEY, DAVID PATRICK, banker; b. Coos Bay, Oreg., Aug. 2, 1950; s. William Patrick and Beverly Ann (Curtis) H.; m. Kathryn Ann McCloskey, Aug. 2, 1975; 1 child, Kristin R. AA, Am. River Coll., 1970; BS, Calif. State U., Sacramento, 1974; MBA, Chico State U., 1978. V.p. Bank of Am. N.T. and S.A., Sacramento, 1974-85; exec. v.p. Sunrise Bank Calif., Curtis Heights, 1985-90, pres., chief exec. officer Sunrise Bancorp, 1986-90; exec. v.p. Sacramento 1st Nat. Bank. subs. West Coast Bancorp, 1990-92, Sacramento First Nat Bank, 1990-92; exec. v.p., CFO, bd. dirs. Step Ahead Investments Inc., North Highlands, Calif., 1992-95; pres., CEO, bd. dirs. Sentinel Savs. & Loan, A Fed. Assn., 1995-96; investment broker AG Edward & Sons Inc., Roseville, Calif., 1996-99; v.p. investments Wachovia Securities, Folsom, Calif., 1999—. Chmn. bd. dirs. Data Corp., Roseville, Western Sunrise Mortgage Corp., Rancho Cordovia, Calif. Advisor Sch. Bus. Calif. State U., Sacramento, 1987. Named Outstanding Alumni Calif. State U., 1987. Republican. Office: Wachouia Securities 620 Coolidge Dr Ste 300 Folsom CA 95630-3183 Home: 4037 Royal Troon Dr El Dorado Hills CA 95762-7688 Fax: 916-351-5783. E-mail: dpath@sbcglobal.net., phennes@wachoviasec.com.

HENNESSEY, JAMES VINCENT, physician, educator; b. Middletown, Conn., Dec. 29, 1949; s. James Michael and Genevieve Marie Hennessey; m. Katherine Valk, Aug. 19, 1977; children: James Michael, Ian Thomas, Patrick William. BA cum laude, St. Michael's Coll., Winooski, Vt., 1971; MD, U. Graz, Austria, 1977. Commd. 2d lt. USAF, 1971, advanced through grades to col., 1998; intern, resident in internal medicine New Britain (Conn.) Gen. Hosp., 1978-81; internist USAF, Cannon AFB, N.Mex., 1981-83; fellow Walter Reed Army Med. Ctr., Washington, 1983-85; endocrinologist USAF Med. Ctr., Wright-Patterson AFB, 1985-93; clerkship dir. Wright State U., 1988-93; assoc. prof. medicine, assoc. dir. for clin. edn., sect. leader student pathophysiol. course in endocrinology Brown U., 1993—; physician R.I. Hosp., Providence. Air surgeon State of R.I. Air Nat. Guard, 1997—. Recipient Bailey K. Ashford award Walter Reed AMC, 1985. Fellow ACP; mem. Am. Thyroid Assn., Internat. Soc. Clin. Densitometry, Endocrine Soc. Avocations: sailing, golfing, skiing. Office: Divsn Endocrinology Hallet Ctr Diabetes and Endocrinology 1 Hoppin St Providence RI 02903-4923 E-mail: jhennessey@lifespan.org.

HENNESSEY, JOHN WILLIAM, JR., academic administrator, educator; b. Danville, Pa., Mar. 25, 1925; s. John William and Martha Scott (Braun) H.; m. Jean Marie Lande, June 26, 1948; children: John William III, Martha Scott. AB, Princeton U., 1948; MBA, Harvard U., 1950; PhD, U. Wash., 1956; MA (hon.), Dartmouth Coll., 1959; LHD (hon.), York Coll. of Pa., 1978, U. N.H., 1981. From instr. to assoc. prof. orgn. and adminstrn. Coll. Bus. Adminstrn., U. Wash., 1950-57; prof. Amos Tuck Sch. Bus. Adminstrn., Dartmouth Coll., 1957-87, assoc. dean, 1962-68, dean, 1968-76, Charles H. Jones 3d Century prof. mgmt., 1976-87, now emeritus; provost U. Vt., Burlington, 1987-89, interim pres., 1990. Prof. Inst. pour l'Etude des Methodes de Direction de l'Enterprise, Lausanne, Switzerland, 1959. Author: (with Austin Grimshaw) Organizational Behavior, 1960, (with others) Hospital Policy Decisions, 1966. Trustee Mary Hitchcock Meml. Hosp., Hanover, 1963-86, chmn. bd. 1977 83; trustee Ednl. Testing Svc. 1975-80, 81-85, chmn. bd. 1978-80, 84-85; chmn. governing coun. Dartmouth Hitchcock Med. Ctr., 1977-83, trustee, 1983-86, 91—, chmn. bd. trustees, 1992-95; bd. visitors Grad. Sch. Bus., U. Pitts., 1970-76, 79-88; mem. Pres.'s Coun. on Bus. Sch., U. Vt., 1982-87; dir. Milbank Meml. Fund, 1982-87; trustee U. Vt., 1985-87, Med. Ctr. Hosp. Vt., 1988-90, Vt. Law Sch., 1999—; bd. dirs. Kendal at Hanover, 1995-2001, chmn., 1998-2001; bd. dirs. Ams. for Campaign Reform, 2003—. 1st lt. U.S. Army, 1943-46. Mem. Am. Assembly Collegiate Schs. Bus. (dir. 1970-77, pres. 1975-76), Phi Beta Kappa. Home: 80 Lyme Rd Apt 1038 Hanover NH 03755 E-mail: john.hennessey@dartmouth.edu.

HENNESSEY, MICHAEL PETER, mechanical engineer, educator; b. Mankato, Minn., Apr. 14, 1957; s. Patrick Eugene and Rachel Marie (Alfs) Hennessey; m. Catherine Marie Carlson, June 28, 1980; children: Lisa Marie, David Michael. BS in Math., U. Minn., 1980; MSME, MIT, 1982; PhD in Mech. Engring., U. Minn., 1993. Advanced engr. 3M Corp., St. Paul, 1982—85; staff engr. FMC Corp., Mpls., 1985—90; postdoctoral/rsch. assoc. U. Minn., Mpls., 1993—95; prof. Rochester Inst. Tech., NY, 1995—98; asst. prof. Minn. State U., Mankato, 1998—2000, U. St. Thomas, St. Paul, 2000—. Contbr. Mem.: ASME, Am. Soc. Engring. Edn. (Best Paper award 2001), Soc. for Indsl. and Applied Math. Lutheran. Avocations: golf, sailing, fishing, camping. Home: 4662 Parkwood Dr Se Prior Lake MN 55372-3358 Office: Univ of Saint Thomas 2115 Summit Ave Saint Paul MN 55105-1079

HENNESSEY, WILLIAM JOSEPH, physician; b. Troy, N.Y., Mar. 8, 1947; BS, Rensselaer Poly. Inst., 1969; MD, Albany Med. Coll., 1973. Resident in ob-gyn Albany (N.Y.) Med. Ctr. Hosp., 1973—76; pvt. practice specializing in gynecology Green Island, NY, 1976—. E-mail: whennessey@aol.com.

HENNESSY, CHARLENE C. retired library director; b. Avoca, Pa., Apr. 26, 1928; d. Joseph P. and Mildred (Dever) Curley; m. F. D. Hennessy Jr., May 17, 1952; children: Jefferson D., Meg M., Bonnie E. BA, Marywood Coll., 1949; MS, Villanova U., 1977. Cert. pub. libr., N.Y., Pa. Children's libr. Bklyn. Pub. Libr., 1949-51; mem. army libr. svc. U.S. Army, Camp Kilmer, N.J., 1951-53; libr. Haverford (Pa.) Coll., 1954-55; asst. libr. Pa. RR, Phila., 1955-57; libr. Villanova (Pa.) U., 1957-59, 1982-87; libr. system coord. County of Delaware, Media, Pa., 1978-81; dir. Harcum Jr. Coll., Bryn Mawr, Pa., 1987-94. Cons. in field. Mem. Lansdowne Borough Planning Com., 1982-84; mem. Lansdowne Borough Coun., 1987-95, v.p., 1994-95. Mem. Pa. Libr. Assn., Del. County and Pa. State Lawyers' Wives (pres.). Republican. Roman Catholic. Avocation: genealogy.

HENNESSY, DANIEL KRAFT, lawyer; b. Summit, N.J., Jan. 4, 1941; s. Robert Emmett and Agnes Lyons (Lindle) H.; m. Susan Elizabeth (Bettina) Ware, June 17, 1972; children— Mary Elise, Daniel Joseph, Michael Ware, Catherine Anne. BS with highest honors, U.S. Naval Acad., 1963; JD cum laude, Harvard U., 1970. Bar: Tex. 1970. Commd. ensign U.S. Navy, 1963, advanced through grades to lt., 1966; service in Vietnam; resigned, 1967; ptnr. Hughes & Luce (formerly Hughes & Hill), 1973—. Editor: Harvard Law Rev, 1969-70. Mem. bd. advisers Jesuit Coll. Prep. Sch., Dallas, 1975-88; bd. dirs. Dallas-North Tex. region NCCJ, 1976-83, Catholics United for Faith, Inc., 1982-99, Greater Dallas Right to Life Ednl. Found., 1974-86, Cath. Pro-life Com. of North Tex., 2001—, The Highlands Sch., 1986—. Decorated knight grand cross Equestrian Order of Holy Sepulchre of Jerusalem, Knight of Malta. Mem. Dallas Bar Assn., State Bar of Tex. Roman Catholic. Home: 4405 Beverly Dr Dallas TX 75205-3001 E-mail: hennesd@hughesluce.com.

HENNESSY, DAVID V. literature educator; b. Danbury, Conn., Sept. 24, 1974; s. Vincent Charles and Jane Clark Hennessy; m. Nathaniel B. King, May 22, 1978. BA in English/Edn., U. Miami, 1995, MA in English, 2001. Instr. English St. Brendan H.S., Miami, 1995—99; grad. asst. instr. English U. Miami, Coral Gables, Fla., 1999—2001; adj. instr. English Keiser Coll., Fort Lauderdale, Fla., 2001—, Broward C.C., Fort Lauderdale, 2001—. Scholar, U. of Miami, 1999—2001; Henry King Stanford scholar, U. Miami, 1992—95, Fla. Undergraduate Merit scholar, State Fla., 1992—95. Mem.: MLA. Democrat. Office: Broward Community College Fort Lauderdale FL Personal E-mail: davidvhennessy@aol.com.

HENNESSY, DEAN MCDONALD, lawyer, multinational corporation executive; b. McPherson, Kans., June 13, 1923; s. Ernest Weston and Beulah A. (Dunn) H.; m. Marguerite Sundheim, Sept. 6, 1946 (div. Sept. 1979); children: Joan Hennessy Wright, John D., Robert D. (dec.), Scott D. (dec.); m. Darlene MacLean, Apr. 4, 1981. AB cum laude, Harvard U., 1947, LLB, 1950; MBA, U. Chgo., 1959. Bar: Ill. 1951. Assoc. Carney, Crowell & Leibman, Chgo., 1950-53; atty. Borg-Warner Corp., Chgo., 1953-62; with Emhart Corp., Farmington, Conn., 1962-88, asst. sec., 1964-67, sec., gen. counsel, 1967-74, v.p., sec., gen. counsel, 1974-76, v.p., gen. counsel, 1976-86, sr. v.p., gen. counsel, 1986-88, ret., 1988. Incorporator Ill. Citizens for Eisenhower, 1952; chmn. Citizens Activities, Ill. Citizens for Eisenhower, 1952, 56; Justice of the peace, mem. bd. suprs. Proviso Twp., Ill., 1952-56; vice chmn. Jr. Achievement Chgo., 1959; program chmn. trade and industries divsn. United Rep. Fund Ill., 1961; trustee West Hartford Bicentennial Trust, Inc., 1976-77, Friends and Trustees of Bushnell Meml., Hartford, 1978-84; bd. dirs. Royal Homestead Condominium Assn., Juno Beach, Fla., 1990-93. Served to lt. (j.g.) USNR, 1943-46. Sheldon fellow Harvard U., 1947. Mem. ABA, Mfrs. Alliance for Productivity and Innovation (vice chmn. law coun. 1984-87, chmn. 1987, 88), John Harvard Soc. Republican. Presbyterian.

HENNESSY, ELLEN ANNE, lawyer, benefits compensation analyst, educator; b. Auburn, N.Y., Mar. 3, 1949; d. Charles Francis and Mary Anne (Roan) H.; m. Frank Daspit, Aug. 27, 1974. BA, Mich. State U., 1971; JD, Cath. U., 1978; LLM in Taxation, Georgetown U., 1984. Bar: D.C. 1978, U.S. Ct. Appeals (D.C. cir.) 1978, U.S. Supreme Ct. 1984. Various positions NEH, Washington, 1971-74; atty. office chief counsel IRS, Washington, 1978-80; atty.-advisor Pension Benefit Guaranty Corp., Washington, 1980-82; assoc. Stroock & Stroock & Lavan, Washington, 1982-85, Willkie Farr & Gallager, 1985-86, ptnr., 1987-93; dep. exec. dir. and chief negotiator Pension Benefit Guaranty Corp., Washington, 1993—98; sr. v.p and dir. Actuarial Sci. Assoc., 1998—2000; sr. v.p. Aon Cons. Inc., Washington, 2000—03; pres. Fiduciary Counselors, Inc., 1999—. Adj. prof. law Georgetown U., Washington, 1985—; mem. com. on continuing profl. edn. Am. Law Inst./ABA, 1994—97. Mem. ABA (supervising editor taxation sect. newsletter 1984-87, mem. standing com. on continuing edn. 1990-94, chair joint com. on employee benefits 1991-92), Worldwide Employee Benefits Network (pres. 1987-88), D.C. Bar Assn. (mem. steering com. tax sect. 1988-93, chair continuing legal edn. com. 1993-95), Am. Coll. Employee Benefits Counsel (bd. govs. 2000—).mem. standing com. on tech. and info. sys. 2002—, mem. taskforce on corp. responsiblity, 2002— . Democrat. Avocation: whitewater canoeing. Home: 1926 Lawrence St NE Washington DC 20018-2734 Office: South Bldg Ste 900 601 Pennsylvania Ave NW Washington DC 20004-2601 E-mail: nell.hennessy@fiduciarycounselors.com.

HENNESSY, JOHN FRANCIS, III, engineering executive, mechanical engineer; b. N.Y.C., Nov. 27, 1955; s. John Francis Jr. and Barbara (McDonnell) H. AB, Kenyon Coll., 1977; BSME, Rensselaer Poly Inst., 1978; MS, MIT, 1988. Registered profl. engr., N.Y., N.J., Mass., Va., Del., Calif. Project engr. Syska & Hennessy, N.Y.C., 1978-83, project mgr. San Francisco, 1983-86, v.p. L.A., 1986-87, Cambridge, Mass., 1987-88, sr. v.p., 1988-89, CEO N.Y.C., 1989—, chmn., 1989—. Chmn., bd. dirs. N.Y. Bldg. Congress, N.Y.C., 1992-96; chmn. Times Square Subway Sta. Improvement Corp., N.Y.C., 1989—. Mem. USO of Met. N.Y.; chmn. Salvation Army of N.Y., 2001—; mem. Bldg. Futures Coun.; bd. dirs. Internat. Alliance for Interoperability, 1998—; trustee Nat. Bldg. Mus., 2000—. Sloan fellowship, 1987. Mem. ASHRAE, NSPE, ASME, Coun. on Tall Bldgs. and Urban Habitat, Univ. Club, Olympic Club, Union League Club, Met. Club (Washington), Lyford Cay Club (Nassau), Winged Foot Golf Club (Mamaroneck, N.Y.), Nat. Golf Links of Am., Princeton Club, The Links. Roman Catholic. Avocations: golf, tennis, skiing, squash. Office: Syska & Hennessy 11 W 42nd St New York NY 10036-8002

HENNESSY, JOHN L. academic administrator; B in Engring. in Elec. Engring., Villanova U., 1973; MS in Computer Sci., SUNY, Stony Brook, 1975, PhD in Computer Sci., 1977. Asst. prof. elec. engring. Stanford U., Calif., 1977—83, assoc. prof. elec. engring., 1983—86, prof. elec. engring. and computer sci., 1986—, chmn. dept. computer sci., 1994—96, dean Sch. Engring., 1996—99, provost, 1999—2000, pres., 2000—. Founder, chief scientist MIPS Computer Sys., 1984—92; chief arch. Silicon Graphics Computer Sys., 1992—98; founder MIPS Techs. (formerly MIPS Computer Sys.), 1998—; chmn. bd. dirs. T-span; mem. com. study internat. devels. in computer sci. and tech. NRC, 1988, mem. computer sci. and tech. bd., 1989—94, mem. com. study acad. careers for exptl. computer scientists, 1992—93, mem. statttus and direction of high performance computing and comm. initiative, 1995, mem. commn. phys. scis., math. and applications, 1998—99; mem. adv. com. computer and info. sci. and engring. NSF, 1992—96, chair oversight rev. of computer and info. sci. and engring. instnl. infrastructure program, 1992, mem. task force on future supercomputer ctrs. program, 95; tech. adv. bd. Microsoft Corp., 1992—96, Virtual Machine Works, 1995—96, Tensilica, 1998—99; strategic adv. bd. NetPower, 1992—95; mem. fellowship sel. com. Sloan Found., 1993—96; chmn. info. sci. and tech. Def. Advances Rsch. Projects Found., 1993—96, chair, 1994—95; mem. com. study investment strategy DARPA Def. Sci. Bd., 1998—99; mem. various conf. coms.; spkr. in field. Co-author (with D.A. Patterson): Computer Organization and Design: The Hardware/Software Interface, 1993, Computer Organization and Design: The

Hardware/Software Interface, 2d edit., 1998; co-author: Computer Architecture: A Quantitative Approach, 1990; contbr. articles to profl. jours. Named Profl. Young Investigator, NSF, 1984; recipient Disting. Alumnus award, SUNY, Stony Brook, 1991, J. Stanley Morehouse Meml. award, Villanova U., 1997. Fellow: IEEE (Emmanuel R. Piore award 1994, John Von Neumann medal 2000), Am. Acad. Arts and Scis., Assn. Computing Machinery; mem.: Nat. Acad. Engring. (peer selection com. computer sci. and engring. 1996—99, chair 2000), Pi Mu Epsilon, Eta Kappa Nu, Tau Beta Pi. Office: Stanford U Office of the Provost Bldg 10 Stanford CA 94305-2061 Fax: 650-724-4062. E-mail: hennessy@stanford.edu.*

HENNESSY, THOMAS CHRISTOPHER, clergyman, educator, retired university dean; b. NYC, Nov. 3, 1916; s. Thomas C. and Anna E. (Regan) H. AB, Georgetown Coll., 1940; MA in Latin and Greek Classics, Fordham U., 1947, MS in Edn., 1957, PhD, 1962. Joined S.J., 1934, ordained priest Roman Cath. Ch., 1947. Tchr. Fordham Prep. Sch., NYC, 1941-44, 49-52, high sch. counselor, 1952-61; counselor educator Fordham U. at Lincoln Ctr., N.Y.C., 1961-81; dean, prof. counselor edn. Sch. Edn. Marquette U., Milw., 1981-85. Editor: The Inner Crusade: The Closed Retreat in the US, 1965, The High School Counselor Today, 1966, The Interdisciplinary Roots of Guidance, 1966, Values and Moral Development, 1976, Value-Moral Education: The Schools and the Teachers, 1979, Fordham: The Early Years, 1998; How the Jesuits Settled in NY, A Documentary Account, 2003; cons. editor: Pers. and Guidance Jour., 1978-81; contbr. numerous articles to profl. jour. Mem. APA. Office: Fordham U Loyola Hall Bronx NY 10458

HENNESY, GERALD CRAFT, artist; b. Washington, June 11, 1921; s. Gerald Craft and Frances Lee (Moore) H.; m. Elizabeth Ann Lovering, Mar. 4, 1950; children: Kathleen, Paul, Brian, Shawn, Hugh, Craig. Student, Corcoran Sch. Art, 1939, George Washington U., 1940; BS, U. Md., 1948. Enlisted U.S. Navy, 1942, advanced through grades to comdr., 1956; mgmt. analyst U.S. Air Force Hdqrs., Pentagon, Washington, 1948-52, 53-56; asst dir. for orgn. and mgmt. AEC, 1956-72; artist, dir. Studio of Hennesy, Clifton, Va., 1972—. One man shows include PLA Gallery, McLean, Va., 1967, Tolley Galleries, Washington, 1983, Venable Neslage Galleries, Washington, 1993, Marin-Price Galleries, Chevy Chase Md., 1995-96, 98, 2000, 02, Prince Royal Gallery, Alexandria, Va., 1999; exhibited works at Corcoran Gallery Art, Washington, 1957, 59, 67, Smithsonian Inst., Washington, 1962, 64, Allied Artists of Am., N.Y.C., 1974, 75; represented in permanent collections at U.S. Ho. of Reps., Washington, Md. State Exec. Mansion, Annapolis, Nat. Hdqrs. Am. Legion, Washington, Nat. Hdqrs. DAR, Washington, Hdqrs. FDIC, Washington, others. Decorated Air medal with one star. Republican. Home and Office: 6811 White Rock Rd Clifton VA 20124-1434 E-mail: hennesy@erols.com.

HENNEY, JANE ELLEN, health administrator, oncologist; b. Kendallville, Ind., Mar. 26, 1947; d. Harry H. and Jeanette (Park) H.; m. J. Robert Graham, June 6, 1975. BS, Manchester Coll., North Manchester, Ind., 1969; MD, Ind. U.-Indpls., 1973. Intern St. Vincent's Hosp., Indpls., 1973-74; with Nat. Cancer Inst., Bethesda, Md., 1976—85, dep. dir., 1980—85; assoc. prof. medicine U. Kans. Med. Ctr., Kansas City, Kans., 1985—92, assoc. vice chancellor, acting dir. Mid Am. Cancer Ctr., 1985—92; prof. medicine, v.p. for health svcs. U. N.Mex., 1994—98; dep. commr. for ops. U.S. FDA, 1992—94, commr. food and drugs, 1998—2001. Scholar in residence Assoc. Acad. Health Centers. Served with USPHS, 1976-86. Recipient commendation USPHS, 1979, 81, Sec.' Recognition award HHS, 1985. Mem.: Inst. Medicine. Office: Assoc Acad Health Ctrs 1400 16th St NW Ste 720 Washington DC 20036

HENNIES, CLYDE ALBERT (LOU HENNIES), military officer, state official, military academy administrator; b. Manly, Iowa, Oct. 31, 1935; s. William Albert and Dorothy Lucille (Harrington) H.; m. Connie Lee Baker, June 12, 1974; children: David Lowthian. BGS in Polit. Sci., U. Nebr., Omaha, 1972; MA in Journalism, U. Nebr., Lincoln, 1983; MS in Pub. Adminstrn., Shippensburg (Pa.) U., 1983. Commd. 2d lt. U.S. Army, 1963—, advanced through grades to major gen., 1996; comdr. 4 Units and S-3, 3 combat tours RVN 7th Squadron, 17th Cavalry, 17th Aviation Group, Vietnam, 1966—71; chief pub. affairs hdqrs. U.S. Army Europe and Seventh Army, 1983-84; comdr. TF160 Army Spl. Ops. Aviation, 1985-86; dep. chief pub. affairs Office Chief of Pub. Affairs, Washington, 1986-89; commanding gen. U.S. Army Safety Ctr./Dir. Army Safety, Ft. Rucker, Ala., 1989-91; adj. gen. hdqrs. State Area Command, Ala. Army N.G., Montgomery, 1995-99; pres. Lyman Ward Mil. Acad., Camp Hill, Ala., 1999—. Co-owner Hennies Group, Inc., Ozark, Ala., 1991—; advisor film industry on Firebird, 1989—90; mem. Gov.'s Nat. Guard Adv. Commn. Pres. Broad St. Assn., Ozark, Ala., 1990—; charter mem. exec. bd. Boys and Girls Club of Am., Ozark, 1994—; mem. exec. bd. Army Aviation Heritage Found.; trustee Nat. Def. Indsl. Assn.; bd. dirs. Army Aviation Mus., Lyman Ward Mil. Acad. Decorated D.S.M. with oak leaf cluster, Silver Star, Legion of Merit with oak leaf cluster, D.F.C., Soldiers medal, Bronze Star with 7 oak leaf clusters, Air medals with 2 V devices, Air medals (27), Purple Heart, Army Commendation medal with oak leaf cluster, Vietnam Svc. medal, Vietnam medal of honor, Vietnam Gallantry Cross, others; named to Order of Mil. Merit, Republic of Korea, The Hon. Order of St. Michael, Infantry Officer Candidate Sch. Hall of Fame, Order of St. Maurice, Primicerius (Infantry), mem. Gathering of Eagles Class of 2000. Mem. Army Aviation Assn. Am. (exec. v.p., nat. exec. bd.), Assn. U.S. Army, Nat. Wild Turkey Fedn., Rotary Internat. Methodist. Avocations: training gun dogs, hunting, music/performing arts, golf, handball. Home: 461 E Broad St Ozark AL 36360 E-mail: lou.henn@aol.com.

HENNIG, BERTRAND RANDY, journalist, commentator; b. Beaver Dam, Wis., Jan. 12, 1952; s. Walter A. and Marie B. Hennig. BJ, U. Wis., Oshkosh, 1974. Supervising radio news editor Voice of Am., Washington, 2001—; news anchor WTOP News Radio, Washington, 1998—2001. Contract news reporter Sta. WBAY-TV and WFRV-TV, Green Bay, 1980-83; state desk corr. Milw. Jour. and Milw. Sentinel, 1980-83; anchor, news editor WILM All-News Radio, Phila., 1986-87; Washington corr. 6PR New Radio, Perth, Australia, 1998-2002; internat. news editor, anchor Feature Story News Agy., Washington, 1999—; newswriter, editor Voice Am., Washington, 2001—; creator, instr. radio broadcasting course U. Wis., 1980. Prodr.: (continuing radio news coverage) Gulf War Reporting, 1991 (First place: Pennsylvania Associated Press Competition, 1992). Recipient various awards for news reporting AP Broadcasters Assn., 1984-92, 1st place award for radio editl., 1992. Mem. Soc. Profl. Journalists (v.p. Ctrl. Pa. chpt. 1992). Home: 2401 Calvert St NW Washington DC 20008 Office: Voice of America Independence Ave SW Washington DC 20008 Personal E-mail: randyhennig@webtv.net.

HENNIG, CHARLES WILLIAM, psychology educator; b. Queens, N.Y., May 7, 1949; s. Charles Joseph and Evelyn Mary (Gerstel) H.; m. Mary Christina Shamrock, Jan. 9, 1982; 1 child, Brian Steve. BA, SUNY, Buffalo, 1971; MS, Tulane U., 1976, PhD, 1978. Grad. teaching asst. Tulane U., New Orleans, 1974-78; vis. asst. prof. psychology U. Okla., Norman, 1978-79, Centre Coll. Ky., Danville, 1979-80; asst. prof. Salem (W.Va.) Coll., 1980-83, assoc. prof., 1983-88, prof., 1988-89, chair psychology, 1983-89; prof. McMurry U., Abilene, Tex., 1989—2003, chair psychology, 1989—2003. Contbr. articles to profl. jours. Bd. dirs. client advocacy coun. Betty Hardwick MH/MR, 1996—, chair, 1998—2000, mem. human rights com., 1998—; bd. dirs. Family Outreach Abilene, 1999—2002, v.p., 2000, pres., 2001, treas., 2002. Mem. APA, Am. Psychol. Soc., Animal Behavior Soc., Psychonomic Soc., Midwestern Psychol. Assn., Southeastern Psychol. Assn., Abilene Psychol. Assn. (sec.-treas. 1990-91, 94-95, pres. 1992-93, 96-97, 2001-02), Psi Chi. Republican. Roman Catholic. Avocations: travel, reading. Home: 4701 Stonehedge Rd Abilene TX 79606-3429 Office: McMurry U Dept Psychology PO Box 86 Abilene TX 79697-0086 E-mail: hennigc@mcmurryadm.mcm.edu.

HENNIGAR, DAVID JOHN, investment broker; b. Windsor, N.S., Can., July 5, 1939; s. Dean S. and Jean B. (Jodrey) H.; m. Carolyn Hiltz, June 8, 1964; children: Brian, Jan. B of Commerce, Mt. Allison U., 1960; MBA, Queen's U., 1962. Investment analyst Burns Fry Ltd. and predecessor co., Toronto, Ont., Can., 1963-66, br. mgr. Halifax, N.S., Can., 1966-71, Atlantic regional dir., 1971-93. Chmn. bd. dirs. Annapolis Group Inc., Extendicare Inc., Acadian Securities Inc., Aquarius Coatings Inc., Highliner Foods, Inc.; bd. dirs. Crown Life Ins. Co., Minas Basin Pulp & Power Co. Ltd., Scotia Investment Ltd., Cromie Properties, Ltd., Maritime Paper Products Ltd., Sentex Systems Ltd., CentrSource Corp., KLI Field Svcs., Inc., Thinc, Information Management Inc; chmn. VR Interactive Inc.; pres., chmn. bd. dirs. Landmark Global Fin. Inc. Bd. dirs., treas. Izaak Walton Killam Hosp. for Children, Halifax, 1976-82; bd. dirs. Inst. for Rsch. on Pub. Policy, 1983-89; active Trilateral Commn., 1988-94; bd. govs. Dalhousie U., 1983-90; dir. Hope Air Inc. Mem. Investment Dealers Assn. Can. (nat. bd. dirs. 1985-87), Internat. Oceans Inst. (chmn.), Halifax Club. Home: 51 Forest Ln Bedford NS Canada B4A 1H8 Office: 3 Bedford Hills Rd Bedford NS Canada B4A 1J5 also: Extendicare 3000 Steeles Ave E Ontario ON Canada L3R 9W2

HENNIGAR, WILLIAM GRANT, JR., dentist; b. Buffalo, Dec. 25, 1947; s. William Grant and Donnette (Glaeser) H.; m. Jennie Carcaud, Mar. 22, 1975 (div.); children: William Grant III, Charlotte Carcaud, Travis Welshofer(dec.), Brittany Lines. AB, Colgate U., 1970; DMD, U. Pa., 1973; cert., U. Rochester, 1975; JD, Cleve. State U., 1992. Bar: Mass., N.Y. 1993. With Harvard U. Health Inc., Cambridge, Mass., 1974; ptnr. Am. Family Dental Group, P.C., Cheektowaga, N.Y., 1982-97; pres. Grand Island, Cheektowaga, N.Y., 1988—. Bd. dirs. West River Homeowners Assn., Grand Island, 1985-88, Alumni Bd. Nichols Sch., Buffalo, 1988-89. Lic. capt. U.S. Coast Guard, 1989—. Fellow Acad. of Gen. Dentistry, ADA, Town of Grand Isl. Long Range Planning Com., 1998; mem. ABA, N.Y.State Bar Assn., Internat. Assn. for Orthodontics, Am. Acad. Dental Group Practice, U.S. Dental Inst. (cert. 1985), Erie County Bar Assn.,Buffalo Launch Club (Grand Island), Phi Kappa Psi, Psi Omega, U.S. Power Squadron. Libertarian. Episcopalian. Avocations: volleyball, boating, softball, geneology, running. Home: PO Box 691 Grand Island NY 14072-0691 Office: Am Family Dental Group 2025 Whitehaven Rd Grand Island NY 14072-2024

HENNING, ANGELA E. controller; d. Robert L. and Barbara J. Henning; life ptnr. Eric J. Scott. BS, BA, U. Nebraska, 1996. CPA Nebr. Sr. acct. Nat. Indemnity Co., Omaha, 1997—2001; contr. No. States Agy., Inc., St. Paul, 2001—. Mem.: Minn. Soc. CPAs, Jaycees (chair cmty. involvement 2002). Office: Northern States Agency Inc 2145 Ford Parkway Suite 202 Saint Paul MN 55116 Office Fax: 651-646-1971. E-mail: ahenning@nsa-mga.com.

HENNING, GEORGE THOMAS, JR., steel company executive; b. West Reading, Pa., Sept. 26, 1941; s. George Thomas and Helen Virginia (Spangler) H.; m. Susan Young, July 21, 1962; children: George Thomas III, Michael Kevin. BA, Pa. State U., 1963; MBA, Harvard, 1965. Mgr. econ. analysis Eastern Gas & Fuel, Boston, 1967; mgr. gen. acctg. Ohio River Co., Cin., 1968; asst. to contr. Eastern Gas & Fuel Assos., Boston, 1969; dir. corp. planning Boston Gas Co., 1970; contr. Eastern Assoc. Coal Corp., Pitts., 1971-74; v.p., contr. Lykes Resources, Inc., 1974-78; asst. contr. Jones & Laughlin Steel Corp., 1979-85; gen. mgr. coal mine ops. and raw materials sales LTV Steel Co., Cleve., 1986, gen. mgr. asset mgmt., 1986-89; v.p., chief fin. officer Pioneer Chlor Alkali Co., Inc., Houston, 1988-95; v.p., CFO Pioneer Cos., Inc., 1995; v.p., contr. The LTV Corp., Cleve., 1995-99, v.p., CFO, 1999—2001, ret., 2001; bus. cons., 2002—. Mem. Pa. State Alumni Council. Mem. Omicron Delta Kappa, Pi Gamma Mu. Methodist. E-mail: shenning@penn.com.

HENNING, JOEL FRANK, lawyer, author, publisher, consultant; b. Chgo., Sept. 15, 1939; s. Alexander M. and Henrietta (Frank) H.; m. Grace Weiner, May 24, 1964 (div. July 1987); children: Justine, Sarah-Anne, Dara; m. Rosemary Nadolsky, June 21, 1992; 1 child, Alexandra. AB, Harvard U., 1961, JD, 1964. Bar: Ill. 1965. Assoc. Sonnenschein, Levinson, Carlin, Nath & Rosenthal, Chgo., 1965-70; fellow, dir. program Adlai Stevenson Inst. Internat. Affairs, Chgo., 1970-73; nat. dir. Youth Edn. for Citizenship, 1972-75; dir. profl. edn. Am. Bar Assn., Chgo., 1975-78; asst. exec. dir. comm. and edn. ABA, 1978-80; ptnr. Joel Henning & Assocs., 1980-87; sr. v.p., gen. counsel, mem. exec. com. Hildebrandt, Internat., Inc., 1987—; pres., pub. LawLetters, Inc., 1980-89; pub. Lawyer Hiring and Tng. Report, 1980-89; Chgo. theater critic Wall St. Jour., 1989—; pub. Almanac of Fed. Judiciary, 1984-89; editor Bus. Lawyer Update, 1980-87. Mem. faculty Inst. on Law and Ethics, Council Philos. Studies; chmn. Fund for Justice, Chgo., 1979-85 Author: Law-Related Education in America: Guidelines for the Future, 1975, Holistic Running: Beyond the Threshhold of Fitness, 1978, Mandate for Change: The Impact of Law on Educational Innovation, 1979, Improving Lawyer Productivity: How to Train, Manage and Supervise Your Lawyers, 1985, Law Practice and Management Desk Book, 1987, Lawyers Guide to Managing and Training Lawyers, 1988, Maximizing Law Firm Profitability: Hiring, Training and Developing Productive Lawyers, 1991-98, also articles. Chmn. Gov.'s Commn. on Financing Arts in Ill., 1970-71; bd. dirs. Ill. Arts Council, 1971-81, Columbia Coll., Chgo.; bd. dirs., v.p., pub. edn. exec. com. ACLU of Ill.; trustee S.E. Chgo. Commn.; mem. Joseph Jefferson Theatrical Awards Com. Fellow Am. Bar Found. (life); mem. Am. Law Inst., ABA (ho. of dels.), Chgo. Bar Assn., Chgo. Council Lawyers (co-founder), Social Sci. Edn. Consortium. Office: 150 N Michigan Ave Ste 3600 Chicago IL 60601-7572 *The hardest question for me to answer is, "What do you do?" I do a lot. Some of it returns money and satisfaction. Some returns more of one than the other. And, I do some things that make me feel fit. The best of what I do helps integrate my various selves and improves my relations with the world. But I have no facile way to say all of this at cocktail parties when, invariably, that question is popped.*

HENNING, NEIL SCOTT, financial consultant; b. S.I., N.Y., Nov. 30, 1961; s. Hugo L. and Janette (Tasker) H.; m. Robyn R. Cooper, Mar. 21, 1987; children: Samantha, Kirsten, Pamela. Retirement specialist Copeland Cos., Clark, NJ, 1983-92; account exec. Cigna, Hackensack, 1992-93, Lincoln Investment Planning, Florham Park, 1993—2002, Frtress Fin., 2002—. Named to Summit Club, Am. Inst. Mgmt., 1992. Mem. Freemasons (sr. warden Nutley, N.J. 2000, chmn. scholarship com. 1997, mem. budget com. 1997, jr. warden 1999, worshipful master 2001). Republican. Avocations: golf, model trains, philately. Home: 31 Terrace Ave Nutley NJ 07110-1139

HENNING, RONI ANITA, printmaker, artist; b. Bklyn., Mar. 19, 1939; d. Margaritis George Michos and Jane Eliza Duggan; m. John Henry Henning, Dec. 28, 1958 (dec. May 18, 1992); children: Dawn, Diane. Cert. in fine art, Cooper Union Sch. Art and Arch., 1970. Dir., masterprinter, tchr. screenprint workshop N.Y. Inst. Tech., Old Westbury, NY, 1977—95; dir., masterprinter Henning Screenprint Workshop, Bklyn., 1994—. Leader screened monotype workshop Rutgers U., New Brunswick, NJ, 1998, New Brunswick, 2000, Lower Eastside Printshop, N.Y.C., 1998—2003, Hunterdon Art Mus., Clinton, NJ, 1999—2001; cons. Photographys Changing Image Frontiers of Photography, Time Life Book, N.Y.C., 1972; cons. waterbased screen printing U. of the West of Eng., Bristol, 1999; leader children's printmaking workshop Goddard-Riverside Cmty. Ctr., N.Y.C., 1990. Author: Screenprinting: Water-based Techniques, 1994; exhibitions include The Art of Women Printmaker, The Womens Mus., Washington, 1991, Represented in permanent collections Lang Comm., NIH, Bethesda, Md. Active print project for Save the Children Columbia Tchrs. Coll., N.Y.C., 1985. Scholar, Cooper Union Sch. Art and Arch., N.Y.C., 1966—70. Achievements include development of quality non-toxic water-based screenprinting system as an alternative to the traditional solvent-based one. Avocations: gardening, travel, protecting wildlife and their environment. Home: 7908 Ridge Blvd Brooklyn NY 11209 Office: Henning Screenprint Workshop 7908 Ridge Blvd Brooklyn NY 11209

HENNING, RUDOLF ERNST, electrical engineer, educator, consultant; b. Hamburg, Germany, Aug. 3, 1923; came to U.S., 1939; s. Ernest P. and Emmy (Rosenfeld) H.; m. Patricia Ann Miklas, Sept. 30, 1961; 1 child, Patricia Emerson Irwin. BSEE, Columbia U., 1943, MSEE, 1947, D Engring. Sci. in EE, 1954. Registered profl. engr., Fla. Jr. engr. Radio Receptor Co., N.Y.C., 1946; project engr., sect. head Sperry Gyroscope Co., Great Neck, N.Y., 1947-58; chief engr. Sperry Microwave Electronics Co., Clearwater, Fla., 1958-70; acting asst. dean U. South Fla. Coll. Engring., Tampa, 1970-71; assoc. dean U. South Fla., Tampa, 1971-82, prof. elec. engring., 1982-95, Disting. Univ. prof., 1995—. Chmn. elect. engring. dept. U. South Fla., Tampa, 1986-87; dept. head Naval Electronics Lab. Ctr., San Diego, 1971; program evaluator Accreditation Bd. Engring. and Tech., N.Y.C., 1988-95; rev. panel NSF, 1989; cons. in field. Devel. coun. Morton F. Plant Hosp., Clearwater, Fla., 1970; bd. dirs. Clearwater Cmty. Concert Assn., 1963-65, S.E. Consortium for Minorities in Engring., Atlanta, 1979-82; founder, dir., adviser Yes We Care! Minority Engring. Program, Pinellas County, Fla., 1983—, Hillsborough County, Fla., 1991—. With U.S. Army, 1944-46, ETO. Recipient Pres.'s Affirmative Action award U. South Fla., 1986, Disting. Svc. award, 1990; named Engr. of Yr. by Tampa Bay Engring. Socs., 1987. Fellow IEEE (Centennial medal 1984, U.S. Activities Bd. Citation of Honor 1992), Microwave Theory and Tech. Soc. IEEE (pres. 1968, chmn. Internat. Microwave Symposia 1965, 79, co-chmn. 1995, Automated Measurement Career award 1986, Disting. Svc. award 1996), Fla. Engring. Soc.; Am. Soc. Engring. Edn., Electromagnetics Acad., Sigma Xi (pres. U. South Fla. chpt. 1977-78). Presbyterian. Avocations: hiking, travel, gardening, orchids. Office: U South Fla Dept Elec Engring Tampa FL 33620

HENNING, SANDRA JEAN, social worker; b. Saginaw, Mich., Oct. 17, 1940; d. Raymond Albert and Gertrude (Busch) H. BA in Social Work, Mich. State U., 1976, MSW, 1978. Cert. social worker, Mich. Mgr. social svcs. Provincial Hosp., Lansing, Mich., 1978-79; clin. social worker Lansing Gen. Hosp., 1979-89; home care social worker Americor Home Health, Lansing, 1986; mental health therapist Sparrow/St. Lawrence Geriatric Psychiatry, Lansing, Mich., 1989—. Social work cons. Roselawn Manor, Lansing, 1986-87. Mem. NASW, Acad. Cert. Social Workers. Home: 1467 Vondel Dr Holt MI 48842-9620

HENNING, TERESA BETH, English educator; b. Princeton, Ill., Dec. 16, 1967; d. John Francis and Diana K. (Parsons) H.; m. Gary Bruce Garcia, May 25, 1996. BA, Ill. State U., 1989; MA, Purdue U., 1991, PhD, 1998. Undergrad. tchg. asst. Ill. State U., Normal, 1988-89; grad. instr. Purdue U., West Lafayette, Ind., 1989-96; lectr. Ind. U./Purdue U., Indpls., 1996-2000; asst. prof., dir. Writing Ctr. Purdue North Central, 2000—. Spkr. in field. Ill. State scholar, State of Ill., 1986-87; Purdue Rsch. Found. Summer grantee Purdue U., West Lafayette, 1994, Purdue North Ctrl. New Faculty Summer grantee, 2001, 2003. Mem. MLA, Internat Writing Ctr. Assn., Nat. Coun. Tchrs. English, Conf. on Coll. Composition and Comm., Ind. Tchrs. Writing, Golden Key. Office: Purdeu North Ctrl Letters and Langs 1401 S US 421 Westville IN 46391 E-mail: thenning@pnc.edu.

HENNING, WILLIAM CLIFFORD, cemetery consulting company executive; b. Kalamazoo, Oct. 21, 1918; s. Russell and Dott Lois (Stauffer) H.; m. Charlotte Conrad, Sept. 14, 1946; children: Peggy Henning Berlin, Helen L. Henning Boddy. BA, Albion Coll. (Mich.), 1940; postgrad., Northwestern U. Law Sch., 1940-42, U. Mich. Law Sch., summer 1941. Sec. Sycamore (Ill.) C. of C., 1945-46; exec. sec. Allegheny County Funeral Dirs. Assn., Pitts., 1946-48, Am. Cemetery Assn., Columbus, Ohio, 1948-56; owner, pres. Am. Cemetery Cons., Inc., Springfield, Ohio, 1961-89; cons., 1989—. Sec., treas., gen. mgr. Rose Hill Burial Park, Springfield, Ohio, 1956-76. Contbr. articles to profl. jours. County chmn. United Appeals Fund, 1962; bd. dirs., 1964-67; moderator Snowhill United Ch. Christ, Springfield, 1958-60. Served to 1st lt. USAAF, 1943-45; PTO. Decorated Air medal with 2 oak leaf clusters. Mem. Am., Central Ohio (pres. 1958), cemetery assns., Ohio Assn. Cemetery Supts. and Ofcls. (pres. 1960), Am. Soc. Profl. Cons. Clubs: Springfield Lit. (pres. 1984). Lodges: Eagles, Kiwanis (pres. Springfield 1963), Masons. Republican. Home: 2714 Rockford Dr Springfield OH 45503-1931

HENNING, WILLIAM THOMAS, curator; b. Denver, Mar. 5, 1937; s. William Thomas Sr. and Rosalee (Bennett) H.; m. Eleanor Ann Whiteley, May 29, 1958; children: Cynthia Diane, Thomas Reed, David Randal. BFA, Phillips U., Enid, Okla., 1959; MA, U. Denver, 1963; postgrad., U. Iowa, 1966-69. Instr. Ariz. Western Coll., Yuma, 1963-66; asst. prof. Phillips U., 1969-75; curator Colorado Springs Fine Art Ctr., 1976-79, Hunter Mus. Art, Chattanooga, 1980-87, Ark. Arts Ctr., Little Rock, 1987-91, U. Ky. Art Mus., Lexington, 1991-96; dir. Rosemount Mus., Pueblo, Colo., 1996—2002; curator of collections Contemporary Crafts Mus. and Gallery, Portland, 2002—. Adj. faculty U. Ark., Little Rock, 1990-91, U. Ky., Lexington, 1995, U. So. Colo., Pueblo, 1997. Author: A Catalogue of the American Collection. Hunter Museum of Art, 1985; co-author: A Spectacular Vision: The George and Susan Proskauer Collection, 1994. Mem. Am. Assn. Museums, Mountain-Plains Mus. Assn., Nat. Trust for Historic Preservation, Rotary Club, Blue Key. Episcopalian. Avocations: reading, research writing. Home: 13838 A NW 10th Ct Vancouver WA 98685-2992 Office: Contemporary Crafts Mus and Gallery 3934 SW Corbett Ave Portland OR 97239

HENNINGER, BRIAN HATFIELD, professional golfer; b. Sacramento, Oct. 19, 1962; m. Catherine Henninger; children: Carlin, Hunter. Degree in psychology, U. So. Calif., 1987. Profl. golfer, 1987—; winner Deposit Guaranty Golf Classic, 1994. Won Queen Mary Open, 1989, Pacific Coast Amateur, 1989, Macon Open, 1992, Tex. Open, 1992, Knoxville Open, 1992, Deposit Guaranty Golf Classic, 1994. Office: PGA Am Box 109601 100 Avenue Of Champions Palm Beach Gardens FL 33410

HENNINGER, KATHERINE, English educator; BA in English, U. Pa., 1988; MA in English, U. Tex., 1994, PhD in English, 1999. Vis. asst. prof. U. Miss., Oxford, 2000—01; asst. prof. English, La. State U., Baton Rouge, 2001—. Artist-in-residence Lillian Smith Ctr. Creative Arts, Clayton, Ga., 2001. Fellow, U. Tex., 1998; rsch. fellow, La. Bd. Regents, 2002. Mem.: MLA, Soc. Study of So. Lit., Phi Beta Kappa. Office: La State U Allen Hall Baton Rouge LA 70803 Business E-Mail: kth@lsu.edu.

HENNINGS, DOROTHY ANN, financial advisor; b. Spokane, Wash., Mar. 23, 1937; d. Theodore Baza LaRue and Florence Irene (Jaeger) Innes; m. Peter L. Sbarbaro Sr., May 16, 1959 (div. 1973); children: Peter L. Jr., David A., John E. AS in Acctg., Napa Valley Coll., 1974; BS, Calif. State U., Sacramento, 1977. Cert. fin. planner. Acctg. asst. Napa (Calif.) County Counsel for Econ. Opportunity, 1972-73; owner, cons. Dash Enterprises, American Canyon, Calif., 1973-78; owner, bookkeeper Reliable Meats, American Canyon, 1973-74; fin. planner IDS Fin. Svcs., Napa, 1983-94, Am. Express Fin. Advisors, Napa, 1995—. Vol. Boy Scouts Am., Am. Canyon PTA, Little League, Pop Warner Football; sponsor T-ball and Babe Ruth Bambino and Babe Ruth League Teams; tax preparer Vita, Napa, 1973-74. Mem. Order Ea. Star, Women of Moose. Republican. Office: Am Express Fin Advisors 3033 California Blvd Napa CA 94558-3304

HENNINGS, DOROTHY GRANT (MRS. GEORGE HENNINGS), education educator; b. Paterson, N.J., Mar. 15, 1935; d. William Albert and Ethel Barbara (Moll) Grant; m. George Hennings, June 15, 1968. AB, Barnard Coll., 1956; MEd (NSF Acad. Yr. Inst. grantee), U. Va., 1959; EdD (Field Enterprise grantee), Columbia, 1965. Tchr. Pierrepont Elem. Sch., Rutherford, N.J., 1956-58, Thomas Jefferson jr. High Sch., Fair Lawn, N.J., 1959-64; prof. edn. Kean U. of N.J., Union, 1965-99, disting. prof. edn., 1999—2002, disting. prof. emeritus, 2002—. Author citation N.J. Inst. Tech., Div. Continuing Edn., 1982; author: (with B. Grant) Teacher Moves, 1971; Content and Craft: Written Expression in the Elementary School, 1973; Smiles, Nods and Pauses: Activities to Enrich Children's Communication Skills, 1974; Mastering Classroom Communication: What Interaction Analysis Tells the Teacher, 1975; (with G. Hennings) Keep Earth Clean, Blue and Green: Environmental Activities for Young People, 1976; Words, Sounds, and Thoughts: More Activities to Enrich Children's Communication Skills, 1977; Communication in Action: Teaching the Language Arts, 1978, 8th edit. 2002 (with D. Russell) Listening Aids Through the Grades, 1979; (with G. Hennings) Today's Elementary Social Studies, 1980, 2d edit., 1989; Written Expression in the Language Arts, 1981; Teaching Communication and Reading Skills in the Content Areas, 1982; (with L. Fay) Star Show, 1989, Grand Tour, 1989, Previews, 1989, Reading with Meaning: Strategies for College Reading, 1990, 5th rev. edit., 2002, Poets Journal, 1991, Beyond the Read Aloud: Learning to Read Through Listening to and Reflecting on Literature, 1992, Vocabulary Growth: Strategies for College Word Study, 2001, Words Are Wonderful: An Interactive Approach to Vocabulary, books 1 and 2, 2003; contbr. articles to Edn., The Record, Lang. Arts, Sci. Tchr., The Reading Tchr., Jour. of Adolescent & Adult Lit., Jour. of Reading, Tchr. to Tchrs., Sci. and Children, Early Years, Reading Rsch. and Instrn., New Eng. Jour. of History, Jour. Reading Edn., others. Recipient Edn. Press award, 1974, Outstanding Article award, 1999. Mem. Nat. Coun. Tchrs. English, N.J. Reading Assn. (Disting. Svc. to Reading award 1993), Internat. Reading Assn. (Outstanding Tchr. Educator in Reading award 1992), Suburban Reading Coun., Phi Beta Kappa, Phi Delta Kappa, Phi Kappa Phi, Kappa Delta Pi. Home: 21 Flintlock Dr Warren NJ 07059-5014 E-mail: hennings@verizon.net.

HENNINGSEN, PETER, JR., diversified industry executive; b. Mpls., Oct. 6, 1926; s. Peter and Anna O. (Kjelstrup) H.; m. Donna J. Buresh, June 19, 1948; children— Deborah, Pamela, James. BBA, U. Minn., 1950. Packaging engr.

govt. and aero. products div. Honeywell, Inc., Mpls., 1950-72; mgr. packaging Internat. Tel. & Tel., N.Y.C., 1972-80; v.p. Raymond Eisenhardt & Son, Inc., 1980-90; ind. packaging and material handling cons., 1990—. Mem. Inst. Packaging Profls. (formerly Soc. Packaging and Handling Engrs.), 1951—, fellow, 1970, pres., 1970-71, chmn. bd., 1972-73, named Man of Yr., 1968. Editl. cons. mags. in field. With USNR, 1944-46. Elected to Packaging Hall of Fame, Packaging Edn. Forum, 1995. Mem. ASTM, Aerospace Industries Assn. (chmn. packaging com. 1967), Masons, Shriners. Methodist. Home and Office: 7610 Smetana Ln # 211 Eden Prairie MN 55344

HENNION, CAROLYN LAIRD (LYN HENNION), investment executive; b. Orange, Calif., July 27, 1943; d. George James and Jane (Porter) Laird; m. Reeve L. Hennion, Sept. 12, 1964; children: Jeffrey Reeve, Douglas Laird. BA, Stanford U., 1965; grad. Securities Industry Inst., U. Pa., 1992. CFP, fund specialist; lic. ins. agt.; registered gen. securities prin. Portfolio analyst Schwabacher & Co., San Francisco, 1965-66; adminstrv. coord. Bicentennial Commn., San Mateo County, Calif., 1972-73; dir. devel. Crystal Springs Uplands Sch., Hillsborough, Calif., 1973-84; tax preparer Household Fin. Corp., Foster City, Calif., 1982; freelance, 1983-87; sales promotion mgr. Franklin Distbrs., Inc., San Mateo, 1984-86, v.p. and regional sales mgr. of N.W., 1986-91, v.p. Mid-Atlantic, 1991-94; v.p. Viatech, Inc., 1986-92; propr. Buncom Ranch, 1990—; v.p. Keypoint Svcs. Internat., 1992—2002; pres. Brock Rd. Corp., 1993—; v.p. Strand, Atkinson, Williams & York, Medford, Oreg., 1994—. Editor: Lest We Forget, 1975. Pres. South Hillsborough Sch. Parents' Group, 1974—75; sec. Vol. Bur. San Mateo County, Burlingame, Calif., 1975; chmn. Cmty. Info. Com., Town of Hillsborough, 1984—86, mem., subcom. chmn. fin. adv. com., 1984—86; mem. adv. com. Rogue Valley Internat. Airport, 1996—2003, vice-chair, 1999—2001, chair, 2001—03; mem. coun. Town of Buncom, Oreg., 1990—; chmn. Jackson County Applegate Trail Sesquicentennial Celebration, 1995—97; founding dir. So. Oreg. Hist. Soc. Found., v.p., sec., 1995—98, pres., 1998—2001; trustee Oreg. Shakespeare Festival Endowment Fund, 1996—2000, sec., treas., 1997—98, pres., 1998—2000; dir. Rogue Valley Manor Cmty. Svcs., 1996—, vice-chair, 1997—; dir. Craterian Performances Co., 1997—, chmn. mem. com., 1998—2001, pres., 2001—03; dir. So. Oreg. Estate Planning Coun., 1997—2003, pres., 1998—99; dir. Oreg. Cmty. Found., 2002—; bd. dirs Pacific N.W. Mus. Natural History, 1995—96, Providence Cmty. Health Found., 1996—2003, chmn. planned giving com., 1997—2000, sec., 1998—2000, v.p., 2000—01, pres., 2001—02; bd. dirs. Chamber of Medford, Jackson Co., 1997—2000, v.p., 1999—2000; bd. dirs. Oreg. Shakespeare Festival, 2002—; mem. So. Oreg. Leadership Coun., 2000—, chmn., 2002—. Recipient awards Coun. for Advancement and Support of Edn., 1981, Exemplary Direct Mail Appeals Fund Raising Inst., 1982, Golden Mic award Frederic Gilbert Assocs., 1993; named Wholesaler of Yr., Shearson Lehman Hutton N.W. Region, 1989, among Top 300 Fin. Advisors, Worth Mag., 1998, Top 250 Fin. Advisors, 1999, 2001, Among 10 Outstanding Brokers Registered Rep. Mag., 2000. Mem. So. Oreg. Estate Planning Coun., Buncom Hist. Soc., Oreg. Shakespeare Festival, Britt Festivals, So. Oreg. Hist. Soc., Jr. League, Medford Rogue Rotary, Craterian Performances Co. Republican. Home: 3232 Little Applegate Rd Jacksonville OR 97530 9303 Office: Strand Atkinson Williams & York 2495 E Barnett Ste A Medford OR 97504 E-mail: lhennion@strandatkinson.com.

HENNION, REEVE LAWRENCE, communications executive; b. Ventura, Calif., Dec. 7, 1941; s. Tom Reeve and Evelyn Edna (Henry) H.; m. Carolyn Laird, Sept. 12, 1964; children: Jeffrey Reeve, Douglas Laird. BA, Stanford U., 1963, MA, 1965. Reporter Tulare (Calif.) Advance-Register, 1960-62; reporter UPI, San Francisco, 1963-66, mgr. Fresno, Calif., 1966-68, regional exec. Los Angeles, 1968-69, mgr. Honolulu, 1969-72, San Francisco, 1972-75, Calif. editor, 1975-77, gen. news editor, 1977-81, bus. mgr., 1981-83, v.p., gen. mgr. Pacific div., 1983-85; v.p., gen. mgr. Calif.-Oreg. Broadcasting, Inc., 1985-86; pres. Viatech Inc., 1986-92; propr. Buncom Ranch; pres. Keypoint Svcs. Internat., Inc., Medford, Oreg., 1992—2002; interim exec. dir. Rogue Valley Coun. of Govts., 1998. Editor: The Modoc Country, 1971, Buncom: Crossroads Station, 1995. Chmn. Calif. Freedom of Info. Com., 1983-84; mem. Jackson County Planning Commn., Jackson County Roads Com.; mayor of Buncom, Oreg.; pres. Buncom Hist. Soc. Mem. Am. Planning Assn. (exec. bd. Oreg. chpt.), Delta Kappa Epsilon. Home: 3232 Little Applegate Rd Jacksonville OR 97530-9303

HENRETTY, DONALD BRUCE, history educator; b. Washington, June 12, 1937; s. Malcolm Senseney and Ethel Louise (Kidwell) H.; m. Elizabeth Kathleen Talbot, June 21, 1986. BA, Randolph-Macon Coll., Ashland, Va., 1959; MEd, U. Va., 1967. Cert. secondary tchr., Va. Tchr. history Annandale (Va.) H.S., 1959-90, dir. athletics, 1978-80; tchr. history Centreville (Va.) H.S., 1990-92; coach varsity soccer St. Stephen's and St. Agnes Sch., Alexandria, 1991-96, interim chair dept. history, 1996-97, tchr. history, 1993—. V.p. Va. Edn. Assn., 1972—73; pres. No. Va. Soccer Coaches, Fairfax, 1982—84; mem. regional adv. coun. Hermitage No. Va.; legis. asst. Va. State Senate, Richmond, 1973; lay leader Calvary United Meth Ch., Arlington, Va., 1968—69, 1972—73, 1990—92; bd. dirs. Va. Conf. Higher Edn. Ministries; dir. Camp Pleasant, Dunfries, Va., 1964, Glayden Sch. and Camp, Lucketts, Va., 1967—78; chmn. bd. trustees Fairfax (Va.) Retirement Sys., 1976—77; bd. dirs. Fairfax Edn. Assn., 1969—73, Soc. Alumni Randolph-Macon Coll., 1980—83. Study grantee NEH, 1983. Mem. Va. Hist. Soc. Democrat. United Methodist. Home: 8325 Toll House Rd Annandale VA 22003-4630 E-mail: betdonh@earthlink.net.

HENRI, JANINE JACQUELINE, librarian; b. Washington, Aug. 16, 1955; d. Victor Philippe and Christine (Leuschner) H.; m. David Theron Sanford, July 24, 1982; 1 child, Geoffrey K. Sanford. AB, San Diego State U., 1979; postgrad., UCLA, 1979—82; M of Libr. Info. Sci., U. Calif., Berkeley, 1990. Res. supr. bus. and social sci. libr. U. Calif., Berkeley, 1982-87, monographs, res. supr. environ. design libr., 1987-89, head tech. svcs. environ. design libr., 1989-91; art libr. fine arts libr. U. Tex., Austin, 1991—95, head libr. architecture and planning libr., 1995—. Compilor: 1986-88 Bibliography of South Asian Art, 1990; contbr. articles to profl. jours. Mem. ALA, Art Libraries Soc. North Am. (exec. bd. 1996-97), Am. Com. for South Asian Art, Assn. Architecture Sch. Libr.

HENRICH, WILLIAM JOSEPH, JR., lawyer; b. Phila., Jan. 13, 1929; s. William J. and Helen (Moylan) H.; m. Dorothy Kolsun; children: William III, Michael, David, Richard. BA in Econs., LaSalle U., 1950; JD, Temple U., 1956. Bar: Pa. 1957, Ct. Common Pleas 1957, U.S. Dist. Ct. (ea. dist.) Pa. 1957. Assoc. Dilworth, Paxson, Kalish & Kauffman, Phila., 1957-65, ptnr., 1965-84, sr. ptnr., 1988—; pres., gen. counsel Triangle Pub. Inc., Radnor, Pa., 1985-88. Bd. mgrs. Beneficial Bank, Phila; bd. dirs. Phila. Consolidated Holding Corp. Bd. dirs. LaSalle U., Phila., Pa., 1985—; trustee The Annenburg Sch. Comm., U. Pa., 1985—, The Annenburg Sch. Comm., U. So. Calif., L.A., 1985—; active Union League of Phila. Mem. ABA. Office: Dilworth Paxson LLP 1735 Market St Fl 32 Philadelphia PA 19103-7595

HENRICHS, ALBERT MAXIMINUS, classicist, educator; b. Cologne, Germany, Dec. 29, 1942; came to U.S., 1971; s. Johannes and Berti H.; m. Ingrid Ursula Schaadt, June 4, 1965 (div. Mar. 1990); children: Markus, Helen Felicitas; m. Maura Giles, June 19, 1997 (div. Apr. 2001). Student, U. Cologne, 1962-66, U. Bonn, 1962-63; Dr.phil., U. Cologne, 1966, habilitation, 1969; A.M. (hon.), Harvard U., 1972. Vis. lectr. U. Mich., Ann Arbor, 1967-69; prof. U. Cologne, 1970-71; asso. prof. classics U. Calif., Berkeley, 1971-73; prof. Greek and Latin. Harvard U., Cambridge, Mass., 1973-84, Eliot prof. Greek lit., 1984—, chmn. dept. classics, 1982-88, mem. affiliated faculty Div. Sch., 1982—90; Sather prof. classical lit. U. Calif., Berkeley, 1990. Sr. fellow Ctr. for Hellenic Studies, Washington, 1992-97. Author: Didymos der Blinde Kommentar zu Hiob (Tura-Papyrus), 2 vols., 1968, Die Phoinikika des Lollianos, 1972, Die Götter Griechenlands, 1987, Warum soll ich denn tanzen? Dionysisches im Chor der griechischen Tragödie, 1996; editor: Harvard Studies in Classical Philology, 1975-79, 2001—; adv. bd. Harvard Libr. Bull., 1981-95, Greek, Roman and Byzantine Studies, 1984—; contbr. articles on ancient Greek lit., papyrology, mythology and religion to scholarly jours. Fellow Am. Acad. Arts and Scis.; mem. Am. Philos. Soc., Am. Philol. Assn., Assn. Internationale de Papyrologues., Egypt Exploration Soc. Home: 272 Concord Ave Cambridge MA 02138-1338 Office: Harvard U Dept Classics 212 Boylston Hall Cambridge MA 02138

HENRICHS, W(ALTER) DEAN, dermatologist; b. Smith Center, Kans., Oct. 26, 1939; s. Walter George and Mildred (Kubias) H.; m. Barbara Ann Bremer, Apr. 7, 1967; children: Matthew, Mark, Jonathan. BA, U. Kans., 1961, MD, 1965. Diplomate Am. Bd. Dermatology, Am. Bd. Dermatopathology. Commd. ensign USN, 1964, advanced through grades to capt.; chmn. dept. dermatology Winston-Salem (N.C.) Health Care Plan, 1984—. Methodist. Avocations: golf, reading. Office: Winston Salem Health Care 250 Charlois Blvd Winston Salem NC 27103-1579 Fax: (336) 718-1296. E-mail: wdhenrichs@novanthealth.org.

HENRICK, MICHAEL FRANCIS, lawyer; b. Chgo., Feb. 29, 1948; s. John L. and A. Madeline (Hafner) H.; m. Cissi F. Henrick, Aug. 9, 1980; children: Michael Francis Jr., Derry Patricia. BA, Loyola U., 1971; JD with honors, John Marshall Law Sch., 1974. Bar: Ill. 1974, U.S. Dist. Ct. (no. dist.) Ill. 1974, U.S. Supreme Ct. 1979, Wis. 1985, U.S. Dist. Ct. (ea. dist.) Wis. 1985. Ptnr. Hinshaw & Culbertson, Chgo., Waukegan, Ill., 1974—. Recipient Corpus Juris Secundum award West Publ. Co., 1974. Mem. ABA, Def. Rsch. Inst., Ill. Bar Assn., Lake County Bar Assn., Ill. Hosp. Attys. Assn., Internat. Assn. of Def. Counsel, Ill. Def. Attys. Assn., Soc. Trial Lawyers Def. Rsch. Inst., Am. Inns of Ct. Office: Hinshaw & Culbertson 110 N West St Waukegan IL 60085-4330 E-mail: m.henrick@hinshawlaw.com.

HENRICKS, ROGER LEE, retired social services administrator; b. Wauseon, Ohio, May 16, 1943; s. Clifford Seldon and Annabelle Mae (Perkins) H.; m. Judith Ann Shimp, Aug. 28, 1966 (div. Mar. 1981); children: Wendy, Craig, Joel; m. Helen Elizabeth Dennis, June 6, 1986. BA, Adrian (Mich.) Coll., 1966. Welfare caseworker Dept. Social Svcs., Adrian, Mich., 1966-68, protective svcs. caseworker, 1968-78, supr. protective svcs., 1978-94; exec. dir. Family Awareness Ctr., Adrian, 1994-97; youth specialist Adrian Tng. Sch., 1997-98; ret. Instr. Ea. Mich. U., Ypsilanti, 1977-82, Siena Heights Coll., Adrian, 1987-95, Parent Nurturing Program, Adrian, 1985-97; co-founder Family Awareness Ctr., Adrian, 1982-84; presenter in field. Founder, pres. Child Abuse and Neglect Coun., Adrian, 1977—, Sexual Abuse Task Force, Adrian, 1988-97; pres., bd. dirs. Call Someone Concerned, Adrian, 1972-86, hon. bd. dirs., 1986—. Recipient Nancy Nichols award Office Substance Abuse, 1983, Mich. Pub. Servant of Yr. award Govt. Adminstrs. Assn. Found, 1988, Ray Helfer award Mich. Commn. for Prevention Child Abuse, 1989. Avocations: woodworking, softball, basketball. E-mail: rlhendricks00@attbi.com.

HENRICKSON, CHRISTINE GULDAGER, social worker; b. Detroit, May 15, 1953; BA, Mich. State U., 1975; MSW, U. Mich., 1979. Cert. social worker, Mich. Adminstr. asst. programs for mentally retarded Clinton-Eaton-Ingham Cmty. Mental Health Bd., Lansing, Mich., 1975-76, referral worker Capitol Area Counseling Ctr., 1977; med. social worker St. Lawrence Hosp., Lansing, Mich., 1979-88; clin. social worker Shands Tchg. Hosp., U. Fla., Gainesville, 1988-89; sr. clin. social worker, clin. mgr., chief social worker, interim dir. dept., clin. social worker U. Mich. Health Sys., Ann Arbor, Mich., 1989—. Staff trainer, counselor Listening Ear, Inc., East Lansing, Mich., 1975—84, sexual assault counseling coord., 1976—77, ctr. coord., 1980. Mem. NASW, Assn. Oncology Social Workers, Soc. S.W. Leadership in Healthcare, Mich. Assn. Social Workers in Health Care. Office: D2202 Med Profl Bldg PO Box 0718 Ann Arbor MI 48106-0718 also: Heron Ridge Assoc Plymouth MI

HENRICKSON, EILER LEONARD, retired geologist, educator; b. Crosby, Minn., Apr. 23, 1920; s. Eiler Clarence and Mabel (Bacon) H.; children: Eiler Warren, Kristin, Kurt Eric, Ann Elizabeth. BA, Carleton Coll., 1943; PhD, U. Minn., 1956. Geologist U.S. Geol. Survey, Calif., 1943-44; instr. Carleton Coll., 1946-47, 48-51, asst. prof., 1951-53, 54-56, assoc. prof., 1956-62, prof., 1962-70, Charles L. Denison prof. geology, 1970-87, chmn. dept., 1970-78, wrestling coach, 1946-58, 83-87, Emeritus prof. geology, 1987—; prof. geology, chmn. dept. Colo. Coll., 1987-96, Emeritus prof. geology, 1997—; pres. Concentrating Systems of Am., 1996—, U.S. Vermiculite Products, 1997—, C.S.A. Corp., 1985—. Instr. U. Minn., 1947-48, 53-54; vis. lectr. numerous univs., Europe, 1962; cons. Jones & Laughlin Steel Corp., 1946-58, Fremont Mining Co., Alaska, 1958-61, G.T. Schieldahl Co., Minn., 1961-62, Bear Creek Mining Co., Mich., 1965-66, U. Minn. Messenia Expdn., 1966-75, Exxon Co., 1977-78, Cargill Corp., Mpls., 1983-84, Leslie Salt Co., San Francisco, 1985-86, various other cos.; research scientist, cons. Oak Ridge (Tenn.) Nat. Lab., 1985-86; cons. Argonne Nat. Lab., 1966-78, research scientist, summers, 1966-67; field studies metamorphic areas, Norway and Scotland; dir. young scholars program NSF, 1988-90. Author: Zones of Regional Metamorphism, 1957. Dir. Northfield Bd. Edn., 1960-63; steering com. Northfield Community Devel. Program, 1966-67. Served as 1st lt. USMCR, 1943, AUS, 1944-46. Fulbright research scholar archeol. geology, Greece, 1966-87. Mem. AAAS, Mineral Soc. Am., Nat. Assn. Geology Tchrs., Minn. Acad. Sci (vis. lectr.), Am. Geol. Inst., Geol. Soc. Am., Soc. Econ. Geologists, Rocky Mountain Assn. Geologists, Nat. Wrestling Coaches and Ofcls. Assn., Archaeol. Inst. Am. (vis. lectr.), Sigma Xi. Achievements include research in archaeology and geology of Greece and North Africa, 1977-78, in mineral potential of Greece and Egypt, 1978-79, on ore deposits and archaeology, geology, province of copper and tin in artifacts in N.Am. and world. Home: 2107 Park Pointe Dr Northfield MN 55057-3540 Fax: 507-645-4354.

HENRICKSON, LESLIE ANN, educational consultant, educator; b. Sioux Falls, S.D., May 20; d. Reynolds Keith Henrickson and A. Jeanne Burkhalter; m. Joseph Dairmuid Deely, Jan. 2, 1983 (div. 1993); children: Brenda Kathleen Deely, Brian Seamus Deely. B in Chem. Engring., U. Ill., 1982; M in Physics, San Jose State U., 1990; MPhil, U. Calif., Riverside, 1997; PhD in Edn., UCLA, 2003. Rsch. engr. in advanced tech. Lockheed Missiles and Space Co., Sunnyvale, Calif., 1983—89; rsch./process engr. Censtor Corp., San Jose, Calif., 1989—90; physics and chemistry instr. San Jose City Coll., 1992—94; philosophy and physics instr. San Jose State U., 1993—94; physics instr. Foothill C.C., Menlo Park, Calif., 1993—94; CEO, pres. Tech. Edn. Consulting and Rsch., L.A., 1999—; edn. rschr. Ctr. for Governance, L.A., 2001—, Ctr. for Assessment and Evaluation Student Learning, L.A., 2002—; prof. Touro U. Internat., Cypress, Calif., 2003—. Contbr. articles to profl. jours. Fellow Nat. Sci. fellow for Assn. for Instl. Rsch., NSF, 2000; grantee Doctoral Incentive Program, Calif. State U., 1995; Resident fellow at the Ctr. for Ideas and Soc., U. Calif., Riverside, 1995, Kneller scholar, UCLA, 1999, Nat. Sci. fellow for Ctr. for Assessment and Evaluation of Student Learning Project, NSF, 2002. Mem.: Comparative and Internat. Edn. Soc. (assoc.), Computer Using Educators (assoc.), Assn. Instl. Rsch. (assoc.), Sigma Pi Sigma (life). Methodist. Achievements include copyright pending on Student Technology Assessment Tool (Qwik-STAT) survey; copyright pending on computer program, Higher Education Enrollment Flow Predictor. Avocations: reading, running, needlecrafts. Home and Office: TECR 43 Weepingwood Irvine CA 92426 Office: Touro U Internat 5665 Plaza Dr 3d fl Cypress CA 90630 Personal E-mail: lhenrick@techeder.com.

HENRICSON, BETH ELLEN, microbiologist; b. Johnson City, N.Y., Apr. 22, 1947; d. Clifford Lyle and Margaret Addison (Moore) Hevenor; m. Lawrence Karl Henricson, Aug. 9, 1969; children: Erik Karl, Karen Jeanette. BS in Microbiology, Pa. State U., 1969; postgrad., U. Rochester, 1969-70; MEd, Boston U., Sechenheim, Germany, 1987; PhD in Biomed. Sci., Uniformed Svcs. U. Hlth. Scis., 1992. Registered clin. pub. health microbiologist Am. Acad. Microbiologists. Med. technologist Dept. of Army, Ft. Hood, Tex., 1981-84; microbiologist, med. technician Dept. of Army 5th Gen. Hosp., Stuttgart, Germany, 1986-87; predoctoral rsch. fellow USUHS, Bethesda, Md., 1987-92; NRC fellow FDA Ctr. Biol. Evaluation & Rsch., NIH, Bethesda, Md., 1992-93; postdoctoral rsch. fellow Henry M. Jackson Found., Bethesda, Md., 1993-95; microbiologist supr., quality assurance coord. Va. Dept. Agr. and Consumer Svcs., Warrenton, 1995—2002; adminstrv. officer Vet. Med. Assistance Team-2, Nat. Disaster Med. Sys., 2000—. Contbg. author: Endotoxin Research, 1990, Bacterial Endotoxins, 1995, Bioterrorism Agents: Implications for Animals, 2001, author, editor: VDACS Office of Animal Industry Lab. Svcs. Quality Assurance Guidance Manual; contbr. articles to profl. jours. Leader Boy Scouts Am., Hawaii, 1978—85, Girls Scouts Am., Tex., 1982—87; vol. Washington AIDS Ride, 1996. Scholar N.Y. State Regents, 1965. Mem.: AAUW, ACLU, LWV, AAAS, Am. Acad. Vet. Disaster Medicine, Am. Chem. Soc., Nat. Environ. Health Assn., Internat. Endotoxin Soc., Am. Soc. Microbiology, U.S. Animal Health Assn., Am. Assn. Vet. Lab. Diagnosticians (Bacteriology, Mycoplasmology, Mycology steering com. 1998—, subcom. for antimicrobial susceptibility testing 1998—, co-chair lab. biosafety com. 2002), Assn. Vet. Microbiologists (v.p. Colonial States chpt. 1996—98, pres. 1999—2001), N.Y. Acad. Scis., Phi Kappa Phi, Phi Beta Kappa, Phi Sigma, Iota Sigma Pi. Achievements include research in cellular and molecular mechanism of endotoxic shock and early endotoxin tolerance; systemic inflammatory response to endotoxin analogs; in LPS (lipopolysaccharide)-inducible gene expression; in systemic inflammatory response syndrome; in acyloxyacyl hydrolase contribution to LPS detoxification; in LPS and Taxol or paclitaxel activation of Lyn Kinase autophosphorylation and LPS-induced cytokine production; contribution of C. diphtheriae to wound infection in an equine; contribution in agents of bioterrorism: consequences in animals. Office: VMAT 2 Inc c/o Office of Emer Response/NDMS Office 12300 Twinbrook Pky Ste 520 Rockville MD 20852 E-mail: bhenricson@aol.com.

HENRIKSEN, EVA H. former anesthesiology educator; b. Petaluma, Calif., Jan. 1, 1929; d. Peder Henrik Boas and Karen (Nielsen) Henriksen; m. Daniel Edward MacLean, Aug. 25, 1957 (dec. Dec. 1981); children: Elizabeth, Mary Ann. AA, U. Calif., Berkeley, 1948, BA, 1950; MD, Yale U., 1954. Diplomate Am. Bd. Anesthesiology. Intern, resident Los Angeles County Hosp., L.A., 1954-57; from instr. to asst. prof. anesthesia Loma Linda U. (formerly Coll. Med. Evangelists), L.A., 1957-68; from instr. to assoc. prof. surgery anesthesiology Sch. Medicine U. So. Calif., L.A., 1957-94, assoc. prof. anesthesiology emeritus, 1994—. Anesthesia cons. L.A. Coroner's Office, 1992—2003. Mem. governing coun. Angelica Luth. Ch., 1992—2000, 2002—. Democrat. Avocation: patchwork quilt making. Home: 957 Arapahoe St Los Angeles CA 90006-5703

HENRIKSEN, MELVIN, mathematician, educator; b. N.Y.C., N.Y., Feb. 23, 1927; s. Kaj and Helen (Kahn) Henriksen; m. Lillian Viola Hill, July 23, 1946 (div. 1964); children: Susan, Richard, Thomas; m. Louise Levitas, June 12, 1964 (dec. Oct. 1997). BS, Coll. City N.Y., 1948; MS, U. Wis., 1949, PhD in Math, 1951. Asst. math., then instr. extension div. U. Wis., 1948-51; asst. prof. U. Ala., 1951-52; from instr. to prof. math. Purdue U., 1952-65; prof. math., head dept. Case Inst. Tech., 1965-68; research assoc. U. Calif. at Berkeley, 1968-69; prof., chmn. math. dept. Harvey Mudd Coll., 1969-72, prof., 1972-97, prof. emeritus, 1997—. Mem. Inst. Advanced Study, Princeton, 1956-57, 63-64; vis. prof. Wayne State U., 1960-61; rsch. assoc. U. Man., Winnipeg, Can., 1975-76; vis. prof. Wesleyan U., Middletown, Conn., 1978-79, 82-83, 86-87, 93-94. Author: (with Milton Lees) Single Variable Calculus, 1970; assoc. editor: Algebra Universalis, 1993—, Topology Atlas, 1996-2002, Topological Commentary, 1996-2002; mem. editl. bd. Functiones et Approximatio Commentario Mathematici, 2001—; author articles on algebra, rings of functions, gen. topology. Sloan fellow, 1956-58 Mem. Am. Math. Soc., Math. Assn. Am. (assoc. editor Am. Math. monthly 1988-91, assoc. editor Algebra Universalis 1993—). Office: Harvey Mudd Coll Math Dept Claremont CA 91711 E-mail: henriksen@hmc.edu.

HENRIKSEN, THOMAS HOLLINGER, university official; b. Detroit, Nov. 16, 1939; s. Paul and Irene (Hollinger) H.; m. Margaret Mary Mueller, Sept. 9, 1968; children— Heather Anne, Damien Paul Hollinger BA, Va. Mil. Inst., 1962; MA, Mich. State U., 1966, PhD, 1969. Asst. prof. SUNY, Plattsburgh, 1969-73, assoc. prof., 1973-79, prof., 1979-80; Peace fellow Hoover Instn. on War, Revolution and Peace Stanford (Calif.) U., 1979-80, research fellow, 1980-82, sr. research fellow, 1982 86, sr. fellow, 1986—, assoc. dir., 1983—, exec. sec. nat. fellows program, 1984—, mem. Pres.'s Commn. on White House fellows, 1987-93. Mem. U.S. Army Sci. Bd., 1984-90. Author: Mozambique: A History, 1978, Revolutiona and Counterrevolution: Mozambique's War of Independence, 1964-74, 1983, The New World Order: War, Peace and Military Preparedness, 1992, Clinton's Foreign Policy in Somalia, Bosnia, Haiti, and North Korea, 1996, Using Power and Diplomacy to Deal With Rogue States, 1999; co-author: The Struggle for Zimbabwe: Battle in the Bush, 1981; contbg. author, editor: Soviet and Chinese Aid to African Nations, 1980; Communist Powers in Sub-Saharan Africa, 1981; assoc. editor Yearbook on Internat. Communist Affairs, 1982-91; contbg. author, editor: One Korea? Challenges and Prospects for Reunification, 1994. Trustee George C. Marshall Found., 1993—. Served to lt. U.S. Army, 1963-65 Home: 177 Lundy Ln Palo Alto CA 94306-4563 Office: Stanford U Hoover Instn Stanford CA 94305

HENRIKSON, ARTHUR ALLEN, political cartoonist, educator; b. Oak Park, Ill., June 1, 1921; s. Allen Bernhardt and Florence Ella (Dixon) H.; m. Lois Elizabeth Wessling, July 3, 1943; children: Diane Elizabeth Russell, Janet Christine, Michele Charlene Smetana. Student, Austin Acad. Fine Arts, Chgo., Chgo. Acad. Fine Arts, 1936-37; BS, Northwestern U., 1946, postgrad., 1946-51. With advt. dept. Snips Mag., Chgo., 1947-56; advt. and layout Des Plaines (Ill.) Jour., 1956; with Wessling Svcs., Des Moines. Illustrator: Living the Good Life Microwave Recipebook, 1990, PMS-Solving the Puzzle, 1995; editl. polit. cartoonist for The Daily Herald, Paddock Pubs., Arlington Heights, Ill., 1955-2001, Des Plaines Jour., 1956-69, Rockford Newspapers, Inc., 1959-73, Reporter/Progress, Downers Grove, Ill., 1959-2001, The Doings, Hinsdale, Ill., 1960-73, Ill. Cartoon Svc., 1961-81, Ind. Register, Libertyville, Ill., 1961-75, Suburban Life, Berwyn, Ill., Harvey (Ill.) Tribune, 1962-73, St. Petersburg Times/Brandon Times, Fla., 2003—, others; contbr. cartoons to Modern Medicine, Esquire, Nat. Enquirer, AMA, Christian Sci. Monitor; cartoons reprinted in Today's Cartoon, 1962, Best Gag Cartoons of the Year, 1964, Best Editorial Cartoons of the Year, 1972-2002, also in Chgo. Sun Times, Chgo. Daily News, Chgo. Tribune, L.A. Times, Sacramento Bee, San Diego Union, U.S. News and World Report, numerous others; cartoons exhibited at Columbia U., 1960, Art Inst. Chgo., 1962, White House, Washington, 1963, LWV, Washington, 1963, others; promotional cartoons for NBC-TV, for Motorola; cartoons in permanent collections at Libr. of Congress, Lyndon Baines Johnson Libr., Mus. of Cartoon Art, State Hist. Soc. Mo., others. Mem. bd. deacons First Congl. Ch., United Ch. of Christ, Des Plaines, 1970-74, chmn., 1972, 74, moderator, 1976, also mem. mission bd. and music bd.; bd. dirs. Northwest Cmty. coun. Girls Scouts U.S., 1972-79; pres. Sch. Bd. Caucus, Des Plaines, 1968-72, pres., 1970. Lt. USAF, 1942—46, capt. Med. Adminstrv. Corps USAF, 1946. Recipient numerous awards for cartoons including Sigma Delta Chi Peter Lisagor award, George Washington Honor medal Freedoms Found., 1962, 63, 64, 65, 66, 69. Mem. Assn. Am. Editl. Cartoonists, Ret. Officers Assn. Avocations: music, theatre, art, travel. Home and Office: 27 N Meyer Ct Des Plaines IL 60016-2243 E-mail: lahenrikson@aol.com.

HENRIKSON, DONALD MERLE, forensic pathologist; b. Walla Walla, Wash., May 2, 1947; s. James Christan and Carol Jean (DuBois) H.; m. Eileen Ruth Mikita, Oct. 12, 1980. BA, Harvard U., 1969; MD, U. Calif., Davis, 1981. Diplomate Am. Bd. Pathology. Assoc. pathologist Lab. Medicine Cons., Inc., Auburn, Calif., 1986-87, FPMG, Inc., Auburn, 1987-88; owner, pathologist FFPMG, Auburn, 1989-94; assoc. pathologist NCFP, Inc., Sacramento, 1994—2002; pathologist Placer County Coroner's Office, Auburn, 2002—. Mem. med. staff Sierra Valley Dist. Hosp., Loyalton, Calif., 1992-95, Oroville Hosp. and Med. Ctr., 1986-95, Sierra Nev. Meml. Hosp., Grass Valley, Calif., 1986—, Sutter Auburn Faith Hosp., 1986—; asst. clin. prof. U. Calif. Sch. of Medicine, Davis, 1994—. Mem. Placer County Child Death Rev. Team, Auburn, 1990—; mem., former chair Sacramento County Child Death Rev Team, Sacramento, 1994-2001, mem. Nevada County Child Death Rev. Team, Nevada City, 1996—. Sgt. U.S. Army, 1969-71. Fellow Coll. of Am. Pathologists; mem. AMA, AAAS, Am. Acad. Forensic Scis., Am. Soc. for Clin. Pathology. Avocations: hiking, golfing, playing piano. Office: Placer County Coroner DeWitt Ctr 11500 A Ave Auburn CA 95603

HENRIKSON, LOIS ELIZABETH, photojournalist; b. Lytton, Iowa, Nov. 10, 1921; d. Daniel Raymond and Cora Elizabeth (Thomson) Wessling; m. Arthur Allen Henrikson, July 3, 1943; children: Diane Elizabeth Henrikson Russell, Janet Christine, Michele Charlene Henrikson Smetana. BS, Northwestern U., 1943. Adminstrv. asst. to v.p., dir. ops. bus. comm. divsn. ITT Telecommunications Corp., Des Plaines, Ill., 1980-82; adminstrv. asst. to exec. v.p. Wholesale Stationers' Assn., Des Plaines, 1982-84, membership svcs. coord., editor membership roster, 1984-88; field editor Office World News, BUS Publ. Group, Jericho, N.Y., 1988-92. Copy editor for author Jan Henrikson, 2000—. Contbg. editor: Home World Bus. ICD Publs., Today's Office, FM Bus. Publs., Inc., Office Tech. Mgmt., Bus. Tech. Comms. Inc.; project editor: Dyna Search, Inc., Wallace Offutt Cons.; pub. rels. photographer 1995—; contbr. and appeared on ABC 7 News investigative reports Signed, Sealed and Swindled, 1996, Fraud From Afar, 1998. Chair safety com. Cumberland Sch. PTA, Des Plaines, 1957-58, publicity 1960-61; bd. dirs. Maine West High Sch. Music Boosters, Des Plaines, 1967-69; capt. fin. dr. YMCA, Des Plaines, 1964; mem.

diaconate bd., visitation coord., growth and membership bd. 1st Congl. Ch., Des Plaines; mem. Art Inst. Chgo., Peale Ctr. for Christian Living. Mem. NAFE, AAUW (chair social com. 1983-84, editor newsletter 1984-85, 88-94, newsletter 1st pl. award 1993, membership com. 1988-94, N.W. Suburban Ill. br. Edtl. found. contbn. made in honor 1992, 95), DAR, Am. Soc. Assn. Execs. (cert. membership mktg. 1986), Am. Soc. Profl. and Exec. Women, Am. Assn. Editl. Cartoonists Aux., Chgo. Soc. Assn. Execs. (registrar 1984-85), Soc. Profl. Journalists, Am. Bus. Editors and Writers, Nat. Soc. Magna Charta Dames, Am. of Royal Descent, Northwestern Univ. Guild, Northwestern U. Club Chgo., Northwestern U. Half Century Club, Alpha Gamma Delta. Avocations: theater, music, art, traveling. Home and Office: 27 N Meyer Ct Des Plaines IL 60016-2243 E-mail: LAHENRKSON@aol.com. *Learn from the past, live in the present, plan for the future. Every experience in life and everyone you meet has a positive value to you although it may not be evident at the time.*

HENRION, ROSEMARY P. mental health professional; b. Greenville, Miss., Oct. 2, 1929; d. Vincent and Camille (Portera) Provenza; 1 child, Albert Joseph Henrion, Jr. BSN, U. Tex., 1963; MSN, Vanderbilt U., 1972; MEd, U. South Miss., 1974. Cert. logotherapist diplomate, med. psychotherapist psychodiagnosticians fellow and diplomate; cert. profl. psychotherapist diplomate. Instr. Maternal Child Health Nursing Inst. Miss. Gulf Coast Jr. Coll. Dist., Handsboro, 1964—66; dir. nursing svc. Meml. Hosp. Gulfport, Miss., 1967—68; clin. asst. prof. nursing La. State U., New Orleans, 1973—74; adj. clin. prof. grad. nursing program U. South Miss., Hattiesburg, 1983—92; faculty V.F. Inst. Logotherapy, Berkeley and San Jose, Calif., 1983—92, Abilene, Tex., 1993—; clin. instr. grad. nursing program U. So. Ala., Ala., 1998—99. Co-editor profl. book, 2002; co-author: The Power of Meaningful Intimacy: Key to Successful Relationships, 2003; contbr. articles to profl. jours., chpts. to books. Internat. bd. dirs. Inst. Logotherapy, 1989—. Named Miss. Nurse of Yr., 1988. Mem.: AAUW, Leadership Am. Alumni Assn., MS bd. of Nursing (pres. 1977—79), Wellsley Ctr. for Women, George Bush Presdl. Libr., Charles F. Menninger Soc., Viktor Frankl Inst. Logotherapy (life), Vanderbilt Alumni Assn., Sigma Theta Tau (Iota chpt. 1972—). Home and Office: 19 Wenmar Ave Pass Christian MS 39571-3144 E-mail: ahenrion@ametro.net.

HENRIQUES, DIANA BLACKMON, journalist; b. Bryan, Tex., Dec. 17, 1948; d. Lawrence Ernest and Pauline (Webb) Blackmon; m. Laurence Barlow Henriques, Jr., June 7, 1969. BA with distinction, George Washington U., 1969. Editor Lawrence Ledger, Lawrenceville, N.J., 1969-71; reporter Asbury Park (N.J.) Press, 1971-74; copy editor Palo Alto (Calif.) Times, 1974-76; investigative reporter Trenton (N.J.) Times, 1976-82; bus. writer The Phila. Inquirer, 1982-86; writer Barron's Fin. Weekly, N.Y.C., 1986-89, The New York Times, 1989—. Vis. fellow, cons. Woodrow Wilson Sch., Princeton U., N.J., 1981-82, Guggenheim Found., N.Y., N.J., 1981-82. Author: (books) The Machinery of Greed, 1986, Fidelity's World, 1995, The White Sharks of Wall Street, 2000; contbr. articles to profl. jours. Recipient Bell Prize N.J. Press Assn., 1977, Investigative Reporting prize Deadline Club, 1997; co-recipient Loeb award Deadline Reporting, 1999. Mem. N.Y. Fin. Writers Assn., Phi Beta Kappa, Lectr. Am. Press Inst. Avocations: walking, reading. Office: The New York Times 229 W 43rd St New York NY 10036-3959

HENRIQUES, JEFFREY BARLOW, psychology educator, consulting statistician; b. New Rochelle, N.Y., Nov. 1, 1958; s. Jeffrey Barlow Henriques and Kathryn Loeber; m. Laurie Anne Frost; children: Reuben, Simon. BA, Gettysburg (Pa.) Coll., 1980, SUNY, Purchase, 1985; MS, U. Wis., Madison, 1989, PhD, 1998. Assoc. rschr. N.Y. Hosp./Cornell U. Rsch. Ctr., White Plains, 1985-86; lectr. Edgewood Coll., Madison, 1991, 1998; instr. Madison Area Tech. Coll., 1997; cons. statistician U. Wis. Sch. Nursing, Madison, 1998—; lectr. psychology U. Wis., Madison, 1998—, fellow Tchg. Acad., 2002—. Contbr. articles to profl. jours., chpts. to books (Messerschmitt award 1989). Soccer coach, Madison Area Youth Soccer Assn., 1999—. Mem. APA, Soc. Psychophysiol. Rsch., Am. Psychol. Soc., Midwestern Psychol. Assn. Office: U Wis 600 Highland Ave H6/148 Madison WI 53792 Fax: (608) 263-5332. E-mail: jhenriqu@wisc.edu.

HENRY, BARBARA A. publishing executive; b. Oshkosh, Wis., July 23, 1952; d. Robert Edward and Barbara Frances (Aylesworth) H. BJ, U. Nev. Reporter Reno Newspapers, 1974-78, city editor, 1978-80, mng. editor, 1980-82; asst. nat. editor USA Today, Washington, 1982-83; exec. editor Reno Gazette-Jour., 1981-86; editor, dir. Gannett Rochester Newspapers, Rochester, NY; pub. Great Falls (Mont.) Tribune(part of the Gannett group), 1992-96; pres., pub. Des Moines Register, 1996—2000, The Indianapolis Star, 2000—02; pres. Ind. Newspaper Group, 2002—. Recipient Publisher of the Year, Gannett Newspaper Group, 2001. Mem. Soc. Profl. Journalists, Associated Press Mng. Editors, Am. Soc. Newspaper Editors, Calif.-Nev. Soc. Newspaper Editors (bd. dirs.). Avocation: skiing. Mailing: Indianapolis Star PO Box 145 Indianapolis IN 46206-0145*

HENRY, BRIAN THOMAS, lawyer; b. Chgo., Dec. 25, 1954; s. Thomas Joseph and Shirley Grace (Pfaff) H.; m. Mary Elizabeth Collins, Sept. 17, 1983; children: Kyle Justin, Erin Maureen, Colin Thomas. BA Honors in History magna cum laude, Loyola U., Chgo., 1977; JD, U. Ill., 1980. Bar: Ill. 1980, U.S. Dist. Ct. (no. dist.) Ill. 1980. Ptnr. Pretzel & Stouffe Chtd., Chgo., 1980—; fellow Am. Coll. of Trial Lawyers. Faculty instr. Ill. Assn. of Def. Trial Counsel Trial Acads., 1990-2003; seminar speaker Chgo. Bar Assn. Comparative Negligence Seminar, 1990, '91; cons. health care com. Inst. of Medicine of Chgo.; frequent lectr. med. groups. Editor-in-chief Recent Decisions Sect. of Ill. Bar Jour., 1979-80 Fellow Am. Coll. Trial Lawyers; mem. ASTL, ABA, Ill. Assn. Hosp. Attys., Ill. Assn. Def. Trial Counsel, Internat. Assn. Def. Counsel (faculty instr. trial acad. 2001), Ill. Bar Assn., Phi Alpha Theta, Phi Alpha Delta. Office: Pretzel & Stouffer Chtd 1 S Wacker Dr Ste 2500 Chicago IL 60606-4614

HENRY, C. BRAD, governor; b. Shawnee, Okla., June 10, 1963; m. Kimberley Blain; children: Leah, Laynie. BA, Okla. U., 1985, JD, 1988. Bar: Okla. 1988, U.S. Ct. Appeals (10th cir.), U.S. Dist. Ct. (we. dist.) Okla. Staff researcher Okla. State Senate, Oklahoma City, summer 1984, senator; econs. tchg. asst. U. Okla., Norman, 1983-85; legal asst. Henry Henry & Henry, Shawnee, summer 1985; law clk. Andrews Davis Legg Bixler Milsten & Murrah, Oklahoma City, summer 1987; pres. Brad Henry Oil Co., Inc., Shawnee, 1987-89; legal intern Cleveland County Legal Aid Office, Norman, 1987-88; assoc. atty. Andrews Davis Legg Bixler Milsten & Price, Oklahoma City, 1988-89; atty. City of Shawnee, 1989—2002, state senator, 1989—2002; assoc. Charles T. Henry, Inc. & Assocs., Shawnee, 1989—; gov. State of Okla., Oklahoma City, 2003—. Mng. editor Okla. Law Rev., 1988. Trustee St. Gregory's Coll.; bd. dirs. Gateway to Prevention and Recovery, Inc.; mem. Okla. Acad. for State Goals, First Bapt. Ch., Shawnee; active Muscular Dystrophy Assn.; commr. U. Okla. Election Commn., 1987-88; bd. govs. U. Okla., 1982-84; Okla. and Cleveland County coord. Robert Henry for Atty. Gen. Campaign, 1986. Mem. ABA, ATLA, Okla. Bar Assn., Am. Inn of Ct., Pottawatomie County Bar Assn. (pres. 1991), Shawnee C. of C. (amb.), Lions, Jaycees, Delta Tau Delta (pres. 1984), Phi Delta Phi. Office: Gov Office State Capitol Bldg Ste 212 Oklahoma City OK 73105*

HENRY, CARL NOLAN, lawyer; b. Washington, Sept. 30, 1965; s. Robert Benjamin Covington III and Inola Francis Henry. BA in Polit. Sci., U. Calif., Berkeley, 1987, JD, 1993. Bar: Calif. 1993, U.S. Supreme Ct. 1997, U.S. Ct. Appeal (9th cir.) 1993, U.S. Dist. Ct. (no., ctrl. dists.) Calif. 1993. Dep. atty. gen. Calif. Dept. Justice, L.A., 1994-99, 99—; staff atty. to Hon. Janice Rogers Brown Calif. Supreme Ct., San Francisco, 1999. Career Awareness Acad. scholar Home Savings Am., 1983; Liberal Arts award Bank Am., 1983. Mem. L.A. Angel City Links Assn. (O. J. Simpson Acad. scholar 1983), L.A. Ephebian Honor Soc. Democrat. Methodist. Avocations: sports, politics, music, history, education. Office: Calif Dept Justice 300 S Spring St Ste 5000 Los Angeles CA 90013-1230

HENRY, CARLA L. advertising executive; b. Hartford, Conn., Sept. 26, 1946; d. Robert W. Bresnan and Loretta Godwin; m. Edward J. Henry (div. 1973); children: Travis J., Zachary H., Justine. AA, Pierce Coll., 1989. Sales mgr. 3-I/Duracraft Tools, Northridge, Calif., 1977-84; jr. ptnr., owner DSA Mfg. Reps., Van Nuys, Calif., 1984-86; inside sales mgr. Spacelabs, Chatsworth, Calif., 1986-90; owner PODS Mktg., West Hills, Calif., 1990-91; mktg. mgr. DAMACO, Inc., Chatsworth, 1991-94; advt. specialist Adspec, Chatsworth, 1996—. Instr. Calif. State U., Northridge, 1997-99, Learning Tree U., Chatsworth, 1995, Thousand Oaks, 2001—. Author: Blueline-Poetry Anthology, 2002; (cookbook) Souper Skinny Soups, 1993, Vegetarians in the Fast Lane, 1996. Mem. PEN, Women's Nat. Book Assn. (bd. dirs. 1997-2000), Paradigm Poets, Calif. Writers Club (v.p. membership 1986-2000). Avocations: art, photography, hiking, poetry, reading. Office: Adspec 21818 Lassen St Unit D Chatsworth CA 91311 E-mail: carla@caladspec.com.

HENRY, CHARLES HOWARD, non-commissioned officer; b. Aurora, Ill., Oct. 14, 1966; s. Howard Hufford and Barbara Jeanne (Keller) H.; m. Trisha Barnhisel, May 8, 1999. Personnelman 3d class, USS Guardfish USN, San Diego, 1986-89, yeoman 2d class, comdr. submarine group 5, 1989-92, yeoman 2d class, USS Alabama Silverdale, Wash., 1993-96, pers. officer, cmdr. submarine squadron 22 La Maddalena, Sardinia, Italy, 1996-98, yeoman divsn. leading petty officer USS Jefferson City San Diego, 1998-2000; comdr. submarine force U.S. Pacific Fleet, shipyard representative Puget Sound Naval Shipyard, 2000—. Mem. U.S. Naval Inst., 1991-98. Named Sr. Sailor of Yr., Cmdr. Submarine Squadron 22, USN, 1997. Mem. Non-Commissioned Officers Assn., Warren G. Harding Lodge. Republican. Lutheran. Avocations: investing, current events, reading, music. E-mail: billiebighead@aol.com.

HENRY, DAVID HOWE, II, retired diplomat; b. Geneva, N.Y., May 19, 1918; s. David Max and Dorothy (Buley) H.; m. Margaret Beard, Nov. 16, 1946; children: David Beard, Peter York, Michael Max, Susan. Student, Hobart Coll., 1935-37, Sorbonne, 1937-38; AB, Columbia U., 1939; student, Russian Inst., 1948-49, Harvard U., 1944-45, Nat. War Coll., 1957-58. Ins. agt., 1939-41; mem. fgn. svc. Dept. State, 1941-71, assigned Montreal, 1941—42, assigned Beirut, 1942-44, Washington, 1944-45, 48-52, 57-66, 70, Moscow, 1945-48, 52-54, Vladivostok, 1945-46, Berlin, 1955-57; acting dir. Office Research and Intelligence Sino-Soviet bloc, 1958-59; dir. dept. polit. affairs Nat. War Coll., 1959-61; dep. dir. Office Soviet Affairs, 1961-64, dir., 1964-65; mem. Policy Planning Council, 1965-66; dep. chief of mission Am. embassy, Reykjavik, Iceland, 1966-69; information systems specialist, 1970; polit. and security council affairs UN, N.Y.C., 1971—79. Mem.: Rotary, Kappa Alpha. Presbyterian. Home: 2551 SW Brookwood Ln Palm City FL 34990-4752

HENRY, DEWITT PAWLING, II, creative writing educator, writer, arts administrator; b. Wayne, Pa., June 30, 1941; s. John and Kathryn (Thralls) Henry; m. Constance Joy Sherbill, Aug. 25, 1973; children— Ruth Kathryn, David Jung Min. AB, Amherst Coll., 1963; A.M., Harvard U., 1965, PhD, 1971; postgrad., U. Iowa-Iowa City, 1964-66. Editor Ploughshares, dir. Ploughshares, Inc., Watertown, Mass., 1971-89, exec. dir., 1989-95; dir. Book Affairs, Inc., Watertown, 1975-85. Adj. prof. Emerson Coll., Boston, 1982-83, asst. prof. creative writing and lit., 1983-89, assoc. prof., 1989—, acting chair div. writing, pub. and lit., 1987-88, chair, 1989-93; mem. adv. panel Mass. Coun. on the Arts, Boston, 1981-83; literature panelist Nat. Endowment for the Arts, Washington, 1982-85, 92-93; mem. adv. bd. New England Found. for Arts, 1983-85; mem. Watertown Arts Lottery coun., 1987-92; bd. dirs., treas. Associated Writing Programs, 1988-90, pres., 1990-91. Author: The Ploughshares Reader, New Fiction for the 80s, 1985, Other Sides of Silence, New Fiction from Ploughshares, 1993, Fathering Daughters, 1998, Breaking Into Print, 2000, Sorrow's Company: Writers on Loss and Grief, 2001, The Marriage of Anne Maye Potts, 2001; columnist Wilson Libr. Bull., 1979-81; staff editor The Pushcart Prize, 1978—. Fellow Woodrow Wilson found., 1963; fellow Coordinating Council of Literary Mags., 1979, Nat. Endowment for Arts, 1979 Mem. Associated Writing Programs, Phi Beta Kappa Presbyterian. Home: 33 Buick St Watertown MA 02472-2176 Office: Emerson Coll Writing Lit Pub Divsn 120 Boylston St Boston MA 02116-4624 E-mail: bakofpak@aol.com.

HENRY, DONNA EDWARDS, educator; b. Washington, Oct. 1, 1949; d. Conard Paul and Jean Marie (Kemp) E. BS, D.C. Tchrs. Coll., 1971; MA, Columbia U., 1974. Cert. tchr., Md. Tchr. Binghamton (N.Y.) Sch. System, 1971-73; group tchr., supr., acting dir. N.Y.C. Coll. Day Care Ctr., 1974-76; tchr., supr. student tchrs. Balt. City Schs., 1976-87, Prince George's County Schs., Laurel, Md., 1987—, Bowie, Md., 1996—. Asst. volley-ball coach Binghamton Sch. System, 1973; project dir. Fund for Ednl. Excellence, Balt., 1986-87 (ednl. grant); participant Gov.'s Acad. Sci., Math., and Tech. Towson (Md.) State U., 1991. Contbr. articles and photographs to mags.; co-writer nat., state and nat. awards. Coach Balt. City Volleyball League, 1979-80; vol. Balt. Neighborhoods, Inc., 1980-87. Winner Washington Post Grants for Edn., 1995. Mem. NAFE, NEA (Vol. conv. comms. com.), Md. Assn. Sci. Tchr. Avocations: photography, racquetball, volleyball.

HENRY, EDWARD FRANK, computer accounting service executive; b. East Cleveland, Ohio, Mar. 18, 1923; s. Edward Emerson and Mildred Adelia (Kulow) H.; m. Nicole Annette Peth, June 18, 1977. BBA, Dyke Coll., 1948; postgrad., Case Western Reserve U., 1949, Cleve. Inst. Music, 1972. Cert. Notary Public Ohio. Internal auditor E.F. Hauserman Co., 1948-51; sales and radio announcer Sta. WSRS, 1951; office mgr. Frank C. Grismer Co., 1951-52, Broadway Buick Co., 1952-55; sec., treas. Commerce Ford Sales Co., 1955-65; nat. mgr. Auto Acctg. divsn. United Data Processing Co., Cin., 1966-68; v.p. Auto Data Sys. Co., Cleve., 1968-70; pres. Profl. Mgmt. Computer Sys., Inc., Cleve., 1970—2003, Profl. Mgmt. Computer Sys. Becane Internat., 1999—2003, ComputerEASE, Small Bus. Computer Ctrs. divsn. Profl. Mgmt. Computer Sys., Inc., 1985—2003, VideoEASE CompuAIDE Computerized Video Rental Sys. divsn. Profl. Mgmt. Computer Systems, Inc., 1987-89; pres. CompuPRINT divsn. Profl. Mgmt. Computer Sys., Inc., 1995—, pres. TravelEASE divsn., 1996—. Drum maj., musician Wurlitzer Marching Band, Cleve., 1939—42, The Ed Henry Dance Band, 1939—42; with USAF Marching Band, Kearns, Utah, 1943; dramatic dir., actor Euclid Little Theatres, Jewish Cmty. Ctr. ; actor Cleve. Playhouse, 1961—63; dramatic dir., actor various other theatres; exec. artistic dir. NorthCoast Cultural Ctr., 1989—. Contbr. photography, Travel Agents Internat. mag., 1990 (hon. mention, 1990); prodr., dir. (Jesters) (plays) National Book of the Play Acapulco, Mexico, 1985, nat. prodr., dir. (Jesters) Nat. Book of the Play Reno, 1988—, Bally's Celebrity Rm., Las Vegas, 1989—96, Hyatt Regency O'Hare, 1998, Millennium, 2000, Nat. Book of the Play Bally's Las Vegas. Charter pres. No. Ohio Coun. Little Theatre, 1954—56; founder, artistic and mng. dir. Exptl. Theatre, Cleve., 1959—63; bd. dirs. Cleve. Philharm. Orch., 1972—74, Cleve. Jazz Orch., 1991—, Cleve. Opera League, Back on Board, 2002. 1st lt. USAF, 1943—46, PTO, capt. USAF, 1946—57. Decorated Bronze Star with 3 oak leaf clusters; named in Showtime in Cleveland: The Rise of A Regional Theater Center (John Vacha). Mem.: APA, Res. Officers Assn., Internat. Soc. Photographers, Associated Photographers Internat., Internat. Platform Assn., Am. Soc. Profl. Cons., Nat. Assn. Profl. Cons., Data Processing Mgmt. Assn., Mil. Order World Wars (commdr. Cleve. chpt. 1994—95, adjutant 2001, dept. commdr. State of Ohio 2001), Inst. Mgmt. Accts., Am. Mgmt. Assn., Air Force Assn. (life), Art Inst. Chgo., Cleve. Mus. Art, Nat. Assn. Met. Mus. Art of N.Y., Mayfield Area C. of C., Ky. Cols., Rotary, Univ. Club, Acacia Country Club, Hermit Univ. Club, Cleve. Grays Club, Deep Springs Trout Club, Jesters (dramatic dir. 1971—, dir. 1981, impresario 1984—99, impresario emertus 2000, Cleve. Ct. # 14, SOBIB, Kachina), Grotto, Scottish Rite (dramatic dir. 1967—, thrice potent master 1982—84, class named in his hon. 1994), DeMolay (master Cleve. Chpt. 1942, Legion of Honor 1970), Sojourners (Nat. President's cert. 1977—78, pres. Cleve. chpt. #23 1978), Masons (50 yr. hon. 1994, hon. 33d degree St. Bernard lodge, Doge City), Am. Legion, VFW, KT, Heroes of '76 (comdr. Cleve. 1977), Cuyahoga County Meml. Lodge (worshipful master 1993—94), Shriners (dramatic dir. 1968—88), Phi Kappa Gamma (charter pres., past nat. pres.). Republican. Presbyterian. Home: 666 Echo Dr Gates Mills OH 44040-9606 Office: Profl Mgmt Computer Systems Inc 19701 S Miles Rd Cleveland OH 44128-4257 Fax: 216-663-9822. E-mail: pmcscomputerease@aol.com.

HENRY, ELAINE OLAFSON, artist, educator; b. Marshall, Minn., Aug. 25, 1945; d. Norman Jonas and Isfold Sigurdur (Josefson) Olafson; m. James Edward Henry, Sept. 30, 1967 (div. Dec. 1978); children: Julie Lynn, Cheryl Anne Henry Fields; m. Richard Story Garber, July 25, 1992. BFA, U. Wyo., 1992; MFA, So. Ill. U., 1995. Mktg. coord. Cannon Design, Inc., Grand Island, N.Y., 1978-82; mktg. cons. Mpls., 1982-83; mktg. dir. Campbell City C. of C., Gillette, Wyo., 1983-86; owner J&J Awards and Ad Concepts, Gillette, 1986-89; grad. asst. So. Ill. U., Carbondale, 1992-95; asst. prof. Emporia (Kans.) State U., 1996—2002, chair dept. art, 2000—, assoc. prof., 2002—. Pres. Nat. Coun. on Edn. for the Ceramic Arts, Erie, Colo., 2002—; pres. Emporia Arts Coun., 1997-99; pres. Kans. Artist Craftsman Assn., 1999-2000. Featured artist/sculptor Ceramics: Mastering the Craft, 2001, Studio Potter Mag., 1999, Ceramic Design Book, 1998; featured artist and author Ceramics Monthly Mag., 1996. Emporia State U. grantee, 1997, 99; recipient awards. Mem. Kans. Artist Craftsmen Assn. (pres. 1999). Avocations: travel, books, music. Office: Emporia State U Campus Box 4015 1200 Commercial St Emporia KS 66801-5087

HENRY, FRANCES ANN, journalist, educator; b. Denver, July 23, 1939; d. Lewis Byford and Betsy Mae (Lancaster) Patten; m. Charles Larry, June 28, 1963 (div. May 1981); children: Charles Kevin, Tracy Diane. BA in English, Carleton Coll., 1960; MA in Social Sci., U. Colo., Denver, 1988; MA in Journalism, Memphis State U., 1989. Cert. tchr. Lang. arts tchr. Rolla (Mo.) Pub. Schs., 1963-66; journalism/English tchr. Douglas County Pub. Schs., Castle Rock, Colo., 1976-99, retired, 1999, chmn. English dept., 1992-98; asst. prof. Memphis State U., 1991-92; mng. editor Douglas County News-Press, Castle Rock, 1986-87; editor Fourth World Bulletin, 1988; exec. editor Daily Helmsman Memphis State U., 1988-89, gen. mgr. Daily Helmsman, 1991-92; sole proprietor The Editor's Desk, 1997—. Contbr. articles to profl. jours. Recipient Gov.'s award for excellence in edn. Colo. Endowment for Humanities, 1997. Mem. ACLU, Colo. H.S. Press Assn. (sec. 1981-83, pres. 1983-91, bd. dirs., named Colo. Journalism Tchr. of Yr. 1985), Mensa, Kappa Tau Alpha. Democrat. Episcopalian.

HENRY, FREDERICK EDWARD, lawyer; b. St. Louis, Aug. 28, 1947; s. Frederick E. and Dorothy Jean (McCulley) H.; m. Vallie Catherine Jones, June 7, 1969; children: Christine Roberta, Charles Frederick. AB, Duke U., 1969, JD with honors, 1972. Bar: Ill. 1972, U.S. Dist. Ct. (no. dist.) Ill. 1972, Calif. 1982. Assoc. Baker & McKenzie, Chgo., 1972-79, ptnr., 1979—. Elder, session mem. Fourth Presbyn. Ch., Chgo., 2000—02; bd. dirs. Lincoln Park Conservation Assn., 1983—85, Old Town Triangle Assn., Chgo., 1980—83, pres., 1984. Recipient Willis Smith award, Duke U. Law Sch., 1972. Mem.: ABA, Calif. State Bar, Chgo. Bar Assn., Order of Coif. Home: 164 W Eugenie St Chicago IL 60614-5809 Office: Baker & McKenzie 1 Prudential Plz 130 E Randolph St Ste 3700 Chicago IL 60601-6342 E-mail: frederick.e.henry@bakernet.com.

HENRY, GARY NORMAN, air force officer, astronautical engineer; b. Fort Wayne, Ind., Nov. 3, 1961; s. Norman Thomas and Elaine Cathrine (Schabb) H. BS in Astro. Engrng. with distinction, USAF Acad., 1984; MS in Aero./Astronautical Engrng., Stanford U., 1988; grad., USAF Test Pilot Sch., 1994, USAF Air Command & Staff Coll., 1997; student, Air War Coll., Air U., Maxwell AFB, Ala., 2002—03. CFP. Commd. 2d lt. USAF, 1984, advanced through grades to lt. col., 2000; project engr. USAF Weapons Lab., Kirtland AFB, N.Mex., 1984-87; asst. prof. astronautics USAF Acad., Colorado Springs, 1989-93; flight test engr. 418 Flight Test Squadron, Edwards AFB, Calif., 1993-94, chief flight dynamics br., 1994-95; exec. officer USAF Flight Test Ctr., Edwards, 1995-96; dep. dir. test and evaluation Airborne Laser Sys. Program Office, Kirtland AFB, N.Mex., 1997-99; lead airborne laser (PEM) Air Staff, The Pentagon, 1999-2001; dep. divsn. chief for counter air directorate global power Asst. Sec. of the Air Force, The Pentagon, 2001—02; chief advanced tech. divsn. Space Superiority Sys. Program Office, Los Angeles AFB, Calif., 2003—; sole propr. Polaris Fin. Svcs., 1987—. Editor: (textbook) Space Propulsion Analysis and Design, 1995; contbr. articles to profl. jours. Recipient sci. and engrng. award USAF, 1993. Mem. AIAA (sr. mem., hybrid rocket tech. com. 1993-94, Young Engr. of Yr. Rocky Mountain region 1993), Fin. Planning Assn. Achievements include research director of 1st successful Department of Defense land-based hybrid sounding rocket flight. E-mail: gary.genry@losangeles.af.mel.

HENRY, HELGA IRMGARD, liberal arts educator; b. Soppo, Buea, Cameroon, May 30, 1915; d. Carl Jacob and Hedwig (Kloeber) Bender; m. Carl F.H. Henry, Aug. 17, 1940; children: Paul Brentwood (dec. 1993), Carol Jennifer. BA, Wheaton Coll., Ill., 1936, MA, 1937; M of Religious Edn., No. Bapt. Theol. Sem., 1945. Dean of women, instr. in German State Tchrs.' Coll., Ellendale, N.D., 1937-40; librarian, instr. in lit., religious edn. No. Bapt. Theol. Sem., Chgo., 1940-47; instr. German Wheaton Coll., 1945-47; assoc. prof. edn. Pasadena (Calif.) Coll., 1951-60; vis. instr. religious edn. Ea. Bapt. Theol. Sem., Phila., 1963-66. Chmn., treas. The Elmer Bisbee Found., 1986-91. Author: Mission on Main Street, 1955, Cameroon on a Clear Day, 1999; translator: Paulus Scharpff, History of Evangelism, 1966. Trustee Ea. Bapt. Theol. Sem., 1971-73. Home: 1141 Hus Dr Apt 206 Watertown WI 53098-3258

HENRY, J. MYRLE, pharmacist; b. Jacksonville, Fla., Aug. 30, 1938; s. Joseph Mason and Ovieda Ida (Dossey) H.; m. Tommie Claire Williams, Aug. 28, 1959; children: Cheri Kim, Kathy Lynn. BSP, U. Fla., 1961. Registered pharmacist Fla. Pharmacist Barwick Drugs, Plant City, Fla., 1961, Magnolia Pharmacy, Plant City, 1962-66, pharmacist, co-owner, 1966-80; co-owner H&R Drug Ctr., Plant City, 1973-85, owner, 1985-93, Herring Drug, Plant City, 1977-86; pharmacist, owner Magnolia Pharmacy, 1980-2000; pharmacist Kash n Karry Pharmacy, Plant City, 2000—. Past mem. Hillsborough County Citizens Adv. Com.; pres. The Fla. Opry; past pres. East Hillsboro Hist. Soc.; Plant City Down Town Bus. and Merchants Assn.; founder, pres. Bapt. Towers Plant City, Inc.; deacon 1st Bapt. Ch.; pres. Christian Living Ctr., Inc.; trustee So. Fla. Bapt. Hosp.; past bd. dirs. Hillsborough County unit Am. Cancer Soc., past chmn. Plant City br.; founder, past chmn. Strawberry Classic Car Show. Named Plant City's Citizen of Yr., 2001. Mem.: East Hillsborough C. of C. (past bd. dirs., past treas.), Fla. State Pharm. Assn., Am. Pharm. Assn., Hillsborough County Pharmacy Assn. (past pres.), Plant City Lions Club, Kappa Psi. Avocations: swimming, tennis, gardening. Office: Kash n Karry Pharmacy Wheeler St Plant City FL 33566

HENRY, JACK ALLEN, JR., music educator; b. Roswell, N.Mex., June 21, 1950; s. Jack Allen, Sr. and Dalphna Lee Henry; m. Esther Deann Shaw, Aug. 23, 1975; children: Austin Lee, Joseph Charles. BA in Music Edn., SW Mo. State U., 1975; MusM, Boston U., 1986; DMA, U. Mo., Kansas City, 2002. Cert. min. BBFI, 1972; music tchr. Mo. Chmn. music dept. Boston Bapt. Coll., 1981—89, Bapt. Bible Coll., Springfield, 1998—; min. of music Pk. Crest Bapt. Ch., Springfield, Mo., 1994—. Adjudicator for music competitions Mo. Music Educators Assn., 2001—; music cons./seminarian, 1981—. Composer: (oratorio) The Seven Seals, (numerous compositions for orchestra) Fixed Form, Atmospheres for Strings, 2000, (chamber work) Regroup. Coord. Springfield Choir Festival, 1999—. Fellow, U. Mo.-Kansas City, 1996. Mem.: ASCAP, Am. Composers Forum, Am. Choral Directors Assn., Soc. of Composers, Inc., Mo. Assn. Depts. and Schs. of Music. Republican. Baptist. Avocations: painting, distance running, gardening. Office: Baptist Bible Coll 628 E Kearney St Springfield MO 65803 E-mail: jhenry@bbcnet.edu.

HENRY, JOHN BERNARD, pathologist, university president; b. Elmira, N.Y., Apr. 26, 1928; m. Georgette Boughton, June 10, 1953; children: Maureen Anne, Julie Patricia, William Bernard, Paul Bernard, John Bernard, Thomas David. AB, Cornell U., 1951; MD, U. Rochester, 1955. Diplomate: Am. Bd. Pathology (v.p. 1974-75, 76-79, pres. 1976-78, trustee). Intern ward med. service Barnes Hosp., St. Louis, 1955-56; resident pathology Presbyn. Hosp., N.Y.C., 1956-58, New Eng. Deaconess Hosp., Boston, 1958-60; trainee Nat. Cancer Inst., NIH, 1958-60; clin. pathologist, chmn. clin. lab. com., dir. Blood Bank and Clin. Labs. Teaching Hosp. and Clinic, U. Fla., 1960-64; asst. medicine Washington U. Sch. Medicine, St. Louis, 1955-56; asst. pathology, then instr. pathology Columbia Coll. Phys. and Surg., 1956-58; teaching fellow pathology Harvard U. Med. Sch., 1959-60; asst. prof., then asso. prof. pathology U. Fla. Coll. Medicine, 1960-64; prof. pathology Coll. Medicine; dir. clin. pathology SUNY, Upstate, Syracuse, 1964-79; dean Coll. Health Related Professions SUNY Upstate Med Ctr., 1971-77; dean, prof. pathology Georgetown U. Sch. Medicine, Washington, 1979-84; pres. SUNY Upstate Med. U., Syracuse, 1985-92, prof. pathology, past pres., 1992—. Author numerous articles on chemistry, med. edn. and immunopathology field. Bd. dirs. FACT, 1985-90. With USN, 1946-48, capt. USNR, 1967-95. Recipient S.C. Dyke Founder award Assn. Clin. Pathologists, 1979. Fellow Coll. Am. Pathologists, Am. Soc. Clin. Pathologists (bd. dirs. 1974-82, pres. 1980-81, Distinguished Serv. Clin. Pathology award 1993), Am. Coll. Physician Execs.; mem. Am. Acad. Clin. Toxicology, AAAS, Am. Blood Commn. (pres. 1978-80), Am. Assn. Blood Banks (pres.), Am. Assn. Clin. Chemists, Am. Assn. History Medicine, Am. Assn. Med. Writers, Am. Chem. Soc., Am. Mgmt. Assn., AMA, Assn. Am. Med. Colls., Soc. Advanced Med. Systems, Am. Assn. Pathologists, Am. Soc. Histocompatibility and Immunogenetics, Internat. Soc. Blood Transfusion, Soc. Med. Consultants to Armed Forces, World Assn. Socs. Pathology, Med. Soc.

D.C. (exec. bd. 1982-84), CAP (chmn. future tech. com. 1985-92, bd. dirs. council on edn. and pubs. 1986-92), Onondaga Med. Soc. (bd. dirs.), Alpha Omega Alpha. Office: SUNY Upstate Med Ctr Dept Pathology 750 E Adams St Syracuse NY 13210-1834

HENRY, JOHN COOPER, journalist; b. San Antonio, Sept. 18, 1948; s. Deck Houston and Ruth Brophy (Cooper) H.; m. Patricia Mayer, Oct. 3, 1981. BS in History, Miss. State U., 1975. Photographer Starkville (Miss.) Daily News, 1975; politics and govt. reporter Delta Dem. Times, Greenville, Miss., 1975-79; reporter Austin (Tex.) Am.-Statesman, 1979-85, asst. state editor, 1985-86, state capitol bur. chief, 1986-88, asst. bus. editor, 1989-90; asst. city editor Houston Chronicle, 1990-93, night city editor, 1993-95, polit. editor, 1995—97, Washington bur. reporter, 1997—99, asst. Washington bur. chief, 1999—2000, Washington bur. chief, 2000—. Mem. steering com., reporters com. Freedom of the Press, Washington, 1985—, mem. exec. com., 1992-94; mem. steering com. Tex. Media: A First Amendment and Freedom of Info. Coalition, Austin, 1986-95. Asst. comm. dir. Gil Carmichael for Gov. campaign, Meridian, Miss., 1975. Staff Sgt. USAF, 1967-71. John S. Knight Journalism fellow, Stanford (Calif.) U., 1988-89. Mem. Soc. Profl. Journalists, Freedom of Info. Found. Tex. (bd. dirs. 1990-96), U.S. Golf Assn., Houston Press Club. Presbyterian. Avocations: golf, hiking. Office: Houston Chronicle Pub Co 1850 K St NW Ste 10009 Washington DC 20006

HENRY, JOHN W. professional sports team executive; b. Quincy, Ill. m. Peggy Henry; 1 child. Founder, chmn. John W. Henry & Co., Inc., Boca Raton, Fla., 1981—, Westport, Conn., 1981—; chmn., majority owner Class AAA Tucson Toros, Pacific Coast League, 1989-97; co-owner W. Palm Beach Tropics, Sr. Baseball League, 1989—; limited ptnr. N.Y. Yankees, 1992—; chmn. Fla. Marlins Baseball Club, Miami, 1999—2002; majority owner Boston Red Sox, 2002—. Mem. Nat. Assn. Futures Trading Advisors (bd. dirs.), Managed Futures Trade Assn. (bd. dirs.), Nat. Futures Assn. (mem. nominating com.), Futures Industry Assn. (bd. dirs.). Office: Boston Red Sox 4 Yawkey Way Boston MA 02215-3496

HENRY, JOSEPH LOUIS, university dean; b. New Orleans, May 2, 1924; s. Varice S. and Mabel (Mansion) H.; m. Dorothy L. Whittle, July 28, 1954 (dec. 1991); children: Joseph Louis, Ronald Maurice, Joan Alison, Leilani Cecile (Mrs. P. Smith), Peter Donald; m. Gracia Bautista Cua, Jan. 1995. D.D.S., Howard U., 1946; BS, Xavier U., 1948, Sc.D., 1975; MS, Ill. U., 1949, PhD, 1951; D.H.L., Ill. Coll. Optometry, 1973; MA (hon.), Harvard U., 1975. Diplomate Am. Bd. Oral Medicine. Instr. oral medicine Coll. Dentistry, Howard U., Washington, 1946-48, assoc. prof. oral medicine, 1951-53, supt. clinics, 1953-65, prof. oral medicine, 1958-66, dir. clinics, 1965-66, dean, 1966-75, dean emeritus, 1981—; chmn., prof. oral diagnosis and radiology Sch. Dental Medicine, Harvard U., 1975—, prof. emeritus, 1995, assoc. dean, 1978-93, interim dean, 1990-91. Nat. adv. coun. dental rsch., HHS, 1991—; Joseph N. Pew Charitable Trust health prof. com. adv. panel for dent., 1991—; nat. adv. coun. on health professions edn. HHS, 1990-92, IOM Commn. on Educating Dentists for Future 1993-95, Nat. Affairs Commn., 1993—; minority audit panel mem. Clinton Health Care Program, 1993; rsch. fellow U. Ill.; extern U. Ill. Rsch. and Ednl. Hosp., Chgo., 1948-51; cons. Freedmen's Hosp., 1951—, Tuskegee VA Hosp., 1951—, Crownsville (Md.) State Hosp., 1960—; trustee Ill. Coll. Optometry, 1972—, chmn. bd. trustees, 1982-86; cons. Essex Community Coll., 1972, Roxbury Med.-Tech. Inst., 1969—, Bakers Dozen Youth Center, Project Headstart, Peace Corps, Mt. Altoe Vets. Hosp.; bd. govs. D.C. Gen. Hosp., 1971-72; mem. dental editorial award com. William J. Gies Found. Advancement Dentistry; mem. adv. panel for dentistry Pew Health Professions Commn., 1991—; mem. nat. adv. coun. for dental rsch. HHS, 1991—; adj. prof. dental practice Sch. Dentistry, U. Pacific, 2000—. Contbr. to: Optometry: Education for the Profession, 1973, Optometric Education, A Summary Report, 1973, also articles in profl. jours. Mem. White House Conf. Internat. Relations, 1965; cons. White House Conf. Employment Handicapped, 1967, Nat. Urban Coalition, 1971, Nat. Commn. on Optometry, 1971-72; sponsor Boys Town, 1955— ; life mem. NAACP; sponsor Urban League, 1953— ; program dir. YMCA, 1950-51; mem. St. Gabriel's PTA, 1960— ; trustee D.C. div. Am. Cancer Soc., Ill. Coll. Optometry; bd. dirs. Inst. Myofunctional Therapy, 1973, Symposia and Seminars, Inc., 1974; mem. Commn. Ednl. Credit Am. Council Edn., 1974; trustee Roxbury Latin Sch.; bd. dirs. W.E.B. DuBois Inst. Harvard U. Afro-Am. Research, 1976, Urban Health Project, 1997. Served to 2d lt. ASTP, 1942-43. Recipient Student Body and Student Council Faculty award, 1964, Achievement award Howard U. Dental Coll., 1967, Wisdom award Honor, 1970, Dental Alumni award, 1971, Inter-Alumni award United Negro Coll. Fund, 197O, Pub. Service award Urban League, 1970, awards Nat. Dental Assts., 1970, awards Nat. Naval Dental Sch., 1971, awards Roxbury Med.-Tech. Inst., 1972, Founders award Nat. Optometric Assn., 1973, Triennial award Nat. Dental Assn., 1973, award services D.C. govt., 1975, Disting. Svc. award Am. Assn. Dental Schs., 1995, Disting. Friend award Ill. Coll. Optometry, 1995, Carel C. Koch Meml. Medal award Am. Acad. Optometry, 1996, Orgn. of Tchrs. of Oral Diagnosis award, Presdl. Medal of Honor, Ill. Coll. Optometry, 1999, Koch Meml. award for outstanding contbns. to the profession Am. Acad. Optometry, 1999; named Dentist of Year D.C. Dental Soc., 1973 Fellow AAAS (v.p., chmn. sect. on dentistry, mem.-at-large sect. dentistry), Internat., Am. Coll. Dentists, Royal Soc. Health; mem. Nat. Dental Assn. (Achievement award 1967, dentist of year award 1972, Presdl. award 1976), ADA (Quiz bowl champion trophy 1970, chmn. sect. periodontics ann. meeting 1976), Am. Acad. Oral Medicine (Robert T. Freeman award 1972, numerous others), Inst. Medicine, D.C. Dental Soc., Maimonides Dental Soc., Internat. Assn. Dental Research, Nat. Acad. Scis., Washington Acad. Sci., N.Y. Acad. Scis., Am. Acad. Polit. and Social Scis., Am. Assn. Tchrs. Practice Adminstrn. (pres., v.p., mem. exec. com.), Greater Washington Periodontal Soc. (pres. 197O), Am. Acad. Periodontology, AAUP, Am. Assn. Dental Schs., Acad. Dental Practice Adminstrn. (chmn. profl. liaison com. 1972), Acad. History of Dentistry, Am. Coll. Health Orgn., Howard U., U. Ill., Xavier U. alumni clubs, Sigma Xi, Alpha Eta Epsilon, Alpha Kappa Mu, Chi Delta Mu, Chi Lambda Kappa, Omicron Kappa Upsilon. Roman Catholic. Address: 60 Marinita Avenue San Rafael CA 94901 *My success is primarily attributable to "the way the twig was bent" by my parents. They provided a home in which love for God, each other and our fellow man prevailed.*

HENRY, JOSEPH PATRICK, chemical company executive; b. Mansfield, Ohio, Mar. 3, 1925; s. Harold H. and Louise A. (Droxler) H.; student Bowling Green State U., 1943-44; B.S., Ohio State U., 1949; m. Jeanette E. Russell, Oct. 26, 1957; 1 dau., Jeanette Louise. Ohio sales mgr. NaChurs Plant Food Co., Marion, Ohio, 1949-55; organizer, pres. Growers Chem. Corp., Milan, 1955—, Sandusky Imported Motors, Inc. (Ohio), 1958-78; pres. Homestead Motors, Inc., 1978-83; co-owner Homestead Inn Restaurant, Homestead Farms; v.p. Homestead Inn, Inc. Motels, 1963—, South Avery Corp. Motels, 1961—; dir. Erie County Bank, Vermilion, Ohio., Soc. Bank of Firelands. Served with USMCR, 1943-46; PTO. Named to Lakewood (Ohio) H.S. Athelctic Hall Fame, 1997—; recipient Businessman of the Year award Republican Congressional Com., 1999. Mem. Nat. Fedn. Ind. Bus. (nat. adv. council), AAAS, Ohio Farm Bur. Fedn., Milan C. of C., Aircraft Owners and Pilots Assn., Internat. Flying Farmers, Ohio Restaurant Assn., Ohio Motel-Hotel Assn., Ohio Licensed Beverage Assn., Am. Horse Show Assn., Nat. Trust for Historic Preservation, N.A.M., Internat. Platform Assn., Huron County Hist. Soc., Ohio Farm Bur., (pres.), Ohio, Internat. (dir. 1978-84) Arabian horse assns. Clubs: Antique Automobile Am., Sports Car Am., N. Am. Yacht Racing Union, Sandusky Yacht, Sandusky Sailing, Catawba Island. Developer (with V.A. Tiedjens) foliage fertilization and direct to seed fertilization of comml. field crops. Home: 128 Center St Milan OH 44846-9757 Office: Growers Chem Corp PO Box 1750 Milan OH 44846-1750 also: Homestead Farms RR 1 Milan OH 44846-1700

HENRY, KATHLEEN MARIE, marketing executive; b. Stillwater, Okla., Sept. 24, 1950; d. Irl Wayne and Hulda Mary Henry. BS, U. Cen. Okla., Edmond, 1972. Community relations dir./account exec. Lowe Runkle Advt., Oklahoma City, 1972-74, account coordinator, 1975; sales promotion cons. McDonald's Corp., Houston, 1974, regional advt. supr. Southfield, Mich., 1975, regional advt. mgr., 1976-78, local store mktg. mgr. Oak Brook, Ill., 1978-80, staff dir., store mktg./sales promotion, 1980-82, home office dir. store mktg./sales promotion, 1982-83, dir. nat. sales promotion, 1983-84, internat. mktg. dir., 1984-85; mktg. dir. McDonald's System France, 1985-86, McDonald's System Europe, 1985-88, v.p. mktg., 1988-97; pres. Henry Jamieson Assocs., Tulsa, Okla., 1997—. Publicity chmn. Keep Okla. Beautiful, 1973-74; publicity chmn. Muscular Dystrophy Assn. Am., Okla. chpt., 1973-74; bd. dirs. Southfield Arts Coun., Mich., 1976-78; commr. Lake Keystone Planning and Zoning Commn., 1999—; bd. dirs. Perry High Sch. Alumni Assn., 1999-; bd. dirs sec. Keystone Peninsula Property Owners Assn., 1998-. Recipient Chgo. YWCA Leadership award, 1978, Disting. Former Student award U. Ctrl. Okla., 1979, Bronco award U. Ctrl. Okla. Centennial, 1991; named Outstanding Sr. Woman U. Ctrl. Okla., 1972, Outstanding Greek Woman, 1972. Mem. U. Ctrl. Okla. Alumni Assn. (dir. 1974, 1998-2002, found. bd. dirs. 1999—), U. Ctrl. Okla. Centennial Commn., Sigma Kappa. Office: Henry Jamieson Assocs Rte 3 Box 150A Cleveland OK 74020

HENRY, KENNETH ALAN, lawyer; b. Chgo., Jan. 21, 1951; s. Marvin David and Diane Dina (Kraft) H.; m. Amyra Weissberg, July 1, 1979; children: Oren Meron, Orly Michal. BS with distinction, U. Wis., Madison, 1972; JD, Ill. Inst. Tech., 1976; postgrad., Northwestern U., 1982-87. Bar: Ill. 1976, U.S. Dist. Ct (no. dist.) Ill. 1976, U.S. Ct. Appeals (7th cir.) 1976, U.S. Supreme Ct. 1981, U.S. Ct. Appeals (fed. cir.) 1986. Assoc. Edes & Rosen, Chgo., 1976-78; trial atty. office of solicitor region 5 U.S. Dept Labor, Chgo., 1978-85; ptnr. Weissberg & Henry, Ltd., Chgo., 1985-87; pvt. practice law Chgo., 1987—. Arbitrator Am. Arbitration Assn., Chgo., 1982—; hearing officer Ill. State Bd. Edn., Chgo., 1982—; mem. Ill. Pub. Employee Mediation-Arbitration Roster, Chgo., 1986—; adj. asst. prof. health policy and adminstrn. divsn. Sch. Pub. Health, U. Ill., Chgo., 1998—. Author: The Labor Handbook, 1984, 2nd edit., 1986. Mem. Environ. Control Commn., Highland Park, Ill., chmn., 1989—91; mem. North Shore Sch. Dist. 112, Highland Park, 1995—99, Highwood-Highland Park Sch. Dist. 111, 1992—93, Human Rels. Commn., Highland Park, 2002—, chmn., 2003—; bd. dirs. Suburban Fine Arts Ctr., 2001—02, Temple Beth El, Northbrook, Ill., 1985—, adminstrv. v.p., 2000—02, chmn., 2002—03. Mem. ABA, Chgo. Bar Assn., Decalogue Soc. Lawyers. Jewish. Avocations: athletics, theater, dance, symphony, reading. Home: 2847 Idlewood Ln Highland Park IL 60035-1125 Office: 120 W Madison St Ste 600 Chicago IL 60602-4106 Fax: (312) 857-1157. E-mail: khenry@kahlaw.com.

HENRY, KEVIN GUDGEL, lawyer; b. Lexington, Ky., June 23, 1953; s. Edward Joseph and Sue H.; m. Ann M., Apr. 23, 1983. BA in History, Ctr. Coll., 1975; JD, U. Ky., 1978. Bar: Ky. 1978, U.S. Supreme Ct. 1992. Law clerk Chief Justice, Supreme Ct. Ky., Frankfort, 1978-79; assoc. atty. Trimble, Stapleton, Reaves, Slone & Driesler, Lexington, Ky., 1979-80; mem. Trimble & Henry, Lexington, 1980-91, Sturgill, Turner, Barker & Moloney, Lexington, 1991—. Editor It's A New Age For You, 1990-91 (Ky. Bar Found. award 1990). Mem. Leadership Lexington, 1983-84; bd. mgrs. Beaumont Family YMCA, Lexington, 2000-2001. Mem. Ky. Acad. Trial Lawyers (bd. govs. 1987-90),, Ky. Def. Counsel, Def. Rsch. Inst., Fayette County Bar Assn. (pres. 1991-92), Employment Law Alliance. Episcopalian. Avocations: golf, women's basketball. Office: Sturgill Turner Barker Moloney PLLC 155 E Main St # 400 Lexington KY 40507

HENRY, LAURIN LUTHER, public affairs educator; b. Kankakee, Ill., May 23, 1921; s. Laurimer Luther and Jeanette Belle (Wagner) H.; m. Kathleen Jane Stephan, May 18, 1946; children— Stephanie Jane, Robin Leigh. BA, DePauw U., 1942; MA, U. Chgo., 1948, PhD, 1960. Staff asst. Public Adminstrn. Clearing House, Chgo. and Washington, 1950-55; research asso., sr. staff mem. Brookings Instn., Washington, 1955-64; prof. govt. and fgn. affairs U. Va., 1964-78; dean Sch. Community and Public Affairs, Va. Commonwealth U., Richmond, 1978-86, prof., 1986-87, prof. emeritus, 1987—. Guest scholar U. Va., 1988-95; vis. prof. Johns Hopkins U.; cons. to govt. Author: Presidential Transitions, 1960, The NASA-University Memorandum of Understanding, 1967; co-author: Presidential Election and Transition of 1960-61, 1961; contbr. articles profl. publns. Served with USNR, 1942-46. Recipient L.D. White prize Am. Polit. Sci. Assn., 1961. Fellow Nat. Acad. Pub. Adminstrn. (sr.); mem. Nat. Assn. Schs. Public Affairs and Adminstrn. (pres. 1971-72), Am. Soc. Pub. Adminstrn., Phi Beta Kappa, Phi Kappa Phi. Home: 500 Crestwood Dr Apt 1204 Charlottesville VA 22903-4853

HENRY, LOIS HOLLENDER, psychologist; b. Phila., Jan. 19, 1941; d. Edward Hubert and Frances Lois (Nesler) Hollender; m. Charles L. Henry, Oct. 24, 1964 (div. 1971); children: Deborah Lee, Randell Huitt, Andrew Edward. BA, Thomas A. Edison Coll., 1979; MSW, Fordham U., 1981; PhD in Indsl. Psychology, City U. L.A., 1992. Diplomate cert. neurofeedback provider; cert. social worker, Ariz., N.Y., N.J., EEG Biofeedback Practitioners; lic. svc. profl., career counselor, Ariz. Pers. asst., sec. IBM, Paterson, N.J., St. Louis, 1964-66; min.'s asst. Grace Luth. Ch., St. Cloud, Fla., 1966-68; adminstr., tchr. Fla. Finishing Acad., St. Cloud, 1968-70; adminstv. asst. Newark Book Ctr., 1972-77; intern, med. social worker Jersey City Med. Ctr., 1979-80; intern, psychiat./med. social worker VA Med. Ctr., Lyons, N.J., 1980-81; sch. social worker Lakeview Learning Ctr., Budd Lake, N.J., 1981-82; mgr. human resources Terak Corp., Scottsdale, Ariz., 1982-85; v.p. counseling and bus. devel. Murro & Assocs., Phoenix, 1985-88, exec. v.p. cons., 1988-91; prin. career cons. Henry & Assocs., Scottsdale, 1982-97; staff psychologist Nelson O'Connor & Assocs., Phoenix, 1993-97; v.p. dir. profl. svcs. Lee Hecht Harrison, Phoenix, 1997-98; cert. neurotherapist Forensic Psychol. Svcs., Phoenix, 1995-96; career cons., individual/family counselor/psychotherapist/neurotherapist, spkr. Henry & Assocs., Scottsdale, 1982-97. Adj. prof. Ottawa U.; mem. employers com. Ariz. Dept. Econ. Security; cons. in field. Coord.-vol. Job-A-Thon, Phoenix, 1983. Fellow Am. Orthopsychiat. Assn., Internat. Assn. Outplacement Profls. (treas. Ariz. region 1992-95, assoc. editor Internation Jour. Neuronal Regulation), Nat. Registry of Soc. Neuronal Regulation (diplomate, charter mem.); mem. NASW, Soc. Human Resource Mgmt., Am. Assn. Psychophysiology.

HENRY, LOUISE L. educational association administrator; b. Larned, Kans., Nov. 11, 1954; d. Charles Ronald and Grace Marybelle Schreiner; m. Robert M. Henry, Aug. 13, 1973; children: Susan R., Lynne N. BJ, U. Kans., 1976; MBA, Loyola U., 1982. Cert. APR, 1996. Reporter, news anchor KANU, Lawrence, Kans., 1975—76, KAYQ, Kansas City, Mo., 1977; adminstr. asst. Leydig, Voit, Osann, Mayer & Holt Medicus Microsys., Chgo., 1977—78, Evanston, Ill., 1978—79; mgr. ednl. adminstrn. svs. Am. Hosp. Assn., Chgo., 1979—83; asst. to exec. dir. Cable Access, St. Paul, 1985—87; ptnrs. in edn. coord. Round Rock Ind. Sch. Dist., Tex., 1990—95; dir. devel. and sch. cmty. rels. Grapevine-Colleyville Ind. Sch. Dist., Tex., 1995—2003; dir. cmty. rels. Region V Edn. Svc. Ctr., Houston, 2003—. Pres., treas. 1st v.p. area coord. Tex. Assn. Ptnrs. in Edn., Austin, 1992—99; parliamentarian, com. chair Tex. Sch. Pub. Rels. Assn., Austin, 1994, 2001; v.p. so. ctrl. region Nat. Sch. Pub. Rels. Assn., Rockville, Md., 2002—. Author (prodr.): (promotional CD) Virtual Brochure, 2000 (2 nat., 2 state awards, 2000, 2002). Hon. life mem. Friend of Children, Tex. PTA Round Rock Coun. and Opine-Colleyville Coun., 1995—2001. Recipient Silver, Gold, and Crystal awards, Tex. Sch. Pub. Rels. Assn., Austin, Tex., 1992—2003, Golden Achievement Award of Excellence, Nat. Sch. Pub. Rels. Assn., Rockville, Md., 1998—2002. Mem.. Colleyville Women's Club, Grapevine C. of C. (amb. 1999—2003), Grapevine Rotary Club (vocat. dir. 1996—98, Paul Harris fellow 2002). Avocations: singing, sewing, gardening, reading. Office: Region IV Edn Svc Ctr 7145 West Tidwell Houston TX 77092 Office Fax: 713-744-6514.

HENRY, MARGARET ROSE, state legislator; b. Rayne, La., June 20, 1944; BA, Tex. So. U.; MA, Springfield Coll. Mem. Dist. 2 Del. Senate, Dover, 1994—, mem. joint fin. com., children, youth and their families, mem. health and social svcs., chmn. pub. safety coms.; chmn. Combat Drug Abuse Coms. Trustee Med. Ctr. Del.; exec. dir. of Girls, Inc., Del. Mem. Brandywine Profl. Assn. E-mail: mrh9220@aol.com.

HENRY, MARIE ELAINE, poet; b. San Francisco, Oct. 4, 1948; d. Norbert Francis and Katharyne Elizabeth (Hedman) H. BA in English with honors, San Jose State U., 1970; MA in Creative Writing, San Francisco State U., 1972. Contbg. poet/short fiction: The Reed, Panjandrum, Gallimaufry, Beautitude, Alcatraz, Center, Boulevards, Rapscallions Dream, Yellow Silk, Another Small Magazine, California Oranges, Peace or Perish: A Crisis Anthology, Co-Evolution Quar., Apalachee Quar., Squaw Valley Community of Writers Poetry Anthology, Canvass, Noe Valley Voice, Only Morning in Her Shoes, Pudding Mag., Sacred River, Out of Season, Disability Rag, Range of Motion, Watch Out! We're Talking, Through the Mill, Bite to Eat Place, Poetry at the 33 Review, Dream Machinery, Buffalo Bones, Convolvulus, Exquisite Corpse, Full Court: A Literary Anthology of Basketball, Barnabe Mountain Rev., Beside the Sleeping Maiden, Marin Poetry Ctr. Anthology, GRRRRR: A Collection of Poems About Bears, To Honor a Teacher, The Blue Violin. Recipient James D. Phelan writing awards San Jose State U., 1970, Bukowski Poetry Contest award, 1999. Mem. Marin Poetry Ctr., Bay Area Folk Harp Soc. Avocations: playing harp, guitar and blues harmonica, swimming. Home: 855 C St Apt 408 San Rafael CA 94901-2853

HENRY, MARTIN DANIEL, university president; b. Pitts., Dec. 13, 1940; s. Martin A. and Margaret (Fisher) H.; m. Aimee Monteverde, Nov. 21, 1973; children: Donna, Nicholas, Bryan. BA, St. Vincent Coll., 1962; MEd, Duquesne U., 1965; MBA, Barry U., 1973; PhD, U. Pitts., 1979; JD, U. Dayton, 1984. Bar: Ohio, 1984. Tchr. South Hills Cath. High Sch., Pitts., 1963-65; adminstr. U. Pitts., 1966-71; dean LaRoche Coll., Pitts., 1971-74; v.p. acad. affairs Barry U., Miami, Fla., 1974-79; v.p. adminstrn., asst. to pres. U. Dayton, Ohio, 1979-85; pres. St. Leo (Fla.) Coll., 1985-87, Gannon U., Erie, Pa., 1987-91. Speaker numerous univs., sems., confs. Author: The Practice of Management, 1980; author invited and juried papers. Chmn. bd. dirs. Sta. WETG TV, Erie, 1987—; trustee St. Vincent Health System, Erie, 1987—; bd. dirs. United Way of Erie, 1987—. Recipient Disting. Alumnus award St. Vincent Coll., Latrobe, Pa., 1985, Bicentennial Medallion of Distinction U. Pitts, 1987. Mem. Ohio State Bar Assn., Erie County Bar Assn. (assoc.), Nat. Assn. Coll. & Univ. Attys., Soc. Coll. & Univ. Planning, Rotary (bd. dirs. local chpt.). Clubs: Erie, Kahkwa (Erie). Roman Catholic. Avocations: racquet sports, spectator sports, movies, travel. Home: 2095 S Woodshire Dr New Berlin PA 53151-2377 Office: Gannon U Office of Pres University Sq Erie PA 16507

HENRY, MARY LOU SMELSER, elementary education educator; b. Russellville, Ala., Mar. 2, 1953; d. Jessie Clifton and Margie Lou (Willingham) Smelser; m. Don M. Henry, Aug. 26, 1972; children: Aaron, Nathan. Student, N.W. Ala. State Jr. Coll., 1971-72; BS, Middle Tenn. State U., 1975; MA, Tenn. Tech. U., 1986, postgrad., 1998. Cert. elem. tchr., secondary tchr. history and sociology, Tenn., Ala. Substitute tchr. Warren County Bd. Edn., McMinnville, Tenn., 1979-82; tchr. LaPetite Acad., McMinnville, 1982-83; tchr. 2d grade Grundy County Bd. Edn., Altamont, Tenn., 1983—. Coord. Drug Awareness Task Force, 1990-92; mem. Grundy County Edn. Assn. Recipient Tchr. of Yr. award 1987-88, Trophy award 4H, 1988-91. Mem. NEA, Grundy County Edn. Assn. (sec. 1989-90, chmn. pub. rels. 1990-91, rep. North Elem. 1990-91, editor Tchr. Times 1989-91, pres. 1993-94, chair grievance com. 1994-95, negotiations com. 1993-99, sec. 2000-01, sec.-treas. 2001—), Tenn. Edn. Assn. (Cert. of Appreciation 1991, women status com. 1994-96). Home: 212 Forest Dr Mc Minnville TN 37110-2333

HENRY, NICHOLAS LLEWELLYN, public administration educator; b. Seattle, May 22, 1943; s. Samuel Houston and Ann (Connor) H.; m. Muriel Bunney; children: Adrienne Richardson, Miles Houston. BA, Centre Coll. Ky., 1965; MA, Pa. State U., 1967; M.P.A., Ind. U., 1970, PhD, 1971. Asst. to dean Coll. Arts and Scis.; instr. Ind. State U., 1967-69; vis. asst. prof. U. N.Mex., 1971-72; asst. prof. polit. sci. U. Ga., 1972-75, assoc. prof., 1975-78, prof., 1978-87, dir. Ctr. Pub. Affairs, 1975-80, dean Coll. Pub. Programs, 1980-87; prof., pres. Ga. So. U., Statesboro, 1987-98, prof. polit. sci., 1998—. Author or editor 12 books; contbr. numerous articles to profl. jours. Recipient Author of Yr. award Assn. Sci. Jours., Laverne Burchfield award ASPA, 2002; named One of 100 Most Influential People in Ga., Ga. Trend, 1994. Fellow Nat. Acad. Pub. Adminstrn.; mem. Cosmos Club (Washington). Office: Ga So U PO Box 8009 Statesboro GA 30460-1000

HENRY, PAUL EUGENE, JR., minister; b. Summit, N.J., Jan. 10, 1941; s. Paul Eugene and Arline Anita (Ferns) H; m. Carolyn Sandra Haas, July 16, 1966; children: Susan Beth, Thomas Paul, Carol Lee. BA, Gettysburg (Pa.) Coll., 1963; MDiv, Luth. Theol. Sem., Gettysburg, 1966. Ordained to ministry Luth. Ch. Am., 1966. Asst. pastor 1st Luth. Ch., Albany, N.Y., 1966-67; pastor St. John's Luth. Ch., Canajoharie, N.Y., 1967-70, Mamaroneck, N.Y., 1970-77, Faith Luth. Ch., East Hartford, Conn., 1977—. Chmn. Lay Workers Conf. Met. N.Y. Synod, 1974; sec. Capitol Dist., Upper N.Y. Synod, 1966-67; mem. worship com. Met. N.Y. Synod, 1975-76; mem. exec. bd. New Eng. Synod, 1979-85; mem. Common. on Budget and Fin., 1979-85, chmn., 1980-82; coord. Area V, No. Conn., 1979-85; chmn. New Eng. Synod Conv., 1991. Chaplain Mamaroneck Vol. Fire Dept, 1970-77, East Hartford Police Dept., 1982—; dean Greater Hartford Conf., New Eng. Synod, Evang. Luth. Ch. in Am., 1979—, seminarian intern supr., 1990-95; mem. East Hartford Town Bd. Ethics, 1999—; bd. dirs. East Hartford Cmty. Property Co., Inc., 2001—. Mem.: East Hartford Clergy Assn. (pres. 1986—). Home: 22 Dartmouth Dr East Hartford CT 06108-1426 Office: 1120 Silver Ln East Hartford CT 06118-1329

HENRY, PAULA LOUISE (PAULA LOUISE HENRY COOVER), academic administrator; b. White Plains, NY, Mar. 5, 1947; d. Raymond Francis and Carolyn Louise (Landis) Henry; m. John David Coover, Nov. 18, 1967 (div. Jan. 1992); children: Jeffrey Darren, Robert Benson, Jennifer Danielle (dec.). AA in Psychology, Monmouth U., 1967; student, Pace U., 1972-76; BA in Psychology, Monmouth U., 1993. Chair gifted and talented com., then pres. Hunterdon County (N.J.) Coun. PTAs, 1980-86; chmn. county pres. group, nat. conv. del., gen. conv. chmn. N.J. Congress Parents & Tchrs., Trenton, 1985-87, field svc. chmn., 1985-89, pres., 1989-91, immediate past pres., 1991-93, hon. v.p., 1991—; asst. to dean Rutgers Bus. Sch., Newark and New Brunswick, 1995—2002; campus adviser Office Student Jud. Affairs, Rutgers U., Newark and New Brunswick, 1996—, sr. exec. asst. univ. rel. New Brunswick, 2002—. Sch. bd. Union Twp. Bd. Edn., N.J., 1983-86, assembly del., 1984-86, legis. chmn. 1984-86, policy chmn. 1986, edn. chmn. 1984-85; trustee Jennie M. Haver Scholarship Fund, 1984-89; active Hunterdon County Edn. Coalition, 1984-88, Child Abuse and Missing Children Com., Hunterdon, 1987-98, Hunterdon County Youth Svcs. Commn., Flemington, 1987-98, N.J. Gov.'s Commn. on Quality Edn., 1991-93; treas. Fannie B. Abbott Student Loan Found., 1985-90, trustee, 1985-80; v.p. Hunterdon County Child Assault Protection Program, 1986-90; strategic planning com. United Way of Essex and West Hudson, 1994-95; trustee Good News Home for Women, 1997-2002, sec., 1999-2002; governing bd. Quality Edn. N.J., 1998—, co-chair, 2000-02, immediate past chair 2002; bd. dirs. Recordings for the Blind and Dyslexic, NJ, 2001-02, Bus. and Edn. Partnership Somerset/Hunterdon Counties, 2002—; mem. Raritan Millstone Heritage Alliance Bd., 2002—. Democrat. Methodist. Home: PO Box 5228 Clinton NJ 08809-0228 Office: Rutgers Univ Univ Relations New Brunswick NJ 08901-1281 E-mail: pauhen@yahoo.com., phenry@oldqueens.rutgers.edu.

HENRY, PHILIP LAWRENCE, marketing professional; b. Los Angeles, Dec. 1, 1940; s. Lawrence Langworthy and Ella Hanna (Martens) H.; m. Claudia Antonia Huff, Aug. 9, 1965 (div. 1980); children: Carolyn Marie, Susan Michelle; m. Carrie Katherine Hoover, Aug. 23, 1985. BS in Marine Engring., Calif. Maritime Acad., 1961. Design engr. Pacific Telephone Co., San Diego, 1963-73; service engr. Worthington Service Corp., San Diego, 1973-78; pres. Realmart Corp., San Diego, 1978-81; dir. mktg. Orbit Inn Hotel and Casino, Las Vegas, 1981-84; pres. Comml. Consultants, Las Vegas, 1984—, Gray Electronics Co., Las Vegas, 1986—. Chmn. bd. dirs. Las Vegas Accomodations Unltd., 1997-2000; mng. mem. G/Tracker Techs., LLC, 1998, Strobe Detector Techs., LLC, 1998; bd. dirs. Silver State Classic Challenge, Inc. Inventor electronic detection devices, 1986—. Served to lt. (j.g.) USNR, 1961-67. Republican. Avocations: amateur radio, open road auto racing, storm chasing. E-mail: info10@philhenry.com.

HENRY, RANDOLPH MARSHALL, investments executive, real estate broker; b. Houston, Jan. 23, 1946; s. Marshall Gambrell and Merriem Rue (Evans) H.; m. Janis Kay Frank, Apr. 5, 1979; children: Vernon Clark, Clark Marshall. BA, So. Meth. U., 1968; Diploma in Hist. Studies, Cambridge (Eng.) U., 1969; MBA, U. Pa., 1971. Lic. real estate broker. Asst. to pres. Surfcoat Inc., Houston and Fairbanks, Alaska, 1971-72; mgr. Gerald D. Hines Interests, Houston, 1972-75; pres. Randolph Henry Co., Houston, 1975—, EcoPoly, Inc., 1993-98, AllPoly Corp., 1999-2001, Med-Shred, Inc., 2003—; ptnr. Investline Group. Pres. MGP Mgmt. Inc., Houston, 1976-87; adv. dir. Tex. Commerce Bank, Houston, 1982-96; v.p., bd. dir. Brazos Mgmt. Co., 1976-90, Skyline Condominium Corp., 1983-90; co-chmn. bd. dir. Pvt. Sector Initiatives, Houston; mem. adv. com. New Founds. for Neighborhoods, mem., Nat. Bd. of Dir., Rebuilding Together. Mktg. network Houston Econ. Devel. Coun., 1987—; chmn. Post Oak Sch., Houston, 1987-89; founding pres. City of Post Oak Assn., 1974-75; Rep. precinct chmn., Houston, 1979; adminstrv. bd.

Chapelwood Meth. Ch., 1987—, chmn. bldg. com., treas. Mem. Reusable Indsl. Packaging Assn. (chair plastic drum products group, bd. dirs.), Wharton Alumni Assn., Houston C. of C. (aviation com.), Univ. Club. Methodist. Avocations: astronomy, skiing, cattle ranching, basketball. Home: 640 Pifer Rd Houston TX 77024-5434 Office: Ste 408 5858 Westheimer Rd Houston TX 77057-5647

HENRY, RENE ARTHUR, author, consultant; b. Charleston, W.Va., June 13, 1933; s. Rene A. and Lillian E. (Reveal) H.; children: Deborah Marie, Bruce Rexford. AB, Coll. William and Mary, 1954; postgrad., W.Va. U., 1954-56. Account exec. Flournoy & Gibbs, Toledo, 1956-59; publicity dir. Lennen & Newell, Inc., San Francisco, 1959-67; sr. v.p., dir. Daniel J. Edelman, Inc., Los Angeles, 1967-70; pres. Rene A. Henry, Jr., Inc., L.A., 1970-74; ptnr. Allen, Ingersoll, Segal & Henry, Inc., L.A., 1974-75; prin. ICPR, L.A., 1975-81; pvt. practice mgmt. and sports mktg. cons., 1981-86, 90-91; pres., chief exec. officer Nat. Inst. Bldg. Scis., Washington, 1986-88; confidential asst. to adminstr. Farmers Home Adminstrn. USDA, 1989; cons., designate asst. adminstr. AID, Dept. State, 1989-90; spl. asst. to dir. Office of Fed. Contract Compliance Programs, U.S. Dept. Labor, Washington, 1991; exec. dir. univ. rels. Tex. A&M U., College Station, 1991-96; dir. Office of Comm. and Govt. Rels. U.S. EPA, Phila., 1996—2001; cons. Innovative Comm. Corp., St. Croix. Exec. sec. to bd. dirs. Coun. Housing Producers, 1968-78; spl. advisor The Pres.'s Coun. on Phys. Fitness and Sports, 1981-89; spl. cons. Nat. Fitness Found., 1981-89; cons. Innovative Comm. Corp., W. Palm Beach, Fla., 2003—. Author: How to Profitably Buy and Sell Land, 1977, Marketing Public Relations, 1995, You'd Better Have a Hose If You Want to Put Out the Fire: The Complete Guide to Crisis and Risk Communications, 1999, Offsides!: Fred Wyant's Provocative Look Inside the National Football League, 2001; co-author: MIUS and You--The Developer Takes a Look at a New Utility Concept, 1980, Bears Handbook, 1996. Adv. bd. Arthur R. Marshall Found.; asst. to. pres., mem. coms. internat. rels., pub. rels., long range strategic planning task force U.S. Olympic Com., 1984—89; campaign dir. for athletes and entertainers Bush for Pres. and Bush/Quayle '88 presdl. election campaigns; mem. adv. bd. Ctr. Crisis Pub. Rels. and Litigation Lehigh U. With U.S. Army, 1956—58. Named San Francisco Bay Area Pub. Relations Man of Year, 1963; recipient Clarion award for human rights Women in Communication, 1980; inductee Granby H.S. Hall of Fame, Norfolk, Va., 2001. Mem.: Acad. Motion Picture Arts and Scis., Pub. Rels. Soc. Am. (mem. global initiatives com., exec. com. environ. sect., chmn. Coll. Fellows 2001, Disting. Citizen award L.A. chpt. 1979, 3 Silver Anvils), Inst. Residential Mktg., Nat. Assn. Home Builders, Acad. TV Arts and Scis. (past chair bld. com.), Sigma Nu. Episcopalian. Office: Innovative Comm Corp Phillips Point East Tower 777 S Flagler Dr # 1201-E West Palm Beach FL 33401 E-mail: sail2gold@aol.com.

HENRY, ROBERT HARLAN, federal judge, former attorney general; b. Shawnee, Okla., Apr. 3, 1953; BA, U. Okla., 1974, JD, 1976. Bar: Okla. 1976. Atty. Henry, West, Still & Combs, Shawnee, Okla., 1977—83, Henry, Henry & Henry, Shawnee, 1983—87; mem. Okla. Ho. of Reps., 1976—86; atty. gen. State of Okla., Oklahoma City, 1987—91; dean, prof. Okla. City U. Law Sch., 1993—94; judge U.S. Ct. Appeals (10th cir.), Oklahoma City, 1994—. Mem. Nat. Conf. Commrs. on Uniform State Law. Fellow: Am. Bar Found.; mem.: Nat. Assn. Attys. Gen. (chmn. state constl. law adv. com., vice-chmn. civil rights com.), Am. Coun. Young Polit. Leaders, Okla. Bar Assn. Office: US Ct Appeals 10th Cir 200 NW 4th St Rm 2021 Oklahoma City OK 73102-3026 also: Byron White US Cthse 1823 Stout St Denver CO 80257

HENRY, ROBERT E. dean, educator; s. Hiram H. and Wanda J. Henry; m. Anna M. Whitlock, May 0, 1989; 1 child, Scott A. PhD, U. North Tex., 1987; MEd.-Music, U. Mo. Columbia, 1978; BME, Okla. State U., 1972. Cert. tchr. Am. Orff-Schulwerk Assn., 1990, Orgn. Am. Kodaly Educators, 1990. Assoc. dean Coll. Visual and Performing Arts Tex. Tech U., Lubbock, Tex., 2002—, assoc. dir. Sch. Music, 1987—2002, prof. music edn., 1985—. Pres. Tex. Music Educators Assn., Austin, Tex., 1999—2001. Musician: (profl.) Symphony, Jazz.

HENRY, ROBERT JOHN, lawyer; b. Chgo., Aug. 1, 1950; s. John P. and Margaret P. (Froelich) Henry; m. Sara Mikuta; children: Cherylyn, Deanna, Laurin, Joseph Mikuta, Nicholas Mikuta. BA cum laude, Loyola U., Chgo., 1973, JD cum laude, 1975. Bar: Ill 1975, U.S. Dist. Ct. (no. dist.) Ill. 1975. Atty. Continental Ill. Nat. Bank, Chgo., 1975-77, Allied Van Lines, Inc., Chgo., 1977-81, assoc. gen. counsel, 1981-88, gen. counsel, 1988-90, v.p. adminstrn., gen. counsel, 1990-93, v.p. gen. counsel, 1993-99; v.p., assoc. gen. counsel SIRVA, Inc., Chgo., 1999—. Gen. counsel NFC N.Am., 1996-99. Alt. scholar Weymouth Kirkland Found., 1971. Mem. Chgo. Bar Assn., Am. Corp. Counsel Assn. Office: SIRVA Inc PO Box 4403 Chicago IL 60680-4403 E-mail: robert.henry@sirva.com.

HENRY, RONALD GEORGE, lawyer, consultant; b. Beaver Falls, Pa., May 14, 1949; s. Ronald S. and Alice H.; m. Linda Callahan, Aug. 28, 1976; 1 child, Elizabeth Walton. AB with honors, Georgetown U., 1971, JD, 1974. Bar: Pa. 1974, D.C. 1978, U.S. Supreme Ct. 1977. Asst. atty. gen. Pa. Dept. Commerce, Harrisburg, Pa., 1974-76; counsel to lt. gov. State of Pa., Harrisburg, 1976-79; assoc. Ballard, Spahr, Andrews & Ingersoll, Phila., 1979-83; v.p. pub. fin. Prudential Bache, Inc., Phila., 1983-85, Smith Barney, Harris Upham & Co., Phila., 1985-90; chief counsel Phila. Regional Port Authority, 1990-91; exec. dir. Pa. Intergovtl. Coop. Authority, Phila., 1991-94, coord. spl. projects, 1994-95; pvt. practice Bryn Mawr, Pa., 1995—; mng. dir. The Harriton Group, Inc., Broomall, Pa., 1997-99. Author: (with others) Financing Colleges and Universities, 1983. Mem. task force on econ. devel. fin. alternatives Pa. Dept. Commerce, 1987; mem. water supply adv. com. Pa. Dept. Environ. Resources, 1990; trustee Internat. Visitors Coun. Phila., 1991—, chmn., 1997-2001. Mem. ABA, Pa. Bar Assn., D.C. Bar Assn., Phila. Bar Assn. Office: 711 Pennstone Rd Bryn Mawr PA 19010-2939 E-mail: rhenry1949@aol.com.

HENRY, RONALD JAMES WHYTE, university official; b. Belfast, No. Ireland, Feb. 5, 1940; came to U.S., 1965; s. William James Louis and Mary Ann (Whyte) H.; children: Norah Lynn, Andrea Marie. BSc, Queen's U., Belfast, 1961, PhD, 1964. Asst. lectr. Queen's U., 1964-65; rsch. assoc. Goddard Space Flight Ctr., Greenbelt, Md., 1965-66; asst. physicist Kitt Peak Nat. Obs., Tucson, 1966-69; assoc. prof. La. State U., Baton Rouge, 1969-73, prof., 1973-89, chmn. dept. physics and astronomy, 1976-82, dean basic scis., 1982-89; v.p. acad. affairs Auburn (Ala.) U., 1989-91; provost, exec. v.p. for acad. affairs Miami U., Oxford, Ohio, 1991-94; provost, v.p. acad. affairs Ga. State U., Atlanta, 1994—. Com. on undergrad. sci. edn. Nat. Rsch. Coun., 1998—. Fellow Am. Physics Soc. Republican. Avocation: golf. Office: Ga State U Atlanta GA 30303 E-mail: rhenry@gsu.edu.

HENRY, RONALD O. academic administrator; b. Waterloo, Iowa, Mar. 21, 1936; s. Orlin E. and Mabel M. Henry; m. Willa Lucia Leidy, May 31, 1958; children: Denise Michelle Heffelfinger, Monica Dee Wayne. BA, Grace Coll., Winona Lake, Ind., 1958; MDiv, Grace Theol. Sem., Winona Lake, 1962; MA, Ind. U., 1963. Instr. Grace Coll., Winona Lake, Ind., 1962—64, asst. prof., 1964—66, assoc. prof., 1966—, dean of admissions, 1965—2001, asst. to the pres., 2001—. Chmn. bd. Cardinal Ctr., Warsaw, Ind., 1990. Mem.: Orgn. Am. Historians, Warsaw Optimist Club (pres. 1988—89). Republican. Grace Brethren. Home: 407 Kings Hwy Winona Lake IN 46590

HENRY, SHERRYE P. former political advisor; b. Memphis, July 13, 1935; Grad. magna cum laude, Vanderbilt U.; MBA, Fordham U. Asst. adminstr. Office Women's Bus. Ownership SBA; sr. adv. to congresswoman Louise M. Slaughter, 2000—. Vice-chair interagy. com. on women's bus. enterprise. Author of 2 books including The Deep Divide: Why American Women Resist Equality; contbr. numerous articles to nat. mags.; creator, host Woman! program on Sta. WCBS-TV, N.Y.C.; ind. prodr., broadcaster Sherrye Henry Program WOR Radio, N.Y.C. Active Group for the South Fork, eastern end of L.I., N.Y.; Fedn. Protestant Welfare Agys. N.Y., The Retreat, East Hampton, N.Y. Mem. Women's Forum N.Y. (founding mem.).

HENRY, STEPHEN LEWIS, lieutenant governor, orthopedic surgeon, educator; b. Owensboro, Ky., Oct. 8, 1953; s. Virgil Lewis and Wanda (Harper) Henry; m. Heather Reneé French, Oct. 27, 2000. BS, We. Ky. U., 1976; MD, U. Louisville, 1981. Diplomate Am. Bd. Orthopaedic Surgery. Intern gen. surgery U. Louisville Med. Ctr., 1981-82, resident, 1982-86, instr. orthopedic surgery, 1986—; lt. gov. Commonwealth of Ky., 1995—. Clin. investigator Richards Med. Co., Memphis, 1986—; athletic physician football teams U. Louisville, 1987—, Seneca High Sch., 1987—, Ky. State Football Championships, 1986—; commr. "A" dist. Jefferson County, 1992-95. Editor: Sports Medicine; contbr. abstracts and articles to profl. jours., chpts. to books. Treas. Louisville Tyler Park Neighborhood Assn., 1983-88, pres., 1988-89 Recipient best paper award So. Med. Assn., 1985, best clin. rsch. award U. Cin., 1986, outstanding resident rsch. award U. Louisville, 1988, Edwin G. Bovill rsch. award Orthopaedic Trauma Assn., 1989, Bell award for outstanding vol., Louisville, 1989, Presdl. recognition Nat. Vol. Week, The White House, 1989; named Outstanding Young Leader in Ky., 1988, One of 10 Outstanding Young Ams., U.S. Jaycees, 1989, Bell award, 1989, Jefferson award, 1989, Owensboro award for excellence, 1990, Lawrence-Grever award, 1990; grantee Richards Med. Co., 1986, Dept. Navy, 1989. Mem. Jefferson County Med. Soc., So. Orthopedic Assn., Ky. Med. Assn., U. Louisville House Staff Assn. (com. on health, phys. edn. and med. aspects of sports 1987—). Democrat. Home: 2550 Ransdell Ave Louisville KY 40204-1539 Office: 700 Capitol Ave Frankfort KY 40601-3410 E-mail: shenry@mail.st.ky.us.*

HENRY, STEPHEN RAY, director; b. Ft. Worth, July 17, 1965; s. Ray Harper and Melba Ruth Henry; m. Maria Gomez, Aug. 18, 1990; children: Ray, Jake. B of Music Edn., Angelo State U., 1987. Cert. tchr. music Tex., 1987. Band dir. Floydada Jr. H.S., Tex., 1987—88; tchg. asst. U. North Tex., Denton, 1988—90; band dir. Winters H.S., Winters, 1990—93, Lincoln Jr. H.S., San Angelo, 1993—96, Grape Creek H.S., 1996—99, Indsl. H.S., Vanderbilt, 1999—. Vol. ambulance svc. Vanderbilt EMS, 2002—02. Mem.: MENC, Assn. Tex. Small Sch. Bands (region coord. 2002—02), Tex. Music Educators Assn. (band divsn. chair 2000—02), Phi Mu Alpha. Achievements include State Finalist in the Association of Texas Small School Bands Outstanding Performance Series.

HENRY, SUE, social worker, educator; b. Marion, Ind., Aug. 25, 1934; d. William Floyd and Mildred Ethel (Schwark) H. AB, Earlham Coll., 1956; MSc in Social Adminstrn., Western Res. U., 1964; DSW, U. Denver, 1972. Teenage program dir. YWCA, Lima, Ohio, 1956-62; br. exec. YWCA Met. Cleve., 1964-67; spl. svcs. dir. YWCA Met. Denver, 1967-70; asst. prof. U. Pa., Phila., 1972-76; assoc. prof. U. Denver, 1976-82; faculty fellow Colo. Divsn. Mental Health, Denver, 1984-85; adj. faculty Met. State Coll., Denver, 1985-89; prof. U. Denver, 1982-99, prof. emerita, 2000—. Cons. Denver Internat. Program, 1977—; rsch. assoc. Applied Social Sci. Cons., Denver, 1982-87. Author: Group Skills in Social Work, 1981, revised edit., 1992; sr. editor: Social Work with Groups Mining the Gold, 2002; mem. editl. bd. Social Work with Groups, 1981—; contbr. articles to profl. jours. Com. chair Am. Friends Svc. Com., Phila., 1972-76; mem. Planning Commn., Gilpin County, Colo., 1985-88, chair Citizen Adv. Bd. Health and Human Svcs., 1997-2002; bd. pres. Columbine Family Health Ctr., 1988-92. W.T. Grant fellow YWCA of U.S.A., N.Y.C., 1962-64, doctoral tng. grantee Children's Bur., U.S. Govt., 1970-72; recipient Contbn. to Profl. Lit. award Assn. Social Group Workers, 1986. Mem. AARP (mem. nat. legis. coun. 2002—), Coun. Social Work Edn. (ho. of dels. 1981-83), Assn. for Advancement Social Work with Groups. Democrat. Avocations: travel, skiing, weaving, internat. cuisine cooking. E-mail: shenry@du.edu.

HENRY, THORNTON MONTAGU, lawyer; b. Bermuda, May 8, 1943; s. Otis R. and Barbara M. Henry; m. Ann Portlock, Aug. 28, 1971; children: Ruth Montagu, Thornton Bradshaw, John Gordon. BA, Washington and Lee U., 1966, LLB, 1969; LLM, Georgetown U. Bar: Fla. 1972, U.S. Dist. Ct. (so. dist.) Fla., U.S. Ct. Appeals (11th cir.), U.S. Tax Ct., U.S. Ct. Claims; cert. in taxation, Fla. Tax law specialist IRS, Washington, 1972-74; chmn., pvt. client svcs. group Jones, Foster, Johnston & Stubbs, PA, West Palm Beach, Fla., 1974—. Counsel, bd. profl. adv. Cmty. Found. for Palm Beach and Martin Counties; bd. dirs., 1st v.p., counsel Internat. Children's Mus. Pres., elder Meml. Presbyn. Ch.; chmn. scholarship fund Benjamin Sch.; bd. dirs., past pres. Rehab. Ctr. Children and Adults, Inc., Palm Beach; past pres. Planned Giving Coun., Palm Beach County; mem. adv. com. Habitat for Humanity; mem. planned giving com. Norton Mus. Art; bd. dirs. Palm Beach Roundtable. Capt. C.E., U.S. Army, 1970-72. Mem. ABA (tax com.), Fla. Bar Assn., Fla. Bar (tax sect.), East Coast Estate Planning Coun. (past pres.), Palm Beach Tax Inst., Kiwanis (past pres.). Order St. John of Jerusalem (chmn.-elect., knight). Republican. Avocations: jogging, furniture restoration, reading, photography, missionary work. Office: Jones Foster Johnston & Stubbs 505 S Flagler Dr Ste 1100 West Palm Beach FL 33401-5923 E-mail: thenry@jones-foster.com.

HENRY, VIC HOUSTON, lawyer; b. Big Spring, TX, Apr. 23, 1958; s. Don Vernor and Patricia Jean (Ezell) H.; m. Candace Lee McComb, Dec. 27, 1980; children: Taylor McComb, Lee Houston. BA with highest honors, U. Tex., 1980; JD cum laude, Georgetown U., Washington, 1983. Bar: Tex. 1983, U.S. Ct. Appeals (5th, 8th, 10th and D.C. cirs.) 1985, U.S. Ct. Appeals (fed. cir.) 1987, U.S. Dist. Ct. (no. dist.) Tex. 1983, U.S. Dist. Ct. (ea. and we. dists.) Tex. 1985, U.S. Dist. Ct. (ea. and we. dists.) Okla. 1985, U.S. Dist. Ct. (ea. and we. dists.) Ark. 1985, U.S. Dist. Ct. (no. dist.) Ala. 1985, U.S. Claims Ct. 1986, U.S. Supreme Ct. 1985. Law clk. to presiding justice U.S. Dist. Ct., Dallas, 1983—84; assoc. Storey Armstrong Steger & Martin, Dallas, 1984—88, ptnr., 1989—97, Henry Oddo Austin & Fletcher, P.C., Dallas, 1997—. Mem. faculty U. Tex. Arlington Asbestos Abatement, 1987; mem. adv. group Civil Justice Reform, U.S. Dist. Ct. (no. dist.) Tex., 1990; speaker seminars including Am. Corp. Counsel Assn., 1987, Notre Dame U. Sch. of Law, 2000-02, Georgetown U. Law Ctr., 2001. Adminstrv. asst. Tex. senate, Austin, 1976-78, Tex. Ho. of Reps., Austin, 1979-80, U.S. Ho. of Reps., Washington, 1980-82; chmn. deacons Gaston Ave. Baptist Ch., Dallas, 1988, 02. Mem. ABA (labor-OSHA subcom. 1985-86, 90—, mem. ins. environ. com., chmn. litig. subcom. firms 5-15 lawyers), Tex. State Bar, Dallas Assn. Young Lawyers (chmn. fed. casenotes com. 1985-87), Conf. Freight Counsel, Dallas Inn Ct. (barrister 1988-91). Avocations: basketball, travel, fly fishing. Home: 4903 Heritage Cir Sachse TX 75048-4560 Office: Henry Oddo Austin & Fletcher PC 1700 Pacific AVe Ste 2700 Dallas TX 75201-7353 E-mail: vhhenry@hoaf.com.

HENRY, WILLIAM LOCKWOOD, former food products executive, brewery executive; b. Pasadena, Calif., July 2, 1948; s. Edward Lockwood and Jane (Post) Henry; m. Pamela Ann Henry; children: Thomas Edward, Michael Lockwood. BS, UCLA, 1971, MS, 1973. Fin. exec. Ford Motor Co., Dearborn, Mich., 1973-81; dir. fin. Stroh Brewery Co., Detroit, 1981-82, v.p., fin. planner, 1982-84, v.p., sales, mktg. adminstr., 1985-1986, v.p. mktg. and planning, 1987-89; exec. v.p. Stroh Brewery Co, Detroit, 1989-91; pres., CEO Stroh Brewery Co., Detroit, 1991-99. Bd. dirs. Met. Affairs Corp., Century Coun. Mem.: Detroit Athletic Club. Office: The Stroh Brewery Co 100 River Place Dr Ste 100 Detroit MI 48207-4291

HENRY, WILLIAM OSCAR EUGENE, lawyer; b. Ocala, Fla., Mar. 30, 1927; s. Jesse Dawson and Alice M. (Johnson) H.; m. Bobbie Moorhead, May 9, 1952 (div.); children: Carol Ann, Robert Dawson, Jean Elizabeth; m. Mary Goode Croft, Dec. 1, 2000. BS in Journalism, U. Fla., 1950, JD, 1952. Bar: Fla. 1952, U.S. Dist. Ct. (mid. dist.) Fla., 1954; cert. cir. mediator Supreme Ct. Fla., tax lawyer Fla. Bd. Legal Specialization. Newspaperman The Marion Sun, Ocala, 1952-53; assoc. Holland, Bevis, McRae & Smith, Bartow, Fla., 1953-55; ptnr. Holland & Knight LLP (and predecessor firms), Bartow, Lakeland and Orlando, Fla., 1955—. Bd. dirs. Consol.-Tomoka Land Co., Daytona Beach, Fla.; arbitrator, mem. panel Am. Arbitration Assn. Contbr. articles to profl. jour. Legis counsel Office of Gov. of Fla., Tallahassee, 1963; bd. dirs. U. Fla. Found., Inc., 1977-87, Holland and Knight Found., Lakeland, 1982-97; v.p. Ctrl. Fla. coun. Boy Scouts Am., 1990-95; trustee Fla. Bar Found. Endowment Trust, 1991-99. Recipient Disting. Eagle Scout award, 1990, Silver Beaver award, 1992; named Outstanding Past Pres. Vol. Bar Assn. award Fla. Coun. Bar Assn. Pres., 1991-92. Fellow Am. Bar Found., Am. Coll. Trusts and Estates Coun., Am. Coll. Tax Coun., Am. Judicature Soc., Nat. Health Lawyers Assn., Fla. Bar Found. (bd. dirs. 1983-89, pres. 1988-89, Medal of Honor 1996); mem. ABA (ho. of dels. 1984-89, 93-99, exec. com. sect. officers conf. 1997-98), Fla. Bar (pres. 1983-84, Fla. Outstanding Tax Atty. award 1986), U. Fla. Nat. Alumni Assn. (bd. dirs., pres. 1968, Disting Alumnus award 1972, Alligator Hall of Fame 2000), Univ. Club, Citrus Club, Elks, Sigma Alpha Epsilon (pres. Fla. Upsilon alumni 1993—). Methodist. Home: 2150 Huron Trl Maitland FL 32751-3929 Office: Holland & Knight LLP 200 S Orange Ave Ste 2600 Orlando FL 32801-3453 E-mail: whenry@hklaw.com.

HENRY, WILLIAM RAY, business administration educator; b. Russellville, Ark., Dec. 30, 1925; s. Mace Leon and Violet May (Shinn) H.; m. Norma Talmadge Wright, Nov. 27, 1954; children— William Ray, Lisa Carolyn, Linda Carol, Lara Carlene. BS, U. Ark., 1948, MS, 1953; PhD, N.C. State U., 1957. Asst. prof., then asso. prof., prof. N.C. State U., Raleigh, 1956-70; prof. bus. adminstrn. Ga. State U., Atlanta, 1970—, prof. emeritus fin., 1993—. Author: (with others) Managerial Economics, 1978; contbr. (with others) articles to profl. jours. Served with USAAF, 1944-45. Recipient award of merit Am. Agrl. Econs. Assn., 1957, 61

HENRY-BEAUCHAMP, LEAH ALEXANDRA, special education educator; b. Phila., May 23, 1968; d. Helen Smith and Ragan Augustus Henry; m. Brian Thomas Beauchamp, Dec. 9, 1994; children: Nicholas Henry Beauchamp, Olivia Helen Beauchamp. PhD, Syracuse U., 1994. Asst. prof. U. South Fla., Tampa, 1994—96, Wagner Coll., S.I., NY, 1996—2001; assoc. prof. Montclair (NJ) State U., 2001—. Bd. dirs. Pilgrim Nursery Sch., Glen Ridge, NJ, 2002; alumni bd. mem. Whittier (Calif.) Coll., 2002.

HENSARLING, JEB, congressman; b. Stephenville, Tex., May 29, 1957; m. Melisa Fore; 1 child, Claire; m. Melissa Fore. BA in Econs. magna cum laude, Tex. A&M, 1979; JD, U. Tex., 1982. Atty. Oppenheimer, Harrison, Blend and Tate, San Antonio; v.p. Maverick Capital, Dallas; prin.-owner F-H and Assocs., Dallas; congressman 5th Dist. Tex. U.S. Ho. Reps., 2003—. Bd. dirs. IMCO Recycling Inc. Co-founder Family Support Assurance Corp.; mem. adv. bd. Children's Edn. Fund; exec. dir. Nat. Rep. Senatorial Com., 1991—93; Tex. dir. U.S. Senator Phil Gramm, 1985—89, chair re-election campaign, 1990; bd. dirs. Am. Cancer Soc.-Dallas Metro Area, Tex. Pub. Policy Found. Republican. Episcopalian. Office: 423 Cannon House Office Bldg Washington DC 20515*

HENSCHEL, SHIRLEY MYRA, licensing agent; b. N.Y.C., Dec. 18, 1932; d. Joseph and Leah Rose (Cooper) H. BA, Barnard Coll., 1954. Pub. rels., sales promotion exec. Louis Marx & Co., Inc., N.Y.C., 1954-59; acct. exec. Harold J. Siesel Co., N.Y.C., 1959-62; pres. U.S. Motor Sport Promotions, Inc., N.Y.C., 1962-66; v.p. Flora Mir Candy Corp., N.Y.C., 1966-71, Marden-Kane, Inc., N.Y.C., 1971-79; pres. Alaska Momma, Inc., N.Y.C., 1979—. Mem. Sch. and Home Products Assn. (assoc.), Licensing Industry and Merchandisers Assn. (charter mem. Achievement award 1988, nominee Hall of Fame 1994, 98, 99, 2000), Women Inc., Women in Toys (charter mem.). Democrat. Jewish. Avocations: cooking, travel, reading, theatre, investing. Office: Alaska Momma Inc 303 5th Ave Rm 2009 New York NY 10016-6652 Fax: 212 696 1340. E-mail: licensing@alaskamomma.com.

HENSE, DONALD LANGFORD, educational association administrator; b. St. Louis, July 4, 1942; s. Fred Hense and Lillie Ivy H.; 1 child, Dana. AB, Morehouse Coll., 1970; postgrad., Stanford U., 1973. Dir. govtl. rels. Howard U., Washington, 1973-79, Boston U., 1979-81, Dartmouth Coll., Hanover, N.H., 1984-86; v.p. for devel. and univ. rels. Prairie View (Tex.) A&M U., 1986-88; v.p. for devel. Nat. Urban League, N.Y.C., 1988-90. Dir. Nat. Fedn. of Interfaith Vol. Caregivers, Kansas City, Mo., 21st Century Found., N.Y. Pres., CEO Friendship House Assn.; chmn., founder Edison Friendship Pub. Charter Sch. Merrill scholar Charles E. Merrill Trust, U. Ghana, 1969, Rockefeller Intern in Econs., Rockefeller Found., Cornell U., 1968, Ford Found. Dissertation fellow, Stanford U., 1973, NDEA fellow, 1970-72. Mem. Nat. Soc. Fundraising Exec. (DC chpt. bd. dirs. 1993-96, Fundraising Exec. of Yr. 1999), Kappa Alpha Psi. Baptist. Office: Friendship House Assn 619 D St SE Washington DC 20003 E-mail: dhense@friendshiphouse.net.

HENSEL, ROBIN ANN MORGAN, mathematics and computer science educator; b. Buffalo, Dec. 1, 1960; d. Robert R. and Vivian J. (Kline) Morgan; m. John Peter Max Hensel; 1 child, Jonathan Peter. BS in Math., Wheaton Coll., 1981; MA in Math., SUNY, Buffalo, 1983; EdD in Higher Edn. Tchg., W.Va. U., 1988. Mathematician Morgantown (W.Va.) Energy Tech. Ctr. U.S. Dept. Energy, 1983-88; computer sys. analyst Morgantown (W.Va.) Energy Tech. Ctr., U.S. Dept. Energy, 1988-90; asst. prof. math. and computer sci. Salem Internat. U., Salem, W.Va., 1990-95, assoc. prof., 1995—. Violinist Morgantown Cmty. Arts Orch., 1984-89, Amherst Symphony, N.Y., 1981-83, Morgantown Christian and Missionary Alliance Ch. Orch., 1992—; instr. ARC, 1982; mem. Christian and Missionary Alliance; trustee Alliance Christian Sch., 1995—, pres. bd. trustees, 1997-2003. Recipient Joseph K. Bailey Tchg. Excellence award, 1998, Irving A. Barret prize for outstanding achievement in math. and sci., 1978; N.Y. State Regents scholar, 1978. Mem. Am. Math. Soc., Nat. Coun. Tchrs. Mathematics, Cum Laude Soc., Assn. Women in Math., Math. Assn. Am., Assn. for Christians in the Math. Scis., Am. Statis. Assn., Phi Delta Kappa. Republican. Avocations: swimming, music, camping. Home: 163 Scenery Dr Morgantown WV 26505-2534 Office: Salem Internat Univ Dept Math and Tech Studies Salem WV 26426 E-mail: hensel@salemiu.edu.

HENSEL, WILLIAM ARTHUR, family physician; b. Hackensack, N.J., June 1, 1954; s. John William Hensel and Jean Darlene Powers; m. Bonnie Patten Hensel, June 14, 1975; children: Craig Patrick, Carly Elyse. BA, MD, Ohio State U., 1978. Diplomate Am. Bd. Family Practice. Family practice resident, chief resident U. Tex. Med. Sch., Houston, 1978-81, instr., 1981-83, asst. prof., 1983-84, U. N.C., Chapel Hill, 1984-91, clin. assoc. prof., 1991-97, prof., 1997—. Assoc. dir. Moses Cone Family Practice Residency, Greensboro, N.C., 1996-2002; assoc. med. dir. Hospice at Greensboro, 1998—, profl. adv. com., 1995-99. Contbr. articles to profl. jours. Chmn. Aquatic Life Ctr., Greensboro, 1995-2000. Named Physician of Yr. Mayors Coun. on Handicapped, 1985 Mem. AMA (instr. educating physician on end-of-life care project 1999), Am Heart Assn. (N.C. chpt. affiliate faculty 1986—), Sports Medicine Soc. (U.S swimming chpt.), Greensboro Swimming Assn. (pres. 2000-03). Democrat Presbyterian. Avocations: sports, swimming. Home: 5590 Anson Rd Greensboro NC 27407-7200 Office: Moses Cone Family Practice Ctr 1125 N Church St Greensboro NC 27401-1007 E-mail: bill.hensel@mosescone.com.

HENSELER, CHRISTINE, language educator; b. London, Mar. 31, 1969; d Klaus Henseler and Trin-Madlen Winden. BA with honors, BSJ in Advt., U Kans., 1993, MA, 1995; PhD, Cornell U., 1999. Asst. prof. SUNY, Fredonia 1999—2001, Union Coll., Schenectady, NY, 2001—. Editor: Escritoras Españolas ante el Mercado Literario, 2003; author: Contemporary Spanish Women's Narrative and the Publishing Industry. Named John T. and Catherine MacArthur jr. prof., Union Coll., 2002; grantee, NEH, 2000, NEH summer seminar, 2002 Mem.: MLA, Am. Assn. Tchrs. Spanish and Portuguese, Am. Coun. Tchg. Fgn Lang., Soc. for History Authorship, Reading and Pub., Twentieth Century Spanish Assn. Am., Sigma Delta Pi, Phi Beta Kappa.

HENSELMANN, CASPAR GUSTAV FIDELIS, sculptor; b. Mannheim Germany, Mar. 13, 1933; came to U.S., 1950; s. Albert Edward and Lor Elfriede (Feist) Henselmann; m. Evangeline Karantzaki, Dec. 30, 1961 children: Xavier, Samuel. Student, Northwestern U., 1950-52; diploma in med art, U. Ill. Coll. Medicine, 1955; BFA, Art Inst., Chgo., 1956; postgrad. studies Wayne State U., Columbia U., 1958-61. Fellow W. B. Saunders Pub. Co., Phila 1956; med. illustrator pvt. practice, N.Y.C., 1968—; art dir. Aron & Falcon Advtg., Chatham, N.J., 1972-73; assoc. prof. sculpture CW Post Ctr. Long Island (N.Y.) Univ., 1976-77, Hofstra Univ., Hempstead, N.Y., 1987-88; assoc prof. Long Island U., Brooklyn, 1996—. Vis. artist St. Cloud (Minn.) State Coll., 1975, Ox-Bow Sch. of Painting, Sugatuck, Mich., 1976, Memphis Acad Fine Arts, 1982, Md. Art Inst., 1982, Univ. N.C., Chapel Hill, 1983; lectr. and critic Grad. Sch. of Architecture, U. Pa., Phila., 1993, Grad. Sch. Architecture Columbia U., N.Y.C., 1994; mem. Berlin-Spandau Internat. City Planning Project Team, Columbia U., 1993. One-man shows include Rice Gallery N.Y.C., 1961, 63, Kern County Mus., Bakersfield, Calif., 1965, Stable Gallery 1968, 55 Mercer Gallery, 1972, 74, 75, 76, 77, Sculpture Now, NYC, 1979 Fredericsburg (Va.) Ctr. for Creative Arts, 1979, Walter Bischoff Gallery, Chgo 1986, Drothea Van Der Koelen, Mainz, Germany, 1989, Walter Bischof Stuttgart, Berlin, Germany, 1990, 94, 97, Kunstverein Bielefeld Mus. i Waldhof, Germany, 1991, Bill Bace Gallery, N.Y.C., 1992, 95, Stadt Gallery Lahr, Germany, 1993, Offenberg Mus., Germany, 1994, View Pardo Gallery N.Y.C., 1996, Kingsborough C.C., Bklyn., 1997, Lindenau Mus., Altenburg Germany, 1991, Rosenberg & Kaufman Gall., NYC, 1995, Villa Haiss Mus Altenburg, Neuberger Mus., Purchase, N.Y., 1999, Robert Pardo Gallery, 1999 exhibited in group shows Am. Painting and Sculpture Annual, Phila., 1964, Nat Design Ctr., Chgo., 1964, New Eng. Artists Annual, Silvermine, Conn., 1964 Arts Coun. of Great Britain, Whitechapel Gallery, London, 1970, Marik

Malacorda Gallery, Geneva, 1976, Memphis (Tenn.) Acad. Fine Arts, 1982, Nina Owen Gallery, Chgo., 1987, U. Mass., Amherst, 1989, Bischoff Gallery, 1998, U. L.I., 1998, Pardo Gallery, 1999-2002, Chelsea Studio Gallery, N.Y.C., 2002, Berlin, 2002; represented in collections in Marshall-Isley Bank Lobby, Milw., 1971, Mannesmann Internat. Hdqrs., Dusseldorf, Germany, 1985, Deutsche Bank, N.Y.C., 1990, Julius Baer Bank, N.Y.C., 1992, Kunsthalle, Bremen Germany, 1993, Collection Hurrle, Durbach, Germany, 1994, Lindenau Mus., Villa Haiss Mus., Neuberger Mus., Swiss Paraplegic Ctr., Nottwil. Home: 21 Bond St New York NY 10012-2451 E-mail: chenselmann@earthlink.net.

HENSELMEIER, SANDRA NADINE, retired training and development consulting firm executive; b. Indpls., Nov. 20, 1937; d. Frederick Rost Henselmeier and Beatrice Nadine (Barnes) Henselmeier Enright; m. David Albert Funk, Oct. 2, 1976; children: William H. Jr. Stolz, Harry Phillip II Stolz, Sandra Ann Stolz. AB, Purdue U., 1971; MAT, Ind. U., 1975. Exec. sec. to dean Ind. U. Sch. Law, Indpls., 1977—78; adminstrv. asst. Ind. U.-Purdue U., Indpls., 1978—80, assoc. archivist, 1980—81; program and comm. coord. Midwest Alliance in Nursing, Indpls., 1981—82; tng. coord. Coll./Univ. Cos., Indpls., 1982—83; pres. Better Bus. Comms., Indpls., 1983—. Adj. lectr./lectr. U. Indpls. Ctr. Continuing Mgmt. Devel. and Edn., Indpls., 1984—. Author: Successful Customer Service Writing, Winning with Effective Business Grammar, Successful Telephone Communication and Etiquette, Management Writing; contbr. Mem.: Am. Soc. Indexers, Econ. Club of Indpls. Republican. Presbyterian. Avocations: travel, walking, reading, learning new ideas.

HENSEN, STEPHEN JEROME, lawyer; b. Durango, Colo., Nov. 8, 1961; s. Ronald Jerome and Sandra Lucille (Monroe) H.; m. Janice Lynn Lamunyon; children: Amanda, Stephanie, Cory. BS in Econs., Colo. State U., 1984; JD, Gonzaga U., 1987. Bar: Colo. 1987, U.S. Dist. Ct. Colo. 1987, U.S. Ct. Appeals (10th cir.) 1988, U.S. Supreme Ct. 1994. Atty. Cortez Friedman, P.C., Denver, 1987-93; atty. McKenna & Cuneo, Denver, 1993-95; ptnr. Richman & Hensen, P.C., Denver, 1995-99, Hensen & Drake, Denver, 1999—. Mem. Colo. Bar Assn., Denver Bar Assn., Colo. Supreme Ct. Bar Com. Republican. Office: Ste 1515 1515 Arapahoe St Denver CO 80202-2115

HENSEY, CHARLES MCKINNON, retired lawyer; b. Ft. Bragg, N.C., Aug. 20, 1934; s. Charles Walter and Sarah McQueen (McKinnon) H.; m. Edna May Railey, July 9, 1966; children: Charles Gordon, Walter Thomas. BA in Bus. Adminstrn., Duke U., 1957; JD, U. N.C., 1962. Bar: N.C. 1962, U.S. Ct. Appeals (4th cir.) 1984, U.S. Supreme Ct. 1972. Assoc. Johnson, Biggs & Britt, Lumberton, N.C., 1962-65; asst. atty. gen. N.C. Dept. Justice, Raleigh, 1965-85, spl. dep. atty. gen., 1985-86, mem. spl. litig. counsel, 1985-91, counsel N.C. State Bd. Elections, 1991-97. Bd. dirs. Montessori Sch., Raleigh, 1978. Lt. (j.g.) USNR, 1957-59; capt. USNR ret. Mem. N.C. Bar Assn., N.C. State Bar. Democrat. Avocations: genealogy, historical research. Home: 2051 White Oak Rd Raleigh NC 27608-1449

HENSGEN, HERBERT THOMAS, medical technologist; b. Cin., May 28, 1947; s. Herbert and Carolyn Elizabeth (Stites) H. BS, U. Cin., 1973, MS, 1978; AAS, Cin. State Tech. and C.C., 1981. Reg. med. technologist. Grad. tchg. asst. U. Cin., 1976-77; lectr. Xavier U. (formerly Edgecliff Coll.), Cin., 1977-78; tech. Our Lady of Mercy Hosp. (now Mercy Hosp. Anderson), Cin., 1979-81; med. lab. tech. Our Lady of Mercy Hosp., Cin., 1981-84, med. technologist, 1984-86; rsch. asst. Children's Hosp. Med. Ctr., Cin., 1986—. Instr. Cin. State Tech. and C.C., 1984-85. Contbr. article to Gen. and Comparative Endocrinology; co-author abstracts for Soc. for Pediat. Rsch., Endocrine Soc. Deacon Madisonville Bapt. Ch., 1977. Mem. Am. Soc. Clin. Pathologists, Triple Nine Soc., Am. Mensa, Ltd., N.Y. Acad. Scis. Achievements include production of data suggesting lack of insulin-like growth factor-1 (IGF-I) may mediate growth retardation in the neonatal rat; discovery of evidence that IGF-I may be one of several growth factors regulating differentiation of the fetal brain; demonstration that the antigonadal effect of prolactin in the lizard Anolis carolinensis is directed toward the smaller ovarian follicles; research on effects of IGF-I and its binding proteins on fetal and neonatal development. Home: 7420 Drake Rd Cincinnati OH 45243-1422 Office: Children's Hosp Med Ctr Dept Endocrinology 3333 Burnet Ave Cincinnati OH 45229-3026

HENSHAW, BEVERLY ANN HARSH, women's health nurse, consultant; b. Jasper, Mich., Aug. 26, 1937; d. Arthur Estol and Doris Ione (Lindsay) Harsh; m. Robert E. Henshaw, Aug. 30, 1958 (div.); children: Kit, Kim, Brad; m. Kenneth P. Wilkinson, Apr. 8, 1978; children: Jeff Wilkinson, Brian Wilkinson, David Wilkinson. BSN, U. Mich., 1960; cert. in ob-gyn. nurse practitioner, Johns Hopkin's U., 1973; MSN, Pa. State U., 1983. RN Pa., cert. nurse practitioner, sexual assault forensics examiner. Instr. Sch. Nursing Pa. State U., University Park, NP women's health; NP, clinic mgr. Family Health Svcs., Inc., State College, Pa.; pvt. practice cons. State College. Care coord. Health Beginnings Plus Project; coord. S.A.F.E. program Pa. State U., Univeristy Park; cons. in field. Mem.: NANPRH, ANA, Lamaze Internat., Assn. Reproductive Health Profls., Jacobs Inst. Women's Health, Internat. Assn. Forensic Nurses, Assn. Women's Health, Obstetrics and Neonatal Nurses, Am. Acad. Nurse Practitioners. Home: 1889 Huntington Lane State College PA 16803 E-mail: bevhenshaw@aol.com.

HENSHAW, GUY RUNALS, management consultant; b. Moscow, Idaho, Sept. 27, 1946; s. Paul C. and Helen E. Henshaw; m. Susan S. Seigel, Dec. 29, 1968; children: Christine, Victoria. BA, Ripon Coll., 1968; MBA, U. Pa., 1970. V.p. Security Nat. Bank, Walnut Creek, Calif., 1970-80, Bank Am., San Francisco, 1980-84; pres., dir. CivicBan Corp., Oakland, Calif., 1984-93; chmn. Payday Payroll Co., San Francisco, 1993-96; mng. dir. Henshaw/Vierra, LLC, San Francisco, 1996—. Dir. Calif. Banker's Ins. Svcs., Inc., San Francisco, 1989-92, Fair Isaac & Co., San Rafael, Calif., 1994—, R&D Diagnostic Antibodies, Benicia, Calif., 1997, Sleepy Cat Software, Boston, 2001. Chmn. bd. trustees Head Royce Sch., Oakland, 1982-90; trustee Ripon (Wis.) Coll., 1994—; dir. John Muir Health Sys., Walnut Creek, 1999—. Lt. col. U.S. Army, 1968-96. Mem.. Diablo Country Club, Pacific Union Club. Episcopalian. Avocations: tennis, travel. Office: Henshaw/Vierra LLC 400 Montgomery St Ste 820 San Francisco CA 94104-1221 E-mail: guy@henshawvierra.com.

HENSHAW, JOHN LESTER, federal agency administrator; B, Appalachian StateU.; M, U. Mich. Various positions including corp. dir. quality and compliance assurance, corp. stewardship environ. safety and health, corp. indsl. hygiene dir. Monsanto Co., 1975—95; dir. environ., safety and health Astaris, LLC, St. Louis, 1995—2001; asst. sec. occupational safety and health adminstrn. U.S. Dept. Labor, Washington, 2001—. Office: US Dept Labor 200 Constitution Ave NW Washington DC 20210

HENSHAW, JONATHAN COOK, manufacturing company executive; b. Dobbs Ferry, N.Y., Jan. 29, 1922; s. Elmer Ellsworth and Leonora Agnes (Scott) H.; m. Martha Emily Stock, July 14, 1948; children: William, Jane, Mary, Thomas, Daniel, Anne. BS, Fordham U., 1950; MBA, NYU, 1952; AA in Real Estate, Bucks County Community Coll., 1988. C.P.A., N.Y. Staff accountant Coopers & Lybrand, N.Y.C., 1951-55, 68-69; v.p., treas. J.A. Ewing & McDonald, Inc., N.Y.C., 1955-62; asst. treas. Block Drug Co., Jersey City, 1962-64; controller, asst. treas. Turner Jones Co., Inc., N.Y.C., 1964-68; treas. Visual Electronics, N.Y.C., 1969—, Crane Co., N.Y.C., 1970-80; assoc. broker Fox & Lazo Realtors, 1980-83, John T. Henderson, Inc., 1983-87, Richard A. Weidel Corp., Newtown, Pa., 1987—2002; ret., 2002. Served as sgt. AUS, 1943-46. Decorated Purple Heart. Roman Catholic. Home: 48 Falcon Rd Levittown PA 19056-1906

HENSHAW, NATHANIEL VENABLE, venture capitalist; b. Boston, May 8, 1961; s. Weld Stevens and Dalene (Powers) Henshaw; m. Michelle Rocheleau, Aug. 2, 1986; children: Nicholas Townsend Rocheleau, Lyse Anna. BA in Econs., Duke U., 1984, MBA, 1988. Cert. venture capitalist Nat. Venture Capitalist Assn. Asst. to pres., analyst Chem. Venture Capital Corp., N.Y.C., 1984—86; assoc. Intersouth Ptnrs., Research Triangle Park, NC, 1986—87, Kitty Hawk Capital, Charlotte, 1987; loan and investment officer Coastal Enterprises, Inc., Wiscasset, Maine, 1988—93; pres. CEI Ventures, Inc., Portland, Maine, 1993—. Co-founder, bd. dirs. Cmty. Devel. Venture Capital Alliance; bd. dirs. Maine Investment Exch. Contbr. articles to profl. jours. Trustee Maine Episcopal Diocesan Funds, Portland, 1996—; bd. dirs. Ctr. Environ. Enterprise South Portland, 1997—. Mem.: Hannaseeket Yacht Club (Named Commodore 1995). Avocations: sailing, sailboat racing, skiing, photography. Home: 362 Bunganuc Rd Brunswick ME 04011 Office: CEI Ventures Inc 2 Portland Fish Pier Ste 201 Portland ME 04101 Office Fax: 207-772-5503. Business E-Mail: nvh@ceimaine.org.

HENSHAW, STANLEY K. sociologist researcher, consultant; b. Cin., Oct. 21, 1938; s. Lewis Johnson and Dorothy Henshaw; m. Charlotte Virginia Eakin, May 6, 1972; children: Stephanie Kirsten, Emily Marisa. BA, Harvard Coll., 1960; PhD, Columbia U., 1971. Rsch. assoc. Columbia Sch. of Pub. Health, New York, NY, 1969—71, Cornell Med. Coll., New York, 1971—76; sr. analyst Roger Seasonwein Associates, New Rochelle, NY, 1977—78, Zanes and Associates, Inc., Fort Lee, NJ, 1978—79; sr. rsch. assoc. The Alan Guttmacher Inst., New York, NY, 1979—85, dep. dir. of rsch., 1985—2000, sr. fellow, cons., 2000—. Mem., bd. of dirs. Nat. Abortion Fedn., Wash., 1989—95. Author: (articles) various scientific jours. Recipient Outstanding Sci. Contbn., Nat. Family Planning and Reproductive Health Assn., 2000, Best Clin. Paper, Nat. Abortion Fedn., 1986. Mem.: APHA, Population Assn. of Am., Internat. Union for the Sci. Study of Population. Liberal. Episcopal. Achievements include research in on abortion and family planning. Avocations: travel, current affairs, financial markets. Home: 140 Christie St Leonia NJ 07605 Office: The Alan Guttmacher Inst 120 Wall St New York NY 10005 Personal E-mail: shenshaw@concentric.net. E-mail: shenshaw@guttmacher.org.

HENSHAW, WILLIAM RALEIGH, retired middle school educator; b. Richmond, Va., Apr. 28, 1932; s. Edmund James Jr. and Dorothy Varnes (Carrier) H.; m. Joyce Winston Kuhn, Mar. 24, 1956; children: Mark Hutson, Marcia Lynne, Matthew Harrison. BA, Randolph-Macon Coll., 1957; postgrad., Va. Commonwealth U., 1964-89, Coll. William and Mary. Cert. collegiate profl. tchr. with endorsements, Va. Securities clk. Fed. Res. Bank, Richmond, 1960-62; mid. sch. tchr. Hanover County Pub. Schs., Ashland, Va., 1963-99, adviser, yearbook specialist, 1988-99; ret., 1999. Author instrnl. manuals. Vice pres., pres. Pearson's Corner Elem. Sch. PTA, Mechanicsvillle, Va., 1980-84. With U.S. Army, 1952-60, Korea. Mem. NEA, Va. Edn. Assn., Hanover Edn. Assn., Va. Assn. Sci. Tchrs. (exec. bd.), Greater Richmond Assn. Sci. Educators, U.S. Boomerang Assn. Avocations: boomerangs, making custom knives. Home: 6450 Birch Tree Trce Mechanicsville VA 23111-5306

HENSHEL, HARRY BULOVA, watch manufacturer; b. N.Y.C., Feb. 5, 1919; s. Harry D. and Emily (Bulova) H.; m. Joy Altman, Nov. 4, 1948; children—Dale, Patti, Diane, Judith. AB, Brown U., 1940; grad., U.S. Army Command and Gen. Staff Sch., 1945; MBA, Harvard U., 1951. With Bulova Watch Co., Inc., Flushing, N.Y., 1938—, asst. sec., 1950, sec., 1951, v.p. finance, 1957, exec. v.p., 1958, pres., 1959-74, chmn., 1973-96, vice-chmn., 1996—. Bd. dirs. Ampal Corp., mem. audit com., Universal Holdings Corp., mem. audit com.; chmn. bd. dirs. Bulova Internat., Ltd., 11961-81; chmn. Atlantic Time Products Corp., 1991—; chmn. chief execs. coun. The Omega Group, 1991; chmn. Bulova Watch Co., 1973-96, vice chmn., 1991—. Vice chmn., trustee Adelphi U., 1955-88, emeritus trustee, 1989—; bd. overseers parsons Sch. Design; bd. dirs. U.S. Com. for UNICEF, 1979-87, Fedn. Employment and Guidance Svcs., Westchester Philharm. Orch., 1990; mem. bus. coun. UN Bus. Adv. Com., policy study com. Heller Inst., 1979-85; mem. adv. bd. N.Y.C. chpt. Am. Cancer Soc., N.Y. State Bus. Venture Partnership. Mem. Amateur Athletic Union U.S. (timing com.), N.Y. C. of C. (dir.), Am. Ordnance Assn (life), Newcomen Soc. N.Am., UN Assn. U.S. (dir.), Thoroughbred Owners and Breeders Assn., Sigma Chi (Significant Sig medal) Clubs: Harvard Business School, Sales Executives, New York (dir.), Brown Univ, Harmonie, Economic; Army and Navy (Washington); Old Oaks Country (Purchase, N.Y.); Turf and Field; Town (Scarsdale). Republican. Home: 24 Murray Hill Rd Scarsdale NY 10583-2828 Office: Bulova Corp 1 Bulova Ave Flushing NY 11377-7826

HENSINGER, ROBERT NEIL, pediatric orthopaedist; AB, U. Mich., 1960, MD, 1964. Pediatric orthopaedist U. Mich. Health Sys., Ann Arbor, Mich., 1974—, sect. head orthopaedics, 1996—2001, chmn., 2001—. Office: U Mich Health Sys Taubman Ctr 2912/0328 1500 E Medical Center Dr Ann Arbor MI 48109-0328

HENSLEIGH, HOWARD EDGAR, lawyer; b. Blanchard, Iowa, Oct. 29, 1920; s. Albert Dales and Eula Fern (Bair) H.; m. Janice Lee Pedersen, Aug. 15, 1948; children: Susan Lee Hensleigh Harvey, Nancy Ann Hensleigh-Quinn, Jonathan Blair. BA, Iowa U., 1943, JD, 1947; postgrad., Columbia U., 1954-55. Bar: Iowa 1947, N.Y. 1955, Mass. 1968. Commd. U.S. Army, 1943, advanced through grades to col., 1965, ret., 1973; legal adviser U.S. Mission to NATO, Paris, 1958-60; dep. asst. gen. counsel office of Sec. Def. U.S. Govt., Washington, 1960-67, dep. asst. to sec. treas., 1967-68; asst. gen. counsel Raytheon Co., Bedford, Mass., 1968-91, ret., 1991; pvt. practice Carlisle, Mass., 1991—. Participated in U.S. Italy Internat. Ct. Justice, The Hague, 1989. Chmn. town com. Carlisle Reps., 1972-80, sch. com. Carlisle, 1973-75, bd. selectmen, 1977-80, Pres. 517th Parachute Regimental Combat Team Assn. Inc. (2003-). Mem. ABA (chmn. region I), Fed. Bar Assn., Am. Soc. Internat. Law Home and Office: 479 West St Carlisle MA 01741-1439 E-mail: hhensleigh@earthlink.net.

HENSLEY, ELIZABETH CATHERINE, nutritionist, educator; b. Mpls., Feb. 27, 1921; d. Erich Christian and Lulu Mabel (Elliott) Selke; m. Eugene B. Hensley, June 10, 1954 (dec. 1992). BS in Edn., U. N.D., 1942; MS, Cornell U., 1944, postgrad., 1950-51. Instr. food and nutrition U. Del., 1944-47; asst. prof. Okla. A&M U., 1947-50; mem. faculty U. Mo., Columbia, 1951—, prof. food and nutrition, 1954-84, prof. emeritus, 1984—, chmn. dept. home econs., 1954-55, head dept. food and nutrition, 1955-65, co-chmn. dept. human nutrition, 1973-76. Author: Basic Concepts of World Nutrition, 1981. Mem. Am. Home Econs. Assn., Nutrition Today Soc., Mo. Home Econs. Assn., Boone County Hist. Soc., PEO, Pi Lambda Theta, Omicron Nu, Phi Upsilon Omicron, Gamma Sigma Delta, Kappa Alpha Theta Mem. Christian Ch. (Disciples Of Christ). Home: 802 Greenwood Ct Columbia MO 65203-2841

HENSLEY, JOHN CLARK, religious organization administrator, minister; b. Sullivan County, June 16, 1912; s. Truman and Ivan (Moddrell) H.; m. Margaret Sipes, Nov. 24, 1946; children: Gary, Clark, Dana. Ordained to ministry So. Bapt. Conv., 1930. Pastor, Moberly and Kansas City, Mo., 1935-46, Nashville and Pulaski, Tenn., 1947-58; supt. missions Hinds County Bapt. Assn., Jackson, Miss., 1958-66; exec. dir. Christian Action Commn. Miss. Bapt. Conv., Jackson, 1966-82, exec. dir. emeritus, 1982—, cons. family life, 1982-90, rec. sec., 1982-90. Assoc. prof. Cen. Bapt. Theol. Sem., 1943-46. Author: The Pastor as Educational Director, rev. edit., 1950, My Father is Rich, 1956, In the Heart of the Young, 1952, Behaving at Home, 1972, 99, Help for the Single Parents and Those Who Love Them, 1973, Coping With Being Single Again, 1978, Preacher Behave! Pointers on Ministerial Ethics, 1978, 99, rev., 2001, Good News for Todays Single, 1985, The Autumn Years, 1987, The Pastor in Family Ministry, 1990. Pres. bd. CONTACT, 1973—; trustee Radio and TV Commn. So. Bapt. Conv., 1980-88; mem. Gov. Miss. Com. Alcohol Abuse and Alcoholism, 1972—; mem. bd. Am. Coun. Alcohol Problems, 1972—; trustee Hannibal, Mo. LaGrange Coll., 1939-45. Recipient Disting. Svc. award for leadership in Christian ethics Christian Life Commn., 1975, Disting. Svc. award Family Ministry Bapt. Sunday Sch. Bd., 1988, Brooks Hays Christian Citizenship award, 1992, Ctrl. Bapt. Theol. Sem. Alumnus of the Yr. award, 1996. Mem. Nat. Coun. Family Problems, Southeastern Coun. Family Problems, Miss. Couns. Family Problems, Am. Judicature Soc., Am. Acad. Polit. Assn., Am. Assn. Sex Educators and Counselors. Home: 130 Caribbean Cv Clinton MS 39056-6101 E-mail: j.clarkhen@aol.com. *God must have intended that we have enough of Heaven in our homes here to get us a little bit prepared for what Heaven is like. The spiritual temperature of our churches is controlled by thermostats in the homes of the members.*

HENSLEY, KIMBERLY SUE, counselor; b. Lawrenceburg, Ind., Aug. 6, 1965; d. William Edwin and Yvonne Mittendorf; m. David Wayne Hensley, May 25, 1996. MA in Edn., Mt. St. Joseph, Cin., 1996, BFA in Theater, 1987; MA in Cmty. Counseling, U. Cin., 2002. Coord. consumer affairs Clermont Counseling Ctr., Amelia, Ohio, 1997—. Named Lilly scholar, 1997. Mem.: ACA, Chi Sigma Iota. Avocations: reading, walking, writing. Home: 3745 Fox Point Ct Amelia OH 45102 Office: Clermont Counseling Ctr Amelia OH 45102 E-mail: khensley@clermontcounseling.org.

HENSLEY, MARBLE JOHN, SR., civil engineer, consultant; b. Ball Ground, Ga., Nov. 6, 1922; s. C. Paul and Ober Odel (Penland) H.; m. Ruth Ann Collins, Sept. 11, 1948; children: Carol Hensley Hastey, Sandra Hensley Wise, Kathy Hensley McFarlane, Marble John Jr. BS in Civil Engring., Ga. Inst. Tech., 1950. Registered profl. engr., Ala., Ga., Ind., Ky., La., Miss., NC, SC, Tenn., Va., W.Va., NJ, Pa.; registered land surveyor, Ga., Ky., Tenn., La. Aviation loftsman Bell Aircraft, Marietta, Ga., 1942-44; jr. engr. Ga. Hwy. Dept., 1949-50; asst. traffic engr. City of Atlanta, Ga., 1950-54; traffic engr. City of Chattanooga, Tenn., 1954-58, city coord., 1958-63; pres. Hensley & Assocs., Marietta, Ga., 1957-63, Hensley-Schmidt, Inc., Chattanooga, 1963-81, chmn. of bd., 1981-91; dir. Piedmont Olsen Hensley, Chattanooga, 1991—95; sr. v.p. Arcadis, Chattanooga, 1995—. Del. President's Hwy. Conf., Miami, Fla., 1957; col., aide de camp Govs. Staff State of Tenn., Nashville, 1989—,dir. Interfed Saving and Loan, (later First Fed. Savings and Loan, then Am. South Bank of TN), 1981-1995. Trustee Bryan Coll. Dayton, Tenn., 1983—, Memphis Theol. Sem., 1981-89; elder First Cumberland Presbyn. Ch., Chatanooga, 1961-89, Brainerd Presbyn. Ch., Chatanooga, 1989—; bd. dir. Chatanooga Automobile Club, 1955-59, Chatanooga Kiwanis Club, 1962-63. With US Navy, 1944-46. Marble J. Hensley award created in his honor by So. Dist. Inst. Transp. Engrs.; named Engr. of Yr. Chattanooga Engr. Club, 1961. Fellow ASCE, Inst. Transp. Engr. (mem. tech. coun. 1959-64, chm. tech. program annual meeting 1964, pres. 1969), Consulting Engr. Coun. (pres. consulting engr. Tenn., del. nat. coun. 1970). Office: Arcadis G&M Inc 1210 Premier Dr Chattanooga TN 37421

HENSLEY, STEPHEN ALLAN, insurance executive; b. Portsmouth, Va., July 29, 1950; s. Theodore Allen and Lillie Mae (Costner) H. BA, U. W. Fla., 1976. Mgr. Carlyle & Co. Jewelers, Killeen, Tex., 1977-83; owner L.T., Ltd. Property, Killeen, 1983—; claims specialist State Farm Ins., Austin, 1985—. Disaster rep. State Farm Fire & Casualty Ins. Co., Austin, 1989—; investigator State Farm Life Ins. Co., 1986—; chmn. Computers for Freedom project Amnesty Internat., 1998—; mem. Pitsco Ask an Expert Group, 1997—. Univac focus group Brasenose Coll., Oxford, England, 1993; contbr. articles to profl. jours. Active Friends of KNCT-TV, Belton, 1985—, Viva Les Arts Societe, Killeen, 1988—. Decorated Knight Grand Comdr., Order of the Commonwealth, Can., 1990, Knight Grand Cross, Order of St Joseph, B.C., 1994, Count, Order of the Sursum Corda, Belgium, 1991, Baron, Sovereign Order von Liechtenstein, 1991, Keeper of the Tomes Principality of St. Michel de Clermont, 1991, Adm., Tex. Navy, 1991, Knight Comdr., Mil. and Chivalric Order of Sword of Eng., 1996, Chevalier Comdr. Order St. Raphael, Eng., 1997, Comdrs. Cross Order of St. Stanislas, Poland, 1997, Gold Cross of Merit Order of St. Stanislas, Poland, 1999; named lt. col. Legion of Frontiersmen Legion of Horse of the Brit. Commonwealth, 1999. Mem. Lake Belton Yacht Club, Am. Legion. Avocations: golf, sailing, fencing, tennis, english riding. E-mail: baronkge@bigfoot.com.

HENSLEY, WILLIAM MICHAEL, lawyer; b. Fresno, Calif., Apr. 25, 1954; s. Goldie Reeves and Allene (Watson) H.; m. Mari Bordona Calabrese, May 1981 (div. Jan. 1984); 1 child, Gilliann Mar; m. Anne Fields, Nov. 20, 1988. BA in Speech Comm., U. So. Calif., 1976; JD, Rutgers U., Camden, N.J., 1979. Bar: Calif. 1979, U.S. Dist. Ct. (no., ea., ctrl. and so. dists.) Calif., U.S. Ct. Appeals (9th cir.), U.S. Supreme Ct. Law clk. to Hon. Zenovich Calif. Ct. Appeals, 5th Appellate Dist., Fresno, 1979-81; assoc. Kadison, Pfaelzer, Woodard, Quinn & Rossi, L.A., 1981-87, Irell & Manella, L.A., 1987-92, Menke, Fahrney & Carroll, Costa Mesa, Calif., 1992-95; atty. Jackson, DeMarco & Peckenpaugh, Irvine, Calif., 1995—. Mem. editl. bd. Matthew Bender Calif. Real Estate Reporter, 1993—; contbr. articles to profl. jours. Mem. Orange County Bar Assn. Democrat. Mem. Ch. of Christ. Achievements include arguing more than 80 appellate cases in Calif. state and federal courts. Home: 25 Pacific Crst Laguna Niguel CA 92677-5314 Office: Jackson DeMarco & Peckenpaugh 2030 Main St Ste 1200 Irvine CA 92614 E-mail: mhensley@jdplaw.com.

HENSON, ANNA MIRIAM, retired otolaryngologist, retired medical educator; b. Springfield, Mo., Nov. 7, 1935; d. Bert Emerson and Esther Miriam (Crank) Morgan; m. O'Dell Williams Henson, Aug. 1, 1964; children: Phillip, William. BA, Park Coll., Parkville, Mo., 1957; MA, Smith Coll., 1959; PhD, Yale U., 1967. Instr. Smith Coll., Northampton, Mass., 1960-61; rsch. assoc. Yale U., New Haven, 1967-74; instr. U. N.C., Chapel Hill, 1975-78, rsch. asst. prof., 1978-83, rsch. assoc. prof., 1983-86, prof. Sch. Medicine dept. otolaryngology, 1986—2001; ret., 2001. Mem. study sect. on hearing rsch. NIH, Bethesda, Md., 1990-93. Contbr. articles to profl. jours. Fulbright scholar, Australia, 1959-60; NIH grantee, 1975—. Mem. Assn. for Rsch. in Otolaryngology, Sigma Xi. E-mail: mmhenson@med.unc.edu.

HENSON, DANIEL P., III, real estate developer; b. Balt. m. Del Carter; children: Darren, Dana. AB in History and Polit. Sci., Morgan State U., 1966; postgrad. in bus. and ins., Johns Hopkins U., 1967—70. Jr. h.s. and spl. edn. tchr. Balt. City Pub. Schs., 1966-67; agt., sales mgr. Met. Life Ins. Co., Balt., 1967-74; gen. agt. Guardian Life Ins. Co. Am., Inc., Balt., 1974-77; regional adminstr. U.S. SBA, Phila., 1977-79; dir. Minority Bus. Devel. Agy., U.S. Dept. Commerce, Washington, 1979-81, Greater Balt. Com., Inc., 1981-82; v.p., mktg. G & M Oil Co., Inc., Balt., 1982-84; v.p., ptnr., sr. devel. mgr. Struever Bros. Eccles & Rouse, Inc., Balt., 1984-93; commr., exec. dir., CEO Balt. City Dept. Housing and Cmty. Devel. and Housing Authority Baltimore City, 1993-99; pres. Henson Devel. Co., Inc., Balt., 2000—. Sr. fellow U. Md. Sch. Pub. Affairs, College Park, 2000. Past co-host (TV series) City Line, Balt. bd. dirs. Balt. Urban League, 1988—92; bd. dirs. Balt. br. Home Builders Assn. Md, 1988—93; bd. dirs., chmn. Balt. chpt. Fed. Res. Bank Richmond, 1981—93; bd. dirs. Balt. Mental Health Sys., Balt. Delta Alumnae Found., 1987—93, Ctr. Ethics and Corp. Policy, Balt., 1987—91; chmn. bd. dirs. Balt. Sch. Arts, 1985—, Investing in Balt. Com., 1985—90, Nat. Orgn. African Ams. in Housing, 1999—. Office: Henson Devel Co 5517 Groveland Ave Baltimore MD 21215-4243

HENSON, DAVID B. university administrator; b. Orlando, Fla. m. Earlene V. Ovletrea; children: Mary, Charles. BS in Biology, Fla. A&M U., 1961; MSEd in Chemistry, Tuskegee U., 1968; PhD in Biochemistry, U. Iowa, 1972. Acting chmn. dept. biochemistry, asst. dean student affairs Howard U. Coll. Medicine, assoc. prof. biochemistry; dean student affairs, assoc. dean Yale Coll.; lectr. molecular biophysics and biochemistry, fellow Timothy Dwight Coll., Yale U.; provost, prof. chemistry Fla. Atlantic U., Broward; vice chancellor acad. svcs./student support svcs. U. Colo., Boulder; pres., prof. chemistry Ala. A&M U., Huntsville; v.p. student svcs. Purdue U., West Lafayette, Ind.; pres., prof. biochemistry Lincoln U., Jefferson City, Mo., 1997—. Contbr. articles to profl. publs. Treas. Coun. on Pub. Higher Edn. Mo.; bd. dirs. Jefferson City C. of C.; bd. govs. Capital Region Med. Ctr.; mem. steering com. River Rendezvous. Diabetes rsch. fellow U. Tex. Med. Sch., Houston, fellow Am. Coun. Edn. Mem. Sigma Xi, Beta Kappa Chi, Alpha Phi Alpha. Office: Lincoln U 340 Tomahawk Rd Jefferson City MO 65101-4463

HENSON, ELIZABETH K. accountant; b. Urbana, Ill., Dec. 19, 1972; d. Woodrow Calvin and Ora Sue Chenault; m. Dennis Eugene Henson, Apr. 26, 1997. BS, U. Ill., 1995. CPA, Mo. Staff accountant Clifton Gunderson LLC, Champaign, Ill., 1994-97; mgr. Kraft, Miles & Tatum LLC, Poplar Bluff, Mo., 1997—. Avocations: rodeo, horses, landscaping, interior decorating. Home: 20140 Hwy 51 Puxico MO 63960 Office: Kraft Miles & Tatum LLC 1650 W Harper St Poplar Bluff MO 63901-4119

HENSON, GENE ETHRIDGE, retired legal administrator; b. Lawrenceville, Ga., Sept. 26, 1924; d. Fred Golden and Cora Jewell (Smith) E.; m. James Arthur Henson, May 2, 1948 (dec.); 1 child, Gena Arlene Cauthen. Grad. Interior Design, Gwinnett Tech. Inst., 1991. With Smith, Currie & Hancock, Atlanta, 1959-90, adminstr., 1965-90; chair fashion & design adv. com. Gwinnett Tech. Inst., 1992-93; owner Gene Henson Interiors. Ofcl. hostess for State of Ga., So. Gov's Conf., Atlanta, 1971; past adult tchr. First Baptist Ch., Lawrenceville; mem. adv. coun. Ctr. for Profl. Edn. Ga. State U., 1980-84. Actress Steel Magnolias, The Foreigner, Harvey, Our Town, Dearly Departed; bd. dirs. Gwinnett Coun. for Arts, 1993—99, sec., 1997—98; bd dirs. County Seat Players Theatre Group, 1993—2002, treas., 1999—2001. Mem. Atlanta Assn. Legal Execs. (1st pres. 1975), Assn. Legal Adminstrs. (life, nat. v.p. 1979—, bd. dirs. 1979-83, v.p. Atlanta chpt., pres.-elect, 1986-87, pres. 1987-88). Home and Office: 74 Scenic Hwy Lawrenceville GA 30045-5729

HENSON, JAMES BOND, veterinary pathologist; b. Colorado City, Tex., Nov. 13, 1933; s. John Lee Henson and Beatrice (Porter) Walls; m. Janet Christine Noel; children: Sarah, Ben, James. BS in Animal Sci., Tex. A&M U., 1956, DVM, 1958, MS, 1959; PhD, Wash. State U., Pullman, 1962. Diplomate Am. Coll. Vet. Pathologists. Assoc. prof. Wash. State U., Pullman, 1962-68, prof., chair vet. pathology, 1968-73; dir. rsch. grad. edn. Coll. Vet. Medicine, Pullman, 1973-74, dir. internat. program devel., prof. vet. pathology, 1978-98. Dir. internat. programs, Wash. State U., 1992-99; prof. exptl. animal medicine U. Wash., Seattle, 1968-74; dir. Internat. Lab. Research in Animal Diseases, Nairobi, Kenya, 1974-78; project dir. Western Sudan Agrl. Research Project, 1979-83; cons. U.S. AID, WHO, FAO, others, also various developing countries; mem. sci. and tech. adv. com. Spl. Program on Tropical Diseases, WHO, 1978-82; trustee Consortium Internat. Devel., 1979-2002; mem. exec. com. Small Ruminant Collaborative Research Support Project, 1981-84, 90-93, chair, 1993. Contbr. articles to profl. jours., chpts. to books. Recipient Outstanding Tchg. award Tex. A&M U., 1964, Mary K. Dunkle award Mich. State U., 1966; NIH fellow, 1965. Mem. Assn. Internat. Agrl. Rsch. and Devel. (pres.). Home: PO Box 2684 Pullman WA 99165-2684 Office: Wash State U 206 Bryan Hall Pullman WA 99164-0001

HENSON, JANE ELIZABETH, information management professional, adult educati; b. Ft. Wayne, Ind., Dec. 1, 1946; d. Robert Eugene and Lucile Catherine (Feeney) Tucker; m. Phillip Likins Henson, Aug. 23, 1971; 1 child, Robert Likins. BS in Edn., Ind. U., 1970, MS in Edn., 1973, MLS, 1976. Tchr. pub. schs., Ft. Wayne, 1970-71, Nevada, Mo., 1971-72; libr., cataloger Ctrl. Conn. State U., New Britain, 1976-77; libr. numeric data U. Wis., Madison, 1978-80; adj. prof. libr. Navy Safety Sch. Ind. U., Bloomington, 1981-83, reference libr. Vocat. Edn. Project, 1984-86; asst. dir. ERIC Clearinghouse, Bloomington, 1988-95, assoc. dir., 1995-98, co-dir., 1999—. Co-author: Rising Expectations: A Framework for ERIC's Future in the National Library of Education, 1997; editor: Libraries Link to Learning: Final Report on the Indiana Governor's Conference on Libraries and Information Services, 1990. Chair ERIC tech. com. U.S. Dept. Edn. ERIC Program, Washington, 1990—, mem. ERIC exec. com., 1990—. Mem. Am. Soc. Info. Sci. (dept. dir. SIG cabinet 1993, chair behavioral and social sci. SIG 1994, cert. of appreciation 1993). Roman Catholic. Avocations: officiating track and field events (cert.), reading, travel. Office: ERIC Clearinghouse for Social Studies Social Sci Edn 2805 E 10th St Ste 120 Bloomington IN 47408-2601 E-mail: henson@indiana.edu.

HENSON, KENNETH TYRONE, education educator; b. Anniston, Ala. s. Roscoe Randall and Icie Ola Camp Henson; m. Sharon Kay Worley, Dec. 25, 1964; children: James Randall, Kenneth Allen. BS, Auburn U., 1963; MEd, U. Fla., 1967; EdD, U. Ala., 1969. From asst. prof. to assoc. prof. Ind. State U., Terre Haute, 1969-75; assoc. prof. U. Miami, Coral Gables, Fla., 1975-78, Tex. A&M U., College Station, 1978-81; prof., dir. doctoral studies Delta State U., Cleveland, Miss., 1981-83; prof., dept. head U. Ala., Tuscaloosa, 1983-88; dean Coll. Edn. Ea. Ky. U., Richmond, 1988-99, prof., 1999-2001; prof., dean of edn. The Citadel, Charleston, S.C., 2001—. Workshop leader on writing for publication. Author: (books) Writing for Professional Publication, 1999, Curriculum Planning: Integrating Multiculturalism, Constructivism and Education Reform, 2nd edit., 2001; co-author: (books) Educational Psychology for Effective Teaching, 1999, Education Today, 6th edit., 2001. NSF grantee, 1966-67; Fulbright fellow, 1971-72. Mem. ASCD, Am. Assn. Colls. for Tchr. Edn., Assn. Tchr. Educators (Top 70 Educators in U.S. 1990, Disting. Tchr. Educator 2000), Phi Delta Kappa, Kappa Delta Pi (editl. bd.), Phi Kappa Phi. Home: MSC 57 The Citadel 171 Moultrie St Charleston SC 29409 Office: Edn Sch 171 Moultrie St Charleston SC 29409-0063 E-mail: kenneth.henson@citadel.edu.

HENSON, KRISTIN L. veterinary pathologist; b. Salisbury, Md., Dec. 31, 1966; d. Ernest Lester and Ella Ruth Lamberth; m. William Edwin Henson, Apr. 24, 1993. BS in Chemistry, U. Montevallo, 1988; DVM, Miss. State U., 1992; MS in Environ. Toxicology, U. Fla., 2000. Diplomate Am. Coll. Vet. Pathology. Assoc. veterinarian Meridian (Miss.) Animal Clinic, 1992-95; resident in clin. pathology Coll. Vet. Medicine U. Fla., Gainesville, 1995-98, grad. rsch. asst., 1998-2000, clin. pathology instr., 1999; clin. pathologist Mid Atlantic Med. Labs. Inc., Richmond, Va., 2001; owner, clin. pathologist Vet. Cytopathology Svcs., Richmond, Va., 2001—. Contbr. articles to profl. jours. including Vet. Clin. Pathology, Jour. Vet. Med. Assn. Recipient scholarship C.L. Davis Found., 1997. Mem. AVMA, Am. Soc. Vet. Clin. Pathology, Am. Coll. Vet Pathology, Soc. Toxicology. Avocations: travel, reading, needlecrafts, tennis. Home: 2900 Kensington Ave # 702 Richmond VA 23221 Office: 1596 Hockett Rd Manakin Sabot VA 23103 E-mail: hensonwk@cavtel.net.

HENSON, O'DELL WILLIAMS, JR., anatomy educator; b. Kansas City, Mo., Jan. 11, 1934; s. O'Dell Williams and Natalie (Smith) H.; m. Miriam Morgan, Aug. 1, 1964; 1 child, Phillip William. BA, U. Kans., 1957, MA, 1960; PhD, Yale U., 1964. From instr. to assoc. prof. Dept. Anatomy, Yale U., New Haven, 1964-74; prof. Dept. Cell Biology and Anatomy U. N.C., Chapel Hill, 1974—. Chmn. Commn. Anatomy, N.C., 1982-2003. Recipient Phi Sigma award 1960, Alexander Von Humbolt award 1982, Cen. Carolina Bank Excellence in Teaching award 1982, NIH-Nat. Inst. Deafness and Other Communicative Disorders Claude Pepper award, 1989. Fellow AAAS. Home: 317 Reade Rd Chapel Hill NC 27516-1509 Office: U NC Dept Cell and Developmental Biology Taylor Hall Cb 7090 Chapel Hill NC 27599-0001 E-mail: owh@med.unc.edu.

HENSON, PAMELA TAYLOR, secondary education educator; b. Mobile, Ala., Aug. 31, 1958; d. Richard Dowdy and Martha Jo (Hanson) Taylor; m. Thomas Baird Henson III, Mar. 7, 1987; 1 child, Joshua Taylor. BS in Secondary Edn./Biology, U. South Ala., 1983; MS in Secondary Edn./Biology, U. Mobile, 1989, Adminstrv. Cert., 1990; Edn. Specialist Adminstrn., Ala. State U., 1995; postgrad., U. West Fla. Cert. secondary edn. educator. Sci. tchr. Fairhope (Ala.) Middle Sch., 1984-91, Foley (Ala.) H.S., 1991-97; sci. supr., grant writer Baldwin County Schs., 1994—. Christa McAuliffe fellow State Dept. of Edn., 1994, Outstanding Biology tchr. Nat. Assn. Biology Tchrs., 1994, Outstanding Instr. in Environ. Edn., Legacy Found., 1995, Outstanding Sci. Supr. award, 2002, Mobile Bay NEP award, 2002, YWCA Woman of Profl. Achievement award, 2002; recipient Presdl. award NSTA, 1994, Melvin Paul Jones award Tuskegee U., Outstanding Svc. to Edn. award. Mem. NSTA, Nat. Assn. Biology Tchrs., Ala. Sci. Tchrs. Assn., Nat. Marine Educators Assn., Baldwin County Assn. Profl. Educators (pres. 1994—), Alpha Delta Kappa (treas. 1994-96). Republican. Baptist. Avocations: travel, walking, outdoor summer sports. Home: PO Box 1676 810 Juniper Ct Daphne AL 36526-4358

HENSON, PHILLIP RICKMAN, religious organization administrator, minister; b. Sylva, N.C., Aug. 8, 1955; s. William R. and Lizzie M. (Nicholson) Henson; m. Deborah Jean Carter, Aug. 24, 1976 (div. May 20, 1984); children: Phillip Randall, Wilma Regina, James Michael; m. Shirley Ann Smith, Jan. 5, 1999; children: Jim Newcomer, Phillip Newcomer. AAS in Drug and Alcohol Tech., Southwestern Coll., 1988; BSW, Western Carolina U., 1991; M in Bibl. Studies, Promise Ministries Inst. for Bibl. Studies, Battle Creek, Mich., 2001. Counselor Oconaluftee Job Corp, Cherokee, NC, 1990—2001; resident social worker Cherokee Childrens Home, Cherokee, 1991—92; asst. pastor, evangelist Miracles of Faith, Jacksonville, Fla., 1998—99; min., evangelist Sonlight Ministries, Ft. Walton, Fla. and Cashiers, N.C., 1993—98, adminstr., evangelist Cashiers, 1998—. Owner Miracle Works Constrn., Cashiers. L/Cpl. USMC, 1970—73. Recipient Govs. Citizenship award, N.C., 1992, Commdrs. award, CAP, 1991—92, N.C. Vol. award, N.C., 1989. Mem.: NASW, Pi Gamma Mu. Pentecostal. Avocations: hiking, photography, writing, camping, helping the needs of the destitute. Home: 107 Fresno Ln Cashiers NC 28717 Fax: 828-743-5564. E-mail: sonlightministrync@yahoo.com.

HENSON, RAY DAVID, law educator, consultant; b. Johnston City, Ill., July 24, 1924; s. Ray David and Lucile (Bell) Henson. BS, U. Ill., 1947, JD, 1949. Bar: Ill. 1950, U.S. Supreme Ct. 1960. Assoc. CNA Fin. Corp., Chgo., 1952-70; prof. law Wayne State U., 1970-75, Hastings Sch. Law, U. Calif., San Francisco, 1975—95, prof. emeritus, 1995—. Author: Landmarks of Law, 1960, Secured Transactions, 1973, 2d edit., 1979, Documents of Title, 1983, 2d edit., 1990, The Law of Sales, 1985; also various other books and numerous articles; editor: The Business Lawyer, 1967-68. Mem. legal adv. com. N.Y. Stock Exch., 1971-75. Served with USAAC, 1943-46. Mem. Am. Law Inst. (life), ABA (chmn. bus. law sect. 1969-70, adv. bd. jour. 1974-80), Ill. Bar Assn. (chmn. comml. banking and bankruptcy law sect. 1963-65), Chgo. Bar Assn. Clubs: Univ. (San Francisco). Home: 1400 Geary Blvd San Francisco CA 94109-6561 Office: U Calif Hastings Sch Law 200 Mcallister St San Francisco CA 94102-4707

HENSON, ROBERT FRANK, lawyer; b. Jenny Lind, Ark., Apr. 10, 1925; s. Newton and Nell Edith (Kessinger) H.; m. Jean Peterson Henson, Sept. 14, 1946; children: Robert F., Sandra Henson Curfman, Laura, Thomas, David, Steven. BS, U. Minn., 1948, JD, 1950. Bar: Minn. 1950, U.S. Supreme Ct. 1972. Atty. Soo Line R.R., 1950-52; ptnr. Cant, Haverstock, Beardsley, Gray & Plant, Mpls., 1952-66; sr. ptnr. Henson & Efron, Mpls., 1966-94, of counsel, 1995—; !. Chmn. Minn. Lawyers Profl. Responsibility Bd., 1981-86; co-chmn. Supreme Ct. Study Com. on Lawyer Discipline, 1992-94. Trustee Mpls. Found., 1974-85, Emma Howe Found, 1986-90; chmn. Hennepin County Mental Health and Mental Retardation Bd., 1968-70. Served with USN, 1943-46. Fellow Am. Bar Found.; mem. ABA, Hennepin County Bar Assn. (pres. 1968-69), Minn. Bar Assn., Order of Coif. Unitarian Universalist. Office: 220 S Sixth St Ste 1800 Minneapolis MN 55402-4503 Personal E-mail: rhenson@mn.rr.com. Business E-Mail: rhenson@hensonefron.com.

HENSON SCALES, JEFFREY C. photographer, photo editor; b. San Francisco, July 18, 1954; s. Emmett Thomas and Barbara Jean Scales; m. Meg D. Henson, Dec. 16, 1985; 1 child, Coco Henson. Student, Art Inst. San Francisco, 1974-75. Road mgr. Minnie Riperton, L.A., 1975-77; freelance comml. photographer L.A., 1977-84; photo editor L.A. Weekly, 1978-79, N.Y. Times, 1998—; comml. photographer Henson Scales Prodns., N.Y.C., 1984-98. Staff photographer Black Panthers, Oakland, Calif., 1968-70. Contbr., photographer: The African Americans, 1993, The Family of Black America, 1966, Exploring Color Photography, 1996, Reflections in Black: A History of Black Photographers 1840 to Present, 2000, Open Ends: Museum of Modern Art, 2000, Committed to the Image: Contemporary Black Photographers, 2001, A Day In the Life of Africa, 2002. Founding mem. Com. for Rational African Ams. Against the Parade, N.Y.C., 1995, African Ams. Against Violence, N.Y.C., 1995. Mid-Atlantic Arts Orgn. photographer's fellow, 1991, N.Y. Found. for Arts fellow, 1996; recipient Dorothea Lange/Paul Taylor award for collaborative projects Ctr. for Documentary Studies, Duke U., 1991; W. Eugene Smith grantee in humanistic photography Internat. Ctr. Photography, 1991. Mem. Comm. Workers Am., Newspaper Guild N.Y. Avocations: lighting design, audio, speaker building, guitar. Office: NY Times 229 W 43d St New York NY 10026 E-mail: scales@hensonscales.com.

HENSON SCALES, MEG D(IANE), artist, writer, publisher; b. Portland, Oreg., Oct. 16, 1953; d. Kenneth Jack and Jessie Louise (Mott) Henson; m. Jeffrey Charles Henson Scales, Dec. 16, 1985; 1 child, Coco Tigre Roja. Student, San Francisco State U., 1972-73, 74-75, Friends' World Coll., Guatemala, 1974. Founding mem. Black Edn. Ctr., Portland, Oreg., 1970-71; mng. editor Woman's Bldg., L.A., 1979-81; pvt. investigator Kleinbauer Investigations, L.A., 1981-83; tchr. CUNY, N.Y.C., 1987-89, Mindbuilders, Bronx, NY, 1987-89; painter, writer, strategist Henson Scales Prodns., N.Y.C., 1989—; founder Com. for Rational African Americans Against the Parade, N.Y.C., 1995; pub., editor The Harlem Howl, N.Y.C., 1995—; freelance photographer N.Y. Times, The Oregonian, The Internat. Herald Tribune, The LA Weekly, 2001—; freelance writer N.Y. Times, 2001—. Commn. Sacred banners for Grace Methodist Ch., Wilmington, Del., 1997; spkr. in field. Author: The Book of Love, 1988, Melisma, 1989 (Deming award 1989); co-creator, performer Tragedy in Black and White/A Race Record in One Act, 1981; dir., prodr. video documentary Class, 1989, Action/Reaction, 1998; author essays Tenderheaded; Man, God and the Okey-Doke; Be/Held; contbg. author: Divine Mirror: The Maddonna Revealed, 2001, Tenderheaded, 2001, Internat. Rev. of African Am. Art, 2001, Davis Mus./Wellesley Coll., 2000; one-woman show U. Fla. at Gainesville Univ. Gallery, 1998, Smithsonian Anacostia Mus. and Ctr. for African Am. History and Culture, 1999. Founding mem. African Am. Against Violence, N.Y.C., 1995. Recipient N.Y. Found. Arts fellowship, N.Y.C., 1989, honorable mention Dorothea Lange/Paul Taylor prize in photojournalism, 1993. Avocations: creation myths, prayers, piano, flute. E-mail: mhensons@yahoo.com.

HENTGES, DAVID JOHN, microbiology educator; b. LeMars, Iowa, Sept. 18, 1928; s. Romaine Francis and Geneva Mae (Kruger) H.; m. Kathleen Edwina Mullan, Dec. 28, 1957; children: Stephen Edward, Kathleen Marie, Margaret Ann. BS, U. Notre Dame, 1953; MS, Loyola U., Chgo., 1958, PhD, 1961. Asst. prof. Creighton U. Sch. Medicine, Omaha, 1964-67, assoc. prof., 1967-68, U. of Mo. Sch. of Medicine, Columbia, 1968-72, prof., 1972-81, interim chmn., 1976-79; prof., chmn. Tex. Tech. U. Sch. Medicine, Lubbock, 1981-96, vice provost for rsch., dean grad. sch. biomed. scis., 1996-98, assoc. dean basic scis., 1996-98, dean emeritus, 1998—. Editor: Human Intestinal Microflora, 1983, Medical Microbiology, 1986, Microbiology and Immunology, 2d edit., 1995; regional editor Microbial Ecology in Health and Disease, 1987-96; mem. editl. bd. Infection and Immunity, 1983-92, Anaerobe, 1998—; contbr. chpts. to books and articles to profl. jours. Lay gen. chmn. Diocesan Cath. Appeal, Lubbock, 1989, 1997; co-exec. dir. Cath. Found. Diocese of Lubbock, 1998—2002. Named Knight Grand Cross Order of the Holy Sepulchre, 2003, Knight of Merit with star Constantinian Order of St. George, 2000. Fellow Am. Acad. of Microbiology (emeritus); mem. Cath. Acad. of Scis., Soc. for Microbial Ecology and Disease (pres. 1987-89), Serra Internat. (dist. gov. 1987-88), Sigma Xi. Republican. Roman Catholic. Avocations: gardening, fly fishing. Home: 4601 88th St Lubbock TX 79424-4107

HENTIC, YVES FRANK MAO, investment banker, industrial engineer; b. Paris, Dec. 7, 1946; came to U.S., 1947; s. Pierre Yves and Alberta Dorothy (Smith) H.; m. Donna May Woods, Aug. 3, 1981 (div. Dec. 1990); 1 child, Frank Hilton Wadsworth Hentic; m. Pandora Duke Biddle, Jan. 19, 1991; 1 child, Katherine Yvette Biddle Hentic. AB in Econs., Georgetown U., 1970; AS in Engring., Fashion Inst. Tech., N.Y.C., 1972; MBA, Harvard U., 1975. Plant engr. Lynn Lee Fabrics, N.Y.C., 1972-73; cons. Emanuel Weintraub Assocs., N.Y.C., 1974; securities analyst Wertheim & Co., N.Y.C., 1975-77; arbitrage analyst Colin Hochstin & Co., N.Y.C., 1977-78; rsch. ptnr. Bodkin, DePaolis, Hentic, Satloff & Co., N.Y.C., 1978-80; mng. ptnr. Y.H. Assocs., N.Y.C., 1980-95; pres. Yves Hentic & Co., Jersey City, 1983-86, Merger, Inc., Reno, 1987-95, Send It In, Mex., 1993-95, Archimedes Mgmt. Inc., 1995-97, OX Pasture Devel., Inc., Southampton, 1997—. Pres. 18 pub. cos. for Merger Inc., Reno, 1987-92; mem. N.Y. Stock Exch., 1983-86. Mem. Southampton (N.Y.) Assn., 1992—. Mem. St. Nicholas Soc. (treas. 1990-95), Soc. Colonial Wars N.Y. (3d v.p. 1992-94), U.S. Croquet Assn., Kane Lodge, Colonial Order of the Acorn, Sons of the Revolution N.Y. Avocations: croquet (3rd 1st flight doubles Nat. Championship 1998), mineralogy, game fishing (holder world record for big eye trevally, Costa Rica 1983), technical scuba diving, cave exploring. E-mail: yves@hamptons.com.

HENTON, MELISSA KAYE, analyst; b. Bossier City, La., Apr. 6, 1968; d. Harold Hayes and Nancy Lee Henton. BA, Creighton U., 1990; MA, George Washington U., 1995. Asst. dir. civil-mil. rels. Atlantic Coun. of U.S., Washington, 1991-93, dep. dir. civil-mil. rels., 1993-95, dep. dir. ops., 1995, dir. of planning, 1996-98; analyst strategic technol. and arms control analysis divn. Dyn Meridian, 1998-2000; analyst Ctr. for Naval Analyses, 2000—. Home: 5306 Chieftain Cir Alexandria VA 22312-2308

HENTON, WILLIS RYAN, retired bishop; b. McCook, Nebr., July 5, 1925; s. Burr Milton and Clara Vaire (Godown) H.; m. Martha Somerville Bishop, June 7, 1952; 1 son, David Vasser. BA, U. Nebr., 1949; S.T.B., Gen. Theol. Sem., N.Y.C., 1952, D.S.T., 1972; D.D., U. of South, Sewanee, Tenn., 1972. Ordained priest Episcopal Ch., 1953; missionary St. Benedicts Mission, Besao, Mountain Province, Philippines, 1952-57; mem. staff St. Lukes Chapel, N.Y.C., 1957-58; rector Christ Ch., Mansfield, La., 1958-61, St. Augustine's Ch., Baton Rouge, 1961-64; archdeacon Diocese of La., 1964-71; bishop coadjutor Diocese N.W. Tex., 1971-72; bishop N.W. Tex. Lubbock, 1972—80; bishop Western La., 1980—90; ret., 1990. Pres. Tex. Conf. Chs., 1978-80; pres. La. Inter-Ch. Conf., 1985-86. Served with inf. AUS, 1944-46. Decorated Bronze Star. Episcopalian. Office: PO Box 10108 New Iberia LA 70562-0108

HENWOOD, WILLIAM SCOTT, lawyer; b. Toronto, Ont., Can., May 24, 1949; s. William John and Muriel Mae (Scott) H.; m. Carol Elizabeth Nichols, Nov. 17, 1973; children: William Scott Jr., Cameron Nichols. BBA, Ga. State U., 1976; JD, Woodrow Wilson Coll. Law, 1978. Bar: Ga. 1979. Law clk. to reporter of decisions Supreme Ct. Ga., Atlanta, 1974-80, asst. reporter of decisions, 1980-84, reporter of decisions, 1984—. Co-author: Georgia's Appellate Judiciary: Profiles and History, 1987. Pres. Leafmore-Creek Park Civic Assn., Decatur, Ga., 1982-83, Briarcliff Cmty. Sports, Decatur, 1986-87; mem. Sesquicentennial Com., Supreme Ct. of Ga. With Army N.G., 1968-74. Fellow Ga. Bar Found.; mem. Assn. of Reporters of Jud. Decisions (pres. 1988-89), Ga. Legal History Found. (treas. 1984-96), Gridiron Secret Soc., Lawyers Club Atlanta (exec. com. 1998-2003, pres. 2003—), Advocates Club (exec. bd. 1996-98, treas. 2003—), Burns Club (sec. 1992-93), Old War Horse Lawyers Club. Democrat. Presbyterian. Avocations: travel, hunting, sports car racing. Home: 2247 Springwood Dr Decatur GA 30033-2722 Office: Supreme Ct Ga Judicial Bldg Atlanta GA 30334 E-mail: henwoods@supreme.courts.state.ga.us.

HENZE, DAVID CARLETON, pharmaceutical company executive; b. Elk Grove, Ill., July 14, 1969; s. John Carlton and Joanna Lillian Henze; m. Laura Anne Henze, Oct. 19, 1996. BBA, St. Norbert Coll., DePere, Wis., 1991. Profl. sales rep. Boehringer Ingelheim, Ridgefield, Conn., 1992-96; terr. mgr. Bristol Myers-Squibb, Princeton, N.J., 1996-97; med. sales specialist EISAI, Inc., Teaneck, N.J., 1998-99, dist. mgr., 1999—2001, regional sales dir., 2001; region Chgo. Immunex Corp., Seattle, 2001—, Amgen, Inc., Thousand Oaks, Calif., 2001—. Mem. com. Alzheimer's Assn., Rockford Ill. Avocations: golf, skiing, music, travel.

HENZE, WILLIAM F., II, lawyer; b. Cleve., Apr. 20, 1949; BA, Ohio Wesleyan U., 1971; JD, U. Ariz., 1974; LLM, NYU, 1976. Bar: Ariz. 1974, N.Y. 1977, Tex. 1984. Ptnr. Jones, Day, Reavis & Pogue, N.Y.C. Instr. in law NYU, 1974-76. Mem. Phi Beta Kappa. Office: Jones Day Reavis & Pogue 599 Lexington Ave Fl C1A New York NY 10022-6030

HENZLIK, RAYMOND EUGENE, zoophysiologist, educator; b. Casper, Wyo., Dec. 20, 1926; s. William H. Henzlik and Adeline Adele (Brown) Wolff; m. Wilma Louise Bartels, Oct. 1, 1950; children: Randall Eugene, Nancy Jo. BS, U. Nebr., 1948, MS, 1952, PhD, 1960; postgrad., Cornell U., 1961-62. Tchr. biology and chemistry York (Nebr.) High Sch., 1948-50; sci. edn. supr. Tchrs. Coll., U. Nebr., Lincoln, 1951-53; tchr. biology Omaha North High Sch., 1953-56; instr. biology Nebr. Wesleyan U., Lincoln, 1957-59; asst. prof. zoology and biology U. Nebr., Lincoln, 1959-61; asst. prof. biology Ball State U., Muncie, Ind., 1962-67, assoc. prof. physiology, 1967-69, prof. physiology, 1970—. Adj. vis. prof. vet. physiology Tex. A&M U., College Station, 1984-85; anatomy cons. Nat. Prescription Footwear Applicators Assn., Muncie, 1962—; lectr. Pedorthics Tech. Program, Muncie, 1977—; cons. ednl. affairs Argonne (Ill.) Nat. Lab., 1970-76; dir. ednl. program Am. Diabetes Assn., Muncie, 1979-83; vis. prof. health sci. USAF European Ctr., Ramstein and Rhein Main, Germany, 1977-78; lectr. Ind. Health Care Assn., 1985-91. Author: Human Physiology Lab Manual, 1976-92; contbr. articles to profl. jours. Pres. Muncie Tech. Soc., 1975-80; mem. bd. Am. Diabetes Assn. Delaware County, Muncie, 1979-85. Radiation biology fellow NSF/AEC, U. Mich., 1960, Radiobiology fellow AEC/NSF, Cornell U., 1961-62, Radiation Biology Rsch. fellow U.S. Radiobiology Lab N.C. State U., 1965, P.R. Nuclear Ctr., 1967. Mem. AAAS, Nutrition Today Soc., Ind. Acad. Sci., Muncie Tech. Soc., Mensa, Sigma Xi, Phi Delta Kappa. Avocations: renting houses, reading, book collecting. Home: 5009 N Somerset Dr Muncie IN 47304-6501

HEO, MOONSEONG, statistician, researcher; arrived in U.S., 1989; s. Kyu Won Heo and Jae-Eun Ryang; m. Mi-Seon K. Kim, Apr. 30, 1989; children: Jee-Eun Grace, Yeh-Eun Joan. BA, Yonsei U., Republic of Korea, 1985, MA, 1987; PhD, U. Rochester, 1996. Post-doctoral fellow N.Y. Obesity Rsch. Ctr., N.Y.C., 1996—99, assoc. rsch. scientist, 1999—2002; asst. rsch. prof. Weill Med. Coll. of Cornell U., White Plains, NY, 2002—. Statis. svc./obesity rsch. N.Y. Obesity Rsch. Ctr., N.Y.C., 1996—2002; rsch. collabortion in geriatric psychiatry Weill Med. Coll. of Cornell U., White Plains, 2002—. Contbr. articles to acad. jours. Recipient Young Investigator award, NIH, 1997. Mem.: N.Am. Assn. for Study of Obesity, Am. Statis. Assn. Avocation: running. Home: 132 Continental Ave River Edge NJ 07661 Office: Weill Med Coll Cornell Univ 21 Bloomingdale Rd White Plains NY 10605 Office Fax: 914-682-6967. E-mail: moh2002@med.cornell.edu.

HEO, UK, political scientist, educator; b. Seoul, Korea (South), July 20, 1962; arrived in U.S., 1986; s. Mansik Heo and Sunok Chang; m. Sooho Song, Dec. 25, 1994; children: Min, Jieun. BA in Polit. Sci., Yonsei U., 1986; MA in Polit. Sci., U. Wyo., 1988; PhD, Tex. A&M U., 1996. Asst. prof. U. Wis., Milw., 1996—2000, assoc. prof., 2000—. Author: The Political Economy of Defense Spending Around the World, 1999; editor: The Political Economy of International Financial Crisis, 2001; contbr. articles to profl. jours. Mem.: Am. Polit. Sci. Assn. Office: University of Wisconsin-Milwaukee 3210 N Maryland Ave Milwaukee WI 53201 Office Fax: 414-229-5021. Personal E-mail: heouk@uwm.edu. Business E-Mail: heouk@uwm.edu.

HEPBURN, JEANETTE C. home health nurse; b. Provo, Utah, Nov. 7, 1952; d. George Blaine Clay, Sr. and E. Joan Clay; m. David Smiley, Feb. 15, 1975 (div. Aug. 1991); children: Peter David, Paul William, Adam George; m. Moller Boon, June 10, 1994 (dec. Sept. 1994); m. Charles Raymond Hepburn, June 3, 2000. Nursing diploma, Crouse Irving Meml. Hosp. Sch. Nursing, Syracuse, N.Y., 1972; BSN, Rockhurst Rsch. Coll., Kansas City, Mo., 1997; postgrad., Bowie State U. RN, cert. tech., ARC Disaster Health Svcs. Nursing asst. Crouse-Irving Meml. Hosp., Syracuse, NY, 1970—72; nurse RR, emergency rm., ICU Tompkins County Hosp., Ithaca, NY, 1972—75; ICU staff nurse II George Washington Hosp., Washington, 1975—78; ICU staff nurse Prince William Hosp., Manassas, Va., 1978—79; office nurse Romaker & Assocs. Kansas City, Mo., 1992—95; home health nurse Glen Burnie, Md., 1995—; served with disaster relief Pentagon Anne Arundel County, 2001, Am. Red Cross disaster nurse, 1998—2003, served with disaster relief Pentagon Hyattsville, Md., 1998—2003. Com. mem. to implement primary nursing George Washington Hosp., Washington, 1976. Sem. tchr. Ch. LDS, Adelphi, Md., 1999—2000, relics soc. counselor Adelphi, Glen Burnie, Md., 1996—98, relief soc. counselor, 2000—01. Scholar Senatoral scholar, Md., 2001—03. Mem. Bowie Student Nurses Assn., Phi Sigma Tau. Mem. Lds Ch. Avocations: cross stitch, dog training, swimming. Home and Office: 312 Oak Manor Dr Glen Burnie MD 21061 E-mail: crhepburn@msn.com.

HEPBURN, LAIRD, financial consultant; b. Memphis, Dec. 18, 1962; s. Wayne Hepburn and Sharron Molaison; m. Monica East, Jan. 6, 1990; children: Haley, Ashton, Zane. BS in Computer Sci., Tex. A&M U., 1984; MS in Ops. Rsch., Naval Postgraduate Sch., 1992. Aviation safety officer Dept. of the Navy 1989, assoc. safety profl. Bd. Cert. Safety Profls., 1996. Commd. officer USN 1985, advanced through grades to lt. comdr., ret., 1995; cons. KPMG, LLP Washington, 1995—98; strategy cons. Arthur D. Little, Inc., Cambridge, Mass. 1998—2000; bus. strategy advisor Internat. Bus. Machines, San Diego 2000—02; mng. bus. advisor DuPont Safety Resources, Newark, Del., 2002—. Exec. bd. mem. L.A. Econ. Devel. Corp., 2002—; boad mem. Ctrl. City Assn. L.A., 2002—. Editor: (aviation safety newsletter) RotorView, author reports Worship leader Plymouth Haven Ch., Alexandria, Va., 1996—99. Mem.: Inst for Ops. Rsch. and Mgmt. Sci., Am. Soc. Safety Engrs. (mem. chair 1996—98) Avocations: flying, sailing, scuba diving, motorcycles, woodworking. Personal E-mail: lwhepburn@yahoo.com. E-mail: laird.w.hepburn@usa.dupont.com.

HEPLER, KENNETH RUSSEL, manufacturing executive; b. Canton, Ohio Mar. 31, 1926; s. Clifton R. and Mary A. (Sample) H.; m. Beverly Best, Jun 9, 1945; 1 child, Bradford R. Student, Cleve. Art Inst., 1946-47, Case Wester Res. U., 1948-50. V.p., adminstr. A. Carlisle and Co., San Francisco, 1954-67 pres. K.R. Hepler and Co., Menlo Park, Calif., 1968-73, Paramount Press Jacksonville, Fla., 1974-75; pvt. practice printing broker, 1976-80; chmn Hickey and Hepler Graphics Inc., San Francisco, 1981—. Instr. printing prodn. San Francisco City Coll. With USAAC, 1943-45. Mem. San Francisco Litho Club (pres. 1972), Phila. Litho Club (sec. 1975-76), Newtown Exchange Club (pres. 1976), Elks. Republican. Presbyterian. Office: Hicky & Hepler Graphic Inc PO Box 4336 Scottsdale AZ 85261-4336

HEPLER, MERLIN JUDSON, JR., real estate broker; b. Hot Springs, Va., May 13, 1929; s. Merlin Judson and Margaret Belle (Vines) H.; m. Lanova Helen Roberts, July 25, 1952; children: Nancy Andora, Douglas Stanley. BS in Bus., U. Idaho, 1977; grad., Realtors Inst., 1979. Cert. residential specialist. Enlisted USAF, 1947, advanced through grades to sgt., 1960, ret., 1967; service mgr. Lanier Bus. Products, Gulfport, Miss., 1967-74; sales assoc. Century 21 Singler and Assn., Troy, Idaho, 1977-79; broker B&M Realty, Troy, 1979—. Mem. Nat. Assn. Realtors, Am. Legion, U. Idaho Alumni Assn., Air Force Sgts. Assn. Lodges: Lions. Republican. Avocations: hunting, fishing. Home: 1081 Driscoll Ridge Rd Troy ID 83871-9605 Office: B&M Realty W 102 A St PO Box 187 Troy ID 83871-0187 E-mail: mhepler@idaho.tds.net.

HEPNER, MICHAEL JULES, allergist; b. Pitts., Oct. 1, 1952; BS, U. Mich., 1974; MD, U. Pitts., 1978. Diplomate Am. Bd. Internal Medicine, Am. Bd. Allergy and Immunology. Intern Washington (D.C.) Hosp. Ctr., 1978-79, resident, 1979-81; fellow in allergy Henry Ford Hosp., Detroit, 1981-83, mem. staff allergy div., 1983-89; pvt. practice West Bloomfield, Mich., 1995—. Fellow Am. Coll. Allergy, Asthma, and Immunology; mem. AMA, ACP, Am. Acad. Allergy, Asthma and Immunology. Office: 6900 Orchard Lake Rd Ste 215 West Bloomfield MI 48322-3425

HEPP, JOHN HENRY, IV, historian, lawyer; b. West Chester, Pa., Oct. 21, 1959; s. John Henry Hepp, III and Rose Hunt Hepp; m. Julie Kay Benigni, Dec. 29, 1984; 1 child, John Henry V. BA, Temple U., 1982; JD, U. of Pa., 1986; PhD in History, U. of NC, 1997. Bar: Pa. 1986. Atty. Dechert Price and Rhoads, Phila., 1986—91; lectr. U. of NC, Chapel Hill, NC, 1998—99; asst. prof. Wilkes U., Wilkes-Barre, Pa., 1999—. Author: The Middle-Class City: Transforming Space and Time in Philadelphia, 1876-1926, 2003. Mem.: Soc. for Historians of the Gilded Age and Prog. Era (mem. H-SHGAPE editl. bd. 1997—2000), Orgn. of Am. Historians, Am. Studies Assn., Am. Hist. Assn., Athenaeum of Phila., Order of the Coif. Home: 437 Rutter Avenue Kingston PA 18704 Office: Wilkes U Dept History Wilkes Barre PA 18766 Office Fax: 570-408-7829. Personal E-mail: jhhepp@epix.net. E-mail: heppj@wilkes.edu.

HEPPA, DOUGLAS VAN, computer specialist; b. Bklyn., May 26, 1945; s. Joseph Charles and Antoinette Palmer (Vanasco) H.; m. Barbara Zanlunghi. BS in Social Sci., Poly. Inst. N.Y., 1968, BS in Math., 1971, MS Insl. & Applied Math., 1973, postgrad., 1983—. Assoc. engr. Raytheon Co., Portsmouth, R.I., 1968-70; systems engr. PRD Electronics, Syosset, N.Y., 1970-71; mathematician USN, New London, Conn., 1971; asst. computer engr. George Sharp, N.Y.C., 1972-73; programmer N.Y.C. Dept. Social Svcs., 1975; quantitative analyst N.Y.C. Fire Dept., 1976-80, assoc. staff analyst, 1980-81, computer specialist, 1991—99; with Algorithm Devel. Co., Maspeth, NY, 1999—. Pres. Algorithim Devel. Co., Queens, N.Y., 1985—. Mem. Math. Assn. Am., Am. Mgmt. Assn., Soc. for Indsl. & Applied Math., Assn. for Computing Machinery, IEEE, Am. Math. Soc. Avocations: fishing, swimming, boating, amateur radio, astronomy. Home: 64-08 60 th Rd Maspeth NY 11378 Office: Algorithm Devel Co 64-08 60th Rd Maspeth NY 11378-3433

HEPPE, KAROL VIRGINIA, lawyer, educator; b. Vinton, Iowa, Mar. 14, 1958; d. Robert Henry and Audry Virginia (Harper) Heppe. BA in Law and Society, U. Calif., Santa Barbara, 1982; JD, People's Coll. Law, 1989. Cmty. organizer Oreg. Fair Share, Eugene, 1983; law clk. Legal Aid Found. L.A., summer 1986; devel. dir. Ctrl. Am. Refugee Ctr., L.A., 1987-89; exec. dir. Police Watch-Police Misconduct Lawyer Referral Svc., L.A., 1989-94; instr. People's Coll. Law, L.A., 1992-94; dir. alternative sentencing project Ctr. Juvenile and Criminal Justice, 1994-95; cons. Bay Area Police Watch, 1996; investigator Office Citizen Complaints City and County of San Francisco, 1998—. Vol. law clk. Legal Aid Found. L.A., 1984—86, Lane County Legal Aid Svc., Eugene, 1983. Editor: (newsletter) NLG Law Students Action, 1986, Ctrl. Am. Refugee Ctr., 1986—89, Prison Break, 1994. Mem. Coalition Human Immigrants Rights, 1991—92, So. Calif. Civil Rights Coalition, 1991—92; bd. dirs. Nat. Police Accountability Project Adv. Bd., 1999—2003, People's Coll. Law, 1985—90, Law Student Civil Rights Rsch. Coun., N.Y.C., 1986. Scholar, Kramer Found., 1984—88, Law Students' Civil Rights Rsch. Coun., 1986, Davis-Putter Found., 1988, Assn. Cmty.-Based Edn. Prudential, 1988. Avocations: reading, travel. E-mail: karol_heppe@ci.sf.ca.us.

HEPPER, IONA LYDIA, gallery owner, retired; b. Eureka, S.D., Mar. 10, 1918; d. Emanuel E. and Lydia (Koerner) Voll; m. Kenneth Melvin Hepper, May 1, 1938 (dec. Feb. 1998); children: Judy, Rod. Student, Calif. Sch. Arts & Crafts, 1936-37. Owner Flair Gifts & Interiors, Stockton, Calif., 1951-81, tchr. art, 1965—, designer, 1971—; owner GAlerie Iona, Stockton, Calif., 1993-99. Cover designer (book) The Concepts of Bodily Objects, 1997. Named Millennium Artist of Yr. Haggin Mus., 2000. Mem. Nat. Watercolor Soc., Pastel Soc. Am., Pastel Soc. West Coast, Stockton Art League. Republican. Presbyterian. Avocations: painting, travel, reading. Home: 5469 Covey Creek Cir Stockton CA 95207-5329

HEPPLER, ROBIN LEE, science administrator; b. Detroit, Aug. 12, 1953; d. Warren G. and Maurida (Tillie) H. Student, Glendale Community Coll., 1971-74, 82, Ariz. State U., 1975, 81, U. Wis., 1981. Various positions Valley Nat. Bank, Phoenix, 1971-78; project bus. regional dir. Jr. Achievement, Inc., Phoenix, San Jose, Atlanta, 1978-81; asst. v.p., ctr. mgr. 1st Tenn. Bank, Memphis, 1981-83; customer svc. mgr., ops. analyst Wells Fargo Credit Corp., Phoenix, 1983-84; officer Citibank, Ariz., Phoenix, 1984-85; ops. mgr., asst. v.p. MeraBank, Phoenix, 1985-89; lending officer, policy analyst 1st Interstate Bank, Phoenix, 1989; project mgr. Colo. Nat. Bank, 1991-93; project mgr. Ctr. of Excellence for Project Mgmt. US West Techs., Denver, 1993—2000; lotus notes developer and project mgr. EDS at Western Union, 2000—. Precinct bd. Maricopa County Election Dept., Phoenix, 1990; fundraiser Fiesta Bowl Com., Tempe, Ariz., 1990-92; bd. sec. Ariz. Easter Seal Soc., Phoenix, 1989-90; bd. dirs. Cen. Ariz. Arthritis Found., Phoenix, 1989-90, chmn. jingle bell run, 1989, active Fiesta Bowl Parade Com., 1983-92; chmn. jail-athon Am. Cancer Soc., 1989; coord. Andre House Diocese of Phoenix, 1987 90; sec. bd. dirs. Human Svcs. Inc., Denver, 1991-95; chmn. Festival of Kites, Denver, 1992, chmn. champagne and chocolate black tie silent auction, 1994, Denver Jr. League, 1994-2000; chair holiday mart solicitations, 1996, safehouse Denver 5K run, corporate teams chair, 1994, 95. Named one of Outstanding Young Women Am., 1979; recipient award for outstanding contbn. Arthritis Found., 1990, award for outstanding achievement Am. Cancer Soc., Phoenix, 1989. Mem. Fin. Women Internat. (bd. dirs. 1988-90), Soc. Tech. Communicators. Avocations: calligraphy, guitar, snow skiing, hot air ballooning. Home: 3635 S Carr St Denver CO 80235-1801

HEPPNER, DONALD GRAY, JR., immunology research physician, army officer; b. Lynchburg, Va., Jan. 17, 1956; s. Donald Gray Sr. and Nathalie (Ward) H., m. Mary Virginia Leach, June 12, 1983; children: Charlotte Nathalie, Virginia Dearing, William Lynch. BA in Biochemistry/German Lit., U. Va., 1978, MD, 1983. Diplomate Am. Bd. Internal Medicine, Am. Bd. Infectious Diseases. Commd. capt. U.S. Army, 1987, advanced through grades to col., 2002; intern in internal medicine U. Minn. Hosps. and Clinics, Mpls., 1983-84, resident in internal medicine, 1984-86; rsch. assoc. Dight Lab., U. Minn., Mpls., 1987; with emergency medicine dept. Abbot North Western Hosp., Mpls., 1986-88; fellow infectious diseases U. Md., Balt., 1988-90; infectious disease officer Dept. Immunology, Walter Reed Army Inst. of Rsch., Washington, 1990-93; asst. chief dept. immunology Armed Forces Rsch. Inst. Med. Scis., 1993-94, chief dept. immunology and medicine, 1994-97; overseas malaria vaccine trial coord. dept. immunology Walter Reed Army Inst. Rsch., Forest Glen, Md., 1997-99, chief dept. immunology, 1999—; dir. U.S. Army Malaria Vaccine Program, 2001—. Attending physician Walter Reed Army Med. Ctr., Washington, 1991-93, 2003—; advisor NRC, 1995-97; mem. Fed. Malaria Vaccine Steering Com. Contbr. articles to profl. jours. Mem. Com. on Fgn. Rels., Charlottesville, Va., 1983—. Fellow ACP; mem. Am. Soc. Tropical Medicine and Hygiene, Multilateral Initiative n Malaria, Armed Forces Infectious Disease Soc. Achievements include development and testing of human malaria vaccines. Office: Walter Reed Army Inst Rsch Dept Immunology 503 Robert Grant Ave Silver Spring MD 20910 E-mail: donald.heppner@na.amedd.army.mil.

HEPPNER, GLORIA HILL, medical science administrator, educator; b. Gt. Falls, Mont., May 30, 1940; d. Eugene Merrill and Georgia M. (Swanson) Hill; m. Frank Henry Heppner, June 6, 1964 (div. 1975); 1 child, Michael Berkeley. BA, U. Calif., Berkeley, 1962, MA, 1964, PhD, 1967. Damon Runyon postdoctoral fellow U. Wash., Seattle, 1967-69; asst. and assoc. prof. Brown U., Providence, 1969-79, Herbert Fanger meml. lectr., 1988; chmn. dept. immunology, dir. labs., sr. v.p. Mich. Cancer Found., Detroit, 1979-91; dir. breast cancer program Karmanos Cancer Inst., 1991—2003, dep. dir., 1994—2003; assoc. chair for rsch. dept. internal medicine Wayne State U. Sch. Medicine, Detroit, 1991—2001, asst. dean cancer program, 2002—, pres. Karmanos Cancer Inst., spl. asst. to dean, 2003—. Mem. external adv. com. basic sci. program M.D. Anderson Hosp. and Tumor Clinic, Houston, 1984-94; mem. external adv. com. Case Western Res. U. Cancer Ctr., Cleve., 1988—, Roswell Park Meml. Inst., Buffalo, 1991-98; Sarah Stewart meml. lectr. Georgetown U., Washington, 1988; bd. sci. counselors Nat. Inst. Dental Rsch., 1993-97. Editor: Macrophages and Cancer, 1988; mem. editl. bd. Cancer Rsch., 1989-93, Jour. Nat. Cancer Inst., 1988, Sci., 1988-92; contbr. over 200 articles to sci. jours. Bd. dirs. Lyric Chamber Ensemble, 1996-99. Recipient Mich. Sci. Trail-Blazer award State of Mich., 1987; fellow Damon Runyon-Walter Winchell Found., 1967-69. Mem. AAAS, Am. Assn. for Cancer Rsch. (bd. dirs. 1983-86, chmn. long-range planning com. 1989-91), Am. Assn. Immunologists, Metastasis Rsch. Soc. (bd. dirs. 1985-89), Women in Cancer Rsch. (nat. pres.), Internat. Differentiation Soc. (v.p. 1990-92, pres. 1992-94), LWV (bd. dirs. Grosse Pointe, Mich. 1989-95). Democrat. Avocations: music, theater. Office: Karmanos Cancer Inst 110 E Warren Detroit MI 48201

HEPTINSTALL, DEBRA LOU, marketing professional; b. Tacoma, Mar. 5, 1952; d. Fred Bernard and June Isabella (Carter) H.; m. Michael Emory Smith, Sept. 26, 1980. Cert., Ctrl. Va. C.C., 1970, AAS cum laude, 1973. Advt. mgr. Times Record/Roane County Reporter, Spencer, W.Va., 1976-78; advt. clk., sales asst. The Washington Post, Washington, 1978-79, ind. sales contractor, 1980-81, advt. sales rep., 1981-85, mktg. analyst pricing, 1985-87; advt. mgr. The Reston (Va.) Times, 1979-80, The Springfield (Va.) Connection Newspaper, 1988; mktg. promotional mgr. Def. News, Springfield, 1988; asst. rsch. dir. Army, Navy and AF divsn. The Times Jour. Co., Springfield, 1988-91; mktg. analyst B&W Nuclear Environ. Svcs., Inc., Lynchburg, Va., 1993-94; adminstr., receptionist Indsl. Products, Co., Lynchburg, Va., 1994—. Methodist. Avocations: playing classical piano, tae kwon do karate. Home: 404 College Park Dr Lynchburg VA 24502-2410

HEPTINSTALL, ROBERT HODGSON, physician; b. Keswick, Eng., July 22, 1920; s. James A. and Mabel (Sanders) H.; m. Ann Enraght Porter, Jan. 25, 1950; children: Bridget, Gillian, Jonathan, James, Caroline, Christopher. MB, BS, London U., 1944, MD, 1948. Intern, house surgeon Charing Cross Hosp., London, 1944; jr. lectr. pathology St. Mary's Hosp., London, 1947-50, sr. lectr. pathology, 1950-60; vis. prof. pathology Washington U., St. Louis, 1960-62; assoc. prof. pathology Johns Hopkins Med. Sch., Balt., 1962-67, prof. pathology, 1967-69, 88—, Baxley prof. pathology, dir. dept., 1969-88; pathologist in chief Johns Hopkins Hosp., 1969-88; disting. svc. prof. pathology, 1992—. Pathology study sect. NIH, 1963-67, pathology tng. com., 1967-71; sci. adv. bd. Nat. Kidney Found., 1969-73. Author: Pathology of the Kidney, 1966, 5th edit., 1998; editor Lab. Invest, 1976-81; mem. editl. bd. Kidney Internat., Lab Investigation. With M.C., Royal Army, 1944-47. Recipient gold medal Danish Surg. Soc., 1984, David M. Hume Meml. award Nat. Kidney Found., 1986. Mem.: Renal Pathology Soc. (pres. 1980—83), Internat. Soc. Nephrology (v.p. 1981—84, Jean Hamburger award 1999), Am. Soc. Nephrology (pres. 1972—73, John P. Peters award 1993), Internat. Acad. Pathology (Maude Abbott lectr. 1983, Disting. Pathologist award 2002), Danish Soc. Nephrology (hon.), Alpha Omega Alpha.

HEPWORTH, JOHN LEONARD, chemist, researcher; b. Salt Lake City, Nov. 2, 1927; s. Peter Leonard and Flora Victoria (Burningham) H.; m. Caryl Peterson, Mar. 19, 1951; children: Dale, Diana, Vicki, Joseph, James, John T. BS, U. Utah, 1952; MS, U. Idaho, 1958. Chemist GE Co., Richland, Wash., 1953-57, Am. Potash and Chem. Corp., Henderson, Nev., 1957-58; sr. chemist Thiokol Corp., Brigham City, Utah, 1958-90, supr. propellant devel. sect., 1960, sr. scientist, 1967, dept. mgr. asst., 1970. Instr. propellant chemistry Utah State U., Logan, 1962; cons. Battelle Inst., Hanford, Wash., 1965-68, McGraw-Hill, Inc., 1968-90; vol. substitute tchr. math., chemistry, physics, religion Box Elder H.S., Brigham City, Utah, 1998—; vol. tchr. for young adults with spl. needs, 1999—. Author: A Review of Hydrazinium Diperchlorate, 1967; contbr. articles to profl. publs. Missionary LDS Ch., 1948-50, 90-93; instr. Early Morning Seminary, 1954-57; officer PTA, 1960-62; coach Little League Sports, 1964-75; H.S. athletic officiator, 1972-92. With USN, 1946-48. Republican. Achievements include patents for development of separation process of Uranium and Plutonium from fission products, separation of radioactive Cesium from fission products, development of first stage propellant for Minuteman, C-4 and C-5 Trident, and Peacekeeper missiles, supervision of space shuttle development, development of delayed quick-cure catalyst employed in all three stages of Trident missiles; effect of di-n-butyl phosphate on the partition of zirconum between aqueous solutions and 2.2.4. trimethylpentane. Home: 560 Holiday Dr Brigham City UT 84302-2387 E-mail: jhepworth@favorites.com.

HEPWORTH-WOOLSTON, CONNIE JO, choreographer; Dancer Ririe-Woodbury Dance Co.; choreographer U. Utah; bd. govs. AAHPERD. Dancer educator, chair dance dept. East H.S., Salt Lake City; artistic dir. East H.S. Dance Co.; cons. U. New Mex. Contbr. Achievements include Connie Jo Hepworth-Woolston scholarship awarded to East H.S. Grad. outstanding in dance. Office: AAHPERD 1900 Association Dr Reston VA 20191-1598

HERAKOVICH, CARL THOMAS, civil engineering, applied mechanics educator; b. East Chicago, Ind., Aug. 6, 1937; m. Marlene Vukowich, Apr. 23, 1960; children: Bradley, Douglas, Kristine, Russell. BSCE, Rose-Hulman Inst. Tech., 1959; MS in Mechanics, U. Kans., 1962; PhD in Mechanics, Ill. Inst. Tech., 1968. Registered profl. engr., Va. Prof. Va. Poly. Inst. and State U., Blacksburg, 1967-87; prof. civil engring. and applied mechanics U. Va., Charlottesville, 1987-98, Henry L. Kinnier prof. civil engring., 1990-98, prof. emeritus, 1998—, dir. applied mechanics, 1987-98; co-dir. NASA composites program Va. Poly. Inst. and State U., Blacksburg, 1974-87. Dir. Ctr. for Innovative Tech., Inst. for Materials Sci. and Engring., 1984-86, Ctr. for High Temp. Composites, 1993-98. Editor: Handbook of Composites No. 2, 1989; author: Mechanics of Fibrous Composites, 1998. Fellow ASME (chmn. com. composite materials 1989-92, exec. com. 1992-97, divsn. chair 1996-97, vp. basic engr. 2001—), ASCE, Am. Acad. Mechanics; mem. Internat. Union Theoretical and Applied Mechanics (gen. assembly 2000—), U.S. Nat. Com. on Theoretical and Applied Mechanics (sect. rep. 1996-2000, sec. 2000--), Soc. Engring. Sci. (sec. 1983-90, bd. dirs. 1989-92, v.p. 1991, pres. 1992), Soc. Exptl. Mechanics, Soc. Advancement Materials Processing and Engring.

HERALD, GEORGE WILLIAM, news correspondent; b. Berlin, Jan. 3, 1911; arrived in U.S., 1941; s. Bruno H. and Paula J. (Levy) Herald; m. Martha A. Dubois, Mar. 24, 1948; children: Steve Andrew, Patricia Claudia. LLD cum laude, Basle (Switzerland) U., 1934; postgrad., Columbia U., 1950-52. Staff corr. INS, N.Y.C., London, Paris, 1945-46, bur. chief Berlin and Vienna, 1946—49; spl. writer United Features, N.Y.C., 1949-52; assoc. editor UN World mag., N.Y.C. and Europe, 1952-55; head bur. Vision, Inc., Paris, 1955—. Author: My Favorite Assassin, 1943, The Big Wheel, 1963; author: (with others) Off the Record, 1952, Tatiana, 1955; author: (with Soraya Esfandiary) My Life as an Empress, 1962; contbg. editor: Am. Peoples Ency., 1952—62; contbr. articles to mags. including: Capt. U.S. Army, 1942—45. Recipient Best Spl. Reporting from Abroad award, Mex. Press, 1989. Mem.: Anglo-Am. Press Club, Overseas Press Club Am., Internat. Arts Coun., Authors League Am. Office: Vision Inc Vision Bldg 310 Madison Ave Rm 1412 New York NY 10017-6006

HERALD, J. PATRICK, lawyer; b. Latrobe, Pa., Sept. 27, 1947; s. John P. and Doris Faye (Galvin) H.; m. Bridget Grace Tobin, Aug. 17, 1973; children: Brian Michael, Matthew Patrick, Molly Bridget, John Francis. AB in History, John Carroll U., 1969; JD, U. Notre Dame, 1972. Bar: Ill. 1972, U.S. Dist. Ct. (no. dist.) Ill. 1972, U.S. Ct. Appeals (7th cir.) 1975, U.S. Supreme Ct. 1978. Assoc. Baker & McKenzie, Chgo., 1972-79, ptnr., 1979—. Fellow Am. Coll. Trial Lawyers, Internat. Acad. Trial Lawyers; mem. ABA, Ill. Bar Assn., Chgo. Bar Assn., 7th Cir. Bar Assn., Soc. Trial Lawyers (bd. dirs. 1987-89), Internat. Assn. Def. Counsel, Chgo. Trial Lawyers Club (pres. 1982-83). Roman Catholic. Home: 1721 N Normandy Ave Chicago IL 60707-3925 Office: Baker & McKenzie 1 Prudential Plz 130 E Randolph St Fl 3500 Chicago IL 60601-6213 E-mail: j.patrick.herald@bakernet.com.

HERALD, SARA BARLI, bank executive; b. Miami, Fla., June 25, 1955; d. John and Norma (Gavilan) Barli; m. James P. Herald, Aug 14, 1976; children: Maria, Brandon, Annie, Amanda. Student, Vanderbilt U., 1973—74; BA cum laude, U. Fla., 1976; JD, U. Miami, 1979. Shareholder Fine, Jacobson, Schwartz, et. al., 1979—90; pvt. practice, 1990—92; disaster relief coord. State of Fla. Dept. Health & Rehabilitative Svcs., 1992—93; exec. dir. Coconut Grove Arts Festival, 1994—95; exec. dir. southeastern divsn. Children's Home Soc. Fla., Inc., 1995—98, v.p. Region 5, 1998—2000; exec. v.p. human & orgnl. excellence Union Planters Bank, N.A., Coral Gables, Fla., 2000—01, chief adminstrv. officer, 2001—, mem. Orange Bowl com., 2001—. Chairperson Project Fresh Start State of Fla. Dept. Health & Rehabilitative Svcs., 1992; acting dist. adminstr. Dist. 11 State of Fla. Dept. Children & Families, 1999; bd. advisor St. Thomas U., 2002—. Mem. program adv. com. Dade County Cable TV Access Project, 1991—94, mem. adv. bd. VIVE Mag., 2001—. Bd. dirs. Children's Genetic Disease Found., 1984—88; vol. Girl Scouts U.S., Tropical, Fla., 1986—; chairperson Dade County Citizen's Adv. Com. Sch. Based Health Clinics, 1986—88; trustee United Way, 2001—; bd. dirs. YWCA Greater Miami, 1988—94, pres.-elect, 1989—90, pres., 1990—92; facilitator strategic planning and orgnl. structure Temple Beth Am; guardian ad-litem children in state custody; pro bono atty. CHARLEE Dade County, Inc.; social svc. policy coord. transition team Gov. Jeb Bush, Fla., 1998—99, co-chair strengthening families workgroup 2d term transition; pre-marital inventory ministry co-coord. St. Louis Cath. Ch., 1983—88, Cath./Jewish dialogue ministry co-coord., 1989—93, dialoge ministry co-coord., 1989—92; bd. dirs. Dade County Women's Fund, 1993—95. Named Outstanding Woman, Greater Miami Opera, 1992, Champion for Children, Miami Dade CC, 1995; recipient Women in Bus. and Industry award, YWCA, 1986, Rebekah Herndon Bush Cmty. Svc. award, Jr. League Miami, 1988, Cmty. headliner award, Women in Comm., 1989, Leadership award, S. Fla. Perinatal Network, 1991, Young Leadership award, Greater Miami Opera, 1992, Lollipop award, Amigos Together for Kids, 2000, Woman of Valor award, Children's Home Soc., 2003. Mem.: Phi Beta Kappa. Office: Union Planters Bank 2800 Ponce de Leon Blvd Coral Gables FL 33134

HERAUF, WILLIAM ANTON, lawyer; b. Dickinson, N.D., Feb. 26, 1957; s. Herbert Henry and Nancy Dann (Rabe) H.; m. Joan Thompson, May 17, 1986. BSBA, U. N.D., 1979, JD, 1982. Bar: N.D. 1982, Minn. 1982, U.S. Dist. Ct. N.D. 1982. Assoc. Mackoff, Kellogg, Kirby & Kloster, Dickinson, 1982-84; corp. atty. Multi Nat. Diving Educators Assn., Marathon, Fla., 1984-89; asst. city atty. City of Dickinson, 1985-90; assoc. Ficek Law Office, Dickinson, 1985-90; state's atty. Slope County, N.D., 1985-87. Fireman Dickinson Vol. Fire Dept., 1985-88; bd. dirs. Dickinson Underwater Search and Recovery Team, 1985-88. Mem. ABA (Bronze Key 1982, bd. govs. cert. 1982), N.D. Trial Lawyers Assn. (bd. dirs. 1985—, treas. 1988-89, sec. 1989-90, pres. elect 1990-91, pres. 1991-92), Assn. Trial Lawyers Am., Stark County Bar Assn. Lodges: Elks. Methodist. Avocations: skiing, scuba diving, running, swimming, reading. Home: 1055 5th Ave W Dickinson ND 58601-3836 Office: Reichert Herauf PC 34 1st St SE # K Dickinson ND 58601-5612

HERAVI, MEHDI, economist; BA, Utah State U., 1963, MA, 1964; Phd, Am. U. Sch. Internat. Svc., 1967. Asst. prof. polit. sci. Tenn. Technol. U., Cookeville, 1967-70, assoc. prof. govt., 1970-72; assoc. prof. polit. sci. Nat. U. Iran, Tehran, 1972-74, prof. polit. sci., 1976-81; editor Shabaviz Press, Tehran, 1981-92; cons., rschr. Econs. Inst., Boulder, Colo., 1999—. Dir. gen. in charge of internat. affairs Nat. U. Iran, 1972-74, v.p. in charge of rsch. & devel., 1976-79; v.p. acad. & student affairs Razi U., Kermanshah, Iran, 1974-76. Author: Iranian-American Diplomacy, 1969; editor: Encyclopedia of the Middle East, 1973; contbr. articles to profl. jours. Mem. Am. Polit. Sci. Assn., Am. Acad. Polit. & Social Scis., Mid. East Studies Assn. N.Am., Am. Soc. Pub. Adminstrn., AAUP, Internat. Polit. Sci. Assn., Mid. East Inst., Iranian Polit. Sci. Assn., Iranian Nat. Prof.'s Orgn., Cosmos Club. Address: 4201 Cathedral Ave NW Apt 415W Washington DC 20016-4902 E-mail: behjal@msn.com.

HERB, EDMUND MICHAEL, optometrist, educator; b. Zanesville, Ohio, Oct. 9, 1942; s. Edmund G. and Barbara R. (Michael) H.; divorced; children: Sara, Andrew; m. Jeri Herb. OD, Ohio State U., 1966. Pvt. practice optometry, Buena Vista, Colo., 1966—; past prof. Timberline campus Colo. Mountain Coll.; past clin. instr. Ohio State U. Sch. Optometry. Mem. Am. Optometric Assn., Colo. Optometric Assn. Home: 16395 Mt Princeton Rd Buena Vista CO 81211-9505 Office: 115 N Tabor St Buena Vista CO 81211 also: Leadville Colorado Med Ctr Leadville CO 80461

HERB, F(RANK) STEVEN, lawyer; b. Cin., Nov. 9, 1949; s. Frank X. and Jean M. (Zurcher) H.; m. Jean L. Jeffers, June 21, 1971; children: Tracy Lynn, Jacquelyn Anne. BS, Bowling Green U., 1971; JD, U. Cin., 1974. Bar: Ohio 1974, Fla. 1978, U.S. Dist. Ct. (no., mid., and so. dists.) Fla., U.S. Ct. Appeals (11th cir.); cert. county and cir. ct. mediator, Fla. Supreme Ct. Assoc. Connaughton Law Offices, Hamilton, Ohio, 1974; jud. advocate gen., chief of civil law USAF, Tyndall AFB, Fla., 1975—78; ptnr. Nelson Hesse, Sarasota, Fla., 1979—. Author: (with others) Bennedicts on Admiralty, 1996, 97, 98; contbr. chpts. to books. Bd. dirs. Brock Wilson Found., Sarasota, 1983-92; pres. Riegels Landing Assn., Sarasota, 1986-90, 98-2000; dir., chmn. Siesta Key Utilities Assn., 1994—; mem. govt. rels. com. Nat. Marine Mfrs. Assn. Capt. JAGC USAF, 1975-78. Decorated USAF Meritorious Svc. medal. Mem. Ohio Bar Assn., Fla. Bar Assn. (chmn. 12th Jud. cir. unauthorized practice of law com. 1986-93, fee arbitration com. 12th jud. cir. 1996—), Sarasota Bar Assn., Def. Rsch. Inst., Maritime Law Assn., Am. Boat and Yacht Counsel, Nat. Marine Mfrs. Assn. (govt. rels. com.), The Field Club (commodore, dir. exec. com.). Republican. Roman Catholic. Avocations: boating, woodworking, skiing, tennis, golfing. Office: Nelson Hesse 2070 Ringling Blvd Sarasota FL 34237-7002 E-mail: Falcon71@aol.com.

HERB, SAMUEL MARTIN, manufacturing company executive; b. Yeadon, Pa., Nov. 29, 1938; s. Samuel F. and Mildred V. (Reitz) H.; m. Judith Ann Oesch, July 2, 1966 (dec.); children: Samuel S., Corinne M., David M. (dec.), Elizabeth A. BEE, Drexel U., 1969. Registered profl. engr., Calif. Tech. writer Honeywell Corp., Ft. Washington, Pa., 1964—73, applications engr., 1973—76, project engr., 1976—79; from product application specialist to mkt. mgr. Leeds & Northrup, North Wales, 1979—93, market mgr. control applications, 1993—94; dir. mktg. Procon Sys., Inc., Lansdale, 1994—95, Siemens Energy & Automation, Inc., Spring House, 1996—2002; owner JAOMAD Cons., New Britain, 2002—. Mem. faculty Spring Garden Coll., Chestnut Hill, Pa., 1976-82; columnist Intech mag. Author: Understanding Distributed Process Control, 1983, Control System Architectures, 1994, Implementing Control Systems, 1995, Understanding Distributed Processor Systems for Control, 1999, Human-Machine Interfaces for Plant Automation, 2000, Distributed Controller Hardware and Software Basics, 2000, Alarms and Plant Upsets in Distributed Control, 2000, Network for Plant Automation, 2000, Implementing Distributed Control of Processes, 2000, Glossary of Industrial Computing Acronyms and Terminology, 2000, System Security in Distributed Control, 2001; author 5 on-line/CD courses, 2002; contbr. articles to profl. jours. Commr. Boy Scouts Am., 1961—. Named to Legion of Honor Chapel of Four Chaplains, 1985; recipient Woodbadge, 1989, Disting. Commissioner Awd., Silver Beaver award, 1990, Boy Scouts Am. Mem. Instrument Soc. Am. (sr., Donald P. Eckman Edn. award 1999, Golden Eagle award 2001), Indsl. Computing Soc., Engrs. Club (Phila.). Republican. Roman Catholic. Avocations: travel, swimming, outdoors, model railroading, house projects. Home: 117 Pawnee Rd New Britain PA 18901-5142

HERBAUGH, ROGER DUANE, computer and software company executive; b. Mt. Vernon, Wash., May 20, 1957; s. Donald Lloyd and Kathleen Joyce (Anderson) H.; m. Anne Louise Finlayson, May 8, 1993; children: Andrew David Miller, Celeste Jane Miller, Trevor Allan Miller, Vanessa Anne Herbaugh, Deirdre Rose Herbaugh. AA, Skagit Valley Coll., 1984; BA, Western Wash. U., 1986. Cert. microsoft profl. Computer programmer Stockmar Northwestern, Mt. Vernon, 1986-87; CEO, computer cons. Herbaugh & Assocs., Inc. Computer Support Group, Mt. Vernon, 1987—; also pres. bd. dirs. Herbaugh & Assocs., Inc., Mt. Vernon. Cons. Mobil, Ferndale, Wash., 1985-86, Shell Oil Co., Anacortes, Wash., 1986-98, BP Oil Co., Ferndale, 1986-93, Blaine, Wash., 2000-01, ARCO, Blaine, 1989-2000, Tosco, Ferndale, 1993-97, Tosco, Seattle,

1993-97, Tesoro, Anacortes, 1998—; bd. dirs., pres. Software Plus, Inc., Mt. Vernon, 1991-99; mem. tech. adv. coun. Mt. Vernon H.S.; trainer Kiwanis. V.p. Shangrila Cmty. Ctr., 1999-2001; grade 8 soccer referee USSF, 1999—, Skagit/Island County area referee adminstr. Sgt. U.S. Army, 1975-81. Mem. Burlington C. of C., Mt. Vernon C. of C., Kiwanis (past lt. gov., past pres. Mt. Vernon chpt., past K-kids dist. adminstr., mem. internat. com. on K-kids 2001-02, dist. webmaster), Skagit Valley Referee Assn. (bd. dirs. 2001—), Skagit Soccer Referee Assn. (pres. 2003--). Republican. Mem. Lds Ch. Avocations: boating, fishing, travel, soccer. Office: Herbaugh & Assocs Inc Computer Support Group PO Box 1665 Mount Vernon WA 98273-1665 E-mail: roger@herbaugh.com.

HERBECK, DALE ALAN, educator; b. Chgo., June 14, 1958; s. Delbert George and Virginia (Gerke) H.; m. Edith Haffenreffer, Aug. 15, 1997. BA, Augustana Coll., 1980; MA, U. Iowa, 1982, PhD, 1988. Instr., dir. forensics Boston Coll., Chestnut Hill, Mass., 1985-88, asst. prof., dir. forensics, 1988-91, assoc. prof., dir. forensics, 1991-94, assoc. prof., 1994-98, assoc. prof., chmn., 1998—2002, prof., chmn., 2002—. Author: Freedom of Speech in the United States; editor: Free Speech Yearbook, 1992-94, Argumentation and Advocacy, 2001-04; contbr. chpts. to books, articles to profl. jours. Recipient Midwest Forensic Assn. Rsch. award, 1987, Trzazka Student Advising award, 1989, Robert M. O'Neil award for rsch. on freedom of expression, Nat. Comm. Assn., 1993, Svc. award, Am. Debate Assn., 1994, Ea. Comm. Assn. Past Pres. award, 1995, James Madison award for scholarly rsch., So. State Comm. Assn., 2001, McGuffy award for excellence and longevity of textbook, Textbook and Acad. Authors Assn., 2002. Mem. Am. Forensic Assn. (pres. 1992-94, v.p. 1990-92), Am. Comm. Assn. (exec. bd. 1994-99, pres. 1997-98), Ctrl. States Comm. Assn., Ea. Comm. Assn., Internat. Comm. Assn., Nat. Comm. Assn. (chair commn. on freedom of expression, 1998-2000), Mortarboard, Phi Beta Kappa (Tchg. award 2000), Delta Sigma Rho, Omicron Delta Kappa, Tau Kappa Alpha. Democrat. Lutheran. Home: 15 Dover Farm Rd Medfield MA 02052-1130

HERBEL, LEROY ALEC, JR., telecommunications engineer; b. Ft. Carson, Colo., July 24, 1954; s. LeRoy Alec and Mabel Bertha (Huffman) H. BS, S.W. Mo. State U., 1976; MEd, Ga. So. U., 1978; MS in Telecommunications, Golden Gate U., 1987; MBA, 1990. Asst. mgr. toy dept. Dillard's Dept. Store, Springfield, Mo., 1971-76; material controller GTE of the South, Durham, N.C., 1979-80; asst. prof. mil. sci. Army ROTC, U. N.H., Durham, 1982-85; tech. instr., course developer Northern Telecom Inc., Raleigh, N.C., 1988-91; sr. engr. No. Telecom Inc., Raleigh, N.C., 1991-93; field engr. mgr. Western Wireless Corp., Bellevue, Wash., 1994-95; switch supr. Palmer Wireless (CellularOne), Ft. Myers, Fla., 1995-96; sr. network analyst Sprint PCS, Lenexa, Kans., 1996-97; instrl. sys. specialist Dept. Def., Fort Gordon, Ga., 1997—. Adj. prof. DeKalb (Ga.) C.C., 1978-79, N.C. Wesleyan Coll., Rocky Mount, 1991. Dist. commr. Kiokee dist. Ga. Carolina Coun., Augusta, Ga., 2000—; scoutmaster Troop 213 Boy Scouts Am., Cary, N.C., 1990-93, asst. dist. commr. Dan Beard dist., 1992-96, mem. merit badge staff Nat. Jamboree, 1993, 2001, mem. troop 213 com., 1993—. Capt. U.S. Army, 1980-88; maj., USAR, 1988—. Recipient Scoutmaster award of merit Boy Scouts Am., 1991, Disting. Leadership citation Boy Scouts Am., 1991, Scoutmaster Key award Boy Scouts Am., 1992, Dist. Order of Merit Boy Scouts Am., 1994, Boy Scout Commr. Key award, 1995, Disting. Commr. Svc. award, 2002. Mem. Telephone Pioneers of Am., Phi Delta Kappa. Avocations: golf, running, trains, camping, music.

HERBERS, TOD ARTHUR, publisher; b. Cin., Sept. 11, 1948; s. Walter Fred and Jeanette Ruth (Dalton) H.; m. Suzanne Jeannine Daly, Sept. 7, 1974. BA, Catholic U. Am., 1970. With Nation's Bus. mag., Washington, 1972-75, promotion dir., 1974-75, Washingtonian mag., Washington, 1975-76, circulation and promotion dir., assoc. pub., 1976-77; pub. Am. Film mag., Washington, 1977-82; mng. pub. Science 86 Mag., Washington, 1982-86; pub. Sci. Illustrated Mag., Washington, 1987-89; pres. Jour. NIH Rsch., Washington, 1989-94; pub. On Target Media, Inc., Washington, 1994—2003; pub., pres. Home & Design Mag., Homestyles Media Inc., Silver Spring, Md., 2002—. Home: 8428 Holly Leaf Dr Mc Lean VA 22102-2224 Office: Homestyles Media Inc Ste 150 12501 Prosperity Dr Silver Spring MD 20904 E-mail: therbers@homeanddesign.com.

HERBERT, ADAM WILLIAM, JR., academic administrator, educator; b. Muskogee, Okla., Dec. 1, 1943; s. Addie (Hibler) H.; m. Karen Y. Lofty, Apr. 1980. BA, U. So. Calif., 1966, MPA, 1967; PhD, U. Pitts., 1971. Instr., asst. prof., coord. acad. programs Ctr. Urban Affairs Sch. Pub. Adminstrn., U. So. Calif., L.A., 1969-72; assoc. prof., chmn. urban affairs program div. environ. and urban systems Va. Poly. Inst. State U., Blacksburg, 1972-75, prof., dir. North Va. programs, Ctr. for Pub. Adminstrn. and Policy, 1978-79; White House fellow, spl. asst. sec. HEW, Washington, 1974-75; spl. asst. to under sec. HUD, Washington, 1975-77; prof., dean Fla. Internat. U., Miami, 1979-87, assoc. v.p. for acad. affairs, chief acad. officer North Miami campus, 1985-88, v.p., chief adminstrv. officer, 1987-88; pres. U. North Fla., Jacksonville, 1989—98; chancellor State Univ. Sys. of Fla., 1998—2001; Regents prof., exec. dir. Fla. Ctr. for Pub. Policy and Leadership U. North Fla., Jacksonville, Fla.; pres. Indiana Univ. System, Bloomington, Ind., 2003—. Office: Indiana Univ System Bloomington IN 47405*

HERBERT, ALBERT EDWARD, JR., interior and industrial designer; b. Detroit, June 12, 1928; s. Albert Edward and Gladys Mae (Speechley) H. Student, Pratt Inst., 1947-50. Owner, operator Albert Herbert Designs, 1957—; designer for V'Soske, Inc. Baker Furniture. Author: (with Roger P. Myers) The Last Survivor, 1976, Killer Pack, 1976, The Skytower Disaster, 2000, The Quest, 2001; contbr. articles to mags. Served with USAF, 1952-56. Fellow Am. Soc. Interior Designers (life). Home: Fords Colony 104 Baltusrol Williamsburg VA 23188

HERBERT, AMANDA KATHRYN, special education educator; b. Cleve., Apr. 10, 1948; d. Ralph Earle and Nina Kathryn (Burkey) Herbert; m. John Davis Reeves, June 26, 1971 (div. 1978). Student, Coll. of Wooster, Ohio, 1966-68; BA, Defiance Coll., 1971; MEd, Lynchburg Coll., 1982. Cert. tchr., Va. Elem. tchr. Napoleon (Ohio) City Schs., 1970-72; substitute tchr. Juvenile Boys Correction Ctr., Maumee, Ohio, 1972-73; Title I reading tchr. Defiance City Schs., 1973-76, tchr. 4th grade, 1976-78; tchr. 4th to 6th grades Platte Valley Schs. RE3, Ovid, Colo., 1978-81; tchr. elem. and secondary spl. edn. Amherst County (Va.) Schs., 1982—. Tchr. Camp Little Indian, Defiance, 1967-77. Contbr. to book. Deacon, elder First Presbyn. Ch., Defiance, 1973-78; singer Defiance Community Choir, 1972-77; actor, singer Fine Arts Ctr., Lynchburg, Va., 1983—; mem. choir Parkland United Meth. Ch., Lynchburg, 1982—. Mem. NEA, Coun. for Exceptional Children (div. learning disabilities), Va. Edn. Assn., People to People Citizen Ambassador Program to Peoples' Rep. China, Amherst Edn. Assn., Alpha Chi. Methodist. Avocations: travel, reading, swimming, acting, instrumental and vocal performance. Office: Amherst County High Sch 139 Lancer Ln Old Rt 29 Amherst VA 24521 E-mail: aher410@aol.com.

HERBERT, BRITTNEY-SHEA, cancer biologist; b. Hartford, Conn., Aug. 16, 1971; d. Robert Frank Jr. and Carol Suzanne Herbert. BA in Biology, U. Tex., 1993, PhD in Biol. Scis., 1998. Instr. dept. cell biology U. Tex. Southwestern Med. Ctr., Dallas, 2002—03; asst. prof. dept. med. and molecular genetics IU Sch. of Medicine, 2002—03. Postdoctoral trainee congressionally directed med.-breast cancer rsch. program Dept. Def., 2000-2003. Contbr. articles to sci. jours., including Jour. Nat. Cancer Inst., Procs. NAS, Nutrition and Cancer, Genes and Devel., Oncogene, Cancer Rsch., Jour. Biol. Chemistry. Predoctoral fellow NASA, 1994-97, univ. continuing fellow U. Tex., Austin, 1997-98, postdoctoral fellow Susan G. Komen Breast Cancer Found., 1999-2002. Mem.: Women in Cancer Rsch., Am. Assn. Cancer Rsch. (Scholar-in-Tng. award 2002), U. Tex. at Austin Friar Soc., Sigma Xi, Omicron Delta Kappa, Phi Kappa Phi. Avocations: astronomy, soccer, scuba diving, travel. Office: U Tex Southwestern Med Ctr 5323 Harry Hines Blvd Dallas TX 75390-9039

HERBERT, CAROL SELLERS, farming executive, lawyer; b. Durham, N.C., Mar. 2, 1943; d. George Grover and Mae (Savage) Sellers; m. James Keller Herbert, Nov. 13, 1980; children: John, Katherine, Paul, Barry. BA, Duke U., 1964; JD cum laude, Whittier Coll., 1976. Bar: Calif. 1976, U.S. Dist. Ct. (cen. dist.) Calif. 1976. Tchr. h.s. Wasatch Sch. Dist., Heber, Utah, 1964-67; dir., tchr. Pinedale (Mont.) Sch. Dist., 1967-71; adminstr. Whittier Law Sch., L.A., 1971-76; lawyer Katz Granof Palarz, Beverly Hills, Calif., 1976-79; exec. dir. MBJ Legal and Profl. Pub., Inc., L.A., 1979-83; dean San Joaquin Coll. Law, Fresno, Calif., 1981-85; pres., co-founder Barrister Project, L.A., 1985-90, Herbert Found., Fresno and Lindsay, Calif., 1990—; dir., CFO HerCal Corp., Lindsay, Calif. Trustee Domus Mitus Found., Fresno, 1994-96; founder Beverly Hills Bar Assn. Com. on Women and Law, 1977; dir. CLI DreamWeavers Divsn., Lindsay, Calif., 1995; Reiki Master Usui Shiki Ryoho, 1996; advisor Mock Trial Project, 2000—. Prodr. Lang. of Dreams (video series), 1994-97. Trustee ARAS, C.G. Jung Inst. L.A., Libr. and Bookstore com., 1989—, chair endowment com. Mem. ABA, Calif. Bar Assn.

HERBERT, CATHERINE DEMING, English educator; b. Charlottesville, Va., July 30, 1968; d. Robert Beverley and Jennette (Campbell) H. BA, U. Va., Charlottesville, 1990; MA, James Madison U., 1994; postgrad., U. Paul Valéry, Montpellier, France, 1999—. Sec. sr. dept. urology U. Va., Charlottesville, 1990-92; tchg. asst. dept. English, James Madison U., Harrisonburg, Va., 1993-94, instr., 1994-95; vol., English tchr./trainer Peace Corps, Madagascar, 1995-98. EMT, Western Albemarle Rescue Squad, Crozet, Va., 1989-95; incident comdr. for search and rescue Appalachian Search and Rescue Conf., Va., 1986-95. Episcopalian. Avocations: reading, cooking, hiking. Home: 7 rue du Generale Rene 34000 Montpellier France E-mail: demingo@hotmail.com.

HERBERT, CHESLEY C. psychiatrist, educator; b. Charlotte, N.C., June 7, 1943; m. Marie Genevieve Groszko, Aug. 10, 1975; Rachel G., Andrew G. AB in History, Duke U., 1961-65; MD, Columbia U., 1965-69. Diplomate Am. Bd. Psychiatry and Neurology; lic. physician and surgeon, Calif., Nat. Bd. Med. Examiners, DEA. Intern Harlem Hosp. Ctr., N.Y.C., 1969-70; resident in psychiatry U. Calif., San Francisco, 1970-73, fellow in social psychiatry, 1973-75; pvt. practice San Francisco, 1973—; asst. clin. prof. psychiatry U. Calif., San Francisco, 1975-83, assoc. clin. prof., 1983—; staff psychiatrist On Lok Sr. Health Svcs., San Francisco, 1980—. Cons. Psychopathic divsn. Superior Ct., San Francisco, 1974-78, North of Market Sr. Alcohol Program, San Francisco, 1979-80; psychiatrist srs. unit N.E. Mental Health Ctr., San Francisco, 1975-79; chief divsn. psychiatry and psychology dept. medicine Davies Med. Ctr., San Francisco, 1996-98; mem., active staff, Calif. Pacific Med. Ctr., courtesy staff mem. St. Francis Meml. Hosp. Contbr. articles to profl. jours. Mem. Am. Psychiat. Assn., No. Calif. Psychiat. Soc., Calif. Med. Assn., San Francisco Med. Soc. Office: 45 Castro St Ste 302 San Francisco CA 94114-1029

HERBERT, CHRISTOPHER JAY, marketing professional, management consultant; b. Flint, Mich., May 8, 1953; s. Clarence LaVern and Doris Julia (Potter) H.; m. Nancy Ellen Welch, Dec. 19, 1987. BA, Lewis and Clark Coll., 1975; MBA, Ariz. State U., 1984. Cert. neurolinguistic programming master practitioner, LAB Profile cons./trainer. Planner Maricopa Employment and Tng. Adminstrn., Phoenix, 1977-78; asst. dir. for planning and program devel. Maricopa County Human Resources Dept., Phoenix, 1978-81, CETA adminstr., 1981; v.p. Cons. Assocs., Inc., Phoenix, 1981-82; pres. C.J. Herbert & Co. Inc., Scottsdale, Ariz., 1982-85; v.p. Behavior Rsch. Ctr., Inc., Phoenix, 1985-89; pres. The Insight Group Inc., Tempe, Ariz., 1989—; rsch. dir. Success Strategies Ltd., Burlington, Ont., Can., 2001—. Mktg. com. Phoenix Symphony, 1988-90. Bd. dirs. Grand Canyon Assn., 1992-98, 2000-02, pres., 1994-96, chair governance com., 1996-97, chair strategic planning com., 1997-98, 2001; bd. dirs. Grand Canyon Nat. Park Found., 1995-2001, chair pers. com. 2000-01, v.p., 1995-99; bd. dirs. The Phoenicians, 1994, Grand Canyon Music Festival, 1998-2000. Mem. Qualitative Rsch. Cons. Assn. (professionalism com. 1991—, chmn. 1992-95, conv. spkr. 1993-95, treas. bd. dirs. 1995), Am. Assn. Pub. Opinion Rsch., Am. Inst. Wine and Food (chmn. Ariz. chpt. 1993, mem. nat. membership com. 1994), Brotherhood of Knights of the Vine (Master Knight, bd. dirs. Phoenix chpt. 1991-95), Phoenix C. of C. (bd. dirs. 1987-89, chmn. small bus. coun. 1986-87, health coun. 1993-97), Rocky Mountain Elk Found. (habitat coun. 1999—, strategic vision com. 2002—, bd. dirs. 2003—, awards com. 2003—, fin. com. 2003—, governance com. 2003—, pers. com. 2003—,), Fedn. Fly Fishers (Eastern Rocky Mountain coun. native trout task force 2002--). Avocations: music, fly fishing, gastronomy, book collecting, bicycling. Office: The Insight Group Inc 2105 E Vaughn St Tempe AZ 85283-3343 E-mail: contactcjh@earthlink.net.

HERBERT, DAVID LEE, lawyer, author; b. Cleve., Oct. 1, 1948; s. William Clayton and Virginia Margaret (Battersby) H.; m. Lynda Jane Rosenkranz, Aug. 23, 1970; children: Laurance, Jason, Meredith. BBA, Kent State U., 1971; JD, U. Akron, 1974. Bar: Ohio 1974, U.S. Dist. Ct. (no. dist.) Ohio 1974, U.S. Ct. Appeals (6th cir.) 1984. Asst. prosecutor Stark County Prosecutors Office, Canton, Ohio, 1974-80; ptnr. Herbert & Benson, Canton, Ohio, 1975—. Pres. Profl. Reports Corp., 1986—; assoc. prof. Kent State U., Ohio, 1980-87; sec., asst. chmn. Ohio Govs. Organized Crime Law Enforcement Cons. Com., Columbus, 1976-78; sec. Stark County Pub. Defender Com., Canton, 1982-87. Author: Attorneys' Master Guide to Psychology, 1980, Legal Aspects of Preventive and Rehabilitative Exercise Programs, 1984, Corporations of Corruption: The Systematic Study of Organized Crime, 1984, Legal Aspects of Sports Medicine, 1990, others; editor The Exercise Stds. and Malpractice Reporter, 1986—, The Sports Medicine Stds. and Malpractice Reporter; contbr. articles to profl. jours. Pres., trustee Lake Twp. Trustees, Hartville, Ohio, 1983-87; bd. dirs. Stark County Jr. Achievement, Canton, 1983; mentor pupil enrichment program Lake Local Sch. Bd., Hartville, 1981-85. Recipient Continuing Legal Edn. award ABA/Am. Law Inst., 1975 Mem. ABA (liaison to jud. adminstrn. divsn. 1972-73), Am. Arbitration Assn. (comml. arbitrator 1983—), Def. Rsch. Inst., Am. Coll. Sports Medicine, Stark County Trustees and Clks. Assn., Stark County Bar Assn. (exec. com. 1984, grievance com. 1979-82), Akron/Canton Def. Lawyers Assn., Ducks Unltd., North Canton Jaycees (com. chmn. 1975-76). Home: 1055 Clearvale St NE Hartville OH 44632-9463 Office: Herbert & Benson 4571 Stephen Cir NW Canton OH 44718-3633 E-mail: herblegal@aol.com.

HERBERT, EDWARD FRANKLIN, public relations executive; b. N.Y.C., Jan. 30, 1946; s. H. Robert and Florence (Bender) H.; m. Rhonda J. Scharf, Aug. 20, 1967; children: Jason Dean and Heather Ann (twins). B.S. in Comm., Syracuse U., 1967, M.S., 1969. Assoc. dir. pub. relations Am. Optometric Assn., Washington, 1971; community relations specialist Gen. Electric Co., Columbia, Md., 1971-73, pub. relations account supr., 1973-75; dir. pub. affairs Nat. Consumer Fin. Assn., Washington, 1975-78; regional dir. pub. relations Montgomery Ward Co., Balt., 1978-80, fin. info. services dir., Chgo., 1980-81, internal comm. dir., 1981-82, corp. comm. dir., 1982-83; regional dir. pub. relations MCI Comm. Corp., Chgo., 1983-84; dir. comm. MCI Midwest, MCI Telecom. Corp., 1985-93; prin. Edward F. Herbert & Assoc., 1993—; Bd. dirs. United Cerebral Palsy of Chgo., Better Bus. Bur. Served with U.S. Army, 1969-71. Mem. Pub. Relations Soc. Am., Execs. Club of Chgo., Info. Industry Council. E-mail: efherbert@aol.com. Home and Office: 830 Timberhill Ln Highland Park IL 60035-5121

HERBERT, GAVIN SHEARER, health care products company executive; b. L.A., Mar. 26, 1932; s. Gavin and Josephine (D'Vitha) H.; children by previous marriage Cynthia, Lauri, Gavin, Pam; 2d. m. Ninetta Flanagan, Sept. 6, 1986. BS, U. So. Calif., 1954. With Allergan, Inc., Irvine, Calif., 1950—, v.p., 1956-61, exec. v.p., pres., 1961-77, chmn. bd., CEO, 1977-91, chmn. bd., 1992-95, chmn. emeritus; pres. Eye and Skin Care Products Group Smith Kline Beckman Corp., 1981-89. Exec. v.p Smith Kline Beckman Corp., 1986-89; bd. dirs. Beckman Instruments, Inc., Calif. Healthcare Inst. Mem. Rsch. to Prevent Blindness (bd. dirs.), Big Canyon Country Club, Newport Harbor Yacht Club, Pacific Club, Beta Theta Pi. Republican.

HERBERT, JAMES ALAN, writer; b. Burlington, Vt., July 29, 1945; s. Alan Wells and Rose Marion H.; m. Martha Lebedzinski, June 20, 1976 (div. 1983); children: Denise M., Jeni Ayn; m. Margaret Harris, Oct. 20, 1992; 1 child: Alicia Ayn. Student, Wittenberg U., Springfield, Ohio, 1963-65, SUNY, Buffalo, 1986, Niagara U., 1991. McLean Trucking Co., 1969-86; author, 1986—. Author: The Third Testament, 1988, Rock and Roll Politics, 1992. Committeeman Conservative Party, N.Y., 1971; pub. rels. Vietnam Vets. of Am., 1989-91. Served to cpl. USMC, 1966-69, Vietnam. Recipient conspicuous svc. award State of N.Y., 1991. Mem. Toastmasters Internat. (treas. Buffalo chpt. 1988-90), Niagara Falls Transp. Club, Buffalo Transp. Club. Avocations: boating, golf, swimming. Office: PO Box 83 North Boston NY 14110-0083

HERBERT, JAMES ARTHUR, artist, filmmaker; b. Boston, Feb. 13, 1938; s. James Arthur and Bernice Frances (Burns) H. AB magna cum laude, Dartmouth Coll., 1960; M.F.A., U. Colo., 1962. Instr. U. Colo., 1962; artist-in-residence Yale Summer Sch. Art and Music, 1965; mem. faculty dept. art U. Ga., Athens, 1962—, prof., 1973—, rsch. prof., 1992—, disting. rsch. prof. art, 1999—. One-man shows include Babcock Galleries, N.Y.C., 1967, U. Colo., Boulder, 1972, Poindexter Gallery, N.Y.C., 1972, 1973, 1974, 1976, Mus. Modern Art, 1970, 1972, 1974, 1977, 1981, 1988, 1994, 1998, 1999, Walker Art Ctr., Mpls., 1973, 1982, Harvard U., 1973, High Mus. Art, Atlanta, 1979, Kennedy Ctr., Washington, 1981, Libr. of Congress, 1983—, Museu Tropical, Lisbon, Lisbon, Portugal, 1993, Art Gallery Toronto Can., 1994, Oberhausen Internat. Film Festival, Germany, 1999, Brit. Coun., Cologne, Germany, 1999, Film Mus. Munich, 1999, Atl. Contemporary Art Ctr., 2000, exhibited in group shows at Krannert Art Mus., Urbana, Ill., 1974, New Orleans Mus. Art, 1975, 1980, 1989, Whitney Mus. Am. Art, 1969, 1973, 1974, 1983, Westdeutsche Kurzfilmtage, Oberhausen, W. Ger., 1970, 1972, 1989, 1992, 2001, La Cinémathèque Royale de Belgique, Knokke-Heist, Belgium, 1974—75, Mus. Modern Art, 1979, P.S. 1, N.Y.C., 1979, Stedelijk Mus., Amsterdam, 1982, Kennedy Ctr., Washington, 1983, Monique Knowlton Gallery, N.Y.C., 1983, IRCAM, Pompidou Ctr., Beaubourg, France, 1984, Cinémateque Française, Beaubourg, 1985, Bibliotheque Nat., Avignon, France, 1985, Mus. Modern Art, N.Y.C., 1986, 1991, L.A. County Mus. Art, 1988, Carnegie-Mellon U. Art Gallery, Pitts., 1988, Va. Mus. Fine Art, Richmond, Va., 1988, Southeastern Ctr. for Contemporary Art, Winston-Salem, N.C., 1988, Corcoran Gallery of Art, Washington, 1989, Kuznetsky Most Exhbn. Hall, Moscow, 1989, Art Gallery of Ont., 1989, Long Beach Mus. Art, Calif., 1989, 1991, Norton Galley Art, Palm Beach, 1989, Sheridan Opera House, Telluride, Colo., 1989, 1991, 1993, Mus. Fine Arts, Boston, 1990, Art Inst., Chgo., 1990, Pacific Film Archive, Berkeley, Calif., 1991, Walker Art Ctr., Mpls., 1991, Sundance Theatre, Park City, Utah, 1992, Melbourne Internat. Film Theatre, Australia, 1992, European Media Art Theatre, Osnabrück, Germany, 1992, Toronto (Can.) Film Festival Theatre, 1992, N.Y. Film Festival at Lincoln Ctr., 1992, Inst. de Estadios Norteamericanos, Barcelona, Spain, 1992, Eldorado Theatre, Royal Palace, Antwerp, Belgium, 1993, Odense (Denmark) Internat. Film Theater, 1993, Fifth Media Festival Theatre, Hertogenbosch, The Netherlands, 1993, Vienna Shortfilm Mus., Antwerp (Belgium) Sinema festival Theatre, 1993, Rio Internat. Festival Hall, Rio de Janiero, Brazil, 1993, Melbourne (Australia) Internat. Film Mus., 1992, Sydney (Australia) Internat. Film Mus., 1994, Vherskě Hradiště, Czech Republic, 1994, Kunstencentrum, Leuveen, Netherlands, Gaumont Marignan Theater, Paris, 1995, Toronto Internat. Film Festival, 1997, 1999, Sundance Film Festival Theater, Park City, Utah, 1998, 1999, Rotterdam Internat. Film Festival, The Netherlands, 1998, 1999, 2000, Mus. Nat. Ctr. de Arte Reina Sofia, Madrid, Spain, Edinburgh (Scotland) Internat. Film Festival, 1999, Rio Internat. Film Festival, Brazil, 1999, Sao Paulo (Brazil) Internat. Film Festival, 1999, Film Theatre Brit. Coun., Cologne, Germany, 1999, Staatliche Galerie Moritzburg, Halle, Germany, 1999, Represented in permanent collections NYU, Am. Fedn. Arts, Royal Film Archives Belgium, Centre Beaubourg, Paris, Mus. Modern Art, Whitney Mus. Am. Art, Cornell U., Am. Film Inst., Chase Manhattan Bank, Coca Cola USA, Herbert F. Johnson Mus. Art at Cornell U., Walker Art Ctr., Mpls., Anthology Film Archives, N.Y.C.; author: Stills: Photographs by James Herbert, 1992. Recipient Awards in the Visual Arts, Rockefeller Found., 1987; Woodrow Wilson fellow, 1960-62, Guggenheim Found. fellow, 1971-72, 89-90; grantee Am. Film Inst., 1969, Nat. Endowment Arts, 1975, 78, 81, 82, Louis Comfort Tiffany Found., 1980, Rockefeller Found., 1993; commn. Libr. of Congress, 1983, Adolph and Esther Gottlieb Found., 1991. Office: U Ga Sch Art Athens GA 30602

HERBERT, JAMES CHARLES, educational association administrator; b. Dayton, Ohio, Nov. 22, 1941; s. Charles August and Helen Louise (Korte) H.; m. Sandra Lynn Swanson, June 4, 1966; children: Kristen, Sonja. BA, U. Dayton, 1963; MA, Brandeis U., 1965, PhD in History of Ideas, 1970. Instr. history Cath. U. Am., Washington, 1967-69; asst. prof. history and philosophy U. D.C., Washington, 1971-73; asst. prof. gen. honors program U. Md., College Park, 1973-79; Am. Coun. on Edn. fellow U.S. Dept. Edn., Washington, 1979-80; dir. governance study Carnegie Found. for Advancement Teaching, Washington, 1980-82; dir. acad. rels. Coll. Bd., N.Y.C., 1982-84, exec. dir. acad. affairs, 1984-89; dir. edn. programs NEH, Washington, 1989-95, dir. rsch. and edn. programs, 1995-99, dir. rsch. programs, 1999—. Mem. Nat. Performance Review, Office of V.P. of U.S., 1993; vis. rsch. scholar Inst. for Philosophy and Pub. Policy, U. Md., 1998-99; acting chmn. NEH, 2001. Gen. editor Academic Preparation Series, 6 vols., 1985-86; editor, writer: Academic Preparation for College, 1983; writer: Control of the Campus, 1982. GM scholar, 1959-63, NDEA fellow, 1963-66, Folger Shakespeare Libr. fellow, 1971, Am. Coun. on Edn. fellow, 1979-80. Mem. Am. Philos. Assn., AAUP, Nat. Collegiate Honors Coun. (exec. com. 1978-80, 81-84, pres. N.E. region 1978-79), D.C. Edn. Licensure Commn. Avocations: writing, swimming, travel, gardening. Office: NEH 1100 Pennsylvania Ave NW Washington DC 20506 E-mail: jherbert@neh.gov., jcherbert@att.net.

HERBERT, JOHN DAVID, urban planner; came to U.S., 1956; s. Redvers Buller and Ruby Kathleen H.; m. Marian Naomi Macbaisey. 1960; children; Rachel Anna, Devorah Jessica. BArch, Auckland U., New Zealand, 1953; PhD, U. Pa., 1964. Faculty U. Calif., Berkeley, 1961-63; advisor urban devel. Ford Found., Calcutta, India, 1964-67; sr. v.p. Planning and Devel. Collaborative Internat. (PADCO), Washington, 1967-81; mgr. urban devel. tng. program World Bank, Washington, 1981-88, sr. urban specialist Asia Tech. Dept., 1988-90; chief tech. advisor UN Devel. Program, Jakarta, Indonesia, 1990-93; spl. advisor to deputy min. Nat. Devel. Planning Bd., Jakarta, Indonesia, 1993-95; sr. fellow Planning & Devel. Collaborative Internat. (PADCO), Washington, 1995—; planning commr. Catoctin Dist., Loudoun County, Va., 2000—; advisor Inst. for Planned Air Rights Comtys., 2003—. Fellowship com. Fulbright-Hayes Fellowships, Urban Planning and Architecture, 1963; external examiner U. New Zealand, 1968, doctoral program Inst. Tech., Bandung, Indonesia, 1993. Contbr. articles to profl. jours. James Sutton fellow, U. Calif., Berkeley, 1957-58, Univ. fellow and Samuel S. Fels fellow, U. Pa., Phila., 1960-61, George Leib Harrison fellow, U. Pa., Phila., 1958-59, 59-60. Hon. fellow Pakistan Inst. Town & Country Planning; mem. Regional Sci. Assn., Cosmos Club. Avocations: poetry, tennis, squash. Office: Planning & Devel Collaborative Internat Ste 170 1025 Thomas Jefferson St NW Washington DC 20007-5201

HERBERT, KEVIN BARRY JOHN, classics educator; b. Chgo., Nov. 18 1921; s. William Patrick and Margaret (Lomasney) H.; m. Margaret Frances Lambin, Dec. 28, 1946; children: John Barry (dec.), Catherine Ann (Mrs. John Reilly). BA, Loyola U., Chgo., 1946; MA, Harvard U., 1949, PhD, 1954. Instr classics Marquette U., Milw., 1948-52; instr. Ind. U., Bloomington, 1952-54 master St. Paul's Sch., Concord, N.H., 1954-55; asst. prof. Bowdoin Coll. Brunswick, Maine, 1955-62; asso. prof., prof. Washington U., St. Louis 1962-92, chmn. dept., 1982-92, prof. emeritus, 1992—, curator emeritus 1994—; reader Advanced Placement Latin, 1962-68, chief reader, 1969-73 mem. Latin test com. Coll. Entrance Exam. Bd., 1968-73; dir. tours to Europe and Middle East, 1973-96; referee Am. Coun. of Learned Socs., 1990-94; mem editorial and adv. bd. Internat. Jour. of the Classical Tradition, 1993—. Author Hugh of St. Victor: Soliloquy on the Earnest Money of the Soul, 1956, Ancient Art in Bowdoin College, 1964, Greek and Latin Inscriptions in the Brooklyn Museum, 1972; co-editor: Ancient Collections in Washington University, 1973 contbr. to: Great Events from History, 2 vols., 1972, Greek Coins in the Wulfing Collection of Washington University, 1979, Maximum Effort The B-29s Against Japan, 1983, Roman Republican Coins in the Wulfing Collection of Washington University, 1987, Roman Imperial Coins in the Wulfing Collection of Washington U.: 31BC-AD180, 1996; prodr. exhbns. and descriptive catalogs Washington U. Gallery of Art: Greek Coins, Fall term, 1989, Roman Republican Coins, Fall term, 1990, Goddesses, Queens and Women of Achievement: 55 B.C.-A.D. 1979, Spring Term, 1993; guest editor Classical Bull., 1998, 99 translator (Greek and Latin commentaries) St. Paul Epistle to the Romans 1999-2000; contbr. articles and revs. to profl. jours. With USAAF, 1942-45 Decorated DFC, Air medal with two silver oak leaf clusters, others; recipient dean's award for outstanding teaching Univ. Coll., Washington U., 1985 Mentoring award, Grad. Sch., Wash. U., 2000; Wilbour fellow Bklyn. Mus 1967. Fellow Am. Numis. Soc.; mem. Am. Philol. Assn., Classical Assn. Middle West and South. Home: 1124 Basswood Ln Saint Louis MO 63132-300 E-mail: kherbert@artsci.wustl.edu.

HERBERT, LEROY JAMES, retired accounting firm executive; b. Long Branch, N.J., Aug. 3, 1923; s. LeRoy J. and Edna Hazel (Keller) H. BS, U. Md., 1950. CPA, N.J., N.Y., Ohio, Tenn., La., N.C., Va.; chartered acct. South Africa. Profl. staff mem. Ernst & Ernst, Balt., 1950-58, asst. mgr., 1958-60, mgr. internat. ops. N.Y.C., 1960-63, ptnr., 1963-67; sr. U.S. ptnr. Whinney Murray Ernst & Ernst, London and Paris, 1967-70; ptnr. in charge internat. ops. N.Y.C., 1970-78; internat. exec. ptnr. Ernst & Whinney Internat., N.Y.C., 1979-83. Bd. dirs. U. Md. Found., St. Barnabas Health Care Sys., Ronald McDonald House, Long Branch, N.J., Monmouth Health Care Found.; past chmn. Monmouth Med. Ctr., Long Branch. With U.S. Army, 1942-46. Recipient Disting. Alumnus award U. Md. Coll. Bus. and Mgmt., 1980, Disting. Acctg. Alumnus award, 1991; named to Long Branch H.S. Disting. Alumni Hall of Fame, 1996. Mem. AICPA, N.Y. Assn. CPAs, Ohio Assn. CPAs, Md. Assn. CPAs, Transvaal Soc. Accts. (South Africa), Deal Country Club, Harpoon and Needle Club, Pres.'s Club (U. Md.), Beta Alpha Psi Episcopalian. Home: Channel Club Tower Monmouth Beach NJ 07750

HERBERT, MARC LOUIS, software engineer; b. Kew Gardens, N.Y., Sept. 2, 1948; s. Charles David and Lee (Laufer) H.; m. Judith Lee Leichman, Mar. 27, 1982; children: Dina Rachel, Arielle Norit. BA in Physics, Harpur Coll., 1969; MS in Physics, Purdue U., 1971; PhD in Physics, U. Pitts., 1978. Sr. software engr. Singer-Kearfott, Wayne, NJ, 1978-82, Lockheed Martin Corp., Great Neck, NY, 1982—2002, master software engr., 2000—02; sr. software engr. Bloomberg, L.P., N.Y.C., 2002—. Mem. Am. Phys. Soc., IEEE. Home: 3450 Manchester Rd Wantagh NY 11793-3058 Office: Bloomberg LP 499 Park Ave New York NY 10022

HERBERT, MARILYNNE, public relations executive, freelance photographer; b. Columbus, Ga., Aug. 12, 1944; d. Herbert Paul and Victoria (Raskin) Gruber; m. Victor Daniel Herbert, June 23, 1968 (div. 1990), remarried Oct. 6, 2001; children: Alissa, Laura. BA, Colo. Woman's Coll., 1966. Adminstrv. asst. pub. rels. dept. Mt. Sinai Med. Ctr., N.Y.C., 1966-68; freelance photographer N.Y.C., 1977—; sr. account exec. Ruder-Finn, Inc., N.Y.C., 1986-93; dir. pub. rels. Iona Coll., New Rochelle, N.Y., 1993-94; sr. account exec. Coll. Connections Inc., N.Y.C., 1994-96; sr. mgr. media rels. Halstead Comm., N.Y.C., 1997—2002, exec. v.p., 2002—; cmty. rels. coord. Osborn Retirement Cmty., 1995—2003. Bd. dirs. Women of Westchester, White Plains, N.Y., 1977—, Byrdcliffe Performing Arts Orgn., New Rochelle, 1987-91, Nat. Women's Polit. Caucus, Westchester County, 1988—, Sr. Pers. Placement Bur., Inc., 1989-92; bd. dirs., sec. New Rochelle Cmty. Fund, 1986-91. Recipient Spl. Recognition award Nat. Women's Polit. Caucus, 1989. Mem. Am. Soc. Mag. Photographers, Assn. for Women in Comm., Lake Katonah Club (bd. govs. 1995-98). Jewish. Home: 77 Upper Lake Shore Dr Katonah NY 10536-2646 Office: Halstead Comms 329 E 82d St New York NY 10028 E-mail: halstead@halsteadpr.com.

HERBERT, MARY KATHERINE ATWELL, writer; b. Grove City, Pa., Dec. 9, 1945; d. Stewart and Luella Irene (Brown) Atwell; m. Roland Marcus Herbert; children: Stephen Todd, Amy Elizabeth, Jill Anne. BA, Ariz. State U., 1968, MA, 1973; film cert., U. So. Calif., 1978. Film writer Scottsdale Daily Progress, 1976-79; dir. pub. relations Phoenix Theatre, 1980-85; script analyst, 1985-86; exec. asst. to v.p. prodn. DeLaurentiis Entertainment Group, 1986; producer's assoc. film TRAXX, 1986-87; dir. of devel. Devin/DeVore Prodns., 1988-89; free-lance script analyst and writer Glendale, Calif., 1989-97. Dir. motion picture TV program Scottsdale (Ariz.) Coll., 2000—. Script writer: (TV shows) Trial By Jury, Dick Clark Prodn., (feature films) Dry Heat, Blind Desire, others; author: Writing Scripts Hollywood Will Love, 1994, 2d edit., 2000, Selling Scripts to Hollywood, 1999. Mem. bd. mgrs. Hollywood-Wilshire YMCA, 1992-96. Mem. Kappa Delta Pi, Pi Lambda Theta.

HERBERT, TERI LYNN, librarian; b. Cedar Falls, Iowa, May 31, 1948; d. Richard Morris and Helene Kathryn (Zarecky) H. BS, Memphis State U., 1970; MS, U. N.C., 1975, MLS, 1978. Chem. technician marine lab. Duke U., Beaufort, N.C., 1972-75, sr. rsch. technician in biopaleontology marine lab., 1975-76, biomed. rsch. technician, info. specialist biomed. lab., 1978-83; rsch. technician in marine mycology U. N.C., Morehead City, 1975-77; food technologist asst. N.C. State U., Morehead City, 1976-77; dir. libr. Skidaway Inst. Oceanography, Savannah, Ga., 1983-85; reference libr., info. specialist Med. U. S.C., Charleston, 1985—. Avocations: sailing, gardening, reading, cultural affairs, historic house preservation. Home: 1726 Brantley Dr Charleston SC 29412-3503 Office: Library of Med U SC 171 Ashley Ave Charleston SC 29425-0001

HERBERT, VICTOR JAMES, foundation administrator; b. Follansbee, W.Va., Aug. 6, 1917; s. Oliver James and Gertrude Mae (Lazear) H.; m. Dorothy Clara Johnson, Sept. 2, 1942 (dec. 1997); children: Victor J., Dorothy Constance; m. Venita Foster, Oct. 10, 1998. AB, Bethany (W.Va.) Coll., 1940. Adminstr., negotiator, airline employee orgns.; a founder Air Line Stewards and Stewardesses Assn., Internat., 1946, acting pres., 1946-51, asst. to pres., 1951-59; in charge edn. and orgn. dept. Air Line Pilots Assn. A.F.L., 1946—2002. Pres. Airline Employees Assn., 1962-2002. Editor: Air Line Employee. Pres. bd. dirs. Bus. Indsl. Ministry. Mem. Beta Theta Pi. Clubs: Mason. Presbyterian. Home: 14730 Greenview Rd Orland Park IL 60462-1992 E-mail: aleaintl@aol.com.

HERBERT, WILLIAM CARLISLE, lawyer; b. Gainesville, Fla., Aug. 25, 1947; s. Thomas Walter and Jean Elizabeth (Linton) H.; m. Mary Lee Dedinsky. AB, Princeton U., 1969; MSJ, Northwestern U., 1970, JD cum laude, 1976. Bar: Ill. 1976, U.S. Ct. Appeals (7th cir.) 1977, Fla. 1978, U.S. Dist. Ct. (no. dist.) Ill. 1978, U.S. Supreme Ct. 1980, U.S. Tax Ct. 1982. Law clk. to Hon. Latham Castle U.S. Ct. Appeals (7th cir.), 1976-77; ptnr. Foley & Lardner, Chgo. Exec. editor Northwestern U. Law Rev., 1976. Mem. ABA, Ill. State Bar Assn., Fla. Bar, Chgo. Bar Assn., Legal Club Chgo., U. Club Chgo. Presbyterian. Office: Foley & Lardner 3 1st National Plz Chicago IL 60602

HERBIG, GEORGE HOWARD, astronomer, educator; b. Wheeling, W.Va., Jan. 2, 1920; s. George Albert and Glenna (Howard) H.; m. Delia Faye McMullin, Oct., 1943 (div. 1968); children: Marilyn, Lawrence, John, Robert; m. Hannelore Helene Tillmann, Sept. 3, 1968. AB, UCLA, 1943; PhD, U. Calif., Berkeley, 1948. From jr. astronomer to assoc. astronomer Lick Obs., U. Calif., Mt. Hamilton, 1948-60, astronomer, 1960-67; prof. astronomy U. Calif., Santa Cruz, 1967-87; astronomer Inst. for Astronomy, U. Hawaii, 1987—2001, emeritus, 2001—. Asst. dir. Lick Obs., 1960-63, acting dir., 1970-71. Editor: Non-Stable Stars, 1955, Spectroscopic Astrophysics, 1970; author over 230 sci. papers, articles, revs. Martin Kellogg fellow U. Calif., Berkeley, 1946-48, NRC fellow Pasadena and U. Chgo., 1948-49, Washington, 1948-49; recipient Medaille U. de Liège, Belgium, 1970, Catherine Wolfe Bruce Gold medal Astron. Soc. Pacific, 1980, Petrie prize and lecture Can. Astron. Soc., 1995. Fellow Am. Acad. Arts and Scis; mem. Nat. Acad. Scis., Internat. Astron. Union, Am. Astron. Soc. (Warner prize 1955, Henry Norris Russell lectr. 1975), Max Planck Inst. für Astronomie (fgn. sci. mem.), Soc. Royale des Scis. de Liège (corr.). Democrat. Office: U Hawaii Inst Astronomy 2680 Woodlawn Dr Honolulu HI 96822-1839

HERBIG, GÜNTHER, conductor; b. Aussig, Germany, Nov. 30, 1931; s. Emil and Gisela (Hieke) H.; m. Jutta Czapski, Oct. 30, 1958; children: Beate, Thomas. Diploma, Franz Liszt Hochschule, Weimar, Germany, 1956. Mus. asst. Erfurt Theatre, 1956-57; condr. German Nt. Theatre, Weimar, 1957-62; prin. condr. Potsdam (Germany) Theatre, 1962-66; condr. Berlin Symphone Orch., 1966-72, chief condr., artistic dir., 1977-83, Dresden (Germany) Philharm. Orch., 1972-77; prin. guest condr. Dallas Symphony Orch., 1979-81, BBC Philharm., 1982-85; music dir. Detroit Symphony Orch., 1984-90; artistic advisor Toronto (Ont., Can.) Symphony Orch., 1988, music dir., 1988-94; chief condr. Saarbrücken (Germany) Radio Symphony Orch., 2001—. Recipient Theodor Fontane Arts prize, 1975; arts prize Govt. of German Dem. Republic, 1970, nat. prize, 1977. Roman Catholic.

HERBISON, PRISCILLA JOAN, public policy and law educator, consultant; b. Mpls., Sept. 13, 1943; d. Charles W. and Vonda C. (Rogers) H. BA, Coll. St. Catherine, St. Paul, 1965; MSW, U. Ill., Urbana, 1969; JD, U. Minn., 1982. Social worker Cath. Social Svc., St. Paul, 1965-67, Cath. Welfare Svc., Mpls., 1969-71; prof. social work U. W.V., 1971-74; prof., dir. social work program St. Cloud (Minn.) State U., 1974—, chmn. dept. sociology, anthropology and social work, 1987—. Prof., dir. human devel. and psychology St. Mary's U. Minn., 1987—; cons., researcher in law; staff aide to speaker of Ill. Ho. of Reps., 1968-69; founder, dir. early childhood ctrs. in rural Appalachia, 1971-72. Author: God Knows We Get Angry, 2002, God Knows Grandparents Make a Difference: Sharing Grandparent's Wisdom, 2003. Recipient Grad. Advisor of Yr. award, 1996, George R. Christenson award for Excellence in Edn., 1998; Fairchild fellow, 1980. Mem. NASW, Acad. Cert. Social Workers (cert.), Conf. Social Work End., Delta Theta Phi. Roman Catholic. Home: 5905 Columbus Ave Minneapolis MN 55417-3107 Office: St Mary's U 2500 Park Ave Minneapolis MN 55404-4403 E-mail: pherbiso@smumn.edu., pjwrites2@aol.com.

HERBITS, STEPHEN EDWARD, strategic consultant; b. Pittsfield, Mass., Mar. 13, 1942; s. Nathaniel R. and Esther (Levin) H. AB, Tufts U., 1964; JD, Georgetown U., 1972. Adminstrv. asst. for rsch. U.S. Senator Edward W. Brooke of Mass., 1966; staff asst., staff dir. Wednesday Group, U.S. Ho. of Reps., 1967-68; commr. President's Commn. All-Vol. Armed Forces, 1969-70; cons. Bailey, Deardourff & Assocs., Inc., Washington, 1969, 73, 74, 77; v.p. fin. devel. Sabre Found., Fond-du-Lac, Wis., 1970; legis. asst. to U.S. Senator Robert T. Stafford of Vt., 1971-73; spl. asst. to asst. sec. def. manpower and res. affairs Dept. of Def., 1973-74; spl. asst. to dir. Presdl. Pers. Office, White House, Washington, 1974-75; counsel U.S. del. Multilateral Trade Negotiations Office Spl. Rep. for Trade Negotiations, 1975-76; spl. asst. to sec. and dep. secs. def. Dept. Def., 1976-77; v.p. Seagram Overseas Sales Co., 1977-79; mng. dir. Kirin-Seagram, Japan, 1977-79; v.p. Seagram Europe, 1979-80; pres. Browne Vintners, Joseph E. Seagram & Sons, Inc., N.Y.C., 1980-82; mng. dir. Seagram Far East, 1982-83; v.p. corp. devel. Seagram Co. Ltd., 1983-86. Exec. v.p. external affairs and corp. policy Seagram Co. Ltd., 1986—97; cons. to Sec. of Def., 2001—02. Contbr. articles to profl. publs. Bd. dirs. The Century Coun., 1993-94. Mem. D.C. Bar Assn. Home and Office: 1000 Venetian Way Apt 904 Miami FL 33139-1008

HERBORG-NIELSEN, THORKILD, retired business educator; b. Skjern, Jutland, Denmark, Apr. 6, 1921; s. Jens Jacobi and Anine Jacobi (Petersen) N.; m. Edith Herborg-Nielsen, Dec. 15, 1946; children: Bente, Hanne. M of Econs., U. Aarhus, Denmark, 1947. Econ. sec. Jutland Telephone Co., Aarhus, 1947-54, head budgeting, 1954-59; mng. dir. C.W. Obel Tobacco Mfg., Aalborg, Denmark, 1959-62; prof. The Aarhus Sch. Bus., 1962-90. Econ. mgr. Regnecentralen Copenhagen, 1962-65; mem., past chmn. Total Harvest Project, Viborg, Denmark, 1986-92, Danish Social Sci. Rsch. Coun., Copenhagen, 1968-76; dep. chmn. expert com. for The EEC Found. of Improvement of Living and Working Conditions in Europe, Dublin, Ireland, 1976-91; chmn. EDP rsch. group IFIP, Ljubhana World Conf., 1971. Chmn., initiator The Hudson Report, Denmark in Europe, 1976. Chmn., mem. various Danish govtl. coms., 1965-90. Recipient Silver Core award Internat. Fedn. Info. Processing, 1971. Mem. Danish Soc. for Future Rsch., Danish Acad. Tech. Scis., Rotary Internat. (gov. dist. 1450 1990-91, Paul Harris fellow 1987), Danish Info. Application Group (founder 1968, mem. of honor 1985). Lutheran. Avocations: yachting, fishing, hunting, music. Home: Elsdyrvej 20 B Hojberg 8270 Aarhus Jutland Denmark E-mail: THerborg@worldonline.dk.

HERBRUCKS, STEPHEN, food products executive; b. 1950; m. Harry Herbrucks. Pres. Herbruck Poultry Ranch Inc., Saranac, Mich., Poultry Mgmt. Systems, Saranac, Mich., 1980—. Office: Herbruck Poultry Ranch Inc 6425 W Grand River Ave Saranac MI 48881-9669

HERBST, ABBE ILENE, lawyer; b. NYC, June 19, 1955; d. Seymour and Charlotte (Wolper) H. BA summa cum laude, Fordham U., 1976, JD, 1979. Bar: N.Y. 1980, N.J. 1980, U.S. Dist. Ct. (so. dist.) N.Y. 2002, U.S. Supreme Ct. 1986. Law clk. Keenan, Powers & Andrews, N.Y.C., 1978-79, assoc., 1980-83, DeForest & Duer, N.Y.C., 1983-90, ptnr., 1991—2001; shareholder Anderson Kill & Olick, PC, N.Y.C., 2002—. Editor: Fordham Urban Law Jour., 1978—79, AKO Estate Planning & Tax Advisor, 2002—. Recipient Outstanding Presentation award, Cmty. Svc. Soc., 1986. Mem. ABA, N.Y. State Bar Assn., N.J. State Bar Assn., N.Y. County Lawyers Assn., Fin. Women's Assn. N.Y., Riverdale Mental Health Assn., Phi Beta Kappa. Avocations: travel, collecting miniature cat figurines. Office: Anderson Kill & Olick PC 1251 Ave of the Americas New York NY 10020

HERBST, ARTHUR LEE, obstetrician, gynecologist; b. NYC, Sept. 14, 1931; s. Jerome Richard and Blanche (Vatz) H.; m. Lee Ginsburg, Aug. 10, 1958. AB magna cum laude, Harvard Coll., 1953, MD cum laude, 1959; DSc (hon.), N.E. Ohio U., 2001. Diplomate Am. Bd. Ob-gyn. (bd. dirs. 1985-93, dir. div. gynecol. oncology 1989-91). Intern Mass. Gen. Hosp., Boston, 1959—60, resident, 1960—62; resident in ob-gyn. Boston Hosp. for Women, 1962—65; instr., assoc. prof. ob-gyn. Mass. Gen. Hosp. and Harvard U. Med. Sch., Boston, 1965—76; Joseph B. DeLee prof. ob-gyn. U. Chgo., 1976—84, Joseph B. DeLee Disting. Service prof., 1984—; chmn. dept. ob-gyn. Chgo. Lying In Hosp., 1976—2001; chmn. exec. com. U. Chgo. Hosps. and Clinics, 1980. Contbr. articles to profl. jours. Fellow Royal Coll. Obstetricians and Gynecologists (hon.), Inst. Med., Nat. Acad. Scis.; mem. AMA, ACS, ACOG, Am. Gynecol. and Obstet. Soc. (pres. 1997-98), Am. Assn. Profs. Ob-Gyn., Ctrl. Assn. Obstetricians and Gynecologists, Chgo. Gynecologic Soc., Soc. Pelvic Surgeons, Endocrine Soc., Infertility Soc., Soc. Gynecologic Oncologists. Home: 1234 N State Pkwy Chicago IL 60610-2219 Office: U Chgo Med Ctr 5841 S Maryland Ave Chicago IL 60637-1463

HERBST, EDWARD IAN, brokerage firm executive; b. N.Y.C., Aug. 22, 1945; s. Samuel B. and Grace Ann (Ballin) H.; m. Lois Gabbe (div. 1983); children: Sandra, Brian. AB, George Washington U., 1967; MBA, NYU, 1970. Corp. 1st v.p. Drexel Burnham Lambert, N.Y.C., 1970-83; mng. dir. Cowen & Co., N.Y.C., 1983—98, SG Cowen Securities Corp., N.Y.C., Capital Mgmt. Assocs., N.Y.C., 1998—. Mem. Chgo. Bd. Trade; mem. nominating com. for bd. govs. Am. Stock Exch., N.Y.C., 1991—; mem. nominating com. for bd. dirs. Options Clearing Corp., N.Y.C., 1991—; mem. permanent faculty com. on continuing edn. Am. Law Inst., N.Y.C., 1986—, AICPA, N.Y.C., 1986—. Chmn. Young Dem. Party, Harrison, N.Y., 1961-63; bd. dirs. Westchester Shore Humane Soc., White Plains, N.Y., 1970-74, George Washington U. Nat. Coun. for Arts and Scis., 1995—; Am. Italian Found. for Cancer Rsch., 1993—; bd. trustees Second Stage, 1991—. Mem. Securities Industry Assn. (com. on options and derivative products 1982-84), Metropolis Country Club (White Plains). Avocations: photography, antique cars. Office: Capital Mgmt 140 Broadway New York NY 10005

HERBST, ERIC, physicist, astronomer, chemist; b. N.Y.C., Jan. 15, 1946; s. Stuart Karl and Dorothy (Polakoff) H.; m. Judith Strassman, Oct. 15, 1972; children: Elisabeth, Andrea, Seth. AB, U. Rochester, 1966; MA, Harvard U., 1969, PhD, 1972. Asst. prof. chemistry Coll. of William and Mary, Williamsburg, Va., 1974-79, assoc. prof.chemistry, 1979-80; assoc. prof. physics Duke U., Durham, N.C., 1980-86, prof. physics, 1986-91, Univ. zu Köln, Cologne, Germany, 1988-89, Ohio State U., Columbus, 1991—, prof. astronomy, 1992—, prof. chemistry, 2003—. Cons. NASA, Washington, 1985-90, NSF, Washington, 1989-92. Contbr. over 240 articles and 25 revs. to profl. jours. Recipient Humboldt award Humboldt Found., 1988, Max Planck prize Max Planck Soc., 1993. Fellow Am. Phys. Soc.; mem. Am. Astron. Soc., Am. Chem. Soc. Achievements include theory of how organic molecules are formed in space; theory of floppy molecules. Office: Ohio State U Dept Physics 174 W 18th Ave Columbus OH 43210-1106 E-mail: herbst@mps.ohio-state.edu.

HERBST, JAN FRANCIS, physicist, researcher; b. Tucson, May 1, 1947; s. Alva and Frances Theresa (Feler) H.; m. Margaret Mae Priest, July 24, 1982; children: Helen, John, Mary. BA in Physics, MS, U. Pa., 1968; PhD, Cornell U., 1974. Postdoctoral rsch. assoc. Nat. Bur. Standards, Gaithersburg, Md., 1974-76; asst. physicist Brookhaven Nat. Lab., Upton, N.Y., 1976-77; assoc. sr. rsch. physicist GM Rsch. Labs., Warren, Mich., 1977-81, staff rsch. scientist, 1981-85, mgr. magnetic materials sect., 1984—, sr. staff rsch. scientist, 1985-93, prin. rsch. scientist, 1993—. Mem. basic energy scis. adv. com. Dept. Energy, 1996-2000, panel chair workshop on devel. of secure energy future, 2002; mem. panel for physics Nat. Rsch. Coun. bd. assessment NIST Programs, 2000—. Contbr. articles over 95 to profl. jours. Recipient Campbell award GM Rsch. Labs., 1983, McCuen award GM Rsch. Labs., 1987, Kettering award GM Corp., 1987. Fellow Am. Phys. Soc. (sec.-treas. div. condensed matter physics 1985-90, nominating com. 1996-98, Internat. prize for new materials 1986). Achievements include patents for in field. Avocations: reading, numismatics. Office: GM R&D Ctr MC 480-106-224 30500 Mound Rd Warren MI 48090-9055

HERBST, JOHN EDWARD, diplomat; b. Rockville Center, N.Y., Aug. 12, 1952; s. Christopher and Mary Rose (Vaccheli) H.; m. Nadezda Christoff, May 22, 1977; children: Maria, Ksenia, Aleksandra. BSFS, Georgetown U., 1974; MA, Tufts U., 1978; MALD, Fletcher Sch., Medford, Mass., 1979. Staff asst. Am. Embassy, Jidda, Saudia Arabia, 1980-82, polit. officer Moscow, 1985-87, Office of Israel, Arab-Israeli Affairs, 1982-84; dir. policy devel. NSC, Washington, 1977-88; dep. dir. econs. Office Soviet Affairs, U.S. State Dept., Washington, 1988-97; consul gen. Am. Consulate, Jerusalem, 1997-2000; amb. to Republic of Uzbekistan U.S. Fgn. Svc., 2000—03; amb. to Ukraine U.S. Dept. State, Washington, 2003—. Contbr. articles to profl. publs. Mem. Phi Beta Kappa, Phi Alpha Theta. Avocations: reading, sports. Office: Dept of State 5850 Kiev Pl Washington DC 20521-5850*

HERBST, JURGEN, history and education educator; b. Braunschweig, Germany, Feb. 22, 1928; came to U.S., 1954, naturalized, 1957; s. Hermann and Annemarie (Otto) H.; m. Susan Lou Allen, Sept. 16, 1951; children— Christian, Annemarie, Stephanie. Student, U. Gottingen, 1947-48; BA, U. Nebr., 1950; MA, U. Minn., 1952; PhD, Harvard U., 1958. Instr. edn. and history Wesleyan U., Middletown, Conn., 1958-59, asst. prof., 1959-65, asso. prof., 1965-66; assoc. prof. ednl. policy studies and history U. Wis., 1966-69, prof., 1969-94, prof. emeritus, 1994—; profl. assoc. Ft. Lewis Coll., Durango, Colo., 1999—. Author: The German Historical School in American Scholarship, 1965, The History of American Education, 1973, From Crisis to Crisis: American College Government, 1636-1819, 1982, And Sadly Teach: Teacher Education and Professionalization in American Culture, 1989, The Once and Future School: 350 Years of American Secondary Education, 1996, Requiem for a German Past: A Boyhood among the Nazis, 1999; editor: Our Country, 1963, History of Elementary School Teaching Curriculum, 1990, Aspects of Antiquity in the History of Education, 1992, German Influences on Education in the United States to 1917, 1995, Mutual Influences on Education: Germany and the United States in the Twentieth Century, 1997. Am. Coun. Learned Socs. grantee, 1960; Fulbright Commn. grantee, 1963, 81; Nat. Endowment for Humanities grantee, 1972-73; Nat. Inst. Edn. grantee, 1973-76; Internat. Research and Exchanges Bd. grantee, 1977; Guggenheim Found. grantee, 1978-79; Wis. Inst. Research in Humanities grantee, 1978-79; Spencer Found. grantee, 1986, 99. Mem. Nat. Acad. Edn., Am. Hist. Assn., Orgn. Am. Historians, History of Edn. Soc. Historische Kommission der Deutschen Gesellschaft für Erziehungswissenschaft, Internat. Standing Conf. for the History of Edn. (mem. exec. com., pres. 1988-91). Democrat.

HERBST, KAREN LOUISE, endocrinologist, researcher; b. Drexel Hill, Pa., June 23, 1961; d. Frank Herbst; life ptnr. John Thomas Arndt, July 23, 1964; 1 child, Sarah Inger Arndt. BA, U. of Iowa, 1983, PhD, 1990—90; MD, Rush U., 1996. Diplomate Am. Bd. of Internal Medicine, 2001. Howard hughes rsch. fellow U. of Utah, Salt Lake City, Utah, 1990—92; med. resident U. of Wash., Seattle, Wash., 1996—98; chief med. resident Dept. of Vet. Affairs Puget Sound Health Care Sys., Seattle, Wash., 1999—2000; endocrinology fellow U. of Wash., Seattle, Wash., 2000—02; asst. prof. Charles R. Drew U., Los Angeles, Calif., 2002—. Cons. Nat. Inst. of Child Health and Human Devel., Bethesda, Md., 1999—2000, Merck, Seattle, 2000—02. Recipient Cardiology prize, Rush U., 1996, Endocrine Scholar award, Pfizer, 2002; fellow Howard Hughes fellowship, U. of Utah, 1990—92; grantee, Adam Tuke Lipodystrophy Found., 2001—; scholar, Am. Med. Women's Assn., 1996. Mem.: AMA (assoc.), Am. Fedn. for Med. Rsch. (assoc.), Endocrine Soc. (assoc. Women in Endocrinology Travel award 2001), Mortar Bd. (hon.), Omicron Delta Kappa (hon.), Alpha Omega Alpha (hon.; pres. 1994—96). Avocations: painting, photography, walking, travel, reading. Office: Charles R Drew University 1731 East 120th Street Los Angeles CA 90059 Office Fax: 323-563-9352. E-mail: kaherbst@cdrewu.edu.

HERBST, RENATE DIANE, lawyer; b. Kitchener, Ont., Can., May 22, 1958; d. Karl and Helma (Eppich) Herbst. Grad., Can. Jr. Coll., Lausanne, Switzerland, 1977; student, Wilfrid Laurier U., Waterloo, Can., 1979; LLB, U. Western Ont., London, 1982. Bar: Ont. 1984. Ptnr. Robins, Appleby & Taub, Toronto, Canada, 1984-89; assoc. Goodman & Goodman, Toronto, 1989-93; ptnr. Bennett Jones, Toronto, 1993-99, Cassels Brock & Blackwell LLP, Toronto, 1999—. Mem.: Can. Inst. Internat. Affairs (hon. solicitor), Assn. Corp. Growth (internat. dir. 2001—), Mayfair Racquet and Tennis Club. Roman Catholic. Avocations: skiing, squash, sailing, golf. Home: 2114-2285 Lakeshore Blvd W Toronto ON Canada M5V 3X9 Office: Cassels Brock & Blackwell LLP 40 King St W Ste 2100 Toronto ON Canada M5H 3C2

HERBST, ROBERT LEROY, organization executive; b. Mpls., Oct. 5, 1935; s. Walter Peter and Bernice Mickey (Mikkelson) H.; m. Evelyn Clarice Elford, Sept. 22, 1956; children— Eric Elford, Peter Robert, Amy Jo. BS in Forest Mgmt, U. Minn., St. Paul, 1957. Dep. commnr. Minn. Conservation Dept., 1966-69; nat. exec. dir. Izaak Walton League Am., 1969-70; commr. natural resources State of Minn., 1971-77; asst. sec. fish, wildlife and parks Dept. Interior, Washington, 1977-81, sec., Jan. 20-26, 1981; exec. dir. Trout Unltd., 1981-90; pres. Lake Superior Ctr., Washington, 1990-92, A-S5 Energy Co., Reno, Nev., 1997-98; Washington rep. TVA, Washington, 1992-96; CEO, chmn. bd. dirs. Global Environment & Tech. Found., Annandale, Va., 1996—. Instr. U. Minn., 1954; mem. adv. faculty N. Am. Sch. Conservation, 1969-77; chmn. Gt. Lakes Fisheries Commn., 1978-80, steering com. Nat. Fishing Week, 1991; mem. U.S. Commn. UNESCO, 1978-79, Pres. Carter's Interagency Coun., 1978-80; co-chmn. Nat. Adv. Coun. Environ. Edn., 1989, chmn., 1990-92; mem. U.S. bd. Environ. Ctr. for Ctrl. and Ea. Europe, 1997—, chmn. bd. dirs.; chmn. bd. dirs. Nat. Wildlife Refuge Assocs., 1998-2001. Author: Careers in Environment, 1973; contbr. articles to profl. jours. Mem. nat. bd. Boy Scouts Am., 1969—77; exec. bd. Viking Coun., 1975—76; bd. govs. African Inst. Econs. Edn. and Devel., 1980; pres. Nat. Watershed Protection Ctr., 1994; U.S. rep. Regional Environ. Ctr. for Ctrl. and Ea. Europe, chair bd. dirs.; chmn. bd. Nat. Reach Coun.; mem. Annandale United Meth. Ch., 1969—77. Recipient Nat. Svc. award Izaak Walton League Am., 1971; Silver Beaver award Boy Scouts Am., 1977; Disting. Svc. award U. Minn., 1969; named Pub. Adminstr. of Yr. in Minn. Am. Soc. Pub. Adminstrn., 1976; elected Nat. Fresh Water Fishing Hall Fame, 2003. Mem. Natural Resource Coun. Am. (chmn. 1989-91, Honor award 1994), Land Between Lakes Assn.(chmn. 1982-91, trustee 1981-91). Democrat. Office: Global Environment & Tech Found Ste 460 7010 Little River Tpke Annandale VA 22003-3241 E-mail: bherbst@getf@org.

HERBST, TODD L. lawyer; b. N.Y.C., July 15, 1952; s. Seymour and Charlotte (Wolper) H.; m. Robyn Beth Kellman, June 3, 1979; children: Scott Marshall, Carly Nicole. BA, CUNY, 1974; JD, John Marshall Law Sch., 1977. Bar: NY 1978. Assoc. Max E. Greenberg, Cantor & Reiss, N.Y.C., 1977-83, mng. ptnr., 1984-87; sr. ptnr. Greenberg, Trager & Herbst LLP, N.Y.C., 1988—. Bus. cons. Gottlieb Skanska, Inc., N.Y.C., 1980—, Shimizu Corp., U.S., 1983—, Dillingham Constrn. Holdings, Inc., San Francisco, 1987—2001, Jolly Hotels, Italy, 1993—, NTT Internat. Corp., Japan and U.S., 1996—, Legal Commentary UPN News, N.Y.; lectr. Nat. Assn. Corp. Real Estate Execs. Exec. editor: John Marshall Law Rev. Mem. ABA (A/V rated), Am. Inst. Archs., N.Y. State Bar Assn., Am. Corp. Counsel Assn., N.Y. County Lawyers Assn. Avocations: poetry, automobiles. Home: 7 Brookwood Ln New City NY 10956-2203 Office: Greenberg Trager & Herbst LLP 12th Fl 767 Third Ave New York NY 10017-2023 E-mail: therbst@ghtny.com.

HERBSTMAN, LORETTA, sculptor, painter; b. Bklyn., June 14; d. Berardino and Sabina (Senelli) Guicciardini; m. Martin Herbstman, Aug. 28; children: Jason, Dana. Instr. stone sculpture J. Reid Sch. Art, Buford, Ga.; instr. art Brimarsh Acad., Roswell, Ga. Sculptor in stone, cast bronze, cast resins and wire mesh; exhbns. include galleries throughout Manhattan, L.I., Staten Island, Ga., Fla. and shown on Joe Franklin TV Show, as well as Smithtown Art Coun. Mill Pond House, C.W. Post U. Hutchins Gallery, Gallery North, Suffolk County Bald Hill Cultural Ctr., Falconaire's Gallery, N.Y. Design Ctr.; jewelry designer/maker. Founder, pres. Farmingville (N.Y.) Improvement Coun.; mem. East End Arts Coun., Huntington Town Art League, Smithtown Art League,

Westhampton Cultural Consortium. Recipient 1st prize for sculpture in a mixed-media juried show East Islip Arts Coun., numerous others. Mem. Nat. Sculpture Soc., Ga. Artists Registry. Home: 1490 S Orlando Ave Cocoa Beach FL 32931-2334

HERCAMP, RICHARD DEAN, chemical engineer; b. Seymour, Ind., Apr. 5, 1935; s. Carl A. and Elsie Sophia (Rotert) H.; m. Joan Ruth Noblitt, June 9, 1957; children: Gregory Lynn, Tamara Jo. BSChE, Purdue U., 1957, MSE, 1969. Registered profl. engr., Ind. Rsch. engr. Arvin Industries, Columbus, Ind., 1957-61, chief engr., 1961-63, mgr. engring., 1963-66; sr. engr. Cummins Engine Co., Columbus, Ind., 1966-71, tech. specialist, group leader, 1971-76, engring. mgr., 1976-80, tech. advisor, 1980-87, cons. engr., 1987—. Contbr. numerous articles to Jour. ASTM, Soc. Automotive Engrs. Jour. Past mem. Bd. of Zoning Appeals, Jackson County, Ind.; bd. dirs. Quinco Behavior Health Systems, Columbus. Recipient Tech. Svc. award Nat. Automotive Radiator Svc. Assn., 1989, Dr. Julius P. Perr Innovation award Cummins, Inc., 2002. Mem. ASTM (chmn. D15.92 1991-94, award of appreciation 1997, Raymond H. Rudisill award 1999), Soc. Automotive Engrs. (Excellence in Oral Presentation award 1982, Forest R. McFarland award 1999), Tau Beta Pi. Republican. Lutheran. Achievements include patent for Diesel Engine Cooling System Compositions. Home and Office: 55 E 1100 S Columbus IN 47201-9314

HERCHENROETHER, PETER YOUNG, lawyer; b. Pitts., Apr. 14, 1954; s. Henry C. and Nell E. (Young) H.; m. Susan E. Suomi, Aug. 4, 1979; children: Gregory A., Emily A. BA, Westminster Coll., 1976; JD, Vanderbilt U., 1979. Bar: Pa. 1979, U.S. Dist. Ct. (we. dist.) Pa. 1979, U.S. Ct. Appeals (3d cir.) 1984, U.S. Supreme Ct. 1985. Mem. Alter, Wright & Barron, Pitts., 1979-90, Sherrard, German & Kelly, P.C., Pitts., 1990—. Mem. Pa. Bar Assn., Allegheny County Bar Assn. Republican. Presbyterian. Office: Sherrard German & Kelly PC FreeMarkets Ctr 35th Fl Pittsburgh PA 15222-2600

HERCKIS, CHARLES Y. civil engineer; b. Chgo., Nov. 7, 1946; s. Oscar and Rose T. (Pagowsky) H.; m. Rosa Maria Cervantes, Apr. 5, 1974; children: Holly, Gayle, Saul, Arian. BSCE, Ill. Inst. Tech., 1968, MPA, 1994, MPW, 1997. Profl. engr., Ill., Costa Rica. Drainage and irrigation engr. Peace Corps, Linares, Chile, 1968-71, village engr., 1971-73; dir. civil engring. Vidiera Centro Americana, San Jose, Costa Rica, 1974-76; dir. consul. & inspection Fertica Industries, Costa Rica, 1976-78; owner Herckis Ltd., San Jose, 1978-89; pub. works dir. Village of Maywood, Ill., 1989-91; cmty. devel. engr. Village of Morton Grove, Ill., 1991-93; head civil/structural div. Great Lakes Naval Tng. Ctr., Ill., 1994-97; civil engr. Harza Engring. Co. (merged with Montgomery, Watson, now MWH), Chgo., 1997—. Cons. Agy. for Internat. Devel., San Jose, 1984-89. Mem. ASCE. Home: 201 S Maple Ave Oak Park IL 60302-3076 Office: MWH 175 W Jackson Blvd Chicago IL 60604

HERCULES, DAVID MICHAEL, chemistry educator, consultant; b. Somerset, Pa., Aug. 10, 1932; s. Michael George and Kathryn (Saylor) H.; m. Nancy Catherine Miller, Sept. 23, 1957 (div. 1968); 1 dau., Kimberly Ann; m. Shirley Ann Hoover, Dec. 14, 1970; children: Sherri Kathryn, Kevin Michael. BS, Juniata Coll., 1954; PhD, MIT, 1957. Asst. prof. Lehigh U., 1957-60; assoc. prof. Juniata Coll., Huntington, Pa., 1960-63; asst. prof. MIT, 1963-68, assoc. prof., 1968-69, U. Ga., Athens, 1969-74, prof., 1974-76; prof. dept. chemistry U. Pitts., 1976-94, chmn., 1980-89, Miles prof., 1990-94; Centennial prof. Vanderbilt U., Nashville, 1995—, chmn. dept., 1995—2003. Mem. vis. com. for chemistry Lehigh U., 1980-84 ; vis. prof. Mich. State U., 1972; chmn. Gordon Research Conf. on Electron Spectroscopy, 1974, Gordon Research Conf. on Analytical Chemistry, 1966; co-chmn. Internat. Conf. Chemiluminescence, 1972; univ. rep. Council on Chem. Research, 1980-88 ; mem. program com. Pitts. Conf. on Analytical Chemistry and Applied Spectroscopy, 1977-94; mem. vis. scientist program NSF, 1964-76 Mem. editorial bds.: Applied Spectroscopy, 1963-65, Analytical Chemistry, 1964-67, Jour. Electron Spectroscopy, 1971-77, Environ. Analytical Chemistry, 1973—, Spectrochimica Acta, 1973-83, Talanta, 1974-80, Spectroscopy Letters, 1975—, The Scis., 1979-84, Trends in Analytical Chemistry, 1980-88, Jour. Trace and Microprobe Techniques, 1980-93, Fresenius Zeitschrift für Analytische Chemie, 1987-; patentee (in field). Recipient Benedetti-Pichler award Am. Microchem. Soc., 1987, Achievement in Analytical Chemistry award Ea. Analytical Symposium, 1988, prize Alexander von Humboldt Found., 1984, Disting. Alumnus award Juniata Coll., 1989, Pres.'s Disting. Rsch. award U. Pitts., 1990; John Simon Guggenheim Meml. fellow, 1973. Mem. Am. Chem. Soc. (Petroleum Research Fund adv. bd. 1978-80, chmn. div. analytical chemistry 1977-78, analytical chemistry award 1986, Arthur W. Adamson award disting. svc. in advancement of surface chemistry 1993, Pitts. sect. award 1997), Soc. Applied Spectroscopy (Lester W. Strock medal New Eng. sect. 1981, Pitts. Spectroscopy award 1996), Am. Vacuum Soc., Photoelectric Spectrometry Group, Pa. Acad. Scis., Spectroscopy Soc. Pitts. (award 1996), Soc. Analytical Chemists Pitts., Sigma Xi Home: 200 Olive Branch Rd Nashville TN 37205-3220 Office: Vanderbilt U Dept Chemistry Box 1822, Sta B Nashville TN 37235

HERD, JOANNE MAY BEERS, infusion therapy nurse, educator; b. Nazareth, Pa, Nov. 28, 1934; d. Robert Albert and Marguerite (Small) Beers; m. Robert Von Steuben Herd, Oct. 25, 1958; 1 child, Scott Robert. Diploma, Allentown (Pa.) Hosp., 1955. Cert. infusion nurse. Asst. instr. sci. Allentown Hosp., 1956-57, recruitment dir., 1957-58; staff nurse Tidewater Blood Bank Svc., ARC, Norfolk, Va., 1950—60, Sentara Virginia Beach Gen. Hosp., Va., 1979—86, staff educator, 1986—2003, ret., 2003. Infusion nurse educator, cons., 1997—. Designer intravenous nurse emblem lapel pin, mobile teaching unit. Mem. League Intravenous Therapy Edn., Infusion Nurses Soc. (chmn. Ea. Va. chpt. 1983-85, pres. elect 1993-94, pres. 1994-95, presdl. advisor 1995-96, bd. mem. at large 1996—), Allentown Hosp. Alumni Assn. (life).

HERDEG, HOWARD BRIAN, physician; b. Buffalo, Oct. 14, 1929; s. Howard Bryan and Martha Jean (Williams) H.; m. Beryl Ann Fredricks, July 21, 1955; children: Howard Brian III, Erin Ann Kociela. Student, Paul Smith's Coll., 1947-48, U. Buffalo, 1948-50, Canisius Coll., 1949; DO, Phila. Coll. Osteo. Medicine, 1954; MD, U. Calif., Irvine, 1962. Diplomate Am. Acad. Pain Mgmt. Intern Burbank (Calif.) Hosp., 1954-55; practice medicine specializing in gen. medicine, surgery and pain mgmt., Woodland Hills, Calif., 1956—. Chief med. staff West Park Hosp., Canoga Park, Calif., 1971-72, trustee, 1971-73; chief family practice dept. West Hills Hosp. and Med. Center (formerly Humana Hosp. West Hills, 1982-83, 84-85, 88-89), mem. exec. com., 1984-85, 88-89. Mem. Hidden Hills (Calif.) Pub. Safety Commn., 1978-82; bd. dirs. Hidden Hills Cmty. Assn., 1971-73, pres. 1972; bd. dirs. Hidden Hills Homeowners Assn., 1973-75, pres. 1976-77; bd. dirs. Woodland Hills Freedom Season, 1961-67, pres. 1962; mem. Hidden Hills City coun., 1984-2001, mayor pro tem, 1987-90, mayor, 1990-92. Recipient Disting. Svc. award Woodland Hills Jr. C. of C., 1966. Mem. Woodland Hills C. of C. (dir. 1959-68, pres. 1967), Calabasas C. of C., Calabasas-Agoura Hills Rotary Club, Theta Chi, Gamma Pi. Republican. Home: 24530 Deep Well Rd Hidden Hills CA 91302-1210 Office: 22600 Ventura Blvd Woodland Hills CA 91364-1414

HERDEG, JOHN ANDREW, lawyer; b. Buffalo, Sept. 15, 1937; s. Franklin Leland and Susannah Estelle (Clark) H.; m. Judith Coolidge Carpenter, June 24, 1961; children: Judith Leland Herdeg Wilson, Andrew Carpenter Herdeg, Fell Coolidge Herdeg. BA, Princeton U., 1959; LLB, U. Pa., 1962. Bar: Conn. 1963, Del. 1964. Atty. Wilmington (Del.) Trust Co., 1963-75, sr. v.p. in charge of trust dept., 1975-85, bd. dirs., chmn. trust com., corp. sec., 1977-85; pres. Herdeg & Assocs., Wilmington, 1986-98; ptnr. Herdeg, duPont & Dalle Pazze, LLP, Wilmington, 1999—. Co-founder, chmn. bd. dirs. Christiana Bank & Trust Co., Greenville, Del., 1992—. Bd. trustees Henry Francis duPont Winterthur (Del.) Mus., 1970—, chmn., 1977-86; trustee Med. Ctr. of Del., Stanton, 1965—; supr. Pennsbury Twp., Chester County, Pa., 1968-74; mem. Westminster Presbyn. Ch. Mem.: Confrerie des Chevalier du Tastevin, Walpole Soc., Mill Reef Club, West Chop Club, Vicmead Hunt Club (bd. govs. 1977—84), Wilmington Club (bd. govs. 1997—, treas. 1999—2003, v.p. 2003—). Avocations: tennis, photography, decorative arts. Home: PO Box 216 Mendenhall PA 19357-0216 Office: Herdeg DuPont & Dalle Pazze LLP 12th & Orange St Ste 500 Wilmington DE 19801-1140 E-mail: jherdeg@dellaw.com.

HERDENDORF, CHARLES EDWARD, III, oceanographer, limnologist, consultant; b. Lorain, Ohio, Oct. 2, 1939; s. Charles Edward, Jr. and Esther Kathryne Herdendorf; m. Ricki Sue Crowl, May 22, 1993. BS, Ohio U., 1961, MS, 1963; PhD, Ohio State U., 1970. Cert. profl. geologist, Am. Inst. Profl. Geologists. Geologist, section head Ohio Dept. Natural Resources, Sandusky, Ohio, 1960-71; assoc. prof. geol. scis. and zoology Ohio State U., 1971-76, prof., 1976-88, prof. emeritus, 1988—. Dir. Franz Theodore Stone Lab. and Ctr. for Lake Erie Area Rsch., Put-in-Bay, Ohio, 1971-88; dir. Ohio Sea Grant Coll. program Ohio State U., Columbus, 1978-88; sci. dir. Columbus-Am. Discovery Group, Columbus, 1988-95; apptd. by Ohio Gov. to Acid Rain Task Force, 1984, Ohio Maritime Adv. Coun., 1999; founder, CEO, EcoSphere Assocs., Gt. Lakes and Oceanographic Cons. Author: Ohio's Natural Heritage, 1979 (Ohioana Book Award 1980), Journal of Great Lakes Research, 1997; Author/Editor: Large Lakes of the World, 1990, Lake Erie Handbook, 1993, Science on a Deep-Ocean Shipwreck, 1995. Vol. naturalist Ohio Divsn. Nat. Areas and Preserves, Huron, Ohio, 1988—; pres. Beachwood Villas Assn., Huron, 1989-90, Rep. candidate for mayor, Sheffield, Ohio, 2003; advisor Nat. Maritime Hist. Soc., Peekskill, N.Y., 1989—; trustee Ohio Hist. Soc., Columbus, 1995-96, Great Lakes Hist. Soc., Vermilion, Ohio, 1999—; coord. Lake Erie Shipwreck Rsch. Ctr., Vermilion, 1999—. With ROTC, USAF, 1957-58. Recipient Citizenship medal SAR, 1990; named to Hall of Fame F. T. Stone Lab., Ohio State U., 1996, Diver of Year Bay Area Divers, 1998; new species of golden coral named Chrysogorgia herdendorfi in his honor, 2001. Fellow Geol. Soc. Am., Explorers Club; mem. Ohio Acad. Sci. (pres. 1995-96, Centennial Honoree 1991), Internat. Assoc. for Great Lakes Rsch. (bd. dirs. 1977-80, v.p. 1979-80, Best Paper of Yr. 1998), Am. Inst. Profl. Geologists (cert. profl. geologist), Am. Fisheries Soc. (cert. fisheries scientist), Ohio Office Hist. Preservation and U.S. Nat. Park Svc. (cert. underwater archeologist) Republican. Methodist. Avocations: photography, scuba diving, boating, aircraft piloting, hiking. Home: 585 West Shore Blvd Put In Bay OH 43456 Office: Garfield Farms 4921 Detroit Rd Sheffield Village OH 44054 E-mail: herdendorf.1@osu.edu.

HERDER, PAUL O. secondary school educator; b. Duluth, Minn., Sept. 24, 1956; s. Merill Otto and Irma Sophia Herder; m. Joan Marie Evansen, Oct. 4, 1986; children: Emily Anne, Samuel Paul, Daniel John. BS in Geology, U. Wis., Oshkosh, 1982; MA in Tchg., U. Wis., River Falls, 1991. Secondary sci. tchr. Marshfield (Wis.) Sch. Dist., 1985—. Owner What If? Sci. Edn. Supply Co., Marshfield, 1998—; coach Marshfield's Nat. Ocean Sci. Bowl Team. Active Groundwater Guardians, Marshfield, 1998—. Named Tchr. of the Yr., Marshfield Tchrs. Assn., 2003. Mem.: Nat. Soc. Sci. Tchrs., Wis. Soc. Earth Sci. Tchrs., Wis. Soc. Sci. Tchrs., Heart of Wis. Gem and Mineral Soc. (v.p. 1993—). Achievements include invention of density flow model; density flow model junior. Avocations: hunting, fishing, golf. Home and Office: 754 Hanson Rd Spencer WI 54479

HERDLEIN, RICHARD JOSEPH, III, college official and dean, educator; b. Valdosta, Ga., Dec. 8, 1944; s. Sharon L. Herdlein; 1 child, Richard J. IV. BA, St. John Fisher Coll., 1966; MA, Niagara U., 1970, MS, 1976; PhD, U. Pitts., 1985. Gen. mgr. Schmitt Sales, Inc., Amherst, NY, 1964-68; dir. residence Kent (Ohio) State U., 1969-72; dir. student ctr. D'Youville Coll., Buffalo, 1974-76; dir. student activities Eckerd Coll., St. Petersburgh, Fla., 1976-77; asst. dir. univ. ctr. Adelphi U., Garden City, NY, 1978-80; dean student affairs U. Pitts., 1980-87; v.p. Thomas More Coll., Crestview Hills, Ky., 1987-90; v.p. student affairs, dean, assoc. prof. history Medaille Coll., Buffalo, 1990-2001; assoc. prof. Grad. Sch. Higher Edn. and Student Pers. Admin. SUNY Coll. at Buffalo, 2001—. Councilman Amherst Rep. Com., 1993-96; chmn. jingle bell run Arthritis Found., Tonawanda, N.Y., 1991-95; bd. dirs., chmn. fundraising com. Leadership Buffalo, 1997—; bd. dirs. Buffalo Coun. on World Affairs; alumnus Ctr. for Entrepreneurial Leadership, SUNY, Buffalo, 1996. Sgt. USAR, 1967-73. Named Person of Yr. Adelphia U., 1980, Most Respected Dr., Ctr. for Entrepreneurial Leadership SUNY Buffalo, 1996, Adminstr. of Yr., Medaille Coll. Student Govt. Assn., 1999; named one of Outstanding Young Men of Am., 1976. Mem.: Amvets. Republican. Roman Catholic. Avocations: golf, racquetball, running, reading, arts. Office: Buffalo State Coll Bacon Hall 1300 Elmwood Ave Buffalo NY 14222 Home: 19 Sargent Dr Buffalo NY 14226-4038 E-mail: herdlerj@buffalostate.edu.

HERDMAN, ROGER C. physician, policy analyst; b. Newton, Mass., Sept. 22, 1933; s. Gordon Walker Herdman and Florence Elizabeth Watson; m. Ellen Tifft, May 13, 1957; children: Jennifer, Lisa, Prudence, Betsey. BS, Yale U., 1955, MD, 1958. Resident in pediat. U. Minn., Mpls., 1958-61, fellow in pediat., 1962-65, asst. prof., 1965-69; prof. pediat. Albany (N.Y.) Med. Coll., 1969-79; dep. health commr. N.Y. State Dept. Health, Albany, 1969-77, dir. pub. health, 1977-79; v.p. profl. affairs Meml. Sloan-Kettering Cancer Ctr., N.Y.C., 1979-83; asst. dir. Congl. Office Tech. Assessment, Washington, 1984-92, dir., 1993-96; sr. scholar Inst. Medicine-NAS, Washington, 1996-2000, dir. nat. cancer policy bd., 2000—. Author: Organ Transplantation, 1997, Safety of Silicone Breast Implants, 1999; contbr. numerous articles to med. jours. Lt. USNR, 1959-61. Office: Inst Medicine NAS 2101 Constitution Ave NW Washington DC 20418-0007

HERDMAN, SUSAN, art educator, artist; b. Yonkers, NY, May 29, 1941; d. Raymond Charles and Ellen (Saunders) Herdman; m. John C. Barker, June 12, 1965 (dec.); children: Jennifer, Carrie, John. BFA, Alfred U.; MA, U. Iowa. Artist, owner Herdman Archive, Bettendorf, Iowa, 1992—; art educator Davenport (Iowa) Cmty. Sch., 1985—, Scott C.C., Davenport, 1997—. Group shows include Quincy (Ill.) Art Ctr., 1992, Walton Art Ctr., Fayetteville, Ark., 1992, 93, Alias Gallery, Atlanta, 1992, Ga. Tech., Atlanta, 1992, Lincoln (Colo.) Art Ctr., 1992, 93, Davenport Mus. Art, 1992, Mus. Anthropology U. Calif., Chico, 1992, Red Mesa Art Gallery, Gallup, N.Mex., 1992, Putnam County Arts Coun., Mahopac, NY, 1992, Near Northwest Arts Coun., Chgo., 1993, North Platte Valley Art Guild, Scottsbluff, Nebr., 1993, U. Iowa, 1993, Chatauqua Art Assn. Galleries, 1993, Greater Harrisburg (Pa.) Arts Coun., 1993, 94, Fla. Soc. Fine Arts, Miami, Fla., 1993, Columbia Arts Ctr., Vancouver, Wash., 1993, Eiteljorg Mus. Am. Indian and Western Art, Indpls., 1994, Maude Kerns Art Center, Eugene, Oreg., 1994, Soc. Contemporary Photography, Kansas City, 1994, Mus. Northwest Colo., Craig, 1994, Fuller Mus. Art, Brockton, Mass., 1994, Perry House Galleries (Silver medal), Alexandria, Va., 1995, No. Colo. Artists Assn., Fort Collins, Colo., 1996, Photo Nat. 96 (2nd place award), Mo., 1996, Oscar Howe Art Ctr., S. Dakota, 1996; one-person show Cornell Coll., Mt. Vernon, Iowa, 1997, 2000; permanent collections include Am. Indian Art Ctr., Chgo., Mus. Anthropology U. Calif., Chico, Deere and Co., Moline, Ill, Eiteljorg Mus. Native Am. and Western Art, EverColor Corp., Wooster, Mass., Heard Mus. Libr. and Archives, Phoenix. Mem. Nat. Mus. Am. Indian, Nat. Mus. Women in Arts, Davenport Indian Parent Adv. Com., 1991-95. Recipient Best of Photography Ann. Photographers Forum Mag., 1993, Best of Show, The Camera's Eye, Mus. N.W. Colo., 1994, Photo '96, Nat. 2d Pl., S.E. Mo. Arts Coun., others; grantee Iowa Arts Coun., 1995, 99, 2000. Home: 4639 Sunset Ridge Santa Fe NM 85707

HERDZIK, ARTHUR ALAN, lawyer; b. Buffalo, June 6, 1950; s. Arthur Chester and Lottie Marie (Kowalczyk) H.; m. Jean Marie Rozler, Aug. 3, 1973; children: Julie, Karen, Lisa, Molly. BA magna cum laude, SUNY-Buffalo, 1972, JD, 1975. Bar: N.Y. 1976, U.S. Dist. Ct. (we. dist.) N.Y. 1976. Assoc. Miles, Cochrane, Grosse, Rossetti & Chelus, P.C., Buffalo, 1976-84; mem. Chelus, Herdzik & Speyer, P.C., Buffalo, 1985—. Acting judge Village of Lancaster, N.Y., 1980-82, village prosecutor, 1982-92, village atty., 1988—. Sr. editor Buffalo Law Rev., 1975. Committeeman Erie County Dem. Com., 1978-80, 82—, Lancaster chpt. chmn., 1998-2000, mem. exec. com., 1998-2000. Mem. ABA, N.Y. State Bar Assn., Erie County Bar Assn. (negligence com. 1990-93), Trial Lawyers Assn. Erie County, Am. Bd. Trial Advocates, Lions (pres. 1998-99, treas. 2000--), Phi Beta Kappa Democrat. Home: 68 Church St Lancaster NY 14086-2638 Office: Chelus Herdzik Speyer Monte & Pajak PC 1000 Main Court Bldg 438 Main St Buffalo NY 14202-3208

HEREFORD, FRANK LOUCKS, JR., physicist, educator; b. Lake Charles, La., July 18, 1923; s. Frank L. and Marguerite (Roussel) H.; m. Ann Lane, Jan. 3, 1948; children— Frank, Sarah, Robert. BA, U. Va., 1943, PhD in Physics, 1947; DSc, Fla. Inst. Tech., 1974; LLD, Hampden-Sydney Coll., 1974. Physicist Bartol Research Found., Swarthmore, Pa., 1947-49; mem. faculty U. Va., 1949-92, prof. physics, 1952-92; dean U. Va. (Grad. Sch. Arts and Scis.), 1962-66, Robert C. Taylor prof. physics, 1966-92, provost, v.p., 1966-71, pres., 1974-85. Vis. prof. U. St. Andrews, Scotland, 1971-72; dir. Gould, Inc., Rolling Meadows, Ill., 1980-88. Contbr. profl. jours. Bd. govs. Belfield Sch., Charlottesville, 1959-62, 63-65, chmn. bd., 1962; bd. dirs. St. Anne's Sch., Charlottesville, 1966-70; trustee Woodberry Forest Sch., 1968-74, Mariner's Mus., Newport News, Va., 1975-85. Fulbright scholar U. Birmingham, Eng., 1957-58; recipient Devel. award USN Ordnance Dept., 1945, Horsley Rsch. prize Va. Acad. Sci., 1953. Fellow Am. Phys. Soc. (chmn. Southeastern sect. 1961-62), Phi Beta Kappa, Sigma Xi, Omicron Delta Kappa, Alpha Tau Omega.

HEREMANS, JOSEPH PIERRE, physicist; b. Leuven, Belgium, Jan. 8, 1953; came to U.S., 1984; s. Joseph Felix Heremans and Marie Therese Bracke; m. Claire Pierre Mali, July 1, 1978; children: Hilde Anne, Joseph Paul. Elec. Engr., U. Louvain, Belgium, 1975, PhD in Applied Physics, 1978. Aspirant Belgium Nat. Sci. Found., Louvain, 1978-80, charge de recherche, 1980-83; rsch. scientist GM Rsch. and Devel. Ctr., Warren, Mich., 1984-85; group leader GM Rsch., Warren, Mich., 1985-87, sect. mgr., 1987-99; rsch. fellow Delphi Rsch. Labs., Shelby Township, 1999—. Invited prof. U. Louvain, 1989; vis. scientist U. Tokyo, 1982, MIT, Cambridge, 1980-81. Editor: Growth, Characterization and Properties of Ultrathin Magnetic Films and Multilayers, 1989, Survey of Semiconductor Physics, 2002; contbr. articles to profl. jours. Fellow Am. Phys. Soc.; mem. AAAS, Materials Rsch. Soc., Sigma Xi. Achievements include patents in field. Office: Delphi Rsch Labs 51786 Shelby Pkwy Shelby Township MI 48315 E-mail: joseph.p.heremans@delphi.com.

HERENTON, WILLIE W. mayor; b. Memphis, Apr. 23, 1943; divorced; children: Errol, Rodney, Andrea. BS, LeMoyne-Owen Coll., 1965; MA, Memphis State U., 1966; PhD, So. Ill. U., 1971, Rhodes Coll., Christian Brother's Coll. Elem. sch. tchr. Memphis City Sch. System, 1963-67, elem. sch. prin., 1967-73; dept. supt. Memphis City Schs., 1974-78, supt. of schs., 1979-91; mayor Memphis, 1991—. Bd. dirs. Nat. Urban League Edn. Adv. Coun., 1978, Nat. Jr. Achievement, Jr. Achievement of Memphis 1979—, United Way Greater Memphis, 1979—; mem. Nat. Alliance of Black Educators, 1974—, Am. Assn. Sch. Adminstrs., Am. Mgmt. Assn.; mem. bd. Promous Cos., Inc., First Tenn. Nat. Corp.; mem. exec. bd. Nat. Conf. Christians and Jews. Named one of Top 100 Sch. Adminstrs. in U.S. and Can., Exec. Educator Jour., 1980, 84. Fellow Rockefeller Found., 1973. Baptist. Office: Office of the Mayor 125 N Main St Ste 700 Memphis TN 38103-2017*

HERETH, LYLE GEORGE, electrical engineering technologist; b. Everett, Wash., Oct. 14, 1947; s. L. Walter and Alvina Katharina (Weber) H.; m. Margaret Sue Brewer, Dec. 19, 1978; children: Christopher, Walter, Emilie, Jennifer, Jacob. BS in Elec. Engring. Tech., Weber State Coll., 1975; M of Engring. Adminstrn., U. Utah, 1981. Quality engr. Nat. Semiconductor, Salt Lake City, 1975-78, Beehive Internat., Salt Lake City, 1978-80; quality mgr. Sperry Univac, Salt Lake City, 1980-82; sys. devel. mgr. LDS Ch., Salt Lake City, 1982-85, dir. tech., arch., 1985-90, asst. coord., 1990-93, cons. emerging tech., 1993-99, mgr. info. tech., 1999—. Mem. Internat. Coun. on Archives com. current records in electronic environment, chmn. info. sys. VIM, CDC Corp., Minn., 1984-89; project mgr. geneal. sys. FamilySearch, 1987 (Smith award 1992, 95). Chmn. planning and zoning South Salt Lake City Govt., 1986-94; chaplain South Salt Lake Police and Fire Depts. Recipient Pub. Svc. awards South Salt Lake Govt., 1983, 94. Mem. Assn. for Info. and Image Mgmt. Mem. Lds Ch. Avocations: reading, camping, cooking, acting. Office: LDS Ch Fhd 50E N Temple Salt Lake City UT 84150-0001 E-mail: herethlg@ldschurch.org.

HERGE, DONNA CAROL, secondary school educator; b. Rockford, Ill., Nov. 11, 1948; d. William Carl and Grace Wilma Kling; m. John Arthur Herge, June 9, 1973; 1 child, Thomas William. BA in Math. and Philosophy, Rockford Coll., 1970; MS in Math., Wright State Univ., 1973; PhD and MS in Stats., Fla. State Univ., 1992. Commd. 2d lt. USAF, 1971, advanced through grades to lt. col., 1989, comdr. Detachment 1, 6th Weather Squadron, 1974—75, contract monitor 16th Surveillance Squadron Shemya AFB, Alaska, 1975—76, asst. prof. math USAF Acad. Colorado Springs, Colo., 1976—80, comm.-electronics br. chief Offutt AFB, Nebr., 1980—83; dir. rsch. and analysis AF Quality Inst., Maxwell AFB, Ala., 1991—95; stats. br. chief Air Force Inst. Tech. USAF, Wright Patterson AFB, Ohio, 1986—91; dir. rsch. and analysis AF Quality Inst., Maxwell AFB, Ala., 1991—95; ret. USAF, 1995; math tchr. Cath. H.S., Montgomery, Ala., 1996—. Adj. prof. stats. Troy State U., Montgomery, 1995—96, Auburn U., Montgomery, 1995—96. Editor: (book) Process Improvement Guide: Tools for Today's Air Force, 1992. Alto St. Bede Ch. Adult Choir, Montgomery, 1995—2002. Decorated Commendation medal USAF, Meritorious Svc. medal; recipient Comm. Electronics Profl. Achievement award, Aerospace Def. Command, 1976. Mem.: Am. Soc. for Quality, Am. Statis. Assn., Phi Beta Kappa (hon.).

HERGE, HENRY CURTIS, SR., education educator, dean emeritus; b. Bklyn., June 29, 1905; s. Henry John and Theresa (Maaz) H.; m. Josephine E. Breen, July 2, 1931 (dec. Oct. 8, 1975); children: Joel Curtis, Henry Curtis; m. Alice V. Wolfram, Apr. 21, 1976. BS, NYU, 1929, MA, 1931, EdD, 1942; MA (hon.), Wesleyan U., 1946; PhD, Yale U., 1956. Instr. English Sr. High Sch., Port Washington, N.Y., 1928-38; dist. prin. Bayville, N.Y., 1938-41, Bellmore, N.Y., 1941-45; asst. dir. study on implication of armed svcs. edn. programs Am. Council Edn., Washington., 1945-46; dir. higher edn., tchr. edn. cert. Conn. State Dept. Edn., 1946-53; adjunct prof. Hartford U., 1950-52, Fairfield U., 1950-53; dean, prof. edn. Rutgers U., 1953-64; adjunct prof. U. So. Calif., summer 1964, NYU, 1964-65; prof. edn., assoc. dir. Rutgers Ctr. for Internat. Programs, 1964-75. Del. White House Conf. Edn., 1957; edn. cons. USOM Asuncion and ICA dir. ednl. priorities study for Ministry of Edn., Paraguay, 1961; team leader Rutgers-U.S. AID field survey, Zambia and Malawi, 1961-62; chief edn. devel. officer U.S. AID, Jamaica, 1966-68; Fulbright rapporteur Seminar in Univ. Adminstrn., U.S. and Italy, 1970; OAS sr. rsch. fellow, Paraguay and Jamaica, 1972-73. Author: Wartime College Training Programs of Armed Services, 1948; The College Teacher, 1966, Navy V-12, 1996; editor: Disarmament in the Western World, 1968; Common Concerns in Higher Education: An Italian-American Universities Project, Phase I, 1970; contbr. numerous articles to profl. publs. Pres. Shadow Lake Assn., Vt., 1976-78; sec. Fed. Lake Assns., No. Vt., 1980-84; project dir. Hilton Head Plantation Public Forum for Humanities, 1980-81; chmn. bd. trustees Coll. Hilton Head (S.C.), 1984-86, Town Council Com. for Higher Edn., 1986-88. Served as comdg. officer Wesleyan U.S. Navy V-12 unit 1943-45; lt. comdr. USNR (Ret.). Recipient cert. of recognition NCCJ, 1958, Honor citation, Rutgers Grad. Sch. Edn., 1993. Mem. N.J. Congress Parents and Tchrs. (hon. life), N.J. Secondary Sch. Tchrs. Assn. (trustee 1954-66, merit award 1966), N.J. Coun. on Edn., N.J. Schoolmasters Club, Fulbright Alumni Assn. (v.p. S.C. chpt. 1983-91), Naval Res. Assn. (life), Retired Officers Assn. (life), Phi Delta Kappa (emeritus), Epsilon Pi Tau (laureate trustee), Kappa Delta Pi (award 1976).

HERGE, HENRY CURTIS, JR., consulting firm executive; b. Hartford, Conn., Sept. 13, 1950; s. Henry Curtis and Josephine (Breen) Herge; m. Donna Gay Takeda, Dec. 20, 1974 (div. Dec. 1982); m. Madge Lynn Henley, Feb. 19, 1983; children: H. Curtis III, Erica Ainsley, Alyssa Taylor, Whitney Meghan. BSME, Rutgers U., 1972, BA, 1972. Prodn. splst. GE, Columbia, Md., 1972-73, engring. foreman med. sys. divsn. Milw., 1973-74, buyer internat. sales divsn. N.Y.C., NY, 1974-76; sr. sys. analyst Arthur Andersen & Co. (now Accenture), N.Y.C., 1976-78, cons. mgr. Stamford, Conn., 1978-85, ptnr., 1985—, practice dir. cons. divsn. Rochester (N.Y.) office, 1987-92. Sr. v.p. Tech. Solutions Co., 1992—94; ptnr. Diamond Tech. Ptnrs., Chgo., 1994—95; prin. A. T. Kearney divsn. Electronic Data Sy., Plano, Tex., 1995—, global contracts mgr., 1997—, svc. delivery quality, 1998—; cons. strategic devel. mgr.. Electronic Data Sys., 2002—, strategic devel. mgr. solutions cons. N.E. USA; dir. Value-2-Xerox Corp., 2000—. Mem.: Am. Prodn. and Inventory Soc. (v.p. 1985). Presbyterian. Avocations: skiing, travel, canoeing, kites. Home: 16 Lancashire Way Pittsford NY 14534-9786

HERGE, J. CURTIS, lawyer; b. Flushing, N.Y., June 14, 1938; s. Henry Curtis and Josephine E. (Breen) H.; m. Joyce Dorean Humbert, Aug. 20, 1960 (div. 1988); children: Cynthia Lynda, Christopher Curtis; m. Shirley Brooks Labonte, Dec. 22, 1989. Student, Cornell U., 1956-58; BA, Rutgers U., 1961, JD, 1963. Bar: N.Y. 1964, U.S. Supreme Ct. 1970, U.S. Ct. Claims 1974, D.C. 1974, Va. 1976. Assoc. Mudge Rose Guthrie & Alexander, N.Y.C., 1963-71; spl. asst. to atty. gen. U.S. Dept. Justice, Washington, 1973; assoc. solicitor conservation and wildlife U.S. Dept. Interior, Washington, 1973-74, asst. to sec. and chief staff, 1974-76; ptnr. Sedam & Herge, McLean, Va., 1976-85, Herge, Sparks & Christopher LLP, McLean, Va., 1985—. Bd. dirs. Diversified Labs., Inc., Am. E.W. Stone & Assocs., Inc., Palmer Tech. Svcs., Inc., Eaton Design Group, Inc., George Washington Banking Corp., Eaton Purchase Mgmt., Inc., Georg

Washington Nat. Bank, Congl. Inst. Inc., Citizens United for Am., Am. Def. Lobby, Coun. Nat. Def., Renascence Found., The Am. Lobby Econ. Recovery Taskforce, Nat. Bank No. Va., Am. Freedom Found., Creative Response Concepts Inc., Congl. Inst., Inc.; spkr. in field. Adv. bd. Washington Legal Found., Nat. Taxpayers Legal Fund; Va. Commonwealth escheator Loudoun County and City of Fairfax, 1979-83; co-dir. spokesmen resources Com. for Re-election of Pres., 1971-72; mem. No. Va. Estate Planning Council; mem. natural resources coun. Rep. Nat. Com.; mem. Fairfax County Rep. Com., Conservative Rep. Com.; mem. Office Pres.-Elect Fed. Election Commn. Transition Team, 1980; co-chmn. N.Y. Honor Am. Day, 1970; expert witness, charitable fund-raising, U.S. Tax Ct. Sebastian Gaeta scholar Rutgers U., 1963. Mem. ABA, N.Y. State Bar Assn., Va. Bar Assn., D.C. Bar Assn., Capital Hill Club, Phi Kappa Sigma. Clubs: Capitol Hill. Home: 35 Rutherford Cir Potomac Falls VA 20165-6221 Office: Herge Sparks & Christopher LLP 6862 Elm St Ste 360 Mc Lean VA 22101-3867

HERGENHAN, JOYCE, public relations executive; b. Mt. Kisco, N.Y., Dec. 30, 1941; d. John Christopher and Goldie (Wago) H. BA, Syracuse U., 1963; MBA, Columbia U., 1978. Reporter White Plains Reporter Dispatch, 1963-64; asst. to Rep. Ogden R. Reid Washington, 1964-68; reporter Gannett Newspapers, 1968-72; with Consol. Edison Co. of N.Y., Inc., N.Y.C., 1972 82, v.p., 1977 79, sr. v.p. pub. affairs, 1979-82; v.p. corp. pub. relations General Electric Co., Fairfield, Conn., 1982-98; pres. GE Fund, 1998—. Trustee Syracuse U., 1996-; bd. dirs. Civilian Pub. Affairs Coun., U.S. Mil. Acad. at West Point, 1990-, Jackie Robinson Found. 2001, Inner City Found. for Edn. and Charity; past chmn. Pub. Rels. Seminar. Recipient Lifetime Achievement award, Women in Communications, 1999. Mem.: Conn. Audubon Soc. (bd. dirs. 2002—). Office: GE 3135 Easton Tpke Fairfield CT 06431-0002

HERGENHAN, KENNETH WILLIAM, lawyer; b. N.Y.C., Apr. 21, 1931; w. William Otto and Neva H.; m. Jane Steinruck Stahl, Aug. 24, 1959; children: Lisa Fevery, Susan Mitchell, William, John. BS, Lehigh U., 1953; LLB, Harvard U., 1958. Bar: Oreg. 1958, U.S. Dist. Ct. Oreg. 1958. Assoc., then ptnr. Miller Nash and predecessors, Portland, Oreg., 1958-96; dir. Willamette Industries, Inc., Portland, 1997-2001. Contbr. articles to legal publs. 1st lt. U.S. Army, 1953-55. Mem. Oreg. Bar Assn., Multnomah Athletic Club. Democrat. Episcopalian. Avocations: aviation, gardening. Home: 4237 SW Arthur Way Portland OR 97221-3203

HERGER, WALLY W. congressman; b. Yuba City, Calif., May 20, 1945; Formerly mem. Calif. State Assembly; mem. U.S. Congress from 2nd Calif. dist., 1987—; mem. ways and means com.; mem. human srvc. subcom.; owner Herger Gas, Inc. Republican. Office: US Ho of Reps 2268 Rayburn Bldg Washington DC 20515-0502*

HERGO, JANE ANTOINETTE, piano educator, composer; b. Dayton, Ohio, Apr. 16, 1946; d. Frank Gustav and Antoinette Rosalyn (Jean) Hergo. BMus, U. Dayton, 1968, BS in Music Edn., 1975; MMus, Wright State U., 1980. Cert. music tchr., Ohio. Kindergarten tchr., Englewood, Ohio, 1971-73; elem. tchr. Dayton, Ohio, 1976-77, 78-81; class piano instr. Sinclair C.C., Dayton, Ohio, summer 1981, piano accompanist for ballet and modern dance, 1983-84; ind. piano tchr. Dayton, Ohio, 1964—. Composer (book) Five Finger Frolics, 1988, Keyboard Confections, 1992 (sheet music) Gems on the Lake, 1991 (Ohio Music Tchrs. Assn. award 1990), Skeleton Skedaddle, 1993 (hon. mention award composition contest), Forest in the Rain (hon. mention award composition contest), Jazz Spooks (hon. mention award composition contest), Ghostly Gatherine, 1991, Chilipeppers, 1998, Snowswirls, 2002 (hon. mention award composition contest). Piano soloist Dayton Philharm. Designer Show House, 1985, 87; adjudicator Jr. Music Club Festivals, Dayton, 1989—. Recipient Jr. Composer award Ohio Fedn. Music Club, 1998, Piano Compositions awards Key Piano Mag., 1990, 93, Merit award Nat. Fedn. Music Clubs, 1990. Mem. ASCAP, Music Tchrs. Nat. Assn. (nat. cert.), Ohio Music Tchrs. Assn. (officer student composition sect. Western dist. 1988 90, composition panel 1989, state conv. 1992), Jr. Music Club, Dayton Music Club (composer), Sigma Alpha Iota. Avocations: emboidery, drawing, sewing, reading, flower gardening.

HERGUTH, ROBERT JOHN, columnist; b. Chgo., Apr. 4, 1926; s. Harry Conrad Herguth and Loretta (Oberreither) Herguth-Slimmer; m. Margaret Ann Silsbee, Apr. 16, 1966; children: Amy Rene, Robert Charles, Mary Jennifer BA in Journalism, U. Mo., 1948. Copy editor, reporter Peoria Star, Ill., 1948-54; reporter, feature writer, columnist Chgo. Daily News, 1954-78; columnist Chgo. Sun Times, 1978-97, freelance weekly columnist, 1997-2001. Mem. editl. bd. Chgo. Sun Times., 1985-86. With U.S. Army, 1950-52. Inducted into Chgo. Journalism Hall of Fame, 1996. Mem. Chgo. Newspaper Guild (Page One award 1973), Chgo. Press Club (v.p. 1984-87, pres. 1987). Democrat. Roman Catholic.

HERING, DORIS MINNIE, dance critic; b. N.Y.C., Apr. 11, 1920; d. Harry and Anna Elizabeth (Schwenk) H. BA cum laude, Hunter Coll., 1941; MA, Fordham U., 1985. Freelance dance writer, 1946-52; assoc. editor, prin. critic Dance mag., N.Y.C., 1952-72; exec. dir. Nat. Assn. for Regional Ballet, N.Y.C., 1972-87; adj. assoc. prof. dance history NYU, 1968-78; freelance dance writer, lectr., cons., 1987—. Mem. dance panel NEA, 1972-75, cons., 1991—; mem. dance panel N.Y. State Coun. Arts, 1992-96, program auditor, 1997—; bd. dirs. Walnut Hill Sch., 1975—, Internat. Ballet Competition, 1981—; hon. bd. dirs. Phila. Dance Alliance, 1980—; cons. Regional Dance Am.; adj. assoc. prof. dance history NYU Grad. Sch. Edn. Author: 25 Years of American Dance, 1950, Dance in America, 1951, Wild Grass, 1965, Giselle and Albrecht, 1981; sr. editor Dance mag., 1989—. Howard D. Rothschild Rsch. fellow Harvard U., 1991-93; recipient 33d ann. Capezio Dance Found. award for lifetime svc., 1985, Award of Distinction Dance mag., 1987, Sage Cowles Land Grant chair in dance U. Minn., 1993, Sr. Critics tribute Dance Critics Assn., 2002, Annual award, Martha Hill Dance Fund, 2002; named to Hunter Coll. Alumni Hall of Fame, 1986. Mem. Dance Critics Assn., Assn. Dance History Scholars, Phi Beta Kappa, Chi Tau Epsilon (hon.).

HERING, HELEN DORA, controller; b. Birnamwood, Wis., Mar. 19, 1921; d. August Ferdinand Grosinske and Bertha Wilhelmina Kraege; m. Edwin R. Baeseman (dec. Sept. 18, 1962); 1 child, Randall Layne Baeseman; m. Alfons Frank Hering, Sept. 10, 1972 (dec. Aug. 10, 1991). Tchrs. diploma, Marathon County Norman Sch., Wausau, Wis., 1940. Grade sch. tchr. Marathon County Schs., Wausau, 1940—45; mem. statis. dept. Employers Mut. Ins. Co., Wausau, 1946—48; cashier, bookkeeper Employers Mut. Credit Union, Wausau, 1948—53; ptnr., bookkeeper Baeseman's Shoe & Clothing, Wausau, 1953—79; antiques dealer Hering House Antiques, Wausau, 1972—99; English editor Gwiazda Polarna (Polish lang. weekly newspaper), Stevens Point, Wis., 1993—95. Pub.: So You Wanted America, 1996, author poetry. Recipient Valley Forge Honor cert., Freedoms Found., Milw., 1978, monetary prize, World of Poetry, Anaheim, Calif., 1988, World of Poetry, Las Vegas, 1990. Republican. Lutheran. Avocations: poetry, entering contests. Home: 8301 S Mountain Rd Wausau WI 54401

HERING, WILLIAM MARSHALL, medical organization executive; b. Indpls., Dec. 26, 1940; s. William Marshall and Mary Agnes (Clark) H.; m. Suzanne Wolfe, Aug. 10, 1963. BS, Ind. U., 1961, MS, 1962; PhD, U. Ill., Urbana, 1973. Tchr. Indpls. pub. schs., 1962-66; asst. dir. sociol. resources project Am. Sociol. Assn., 1966-70; dir. social sci. curriculum Biomed. Interdisciplinary Project, Berkeley, Calif., 1973-76; staff assoc. Tchrs. Ctrs. Exch., San Francisco, 1976-82; dir. rsch. Far West Lab. Ednl. R&D, San Francisco, 1979-85; mgr. human resource devel. Bank Am., San Francisco, 1985-94; dir. programs Am. Acad. Ophthalmology, San Francisco, 1994—. Mem. Nat. Adv. Bd. Educ. Resource Info. Ctr.; cons. U.S. Dept. Edn.; pres. Social Sci. Educ. Consortium, 1981-82, bd. dirs., 1979-81. Contbr. over 100 articles, book chpts. Bd. dirs. San Francisco Chamber Orch., 1986-94. Nat. Inst. Edn. grantee, 1979-82. Mem. ASTD (v.p. 1986), Alliance Continuing Med. Edn., Alpha Tau Omega, Phi Delta Kappa. Republican. Episcopalian. Home: 31 Duboce Ave San Francisco CA 94117-3214 Office: 655 Beach St San Francisco CA 94109-1336 E-mail: bhering@aao.org.

HERINGTON, LEIGH ELLSWORTH, state legislator, lawyer; b. Rochester, N.Y., Aug. 8, 1945; s. Donald G. and Ethel (Buck) H.; m. Anita Dixon, Dec. 12, 1970; children: Laurie, Tanya. AAS, Alfred State Coll., 1965; BBA, Kent State U., 1967, MBA, 1971; JD, U. Akron, 1976. Bar: Ohio 1976. Asst. sports info. dir. Kent State U., Ohio, 1969-70, asst. coord. internal comm., 1970-71, asst. dir. alumni rels., 1971-72; dir. pub. rels. Walsh Coll., Canton, Ohio, 1972-73; dir. comm. Hiram Coll., Ohio, 1973-77; sole practice Aurora, Ohio, 1977-78; ptnr. Christley, Herington & Pierce, Aurora, 1978—; mem. Ohio Senate from 28th dist., Columbus, 1994—. Instr. law Hiram Coll., 1978— . Pres. Crestwood Bd. Edn., Portage County, Ohio, 1981, Portage County United Way, 1984; chmn. crusade Am. Cancer Soc., Portage County. Served with U.S. Army, 1968-69. Recipient Pres.'s award Portage County United Way, 1983; named Alumnus of Yr., Kent State U. Bus. Coll., 1984, Vol. of Yr., Portage County, 1986. Mem. ABA, Ohio State Bar Assn., Portage County Bar Assn., Ohio Coun. Sch. Bd. Attys., Pub. Rels. Soc. Am., Aurora-Streetsboro Club (charter), Rotary. Democrat. Office: Christley Herington & Pierce 215 W Garfield Rd Aurora OH 44202-8849 Address: 4039 Hardin Rd Ravenna OH 44266-9313 Office: Ohio Senate Senate Bldg Columbus OH 43215

HERIOT, RUTHANNE, librarian; b. Pitts., July 11, 1948; d. James Fairgrieve and Mary Louise (Kloss) H.; 1 child, P. Andrea. BA cum laude, Wheeling (W.Va.) Jesuit Coll., 1970; MA, Sangamon State U., Springfield, Ill., 1976; MLS, U. Pitts., 1977. Park ranger, historian Nat. Park Svc., 1970-76; libr. Mary H. Weir Pub. Libr., Weirton, W.Va., 1977-81; libr. cons. Libr. Corp., Charlestown, W.Va., 1985-86; libr. Harpers Ferry (W.Va.) Ctr. Nat. Park Svc., 1981-88, NOAA Ctrl. Libr., Silver Spring, Md., 1988-95. Contbr. articles to profl. jours. Mem., subdeacon Order of Jerusalem, Diocese of W.Va., 1982-89. Episcopalian. Avocations: flute, church activities, gardening, cats. Home: RR 3 Box 934 Harpers Ferry WV 25425-9324

HERKNER, BERNADETTE KAY, occupational health nurse; b. East Liverpool, Ohio, Apr. 29, 1947; d. Charles R. and Anna G. (Parr) Geon. Diploma in nursing, East Liverpool City Hosp., 1973; BS in Applied Sci., Youngstown (Ohio) State U., 1976. RN, Ohio, Mich., Fla; cert. in audiometrics, sipromety, ICD-9-CM; cert. case mgr.; cert. occupl. health nurse specialist. Charge nurse emergency rm. East Liverpool City Hosp., 1976-78; sr. occupl. health nurse specialist Dow Chem. N.Am., Midland, Mich., 1978-2000. Active Vol. Action Ctr. Midland County. Recipient Best Bedside Nurse, Centennial award for svc. to humanity, 1973, Ctrl. Mich. Outstanding Occupl. Health Nurse of Yr. award, 1993; named Miss Hope Columbiana County unit Am. Cancer Soc., 1977. Mem. Am. Assn. Occupl. Health Nurses (cert.), Mich. Assn. Occupl. Health Nurses (bd. dirs.), Emergency Nurses Assn., Mich. Nurses Assn., Ctrl. Mich. Assn. Occupl. Health Nurses (bd. dirs., corr. sec. 1986-90, rec. sec. 1990-91, pres. 1991-95, legis. chmn. 1995-96), East Ctrl. Mich. Emergency Nurses, Ohio Emergency Nurses Assn. (membership sec.), Case Mgmt. Soc. Am.

HERLEMAN, LAURA ANN, nursing administrator; b. Allegheny County, Pa., Mar. 27, 1949; d. Frank K. and Ellen Louise (Hogg) Sweeny; m. William H. Herleman, Aug. 22, 1970 (dec.); children: William H. Jr., Amy S. Diploma in nursing, Allegheny Valley Hosp., Natrona Heights, Pa., 1970; BSN, La Roche Coll., Pitts., 1995; postgrad., Duquesne U., 1998—. RN, Pa. Staff nurse med.-surg. units Allegheny Valley Hosp., Natrona Heights, Pa., 1970-76, 79-86, supr. nursing, 1986-91; staff nurse med.-surg. unit St. Clair Meml. Hosp., Pitts., 1977-79; asst. DON Allegheny Gen. Hosp., Pitts., 1990-93; staff nurse Allegheny Homecare, 1993-95, coord., 1995-96, mgr., 1996—; nursing supr. Forbes Nursing Ctr., Pitts., 1995-96. Substitute sch. nurse Freeport (Pa.) Area Sch. Dist., Highlands Sch. Dist., Natrona Heights, 1988-94. Office: Allegheny Home Care 500 Finley St 2nd Fl Pittsburgh PA 15206

HERLIHY-CHEVALIER, BARBARA DOYLE, mental health nurse; b. Cambridge, Mass., June 28, 1935; d. William A. and Aloyse V. (Mahoney) Doyle; m. Timothy J. Herlihy, Aug. 20, 1955 (dec. Oct. 1983); children: Michael, Ann-Marie, Sharon, Ellen, Stephen, Kathleen, James; m. Robert J. Chevalier, May 28, 1994 (dec. Oct. 1995); 1 stepchild, Ron. RN, Mass. Gen. Hosp., 1956; BS in Human Svcs., N.H. Coll./So. N.H. U., 1983; MS in Nursing, Anna Maria Coll., 1987. Nat. cert. instr. and coord. remotivation therapy. Pvt. duty nurse N.E. Bapt. Hosp., MGH, Boston, 1956-58, St. John's Hosp., Lowell, Mass., 1966-70; charge nurse Tewksbury (Mass.) Hosp. Mass. Dept. Pub. Health, 1970-76; coord. remotivation therapy Danvers (Mass.) State Hosp., 1976-79; registered community mental health nurse Mass. Dept. Mental Health, Lawrence, 1979-91; mental health nurse Lowell (Mass.) Adult Day Treatment, 1991-94. Fellow Nat. Remotivation Therapy Orgn. (nat. instr., coord., Dorothy Hoskins Smith honorarium 2001); mem. Internat. Adv. Coun. Remotivation Therapy, Bay State Remotivation Coun. Home: 142 Trull Rd Tewksbury MA 01876-1705

HERLING, MICHAEL, steel company executive; b. Cernauti, Romania; arrived in Canada, 1950; m. Marta Klein; children: Dorothy Herling Chaikelson, Joyce Herling Saifer. B in Econs., U. Vienna, Austria, 1933; D in Econs., U. Florence, 1935. Sr. v.p. Ivaco, Inc., Montreal, Que., Can., 1969—. Office: Ivaco Inc 770 Rue Sherbrooke Ouest Montreal QC Canada H3A 1G1

HERMACH, FRANCIS LEWIS, consulting engineer; b. Bridgeport, Conn., Jan. 8, 1917; s. Frank and Barbara (Dauenheimer) H.; m. Frances M. Roberts, June 22, 1940 (dec. Feb. 1996); children: George, William (dec.); m. Friede Groen, Oct. 11, 1998. B.E.E., George Washington U., 1943. Sci. aid Nat. Bur. Standards, Washington, 1939-42; elec. engr., 1942-63; chief elec. instruments sect., 1963-72; dep. chief electricity div., 1970-72; cons., 1972-76; cons. engr. Elec. Measurements, Silver Spring, Md., 1976—. Contbr. articles on elec. measurements to profl. jours. Served with USNR, 1945-46. Recipient Disting. service award Dept. Commerce, 1954; Morris E. Leeds award IEEE, 1976, Centennial medal, 1984; Engr. Alumni Achievement award George Washington U., 1985 Fellow IEEE, Instrument Soc. Am., Washington Acad. Scis.; mem. Precision Measurements Soc., Philos. Soc. Washington. Methodist. Achievements include patents in field. Home: 2850 Aquarius Ave Silver Spring MD 20906-1811

HERMALIN, BENJAMIN E. economics educator; b. N.Y.C., Jan. 14, 1962; s. Albert I. and Jolene C. Hermalin; m. Ruth Ann Konoff, June 26, 1988; children: Rose A., Noah M. AB summa cum laude, Princeton U., 1984; PhD, MIT, 1988. Asst. prof. U. Calif., Berkeley, 1988-94, assoc. prof., 1994—98, Booth prof. of banking and fin., 1999—. Vis. prof. MIT, Cambridge, Mass., 1993. Contbr. articles to profl. jours. Grad. fellow NSF, 1984-87, John M. Olin Faculty Rsch. fellow Yale U. Law Sch., 1992-93; grantee NSF, 1991-93. Mem. Phi Beta Kappa. Office: U Calif Haas Sch Bus 545 Student Services Bldg Berkeley CA 94720-1900

HERMALYN, DOC, historian, writer; b. Bronx, N.Y., Aug. 3, 1953; s. Sol Montcalm and Isabelle Lee Hermalyn; m. Elizabeth Beirne. BA, CCNY, 1971; MA, L.I. U., 1982; EdD, Columbia U., 1985. Exec. dir. The Bronx County Hist. Soc., 1974—; pres. History of N.Y.C. Project, Inc., Bronx, 1981—. Prodr., writer Out of the Past radio show, N.Y.C., 1974—91; tour leader, lectr., NY, 1974—; expedition leader, N.Y.C. area, 1980—; expedition cons. Planetary Studies Assn., Urbana, Ill., 1998—; leader exploration of bygone waterways and pathways, 1977—; author, dir. Yankee Stadium Tour, N.Y.C., 1980—. Author: Morris High School and the Creation of the New York Secondary School System, 1995, (book and planetarium show) Time and the Calendar, 2002; author and editor: 4 vol. series Life in the Bronx; editor: Roots of the Republic, 6 vols., 1994, The U.S. Supreme Court, 10 vols., 1993; assoc. editor: The Ency. of NYC, publisher: of 125 publs. Founding dir. Armory H.S. Sports Edn. of N.Y., N.Y.C., 1985—; advisor Bronx Dance Theater, 1990—; sponsor New Pub. H.S.-New Explorers High. Named a Centennial Historian of N.Y.C., Mayor of N.Y.C., 1998; recipient Edgar Allan Poe award, Bronx Hist. Soc., 1985. Fellow Explorers Club (chmn. centennial com. 2002—, chmn. millennium dinner); mem.: 100 Yr. Assn. of N.Y. (bd. dirs. 1995—), Author's Guild. Avocations: kayaking, percussionist, bamboo cultivation. Office Fax: 718-881-4827. Business E-Mail: dochermalyn@bronxhistoricalsociety.org.

HERMAN, ALEXIS M. former labor secretary; b. Mobile, Ala., July 16, 1947; BA, Xavier U., New Orleans, 1969. Founder, CEO A.M. Herman & Assocs., Washington; nat. dir. Minority Women's Employment Program, Washington, until 1977; dir. Women's Bur. Dept. Labor, Washington, 1977-81; chief staff, then dep. chair Dem. Nat. Conv. Com., Washington, until 1991, CEO, 1991-92; dep. dir. Clinton-Gore Presdl. Transition Office, Washington, 1992-93; asst. to President U.S., Pub. Liaison dir. White House, Washington, 1993-96; sec. labor U.S. Dept. Labor, Washington, 1997-2001; chmn. & CEO New Ventures, Inc., DC, 2001—; chairperson Coca-Cola Human Resources Diversity Task Force, Ga., 2001—; chmn. Toyota North Amer. Diversity Bd., 2002—. Recipient Sara Lee Front Runner award, 1999. Mem. Nat. Coun. Negro Women, Delta Sigma Theta. Democrat. Office: 1501 M St NW Ste 1175 Washington DC 20005

HERMAN, ALLEN IAN, foundation administrator; b. Pitts., June 16, 1950; s. Harry W. and Ann (Burke) H.; m. Jacqueline Wadler, July 5, 1981; children: Zvi, Ari, Michal. BA, U. Pitts., 1972; MBA, U. Pa., 1974. Cancer coordinator Jamaica (N.Y.) Hosp., 1975-76; asst. adminstr. SUNY-Downstate Med. Ctr., Bklyn., 1976-79, assoc. adminstr., 1979-83; chief exec. officer Nephrology Found. Bklyn., 1983—. Lectr. Ctr. Health Related Professions SUNY-Downstate Med. Ctr., Bklyn., 1983—; mem. coun. ESRD Network # 25, N.Y.C., 1980—88. Mem. editorial bd.: Jour. Greater N.Y. Med. Records Assn., 1984; contbr. articles to profl. jours. Coach little league baseball, 1990—98; chmn. youth dept. Young Israel of Kew Gardens Hills, 1998—2000, v.p., 2000—01, 2002, exec. v.p., 2002—03; bd. dirs. Hebrew Acad. West Queens, Jackson Heights, NY, 1987—. Fellow Am. Coll. Healthcare Execs.; mem. Am. Hosp. Assn., Nat. Dialysis Assn. (bd. dirs. 1985-87, v.p. 1988, pres. 1989-90), Nat. Renal Adminstrs. Assn., Wharton Health Care Alumni Assn. Democrat. Jewish. Avocations: sports, music, photography. Office: Nephrology Found Bklyn 342 Flatbush Ave Brooklyn NY 11238-4902 E-mail: allenih@aol.com.

HERMAN, ANDREA MAXINE, newspaper editor; b. Chgo., Oct. 22, 1938; d. Maurice H. and Mae (Baron) H.; m. Joseph Schmidt, Oct. 28, 1962. BJ, U. Mo., 1960. Feature writer Chgo.'s Am., 1960-63; daily columnist News Am., Balt., 1963-67; feature writer Mainichi Daily News, Tokyo, 1967-69; columnist Iowa City Press-Citizen, 1969-76; music and dance critic San Diego Tribune, 1976-84; asst. mng. editor features UPI, Washington, 1984-86, asst. mng. editor news devel., 1986-87; mng. editor features L.A. Herald Examiner, 1987-91; editor/culture We/Mbl Newspaper, Washington, 1991—. Recipient 1st and 2d prizes for features in arts James S. Copley Ring of Truth Awards, 1982, 1st prize for journalism Press Club San Diego, 1983. Mem. Soc. Profl. Journalists, Am. Soc. Newspaper Editors, AP Mng. Editors, Women in Communications. Avocations: music, art. Office: We Mbl Newspaper 1350 Connecticut Ave NW Washington DC 20036-1722

HERMAN, BARBARA ROSE, interior decorator; b. Worcester, Mass., Feb. 14, 1938; d. Albert H. and Mary Margaret (Convery) Garnache; children: Diane G. Herman Johnson, Mary E. Herman Thurston, Tracy A., Barry J. Cert., N.Y. Sch. Interior Design, N.Y.C., 1972, RISD, Providence, 1974. Owner Decorating Barn, Auburn, Pa., 1970-79, Barbara Herman Ineriors, Worcester, Mass., 1979—. Tchr. Worcester Night Life Continuing Edn., Worcester, 1970-89, Becker Jr. Coll., Worcester, 1982; participant in show houses for Jr. League fundraisers; lectr. in field. Work appeared in Womens Day Mag., 1987, Condo Media Cover, 1989, Condo Media Cover, 1992. Mem. Worcester Exec. Assn. (pres. 1984). Roman Catholic. Avocations: tennis, art. Home: 104 June St Worcester MA 01602-2950 Office: Barbara Herman Interiors 104 June St Worcester MA 01602-2950 E-mail: bh1438@aol.com.

HERMAN, BARRY MARTIN, international economist; b. Bklyn., June 27, 1943; s. Aaron and Fannie Herman; m. Martha Feldman, Mar. 19, 1967; children: Alicia, Mark. AB, Columbia U., 1965; MBA, U. Chgo., 1967; PhD, U. Mich., 1974. Mgmt. analyst U.S. Bur. of the Budget, Washington, 1967; lectr. in econs. U. Mich., Dearborn, 1972-73; asst. prof. Dickinson Coll., Carlisle, Pa., 1973-75; instr. Lehman Coll., CUNY, Bronx, 1975-76; econs. affairs officer UN, N.Y.C., 1976-89, chief developed economies sect., 1989-95, chief internat. econ. rels. br., 1995-99, chief fin. and devel. br., 1999—2002, chief policy analysis and devel., 2003—. Adv. Financing for Devel. Summit Conf. Preparations, Monterrey, Mexico, 2002. Editor, author: International Finance and Developing Countries in a Year of Crisis, 1998, Financial Turmoil and Reform, 1999, Financing for Development: Proposals From Business and Civil Society, 2001; contbr. articles to profl. jours. Conf. planning com. Global Interdependence Ctr., Phila., 1995-8. Mem. Am. Econs. Assn. Office: Dept Econs and Social Affairs UN New York NY 10017 E-mail: herman@un.org.

HERMAN, CHARLES JACOB, lawyer, accounting firm executive; b. Balt., May 31, 1937; s. Jacob and Edna M. (Hackett) H.; m. Frances L. Leonard, Oct. 25, 1958; children— Alison, Charles J., Leonard. B.A., U. Balt., 1958, J.D., 1961. Bar: Md. 1961. Atty. Fidelity & Deposit, N.Y.C., 1958-69, Aetna Ins. Co., Hartford, Conn., 1969-71, INA, Phila., 1971-76; officer Home Ins. Co., N.Y.C., 1976-80; nat. ptnr., dir. litigation support services Laventhol & Horwath, Phila., 1980—; ptnr. Margolis Edelstein Scherles and Kraemer; founder, chief exec. officer Curtis Cons. Group Ltd. Co-author: (manual) Bonds on Public Works, 1986. Past pres. St. John's Lutheran Ch., Morrisville, Pa.; bd. dirs. Luth. Home, Germantown, Germantown Home. Served to sgt. U.S. Army, 1961-66. Mem. ABA, Internat. Assn. Ins. Counsel, Am. Arbitration Assn., Md. Bar Assn. Republican. Lutheran. Home: 957 Randolph Dr Morrisville PA 19067-4207 Office: Curtis Cons Group Ltd The Curtis Ctr 4th Fl Independence Sq W Philadelphia PA 19106

HERMAN, CHARLES WENDELL, history educator; b. Storm Lake, Iowa, Jan. 22, 1940; s. Verne Ernest and Bernice Leona Herman; m. Rosanne Marie Raygor, June 13, 1964; children: Margret Annalee Kracinski, Amy Kate Herman-Roloff. BA, Trinity Coll., Deerfield, Ill.; MA, PhD, U. Minn. Asst. prof. history Northwestern Coll., Roseville, Minn., 1972—86; assoc. prof.history Roberts Wesleyan Coll., Rochester, NY, 1986—90; prof. history U. Sioux Falls, SD, 1990—. Fellow Summer Seminar/Inst. Coll. Teachers, Nat. Endowment Humanities, 1978, 1988, 1990, 1995. Mem.: Conf. Faith and History, Soc. French Hist. Studies, Am. Hist. Assn. (life), Phi Alpha Theta. Christian. Home: 411 S Summit Ave Sioux Falls SD 57104 Office: U Sioux Falls 1101 W 22nd St Sioux Falls SD 57105 Office Fax: 605-331-6615. E-mail: charles.herman@usiouxfalls.edu.

HERMAN, DAVID HENRY, artist, violin restorer and dealer; b. N.Y.C., Apr. 28, 1940; s. Morris and Elsie (Lass) H.; m. Sandra Lois Pinker, June 27, 1972; children: Lori, Tammy, Deanne. BS, NYU, 1961; MA, Bklyn. Coll., 1970. Tchr. orchestral music J.H.S. 210, N.Y.C., 1961-64, Elmont (N.Y.) Meml. H.S., 1964-94; violin restorer, dealer East Meadow, N.Y., 1975—; painter L.I. and N.Y.C., 1991—. Mem., organizer Rudolf Baranik Art Seminar, N.Y.C., 1996—; panelist Fitting into 21st Century Heckscher Mus., Huntington, N.Y., 1996. One-man shows include Denise Bibro Gallery, N.Y., 1999, 2001, 02, 03, Hewlett-Woodmere Libr., N.Y., 1994, Gallery Swan, Soho, N.Y., 1995, Gallery Emanuel, Kings Point, N.Y., 1996, Nexus Gallery, N.Y.C., 1998, Caelum Gallery, 1998, 99, Fairleigh Dickinson U., N.J., 2000, Molloy Coll., Rockville Centre, N.Y., 2002; group exhbns. include Nassau County Mus. Annex, 1993, Heckscher Mus., Huntington, N.Y., 1997, Mills Pond House, St. James, N.Y., 1998, 2002, Amos Eno Gallery, N.Y., Denise Bibro Gallery, N.Y.C., 1999, 2003, Muscarelle Mus. Art, Williamsburg, Va., 2000, Knox Mus., Buffalo, N.Y., 2000, B.J. Spoke Gallery, Huntington, N.Y., 2001, Albright-Knox Mus., Buffalo, 2000-01, 03—. With USAR, 1961. Mem. Appraisers Assn. Am. Jewish. Avocations: walking, reading, playing the piano.

HERMAN, DAVID JAY, orthodontist; b. Rome, N.Y., Oct. 4, 1954; s. Maurice Joseph and Bettina S. (Stiener) H.; m. Mary Beth Appleberry, Apr. 11, 1976; children: Jeremiah D., Kellin A. BA in Biology, San Jose State U., 1976; DDS, Emory U., 1981; MS in Orthodontics, MPH, U. N.C., 1992. Comdr. USPHS, 1981-97; advanced gen. practice resident Gallup (N. Mex.) Indian Med. Ctr., 1983-84; Navajo area dental br. chief Window Rock, Ariz., 1986-89; mem. grad. residency com. U. N.C., Chapel Hill, 1990-91; Navajo area orthodontic specialist Shiprock, N. Mex., 1992-97; clin. dir. Nizhoni Smiles Inc., 1997-99; pvt. practice Farmington, N.Mex., 1998—; pres. Four Corners Orthodontics, Inc., 1998—. Mem. health adv. bd. Navajo Reservation Headstart, 1986—89; health promotion/disease prevention cons. USPHS/Indian Health Svc. Navajo Area, Window Rock, 1986—89; cons. Ariz. IHS Periodontal Health Task Force, 1986—90. Asst. wrestling coach Winslow (Ariz.) H.S., 1984-86, Gallup High Sch., 1987-89, Chapel Hill H.S., 1991-92, Farmington H.S., 1992-2002, Aztec H.S., 1998-2000; mem. H.S. Youth Wrestling Program, 1992-2000; mem. corp. bd. San Juan Reg. Med. Ctr., 1996—. Recipient Healthy Mothers/Healthy Babies Disease Prevention award, 1988, USPHS Achievement medal, 1985, Headstart Achievement award, 1989, Ariz. Pub. Health Assn. Hon. award, 1989; Nat. Health Svc. Corp. scholar Emory U., 1977-81. Mem. ADA, Am. Assn. Orthodontists, Rocky Mountain Soc. Orthodontists, N.Mex. Soc. Orthodontists

(pres. 1998-99), Northwestern N.Mex. Sco. Orthodontists (pres. 1999-00), Navajo Area Dental Soc. (pres. 1985), Am. Assn. Mil. Orthodontists (sec.reas. 1992, v.p. 1993-94, pres. 1995-97). Avocations: wrestling, weight lifting, jogging, skiing, backpacking.

HERMAN, EDITH CAROL, journalist; b. Edgewood, Md., July 1, 1944; d. Herbert R. and Thirza E. (Simmons) H.; m. Leonard Wiener. BA, Purdue U., 1966. Reporter Hollister Newspaper Chain, Wilmette, Ill., 1966-68, Chgo. Tribune Newspaper, 1968-79, edn. editor, 1971-74, feature writer, 1976-79; sr. editor TV Digest Inc., 1980-83; pub. rels. mgr. AT&T, 1983-90; pub. rels. cons. Bethesda, 1990—93, Warren Comm., 1994—, assoc. mng. editor, 2001—. Bd. dirs. Sigma Delta Chi Found. of Washington, 1990-92. Recipient Journalism award Ill. Edn. Assn., 1969-70; Editorial award Ill. Automatic Merchandising Council, 1977 Mem. Soc. Profl. Journalists. Home: 5501 Burling Ct Bethesda MD 20817-6309 E-mail: eherman@warren-news.com.

HERMAN, ELAINE, non-profit theatre artistic director; b. Wildwood, N.J., July 31, 1933; d. Edward and Mae (Levinson)Seigle; m. George Herman, Dec. 8, 1953; children: Laurie, Rhonda, Marcie. BA in Theatre Arts magna cum laude, Calif. State Coll., 1972; MA in Theatre Arts, Calif. State U., Long Beach, Calif., 1974. Cert. tchr., Calif. Theatre dir. various states, 1956—, scenic designer freelance, 1963—; arts adminstr. Pub. Corp. for the Arts, Long Beach, Calif., 1977-87; mng. dir. Long Beach (Calif.) Playhouse, 1987-98, artistic dir., 1998—. Directing panelist So. Calif. Edn. Theatre Assn., Palm Springs, Calif., 1991; producing panelist Showbiz Expo, L.A., 1992; panelist Women in Theatre, L.A., 1992; keynote spkr. Congress of Arts, Pub. Corp. for the Arts, Long Beach, 1993. Author: (handbook) Production Planning for the Theatre Director, 1974, (annotated textbook) Theatre Technology and Design, 1984; stage dir. for over 50 plays (12 "Best Dir." awards), L.A. Johnston's Outstanding Women Dirs. award 1983); scenic designer for 34 plays, 1963—. Arts adv. com. City of Long Beach, 1984-88, strategic plan task force, 1985-86, cultural arts facilities task force, 1985-86, cultural master plan steering commn., 1993-94. Recipient Disting. Artist award City of Long Beach and County of L.A., 1992. Mem. Pub. Corp. for Arts, Long Beach Conv. & Visitors Bur., Long Beach C. of C. Avocations: travel, camping, fgn. langs., gourmet cooking, interior design. Home: 1340 Park Plaza Dr Long Beach CA 90804-3201 Office: Long Beach Playhouse 5021 E Anaheim St Long Beach CA 90804-3214

HERMAN, ELVIN E. retired consulting electronic engineer; b. Mar. 17, 1921; s. John Lawrence and Martha Elizabeth (Conner) H.; m. Grace Winifred Eklund, Sept. 29, 1945; 1 child, Jane Ann Herman Fischer. BSEE, State U. Iowa, 1942. Engr., sect. head Naval Rsch. Lab., Washington, 1942-51; sect. head Corona (Calif.) Labs., Nat. Bur. Stds., 1951-53; sect. head, lab. mgr., tech. dir. radar sys. group Hughes Aircraft Co., El Segundo, Calif., 1953-83; cons. electronic engr., Pacific Palisades, Calif., 1983-88; ret., 1988. Recipient Meritorious Civilian Svc. award Naval Rsch. Lab., 1946. Fellow IEEE. Achievements include 24 patents in field. Home: 1200 Lachman Ln Pacific Palisades CA 90272-2228 E-mail: alherm@earthlink.net.

HERMAN, GEORGE, speech educator; b. New York, Apr. 19, 1922; s. Leo and Sara (Geller) Herman; m. Fern Reissig Herman, June 29, 1946; children: Lee D., Linda Jo Donovan. BA, Bklyn Coll., 1941; MA, U. Mich., 1943, PhD, 1952. Asst. prof. speech Wayne U., Detroit, 1946—52, U. Mich., Ann Arbor, 1952—58, Bowling Green State U., Ohio, 1958—64, assoc. prof. speech, 1964—66, prof. speech, 1966—81, vice provost, 1971—75, prof. emeritus, 1981—. Editor numerous jor. publs. Mem. ACLU So. N.Mex, Las Cruces, 1954—56. Mem.: Acoustical Soc. Am., Cruces Apple User Group (treas. 2001—02), Phi Kappa Phi. Jewish. Avocation: computers. Home: 2861 Buena Vida Court Las Cruces NM 88011-5056

HERMAN, GEORGE ADAM, retired writer and educator; b. Norfolk, Va., Apr. 12, 1928; s. George Adam and Minerva Nevada (Thompson) H.; m. Patricia Lee Glazer, May 26, 1955 (div. 1989); children: Kurt, Erik, Karl, Lisa, Katherine, Christopher, Jena, Amanda; m. Patricia Jane Piper Dubay, Aug. 25, 1989; children: Lizette, Paul, Kirk, Victoria. PhB, Loyola Coll., 1950; MFA, Cath. U., 1954; Cert. fine arts, Boston Coll., 1951,52,53. Asst. prof. Clarke Coll., Dubuque, Iowa, 1955-60, Villanova (Pa.) U., 1960-63; asst. prof., playwright in residence Coll. St. Benedict, St. Joseph, Minn., 1963-65; chmn. theatre dept. Coll. Great Falls, Mont., 1965-67; media specialist Hawaii State Dept. Edn., Honolulu, 1967-75, staff specialist, 1975-83; sr. drama critic Honolulu Advertiser, 1975-80; artistic dir. Commedia Repertory Theatre, Honolulu, 1978-80; freelance writer, lectr., composer Portland, Oreg., 1983—. Author: (plays) Company of Wayward Saints, 1963 (McKnight Humanities award 1964), Mr. Highpockets, 1968, A Stone for Either Hand, 1969, Tenebrae, 1984, (novels) Carnival of Saints, 1994 (finalist Oreg. Book Awards 1994), A Comedy of Murders, 1994, Tears of the Madonna, 1995, The Florentine Mourners, 1999, The Toys of War, 2002, Little Rome, Iowa, 2003, Nine Dragons, 2003, Necromancer, 2003; composer (ballets) The Dancing Princesses, Fraidy Cat. Pres. local chpt. Nat. Sch. Pub. Rels. Assn., Honolulu, 1981-83; bd. dirs. Honolulu Community Theatre, 1981-82, Hawaii State Theatre Coun., Honolulu, 1981. With U.S. Army, 1950-52. Recipient Hartke Playwrighting award Cath. U., 1954, Humanities award McKnight Found., 1963, Excellence award Am. Security Coun., 1967. Avocations: directing theatre, lecturing. E-mail: gadamo@aol.com.

HERMAN, GEORGE EDWARD, radio and television correspondent; b. N.Y.C., Jan. 14, 1920; s. Sydney H. and Tessie Samuels (Dryfoos) H.; m. Patricia Kerwin, Feb. 19, 1955; children— Charles, Scott, R. Douglas. AB cum laude, Dartmouth Coll., 1941; MS, Columbia U., 1942. Night news editor radio sta. WQXR, N.Y.C., 1942-44; joined CBS, 1944, Tokyo bur. mgr., 1950-53, Washington corr., 1954-87; moderator Face the Nation, 1969-84; also lectr.; free-lance corr., contbr. Nat. Pub. Radio and World Monitor TV, 1987—. Contbr. articles to mags. Mem. AFTRA (v.p. 1970-78), Am. Automobile Assn., Press Club (Tokyo), Cosmos Club. Home: 4500 Q Ln NW Washington DC 20007-2569

HERMAN, HANK, writer; b. N.Y.C., Nov. 13, 1949; s. Philip and Stella (Rubenfeld) H.; m. Carol K. Korngut, Dec. 30, 1972; children: Matt, Greg, Robby. BA, U. Pa., 1971. Advt. copywriter Prentice-Hall, Englewood Cliffs, N.J., 1972-73; assoc. editor Travel Mgmt. Daily, N.Y.C., 1973-74; mng. editor TravelScene, N.Y.C., 1975-77, Health Mag., N.Y.C., 1978-79, editor in chief, 1980-88; freelance writer, 1989—. Health reporter Sta. WINS-Radio, N.Y.C., 1987-90. Award-winning columnist Westport News, 1993—; author numerous mag. articles and youth sports fiction books, 1973—. Avocations: running, tennis, skiing, coaching youth sports.

HERMAN, J. CLAYTON, retired adult education educator; b. Bellaire, Kansas, Sept. 6, 1930; s. Ezra George and Lora Rosella Herman; m. Marilyn Ruth Kattenberg, Aug. 28, 1955 (dec. Oct. 1997); 1 child, Lisa Dianne Miles; m. Sofia de Oliveira, Sept. 6, 2002. BS in Agrl. Journalism, Kans. State U., 1957; MS in Rural Sociology, U. Ark., 1962. Asst. editor experiment sta. U. Ark., Fayetteville, 1957—61; comm. specialist Iowa State U., Ames, 1961—90. Cattle prodr., Lebanon, Kans., 1990—2000; ret. vol. worker RSVP, Marysville, Kans., 2001—. Contbr. ; author: (novel) License to Steal, 2003. Vol. Habitat for Humanity, Marysville, Kans., 1960—. Airman 1st Class USAF, 1949—52, Japan. Mem.: Heart of Am. Christian Writers Network, Singles in Agr. (sec. Kans. chpt. 2001—), Moose Lodge. Republican. Mem. Ch. Of Christ. Avocations: recycling scrap metal, writing. Home: 407 S 13th St Marysville KS 66508-2020

HERMAN, JOAN ELIZABETH, healthcare company executive; b. N.Y.C., June 2, 1953; d. Roland Barry and Grace Gales (Goldstein) H.; m. Richard M. Rasiej, July 16. 1977. AB, Barnard Coll., 1975; MS, Yale U., 1977. Actuarial student Met. Life Ins. Co., N.Y.C., 1978-82; asst. actuary Phoenix Mut. Life Ins. Co. (now Phoenix Life Ins.), Hartford, Conn., 1982-83; assoc. actuary, dir. underwriting research Phoenix Mut. Life Ins. Co., Hartford, Conn., 1983-84, 2d v.p., 1984-85, v.p., 1985-89, sr. v.p., 1989-98; pres. splty. bus. WellPoint Health Networks, Woodland Hills, Calif., 1998, group pres., 1999—2001, pres., sr., splty. and state sponsored programs divsn., 2002—. Bd. dirs. PM Holdings, Inc., Phoenix Group Holdings, Inc., Phoenix Am. Life Ins. Co., Emprendimiento Compartido, S.A., v.p., BC Life & Health Co., Profl. Claims Svcs Inc., Proserv., MEDIX. Contbr. articles to profl jours. Capt. fundraising team Greater Hartford Arts Coun., 1986; bd. dirs. Hadassah, Glastonbury, Conn., Temple Beth Hillel, South Windsor, Conn., 1983-84, Children's Fund Conn., 1992-98, My Sister's Place, Shelter, Hartford, 1989-94, Western Mass. Regional Nat. Conf. Conn., 1995-98, Greater Hartford Arts Coun., 1997-98; bd. dirs. Hartford Ballet, 1989-95, corporator, 1995-98; bd. dirs. Leadership Greater Hartford, 1989-94, chmn. bd. dirs., 1993-94, bd. dirs. Health Ins. Assn. of Am., 2002—; mem. bd. founders Am. Leadership Forum of Hartford, 1991-98; corporator Hartford Sem., 1994-98. Fellow Soc. Actuaries (chairperson health sect. coun. 1994-95); mem. Am. Acad. Actuaries (bd. dirs. 1994-97), Am. Leadership Forum, Home Office Life Underwriters Am. Jewish. Avocations: reading, swimming, bicycling, jogging, aerobic dancing, hiking. Office: Wellpoint Health Networks 1 Wellpoint Way Thousand Oaks CA 91362-3893 E-mail: joan.herman@wellpoint.com.

HERMAN, KENNETH BEAUMONT, lawyer; b. Medford, Mass., Jan. 23, 1944; s. Beaumont Alexander and Winifred (Small) H.; m. Agnes Anne Burch, Sept. 18, 1976; children: Alexander Beaumont, Juliana Burch. AB, Harvard U., 1966; JD, Harvard Law Sch., 1969. Bar: N.Y. 1971. Tchr. St. Dominic Savio High Sch., East Boston, Mass., 1969-70; assoc., then ptnr. Fish & Neave, N.Y.C., 1970—. Mem. Larchmont (N.Y.) Recreation Com., 1983-94, trustee Larchmont Hist. Soc., 1987-88. Mem. ABA, N.Y. State Bar Assn., N.Y. Intellectual Property Law Assn. (chmn. com. on incentives for innovation 1987-88), Licensing Execs. Soc., Internat. Trade Commn. Trial Lawyers Assn., Fed. Cir. Bar Assn., Am. Intellectual Property Law Assn., Assn. Bar of City of N.Y., Am. Arbitration Assn. (panel arbitrators). Avocations: sailing, skiing, kayaking, reading. Home: 810 Pirates Cv Mamaroneck NY 10543-4717 Office: Fish & Neave 1251 Sixth Ave Avenue of the Americas New York NY 10020-1105

HERMAN, LLOYD ELDRED, curator, consultant, writer; b. Corvallis, Oreg., Mar. 19, 1936; s. Raymond R. and Luella Jane (McNabb) H. BS, Am. U., 1960. Pub. rels. mgr. Nat. Housing Ctr., Nat. Assn. Home Builders, Washington, 1965-66; adminstrv. officer Office Dir. Gen. Mus. Smithsonian Instn., Washington, 1966-71; dir. Renwick Gallery, Smithsonian Instn., 1971-86, dir. emeritus, 1993; dir. Can. Craft Mus., Vancouver, B.C., 1988-91. Mem. adv. bd. Internat. Tapestry Network, 1991-99, Friends Fiber Art Internat., 1991—. Author: Art that Works: The Decorative Art of the 80's, Crafted in America, 1990, Clearly Art: Pilchuck's Glass Legacy, 1992, Trashformations: Recycled Materials in Contemporary American Art and Design, 1998; co-author: Tales and Traditions: Storytelling in 20th Century American Craft, 1993. Chair Mcpl. Arts Commn., Bellingham, Wash., 1995. With USN, Pacific Fleet, 1956-58. Decorated chevalier Order of Daneborg, Order Leopold II. Mem. Am. Craft Coun. (hon. fellow, 1991), Am. Assn. Mus., Internat. Coun. Mus. Democrat. Avocations: swimming, theatre, travel. Home: 8500 32nd Ave NW Seattle WA 98117-3901

HERMAN, LYNN BRIGGS, state legislator; b. Philipsburg, Pa., Oct. 30, 1956; s. Frederick Jr. and Barbara Ann (Briggs) H. BA, U. Pitts., Johnstown, 1978; MPA, U. Pitts., 1980. Adminstrv. asst. Pa. Dept. Edn., Harrisburg, 1980-81; adminstrv. analyst Pa. Dept. Transp., Harrisburg, 1981-82; mem. Pa. Ho. of Reps., Harrisburg, 1982—. Chmn. local govt. com. Pa. Ho. of Reps., 1997—, chmn. legis. data processing com., 1994—. Elected pres. Centre County's 148th Pa. Vol. Inf. Regiment Civil War reenactment group. Named Outstanding Legislator, Pa. Rifle and Pistol Assn., 1987, named to Outstanding Young Men of Am.; recipient Presdl. Recognition award Moshannon Valley Econ. Devel. Partnership, 1990, Champion of Good Govt. award Common Cause of Pa., 1999, Disting. Svc. award Pa. Mcpl. Authorities Assn., 2002. Mem. Frat. Order Police, Pa. State Alumni Assn., Ctr. County Hist. Assn., Ctrl. Pa. Civil War Round Table, State Coll. Quarterback Club, Grange, Pa. State Club, Elks, Kiwanis, Masons. Republican. Office: Pa Ho of Reps State Capitol Rm 312 Harrisburg PA 17120

HERMAN, MARK NORMAN, translator; b. Bklyn., Dec. 9, 1942; s. Joseph and Sylvia (Shapiro) H.; m. Ronnie Susan Apter, June 18, 1967; children: Daniel Arthur, Jeffry Michael. BS, Columbia U., 1963; MS, U. Calif., Berkeley, 1965. Pvt. practice, Shepherd, Mich. Translator (with Ronnie Apter) of nineteen operas and operettas performed in the U.S., Can., and Eng.; author or translator numerous poems; contbr. articles to profl. jours.; pub. 1st Performing Edition of Alessandro Scarlatti's Eraclea. Mem. Am. Translators Assn., Am. Literary Transl. Assn. Home and Office: 5748 W Brooks Rd Shepherd MI 48883-9202 E-mail: hermanapter@earthlink.net.

HERMAN, MARY MARGARET, neuropathologist; b. Plymouth, Wis., July 26, 1935; d. Elmer Fredolein and Esther Lydia (Bross) H.; m. Lucien Jules Rubinstein, Jan. 31, 1969. BS in Med. Sci., U. Wis., 1957, MD, 1960. Diplomate Nat. Bd. Med. Examiners, Am. Bd. Anatomic Pathology, Am. Bd. Neuropathology. Intern Mary Hitchcock Meml. Hosp., Hanover, N.H., 1960-61; resident in neurology U. Wis. Hosps., 1961-62; intern in pathology Yale U., New Haven, 1962-63, asst. resident in pathology, 1963-64, fellow neuropathology, 1964-65, rsch. assoc. pathology, 1967-68; fellow neuropathology Stanford U., Palo Alto, Calif., 1965-66, fellow, acting instr. neuropathology, 1966-67, asst. prof. pathology, 1967-74, assoc. prof., 1974-81; prof., co-dir. divsn. neuropathology U. Va. Sch. Medicine, Charlottesville, 1981-91, prof. clin. pathology, 1991-92; spl. expert neuropathology in clin. brain disorders br. NIMH, Washington, 1991-96, sr. staff scientist, 1996—; neuropathologist NIMH Brain Collection, 1992—, Stanley Fund Brain Collection, 1992—2002. Vis. asst. prof. Albert Einstein Coll. Medicine, Bronx, NY, 1971—72; mem. program project rev. com. Nat. Inst. Neurol. and Communicative Diseases NIH, 1973—77; cons. lab. svc. VA Hosp., Salem, Va., Ctrl. Va. Tng. Ctr., Lynchburg, 1982—92, ad hoc mem. pathology A study sect., 1986—91; cons. neuropathologist D.C. Med. Examiner's Office, Washington, 1992—, Med. Examiner's Office, No. Va. Dist., Fairfax, 2000—, D.C. Gen. Hosp., 1992—2002; mentor scientist NIH Intramural Rsch. Tng. award, Fogarty Fellows, Howard Hughes Med. Inst./MCPS/NIH student and tchr. internships program, Stanley Found. scholar's program. Mem. editl. bd.: Jour. Neuropathology and Exptl. Neurology, 1989—93, 2001—; contbr. over 180 articles to profl. jours. Recipient Rsch. Career Devel. award, NIH, 1967—72, Staff Recognition award, 2000—02, Faculty Devel. award, Merck Found., 1969. Mem. AAAS, AMA, Am. Assn. Anatomists (trust fund com.), Soc. Biol. Psychiatry, Am. Assn. Neuropathologists (Weil award 1974), Am. Soc. for Investigative Pathology, Soc. for Devel. Biology, Internat. Soc. Neuropathology, Am. Soc. Cell Biology (rsch. fellowship program, mentor scientist summer tchr. 1994), Internat. Acad. Pathology, Soc. In Vitro Biology, Soc. Neurosci. Achievements include research in neuropathology of serious mental disorders, neurodegeneration and aluminum neurotoxicity, and embryonal tumors of the CNS. Avocations: tennis, gardening, music. Home: 10008 Stedwick Rd Apt 304 Montgomery Village MD 20886-3718 Office: Clin Brain Disorders Br NIMH NIH Msc 4091 Bethesda MD 20892-4091 E-mail: mh230t@nih.gov.

HERMAN, RAYNA S. pharmaceutical consultant; b. Kokomo, Ind., Apr. 5, 1970; d. Ashok Kumar and Meena Kumar Sethi; m. Christopher R. Herman, May 14, 1994. BA in Chemistry, Ind. U., 1991; MBA, Washington U., 1996. Sales/mktg. staff Merck & Co., Inc., West Point, Pa., 1991-99; prin., owner Health Strategies Group, Lambertville, N.J., 1999—. Bd. dirs. Big Bros. Big Sisters, Montgomery County, 1999-2001; collegiate advisor Sigma Sigma Sigma, 2002-03; active Jr. League, 2002—.

HERMAN, RICHARD GERALD, research chemist, consultant, educator; b. Springville, N.Y., Mar. 11, 1944; s. Richard Arthur and Mary Ann (Hoffman) H.; m. Helen Lynn Ramer; children: Richard David, Sarah Louise, Jonathan Garett. BS, SUNY, Fredonia, 1966; PhD, Ohio U., 1972. Cert. secondary edn. tchr., N.Y. Postdoctoral fellow Lund (Sweden) U., 1972-73, Tex. A&M U., College Station, 1973-75; rsch. scientist I Lehigh U., Bethlehem, Pa., 1975-82, rsch. scientist II, 1982-89, prin. rsch. scientist, 1989—, interim dir. Zettlemoyer Ctr. for Surface Studies, 1989; exec. dir. Zettlemoyer Ctr. for Surface Studies, Bethlehem, Pa., 1995-2001. Adj. assoc. prof. dept. chemistry Lehigh U., 1980—81, adj. prof. dept. chem. engring., 2002—03. Editor: Catalytic Conversions of Synthesis Gas and Alcohols to Chemicals, 1984, Advances in Clean Fuel Technology and Control of Atmospheric Emissions, 2000, Catalytic Surface Centers and Mechanisms, 2002; contbg. author: New Trends in CO Activation, 1991, also others; contbr. over 110 articles to Catalysis, Chem. Engring. Sci., Inorganic Chemistry, Chem. Comm., also others. Tchr. Bible class Christ Evang. Luth. Ch., Schoenersville, Pa., 1981—, youth retreat asst., 1987-90; asst. coach Tri-Boro Youth Soccer, Whitehall, Pa., 1987-92. Recipient Outstanding Achievement award SUNY, Fredonia, 1991, Disting. Svc. award Tri-Boro Youth Soccer, 1995. Mem.: Ill. Mining Inst., Catalysis Soc. N.Am., Am. Chem. Soc. (chmn. Lehigh Valley chpt. 1989), Sigma Xi. Republican. Achievements include 5 patents for methanol synthesis, amine synthesis and water gas shift; development of new process for obtaining high cetane liquid fuels from alcohols; development of new catalytic process for low temperature abatement of NOx emissions. Office: Lehigh U Dept of Chemistry 6 E Packer Ave Bethlehem PA 18015-3102 E-mail: rgh1@lehigh.edu.

HERMAN, RICHARD J. marine life administrator; Mng. dir. Harbor Br. Oceanographic Inst., Inc., Fort Pierce, Fla., ocean R&D CEO, COO. Office: Harbor Br Oceanographic Inst Inc 5600 US Highway 1N Fort Pierce FL 34946-7320 Fax: 561-465-5415. E-mail: herman@hboi.edu.

HERMAN, R(OBERT) THOMAS, journalist; BA, Yale U., 1968. Intern Washington bur. Wall St. Jour., 1967, reporter N.Y. bur., 1968—69, reporter Atlanta bur., 1969—74, reporter N.Y. bur., 1974—76, reporter Asian edit., 1976—77, taxes, personal fin. and fin. markets reporter, 1978—. Co-author: The Flat-Tax Primer, others; contbr. columns in newspapers. Office: Wall St Jour 200 Liberty St New York NY 10281-1003

HERMAN, ROBERT JOHN, artist manager, producer, author, music industry advisor; b. Aug. 30, 1955; Stage hand, asst. house mgr., talent booker Ungano's/Ritz Theatre, S.I., N.Y.; talent booker, from mid-1970s; co-founder the factory a music club, mid 1970s; exec. v.p. Moviola/J&R Film Co., N.Y.C., 1980-92; founder, pres. Consol. Video Svcs., from 1992; campaigned to save Fillmore East Theatre, N.Y.C.; Am. music corr. BBC Radio, London; pres. Pinnacle Artists; exec. prodr. Pinnacle Artists Concert, Music, Film and Video Prodn. Concert promoter music prodns. Author articles and music revs. for various publs. Home: 15 Egbert Ave Staten Island NY 10310-2617 E-mail: pinnacleartists@yahoo.com.

HERMAN, ROBERT LEWIS, cork company executive; b. N.Y.C., July 16, 1927; s. Nat W. and Ruth (Stockton) H.; m. Susan Marie Volper, Dec. 10, 1966; children: Candia Ruth, William Neal. AB, Columbia U., 1948, BS, 1949. V.p. Joseph Samuels & Sons, Inc., Whippany, N.J, 1953-62; pres. Dependable Cork Co., Inc., Morristown, N.J, 1962—. Sr. chmn. Amorim Indsl. Solutions, Inc., Trevor, Wis., 1999—; bd. dirs. Concorco LDA, Lisbon, Portugal, Oporto, Portugal, Amorim Indsl. Solutions, LDA, Oporto, Portugal. Inventor Corticiera natural cork wallcovering. Comdr. C.E. Corps, USNR, 1949-53. Mem. N.J. Mfrs. Assn., Naval Res. Assn., U.S. C. of C., Navy League Club, Columbia U. Club, Princeton Club (N.Y.C.). Home: PO Box 1023 Morristown NJ 07962-1023 Office: PO Box 1102 Morristown NJ 07962-1102

HERMAN, ROBERT S. former state official, economist, educator; b. Newburgh, N.Y., Dec. 18, 1919; s. Bernard O. and Leona (Gottlieb) H.; m. Beatrice Hirsch, June 20, 1942; children: Gerald W., Arthur P. AB, Union Coll., 1941; MA, U. Cin., 1942; PhD, NYU, 1950. Lectr. Syracuse U., 1947-60; vis. prof. Russell Sage Coll., 1948-57, SUNY, 1960-62; vis. lectr. Econ. Devel. Inst., Washington, 1958-69; dir. research and fiscal policy div. budget N.Y. State Exec. Dept., Albany, 1950-63, dir. budget planning and devel., 1963, asst. budget dir., 1963-66; exec. dir. Commn. on Constl. Conv., 1966-67; exec. asst. to pres. N.Y. State Constl. Conv., 1967; dir. N.Y. Senate Com. on Higher Edn., 1968-72; prof. CUNY, 1968, SUNY, Albany, 1968-69, vis. prof., 1970—; prof. econs. and pub. adminstrn., chmn. dept. Union Coll., Schenectady, 1969-74; spl. adviser N.Y. State Assembly, 1974-80; chmn. Kennerman Assos., 1979-89, Ednl. Planning and Mgmt. Assocs., 1982-86. Spl. adv. N.Y. State Assembly, 1974-80; cons. UN; former U.S. adviser to, Venezuela, Peru, India, Greece, Ecuador, Nigeria, Turkey, Iran, Guatemala, Iran, U.S. State Dept. lectr. in field. Columnist: Overseas English, English Salon, 2002—; author: numerous poems; contbr. articles to profl. jours. Mem. adv. com. Nat. Planning Assn., Ctr. for Econ. Projections, Rand Corp., Ford Found.; adviser Assoc. Arts Councils, Inst. Man and Sci.; staff v.p. Nat. Conf. State Legislatures, 1974-99; dir. Traffic Safety Inst., bd. dirs. Albany Symphony Orchestra, 1999—. Recipient Charles Evans Hughes award for excellence in pub. svc., 1991, award for excellence in hwy. safety rsch. U.S. Dept. Transp., 1992. Mem.: Acad. Am. Poets, Phi Beta Kappa. Home: 2 Creekside Ct Slingerlands NY 12159-9335 Office: SUNY 80 Wolf Rd Albany NY 12205-2608 E-mail: hermsling@aol.com.

HERMAN, ROBERT STEPHEN, lawyer; b. Pitts., Aug. 1, 1954; s. Earl and Lena Herman; children: Kelsey, Brian, Kaley. Student, Tulane U., 1972-74; BA, U. Fla., 1976; JD, Loyola U., 1981. Bar: La. 1982, Tex. 1984, Mo. 1987. Assoc. Newman Drolla, New Orleans, 1982-84, Howard Abramson, Dallas, 1984-86, McDowell Rice, Kansas City, Mo., 1987-92; of counsel Kurlbaum Stoll, Kansas City, 1992-98; atty. Norris Keplinger & Herman LLC, Overland Park, Kans., 1998—2002; shareholder King Hershey, P.C., Kansas City, Mo., 2003—. Approved agt. The Bar Plan Title Ins. Co., Kansas City, 1997—; spkr. Paine Webber Fin. Planning Seminars, Overland Park, Kans., 1998—, Nat. Bus. Inst.; spkr. in field. Coach Blue Valley Soccer Club, Overland Park, 1993-98; scout leader Boy Scouts Am., Leawood, Kans., 1998. Mem. ABA, Nat. Network Estate and Fin. Planning Attys., The Midwest Estate Planning Inst., Kansas City Metro. Bar Assn. Avocations: tennis, golf, scuba, travel. Office: King Hershey PC 2345 Grand Blvd Ste 2100 Kansas City MO 64108

HERMAN, ROGER ELIOT, professional speaker, consultant, futurist, writer; b. San Francisco, Dec. 11, 1943; s. Carlton Martin and Estelle (Nadler) H.; m. Janet I. Meyer, June 22, 1969 (div. Feb. 1974); 1 child, Scott Philip; m. Sandra Jean Steckel, May 2, 1974 (div. Sept. 1997); Jennifer; m. Joyce L. Gioia, Dec. 27, 1997. BA in Sociology, Hiram Coll., 1969; MA in Pub. Adminstrn., Ohio State U., 1977. Cert. mgmt. cons.; cert. speaking profl. Mgr. Rayco, Inc., Kent, Ohio, 1970-72; pvt. practice sales Stow, Ohio, 1972-76; pub. service dir. City Hilliard, Ohio, 1976-78; city mgr. City Rittman, Ohio, 1978-80; pres. The Herman Group, Greensboro, N.C., 1980—. Author: Disaster Planning for Local Government, 1982, Emergency Operations Plan, 1983, The Process of Excelling, 1988, Keeping Good People, 1990, 99, Turbulence!, 1995, Lean & Meaningful, 1998, Signs of the Times, 1999, Workforce Stability, 2000, How to Become an Employer of Choice, 2000, How to Choose Your Next Employer, 2000, Impending Crisis, 2002; contbg. editor: Workforce and Workplace Trends, The Futurist mag.; contbr. mag. columns, articles to profl. jours. Commr. Ohio Boy Scouts Am., 1970, scoutmaster Texas (Ohio) Boy Scouts Am., 1966-70; mem. bd. visitors Hiram (Ohio) Coll., 2002--. Served with U.S. Army, 1965-68. Named Most Interesting Person In Northeast Ohio, Cleve. mag., 1981, named one of Outstanding Young Men Am., 1976, 77, 78, 79; recipient Arrowhead award Boy Scouts Am., Ohio, 1969. Fellow Inst. Mgmt. Cons. (cert. mgmt. cons., pres. Ohio chpt. 1991-95, nat. bd. dirs. 1996-2000, vice chair 1999-2000); mem. ASTD (chmn. profl. devel. 1987-88, program chmn. 1985-86, newsletter editor N.E. Ohio chpt. 1985-86), Nat. Spkrs. Assn. (cert. speaking profl.), World Future Soc., Assn. Profl. Futurists (charter mem.), Ohio Jaycees (Hilliard pres. 1976-77, Blue Chip Disting. Svc. award 1977), Toastmasters (dist. lt. gov. Texas, Ohio 1965-80, Able Toastmaster award 1969). Republican. Jewish. Avocations: writing, traveling. Office: The Herman Group Ste 403 3300 Battleground Ave Greensboro NC 27410-2447 E-mail: roger@herman.net.

HERMAN, SIDNEY N. lawyer; b. Chgo., May 14, 1953; s. Leonard M. and Suzanne (Nierman) H.; m. Meg Dobies. BA, Haverford Coll., 1975; JD, Northwestern U., 1978. Bar: Ill. 1978, U.S. Dist. Ct. (no. dist.) Ill. 1978, U.S. Ct. Appeals (7th cir.) 1982, U.S. Supreme Ct. 1983. Assoc. Kirkland & Ellis, Chgo., 1978-84, equity ptnr., 1984-93; founding ptnr. Bartlit Beck Herman Palenchar & Scott, Chgo., 1993—. Bd. dirs. Todd Shipyards Corp., Sigmatron Inc., Chgo., Global Material Techs., Chgo. Lawyers' Com. for Civil Rights Under Law, Inc.; mem. law bd. Northwestern U. Sch. Law. Articles editor Northwestern U. Law Rev. Trustee Francis W. Parker Sch.; bd. mem. Chgo. Lawyers' com. for Civil Rights Under Law. Mem. ABA, Ill. Bar Assn. Jewish. Office: Bartlit Beck Et Al Courthouse Pl 54 W Hubbard St Ste 300 Chicago IL 60610-4668

HERMAN, STEVEN DOUGLAS, cardiothoracic surgeon, educator; b. Budapest, Hungary, Apr. 7, 1945; came to U.S., 1949; s. Frank Elroy and Martha (Fischer) H.; m. Jacqueline Lee Forman, Aug. 14, 1983; children: Andrew Scott, Rebecca Sue. Student, Cornell U., 1962-64; BA, Johns Hopkins U., 1966, MD,

1969. Diplomate Am. Bd. Surgery, Am. Bd. Thoracic Surgery. Intern, resident, chief resident in surgery N.Y. Hosp.-Cornell Med. Ctr., N.Y.C., 1969-75, resident, chief resident in cardiovasc. and thoracic surgery, 1975-77; fellow in thoracic surgery Meml.-Sloan Kettering Cancer Ctr., N.Y.C., 1975; asst. prof., attending surgeon adult and pediatric cardiothoracic surgery Hahnemann Med. Sch. and Hosp., Phila., 1977-79; chief cardiovasc. and thoracic surgery St. Vincent's Med. Ctr., Bridgeport, Conn., 1979-88; attending cardiothoracic surgeon St. Michael Med. Ctr., Univ. Hosp., Newark, 1990—; attending thoracic surgery Mt. Sinai Med. Ctr., N.Y.C., 1997—; clin. asst. prof. surgery Univ. Medicine and Dentistry N.J., Newark, 1991-94, clin. assoc. prof., 1994—. Adj. assoc. prof. cardiothoracic surgery Mt. Sinai Med. Sch., 1997—; mem. cardiovasc. task force Health Sys. Agy., Fairfield County, Conn., 1980-81; mem. exec. com. St. Michael's Med. Ctr., 1993-96; presenter in field. Contbr. articles to profl. jours. Trustee Congregation Ahavath Achim, Fairfield, Conn., 1983-90, Hillel Acad. Sch., 1984-87, Aleh Found., Bnai Brak, Israel. Fellow ACS, Am. Coll. Cardiology, Coll. Physicians Phila.; mem. Am. Heart Assn. (mem. cardiovasc. coun., bd. dirs. Fairfield County br. 1980-83, program chmn. Ea. Fairfield County region 1985), N.Am. Soc. Pacing and Electrophysiology, N.J. Soc. Thoracic Surgeons, N.Y. Acad. Scis., N.J. Med. Soc., Essex County Med. Soc. (mem. spkrs. bur. com. 1992—), Soc. Thoracic Surgeons, Internat. Soc. Cardiothoracic Surgeons, Internat. Soc. Heart Transplantation, Internat. Assn. Cardiac Biol. Implants, Assn. Acad. Surgery, C. Walton and Richard C. Lillehei Surg. Soc., Johns Hopkins Med. and Surg. Soc., Gen. Thoracic Surg. Club. Republican. Jewish. Avocations: skiing, tennis, computers. Home: 160 E Linden Ave Englewood NJ 07631-3622 Office: 268 Dr Martin Luther King Newark NJ 07102

HERMAN, WILLIAM GEORGE, municipal government executive; b. West Chester, Pa., Sept. 2, 1956; s. Albert William Jr. and Beverly Lou (Marshall) H.; m. Mary Jo Batchelder, July 7, 1983; children: Brian William, Andrew Albert. Grad. H.S., Weare, N.H., 1974. Cert. pub. mgr. Reporter, photographer Union Leader Corp., Manchester, N.H., 1973-80; prin., owner Herman Assocs. P.R., Manchester, 1980-82; press sec. Gov. John H. Sununu, Concord, N.H., 1982-83; programs info. officer N.H. Divsn. Human Svcs., Concord, 1984-86, Divsn. Econ. Devel., Concord, 1986-92; pub. info. officer Fed. Emergency Mgmt., Boston, 1992—; town adminstr. Town of Milton, N.H., 1993-95, Town of New Durham, N.H., 1995—. Affiliate, cons. Mcpl. Resources, Inc., Meredith, 1995—; bd. dirs. N.H. Sch. Health Care Coalition, treas., 2002—, NH Pub. Works Mut. Aid Program, 1999—, N.H. Pub. Works Stds. and Tng. Coun., 2000—, vice-chmn., 2000-03, chmn., 2003—; mem. U.S. Selective Svc. #4, Merrimack County, 1999—. Vice chmn. U.S. Selective Svc. #10, Hillsborough County, 1982-98; chmn. Bd. Selectmen, Weare, N.H., 1984-96; commr., officer So. N.H. Planning Commn., Manchester, 1984-96; chmn. Concord Regional SW/RRC, Corcord, 1987—; dir. Greater Manchester ARC, 1988-94; trustee YMCA Camp Coniston, Grantham, N.H., 1989-93; dir. ARC Blood Svc., Dedham, Mass., 1989-98. Recipient George Washington honor medal Freedom Found., Valley Forge, Pa., 1973, Svc. award Town of Weare, 1996, Grassroots govt. leadership award Nat. Assn. Towns & Twps., Washington, 1991. Mem. Am. Acad. Cert. Pub. Mgrs. (ho. of dels. 2000—, chmn. integrated mktg. com. 2001—, bylaws com. 2001—, bd. dirs. mem.-at-large, 2002-), Internat. City/County Mgmt. Assn. (small cmtys. task force 1999-2001), N.H. Assn. Cert. Pub. Mgrs. (officer, sec. 1999-2001, treas. 2001—), N.H. Mcpl. Mgmt. Assn., N.H. Govt. Fin. Officers. Republican. Avocations: reading, travel, computers. Home: 203 Loudon Rd Unit 721 Concord NH 03301 Office: Town of New Durham PO Box 207 New Durham NH 03855-0207

HERMAN, WILLIAM ARTHUR, engineering and physics laboratory director; b. Washington, Mar. 9, 1947; s. William Jackson and Alma Rebecca (Wattwood) H. BSEE, George Washington U., 1968. Chief microwave sect. Southeastern Radiol. Health Lab., Montgomery, Ala., 1968-70; chief microwave measurements unit FDA, Rockville, Md., 1970-73, dep. chief. electromagnetics br., 1973-74, sr. engr. electromagnetics br., 1974-79, assoc. dir. divsn. electronic products, 1979-83, dir. divsn. phys. scis., 1983—. Mem. Interagy. Group on Sic. Performance Measures, Rockville, 1994 -96; staff mem. blue ribbon panel FDA, Washington, 1990; coord. scholar-in-residence program NSF/FDA, 2003; expert panelist NAS Symposium on Video Display Terminals and Vision, 1981, NIH Bioengring. Symposium: Bldg. the Future of Biology and Medicine, Instruments and Devices Panel, 1998; expert bioengring. panelist NSF, 1999—2003. Contbr. articles to profl. jours.; patentee in field. With USPHS, 1968-74. Mem. IEEE (sr.), World Future soc., Mensa, Tau Beta Pi, Amnesty Internat., Sigma Tau, Omicron Delta Kappa, Phi Eta Sigma, Alpha Theta Nu.

HERMAN, WILLIAM CHARLES, lawyer; b. N.Y.C., Nov. 6, 1935; s. Milton and Hortense (Rosenthal) H.; m. Elizabeth Leitner; children: Howard, Sarah Jane (dec.). BA, CCNY, 1958; LLB, Columbia U., 1959. Bar: N.Y. 1960, U.S. Dist. Ct. (so. and ea. dists.) 1964, U.S. Ct. Appeals (2d cir.) 1964, U.S. Supreme Ct. 1964. Assoc. Howard H. Spellman, N.Y.C., 1960-61; pvt. practice law N.Y.C., 1962-65; assoc. Gilbert S. Rosenthal, N.Y.C., 1965-70; ptnr. Rosenthal & Herman, N.Y.C., 1970-82, Rosenthal, Herman & Mantel, P.C., N.Y.C., 1982-94, Rosenthal & Herman, P.C., N.Y.C., 1994—2002, Herman Sloan Robarge & Sullivan, LLP, 2002—. Bd. dirs., Camphill Spl. Schs., Inc., Glenmoore, Pa., 1980—; bd. dirs. Camphill Found., Kimberton, Pa., 1987—; trustee Camphill Assn., N.Am., Copake, N.Y., 1982—. With U.S. Army, 1959-60. Fellow Am. Acad. Matrimonial Lawyers; mem. ABA, N.Y. State Bar Assn., N.Y. County Lawyers Assn. (bd. dirs. 1979-85, chmn. matrimonial law com. 1982-84), Am. Coll. Family Trial Lawyers (diplomate). Avocations: charitable activities, fishing, platform tennis. Home: 95 Lord Kitchner Rd New Rochelle NY 10804-2230 E-mail: wherman@hsrslaw.com.

HERMANCE, LYLE HERBERT, retired college official; b. Lincoln, Nebr., Dec. 10, 1939; s. Milo Lee Sr. and Amelia Henrietta (Schoneman) H.; m. Dorothy Kay Stanislav, June 12, 1960 (div.); children: Lane Alan, Lori Ann, Russell Joel; m. Janette Kay Sims, Oct. 11, 1986 (dec.). BS, U. Nebr., 1964, MS, 1970. Cert. agr. edn. tchr., Nebr. Tchr. vocat. agr. and indsl. arts Emerson (Nebr.)-Hubbard Pub. Schs., 1964; tchr. vocat. agr. Waverly (Nebr.) Pub. Schs., 1964-79, chmn. dept. vocat. edn., 1973-79; coord. adult agr. program area cmty. svcs. div. S.E. C.C., Lincoln, 1979—, dir. Adult Edn. Ctrs. area cmty. svcs. div., 1991—, interim dir. div., 1992-94, dir. div., 1994-96, dir. continuing edn., 1996—2002; vol. tng. engr. Folsom Children's 200 and Bot. Garden, 2003—. Rep. Nebr. Turkey Coun., 1968-72, Nebr. Grassland and Forage Coun., 1969—; nat. coord. computers in agr. demonstration contest Future Farmers Am. 1990-93; mem. adult edn. task force Nat. Coun. for Argl. Edn., 1991—; mem. adv. coun. agrl. edn. dept. U. Nebr., 1987—; mem. S.E. Rsch. and Ext. Ctr. adv. team Inst. Agr. and Natural Resources, 1992—; asst. supt. Future Farmers Am. div. sheep show Nebr. State Fair, 1988-90, supt., 1990—; pres. Nebr. Vocat. Agrl. Found., 1970-71, bd. dirs., 1991-92. Mem. Lancaster County Ext. Bd., 1990—95, pres., 1992—95; mem. Nebr. affiliate task force Am. Heart Assn., 1992—98; mem. spl. com. on agrl. edn. Nebr. Coun. Vocat. Edn., 1986—88; charter bd. dirs., advisor Nebr. Agrl. Leadership Coun., Inc., 1980—82; charter mem. Nebr. Coalition for Agrl. Fin. Mgmt. Edn., 1990—99, state co-chmn., 1991—99; bd. dirs. Nebr. Assn. Vocat. Indsl. Clubs Am., 1995—2000, state coord. leadership and skills contest, 1996—2000; Bd. dirs. Lancaster County Pub. Nursing Adv. Com., 1972—76. Recipient hon. degree Future Farmers Am., 1970, 71, 94, Nebr. Disting. Svc. award, 1994, Nebr. Lifetime Svc. award, 1996, Disting. Svc. award Nat. Farm Ranch Bus. Mgmt. Edn. Assn., 1997. Mem.: Nebr. Agrl. Educators Assn., Am. Vocat. Assn., Nat. Assn. Agrl. Educators, Assn. for Career and Tech. Edn., Nebr. Assn. for Adult Agrl. Educators (charter, pres. 1988-89)), Nat. Farm Ranch Bus. mgmt. Edn. Assn., Nebr. Vocat. Assn., Nebr. Vocat. Agrl. Assn. ((offices: dist. chmn. 1966-67, 87-89, 97-2001, state pres. 68-69), exec. dir. 2002—), Lancaster County Agrl. Soc., Waverly Edn. Assn., Nebr. Edn. Assn., NEA, Kiwanis ((pres. elect 2001-02)). Home: 13305 N 112th St Lincoln NE 68517-9769

HERMANCE, JR. MYRON E. conductor, educator; b. Hudson, Ny, May 7, 1928; s. Myron Erastus and Thelma Evelyn Hermance; m. Alicia Van Zoeren Hermance, June 21, 1952; children: Susan Adella Hermance, Dirk Edward Hermance, Melanie Jo Hermance, Peter Alan Hermance, Gay Marie Hermance, Rhonda Kay Hermance, Philip Jon Hermance. MusM, Ind. U., 1956; BA, Hope Coll., 1950. Cert. Secondary Teaching Mich., 1950, Music Education NY State, 1961. Profl. vocalist chs., colls. and theater, Western Mich. and Ea. NY, 1952—; pvt. voice educator NY, 1952—; vocal and instrumental educator Fremont (Mich.) H.S., 1952—57; music supr. Holton (Mich.) Pub. Schs., 1957—60; condr., pvt. educator chs., sr. citizen homes and cmty. theatre, Albany, NY, 1960—; vocal music educator Schenectady (NY) City Schools, 1960—87. Orchestral condr. Albany and Schenectady Sr. Ctrs., 1994—; ch. music ministry Ref. Chs., Schenectady and Albany, NY, Congl. Ch., Fremont, Mich., 1952—60. Recipient Teacher's Performance Inst., Rockefeller Found., Oberlin Coll., 1968. Mem.: NY State Sch. Music Assn. (all-state voice judge 1997—), Music Educators Nat. Conf., NY State Fedn. Tchrs., Nat. Assn. Tchrs. of Singing. Democrat-Npl. Reformed Church In America. Avocations: lay preacher, civil war historian, geneologist, theology, artist. Home: 25 Alvey Street Schenectady NY 12304

HERMAND, JOST, German language educator; b. Kassel, Germany, Apr. 11, 1930; came to U.S., 1958; s. Heinz and Annelies Hermand; m. Elisabeth Jagenburg, Mar. 16, 1956. Dr phil, U. Marburg, Germany, 1955, Staatsexamen, 1956. Asst. prof. German U. Wis., Madison, 1958-61, assoc. prof., 1962-63, prof., 1964-67, rsch. prof., 1968—. Mem. Saxon Acad. Sci., Leipzig, Germany, 1985; hon. prof. Humboldt U., Berlin, 2003. Author: Cultural History of Germany, 8 vols., 1959-88, A Hitler Youth in Poland, 1994, Geschichte des Germanistik, 1994. Fellow Am. Coun. Learned Socs., 1963, Internationales Kulturwissenschaftliches Institut, Vienna, 1994, 97.

HERMAN-GIDDENS, GREGORY, lawyer; b. Birmingham, Ala., Aug. 8, 1961; BA, U. N.C., 1984; JD, Tulane U., 1988; LLM in Estate Planning, U. Miami, 1993. Bar: N.C. 1988, U.S. Dist. Ct. (mid. dist.) N.C. 1988, Fla. 1992, U.S. Tax Ct. 2001, U.S. Supreme Ct. 1998, U.S. Tax Ct. 2001; cert. specialist in estate planning and probate law, N.C. State Bar Bd. Legal Specialization; grad. leadership triangle program 1996. Assoc. N. Joanne Foil, Atty. at Law, Durham, N.C., 1988-92, Catalano, Fisher, Gregory & Crown, Chartered, Naples, Fla., 1993, Northen, Blue, Rooks, Thibaut, Anderson & Woods, L.L.P., Chapel Hill, N.C., 1994-96; pvt. practice Chapel Hill, 1996—. Profl. adv. com. Triangle Cmty. Found., 1999—. Mem. Chapel Hill Bd. Adjustment, 1989—92; bd. dirs. Friends of Chapel Hill Sr.Ctr., 1994—97; mem. Orange County Adv. Bd. on Aging, 1994—97, vice chair, 1996—97; treas., bd. dirs. Orange County Literacy Coun., Carrboro, NC, 1994—98. Mem.: Durham/Orange Estate Planning Coun., Nat. Acad. Elder Law Attys., N.C. Bar Assn. (career devel. com. young lawyers divsn. 1990—91, law and aging com. young lawyers divsn. 1994—98, dir. young lawyers divsn. 1997—98, endowment com. 1997—, elder law sect. coun. 1998—2001, newsletter editor 2001—), ABA (probate and trust sect. 1996—, coms. on stds. of tax practice and tax practice mgmt. of tax sect., coms. on lifetime and testamentary charitable gift planning, com. on planning for execs. and profls. of real property), Psi Chi, Phi Beta Kappa. Office: 1829 E Franklin St Ste 700D Chapel Hill NC 27514-5867 E-mail: ghgiddens@trust-specialist.com.

HERMANIES, JOHN HANS, retired lawyer; b. Aug. 19, 1922; s. John and Lucia (Eckstein) H.; m. Dorothy Jean Steinbrecher, Jan. 3, 1953 AB, Pa. State U., 1944; JD, U. Cin., 1948, D of Law (hon.), 1992. Bar: Ohio 1948. Atty. Indsl. Commn. Ohio, 1948-50; asst. atty. gen. State of Ohio, 1951-57, asst. to gov., 1957-59; ptnr. Hermanies & Major (formerly Beall, Hermanies, Bortz & Major), Cin., 1958-99; mem. bd. grievances and discipline Supreme Ct. Ohio, 1976-82; ret., 1999. Mem. Ohio Bd. Bar Examiners, 1963-68. Mem. Southwest Ohio Regional Transit Authority, 1973-76; trustee U. Cin, 1977-92, Found. Bd., 1992-99, trustee emeritus, 1999—; mem. bd. elections Hamilton County, Ohio, 1984-88; chmn. exec. com. Hamilton County Rep. Party, 1974-88. With USMC, WWII. Mem. ABA, Ohio Bar Assn., Cin. Bar Assn., Queen City Club, Highland Country Club, Hyde Park Golf and Country Club. Home: 1201 Edgecliff Pl Cincinnati OH 45206-2847

HERMANN, ALBERT JOSEPH, oceanographer; b. Pittsfield, Mass., July 3, 1954; s. Gerald Paul and Aleta Marjorie Hermann; m. Theresa Marie Thees, Aug. 24, 1985; 1 child, Sophia. B.Sc. Engring. (Ecol. Modeling), Cornell U., Ithaca, NY, 1977; MSc in Systems Ecology, U. of Fla., Gainesville, 1980; PhD in Oceanography, U. of Wash., Seattle, 1988. Postdoctoral investigator Woods Hole Oceanog. Instn., Falmouth, Mass., 1989—91; oceanographer JISAO/Univ. Wash., Seattle, 1991—. Mem.: Am. Geophys. Union, Am. Meterol. Soc. Achievements include research in numerical modeling of coastal circulation and biology; low-cost virtual reality techniques for data visualization. Avocations: hand percussion, skiing. Office: JISAO/Pacif Marine Environ Lab 7600 Sand Point Way NE Seattle WA 98115 Business E-Mail: hermann@pmel.noaa.gov.

HERMANN, ALLEN MAX, physics educator; b. New Orleans, July 17, 1938; s. Edward Frederick and Miriam (Davidson) H.; m. Leonora Christopher, May 19, 1979 ; children: Miriam, Mary, Neil, Scott. BS with honors in Physics, Loyola U., New Orleans, 1960; MS in Physics, U. Notre Dame, 1962; PhD in Physics, Tex. A&M U., 1965. Sr. research scientist Jet Propulsion Lab, Pasadena, Calif., 1965-67, tech. mgr., 1985-86; asst. prof. physics Tulane U., New Orleans, 1967-70, assoc. prof. physics, 1970-75, prof. physics, 1975-81; task mgr. Solar Energy Research Inst., Golden, Colo., 1980-85; prof., chmn. dept. physics U. Ark., Fayetteville, 1986-89, Disting. prof., 1989; prof. dept. physics U. Colo., Boulder, 1990—. Cons. Jet Propulsion Lab., 1978-81, 86-87, NASA-Lewis Rsch. Ctr., Cleve., 1978-80, Cardiac Pacemakers Inc., Mpls., 1976-79, Radiation Monitoring Devices, Newton, Mass., 1990-93, Superconducting Core Techs., Denver, 1989-95, Sumitomo Electric Industries, Osaka, Japan, 1991-98, MV Sys., Inc., Golden, 1999—. Founding co-editor Applied Physics Communication; editor: Applied Physics Book Series; contbr. numerous articles to profl. jours. Bd. dirs. Colo. Assn. Retarded Citizens, Denver, 1983-85. Recipient NASA Outstanding Achievement award 1970, 72, Disting. Scientist award Am. Assn. Physics Tchrs., 1987; named Hero, State of Ark., Ark. Times mag.; named Person of the Yr., Superconductivity Week, 1989; elected to Acad. Disting. Grads., Coll. Sci., Tex. A&M U., 1999. Fellow Am. Phys. Soc.; mem. IEEE (sr.), Materials Rsch. Soc. Home: 2704 Lookout View Dr Golden CO 80401-2520 Office: U Colo PO Box 390 Boulder CO 80309-0390

HERMANN, DONALD HAROLD JAMES, lawyer, educator; b. Southgate, Ky., Apr. 6, 1943; s. Albert Joseph and Helen Marie (Snow) H. AB (George E. Gamble Honors scholar), Stanford U., 1965; JD, Columbia U., 1968; LLM, Harvard U., 1974; MA, Northwestern U., 1979, PhD, 1981; MA in Art History, Sch. Art Inst. Chgo., 1993; MLA, U. Chgo., 2001. Bar: Ariz. 1968, Wash. 1969, Ky. 1971, Ill. 1972, U.S. Supreme Ct. 1974. Mem. staff, directorate devel. plans U.S. Dept. Def., 1964-65; With Legis. Drafting Research Fund, Columbia U., 1966-68; asst. dean Columbia Coll., 1967-68; mem. faculty U. Wash., Seattle, 1968-71, U. Ky., Lexington, 1971-72, DePaul U., 1972—, prof. law and philosophy, 1978—, dir. acad. programs and interdisciplinary study, 1975-76, assoc. dean, 1975-78, dir. Health Law Inst., 1985—2000; lectr. dept. philosophy Northwestern U., 1979-81; counsel DeWolfe, Poynton & Stevens, 1984-89. Vis. prof. Washington U., St. Louis, 1974, U. Brazilia, 1976, U. P.R. Sch. Law, 1993; lectr. law Am. Soc. Found., 1975-78, Sch. Edn. Northwestern U., 1974-76, Christ Coll. Cambridge (Eng.) U., 1977, U. Athens, 1980; vis. scholar U. N.D., 1983; mem. NEH seminar on property and rights Stanford U., 1981; participant law and econs. program U. Rochester, 1974; mem. faculty summer seminar in law and humanities UCLA, 1978; Bicentennial Fellow of U.S. Constitution Claremont Coll., 1986; Law and Medicine fellow Cleve. Clinic., 1990; bd. dirs. Coun. Legal Edn. Opportunity, Ohio Valley Consortium, 1972, Ill. Bar Automated Rsch. Corp., 1975-81, Criminal Law Consortium Cook County, Ill., 1977-80; cons. Adminstrv. Office Ill. Cts., 1975-90; reporter cons. Ill. Jud. Conf., 1972-90; mem. Ctr. for Law Focused Edn., Chgo., 1977-81; faculty Instituto Superiore Internazionale Di Science Criminali, Siracusa, Italy, 1978-82; cons. Commerce Fedn., State of São Paulo, Brazil, 1975; residential scholar Christ Ch., Oxford, 1999. Editor: Jour. of Health and Hosp. Law, 1986-96, DePaul Jour. Healthcare Law, 1996—, AIDS Monograph Series, 1987—. Mem. Cook County States Atty. Task Force on Gay and Lesbian Issues, 1990—, Contemporary Arts Coun. Chgo., 1999—; bd. dirs. Ctr. Ch.-State Studies, 1982—, Horizons Cmty. Svcs., 1985—88, Chgo. Area AIDS Task Force, 1987—90, Howard Brown Health Ctr., 1994—; v.p. Inst. Genetics, Law and Ethics, Ill. Masonic Hosp., 1993—2000; trustee 860 N. Lakeshore Trust, Chgo., 1993—95; bd. visitors Oriental Inst. U. Chgo., 1995—; co-chair parity and inclusion com. Ill. HIV Prevention Cmty. Group Ill. Dept. Pub. Health; dir. Inst. Genetics, Law and Ethics, Ill. Masonic Hosp., 1993—2000; bd. dirs. Gerber-Hart Libr. and Archives, Mostly Music of Chgo., 1998—2001; mem. scholars' group ethics and med. rsch. NIH/U. Ill. Med. Sch. John Noble fellow Columbia U., 1968, Internat. fellow, NEH fellow, Law and Humanities fellow U. Chgo, 1975-76, Law and Humanities fellow Harvard U., 1973-74, Northwestern U., 1978-82, Criticism and Theory fellow Stanford U. 1981, NEH fellow Cornell U., 1982, Judicial fellow U.S. Supreme Ct., 1983-84, U. Ill. fellow med. ethids rsch. group; Dean's scholar Columbia U., 1968, Univ. scholar Northwestern U., 1979. Mem.: ABA, Am. Inn of Ct. (Abraham Lincolm Marowitz chpt.), Chgo. Coun. Fgn. Rels., Ill. Assn. Hosp. Attys., Am. Acad. Healthcare Attys., Am. Assn. Law Schs. (del., sect. chmn., chmn. sect. on jurisprudence), Soc. Am. Law Tchrs., Internat. Penal Law Soc., Soc. Writers on Legal Subjects, Soc. Phenomenology and Existential Philosophy, Soc. Bus. Ethics, Am. Philos. Assn., Am. Judicature Soc., Nat. Health Lawyers Assn., Internat. Assn. Philosophy of Law and Soc., Am. Soc. Polit. and Legal Philosophy, Am. Soc. Law, Medicine and Ethics, Am. Law Inst., Am. Acad. Polit. and Social Sic., Chgo. Bar Assn., Ill. Bar Assn., Soc. Contemporary Art Art Inst. Chgo., Evanston Hist. Soc., Northwestern U. Alumni Assn., Chgo. Literary Soc., Quadrangle Players, Renaissance Soc. (bd. dirs. 1995—), Lawyers Club Chgo., Arts Club Chgo., Cliff Dwellers Club, Tavern Club, Quadrangle Club, University Club, Hasty Pudding Club, Signet Club Harvard. Episcopalian.

HERMANN, EDWARD ROBERT, health engineer, educator, writer, consultant, hygicologist; b. Newport, Ky., Oct. 9, 1920; s. Joseph George and Beatrice Bluebell (Beyland) H.; m. Eleanor Marie Hill, June 10, 1946; children: Mary, Carolyn, Catherine, Georgia, Joseph, Michael, John. BSCE, U. Ky., 1942; SM in Sanitary Engring., MIT, 1949; CE, U. Ky., 1953; PhD in Engring. and Health Scis., U. Tex., 1957. Lic. profl. engr., Ill.; lic. indsl. hygienist, Ill.; diplomate Am. Acad. Environ. Engrs., Am. Bd. Indsl. Hygiene. Jr. engr. TVA, Knoxville, 1942; instr. U. Ky., 1943-44; pub. health engr. U.S. Atomic Energy Commn., Los Alamos, N.Mex., 1950-51, chief sanitary engr., chief pub. health and sanitation, 1951-54; rsch. engr. U. Tex., 1954-57; indsl. health engr. Humble Oil & Refining Co., 1957-62; from assoc. to prof. Northwestern U., Evanston, Ill., 1963-75; prof. occupl. and environ. medicine, environ. and occupl. health scis., dir. indsl. hygiene programs U. Ill., Chgo., 1975-88, prof. emeritus Sch. Pub. Health, 1988—. Rsch. advisor, litigation cons., expert witness in field; judge sch. sci. fairs; mem. space sci. bd. on mgmt. waste in space NAS, also others; chmn. subcom. on toxicology and occupational health; evaluator, reviewer grad. indsl. hygiene programs in U.S. univs. for Accreditation Bd. for Engring. and Tech., 1991—; keynote spkr. profl. conf. indsl. hygiene Am. Acad. Indsl. Hygiene, Balt., 1997. Contbr. book chpts. and articles to profl. jours. Pres. Bayside Ter. Civic Orgn.; pres. bd. dirs. Bayshore Mcpl. Utility Dist., Harris County, Tex.; mem. adv. com. Ill. Gov.'s Safety and Edn. Commn.; contbr. Pres. Kennedy's Energy Study Group; chmn. subcom. on toxicology and occupational health. With USN, 1944-46; lt. comdr. USPHS, 1956, capt. Res., 1976—. Recipient award Am. Water Works Assn. Resources Div., 1960, award Mich. Indsl. Hygiene Soc., 1964, merit award Chgo. Tech. Socs. Coun., 1978, award Borden Found., 1988, Outstanding Civil Engring. Alumnus award U. Ky., 1995, Donald Eddy Cummings Meml. award. Fellow AAAS, ASCE, APHA, Am. Indsl. Hygiene Assn. (Outstanding Tech. Publ. award 2000); mem. Am. Conf. Gov. Indsl. Hygienists (emeritus), Chgo. Acad. Tech., Water Environ. Fedn. (Harrison Prescott Eddy medal 1959, Radebaugh award Ctrl. States 1976), Sigma Xi, Tau Beta Pi. Democrat. Roman Catholic. Avocations: sailing, investing, grandchildren, great grandchildren, aerobatic kites. Home: 117 Church Rd Winnetka IL 60093-3903

HERMANN, JOHN ROBERT, political science educator; b. N.Y.C., Apr. 6, 1966; s. Arthur L. and Susan (Leibow) H.; m. Elizabeth H. Minnella, June 24, 1990 (div. Mar. 1996); m. Ming Hua Lee, Sept. 5, 1999. BA in Polit. Sci., Wash. U., 1989; PhD in Polit. Sci., Emory U., 1995. Legal asst. Legal Aid Soc., N.Y.C., 1989-90; account mgr. Gutenberg Printing, N.Y.C., 1990-91; prof. Trinity U., San Antonio, 1995—; aerobics instr. Racquetball & Fitness, San Antonio, 1997—2002. Polit. cons. KPOZ Radio AM, San Antonio, 1997; sec. Am. polit. sci. profl. rev., assoc. Allyn Bacon, Boston, 1996—. Contbr. chpts. to books, articles to profl. jours., including Am. Politics Quar., Judicature, Social Sci. Jour., Social Sci. Quar. Mem. Nat. Am. Rights, Boulder, 1995—; mem. exec. faculty devel. com. Trinity U., San Antonio, 1997. Recipient scholarship Emory U., 1991-95, grantee, 1993-94; grantee Am. Bar Found., 1993, Trinity U., 1995, 97. Mem. Am. Polit. Sci. Assn. (mem. steering com. Native Am. sect. 1996—), Am. Judicature Soc., Pre-Law Soc., Sigma Theta Tau. Democrat. Home: 3122 Fall Creek Dr San Antonio TX 78247 Office: Trinity U Dept Polit Sci 715 Stadium Dr San Antonio TX 78212-7200 E-mail: jhermann@trinity.edu.

HERMANN, MILDRED L. artist; b. Bklyn., Mar. 8, 1920; d. Philip and May Atkin Lipskin; m. Arthur E. Hermann, June 27, 1942; children: Laurie Schwartzer, Elizabeth Schoenfeld, Jane Simons. Student, Bklyn. Coll., 1937—40, Artists in Am. Sch. Painting. One-woman shows include over 21 solo shows, Represented in permanent collections Albright-Knox Gallery, Buffalo, N.Y., Norton Mus. Art, West Palm Beach, Fla. Recipient Childe Hassam Purchase award, Am. Acad. Arts and Letters, 1978. Mem.: Audubon Artists (Mixed Media Painting award 1981), Nat. Assn. Women Artists.

HERMANN, NAOMI BASEL, librarian, interior decorator; b. N.Y.C., Feb. 12, 1918; d. Alexander and Rebecca (Deinard) Basel; m. Henry I. Almour, June 26, 1938 (dec.); 1 child, Jay Alexander; m. Stanford Leland Hermann, Dec. 20, 1951. BS in Edn., NYU, 1937, MS in Psychology, 1939; MLS, Columbia U., 1963; postgrad., Vassar Coll., Cornell U., Hunter Coll. Newspaper reporter Times Picayune, New Orleans, 1935; tchr. gifted children N.Y.C. Schs., 1946-58; libr. supr. 22 elem., jr. and sr. high schs., N.Y.C., 1958-72; libr. Brandeis High Sch., 1972-75. Interior decorator, pvt. practice, N.Y.C., 1946—; instr. Children's Literature, N.Y.C. Bd. Edn., 1969-73; libr. examiner, N.Y.C. Bd. of Edn., 1967-72. Pres. Hadassah, N.Y.C., 1939-41, life mem.; life mem. Coun. Jewish Women, 1974—; charter mem. Eleanor Roosevelt Fund for Women and Girls; established adult library Temple Beth El, Boca Raton, Fla. Mem. AAUW (pres. Boca Raton chpt. 1987-89), Boca Raton Noontime Ladies Club (pres.). Avocations: world travel, bridge, music, finance. Home: 23343 Blue Water Cir B309 Boca Raton FL 33433

HERMANN, PAUL DAVID, retired association executive; b. Chgo., Feb. 1, 1925; s. Edgar Paul and Marjory (Alexander) H.; m. Joan Louise Mullin, Nov. 10, 1948; children: Bruce Phillip, Susan Marie. Student, Lawrence U., 1942-45; BS in Bus. Adminstrn, Northwestern U., 1948. Cert. assn. exec. Asst. dir. news bur. Ill. Inst. Tech., Chgo., 1945-48; editor Constrn. Equipment News, Chgo., 1948-49; exec. v.p. Assn. Equipment Distbrs., Oak Brook, Ill., 1950-90; pres. AED Research & Services Corp., 1974-90. Contbr. articles on assn. mgmt. to various jours. Mem. Am. Soc. Assn. Execs. (hon., pres. 1974, Key award 1985), Chgo. Soc. Assn. Execs. (life, pres. 1969), U.S. C. of C. (dir. 1980-82, chmn. assn. com. 1981-86, small bus. council 1976-82), Nat. Chamber Alliance for Politics (adv. council 1978-82), Inst. Orgn. Mgmt. (mem. bd. regents 1969-72), Delta Tau Delta (Alumni Achievement award 1982) Home: 411 S Prospect St Galena IL 61036-2159 E-mail: pdh@galenalink.com.

HERMANN, PHILIP J. lawyer; b. Cleve., Sept. 17, 1916; s. Isadore and Gazella (Gross) H.; m. Cecilia Alexander, Dec. 28, 1945; children: Gary, Ann. Student, Hiram Coll., 1935-37; BA, Ohio State U., 1939; JD, Western Res. U., 1942. Bar: Ohio 1942. With Hermann Cahn & Schneider and predecessors, Cleve., 1946 86. Founder, former chmn. bd. Jury Verdict Rsch., Cleve.; pres. Legal Info. Pubs. Author: 1956, Better Settlements Through Leverage, 1965, Do You Need a Lawyer?, 1980, Better, Earlier Settlements through Economic Leverage, 1989, Injured? How to Get All the Money You Deserve, 1990, The 96 Billion Dollar Game: You are Losing, 1993, How to Select Competent Cost-effective Legal Counsel, 1993, Profit With the Right Lawyer, I Was Raised by a St. Bernard, 2003; contbr. articles to profl. jours. Served to lt. comdr. USNR, 1942-46, PTO. Mem. ABA (past vice chmn. casualty law com., past chmn. use of modern tech. com.), Ohio Bar Assn. (past chmn. ins. com., past chmn. fed. ct. com., past mem. ho. of dels.), Cleve. Bar Assn. (past chmn. membership com.), Am. Law Firm Assn. (past chmn. bd.), Fedn. Ins. Counsel. Home: Hunters Run Golf & Tennis Club 34F Southport Ln Boynton Beach FL 33436-6429 *Being what some people label "a perfectionist" is not easy and certainly not popular. It takes time and effort to collect information, to analyze it, to apply these to decisions and to insist upon careful work, but in the long run it is rewarding.*

HERMANN, ROBERT BELL, physical chemist, consultant; b. Bellevue, Pa., Dec. 12, 1930; s. Gustave Adolph and Alida Hermann; m. Phyllis Ann Halley, Aug. 7, 1958 (div. Feb. 1982); children: Deborah, David, Stephen; m. Carol Sue Lester, June 12, 1985. BS in Chemistry, U. Mich., 1953; MS, Wayne State U.,

1960, PhD, 1962. Organic chemist Parke-Davis & Co., Detroit, 1953-58; NSF postdoctoral fellow U. Wis., Madison, 1962-63; postdoctoral fellow Ill. Inst. Tech., Chgo., 1963-64; computational chemist Eli Lilly & Co., Indpls., 1964-93. Vis. prof. Ind. U.-Purdue U. Ind., Indpls., 1994—; cons. Eli Lilly & Co., 1994—. Contbr. articles to profl. jours. Presbyterian. Achievements include research of relationship between molecular surface area and solubility especially with regard to hyrdophobic interactions; patent for inhibitors of phospholipase A2. Office: Ind U Purdue U Indpls Dept Chemistry 402 N Blackford St Indianapolis IN 46202-3217 E-mail: herm@lilly.com.

HERMANN, ROBERT EWALD, surgeon; b. Highland, Ill., Jan. 28, 1929; s. Ewald E. and Erna (Pabst) H.; m. Barbara Bower, Aug. 23, 1952 (dec. Aug. 1980); m. Polly Dreher, Mar. 8, 1986; childrn: Robert Jr., Barry, Monty. AB cum laude, Harvard U., 1950; MD, Washington U., St. Louis, 1954. Diplomate Am. Bd. Surgery. Intern, resident Univ. Hosps., Cleve., 1954-61; chmn. gen. surgery Cleve. Clinic, 1969-94, emeritus cons. dept. gen. surgery, 1994—; clin. prof. surgery Case Western Res. Sch. Medicine, Cleve., 1970—. Dir. Am. Bd. Surgery, Phila., 1975-81; mem. Residency Rev. Com., Chgo., 1975-81. Author: Surgery of Gallbladder, Bile Ducts, Pancreas, 1979, Surgical Practice of Cleveland Clinic, 1985; contbr. over 180 articles to med. jours., 53 chpts. to books. Trustee Cleve. Clinic Found., 1976-77. Capt. M.C. U.S. Army, 1956-57. Recipient Roswell Park Gold medal Buffalo Surg. Soc., 1993. Mem. ACS (gov. 1981-87, v.p. 1996-97, Disting. Svc. award 1994), Am. Surg. Soc., German Surg. Soc. (hon.), Internat. Surg. Soc., Internat. Coll. Surgeons (hon.), Soc. Surg. Oncology, Soc. Surgery Alimenatary Tract (pres. 1988-89), Assn. Program Dirs. Surgery (pres. 1979-81), Ea. Surg. Soc. (pres. 1985-86), Pan-Pacific Surg. Assn. (v.p. 1991-93), Joint Commn. on Accreditation of Healthcare Orgns. (bd. commrs. 1997-2002). Republican. Avocations: tennis, golf, sailing, music. Home: 1 Bratenahl Pl Apt 1403 Bratenahl OH 44108-1156 Office: Cleve Clinic A-80 9500 Euclid Ave Cleveland OH 44195-0001 E-mail: rhermannmd@aol.com.

HERMANN, ROBERT JAY, manufacturing company engineering executive, consultant; b. Sheldahl, Iowa, Apr. 6, 1933; s. John and Ellen Melinda (Ericson) H.; m. Darlene Velda Lowman, Mar. 20, 1954; children: Scott Alan, Sherie Lynn. BSEE, Iowa State U., 1954, MSEE, 1959, PhD, 1963. Dep. dir. research and engring. Nat. Security Agy., Ft. Meade, Md., 1973-75; spl. asst. to supreme allied comr. Europe SHAPE, Casteau, Belgium, 1975-77; dep. under sec. of def. for research and engring. Dept. Def., Washington, 1977-79, asst. sec. of Air Force for research, devel. and logistics, 1979-81; dir. Nat. Reconnaissance, 1979-81; spl. asst. for intelligence to under sec. of def. for research engring. Dept. Def., Washington, 1981-82; v.p. systems tech. and analysis United Techs., Hartford, Conn., 1982-84, v.p. advanced systems def. and space group, 1984-87, v.p. sci. and tech., 1987-92, sr. v.p. sci. and tech., 1992-98; sr. ptnr. Global Tech. Partners, LLC, 1998—. Cons. Def. Sci. Bd.; mem. vis. com. advanced tech. Nat. Inst. Stds. and Tech., 1992-97; mem. Pres. Fgn. Intelligence Adv. Bd., 1993-01; mem. commn. on phys. scis., math. and applications NRC, 1993-98; bd. dirs. Draper Labs., 1992-2001, Am. Nat. Stds. Inst., 1994-2002. 1st lt. USAF, 1955-57. Recipient Arthur Fleming Washington Jaycees, 1972; recipient Nat. Capital Nat. Capital Area Architects and Engrs., Washington, 1967, Air Force Disting. Service medal USAF, Washington, 1980, Disting. Grad. award Iowa State U., 1995. Mem. NAE, AIAA, Armed Forces Comms. and Electronics Assn. (bd. dirs. 1979-83), Security Affairs Support Assn. (pres. 1983-86, award 1994), Navy League (chmn. indsl. exec. bd. 1989). Home: 5 Stonepost Simsbury CT 06070-2511 Office: Global Tech Ptnrs LLC 14th Fl 100 Pearl St Hartford CT 06103 E-mail: rjhinct@aol.com.

HERMANN, WILLIAM M. finance company executive; Part-time positions Plante and Moran, Grand Rapids, Mich., 1971, various positions, 1972—81, ptnr., 1981, office mng. ptnr. Ann Arbor, 1982, group mng. ptnr., 1995—2000, mng. ptnr., 2000—. Mem.: Mich Assn. CPA, Inst. CPAs. Office: Plante & Moran Bridgewater Pl 333 Bridge St NW Ste 600 Grand Rapids MI 49504 Office Fax: 616-774-0702.

HERMANOWICZ, JOSEPH CRAIG, sociologist, educator; b. Normal, Ill., Mar. 11, 1969; m. Erika Jean Thorgerson, June 16, 2001. AB, U. Chgo., 1990, AM, 1993, PhD, 1996. Lectr. U. Chgo., 1996, rsch. analyst, 1997-99; asst. prof. sociology U. Ga., Athens, 1999—. Author: The Stars Are Not Enough: Scientists-Their Passions and Professions, 1998, College Attrition at American Research Universities: Comparative Case Studies, 2003. Mem. AAAS, Am. Sociol. Assn., Am. Ednl. Rsch. Assn. Office: U Ga Dept Sociology Athens GA 30602

HERMANSEN, JOHN CHRISTIAN, computational linguist; b. Athens, Greece, Oct. 21, 1949; s. John Theodore and Lois Ann Hermansen; m. Sharyl Lynn Miner (div. 1994); children: John Theodore, Janet Lois. BA in Speech, BA in Linguistics, Pa. State U., 1975; PhD in Computational Linguistics, Georgetown U., 1985. Cert. knowledge engr., 2002. Propr. CompAssociates, Inc., Washington, 1974-78; lectr., univ. fellow computational linguistics Georgetown U., Washington, 1980-83, dir. Lang. Processing Ctr., Sch. Langs. and Linguistics, 1982-85; artificial intelligence rsch. scientist Planning Rsch. Corp., McLean, Va., 1985-88, computational linguistics cons., 1988-90; cons. knowledge engring. Sterling Software, Inc., McLean, Va., 1991-95; lead scientist linguistics analysis team State Dept. CLASS Project, Lang. Analysis Systems, Inc., Herndon, Va., 1986—; computational linguistics cons. Ctr. for Applied Linguistics, Washington, 1985-94; CEO Lang Analysis Systems, Inc., Herndon, Va., 1991—. Spkr. Beijing Conf. Asian Organized Crime, 2000; instr. effects of Asian organized crime on U.S., Fla. NG, 2000. Co-author: Southeast Asia Refugee Testing Report, Vols. I and II, 1985, Report on the Evaluation of Kenya Radio Language Arts Project, 1985, PAKTUS Version 1 User's Guide, 1986, Building NLU Systems in the PAKTUS Environment: Developer's Introduction, 1987, Message Processing Systems: Evaluation Factors, 1987, Meronomy, Word Experts and Prepositional Phrase Attachment in PAKTUS, 1989, Techniques in Multilingual Name Searching, 1989, The Automated Templating System for Database Update from Unformatted Message Traffic, 1995, The On-Line Name Reference Library Project, 1999, Combatting Asian Organized Crime, 2001, Advanced Name Matching for Enhanced Airline Security, 2002, Predictive Technology and Border Security, 2002, Name Recognition Tech., 2003, Names Have Currency Fin. Tech., 2003; contbr. articles to profl. jours.; patentee in field; co-author: Names Have Currency, Technology for Finance, 2003. Recipient Fast 50 Champion CEO, Fast Co. magazine, 2003. Mem. IEEE, Assn. for Computational Linguistics, Internat. Assn. Knowledge Engrs., Data Adminstrn. Mgmt. Assn. Home: 12012 Robin Dr Catharpin VA 20143-1307 Office: Lang Analysis Systems Ctr for Innovative Tech 2214 Rock Hill Rd Herndon VA 20170-4214

HERMANSON OGILVIE, JUDITH, foundation executive; b. London, Oct. 16, 1945; d. John Herbert and Estella Barbara (Osborne) Hermanson; m. Keith William Ogilvie, Nov. 19, 1976. AB magna cum laude, Smith Coll., Northampton, Mass., 1967; student, Am. U., Paris, 1965; MA, George Washington U., 1968, PhD, 1984. Ops. tng. officer Peace Corps, Washington, 1968-70, assoc. dir., 1970-71, 1971-72; policy analyst VISTA, Washington, 1972-73; spl. asst. to commr., vice chair Consumer Product Safety Commn., Washington, 1973-76; dir. program devel. evaluation Dept. HUD, Washington, 1976-77; co-founder, exec. v.p. Newman & Hermanson Co., Washington, 1977-83; dep. regional dir. African region Coop. Housing Found., Washington, 1984; program and tng. chief Peace Corps, Washington, 1984-86, regional dir. for Europe, Africa, Middle East, 1986-92; exec. v.p. internat. programs Coop. Housing Found. Internat., Washington, 1992—; v.p., COO CHF Internat. (formerly Coop. Housing Found.), Washington, 1996—. Cons. World Bank, U.S. AID; bd. dirs. Overseas Coop. Devel. Coun., 1992—, vice chair, 2000—01, chair, 2001—02; trustee Am. U. Paris, 1999—, chair bd. com. on acad. policy, 2002—. Contbr. articles to profl. jours. Mem. Montgomery County Housing and Community Devel. Adv. Com. Recipient Spl. Achievement award Peace Corps, 1986, John D Lange Internat. award Nat. Assn. Housing and Redevel. Ofcls., 1995, Disting. Alumni Profl. Achievement award Am. U. Paris, 1999. Mem. Phi Beta Kappa, Smith Club, George Washington U. Club. Episcopalian. Office: CHF Internat 8601 Georgia Ave Silver Spring MD 20910-6225 E-mail: jho@chfhq.org.

HERMES, MARJORY RUTH, machine embroidery and arts educator; b. Caldwell, Kans., June 28, 1931; d. Truman Homer and Olive Ruth (Ridings) Brown; m. Ogden S. Jones, Jr., Dec. 17, 1949 (div. Aug. 1956); m. Richard Lawrence Hermes, July 18, 1963; children: Penelope, Peter, Deborah, Patricia, Pamela, Kristin. Student, U. Kans., 1949-50, Arkansas City Jr. Coll., 1953-54. Sec. Maurer-Neuer Corp., Arkansas City, Kans., 1954-56, Lesh, Bradley & Barrand, Lawrence, Kans., 1959-60; exec. sec. Houston Corp., Wichita, Kans., 1956-57; mgr. Ind. Ins. Co., Landstuhl, Fed. Republic Germany, 1960-62; sec. U. Kans., Lawrence, 1962-63; photograph restorer Herb's Studio, Lawrence, 1977-78; ptnr., agt. Hayes-Richardson-Santee Inc., Lawrence, 1978-83; instr. sewing and machine embroidery Self & Bob's Bernina, Lawrence, 1985-95. Mem. Lawrence Ins. Bd., 1980-83. Bd. dirs. United Way, Lawrence, 1981-83; treas. local polit. campaigns, host Am. Indian Athletic Hall of Fame, 1980-82; treas. local polit. campaigns, 1984, 88; leader Therapeutic Horse Riding Instrn., Lawrence, 1992-95; vol. Lawrence Sr. Ctr., 1999-2001. Mem. Nat. Machine Embroidery Instrs. Assn. (bd. dirs. for N.D., S.D., Nebr., Iowa, Mo., Minn. and Kans. 1987-90), Am. Sewing Guild, Am. Bus. Women's Assn. (v.p. Lawrence 1980-81, pres. 1981-82, Inner Circle award 1982, Woman of Yr. award 1984), Lawrence C. of C. (envoy 1978-83). Republican. Avocations: horsemanship, travel, sailing. Home: 2513 W 24th Ter Lawrence KS 66047-2818

HERMINGHOUSE, PATRICIA ANNE, foreign language educator; b. Melrose Park, Ill., Mar. 13, 1940; m. 1964; 2 children. BA, Knox Coll., 1962; MA, Washington U., 1965, PhD in German, 1968. Asst. prof. German U. Mo.-St. Louis, 1966-67, vis. lectr., 1968-69; asst. prof. Washington U., St. Louis, 1967-78, assoc. prof. German, 1978-83; Fuchs prof. German studies U. Rochester, N.Y., 1983—, chmn. dept. fgn. flangs., lits. and linguistics, 1983-89. Lectr. German, Fontbonne Coll., 1965-66. Internat. Research & Exchanges Bd. ad hoc grantee, 1976. Editor or co-editor: Literatur der DDR in den siebziger Jahren, 1983, Literatur und Literaturtheorie in der DDR, 1976, Frauen im Mittelpunkt, 1987, Gender and Germaness, 1997, Ingeborg Bachmann and Christa Wolf, 1998, German Feminist Writings, 2000; editor GDR Bull., Newsletter Lit. and Culture in German Dem. Republic, 1975-83; co-editor: Women in German Yearbook, 1994-2002. Recipient Susan B. Anthony Lifetime Achievement award, 2003; sr. fellow, NEH, 1991. Mem. MLA, Am. Assn. Tchrs. German (exec. coun. 1979-81), German Studies Assn. (exec. com., v.p./pres. 2001-02, pres. 2003—), Coalition Women German (coord. 1974-75, nat. steering. com. 1976-79, 94-2002), Assn. Depts. Fgn. Langs. (exec. com.), Address: U Rochester Dept Modern Lang and Cultures Rochester NY 14627 E-mail: pahe@troi.cc.rochester.edu.

HERMSEN, JAMES R. lawyer; b. Orange, Calif., Oct. 2, 1945; BA, U. Wash., 1967, JD, 1970. Bar: Wash. 1971. Mem. Bogle & Gates, PLLC, Seattle, Dorsey & Whitney, Seattle, 2000—. Mem. Bur. of Competition Fed. Trade Commn., 1971-73. Mem. ABA, Seattle-King County Bar Assn., Wash. State Bar Assn., Phi Beta Kappa, Omicron Delta Epsilon, Phi Delta Phi. Office: Dorsey & Whitney 1420 5th Ave Ste 3400 Seattle WA 98101-4010

HERNANDEZ, AILEEN C(LARKE), urban consultant; b. Bklyn., May 23, 1926; d. Charles Henry and Ethel Louise (Hall) Clarke; divorced. AB in Sociology and Polit. Sci. magna cum laude, Howard U., 1947; MA in Pub. Adminstrn. with honors, Calif. State U., L.A., 1961; LHD (hon.), So. Vt. Coll., 1979. From organizer to dir. edn. and pub. rels. Internat. Ladies' Garment Workers' Union, Calif., 1950-61; asst. chief Calif. div. Fair Employment Practices, 1962-65; appointed commr. U.S. EEOC, Washington, 1965-66; prin. Aileen C. Hernandez Assocs., San Francisco, 1966—. Rsch. asst. dept. govt. Howard U., 1948; specialist in labor edn., lectr. U.S. Dept. State, 1960; mem. internat. conf. on minorities and the metropolis Konrad Adenauer Found./U.S. Dept. State, 1975; mem. Nat. Commn. on Study of People's Republic of China, 1978, Nat. Commn. on Am. Fgn. Policy Towards South Africa, 1981; advisor BART impact study com. Nat. Acad. Engring.; commr. Bay Vision 2020, 1990-93; vice chair San Francisco 2000; lectr. polit. sci. U. Calif., Berkeley, UCLA, San Francisco State U. Columnist Washington Tribune, 1946-47; contbr. commn. report South Africa: Time Running Out, 1981. Coord. Senator Alan Cranston's campaign for State Controller of Calif., 1961; chair Working Assets Money Fund; co-chair Nat. Urban Coalition, bd. dirs. Death Penalty Focus; vice chair nat. adv. couns. ACLU; coord. San Francisco African Am. Agenda Coun.; mem. adv. bd. Program for Rsch. on Immigration Policy; mem. nat. adv. coun. Nat. Inst. for Women of Color; bd. dirs. Ctr. for Women Policy Studies; mem. Citizens Commn. on Civil Rights; treas. Eleanor R. Spikes Meml. Fund; active San Franciscans Seeking Consensus, 1982—; founding mem., chair Coalition for Econ. Equity; chair Sec's. Adv. Com. on Rights and Responsibilities of Women; officer, bd. dirs. Mt. Zion Hosp.; bd. dirs. Westside Community Mental Health Ctr.; chair Calif. Coun. Humanities; founding mem. Nat. Women's Polit. Caucus, Black Women Organized for Action, Bay Area Black Women United, Nat. Hook-Up of Black Women; bd. dirs., project dir. Nat. Com. Against Discrimination in Housing; mem. housing com. Assn. Bay Area Govts.; chmn. Ctr. Common Good, Calif. Women's Agenda; bd. dirs. Wellesley Ctrs. for Rsch.; bd. Ctr. Govtl. Studies. Named Woman of Yr., Cmty. Rels. Conf. So. Calif. 1961, One of Ten Most Disting. Women in the San Francisco Bay Area, San Francisco Examiner, 1969, One of Ten Women Who Make a Difference, San Francisco LWV, 1985; recipient Disting. Postgrad. Achievement award Howard U., 1968, disting. svcs. to urban cmtys. award Nat. Urban Coalition, 1985, Bicentennial award Trinity Bapt. Ch., 1976, humanitarian svcs. award Glide Meml. United Meth. Ch., 1986, appreciation awards Nat. Inst. for Women of Color, 1987, Western Dist. Conf. of Nat. Assn. Negro Bus. and Profl. Women's Clubs, 1988, San Francisco Conv. and Visitors Bur., Parren J. Mitchell award San Francisco Black C. of C., 1985, Silver Spur award, Wise Woman award Ctr. for Women Policy Studies, Women of Achievement award, Vison and Excellence award, others. Mem. NAACP (life), NOW (past nat. pres.), Ms. Found. for Women (bd. dirs.), Bay Area Urban League (past bd. dirs.), Urban Inst. (life trustee), Gamma Phi Delta (hon.), Alpha Kappa Alpha. Office: Aileen C Hernandez Assocs 818 47th Ave San Francisco CA 94121-3208

HERNANDEZ, ANTONIO, gynecologist; b. Granada, Spain, June 8, 1934; arrived in U.S., 1964; s. Antonio and Angustias Hernandez. MD, U. Buenos Aires, 1962; ECFMG (hon.), Amecan Embasy, Buenos Aires, 1964. Cert. Am. Bd. of Medicine 1973, Am. Bd. Ob-Gyn 1977. Resident ob-gyn San Martin Hosp., Buenos Aires, 1964; intern East Orange (NJ) Hosp., 1964—65; pvt. practice Alexandria, Va., 1978—99; ret., 2000. Mailing: Apt 250 5501 Seminary Rd Falls Church VA 22041-3903

HERNANDEZ, DAVID N(ICHOLAS), lawyer; b. Albuquerque, Nov. 5, 1954; s. B.C. and Evangeline (C De Baca) H.; m. Alice A. McLish, June 7, 1975. BA, U. N.Mex., 1975, MBA, 1978, JD, 1979. Bar: N.Mex. 1979, U.S. Dist. Ct. N.Mex. 1979. Law clk. to presiding justice N.Mex. Supreme Ct., Santa Fe, 1979-80; assoc. Knight, Custer & Duncan, Albuquerque, 1980-82; sole practice David N. Hernandez & Assoc., Albuquerque, 1982—; of counsel Western Glass & Panels, Albuquerque. Mem. com. rules appellate ct. procedure N.Mex. Supreme Ct., 1984—; bd. dirs. Delta Dental N.Mex., Albuquerque. Mem. Environ. Planning Commn., Albuquerque, 1984-86, PHS assocs. Presbyn. Healthcare Found., 1985—. Named one of Outstanding Young Men Am., 1980. Mem. ABA, N.Mex. Bar Assn. (pres. 2000-01), Albuquerque Bar Assn., Am. Judicatur Soc., Greater Albuquerque C. of C. (bd. dirs. 1982-86, polit. action com. 1983-85). Avocations: tennis, golf, reading, fishing, politics.*

HERNANDEZ, ENRIQUE, gynecologist, educator; b. Vega Baja, P.R., Oct. 25, 1951; s. Nathaniel and Ana Luisa (Lopez) H.; children: David Enrique, Daniel Antonio. BS, U. P.R., Rio Piedras, 1973, MD, 1977. Diplomate Am. Bd. Med. Examiners, Am. Bd. Ob-Gyn, Am. Bd. Gynecol. Oncology. Resident in ob-gyn Johns Hopkins Hosp., Balt., 1977-81, fellow in gynecol. oncology, 1981-83; instr. ob-gyn Johns Hopkins U., Balt., 1981-82, asst. prof., 1982-83; chief gynecol. oncology service Tripler Army Med. Ctr., Honolulu, 1983-87, asst. dir. intern tng., 1984-87; assoc. prof. Med. Coll. of Pa., Phila., 1987-89, prof., 1989-98; dir. divsn. gynecologic oncology Med. Coll. Pa./Hahneman Univ., Phila., 1987-98; vice chair dept. ob-gyn. Med. Coll. Pa./Hahneman U., Phila., 1995-98. Pres. med. and dental staff Med. Coll. Pa. Hosp., 1992—93; chief ob-gyn. svc. Allegheny U. Hosp. for Women, 1997—98, Allegheny U. Hosps./Med. Coll. Pa., 1997—98; prof. ob-gyn. Temple U. Sch. Medicine, 1998—, prof. pathology and lab. med., 1998—, chmn., dept. obstetrics and gynecology, 2002—, dir. divsn. gynecol. oncology, 1998—, Abraham Roth prof., 2002—; dir. ob/gyn. residency program Temple U. Hosp., 1998—. Author: Manual of Gynecologic Oncology, 1989; editor: Clinical Gynecologic Pathology, 1995; contbr. articles to profl. jours. Bd. dirs. Allegheny Health, Edn. and Rsch. Found., 1992—93, Found. Obstet. Soc. Phila., 1998—2000; bd. dirs. Pa. divsn. Am. Cancer Soc., 2002—. Maj. U.S. Army, 1983—87. Recipient Bristol award P.R. Med. Assn., 1977. Fellow: ACOG, ACS (treas. met. Phila. chpt. 1995—99, pres.-elect 2000—01, pres. Phila. chpt. 2001—02); mem.: Phila. County Med. Soc. (bd. dirs. 1999, treas. 2001—03, pres.-elect 2003—, chmn. pub. health and edn. com. 2003), Pa. Med. Soc. (ho. of dels. 1998—), Am. Coll. of Surgeons (v.p. met. Phila. chpt. 1999—2000, pres.-elect 2000—01, pres. 2001—02), Soc. Ibero Latin Am. Med. Profls. (pres.-elect 1999—2001, pres. 2001—03, pres.-elect 2003—), Colposcopy Soc. of Phila. (pres. 1999—2001), Am. Cancer Soc. (mem. adv. bd. Southeastern Pa. chpt. 1998—), Mid-Atlantic Gynecologic Oncology Soc. (pres. 1996—97), Obstet. Soc. Phila. (sec. 1994—96, pres.-elect 1996—97, pres. 1997—98), Soc. Gynecologic Oncologists, Am. Soc. Clin. Oncology. Roman Catholic. Avocation: long distance running. Office: Temple Univ Hosp 3401 N Broad St Philadelphia PA 19140-5189

HERNANDEZ, FERNANDO VARGAS, lawyer; b. Irapuato, Mex., Sept. 8, 1939; came to U.S., 1942, naturalized, 1957; s. José Espinosa and Ana Maria (Vargas) H.; m. Bonnie Corrie, Jan. 8, 1966 (div. Feb. 1991); children: Michael David, Alexandra Rae, Marcel Paul. BS, U. Santa Clara, 1961; MBA, 1962; JD, U. Calif., Berkeley, 1966. Bar: Calif. 1967, U.S. Dist. Ct. (no. dist.) Calif. 1967. Sole practice law, San Jose, Calif., 1967—. Lectr. law Lincoln U.; lectr. bus. U. Santa Clara. Mem. San Jose Housing Bd., 1970-73; arbitrator Santa Clara County Superior Cts., 1979-2003, judge pro tem, 1979—. Contbg. editor to legal pleadings books. Mem. San Jose Civic Light Opera, 1981-83; founder Greater San Jose Hispanic C. of C.; bd. dirs. Tapestry in Talent, 2001—. Served with AUS, 1962-63. Mem. Calif. State Bar Assn., Santa Clara County Bar Assn. (chmn. torts sect. 1977-78, features editor In Brief mag. 1990-93), Calif. Trial Lawyers Assn. (bd. govs. 1979-82), Santa Clara County Trial Lawyers Assn., La Raza Lawyers Assn., Tapestry in Talent (bd. dirs. 2000—), Greater San Jose Hispanic C. of C. (founder, corp. counsel, bd. dirs. 2003—), Silicon Valley Capital Club, Silicon Valley Capital Club. Democrat. Roman Catholic. Office: 46 S 1st St San Jose CA 95113-2406 E-mail: fvhlaw@pacbell.net.

HERNANDEZ, GILBERTO JUAN, accountant, auditor, management consultant; b. Havana, Cuba, July 12, 1943; came to U.S., 1960; s. Gilberto E. and Zoila M. (Mendez) H.; m. Maria-Elena Diaz Lugo, Jan. 19, 1968 (div. 1971); 1 child, A. Patrick; m. Maria-Carmen Marcet, Dec. 23, 1972; children: Martin J., David J., Thomas J. BBA, Pace U., 1968. CPA, N.Y., Fla. Auditor sr. Arthur Andersen LLP, N.Y.C., Tampa, Fla., 1968-73; v.p., treas. Coaxial Comms., Inc., Sarasota, Fla., 1973-81; tax mgr. Laventhol & Horwath, Tampa, Fla., 1981-83; mem. firm ValienteHernandez P.A., CPAs, Auditors and Consultants, Mems. Independent Accts. (IA), Internat., Tampa and Tallahassee, Fla., 1983—. Chmn. N.Am. region IA Internat.; dir. IA Internat. World Bd. Commr. City of Tampa Housing Authority, 1981-95; treas., bd. dirs. Ybor City Devel. Corp., Tampa, 1988—; past chmn. Tampa Bay Econ. Devel. Corp. Mem. AICPA, N.Y. State Soc. CPAs, Fla. Inst. CPAs (bd. dirs., pres. West Coast chpt., past chmn. com. on unauthorized practice of pub. accountancy 1993-94, Outstanding Chmn. of Yr. 1994), Nat. Assn. Housing and Redevel. Ofcls. (bd. govs. 1988-94), Govt. Fin. Officers Assn., Fla. Assn. Govt. Fin. Officers, Ybor City C. of C. (chmn. 1997-98, chmn. 1998-99), Ybor City Rotary Club (pres. 1990-91). Avocations: geography, travel, hiking. Office: ValienteHernandez PA 1715 N Westshore Blvd Ste 950 Tampa FL 33607-3920 E-mail: ghernandez@vhcpa.com.

HERNANDEZ, JEANNE TAYLOR, psychologist, human services researcher, personal/professional coach; b. Rochester, N.Y., Feb. 5, 1946; d. Millard Benjamin and Marie Jeanne (Capasso) Taylor; m. John Peter Hernandez, 1966 (div. 1992); children: John Benjamin, Peter Rob. Student, Tufts U., 1963-65; BS cum laude, U. Rochester, 1967; MSPH, U. N.C., 1971; PhD, N.C. State U., 1988; postgrad., U. N.C., 1991-93, Ericksonian Hypnosis Tng., 1992-97; student, Coach U., 1998—2000. Lic. practicing psychologist health svcs. provider N.C., cert. med. hypnotherapy, lic. clin. psychologist Calif., approved cons. in med. hypnosis, cert. Nat. Register Health Svcs. Providers in Psychology. Rsch. asst. dept. psychiatry U. N.C., Chapel Hill, 1982-88, rsch. asst. prof. dept. psychiatry, 1988-95, asst. clin. prof. dept. anesthesiology, 1995—, dir. behavioral medicine in pain medicine divsn., 1995—. Personal and profl. coach, medical psychologist, tchr. profl. workshops, clin. cmty. psychology in health and mental health clinics; Coach U., 1998-01. Contbr. articles to profl. jours. Mem.: APA, Assn. Med. Sch. Psychologists, Am. Soc. Clin. Hypnosis. Office: U NC Dept Anesthesiology CB 7010 Chapel Hill NC 27599-7010 E-mail: jhernandez@aims.unc.edu., coachjeanne@msn.com.

HERNANDEZ, JO FARB, music director, consultant; b. Chgo., Nov. 20, 1952; BA in Polit. Sci. & French with honors, U. Wis., 1974; MA in Folklore and mythology, UCLA, 1975; postgrad., U. Calif., Davis, 1978, U. Calif., Berkeley, 1978-79, 81. Registration Mus. Cultural History UCLA, 1974-75; Rockefeller fellow Dallas Mus. Fine Arts, 1976-77; asst. to dir. Triton Mus. Art, Santa Clara, Calif., 1977-78, dir., 1978-85; adj. prof. mus. studies John F. Kennedy U., San Francisco, 1978; grad. advisor arts adminstrn. San Jose (Calif.) State U., 1979-80; dir. Monterey (Calif.) Peninsula Mus. Art, 1985-93, cons. curator, 1994—2000; prin. Curatorial and Mus. Mgmt. Svcs., Watsonville, Calif., 1993—. Cons.SPACES (Saving and Preserving Art and Cultural Environ.), 2000—; nominator Creative Works Fund, 2001; adj. prof. gallery mgmt. art dept. U. Calif., Santa Cruz, 1999—; cons. Archives Am. Art., 1998—2000; dir. Thompson Gallery, San Jose State U., 2000—; lectr., panelist, juror, panelist in field USIA, Calif. Arts Coun., Calif. Confedn. for Arts, Am. Assn. Mus. Western Mus. Assn., Am. Folklore Soc., Calif. Folklore Soc., Internat. Coun. on Mus., others; vis. lectr. U. Wis., 1980, U. Chgo., 1981, Northwestern U., 1981, San Jose State U., 1985, UCLA, 1986, Am. Cultural Ctr., Jerusalem, 1989, Tel Aviv, 89, Binational Ctr., Lima, Peru, 1988, Daytona Beach Mus. Art, 1983, UCLA, 1986, Israel Mus., 1989, Mont. State U., 1991, Oakland Mus., 1996, High Mus. Art, Atlanta, 1997, Mus. Am. Folk Art, NY, 1998, San Francisco Mus. Modern Art, 1998, U. Calif., 1998, Grinnell Coll., Iowa, 1999, Arts Coun. Silicon Valley, 2000, U. Calif., Santa Cruz, 2000, ICOM, Barcelona, 2001; guest curator San Diego Mus. Art, 1995—98; guest on various TV and radio programs. Author: (mus. catalogs) The Day of the Dead: Tradition and Change in Contemporary Mexico, 1979, Three from the Northern Island: Contemporary Sculpture from Hokkaido, 1984, Crime and Punishment: Reflections of Violence in Contemporary Art, 1984, The Quiet Eye: Pottery of Shoji Hamada and Bernard Leach, 1990, Alan Shepp: The Language of Stone, 1991, Wonderful Colors: The Paintings of August Francois Gay, 1993, Jeannette Maxfield Lewis: A Centennial Celebration, 1994, Armin Hansen, 1994, Jeremy Anderson: The Critical Link/A Quiet Revolution, 1995, A.G. Rizzoli: Architect of Magnificent Visions, 1997 (one of 10 Best Books in field Amazon.com), Misch Kohn: Beyond the Tradition, 1998, Fire and Flux: An Undaunted Vision/The Art of Charles Strong, 1998, Mel Ramos: The Galatea Series, 2000, Holly Lane: Small Miracles, 2001, Irvin Tepper: When Cups Speak/Life with the Cup, 2002; co-author: Sam Richardson: Color in Space, 2002, Marc D'Estout: Domestic Objects, 2003; mem. internat. editl. bd. Raw Vision Mag., 2001--; contbr. articles to profl. publs. Bd. dirs. Bobbie Wynn and Co. of San Jose, 1981-85, Santa Clara Arts and Hist. Consortium, 1985, Non-Profit Gallery Assn. 1979-83, v.p., 1979-80; mem. nat. adv. bd. The Fund for Folk Culture, Santa Fe, 1995-98; mem. founding and exec. bd. Alliance for Calif. Traditional Arts, 2002—; mem. founding internat. adv. bd. Friends of Fred Smith, 2002—. Recipient Golden Eagle award, Coun. Internat. Non-theatrical Events, 1992, Leader of Decade award, Arts Leadership Monterey Peninsula, 1992, mer. award, N.Y. Book Show, 1997; grantee Rsch., Calif. State U., 2001, 2002, 2003, Dean's grant, 2001. Mem.: Nat. Coun. for Edn. in Ceramic Arts, Western Mus. Conf. (bd. dir., exec. com. 1989—91, program chair 1990), Am. Folklore Soc., Art Table, Calif. Assn. Mus. (bd. dirs. 1985—94, v.p. 1987—91, chair nominating com. 1988, chair ann. meeting 1990, chair nominating com. 1990, pres. 1991—92, chair nominating com. 1993), Am. Assn. Mus. (lectr. 1986, mus. assessment program surveyor 1990, nat. program com. 1992—93, mus. assessment program surveyor 1994), Phi Beta Kappa. Office: Curatorial Mus. Mgmt Svcs 345 White Rd Watsonville CA 95076-0429 E-mail: jfh@cruzio.com.

HERNANDEZ, JOEL THOMAS, writer; b. Duluth, Minn., June 11, 1968; s. Ronald Earl Turnipseed and Cathleen Ann (Cox) Wilson. Student, U. Minn., 1988-95. Staff writer Minn. Spectator, Mpls., 1988-89, editor, 1989-90; pres. editor-in-chief Hotel Zero: Arts and Literature on the Web. Founder, chief tech. officer Archemedia; creative writing resident The Loft, Mpls., 1996. Contbr. essays, revs. to profl. publs. Author: Baghdad Express, 2003. State del. Minn. Rep. Party, Bloomington, 1990; charter mem. Students and Cmty. Organized fo

Reflective Effort, Mpls., 1991-93. Cpl. USMC, 1990-91. Scholar Bread Loaf Writers' Conf., 1996, 98. Fellow Minn. State Arts Bd. Avocations: book collecting, stamp collecting, running, skiing, fly fishing.

HERNANDEZ, JOHN E. musician, music educator; arrived in U.S., 2001; s. Gerardo E. Hernandez and Dolores Ludena de Hernandez. Bachelor's Degree, Conservatory Salvador Bustamante Celi, Loja, 1992; Bachelor's Degree with honors and excellence, Conservatory Rimsky-Korsakov, Ecuador, 1999; MusM, U. Louisville, 2003. Tchr. Conservatory Salvador Bustamante Celi, Loja, 1990—94, Conservatory Rimsky-Korsakov, Guayaquil, Ecuador, 1997—2001, Ctr. for the Arts, Guayaquil, 1998—99; pianist Home of Culture Chamber Ensemble, Loja, 1992—94; pianist, soloist, accompanist Symphony Orch. Guayaquil, 1990—2001; grad. asst. U. Louisville, 2002—. Arranger, pianist: recording Te Voy a Dejar Vivir, 1991, Que Bonita Es La Vida, 1992, Un Lugar en La Musica, 2000. Recipient Cultural Merit award, City Hall Loja, 1990, first prize nat. contest, German-Ecuadorian Cultural Ctr., 1993. Mem.: Casa de la Cultura, Music Tchrs. Nat. Assn. Avocations: reading, soccer, movies, theater, gardening. Office: Univ Louisville Belnak Campus Louisville KY 40292

HERNANDEZ, JOSE, baseball player; b. July 14, 1969; m. Melanie Hernandez; children: Jolanie, Jose Orlando. Short stop Milw. Brewers, 2000—. Office: Milw Brewers 1 Brewers Way Milwaukee WI 53214

HERNANDEZ, JOSE YOLANDO BALAGTAS, physician, surgeon; b. Manila, Philippines, Dec. 30, 1938; came to U.S., 1964; s. Pablo Manio and Leoncia (Balagtas) Hernandez; m. Minerva Cuadrante, Dec. 17, 1966; children: Jay, Myra, Maureen. MD, U. St. Thomas, Manila, Philippines, 1962. Diplomate Am. Bd. Surgery, Am. Bd. Colon-Rectal Surgery, Internat. Bd. Proctology. Fellow: Soc. Philippine Surgeons in Am., Southeastern Surgical Congress, Internat. Acad. Proctology, InterAm. Coll. Physicians and Surgeons, Internat. Coll. Surgeons, Am. Soc. Colon Rectal Surgeons, Am. Soc. Abdominal Surgeons; mem.: AMA, Coll. Internat. Chirurgiae Digestiva, Endoscopic Surgeons, Am. Gastroent. Roman Catholic. Avocations: ballroom dancing, golf, music. Home and Office: 3053 Carlow Cir Tallahassee FL 32309-3302

HERNANDEZ, MACK RAY, lawyer; b. Austin, Tex., Sept. 8, 1944; s. Mack and Mary (Prado) Hernandez; 1 child, John Christopher; m. Jayne Webb Barrett, Aug. 2, 2001. BA, U. Tex., 1967, JD, 1970. Bar: Tex. 1970, U.S. Dist. Ct. (we. dist.) Tex. 1972. Staff atty. Travis County Legal Aid Soc, Austin, 1970-71; pvt. practice Austin, 1971—. Bd. dirs. Austin C. of C., 1983-86, Meals on Wheels, Austin, 1972-76; trustee Austin C.C., 1988—; vice-chair, 1990-92, chair, 1992-94; chmn. bd. dirs. Am. Cancer Soc., Austin, 1988-95; trustee Austin Mus. Art, 2000—. Mem. Tex. Bar Assn., Travis County Bar Assn., Coll. of State Bar, Tex. Bar Found. Avocations: travel, jogging, hiking, backpacking. Office: 524 N Lamar Blvd Ste 202 Austin TX 78703-5422 E-mail: mrhernandez@hernandezlaw.com.

HERNANDEZ, MARISSA, physicist; b. Manila, Dec. 26, 1964; came to the U.S., 1989; d. Juan and Josefina (Timbol) H. BS in Physics, Ateneo de Manila U., 1985; MS in Physics, Tex. Tech. U., 1992; MS in Radiol. Physics, Wayne State U., 1993. Physics instr. U. Philippines, Manila, 1985-89; teaching asst. Tex. Tech. U., Lubbock, 1989, rsch. asst., 1990-92, Wayne State U., Detroit, 1992-93; med. physicist Med. Coll. Pa., Phila., 1994-2000, Morristown (N.J.) Meml. Hosp., 2000—. Contbr. articles to profl. jours. Scholar Philippine VA Office, 1981-85; fellow Robert A. Welch Found., 1990-92; scholarship grantee PEO, 1993. Mem. Ateneo Physics Soc. (pres. 1984-85), Am. Phys. Soc., Am. Assn. Physicists in Medicine, Am. Coll. Radiology, Soc. Nuclear Medicine, Health Physics Soc., Laser Inst. Am., Radiol. Soc. N.J., Soc. Computer Applications in Radiology. Office: Diagnostic Imaging Physics 100 Madison Ave Morristown NJ 07960-6136 E-mail: marissa.hernandez@ahsys.org.

HERNANDEZ, MARK ALAN, Latin American/Latino literary and cultural studies educator; b. San Antonio, May 29, 1964; s. John C. and Mary Antonieta (Gonzalez) H. BA, Yale U., 1986; postgrad. studies, Duke U., 1987-88; MA, U. Kans., 1990, PhD, 1996. Mng. editor Intercultural Devel. Rsch. Assn., San Antonio, 1986-87; instr. in Spanish Duke U., Durham, N.C., 1987-88; grad. tchg. asst. U. Kans., Lawrence, 1988-94; dissertation fellow Grinnell (Iowa) Coll., 1994-96, asst. prof. Spanish, 1996-98, Bowling Green State U., 1998-2001, Tufts U., Medford, Mass., 2001—. Duke Endowment fellow, Duke Univ., 1987-88, fellow U. Kans., 1989-91, Grad. Tchg. Asst. award, 1993, Dissertation fellow Grinnell Coll., 1994-96; Nat. Hispanic Scholarship Fund scholar, 1987-94. Mem. MLA, Am. Assn. Tchrs. of Spanish and Portugese, Latin Am. Studies Assn., Am. Studies Assn. Avocations: travel, Latin Am. music, tennis, basketball. Office: Tufts U Dept Romance Langs Olin Ctr Medford MA 02155 E-mail: mark.hernandez@tufts.edu.

HERNANDEZ, MICHAEL VINCENT, law educator; b. Richmond, Va., Apr. 29, 1962; s. Henry Vincent and Betty Jane (Fulwider) H.; m. Laura Ruth Brown, Sept. 16, 1989; children: Justin Michael, Nathan Marc, Alicia Joy, Brent Matthew. BA in Govt. with high distinction, U. Va., 1984, JD, 1987. Bar: Va. 1987, U.S. Dist. Ct. (ea. and we. dists.) Va., 1987, U.S. Ct. Appeals (4th cir.) 1987, U.S. Supreme Ct. 1990. Assoc. McGuire, Woods, Battle & Boothe, Richmond, 1987-89, McSweeney, Burtch & Crump, Richmond, 1990-92; adj. asst. prof. Regent U. Sch. Law, Virginia Beach, Va., 1992, asst. prof., 1992—98, faculty advisor moot ct., 1994—2002, assoc. prof., 1998—2002, prof., 2002—. Mem. Tidewater Va. Tchg. Consortium, spring 1995; counsel for State of N.C. re interstate dispute over Coastal Zone Mgmt. Act, 1994, and challenge to fed. fishing regulations, 1995-98. Contbr. articles to law jours., chpt. to book. Pro bono counsel tenants coalition and lead com. Washington Park, Portsmouth, Va., 1992-2000; gen. counsel Richmond AIDS Ministry, 1992; vol. Strategies To Elevate People, Richmond, 1987-92; asst. homegroup leader, Sunday sch. tchr. Southside Ch. Richmond, 1990-92; asst. homegroup leader, nursery vol., lector, Eucharistic minister Episcopal Ch. of Messiah, Chesapeake, Va., 1993-95, 98—; nursery vol. Kempsville Presbyn. Ch., Virginia Beach, 1994-98; children's Sunday sch. tchr., substitute lector, chalice minister, Christ Covenant Ref. Episcopal Ch., Virginia Beach, 1996-97; bd. dirs. Bethany Christian Svcs. of Hampton Roads, 1999-2002, pres., 2001-02. Mem. ABA, Va. State Bar, Va. Bar Assn. Avocations: golf, tennis, basketball. Office: Regent U Sch Law 1000 Regent University Dr Virginia Beach VA 23464-5037 E-mail: michher@regent.edu.

HERNANDEZ, PATRICIA B. biologist, educator; b. Del Rio, Tex., Sept. 9, 1954; d. Preciliano DeLeon and Berta (Borrego) Hernandez. PhD, Tex. Woman's U., 1989. Prof. biology ACU, Abilene, Tex., 1989—. Pres., bd. dirs. The House That Kerry Built, Abilene, 2001—02. Mem.: Sci. Tchrs. Assn. Tex., Soc. Neurosci. Avocation: gardening. Office: ACU Dept Biology Box 27868 Abilene TX 79699-0001

HERNANDEZ, RAMON ROBERT, retired clergyman and librarian; b. Chgo., Feb. 23, 1936; s. Eleazar Dario and Marie Helen (Stange) H.; m. Fern Ellen Muschinske, Aug. 11, 1962; children: Robert Frank, Maria Marta. BA, Elmhurst (Ill.) Coll., 1957; BD, Eden Theol. Sem., St. Louis, 1962; MA, U. Wis., 1970. Co-pastor St. Stephen United Ch. Christ, Merrill, Wis., 1960-64; dir. youth work Wis. Conf. United Ch. Christ, Madison, 1964-70; dir. T.B. Scott Free Library, Merrill, 1970-75, McMillan Meml. Library, Wisconsin Rapids, Wis., 1975 83, Ann Arbor (Mich.) Pub. Library, 1983-94; pastor Comty. Congl. Ch., Pinckney, Mich., 1994-98. Seminar leader on pub. libr. long-range planning, budgeting and handling problem patrons. Editl. com. mem. Songs of Many Nations Songbook, 1970; contbr. articles to profl. jours. Treas. Ann Arbor Homeless Coalition, 1985-88; bd. dirs., sec., v.p. Riverview Hosp. Assn., Wisconsin Rapids, 1977-83; bd. dirs. Hist. Soc. Mich., 1988-90, Ind. Living, Inc., Dame County, Wis., 2001—; bd. trustees Madison Pub. Libr, Wis., 2000—. Mem. ALA, Wis. Libr. Assn. (Leadership award 1980, pres. 1980), Rotary (pres. Merrill chpt. 1974-75, Community Svc. award 1975, pres. Ann Arbor chpt. 1990-91, Paul Harris fellow 1994).

HERNANDEZ, ROBERTO, professional baseball player; b. Santurce, P.R., Nov. 11, 1964; Student, U. S.C. Pitcher CHW, 1991-97, SF, 1997, Tampa Bay Devil Rays, 1998—2000; pitcher Kansas City Royals, 2001—. Office: Kansas City Royals One Royal Way Kansas City MO 64129

HERNANDEZ, ROBERTO REYES, secondary school educator, educator; b. Juarez, Chihuahua, Mex., Apr. 30, 1950; came to U.S., 1953; s. Felipe de Jesus and Juanita (Reyes) H.; m. Joanne Dora Richard; adopted children: Rosellor, Ledores, Joetta, Harriett, Barbara, Richard, Ray. AA in Edn., El Paso C.C., 1976; BS in Psychology, U. Tex., El Paso, 1978, BE in Secondary Edn., 1981, BS in Biology, 1982, MS in Biology, 1986; grad. sci. fellow, Baylor Coll. Medicine, 1984-85. Cert. secondary edn. teacher, Tex. Pharmacy technician Southwestern Gen. Hosp., El Paso, 1974-79, William Beaumont Army Med. Ctr. U.S. Civil Svc., Ft. Bliss, Tex., 1979-81; tchr. life and earth sci. Houston Ind. Sch. Dist., 1984-85; tchr. phys. sci., anatomy, physiology, biology Socorro Ind. Sch. Dist., El Paso, 1981-84; tchr. phys. sci., biology, astronomy, chemistry, computer sci., psychology, sociology and GED Ysleta Ind. Sch. Dist., El Paso, 1985—. Instr. English El Paso C. C., spring, 1986; grad. asst. interdisciplinary edn. Tex. A & M U., summer, 1989, 90; mem. evaluation team So. Assn. of Accreditation, El Paso, 1984; mem. textbook adoption team Tex. Biology Textbook Adoption Com., El Paso, 1983-84. Pres. Tex. Student Edn. Assn., El Paso, 1980-81; vol. instr. ESL The Westin Paso Del Norte Hotel, El Paso, 1990; den leader Wolf and Bear Cub Scout Pack 201, 1994-95. Recipient Hidalgo award Heftel Broadcasting Corp., 1997. Mem.: NEA, Ysleta Tchrs. Assn. (area rep. 1994—97), Tex. State Tchrs. Assn., Blue Jackets Cmty. Svc. Orgn. (faculty sponsor 2001—), Eastwood Stargazers Club (faculty sponsor 2001—01), Bow and Arrow Sci. Club (faculty sponsor 1985—96), Vista Hills Lions Club (lion tamer 1992—94, LEO Advisor 1992—2001, editor newsletter 1993—95, 2d v.p. 1994—95, dir. 1995—96, chair dist 2—T3 Leo Clubs 1997—2001, exec. v.p. 1998—99, sec. 2001, Lion of Yr. 1992—93, 1996—97, 1999—2000). Home: 10310 Kellogg St El Paso TX 79924-2902 Office: Eastwood HS 2430 Mc Rae Blvd El Paso TX 79925-6097 E-mail: RobertHernandez67@hotmail.com.

HERNANDEZ, ROLAND, broadcast executive; Pres., CEO Telemundo Group, Inc., Hialeah, Fla., chmn. bd., CEO. Office: Telemundo Group Inc 2290 W 8th Ave Hialeah FL 33010-2017 also: 1130 Air Way Glendale CA 91201-2404

HERNANDEZ-DENTON, FEDERICO, supreme court justice; b. Santurce, P.R., Apr. 12, 1944; s. Federico and Teresa (Denton) Hernandez-Morales; m. Isabel Pico, 1966. BA, Harvard U., 1966, JD, 1969. Bar: P.R. 1971. Dir. Consumer Rsch. Ctr. and Bus. Adminstrn. Rsch. Ctr. U. P.R., 1970-72; dir. P.R. Consumer Svc. Adminstrn., 1973; sec. P.R. Dept. Consumer Affairs, 1973-76; asst. prof. Law Sch. Interam. U., P.R., 1977-84, dean, 1984-85; now justice Supreme Ct. P.R, San Juan. Chair Bd. Bar Examiners. Mem. ABA, Am. Law Inst., P.R. Bar Assn. Office: Supreme Ct of PR PO Box 9022392 San Juan PR 00902-2392

HERNANDEZ-RODRIGUEZ, RAFAEL, language educator, writer; b. Mexico City, Mar. 17, 1963; s. Rafael Hernandez and Esther Rodriguez. PhD, NYU, 1998. Lectr. NYU, 1996—98; asst. prof. So. Conn. State U., New Haven, 1998—. Mgr. translating dept. YAR Comm., N.Y.C., 1994. Author, co-editor Una poetica de la despreocupacion, Agitese bien: A New Look at the Hispanic Avant-Gardes. Mem.: MLA (assoc.; del. 2002—). Avocations: travel, photography. Home: 169 Sullivan St # 13 New York NY 10012 Office: So Conn State U 501 Crescent St New Haven CT 06515 Home Fax: 203-392-6136; Office Fax: 203-392-6136. Personal E-mail: rafah63@netscape.net. E-mail: hernandezr3@southernct.edu.

HERNDON, ALICE PATTERSON LATHAM, public health nurse; b. Macon, Ga., Dec. 18, 1916; d. Frank Waters and Ruby (Dews) Patterson; m. William Joseph Latham, July 21, 1940 (dec. Apr. 1981); children: Jo Alice Latham Miller, Marynette Latham Herndon, Lauruby Latham Herndon; 1 adopted child, Courtney Marie Herndon; m. Sidney Dumas Herndon, Apr. 26, 1985. Diploma, Charity Hosp. Sch. Nursing, New Orleans, 1937; student, George Peabody Tchrs. Coll., 1938-39; BS in Pub. Health Nursing, U. N.C., 1954; MPH, Johns Hopkins U., 1966. Staff pub. health nurse assigned spl. venereal disease study USPHS, Darien, Ga., 1939—40; county pub. health nurse Bacon County, Alma, Ga., 1940—41; USPHS spl. venereal disease project Glynn County, Brunswick, 1943—47, county pub. health nurse, 1949—51, Ware County, Waycross, 1951—52; pub. health nurse surp. Wayne-Long-Brantley-Liberty Counties, Jesup, 1954—56; dist. dir. pub. health nursing Wayne-Long-Appling-Bacon-Pierce Counties, Jesup, 1956—70; dist. chief nursing S.E. Ga. Health Dist., 1970—79, organizer mobile health svcs., 1973—. Founder, exec. dir. Wayne County Home Health Agy., 1968—80; exec. dir. Ware County Home Health Agy., 1970—79, mem. exec. com., 1978—85; mem. governing bd. S.E. Ga. Health Sys. Agy., 1975—82; organized and mem. governing bd. Health Dept. Home Health Agy., 1978—, also author numerous grant proposals; governing bd. Brunswick Civic Orch., 1993—97. Contbr. to state nursing manuals. Mem. adv. coun. Ware Meml. Hosp. Sch. Practical Nursing, Waycross, Ga., 1958; mem. Altar Guild St. Paul's Episc. Ch., 1979—86, vestrywoman, 1981—82; mem. Altar Guild St. Marks Episcopal Ch., Brunswick, Ga., 1994—2001; bd. dirs. Wayne County Mental Health Assn., 1959—61, 1981—82, Wayne County Tb Assn., 1958—62, a non-alcoholic organizer Jesup group Alcoholics Anonymous, 1962—63. Recipient recognition Gen. Svc. Bd., Alcoholics Anonymous, Inc. Fellow APHA; mem. ANA, 8th Dist. (pres. 1954-58, sec. 1958-60, dir. 1960-62, 1st v.p. 1962), Ga. Nurses Assn. (exec. bd. 1954-58, program rev. continuing edn. com. 1980-86, Dist. 21 Excellence in Nursing award 1994), Ga. Pub. Health Assn. (chmn. nursing sect. 1956-57), Ga. Assn. Dist. Chiefs Nursing (pres. 1976). Home: 192 Bluff Dr Brunswick GA 31523-6225

HERNDON, CATHY CAMPBELL, artist, educator; b. Richmond, Va., Sept. 25, 1951; d. Kenneth Holcomb and Grace (Brooks) Campbell. BS in Art and Drama, Radford (Va.) U., 1973; MS in Art Edn., Va. Commonwealth U., 1980. Tchr. art Hanover County Schs., Va., 1973-76, Stafford County Schs., Va., 1976-86, Fredericksburg City Schs., 1991—; exch. tchr. Kingston U., Eng., 1995; neon mixed media constrn. artist, signmaker Fredericksburg, Va. Artist, tchr. Rappahannock Security Ctr., Fredericksburg Ctr. for Creative Arts; tchr. Inst. of Contemporary Art, Chgo. Art Inst. One-woman shows include Fredericksburg Ctr. for Creative Arts, Southside Va C.C., Art First Gallery, Fredericksburg, Shenandoah Valley Art Ctr., Geico Corp. Hdqrs., Fredericksburg, Riverby's Gallery, Frejuis, France, 1997, e.e. smith Gallery, others, exhibited in group shows at Karpathos, Greece, London, Stafford Eng., Rocquebrune and Frejuis, France, Montross Gallery, Zenith Gallery, Washington, Va. Ctr. Creative Arts, Exposure Unltd. Art Group, various murals. Mem. Fredericksburg/Frejus Sister City Assn., 1992—; pres., bd. dirs. Fredericksburg Ctr. for Creative Arts, 1984—. Named Best in Show, Hanover Arts Festival, 1995, Geico Educator of Yr., 1996, Educator of Yr., Fredericksburg Jaycees, 1998; Fulbright Meml. scholar, Japan, 2000; recipient TICA award Chgo. Art Inst., 2003. Mem.: Nat. Art Edn. Assn. Avocations: beach, travel, dancing. Home: 408 Frederick St Fredericksburg VA 22401-6028 E-mail: cherndon@cityschools.com.

HERNDON, CHRISTOPHER M. clinical pharmacist, medical educator; s. Frank M. and Beth L. Herndon; m. Angela D. Riddle, June 13, 1998; 1 child, Benjamin G. PharmD, St. Louis Coll. of Pharm., St. Louis, MO 63110, 1991—98. Cert. Pharmacotherapy Specialist MD, 2000. Sci. liaison Ortho-McNeil / Johnson & Johnson, Raritan, NJ, 2001—; asst. prof. Tex. Tech U., Amarillo, Tex., 1999—2001; splty. resident U N.Mex, Albuquerque, 1998—99. Co-chmn. Bd. of Dir., Mo. Pain Initiative, St. Louis, 2002—. Author: (medical publication) Jour. Pain and Symptom Mgmt. Profl. advisor Hospice of So. Ill., Belleville, Ill., 2001—02. Recipient Award for Excellence in Med. Writing, Profl. Drug Systems, 1998. Achievements include patents for Computer related patent-pending. Home Fax: 618 622 3325.

HERNDON, JAMES HENRY, orthopedic surgeon, educator; b. L.A., Oct. 31, 1938; s. James Greene and Kathleen Theresa (Murphy) H.; m. Geraldine Grace Armiger, Feb. 26, 1971; children: Jennifer, Jonathan. BS, Loyola U., L.A., 1961; MD, UCLA, 1965; MA, Brown U., 1979; MBA, Boston U., 1990; MA (hon.), Harvard U., 1999. Diplomate Am. Bd. Orthopaedic Surgery (bd. dirs., pres. 1991-92). Intern Hosp. of U. Pa., Phila., 1965-66, resident in surgery, 1966-67; resident in orthopaedics Mass. Gen. Hosp., Boston, 1970, chief resident in orthopaedics, 1967-70; asst. clin. prof. orthopaedic surgery Mich. State U., Grand Rapids, 1974-77, assoc. clin. prof., 1977-78; prof., chmn. dept. orthopaedics Brown U., Providence, 1979-88; surgeon-in-chief dept. orthopaedic surgery R.I. Hosp., Providence, 1979-88; Silver prof., chmn. dept. orthopaedic surgery U. Pitts., Pitts.; chief orthopaedics, 1988-98; chief dept. orthopeadics and rehab. Presbyn. U. Hosp., Pitts., 1988-98; assoc. sr. vice chancellor Health Svcs. U. Pitts. Med. Ctr., 1995-98, v.p. med. svcs., 1995-98; chmn. ptnrs. dept. orthopaedic surgery Mass. Gen. Hosp., 1998—, Brigham Women's Hosp., 1998—. Examiner Am. Bd. Orthopaedic Surgery, Chgo., 1977—, pres., 1990-91; William H. and Johanna A. Harris prof. Harvard Med. Sch., 1998—. Reviewer Jour. Bone and Joint Surgery, 1975—; contbr. articles to profl. jours., chpts. to books; author books in field. Trustee Meeting St. Sch., Providence, 1984-88, Harmarville Rehab. Hosp., Pitts., 1989-95; mem. bd. govs. Arthritis Found., Providence, 1984-88, Pitts., 1989—; bd. dirs. Make A Wish Found., chmn., 1998-99. Recipient Edith and Carl Lasky Meml. award UCLA Med. Sch., 1965, Bronze award Am. Congress Rehab. Medicine, 1972, Clin. Rsch. award N.Y. Med. Soc., 1974. Fellow ACS, Am. Acad. Orthopaedic Surgeons (treas. 1994-97, pres. 2003—); mem. Am. Orthopaedic Assn. (pres. 1999-00), Orthop. Rsch. Soc., Residence Rev. Com. Orthopaedic Surgery (past chmn.), Am. Soc. Surgery of Hand, Internat. Soc. for Quality in Health Care. Office: Massachusetts Gen Hosp Gray 624 55 Fruit St Boston MA 02114-2696

HERNDON, JOHN WYATT, otolaryngologist; b. Waxahachie, Tex., Sept. 6, 1929; s. John Wyatt and Hattie Belle (Evans) H.; m. Roblyn M. Markham, Oct. 15, 1955; children: Sally Wyatt Herndon Lombardo, John Wyatt III. MD, Baylor U., 1953. Intern Hermann Hosp., Houston, 1953-54; resident in otolaryngology Baylor Affiliated Hosps., Houston, 1954-56, 58-59; fellow in otolaryngology Dr. F.R. Guilford, Houston, 1959-60; with Meth. Hosp., Houston. Mem. Am. Acad. Otolaryngology, Head and Neck Surgery, AMA, Tex. Med. Assn. Office: Med Ctr ENT Assocs 6624 Fannin St Ste 1500 Houston TX 77030-2327 E-mail: mcenta@aol.com.

HERNDON, ROY CLIFFORD, physicist; b. Washington, Sept. 25, 1934; BS, Washington and Lee U., 1955; PhD, Fla. State U., 1962. Staff physicist Lawrence Livermore (Calif.) Lab., 1962—67; prof. Nova U., Ft. Lauderdale, 1967—75; dir. CBTR Ctr. for Biomed. & Toxicol. Rsch., Fla. State U., Tallahassee, 1983—. Dir. Inst. Internat. Coop. Environ. Rsch.; exec. dir. Fla. Hazardous Waste Adv. Coun., Tallahassee, 1980-82; mem. adv. bd. Fla. State U. System, Tallahassee, 1988—; hon. prof. Tech. U. Budapest, 1992. Author: (with others) Methods of Computational Physics, 1966, Land Use: A Spatial Approach, 1980, Theories of Electrons in Disordered Systems, 1982; contbr. over 100 articles to profl. jours. Mem. AAAS, Am. Inst. Biol. Scis., Fla. Acad. Sci., Phi Beta Kappa. Office: CBTR Fla State U 226 Morgan Bldg 2035 E Paul Dirac Dr Tallahassee FL 32310-3713

HERNDON, WALLACE EUGENE, JR., human resources manager; b. Hopkinsville, Ky., June 12, 1945; s. Wallace Eugene Sr. and Cornelia (Edwards) H.; m. Jane Macomber, Aug. 16, 1969; children: Bradford Colby, Jane Allison. BS in Pers. Mgmt., U. Ky., 1963; postgrad., W.Va. U., 1967-69. Employee and community rels. specialist GE, Memphis, 1969-72, employee and community rels. mgr. Jefferson, Ohio, 1972-76, hourly rels. specialist Murfreesboro, Tenn., 1977; human resources mgr. Bristol Myers Squibb, Franklin, Ky., 1977-93; corp. human resource mgr. Fruit of the Loom, Bowling Green, Ky., 1993-98, dir. human resources, 1998-99; human resources cons. Leadership Strategies, Internat., 1999—. Bd. dirs. Franklin-Simpson Arts Coun., 1987-89, United Way So. Ky., Bowling Green, 1991-93, Franklin-Simpson Literacy Coun., 1983-86, pres., 2000-2003, Franklin-Simpson Sch. Cmty. Partnership Com., 1985-88. Recipient Outstanding Community Vol. award Bristol-Myers Squibb, 1992; named Ky. Outstanding Vol. of Yr., United Way Ky., Louisville, 1992. Mem. Soc. Human Resource Mgmt., So. Ky. Pers. Assn., Franklin Pers. Assn. (pres. 1980-81), U. Ky. Nat. Alumni Assn. (life mem., bd. dirs. 1991-96), U. Ky. Logan-Simpson-Warren County Alumni Club (pres. 1985-86, U. Ky. fellow), Franklin-Simpson C. of C. (bd. dirs. 1981-83), Rotary (v.p. Franklin club 1988-89, Paul Harris fellow 1992). Methodist. Avocations: piano, travel. Home: 1113 Bennington Pl Franklin KY 42134

HERNLY, SHARON KELLEY, geriatrics nurse practitioner, consultant, educator; b. Wolfeboro, N.H., Mar. 27, 1947; d. Charles William and Dorothy (Brown) Kelley; m. Thomas Knight Hernly, June 25, 1967; children: Thomas Knight II, Gregory, Sharon Marie. Diploma, Flushing (N.Y.) Hosp., 1968; BSN, Western Conn. State U., 1985; MSN, Columbia U., 1989. RN, Conn., N.Y., Ariz.; cert. geriatric nurse practitioner; adult nurse pr. Staff nurse Flushing Hosp., 1968, St. Lukes, N.Y.C., 1968-69; supr. long term care Danbury (Conn.) Pavilion, 1977-82; substitute sch. nurse Danbury Edn. Dept., 1981-82; psychiat. nurse Danbury Hosp., 1982-85, asst. dir. nursing, 1985-87, nurse mgr. geriatrics, 1987-89, geriatric nurse practitioner, 1989-90, Sound Shore Med. Ctr., 1991-97, Horizon Med. Clinic, Sun City West, Ariz., 1997—2002, Sunrise Med. Ctr., 2002—. Program developer satellite clinics and geriatric med. home visit program, urinary incontinence, sexual dysfunction in elderly, geriatric gynecology, diabetes and pulmonary medicine; mem. adv. bd. Westchester Office of Aging, White Plains, N.Y., 1991-97; cons. long term care; instr. case mgmt. to hosps.; adj. faculty Ariz. State U., NYU, 1995-97. Contbr. articles to profl. jours. and text; poster presenter GSA, Am. Geriatrics Soc. and Coalition Nurse Practitioners. Mem. ANA, Am. Coll. Nurse Practitioners, Gerontol. Soc. Am., Am. Geriatrics Soc., Ariz. Assn. Nurse Practitioners, Ariz. Geriatric Soc., Sigma Theta Tau. Avocations: writing, reading, art, travel. Home: PO Box 20849 Wickenburg AZ 85358-5849 Office: Sunrise Med Ctr 14300 W Granite Valley Dr A-1 Sun City West AZ 85375 E-mail: thernly@primenet.com.

HERNON, PETER, library science educator; b. Kansas City, Mo., Aug. 31, 1944; s. Robert M. and Ethel S. (Grazier) H.; m. Elinor Hernon, Dec. 30, 1972; children: Alison K., Linsay C. BA, U. Colo., 1966, MA, 1968, U. Denver, 1971; PhD, Ind. U., 1978. From asst. prof. to assoc. prof. Simmons Coll., Boston, 1978-83; from assoc. prof. to prof. U. Ariz., Tucson, 1983-85; prof. Simmons Coll., 1986—. Vis. prof. Victoria U., Wellington, New Zealand, 1995-96. Author: Federal Information Policies, 1987 (Best Book award 1988), Service Quality in Academic Libraries, 1996, Assessng Service Quality (Best Book award ALA), U.S. Government on the Web, 1999, 3d edit., 2003, also others; editor Govt. Info. Quar., 1984-2000, Jour. Acad. Librarianship, 1993-2002; co-editor Libr. & Info. Sci. Rsch., 1992—. Recipient Best Article award Coll. & Rsch. Libraries, 1993. Avocation: jogging. Home: 23 Westgate Rd Framingham MA 01701-8843 Office: Simmons Coll 300 Fenway Boston MA 02115-5820

HERNON, RICHARD FRANCIS, civil engineer; b. N.Y.C., July 14, 1940; s. Francis Augusta and Mary Columba (Francis) H.; m. Susan Teresa Hartnett (dec. Jan. 1975); m. Jane Margaret Murphy, June 12, 1977; children: Robert Elizabeth, Richard Jr., Patrick. BCE, Rutgers U., 1962; MCE, N.J. Inst. Tech. (formerly Newark Coll. Engring.), 1969. Registered profl. engr., N.J. Constrn. engr. N.J. Dept. Transp., Trenton, 1964-74, fleet mgr., 1974-76; county engr. Hudson County, Jersey City, 1976-80; dir. N.J. Transit Waterfront Transp., Jersey City, 1980-2000; mgr. transp. engring. T&M Assocs., Middleton, N.J., 2000—, sr. v.p., 2000—. Pres. Rutgers Engring. Soc., New Brunswick, 1977, Island Heights (N.J.) Voters and Taxpayers, 1973-75; chmn. Island Heights Planning Bd., 1973-75. Served to 1st Lt. U.S. Army, 1962-64. Mem. ASCE. Roman Catholic. Home: 69 Hadley Ave Toms River NJ 08753-7769 Office: T&M Assoc 11 Tindale Rd Middletown NJ 07748-2792 E-mail: rhernon@jamace.com.

HERNREICH, NANCY, federal official; b. State College, Miss., July 27, 1946; d. Bernard Francis and Nancy Davis (Martin) McAvoy; m. Robert Eastman Hernreich, Sept. 21, 1968 (div. 1979); 1 child, Ashley Proulx. BA, Webster Coll., 1968; postgrad., Ark. State U. Social worker Jonesboro (Ark.) Sch. Dist., 1970-76; scheduling sec. Gov. of Ark., Little Rock, 1985-92; dep. asst. to pres., dir. Oval Office White House, Washington, 1993—. Mem. Ft. Smith Jr. League, Little Rock Jr. League; chmn. bd. Ft. Smith Pride, social worker, Jonesboro; bd. dirs. Big Bros./Big Sisters Ft. Smith, Spl. Olympics; mem. state steering com. Mondale for Pres.; mem. state Dem. Exec. Com.; del. Dem. Nat. Conv., 1980; election commr. Sebastion County; coord. Sebastion County Clinton Campaign, 1980, 82, 84; dir. March of Dimes Telethon, 1985; head state pub. affairs com. Jr. League. Democrat. Avocations: running, cooking. Office: White House 1600 Pennsylvania Ave NW Washington DC 20500-0004

HERNSTADT, JUDITH FILENBAUM, city planner, real estate executive, broadcasting executive; b. N.Y.C., Nov. 18, 1942; d. Alex and Ruth Selena (Silberman) Filenbaum. BA, NYU, 1964, M Urban and Regional Planning, 1966; cert. smaller co. mgmt. program, Harvard Bus. Sch., 1977. With Office

Planning Coordination, State of N.Y., 1966-68; ptnr. Devel. Planning Assocs., N.Y.C., 1967-68; with engring. scis. dept. Svc. Bur. Corp., N.Y.C., 1968-69; planning cons. Llewelyn-Davies Assocs., N.Y.C., 1969-71, Arlen Realty & Devel. Corp., N.Y.C., 1971-73; ptnr. Planning & Devel. Team, N.Y.C. and Las Vegas, 1974—; v.p. Sta. KVVU-TV Nev. Ind. Broadcasting Corp., Las Vegas, 1974-75, pres., 1976-77, Hernstadt Broadcasting Corp., 1978-81. Chmn. adv. bd. Internat. Film and TV Exch., Inc.; mem. coun. Rockefeller U., 1998—. Condr. TV interview programs. Bd. dirs. Nat. Com. on Am. Fgn. Plicy, Decorative Arts Trust, 1980—98, Eastside Internat. Cmty. Ctr., 1988—96; bd. advisors ACORN Found.; mem. fine arts com. U.S. Dept. State, 1976—; del. Fine Arts Fedn. N.Y., 1970—90; mem. Hudson Inst., 1980—92. Mem. Internat. Film and TV Exch. (bd. dirs.), Harvard Club (N.Y.C.), Hadji Baba Soc., Lotos Club, Explorers Club. Home: 927 5th Ave New York NY 10021-2650

HERO, BARBARA FERRELL, visual and sound artist, writer; b. LA, Jan. 3, 1925; d. Paul C. and Lucile (Evans) Ferrell; children: Alfred O. III, Barbara Ann, Michelle Claire, David Evans. BA in Art, George Washington U., 1950; EdM in Math., Boston U., 1980; cert. in techniques of computer sound Synthesis, MIT, 1981. Art tchr. Marjory Webster Jr. Coll., Washington, 1953-54; printmaker, painter, 1948—. Vis. artist, lectr. U. Mass., Amherst, 1970s, Rochester (N.Y.) Inst. Tech., 1970s, U.S. Psychotronics Assn., Chgo., 1981-89; mus. sound creator Acoustic Brain Rsch., N.C., 1989; founder, dir. Internat. Lambdoma Rsch., Wells, Maine, 1994. Inventor Lambdoma Harmonic Keybd.; exhibited in Contemporary Am. Artist series Corcoran Gallery of Art, 1950; paintings represented in collections at Chase Manhattan Bank, N.Y.C., 1960s, Miami (Fla.)-Dade U., 1960s; author: Lambdoma Unveiled (The Theory of Relationships), The Glass Bead and Knot Theory of Relationships, The Lambdoma Resonant Harmonic Scale (P, Q, R, S, T, U, V and W); contbr. articles to profl. jours. Recipient Davina Winslow Meml. prize Nat. Soc. Painters in Casein, 1964, Cert. of Achievement, Interant. Assn. Colour Healers, London, 1982, J.A. Gallimore cert. for tech. R&D in psychotronics U.S. Psychotronics Assn., Chgo., 1994. Mem. IEEE, Math. Assn. Am., U.S. Ptychotronics Assn. (v.p. 1998-2003). Office: Internat Lambdoma Rsch Inst 496 Loop Rd Wells ME 04090-7622 Business E-Mail: hero@lambdoma.com.

HEROLD, JEFFREY ROY MARTIN, retired library director; b. Chgo., Aug. 9, 1941; s. Roy George and Anne (Polacek) H.; m. Carol Ann Courtial, June 20, 1964; children: Kristin Ann, Timothy Scott. MEd, SUNY, Buffalo, 1966; PhD, Ohio State U., 1969; MLS, Kent State U., 1986. Teaching assoc. Ohio State U., Columbus, 1965-69; asst. prof. edn. SUNY, Cortland, 1969-74, Ind. U. Pa., 1974-75; lectr. in edn. Kelvin Grove Coll., Brisbane, Australia, 1976-78; assoc. dir. office continuing edn. Ohio State U., Columbus, 1979-84; extension libr. Columbus Pub. Libr., 1985-87; dir. Bucyrus (Ohio) Pub. Libr., 1987-2000, Bucyrus Libr. Consortium, 1989-2000; mem. adv. coun. Nat. Multiple Sclerosis Soc., Idaho, 2002—. Book reviewer: Libr. Jour., 1988-97. Chair McGovern for Pres. Com., Cortland County, N.Y., 1972; founder and pres. SUNY Founds. of Edn. Assn., 1971-72; adv. coun. Idaho divsn. Nat. Multiple Scelorsis Soc., 2002—. Grantee Timken Found., 1989, 96, Ohio Humanities Coun., 1994, 95, 97, Libr. Svcs. and Tech. Act, 1998. Avocations: reading, walking.

HEROLD, JILL MEHLHOP, public administrator; b. Key West, Fla., Dec. 24, 1943; d. Donald Leigh and Evelyn Chapman Mehlhop; m. James B. Herold, June 13, 1965 (div. June 1991); children: Gretchen Nelson, Erica Senna. BS, U. Md., 1965; M in Pub. Adminstrn., Harvard U., 1989. Adminstr. Agassiz Cmty. Children's Sch., Cambridge, 1970-72; co-dir. Child Care Resource Ctr., Cambridge, Mass., 1972-78; divsn. head for human svcs. planning City of Cambridge, 1978-80, asst. city mgr. human svcs., 1980—. V.p., bd. dirs. U.S. Conf. of City Human Svcs. Offcls., Washington, 1985—; treas., trustee Pub. Employees Dental and Vision Fund, Cambridge, 1985—; evaluator Innovations in Govt., Ford Found. and Kennedy Sch. of Govt., Cambridge; gov.'s appointee Office for Children Adv. Coun. Gov. of Mass., 1975-78. Mem. Internat. City/County Mgmt. Assn. Episcopalian. Avocations: scuba diving, golf. Home: 10 Rogers St Unit 806 Cambridge MA 02142 Office: City of Cambridge 51 Inman St 3rd Fl Cambridge MA 02139 Fax: 617-349-6248. E-mail: jherold@ci.cambridge.ma.us.

HEROLD, KARL GUENTER, lawyer; b. Munich, Feb. 3, 1947; came to U.S., 1963; s. Guenter K.B. and Eleonore E.E. H.; children: Deanna, Donna, Nicole, Jessica, Christine, Karl-Matthäus. BS, Bowling Green State U., 1969; JD, Case Western Res. U., 1972. Bar: Ohio 1972, N.Y. 1985; avocat, France, 1992; mem. Anwaltskamer, Frankfurt, Germany. Ptnr.-in-charge, European bus. practice coord. Jones Day, Frankfurt, Germany, 1972—; coord. bus. practice Europe and Ctrl. and Ea. Europe Jones, Day. Trustee Internat. and Comparative Law Ctr. Southwest Legal Found., Dallas, 1983; bd. dirs. Didier Taylor Refractories Corp., Cin., Redland Corp., San Antonio, v.p., Redland Credit Corp., San Antonio, v.p., Redland Fin. Inc., San Antonio, v.p., 1979-86, Zircoa Inc., Solon, Ohio, 1988-92. Contbr. numerous articles to legal jours. Trustee Cleve. Internat. Program, 1982-88; chmn. bd. dirs. Frankfurt Internat. Sch., 1991-93; Am. councilor Germany-Am. adv. com., 1995-, Atlantik Bricke, Berlin, 1992-. Mem. ABA, Internat. Bar Assn., Order of Coif, Omicron Delta Kappa. Office: Jones Day 222 E 41st St New York NY 10017 also: Jones Day Hochhaus am Park Grueneburg Weg 60323 Frankfurt Germany E-mail: KGHerold@JonesDay.com.

HEROLD, ROCHELLE SNYDER, early childhood educator; b. Bklyn., Oct. 6, 1941; d. Abe and Anna (Chazen) Snyder; m. Frederick S. Herold, May 7, 1966; children: David Marc, Caryn Michele. BA, Bklyn. Coll., 1963; MS, CCNY, 1968. Cert. tchr., N.Y.; cert. child-care provider, Fla. Tchr. N.Y.C. Pub. Schs., 1963-68; tchr., adminstr. Chanute AFB Pvt. Sch., Rantoul, Ill., 1970-72; dir. early childhood edn. Temple Solel, Hollywood, Fla., 1974-99, dir. social and ednl. programs for young couples, families and singles, 1995-99. Cons. bd. dirs. Temple Solel, 1982-99; nursery sch. com. PTO, 1982-89; lectr., coord. at tchr. seminars, parenting lecture series; freelance writer parenting mags. Author, illustrator: A Family Seder Through a Child's Eyes, 1984, Celebrating Shabbat in the Home, 1992, The Seven Secrets of Perfect Parenting, 1994, Choosing Chessie, 2000, Baby Bear Learns to Share, 2001, A Bear in the Brook, 2001. Mem. AMA Aux., Fla. Med. Assn. Aux., Temple Solel Sisterhood. Avocations: ventriloquism, arts and crafts, writing, interior design, directing children's musical productions. E-mail: rsherold@aol.com.

HERON, DAVID WINSTON, librarian; b. Los Angeles, Mar. 29, 1920; s. Charles Morton and Elizabeth (Atsatt) H.; m. Winifred Ann Wright, Aug. 24, 1946; children— Holly Winston, James, Charles. AB, Pomona Coll., 1942; B.L.S., U. Calif. at Berkeley, 1948; MA, U. Calif. at Los Angeles, 1951. Reference asst. U. Calif. at Los Angeles Library, 1948-52; librarian Am. embassy, Tokyo, Japan, 1952-53; staff asst. to librarian Grad. Reading Room U. Calif. at Los Angeles, 1953-55; asst. to dir. Stanford Libraries, 1955-57, asst. dir., 1959-61; asst. librarian Hoover Instn., Stanford, 1957-59; dir. libraries U. Nev., Reno, 1961-68, U. Kans., Lawrence, 1968-74; univ. librarian U. Calif. at Santa Cruz, 1974-78, emeritus librarian, 1979—; sr. lectr. Sch. Library and Info. Studies, 1978-79; head reader services Hoover Instn., 1980-86. Library adviser U. Ryukyus, Naha, Okinawa, 1960-61; mem. Kans. Library Adv. Commn., 1973-74 Author: Forever Facing South, 1991, Night Landing, 1999; editor: A Unifying Influence, 1981; mem. editorial bd. Coll. and Rsch. Librs.; contbr. articles to gen. and profl. jours. Served as 1st lt. AUS, 1942-46, ETO. Mem. ALA (exec. bd.), Kans. Library Assn., Nev. Library Assn. (pres. 1963-65), Assn. Research Libraries (bd. dirs. 1974), ACLU, Assn. Coll. and Research Libraries (editor monographs; chmn. U. libraries sect. 1970-71). Democrat. Home: 120 Las Lomas Dr Aptos CA 95003-3221

HERON, JULIAN BRISCOE, JR., lawyer; b. Washington, Dec. 17, 1939; s. Julian B. Sr. and Doris S. (Strange) H.; m. Kathleen Ann Sweeney, Aug. 13, 1983; children: Kimberle, Melissa, Julian III, Kevin, Kathleen. BS, U. Ky., 1962, LLB, 1965. Bar: Ky. 1965, D.C. 1966, U.S. Dist. Ct. D.C. 1966, Md. 1968, U.S. Ct. Appeals (D.C. cir.) 1968, U.S. Supreme Ct. 1968. Ptnr. Pope, Ballard & Loos, Washington, 1968-81, Heron, Burchette, Ruckert & Rothwell, Washington, 1981-90, Tuttle, Taylor & Heron, Washington, 1990—. Chmn. U.S. Agrl. Export Devel. Coun., 1983-85. Pres. Washington Internat. Horse Show, 1984, 85, Nat. Horse Show, 1994-96; mem. Dominican 3d Order Preachers. Capt. USAF, 1965-68. Fellow: ABA (chmn. agr. com. of adminstrv. law sect.); mem.: Bar Assn. D.C., Md. Bar Assn., Ky. Bar Assn., D.C. Bar Assn. (chmn. ethics com.), Va. Angus Assn. (bd. dirs., treas. 2000—), Barristers, Legatus, Knight of the Equestrian Order of the Holy Sepulchre of Jerusalem Legatus, KC, The Golf Club Va. Republican. Roman Catholic. Office: Tuttle Taylor & Heron Ste 502 1025 Thomas Jefferson St NW Washington DC 20007-5201

HERON, TIMOTHY EDWARD, special education educator, consultant; b. Ridley Park, Pa., Sept. 20, 1948; s. Raymond Charles and Bernice Marie (Dougherty) H.; m. Marguerite Agnes Campiglia, Aug. 19, 1972; children: Kathleen Marie, Christine Noel. BA, Temple U., 1970, MEd, 1972, EdD, 1976. Cert. flight instrument (CFI-I) Ohio State U. Airport. Devel. supr. United Cerebral Palsy Delaware County, Boothwyn, Pa., 1970-71; tchr. Delaware County Intermediate Unit, Media, Pa., 1971-73; teaching asoc. Temple U., Phila., 1973-76; asst. prof. Ohio State U., Columbus, 1976-81, assoc. prof., 1981-86, prof., 1986—. Ednl. cons. Children's Hosp. Behavior and Learning Disability Clinic, Columbus, 1982-96. Co-author: Applied Behavior Analysis, 1987, Focus on Behavior Analysis in Education, 1984, rev. edit., 1994, The Educational Consultant, 1982, 4th rev. edit., 2001; contbr. articles to profl. jours. Mission pilot, capt. Ohio CAP, Columbus, 1988—; pilot Airlifeline, Sacramento, 1990—2003. Doctoral fellow U.S. Office Edn., Washington, 1974, 75. Mem. Coun. Learning Disabilities (leadership chairperson 1984-86, Ohio pres. 1998—), Assn. Behavior Analysis, Coun. Exceptional Children, Ohio Coalition for Edn. of Handicapped Children (chpt. pres. 1979-81). Republican. Roman Catholic. Avocations: flying, sports, coin collecting, reading, playing guitar. Office: Ohio State Univ 1945 N High St Columbus OH 43210-1120 E-mail: heron.2@osu.edu.

HEROS, ROBERTO COSME, neurosurgeon; b. Havana, Cuba, Sept. 27, 1942; m. Deborah O.; children: Elsa, Rob, Carlos. MD, U. Tenn., Memphis, 1968. Diplomate Am. Bd. Neurol. Surgery. Intern in surgery Mass. Gen. Hosp., Boston, 1968-69; asst. resident gen. surgery, 1969-70; resident in neurosurgery, 1972-77; asst. in neurosurgery, 1976-77; attending neurosurgeon Presbyn. U. Hosp., Pitts., 1977-79; assoc. chief neurosurgery, 1979-80; asst. prof. neurosurgery U. Pitts., 1977-80, dir. neurosurgery residents ednl. program, 1979-80; asst. prof. surgery Harvard Med. Sch., Boston, 1980-83; assoc. prof. surgery, 1983-89; prof. surgery, 1989-90; Lyle A. French prof., chmn. dept. neurosurgery U. Minn., 1990-95; prof., chair dept. neurol. surgery U. Miami, 1995—. Dir. U. Miami Internat. Health Ctr. Chmn. editl. bd. Neurosurgery, 1988; contbr. articles to profl. jours. Chmn. Brain Attack Nat. Coalition, neurovasc. com. World Fedn. Neurosurg. Soc. Recipient Medal of Surgery U. Tenn., 1968, Dean's medal, 1968. Fellow: ACS; mem.: Congress Nuerol. Surgeons (v.p. 1986—87), Neurosurg. Soc. Am., Am. Acad. Neurol. Surgeons (pres. 2001), Am. Assn. Neurol. Surgeons (pres. 2002), Alpha Omega. Office: U Miami Med Sch 1095 NW 14th Terr Miami FL 33136-1407 E-mail: rheros@med.miami.edu.

HERPE, DAVID A. lawyer; b. Chgo., May 2, 1953; s. Richard S. and Beverly H.; m. Tina Demsetz, Aug. 21, 1977; children: Lauren E., Stacy P. BA in Econs., U. Ill., 1975; JD, U. Chgo., 1978. Bar: Ill. 1978, U.S. Dist. Ct. (no. dist.) Ill. 1979, U.S. Tax Ct. 1991. Assoc. then ptnr. Schiff, Hardin & Waite, Chgo., 1978-1996; ptnr. McDermott, Will & Emery, Chgo., 1996—. Co-author: Illinois Estate Planning, Will Drafting and Estate Administration Forms-Practice, 2nd edit., 1994; contbr. articles to legal jours. Mem. and dir. Chgo. Estate Planning Coun. (pres. 2000-01). Fellow Am. Coll. of Trust and Estate Counsel; mem. ABA. Office: McDermott Will & Emery 227 W Monroe St Ste 3100 Chicago IL 60606-5096

HERPEL, GEORGE LLOYD, marketing educator; b. St. Louis, Aug. 31, 1921; s. George Martin and Irene (Lloyd) H.; m. June L. Stamm, Nov. 22, 1949; children: John, Mark. BA, Vanderbilt U., 1943, MBA, 1955; PhD, St. Louis U., 1958. Gen. sales mgr., dir. pub. relations C.V. Mosby Pub. Co., St. Louis, 1947-54; dir. mgmt. devel. Internat. Shoe Co., St. Louis, 1954-62; sr. prof. mktg. Temple U., Phila., 1962-83, prof. emeritus, 1988—; prof. bus. adminstrn. Villanova U., 1983-88. Pres. Hedgerow Theatre Corp., 1971-76; chmn. bd. trustees Sales Mktg. Execs. Grad. Sch. Sales and Mktg. Mgmt., Syracuse U., 1962-64, dean faculty, 1964-83; nat. ednl. cons. Splty. Advt. Assn., Dallas, 1972-89; trustee Accreditation Inst., Sales Mktg. Execs., 1986-90; chmn. Midwest Pres.' Conf. for Small Bus. Author: Specialty Advertising in Marketing, 1972, New Dimensions in Creative Marketing, 1983. Mem. Regional Export Expansion Com., 1966-74, U.S. Dept. of Commerce; chmn. Export Planning Com., Phila. With USNR, 1943-46. Recipient Educator of Yr. award Internat. Sales Mktg. Execs., 1985; named to Hall of Fame, Splty. Advt. Assn. Internat., 1991. Mem. Am. Mktg. Assn. (pres. St. Louis 1957-58, nat. v.p. 1963-65, chpt. bd. dirs. 1999—), Am. Soc. Internat. Execs. (bd. dirs., sec. 1975-94), Sales Mktg. Execs. Internat. (bd. dirs., v.p., exec. com. 1964-64), Nat. Spkrs. Assn. (charter), Sales Execs. Assn. St. Louis (pres. 1954-56), Vanderbilt U. Alumni Assn. (pres. St. Louis 1950), Pi Sigma Epsilon (bd. dirs. 1960-69), Beta Theta Pi (pres. St. Louis 1949). Home: 5323 Bermuda Vlg Advance NC 27006-9455

HERPST, ROBERT DIX, lawyer, optics and materials technology executive; b. Teaneck, N.J., Jan. 23, 1947; s. Harold Dix and Anita Augusta (Adams) H.; children: Katherine Elizabeth, Lauren Gabrielle, Sarah Elizabeth; m. Theresa M. Jacobini, Oct. 24, 1987. BS, NYU, 1969; JD, Rutgers U., 1972. Bar: N.J., U.S. Supreme Ct. Assoc. Pitney, Hardin & Kipp, Morristown, N.J., 1972-77, BOC Group, Inc., Montvale, N.J., 1977-89, div. counsel, 1978-82, corp. counsel, asst. sec., 1982-88. Pres. Internat. Crystal Labs., Garfield, N.J., 1982-88, mng. dir., chmn. bd. dirs., 1988—; chmn. bd. suprs. Solaris Optics, S.A., Warsaw, Poland. Patentee in field. Avocations: golf, politics, stock market, graphic arts. Office: Internat Crystal Labs 11 Erie St Garfield NJ 07026-2307

HERR, SISTER ANNETTE ELLEN, pharmacist; b. Sheboygan, Wis., Jan. 2, 1930; d. George E. and Mollie (Rammer) H. BS, St. Louis Coll. Pharmacy, 1953; MA, St. Mary's U., 1973. Staff pharmacist St. Agnes Hosp., Fond du Lac, Wis., 1953-62, pharmacy dir., 1962-68, St. Anthony Hosp., Hays, Kans., 1968-71; staff pharmacist Med. Ctr. U. Tex. Health Sci. Ctr., San Antonio, 1973-84, St. Joseph's Regional Med. Ctr., Milw., 1984—. Adj. instr. U. Tex. Health Sci. Ctr., 1979-83; pharmacy preceptor St. Agnes Hosp., Fond du Lac, 1958-68, Med. Ctr. Hosp., San Antonio, 1974-84. Vol. tchr. Milw. Achiever Program, 1992—; vol. pharmacist S.E.T. Ministry, Milw., 1985—; active mem. Congregation of Sisters of St. Agnes. Mem. Am. Soc. Health Systems Pharmacists, Am. Pharm. Assn., Pharmacy Soc. Wis. (sec. 1961-63, treas. 1963-65, pres. 1966-67). Roman Catholic. Home: 1210 S 45th St Milwaukee WI 53214-3614

HERR, BRUCE, lawyer; b. Chgo., Aug. 12, 1943; s. Ross and Emilie (Robert) H.; m. Ellen Epstein, Feb. 22, 1968; children: Sarah, Rachel. BA cum laude, Harvard U., 1965, JD, 1968. Bar: N. Mex. 1969, Ill. 1970, U.S. Dist. Ct. N. Mex. 1969, U.S. Ct. Appeals (10th cir.) 1969, U.S. Supreme Ct. 1973. Staff atty. DNA Legal Svcs., Shiprock, N. Mex., 1969-70, Appellate Defender Project, Springfield, Ill., 1970-73; legal dir. Office of Ill. Appellate Defender, Springfield, 1973; appellate defender N. Mex. Pub. Defender Dept., Santa Fe, 1973-76; assoc., shareholder Montgomery & Andrews, PA, Santa Fe, 1976-99, of counsel, 1999-2000; with Office Lab. Counsel, Los Alamos Nat. Lab., 2000—. Mem. N. Mex. Supreme Ct. Com. on Civil Procedure Rules, 1983-98, chair, 1996-98, chair task force on electronic filing, 1994-96, mem. disciplinary bd., 2003—; mem. ethics adv. com. N. Mex. State Bar, 1985-88, 96-2002, chair employment and labor law sect., 1994-95; mem. legal com. Santa Fe Cmty. Fdn., 2002—. Pres. Friends of Santa Fe Pub. Libr., 1997-98; tutor Literacy Vols. Santa Fe, 1996-2001; bd. dirs. Santa Fe Bus. Incubator, Inc., 1995-96; v.p. Santa Fe Econ. Devel., Inc., 1999-2000. Lifetime hon. bd. mem. Santa Fe Bus. Incubator, Inc., 1996. Mem. ABA, First Jud. Dist. Bar Assn., Oliver Seth Am. Inn of Ct., Santa Fe County C. of C. (dir. 1992-96, chair 1995-96, Bd. Mem. of Yr. 1993-94). Avocations: running, hiking, reading, community activities. Home: 148 Elena St # A Santa Fe NM 87501-6528 Office: Los Alamos Nat Lab PO Box 1663 MS A-187 Los Alamos NM 87545-0001 E-mail: herr@lanl.gov.

HERR, EDWIN LEON, educator, academic administrator; b. Carlisle, Pa., Nov. 23, 1933; s. Samuel Leon and Ruth Estelle (McGonigal) H.; m. Patricia Ann Green, July 27, 1963; children: Amber Leigh, Christopher Alan, Alicia Estelle. BS in Bus. Edn., Shippensburg State Tchrs. Coll., 1955; MA in Psychol., Columbia U., 1959, Profl. Diploma, 1961, EdD, 1963. Lic. counseling psychologist, Pa.; lic. prof. counselor, Pa. Instr. Columbia U. Tchrs. Coll., N.Y.C., 1959-63; from asst. to assoc. prof. dept. counselor edn. SUNY, Buffalo, 1963-66; dir. bur. guidance svcs., dir. bur. pupil pers. Pa. Dept. Pub. Instrn., Harrisburg, 1966-68; prof. edn. Pa. State U. Coll. Edn., State College, 1968-89, disting. prof. edn. University Park, 1989—. Dept. head counselor edn., counseling psychology & rehab. svcs. Pa. State U. Coll. Edn., State College, 1968-92, acting asst. dean for grad. studies, 1972-74, dir. vocat. edn., 1972-77, 85-90, acting dir. divsn. edn. policy studies, 1973-76, interim dean Coll. Edn., 1974, 98-99, dir. addictions prevention lab., 1978-79, assoc. dean grad. programs, rsch. and tech., 1992-2001; dir. Coll. Edn. Counseling Ctr., 1974-92; vis. prof. Inst. for the Devel. Nations/U. Reading, Eng., 1967, U. British Columbia, Vancouver, Can., 1989; ext. prof. Temple U., 1967-68; aux. prof. psychology adolescence Lebanon Valley Coll., 1967-68; faculty Nat. Ctr. for Rsch. in Vocat. Edn./Ohio State U., 1978-85. Co-author: (with Evans) Foundations of Vocational Education, 1978, Guidance and Counseling in the Schools: Perspectives on the Past, Present, and Future, 1979; (with Pinson), Foundations of Policy for Guidance and Counseling, 1982; (with Long) Counseling for Youth Employability, 1983; (with Cramer) Career Guidance and Counseling Through the Life Span: Systematic Approaches, 2004, sixth edit., 1996, Controversies in the Mental Health Professions, 1989, Multicultural Diversity in Britain and the U.S.: Implications for Counseling, 1990, (with Rayman and Garis) Handbook for the College and University Career Center, 1993, Counseling Employment-Bound Youth, 1995; (with K. Gray) Other Ways to Win. Creating Alternatives for High School Graduates, 1995, 2d edit., 2000 (with K. Gray) Workforce Education: The Basics, 1998, Counseling in a Dynamic Society, Contexts and Practices for the 21st Century, 1998, (with Locke and Myers) The Handbook of Counseling, 2001; editor Jour. Counseling and Devel., 1992-96; mem. various editl. bds.; contbr. articles to profl. jours. Co-chmn. Centre County Cancer Crusade, State College, 1978-79; lay leader St. Pauls United Meth. Ch., State College, 1978-81, chmn. adminstrv. bd., 1978-81, chmn. edn. commn., 1975-78, pastor-parish com., 1981-83; active State College Mcpl. Band, 1989—; active Sr. Citizens Dance Band, 1998—, Jazz Band, 2000—l asst. baseball coach Teener League, 1982-83; bd. dirs. Gen. Alumni Assn. of Shippensburg U., 2002—. Capt. Pa. Air Nat. Guard, USAFR, 1952-68. Ditchley Found. fellow Eng., 1972, Rsch. fellow Japan Soc. for Promotion Sci., Sophia U., Tokyo, 1979, Vis. fellow Nat. Inst. for Careers Edn. and Counseling, Cambridge, Eng., 1976, Overseas fellow, 1997—; Disting. scholar Chi Sigma Iota, 1993; recipient Jesse S. Heiges Disting. Alumni award Shippensburg U., 1984, Govt. Rels. award Am. Counseling Assn., 1993, Career Achievement award Pa. State U. Coll. Edn., 1996, Cotterill Sr. Leadership Enhancement award, 2000, Howard B. Palmer Faculty Mentoring award, 2001. Fellow Am. Assn. Applied and Preventive Psychology (com. mem.), Am. Psychol. Assn. (com. mem., disting. sr. contbr. 2000), Am. Psychol. Soc. (com. mem.), Pa. Psychol. Assn. (com. mem.); mem. AACD (pres. 1983-84, Profl. Devel. award 1990), Nat. Vocat. Guidance Assn. (pres. 1978-81, Merit award 1976, Outstanding Svc. award 1990), Internat. Round Table for the Advancement Counseling (bd. dirs. 1976-84), Internat. Assn. for Ednl. and Vocat. Guidance (bd. dirs. 1991-99), Assn. for Counselor Edn. and Supervision (pres. 1974-75, pres. North Atlantic region 1969-70, Outstanding Svc. award 1975, Profl. Leadership award 1990), Am. Pers. and Guidance Assn. (bd. dirs. 1975-78, 82-85, Arthur A. Hitchcock Disting. Profl. Svc. award 1980), Am. Sch. Counselor Assn., Am. Vocat. Assn., Assn. for Multi-Cultural Counseling and Devel., Nat. Career Devel. Assn. (pres. 1978-81, Eminent Career award 1986, Pres. award 2000), Assn. for Measurement and Evaluation in Guidance, Am. Mental Health Counselors Assn., Internat. Assn. for Applied Psychology, World Future Soc., Am. Counseling Assn. (life, pres. 1982-85, Profl. Devel. Leadership award 1990, Extended Rsch. award 2003), Pa. Counseling Assn. (life, Presdl. award 1993), Nat. Cert. Coun., Nat. Cert. Career Counselor (cert.), Am. Assn. Christian Counselors, Phi Delta Kappa, Chi Sigma Iota (pres. 1998-2001), Phi Kappa Phi. Republican. United Methodist. Avocations: fishing, flying (lic. pilot), travel, music. Home: 860 Saxton Dr State College PA 16801-4236 Office: The Pa State Univ College Edn 241 Chambers Bldg University Park PA 16802-3206 E-mail: elh2@psu.edu.

HERR, PETER HELMUT FRIEDERICH, sales executive; b. Hamburg, Germany, Apr. 23, 1951; came to U.S., 1978; s. Helmut and Ellen (Schmidt) H.; m. Kim Lovett, Sept. 29, 1984 (div. Nov. 1991); 1 child, Andrew; m. Monika Berns, Nov. 19, 1991; children, Jan, Maximilian. BS in Mech. Engring., U. Braunschweig, 1974, MS in Aero. Engring., 1978. Aero. engr. R&D Beech Aircraft Corp., Wichita, Kans., 1978-81, regional mgr., 1981-86, sr. regional mgr., 1987-92, dir. internat. market devel., 1992-93, regional dir. western Europe and Africa, 1993-94; v.p. internat. sales for Europe, Africa Middle East, Raytheon Aircraft, Wichita, 1994—. Sec., treas. Euroflight, Inc., Wichita, 1985—. Cpl. German Air Force, 1970-72. Lutheran. Avocations: flying, comml. and instrument rated multi engine pilot, golf, boating. Home: 15229 E Zimmerly Ct Wichita KS 67230-9244 Office: Raytheon Aircraft Co 10511 E Central Ave Wichita KS 67206-2557 also: Raytheon Internat Inc Schwedenpfad 16 61348 Bad Homburg Germany

HERR, PHILIP MICHAEL, lawyer, accountant; b. N.Y.C., June 22, 1955; s. Norman and Grace (Sporn) H.; m. Lorrie Wiener, Nov. 23, 1978; children: Gabrielle, Nicole, Adam. BS, BA magna cum laude, L.I. U., 1977; JD, Ohio No. U., 1980. Bar: N.Y. 1981, U.S. Tax Ct. 1982; CPA, N.Y. 1995; registered rep. 1998. Tax staff Ernst & Young, N.Y.C., 1980-83; tax supr. Wiss & Co., Livingston, N.J., 1983-88; tax mgr. Goldstein Golub Kessler & Co., N.Y.C., 1988-93; cons. N.Y.C., 1992-95; cons. estate bus. and fin. planning Guardian Life Ins. Co. of Am., N.Y.C., 1995-98; dir. advanced underwriting Kingsbridge Fin. Group, Inc., Pt. Pleasant Beach, NJ, 1998—; registered rep. AXA Advisors, LLC, 1998—. Adj. prof. bus. Ohio No. U., Ada, 1978-80, Fairleigh Dickinson U., Teaneck, N.J., 1983—, NYU Sch. Continuing Edn., N.Y.C., 1992-95. Contbr. articles to profl. jours., chpt. to book. Mem.: N.Y. State Soc. CPAs, N.Y. State Bar Assn., Assn. Advanced Life Underwriting. Jewish. Avocations: racquetball, tennis, power walking. Office: Kingsbridge Financial Group Inc 501 Broadway Point Pleasant Beach NJ 08742

HERR, RICHARD, history educator; b. Guanajuato, Mexico, Apr. 7, 1922; s. Irving and Luella (Winship) H.; m. Elena Fernandez Mel, Mar. 2, 1946 (div. 1967); children: Charles Fernandez, Winship Richard; m. Valerie J. Jackson Aug. 29, 1968; children: Sarah, Jane. AB, Harvard U., 1943; PhD, U. Chgo. 1954; Doctorate (hon.), U. Alcalá de Henares, Spain, 2001. Instr. Yale U. 1952-57, asst. prof., 1957-59; assoc. prof. U. Calif., Berkeley, 1960-63, prof history, 1963-91, prof. emeritus, 1991—, chancellor's fellow, 1987-90. Directeur d'études associé, sixième sect. Ecole Pratique des Hautes Etudes, Paris 1973; dir. Madrid Study Ctr., U. Calif., 1975-77; chair Portuguese Studies Program, U. Calif., Berkeley, 1994-98, chair Spanish Studies Program, U. Calif Berkeley, 2002—; vis. life mem. Clare Hall, Cambridge, Eng., 1985—; vis prof. U. Alcalá. Henares, Spain, 1991; bd. dirs. Internat. Inst. Found. in Spain Boston, 1997-2000; fellow Ctr. for History of Freedom, Washington U., St Louis, 1994. Author: The Eighteenth Century Revolution in Spain, 1958 Tocqueville and the Old Regime, 1962, Spain, 1971, Rural Change and Roya Finances in Spain at the End of the Old Regime, 1989 (Leo Gershoy award Am Hist. Assn. 1990); co-author: An American Family in the Mexican Revolution 1999; editor: Memorias del cura liberal don Juan Antonio Posse, 1984 co-editor, contbr.: Ideas in History, 1965, Iberian Identity, 1989; editor, contbr. The New Portugal: Democracy and Europe, 1993, Themes in Rural History o the Western World, 1993; asst. editor: Jour. Modern History, 1949-50; mem editl. bd. French Historical Studies, 1966-69, Revista de Historia Economica 1983-91. With AUS, 1943-45. Decorated Comendador of the Orden de Isabel l Católica (Spain); recipient Bronze medal Collège de France, Paris, Th Berkeley citation U. Calif., 1991; Social Sci. Rsch. Coun. grantee, 1963-64 Guggenheim fellow, 1959-60, 84-85; NEH sr. fellow, 1968-69. Fellow Am Acad. Arts and Scis.; mem. Am. Philos. Soc., Real Academia de la Histori Madrid (corr.), Soc. for Spanish and Portuguese Hist. Studies. Office: U Cal Dept History Berkeley CA 94720-2550

HERR, RICHARD JOSEPH, sculptor, educator; b. Sheboygan, Wis., Jan. 17 1937; s. George E. and Mollie (Rammer) H.; m. Anya Van Dulm, Dec. 21, 1995 children: Gretchen, Kurt, Eric. Pvt. instrn., Oscar Binder, Stuttgart, German 1955-58; student, Layton Sch. Art, Milw., 1959-61, Marquette U., 1960-61, U Wis., Milw., 1961-62. Prin./dir. Art Independent Gallery, Lake Geneva, Wis 1968-84; artist-in-residence The Prairie Sch., Racine, Wis., 1970-71, art instr 1971-76, U. Wis. Parkside, Kenosha, 1972-73, Santa Barbara (Calif.) City Coll 1983-88; prin./dir. The New Gallery, Santa Barbara, 1985-87; pres. Richard Herr Corp. Fine Art Acquisition, Milw., 1995—. Mem. Visual Art in Pub. Place com. appointed by Santa Barbara city coun., 1983-85; bd. dirs. Wis. Art Ed Assn., 1974-75, Artists Equity Santa Barbara (v.p. 1984-86); exec. bd. A

Affiliates U. Calif. Santa Barbara, 1986-87. Exhbns. include Painters and Sculptures Show, Milw. Art Ctr., 1965, Old Orchard Invitational Show, Skokie, Ill., 1972, group show Artists Equity, Santa Barbara, 1984, Art Milw., Pfister Hotel, 1995; sculpture reproduced in Milw. Sentinel, Chgo. Sun-Times, Playboy others; lectr., workshop presenter in field. Bd. dirs. Repertory West Dance Co., Santa Barbara, 1986-87 Recipient numerous awards including Marquette U. Fine Arts Festival award for sculpture, 1967, 1st award for sculpture Racine Invitational, Wustum Mus., 1970, 1972, Duo Critic's award Chgo. Tribune, Chgo. Art Inst., 1972. Mem. Am. Internat. Sculptors. Home: W5284 Wisconsin Dr Elkhorn WI 53121

HERR, SHARON MARIE, librarian; b. St. Cloud, Minn., June 23, 1950; d. Lawrence James and Avis Christina (Klein) Blenkush; m. Dennis Wilfred Herr, June 8, 1985. BA cum laude, Coll. St. Benedict, 1972; MA in LS, U. Mich., 1974. Scheduling asst. South Jr. H.S., St. Cloud, 1968; asst. to libr. Coll. of St. Benedict, St. Joseph, Minn., 1972-73; sci. libr. Ohio No. U., Ada, 1974-78, cataloging libr., 1978—. Mem. univ. coun. Ohio No. U., Ada, 1989-91, 97-2001, mem. pers. com., 1979-80. Author essay. Judge elections Hardin County Bd. Elections, Kenton, Ohio, 1995-2001. Recipient Betty Crocker Homemaker award Gen. Mills, 1968. Mem.: ALA, Assn. Libr. Collections and Tech. Svcs., Assn. Coll. and Rsch. Librs., Ohio Hist. Soc., Smithsonian Instn. Democrat. Avocations: antiques, gardening, christmas tree ornament collecting, investing. Home: 822 S Johnson St Ada OH 45810-1521 Office: Ohio No U Ada OH 45810

HERRANEN, KATHY, artist, graphic designer; b. Zelienople, Pa., Dec. 22, 1943; d. John and Helen Elizabeth (Sayti) D'Biagio; m. John Warma Herranen, Dec. 31, 1974 (div. Feb. 1994); 1 child, Michael John. Student, Scottsdale (Ariz.) C.C., 1990—. Cert. tchr. art, State Bd. Dirs. for Cmty. Coll. of Ariz. Horseback riding instr. Black Saddle Riding Acad., Lancaster, Calif., 1960—65; tel. company supr. Bell Tel., Bishop, Calif., 1965; reporter, part-time photographer Ellwood City (Pa.) Ledger, 1967—70; back-country guide and cook Mammoth Lakes (Calif.) Pack Outfit, 1970; motel mgr. Mountain Property Mgmt., Mammoth Lakes, 1970—72; reporter, bookkeeper Hungry Horse (Mont.) News, 1973—74; pig farmer Columbia Falls, Mont., 1973—75; fine artist, illustrator, graphic designer Mont., Calif., and Ariz., 1980—; fine arts cons. Collector's Gallery, Galleri II, Yuma, Ariz., 1983—84; wind chime designer, creator Phoenix, 1995—; represented by Marcella's Ariz. Collection, Phoenix, 1995—, Backstreet Furniture and Art, Phoenix, 1995—2001, Hohn Gallery Fine Arts, Ltd., Scottsdale, 1997—, Magickal Paths, Tempe, Ariz., 2003—, Coomers Mall, Phoenix, 2003—. Guest lectr. Paradise Valley Tchrs Acad., Phoenix, 1993, Sr. Adult Edn. Program, Scottsdale (Ariz.) Cmty. Coll., 1994, pastel painting instr., 1996—; guest demonstrator Binder's Art Ctr., Scottsdale, 1995, Backstreet Furniture and Art, Phoenix, 1995-96; guest lectr., demonstrator Summer Edn. Program Paradise Valley Sch. Dist., 1996, 99, 2000; guest demonstrator Phoenix Artists Guild, 2000, Paradise Valley Artists, 2000. Solo shows include Pinnacle, Phoenix, 1993, Villas of Sedona, Ariz., 1995. Sec. Young Dems., Ellwood City, Pa., late 1960's, Vistas Home Owners Assn., Phoenix, 1995—; troubleshooter Maricopa County Elections Dept., Phoenix, 1994-96, 2000, 2002. Recipient 1st place award, Potpourri Artists, Yuma, Ariz., 1981, Subscriber award, Butte (Mont.) Arts Coun., 1981, 2d place award, Desert Artists, Yuma, 1982, hon. mention, Yuma County Fair, 1983, Wildlife Painting Exhibit, Scottsdale, 1993, Fountain Festival Juried Competitive exhbn. Fine Arts, 1993, Scottsdale Studio 13, 1991, 1992, Spl. award, 1993, Merit award, 1993, 2 Merit awards, 1994, 1st Pl. award, Phoenix Ctr. for the Arts, 2003. Mem. Nat. Assn. Sr. Friends Fine Artists (chair 1995-2003, honorable mention 1993, People's Choice award 1996, 1st place award, hon. mention, 2001), Women's Caucus for Art, Phoenix Artists Guild (hon. mention 2003), Ariz. Pastel Artists Assn. (charter mem., membership chair 1995-96, 2002—, 2d v.p., show chair 1996, guest demonstrator 1995, guest lectr. 1998, Merit award 1995), Ariz. Art Alliance (juried mem., publicity chmn. 2000—), Artists and Craftsmen of Flathead Valley (founder, charter mem., pres. 1981-82), Desert Age Artists (charter mem., v.p. 2003-), Phi Theta Kappa. Republican. Lutheran. Avocations: public speaking and acting, dancing, stamp collecting, photography, interior decorating. E-mail: kathyherranen@aol.com.

HERRANS-PEREZ, LAURA LETICIA, psychologist, educator, research consultant; b. Vega Baja, P.R., June 16, 1935; d. Juan B. and María T. (Pérez) Herrans. BA, U. P.R., 1955; MA, Cath. U. Am., 1957, PhD, 1969. Lic. psychologist, P.R. Psychologist I, Dept. Health, San Juan, P.R., 1957-60, rsch. cons. mental health secretariat, 1983—; prin. investigator WISC-R rsch. project U. P.R., Rio Piedras, 1960-63, instr. psychology, 1963-69, assoc. prof., 1969-77, prof., 1977—, prin. investigator, WISC-R rsch. project San Juan, P.R., 1987-92. Prin. investigator WISC-R-P.R. Transl., Adaptation to Puerto Rican Culture and Standardization, 1992. Author: Psicologia y Medición, 1985, 2d edit., 2000, Manual of Instructions for the Puerto Rican WISC-R, 1992; co-author: Dos Modelos Psicometricos para el Diagnostico Diferencial, 1989, Manual WISC-R, 1992. Pres. ICPE de P.R., Inc., 1989—. Mem. APA, Assn. Psychologists P.R. (pres. 1970-71), Assn. Univ. Profs. Roman Catholic. Avocations: sailing, swimming. Office: ICPE de PR Inc Ste 107 Med Ophthalmic Pla Hnas Davila Bayamon PR 00959 E-mail: icpedeprinc@hotmail.com.

HERREGAT, GUY-GEORGES JACQUES, banker; b. Oostende, West Flanders, Belgium, July 22, 1939; came to U.S., 1966; s. Georges-Albert Maurice and Marie-Gerard S. (Elleboudt) H. Licence en philosophie, U. Louvain, 1961, licence en philosophie et lettres, 1964; postgrad., Yale U., 1966-67, PhD in Econs., 1972. Rsch. asst. U. Louvain (Belgium), 1964-66; rsch. assoc. Nat. Bur. Econ. Rsch., N.Y.C., 1967-72; internat. economist Brown Bros. Harriman & Co., N.Y.C., 1973-74; asst. v.p. Chem. Bank, N.Y.C., 1974-76; dep. chief economist European Am. Bank, N.Y.C., 1977-80; sr. advisor, sr. v.p. Societe Generale de Banque, N.Y.C., 1980-85; mgr. Banque Worms, N.Y.C., 1985-86; sr. v.p., dep. gen. mgr. Credit du Nord, N.Y.C., 1986-93; sr. v.p. Banque Paribas, N.Y.C., 1993-2000; mgr. dir. risk mgmt. BNP Paribas, N.Y.C., 2000—. Cons. Am. Bankers Assn., N.Y.C., 1971, SEIDEIS-Futuribles, Paris, 1967-80, Ford Found., N.Y.C., 1972-73. Author: Managerial Profiles and Investment Patterns, 1972, (with others) The Diffusion of New Industrial Processes, 1974, THe Finances of the Performing Arts, 1974; contbr. articles to profl. jours. Yale U. fellow, 1966-67, Nat. Bur. Econ. Rsch. fellow, 1971-72; named Aspirant de Recherches Fonds National Belge de la Recherche Scientifique, 1967-72. Mem. Am. Econ. Assn., Acad. Polit. Sci., Yale Alumni Assn., Japan Soc., Inst. Internat. Bankers, Belgian-Am. C. of C. (bd. dirs. 1986—). Home: 30 E 81st St New York NY 10028-0222 also: 253 Atlantic Fire Island Pines NY 11782 also: 800 West Ave Miami Beach FL 33139-5542 Office: BNP-Paribas 787 7th Ave 31st Fl New York NY 10019-6018

HERRELL, VIRGIL LEE, county official; b. Jefferson City, Tenn., Apr. 25, 1962; s. Virgil and Mattie Lee (Stansberry) H.; m. Pamela Kay Lowe, Oct. 22, 1994. BA, Lincoln Meml. U., 1983. Profl. cert. Tenn. State Bd. Edn Tchr. Claiborne County H.S., Tazewell, Tenn., 1983—2002; county exec. Claiborne County, Tenn., 2002—. Instr. Walter's State C.C., Morristown, Tenn., 1997—2002. Bd. mem. Spl. Olympics, Tazewell, 1985-93. Named Ky. Col., Tenn. Col. Mem. Tenn. Assn. County Execs., Tenn. County Svcs. Assn., Masons (32d degree). Democrat. Baptist. Avocations: music, reading, theater. Office: Claiborne County Courthouse 1740 Main St Tazewell TN 37879

HERREMA, ROBERT DALE, music educator; b. Grand Rapids, Mich., Apr. 2, 1941; s. Ted and Mae Herrema; m. Joyce A Peuler, Aug. 10, 1962; children: Robert Todd, Christi L Petersen, Kevin Michael. AB in Secondary Vocal Music, Calvin Coll., Grand Rapids, 1964—64; MM, U. of Mich., 1966—66. Choirmaster/organist Numerous churches, Grand Rapids, Mich., 1958—66; vis. lectr. Stillman Coll., Tuscaloosa, Ala., 1967—70; asst. prof. Elmira Coll., NY, 1970—73; assoc. prof. Marywood U., Scranton, Pa., 1973—. Guest condr. various schs. and chs., Pa., 1973—95; tchr. South Chrstian H.S., Cutlerville, Mich., 1964—65; choir dir. Covenant Presbyn. Ch., Tuscaloosa, Ala., 1968—70; founder, musical dir. Cmty. Singers, Tuscaloosa, Ala., 1968—70; music dir. Cantata Singers of Elmira, NY, 1971—75; music critic Scranton Tribune, 1973—81; choirmaster St. Peter's Cathedral, Scranton, 1975—77; min. of music First Presbyn. Ch., Clarks Summit, Pa., 1977—85; founder, artistic dir. Robert Dale Chorale, Clarks Summit, 1978—; choirmaster St. Luke's Episc. Ch., Scranton, 1986—95. Musician (conductor, composer, author/critic). Pres. Lackawanna Arts Coun., Scranton, 1978—80; founder and musical dir. Robert Dale Chorale, Scranton, 1977—2003. Recipient William L. Connell award, Lackawanna Arts Coun., 1978; grantee Outstanding Tchg. fellow, Stillman Coll., 1968, Marywood U. grantee, 1998. Mem.: Chorus Am. (assoc.), Internat. Fedn. for Choral Music (assoc.), Coll. Music Soc. (life), Am. Choral Dir. Assn. (life). Home: 204 Skyline Dr N Clarks Summit PA 18411 Office: Marywood University 2300 Adams Ave Scranton PA 18509 Office Fax: 570-962-4721. Personal E-mail: rherrema@aol.com. E-mail: herrema@es.marywood.edu.

HERREN, MICHAEL WAYNE, classical studies educator; b. Santa Ana, Calif. s. Cecil Ray Herren and Carol Jean McCollum; m. Dana Tenny, Aug. 28, 1962 (div. Feb. 1975); m. Shirley Ann Brown, Apr. 12, 1975; children: Sarah, Michael Aidan. BA, Claremont McKenna Coll., 1962; MSL, Pontif. Inst. Mediaeval Studies, Toronto, Can., 1967; PhD, U. Toronto, 1969. Asst. prof. classics York U., Toronto, 1969-74, assoc. prof. classics, 1974-78, prof. classics, 1978-98, disting. rsch. prof. classics, 1998—. Adj. prof. medieval studies U. Toronto, 1990—; cons. Royal Irish Acad. Latin Texts, Dublin, 1995—. Author: Chirst in Celtic Christianity, 2002; editor, translator: The Hisperica Famina, 2 vols., 1974, 87, Social Sciences and Humanities Research Coun., 1974, 87, Aldhelm the Prose Works, 1979, Iohannis Scotti Eriugenae Carmina, 1993, Latin Letters in Early Christian Ireland, 1996, Latin Culture in the Eleventh Century, 2002; editor Jour. Medieval Latin, 1991-2001, gen. editor, pub., 1996—; mem. adv. bd. Filologia Mediolatina Spoleto It jour., 1994—. Bd. dirs. Mozart Soc., Toronto, 1990—. Sr. Rsch. fellow Kings Coll., London, 1987-88, Alexander von Humboldt fellow, 1981-82, 88-89, Killam Rsch. Can. Coun. fellow, 1995-97, Guggenheim Rsch., 1998-99. Fellow Royal Soc. Can.; mem. Medieval Acad. Am., Classical Assn. Can., Soc. for Promotion of Eriuenian Studies, Hon. mem. Royal Irish Acad. Avocations: classical music vocalist, opera and lieder. Office: Atkinson Coll York U 2300 Toronto ON Canada M3J 1P3 E-mail: aethicus@yorku.ca.

HERRENKOHL, ROY CECIL, psychology educator; b. Huntington, W.Va., Aug. 26, 1932; s. Roy Cecil and Anna Marie (Ashworth) H.; m. Ellen Madeline Cohen, Nov. 27, 1964; children: Eric Brian, Todd Ian, Joshua David. BA, Washington and Lee U., 1954; postgrad., Reading (Eng.) U., 1954-55, Union Theol. Sem., N.Y.C., 1955-57; PhD in Psychology, NYU, 1966. Assoc. sec. W.T. Grant Found., N.Y.C., 1957-62; lectr. in psychology Long Island U., N.Y.C., 1964-66; asst. prof. social rels. Lehigh U., Bethlehem, Pa., 1966-69, assoc. prof., 1969-75, prof., 1975-96, dir. Ctr. for Social Rsch., 1974-90, vice provost for rsch., 1990-96, Disting. Univ. Svc. prof., 1996—. Cons. Computing Devices Internat., Mpls., 1995-97. Author: Becoming a Team, Achieving a Goal, 2004; contbr. articles to profl. jours. Recipient Outstanding Rsch. Article award Am. Profl. Soc. on the Abuse of Children, 1998. Mem. APA, Am. Psychol. Soc. Avocation: carpentry. Office: Lehigh U Dept Sociol & Anthropol Price Hall Bethlehem PA 18015-3008 E-mail: rch1@lehigh.edu.

HERRERA, ARTURO, artist; b. Caracas, Venezuela, 1959; BFA, U. Tulsa, 1982; MFA, U. Ill., Chgo., 1992. Resident ArtPace, San Antonio, 1999—. One-man shows include MWMWM Gallery, Chgo., 1993, 1994, The Ctr. Contemporary Arts, Santa Fe, 1993, Randolph St. Gallery, Chgo., 1995, Hermetic Gallery, Milw., 1995, Mus. Contemporary Arts, Chgo., 1995, Revolution Gallery, Ferndale, Mich., 1996, Univ. Club., Chgo., 1996, Gahlberg Gallery Coll. DuPage, Glen Ellyn, 1996, Brent Sikkema/Wooster Garden, N.Y.C., 1998, The Renaissance Soc. U. Chgo., 1998, Worcester (Mass.) Art Mus., 1998, The Art Inst. Chgo., 1998, Dia Ctr. Arts, 1998, exhibited in group shows at Gallery 400, Chgo., 1992, Nomadic Site, L.A., 1992, MWMWM Gallery, Chgo., 1993, Klein Art Works, 1993, Sch. Art and Design U. Chgo., 1994, Sotheby's Inc., Chgo., 1994, The Drawing Ctr., N.Y.C., 1994, Layton Gallery Milw. Inst. Art and Design, 1994, Feature, N.Y.C., 1994, 1995, PS 122, 1994, Ten in One Gallery, Chgo., 1994, LACE, L.A., 1995, 213 Inst. Pl., Chgo., 1995, TBA Exhbn. Space, 1995, Chgo. Cultural Ctr., 1996, NIU Gallery, Chgo., 1996, Randolph St. Gallery, 1996, Thread Waxing Space, N.Y., 1996, Gallery 312, Chgo., 1996, Gallery 16, San Francisco, 1997, Real Art Ways, Hartford, Conn., 1997, Stephen Friedman Gallery, London, 1998, Brent Sikkema, N.Y., 1999. Recipient award, Art Matters, Inc., 1995, The Marie Walsh Sharpe Art Found., 1997, Louis Comfort Tiffany Found., 1997, Pollock-Krasner Found., 1998; visual arts fellow, Ill. Arts Coun., Chgo., 1996, CAAP grantee, Dept. Cultural Affairs, Chgo., 1995, SA grantee, Ill. Arts Coun., Chgo., 1995. Office: c/o Brent Sikkema 530 W 22nd St New York NY 10011-1108

HERRERA, CARMEN, painter; b. Havana, Cuba, May 1915; d. Antonio Xavier and Carmen (Nieto) Herrera; m. Jesse Loewenthal, July 10, 1939. Student, Marymouth Coll., Paris, Havana U., Art Students League, N.Y.C. Painter living in, Paris, 1948-53, N.Y.C., 1954—. One-man shows include Eglinton Gallery, Toronto, 1955, Galeria Sudamericana, N.Y.C., 1956, Cisneros Gallery, 1965, Alternative Mus., 1984—85, Rastovski Gallery, 1987, 1988, exhibited in group shows at Salon d'Art Moderne, Zurich, 1952, Galerie Olga Bogroff, Paris, 1953, Rastovski Gallery, 1986, 1987, 1989, Jadite Galleries, N.Y.C., 1992, Artists Space, 1993, Museo Del Barrio, 1998—, World Artists at the Millennium, UN, 1999, others, Represented in permanent collections Museo de la Habana, Museo de Santiago de Cuba, Cintas Found. Collection, Museo Del Barrio, others. Cintas Found. grantee; Creative Artists Pub. Svc. Program grantee, 1977-78. Bd. dirs. INTAR, Hispanic Am. Arts Ctr., N.Y.C. Roman Catholic. Home: 37 E 19th St New York NY 10003-1313

HERRERA, CLARITA, medical association administrator; Rsch. fellow in cardiopulmonary physiology Manhattan Veterans Adminstrn. Med. Ctr., NYU Med. Ctr.; pvt. practice in internal medicine N.Y.C.; faculty mem. N.Y. Med. Coll., Office of Primary Care Edn., Lenox Hill Hosp.; past pres. Women's Med. Assn. of N.Y.C.; chair Health Planning Com., N.Y. County Med. Soc.; pres. Am. Med. Women's Assn., 1997—. Office: Am Med Womens Assn 801 N Fairfax St Ste 400 Alexandria VA 22314

HERRERA, GILBERT VICTOR, engineering executive; b. Albuquerque, Mar. 23, 1959; s. Carlos Placido and Martha Trujillo Herrera; m. Cynthia Villareal, Sept. 1, 1984; children: Aubrey Victoria, Brian Edward. Cadet, U.S. Mil. Acad., 1977—79; BS in Computer Engring., U. N.Mex, 1981; MS in Elec. and Computer Engring., U. Calif., Berkeley, 1982. Mem. tech. staff Sandia Nat. Labs., Albuquerque, 1982—88, supr. radiation-hardened semiconductors divsn., 1988—91, mgr. govt. rels., 1992—93, program mgr. electronic packaging, 1993—97, mgr. electronic and optical materials rsch., 1999—2000, dep. dir. corp. bus. devel. and partnerships, 2000—03, dir., mfg. S&T, 2003—; AAAS/Sloan White House sci. fellow White Ho. Office Sci. and Tech. Policy, Washington, 1991—92; COO SEMI/SEMATECH, Austin, Tex., 1997—99. Adj. asst. prof. U. N.Mex., Albuquerque, 1983—84, mem. external adv. bd. elec. and computer engring. dept., 1989—96, mem. faculty search com. elec. and computer engring., 1996—96; mem. AAAS Nat. Sci. Journalism Award Tech. Rev. Com., Washington, 1991—; mem., chair SEMATECH Tech. Adv. Bd., Electronic Packaging, Austin, Tex., 1993—97; mem. Semiconductor Industry Assn./Nat. Tech. Roadmap for Semiconductors Packaging Working Group, San Jose, 1994—97, Nat. Electronic Mfg. Initiative Packaging Tech. Working Group, Washington, 1995—96, Hispanic Engr. Nat. Achievement Award Selection Com., L.A., 1995—95, Army Sci. Bd., Washington, 1999—, co-chair summer study on force protection, 2002—; mem. AAAS DoD Fellowship Selection Com., Washington; presenter in field. Contbr. articles to profl. jours. Pres. Thomas Village Neighborhood Assn., Albuquerque, 1990—91; mentor Stay in Sch. Program Albuquerque Hispano C. of C., 1987—89; precinct chmn. Rep. Party, Albuquerque, 1980—81; mem., players rep. Altamont Little League, Albuquerque, 1999—99. Recipient Ann. Rising Star in Engring. award, Albuquerque Tribune, 1989; fellow, Am. Ctr. for Internat. Leadership, 1992; scholar, grantee, Minority Access for Rsch. Careers, 1980—81, White Ho. Sci. fellow, AAAS/Sloan Found., 1991—92. Mem.: AAAS, IEEE, Mexican Am. Engring. Soc., Assn. of the U.S. Army, Materials Rsch. Soc., Kappa Mu Epsilon, Etta Kappa Nu, Tau Beta Pi. Republican. Roman Catholic. Achievements include patents pending for Fringing Field Effect Transistor with Integrated Memory Function. Avocations: military history, basketball, science history, science and public policy, singing. Home: 10522 City Lights Dr NE Albuquerque NM 87111 Office: Sandia Nat Labs PO Box 5800 Albuquerque NM 87185-0157 Office Fax: 505-844-2977. E-mail: herrergv@sandia.gov.

HERRERA, GUILLERMO ANTONIO, pathologist, educator, researcher; b. Havana, Cuba, Mar. 16, 1952; came to U.S., 1967; s. Guillermo S. and Olga (Del Castillo) H.; m. Elba A. Turbat, Dec. 23, 1972; 1 child, Marlene F. Student, Columbia U., 1970, U. Miami, 1970; MD cum laude, U. P.R., 1975. Diplomate Am. Bd. Pathology, Am. Bd. Anatomic and Clin. Pathology; cytopathology added qualification bd.; lic. physician Fla., N.Mex., Ala., Miss., La. Intern categorical pathology Brooke Army Med. Ctr., Ft. Sam Houston, Tex., 1975-76, resident pathology, anatomic and clin., 1975-79, chief resident, 1978-79; asst. prof. dept. pathology Sch. Medicine and Dentistry U. Ala., Birmingham, 1982-87, scientist II Nephrology Rsch. and Tchr. Ctr. Sch. Medicine, 1982-88, dir. nephropathology Schs. Medicine and Dentistry, 1987-88, assoc. prof. dept. pathology, 1987-88, prof. pathology, head surg. pathology, 1991-95, sr. scientist Comprehensive Cancer Ctr., 1991-95; assoc. prof., head surg. pathology U. Miss. Med. Ctr., 1989-91; acting med. dir. Sch. Cytotech. U. Ala., Birmingham, 1991-93, faculty mem. Grad. Sch., 1991-95; prof. pathology/medicine/cell biology, chmn. dept. pathology Sch. Medicine La. State U., Shreveport, 1996—, chmn. dept. pathology, 1996—; head surg. pathology, attending pathologist VA Hosp., Birmingham, 1991-95; sr. scientist, co-dir. EM Core Facility Comprehensive Cancer Ctr. Ala., 1991-95. Assoc. pathologist Palm Beach Pathology, Good Samaritan Hosp., West Palm Beach, Fla., 1988-89; faculty Grad. Sch. U. Miss., 1989-91; cons. pathologist VA Hosp., Jackson, 1990-91; attending pathologist, head surg. pathology VA Hosp., Birmingham, 1991-95; acting med. dir. Sch. Cytotech., U. Ala., Birmingham, 1991-93, acting head cytopathology, 1991-93, faculty mem. Grad Sch., 1991-95; sr. scientist Comprehensive Cancer Ctr. Ala., co-dir. EM Core facility, 1991-95; prof., chair dept. pathology La. State U., Shreveport, 1996—, prof. depts. of medicine and cellular biology and anatomy, faculty mem. Grad. Sch., 1996—; cons. Oberton Brooks VA Hosp., Shreveport, La. Mem. editl. bd. Ultrastructural Pathology and Pathology Case Revs, 1995—, Human Pathology and Applied Immunohistochemistry and Molecular Morphology, 2001—; manuscript reviewer Applied Pathology, Diagnostic Cytopathology, Am. Jour. Medicine, Am. Jour. Kidney Diseases, Archives Pathology and Lab. Medicine, Ultrastructural Pathology, Stain Tech. and Histochemistry, Am. Jour. Clin. Pathology, Pathobiology, Human Pathology, Cancer, Kidney Internat., Pathology Rsch., Practice and Annals of Saudi Medicine, Am. Jour. Pathology; contbr. articles to profl. jours., chpts to books. Maj. M.C., U.S. Army, 1974-82, col. USAR, 1988-96, ret. Grantee U. P.R., 1972-75, Brooke Army Med. Ctr., Ft. Sam Houston, 1978-79, U. Ala., Birmingham, 1983-86, 87-88, Universita Degli Studi di Milano, 1984, VA, 1986—, Nat. Cancer Inst., 1991—, NIH, 1992—, Ala. Kidney Found., 1992-93, Leukemia Soc. Am., 1997-99. Mem.: Alpha Omega Alpha, N.Y. Acad. Scis., Birmingham Soc. Pathologists (v.p. 1987—88), Tex. Electron Microscopy Soc., Internat. Acad. Pathology, Arthur Purdy Stout Soc. Surg. Pathologists, Am. Soc. Nephrology, Rsch. Soc., Soc. Advancement Sci., Renal Pathology Soc. (chmn. tng. com. 1996—98, sec.-treas. 1999—), Soc. Ultrastructural Pathology (sec.-treas. 1988—91, treas. 1991—99), Electron Microscopy Soc. Am., Armed Forces Soc. Lab. Scientists, Am. Soc. Clin. Pathology. Roman Catholic.

HERRERA, JESSICA RAE, lawyer, educator; b. Port Arthur, Tex., Aug. 28, 1970; d. Leonel and Virginia Ann Herrera. B.A. in Am. Studies, Yale U., 1992; JD, Harvard U., 1995. Bar: Tex. 1995, D.C. 1996. Atty. Crowell & Moring LLP, Washington, 1995—99; sr. counsel computer crime and IP sect. U.S. Dept. of Justice, Washington, 1999—2003; professorial lectr. Am. U., Wash. Coll. Law, Washington, 2001—; spl. asst. U.S. atty. U.S. Attorney's Office for D.C., Washington, 2002; counsel/staff, house sel.com. Homeland Security, 2003—. Adj. prof. Am. Mil. U.; election bd. mem. DC Bar, Washington. Author: (chapter) International Aspects of Computer Crime in The Investigation, Prosecution, and Defense of a Computer Crime. Mem. Women Under Forty Polit. Action Com., Washington, 1998—99; bd. dirs. Books for Am., Washington. Named one of 100 Most Influential Hispanics in US, Hispanic Bus., 2000, 2002. Mem.: ABA, Hispanic Bar Assn. of DC (pres. 2001—02, v.p. 1998—2001, bd. dirs. 1996—98, 2003—), Pi Beta Phi (directory chair 1998—99, No. Va. alumni chpt.). Roman Catholic. Avocations: Tae Kwon Do, studying American west, writing poetry. Office: House Select Committee Homeland Security 1413 B Longworth HOB Washington DC 20515 Office Fax: 202-226-4499. Personal E-mail: jessica.herrera@mail.house.gov. E-mail: jessica.herrera@usdoj.gov.

HERRERA, JOHN, professional football team executive; married; 9 children. BA in History, U. Calif., Davis. Tng. camp asst. Oakland Raiders, 1963-68, pub. rels. asst., 1968, dir. pub. rels., 1978-80, sr. exec., 1985—; dir. player pers. B.C. Lions, 1981-82; gen. mgr. Sask. Roughriders, 1983-84; with scouting depts. Tampa Bay Buccaneers, 1975-76, Washington Redskins, 1977. Office: Oakland Raiders 1220 Harbor Bay Pkwy Alameda CA 94502-6570 E-mail: jherrera@raiders.com.

HERRERA, PALOMA, dancer; b. Buenos Aires, Dec. 21, 1975; d. Alberto Oscar and Diana Lia (Rube) H. Attended, Olga Ferri Studio, 1982, Ballet Sch. of Minsk, 1987, English Nat. Ballet, London, 1990, Sch. Am. Ballet, N.Y.C., 1991; diploma, Inst. Superior Art at The Colon Theatre, Buenos Aires, 1991. Soloist Am. Ballet Theatre, N.Y.C., 1992-95, prin. dancer, 1995—. Dancer (ballets) Don Quixote, 1987, 88, soloist La Bayadere, The Sleeping Beauty, Don Quixote, Met. Opera, N.Y.C., 1992, Etudes, The Sleeping Beauty, Swan Lake, Symphonie Concertante, Voluntaries, 1993, prin. Symphonie Concertatne, Symphonic Variations, 1993; prin. Peasant Pas de Deux in Giselle, Colon Theatre, Buenos Aires, 1992, La Bayadere, 1993; prin. Don Quixote, soloist Etudes, Voluntaries, Theme and Variations, Kennedy Ctr., Washington, 1993; prin. The Nutcracker, Dorothy Chandler Pavilion, L.A.., 1993, Palace Theatre, Stamford, Conn., 1993; repertoire Met. Opera House Symphonic Variations, Theme and Variations, The Nutcracker, Cruel World, Symphonie Concertante, Gala Performance, 1994, La Bayadera, Don Quixote, Paquite, How Near Heaven, Les Sylphides, Cruel World, Tchaikovsky Pas de Deux, Romeo and Juliet, 1995; guest artist Ballet Gala, Toronto, 1993, Colon Theatre, Buenos Aires, 1993, Gala Ballet of Aix-En-Provence, France, 1993, New Generation Ballet, Moscow, Gala Tribute to Nureyev, Toronto, Le Gala des Etoiles, Montreal, Internat. Evenings of Dance, Vail, Colo., Don Quixote, Kremlin Palace, Moscow, 1995. Recipient First prize Latino Am. Ballet Contest, Lima, Peru, 1985, Coca-Cola Contest of Arts and Scis., 1986, Finalist diploma XIV Varna (Bulgaria) Internat. Competition of Ballet, 1990; scholar Colon Theatre Found., 1989; Dance scholar Antorchas Found., 1991. Home: One Lincoln Plz 20 W 64th St Apt F New York NY 10023-7129 also: Billinghurst 2553 10 Piso Dto CP 1425 Buenos Aires Argentina Office: American Ballet Theatre 890 Broadway Fl 3 New York NY 10003-1278

HERRERA, SHIRLEY MAE, personnel and security executive; b. Lynn, Mass., Apr. 5, 1942; d. John Baptiste and Edith Mae Lagasse; m. Christian Yanez Herrera, Apr. 30, 1975; children: Karen, Gary, Ivan, Iwonne. AS in Bus., Burdette Bus. Coll., Lynn, 1960; student, Wright State U., 1975-78. Cert. facility security officer, med. asst. in pediatrics. Med. asst. Christian Y. Herrera, M.D., Stoneham, Mass., 1972-74; human resource adminstr. MTL Systems, Inc., Dayton, Ohio, 1976-79; dir. pers. and security Tracor GIE, Inc., Provo, Utah, 1979-95; health professions vol. PHS/IHS Hosp., Rosebud, S.D., 2001—. Cons. on family dynamics family enrichment program Hill AFB, Utah, 1980-82; cons. on health care mgmt. Guam 7th Day Adventist Clinic, 1983; cons. on basic life support and CPR, Projecto Corazon, Monterrey, Mex., 1987—; faculty mem. Inst. for Reality Therapy, 1991—. Contbg. editor Inside Tracor, 1991—. Chmn. women's aux. YMCA Counselling Svcs., Woburn, Mass., 1970; chmn. youth vols. ARC, Wright-Patterson AFB, Dayton, 1974-76; trustee Quail Valley Homeowner's Assn., Provo, 1988-89; rep. A Spl. Wish Found., Provo, 1989. Recipient James S. Cogswell award Def. Investigative Svc., Dept. Def., 1987. Mem. Inst. for Reality Therapy (cert.), Pers. Assn. Ctrl. Utah, Women in Mgmt. (coun. 1991-95), Nat. Classification Mgmt. Soc. (chairperson Intermountain chpt. 1992-94). Republican. Avocations: writing, skiing, reading. Home: 3824 Little Rock Ln Provo UT 84604-5234

HERRERA TELLO, MARIA TERESA, secretary of agrarian reform for Mexico; b. Villa de Santiago, Nuevo León, Mex., Oct. 15, 1956; Law degree, Autonomous U. Nuevo Leon, Mex. Head Jud. Br.; chief magistrate Hon. Superior Ct. Justice Nuevo León; sec. agrarian reform Govt. of Mexico, 2000—. Office: Ave H Escuela Naval Militar No 701 Col Presidentes Eiidales 04801 Mexico City Mexico*

HERRERIAS, CARLA TREVETTE, epidemiologist, health policy analyst; b. Chgo., Apr. 8, 1964; d. Ludvik Frank and Carlotta Trevette (Walker) Koci; m. Jesus Herrerias, Feb. 25, 1989; children: Elena Mikele, Coco Trevette. BS in Med.Tech., Ea. Mich. U., 1987; MPH in Molecular and Hosp. Epidemiology, U. Mich., 1991. Med. clk. hydramatic divsn. GM, Ypsilanti, Mich., 1983-86; researcher, support staff dept. human genetics U. Mich., Ann Arbor, 1987-91;

program mgr. Am. Acad. Pediatrics, Elk Grove Village, Ill., 1991-99; sr. health policy analyst Am. Acad. Pediats., Elk Grove Village, Ill., 1999—. Project mgr., contbr.: Clinical Practice Guideline: Otitis Media with Effusion in Young Children, 1994. Mem. APHA, Ill. Pub. Health Assn., Acad. Health Svcs. Rsch. and Health Policy, U. Mich. Alumni Soc., U. Mich. Club Chgo. Avocations: reading, biking, needlework, horseback riding. Office: Am Acad Pediatrics 141 NW Point Blvd Elk Grove Village IL 60007-1019 E-mail: cherrerias@aap.org.

HERRERO RODRIGUEZ DE MIÑON, MIGUEL, former Spanish member of parliament, lawyer, international legal consultant; b. Madrid, June 18, 1940; s. Miguel Herrero and Carmen Rodriguez de Miñon; m. Cristina de Jauregui Segurola, Nov. 6, 1975; children: Miguel, Cristina, Amaya. Student, U. Oxford, England, 1958, U. Luxembourg, 1962, U. Geneva, 1964; LLD, U. Madrid, 1965; BA, Licentiate Philosphy, U. Louvain, Belgium, 1966, 68; Licentiate Literature, U. Madrid, 1969. Sr. legal advisor Spanish Adminstrn. (Conejo de Estado), Madrid, 1966—; gen. sec. Ministry of Justice, Madrid, 1976-77; mem. parliament, 1977—93; leader parliamentary majority, 1980-81; leader opposition parliamentary group, 1982-87; spokesman fgn. affairs opposition parliamentary group, 1987—91. Drafter Spanish Constitution, 1977—78; mem. Trilateral Commn., 1982—, Real Acad. Ciencias Morales y Politicas, 1991—; pres. Constitutional Ct. (Andorra). Author: numerous books on constitutional law; contbr. articles to profl. jours. Decorated Encomienda Merito Civil, Gran Cruz San Raimundo de Peñafort, Gran Cruz Isabel La Catolica, Orden del Merito Constitucional (Spain); Order of Merit (Italy). Mem. Bar Assn. Madrid, Nuevo Club, Gran Peña, Casino de Madrid Club de Campo. Mem. Popular Party. Roman Catholic. Avocations: hunting, collecting antique books. Office: Mayor 70, bajo izq 28013 Madrid Spain

HERRES, ROBERT TRALLES, financial services executive; b. Denver, Dec. 1, 1932; s. F. Willard and Edna Margaret (Tralles) H.; m. Shirley Jean Sneckner, Apr. 16, 1957; children: Julie Latenser, Michael, Jennifer Babeon. BS, U.S. Naval Acad., 1954; MS in Elec. Engring., Air Force Inst. Tech., 1960; MPA, George Washington U., 1965. Commd. 2d lt. U.S. Air Force, 1954, commdr. comms. command, 8th air force, dir. command, control and comms. sys., joint chiefs of staff; astronaut designate chief flight crew divsn. DOD Manned Orbiting Lab., 1967; commdr. in chief NORAD; 1st commdr. in chief U.S. Space Command; advanced to 4 star gen. U.S. Air Force, 1984; vice chair Joint Chiefs of Staff, 1987; ret., 1990; pres. property and caualty divsn. United Svcs. Automobile Assn., 1990, pres., COO, 1992, chmn., CEO, 1993-2000, chmn. bd. dirs., 1993—. Chmn. Nat. Bd. Junior Achievement, 1999; mem. Neighboring Housing Svcs. Am., Atlantic Coun.; mem. nat. exec. bd. Boy Scouts Am.; trustee Trinity U., San Antonio.; nat. adv. coun. Fannie Mae, 1999-2000. Mem. Nat. Assn. Ind. Insurers (chmn. 2000), Am. Inst. Chartered Property Casualty Underwriters (bd. dirs.), Ins. Inst. for Hwy. Safety (chmn. 1998-99), Ins. Info. Inst. (chmn. 1999), Nat. Mentoring Partnership, Naval Acad. Endowment Trust, USNA Found., Air Force Acad. Found. Office: United Svcs Automobile Assn 9800 Fredericksburg Rd San Antonio TX 78288-3025

HERRETT, RICHARD ALLISON, agricultural research institute administrator; b. Buffalo, Aug. 4, 1932; s. Wilbert Atherton and Loys (Richards) H.; m. Virginia Walker, July 28, 1958 (div. July 1978); children: Steven Jay, Jeffrey James, William Allan; m. Joan Hanhauser Maurer, Aug. 26, 1978; 1 child, Maxwell. BS in Agrl. Rsch., Rutgers U., 1954; MS in Agronomy/Organic Chemistry, U. Minn., 1956, PhD in Plant Biochemistry/Organic Chemistry, 1959; postgrad., George Washington U., U. Calif., Berkeley. Leader rsch. team Boyce Thompson Inst., Yonkers, N.Y., 1959-61, Union Carbide Corp., Clayton, N.C., 1961-70; tech. mgr. ICI Ams. Inc., Wilmington, Del., 1970-75, dir. rsch. and devel., 1975-87, mem. govt. rels., sci. liaison, 1987-92; pres., cons. EnvirAg Assocs., Bethesda, Md., 1992-94; exec. dir. Agrl. Rsch. Inst., Bethesda, 1995—. Bd. dirs., treas., trustee N.C. Biotech Ctr., Research Triangle Park; bd. dirs. Agrl. Rsch. Inst./Bio, Washington; treas. C.V. Riley Found., Washington, 1988-92; vice chmn. exec. bd. Bus. Coun. on Indoor Air; appointee N.C. Bd. Sci. and Tech.; presenter in field. Contbr. chpts. to books, articles to profl. jours.; patentee in field. Upton Meml. scholar Rutgers U. Mem. AAAS, Internat. Union of Pure and Applied Chemists (fin. chmn.), Nat. Agrl. Chems. Assn. (chmn., mem. rsch. dirs. com.), Am. Chem. Soc., Weed Sci. Soc. Am., Sigma Xi, Inst. Food Technologists. Avocations: racquetball, skiing. Home: 23 Sonneborn Ln Severna Park MD 21146-4803 Office: Agrl Rsch Inst 505 Capitol Ct Ste 200 Washington DC 20002 E-mail: ariherrett@aol.com.

HERRICK, GREGORY EVANS, technology corporation executive; b. Ottumwa, Iowa, Nov. 23, 1951; s. Walter Edward and Doris Ann (Evans) H. BS, U. Iowa, 1974. Gen. mgr. retail stores Amana (Iowa) Soc., 1975-77; mktg. mgr. Meredith Corp., Des Moines, 1977-80; mktg. devel. mgr. Fingerhut Corp., Minnetonka, Minn., 1980-82; founder, pres., chief exec. officer, chmn. Zeos Internat., Mpls., 1982-95; CEO Yellowstone Aviation, Inc., Jackson, Wyo., 1996—; founder, mgr. Golden Wings Flying Mus., Mpls., 1998—; pres. Sky Media Historic Aviation and Flying Books, 1999—; founder Aviation Found. Am., 2002—. Editor: Complete Desk Reference, 1973; patentee and inventor electronics equipment. Mem. Inst. Am. Entrepreneurs (Minn. Entrepreneur of Yr., 1991). Republican. Roman Catholic. Avocations: flying, skiing, sailing. Address: PO Box 6291 Jackson WY 83002-6291

HERRICK, JOHN DENNIS, financial consultant, former law firm executive, retired food products executive; b. St. Paul, Oct. 8, 1932; s. Willard R. and Gertrude (O'Connor) H. BA, U. St. Thomas, 1954; MBA (hon.), U. Laval, 1969. Field auditor Gen. Mills, Inc., Mpls., 1954-59, acctg. supr. Kankakee, Ill., 1959-61, adminstrv. mgr. Chgo., 1961-62, mgr. auditing Mpls., 1962-65, mgr. new bus. devel., 1965-66, dir. adminstrn. and controller Smiths Food Group (subs.), 1966-68; pres. Gen. Mills Cereals Ltd., Toronto, Ont., Can., 1969-71; chmn. bd., pres., chief exec. officer Gen. Mills Canada, Inc., Toronto, Ont., Can., 1971-86; chief operating officer Borden & Elliot, Toronto, 1986-89; cons. Palm Beach Gardens, Fla., 1989—; pres. J.D. Herrick Found. Past chmn. Grocery Products Mfrs. of Can., Toronto; dir. CP Express & Transport, Toronto. Past pres. Jr. Achievement Can., Toronto, 1970-71; past chmn. Toronto Area Inds. Devel. Bd.; past pres., mem. coun. Bd. Trade Met. Toronto; past chmn. Emmanuel Convalescent Found., Toronto; past pres. Am. Club; past vice-chmn. Nat. Theater Sch. Can., Montreal; past chmn. Toronto Harbour Commn.; bd. dirs., pres. Cath. Charities Palm Beach; bd. dirs. Pub. Voice for Food and Health Policy, Washington; mem. pres.'s coun. U. St. Thomas; chmn.'s adv. bd. Rep. Nat. Com., pres. Roundtable NRSC; bd. dirs., pres. DePorres P.L.A.C.E.; bd. dirs., v.p. Liberty Ednl. Forum; bd. govs. U. St. Thomas Law Sch. Capt. USAF, 1954-57. Decorated knight grand cross Knights of Holy Sepulchre, Order of St. John, knight comdr. Order of Polonia Restituta; recipient Queen's Silver Jubilee medal, 1978, Queen's Golden Jubilee medal, 2003. Mem.: Can. C. of C. (past chmn., gov.), Palm Beach Yacht Club, Palm Beach Yacht Club, Capital Hill Club (Washington), KC, Accademia Italiana Della Cucuna Club, Hot Stove Club, NY Athletic Club, Gov. Club, Lambton Golf and Country Club, Royal Can. Yacht Club, Empire Club, Beefeater Club. Roman Catholic. Home: 529 S Flagler Dr 2 H West Palm Beach FL 33401-5933

HERRICK, KATHLEEN MAGARA, social worker; b. Mpls., Oct. 18, 1943; d. William Frank and Mary Genevieve (Gill) Magara; m. John M. Herrick, Feb. 5, 1966; children: Elizabeth Jane, Kathryn Mary. BA in Social Work and French, Coll. St. Benedict, St. Joseph, Minn., 1965; MSW (Mildred B. Erickson fellow), Mich. State U., 1976. Cert. diplomate Am. Psychotherapy Assn., 1998; cert. Acad. Cert. Social Workers. Social worker II Carver County Social Svcs., Chaska, Minn., 1965-70; therapist St. Lawrence Cmty. Mental Health Ctr., Lansing, Mich., 1974-75; sch. social worker Ingham Intermediate Sch. Dist., Mason, Mich., 1975-76; home/sch. coord. Eaton Intermediate Sch. Dist., Charlotte, Mich., 1976-81; sch. social worker, 1994—. Caseworker St. Vincent Home for Children, Lansing, 1979-80; tchr. cons. for severely emotionally impaired, 1981-83; behavior disorder cons., 1983-85; sch. social work cons., 1985-87, prevention splst. profl. and program svcs., 1987-94. Chmn. bd. dirs. Eaton CountyChild Abuse and Neglect Prevention Coun., 1986—; Dem. precinct del.; bd. dirs. Cath. Socia Svcs., Lansing; splst. substance abuse prevention region XIII SAPE, 1987-94. Recipient Eaton County Svc. to children award Eaton County Child ABuse and Neglect Prevention Coun., 1997. Mem.: NOW, NEA, NASW, Am. Orthopsychiat. Assn., Mich. Assn. Emotionally Disturbed Children, Mich. Assn. Sch. Social Workers, Mich. Edn. Assn., Nat. Women's Health Network, Amnesty Internat., Glasser Inst. Reality Therapy & Choice Theory, Mich. Assn. Suicidology, Phi Alpha, Phi Kappa Phi. Democrat. Home: 2113 Long Leaf Trl Okemos MI 48864-3210 Office: 1790 Packard Hwy Charlotte MI 48813-9717 E-mail: kherrick@eaton.k12.mi.us.

HERRICK, KRISTINE FORD, graphic design educator; b. Bryn Mawr, Pa., Feb. 7, 1947; d. Charles Burton and Leah (Bosler) Ford; m. Stephen Wickes Herrick, Oct. 11, 1969 (div. Apr. 1982); 1 child, Katharine Wickes; m. Lee M. Smith, June 6, 1987; 1 stepchild, Suzannah Stuart Smith. BS, Skidmore Coll., 1969; MFA, Temple U., 1983. Cert. art tchr., N.Y. Layout artist Capital Newspapers, Albany, N.Y., 1969-70; designer Slocum House Pub., Albany, N.Y., 1970; asst. art dir. Gen. Electric Co., Schenectady, N.Y., 1970-72; art dir. Kirkman 3 Advt., Albany, 1972-75; from instr. to asst. prof. Tyler Sch. Art Temple U., 1980-85; design cons. Springhouse (Pa.) Corp., 1983-85; asst. prof., program coordinator graphic design Coll. St. Rose, Albany, 1985-92, assoc. prof., 1992—. Author: Trademarks, A History, 1982, Trademarks, An Evolution, 1983. V.p. Ctr. Sq. Assn., Albany, 1972—; founding mem. Historic Albany Assn., 1974—; bd. dirs. Berkshire Ballet Co., Albany, 1988—. Grantee for excellence in teaching Sears Roebuck Found., 1990. Mem. Am. Inst. of The Graphic Arts, Univ. and Coll. Designers Assn., Graphic Design Edn. Assn., The Creative Club (bd. dirs. 1997—). Office: Coll St Rose 432 Western Ave Albany NY 12203-1419 E-mail: herrickk@strose.edu.

HERRICK, STEWART THURSTON, lawyer; b. Grenada, Miss., July 30, 1945; s. Samuel Thurston and Elizabeth Glenn (Stewart) H.; m. Gretchen Ann Schein, Sept. 9, 1967; children: Alisa, Craig, Ashlie. BA, Syracuse U., 1967; JD cum laude, Suffolk U., 1974. Bar: Mass. 1974, U.S. Dist. Ct. Mass. 1975, U.S. Ct. Claims 1975, U.S. Ct. Appeals (1st cir.) 1976, U.S. Supreme Ct. 1984. Assoc. atty. Law Offices of F. Lee Bailey, Boston, 1974-76; ptnr. Harrison & Maguire, Boston, 1976-85, Catanzaro, Effron & Herrick, Ashland, Mass., 1985-90, Stewart T., Herrick & Assocs.; pvt. practice law, Framingham, Mass., 1990—. Mem. Ashland (Mass.) Dem. Town Com., 1982-83; troop leader Patriots Trail council Girl Scouts Am., 1984; bd. dirs., coach Ashland Youth Soccer, 1986-92. Lt. (j.g.) USN, 1967-70. Mem. ATLA, ABA, Mass. Bar Assn., Boston Bar Assn., Mass. Trial Lawyers Assn., Mass. Assn. Bank Counsel, Internat. Platform Assn., Mass. Conveyancer's Assn., Lions (bd. dirs. Ashland chpt. 1993—). Office: 1661 Worcester Rd Ste 303 Framingham MA 01701-5405

HERRICK, SYLVIA ANNE, health service administrator; b. Minot, N.D., Oct. 5, 1945; d. Sylvester P. and Ethelina (Harren) Theis; m. Michael M. Herrick, Nov. 8, 1969; children: Leo J., Mark A. BSN, U. N.D., 1967; MS in Pub. Health Nursing, U. Colo., Denver, 1970; sch. nurse credential, San Jose State U., 1991; postgrad., Golden Gate U. RN, Calif.; cert. pub. health nursing, health svc. Pub. health nurse Dept. Pub. Health City of Mpls.; instr. nursing San Francisco State U., 1975-88; cons. exec. search Med-Power Resources, Alameda, 1988; coord. health svcs. Alameda Unified Sch. Dist., 1988-91; team mgr. home care nursing and program devel. coord. Vis. Nurse Assn. and Hospice of No. Calif., 1991-99; mgr. disease mgmt. and health awareness East Bay Med. Network, Emeryville, Calif., 1999-2000, interim dir. med. mgmt., 2000; dir. utilization and quality mgmt. Children First Health Network, Oakland, Calif., 2001—. Spkr. in field. Mem. Nat. Nurses Bus. Assn., Calif. Sch. Nurses Orgn. (bd. dirs., chair edn Bay Coast sect.), Delta Kappa Gamma. Home: 1711 Encinal Ave Alameda CA 94501-4020 Fax: (510) 450-5868. E-mail: sherrick@mail.cho.org.

HERRICK, TODD W. manufacturing company executive; b. Tecumseh, Mich., 1942; Grad., U. Notre Dame, 1967. Pres. Tecumseh (Mich.) Products Co., 1984—, CEO, 1987—, chmn. bd., 2003—. Office: Tecumseh Products Co 100 E Patterson St Tecumseh MI 49286-2087

HERRICK, TRACY GRANT, fiduciary; b. Cleve., Dec. 30, 1933; s. Stanford Avery and Elizabeth Grant (Smith) Herrick; m. Maie Kaarsoo, Oct. 12, 1963; children: Sylvi Anne, Alan Kalev. BA, Columbia U., 1956, MA, 1958; postgrad., Yale U., 195-57; MA, Oxford U., England, 1960. Economist Fed. Res. Bank, Cleve., 1960-70; sr. economist Stanford Rsch. Inst., Menlo Park, Calif., 1970-73; v.p., sr. analyst Shuman, Agnew & Co., Inc., San Francisco, 1973-75; v.p. Bank of Am., San Francisco, 1975-81; pres. Tracy G. Herrick, Inc., 1981—. Lectr. Stonier Grad. Sch. Banking Am. Bankers Assn., 1967—76; commencement spkr. Memphis Banking Sch., 1974; bd. dirs. Jefferies Group, Inc., chmn. bd. audit com., 1989—96, chmn. bd. compensation com., 1991—96, dir., 1983—99; bd. dirs. Jefferies & Co., Inc.; dir. Com. Monetary Rsch. and Edn., Inc. Author: Bank Analyst's Handbook, 1978, Timing, 1981, Power and Wealth, 1988; contbr. Mem. adv. bd. San Xavier Found., Monterey, Calif., Kara Found., Palo Alto, Calif. Fellow: Fin. Analysts Fedn.; mem.: San Francisco Soc. Security Analysts, Assn. Investment Mgmt. Rsch. Republican. Congregationalist. Home: 1150 University Ave Palo Alto CA 94301-2238

HERRIFORD, ROBERT LEVI, SR., army officer; b. Lewistown, Ill., May 4, 1931; s. John and Lola (Braden) H.; m. Muriel Jean Davis, July 10, 1949; children: Robert Levi, Thomas Merle, David William, Deborah S., Traci Ann. BS, U. Ariz., 1966, MBA, 1968. Enlisted in U.S. Army, 1948, commd. 2d lt., 1952, advanced through grades to maj. gen., 1979; service in Vietnam, 1966-67; comdr. 269th Ordnance Group, 1969-71; chief spl. items mgmt. Tank Automotive Command Detroit, 1971-72; comdr. Korean Procurement Agy. Seoul, 1973-74; dir. procurement Armaments Command Rock Island, Ill., 1974-76; comdr. Def. Contracts Region, 1976-78; asst. dep. chief of staff logistics, 1978-80; dir. procurement and prodn. Devel. and Readiness Command Alexandria, Va., 1980-83; assoc. chief ops. officer, dir. support services Argonne Nat. Lab., 1983-95. Chmn. Minority Bus. Opportunity Council, N.Y.C., 1976-78. Decorated Legion of Merit, D.S.M., Def. Superior Service medal, Bronze Star, Airmedal, numerous others. Mem. Am. Def. Preparedness Assn., Assn. U.S. Army, Am. Legion, Nat. Contracts Mgmt. Assn. (chpt. pres. 1975-76) Office: 104 N Pittsburg Lndg Springfield IL 62707-7959 E-mail: RobLHerr@aol.com. *There is no substitute in any career, but particularly in an Army officer's career, for hard work, dedication and absolute integrity. Subordinates, peers, and superiors can sense it in training, in garrison, and in battle. Many people, in all pursuits and professions, are created equal in talent. Only a very few are willing to give to that talent all the care and dedication that is required to bring it to the top of their chosen field. It is often easier to explain why you didn't make it than to devote all that is required to develop this talent.*

HERRIGES, GREG C. literature educator, writer; b. Evanston, Ill., Apr. 16, 1950; s. Raymond Charles Herriges and Charlotte Catherine Poggioli; m. Durschlag Cara Herriges, June 22, 1970 (div. July 1977); m. Carmen Nereida Perez, Jan. 22, 1983; 1 child, Jeremy Charles. BA English and Edn., Northeastern Ill. U., 1972, MA Lit., 1975. Tchr. Tuley HS, Chgo., 1972—74, Roberto Clemente HS, Chgo., 1974—88, Taft HS, Chgo., 1988—89; prof. William Rainey Harper Coll., Palatine, Ill., 1989—. Author: (novels) Someplace Safe, 1984, Secondary Attachments, 1986, The Winter Dance Party Murders, 1998. Recipient Disting. Alumni award, Kendall Coll., 1979. Mem.: PEN U.S. West. Office: William Rainey Harper Coll 1200 W Algonquin Rd Palatine IL 60067-7373 Office Fax: 847-925-6039. E-mail: herriges3@aol.com.

HERRIN, DAVID LESLIE, educator; b. Waycross, Ga., Aug. 15, 1955; s. Leslie Edgar and Betty Louise (Cochran) H.; m. Amy L. Schomer, May 1, 1982; children: Alex J., Joey P. BS, U. Miami, 1977; MA, U. South Fla., 1980, PhD, 1985. Rsch. assoc. U. Ga., Athens, 1985-88; asst. prof. U. Tex., Austin, 1988-94, assoc. prof., 1994—2000, prof., 2001—. Contbr. articles to profl. jours. Democrat. Avocations: golf, fishing. Office: U Tex Sch Biolog Scis Molecular Cell and Devel Biology Sect Austin TX 78713

HERRIN, MARK MALACHI, military officer; b. Columbia, S.C., Nov. 13, 1963; s. Leslie E. Herrin, Jr. and Betty L. (Cochran) Herrin; m. Jean M. Jackson, July 4, 1998; children: Synnove K., William H. AA in Gen. Studies, Hillsborough C.C., Brandon, Fla., 1988; BS in Fin., U. of Tampa, 1990; MS in Logistics Mgmt., Naval Postgrad. Sch., Monterey, Calif., 1999; student, U.S. Army Command and Gen. Staff Coll., Ft. Leavenworth, Kans., 2003. Sgt. U.S. Army, Fort Belvoir, Va., 1984—86; served with 3d Armored Divsn., 8th Inf. Divsn., and 1st Armored Divsn., Hanau, Germany, 1990—93; S4, served with Support Squadron, 11th Armored Cav. Rgt. (OPFOR), Fort Irwin, Calif., 1994—95; served with Maintenance Troop, 11th Armored Cav. Rgt. (OPFOR), Fort Irwin, Calif., 1995—97, Def. Logistics Agy., Def. Supply Ctr. Columbus, Ohio, 1999—2002. Maj. U.S. Army, 1983. Decorated Bronze Star, Def. Meritorious Svc. medal, Meritorious Svc. Medal, Nat. Def. Svc. medal. Mem.: Assn. of U.S. Army Quartermasters, Leadership Devel. Assn., Packhorse Assn. (pres. 1994—95, Support Squadron, 11th ACR (OPFOR)), Blackhorse Assn. (11th Armored Cav. Rgt.), Assn. of the U.S. Army, Acad. of Mgmt., Youth Coun. of Cen. Bapt. Ch. (pres. 1981—82), Woods Chapel (singles class pres. 1982—83), Leaders Club Coun. Avocations: motorcycling, world travel, photography, technology. Office: USAG-J Unit 45013 Box 3207 Apo AP 96338-5023 Personal E-mail: mark.herrin@us.army.mil.

HERRING, CHARLES DAVID, lawyer, educator; b. Muncie, Ind., Mar. 18, 1943; s. Morris and Margaret Helen Herring; children: David, Margaret, Christopher. BA, Ind. U., 1965, JD cum laude, 1968. Bar: Ind. 1968, U.S. Dist. Ct. (so. dist.) Ind. 1971, Calif. 1971, U.S. Dist. Ct. (so. dist.) Calif. 1971. Rsch. assoc. Ind. U., 1965-68; intern Office of Pros. Atty., Monroe County, Ind., 1967-68; ptnr. Herring, Stubel & Lehr and predecessor Hering and Stabel, San Diego, 1972—92; pvt. practice San Diego, 1972—. Prof. law Western State U., 1972—91. Author: (with Jim Wade) California Cases on Professional Responsibility, 1976. Vice chmn. Valle de Oro Planning Com., Spring Valley, Calif., 1972-75; chmn. Valle de Oro Citizens Exec. Com. for Community Planning, Spring Valley, 1975-78. Served with JAGC, U.S. Army, 1968-72. Mem.: ABA (Best Brief award 1968), Calif. Trial Lawyers Assn., Conf. Spl. Ct. Judges, San Diego County Bar Assn., Calif. Bar Assn., Ind. Bar Assn., San Diego Lions Club (dir., bd. trustees, past pres.), Order of Coif. Republican. Avocations: computers, gardening, swimming, golf. Home: 284 Sunnybrook Ln El Cajon CA 92021-7801 Office: Herring & Herring 755 Broadway Cir 2d Fl San Diego CA 92101-6160 E-mail: dherring@herringlaw.net.

HERRING, JACKSON REA, physicist; b. Ashland, Ky., Oct. 2, 1931; s. Ralph Alderman and Willeen (Tull) H.; m. Betty Jean Pegram, Jan. 31, 1959; children: Peter, Christopher. BS in Physics, Wake Forest U., 1953; MS in Physics, U. N.C., 1956, PhD in Physics, 1959. Theoretical physicist theoretical divsn. Goddard Space Flight Ctr. NASA, Washington, 1959-61, theoretical physicist Goddard Inst. for Space Studies NASA, N.Y.C., 1961-64, theoretical physicist Goddard Space Flight Ctr. Greenbelt, Md., 1964-72; sr. scientist Nat. Ctr. Atmospheric Rsch., Boulder, Colo., 1972-98, sr. scientist emeritus, 1998—. Mem. adv. com. NASA Ames-Stanford Ctr. for Turbulence Rsch., 1988-89; sr. postdoctoral fellow Nat. Ctr. for Atmospheric Rsch., Advanced Study Program, Boulder, 1972; invited prof. U. Pierre-Marie Currie, Paris, 1995. Editor: (with McWilliams) Lecture Notes on Turbulence, 1989. Green scholar U. Calif. San Diego Inst. of Geophysics and Planetary Physics, 1978. Fellow: AAAS (fellowship com. 2001), Am. Phys. Soc. Home: 2581 Briarwood Dr Boulder CO 80305-6803 Office: Nat Ctr Atmospheric Rsch PO Box 3000 Boulder CO 80307-3000

HERRING, JAMES H. political organization administrator, lawyer; b. 1938; BA, U. Miss., 1960, JD, 1963. Dist. atty. Counties of Madison and Rankin, 1970—75; partner Perry, Phillips, Crockett, Morrison & Herring, 1975—76; instructor Miss. College School of Law, 1975—76; partner Herring, Long & Crews, P.C., Canton, Miss., 1979—97; judge Miss. Court of Appeals, 1997—99; chmn. Republican Party of Miss., Miss., 2001—. Republican. Office: 415 Yazoo St Ste 200 Jackson MS 39201 also: Herring, Long & Crews 129 E Peace St PO Box 344 Canton MS 39046

HERRING, JERONE CARSON, lawyer, bank executive; b. Kinston, N.C., Sept. 27, 1938; s. James and Isabel (Knight) H.; m. Patricia Ann Hardy, Aug. 6, 1961; children— Bradley Jerone, Ansley Carole. AB, Davidson Coll., 1960; LL.B., Duke U., 1963. Bar: N.C. 1963. Assoc. McElwee & Hall, North Wilkesboro, N.C., 1965-69; ptnr. McElwee, Hall & Herring, North Wilkesboro, 1969-71; exec. v.p., sec., gen. counsel Br. Banking & Trust Co., Winston-Salem, N.C., 1971—, BB&T Corp., Winston-Salem, 1995—. Bd. advisors, steering com. U. N.C. Ctr. Banking and Fin.; bd. visitors Davidson Coll. Served to capt. U.S. Army, 1963-65. Mem. ABA, N.C. Bar Assn., Am. Soc. Corp. Secs., Am. Corp. Counsel Assn. Presbyterian. Office: 200 W 2d St Winston Salem NC 27101 E-mail: jherring@bbandt.com.

HERRING, LINDA, pianist, music educator; b. Hong Kong, Oct. 28, 1968; d. Warren Hsiung and Chiu Lan Shui; m. Todd Brian Herring, Jan. 8, 1994; children: Ryan, Andrew. Assoc. Performer diploma, Trinity Coll. of Music, London, 1988; B of Music magna cum laude, Southwest Tex. State U., 1991; M of Music, U. Houston, 1993. Tchr. piano Comml. Piano Studio, Hong Kong, 1985-88, Earline Sneed Piano Studio, Lockhart, Tex., 1989-91, Linda Herring Piano Studio, Houston, 1992—. Mem. Nat. Guild Piano Tchrs., Music Tchrs. Nat. Assn., Cypress Creek Music Tchrs. Assn. (3d v.p. 1996-99), Golden Key Soc., Alpha Chi. Home: 12707 Big Stone Dr Houston TX 77066-1602

HERRING, MARK YOUNGBLOOD, librarian, university dean; b. Dothan, Ala., Oct. 10, 1952; s. Reuben and Dorothy Lavina (McCorvey) H.; m. Brenda Carol Lane, Aug. 11, 1972; children: Adriel, Areli Allene. BA, George Peabody Coll. Tchrs., 1974; MLS, Vanderbilt U., 1978; EdD, East Tenn. State U., 1990. Libr. dir. King Coll., Bristol, Tenn., 1979-87; instr. East Tenn. State U., Johnson City, 1990; dean libr. svcs. Okla. Bapt. U., Shawnee, 1992-99; dean Winthrop U., Rock Hill, S.C., 1999—. Exec. dir. Am. 21, Bristol, Tenn., 1990-92; founder, pres. Electronic Conservative Clearinghouse Libr., Shawnee, 1998—. Author: (monographs) Controversial Issues in Librarianship, 1986, Ethics and the Professor, 1988, Organizing Friends Group, 1993, Historic Guide to the Pro-Life Pro-Choice Debate, 2003, At the Core of the Problem-Reforming Teacher Education in Oklahoma, 2001. Fellow East Tenn. State U., 1987-90; grantee Noble Found., Okla., 1999, S.C. Humanities Found. Mem. Nat. Assn. Scholars, Assn. Libr. and Learning Ctr. Dirs. (pres. 1996-97), Okla. Libr. Assn. (exec. bd. 1993-95), Okla. Assn. Scholars (pres. 1997-99). Republican. Presbyterian. Avocations: reading, running, hiking. Office: Winthrop U Dacus Libr Rock Hill SC 29733-0001 Fax: 803-323-2215. E-mail: herringm@winthrop.edu.

HERRING, MARSHA KATHLINE, health services marketing administrator b. June 23, 1958; B in Gen. Studies, U. Mich., 1980, M. in Pub. Policy, 1983 Press asst. U.S. Senator Carl Levin, Washington, 1980-85; mktg. dir. Humana Hosp.-Brazos Valley, College Station, Tex., 1985-89; dir. mental health mktg Christ Hosp., Oaklawn, Ill., 1991-93; mktg. dir. U. Ill. Chgo. Med. Ctr. 1993-2000; prin. M Powered Comm., 2000—. Social mktg. cons. to state and fed. agys. and not-for-profit orgns. Contbr. articles to profl. jours. Office: 6 Richwood Ter Flossmoor IL 60422-1683

HERRING, MIKE, information technology executive; B in Acctg., UCLA CPA. Contr. biotech. co.; auditor Ernst & Young; v.p. fin. ThirdAge Media, Inc (acquired by MyFamily.com, Inc.); now CFO MyFamily.com, Inc., Provo Utah. Office: MyFamily dot com Inc 360 W 4800 N Provo UT 84604 Office Fax: 801-705-7001.

HERRING, OLIVER, artist; b. Germany; BFA, U. Oxford, Eng., 1988; MFA Hunter Coll., 1991. One-man shows include work Space Gallery, New Mus Contemporary Art, N.Y.C., 1993, Mannheimer Kunstverein, Mannheim, 1993 Max Protetch Gallery, N.Y.C., 1994, 1996, 1997, 1998, Space Untitled, N.Y 1994, Bernard Toale Gallery, Boston, 1994, Solomon R. Guggenheim Mus N.Y., 1996, Mus. Modern Art, N.Y.C., 1996, Manfred Baumgartner Gallery Washington, 1996, Newlyn Art Gallery, Penzance, Eng., 1997, Camden Art Ctr London, 1997, Ace Galleries, L.A., 1999, exhibited in group shows at List Ar Ctr., Brown U., Providence, 1995, Queens (N.Y.) Libr. Gallery, 1996, New Mus Contemporary Art, N.Y., 1996, Randolph St. Gallery, Chgo., 1996, Th Contemporary Mus., Honolulu, 1996, Max Protetch Gallery, N.Y.C., 1997 Galerie Thaddaeus Ropac, Paris, 1997, numerous others. Mass. Arts Lotter grantee, 1989, N.Y. Found. Arts grantee, 1995. Office: care Max Protetc Gallery 511 West 22d St New York NY 10011

HERRING, RAYMOND MARK, marketing professional, researcher; b Nashville, Sept. 23, 1952; s. Raymond Benjamin and Alma Ruth (Murrell) H BA, Baylor U., 1974, MA, 1976, EdD, 1983. Rsch. and evaluation speciali McLennan County Med. Edn. and Rsch. Found., Waco, Tex., 1979-82; dir. edn pub. rels. Providence Hosp., Waco, 1982-85, dir. ctr. for health promotio 1983-85; v.p. John Leifer, Ltd., Shawnee Mission, Kans., 1985-86; pres. Ma Herring Assocs., Inc., Malvern, Pa., 1986—. Mem. editl. bd. Healthcare Mgm

Rev., 1986-90; contbr. articles to profl. jours. Bd. dirs. Am. Diabetes Assn., Waco, 1984—85, Tex. Soc. Hosp. Educators, 1983—85. Mem. Qualitative Rsch. Cons. Assn. (Phila. chpt. bd. dirs. 2001—, MRA/QRCA joint com. 2002—). Office: Mark Herring Assocs Inc 2150 Diamond Rock Hill Rd Malvern PA 19355

HERRING, SUSAN WELLER, dental educator, oral anatomist; b. Pitts., Mar. 25, 1947; d. Sol W. and Miriam (Damick) Weller; m. Norman S. Wolf, May 27, 1995. BS in Zoology, U. Chgo., 1967, PhD in Anatomy, 1971. NIH postdoctoral fellow U. Ill., Chgo., 1971-72, from asst. prof. to prof. oral anatomy and anatomy, 1972-90; prof. orthodontics U. Wash., Seattle, 1990—. Vis. assoc. prof. biol. sci. U. Mich., Ann Arbor, 1981; cons. NIH study sect., Washington, D.C., 1987-89; sci. gov. Chgo. Acad. Sci., 1982-90; mem. pub. bd. Growth Pub. Inc., Bar Harbor, Maine, 1982—. Mem. editl. bd. Cells, Tissues, Organs, 1989—, Jour. Dental Rsch., 1995-98, 2003—, Jour. Morphology, 1997—, Integrative Biology 2000—;, Archives of Oral Biology, 2003-; contbr. articles to profl. jours. Predoctoral fellow NSF, 1967-71; rsch. grantee NIH, 1975-78, 81—, NSF, 1990-92, 94-95. Fellow AAAS; mem. Internat. Assn. Dental Rsch. (dir. craniofacial biology group 1994-95, v.p. 1995-96, pres.-elect 1996-97, pres. 1997-98, Craniofacial Biology Rsch. award 1999), Soc. Integrated Comp. Biol.(chmn. vertebrate zoology 1983-84, exec. com. 1986-88), Am. Soc. Biomechanics, Am. Assn. Anatomists (chmn. Basmajian com. 1988-90), Soc. Vertebrate Paleontology, Internat. Soc. Vertebrate morphology (convenor 4th congress 1994, pres. 1994-97), Sigma Xi. Avocation: semi-profl. violin. Office: U Wash Box 357446 Seattle WA 98195-7446 E-mail: herring@u.washington.edu.

HERRING, WILLIAM CONYERS, physicist, emeritus educator; b. Scotia, N.Y., Nov. 15, 1914; s. William Conyers and Mary (Joy) H.; m. Louise C. Preusch, Nov. 30, 1946; children— Lois Mary, Alan John, Brian Charles, Gordon Robert. AB, U. Kans., 1933; PhD, Princeton, 1937. NRC fellow Mass. Inst. Tech., 1937-39; instr. Princeton, 1939-40, U. Mo., 1940-41; mem. sci. staff Div. War Research, Columbia, 1941-45; prof. applied math. U. Tex., 1946; research physicist Bell Telephone Labs., Murray Hill, N.J., 1946-78; prof. applied physics Stanford (Calif.) U., 1978-81, prof. emeritus, 1981—. Mem. Inst. Advanced Study, 1952-53 Recipient Army-Navy Cert. of Appreciation, 1947; Distinguished Service citation U. Kans., 1973; J. Murray Luck award for excellence in sci. reviewing Nat. Acad. Scis., 1980; von Hippel award Materials Rsch. Soc., 1980, Wolf prize in Physics, 1985. Fellow Am. Phys. Soc. (Oliver E. Buckley solid state physics prize 1959), Am. Acad. Arts and Scis.; mem. AAAS, NAS, Am. Soc. Info. Scis. Home: 3945 Nelson Dr Palo Alto CA 94306-4524 Office: Stanford U Lab for Advanced Materials MS 4045 Stanford CA 94305-4045

HERRINGER, FRANK CASPER, diversified financial services company executive; b. N.Y.C., Nov. 12, 1942; s. Casper Frank and Alice Virginia (McMullen) H.; m. Maryellen B. Cattani; children: William, Sarah, Julia. AB magna cum laude, Dartmouth, 1964, MBA with highest distinction, 1965. Prin. Cresap, McCormick & Paget, Inc. (mgmt. cons.), N.Y.C., 1965-71; staff asst. to Pres., Washington, 1971-73; adminstr. U.S. Urban Mass Transp. Adminstrn., Washington, 1973-75; gen. mgr. San Francisco Bay Area Rapid Transit Dist., 1975-78; exec. v.p. Transam. Corp., San Francisco, 1979-86, pres., dir., 1986-99, CEO, 1991-99, chmn., 1996—; mem. exec. bd. AEGON N.V., 1999-2000; chmn. AEGON USA, 1999-2000. Bd. dirs. AT&T Corp., Unocal Corp., Charles Schwab & Co., Mirapoint, Inc., Calif. Pacific Med. Ctr. Mem. Cypress Point Club, San Francisco Golf Club, Olympic Club, Claremont Country Club, Pacific Union Club, Stock Farm Club, Phi Beta Kappa. Office: Transam Corp 600 Montgomery St San Francisco CA 94111-2702

HERRINGER, MARYELLEN CATTANI, lawyer; b. Bakersfield, Calif., Dec. 1, 1943; d. Arnold Theodore and Corinne Marilyn (Kovacevich) C.; m. Frank C. Herringer; children: Sarah, Julia. AB, Vassar Coll., Poughkeepsie, N.Y., 1965; JD, U. Calif. (Boalt Hall), 1968; Exec. Program, Stanford Grad. Sch. Bus., 1994. Assoc. Davis Polk & Wardwell, N.Y.C., 1968-69, Orrick, Herrington & Sutcliffe, San Francisco, 1970-74, ptnr., 1975-81; v.p., gen. counsel Transamerica Corp., San Francisco, 1981-83, sr. v.p., gen. counsel, 1983-89; ptnr. Morrison & Foerster, San Francisco, 1989-91; sr. v.p. gen. counsel APL Ltd., Oakland, Calif., 1991-95, exec. v.p., gen. counsel, 1995-97; gen. counsel allied bus. Littler & Mendelson, San Francisco, 2000. Bd. dirs. Golden West Fin. Corp., World Savs. Bank, ABM Industries Inc. Author: Calif. Corp. Practice Guide, 1977, Corp. Counselors, 1982. Regent St. Mary's Coll., Moraga, Calif., 1986—, pres., 1990-92, trustee, 1990-99, chmn., 1993-95; trustee Vassar Coll., 1985-93, The Head-Royce Sch., 1993-2002, Mills Coll., 1999—, The Benilde Religious & Charitable Trust, 1999—, Alameda County Med. Ctr. Hosp. Authority, 1998-2002, Univ. Calif. Berkeley Art Mus., 2001—; bd. dirs. The Exploratorium, 1988-93. Mem. ABA, State Bar Calif. (chmn. bus. law sect. 1980-81), Bar Assn. San Francisco (co-chair com. on women 1989-91), Calif. Women Lawyers, San Francisco C. of C. (bd. dirs. 1987-91, gen. counsel 1990-91), Am. Corp. Counsel Assn. (bd. dirs. 1982-87), Women's Forum West (bd. dirs. 1984-87). Democrat. Roman Catholic. E-mail: mherringer@aol.com.

HERRINGTON, JAMES PATRICK, secondary education educator; b. East St. Louis, Apr. 10, 1950; s. James Lindsey and Anna (Kotras) H.; m. Therisa Marie Hawk, July 31, 1981. BS in Math. Edn., Northwestern U., 1972; MS in Math. Edn., So. Ill. U., 1974, EdD in Instructional Process, 1980. Cert. secondary tchr., gen. adminstr., supt., Ill. Grad. rsch. asst. So. Ill. U., Edwardsville, 1972-74, 78-79; math. and sci. tchr. Pontiac Sch. Dist. #105, Fairview Heights, Ill., 1974-78; math. tchr. O'Fallon (Ill.) Twp. High Sch., 1979—, chmn. math. dept., 1986—, chmn. sci. dept., 1993-99. Contbr. articles to profl. pubs. Mem. S.W. Math. Conf. (bd. dirs. 1985-98), Nat. Coun. Tchrs. Math., Ill. Coun. Tchrs. Math. (bd. dirs. 1989-92), Math. Assn. Am., Belleville Weightlifting Club (bd. dirs. 1975—), Kappa Delta Pi. Avocations: weight training, basketball. Office: O'Fallon Twp High Sch 600 S Smiley St O Fallon IL 62269-2399 E-mail: herringtonp@oths.k12.il.us.

HERRINGTON, JOHN B. astronaut, military officer; b. Wetumka, Okla., Sept. 14, 1958; s. James E. and Mrs. Harrington; m. Debra Ann Farmer; 2 children. BS in Applied Math., U. Colo., Colo. Springs, 1976; MS in Aeronautical Engring., USN Postgrad. Sch., 1995. Commd. ensign USN, 1984, student pilot, 1984—85; from student pilot to patrol plane commdr., instr. pilot USN Pacific Theater, 1985—89; student USN Test Pilot Sch., Patuxent River, Md., 1990; test pilot USN Force Warfare Aircraft Test Directorate, 1991—93; student USN Postgrad Sch., Monterey, Calif., 1993—95; astronaut NASA Johnson Flight Ctr., Houston, 1996—. Fellow: Am. Indian Sci. and Engring. Soc.; mem.: Sequoyah, Assn. Naval Aviation (life), U. Colo. at Colo. Springs Alumni Assn. Avocations: bicycling, rock climbing, skiing, running. Office: Astronaut Office/CB Johnson Space Ctr Houston TX 77058

HERRINGTON, JOHN DAVID, III, lawyer, director; b. Warren, Ohio, Nov. 19, 1934; s. John David Jr and Gertrude Francis (Herlinger) Herrington; m. Phoebe Jane Henderson, Mar. 16, 1957; children: Gay Annette, Joy Ann, Jennifer John. BSBA, Ohio State U., 1956. CPA Pa. With Price Waterhouse & Co., Pitts., 1956-63; asst. to sec.-treas. Fisher Sci. Co., Pitts., 1963-65, controller, 1965-71, v.p. fin., treas., 1971-78, sr. v.p. fin., treas., 1979-82; exec. dir. Reed Smith Shaw & McClay, Pitts., 1982-86; ret., 1986. Dir Hi Pure, Inc, Rochester Sci, Pfeiffer Glass, E & A Bldg Corp, F S de Mex, Conco Inc. Bd dirs Family and Children Serv Pittsburgh. With AUS, 1957—58. Mem.: Asn Legal Adminrs, Pa Soc CPAs, Am Inst CPAs, Planning Execs Inst, Tax Execs Inst, Fin Execs Inst. Home: 9402 Babcock Blvd Allison Park PA 15101-2011 also: 9721 S Old Oregon Inlet Rd Nags Head NC 27959-9376

HERRINGTON-BORRE, FRANCES JUNE, sign language school director; b. Austin, Tex., June 14, 1935; d. George Wilmas Neill and Mildred Lucille (Alexander) Williamson; m. Harold M. Herrington, June 6, 1953 (dec. Dec. 1978); children: Harold M.(dec.), Cheryl Anne Calhoun; m. Thomas Raymond Borre, Apr. 5, 1985. Student, U. Tex., 1967-71. With Tex. Dept. Human Svcs., Austin, 1961-90, adminstrv. technician, 1967-71, field rep., 1971-81, asst. pers. dir., 1981-88, labor rels. dir., 1988-89, judge adminstrv. law, 1989-90; freelance profl. interpreter for deaf, 1964—; dir. Austin Sign Lang. Sch., 1964—. Gov.'s appointee Joint Adv. Com. on Ednl. Svcs. to Deaf, Austin, 1977—79; project dir. Gov.'s Office, 1980; chmn. Tex. Commn. for Deaf Bd. Evaluation of Interpreters, 1981—84, Tex. State Agy. Liaisons to Gov.'s Commn. for Women, 1985; legis. liaison Symposium Deaf and Hard-of-Hearing Texans, 1991—99; cons. in field. Co-recipient Lyndon B. Johnson award, Tex. Assn. for the Deaf and the Gallaudet U. Regional Ctr., 1992; named Person of the Week for Outstanding Cmty. Svc., Fox 7 KTBC-TV, Austin, 2000; named an Outstanding Woman Ctrl. Tex., AAUW, 1982; recipient Tex. Rehab. Commn. Merit award, 1977, Gov.'s citation, 1978, Significant and Meritorious Svc. to Mankind award, Capitol Sertoma Club, 1976, Disting. Svc. as Adv. and Interpreter award, Dal-Tar Lions Club, 1977. Mem. Nat. Assn. of Deaf (Golden Hand award 1987), Tex. Assn. of Deaf (Svc. citation 1967, Vol. Svc. award 1971, 91-93, Presdl. citation 1989, Friendship award 1995, Gratitude for Vol. Svcs. award 1993-95, Appreciation award 1996), Tex. Soc. Interpreters for the Deaf (Interpreter of Decade award 1981, Bob Alcorn award 2000), Austin Interpreters for Deaf. Mem. Ch. of Christ. Home: 2404 Laramie Trl Austin TX 78745-3664 E-mail: franhborre2@cs.com.

HERRIOTT, DAVID NEIL, aerospace engineer; b. Pasadena, Calif., Dec. 26, 1967; s. Gerald Don and Mildred Violet (Herforth) H.; m. Pamela Jo Burke, July 2, 1994. B in Aerospace Engring., U. So. Calif., 1989; M in Orgnl. Mgmt., U. Phoenix, Diamond Bar, Calif., 1994. Cert. unigraphics instr. Rsch. asst. U. So. Calif., L.A., 1985-89; structural designer McDonnell Douglas, Long Beach, Calif., 1990-94, CAD tools process leader, 1994-95, instr. unigraphics, 1994-95; pres., CEO, Jovian Techs., Inc., 1996-98; prin. engr. GB Tech., Inc., 2000-01; staff engr. Bastion Techs., Inc., 2001—. Vol. Am. Cancer Soc., Long Beach, 1991-95, Big Sisters, L.A., 1991-96, Long Beach Meml. Hosp., 1990-91. Mem. AIAA, Sigma Xi. Republican. Methodist. Avocations: volleyball, bowling, computers, fishing, travel.

HERRIOTT, DONALD RICHARD, optical physicist; b. Rochester, N.Y., Feb. 4, 1928; s. William T. and Lois Emily (Denton) H.; m. Karis Kernow Smith, Feb. 3, 1951; children— Jean Elizabeth, Ann Barbara, Nancy Jane, Donald Richard, Jr. Student, U. Richmond, 1945; student, Duke U., 1945-49, U. Rochester, 1950-51, Poly. Inst. Bklyn., 1961-63. Optical engr. Bausch & Lomb Co., Rochester, N.Y., 1949-56; mem. tech. staff Bell Telephone Lab., Murray Hill, N.J., 1956-68, head dept., 1968-81; sr. sci. advisor Perkin-Elmer, Norwalk, Conn., 1981-91. Patentee in field Served with USN, 1945-46 Recipient Patent of Yr. award N.J. Research Council, 1978, Thomas Alva Edison Patent award N.J. Research Council, 1986. Fellow Optical Soc. Am. (Fraunhofer award 1983); mem. Nat. Acad. Engring., IEEE (sr.; Cledo Brunetti award 1980), Beta Theta Pi Republican. Presbyterian. Avocations: bird photography, sailing, skiing. Home: 14480 Laguna Dr West Fort Myers FL 33908

HERRLING, ANTHONY CARL, public relations executive; b. N.Y.C., Dec. 30, 1952; s. Francis Anthony Herrling; m. Jane Ellen Haburay; 1 child, Eliza. AB, Columbia Coll., 1974. Pres. Herrling & Assocs., Montclair, N.J., 1991-93; sr. v.p. Edelman Pub. Rels., N.Y.C., 1993-96; mng. dir. Burson-Marsteller, N.Y.C., 1996—. Office: Burson-Marsteller 230 Park Ave S New York NY 10003-1513 E-mail: anthony_herrling@nyc.bm.com.

HERRLINGER, STEPHEN PAUL, flight test engineer, air force officer, educator; b. Louisville, Ky., Nov. 23, 1959; s. John Howard and Josephine Doris (Martin) H.; m. Julie Louise Nelson, Feb. 4, 1989; children: Kyle H., Heidi K. BS in Chemistry, U. Akron, 1981; BS in Aero. Engring., USAF Inst. Tech., 1985; MS in Engring. Mgmt., Golden Gate U., 1989; M in Aero. Sci., Embry Riddle Aero. U., 1992. Registered Engr. in Tng., Ohio. Commd. 2d lt. USAF, 1981, advanced through grades to lt. col., 1998; rsch. chemist USAF Rocket Propulsion Lab., Edwards AFB, Calif., 1981-83; aerodynamic engr. advanced cruise missile 4200 Test and Evaluation Squadron USAF, Edwards AFB, 1985-86; chief advanced cruise missile aerodynamics sect. 31st Test and Evaluation Squadron USAF, Edwards AFB, 1986-87, chief advanced cruise missile performance, environ. sect., 1987-89; projct mgr E-9A surveillance aircraft program 4484th Test Squadron, Tyndall AFB, Fla., 1989-91, missile scoring flight test dir., 1991-92; dir. C-27A operational flight test 84th Test Squadron USAF, Tyndall AFB, 1992-94; chief of advanced testing ESC/ZJ USAF, Hanscom AFB, 1994-95, advanced sensor TBM program mgr., 1995-98, sys. program office dir. range threat sys. SM-ALC/LHR McClellan AFB, Calif., 1998—. Adj. instr. Gulf Coast C.C. U. West Fla., Embry Riddle Aero. U., 1991-99. Contbr. articles to Jour. Organic Chemistry, Soc. Flight Test Engrs. Jour., Jour. Aircraft. Leader youth group Calif. Luth. U. Chapel, Thousand Oaks, 1986-89; guitarist Luth. Ch. of the Savior, Bedford, Mass., 1995-97. Decorated USAF Meritorious Svc. medal with one oak leaf cluster, USAF Commendation medal, USAF Achievement medal with 1 oak leaf cluster, USAF Aerial Achievement medal, Spl. Achievement award Internat. Test and Evaluation Assn., 1994, Electronic Systems Ctr.'s Lt. Gen. O'Neill award for Acquisition Excellence, 1995. Achievements include U.S. patent for aerodynamic fairing /nose cone for M-130 chaff/flare dispenser design.

HERRMAN, JOHN CLINTON, surgeon; b. Phila., Oct. 26, 1927; s. Clinton Simon and Juliet Katz (Kind) H.; m. Mary Murray, May 20, 1960 (separated); children: Kathleen, Kimberly H. Berry, Lisa H. Coming. BA, Lafayette Coll., Easton, Pa., 1949; MD, Jefferson Med. Coll., Phila., 1953. Diplomate Am. Bd. Surgery, Am. Bd. Forensic Medicine, Am. Bd. Medicolegal Death Investigators. Rotating intern Jefferson Hosp., Phila., 1953-54; resident surgery Huron Rd. Hosp., Cleve., 1958-59; fellow surgery Cleve. Clinic, 1959; fellow gen. surgery Mayo Clinic, Rochester, Minn., 1955-57; mem. staff Lewis County Gen. Hosp., Lowville, N.Y., 1964-95, emeritus, trustee, 1997—; lt. Lewis County Sheriff's Dept., Lowville, N.Y., 1992—; clin. asst. prof. surgery SUNY, Syracuse, 1973-96; ret., 1996. Chief dep. coroner Lewis County, Lowville, 1965—; med. dir. Lewis County Pub. Health, Lowville, 1988—; mem. med. adv. bd. N.Y. Dept. Motor Vehicles. Chmn. No. Country Regional EMS Coun., Watertown, N.Y., Lewis County Traffic Safety Coun., Lowville; mem. N.Y. State EMS Coun., Albany, 1979-97. Fellow ACS, Am. Acad. Forensic Scis., Internat. Coll. Surgeons; mem. AMA, Eastern Assn. Surg. Trauma, N.Y. State Soc. Surgeons (pres. 1997-99), N.Y. State Assn. County Coroners and Med. Examiners (exec. v.p. 1986—), Internat. Assn. Coroners and Med. Examiners (1st v.p. 1997-98, pres. 1998-99), Am. Legion, Internat. Homicide Investigators Assn. Office: Lewis County Sheriff Dept PO Box 233 Lowville NY 13367-0233 Fax: 315-376-5232. E-mail: jherrman@lewiscountyny.org.

HERRMAN, MARGARET SUSAN, university official, sociologist; b. Columbia, S.C., Nov. 4, 1944; d. Henry and Frances (Smith) H.; m. Eugene Carl Bianchi, May 1, 1993. BA, Emory U., 1966, MA, PhD, 1977. Lectr. dept. sociology Ga. State U., Atlanta, 1971-77; lectr., temp. asst. prof. dept. sociology U. Ga., Athens, 1978-83, from pub. svc. asst. to assoc., 1983-93, sr. pub. svc. assoc. Carl Vinson Inst. Govt., 1993—. Cons. Carter Ctr., Emory U., Atlanta, 1985; founder, exec. dir. Nat. Conf. on Peacemaking and Conflict Resolution, Washington, 1979-87, chmn. bd. dirs., 1987-89; keynote spkr. nat. confs.; participant numerous nat. and statewide profl. meetings. Contbr. articles to profl. jours., chpts. to books. Recipient numerous grants. Mem.: Assn. Conflict Resolution, Alpha Kappa Delta. Avocations: gardening, travel, family. Home: 400 Red Fox Run Athens GA 30605-4476 Office: U Ga Carl Vinson Inst Govt 201 N Milledge Ave Athens GA 30602-5027 E-mail: herrman@cviog.uga.edu.

HERRMANN, ANDREW WILLIAM, consulting engineer; b. N.Y.C., Aug. 25, 1951; s. Henry Joseph and Joyce Helen (Davis) H.; m. Linda Tirelli, Apr. 24, 1976; children: Christina, Leslie. BCE, Valparaiso U., 1973; MCE, Polytech Inst. N.Y., 1980. Registered profl. engr., 26 states and Ont. From project designer to assoc. engr. Hardesty & Hanover Consulting Engrs., N.Y.C., 1973-89, ptnr., 1989—. Recipient Arc Welding award, James F. Lincoln, N.Y.C., 1987. Fellow ASCE (chmn. steel bridge com. 1990-93, chmn. bridge com. 1994-98, pres. met . sect. 1991-92, chmn. emeritus heavy movable structures); mem. NSPE, Am. Welding Soc., Am. Ry. Engring. Assn., Am. Cons. Engrs. Coun., St. Mary's Rehab. Ctr. for Children. Avocation: cross country skiing. Office: Hardesty & Hanover 1501 Broadway Ste 310 New York NY 10036-5587

HERRMANN, BENJAMIN EDWARD, former insurance executive; b. Bensonhurst, N.Y., May 9, 1919; s. Benjamin Edward and Ethel (Cuff) H.; m. Jean Clare Yancey, Oct. 19, 1946 (dec. Mar. 1, 1994); children: Benjamin E., Elizabeth M.; m. Mary Anne O'Connor, Oct. 20, 1995. BS, Columbia, 1941. C.L.U. With Home Life Ins. Co. N.Y., N.Y.C., 1941-68; regional v.p. Northeastern U.S., P.R., 1960-68; agy. v.p. Acacia Mut. Life Ins. Co., Washington, 1968-75; exec. com., dir. Acacia Nat. Life Ins. Co.; Acacia Equity Sales Corp. regional v.p. Met. N.Y., Home Life Ins. Co., N.Y.C., 1975-78, v.p. sales adminstrn., 1978-80, v.p. mktg., 1980-84; pres. Nat. Benefit Plans Inc., Norfolk, Va., 1986-93. Mem. Planning Bd., Madison, N.J., 1963-68, chmn., 1967-68; mem. Zoning Bd. Adjustment, 1964-68, chmn., 1966. Served to 1st lt. USAAF, 1943-46, PTO. Fellow Life Mgmt. Inst.; mem. Life Ins. Mgmt. and Rsch. Assn. (exec. devel. com., chmn. agy. officers roundtable com. 1968-76, chmn. 1976, chmn. tng. dirs. subcom. 1974-76, grad. sch. agy. mgmt., agy. officer sch., sr. mktg. officers' seminar), Soc. CLUs, Golden Key Soc., U.S. Squash Racquets Assn. (bd. dirs. 1986-95), Va. Squash Racquets Assn. Inc. (pres. 1986-91, chmn. 1991-95), Intertel, Mensa, Kingsmill Golf Club, The Jesters Club, Nat. Eagle Scout Assn. Republican. Presbyterian. Home: 105 Elizabeth Page Williamsburg VA 23185-5108

HERRMANN, DEBRA MCGUIRE, chemist, educator; b. Ft. Benning, Ga., Dec. 28, 1955; d. Delbert Wayne and Twyla Pauline (Moran) McGuire; m. David Read Herrmann, Aug. 2, 1980; children: Adam James, Jesse Read, Aaron Matthew. BS in chemistry, U. Tex., 1979, U. Ark., 1989. Rsch. chemist Dow Chem., Oyster Creek, Freeport, Tex., 1980-84; chemist Aluminum Co. Am., Bauxite, Ark., 1984-87; tchr. Little Rock (Ark.) Sch. Dist., 1987-90; tchr. chemistry and integrated physics and chemistry Carroll Ind. Sch. Dist., Southlake, Tex., 2002—. Pres., bd. dirs. Little Peoples Acad. Sch. Montessori, Ottumwa, Iowa, 1990-93; den leader Cub Scouts. Mem. PEO, Phi Beta Kappa. Democrat. Presbyn. Avocations: walking, watercolor, dogs, sailing, gardening. Home: 1100 Harbor Haven St Southlake TX 76092-2811

HERRMANN, GEORGE, mechanical engineering educator; b. USSR, Apr. 19, 1921; Diploma in Civil Engring., Swiss Fed. Inst. Tech., 1945, PhD in Mechanics, 1949. Asst., then asso. prof. civil engring. Columbia, 1950-62; prof. civil engring. Northwestern U., 1962-69; prof. applied mechanics Stanford, 1969-, prof. emeritus. Cons. SRI Internat., 1970-80 Contbr. 260 articles to profl. jours.; editl. bd. numerous jours. Fellow ASME (hon. mem. 1990, Centennial medal 1980); mem. ASCE (Th. v. Karman medal 1981), Nat. Acad. Engring., AIAA (emeritus). Office: Stanford U Divsn Mechanics Computation Durand Bldg 281 Stanford CA 94305-4040

HERRMANN, JOHN, writer, editor, journalist; b. Berkeley, Calif., May 17, 1931; s. John Phillip Herrmann and Roberta Louise (Neuwohner) Liberto; m. Dolores Mae Arvin, Sept. 15, 1956 (div. 1965); children: Debora Autsen, Linda West, Kathryn Anne Topper; m. Andrea Bess Watson, May 25, 1968 (div. 1993). BA, San Francisco State U., 1960, MA, 1961; MFA, U. Iowa, 1964. Founding editor Chrysalis Rev., San Francisco, 1959-63; sect. head InfoWeek, Manhasset, NY, 1982-83; assoc. editor Mgmt. Technology Mag., N.Y.C., 1983-84; mng. editor Direct Mktg. Mag., Garden City, 1984-85, asst. editor Health Systems Rev. Mag., Little Rock, 1985-88, exec. editor, 1988-95. Dir. creative writing U. Mont., Missoula, 1963—66; asst. prof. English U. N.Y., Oswego, 1966—69; vis. prof. Pahlavi U., Shiraz, Iran, 1969—70; writer-in-residence Cedar Crest Coll., Allentown, Pa., 1971—78; lectr. creative writing U. Ark., Little Rock, 1989—93; vis. prof. lit. Lodz (Poland) U. Internat. Studies, 2003—. Author: (short stories) Summer Will Rise and Other Stories, 1975, (book) Office Automation, 1984, Murder at the Red Dog, 2001. With USN, 1951—54. Named to Roll of Honor, Best Am. Short Stories, 1973; recipient Hart Crane award in poetry, Am. Weave Press, 1969, Disting. Story, Best Am. Mystery Stories, 1999; Residency grantee, Edward MacDowell Colony, Peterborough, N.H., 1968, Yaddo, Saratoga Springs, N.Y., 1968, 1969. Mem.: Mystery Writers Am., Assoc. Writing Programs. Independent. Avocation: trainer border collies for sheep dog trialing. E-mail: jherrmannmt@hotmail.com.

HERRMANN, LACY BUNNELL, investment company executive, financial entrepreneur, venture capitalist; b. New Haven, May 12, 1929; s. James Joseph and Helen Georgia (Bunnell) H.; m. Elizabeth Ocumpaugh Beadle, May 23, 1953; children: Diana Parsons, Conrad Beadle. AB, Brown U., 1950; postgrad., London Sch. Econs., 1953-54; MBA, Harvard U., 1956. Asst. to purchasing mgr. and buyer Westinghouse Elec. Corp., Metuchen, N.J., 1956-60; asst. v.p. Douglas T. Johnston & Co., Inc., N.Y.C., 1960-66; v.p. Johnston Mut. Fund, Inc., N.Y.C., 1964-66; gen. ptnr. Tamarack Assocs., N.Y.C., 1966-84; chmn. bd., pres. Family Home Products, Inc., N.Y.C., 1972-84, Buxton's Country Shops, Jamesburg, N.J., 1973-86. Founder, pres. STCM Corp., moneymarket fund, N.Y.C., 1974-76; vice chmn. bd. trustees, v.p. Centennial Capital Cash Mgmt. Trust, N.Y.C. successor to STCM Corp., 1976-81; chmn. bd. trustees, pres. successor fund Capital Cash Mgmt. Trust, 1981—; founder, chmn. bd. trustees, pres. Trinity Liquid Assets Trust, 1982-85, Oxford Cash Mgmt. Fund, 1982-88, Prime Cash Fund, 1982—; chmn., CEO, Aquila Mgmt. Corp., 1983—; founder, sponsor, mgr. Pacific Capital Cash Assets Trusts, 1984—, Hawaiian Tax-Free Trust, 1985—, Churchill Cash Reserves Trust, 1985—, Tax-Free Trust Ariz., 1986—, Tax-Free Trust Oreg., 1986—, Tax-Free Fund Colo., 1987—, Churchill Tax-Free Fund of Ky., 1987—, Pacific Capital Tax-Free Cash Assets Trusts, 1988—, Pacific Capital U.S. Govt. Securities Cash Assets Trust, 1988—, Narragansett Insured Tax-Free Income Fund, 1992—, Tax-Free Fund for Utah, 1992—, Aquila Rocky Mountain Equity Fund, 1994—, Aquila Cascadia Equity Fund, 1996—, VP Aquila Distributors, Inc.; bd. dirs. Quest for Value Fund Investment Trust, Quest for Value Accumulation Trust, Quest Cash Res., Inc.; trustee Oppenheimer/Quest group funds global Value Fund, 1994—, Oppenneimer Rochester Funds; organizer, bd. dirs. and/or cons. to numerous sml. to medium sized-corps. and orgns.; founding dir. mgmt. cons. firm merged with Towers, Perrin, Forster & Crosby; instr. Rutgers U., 1958-59; chmn., pres. bd. dirs. In-Cap Mgmt. Corp, 1984-98; speaker various profl. investment orgns. Contbr. articles to profl. jours. Organizer, trustee endowed award Internat. div. Grad. Sch. Journalism, Columbia U., 1962—; trustee Meml. and Endowment Trust of St. Paul's Ch., Westfield, N.J., 1968-96; mem. capital devel. com. St. Luke's Ch., Darien, Conn., 1978-85, mem. coll. scholarship fund com., 1976-85; trustee Brown U., 1990-96, trustee emeritus, 1996—, Hopkins Sch., New Haven, 1993-2003. Lt. (j.g.) USN, 1951-54, Korea; lt. USNR ret. Mem. N.Y. Soc. Security Analysts, Harvard Bus. Sch. Club N.Y. (bd. dirs., officer, 1958-71), Assoc. Alumni Brown U. (bd. dirs. 1978-87, exec. com. 1980-85, pres. 1983-85), Harvard Club, N.Y. Athletic Club, Brown U. Club, Brown U. of Fairfield Country Club (pres. 1977-82, bd. dirs. 1977—), Univ. Club (R.I.), Faculty Club Brown U., Stratton Mountain Country Club, Orleans Yacht Club, Ariz. club, Outrigger Canoe Club (Honolulu), Lahaina Yacht Club (Maui). Republican. Episcopalian. Home: 6 Whaling Rd Darien CT 06820-5930 Office: 380 Madison Ave New York NY 10017-2513

HERRMANN, LORENA JOYCE, retired music educator; b. Atchison, Kans., Feb. 2, 1925; d. William Edward and Mary Magdalena (Hodson) Brown; m. William Ernest Herrmann, May 31, 1953; children: Darrell Ernest, Charles Edward, Martha Ellen. Diploma in organ and piano, B of Music Edn., Coll. Emporia, 1947; M of Music Edn., U. Okla., 1950. Tchr. vocal music Jefferson Elem. Sch., Ponca City, Okla., 1947-49, Sr. High & Fogarty Jr. High, Guthrie, Okla., 1950-53; from instr. to assoc. prof. music St. Mary of the Plains Coll., Dodge City, Kans., 1968-92, chmn. dept. music, 1990-92, faculty advisor, 1981-92; ret., 1992. Music dir., organist Kans. LWML Convention and Pageant, Dodge City, 1964, 94. Contbr. articles to profl. jours.; editor: Zion Lutheran Church, 1978; music critic concert reviews SMPC Advance, 1988-90. Mem., officer, former pres. Zion Luth. Ladies Aid, Offerle, Kans., 1954—, pres., 2001-02, treas., 2003—; cmty. leader Trenton Workers 4-H Club, Edwards County, Kans., 1973-78; organist 1st Presbyn. Ch., Ponca City, 1947-49, 1st Unitarian Ch., Oklahoma City, 1949-50, Zion Luth. Ch., Offerle, 1956—; choir dir. 1st Christian Ch., Guthrie, 1950-53; adjudicator piano festivals for various towns and schs., Kans., 1981—. Mem. Music Educators Nat. Conf., Music Tchrs. Nat. Assn., Kans. Music Tchrs. Assn., Kans. Music Educators Assn., Am. Guild Organists, Dodge City Piano Tchrs. League (pres. 1986-87), Dodge City Cmty. Concert Assn. (bd. dirs., v.p. 1993-94, pres. 1995 2000), Minerva Study Club (several offices, pres. 1993-94), Kans. Author's Club (membership chair 1997—), Mu Phi Epsilon (Phi Epsilon chpt. del. nat. conv. 1946, scholar 1947, Scholarship and Achievement award), Phi Delta Kappa. Lutheran. Avocations: photography, creative writing, travel, reading, composing music. Home and Office: 10508 135 Rd Offerle KS 67563-9204

HERRMANN, PAUL C. physician, chemist; b. Radford, Va., Oct. 7, 1968; s. E. Clifford and Marilyn H.; m. Sarah E. Herrmann, July 7, 1996. BS in Chemistry, Andrews U., 1991; PhD in Chemistry, Stanford U., 1996; MD, Loma Linda U., 2000. Printer's apprentice Quick Print, Loma Linda, Calif., 1983-87; waste water lab. analyst Andrews U., Berrien Springs, Mich., 1987-89, boiler rm. water analyst, 1987-89; rsch. indsl. coop. LECO Corp., St. Joseph, Mich., 1989; sci. and engring. rsch. participant Oak Ridge (Tenn.) Nat. Lab., 1990;

tchg. and rsch. asst. Stanford (Calif.) U., 1991-96, rsch. assoc., 1997; clin. fellow NIH, Bethesda, Md., 2000—. Contbr. articles to profl. jours.; lectr. in field. Mem. AMA, AAAS, N.Y. Acad. Scis., Phi Kappa Phi, Phi Lambda Epsilon, Pi Mu Epsilon, Sigma Xi. Avocations: archery, history, literature, hiking. Home: PO Box 437 Loma Linda CA 92354-0437 Address: PO Box 437 Loma Linda CA 92354-0437 E-mail: herrmannp@mail.nih.gov.

HERRMANN, ROBERT LAWRENCE, biochemist, educator; b. N.Y.C., July 17, 1928; s. Philip Charles and Florence Gertrude (Benn) Herrmann; m. Elizabeth Ann Cook, Aug. 12, 1950; children: Stephen, Karen, Holly, Anders. BS in Chemistry, Purdue U., 1951; PhD in Biochemistry, Mich. State U., 1956. Postdoctoral fellow MIT, 1956-59; from asst. prof. to assoc. prof. biochemistry Boston U. Sch. Medicine, 1959-76; prof., chmn. dept. biochemistry Oral Roberts U. Sch. Medicine and Dentistry, Tulsa, 1976-81, assoc. dean biomed. sci., 1978-79; lectr. chemistry Gordon Coll., Wenham, Mass., 1981, adj. prof., 1982-97; exec. dir. Am. Sci. Affiliation, 1981-93; program dir. John Templeton Found., 1992—. Judge Templeton Prize Progress in Religion, 1999—2001. Editor: Prog. in Theology newsletter of John Templeton Found., 1992—2000; contbr. chapters to books, articles to profl. jours. Mem. Bd. Health, Bedford, Mass., 1975—76; trustee Christian Med. Soc., 1976—79, Barrington Coll., 1975—78, Templeton Found., 1987—95, 1996—2002, Southeastern Mass. U., 1988—91. With USN, 1946—48, with USN, 1951—52. Fellow: AAAS, Gerontol. Soc.; mem.: Am. Sci. Affiliation, European Soc. Study Sci. and Theology, Sci. and Religion Forum, Am. Soc. Biochem. and Molecular Biology. Evangelican Christian. Home: 12 Spillers Ln Ipswich MA 01938-2430 Office: Gordon Coll 255 Grapevine Rd Wenham MA 01984-1813 E-mail: herrmann@gordon.edu.

HERRMANNSFELDT, WILLIAM BERNARD, physicist; b. Chgo., Apr. 22, 1931; s. Bernard Ernst and Carolyne (Mueller) H.; m. Marcia Esther Bowman, June 12, 1954; children: Glen A., Paul W. AB, Miami U., 1953; PhD, U. Ill., 1958. Physicist Los Alamos (N.Mex.) Nat. Lab., 1958-62, Stanford (Calif.) Linear Accelerator, 1962-74, 76—; acting sect. leader US AEC, Washington, 1974-76. Ptnr. Electron Optics Simulations, Los Altos, Calif., 1987—; mem. fusion policy adv. com. DOE, Washington, 1990, mem. FEAC panel in inertial fusion energy, 1992. Contbr. articles to profl. jours. Fellow Am. Phys. Soc. (exec. com. divsn. physics beams 1991-94, chmn. divsn. physics beams, 1998-99). Achievements include experimental determination of the nature of beta decay; laser alignment of the 2-mile linear accelerator; electron optics simulation program. Office: Stanford Linear Accelerator 2575 Sand Hill Rd Menlo Park CA 94025 E-mail: wbhap@slac.stanford.edu.

HERRNSTADT, RICHARD LAWRENCE, American literature educator; b. N.Y.C., Nov. 4, 1926; s. Oscar Edward and Helen (Lidz) H.; m. Helen Lea Appel, June 18, 1950; children— Steven, Ellen Sara, Owen BS, U. Wis., 1948, MS, 1950; PhD, U. Md., 1960. Instr. English Iowa State U., Ames, 1954-58, asst. prof., 1958-61, assoc. prof., 1961-65, prof., 1965-92, prof. emeritus, 1992—. Editor: The Letters of A. Bronson Alcott, 1969; contbr. articles to profl. jours. Bd. dirs. Ames Cmty. Sch. Dist., 1967-74, Iowa Humanities Programs, 1973-79, v.p., 1978-79; bd. dirs. Area Edn. Agy. 11, Johnston, Iowa, 1977-91, v.p., 1980-84, pres., 1984-87; bd. dirs. Youth and Shelter Svcs., Ames, 1980-91, v.p., 1984-85, pres., 1985-87; bd. dirs. Joint Action in Cmty. Svc., 1994—. Served with USN, 1945-46. Recipient faculty citation Iowa State U. Alumni Assn., 1983 Mem. MLA, Am. Studies Assn. (exec. council 1969-76), Thoreau Soc., Mid-Am. Studies Assn. (v.p. 1961-62, pres. 1962-63), AAUP. Democrat. Jewish. Home: 5320 N Via Sempreverde Tucson AZ 85750-5970

HERRO, JOHN JOSEPH, software specialist; b. Watertown, Wis., Oct. 3, 1945; s. Alexander Chris and Lyla Victoria H.; m. Beverly Lynn Franz, June 26, 1976; children: Carla Lynn, Brian Peter, Emily Anne. BS, Ill. Inst. Technology, Chgo., 1967; MS, Ill. Inst. Technology, 1968, PhD, 1973. Electronic engr. Motorola, Inc., Schaumburg, Ill., 1968-71; assoc. engr. Ill. Inst. Technology Rsch. Inst., Chgo. and Dayton, Ohio, 1972-75; tech. staff Logicon, Inc., Dayton, 1975-77; systems analyst Cin. Electronics Corp., 1977-78; sr. software engr. GE Co., Cin., 1978-86; staff software engr. Grumman Aerospace, Melbourne, Fla., 1986-88, Harris Corp., Palm Bay, Fla., 1988-89; software specialist Golden Voice, Melbourne, Fla., 1989—2001. Pres. Software Innovations Technology, Palm Bay, Fla., 1988—; bd. dirs. Wheel Strobe Inc., Palm Bay, Fla., 2002—; tchr. SUNY at Binghamton, 1985-86, Fla. Inst. Technology, Melbourne, 1988-89; bd. dirs. Wheel Strobe, Inc. Author: ADA Tutor, 1988. Recipient Spl. Fellowship Ill. Inst. Technology, 1969, Traineeship NSF, 1971. Mem. Tau Beta Pi, Sigma Xi, Sig-ADA, Four Sigma Soc. Roman Catholic. Avocations: amateur radio, home computing, classical music. Home: 1083 Mandarin Dr NE Palm Bay FL 32905-4706 E-mail: john@wheelstrobe.com.

HERROD, HENRY GRADY, III, dean, allergist, immunologist; b. Oakland, Calif., Apr. 30, 1945; MD, U. Ala., 1972. Cert. allergy and immunology; cert. pediats. Intern U. Wash., Seattle, 1972-73, resident in pediats., 1973-74; resident rsch. assoc. in allergy and immunology NIH, Bethesda, Md., 1974-76; fellow in allergy and immunology Duke U., Durham, 1976-78; physician Le Bonheur Childrens Med. Ctr., Memphis; prof. U. Tenn., Memphis, dean, 1998—. Mem. AAAI, AAI, AAP, APS. Office: Dean Coll Medicine U Tenn 62 S Dunlap St Ste 400 Memphis TN 38163-0001 E-mail: hherrod@utmem.edu.

HERROLD, DAVID HENRY, lawyer; b. Corpus Christi, Texas, Sept. 4, 1969; s. Donald Erwin and Mary Louise H.; m. Amy Lynn (Fisher), Aug. 14, 1993. BA in Liberal arts, U. Tex., 1992; JD, U. Tulsa, Okla., 1996. Bar: Okla. 1996, U.S. Dist. Ct. (no., and ea. dists.) Okla. 1996, U.S. Dist. Ct. (we. dist.) Okla. 1997, U.S. Ct. Appeals (10th cir.) 1997, U.S. Ct. Appeals (11th cir.) 1999, U.S. Supreme Ct. 2000. Law clk. Herrold, Herrold, and Davis, Tulsa, Okla., 1992-94, Huffman, Arrington, Tulsa, Okla., 1994-95; law clk., summer assoc. Conner and Winters, P.C., Tulsa, Okla., 1995-96, assoc., 1996—2001; shareholder Herrold, Herrold and Co., Tulsa, Okla., 2002—. Mem. ct. op. com. Tulsa Bar, 1997-98, 2001-02, profl. responsibility com., 2002-03; mem. bankruptcy sect. Okla. Bar, 1997-98; mem. civil procedure sect. Okla. Bar, 1999—. Articles editor Tulsa Jour. of Comparative and Internat. Law, 1993-95; staff mem. Tulsa Law Jour., 1993-94. Tulsa Bus. Forum, 1996-2000. Recipient Am. Jurisprudence Award Contract I, Tulsa, 1992; First Pl. Award St. Francis Corp. Challenge, Tulsa, 1997-98. Mem. ABA; Okla. Bar Assn. (mem. litigation sect. 2001—); Tulsa County Bar Assn.; The Summit Tulsa Tex. Exec. (pres. 1996-98); The Res. Homeowners' Assn. (dir. and officer); Villages of Highland Pk. Homeowners' Assn.;Am. Inns Ct.; Phi Delta Phi. Republican. Presbyterian. Avocations: swimming, water sports, running, racquetball. Office: Herrold Herrold and Co Penthouse Ste II 5310 E 31st St Tulsa OK 74135-4304 Office Fax: 918-621-1141. E-mail: davidherrold@h2law.net.

HERRON, CHARLES KYLE, music educator; b. Clintwood, Va., Jan. 2, 1950; s. Charlie Kyle and Lillie Tipton Herron; m. Susan Kaye Geiger, Jan. 21, 1972; children: Charlie Kyle, Laura Susan. BS, East Tenn. State U., Johnson City, TN, 1971, ME, 1983. Band dir. Unicoi County H.S., Erwin, Tenn., 1972—74, Robinson Mid. Sch., Kingsport, Tenn., 1974—; choir master St. Paul's Episcopal Ch., Kingsport, Tenn., 1981—. Band clinician Honor Bands, Many Cities, 1980—. Recipient Citation of Excellence, Nat. Band Assn., 1994, Outstanding Tchr. Award, Tenn. Governor's Sch. for the Arts. Mem.: Tenn. Music Edn. Assn., Music Educators Nat. Conf., Precussive Arts Soc., Phi Kappa Phi, Phi Mu Alpha Sinfonia. Achievements include endorser for the Drumometer by DrumDial. Avocation: collecting vintage drums. Home: 3908 Lake Valley Court Kingsport TN 37664 Office: Robinson Middle School Band 1517 Jessee Street Kingsport IN 37664 Home Fax: 423-378-2220.

HERRON, DAVID K. brokerage house executive; Floor reporter Pacific Stock Exch., mem. and specialist, Boston Stock Exch., 1982—84; various positions Fidelity Investments, 1984—98; v.p. listed equities Charles Schwab & Co., Inc., 1998—; CEO Chgo. Stock Exch., 2002—. Gov. Boston Stock Exch., 1991—; trustee Cin. Stock Exch., 1996—2001; ofcl. Am. Stock Exch. Office: Chgo Stock Exch One Financial Pl 440 S LaSalle St Chicago IL 60605

HERRON, EDWIN HUNTER, JR., energy consultant; b. Shreveport, La., June 7, 1938; s. Edwin Hunter and Helen Virginia (Russell) H.; m. Frances Irvine Hunter, June 27, 1959; children: Edwin, David, Ashley. BS in Chem. Engring., Tulane U., 1959, MS, 1963, PhD (NSF fellow 1963-64), 1964. Rsch. engr. Exxon Rsch. & Engring. Co., Linden, N.J., 1959-61; sr. rsch. egnr. Exxon Prodn. Rsch. Co., Houston, 1964-66; corp. planning advisor Esso Europe, London, Eng., 1966-74; fin. analyst Exxon Corp., N.Y.C., 1974-78; v.p. Gruy Petroleum Tech., Inc., McLean, Va., 1978-84; pres. Petro-Analysis, Inc. (named changed to Hunter Trading Co. Inc.), 1984—, Petroleum Equities, Inc., 1987—; dir. petroleum projects CORE Internat., Inc., 1989—; pres. Petroleum Holdings, Inc., 1993—; dir. World Energy Sys. Inc., 1999—. Contbr. articles to profl. publs. Recipient Levey award Tulane U., 1970. Mem. Soc. Petroleum Engrs., Am. Inst. Chem. Engrs., Sci. Rsch. Soc., Soc. Tulane Engrs., Tau Beta Pi. E-mail: hunter.herron@petroleum.equities.com.

HERRON, ELLEN PATRICIA, retired judge; b. Auburn, N.Y., July 30, 1927; d. David Martin and Grace Josephine (Berner) H. AB, Trinity Coll., 1949; MA, Cath. U. Am., 1956; JD, U. Calif.-Berkeley, 1964. Bar: Calif. 1965. Asst. dean Cath. U. Am., 1952-54; instr. East H.S., Auburn, 1955-57; asst. dean Wells Coll., Aurora, N.Y., 1957-58; instr. psychology and history Contra Costa Coll., 1958-60; dir. row Stanford, 1960-61; assoc. Knox & Kretzmer, Richmond, Calif., 1964—65; ptnr. Knox & Herron, Richmond, 1965-74, Knox, Herron and Masterson, Richmond, 1974-77; judge Superior Ct. State of Calif., Contra Costa, Calif., 1977-87; pvt. judge, 1987—90, JAMS, Walnut Creek, Calif., 1990—2002. Ptnr. Real Estate Syndicates, Calif., 1967-77; owner, mgr. The Barricia Vineyards, 1978—. Active numerous civic orgns. Home: 15700 Sonoma Hwy Sonoma CA 95476-3025 also: 51 Western Dr Point Richmond CA 94801 Fax: 707-938-0544. E-mail: patherron@vom.com.

HERRON, GAYLE ANN, forensic master psychologist, mental health consultant, psychotherapist, health facility administrator, columnist; b. L.A., Sept. 21, 1953; d. Robert Owen Sr. and Rachel Rebecca (Lemley) Colvin; m. Curtis William Sr. Herron, Feb. 14, 1997. AA in Psychology, Okla. City C.C., Oklahoma City, 1986; BS in Sociology, Okla. State U., 1990, BS in Psychology, 1991, MS in Counseling, 1992; postgrad., U. Okla., 1994—95, U. Nev., Las Vegas, 1995—96. Lic. profl. counselor N.C., Mo., Nebr., cert. master psychologist, forensic clin. counselor. Adminstr., fin. cons. Security Fin. Cons., Oklahoma City, 1980-88; case worker Big Bros./Big Sisters, Stillwater, Okla., 1988-89; counselor Payne County Family Practices, Stillwater, 1989; social worker Dept. Human Svcs. Child Welfare, Stillwater, 1990-91; asst. to v.p. bus. and fin. Okla. State U., Stillwater, 1990-91; adj. instr. Langston (Okla.) U., 1992, counselor Christian Counseling Assocs., Stillwater, 1993-95; social worker Clark County, Las Vegas, Nev., 1995—96; counselor Payne County Health Dept. Child Guidance Clinics, Stillwater and Cushing, Okla., 1992—95; clin. dir., clin. psychotherapist New Beginnings Clin. Svcs. Corp., Las Vegas, 1995-2000; clin. dir., master psychologist/psychotherapist New Beginnings Diagnostic and Clin. Svcs., Brunswick City, N.C., 1997-2001, clin. dir., psychotherapist Branson, Mo., 1999-2001; forensic master psychologist, clin. dir. Crisis Intervention Svcs., Branson, Mo., 2001—02; cons. master psychologist Tri-Lakes Primary Care, Hollister, Mo., 2001—02; dir., forensic clin. counselor, masters psychologist Ozark Child, Adolescent and Adult Counseling, Branson, 2002—. Vol. mental health clinician Crisis Incident Response Team, S.W. Mo., 2001-03. Columnist Brunswick County News, 1997-98. Disaster vol. ARC, Oklahoma City, 1987-88; vol. disaster inquiry team, Oklahoma City, Las Vegas, 1995; vita site coord. IRS, Oklahoma City, 1982-84; emergency room EMT Hillcrest Hosp., Oklahoma City, 1994; EMT/intermediate paramedic Amcare Ambulance Svcs., 1994. Mem. ACA, APA, NASW, Am. Assn. for Christian Counselors, Nat. Assn. Social Workers, Okla. Psychol. Assn., Okla. Assn. Counseling and Devel., Assn. for Humanist Psychology, N.C. Assn. Lic. Counselors and Therapists, Golden Key Soc., Phi Theta Kappa, Psi Chi. Democrat. Mem. LDS Ch., Roman Catholic. Avocations: traveling, drafting, hiking, flying, sports. Address: PO Box 1855 Hollister MO 65673-1855 Fax: 417-335-5177. E-mail: gayleannherron@wmconnect.com., ozarkcounseling@wmconnect.com.

HERRON, JANET IRENE, industrial manufacturing engineer; b. Zanesville, Ohio, Oct. 14, 1949; d. Lincoln and Freda Louise (Nolan) Estep; m. Wade Harold Herron, June 10, 1967; children: Toni Renee, Dawnise Renee. AAS, Muskingum Area Tech. Coll., 1978; BS, Ohio U., 1990. Elec., mech. designer Nat. Cash Register, Cambridge, Ohio, 1978-83; restructuring engr. Cooper Ind., Zanesville, 1983-87; sr. product engr., quality mgr. Tomkins Ind., Malta, Ohio, 1990-93; pres., owner Herron Engring., Ltd., Chandlersville, Ohio, 1993—; co-owner Herron Renovations, Ltd., 1999—. Engring. instr. Mid-East Ohio Joint Vocat. Sch., 1987-88, Ctrl. Ohio Tech. Coll., 1987-88, Muskingum Area Tech. Coll., 1990—; mfg. outreach engr. Edison Welding Inst. Columbus, Ohio, 1996-98. Mem. NAFE, AAUW, Am. Soc. Quality, Am. Soc. Home Inspectors, Inst. Indsl. Engrs., Soc. Mfg. Engrs., Soc. Engrs. in Mfg., Soc. Women Engrs., Mid-East Ohio Women's Entrepreneurs. Democrat. Presbyterian. Avocations: hosting foreign exchange students, attending concerts, travel, home restoration. Home: 9945 Claysville Rd Chandlersville OH 43727-9765

HERRON, ORLEY R. college president; b. Olive Hill, Ky., Nov. 16, 1933; s. Orley R. and Hyllie W. (Weaver) H.; m. Donna Jean Morgan, Aug. 24, 1956; children: Jill Donette, Morgan Niles, Mark Weaver. BA, Wheaton Coll., 1955; MA, Mich. State U., 1959, PhD, 1965; LittD (hon.), Houghton Coll., 1972; LHD (hon.), Lesley Coll., 1983. Dean of students Westmont Coll., Santa Barbara, Calif., 1961-67; dir. doctoral program/student pers. U. Miss., 1967-68; asst. to pres. Ind. State U., 1968-70; pres. Greenville (Ill.) Coll., 1970-77, Nat Louis U. (formerly Nat. Coll. Edn.), Evanston, Ill., 1977-97; chmn., pres. ORH group eBooks Interactive, 1998—; founder AutoeDirect.com, Inc., 2000—; chmn., CEO Herron Multimedia, 2001—. Mem. Ill. Commn. for Improvement Elem. and Secondary Edn., 1983-1985; chmn. bd. Harris Bank, Wilmette, Ill., 1991—. also bd. dirs.; bd. dirs. Corp. Cmty. Schs. Am., 1989—. Author: Role of the Trustee, 1969, Input-Output, 1970, New Dimensions in Student Personnel Administration, 1970, A Christian Executive in a Secular World, 1979, Who Controls Your Child?, 1980, Words to Live By, 1997, Notes for the New Millennium, 2000; (cassette) Governing Higher Education in the 70's, 1970; exec. prodr., composer, songwriter (CD) I Love You My Dearest Darling, 2001; songer, exec. prodr. (CD) OrLey And His Hollywood Friends, 2003. Rep. of Pres. U.S. 25th Anniversary UNESCO, 1971; adv. bd. Expt. on Internat. Living, Santa Barbara, 1961-67; mem. Gov.'s Task Force on Encouraging Citizen Involvement in Edn., 1986-87; nat. dir. educators for reelection of Pres., 1972; bd. dirs. Ch. Centered Evangelism; mem. Chgo. Sun. Evening Club, 1987-97; founder Santa Barbara Industries. Lt. comdr. U.S. Naval Res., 1973-77. Recipient Crusader Christian Contbn. award Wheaton Coll., 1955, 74, Outstanding Citizen award Greenville Jaycees, 1971, Outstanding Educator award Religious Heritage of Am., 1987, Disting. Alumnus award Wheaton Coll., Outstanding Alumnus award New Philadelphia H.S., Amicus Polonae award, 1996. Mem. SAG, AAUP, Am. Assn. Higher Edn., Coun. on Inter-Instnl. Cooperation (pres.), Council Advancement Small Colls. (sec.), Christian Coll. Consortium (exec. com.), Fedn. Ind. Ill. Colls. (exec. bd. 1971-97), Assn. Free Meth. Edn!. Instns. (pres. 1973-75), Rotary, Kiwanis. Office: One Westminster Pl Ste 101 Lake Forest IL 60045 E-mail: orley@orhgroup.com.

HERRON, ROBERT WILBURN, JR., academic administrator, educator; s. Robert Wilburn and Juanita Eleanor (Green) Herron; m. Diane Elaine James, July 8, 1978; children: Robert Wilburn III, Tiffany Danielle. BA, Lee U., Cleve., Tenn., 1977; MA, Western Ky. U., Bowling Green, 1979, Rice U., Houston, 1987, PhD, 1989. V.p. academic affairs Southeastern Coll., Lakeland, 1983—84; prof. religion Lee U., Cleve., Tenn., 1985—94, v.p. exec. asst. to pres., 1994—99; v.p. academic affairs So. Bible Coll., Houston, 1999—. Author: (books) Complete Bible Libr.:Gospel of Mark, 1988, Peter's Denial of Jesus, 1990, Salt and Light. Bd. dir. Crisis Pregnancy Ctr., Cleve., Tenn., 1987—89, Boys and Girls Club, Cleve., Tenn., 1997—99. Avocations: travel, jogging. Office: Southeastern Coll 1000 Longfellow Blvd Lakeland FL 33801 Office Fax: 863-667-5200. Business E-Mail: rherron@secollege.edu.

HERRON, SHERRY SHELTON, biology educator; b. Hattiesburg, Miss., Sept. 4, 1954; d. John Joseph III and Alice English Shelton; m. John Larkin Herron, June 1, 1974; children: Alicia Hope, John Lark, Forrest Boyd, Lauren Guess. BS, U. South Ala., 1975, MEd, 1988; PhD, U. So. Miss., 1999. Sci. tchr. Baldwin County Sch. Sys., Fairhope, Ala., 1975-80, Bayside Acad., Daphne, Ala., 1981-83, Baldwin County Sch. Sys., Bay Minette, Ala., 1983-93; freshman biology program coord. U. So. Miss., Hattiesburg, 1993-2000, dir. Biol. Scis. Freshman Ctr., 1995-2000; staff biologist Biol. Scis. Curriculum Study, Colorado Springs, Colo., 2001—. Author: General Biology Laboratories: Investigations Into the Unity and Diversity of Life, 1998, 2nd edit., 2000, Investigations Into the Issues of Human Biology, 1998, Inquiries into Introductory Biology, 1999. Officer Alpha Delta Gamma, Bay Minette, Ala., 1984-95. Recipient award USM Coll. Discovery, Inst. Higher Learning, 1993-95, award Using Constructivist-Based Investigations and Cooperative Learning in Introductory Coll. Biology, NSF, 1999-2001. Mem. AAAS, Nat. Assn. for Rsch. in Sci. Tchg., Miss. Acad. Sci. (corp. coord. 2000), Sigma Xi, Gamma Beta Phi. Methodist. Avocations: piano, organ. Office: Biol Scis Curriculum Study 5415 Mark Dabling Blvd Colorado Springs CO 80918-3842 Office Fax: 719-531-9104. E-mail: sherron@bscs.org.

HERSCH, BRYAN L. surgeon; b. Detroit, Mich., Oct. 17, 1973; s. Marshall Robert and Marilyn Adele-Jaffe Hersch; m. Stacey Rae Dewitt, Feb. 14, 2003. BS zoology, Mich. State Univ., East Lansing, Mich., 1995; BS Biomedical Sci., Sch. Coll. of Podiatric Medicine, Chgo., 1997, DPM, 1999. Cert. ankle arthroscopy with the Holmium YAG laser, MBA implants. Assoc. Dr. Foot and Ankle Clin. of Am., Chgo., 2001—. Fellowship dir. Foot and Ankle Clin. of Am., Chgo., 2002—. Contbr. articles to profl. jour. Mem.: Ill. Podiatric Med. Assn., Am. Podiatric Med. Assn., Am. Bd. of Podiatric Surgeons. Avocations: guitar, rollerblading, boating, travel. Home: 657 N Peoria #2 Chicago IL 60622

HERSCH, JONI, economist, educator; b. Chicago, Ill., 1956; d. Lawrence Hersch; m. W. Kip Viscusi. PhD, Northwestern U., Evanston IL, 1977—81. Lectr. on law Harvard Law Sch., Cambridge, Mass., 1999—; prof. of economics U. of Wyo., Laramie, Wyo., 1995—99, assoc. prof. of economics, 1989—95; vis. prof. of economics Harvard U., Cambridge, Mass., 1998—98, Duke U., Durham, NC, 1995—96; vis. assoc. prof. of economics Calif. Inst. of Tech., Pasadena, Calif., 1992—93. Author: (journal articles) Am. Econ. Rev., Rev. of Economics and Stats., Jour. of Human Resources, Jour. of Risk and Uncertainty, Indsl. and Labor Rels. Rev., Econ. Inquiry, Managerial and Decision Economics. Fellow Vis. Professorship for Women, NSF, 1992-93. Mem.: Am. Econ. Assn. (bd., com. on the status of women in the economics profession 1994—96). Office: Harvard Law School Lewis 425 Cambridge MA 02138

HERSCHBACH, DUDLEY ROBERT, chemistry educator; b. San Jose, Calif., June 18, 1932; s. Robert Dudley and Dorothy Edith (Beer) Herschbach; m. Georgene Lee Botyos, Dec. 26, 1964; children: Lisa Marie, Brenda Michele. BS in Math., Stanford U., 1954, MS in Chemistry, 1955; AM in Physics, Harvard U., 1956, PhD in Chem. Physics, 1958; DSc (hon.), U. Toronto, 1977, Cornell Coll., 1988, Framingham State Coll., 1989, Adelphi U., 1990, Dartmouth Coll., 1992, Charles U., Prague, 1993, U. Ill., Chgo., 1994, Wheaton Coll., 1995, Franklin & Marshall Coll., 1998. Jr. fellow Harvard U., Cambridge, Mass., 1957—59, prof. chemistry, 1963—76, Frank B. Baird prof. sci., 1976—2002, mem. faculty coun., 1980—83, master Currier House, 1981—86, rsch. prof., 2002—; asst. prof. U. Calif., Berkeley, 1959—62, assoc. prof., 1961—63. Cons. editor W.H. Freeman lectr. Haverford Coll., 1962; Falk-Plaut lectr. Columbia U., 1963; vis. prof. Göttingen (Germany) U., 1963, U. Calif., Santa Cruz, 1972; Harvard lectr. Yale U., 1964; Debye lectr. Cornell U., 1966; Rollefson lectr. U. Calif., Berkeley, 1969; Reilly lectr. U. Notre Dame, 1979; Phillips lectr. U. Pitts., 1971; disting. vis. prof. U. Ariz., 1971, U. Tex., 1977, U. Utah, 1978; Gordon lectr. U. Toronto, 1971; Clark lectr. San Jose State U., 1979; Hill lectr. Duke U., 1988; Priestly lectr. Pa. State U., 1990; Kaufman lectr. U. Pa., 1990; Polanyi lectr. U. N.C., 1991; Dreyfus lectr. Dartmouth Coll., 1992; Pauling lectr. Calif. Inst. Tech., 1993; Bernstein lectr. UCLA, 1994; Brown lectr. Rutgers U., 1995. Assoc. editor Jour. Phys. Chemistry, 1980—88. Named to Calif. Pub. Edn. Hall of Fame, 1987; recipient pure chemistry award, Am. Chem. Soc., 1965, Centenary medal, 1977, Pauling medal, 1978, Spiers medal, Faraday Soc., 1976, Polanyi medal, 1981, Langmuir prize, 1983, Nobel Prize in chemistry, 1986, Nat. Medal of Sci., NSF, 1991, Heyrovsky medal, 1992, Sierra Nevada Disting. Chemist award, 1993, Kosolapoff medal, 1994, William Walker prize, 1994, Council of Scientific Society President's award for support of science, 1999; fellow Guggenheim fellow, U. Freiburg, Germany, 1968, vis. fellow, Joint Inst. for Lab. Astrophysics, U. Colo., 1969, Sloan fellow, 1959—63, Exxon Faculty fellow, 1980—96, Miller fellow, U. Calif. Berkeley, 1997; scholar Fairchild Disting. scholar, Calif. Inst. Tech., 1976. Fellow: Am. Acad. Arts and Scis., Am. Phys. Soc. (chmn. chem. physics divsn. 1971—72), N.Y. Acad. Sci. (hon.; life); mem.: Am. Philos. Soc., NAS, Royal Soc. Chemistry (fgn.) (hon.), Am. Chem. Soc., AAAS, Sigma Xi, Phi Beta Kappa (orator Harvard U. 1992). Office: Harvard U Dept Chemistry Mallickrodt Lab 035 12 Oxford St Cambridge MA 02138-2902*

HERSCHBERGER, RUTH MARGARET, writer; b. Philipse Manor, N.Y., Jan. 30, 1917; d. Clarence Bertram and Grace Josephine (Eberhart) H. Student, U. Chgo., 1935-38, Black Mountain (N.C.) Coll., 1938-39, U. Mich., others. Mem. adv. bd. Women's Interart Ctr., N.Y.C., 1971-73. Author: (poems) A Way of Happening, 1948, Nature and Love Poems, 1969 (Midland Authors award 1969), (nonfiction) Adam's Rib, 1948, paperback edit., 1970, (Vet. Feminists Am. award 1998, 2002); contbr. short story to Best Am. Short Stories, 1949; poems recorded and pub. by Libr. of Congress, 1960; poetry editor The Humanist, 1944-46; contbr. poems to jours. and anthologies. Recipient Hopwood award in poetry U. Mich., 1941, Harriet Monroe Meml. prize Poetry Mag., 1953, Grace Thayer Bradley award for poetry Friends of Lit., 1957; Rockefeller grantee, 1951-53; Bollingen Found. grantee, 1970. Home: 463 West St New York NY 10014-2010

HERSCHENSOHN, BRUCE, film director, writer; b. Milw., Sept. 10, 1932; Ed., Los Angeles. With art dept. RKO Pictures, 1953-55; dir., editor Gen. Dynamics Corp., 1955-56; dir., writer, editor Karma for Internat. Communications Found.; editor, co-dir. Friendship Seven for NASA; dir., editor Tall Man Five-Five for Gen. Dynamics Corp. and SAC; dir. motion picture and TV Service USIA, 1968-72, spl. cons. to dir., 1972—; staff asst. to Pres. U.S., 1972; dep. spl. asst. to Pres., 1973-74, mem. transition team, 1981; sr. fellow Claremont (Calif.) Inst., 1993; Rep. nominee U.S. Senate (Calif.), 1992. Tchr. U.S. fgn. policy Pepperdine U., 1998—; tchr. U. Md., 1972; spl. cons. to Rep. Nat. Conv., 72; polit. analyst KABC-TV and KABC Radio, 1978—91. Directed and wrote films for USIA, including Bridges of the Barrios, The Five Cities of June, The President, John F. Kennedy: Years of Lightning, Day of Drums, Eulogy to 5:02; recipient Acad. award for Czechoslovakia 1968 as best documentary short 1969; author: The Gods of Antenna, 1976; contbg. editor: Conservative Digest. Bd. govs. Charles Eldon Meml. Youth Fund; Rep. nom. U.S. Senate, Calif., 1992. Served with USAF, 1951-52. Recipient Arthur S. Flemming award as 10 of 10 outstanding young men in fed govt., 1969, Disting. Svc. medal, USIA, 1972, Ann. award, Coun. Against Communist Aggression, 1972; fellow, JFK Sch., Harvard U., 1996. Office: Pepperdine Univ 24255 Pacific Coast Hwy Malibu CA 90263

HERSCHER, SUSAN KAY, English language educator; b. Wisconsin Rapids, Wis., Nov. 11, 1949; d. Martin Joseph and Marian Margie (Hentz) Arnold; m. Walter Ray Herscher, June 12, 1976; children: Anne, Brian. BS in Edn., U. Wis., Stevens Point, 1971; MS in Reading Edn., U. Wis., Oshkosh, 1983. Elem. tchr. Wausaukee (Wis.) Pub. Schs., 1971-73; elem. tchr., unit leader Hortonville (Wis.) Pub. Schs., 1974-82; adult basic edn. instr., dept. chair Fox Valley Tech. Coll., Appleton, Wis., 1983—. Master tchr., facilitator for Wis. Adult Basic Edn./ESL Summer Inst., 1993; presenter in field. Recipient Quality Improvement award Fox Valley Tech. Coll., 1994. Mem. Tchrs. of English to Speakers of Other Langs., Wis. Tchrs. of English to Speakers of Other Langs., Wis. East Cen. Assn. for Vocat. Edn., Wis. Edn. Assn., NEA. Avocations: travel, reading, cross country skiing. Home: 1341 W Cloverdale Dr Appleton WI 54914-5815 Office: Fox Valley Tech Coll PO Box 2277 Appleton WI 54912-2277

HERSCHMAN, JEFFREY D. lawyer; b. Chgo., Sept. 30, 1948; BS, Drake U., 1970; JD with honors, U. Ill., 1973. Bar: Md. 1973. Mem. Piper Rudnick LLP, Balt. Address: Piper Rudnick e LLP 6225 Smith Ave Baltimore MD 21209-3600

HERSEY, GEORGE LEONARD, art history educator, retired; b. Cambridge, Mass., Aug. 30, 1927; s. Milton Leonard and Katharine (Page) H.; m. Jane Maddox Lancefield, Sept. 2, 1953; children: Donald, James. BA, Harvard U., 1951; M.F.A., Yale U., 1954, MA, 1961, PhD, 1964. Instr. art Bucknell U., Lewisburg, Pa., 1954-55, asst. prof., 1955-59, acting chmn., 1958-59; instr. Yale U., New Haven, Conn., 1963-65; asst. prof. Yale, 1965-68; assoc. prof. Yale U., 1968-74, prof., 1974-98, ret., 1998. Mem. adv. bd. Conn. Preservation Trust, 1977-79; mem. Conn. State Commn. Capitol Restoration, 1977-79; lectr. Princeton U., Columbia U., other univs., orgns. Author (all books have been translated into German, Italian, Japanes, Turkish, and Russian): Alfonso II and

the Artistic Renewal of Naples, 1969, The Aragonese Arch at Naples, 1443-1475, 1973; High Victorian Gothic: A Study in Associationism, 1972, Pythagorean Palaces: Magic and Architecture in the Italian Renaissance, 1975, Architecture, Poetry and Number in the Royal Palace at Caserta, 1983, The Lost Meaning of Classical Architecture, 1988, (with R. Freedman) Possible Palladian Villas, 1992, High Renaissance Art in St. Peter's and the Vatican, 1993, The Evolution of Allure, Sexual Selection from the Medici Venus to the Incredible Hulk, 1996, The Monumental Impulse: Architecture's Biological Roots, 1999, Architecture and Geometry in the Age of the Baroque, 2001, Falling in Love with Statues: Artificial Humans from Pygmalion to the Present, 2003; also numerous articles and revs.; co-editor: Architectura, 1971—; editor: Yale Publ. in History of Art, 1974-90; art exhbn. co-organizer The Taste of Angels: Neapolitan Paintings in North America, 1650-1750, Yale Univ. Art Gallery and other museums, 1987-88. With U.S. Merchant Marine, 1945-46, U.S. Army, 1946-47. Recipient Monticello prize, 1961; Fulbright scholar, Italy, 1962; Morse fellow, London, 1966, Schepp fellow, Florence, Italy, 1972; resident Am. Acad. Rome, 1994. Mem.: Soc. Archtl. Historians (bd. dirs. 1971—73), Dunky Club (hon.). Democrat. Home: 167 Linden St New Haven CT 06511-2407 E-mail: glherse@aol.com.

HERSH, BURTON DAVID, author; b. Chgo., Sept. 18, 1933; s. Maurice Henry and Florence Nita Hersh; m. Ellen Eiseman, Aug. 3, 1957; children: Leo Joseph, Margery Clara. BA, Harvard Coll., 1955. Cons. Sundance Inst., Park City, Utah, 1991. Elected to Acad. Sr. Profls. at Eckerd Coll., St. Petersburg, Fla., 1993. Author: (novel) The Ski People, 1968, (novel) The Nature of the Beast, 2002, (nonfiction books) The Education of Edward Kennedy 1972 (Book Find Club award 1972), The Mellon Family (Fortune Club award 1978, Book of the Month Club award), The Old Boys, 1992, The Shadow President: Ted Kennedy in Opposition, 1997. Dir. N.H. Civil Liberties Union, Concord, 1983-86; founding chmn. Bradford Conservation Com., N.H., 1970s; fin. com. N.H. Dem. Party, 1970s. With U.S. Army, 1957-59, Germany. Fulbright scholar U.S. Govt., 1955-56; Bread Loaf fellow Bread Loaf Writer's Workshop, Middlebury, Vt., 1964, others. Mem. Authors Guild Am., Am. Soc. Journalists and Authors, Assn. Former Intelligence Officers (bd. dirs. New Eng. br. 1992—), Internat. Soc. for Comparative Lit. and Theatre, PEN, Phi Beta Kappa. Democrat. Jewish. Avocations: print collecting, skiing, tennis, investing.

HERSH, ELLEN E. poet; b. N.Y.C., Mar. 17, 1935; d. James and Margery Kaufmann Eiseman; m. Burton D. Hersh, Aug. 3, 1957; children: Leo J., Margery C. BA, Radcliffe Coll., 1957; MAT, Yale U., 1965; MFA, Norwich U., 1994. French tchr. Etan Preparatory Sch., N.Y.C., 1961—62; French and German tchr. Rosemary Hall, Greenwich, Conn., 1962—64; asst. prof. modern langs. New Eng. Coll., Henniker, NH, 1965—72. Poet-in-residence N.H. State Coun. on the Arts, Concord, 1980—, Fla. Arts Coun., Tallahassee, 1999—; treas. Tree Farm Books, St. Petersburg, Fla., 2001—; presenter poetry to librs., mus. and cultural ctrs. Author: The Best of German Cooking, 1960, poetry. Rep., vice chair Kearsarge Regional Sch. Bd., New London, NH, 1984—93; poetry tchr. Polk County Jail, Bartow, Fla., 2001—; religious sch. tchr. Temple Beth Jacob, Concord, 1975—83. Mem.: Brandeis U. Women's Group (leader poetry group 1996—), Acad. Sr. Profls. Eckerd Coll. (co-chair poetry group 1994—), Am. Literary Translators Assn. Avocations: running, tennis, language study, skiing. Home: 6673 30th St South Saint Petersburg FL 33712 Home (Summer): PO Box 433 43 W Main St Bradford NH 03221

HERSH, IRA PAUL, tax and financial planning consultant; b. Bklyn., July 14, 1948; s. Saul and Mildred (Leibowitz) Hershkowitz; m. Jan Bennett; children: Marcy Fay, Gregory Alexander, Carrie Elizabeth. Tax mgr. Wiss and Co., N.Y.C., 1970-77; contr. Assets Adminstrn. and Mgmt., Stamford, Conn., 1978-79; tax mgr. Exec. Monetary Mgmt., Inc., N.Y.C., 1980-84; pvt. practice Wilton, Conn., 1985—. Pres. MacArthur Equities Ltd., 1985—. Mem. Rolling Hills Country Club. Home and Office: 20 Branch Brook Rd Wilton CT 06897-1520 E-mail: taxplan@optonline.net.

HERSH, RICHARD H. academic administrator; b. N.Y.C. m. Judith C. Meyers. BA in Polit. Sci. and History, Syracuse U., 1964, MA in Social Sci. Edn., 1965; EdD, Boston U., 1969. Prof., chmn. secondary edn. Coll. Edn. U. Toledo, Ohio, 1968-75; assoc. dean tchr. edn., prof. edn. Coll. Edn. U. Oreg., 1976-80, dean grad. sch., assoc. provost rsch., 1980-83, v.p. rsch., 1983-85; v.p. acad. affairs U. N.H., Durham, 1985-89; v.p. acad. affairs, provost Drake U., Des Moines, 1989-91; pres. Hobart and William Smith Coll., Geneva, N.Y., 1991-99; dir. grants program Christian A. Johnson Endeavor Found., 1999—2000; sr. advisor C.A. Johnson Endeavor Found., New York, NY, 2000—02; sr. fellow Council for Aid to Education, 2000—02; pres. Trinity College, Hartford, Conn., 2002—03. Vis. prof., dir. moral edn. project Ont. Inst. Studies Edn. U. Toronto, 1975-76, Ctr. Moral Devel., Harvard U., Cambridge, Mass., 1975-76; vis. prof. Western Australia Inst. Tech., Perth, 1978; speaker in field. Co-author: No G.O.D.'s in the Classroom: Inquiry into Inquiry, 1972, Inquiry and Elementary Social Studies, 1972, Inquiry and Secondary Social Studies, 1972, Perspectives in Moral and Values Education, 1976, Promoting Moral Growth: From Piaget to Kohlberg, 1979, 83, Models of Values and Moral Education, 1980, The Structure of School Improvement, 1983. Stanford U. fellow, 1979, Congl. fellow, 1982-83, Ger. Acad. Exch. Svc. fellow, 1983. Avocations: skiing, tennis, rowing (mem. U.S. rowing team competed World Championships, Bled, Yugoslavia, 1966).

HERSH, STEPHEN PETER, psychiatrist, psycho-oncologist, educator; b. NYC, Aug. 11, 1940; s. Joseph Harrison and Lillian (Berk) H.; m. Jean Ann Lehrke, Apr. l0, l969; children: Damon, Katharine, Justin, Tessa. BA, Amherst Coll., 1962; MD, NYU, 1967. Diplomate Am. Bd. Psychiatry and Neurology. Pediatric intern NYU-Bellevue Med. Ctr., N.Y.C., 1967-68, fellow in child psychiatry, l970-72; resident in psychiatry U. Pa., Phila., l968-70; chief Ctr. for Studies in Child and Family Mental Health, NIMH, Rockville, Md., 1972-73, spl. asst. to dir., 1973-74, asst. dir., 1975-79; dir. div. children and youth St. Elizabeths Hosp., Washington, l981; co-founder, co-dir., chmn. bd. Med. Illness Counseling Ctr., Chevy Chase, Md., 1982-94, exec. and med. dir., 1995—; behavioral health and medicine cons. Marriott Internat., 1996—99. Clin. prof. psychiatry and pediat. George Washington U. Med. Ctr., Washington, 1989—; cons. pediat. br. Nat. Cancer Inst., Bethesda, Md., 1972-99; nat. adv. coun. Nat. Anthrop. Film Ctr., Smithsonian Instn., Washington, 1979-81; chmn. sci. adv. bd. St. Jude Children's Rsch. Hosp., Memphis, 1980-82; attending physician, 1993—; dir., prin. investigator HIV R&D project Nat. Cancer Inst., 1988—; med. staff clin. ctr., NIH, 1992-99; dir. rsch. grant J.W. and Alice S. Marriott Found., 2002—. Author: The Executive Parent, 1979, The Physician and the Mental Health of the Child, 1981, Beyond Miracles, 2000; contbg. editor Journeys, 1994-96; contbr. articles to profl. jours., chpts. to books. Mem. svcs. com. Am. Cancer Soc., Washington, 1974-79; mem. com. on traffic Somerset (Md.) Town Coun., 1975-78; bd. dirs. Barker Found., Washington, 1984-87; mem. med. bd. Lupus Found. Greater Washington, 1988—, My Image After Breast Cancer, 1995—; bd. med. advisors Multimedia Med. Sys., 1997; vol. emergency response physician Md. Dept. Health and Mental Hygiene, 2003 . Recipient spl. award Nat. Consortium for Child Mental Health Svcs., 1979. Fellow, Am. Psychiat. Assn. (disting. life, commendation 1983, Significant Achievement award 1993); mem. AAAS, Am. Pain Soc., Internat. Assn. Study Pain. Democrat. Home: 421 Kent Square Rd Gaithersburg MD 20878-5711 Office: Med Illness Counseling Ctr 2 Wisconsin Cir Chevy Chase MD 20815-7003 *We all should engage in healing. Healing involves helping ourselves or another gain an improved sense of well-being and control. Joyful moments then become more available, involvement with others through love more possible, and life itself more a celebration.*

HERSH, STEVEN LANCE, clinical hypnotherapist, hypnocounselor, author; BA in English, Upsala Coll., 1976. Cert. advanced clin. hypnotherapist, master hypnocounselor Inst. of Hypnotherapy. Dir. mktg. Monmouth County Arts Coun.-Count Basie Theatre, Red Bank, NJ, 1990—91; entertainment columnist The Two River Times, 1991-93; founder, exec. dir. Silent Running Soc., 1985—; with Meridian Healthcare Sys./Jersey Shore Med. Ctr., Neptune, NJ. Host Names in the News, WHTG (FM), Eatontown, N.J., 1993-96. Author: Written Out of Television: The Encyclopedia of Cast Changes and Character Replacements, 1945-94, 1996, Written Out of Television: A TV Lover's Guide to Cast Changes 1945-94, 1996; rsch. asst. (Vincent Terrace) Television Character and Story Facts, 1993, Television Specials, 1995; (James Robert Parish) Rosie: Rosie O'Donnell's Biography, 1997, others; actor Star Trek: The Motion Picture, 1980, Stardust Memories, 1981. Office: Inst Integrated Health and Wellness 1820 Corlies Ave Ste 1B Neptune NJ 07753 Office Fax: 732-775-9987. E-mail: stevenlance@netscape.net.

HERSHAFT, ALEX, organization executive; b. Warsaw, July 1, 1934; came to the U.S., 1951; s. Jozef and Sabina (Kalina) H.; m. Eugenie Crystal, Oct. 1, 1962; 1 child, Monica. BA in Chemistry, U. Conn., 1955; PhD in Chemistry, Iowa State U., 1961. Lectr. Israel Inst. Tech., Haifa, 1961-63; ops. analyst Ctr. for Naval Analyses, Arlington, Va., 1963-65; staff analyst Avco Corp., Wilmington, Mass., 1965-68; rsch. scientist Grumman Corp., Bethpage, N.Y., 1968-72; prin. scientist Booz Allen & Hamilton, Bethesda, Md., 1972-74; dir. environ. studies Enviro Control, Rockville, Md., 1974-76; sr. scientist MITRE Corp., McLean, Va., 1977-81. Founder League for Abolition of Religious Coercion in Israel, 1961, Environ. Tech. Seminar, 1969, Vegetarian Info. Svc., 1976, Farm Animal Reform Movement, 1981; co-founder U.S. animal rights movement, 1981; launched nat. animal rights confs., 1981, the Great Am. Meatout, 1985, World Farm Animals Day, 1983. Contbr. articles to profl. jours. Pres. Farm Animal Reform Movement, 1981—. Named to Vegetarian Hall of Fame, 1998; recipient Animal Rights Hall of Fame, 2001. Home: PO Box 5888 Bethesda MD 20824-5888 E-mail: farm@farmusa.org.

HERSHAFT, ELINOR, space planner, interior designer; b. N.Y.C., Aug. 12, 1940; d. Solomon and Rose (Cohen) Klausner; m. Arthur Hershaft, June 21, 1959 (div. 1983); children: Karin, Peter; m. Alan J. Hoffman, Sept. 2, 1990. Student, Skidmore Coll., 1956-58; BA, N.Y.U., 1960; postgrad., N.Y. Sch. Interior Design, 1977-78. Lic. home improvement contractor, Conn. Interior designer Elinor Hershaft Interiors, Greewich, Conn., 1979—. Major projects house constrn. with interior design, 1985-87, additions, 1982—; projects pub. in House Beautiful, 1988, Tile News, 1988, Kitchen and Bath Concepts, 1989; numerous comml. and residential interior design projects in Fairfield, Conn. and Westchester, N.Y. Counties, Mass., So. Fla., Boulder, Colo., Wilmington, N.C.; also custom furniture design and fabrication. Creative dir. Greenwich Jewish Fedn., 1983—86; creator logo Bobbie Silverman Inst. for Jewish Culture, Greenwich, Conn., 2001; developer design format, logo and calligraphy spl. fund raising campaign Temple Sholom, Greenwich, 1994—95; pro bono office design and space planning Jewish Cmty. Svcs. Recipient Svc. award Jewish Community Svcs. of Greenwich, 1985, Greenwich Jewish Fedn., 1983, 84, 85. Mem. ASID (allied mem.), Allied Bd. Trade, AIA (allied individual), AAF (allied individual). Jewish. Avocations: calligraphy, reading, swimming, piano. Studio: 115 Old Mill Rd Greenwich CT 06831-3015

HERSHATTER, RICHARD LAWRENCE, lawyer, writer; b. New Haven, Sept. 20, 1923; s. Alexander Charles and Belle (Blenner) Hershatter; m. Mary Jane McNulty, Aug. 16, 1980; 1 stepchild, Kimberly Ann Matlock Kleiman-;children from previous marriage: Gail Brook, Nancy Jill, Bruce Warren. BA, Yale U., 1948; JD, U. Mich., 1951. Bar: Conn 1951, Mich 1951, US Supreme Ct 1959. Pvt. practice, New Haven, 1951-85, Clinton, Conn., 1985—99; state trial referee, 1984—. Author: The Spy Who Hated Licorice, 1966, The Spy Who Hated Caramel, 1968, The Spy Who Hated Fudge, 1970; : 2d edit., 2001, Hung Jury, 2001, The Spy Who Hated Taffy, 2001. Mem. Branford Bd. Edn., Conn., 1963—71; mem. Clinton Rep. Town Com., Conn., 1982—2000, chmn., 1984—88. With Air Corps U.S. Army, 1942—44, With U.S. Inf., 1944—46. Mem.: Mystery Writers Am, Middlesex County Bar Asn, Conn. Sch. Attys. Coun. (pres. 1977), Banyan Bay Club (v.p., bd dirs 1988—), Masons. E-mail: hershatter@aol.com.

HERSHBERG, JAMES GORDON, historian, educator; b. N.Y.C., N.Y., May 13, 1960; s. David Emmet and Arline Ackerman Hershberg; m. Annie Brown, Aug. 11, 1969; 1 child, Gabriel William. AB, Harvard Coll., 1982; M of Internat. Affairs, Columbia U., 1985; PhD, Tufts U., 1989. Lectr. Tufts U., Medford, Mass., 1988—90; vis. fellow, lectr. Calif. Inst. of Tech., Pasadena, 1990; dir. cold war internat. history project; editor CWIHP bull. Woodrow Wilson Internat. Ctr. for Scholars, Washington, 1991—97; asst. prof. of history and internat. affairs George Wash. U., Washington, 1997—2000, assoc. prof. of history and internat. affairs, 2000—. Cons. Nat. Security Archive, Washington, 1987—. Author: (non-fiction book) James B. Conant: Harvard to Hiroshima and the Making of the Nuclear Age, 1993 (Bernath prize, 1994), 1995; contbr. articles to profl. jours. Recipient vis. fellowship, Calif. Inst. of Tech., Sci. and Pub. Policy Program, 1990, Norwegian Nobel Inst., 1999. Mem.: Soc. for Historians of Am. Fgn. Rels. Office: George Washington Univ History Dept Phillips Hall 326 Washington DC 20052 Office Fax: 202-994-6231. Personal E-mail: jhershb@gwu.edu.

HERSHBERGER, ROBERT GLEN, architect, educator; b. Pocatello, Idaho, Apr. 4, 1936; s. Vernon Elver and Edna Syvilla (Kinsley) H.; m. Deanna Marlene Van Dyke, Mar. 25, 1961; children: Vernon, Andrew. AB, Stanford U., 1958; BArch, U. Utah, 1959; MArch, U. Pa., 1961, PhD, 1969. Registered architect, Idaho, Ariz. Project architect Spencer & Lee, Architects, San Francisco, 1961-63; project designer GBQC Architects, Phila., 1967-69; asst. prof. Idaho State U., Pocatello, 1963-65; adj. asst. prof. Drexel U., Phila., 1967-69; practicing architect Archtl. & Planning Cons., Tempe, Ariz., 1969-87; prof. Sch. of Architecture Ariz. State U., Tempe, 1969-87, acting dir. Sch. Architecture, 1986-87, assoc. dean. Coll. of Architecture and Environ. Design, 1987; prof. U. Ariz. Coll. Arch., Tucson, 1988—2001, dean, 1988-96; ptnr. Hershberger and Nickels Archs./Planners, 1998—. Chmn. Environ. Design Rsch. Assoc., Washington, 1976-79, chair Archs. in Edn. Com. AIA, Washington, 1983-85; v.p. Arch. Rsch. Ctrs. Consortium, 1994-96; prin. Hershberger, Arch. and Planner, Payson, Ariz., 2002—. Prin. works include Covenant Bapt. Ch. (AIA Excellence award), Urban Renewal Plan Downtown Tempe (AIA Citation), Hershberger residence (AIA honor 1990); author: Architectural Programming and Predesign Manager, 1999; Archtl. Programming in Architect's Handbook of Professional Practice, 2001, Handbook of Environmental Psychology, 2002. Bd. dirs. Rio Salado Found.; mem. Tempe Design Rev. Com., 1985-87, Tempe Elec. Adv. Com., 1982-85, Pocatello Planning Commn., 1962-65; mem. Tucson Planning Commn., 2000-02; mem. pub. arts com. U. Ariz., 1988-96, chmn., 1994-96, mem. campus design rev. adv. com., 1990-96, chmn., 1990-93; chair staff parish com. Catalina United Meth. Ch., 1995; bd. dirs. Catalina Day Care Ctr., 1990-93, So. Ariz. chpt. Make-A-Wish Found., 1995-96; mem. fin. com. Christ Ch. United Meth., 2000-01; conservation commn. Payson Hist. Preservation, 2003—; archtl. rev. com. Portal 4, Pine, Ariz., 2003—; mem. Payson Design Rev., 2003—. Recipient Crescordia Environ. Excellence award Valley Forward Assn., 1986, Hon. Mention award Ariz. Hist. Mus. competition, 1985. Fellow AIA (pres. Rio Salado chpt. 1981, 74-88, bd. dirs. So. Ariz. chpt. 1988-96, pres., 1993, Gold medal adv. bd. 1992-95). Democrat. Methodist. Avocations: fly fishing, skiing, hunting, tennis, golf, photography. Office: PO Box 2266 Payson AZ 85547 Home: 204 N Forest Park Dr Payson AZ 85541 E-mail: hershberger@cybertrails.com.

HERSHCOPF, GERALD THEA, lawyer; b. Feb. 8, 1922; s. Paul and Rose (Thea) Hershcopf; m. Elaine Yeckes, June 10, 1950; 1 child, Jane. AB, Columbia U., 1943; cert. in French Civilization, U. Paris, 1945; JD, Harvard U., 1949. Bar: N.Y. 1949, U.S. Dist. Ct. (so. dist.) N.Y. 1960, U.S. Supreme Ct. 1981. Assoc. Marshall, Bratter, Greene, Allison & Tucker, N.Y.C., NY, 1949—54; ptnr. Starr & Hershcopf, N.Y.C., 1954—56, Hershcopf, Stevenson, Tannenbaum, San Filippo, Donovan & Korn, 1956—91, Eisen, Hershcopf & Schulman, 1991—. Gen. ptnr. Norfolk Realty Corp., N.Y.C., 1961—86; chmn. bd. N.Am. Planning Corp., N.Y.C., 1968—71; pres. Consortium Met. Law Schs., N.Y.C., 1983—. B. dirs. N.Y. divsn. Am. Cancer Soc., 1997—98. Served with U.S. Army, 1943—46, ETO. Mem.: Real Estate Bd. N.Y., Judge Advs. Assn., N.Y. State Bar Assn. (gen. practice sect.), Assn. Bar City N.Y., Doubles Club (N.Y.C.), French-Am. C. of C., Harvard Club, N.Y. Athletic Club, Columbia U. Tennis Club, Beta Sigma Rho. Home: 737 Park Ave New York NY 10021-4256 Office: 609 5th Ave Fl 6 New York NY 10017-1021

HERSHENHORN, ROBERT GENE, bank executive; b. St. Louis, Nov. 2, 1943; s. Isadore and Dorothy Hershenhorn; m. Dittany R. Felker, June 11, 1963 (div. Feb. 1975); children: Lindsay, Alexis; m. Judith Marie Holmberg, Aug. 5, 1995; 1 child, Sarah. BA, Washington U., 1965; JD, Chgo.-Kent Coll. of Law, 1968. Chmn. of the bd. First Bank of Ill., 1976—. Owner Hershenhorn Bancorp. holding co.; past chmn. bd. dirs. Chgo. Econometrics & Forecasting Assocs.; past chmn. bd., prin. Petrocco, Sierra Hotel, Concoco; past prin. Yellow Pages of Hungary. Bd. dirs. Joffrey Ballet, Chgo., 1996-97, Lincoln Park Zoo, Chgo., 1998—; founding mem. fin. com. Peter Fitzgerald for U.S. Senate, 1998; trustee Barat Coll., Lake Forest, Ill., Chgo. Acad. of Sci. and Museum; bd. dirs. Little City, Devel. Office of Chgo. Province of the Soc. of Jesus, Chgo. Hearing Soc., Chgo. Internat. Film Festival, U. Chgo. Cancer Rsch. Found., Lake Forest Symphony, United Way, Northlight Theater, Touchstone Theater, Drexel Hom for the Aged, others. Mem. ABA, Ill. Bar Assn., Chgo. Bar Assn., Ind. Bankers of Am., Am. Bankers Assn., Banker's Club of Chgo. Jewish. Avocations: travel, tennis, biking. Home: 808 E Deerpath Rd Lake Forest IL 60045-2273 Office: First Bank & Trust Co of Ill 300 E Northwest Hwy Palatine IL 60067-8133

HERSHENOV, BERNARD ZION, electronics research and development company executive; b. N.Y.C., Sept. 22, 1927; s. Joseph and Rebecca (Landes) H.; m. Miriam Leah Gold, Oct. 27, 1950; 1 dau., Ruth Lois. BS, U. Mich., 1950, MS, 1952, PhD, 1959. Asso. research engr. U. Mich., Ann Arbor, 1951-59; devel. engr. Gen. Electric Co., Schenectady, 1959-60; mem. tech. staff, head microwave integrated circuits RCA Research Labs., Princeton, N.J., 1960-72; dir. Research Labs., Tokyo, 1972-75, head energy systems Princeton, 1976-79, dir. Solid State Devices Lab., 1979-83, dir. Optical Systems and Display Materials Lab., 1983-84, dir. Optoelectronics Research Lab., 1984-87; dir. mktg. coordination David Sarnoff Research Ctr. (subs. of SRI Internat.), Princeton, 1987-88; dir. internat. bus. devel., 1989-93; sr. advisor Sarnoff Research Ctr. (subs. of SRI Internat.), Princeton, 1994-95; cons., 1993-95. Contbr. articles in field. V.p. Jewish Community Center, Princeton, 1970-71, pres., 1971-72, trustee, 1977-79; mem. physics adv. com. U. Mich., 1988—. Served with USN, 1946-47. Recipient RCA Outstanding Achievement awards, 1963, 66, Microwave Application award Microwave Theory and Techniques Soc. of IEEE, 1992. Fellow IEEE; mem. Sigma Xi, Phi Kappa Phi. Jewish. Home: 22 Raleigh Rd Kendall Park NJ 08824-1007 E-mail: bhershey@bellatlantic.net.

HERSHENSON, GERALD MARTIN, lawyer; b. Revere, Mass., May 14, 1941; s. Morris and Ida Rita (Engorn) H.; m. Sarah Shirley Knobel, June 15, 1969; children: David, Rachel. BSBA, Boston U., 1963, LLB, 1966. Bar: Mass. 1966, Pa. 1969, U.S. Dist. Ct. (ea. dist.) Pa. 1970, U.S. Supreme Ct. 1979. Law clk. Judge E. Hettrick, Boston, 1966-67; ptnr. Curtin & Heefner, Morrisville, Pa., 1969-88; pvt. practice, Morrissville, 1988—. Mem. Dem. Nat. Com., Washington, 1983, Mideast Trade Mission, 1983; officer Bucks County Dem. Com., Doylestown, Pa., 1984; mem. fin. com. Bob Edgar for Pa. Senate, 1986. Capt. U.S. Army, 1967-69. Decorated Army Commendation medal. Mem. Assn. Trial Lawyers Am., Pa. Bar Assn., Pa. State Dem. Fin. Com., Am. Arbitration Assn., Pa. Trial Lawyers Assn., Bucks Bar Assn. (treas. 1980-82), Syda Found., Comml. Law League Am., Jewish Fedn. Delaware Valley (Young Leadership award 1982, v.p. Bucks County chpt. 1980-86). Home: 1637 Bluebird Dr # B Yardley PA 19067-6320 Office: 81 Big Oak Rd Morrisville PA 19067-7801

HERSHENSON, MIRIAM HANNAH RATNER, librarian; b. Springfield, Mass., July 23, 1944; d. David and Thelma (Wasserman) Ratner; children: Trent M., Scott D. AB, Syracuse U., 1966; MS, Simmons Coll., 1967; postgrad., Nova U., 1987-89. Cert. tchr./librarian, Mass. Media specialist Quincy (Mass.) Pub. Schs., 1967-71, Virginia Beach (Va.) Pub. Schs., 1982-84, Portsmouth (Va.) Pub. Schs., 1984; regional children's coord. Broward County Libr., Ft. Lauderdale, Fla., 1985-88, br. liaison, 1988-89, br. librarian, 1989-93, regional br. supr., 1993-2001; head pub. svc. Nova Southeastern U./ Broward County Libr., 2001—03; pub. svc. adminstr. Broward County Libr., 2003—. Mem. ALA, Pub. Libr. Assn., Fla. Libr. Assn. (caucus chair 1990-91), Broward County Libr. Assn. (pres. 1994-95), Hadassah (life, chpt. pres. 1983-84), Nat. Coun. Jewish Women (life), Jewish Women Internat. (life), Brandeis Univ. Women (life). Office: Broward County Libr 100 South Andrews Ave Fort Lauderdale FL 33301 E-mail: mhershen@browardlibrary.org.

HERSHENSON, ROBERTA MANTELL, writer, photographer; b. Newark, Nov. 24, 1940; d. Milton A. and Florence (Braun) Mantell; children: Nina, Michael. BS in Edn., Simmons Coll., Boston, 1962. Freelance writer and photographer, N.Y., 1983—; contbr. N.Y. Times, N.Y.C., 1983—. Lectr. Westchester Photog. Soc., Valhalla, N.Y., 1997; pres. Ground Glass, Irvington, N.Y., 1980s, Film Workshop of Westchester, Tarrytown, N.Y., 1970s. Author news and feature articles N.Y. Times, Opera News, Wildlife Conservation Mag. Recipient Clarion award Women in Comms., 2001. Mem. Am. Soc. Journalists and Authors, Oratorio Soc. of N.Y. Avocations: music, fiction, choral singing. Office: 132 E 35th St New York NY 10016

HERSHER, RICHARD DONALD, management consultant; b. Atlantic City, May 24, 1942; s. Mayo Lawrence and Adele (Dahlman) H.; m. Betsy R. Schnitz, Mar. 15, 1970 (div. June 1983); children: Erin, Laura; m. Roza Khazina, Sept. 4, 1993. BS, U. Cin., 1966; MBA, U. Chgo., 1973. Indsl. engr. U.S. Steel Corp., Chgo., 1966-68; mfg. engr. Westinghouse Electric Corp., Chgo., 1968-73; sr. indsl. engr. Abbott Labs., North Chicago, Ill., 1973-76; plant mgr. DeMert & Dougherty, Chgo., 1976-79; pres. Hersher Assocs., Deerfield, Ill., 1979-83; exec. cons. Inst. Mgmt. Resources, Westlake Village, Calif., 1983-87; v.p. ops. Rex Precision Products, Gardena, Calif., 1987; sr. cons. Morris Anderson & Assocs., Rosemont, Ill., 1987-92; pres. Hersher Cons., Glenview, Ill., 1992—. Mem. Inst. Mgmt. Cons., Inst. Indsl. Engrs., Am. Prodn. Inventory Control Soc.

HERSHEY, DALE, lawyer, educator; b. Pitts., Mar. 24, 1941; s. Henry E. and Elizabeth (Loeffler) H.; m. Susanne Jarrett Wilson, July 8, 1967; children: Lauren Dixon, Justin Alexander. BA, Yale U., 1963; LLB, Harvard U., 1966. Bar: Pa. 1966, U.S. Dist. Ct. (we. dist.) Pa. 1966, U.S. Ct. Appeals (3d cir.) 1971, U.S. Tax Ct. 1978, U.S. Supreme Ct. 1979, Ct. Internat. Trade 1999. Assoc. Eckert Seamans Cherin & Mellott, LLC, Pitts., 1966-75, mem., 1975—. Sr. lectr. law Grad. Sch. Indsl. Adminstrn. Carnegie Mellon U., 2001—; pres. Charleston Trust/U.S.A.; vis. prof. E.M. Lyon, Ecully, France, 2003. Bd. dirs. Legal Aid Soc. Pitts., pres., 1983-89; hon. pres. Gateway to the Arts, Inc.; bd. dirs. Friends of Carnegie Libr., Pitts. Chamber Music Soc., pres., 1992-94; active Leadership Pitts., 1989-90. Mem. ABA, Internat. Bar Assn., Pa. Bar Assn. (Pro Bono award 1988), Allegheny County Bar Assn. (bd. dirs. Bar Found., mem. judiciary com. 1997-2000), Am. Law Inst., Harvard Law Sch. Assn. Western Pa. (pres. 1985-86), Harvard-Yale-Princeton Club, Yale Club (Pitts.) (pres. 1987-89). Unitarian Universalist. Home: 311 Dorseyville Rd Pittsburgh PA 15215-1022 Office: Eckert Seamans Cherin & Mellott LLC 600 Grant St Ste 4400 Pittsburgh PA 15219-2702

HERSHEY, DAVE MICHAEL, musician, music educator; b. York, Pa., Nov. 25, 1952; s. Dave Samuel Hershey and Janet Romaine Forry; m. Katherine Mary Pratt, Dec. 15, 1982; 1 child, Michael Holmes. BS in Music Edn., Austin Peay State U., 1975; M in Music Performance, Western Ky. U., 1977; pvt. student Leigh Howard Stevens, 1979—85. Percussion instr. Hershey Percussion Studio, York, 1976—; percussion shop owner Hershey Percussion Shop, York, 1976—; prin. percussionist York Symphony Orch., 1976—, Harrisburg (Pa.) Symphony Orch., 1979—97; freelance performing percussionist Pa., 1976—; prof. percussion York Coll. Pa., 1978 ; pub. sch. percussion educator Pa. Coun. on the Arts, Harrisburg, 1982—88. Mem.: The Residents of York Coll. (founder), Jaquar Club N.Am. Office: York Coll Pa Music/Art/Comm Dept PO Box 15199 York PA 17405-7199

HERSHEY, GERALD LEE, psychologist, educator; b. Detroit, Mar. 7, 1931; s Von Waltz and Clementine H.; m. Shirley Gauld, Oct. 2, 1954; children: Bruce, Dale, James. Student, UCLA, 1949-54; BA with honors, Mich. State U., 1957, MA, 1958, PhD, 1961. Asst. instr., research assoc. Mich. State U., East Lansing, 1958-61; mem. faculty dept. psychology Fullerton Coll., Calif., 1961—, prof., 1965—, chmn. dept., 1980—; vis. prof. Chapman Coll., Calif., 1962-69. Co-author: Human Development (2d edit.), 1978, Living Psychology (3d edit.), 1981. Served to 1st lt. AUS, 1954-56. Mem. Am. Psychol. Assn., Assn. Humanistic Psychology, NEA Lodges: Lions. Office: Fullerton Coll 321 E Chapman Ave Fullerton CA 92832-2011

HERSHEY, JODY HENRY, public health physician; b. Roanoke, Va., Nov. 1, 1956; s. Jay Henry Hershey and Maryann (Thomas) Shane. BS, Roanoke Coll., 1978; MD, Ea. Va. Med. Sch., 1982; MPH, Johns Hopkins U., 1987. Diplomate Am. Bd. Family Practice; bd. cert. pub. health and gen. preventive medicine. Pub. health officer Piedmont Health Dist. Va. Dept. Health, Farmville, 1987-89, genetics program dir. Richmond, 1989-90; med. dir. Va. Dept. Corrections, Richmond, 1990-92; adminstrv. dir., family/ambulatory care physician Carilion

Healthcare Corp., Roanoke, 1992-95; pub. health dir. New River Health Dist. Va. Dept. Health, Christiansburg, 1995—. Vis. cons., prof. The Second Clin. Coll., People's Hosp. Beijing Med. U., 1995—; mem. steering com. Inst. for Cmty. Health, Blacksburg, Va., 1995—, Ctrl. Highlands Appalachia Leadership Initiative on Cancer, Abingdon, Va., 1996—; mem. steering com. Inst. Cmty. Health; mem. steering com. and adv. bd. S.E. Regional Pub. Health Inst.; bd. dirs., adv. bd. HAWA Comm. Inc., Nutrition Superstores Inc., Waldron Coll. Health and Human Svcs., Radford U.; med. advisor ARC, disaster health svc. vol, med. cons.; adj. faculty U. Va., Radford U., Va. Tech., Va.-Md. Regional Coll. Vet. Medicine; assoc. prof., discipline leader pub. health Va. Coll. Osteopathic Medicine. Contbr. articles to profl. jours. Bd. dirs. Mill Mountain Theatre, Roanoke, 1994-2001, New River Valley Hospice, Christiansburg, 1995-99, The New Century Coun., Roanoke, 1995—; Montgomery Regional Hosp., 1998—, Health Planning Agy. Southwest Va., 2000—; mem. exec. com. Turning Point. Recipient Leadership award Luth. Brotherhood, 1993, Leadership and Scholarship award Lions Club, 1994, Outstanding Cmty. Svc. and Leadership award Kiwanis Club, 1995, Pub. Health Leadership Inst. award The Ctrs. for Disease Control and Prevention, Atlanta, 1996-97, Nat. Assn. City and County Health Officers 2000 Environ. Health award. Fellow Am. Coll. Preventive Medicine; mem. APHA (com. chmn./adv. bd. 1988-2000, adv. bd./steering com. 1996-2000), Am. Acad. Family Physicians, Va. Acad. Family Physicians, Nat. Assn. City and County Health Officers (bd. dirs. 1998-2001, pub. policy com. chmn. 2000-02, v.p. 2001-02, fin. com. chmn. 2001—, pres.-elect 2002-03, pres. 2003, award for excellence in creating healthy cmty. 2001, award for excellence in maternal and child health 2002, Howard Read award 2002), Pub. Health Leadership Soc. and Coun. (sec.-treas. 1997-2001), Hollins Comm. Rsch. Inst. (trustee and bd. dirs. 2000—, sec.-treas. 2001—), Va. Acad. Preventive Medicine and Pub. Health (adv. bd.), S.W. Va. Med. Soc. (bd. dirs., adv. bd., sec.-treas. 2001—). Avocations: triathlete, gentleman farmer. Office: New River Health Dist 210 Pepper St S Ste A Christiansburg VA 24073-3522 E-mail: jhershey@vdh.state.va.us.

HERSHEY, NATHAN, lawyer, educator; b. N.Y.C., Apr. 28, 1930; s. Harry and Hannah (Horwitz) Hershey; m. Carol Fine, July 13, 1958; children: Suzanne, Madeleine. AB, NYU, 1950; LLB, Harvard U., 1953. Bar: D.C. 1953, Pa. 1977. Individual practice law, N.Y.C., 1955—56; rsch. assoc. in health law U. Pitts., 1956—58, asst. prof., 1958—63, assoc. prof., 1963—68, prof., 1968—; mem. Pa. Bd. Med. Edn., 1974—80; of counsel Markel, Schafer, and Goldman P.C., Pitts., 1977—, Post & Schell, Phila., 1984—94. Cons. Pa. State Com. on Pub. Health and Welfare, 1973—80; v.p. U. Pitts. Senate, 1995—98, pres., 1998—2001. Author (with others): Hospital Law Manual, 1959; author: (with Robert D. Miller) Human Experimentation and the Law, 1976; author: Hospital-Physician Relations, 1982; editor: Hosp. Law Newsletter; contbr. articles to profl. jours. Bd. dirs. Women's Health Svcs., 1976—91, bd. v.p., 1982—91; bd. dirs. Hill House Assn., Pitts., 1964—71. Served with U.S. Army, 1953—55. Mem.: Am. Pub. Health Assn., Soc. Hosp. Attys. Western Pa. (dir. 1974—85, past pres.), Am. Soc. Hosp. Attys. (past pres.), Inst. Medicine of NAS. Democrat. Jewish. Home: 5423 Northumberland St Pittsburgh PA 15217-1128 Office: 2200 Lawyers Bldg Pittsburgh PA 15219

HERSHEY, ROBERT LEWIS, mechanical engineer, management consultant; b. Chgo., Dec. 18, 1941; s. Maurice and Rose Beverly (Barrish) H. BSME summa cum laude, Tufts U., 1963; MSME, MIT, 1964; PhD in Engring., Cath. U. Am., 1973. Registered profl. engr., D.C., N.Y.; cert. mfg. engr. Engr. Bell Telephone Labs., Whippany, N.J., 1963-67; acoustics mgr. Weston Instruments, Inc., Poughkeepsie, N.Y., 1967-68; sr. scientist Bolt Beranek & Newman, Washington, 1968-71; acoustics program mgr. Booz Allen & Hamilton, Bethesda, Md., 1971-79; program v.p. Sci. Mgmt. Corp., Washington, 1979-80, divsn. v.p., 1980-88; exec. engr. O'Donnell Cons. Engrs., Inc., Washington, 1988—. Sec. Engring. Registration Bd., D.C., 1987-98, D.C. Profl. Coun., Washington, 1974; mem. coordinating com. on productivity Am. Assn. Engring. Socs., Washington, 1984-88. Author: How to Think With Numbers, 1982, All the Math You Need to Get Rich, 2001. Sci. policy analyst George Bush Presdl. Campaign, Washington, 1988, 92, Bob Dole Presdl. Campaign, Washington, 1996; pres. Hamilton House Assn. Resident Tenants, Washington, 1987-88, 90—; mem. Joint Bd. on Sci. Engring. Edn., Washington, 1972-78. Recipient Design award Machinery Mag., 1963; fellow Nat. Soc. Profl. Engrs., 1973-75. Fellow ASME (chmn. Washington chpt. 1978-79; Dedicated Svc. award 2001); mem. AAAS, D.C. Sci. Writers Assn., Philos. Soc. Washington (v.p., corr. sec.), Capital PC User Group, Acoustical Soc. Am. (chmn. Washington chpt. 1982-83), D.C. Soc. Profl. Engrs. (pres. 1975-76, 2002-03, nat. dir. 1980-86, Young Engr. of Yr. 1974), D.C. Coun. Engring. and Archtl. Socs. (del. 1969—, pres. 1978-79, Pres.'s award 1989, Nat. Capital award 1974), Soc. Mfg. Engrs. (chmn. Washington Robotics Internat. chpt. 1986-87), Mensa, Washington Coal Club, MIT Club of Washington (pres. 1979-80), Washington Tufts Alliance (v.p. 1970-71, mem. steering com. 1999—), Tau Beta Pi (pres. Tufts student chpt. 1962-63, v.p. Washington alumni chpt. 1988-89), Sigma Xi. Republican. Avocations: chess, tennis, sports cars, golf. Home: Apt 1033 1255 New Hampshire Ave NW Washington DC 20036-2328 E-mail: hershey@cpcug.org.

HERSHISER, OREL LEONARD, IV, professional baseball player; b. Buffalo, Sept. 16, 1958; s. Orel Leonard H. III and Millie H. Hershiser; m. Jamie Byars, Feb. 7, 1981; children: Orel Leonard V, Jordan Douglass. Student, Bowling Green State U. Pitcher minor league teams, Clinton, Iowa, 1979,, San Antonio, 1980—81, Albaqueque, N.Mex., 1982—83; with L.A. Dodgers, 1983—94, Cleve. Indians, 1995—97; pitcher San Francisco Giants, 1997—98, N.Y. Mets, 1998—99; with L.A. Dodgers, 1999—. Named Most Valuable Player, World Series, 1988, Major League Player of Yr., Sporting News, 1988, Pitcher of Yr., 1988; named to All-Star Team, Nat. League, 1987, 1988, Sporting News Nat. League, 1988, Silver Slugger Team, Sporting News, 1993, All-Star Games, 1987—89; recipient Cy Young award, Nat. League, 1988, Gold Glove award, 1988. Achievements include playing in the World Series, 1988. Office: Los Angeles Dodgers 1000 Elysian Park Ave Los Angeles CA 90012-1199

HERSHKOWITZ, ALLEN J. waste management specialist, researcher; married; 3 children. Cert. d'assiduite, U. Grenoble, 1975; BA cum laude, CCNY, 1977; M.Phil. in Polit. Econs., CUNY, 1984, PhD in Polit. Econs., 1986. Instr. CUNY, 1979—82; dir. solid waste rsch. INFORM, 1982—86; prin. contractor U.S. Congl. Office Tech. Assessment, 1986—88; sr. scientist Nat. Resources Def. Coun., 1988—. Mem. nat. rsch. coun. com. on health effects of waste incineration NAS; chmn. commr.'s adv. bd. operating requirements for mcpl solid waste incinerators N.Y. State Dept. Environ. Conservation; mem. regulatory negotiations on fugitive emissions U.S. EPA; mem. sci. adv. bd. subcom. sludge incineration EPA; mem. peer rev. panel Agy. Toxic Substances and Disease Registry; advisor Orgn. Am. States, World Bank, others; invited lectr. Yale U., Harvard U., MIT, Columbia U., Princeton U., U. London, U. Pa., NYU, Tufts U.; del. U.N. Treaty Conv. on Transboundary Movements of Hazardous Wastes, 1989; leader Congl. fact-finding mission to Europe to study recycling, 1992; govt. advisor U.S., Europe, Japan. Author: Garbage Burning: Lessons from Europe, 1986, Garbage Management in Japan, 1987, Too Good to Throw Away: Recycling's Proven Record, 1997, Bronx Ecology: Blueprint for a New Environmentalism, 2002; contbr. articles on energy and solid waste issues to profl. jours. including Tech. Rev., N.Y. Times, Amicus Jour., others; TV appearances on CNN, ABC, NBC, CBS, Larry King Live, Crossfire, others; featured in New Yorker, July, 1995. Pres. Bronx Cmty. Paper Co., originator, co-chair bd. dirs. Office: NRDC 40 W 20th St New York NY 10011

HERSHMAN, BRANDT, state legislator; m. Lisa Hershman. Dist. ops. dir. U.S. Rep. Steve Buyer; mgr. Hershman Farms; ptnr. Wilkes Innovative Techs.; mem. Ind. State Senate, 2000—, mem. edn. com., pensions and labor com., others. Mem. governing bd. Ind. Rural Devel. Coun.; bd. dirs., v.p. Pi Kappa Phi. Mem. Ind. Econ. Devel. Assn. Republican. Office: 200 W Washington St Indianapolis IN 46204

HERSHMAN, JACK IRA, urologist; b. Bklyn., Oct. 7, 1955; s. Seymour and Sonia Elaine (Kamins) H.; m. Ingrid Gail Bernstein, Aug. 25, 1986; children: Melissa Paige, Jennifer Whitney, Neil Ross. BA in Biology magna cum laude, U. Rochester, 1977; MD, Mt. Sinai Sch. Medicine, 1981. Diplomate Am. Bd. Urology. Resident in surgery Lenox Hill Hosp., N.Y.C., 1981-83; resident in urology Montefiore Med. Ctr., Bronx, N.Y., 1983-86; chief urology Phelps Meml. Hosp., North Tarrytown, N.Y., 1986—; attending urologist Dobbs Ferry (N.Y.) Hosp., 1986—, Westchester County Med. Ctr., Valhalle, N.Y., 1986—, No. Westchester Hosp., Mt. Kisco, N.Y., 1998—; clin. instr. urology N.Y. Hosp., N.Y.C., 1987—. Chief section urology Phelps Meml. Hosp., North Tarrytown, 1990—. Fellow Am. Coll. Surgeons; mem. Am. Urologic Soc., N.Y.S. Urologic Soc., N.Y. State Med. Soc., Westchester County Med. Soc., Phi Beta Kappa. Office: 777 N Broadway Ste 309 Sleepy Hollow NY 10591-1040 Fax: 914-631-5838. E-mail: fish5facts@aol.com.

HERSHMAN, JEROME MARSHALL, endocrinologist; b. Chgo., July 20, 1932; s. Maurice and Gertrude (Zemel) H.; m. Fleurette Kram, Dec. 22, 1957; children: Daniel, Michael, Jeffrey. BS, Northwestern U., 1952; MS, Calif. Inst. Technology, 1953; MD, U. Ill., 1957. Diplomate Am. Bd. Internal Medicine, Endocrinology & Metabolism. Fellow in endocrinology New England Ctr. Hosp., Boston, 1961-63; clin. investigator Northwestern U. Med. Sch., Chgo., 1964-67; chief clin. nuclear medicine Birmingham (Ala.) VA Hosp., 1967-71, chief endocrine sect., 1971-72; prof. Sch. Medicine U. Ala., Birmingham, 1967-72, UCLA, 1972—; chief endocrinology and metabolism West L.A. VA Med. Ctr., 1972—2002, assoc. chief endocrinology and diabetes, 2002—. Editor: Endocrine Pathophysiology, 1977, 2d edit., 1982, 3d edit., 1988; editor Thyroid, 1991-2000, Jour. Clin. Endocrinology and Metabolism, 1978-83; mem. editl. bd. Am. Jour. Medicine, 1989-95. Capt. USAF, 1959-61, col. USAR, 1985-91. Mem. Am. Thyroid Assn. (dir. 1989-92, pres. 1992-93). Jewish. Achievements include demonstration of thyrotropin-releasing hormone for diagnosis of pituitary and thyroid disease in 1969; discovered thyroid-stimulating activity of human chorionic gonadotropin. Home: 15970 Meadowcrest Rd Sherman Oaks CA 91403-4714 E-mail: jhershmn@ucla.edu.

HERSHMAN, JUDITH, advertising executive; b. Boston, Sept. 16, 1949; d. Max and Mollie (Cohen) H. BFA, Boston U., 1971. Pres., owner Hershman Advt. & Design, Foxboro, Mass., 1979—. Executed mural Kenmore Subway Sta., Boston, 1970. Adv. com. Tri-County Vocational Tech. High Sch. Recipient cert. merit Printing Industries of Am., 1997. Avocations: sewing, volleyball, softball, crewel embroidery, refinishing furniture. Home and Office: 41 Mechanic St Foxboro MA 02035-2027

HERSHMAN, MORRIS, writer; b. N.Y.C., Jan. 31, 1936; s. Banjamin Hershman and Ida Malinski; m. Florence Verbell Brown, Sept. 16, 1960. Student, CCNY, 1955—56, NYU, 1957—59. Asst. editor H and H Pubs., N.Y.C., 1954—56; editl. asst. Topics Pubs., 1957—59. Author (87) novels; author: (311) short stories. Mem.: Mystery Writers Am. (bd. dirs. 1955—56, 1957—59, 1969—71). Avocations: book collecting, fishing, travel. Mailing: c/o Mystery Writers Am 17 E 47th St 6th Fl New York NY 10017

HERSHMAN, SCOTT EDWARD, lawyer; b. N.Y.C., Mar. 31, 1958; s. Harold Martin and Barbara (Goldberg) H. BA, Am. U., 1980; JD, Yeshiva U., 1983. Bar: N.Y. 1984, U.S. Dist. Ct. (so. and ea. dists.) N.Y. 1986, U.S. Supreme Ct. 1994. Asst. dist. atty. N.Y. County Dist. Atty.'s Office, N.Y.C., 1983-86; ptnr. Graubard, Mollen & Miller, N.Y.C., 1986-2000, Hunton & Williams, N.Y.C., 2001—. Mem. ABA, N.Y. State Bar Assn., Assn. Bar City of N.Y. Office: Hunton & Williams 200 Park Ave New York NY 10166-0136 E-mail: shershman@hunton.com.

HERSHNER, ROBERT FRANKLIN, JR., judge; b. Sumter, S.C., Jan. 21, 1944; s. Robert Franklin and Druie (Goodman) H.; m. Sally Sinclair, May 19, 1990; children: Bryan, Andrew. AB, Mercer U., 1966, JD, 1969. Bar: Ga. 1971, U.S. Dist. Ct. (mid. dist.) Ga. 1971, U.S. Dist. Ct. (so. dist.) Ga. 1979, U.S. Ct. Appeals (11th cir.) 1981, U.S. Supreme Ct. 1978. Atty. Ga. Legal Svcs. Corp., Macon, 1972; assoc. Adams, O'Neal, Hemingway & Kaplan, Macon, 1972-76; ptnr. Kaplan & Hershner, P.A., Macon, 1976-80; judge U.S. Bankruptcy Ct. for Mid. Dist. Ga., Macon, 1980—, chief bankruptcy judge, 1986—. Active Fed. Jud. Ctr. Com. on Bankruptcy Edn., 1990—99, chmn., 1994—99; elected mem. bd. Fed. Jud. Ctr., 2001—. Contbr. Georgia Lawyers Basic Practice Handbook, 2d edit., Post-Judgment Procedures, 1979; cons. Norton Bankruptcy Law and Practice. V.p. Macon Heritage Found., 1977-78. Capt. U.S. Army, 1970-75. Mem. Ga. Bar Assn., Macon Bar Assn., Nat. Conf. Bankruptcy Judges (gov., v.p. 1996-97, pres. 1997-98), Blue Key, Phi Eta Sigma. Methodist. Office: US Bankruptcy Ct PO Box 86 Macon GA 31202-0086

HERSKOVIC, ARNOLD MANFRED, physician, oncologist; b. Balt., July 30, 1943; s. James Issac and Helen H.; children: Joshua, Daniel, Michael, Katherine, Alexander. BS, U. Md., 1964, MD, 1969. Asst. prof. Cornell U., 1974-75, U. So. Calif., 1975, George Washington U., 1977-80; assoc. prof. Duke U. Med. Ctr., 1980-82; prof. Wayne State U., 1982-98. Med. dir. radiation oncology N.W. Cmty. Hosp., Arlington Heights; vice chief, dir. radiation oncology Wayne State U., Detroit; prin. investigator Radiation Therapy Oncology Group. Contbr. articles to profl. jours; patentee in field. Fellow Am. Coll. Radiology, Am. Coll. Radiation Oncology; mem. AMA, Am. Soc. Clin. Oncology, Am. Radium Soc., Am. Bradytherapy Soc. Jewish. Avocations: pilot, model trains. Home: 77 S Evergreen #807 Arlington Heights IL 60005 Office: Radiation Oncology 800 W Central Arlington Heights IL 60005

HERSKOVITZ, S(AM) MARC, lawyer; b. Munich, Jan. 1, 1949; came to U.S., 1949; s. Max and Bella Herskovitz; 1 child from previous marriage, David Michael; m. Barbara Hobbs, Nov. 28, 1990; 1 child, Daniel Max. BA, Pa. State U., 1970; MS in Edn. with highest honors, So. Ill. U., 1974; JD with honors, Fla. State U., 1987. Bar: Fla. 1987, U.S. Dist. Ct. (mid. dist.) Fla. 1988, U.S. Ct. Appeals (11th cir) 1988. Agy. mgr. Sun Personnel Svcs., Inc., Sarasota, Fla., 1978-80; claims adjuster Allstate Inc. Co., Lake Worth, Fla., 1980-84; sr. litigation atty. Fla. Dept. Fin. Svcs., Office of Ins. Reg., Tallahassee, 1987—. Mem. ABA, ATLA, Phi Kappa Phi. Democrat. Avocations: softball, reading. Home: 707 Lothian Dr Tallahassee FL 32312-2858 Office: Fla Dept Fin Svcs Office of Ins Reg 612 Larson Bldg Tallahassee FL 32399-0333

HERSLEY, DENNIS CHARLES, environmentalist, software systems consultant; b. Idaho Falls, Idaho, July 11, 1947; s. Cyril R. and Bardella (Webb) H.; m. Jane Anne Lilly, Jan. 16, 1993; children: Cary Connolly, Laura Lilly, Claire Lilly. Student, U. So. Calif., 1964-65; electronics tech. cert., Idaho State U., 1970; postgrad., U. Santa Clara, 1979. Cert. FCC 1st class radio engr. with TV and radar endorsements. Ptnr. Intensive Care Tech. Svcs., Pocatello, Idaho, 1972-74; test engring. mgr. Nat. Semiconductor, Sunnyvale, Calif., 1975-76; test ops. mgr. Amdahl Ireland, Ltd., Dublin, 1978; engr., planner, analyst Amdahl Corp., Sunnyvale, 1979-85; CFO, chmn. Provista Software Internat., San Jose, Calif., 1985-86; pres. Almaden Consulting, Santa Cruz, Calif., 1985—; co-founder, pres., dir. non profit sci. rsch. Citizens United for Responsible Environmentalism, Inc., Santa Cruz, Calif., 1994—; CFO Rsch. Consultation, Inc., Santa Cruz, Calif., 1998—. Planner, sponsor Fusewest Regional Tech. Conf., Scottsdale, Ariz., 1988-89; tech. curriculum advisor Idaho State U., 1970-75; featured on KKUP radio talk show "Mold Can Make You Sick," 2001; participant 3d Internat. Conf. on bioaerosols, Fungi and Mycotoxins, 1998. Inventor calculator design, 1975, featured on BBC documentary, 1998. Recipient Outstanding Alumnus award Idaho State U., 1975, Honored Donor award Monterey Bay Aquarium, 1996. Mem. Calif. Assn. Non-Profits, No. Calif. Focus Users Group (asst. editor 1988-90), Santa Cruz Tech. Alliance. Office: CURE 2375 Benson Ave Santa Cruz CA 95065-1674

HERSMAN, FERNANDO WILLIAM (FERD HERSMAN), retired engineering executive; b. Cin., Apr. 27, 1922; s. Fernando William and Eliza Ann (Garforth) H.; m. Jill Ann Becker, June 30, 1951; children: Michael S., John A., F. William, Christopher B., Jan (dec.). BSChemE, U. Cin., 1949. Registered profl. engr., Ohio. Process engr. Frigidaire div. Gen. Motors, Dayton, Ohio, 1949-51; project engr. Vulcan-Cin., 1951-57; R&D engr. U.S. Indsl. Chems. div., Cin., 1957-61; v.p. Fischer Indsl. Equipment, Inc., Cin., 1961-83, pres., owner, 1983-89. Mem. Mayor's Fin. Com., Greenhills, Ohio, 1983, Charter Commn., Greenhills, 1988-89; elder Blue Ash. Presbyn. Ch., 1996-98. Staff sgt. U.S. Army, 1942-45, PTO; lt. USNR, 1950-67. Decorated Bronze Star with one oak leaf cluster. Mem. AIChE (chmn. Ohio Valley chpt. 1966-67), Ret. Engrs. and Scientists Cin., SAR, Am. Legion. Republican. Presbyterian. Avocations: golf, photography, travel, poetry. Home: 46 Carpenter's Ridge Rd Cincinnati OH 45241-3274

HERSMAN, MARION FRANK, professional administrator, lawyer; b. Huntington, W.Va., Nov. 12, 1932; s. Marion Rockefeller and Frances Mae (Peabody) H.; m. Carole Anne Birthright, Oct. 1960 (div.); 1 child, Frank Eric Birthright; m. Nina Claire Mohay, Dec. 24, 1976 (div.); 1 child, Alicia Claire; m. Eleonora Georgi Hivrina, April 11, 1995; children: Elizabeth Anne, Diana Frances. BS in Chemistry, Physics and Math, Ohio State U., 1953; PhD in Chemistry (Victor Chem. fellow, Colgate Palmolive-Peet fellow, Univ. fellow), U. Ill., 1956; JD, George Washington U., 1958, LL.M., 1960; MA, New Sch. for Social Research, 1964. Bar: Va. 1958, N.Y. 1959, D.C. 1960, U.S. Supreme Ct. 1960, U.S. Ct. Appeals (D.C. cir.) 1960. Teaching fellow U. Ill.; patent examiner U.S. Patent Office, Washington, 1956-57; assoc. firm Burns Doane, Benedict & Irons, Washington, 1957-59, Arthur, Dry & Dole, N.Y.C., 1959-60, Fish, Richardson & Neave, N.Y.C., 1960-64; staff assoc. office sci. resources planning NSF, Washington, 1964-67, office of planning and policy studies, 1967-69, head office intergovtl. sci. programs, 1969-72, dir. office intergovtl. sci. and research utilization, 1972-75; exec. dir. Colo. Planning Coordinating Council, 1976; spl. asst., sci. and tech. advisor to Gov. Colo., 1976; sci. and tech. advisor Fedn. Rocky Mountain States, Denver, 1977; dir. Rocky Mountain Tech. Sharing Task Force, 1977; dir. Div. Water Resources Hillsborough County, Tampa, Fla., 1977, dir. Div. Pub. Utilities, 1977-78, dir. Office of Planning and Intergovtl. Relations, 1978-79; asst. county adminstr. Hillsborough County (Fla.) Div. Pub. Utilities, 1978-79; vice chmn. Hillsborough Intergovtl. Resource Recovery Mgmt. Com.; mem. Fla. Community Conservation Com., 1978-80, Urban Consortium, 1978-80; spl. asst. to pres. U. South Fla., 1979-80; atty. NSF, 1980-82; dir. com. on hazardous materials Fed. Emergency Mgmt. Agy., 1981-83; vis. disting. prof. Nova U., 1982, spl. asst. to pres. for program devel., 1982; asst. city mgr. for health and human services City of Austin, (Tex.), 1982-84; exec. v.p. Lawyers Title of Ky., 1983-85; ptnr. LTK Enterprises, 1983-85; exec. v.p., chief operating officer Automation Telecommunications and Management Inc., Austin, Tex., 1984-85; dir. research and state services The Council of State Govts., Lexington, Ky., 1985-87; town mgr. Town of Snow Hill, Md., 1988; county mgr. Nye County, Nev., 1988-90; dir. social svcs. Louis Berger Internat. Cons., Sasatov Oblast, Russia, 1996—98; pres. RH Mgmt. Assocs., 1990—; town mgr. Town of Pahrup, Nev., 2000—01. Spkr. in field; tchg. assoc. George Washington U., 1957-59; chmn., exec. dir. com. on intergovtl. sci. rels. Fed. Coun. Sci. and Tech., Exec. Office of Pres., 1979-83; mem. Agrl. Yearbook adv. bd. USDA, 1979, mem. tech. adv. bd. nat. rural cmtys. facilities assessment, 1978; chmn. com. on policy mgmt. and assistance U.S. Office Mgmt. and Budget, Washington, 1974-75; mem. com. on tech. sharing President's Office Sci. and Tech., 1972-74; chmn. So. Nev. Rural Health Fair, 1991; prof. urban engring. Nat. U. Mex., Mexico City, 1975; vis. faculty CSC, Kings Point, N.Y., 1975, Fed. Exec. Inst., Charlottesville, Va., 1977, Golden Gate U., 1979-80; vis. prof. U. Colo. Grad. Sch. Pub. Affairs, 1976-77, U. South Fla., 1978, Martin Sch., U. Ky., 1986-88; spl. asst. to dir. NSF, 1976-80; cons. Office Sci. and Tech., Exec. Office of Pres., 1976-80, Western Govs.' Task Force on Regional Policy Mgmt., 1976-77; cons. USDA, 1978; mem. Subcom. on Rsch. Itilization Transp. Rsch. Bd./NRC/NAS, 1981-82; adminstr. Pahrump Valley Med. Ctr., 1991-92; pres. Nev. Health and Med. Found., 1991-92; U.S. exec. advisor mayor and city coun. City of Narva, Estonia, 1994-96; U.S. exec. advisor City of Tartu, Estonia, 1994, Internat. Exec. Svcs. Corps, 1994; U.S. trade rep. City of Narva, Estonia, 1994—; exec. advisor Internat. Exec. Svc. Corps, City of Vladimir, Russia, 1995-96; dir. social svcs. Louis Berger Internat., Inc., 1996-98; exec. advisor Saratov, Russia, 1996-98. Contbg. author: Science and Technology Policies, 1973; bd. editors and consultants: Scholar and Educator, 1977; mem. editorial bd.: Jour. Edn. and Scholar, 1977-87; contbr. articles to profl. jours. Bd. dirs. Warwick Assn., 1980-81; chmn. consumers and bus. affairs com. D.C. Area Neighborhood Council; mem. Washington Mayor's Planning and Budget Adv. Com., 1980-82; vol. exec. Internat. Exec. Svcs. Corps., 1994—; Pahrump Arts Coun., 1994-96. Recipient Pub. Service award states of Ga., La., Ala., Pa., Okla., N.C., Pub. Service award So. Interstate Nuclear Bd., Pub. Service award Nat. Conf. State Legislatures; Picatinny Arsenal fellow, Victor Chem. fellow, Colgate Palmolive-Peet fellow, Ohio State Univ. fellow; U.S. Govt. grantee. Mem. Va., D.C., Fed. bar assns., Am. Chem. Soc., Am. Soc. Pub. Adminstrn. (chmn. sect. on intergovtl. adminstrn. and mgmt. 1977-79, Public Service award), AAAS, Sigma Xi, Phi Lambda Upsilon, Delta Theta Phi (chmn. scholarships), Alpha Chi Sigma, Kappa Sigma. Home and Office: PO Box 3434 2070 S Page St Pahrump NV 89041

HERSON, ARLENE RITA, producer, journalist, television program host, radio commentator and panelist; b. N.Y.C. d. Sam and Mollie (Friedman) Hornreich; m. Milton Herson, June 16, 1963; children: Michael, Karen. Student, Queens Coll., 1957, New Sch. for Social Rsch., N.Y.C., 1960. Exec. sec. Tex McCrary, Inc., N.Y.C., 1958-60; asst. to William L. Safire, Safire Pub. Rels., N.Y.C., 1960-62; columnist The Advisor, Inc., Middletown, NJ, 1974-78; prodr., host The Arlene Herson Show, N.Y.C., 1978—. Syndicated on Tempo TV, 1988, Channel Am., 1989-93; spokesperson Storer Cable TV, Monmouth County, 1989-91, Nutri/Systems, Monmouth and Ocean Counties, 1989-90; news anchor Nostalgia Cable TV Network at Rep. Nat. Conv., 1993; cons., talent coord. Super Annuities, 1993-94; moderator debate on capital punishment, 1998; moderator panel on assisted suicide, 1999; panelist, interviewer The Am. Sr. Side-WXEL-Nat. Pub. Radio, 1999—; co-host radio sta. WJNA, Lunch Bunch; entertainment chmn. Polo Club, 2001—; master of ceremonies Calvacade of Stars, 2002—; mem. grievance com. Fla. Bar, 2003—; lectr., spkr. in field. Contbg. writer The Washington/Hampton Connection Dan's Papers, 1993-98, The Hill Newspaper, 1994-98; exec. producer The Magic Flute, conductor Victor Borge, DAR Constitution Hall, Washington, 1995, 1776, 1997; exec. producer, casting dir. (musical) 1776, DAR Constitution Hall, Washington, 1996, encore prodn., 1998; prodr. 1776 (featuring current mems. of Congress), 1998; interviewer Steven Spielberg's Shoah Found., 1997-99; co-host radio program Changing Times, 1999; host WXEL-TV Pledge Drive, 2000. 92d St. Y benefit com. Variety-The Children's Charity; active Women's Project and Prodns., 1992; com. mem. Children's Psychiat. Ctr., 1971-90, Monmouth Park Charity Fund, 1980-90; corp. exec. bd. Family and Childrens Svcs., 1985—90; life mem. N.Y. chpt. Brandeis U. Libr. Fund; dir.'s resource coun. Nat. Women's Econ. Alliance; social com. Westbridge Condominium; fin. chmn. Mike Herson for Congress, 1994, fin .com. March of Dimes, 1995; profl. women's coun. Nat. Mus. of Women in the Arts, 1994; com. mem. Vicent T. Lombardi Cancer Rsch. Ctr., 1994-98, Parkinson's Action Network, 1996; publicity chmn.exhbn. for Israel Tennis Ctrs. Excalibur Soc. of Lyn U., 1996—; adv. coun. to co-chmn. Rep. Nat. Com., 1997—2000; active Power of Women Effecting Renewal, 1997; 2d decade coun. Am. Film Inst., 1998; bd. dirs. A Healing Among Nations, 1999; active Soc. of 100, Fla. Philharm. Orch., 1999; benefit com. Caldwell Theatre, 1999; bd. dirs. Miami City Ballet, 1999—2000; founder Israel Children's Ctrs., 2000; gubernatorial appointee, bd. dirs. Fla. Film and Entertainment Adv. Coun., 2001—; mem. com. Shaare Zedek Med. Ctr., 2001; honors bd. dirs. Miami City Ballet, 2000—; com. mem. Ctr. for the Arts, 2001—, Palm Beach Cultural Coun., 2001—; corp. exec. com. Ctrl. Park Conservancy, Women of Washington; corp. exec. com. mentor program Women's Econ. Devel. Coun.; gubernatorial appointee, bd. dirs. Miami City Ballet Sch., 2001—; exec. com. Cmty. Rels. Coun., 2001—; leadership coun., exec. com. Rep. Jewish Coalition, 2002—; life mem. Boca Raton cancer unit Papanicolau Corps for Cancer Rsch., 2002—; mem. Boca Raton Mus. Art, 2002, coun. trustees, 2001—; bd. dirs. women's activities campaign Sen. Jacob J. Javits, N.Y.C., 1968, Monmouth (N.J.) Mus., 1982—86, Will Rogers Inst., 1992—, Washington Symphony Orch., 1994—98, v.p., 1994; bd. dirs. Boca Raton Ednl. TV, 2001—, Palm Beach Internat. Film Festival, 2000. Recipient CAPE award for best talk show on Cable TV Network, 1984-93, Woman of Achievement in Comm. award Adv. Commn. on Status of Women, 1986, Pub. and Leased Access (PAL) award for best talk show Paragon Cable TV, N.Y.C., 1988, spl. resolution N.J. Assembly, 1988, Willie award for outstanding svc. Will Rogers Inst., 1992; named Disting. Alumni mem. Waldorf Astoria, 1998. Mem. NAFE, NATAS, Nat. Acad. Cable Programming, Nat. Assn. Profl. Women, Women in Comm., Women in Cable, Women in Film and Video, Am. Women in Radio and TV, Power Women Effecting Renewal, Internat. Radio and TV Soc., Internat. Newswoman's Assn., Rep. Gov's Assn., Nat. Press Club, Friends for Life, Friars Club (house com. 1993, admissions com. 1994—), Bethesda Country Club, Lotos Club, East River Tennis Club, Excalibur Soc. of Lynn U., Seagate Beach Club, Polo Club (cmty. rels. com. 1998-99, social com. 2000, entertainment chmn. 2001), Profl. Bus. Forum, Boca Raton Roundtable. Avocations: tennis, swimming, reading. Fax: 561-998-4776. E-mail: aherson123@aol.com.

HERSON, KAREN J. writer, audio producer, freelance writer; b. Lima, Ohio, Oct. 12, 1962; d. David Wolf and Dorothy Norma (Richman) H. AA in Comm., Miami-Dade C.C., 1982; BFA in Scriptwriting and Cinema Studies, SUNY, Purchase, 1986. Coord. advt. Towne Pub. & Advt., Coral Gables, Fla.,

1987—90; coord. advt. and mktg. Reed Travel Group, Reed Electronic Pub., Miami, Fla., 1990—92; freelance writer Key West (Fla.) Citizen, 1992—93; dir. advt. Action Comm. Network, Miami, 1993—96; writer, audio prodr. Am. TelNet, Inc., Plantation, Fla., 1996—2000. Apprentice, asst. casting dir. feature film project Brighton Beach Memoirs, 1984. Democrat. Jewish. Avocations: theatre, film, concerts, galleries, dance.

HERSON, LAWRENCE J.R. social sciences educator, consultant; b. Chgo., Ill., Oct. 21, 1923; m. Libby (Elizabeth) Kormunda, June 30, 1951; children: Eric Sebastian, Viktoria Sydney. BS, Northwestern U., Evanston, Ill., 1948, MA, 1949; AM, Yale U., 1951, PhD, 1955. Instr. Northwestern U., Evanston, Ill., 1952—55; prof. Ohio State U., Columbus, 1955—, chair dept. polit. sci., 1962—69, dean arts and sci., 1968—71, Ralph Mershon prof. pub. policy, 1970—76, prof. emeritus, 1988—. Disting. vis. lectr. Baylor U., 1987, Wis. U., 1986; election analyst CBS and PBS, 1962—; lectr. Wilton Park Brit. Fgn. Office, 1964—; cons. Ford Found., NSF, Citizenship Clearinghouse; curricula advisor to several colls. and univs.; planning cons. to several U.S. towns and cities; Russian Acad. Sci. invited lectr. various Russian Univ., 1995; frequent lectr. to various groups worldwide. Author: The Politics of Ideas, La Politique Publique Aux Etats-Unis, 1987, Siyaasaat Wa Afkaar, 1988; co-author: The Urban Web, 1990, 1998; contbg. author, editor (11 books); contbr. articles to profl. jour. Forward observer U.S. Air Corps, 1942—45, PTO. Fellow Social Sci. Rsch. fellow, 1950, German Parliamentary fellow, 1964; grantee grant, Nat. Def. Instnl., 1963—68, Ford Found., 1964—87, Soros Found., 1995. Mem.: Whigs, Am. Polit. Sci. Assn., Capital Club, Phi Beta Kappa. Office: Ohio State U Dept Polit Sci Derby Hall Columbus OH 43210

HERSTAND, THEODORE, theatre artist, educator; b. N.Y.C., May 14, 1930; s. Max Arthur and Rose (Shyatt) H.; m. Jo Ellen Gillette, Aug. 23, 1957; children: Sarah Ellen, Michael Simpson. Cert. Advanced Studies, U. Birmingham (Eng.), 1951; BA, U. Iowa, 1953, MA, 1957; PhD, U. Ill., 1963. Instr. theatre Parsons Coll., Fairfield, Iowa, 1953-54, Eastern Ill. U., Charleston, 1957-59; asst. prof. SUNY, Plattsburgh, 1960-64, asso. prof., 1963-64; asst. prof. U. Ill., 1964-66; asso. prof. U. Minn., Mpls., 1966-70; prof., chmn. dept. theatre, drama and dance Case Western Res. U., Cleve., 1970-77, chmn. faculty senate, 1975-76; dir. Sch. Drama, U. Okla., Norman, 1977-79, prof., 1979-92; prof. emeritus U. Okla., Norman, 1992—; artistic dir., actor Okla. Profl. Theatre, 1978. Vis. prof. Mpls. Coll. Art and Design, 1969; vis. dir. Colo. Shakespeare Festival, Boulder, 1968, 82; theatre bldg. cons. Eastern Ill. U., Charleston, Ill. State U., Bloomington, Jewish Community Center Theater, Mpls.; ednl. cons. in arts; spl. contbr. Silver Burdett Music Series. Profl. actor, dir. over 70 plays; author: (plays) Sugar and Lemon, 1968; new version Oedipus, 1978, Dov, 1982, The Emigration of Adam Kurtzik, 1985, 89, It Should Be So, 1989, The Minor Matter of Cynthia Smith, 1990, Bittersweet, 1996, others; assoc. editor: Drama Survey, 1967-70; contbr. revs., articles to profl. jours.; founder Klein Nat. Playwriting award, 1974, Bliss Nat. Playwriting award, 1980. Bd. dirs. Theater-in-the-Round, Mpls., 1968, v.p., 1969; bd. dirs. Gt. Lakes Shakespeare Festival, 1970-71, Okla. Arts Inst., mem. theatre panel, 1991-2003, chair 1994-2003; chmn. bd. dirs. Okla. Hillel Found., 1981-82; trustee Karamu House, 1975-77, Temple B'nai Israel, Oklahoma City, 1989-92, 1999—; chmn. new plays program S.W. Theatre Assn., 1985-89; bd. dirs. Okla. Israel Exch., 2003—. Mem. Jewish Theatre Assn., Nat. Theatre Conf., Dramatists Guild, Omicron Delta Kappa. Home: 4418 Manchester Ct Norman OK 73072-3915

HERSTEIN, HOWARD JOSEPH, author; b. Regent, N.D., Sept. 20, 1927; s. Oliver Daniel and Mantie Esther (Bratcher) H. Student, Mankato (Minn.) Comml. Sch., 1946-47, MacPhail Sch. Drama, Mpls., 1947-49. Supply clk. U.S. Army, Mpls., 1959-63, supply supr. Grand forks, N.D., 1963-71; supply mail supr. Traveler's Ins., Des Moines, 1971-87. Author: (radio plays) Rejection Slip Theatre "WHO", 1995-96, Iowa Radio Project WOI, 1993-94, (quizes) Sky-Delta Airlines Mag., 1987-89. With USN, 1945-46. Mem. Iowa Scriptwriters Alliance, Rosicrucian Order, Am. Legion. Episcopalian.

HERSTEIN, LOUIS ARTHUR, III, physicist; b. Balt., Nov. 15, 1926; s. Nathan Sommerfeld and Ruth (Sachs) H.; m. Natalie Jacoby, Oct. 5, 1952; children: Robert, Jerald, Miriam. BS in Mech. Engring., U. Md., 1950; MA in Judaic Studies, Balt. Hebrew U., 1990. Gen. engr. USN Bur. Ships, Washington, 1951-62; physicist Ship Silencing Divsn. Naval Seas Sys. Command, Washington, 1962-89; cons. Tracor Applied Scis., Washington, 1989—. Mem., chair several stds. writing coms. on acoustical measurements, fed. coms., nat. coms., internat. coms. Active Boy Scouts Am., Balt. area coun., 1960-90. Tech. sgt. U.S. Army, 1944-47, 51-52. Recipient Silver Beaver award Boy Scouts Am., 1974. Fellow Acoustical Soc. Am. (mem. tech. com. on structural acoustics 1980—, com. on stds. 1994—, working group chair), Am. Legion (comdr. 1975-78), Jewish War Vets. (comdr. post 1970-72). Democrat. Jewish. Avocations: philately, camping. Home: 2722 Hanson Ave Baltimore MD 21209-3911 Office: 877 N Howard St Baltimore MD 21201-4605 E-mail: lhers61443@cs.com.

HERTA, BRYAN, race car driver; b. Warren, Mich., May 23, 1970; s. Toma and Nina Herta; m. Janette Herta; 1 child, Calysta. Student, U. Calif., Irvine, Ohio State U. Driver Chip Ganassi Racing, 1995—98; pilot Shell Ford-Cosworth/Reynard Championship car Team Rahal, Indpls, 1998—99; owner/driver Bryan Herta Racing, 1999—; with A.J. Foyt Ent., Indpls. Named Most Import Driver by fellow drivers, 1996; recipient Am.'s Choice award as one of N.Am.'s top young drivers, 1992. Achievements include captured Indy Lights title, 1993; winner Barber-Saab Pro Series championship, 1991; 1989 Skip Barber Formula Ford Series title; 1987 World Karting Assn. championship; scored first career pole position, 1995; earning CART victory from the pole Grand Prix of Monterey at Laguna Seca Racway, 1998; pole positions and podium finishes Long Beach, Portland; finished 8th in championship standings with career-best 97 PPG Cup points. Office: c/o Forsythe Championship Racing 4811 Northwest Pkwy Hilliard OH 43026-1128

HERTEL, SUZANNE MARIE, training and development specialist; b. Hastings, Neb., Aug. 8, 1937; d. Louis C. Hertel and W. Lenore (Cross) Budd. BA, Doane Coll., Crete, Neb., 1959; MSM, Union Theol. Sem., 1961; postgrad., U. Hartford, 1966, U. Conn., 1975; MA, Merrill Palmer Inst., 1977; EdD, Boston U., 1982. Music tchr. Pub. Sch., Wethersfield, Conn., 1962-63; serials libr. Hartford (Conn.) Sem. Found., 1963-64; elem. tchr. Pub. Sch., Glastonbury, Conn., 1965-79; asst. prof. Univ. Northern Iowa, Cedar Falls, Iowa, 1979-81; training mgr. Focus Research Systems Inc., W. Hartford, Conn., 1982-89; pers. adminstr. City of Hartford, 1989-99; cons., 1999—2002. Mem. leadership educators program John F. Kennedy Sch. Govt., Harvard U., 1999; mem. Human Resource Mgmt. Del., Russia and Estonia, 1992, Initiative Edn., Sci. and Tech., South Africa, 1995. Recipient Maria Miller Stewart award, 1992. Mem.: Am. Guild Organists. Democrat. E-mail: smher82@aol.com.

HERTEL, WILLIAM JOHN, music educator; b. Chgo., Jan. 31, 1946, s. John Joseph and Caroline Theresa (Schmidt) Hertel; m. Janet Sue Hudson, June 14, 1969; 1 child, John William. B in Music Edn., Ill. Wesleyan U., 1968; M in Music Edn., Ill. State U., 1974; M in Edn. Adminstrn., No. Ill. U., 1985. Cert. music tchr. grades K-12 Ill., adminstrn. grades K-12 Ill. Band dir., fine arts chair El Paso (Ill.) Cmty. Unit Dist. #375, 1968—73; band dir., music coord. Sterling (Ill.) Cmty. Unit Dist. #5, 1973—96; band dir. Mattoon (Ill.) Cmty. Unit Dist. #2, 1996—2001; instr., cons. Kidder Music Svc., Inc., Sterling, 2001—. Founder, chmn. Sterling Festival of the Arts, 1974—96; cons. Ill. State Bd. Edn., 1975—80; state chmn. Am. Guild English Handbell Ringers, Ill., 1980—83; guest lectr. in field; guest condr., adjudicator, Ill. Named Educator of the Month, WAND-TV, Decatur, Ill., 2000; recipient Those Who Excel award, Ill. State Bd. Edn., 1994. Mem.: Ill. Music Educators Assn., Assn. Am. Educators, Music Educators Nat. Conf. Lutheran. Avocations: church musician, bicycling, photography. Home: 1666 Hill Dr Dixon IL 61021

HERTELENDY, PAUL, critic, writer, poet; b. Budapest, Hungary, June 10, 1932; arrived in U.S., 1940; s. Andor and Elizabeth (Hitt) Hertelendy; m. Martha M. Sam; children: Glen, Ann, Ralph. BSE, Princeton (N.J.) U., 1953; MSE, Stanford (Calif.) U., 1957; PhD, U.Calif., Berkeley, 1965. Rsch. engr. Nat. Bur. of Standards, Washington, 1958—64; music and dance critic Oakland (Calif.) Tribune, 1964—79, San Jose (Calif.) Mercury News, 1979—99; webmaster, CEO artssf.com, Berkeley, Calif., 1999—2002; poet laureate Smithsonian Instn. Nat. Bd., Washington, 2000—. Nat. bd. mem. Smithsonian Instn., Washington, 1995—2001; chair of adv. coun. Lawrence Hall of Sci., Berkeley, Calif., 1999—2003; mem., bd. dirs. SAM Tech., San Francisco, 1997—; bd. mem.; bd. chair Chinese Culture Ctr., San Francisco, 1980—93. Author: (book of poetry) The Very Slender Volume, 1999, Vietnam, Venice, Varied Vales, 2000, Poetrose in the 'Oughtics, 2001, Glaciers and Butterflies, 2002; contbr. articles to Performing Arts, Dance Mags, Contra Costa Times, others. Ensign US Coast and Geod. Survey, 1953—56, Washington, DC. Mem.: U. of Calif. (Berkeley) Alumni Assn. (life). Roman Catholic. Avocations: hiking, tennis, travel, language study, soccer refereeing. Office: artssf dot com Box 1290 Berkeley CA 94701 Personal E-mail: phertelend@aol.com.

HERTENSTEIN, MYRNA LYNN, publishing executive; b. Detroit, July 19, 1937; d. Bernard Franklin and Alice Agnes (Stewart) Aller; m. George Ronald Hertenstein, June 21, 1958 (div. July 1979); children: Dale Ronald, Robert Mark. AS in Bus., Wayne State U., 1957; student, Huntingdon Coll., 1980-84. Departmental sec. Sch. of Bus. Wayne State U., Detroit, 1957-59; county and vol. coord. Montgomery (Ala.) Area Coun. on Aging, 1977-80; admissions counselor Coastal Tng. Inst., Montgomery, 1981-83; rural volunteerism coord. State of Ala., Montgomery, 1983-84; account exec. Ala. Bus. Rev., Montgomery, 1984-85, Sta. WRJM-FM, Montgomery, 1985-86; asst. local sales mgr. Sta. WCOV-TV Fox Affiliate, Montgomery, 1986-90; owner, assoc. pub. TRAVELHOST of Cen. Ala., Montgomery, 1990—. Mem. Dirs. of Vols. in Agys., Montgomery, 1978-82, Montgomery County Health Coun., 1979-81, Area Agy. on Aging Adv. Coun., Montgomery, 1981-83, Pres.' Coun. Montgomery, 1983, 84; asst. to instr. Dale Carnegie & Assocs., Montgomery, 1978-83. Editor (newsletter) Montgomery Area Coun. on Aging, 1978-80; dir., writer (commls.) Sta. WCOV-TV, 1986-90; writer (commls.) Sta.WRJM-FM, 1985-86. Mem. adminstrv. coun. Whitfield United Meth. Ch., Montgomery, 1977, coord. Meals-on-Wheels, 1978-86; mem. pub. rels. coun. First United Meth. Ch., Montgomery, 1992-94, mem. comms. com. 1995—, vice chmn., 1997, chmn., 1998, mem. coun. of ministries, 1998, mem. adminstrv. bd., 1998; den leader coach Boy Scouts Am., Bellevue, Nebr., 1969-71; editor Capitol Jr. Woman's Club, Montgomery, 1975-82; pres. Parents Without Ptnrs., 1983-85; bd. dirs. Arthritis Found., 1992—, vice chair, 1995, chair, 1996, mem. Ala. chpt. exec. com., 1996; dance com. Ala. Dance Theatre, 1996—; bd. dirs. Montgomery chpt. Am. Cancer Soc., 1998-2000, Hospice of Montgomery, 1999—, mem. exec. com., 2000—. Recipient Emerging 30 award Montgomery Area C. of C., 1992, small business of yr. award, 1994, corp. vol. of yr. award Voluntary Action Ctr., Montgomery, 1992, award Montgomery Com. for Arts, 1993, Spl. Achievement award U.S. Small Bus. Adminstrn., 1995, Silver Medal award Montgomery Advt. Fedn. and Am. Advt. Fedn., 1996. Mem. Pub. Rels. Coun. Ala., Ala. Travel Coun., Montgomery Restaurant Assn., Montgomery Hotel/Motel Assn. (bd. dirs. 1992-94, 99—), Sales and Mktg. Execs. (editor newsletter 1995-98, bd. dirs. 1998-99), Montgomery Assn. Bus. Communicators, Montgomery Advt. Fedn. (bd. dirs. 1985-92, 96-2001, newsletter editor 1996-97), Montgomery C. of C. (vice chmn. ambs. 1992, chmn. ambs. 1993, chmn. advt. promotions and publs. 1994, hospitality devel. and mktg. task force 1995—, chmn. spl. projects com. 1996), Montgomery Civitans. Avocations: ballroom dancing, photography, ceramics. Home: 3005 Baldwin Brook Dr Montgomery AL 36116-3803 Office: Travelhost of Cen Ala PO Box 20666 Montgomery AL 36120-0666

HERTER, FREDERIC PRATT, university administrator; b. Bklyn., Nov. 12, 1920; s. Christian Archibald and Mary Caroline (Pratt) H.; m. Annabel Toland, May 27, 1942 (dec. Dec. 1946); m. Harriet Ames Conel, Nov. 22, 1947 (div.); m. Solange Batsell, May 31, 1978; children: Frederic Pratt Jr., Caroline Ames, Brooke. BS, Harvard U., 1941, MD, 1944. Diplomate Am. Bd. Gen. Surgery. Intern Presbyn. Hosp., N.Y.C., 1944-45, resident, 1947-53, attending surgeon, 1954—; from asst. prof. to prof. Columbia U., N.Y.C., 1954—, Auchincloss Prof. of Surgery, 1970—; pres. Am. U., Beirut, 1987-93. Chmn. bd. trustees Am. U., Beirut, 1985-87; trustee Mary Imogene Bassett Hosp., Cooperstown, N.Y., 1970—, Jackson Labs., Bar Harbor, Maine, 1975-85, ANERA, Washington, Cathedral of St. John The Devine, N.Y.C., 1995—, Episc. Social Svcs., N.Y.C., 1997; bd. govs. Middle East Inst., Washington. Contbr. more than 75 articles to profl. jours. Served to capt. M.C. AUS, 1945-47, PTO. Mem. Coun. Fgn. Rels., Century Club, Knickerbocker Club N.Y.C. Republican. Episcopalian. Home: 784 Park Ave New York NY 10021-3553

HERTING, CLAIREEN LAVERN, financial planner; b. Chgo., Sept. 7, 1929; d. Ernst and Louise Caroline (Wagner) Molzan; m. Robert L. Herting, June 5, 1954; 1 son, Robert L. Jr. BS, U. Ill.-Champaign, 1951; MBA, Northwestern U., Chgo., 1953; JD, John Marshall Law Sch., 1960. Bar: Ill. 1960; CPA Ill. With PricewaterhouseCoopers, L.L.P., Chgo., 1951—, audit sr., 1951-58, audit supr., 1959-64, tax supr., 1964-75, dir. personal fin. planning, 1974—, tax mgr., 1985—. Adj. prof. Masters of Taxation program, John Marshall Law Sch., 1987-2001. Contbr. articles to profl. jours. Bd. dirs., sec., v.p., treas. Easter Seal Soc. Met. Chgo., 1974—; bd. dirs. Chgo. Soc. Contemporary Composers, 1979-84; sec., treas., mem. exec. com., bd. trustees John Marshall Law Sch., Chgo., 1984—; vice chmn. Ill. Dept. Registration and Edn., Springfield, 1984-94; mem. planned giving com. Art Inst. Chgo., 1990—; bd. dirs., treas. Free Arts for Abused Children, 1998—; bd. dirs. Ill. CPA Endowment Found., 1999—; chmn. Ill. Bd. Examiners for CPA Exam., 2000—. Recipient Disting. Svc. award John Marshall Alumni Assn., Chgo., 1983. Mem. ABA, AICPAs, Am. Soc. Women CPA, Ill. State Bar Assn., Ill. CPA Soc. (bd. dirs. 1974-75, 87-89, treas. 1987-89, hon. mem. 1993, Pub. Svc. award 1998), Chgo. Estate Planning Coun. (past pres., bd. mem. 1976-84, Austin Flemin Disting. Svc. award 1990), Chgo. Assn. Soc. Execs., Chgo. Bar Assn. (chmn. estate and gift taxation 1990-91, fin. tax law, fed. taxation com.), Am. Women Composers Midwest, Inc. (bd. dirs., treas. 1992-94). Home: 1281 N Northwest Hwy Park Ridge IL 60068-1662 Office: PriceWaterhouseCoopers LLP 1 N Wacker Dr Chicago IL 60606 E-mail: claireen.l.herting@us.pwcglobal.com.

HERTING, ROBERT LESLIE, pharmaceutical executive; b. Aurora, Ill., Jan. 26, 1929; s. Herold Edward and Marie Christine (Parr) H.; m. Claireen LaVern Molzan, June 5, 1954; 1 son, Robert Leslie. BS, U. Ill., 1950, MD, 1954; MS in Biochemistry, Ill. Inst. Tech., 1961, PhD in Biology, 1970. Diplomate Am. Bd. Internal Medicine. Intern Ill. Central Hosp., Chgo., 1954-55; from assoc. dir. clin. rsch. to divsnl. v.p. Abbott Labs., North Chicago, Ill., 1957-76; v.p. med. rsch. Schering-Plough Corp., Bloomfield, N.J., 1977-80; v.p. internat. clin. rsch. and med. affairs G.D. Searle & Co., Skokie, Ill., 1980-84, v.p. clin. rsch., 1984-94, sr. dir. R & D clin. safety, 1994-98; ret., 1998; v.p. Specialized Med. Cons., Ltd., 1998—. Clin. assoc. prof. medicine U. Ill., 1957-77; mem. research adv. com. Agy. for Internat. Devel. U.S. Dept. State, 1986-92. Mem. editorial bd.: Antimicrobial Agents and Chemotherapy, 1963-65. Served with U.S. Army, 1955-57. Fellow ACP; mem. AMA, Chgo. Soc. Internal Medicine, Am. Soc. Microbiology, Am. Soc. Clin. Pharmacology and Therapeutics, Sigma Xi. Home: 1281 N Northwest Hwy Park Ridge IL 60068-1662

HERTLE, RICHARD WILLIAM, pediatric ophthalmologist, educator; b. Bklyn., N.Y., Oct. 23, 1957; s. Richard Henry and Anna Leena Hertle; m. Gloriann Donahue, Sept. 4, 1994; children: Jamie Defrancesco, Jessika Defrancesco. BA, Ohio State U., 1979; MD, Northeastern Ohio U., 1984. Sr. scientist NIH, Nat. Eye Inst., Bethesda, Md., 1998—2001; prof. of ophthalmology Ohio State U. and Columbus Children's Hosp., 2001—. Asst. prof. of ophthalmology Childrens Hosp. of Phila. and U. of Pa, 1991—98; dir. Lab. Visual and Ocular Motor Physiology. Editor: (textbook) Pediatric Eye Disease: Color Atlas and Synopsis, 2002. Ice hockey coach USA Hockey, Columbus. Recipient award, Am. Acad. of Ophthalmology, 1998. Fellow: ACS (life). Office: Pediat Ophthalmology Assocs Inc Ste 4C 555 S 18th St Columbus OH 43205 Office Fax: 614-224-5232. E-mail: hertler@chi.osu.edu.

HERTNEKY, RANDY LEE, optometrist; b. Burlington, Colo., Jan. 9, 1955; s. Harry Francis and Darleen Mae (Walters) H.; m. Laura Ann Ciaccio, Nov. 28, 1981; children: Lisa Kay, Erin Elizabeth. BA, U. Colo., 1977; OD, So. Calif. Coll. Optometry, Fullerton, 1981. Pvt. practice optometry, Yuma and Wray, Colo., 1982—. Precinct committeeman Yuma County Rep. Com., 1986—; mem. bd. rev. Boy Scouts Am., Yuma, 1982—; chmn. bldg. com. Yuma H.S., 1987-89; bd. dirs. Yuma Hosp. Found., 1990-97, vice chmn., 1994-97; chmn. Yuma Sch. Curriculum Com., 1993. Mem. APHA, KC (sec. 1990-95, dep. grand knight 1995-96, grand knight 1996-98), Am. Optometric Assn. (coord. Colo. Polit. Action Com. 1995—, nominee Keyperson of Yr. 1999, 2000), Colo. Optometric Assn. (trustee 1989-90, vice chmn. legis. com. 1994—, nominee Optometrist of Yr. 1996, 2000, 01, named Optometrist of Yr., 2003), Coll. Optometrists in Vision Devel. (assoc.), Yuma C. of C. (Bus. of Yr. 1996), Wray C. of C., Lions (treas. 1987-88, pres. 1991-92, Lion of Yr. award 1992). Roman Catholic. Avocations: golf, coin collecting, skiing. Office: 105 S Main St Yuma CO 80759-1913

HERTWECK, E. ROMAYNE, psychology educator; b. July 24, 1928; s. Garnett Perry and Nova Gladys (Chowning) H.; m. Alma Louise Street, Dec. 16, 1955; 1 child, William Scott. BA, Augustana Coll., 1962; MA, Pepperdine U., 1963; EdD, Ariz. State U., 1966; PhD, U.S. Internat. U., 1978. Cert. sch. psychologist, Calif. Night editor Rock Island (Ill.) Argus Newspaper, 1961; grad. asst. psychology dept. Pepperdine Coll., L.A., 1962; counselor VA Ariz. State U., Tempe, 1963; assoc. dir. Conciliation Ct., Phoenix, 1964; prof. Phoenix Coll., Phoenix, 1965, Mira Costa Coll., Oceanside, Calif., 1966—2003. Mem. senate coun. Mira Costa Coll., 1968-70, 85-87, 89-91, chmn. psychology-counseling dept., 1973-75, chmn. dept. behavioral sci., 1976-82, 87-88, 90-91; part-time lectr. dept. bus. adminstrn. San Diego State U., 1980-84, Sch. Human Behavior U.S. Internat. U., 1984-89; prof. psychology Chapman Coll. Mem. World Campus Afloat, 1970; pres. El Camino Preschs., Inc., Oceanside, Calif., 1985—; CEO Nutri-Cal, Inc., Oceanside, Calif., 1996-2003. Bd. dirs. Lifeline, 1969, Christian Counseling Center, Oceanside, 1970-82; mem. City of Oceanside Childcare Task Force, 1991—1992; mem. City of Oceanside Community Rels. Commn., 1991-96, vice chair, 1994; mem. steering com. Healthy Cities Project City of Oceanside, Calif., 1993-95. Mem. Am. Western, North San Diego County (v.p. 1974-75) psychol. assns., Am. Assn. for Counseling and Devel., Nat. Educators Fellowship (v.p. El Camino chpt. 1976-77), Am. Coll. Personnel Assn., Phi Delta Kappa, Kappa Delta Pi, Psi Chi, Kiwanis (charter mem. Carlsbad club, dir. 1975-77). Home: 2024 Oceanview Rd Oceanside CA 92056-3104 also: El Camino Preschs Inc 2002 California St Oceanside CA 92054-5673 Office: Mira Costa Coll 3210 Bernie Dr Oceanside CA 92056-3816 E-mail: rhertweck@cox.net.

HERTZ, ARTHUR HERMAN, business executive; b. Bklyn., Sept. 10, 1933; s. Edwin Carl and Blanche H.; Stephen R., Andrew P. BBA, U. Miami, Fla., 1955, postgrad., 1955-56. Acct. Aetna Mortgage Co., Miami, Fla., 1955, Wometco Enterprises, Inc., Miami, 1955-60, contr., v.p., 1960-64, sr. v.p., 1964-71, exec. v.p., treas., CFO, 1971-81, COO, 1981-84, chmn., CEO, 1985—; exec. v.p., COO WEI Enterprises Corp., Miami, 1984-85; exec. v.p. Wometco Broadcasting Co., Inc., Miami, 1984-85. Past pres. Orange Bowl Com.; past chair City of Miami Off St. Parking Authority; past chair Pub. Health Trust, Miami Dade County; chmn. audit com. bd. trustees U. Miami. Mem. AICPA, Fla. Inst. CPAs, Greater Miami C. of C. (gov. 1975-78), Iron Arrow, Phi Kappa Phi, Omicron Delta Kappa, Phi Eta Sigma. Home: 610 Fluvia Ave Coral Gables FL 33134-7016 Office: Wometco Enterprises Inc PO Box 141609 Coral Gables FL 33114-1609 E-mail: Arth@wometcoent.com.

HERTZ, DANIEL LEROY, JR., entrepreneur; b. Montclair, N.J., Feb. 27, 1930; s. Daniel Leroy and Elizabeth Nielsen (Beet) H.; m. Valerie A. Smith, Mar. 15, 1956 (div. 1962); m. Isabel Waud Hurd, Apr. 18, 1970; children: Valerie H. Boyle, Suzanne E., Daniel L. III, Seana L. Burdge. Degree in mech. engring., Stevens Inst. Tech., 1952, MSME (hon.), 1982. Sales engr. C.E. Conover & Co., Fairfield, N.J., 1953-58; founder, pres. Seals Eastern, Red Bank, N.J., 1958—. Adv. bd. polymer tech. cons. Tex. A&M U., College Station, 1990-94, CHEMTECH, Washington, 1983-91, Elastomerics, Atlanta, 1984-92. Contbr. chpts. to Intermediate Rubber Technology, 1983, Handbook of Elastomers, 1988, 2d edit., 2000, Vanderbilt Handbook, 1990, 14th edit., 2000, Engineering with Rubber, 1992, 2d edit., 2000, Rubber Products Manufacturing Technology, 1993, Rubber Technology, 2001, Elastomer Technology- Special Topics, 2003; contbr. articles to profl. jours. Vis. com. mech. engring. dept. Stevens Inst. Tech., 1992-96; sec. Riverside Dr. Assn., Red Bank, 1980-85. Cpl. U.S. Army, 1950-51, Korea. Mem. Am. Chem. Soc. (treas. rubber divsn. 1988-90, chmn. 1996, Disting. Svc. award 2000), N.Y. Rubber Group (chmn. 1983), Rumson Country Club, Nassau Club, Seabright Tennis Club. Republican. Episcopalian. Achievements include 5 U.S. patents. Home: 8 Hasler Ln Little Silver NJ 07739-1650 Office: 134 Pearl St Red Bank NJ 07701-1525 E-mail: dhertz@sealseastern.com.

HERTZ, DAWN LESLIE, lawyer; b. Michigan City, Ind., June 15, 1946; d. Wilbur Tracy and Norma (Elaine) Scrivnor; m. Ted Torpo Phillips, July 7, 1969 (div. Dec. 1988); 1 child, Kristin Ann; m. Roger Helmut Hertz, Aug. 5, 1989. BA, U. Mich., 1968, JD, 1971. Bar: Mich. 1971. Law clerk U.S. Dist. Ct., Detroit, 1971-73; assoc. Dickinson, Wright, Detroit, 1973-78; ptnr. Keywell and Rosenfeld, Troy, Mich., 1978-90; pvt. practice Ann Arbor, Mich., 1990—. Gen. counsel Mich. Press Assn., Lansing Mich., 1980—. Author: Michigan Media Law, 1998. V.p. Mich. Edn. Trust, Lansing, 1991—; pres. Creative Arts Center, Pontiac, Mich., 1993—. Fellow Mich. Bar Found.; mem. ABA (co-chair com. 1997-99), Mich. Bar Assn., Women In Comm. Methodist. Avocations: golf, travel. Home: 7844 Fischers Way Dexter MI 48130-9405 Office: 301 E Liberty St Ste 250 Ann Arbor MI 48104-2266 E-mail: dlph@lawyers.com.

HERTZ, HARRY STEVEN, government official; b. N.Y.C., Feb. 25, 1947; s. Marcus and Alice (Oppenheimer) H.; m. Francine Turkowitz, June 21, 1969; children: Matthew Adam, Joshua Lee BS in Chemistry, Poly. Inst. Bklyn., 1967; PhD in Organic Chemistry, MIT, 1971. Alexander von Humboldt fellow U. Munich, Fed. Republic Germany, 1971-73; research chemist Nat. Bur. Standards (now Nat. Inst. Standards and Tech.), Gaithersburg, Md., 1973-78, chief organic analytical rsch. div., 1978-83; dir. Ctr. for Analytical Chemistry Nat. Bur. Standards, Gaithersburg, Md., 1983-91, acting dir. Nat. Measurement Lab., 1989, dir Chem. Sci. and Tech. Lab., 1991-92, dep. dir. Office Quality Programs and Malcolm Baldrige Nat. Quality Award, 1992-96; dir. Baldrige Nat. Quality Program and Malcolm Baldrige Nat. Quality award, 1996—. Mem. health environ. research adv. com. Dept. Energy, Washington, 1984-89, good mfg. practices adv. com. FDA, 1988-90; mem. steering com. conf. bd. Global Ctr. Performance Excellence, 1996—2000; mem. nat. quality com. United Way Am., 1997—2000; mem. operating com. Juran Ctr. for Leadership in Quality. Co-editor: Trace Organic Analysis, 1979; mem. editorial adv. bd. Analytical Chemistry, 1984-86, Chem. and Engring. News, 1990-92; contbr. numerous articles to profl. jours. Recipient Bronze medal Dept. Commerce, 1981, Arthur S. Flemming award for Outstanding Fed. Service, 1985, Silver medal Dept. Commerce, 1986, Gold medal Dept. Commerce, 1998. Fellow AAAS, mem. Am. Soc. for Mass Spectroscopy (sec. 1983-85), Am. Chem. Soc., Nat. Com. for Clin. Lab. Standards (pres. 1986-88), Sigma Xi. Avocations: racquetball, hiking. Office: Nat Inst Standard & Tech A600 Adminstrn Bldg Gaithersburg MD 20899-0001 E-mail: harry.hertz@nist.gov.

HERTZ, KENNETH THEODORE, health care executive; b. Jackson Heights, N.Y., Aug. 19, 1951; s. Irwin R. and Dorothy S. H.; m. Debra Pitre, July 12, 1997. BA in Spl. Studies, SUNY, Fredonia, 1974; cert. med. and dental practice mgmt., Loyola U., 1992. Cert. med. practice exec. Am. Coll. Med. Practice Executives, 2001. Gen. mgr. Cape Cod Symphony, West Barnstable, Mass., 1974-75; mng. dir. Tulsa Philharm., 1975-78; pres., gen. mgr. Atlanta Ballet, 1979-89; instr. continuing edn. Oglethorpe U.; dir. Atlanta Great Artists Series, 1989-90, Atlanta Arts Devel. Svcs., 1989-90; exec. dir. New Orleans Symphony, 1990-91; adminstr. M.D. Care, Inc., New Orleans, 1991-95; dir. acquisitions and network devel. Tenet Healthcare, New Orleans, 1995-96, area mgr. practice ops., 1996-97; adminstr. MacArthur Surg. Clinic, Alexandria, La., 1977—2002, KH Cons. LLC, 2003—. Mem. dance panel City of Atlanta, 1983-89, Ga. Coun. for Arts, 1984-88, NEA, 1985-87; dir. Dance/USA, 1985-89; mem. adv. bd. cert. program in med./dental practice mgmt. Loyola U., 1993—; mem. Pres.'s Adv. Coun., De La Salle H.S., 1993-2000. Chmn. Atlanta C. of C. Cultural Programming Task Force, 1987—89, Atlanta C. of C. "Arts Alive", art celebration, 1986, Ga. Profl. Arts Caucus, 1983—85; bd. dirs. Big Bros./Big Sisters, 1988—89, Arts Festival Atlanta, BVA, 1986—90, Bus. Vols. for Arts, New Orleans Ballet Assn., 1996—98, Rapides Symphony Orch., 1998—2000, Ballet Alexandria, 2000—, Louisiann Med. Group Mgmt. Assn., 2001—; v.p. Ctrl. Louisiann Med. Group Mgmt. Assn., 2001—02; pres. Ctrl. La. Med. Group Mgmt. Assn., 2002—; bd. dirs. Am. Jewish Com., Atlanta, 1967. Mem. Midtown Bus. Assn. (dir. 1984-89), Ga. Citizens for Arts, Am. Symphony Orch. League, Alpha Phi Omega

HERTZ, LEON, publishing executive; b. Perth, Australia, Aug. 1, 1938; came to U.S., 1975; s. A. and Rose (Traub) H.; m. Linda Paula Cooper, June 1, 1980; 1 child, Monique. Student, U. Western Australia, Perth. Dir. Mirror Newspapers News Ltd., Sydney, Australia, 1967-75; gen. mgr., dir. Australian Nationwide

News, Sydney, Australia, 1969-75; v.p., gen. mgr. Express News Corp. Am., San Antonio, 1975-80; v.p., assoc. pub., gen. mgr. N.Y. Post Am., N.Y.C., 1980-86; gen. mgr., dir. News Internat., London, 1986-87; exec. v.p. in charge global mktg. News Corp. Ltd., N.Y.C., 1987; exec. v.p. News Am., N.Y.C., 1987—. Bd. dirs. Media Council of Australia, Sydney, 1970-75; chmn. Australian Newspaper Council, Sydney, 1973-75. Mem. Am.-Scandinavian Found., Am. Australian Assn. (dir.). Clubs: Cruising Yacht (Sydney); Friars (N.Y.C.), Metro. Club (N.Y.C.). Avocation: sailing. Home: 4 E 88th St New York NY 10128-0509 Office: News America Inc Ste 303 1211 Avenue Of The Americas New York NY 10036-8701

HERTZ, NATALIE ZUCKER, retired lawyer; b. Cleveland, Ohio, Sept. 23, 1934; AB, Cornell U., SUNY, 1956; JD, N.Y.U., 1976. Bar: NY 1976, US Dist. Ct. (so. dist.) NY. Pvt. practice, Harrison, NY, 1976—2003; ret., 2003. Mem. Order of Coif; asst. in legal writing NYU Sch. Law, 1975-76. Assoc. editor: Annual Survey of American Law, NYU, 1974-75; Author: The National Environmental Policy Act, 1974. Recipient Pomeroy prize, 1974, 75. Past mem. Westchester County and NY State Bar Assn., Westchester Women's Bar Assn. (v.p. 1987-89, dir. 1989-91, chairperson Trusts and Estates com., 1989-91, chairperson Real Property com. 1984-86), Women's Bar Assn. of State NY (dir. 1991-94), Westchester County Bar Assn. (ethics com. 1991-2002). Office: 451 Harrison Ave Harrison NY 10528-2119

HERTZBERG, ABRAHAM, aeronautical engineering educator, university research scientist; b. N.Y.C., July 8, 1922; s. Rubin and Paulien (Kalif) H.; m. Ruth Cohen, Sept. 3, 1950 (dec.); children: Eleanor Ruth, Paul Elliot, Jean R. BS in Aero. Engring., Va. Poly. Inst., 1943; MS in Aero. Engring., Cornell U., 1949; postgrad., U. Buffalo, 1949-53. Engr. Cornell Aero. Lab., 1949-57, asst. head aerodynamics research, 1957-59, head aerodynamics research, 1959-65; dir. aerospace & energetic rsch. program U. Wash., 1966-93, prof. astronautics, 1966-93; prof. emeritus astronautics, 1993—. Prin. investigator numerous federal rsch. grants; cons. Aerospace Corp., past mem. sci. adv. bd. USAF, Olin-Rocket Rsch., STI Optronics; past mem. electro-optics panel SAB, mem. various ad hoc coms.; mem. space sys. and tech. adv. com., rsch. and tech. subcom., past mem. rsch. and tech. adv. coun. NASA; mem. plasma dynamics rev. panel NSF, U.S. Army; honored spkr. Laser Inst. Am., 1975, Citizens of Sendai, 1991; past mem. theory adv. com. Los Alamos Nat. Lab.; vis. lectr. Chinese Acad. Scis., Beijing, 1983, 88, 97; Paul Vieille lectr. 7th Internat. Shock Tube Symposium, 1969, 89, 17th Internat. Symposium on Shock Waves and Shock Tubes, 1989; Irvine I. Glass Meml. lectr. U. Toronto, 1996. Editor Physics of Fluids, 1968-70; contbr. numerous articles on modern gas dynamics, high powered lasers, controlled thermonuclear fusions processes, space laser solar energy concepts, space energy concepts and new ultra velocity propulsion concepts to profl. jours. Served with AUS, 1944-46. Honored speaker Laser Inst. Am. Fellow AIAA (Dryden lectr. 1977, Agard lectr. 1978, Plasmadynamics and Lasers award 1992), Internat. Acad. Astronautics; mem. AAAS, NAE, Am. Phys. Soc., Sigma Xi. Achievements include patents in field. Office: U Wash Aerospace & Energetics PO Box 352250 Seattle WA 98195-2250

HERTZBERG, ARTHUR, rabbi, educator; b. Lubaczow, Poland, June 9, 1921; s. Zvi Elimelech and Nehamah (Alstadt) H.; m. Phyllis Cannon, Mar. 19, 1950; children: Linda, Susan. AB, Johns Hopkins U., 1940; M.H.L., Jewish Theol. Sem., 1943; PhD, Columbia U., 1966; D.D., Lafayette Coll., 1970; D.H.L., Balt. Hebrew Coll., 1974, Jewish Theol. Sem., 1987, Balt. Hebrew U., 1997, Boston Hebrew Coll., 1999, Hebrew Union Coll., Cin., 2000, CUNY Grad. Ctr., 2001. Rabbi, 1943; Hillel dir. Mass. State and Smith Coll., 1943-44; rabbi Congregation Ahavath Israel of Oak Lane, Phila., 1944-47, West End Synagogue, Nashville, 1947-56, Temple Emanu El, Englewood, N.J., 1956-85, rabbi emeritus, 1985—; prof. religion Dartmouth Coll., 1985-91, prof. emeritus, 1991—. Lectr. Columbia U., 1961-68, adj. prof. history, 1968-90; vis. scholar Mideast Inst., 1991—; vis. assoc. prof. Jewish studies Rutgers U., 1966-68; lectr. religion Princeton U., 1968-69; vis. prof. history Hebrew U., Jerusalem, 1970-71; vis. prof. Ecole des Hautes Etudes, Paris, 1989; vis. scholar St. Antony's Coll., Oxford, 1989; pres. Conf. Jewish Social Studies, 1967-72; mem. exec. com. World Zionist Orgn., 1969-78, Jewish Agy. for Israel, 1969-71, bd. govs., 1971-78; pres. Am. Jewish Congress, 1972-78, Am. Jewish Policy Found., 1978—; v.p. World Jewish Congress, 1975-91, co-chmn. adv. coun., 1991—; vis. prof. humanities NYU, 1991—. Author: The Zionist Idea, 1959; (with Martin Marty and Joseph Moody) The Outbursts that Await Us, 1963, The French Enlightenment and the Jews, 1968, Being Jewish in America, 1979, The Jews in America: Four Centuries of an Uneasy Encounter, 1989, Jewish Polemics, 1992; (with Aron Hirt-Manheimer) Jews: The Essence and Character of a People, 1998, A Jew in America, 2002, The Fate of Zionism, 2003; editor: Judaism, 1961, 2d rev. edit., 1991; introduction author At Home Only With God, 1992; sr. editor: Ency. Judaica, 1972; contbr.: Ency. Britannica, 1975. Vice pres. bd. dirs. Meml. Found. for Jewish Culture, 1965-98. Served 1st lt., chaplain USAF, 1951-53. Recipient Amram award, 1967, award for Lifetime Achievement Present Tense, 1989, Jewish Cultural Achievement award Nat. Found., 2001; Inst. Advanced Studies fellow, Jerusalem, 1982 Jewish. Home: 83 Glenwood Rd Englewood NJ 07631-1909 Office: NYU 726 Broadway Rm 603 New York NY 10003-9502 *I cannot even imagine improving on Hillel's dictum, nearly 20 centuries ago; what is hateful to you, don't do to your fellow man.*

HERTZBERG, DAVID GORDON, retired lawyer; b. Detroit, Feb. 21, 1918; s. Harry Aaron and Sarah Silk Hertzberg; m. Millicent Brower, Aug. 28, 1942 (dec. Oct. 2000); children: Richard York, Jane Elyse Litin. BBA, U. Mich., 1939; LB, Harvard Law Sch., 1942, JD (hon.), 1969. Bar: Mich. 1946, U.S. Supreme Ct. 1958. Estate tax agt. U.S. IRS, Detroit, 1946; tax atty. Hertzberg & Noveck, Detroit, 1947—88; ret., 1989. Trustee, v.p. Sigmund and Sophie Rohlik Found., Southfield, Mich., 1990—2003. Sr. lt. USN, 1942—46. Mem.: Masons (32 degree), Phi Beta Kappa. Avocations: sailing, skiing, running. Home: 22855 Shagbark Beverly Hills MI 48025-4771

HERTZBERG, HENRY, retired radiologist; b. Bklyn., Oct. 21, 1933; s. Louis and Bessie (Eisman) H.; m. Dori Balter, June 10, 1962; children: Richard, Lisa. BS, CCNY, 1955; MD, SUNY, Bklyn., 1959. Diplomate Am. Bd. Radiology. Intern Kings County Med. Ctr., Bklyn., 1959-60; resident Roosevelt Hosp., N.Y.C., 1960-63; dir. radiology Fort Gordon (Ga.) Army Hosp., 1963-65; pvt. practice Green Brook, N.J.; assoc. dir. dept. radiology Somerset Med. Ctr., Somerville, N.J., 1975-85; dir. dept. radiology Muhlenberg Med. Ctr., Plainfield, NJ, 1985-92, attending radiologist, 1992—2002. Clin. asst. prof. radiology Rutgers U. Med. Ctr., 1985—. Capt. M.C., U.S. Army, 1963-65. Mem. AMA. Avocation: travel. Home: 182 Deer Run Watchung NJ 07069-6222 Office: Assoc Radiologists PA 239 Us Highway 22 Green Brook NJ 08812-1916

HERTZBERG, RICHARD WARREN, materials science and engineering educator, researcher; b. N.Y.C., Aug. 17, 1937; s. Nelson Bert and Alice (Sobin) H.; m. Linda Judith Wishnow, June 18, 1961; children: Michelle, Ilyce, Jason Lyle. BSME, CCNY, 1960; MS in Metallurgy, MIT, 1961; PhD in Metallurgy, Lehigh U., 1965. Research asst. MIT, 1960-61; research scientist United Aircraft Corp., East Hartford, Conn., 1961-64; dir. mech. behavior Lehigh U., Bethlehem, Pa., 1964-98, N.J. Zinc prof. emeritus metallurgy, 1978-98, short course organizer, 1977—, chmn., 1987-92. Vis. prof. Ecole Polytechnique Fédérale de Lausanne (Switzerland), 1976; v.p. Del Rsch. Corp., Hellertown, Pa., 1969-74. Author: Deformation and Fracture Mechanics of Engineering Materials, 1976, 83, 89, 96, (with John A. Manson) Fatigue of Engineering Plastics, 1980; co-editor: Conference on In Situ Composites II, 1980. Bd. dirs. Temple Beth El, Allentown, Pa., 1973-76; sec. Temple Beth El Endowment Found., 1979-84; bd. dirs. Congregation Am Haskalah, Allentown, 1982-88. Recipient award for outstanding rsch. Alcoa Found., Bethlehem, 1972, 73, Bradley Stoughton award Lehigh Valley chpt., 1992, R.R. and E.C. Hillman award for advancing the interests of Lehigh U., 1994; co-recipient Eleanor and Joseph Libsch award for outstanding achievement and distinction in rsch. Lehigh U., 1983, award for teaching excellence Lehigh U., 1991, Educator award The Metall. Soc., 2000. Fellow Am. Soc. Metals (chmn. nat. young mems. com. 1969-72, Phila. chpt. Notable Achievement award, Lehigh Valley chpt. Bradley Stoughton award 1992); mem. ASTM, AIME. Office: Lehigh U Dept Material Sci 5 E Packer Ave Bethlehem PA 18015-3102 E-mail: rwh1@lehigh.edu.

HERTZBERG, ROBERT M. former state legislator; m. Cynthia Telles; children: Daniel, David, Raymond. Graduated magna cum laude, U. Redlands, 1976; JD magna cum laude, U. Calif., 1979. Mem. Calif. State Assembly, 1996—, spkr., 2000—02, spkr. emeritus, 2002—. Chmn. Calif. Assembly Rules Com., 1998—. Mem. L.A. County Quality and Productivity Commn., Calif. State Bd. Pharmacy, 1984-88; chmn. Calif. Adv. Commn. on Youth, 1978-79, dean's coun. Hebrew Union Coll., 1991-95, v.p. Am. Jewish Com.; bd. dirs. CORO Assocs., Chinatown Svc. Ctr., Mulholland Tomorrow.; mem. exec. com. Jewish Cmty. Rels. Com. of Valley Alliance, state issues com. Valley Industry and Commerce Assn., Sherman Oaks Town Coun. Commerce Assn. Recipient Paul Harris fellow Rotary Found. Rotary Internat, Joe Farber Legis. award Peace Officers Rsch. Assn. Calif., Gold Key award L.A. Opportunities Industrialization ctr., PTA award 31st Dist. PTSA, Disting. Svc. award Planned Parenthood. Office: Calif State Assembly Van Nuys State Bldg 6150 Van Nuys Blvd Ste 305 Van Nuys CA 91401-3345 also: State Capitol Rm 319 Sacramento CA 95814

HERTZEL, DOROTHY, librarian; b. Cleve., Aug. 5, 1915; d. Walter and Helen (Metz) Hoffstetter; m. Franklin William Hertzel, July 22, 1944 (dec. May 1987); children: Franklin Dale, Brian James. BS, Baldwin-Wallace Coll., 1938; MLS, Case Western Res. U., 1965, DPhil, 1985. Tchr. math. Garfield Heights High Sch., 1939-49; asst. children's libr. Cuyahoga County Pub. Libr., Parma, Ohio, 1960-64, children's libr., 1964-65, Brooklyn, Ohio, 1965-66, libr. mgr., 1966-79. Founder Friends of Bklyn. Br. Cuyahoga County Pub. Libr., 1973—, trustee; vol. Brooklyn Sr. Ctr., 1979—; mem. Bklyn. City Sch. Vol. Tutor com., 1980-88; mem. Bklyn. City Sch. Bd. Edn., 1990-93, v.p., 1992, pres., 1993; mem. Brooklyn City Sch. Fin. com., 1993-97, Cmty. Edn. Adv. Com., 1987-90. Mem. Ohio Libr. Coun., Brooklyn Hist. Soc. (co-founder 1970, v.p. 1970-73, corr. sec. 1973-78), Soc. Ohio Archivists, Mid-Atlantic Regional Archives Conf., Greater Cleve. Genealogical Soc., Ohio Hist. Soc., Cleve. Archival Roundtable, Brooklyn Genealogical Soc. (founder 1996, pres.1996-2001, program chair 2003).

HERTZIG, MARGARET E. psychiatrist; b. N.Y.C., Feb. 9, 1935; d. Morris and Grace Koenig Hertzig; m. Herbert George Birch, Dec. 11, 1961 (dec. Feb. 5, 1973); children: Susan Ellen Birch, Martin Lawrence Birch. AB, Vassar Coll., 1956; MD, NYU, 1960. Diplomate psychiatry Am. Bd. Psychiatry and Neurology, 1968, child psychiatry Am. Bd. Psychiatry and Neurology, 1977. Assoc. prof. psychiatry Cornell U. Med. Coll., N.Y.C., 1977—95; assoc. attending psychiatrist N.Y. Hosp.-Cornell Med. Ctr., N.Y.C., 1977—95; dir. child and adolescent outpatient dept. Payne Whitney Clinic-The N.Y. Presbyn. Hosp., N.Y.C., 1977—; prof. psychiatry Weill Med. Coll. Cornell U., N.Y.C., 1995—, interim vice-chair child and adolescent psychiatry, 2002—; attending psychiatrist N.Y. Presbyn. Hosp., Weill Cornell Med. Ctr., N.Y.C., 1995—. Cons. Spl. Citizens Inc., N.Y.C., 1980—. Fellow: Am. Acad. Child and Adolescent Psychiatry. Office: Weill Med Coll Cornell Univ 525 East 68th St New York NY 10021 Office Fax: 212-746-5944. E-mail: mehertzi@med.cornell.edu.

HERTZOG, ROBERT WILLIAM, pathologist, consultant, educator; b. Danville, Pa., Oct. 31, 1939; s. Robert Lee and Thelma Isabelle H.; m. Florence Rebecca Smoot, May 26, 1962; children: Brian, Sheryl, Brent. BS, Morgan State U., Balt., 1963; MD, U. Md., Balt., 1967. Diplomate in cytopathology, forensic, anatomic and clin. pathology Am. Bd. Pathology. Staff pathologist Armed Forces Inst. Pathology, Washington, 1973-76; chief accident pathology sect., registrar Am. Registry Accident Pathology, 1974-75, chief missile trauma pathology, 1975-76, chief forensic pathology, 1976; attending pathologist Millard Fillmore Hosp./Kaleida Health, Buffalo, 1976—; clin. asst. prof. dept. pathology Sch. Medicine SUNY, Buffalo, 1977—. Dir. Sch. Med. Tech., Millard Fillmore Hosp., 1982-89. Contbr. articles to profl. jours. Lt. col. U.S. Army, 1967-76. Fellow Am. Coll. Pathologists, Am. Soc. Clin. Pathologists, Am. Acad. Forensic Scis., Am. Soc. Cytopathology. Home: 34 Ruskin Ct East Aurora NY 14052-1419 Office: Ctr for Lab Medicine 115 Flint Rd Williamsville NY 14221-3097

HERVEY, HOMER VAUGHAN, retired federal agency administrator; b. Texarkana, Tex., Sept. 27, 1936; s. Charles Ethelbert and Ambolyn (Vaughan) H.; m. Nancy McDonald, July 7, 1962; children: Nancy Vaughan, H.V. Jr. BS in Social Scis., Georgetown U., 1958, MA, 1962. Executive trainee Riggs Nat. Bank, Washington, 1958-61, U.S. Govt. Office of Edn., Washington, 1961-63; program officer Exec. Office of the Pres., Washington, 1963-73, Dept. of the Treasury, Washington, 1973-77, Fed. Preparedness Agy., Washington, 1977-79, Fed. Emergency Mgmt. Agy., Washington, 1979-85, asst. assoc. dir., dir. ops., 1985—, ret., 2001. Mem. exec. com. Georgetown U. Library, Washington, 1982—. Mem.: Chevy Chase. Avocations: motion pictures, tennis, golf, reading. E-mail: saxa3@aol.com.

HERWIG, JOAN EMILY, developmental education educator, researcher; b. Apr. 7, 1943; Student, Merrill-Palmer Inst., 1964; BS, U. Wis., Stout, 1965; MS, Iowa State U., 1971; PhD, Purdue U., 1978. Tchr. jr. h.s., Pt. Huron, Mich., 1965—69; dir.-tchr. Head Start, Pt. Huron, Mich., 1965—69; tchg. asst. Iowa State U., 1969—70, assoc. prof. child devel., 1971—, chmn. dept., 1983—86, faculty senate, 1997—2003. Rsch. asst. Purdue U., 1976—78; dir. Child Devel. Lab. Sch., 1993—2001; early childhood spl. edn. tchr. Licensure Com. Iowa Dept. Edn., 1993—; cons. child devel., early childhood edn.; mem. conf. U.S./China on Early Childhood Edn. to People's Republic of China, 1993. Cons. editor: Early Childhood Rsch. Quar., 1990—93, Young Children, 1990—, Jour. Family and Consumer Svcs., 1981—, mem. editl. bd.: Jour. Early Childhood Tchr. Edn., 1995—; contbr. chpts., articles to profl. jours. Named David Ross fellow, Purdue U., 1978; recipient Fulbright scholarship, India, 1991—92, Outstanding Tchr. award, Amoco, 1982—83, Disting. Alumni award, U. Wis., 1985, Outstanding Acad. Advisor award, 1982, Midwest Shirley Dean Early Childhood Educator award, 1993, Outstanding Internat. Achievement award, Coll. Family and Consumer Scis., Iowa State U., 1997, Faculty award, Iowa State U. Alumni Assn., 2002. Mem.: World Orgn. of Children, Soc. Internat. Devel., Internat. Fed. Home Econ., Am. Edn. Rsch. Assn., Nat. Assn. Early Childhood Tchrs. Educators, Am. Assn. Family and Consumer Scis. (sec.-treas. family rels. child devel. sect. 1988—90, fellowship com. 1990—91, recognition and honors com. chair 1994—96), Iowa Assn. Edn. Young Children (sec. 1979—82, v.p. 1982—83, pres. 1983—84), Iowa Assn. Early Childhood Tchr. Educators (founder), Midwestern Assn. Edn. Young Children (Iowa rep. coun. 1985—92, v.p. 1986—87, pres. 1987—90), Nat. Assn. Edn. Young Children (pres.-elect 1995—97, pres. 1997—99), Soc. Rsch. in Child Devel., Phi Beta Delta, Phi Delta Kappa, Kappa Omicron Nu. Achievements include research in cognitive development of young children's play, parent involvement and early childhood teacher education. Office: Iowa State U 2356 Palmer HDFS Bldg Ames IA 50011-4380 E-mail: jherwig@iastate.edu.

HERZ, ANDREW LEE, lawyer; b. N.Y.C., Nov. 12, 1946; s. John W. and Elise J. H.; m. Jill K. Herz; children: Adam, Matthew, Daniel, Michael. BA, Columbia U., 1968, JD, 1971. Bar: N.Y. 1972. Assoc. Milbank, Tweed, Hadley & McCloy, N.Y.C., 1971-75, Nickerson, Kramer, Lowenstein, Nessen, Kamin & Soll, N.Y.C., 1975-76, Marshall, Bratter, Greene, Allison & Tucker, N.Y.C., 1977-80; gen. counsel N.Y. State Mortgage Loan Enforcement and Adminstrn. Corp., N.Y.C., 1980-81; ptnr. Richards & O'Neil, LLP, N.Y.C., 1981-2001, Bingham McCutchen LLP, N.Y.C., 2001—. Lectr. Real Estate Inst., NYU, 1988-93; cons. N.Y. Real Property Svcs., 1987. Author: Office Lease Operating Expense Clauses-Definitional Problems, 1986, Renegotiating Commercial Leases, 1993, Liability Risks for Ducking Loan Commitments, 1995; co-author: Japanese Yen Financing of U.S. Real Estate, 1989, Real Estate Management Agreements, 1990, Subleases: The Same Thing as Leases, Only Different, 2000; contbr. articles to profl. jours. Chmn. zoning bd. appeals Village of Ossining, N.Y., 1980-88; bd. dirs. Planned Parenthood N.Y.C., 1987-94, AIDS Resource Ctr., 1991-94, Commercial Real Estate Law Advisor, Realcomm, 2001-02. Harlan Fiske Stone Scholar, 1971. Mem.: ABA (vice chmn. 1988—90, chair real estate mgmt. com. 1990—91, co-chair real estate asset mgmt. com. 1992—94, chair real estate asset mgmt. com. 1994—95, lending and financing subcom. 1997—99, comml. office leasing com. 1999—2001, co-chair comml. leasing com. 1999—2001, real property divsn.), Urban Land Inst. (dir.), Real Estate Bd. N.Y., Assn. Bar City N.Y., N.Y. State Bar Assn. (co-chmn. comml. leasing com. 1991—96, exec. com. 1991—96, editor N.Y. Real Property Jour. 1996—97, real property sect.), Am. Coll. Real Estate Lawyers (vice chair office leasing com. 1997—98, chair office leasing com. 1999—2001), Columbia Law Sch. Alumni Assn. (dir.). Democrat. Home: 31 Flint Ave Larchmont NY 10538-3807 Office: Bingham McCutchen LLP 399 Park Ave New York NY 10022-4689 E-mail: andrew.herz@bingham.com.

HERZ, MARVIN IRA, physiatrist, educator; b. N.Y.C., Dec. 24, 1927; s. Jules Edward and Vivian M. (Becker) Herz; m. Beatrice Leslie Mittelman, Sept. 13, 1952; 3 children. BA, U. Mich., 1949; MS in Psychology, Yale U., 1950; MD, Chgo. Med. Sch., 1955; cert. in psychoanalysis, Columbia U., 1968. Diplomate Am. Bd. Psychiatry and Neurology (sr. examiner). Intern U. Ill. Rsch. and Ednl. Hosps., 1955-56; resident in psychiatry Michael Reese Hosp., Chgo., 1956-59; dir. inpatient service div. psychiatry Montefiore Hosp., N.Y.C., 1961-63; dir. Westchester Sq. Day Hosps., N.Y.C., 1963-65; asst. prof. psychiatry Albert Einstein Coll. Medicine, N.Y.C., 1963-65; assoc. in psychiatry Columbia U., 1965-68, asst. prof., 1968-72, assoc. prof., 1972-77; ward adminstr. Washington Heights Cmty. Svc., N.Y. State Psychiat. Inst., 1965-68, dir., 1968-72; asst. attending psychiatrist Vanderbilt Clinic, Presbyn. Hosp., N.Y.C., 1965-68; dir. cmty. services N.Y. State Psychiat. Inst., 1972-77, acting clin. dir., 1975-76; med. dir. Ga. Mental Health Inst., Atlanta, 1977-78, dir. ops. rsch., 1977-78; prof. Emory U., 1977-78; prof., chmn. dept. psychiatry SUNY Sch. Medicine, Buffalo, 1978-91; dir. psychiatry Erie County Med. Center, Buffalo, 1978-91; head dept. psychiatry Buffalo Gen. Hosp., 1978-91; prof., dir. Mental Health Svcs. Rsch. U. Rochester, NY, 1991—2002, prof. emeritus, 2002; prof. U. Miami, Fla., 2003. Cons. Task Panel Pres.'s Commn. Rsch. Mental Illness, 1977, Robert Wood Johnson Found., 1992, Nat. Heart and Lung Inst.; cons. psychiatry VA Hosp., Buffalo, 1978—91; sr. sci. advisor to dir. NIMH, 1989—91; cons. psychiatry edn. br., 1978; chmn. psychiat. adv. com. N.Y. State Office Mental Health, 1980—87. Contbr. articles to med. jours. Served to lt. comdr. USNR, 1959—61. Recipient award for outcomes rsch., World Assn. Psychosocial Rehab., U.S. Br., 1994, Heinz Lehmann Rsch. award, N.Y. State Office Mental Health, 1994, award for svcs. rsch., 2002. Fellow: Am. Coll. Psychoanalysts (treas. 1991—95, v.p. 1996—97, pres. elect 1997—98, pres. 1998—99), Am. Coll. Psychiatrists (bd. regents 1990—93, 2d v.p. 1994—95, v.p. 1995—96, pres. elect 1996—97, pres. 1997—98, Dean award for Rsch. in Schizophrenia 1993), Am. Psychiat. Assn. (life; chmn. com. to develop practice guidelines schizophrenia 1992—97, chair rsch. prize com. 1996—2000, prize in hosp. psychiatry rsch. 1988, Alexander Gralnick award for Rsch. in Schizophrenia 2003); mem.: Am. Psychopathol. Assn., Assn. Psychoanalytic Medicine (chmn. com. comm. psychiatry 1975—76), Assn. Clin. Psychosocial Rsch. (pres. 1993—95), Alpha Omega Alpha. Address: Strong Ties 1650 Elmwood Ave Rochester NY 14620-3427 Home: 255 Evernea Street Apt 806 West Palm Beach FL 33401 Personal E-mail: marvles@aol.com. E-mail: marvin_herz@urmc.rochester.edu.

HERZ, MICHAEL B. accountant, management consultant; b. Forest Hills, N.Y., June 21, 1957; s. Leonard and Sally (Jampolsky) H.; m. Sherrie-Sue Greenberg, June 14, 1981; children: Elyse, Rachel, Elliott. BBA in Acctg., Pace U., Pleasantville, N.Y., 1979; MBA in Fin., Pace U., N.Y.C., 1985. CPA, N.Y. Staff auditor Coopers and Lybrand, CPAs, N.Y.C., 1979-81; audit mgr. Mann Judd Landau, CPAs, N.Y.C., 1981-85; controller, treas., CFO Nutri-Bevco, Inc., Middletown, N.Y., 1985-86; controller, treas. Fingermatrix, Inc., North White Plains, N.Y., 1986-88; corp. controller, treas. PPI Enterprises (U.S.), Inc., N.Y.C., 1988-90, v.p. fin., 1991-92; mng. dir. Herz and Herz, Armonk, N.Y., 1992—. Co-founder, dir. Network Alliance of Westchester Bus., 2000—. Mentor Pace U. Alumni, N.Y.C., 1996—. Mem. AICPA (mgmt. consulting divsn.), N.Y. State Soc. CPA, Faculty Bank Found. Acctg. Edn., Danbury Bowling Assn. (dir., v.p., chmn. Hall of Fame com. 1999—, chmn. audit com., chmn.pub. rel. com.). Avocations: golfing, bowling. Home: 6 Carpenter Way Armonk NY 10504-1451 E-mail: herz1herz@aol.com.

HERZ, MICHAEL JOSEPH, marine environmental scientist; b. St. Paul, Aug. 12, 1936; s. Malvin E. and Josephine (Daneman) H.; m. Joan Klein Levy, Feb. 3, 1962 (div. 1982); children: David M., Daniel J., Ann K.; m. Naomi Brodie Schalit, Aug. 21, 1984 (div. 1996); children: Nathaniel B., Hallie R.; m. Kate Pearson Josephs, Sept. 27, 1998. BA, Reed Coll., 1958; MA, San Francisco State U., 1962; PhD, U. So. Calif., 1966. Program coord. postdoctoral tng. program U. Calif., San Francisco, 1969-73, asst. prof., 1969-73, assoc. prof. in residence, 1973-74; exec. dir., dir. water quality tng. program San Francisco Bay. chpt. Oceanic Soc., 1974-77; exec. v.p., co-dir. rsch. and policy Oceanic Soc., San Francisco, 1977-84; sr. rsch. scientist San Francisco State U., 1984-88; exec. dir. and baykeeper San Francisco BayKeeper, 1989-95; pvt. cons. Alna, Maine, 1995—. Chmn. bd. govs. Tiburon Ctr. Environ. Studies, San Francisco State U., 1985-86; NRC com. mem. Effectiveness of Oil Spill Disperants, Washington, 1985-87, Risk Assessment Mgmt. Marine Systems, Washington, 1996-98; mem. com. on ocean disposal of radwaste Calif. Dept. Health, Sacramento, 1985-92; mem. tech. adv. com. Calif. Office of Oil Spill Prevention and Response, 1992-95; bd. dirs. Friends of the Earth, Washington, 1989—, chmn. bd. dirs., 1997-99; bd. dirs. Oceanic Soc., 1984-89; chmn. bd. dirs. Aquatic Habitat Inst.; mem. Alaska Oil Spill Commn., 1989-90; mem. NRC com. Risk Assessment and Mgmt. of Marine Systems, Washington, 1996—. Author, co-editor: Memory Consolidation, 1972, Habituation I & II, 1973;co-author: Cruise Control: A Report on How Cruise Ships Affect the Marine Environment, 2002; editor: Protection and Restoration of Salmon Habitat, 2001; contbr. reports to profl. publs. Chmn. cmty. adv. bd. Sta. KQED (Pub. Broadcast Sys. affiliate), 1979—85; San Francisco citizens adv. com. San Francisco Bay Conservation and Devel. Commn., 1979—94, chmn., 1984; mem. tech. adv. com. San Francisco Bay Regional Water Quality Control Bd., Oakland, Calif., 1979—82, Assn. Bay Area Govts., Oakland, 1983—84; mem. Bay area adv. com. Sea Grant Marine Adv. Program, San Francisco, 1983—89; mem. com. Bur. Land Mgmt., Pacific States Regional Tech. Working Group, 1979—83; bd. dirs. Maine Initiatives, 1996—2000, Sheepscot Valley Conservation Assn., 1994—, pres., 1999—; bd. dirs. Citizens for a Better Environment, 1986—94, Oceanic Soc., 1984—89, Maine Rivers, 2002—. With U.S. Army, 1958—59. Predoctoral fellow NIMH, U. So. Calif., 1963-64; postdoctoral fellow NIMH, UCLA Brain Research Inst, 1966-68. Mem. AAAS, Calif. Acad. Scis., San Francisco Bay and Estuarine Assn. E-mail: mherz@lincoln.midcoast.com.

HERZ, RACHEL SARAH, research psychologist; b. Ithaca, N.Y., Apr. 20, 1963; d. Carl Samuel and Judith Emily (Scherer) Herz. BA with honors, Queen's U., Kingston, Ont., Can., 1985; MA, U. Toronto, 1987, PhD, 1992. NSERC postdoctoral fellow in psychology U. B.C., Canada, 1992-94; asst. mem. Monell Chem. Senses Ctr., Phila., 1994-2000; asst. prof. dept. psychology Brown U., Providence, 2000—. Co-author: (book) Memory for Odors, 1995, Advances in Chemical Signals in Vertebrates, 1999, Olfaction, Taste and Cognition, 2002; contbr. articles to profl. jours. Recipient Life Scis. Grad. Student summer award, 1991—92, Life Scis. Grad. Degree Completion award, 1991—92, Ajinomoto USA Inaugural award to Promising Young Rschrs. in Olfaction, 1994, Mscowitz-Jacobs award, 2002; fellow Open, U. Toronto, 1987—89, Morley R. Kare, 1998; scholar Ont. Grad. Student, 1989—91; postdoctoral fellow, NSERC, 1992—94. Mem.: Human Behaviour and Evolution Soc., Cognitive Neurosci. Soc., Assn. Chemoreception Scis., Psychonomic Soc., Am. Psychol. Soc. Office: Brown U PO Box 1853 Providence RI 02912-1853

HERZBERG, DOROTHY CREWS, secondary education educator; b. N.Y.C., July 8, 1935; d. Floyd Houston and Julia (Lesser) Crews; m. Hershel Zelig Herzberg, May 22, 1962 (div. Apr. 1988); children: Samuel Floyd, Laura Jill, Daniel Crews. AB, Brown U., 1957; MA, Stanford U., 1964; JD, San Francisco Law Sch., 1976. Legal sec. various law firms, San Francisco, 1976-78; tchr. Mission Adult Sch., San Francisco, 1965-66; tchr. secondary and univ. levels Peace Corps, Nigeria, 1961-63; investigator Office of Dist. Atty., San Francisco, 1978-80; sr. adminstr. Dean Witter Reynolds Co., San Francisco, 1980-83; registered rep. Waddell and Reed, 1983-84; fin. services rep. United Resourceds, Hayward, Calif., 1984-86; tax preparer H&R Block, 1987; revenue officer IRS, 1987-89; tchr. ESL West Contra Costa Sch. Dist., Richmond, Calif., 1991—. Sponsor debate team and Close UP, Richmond H.S., 2001—. Editor: (newsletters) Coop. Nursery Sch. Council, 1969-71, Miraloma Life, 1976-82. Bd. dirs. LWV, San Francisco, 1967-69, mem. speakers bur., 1967-80; pres. Council Coop. Nursery Schs., San Francisco, 1969-71; bd. dirs. Miraloma (Calif.) Improvement Club, 1977-88, pres., 1980-81; alt. for supr. San Francisco Mayor's Commn. on Criminal Justice, 1978; chairperson social justice coun. Unitarian Universalist Ch. Berkeley, 1997—. Democrat. Achievements include raised $54,000 to send Richmond H.S. students to Washington, 2002, 03. Home: 1006 Richmond St El Cerrito CA 94530-2616

HERZBERG, PETER JAY, lawyer; b. Newark, Feb. 3, 1950; s. Arno and Annelle (Baruch) Herzberg; m. Lisa F. Chrystal, Mar. 13, 1982. BA, Haverford Coll., 1972; JD, U. Pa., 1975. Dep. atty. gen. N.J. Dept. Law and Pub. Safety, Trenton, 1975-78, 80, 82-83; staff atty. Sierra Club Legal Def. Fund, Washington, 1978-80; acting asst. counsel to gov. of N.J. Trenton, 1981; John F. Baker scholar, 1971; atty. Pitney Hardin Kipp & Szuch, Morristown, N.J. Mem. Phi Beta Kappa. Office: Pitney Hardin Kipp & Szuch PO Box 1945 Morristown NJ 07962-1945 E-mail: pherzberg@pitneyhardin.com.

HERZBERG, STEVEN MICHAEL, physician; b. Newark, May 21, 1944; s. Arno and Annelie Babette (Baruch) H.; m. Wendy Paula Kotler, Dec. 23, 1984; children: Rachel Elizabeth, Gary Robert. AB, Columbia U., 1965; MD, Yale U., 1969. Diplomate Am. Bd. Dermatology. Intern St. Luke's Hosp., N.Y.C., 1969-70, resident in internal medicine, 1970-71; resident in dermatology Boston U.-Tufts U., Boston, 1973-75; clin. assoc. NIH, Bethesda, Md., 1971-73; pvt. practice Roselle Park, NJ, 1976—. Clin. asst. prof. dermatology NYU, N.Y.C., 1984—2002. Contbr. articles to profl. jours. Surgeon (R) (T), USPHS, 1971-73. Fellow Am. Acad. Dermatology; mem. Med. Soc. N.J., Dermatol. Soc. N.J., Union County Med. Soc. Office: 236 E Westfield Ave Roselle Park NJ 07204-2084

HERZBERG, THOMAS, artist, illustrator; b. Chgo., Feb. 3, 1954; s. Carroll Alexander and Victoria Herzberg; m. Rosemary Ann Morrissey, Aug. 11, 1979; 1 child, Kyli Rose. BA, Northeastern U., 1975; MFA, Northern Ill. U., 1979. Instr. Am. Acad. Art, Chgo., 2000—. Illustrations appeared in Chgo. mag., Advertising Age, Playboy mag., World Book, Chgo. Tribune, Washington Post, Art Inst. Chgo., Goodman Theatre, Chg. Exhibited Art Inst. Chgo., 1978, 84, De Cordova Mus., Lincoln., Mass., 1978, 79, 83, Silvermine Guild Artists, New Canaan, Conn., 1980, Met. Mus. and Art Ctr., Coral Gables, Fla., 1980, 82, Hunterdon Art Ctr., Clinton, N.J., 1982, U. Dallas, 1983, 10th, 12th and 13th Ann. Soc. Newpaper Design, Am. Soc. Illustrators 28th, 39th and 41st Ann. Exhbns.; represented in permanent collections De Cordova Mus., Terrance Gallery, Palenville, N.Y., Met. Mus. and Art Ctr., Silvermine Guild Artists, Carnegie Inst., Art Inst. Chgo., Lincoln Park Zoo, Chgo. Symphony Orch.; over 1900 illustrations in newspapers, mags., books, mus. graphics, 1981—. Mem. Air Force Art Program, 1998—. Named Best of Show 3 Ann. Ill. Regional Print Show, 1980; recipient Award of Excellence New Horizons in Art North Shore Art League, 1980-82, Weston Press and Gallery award 8th Internat. Miniature Print Exhbn. Pratt Graphic Ctr., 1981, Cert. of Design Excellence Print's Regional Design Ann., 1994-96, 97, also numerous awards Art Direction mag. creativity show, 1992-93, Soc. Newspaper Design, Cert. of Merit Soc. Illustrators.

HERZECA, LOIS FRIEDMAN, lawyer; b. July 7, 1954; d. Martin and Elaine Shirley (Rapoport) Friedman; m. Christian S. Herzeca, Aug. 15, 1980; children: Jane Leslie, Nicholas Cameron. BA, SUNY-Binghamton, 1976; JD, Boston U., 1979. Bar: N.Y. 1980, U.S. Dist. Ct. (so. and ea. dist.) N.Y. 1980. Atty. antitrust div. U.S. Dept. Justice, Washington, 1979-80; assoc. Fried, Frank, Harris, Shriver & Jacobson, N.Y.C., 1980-86, ptnr., 1986—. Editor: Am. Jour. Law and Medicine, 1978-79. Mem. ABA, N.Y.C. Bar Assn. Office: Fried Frank Harris Shriver & Jacobson 1 New York Plz Fl 22 New York NY 10004-1980

HERZENBERG, ARVID, physicist, educator; b. Vienna, Apr. 16, 1925; s. Harry and Wilhelmine (Pfeiffer) H.; m. Marjorie Swift, Nov. 30, 1949; children: Catherine, Anne, Stephen. BS, U. Manchester, Eng., 1949, D.Sc., 1964. Mem. faculty U. Manchester, 1952 69; prof. applied physics Yale, 1969—. Contbr. articles to profl. jours. Fellow Brit., Am. phys. socs. Home: 6 Legrand Rd North Haven CT 06473-1013 Office: 329 Becton Ctr Yale University New Haven CT 06520 E-mail: arvid.herzenberg@yale.edu.

HERZENBERG, CAROLINE STUART LITTLEJOHN, physicist; b. East Orange, N.J., Mar. 25, 1932; d. Charles Frederick and Caroline Dorothea (Schulze) L.; m. Leonardo Herzenberg, July 29, 1961; children: Karen Ann, Catherine Stuart. SB, MIT, 1953; SM, U. Chgo., 1955, PhD, 1958; DSc (hon.), SUNY, Plattsburgh, 1991. Asst. prof. Ill. Inst. Tech., Chgo., 1961-66, research physicist ITT Research Inst., 1967-70, sr. physicist, 1970-71; lectr. Calif. State U., Fresno, 1975-76; physicist Argonne (Ill.) Nat. Lab., Ill., 1977-2001. Prin. investigator NASA Apollo Returned Lunar Sample Analysis Program, 1967-71; producer and host TV sci. series Camera on Sci.; disting. vis. prof. SUNY, Plattsburgh, 1991; mem. final selection com. 1993 Bower award and Prize for Achievement in Sci., 1993-94; bd. adv. the Bower award and Prize for Achievements in Sci.; mem. nat. panel of advisors PBS TV sci. series Bill Nye the Sci. Guy, 1991-95; steering com. mem. Midwest Consortium for Internat. Security Studies, 1994-95. Author: Women Scientists from Antiquity to the Present: An Index, 1986; co-author: (with R.H. Howes) Their Day in the Sun: Women of the Manhattan Project, 1999; contbr. articles to profl. jours. Candidate for alderman, Freeport, Ill., 1975; past chmn. NOW chpt., Freeport Am. Phys. Soc. Congl. Scientist fellow finalist, 1976-77; recipient award in sci. Chgo. Women's Hall of Fame, 1989. Fellow AAAS, Am. Phys. Soc. (past chmn. com., past sec.-treas. forum on Physics and Soc., past exec. bd. Forum on the History of Physics, panel pub. affairs), Assn. Women in Sci. (nat. sec. 1982-84, pres. 1988-90); mem. Sigma Xi. Home and Office: 1700 E 56th St Apt 2707 Chicago IL 60637-5092 E-mail: carol@herzenberg.net.

HERZER, MARIAN DAY, not-for-profit developer, educator; b. Williston, N.D., July 1, 1933; d. Joseph Rollin and Catherine Elizabeth (Bissett) Day; m. Kaye H. Herzer, June 12, 1954; children: Scott Kaye, Kent Day, Brett Herbert. BS in Music, Drama, Business, U. N.D., 1955; AA in real estate, Whatcom Cmty. Coll., 1979. Cert. mgmt. tng. Spokane (Wash.) Leadership Inst., 1975, lic. real estate Wash., 1976, real estate instr. Wash., 1977. Program dir. YWCA, Grand Forks, ND, 1954—56; tchr. secondary ed. Montgomery, Ala., 1957—67, Schertz, Tex., 1957—67, Redondo Beach, Calif., 1957—67; exec. dir. Sinto Ctr., Project JOY, Spokane, Wash., 1969—75; realtor Arnasons & Century 21, Bellingham, Wash., 1976—85; corp. sales mgr. Fairwood Village, Spokane, 1985—87; devel. dir., vol. mgr. Hospice of North Idaho, Coeur d'Alene, Idaho, 1987—89; vol. mgr. Wash. County, Hillsboro, Oreg., 1989—95; retired, 1995. Pres. Prevention, Edn. and Devel., Spokane, 1995—, Spokane, 2000—03; sec. N.W. Regional Mental Health Bd., Bellingham, Wash., 1978—82, Whatcom County Bd. of Realtors, Bellingham, 1976—82; generalist com. Health Improvement Partnership, Spokane, 1997—99. Editor: Living, Loving, Letting Go, 2002; author: Six Scripts for Seniors, 1988. Chair War on Poverty Coalition, Montgomery, Ala., 1958—61; sec. No. Va. Action Com., Wash., DC, 1967; mem. So. Poverty Law Ctr., Montgomery, 1993—2002, Poor People's Campaign; bd of dir. Citizens League, Spokane, 1997—2001. Recipient Disting. Svc. award, ACTION - Region X, 1993, Marian Herzer award, Spokane Parks & Recreation, 1985, Outstanding Vol. Mgr. award, Retirement and Sr. Vol. Program, 1998, Ethel Percy Andrus Award for Cmty. Svc., Wash. State, 2002, Spokane Women of Achievement Award for Community Svc., 2002, Outstanding Vol. award, Retirement and Sr. Vol. Program, 2002, Outstanding Cmty. Svc. Award, DAR, 2003. Mem.: AARP, Sr. Svc. of Wash. Achievements include founder numerous civc orgns. Avocations: music, reading, travel, art collecting, writing. Home: 8230 No Pamela St Spokane WA 99208 Office: Prevention Education and Devel Inc 315 W Mission Ste 22 Spokane WA 99201 Home Fax: 509-326-1472. E-mail: dayher@msn.com.

HERZFELD, CHARLES MARIA, physicist, educator; b. Vienna, June 29, 1925; came to U.S., 1942, naturalized, 1949; s. August Alfred and Frieda Auguste (Poehlman) H.; children: Charles Christopher, Thomas Augustine, Paul Vincent; m. Shannon Stock Shuman, June 9, 1990. BS in Chem. Engring. cum laude, Cath. U. Am., 1945; PhD (Carnegie Found. fellow), U. Chgo., 1951. Lectr. chemistry Cath. U. Am., 1946; lectr. gen. sci. Coll. U. Chgo., 1946-47; lectr. physics DePaul U., Chgo., 1948-50; physicist Ballistic Research Lab., Aberdeen, Md., 1951-53, Naval Research Lab., Washington, 1953-55; lectr. physics U. Md., 1953-57, prof. physics, 1957-61; cons. chief heat and power div. Nat. Bur. Standards, 1955-56, acting asst. chief, 1956-57, chief heat div., 1957-61, asso. dir. bur., 1961; asst. dir. Advanced Research Project Agy., Dept. Def., 1961-63, dir. ballistic missile def., 1963; dep. dir. Advanced Research Projects Agy., 1963-65, dir., 1965-67; tech. dir. def. space group ITT, Nutley, N.J., 1967-74, tech. dir. aerospace-electronics-components-energy group, 1974-76, tech. dir. telecommunications and electronics group N.Am., 1978-79; v.p., dir. research ITT Corp., 1979-83, v.p., dir. research and tech., 1983-85; vice chmn. Aetna, Jacobs and Ramo, N.Y.C., 1985-90; dir. def. rsch. and engring. Dept. Def., Washington, 1990-91; cons. to Office Sci. and Tech. Policy, Exec. Office Pres. of U.S., Washington, 1991. Chmn. bd. Westronix Co., Midvale, Utah, 1985-88; mem. Def. Sci. bd., 1968-83, Def. Policy Bd., 1985-90, Nat. Commn. on Space, 1985-86; cons. in field; fellow Hudson Inst., 1970-90; mem. Brookings Inst. 5th Conf. for Career Execs. in Fed. Govt., 1958, mem. chief of Naval Ops. exec. panel, 1970-2000; mem. Tech. Review Bd. Hong Kong, 1993-94, Nat. Security Advisory Bd., Los Alamos Nat. Lab.; adj. fellow Ctr. Strategic and Internat. Studies, Washington, 1995—. Editor: Temperature, Its Control in Science and Industry, vol. III, 1962; contbr. articles to profl. jours. Recipient Flemming award, 1963; Meritorious Civilian Service medal Dept. Def., 1967 Fellow AAAS, Am. Phys. Soc., Conf. on Sci., Philosophy and Religion, Coun. Fgn. Rels., Ctr. for Strategic and Internat. Studies (Washington); mem. Explorers Club, Inst. for Strategic Studies (London), Cath. Assn. Internat. Peace (pres. 1959-61), Cosmos Club (Washington).

HERZFELD, GARSON, rabbi; b. Cleve., May 2, 1951; s. Jacob L. Herzfeld and Lila (Bloomberg) Held. BA, Hobart and William Smith Coll., Geneva, N.Y., 1973; MA in Hebrew Letters, Hebrew Union Coll., 1979. Ordained rabbi, 1979. Rabbi Congregation Rodeph Shalom, Dollard Des Ormeax, Que., 1979 81, Temple Beth-El, Geneva, N.Y., 1981-86; campus rabbi Hobart & William Smith Colls., Geneva, N.Y., 1981-86; Jewish chaplain Willard (N.Y.) Psychiatric Ctr., 1983-86; rabbi Temple Israel, Brockton, Mass., 1986-88; rabbi, dir. B'nai Brith Hillel Found., Tampa, Fla., 1988-93; dir. Israel Programs, Marblehead, Mass., 1993-94; asst. dir. Windsor (Ont., Can.) Jewish Cmty. Ctr./Fedn., 1995-98; exec. dir. Toledo Bd. Jewish Edn., 1998-99; rabbi Beth El Congregation, Winchester, Va., 1999—; adj. asst. prof. Rel. Shenandoah U., Winchester, Va., 2000—; mentoring staff Northwest Cmty. Svcs., Winchester, Va., 2000—. Adj. Hebrew instr. U. South Fla., Tampa, 1989-93; mem. steering com. Jewish Cmty. Rels. Coun., Tampa, 1989-93, Operation Exodus task force, Tampa, 1990-93; leadership v.p. Young Adults div. Tampa Jewish Fedn., 1990-91. Contbr. articles to profl. jours. Mem. Tampa Gen. Hosp. Pastoral Edn. Steering Com., 1990-93; mem. Wellness Com. U.S. Fla., 1989-91. Mem. Cen. Conf. Am. Rabbis, Coalition for Advancement of Jewish Edn., Am. Psychol. Assn., Greater Washington D.C. Bd. Rabbis, Winchester-Frederick County Ministerial Assn., Coalition for Racial Unity, Kappa Delta Pi. Home: 413 Lanny Dr Winchester VA 22601-3013 E-mail: rabgar@hotmail.com.

HERZFELD-KIMBROUGH, CIBY, mental health educator; b. Mobile, Ala., Oct. 10, 1941; d. Julius Sr. and Nettie (Fraizer) Herzfeld; m. Charles C. Kimbrough, Nov. 28, 1964; children: Carolos R., Choron F. BS, U. Mo., 1970; MA, Wash. U., 1980; MAT, AGC, Webster U., 1982. Cert. tchr., Mo. Coord. children-adolescent svcs. Metro Comprehensive Mental Health Ctr., St. Louis; cons. C. Kimbrough and Assocs.; instr. minority mental health Wash. U., St. Louis; founder, exec. dir. Creative Inovative and Behavioral Experences, CIBE; mng. dir. CKAN Ltd., Nigeria; project coord. Children's Devel. Ctr., Lagos, Nigeria; intervention specialist, counselor Ferguson Florissant Schs. Adj. instr. St. Louis U.; developer Children's Treatment Program; established Metroties Day Treatment Sch., 1987. Creator (line of African greeting cards) KenteKards. Trustee Children's Devel. Ctr., Lagos, Nigeria. Knoxville Coll. acad. scholarship, 1961; NIMH fellow, 1979; recipient Outstanding Leadership award Woman's Collaboration Conf., 1985, Exceptional Tchr. award INROADS Pre-Coll. Inst., 1986, Devel. award MTS, Lagos, Nigeria. Mem. Am. Women's Assn. Singapore, Nat. Black Child Devel. Inst. (pres. St. Louis affiliate, Outstanding Svc. award), St. Louis Assn. of Black Psychologists (membership chair), St. Louis Mental Health Assn. (children's svcs. coun., membership chair), Mo. Psychol. Assn. (St. Louis network for women psychologists sec.), Nigerian Field Soc. (membership chair), Internat. Platform Soc., 100 Black Women, Nigerian Federated Women, Am. Women Assn. Singapore, Am. Woman's Club, Nigerians U.S.A. Home: 11752 Russet Meadow Dr Saint Louis MO 63146-4231

HERZIG, DAVID JACOB, pharmaceutical company executive, consultant; b. Cleve., Dec. 13, 1936; s. Marvin Laurence and Lillian Gertrude (Blaine) H.; m. Phyllis Glicksberg, Sept. 2, 1962; children: Michael, Pamela, Roberta, Karen. BA, Oberlin Coll., 1958; PhD in Chemistry, U. Cin., 1963. Vis. scientist NIH, Bethesda, Md., 1963-65, staff fellow, 1965-67; sr. rsch. assoc. NYU Sch. Medicine, N.Y.C., 1967-68, Warner Lambert, Parke-Davis Co., Ann Arbor, Mich., 1968-77, dir. immunopharmacology, 1977-81, dir. sci. devel., 1981-99; v.p. drug devel. and sci. devel. Mich. Biotechnology Inst., also bd. dirs. Bd. dirs. Metabasis, Inc. Contbr. articles to profl. jours. Bd. dirs. Mich. Ctr. High Tech., 1992-95. Fellow Damon Runyon Meml. Fund. Mem. AAAS, Am. Soc. Pharmacology and Exptl. Therapeutics, Am. Acad. Allergy Immunology, Mich. Biotech. Assn. (bd. dirs. 1993-96, pres. 1994-96), N.Y. Acad. Scis., N.Y. Fencers Club (bd. dirs. 1970-77), Sigma Xi. Avocations: squash, fencing, furniture building. Home and Office: 3540 Windemere Dr Ann Arbor MI 48105-2842 E-mail: davidjhherzig@world.oberlin.edu.

HERZIG, JULIE ESTHER, designer; b. N.Y.C., Jan. 23, 1951; d. Philip R. and Helene J. (Phillips) H.; m. Robert J. Desnick, Oct. 23, 1988; 1 child, Jonathan Phillips. BA, Mt. Holyoke Coll., 1973; BArch with honors, Pratt Inst., 1983. With Red Roof Design, N.Y.C., 1977-80, Phillips Janson Group, N.Y.C., 1983-84, Herzig, Knechtel Assocs., N.Y.C., 1984-85, Herzig Design, N.Y.C., 1985—. Mt. Holyoke Coll. grantee, 1972. Mem. AIA, Mt. Holyoke Club.

HERZLICH, HAROLD J. chemical engineer; b. Bklyn. m. Carol Ast; children: Amy, Adam. BSChemE, NYU, 1956; student, So. Conn. Coll., Quinnipiac Coll. Mem. prodn. squadron Goodyear Tire & Rubber Co., Akron, Ohio, 1956-57, mem. process devel., 1957-58; prodn. compounder Armstrong Rubber Co., New Haven, 1958-61, sr. compounder, 1961-62, divsn. compounder, 1962-65, mgr. pass tire comp. devel., 1965-66, mgr. auto tire comp. devel., 1966-68, mgr. pass car tire comp. devel., 1968-70, sr. rsch. chemist, 1970-73, mgr. compound rsch., 1973-75, mgr. compound devel., 1975-85, dir. tire engring., legal matters and product reliability, 1985-88, Pirelli Armstrong Tire Co., New Haven, 1988-90; consulting tire engr. Tire Engring., Chemistry and Safety, Las Vegas, 1990—. Pres. Elasphalt Corp.; chmn. Internat. Tire Conf.; speaker in field. Tech. editor Rubber and Plastics News. With USCG. Mem. ASTM (mem. E-40), Am. Chem. Soc. (chmn. rubber divsn. 1982—, chmn.-elect 1981, mem. membership com., mem. edn. com., mem. budget and fin. com., treas. rubber divsn. 1978 81, bus. mgr. rubber chemistry and tech., mem. divsn. chemistry and law, hon. life), Soc. Automotive Engrs., Acad. Forensics Sci. (engring. divsn.), Tire Soc., Conn. Rubber Group (edn. chmn., vice chmn., chmn. 1966, hon. life). Avocations: sports, community svc., travel. Home and Office: Tire Engring Chemistry & Safety 8908 Desert Mound Dr Las Vegas NV 89134-8801

HERZOG, ALFRED, psychiatrist, health facility executive; b. Degernau, Germany, Jan. 5, 1941; came to U.S., 1953; m. Katharine Winslow, Aug. 20, 1966; children: Trina, Anne. BA, Amherst Coll., 1963; MD, U. Pa., 1967; D Psychiatry, Yale U., 1974. Diplomate Am. Bd. Psychiatry and Neurology. Pvt. practice Hartford Hosp., 1974—, v.p., med. affairs, 1991—. Trustee Commn. Accrediting Rehab. Facilities, Tuscon, 1999—, New Eng. Healthcare Assembly, Boston, 1994—2000; v.p. Conn. Med. Soc., pres.-elect, 2000—01, pres., 2001—02; spkr. APA, Washington, 1999—2000. Lt. Cmdr., USN, 1969-71. Recipient Disting. Svc. award, Hartford County Med. Assn., Hartford, 1995. Fellow APA, 1984, Soc. Clin. Exptl. Hypnosis; mem. Exchange Club. Unitarian Universalist. Avocations: tennis, golf, running, reading. Office: Hartford Hosp 80 Seymour St Hartford CT 06102-8000 E-mail: herzog@harthosp.org.

HERZOG, ARTHUR, III, author; b. N.Y.C., Apr. 6, 1927; s. Arthur Jr. and Elizabeth Lindsay (Dayton) H.; 1 son by previous marriage, Matthew Lennox. Student, U. Ariz., 1945-46; BA, Stanford U., 1950; MA, Columbia U., 1956. Editor Fawcett Pubs., 1957-59. Cons. Peace Corps, 1967-68; polit. cons., 1969-71; bd. dirs. Leslie Mandel Enterprises, Mandel Airplane Funding and Leasing Co. Author: (with others) Smoking and the Public Interest, 1963, The War-Peace Establishment, 1965, The Church Trap, 1968, McCarthy for President, 1969, The B.S. Factor, 1973, The Swarm, 1974, Earthsound, 1975, Orca, 1977, Heat, 1977, rev. edit., 1989, IQ 83, 1978, Make Us Happy, 1978, Glad to be Here, 1979, Aries Rising, 1981, The Craving, 1982, L.S.I.T.T., 1983, Vesco-From Wall Street to Castro's Cuba, The Rise, Fall and Exile of the King of White Collar Crime, 1987, Takeover, 1987 (formerly L.S.I.T.T.), The Woodchipper Murder, 1989, Seventeen Days: The Katie Beers Story, 1993, How to Write Almost Anything Better and Faster, 1995, Body Parts, 2001, Imortalon, 2003, (almost all works transl. and published in Hungary); contbr. articles profl. jours. Campaign mgr. Oreg., nat. pub. rels. dir. Eugene McCarthy Presdl. Campaign, 1968; founder New Democratic Coalition, N.Y. and nationally, 1968-69, Lexington Dem. Club, 1974. With USNR, 1944-45. Mem.: PEN, Authors League, Authors Guild, Pigeon Point Club Tobago. Address: PO Box 294 Wainscott NY 11975-0294 E-mail: artherz@aol.com. *I do not believe that money and success should figure as strongly as it does in our estimate of what is a good life. Since it often does, though, I would point to perseverance as a major element of success. Another, mostly overlooked, is a lack of dogmatism and a belief in skepticism and personal happiness as ends in themselves.*

HERZOG, BARBARA JEAN, secondary school educator, administrator; b. Fond du Lac, Wis., d. Charles Victor and Helen Jean (Gutsch) H. BS in Social Studies, U. Wis., Oshkosh, 1970, MS in Teaching in History-Social Sci., 1975; PhD in Ednl. Adminstrn., U. Wis., Madison, 1984. Cert. tchr., Wis.; cert. prin., Wis. Tchr. Woodworth Jr. H.S., Fond du Lac, 1970-75, 76-81; adminstrv. intern Fond du Lac Pub. Schs., 1983, mem. insvc. edn. coun., 1978-84; grad. asst. U. Wis., Madison, 1982-83; tchr. Sabish Jr. H.S., Fond du Lac, 1981-82, 83-84, Shattuck Jr. H.S., Neenah, 1984-87; asst. prin. Neenah Jr. H.S. Dist., 1984-87; tchr., curriculum dir. Oshkosh Area Sch. Dist., 1987-97, asst. supt. instrn., 1997—. Ad hoc prof. U. Wis. Oshkosh Coll. Edn., 1977—; presenter U. Wis. Oshkosh NSF Conf., 1976, Wis. Ednl. Rsch. Assn., Milw., 1976, Nat. Coun. for the Social Studies Conf., Mpls., 1978, Tex., 1978, Wis. Coun. for the Social Studies, Oconomowoc, 1978, 83,, 84, 86, Milw. Tchrs. Edn. Assn., 1978, Great Lakes Regional Social Studies Conf., Chgo., 1979, Nat. U. Extension Assn. Region IV Conf., Kalamazoo, 1979, Wis. Edn. Assn. Coun., Milw., 1979, Assn. Tchr. Educators, Washington, 1980, San Diego, 1988, Nat. Coun. on States on Insvc. Edn., San Diego, 1980, 14th Annual Mid. and Jr. H.S. Conf., U. Wis., Oshkosh, 1986, 15th Annual Conf., 1987, Assn. Tchr. Educators Regional Spring Miniclinic, Oak Brook, Ill., 1986, Globescope Wis. 88, Oshkosh, 1988, Assn. Wis. Sch. Adminstrs., Madison, 1988, U. Wis. Oshkosh and Green Bay, 1990, 91, among others; presenter NAESP, 2003. Co-author: (with others) Programming for Staff Development: Fanning the Flame, 1990; contbr. articles to profl. jours. Mem. exec. com. Oshkosh Human Rels. Coun., 1993-96; chairperson, mem. faith formation com. St. Peter Cath. Ch., Oshkosh, 1993-95, communion min., 1982—; mem. South Winnebago pub. edn. com. Am. Cancer Soc., Oshkosh, 1992-96; bd. dirs. Silvercrest Girls' Group Home, Neenah, 1986 87, So. Fox Valley Child Svcs. Soc., Oshkosh 1990-96; mem. ednl. outreach subcom. Oshkosh Cmty. U. Human Rels. Coun., 1989—; alt. Oshkosh Addictions Coord. Bd., 1990-92; mem. bd. visitors Sch. Edn. U. Wis., Madison, 1997-2001; bd. dirs. Paine Art Ctr. and Gardens, 1999--. Recipient Advocacy award Wis. Sch. Counselors Assn., 1992, Best Overall Paper award Wis. Ednl. Rsch. Assn., 1986, Rsch. award Wis. Improvement Program, 1986, U. Wis. Sch. Edn. Alumni Achievement award, 1995, Citation award Wis. AHPERD, 1997, Adminstr. of Yr. award Oshkosh Area Sch. Dist., 1995. Mem. ASCD, Assn. Am. Sch. Adminstrs., Wis. Coun. for the Social Studies (exec. com. 1980-87), Oshkosh Area Sch. Dist. Adminstrs. Assn., TESOL, Wis. ASCD, Wis. Staff Devel. Coun., Oshkosh Area United Way, Oshkosh Southwest Rotary, Oshkosh C. of C. (edn. com. 1987-96), Phi Delta Kappa (chpt. pres. 1989-90), Delta Kappa Gamma (Helen Duling scholarship 1982). Home: 925 E Bent Ave Oshkosh WI 54901 Office: Oshkosh Area Sch Dist 215 S Eagle St Oshkosh WI 54902-5624

HERZOG, BEVERLY LEAH, hydrogeologist; b. Fond du Lac, Wis., Aug. 27, 1954; d. Charles Victor and Helen Jean (Gutsch) H.; m. Craig Warren Cutbirth, June 2, 1979. BS in Geology, U. Wis., Oshkosh, Wis., 1976; MS in Hydrology, Stanford U., 1978. Cert. groundwater profl., cert. profl. geologist. Asst. hydrogeologist Donohue & Assocs., Sheboygan, Wis., 1977; cons. Hydrocomp Internat., Palo Alto, Calif., 1977-78; asst. hydrogeologist Camp, Dresser & McKee, Champaign, Ill., 1978-79; asst. geologist Ill. State Geol. Survey, Champaign, 1980-84, assoc. hydrogeologist, 1985-90, sr. hydrogeologist, head groundwater resources & protection, 1991-98, head environ. geosci. ctr., 1997—. Mem. editorial bd. Ground Water, 1985-90, Ground Water Monitoring Rev., 1987-97; contbr. numerous articles on ground water in profl. jours. and symposium procs. Bd. dirs. DeWitt County chpt. ARC, Clinton, Ill., 1984-90, CPR and first aid instr. Champaign County ARC, 1978-93; bd. dirs. Green Meadows coun. Girl Scouts U.S., 1994-99, 2d v.p., 1997-99, camp counselor Fox River Area coun., Appleton, Wis., 1972, 73, 76; bd. dirs. Ctr. for Women in Transition, 1999-2002. Named outstanding vol. Champaign County ARC, 1987; recipient best paper award Ground Water Monitoring Rev., 1988, disting. achievement award Ill. State Geol. Survey, 1989; named woman of distinction Green Meadows Girl Scout Coun., 1994. Mem. Assn. Ground Water Scientists and Engrs. (bd. dirs. 2000-03, sec.-treas. 2003--), Am. Inst. Profl. Geologists (sec. Ill.-Ind. sect. 1992-93), Geol. Soc. Am., Ill. Groundwater Assn. (bd. dirs. 1991-94, vice-chmn. 1992, chmn. 1993), Altrusa (bd. dirs. Champaign-Urbana club 1996-98, pres.-elect 1998-2000, pres. 2000-02, dist. six bd. 2003-05), Sigma Xi. Avocations: racquetball, travel, companion animals. Home: 37857 E 100 North Rd Bellflower IL 61724-9721 Office: Ill State Geol Survey 615 E Peabody Dr Champaign IL 61820-6918 E-mail: herzog@isgs.uiuc.edu. *When we are striving for success, however we define it, we must take care not to lose our humanity or integrity. Without these, success means nothing. We must still be able to look in the mirror and like the person looking back.*

HERZOG, CHARLES A. cardiologist, researcher; b. Baton Rouge, May 7, 1953; s. Robert and Justine Schmertz Herzog; m. Jeanne Goodman Herzog, June 30, 1974; children: Jocelyn Rose, Linnea Elizabeth. BS, Yale U., 1974; MD, U. Rochester, 1978. Intern U. Iowa, Iowa City, 1979; resident U. Minn., Mpls., 1979—81, fellow cardiology, 1981—84, asst. prof. medicine, 1984—98, assoc. prof. medicine, 1999—; staff physician emergency dept. U. Minn. Hosp., Mpls., 1982—84; dir. cardiac catherization lab. Hennepin County Med. Ctr., Mpls., 1984—91, dir. cardiac ultrasound lab., 1997—. Dir. Cardiovasc. Spl. Studies Ctr. U.S. Renal Data Sys., Mpls., 1999—; chmn. critical events com. Chorus Trial (Bayer), 2000—01; mem. critical events com. Choir Trial (Ortho), 2001—. Fellow: Am. Coll. Cardiology; mem.: Am. Heart Assn., Am. Soc. Nephrology, Phi Beta Kappa. Avocation: photography. Office: Hennepin County Med Ctr Cardiology Divsn 701 Park Ave South Minneapolis MN 55415

HERZOG, CYNTHIA ELAINE, physician, educator; b. Houston, Nov. 3, 1956; d. Frank and Bessie Pearl Herzog; m. James Roscoe High; 1 child, Magdalena Elise High. BA, Rice U., 1979; MD, U. Tex., Galveston, 1985. Resident in pediatrics Children's Hosp., Dallas, 1985-88; fellow in pediatric hematology/oncology Nat. Cancer Inst., Bethesda, Md., 1988-92; asst. prof. pediatrics U. Tex./M.D. Anderson Cancer Ctr., Houston, 1992—. Contbr. articles to Cancer Rsch., Clin. Cancer Rsch., Jour. Biol. Chemistry. Mem. AAAS, Am. Assn. for Cancer Rsch., Am. Soc. for Clin. Oncology, Am. Soc. for Pediatric Hematology/Oncology. Office: U Tex/MD Anderson Cancer Ctr 1515 Holcombe Blvd Houston TX 77030-4009

HERZOG, DOUG, broadcast executive; Pres. entertainment Fox Broadcasting, L.A. Office: Fox Broadcasting 10201 W Pico Blvd Los Angeles CA 90064-2606

HERZOG, FRED F. law educator; b. Prague, Czech Republic, Sept. 21, 1907; s. David and Anna (Reich) H.; m. Betty Ruth Cohen, Mar. 27, 1947 (dec. Sept. 1984); children: Stephen E., David R. Dr. Juris, U. Graz (Austria), 1931; JD with high distinction U. Iowa, 1942; LL.D. (hon.), John Marshall Law Sch., 1983. Bar: Iowa 1942, Ill. 1946, U.S. Supreme Ct. 1965. Judge, Vienna, Austria, 1937-38; prof. and dean Chgo.-Kent Coll. Law, 1947-73; spl. atty. Met. San. Dist. Greater Chgo., 1962-70; 1st asst. atty. gen. Ill., 1973-76; dean John Marshall Law Sch., Chgo., 1976-83, prof., 1976—. Recipient Americanism award DAR, 1978; Golden Doctor diploma U. Graz, 1981; award of Excellence, John Marshall Law Sch. Alumni Assn., 1981; cert. of Appreciation, Ill. Dept. Registration and Edn., 1978; Ill. Atty. Gen.'s award for Outstanding Pub. Service, 1976; Torch of Learning award Am. Friends of the Hebrew U., 1986; named to Sr. Citizens Hall of Fame, City of Chgo., 1983. Mem. ABA, Ill. Bar Assn., Chgo. Bar Assn., Ill. Appellate Lawyers Assn., Decalogue Soc. Lawyers, Mid-Am. Club, Internat. Club (Chgo.), Union League Club (Chgo.). Contbr. articles to legal jours. Office: John Marshall Law Sch 315 S Plymouth Ct Chicago IL 60604-3969

HERZOG, JOHN E. securities dealer; b. N.Y.C., Mar. 18, 1936; s. Robert I. and Norma (Englander) H.; m. Diana E. Rigby; children: Mary, Sarah. BA, Cornell U., 1957; postgrad., N.Y. Inst. Fin., 1958; MBA, NYU, 1970. With Eastman Dillon (Paine Weber), Phila., 1957-59; chmn. Herzog, Heine, Geduld, N.Y.C., 1959—2002, R.M. Smythe & Co. Inc., 1996—. Charter mem. regula-

tory policy adv. com. N.Y. Stock Exchange, 1981—, mem. regional firms adv. com.; trustee Securities Industry Inst. Bd. dirs. Resources for Children with Spl. Needs, N.Y.C.; trustee The Knox Sch., 1986-91, Randolph Macon Woman's Coll., Securities Industry Inst.; bd. regents L.I. Coll. Hosp., Bklyn.; founder, chair Mus. Am. Fin. History. Mem.: Cornell Libr. (adv. coun.), N.Y. Univ. Stern Sch. of Bus. (bd. of overseers), Smithsonian Nat. Bd., Securities Industry Assn. (chmn. N.Y. Area firms com., econ. edn. com. N.Y.dist.).

HERZOG, JOHN LANFIELD, public policy, advertising and public relations executive; b. Portland, Oreg., Oct. 30, 1938; s. Ralph B. and Rose (Weinstein) H.; m. Leslie Ann Keck, Sept. 6, 1983; children: Catherine, Peter, Dana. BS, U. Colo., 1961; MS, UCLA, 1962. Trainee Carson/Roberts Advt., L.A., 1962; copywriter Rexall Drug Co., L.A., 1962-63; account exec., copywriter Richard N. Meltzer Advt., San Francisco, 1963-64, Gross, Roberts & Rockey Advt., San Francisco, 1964-66; advt. promotion mgr. Dow Jones & Co., San Francisco, 1966-67, copy chief advt. promotion dept. N.Y.C., 1967-69; dir. advt. and pub. rels. Woodmoor Corp., Monument, Colo., 1969-70; owner Herzog Advt. and Pub. Rels., Colorado Springs, Colo., 1970-91; apptd. spl. asst. mktg. and comms. Fed. Emergency Mgmt. Agy., Washington, 1991-93; v.p. Strategic Advocacy Group, Washington, 1995-98; v.p. pub. policy Air Conditioning Contractors Am., 1998—. Part-time tchr. U. Colo., Colorado Springs, 1988-91, National Coll., Colorado Springs, 1988, U. of Phoenix, Colorado Springs, 1989-91. Author, editor: Daddy Won't Be Home For A Long Time, 1971; contbr. articles to newspapers and mags. Bd. dirs. Cheyenne Mountain Sch. Dist., Colorado Springs, 1977-80; mem. Colo. Ho. of Reps., Denver, 1980-86; bd. dirs. Ctr. for Prevention of Domestic Abuse, Very Spl. Arts, Colo., DaVinci Quartet, Pikes Peak Found. for Mental Health; mem. adv. bd. Coll. Letters, Arts & Scis., U. Colo.; mem. adv. bd. Salvation Army ARC. With USNR, 1957-61. Recipient Outstanding Legislator award Delta Kappa Gamma, 1985, Letter of Recommendation, Delta Kappa Gamma, 1986, Outstanding State Legislator award Colo. chpt. Assn. for Retarded Citizens, 1985, numerous others. Mem. Am. Advt. Fedn. (gov. dist. 12 1985), Pikes Peak Advt. Fedn. (pres. 1981). Republican. Avocations: mountain climbing, running, scuba diving. E-mail: john.herzog@ms.acca.org.

HERZOG, LESTER BARRY, lawyer, educator; b. Presov, Slovakia, July 3, 1953; came to U.S., 1965; s. Alexander and Flora (Braun) H.; m. Terry Lynn Hochhauser, Feb. 6, 1979; children: Simcha, Sarah, Chaim, Judah, Leah. BA, Rabbinical Sem. Belz, Bklyn., 1974; MBA with distinction, L.I. U., 1977; JD cum laude, Bklyn. Law Sch., 1983. Bar: N.Y. 1984, U.S. Dist. Ct. (ea. and so. dists.) N.Y. 1984; CPA, N.Y. Sr. auditor Seidman & Seidman, N.Y.C., 1977-83; sr. trial atty. Office Corp. Counsel N.Y.C. Law Dept., Bklyn., 1983-89; pvt. practice N.Y.C., 1989—. Adj. assoc. prof. law and acctg. L.I. U., Bklyn., 1985—. Contbr. articles to profl. jours. Mem. ABA, AICPA (exam grader 1981-83), N.Y. State Bar Assn. Democrat. Jewish. Avocations: chess, fishing, gardening. Home and Office: 1729 E 15th St Brooklyn NY 11229-2084

HERZOG, PETER EMILIUS, retired legal educator; b. Vienna, Dec. 25, 1925; came to U.S., 1950, naturalized, 1955; s. Paul and Leopodine (Mannhart) H.; m. Brigitte Ecolivet, June 29, 1970; children: Paul, Elizabeth Ann. Student, U. Vienna, 1949-50; BA, Hobart Coll., 1952; LLB summa cum laude, Syracuse U., 1955; LLM, Columbia U., 1956. Bar: N.Y. 1957. Dep. asst. atty. gen. N.Y. State Dept. Law, Albany, 1955-57, asst. atty. gen., 1957-58; asst. prof. law Syracuse U. Coll. Law, 1958-62, assoc. prof., 1962-66, prof., 1966-83, Crandall Melvin prof., 1983-94, Crandall Melvin prof. emeritus, 1995—, law librarian, 1960-68; staff mem. Columbia U. Project on Inter Procedure, 1960-63; assoc. dir. Project on European Legal Instns., 1968-73; ret. Staff mem. UN Commn. on Internat. Trade Law, 1968-69; rsch. fellow Procedural Aspects Internat. Law Inst., 1968-71; lectr. Hague (Netherlands) Acad. Internat. Law, 1992; cons. N.Y. State Eminent Domain Commn., 1971; vis. prof. U. Paris, 1976-77, U. Dijon, France, 1987, U. Fribourg, Switzerland, 1987. Author: (with Martha Weser) Civil Procedure in France, 1967, (with Ivan Head and Frank Dawson) International Law, National Tribunals and the Rights of Aliens, 1971, (with Hans Smit) The Law of the European Economic Community, A Commentary, 1976, (with Schlesinger, Baade and Wise) Comparative Law, 6th edit., 1998; contbr. articles to legal publs. Jervey fellow Columbia U., 1956. Mem. Am. Soc. Internat. Law, Soc. de Législation Comparée, Internat. Law Assn., Internat. Acad. Comparative Law (assoc.), Wissenschaftliche Gesellschaft für Verfahrensrecht, Order of Coif, Phi Beta Kappa. Roman Catholic. Home: 112 Erregger Rd Syracuse NY 13224-2220 E-mail: 72560.1122@compuserve.com.

HERZOG, TOBEY CHURCH, English educator; b. Peru, Ill., Oct. 16, 1946; s. Robert F. and Anna Church Herzog; m. Peggy Miller, Sept. 2, 1967; children: Robert M., Joseph M. BA in English, Ill. Wesleyan U., 1968; MA in English, Purdue U., 1972, PhD in English, 1975. Vis. instr. Purdue U., West Lafayette, Ind., 1975-76; asst. prof. Wabash Coll., Crawfordsville, Ind., 1976-82, assoc. prof., 1982-91, prof. English, 1992—, chmn. English dept., 1994—97, chmn. divsn. humanities and fine arts, 1998—2001. Writing cons. to various bus. and industries, 1985—; McLain-McTurnan-Arnold rsch. scholar Wabash Coll., 1988—89. Author: Vietnam War Stories: Innocence Lost, 1992, Tim O'Brien, 1997; contbr. articles to profl. jours. With U.S. Army, 1969-70, Vietnam. Decorated Bronze Star; recipient Outstanding Young Alumnus award Ill. Wesleyan U., 1982. Avocations: travel, sports. Office: Wabash Coll PO Box 352 Crawfordsville IN 47933 E-mail: herzogt@wabash.edu.

HERZSTEIN, ROBERT ERWIN, lawyer; b. Denver, Feb. 26, 1931; s. Sigmund Edwards and Estelle Ruth (Borwick) H.; m. Priscilla Holmes, July 11, 1956; children: Jessica Anne, Emily Holmes, Robert Holmes. AB, Harvard U., 1952, LLB, 1955. Bar: Colo. 1956, D.C. 1959, U.S. Supreme Ct. 1962. Sr. ptnr., other positions Arnold & Porter, Washington, 1958-80, sr. ptnr., 1981-89; undersec. for Internat. Trade U.S. Dept. Commerce, Washington, 1980-81; ptnr. Shearman & Sterling, Washington, 1989-95, counsel, 1995-99; mem. Miller & Chevalier, Washington, 1999—. Contbr. articles to profl. jours. Trustee Internat. Law Inst., Washington, 1974—; bd. dirs. Ptnrs. for Dem. Change, Appleseed Found., Washington, Coun. of Ams., NY, Internat. Human Rights Law Group, Washington, 1986—91; bd. dirs., mem. faculty Salzburg Seminar in Am. Studies, 1986—93. Mem. ABA, Am. Soc. Internat. Law (exec. coun. 1981-84), Coun. on Fgn. Rels. Home: 4710 Woodway Ln NW Washington DC 20016-3241 Office: 655 15th St NW Ste 900 Washington DC 20005-5701 E-mail: RHerzstein@milchev.com.

HESELTON, KENNETH EMERY, energy engineer; b. Corning N.Y., Nov. 17, 1943; s. Richard Linsmore and Dorothy Bertha (Schoonover) H.; m. Susan L. Benkert, July 4, 1965. BS in Marine Engring., USMMA, 1965. Registered profl. engr., Md., Pa., Del.; cert. energy mgr. Engr. Hercules Inc., Wilmington, Del., 1968-72, Power and Combustion, Inc., Balt., 1972-94, v.p., 1989-94. Pres. Md. Nat. Cert. Pipe Welding Bur., 1989-92. Office: KEH Energy Engring Baltimore MD 21237 E-mail: KHeselton@cs.com.

HESER, CHERYL J. library director; b. Iowa City, Mar. 14, 1948; d. Eugene W. and Myrtle A. Elliott; m. Douglas C. Heser, June 8, 1974; children: Clinton D., Anne J. Heser Robinson, Joshua R. BA, Ea. Mont. Coll., 1970, tchg. cert., 1972; postgrad., Western Mont. Coll., 1995. Tchr. Rosebud (Mont.) Schs., 1986—91, tchr., sch. libr., 1993—98; advt. mgr. Ind. Enterprise, Forsyth, Mont., 1991—93; dir. Rosebud County Libr., Forsyth, 1997—. Author: Lewis & Clark Activity Book, 2003. Judge speech and drama meets, Forsyth, 1997—; mem. Immaculate Conception Ch., Forsyth, 1986—. Mem.: Mountain Plains Libr. Assn., Mont. Libr. Assn. (dir. at large 1997—99, chair Lewis & Clark task force 1999—, Mountain Plains Libr. Assn. rep. 2000—, Media award 2002). Roman Catholic. Avocations: writing, music, backpacking. Office: Rosebud County Libr 201 N Ninth Ave Forsyth MT 59327

HESHMAT, HOOSHANG, manufacturing executive; b. Tabriz, Iran, Aug. 20, 1950; BS, Pa. State U., 1977; MS, Rensselaer Poly. Inst., 1979, PhD in Mech. Engring., 1988. With Reliance Electric Co.; co-founder, pres., tech. dir. Mohawk Innovative Tech., Inc. Co-author: (chpt.) Compressor Handbook; contbr. over 110 articles to profl. jours.; Patentee in field. Recipient Tech. Creativity award Mech. Tech. Inc., 1990; Thomas A. Edison Patent award, 2002. Fellow Soc. Tribologists and Lubrication Engrs./ASME (chmn. internat. joint conf. 1994, vice chmn. rsch. com. tribology, tribology divsn. exec. com., Wilbur Deutsch Meml. award 1983, Burt L. Newkirk award 1985, Capt. Alfred E. Hunt award 1993, Creative Rsch. award 1995, Al Sonntag award 1996, Thomas A. Edison Patent award 2002, Frank P. Bussick award 2003). Office: Mohawk Innovative Tech Inc 1037 Watervliet Shaker Rd Albany NY 12205-2033

HESLIN, CATHLEEN JANE, artist, designer, entrepreneur; b. Bklyn., Feb. 24, 1929; d. Charles Jenkins and Katherine (Bauer) Hunter; m. John Thomas Heslin, June 24, 1950. AA, Packer Collegiate Inst., Bklyn., 1950; postgrad., Duke U., 1952, Pratt Inst., 1952. Sr. artist, designer Klopman Mills, Rockleigh, N.J., 1966-72; free-lance designer, 1972-90; propr. Quilters Corner, Tappan, N.Y., 1978-90. Author: History of Rockleigh, N.J., 1648-1973, 1973, Old Order Amish-The People and Their Quilts, 1988; inventor Quilters Quarter measuring device. Councilwoman Borough of Rockleigh, 1973-85, 90-92, pres. coun., 1983-85, historian, 1973-90, chmn. anniversary dedication com., 1973, environ. com., 1974, action com., 1974-75, borough hall com., 1975, acquisition com., 1975, chmn. bicentennial com., 1974-76, chmn. fin. com., 1977-78, chmn. hist. adv. com., 1977-86, liaison to Bergen County hist. programs, 1978, pub. safety com., 1979-84, chmn. bldg. com., 1983-85, housing commn., 1984, Hist. Preservation Commn., 1987-90, ins. com., 1990, liaison to planning bd., 1990, designs for Rockleigh Commons; mem. Rockleigh Planning Bd., 1973, 87-89; Rep. mayoral nominee Borough of Rockleigh, 1988; founder Cathleen Heslin Found., 1990; trustee Abram Demaree Homestead, 1982-84; established Rockleigh Wildlife Sanctuary and Land Preserve. Recipient various certs. of appreciation. Mem. Tappantown Hist. Soc. (dir.), Soc. Archtl. Historians, Am. Soc. Planning Ofcls., Bergen County Hist. Soc. (trustee 1984-90), Historic Homes Assn. N.J. Achievements include being obtained State and Nat. Historic Dist. status for Borough of Rockleigh, 1976. Home and Office: PO Box 115 Northvale NJ 07647-0115

HESS, CHARLES EDWARD, environmental horticulture educator; b. Paterson, N.J., Dec. 20, 1931; s. Cornelius W. M. and Alice (Debruyn) H.; children: Mary, Carol, Nancy, John, Peter; m. Eva G. Carroad, Feb. 14, 1981. BS, Rutgers U., 1953; MS, Cornell U., 1954, PhD, 1957; DAgr (hon.), Purdue U., 1983; DSc (hon.), Delaware Valley Coll., Doylestown, Pa., 1992. From asst. prof. to prof. Purdue U., West Lafayette, Ind., 1958-65; rsch. prof., dept. chmn. Rutgers U., New Brunswick, N.J., 1966, assoc. dean, dir. N.J. Agrl. Exptl. Sta., 1970, acting dean Coll. Agrl. and Environ. Sci., 1971, dean Cook Coll., 1972-75; assoc. dir. Calif. Agrl. Exptl. Sta., 1975-89; asst. sec. sci. and edn. USDA, Washington, 1989-91; dean Coll. Agrl. and Environ. Scis. U. Calif., Davis, 1975-89, prof. dept. environ. horticulture, 1975-94; prof. emeritus, 1994—; dir. internat. programs Coll. Agrl. and Environ. Scis. U. Calif., Davis, 1992-98, spl. asst. to provost, 1994—2003. Cons. U.S. AID, 1965, Office Tech. Assessment, U.S. Congress, 1976-77; chmn. study team world food and nutrition study NAS, 1976; mem. Calif. State Bd. Food and Agr., 1984-89; mem. Nat. Sci. Bd., 1982-88, 92-98, vice-chmn., 1984-88; co-chmn. Joint Coun. USDA, 1987-91. Mem. West Lafayette Sch. Bd., Ind., 1963-65, sec., 1963, pres., 1964; mem. Gov.'s Commn. Blueprint for Agr., 1971-73; bd. dirs. Davis Sci. Ctr., 1992-94; trustee Internat. Svc. for Nat. Agrl. Rsch., The Hague, The Netherlands, 1992-98, bd. chmn., 1995-96. Mem. U.S. EPA (mem. biotech. sci. adv. com. 1992-96), AAAS (chmn. agriculture sect. 1989-90), Am. Soc. Hort. Sci. (pres. 1973), Internat. Plant Propagators Soc. (pres. 1973), Agrl. Rsch. Inst., Phi Beta Kappa, Sigma Xi, Alpha Zeta, Phi Kappa Phi. Office: U Calif Coll Agrl Environ Scis Dept Environ Horticulture Davis CA 95616 E-mail: cehess@ucdavis.edu.

HESS, CHARLES T. education educator; b. Cin., Nov. 21, 1940; s. Louis C. and Freida E. Hess; m. Anna L. Hess, Aug. 30, 1966; 1 child, Samuel T. BA, Wabash Coll., Crawfordsville, Ind., 1962; PhD, Ohio Univ., Athens, Ohio, 1967. Post doctoral Ohio Univ., Athens, Ohio, 1962—68, Fla. State Univ., Tallahassee, 1969; asst. prof. Univ. Maine, Orono, Maine, 1969—80; assoc. prof. Univ. Texas, Houston, 1980—81; prof. Univ. Maine, Orono, Maine, 1981—. Contbr. articles to profl. jour. Mem.: Health Physics Soc., Am. Physical Soc., Sigma XI. Home: 103 Spring St Orono ME 04469 Office: Univ Maine Dept Physics Bennett Hall Orono ME 04469

HESS, DALE ESHLEMAN, geneticist, educator; b. Shirati, Tanzania, June 12, 1954; s. Mahlon Murray and Mabel Eshleman Hess; m. Ursula Maria Hilbert, July 27, 1984; children: Markus Edgar, Hans-Martin, Karsten Adrian. BA, Millersville U., Pa., 1976; MSc, Purdue U., West Lafayette, Ind., 1984; PhD, Purdue U., 1989. Prin. scientist pathology I.C.R.I.S.A.T., Niamey, Niger, 1990—95, Bamako, Mali, 1996—2001; vis. asst. prof. Agronomy Dept., Purdue U., West Lafayette, Ind., 2001—. Editor books; contbr. Choir mem. Faith Presbyn. Ch., West Lafayette, Ind., 2001—03; Sun. sch. tchr. Bamako Christian Fellowship, Bamako, Mali, 1996—99; elder Internat. Evang. Ch., Niamey, Niger, 1990—95, choir mem., 1990—95; vol. biologist Mennonite Ctrl. Com., Ouagadougou, Burkina Faso, 1978—81. Recipient George D. Scarseth award, Agronomy Dept, Purdue U., 1988. Mem.: Internat. Found. for Sci., AAAS, Crop Sci. Soc. of Am., Am. Soc. of Agronomy, Am. Phytopathological Soc., Gamma Sigma Delta. Avocations: music, reading, photography, bicycling, stamp collecting. Office: Purdue University Dept Agronomy 1150 Lilly Hall West Lafayette IN 47907 Office Fax: 765-496-2926. E-mail: dhess@purdue.edu.

HESS, DARLA BAKERSMITH, cardiologist, educator; b. Valparaiso, Fla., June 4, 1953; d. James Barry and Irma Marie (Baker) Bakersmith; m. Leonard Wayne Hess, July 20, 1988; 1 child, Ever Marie. BS, Birmingham So. Coll., 1975; MD, Tulane U., 1979. Diplomate Am. Bd. Internal Medicine, Am. Bd. Cardiovascular Disease. Commd. ensign USNR, 1979, advanced through grades to lt. comdr., 1988; resident in internal medicine Portsmouth (Va.) Naval Hosp., 1979-82, cardiologist, head non-invasive cardiology, 1986-88; fellow in cardiology San Diego Naval Hosp., 1982-84; cardiologist, head med. officer in charge ICU Camp Lejeune (N.C.) Naval Hosp., 1984-85; asst. prof. medicine U. Miss. Med. Ctr., Jackson, 1988-91, asst. prof. ob/gyn., 1990-91; dir. noninvasive sect. cardiology, dir. fetal echocardiography U. Mo., Columbia, 1991—99, co-dir. Adult Cogenital Heart Disease Clinic, 1991—99, assoc. prof. medicine, assoc. prof. ob/gyn., 1998—2001. Author: (with others) Obstetrics and Gynecology Clinics, 1992, Clinical Problems in Obstetrics & Gynecology, 1993, General Medical Disorders During, 1991; co-editor: Fetal Echocardiography, 1999; contbr. articles to So. Med. Jour., Ob/Gyn. Clinics N.Am., Soc. Perinatal Obs., Jour. Reproductive Medicine, others. Fellow Am. Coll. Cardiology, Fellow Am. Heart Assn. (fellow stroke coun.), Fellow Am. Soc. Echocardiography; mem. Am. Assn. Nuclear Cardiology, Phi Beta Kappa, Alpha Omega Alpha. Republican. Episcopalian. Home: 7945 Springhouse Rd New Tripoli PA 18066

HESS, DAVID CHARLES, neurologist, educator; b. Summit, N.J., Dec. 17, 1956; s. Raymond Charles and Eleanor Hanson Hess; m. Diane Lynn DeGrandis, Oct. 12, 1984; children: Matthew Charles, Sara Alexandra children: Lisa Alexandra, Daniel Louis. MD, U. Md., Balt., 1983; student, Johns Hopkins U., 1979. Bd. cert. Am. Bd. Psychiatry and Neurology, 1990, Am. Bd. Internal Medicine. Resident neurology Med. Coll. Ga., prof., chmn. dept. neurology, 2001—. Med. dir. Neurosci. Ctr. Med. Coll. Ga., Augusta, 2001—. Fellow: ACP. Roman Catholic. Home: 434 Wexford Ct Martinez GA 30907 Office: Dept Neurology Med Coll Ga Augusta GA 30912 Home Fax: 706-721-7619. Personal E-mail: dhess@mail.mcg.edu. E-mail: dhess@neuro.mcg.edu.

HESS, DAVID GRAHAM, engineering administrator; b. Phila., June 20, 1957; s. Carleton and Irene Florence (Ehrle) H.; m. Karen Denise Alke, Apr. 21, 1984; children: Laura Christine, Sarah Elizabeth, Kayla Rose. BS in Engring., Drexel U., 1980; postgrad., John Hopkins U., 1982-83, U. So. Calif., 1984-85. Metallurgist Howmet Aluminum Corp, Lancaster, Pa., 1976-80; composites engr. Martin Marietta Aerospace, Denver, 1980-81, program mgr. Balt., 1981-82, liaison engr., 1982-83; mantech sr. engr. Northrop Corp., Pico Rivera, Calif., 1983-84, mfg. tech. specialist, 1984-86, quality assurance specialist, 1986, mgr. div. advanced systems and quality assurance R & D, 1986-88; mfg. engr., mgr. Rayproof Absorber Products, Amesbury, Mass., 1988-90; program mgr. BF Goodrich Aerospace, Marlboro, Mass., 1991-96; owner Hess Integrated Svcs. Co., Atkinson, N.H., 1996—; engring. mgr. ARC Technologies, Inc., 1996—. Cons. Aero Visions Inc., Irvine, Calif., 1986-87, Rosene Design Inc., Fountain Valley, Calif., 1987—. Contbr. Composites Engineering, 1987; inventor in field. Home donor Life Support for Unwed Mothers, Anaheim, Calif., 1987. Recipient Kerr Cup award Schuylkill Navy, Phila., 1980. Mem. Am. Soc. for Metals, Soc. for Advancement Materials and Process Engrs. Republican. Avocations: scuba diving, computers, photography, gardening, fine woodworking. Home and Office: 25 Summit Dr Atkinson NH 03811-2339

HESS, DENNIS JOHN, investment banker; b. Manila, July 7, 1940; s. Carl and Anna (Harris) H.; m. Marilyn Golchert, July 7, 1977; children: Whitney, Christine, Craig. BS, U. Calif., Berkeley, 1962. With Merrill Lynch & Co., 1969—, v.p., 1977-80; chmn. bd., chief exec. officer Merrill Lynch, Hubbard, Inc., N.Y.C., 1980—; dir. diversified fin. svcs. Merrill Lynch, Pierce, Fenner & Smith, 1985-2000; pres., chief oper. officer ML Realty, 1983-2000; chmn., CEO, ML Equity Mgmt. Corp., 1984-2000, Paine Webber Life Ins. Co.; chmn. bd. Tandem Fin. Corp.; CEO, Merrill Lynch Ins. Group, 1986-2000; pres. DJH, Inc., Greenwich, Conn.; ret. Bd. dirs. United First Mortgage Corp., M.L. Huntoon Paige, Inc., MLH Puerto, SA, Family Life Ins. Co., DJH, Inc.; exec. v.p. Payne Webber Inc.; chmn., CEO Paine Webber Life Ins. Co. Served to 1st lt. USAF, 1962-66. Mem. Greenwich Country Club. Republican. Roman Catholic.

HESS, DENNIS WILLIAM, chemical engineering educator; b. Reading, Pa., Mar. 1, 1947; s. John William and Dorothy E. (Miller) H.; m. Patricia Ruth Weidner, June 1, 1968; children: Amy R., Sarah E. BS in Chemistry, Albright Coll., 1968; MS in Phys. Chemistry, Lehigh U., 1970, PhD in Phys. Chemistry, 1973. Staff researcher Fairchild Semiconductor, Palo Alto, Calif., 1973-77; from asst. prof. to prof. chem. engring. U. Calif., Berkeley, 1977-91; prin. investigator Materials and Molecular Research div. Lawrence Berkeley Lab., 1978-84, Ctr. for Adv. Materials, Lawrence Berkeley Lab., 1983-85; asst. dean Coll. Chemistry U. Calif., Berkeley, 1982-87; vice chmn. dept. chem. engring U. Calif., Berkeley, 1988-91; chmn. dept. chem. engring. Lehigh U., Bethlehem, Pa., 1991-96; William W. LaRoche Jr. prof. chem. engring. Ga. Inst. Tech., Atlanta, 1996—. Contbr. articles to profl. jours. Mem. The Electrochem. Soc. (pres. 1996-97). Office: Ga Tech Sch Chem Engring 311 Ferst Dr Atlanta GA 30332-0100 E-mail: dennis.hess@che.gatech.edu.

HESS, EMERSON GARFIELD, lawyer; b. Pitts., Nov. 13, 1914; AB, Bethany Coll., 1936; JD, U. Pitts., 1939. Bar: Pa. 1940. Sr. ptnr. Hess, Reich, Georgiades, Wile & Homyak and predecessor firm Emerson G. Hess & Assocs., Pitts., 1940-92; of counsel DeMarco & Assocs., Pitts., 1992—. Solicitor Scott Twp. Sch. Bd., 1958-65; legal counsel Judiciary com. Pa. Ho. of Reps., 1967-69; solicitor Scott Twp., 1968-69, Crafton Borough, 1974-78, Authority for Improvements in Municipalities of Allegheny County, 1977-80. Bd. dirs. Golden Triangle YMCA, Pitts., 1945—, WQED Ednl. TV, Pitts., 1952-68; pres., dir. Civil Light Opera Assn., Pitts., 1967-68; mem. internat. com. YMCA World Svc., N.Y.C., 1968-78; trustee, chmn. Cen. Christian Ch., Pitts., 1962-63; pres. Anesthesia and Resuscitation Found., Pitts., 1964-88, Pa. Med. Rsch. Found., 1960-88. Mem. ABA, Pa. Bar Assn., Allegheny County Bar Assn. Home: 43 Robin Hill Dr Mc Kees Rocks PA 15136-1238 Office: DeMarco & Assocs 946 Gulf Tower 707 Grant St Pittsburgh PA 15219-1908

HESS, EVELYN VICTORINE (MRS. MICHAEL HOWETT), medical educator; b. Dublin, Nov. 8, 1926; arrived in U.S., 1960, naturalized, 1965; d. Ernest Joseph and Mary (Hawkins) H.; m. Michael Howett, Apr. 27, 1954. MB, B.Ch, BAO, U. Coll., Dublin, 1949; MD, Univ. Coll., Dublin, 1980. Intern West Middlesex Hosp., London, Eng., 1950; resident Clare Hall Hosp., London, 1951-53, Royal Free Hosp. and Med. Sch., London, 1954-57; rsch. fellow in epidemiology of Tb Royal Free Med. Sch., London, 1955; asst. prof. internal medicine U. Tex. Southwestern Med. Sch., 1960-64; assoc. prof. dept. medicine U. Cin. Coll. Medicine, 1964-69, McDonald prof. medicine, 1969—, dir. div. immunology, 1964-95. Sr. investigator Arthritis and Rheumatism Found., 1963-68; attending physician Univ. Hosp., VA Hosp.; cons. Children's Hosp., Cin., 1967—, Jewish Hosp., Cin., 1968—; mem. various coms., mem. nat. adv. coun. NIH; mem. various coms. FDA, Cin. Bd. Health. Contbr. articles on immunology, rheumatic diseases to jours., chpts. to books. Active Nat. Pks. Assn., Smithsonian Instn., others. Recipient Arthritis Found. award, 1973, 78, 83, Am. Lupus Soc. award, 1979, Am. Acad. Family Practice award, 1980, award for AIDS work State of Ohio, 1989, Spirit of Am. Women award, 1989, Daniel Drake medal U. Cin., 2001; travel fellow Royal Free Med. Sch., Scandinavia, 1956, Empire Rheumatism Coun., 1958-59. Master ACP (gov. Ohio chpt. 1999-2003, Master Tchr. award 1995); fellow AAAS, Am. Acad. Allergy, Royal Soc. Medicine, ACR (master, Disting. Rheumatologist award 1996); mem. Heberden Soc., Am. Coll. Rheumatology, Pan-Am. League Assns. for Rheumatology (Gold medal), Ctrl. Soc. Clin. Rsch., Am. Fedn. Clin. Rsch., Am. Assn. Immunologists, Am. Soc. Nephrology, Am. Soc. Clin. Pharmacology and Therapeutics, Transplantation Soc., N.Y. Acad. Scis., Soc. Exptl. Biology and Medicine, Rheumatological Soc. Colombia (hon.), Rheumatological Soc. Peru (hon.), Rheumatological Soc. Italy (hon.), Clin. Immunol. Soc. Japan (hon.), Cuban Soc. Rheumatology (hon.), Alpha Omega Alpha. Home: 2916 Grandin Rd Cincinnati OH 45208-3418 Office: U Cin Med Ctr ML 563 ML 563 MSB Cincinnati OH 45267-0001 E-mail: hessev@email.uc.edu.

HESS, FREDERICK J. lawyer; b. Highland, Ill., Sept. 22, 1941; s. Fred and Matilda (Maiden) H.; m. Mary V. Menkhus, Nov. 13, 1976; children—Frederick, M. Elizabeth. BS in Polit. Sci. and History, St. Louis U., 1963; JD, Washburn Sch. Law, Topeka, 1971. Bar: Kans. 1971, Ill. 1975, U.S. Supreme Ct. 1975, D.C. 1977, U.S. Tax Ct. 1977. Asst. U.S. atty. Dept. Justice, East St. Louis, Ill., 1971-73, 1st asst. U.S. atty., 1973-76; ct. appt. U.S. Atty. E. Dist. of Ill., 1977; ptnr. Stiehl & Hess, Belleville, Ill., 1977-82; U.S. atty. U.S. Dist. Ct. (so. dist.) Ill., East St. Louis, 1982-93; pvt. practice Lewis Rice & Fingersh, Belleville, 1993—. Bd. dirs., past pres. Nat. Assn. Former U.S. Attys., 1996; part-time judge Ill. Ct. of Claims, 1997—. Served to capt. USAF, 1964-68. Fellow ABA Found., ISBA Found., Ill. Bar Assn., Ill. Bar Found.; mem. Kans. Bar Assn., D.C. Bar Assn., Tamarac Golf Club (Shilo, Ill.), Stone Wolf Club (Fairview Heights, Ill.). Republican. Office: Lewis Rice & Fingersh 325 S High St Belleville IL 62220-2116

HESS, FREDERICK SCOTT, artist; b. Balt., July 12, 1955; s. Charles Stevens and Katherine Ruth Hess; m. Gita Tabatabai, Dec. 28, 1989; children: Ava Katarina, Atiyeh Mehri. BS, U. Wis., 1977; postgrad., Vienna Acad. Fine Art, 1979-84. Artist in residence Bahman Cultural House, Tehran, Iran, 1992, Cité Internat. des Arts, Paris, 1993. Solo exhibitions include Gallery Herzog, Vienna, Austria, 1979, Galerie im Tabak Museum, Vienna, Austria, 1982, Ovsey Gallery, L.A., Calif., 1985, 86, 88, 89, 90, 92, 94, U. So. Calif. Fisher Art Gallery, 1987-88, Santa Clara U. de Saisset Mus., Santa Clara, Calif., 1987-88, Mt. San Jacinto Coll., San Jacinto, Calif., 1989, Fresno (Calif.) Art Mus., Calif., 1991, Underground Exhibition, Tehran, Iran, 1993, Art Inst. So. Calif., Laguna Beach, 1996, Mt. S. Antonio Coll. Walnut, Calif., 1997, Hackett-Freedman Gallery, San Francisco, 1999, Orange County Mus. Art, Newport Beach, 2001, Loyola-Marymount U., L.A., 2002; exhibited in group shows at Taipei (Taiwan) Fine Arts Mus., 1987, U. So. Calif., L.A., 1987-88, Laguna Art Mus., Laguna Beach, Calif., 1988, Henry Art Gallery, U. Washington, Seattle, 1988, Fresno (Calif.) Art Mus., 1988-89, Flint (Mich.) Inst. Art, 1991, San Diego Mus. Art, 1991, Triton Mus., Santa Clara, Calif., 1992, Oakland (Calif.) Mus., 1992, Flint (Mich.) Inst. Art, 1992, Nev. Inst. Contemporary Art, Las Vegas, 1995, L.A. County Mus. Art, 1997, Armory Ctr. for Arts, Pasadena, 1997, Laband Art Gallery, L.A., 1998, Frye Art Mus., Seattle, 2000. Recipient Theodor Koerner award Austrian Min. Culture, Vienna, 1981, WESTAF award Nat. Endowment for the Arts, 1990; fellow J. Paul Getty Trust, 1991, Nat. Endowment for the Arts, 1991. Mem. The Drawing Group. Avocations: writing, polo, sailing. Address: 1830 Lake Shore Ave Los Angeles CA 90026-1716 E-mail: shess@artcenter.edu.

HESS, GEORGE FRANKLIN, II, lawyer; b. Oak Park, Ill., May 13, 1939; s. Franklin Edward and Carol (Hackman) H.; m. Diane Ricci, Aug. 9, 1974; 1 child, Franklin Edward. BS in Bus., Colo. State U., 1962; JD, Suffolk U., 1970; LLM, Boston U., 1973. Bar: Pa. 1971, Fla. 1973, U.S. Tax Ct. 1974, U.S. Dist. Ct. (so. dist.) Fla. 1975. Assoc. Hart, Childs, Hepburn, Ross & Putnam, Phila., 1970-72; instr. Suffolk U. Law Sch., Boston, 1973-74; ptnr. Henry, Hess & Hoines, Ft. Lauderdale, Fla., 1974-79, Mousaw, Vigdor, Reeves & Hess, Ft. Lauderdale, Fla., 1979-94; pvt. practice Ft. Lauderdale, Fla., 1995—. Bd. dirs. Childrens Home Soc., Ft. Lauderdale, 1985-89, Nadeau Charitable Found., 1985-2000; trustee endowment fund All Sts. Ch., 1995—. Lt. USNR, 1963-66.

Mem. ABA, SAR, Fla. Bar Assn., Broward County Bar Assn., Lauderdale Yacht Club, USN League, Phi Alpha Delta. Episcopalian. Home: 2524 Castilla Is Fort Lauderdale FL 33301-1505 Office: 333 N New River Dr E Fort Lauderdale FL 33301-2241

HESS, GEORGE PAUL, biochemist, educator; b. Vienna; came to U.S., 1938; s. Henry Steven Hess and Edith Muller; children: Alvis, Peter, Richard, Paul, David. AB, U. Calif., Berkeley, 1951, PhD, 1953. Postdoctoral fellow MIT, 1953—55, Nat. Infantile Paralysis, 1953-55; instr. Cornell Med. Sch., 1955; asst. prof. biochemistry Cornell U., Ithaca, N.Y., 1956-60, assoc. prof., 1960-64, prof., 1964—. Vis. fellow chemistry Yale U., 1960, U.S. Dept. State Cultural Exchange prof. to Europe, 1963, 70; vis. prof. biophysics U. Pa., Phila., 1964-65, biochemistry U. Hawaii, Honolulu, Jan. 1966, chemistry U. Ariz., Tucson, Feb. 1968, biology MIT, 1990; lectr. Naito Found., Japan, 1988. Mem. Biochemistry Editl. Adv. Bd.; adv. bd. Ctr. Molecular and Behavioral Neuroscis., Universidad del Caribe Ctr., P.R. With U.S. Army, 1945-47. Recipient Alexander von Humboldt Sr. Scientist award U. Konstanz, 1982, Outstanding Educator Recognition award Cornell Merrill Presdl. scholar, 1994, 97, Wellcome vis. professorship, 1998; Guggenheim fellow, sr. Fulbright grantee Max-Planck-Inst. fur physikalische Chemie, 1962-63; spl. NIH fellow Med. Rsch. Coun. Lab Molecular Biology, 1969-70; Churchill Coll. U. Cambridge vis. fellow 1969-70; NIH Nat. Inst. of Neurol. Diseases and Stroke Fogarty scholar, 1999-2000. Fellow AAAs, Am. Acad. Microbiology; mem. NAS, Am. Soc. Cell Biol.; Am. Chem. Soc., Biophys. Soc., Fedn. Am. Soc. of Exptl. Biologists, N.Y. Acad. Scis., Soc. Neurosci., Protein Soc. Home: 123 Heights Ct Ithaca NY 14850-2450 Office: Cornell Univ 216 Biotechnology Bldg Ithaca NY 14853-2703 E-mail: gph2@cornell.edu.

HESS, H. OBER, lawyer, director; b. Royersford, Pa., Nov. 8, 1912; s. Samuel Harley and Annamae (Wenger) H.; m. Dolores Groke, May 18, 1940; children: Antonine (Mrs. Joseph J. Gal), Roberta (Mrs. Edward S. Trippe), Liesa (Mrs. Arleigh P. Helfer, Jr.), Kristina (Mrs. Charles H. Bonner). AB, Ursinus Coll., 1933, LL.D. (hon.), 1979; LL.B., Harvard U., 1936; LL.D. (hon.), Muhlenberg Coll., 1964; D.F.A. (hon.), Phila. Coll. Art, 1981. Of counsel to Ballard, Spahr, Andrews & Ingersoll, Phila. Editor: Fiduciary Rev. monthly, The Nature of a Humane Society, 1976. Former mem. exec. coun. Luth. Ch. in Am.; trustee Lankenau Hosp., Phila. U. of the Arts; former chmn. Mary J. Drexel Home, Lankenau Med. Rsch. Ctr.; former bd. dirs., sec. Phila. Orch. Assn., Acad. Music Phila.; former mem. Harvard Overseers Com. to Visit Law Sch.; former nat. chmn. Harvard Law Sch. Fund. Mem. ABA, Pa., Phila., Montgomery County bar assns., Harvard Law Sch. Assn. Clubs: Philadelphia, Union League, Philadelphia Country (Phila.). Home: 1400 Waverly Rd Muirfield 244 Gladwyne PA 19035-1254 Office: 1735 Market St Fl 51 Philadelphia PA 19103-7501

HESS, JOHN, education educator, counselor; b. Hume, Mo., Mar. 13, 1947; s. John D. and Mary L. Hess; m. Gloria D. Stocklaufer; 1 child, Misty D. BA, Pittsburg (Kans.) U., 1969, MS, 1970, EdS, 1976. Instr. psychology Highland (Kans.) C.C., 1970—91, dir career info. ctr., 1980—91; chair social sci. divsn. Ozarks Tech. C.C., Springfield, Mo., 1995—99, instr. psychology, 1991—2003. Bd. dirs. CAP, Horton, Tex., 1978—84. Bd. dirs. CAP, Horton, Kans., 1978—84. Recipient Gov.'s award for Excellence in Tchg., State of Mo., 1999, Excellence in Edn. award, 1999—2000, NISOD Excellence award, Austin, Tex., 2000. Mem.: ACA, Psychology Tchrs. in the C.C., Am. Psychol. Soc. Avocation: travel. Office: Ozarks Tech CC 1020 E Brower PO Box 5958 Springfield MO 65801

HESS, JOHN B. oil industry executive; Chmn., CEO Amerada Hess Corp., N.Y.C., 1995—. Office: Amerada Hess Corp 1185 Avenue Of The Americas New York NY 10036-2601

HESS, JOHN WARREN, professional society administrator; b. Lancaster, Pa., May 6, 1947; s. John Warren and Barbara Kathryn (Spencer) H.; m. Letitia Jean Schrantz, Mar. 20, 1971; children: Nathan James, Joshua Kyle. BS in Geol. Scis., Pa. State U., 1969, PhD in Geology, 1974. Asst. rsch. prof. water resources ctr. Desert Rsch. Inst., Las Vegas, Nev., 1974-78, assoc. rsch. prof., 1978-86, rsch. prof., 1985—2001, dir. environ. isotope lab., 1981-87, dep. dir., 1987-89, exec. dir., 1989-2000, interim v.p. rsch., 1994-95, v.p. acad. affairs, 1995—2001, congrl. fellow, 2000—01; exec. dir. Geol. Soc. Am., Boulder, Colo., 2001—. Chmn. bd. dirs. Karst Waters Inst., Charlestown, W.Va. Contbr. over 85 articles to profl. jours. Adult leader Boy Scouts Am., Las Vegas, 1978—2001, Boulder, Colo., 2002—. Hon. Rsch. fellow U. Glasgow, Scotland, 1980-81; Centennial fellow Coll. Earth and Mineral Scis., Pa. State U. Fellow Geol. Soc. Am. (2nd vice chmn. 1993-94, 1st vice chmn. 1994-95, chair 1995-96), Nat. Speleological Soc.; mem. AAAS, Am. Geophys. Union, Internat. Assn. Hydrogeologists, Geochem. Soc. Office: Geol Soc Am 3300 Penrose Pl Boulder CO 80301

HESS, KARL, electrical and computer engineering educator; b. Trumau, Austria, June 20, 1945; came to U.S. 1977; naturalized 1988; s. Karl Joseph and Gertrude (Resch) H.; m. Sylvia Horvath, Sept. 1967; children: Ursula, Karl PhD, U. Vienna, Austria, 1970. Rsch. asst. U. Vienna, 1969-71, asst. prof., 1971-77, univ. lectr., 1977; vis. assoc. prof. U. Ill., Urbana, 1977-80, prof. elec. and computer engring., 1988—, adj. prof. supercomputing applications, 1990—, Swanlund Endowed chair, 1996—, prof. physics. Contbr. articles to profl. jours.; patentee in field Univ. scholar U. Ill., 1982-83; Fulbright scholar, 1973-74. Fellow AAAS, IEEE (J.J. Ebers award 1994, David Sarnoff field award 1995, H. Welker Meml. medal 2001), NAS, NAE, Am. Phys. Soc., Am. Acad. Arts and Scis. Avocations: classical music, chess. Home: 1805 Bentbrook Dr Champaign IL 61822-9220 Office: U Ill Beckman Inst 405 N Mathews Ave Urbana IL 61801-2325 E-mail: k-hess@uiuc.edu.

HESS, LEONARD WAYNE, obstetrician gynecologist, perinatologist; b. Richlands, Va., Nov. 23, 1949; s. Ralph Eugene and Lucille Cindy (Kennedy) H.; m. Sarah Mahala Leedy, Nov. 27, 1969 (div. July 1988); children: Gregory Scott, Lauren Ashley; m. Darla Irma Bakersmith, July 20, 1988; 1 child, Ever Marie. BSChemE, Va. Poly. Inst., 1973; MD, Va. Commonwealth U., 1977. Diplomate Nat. Bd. Med. Examiners, Am. Bd. Ob-Gyn., also sub.-bd. Maternal-Fetal Medicine. Intern U.S. Naval Hosp., Portsmouth, Va., 1977-78, resident in ob-gyn., 1978-81; fellow in maternal-fetal medicine Naval Med. Command, Walter Reed Army Med. Ctr., Washington and Bethesda, 1981-83; staff dept. ob-gyn. U. Health Scis., Bethesda, 1981-85; dept. ob-gyn. U.S. Naval Hosp., Portsmouth, 1985-87; comdr. USNR, 1987-88; asst. prof. dept. ob-gyn. U. Miss. Med. Ctr., Jackson, 1987-91; assoc. prof. ob-gyn. U. Mo. Med. Ctr., Columbia, 1991-96, head obstetrics and maternal-fetal medicine, 1991-96, prof., chmn. ob-gyn., 1996—2001; chmn. ob-gyn. Lehigh Valley Hosp. and Health Network, 2001—; prof. ob/gyn. Pa. State U. Sch. Medicine. Mem. Med. Ethics Com., U.S. Naval Hosp., Portsmouth, 1985-87; mem. Patient Care Com., U. Miss. Med. Ctr., Jackson, 1988-91, Infection Control Com., 1988-91; bd. examiner Am. Bd. Ob-Gyn., 1997—. Author: Fetal Echocardiography, 1999; cons. editor Obstetrics and Gynecology, 1988—, Am. Jour. Obstetrics and Gynecology, 1988—, Am. Jour. Med. Genetics, 1989—; contbr. numerous articles to profl. jours. Mem. AMA, USP (ob-gyn. adv. panel 1995-2001), Am. Coll. Obstetricians and Gynecologists, Soc. Perinatal Obstetricians, Am. Inst. Ultrasound in Medicine, Assn. Profs. Gynecology and Obstetrics, Cen. Assn. Obstetricians and Gynecologists, Am. Soc. Human Genetics, So. Med. Assn., Winifred L. Wiser Soc., Miss. State Obstet. and Gynecol. Soc., Cen. Med. Soc., Gynecol. Soc., Med. Soc. Va., Portsmouth Acad. Medicine, Med. and Surgical Soc. of Md., Miss. State Med. Assn., Assn. Mil. Surgeons, Miss. Perinatal Assn., So. Perinatal Assn. Republican. Episcopalian. Office: Lehigh Valley Hosp 17th and Chew Sts Allentown PA 18105

HESS, MARCIA WANDA, retired educator; b. Cin., Mar. 15, 1934; d. Edward Frederick Lipka and Rose (Wirtle) Lipka Stanley; m. Edward Emanuel Grenier, Aug. 9, 1952 (div.); m. Thomas Benton Hess, Mar. 25, 1960; children: Kathleen Ann, Cynthia Jean, Thomas Allen. Grad. high sch., Cin. Instr. asst. Cin. Pub. Schs., 1970-95, also mem. staff desegregation workshop and unified K-12 reading communication arts program staff tng. com.; ret., 1995. Contbr. tchr.-instr. asst. handbook, instr. asst. tng. film. Mem. Winton Place Vets of World War II Women's Aux. (pres. 1982-84, bd. dirs. 1982-86, 89-91, v.p. 1997-99). Republican. Roman Catholic. Avocations: travel, reading. collecting first editions, needlepoint, photography. Home: 157 Palisades Pt Apt 4 Cincinnati OH 45238-5660

HESS, MARGARET JOHNSTON, religious writer, educator; b. Ames, Iowa, Feb. 22, 1915; d. Howard Wright and Jane Edith (Stevenson) Johnston; m. Bartlett Leonard Hess, July 31, 1937; children: Daniel, Deborah, John, Janet. BA, Coe Coll., 1937. Bible tchr. Cmty. Bible Classes, Ward Presbyn. Ch., Livonia, Mich., 1959-96, Christ Ch. Cranbrook (Episcopalian), Bloomfield Hills, Mich., 1980-93, Luth. Ch. of the Redeemer, Birmingham, Mich., 1993-99. Co-author: (with B.L. Hess) How to Have a Giving Church, 1974, The Power of a Loving Church, 1977, How Does Your Marriage Grow?, 1983, Never Say Old, 1984; author: Love Knows No Barriers, 1979, Esther: Courage in Crisis, 1980, Unconventional Women, 1981, The Triumph of Love, 1987; contbr. articles to religioous jours. Home: 15191 Ford Rd Apt 302 Dearborn MI 48126-4696 *A lifetime of teaching the Bible, mainly to women, has shown me how it meets people's needs, in the home, in the work place, in the world.*

HESS, MARILYN ANN, state legislator; m. Dennis J. Hess; children: Christine, Craig. AA, NYU, 1977; BBA in Mgmt. cum laude, Pace U., 1980. Assoc. Merrill Lynch, N.Y.C., 1972-77; home improvement contractor Conn., 1982-90; mem. Conn. Ho. of Reps., 1993-2001; rep. 150th Assembly Dist., Conn., 1993—2001. Dir. Rep. Town Com., 1989—2001; mem. Conn. Reps. for Choice, 1992—, Rep. Roundtable of Greenwich, 1993—2001, Amb. Roundtable, 1994—2001; chmn. Conn. Internat. Trade Coun., 1995—2001. Organizer pack 516 Boy Scouts Am., N.Y.C., 1976; alt. Greenwich Planning and Zoning Commn., 1990—93; bd. dirs. Friends of the Byram Shubert Libr., 1989—93; founding trustee Byram Scholarship Fund, 1991—; bd. dirs. YMCA, Greenwich, 1997—; fund raiser, chmn. Lewisboro Neighbor's Club, South Salem, 1979; sec. Ridgefield Hist. Dist. Commn., 1984—85, Greenwich Hist. Dist. Commn., Greenwich, 1988—90; del. Parents Together, 1980; underwriting com. Bruce Mus. Ball, 1990—91; co-founder Byram River Watershed Alliance, 1995—. Named Mother of the Yr., Town and Village Newspaper, 1974. Home: 660 Lake Ave Greenwich CT 06830-3854

HESS, P. GREGORY, lawyer; b. Wheeling, W.Va., Sept. 15, 1946; s. Philip Tilman and Virginia Lamberton (Jackson) H.; m. Susan Marion Kyff, Aug. 16, 1969; children: Philip Andrew, Peter Gregory, Michael Trevor, Aimee Suzanne. AB, Princeton U., 1968; JD, Yale U., 1971; LLM in Taxation, NYU, 1976. Bar: N.Y. 1972, Fla. 1976. Assoc. Breed, Abbott and Morgan, N.Y.C., 1971-73; ptnr. Williamson and Green, N.Y.C., 1973-76, Williamson and Hess, N.Y.C., 1976-80; of counsel Christy & Viener, N.Y.C., 1980, ptnr., 1980-98, Salans, N.Y.C., 1999—2002, Schiff Hardin & Waite, N.Y.C., 2002—. Bd. dirs. Barr and Barr, Inc., N.Y.C. Trustee N.Y. Sch. for Deaf, White Plains, 1982—, pres., 1990-93, chmn., 1993-2002; bd. dirs. Ruby Bridges Found., Inc., 2001—, treas., 2001—; bd. dirs. Pro Mujer, Inc., 2001—, sec., 2002—; trustee Princeton (N.J.) Campus Club, 1972-97, NTID Found., Rochester, N.Y., 1999—; bd. dirs. Greater Westchester Youth Orchs. Assn., Inc., Millwood, N.Y., 1986-91, chmn., 1988-91; bd. dirs., v.p. Westchester Found. for the Deaf, Inc., Hawthorne, N.Y., 1997-2003. Mem. Princeton Club N.Y. Home: 47 Quaker Bridge Rd Ossining NY 10562-1624 Office: Schiff Hardin & Waite 623 5th Ave NW New York NY 10022 Business E-Mail: ghess@schiffhardin.com.

HESS, PATRICK HENRY, chemist, researcher; b. Albia, Iowa, Aug. 6, 1931; s. John Henry and Mary Ellen (Judge) H.; m. Ann Marie Malone, June 6, 1959; children: Michelle, Maria, Margaret, Catherine, John. BS in Chemistry, U. Iowa, 1953; MS in Organic Chemistry, U. Nebr., 1958, PhD in Organic Chemistry, 1960. Chemist Iowa State Hygienic Labs., 1953-54; teaching asst. U. Nebr., 1956-57, rsch. asst., 1957-58, rsch. fellow, 1958-60; rsch. chemist Chevron Research Co., Richmond, Calif., 1960-64, Chevron Oil Field Rsch. Co., La Habra, Calif., 1964-65; sr. rsch. chemist Chevron Oil Field Research Co., La Habra, Calif., 1965-69, sr. rsch. assoc., 1969-92; ret., 1992. Rsch. group supr. Chevron Corp. Contbr. articles to profl. jours.; patentee crude oil recovery. Active youth sports PTA. Served with USAF, 1954-55. Rsch. fellow 3-M, 1958-59, Monsanto, 1959-60. Mem. Am. Chem. Soc., Soc. Petroleum Engrs., Sigma Xi, Alpha Chi Sigma, Alpha Tau Omega Republican. Roman Catholic. Home: 12463 Jeremiah Dr Auburn CA 95603-9051 *Retirement is great - so long as one doesn't become too retired.*

HESS, RICHARD CHRISTIAN, JR., obstetrician/gynecologist, educator; b. Bethlehem, Pa., June 21, 1943; MD, Johns Hopkins U., 1967. Diplomate Am. Bd. Ob Gyn. Intern Cleve. Metro Gen. Hosp., 1967-68; resident ob-gyn U. Wash. Hosp., Seattle, 1968-72; ob-gyn USN, Keflavik, Iceland, 1972-74, Fairbanks (Alaska) Meml. Hosp., 1974—. Clin. instr. U. Wash., 1978—. Fellow Am. Coll. Ob-Gyn; mem. AMA, Alaska Med. Assn. Office: Tanana Valley Med-Surg Group 1001 Noble St Fairbanks AK 99701-4978 E-mail: richard.hess@acsalaska.net.

HESS, RONALD ANDREW, aerospace engineer, educator; b. Norwalk, Ohio, Mar. 12, 1942; s. Robert Andrew and Catherine Ann (Caruso) H.; m. Connaught Ann McCormack, Sept. 7, 1967; children: Christian Anthony, Catherine Ann. BS in Aerospace Engring., U. Cin., 1965, MS in Aerospace Engring., 1967, PhD in Aerospace Engring., 1970. Registered profl. engr., Calif. Asst. prof. dept. aero. Naval Postgrad. Sch., Monterey, Calif., 1970-76; rsch. scientist NASA Ames Rsch. Ctr., Moffet Field, Calif., 1976-82; assoc. prof. dept. mech., aero. and materials engring. U. Calif., Davis, 1982-84, prof., 1984—, vice chmn. dept., 1998—. Assoc. editor Jour. Aircraft, 1977—; contbr. over 70 articles to profl. jours. Mem. AIAA (assoc. fellow, tech. com. guidance navigation and control 1984-86, tech. com. atmospheric flight mechanics 1988-90, Mechanics and Control of Flight award 2000), IEEE (sr.), Systems, Man and Cybernetics Soc. (v.p. 1989-91, chmn. manual control tech. com. 1986-2003, assoc. editor IEEE Transactions Systems, Man and Cybernetics 1979—, Jour. Aero. Engring. 1998—), Sigma Xi, Tau Beta Pi. Achievements include rsch. on developing models of human pilot behavior, aircraft control system design, aircraft handling qualities assessment. Office: Mech and Aero Engring Univ Calif Davis CA 95616 E-mail: rahess@ucdavis.edu.

HESS, SHARON MARIE, computer programmer; b. Appleton, Wis., Aug. 28, 1959; d. John Nicholas and Marjorie Ann Kramer; m. Mark Eric Hess, May 16, 1987; children: Megan, Rachel, Eric. AAS in Data Processing, Fox Valley Tech. Inst., Appleton, 1980; BBA and Computer Sci., Lakeland Coll., Sheboygan, Wis., 1989. Analyst, programmer SECURA Ins., Appleton, 1980—. Mem.: Wis. Assn. Bus. Profls. Am. (pres. 1993—94, sec.-treas. 1995—2001, pres.-elect 2001—02, pres. 2002—). Avocations: camping, 4-h. Office: SECURA Ins 2401 S Memorial Dr Appleton WI 54915-1406

HESS, SIDNEY J., JR., lawyer; b. Chgo., June 26, 1910; s. Sidney J. and Alma (Katz) Hess; m. Jacqueline Engelhardt, Aug. 28, 1948; children: Karen E. Hess Freeman, Lori Hess Pleiss. PhB, U. Chgo., 1930, JD, 1932. Bar: Ill. 1932. Practiced in, Chgo., 1932—; mem. firm Aaron, Schimberg & Hess, 1933—84, D'Ancona & Pflaum, 1985—. Bd. dirs., legal counsel Jewish Fedn. of Met. Chgo., 1968-95, v.p., 1972-74, pres., 1974-76; dir., legal counsel Jewish United Fund Met. Chgo., 1971-95, pres., 1974-76; legal counsel Jewish Welfare Fund Met. Chgo., 1969-73; bd. dirs. S. Silberman & Sons, Chgo. Metallic Products, Inc., Vienna Sausage Mfg. Co. Mem. exec. com. Anti-Defamation League, 1954-57, HIAS, 1974-90; mem. nat. devel. coun., aims com., citizens bd. U. Chgo.; bd. dirs. Schwab Rehab. Hosp., 1954-65, pres., 1959-64; trustee Michael Reese Founds., 1991—. Recipient Judge Learned Hand Human Rels. award Am. Jewish Com., 1979, Julius Rosenwald Meml. award Jewish Fedn. Met. Chgo., 1994, Army Commendation Medal (USAF); elected to Jewish Cmty. Ctrs. Hall of Fame, 1985, City of Chgo. Sr. Citizens Hall of Fame, 1987. Mem. ABA, Ill. State Bar Assn., Chgo. Bar Assn., Am. Judicature Soc., U. Chgo. Law Sch. Assn. (dir.), Std. Club (past pres., dir.), Mid-Day Club (Chgo.), Northmoor Country Club (Highland Park, Ill.), Tamarisk Country Club (Rancho Mirage, Calif.), Phi Beta Kappa, Pi Lambda Phi. Home: 1040 N Lake Shore Dr Chicago IL 60611-1165 Office: 111 E Wacker Dr Chicago IL 60601-3713 Fax: 312-602-3162. *In my judgment the principles and standard of conduct which one must observe in daily life include a clear recognition of the rights and privileges of others, coupled with a desire to provide assistance to those who are less fortunate and unable to provide for themselves. No conduct of one's affairs can be adequate and fulfilling without recognition and observance of relationships with family. In all dealings, one must act with the highest degree of integrity and conscientious application.*

HESS, SIDNEY WAYNE, management consultant, educator; b. Ames, Iowa, Oct. 21, 1932; s. Edwin M. and Mina Hess; m. Grayce Ann Medici, Oct. 9, 1954; children: Debra, Peter, Diana. BS, M.I.T., 1953; postgrad., Delft Technische Hogeschool, 1953-54; PhD, Case Inst. Tech., 1960; MA (hon.), U. Pa., 1971. Mgr. ops. research Atlas Chem. Industries, Inc., Wilmington, Del., 1959-66; assoc. prof., dir. Mgmt. and Behavioral Sci. Center, U. Pa., 1966-75; dir. pharm. program devel. ICI Americas, 1974-76, v.p. planning and rsch., 1976-80, v.p., gen. mgr. aerospace div., 1980-86; v.p. mfg. Synthes Ltd. (USA), 1986; sr. v.p. Chase Enterprises, 1987-89; prof. mgmt. Drexel U., Phila., 1989-94; pres. Hess Assoc., 1986—. Bd. dirs. Ketron, Inc.; prin. Becknell, Frank, Gross & Hess, Inc., 1968-71 Contbr. articles to profl. jours. Bd. dirs. Girls Inc. of Del., 1980-96, 98—, also treas., former sec.; trustee Concord Presbyn. Ch., 1978-80; mem. Adv. Com. on Indsl. Innovation, Dept. Commerce, 1978-79. Served to 1st lt. U.S. Army, 1954—56. Fulbright fellow, 1953 Mem. Inst. Mgmt. Sci. (past internat. sec. and pres., Disting. Svc. medal 1992), Ops. Rsch. Soc. Am. (past pres. Delaware Valley sect.), Am. Def. Preparedness Assn. (past bd. dirs. Phila. sect.), Chem. Mktg. Rsch. Assn. (Meml. award), Inst. for Ops. Rsch. and Mgmt. Sci. (pub. info. com.), Coun. of Ringfield Pvt. Resdl. Devel. (past pres.), Greenville Country Club, MIT Club of Delaware Valley (bd. dirs., pres.), Tau Beta Pi, Theta Chi.

HESS, STANLEY O. retired art educator; b. Weatherford, Okla., July 8, 1923; s. Otto Mathias Hess and Julia Telford Claunch; m. Mildred Ann Elmenhorst, Jan. 26, 1948 (dec. Apr. 1991); children: Patricia, Catherine, Thomas, Rebecca, Mary, Michael; m. Joanne Lenore Gravelin, June 6, 1992. BFA in Art, U. Okla., 1948, MFA in Art, 1950. Spl. instr. art U. Okla., 1948—50; instr. art William Woods Coll., 1951; prof. art Drake U., 1951—85. Supt. Iowa State Fair Art Salon, 1952—70. One-man shows include U. Okla., 1950, 1956, Sioux City Art Ctr., 1958, Des Moines Art Ctr., 1958, Mabee-Gerrer Mus. Art, St. Gregory's U., Shawnee, Okla., 1994, exhibited in group shows at Renwick Gallery, Washington, 1978, Okla. Arts Workshop, Tulsa, 1993—95, Tulsa Mayfest Gallery, 1994—2000, Leslie Powell Found., Lawton, Okla., 1995, Holliman Gallery, Tulsa, 1996, Mabee-Gerrer Mus. Art, 1997, Anderson Gallery, Des-Moines, 1997, Okla. Artists Painting Biennial, 1997, Okla. Forestry Mus., Idabel, 1998, Okla. City Art Ctr., 1999, Drake U. Beinnial Faculty Exhbn., Butler Inst. Am. Art, others; contbr. articles to profl. jours. 1st lt. U.S. Army, 1942—45, PTO. Avocations: reading, bridge. Home: 5412 S 76th East Ave Tulsa OK 74145-7819

HESS, STEPHEN, political scientist, author; b. NYC, Apr. 20, 1933; s. Charles and Florence (Morse) Hess; m. Elena Shayne, Aug. 23, 1959 (div. 1979); children: Charles P., James R.; m. Beth Amster, Aug. 22, 1982. Student, U. Chgo., Ill., 1950-52; BA, Johns Hopkins U., 1953. Jr. instr. polit. sci. Johns Hopkins U., 1953-55; staff asst. to US Pres., 1959-61; asst. to minority whip US Senate, 1961; assoc. fellow Inst. for Policy Studies, 1964-65; fellow Inst. Politics J.F. Kennedy Sch. Govt., Harvard, 1967-68; dep. asst. to US Pres. for urban affairs, 1969; nat. chmn. White House Conf. on Children and Youth, 1969-71; sr. fellow Brookings Instn. Washington, 1972—. Mem. Washington regional selection panel Pres.'s Commn. White Ho. Fellows, 1973; cons. Ford Found., 1974—76; mem. DC Bd. Higher Edn., 1973—76; chmn. DC Coun. Home Rule Transition Commn., 1974; U.S. alt. rep. UNESCO Gen. Conf., 1974; mem. Alumni fellows adv. com. Inst. Politics, J. F. Kennedy Sch. Govt., Harvard U., 1974—; mem. 20th Century Fund Task Forces, 1975, 78, US Nat. Commn. UNESCO, 1975—77; editor-in-chief Nat. Rep. Platform, 1976; mem. adv. coun. gen. govt. Rep. Nat. Com., 1978—81; U.S. alt. rep. UN Gen. Assembly, 1976; cons. USIA, 1976, US Office Mgmt. and Budget, 1977; mem. vis. com. Gerald R. Ford Inst. Pub. Svc., Albion Coll., 1979—82; fellow faculty govt. Harvard U., 1979—82; mem. adv. com. Fund Investigative Journalism, 1981—; mem. sr. adv. bd. ctr. for press, politics and pub. policy John F. Kennedy Sch. Govt., Harvard U., 1987—; vis. prof. Johns Hopkins U., 1990, UCLA, Washington Program, 1990. Author (with Malcolm Moos): (novels) Hats in the Ring: The Making of Pres. Candidates, 1960, (book) America's Polit. Dynasties, 1966; author: (with David S. Broder) The Rep. Establishment, 1967; author: (with Milton Kaplan) The Ungentlemanly Art: A History of Am. Polit. Cartoons, 1968; author: (with Earl Mazo) Nixon: A Polit. Portrait, 1968, Nixon: A Polit. Portrait, rev. edit., 1969, The Presdl. Campaign, 1974; author: (with Milton Kaplan) The Ungentlemanly Art: A History of American Political Cartoons, rev. edit., 1975; author: Organizing the Presidency, 1976; author: (with Earl Mazo) The Washington Reporters, 1981; author: The Government/Press Connection: Press Officers and Their Offices, 1984, The Ultimate Insiders: U.S. Senators in the National Media, 1986, The Presdl. Campaign, rev. edit., 1987, Live from Capitol Hill! Studies on Congress and the Media, 1991, Internat. News & Fgn. Correspondents, 1995, Presidents & The Presidency, 1995, News & Newsmaking, 1995; author: (with Sandy Northrop) Drawn & Quartered, 1996; author: America's Polit. Dynasties, rev. edit., 1996, International News & Foreign Correspondents, rev. edit., 1997, The Little Book of Campaign Etiquette, 1998; author: (with Sandy Northrop) The Little Book of Campaign Etiquette, rev. edit., 2000; author: Organizing the Presidency, rev. edit., 2002; editor (with Marion Kalb): (novels) The Media and the war on Terrorism, 2003. With AUS, 1956—58. Fellow: Nat. Acad. Pub. Adminstrn. Home: 2801 New Mexico Ave NW Washington DC 20007 Office: Brookings Instn 1775 Massachusetts Ave NW Washington DC 20036-2103 E-mail: shess@Brookings.edu.

HESS, TERESA, fine arts educator; BFA, Kansas City Art Inst., 1985; MFA, Queens Coll. of CUNY, 1987. Instr. Hutchinson (Kans.) C.C., 1989-96; assoc. prof. Lakeland C.C., Kirtland, Ohio, 1996—. Exhbn. judge N.E. Ohio Art Edn. Assn., 1996; awards juror Euclid Art Assn., Cleve., 1998-2000; juror Nat. Coll. Soc., Kent State U., Hudson, Ohio, 1999, The Congl. H.S. Art Exhbn., 19th Congl. Dist., 1999, 2000; awards selection judge Lake/Geauga County Jr./Sr. H.S. Exhbn., 1999, 2000; chmn. fine arts dept. Lakeland Cmty. Coll., 2001-. Artist over 30 art exhbns., 1983—. Mem.: NEA, Nat. Collage Soc., Willoughby Fine Arts Assn., Coll. Art Assn., Cleve. Mus. Art, Ohio Edn. Assn. Office: 7700 Clocktower Dr Kirtland OH 44094-5198 E-mail: thess@lakeland.cc.oh.us.

HESS, TERRY LEE, writer, educator; b. Balt., July 22, 1954; d. Lee Hess Ray and Ruth Carol Smith, Iva Estelle Teague (Stepmother). MA in English Creative Writing Nonfiction, U. Ctrl. Fla., 2002, postgrad. Program mgr., logistic engr. TRW Aerospace, Redondo Beach, Calif., 1982—89; sr. logisitics engr. Boeing/McDonnell Douglas, Kennedy Space Ctr., Cape Canaveral, Fla., 1990—97; mng. editor Fla. Rev., Orlando, 1999—2002, non-fiction editor, 2001—02; sr. proposal specialist Johnson Controls, Inc., Cape Canaveral, 2003—. Instr. U. Ctrl. Fla., 2001—03. Author: (Memoir) Bellingham Review, 2002 (AWP Intro Award for Creative Nonfiction, 2001), Cypress Dome, 2000, 4th edit., 2003. Fin. advisor 53rd Assembly Dist., 27th Congl. Dist., Rep. Party, L.A., 1985—87. With USAF, 1972—76, with USMC, 1978—82. Recipient United Arts Emerging Writers award, First Place Nonfiction and Second Place Fiction, United Arts, Orlando, Fla., 1999. Home: 3242 Angelica St Cocoa FL 32926 Office: Johnson Controls Inc 7315 N Atlantic Ave Cape Canaveral FL 32926 Personal E-mail: hes1of6@bellsouth.net.

HESS, WANDA JEAN, health facility administrator; b. Rochester, N.Y., June 30, 1949; d. Edwin and Irene (Miller) H. BS in Speech and Hearing Sci., SUNY, Geneseo, 1972; MS in Speech Pathology, U. Kans., 1974, MS in Audiology, 1975; postgrad., SUNY, Buffalo, 1982-83. Cert., lic. speech pathologist, audiologist, N.Y., Pa., speech lang. impaired tchr., Pa., N.Y. Instr. SUNY, Geneseo, 1976-77, area chmn., speech pathology Brockport, 1978-82; pres., CEO Northwest Hearing and Speech Ctr., Rochester, N.Y., 1983-94; dir. speech pathology IHS Nursing Home, 1995-96; supr. and speech pathologist DMA, Multicare & Genesis Elder Care, 1996—2001, Pacific Rehab., 2001—. Chmn. Alexander Graham Bell Assn. Conv. 1994. Author: (workbook) Basic Amplication System, 1982 (policy manual) Staffing Procedures Manual United Cerebral, 1977. Bd. dirs. St. Mary's Hosp., Rochester, 1992—, DePaul Mental Health Clin., Rochester, 1990—, Health Care Rsch., Rochester, Epilsey Assn., Rochester, 1982-85; chmn. Jefferson Ave. Bus. Assn., Rochester, 1990—. Grantee Daisy, Marquis Jones Found., State Dept. of Health, Conrad Hilton Fund, Gannett Found., Davenport Hatch Found. Fellow Am. Acad. Audiology; mem. Am. Speech/Lang./Hearing Assn. (cert.), N.Y. State Speech and Lang. Assn., Alexander Graham Bell Assn., Acoustical Soc. Roman Catholic. Avocations: sports, reading. Home: Green Valley Manor 150 Ridge Pike Apt A308 Lafayette Hill PA 19444-1929

HESSE, CAROLYN SUE, lawyer; b. Belleville, Ill., Jan. 12, 1949; d. Ralph H. Hesse and Marilyn J. (Midgley) Hesse Dierkes; m. William H. Hallenbeck. BS, U. Ill., 1971; MS, U. Ill., Chgo., 1977; JD, DePaul U., 1983. Bar: Ill. 1983, U.S. Dist. Ct. (no. dist.) Ill. 1983. Rsch. assoc. U. Ill., Chgo., 1974-77; tech. adviser

Ill. Pollution Control Bd., Chgo., 1977-80; environ. scientist U.S. EPA, Chgo., 1980-84; assoc. Pretzel & Stouffer, Chartered, Chgo., 1984-87, Coffield Ungaretti Harris & Slavin, Chgo., 1987-88; ptnr. McDermott, Will & Emery, 1988-99; pvt. practice Chgo., 1999-2001; with Barnes & Thornburg, 2001—. Frequent spkr. seminars on environ. issues. Contbr. articles on environ. sci. to profl. jours. Mem. ABA, Chgo. Bar Assn. Office: Barnes & Thornburg 2600 Chase Plaza 10 S LaSalle St Chicago IL 60603 E-mail: chesse@btlaw.com.

HESSE, DOUGLAS DEAN, English educator; b. DeWitt, Iowa, July 25, 1956; s. Donald Glen and Coral Ardis (Krukow) H.; m. Dawn Dannenbring, June 7, 1981 (div. 1996); children: Monica, Andrew; m. Becky Bradway, Mar. 7, 1998. BA, U. Iowa, 1978, MA, 1980, PhD, 1986. Editor ACT, Iowa City, 1978-80; instr. English Findlay (Ohio) Coll., 1980-83; prof., dir. Ill. State U. Ctr. for Advacement of Tchg., Normal, 1986; editor WPA, 1994-98; Wiepking disting. prof. Miami U., Oxford, Ohio, 2001—02. Actor, bd. mem., stage mgr. cmty. theatre, Bloomington, Ill., 1991—; vol. Metcalf Sch. Univ. H.S., Normal, 1988—. Mem. MLA, Assn. Tchrs. Advanced Composition, Coun. Writing Program Adminstrs. (pres.), Conf. Coll. Composition (exec. com., v.p.), Am. Assn. Higher Edn., Nat. Coun. Tchrs. English, Rhetoric Rev. Soc. Democrat. Lutheran. Avocations: acting, singing, swimming, tennis. Home: 204 William Dr Normal IL 61761-1851 Office: Ill State U 3990 Ctr Advancement Teaching Normal IL 61790-4240

HESSE, KAREN (KAREN SUE HESSE), writer, educator; b. Balt., Md., Aug. 29, 1952; d. Alvin Donald and Frances Broth Levin; m. Randy Hesse; children: Kate, Rachel. BA, U. Md., 1975. Reference libr. U. Md., 1973-75, leave benefit coord., 1975-76; advt. sec. Country Journal mag., 1976-77, typesetter, proofreader, 1978-88; mental health care provider, 1989-91; children's lit. reviewer, 1993-94. Author: (children's books) Wish on a Unicorn, 1991 (Hungry Mind Rev. Children's Book of Distinction 1992), Letters From Rifka, 1992 (Nat. Jewish Book award 1993, IRA Children's Book award 1993, Christopher award 1992, Sydney Taylor Book award 1992, ALA Notable Book 1992, ALA Best Book for Young Adults 1992, Sch. Libr. Jour. Best Book of Yr. 1992, Horn Book Outstanding Book of Yr. 1992, Booklist Editors' Choice 1992, NY Pub. Libr. 100 Titles for Reading and Sharing 1992), Poppy's Chair, 1993 (Am. Booksellers Assn. Pick of List 1993), Lester's Dog, 1993 (Best Book of Yr. Sch. Libr. Jour. 1993, Notable Children's Trade Book in Field of Social Studies 1993), Lavender, 1993, Sable, 1994 (Sch. Libr. Jour. Best Book of Yr. 1994, NY Pub. Libr. 100 Titles for Reading and Sharing 1994, Boston Globe 10 Best Trade Books 1994, Parenting Mag. 40 Outstanding Children's Books 1994), Phoenix Rising, 1994 (Sch. Libr. Jour. Best Book of Yr. 1994, IRA Tchr.'s Choice 1995, NY Pub. Libr. Books for the Teenage 1995, Best Book for Young Adults ALA 1995, Notable Book, 1995, Wilson Libr. Bull. 33 Favorite Reads 1994 (S.C. Jr. Book award, 1996, 97, others), A Time of Angels, 1995 (IRA Tchr's Choice 1996, IRA Young Adults' Choice, 1997, NY Pub. Libr. Books for the Teenager 1995), The Music of Dolphins, 1996 (Pub.'s Weekly Best Book of Yr. 1996, Best Book of Yr. Sch. Libr. Jour. 1996, Book Links, 100 Titles for Reading and Sharing NY Pub. Libr. Children's Book 1996, Best Books for Young Adults ALA, 1997, Golden Kite Honor Book, 1997), Out of the Dust, 1997 (Newbery medal 1998, Scott O'Dell award 1998), Just Juice, 1998 (100 Titles for Reading and Sharing NY Pub. Libr. 1998, Notable Children's Trade Book in the Field of Social Studies 1998), Come On, Rain! (BCCB Blue Ribbon Book, NYPL 100 Books for Reading & Sharing, Jr. Library Guild selection, Book of the Month Club selection), 1999; contbr. When I Was Your Age, Vol. II, 1999 (2000 Books for the Teen Age), A Light in the Storm, 1999 (Notable Children's Trade Book in the Field of Social Studies 1999, Kennedy Ctr. Stage Adaptation, 2001), Stowaway, 2000 (SLJ Book of Yr., 2001, Capitol Choice Noteworthy Books for Children (10-14), 100 Titles for Reading and Sharing NY Pub. Libr., 2000, Jr. Libr. Guild Selection), Witness (NY Pub. Libr. 100 Books for Reading and Sharing, ALA Notable Children's book, LA 100 Best Books 2001, 2002 IRA Notable, 2002 CBC Choice, 2002 Myers Award, 2002 NCTE Notable, Christopher award, 2002, Parents Guide to Children's Media award); MacArthur Found. Fellowship, 2003, Aleutian Sparrow (Jr. Libr. Guild selection); contbr. articles to profl. jour. Chmn. Sch. Bd., 1989; sec. bd. dirs. Moore Free Libr., 1989-91; active Hospice, 1988—. MacArthur fellow, 2003—. Mem. Soc. Children's Book Writers and Illustrators, So. Vt. Soc. Children's Book Writers (leader 1985-92), Ctr. for Children's Environ. Lit., Author's Guild. Avocations: reading, hiking, cultivating friendships, music. Office: Scholastic 555 Broadway New York NY 10012-3919

HESSE, MARTHA O. natural gas company executive; b. Hattiesburg, Miss., Aug. 14, 1942; d. John William and Geraldine Elaine (Ossian) H. BS, U. Iowa, 1964; postgrad., Northwestern U., 1972-76; MBA, U. Chgo., 1979. Research analyst Blue Shield, 1964-66; dir. div. data mgmt. Am. Hosp. Assn., 1966-69; dir., chief operating officer SEI Info. Tech., Chgo., 1969-80; assoc. dep. sec. Dept. of Commerce, Washington, 1981-82; exec. dir. Pres.' Task Force on Mgmt. Reform, 1982; asst. sec. mgmt. and adminstrn. Dept. of Energy, Washington, 1982-86; chmn. FERC, Washington, 1986-89; sr. v.p. 1st Chgo. Corp., 1990; now pres. Hesse Gas, Houston. Bd. dirs. Pinnacle West Capital Corp., Ariz. Pub. Svc. Co., Mut. Trust Life, Laidlaw, AMEC plc, Terra Industries, Enbridge Energy Prnrs. Home: 4171 Autumn Hills Dr Winnemucca NV 89445

HESSE, RICHARD JOSEPH, construction engineer; b. Hartington, Nebr., Aug. 5, 1921; s. Joseph and Mary Wortmann Hesse; widowed; children: Katherine, Daniel, Maria, Patricia, Jeanne. AB, Wayne State U., 1942; BS, U.S. Mil. Acad., 1945; MS, Iowa State U., 1949. Registered profl. engr., Wis., D.C., Pa. Commd. 2d lt. U.S. Army Corps Engrs., 1945, advanced through grades to col., 1966, ret., 1975; mgr. Harza Engring. Co., Great Falls, Va., 1977—. Fellow ASCE, Am. Cons. Engrs. Coun., Soc. Am. Mil. Engrs. Roman Catholic. Home and Office: 1060 Leigh Mill Rd Great Falls VA 22066

HESSELBEIN, FRANCES RICHARDS, foundation executive, consultant, editor; b. South Fork, Pa. d. Burgess Harmon and Anne Luke (Wicks) Richards; widowed, 1978; 1 child, John Richards. DHL (hon.), Buena Vista Coll., 1987, Juniata Coll., 1990, Hood Coll., 1991; D Mgmt. (hon.), GM Inst., 1990; LLD (hon.), Wilson Coll., 1991; LHD (hon.), Marymount-Tarrytown Coll., 1993; DHL (hon.), Boston Coll., 1994, U. Nebr., Kearney, 1994, Lafayette Coll., 1995, Carroll Coll., 1996, Fairleigh Dickinson U., 1996, Muhlenburg Coll., 1996; LLD (hon.), Moravian Coll., 2000; D in Pub. and Internat. Affairs, U. Pitts., 2001; DHL (hon.), Mt. Mary Coll., 2002. CEO Talus Rock Girl Scout Coun., Johnstown, 1970-74, Penn Laurel Girl Scout Coun., York, Pa., 1974-76, Girl Scouts U.S., N.Y.C., 1976-90; pres., CEO Peter F. Drucker Found. Nonprofit Mgmt., N.Y.C., 1990-99, chmn., 1999—2003, Leader To Leader Inst., N.Y.C., 2003—. Chmn. Nat. Bd. Vols. Am.; bd. dirs. Mut. of Am. Ins. Co., N.Y.C.; nat. bd. visitors Peter F. Drucker Grad. Mgmt. Sch. Claremont (Calif.) Grad. Sch., 1987—; chmn. bd. govs. Josephson Ethics Inst., 1989-99; adv. com. to bd. dirs. N.Y. Stock Exch., 1988-91; bd. govs. Ctr. for Creative Leadership, Greensboro, N.C., 1992-98; adv. bd. Harvard Bus. Sch.'s Initiative on Social Enterprise, Harvard's Kennedy Sch. Hauser Ctr. Nonprofit Policy and Leadership Program; chmn. Vols. Am., 2002-, Leader to Leader Inst., 2003—. Editor-in-chief Leader to Leader; co-editor The Leader of the Future, The Organization of the Future, The Community of the Future, Drucker Found. Future Series, Leader to Leader Book, 1999, Leading Beyond the Walls, 1999; author: Hesselbein on Leadership, 2002. Trustee Juniata Coll., Huntingdon, Pa., 1988—, Allentown (Pa.) Coll., 1988-97; mem. Pres.'s Adv. Com. on Points of Light Initiative Found., 1989; bd. dirs. Nat. Exec. Svc. Corps., N.Y., Commn. on Nat. and Cmty. Svc., 1991-94, Village Found., also vice-chmn.; adv. bd. The Leadership Inst., U. So. Calif., 1991, Harvard U.'s John F. Kennedy Sch. Govt. Nonprofit Policy and Leadership Program. Recipient Outstanding Achievement award Inter-Svc. Club Coun., Johnstown, 1976, Entrepreneurial Woman award Women Bus. Owners of N.Y., 1984, Nat. Leadership award United Way of Am., Washington, 1985, Disting. Cmty. Svc. award Mut. of Am. Ins. Co., 1985, Dir.'s Choice-award Nat. Women's Econ. Alliance, 1989, Pa. Soc. Disting. Citizen award, 1991, Wilbur M. McFeeley award Internat. Mgmt. Coun. YMCA, 1993, U. Pitts. Legacy Laureate award, 2000, Internat. Leadership award Athena Found., 2001, Henry Russo award Ind. U. Ctr., 2001, Dwight D. Eisenhower Series Nat. Security award, 2002; named to Bus. Hall of Fame, Johnstown, 1995; named Outstanding Exec., Savvy Mag., 1985, Disting. Alumni Fellow U. Pitts., 1999, Disting. Dau. of Pa., Gov. Ridge, 1999, Woman of Yr., Boy Scouts of Greater N.Y., Legacy Laureate, U. Pitts., 2000; on cover BusinessWeek, 1990, Presdl. Medal of Freedom, 1998; featured in Chief Exec. mag., 1995, Fortune, 1995-96, Chapel of Four Chaplains Gold Legion of Hon. medal, 1999, Athena Found.-Internat. Leadership award, 2001, Henry Rosso award for lifetime ethical fundraising Ind. U. Ctr., 2001-02. Mem. Sky Club, Pa. Soc. Office: Leader to Leader Inst 320 Park Ave 3d Fl New York NY 10022-6815 Office Fax: 212 224-2508. E-mail: frances@leadertoleader.org.

HESSELINK, ANN PATRICE, financial executive, lawyer; b. Tokyo, July 20, 1954; d. Ira John Jr. and Etta Marie (Ter Louw) H.; 1 child, Katherine Marie Hesselink Hicks. AB in Psychology, Hope Coll., 1975; JD, St. Johns U., 1980; advanced profl. cert. in fin., NYU, 1983. Bar: N.Y. 1981; CPA, N.Y. Tax mgr. Coopers & Lybrand, N.Y.C., 1980-82; asst. v.p. Bankers Trust Co., N.Y.C., 1982-83; dir. internat. taxes PepsiCo, Inc., Purchase, N.Y., 1983-85; sr. v.p., dir. taxes Young & Rubicam Inc., N.Y.C., 1986-94; v.p. taxes, tax counsel AT&T Capital Corp., Morristown, N.J., 1994-97; cons., 1997—2002; dir. taxation Gentek Inc., Parsippany, NJ, 2002—. Trustee, v.p. Blue Rock Sch., Palisades, N.Y., 1987-89; treas., bd. dirs. Plays for Living, 1991-98; trustee New Brunswick Sem., 1993-98; bd. trustees Ctrl. Coll., 1999—. Mem. ABA, N.Y. State Bar Assn., AICPA, Am. Sch. in Japan Alumni Assn. (chmn. N.Y. region). Democrat. Presbyterian. Home: 27 Ballantine Rd Mendham NJ 07945-3004 E-mail: ahesselink@gentek-global.com.

HESSELINK, LAMBERTUS, electrical engineering and physics educator; b. Enschede, The Netherlands, Dec. 4, 1948; came to U.S., 1971; s. Lambertus and Wilhelmina (ten Tye) H. BSME, Twente Inst. Tech., Enschede, 1970, BS in Applied Physics, 1971, postgrad., 1974; MSME, Calif. Inst. Tech., 1972, PhD in Applied Mechs., Physics, 1977. Rsch. fellow Calif. Inst. Tech., Pasadena, 1977-78, instr. applied physics, 1978-80, sr. rsch. fellow fluid mechs., 1979-80; asst. prof. aeros. and astronautics Stanford (Calif.) U., 1980-85, asst. prof., 1985—, assoc. prof. elec. engring., 1980-85, asst. prof., 1985-90, prof. electrical engring. and aeronautics/astonautics, 1990—. Cons. Hughes Aircraft Corp., Culver City, Calif., 1978-79, MCC Corp., 1986-92; invited scientist mem. image processing work group for Hubble Space Telescope, 1990; assoc. editor Jour. Applied Sci. and Applied Optics, 1990; founder Siros Technologies, Inc.; cons. to industry and govt.; mem. scientific adv. bd. USAF, 1995—; founder Senvid, Inc. Patentee in field. Recipient Stheeman prize Twente Inst. Tech., 1970; Fulbright fellow 1971-74; Josephine de Karman fellow, 1974-75. Fellow Optical Soc. Am.; mem. AIAA (Engr. of Yr. 1982), Soc. Photo-Optical Instrumentation Engrs. Optical Soc. Am., Am. Phys. Soc., Royal Dutch Acad. Arts and Scis. (corr.), Sigma Xi. Office: Stanford U Mail Code 4075 CISX Bldg Rm 325 Stanford CA 94305-4075 E-mail: bert@kaos.stanford.edu.

HESSERT, WILFRED O. military officer; BS in Acctg. magna cum laude, Husson Coll., 1969; M in Bus. Adminstrn., Auburn U., 1974; grad., Air Command and Staff Coll., 1974, Air War Coll., 1982, CAPSTONE, 1997. Commd. 2d lt. USAF, 1968, advanced through grades to maj. gen., 1997; pilot 132d Fighter Inceptor Squadron, Maine Air N.G., Dow AFB, Maine, 1967-72; aircraft maintenance and flight test officer Maine Air N.G., Bangor Internat. Airport, 1972-76, chief of maintenance, 1976-79; comdr. 101st Consol. Aircraft Maintenance Squadron Maine Air N.G., Bangor Air N.G. Base, 1979-84, dep. comdr. for maintenance 101st Consol. Aircraft Main. Sq., 1984-87, dep. comdr. for ops. Hdqs., 1987-91, vice wing comdr. 101st Air Refueling Wing, 1991, wing comdr. 101st Air Refueling Wing, 1991-96; Air N.G. asst. to comdr. U.S. Air Forces in Europe, Ramstein Air Base, Germany, 1996-97; dep. inspector gen. Hdqs. USAF, Washington, 1997—; mil. exec. Res. Forces Bd. Policy, Arlington, Va., 1999—. Decorated Legion of Merit, Meritorious Svc. medal with oak leaf cluster.

HESSLER, DAVID WILLIAM, information and multimedia systems educator; b. Oak Park, Ill., May 9, 1932; s. William Wigney and Gwendolyn Eileen (Butler) H.; m. Helen Montgomery, Aug. 27, 1955; children: Leslie Susan, Laura Lynne. BA, U. Mich., 1955, MA, 1961; PhD, Mich. State U., 1972. Comml. photographer Oscar & Assocs., Chgo., 1950; equipment engr. Western Electric Co., Chgo., 1958-59; dir. libs. and media Ann Arbor (Mich.) Pub. Schs., 1966-67; asst. prof. edn. Western Mich. U., 1967-72, assoc. prof., 1974-77; dir. instrnl. svcs., dir. broadcasting, prof. edn. U. S.C., 1973-74; cons., asst. dir. Audio-Visual Edn. Ctr. U. Mich., Ann Arbor, 1960-66, prof. Sch. Info., 1977-98, prof. emeritus, 1998—, dir. instrnl. strategy svcs. for schs. of edn., libr. sci., 1979-81, pres. Ann Arbor sys. and tech., 1987—, exec. dir. for info. svcs. Info-Span, 1991-92; exec. v.p. Infotronix, Ann Arbor, 1993-97. Cons. Presdl. Commn. on World Hunger; cons. media and tech.; instrnl. designer and evaluator; bd. dirs. Kirsch Techs.; vis. prof., cons. dept. biblioteconomia U. Brazil, 1981. Author: (with J. Smith) Student Production Guide, 1975, Technology for Communication and Instruction, 1983; producer/dir. numerous films, filmstrips, TV programs and sound/slide programs for various ednl. levels. Lt. USAF, 1955-58; capt. Res. ret. Decorated Air Force Commendation medal; named Mich. Most Valuable Tchr. Chrysler Corp., 1965; Ednl. Profl. Devel. Act fellow, 1968-69. Mem. ALA, ASTD, Assn. Image and Info. Mgmt., M Club, Phi Kappa Phi. Home: 3677 Frederick Dr Ann Arbor MI 48105-2887 Office: Univ Mich Sch Info W Hall 550 E University Ave Ann Arbor MI 48109-1092 E-mail: dwh@umich.edu.

HESSLER, DOUGLAS SCOTT, screenwriter; b. Hagerstown, Md., July 22, 1948; s. Chester Scott (dec.) and Betty Jane (Martin) H.; m. Fumiko Hamada, June 11, 1993. BFA, Va. Commonwealth U., 1971; MFA, Md. Inst. Coll. of Art, 1974; Postgrad. Degree, Am. Film Inst., L.A., 1985. Painter, filmmaker, N.Y.C., 1974-82; creative dir. J. Walter Thompson Advt., N.Y.C., 1977-83; prodn. exec. Cannon Films, L.A., 1985-88, Walt Disney Co., L.A., 1988-90; artistic dir. Landmark Entertainment, L.A., 1990-92; with German TV and feature film prodn. cos., TV networks. Condr. screenwriting workshops, L.A., Germany, 1995-96, guest lectr, Shepherd Coll., Shepherdstown, W.V., 2003. Screenwriter: Out of Nowhere, Over the Line, 1993, Eye of the Storm, 1993, Judgement Day, 1994, Adrenaline, 1995, Code Red, 1996, Side Swipe, 1996, (TV movie) Extreme; prodr. Intruder, Paramount Pictures, 1990, Because the Night, Penthouse German film sub., 1998; (German TV movies) GUN, 1998, Extreme, 1998, The Bitch, 1998. Staff sgt. USAFR, 1967-72. Recipient Adolf-Grime award, Germany, 1995, award Houston Film Internat. Festival, 1996, N.Y. Film Festival, 1996; N.Y. State Arts grantee N.Y. State Coun. on Arts, 1979, 80, 81; Am. Film Inst. Writer/Dir. fellow, 1984-85. Avocations: fly fishing, traveling, writing. Address: 32 W Potomac St Williamsport MD 21795-1036

HESSLER, GENE JOSEPH, museum curator, retired musician; b. Cin., July 13, 1928; s. Joseph August and Clara (Schmidt) H. BS in Music Edn., U. Cin., 1955; MM in Musicology, Manhattan Sch. Music, 1957. Trombonist Band of Elliot Lawrence, 1949-51, Band of Billy May, 1954, Band of Woody Herman, 1955, Band of Sauter-Finnegan, 1956, Band of Buddy Rich, 1959; prin. trombonist San Antonio Symphony, 1957-59, Cin. Symphony World Tour, 1966; trombonist various Broadway musicals, N.Y.C., 1959-67; curator Chase Manhattan Bank Money Mus., N.Y.C., 1967-77, St. Louis Mercantile Bank Money Mus., 1986-88. Author: The Comprehensive Catalog of U.S. Paper Money, 6th edit., 1997, U.S. Essay, Proof and Specimen Notes, 1979, 2d edit., 2002, An Illustrated History of U.S. Loans, 1988, The Engraver's Line, 1993; editor: Paper Money, 1985-98; contbg. editor: The Numismatist, 1986—; columist Numismatist, 1992—, Coin World, 1993—. Mem. sch. bd. St. Louis Cathedral Sch., 1994-96, vol. tchr., 1990-96; vol. tchr. St. Boniface Sch., 1997-99, vol. tchr. St. Catherine Sch., 1999-2003, instr. Am. Numismatic Assn. Summer Seminar, 1997, 98, 2000-01. Recipient Medal of Merit, Soc. Internat. Numismatics; named Numismatic Amb., Numismatic News. Fellow Am. Numismatic Soc.; mem. Am. Numismatic Assn. (Heath Literary award, Medal of Merit, Catherine Sheehan Lit. award), Internat. Bank Note Soc. (recipient Silver Medal for Contrbn. to 40th Anniversary, 2001), Soc. Paper Money Collectors (hon. life). Avocations: photography, cooking, wine. Office: PO Box 31144 Cincinnati OH 45231-0144

HESSLER, THOMAS JOHN, community activist; b. Cin., Apr. 25, 1937; s. Carl Bernard and Marcella Christina (Hoffmeier) H.; m. Nancy Ann Eshman, Sept. 21, 1963; children: Susan, Cara Snyder, Thomas, Angela Daddario. BSEE, U. Dayton, 1959; MSEE, Ga. Inst. Tech., 1968. Commd. 2d lt. U.S. Army, 1959, advanced through grades to col., 1980, ret., 1985; sr. engr. Planning Rsch. Corp., Sierra Vista, Ariz., 1985-88, TechDyn Corp., Sierra Vista, 1988-93, EDSI, Sierra Vista, 1993-95. Vice mayor City of Sierra Vista, 1994-95, mayor, 1999—, mem. coun., 1992-94; mem. Sierra Vista Planning and Zoning Commn., 1995-99. Mem. Joint Svc. Clubs of Greater Sierra Vista (founder, pres. 1995—),Rotary Club of Sierra Vista (pres. 1998-99), Assn. U.S. Army (adv. dir. 1997-2001), Ret. Officers Assn. (pres. 1992-93, 95-96), Armed Forces Comms. and Electronics Assn. (pres 1994-95). Republican. Roman Catholic. Avocations: downhill skiing, travel. Home: 2000 Golf Links Rd Sierra Vista AZ 85635-4837 E-mail: ThomasJHessler@cs.com.

HESSLER, WILLIAM GERHARD, tax consultant; b. Chgo., May 20, 1926; s. William Gerhard and Rosemary (Kalb) Hessler; m. Kazuko Yonetsu, June 2, 1956 (dec. Mar. 1995); children: Martha, George, Kay, Emmy. BSEE, Purdue U., 1946; MBA, Northwestern U., 1956. Cert. data processor, individual tax profl. Tech. intelligence investigator U.S. Army, Tokyo, 1947-50, electronics engr. signal corps. Yokohama, Japan, 1952-54; mfg., devel. engr. Western Electric, Chgo., 1955-61; engring. specialist Goodyear Aerospace Corp., Akron, Ohio, 1961-65; computer applications programmer analyst Goodyear Tire & Rubber Co., Akron, 1965-83, computer operating systems programmer, 1983-87; cons. Cutler-Williams, Independence, Ohio, 1987; systems engineer Profl. Support, Inc., Brecksville, Ohio, 1989. Tax cons. and return preparer H & R Block, Greater Akron, 1969—80, Akron Nat. Tax & Notary, 1981, Tax Ctr. and Fin. Solutions, Inc. (formerly Hammer Tax Ctr.), Akron, 1982—2001; cons. in field; agt. enrolled to practice U.S. Dept . Treasury IRS, 1984—2002. Scoutmaster Boy Scouts Am., Silver Lake, Ohio, 1972—77. With U.S. Army, 1950—52, Japan. Mem.: AARP (pres. chpt. 3515 2003). Roman Catholic. Avocation: amateur radio (w8dxt). Home: 3046 Lake Rd Stow OH 44224-3814 E-mail: J2QBI@aol.com.

HESSONG, CINDY HOCH, music educator; b. Refugio, Tex., Mar. 6, 1964; d. Edgar Louis and Linda Ruth (Andersson) Hoch; m. Donald Wayne Hessong, Dec. 28, 1985; children: Samantha Anne, Jessica Gayle. Student, Bee County Coll., Beeville, Tex., 1983-84, U. Tex., 1985, Tex. A&I U., 1986-91. Owner Hessong Piano Studio, Kingsville, Tex., 1986-98; dir., owner Hessong Sch. Music, Kingsville, Tex., 1998—. Performer (CD recording) Watercolors: A Piano Portrait, 1999. Guest artist Tex. Atty. Gen. Rep. Orgn., Austin, 1999. Mem. Am. Coll. Musicians (Approved Music Tchr. award 1999), Music Tchrs. Nat. Assn., Tex. Music Tchrs. Assn., Corpus Christi Music Tchrs. Assn. (1st v.p. 1997-99). Republican. Baptist. Avocations: gardening, traveling. Home and Office: 227 E Fm 772 Kingsville TX 78363-2647 E-mail: hessongmusic@hotmail.com.

HESTAD, MARSHA ANNE, educational administrator; b. Evanston, Ill., Apr. 25, 1950; d. Bjorn Mark and Florence Anne (Ragusi) H. BS, U. Ill., 1972; MEd, Nat. Coll. Edn., Evanston, Ill., 1978; postgrad., Purdue U., 1985; PhD, Loyola U., Chgo., 1991. Cert. in elem. edn., spl. reading, gifted edn., gen. adminstrn., Ill., Ind. Tchr. 5th grade Deerfield (Ill.) Sch. Dist. 109, 1972-78; head tchr. North Aegean Acad., Kavala, Greece, 1978-81; gifted resource tchr. Alief Ind. Sch. Dist., Houston, 1983-84, TeKoppel, Evansville, Ind., 1984-85; field supr. Purdue U., West Lafayette, Ind., 1987; gifted coord. MSD Mt. Vernon, Ind., 1985-88; gifted resource Libertyville (Ill.) Sch. Dist. 70, 1988-91; instr. Coll. Lake County, Grayslake, Ill., 1991; clin. prof. Loyola U., Chgo., 1991; prof. Ind. State U., Terre Haute, 1992-93; tchr. lang. arts/lit. 7th grade, co-dir./prin. summer sch. Libertyville (Ill.) Sch. Dist. 70, 1993-94; prin. Chippewa Sch., Bensenville (Ill.) Dist. 2, 1994-96, Rockland Sch., Libertyville Ill., 1996—. Adj. prof. Loyola U., Chgo., 1998-99, Lake Forest Coll., 2003—; bd. dirs. Odyssey of the Mind, Ind. and Ill.; cons. in field. Co-prodr.: Countdown Interactive (cable program), 1995—96; exec. prodr.: Blast Off (cable program), 1997—2001; contbr. articles to profl. jours. Dist. 70 coord. Learn and Serve, Am. Grant Activities. Mem. ASCD, Nat. Coun. Staff Devel., Ill. Assn. for Gifted Children (v.p. 1998, pres.-elect 1999, pres. 2000-2002, past pres. 2002-04), Phi Delta Kappa. E-mail: mhestad@d70k.12.il.us.

HESTAND, JOEL DWIGHT, minister, evangelist; b. Henrietta, Tex., May 23, 1939; s. Dee Lathell and Jack Fern (Gamble) H.; m. Carolyn Somers, June 12, 1959; children: Paul Daniel, Joe Randall. Student, Odessa (Tex.) Coll., 1963-66; diploma, Brown Trail Sch. Preaching, Ft. Worth, Tex., 1968-70, Sunset Sch. Missions, Lubbock, 1973. Evangelist Ch. of Christ, various locations, 1968—; missionary Tanzania, E. Africa, 1973-75, Chimala Mission and Hosp., Mbeya, Tanzania, 1994-95. Police chaplain Naperville (Ill.) Police Dept., 1977-83; ednl. dir. Rockford (Ill.) Christian Camp, 1977-82, bd. dirs., 1977-82; instr. Fishers of Men Evangelism, Frankfort, Ky., 1984—. With USAF, 1957-66. Republican. Office: Myrtle Ave Ch of Christ 134 Myrtle Ave Frankfort KY 40601-3114 E-mail: jdhestand@aol.com. *"Now all has been heard; here is the conclusion of the matter: Fear God and keep His Commandments, for this is the whole of man." Ecclesiastes 12:13.*

HESTER, BRUCE EDWARD, library media specialist, lay worker; b. Clarksville, Tenn., June 26, 1956; s. Edward Vaughan and Mabel Sarah (Chandley) H. BS, Middle Tenn State U., 1978; MEd, Trevecca Nazarene Coll., 1987. Cert. elem. tchr., cert. secondary tchr. and libr., Tenn. Tchr. Met.-Davidson County Schs., Nashville, 1993-98; libr. Clarksville/Montgomery County Schs., Clarksville, Tenn., 1998—. Adj. faculty-vol. State C.C., Gallatin, Tenn., 1993-2001; choir dir. First Christian Ch., Dover, Tenn., 1983-95, Sunday sch. tchr., deacon, 1988-93, chmn. bd. dirs., 1989-95; dir. Stewart County Cmty. Choir, 1987-89. Co-chmn. Stewart County Rep. Party, 1986-89. Recipient Vol. Svc. award Cystic Fibrosis Found., 1984, Mayor's Acts of Excellence award, 1994; named E. Middle Sch. Tchr. of Yr., 1996. Mem. ALA, NEA, Tenn. Edn. Assn., Tenn. Assn. Sch. Librs. (conf. coord.), Tenn. Assn. Mid. Schs., Clks. Montgomery County Edn. Assn. (editor The Collective Voice, mem. CMCEA negotiations team 2002-, East Mid. Sch. Tchr. of Yr. 1995, N.E. Mid. Sch. Tchr. of Yr. 2000). Mem. Christian Ch. (Disciples Of Christ). Home: 1724 Valley Rd Clarksville TN 37043-4537 Office: Northeast Middle Sch 3703 Trenton Rd Clarksville TN 37040-5622 Home Fax: 931-506-5690. E-mail: amn2bks@aol.com. *Our heritage is the foundation of our future. As children, our parents help to build us to be able to meet the challenge of life and embrace the future. The option is ours; to add to that foundation or remain unfinished.*

HESTER, D. MICAH, education educator; b. Pomona, Calif., July 16, 1966; s. James D. and Darylin J. Hester; m. Kelly Nugent Sherman, Oct. 1, 1993; children: Emily Sherman, Joshua Davis. BA, Pomona Coll., Calif., 1988; MA, Vanderbilt U., Nashville, 1995, PhD, 1998. Adj. asst. prof. philosophy Tenn. State U., Nashville, 1993—99; asst. prof. biomedical ethics and humanities Mercer Univ. Sch. of Medicine, Macon, Ga., 1999—. Sec. treas. William James Soc., Macon, Ga., 2001—. Author: (scholarly monograph) Community As Healing, 2001, On James, 2003; editor: (textbook anthology) Computers and Ethics in the Cyberage, 2001, (scholarly anthology) Dewey's Logical Theory, 2002. Trustee Ga. Health Decisions, Atlanta, 1999—2003. Fellow: Soc. of Philosophers in Am. Office: Mercer U Sch of Medicine 1550 College St Macon GA 31207-0001 Office Fax: 478-301-5487. Personal E-mail: hesterdm@alum.pomona.edu. E-mail: hester_dm@mercer.edu.

HESTER, DONALD DENISON, economics educator; b. Cleve., Nov. 6, 1935; s. Donald Miller and Catherine (Denison) H.; m. Karen Ann Helm, Oct. 24, 1959; children: Douglas Christopher, Karl Jonathan. BA, Yale U., 1957, MA, 1958, PhD, 1961. Asst. prof., assoc. prof. Yale U., New Haven, Conn., 1961-68; jr. vis. prof. Bombay Univ., India, 1962-63; econs. prof. U. Wis., Madison, 1968-2000, dept. chmn., 1990-93. Cons. Fed. Res., 1969-84; vis. prof. People's U. China, Beijing, 1987. Author: Indian Banks: Their Portfolios, Profits and Policy, 1964; co-author: Bank Management and Portfolio Behavior, 1975, Banking Changes in the European Monetary Union: An Italian Perspective, 2002; co-editor: Risk Aversion and Portfolio Choice, 1967; contbr. numerous articles to profl. jours. Mem. Wis. Coun. Econ. Affairs, 1983-87. Guggenheim fellow 1972, Econometric Soc. fellow, 1977; recipient faculty fellowship Ford Found., 1967, other rsch. awards. Avocations: classical music, art, hiking, traveling. Home: 2111 Kendall Ave Madison WI 53726-3915 Office: U Wis Dept Econs 1180 Observatory Dr Madison WI 53706-1320

HESTER, DOUGLAS BENJAMIN, lawyer, federal official; b. McKenzie, Ala., Sept. 18, 1927; s. Mack Ellis and Carrie Lottie (Taylor) H.; m. Melissa Hood Fuller, Apr. 16, 1960; children: Carlotta Marie, Benjamin Alexander. BS, U. Ala., 1950, LL.B., 1952. Bar: Ala. 1952, D.C. 1960, U.S. Supreme Ct. Law asst. Office Legis. Counsel-U.S. Senate, Washington, 1952-54, asst. counsel, 1954-69, sr. counsel, 1969-80; legis. counsel U.S. Senate, 1980-91; mem., liaison between Ala. and U.S. Congress Svc. Corps. of Retired Execs., 1992-93. Trustee Centro Anglo-Espanol, Washington, 1990. Served with AUS, 1945-47.

Mem. ABA, D.C. Bar Assn., Ala. Bar Assn., Farah Order of Jurisprudence, Pi Alpha Delta, Omicron Delta Kappa, Sigma Delta Pi, Pi Kappa Phi. Home: 2171 Vaughn Ln Montgomery AL 36106-3252

HESTER, FRANCIS BARTOW, III, (FRANK HESTER), lawyer; b. Interlachen, Fla., Oct. 13, 1920; s. Francis Bartow Jr. and Flora McRae H.; m. Joyce Slate, Dec. 21, 1946; children: Susan Hester Elmore, Blanche Hester Wolfson, F. Bartow Hester Jr. Student, Ga. Inst. Tech., 1938-42, U. Ga., 1946; LLB, Emory U., 1948. Bar: Ga. 1952, U.S. Dist. Ct. (no. dist.) Ga. 1952, U.S. Ct. Appeals (4th cir.) 1990, U.S. Ct. Appeals (5th cir.) 1955, U.S. Ct. Appeals (6th cir.) 1967, U.S. Ct. Appeals (7th cir.) 1994, U.S. Ct. Appeals (11th cir.) 1981, Ga. Supreme Ct. 1952, Ga. Ct. Appeals 1952, U.S. Bd. Immigration Appeals 1985, U.S. Supreme Ct. 1960. Spl. agt. FBI, Cleve., Phila., Atlanta, 1948-51; criminal case trial lawyer Hester & Hester, 1952-99. Spl. investigator of fraud in Ga. State Govt., 1958-59. With Air Corp., U.S. Army, 1942-45. Recipient Commendation, Ga. Ho. of Reps., 1997. Mem. Ga. Bar Assn., Ga. Assn. Criminal Def. Lawyers, Former Spl. Agts. of FBI Assn., Inc., Atlanta Bar Assn., Mason (32d degree), 6th Bomb Group Assn. (Tinian 1945), Cherokee Town & Country Club, Shriner (Yaarab temple), Sigma Alpha Epsilon. Democrat. Avocation: boating. Home and Office: 5350 Larch Ln Gainesville GA 30506-6282

HESTER, GAIL, receptionist, writer; b. Stevens, Ark., Oct. 20, 1950; d. Clifton and Ruby Jewel H.; 1 child, Kim. Grad. H.S., Ogden, Utah, 1968. Mail clk. IRS, Ogden, 1985-87; receptionist Merisel Computer Products, L.A., 1987-92, Levolor Home Fashions, L.A., 1993-96, R.T.V. Video, L.A., 1997, Career Strategies, L.A., 1998—. Contbr. poetry to various publs. Avocations: vol. work with abused children, writing, basketball. Home and Office: 1601 Venice Blvd Apt 303 Venice CA 90291-5904

HESTER, JAMES MCNAUGHTON, foundation administrator, artist; b. Chester, Pa., Apr. 19, 1924; s. James Montgomery and Margaret (McNaughton) H.; m. Janet Rodes, May 23, 1953; children: Janet McN., Margaret, Martha. BA, Princeton U., 1945, LL.D. (honoris causa), 1962; BA (Rhodes scholar 1947-50), Oxford (Eng.) U., 1950, D.Phil., 1955; LL.D., Lafayette Coll., 1964, Morehouse Coll., 1967; L.H.D., Hartwick Coll., 1964; LHD (hon.), Pace U., 1971, U. Pitts., 1971, Colgate U., 1974; L.H.D., N.Y. U., 1977; DCL, Alfred U., 1965; LLD (hon.), Hofstra U., 1967, Hahnemann Med. Coll., 1967, Fordham U., 1971, Amherst Coll., 1975, New Sch. for Social Rsch., 1975, Union Coll., 1983. Civil information officer Fukuoka Mil. Govt. Team, Japan, 1946-47; asst. to Am. sec. to Rhodes Trustees, 1950; asst. to pres. Handy Assocs., Inc. (mgmt. cons.), N.Y.C., 1953-54; account supr. Gallup and Robinson, Inc., Princeton, N.J., 1954-57; provost Bklyn. center L.I. U., 1957-60, v.p., 1958-60; prof. history, exec. dean arts and sci., dean Grad. Sch. Arts and Sci. N.Y.U., 1960-61, pres., 1962-75; rector UN U., Tokyo, 1975-80; pres. N.Y. Bot. Garden, 1980-89, The Harry Frank Guggenheim Found., N.Y.C., 1989—, also bd. dirs. Bd. dirs. various Alliance Funds. Trustee Lehman Found. Served with USMCR, 1943-46, 51-52. Mem. Assn. Am. Rhodes Scholars Clubs. Century Assn., University, Pretty Brook Tennis. Office: H Frank Guggenheim Found 527 Madison Ave New York NY 10022-4304

HESTER, JULIA A. lawyer; b. L.A., Nov. 14, 1953; d. Robert William and Bertie Ella (Gilbert) Hester; children: Allison Hester-Haddad, Nancy Hester-Haddad. BA, Fla. Atlantic U., 1984; JD, Nova U., 1990. Bar: Fla. 1990, U.S. Dist. Ct. (mid. dist.) Fla. 1993. Asst. pub. defender Broward Pub. Defender, Ft. Lauderdale, Fla., 1990-93; atty., ptnr. Haddad & Hester, Ft. Lauderdale, 1993-95, 97—. Bd. dirs. St. Anthony Found., Ft. Lauderdale, Ft. Lauderdale Billfish Tournament, 1992—96; bd. dirs., mem. exec. bd. St. Thomas Aquinas Found.; mem. Sunrise Intercoastal Bd., Ft. Lauderdale, 1995; bd. dirs., officer Kids Inn Distress Aux., Ft. Lauderdale, 1984—87. Office: 1 Financial Plz Ste 2612 Fort Lauderdale FL 33394-0061

HESTER, LINDA HUNT, retired dean, counseling administrator; b. Winston-Salem, NC, June 16, 1938; d. Hanselle Lindsay and Jennie Sarepta (Hunt) H. BS with honors, U. Wis., 1960, MS, 1964; PhD, Mich. State U., 1971. Lic. ednl. counselor, Wis. Instr. health and phys. edn. for women U. Tex., Austin, 1960—62; asst. dean women U. Ill., Urbana, 1964—66; dean of women, asst. prof. sociology and phys. edn. Tex. Woman's U., Denton, 1971—73. Rsch. assoc. bur. higher edn. Mich. Dept. Edn., Lansing, 1969-70; vol. counselor Dallas Challenge and Dallas Ind. Sch. Dist., 1989-90 Stradivarious mem. Dallas Symphony, 1991—; assoc. mem. Dallas Mus. Art, 1991—; friend of Kimbell Art Mus., com. of 1000 Philharmonic Ctr. for Arts, Naples, Fla.; founder Women's Mus., Dallas; mem., donor Naples Mus. Art; bd. dirs. Dallas Opera, Dallas, 1986—; bd. dir. Disting. Svc. Registry in Counseling and Devel. Fellow coll. edn. Mich. State U., 1968. Mem. Am. Counseling Assn., Am. Coll. Pers. Assn., Nat. Assn. Women in Edn. (named one of 100 Notable Women in Tex. 2003), Brookhaven Country Club, Wyndemere Country Club, Delta Kappa Gamma, Alpha Lambda Delta. Republican. Presbyterian. Avocations: golf, reading, sailing, cooking, travel. Home: 7606 Wellcrest Dr Dallas TX 75230-4857

HESTER, NANCY ELIZABETH, county government official; b. Miami, Fla., Jan. 20, 1950; d. George Temple and Lorraine Patricia (Cluney) Hester. BA, Bucknell U., 1972; MIA, Columbia U., 1974; MBA, Fla. Internat. U., 1979; PhD, Fla. Atlantic U., 2003. Treasury rep. Westinghouse Elec. Co., N.Y.C., 1974-76; adminstrv. officer serving in bldg. and zoning, gen. svcs. and corrections and rehab. depts. Metro Dade County, Fla., 1979-2000, bur. comdr. corrections and rehab. dept., 1990-2000. Adj. prof. Fla. Internat. U., Miami, 1980-83. Bd. dirs. YWCA Greater Miami, 1988-92, LWV Dade County, 1993-98; pres. bd. dirs., pres. bd. turstees edn. fund, 1994-96; mem. adv. bd. SafeSpace, 1995-2001, v.p. adv. bd., 2000.

HESTER, NORMAN ERIC, chemical company technical executive, chemist; b. Niangua, Mo., Dec. 16, 1946; s Eric Ira and Norma Josephine (Wright) H.; m. Sylvie Jean Hunt, June 16, 1973; children: Jenay Aimee, Yvette Joy, Trinity Marie. AA, El Camino Coll., 1966; BS, Calif. State U., Long Beach, 1968; MS, U. Calif., Riverside, 1971, PhD, 1972. Postdoctoral rsch. chemist U. Calif. Air Pollution Ctr., Riverside, 1972-74; air quality chemist EPA, Las Vegas, Nev., 1974-77; program mgr. Rockwell Internat., Newbury Park, Calif., 1977-80; group head Occidental Petroleum Rsch. Ctr., Irvine, Calif., 1980-83; tech. dir. Truesdail Labs. Inc., Tustin, Calif., 1983—. Pvt. environ. cons., Mission Viejo, Calif., 1983. Contbr. articles to profl. jours. Mem. Am. Chem. Soc., Assn. Ofcl. Racing Chemists. Republican. Avocations: growing hybrid roses, hiking, travel. Office: Truesdail Labs Inc 14201 Franklin Ave Tustin CA 92780-7008 E-mail: norman@truesdail.com.

HESTER, PAUL V. career officer; BSBA in Accountancy, U. Miss., 1969, MBA in Accountancy, 1970; student pilot tng., Columbus AFB, Miss., 1971; student, Squadron Officer Sch., 1974, Air Command and Staff Coll., 1979; M in Mil. Arts and Scis., U.S. Army Command and Gen. Staff Coll., 1980; student, Nat. War Coll., 1990, Harvard U., 1992, sr. def. fellow, 1993. Commd. 2d lt. USAF, 1970, advanced through grades to maj. gen., 1998; stationed at Davis-Monthan AFB, Ariz., 1972, 73-74; aircraft comdr. 354th Tactical Fighter Squadron, Korat Royal Thai AFB, Thailand, 1973; various positions Luke AFB, Ariz., 1974-76; F-15 instr., flight examiner 525th Tactical Fighter Squadron, Bitburg Air Base, W. Germany, 1977-79; stationed at Langley AFB, Va., 1980-86; chief Ho. of Reps. liaison, sec. Air Force legis. liaison Hdqs. USAF, Washington, 1986-89; stationed at Kadena Air Base, Japan, 1990-92; div. chief weapons tech. control div. Joint Chiefs of Staff, Washington, 1993-94; Joint Chiefs of Staff rep. Com. Security and Cooperation Europe, Vienna, Austria, 1994-95; comdr. 35th Fighter Wing, Misawa Air Base, Japan, 1995-97, 53rd Wing, Eglin AFB, Fla., 1997; dir., legis. liaison Office Sec. Air Force, Washington, 1997-99; comdr. U.S. Forces in Japan, 5th Air Force, Yokota Air Base, Japan, 1999—. Decorated Legion of Merit with oak leaf cluster, Air medal with four oak leaf clusters; Vietnam Gallantry Cross with palm. Office: Commander USFJ/5 AF Apo AP 96328

HESTER, ROSS WYATT, retired business forms manufacturing executive; b. Amarillo, Tex., Aug. 23, 1924; s. Wyatt Langford and Nettie Estelle (Horne) H.; m. Elizabeth Ruth Hobbs, May 28, 1948 (div. Aug. 1984); children: Sherry Gail, Randal Ross, Debra Renee, Stephen Keith, Jeffry Wyatt. BA, Austin Coll., Sherman, Tex., 1947. Vice pres. Hester's Office Supply, Inc., Lubbock, Tex., 1947-60; pres. Caprock Bus. Forms, Inc., Lubbock, 1960-90, chmn. bd., 1990-96; ret., 1996. Trustee Austin Coll., 1987-99. With USAAF, 1943-46, CBI. Recipient Disting. Alumnus award Austin Coll., 1984. Mem. Printing Industry Assn. Tex. (pres. 1988-89). Republican. Presbyterian. Avocations: tennis, reading, travel. Office: Hester Books 3504 34th St Lubbock TX 79410-2832

HESTERBERG, LARRY ALLEN, aerospace engineer; b. Springfield, Ill., June 20, 1964; s. Harold August Walter and Ruth Helen Folkerts Hesterberg, Jo Ashbaugh (Stepmother). BS Aerospace Studies, minors: Space Studies, Computer Sci., Humanities, Embry-Riddle Aero. U., Daytona Beach, FL, 1998. Computer operator Direct Mail Express, Daytona Beach, Fla., 1993—95; sr. database specialist Mktg. Gen., Inc., Alexandria, Va., 1996—98; satellite systems engr. Lockheed Martin Tech. Support Group, Springfield, Va., 1998—2000; command & control subsytem engr. ASRC Aerospace, Greenbelt, Md., 2000—01; sr. systems engr. AERA, Inc., Alexandria, Va., 2001—03, Lockheed Martin Mgmt. and Data Sys., Gaithersburg, Md., 2003—. Commn. mem. City of Alexandria, VA, Pub. Records Adv. Commn., Alexandria, Va., 1997—99. Recipient Honor Roll, Embry-Riddle Aero. U., Spring 1993, Dean's List, Daytona Beach C.C., 1990 & 1992. Mem.: AIAA, Aircraft Owners and Pilots Assn., Ill. State Soc., Fla. State Soc., Sigma Chi Frat. (life Cert. of Appreciation 1996, Outstanding Alumni Rels. Award 1992), Eta Iota Ho. Corp. (life; corp. sec. 1991—92, trustee 1995—96). Home: 7121 Rock Ridge Ln #E Alexandria VA 22315 Office: Lockheed Martin Mgmt and Data Sys 200 N Frederick St Gaithersburg MD 20877 E-mail: larry.hesterberg@verizon.net.

HESTERMAN, PHILLIP KARL, music educator; b. Sheboygan, Wis., Nov. 3, 1961; s. Marvin Henry Hesterman and Karilyn Marie Heermann, June Carole Kastens (Stepmother); m. Rebecca Lynn Metzger; children: Micah, Andrea, Bryce. BS in Edn., Concordia Teachers Coll., 1984; MA in Ch. Music, Concordia U., 1994; MA in Tchg., Hastings Coll., 2000. Tchr. Trinity Luth. Sch., Janesville, Minn., 1984—85; tchr. and music dir. St. John Luth. Ch. and Sch., Chaska, Minn., 1985—89; music dir. and tchr. Trinity Luth. Ch. and Sch., Sheboygan, 1989—95; asst. prof. of music Concordia U., Austin, 1995—97; choral dir. Bastrop H.S., Tex., 1997—98; min. of music Trinity Luth. Ch. and Sch., Grand Island, Nebr., 1998—. Dir. Austin Children's Choir, 1995—96; asst. dir. South Ctrl. Nebr. Children's Chorale, Hastings, 1999—; adj. instr. in music Hastings Coll., 1999—. Composer: (partita for organ) Partita on "Good Christian Friends, Rejoice and Sing", 1996. Mem.: Music Educators Nat. Conf., Nebr. Music Educators Assn., Am. Choral Dirs. Assn., Nebr. Choral Dirs. Assn. (chmn. children's choirs repertoire and stds. 2003), Choristers Guild. Lutheran. Avocation: travel, reading, computers. Office: Trinity Luth Ch and Sch 212 W 12th St Grand Island NE 68801 Home Fax: 308-384-6722; Office Fax: 308-384-6722. Business E-Mail: phil@trilutlgi.org.

HESTHAVEN, JAN SICKMANN, mathematician, educator; b. Odense, Denmark, Dec. 10, 1965; arrived in U.S., 1995; s. Finn Sickmann Hesthaven, Karen Margrete Hesthaven; m. Aminia Maria Brueggemann; 1 child, David. MSc, Tech. U., Denmark, 1991, PhD, 1995. Vis. asst. prof. Brown U., Providence, 1995—99, asst. prof. applied math., 1999—2002, Manning asst. prof., 2001—02, assoc. prof. applied math., 2003—. Cons. Inst. for Computer Applications in Sci. and Engring./NASA Langley Rsch. Ctr., Hampton, 1996—2002. Fellow, NSF, 1995; grantee, 2002; Rsch. fellow, Alfred P. Sloan Found., 2000. Office: Brown Univ 182 George St Providence RI 02912 Business E-Mail: jan.hesthaven@brown.edu.

HESTON, THOMAS J. education educator; b. Bethesda, Md., Nov. 2, 1945; s. Walter Enoch and Vivian Janney Heston; m. Susan Luella De Voice, Oct. 14, 1969. AB, Gettsburg Coll., 1967; MA, Case Western Res., 1972, PhD, 1975. Grad. fellow Case Western Res., 1970—74; veterans benefits counselor VA, Cleve., 1974—75; asst. prof. West Chester State Coll., Pa., 1975—81; assoc. prof. West Chester U., Pa., 1981—86, prof., 1986—. Acting asst. dean Coll. of Arts & Sci., West Chester U., 1986—87. Author: (article) Diplomatic History, 1982, (book) Sweet Subsidy, 1987. With U.S. Army, 1968—70. Grantee Bernadette E. Schmitt fellowship, Case Western Res. U., 1973. Mem.: Soc. of Mil. History, US Naval Inst., Soc. of Historians of Am. Fgn. Rels., Orgn. of Am. Historians. Office: Dept of History West Chester U West Chester PA 19383

HETH, DIANA SUE, therapist; b. Robinson, Ill., Sept. 25, 1948; d. Quentin Wilson and Marguerite (Byrd) Abraham; m. Kenneth Lewis Greider, Aug. 16, 1970 (div. Mar. 1985); children: Kathryn Elizabeth, Susan Nicole, Jonathan Abraham; m. Harold Eugene Heth; children: Joseph Brockwell, Kiley Joy, Mark Quentin. BSE, Eastern Ill. U., 1970; MSW, U. Ill., 1992. Lic. clin. social worker; cert. criminal justice specialist. Exec. dir. Nat. Assn. Downs Syndrome, Chgo., 1977—78, Heartland Hospice, Effingham, Ill., 1983—88; office adminstr. Am. Family Life Assurance, Effingham, Ill., 1988—90; sec. design engring. dept. Fedders N.Am., Effingham, Ill., 1990; co-owner H&S Vending, 1990—98; therapist sexual abuse Heartland Human Svcs., Effingham, Ill., 1992—94; child protection advanced specialist Ill. Dept. of Children and Family Svcs., Effingham, 1994. Profl. adv. com. Hospice Lincolnland. Author: One Gift to the Next, 1983, Sundance Lady, 1990. Vol. Belleville (Ill.) Hospice, 1981-83; co-chmn. svc. and rehab. com. Am. Cancer Soc.; mem. parent adv. bd. Ill. State U., 1996-99; social work cons. Effingham County Health Dept., 1995—; steering com. Coun. on Domestic Violence, 1998. Mem. NASW, Assn. for Christian Counselors, Ill. State Hospice Orgn. (bd. dirs. 1985-86), Ill. Pub. Health Assn., County Orgn. Svc. Providers, Newcomers Club (pres. 1984-85), Compassionate Friends Club (bd. dirs. 1985-86), Topnotcher's 4-H Club (leader), Nat. Assn. for Forensic Counselors. Republican. Methodist. Avocations: bridge, bowling, needlework, gardening, cooking. Home: 9973 E 1735th Ave Shumway IL 62461-2229 Office: Effingham Field Office Ill Dept Child/Family Svcs 401 Industrial Ave Ste 2 Effingham IL 62401-2835 Fax: (217) 868-5082. E-mail: mkjj9973@effingham.net.

HETHERINGTON, BONITA ELIZABETH, elementary education educator; b. Sully, Iowa, May 27, 1946; d. Marion Peter and Florence Lucille Swank; m. Thomas Olson Hetherington, Aug. 17, 1968; children: Eric Hunter, Cori Joanne. BA, Cen. Coll., Pella, Iowa, 1968; postgrad., Tex. A&M U., 1979, Tex. Tech U., 1983-87, Clarion (Pa.) U., 1990, Carlisle U., Millersville U.; Pa. Master's equivalency, Ind. U. of Pa., 1992, Ind. U., 2001. Cert. tchr., Pa., Tex. Elem. tchr. Schley County Schs., Ellaville, Ga., 1968-71; 3d grade tchr Montezuma Ind. Sch., Buena Vista, Ga., 1971; 2d grade tchr. Bryan (Tex.) Ind. Schs., 1979-82; tchr. Lubbock (Tex.) Ind. Sch., 1982-88; 3d grade tchr. Lewisburg (Pa.) Area Schs., 1989-91, K-12 lang. arts instnl. specialist, 1991—, 4th grade tchr., 1991-2001, tchr. K-5 gifted, 2001—. Supr. student tchrs. Ga. S.W. Coll., 1971, Tex. A&M U., 1978-82, Tex. tech., 1987, Susquehanna U., 1992, Bloomsburg U., 1993-94, 96-99, Bucknell U., 1999; cons. Lubbock Schs., 1983-88, Muleshoe (Tex.) Ind. Schs., 1986-88, Region XI Ext. Day Insvc., Mason, Tex., 1987; instr. Inst. for Tchrs. of Disadvantaged Gifted, Lubbock, 1987-88; bd dirs. Regional Insvc. Bd., Montandon, Pa., 1989-2000, chmn., 1996-2000, Act 48 Design Team, 2000-; strategic planning steering com., sec. Lewisburg Area Sch. Dist., 1993-98, 2000—, policies and procedures com., 1992-97, act 178 profl. devel. com., 1991-93, 94, 2002-, act 48 com. 2000—, insvc. presenter, 1994—, sch. improvement team, 1995—, Blue Ribbon sch. prep. com., 1996-98, Goals 2000 Consortium, 1996-98, Educate Am. Consortium, 1998—; Foreign Lang. Dist. com., 1999; faculty rep. LAEA, 1999, negotiations team, 1999—, chair sick bank com.—, 2001—. Leader Brownies, Girl Scouts U.S., Lubbock, 1983-86, Cub Scouts, Bryan, 1979-81; pres. PTA, Canton, Tex., 1975-76, PTO, Lubbock, 1985-86; edn. com. Union County Hist. Soc.; mem. Packwood House Mus. Vols., vol. Am. Heart Assn., Am. Cancer Soc.; lector, usher, mem. social concern com., substitute tchr. for Sunday sch. nursery to adult Luth. Ch. Named one of 17 showcased tchrs. Pa. Assn. Childhood Edn. Internat., 1993; named one of Outstanding People of 20th Century Internat. Biog. Ctr., Cambridge, Eng., 1998. Fellow Internat. Biog. Assn.; mem. NEA, NAGC, AAUW, PA Assn. Gifted Edn., Pa. State Edn. Assn., Lewisburg Edn. Assn. (Linntown bldg. rep. 1999-2001), Alpha Delta Gamma, Epsilon Sigma Alpha. Republican. Avocations: reading, travel, cooking, crafts, personal computing. Home: 1615 Market St Lewisburg PA 17837-1231 Fax: 570-524-4120. E-mail: boto2@yahoo.com.

HETHERINGTON, EILEEN MAVIS, psychologist, educator; b. Nov. 27, 1926; BA, U. B.C., 1947, MA, 1948; PhD in Psychology, U. Calif.-Berkeley, 1958. Clin. psychologist B.C. Child Guidance Clinic, 1948-51, sr. psychologist, 1951-52; clin. internship Langley Porter Clinic, 1956-57; instr. psychology San Jose State Coll., 1957-58; asst. prof. Rutgers U., 1958-60; from asst. prof. to prof. U. Wis., 1960-70; prof. psychology U. Va., Charlottesville, 1970-99, James Page prof. psychology, 1976-99, prof. emeritus, 1999—, dept. chmn., 1980-84. Editor Child Devel., 1971-77; rschr. in personality devel. and childhood psychopathology, the role of family process and parent characteristics on normal and deviant behavior in children, the effects of divorce and remarriage on families, parents and children. Bd. dirs. Found. for Child Devel. Recipient Disting. Scientist award Am. Assn. for Marriage and Family Therapy, 1988, Am. Family Therapy Assn., 1992, Burgess award Nat. Coun. on Family Rels., 2000. Mem. APA (pres. divsn. 7, 1978-79, Stanley Hall Disting. Scientist award 1987, Disting. Scientist award 1993), Soc. Rsch. in Child Devel. (pres. 1985-87, Disting. Scientist award 1995), Soc. Rsch. in Adolescents (pres. 1986-88, Disting. Scientist award 1988, William James Disting. Scientist award 1994), Am. Psychol. Soc. Office: U Va Dept Psychology Gilmer Hall PO Box 400400 Charlottesville VA 22904-4400

HETHERWICK, GILBERT LEWIS, lawyer; b. Winnsboro, La., Oct. 30, 1920; s. Septimus and Addie Louise (Gilbert) H.; m. Joan Friend Gibbons, May 31, 1946 (dec. Aug. 1964); children: Janet Hetherwick Pumphrey, Ann Hetherwick Lyons Winegeart, Gilbert, Carol Hetherwick Sutton, Katherine Hetherwick Hummell; m. Mertis Elizabeth Cook, June 7, 1967 (dec. May 2003). BA summa cum laude, Centenary Coll., 1942; JD, Tulane U., 1949. Bar: La. 1949. With legal dept. NorAm Energy Corp., Shreveport, La., 1949-53; dir. Blanchard, Walker, O'Quin and Roberts, PLC, Shreveport, 1953-99, of counsel, 2000—. Mem. Shreveport City Charter Revision Com., 1955; mem. Shreveport Mcpl. Fire and Police Civil Svc. Bd., 1956-92, vice chmn., 1957-78, chmn., 1978-88. Served with AUS, 1942-46. Recipient Tulane U. Law Faculty medal, 1949. Mem. ABA, La. Bar Assn., Shreveport Bar Assn. (pres. 1987), Energy Bar Assn., Order of Coif, Phi Delta Phi, Omicron Delta Kappa. Episcopalian. Home: 4604 Fairfield Ave Shreveport LA 71106-1432 Office: Bank One Tower Shreveport LA 71101

HETHMON, ROBERT H. writer, educator; b. Paducah, Ky., Oct. 19, 1925; s. Robert Henry and Ruth Hummel H.; m. Charlotte F. Hethmon, July 19, 1952 (div. Feb. 1977); children: Michael M., Mark A., Thomas A.; m. Märta Leijonhufvud June 1977. BA, U. Tenn., 1946; MA, Cornell U., 1948; PhD, Stanford U., 1956. Tchr. U. Colo., Boulder, 1948-51, U. Calif., Riverside, 1955-56, U. Wis., Madison, 1956-62, UCLA, 1963-93, ret., 1993. Editor: Strasberg at the Actors Studio, 1965; contbr. articles to profl. jours. With U.S. Army, 1951-53. Mem. ACLU, So. Poverty Law Ctr., Amnesty Internat., Sierra Club. Democrat. Avocation: mountain climbing. Home and Office: 8967 Wonderland Park Ave Los Angeles CA 90046-1429 E-mail: rhethmon@aol.com.

HETLAND, JAMES LYMAN, JR., banker, lawyer, educator; b. Mpls., June 9, 1925; s. James L. and Evelyn E. (Lundgren) H.; m. Barbara Anne Taylor, Sept. 10, 1949; children: Janice E., James E., Nancy L., Steven T. BSL., U. Minn., 1948, JD, 1950. Bar: Minn. 1950. Law clk. Minn. Supreme Ct., 1949—50; asso. firm Mackall, Crounse, Moore, Helmey & Palmer, Mpls., 1950-56; prof. U. Minn. Coll. Law, 1956-71; v.p. urban devel. First Nat. Bank Mpls., 1971-75, sr. v.p. law and urban devel., 1975-82, sr. v.p., gen. counsel, sec., 1982-88; sr. v.p. First Bank System, 1987-88; counsel to bd. and sec. First Bank, N.A., 1988-90; of counsel Rasmussen & Assocs., Ltd., 1990-99, Leighton, Hetland & Stein, PLLP, Mpls., 2002—. Adj. prof. Hubert Humphrey Inst., U. Minn., 1976—90, regents adv. com., 1982—90; adj. prof. Bus. Coll. ext., 1975—81, Coll. Law, 1980—90; labor arbitrator, 1967—; chmn. Minn. Citizens Coun. Crime and Delinquency, 1978—83; chmn. adv. coms. Minn. Supreme Ct., 1958—90; chmn. Telecommuters, Inc., 1992—96. Co-author: Minnesota Jury Instruction Guides, 1963, 2d edit., 1974, Minnesota Practice, 3 vols., 1970. Chmn. Met. Coun. Twin Cities, St. Paul, 1967-71, Mpls. Charter Commn., 1963-70; chmn. Mpls. Citizens League, 1963-64, bd. dirs., 1953-67; bd. dirs. Mpls. Downtown Coun., 1971—, vice chmn., 1978-82, chmn., 1982-83; chmn. bd. Minn. Zool. Garden, 1978-83; nat. v.p., mem. exec. com. Nat. Mcpl. League, 1979-82, pres., 1982-85, chmn. bd., 1985-87; vice chmn. Minn. Press Coun., 1973-81; vice chmn. bd. Minn. Health Care Cost Coalition, 1980; bd. dirs. Interstudy, 1972-79, chmn., 1974; mem. Bus. Urban Issues Coun., Conf. Bd., 1980-89; bd. dirs. Freshwater Biol. Rsch. Found., 1971-85, adv. bd., 1985—; bd. dirs. Mpls. Community Coll. Found., 1978-83, Minn. Exptl. City, 1972-75, Minn. Campfire Girls, 1974-79, Mpls. YMCA, 1957-76; bd. dirs. Health Central, Inc., 1973-87, exec. com., 1977-87; bd. dirs. Citizen Coun. on Crime and Justice, 1977—, chmn., 1979-82; bd. dirs. Ctr. for Policy Studies, 1983—, Twin Cities Habitat for Humanity, 1988-95; mem. exec. com. Partnership Dataline U.S.A., 1983; bd. dirs., exec. com. Health One, 1987-93; trustee Metro State U., 1989-98, Mpls. United Way, 1988-99; chmn. Mpls. Urban Tennis, 1987-94. With AUS, 1943-46. Mem.: ABA, Hennepin County Bar Assn., Minn. Bar Assn., Am. Bankers Assn., N.W. Tennis Assn., Rotary. Republican. Lutheran. E-mail: jbh1and@aol.com. *Seeking to improve services for urban citizens through new public and private service delivery systems has been a keystone for setting involvement priorities. Effective service delivery systems are essential if an urban society is to preserve a free public-private economic democracy. Involvement and change in the private sector is as important as in the public sector.*

HETLAND, JOHN ROBERT, lawyer, educator; b. Mpls., Mar. 12, 1930; s. James L. and Evelyn (Lundgren) H.; m. Mildred Woodruff, Dec. 1951 (div.); children: Lynda Lee Catlin, Robert John, Debra Ann Allen; m. Anne Kneeland, Dec. 1972; children: Robin T. Willcox, Elizabeth J. Pickett. BSL., U. Minn., 1952, JD, 1956. Bar: Minn. 1956, Calif. 1962, U.S. Supreme Ct, 1981. Practice law, Mpls., 1956-59; prof. law U. Calif., Berkeley, 1959-91; prof. emeritus, 1991—; prin. Hetland & Kneeland, PC, Berkeley, 1959—. Vis. prof. law Stanford U., 1971, 80, U. Singapore, 1972, U. Cologne, Fed. Republic Germany, 1988. Author: California Real Property Secured Transactions, 1970, Commercial Real Estate Transactions, 1972, Secured Real Estate Transactions, 1974, 1977; co-author: California Cases on Security Transactions in Land, 2d edit., 1975, 3d edit., 1984, 4th edit., 1992; contbr. articles to legal, real estate and fin. jours. Served to lt. comdr. USNR, 1953 55. Fellow Am. Coll. Real Estate Lawyers, Am. Coll. Mortgage Attys., Am. Bar Found.; mem. ABA, State Bar Calif., State Bar Minn., Order of Coif, Phi Delta Phi. Home and Office: 20 Red Coach Ln Orinda CA 94563-1112 E-mail: hetlandj@law.berkeley.edu.

HETNARSKI, RICHARD BOZYSLAW, mechanical engineering educator; b. Stopnica, Poland, May 31, 1928; came to U.S., 1969; s. Jan and Izabela Hetnarski; m. Leokadia Elizabeth Lalak, Sept. 24, 1960; children: Eve M., Adam P. MSME, Tech. U. Gdansk, Poland, 1952; MS in Math., U. Warsaw, Poland, 1960; PhD in Mechanics, Polish Acad. Scis., Warsaw, 1964. Registered profl. engr., N.Y. Vis. assoc. prof. Cornell U., Ithaca, N.Y., 1969-70; dist. vis. prof. mech. engring. Rochester (N.Y.) Inst. Tech., 1970-71, prof., 1971-92, James E. Gleason prof., 1992-98; prof. emeritus, 1998—. Founder, pres. Lastran Corp.; pub. books on mechanics, 1998—; vis. prof. U. Paderborn, Germany, 1980; organizer internat. sci. congresses. Editor: Thermal Stresses, vol. I, 1986, vol. II, 1987, vol. III, 1989, vol. IV, 1996, vol. V, 1999; editor-in-chief Jour. Thermal Stresses, 1978—; assoc. editor Applied Mechanics Revs., 1988-2001—; editor various books on mechanics translated from Russian and Polish; contbr. over 50 articles and three books in field. Fellow Columbia U., 1964-65, NASA Lewis Rsch. Ctr., 1979. Fellow ASME; mem. Am. Acad. Mechanics Office: Dept Mechanical Engineering Rochester Inst Technology Rochester NY 14623

HETRICK, CHARLES BRADY, county official; b. Linton, Ind., Jan. 16, 1932; s. Norman Charles and Emma (Klinger) H.; divorced; children: Keith Charles, David Kent, Steven John. BA, Ind. U., 1953; MPA, U. Mich., 1957. Adminstrv. asst., asst. to city mgr., asst. city mgr. City of Park Ridge (Ill.), 1956-68; exec. dir. Miami Valley Coun. Govts., Dayton, Ohio, 1968-69; cons. to pres., div. mgr., dir. corp. planning Dayton Progress Corp., 1969-71, 73-74; exec. v.p., gen. mgr. Ft. Worth Area C. of C., 1971-73; sr. assoc. Louis A Allen Assocs., Inc., Palo Alto, Calif., 1974-75; econ. devel. coord. State of Wis., Madison, 1975-76; asst. county mgr. Volusia County, Daytona Beach and Deland, Fla., 1975-80; county adminstr. Rock County, Janesville and Beloit, Wis., 1980-84, Charleston County, Charleston, S.C., 1984-85, Hernando County, Brooksville, Fla., 1985-97; cmty. devel. coord. Fla. Dept. Cmty. Affairs, Tallahassee, Fla., 1997-2000. Adj. instr. bus. and pub. svc. program Tallahassee C.C. Contbr. articles on mcpl. problems and urban affairs to various publs. 1st lt. U.S. Army, 1953-55. Recipient resolution S.C. Ho. of Reps. and Senate, 1985; U. Mich.

Met. Community fellow, 1955-56. Mem. Internat. City Mgmt. Assn., Am. Soc. for Pub. Adminstrn. Home: PMB 251 400 Capital Cir SE Ste 18 Tallahassee FL 32301-3802 E-mail: chetrick9@comcast.net.

HETRICK, JOAN WILLETTE, critical care nurse, administrator; b. Oct. 14, 1959; d. Wilbert D. Sproul and Lois Diane (Wilson) Pinette Anderson; m. Charles Vance Frum, Mar. 21, 1981. B in Health Scis., Fla. Atlantic U., 1996; ASN, Miami-Dade Med. Ctr., 1998. RN, Fla., Ga. Adminstrv. asst., cons. Holiday Prime Foods, 5 Star Mktg. Group, Davie, Fla., 1996—; RN critical care Aventura (Fla.) Hosp., 1999; RN Meml. Reg. Hosp., Hollywood, Fla., 1999, Hollywood Med. Ctr. Telemetry and Progressive Care, 1998-99; charge nurse Hallandale Rehab. Ctr., 2000—02; ER nurse Plantation Gen. Hosp., 2001—02; RN specialist Agy. for Health Care Adminstrn., Fla., 2001—02; RN Agy., 2002—; oncology nurse Kennestone Hosp., Ga., 2003—. Health instr. Miami Book Fair Internat., Miami-Dade C.C., 1997; health care rschr. for 104th Congress, 1995. Mem. Internat. Thespian Soc., Fla. Nurses Assn., Kappa Delta Pi, Alpha Phi Omega. Republican. Avocations: critical care nursing studies, business studies, real estate studies, pets, surfing the internet. Home: 282 Hood Pkwy Kennesaw GA 30152-

HETRICK, THEODORE LEWIS, JR., emergency medicine physician; b. Danville, Pa., Nov. 5, 1949; s. Theodore Lewis and Betty Jane (Saylor) H.; m. Cynthia Ellen Smith, June 14, 1986; children: Keturah Ellen, Kimberly Lauren. BS summa cum laude, Dickinson Coll., 1971; MD, Temple U., 1975. Family practice resident Geisinger Med. Ctr., Danville, Pa., 1975-78; emergency room physician Sunbury (Pa.) Cmty. Hosp., 1979—, med. dir. paramed. svcs., 1989—; staff physician Yellowstone Nat. Park (Wyo.) Med. Svcs., 1984—; emergency room physician Shamokin Area Cmty. Hosp., Coal Twp., Pa., 1994—. Med. dir. Rescue Hose Co., Beavertown, Pa., 1991—. Contbr. wildlife photographs to numerous mags. Mem. Phi Beta Kappa, Alpha Omega Alpha. Home: RR 1 Box 1029 Beavertown PA 17813-9707 Office: Sunbury Cmty Hospital Emergency Room 350 N 11th St Sunbury PA 17801-1600

HETRICK, WILLIAM P. marketing professional, educator; b. Sharon, Pa., Jan. 24, 1939; s. James Roger and Gail Hetrick. BSBA, Youngstown State U., 1981, MBA, 1984; ABD, U. Ky., 1988. Asst. prof. Loyola Marymount, L.A., 1988—91, Slippery Rock U., Pa., 1991—93; assoc. prof. Bethel Coll., McKenzie, Tenn., 1998—. Contbr. Office: Bethel College 325 Cherry Ave McKenzie TN 38201*

HETT, JOAN MARGARET, ecological consultant; b. Trail, B.C., Can., Sept. 8, 1936; d. Gordon Stanley and Violet Thora (Thors) Hett. BSc, U. Victoria, B.C., Can., 1964; MS, U. Wis., Madison, 1967; PhD, U. Wis., 1969. Ecologist Eastern Deciduous Forest Biome, Oak Ridge Nat. Lab., 1969-72; coord. sites dir. Coniferous Forest Biome, Oreg. State U. Corvallis and U. Wash., Seattle, 1972-77; ecol. cons. Seattle, 1978-84; plant ecologist Seattle City Light, 1986-91, vegetation mgmt. mgr., 1991-2000, ecol. cons., 2000—. Contbr. articles to profl. jours.; rsch. in plant population dynamics, land use planning, and forest succession. Mem. Ecol. Soc. Am., Brit. Ecol. Soc., Am. Inst. Biol. Scis., Am. Forestry Assn., Sigma Xi.

HETTCHE, L. RAYMOND, research director; b. Balt., Mar. 24, 1938; s. Leroy and Dorothy (Curtain) H.; m. Patricia Durkan, July 1965; children: Lisa, Kathleen, Matthew, Craig. BSCE, AB in Math., Bucknell U., 1961; MSCE, Carnegie-Mellon U., 1961, PhD in CE, 1965. Asst. prof. Rutgers U., New Brunswick, N.J., 1964-66; resident rsch. assoc. Nat. Bur. Standards, Washington, 1966-68; structural engr. metallurgy div. Naval Rsch. Lab., Washington, 1968-71, head thermomech. effect sect., 1971-73, head mech. br. metallurgy div., 1973-75, supt. materials sci. div., 1975-81; now, dir. Applied Rsch. Lab. Pa. State U., State College, 1981—2002, prof. engrng. rsch., 2002—. Navy rep. Tech. Working Group Export Control, Washington, 1979-81; navy rep. subgroup P materials panel for metals Tech. Cooperation Program, Washington, 1977-81; session chmn. Submarine Tech. Symposium, Columbia, Md., 1990. Contbr. numerous articles to profl. jours. Tau Beta Pi Nat. fellow, 1961-63; NSF fellow, 1963; recipient Outstanding Achievement award Am. Def. Preparedness Assn., 1986. Office: Pa State U Applied Rsch Lab PO Box 30 State College PA 16804-0030

HETTMANSPERGER, SUE, artist, art educator; b. Akron, Ohio, Nov. 20, 1948; d. Hilton E. Hettmansperger and Dorothy E. Stone. Student, Yale U., summer 1971; BFA in Lithography and Drawing cum laude, U. N.Mex., 1972, MA in Lithography and Drawing, 1974. Grad. tchg. asst. U. N.Mex., 1972-74; instr. lithography, intaglio and drawing Pa. State U., State Coll., 1974-75; prof. painting and drawing U. Iowa, Iowa City, 1977—. Vis. lectr. U. N.Mex., Albuquerque, 1985; invited artist in residence in painting and drawing Roswell Art Mus., N.Mex., 1990; artist in residence in drawing U Cross Found., Wyo., 1992; curator of prints Tyler Graphics, Bedford Village, N.Y., 1976; nat. affiliate A.I.R. Gallery, N.Y.C., 1989—; lectr. in field. One-woman shows include, Frumkin & Struve Gallery Chgo., 1981, A.I.R. Gallery, NYC, 1990, 1994, 1999, 2003, CSPS Alternative Space, Cedar Rapids, Iowa, 1992, U. No. Iowa Gallery, Cedar Falls, 1994, Artemisia Gallery C, Chgo., 1995, exhibited in group shows, Artemisia Gallery, Chgo., 1996, Arts Iowa City Gallery, Iowa, 1998, Galeria Article 26, Carer de Ferlandina, Barcelona, Spain, 1999, U. Tex. San Antonio Gallery, 2002, numerous others, represented in pub. and pvt. collections. MacDowel Colony Drawing fellow, 1977; NEA fellow in drawing, 1983; recipient Faculty Scholar award U. Iowa, 1997-99; arts and humanities interdisciplinary grantee U. Iowa, 2001. Office: U Iowa E 100 AB Riverside Dr Iowa City IA 52242

HETTRICK, GEORGE HARRISON, lawyer; b. Piney River, Va., Aug. 15, 1940; s. Ames Bartlett and Frances Caryl (O'Brian) H.; children: Heather White Hettrick Brugh, Edward Lord. BA, Cornell U., 1962; JD, Harvard U., 1965. Bar: Va. 1965. Assoc. Hunton & Williams, Richmond, Va., 1965-73, ptnr., 1973—. Ptnr. in charge Church Hill Neighborhood Law Office Hunton & Williams, 1990—, chmn. Community Svc. com.; dir. Richmond Community Hosp., 1992—. Contbr. articles to profl. jours. Pres. bd. trustees Va. Episcopal Sch., Lynchburg, 1978—81; spl. counsel Gov. of Va., Richmond, 1971—72; vice-chmn. bd. dirs. Va. Port Authority, Norfolk, 1970—75, former commr., vice-chmn.; Va. State adv. com. Neighborhood Assistance Program; past dir., chmn. Peter Paul Devel. Ctr., Inc.; bd. dirs. Lawyers Helping Lawyers, St. Mary's Hosp., Stuart Circle Hosp., Regional Meml. Med. Ctr; bd. dirs., pres. Greater Richmond Bar Found., 2003—; active Henrico County (Va.) Cmty. Svcs. Bd., 1997—, chmn., 2002—; bd. dirs. Chesterfield/Colonial Heights Drug Ct. Found., 2002—. Capt. U.S. Army, 1966—68. Fellow Va. Law Found.; mem. ABA, Va. Bar Assn. (chmn. substance abuse com. 1995-96), Va. State Bar, Richmond Bar Assn. (chmn. pro bono com. 1998-2001). Republican. Episcopalian. Home: 6350 Memorial Dr Sandston VA 23150-6307 Office: Hunton & Williams PO Box 1535 Richmond VA 23218-1535 E-mail: ghettrick@hunton.com.

HETTRICK, JANE SCHATKIN, music educator, classical musician; b. N.Y.C. d. Sidney B. and Amy Wheeler (White) Schatkin; m. William E. Hettrick III, June 5, 1966. BA, CUNY, 1963; student, Acad. Music, Vienna, Austria, 1964-65; MusM, U. Mich., 1966, Mus D, 1972. Asst. prof. music St. Peter's Coll., Jersey City, 1970-71; music lectr. Hofstra U., Hempstead, N.Y., 1971-74; dir. music Redeemer Lutheran Ch., Bayside, N.Y., 1972-86; from asst. to full prof. music Rider U., Lawrenceville, NJ, 1974—; prof. organ Hofstra U., 2003—. Numerous solo organ recitals, dir. numerous choral performances. Author: Antonio Salieri, Concerto per l'organo, 1981, Antonio Salieri, Three Symphonies, vol. 2, series B of The Symphony, 1720-1840, 1983, Antonio Salieri, Messe in B Dur, vol. 146, Denkmäler der Tonkunst in Österreich, 1988, Antonio Salieri, Missa stylo a cappella, 1993, Antonio Salieri, Mass in D Major, 1994, Pietro Sales, Concerto in G Major, 1996, Anna Bon, Six Sonatas for Keyboard, 1997, Antonio Salieri, Mass in D Minor, 2002; editor: Lutheran Worship; contbr. articles to profl. jours., to music mags. Fulbright-Hays scholar, 1964, Nat. Endowment for the Humanities fellow, 1983; grantee D.C. chpt. Am. Guild Organists Found., 1986, San Francisco chpt. Am. Guild Organists Found. Spl. Projects Fund, 1991, The Thanks Be to Grandmother Winifred Found., 1999; mem. Gesellschaft zur Herausgabe von Denkmälern der Tonkunst in Österreich, 1988. Mem. Am. Guild Organists, Am. Musicological Soc., Am. Musical Instrument Soc., Soc. for 18th Century Music, Mozart Soc. Am., Phi Alpha Theta, Phi Beta Delta. Home: 48 21 Glenwood St Little Neck NY 11362-1422

HETTRICK, WILLIAM EUGENE, music educator; b. Toledo, Nov. 15, 1939; s. William E., Jr. and Marian (Morse) H.; m. Jane Helen Schatkin, June 5, 1966. B.Mus., U. Mich., 1962, M.A., 1964, Ph.D., 1968. Asst. prof. music Hofstra U., 1968-75, assoc. prof., 1975-81, prof., 1981—; dir. Hofstra Collegium Musicum, 1969—. Author: Musica instrumentalis deudsch of Martin Agricola: A Treatise on Musical Instruments, 1529 and 1545, 1994; editor: Gregor Aichinger: Cantiones Ecclesiasticae (1607), 1972, Bernhard Klingenstein: Rosetum Marianum (1604), 1977, Jour. Am. Mus. Instrument Soc., 1979-85, 92, Musica Selecta, 1979-85, Gregor Aichinger: The Vocal Concertos (2 vols.), 1986, Am. Mus. Instrument Soc. Newsletter, 1997, 99-2003; mem. editl. bd. The American Recorder, 1979-89, Jour. Am. Mus. Instrument Soc., 1986—. Contbr. articles to profl. jours. Fulbright grantee, 1966-67; NEH stipend, 1971, NEH summer Inst., 1985, NEH Travel to Collections award, 1987. Mem. Am. Musicol. Soc., Am. Mus. Instrument Soc. (bd. govs. 1988-94, pres. 1995-99), Gesellschaft fuer Bayerische Musikgeschichte, Internat. Musicol. Soc., Phi Beta Kappa, Pi Kappa Lambda. Home: 48-21 Glenwood St Little Neck NY 11362-1422 Office: 112 Hofstra U Emily Lowe Hall Hempstead NY 11549 E-mail: musweh@hofstra.edu.

HETZEL, ALICE M. statistician, researcher; b. Guthrie, Okla., Feb. 9, 1922; d. Eugene Tilden and Ina (Pence) H. BS, Okla. State U., 1942; postgrad., Georgetown U., 1945. Economist Navy Dept., Washington, 1943-46; statistician USPHS, Washington, 1946-50, U.S. Navy Dept., Washington, 1950-61; spl. asst. to chief Nat. Office Vital Stats., Washington, 1961-68, chief marriage and divorce stats., 1968-74; dep. dir. divsn. vital stats. NCHS, Washington, 1974-83; rschr. self employed, Silver Spring, Md., 1983—. Author: U.S. Vital Statistics System 1950-1995, 1997, Marriage and Divorce Statistics and the Health Department, 1971, Health Survey of the Trust Territory of the Pacific Islands, 1959; co-author: Vital Statistics Rates in the U.S. 1940-1960, 1968. Recipient Exemplary Svc. award Nat. Vital Statistics Program, 1983. Mem. Argyle Country Club. Home: 1300 Ednor Rd Silver Spring MD 20905-5110

HETZEL, FREDRICK WILLIAM, biophysicist, educator; b. Toronto, June 28, 1946; came to U.S., 1974; BS, U. Waterloo, Ont., Can., 1970, MS, 1971, PhD, 1974; JD, Wayne State U., 1994. Sr. CA rsch. scientist Radiation Med. Dept. Div. Radiology, Buffalo, N.Y., 1976-78; asst. prof. Biophysics Dept. SUNY, Buffalo, N.Y., 1977-78; rsch. prof. Grad. Div. Niagra (N.Y.) U., 1978; sr. radiation biologist Therapeutic Radiology, Henry Ford Hosp., Detroit, 1978-82; adjunct asst. prof. Biology Dept. Wayne State U., Detroit, 1979-85; clin. assoc. prof. Physics Dept. Oakland U., Rochester, Mich., 1982-85, assoc. prof., 1985-87; dir. radiobiology Neurology Dept. Henry Ford Hosp., Detroit, 1982-90; prof. Physics Oakland U., Rochester, Mich., 1987-93, dir. radiation oncology rsch., 1991-93; dir. R & D Presbyn./St. Luke's Med. Ctr., Denver, 1993-94; dir. R&D HealthOne, Denver, 1994-96, v.p., dir. rsch., 1996—. Co-organizer, guest faculty Hyperthermia and Cancer Therapy, Seattle, 1984, Madison, Wis., 1985, Durham, N.C., 1987; profl. cons. hyperthermia FDA Regulations, Protocol Design, 1986; mem. med. staff bylaws com. Henry Ford Hosp., 1989; mem. radiation study sect. DHHS/NIH/DRG, 1989-93. Assoc. editor: Radiation Rsch., 1987-91. Grantee NIH, 1979-88, 86-90 (2), 87-90, 92—. Mem. N.Am. Hyperthermia Group (memberhsip com. 1987-88, sec.-treas. 1989-91), Am. Assn. Physicians in Medicine (chmn. task group), Am. Soc. Clin. Oncology, Am. Coll. Med. Physics. Home: 201 Locust Ln Denver CO 80220-5973 Office: HealthOne Rsch 1850 High St Denver CO 80218-1308 E-mail: fwhetzel@aol.com.

HETZEL, WILLIAM GELAL, executive search consultant; b. New Rochelle, N.Y., May 19, 1933; s. William Gelal and Nan (Sanes) H.; m. Karen Marie Ross; children: William Gelal III, Tara L., John F., Janda B. Student, Washington Coll., 1949-51; BBA, U. Miami, 1953; postgrad., Xavier U., 1957-58; MBA, Northwestern U., 1962. Cons. McKinsey & Co., Inc., Chgo., 1961-64; various sales mgmt. positions Xerox Corp., Chgo., Rochester, N.Y., Louisville, 1964-69; dir. mktg. Maremont Corp., Chgo., 1969-70; pres. Medelco, Inc., Schiller Park, Ill., 1970-72; div. gen. mgr., v.p. ITT Service Industries Corp., Cleve., 1972-74; v.p. Lamalie Assos., Inc., Chgo., 1974-78; sr. v.p. Eastman & Beaudine, Chgo., 1978-81; pres. The Hetzel Group, Inverness, Ill., 1981—. Speaker in field. Contbr. numerous articles on exec. recruitment to profl. jours. Mem. found. bd. Northeastern Ill. U., 1993—. Served to lt. (j.g.) USN, 1953-56. Mem. Internat. Assn. Corp. and Profl. Recruitment, Am. Assn. Exec. Search Cons., Northeastern Ill. U. Found. Bd. Republican. Lutheran. Office: 157 K Helm Rd Barrington IL 60010-7632

HETZLER, SUSAN ELIZABETH SAVAGE, educational administrator; b. Monticello, Iowa, Mar. 18, 1947; d. Robert Engelbert and Josephine May (Ricklefs) Savage; children: Stephanine, Michael. BS in Edn., Rockford (Ill.) Coll., 1971; 2MS in Edn., No. Ill. U., 1978, cert. advanced study, 1984; PhD, Walden U., Mpls., 1989. Cert. elem. tchr., adminstr., Ill., Iowa; supr., sociology tchr., Ill. Elem. tchr. Freeport (Ill.) Sch. Dist., 1971-86; prof. elem. edn. Iowa State U., Ames, 1986-90; dir. tchr. edn. and devel. Iowa Dept. Edn., Des Moines, 1990-96; prof. edn., dean sch. edn. Buena Vista U., Storm Lake, Iowa, 1996-99; program admin. for educator preparation Tex. State Bd. for Educator Certification, Austin, 1999—2001; dir. tchr. edn. Tex. Higher Edn. Coord. Bd., Austin, 2001—. Curriculum cons. Ames Sch. Dist., 1985-90, Des Moines Sch. Dist., 1985-90; mem. ISU adv. bd., Ames, 1991—. Author: Elementary Education Practicum Teaching, 1988, Learning Centers, 1989. Comsnr. Drug and Alcohol Prevention Project, Freeport, 1976-85; chairperson Stephenson County (Ill.) Cancer Soc., 1976-78, small bus. dvsn. United Way, Freeport, 1980-85; vol. BSA and GSA, Freeport, 1974-85. Recipient Excellence in Teaching award Iowa State U., 1989-90, Outstanding Elem. Tchrs. Am. Ill., 1974, 81. Mem. AAUP, ASCD, NEA, Iowa ASCD, Am. Assn. Colls. of Tchr. Edn., Iowa Assn. Colls. of Tchr. Edn., Iowa Ednl. Rsch. and Eval. Assn., Assn. Tchr. Educators, Tex. Tchr. Educators, Tex. Coun. Women Sch. Execs., Delta Kappa Gamma, Phi Delta Kappa, Rotary, Kiwanis. Presbyterian. Avocations: reading, skiing, tennis, piano, antiques, golf. Home: 1107 Chardonnay Crossing Leander TX 78641 Office: Tex Higher Edn Coord Bd 1200 E Anderson Ln Austin TX 78752 E-mail: susan.hetzler@thecb.state.tx.us.

HETZNER, DONALD RAYMUND, social studies educator, forensic social scientist; b. Ottawa, Ill., Jan. 1, 1938; s. James Hyatt and Thelma Margaret (Sheedy) H.; m. Coralia Josefina Lora, July 9, 1966; children: Sean, Matthew. AA, LPO Jr. Coll., 1957; BA in Social Sci., Shimer Coll., 1961; MA in Polit. Sci., No. Ill. U., 1965; EdD in Social Studies, SUNY, Buffalo, 1972. Cert. tchr. social studies, N.Y. Tchr. English, social studies Medina (N.Y.) Pub. Sch. System, 1966-68; tchr. Kenmore-Tonawanda (N.Y.) Union Free Sch. Dist. 1, 1968-69; prof. SUC, Buffalo, 1970—. Scholar in residence Am. Assn. Cmty. and Jr. Colls., Washington, 1986-87; cons. restructuring post-secondary edn. in The Acad. Namibia, Southwest Africa, 1989; founder Applecore Consulting. Co-author: Practical Methods for the Social Studies, 1977, Working in America, 1976, Historian: Building a New Nation in 1789; editor: The Social Science Record, 1975-78; contbr. articles to ednl. jours. Mem. World Assn. for Case Rsch. and Application, Nat. Coun. for Social Studies, N.Y. State Coun. for Social Studies (exec. bd. dirs. 1975-78, jour. editor), Rsch. and Planning for the Future (founder). Democrat. Avocations: travel, historical research. Home: 67 Lancaster Ave Buffalo NY 14222-1403 Office: SUC Dept History & Social Studies 1300 Elmwood Ave Buffalo NY 14222-1004

HETZNER, MARC A. lawyer; b. Logansport, Ind., Apr. 24, 1953; s. John R. and Nelma L. (Byrt) H.; m. Rosalie M.; children: Collette N., Christopher R., Kimberly A. BA, Ind. U., 1975, MBA in Taxation, JD, Ind. U., 1983. Bar: Ind. 1983, U.S. Dist. Ct. (so. dist.) Ind. 1983, U.S. Tax Ct. 1983, U.S. Ct. Appeals (7th cir.) 1988. Ptnr. Krieg DeVault LLP, Indpls., 1989—. Contbr. articles to profl. jours. 1st lt. U.S. Army, 1975-79. Fellow Am. Coll. Trust & Estate Counsel, Ind. State Bar Found. (coun. tax sect.); mem. Indpls. Estate Planning Coun. Office: Krieg DeVault LLP Ste 2800 1 Indiana Sq Indianapolis IN 46204-2079

HEUBAUM, WILLIAM LINCOLN, retired lawyer; b. Chgo., Jan., 1938; s. Lincoln William and Hazel Lillian Heubaum; m. Mary Lynn Gilbert, June 19, 1965; children: Karl Franz, Joy Ann. BS (Forrestel scholar), Northwestern U., 1959, JD (Kosmerl scholar), 1965. Bar: Ill. 1965, Iowa 1973, Nebr. 1982. Atty. Hopkins & Sutter, Chgo., 1965-72; v.p., sec., gen. counsel IBP (formerly Iowa Beef Processors, Inc.), Dakota City, Nebr., 1972-82; ptnr. Bikakis, Heubaum, Vohs & Storm, Sioux City, Iowa, 1983-85; founder, mem. Crime Stoppers, 1982-98. Lectr. Chgo. Bar Assn. Continuing Legal Edn. Com. Mem. Local Bd. 12; asso. govt. appeal agt. Local Bd. 30, Ill. Selective Service System, 1967-72. Served to lt. Supply Corps USNR, 1959-62. Mem. Acacia, Masons, Moose, Rotary, Phi Alpha Delta. Republican. Methodist. Home: 204 Calumet Dr Yankton SD 57078-6751

HEUBEL, WILLIAM BERNARD, lawyer, international contract consultant; b. Sharon, Pa., Mar. 7, 1928; s. Herman J. and Margaret (Becker) H. Student, Gannon U., 1948-49; BS, Purdue U., 1952; JD, Ind. U., 1954. Bar: Ind. 1955, U.S. Dist. Ct. (so. dist.) Ind. 1955. Mem. profl. mgmt. staff AT&T Long Lines, 1955-61; contract adminstr. nuclear and def. Westinghouse Electric Corp., Pitts., 1961-68, mgr. mktg. adminstrn. nuclear, 1968-73, contract mgmt. cons. corp. mktg., 1973-81, contract cons. internat. sales contracts-law dept., 1981-87; pvt. practice, 1988—. Served with AUS, 1946-48. Mem. Internat. Bar Assn. Roman Catholic. Office: 123 Franklin Dr Greensburg PA 15601-1304

HEUBI, JAMES EDWARD, pediatrician, educator; b. Indpls., Nov. 13, 1948; s. John Edward and Elizabeth Ruth Heubi; m. Margo A. Hungerford; children: Elizabeth C., Christine H. BS, Ind. U., 1970; MD, Ind. U., Indpls., 1973. Asst. prof. pediat. U. Cin. Coll. Medicine, 1979—83, assoc. prof. pediat., 1983—89, prof. pediat., 1989—, assoc. dean clin. rsch., 2003—; program dir., Gen. Clin. Rsch. Cin. Children's Hosp. Med. Ctr., 1988—. Contbr. articles to med. rsch. jours. Mem.: Am. Gastroenterol. Assn., Am. Assn. Study Liver Disease, Am. Pediat. Soc., Alpha Omega Alpha, Phi Beta Kappa. Achievements include research in finding new defects of bile acid synthesis which could be treated medically with liver transplantation; instrumental in increasing understanding of importance of early recognition of Reyes Symdrome and its effect on prognosis. Avocations: indoor soccer, reading, water sports. Office: Cincinnati Childrens Hosp Med Ctr 3333 Burnet Ave Cincinnati OH 45229

HEUER, ARTHUR HAROLD, ceramics engineer, educator; b. N.Y.C., Apr. 29, 1936; s. William Jacob and Hannah (Kaye) H.; m. Roberta Feinstein, Dec. 22, 1956 (div. 1974); children: Howard, Michael, James; m. Joan McKnee Hulburt, May 8, 1976. BS, CCNY, 1956; PhD, U. Leeds, Eng., 1965, DSc, 1977. Rsch. chemist Ind. Gen. Corp., Keasbey, N.J., 1956-60; rsch. engr. Electron Tube Div. Bendix Co., Eatontown, N.J., 1960-61, staff scientist AVCO Space Systems Div., Lowell, Mass., 1965-67; asst. prof. ceramics div. metall. and materials Case Western Res. U., Cleve., 1967-70, assoc. prof., 1970-74, prof., 1974—, dir. materials rsch. lab. Case Inst. Tech., 1974-80, Kyocera Prof. Ceramics, 1985—. External sci. mem. Max-Planck Inst. fur Metalforschung, Germany, 1990—. Editor: Zirconia I, Zirconia II; contbr. over 420 articles to profl. jours. Recipient Alexander von Humboldt award Max-Planck Inst., 1983, Gold Medal award ASM. Fellow Am. Ceramic Soc. (chmn. basic sci. com., Sosman Meml. lectr. 1986, editor jour. 1988-90, John Jeppson award 1990, Orton lectr. 1991, Disting. Life mem. 1996), U.K. Inst. Physics; mem. AAAS, NAE, ASM (Gold medal). Achievements include research in transformation toughening in Zirconia, electron microscopy in ceramics, dislocations in ceramics, phase transformations in ceramics, biomimetic processing of materials, materials science aspects of MEMS, rapid prototyping technology/solid freeform fabrication of engineering materials, mechanical properties of hard and soft tissue; co-founder CAM-LEM Inc. Home: 2043 Random Rd Apt 303 Cleveland OH 44106-5916 Office: Case Western Res U Materials Sci and Engring 10900 Euclid Ave Cleveland OH 44106-7204 E-mail: heuer@cwru.edu.

HEUER, BETH LEE, music educator, composer; b. Rockford, Ill., May 13, 1957; d. Stanton Lee and Gladys Mae Heuer. BA in Music, 1980, BFA in Music Edn., 1981, M in Music Edn., 2001. Vocal music tchr. Boylan Cath. H.S., Rockford, Ill., 1981—82, Pecatonica (Ill.) H.S., 1982—83; band dir. Boylan Cath. H.S., 1983—, chmn. dept. music, 1987—. Pvt. music tchr., Rockford, 1982—. Music arranger, composer, 1985—. Mem.: Ill. Music Educators Assn., Music Educators Nat. Conf., Internat. Jazz Educators Assn. Avocations: gardening, reading, traveling. Office: Boylan Cath HS 4000 St Francis Dr Rockford IL 61103

HEUER, GERALD ARTHUR, mathematician, educator; b. Bertha, Minn., Aug. 31, 1930; s. William C. F. and Selma C. (Rosenberg) Heuer; m. Jeanette Mary Knedel, Sept. 5, 1954; children: Paul, Karl, Ruth, Otto. BA, Concordia Coll., 1951; MA, U. Nebr., 1953; PhD, U. Minn., 1958. Math. instr. Hamline U., 1955-56, Concordia Coll., Moorhead, Minn., 1956-57, asst. prof., 1957-58, assoc. prof., 1958-62, prof., 1962-95, Sigurd and Pauline Prestegaard Mundhjeld prof., 1988-95, chmn. dept., 1963-70, research prof., 1970-71, prof. emeritus, mathematician-in-residence, 1995—; mathematician Remington Rand Univac, summer 1958. Vis. prof. U. Nebr., Lincoln, 1960—61, Wash. State U., Pullman, 1980—81; mathematician Control Data Corp., 1960—62, cons., 1960—63; vis. lectr. Math. Assn. Am., 1964—66; cons. NSF-AID, India, 1968—69; guest spkr. Minn. sect. Math. Assn. Am., 1956, Nebr. sect. Math. Assn. Am., 1961, No. Ctrl. sect. Math. Assn. Am., 1974; vis. prof., scholar Math. Inst. Cologne (Germany) U., 1973—74; vis. prof., scholar Inst. Stats., Econs. and Ops. Rsch. Graz U., Austria, 1987—88, rsch. prof., Austria, 1990, vis. prof., Austria, 94, Austria, 97; dir. U.S. Math. Olympiad Tng. Session; leader U.S. team Internat. Math. Olympiad, 1988—90; invited plenary spkr. Internat. Symposium Ops. Rsch., Passau, Germany, 1995. Author (with Ulrike Leopold-Wildburger): (book) Balanced Silverman Games on General Discrete Sets, 1991, Silverman's Game, 1995; contbr. articles to profl. jours.; reviewer: Zentralblatt für Mathematik, 1967—, Math. Revs., 1978—. Fellow Faculty, NSF, 1966—67; grantee Rsch., 1963, 1964, 1966; scholar Bush Rsch., Concordia Coll., 1983—84, Centennial Rsch., 1992, 1993, 1994, 1995. Mem.: Österreichische Math. Gesellschaft (Vienna), Deutsche Math.-Vereinigung e.v. (Berlin), Nat. Geographic Soc., Am. Math. Soc., Math. Assn. Am. (com. Am. math. competitions 1988—, nat. bd. govs. 1971—73, com. Putnam prize 1987—90, pres. Minn. sect. 1959—60, cert. meritorious svc. 1994), Sigma Xi. Lutheran. Home: 1216 Elm St S Moorhead MN 56560-4049 Office: Concordia Coll Dept Math Moorhead MN 56562-0001 E-mail: heuer@cord.edu.

HEUER, MARGARET B. retired microcomputer laboratory coordinator; b. Juneau, Alaska, Sept. 12, 1935; d. William George and Flora (Rusk) Allen; m. Joseph Louis Heuer; children: Leilani, Joseph (dec.), Daniel, Suzanne, Karen, Mark, Jerina. AA, San Bernardino Valley Coll., 1980. Cert. data processing, computer repair and maintenance, microcomputer support specialist. Coord. microcomputers lab. Oakton Community Coll., Skokie, Ill., 1981-93; ret., 1993; switchboard oper. Coll. Am. Pathologists, 2000—.

HEUER, MARVIN ARTHUR, physician, research and industry consultant; b. Mankato, Minn., Mar. 11, 1947; s. Marvin Ernst and Elaine Olive (Melahn) H.; children: David Walter, Michael Arthur. BA, Mankato State U., 1969; BS, MD, U. Minn., Mpls., 1973. Intern, resident family practice St. John's Hosp., St. Paul, 1973-80; ptnr. Family Med. Group practice Park Rapids (Minn.)/Walker Clin. LTD, 1980-81; assoc. med. dir. Smith Kline & French Corp., Phila., 1981-82, group dir. clin. rsch., 1982-84, acting v.p. worldwide ops., 1984-87; v.p. med. affairs, v.p. clin. rsch. worldwide Am. Home Products, N.Y.C., 1987-89; v.p. R&D Wallace Labs., Cranbury, N.J., 1989-91; v.p., dir. clin. rsch. Worldwide Smithkline Beecham Corp., London, 1990-92; CEO Heuer Assocs., Gainesville, Fla., 1992—; physician Westview Clinic, West Saint Paul, Minn., 1991-97; dir. clin. rsch. Allina Corp., Mpls., 1993; v.p. clin. rsch. IntegraMed Am., Purchase, N.Y., Gainesville, Fla., 1997-98, Women's Med. & Diagnostic Ctr., Gainesville, Fla., 1997-98; pres. Fla. Med. and Rsch. Inst., PA, Gainesville, 1998-2001, Clin. Sci. Internat., Inc., Williston, Fla., 2001—. Clin. asst. prof. Robert Wood Johnson Med. Sch., Dept. of Family Medicine, New Brunswick, N.J., 1981-91; clin. assoc. prof. family practice U. Minn. Med. Sch., 1992-96, U. Fla., Gainesville, 1997—; mem. biotech. adv. bd. Mankato State U.; mem. drug utilization rev. panel Dept. Health, Minn., 1992-98. Contbr. 12 articles on drugs to profl. jours., tng. manual, Med. Monitors Guide 1983. Dir. youth activities St. Matthews Luth. Ch., Moorestown, N.J., 1981-86, trustee 1983-92, coun. mem., 1984-87, alt. bd. mem. 1986; fin. com. Incarnation Luth. Ch., St. Paul, Minn., 1991-97, property com., 1991-97. Fellow Am. Bd. Family Practice; mem. AMA, ACP, Am. Assoc. Physician Execs., Am. Acad. Family Physicians, Minn. Med. Soc., Pharm. Mfrs. Assn., Minn. Acad. Family Practice, Am. Coll. Cardiology, Am. Rheumatol. Assn., Med. Alley Assn., Nat. Geog. Soc., Drug Info. Assn., Soc. Clin. Trials. Avocations: private pilot, scuba, skydiving, surfing, tennis. Home: 17072 NW 86th Terr Reddick FL 32686 Office: Clin Sci Internat Inc # 151 3324 W University Ave Gainesville FL 32607

HEUER, MICHAEL ALEXANDER, dean, endodontist educator; b. Grand Rapids, Mich., Apr. 27, 1932; s. Harold Maynard and Gwendolyn Ruth (Kremer) H.; m. Barbara Margaret Naines, Nov. 23, 1955; children— Kristan M., Karin E., Katrina A. DDS, Northwestern U., 1956; MS, U. Mich., 1959. Pvt. practice, Chgo., 1959-86; asst. prof. Northwestern U., 1960-66; assoc. prof. Loyola U., Chgo., 1968-73; prof., chmn. dept. endodontics Northwestern U., 1974-83, assoc. dean acad affairs, 1983-88, sr. assoc. dean, 1988-93, dean, 1993-98, prof. emeritus, 1999—. Dir. Am. Bd. Endodontics, 1971-77, sec.-treas., 1973-76, pres., 1976-77; chmn. subcom. Am. Nat. Standards Inst.; mem. com. on advanced edn. Commn. on Accreditation of Dental Edn., 1974-77, endodontic cons., 1986-91, curriculum cons., 1986-92. Contbr. articles in field to profl. jours. Served with USNR, 1956-58. Recipient Northwestern U. Alumni Merit award, 2001. Fellow Am. Coll. Dentistry (life, sec.-treas. Ill. sect. 1986-92, vice chair 1992-94, chair 1994-96), Internat. Coll. Dentistry, Am. Assn. Endodontists (life; exec. coun. 1967-71, sec. 1979-84, v.p. 1984-85, pres.-elect 1985-86, pres. 1986-87); mem. AAAS, ADA (life; coun. dental materials and devices 1972-78, chmn. 1977-78, sci. coun. 1980-97), Internat. Assn. Dental Rsch., Am. Assn. Dental Schs., Chgo. Odontographic Soc. (pres. 1982-84), Edgar D. Coolidge Endodontic Soc. (life, charter sec. 1961, pres. 1964, trustee), Phi Eta Sigma, Omicron Kappa Upsilon, Chi Psi, Delta Sigma Delta. Home: 1552 Treeline Ct Naperville IL 60565-2015 E-mail: mikeaheuer@aol.com.

HEUER, ROBERT MAYNARD, II, opera company executive; b. Detroit, Nov. 27, 1944; s. Robert Maynard and May Elizabeth (Quinn) H. Student, Capital U., 1963-64; BA, Wayne State U., 1976. Youth dir. Grace Luth. Ch., Detroit, 1964-66; costume designer, prodn. mgr. U. Windsor, Ont., Can., 1967-69; program coord. Detroit Youtheatre, Detroit Inst. Arts, 1970-71; mng. dir. Mich. Opera Theatre, Detroit, 1971-79; prodn. dir. Fla. Grand Opera (formerly Greater Miami Opera), 1979-83; asst. gen. mgr. Greater Miami Opera, 1984-85, gen. mgr., CEO, 1986-97, gen. dir., CEO, 1997—. Mem. Performing Arts Ctr. Found. Greater Miami. Recipient Narot Humanitarian award, 2001. Mem.: Opera Am., Greater Miami C. of C. Home: 547 Navarre Ave Coral Gables FL 33134-4231 Office: Fla Grand Opera 1200 Coral Way Miami FL 33145-2927 E-mail: rmheuer@fgo.org.

HEUER, SAM TATE, lawyer; b. Batesville, Ark., July 11, 1952; s. Albert A. and Mary (Baker) H.; children: Noal Tate, Polly Anna, Charles Albert; m. Max Parker. BBA in Banking and Fin., U. Miss., 1974; JD, U. Ark., 1978. Bar: Ark. 1979, U.S. Dist. Ct. (ea. and we. dist.) Ark. 1979, U.S. Ct. Appeals (8th cir.) 1980. Dep. pros. atty. 4th Jud. Dist., Fayetteville, Ark., 1979-80; assoc. Davis Bracey & Heuer, Springdale, Ark., 1980-81; pvt. practice, Batesville, 1981-86; pros. atty. 16th Jud. Dist., Batesville, 1983-86; assoc. salesman Crews & Assocs., Little Rock, 1987-88; assoc. John Wesley Hall P.C., Little Rock, 1988-93; ptnr. Heuer Law Firm, Little Rock, 2000—. Mem. ATLA, Ark. Prosecutor's Assn. (bd. dirs. 1984-86, v.p. 1985-86), Ark. Trial Lawyers Assn., Am. Trial Lawyers Assn., Pulaski County Attys. Assn. Democrat. Episcopalian. Office: Heuer Law Firm 124 W Capitol Ave Ste 1650 Little Rock AR 72201-3758

HEUISLER, CHARLES WILLIAM, lawyer; b. Phila., May 24, 1941; s. Isaac Kilner and Mary Gertrude (Smith) H.; m. Judith Ann Hargadon, June 26, 1965; children: Karen L. Heuisler Murphy, Susan M. Heuisler McCabe, Charles W. Jr. BA in Modern Lang., Coll. of Holy Cross, 1963; JD, Villanova U., 1966. Bar: N.J. 1966, U.S. Dist. Ct. N.J. 1966, U.S. Ct. Appeals (3d cir.) 1970, U.S. Supreme Ct. 1972; cert. civil trial atty. Am. Bd. Trial Advs. Law clk. to Hon. John B. Wick, Superior Ct. of N.J., Chancery Divsn., Camden, 1966-67; shareholder Archer & Greiner, Haddonfield, N.J., 1972—. Counsel, mem. adv. bd. Haddonfield Symphony Soc., 1980—; chmn. South Jersey Performing Arts Ctr., 1992-98. Mem. FBA, N.J. Bar Assn. (trustee from Camden County 1989-93), Camden County Bar Assn. (pres. 1985-86, Peter J. Devine award 1991), Rotary (pres. Order of Camden 1987-88). Avocations: tennis, sailing. Home: 1236 Folkestone Way Cherry Hill NJ 08034-3021 Office: Archer & Greiner PC One Centennial Sq Haddonfield NJ 08033 E-mail: cheuisler@archerlaw.com.

HEVENER, FILLMER, JR., English language educator, writer, portrait artist; b. Churchville, Va., May 14, 1933; s. Fillmer Sr. and Estie (Harper) H.; m. Celia Achenbach, Aug. 27, 1954; children: Dennis Lyle, Yolanda Mae. BA, Columbia Union Coll., 1954; MA, James Madison U., 1957; EdD, U. Va., 1973. Cert. tchr., Va.; ordained pastor, 2001. Secondary English tchr. State of Va., 1954-55, Shenandoah Valley Acad., New Market, Va., 1955-57; tchr. ESL Bugema Missionary Coll., Kampala, Uganda, 1957-58; secondary English tchr. State of Mich., 1958-60; asst. prof. English Frostburg (Md.) State Coll., 1960-64, LaSierra Coll., Riverside, Calif., 1965-66; assoc. prof. English edn. Longwood Coll., Farmville, Va., 1966-92; owner Fillmer Hevener Studio-Gallery, Farmville, Va., 1995—; owner, pres. health food divsn. Fillmer Hevener Studio, Inc., 1997—; owner Green Meadows Farm and Village, 1997—; owner, mgr. Blue Ridge Boys, 1999—. Cons. student tchrs. Longwood Coll., Farmville, Va.; pres., owner Fillmer Hevener Studio, Inc., Farmville, 1992—; presenter seminar on home schooling, Farmville, 1997; interim pastor Farmville S.D.A. Ch., 1999-00; lectr. on vegetarianism Southside Cmty. Hosp. Farmville, 2000—; founder Good Samaritan Soc., 2003. Author: Successful Student Teaching: A Handbook for Elementary and Secondary Student Teachers, 1981, Hot Tips for Student Teachers, 1985, Technical Writing: A Theoretical Basis, 1991, Tithing: Not Required After the Cross, 1993; contbr. articles to profl. publs.; one-man shows include Eisenhower Sch., Ft. Leavenworth, Kans., Richmond (Va.) Pub. Libr., Appomattox (Va.) Pub. Libr., Jefferson Hotel Gallery, Richmond; portraits exhibited at Mayflower Hotel Gallery, Washington, New England Fine Arts Inst., Boston Trade Ctr., Chateau Elan Gallery, Braselton, Ga.; commd. portraits include H. Ross Perot, Gen. Douglass MacArthur, Gen. Robert E. Lee, Pres. George Bush, Pres. Bill Clinton, Pres. J.F. Kennedy, Will Rogers, Pres. Thomas Jefferson, Sir Winston Churchill, Pres. Abraham Lincoln, Pres. Dwight D. Eisenhower, Pres. Woodrow Wilson, Stone Mountain (Ga.) carving; portrait of Mayor Rudolph Giuliani, 2002.. Mem. bd. regents Gen. Conf. Seventh Day Adventists, 1977-80; supr. Buckingham County (Va.). 1984-87; pres. Lower Francisco Fire Assn., Buckingham County, 1981—; vice chair Crossroads Mental Health Svcs., Va., 1985-87; elected sec. Ctrl. Va. Fine Arts Assn., 1993-94, 94—; chair Farmville Post Office Adv. Com., 1997—; bd. dirs. Va. Arts., 1996-97, 2001—, pres. 2000-01; pres. Ctrl. Va. Arts, Inc., 2000-01; bd. dirs. Longwood Ctr. Visual Arts, 2000-01; founder Hevenerites, 2001, Good Samaritan Soc., 2002; pastor Guthrie Meml. Adventist Chapel, Cumberland, Va., 2002. Mem. ASCD, Va. Conf. English Educators (chmn. 1988-90), Nat. Coun. Tchrs. English, Va. Assn. Tchrs. English, Univ. Profs. for Acad. Order, Internat. Platford Assn., Am. Culture/Popular Culture Assn. (presenter 1990), Good Samaritan Soc. (founder 2002), Lions Club Internat. Avocations: playing mandolin and violin, travel. Home and Office: RR 2 Box 1425 Farmville VA 23901-9502 Fax: 434-392-6255. E-mail: fhevener@oilart.com.

HEVERLY, JOHN C. writer, journalist; b. Lock Haven, Pa., Aug. 17, 1963; s. Clifford W. and Margaret A. Heverly. BA in English Lit., Lock Haven U., Pa., 1990. Journalist various newspapers, 1991—. Debate panelist Tioga County Devel. Corp. Congl. Debate, Wellsboro, Pa., 1996, Ronald Reagan Club Congl. Debate, Williamsburg, Va., 2000. Author: (novels) The Truth of Sport, 2002, (poetry) This is NOT a Bill, 2003; playwright A Life of Parties, 2001. Founding mem., participant global issues com./conf. Mansfield U., Pa., 1996—; study participant Stanley Ctr. for Bipolar Rsch., 1997—. Recipient Keystone award, Pa. Newspaper Pubs. Assn., 1995. Mem.: Nat. Depressive and Manic Depressive Assn., Nat. Alliance of the Mentally Ill. Avocations: reading, hiking, travel, cinema.

HEVERN, VINCENT WILLIAM, psychologist, priest; b. N.Y.C., June 28, 1948; AB, Fordham Coll., 1971; MDiv, Weston Sch. Theology, 1976; MA, Fordham U., 1979, PhD, 1985. Lic. psychologist NY; ordained priest Roman Cath. Ch. Tchr. Xavier H.S., N.Y.C., 1971—73; pastoral assoc. St. Ann's Ch., Sommerville, Mass., 1976—77; prof. psychology LeMoyne Coll., Syracuse, NY, 1991—, chmn. psychology, 1997—2001. Internet editor Soc. for Tchg. of Psychology, Washington, 1998—; Marchetti Jesuit lectr. St. Louis U., 2002. Editor: (website) Psych Ref, 1996—, Narrative Psychology: Resource Guide, 1997—. Fellow: APA; mem.: Sigma Xi. Roman Catholic. Avocation: photography. Office: LeMoyne Coll 1419 Salt Springs Rd Syracuse NY 13214 Office Fax: 315-445-4722. E-mail: hevern@lemoyne.edu.

HEVNER, ALAN RAYMOND, educator, consultant; b. Marion, Ind., Dec. 9, 1950; s. Raymond Leland and Pauline Honora (Roach) H.; 1 child, Caitlin Marie. BS, Purdue U., 1973, MS, 1976, PhD, 1979. Asst. prof. U. Minn., Mpls., 1979-81; prof. U. Md., College Park, 1981-94, chmn. Info. Sys. Dept., 1987-93; prof. U. South Fla., 1994—. Endowed chair Salomon Bros. Dist. Tech.; eminent scholar U. Fla. Sys. Author: Principles of Information Systems Analysis and Design, 1986; contbr. articles to profl. jours. Lt. U.S. Army, 1973-75. Mem. Computer Soc. of IEEE (Cert. of Appreciation 1985), Assn. Computing Machinery, Assn. Info. Systems, Inst. Ops. Rsch. and Mgmt. Sci. Christian (Disciples of Christ). Avocations: tennis, basketball, baseball. Office: Info Systems College of Business Admin University of South Florida Tampa FL 33620-7800 E-mail: ahevner@coba.usf.edu.

HEWES, GEORGE POINDEXTER, III, lawyer; b. Jackson, Miss., Oct. 25, 1928; s. George P. Jr. and Gertrude (Turner) H.; m. Helen Elizabeth Morrison, Nov. 19, 1954 (dec. July 1997); children: George P. IV, Laura L. Hewes Bell, Robert Russelll m. Joan Dean, Dec. 27, 1998. BBA, U. Miss., 1950, JD, 1954. Bar: Miss. 1954, U.S. Dist. Ct. (so. and no. dists.) Miss. 1954, U.S. Ct. Appeals (5th cir.) 1954, U.S. Supreme Ct. 1970. Enlisted U.S. Marine Corps, 1950, advanced through grades to lt. col., ret., 1975; sr. ptnr. Brunini, Grantham, Grower & Hewes, Jackson, 1955—2002. Bd. dirs. Trustmark Nat. Bank, Jackson. Chmn. United Way Campaign, 1985; chmn. bd. dirs. Magnolia Speech Sch. Deaf, 1986-87; chancellor Episc. Diocese Miss., 1984-2002. Fellow Am. Coll. Trial Lawyers (regent 1984-88); mem. ABA, Miss. State Bar Assn. (pres. young lawyers sect. 1963-64), Hinds County Bar Assn., Nat. Conf. Commrs. Uniform State Laws, Jackson Symphony Orch. Assn. (past pres.), Met. YMCA (past pres.), Jackson Jr. C. of C. (Young Man Yr. local and state 1962), Jackson Country Club, One Hundred Club Jackson (sec. 1984—, past pres.). Republican. Home: 4 Rivers Creek Dr Jackson MS 39211-5900 Office: Brunini Grantham Grower & Hewes PO Box 119 Jackson MS 39205-0119 E-mail: ghewes@brunini.com.

HEWES, LAURENCE ILSLEY, III, lawyer, management, development, legal consultant; b. Palo Alto, Calif., Sept. 18, 1933; s. Laurence Ilsley, Jr. and Patricia Esther (Jackson) H.; m. Mary Clarke Darling, Oct. 1, 1960; children: Laurence Ilsley IV, Henry Patrick Darling, Mary Clarke Danforth. AB, Yale U., 1956, LLB, 1959. Bar: D.C. 1961, U.S. Dist. Ct. D.C., 1961, U.S. Ct. Appeals (D.C. cir.) 1961, U.S. Supreme Ct. 1966. Assoc. counsel U.S. Senate Comm. Labor and Human Resources, Washington, 1961; assoc. counsel Econ. Devel. Adminstrn. U.S. Dept. Commerce, Washington, 1961-62; staff dir., counsel Pres.'s Com. on Equal Opportunity in Armed Forces, Washington, 1962-63; assoc. then ptnr. Hydeman & Mason and successor firms, Washington, 1963-72; ptnr. Boasberg & Hewes (and successor firms), Washington, 1972-80, Wald Harkader & Ross, Washington, 1980-85; exec. dir., gen. counsel The Support Ctr., 1985-88; pres., chief exec. officer, gen. counsel Corp. Against Drug Abuse, 1989-93; legal, devel. and mgmt. cons. Washington, 1994—. Bd. dirs., Officer Taft Corp., Washington and N.Y.C., 1967-72; bd. dirs., mgr. Grants Mgmt. Adv. Svc., Inc., 1975-80; lectr. non-profit orgn. field. Contbr. articles to profl. jours., chpts. to books. Bd. trustees, Wooster Sch., Danbury Conn., 1981-89, Friends of Superior Ct. of D.C., 1973-87. Served with USAFR, 1959-66. Mem. ABA, D.C. Bar Assn., Cosmos Club, Yale Club (N.Y.C.), Mountain View Country Club. Democrat. Avocations: music, reading, bicycling, fly fishing, tennis.

HEWES, ROBERT CHARLES, radiologist; b. Balt., Feb. 14, 1953; s. Gordon Cecil and Gladys Dorothy (Barringham) H.; m. Judith Renee Lacy, Mar. 23, 1975; children: Christy, Amy, Jeremy. Student, Columbia Union Coll., 1973, Kettering Coll. of Med. Arts, 1971; BS, Loma Linda U., 1976, MD. Diplomate Am. Bd. Med. Examiners, Am. Bd. Radiology with subspecialty in vascular and interventional radiology. Resident in radiology Loma Linda (Calif.) U., 1978-81, asst. prof. radiology, 1983-84; fellow in orthopedic radiology Hosp. for Spl. Surgery Cornell U. Med. Ctr., N.Y.C., 1981-82; fellow in interventional radiology Johns Hopkins U. Hosp., Balt., 1982-83; assoc. prof. Wright State U.; mem. staff Kettering (Ohio) Med. Ctr., 1984—2002, vice chmn. dept. radiology, 1985-87, chmn., 1988-95; pres. Patient First Imaging Network, 1994-95, med. dir., 1996-98; radiologist Hilton Head Med. Ctr. and Clinics, 1999—, mem. med. staff, 1999—. Pres. Kettering Radiologists, Inc., 1987-95, 97-99; bd. dirs. Spring Valley Acad., chmn. fin. mgmt. com., 1998-99; pres. Alumni Assn. Spring Valley Acad., 1987-89. Contbr. articles on radiology to profl. jours. Bd. dirs. Seventh Day Adventist Ch., Kettering, Ohio, Hilton Head Island, SC. Recipient Cert. of merit Am. Roentgen Ray Soc., 1983, Disting. Alumnus award Kettering Coll. of Med. Arts, 1990. Mem.: Miami Valley Radiol. Soc. (pres. 1994), Soc. of Interventional Radiology, Radiol. Soc. N.Am., AMA, Alpha Omega Alpha (award). Republican. Adventist. Avocations: golf, travel, water-sports. Office: Hilton Head Hosp Dept Radiology PO Box 21117 Hilton Head Island SC 29925-1117 E-mail: bobhewes@aol.com.

HEWES, THOMAS FRANCIS, physician; b. Boston, Mar. 5, 1929; s. Walter Raymond and Margaret Frances (Fallon) Hewes; m. Catherine Rene Lemaitre, June 29, 1958; children: Christine, Philip, Gerald, Nancy. AB, Coll. of the Holy Cross, 1950; MD, Tufts U., 1954. Diplomate Am. Bd. Internal Medicine. Intern U. Rochester (N.Y.) Strong Meml. Hosp., 1954-55, resident, 1955-56; sr. med. resident VA Hosp., Boston, 1958-59; clin. and rsch. fellow in gastroenterology Mass. Gen. Hosp., Boston, 1959-60; physician Am. Hosp. Paris, Neuilly-sur-Seine, France, 1961-98, dir. ICU, 1968-87, v.p. med. staff, 1978-80, 82-85, pres. med. staff, 1980-82, 85-87, chmn. dept. medicine, 1978-92. Adj. clin. prof. medicine Tufts U. Sch. Medicine, Boston, 1993—2001; bd. govs. Am. Hosp. Paris, 1976—87; trustee Am. Sch. Paris, Garches, France, 1971—80. Pres. bd. regents Marymount Internat. Sch., Neuilly-sur-Seine, 1997—2000, v.p., trustee, 2000—01. Capt. U.S. Army, 1956—58. Recipient Profl. Svc. citation, FAA, 1994. Mem.: AMA, Mass. Med. Soc. Democrat. Roman Catholic. Avocation: Avocations: sailing, gardening, travel. Home: 46 Blvd Inkermann 92200 Neuilly-sur-Seine France E-mail: tomfhewes@yahoo.com.

HEWITSON, WILLIAM CRAIG, physician, career officer; b. Park City, Utah, July 4, 1961; s. William Glenn and Darlene Marie Hewitson; m. Deanne Gomm, July 15, 1983; children: William Brent, Staci Anne. BA with honors, U. Utah, 1986; MD, USUHS, 1991; MPH, Johns Hopkins U., 1995. Diplomate Am. Bd. Preventive Medicine. Officer U.S. Army, advanced through grades to lt. col., 1986; transitional intern Fitzsimons Army Med. Ctr., Aurora, Colo., 1991-92; 2d brigade surgeon 7th Inf. Divsn., Ft. Ord, Calif., 1992-93, divsn. surgeon Ft. Lewis, Wash., 1993-94; resident in general preventive medicine Walter Reed Army Inst. Rsch., Washington, 1994-96; chief injuries and occupation illnesses U.S. Army Ctr. for Health Promotion and Preventive Medicine, Aberdeen Proving Grounds, Md., 1996-98; chief preventive medicine divsn. Gen. Leonard Wood Army Cmty. Hosp., Ft. Leonard Wood, Mo., 1998-2000; healthcare adminstrv. fellow Baylor U., Ft. Sam Houston, Tex., 2000—02; chief epidemiology and disease surveillance Brooke Army Med. Ctr., Ft. Sam Houston, Tex., 2002—03; chief cmty. health practices br. AMEDD Ctr. & Sch., Ft. Sam Houston, Tex., 2003—. Dir. The Preventive Health Care Mgmt. Group, Salt Lake City, 1996-97; cons. Med. Adv. Sys., Owings, Md., 1995-98. Contbr. articles to profl. jours. Advancement chmn. Big Piney dist. Boy Scouts Am., Waynesville, Mo., 1999, Four Rivers dist. health and safety com., 1998, Pack com. chmn., Ft. George G. Meade, 1995-97, health and safety com. Eagle dist., 2001-02; missionary LDS Ch., Argentina, 1980-82. Fellow Am. Coll. Preventive Medicine; mem. AMA (Physician Recognition award 1997, 2000, 03), Assn. Mil. Surgeons U.S., Masons. Avocations: running, fitness, flying, golf, tennis. Office: 2250 Stanley Rd # 574 Fort Sam Houston TX 78234-2641 E-mail: whewitson@satx.rr.com.

HEWITT, BENJAMIN ATTMORE, psychologist, consultant; b. Westerly, R.I., Dec. 20, 1921; s. Benjamin Henry and Anne Mildred (Wangelin) H. BA, Yale U., 1943, MA, 1950, PhD, 1952. Lic. psychol., Conn. Dean Mitchell Coll., New London, Conn., 1948-51; dir. counseling Wesleyan U., Middletown, Conn., 1952-53; pres. Psychol. Svcs., Inc., New Haven, Conn., 1958-70; rsch. assoc. Yale U., New Haven, 1960-68; cons. psychologist New Haven, 1969-92; furniture cons. Wakefield, R.I. Guest curator Work of Many Hands; Card Tables in Fed. Am. Yale U. Art Gallery, New Haven, 1981-82; furniture researcher, 1965—. Author: The Work of Many Hands: Card Tables in Federal America, 1982. With U.S. Army, 1943-46, PTO. Mem. APA, Conn. State Psychol. Assn. (coun. 1960-64, ethics com. 1983-84), Friends of Am. Arts at Yale (sec. 1969-83, exec. com. 1969-92). Avocations: gardening, furniture collecting, boating.

HEWITT, DENNIS EDWIN, financial executive; b. Los Angeles, Apr. 9, 1944; s. Robert Sherwood and Anna Marie (Linge) H.; m. Kathryn Dale Lefler, June 11, 1966; children— Denise, Dawn BS, UCLA, 1966; MBA, U. So. Calif., 1968. Fin. analyst Rockwell Internat., L.A., 1967-72; div. contr. Arcata Co., N.Y.C., 1972-76; v.p., contr. Weeden Co., N.Y.C., 1976-78; sr. v.p., treas. Young & Rubicam Inc., N.Y.C., 1979-88; treas. Omnicom Group Inc., N.Y.C., 1988—; pres., CEO Omnicom Capital Inc., N.Y.C., 2000—. Republican. Avocations: golf, tennis. Home: 1 Richmond Dr Old Greenwich CT 06870-1413 also: 2794 Bayside Walk San Diego CA 92107 Office: Omnicom Capital Inc 1 E Weaver St Greenwich CT 06831-5146 E-mail: parents@mindspring.com.

HEWITT, DON S. television news producer; b. N.Y.C., Dec. 14, 1922; s. Ely S. and Frieda (Pike) H.; children: Jeffrey, Steven, Jill, Lisa; m. Marilyn Berger, Apr. 14, 1979. Student, NYU, 1941; hon. degree, Brandeis U., 1990; DFA (hon.), Am. Film Inst., 1993. War corr., World War II; prodr. 1st Kennedy-Nixon TV debate, 1960; exec. prodr. CBS Evening News with Walter Cronkite, 1960-65, 60 Minutes, 1968—. Delivered 1st ann. William S. Paley lectr. Mus. of TV and Radio, 1993. Recipient Paul White award Radio and TV News Dirs. Assn., 1987; Gold medal Internat. Radio and TV Soc., 1987, Broadcaster of Yr. award, 1980; Gold Baton award Columbia DuPont, 1988, Peabody award, 1989, Lowell Thomas Centennial award, 1992, 1st ann. Goldsmith award for Investigative Reporting, John F. Kennedy Sch. Govt. Harvard U., 1992, Lifetime award Prodrs. Guild Am., 1993, Founders award Internat. Coun. of TV Acad. Arts and Scis., 1995, Com. to Protect Journalists 9th Ann. Burton Benjamin Meml. award Internat. Press Freedom, 1999; named to Hall of Fame, NATAS, 1990. Office: CBS News/60 Minutes 524 W 57th St New York NY 10019-2924 *Sometimes I think I am not sure of what I absolutely know is so.*

HEWITT, EMILY CLARK, judge, minister; b. Balt., May 26, 1944; d. John Frank and Margaret Genevieve (Gray) H. AB, Cornell U., 1966; MPhil, Union Theol. Sem., 1975; JD, Harvard U., 1978. Bar: Mass. 1978, U.S. Dist. Ct. Mass. 1979, U.S. Ct. Appeals (1st cir.) 1984, U.S. Ct. Appeals (fed. cir.) 1999, U.S. Supreme Ct. 2003; ordained priest Protestant Episcopal Ch. 1974. Adminstr. Upward Bound Programs Cornell and Hofstra U., N.Y.C., 1967-69; asst. min. St. Mary's Episcopal Ch., Manhattanville, N.Y., 1972-73; lectr. Union Theol. Sem., N.Y.C., 1972-73, 74-75; asst. prof. Andover Newton Theol. Sch., Newton Centre, Mass., 1973-75; assoc. Hill & Barlow, Boston, 1978-85, ptnr., 1985-93; gen. counsel GSA, 1993 98; judge U.S. Ct. of Fed. Claims, Washington, 1998—. Co-author: Women Priests: Yes or No?, 1973; contbr. works in field. Bd. dirs. Mass. Found. for Humanities and Pub. Policy, South Hadley, 1983-89. Mem.: Mass. Conveyancers Assn. (exec. com. 1990—93), New Eng. Women in Real Estate (dir. 1985—89), ABA (vice chair Bid Protest com. sect. pub. contract law 2000—02). Office: National Courts Bldg 717 Madison Pl NW Washington DC 20005

HEWITT, EMMETT CLYDE, III, software acquisition executive; b. Statesville, N.C., Apr. 29, 1955; s. Emmett Clyde Jr. and Leta Joye (Elmore) H.; m. Linda Kay Lavender, July 12, 1986; children: Amanda Nicole, Megan Alyssa, Amy Lauren. BA in Internat. Rels., U. N.C., 1977; MS in Ops. Mgmt., U. Ark., 1985; grad., Air Command and Staff Coll., Maxwell AFB, Ala., 1985, Air War Coll., 1994; grad. PMC, Def. Sys. Mgmt. Coll., Ft. Belvoir, Va., 1994. Commd. 2nd lt. USAF, 1977, advanced through grades to lt. col., 1993; flight examiner navigator C-130 Tactical Flight Sch., Little Rock, 1982-86; chief command and control modernization program divsn. Mil. Airlift Command, Scott AFB, Ill., 1986-90, program mgr. worldwide mil. command and control sys. Electronic Sys. Ctr., Hanscom AFB, Mass., 1990-92, chief Air Force shelter tech. divsn., 1992-93, program mgr. advanced theater battle mgmt. sys., 1993-94; prof. engring. mgmt. Def. Sys. Mgmt. Coll., Ft. Belvoir, Va., 1994-96; asst. program exec. officer Hdqrs. Air Force, Washington, 1996—; cons. NC Dept. Health and Human Svcs., 1998—2001; prin. Phoenix Health Sys., Montgomery Village, Md., 2001—. Cons. UN Spl. Commn. on Baghdad, N.Y.C., 1993, Data Processing Modernization Program, Thailand Chiefs of Staff, Bangkok, 1989; program coord. year 2000 N.C. Dept. Health and Human Svcs., Raleigh, 1998—. Contbr. articles to profl. jours.; contbg. author Guide to Medical Privacy and HIPAA. Decorated Air Force Commendation medal, Meritorious Svc. medal with three oak leaf clusters, Def. Meritorious Svc. medal. Mem.: NC Healthcare Info. and Comm. Alliance, Def. Acquisition U. Alumni Assn. Methodist. Avocations: snow skiing, bicycling, running. Office: Phoenix Health Sys 9400 Wightman Rd Ste 400 Montgomery Village MD 20886

HEWITT, JAMES WATT, retired lawyer; b. Hastings, Nebr., Dec. 25, 1932; s. Roscoe Stanley and Willa Manners (Watt) H.; m. Marjorie Ruth Barrett, Aug. 8, 1954; children: Mary Janet, William Edward, John Charles, Martha Ann. Student, Hastings Coll., 1950-52; BS, U. Nebr., 1954, JD, 1956, MA, 1994, PhD, 2003. Bar: Nebr. 1956. Practice, Hastings, 1956—57, Lincoln, Nebr., 1960—2003; v.p., gen. counsel Nebco, Inc., Lincoln, 1961—2003. Vis. lectr. U. Nebr. Coll. Law, 1970—71; adj. prof. Am. history Nebr. Wesleyan U., 2001—. Mem. state exec. com. Rep. Party, 1967-70, mem. state ctrl. com., 1967-70, legis chmn., 1968-70; bd. dirs. Lincoln Child Guidance Ctr., 1969-72, pres., 1972; bd. dirs. Lincoln Cmty. Playhouse, 1967-73, pres., 1972-73; trustee Bryan Meml. Hosp., Lincoln, 1968-74, 76-82, chmn., 1972-74; bd. dirs. Lincoln Libr., 1990-97; trustee U. Nebr. Found., 1979—; dir. Bryan Meml. Hosp. Found., Lincoln, 1994—; pres, dir. Nebr. State Hist. Soc. Found., Lincoln, 1994—; dir. Nebr. state chpt. The Nature Conservancy, 1993-97. Capt. USAF, 1957-60. Fellow Am. Bar Found. (Nebr. state chmn. 1988-92, 99-2003, chmn. 1994-95); mem. ABA (Nebr. state del. 1972-80, bd. govs. 1981-83), Nebr. State Bar (chmn. ins. com. 1972-76, chmn. pub. rels. com. 1982-84, pres. 1985-86), Fed. Bar Assn., Lincoln Bar Assn., Newcomen Soc. (Nebr. chair 1995-03), Am. Rose Soc., Nebr. Rose Soc., Lincoln Rose Soc., Nebr. Club, Country of Lincoln Club, Round Table, Beta Theta Pi, Phi Delta Phi. Congregationalist. Home: 2990 Sheridan Blvd Lincoln NE 68502-4241 Office: PO Box 80268 1815 Y St Lincoln NE 68508-1233

HEWITT, PAUL BUCK, lawyer; b. St. Louis, July 27, 1949; s. John York and Kathryn Louise (Buck) H.; m. Marla Ivy Zimmers, Feb. 17, 1985; children: Anna Ruth, Rachel Elizabeth. BA in Econs., Northwestern U., 1971; JD cum laude, U. Wis., 1974. Bar: D.C. 1979, Wis. 1974. Law clk. to chief justice Wis. Supreme Ct., Madison, 1974-75; atty. Bureau of Competition FTC, Washington, 1975-78; assoc. Akin Gump Strauss Hauer and Feld, Washington, 1978-82, ptnr., 1983—. Articles editor Wis. Law Rev., Madison, 1973-74. Mem. ABA, D.C. Bar, Wis. Bar Assn. Office: Akin Gump Strauss Hauer and Feld LLP Ste 400 1333 New Hampshire Ave NW Washington DC 20036-1564

HEWITT, TIMOTHY MARTIN, museum curator; b. Lakewood, Ohio, Nov. 16, 1963; s. Martin Alexander Hewitt and Janet Natalie Steinke. BA in History/Anthropology, Pacific Luth. U., 1986. Mus. curator The Presdl. Mus., Odessa, Tex., 1992—. Author exhibit texts; composer chamber music, 1982—; arranger sml. ensemble music, 1992—. Youth counselor Redeemer Luth. Ch., Odessa, 1992—, dir. handbell choir, 1993-2001, leader brass ensemble, 1995—, dir. youth bd., 1998-2002, treas., 1995—; mem. French Horn sect. Odessa Coll. Concert Band, 1992—. Recipient Don Jerke Leadership award Pacific Luth. U., Tacoma, Wash., 1985, John Philip Sousa Band award Mead H.S. Band, Spokane, 1982, mem. All-State H.S. Band, Wash. State Music Educators Assn., Richland, 1982. Mem. Aid Assn. Luths. (treas. local br. 1996-03, v.p. 1995). Avocations: playing piano and french horn, composing music, genealogy, bicycle touring. Office: The Presdl Mus 4919 E University Blvd Odessa TX 79762-

HEWITT, VIVIAN ANN DAVIDSON (MRS. JOHN HAMILTON HEWITT JR.), retired librarian; b. New Castle, Pa., Feb. 17, 1920; d. Arthur Robert and Lela Luvada (Mauney) Davidson; m. John Hamilton Hewitt, Jr., Dec. 26, 1949; 1 son, John Hamilton III. AB with honors, Geneva Coll., 1943, LHD, 1978; BSLS, Carnegie Mellon U., 1944; postgrad., U. Pitts., 1947-48. Sr. asst. libr. Carnegie Libr., Pitts., 1944-49; instr., libr. Sch. Libr. Sci. Atlanta U., Atlanta U., 1949-52; with Readers Reference Svce., Crowell-Collier Pub. Co., N.Y.C., 1953-55; libr. Rockefeller Found., N.Y.C., 1955-63; librarian Carnegie Endowment Internat. Peace, N.Y.C., 1963-83; librarian Mexican Agrl. Program, Rockefeller Found., summer 1958; dir. libr. and info. svcs. Katherine Gibbs Sch., N.Y.C., 1984-86; reference asst. Coun. on Fgn. Rels., 1986-89. Lectr. spl. librarianship at grad. schs. of L.S. and info. throughout U.S. and Can., 1968-88; condr. profl. seminars Am. Mgmt. Assn., 1968-69, UN Inst. Tng. and Rsch., 1973, 74, Grad. Sci. Libr. and Info. Sci., Rutgers U., 1986; mem. faculty Grad. Sch. Libr. and Info. Sci., U. Tex., Austin, summer 1985; SLA rep. to Internat.

Fedn. Libr. Assns., 1970-73, 73-75, 75-77; mem. nat. adv. com. Ctr. for the Book, Libr. of Congress, 1979-84; mem. adv. bd. Who's Who Among African Ams., 1975—. Contbr. chpt. to: The Black Librarian in America, 1970, What Black Librarians Are Saying, 1972, New Dimensions for Academic Library Service, 1975, A Century of Service, 1976, Handbook of Black Librarianship, 1977, 2d edit., 2000, The Black Librarian in America Revisited, 1994, Notable Black American Men, 1999. Bd. dirs. Graham-Windham, 1967, sec., 1980-87; bd. dirs. Laymen's Club, Cathedral Ch. of St.John the Divine, 1975-82, sec., 1986-93. Recipient Outstanding Cmty. Svc. awards, United Fund N.Y., 1965—77, Disting. Alumna award, U. Pitts.-Carnegie Mellon U. Alumni Assn., 1978, Merit award, Carnegie Mellon U. Alumni Assn., 1979, Leadership award, Carnegie Mellon U. Black Alumni, 2001. Mem.: ALA (Disting. Svc. to Librarianship award Black Caucus 1978, Leadership in Profession award Black Caucus 1992), Jack and Jill Am., Inc. (ea. regional dir. 1967—69), Spl. Librs. Assn. (pres. N.Y. chpt. 1970—71, nat. pres. 1978—79, rep. to Pacem in Terris Convocation 1965, rep. to White House Conf. Internat. Coop. Ur. 1965, Hall of Fame 1984, Leadership award 2001), Am. Soc. Order of St. John, Pierians, Inc. (hon.), Alpha Kappa Alpha, Tower Soc. Geneva Coll. Democrat. Episcopalian. Home: 862 West End Ave New York NY 10025-4959 E-mail: jhh2nyc@aol.com.

HEWLETT, RICHARD GREENING, historian; b. Toledo, Feb. 12, 1923; s. Timothy Younglove and Gertrude Josephine (Greening) H.; m. Marilyn Eloise Nesper, Sept. 6, 1946. Student, Dartmouth, 1941-43, Bowdoin Coll., 1943-44; MA, U. Chgo., 1948, PhD, 1952. Intelligence specialist USAF Hdqrs., Washington, 1951-52; reports analyst AEC, Washington, 1952-57, chief historian, 1957-75, ERDA, Washington, 1975-77, U.S. Dept. Energy, 1977-80; sr. assoc., sr. v.p., chmn. bd. History Assoc., Inc., Rockville, Md., 1980—. Regents' lectr. U. Calif., 1982; historiographer Episcopal Diocese of Washington, also Washington Cathedral, 1978—, honorary canon, 2003-; chmn. fed. govt. resource group Nat. Coordinating Com. for Promotion of History, 1977-81; mem. U.S. Del. 2d UN Internat. Conf. on Peaceful Uses Atomic Energy, 1958. Author: Jessie Ball du Pont, 1992; co-author: The New World, 1939-46, 1962, Atomic Shield, 1947-52, 1969, Nuclear Navy, 1946-52, 1974, Atoms for Peace and War, 1953-61, 1989. Served with USAAF, 1943-46. Recipient David D. Lloyd prize Harry S. Truman Libr. Found., 1970; Distinguished Service award AEC, 1973. Mem. Am. Hist. Assn., Orgn. Am. Historians (Richard W. Leopold prize 1970), Soc. History Tech., Hist. Soc. Episc. Ch., Nat. Coun. Pub. History, Soc. for History in Fed. Govt. (v.p. 1983-85, Henry Adams prize 1990, Franklin D. Roosevelt award 1994), Cosmos Club. Episcopalian. Home: 7909 Deepwell Dr Bethesda MD 20817-1927 Office: History Assocs Inc 300 N Stonestreet Ave Rockville MD 20850 E-mail: rhewlett6@cs.com.

HEY, NANCY HENSON, educational administrator; b. Cleve., Apr. 1, 1935; d. Henry Brumback Henson and Isabelle (Smock) Selverstone; m. Robert Pierpont Hey, July 4, 1959; 1 child, Julie Dean. AB, Bates Coll., 1957; MS in Edn., Bank Street Coll. Edn., 1961. Cert. advanced profl. in early childhood nursery thru grade 3, Md. Primary tchr. Concord Pub. Sch., Mass., 1958-59; tchr. The Potomac Sch., McLean, Va., 1959-60, Galloway Sch., Atlanta, 1968-69; head tchr. Beauvoir Sch. Nursery Dept., Washington, 1969-70; supr. student tchr. U. Md. Coll. Edn., Coll. Pk., Md., 1973-76, Tufts U., Medford, Mass., 1978-79; head tchr. Newton Ctr. Day Care Ctr., 1980-81, Cmty. Child Devel. Ctr., Peabody, Mass., 1981-82; dir. Greater Lawrence YWCA Children's Ctr., Mass., 1982-86; tchr. Prince George's County Pub. Sch., Md., 1986-88; dir. Child Devel. Ctr., FTC, Washington, 1988-92; dir. Chevy Chase Plz. Children's Ctr., Washington, 1992-93; assoc. dir. Ctr. for Young Children, U. Md., Md., 1994—. Supr. student tchrs. Simmons Coll., Boston, 1965-67; teaching asst. to head of lower sch.Shady Hill Sch., Cambridge, Mass., 1960-61; mem. task force com. Region III Dept. of Social Svcs., Middleton, Mass., 1984-86; bd. dirs. Greater Lawrence Coun. for Children, 1984-86. Mem. Nat. Assn. for Edn. of Young Children, Congressional and Fed. Child Care Dir. Assn. (Sec., 1990-92) Dirs. Exch., Nat. Coalition for Campus Children's Ctrs. Home: 10908 Candlelight Ln Potomac MD 20854-2756 Office: U Md Ctr for Young Children Valley Dr College Park MD 20742-0001

HEY, RICHARD NOBLE, marine geophysicist; b. Lebanon, Tenn., June 2, 1947; s. Richard and Miriam (Jennings) Hey; m. Donna Dale, 2003. BS, Calif. Inst. Technology, 1969; PhD, Princeton U., 1975. Rsch. assoc. U. Tex., Galveston, 1974-75; from asst. to geophysicist Hawaii Inst. Geophysics, Honolulu, 1975-80; from asst. to assoc. rsch. geophysicist Scripps Inst. Oceanography, La Jolla, Calif., 1981-86; prof. U. Hawaii, Honolulu, 1986—. Adj. lectr. Scripps Inst. Oceanography, La Jolla, 1983-90. Fellow Geol. Soc. Am., Am. Geophys. Union; mem. AAAS. Office: U Hawaii at Manoa Inst Geophysics Planetology Honolulu HI 96822 E-mail: hey@soest.hawaii.edu.

HEY, ROBERT PIERPONT, retired editor; b. East Providence, R.I., Jan. 24, 1935; s. Daniel Chase and Grace (Pierpont) H.; m. Nancy Henson, July 4, 1959; 1 dau., Julie. AB, Harvard U., 1955. Gen. assignment reporter, local edn. reporter Christian Sci. Monitor, Boston, 1960-64, asst. to Am. news editor, then asst. Am. news editor, 1964-67, S.E. U.S. corr., then Washington corr., 1967-76, asst. mng. editor, 1976-79, mng. editor features, 1979-83, editorial writer, 1983-86, Washington Corr., 1986-91; mng. editor AARP Bull., 1991-2000; purchasing agt. Arkell Safety Bag Co., N.Y.C., 1956-58; with public relations dept. U. Pitts., 1964. Served with AUS, 1958-60.

HEYCK, JOSEPH GIRAUD, JR., lawyer; b. Lake Charles, La., Sept. 25, 1935; s. Joseph G. Sr. and Frances (Hunter) H.; m. Marilyn C. Grace, Dec. 26, 1964; children: Laura Frances, Thomas Michael. B in Indsl. Engring., U. Fla., 1958, JD, 1963. Bar: Fla. 1964, U.S. Dist. Ct. (mid. dist.) Fla. 1965, U.S. Ct. Appeals (5th and 11th cirs.) 1968. Law clk. to presiding judge U.S. Dist. (mid. dist.) Fla., Tampa, 1963-64; ptnr. Allen, Dell, Frank & Trinkle, Tampa, 1964—. Active parish council Our Lady of the Rosary Cath. Ch., Land O'Lakes, Fla., 1975; bd. dirs. Am. Cancer Soc., Hillsborough County, Fla., 1972. Capt. USNR, 1958-81, ret. Mem. ABA, Fla. Bar Assn., Hillsborough County Bar Assn., Am. Judicature Soc., Tampa Yacht and Country Club (bd. dirs. 1978), Tampa Bay Bankruptcy Bar Assn. Avocations: fishing, golf. Home: 3624 Crenshaw Lake Rd Lutz FL 33548-4755 Office: Allen Dell PA 202 S Rome Ave Ste 100 Tampa FL 33606

HEYCK, THEODORE DALY, lawyer; b. Houston, Apr. 17, 1941; s. Theodore and Richard and Gertrude Paine (Daly) H. BA, Brown U., 1963; postgrad., Georgetown U., 1963-65, 71-72; JD, N.Y. Law Sch., 1979. Bar: N.Y. 1980, Calif. 1984, U.S. Ct. Appeals (2d cir.) 1984, U.S. Supreme Ct. 1984, U.S. Dist. Ct. (so. and ea. dists.) N.Y. 1980, U.S. Dist. Ct. (we. and no. dists.) N.Y. 1984, U.S. Dist. Ct. (cen. and so. dists.) Calif. 1984, U.S. Ct. Appeals (9th cir.) 1986. Paralegal dist. atty., Bklyn., 1975-79; asst. dist. atty. Bklyn. dist., Kings County, N.Y., 1979-85; dep. city atty. L.A., 1985—. Bd. dirs. Screen Actors Guild, N.Y.C., 1977-78. Mem. ABA, ATLA, AFTRA, NATAS, SAG, Bklyn. Bar Assn., N.Y. Trial Lawyers Assn., N.Y. State Bar Assn., Calif. Bar Assn., Fed. Bar Coun., L.A. Coun. Bar Assn., Actors Equity Assn. Home: 2106 E Live Oak Dr Los Angeles CA 90068-3639 Office: Office City Atty City Hall E 200 N Main St Los Angeles CA 90012-4110

HEYDE, MARTHA BENNETT (MRS. ERNEST R. HEYDE), psychologist; b. New Bern, N.C., Jan. 31, 1920; d. George Spotswood and Katherine (McIntosh) Bennett; m. Ernest R. Heyde, Aug. 17, 1946. AB, Columbia U., 1941, MA, 1949, PhD, 1959. Instr. psychol. founds and svcs. Tchrs. Coll., Columbia U., N.Y.C., 1957-59, rsch. assoc., 1960-70, cons., 1970-73. Contbg. author: (rsch. monograph) The Vocational Maturity of Ningh Grade Boys, 1960, Floundering and Trial After High Sch., 1967; co-author: Vocational Maturity During the High School Years, 1979. Mem. Barnard Coll. alumnae coun. Columbia U., 1956-61, 69—, pres. class, 1956-61, trustee, 1974-79, hon. vice chmn. Barnard Coll. Centennial, 1987-89. Mem. APA, Sigma Xi, Kappa Delta Pi, Pi Lambda Theta. Home: 530 E 23rd St Apt 8E New York NY 10010-5030

HEYDEBRAND, WOLF VON, sociology educator; b. Kl. Tschunkawe, Germany, June 15, 1930; came to U.S., 1954; s. Georg Von and Sigrid Von (Waldersee) H.; m. Ruth Keiling, Sept. 1954 (div. 1973); 1 child, Gitry V.; m. Sarah Rosenfield, June 1974 (div. 1979); m. Elizabeth Robinson, Mar. 1987; children: Daniel Adam V., Sophia Ingrid V. MA, U. Chgo., 1961, PhD, 1965. Asst. prof. sociology U. Chgo., 1964-67; assoc. prof. Washington U., St. Louis, 1967-71; prof. NYU, N.Y.C., 1973—. Vis. assoc. prof. Columbia U., 1972-73, 85; co-dir. Comparative Orgn. Rsch. Program, U. Chgo., 1964-67; rsch. assoc. Med. Care Rsch. Ctr., St. Louis, 1967-71; co-prin. investigator Explorat's Health Svc., N.Y.C., 1972-74; prin. investigator Adjudication vs. Adminstrn., Russell Sage Found., 1974-75; Max Weber prof. U. Heidelberg, 1996. Author: Hospital Bureaucracy, 1973; (with others) Rationalizing Justice: The Political Economy of Federal District Courts, 1990; editor: Comparative Organizations, 1973, Max Weber, 1994; assoc. editor Am. Jour. Sociology, 1964-67, Contemporary Sociology, 1972-74, Social Problems, 1981-84, Law and Soc. Rev., 1985-87. Grantee NSF, 1964; grantee USPHS, 1967, Nat. Ctr. Health Service, 1972, Russell Sage Found., 1974-75 Mem. Am. Sociol. Assn. (pres. sect. orgns. and occupations 1987-88), Ea. Sociol. Assn. (exec. coun. 1979-82), Law and Soc. Assn. (trustee), Internat. Sociol. Assn. Jewish. Office: NYU Dept Sociology 269 Mercer St Rm 411 New York NY 10003-6633 E-mail: wolf.heydebrand@nyu.edu.

HEYDERMAN, ARTHUR JEROME, engineer, civilian military employee; b. Bklyn., Jan. 1, 1946; s. Herbert Robert and Sally (Baron) H.; m. Renee Linda Pearlman, July 4, 1967; children: Brian Douglas, Deborah Ann, Cathy Ruth. BS in Applied Math., Poly. Inst. Bklyn., 1966, MS in Applied Math., 1973; postgrad., Stevens Inst. Tech., 1982, Brookings Inst., 1992, Wharton Sch. Bus., U. Pa., 1993. Nuclear weapons engr. U.S. Army Armaments R&D Ctr., Picatinny Arsenal, N.J., 1971-83, asst. tech. dir., 1983-84, chief prodn. program planning, 1984, assoc. tech. dir., 1984-86; armaments rsch. and devel. prog. mgr. U.S. Army Armaments Munitions and Chem. Command, Rock Island, Ill., 1986-93, chief of rsch. devel., test and evaluation integration, 1993-94; chief improved armor engring. U.S. Army Armaments Rsch., Devel. and Engring. Ctr., Rock Island, Ill., 1994-96; chief armor engring. U.S. Armaments Rsch. Devel. & Engring. Ctr., Rock Island, Ill., 1996-98, chief arty. sys. & armor divsn., 1998—99; chief prodn. and logistics engring. support U.S. Armaments Rsch. Devel. and Engring. Ctr., Rock Island, Ill., 1999—. Bd. dirs., sec./treas., pres. Iowa-Ill. chpt. Am. Def. Preparedness Assn., Rock Island; lt. col. nuclear weapons officer USAR, Ft. Sheridan, Ill., 1989-93; pres. OPICON, Bettendorf, Iowa, 1989—; nat. coun. Am. Def. Preparedness Assn.; coun. mem. Quad-Cities Engring. and Sci. Coun.; adj. faculty U.S. Army Command and Gen. Staff Coll., Ft. Leavenworth, Kans., 1981-89, Scott C.C., 1997. Contbr. column to Rock Island Argus/Moline Dispatch; guest editor Quad Cities Times; contbr. tech. papers on weapons and weaponry assessment to profl. meetings. Pres., bd. dirs. Sussex County Jewish Ctr., Newton, N.J., 1979-86; fundraiser United Jewish Fedn., Davenport, Iowa, 1986-99, mem. Rock Island Arsenal Com. for Disabled, 1987-93, Quad Cities Coalition for Choice; dir. intake Quad City chpt. ACLU; mem. platform com. Scott County Dem. Ctrl. Com., 1994—; mem. 1st dist. Iowa Dem. Ctrl. Com., 1994—; mem. platform com. Iowa State Dem. Party; chmn. Quad Cities WWII Commemoration Com., 1995, Quad Cities Vietnam Wall Com., 1997; mem. Iowa Sesquecentennial Commemoration Com., 1995, Rock Island County, Ill. C. of C. Spkrs. Bur., 1996; bd. dirs. Jewish Fedn. of Quad Cities, 1996-99; funds distbn. panelist United Way of Quad Cities, 1999-2000; bd. dirs. Iowa Civil Liberties Union, 1997—, Iowa Civil Liberties Found., 1997—; mem. Scott County Foster Care Citizens Rev. Bd., 2000-2001. Capt. U.S. Army, 1968-71, Vietnam; maj./lt. col. USAR, 1971-93. Decorated Bronze Star; Cross of Gallantry (Vietnam); named to Hon. Order St. Barbara, U.S. Army Field Arty. Assn.; recipient Civilian of Yr. award Fifth Region Assn. of the U.S. Army, 1998; recipient Nat. President's award, Women in Def., 2003. Mem. VFW, ACLU (nat. bd. dirs. 1998—), NAACP (bd. dirs. Quad Cities chpt. 1996-2001), U.S. Army Acquisitions Corps, U.S. Army Engr. Assn., Assn. U.S. Army (v.p. Ft. Armstrong chpt. 1993—, acting pres. chpt. 1996-97), Soc. Am. Mil. Engrs. (scholar 1966), Soc. Am. Mil. Comptrs., Federally Employed Women, Planned Parenthood (mem. cmty. coun.), Nat. Soc. Scabbard and Blade (chpt. v.p. 1965-66), Nat. Def. Indsl. Assn. (pres. Iowa Ill. chpt.), Res. Officers Assn., Women in Defense, Poly. Alumni Assn. (pres. Quad City chpt. 1989—), Mensa, Intertel, Vietnam Vets. Jewish. Avocations: horticulture, art, bonsai, cooking, photography. Home: 1430 Grappler Ct Bettendorf IA 52722-1847

HEYDMAN, ABBY MARIA, academic executive; b. Des Moines, June 1, 1943; d. Frederick Edward and Zeta Margaret (Harrington) Hitchcock; m. Frank J. Heydman, Dec. 20, 1967; 1 child, Amy Lee. BS, Duchesne Coll., 1967; MN, U. Wash., 1969; PhD, U. Calif., Berkeley, 1987. Registered nurse, Calif. Staff nurse Bergan Mercy Hosp., Omaha, 1964—65; student health nurse St. Joseph's Hosp., Omaha, 1965—66, instr. sch. nursing, 1966—68; staff nurse Ballard Community Hosp., Seattle, 1968—69; instr. Creighton U., Omaha, 1969—70, asst. prof., 1970—74, acting dean, 1971—72; chairperson nursing dept. St. Mary's Coll., Moraga, Calif., 1978—85; dean nursing program Samuel Merritt-Saint Mary's Coll., Oakland and Moraga, Calif., 1985—93; acad. dean Samuel Merritt Coll., Oakland, 1989—99, acad. v.p., provost, 1999—2002, spl. asst. to pres., 2002—. Lectr. U. Calif., San Francisco, 1974-75. Contbr. articles to profl. jours. Chmn. Newman Hall Community Council, Berkeley, 1985-87; bd. dirs. Oakland YMCA, 1981-83. Mem.: ACAD, ANA, AAHE, Phi Kappa Delta, Sigma Theta Tau (chair fundraising com. Nu Xi chpt. 1998—2001, pres.-elect 2001—03, pres. 2003—). Roman Catholic. Avocations: swimming, writing, travel, reading. Home: 78629 Rainswept Way Palm Desert CA 92211 Office: Samuel Merritt Coll 450-30 St Oakland CA 94609-3108 E-mail: aheydman@samuelmerritt.edu.

HEYDON, PETER NORTHRUP, farmer, educator, philanthropist; b. Hackensack, N.J., Nov. 25, 1940; s. Clark A. and Elizabeth VanFleet (Northrup) H.; m. Henrietta M. Heydon, Aug. 24, 1968. BA, Princeton U., N.J., 1962; MA, U. Mich., Ann Arbor, 1963, PhD, 1970. Lectr. in humanities & English U. Mich., Ann Arbor, 1963-80, adj. prof., 1980-86. Chmn. The Clements Library Assocs., Ann Arbor, 1970-2001; trustee Folger Shakespeare Libr., Washington D.C., 1986-99, Nat. Pub. Radio Found., 1994—; dir. Farrar, Straus & Giroux, N.Y.C., 1970-94; pres. The Browning Inst., N.Y.C., 1971-85, Firenze, N.Y.C., 1971-85, Beacon Theatre Assocs., N.Y.C., 1990—. Founder, bd. dirs. The Mosaic Found., 1989—. Mem. The Lotos Club, The Grolier Club, The Century Assn., Maitre, Commanderie de Bordeaux á Detroit, Commandeur Chevaliers du Tastevin. Avocations: restoration of classic and special interest automobiles, historic preservation of national register buildings, wine, food, horse breeding. Office: Heydon Washington St Prop 324 E Washington St PO Box 7801 Ann Arbor MI 48107-7801

HEYDT, WILLIAM, former mayor; b. Allentown, Pa., June 11, 1938; married. 2 children. Cer: CLU. Pres. Heydt Ins. Agy., Inc.; mayor City of Allentown, Pa., 1994—2001; pres. Heydt Ins. Agy., Inc., Allentown, 1997—. Instr. Allentown Coll. of St. Francis de Sales Center Valley, Pa., Northampton C.C., Bethlehem, Pa. Past cantor, choir mem. St. Thomas Moore Cath. Ch.; performer Allentown Mcpl. Opera Co., Civic Little Theater; past pres. Mcpl. Opera Co. Allentown; chmn. Lehigh County Drug and Alcohol Commn., Corp. Gifts for Ctrl. Cath. High Sch., South Whitehall Twp. Authority; divsn. chmn. Cath. Charities Appeal; assoc. chmn. United Fund.; vice chmn. City of Allentown Planning Commn. With USMC. Mem. Am. Planning Assn., Pa. Assn. Life Underwriters (past pres.), Lehigh Valley Assn. Life Underwriters (past pres.), Lehigh Valley CLU and ChFC Assn. (past pres.), Allentown Jaycees (dir., v.p.), Parkland Area Jaycees (dir., pres.), Pa. Jaycees (state dir.). Roman Catholic. Avocations: golf, plate collecting.

HEYEN, BEATRICE J. psychotherapist; b. Chgo., June 23, 1925; d. Carl Edwin and Anna W. (Carlson) Lund; m. Robert D. Heyen, June 16, 1950 (dec. Feb. 1981); children: Robin, Jefferson, Neil; m. Robert Christiansen, Nov. 24, 1984. BS, U. Chgo., 1949. Instr. Boone (Iowa) Jr. Coll., 1959-64, Rochester (Minn.) Jr. Coll., 1967-68, Winona (Minn.) State Coll., 1965-68; dir. social svc. State Clinic, Kirksville, Mo., 1968-71; supr., dir. Family Counseling Agy., Joliet, Ill., 1971-85; pvt. practice Muskegon, Mich., 1985—. Cons. Homes for Aged, Programs for Aged, Winona, 1965-68, Spl. Programs and Individuals in Psychotherapy, Muskegon, 1984—; dir. Christiansen Fine Art Gallery, North Muskegon. Mem. Gov.'s Com. on Status of Women, Iowa, 1957-62, Gov.'s Com. on Aging, Minn., 1966-68; bd. mem. Mission for Area People, Muskegon, 1998. Grantee for Pilot Projects in Svc. to Women 1971-84. Mem. AAUW, NASW, Acad. Cert. Social Workers, C.G. Jung Inst. (Chgo.). Methodist. Avocations: ecological interests, day lily gardening, contemporary art. Home: 1610 N Weber Rd North Muskegon MI 49445

HEYEN, WILLIAM H. literature educator, poet; b. Bklyn., Nov. 1, 1940; s. Henry Jurgen Heyen and Wilhelmina Auguste Else Wörmke; m. Hannelore Irene Greiner, July 7, 1962; children: William, Kristen. BSEd, SUNY, Brockport, 1961; MA in English, Ohio U., 1963, PhD in English, 1967. Instr. English Springville (NY) Jr. HS, 1961—62, SUNY Coll., Cortland, 1963—65; grad. asst., tchg. fellow Ohio U., 1963—67; from asst. prof. to prof. English SUNY, Brockport, 1967—. Sr. Fulbright lectr. Hannover (Germany) U., 1971—72; vis. writer U. Wis., Milw., 1980; vis. writer, poetry workshop leader Hofstra U., NY, 1981, 83, Southampton Coll., 1984—85, 1987, 89, 91; vis. prof. English, creative writing U. Hawaii, Manoa, 1985; leader poetry workshop Chautauqua Instn., 1993, 95. Editor: A Profile of Theodore Roethke, 1971, American Poets in 1976, 1976, The Generation of 2000: Contemporary American Poets, 1984 (Outstanding Book of 1984 Booklist of Am. Libr. Assn.), September 11, 2001: American Writers Respond, 2002; author: Depth of Field: Poems, 1970, Noise in the Trees: Poems and a Memoir, 1974 (One of 30 Notable Am. Books of 1974 Am. Libr. Assn.), The Swastika Poems, 1977, Long Island Light: Poems and a Memoir, 1979, The City Parables, 1980 (main selection Small Press Book Club, 1981), Lord Dragonfly: Five Sequences, 1981, Erika: Poems of the Holocaust, 1984, Vic Holyfield and the Class of 1957: A Romance, 1986, The Chestnut Rain: A Poem, 1986, Brockport, New York: Beginning with And, 1988; author: (with Louis Daniel Brodsky) Falling from Heaven: Holocaust Poems, 1991; author: Pterodactyl Rose: Poems of Ecology, 1991, Ribbons: The Gulf War-A Poem, 1991, The Host: Selected Poems 1965-1990, 1994, With Me Far Away: A Memoir, 1994, Crazy Horse in Stillness: Poems, 1996 (Nat. Small Press Book award, 1997, Lillian Fairchild Meml. award, 1996), Pig Notes & Dumb Music: Prose on Poetry, 1998, Shoah Train: Poems, 2003; contbr. prose and poetry to lit. jours., mags. and anthologies. Recipient Borestone Mountain Poetry prize, 1965, Poetry prize, Ont. Rev., 1977, Outstanding Alumni award, SUNY Brockport, 1977, Eunice Tietjens Meml. award, Poetry mag., 1978, Medal of Merit, Ohio U. Alumni Assn., 1982, Witter Bynner prize, Am. Acad. and Inst. Arts and Letters, 1982; fellow Creative Writing, Nat. Endowment for Arts, 1973—74, 1984—85, John Simon Guggenheim Meml Found., 1977—78, NY Found for Arts, 1984—85. Home: 142 Frazier St Brockport NY 14420

HEYER, CAROL ANN, illustrator; b. Cuero, Tex., Feb. 2, 1950; d. William Jerome and Merlyn Mary (Hutson) H. BA, Calif. Lutheran U., 1974. Freelance artist various cos., Thousand Oaks, Calif., 1974-79; computer artist Image Resource, Westlake Village, Calif., 1979-81; staff writer, artist Lynn-Davis Prodns., Westlake Village, Calif., 1981-87; art dir. Northwind Studios Internat., Camarillo, Calif., 1988-89; illustrator Touchmark, Thousand Oaks, 1989—. Cons. art dir., writer Lynn-Wenger Prodns., 1987-89; guest spkr. Ariz. Kidney Found. Children's Art and Lit. luncheon 2000, Thousand Oaks Libr., Author's Faire, Calif. Luth. U., Soc. Children's Book Writers and Illustrators, Illustrators Day, Ventura County Reading Assn.'s Author's Faire; guest artist/spkr. Oxnard Libr.; booksignings/appearances Anaheim Conv. Ctr., L.A. Conv. Ctr., Am. Booksellers Assn.; guest 1996 Readout, grand opening Barnes and Noble, Thousand Oaks; represented by Art Works, N.Y.C.; invited artist Ann. Art Show, Chemers Gallery; spkr. in field. Illustrator (children's books) Down the Grand Canyon Harcourt, A Star in the Pasture, 1988, The Dream Stealer, 1989, The Golden Easter Egg, 1989, All Things Bright and Beautiful, 1992, Rapunzel, 1992, The Christmas Carol, 1995, Prancer, Gift of the Magi, Black Beauty, Dinosaurs Strange and Wonderful, Down the Great Unknown, 1999, Abraham Lincoln, 2002, Teacher of the Year, Two Fridas, Down the Grand Canyon, The First Easter, 2003, The First Christmas, 2003, Flame and Clay (teachers' big book) 1998, 3 Repeat Jobs for Hampton/Brown (teacher's big book), (illustrator) Night Journey, 1999, Here Come the Brides, (adult book) The Artist's Market, also L.A. Times, Daily News, The Artist's Mag., News Chronicle; also cover art for Troll Assoc., Top Secret, The Loveless Cafe (cookbook), Ellery Queen's Mystery Mag., Frontispiece Collectors Leather Bound Edition, Crippen and Landru Mystery Covers, Dragon mag., Dungeon mag., Aboriginal Sci. Fiction mag., Wizards of the Coast, (game covers) F.X. Schmid - Puzzle Wizards of the Coast (fantasy collector cards, Dune and Hobbit), 4 covers, frontispieces and chpt. headings for Henry Winkler's Hank Zipzer series, Georgw W. Bush Scholastic, 2003, also various novels, books and games; illustrator Bugs Bunny Coloring Book, Candyland Work Book, The Dragon Sleeps Step Ahead Workbook, City of Sorcers, CD-ROM cover for Memorex/Roaring Mouse Prodns., George W. Bush Scholastic; interior art for various publs. including (mags.) Amazing Stories two covers, Interzone, Aboriginal Sci. Fiction Mag., Alfred Hitchcocks Mystery Mag., Ideals mag., Ellery Queen's Mystery mag. two covers, Realms of Fantasy mag., Sci. Fiction Age mag., Tomorrow mag., (book) Tome of Magic, Spider Magazine, (book) Top Secret, (book, interiors) Star Trek Next Generation, (also art for game cards), (repeat covers) Crippen and Landru, (game book cover) Wizards of the Coast; writer (screenplay) Thunder Run, 1986; illustrator, writer (children's books) Black Beauty, Beauty and the Beast, 1989, The Easter Story, 1989, Excalibur, Robin Hood, 1993, Sleeping Beauty in the Wood, 1996, The Christmas Story, 1996, Down the Great Unknown, 1999, Flame and Clay, 1998, Black Beauty, The First Easter, 2003, The First Christmas, 2003; paintings for line of Fantasy Art Prints, Scafa/Tornabene, religious art prints; rep. by Every Picture Tells a Story Gallery, Worlds of Wonder; cover art/bookmark for Antioch Pub.; new cover for Baen Books; art for Maruri USA Corp.; 2 covers for young adults Hyperion/Disney Press; one-woman show Adventures for Kids Gallery; illustrator poster for motion picture and TV fund; writer Disney ednl. prodns., others; freelance artist Disney Interactive. Guest spkr. Ariz. Kidney Found. Recipient Lit. award City of Oxnard Cultural Arts Commn. and Carnegie Art Inst., 1992, Best Cover Art Boomerang award, 1989, Cert. of Merit, Career Achievement award Calif. Luth. U., 1993, Cert. of Excellence Alumni Career Achievement award, 1993, Print's Regional Design Ann. award, 1992, Best Paper Backs award Internat. Reading Assn. Children's Book Coun. Joint Com., 1994, Spectrum Internat. Competition for Best in Contemporary Fantastic Art, Spectrum 7 award, Spectrum 9 Art Competition award, award Ventura Soc. of Children's Bookwriters and Illustrators, 2002. Mem. Soc. Children's Book Writers (judge 1990, Mag. Merit award 1988, Keynote spkr.), Assn. Sci. Fiction and Fantasy Artists (nominated for Chelsey award), Soc. Illustrators (Cert. of Merit 1990-92, winner Ann. Illustration West show, award L.A. chpt. 1998). Achievements include being featured in articles. Home and Office: Touchmark 925 Ave Arboles Thousand Oaks CA 91360

HEYERDAHL, JENS P. business executive; b. Oslo, Feb. 17, 1943; s. Jens and Sessan (Lyche) H.; widowed; 2 children. Student, Cavalry Officers Sch., 1961-63; degree in law, Oslo U., 1968; MBA, European Inst. Adminstrn. Affairs, Fontainebleau, France, 1970. Atty. Thommessen, Karlsrud, Heyerdahl & Brunsvig, Oslo, 1968; staff Directorate for Legal Harmonization, EEC, Brussels, 1969; legal cons. Insp. of Taxes, Oslo, 1970-71; dep. judge of Lier Røyken and Hurum Magistrate, 1971-72; co. sec. Dyno Industrier A.S., Oslo, 1972-75; v.p. indsl. devel. and investments Orkla Industrier A/S, 1975-79, CEO, 1979—2001. Bd. dirs. BASF Norge, Hafslund ASA, Oslo, subs. cos. Orkla ASA. Avocation: riding (internat. awards in Grand Prix show-jumping events). Office: Orkla ASA PO Box 423 Skøyen N-0213 Oslo Norway E-mail: jens.p.heyerdahl@orkla.no.

HEYL, ALLEN VAN, JR., geologist; b. Allentown, Pa., Apr. 10, 1918; s. Allen Van and Emma (Kleppinger) H.; m. Maxine LaVon Hawke, July 12, 1945; children: Nancy Caroline, Allen David Van. BS in Geology, Pa. State U., 1941; PhD in Geology, Princeton U., 1950. Field asst. major regional exploration, govt. geologist Nfld. Geol. Survey, summers 1937-40, 42; jr. geologist U.S. Geol. Survey, Wis., 1943-45, asst. geologist, 1945-47, assoc. geologist, 1947-50, geologist, 1950-67, staff geologist Denver, 1968-90; cons. geologist, 1990—. Disting. lectr. grad. coll. Beijing, China and Nat. Acad. Sci., 1988; disting. invited lectr. Internat. Assn. Genesis Ore Deposits 9th Symposium, Beijing, 1994; chmn. Internat. Commn. Tectonics of Ore Deposits. Contbr. numerous articles to profl. jours., chpts. to books. Fellow Instn. Minin and Metallurgy (Gt. Brit.), Geol. Soc. Am., Am. Mineral Soc., Soc. Econ. Geologists, Inst. Genesis of Ore Deposits (hon., life), Geol. Soc. Wash., Colo. Sci. Soc., Rocky Mountain geol. Soc., Friends of Mineralogy (hon., life), Evergreen Naturalist Audubon Soc., Sigma Xi, Alpha Chi Sigma. Lutheran. Home: PO Box 1052 Evergreen CO 80437-1052

HEYL, GUY CARLISLE, JR., orthopedic surgeon; b. Chester, Pa., Sept. 23, 1929; s. Guy Carlisle and June Bryte (Black) H.; m. Mary Lynn Idleman, Sept. 7, 1952; children: Barbara Lynn, Stephen Scott, Douglas Guy. BA, U. Va., 1951, MD, 1954. Diplomate Am. Bd. Orthop. Surgery. Pvt. practice, Herscher, Ill., 1958-61; resident physician Med. Coll. Ga., Augusta, 1961-64; pvt. practice Aiken, S.C., 1964-94; ret., 1994. Chief of staff Aiken County Hosp., 1974; trustee Aiken Cmty. Hosp., 1983-86. Capt. USAF, 1954-58. Fellow ACS, Am. Acad. Orthop. Surgeons. Democrat. Episcopalian. Avocations: scuba diving, model railroading. Home: 3415 Meadow Dr Aiken SC 29801-2883

HEYLER, GROVER ROSS, retired lawyer; b. Manila, June 24, 1926; s. Grover Edwin and Esther Viola (Ross) H.; m. Caroline Yarbrough, Aug. 10, 1949; children: Richard Ross, Sue Louise, Randall Arthur BA, UCLA, 1949; LLB, U. Calif., Berkeley, 1952. Bar: Calif. 1953. Assoc. Latham & Watkins, L.A., 1952-60, ptnr., 1960-93, chmn., corp. securities dept., 1967-89. Chmn. Nat. Alliance for Rsch. into Schizophrenia and Depression, NYC. Mem. Calif. Bar Assn. (com. on drafting Calif. corps. code 1971-75), Order of Coif, UCLA ALumni Assn. (bd. dirs. 1966-70, 1988-90), L.A. Country Club. Home: 491 Homewood Rd Los Angeles CA 90049-2713

HEYMACH, GEORGE JOHN, III, physician, educator, health facility administrator, consultant; b. N.Y.C., Nov. 17, 1942; s. George John and Bertha Vina (Floerke) H.; m. Barbara Lynne Lerew, Oct. 26, 1968; children: Brooke Lerew, G. John IV, Bria Lerew. BS in Chem. Engring., CCNY, 1964; MS, U. Pa., 1966, PhD, 1969; MD, Jefferson Med. Coll., 1976; MBA, U. Pitts., 1997. Diplomate in internal medicine, pulmonary medicine, critical care medicine, geriatrics Am. Bd. Internal Medicine. Asst. prof. chem. engring. Kans. State U., Manhattan, 1969-72; resident in medicine Thomas Jefferson U. Hosp., Phila., 1976-79; fellow in medicine Washington U., St. Louis, 1979-81; physician Pitts. Pulmonary Assn. Ltd., 1981-96; v.p. med. affairs Bapt. Med. Ctr., Kansas City, Mo., 1997-98; med. dir. Health Midwest, Kansas City, Mo., 1998—2000; sr. v.p. healthcare Fleishman-Hillard, 2000—01; pres. Physicians' Health Care Cons., 2001—. Clin. asst. prof. medicine U. Pitts., 1982-2003; adj. prof. biomed. engring. Carnegie-Mellon U., Pitts., 1982—96. Contbr. articles to profl. jours. Fire surgeon Fox Chapel (Pa.) Vol. Fire Dept., 1984-92; Tb physician Allegheny County Health Dept., Pitts., 1986-90. Served to capt. U.S. Army, 1970-72. Grantee in field. Fellow ACP, Am. Coll. Chest Physicians. Avocations: boating, travel, racketball, music. Home: 801 W 57th Ter Kansas City MO 64113-1166 Office: 801 W 57th Terr Kansas City MO 64113 Fax: 816-333-0224. E-mail: Breathdoc@aol.com.

HEYMAN, GENE MORRIS, research psychologist, educator; b. Fayetville, N.C., June 26, 1945; s. Philip and Florence Ehrlich Heyman; m. Martha Lynn Pott, May 11, 1987; 1 child, Phoebe Lily Ehrlich Pott-Heyman. BA, U. Calif., Riverside, 1966; PhD, Harvard U., 1977. Postdoctoral fellow U. Chgo., 1981-83; rsch. scientist Lederle Labs., Pearl River, N.Y., 1983-88; assoc. prof. psychology Harvard U., Cambridge, Mass., 1989-98; rsch. psychologist McLean Hosp., Belmont, Mass., 1998—; lectr. Harvard U. Med. Sch., Boston, 1998—. Cons., 1998—. Bd. editors, Jour. Exptl. Analysis of Behavior, 1978-83, 95-98; contbr. articles to profl. jours. and ency. Grantee NSF, 1995-98, Nat. Inst. Drug Abuse, 1998—, Nat. Inst. Alcoholism and Alcohol Abuse, 1995-98, 2002—, Russell Sage Found., 1995-98. Mem. Am. Psychol. Soc., Behavioral Pharmacol. Soc., Soc. Quantitative Analysis of Behavior. Avocations: tennis, skiing. Office: McLean Hosp 115 Mill St Belmont MA 02478-1048

HEYMAN, IRA MICHAEL, federal agency administrator, museum executive, law educator; b. N.Y.C., May 30, 1930; s. Harold Albert and Judith (Sobel) H.; m. Therese Helene Thau, Dec. 17, 1950; children: Stephen Thomas (dec.), James Nathaniel. AB in Govt., Dartmouth Coll., 1951; JD, Yale U., 1956; LLD (hon.), U. Pacific, 1981, Hebrew Union Coll., 1984, U. Md., 1986, SUNY, Buffalo, 1990, Dartmouth Coll., 2001. Bar: NY 1956, Calif. 1961. Legis. asst. to U.S. Senator Ives, 1950-51; assoc. Carter, Ledyard & Milburn, N.Y.C., 1956-57; law clk. to presiding justice U.S. Ct. Appeals (2d cir.), New Haven, 1957-58; chief law clk. to Supreme Ct. Justice Earl Warren, 1958-59; acting assoc. prof. law U. Calif., Berkeley, 1959-61, prof. law, 1961—93, prof. city and regional planning, 1966-93, prof. emeritus, 1993—, vice chancellor, 1974-80, chancellor, 1980-90, chancellor emeritus, 1990—; counselor to Sec. of Interior Dept. Interior, Washington, 1993-94; sec. Smithsonian Inst., Washington, 1994-99, sec. emeritus, 2000—; mem. Citizens' Stamp Adv. Com., 2000—. Vis. prof. Yale Law Sch., 1963—64, Stanford Law Sch., 1971—72; bd. dirs. Presicio Trust. Editor Yale Law Jour.; contbr. articles to profl. jours. Sec. Calif. adv. com. U.S. Commn. Civil Rights, 1962-67; trustee Dartmouth Coll., 1982-93, chmn., 1991-93; mem. Lawyers' Com. for Civil Rights under Law, 1977-95, Citizens Stamp Advisory Com., USPS, 2000-; chmn. exec. com. Nat. Assn. State Univs. and Land Grant Colls., 1986; bd. regents Smithsonian Instn., 1990-94; bd. dirs. Presidio Trust, 2000—. 1st lt. USMC, 1951-53, capt. Res. ret. Decorated chevalier Legion of Honor (France). Mem. Am. Acad. Arts and Sci. E-mail: mheyman@law.berkeley.edu.

HEYMAN, LAWRENCE MURRAY, printmaker, painter; b. Washington, June 30, 1932; s. Philip I. and Gertrude B. H. BFA, Tyler Sch. Fine Arts, Temple U., 1954, BS in Edn., 1955; MFA, Am. U., 1972. Instr. fine arts in printmaking R.I. Sch. Design, 1967-69, asst. prof. fine arts and printmaking, 1972-79, dir. printmaking program, 1976-79; lectr. Am. U., 1971-72. Exhibited in one-man shows, Mickelson Gallery, Washington, 1966, 77, R.I. Sch. Design, 1969, 79, St. John's U., St. Paul, 1980, Mus. City of N.Y., 1984, Starr Gallery, Newton, Mass., 1985, Plum Gallery, Kensington, Md., 1986, 88, NIH, Bethesda, Md., 1990, Vets.' Meml. Auditorium, Providence, 1991; group shows including, Providence Art Club, (prize 1974, 76), Bibliotheque Nationale, Paris, 1977 (purchase honor 79), San Francisco Art Museum, 1977, Plum Gallery, Kensington, Md., 1985, 86, 89, Starr Gallery, Newton, Mass., 1991; represented in permanent collections Bibliotheque Nationale, Paris, Bklyn. Mus., Brooks Meml. Mus., Tenn., Mus. City of N.Y., Portland (Oreg.) Art Mus.; U.S. rep. Art in Embassies program exhbn., Istanbul, Turkey, 1976; Commd.: print edits. for Associated Am. Artists, N.Y.C., 1964, 68, 69, Antares Editions d'Art, Paris, 1970, 71, 72, Judith Selkowitz Fine Arts, N.Y.C., 1978; featured in book Painting the Town, 2000. Served with U.S. Army, 1955-57. Nominee and finalist for Nat. Arts medal Nat. Endowment for Arts, 1987; finalist 1989 Portrait Painting Competition Artist's Mag. Mem. Whitegate Features Syndicate Fine Arts. Office: 71 Faunce Dr Providence RI 02906-4805

HEYMAN, MELVIN BERNARD, pediatric gastroenterologist; b. San Francisco, Mar. 24, 1950; s. Vernon Otto and Eve Elsie Heyman; m. Jody Ellen Switky, May 8, 1988. BA in Econs., U. Calif., Berkeley, 1972; MD, UCLA, 1976, MPH in Nutrition, 1981. Diplomate Am. Bd. Pediatrics (assoc. 1997—), Am. Bd. Pediatric Gastroenterology (assoc. 1997—). Intern, resident Los Angeles County-U. So. Calif. Med. Ctr., 1976-79; fellow UCLA, 1979-81; asst. prof. U. Calif., San Francisco, 1981-88, assoc. prof., 1988-94, prof., 1994—, chief pediatric gastroenterology, hepatology and nutrition, 1990—; dir. UCSF Tng. Program Pediatric Gastroenterology/Nutrition, 1997—; dir. UCSF/Stanford Combined Tng. Program Pediatric Gastroenterology/Nutrition, 1998—2002. Assoc. dir. Pediatric Gastroenterology/Nutrition, San Francisco, 1986-89; mem. cons. staff San Francisco Gen. Hosp., Natividad Med. Ctr., Salinas, Calif., Scenic Gen. Hosp., Modesto, Calif.; assoc. dir. Pediatric IBD Consortium 2000—. Contbr. articles to profl. jours. Chmn. scientific adv. com. San Francisco chpt. Crohn's and Colitis Found. Am., 1987-94, bd. dirs., 1986—. Recipient Investigator award, NIH-NIDDK, 2002—, rsch. grantee, Children's Liver Found., 1984—85, John Tung grantee, Am. Cancer Soc., 1985—89; grantee, NIH-NIDDK, 1998—. Mem.: Assn. Food and Drug Ofcls., Am. Bd. Pediatric Gastroenterology (chair sub-bd. 2000—01), Am. Soc. Parenteral Enteral Nutrition, Soc. Clin. Nutrition, Am. Gastroenterol. Assn., Am. Inst. Nutrition (exec. com. on pediat. gastroenterology and nutrition 1999—), Am. Acad. Pediat. (com. on nutrition 1999—, exec. com. sect. on pediat. gastroenterology and nutrition 1999—), N.Am. Soc. Pediat. Gastro Nutrition (chair patient care com. 1997—2000). Avocations: skiing, swimming, hiking, tennis, biking. Office: U Calif Dept Pediat PO Box 0136 San Francisco CA 94143-0136

HEYMAN, RALPH EDMOND, lawyer; b. Cin., Mar. 14, 1931; s. Ralph and Florence (Kahn) H.; m. Sylvia Lee Schottenstein, Jan. 2, 1984; children: Michael Cary, Cynthia Ann Heyman Eeg, Ginger Florence. AB magna cum laude (Rufus Choat scholar), Dartmouth Coll., 1953; LLB cum laude, Harvard U., 1956; LLM, U. Cin., 1957. Bar: Ohio 1956, Ill. 1957. Pvt. practice, Cin., 1956-58, Dayton, 1958—; assoc. Freiden & Wolf, 1956-58; from assoc. to ptnr. Smith & Schnacke, 1958-88; ptnr. Chernesky, Heyman & Kress, Dayton, Ohio, 1988—. Lectr. estate planning U. Cin., 1958-61; lectr. participant Southwestern Ohio Tax Inst., 1957-65; lectr., moderator Dayton Bar Assn. Tax Insts., 1975-79, 94; lectr. continuing edn. program U. Dayton, 1989; lectr. estate planning Dayton Area Tax Profls., 1993; lectr. on venture capital Miami Valley Venture Assn., 1998; dir., gen. counsel Towne Properties, Ltd., Sachs Mgmt. Corp., Inc., Aristocrat Products, Inc., K.k. Motorcycle Supply, Inc., The Sportsman's Guide. Recipient Robert A. Shapiro Vol. award 1998. Commr. Bd. Rural Zoning Commn. Montgomery County, 1969-71; bd. dirs., pres. Jewish Fedn. Dayton, 1993-97; nat. trustee NCCJ; past pres. Temple Israel; pres. Temple Israel Found., 1999-2001; dir. United Way Greater Dayton Area, 1999. Recipient Humanitarian award NCCJ, 1997, Robert A. Shapiro Vol. award, 1998. Mem. ABA, Ohio Bar Assn., Dayton Bar Assn. (chmn. tax com.), Cin. Bar Assn., Lawyers Club, Bicycle Club, Meadowbrook Club, Dayton City Club (past pres.), B'nai Brith, Phi Beta Kappa. Jewish. Office: Chernesky Heyman & Kress PLL PO Box 3808 1100 Courthouse Plz SW Dayton OH 45401-3808

HEYMAN, RICHARD E. psychology educator; b. Washington, Sept. 10, 1964; s. Victor Kenneth and Reba Renee Heyman; m. Maria Valli Vanoni, Jan. 18, 1963. BS, Duke U., 1986; PhD, U. Oreg., 1992. Lic. psychologist. Psychology intern Ea. Pa. Psychiat. Inst., Phila., 1991-92; rsch. assoc. prof. SUNY, Stony Brook, 1992—. Author: Couples Psychotherapy Treatment Planner, 1998. Office: SUNY Dept Psychology Stony Brook NY 11794-2500

HEYMAN, SAMUEL J. building materials manufacturing company executive; b. N.Y.C., Mar. 1, 1939; s. Lazarus S. and Annette (Silverman) H.; m. Ronnie Feuerstein, Nov. 1970; children: Lazarus, Eleanor, Jennifer, Elizabeth BS magna cum laude, Yale Coll., 1960; LLB, Harvard U., 1963. Bar: Conn. 1963. Atty. U.S. Dept. Justice, Washington, 1963-64; asst. U.S. atty. Dist. of Conn., New Haven, 1964-67; chief asst. U.S. atty. New Haven div., 1967-68; pres. Heyman Properties, Westport, Conn., 1968-83; chmn., CEO Internat. Specialty Products Inc., Wayne, NJ, 1991—99, chmn. only, 1999—; chmn. G-I Holdings Inc. (formerly GAF), Wayne, NJ, 1983—. Office: GAF 1361 Alps Rd Wayne NJ 07470*

HEYMAN, SIDNEY, lawyer, educator; b. Riga, Latvia, Feb. 1, 1925; came to U.S., 1927; s. Seymour and Paula H.; m. Doris A. Groudine, Sept. 9, 1-51; children: Susan Cohn, Sharon McDermott. BS, L.I. U., 1949; LLB, Bklyn. Law Sch., 1953, JD, 1967. Trial atty. Great Am. Ins., N.Y.C., 1953-59, Julius Diamond, N.Y.C., 1959-68, Chikovsky, Snyder & Heyman, Rochester, N.Y., 1969-82; ptnr. Cory & Heyman, Staten Island, 1969; pvt. practice Rochester, 1983—. Tchr. polit. sci. SUNY, Geneseo, 1989, 95. Staff sgt. U.S. Army, 1943-46, PTO. Avocation: competitive swimming. Office: 36 W Main St Ste 604 Rochester NY 14614-1701

HEYMAN, WILLIAM HERBERT, financial services executive; b. N.Y.C., Apr. 20, 1948; s. George Harrison and Edythe Jane (Forman) H., Jr. AB magna cum laude, Princeton U., 1970; JD cum laude, Harvard U., 1973. Bar: N.Y. 1974, D.C. 1991. Assoc. Cravath, Swaine & Moore, N.Y.C., 1975-78, White & Case, N.Y.C., 1973-75, Stroock & Stroock & Lavan, N.Y.C., 1978-79; gen. ptnr., COO Mercury Securities, N.Y.C., 1979-88; mng. dir. Smith Barney, Harris Upham & Co., Inc., N.Y.C., 1989-91; dir. divsn. market regulation SEC, Washington, 1991-93; mng. dir. Salomon Bros. Inc., Washington, 1993-95; exec. v.p. Citigroup Investments, Inc., N.Y.C., 1995—2000, chmn., 2001—02; CEO Tribeca Investments LLC, N.Y.C., 1996—2002; exec. v.p., chief investment officer St. Paul Cos., 2002—. Bd. dirs. Max Re Capital Holdings Ltd., Max Re Ltd., Nuveen Investments Inc. Trustee Mt. Sinai-NYU Med. Ctr., 1994-99, Hosp. for Joint Diseases, 1994-98; mem. N.Y. area firms adv. com. N.Y. Stock Exch., 1996-2002; mem. adv. bd. fin. math. Courant Inst. Math. Scis. NYU; bd. dirs. Student/Sponsor Partnership of N.Y., 1989-91, 93 ; bd. dirs. 92d St. YM&YWHA, N.Y.C., 1979-90, hon. bd. dirs., 1991—; coun. overseers United Jewish Appeal-Fedn. N.Y., 1986-88; mem. fin. com. N.Y. State Reps., 1986-90, v.p. N.Y. County Reps. Com., 1987-90; mem. nat. fin. com. George Bush for Pres., 1987-88; hon. chmn. Bicentennial Presdl. Inaugural, 1989, pub. mem. Adminstrv. Conf. of the U.S., 1989-90; mem. N.Y. regional panel for selection of White House Fellows, 1989; mem. fin. products adv. com. Commodity Futures Trading Commn., 1992-93. Mem. Harvard Law Sch. Assn. (nat. coun. 1986-90), Econ. Club N.Y., Century Country Club (Purchase, N.Y.), Army and Navy Club (Washington), Univ. Club (N.Y.), Midland Hills Country Club (St. Paul), Mid Ocean Club (Bermuda), Phi Beta Kappa. Jewish. Office: St Paul Cos 385 Washington St Saint Paul MN 55102-1396 E-mail: wheyman103@aol.com., bill.heyman@stpaul.com.

HEYMANN, C(LEMENS) DAVID, author; b. N.Y.C., Jan. 14, 1945; s. Ernest Frederick and Renee K. (Vago) H.; m. Jeanne Ann Lunin, Nov. 10, 1974 (div. 1995); children: Chloe Colette, Paris Kent Fineberg-Heymann; m. Rebecca Ellen Coughlan, 1995 (div. 1996). BS, Cornell U., 1966; MFA, U. Mass., 1969. Lectr. English lit. SUNY-Stony Brook, 1969-74, Antioch Coll., N.Y.C. campus, 1975. Mem. judges panel Am. Book Awards, 1979-80, Nat. Book Critics Circle, 1978-79 Author: (poetry) The Quiet Hours, 1969; Ezra Pound: The Last Rower, 1976, American Aristocracy: The Lives and Time of James Russell, Amy and Robert Lowell, 1980, Poor Little Rich Girl: The Life and Legend of Barbara Hutton, 1983, A Woman Named Jackie: An Intimate Biography of Jacqueline Bouvier Kennedy Onassis, 1989, Liz: An Intimate Biography of Elizabeth Taylor, 1995, RFK: A Candid Biography of Robert F. Kennedy, 1998, The Georgetown Ladies' Social Club: Power, Passion, and Politics in the Nation's Capital, 2003; also book revs. and articles for nat. mags. and newspapers. Israeli govt. writer's grantee, 1984-85 Address: William Morris Agy 1325 Avenue Of The Americas New York NY 10019-6026

HEYMANN, PHILIP BENJAMIN, law educator, academic director; b. Pitts., Oct. 30, 1932; BA, Yale U., 1954; LL.B., Harvard U., 1960. Bar: D.C. 1960, Mass. 1969. Trial atty. gen. Dept. Justice, Washington, 1961-65, asst. atty. gen. criminal div., 1978-81, dep. atty. gen., 1993-94; dep. adminstr. Bur. Security and Consular Affairs, Dept. State, Washington, 1965, acting adminstr., to 1967; dep. asst. sec. of state for Bur. Internat. Orgns., 1967, exec. asst. to under sec. of state, 1967-69; with Legal Aid Agy. of D.C., 1969; faculty law Harvard U., 1969—, James Barr Ames prof. law, dir. Harvard Law Sch. Ctr. for Criminal Justice. Assoc. prosecutor and cons. to Watergate Spl. Prosecution Force, summers 1973-75 Served with USAF, 1955-57.

HEYMANN, S. RICHARD, lawyer; b. Chgo., Sept. 18, 1944; s. Samuel R. and Ann (Menning) H.; m. Jane Ann Gebhart, June 14, 1980; children: Elizabeth Jane, Catherine Claire. BS, U. Wis., 1966; JD, U. Mich., 1969. Bar: Mo. 1969, Wis. 1988. Law clk. Minn. Supreme Ct., St. Paul, 1970-72; assoc. Bryan, Cave, McPheeters & McRoberts, St. Louis, 1972-79, ptnr., 1980-87, Foley & Lardner, Madison, Wis., 1987-99; dir. Inst. for Environ. Studies U. Wis., Madison, 1996—. Adj. prof. U. Wis. Law Sch.; fellow U. Wis. Bus. Ctr.Urban Land Econs. Rsch. Fellow, Ctr. for Urban Land Econs. Mem. U. Wis. Found., Wis. Alumni Assn. (bd. dirs. 1985-87), Madison Club, Maple Bluff Country Club. Office: Univ Wis Inst Environ Studies 550 N Park St Rm 70 Madison WI 53706-1404 E-mail: srheymann@wisc.edu.

HEYN, ARNO HARRY ALBERT, retired chemistry educator; b. Breslau, Germany, Oct. 6, 1918; s. Myron and Margarete M.E.C. (Cierpinski) H.; m. Helen A. Pielemeier, Mar. 14, 1942; children: Evan A., Margaret L., Robert E. BS, U. Mich., 1940, MS, 1941, PhD in Analytical Chemistry, 1944. Exptl. chemist Sun Oil Co., Norwood, Pa., 1944-47; from instr. to prof. chemistry Boston U., 1947-84, prof. emeritus, 1984. Vis. scientist Brookhaven Nat. Lab., summers 1954-56; acad. guest Eidg. Techn. Hochschule, Zurich, 1965, Gesellschaft F. Kernforschung, Karlsruhe, 1973, 80, 81, 82, Landesanst. F. Wasserbiologic, Vienna, 1973; sci. adviser Boston Dist. U.S. FDA, 1967-72 Contbr. articles to profl. jours. Fellow AAAS; mem. Am. Chem. Soc. (councilor 1967-97, alt. councilor 1998—, chmn. coun. com. on constn. and bylaws 1983-85, coun. policy com. 1986-91, vice-chmn. 1987-88, com. on coms. 1992-94, Henry Hill award N.E. sect. 1986, editor Nucleus 1989—), AAUP (treas. Boston U. chpt. 1979-83), Sigma Xi, Phi Lambda Upsilon, Sub Sig Outing Club (Boston). Avocation: locksmithing. Home: 21 Alexander Rd Newton MA 02461-1830 E-mail: aheyn1@juno.com.

HEYNEMAN, DONALD, parasitology and tropical medicine educator; b. San Francisco, Feb. 18, 1925; s. Paul and Amy Josephine (KLauber) H.; m. Louise Davidson Ross, June 18, 1971; children: Amy J., Lucy A., Andrew P., Jennifer K., Claudia G. AB magna cum laude, Harvard U., 1950; MA, Rice U., 1952, PhD, 1954. Instr. zoology UCLA, 1954-56, asst. prof., 1956-60; head dept. parasitology U.S. Navy Med. Research unit, Cairo, also co-dir. Malakal, Sudan, 1960-62; assoc. research parasitologist Hooper Found. U. Calif., San Francisco, 1962-64, assoc. prof., 1966-68, prof., 1968-91, prof. emeritus, 1991—, asst. dir. Hooper found., 1970-74, acting chmn. dept. internat. health, 1976-78, assoc. dean Sch. Pub. Health Berkeley and San Francisco, 1987-91, assoc. dean emeritus, 1991—, chmn. joint med. program, 1987-91, chmn. emeritus, 1991—. Research coordinator U. Calif. Internat. Ctr. Med. Research and Tng., Kuala Lumpur, Malaysia, 1964-66; cons. physiol. processes sect. NSF, 1966-91; environ. biology div. NIH, 1968-91; mem. tropical medicine and parasitology study sect. NIAID-NIH, 1973-76; mem. adv. sci. bd. Gorgas Meml. Inst., 1967-90; cons. WHO, 1967, mem. sci. tech. rev. com. on Leishmaniases, 1984; cons. UN Devel. Program, 1978-91, US-AID, others; panel reviewer Internat. Nomenclature of Diseases, 1984—; Am. cons. and U.S. prin. investigator U. Linkage Project, Egypt-U.S., 1984—; mem. Calif. Health Adv. Com., 1983—. Author: (with R. Boolootian) An Illustrated Laboratory Text in Zoology, 1962, An Illustrated Laboratory Text in Zoology, A Brief Version, 1977, International Dictionary Medicine and Biology, (with R. Goldsmith) Textbook of Tropical Medicine and Parasitology, 1989;co-author, contbg. editor Phytolacca dodecandra: Endod, 1984, Endod II, 1987; contbr. articles to jours., chpts. to books.; editorial cons. Am. Jour. Tropical Medicine and Hygiene, Jour. Parasitology, Jour. Exptl. Parasitology, Sci., 1968—, other jours. Served with AUS, 1943-46. NIH grantee, 1966-85. Mem. Am. Soc. Parasitologists (council 1970-74, pres. 1982-83), Am. Micros. Soc. (exec. com. 1971-75), Am. Soc. Tropical Medicine and Hygiene (councilor 1981-84), So. Calif. Parasitol. Soc. (pres. 1957-58), No. Calif. Parasitologists (sec.- treas. 1969-72, pres. 1977-78), Phi Beta Kappa. Home: 1400 Lake St San Francisco CA 94118-1036 Office: U Calif Dept Epidemiology Biostat PO Box 0560 San Francisco CA 94143-0001 E-mail: dheyneman@epi.ucsf.edu.

HEYWARD, ANDREW JOHN, television producer; b. Roslyn, N.Y., Oct. 29, 1950; s. E.J.R. and Elisabeth Heyward; m. Jody Gaylin Heyward, May 23, 1976; children: David, Emily, Sarah. BA, Harvard U., 1972. Producer Sta. WNEW-TV News, N.Y.C., 1974-76, Sta. WCBS-TV News, N.Y.C., 1976-78, exec. producer, 1978-81; producer CBS Evening News CBS News, N.Y.C., 1981-84, sr. producer, 1984-87; exec. producer 48 Hours, N.Y.C., 1987-93, Eye to Eye, 1993-94; v.p. CBS News, 1994-96; exec. producer CBS Evening News, 1994-96; pres. CBS News, 1996—. Mem. NATAS (Emmy award 1977-78, 84, 88-93, 95). Office: CBS News 524 W 57th St New York NY 10019-2924

HEYWOOD, ANNE, artist, educator, author; b. Newport, RI, Sept. 15, 1951; d. Albert Paul and Eileen Frances (Laforest) Boretti; m. Ciro DiGiovanni, May 24, 1969 (div. 1980); 1 child, Carlo; m. Henry Robert Heywood, Nov. 9, 1985. BA in Art summa cum laude, Bridgewater (Mass.) State Coll. Tchr. drawing and pastels Silver Lake Reg. H.S. Adult Edn., Kingston, Mass., 1991—95; art educator pastels, drawing South Shore Art Ctr., Cohasset, Mass., 1996—; art educator pastels Fuller Mus. Art, Brockton, Mass., 1996—, Pastel Painters Soc. Cape Cod, Barnstable, Mass., 1997; art educator drawing Swinburne Sch., Newport, RI, 1995, Round Top Ctr. for Arts, Damariscotta, Maine, 1996; workshop instr. Northwest Pastel Soc., Gig Harbor, Wash., 2002. Pastel demonstrator, spkr. in field; artist residency Carillon Beach Inst., Panama City, Fla., 2002; juror Renaissance in Pastel, 1999; juror N.W. Pastel Soc., 2002, workshop instr., Wash., 02. Author: Pastels Made Easy, 2003; contbg. artist: Best of Pastel, 1996, Landscape Inspirations, 1997, Best of Sketching and Drawing 1999; one-woman shows include East Bridgewater (Mass.) Pub. Libr., 1992, 95, Mass. Audubon Soc., Marshfield, 1992, South Shore Natural Sci. Ctr., Norwell, Mass., 1993, Marion (Mass.) Art Ctr., 1994, Fuller Art Mus., Brockton, Mass., 1995, 2000, Passage Gallery, South Shore Art Ctr., Cohasset, Mass., 1996, 98, Sparrow House, Plymouth, Mass., 1997, 2000, Landmark Bldg., Boston, 1999; exhibited in group shows at Duxbury Art Assn., Mass., 1993, Trenton (N.J.) State Coll., 1994, Bridgewater State Coll., 1994, Zullo Gallery, Medfield, Mass., 1995, 99, 2001, Maine Art Gallery, Wiscasset, 1995, Pastel Soc. Am., N.Y.C., 1995, 97, Internat. Assn. Pastel Socs., 1997, 99 (Convention Image award), Left Bank Gallery, Wellfleet, Mass., 1997, Gallery at C3TV, South Yarmouth, Mass., 1997, Salmagundi Club, N.Y. 1999 (George Inness Jr. Meml. award for pastel), Nat. Biennial Exhbn. Degas Soc., La. (La. Watercolor Soc. award of merit), Colo. History Mus., Fla. Pastel Soc., Soc. Western Artists, Mass., 1999, Pastel Soc. of the West Coast, 2001, Audubon Artists Exhbn., 2001, Newington-Cropsey Found., N.Y., 2001; also pvt. collections; contbr. articles to profl. jours.; editor Pastel Painter's Soc. Cape Cod newsletter, 1998-99, bd. dirs., 1999—. Sec. East Bridgewater Arts Coun., 1992-97, Artists Cir. at Fuller Mus., Brockton, Mass., 1995-97; juror Renaissance in Pastel, 1999, Northwest Pastel Soc., Harbor, Wash., 2002. Recipient 1st pl. drawing East Bridgewater Art Festival, 1991, 1st pl. awards Wickford (R.I.) Art Assn., 1992, Taunton (Mass.) Art Assn., 1993, South Shore Art Ctr. Blue Ribbon Members Show, Cohasset, 1994, Fuller Art Mus., Brockton, 1994, 1st pl. pastels Plymouth Guild May Members Show, 1994, award Providence Art Club, 1996, award of distinction All New Eng. Color Show, Cohasset, 1996; Vt. Studio Ctr. Residency fellow, 1999. Mem.: Nat. Assn. Women Artists (D.Wu and Elsie Jeck-Key Meml. award 2000), Oil Pastel Assn./United Pastellists Am. (signature mem.), Pastel Soc. Am. (Holbein award 1995), Conn. Pastel Soc. (signature mem.), Pastel Painters Soc. Cape Cod (signature mem., Canson-Talens award 1997), Allied Artists of Am., Associated Pastelists on Web (signature mem.), Am. Artists Profl. League, Internat. Assn. of Pastel Socs., Salmagundi Club. Roman Catholic. Avocations: reading, walking, biking, choir. Home: 85 Ashley Dr East Bridgewater MA 02333-1703 E-mail: aheywood@anne-heywood.com.

HEYWOOD, ELIZABETH ZONA, nurse educator; b. Gardner, Mass, Feb. 13, 1941; Student, Johnson County Vocat. Nursing, Cleburne, Tex., 1971; BSN, U. Tex., Austin, 1986. Cert. emergency med. technician, BLS, ACLS. Staff nurse Stephenville Gen. Hosp., Tex., 1983, Lea Regional Hosp., Hobbs, N.Mex., 1983; staff nurse med.-surg. unit South Austin Cmty. Hosp., Austin, Tex., 1983-86; staff nurse on neuro-respiratory unit Ctrl. Meth. Med. Ctr., Dallas, 1986—87; staff nurse post cardiac unit Mary Washington Hosp., Fredericksburg, Va., 1987-89; staff nurse and night shift supr. Summers County Hosp., Hinton, W.Va., 1990-94; edn. coord., nursing supr. Summers County Appalachian Regional Hosp., 1994—. Founder Follow the Son Ministries Inc; mem. Son Seekers Gospel Group. Adminstr. Peace in the Valley Praise Ctr. Mem. Phi Theta Kappa.

HEYWOOD, JOHN BENJAMIN, mechanical engineering educator; b. Sidcup, Kent, Eng., Jan. 11, 1938; s. Harold and Frances Dora (Weaver) H.; m. Marguerite Gilkerson, Dec. 28, 1961; children: James, Stephen, Benjamin. BA, Cambridge U., 1960, DSc, 1984; MS, MIT, 1962, PhD, 1965; DTech (hon.), Chalmers U. Tech., 1999. Lectr. Northeastern U., Boston, 1963-65; rsch. assoc. mech. engring. dept. MIT, Cambridge, 1964-65, asst. prof. mech. engring., 1968-70, assoc. prof., 1970-76, prof., 1976-92, dir. Sloan Automotive Lab., coord. transp. programs in Energy Lab., 1972—, co-dir. leaders for mfg. program, 1991-93; Sun Jae prof. mech. engring., 1992—; rsch. officer Cen. Electricity Generating Bd., Leatherhead, Eng., 1965-67, group leader, 1967-68; co-dir. Ford-MIT Alliance, 2003—. Co-dir. Ford-MIT Alliance, 2003—; cons. in field. Author, editor: (with others) Open-Cycle MHD Power Generation, 1969; author: (with others) The Automobile and the Regulation of its Impact on the Environment, 1975, Internal Engine Combustion Fundamentals, 1988, (with E. Sher) The Two-Stroke Engine, 1999; contbr. Ency. Britannica, chpts. to books, numerous articles, papers to profl. jours., confs., symposia U.S.A, Eng., Europe. Recipient Ayerton Premium Inst. Elec. Engrs., U.K., 1969; Fulbright travel scholar, 1960; Richard C. Mellon Overseas fellow Churchill Coll., Cambridge, Eng., 1976-77; recipient Nat. award for Advancement of Motor Vehicle R&D, US DOT, 1996. Fellow U.K. Instn. Mech. Engrs. (George Stephenson Internat. Lectr. 1997); mem. Soc. Automotive Engrs. (Ralph R. Teeter Outstanding Young Engr. award 1971, Arch T. Colwell Merit award 1973, 81, 89, Outstanding Oral Presentation award 1980, 2001, Horning Meml. Best Paper award 1984, Rsch. on Automotive Lubricants award 2001), ASME (Freeman scholar 1986, Honda lectr. 1990, Honda medal 1999), Nat. Acad. Engring., Am. Acad. Arts and Scis. Achievements include rsch. interests in thermodynamics, combustion, energy, power and propulsion, performance, efficiency and emissions of spark-ignition and diesel engines, control of air pollution, engine design and manufacture. Office: MIT Dept Mech Engring 77 Mass Ave # 3-340 Cambridge MA 02139-4307

HEYZER, NOELEEN, international organization official; BS, U. Singapore; PhD in social scis., Cambridge U. Exec. dir. UN Devel. Fund for Women, 1994—. Keynote spkr. for numerous univs. and orgns. Office: UNIFEM 304 E 45th St 15th fl New York NY 10017

HEZEL, FRANCIS XAVIER, clergy member, educator; b. Buffalo, N.Y., Jan. 29, 1939; arrived in Micronesia, 1963; s. Francis Xavier Hezel and Patricia Mary Kolb. BA, Fordham U., N.Y.C., 1962; MA, Fordham U., 1963, HHD

(hon.), 1994; MDiv, Woodstock (Md.) Coll., Md., 1969; MST, Woodstock Coll., 1970; HHD (hon.), U. Guam, 1986, Fordham U., 1995. Ordained priest Roman Cath. Ch., 1969. Tchr. Xavier H.S., Chuuk, Micronsia, 1963-66, 69-73, prin., 1973-75, dir., 1976-82, Micronesian Seminar, 1972—. Regional superior Jesuits of Micronesia, 1992-98; dir. Med. Grad. Support Program, Micronesia, 1996-2000; mem. com. evaluate health svcs. in Pacific Inst. Medicine, Washington, 1996-97; assoc. Micronesia Area Rsch. Ctr. Author: First Taint of Civilization, 1983, Strangers in Their Own Land, 1995, New Shape of Old Island Cultures, 2001; prodr. (TV documentaries) Island Topics, 1994-98; corr. Jour. Pacific History; contbr. arricles to profl. jours. Mem. Chuuk State Bd. Edn., 1987-90, Com. Primary Health Care, Chuuk, 1987-88, Pohnpei (Micronesia) Econ. Coun., 1996-99. Mem. Pacific Islands Assn. Libr. Archives, Assn. Social Anthropologists Oceania. Roman Catholic. Avocations: basketball, tennis, writing. Home and Office: Micronesian Seminar PO Box 160 Pohnpei FM 96941-0160 E-mail: fxhezel@mail.fm.

HEZIR, JOSEPH S. energy and environmental company executive; b. Pitts., Aug. 27, 1950; s. Joseph F. and Elizabeth G. F.; m. Joyce Ann Martincic, May 12, 1979; children: Alexandra M., Damjan S. BS, Carnegie-Mellon U., 1972, MS, 1974. Rsch. engr. St. Joe Minerals Corp., Monaca, Pa., 1971, Carnegie-Mellon U., Pitts., 1972; planning analyst City of N.Y., 1973; budget examiner U.S. Office Mgmt. and Budget, Washington, 1974-82, dep. assoc. dir., 1986-92; sr. corp. analyst Exxon Rsch. and Engring. Corp., Florham Park, N.J., 1982; mng. ptnr. The EOP Group, Inc., Washington, 1992—. Mem. adv. bd. Competitiveness Policy Coun., Washington, 1992-94, NASA Adv. Coun., Washington, 1992-93. Dir. nat. capital chpt. ARC, Washington, 1987-90. Fellow Coun. Excellence in Govt.; mem. NAS (mem. study bds.), Croatian Fraternal Union Am. Roman Catholic. Home: 1509 Pennycress Ln Vienna VA 22182-1473 Office: EOP Group Inc 819 7th St NW Washington DC 20001-3762 E-mail: jshezir@819eagle.com.

HIAPO, PATRICIA KAMAKA, lay worker; b. Honolulu, May 18, 1943; d. Ward Charles and Violet Kaopua (Nicholas) McKeown; m. Bernard Joseph Hiapo, July 9, 1960; children: Bernard Jr., Beatrice, Jacqueline, Mary-Louise. Grad. high sch., Honolulu. Cert. catechist, 1988. Area del. St. John Apostle and Evangelist, Mililani, Hawaii, 1981-84, eucharistic min., 1981-88; hospice and bereavement ministry St. Francis Hosp., Honolulu, 1983, eucharistic min., 1983-88; religious edn. coord. Resurrection of The Lord, Waipahu, Hawaii, 1984-88, dir. religious edn. St. Jude, Ewa Beach, Hawaii, 1988-91; home visitor Hana Like, Honolulu, 1990-98; parent educator Alu Lke Pulama I Na Keiki/Lee Town Ctr., Waipahu, Hawaii, 1998—. Mem. marriage encounter team Cath. Ch., Honolulu, 1981-83. Recipient award Our Lady of Peace, 1991. Office: 87-117 Pulapa Pl Waianae HI 96792 also: Parents and Children Together-Hana Like 45-955 Kamehameha Hwy Ste 404 Kaneohe HI 96744-3222

HIATT, ARNOLD, shoe manufacturer, importer, retailer; b. May 26, 1927; s. Alexander and Dorothy H.; m. Anne Wechsler. BA, Harvard U., 1948. Pres., founder Blue Star Shoe Co., Lawrence, Mass., 1952-69; pres., chief exec. officer Stride Rite Corp., Boston, 1969-89, chmn. bd., 1982-92; chmn. Stride Rite Found., Boston, 1982—. Bd. dirs. Dreyfus Fund. Former mem. bd. regents of higher edn. Commonwealth of Mass.; mem. bd. trustees Isabela Stewart Gardner Mus., The John Merck Found.; former mem. vis. com. Boston U. Sch. Medicine; bd. overseers Harvard U., 1984-90; chair Bus. for Social Responsibility. Mem. Am. Footwear Industries Assn. (dir., chmn. 1980).

HIATT, FRED, editorial editor; b. Washington, 1955; BA in History, Harvard U., 1977. City Hall reporter Atlanta Jour.-Constitution, 1979—80; reporter The Washington Star, 1981; Va. reporter The Washington Post, 1981—83, Pentagon reporter, 1983—86, Northeast Asia co-bur. chief, 1987—90, Moscow co-bur. chief, 1991—95, editl. writer, 1996—. Author: (novels) The Secret Sun, 1992, (children's book) If I Were Queen of the World, 1997, Baby Talk, 1999. Office: The Washington Post 1150 15th St NW Washington DC 20071-0001

HIATT, HOWARD H. physician; b. Patchogue, N.Y., July 22, 1925; s. Alexander and Dorothy (Askinas) Hiatt; m. Doris Bieringer, Nov. 29, 1947; children: Jonathan, Deborah, Frederick. MD, Harvard U., 1948. Intern, then resident medicine Beth Israel Hosp., Boston, 1948—50; research fellow Cornell U. Med. Coll., 1950—53; clin. investigator USPHS, 1953—55; mem. faculty Med. Sch., Harvard U., 1955—, H.L. Blumgart prof. medicine, 1963—72, prof. medicine, 1972—, prof. medicine Sch. Pub. Health, 1984—92, dean Sch. Pub. Health, 1972—84; physician-in-chief Beth Israel Hosp., 1963—72; sr. physician, divsn social medicine and health inequalities Brigham Women's Hosp., Boston, 1984—. Mem.: NAS Inst. Medicine, Partners in Health, Bd. Physicians for Human Rights (vice chair 2001—, bd. dirs. 1996—2002), Am. Acad. Arts and Scis. (sec. 1992—97, dir. Initiatives for Children 1992—2002), Assn. Am. Physicians, Am. Soc. Clin. Investigation, Alpha Omega Alpha. Home: 130 Mt Auburn St Cambridge MA 02138-5757 Office: Brigham and Women's Hosp Boston MA 02115 E-mail: HHiatt@partners.org.

HIATT, JANE CRATER, arts agency administrator; b. Winston-Salem, N.C., May 26, 1944; d. Howard Rondthaler Jr. and Irene (Sides) Crater; m. K.W. Everhart Jr. (div. June 1973); m. Wood Coleman Hiatt, May, 1978; 1 child, Jonathan David. BA, U. N.C., 1966; MA, Wake Forest U., 1972. Eng. tchr. Winston-Salem (N.C.)/Forsyth County Schs., 1966-70; exec. dir. Tenn. Com. for the Humanities, Nashville, 1973-77; cons. various ednl. and cultural agys. Ocean Springs, Miss., 1978-80; asst. dir. Miss. Humanities Coun., Jackson, Miss., 1981-85; exec. dir. Arts Alliance of Jackson and Hinds County, Miss., 1985-89, Miss. Arts Commn., Jackson, 1989-95; interim dir. Miss. Mus. Art, 2001. Participant Arts Leadership Inst. of Humphrey Inst. for Pub. Affairs, Mpls., 1986, Leadership, Jackson, 1987; interim exec. dir. Miss. Mus. Art, 2001. Co-editor Peoples of the South, 1976; exec. producer (TV series) The South with John Siegenthaler, 1976; host, reporter Miss. Ednl. TV, Jackson, 1981-87. Mem. Miss. Econ. Coun., 1986—87, Miss. R&D Coun., 1984—88; pres. Mental Health Assn. of Hinds County, Jackson, 1986; treas. Miss. for Ednl. Broadcasting, 1987, 1988, 1989, Premier Class Leadership, Jackson, 1987, 1988; mem. cmty. adv. coun. Jr. League of Jackson, 1995—2002; mem. representing Miss. Friends of Art and Preservation in Embassies Millennium Com.; bd. dirs. Miss. Mus. Art, 2000—; bd. dirs. Miss. state com. Nat. Mus. Women in Arts. Recipient Heritage award City of Biloxi, 1984. Mem.: Greater Jackson Found. (bd. dirs. 1996—, chmn. 2002—), Pub. Edn. Forum (bd. dirs. 1993—), Miss. Ctr. for Nonprofits (vice chmn., bd. dirs. 1993—96, adv. bd. 1997—), So. Arts Fedn. (bd. dirs. 1989—95), Nat. Assembly State Arts Agys. (bd. dirs. 1992—95, 2d v.p. 1995), Nat. Coun. on Arts, Nat. Assembly Local Arts Agys., Phi Beta Kappa. Home: 507 Roses Bluff Dr Madison MS 39110-7545 E-mail: janewoodhiatt@aol.com.

HIATT, PETER, retired librarian studies educator; b. N.Y.C., Oct. 19, 1930; s. Amos and Elizabeth Hope (Derry) H.; m. Linda Rae Smith, Aug. 16, 1968; 1 child, Holly Virginia. BA, Colgate U., 1952; M.L.S., Rutgers U., 1957, PhD, 1963. Libr. intern Elizabeth (N.J.) Pub. Libr., 1955-57; head Elmora Br. Libr., Elizabeth, 1957-59; instr. Grad. Sch. Libr. Service, Rutgers U., 1960-62; libr. cons. Ind. State Libr., Indpls., 1963-70; asst. prof. Grad. Libr. Sch., Ind. U., 1963-66, assoc. prof., 1966-70; dir. Ind. Libr. Studies, Bloomington, 1967-70; dir. continuing edn. program for library pers. Western Interstate Commn. for Higher Edn., Boulder, Colo., 1970-74; dir. Grad. Sch. Libr. and Info. Sci., U. Wash., Seattle, 1974-81, prof., 1974-98; prin. investigator Career Devel. and Assessment Ctr. for Librarians, 1979-83, 90-93; dir. library insts. at various colls. and univs.; adv. projects U.S. Office Edn.-ALA, 1977-80; prof. emeritus U. Wash., 1998—. Bd. dirs. King County Libr. Sys., 1989-97, pres., 1991, 95, sec., 1993, 94; prin. investigator Career Devel. and Assessment Ctrs. for Librs.: Phase II, 1990-93. Author: (with Donald Thompson) Monroe County IN Public Library: Planning for the Future, 1966, The Public Library Needs of Delaware County, 1967, (with Henry Drennan) Public Library Services for the functionally Illiterate, 1967 (with Robert E. Lee and Lawrence A. Allen) A Plan for Developing a Regional Program of Continuing Education for Library Personnel, 1969, Public Library Branch Services for Adults of Low Education, 1964; dir., gen. editor: The Indiana Library Studies, 1970-74; author: Assessment Centers for Professional Library Leadership, 1993; mem. editorial bd. Coll. and Rsch. Librs., 1969-73; co-editor Leads: A Continuing Education Newsletter for Library Trustees, 1973-75, Octavio Noda; author chpts., articles on library continuing edn., staff devel. and libr. adult svcs. Mem. selection com. Jefferson County Pub. Libr., Washington, 2000—01; pres. Port Townsend Pub. Libr. Found., 2002—; mem. bd. dirs. Turtle Bluff Chamber Orch., Jefferson County, Wash., 2000—, mem. soloist competition jury, 2000—, mem. scholarship com., 2000—, chair spl. fundraising com., 2002—03; bd. dirs. Turtle Bluff Chamber Orch, 2000—03. Mem. ALA (officer), Pacific N.W. Libr. Assn., Assn. Libr. and Info. Sci. Educators (officer, Outstanding Svc. award 1979), ACLU. Home: 20 Sequim Pl Port Townsend WA 98368-9414 E-mail: phiatt@cablespeed.com. *I know of no other profession which helps so many people and organizations change and grow--from pre-school years through retirement, as does librarianship. It is a joy to be part of that.*

HIBBARD, CARL ROGER, social services administrator; b. Charlotte, N.C., Aug. 21, 1944; s. Carl Hiram and Doris May (Foster) H.; m. Nancy Rosalyn Cude, June 18, 1967; children: Alison Elizabeth Hibbard Hager, Christopher Roger. BA in Bus. Adminstrn., Furman U., 1966; MEd in Cmty. Leadership and Devel., Springfield Coll., 1967. Cert. camp dir. Am. Camping Assn.; cert. YMCA sr. dir. Phys. dir. Johnston Meml. YMCA, Charlotte, 1967-68; exec. dir. YMCA Camp Cheerio, High Point, N.C., 1970-74; asst. gen. dir. Durham (N.C.) YMCA, 1974-76; adminstrv. dir. YMCA Blue Ridge Assembly, Black Mountain, N.C., 1976-85, exec. dir., 1985—. Contbr. articles to profl. jours. Mem. Black Mountain Recreation Commn., 1986-98, chmn., 1989-91; mem. Buncombe County Recreation Adv. Com., Asheville, N.C., 1991-99, chmn., 1993-96, 97-99; mem. Black Mountain Correctional Ctr. for Women Cmty. Resource Coun., 1996-2002, chmn., 1998-2001; exec. bd. Daniel Boone Coun. Boy Scouts Am., 1997—, v.p. program, 2000-01, v.p. adminstrn., 2002—; bd. dirs. Asheville Mountain Area chpt. ARC, 1998—2003, exec. com., 2000—03. 1st lt. USAR, 1968—70. Mem. Internat. Assn. Conf. Ctr. Adminstrs. (first v.p. 1984-86), Acad. Cert. Profl. Dirs. YMCAs, Assn. Profl. YMCA Dirs. (cert., pres. Carolinas' chpt. 1981-84, dist. v.p. S.E. dist. 1984-87, dist. v.p. S.E. dist. adminstrn. sect. 1991-93, chmn. N.C. YMCA's pub. policy com. 1999—), Black Mountain-Swannanoa C. of C. (bd. dirs. 1980-81, 85-88, 93-98, pres. 1987), Rotary Club (pres. 1980-81, Paul Harris fellow). Methodist. Home and Office: YMCA Blue Ridge Assembly Inc 84 Blue Ridge Cir Black Mountain NC 28711-9750

HIBBARD, JUDITH HOFFMAN, health services researcher; b. L.A., Nov. 30, 1948; d. Arnold Mandel and Marian (Carob) Hoffman; m. Michael John Hibbard, Aug. 1, 1968; 1 child, Johanna. BS, Calif. State U., Northridge, 1974; MPH, UCLA, 1975; DrPH, U. Calif., Berkeley, 1982. Asst. prof. U. Oreg., Eugene, 1982-88, assoc. prof., 1988-94; prof., 1994—. Adj. investigator Ctr. Health Rsch., Portland, 1982—; clin. prof. pub. health & preventive medicine Oreg. Health Scis. U., Portland, 1993—. Contbr. articles to profl. jours. Recipient New Investigator Rsch. award Nat. Inst. Aging, 1983-86, Dissertation Rch. award Nat. Ctr. Health Svcs. Rsch., 1981-82; grantee NIA, 1988-91, Robert Wood Johnson Found., 1995—; grantee Agy. for Health, Rsch. and Quality, 1995—. Mem.: Nat. Quality Forum (mem. strategic adv. com.). Avocations: bicycling, horseback riding. Office: U Oregon 119 Hendricks Hall Eugene OR 97403-1209 E-mail: jhibbard@oregon.uoregon.edu.

HIBBARD, RICHARD PAUL, industrial ventilation consultant, educator; b. Defiance, Ohio, Nov. 1, 1923; s. Richard T. and Doris E. (Walkup) H.; m. Phyllis Ann Kirchoffer, Sept. 7, 1948; children: Barbara Rae, Marcia Kae, Rebecca Ann, Patricia Jan, John Ross. BS in Mech. Indsl. Engring., U. Toledo, 1949. Mech. engr. Oldsmobile divsn. GM, Lansing, Mich., 1950-56; design and sales engr. McConnell Sheet Metal, Inc., Lansing, 1956-60; chief heat and ventilation engr. Fansteel Metall. Corp., North Chicago, Ill., 1960-62; sr. facilities and ventilation engr. The Boeing Co., Seattle, 1962-63; ventilation engr. environ. health divsn. dept. preventive medicine U. Wash., Seattle, 1964-70, lectr. dept. environ. health, 1970-82, lectr. emeritus, 1983—. Prin. Indsl. Ventilation Cons. Svcs., 1983—; chmn. Western Indsl. Ventilation Conf., 1962; mem. com. indsl. ventilation Am. Conf. Govtl. Indsl. Hygienists, 1966—; mem. staff Indsl. Ventilation Conf., Mich. State U., 1955—. Contbr. articles on indsl. hygiene and ventilation to profl. jours. With USAAF, 1943-45; maj. C.E., USAR ret. Recipient Disting. Svc. award Indsl. Ventilation Conf., Mich. State U., 1975, 93. Mem.: VFW, ASHRAE, Am. Foundrymen's Soc., Am. Indsl. Hygiene Assn. (J.M. Dallevalle award 1977), Am. Inst. Plant Engrs., Am. Soc. Safety Engrs. (R.M. Gillmore Meml. award Puget Sound chpt.), Elks, Masons. Home: 41 165th Ave SE Bellevue WA 98008-4721

HIBBARD, WALTER ROLLO, JR., retired engineering educator; b. Bridgeport, Conn., Jan. 20, 1918; s. Walter R. and Helen S. (Kenworthy) H.; m. Charlotte H. Tracy, Mar. 21, 1942 (dec. 1970); children: Douglas, Lawrence, Diana; m. Louise A. Brembeck, Jan. 29, 1972. AB, Wesleyan U., 1939; DEng, Yale U., 1942; LLD (hon.), Mich. Tech. U., 1968; DEng (hon.), Mont. Coll. Mineral Scis. and Tech., 1970. Asst., then assoc. prof. Yale U., New Haven, 1946-51; rsch. assoc., then mgr. metallurgy and ceramics GE Rsch. Lab., Schenectady, N.Y., 1951-65; dir. U.S. Bur. Mines, Washington, 1965-68; v.p. Owens Corning Fiberglass Corp., 1968-74; prof. engring. Va. Poly Inst. and State U., Blacksburg, 1974-87, prof. emeritus, 1987—. Dir. Va. Ctr. for Coal and Energy Research, Blacksburg, 1977-87. Contbr. numerous articles to profl. publs. Lt. comdr. USNR, 1942-46. Recipient Yale U. Engring. Alumni award, 1955, Wesleyan U. Disting. Alumnus award, 1979. Mem. AIME (R.W. Raymond award 1950, J. Douglas medal 1969, Mineral Econs. award 1983), Nat. Acad. Engring., Am. Soc. Metals, Am. Ceramic Soc. Home: Apt 54 890 A1A Beach Blvd Saint Augustine FL 32080-6746 E-mail: walter.hibbard.eng.42@aya.yale.edu.

HIBBETT, ROBERT NELAND, lawyer; b. Nashville, July 14, 1960; s. Neland Carver and Jenny Bess (Goggin) H. BBA, U. Tenn., Martin, 1982; JD, U. Tenn., Knoxville, 1985. Bar: Tenn. 1985, U.S. Dist. Ct. (ea. dist.) Tenn. 1987. Assoc. Wortley and Hibbett, Knoxville, Tenn., 1986-88; asst. dist. atty. gen. 15th jud. dist., Lebanon, Tenn., 1989—. Mem. Boys Scouts of Am. Mem. ABA, Tenn. Bar Assn., N.G. Assn. U.S., Young Life, Maj. TNARNG. Democrat. Baptist. Office: Dist Atty Gen Office 119 South College St Lebanon TN 37087 E-mail: bhibbett@tndagc.com.

HIBBS, CLAIR M. retired pathologist; b. Lucerne, Mo., Oct. 10, 1923; s. Grover Clarence and Bertha Cassiday H.; m. Ann Elisabeth Robinson, Dec. 28, 1946; children: Drew Robinson, Gerald Wayne. BS in Agr., U. Mo., Columbia, 1949, DVM, 1953; MS in Pathology, Kans. State U., Manhattan, 1962, PhD in Pathology, 1965. Gen. vet. practice Philips Magilton & Hibbs, David City, Nebr., 1953—60; instr. Kans. State U., Manhattan, 1960—62, 1968—69, assoc. prof., 1968—69, U. Nebr., North Platte, 1969—73, prof., 1973—79; dir. N.Mex. Diagnostic Lab N.Mex. State U., Albuquerque, 1979—90. Advisor Norden Labs. (divsn. SmithKline), Lincoln, Nebr., 1988—89; cons. Triple J Zahnis Lab., Bellingham, Wash., 2000—01; bd. dirs. Nebr. Med. Rsch. Com., 1977; pres. Western Vet. Conf., 1997—98. Contbr. articles. Mm3/c USN, 1943—46. Recipient Disting. Svc. award, Nebr. Vet. Med. Assn., 1978—79, N.Mex. Vet. Assn., 1986, N.Mex. Dept. Agr., 1986; fellow kidney rsch. fellow, Mark Morris Found., 1962. Mem.: We. Vet. Med. Assn. (past pres. 1998), Rotary (past pres. 1977), Am. Legion (comdr. 1958). Home: 1172 Edgewater Ln Lynden WA 98264-1079

HIBBS, DAWN WILCOX, elementary school educator; b. Buffalo, Sept. 30, 1940; d. Alfred and Helena Pavone; m. Leroy Wilcox, July 18, 1964 (div. June 1981); children: Brett Alan, Dana Lee; m. Harold Keith Hibbs, Dec. 27, 1986. Tchr. 5th grade North Tonawanda (N.Y.) Schs., 1961-63, Los Alamos (N.Mex.) Schs., 1963-64; tchr. 6th grade Kenmore (N.Y.) Schs., 1965-69; caseworker Erie County Dept. Social Svcs., Buffalo, 1980-84; elem. tchr. Lynwood (Calif.) Schs., 1986-88, Santa Ana (Calif.) Schs., 1988-96, intermediate tchr., 1996—2002, textbook advisor, grant writer, 1996-97. Mentor new tchrs. Santa Ana Schs., 1991-92, instr. Reading to Learn programs, 1999-2000, tchr. cabinet rep., 1998-2000, mem. sch. site coun., 2000-2001, mem. Oreg. project, 2000-02. Patentee eyewear identification labels and design. Pres. Parents Without Ptnrs., Tonawanda, 1983. Mem. AAUW (treas. 1995-96, EF fund prize chmn. 1997, membership v.p. 1997-2000, mem. membership com. Calif. 1998-2001, co-pres. Orange County Interbr. 1999—, tech. trek coord., 1999-2001, v.p. Mission Viejo-Saddleback Valley br. LAF 2000-2001, pres. 2003-), Class Act Investors (treas. 1999—).

HIBBS, JOHN DAVID, software executive, engineer, business owner; b. Del Norte, Colo., Jan. 26, 1948; s. Alva Bernard and Frances Ava (Cathcart) H.; m. Ruthanne Johnson, Feb. 28, 1976. BSEE, Denver U., 1970. Elec. engr. Merrick and Co., Denver, 1972-73; lighting engr. Holophane div. Johns Manville, Denver, 1973-79; lighting products mgr. Computer Sharing Svcs., Inc., Denver, 1979-83; pres., owner Computer Aided Lighting Analysis, Boulder, Colo., 1983-86, Hibbs Sci. Software, Boulder, Colo., 1986—; chmn. bd. Sport Sail Inc., 1996-97. Co-founder Sport Sail, Inc. Author CALA, CALA/Pro and PreCALA lighting programs; patentee in field. With USNR, 1970-72. Recipient 1st prize San Luise Valley Sci. Fair, 1963. Mem. IEEE, Illuminating Engring. Soc. North Am. (chmn. computer com. 1988-91), Computer Soc. IEEE (chmn. computer problem set com. 1991-95). Avocations: woodworking, bicycling, sailing, skiing. Home and Office: PO Box 400 Fraser CO 80442-0400 E-mail: jdhibbs@ieee.org.

HIBBS, LOYAL ROBERT, lawyer; b. Des Moines, Dec. 24, 1925; s. Loyal B. and Catharine (McClymond) H.; children: Timothy, Theodore, Howard, Dean. BA, U. Iowa, 1950, LLB, JD, 1952. Bar: Iowa 1952, Nev. 1958, U.S. Supreme Ct. 1971. Ptnr. Hibbs Law Offices, Reno, 1972—. Moderator radio, TV Town Hall Coffee Breaks, 1970-72; mem. Nev. State Bicycle Adv. Bd., 1996-2000, Reno Bicycle Coun., 1995-99; mem. Reno Parks, Restoration and Cmty. Svc. Commn., 1998--, chmn., 2001--. Fellow Am. Bar Found. (Nev. chmn. 1989-94); mem. ABA (standing com. Lawyer Referral Svc. 1978-79, steering com. state dels. 1979-82, consortium on legal svcs. and the pub. 1979-82, Nev. State Bar del. to Ho. of Dels. 1978-82, 89-90, bd. govs. 1982-85, mem. legal tech. adv. coun. 1985-86, standing com. on nat. conf. groups 1985-91, chmn. sr. lawyers divsn. Nev. 1988—), Nat. Conf. Bar Pres.'s Iowa Bar Assn., Nev. Bar Assn. (bd. govs. 1968-78, pres. 1977-78), Washoe County Bar Assn. (pres. 1966-67), Nat. Jud. Coll. (bd. dirs. 1986-92, sec. 1988-92), Assn. Def. Counsel No. Calif., Assn. Def. Counsel Nev., Assn. Ski Def. Attys., Aircraft Owners and Pilots Assn. (legal svcs. plan 1991—), Washoe County Legal Aid Soc. (co-founder), Lawyer-Pilots Bar Assn. (chmn. Nev.), Greater Reno C. of C. (bd. dirs. 1968-72), Phi Alpha Delta. Home: 3600 Salerno Dr Reno NV 89509 Office: 290 S Arlington Ave Ste 100 Reno NV 89501-1793 E-mail: loyalhibbs@aol.com.

HIBIKI, TAKASHI, nuclear scientist, educator; b. Miyazu, Kyoto, Japan, Mar. 3, 1963; s. Yoshitami and Masako Hibiki; m. Kazue Hibiki, June 13, 2003. PhD, Osaka U., 1990. Assoc. prof. Kyoto U., Kumatori, Japan, 1990—. Adj. assoc. prof. High Energy Accelerator Rsch. Orgn., Tsukuba, Japan, 1998—99; vis. assoc. prof. Purdue U., West Lafayette, Ind., 2001—; adj. assoc. prof. Osaka U., Toyonaka, Japan, 2001—03. Scientist (research) Nuc. Engring. (Am. Nuc. Soc. Young Mem. Engring. Acievement Award, 2001), (Preeminent Monograph Award, Japanese Soc. for Multiphase Flow, 2001), (Cert. of Merit for Outstanding Presentation, Power and Energy Sys.Divsn., Japan Soc. of Mech. Engrs., 2001), (Promising Endeavor Award, Atomic Energy Soc. Japan, 1996). Mem.: The Heat Transfer Soc. Japan, The Japanese Soc. for Multiphase Flow, Soc. Chem. Engrs. Japan, Japan Soc. Mech. Engrs., Atomic Energy Soc. Japan, Am. Nuc. Soc. (life). Buddhist. Achievements include development of Development of High-Frame-Rate Neutron Radiography System; first to Development of Interfacial Area Transport Equation. Home: Kyoto University Staff Dormitry 1044 Osaka Kumatori 590-0451 Japan Office: Kyoto University Rsch Reactor Inst Noda Sennan Kumatori, Sennan Osaka 590-0494 Japan Home Fax: +81-724-52-9876; Office Fax: +81-724-51-2461. E-mail: hibiki@rri.kyoto-u.ac.jp.

HIBL, VERONICA KATHERINE, physician assistant; b. Pompano Beach, Fla., June 29, 1965; d. William Leo and Peggy Joan Haga. BS in Med. Sci., Alderson-Broaddus Coll., Philippi, W.Va., 1988. Cert. physician asst., Nat. Commn. Cert. Physician Assts.; lic. physician asst., Nebr. Bd. Medicine; cert., ACLS, BCLS. Physician asst. Marion (Ohio) Surg. Assocs., 1989-90, George L. Mueller MD, P.A., Boynton Beach, Fla., 1990-91, Ctrl. Bapt. Hosp., Lexington, Ky., 1991, CVT Assocs., Lexington, 1991—2002, Faith Regional Health Svcs. Cardiovasc. Inst., Norfolk, Nebr., 2002—. Fellow Am. Acad. Physician Assts., Assn. Physician Assts. in Cardiovasc. Surgery. Avocations: movies, travel, oil painting, piano. Home: 1600 Longhorn Dr Norfolk NE 68701 Office: Faith Regional Health Svc 2700 Norfolk Ave Norfolk NE 68701

HIBLER, ROBERT BENNETT, construction executive; b. Teaneck, N.J., Apr. 8, 1944; s. Rudolph Frederick and Cornelia Jacoba (Lems) H.; m. Joan Irene Eagen, July 15, 1967. BSBA, U. S.C., 1968. Gen. mgr. Gen. Trading & Equipment, Al Khobar, Saudi Arabia, 1976-78; ops. mgr. Contractors Supply Corp., Roslyn, N.Y., 1967-88; ops. v.p. Viking Reps., Old Bridge, N.J., 1988-90; product mgr. Patent Constrn. Systems, Paramus, N.J., 1990—. Editor Patent Works, 1991—; contbr. articles and photographs to profl. jours. Pres. Bd. of Health, Westwood, N.J., 1993—; rec. sec. Westwood Rep. Club, 1993—; del. N.E. Rep. Orgn., Bergen County, N.J., 1993—; trustee Wash. Twp. Columbian Club, 1991—, Picarella Trust Scholarship Fund, 1991—, Thomas J. Riley Sr. Ctr., Westwood, N.J., 1998—; fund raiser St. Andrew's Roman Cath. Ch. Ministry, 1993—. Recipient resolution and commendation N.J. Gen. Assembly, 1994, Crystal award for newsletter excellence Communicator Awards, 1996, 97, 98. Mem.: Roxbury Condominium Assn., KC (officer Twp. of Washington, N.J. 1991—). Avocations: arabic and spanish languages, clarinet, flute, harmonica, motorcycle touring. Office: Patent Constrn Systems Divsn Harsco 1 Mack Centre Dr Paramus NJ 07652-3906 E-mail: robert_hibler@hotmail.com.

HIBNER, RAE A. risk management consultant, director, nursing; b. Libertyville, Ill., Jan. 31, 1956; d. Richard Douglas (dec.) and Raelene Ann (Warren) Lyons; m. John Paul Hibner, June 21, 1986; children: Kevin John, Thomas Ivan. Diploma, Luth. Gen. Hosp. Sch. Nursing, Park Ridge, Ill., 1979; BS in Nursing, U. Ill., Chgo., 1984; MS, No. Ill. U., 1987. RN. Staff nurse Cardiac Telemetry Luth. Gen. Hosp., 1979-81, staff nurse CCU, 1981-82; staff nurse coronary ICU U. Ill. Hosp., Chgo., 1982-83, asst. head nurse coronary ICU, 1983-86, head nurse coronary ICU, 1986-88, staff nurse coronary-med. ICU, 1988-90; coord. utilization rev. Parkside Health Mgmt. Corp., Chgo., 1989-91; asst. dir. utilization mgmt. U. Ill., Chgo., 1991-93; risk mgr. Rush-Presbyn.-St. Lukes Med. Ctr., Chgo., 1993-96; claims cons. CNA Ins. Cos., Chgo., 1996; dir. claims corp. accts. CNA Health Pro, Chgo., 1996-2001; claims cons. CNA, HealthPro, 2001—02; dir. risk mgmt. Loyola Univ. Med. Ctr., Maywood, Ill., 2002—. Roman Catholic. Avocations: needlepoint, crochet, swimming, camping.

HICE, CHRISTINE LORRAINE, research scientist; b. Vicksburg, Mich., Apr. 5, 1968; d. Dennis Lee and Joanne Lillian Hice. AS, Kalamazoo (Mich.) Valley C.C., 1988; BS, U. Ctrl. Fla., 1992; MS, Tex. A&M U., 1996; PhD, Tex. Tech. U., 2003. Rsch. asst. Tex. A&M U., Coll. Sta., Tex., 1993—96; rsch. assoc. U. Tex. Med. Br., Galveston, Tex., 1997—98; rsch. asst. Tex. Tech. U., Lubbock, 1999—2001; rsch. assoc. U. Tex. Med. Br., Galveston, 2001—. Cons. U.S. Army, Iquitos, Peru, 1999. Contbr. scientific papers. Mem.: Am. Soc. Mammalogists (bd. dirs. 2001—), Assn. Women in Sci. (fellowship 2000), Phi Kappa Phi (fellowship 2001). Avocations: reading, weightlifting, gardening, exotic pets. Office: Texas Tech Univ Dept Biology Lubbock TX 79409-3131 E-mail: chris.hice@ttu.edu.

HICK, KENNETH WILLIAM, marketing company executive; b. New Westminster, B.C., Can, Oct. 17, 1946; s. Les Walter and Mary Isabelle (Warner) H. BA in Bus., Ea. Wash. State coll., 1971; MBA, U. Wash., 1973, PhD, 1975. Regional sales mgr. Hilti, Inc., San Leandro, Calif., 1976-79; gen. sales mgr. Moore Internat., Inc., Portland, 1979-80; v.p. sales and mktg. Phillips Corp., Anaheim, Calif., 1980-81; owner, pres., CEO K.C. Metals, San Jose, Calif., 1981-87, Losli Internat., Inc., Portland, 1987-89; pres. Resources N.W., Inc., Portland, 1989—. Communications cons. Asso. Pub. Safety Communication Officers, Inc., State of Oreg., 1975-93; numerous cons. assignments, also seminars, 1976-2000. Contbr. articles to numerous publs. Mem. Oreg. Gov.'s Tax Bd., 1975-76; pres. Portland chpt. Oreg. Jaycees, 1976; bd. fellows U. Santa Clara, 1983-90. With USAF, 1966-69. Decorated Commendation medal; U. Wash. fellow, 1973. Mem. Am. Mgmt. Assn., Am. Mktg. Assn., Assn. MBA Execs., Assn. Gen. Contractors, Soc. Advancement Mgmt., Home Builders Assn. Roman Catholic. Home: 25659 Cheryl Dr West Linn OR 97068-4589 Office: Resources Northwest Inc 8415 SW Seneca # 210 Tualatin OR 97062

HICKEL, WALTER JOSEPH, investment firm executive, forum administrator; b. nr. Claflin, Kans., Aug. 18, 1919; s. Robert A. and Emma (Zecha) H.; m. Janice Cannon, Sept. 22, 1941 (dec. Aug. 1943); 1 child, Theodore; m. Ermalee Strutz, Nov. 22, 1945; children: Robert, Walter Jr., Jack, Joseph, Karl. DEng(hon.), Stevens Inst. Tech., 1970, Mich. Tech. U., 1973; LLD (hon.), St. Mary of Plains Coll., St. Martin's Coll., U. Md., Adelphi U., U. San Diego, Rensselaer Poly. Inst., 1973, U. Alaska, 1976, Alaska Pacific U., 1991, Benedictine Coll., Kans., 2003; D in Pub. Adminstrn. (hon.), Willamette U. Founder Hickel Investment Co., Anchorage, 1947—; gov. State of Alaska,

1966-69, 90-94; sec. U.S. Dept. Interior, 1969-70; sec. gen. The Northern Forum, 1994—. Former mem. world adv. coun. Internat. Design Sci. Inst.; former mem. com. on sci. freedom and responsibility AAAS; nominated for pres. at Rep. Nat. Convention, 1968; co-founder Yukon Pacific Corp.; founder Inst. of the North, 1996—. Author: Who Own's America?, 1971, Crisis in the Commons--The Alaska Solution, 2002; contbr. articles to newspapers. Mem. Republican Nat. Com., 1954-64; bd. regents Gonzaga U.; bd. dirs. Salk Inst., 1972-79, NASA Adv. Coun. Exploration Task Force, 1989-91; mem. Governor's Econ. Com. on North Slope Natural Gas, Alaska, 1982, USAR amb. representing Alaska. Named Alaskan of Year, 1969, Man of Yr. Ripon Soc., 1970; recipient DeSmet medal Gonzaga U., 1969, Horatio Alger award, 1972, Grand Cordon of the Order of Sacred Treasure award His Imperial Majesty the Emperor of Japan, 1988. Mem. Pioneers of Alaska, Alaska C. of C. (former chmn. econ. devel. com.), Equestrian Order Holy Sepulchre, KC. Achievements include leading the first Alaska Chamber economic trade mission to Japan. Home: 1905 Loussac Dr Anchorage AK 99517-1225 Office: PO Box 101700 Anchorage AK 99510-1700 *We shall never understand peace, justice and the living of life until we recognize that all people are human and that humans are the most precious things on earth.*

HICKEN, JEFFREY PRICE, lawyer; b. Macomb, Ill., Oct. 25, 1947; s. Victor and Mary Patricia (O'Connell) H.; m. Mary Sarah Schmidt, Aug. 23, 1969; children: Andrew, Molly, Elizabeth. BA, Cornell Coll., 1969; JD, U. Ill., 1972. Bar: Minn. 1972, U.S. Dist. Ct. Minn. 1980, U.S. Ct. Appeals (8th cir.). Assoc. Weaver, Talle & Herrick, Anoka, Minn., 1972-77; sr. ptnr. Hicken, Scott & Howard, P.A., Anoka, 1977-00, 1998—. Mem. Minn. Family Law Certification Commn., 1999. Bd. dirs. Anoka Lyric Arts; precinct chair Dem. Farmer-Labor Party, Anoka, 1976—. Capt. U.S. Army, 1969-77. Recipient J. Franklin Littel scholarship Cornell Coll., Mt. Vernon, Iowa, 1969 Fellow Am. Acad. Matrimonial Lawyers (cert. arbitrator, bd. mgrs. 1992--); mem. Minn. State Bar Assn., Anoka County Bar Assn. (pres. 1990-91), City of Anoka Charter Commn. (chmn. 1978—). Democrat. Avocations: running, violin. Home: 1700 West Ln Anoka MN 55303-1923 Office: Hicken Scott & Howard PA 2150 3rd Ave Ste 300 Anoka MN 55303-2200

HICKEN, RUSSELL BRADFORD, art dealer, appraiser; b. Jacksonville, Fla., Dec. 24, 1926; s. Leslie Adames and Nettie Bradford (Frazee) H.; m. Margot Louise Ward, Apr. 14, 1978. BS in Housing and Interior Design, U. of Mo., Columbia, 1974, MA, 1978. Tchr. Fletcher H.S., Jacksonville, 1951-57; dir. Jacksonville Art Mus., 1957-64, 69-75, Tampa (Fla.) Art Inst., 1964-67, Mint Mus. Art, Charlotte, 1967-69, Hollywood (Fla.) Art & Culture Ctr., 1975-77; art dealer Russell B. Hicken, Fine Arts Ltd., Tampa, Miami, 1977—. Sr. cons. Koger Gallery and Gardens, Jacksonville, 1999—. Mem. Bakehouse Art Ctr., Miami, 1996—, Sesquicentennial Commn., Jacksonville, 1972. With U.S. Army, 1944-46, ETO. Mem. Am. Assn. Mus., S.E. Mus. Conf. (pres. 1969-70, AAM rep. 1970-76). Democrat. Avocations: chess, backgammon, travel. Home and Office: 5403 Widefield Dr Tallahassee FL 32309-6454 Fax: 850-907-0066. E-mail: artra@nettally.com., hickenr@earthlink.net.

HICKENLOOPER, JOHN W. mayor; m. Helen Thorpe; 1 child, Teddy. BA in English, Wesleyan U., 1974, MS in English, 1980. Exploration geologist Buckhorn Petroleum, Denver, 1981 86; developer The Wynkoop Brewing Co., 1986—; mayor City of Denver, 2003—. Co-founder CultureHaus, Chinook Fund; bd. dirs. Colo. Bus. Com. for the Arts, Denver Metro Conv. and Visitors Bur., Denver Art Mus., Denver Civic Ventures, Volunteers for Outdoor Colo. Office: 11437 Dannock St Ste 350 Denver CO 80202*

HICKERSON, DIANNE, artist, former educator; b. Rochester, N.Y., May 20, 1942; d. Harold Wadsworth Dobson and Ruth Stock Dobson; m. J. Douglas Hickerson, June 23, 1984; children: Cherie, Timothy, Anne, Alice. BS, SUNY, Brockport, 1964, MS, 1969. Tchr. Brockport (N.Y.) Cen. Sch., 1964-96; free-lance artist, 1996—. Recipient awards in, nat. and regional juried exhbns. Mem. Am. Watercolor Soc. (assoc.), Midwest Watercolor Soc. (assoc.), Niagara Frontier Watercolor Soc. (signature mem.). Avocations: skiing, biking, gardening. Home: 231 Hollybrook Rd Brockport NY 14420 E-mail: DianneHickerson@aol.com.

HICKERSON, GLENN LINDSEY, leasing company executive; b. Burbank, Calif., Aug. 22, 1937; s. Ralph M. and Sarah Lawson (Lindsey) H.; m. Jane Fortune Arthur, Feb. 24, 1973. BA in Bus. Adminstrn., Claremont McKenna Coll., 1959; MBA, NYU, 1960. Exec. asst. Douglas Aircraft Co., Santa Monica, Calif., 1963; sec., treas. Douglas Fin. Corp., Long Beach, Calif., 1964-67, regional mgr. customer financing, 1967; exec. asst. to pres. Universal Airlines, Inc., Detroit, 1967-68, v.p., treas., asst. sec., 1968-69, pres., 1969-72; v.p., treas., asst. sec. Universal Aircraft Service, Inc., Detroit, 1968-69, chmn. bd., 1969-72; v.p., treas. Universal Airlines Co., Detroit, 1968-69, pres., 1969-72; group v.p. Marriott Hotels, Inc., Washington, 1972-76; dir. sales Far East and Australia Lockheed Calif. Co., 1976-78, dir. mktg. Americas, 1978-79, dir. mktg. Internat., 1979-81, v.p., internat. sales, 1981-83; v.p. comml. mktg. internat. Douglas Aircraft Co., McDonnell Douglas Corp., 1983-89; mng. dir. GPA Asia Pacific, El Segundo, Calif., 1989-90; exec. v.p. GATX Air Group, San Francisco, 1990-95, pres., 1995-98, chmn., dir. adv. bd., 1998—, GATX Capital Corp., San Francisco, 1998—; pres. Hickerson Assocs., 1998—, Quality Aerospace, Inc., 2000—. Bd. dirs. Willis Lease Fin. Corp. Lt. (j.g.) USCGR, 1960—62. H.B. Earhart Found. fellow, 1962 Mem.: St. Francis Yacht Club, Pacific Union Club. E-mail: ghickers@gatxcap.com.

HICKEY, BRUCE WILLIAM, lawyer; b. Washington, Mar. 2, 1973; s. Lien Huong H. AB, Princeton U., 1995; BA, MSt, Oxford U., England, 1998; JD, Harvard U. Bar: N.Y. 2001, D.C., 2002. Editor Harvard Law Review, Cambridge, Mass., 1999-2001; atty. Sullivan & Cromwell, Washington, 2001—. Dir. Washington-Lee H.S. Edn. Found., Inc., Arlington, Va., 1999—. Marshall scholar, 1995-98. Mem. ABA, Phi Beta Kappa. Home: 1302 N Utah St Arlington VA 22201-4822 Office: Sullivan & Cromwell 1701 Pennsylvania Ave NW Washington DC 20006 Fax: 202-293-6330. E-mail: bwhickey@alumni.princeton.edu., hickeyb@sullcrom.com.

HICKEY, DAMON DOUGLAS, library director; b. Houston, Oct. 30, 1942; s. Thomas Earl and Ethel Elizabeth (Place) Hickey; m. Mary Lyons Temple, May 27, 1967; 1 child, Doralyn Temple Hickey Rossmann. BA, Rice U., 1965; MDiv, Princeton (N.J.) Theol. Sem., 1968; cert. in clin. pastoral care, Inst. of Religion, Houston, 1969; MSLS, U. N.C., 1975; MA, U. N.C., Greensboro, 1982; PhD, U. S.C., 1989. Assoc. pastor First Presbyn. Ch., Irving, Tex., 1969-71, Southminster Presbyn. Ch., Oklahoma City, 1971-72; pastor First Presbyn. Ch., Moore, Okla., 1971—72; catalog librarian U. N.C., Chapel Hill, 1972-73; acting curator rare books Duke U., Durham, N.C., 1973-74; assoc. libr. dir. Guilford Coll., Greensboro, N.C., 1975-91, curator Friends Hist. Collection, 1980-91; dir. libr. Coll. Wooster, Ohio, 1991—. Adj. asst. prof. history Guilford Coll., 1990—91. Author: Sojourners No More: The Quakers in the New South, 1865-1920, 1997, When Chage is Set in Store: An Analysis of Seven Academic Libraries, 2001, Learn Library Management, 2003; editor: (jour.) The Southern Friend, 1983—91; contbr. chapters to books, articles and book revs. to profl. jours. Chair fund distbn. com. United Way Wooster, 1998-99. Recipient Twiford Religious History Book award N.C. Soc. of Historians, Inc., 1998. Mem.: ALA, Assn. Coll. and Rsch. Librs., Hist. Soc. N.C. (elect), Friends Hist. Assn., So. Hist. Assn., Orgn. Am. Historians, N.C. Friends Hist. Soc. (bd. dirs. 1977—91), Beta Phi Mu, Phi Alpha Theta. Democrat. Espicopalian. Avocations: church work, baseball. Office: Coll of Wooster Libraries Wooster OH 44691-2364 E-mail: dhickey@wooster.edu.

HICKEY, DAVID C. art historian; BA, Tex. Christian U., 1961; MA, U. Tex., 1963. Owner, dir. Clean Well-Lighted Pl. gallery, Austin, Tex.; dir. Reese Palley Gallery, N.Y.C.; curator SITE Santa Fe's Fourth Internat. Biennial, 2001—02; Cullinan chair arch. Rice U., Houston, 1997; prof. art theory and criticism U. Nev., Las Vegas, 1992—. Vis. prof. Harvard U., Rice U., Otis Parsons Inst., L.A., U. Tex., Austin, U. Calif., Santa Barbara; vis. prof. Grad. Sch. Design Harvard U., Cambridge, Mass.; lectr. in field. Author: (book) The Invisible Dragon: Four Essays on Beauty, 1993, Air Guitar: Essays in Art and Democracy, 1997, Stardumb, 1999, Prior Convictions, mus. exhbn. catalog essays; contbr. articles to profl. jours.; editor (exec. editor): Art in Am. mag.; contbg. editor: The Village Voice; one-person shows, for artists including David Reed, Peter Alexander, Karen Carson, Scott Grieger, Lynton Wells, Jim Shaw, others; subject of personal profile N.Y. Times, L.A. Times, U.S. News and World Report, Tex. Monthly mag., interview appearances L.A. Times, Bomb, New Art Examiner, PBS-TV, Nat. Pub. Radio. Recipient Frank Jewett Mather award for distinction in art or archtl. criticism, Coll. Art Assn., 1993; grantee, NEA, 1969. Office: U Nev Las Vegas Dept Art HFA-274 4505 Maryland Pky Las Vegas NV 89154

HICKEY, DELINA ROSE, retired education educator; b. N.Y.C., Mar. 25, 1941; d. Robert Joseph and Marie (Ripa) Hickey; m. David Andrews; 1 child, Jon Robert. BS in Edn., SUNY, Oneonta, 1963; MA, Manhattan Coll., 1967; EdD in Counselor Edn. and Psychology, U. Idaho, 1971; postgrad., Harvard U., 1995. Sch. tchr., counselor pub. schs., Westchester, NY, 1963-68; part-time instr. psychologist St. Thomas Aquinas Coll., Sparkhill, NY, 1971-72; asst. prof. edn. Nathaniel Hawthorne Coll., Antrim, NH, 1972-75; mem. faculty Keene (N.H.) State Coll., 1975—2000, assoc. prof. edn., 1978-87, prof., coord. faculty, 1987-2000, interim dean profl. studies, 1887, v.p. student affairs, 1990-2000; ret., 2000. Mem. adv. coun. Title IV, 1979—82; assoc. in edn. Harvard U., 1984—85, Inst. Ednl. Mgmt., 1995; chmn. curriculum Acad. Life Long Learning U. S.C., Aiken, SC, 2003—; presenter in field. Contbr. Bd. trustees Hist. Aiken Found., 2002—, Smart Growth Aiken, 2000—; mem. N.H. Ho. of Reps., 1981—85; trustee Big Bros.-Big Sisters, Keene, 1978—80, Family Planning Svcs. S.W. N.H., 1976—85, Monadnock Family Svcs., 1995—97, Monadnock Hospice, 1994—96, chmn. pers. com.; mem. N.H. Juvenile Conf. Com., 1976—81; bd. dirs. Cheshire Med. Ctr.; trustee Cheshire Med. Assn., 1996—2001; pres. bd. dirs. CHESCO; trustee Home Health Care, 1998—2001; CEO HMS Ednl. Cons., 2000—. Fellow, Nat. Ctr. Rsch. in Vocat. Edn., 1984—85; grantee, Marion Jasper Whitney Found. Mem.: AAUW (vice chmn. programs 2002—), N.H. Assn. Student Pers. Adminstrs. (adv. bd.), N.H. Pers. and Guidance Assn., New Eng. Rsch. Orgn., New Eng. Assn. Tchrs. and Educators, Am. Vocat. Assn., Nat. Assn. Student Pers. Adminstrs. (adv. com. region I, editor, chief Net Results electronic mag. 1997-99), N.H. Order Women Legislators. Office: HMS Ednl Cons Keene NH 03431 E-mail: dhickey@atlantic.net.

HICKEY, ELIZABETH LOUISE, advertising agency executive; b. N.Y.C., Nov. 6, 1958; d. Louise Anthony and Josephine Morgan (Stancisko) Piccoli; m. Mark Hickey, Oct. 15, 1983; children: Caitlin, John, Alanna, Shannon. BA, U. Rochester, 1979; Cert. in Graphic Design, Mass. Coll. Art, 1984. Art and recreation therapist Fernald State Sch., Waltham, Mass., 1979-82; art dir. Wizard of Adz, Dedham, Mass., 1984-89; graphic designer Imageworks, Waltham, 1984-92; pres., mktg. dir. Limo Dreams, Inc., Waltham, 1985-90; creative dir. Wizard of Adz, Dedham, Mass., 1989; art dir. Emerson Lane Fortuna, Boston, 1989—. Faculty mem. Mass. Coll. Art, 1987—, mem. portfolio rev. com.; faculty mem. Emerson Coll., 2002—; art dir. Arnold Fortuna Lane, Boston, 1991-93; sr. art dir. Hill Holliday, 1993-94; creative dir. Holland Mark Martin, 1994-96, Heater Advt. 1997-98; sr. v.p. assoc. creative dir. Arnold Advt., 1996-97; CEO, creative dir. Velocity Inc., 1999—. Author: Design Secrets Advertising, 2002. Recipient Alcoholism and Communications Mktg. Achievement award, 1986, New Eng. Best of Broadcast award, 1991, 1993, 1997, 1999, Francis J. Hatch award, 1991, 1993, 1994, 1996, 1999, 2000, Cannes Internat. advt. award, 1994, Clio Nat. Advt. award, 1994, MCIcon award, 2001, award, The London Show, 1994. Mem.: Big Idea Group. Democrat. Roman Catholic. Avocations: white water rafting, skiing. Home and Office: 306 Dartmouth St Boston MA 02116 E-mail: lisa@velocityadvertising.com.

HICKEY, FRANCIS ROGER, physicist, educator; b. Troy, N.Y., June 8, 1942; s. Frank R. and Ann M. (O'Malley) H.; m. Paula Williamson, Aug. 29, 1964; children: Sharon Ann, Kevin Derus (dec.). BS, Siena Coll., 1964; MS, Clarkson U., 1967, PhD, 1970. From asst. to assoc. prof. Physics Hartwick Coll., Oneonta, N.Y., 1969-83, prof. Physics, 1983—. Adv. bd. Sci. Discovery Ctr. of Oneonta, 1989—, Oneonta Newman Found, 1988—; nat. councillor Soc. Physics Students, 1974-75. Contbr. articles to profl. jours. Founding mem. Oneonta region chpt. The Compassionate Friends. Mem. Am. Phys. Soc., Am. Assn. Physics Tchrs. Roman Catholic. Achievements include development of Physics Educational Computer Programs. Home: 117 Glen Dr Oneonta NY 13820-3553 Office: Hartwick Coll Physics Dept Oneonta NY 13820 E-mail: hickeyr@hartwick.edu.

HICKEY, GERALD VINCENT, writer; b. Columbus, Ohio, Feb. 28, 1925; s. John Francis Hickey and Florence Conrad; m. Patricia Ann Lehmann, June 15, 1955; 1 child, Julie Lynn McGuire. BS, Ohio State U., 1958. Reporter Free Press, Colorado Springs, Colo., 1967—69, Rev. Jour., Las Vegas, Nev., 1969—73, Ariz. Republic, Phoenix, 1973—88. Author: The Redemption of Charlie Devlin, 2001, Crossing a Rainbow, 2002, The Heart Heals Slowly, 2002. Avocations: singing, hiking, swimming, reading, travel.

HICKEY, GREGORY J. priest, academic administrator; b. Darby, Pa., Aug. 11, 1947; s. Joseph Thomas and Helen Gertrude (Lockard) H. BA in Psychology, Temple U., 1973; MDiv, St. Charles Barromeo Sem., 1979; MA in Edn., Villanova U., 1989. Ordained priest Roman Cath. Ch., 1979. Lay tchr. St. Patrick Sch., Norristown, Pa., 1969—74; deacon intern St. Frances DeSales Ch., Phila., 1978—79; asst. pastor Sts. Simon and Jude Ch., Westtown, 1979—81, St. Augustine Ch., Bridgeport, 1981—82, St. Leo Ch., Phila., 1982—87; resident Our Lady Help of Christians, Phila., 1987—99, St. Helena, Center Square, Pa., 1999—2001; theology tchr. Cardinal Dougherty H.S., 1991—92, 1991—92; sch. min. Bishop Conwell H.S., 1988—90; dir. studies St. Hubert H.S., 1990—91; dir. guidance Roman Cath. H.S., 1992—96; prin. Kennedy-Kenrich Cath. H.S., 1996—99, pres., 1999—2001; chaplain, mem. faculty Immaculata (Pa.) U., 2001—. Advocate Met. Tribunal, 1980—82; tchr. ch. ministry program St. Charles Sem., 1985—87; campus min. Nazareth Acad., 1985—87; mem. Pa. state adv. bd. Mid. States Assn. Secondary Sch., 2000—; chair mid. states DeMatha Cath. H.S., Hyattsville, Md., 2003. Trustee St. Charles Sem. Alumni Assn., 1982—87. Mem. ASCD, Nat. Cath. Edn. Assn., Assn. for Psychol. Type, Ancient Order Hibernians, Kappa Delta Pi. Republican. Roman Catholic. Avocations: reading, travel, music, theater. Mailing: Immaculata Univ PO Box 663 Immaculata PA 19345-0663 Office Fax: 610-251-1668. E-mail: Ghickey@immaculata.edu.

HICKEY, JAMES ALOYSIUS CARDINAL, emeritus archbishop; b. Midland, Mich., Oct. 11, 1920; s. James P. and Agnes (Ryan) Hickey. JCD, Lateran U., Italy, 1950; STD, Angelicum U., Italy, 1951; MA, Mich. State U., 1962. Ordained priest Roman Catholic Ch., 1946, elevated to cardinal 1988. Sec. to Bishop of Saginaw, Mich., 1951—60; rector St. Paul Sem., Saginaw, 1960—68; aux. bishop Saginaw, 1967—69; chmn. bishops' com. on Priestly Formation, 1968—69; rector N.Am. Coll., Rome, 1969—74; bishop of Cleve., 1974—80; archbishop of Washington, 1980—2000; chancellor Cath. U. Am., 1980—2000. Mem. Ctrl. Com. for 1975 Holy Yr., 1973—75; chmn. Bishop's Com. Pastoral Rsch. and Practices, 1974—77, Bishop's Com. for Doctrine, 1979—82, Bishops' Com. Human Values, 1984—87, Bishop's Com. on N.Am. Coll., 1988—92, 1994—97. Episc. moderator Holy Childhood Assn., 1984—93; elected mem. Secretariat Synod of Bishops, 1991—94; chmn. bd. trustees Basilica of the Nat. Shrine of Immaculate Conception, 1980—2000; Episc. advisor Serra Internat., 1981—88. Roman Catholic. Address: Archdiocese Washington Archdiocesan Pastoral Ctr PO Box 29260 Washington DC 20017-0260

HICKEY, JEROME EDWARD, investment company executive; b. Chgo., June 25, 1937; s. Matthew Joseph and Naomi (Pope) H.; m. Denise Coakley, May 20, 1967; children: J. Graham, Matthew, Elizabeth, George, Peter. BS in Econs., Coll. of the Holy Cross, 1959; MA in Philosophy, Boston Coll., 1964. Instr. Cranwell Sch., Lenox, Mass., 1964-66; acct. exec. Paine Webber, N.Y.C., 1966-68; v.p. Hickey & Co., Chgo., 1968-72, Ralph W. Davis, Chgo., 1972-75, Weeden & Co., Chgo., 1975-78; founder, pres. Jerome Hickey Assocs., Chgo., 1979-84; pres. No. Trust Brokerage, Chgo., 1984-87; sr. v.p. Stein Roe & Farnham, Chgo., 1988-93; sr. v.p., mng. dir. SEI Corp., Chgo., 1993-96; founder, mng. dir. Dearborn Ptnrs., Chgo., 1997—. Dir. Western Golf Assn., Golf, Ill., 1979—, chmn. exec. com., 1991-96; trustee St. Ignatius Coll. Prep., Chgo., 1988-93, chmn., 1990-93. Named Outstanding Young Man in Am., 1971. Mem. Knollwood Club (Lake Forest, Ill., dir. 1976-79), Bond Club Chgo. (dir. 1974-75), Econ. Club Chgo., Desert Forest Golf Club, The Boulders. Roman Catholic. Home: 245 Leeds Ct Lake Bluff IL 60044 Office: Dearborn Ptnrs 200 W Madison St Chicago IL 60606-3414 E-mail: jhickey@dearpart.com.

HICKEY, JOHN HEYWARD (JACK HICKEY), lawyer; b. Miami, Fla., Dec. 18, 1954; s. Weyman Park Hickey and Alice Joan (Heyward) Brown. BA magna cum laude, Fla. State U., 1976; JD, Duke U., 1980. Bars: Fla. 1980, U.S. Dist. Ct. (so. dist) Fla. 1980, U.S. Dist. Ct. (mid. dist.) Fla. 1982, U.S. Ct. Appeals (5th cir.) 1982, U.S. Ct. Appeals (11th cir.) 1983, U.S. Supreme Ct. 1985. Trial lawyer Smathers & Thompson, Miami, 1980-85, Hornsby & Whisenand P.A., Miami, 1985—, ptnr., 1988, Hickey & Jones, Miami, 1988—99, Hickey Law Firm, PA, Miami, 1999—. Lectr. securities litigation Internat. Assn. Fin. Planners, 1989, 90, Fla. Inst. CPAs, 1990, Flood Ins. Conf., Columbus, Ohio, 1991, Scottsdale, Ariz., 1992, Orlando, Fla., 1993; lectr. admiralty law, Fla. Bar, 1994, 2000; lectr. slip and fall litigation ATLA, Montreal, Can., 2001-02. Contbg. author: Fla. Bar Jour., 1990, Trial mag., 2000, P&I Internat., 1998. Interviewer of prospective undergrads. Duke U. Alumni Adv. Com., 1984—; arbitrator Miami Marine Arbitration Coun. Mem. ABA (litigation mgmt./econs. com. 1986—, comml. transactions and banking com. 1986—), Fla. Bar (chmn. admiralty law com. 2000-01, chmn. grievance com. 1986-89, vice chmn. 1999—, lectr. Bridge the Gap seminars 1984-85, jud. evaluation com. 1985, chmn. 11th cir. fee arbitration com. 1991—, cert. civil trial lawyer 1990, lectr. admiralty law 1994, chair admiralty law com. 1997—), Dade County Bar Assn. (pres. 2003—, bd. dirs. 1998—, chmn. membership com. 1982-83, chmn. cir. ct. com. 1983-84, dir. 1984-86, chmn. young lawyers sect. meetings and programs com. 1985-86, chmn. young lawyers sect. sports com. 1984-85, exec. com. 1985—, chmn. profl. arbitration subcom. 1986—, cert. of merit 1985, 88, 89, 91, 921, 93, bd. dirs. 1990-93, 97—, chmn. banking and corp. litigation com. 1990, 91, 92, chmn. civil litigation com. 1992-93, exec. com. 1992-93, treas. 1999—, sec. 2000—, v.p. 2001—), Greater Miami C. of C., Coral Gables C. of C., Propellor Club of U.S. (Miami divsn.), Southeastern Admiralty Law Inst. (proctor), Maritime Law Assn., Miami Marine Arbitration Coun., Phi Beta Kappa. Office: Hickey Law Firm PA 1401 Brickell Ave Ste 510 Miami FL 33131-3501 Business E-Mail: hickey@hickeylawfirm.com.

HICKEY, JOHN KING, lawyer, career officer; b. Mt. Sterling, Ky. s. John Andrew and Anna Christine H.; m. Elizabeth Jane Pattavina, Nov. 23, 1944; children: Roger Dennis, John King, Patricia Elizabeth Corsini. JD, U. Ky., 1948; M in Internat. Affairs, George Washington U., 1974. Bar: Ky. 1949, Colo. 1958, U.S. Ct. Military Appeals 1959, U.S. Supreme Ct. 1959. Commd. 2d. lt. U.S. Army Air Forces, 1942; advanced through grades to col. USAF, 1964, ret., 1970; dir. legal judicial adminstrn. Council State Govts., Lexington, Ky., 1971-73; dir. continuing legal edn. U. Ky. Coll. Law, Lexington, Ky., 1973-86; pvt. practice Lexington, Ky., 1986—. Mem. Nat. Assn. Attorneys Gen. (outstanding contributions award 1973, sec.), U. Ky. Law Alumni Assn. (sec., treas. 1973 76, appreciation award 1976), Ctrl. Ky. Knife Club (plaque 1997). Democrat. Roman Catholic. Avocations: machairologist, reading, walking, swimming. Office: 3340 Nantucket Dr Lexington KY 40502-3205

HICKEY, JOHN MILLER, lawyer; b. Cleve., June 4, 1955; s. Lawrence Thomas and Margaret (Miller) H.; m. Sharon Salazar, Aug. 4, 1984; children: Theodore James, John Salazar, Margaret Maureen. Student, U. Wales, U.K., 1975-76, BA, Tulane U., 1977; JD cum laude, Calif. We. Sch. Law, 1981; LLM in tax, NYU, 1982. Bar: Calif. 1981, N.Mex. 1983, U.S. Dist. Ct. N.Mex. 1983, U.S. Tax Ct. 1983, U.S. Ct. Appeals (10th cir.) 1983. Prodn. control mgr. Randall-Textron, Inc., Wilmington, Ohio, 1977-78; assoc. Montgomery & Andrews, Santa Fe, 1983-88; shareholder, dir. Compton, Coryell, Hickey & Ives, Santa Fe, 1988-93, Hickey & Ives, Santa Fe, 1993-97, Hickey & Johnson PA, Santa Fe, 1998-99, White, Koch, Kelly & McCarthy, P.A., Santa Fe, 1999—. Mem. legal com. Santa Fe Cmty. Found., 2000—; mem. adv. bd. Presbyn. Med. Svcs. Found. Mem.: State Bar N.Mex. (bd. dirs. taxation sect. 2002—). Republican. Roman Catholic. Avocations: bicycling, squash, reading. Home: 806 Camino Zozobra Santa Fe NM 87505-6101 Office: White Koch Kelly & McCarthy PA 433 Paseo De Peralta Santa Fe NM 87501-1958

HICKEY, JOHN THOMAS, JR., lawyer; b. Evanston, Ill., July 9, 1952; s. John Thomas and Joanne (Keating) H.; m. Candis Bailey, July 7, 1979; children: Alison, Jack, Patrick, Claire, Matthew. AB, Georgetown U., 1974; JD, U. Chgo., 1977. Bar: Ill. 1977, U.S. Dist. Ct. (no. dist.) Ill. 1977, U.S. Ct. Appeals (7th cir.) 1977, U.S. Ct. Appeals (10th cir.) 1987. Assoc. Kirkland & Ellis, Chgo., 1977-83, ptnr., 1983—. Mem. adv. bd. Leading Lawyers Network. Fellow Am. Coll. Trial Lawyers. Office: Kirkland & Ellis 200 E Randolph St Fl 59 Chicago IL 60601-6609

HICKEY, JOHN THOMAS, retired electronics company executive; b. Chgo., Oct. 28, 1925; s. Matthew J., Jr. and Naomi (Pope) H.; m. Joanne R. Keating, Sept. 17, 1949; children: Kathleen Coakley Barrie, John, Michael, James, Roger. BS in Commerce, Loyola U., Chgo., 1948; MBA, U. Chgo., 1952. With Motorola Inc. (and subs.), 1943-96, gen. mgr. semicondr. div., 1955-58, asst. to pres., 1958-62, dir. long range planning, 1962-65, v.p. planning, 1965-70, v.p. finance, sec., 1970-74, sr. v.p., chief fin. officer, dir., 1974-84, exec. v.p., chief fin. officer, dir., 1984-86, chmn. fin. com., dir., 1986-96. Served with AUS, 1944-46. Mem. Skokie Country Club (Glencoe, Ill.), Ocean Forest Golf Club, Sea Island (Ga.) Club. Home: 2320 Indigo Ln Glenview IL 60025 also: PO Box 31065 Sea Island GA 31561-1065

HICKEY, JOSEPH MICHAEL, investment banker; b. Greenburgh, Pa., June 6, 1940; s. Joseph Michael and Margaret (Nelson) H.; m. Suzanne Klempay, July 2, 1970. BS, Ind. U. Pa., 1963. Sales rep. 3M Co., St. Paul, 1967-69; acct. exec. Hornblower & Weeks, Helphill, Noyes, Cleve., 1970-75; pres. Prescott, Ball & Turben, Cleve., 1976-88; dist. chmn. Nat. Assn. Security Dealers, Cleve., 1979-81; mem. mktg. com. SIA, N.Y.C., 1982-86, mem. regional firms com., 1989; chmn. bd. Canregie Capital Mgmt. Co., Cleve., 1983-86; pres. J.W. Charles Group, Cleve., 1988-90; chmn. Pierman Golf Co., North Palm Beach, Fla., 1991-92; pres. Greyfriar Capital Corp., North Palm Beach, Fla. Bd. dirs. No. Trust Corp. Fla. Capt. U.S. Army, 1963-67. Mem. Kirtland Country Club (Willoughby, Ohio), Loxahatchee club (Fla.), Castle Pines Golf Club (Castle Rock, Colo.), Lost Tree Club (Fla.), The Bear's Club (Jupiter, Fla.).

HICKEY, KEVIN FRANCIS, healthcare executive; b. Bridgeport, Conn., June 20, 1951; s. Herbert Augustine and Anne Therese (Pisani) H.; m. Christine Marie Hackett, June 10, 1973 (div. 1978); m. Eileen Michael O'Gara, July 4, 1981; children: Frances, Augustine. AB, Harvard U., 1973; MHSA, U. Mich., 1976; JD, Loyola U., Chgo., 1984. Bar: Ill. 1984. Dir. Am. Hosp. Assn., Chgo., 1978-83; exec. v.p. First Health Assocs., Chgo., 1983-85; v.p., gen. counsel Metlife Healthcare Mgmt. Corp., St. Louis, 1985-88; sr. v.p. Lincoln Nat. Life Ins. Co., Ft. Wayne, Ind., 1988-92; regional v.p. Aetna Health Plans, Chgo., 1992-94, sr. v.p. ops. Hartford, Conn., 1994-96; pres. Health Plans of Am., Farmington, Conn., 1996-97; exec. v.p. Oxford Health Plans, Norwalk, Conn., 1997-98; chmn., CEO IntelliClaim, Inc., Norwalk, Conn., 1998—. Chmn. NEIC, Secaucus, N.J., 1994-95. Contbr. articles to profl. publs. Office: 20 Glover Ave Norwalk CT 06850-1219

HICKEY, LEO J(OSEPH), museum curator, educator; b. Phila., Apr. 26, 1940; s. James J(oseph) and Helen Marie (Schwarz) H.; m. Judith McKendry, June 29, 1968; children: Geoffrey Alan, Damian Michael, Jason Alexander. BS, Villanova U., 1962; MA, Princeton U., 1964; postgrad., Rutgers U., 1963-65; PhD, Princeton U., 1967; MA (privatim), Yale U., 1983. Postdoctoral fellow NRC-Smithsonian Inst., Washington, 1966-69, assoc. curator, 1969-80; chmn. exhibits com. Natural History Mus., Smithsonian, 1973-75, curator, 1980-82; prof. geology Yale U., New Haven, 1982—; dir. Peabody Mus., Yale U., 1982-87; prof. biology Yale U., 1982-97, chair dept. geology and geophysics, 2003—, curator of paleobotany Peabody Mus. Nat. History, 1982—. Adj. prot. botany U. Md., College Park, 1981-85; adj. prof. geology U. Pa., Phila., 1982-, chmn. dept. geology and geophysics, 2003-; past pres., pres., v.p. Yellowstone-Bighorn Rsch. Assn., Red Lodge, Mont., 1979-86; dir. Mus. of Am. Theatre, New Haven, 1983-87; mem. Mars Lander Sci. Team, 1999—. Author: Stratigraphy and Paleobotany of Golden Valley Formation, 1977; co-author: The Great Dinosaur Mural, 1990; editor: (with D.W. Taylor) Origin, Early Evolution, and Phylogeny of the Flowering Plants, 1996. Recipient H.A. Gleason award NY Bot. Gardens, 1977, Best Paper award Geol. Soc. Washington, 1981, Disting. Alumnus award Villanova U., 1982, Ann. Book award Dinosaur Soc., 1992; grantee Smithsonian Rsch. Found., 1972-76, Nat. Geog. Soc., 1979, 84-85, NSF, 1984, 90, 92, 2000, 03, Bay Found., 1995-96, 2000, Nason Found., 2002.

Fellow Geol. Soc. Am.; mem. AAAS, Bot. Soc. Am., Paleontol. Soc. Democrat. Roman Catholic. Office: Peabody Mus Natural History PO Box 208118 170 Whitney Ave New Haven CT 06520-8118

HICKEY, M. GAIL, education educator; b. Chattanooga, Mar. 20, 1955; d. Earl R. and Rebecca Alvena (Russell) H.; m. Robert Humphreys, 1995. BS, Lee Coll., 1978; MS, U. Tenn., 1983, EdD, 1986. Cert. tchr., gifted edn. tchr., Tenn., Ga. Tchr. elem. edn. Bradley Co. Schs., Tenn., 1978—82; gifted resource tchr. pub. schs. Eton and Chatsworth, Ga., 1982—83; gifted program coord. grades K-8 Chickamauga City Schs., Ga., 1983—84; tchg. asst. U. Tenn., 1984—86; resource tchr. Sevier County Schs., Tenn., 1987; asst. prof. edn. Brewton-Parker Coll., Mt. Vernon, Ga., 1987-88, Ind. U.-Purdue U., Ft. Wayne, 1988—, assoc. prof. edn., 1994—99, prof. edn., 2000—. Vis. rsch. scholar Inst. for Advanced Study, Ind. U., Bloomington, 1994, spring 2001, U. N.C., Asheville, 1997, Ctr. for Study of Ethnicity and Race in Am., U. Colo., 1995, Immigration History Rsch. Ctr., U. Minn., 1995; cons. Scott Foresman Ednl. Pub., 2000—; manuscript reviewer Social Studies and the Young Learner, 1988—, Social Edn., 1988—, Jour. Tchr. Edn., 1993—, Internat. Jour. Ednl. Reform, 1995-97, Jour. for Edn. of the Gifted, 1996—; presenter in field. Author: Challenging the Gifted Reader, Bringing History Home: Local and Family History Projects for Grades K-6, 1999; editor Social Studies Experiences, 1988-90; mem. editl. adv. bd. Social Studies and the Young Learner, 1996—; contbr. numerous articles to profl. jours., chpts. to books. Mem. New Ams. task force Allen County United Way, 2002—; mem. steering com. Ft. Wayne Internat. Day, 2002—; instrnl. com. mem. Allen County/Ft. Wayne Hist. Mus., 2000—; mem. tech. assistance com. Ft. Wayne Cmty. Schs., 2000—; mem. ednl. task force Ft. Wayne Bicentennial Celebration, 1991—94; mem. curriculum task force Ft. Wayne Jr. Achievement, 1990—; mem. Ind. Dist. 4 "We the People" Judges Panel, 1996—2001; mem. social studies textbook adoption com. Ft. Wayne Schs., 1996—97. Recipient Golden Achievement Excellence in Edn. Tchg. award, Jr. Achievement of Ind., 1995; fellow Ind. U. Inst. for Advanced Study Scholar-in-Residence fellow, 2001; grantee numerous grants, Ind. U.-Purdue U.-Ft. Wayne, 1990—, Internat. Travel grantee, Ind. U., 1991, 1994, Nat. Geog. Soc. and Geog. Educators Network of Ind. collaborative grantee, 1992, Foellinger Found. grantee, 1999, Clio grantee, Ind. Hist. Soc., 1999, Ind. Heritage Rsch. grantee. Mem. IRA, ASCD, AAUP, Nat. Coun. for Social Studies (sec. elem. spl. interest group, pres. elem. adv. bd., mem. editl. adv. bd. 1996—, ho. of dels. 1993, bd. dirs. 1997-2000, treas. 1997-2000), Ind. Coun. for Social Studies (pres. elem. spl. interest group, bd. dirs. 1993-97, sec. 1995-97), Nat. Geog. Alliance, World Coun. for the Gifted, Nat. Assn. for Gifted Children, Ind. Assn. for Gifted (rsch. task force 1990-94), Eastern Ednl. Rsch. Assn., Internat. Soc. Exploration Teaching Alternatives (tchr. edn. com. 1991-95, membership com. 1993-95), Textbook Authors Assn., Intellectual Skills Devel. Assn., Oral History Assn. (edn. com. 1994—), Am. Ednl. Rsch. Assn. (tchr. as rschr. SIG 1994—), Assn. for Tchr. Edn., Geog. Educators Network of Ind. (co-dir. summer tchrs. inst. 1991-92), Nat. Ctr. for Excellence in Critical Thinking (social studies and critical thinking com. 1992-94, reading and critical thinking com. 1992-94), Nat. Rsch. Ctr. for Gifted and Talented (rsch. pubs. reviewer and grant critic 1992—, content area expert/cons. social studies and reading 1991—), Phi Kappa Phi, Pi Lambda Theta (voting del. 1989-91, treas. Alpha Chi chpt. 1984-86), Phi Delta Kappa. Office: 2101 E Coliseum Blvd Fort Wayne IN 46805-1445

HICKEY, ROBERT JAMES, III, geologist, geographer, educator; b. Media, Pa., June 12, 1965; s. Robert and Kate H. BS in Geology, Edinboro U. of Pa., 1987; MS in Geology, Wash. State U., 1990; PhD in Geography, U. Idaho, 1994. Tchg. asst. dept. geology Washington State U., Pullman, 1988-90; tchg. asst. dept. geography U. of Idaho, Moscow, 1991-94; assoc. prof. dept. geology State U. of W. Ga., Carrollton, 1994-96; sr. lectr. Sch. of Spatial Scis., Curtin U. Tech., Perth, Australia, 1997—2002; assoc. prof. dept. geography Ctrl. Wash. U., 2000—. Cons. various mining cos., govt. agys. and environ. groups, U.S. and Australia, 1990—. Presenter papers at sci. confs. Recipient Dean's medallion for Excellence in Tchng., Curtin U., 1998, 99, Grad. Student Assn. Tchg. Excellence award, U. Idaho, 1994; grantee Crown Resources Corp., Buckhorn Mt., Wash., 1989, Australian Rsch. Coun., 1997, Curtin U. Tech., 1997, Mem. Am. Assn. Geographers (finalist for Warren Nystrom award 1995), Australasian Surveying and Mapping Lectrs. Assn. (sec. 1997-99), Australian Urban and Regional Info. Systems Assn. (Best Presented Paper ann. conf. 1997), Mapping Scis. Inst. of Australia (councillor WA Australia chpt. 1999-2000, web editor 1997-2000). Avocations: reading, travel, Karate, weightlifting. Home: 315 W 10th Ave Ellensburg WA 98926 Office: Ctrl Wash U Dept Geography/Land Studies Ellensburg WA 98926 E-mail: rhickey@cwu.edu.

HICKEY, SHARON MARIE, middle school educator; b. Chgo., Dec. 23, 1970; d. Daniel J.and Mary A. (Jablonski) T.; m. Gregory M. Hickey; June 12, 1993; children: Megan Elizabeth, Sean Myers, Allison Marie. BS in Elem. Edn. magna cum laude, Ball State U., 1992; MEd Reading Specialist, George Mason U., 1997. Reading, study skills coord. No. Va. C.C., Annandale, Va., 1992-94; reading, lang. arts educator Loudoun County Pub. Schs., Sterling, Va., 1994-98; tutor Sylvan Learning Ctr., 2000—. Faculty advisor Helping Hands Club, Seneca Ridge Mid. Sch., Sterling, Va., 1992-94. Mem. Nat. Coun. Tchrs. of English, Kappa Delta Pi, Phi Mu.

HICKEY, WILLIAM V. manufacturing executive; b. 1945; BS U.S. Naval Acad, MBA Harvard U. With W.R. Grace & Co.; joined Sealed Air Corp., 1980, pres., COO, 1996—2000, pres., CEO, 2000—. Bd. dirs. Universal Foods Corp. Office: Sealed Air Park 80 East Saddle Brook NJ 07663*

HICKEY, WINIFRED E(SPY), former state legislator, social worker; b. Rawlins, Wyo. d. David P. and Eugenia (Blake) Espy; children: John David, Paul Joseph. BA, Loretto Heights Coll., 1933; postgrad., U. Utah, 1934, Sch. Social Svc., U. Chgo., 1936; LLD (hon.), U. Wyo., 1991. Dir. Carbon County Welfare Dept., 1935—36; field rep. Wyo. Dept. Welfare, 1937—38; dir. Red Cross Club, Europe, 1942—45; commr. Laramie County, Wyo., 1973—80; mem. Wyo. Senate, 1980—90; dir. United Savs. & Loan, Cheyenne; active Joint Powers Bd. Laramie County and City of Cheyenne. Pub. Where the Deer and the Antelope Play, 1967; pres. Meml. Hosp. of Laramie County, 1986—88, Wyo. Transp. Mus., 1990—92; pres. county and state mental health assn., 1959—63; trustee U. Wyo., 1967—71; active Gov. Residence Found., 1991—93, Wyo. Transp. Mus., 1993—; trustee St. Mary's Cathedral, 1986—; active Nat. Coun. Cath. Women; pres., bd. dirs. U. Wyo. Found., 1986—87; chmn. adv. coun. div. cmty. programs Wyo. Dept. Health and Social Svcs.; chair Am. Heritage Assocs. of U. Wyo., 1992—96. Named Outstanding Alumna, Loretto Heights Coll., 1959, Woman of Yr., Commn. for Women, 1988, United Med. Ctr., Cheyenne, 1998, Legislator of Yr., Wyo. Psychologists Assn., 1988, Family of the Yr., U. Wyo., 1995, Person of Yr., United Med. Ctr., Cheyenne, Wyo., 1998. Mem.: Altrusa Club (Cheyenne).

HICKLE, WILLIAM EARL, lawyer, judge; b. Ft. Worth, Aug. 23, 1957; s. John Edward Sr. and Jean Gore Hickle; m. Debra Kruse, Jan. 27, 1982; children: David John, Mark Daniel, Nathan William, Sarah Elaine, Rachel Diane. BA in Chemistry, Baylor U., 1979; JD, U. Mo., 1982. Bar: Mo. 1983. Ptnr. Hickle & Calvert, L.L.C., Rolla, Mo., 1983—. Part-time mcpl. judge City of Rolla, 1996—; chmn. Mo. Head Injury Adv. Coun. to Gov., Jefferson City, 1996-98. Mem. Phelps County Bar Assn. (pres. 1988), Rolla Rotary Club (pres. 1992-93). Avocations: basketball, hunting, piano. Home: 1100 Ironhorse Rd Rolla MO 65401-4719 Office: Hickle & Calvert LLC PO Box 698 406 N Main St Rolla MO 65401-3016 E-mail: hickle@rollanet.org.

HICKLIN, EDWIN ANDERSON, lawyer; b. Wapello, Iowa, June 13, 1922; s. Edwin Reichley and Leona Irene (Anderson) H.; m. Carolyn Woods, June 21, 1947 (dec. Aug. 1990); children: Kathryn Hicklin Gerst, Martha Hicklin Remley, Elizabeth Hicklin Barber; m. Margaret H. Weaver, Nov. 23, 1995. BA, U. Iowa, 1946, JD, 1948. Bar: Iowa 1948, U.S. Dist. Ct. (so. dist.) Iowa 1953, U.S. Ct. Appeals (8th cir.) 1964. Ptnr. Hicklin & Hicklin, Wapello, 1948-57, Hicklin & Matthews, Wapello, 1962-90. County atty. Louisa County, Wapello, 1952-56. Active Iowa Ho. of Reps., Des Moines, 1967-68, Iowa State Bd. Tax Rev., Des Moines, 1969-74, chmn., 1969-70. 1st lt. USAF, 1943-45 (B-24 pilot 13th AF); PTO. Mem. ABA, Iowa State Bar Assn. (com. on jud. adminstrn. 1969-73, chmn. 1972-73), Masons, Phi Delta Phi. Republican. Episcopalian. Office: Hicklin & Matthews 326 Van Buren St Wapello IA 52653-1223

HICKLIN, RONALD LEE, music production company executive; b. Burlington, Wash., Dec. 4, 1937; s. Wendell C. and Theodora (Van Voorhis) H.; children: Jennifer Lynn, Mark Allan; m. Trudi Takamatsu, Oct. 23, 1994. Student, U. Wash., 1956-57. Pres. S.A.T.B. Inc., L.A., 1979-98, Killer Music, Inc., San Marino, Calif., 1982—2003, T.T. B.B., Inc., Hollywood, 1989—97. Ptnr. Killer Tracks, Primat Am., Hollywood, 1990-96. Lead tenor The Eligibles, 1958-62; vocal dir., singer Piece of Cake Inc., 1968-81; arranger, producer Calif. Raisin Adv. Bd., 1982 (recipient 2 Clios 1983); producer/co-writer Wheaties, 1983 (Clio award); producer/composer Gatorade, 1983; producer/performer Levi's 501 Blues, 1984. With USAF, 1959-65. Mem. NARAS (MVP award 1973, 75), AFTRA (nat. bd. dirs. 1970-85, local bd. dirs. 1968-85), Screen Actors Guild (nat. bd. dirs. 1975), Am. Fedn. Musicians, Hollywood C. of C. Avocations: golf, tennis, basketball. Home and Office: 1175 Arden Rd Pasadena CA 91106 E-mail: killermusic@earthlink.net.

HICKMAN, BERT GEORGE, JR., economist, educator; b. Los Angeles, Oct. 6, 1924; s. Bert George and Caroline E. (Douglas) H.; m. Edythe Anne Warshauer, Feb. 9, 1947; children: Wendy Elizabeth, Paul Lawrence, Alison Diane. BS, U. Calif.-Berkeley, 1947, PhD, 1951. Instr. Stanford U., 1949-51; research asso. Nat. Bur. Econ. Research, 1951-52; asst. prof. Northwestern, 1952-54; mem. sr. staff Council Econ. Advisers, 1954-56; research assoc. Brookings Instn., 1956-58, mem. sr. staff, 1958-66; prof. Stanford U., 1966-95, prof. emeritus, 1996—. Vis. prof. U. Calif. at Berkeley, 1960, London Grad. Sch. Bus Studies, 1972-73,. Inst. Advanced Studies, Vienna, Austria, 1974, 1975, Kyoto U., 1977; NSF fellow Netherlands Econometric Inst., Rotterdam, 1964-65; Ford Found. Faculty research fellow, 1968-69; mem. com. econ. stability Social Sci. Research Council, 1959-61, chmn., 1962-95; chmn. exec. com. Project Link, 1969—; hon. prof. U. Vienna, 1985—; chmn. Energy Modeling Forum working group on macroecon. impacts of energy shocks Stanford U., 1982-83; Am. coord. US-USSR program on econ.-math. macromodeling Am. Coun. Learned Socs., 1988-90. Author: Growth and Stability of the Postwar Economy, 1960, Investment Demand and U.S. Economic Growth, 1965, (with Robert M. Coen) An Annual Growth Model of the U.S. Economy, 1976; Editor: Quantitative Planning of Economic Policy, 1965, Econometric Models of Cyclical Behavior, 1972, Global International Economic Models, 1983, International Monetary Stabilization and the Foreign Debt Problem, 1984, International Productivity and Competitiveness, 1992; co-editor: Global Econometrics, 1983, Macroeconomic Impacts of Energy Shocks, 1987, Link Proceedings, 1991, 92, Studies in Applied Economics Vol. I 1997; contbr. articles to profl. jours. Served with USNR, 1943-46. Vis. fellow Internat. Inst. Applied Systems Analysis, 1979, 80; resident fellow Rockefeller Found., 1989; named Hon. Prof. U. Vienna. Fellow Econometric Soc.; mem. Am. Econ. Assn. (chmn. census adv. com. 1968-71, tech. subcom. to rev. bus. cycle devels. 1962-68, nominating com. 1978-79, chmn. seminar on global modeling, conf. on econometrics and math. econs. 1975-83), Phi Beta Kappa, Phi Eta Sigma. Home: 904 Lathrop Pl Stanford CA 94305-1060 Office: Stanford U Dept Econs Stanford CA 94305

HICKMAN, ELIZABETH PODESTA, retired counselor, educator; b. Livingston, Ill., Sept. 30, 1922; d. Louis and Della (Martin) Podesta; m. Franklin Jay Hickman, Mar. 17, 1944 (dec.); children: Virginia Hickman Hellstern, Franklin. BE summa cum laude, Ea. Ill. State U.; MA, George Washington U., 1966, EdD (Exxon Found.-Raskob Found. grantee), 1979; postgrad., U. Chgo., 1945, U. Va., 1964-66; postgrad. (fellow), Northeastern U., 1967-68. Lic. counselor, Va. Tchr. pub. schs., Ill., Ohio, 1944-64; dir. coll. transfer guidance Maymount Coll. Va., Arlington, 1964-67, dir. Counceling Ctr., 1974-81, assoc. dean counseling and residence life, 1981-84; cmty. counselor Divsn. Mass. Employment Security, Newton, 1968-69; tchr. English conversation, Fuchu, Japan, 1969-73; placement dir., career counselor Coll. of Gt. Falls, Mont., 1973-74; assoc. rschr. George Washington U., Washington, 1986. Lectr. Far East divsn. U. Md., Fuchu, 1971-73; spl. advisor Internat. Ranger Camps, Denmark and Switzerland, 1974-81; spl. cons. Internat. Quaker Sch., Werkhoven, The Netherlands, 1959-63; mem. steering com. Pres.'s Com. on Employment of Handicapped, 1974-95. Vol., ARC, 1967-68, Family Svcs., 1954-75, White House Agy. Liaison, 1986—, Kennedy Ctr. Adminstrn., Washington, 1984—, Arlington Free Clinic, 2000—. With WAVES, 1943-44. Recipient Distng. Alumnus award Ea. Ill. U., 1984. Mem. Brent Soc., Rose Soc., Potomac (Ill) Soc., Italian Am. Soc., Marymount U. Angels Soc., Women's Com. Nat. Symphony Orch., Washington Opera Guild, Delta Epsilon Sigma, Pi Lambda Theta. Roman Catholic. Home: 4708 38th Pl N Arlington VA 22207-2915

HICKMAN, FREDERIC W. lawyer; b. Sioux City, Iowa, June 30, 1927; s. Simeon M. and Esther (Nixon) H.; m. Katherine Heald, July 15, 1964; children: Mary Sanders, Sara Ridder. AB, Harvard U., 1948, LLB magna cum laude, 1951. Bar: Ill. 1951. Asso. firm Sidley & Austin, Chgo., 1951-55; partner firm Hopkins & Sutter, Chgo., 1956-71, 75-92, sr. counsel, 1993-2001. Asst. sec. for tax policy Dept. Treasury, Washington, 1972-75; draftsman Ill. Income Tax, 1969; author and lectr. on taxation. Mem. Ill. Humanities Council, 1977-82; mem. Citizens Commn. on Public Sch. Fin., 1977-78; chmn. bd. trustees Am. Conservatory Music, 1980-90; pres. Nat. Tax Assn., 1989-90. Served with USN, 1945-46. Mem. ABA (chmn. com. on depreciation 1966-68, com. on capital formation 1976-78, coun. 1980-83, chmn. com. on tax structure and simplification 1991-92, Internat. Fiscal Assn. (dr. 1973-77), Am. Coll. Tax Counsel (regent 1989-92), Comm. Club (Chgo.), Union League (Chgo.), Mid-Day (Chgo.), Cliff Dwellers (Chgo.), Legal (Chgo., pres. 1980-81), Chikaming Country (Lakeside, Mich.) Club. Republican. Methodist. Home: 360 Green Bay Rd # 4E Winnetka IL 60093-4032 Office: Foley & Lardner 321 N Clark St Chicago IL 60610

HICKMAN, HUGH V. science educator, researcher; b. Washington, June 3, 1947; s. Jack Wallis Hickman and Mary Cecelia (Regar) McCoy; m. Kayoko K. Hickman, Dec. 30, 1997; 1 child, Hugh Yamato. BSEE, U. South Fla., 1984, PhD, 1989. Entrepreneur, 1969-80; vis. prof. elec. engring. U. South Fla., Tampa, 1989-90; vis. prof. computer sci. Eckerd Coll., St. Petersburg, Fla., 1990-91; prof. physics Hillsborough CC, Tampa, Fla., 1991—2001. Contbr. articles to profl. jours. Mem. AAAS, IEEE, Am. Assn. Physics Tchrs., Am. Phys. Soc., Ye Mystic Krewe of Gasparilla, Phi Kappa Phi. Republican. Roman Catholic. Achievements include research into temporal dynamics. Home: 5010 W Dante Ave Tampa FL 33629-7513 E-mail: kayoko@tampabay.rr.com.

HICKMAN, J. KENNETH, accounting company executive; b. Bklyn., July 8, 1928; s. Walter E. and Mildred C. (Ehrhardt) Hickman; m. Irene A. Davis, May 12, 1956; children: Patricia, Carolyn, Beth. BS cum laude, Fordham U., 1951. With Arthur Andersen & Co. CPAs, 1953-91, mng. ptnr. N.J. office, 1963-72, ptnr. N.Y. office, 1972-91; sr. mng. dir. Grubb & Ellis Real Estate, 1992—2000. Bd. dir. Gunther Internat., Ltd.; mem. US Coun. for Internat. Bus., Nat. Com. Am. Fgn. Policy, Inc., Carnegie Coun. Ethics and Internat. Affairs; mem. Bus. Coun. UN, mem. Am. Coun. on Germany, mem. Nat. Com. for US-China Rels.; mem. Ireland-US Coun. for Commerce and Industry, 1978—, v.p., 1979—93. Trustee Fordham U., 1983—, Am. Irish Legal Rsch. and Edn. Found., Inc., 1995—. 1st lt. AUS, 1951—53. Mem.: AICPA, NJ Soc. CPAs (trustee 1971—73), Inst. Mgmt. Accts., Beacon Hill Club, Econ. Club NY, Fordham U. Alumni Fedn. (nat. chmn. 1973—75), Am.-Irish Hist. Soc. (exec. coun. 1981—), Beta Gamma Sigma, Alpha Kappa Psi. Home: 45 Templar Way Summit NJ 07901-3730 Office: JKH Assocs 45 Templar Way Summit NJ 07901-3730 *Never fold. Play every hand as it is dealt to you.*

HICKMAN, JAMES CHARLES, finance educator, dean; b. Indianola, Iowa, Aug. 27, 1927; s. James C. and Mabel L. (Fisher) Hickman; m. Margaret W. McKee, June 11, 0950; children: Charles Wallace, Donald Robert, Barbara Jean. BA, Simpson Coll., 1950; MS, U. Iowa, 1952, PhD, 1961. Actuarial asst. Bankers Life Co., Des Moines, 1952-57; from asst. prof. to assoc. prof. dept. stats. U. Iowa, 1961—67, prof., 1967-72; prof. bus. and stats. U. Wis., Madison, 1972-93, dean Sch. Bus., 1985-90, emeritus prof. and dean, 1993—; Warren prof. U. Man., 1990; Bowles prof. George State U., 1996. Mem. panel cons. social security fin. Senate Fin. Com., Ho. Ways and Means Com., 1975—76; mem. adv. com. Joint Bd. Enrollment Acutaries, 1976—78; mem. Actuaries Stds. Bd., 1985—92; dir. Mems. Capital Advisors, Am. Med. Security; vis. prof. Nankai U., Tianjin, China, 1993, Tianjin, 96. Mem. editl. bd. N.Am. Actuarial Jour., 1997—. Mem. bd. pensions Presbyn. Ch. U.S., 1989—. With USAAF, 1945—47. Recipient Alumni Achievement award, Simpson Coll., 1979, David Halmstad award for actuarial rsch., Actuarial Ednl. Rsch. Fund, 1979, 1981, Disting. Alumni award, U. Iowa, 1993; Coll. Liberal Arts Alumni fellow, 1999. Fellow: Actuarial Found. (trustee 1994—2000), Soc. Actuaries (bd. govs. 1971—74, v.p. 1975—77, bd. govs. 1991—94, J. E. O'Connor Disting. Svc. award 2000); mem.: Nat. Acad. Social Ins., Swiss Assn. Actuaries (corr.), Casualty Actuarial Soc. (assoc.), Am. Statis. Assn., Am. Acad. Actuaries (Jarvis Farley award for svc.), Beta Gamma Sigma (bd. govs. 1988—92). Presbyterian. Home: 2822 Marshall Ct #3 Madison WI 53705-2271 Office: U Wis Sch Bus 975 University Ave Madison WI 53706-1324

HICKMAN, JAMES J. research scientist, educator; b. Phila., Nov. 19, 1957; s. James Joseph and Thekla C. Hickman. BS, Pa. State, 1983, MS, 1985; PhD, Mass. Inst. Tech., Cambridge, Mass., 1990. Rsch. chemist plasma tech. devel. SAIC, McLean, Va., 1990—94; adj. prof. George Mason U., Fairfax, Va., 1992—95; biotech. rsch. and applications divsn. SAIC, 1994—98; assoc. rsch. prof. George Washington U., Washington, 1998—2000, adj. assoc. prof., 2000—; sci. adv. Nat. Sci. Found., Washington, 2000—; Hunter Edward assoc. prof. Clemson (SC) U., 2000—. Sci. adv. to dir. info. tech. office DARPA, Washington, 1998—99; sci. adv. Biostream Inc., 2000; sci. adv. to dir. Nat. Sci. Found., Washington, 2000—02, EIA, Washington, 2000—02, CISE, Washington, 2000—02. Contbr. articles to profl. jours. Mem.: AVS (chmn. biomaterials interface tech. group 1995—2000, treas and mem. sec. biomaterials interface tech. group 2000—), Soc. Biomaterials (mem. liaison com. 2000—), Am. Chem. Soc., NY Acad. of Scis. Achievements include patents in field. Office: Clemson University 501 Rhodes Engring Rsch Ctr Clemson SC 29634 Office Fax: 864-656-4466. E-mail: hickman@clemson.edu.

HICKMAN, JANET SUSAN, college administrator, educator; b. Bklyn., Aug. 28, 1948; d. Richard and Frances J. (Falconer) Liberth; m. C. Kennedy Hickman, June 21, 1970; 1 child, Kennedy R. BSN cum laude, U. Bridgeport, 1970; MS, No. Ill. U., 1976; EdD, Temple U., 1987. RN, Ill., Ohio, Pa., Del., N.Y. Instr. St. Joseph Hosp., Joliet, Ill., 1974-77, Wright State U., Dayton, Ohio, 1977-78; asst. prof. Neumann Coll., Aston, Pa., 1979-81; assoc. dean health professions Ea. Coll., St. Davids, Pa., 1982-92; coord. grad. program, prof. West Chester (Pa.) U., 1992—. Author: Mental Health and Psychiatric Nursing, 1992, Health Assessment in Nursing, 1995; author: (with others) Nursing Theories, 5th edit., 2002; author: Fundamentals of Nursing, 2003; contbr. articles to profl. jours. Mem. APHA, ANA, Pa. State Nurses Assn., Assn. Comty. Health Nursing Educators, Temple U. Alumni Assoc., Sigma Theta Tau. Home: 1435 Clover Ln West Chester PA 19380-5906 Office: West Chester Univ Dept Nursing West Chester PA 19383-0001 E-mail: jhickman@wcupa.edu.

HICKMAN, JOHN NORWOOD, marketing professional; b. Sept. 1, 1964; BS in Agrl. Econs., N.C. State U., 1986; MBA, Coll. William & Mary, 1992. Dealer credit mgr. Wachovia, Burlington, N.C., 1986-90; regional mktg. dir. AMF, Atlanta, 1992-93; COO/mgr. E.S. Mktg. Co-op, Melfa, Va., 1993-96; mgr. specialty food products E.S. Enterprises/VESC, Melfa, Va., 1996—2002; dir. ea. region Md. SBDC, 2002—. Home: 33077 Peach Orchard Rd Pocomoke MD 21851 E-mail: bontemps@intercom.net.

HICKMAN, LUCILLE, physical therapist; b. Chgo., July 21, 1949; d. Louis Melvin and Edna (Edwards) H. BA in Sociology, Lake Forest Coll., 1972; BS in Physical Therapy, Chgo. Med. Sch., 1975; MS in Health Sci., Gov.'s State U., 1985. Staff phys. therapist Michael Reese Hosp., Chgo., 1975-79; dir. phys. therapy Provident Med. Ctr., Chgo., 1979-83; instr. phys. therapy Chgo. State U., 1983-87; pres. adminstrv. dir. R.O.C. Phys. Therapy Svcs., Chgo., 1985—93; founder, pres. PhysioCare Ltd., Chgo., 1988—93. Pvt. practice therapy cons., Chgo., 1983—93. Mem. Am. Phys. Therapy Assn., Nat. Soc. Allied Health. Democrat. Episcopalian. Achievements include patents for exercise machine, 1998. Avocations: piano, composing, cooking, writing.

HICKMAN, MARGARET CAPELLINI, advertising executive; b. Hartford, Conn., Sept. 21, 1949; d. Anthony Serafino Capellini and Mary Magdelan (Budash Capellini) Zanardi; m. Richard Lonnie Hickman, Nov. 6, 1982; children: Wilder A., Langdon B. BA, U. Conn., 1971. Mktg. asst. Advo Sys., Inc., Hartford, Conn., 1971-72, mktg. analyst, 1972-75; mktg. asst. Cinamon Assocs., Inc., Brookline, Mass., 1975-77, profn. supr., 1977-81, v.p. prodn., 1981-84, v.p. client svcs., 1984-85, 86; dir. client svcs. Bozell, Jacobs, Jenyon & Eckhardt, Boston, 1985-86; ptnr. Hickman & Hickman, Merritt Island, Fla., 1987; prodn. mgr. Direct Mktg. Aty., Stamford, Conn., 1988-90; v.p. prodn. Martin Direct, Glen Allen, Va., 1990-96, Martin Agy., Richmond, Va., 1996—. Mem. Direct Mktg. Assn. (past sec., treas., v.p.), Cape Ann Child Devel. Programs (past dir.), Am. Legion Aux. Democrat. Roman Catholic. Home: 10717 Wellington St Fredericksburg VA 22407-1272

HICKMAN, PATRICIA, artist, craftswoman; BA, U. Colo., 1962; MA in Design and Textiles, U. Calif., Berkeley, 1977. Prof., head fiber program art dept. U. Hawaii at Manoa, Honolulu. One-woman shows include U. Hawaii, 1991, Contemporary Mus., Honolulu, 1995—96, Banker Gallery, San Francisco, 1996, San Francisco Craft and Folk Art Mus., 1998—99, exhibitions include, Kanezawa, Japan, 1982, Kassel, Germany, 1985, Galerie de Sluis, Leidschendam, The Netherlands, 1984, Maya Behn Gallery, Copenhagen, 1986, Zurich, Switzerland, 1985, Kyoto, Japan, 1987, N.D. Mus. Art tour in Far East, 1988—90, Bradford, Eng., 1990, Philharm. Gallery, Liege, Belgium, 1991—93, Am. Embassy, Warsaw, 1991—93, Africa tour, 1992—94, Represented in permanent collections Contemporary Mus., Honolulu, State Found. Culture and Arts, Honolulu Acad. Art, Ark. Arts Ctr., Little Rock, Am. Craft Mus., N.Y.C., Erie (Pa.) Art Mus., Oakland (Calif.) Mus., Wadsworth Atheneum, Hartford, Conn., Savaria Mus., Smithsonian Instn., Washington, also corp. collections, commns., Maui Arts and Culture Ctr., Kahului, Hawaii, 1991—94, work represented in various publs.; contbr. essays to exhbn. catalogs. Individual artist visual arts fellow, Hawaii State Found. on Culture and Arts, 1998, grantee, NEA, 1986—87.

HICKMAN, RICHARD LONNIE, advertising executive; b. Atlanta, Oct. 18, 1950; s. Lonnie C. and Dean (Wilder) H.; m. Margaret Mary Capellini, Nov. 6, 1982; children: Wilder Anthony, Langdon Bond. BA, MA, U. S.C., 1973. V.p. mktg. Mowbray Pub., Providence, 1977-80; pres. Indianhead Advt., Gloucester, Mass., 1980-87; v.p., dir. prodn. Barry Blau & Ptnrs., Fairfield, Conn., 1987-89; pres. Oxford Direct, Boston, Va., 1990-92; v.p. new bus. NAIM, Fredericksburg, Va., 1993-94, exec. v.p., 1994; sr. cons. Harte-Hanks Direct Mktg., Fredericksburg, 1994-98, developer e-commerce bus., 1998-2000; CEO, chmn. Indian Head Industries, Fredericksburg, 2000—. Author: The Four Color Primer, 1983, The Direct Mail Package from Hell, 1989, Credit Card Retention in a Shark's Feeding Frenzy, 1994; inventor in field. Sgt. U.S. Army, 1969-71, Vietnam. Decorated Bronze star. Republican. Episcopalian. Home and Office: 10717 Wellington St Fredericksburg VA 22407-1272 E-mail: ndianhead@earthlink.net.

HICKMAN, RONALD LEE, media broker, broadcast executive; b. Belmar, N.J., Sept. 23, 1932; s. Charles Alfred and Thelma Hefter Hickman; m. Barbara Alice Sanders; children: Ronald Hickman, II, David, Todd. Student, Pikeville Coll., 1953—55. Announcer, sportscaster, salesman WPKE-AM, Pikeville, Ky., 1952—55; salesman, news dir., gen. mgr. WNNJ-AM & FM, Newton, NJ, 1955—63; gen. mgr., part-owner WKER-AM, Pompton Lakes, NJ, 1963—69; pres., gen. mgr. WKFD-AM, Wickford, RI, 1969—78; founder, gen. mgr., pres. WOTB-FM, Middletown/Newport, RI, 1978—83; media broker Hickman Assocs., Gulf Breeze, Fla., 1984—. Author Hickman Assocs., Gulf Breeze, 1984—. Author: Touching the Stars, 1986, The Media Brokers, 2000. Pres. Newton Country Club, 1995—97; founder Newton (N.J.) Jaycee Chpt., 1959—60; pres. N.J. Broadcasters Assn., 1964; bd. dirs. People's Credit Union, Middletown, RI, 1982—86. Pvt. USAF, 1951—51. Recipient Best News Story, AP to WOTB-FM, 1982. Mem.: Men's Golf Assn. (pres. 1998—2000), Tiger Point Golf and Country Club. Episcopalian. Avocations: golf, music, photography. Home: 48 Timberton Dr Hattiesburg MS 39401 Personal E-mail: RonHickman@BellSouth.net.

HICKMAN, RUTH VIRGINIA, Bible educator; b. Sac City, Iowa, Oct. 15, 1931; d. Ronald Minor and Ida E. (Willcutt) Wilson; m. Charles Ray Hickman, Aug. 25, 1962; children: Ronald Everett, Lisa Michelle. BS in Home Econs., Morningside Coll., 1953. Ordained to ministry Christian Ch., 1985. Instr. Nat. Ednl. TV, 1964-76; staff coord., tchr. Life for Layman, Denver, 1974-77; founder, tchr. Abundant Word Ministries, Lakewood, Colo., 1980—; tchr. Bible

Calvary Temple, Denver, 1980—; sales/trainer Hillestad Internat., Woodruff, Wis., 1978—. Women's com. Billy Graham Assn., Denver, 1986-87. Author: (book) Hope for Hurting People, 1987; spkr., instr. audio and video tape series, 1980—. Leader pilgrimages to Israel, 1984, 87, 94, 96, 98, 2001. Republican. Home: 3043 S Holly Pl Denver CO 80222-7010 Office: Abundant Word Ministries 2109 S Wadsworth Lakewood CO 80227 E-mail: RuthAbundant@c.s.com., abundant_word@hotmail.com.

HICKMAN, TERRIE TAYLOR, administrator; b. Rapid City, S.D., Dec. 2, 1962; d. William Adrian and Carolyn Gene (Habben) T.; children: Matthew, Kalie. BS, Okla. State U., 1985; MEd, Cen. State U., 1988. Cert. elem tchr., presch. tchr., Okla. Mktg. dir. Tealridge Manor, Edmond, Okla., 1989-90; owner Oxford Pointe Jazzercize, Edmond, Okla., 1989-90; adminstr. Retirement Inn at Quail Ridge, Oklahoma City, Okla., 1991-92, Country Club Square, Edmond, 1992-93; planner Areawide Aging Agency, Oklahoma City, 1992-97. Mem. adv. coun., co-chmn. Okla. Bus. and Aging Leadership Coalition, newsletter Networker editor; presenter in field; adv. coun. sr. companion planning com. State of Okla. Conf. on Aging; mem. Oklahoma City Reading Coun. Co-editor Sage Age; contbr. articles to various pubs. Co-chmn. media hosting party Olympic Festival, Norman, Okla., 1989; co-coord. jazzercize for hope Benefit for Hope Ctr., Edmond, The McGruff Safe House Program, Stillwater, Okla.; com. chmn. Coalition for Elderly Concerns, Oklahoma City; vol. Stillwater Domestic Violence Shelter, Payne County Employment Svcs., Stillwater; mem. renter's adv. bd. Okla. State U. Student Senate. Mem. ASCD, Women in Bus., Edmond Area C. of C., Okla. Bus. and Aging Leadership Coalition, Phi Kappa Delta, Alpha Gamma Delta, Sigma Phi Omega, Kappa Delta Pi. Republican. Lutheran. Avocation: biking. E-mail: cityfarmer@worldnet.att.net.

HICKMAN, TRAPHENE PARRAMORE, library director, storyteller, library and library building consultant; b. Dallas, Jan. 31, 1933; d. Redden Travis and Stella (Moore) P.; m. John Robert Hickman, June 9, 1950; children— Lynn Kleifgen, Laurie Ward AA, Mountain View Community Coll.; BA, U. Tex-Arlington; M.L.S., U. North Tex. Cert. librarian, Tex. Librarian Cedar Hill Pub. Library, Tex., 1959-77; dir. Dallas County Library System, Dallas, 1977-93; libr. cons. Dallas County, 1993-95. Chair leadership coun. and family ministries FUMC of Cedar Hill. Editor: History and Directory of Cedar Hill, 1976; editor News and Views newsletter Dallas county Employees, 1986-92. Chmn. Bicentennial Com., Cedar Hill, 1976; del. Dem. Nat. Conv. 9th Senate Dist., Tex., 1976; chmn. Sesquicentennial Com., Cedar Hill, 1984-86; Dallas County Dem. Forum; mem. Electoral Coll., 1988; chairperson Women's Bd. Northwood Inst., Cedar Hill; active Dallas County Sesquicentennial Com., 1996— Recipient Newsmaker of Yr. award Cedar Hill Chronicle, 1976; named Ambassador of Goodwill, State of Tex., 1976 Mem. ALA, Tex. Libr. Assn. (legis. com. 1984-95, councillor 1982-83, trustee com. 1987-95, pub. info. com. 1987-95), Pub. Libr. Adminstrs. of North Tex. (sec., v.p., pres. 1980, 87), Dallas County Libr. Assn., N.E. Tex. Libr. Sys. (legis. commn. 1978-95, Libr. of Yr. 1987), U. North Tes. Sch. Libr. and Info. Scis. Alumni Assn. (pres. 1987-88), Cedar Hill C. of C., Cedar Summit Book Club (officer), Dallas Area Storytelling Guild (pres. 1995-99) Democrat. Methodist. Avocations: writing, reading, storytelling, gardening, bridge, travel, square dancing. Home and Office: 421 Lee St Cedar Hill TX 75104-2697

HICKOK, D. ALICIA, lawyer; b. Whittier, Calif., Oct. 19, 1960; d. Gus J. Gerson, Jr. and Diane E. Gerson; m. Peter K. Hickok, Mar. 16, 1985; children: Samuel, Elonnai, Bennet. BA cum laude, Tex. Christian U., 1979; JD cum laude, U. Pa., 2001. Bar: Pa., N.J., U.S. Dist. Ct. (ea. dist.) Pa., U.S. Dist. Ct. N.J., U.S. Ct. Appeals (3rd cir.). Law clk. to hon. M.O. Rendell 3d Cir. Ct. Appeals, 2001—02; atty. Drinker, Biddle & Reath, Phila., 2002—. Tchg. asst. U. Pa., 1999; coach mem. Jessup Internat. Moot Ct. Team, 1999—2000, 2000—01. Assoc. editor: U. Pa. Law Rev., 1999—2000, tech. editor:, 2000—01. Mem.: ABA (antitrust, internat. law and lit. sects.). Avocations: bridge, bread baking. Office: Drinker Biddle & Reath One Logan Sq 18th and Cherry Philadelphia PA 19103

HICKOK, EUGENE W. federal agency administrator; m. Katharine Pauley; 2 children. BA, Hampden-Sydney Coll., 1972; master's, U. Va., 1978, PhD, 1983. Spl. asst. Office Legal Counsel U.S. Dept. Justice, 1986—87; dir. fin. aid Hampden-Sydney Coll.; Va.; assoc. dir. dept. polit. sci. Miss. State U.; instr. polit. sci. Dickinson Coll., Carlisle, Pa., 1980—, dir. Clarke Ctr. Interdisciplinary Study of Contemporary Issues; sec. edn. Commonwealth of Pa. Dept. Edn., Harrisburg, 1995—2001; under sec. edn. Dept. Edn., Washington, 2001—, acting dep. sec. edn., 2003—. Dir. Clarke Ctr. Interdisciplinary Study of Contemporary Issues. Author books; contbr. articles to profl. jours. Mem. Carlisle Area Sch. Bd. Adj. scholar Heritage Found. Office: Dept Edn Office of Under Sec 400 Maryland Ave SW Rm 7W310 Washington DC 20202-1510*

HICKROD, GEORGE ALAN KARNES WALLIS, educational administration educator; b. Fort Branch, Ind., May 16, 1930; s. Hershell Roy and Bernice Ethel (Karnes) H.; m. Ramona Dell Poole, 1952 (dec.); m. Lucy Jen Huang, 1964 (dec.); 1 stepchild, Goren Wallis Liu (dec.); m. Marcia D. Escott, 1998; stepchildren: Eric David Escott, Beth Ann Escott Newcommer. AB, Wabash Coll., 1954; MA, Harvard U., 1955, EdD, 1966. Asst. prof. ednl. and social scis. Lake Erie Coll., 1962-67; assoc. prof. ednl. adminstrn. Ill. State U., Normal, 1967-71, prof., 1971-83, disting. prof., 1983-95, emeritus disting. prof., 1995—, dir. Ctr. for Study Ednl. Fin., 1974-95. Dir. McArthur/Spencer Ill. Sch. Fin., 1987-92, Joyce Found. Sch. Fin. Study, 1990-92; pres. Coalition for Ednl. Rights Under the Constn., 1989-91, mem. ednl. rights com., 1990-98. With USMC, 1950-52, Korea. Recipient Chgo. Urban League award, 1994, Van Miller Disting. Scholar award U. Ill., 1994; State of Ill. and U.S. Govt. grantee. Mem. Am. Edn. Fin. Assn. (v.p. 1983-84, pres. 1984-85, Disting. Svc. award 1992), Scottish-Am. Soc. Ctrl. Ill. Club (past chief), Clan Wallace Internat. Royal Order of Scotland Masonic, Phi Beta Kappa, Commun Gaidhleach Am., Masons, Elks. Democrat. Unitarian Universalist. Avocations: history, genealogy, travel, cooking, gaelic (albanach) language. Home: 2 Turner Rd Normal IL 61761-4218 E-mail: AlanHickrod@aol.com.

HICKS, ALLEN MORLEY, hospital administrator; b. Toronto, Iowa, May 11, 1928, s. Perle and Grace (Mowry) H.; m. Sue Hicks; children by previous marriage: David, Dennis, Wendy, Patricia. Student, Long Beach City Coll., 1949-50; BS, U. Iowa, 1952, MS, 1954. Adminstrv. resident St. Lukes Hosp., Davenport, Ia., 1953-54; adminstr. Schmitt Meml. Hosp., Beardstown, Ill., 1954-57, Pekin (Ill.) Meml. Hosp., 1957-63, Ill. Masonic Hosp. and Med. Center, Chgo., 1963-72; pres. Community Hosp., Indpls., 1972-84, Meth. Health Care Systems, Memphis, 1984-85, VHA Enterprises, 1985-90; adminstr. Midwest Med. Ctr., Indpls., 1991-93. Sr. advisor St. Vincent's Hosp. and Health Care Corp.; chmn. bd. Vol. Hosps. Am., 1980-84, Multi-Mut. Ins. Cos. of Bermuda and Cayman Islands; bd. dirs. Am. Coll. Testing, Ind. Blue Cross, Am. Health Capital, Indpls. Conv. Ctr.; preceptor masters degree program in health and hosp. adminstrn. U. Iowa; chmn. com. extended care Coun. on Assn. Svc., 1963; pres. Chgo. Hosp. Coun., 1970-71. Campaign chmn., bd. dirs., chmn. indsl. div. United Fund, Pekin, Ill., 1959-64; pres. Tazewell County United Cerebral Palsy, 1960-61; chmn. Cancer Crusade, Pekin, 1960-61; service chmn. Tazewell County, 1958-60; chmn. bd. Tomahawk dist. Creve Coeur council Boy Scouts Am., 1963-64, bd. dirs. Crossroads council; bd. dirs. Cancer Soc., Hosp. Research and Devel. Inst., Inc.; pres. Meth. Health Systems Memphis, 1984-85. H, Served with USNR, 1945- 49, 51-52. Recipient Outstanding Young Man of Year award State Ill., 1960; Distinguished Service award Pekin Jr. C. of C., 1960; Boss of Year award Marquette chpt. Nat. Secs. Assn., 1962 Fellow Am. Coll. Health Adminstrn.; mem. Am. Hosp. Assn. (del. 1971—, chmn. com. community relations), Ill. Hosp.Assn. (trustee, chmn. com. personnel relations), Am. Coll. Hosp. Adminstrs., Am. Assn. Maternal and Infant Health, Ill. Welfare Assn., Ill. C. of C., Am. Legion, Am. Vets., 500 Assn., Beta Gamma Sigma. Presbyterian (elder, trustee). Clubs: Mason, Elks, Kiwanis (bd. dirs. Internat. Found. 1981-85, pres. local chpt. 1983). Address: 202 Wellington Rd Irving TX 75063-7201

HICKS, BETHANY GRIBBEN, judge, commissioner, lawyer; b. N.Y., Sept. 8, 1951; d. Robert and DeSales Gribben; m. William A. Hicks III, May 21, 1982; children: Alexandra Elizabeth, Samantha Katherine. AB, Vassar Coll., 1973; MEd, Boston U., 1975; JD, Ariz. State U., 1984. Bar: Ariz. 1984. Pvt. practice, Scottsdale and Paradise Valley, Ariz., 1984-91; law clk. to Hon. Kenneth L. Fields Maricopa County Superior Ct. S.E. dist., Mesa, 1991-93; commr., judge pro tem domestic rels. and juvenile depts. Maricopa County Superior Ct. Ctrl. and S.E. Dists., Phoenix and Mesa, Ariz., 1993-99; magistrate Town of Paradise Valley, Ariz., 1993-94; judge ctrl. dist. domestic rels. dept. Maricopa County Superior Ct., Phoenix, 1999-2000, presiding judge family ct. dept., 2000—02, judge S.E. dist. civil dept., 2002—. Mem. Jr. League of Phoenix, 1984-91; bd. dirs. Phoenix Children's Theatre, 1988-90; parliamentarian Girls Club of Scottsdale, Ariz., 1985-87, 89-90, bd. dirs., 1988-91; exec. bd., sec. All Saints' Episcopal Day Sch. Parents Assn., 1991-92, pres., 1993-94; active Nat. Charity League, 1995-99, Valley Leadership Class XIX, 1997-98; vol., Teach for Am., 1997—. Mem.: ABA, Nat. Assn. of Women Judges, Assn. Family Ct. Conciliators (bd. dirs. 2001—), Ariz. Women Lawyers' Assn. (steering com. 1998—), Maricopa County Bar Assn., State Bar Ariz. Republican. Episcopalian. Office: 222 E Javelina Ave Mesa AZ 85210- E-mail: bhicks@superiorcourt.maricopa.gov.

HICKS, C. FLIPPO, lawyer; b. Fredericksburg, Va., Feb. 24, 1929; s. Robert A. and Nell (Jones) Hicks; m. Patricia DeHardit (dec. 1983); children: Robert, Patricia Shull, J. Flippo(dec.), Paula Mooradian; m. Martha Kent. BS in Commerce, U. Va., 1950, LLB, 1952. Bar: Va. 1952, U.S. Supreme Ct. 1955. Asst. atty. gen. Commonwealth of Va., Richmond, 1953-59; ptnr. Martin, Hicks, Ingles, Ltd., Gloucester, Va., 1959-91; gen. counsel Va. Assn. Counties, Richmond, 1991—2003; pvt. practice Gloucester, 2003—. Presdl. elector, 1968, 1976, 1980; pres. exec. coun. Episcopal Diocese of Va., 1970—71, mem. standing com., 1971—74. Fellow: Am. Bar Found.; mem.: ABA (Leader of the Yr. award gen. practice sect., Constbar Leader of the Yr. 1992), Defenders Commn. Va., Nat. Assn. Counties Civil Attys. (pres. 1999—, bd. dirs.), Va. State Bar (pres. 1990—91). Democrat. Episcopalian. Avocations: gardening, college sports. Office: PO Box 1300 6517 Main St Gloucester VA 23061 E-mail: counsel@vaco.org.

HICKS, C. THOMAS, III, lawyer; b. NYC, Sept. 14, 1945; s. Charles Thomas and Jeane (Merritt) H.; m. Susan Massie, Dec. 30, 1967 (div. Dec. 1997); children: Melissa, Merritt. BSCE, Va. Tech. U., 1967; JD, U. Ga., 1970; LLM in Tax, Georgetown U., 1975. Bar: Ga. 1970, Va. 1972, D.C. 1981. Assoc. Boothe, Prichard & Dudley, Fairfax, Va., 1975—78; ptnr. Wickwire, Gavin & Gibbs, P.C., Vienna, Va., 1978—83, Shaw, Pittman, Potts & Trowbridge, McLean, Va., 1983—98; shareholder Greenberg Traurig, McLean, Va., 1998—2001; ptnr. Wilmer, Cutler & Pickering, McLean, Va., 2001—03, sr. counsel, 2003—. Gen. counsel Wolf Trap Found. Performing Arts, 1998-2001. Judge advocate USMC, Washington, 1971-75; co-founder, dir. No. Va. Transp. Alliance, McLean, Va., 1987-2001, gen. counsel, 1987-2001. Mem. Va. Bar Assn. (chair bus. law coun.), Va. State Bar (bus. law sec. bd. governors, chmn. 1997-99), Fairfax Bar Assn., Nat. Assn. Bond Lawyers, Va. Assn. Comml. Real Estate (co-founder, pres., dir. 1990-92), Nat Assn. Indsl. and Office Properties (dir. Va. chpt. 1985-91, pres. 1990), No. Va. Tech. Coun. (dir. 2000—, gen. counsel 1996-2000), Greater Washington Bd. Trade, Fairfax County C. of C. (dir. 1998—). Avocations: singing, sailing, tennis, golf. Home: 6643 Madison McLean Dr Mc Lean VA 22101 Office: Wilmer Cutler & Pickering 1616 Anderson Rd Mc Lean VA 22101-2109 Business E-Mail: thomas.hicks@wilmer.com.

HICKS, CADMUS METCALF, JR., financial analyst; b. Hagerstown, Md., Dec. 21, 1952; s. Cadmus Metcalf Sr. and Marie Elizabeth (Keefauver) H.; m. Elizabeth Ann Dressel, May 31, 1980; children: Liza, Alethea, Cadmus III. BA, Wheaton (Ill.) Coll., 1974; MA, U. Chgo., 1976; PhD, Northwestern U., Evanston, Ill., 1980. Chartered fin. analyst. Rsch. analyst John Nuveen & Co. Inc., Chgo., 1980-85, asst. v.p., 1985-90, v.p., 1990—, asst. mgr. rsch. dept., 1993-96, mgr. rsch. dept., 1996-99, market strategist, 1999—. Author: (with others) The Municipal Bond Handbook, 1983, Bond Credit Analysis: Framework and Case Studies, 2001; contbr. articles to profl. jours. Mem. Nat. Fedn. of Mcpl. Analysts (bd. govs. 1991-93), Chgo. Mcpl. Analysts Soc. (pres. 1991-92), Investment Analysts Soc. of Chgo., Assn. for Investment Mgmt. and Rsch. Republican. Office: 333 W Wacker Dr Chicago IL 60606-1220

HICKS, DAVID EARL, writer, inventor; b. Indpls., Jan. 1, 1931; s. John Arthur and Marguerite (Barnes) H.; m. Shirlene Lavan Barlow, Jan. 22, 1958 (div. June 1973); children: Sharon Lynn, Brenda Kay; m. Margaret Leigh Payne, Feb. 17, 1977; children: David Bradley, Leslie Ann, Brian Patrick. Grad., Nat. Radio Inst., 1953; student, Purdue U., 1959-60, Miami-Dade Community Coll., 1971-72. Cert. advanced paramedic. Tech. writer, editor Howard W. Sams, Inc., Indpls., 1958-64; tech. writer Systems Engring. Labs, Inc., Ft. Lauderdale, Fla., 1964-67; publs. mgr. Novatronics, Inc., Pompano Beach, Fla., 1967-69; pres. Datatek, Inc., Ft. Lauderdale, 1969-71; tech. writer Systems Devel. Corp., Colorado Springs, Colo., 1973-74, Ford Aerospace Corp., Colorado Springs, 1974-76; pres. Nutronics Corp., Colorado Springs, 1982-87; tech. writer Digital Equipment Corp., Colorado Springs, 1978-88; pres. Innovation USA Mag., Colorado Springs, 1989; tech. cons., inventor pvt. practice, Colo. Springs, 1964-65, 75-92; novelist Colo. Springs, 1992—. Tech. cons. Japan Electronics, Tokyo, 1962-63, Nutronics Corp., Longmont, Colo., 1987, Gates Motor Corp., Kailua, Hawaii, 2000—. Author of eight tech. books (two made best seller list) including: Citizens Band Radio Handbook, 1961, Amateur Radio-VHF and Above, 1965, CB Radio Operating Procedures, 1976; contbr. articles to electronics jours.; inventor of new electric charging system, 1978, awarded U.S. patent, 1981; lectr. numerous sci. and invention seminars, 1978—. Communications officer CD, Indpls., 1962-63; judge sci. fair Pub. Sch. System, Colorado Springs, 1986-87. Served with USN, 1948. Recipient Red Cross Hall of Fame, Indpls., 1963; grantee U.S. Dept. of Energy, 1984; recipient Nat. Energy Resources Tech. Innovation award, 1989, Disting. Leadership award Am. Biog. Inst. 1990, cert. of merit Internat. Biog. Ctr., 1990 Mem. Soc. of Am. Inventors (bd. dirs., Pres. award 1989), Am. Radio Relay League, Author's Guild, Author's League of Am. Republican. Avocations: traveling, camping, hiking, photography. Office: PO Box 25053 Colorado Springs CO 80936-5053

HICKS, DOLORES KATHLEEN (DE DE HICKS), foundation director; b. Mount Vernon, Iowa, Sept. 22, 1932; d. Edward M. and Olga Marie (Hekl) Staskal; m. Roswell Allen Hicks, Sept. 5, 1952; children: Thomas, Gregory, Bryan, Kevin. Student, Colo. Coll., 1950-52. Exec. women's wardrobe cons. Bullock's, Torrance, Calif., 1985-86; exec. dir. The Vol. Ctr., Torrance, 1986—. Pres. Vol. Ctrs. So. Calif., 1988; coord. First Lady of Calif. Outstanding Vol. Awards, Sacramento, 1993; nat. bd. dirs. Vol. Ctrs.-Points of Light Found., Washington, 1993-96. Pres. LWV, Palos Verdes Peninsula, Calif., 1981-83; chair Year of the Coast, Calif. LWV, Sacramento, 1984; active in state and local polit. campaigns. Named Woman of the Yr., YWCA, Torrance, 1986, Woman of Distinction, Soroptimist, Torrance, 1988, South Bay Woman of the Yr., Switzer Ctr., 2002; recipient Others award Salvation Army, 2003. Mem.: Vol. Ctrs. Calif. (bd. dirs. 1988—, Founders award 1991), So. Bay Prodrs. Guild (Outstanding Interviewer 1995), Pvt. Industry Coun. (bd. dirs. 1994—97), Cmty. Assn. Penisnula (life, pres. 1984—87, Palos Verdes Peninsula Citizen of Yr. 1987, Outstanding Vol. award 1988), Gamma Phi Beta (alumni mem., Internat. Carnation award 1992, Achievement award 1993). Democrat. Roman Catholic. Avocations: gourmet cooking, home decorating, entertaining, reading, traveling.

HICKS, DOUGLAS A. religious studies educator, minister; s. Harry Earl and Susan V. Hicks. AB in Econs. magna cum laude, Davidson Coll., 1990; MDiv summa cum laude, Duke U., 1993; MA in Study of Religion, Harvard U., 1995, PhD in Study of Religion, 1998. Ordained min. of word and sacrament Presbyn. Ch., 1995. Parish assoc. Clarendon Hill Presbyn. Ch., Somerville, Mass., 1995—98, Bon Air Presbyn. Ch., Richmond, Va., 1998—; asst. prof., leadership studies and religion U. of Richmond, Richmond, Va., 1998—. Trustee Duke U., Durham, NC, 1993—96; core seminar Pulpit & Pew: Rsch. on Pastoral Leadership, Durham, 1999—; nat. program adv. bd. Coun. for Am.'s 1st Freedom, Richmond, Va., 2002—; vis. asst. prof. religion and society Harvard U. Divinity Sch., Cambridge, 2003. Author: (book) Inequality and Christian Ethics, 2000, Religion and the Workplace, 2003. Recipient Mellon Dissertation fellowship, Mellon Found. and Harvard U., 1997—98, Summer Rsch. stipend, NEH, 2001. Mem.: Acad. of Religious Leadership, Internat. Leadership Assn., Soc. of Christian Ethics (coord. ethics and polit. economy interest group 2001—), Am. Acad. of Religion (mem. religion and social scis. steering com. 1999—). Presbyterian. Avocations: travel, reading, tennis. Office: U Richmond Jepson Sch Leadership Studies Richmond VA 23173 Office Fax: 804-287-6062.

HICKS, EVA FERN, retired music educator; b. Springer, N.Mex., Sept. 12, 1929; d. Marion Robert and Leila Fern Nimerick; children: Roger, Kenneth, Daniel, Judi. BA in Music Edn., San Jose State U., 1951; MEd, We. State U., Gunnison, Colo., 1980. Cert. tchr. Calif., Fla., Ind. Elem. tchr., Panama City, Fla., 1950—51, 1951—52, various elem. schs., Chowchilla, Calif., 1953—54, Fresno City Schs., Calif., 1959—63, Good News Sch., Fresno, 1971—77; ins. clk. Gunnison Hosp., Colo., 1980—90; payroll clk. St. Joseph Hosp., Orange, Calif., 1990—99. Treas. Aglow Prison Ministry, Orange, Calif., 2003—. Avocation: piano. Home: 755 Highland Ln Anaheim CA 92807

HICKS, GEORGE WILLIAM, mechanical engineer, automotive engineer; b. Ypsilanti, Mich., Jan. 15, 1948; s. Troy Diamond Sr. and Clara (Sehl) H.; m. Carol Ann Kohorst, Aug. 5, 1967; children: Lorelei Lynn, Dawn Marie, Heather Nicole. BSME, U. Mich., 1977. Registered prof. engr., Mich., Ohio, Pa., cert. traffic accident reconstructionist, ACTAR, safety instr., OSHA; diplomate Am. Bd. Forensic Engring. and Tech. Test and devel. engr. Chrysler Corp., Chelsea, Mich., 1976-81; sr. engr. Alexander Proudfoot Co., Chgo., 1981; mech. engr. Polytechnic, Lincolnwood, Ill., 1981-82; mgr. tech. svcs. Shackson Assocs., Ann Arbor, Mich., 1982-84; forensic engr. Joscelyn & Treat, Ann Arbor, 1984-86; staff cons. Packer Engring., Troy, Mich., 1986-90; owner, prin. cons. Ingenium Engring. Svcs., Petersburg, Mich., 1990—. Cons. Backplane Tech., Clinton, 1984-86, Shackson Assocs., Ann Arbor, 1984-86; spkr. ADED Midwest Conf., Cleve., 1992. Author: Anatomy of an Instrumented Generic Quadriplegic Evaluation Van, 1993, Safety Standards and the Rehabilitation Vehicle, 1991; editor: Roll Over Protective Structures Manual, 1989, Safety Belt Components manual (Internal Distribution), 1992-94. Mem. ASME, NSPE, Nat. Mobility Equipment Dealers Assn., Engring. Soc. Detroit, Assn. Driver Educators for the Disabled, Mich. Assn. Traffic Accident Investigators, Soc. Automotive Engrs., Nat. Fire Prevention Assn., Am. Welding Soc., Internat. Assn. Arson Investigators. Office: 4345 Teal Rd Petersburg MI 49270-9304 E-mail: gwhicks@umich.edu.

HICKS, GREGORY STEVEN, marketing professional; b. Ft. Wayne, Ind., Dec. 24, 1959; s. Earl Hoyt and Sarah Helen (Bobo) H.; m. Nita Dawn Noblitt, Nov. 9, 1985. BS in Fin., Ind. U., 1983; MBA, U. Indpls., 1995. Asst. v.p. Fidelity Fed. Savs. and Loan, Seymour, Ind., 1983; fin. dir. Devel. Svcs., Columbus, Ind., 1983-85; account coord. Devel. Services, Columbus, Ind., 1985-86; exec. dir. Jennings County Econ. Devel., North Vernon, Ind., 1986-88; dir. Columbus (Ind.) Econ. Devel. Bd., 1989-91; mgr. nat. devel. PSI Energy, Plainfield, Ind., 1992-95, acct. mgr. comml. and indsl. sales, 1995-97; strategic mktg. rep. Cinergy Power Mktg. and Trading, Cin., 1997-98, mgr. retail aggregation, 1998; v.p. mktg. and bus. devel. Gaylor, 1998-99; v.p. bus. devel. Home Fed. Savs. Bank, Columbus, Ind., 1999—2003; dep. exec. dir. Ind. Dept. Commerce, 2003—. Active Assn. for Retarded Citizens, North Vernon, 1983-86, Jennings County Econ. Devel., 1985-88; head coach Hayden Elem. Girls and Boys Basketball, North Vernon, 1984-86; sec. bd. dirs. Jennings Community Hosp. Found., 1987-88; bd. dirs. Columbus Found. for Youth, 2000—; mem. fin. com. St. Marys Ch., N. Vernon, Ind., 1997—; mem. Columbus Econ. Devel. Bd., 1999—. Mem. South Cen. Savs. and Loan League (v.p. 1983), Columbus Area C. of C. (bd. dirs. 2001—), Rotary (treas. 2000-01), Kiwanis (treas. local chpt. 1985-86, pres. 1987 88, lt. gov. 1991-92), Kappa Delta Rho (bd. dirs. 1984-92). Home: 565 Persimmon Dr North Vernon IN 47265-6730 Office: 501 Washington St Columbus IN 47201-6229

HICKS, HAROLD EUGENE, chemical engineer; b. Mpls., Jan. 20, 1919; s. Julius and Della (Beebe) H.; m. Ruth Esther Nelson, Oct. 4, 1941 (dec. Mar. 1989); children: Barbara H. Young, Charlotte H. Silvia, David H., Douglas E.; m. Virginia C. Hobson, Mar. 31, 1990. B Chem. Engring., U. Minn., 1941; postgrad., U. Del., 1946-47. Chemist Hercules Powder Co., Wilmington, Del., 1941, rsch. chemist, 1941, 46-50, prodn. supr. Hattiesburg, Miss., 1950-64, plant mgr. Chicopee, Mass., 1964-66, Hercules Inc., Franklin, Va., 1966-68, Brunswick, Ga., 1968-76, Louisiana, Mo., 1978-80; tech. advisor Dawood-Hercules, Lahore, Pakistan, 1976-78; vol. exec. Internat. Exec. Svc. Corp., 1986-94; pres. The Book Shop, Inc., Brunswick, 1991—. Bd. dirs. Downtown Devel. Authority, Brunswick. Mem. county cos. Glynn County; dir. St. Mark's Towers, Glynn-Brunswick Navy League of the U.S., Pine Belt Savings & Loan Assn, Hattiesburg, Miss., 1958-64, dir., 1st Nat. Bank of Brunswick, Ga., 1969-76. Maj. U.S. Army, 1941-46, ETO. Mem. AIChE (emeritus), Am. Chem. Soc. (emeritus), Rotary. Methodist. Avocations: computers, photography, travel, reading, gardening. Home: 262 Sutherland Bluff Dr Townsend GA 31331-9239

HICKS, IRLE RAYMOND, retail food chain executive; b. Welch, W.Va., Dec. 21, 1928; s. Irle Raymond and Mary Louise (Day) H. BA, U. Va., 1950. Bus. mgr. Hicks Ford, Covington, Ky., 1952-58; acct. Firestone Plantations Co., Harbel, Liberia, 1958-60; auditor Kroger Co., Cin., 1960-66, gen. auditor, 1966-68, asst. treas., 1968-72, treas., 1972—. Bd. dirs. Old Masons' Home Ky. Served with AUS, 1950-52. Mem. Fin. Execs. Inst., Bankers Club, Alpha Kappa Psi, Phi Kappa Psi. Clubs: Mason, Cincinnati. Episcopalian. Home: 454 Oliver Rd Cincinnati OH 45215-2507 Office: 1014 Vine St Cincinnati OH 45202-1141

HICKS, J. PORTIS, lawyer; b. Detroit, May 16, 1938; s. Livingstone Porter and Mildred (Portis) H.; m. Julie A. Gildersleeve, June 1, 1963 (div. Apr. 1977); children: Darcy A., Tyler P; m. Laura J. Corwin, Oct. 25, 1995. BA in History, U. Mich., 1962, JD, 1964; cert., London Sch. Econs.-Polit. Sci., 1965. Bar: N.Y. 1966, U.S. Dist. Ct. (so. and ea. dists.) N.Y. 1971, U.S. Ct. Appeals (2d cir.) 1972, U.S. Supreme Ct. 1981. Assoc. Kelley Drye & Warren, N.Y.C., 1965-69, Pinheiro Neto, Barros & Freire, Sao Paulo, Brazil, 1969-71; assoc., then ptnr. Wender, Murase & White, N.Y.C., 1971-82; ptnr. Boulanger, Finley & Hicks, N.Y.C., 1982-84, 89-91, Drinker, Biddle, & Reath, N.Y.C., 1984-89, of counsel, 1989-91; ptnr. Boulanger, Hicks, & Churchill, N.Y.C., 1989—96, Winthrop Stimson Putnam & Roberts (now Pillsbury Winthrop), N.Y.C., 1996-2000, sr. counsel, 2000—. Mem.: Assn. Bar City N.Y. Office: Pillsbury Winthrop LLP 54 Lombard St London EC3V 9DH England Home: Borgo Degli Albzi 27 50122 Florence Italy E-mail: phicks@pillsburywinthrop.com.

HICKS, JACK ALAN, library director; b. Ft. Dodge, Iowa, Sept. 14, 1939; s. Thomas D. and Calma J. (Voss) H.; m. Donna Marie Westervelt; children: Maren Lydia, Sarah Marie. BA, Hamline U., 1967; MLS, Rosary Coll., 1972. Librarian Deerfield (Ill.) Pub. Libr., 1972—. V.chmn. Joint Computer Program for Libs., Skokie, Ill., 1988—2001; bd. dir. Ill. Ctr. for the Book. Contbr. articles to profl. publs. Mem. adv. bd. Coll. of Lake County, Highland Park, Ill., 1988-95; fundraiser Girl Scouts U.S., Moraine Coun., 1975—, Historic Pullman Found. Sgt. U.S. Army, 1961-65. Mem. ALA, Ill. Libr. Assn., Ch. and Synagogue Libr. Assn., Deerfield C. of C., Pi Gamma Mu. Episcopalian. Avocations: motorcycles, kayaking. E-mail: jhicks@nslsilus.org.

HICKS, JAMES THOMAS, lawyer, physician; b. Brownsville, Pa. s. Thomas A. and Florence Julia (O'Donnell) H. AB, BS, MS, U. Pitts.; PhD, George Washington U.; MD, U. Ark.; JD, DePaul U.; LLM in Health Law, Loyola U., 1989. Bar: Ill. 1977, Pa. 1977, U.S. Supreme Ct. 1980, N.Y. 1988, D.C. 1988, U.S. Dist. Ct. D.C. 1988, U.S. Ct. Appeals (7th cir.) 1977, U.S. Ct. Appeals (D.C. and Ill. cirs.) 1988; lic. airline transport flight instr.; cert. sports trainer, nutrition, old age and strength devel. Tchr. DePaul U. Coll. Law, Chgo., 1990—; intern USPHS Hosp., Balt.; resident VA Hosp., Pitts.; pvt. practice River Forest, Ill., Oak Brook Terrace, Ill. Contbr. editor Hosp. Mgmt. mag. Asst. surgeon USPHS. Recipient Outstanding Alumnus award De Paul U., 1980. Fellow ACP, Am. Coll. Pathologists, Am. Acad. Forensic Scientists, Am. Soc. Clin. Pathologists, mem. ABA (com. on professionalism and ethics, vice-chmn. health law com. gen. practice sect.), Royal Coll Physicians (Eng.), Assn. Trial Lawyers Am., Pa. Bar Assn., Ill. Bar Assn., Chgo. Bar Assn. (health law com., ethics com.), Ill. Trial Lawyers Assn., D.C. Bar Assn., Pa. Trial Lawyers Assn., N.Y. Bar Assn., N.Y. Acad. Sci., Univ. Club, Carlton Club, Elks, Moose, Oak Park Country Club. Office: Ste 218 17 W 706 Butterfield Rd Oakbrook Terrace IL 60181

HICKS, JERRY, retired systems engineer; b. Bakersfield, Calif., Nov. 28, 1936; s. Fred Henry Hicks and Beverly Louisita Manson; m. Antonia Almeida (div.); children: Kimberly A., Jennifer A., Audrey M.; m. Barbara Weeks (div. 1979). AA, Phoenix Coll., 1962; BS, Ariz. State U., 1972; MS, West Coast U., 1989. Mem. tech. staff Rockwell Autonetics, Anaheim, Calif. Contbr. articles to mags., poetry and fiction to lib. publs.; author: (poems) Even Weeds have Flowers, 1995, Instructions Included, 1996; contbr. columns. Host weekly fiction workshops, 1995—96; host weekly poetry workshops, 1996—2000;

founder South Bay Author's Coalition, 1996—2001; co-host poetry slam Poet's and Writers Mag., Santa Monica, Calif., 1996; co-founder Redondo Poets Collective, 1996—2001; dir. poetry expo. Aloud from the Heart, 1996. With Calif. Nat. Guard, 1955—56, with USAF, 1956—60. Recipient Excellence in Art award for litarary art, Torrance Cultural Arts Commn., 1999. Mem.: West Coast U. Alumni Assn., UCLA Alumni Assn., Ariz. State U. Alumni Assn., Aramco Brats, Pen USA West, Beyond Baroque Found., S.W. Manuscripters. Home: 2614 W 181 St Torrance CA 90504

HICKS, JOHN BERNARD, retired internist; b. Deer Lake, Nfld., Can., Aug. 22, 1933; arrived in U.S., 1960; s. William Francis and Mary Esther (Dalton) Hicks; m. Bernice Elizabeth Algee; children: Ann Elizabeth, Joan Marie, Cathie, John Bernard, Carolyn Andrea. BS, St. Francis Xavier U., Antigonish, N.S., Can., 1953; MD, Dalhousie U., 1958. Intern Dalhousie Affiliated Hosps., 1957-58; gen. practice, 1958-59; resident in pathology Regina (Can.) Hosp., 1959-60; resident in internal medicine Baylor Coll. Medicine Affiliated Hosps., Houston, 1960-62, fellow in renal and hypertensive diseases, 1962-63; pvt. practice Houston, 1964—2001; ret., 2001. Assoc. clin. prof. Baylor Coll. Medicine, Houston, U. Tex. Med. Sch., Houston; attending physician Meth. Hosp., St. Luke's Episcopal Hosp., St. Anthony's Ctr. Mem.: Harris County Med. Soc. (chmn. splty. coun. 1990, exec. com. 1990, med. grievance com. 1993, ethics com. 1994—96), Houston Soc. Internal Medicine (pres. 1988), Tex. Med. Soc., Am. Soc. Internal Medicine. Roman Catholic. Home: 2111 Mcclendon St Houston TX 77030-2109 Office: Med Clinic Houston 1707 Sunset Blvd Houston TX 77005-1713

HICKS, JUDITH EILEEN, nursing administrator; b. Chgo., Jan. 1, 1947; d. John Patrick and Mary Ann (Clifford) Rohan; m. Laurence Joseph Hicks, Nov. 22, 1969; children: Colleen Driscoll, Patrick Kevin. BSN, St. Xavier Coll., Chgo., 1969, U. Ill., 1975. Staff nurse Mercy Hosp., Chgo., 1969-70, nursing supr., 1970-73; cons. continuing edn. Ill. Nurses Assn., Chgo., 1974-75; dir. ob-gyn. nursing Northwestern Meml. Hosp., Chgo., 1975-81; v.p. nursing Children's Meml. Hosp., Chgo., 1981-86; pres. Children's Meml. Home Health, Inc., 1986—2001, Children's Meml. Nursing Svcs., 1986—2001. Pres. Allied & Children's Home Health and Nursing Svcs., 1988, CM Healthcare Resources, Inc., 1988—2001, The Pediat. Pl., Inc., 1994—2001, Focused Health Solutions, Inc., 2000—; dir. Near North Health Corp., Chgo., 1982—85; pres. Pediat. Excellence Program Svc.; bd. dirs. Infant Welfare Soc. Chgo., Nat. Breast Cancer Assn., Children's Meml. Med. Ctr., 1985—. Recipient Jonas Salk Leadership award March of Dimes, 1998, Ernst and Young Outstanding Ill. Nurse Leader award, 1999. Mem. Am. Soc. Nursing Adminstrs., Women's Health Exec. Network (1984-85), Ill. Hosp. Assn. (chmn. coun. on nursing 1982-83), Inst. Medicine. Home: 2206 Beechwood Ave Wilmette IL 60091-1508 Office: CM Health Care Resources Ste 200 1000 Sunset Ridge Rd Northbrook IL 60062-4010

HICKS, M. ELIZABETH (LIZ HICKS), pharmacist; b. Shawnee, Okla., Aug. 16, 1944; d. Joseph Robert and Betty Ruth (Thomas) Coughlin; m. Frank Jack Hicks, July 16, 1965 (dec. 1978); 1 child, Felicia Jeanette. BS, Okla. U., 1967. Lic. pharmacist, cert. menopause educator 2001. Pharmacy intern Liberty Drug, Chickasha, Okla., 1967-68; pharmacist St. Francis Hosp., Wichita, Kans., 1968, Hart Drug, Wichita, 1968-70; pharmacist, dir. Home Drug/PrePrep Med. Div., Wichita, 1970-82; pharmacist, mgr. Revco Drug, Wichita, 1982-87; pharmacist Gessler's Drug, Wichita, 1987—, pharmacist in charge, 1994-95. Author, presentor continuing edn. programs for nursing home adminstrs., dental technicians, nurses, nurses aides, and pharmacists. Author, presenter: Women You'll Wish You Had Known, Parts 1 and 2; host TV show Sexual Assault, Wichita Survivors' Guide; pharmacist presenter The Health Channel. Mem. Commn. on the Status of Women, Wichita Housing Authority, 1989-91; precinct committeewoman Dem. Ctr. Com., Sedgwick County, Kans., 1984—; co-chair Woman Fair, Wichita, 1985; chair Sedgwick County Coun. on Aging, Wichita, 1982-83; mem. Wichita-Sedgwick County Bd. Health, 1992-96, chmn. 1996; pres.-elect Kans. Employee Pharmacists Coun., 1997, pres. 1998; singer Stage One Singers. Recipient Wichita NOW Trophy, 1991. Mem. Wichita Acad. Pharmacists (pres. 1983-84), Kans. Pharmacists Assn. (chair PAC 1986-89), Am. Pharm. Assn., NOW (pres. Wichita Chpt. 1981-82, 2000—, state coord. 1988-90). Avocations: travel, reading mysteries, performing as women from history. Home: 5233 W 1st N Wichita KS 67212-2402 E-mail: catpharm@cisp.ws.

HICKS, MARION LAWRENCE, JR., (LARRY HICKS), lawyer; b. Bethlehem, Pa, Sept. 5, 1945; s. Marion Lawrence and Martha (McCracken) H.; m. Beverly Brickman, Nov. 28, 1970; children: Yale McCracken, Hadley Brook, Kelley Hayden. BA History, Duke U., 1967; JD with honors, U. Tex., 1970. Bar: Tex. 1970. Law clk. 9th cir. US Ct. Appeals, LA, 1970-71; assoc. Thompson, Knight, Simmons & Bullion, Dallas, 1971-77; ptnr. Thompson & Knight, Dallas, 1977—. Dir. The Real Estate Coun.; spkr. in field. Editor Tex. Law Review; contbr. articles to profl. jour. Mem. ABA (real property, trust and probate sect.), Am. Coll. Mortgage Atty. (regent), State Bar Tex., Dallas Bar Assn. (past chmn. real property sect., legal aid and legal svc. com.), Coll. State Bar Tex., Order of Coif, Tower Club (bd. gov.), Phi Delta Phi. Avocations: sports, hunting, fishing. Home: 4310 Throckmorton St Dallas TX 75219-2240 Office: Thompson & Knight LLP 1700 Pacific Ave Ste 3300 Dallas TX 75201-4693 E-mail: larry.hicks@tklaw.com.

HICKS, PATRICK, writer, educator; b. Charlotte, N.C., Apr. 12, 1970; s. James P. and Lynne Hicks; m. Tania Hicks, Jan. 18, 2002. BA, St. John's U.; MA, DePaul U., Queen's U. Belfast; PhD, U. Sussex. Prof. Augustana Coll., U. St. Thomas, U. Sussex. Contbr. articles to mags. Mem.: S.D. Humanities Coun., Am. Conf. Irish Studies. Roman Catholic. Office: Augustana Coll 2001 S Summit Sioux Falls SD 57197

HICKS, PHYLLIS ANN, retired medical, surgical nurse; b. Croghan, N.Y., July 4, 1935; d. Leonard B. and Doris A. (Schack) Bush; m. Patrick Clare, Aug. 1, 1953 (dec. Jan. 1976); m. Charles L. Hicks, May 26, 1979; children: Michael Clare, Maureen (dec.), Martin (dec.); stepchildren: Lynn, Melinda, Kevin. ADN, St. Elizabeth's Hosp., Utica, N.Y., 1988; cert. pharmacology, Bd. Coop. Ednl. Svcs., Verona, N.Y., 1989, phlebotomy cert., 1994; student, Mercy Hosp. Sch. Nursing, Watertown, N.Y., 1952-53. RN, N.Y. Nurse med.-surg. unit Rome (N.Y.) Murphy Meml. Hosp., 1988-90; head nurse geriatrics Stonehedge Nursing Home, Rome, N.Y., 1990; nurse I Mohawk Valley Psychiatric Ctr., Utica, N.Y., 1990-91; charge nurse ventilator unit Oneida (N.Y.) City Hosp., 1993-98; ret., 1998; part-time supr. Sunset Nursing Home, Boonville, NY, ret., 2001. Home: 10276 State Route 26 Ava NY 13303-2213

HICKS, RONALD ALVIN, music educator; b. Cleveland, Tenn., July 22, 1949; BS in Edn., U. Tenn., 1974; MA in Edn., Cumberland U., 2001. Band dir. Sevier County Bd. Edn., Sevierville, Tenn., 1974—. Former cubmaster, asst. scoutmaster Boy Scouts Am.; former referee, chief referee Am. Youth Soccer Orgn.; girls' soccer coach. Recipient Outstanding Tchr. award (2), Tenn. Gov.'s Sch. for the Arts. Mem.: Tenn. Band Assn., Nat. Music Educators Assn., Tenn. Music Educator Assn., East Tenn. Sch. Band and Orch. Assn., Nat. Band Assn., Tenn. Secondary Schs. Band Dirs. Assn. (v.p. to pres.), Pinnacle Nat. Honor Soc.

HICKS, SHERMAN GREGORY, pastor; b. Bklyn., June 22, 1946; s. Charles Sr. and Sarah Mae (Rollins) H.; m. Anna Marie Peck, Sept. 12, 1970 (div.); children: Andrea, Geoffrey, Christopher. BA, Wittenberg U., 1968; MDiv, Hamma Sch. Theology, 1973; DD (hon.), Carthage Coll., 1988, Elmhurst Coll., 1989, Wittenberg U., 1990. Ordained to ministry Luth. Ch., 1973. Pastor Concordia Luth. Ch., Buffalo, 1973-77; co-pastor Holy Trinity Luth. Ch., East Orange, N.J., 1977-79; asst. to bishop Ill. Synod, Luth. Ch. Am., Chgo., 1979-87; bishop Met. Chgo. Synod, Evang. Luth. Ch. in Am., Chgo., 1988-95; sr. pastor First Trinity Luth. Ch., Washington, 1996—2003; mission dir. divsn. outreach Evang. Luth. Ch. Am., 2003—. Pres. of bd. Third World Social Svcs., 1998; bd. dirs. Mission Resource Inst. Pres. Interfaith Coun. for Homeless, Chgo., 1988, AIDS Nat. Interfaith Network, 1991; trustee Carthage Coll., Kenosha, Wis., 1988, Nat. AIDS Fund, 1997; bd. dirs. Luth. Social Svcs. Ill., 1988-95, Bethphage, Omaha; mem. Coun. Religious Leaders, Chgo., 1988-95; bd. dirs. Leadership Coun. for Met. Open Cmty. Named One of Outstanding Young Men in Am., Jaycees, 1974; recipient Alumni Citation, Wittenberg U., 1993. Office: The Luth Ctr 700 Light St Baltimore MD 21230 E-mail: doelca8@aol.com., sgreghicks@aol.com. *In my experiences with life I have discovered that there are three very basic questions that we humans have the need to know answers for: (1) Who am I? (2) For what purpose am I here? (3) What am I going to do? Within the context of our faith we can find the answers.*

HICKS, STEVE L. artist, art educator; b. Fayetteville, Ark. s. Shelby and Lucie H.; m. Cynthia B., March, 1970; children: Jessica, Spencer. BA, U. Ky., 1969; MA, Murray State U., 1972; MFA, U. Ark., 1975. Instr. art La. State U., Eunice, 1978-80; prof. art, chair art divsn. Okla. Bapt. U., Shawnee, 1980—. Adv. conservationist Mabee-Gerver Mus., Shawnee, 1985-95. Mem. Coll. Art Assn. Office: Okla Bapt U Art Divsn #61197 500 University Shawnee OK 74804 E-mail: obuartchair@compuserve.com.

HICKS, THOMAS O. buyout firm executive, professional baseball team executive; b. N.Y.C., 1946; BBA, Univ. of Tex., 1968; MBA, Univ. So. Cali., 1970. Investment officer Morgan Guaranty Trust Co., New York, 1968-74; pres. First Dallas Capital Corp., Dallas, 1974-77; co-mng. ptnr. Summit Ptnrs., Dallas, 1977-83; co-chmn., co-CEO, Hicks & Haas Inc., Dallas, 1983-89; chmn., CEO, Hicks, Muse, Tate & Furst Inc., Dallas, 1989-; chmn., owner Tex. Rangers, Arlington, 1995-; chmn., CEO, Dallas Stars, Dallas, 1996-, AMFM, Inc., Dallas; vice chmn. Clearchannel Comm. Inc., San Antonio, also bd. dirs. Chmn. Chancellor Media Corp., Capstar Broadcasting Corp.; dir. Sybron Intl. Corp., CorpGroup Ltd., Intl. Home Foods., MVS Corp., Olympus Real Estate Corp., Regal Cinemas Inc., Triton Energy Ltd., Viasystems Grp., Home Interiors & Gifts Inc.; bd. of dirs. Crow Family Holdings., adv. bd. Chase Manhattan Corp.; chair., Univ. of Tex. Investment Mgmt. Co. Contributor: United Way, Goodwill, The Dallas Art Museum, The Dallas Symphony Orchestra, The Science Place at Fair Park. Office: Clearchannel Comm Inc Ste 1600 200 Crescent Ct Dallas TX 75201 also: Hicks Muse Tate & Furst 200 Crescent Ct Ste 1600 Dallas TX 75201-1844

HICKS, TYLER GREGORY, publishing company executive, writer; b. N.Y.C., June 21, 1921; s. Ernest Tyler and Mary B. (O'Brien) H.; m. Saretta M. Gratke, Feb. 23, 1946 (dec. Mar. 1974); children: Gregory T., Barbara L., Steven D.; m. Mary T. Shanley, Aug. 29, 1975. B of Mech. Engring., Cooper Union Advancement Sci., 1948. Engr. Merport Realty Co., 1943-46; design engr. Lockwood-Greene Engrs. Inc., 1946-49; editor in chief Profl. and Reference Books div. McGraw-Hill Co., N.Y.C., 1962-85, pres., chmn. bd. dirs. employees fed. credit union, 1970-95, bd. dirs., 1995—. Instr. Cooper Union, N.Y.C.; owner Internat. Engring. Assocs.; pres. Internat. Wealth Success Inc., Rockville Centre, N.Y.; lectr. in field *Tyler Hicks is a publishing executive who has combined several careers into a highly successful business. Starting as a mechanical engineer, he moved into magazine and book publishing for a major U.S. publisher. He writes engineering books, a number of which have become classics in their field. After buying a small business, he quickly learned the many problems faced by small business owners. He then created two business-opportunity newsletters which have been published for more than 35 years. A number of business books also grew out of this small-business experience, one of which has sold more than one million copies.* Author: How To Borrow Your Way to a Great Fortune, 1970, Magic Mind Secrets for Building Riches Fast, 1971, How To Make One Million Dollars in Real Estate in Three Years Starting with No Cash, 2000, Tyler Hicks' Encyclopedia of Wealth-Building Secrets, 1980, How to Borrow Your Way to Real Estate Riches, 1987, Business Capital Sources, 1984, Financial Broker, Finder, Business Broker Complete Success Kit, 1988, Real Estate Riches Success Kit, 1988, Complete Business Borrowers Success Kit, 1988, 101 Ways to 100% Financing of Business and Real Estate, 1997, How to Get Rich on Other People's Money, 1988, Standard Handbook of Engineering Calculations, 1995, Handbook of Mechanical Engineering Calculations, 1998; co-author: Handbook of Electric Power Calculations, 1984, Handbook of Chemical Engineering Calculations, 1984; co-editor: Standard Handbook of Consulting Engineering, 1986, How to Get Rich on Other People's Money, 1988, How to Build A Million Dollar Fortune, 1989, Mail Order Success Secrets, 1990, How to Make Big Money in Real Estate, 2000, 199 Greate Home Businesses You Can Start (and Prosper In), for Under $1,000, 1993, How to Start Your Own Business on a Shoestring and Make Up to $500,000 a Year, 1995, 203 Home-Based Businesses, 1999, Handbook of Civil Engineering Calculations, 2000, Civil Engineering Formulas, 2002. With U.S. Mcht. Marines, 1936-43. Mem. IEEE, ASME, U.S. Naval Inst., Internat. Oceanographic Found. Clubs: Rockville Links Golf, Huntington Yacht. Home: 24 Canterbury Rd Rockville Centre NY 11570-1310 Office: McGraw-Hill 2 Penn Plz Rm 1500 New York NY 10121-1599 E-mail: tyhicks@iwsmoney.com. *The clearest and strongest thought permeating my life is based on my own experience and observation of lives of thousands of people throughout the world. This thought is: Men and women can achieve in life whatever goals they set for themselves if a person combines careful planning and analysis of each objective with mental images of successful achievement. This approach seems to work everywhere— for everyone. Choosing to do what one enjoys also contributes to success because better performance occurs when people like what they're doing. Helping others achieve their goals in life brings great rewards to both the helper and the person assisted.*

HICKS, VIRGINIA HOBSON, bookstore owner, educator; b. Birmingham, Ala., June 15, 1923; d. Earle Pegram and Virginia (Robinson) Calvin; m. John Lewis Hobson, Sept. 9, 1950 (div. 1974); children: John Lewis, Virginia Hobson Watson; m. Harold Eugene Hicks, Mar. 31, 1990. AB, Vanderbilt U., 1948, MS, 1979, PhD; postgrad., Sullins Coll., Memphis State U., Jacksonville U., U. North Fla., George Peabody Coll. Cert. tchr., N.Y. Head gen. cargo Brit. Ministry, N.Y. Ctrl. R.R., N.Y.C., 1944; with United Air Lines, N.Y.C., 1945; tchr. Caldwell Sch., Nashville, 1948-50, Venetia Sch., Jacksonville, Fla., 1950-51, Hutchison Sch., Memphis, 1959-65; owner, operator Lee St. Book and Art Shops, Brunswick, Ga., 1970-74, Golden Isles Book Distbn., Brunswick, 1970-74; tchr. AP English The Webb Sch., Bell Buckle, Tenn., 1974—78; head upper sch., dir. studies K-12, Bartrom Sch. for Girls, Jacksonville, Fla., 1979—82; antiquarian bookseller, 1970—; owner The Book Shop Inc., Brunswick. Bd. dirs. St. Mark's Towers Home for Elderly, Brunswick, 1981—. Recipient Charles S. Haslam award for excellence in bookselling, book appraisal and mktg. Mem. Am. Booksellers Assn., Southeastern Booksellers Assn. (bd. dirs.), Ga. Antiquarian Booksellers Assn., Jr. League Savannah (Sustainer of Yr. 1998). Home: 262 Sutherland Bluff Dr Townsend GA 31331-9239 Office: The Book Shop Inc (Books on the Bluff) Townsend GA 31331-9239 E-mail: bookshop@darientel.net.

HICKS, WALTER JOSEPH, electrical engineer; b. Lawrence, Mass., Mar. 10, 1935; s. Walter Francis and Ethel Mary (Royds) H.; m. Faith Winifred McCrum, Apr. 4, 1959; children: Janet Lee, Walter David, Pamela Jean. BSEE, MSEE, MIT, 1957; PhD in Plasma Physics, N.Mex. State U., 1969. Elec. engr. Raytheon Co., Bedford, Mass., 1957-67, radar system engr., dept. mgr., 1970-74, tech. advisor, 1974-84, cons. engr. Bedford, 1984-98; CEO, Paradox Scientific of Acton, Mass., 1998—. Mem. sci. adv. bd. USAF, Washington, 1983. Patentee in field. Elder United Presbyn. Ch., Newton, Mass., 1978-82. Home: 7 Pinewood Rd Acton MA 01720-4409 E-mail: whicks@paradoxscientific.com.

HICKS, WENDELL LEON, history educator, publisher, political scientist; b. Pitts., July 2, 1946; s. John Verris and Juanita H.; m. Patricia Ann Du Hart, Jan. 15, 1976 (div. Jan. 1980); children: Wendell Leon Jr., Gregory Moore. BA, Fayetteville State U., 1971; MA, N.C. Ctrl. U., 1973. Grad. asst. N.C. Ctrl. U., Durham, 1972; instr. St. Augustine's Coll., Raleigh, NC, 1973—74; grad. asst. U. Toledo, 1974-78; prof. history Bowling Green (Ohio) State U., 1978; pub. Azaka Publs., Pitts., 1983—. Author: The Bloody Flux: The World's No. 1 Killing Disease for the Past Six Centures, 1982, The Ku Klux Klan: A Psychoanalytical and Medical Perspective, 1992, A 2001 Historical Update on Black Holes: The Most Contructive and Destructive Objects in the Universe, 2001. Co-chmn. Operation PUSH, Pitts., 1983; active NAACP, Pitts., Vet. Club, Fayetteville, N.C. With USN, 1965-71. Mem.: AAUP, Phi Alpha Theta (v.p. 1976—77, pres. 1977—78), Pi Gamma Mu. Democrat. Methodist. Avocations: football, track and field, swimming, weightlifting, boxing. Home and Office: Azaka Publs 711 Ledlie St Pittsburgh PA 15219-3631

HICKS, WILLIAM ALBERT, III, lawyer; b. Welland, Ont., Can., Apr. 6, 1942; s. William Albert and June Gwendolyn (Birrell) H.; m. Bethany G. Galvin, May 21, 1982; children: James Christopher, Scott Kelly, Alexandra Elizabeth, Samantha Katherine. AB, Princeton U., 1964; LLB, Cornell U., 1967. Bar: N.Y. 1967, Ariz. 1972, U.S. Dist. Ct. Ariz. 1972. Assoc. Seward & Kissel, N.Y.C., 1967-68, Snell & Wilmer LLP, Phoenix, 1972-75, ptnr., 1976—. Instr. Ariz. State U., 1974-75. Mem. U.S. Olympic Fencing Squad, 1964; mem. bd. advisors Casino USA, Inc., 1981-84; bd. dirs. Scottsdale Arts Ctr. Assn., 1984-88, v.p. devel,. 1985-87; bd. dirs. Valley Leadership, Inc., 1987-91, sec., 1988-89, sec.-treas., 1989-90; bd. dirs. Scottsdale Cultural Coun., 1988-97, vice chmn., 1992-95, chmn., 1995-96; active The Luke's Men, 1992—, bd. dirs., 1993-97, 99-2002, sec., 1993-94, v.p. 1995-96, pres., 1996-97; mem. adv. bd. Scottsdale Arts Ctr., 1988-91, chmn., 1988-90; bd. dirs., vice chmn. Ariz. Coun. on Econ. Edn., 1999-2000, chmn., 2000—. Capt. JAG Corps, USAF, 1968-72. Decorated DSM. Mem. ABA, Ariz. State Bar Assn., N.Y. State Bar Assn., Nat. Assn. Bond Lawyers (vice chmn. com. on fin. health care facilities 1982-83, chmn. com. on fin. health care facilities 1983-86, securities law and disclosure com. 1994—), Assn. for Govtl. Leasing and Fin., Princeton U. Alumni Assn. Ariz. (pres. 1978-81, sec. 1981—), Paradise Valley (Ariz.) Country Club, Princeton Club N.Y. Office: Snell & Wilmer LLP One Arizona Ctr Phoenix AZ 85004-2202 E-mail: whicks@swlaw.com.

HICKS, WILLIAM HAMPTON, pianist, conductor, voice coach; b. Lexington, Ky., Nov. 30, 1956; s. Billy and Betty (Clark) H. Student, U. Cin. Asst. condr. opera cos. including The Cin. Opera, The Omaha Opera, N.Y.C. Opera, The Friends of French Opera, The Met. Opera, Santa Fe Opera, Can. Opera., 1975-91; free-lance voice coach N.Y.C., 1977—; assoc. condr. to John McGlinn, N.Y.C., 1983—2002; assoc. condr., pianist Am. Mus. Theatre Series Library of Congress, Washington, 1984-88; condr. Opera Uptown, N.Y.C., 1984; assoc. condr. New Amsterdam Theatre Co., N.Y.C., 1984-86, Jerome Kern Festival, Carnegie Hall, N.Y.C., 1985; assoc. dir. Natchez Opera Festival, 1991; asst. condr. The Met. Opera, N.Y.C., 1995-2001, asst. chorus master, 1999-2001; assoc. condr., voice coach The Packard Humanities Inst., London, 2001—02; pianist, voice coach Bel Canto Soc., 2001—; condr. Packard Humanities Inst/ London Sinfonietta project, 2002—; musical dir. Nickel City Opera, 2001—. Performed with Roberta Peters, The White House, 1991; voice coach to Luciano Pavarotti, Teresa Stratas, Thomas Hampson, Marcello Giordani, Harolyn Blackwell, Angelina Reaux, Judy Kaye, Israel Vocal Arts Inst., Juilliard Opera Ctr., The Richard Tucker Found.; appeared in master classes with Regina Resnik, Renata Scotto, Carlo Bergonzi and Anna Moffo; music dir. The Singers Devel. Found., 1994—; ofcl. pianist The George London Found., 1998—, The Licia Albanese/Puccini Found., 1989—, Opera Index, 1993—; creative dir. OperaMCY, 1999-2001; cons. mcy.com, 1999-2001. Stage debut in Giordano's Fedora, Met. Opera, 1996; pianist various recordings including The Films of Léonide Massine, 1979-81, Songs of New York, 1984, Kiri Sings Gershwin, 1987, Gershwin Overtures, 1987, Blackwell Sings Bernstein: A Simple Song, 1996, Harolyn Blackwell: All Through the Night, 2001; condr. opera Monteverdi's Il Ritorno d'Ulisse in Patria, 1988-89; soloist PBS telecast Evening at the Pops, 1990; appeared with Luciano Pavarotti on The David Letterman Show, 1993; appeared in recitals with Roberta Peters, Jerry Hadley, Ruth Ann Swenson, Rockwell Blake and Jacques Thibaud String Trio, 1996-2002; pianist, actor Schubert's Winterreise and Mussorgsky's Nursery, Songs and Dances of Death, Pictures at an Exhibition, 2001—, Amherst Coll. staged song cycles project, 2001—. Mem. Am. Lyric Theater Assn., Inc. (co-founder, 1st v.p. 1999-2001), Omega Investment Club (founder, presiding ptnr. 1996-2002).

HICKSON, ERNEST CHARLES, financial executive; b. L.A., July 14, 1931; s. Russell Arthur and Marilyn Louise (Mambert) H.; m. Janice Beleal, Sept. 5, 1959; children: Arthur, Jennifer, Barton. BS, U. So. Calif., 1961; postgrad., UCLA Grad. Sch. of Bus. Admin., 1961-63. Lic. real estate broker Calif., 1956. Credit supr. ARCO (Richfield Oil), L.A., 1955-60; asst. v.p. Union Bank L.A., 1960-64; v.p. County Nat. Bank (now Wells Fargo), Orange, Calif., 1964-67; v.p., sr. loan ofcr. City Bank, Honolulu, 1967-70; pres., CEO Shelter Corp., NYSE, 1968-72; exec. v.p., dir. U.S. Fin., Inc. NYSE, San Diego, 1970-73, pres., CEO USF Investors, 1971-73; exec. v.p. Sonnenblick Goldman, L.A., 1973-76; pres., CEO First Hawaiian Devel., Honolulu, 1976-82; sr. ptnr. TMH Resources and affiliates, Laguna Niguel, Calif., 1982—. Expert witness in fin. Author: (novel) The Developers, 1978; editor: (monthly newsletter) Financial Marketing, 1978-83. Staff sgt. USAF, 1951—54. Recipient Exec. award Grad. Sch. of Credit and Fin. Mgmt., Stanford U., 1964, Assocs. award The Nat. Inst. of Credit, UCLA, 1959. Mem. U. So. Calif. Assocs., U. So. Calif. Pres.'s Circle, Urban Land Inst., Town Hall, Salt Creek Club (charter), Pacific Club (Honolulu), Outrigger Canoe Club (Honolulu), Phi Gamma Delta. Avocations: tennis, walking, writing. Fax: 948-495-9458. E-mail: ernesth541@aol.com.

HICKSON, MARCUS LAFAYETTE, III, communication educator, consultant; b. Macon, Ga., Aug. 10, 1945; s. Marcus Lafayette Jr. and Edna Lucille (Cribb) H.; m. Joyce Horton, Sept. 1, 1968 (div.); m. Nancy Dorman, Dec. 13, 1986. BS, Auburn U., 1966, MA, 1968, Miss. State U., 1981; PhD, So. Ill. U., 1971; JD, Birmingham Sch. Law, 1993. Asst. prof. Miss. State U., Starkville, 1970-71, prof., chmn., 1974-87; prof. comm., chmn. dept. U. Ala., Birmingham, 1987—. Co-author: The Southern Redneck, 1982, NVC: Nonverbal Communication, 1989, Introduction to Communication Theory, 1991, Effective Communication for Academic Chairs, 1993, Organizational Communication in the Personal Context, 1998, Going Public, 2002. With U.S. Army, 1971-74. Home: 1004 Oak Tree Rd Birmingham AL 35244-2604 Office: U Alabama 1612 10th Ave S Birmingham AL 35205-3514

HICKSON, ROBIN JULIAN, mining company executive; b. Irby, Eng., Feb. 27, 1944; s. William Kellett and Doris Matilda (Martin) H.; m. P. Anne Winn, Mar. 28, 1964; children: Richard, Sharon, Nicholas, Steven. BS in Mining Engring. with honors, U. London, 1965; MBA, Tulane U., 1990. Chartered engr., U.K. and Europe. Mining engr. N.J. Zinc Co., Austinville, 1965-70, divisional mgr. Jefferson City, Tenn., 1970-71; spl. project engr. Kerr McGee Corp., Grants, N.Mex., 1971-72; gen. mgr. Asarco, Inc., Vanadium, N.Mex., 1972-78, Gold Fields Mining Corp., Ortiz, N.Mex., 1978-83, Mesquite, Calif., 1982-86; v.p. Freeport Mining Co., New Orleans, 1986-91, Freeport Indonesia Inc., Irian Jaya, 1991-92; pres. Freeport Rsch. and Engring. Co., New Orleans, 1992-93; sr. v.p. Cyprus Climax Metals Co., Tempe, Ariz., 1993-94; pres. Cyprus Amax Engring. and Project Devel. Co., Tempe, 1994-99; exec. officer Cyprus Amax Minerals Co., 1994-99; sr. v.p. engring. and project mgmt. Kvaerner Metals, San Ramon, Calif., 2000—02; pres., COO Gabriel Resources Ltd., Toronto, Canada, 2002—. Bd. dirs. Gabriel Resources Ltd., Rosia Mont. Gold Corp., S.A., Romania. Author (with others): Interfacing Technologies in Solution Mining, 1981, Mineral Processing: Plant Design, Control and Practice, 2002. Recipient Robert Earll McConnell award AIME, 1999. Mem. Instn. Mining and Metallurgy, Am. Inst. Mining and Metallurgy, Mining and Metall. Soc., N.Mex. Mining Assn. (bd. dirs. Santa Fe, N.Mex. chpt. 1975-83), Calif. Mining Assn. (bd. dirs. Sacramento chpt. 1982-86), Beta Gamma Sigma. Episcopalian. Avocations: ornithology, travel. Home: 12246 S Honah Lee Ct Phoenix AZ 85044-3455 Office: 110 Yonge St Ste 1501 Toronto ON Canada M5C 1T4 E-mail: annerobin@worldnet.att.net., rjh@gabrielresources.com.

HIDALGO, HENRY, aerospace engineer, consultant; arrived in U.S., 1944; s. Angel Rafael Hidalgo and Floriza Naranjo; m. Lotte R. Schlumpberger; children: Henry T., John, David A., James M. BS in Mech. Engring., Tri-State U., 1949; MS in Mech. Engring., MIT, 1951. Advanced jet engine devel. United Aircraft Rsch. Dept., East Hartford, Conn., 1951—55; rschr. reentry physics AVCO Lab., Everett, Mass., 1956—62; co-founder Heliodyne Corp., L.A., 1963—64; cons. to sec. of def. Inst. Def. Analysis, Arlington, Va., 1964—80; anti-submarine weapon devel. Gould Inc., Arlington, 1981—84; anti-missile interceptor devel. Rockwell Internat. Corp., Arlington, 1984—90; Israeli arrow missile devel. Ares Corp., Arlington, 1991—96; interceptor devel. SPARTA, Arlington, 1996—. Contbr. articles to profl. jours. Sgt. U.S. Army, 1945—47, Germany. Fellow: AIAA (mem. com.). Roman Cath. Office: SPARTA 1911 Fort Myer Drive Stes 1100 3a Arlington VA 22209 E-mail: henry.hidalgo-contractor@mda.osd.mil.

HIDALGO, ISMAEL J. pharmaceutical scientist; s. Deciderio and Rafaela Hidalgo; m. Margarita Gantes, Aug. 23, 1979; children: Carlos A., Daniel A. BS in Pharmacy, U. Panama, Panama City, 1978; PhD, U. So. Calif., L.A., 1986. Lab. asst. U. Panama, 1978—80; postdoctoral fellow U. Kans., Lawrence, 1986—88, asst. rsch. scientist, 1989—90; rsch. investigator SmithKline Beecham, King of Prussia, Pa., 1990—91, sr. rsch. investigator, 1991—92; rsch. fellow Rhone-Poulenc Rorer, Collegeville, Pa., 1993—95, sr. rsch. fellow, 1995—97; co-founder, chief sci. officer Absorption Systems, Exton, Pa., 1997—. Named Entrepreneur of the Yr. in the Life Scis. for the Phila. area,

Ernst & Young, 2002; fellow, UpJohn Co., 1986—88; scholar, OAS, 1980—82. Mem.: AAAS (assoc.), Am. Assn. Pharm. Scientists (assoc.), Am. Chem. Soc. (assoc.). Roman Catholic. Achievements include patents for device to measure electrical resistance of cell monolayers in side-by-side diffusion apparatus; first to characterizing a cell culture model (Caco-2) of small intestinal permeability. Avocations: golf, travel, music, reading. Office: Absorption Systems LP Ste 300 440 Creamery Way Exton PA 19341 E-mail: hidalgo@absorption.com.

HIDALGO, MIGUEL, transportation company executive; b. Detroit, Nov. 10, 1958; s. Manuel and Ann (Molina) H.; m. Rausdha Nelly Cachoa, Nov. 14, 1992; children: Jesahel, Monica Natasha, Samuel. BA in Communications, Pepperdine U., 1981; MS in Aero. Mgmt., Nat. U., 1992, MBA in Internat. Bus. and Mktg., 2003. Owner Pacific Trans Service, L.A., 1981-83, Disneyland, Anaheim, Calif., 1984; legal adminstr. Hidalgo & Assocs., L.A., 1985-90; ops. and customs Aero Calif. Airlines, San Diego, 1990-91; pres. AeroCargo, San Diego, 1992-96; owner AeroCargo, Inc., Baja AirWest Express, Nelly's Pilot/Aircraft Supply, Brown Field Rental Car Svc., Nelly's Airport Sta.; with U.S. Airways, 1997-99; CEO, pres. Voyager, 2000—. Author: Baja Nelly's Flightguide to Mexico, 1994; contbr. articles to profl. jours. With USN, mem. Res., ret., 1985-91. Mem. Pepperdine Assocs., San Marino Alumni Assn., Huntington Libr. Republican. Roman Catholic.

HIDDING, GEZINUS JACOB, management information systems educator; b. Vlagtwedde, The Netherlands, Apr. 11, 1958; came to U.S., 1982; s. Pieter J. H. and Martje (Veldhuis) H.; m. Antje Kuiper, June 5, 1987. BS in Econometrics, U. Groningen, The Netherlands, 1979, MS in Econometrics/DSS, 1982; MS in Info. Systems, GSIA/Carnegie Mellon U., 1985, PhD in Info. Systems, 1992. Staff Andersen Consulting, Chgo., 1986-87; cons. Andersen Informatique, Paris, 1987-88; various positions Andersen Consulting, Chgo., 1988-94, sr. methodologist, 1994-96; vis. asst. prof. Loyola U., Chgo., 1996-97, asst. prof., 1997-2001, assoc. prof., 2001—. Mem. adv. bd. Eolas Devel. Corp., 1998—2001, Rocketcheck.com, 2000—, Tekchand, 2001—, CentraCom Inc., 2002—; lectr. in U.S., Europe and Japan; chmn. bd. dirs. Verhuur.nl, an Easy2Find B.V. Co. Contbr. articles to profl. jours. and chpts. to book. Mem. Assn. Computing Machinery, Dutch Assn. Informatics, Inst. Ops. Rsch. and Mgmt. Scis. Avocations: playing and listening to music, languages: dutch, french, german. Home: 1237 W Victoria St Chicago IL 60660-3448 Office: Loyola Univ Chgo 25 E Pearson St Chicago IL 60611-2001 E-mail: ghidding@aol.com.

HIDDLESTON, RONAL EUGENE, mining executive; b. Bristow, Okla., Mar. 21, 1939; s. C. L. and Iona D. (Martin) Hiddleston; m. Marvelene L. Hammond, Apr. 26, 1959; children: Michael Scott, Mark Shawn, Matthew Shane. Student, Idaho State U., 1957-58. With Roper's Clothing and Bishop Redi-Mix, Rupert, Idaho, 1960-61; pres., chmn. bd., gen. mgr. Hiddleston Drilling, Rupert, 1961-66, Mountain Home, Idaho, 1966—. Mem. adv. bd. Mountain Home Airport, 1968—; hon. mem. Idaho Search and Rescue. Mem.: Ground Water Inst. (bd. dirs.), Nat. Fedn. Ind. Businessmen, N.W. Mining Assn., Pacific N.W. Water Well Assn., Idaho Ground Water Assn. (hon.; past pres.), Nat. Ground Water Assn. (hon.; past. pres., Oliver award), Nat. Sporting Clays Assn., Aircraft Owners and Pilots Assn., Ducks Unltd., Nat. 210 Owners Club, El Korzh Shrine, Scottish Rites, Royal Arch, Masons. Home: 1730 E 8th N Mountain Home ID 83647-1726 Office: RR 3 Box 610D Mountain Home ID 83647-9206

HIDEN, ROBERT BATTAILE, JR., lawyer; b. Boston, May 8, 1933; s. Robert Battaile Sr. and Clotilda (Waddell) H.; m. Ann Eliza McCracken, Mar. 27, 1956; children: Robert B. III, Elizabeth Patterson, John Hughes. BA, Princeton U., 1955; LLB, U. Va., 1960. Bar: N.Y. 1961, U.S. Ct. Appeals (2d cir.) 1974, U.S. Dist. Ct. (so. dist.) N.Y. 1975. Assoc. Sullivan & Cromwell, N.Y.C., 1960—67, ptnr., 1968—98, of counsel, 1999—2000, sr. counsel, 2001—. Articles editor and contbr. U. Va. Law Rev., 1959-60; contbr., mem. bd. editors Futures Internat. Law Letter, 1987-92. Trustee Hampton (Va.) U. and Hampton Inst., 1984—2003; mem. Dillard scholarship com. U. Va. Law Sch., 1984—98, 2001—02; gov. Ramapo (N.J.) Coll. Found., 2002—; commr. Larchmont (N.Y.) Little League, 1964—68; chmn. Larchmont Jr. Sailing Program, 1977—78; vestry, jr. warden St. John's Episc. Ch., Larchmont, 1982—86, 1999—2002. Served to lt. (j.g.) USNR, 1955—57. Mem. ABA, N.Y. State Bar Assn., Assn. of Bar of City of N.Y., N.Y. County Bar Assn., Am. Judicature Soc., Larchmont U. Club (pres. 1976-77), Larchmont Yacht Club (trustee 1979-85, sec. 1990—), Yale Club (N.Y.C.), Coral Beach Club (Bermuda), Raven Soc., Order of Coif, Omicron Delta Kappa. Democrat. Avocations: skiing, golf, sailing, tennis. Home: 2 Walnut Ave Larchmont NY 10538-4232 Office: Sullivan & Cromwell 125 Broad St Fl 28 New York NY 10004-2489

HIDY, GEORGE MARTEL, chemical engineer, executive; b. Kingman, Ariz., Jan. 5, 1935; s. John William and Margaret (Coqueron) H.; m. Dana Sexton Thomas, Oct. 15, 1958; children— Anne, Adrienne, John; m. 2d, Doris A. Wilson, Sept. 28, 1990. AB, Columbia U., N.Y.C., 1956, BS, 1957; MSE., Princeton U., N.J., 1958; D.Eng., Johns Hopkins U., Balt., 1962. Asst. dir. chemistry and microphysics Nat. Ctr. Atmospheric Rsch., Boulder, Colo., 1967-69; group leader chem. physics Rockwell Internat. Sci. Ctr., Thousand Oaks, Calif., 1969-73, assoc. dir., 1973-74; gen. mgr. Environ. Rsch. & Tech., West Lake, Calif., 1974-76, v.p., 1976-84; pres. Desert Rsch. Inst., Reno, 1984-87; v.p. Electric Power Rsch. Inst., Palo Alto, Calif., 1987-94; assoc. dir. coll. engring. Ctr. Environ. Rsch. and Technol. U. Calif., Riverside, 1994-96; prin. Aerochem Assocs., Riverside, 1995—; Ala. Indsl. prof. environ. engring. U. Ala., Birmingham, 1996-99; prin. Envair Aerochem, 1999—; interim dir. N.Mex. State U. Carlsbad Ctr. for Environ. Monitoring/Rsch., 2001—02. Commr., Calif. Youth Soccer Assn., Los Angeles, 1982-84; bd. dirs. El Pueblo Health Ctr., 2003—. Fellow AAAS, Air and Waste Mgmt. Assn.; mem. AIChE, Am. Meteorol. Soc., Am. Chem. Soc., Am. Geophys. Union. Home: 6 Evergreen Dr Placitas NM 87043-8903 E-mail: dahidy@aol.com.

HIEATT, ALLEN KENT, language professional, educator; b. Indpls., Jan. 21, 1921; emigrated to Can., 1968, returned to U.S., 1986. s. Allen Andrew and Violet Rose (Kent) H.; m. Constance Bartlett, Oct. 25, 1958; children by previous marriage: Alice Allen, Katherine Marsh. AB, U. Louisville, 1943; PhD, Columbia U., 1954. Lectr. Columbia U., N.Y.C., 1944-45, instr., 1945-55, asst. prof., 1956-59, assoc. prof., 1960-69; prof. English U. Western Ont., London, 1969-86, emeritus, 1987—; sr. founding editor Spenser Newsletter, London, Ont., 1970-75. *Allen Kent Hieatt has published 56 shorter pieces, of which an article identifying the subject of, and adding other evidence about, one of the three or four most important German Renaissance paintings in North America (Hans Baldung Grien's Ottawa Eve and its Context, Art Bulletin, 65 (1983)), stands with Short Time's Endless Monument as his most important work.* Mem. editorial bd. Duquesne Studies, Pitts., 1976—, Spenser Studies, 1979—; editorial cons. Spenser Ency., 1990; co-editor: College Anthology of British and American Verse, 1964, Poetry in English: An Anthology, 1987; author: Short Time's Endless Monument, 1960, (with C. Hieatt) The Canterbury Tales of Geoffrey Chaucer, 1964, rev. edit., 1981, Spenser: Selected Poetry, 1970, Chaucer, Spenser, Milton, 1975; translator: (with M. Lorch) Lorenzo Valla, On Pleasure, 1977; co-author: (with C. Hieatt) (children's book) The Canterbury Tales of Geoffrey Chaucer, 1961. Cutting fellow, 1946-47; leave grantee Can. Council, Oxford, Eng., 1977-78; research fellow Social Sci. and Humanities Research Council of Can., 1981-82 Fellow Royal Soc. Can.; mem. MLA (chmn. div. English lit. Renaissance 1978-79, William Riley Parker Prize, 1984), Spenser Soc. (pres.), Renaissance Soc. Am. (chmn. north central div. 1973-79) Home: 335 Essex Mdws Essex CT 06426-1526

HIEATT, CONSTANCE BARTLETT, English language educator; b. Boston, Feb. 11, 1928; d. Arthur Charles and Eleonora (Very) Bartlett; m. Allen Kent Hieatt, Oct. 25, 1958. Student, Smith Coll., 1945-47; AB, Hunter Coll., 1953, AM, 1957; PhD, Yale U., 1959. Lectr. City Coll., CUNY, 1959-60; from asst. prof. to assoc. prof. English Queensborough C.C., CUNY, 1960-65; from assoc. prof. to prof. St. John's U., Jamaica, N.Y., 1965-69; prof. English U. Western Ont., London, Can., 1969-93, prof. emeritus, 1993—. Author: (with A.K. Hieatt) The Canterbury Tales of Geoffrey Chaucer, 1964, rev. edit., 1981, Spenser: Selected Poetry, 1970; The Realism of Dream Visions, 1967, Beowulf and Other Old English Poems, 1967, rev. edit., 1983, Essentials of Old English, 1968, The Miller's Tale By Geoffrey Chaucer, 1970; (with Sharon Butler) Pleyn Delit: Medieval Cookery for Modern Cooks, 1976, rev. edit., 1979; (with Brenda Hosington) rev. 2d edit., 1996, Karlamagnus Saga, Vols. I and II, 1975, Vol. III, 1980; (with Sharon Butler) Curye on Inglysch, 1985; An Ordinance of Pottage, 1988; (with Robin F. Jones) La Novele Cirurgerie, 1990; (with Minnette Gaudet) Guillaume de Machaut's Tale of the Alcrion, 1994, (with Brian Shaw and Duncan Macrae-Gibson) Beginning Old English, 1994; (with Rudolf Grewe) Libellus de Arte Coquinaria, 2001; also children books (with Hieatt) The Canterbury Tales of Geoffrey Chaucer, 1961, Sir Gawain and the Green Knight, 1967, The Knight of the Lion, 1968, The Knight of the Cart, 1969, The Joy of the Court, 1971, The Sword and the Grail, 1972, The Castle of Ladies, 1973, The Minstrel Knight, 1974. Yale U. fellow, and Lewis-Farmington fellow, 1957-59, Vis. fellow Yale U., 1985-86, 89-93; Can. Council and Social Sci. and Humanities Rsch. Coun. grant. Fellow Royal Soc. Can.; mem. MLA, Medieval Acad. Am., Internat. Soc. Anglo-Saxonists, Can Soc. Medievalists. Episcopalian. Home: 335 Essex Mdws Essex CT 06426-1526 E-mail: constance.hieatt@yale.edu.

HIEB, MARIO KIRK, broadcast engineer, inventor, writer, consultant; b. Rapid City, SD, Oct. 22, 1958; s. Harry Melvin and Carolyn (Opp) H. BSEE, S.D. Tech., 1982. Registered profl. engr., Utah. Chief engr. Sta. KIMM/KGGG-FM, Rapid City, 1977-84, Sta. KLTQ-FM, Salt Lake City, 1985-87; engr. Centro Corp., Salt Lake City, 1987-88; chief engineer KXRK-FM, Salt Lake City, 1992-98; audio engr. ESPN TV, 1991, 93; v.p., dir. engring. Acme Broadcasting, Inc., 1998—, frequency coord., 2000—02. Mem. Salt Lake Organizing Com. for 2002 Olympic Winter Games; project engr. Post Perfect, N.Y.C., 1987, Gramercy Broadcast Ctr., N.Y.C., 1988; producer, editor, engr. Wasatch Imagination Ctr., Salt Lake City, 1990; chief engr. Sta. KJQ-FM, Salt Lake City, 1991; audio, video, RF engr. Sydney Olympic Broadcast Orgn., 2000. Patentee in field; contbr. Radio World mag. Com. mem. capital campaign KRCL Radio, 1998-99; co-chmn. radio users com., radio sys. frequency mgr. Olympic Winter Games, Salt Lake City, 2002 Mem. Soc. of Broadcast Engrs. (cert. profl. broadcast engineer, chmn. Utah chpt. 1997, 98), Mensa. Avocations: fly fishing, skiing. E-mail: mario@xmission.com.

HIEBEL, WILLIAM RAYMOND, writer, artist, photographer, composer, retired English educator; b. Chgo. s. Joseph James and Catherine Theresa (Walsh) H. AB, Loyola U., Chgo.; MA, PhD, Northwestern U., Evanston, Ill. Tchg. asst. English Northwestern U.; instr. Ill. Inst. Tech., Chgo., Georgetown U., Washington; asst. prof. Ill. Inst. Tech., Chgo., Loyola U., Chgo., prof. emeritus. Author 5 books of poetry, more than 800 poems; illustrator, cover artist. Avocations: bicycle riding, tennis.

HIEBERT, RAY ELDON, educator, author, consultant; b. Freeman, S.D., May 21, 1932; s. Peter Nicholas and Helen (Kunkel) H.; m. Roselyn Lucille Peyser, Jan. 30, 1955 (div. Apr. 1985); children: David, Steven, Emily, Douglas; m. Sheila Jean Gibbons, Dec. 21, 1985 BA, Stanford U., 1954; MS, Columbia U., 1957; MA, U. Md., 1961, PhD, 1962. Faculty Am. U., 1958- 67, prof. journalism, chmn. dept. journalism, 1962-67; dir. Washington Journalism Center, 1965-68; head dept. journalism U. Md., College Park, 1968-72; dean Coll. Journalism, 1973-79, prof., 1980-98, prof., dean emeritus, 1998—. Pres. Comm. Rsch. Assocs., 1979—; dir. Am. Journalism Ctr., Budapest, Hungary, 1991-95; acad. adv. U.S. Voice of Am., 1983 91; vice chmn. Montgomery County (Md.) Cable-TV Commn., 1973-77; mem. St. Mary's County Cable-TV Commn., 2001—. Author: more than 20 books; editor. Fulbright fellow to Africa, 1982; recipient U. Md. Landmark award for Internat. Svc., 2000. Mem. Soc. Profl. Journalists (pres. Md. chpt. 1977-78), Cosmos Club (Washington), Kappa Tau Alpha, Phi Kappa Phi, Omicron Delta Kappa. Home: 38091 Beach Rd Coltons Point MD 20626-0180 Office: 1220 Watergate S 700 New Hampshire Ave NW Washington DC 20037

HIEGEL, JAMES EDWARD, mechanical engineer; Prin. cons. Blue Sky, Ltd., Plano, Tex., 2000—01; curriculum mgr. Keller Grad. Sch. Mgmt., Plano, Tex., 2001—. Mem. Office: Keller Grad Sch Mgmt 2301 Plano Parkway Suite 101 Plano TX 75075

HIEKEN, CHARLES, lawyer; b. Granite City, Ill., Aug. 15, 1928; s. Samuel and Margaret (Isaacs) H.; m. Donna Jane Clanin, Jan. 6, 1961; children: Tina Jane, Seth Paul. SBEE, SMEE, MIT, 1952; LLB, Harvard U., 1957. Bar: Ill. 1957, Mass. 1958, U.S. Supreme Ct. 1960, U.S. Ct. Customs and Patent Appeals 1961, U.S. Ct. Claims 1963, U.S. Ct. Appeals (fed. cir.) 1982. Patent asst. Lab. Electronics, Boston, 1954-56, Fish, Richardson & Neave, Boston, 1956-57; assoc. Hill, Sherman, Meroni, Gross & Simpson, Chgo., 1957, Joseph Weingarten, Boston, 1957-58, Wolf, Greenfield & Hieken, Boston, 1958-61, ptnr., 1961-70; prin. Charles Hieken Law Offices, Waltham, Mass., 1970-87; ptnr. Fish & Richardson, Boston, 1987-94, prin., 1995—. Mem. Pres. Carter's adv. com. on indsl. innovation, 1979. Mem. pres.'s adv. coun. Bentley Coll., 1993—; mem. coun. Harvard Law Sch. Assn., 1998-02. Served with U.S. Merchant Marine, 1944-47, U.S. Army, 1952-54. Mem.: IEEE (sr.; life), Boston Patent Law Assn. (chmn. pub. rels. com. 1965—66, chmn. antitrust law com. 1966—70, 1978—80, treas. 1970—71, v.p. 1971—72, pres.-elect 1972—73, pres. 1973—74), Ill. State Bar Assn. (privileged mem.), Mass. Bar Assn. (chmn. intellectual property com. 1977—80), Boston Bar Assn. (civil procedure com. 1959—), Down Town Club (bd. govs., v.p. gen counsel), Tau Beta Pi, Eta Kappa Nu. Home: 193 Wilshire Dr Sharon MA 02067-1561 Office: Fish & Richardson PC 225 Franklin St 31st Fl Boston MA 02110-2804 E-mail: hieken@fr.com.

HIEMSTRA, MARVIN ROY, poet, humorist, literary consultant; b. Pella, Iowa, July 27, 1939; s. Martin Jess and Henrietta Catherine Hiemstra. BA with honors, State U. Iowa, 1962; MA, Ind. U., 1966. Poet, humorist, 1967—. Lit. cons., San Francisco, 1967—; book arts cons. Juniper Von Phitzer Press, San Francisco, 1975—. Author: Cats in Charge, 1989, Dream Tees, 1991, Autobiography of Teardrop, 2001, Two-Way Zipper Dream, 2002, Iambic Jam, 2003; author, performer: (CD) In Deepest USA, 1996, (performance video) A Turquoise Coyote Under Your Pillow, 1998. Recipient Narrative Poetry award Browning Soc., 1975, Three Poem prize Montalvo Ctr. for the Arts, 1985, Poet in Performance award Carmel Festival for the Performing Arts, 1998, Edinburgh Festival First, 1999, First pl. Mt. Diablo Poetry Contest, 2000. Mem. Poetry Soc. Am., Acad. Am. Poets, The Dramatists Guild, Inc., MBS Internat. (Disting. Book award 1990). Avocations: piano, folk humor, architecture, horticulture. Office: Zippy Digital 166 Bonview St San Francisco CA 94110-5147 E-mail: drollmarv@aol.com.

HIEMSTRA, ROGER, adult education educator, writer; b. Plainwell, Mich., Sept. 15, 1938; s. Claude and Frances (Anson) H.; m. Janet Louise Wemer, June 23, 1968; children: Nancy, David. AA, Pasadena City Coll., Calif., 1958; BS, Mich. State U., 1964; MS, Iowa State U., 1967; PhD, U. Mich., 1970. Mott Intern Flint (Mich.) Community Schs., 1968-69; program coordinator Wayne State U., Detroit, 1969-70; dept. asst. U. Mich., Ann Arbor, 1969-70; prof. adult edn. U. Nebr., Lincoln, 1970-76; prof., chmn. adult edn. Iowa State U., Ames, 1976-80; prof. adult edn., instrnl. design Syracuse (N.Y.) U., 1980—96, chmn. dept. adult edn., 1980—94, prof. emeritus, 1996—; prof., program dir. of adult edn. Elmira Coll., 1997—. Chmn. Commn. Profs. Adult Edn., Washington, 1981-83; co-dir. adult edn. resource worldwide Kellogg Project, 1986-90, dir., 1991-93. Co-author, editor: Changing Approaches to Studying Adult Education, 1980; co-author: Individualizing Instruction, 1990, Self-Direction in Adult Learning, 1991, Professional Writing, 1994, Toward Ethical Practice, 2003; author editor: Creating Environments for Effective Adult Learning, 1991; co-editor, author Overcoming Resistence to Self-Direction in Adult Learning, 1994; author: The Educative Community, 1972, Lifelong Learning, 1976; sr. editor Lifelong Learning: The Adult Years, 1980-83; editor Adult Edn. Quar., 1985-88. Mem. Commn. of Profs. of Adult Edn. With USNR, 1960-62. Named Tchr. of Yr. for Grad. Studies, Elmira Coll., 1999; inducted into Internat. Adult and Continuing Edn. Hall of Fame, 2000. Mem. Adult Edn. Assn. U.S.A. (exec. bd. 1977-82, svc. award), Am. Assn. Adult and Continuing Edn., Assn. for Continuing Higher Edn. (Nat. Leadership award 1991). Democrat. Unitarian-Universalist. Home: 318 Southfield Dr Fayetteville NY 13066-2253

HIENTON, JAMES ROBERT, lawyer; b. Phoenix, July 25, 1951; s. Clarence J. Jr. and Lola Jean (Paxton) H.; m. Diane Marie DeBrosse, July 22, 1977. BA, U. Ariz., 1972; MBA, JD, Ariz. State U., 1975; LLM, Washington U., St. Louis, 1977. Bar: Ariz. 1975, U.S. Dist. Ct. (Ariz.) 1975. Corp. atty. Ariz. Pub. Service, Phoenix, 1975-76; asst. prof. Ariz. State U., Tempe, 1977; assoc. then ptnr. Gust, Rosenfeld, Divelbess et al, Phoenix, 1978-85; sr. tax ptnr. Evans, Kitchel and Jenckes, Phoenix, 1985-89; ptnr. Jennings, Strouss and Salmon, Phoenix, 1989-93; sr. shareholder Bonnett, Fairbourne, Friedman, Hienton, Miner & Fry, P.C., Phoenix, 1993-95, Ridenour, Hienton, Harper and Kelhoffer, P.C., Phoenix, 1995—. Officer, bd. dirs. Charter Govt., Phoenix, 1978-82; mem. Phoenix Citizens Charter Rev. Com., 1982; participant Phoenix Together; participant lst Phoenix Town Hall, 1981, 2d, 1982, 3d, 1983, recorder, 1983, 85; mem. Balanced Govt. Com., 1983; mem Phoenix Police and Fire Pension Bds., 1982-89; bd. dirs. Ariz. Theater Co., 1979-89; mem. class V, Valley Leadership, 1983-84; founding life mem. Ariz. Mus. Sci. and Industry. Mem. ABA, Ariz. Bar Assn., Maricopa County Bar Assn., Phi Kappa Phi. Clubs: Phoenix City. Republican. Home: 441 W Mclellan Blvd Phoenix AZ 85013-1141 Office: Ridenour Hienton Harper & Kelhoffer PC Ste 3300 201 N Central Ave Phoenix AZ 85004

HIER, DANIEL BARNET, neurologist; b. Chgo., Mar. 23, 1947; BA, Harvard U., 1969, MD, 1973. Medical intern Bronx Mcpl. Hosp., N.Y.C., 1973-74; neurology resident Mass. Gen. Hosp., Boston, 1974-77, neurology fellow, 1977-79; neurologist Michael Reese Hosp., Chgo., 1979-89, chmn. neurology, 1987-89; head neurology U. Ill., Chgo., 1989—, assoc. prof. neurology, 1989-91; prof. Ul. Ill., 1991—. Fellow Am. Acad. Neurology, Am. Heart Assn. (stroke council). Home: 2210 Schiller Ave Wilmette IL 60091-2328 E-mail: dhier01@ameritech.net.

HIER, MARSHALL DAVID, lawyer; b. Bay City, Mich., Aug. 24, 1945; s. Marshall George and Helen May (Copeland) H.; m. Nancy Speed Brown, June 26, 1970; children: John, Susan, Ann. BA, Mich. State U., 1966; JD, U. Mich., 1969. Bar: Mo. 1969. Assoc. Peper, Martin, Jensen, Maichel and Hetlage, St. Louis, 1969-76, ptnr., 1976-95; prin. Bertram, Peper and Hier, P.C., St. Louis, 1996—. Bd. dirs. Gateway Ctr. Met. St. Louis, Mercantile Libr. Assn., St. Louis Soc. Blind and Visually Impaired. Contbr. articles to profl. jours. Mem. St. Louis Bar Assn. (editor jour. 1988—), St. Louis Civil Round Table (former pres.). Baptist. Home: 17141 Chaise Ridge Rd Chesterfield MO 63005-4457

HIERONYMUS, DEBRA JEAN, literature educator; b. El Dorado, Ark., June 1, 1957; d. Bill Eugene and Beverly Ann Linn; m. John Michael Hieronymus, June 2, 1990; 1 child, Judith Anne Nitcy. MFA in Creative Writing, U. Idaho, 2000. Lectr. Fla. State U., Tallahassee, 2000—01, U. Idaho, Moscow, 2001—. Editor: (creative writing jour.) Talking River Rev.; mem. editl. bd.: creative writing jour. Talking River Review, author poems and essays. Panel mem. intergenerational lang. Internat. Exch. Conf., Lewiston, 1996—96; student rep. faculty search com. Lewis Clark State Coll., Lewiston, Idaho, 1996—97; mem. writing curriculum com. U. Idaho, Moscow, 1999—2000, mem. exec. com., 2002—03, mem. writing placement com., 2002—03. Susan P. Schroeder scholar, Lewis Clark State Coll., 1996, Grace N. Nixon scholar, U. Idaho, 1997—98, Estelle Suave scholar, 1998—99, Grace N. Nixon scholar, 1999 2000. Mem.: Associated Writers (assoc.). Independent. Avocations: travel, photography, visual art, working out. Home: 1631 15th Ave Lewiston ID 83501 Office: Univ Idaho English Dept Brink 200 Moscow ID 83844-1102 Personal E-mail: dh@cableone.net. E-mail: debrah@uidaho.edu.

HIERONYMUS, EDWARD WHITTLESEY, lawyer; b. Davenport, Iowa, June 13, 1943; BA cum laude, Knox Coll., 1965; JD with distinction, Duke U., 1968. Bar: Calif. 1969, Iowa 1968. Ptnr. O'Melveny & Myers, LA, 1974—96, of counsel, 1996—99. Contbr. articles on law to profl. jours. Exec. sec. Los Angeles Com. Fgn. Relations, 1975-86. Served with Judge Adv. Gen. U.S. Army, 1965-74. Mem. ABA (award for profl. merit 1968), Calif. Bar Assn. (founding co-chair natural resources subsect., real property sect. 1986-88), Los Angeles County Bar Assn., Iowa Bar Assn. Office: O'Melveny & Myers 400 S Hope St Los Angeles CA 90071-2899

HIERS, RICHARD HYDE, lawyer, educator, writer; b. Phila., Apr. 8, 1932; s. Glen Sefton and Mildred (Douthitt) H.; m. Jane Leslie Gale, Jan. 30, 1954; children: Peter Leslie, Rebecca Hathaway. BA magna cum laude, Yale U., 1954, BD cum laude, 1957, MA, PhD, 1959, 61; JD with high honors, U. Fla., 1983. Bar: Fla. 1984, U.S. Dist. Ct. (we. dist.) Tex. 1988, U.S. Ct. Appeals (5th cir.) 1988. Asst. prof. Coll. Liberal Arts and Scis., U. Fla., Gainesville, 1961-66, assoc. prof., 1966-72, prof., 1972—, affiliate prof. law Coll. Law, 1994—. Jud. law clk. U.S. Ct. Appeals, Austin, Tex., 1987-88. Author: Trinity Guide to the Bible with Apocrypha, 2001, Contbr. numerous articles to law jours. including Cumberland Law Rev., Jour. Coll. and Univ. Law, Fifth Cir. Reporter, George Mason Civil Rights Law Jour., Jour. of Law and Religion, U. Fla. Jour. Law and Pub. Policy, Wayne Law Rev. Mem. Am. Acad. of Religion (pres. southeastern region 1969-70), AAUP (pres. U. Fla. chpt. 1972-74), Soc. of Biblical Lit. (pres. southeastern reg. 1982-83), Fla. Bar Assn. (com. on individual rights and responsiblities 1985-87, 90, pub. interest law sect. 1990-), Bar Assn. of 5th Fed. Cir., Danforth Assocs. in Tchg, Order of Coif, Aurelian Honor Soc., Skull and Bones, Phi Beta Kappa (pres. U. Fla. chpt. 1975-76), Phi Kappa Phi (pres. U. Fla. chpt. 1995-96). Democrat. Avocation: hiking. Office: U Fla 107 Anderson Hall Gainesville FL 32611-7410 *All decisions affecting ourselves, other persons, and other living beings, are basically ethical decisions. And ethical decisions inevitably give expression to our ultimate loyalties and convictions as to the meaning of life that is, ultimately, religious in character.*

HIESTAND, O.S., JR., lawyer; b. 1920. A.B., Ind. U., 1941; LL.B., Northwestern U., 1947. Bar: Ill. 1947, Tenn. 1953, U.S. Supreme Ct. 1964, D.C. 1973, U.S. Ct. Claims 1979, U.S. Ct. Appeals (fed. cir.) 1983. Gen. counsel Commn. on Govt. Procurement, 1970-73; ptnr. Morgan, Lewis, & Bockius, Washington. Office: 1800 M St NW Suite 800 N Washington DC 20036

HIGANO, NORIO, retired internist; b. Seattle, May 6, 1921; s. Hanji and Ura (Kameta) H.; m. Dorothy Wright Taylor; children: Celestia, Priscilla, Stuart. BS, U. Wash., 1943; MD, St. Louis U., 1945. Diplomate Am. Bd. Internal Medicine, Am. Bd. Nuclear Medicine. Intern Boston City Hosp., 1945-46; resident pathology Mass. Meml. Hosp., 1947 48; resident medicine Mt. Auburn Hosp., 1948-49, Boston Lying-In Hosp., PBBH, 1950-51; fellow Thornike Meml. Lab. Harvard Med. Sch., 1951-52; mem. rsch. lab. The Meml. Hosp., Worcester, Mass., 1953-61, chief nuclear medicine lab., 1953-95, attending physician, 1952-99; ret. Fellow ACP, Am. Coll. Endocrinology; mem. AMA, Mass. Med. Soc., Worcester Dist. Med. Soc., Soc. of Nuclear Medicine (pres. New England chpt. 1975-76). Avocations: art, photography. Home: 5 Essex Way Westborough MA 01581-1194

HIGASHIDA, RANDALL TAKEO, radiologist, neurosurgeon, medical educator; b. L.A., Oct. 26, 1955; s. Henry and Alice Higashida; m. Jean Kim, May 17, 1986. BS, U. So. Calif., 1976; MD, Tulane U. Diplomate Am. Bd. Radiology. Intern Harbor UCLA Med. Ctr., 1980-81, resident in radiology, 1981-84, fellow in diagnostic/interventional neuroradiology, 1984-85; asst. prof. radiology UCLA Med. Ctr., 1985-86; assoc. prof. radiology U. Calif. San Francisco Med. Ctr., 1986-94, prof. radiology and neurosurgery, 1994—. Cons. Target Therapeutics Corp., Fremont, Calif., 1989-93, Interventional Therapeutics Corp., Fremont, 1986-93, Cordis Corp., Miami Lakes, Fla., 1993-96; mem. exec. com. stroke rsch. grants Abbott Labs., Chgo., 1994-96. Mem. editl. bd. Jour. Endovasc. Surgery, 1994-96, Jour. Minimally Invasive Neurosurgery, 1994-96; manuscript reviewer Am. Jour. Neuroradiology, 1992—. Recipient rsch. award Am. Heart Assn., Dallas, 1978-79. Mem. AMA, Am. Soc. Neuroradiology (sr. mem., exec. coun. joint section of cerebrovascular neurosurgery), Soc. Cardiovascular and Interventional Radiology, Am. Soc. Interventional and Therapeutic Neuroradiology (exec. com. 1994-96), Internat. Soc. Endovascular Surgery. Republican. Protestant. Avocations: hiking, tennis, biking, photography, travel. Office: UCSF Medical Ctr 505 Parnassus Ave # L352 San Francisco CA 94143-0001

HIGBEE, DALE (STROHE), musician, retired psychologist; b. Proctor, Vt., June 14, 1925; s. Paul Wilbur Higbee and Catherine Ann Strohe; 1 child, Catherine Ann Higbee Mize. AB, Harvard, Cambridge, Mass., 1949; PhD, Univ. Tex. at Austin, Austin, Tex., 1954; studied flute with, Georges Laurent, Artur Lora, Marcel Moyse; studied recorder with, Carl Dolmetsch. Clin. psychologist SC State Hosp., Columbia, SC, 1954—55, VA Med. Ctr., Salisbury, NC, 1955—87; freelance flutist & recorder player NC, 1954—87; music dir. Carolina Baroque, Salisbury, NC, 1988—. Contbr. articles to profl. jour. Pfc. 314th reg., 79th divsn., 1943—45. Home: 412 S Ellis St Salisbury NC 28144 Office: Carolina Baroque 412 S Ellis St Salisbury NC 28144

HIGBEE, DONALD WILLIAM, electronics company executive, lawyer; b. Stonewall, Okla., Jan. 7, 1931; s. James W. and Nannie M. (Driver) H.; m. Joan M. Diamond; children: Bradley, Carter, Phillip, Lisa. AB cum laude, U. So. Calif., 1956, JD, 1962. Bar: Calif. 1963; U.S. Supreme Ct. Quet. Pacific Press, Inc., Los Angeles, 1956-60; sec., treas. Utah Research and Devel. Co., Salt Lake City, 1964; controller Interstate Electronics, Anaheim, Calif., 1960-63, dir. contracts, 1965-74, v.p., sec., 1974-86, also bd. dirs.; pres. Higbee Investments, 1989—. Bd. dirs. Silverado (Calif.) Water Dist., 1965-70, Silverado-Modjeska Recreation and Park Dist., 1965-70. Served with USMC, 1950-51, Korea. Decorated Purple Heart, 1951. Mem. State Bar of Calif., Orange County Bar Assn., Nat. Contract Mgmt. Assn., Nat. Assn. Accts., Machinery and Allied Products Inst., Nat. Security Indsl. Assn., Elks, Masons, Moose, VFW. Republican. Avocations: gardening, computers, tennis, golf. Home: 3502 Cazador Ln Fallbrook CA 92028-9426

HIGBY, EDWARD JULIAN, safety engineer; b. Milw., June 9, 1939; s. Richard L. Higby and Julie Ann (Bruins) O'Kelly; m. Frances Ann Knoodle, 1959 (div. 1962); 1 child, Melinda Ann Mozader. BS in Criminal Justice, Southwestern U., Tucson, 1984. Cert.: county ct. mediator. Tactical officer Miami Police Dept., Fla., 1967-68; intelligence officer Fla. Divsn. Beverages, 1968-72; licensing coord. Lums Restaurant Corp., Miami, 1972-73; legal asst. Walt Disney World, Lake Buena Vista, Fla., 1973-78; loss control cons. R.P. Hewitt & Assocs., Orlando, Fla., 1978-79; safety coord. City of Lakeland, Fla., 1979-94. Author: Safety Guide for Health Care, 1979. Councilman City of Bay Lake, 1974-76, mayor, 1975-76; active Fla. League of Cities, 1974-76, Tri-County League of Cities, 1974-76, Orange County Criminal Justice Coun., 1974-78, Ctrl. Fla. Safety Coun., 1978-79; bd. dirs. Greater Lakeland chpt. ARC, 1980-86, chmn. bd. dirs., 1983-84, 85-86, chmn. health svcs., 1980-86; budget com. United Way Ctrl. Fla., 1983-85; bd. dirs. Tampa Area Safety Coun., 1983-92, pres., 1990-91; bd. dirs. Imperial Traffic Safety Coun., 1983-89, Employers Health Care Group Polk County, 1987-89, Parent Resources and Info. on Drug Edn., 1989-92; mem. Polk County Disaster Coordination Com., bd. dirs., 1984-92, bd. dirs. ARC Polk County chpt., 1990-92, 94-96, coord. Mass Care, 1994-95, chmn. Health and Safety, 1994-95, chmn. Risk Mgmt., 1995-96; active ARC Disaster Svcs. Human Resources Sys., 1994-99; mem. Fla. Adv. Com. Arson Prevention, Local Emergency Planning Com., State of Fla., 1987-92, 94—, chmn. Dist. 7, 1998—, Fla. Disaster Mortuary Team, 1995—; adv. panel Polk County Industry Cmty., 1997-2002; adv com. Charlotte Harbor Nat. Estuary, 1997-2002, chmn. citizen adv. com., mgmt. com., 1999-2002; bd. dirs. Friends of Charlotte Harbor Estuary, 2000-2002; adv. coun. Kingsford Elem. Sch., 1999—; Fla. Emergency Mgmt. Reservist Program, 2001—. With U.S. Army, 1963-64. Named Vol. of Yr., Greater Lakeland chpt. ARC, 1983-84. Mem. NRA (life), World Safety Orgn., Fla. Sheriffs Assn. (hon. life), Internat. Assn. Identification (life, Fla. divsn., Russian divsn.), Nat. Found. Mortuary Care, Automatic Fire Alarm Assn., Disaster Emergency Response Assn. (life), Environ. Assessment Assn., U. Fla. Nat. Alumni Assn. (life), Fla. Pub. Health Assn., Fla. Fedn. Safety, Am. Soc. Safety Engrs. (regional oper. com. 1983-85, 88-90, profl. devel. conf. com. 1983, 85, chpt. bd. dirs. 1983-87, chpt. pres. 1984-85, v.p. profl. devel. region VIII 1988-90, Safety Profl. of Yr. 1984-85, Albert G. Mowson award 1995-96, Davis Productivity award 2001), Heartland Safety Soc. (life, pres. 1982-83, 94-95), Fla. Citrus Safety Assn. (pres. 1981-83), Nat. Fire Protection Assn., Am. Indsl. Hygiene Assn. (Fla. chpt.), Fire Marshals Assn. N.Am., Soc. Fire Protection Engrs. (bd. dirs. Fla. chpt. 1994-99), So. Health Assn., Fla. Affiliation of Ins. Safety Reps., Internat. Critical Incident Stress Found., Critical Incident Stress Debriefers Fla., Nat. Assn. Search and Rescue, Fla. Funeral Dirs. Assn., Fla. Emergency Preparedness Assn., Fla. Assn. Code Enforcement, Fla. Acad. Profl. Mediators, First Amendment Found., Internat. Assn. Arson Investigators, Fla. Cracker Cattle Assn. (life), Harley Owners Group (life), Am. Motorcycle Assn. (life), Lakeland Rifle and Pistol Club. Republican. Avocations: hunting, fishing. E-mail: ed-valeriehigby@webtv.net.

HIGBY, GREGORY JAMES, historical association administrator, historian; s. Warren James and Gertrude H.; m. Marian Fredal, June 2, 1979. BS in Pharmacy, U. Mich., 1977; MS in Pharmacy, U. Wis., 1980, PhD in Pharmacy, 1984. Staff pharmacist Higby's Pharmacy, Bad Axe, Mich., 1977-78; asst. to dir. Am. Inst. of the History of Pharmacy, Madison, Wis., 1981-84, asst. dir., 1984-86, assoc. dir., 1986, acting dir., 1986-88, dir., 1988—; rsch. assoc. U. Wis., Madison, 1984-86. Adj. asst. prof. U. Wis., Madison, 1984-94, adj. assoc. prof., 1994-2000, adj. prof., 2000—; cons. Smithsonian Instn., Washington, 1987, Am. Soc. Hosp. Pharmacists, Bethesda, Md., 1990, U.S. Pharmacopeial Conv., 1992-95, Am. Assn. Colls. Pharmacy, 1993-99; adv. com. Fed. Drug Law Inst., Washington, 1989-90. Author: In Service to American Pharmacy: The Professional Life of William Procter, Jr., U. Ala. Press, 1992; co-author: The Spirit of Voluntarism...The United States Pharmacopeia 1820-1995, 1995; editor: One Hundred Years of the National Formulary, 1989, Pill Peddlers: Essays on the History of the Pharmaceutical Industry, 1990, Historical Hobbies for the Pharmacist, 1994, The History of Pharmacy, A Selected Annotated Bibliography, 1995, The Inside Story of Medicines, 1997, Apothecaries and the Drug Trade, 2001, 150 Years of Caring: A Pictorial History of the APHA, 2002, Drugstore Memories: American Pharmacists Recall Life Behind the Counter, 2002; author poetry; editor: Pharmacy in History Jour., 1986—; contbr. articles to profl. jours. Recipient Edward Kremers award 1995. Mem. Am. Pharm. Assn., Am. Assn. Coll. Pharm., Am. Assn. for History of Medicine, Hist. Sci. Soc., Orgn. Am. Historians, Soc. for History of Tech., Internat. Acad. History of Pharmacy. Avocations: bird watching, cycling, racquetball, musician. Office: Am Inst of the History of Pharmacy 777 Highland Ave Madison WI 53705-2222 E-mail: greghigby@aihp.org.

HIGBY, WAYNE (DONALD HIGBY), artist, educator; b. Colorado Springs, Colo., May 12, 1943; s. Donald W. and Betty (Bates) H.; m. Donna Claire Bennett, Mar. 12, 1966; children: Austin Myles, Sarah Lark. BFA, U. Colo., 1966; MFA, U. Mich., 1968. Prof. art N.Y. State Coll. Ceramics, Alfred U., 1973—; chair divsn. ceramic art, 1983-91. Panelist Task Force for Individual Artists N.Y. State Coun. Arts, 1980-82, chair, 1978, mem. visual arts panel, 1976, 77; mem. NEA Visual Artists Fellowship/Crafts, 1986, NEA Visual Arts Overview Panel, 1989-90; hon. prof. Shanghai U., 2000, ceramic art Jingdezhen Ceramic Inst, People's Republic of China, 1994; bd. dirs. Intrnat. Acad. Ceramics. One-man exhbns. include Helen Drutt Gallery, 1988, 90, Mus. of Art and Design, Helsinki, Finland, 1999; invitational exhbns. include 8th and 13th Chunichi Internat. Exhbn. Ceramic Art, Nagoya, Japan, 1980, 85, respectively, Everson Mus. Art, Syracuse, N.Y., 1981, 87, 89, Am. Craft Mus., N.Y.C., 1982, 89, Jacksonville (Fla.) Mus. Art, 1982, Nelson-Atkins Mus. Art, Kansas City, 1983, Boston Mus. Fine Arts, 1984, Victoria and Albert Mus., London, 1986, Seoul Olympics Arts Festival, 1988, Nat. Mus. Ceramic Art, Balt., 1989, Kanazawa, Ishibkawa Pref, Japan, 1991, Nat. Mus. Modern Art, Tokyo, 1992-93, Met. Mus. Art, N.Y.C., 1999; public collections include Met. Mus. Art, N.Y.C., Mpls. Mus. Art, Phila. Mus. Art, Everson Mus. Art, Joslyn Mus. Art, Omaha, Am. Craft Mus., Victoria and Albert Mus., Boston Mus. Fine Arts, Bklyn. Mus. Art, L.A. County Mus. Art. Bd. dirs. Haystack Mountain Sch. Crafts, Deer Isle, Maine, 1983—, pres., 1989-92, chmn., 2000—. Howard Found. fellow, 1985-86, 89-90; recipient Master Tchr. award U. Hartford, 1990, Chancellor's award SUNY, 1993, Disting. Educator award James Renwick Alliance; named visionary of Am. craft Am. Craft Mus., 1995, Disting. Educator James Renwick Alliance, 2002. Mem. Coll. of Fellows Am. Craft Coun. Office: N Y State Coll Ceramics Alfred U Alfred NY 14802-2207

HIGDON, FREDERICK ALONZO, lawyer, accountant; b. Lebanon, Ky., Aug. 30, 1950; s. William Joseph and Mary Rita Higdon; m. Nancy Lawrence Brents, Aug. 4, 1972; children: Ashley, Matthew, Scott. BS cum laude, Western Ky. U., 1972; JD, U. Louisville, 1975. Bar: Ky. 1975. Staff acct. Coopers & Lybrand, Louisville, 1972-74; tax acct. Peat, Marwick & Mitchell, Louisville, 1974-76; lawyer Spragens, Smith & Higdon, P.S.C., Lebanon, Ky., 1976—. Bd. dirs., vice chair Peoples Bank, Lebanon; asst. county atty. Marion County, Ky., 1992-96. Past pres. Lebanon/Marion County C. of C., Lebanon/Marion County Leadership Alumni Assn., Marion County Jr. Miss, Inc., 2001; past pres., dir. Marion County Pub. Libr., Lebanon, 1993-2001; pres. Marion County Indsl. Found., Lebanon, 1997—. Mem. Ky. Bar Assn., Ky. Soc. CPAs, Marion County Bar Assn. (treas. 1978—). Avocations: snow skiing, hunting, fishing. Office: Spragens Smith and Higdon PSC 15 Court Sq Lebanon KY 40033-1257

HIGDON, JAMES NOEL, lawyer; b. McAlester, Okla., Oct. 20, 1944; s. Wilford Dain and Ida Jean (Douglass) H.; m. Barbara Ann Downing, Feb. 8, 1969; children: Travis Noel, Charles Andrew. BA, U. Tex., 1967; MBA, U. West Fla., 1973; JD, St. Mary's U., 1975. Bar: Tex. 1976; U.S. Dist. Ct. (we. dist.) Tex. 1978, U.S. Dist. Ct. (no. dist.) Tex. 1979, U.S. Dist. Ct. (ea. dist.) Tex. 1980; U.S. Ct. Appeals (5th cir.) 1979, U.S. Supreme Ct. 1979; bd. cert. family law, civil appellate law; trained mediator, arbitrator. Briefing atty. 4th Ct. Civil Appeals, San Antonio, 1976-77; assoc. Wiley, Plunkett, Gibson and Allen, San Antonio, 1977-79; ptnr. Wiley, Garwood, Hornbuckle and Higdon, San Antonio, 1979-81; ptnr., sec., treas. Hornbuckle, Higdon and Young, P.C., San Antonio, 1981-83; ptnr., v.p. Bass, Higdon and Hardy, Inc., San Antonio, 1983-97; ptnr. Higdon, Hardy & Zuflacht, L.L.P., San Antonio, 1997—. Bd. dirs. Alamo Masonic Cemetery Corp. Mem. Alamo Coun., Navy League of U.S.; Troop com. chmn. Boy Scouts Am., 1989—91, cubmaster, treas., den leader, 1982—87; commr City San Antonio AIDS/HIV Commn., 1990—93; bd. dirs. Bexar County Dispute Resolution Ctr., 1997—, San Antonio Pub. Libr. Found., 1997—2001, Scottish Rite Learning Ctr. South Tex., 2000—, Lee Lockwood Scottish Rite Found. Tex., 2000—; chmn. San Antonio Navy Recruiting dist. assistance coun., 1989—91. Fellow Am. Acad. Matrimonial Lawyers, Tex. Bar Found., San Antonio Bar Found.; mem. State Bar Tex. (mem. Tex. Bar Jour. Commn., 1980-95, family law, ADR, vice chmn. mil. law, 2002—, litigation, appellate advocacy secs., vice chair 2002—), San Antonio Bar Assn. (chmn. continuing legal edn. com. 1990-92, bd. dirs. 1992-94, founder, charter chmn. family law sec. 1992-94), San Antonio Family Lawyers Assn. (sec. 1987-88, v.p. 1988-89, pres. 1989-90, bd. dirs. 1986-91, 98-99), Tex. Acad. Family Law Specialists, Rotary (San Antonio Oak Hills, v.p. program chmn. 1989-90, pres. 1991-92, bd. dirs. 1986-93, sec. dist. 5840 1992-93), Masons (pres. lodge 1980-81, chpt. 1983-84, 98-01, coun. 1984-85, commandery 1992, york rite coll. 1994-95, s.a. coun. # 261AMD 1997-98, Ft. Sam Houston chpt. 17 Nat. Sojourners Inc. 2001-02, Alamo camp heroes of '76 2000-01), Masonic Grand Lodge Tex. (dist. deputy grand master-39A 1989-90, dist. Masonic rels. officer-39A 1990-93, civil law com. 1998—), Masonic Grand Royal Arch chpt. Tex. (dist. dep. grand high priest 23 1997-98), Masonic Grand Coun. Royal & Select Masters of Tex. (mem. jurisprudence com. 2000—, chmn. 2002—), dist. dep. grand master 22 1999-2000, Knights Templar of Tex. (grand line officer 1996—, dep. gr. cdr. 2003-04), Sigma Phi Epsilon. Baptist. Home: 10122 N Manton Ln San Antonio TX 78213-1948 Office: Higdon Hardy & Zuflacht LLP 12000 Huebner Rd Ste 200 San Antonio TX 78230-1209

HIGDON, JIMMY, state representative; b. July 15, 1953; BS, Morehead State Univ. State Rep. House of Rep., Dist. 24, 2002—; mcht. Higdon's Foodtown. Mem. Local Gov., Agr. and Small Bus., Health and Welfare. USAR. Caucuses: Former Bd. of Dir.; Lebanon housing Authority; Bd. of Dir., Marion County Econ. Devel. Republican. Catholic. Office: Dist 507 W Main St Lebanon KY 40033*

HIGGENS, WILLIAM JOHN, III, (TREY HIGGENS), sales executive; b. Evanston, Ill., May 26, 1951; s. William John Jr. and Delores May (Fuller) H.; m. Melanie Ann Mayer (div.); children: Melissa Lee, Tracy Ann; m. Barbara Carrie Simcoe, July 8, 1989. BS in Mktg. Mgmt., Miami U., Oxford, Ohio, 1973. Sales rep. A.B. Dick Co., Chgo., 1973-76; dist. sales mgr. McGraw-Hill Pub. Co., Chgo., 1976-85, CMP Publ., Inc., Chgo., 1985-91, McGraw-Hill Pub. Co., Chgo., 1991-96; nat. sales mgr. Lightwave Mag., Oak Brook, Ill., 1996—2003; reg. sales mgr. Security Mag., Bus. News Pub., Bensenville, Ill., 2003—. Mem. Bus. Mktg. Assn. (bd. dirs. 1984—, cert. bus. communicator 1989). Republican. Episcopalian. Avocations: flying, golf, reading, travel, computers. Home: Peregrine Lake Estates 873 W Lukas Ave Palatine IL 60067-2381 Office: PennWell Pub Co 2625 Butterfield Rd Ste 138S Oak Brook IL 60523-1244

HIGGINBOTHAM, EDITH ARLEANE, radiologist, researcher; b. New Orleans, Sept. 14, 1946; d. Luther Aldrich and Ruby (Clark) H.; m. Terry Lawrence Andrews (div. 1979); m. Donald Temple Ford (div. 1989). BS, Howard U., 1967, MS, 1970, MD, 1974. Diplomate Am. Bd. Radiology, Am. Bd. Nuclear Medicine. Intern St. Vincent's Hosp., N.Y.C., 1974-75, resident in diagnostic radiology, 1975-78, resident in nuclear radiology, 1978-79; asst. prof. radiology, chief nuclear medicine Howard U., Howard U. Hosp., Washington, 1979-82; assoc. prof. clin. radiology, dir. nuclear medicine U. Medicine and Dentistry N.J., Newark, 1982-90; locum tenens radiologist Sterling Med., Cin., 1991-94, Med. Nat., San Antonio, 1990-91; diagnostic radiologist Diagnostic Health Imaging Systems, Lanham, Md., 1994-95; locum tenens radiologist, 1995-97; radiologist, dir. radiology N.E. Wash. Med. Group, Colville, Wash., 1997—99; radiologist Mount Carmel Hosp., Colville, 1997-99, Barstow (Calif.) Cmty. Hosp., 1999, Queen of Peace Hosp., Mitchell, SD, 1999—2002, New Ulm Med Ctr., Minn., 2002—, dir. radiology, 2003—. Cons. Biotech. Rsch. Inst., Rockville, Md., 1989-94; profl. assoc. Ctr. for Molecular Medicine and Immunology, Newark, 1984-90; asst. prof. radiology George Washington U., Washington, 1990; presenter in field. Contbr. articles to profl. jours. Named Outstanding Working Woman, Glamour mag., 1981, Hon. Dep. Atty. Gen., State of La., 1982. Mem. Am. Coll. Radiology, Radiol. Soc. N.Am., Soc. Nuclear Medicine, Sigma Xi, Phi Delta Epsilon. Roman Catholic. Avocations: aerobics, reading, self-improvement, music. travel.

HIGGINBOTHAM, JOAN E. astronaut; b. Chgo., Aug. 03; BSEE, So. Ill. U., 1987; M in Mgmt., Fla. Inst. Tech., 1992, M in Space Sys., 1996. Payload elec. engr. divsn. ele. and telecomm. sys. NASA, Kennedy Space Ctr., Fla., 1987, lead orbiter experiments space shuttle Columbia, 1987, exec. staff asst. to dir. shuttle ops. and mgmt., backup orbiter project engr. space shuttle Atlantis, lead orbiter project engr. space shuttle Columbia; astronaut, mission specialist NASA, Johnson Space Ctr., Houston, 1996—. Named Disting. Alumni, Fla. Inst. Tech., 1997, So. Ill. U.; named one of 50 Disting. Scientists and Engrs., Nat. Tech. Assn.; recipient Key to City of Cocoa, Fla., Key to City of Rockledge, Presdl. Sports award in bicycling and weight training, Outstanding Woman of Yr. award. Mem.: Links, Inc., Bronze Eagles, Delta Sigma Theta. Avocations: weightlifting, cycling, music, motivational speaking. Office: Astronaut Office/CB NASA Johnson Space Ctr Houston TX 77058

HIGGINBOTHAM, KENNETH JAMES, financial services executive; b. Phila., Aug. 3, 1942; s. James V. and Elizabeth R. (Roebus) H.; m. Ruth M. Schaffer, Apr. 12, 1969; children: Jennifer K., Scott G. BA, Rutgers U., 1971; MBA, Drexel U., 1973. Cert. sr. advisor. Fin. analyst, discount window Fed. Res. Bank of Phila., 1972-77; corp. cash mgmt. cons. First Pa. Bank NA, Phila., 1977-79; EFT cons. Control Data Corp., Mpls., 1979-84; dist. rep. Aid Assn. for Lutherans, Appleton, Wis., 1984-94; reg. rep. Lincoln Fin. Advisors, Richboro, Pa., 1994-2000; independent fin. planner, 2000—. Adj. faculty LaSalle U., Phila., 1977—. With USN, 1963-67. Mem. AAUP, Fin. Planning Assn., Bucks County Estate Planning Coun. (officer, pres.), Northampton Twp. Bus. and Profl. Assn. Office: Ind Fin Planners 21 Holly Hill Rd Richboro PA 18954-1917

HIGGINBOTHAM, PATRICK ERROL, federal judge; b. Ala., Dec. 16, 1938; Student, U. Ala., 1956, Arlington State Coll., 1957, North Tex. State U., 1958, U. Tex., 1958; BA, U. Ala., 1960, LLB, 1961; LLD (hon.), So. Meth. U., 1989. Bar: Ala. 1961, Tex. 1962, U.S. Supreme Ct. 1962. Assoc. to ptnr. Coke & Coke, Dallas, 1964—75; judge U.S. Dist. Ct. (no. dist.) Tex., Dallas, 1976—82, U.S. Ct. Appeals (5th cir.), Dallas, 1982—. Adj. prof. So. Meth. U. Law Sch., 1971—, adj. prof. constl. law, 1981—, U. Tex. Sch. Law, 1998; M.D. Anderson pub. svc. prof. in residence Tex. Tech. U. Sch. Law, 1999; John Sparkman jurist-in-residence U. Ala. Sch. Law, 1995, 97, 99; conferee Am. Assembly, 1975, Pound Conf., 1976; bd. suprs. Inst. Civil Justice Rand. Contbr. With JAG USAF, 1961—64. Named Outstanding Alumnus, U. Tex., Arlington, 1978, One of Nation's 100 Most Powerful Persons for the 80's, Next Mag.; recipient Dan Meador award, U. Ala., Samuel E. Gates Litigation award, Am. Coll. Trial Lawyers, 1997, A. Sherman Christensen award, 2002. Fellow: Am. Bar Found.; mem.: ABA, Ctr. for Am. and Internat. Law (bd. dirs. 1998—, chmn.), Am. Inns. of Ct. Found. (pres. 1996—2000), Farrah Law Soc., Dallas Inn of Ct., Nat. Jud. Coun. State and Fed. Cts., Am. Judicature Soc., Am. Law Inst., Dallas Bar Found., Dallas Bar Assn., Bench and Bar, Order of Coif (hon.), Omicron Delta Kappa. Office: US Ct Appeals 1302 US Courthouse 1100 Commerce St Dallas TX 75242-1027

HIGGINBOTHAM, PRIEUR JAY, city official, writer; b. Pascagoula, Miss., July 16, 1937; s. Prieur Jay and Vivian Inez (Perez) H.; m. Alice Louisa Martin, June 27, 1970; children: Jeanne-Felicie, Denis Prieur, Robert Findlay. BA, U. Miss.; postgrad. Am. U., CCNY. Asst. clk. Miss. Ho. of Reps., Jackson, 1955-58; tchr. Mobile County Pub. Schs., Ala., 1962-73; head local history Mobile Pub. Libr., 1973-83; dir. Mobile Mcpl. Archives, 1983— . Author: Old Mobile, 1977 (ALA prize 1978), Mauvila, 1990; Fast Train Russia, 1983; 13 other books, articles; contbg. editor The Citizen Diplomat, Gainesville, Fla., 1985— ; adv. editor, contbr. Encyclopedia Britannica, 1989—; editl. dir. Gulf Coast Hist. Rev., 1984— ; book reviewer Library Jour., N.Y.C., 1985— ; bd. dirs. Ala. Records Commn., 1984— . Pres. Mobile Soc. for Soviet-Am. Understanding, 1982-88; chmn. Mobile Com. on Fine Arts, 1985—, Soc. Mobile-Rostov-on-Don, 1988-94; exec. bd. Mobile Internat. Festival, 1984-86, Neighborhood Improvement Coun., 1974-79; pres. Soc. Mobile-La Habana, 1993—; chmn. Mobile Tricentennial Commn., 1994—; pres. Friends of Freedom, 1995—. Served with USAR, 1956-62. Recipient Gen. L. Kemper Williams award La. Hist. Assn., 1977, award of Merit, Miss. Hist. Soc., 1979, Gilbert Chinard prize, Franco-Am. Soc., Duke U., 1979, Elisabeth Gould award Mobile Hist. Devel. Commn., 1981. Mem. Soc. Am. Archivists, Smithsonian Soc., Nat. Geog. Soc., Authors League, Am. Com. on East-West Accord, Sister Cities Internat. Democrat. Methodist. Avocations: tennis; painting; music. E-mail: archives@cl.mobile.al.us. Home: 60 N Monterey St Mobile AL 36604-1348 Office: Mobile Mcpl Archives 457 Church St Mobile AL 36602-2304 E-mail: archives@ci.mobile.al.us.

HIGGINBOTHAM, WENDY JACOBSON, political adviser, writer; b. Salt Lake City, Oct. 23, 1947; d. Alfred Thurl and Virginia Lorraine (LaCom) Jacobson; m. Keith Higginbotham, July 12, 1969; children: Ann Elizabeth Morley, Ryan Keith, Laura Carol Hoopes. Student, Occidental Coll., 1965-66, U. Grenoble, France, 1967; BA cum laude with highest honors, Brigham Young U., 1969. Teaching instr. Brigham Young U., Provo, Utah, 1969-70, editor univ. press, 1970-71; freelance editor Camarillo, Calif., 1971-78; freelance newspaper writer Vienna, Va., 1983-85; mem. profl. staff U.S. Senate Labor Com., Washington, 1985-86; exec. asst. U.S. Senator Orrin G. Hatch, Washington, 1986-88, legis. dir., 1988-91, chief of staff/adminstrv. asst., 1991-94, chief policy adviser, 1994-95; polit. adviser, freelance writer Washington, 1996—. Mem. Profl. Rep. Women, Phi Kappa Phi. Republican. Mem. Lds Ch. Avocations: traveling, hiking. Home: 2022 Willow Branch Ct Vienna VA 22181-2972

HIGGINBOTTOM, SAMUEL LOGAN, retired aerospace company executive; b. North Lawrence, Ohio, Oct. 5, 1921; s. Samuel Bradlaugh and Vera Abbie (Gutchess) H.; m. Fair Steinschneider, Aug. 30, 1947 (dec. May 1997); children: Samuel Logan, Marie Fair, Michele Rowan Maclaren; m. Janaina Dornelles, Aug. 4, 1998. BS in Civil Engring, Columbia, 1943; grad. Advanced Mgmt. Program, Harvard U. Design engr. Parsons, Brinckerhoff, Hogan & McDonald, N.Y.C., 1945-46; v.p. engring., flight, test and inspection Trans World Airlines, Inc., 1946-64; v.p. engring. and maintenance Eastern Air Lines, Inc., 1964-67, v.p. operations group, 1967-69, sr. v.p., 1969, exec. v.p., 1969-70, pres., chief operating officer, 1970-73; chmn., pres., chief exec. officer Rolls-Royce Inc., N.Y.C., 1974-86. Bd. dirs. Heico Corp. Emeritus chmn. bd. trustees Columbia U.; mem. adv. bd. Taub Inst. Capt. USAAF, WWII, ETO. Decorated hon. comdr. Order Brit. Empire; recipient Egleston medal Columbia U. Engring. Sch., 1977 Fellow AIAA; mem. Soc. Automotive Engrs., Conquistadores del Cielo, Wings Club (pres.1980-81), Deering Bay Yacht and Country Club, Tau Beta Pi, Psi Upsilon, Theta Tau. Roman Catholic. Home: 6741 SW 140th St Miami FL 33158-1388 Office: 95 Merrick Way Ste 520 Coral Gables FL 33134-5311

HIGGINS, BRIAN ALTON, art gallery owner, pastel artist; b. Brookline, Mass. s. Gerald and Catherine (Walsh) H.; m. Jane Edgington, July 1, 1975; children: Brenda, Belinda, Devon. Ops. mgr. Sta. WMTW-TV, Portland, Maine, 1965-68; v.p., gen. mgr. Sta. WSMW-TV, Worcester, Mass., 1974-84; pres. Brian Edgington Collection Am. Art, 1974—. Pastel exhbns. include Danforth Mus. Art, For Pastels Only, Pastel Soc. Am., Land, Sea, Earth, San Francisco (PSA sanctioned), 1997, Art on Paper, 21st Ann. (Maryland Fedn. of Art), Pastel Painters' Soc. of Cape Cod, Ann. Exhibition Award, Internat. Assn. of Pastel Socs., 1998, Pastel Soc. of the Southwest, 18th Ann., Renaissance in Pastel, Conn. Pastel Soc., 1999, Art of Northeast, 50th Ann. award; shows Lindenberg Gallery, N.Y.C., Gallery 214, Montclair, N.J., 2000, Ann. Exhbn. Conn. Acad. Fine Arts, Slater Mus., 2000, 01, 02, Reading Between the Lines: A National Exhbn., Constn. Sq. Hist. Site, Ky. (Purchase award 2000), 2000, Pastel Painters of Maine, 2000 (The Merit award 2000), Nat. Pastel Exhbn., Impact Artists Gallery, Buffalo, N.Y., 2000 (award 2000), 50th Nat. Exhbn. Contemporary Realism in Art, Acad. Artists Assn., 2000, 13th Ann. Exhbn. Pastel Soc., Oreg., 2000, Good and Evil, Fredericksburg Ctr. for Creative Arts, Va. Mus. Fine Arts, 2000, 20th Anniversary Miniature Juried Show, Colorado Springs, 2001, Edward Hopper Ctr., N.Y., 2001, Pastel Nat., Wichita, Kans., 2002. Chmn. bd. Ctrl. Mass. Symphony Orch., 1979—, Ctrl. Mass. chpt. Am. Heart Assn.; bd. dirs. Ctrl. Mass. chpt. ARC; mem. coun. YMCA, Worcester Art Mus.; past vice-chmn. Maine Project Hope. Recipient numerous civic awards. Mem. Degas Pastel Soc., Pastel Soc. Am., Conn. Acad. Fine Arts, United Pastelists Am., Acad. Artists Assn. Republican. Home: Ridge Rd West Brookfield MA 01585 Office: PO Box 1011 West Brookfield MA 01585-1011 E-mail: brianhiggins@charter.net.

HIGGINS, DOROTHY MARIE, academic dean; b. Lawrence, Mass., May 1, 1930; d. John Daniel and Mary Jane (Herbertson) H. AB, Emmanuel Coll., 1951; MS, Cath. U., 1961; PhD, Boston Coll., 1966. Assoc. prof. chemistry Emmanuel Coll., Boston, 1966-88, chair chemistry dept., 1974-85; div. chair math., sci., tech. Roxbury Community Coll., Roxbury Crossing, Mass., 1988-90; dean arts and scis. Teikyo-Post U., Waterbury, Conn., 1990-97; part-time instr. organic chemistry & genl. chemistry Naugatuck Valley C.C., 1998—, rsch. assoc., 1999—, instr. intro. to engring., 1998—. Grant cons. N.E. coll. Optometry, Boston, 1986; faculty cons. Zymark Corp., Hopkinton, Mass., 1982; rsch. assoc. U. Mass., Boston, 1975-84. Editor: (workbook) Geometry: Development Students, 1989; editor sci. newsletter, 1989; editorial adv. bd. Jour. Coll. Sci. Teaching, 1984-88, 2001-2005 Instrumentation grantee NSF, 1985, Chautauqua grantee NSF, 1981-82, Instrumentation grantee George Alden Trust, 1985, Boston Globe Found., 1985, Extramural Assoc. grantee NIH, 1984. Mem. Am. Chem. Soc., Nat. Sci. Tchrs. Assn., New Eng. Chem. Tchrs., Soc. Coll. Sci. Tchg. Democrat. Roman Catholic. Avocations: needlework, crocheting, cross-country skiing. E-mail: dhiggins@snet.net.

HIGGINS, E. TORY, psychology educator, research scientist; b. Montreal, Que., Can., Mar. 12, 1946; s. Benjamin H. Higgins and Agnes C. Quamme; m. Robin S. Wells; 1 child, Kayla. PhD, Columbia U., 1972. Prof. psychology NYU, N.Y.C., 1981—89, Columbia U., N.Y.C., 1989—. Chair sci. awards com. APA; co-founder Ontario Symposium on Personality and Social Psychology; assoc. editor Social Cognition; mem. spl. com. on social psychology and aging Nat. Inst. of Aging Task Force ; exec. com. Soc. Exptl. Social Psychology; mem. com. on sci. rev. restructuring NIH; mem. basic behavioral sci. task force NIMH; chair dept. psychology Columbia U., 1994—2001. Author over 15 edited books and monographs, over 50 book chpts.; contbr. numerous articles to profl. jours. Named Stanley Schachter Prof. Psychology, Columbia U., 2001, Univ. Lectr., 2001; recipient Donald T. Campbell award, Soc. for Personality and Social Psychology, 1996, Thomas M. Ostrom award for outstanding contbns. to social cognition, Social Cognition Soc., 1999, William James Fellow award, Am. Psychol. Soc., 2000, award for disting. sci. contbns., Am. Psychol. Assn., 2000, MERIT award, NIMH, 1999; fellow, Ctr. for Advanced Study in the Behavioral Scis., 1986. Office: Columbia U 116th St New York NY 10027 Office Fax: 212-854-1297.

HIGGINS, EDWARD ALOYSIUS, retired newspaper editor; b. St. Louis, Aug. 22, 1931; s. Edward Aloysius and Elsie (Gummersbach) H.; m. Mary Suzanne Vallar, May 15, 1954; children— Nancy Elizabeth, David Francis, Carol Marie. AB, St. Louis U., 1953; Stanford Journalism fellow, Stanford U., 1968-69. Gen. assignment reporter St. Louis Post-Dispatch, 1953-67, editorial writer, 1967-84, editor Commentary Page, 1984-87, asst. editor editorial page, 1986-87, editor editorial page, 1987-97; ret., 1997. Home: 15340 Braefield Dr Chesterfield MO 63017-1832 E-mail: edwhiggins@msn.com.

HIGGINS, GEORGE EDWARD, sculptor; b. Gaffney, S.C., Nov. 13, 1930; BA, U. N.C. Instr. sculpture Parsons Sch. Design, N.Y.C., 1961-62. Vis. prof. Cornell U., 1968, U. Wis., 1968-69, U. Ky., 1969-70, Sch. Visual Arts, N.Y.C., 1964-72 One man shows, Leo Castelli Gallery, N.Y.C., 1960, 63, 66, Richard

Feigen Gallery, Chgo., 1964, Mpls. Inst. Art, 1964, exhibited group shows Art, USA, 1959, Detroit Inst. Art, 1959-60, Carnegie Inst., 1961, Mus. Modern Art, N.Y.C., 1961, 63, Martha Jackson Gallery, N.Y.C., 1960, Andrew Dickson White Gallery, 1960, Bernard Gallery, Paris, France, 1960, Whitney Mus., N.Y.C., 1964, 66, Documenta, Kassel, Germany, 1968, Art Inst. Chgo., Brandeis U., Tate Gallery, London, Phila. Mus. Arts, New Sch. Art Center, N.Y.C., Smithsonian Instn., numerous others; represented in permanent collections, Whitney Mus., N.Y.C., Guggenheim Mus., N.Y.C., Albright-Knox Gallery, Buffalo, Houston Mus. Fine Arts, Mus. Modern Art, N.Y.C., Albright Art Gallery, Chase Manhattan Bank, N.Y.C., others. Address: 2655 Henley Rd Sanford NC 27330-7549

HIGGINS, GINA O'CONNELL, psychologist, writer; b. Bklyn. d. Paul Bernard Patrick Joseph and Virginia Payne (Conrad) O'Connell; m. James T. Higgins, Aug. 5, 1972 (div. June 1997); children: Caitlin, Taryn; m. R.D. Norton, June 13, 1998; children: Maya, Elias. BA magna cum laude, Tufts U., 1972, MEd, 1974; EdD, Harvard U., 1985. Lic. psychologist, Mass. Diagnostician, med. edn. and evaluation clinic North Shore Children's Hosp., 1982-87; psychotherapist, intake diagnostician, case cons. Mental Health Ctr., North Shore Children's Hosp., 1982-86; fellow Clin. Devel. Inst., Belmont, Mass., 1990—2002; staff psychologist Mass. Gen. Hosp., Boston, 1993—2001; pvt. practice psychotherapy and psychodiagnosis, Salem, Mass., 1993—2002. Lectr. Middlesex C.C., Bedford, Mass., 1974-75, Eliot Pearson dept. child study Tufts U., 1974-75; lectr. Lesley Grad. Sch., Cambridge, Mass., 1974-76, asst. prof., 1976-81; clin. assoc. Harvard Med. Sch./Mass. Gen. Hosp., Boston,. 1994-200102. Author: Resilient Adults: Overcoming a Cruel Past, 1994. Recipient scholarship and fellowships. Mem APA, Mass. Psychol. Assn. Office: One Salem Green Ste 555 Salem MA 01970

HIGGINS, HARRIET PRATT, investment advisor; b. Cortland, N.Y., Dec. 18, 1950; d. Edward Frances and Adeline (Bostelmann) Higgins; children from previous marriage: John Higgins MacDonald, Peter Brewster MacDonald. BA, Wells Coll., 1972; MA, Middlebury Coll. Grad. Sch. Langs., 1973; MBA, Columbia U., 1977. Corp. fin. officer Bank Am., N.Y.C., 1978-80; asst. v.p. J. Henry Schroder Bank and Trust Co., N.Y.C., 1980-82; mgr. Royal Bank Can., N.Y.C., 1982-84, sr. mgr., 1984-94; v.p. pvt. client svcs. TCW Group, N.Y.C., 1994-99; mng. dir. Auda Advisor Assocs. LLC, 1999—2000; mgr., CEO Alyssa LLC, 1999—2000; pres. Mayflower Capital, 2000—; mng. dir., ptnr. Fin. Net Boston, 2001—; regulatory rep. Winston, Evans & Crocher, Boston, 2001—. Adj. prof. econs. Pace U., N.Y.C., 1979 –80, NYU, N.Y.C., 1983—84; chmn., CEO, pres. McGraw, NY, 1987—95; alumni bd. Columbia Bus. Sch., 1982—87; trustee, chair investment com. Wells Coll., 1998—. Vol., contbr. Rep. Nat. Com., N.Y.C., 1980—; trustee Boys and Girls Club, Newport County, 2000—. Fellow Carnegie Found., 1974—75. Mem.: Fin. Womens Assn., Preservation Soc. Newport County, Newport Hist. Soc., Desc. of the Mayflower Soc. Republican. Episcopalian. Avocations: skiing, tennis, violin. Office: Mayflower Capital LLC 33 Broad St Ste 700 Boston MA 02109 E-mail: hhiggins@mayflowercapital.net.

HIGGINS, ISABELLE JEANETTE, librarian; b. Evanston, Ill., Dec. 13, 1919; d. Frank LeRoy and Ada Louise (Wilcox) Heck; m. George Alfred Higgins, Jan. 23, 1945 (dec. Sept. 1994); children: Alfred Clinton, Donald Quentin, Heather Higgins Aanes, Laura Higgins Palmer, Carol Higgins. BS, Northwestern U., 1940; MLS, U. Md., 1971. Cert. libr., Md. With Liebermann Waelchli Co., Tokyo, 1940-41, Shanghai Evening Post, 1941-42; editl. asst. Newsweek mag., N.Y.C., 1944; wire editor FBIS/FCC, Washington, 1944-46; rsch. and analysis China desk CIA, Washington, 1946-49; supr. library vols. Westbrook Sch., Bethesda, Md., 1965-69; reference libr. Montgomery County Pub. Librs., Bethesda, 1969-83; libr. Brooks Inst. Photography, Santa Barbara, Calif., 1984-96, ret., 1996. Treas. Friends of Santa Barbara Pub. Libr., 1987-88. Mem. AAUW (bd. dirs. Santa Barbara br. 1988-94, del. nat. conv. 1989), Spl. Librs. Assn., Calif. Libr. Assn., Santa Barbara Little Gardens Club (pres. 1987-89), Floriade Garden Club (pres. 1990-91). Congregationalist. Avocations: reading, swimming, gardening. Home: # 233 3775 Modoc Rd Santa Barbara CA 93105

HIGGINS, JAMES HENRY, III, marketing executive; b. Providence, May 8, 1940; s. James Henry Jr. and Betty (Hall) H. AB, Brown U., 1962. Mem. faculty Gov. Dummer Acad., Byfield, Mass., 1964-66; rsch. assoc. Entelek Inc., 1966-69; mgr. sch. svc. group Sterling Inst., 1969-72; vice pres. Vickerman and Schultz, Inc., Washington, 1985-87; sr. v.p. Complete Comm., Inc., Washington, 1987-90; dir. devel. The Brit. Consortium, Washington, 1990—. Mktg. cons. Time Life Video, NYC, 1972-73, Longman Group Ltd., Eng., 1973-74, McGraw-Hill Publ. Co., NYC, 1975-85. Lectr., contbr. articles to boating publ. Mem. mgmt. com. A.S.K. Brown Mil. Collection, Brown U., 1990-2000; pres. City TavernPreservation Found., 2000. Mem. Am Soc. Assn. Exec., Naval War Coll. Found. (assoc.), Mystic Seaport Mus. (yachting com. 1986-2000), Antique and Classic Boat Soc. (pres., v.p., bd. dir. 1978-94), Lake Placid Inst. (bd. dir. 1996-2001), Adirondack Archtl. Heritage (bd. dir. 2000—), City Tavern Club (bd. gov. 1998-2000, sec. 1998-2000), Agawam Hunt Club, Hope Club, St. Regis Yacht Club. Home: 2807 O St NW Washington DC 20007-3130 Office: 1101 30th St NW Ste 500 Washington DC 20007-3708

HIGGINS, JAMES JACOB, statistics educator; b. Canton, Ill., Oct. 31, 1943; married, 1967; 2 children. BS, U. Ill., 1965; MS, Ill. State U., 1967; PhD in Stats., U. Mo., 1970. Asst. prof. math. U. Mo., Rolla, 1970-74; from asst. prof. to assoc. prof. math. U. South Fla., 1974-80; prof. stats. Kans. State U., Manhattan, 1980—; dept. head, 1990-95. Fellow Am. Statis. Assn.; mem. Inst. Math. Stats. Achievements include research in reliability theory; classical and Bayesian estimation theory; statistical modelling; experimental design; textbook author. Office: Kans State U Stats Lab Dickens Hall Manhattan KS 66506 E-mail: jhiggins@ksu.edu.

HIGGINS, JANE MARGARET, university official; b. Torrington, Conn., Jan. 10, 1954; d. Edward Corbet and Margaret Katherine (Vestali) H. BA, Ea. Conn. State U., 1976; MEd, U. Mo., 1978; PhD, U. Conn., 1998. Residence hall dir. Western Conn. State U., Danbury, 1977-80; asst. to assoc. dir. housing Ctrl. Conn. State U., New Britain, 1980-82, dir. residence life, 1982-98, assoc. dean student affairs, new student programs, 1998—. Contbr. articles to profl. jours. Asst. div. chair United Way, New Britain, 1985, div. chair edn., 1986; corporator New Britain Gen. Hosp., 1985—. Mem. N.E. Assn. Coll. and Univ. Housing Officers (chair women's issues com. 1989-91), Assn. Coll. and Univ. Housing Officers (chair energy com. 1985-87), Conn. Network of Housing Profls. (pres. 1991-92). Democrat. Roman Catholic. Avocations: walking, music, travel, reading. Office: Ctrl Conn State Univ 1615 Stanley St New Britain CT 06053-2439 E-mail: higginsj@ccsu.edu.

HIGGINS, JANICE, social worker, writer; b. Roswell, N.Mex., Mar. 22, 1963; d. Eddie and Algerita Higgins; children: Kenria Howard, Kupid Davis. Student in Cosmetology, Sierra Vista, Calif. CEO Mim and Praise Dance. Author: There Were No Parents Here, 2002. Avocations: softball, public speaking, helping to motivate homeless people. Home: 403 Emerald Ave Apt 1 El Cajon CA 92020-5044

HIGGINS, JAY F. financial executive; b. Gary, Ind., June 25, 1945; s. J. Francis and Veronica (Conroy) H.; m. Gail Marie Joy, Nov. 23, 1979; children: Maura Ellis, Kerry Elizabeth, Erin Leigh, Conor Francis. AB, Princeton U., 1967; MBA, U. Chgo., 1970. With Salomon Bros., N.Y.C., 1970-92, v.p., 1976, gen. ptnr. mergers and acquisitions dept., 1978, head corp. fin. dept., 1986, vice chmn., head global investment banking, 1987-92; mng. ptnr. Cloverleaf Ptnrs., Inc., Greenwich, Conn., 1992—. With USAR, 1967. Mem. Knights of Malta. Roman Catholic. Home: 2 Hope Farms Rd Bedford NY 10506-2102 Office: Cloverleaf Ptnrs Inc 411 W Putnam Ave Greenwich CT 06830-6261

HIGGINS, JOHN PATRICK, lawyer, mediator, educator, lobbyist; b. Beloit, Wis., Feb. 13, 1952; s. John Eugene and Catherine Marie (Beaudry) H. BA cum laude, St. Norbert Coll., 1973; postgrad., DePaul U. Law Sch., 1974-76; JD, U. Wis., Madison, 1977; MBA, Keller Grad. Sch. Mgmt., Milw., 1986; postgrad., U. Wis., Milw. Bar: Wis. 1977, U.S. Dist. Ct. (ea. and we. dists) Wis., 1977, U.S. Ct. Appeals (7th cir.), 1977, U.S. Supreme Ct., 1983. Assessment technician Kenosha County Assessor, Wis., 1973-75; law clk. various firms, Madison, Wis., 1976-77; claims atty. Employers Ins. of Wausau (Wis.), 1977-80, trial counsel, 1980-99; ptnr. Guttormsen, Hartley, Guttormsen, Wilk & Higgins, Kenosha, 2000—; mng. ptnr. Higgins Investment Properties, LLC, 2002—. Part time instr. North Ctrl. Tech. Inst., Wausau, 1980; adj. prof. Marian Coll., Fond du Lac, Wis., 1990-2000, Carthage Coll., Kenosha, Wis., 2000-01; dir., v.p. legal John E. Higgins Appraisal Co., Kenosha, 1977-97; lectr., spkr. various profl. and fraternal groups; mem. dist. 1 investigative com. Office of Lawyer Regulation Wis. Supreme Ct., 2001—; bd. dirs. St. Joseph HS. Author articles and monographs. Bd. dirs., arbitrator Roman Cath. Archdiocese of Milw., 1983-85; mem. human rels commn. City of Kenosha, 1997—, vice chair, 1999-2001; mem. City of Kenosha Zoning Appeals Bd., 2001—, vice chmn., 2002—; bd. dirs. Michael Naidicz Found. Fellow Young Lawyers Assn.; mem. State Bar Wis. (bd. govs. 1990-91, bd. dirs. young lawyers divsn. 1978-87, sec. 1979-82, chmn. law reform com. 1984-87, chmn. planning conf. young lawyers divsn. 1986, chmn. gavel awards com. 1985-87, chmn. comm. com. 1984-87, interprofl. com. 1987-89, conv. & entertainment com. 1988-1992, 94-97, chmn., mem. various coms.), Thomas More Soc., State Bar Assn. Wis., Civil Trial Coun. Wis., Kenosha Bar Assn., St. Norbert Coll. Alumni Assn. (exec. bd. dirs. 1979-87, chpt. liaison, editor chpt. newsletter, class devel. agt. 1998-99), Nat. Assn. State Bar Jours. (bd. trustee 1986-89), Am. Corp. Coun. Assn. (bd. dirs. 1989-98, pres. Wis. chpt. 1997-98), Am. Acad. ADR Attorneys, Phi Alpha Delta. Office: Guttormsen Hartley Guttormsen Wilk & Higgins LLP 600 52d St Ste 200 Kenosha WI 53140 E-mail: JPH@kenoshalawyers.com.

HIGGINS, JOHN RALPH, writer, educator; b. Chicago, Ill., Apr. 5, 1939; s. John Ralph and Florence Mary Higgins; m. Gayle Agnes Higgins, Aug. 20, 1992; m. Alice Venita Theriault, June 0, 1969 (div.); children: Shannon Patricia, Juliane Alice. BA Psychology, San Jose State U., San Jose, California, 1965. Secondary Teaching Certificate State of Calif., 1971. Bus. owner Relay Sta., Quincy, Calif., 1996—2002; pub./owner Gabriel Pub., Santa Cruz, Calif.; bus. owner Calif. Redwood Playscapes, Santa Cruz, Calif., 1995; pub. Chip Publications, Vancouver, Canada; ptnr./owner Scotts Valley Express, Scotts Valley, Calif., Borges and Higgins Software Devel., San Jose, Calif., 2002; educator Andrew Hill H.S., San Jose, Calif., 1969—75. Music edn. cons., San Jose, Calif. Author 60 books in music edn., co-author 3 edni. software programs; author: (novels) Granite Veil, 2000. Conservative. Protestant. Avocations: music, writing, trumpet. Home: 2214 Reef Ct Discovery Bay CA 94514 Personal E-mail: higgins@sbcglobal.net.

HIGGINS, JOHN STUART, JR., lawyer; b. Providence, Nov. 9, 1939; s. John Stuart and Frances Higgins; m. Karon Ellen Brigman, May 30, 1975; children: Jennifer Reyes, Nathan, Christopher, John, Nicholas, Hanna. AB cum laude, Harvard U., 1961, JD, 1964. Bar: Calif. 1966, U.S. Dist. Ct. (no. dist.) Calif. 1966, U.S. Ct. Appeals (9th cir.) 1966, U.S. Dist. Ct. (ea. dist.) Calif. 1975, U.S. Supreme Ct. 1986, U.S. Dist. Ct. (ctrl. dist.) Calif. 1989. Assoc. Chickering & Gregory, San Francisco, 1965-66; staff atty. San Francisco Neighborhood Legal Assistance Found., 1966-67, Tulare County Legal Svcs. Assn., Tulare, Calif., 1972-75; staff atty., then sr. staff atty. Contra Costa Legal Svcs. Found., Richmond, Calif., 1967-71; pvt. practice, Pleasant Hill, Calif., 1971-72; dep. dist. atty. Tulare County, Visalia, Calif., 1975—2001; child support atty. Tulare County Dept. Child Support Svcs., Visalia, 2001—02, supervising child support atty., 2002—. Chmn. appellate com. Calif. Family Support Coun., Sacramento, 1986-2001. Contbr. articles to law publs. Trustee, chmn. bd. St. Paul's Sch., Visalia, 1978-81, 84-92, 2002—; vestryman St. Paul's Episcopal Ch., 1975-77, 92-94, 97-99, treas. 1976-77, sr. warden, 1994. Recipient Outstanding Achievement award, Nat. Child Support Enforcement Assn., 2000. Mem. State Bar Calif., Marines Meml. Assn. Avocations: hiking, bicycling, skiing. Office: Tulare County Dept Child Support Svcs 8040 W Doe Ave Visalia CA 93291-9721

HIGGINS, KATHRYN O'LEARY, non-profit organization executive; b. Sioux City, Iowa, Oct. 11, 1947; d. Paul C. and Mary Kathryn (Callaghan) O'Leary; widowed; children: Liam James, Kevan Paul. BS, U. Nebr., 1969. Manpower specialist U.S. Dept. Labor, Washington, 1969-78; asst. dir. employment policy White House Domestic Policy, Washington, 1978-81; staff dir. minority U.S. Senate Labor & Human Resources Com., Washington, 1981-86; chief of staff U.S. Representative Sander Levin, Washington, 1986-93, Sec. of Labor Robert Reich, Washington, 1993-95; cabinet sec. White Ho. Cabinet Affairs, Washington, 1995-97, dep. sec. of labor, 1997-99; v.p. pub. policy Nat. Trust for Hist. Preservation, Washington, 1999—. Bd. mem. Charles Carroll House, Surface Transp. Dept. Policy Project Bd.; cabinet mem. Balt. Basilica; bd. dirs. Londontown Found.; bd. dirs. project children young leaders U. Md.. Sch. Pub. Affairs; bd. dirs. Bridges to Peace Lay Vol. Corps; adv. coun. Historic Annapolis. Democrat. Roman Catholic. Avocations: cooking, antiques, book club. Home: 151 Duke Of Gloucester St Annapolis MD 21401-2504 Office: Nat Trust for Historic Preservation 1785 Massachusetts Ave NW Washington DC 20036

HIGGINS, KENNETH DYKE, lawyer; b. Benton, Tenn., Aug. 21, 1916; s. Fredrick Dyke and Martha (Dunn) H.; m. Jane Blair Webb; children: Jane Webb, Kenneth Dyke. AA, Tenn. Wesleyan Coll., 1936, LLB (hon.), 1984; AB, Transylvania U., 1938; JD, Tulane U., 1942. Bar: Tenn. 1946. Ptnr. Higgins, Biddle, Chester & Trew, Athens, Tenn., 1946—. Trustee Tenn. Wesleyan Coll. Served to lt. USN, 1942-46, PTO. Named to Hall of Fame Transylvania U., 1998. Fellow Tenn. Bar Found.; mem. ABA, Tenn. Bar Assn. Lodges: Kiwanis (sec.). Home: 1200 Woodacre Dr Athens TN 37303-2743

HIGGINS, LYNN ANTHONY, humanities educator, writer; b. Ann Arbor, Mich., July 21, 1947; d. Edward Mason and Ann Terbrueggen Anthony; m. Roland Louis Higgins; 1 child, Julian Anthony. BA, Oberlin Coll., 1969; PhD, U. Minn., 1976; MA (hon.), Dartmouth Coll., 1991. Vis. instr. Hamline U., St. Paul, 1973; vis. asst. prof. Semester-at-Sea, U. Pittsburgh, 1982; asst. prof. Dartmouth Coll., NH, 1976—83, assoc. prof., 1983—91, prof., 1991—. Chair Dept. of French & Italian, Dartmouth Coll., 1993—99; adv. bd. WEVO-NH Public Radio Humanities Prog., 1984—90; co-chair Women's Studies Prog. Dept. of French & Italian, 1984—87; guest lectr. NEH Summer Inst., Caen, France, 1999. Author: Parables of Theory: Jean Ricardou's Metafiction, 1984, New Novel, New Wave, New Politics: Fiction and the Representation of History in Postwar France, 1996 (Choice Outstanding Academic Book, 1996, MLA Scaglioni prize in French and Francophone Studies, 1997); co-editor (with Brenda R. Silver): Rape and Representation, 1991, 1993. Recipient Parents Distinguished Rsch. Professorship, Dartmouth Coll., 2002—; fellow NEH Summer Seminar, Princeton U., 1979; grantee Camargo Found. Fellowship, Cassis, France, 1981. Mem.: Modern Language Assn. Avocations: quilting, knitting, swimming, gardening, piano. Office: Darthmouth Coll Dept of French & Italian 6087 Dartmouth Hall Hanover NH 03755 E-mail: lynn.higgins@dartmouth.edu.

HIGGINS, MARGARET ANN, home health nurse, operating room nurse; b. Plattsburgh, NY, Nov. 10, 1949; d. Joseph Alexander and Gertrude Jane (Grogan) Gosselin; m. Richard L. Chellis, Aug. 19, 1971 (div. Nov. 13, 1981); children: Tracey Lynn, Terry Lee; m. Michael F. Higgins, Sept. 27, 1985. LPN, AT&T Ctr., Plattsburgh, 1967; AAS in Nursing, Adirondack C.C., 1969; cert. family support facilitator, U. Vt. Cert. bereavement facilitator Am. Acad. Bereavement. ICU staff nurse Champlain Valley Physician's Hosp. Med. Ctr., Plattsburgh, 1967, oper. rm. staff nurse, 1969—74, St. Luke's Hosp., Denver, 1974—77, Med. Ctr. Hosp. Vt., Burlington, 1977—83; staff nurse, mgr. Profl. Nurses Svc., Winooski, Vt., 1983—. Adv. bd. Traumatic Brain Injury, Vt.; conf. planning com. Parent to Parent Vt. Author: (workbook) These Days of Divorce, 1997. Mem. We. Abenaki Elder's Coun., New Eng.; vol. grief councilor CVU HS, Hinesburg, Vt. Democrat. Roman Catholic. Avocations: Native crafts, Native Am. dance and singing, reading, music. Home: 312 Turkey Ln Panton VT 05491 Office: Profl Nurses Svc Inc PO Box 188 96 W Canal St Winooski VT 05404

HIGGINS, MARGARET CHRISTIE, photographer; b. San Francisco, Apr. 10, 1951; d. James Sloane and Rachel Hall H.; 2 foster children, Armengol Cajares, Phoebe Pandura. BA, Calif. Western U., 1974. Jr. counselor, lifeguard Camp Beaverbrook, Clear Lake, Calif., 1969; resident asst. Calif. Western U., San Diego, 1973-74; disabled veteran's rep. Employment Devel. Dept., 1979-82; asst. tchr. Challenge to Learning, San Francisco, 1985-90; water safety instr. San Francisco, 1985. Author of poems. Psychol. counselor Loma Prieta Earthquake San Francisco, 1989; vol. walked and raised funds Breast Cancer Victims, 1999, Friends for the Elderly, Calif. Pacific Med. Ctr. nursing edn., 1999; vol. Strybing Arboretum, Golden Gate Park, San Francisco, 1995; vol. coach Spl. Olympics; vol. Letterman Army Hosp. ARC; vol. Strybing Arboretum, Golden Gate Park, San Francisco, 1995. Recipient Comdrs.'s Cmty. Svc. award Am. Red Cross. Mem., Relief Team of Loma Prieta earthquake, 1989, Neighborhood Emerg. Response, 1999—. Episcopalian. Avocations: singer, gardening, crafts, poetry, pets.

HIGGINS, MARY CELESTE, lawyer, researcher; b. Chgo., Feb. 9, 1943; d. Maurice James and Helen Marie (Egan) H. AB, St. Mary-of-the-Woods Coll., Ind., 1965; JD, DePaul U., 1970; LLM, John Marshall Law Sch., Chgo., 1976; postgrad., Harvard U., 1981—82, MPA, 1982; MPhil, U. Cambridge (Eng.), 1983. Bar: Ill. 1970, U.S. Dist. Ct. (no. dist.) Ill. 1970. Pvt. practice, Chgo., 1970—72, 1979—80; atty. corp. counsel dept. Continental Bank, Chgo., 1972-76; asst. sec., asst. counsel Marshall Field & Co., Chgo., 1976-79; sr. atty. Mattel, Inc., Hawthorne, Calif., 1980-81; rsch. in revitalization and adjustment of U.S. Industries in U.S. and world markets, 1981-83; legal cons., 1983-85; Midwest regional officer Legal Svcs. Corp., 1985-87, assoc. dir., 1986, acting dir. office of field svcs., 1986-87, dir., 1987-89, Meridian One Corp., Alexandria, Va., 1990—. Recipient Am. Jurisprudence awards for acad. excellence, 1966-70. Mem.: Ill. Bar. Assn. Home: 203 Yoakum Pky Apt 508 Alexandria VA 22304-3711

HIGGINS, MICHAEL EDWARD, finance executive; b. Easton, Md., Nov. 15, 1955; s. George Herman and Margaret Jane (Jones) H. AA, Goldey Beacon Coll., 1975; BS, Salisbury State U., 1981, MBA, 1989. Cost acct. Cambridge (Md.) Wire Cloth Co., 1975-82; adminstrv. asst. Air Plaza West, Church Creek, Md., 1983-84; mktg. svcs. mgr. Nationwide Fulfillment, Ridgely, Md., 1984-86; fin. dir. Dorchester County Commn. Aging, Inc., Cambridge, Md., 1987-99; acct. Shore Health Sys., Inc., Easton, Md., 2000—. Instr. bookkeeping Chesapeake Coll., Cambridge, 1992-95. Bd. dirs. United Fund Dorchester, 1996-99; tchr. Sunday sch. Ch. of Jesus Christ LDS, Cambridge, 1983-2000, fin. clk., 1992-97. Democrat. Avocations: gardening, cooking, reading, geneology. Home: 113 Somerset Ave Cambridge MD 21613-1251 Office: Shore Health Syss Inc 219 S Washington St Easton MD 21601 E-mail: skipjackmike@yahoo.com.

HIGGINS, PETER THOMAS, technology consultant; b. Hackensack, N.J., Aug. 17, 1943; s. Joseph Alexander and Rita Barth (Buckley) H.; m. Kathleen Mary Melehan, June 6, 1970; 1 child, Kelton Charles. BS in Math., Marist Coll., 1967; MS in Math., Computer Sci., Stevens Inst. Tech., 1968. Front desk clk. Carlyle Hotel, N.Y.C., 1964-67; sci. programmer CIA, Washington, 1968-74, project engr., 1974-80, ops. engr. mgr., 1981-86; congl. fellow U.S. House of Reps., Washington, 1986-87, U.S. Senate, Washington, 1987; mgr. rsch. and devel. CIA, Washington, 1987-89, chief info. officer, 1989-92; dep. asst. dir. engrng. FBI, Washington, 1992-95; founder & prin. cons. Higgins & Assocs., Washington, 1995—. Speaker in field; instr. UCLA, 2001—03; mem. bd. advs. NexQL Corp., Dallas. Author: Biometrics-Identity Assurance in the Information Age, 2002. Local leader Jaycees, McLean, Va., 1970; vol. Dem. Nat. Conv., Atlantic City, 1964; Sun. sch. tchr. Holy Trinity Ch., Washington, 1983-91; vol. instr. Presdl. Classroom for Young Ams., 1994-97, 99-2002. Recipient Intelligence medal of merit CIA, 1994. Mem. Am. Polit. Sci. Assn. (Fgn. Affairs Congl. fellow 1986), Congl. Fellows Alumni Steering Com., Internat. Assn. Identification (chmn. automated fingerprint identification com. 1996-2000), Assn. Work Process Improvement (industry leadership coun. 1997-2000). Roman Catholic. Avocations: reading, walking, automobiles. Office: Higgins & Assocs Internat Bldg A Unit 7D 3900 Watson Place NW Washington DC 20016 E-mail: peter.higgins@thehhg.com.

HIGGINS, ROBERT (ROBERT WALTER HIGGINS), career officer, physician; b. Uniontown, Wash., Nov. 9, 1934; s. Nelson Leigh and Abbie Elizabeth (Rowe) H.; m. Barbara Jean Wright, Aug. 19, 1956 (dec. Feb. 2002); children: Fred, Colleen, Jay. BS in Pharmacy, Wash. State U., 1957; MD, U. Wash., 1965. Pharmacist Wenatchee (Wash.) Thrifty Drugs, 1957-59; owner Higgins Drug Store, Pullman, Wash., 1959-61; intern L.A. County Harbor Gen. Hosp., Torrance, 1965-66; commd. lt. USN, 1966; ships surgeon USS Tutuila, Vietnam, 1966-68; ptnr. Ludwick, Zook & Higgins Family Medicine, Wenatchee, 1968-72; commd. lt. comdr. USN, 1972, advanced through grades to rear adm., 1988; chmn. dept. family medicine Naval Hosp., Charleston, S.C., 1972-78, Camp Pendleton, Calif., 1978-80, Bremerton, Wash., 1980-86, comdg. officer Camp Pendleton, 1986-87; med. officer USMC Washington, 1987-89; dep. surgeon gen. USN, 1989-93. Specialty advisor surgeon gen. USN, Washington, 1973-86. Contbg. author: Behavioral Disorders, 1984, 90; contbr. articles to profl. jours. Scoutmaster Boy Scouts Am., Charleston, 1974-78, Camp Pendleton, 1978-80; trustee Family Health Found. Am., Wash. State U. Found., 1992-98; bd. visitors Wash. State U. Coll. Pharmacy, 1998—, pres., 2002—. Decorated Disting. Svc. medal, Legion of Merit, Meritorious Svc. medal, Navy Commendation medal; recipient Alumni Achievement award Wash. State. U., 1988, Disting. Alumnus award U. Wash. Sch. Medicine, 1996; bd. regents disting. alumnus award, Wash. State U., 2002. Fellow: Am. Acad. Family Physicians (pres. 1984—85, alt. del. to AMA 1985—91, del. 1992—2000, John G. Walsh award 2001), Philippine Acad. Family Physicians (hon.); mem.: World Orgn. Family Medicine (v.p. 1986—95, pres.-elect 1995—98, pres. 1998—2001), Uniformed Svcs. Acad. Family Physicians (pres. 1974—76), Masons. Avocations: bird watching, fly fishing, model airplanes, stamp collection, jogging. Home and Office: 2303 Highland Dr Anacortes WA 98221-3143 E-mail: rhigginsmd@aol.com.

HIGGINS, ROBERT ARTHUR, electrical engineer, educator, consultant; b. Watertown, S.D., Sept. 5, 1924; s. Arthur C. and Nicoline (Huseth) H.; m. Barbara Jeanne Fagerlie, 1958; children— Patricia Suzanne, Daniel Alfred, Steven Robert BEE with honors, U. Minn., 1948; MSEE, U. Wis., 1964; PhDEE, U. Mo., 1969. Registered profl. engr. Engr. Schlumberger Well Survey Corp., Tex., 1948-57; rsch. technologist Mobil Rsch. and Devel. Corp., Tex., 1958-61; rsch. engr. United Aircraft Rsch. Labs., Conn., 1965; staff specialist Remote Sensing Inst., S.D., 1969-71; asst. prof. elec. engrng. S.D. State U., 1969-74, assoc. dir. Engrng. Expt. Sta., 1973-77, prof. elec. engrng., 1974-79; cons. Mankato State U., 1980; prin. engr. Sperry Univac, 1981-85; prof. elec. engrng. St. Cloud (Minn.) State U., 1985-95, prof. emeritus, 1995—. Cons. Control Data Corp., 1977-80, Lawrence Livermore Lab., 1971-73, USAF Office Sci. Rsch., Fla., 1976, NCR-Comten, 1988-90, FMC Corp., 1991-92, Ontrack Computer Sys., 1993-98; project dir., cons. NSF, 1973-80, 87-89. Contbr. articles to profl. jours. Bd. dirs. Eden Prairie Bd. Edn., Minn., 1982-85, Nat. Storage Industry Consortium, 1995-98. With CE, AUS, 1943-46. NASA fellow, 1966-68; grantee NSF, 1966, 72, 74, 86, AEC, 1971-73, Office Water Resources Research, 1971-74 Mem. IEEE (sr., life), Am. Soc. Engrng. Educators, Sigma Xi, Eta Kappa Nu. Lutheran. Home: 11260 Windrow Dr Eden Prairie MN 55344-4055 E-mail: rahiggins@ieee.org.

HIGGINS, ROBIN L. federal agency administrator; B in English, SUNY, Oneonta; M in English, Long Island U.; postgrad., Hebrew U., Jerusalem. Commd. USMC, advanced through grades to lt. col., ret.; dep. asst. sec., acting asst. sec. Vet.'s Employment and Tng. U.S. Dept. Labor; exec. dir. Fla. Dept. Vet.'s Affairs, 1999—2001; under sec. meml. affairs Dept. Vet. Affairs, Washington, 2001—. Author: Patriot Dreams - The Murder of Colonel Rich Higgins. Recipient Dickey Chapelle award, Marine Corps League, Pub. Spirit award, Am. Legion, Vets. Caucus award, Am. Acad. Physician Assts. Mem.: Marine Corps League, AmVets, Jewish War Vets., Retired Officers' Assn., Disabled Am. Vets., Gold Star Wives, Am. Legion. Office: US Dept Vet Affairs Nat Cemetery Adminstrn 810 Vermont Ave NW Washington DC 20420

HIGGINS, DAME ROSALYN, judge of international court of justice; b. June 2, 1937; d. Lewis Cohenand F. Inberg; m. Terence L. Higgins, 1961; 2 children. Student, Cambridge U., Yale U. Intern Office Legal Affairs UN, 1958; Commonwealth Fund fellow, 1959; vis. fellow Brookings Inst., Washington, 1960; jr. fellow internat. studies L.S.E., 1961-63, vis. fellow, 1974-78; staff specialist internat. law Royal Inst. Internat. Affairs, 1963-74; prof. internat. law U. Kent, Canterbury, Eng., 1978-81, L.S.E., 1981-95; judge Internat. Ct. Justice, The Hague, The Netherlands, 1995—. Mem. com. human rights UN, 1985-95; vis prof. Stanford U., 1975, Yale U., 1977; v.p. Brit. Inst. Internat. Comparative Law, 2002–. Author: The Development of International Law through the Political Organs of the United Nations, 1963, Conflict of Interests, 1965, The Administration of the United Kingdom Foreign Policy through the United Nations, 1966, UN Peacekeeping: Documents and Commentary; editor:

(with James Fawcett) Law in Movement—Essays in Memory of John McMahon, 1974, Problems & Process, 1994, Terrorism & International Law, 1997; contbr. articles to profl. jours. Mem. Ordre Palmes Academiques. Avocations: sports, cooking. Office: Internat Ct Justice Peace Palace 2517KJ The Hague Netherlands

HIGGINS, ROXANNE SNELLING, educational consultant; b. Ft. Eustis, Va., Aug. 17, 1954; d. William Rodman and Anne Louise (Kurtz) Snelling; m. Vincent James Elliott, Oct. 1, 1983 (div.); children: Brian William, Lauren Elizabeth; m. Robert K. Higgins, June 16, 2001. BA, Denison U., 1976; MBA, Syracuse U., 1978. Internat. loan officer First Pa. Bank, Phila., 1978-82; ins. assoc. Ind. Sch. Mgmt., Wilmington, Del, 1982-83, dir. mgmt. insts., 1983-87, cons., exec. dir. consortium, 1984—, v.p., 1986-90, pres., 1990—. Office: Ind Sch Mgmt 1316 N Union St Wilmington DE 19806-2594

HIGGINS, RUTH ANN, social worker, family therapist; b. Rock Valley, Iowa, Sept. 23, 1944; d. Neal and Tillie (Feekes) Vonk; m. 1972 (div. Sept. 1986); children: Ashlie Kay, Steven Grant. BA, Northwestern Coll., 1966; MA, U. Colo., 1978; LCSW, U. Denver, 1983. Cert. profl. tchr., Colo., social worker, Colo. Tchr. Adams County Dist. 12, Northglenn, Colo., 1967-69, Dept. Def., Clark AFB, The Philippines, 1969-70, Jefferson County Schs., Lakewood, Colo., 1970-75; social worker Boulder (Colo.) County Mental Health Ctr., 1977, Boulder Community Counseling Ctr., 1979-81, Columbine Counseling Ctr., Broomfield, Colo., 1981—; sch. social worker Adams County Sch. Dist. 12, Northglenn, Colo., 1985—. Part time social worker Hospice of Metro Denver, 1984-85, Boulder Valley Pub. Schs., 1985, Lutheran Hospice Care, Wheatridge, Colo., 1985. Author, editor: Nothing Could Stop the Rain, 1976. Counselor trainer for Up With People (Worldsmart), 1998-2000. Recipient Hon. Mention Counselor of Yr. award Colo. Sch. Counselors Assn., 1994; named finalist Alteria M. Bryant award Met. Denver Baha'i Ctr., 1996. Mem. Nat. Assn. Social Workers. Democrat. Avocations: stained glass, hiking, reading, music.

HIGGINS, SHAUN O'LEARY, media executive; b. Princeton, Ind., Mar. 22, 1948; s. John Frank and Laura Dorothea (Thompson) H.; m. Ann Glendening, Nov. 23, 1975; children: Flannery Maeve, Ian Dashiell. BA in Comm., DePauw U., 1971. Reporter, city editor Lu-Mar Newspapers, Inc., Bloomington, Ind., 1967-69; mng. editor The Times, Brazil, Ind., 1969-72; congl. cand. 7th Dist. Ind. Dem., Brazil, 1972; cons. Keep's Creek Assocs., Indpls., 1972-73; wire editor Times & Times World, Roanoke, Va., 1973-74; freelance writer, editor self-employed, N.Y.C., 1974-75; news editor, state bur. chief Lee Newspapers, Inc., Billings, Helena, Mont., 1975-79; asst. mng. editor Cowles Pub. Co., Spokane, Wash., 1973-83, mktg. dir., 1983-88, dir. mktg. and sales, 1988—, chief mktg. officer, 1999; pres., COO New Media Ventures, Inc., Cowles Pub. Co., Spokane, Wash., 1993—; chmn., CEO Print Mktg. Concepts, Inc., Houston, 1996—. Cons. in field; instr. in field; owner The Oxalis Group, Spokane, 1979—. Author: Leadership Secrets of Elizabeth I, 2001, The Newspaper in Art, 1997, Movies for Leaders, 2000, Movies for Business, 2003. Bd. dirs., trustee Wash. Commn. for Humanities, Seattle, 1988-93, United Way of Spokane County, 1988-91; trustee Northwest Mus. Arts and Culture, 2001—; mem. pub. rels. adv. bd. DePauw U., 1996—; bd. dirs. Spokane Regional Conv. and Visitors Bur., 1991-94, Spokane Symphony Orch., 1991-96, Cmty. Devel. Bd., Spokane, 1986-88; trustee, chmn. Spokane Area Econ. Devel. Coun., 1983-91, chair, 1990; chmn. Festival of Four Cultures, 1989. Recipient Emmy(s) NATAS, 1987, Telly awards Cin. Broadcasters, 1988, 2000, MAX Best of Show award Spokane Advt. Fedn., 1988, Best of Show award Internat. Newspaper Mktg. Assn., 1987, Silver Strand award INMA-West, 1993; named Spokane Advt. Profl. of Yr., 1988, Northwest Print Media Person of the Year Media, Inc., 1992. Mem. Spokane Advt. Fedn. (pres. 1988-89, Lifetime Achievement award 2000), Direct Mktg. Assn., Pub. Rels. Soc. Am., Soc. Profl. Journalists, Am. Statis. Assn., Internat. Newspaper Mktg. Assn. (trustee, internat. pres. 1993—, Silver Shovel award 1996), Newspaper Assn. Am. (retail coun., bus. devel. com., chair nat. polit. task force), Fedn. Internationale des editeurs des Journaux (exec., dir.), Chautauqua Soc. of Eastern Wash. U., Voltaire Soc. Am. (founding). Vachel Lindsay Assn., Spokane Club. Avocations: book collecting, reading, travel. Home: 428 W 27th Ave Spokane WA 99203-1854 Office: Cowles Pub Co 999 W Riverside Ave Spokane WA 99201-1006 E-mail: shaunh@spokesman.com.

HIGGINS, SISTER THERESE, English educator, former college president; b. Winthrop, Mass., Sept. 29, 1925; d. James C. and Margaret M. (Lennon) H. AB cum laude, Regis Coll., 1947; MA, Boston Coll., 1959, DHL, 1993; PhD, U. Wis., 1963; DHL, Emmanuel Coll., 1977, Lesley Coll., 1991; postgrad. in lit. and theology, Harvard U., 1965-66; LLD (hon.), Northeastern U., 1982, Bentley Coll., 1992, Regis Coll., 1994. Joined Congregation of Sisters of St. Joseph, Roman Cath. Ch., 1947; asst. prof. English, Regis Coll., Weston, Mass., 1963-65, asst. prof., 1965-67, assoc. prof. English lit., 1968—, pres., 1974-92, also trustee, v.p. devel., 2003—. Book reviewer Boston Globe, 1965—. Trustee Waltham (Mass.) Hosp., 1978-85, Cardinal Spellman Philatelic Mus., 1976-92; mem. Mass. Gov.'s Commn. on Status Women, 1977-79, Nat. Com. Ecclesial Role Women, Archdiocesan Fin. Coun., 1991—. U. Wis. research grantee Eng. Mem. Nat. Cath. Ednl. Assn., AAUW, MLA, AAUP, Assn. Ind. Colls. and Univs. Mass. (exec. com.), New Eng. Colls. Fund, NEASC (commn.). Office: Regis Coll 235 Wellesley St Weston MA 02493-1505

HIGGINS, WALTER M., III, electric power industry executive; b. 1945; BS in Nuclear Sci., U.S. Naval Acad., 1966; student, U.S. Nuclear Power Tng. Program, 1966-68, U. Idaho, 1979; MBA, George Washington U., 1975-77. Commd. USN, 1966, advanced through grades; nuclear engr. Charleston Navy Shipyard, until 1974; sr. nuclear engr. Bechtel Power Corp., Washington, 1975; with U.S. Nuclear Regulatory Commn., Washington, 1975-77; various mgmt. and exec. positions Portland (Oreg.) Gen. Electric Co., 1977-91; pres., COO Louisville Gas and Electric Co., 1991—93; chmn., pres. CEO Sierra Pacific, 1993—98, AGL Resources Inc., Atlanta, 1998—2000, Sierra Pacific Resources, Reno, 2000—. Office: Sierra Pacific Resources 6100 Neil Rd Reno NV 89511*

HIGGINS, WILLIAM WOODS, painter, art educator; b. St. Paul, Feb. 19, 1947; s. John Russell-William Higgins and Helen Catherine Woods; children: Alexander, Catherine. MA, U. Toledo, 1971. Painter, 1972—; lectr. art, theology, and philosophy Geologengasse, Vienna, 1987—. Exhibits include Longboat Key (Fla.) Art Ctr., 1973, 75, Sarasota (Fla.) Art Ctr., 1977, 79, Whitney Mus., N.Y.C., 1979, Coconut Grove (Fla.) Art Festival, 1987, 88, 89, 92, Coconut Grove Playhouse, 1988, Spoleto Festival, Charleston, S.C., 1991, 92, 97, 98, XIII Internat. Congress of Vedanta, Oxford, Ohio, 2002. Avocations: swimming, chess, writing screenplays. Office: Geologengasse 8/6 A-1030 Vienna Austria E-mail: utchateye@lowcountry.com.

HIGGINS-BIDDLE, JOHN CHARLES, humanities educator, consultant; b. Chgo., Aug. 8, 1940; s. Arthur Cooper and Elizabeth F. Biddle; m. Lesley Hall Higgins, May 16, 1982; children: Molly Anne, Mark Russell Biddle, Kathleen Elizabeth Muravnick. BA, Miami U., Ohio, 1962, MA, 1967; PhD, Stanford U., Calif., 1972. Asst. & assoc. prof. Yale U. Div. Sch., New Haven, 1972—81; exec. staff United Way of Ea. Fairfield County, Bridgeport, Conn., 1981—91; exec. dir. Conn. Alcohol & Drug Abuse Commn., Hartford, Conn., 1991—93; asst. prof. U. of Conn. Health Ctr., Farmington, 1993—. Author: (book) John Locke: The Reasonableness of Christianity, (manuals) World Health Orgn. Fellow Younger Humanist award, Nat. Endowment for the Humanities, 1974—75; Leverhulme fellow, Trinity Coll., Cambridge, 1969—70. Achievements include development of one of nation's first community partnership to address substance abuse; research in alcohol screening and brief intervention. Avocations: gardening, woodworking. Office: U of Conn Health Ctr 263 Farmington Ave Farmington CT 06030-6302 Personal E-mail: johnhb@adelphia.net. E-mail: johnbh@nso2.uchc.edu.

HIGGINSON, BOBBY, professional baseball player; b. Phila., Aug. 18, 1970; Baseball player Detroit Tigers, 1995—. Office: Detroit Tigers 2100 Woodward Detroit MI 48201

HIGGINSON, JOHN, retired career officer; b. St. Louis, Oct. 24, 1932; s. John and Clara Elizabeth (Lindemann) H.; married; children: Robert, Mark, Patrick, Paul. BA, St. Mary's U., 1954; BS, Naval Postgrad. Sch., 1966; MS, George Washington U., 1968. Ensign USN, advanced through grades to Rear Adm., ret.; comdr. Helicopter Anti-submarine Squadron 2, 1973-74, Helicopter Anti-submarine Squadron 10, 1976-78, USS Inchon, 1979-80, Amphibious Squadron 7, 1981-83, Amphibious Group 3, 1985, Naval Surface Group, Long Beach, 1986, ret., 1990-92; pres. Long Beach C. of C. Prof. mgmt. Naval War Coll., Newport, R.I. Co-author: Sea and Air, The Marine Environment, 1968, 2nd. edit., 1973. Bd. dirs. United Way, L.A., Long Beach Symphony, Long Beach Youth Activities, DARE, Inc., USO, Leadership Long Beach, St. Mary's Med. Ctr., Meml. Med. Ctr. of Long Beach; trustee Long Beach City Coll. Found., Long Beach Civic Light Opera; mem. exec. bd. of Long Beach Boy Scouts of Am.; mem. exec. coun. Industry-Edn. Coun. of Calif.; former chmn. L.A. Combined Fed. Campaign; pres., CEO Am. Gold Star Manor Charitable Trust, 1993—. Mem. Navy Helicopter Assn. (former pres.), Fed. Exec. Bd. (former chmn.), Rotary (commr. Calif., mem. Vets. Meml. Commn.). Home: 5341 Las Lomas Park Estates Long Beach CA 90815 E-mail: jhigginson@mpicomputers.com.

HIGGS, CRAIG DEWITT, lawyer; b. Coronado, Calif., Mar. 19, 1944; s. DeWitt Alexander and Florence (Fuller) H.; children: Marisa DeWitt, Alexander Craig; m. Cynthia Aaron, May 19, 1993. B.S., U. Redlands, 1966; J.D., U. San Diego, 1969. Bar: Calif. 1971, U.S. Dist. Ct. (so. dist.) Calif. 1971. Dept. city atty. San Diego, 1970-71; assoc. Higgs, Fletcher & Mack, San Diego, 1971-76, ptnr., 1976—; del. 9th Cir. Jud. Conf., 1992-94; dir. San Diego Law Ctr., 1983-89. Bd. visitors U. San Diego Sch. Law, 1983—. Mem. San Diego Bar Found. (bd. dirs. 1983-89), Am. Bd. Trial Advocates (pres. 1995), San Diego Inn of Cts. (pres. 1993), State Bar Calif. (chmn. commn. on jud. nominees evaluation 1981), San Diego County Bar Assn. (pres. 1984). Democrat. Home: 12686 Crest Knolls Ct San Diego CA 92130-2411 Office: Higgs Fletcher & Mack 401 W A St Ste 2600 San Diego CA 92101-7913

HIGGS, DAVID LAWRENCE, lawyer; b. Canton, Ill., Aug. 14, 1951; s. Louis Wilson and Lois (Gentle) H.; m. Carolyn Jean Perardi, June 24, 1973; children: Craig, Scott. BS with high honors, Western Ill. U., 1972; JD summa cum laude, So. Ill. U., 1981. Bar: Ill. 1981, U.S. Dist. Ct. (no. dist.) Ill. 1981, U.S. Ct. Appeals (7th cir.) 1982, U.S. Tax Ct. 1982. Ptnr. Sutkowski & Washkuhn Assocs., Peoria, Ill., 1981-91, Husch & Eppenberger, Peoria, 1991—. Contbr. articles to profl. jours. Mem. ABA, Ill. State Bar Assn. (employee benefits sect. coun. 1990-91, Chmn. award 1991), Peoria County Bar Assn., Estate Planning Coun. of Peoria, Peoria-North Rotary. Presbyterian. Avocation: golf. Office: Husch & Eppenberger LLC 401 Main St Ste 1400 Peoria IL 61602-1258

HIGGS, JOHN H. lawyer; b. Balt., Mar. 10, 1934; s. E. Homer and Josephine (Doughty) H.; m. Helen Platt, Aug. 25, 1956; children: Sarah, Anne, Julia, Susan. AB, Dartmouth Coll., 1956; LLB, U. Pa., 1960. Bar: N.Y. 1961. Founder Higgs Pavements Co., Milford, Conn., 1953-56; assoc. Sullivan & Cromwell, N.Y.C., 1960-61, 62-68, Wickes, Riddell, Bloomer, Jacobi & McGuire, N.Y.C., 1968, ptnr., 1969-79, Morgan, Lewis & Bockius, LLP, N.Y.C., 1979-97, counsel, 1997—; ptnr. Skyport Indsl. Park, Newark, N.J. Sec. Ea. States Bankcard Assn., Lake Success, N.Y., 1970-88; bd. dirs. Indsl. Bank Japan Trust Co., N.Y., 1974—, IBJ Found. Inc., N.Y., 1989—; mem. staff adv. com. on comml. bank supervision State N.Y., 1965-66. Contbr. articles to profl. jours. Mayor Village of Pelham Manor, N.Y., 1979-81. Home: John's Island 45 Wax Myrtle Way Vero Beach FL 32963-3721 Office: Morgan Lewis & Bockius 101 Park Ave Fl 44 New York NY 10178-0060

HIGGS, JON SCOTT, computer company executive, researcher; b. Manhasset, N.Y., Dec. 18, 1956; s. Donald Robert and Jean Marie Higgs. BA, Haverford Coll., 1978. Area mgr. U.S. Treasury, U.S. Savings Bonds divsn., Phila., 1978-84; tech. cons. NSTL, Plymouth Meeting, Pa., 1984-89, project mgr., 1989-93; pres. PC Wizards, Wayne, Pa., 1993—. Internat. computer lab. cons. Nat. Software Testing Labs./Groupe Tests, Paris, 1992. Author: Early One Morning, 1995; author, rschr. Software Digest, 1989-98; contbr. articles to profl. jours. Recipient Choreography award County Dance and Song Soc., 1993. Avocation: choral singing. Home: 588 Forest Rd Wayne PA 19087-2322 Office: PC Wizards 588 Forest Rd Wayne PA 19087-2322

HIGH, JEFFREY L. humanities educator; b. Amesburg, Mass., Nov. 25, 1962; s. Joseph Lester and Mary Elizabeth High. BA, U. Mass., Boston, 1988; MA, U. Mass., 1990, PhD, 2001. Vis. lectr. U. Mass., Amherst, 1992—93; assoc. edn. specialist U. Minn., Mpls., 1996—2002; asst. prof. Calif. State U., Long Beach, 2002—. Author: (literary history-book) Die Goethezeit: Werke-Wirkung-Wechselbeziehungen, 2001. Scholar, Fulbright Commn., 1994—95, 1995—96. Mem.: MLA, Am. Soc. for Eighteenth Century Studies, German Schiller Soc.

HIGH, LINDA OATMAN, author; b. Ephrata, Pa., Apr. 28, 1958; d. Robert and Mary (Millard) Haas; m. John David High; four children. Author: Maizie, 1995, Hound Heaven, 1995, A Christmas Star, 1997, A Stone's Throw from Paradise, 1997, Hogwash, History & Horse Sense, 1997, Beekeepers, 1998, The Summer of the Great Divide, 1998, Barn Savers, 1999, Under New York, 2000, The Last Chimney of Christmas Eve, 2000, Winter Shoes for Shadow Horse, 2001, A Humble Life: Plain Poems, 2001, The President's Puppy, 2002, The Girl on the High-Diving Horse, 2003. Mem. Soc. Children's Book Writers & Illustrators, Pennwriters. Home: 1209 Reading Rd Narvon PA 17555-9352 E-mail: lohigh@desupernet.net.

HIGH, S. DALE, diversified company executive; b. Lancaster, Pa., May 2, 1942; s. Sanford H. and Erma (Denlinger) H.; m. Sadie S. Horst; children from previous marriage: Steven D., Gregory A., Suzanne M. BSBA, Elizabethtown Coll., 1963, LDH (hon.), 1993; LDH (hon.), Thaddeus Stevens Coll. Tech., 2002. Exec. v.p. High Steel Structures, Inc., Lancaster, 1963-77; ptnr. High Properties, Lancaster, 1963—; chmn., pres. High Industries, Inc., Lancaster, 1977—; dir. High Employee Svcs., Ltd., Lancaster. Bd. dirs. High Investors, Ltd., Lancaster, High Food Svcs., Ltd., Lancaster, High Hotels Ltd., Lancaster, Pa. Chamber, Inc., 1995—, Penn Sq. Gen. Corp., chmn.; chmn. bd. dirs. Sageworth Holdings, Inc., 2000—; mem. panel of judges Ctrl. Pa. Entrepreneur of the Yr. Award Program, 1994—95, chmn., 1996; bd. dirs. Educators Mutal Life Ins. Co., 1979—2002. Trustee High Found., Lancaster, 1985—, Lancaster County Found., Elizabethtown Coll., Pa., 1974—99, Lancaster Gen. Hosp., 1976—84; vice chmn. High Found., Lancaster, 2003—; mem. Pa. State Rep. com., Harrisburg, 1985; co-chmn. fin. Lancaster County Rep. Com., 1985—88; chmn. Pa. Chamber PAC, 2002; mem. adv. com. Friends of Better Govt. PAC, 2000—; bd. dirs. United Way Lancaster County, 1975—78, Lancaster County Rev. Commn., 1984—86, Pa. Chamber of Bus. and Industry, Harrisburg, 1991—, vice-chair, 2000—02, chmn., 2003—; bd. dirs. Modern Transit Partnership, 1998—2002. Named Outstanding Young Man, Lancaster Jaycees, 1977, Disting. Pennsylvanian, Phila. C. of C., 1981; recipient Exemplar award Lancaster C. of C. and Industry, 1995, Disting. Bus. Alumni award Elizabethtown Coll., 1995, Jr. Achievement Spirit Achievement award, 1997, Pa. Dutch Coun./BSA Disting. Citizen award, 1999; named Ctrl. Pa. Master Entrepreneur of Yr. Ernst & Young, 1999, Pa. Chamber of Bus. and Industry Outstanding Bus. Leader, 1999, Nat. Entrepreneur of Yr., Real Estate, Ernst and Young, 1999, Centennial medal Elizabethtown Coll., 2000, Cmty. Svc. award Lancaster Rotary Club, 2000, Educate for Svc. award Elizabethtown Coll., 2000, Bus. Achievement award West Shore C. of C., 2001, Family Bus. of Yr. award Wharton Enterprising Families Initiative, 2002. Mem. World Pres.'s Orgn., Lancaster C. of C. (bd. dirs. 1976-82, chmn. 1981), Hamilton Club, Lancaster Country Club, Tuesday Club, Delta Mu Delta (hon.). Republican. Presbyterian. Avocations: reading, bicycling, hiking, travel. Office: High Industries Inc PO Box 10008 1853 William Penn Way Lancaster PA 17601-6713

HIGH, TIMOTHY GRIFFIN, artist, educator, curator, writer; b. Memphis, Tenn., Mar. 10, 1949; s. Warren Barrett and Jo Ellen (Wise) H.; m. Cynthia Spikes, Aug. 10, 1973. BFA, Tex. Tech U., 1973, MA, 1975; MFA, U. Wis., 1976. Assoc. prof. U. Tex., Austin, 1976—. Visual artist drawings, serigraphs, papermaking, monoprints, monotypes, water-media painting, installation and papier maché sculpture; free-lance writer. Over 225 solo, invitational and gallery group shows since 1976, including Amarillo (Tex.) Art Mus., 1993, Martin-Rathburn Gallery, San Antonio, 1997, Tarrytown Gallery, Austin, 2001, Gallery W, Sacramento, 2002; group exhbns. include Adair Margo Gallery, El Paso, Tex., 1996, 177th Ann. Exhbn. of NAD, Mus. Visual Art, N.Y.C., 2002; represented in permanent collections including Art Inst. Chgo., Bklyn. Mus., Mus. Fine Art, Boston, Met. Mus. Art, N.Y.C., Fogg Mus., Cambridge, Mass., Mus. Fine Art, Houston, Milw. Mus. Art; curator group invitational exhbns., Tex. Prints, 2001, Tex. Xpress-I, 2001, Border Crossings, 2001, Three Aces, 2002, Bread Upon the Water, 2003. Travel fellow Ford Found., Peruvian Andes, 1978; individual artist fellow Nat. Endowment Arts, 1989, 2001. Mem. So. Graphics Coun. (conf. coord. 1989, 2001), Mid-Am. Coll. Art Assn. (1998 conf. spkr.), Nat. Assn. Scholars (panelist conv. 1993), Tex. Fine Arts Assn., Christians in Visual Art, CIVA Printmakers Network (chair 2003). Avocations: travel, photography, backpacking, fly fishing, reading. Address: care/Terra Rosa Studio 2308 Lawnmont Ave Austin TX 78756-1915 Office: Univ of Tex Austin Dept Art & Art History Austin TX 78712

HIGH, WILLIAM FRAY, lawyer; b. Kansas City, Kans., Nov. 23, 1962; s. Cecil Ray and Kimi Judy (Tsychia) H.; m. L. Brooke High, Aug. 8, 1987; children: Ashley Brooke, Jessica Kimi, Nathan William, Joseph Wesley. BS, U. Mo., 1984; JD, U. Kans., 1988. Bar: Mo. 1988, Kans. 1989, U.S. Dist. Ct. (we. dist.) Mo. 1988, U.S. Dist. Ct. Kans. 1989. Tchr. Independence (Mo.) Pub. Schs., 1981-88; assoc. Blackwell Sanders Matheny Weary & Lombardi, Kansas City, Mo., 1988—2001, Sanders Conkright & Warren, 2001—; pres., gen. counsel Christian Cmty. Found., Kansas City, 2000—. Contbr. articles to profl. jours. Mem. Oak Hills Presbyn. Ch.; precinct committeeman Rep. Orgn., Olathe, 1990—; chmn. Action Com., Olathe, 1991—. Recipient scholarship Johnson County Bar Found., 1989, Student Found., Columbia, Mo., 1983. Mem. Mo. Bar Assn., Kans. Bar Assn., Kans. City Met. Bar Assn., Johnson County Bar Assn. Avocations: running, reading. Office: Christian Cmty Found 1599 Ridgeview Ste 103 Olathe KS 66061

HIGHAM, PAUL H. marketing professional; Sr. v.p. mktg. and sales promotions Wal-Mart Stores, Inc., Bentonville, Ark. Office: Wal-Mart Stores Inc 702 SW 8th St Bentonville AR 72716-6299

HIGHAM, ROBIN, historian, editor, publisher; b. London, June 20, 1925; came to U.S., 1940, naturalized, 1954; s. David and Margaret Anne (Stewart) H.; m. Barbara Davies, Aug. 5, 1950; children: Peter (dec.), Susan Elizabeth (dec.), Martha Anne, Carol Lee. AB cum laude, Harvard U., 1950, PhD, 1957; MA, Claremont Grad. Sch., 1953. Instr. Webb Sch. Calif., 1950-52; grad. asst. in oceanic history Harvard U., 1952-54; instr. U. Mass., 1954-57; asst. prof. U. N.C., Chapel Hill, 1957-63, assoc. prof. history Kans. State U., 1963-66, prof., 1966-98; historian Brit. Overseas Airways Corp., 1960-66, 76-78; editor Mil. Affairs, 1968-88, emeritus; editor Aerospace Historian, 1970-88, emeritus, 1989—; editor, pub. Jour. of the West, 1977—; adv. editor Tech. and Culture, 1967-85; founder, pres. Sunflower Univ. Press, 1977—; mil. adv. editor Univ. Press Ky., 1970-75. Cons. Epic of Flight, Time/Life Books, 1980-82; lectr. in field; mem. publs. com. Conf. Brit. Studies, 1965-93; advisor Core Collection for Coll. Librs., 1971-72; pres., cons. com. Revue Internat. d'Histoire Militaire, 1976-85, mem. mil. archives com., 1990—, acting pres., 1996-2000, sec. gen., 2002—; founder, organizer Conf. Historic Aviation Writers, 1982-98. Author: Britain's Imperial Air Routes, 1918-39, 1960, The British Rigid Airship, 1908-31, 1961, Armed Forces in Peacetime: Britain 1918-39, 1963, The Military Intellectuals in Britain: 1918-1939, 1966, (with David H. Zook) A Short History of Warfare, 1966, Hebrew edit., 1970, Chinese edit., 1985, The Compleat Academic (Macmillan Book Club choice), 1975, Air Power: A Concise History (selection Mil. Book Soc., History Book Club, Flying Book Club), 1973, 2d enlarged edit., 1984, 3d enlarged edit., 1988, The Bases of Air Strategy, 1998, (with Mary Cisper & Guy Dresser) A Brief Guide to Scholarly Editing, 1982, Diary of a Disaster: British Aid to Greece, 1940-41, 1986; editor: Bayonets in the Streets, 1969, 89, Civil Wars in the Twentieth Century, 1972, A Guide to the Sources of British Military History, 1971, A Guide to the Sources of U.S. Military History, 1975, (with Donald J. Mrozek) supplements, 1981, 86, 93, 99 (with Carol Brandt) The U.S. Army in Peacetime: Essays in Honor of the Bicentennial, 1975, Intervention or Abstention, 1975, (with Jacob W. Kipp) Soviet Aviation and Air Power, 1977, Garland Military History Bibliographic Series (with Jacob W. Kipp), 1978-92, Flying Combat Aircraft (with A. T. Siddall) vol. 1, 1975, (with Carol Williams) vol. 2, 1978 and vol. 3, 1981; editor (with George E. Ham) The Rise of the Wheat State: a History of Kansas Agriculture, 1861-1986, 87, (with Thanos Veremis) The Metaxas Dictatorship: Aspects of Greece, 1936-1940. (with John T. Greenwood and Von Hardesty) Russian Aviation & Air Power, 1998, A Handbook of Air Ministry Organization, 1998; ed. Writing Official Military History, 1999, Official Military History, 2 vols., 2000, The Bases of Air Strategy, 2000, (with Frederick W. Kagan) A Military History of Russia, A Military History of the Soviet Union, 2002, (with David A. Graff) A Military History of China, 2002; sr. advisor on Ency. of U.S. Mil. History, Acad. Mil. Scis., Beijing, 1988—; advisory editor Ency. of USAF, 1988-92; mem. aviation editorial adv. bd. Smithsonian Instn. Press, 1989-92; adv. Greenwood Press, 1992—; mem. editl. bd. Defence Analysis, 1984—; cons., contbr.: Dictionary of Business Biography, 1980-86, Encyclopedia of the American Military, 1994; contbr.100 Years of Aviation,Tex. A&M U. Press. Nov. contbr. The New Dictionary of National Biography, 1994-2002; contbr. articles to profl. jours, also papers at internat. confs. Trustee U.S. Commn. on Mil. History, 1993—; mem. Kans. State Aviation Adv. Com., 1986-95, sec., 1992-95. Pilot RAFVR, 1943-46. Vol. res. RAF. Named Disting. Grad., Faculty Kans. State U., 1971; recipient Victor Gondos award Am. Mil. Inst., 1983, Samuel Eliot Morison award for disting. scholarship Am. Mil. Inst., 1986, Stamey Tchg. award, 1996, Aviation Honors award Gov. Kans., 2000; Social Sci. Rsch. Coun. nat. security policy rsch. fellow, 1960-61. Mem. AIAA (standing com. history 1973—), Soc. History Tech., Am. Aviation Hist. Soc., RAF Hist. Soc., Friends of RAF Mus. (life), Burma Star Assn. (life), Air Force Hist. Found. (trustee 1984-98), Soc. Army Hist. Rsch. (corr. mem. coun. 1980-98), Am. Mil. Inst., WWII Studies Assn. (dir. 1973-75, 79-82, 83—, archivist 1977—), Am. Aviation Hist. Soc., U.S. Commn. on Mil. History, Riley County Hist. Soc. (past dir., chmn. long-range planning com. 1980-97).Hist. Book Club, 2003 Home: 2961 Nevada St Manhattan KS 66502-2355

HIGHAM, SCOTT, reporter; BA in History, SUNY Stony Brook; M in Journalism, Columbia U. Reporter Allentown Morning Call, Miami Herald, Balt. Sun, Washington Post, 2000—. Recipient Pulitzer prize for investigative reporting, 2002. Office: Washington Post 1150 15th St NW Washington DC 20071

HIGHBERGER, EDGAR, music educator; b. Greensburg, Pa., Nov. 7, 1943; s. Edgar Schubert and Virginia Elizabeth Highberger; m. Joanne Salvador, Oct. 7, 1972. BS in music edn., Ind. U. of Pa., 1965, MusM in music edn., 1968; MFA, Carnegie-Mellon U., 1972; attended, York Minister, Eng., 1974. Supr., elem. music Hempfield Area Sch., Greensburg, Pa., 1965—66; music tchr. Greensburg-Salem Sch. Sys., 1970—80; asst. prof. of music Seton Hill U., 1980—, univ. organist, 2002—; min. of music First Presbyn. Ch., 1965—; accompanist Westmoreland Choral Soc., 1976—. Organ cons., recitalist, ch. music clin. various churches, 1965—; pre-concert lectr. Westmoreland Symphony Orch. Vol. Redstone Highlands Retirement Ctr., 1980—2000; elder First Presbyn. Ch., 1987—. Recipient Dist. Cmty. Svc to Arts, Greensburg Cultural Coun., 1996. Mem.: Am. Guild of Organists (sub dean 2003), Organ Hist. Soc., Presbyn. Assn. of Musicians. Achievements include development of the sacred music degree and cert. programs at Seton Hill U. Avocations: reading, gardening. Home: 309 Greenview Dr Greensburg PA 15601 Office: Seton Hill U Seton Hill Dr Greensburg PA 15601 E-mail: higberg@setonhill.edu.

HIGHBERGER, WILLIAM FOSTER, lawyer; b. Suffern, N.Y., May 15, 1950; s. John Kistler and Helen Stewart (Foster) H.; m. Carolyn Barbara Kuhl, July 12, 1980; children: Helen Barbara, Anna Mary. AB, Princeton U.; JD, Columbia U. Bar: Calif. 1976, U.S. Dist. Ct. (cen. dist.) Calif. 1976, U.S. Ct. Appeals (2d cir.) 1976, U.S. Ct. Appeals (9th cir.) 1977, U.S. Dist. Ct. (so. and ea. dists.) Calif. 1979, U.S. Supreme Ct. 1980, D.C. 1981, U.S. Dist. Ct. (no. dist.) Calif. 1981, U.S. Dist. Ct. D.C. 1982, U.S. Ct. Appeals (D.C. cir.) 1982, U.S. Ct. Appeals (3d cir.) 1983, N.Y. 1984, U.S. Dist. Ct. (so. dist.) N.Y. 1984, U.S. Dist. Ct. (ea. dist.) N.Y. 1985. Law clk. to judge U.S. Ct. Appeals (2d cir.), Bridgeport, Conn., 1975-76; assoc. Gibson, Dunn & Crutcher, Washington and L.A., 1976-82, ptnr., 1983-98; judge L.A. Superior Ct., 1998—. Notes and comments editor Columbia U. Law Rev., 1974. Mem. Nature Conservatory, Calif., 1981—; active Pacific Palisades (Calif.) Presbhn. Ch., 1987—. James Kent scholar Columbia U., 1973. Fellow: Coll. Labor and Employment Lawyers; mem.: ABA (com. on individual rights and responsibilities in workplace, labor sec), Am. Employment Law Coun., Indsl. Rels. Rsch. Assn., Am. Law Inst., Los Angeles County Bar Assn., Univ. Cottage Club. Republican. Office: LA County Courthouse Dept 32 111 N Hill St Los Angeles CA 90012 Business E-Mail: whighber@lasc.co.la.ca.us.

HIGHFILL, PHILIP HENRY, JR., retired language educator; b. Petersburg, Va., Aug. 12, 1918; s. Philip Henry and Grace (Jones) H.; m. Annabelle Hollowell (Molly), 1943; children: Mary Hollowell, Philip Henry III. BA, Wake Forest Coll., 1942; postgrad., Middlebury Coll., 1946; MA, U. N.C., 1948, PhD, 1950. Reporter Daily Advance, Elizabeth City, N.C., 1942, 46, Shreveport (La.) Times, 1942; instr. U. Rochester, N.Y., 1950-53, asst. prof., 1953-55; assoc. prof. George Washington U., Washington, 1955-61, prof., 1961-89, prof. emeritus, 1989. Cons. lit. Folger Shakespeare Library, Washington, 1964-68. Co-author: (with Kalman A. Burnim and Edward A. Langhans) A Biographical Dictionary of Actors, Actresses, Musicians, Dancers, Managers and Other Stage Personnel in London, 1660-1800, 16 vols., 1973-93; (with George Winchester Stone) In Search of Restoration and 18th-Century Theatrical Biography, 1976, (with Kalman A. Burnim) John Bell, Patron of Theatrical Portraiture, 1998; editor: Shakespeare's Craft, 1982; contbr. numerous articles and revs. to scholarly jours. With U.S. Army, 1942-46. Grantee Huntington Library, 1959, NEH, 1967-68, 70-71, 74-76, 84-87; fellow John Simon Guggenheim Found., 1959-60, Folger Shakespeare Library, 1968, Theodore Stewart fellow Nat. Library Scotland, 1975; fellow Washington Evening Star, 1963; recipient George Freedley award Theatre Library Assn., 1980. Mem. MLA, South Atlantic MLA, Soc. for Theatre Rsch. (Eng.), Am. Soc. Theatre Rsch. (spl. award 1994), Am. Soc. for 18th Century Studies, Am. Handel Soc. (bd. dirs. 1986-93), Lit. Soc. Washington (v.p. 1991, pres. 1992-93), Wafflers Club, George Washington Univ. Club, Cosmos Club (v.p. 1979, pres. 1980, bd. dirs. 1976-81). Avocations: traveling, music, cooking. Home: 5105 Westpath Ct Bethesda MD 20816-2319

HIGHLANDER, RICHARD WILLIAM, communications executive; b. Beckley, W.Va., Feb. 17, 1940; s. Ronald William and Lucille Bernice (Bland) H.; m. Ida Mae Canterbury, June 26, 1965; one child, Alison Renee. BA, Rutgers U., 1963; MA, U. Ga., 1972. Commd. 2d lt. U.S. Army, 1963, advanced through grades to lt. col., 1979, ret., 1984; dir. communications, def. systems group FMC Corp., Santa Clara, Calif., 1984-94; v.p. comm. United Def. LP, San Jose, 1994-99; dir. pub. rels. Calpine, San Jose, 1999—. Contbr. articles to profl. jours., Freedom Found. award 1966, 81. Trustee San Jose Repertory Co., 1985, pres. bd., 1998-99. Decorated Legion of Merit with bronze oak leaf cluster, Bronze Star with two bronze oak leaf clusters, Purple Heart, recipient Rev Gorlow award for lifetime achievement in pub. rels., Arthur W. Page Soc. Mem. PRSA (accredited), Internat. Assn. Bus. Communicators, Calif. Mfrs. Assn. (bd. dirs. 1985, chmn. bd. 1993), Rotary, San Jose Met. C. of C. (bd. dirs. 1989-1995), Chi Psi. Republican. Methodist. Avocations: racquetball, golf. Home: 5906 Gleneagles Cir San Jose CA 95138-2370

HIGHMAN, BARBARA, dermatologist; b. Washington; d. Benjamin and Helen (Wienshienk) H. Student, Northwestern U., 1960—63; MD, U. Mich., 1967. Diplomate Am. Bd. Dermatology. Intern Baylor U. Affiliated Hops., Houston, 1967—68; dermatology residency Henry Ford Hosp., Detroit, 1968—71; fellow in dermatology Johns Hopkins U., Balt., 1971—72; pvt. practice Laurel, Md., 1972—. Staff North Charles Hosp., Balt., 1972-77, Laurel Regional Hosp.; cons. in dermatology U.S. Army, Ft. Myer, Va., 1972-77. Fellow: Am. Acad. Dermatology (continuing med. edn. award given every 3 years 1978—); mem.: AMA (physicians recognition award given every 3 years 1971—), Prince George's Women's Med. Soc., Laurel Med. Soc., Med. and Chirugical Soc. State of Md., Anne Arundel County Med. Soc., Nat. Found. for Dermatology, Soc. for Investigative Dermatology. Office: 3335 Old Line Ave Laurel MD 20724-2234

HIGHSMITH, JASPER HABERSHAM, sales executive; b. Waycross, Ga., Dec. 3, 1940; s. Jasper H. and Linda (Weatherly) H.; m. Constance Orr Fitzgibbons, Aug. 26, 1963 (div. 1969); m. Linda Inez Diaz, Aug. 25, 1979; children: Richard, Eric, Jason. BBA, U. Ga., 1963. Engring. assoc. Western Electric Co., Atlanta, 1964-66; engr. No. Electric Co., Montreal, Que., Can., 1966-68, Gen. Telephone Co., Tampa, Fla., 1969-74; staff engr. No. Telecom, Inc., Tampa, 1974-76, regional mgr., 1977-85, dir. sales, 1986-94; v.p. ea. ops. Goldfield Telecom Inc., Tampa, 1994-97; pres. Marine Tech. Resources Inc., Tampa, 1997—; ptnr. Snug Island Yacht Co., 2002—. Mem. IEEE, U.S. Telephone Assn., Ind. Telephone Pioneers Assn. (mem. adv. coun. mfrs. chpt. 1987-88), Nat. Telephone Coop. Assn., Telephone Assns. of Ga., Fla., N.C., S.C., Tenn., and Ala., Treasure City Jaycees (v.p. 1969, pres. 1971), Orgn. for the Protection and Advancement of Small Telephone Cos., Phi Delta Theta. Methodist. Avocations: flying, boating, water sports. Home: 13714 Halliford Dr Tampa FL 33624-6903 Office: 5364 Ehrlich Rd Ste 114 Tampa FL 33624-6976 E-mail: jhighsmith@aol.com.

HIGHSMITH, SHELBY, federal judge; b. Jacksonville, Fla., Jan. 31, 1929; s. Isaac Shelby and Edna Mae (Phillips) H.; m. Mary Jane Zimmerman, Nov. 25, 1972; children— Holly Law, Shelby. AA, Ga. Mil. Coll., 1948; BA, JD, U. Kansas City, 1958. Bar: Fla. 1958. Trial atty., Kansas City, Mo., 1958-59, Miami, Fla., 1959-70; circuit judge Dade County, Fla., 1970-75; sr. ptnr. Highsmith, Strauss, Glatzer & Deutsch, P.A., Miami, 1975-91; judge U.S. Dist. Ct. (so. dist.) Fla., Miami, 1991—. Chief legal adviser Gov.'s War on Crime Program, 1967-68; spl. counsel Fla. Racing Commn., 1969-70; mem. Inter-Agy. Law Enforcement Planning Counsel of Fla., 1969-70. Served to capt. AUS, 1949-55. Decorated Bronze Star; recipient Outstanding Alumni Achievement Law award, U. Mo., 1998, Korean War Svc. medal, Pres. South Korea on 50th Anniversary of Korean War, Disting. Alumnus award, Ga. Mil. Coll., 2002. Fellow Internat. Soc. Barristers; mem. ABA, Dade County Bar Assn., Bench and Robe, Torch and Scroll, Miami Nat. Golf Club, Wildcat Cliffs Country Club, (Highlands, N.C.), Omicron Delta, Phi Alpha Delta. Republican. Roman Catholic. Office: Fed Justice Bldg 99 NE 4th St Rm 1027 Miami FL 33132-2138

HIGHSMITH, STEFAN, biochemistry educator; b. Santa Barbara, Calif., July 16, 1944; s. Ralph Nolan Highsmith and Sophie Anne Ruminski; m. Evelyn Kawahara, June 21, 1980; children: Mariko, Emily. BA in Chemistry, U. Calif., Berkeley, 1966; PhD in Chemistry, MIT, 1972. Rsch. assoc. Stanford U., Palo Alto, Calif., 1979; asst. prof. U. of the Pacific, San Francisco, 1980-85, assoc. prof., 1986-92, prof., 1992—, dir. biomed. rsch., 1996—. Mem. editl. adv. bd. Biochemistry, 1993—; contbr. articles to profl. jours., chpts. to books. Bd. dirs. Pacific Dental Rsch. Found., San Francisco, 1981—, treas., 1983—. With Peace Corps, Republic of Korea, 1966-68. Scholar NSF, Brandeis U., 1973, NIH, U. Calif., San Francisco, 1974-78; recipient Rsch. Career award NIH, 1980-84; grantee NSF, NIH, Am. Heart Assn. Mem. AAAS, Am. Chem. Soc., Biophys. Soc., Internat. Assn. Dental Rsch. Avocation: poetry. Office: 2155 Webster St San Francisco CA 94115-2333

HIGHSTEIN, JENE ABEL, sculptor; b. Balt., Md., June 16, 1942; s. Gustav and Ada Abel Highstein; m. Alanna Heiss (div.); 1 child, Lokke Abel; m. Katharine Duane; children: Alex, Jesse. BA, U. Md., Md., 1963; post grad., U. Chgo., Ill., 1963-65, NY Studio Sch., NY, 1966, Royal Acad. Sch., London, 1967-70. Vis. artist Emily Carr Coll. Art, Vancouver, B.C., Can., 1979, Tyler Sch. Art, Phila., 1990, RI Sch. Design, Providence, 1991, Vt. Studio Ctr., Johnsonville, Vt., 1993, Brandeis U., Waltham, 1995; instr. Sch. Visual Arts, NY, 1974, NYU, NYC, 1984-86, Parsons Sch. Design, NY, 1983; vis. prof. UCLA, 1987, Cranbrook Acad. Art, Bloomfield Hills, Mich., 1990; vis. lectr. Harvard U., Cambridge, Mass., 1995-96. One-man shows include Baumgartner Galleries, Washington, 1993, Ace Contemporary Exhbns., LA, 1993, Portland (Oreg.) Art Mus., 1993, St. Gauden's Meml., Cornish, NH, 1993, Secca, Winston-Salem, NC, Ace Gallery NY, Art Space, Seoul, 1996, Stark Gallery, NY, 1997, Hill Gallery, Birmingham, Mich., 1998, 5501 Columbia Arts Ctr., Dallas, 1998, Anders Tornberg Gallery, Sweden, 1998, Todd Gallery, London, 1998, Crosby St. Project Space, 1999, Auchincloss Gallery, 1999, Grant Selwyn Fine Art, 2000, U. Hartford Joseloff Gallery, 2000; group shows include Kunstmuseum, Passau, Germany, 1992, Rhona Hoffman Gallery, Chgo., 1992, Anders Tornberg Gallery, Lund, Sweden, 1993, Bklyn. Mus., 1993, Portland Art Mus., 1993, Andre Emmerich Gallery, NYC, 1993, Galerie Art 4, Galerie de l'Explanade, Paris, 1993, Werkstaat Kollerschlag, Austria, 1993, Kunst Halle Krems, Austria, 1993, Caldas Da Rainha, Portugal, 1993, Drawing Ctr., NYC, 1993, Baumgartner Galleries, Washington, 1994, Neuberger Mus. Art, Purchase, NY, 1994, Michael Klein Gallery, NYC, 1995, Galerij S 65, Aalst, Belgium, 1995, Bilboa Guggenheim, Spain, "Snow Show", Roycincmi Finland, others; represented in permanent collections at Balt. Mus. Art, Bklyn. Mus., Collection Panza di Biumo, Varese, Italy, Dallas Art Mus., Detroit Inst. Arts, Musee Pleine Aire, Paris, Met. Mus. Art, NYC, Mus. Contemporary Art, NYC, Mus. Modern Art, NYC, New Mus. Contemporary Art, NYC, NY Pub. Libr., Portland Art Mus., Rose Art Mus., Brandeis U., Waltham, Mass., San Diego Mus. Contemporary Art, La Jolla, Calif., David & Alfred Smart Art Mus., Chgo., Solomon R. Guggenheim Mus., NYC, Victoria and Albert Mus., London, LA County Mus., Harvard U. Mus., Yale Art Mus., others. Grantee Change Inc., 1974, Creative Artists Pub. Svc., 1975, Theo Doran award Ninth Paris Beinnale, 1975, Nat. Endowment for Arts, 1976, 77, 78, 84, 94, Creative Artists Pub. Svc., 1979; recipient John Simon Guggenheim award, 980, St. Gauden's Meml. prize, 1992. Office: 515 W 36th St New York NY 10018-1100

HIGHT, B. BOYD, lawyer; b. Lumberton, N.C., Feb. 15, 1939; s. B. Boyd and Mary Lou (Lennon) H.; m. Mary Kay Sweeney, Mar. 31, 1962; children: Kathryn, Kevin. BA, Duke U., 1960; LLB, Yale U., 1966; diploma in comparative law, U. Stockholm, 1967. Assoc. O'Melveny & Myers, Los Angeles, 1967-74, ptnr., 1974-79, 81-84, 89—; dep. asst. sec. trans. and telecommunications U.S. Dept. State, Washington, 1979-81; exec. v.p., gen. counsel Sante Fe Internat. Corp., Alhambra, Calif., also bd. dirs. Bd. dirs. Planned Parenthood L.A., 1986-95, pres., 1992-94; mem. bd. overseers Rand Ctr. Russian and Eurasian Studies, 1987-2000, chair, 1994-2000; trustee Am. U. Cairo, 1987—, Autry Western Heritage Mus., 2002—; bd. dirs. Calif. Supreme Ct. Hist. Soc., 1993-2001; bd. overseers The Huntington, 1996—. Mem. Coun. Fgn. Rels., Pacific Coun. on Internat. Policy, Calif. Club, Los Angeles Country Club. Democrat. Office: O'Melveny & Myers 400 S Hope St Los Angeles CA 90071-2899 E-mail: bhight@omm.com.

HIGHT, GAYE DEMETRICE, poet; b. Chgo., Oct. 26, 1961; d. Herman Moore and Kitty Shaheed; m. Tim Hight, June 9, 1981; children: Demetrice, Tim, Jr. Student, U. Hawaii. Owner Success, Spokane, 1997—. Contbr. poetry to anthologies; author: (poetry) Comfort, Comfort's Top 42 Poems. Recipient Famous Poet award, 2000, 2001. Mem.: Ahana Profl. Bus. Avocations: swimming, drawing, enjoying the underwater world, writing, speaking. Office: Success 2104 E Heroy Spokane WA 99207 E-mail: blesspoet@msn.com.

HIGHT, TIM EVERETT, company executive, consultant; b. Oklahoma City, Sept. 30, 1950; s. Everett Temple and Oklahoma (Ogan) H.; m. Maria Telega, Dec. 4, 1976; children: Brian Lee Hardcastle, Tad Edward. BS, Ctrl. State U., Edmond, Okla., 1972. Cert. quality auditor; regulatory affairs cert., hazard analysis and critical control point, registered trainer Nat. Environ. Health Assn. Resident in charge U.S. FDA, Shreveport, La., 1978-85; dir. regulatory affairs Luchem Pharms., Shreveport, 1985-87, Procor Techs., Inc., Arden Hills, Minn., 1987-92; mgr. regulatory affairs Solvay Animal Health, Inc., Mendota Heights, Minn., 1992-95; pres. FDA Svcs., Burnsville, Minn., 1995—; dir. regulatory affairs Aveda Corp., Mpls., 1996-2000; v.p. regulatory affairs Bioenergy, Inc., Mpls., 2000—02; mgr. regulatory compliance Land O'Lakes, Inc., 2002—. Cons. FDA Svcs., Burnsville. Mem.: Am. Soc. Quality, Regulatory Affairs Profl. Soc. Avocations: hiking, gardening, camping, fishing, tennis. Home: 435 Meadowood Ln Burnsville MN 55337 E-mail: skywalker1120000@yahoo.com.

HIGHTON, RICHARD TAYLOR, biologist, educator; b. Chgo., Dec. 24, 1927; s. Albert Henry and Helen Irene (Taylor) Highton; m. Kathryn Ann Adams, June 23, 1950; children: Barbara, Kim, Scott, Caitlin Ann. AB, NYU, 1950; MS, U. Fla., 1953, PhD, 1956. Asst. prof. U. Md., College Park, 1956—62, prof., 1962—73, prof. zoology, 1973—98, prof. emeritus, 1998—. Contbr. With U.S. Army, 1946—48. NSF grantee. Fellow: AAAS; mem.: Am. Soc. Ichthyologists and Herpetologists (pres. 1976). Home: 3613 Van Ness St NW Washington DC 20008-3130

HIGHTOWER, JACK ENGLISH, former state supreme court justice, congressman; b. Memphis, Tex., Sept. 6, 1926; s. Walter Thomas and Floy Edna (English) H.; m. Colleen Ward, Aug. 26, 1950; children— Ann, Amy, Alison. BA, Baylor U., 1949; JD, 1951; LLM, Univ. Va., 1992. Bar: Tex. 1951. Since practiced in, Vernon; mem. Tex. Ho. of Reps., 1953-54; dist. atty. 46th Jud. Dist. Tex., 1955-61; mem. Tex. Senate, 1965-75, pro tempore, 1971; mem. 94th-98th Congresses from 13th Tex. Dist., 1975-85; 1st asst. atty. gen. State of Tex., 1985-87; justice Texas Supreme Ct., Austin, 1988-95; ret., 1996. Mem. Tex. Law Enforcement Study Commn., 1957; del. White House Conf. Children and Youth, 1970; alt. del. Dem. Nat. Conv., 1968; bd. regents Midwestern U., Wichita Falls, Tex., 1962-65; trustee Baylor U., 1972-81, acting gov., 1971; trustee Wayland Bapt. U., Plainview, Tex., 1991-2001, Bapt. Children's Home, 1959-62, Tex. Scottish Rite Hosp. Children, 1991—, vice chmn., 2002—; trustee Human Welfare Commn.; bd. dirs. Bapt. Std., 1959-68; mem. Nat. Commn. on Librs. and Info. Sci., 1999—. With USNR, 1944-46. Named Outstanding Dist. Atty, Tex., Tex. Law Enforcement Found., 1959, Disting. Alumnus, Baylor U., 1978; recipient Knapp-Porter award Tex. A&M Univ., 1980. Mem. Tex. Dist. and County Attys. Assn. (pres. 1958-59), Scottish Rite Ednl. Assn. Tex. (exec. com. 1990—), Tex. Supreme Ct. Hist. Soc. (pres. 1991-98), Tex. Bar. Found. (fellow 1992), SAR, U.S. Supreme Ct. Hist. Soc., Tex. State Hist. Assn. (exec. coun. 1998-2002), Masons (grand master Tex. 1972), Lions (pres. Vernon 1961).

HIGHTOWER, JEANNE JACKSON, nursing administrator; b. Saratoga Springs, N.Y., Feb. 27, 1949; d. Billy G. and Jeanne Lois (Sickles) Jackson; m. Paul Dudley Hightower, July 6, 1971; children: Bradley, Brandon. BA in English, Mass Comm., Western Ky. U., 1971, ADN, 1973. RN, Ind., Ky. DON, Holly Hill Health Care Facility, Brazil, Ind., 1983, Sisters of Providence, St. Mary-of-the-Woods, Ind., 1984; staff nurse open heart surgery Columbia Terre Haute (Ind.) Regional Hosp., 1985, head nurse surgery, 1988, dir. surg. svcs., 1988-90, asst. DON, 1990-91, DON skilled transitional care unit, 1991-92, dir. spl. svcs., 1991-94, dir. med.-surg. svcs., 1994-96, coord. centralized scheduling, 1996-98, coord. surg. pre-admission, 1998—. Active troop com. Boy Scouts Am., Terre Haute, 1993-98. Republican. Mem. Lds Ch. Avocations: interior design, travel, biking, scrapbooking. Office: Columbia Terre Haute Regional Hosp 3901 S 7th St Terre Haute IN 47802-5709

HIGHTOWER, JOHN BRANTLEY, arts administrator; b. Atlanta, May 23, 1933; s. Edward A. and Margaret (Kimzey) H.; m. Martha Ruhl, Feb. 25, 1984; children: Amanda, Matthew. BA in English, Yale U., 1955; DFA, Calif. Coll. Arts and Crafts. Asst. to pub. Am. Heritage Pub. Co., Inc., NYC, 1961-63; exec. asst. NY State Coun. Arts, NYC, 1963-64, exec. dir., 1964-70; dir. Mus. Modern Art, NYC, 1970-72; pres. Am. Coun. Arts, NYC, 1972-74, South St. Seaport, 1977-83; dir., vice chmn. So. St. Seaport, 1983-84; exec. dir. Richard Tucker Music Found., 1977-89, Maritime Ctr. at Norwalk, 1984-89; dir. planning and devel. for the arts U. Va., 1989-93; pres., CEO The Mariners' Mus., Newport News, Va., 1993—. Exec. com. WHRO, Norfolk, 1996-99; vice chmn., Newport News Pub. Art Found., 2000—; founder, chmn. Adv. for Arts, 1974-77; instr. arts mgmt. Wharton Sch., U. Pa., 1976-77, New Sch., 1976-77; cultural advisor Rockefeller Mission to Latin Am., 1969; vis. critic in arts adminstrn. Grad. Sch. Drama, Yale U., 1972-77; chmn. Planning Corp. for Arts, Urban Arts Corps. Bd. dir. NY State Coun. on Arts, Poets and Writers. Capt. USMCR, 1955-63. Fulbright fellow; recipient NY State award, 1970. Mem. Century Assn. (NYC), 1805 Club (London). Home: 101 Museum Pkwy Newport News VA 23606-3635 E-mail: jhightower@mariner.org.

HIGINBOTHAM, HARLOW NILES, economist; b. Joliet, Ill., Nov. 25, 1946; s. Harlow Niles and Eleanor (Dickson); m. Linda Anne Hutton, Dec. 12, 1970 (div. July 1985); m. Susan Ellen Spika, Apr. 27, 1991. BA, Harvard U., 1968; MA, U. Chgo., 1972, PhD, 1976. CFA. Statistician Uniroyal Inc., Joliet, 1969-71; assoc. A.T. Kearney Inc., Chgo., 1976-79, mgr., 1979-88, prin., 1989-93, v.p., 1993—2001; sr. v.p. Nat. Econ. Rsch. Assocs., Inc., Chgo., 2001—03. Bd. dirs. Field Mus. Mem. Casino Club. Republican. Episcopalian. Avocations: gardening, skiing. Home: RR 2 1900 E Cass St Joliet IL 60432-9802 Office: Nat Econ Rsch Assocs Inc 875 N Michigan Ave Ste 3650 Chicago IL 60611 E-mail: Harlow.Higinbotham@NERA.com.

HIGINBOTHAM, JACQUELYN JOAN, lawyer; b. Dec. 15, 1951; d. Ivan Lyle and Ruth Harriet (La Point) H.; m. Robert Redditt; children: Altara Roxana, Rigel Rowena. AA, Northeastern Jr. Coll., Sterling, Colo., 1972; BA, U. No. Colo., 1974; JD, U. Colo., 1978. Bar: Colo. 1978, U.S. Dist. Ct. Colo. 1978, U.S. Ct. Appeals (10th cir.) 1983. Staff, mng. atty. Colo. Legal Svcs., Ft. Morgan, 1979—2003; asst. dir. Caring Ministries of Morgan County, Ft. Morgan, 2003—; co-owner Orion Enterprises Document Preparation Svcs. Mem. adv. bd. Caring Ministries Morgan County, 1986-87. Mem. Colo. Bar Assn., Christian Legal Soc., Order of Coif, Order of Daughters of the King. Democrat. Episcopalian. Avocations: astronomy, music, skating. Home: 702 Sherman St # 1123 Fort Morgan CO 80701-3540 Office: Caring Ministries Morgan County 420 E Railroad St Fort Morgan CO 80701

HIGLEY, BRUCE WADSWORTH, orthodontist; b. Iowa City, Dec. 1, 1928; s. Lester Bodine and Harriet (Wadsworth) H.; m. Marta Beatriz Velasco, Sept. 23, 1966. D.D.S., State U. Iowa, 1952, MS, 1953; student, Grinnell Coll., 1946-48, orthodontic certificate, 1953. Diplomate Am. Acad. Pain Mgmt. Research, instr. Iowa Dental U., 1952-53; practice dentistry, specializing in orthodontics South Miami, Fla., 1955—; Owner, chmn. bd. M.B.H. Enterprises, Inc., Miami, Fla., 1960—. Vice chmn. dist. coun. Boy Scouts Am., 1959-62; Mem. Personnel Bd., South Miami, 1959. Served as 1st lt. Dental Corps AUS, 1953-55. Fellow Internat. Coll. Cranio-Mandibnlar ORthopaedics, World Fedn. Orthodontists; mem. Am. Assn. Orthodontics, Fla. Orthodontic Soc., So., Miami socs. orthodontists, Fla., Am. socs. dentistry for children, Fla., Fla. East Coast, Miami dental socs., Am., S. Dade dental assns., Fedn. Dentaire Internat., English Royal Acad., C. of C. (past dir., sec., treas.), Psi Omega, Omicron Kappa Upsilon. Presbyn. (deacon). Clubs: Rotarian (pres. 1961-62), Elk, Coral Reef Yacht, Coral Gables Country, Royal Palm Tennis; Bankers, Executive (Miami); Army-Navy. Home: 2000 Brickell Ave Miami FL 33129-1721 Office: 7210 S Red Rd Miami FL 33143-5321 E-mail: bhigley1@bellsouth.net.

HIGMAN, SALLY LEE, company executive; b. Hinsdale, Ill., Sept. 12, 1945; d. Lee Fulton and Freda Margaret (Doehle) H. AB in Social Scis., Shimer Coll., Mt. Carroll, Ill., 1967; MA in Govt., Claremont (Calif.) Grad. Sch., 1969; M of Planning, U. So. Calif., 1973; Cert. in Higher Studies in Ekistics, Athens Tech. Orgn., Athens Ctr. of Ekistics, 1970. Cons. Doxiadis Assocs., Athens, Greece, 1971; rsch. asst. U. So. Calif., 1971-72; cons. Republic of Ecuador, Quito, 1973-75; tech. expert in the environment UN Devel. Prog., Quito, 1975-76; environ. analyst Tetra Tech Inc., Pasadena, Calif., 1976-78; sr. environ. planner NUS Corp., Sherman Oaks, Calif., 1978-81; project mgr. ACT, Inc., Westminster, Calif., 1981-87; owner Higman Doehle Environ. Cons., L.A., 1987-88; pres. Higman Doehle Inc., L.A., 1988—. Contbr. articles to profl. jours. Ford Found. scholar U. So. Calif., 1971-73, jr. rsch. fellow Athens Ctr. of Ekistics, 1969-71; intern Social Sci. Rsch. Coun., Ford Found., 1973-75. Mem. Shimer Coll. Scholastic Soc.

HIGONNET, MARGARET RANDOLPH, education educator; b. New Orleans, Oct. 2, 1941; d. Guy Adams and Margaret Randolph (Bullitt) Cardwell; m. Patrice Louis-Rene Higonnet, Aug. 14, 1974; 1 child, Ethel Rene. BA, Bryn Mawr Coll., 1963; PhD, Yale U., 1970. Instr. edn. George Washington U., Washington, 1967-68; asst. prof. U. Conn., Storrs, 1970-75, assoc. prof., 1976-80, prof., 1980—. Sec. English Inst., 1976-79; guest prof. U. Munich, 1991-92. Author: (book translation) Horn of Oberon, 1973; editor Children's Lit. Jour, 1985-90 (CHLA award 1987, 94); editor: Representation of Women, 1983, Behind the Lines, 1987, The Sense of Sex, 1993, Borderwork: Feminist Engagements with Comparative Literature, 1994, Reconfigured Spheres: Literary Representations of Feminist Space, 1994, Antifeminism in the Academy, 1996, Nineteenth Century British Women Poets, 1996, Lines of Fire: Women Writers of World War I, 1998, Nurses at the Front, 2001. Fellow Deutsche Akad. Austauschdienst, Tubingen, Fed. Republic of Germany, 1963-64, Rockefeller Found. fellow, Cassis, France, 1985, NEH fellow, 1988, rsch. fellow Inst. Juan March, Madrid, 1989, vis. fellow Rutgers Ctr. for Hist. Analysis, 1995, Bunting fellow, 1995-96; Fulbright scholar, London, 1966-67. Mem. Am. Conf. on Romanticism (pres. 1997-99), Am. Comparative Lit. Assn. (pres. 2003—). Office: U Conn English # U-25 Storrs CT 06269-1025

HIJUELOS, OSCAR, novelist; b. N.Y.C., Aug. 24, 1951; s. Pascual and Magdalena (Torrens) H. BA, CCNY, 1975, MA, 1976. Prof. English Hofstra U., Hempstead, N.Y., 1988-89. Author: Our House in the Last World, 1983, The Mambo Kings Play Songs of Love, 1989 (Pulitzer Prize for fiction 1990), The Fourteen Sisters of Emilio Montez O'Brien, 1993, Mr. Ive's Christmas, 1995 (Pulitzer prize nominee 1996), Empress of the Splendid Season, 1999, A Simple Habana Melody, 2003. Recipient "Outstanding Writer" citation from Pushcart Press for "Columbus Discovering America", 1978; Oscar Cintas fiction writing grantee, 1978-79; Breadloaf Writers conference scholarship, 1980; Creative Artists Programs Service fiction writing grantee, 1982; Ingram Merrill Found. fiction writing grantee, 1983; Creative Writers fellow Nat. Endowment for the Arts, 1985; Am. Acad. in Rome fellow Am. Acad. and Inst. of Arts and Letters, 1985.

HILBERG, RAUL, political science educator; b. Vienna, 1926; came to U.S., 1939. m. Gwendolyn Montgomery, 1980; children: David, Deborah. PhD in Pub. Law and Govt., Columbia U., 1955. Prof. polit. sci. U. Vt., Burlington, 1956-91, now prof. emeritus, 1991. Rsch. specialist War Documentation Project, Alexandria, Va., 1951-52; lectr. Hunter Coll., 1954, U. P.R., 1954-55. Author: The Destruction of European Jews 1961, new edits. and transls., 1983-2003, Perpetrators Victims Bystanders, 1992, transl., 1992-2002, The Politics of Memory, 1996, transl., 1994-98, Sources of Holocaust Research, 2001, transl., 2001-02. Served with U.S. Army, 1944-46. Home: 236 Prospect Pkwy Burlington VT 05401-4148

HILBERRY, CONRAD ARTHUR, humanities educator, poet; b. Melrose Park, Ill., Mar. 1, 1928; s. Clarence Beverly and Leah Ruth (Haase) H.; m. Marion Elizabeth Hilberry, Apr. 21, 1951; children: Marilyn, Jane, Ann. BA, Oberlin Coll., 1949; PhD, U. Wis., 1954; LLD (hon.), Marietta Coll., 1991. From instr. to asst. prof. DePauw U., Greencastle, Ind., 1954-61; from asst. prof. to prof. Kalamazoo Coll., 1962-98. Editor (poetry): Passages North, 1993-95, (anthology) New Poems from the Third Coast, 2000; author: (poetry) Player Piano, 1999, Sorting the Smoke, 1990 (Iowa prize 1990). Fellow NEA, 1974-75, 84-85; recipient Arts award Mich. Found. for the Arts, 1983, Emily Clark Balch prize Va. Quar. Rev., 1984; VCCA Fellow Va. Ctr. for Creative Arts, 1991, 93, 94. Democrat. Baptist. Home: 1601 Grand Ave Kalamazoo MI 49006 E-mail: hilberry@kzoo.edu.

HILBERT, OTTO KARL, II, lawyer; b. Colorado Springs, Colo., Feb. 9, 1962; s. Otto Karl and Mary Rachel (Shine) H.; m. Lucille Megan O'Shaughnessy, Apr. 21, 1995. BA, U. Notre Dame, 1984, postgrad., 1985; JD, U. Colo., 1988. Bar: Colo. 1989, Ariz. 1989, Wis. 1998, U.S. Dist. Ct. (no. dist.) Calif, U.S. Ct. Appeals (9th cir.) 1991, U.S. Tax Ct. 1992, U.S. Ct. Appeals (10th cir.) 1993, U.S. Supreme Ct. 1995, U.S. Dist. Ct. (we. dist.) Mich. 2001. Assoc. Kelly, Stansfield & O'Donnell, Denver, 1988-89, 92-93, Russell Piccoli, Ltd., Phoenix, 1989-92, LeBoeuf, Lamb, Greene & MacRae LLP, Denver, 1993-96; shareholder Reinhart, Boerner, Van Deuren, Norris & Rieselbach PC, Denver, 1996-2000, Robinson Waters & O'Dorisio, PC, Denver, 2000—. Arbitrator Nat. Assn. Securities Dealers, Inc., 1993—, Nat. Futures Assn., 1993—, Nat. Arbitration and Mediator's Internat. div. bds. arbitration. Mem. law sch. adv. coun. U. Notre Dame, 1989—92; cons. Ariz. Spl. Olympics, Phoenix, 1989—92. Mem.: ABA, Wis. Bar Assn., Ariz. Bar Assn., Denver Bar Assn., Colo. Bar Assn., Edward Frederick Sorin Soc., Denver Athletic Club (bd. dirs. 2000—, sec. 2001—02, pres.-elect 2002—03, pres. 2003—), Lakewood Country Club (v.p., bd. dirs. 1998—2001), Notre Dame Club of Denver (bd. dirs. 1995—97), Notre Dame Club of Phoenix (bd. dirs. 1989—92, 1st v.p. 1991—92). Republican. Roman Catholic. Avocations: piano, guitar, golf. Office: Robinson Waters & O'Dorisio PC 1099 18th St Ste 2600 Denver CO 80202 E-mail: ohilbert@rwolaw.com.

HILBERT, RITA L. librarian; b. Orange, N.J., Nov. 1, 1942; d. Ralph P. LaSalle and Arlene (Julian) Strobel; children: Toby Gayle Buchanan, Stacey Giordano, Joseph, Matthew. AA, NYU, 1988, BA, 1990; MLS, Rutgers U., 1992. Merchandising rsch. analyst Burrelle's, Livingston, N.J., 1975-82; teaching asst. Montessori Sch., Millburn, N.J., 1982-84; outreach specialist Rockwood Meml. Libr., Livingston, 1984-90, head spl. svcs., 1990-92; libr. dir. Lincoln Park (N.J.) Pub. Libr., 1992-94, Mount Olive Township Pub. Libr., 1994—. Mem. Adult Sch. Bd., Livingston, 1990—, Lincoln Pk. Bd. of Edn., 1995-98, chair policy com., 1997-98, negotiations com., 1997-98. Member Livingston Adv. Com. for the Handicapped, 1985—, Livingston Coun. for Sr. Citizens, 1985—, Region III Com. for Svcs. to Spl. Populations, sec., 1987-88; elected mem. Lincoln Park Bd. Edn., 1995-98, chair policy and negotiations coms., 1995-98; trustee Lincoln Park Libr., 1997-98. Recipient Founder's Day award NYU, 1990. Mem.: AAUW (scholarship 1987), ALA, Morris Automated Info. Network (sec. 1993—94, v.p. 1995, pres. 1996), NJ Assn. Libr. Assts.

(pres. 1989—90, scholarship in her name 1994), NJ Libr. Assn. (scholarship 1990), Mt. Olive C. of C. (rec. sec. 2002—), Mt. Olive Twp. Hist. Soc. (founding and charter mem.), Kiwanis (bd. dirs. 1999—), Alpha Sigma Lambda. Avocations: walking, painting, traveling. Office: Wolfe Rd Budd Lake NJ 07828

HILBERT, ROBERT S(AUL), optical engineer; b. Washington, Apr. 29, 1941; s. Philip G. and Bessie (Friend) H.; m. Angela Cinel Ferreira, June 19, 1966; children: David M., Daniel S. BS in Optics, U. Rochester, 1962, MS in Optics, 1964. Optical design engr. Itek Corp., Lexington, Mass., 1963-65, supr. lens design sect., 1965-67, asst. mgr. optical engr. dept., 1967-69, mgr. optical engring. dept., 1969-74, dir. optics, 1974-75; v.p. engring. Optical Rsch. Assocs., Pasadena, Calif., 1975-84, sr. v.p., 1985-91, pres., COO, 1991-2000, pres., CEO, 2000—, also bd. dirs. Lectr. Northeastern U., Burlington, Mass., 1967-69; mem. trustees vis. com. Sch. Engring. and Applied Sci., U. Rochester, 1995-97. Patentee in lens systems. Recipient Future Scientist of Am. award, 1957; Am. Optical Co. fellow U. Rochester, 1962. Fellow Soc. Photo-Optical Instrumentation Engrs. (chmn. fellows com.); mem. Optical Soc. Am. (engring. coun. 1990-92, mem. Fraunhofer award com. 1997-98), Lens Design Tech. Group (chmn. 1975-77). Jewish. Avocations: reading, the cinema. Home: 863 San Vicente Rd Arcadia CA 91007 Office: Optical Rsch Assocs 3280 E Foothill Blvd Pasadena CA 91107-3103 Business E-Mail: bob@opticalres.com.

HILBERT, VIRGINIA LOIS, computer consultant and training executive; b. Detroit, June 4, 1935; d. Howard G. and Lois (Garner) Swaggerty; m. James R. Hilbert, Nov. 24, 1958; children: James Jr., Jennifer, Douglas, Alexandra. BA with honors, U. Mich., 1957. Govt. analyst dept. of health City of Detroit, 1957-60; owner, dir. Profl./Tech. Devel., Inc. dba Lansing Computer Inst., 1978—. Contbr. articles to profl. jours. Tech. bd. Capital Region Cmty. Found.; sec. Tennis Patrons Bd., Lansing, 1984-89, Pro Symphony, 1984—; active Lansing Art Gallery, 1978-84; adv. com. for small bus. Mich. Jobs. Commn., 1997; small bus. chmn. Capital City United Way, 1998, bd. dirs., 1999—; bd. dirs. Physicians Health Plan, Local Initiations Support Corp., 2000, Sparrow Hosp. Found., 2002, chair women working wonders, 2003—. Listed in Entrepreneurial mag., Dun & Bradstreet chpt. on woman-owned firms, 1998; named one of Top Ten Women to own firms in the nation. Mem.: ASCD, ASTD, Human Capital (state chmn. 1995, chair region V for implementation 1996—97, Entrepreneurial award for edn. Greater Lansing 1997, Diana award 1999, Athena award 2001), Capital Area Health Alliance (Cmty. Health Info.Network), Bus. Alliance for Progress, Mich. Opportunity Card, Gov.'s Small Bus. Conf. (del. gov.'s work group), Nat. Bus. Edn. Assn., Mich. Tech. Coun., Women Bus.Owners Assn., CEO Network, Nat. Fedn. Ind. Bus. (guardian), Lansing C. of C. (small bus. coun., co-chair info. and seminar Small Bus. Edn.), U.S. C. of C., Zonta, Rotary, Alpha Phi (pres. heart equipment fund bd. 1957—86, alumnae pres.). Episcopalian. Home: 938 Wildwood Dr East Lansing MI 48823-3050 Office: Profl Tech Devel Inc 3001 Coolidge Rd Ste 403 East Lansing MI 48823-6350 E-mail: vhilbert@aol.com.

HILBOLDT, JAMES SONNEMANN, lawyer, investment advisor; b. Dallas, July 21, 1929; s. Grover C. and Grace E. (Sonnemann) H.; m. Martha M. Christian, Sept. 5, 1953; children: James, Katherine Hilboldt Farrell, Susanna Jean, Thomas. AB in Econs., Harvard U., 1952; postgrad., U. Chgo., 1952-53; JD, U. Mich., 1956. Registered investment advisor. With comml. and trust dept. No. Trust Co., Chgo., 1952-53; pvt. practice Kalamazoo, 1956—; pvt. practice as investment advisor, 1971—. Bd. dirs. Lafourche Realty Co., Inc., Kalamazoo, pres., 1971-2002, chmn. bd., 2002-. Bd. dirs. Kalamazoo Tennis Patrons, Inc., 1974-95, Downtown Devel. Authority, Kalamazoo, 1982-88, Downtown Tomorrow, Inc., Kalamazoo, 1985—, sec., treas., 1995, Downtown Kalamazoo Inc., 1988-91; treas., trustee The Power Found., 1967—, sec., 1967-94. Sgt. USMC, 1946-48. Mem. ABA, Mich. Bar Assn., Kalamazoo County Bar Assn., Harvard Club Western Mich. (pres. 1972-74), Kalamazoo Country Club, Park Club, Harvard Club N.Y.C. Avocations: tennis, swimming. Home: 4126 Lakeside Dr Kalamazoo MI 49008-2814 Office: 136 E Michigan Ave Ste 1201 Kalamazoo MI 49007-3936

HILBRECHT, NORMAN TY, lawyer; b. San Diego, Feb. 11, 1933; s. Norman Titus and Elizabeth (Lair) H.; m. Mercedes L. Sharratt, Oct. 24, 1980. BA, Northwestern U., 1956; JD, Yale U., 1959. Bar: Nev. 1959, U.S. Supreme Ct. 1963. Assoc. counsel Union Pacific R.R., Las Vegas, 1962; ptnr. Hilbrecht & Jones, Las Vegas, 1962-69; pres. Hilbrecht, Jones, Schreck & Bernhard, 1969-83, Hilbrecht & Assocs, 1983—, Mobil Transport Corp., 1970-72; gen. counsel Bell United Ins. Co., 1986-94; mem. Nev. Assembly, 1966-72, minority leader, 1971-72; mem. Nev. Senate, 1974-78; legis. commn., 1977-78; oper. mem. Corp. Svcs. Group, 1998—; pres. Corp. Svcs. Co., 1998—, Nev. Incorporating Co., 1998—; mng. mem. Amcorp LLC., 1999—. Asst. lectr. bus. law U. Nev., Las Vegas. Author: Nevada Motor Carrier Compendium, 1990, Nevada Corporation Handbook, 1999. Labor mgmt. com. NCCJ, 1963; mem. Clark County (Nev.) Dem. Ctrl. Com., 1959-80, 1st vice chmn., 1965-66; del. Western Regional Assembly on Ombudsman; chmn. Clark County Dem. Conv., 1966, Nev. Dem. Conv., 1966; pres. Clark County Legal Aid Soc., 1964, Nev. Legal Aid and Defender Assn., 1965-83; assoc. for justice Nat. Jud. Coll., 1993-96. Capt. AUS, 1952-67. Named Outstanding State Legislator Eagleton Inst. Politics, Rutgers U., 1969. Mem. ABA, ATLA, Am. Judicature Soc., Am. Acad. Polit. and Social Sci., State Bar Nev. (chmn. adminstrv. law com. 1991-94, chmn. sect. on adminstrv. law 1996), Nev. Trial Lawyers (state v.p. 1966), Am. Assn. Ret. Persons (state legis. com. 1991-94), Rotary, Las Vegas Rotary Found. (trustee 2002—), Elks, Phi Beta Kappa, Delta Phi Epsilon, Theta Chi, Phi Delta Phi. Lutheran. Office: 723 S Casino Center Blvd Las Vegas NV 89101-6716 E-mail: hilbrecht@lvcm.com.

HILBRINK, WILLIAM JOHN, violinist; b. Cleve., June 16, 1928; s. William and Caroline (Theil) H.; m. Patricia Anne Schultz, Aug. 6, 1955; children: Mark David, Holly Lee. B of Music Edn., Baldwin-Wallace Coll., 1955; MusM, Eastman Sch. Music, 1960. Cert. tchr. Tchr. strings, orch. Cleve. Pub. Schs., 1955-57; tchr. strings, dir. orch. MacMurray Coll., Jacksonville, Ill., 1958-62; tchr. violin, viola, string pedagogy, theory U. N.C., Greensboro, 1962-67; tchr. strings, grades 1-12, dir. orch. Fairfax (Va.) County Schs., 1967-83; asst. condr., assoc. concertmaster Fairfax Symphony Orch., 1977-84; ops. mgr. Fairfax (Va.) Symphony Orch., 1983-84; founder, 1st violinist Fairfax String Quartet, 1983—. Orch. condr. MacMurray Coll. Community Orch., Jacksonville, 1958-62; founding mem. Collegium Musicum, Jacksonville, 1960-62; concertmaster Springfield (Ill.) Symphony Orch., 1962; 1st violinist Piano Trio, String Quartet, U. N.C., Greensboro, 1962-67; freelance violinist Washington area, 1977—. Reviewer of concerts, Civic Music Assn., 1960-62; violinist in several hundred concerts and recitals, 1958—. Organizer, condr. Fairfax All-County Orch., 1977-78; organizer Washington Met. area Spl. Olympics Orch., 1979; music contractor for several choral groups, Washington; adjudicator for music festivals, Va., N.C., and Md. Recipient scholarship Eastman Sch. Music, 1957-58, Suzuki Inst., 1966. Avocations: operating and collecting O-gauge model trains, woodworking, house remodeling. Home: 5112 Forsgate Pl Fairfax VA 22030-4507 E-mail: PAHilbrink@cs.com.

HILD, MATTHIAS, finance educator; b. Oberscheld, Hessen, Germany, Aug. 16, 1968; s. Karl Heinz and Edith Hild; m. Anastasia Dakouri-Hild, July 29, 2000. DPhil, Oxford (Eng.) U., 1997. Jr. rsch. fellow Christ's Coll., Cambridge, England, 1997—2000; rsch. fellow Ctr. for Interdisciplinary Rsch., Bielefeld, Germany, 2000; sr. rsch. fellow Calif. Inst. of Tech., Pasadena, 2000—02; Adam Smith vis. chair Bayreuth (Germany) U., 2001—02; asst. prof. of bus. adminstrn. Darden Grad. Sch. of Bus. Adminstrn., Charlottesville, Va., 2002—. Rschr. in astrobiology Jet Propulsion Lab., Pasadena, Calif., 2000—02. Business E-Mail: matthias@hild.org.

HILDEBRAND, ALICE GRACE, physician; b. Omaha, June 24, 1913; s. Carl Herbert and Effie Jane (Levoy) H. BS in Medicine, U. Nebr., Omana, 1932; MS in Medicine, U. Minn., Mpls., 1940; MD, U. Nebr., Omaha, 1936. Cert. Am. Bd. Internal Medicine, 1947. Pvt. practice, Seattle, 1942-94; retired capt. USPHS. Assoc. prof. clin. medicine U. Washington Sch. Medicine, Seattle, 1947-80. Capt. USPHS, ret. Fellow ACP. Home: 3913 South Bay Loop NE Olympia WA 98504- E-mail: aliceh@quirk.net.

HILDEBRAND, CAROL ILENE, retired librarian; b. Presho, S.D., Feb. 15, 1943; d. Arnum Vance and Ethel Grace (Cole) Stoops; m. Duane D. Hildebrand, Mar. 21, 1970. BA, Dakota Wesleyan U., Mitchell, S.D., 1965; M in Librarianship, U. Wash., 1968. Tchr. Watertown (S.D.) H.S., 1965-67; libr. dir. Chippewa County Libr., Montevideo, Minn., 1968-70, The Dalles (Oreg.)-Wasco County Libr., 1970-72; libr. Salem (Oreg.) Pub. Libr., 1972-73; libr. dir. Lake Oswego (Oreg.) Pub. Libr., 1973-82; asst. city libr. Eugene (Oreg.) Pub. Libr., 1982-91, acting city libr., 1991-92, libr. dir., 1993-2000, libr. project mgr., 2000—03, ret., 2003. Cons., condr. workshops in field. Vice-chair LWV, Lane County, 1987; bd. dirs. People for Oreg. Librs. Polit. Action Com., 1986—; sec. Citizens for Lane County Libr., 1985-88. Named Woman of Yr., Lane County Coun. of Orgns., 1995, Oreg. Libr. of Yr., 1993. Mem. ALA (chpt. councilor 1990-94), AAUW (bd. dirs. 1986, sec. 1995-96), Pacific N.W. Libr. Assn. (pres. 1989-90), Oreg. Libr. Assn. (pres. 1976-77), Rotary, Phi Kappa Phi. Methodist. Avocations: reading murder mysteries, baking. Office: Eugene Pub Libr 100 W 13th Ave Eugene OR 97401-3433

HILDEBRAND, DANIEL WALTER, lawyer; b. Oshkosh, Wis., May 1, 1940; s. Dan M. and Rose Marie (Baranowski) H.; m. Dawn E. Erickson; children: Daniel G., Douglas P., Elizabeth A., Rachel E., Jacob E., Catherine E. BS, U. Wis., 1962, LLB, 1964. Bar: Wis. 1964, U.S. Dist. Ct. (we. dist.) Wis. 1964, N.Y. 1965, U.S. Dist. Ct. (so. and ea. dists.) N.Y. 1967, U.S. Ct. Appeals (2d cir.) 1968, U.S. Dist. Ct. (ea. dist.) Wis. 1970, U.S. Ct. Appeals (7th cir.) 1970, U.S. Supreme Ct. 1970, U.S. Tax Ct. 1986, U.S. Ct. Appeals (8th cir.) 1988, U.S. Ct. Appeals (D.C. cir.) 1991. Assoc. Willkie, Farr & Gallagher, N.Y.C., 1964-68; from assoc. to ptnr. DeWitt Ross & Stevens S.C., Madison, Wis., 1968—. Lectr. U. Wis. Law Sch., Madison, 1972—; mem. Joint Survey Com. on Tax Ememptions Wis. Editor: U. Wis. Law Rev., 1963-64. Pres. Wis. Law Foun., 1993-95, Wis. Jud. Commn., 1992-98, chmn., 1997-98. Fellow Am. Bar Found. (life), Wis. Bar Found. (life); mem. ABA (com. pub. fin. judicial campaigns 2001—, mem. trial practice com. litigation sect., ho. of dels. 1992—, standing com. on ethics 1997-2003, Wis. state del. 1995-2003, bd. govs. 2003—), Wis. Bar Assn. (bd. govs. 1981-85, 86-93, mem. exec. com. 1987-93, chmn. 1988-89, pres. 1991-92), N.Y. State Bar Assn., Dane County Bar Assn. (pres. 1980-81), 7th Cir. Bar Assn., Am. Law Inst., Am. Acad. Appellate Lawyers, James E. Doyle Inn of Ct. Roman Catholic. Office: 2 E Mifflin St Ste 600 Madison WI 53703-2890 E-mail: dwh@dewittross.com.

HILDEBRAND, FRANCIS BEGNAUD, mathematics educator; b. Washington, Pa., Sept. 1, 1915; s. Frank Alonzo and Inez (Paull) H.; m. Eleanor Maclaren Jenkins, Sept. 18, 1943; children— Susan Lee, Robert Craig, Jean Ellen. BS, Washington and Jefferson Coll., 1936, MA, 1938, Sc.D. (hon.), 1969; PhD, MIT, 1940. Mem. faculty MIT, Cambridge, 1938—2002, assoc. prof. math., 1950-67, prof., 1967-84, prof. emeritus, 1984—2002. Author: Advanced Calculus for Applications, 1949, 62, 76; Methods of Applied Mathematics, 1952, 65; Introduction to Numerical Analysis, 1956, 74; Finite-Difference Equations and Simulations, 1968. Mem. Am. Math. Soc., Math. Assn. Am., Sigma Xi, Phi Beta Kappa, Phi Delta Theta. Home: Wellesley, Mass. Died Nov. 29, 2002.

HILDEBRAND, JOHN FREDERICK, newspaper columnist; b. Chgo., Dec. 23, 1940; s. Paul Hedden and Harriet L. (Cummins) H.; m. Vasana Lohitkoopt, June 24, 1972; children: Marisa Cummins, Shana Victoria, Brent Daniel. B Journalism, U. Mo., 1965; MS in Journalism, Columbia U., 1966. Reporter Poplar Bluff (Mo.) Daily Am. Republic, 1963, Joplin (Mo.) Globe, 1964, AP, Jefferson City and Kansas City, Mo., 1965; fgn. svc. officer U.S. Info. Svc., Washington and Bangkok, 1966-70; reporter Newsday, Melville, N.Y., 1970-74, asst. city editor, 1974-76, edn. writer, 1976—. Adj. prof. journalism Chulalongkorn U., Bangkok, 1967; pres. Lloyd Neck (N.Y.) Holding Corp., 1988-91, bd. dirs., 1986-95. Vestryman St. John's Episcopal Ch., Cold Spring Harbor, N.Y., 1992-98. Recipient citation Adelphi U., Garden City, N.Y., 1987, citation Kappa Delta Pi, Oakdale, N.Y., 1988, citation Phi Delta Kappa Suffolk County Chpt., 1999, Newsday Pub.'s. Spl. Achievement award, 1997. Mem. Edn. Writers Assn. (1st prize opinion article 1978, 1st prize article series 1982, 97, 1st prize article package 1992), Phi Gamma Delta (sec. Chi Mu chpt. 1964). Home: 23 Target Rock Dr Huntington NY 11743-1464 Office: Newsday Inc 235 Pinelawn Rd Melville NY 11747-4250 E-mail: john.hildebrand@newsday.com.

HILDEBRAND, JOHN G(RANT), neurobiologist, educator; b. Boston, Mar. 26, 1942; s. John G. and Helen S. Hildebrand; m. Gail Deerin Burd, July 24, 1982. AB, Harvard U., 1964; PhD, Rockefeller U., 1969; Laurea Honoris Causa, U. Cagliari, Italy, 2000. Instr. neurobiology Harvard U. Med. Sch., Boston, 1970-72, asst. prof., 1972-77, assoc. prof., 1977-80, vis. prof., 1980-81; prof. biol. scis. Columbia U., N.Y.C., 1980-85; prof. neurobiol., biochemistry, molecular biophysics and cellular biology, entomology U. Ariz., Tucson, 1985—, Regents prof., 1989—, dir. div. neurobiology, 1985—. Assoc. behavioral biology Harvard U. Mus. Comparative Zoology, Cambridge, Mass., 1980-97; trustee Marine Biol. Lab., Woods Hole, Mass., 1981-89, mem. exec. com., 1981-88; Jan de Wilde lectr. U. Wageningen, The Netherlands, 1992; King Solomon lectr., Hebrew U., Jerusalem, 1995; K.D. Roeder lectr. Tufts U., 1995; Felix Santschi lectr. U. Zurich, Switzerland, 1995; Grandpierre Meml. lectr., Columbia U., 2002, Padydula lectr., Wellesley Coll., 2003. Co-editor: Chemistry of Synaptic Transmission, 1974, Receptors for Neurotransmitters, Hormones, and Pheromones in Insects, 1980, Molecular Insect Science, 1990; devel. neurosci. sect. editor Jour. Neurosci., 1983-88; co-editor Jour. Comparative Physiology A, 1990—; mem. editorial bd. various other jours. Trustee Rockefeller U., N.Y.C., 1970-73. Recipient Javits Neurosci. award Nat. Isnt. Neurol. and Communicative Disorders and Stroke, NIH, 1986-94, Merit award Nat. Inst. Allergy and Infections Diseases, NIH, 1986-97, R.H. Wright award Simon Fraser U., B.C., Can., 1990, Max Planck Rsch. award Max Planck Gesellschaft and Alexander von Humboldt-Stiftung of Germany, 1990, Founder's Meml. award Entomol. Soc. Am., 1997, Humboldt rsch. award, 1997; Helen Hay Whitney Found. fellow, 1969-72, A.P. Sloan Found. fellow, 1973-77. Fellow: AAAS, Royal Entomol. Soc. UK; mem.: Am. Acad. Arts and Sci., Norwegian Acad. Sci. and Letters, Deutsche Akademie der Naturforscher Leopoldina, Internat. Soc. Chem. Ecology (pres. 1998—99), Soc. Integrative and Comparative Biology, Internat. Soc. Neuroethology (pres. 1995—98), Soc. for Neurosci. (treas. 1993—94), Assn. for Chemoreception Sci. (pres. 2002—03, IFF Innovative Rsch. award 1997), Am. Soc. Biochemistry and Molecular Biology. Avocations: music, lower brass instruments. Home: 629 N Olsen Ave Tucson AZ 85719-5136 Office: U Ariz ARL Div Neurobiology PO Box 210077 Tucson AZ 85721-0077 E-mail: jgh@neurobio.arizona.edu.

HILDEBRAND, ROGER HENRY, astrophysicist, physicist; b. Berkeley, Calif., May 1, 1922; s. Joel Henry and Emily (Alexander) H.; m. Jane Roby Beedle, May 28, 1944; children: Peter Henry, Alice Louise, Kathryn Jane, Daniel Milton. AB in Chemistry, U. Calif., Berkeley, 1947, PhD in Physics, 1951. Physicist, U. Calif., 1942-51; physicist Tenn. Eastman Corp., Oak Ridge Nat. Lab., 1945; asst. prof. dept. physics Enrico Fermi Inst., U. Chgo., 1952-55, asso. prof., 1955-60, prof., 1960—, prof. dept. astronomy and astrophysics, 1978—, Samuel K. Allison Disting. Service prof., 1985—, chmn. dept. astronomy and astrophysics, 1984-88; dir. Enrico Fermi Inst., 1965-68, dean coll., 1969-73. Assoc. lab. dir. for high energy physics Argonne (Ill.) Nat. Lab., 1958-64; chmn. sci. policy com. Stanford (Calif.) Linear Accelerator Ctr., 1962-66; mem. physics adv. com. Nat. Accelerator Lab., 1967-69; mem. sci. and ednl. adv. com. Lawrence Berkeley Lab., 1972-80; chmn. com. to rev. U.S. medium energy sci. AEC and NSF, 1974; chmn. airborne obs. users group NASA, 1983-84; chmn. sci. cons. group Stratopheric Obs. for Infrared Astronomy (SOFIA), NASA, 1985-89, mem. sci. working group, 1995-97, sci. coun., 1997—; mem. space astronomy and astrophysics Space Sci. Bd., 1987-90; mem. coun. Columbus Project, 1987-88; mem. sci. and tech. adv. panel for the submillimeter array Harvard/Smithsonian Ctr. for Astrophysics, 1989-95; mem. astronomy and astrophysics survey com. NAS Panel for Infrared Astronomy, 1989-90; chmn. Dannie Helneman prize com. Am. Inst. Physics, 1990; mem. sci. and tech. adv. group Large Millimeter Telescope, 1995—; mem. obs. vis. com. Assn. Univs. for Rsch. in Astronomy, 1993-96, chmn. Stratospheric Obs. Infrared Astronomy sci. coun., 1997—; mem. NASA review panel for Small Explorer (SMEX) Proposals, 2000; mem. NASA/JPL bd. for Planck High Frequency Instrument Detectors, 2000-02; mem. faculty Canary Islands Winter Sch. Astrophysics, 2000. Guggenheim fellow, 1968-69, Alfred P. Sloan Found. fellow, 1975. Fellow Am. Phys. Soc., Am. Acad. Arts and Scis.; mem. Am. Astron. Soc., Internat. Astron. Union, Midwestern Univs. Rsch. Assn. (dir. 19956-58, 62-68), Phi beta Kappa, Sigma Xi. Office: U Chgo Enrico Fermi Inst 5640 S Ellis Ave Chicago IL 60637-1433

HILDEBRAND, VERNA LEE, human ecology educator; b. Dodge City, Kans., Aug. 17, 1924; d. Carrell E. and Florence (Smyth) Butcher; m. John R. Hildebrand, June 23, 1946; children: Carol Ann, Steve Allen. BS, Kans. State U., 1945, MS, 1957; PhD, Tex. Women's U., 1970. Tchr. home econs. Dickinson County H.S., Chapman, Kans., 1945-46; tchr. early childhood Albany (Calif.) Pub. Schs., 1946-47; grad. asst. Inst. Child Welfare U. Calif., Berkeley, 1947-48; tchr. kindergarten Albany Pub. Schs., 1948-49; dietitian commons and hosp. U. Chgo., 1952-53; instr. Kans. State U., Manhattan, 1953-54, 59, Okla. State U., Stillwater, 1955-56; asst. prof. Tex. Tech U., Lubbock, 1962-67; from asst. prof. to prof. Mich. State U., East Lansing, 1967-97, prof. emeritus, 1997—. Legis. clk. Kans. Ho. of Reps., Topeka, 1955. Author: Introduction to Early Childhood Education, 1971, 6th edit., 1997, Guiding Young Children, 1975, 6th edit., 1998, Parenting and Teaching Young Children, 1981, 90, Management of Child Development Centers, 1984, 5th edit., 2002, Parenting: Rewards and Responsibilities, 1994, 2d edit., 1997, 6th edit., 2002; co-author: China's Families: Experiment in Societal Change, 1985, Knowing and Serving Diverse Families, 1996, 2d edit., 1999. Mem. Nat. Assn. for the Edn. Young Children (task force 1975-77), Am. Home Econs. Assn. (bd. dirs., Leader award 1990), Women in Internat. Devel., Nat. Assn. Early Childhood Tchr. Edn. (award for meritorious and profl. leadership 1995).

HILDEBRANDT, FREDERICK DEAN, JR., management consultant; b. Upper Darby, Pa. m. Marjorie Louise Smith, July 27, 1968; children: Frederick Dean III, Elizabeth Florence. AB magna cum laude, Dartmouth Coll., 1954, MS, 1955. Engr. Eastman Kodak Co., Rochester, N.Y., 1957-60; systems mgr. J.T. Baker Chem. Co., Phillipsburg, N.J., 1960-63; assoc. Booz, Allen & Hamilton Inc., N.Y.C., 1963-72, v.p., 1972-78; sr. v.p. Am. Ins. Assn., N.Y.C., 1978-81; v.p. Travelers Ins. Cos., Hartford, Conn., 1981-89; pres. Dean Hildebrandt & Assocs., Simsbury, Conn., 1989—. Adminstr. Ins. Rsch. Coun., 1979, bd. dirs., 1982-88; vice chmn. bd. dirs. Workers Compensation Rsch. Inst., 1987-88 With U.S. Army, 1955-57. Mem. Inst. Mgmt. Cons. (cert. mgmt. cons.), Phi Beta Kappa.

HILDEBRANDT, H(ENRY) M(ARK), pediatrician; b. Ann Arbor, Mich., Oct. 23, 1926; s. Theophil Henry and Dora (Ware) H.; m. Jennie Parker (div. 1974); children: Marian, Carl, Janet, Jonathan, Lisabeth; m. Linda Figen (div. 1984); 1 child, Ursula; m. Deborah Bush-Black, 1986 (div. 1996). BA, U. Mich., 1948, MD, 1952. Diplomate Am. Bd. Pediatrics. Intern, resident in pediatrics City Hosps. Cleve. and Babies and Children's Hosp., 1952-55; clin. asst. prof. U. Mich., Ann Arbor, Mich., 1958-71, clin. assoc. prof., 1971—; pvt practice Ann Arbor, 1955-87, Ypsilanti, Mich., 1987—. Established U. Mich. Hosp. SCAN (Suspected Child Abuse and Neglect) team, 1971; mem. affiliate faculty U. Mich., Ann Arbor, 1978—. Author: The Windows of St. Andrew's, 2003. Commr. Ann Arbor Hist. Dist. Commn., 2000—. Mem. Am. Acad. Pediatrics, Ambulatory Pediatric Assn., Acad. of Breastfeeding Medicine. Episcopalian. Avocations: playing cello in string quartets, rail and trolley history, hist. preservation. Home: 1930 Cambridge Rd Ann Arbor MI 48104-3651 Office: 5333 McAuley Dr Ste R 1104 Ypsilanti MI 48197-1014

HILDEBRANDT, JANELLE DINER, sales executive; b. Little Rock, Dec. 16, 1957; d. Jack and Wilma Canada Diner; m. Kendall C. Russell, May 24, 1981 (div. Dec. 1994); children: K. Clinton, Jr., Adam A.; m. Larry Paul Hildebrandt, July 19, 1997. BEE, BS in Math., Vanderbilt U., 1979; MBA, City Univ., 1982. Engr. Martin Marietta Aerospace, Orlando, Fla., 1979-81; sr. engr. Boeing Aerospace Co., Kent, Wash., 1981-83; dir. Advanced Technology Labs, Bothell, Wash., 1983-92; bus. devel. mgr. 3M, St. Paul, 1992-97, internat. bus. devel., 1997—2002, sales mgr., 2002—. Cons. Custom Interfaces, Bothell, Wash., 1983-87. Patentee in field. Mem. Rotary, Soroptimist. Avocations: swimming, cooking. Office: 3M 5995 Hillcrest Rd Medford OR 97504-6810 also: 68 Galen Lk Oswego OR 97035 E-mail: jdhildebrandt@mmm.com.

HILDEBRANDT, SHARRIE L. legal technology educator, paralegal; b. Berwyn, Ill., Sept. 1, 1940; m. Richard C. Hildebrandt, Dec. 10, 1960; children— Jeffrey, Laura, Douglas. A.A.S., William R. Harper Coll., 1973; B.A., DePaul U., 1975; M.Ed., U. Ill., 1982. Coordinator legal tech. program William R. Harper Coll., Palatine, Ill., 1974— ; owner Adminstrv. Paralegal Services, Arlington Heights, Ill., 1973— ; mem. adv. bd. Legal Asst. Today mag., 1984. Author: Legal Assistant Program Development Guide, 1978. Pres. Regional Bd. Sch. Trustees, Cook County, Ill., 1974-83. Mem. Am. Assn. Paralegal Edn. (bd. dirs. 1982-84), ABA (edn. com.), Am. Fedn. Tchrs., Nat. Fedn. Paralegals, Ill. Paralegal Assn. Club: N.W. Suburban Women's Republican (corr. sec. 1981-82, newsletter editor). Office: William R Harper Coll Algonquin And Roselle Rd Palatine IL 60067

HILDEBRANDT, WILLIS HARVEY, artist, educator; b. Waverly, Iowa, Nov. 28, 1952; s. Harvey Herman and Lavera Louise (Henning) H.; m. Doris Marie O'Connell, June 11, 1954; children: Matthew Karl, Megan Elisabeth. BA, Wartburg Coll., Waverly, 1975; MA, U. No. Iowa, Cedar Falls, 1979. Cert. tchr., Iowa. Elem. art instr. Griswold (Iowa) Schs., 1975-78; high sch. art instr. East Marshall Cmty. Schs., LeGrand, Iowa, 1980—. Participant Tchr. in Contemporary Art, 2003. Exhibited paintings in shows at James and Meryl Hearst Ctr. for the Arts, 1994, Melon Ctr., Wallingford, Conn., 1994, Des Moines Art Ctr., 1994. Recipient art awards, Iowa Secondary Art Tchr. of Yr., Art Educators of Iowa, 2000. Mem. NEA, Iowa State Edn. Assn., Nat. Art Edn. Assn. (Marie Walsh Sharpe fellow 1995), Ctrl. Iowa Art Assn. (mem. bd. control 1994—, instr. high sch. summer workshop), Iowa Alliance for Arts Edn. Democrat. Roman Catholic. Home: PO Box 381 Le Grand IA 50142-0381 E-mail: hils@marshallnet.com.

HILDEBRANDT-WILLARD, CLAUDIA JOAN, banker; b. Ingelwood, Calif., Feb. 12, 1942; d. Charles Samual and Clara Claudia (Palumbo) Hildebrandt; m. I. LeRoy Willard, Nov. 5, 1993 (dec. Oct. 2001). BBA, U. Colo. Head teller First Colo. Bank & Trust, Denver, 1969-70; asst. cashier Frist Nat. Bank, Englewood, Colo., 1975-79, asst. v.p., 1979-83, v.p., 1983-92; owner CJH Enterprises, Inc., Breckenridge, Colo., from 1980, Garden Tea Shop, Georgetown, Colo., Laudiac, Inc., Breckenridge, from 1993, Mgmt. for Ministry, from 1993. Mem.: Am. Inst. Banking, Am. Soc. Pers. Adminstrn., Fin. Women Internat. (pres.-elect 1989—92), Nat. Assn. Bank Women, Mile High Group. Roman Catholic. Home: Georgetown, Colo. Died Oct. 13, 2001.

HILDERBRANDT, DONALD FRANKLIN, II, urban designer, landscape architect, artist; b. Bloomsburg, Pa., Aug. 30, 1939; s. Donald Franklin and Beatrice May (Kirchman) H.; m. M. Caroline Housenick, Aug. 27, 1960; children: Mark Berwind, John Thomas, Johanna Lynn. BS in Landscape Architecture, Pa. State U., 1961; MS in Landscape Architecture, U. Mich., 1963. Registered landscape architect, Md. Sr. designer, assoc. Johnson, Johnson & Roy, Inc., Ann Arbor, Mich., 1963-68; chief landscape architect The Rouse Co., Columbia, Md., 1968-71; co-founder, pres. Land Design/Rsch., Inc. (now LDR Internat., Inc.), Columbia, Md., 1971—2000; nat. design dir. HNTB Archs. Engrs. Planners, Inc. Urban Design and Planning Divsn., Columbia, Md., 2000—02. Vis. lectr. Pa. State U., University Park, 1968-98; vis. critic Harvard U., mem. design arts program panel; cons. NEA, Washington, 1983-88; bd. dirs. Landscape Architecture Found., 1986-93. Author: Cost Effective Site Planning, 1976 (award 1978), New Life for Maryland's Old Towns, 1979 (award 1980), Cuyahoga Valley, 1975 (award 1976), Centennial Park (award 1989). Pa. State U. Alumni fellow, 1983; recipient Design award, spl. mention HUD, 1974. Fellow Am. Soc. Landscape Architects (nat. awards jury mem. 1975, 81), Balt. Watercolor Soc. (life). Democrat. Episcopalian. Home: 11101 Youngtree Ct Columbia MD 21044-2715

HILDING, JEREL LEE, music and dance educator, former dancer; b. New Orleans, Sept. 24, 1949; s. Oscar William and Loeta Dana (Boldra) H.; m. Krystyna Zofia Jurkowski, July 1, 1978; children: Dennis Jozef, Kristopher Jay. BA, La. State U., New Orleans, 1971. Prin. dancer Joffrey Ballet, N.Y.C., 1975-89; dir. arts in edn. N.J. Ballet, 1989-90; assoc. prof., dir. dance U. Kans., 1990—. Avocations: piano, sports. Office: U of Kansas Dept Music and Dance 460 Murphy Hall 1530 Naismith Dr Lawrence KS 66045-0001

HILDNER, PHILLIPS BROOKS, II, lawyer; b. Battle Creek, Mich., June 26, 1944; s. Phillips Brooks and Eva Marie (Burek) H.; divorced; 1 child, Phillips Brooks III. BS, Western Mich. U., 1967; JD, Detroit Coll. Law, 1971. Bar: Mich. 1971. Asst. prosecuting atty. Genesee County, Flint, Mich., 1971-73; ptnr.

Conover, Hildner & Zielinski, Fenton, Mich., 1973-79; sole practice Fenton, 1980—. Sponsoring atty. Law Day Fenton H.S., 1973—. Mem. State Bar Mich., Genesee County Bar Assn., Fenton C. of C., 2d Century Club Detroit Coll. Law, Delta Theta Phi. Episcopalian. Avocations: fly fishing, hunting, running, exercise. Office: PO Box 87 115 W Shiawassee Ave Fenton MI 48430-2005

HILDRETH, EUGENE A. physician, educator; b. St. Paul, Mar. 11, 1924; s. Eugene A. V. and Lila K. (Clator) Hildreth; m. Dorothy Anne Myers, Mar. 23, 1946; children: Jeffrey Reed, William Myers, Anne Sarver, Katherine Clator. BS, Washington Jefferson Coll., 1943; MD, U. Va., 1947. Diplomate Am. Bd. Internal medicine, Am. Bd. Allergy and Immunology. Intern Johns Hopkins, 1947—48; resident in medicine Hosp. U. Pa., 1948—49, USPHS Postdoctoral Research fellow in cardio-vascular disease, 1949—51, chief resident in medicine, 1953—54, fellow in allergy and immunology, 1954—58, faculty, 1954—69, faculty, 1971—; instr. medicine U. Pa., Phila., 1953—54, asso. medicine, 1954—55, asst. prof. medicine, 1955—60, assoc. prof., 1960—69; assoc. dean U. Pa. (Sch. Medicine), 1964—69, prof. clin. medicine, 1971—90, prof. emeritus, 1990—, acting chmn. dept. research medicine, 1960—64. Chmn. dept. medicine Reading (Pa.) Hosp. and Med. Ctr.; cons. project site visitis USPHS, 1965—70; cons. VA Hosp. Phila., 1955—; nat. adv. com. Medic Alert Found. Internat., 1964—83; cons. Citizens' Com. to Study Grad. Med. Edn., 1966; Am. Bd. Med. Spltys. rep. of subsplty. Bd. Allergy and Immunology of Am. Bd. Internal Medicine, 1969—72; mem. Am. Bd. Internal Medicine, 1969—72, 1975—82, cons., com. mem., 1972—75, chmn. certifying exam. com., 1978—81, mem. core exam. com., 1986—87, mem. exec. com., 1978—82, chmn., 1981—82; founding com. Am. Bd. Allergy and Immunology, 1970, mem., 1970—72, 1st co-chmn.; mem. rep. Am. Bd. Med. Spltys., 1976—83, chmn. nominating com., 1979—80; mem. med. adv. bd. Lupus Found. Del. Valley, 1979—; chmn. Federated Coun. Internal Medicine; appeals bd. liaison Coun. of Grad. Med. Edn., 1980—. Co-author: Low Fat Diet, 1953; mem. editl. bd.: Annals Internal Medicine, 1960—68, Postgrad. Medicine, 1969—75, Jour. Berks County Med. Soc., 1969—73, Internal Medicine Digest, 1971—75; contbr. chapters to books, articles to profl. jours. With USNR, 1943—45, with USNR, 1951—53. Grantee, USPHS; scholar John and Mary R. Markle scholar in acad. medicine, 1958—63. Master: ACP (mem. bd. regents 1985—92, chmn. bd. regents 1989—91, pres. 1991—92, immediate past pres. 1992—, mem. ethics com. 1986—90, chmn. com. to delineate privileges of med. procedures, mem. nominating 1997—); fellow: Am. Clin. and Climatologic Assn., Acad. Medicine of Singapore (hon.); mem.: ACGME (mem. residency rev. com. internal medicine), AAAS, Working Group on Disability of U.S. Presidents, Royal Soc. Medicine, Federated Coun. Internal Medicine, Am. Acad. Allergy, Inst. Medicine of NAS (mem. nominating com 1982—84, mem. coun. 1986—90, chmn. nominating com. for coun. memberships 1989—90, mem. fin. com. 1988—90), N.Y. Acad. Scis., Fedn. AM. Socs. for Exptl. Biology, Peripatetic Soc., Phila. Art Mus. Home: 5285 Sweitzer Rd Mohnton PA 19540-8140

HILDRETH, JAMES ROBERT, retired air force officer; b. Pine Bluff, Ark., May 4, 1927; s. William Wilson and Martha Leah (Chidester) H.; m. Beth Dixon Baker, July 12, 1955; children: John Baker, William Reid, Margaret Leah, Mark Dixon, Amy Beth. BA cum laude, La. Poly. Inst., 1952. Commd. 2d lt. USAF, 1952, advanced through grades to maj. gen., 1976; ret., 1981; comdr. 1st Air Commando Sqdn., 1967; comdr. 4th Tactical Fighter Wing, 1970—72; dep. dir. ops. Office of Joint Chiefs of Staff, 1972—73; dep. comdr. 13th Air Force, 1973—75; sr. Air Force rep. Weapons Systems Evaluation Group, Office of Sec. Def., 1975—76; comdr. Tactical Fighter Weapons Center, 1976—79; comdr. 13th Air Force, 1979—81. Pres. So. Nev. Fed. Exec. Agy., 1975-76; mem. adv. bd. United Way, Las Vegas, Nev., 1975-79; bd. dirs. Las Vegas C. of C., 1976-79; dist. chmn. Boy Scouts Am., 1979-81. Decorated D.S.M. (2), Silver Star, Legion of Merit (3), D.F.C. (3), Bronze Star, Air medal (14), Def. Superior Svc. medal, Meritorious Svc. Medal, Air Force Commendation medal (3), Purple Heart, Cross of Gallantry (Vietnam), Rep. Phillipines Legion of Honor. Mem. Kappa Sigma, Phi Kappa Phi, Omicron Delta Kappa, Sigma Tau Delta. Clubs: DAV. Methodist. Home: 315 E Branch St PO Box 897 Spring Hope NC 27882-0897 Office: 9070 Edgerton Rd Spring Hope NC 27882-8916 E-mail: cbhild@aol.com.

HILE, ELIZABETH GWYN, administrative assistant, marketing professional; b. Nashville, Sept. 18, 1970; d. Richard Stanley and Diane Ruth Hile; 1 child, Eric Richard. AAS in Criminal Justice, Guilford Tech. C.C., Jamestown, N.C., 1999; BS in Human Svcs., Gardner Webb U., 2003. V.p. mktg. Hyperhedron, LLC, Kernersville, NC, 1999—; asst. tchr. Guilford County Schs., Greensboro, NC, 1998—2002, secretary, 2002—. Bd. dirs. Hyperhedron, LLc, Kernersville. Team leader Cystic Fibrosis Found., Winston Salem, NC, 1998—2003; pres. criminal justice club Guilford Tech. C.C., Jamestown, 1997—99; founding mem. High Point (N.C.) Police Dept. Youth Acad., 1998—98; bd. mem. student adv. com. Goal Program Gardner Webb U., Boiling Springs, 2001—03; rep. Classified Employees Guilford Coutny Schs., Greensboro, 1998—2000. Mem.: APA, Profl. Educators N.C., N.C. Assn. Tchrs. Assts. (assoc. level II cert. 2000), Am. Psychol. Soc., Psi Chi (life). Avocations: motorcycling, fitness, travel. Office: Hyperhedron LLC PO Box 1563 Kernersville NC 27284 Personal E-mail: elizabeth@hile.org.

HILER, EDWARD ALLAN, agricultural and engineering educator; b. Hamilton, Ohio, May 14, 1939; s. Earl and Thelma (Kolb) H.; m. Patricia Burke; children: Karen, Richard, Scott. BS in Agrl. Engring., MS in Agrl. Engring., Ohio State U., 1963, PhD in Agrl. Engring., 1966. Registered profl. engr., Tex. Asst. prof. Tex. A&M U., College Station, 1966-69, assoc. prof., 1969-73, prof., 1973—, head dept. agrl. engring., 1974-88, dep. chancellor for acad. program planning and rsch., 1989-91, interim chancellor, 1991, exec. dep. chancellor, 1991, dep. chancellor for acad. and rsch. programs, 1991-92; vice chancellor, dean agrl. and life scis., dir. Tex. Agrl. Expt. Sta., 1992—; dir. Tex. Agrl. Ext. Svc., 1998—2002. Cons. on water conservation, environ. quality, energy and biol. processes and future agrl. engring. Office Tech. Assessment, U.S. Congress, Office of Water Rsch. and Tech., Dept. Interior, others. Contbr. over 100 articles to profl. jours. Recipient numerous ednl. and rsch. awards. Fellow AAAS, Instn. Agrl. Engrs. Eng., Am. Soc. Engring. Edn., Am. Soc. Agrl. Engrs. (bd. dirs., pres. 1991-92, trustee Found.); mem. NAE. Presbyterian. Avocations: golf, photography, reading novels.

HILER, MONICA JEAN, reading and sociology educator; b. Dallas, Sept. 3, 1929; d. James Absalom and Monica Constance (Farrar) Longino; m. Robert Joseph Hiler, Nov. 1, 1952; children: Robert, Deborah, Michael, Douglas, Frederick. BA, Agnes Scott Coll., Decatur, Ga., 1951; MEd, U. Ga., Athens, 1968; EdS, U. Ga., 1972, EdD, 1974. Social worker Atlanta Family and Children's Svcs., 1962-63; tchr. Hall County pub. schs., Ga., 1965-67; mem. faculty Gainesville Jr. Coll., Ga., 1968-87, prof. reading and sociology, 1975-87, chmn. devel. studies program, 1973-85, acting chmn. divsn. social scis., 1986-87, prof. emeritus reading and sociology, 1987—. Cons. So. Regional Edn. Bd., 1975-83, Gainesville Coll., 1987-95; apptd. spl. advocate Juvenile Ct. Union County, Ga., 1994-96; ch. organist, pianist, choir dir., 1964-82, 1988—. Pres. Ch. Women United, N.E. Ga., 1992-94, Named Ch. Woman of Yr., N.E. Ga., 2001, Woman of Yr., St. Franics of Assisi Ch., Blairsville, 1996. Mem. ASCD, Internat. Reading Assn., Ga. Sociol. Assn., Gainesville Music Club, Phi Beta Kappa, Phi Delta Kappa, Phi Kappa Phi. Avocations: piano, painting, sewing. E-mail: jeannbob@brmemc.net.

HILES, BRADLEY STEPHEN, lawyer; b. Granite City, Ill., Nov. 11, 1955; s. Joseph J. and Betty Lou (Goodman) H.; m. Toni Jonine Failoni, Aug. 12, 1977; children: Eric Stephen, Nina Catherine, Emily Christine. BA cum laude, Furman U., 1977; JD cum laude, St. Louis U., 1980. Bar: Mo. 1980, U.S. Dist. Ct. (ea. dist.) Mo., 1980, Ill. 1981. From assoc. to ptnr. Blackwell Sanders Peper Martin, St. Louis, 1980—. V.p., sec., gen. counsel Miss. Lime Co., 1992. Editor-in-chief St. Louis Univ. Law Jour., 1979-80; contbr. articles to profl. jours. Mem. Bar Assn. of Met. St. Louis (chmn. environ. and conservation law com. 1993-94). Republican. Baptist. Avocations: gospel singing, cycling. Home: 34 Meditation Way Ct Florissant MO 63031-6535 Office: Blackwell Sanders Peper Martin 720 Olive St Fl 24 Saint Louis MO 63101-2338

HILF, MICHAEL GARY, law administrator, prosecutor; b. Hollis, N.Y., June 11, 1955; s. Victor and Dorothy (Goldwasser) H. AB, Cornell U., 1976; JD, Harvard U., 1979. Bar: N.Y. 1980, U.S. Dist. Ct. (no., ea., and so. dists.) N.Y. 1980. Asst. dist. atty. N.Y. County, N.Y.C., 1979-86; sr. staff atty. N.Y. State Edn. Dept., Office Profl. Discipline, N.Y.C., 1987-89, dep. dir. prosecutions, 1989—. Vis. asst. prof. law Coll. Law, U. Toledo, 1986-87. Mem. Alumni Assn. of Bronx H.S. of Sci. (trustee 1981—, chmn. bd. trustees 1981-86, 87-91, 92-95), Phi Beta Kappa. Office: NY State Edn Dept 2nd Fl 475 Park Ave S New York NY 10016-6901

HILF, RUSSELL, biochemist, educator; b. Bklyn., Aug. 13, 1931; s. Jerome Joseph and Sydel Ruth (Kaufman) H.; m. Beverly Sydelle Polak, May 29, 1955; children: Elise Rachel, Merrill Jean, Lawrence Michael. BS, CCNY, 1952; MS, Rutgers U., 1953, PhD, 1955. Head biochemistry sect., nutrition div. QM Food and Container Inst., Chgo., 1958-59; head, cancer endocrinology sect. Squibb Inst. for Med. Research, New Brunswick, N.J., 1959-69; prof. biochemistry dept. U. Rochester Sch. Medicine and Dentistry, N.Y., 1969—. Chmn. diagnosis working group Breast Cancer Task Force, Nat. Cancer Inst., NIH, 1978-80; mem. merit rev. bd. in oncology VA, 1979-83; mem. cancer edn. rev. com. Nat. Cancer Inst., NIH, 1985-86, mem. reproductive endocrinology study sect., 1986-89, 97-2000; mem. sci. rev. panel Am. Inst. Cancer Rsch., 1990—; mem. N.Y. State Health Rsch. Sci. Bd., 1997—. Editor: (with J.A. Kellen) Influences of Hormones in Tumor Development, 1979; assoc. editor Cancer Rsch., 1967-78, 83-94; mem. editl. adv. bd. Biochem. Pharmacology, 1973-83; mem. internat. adv. bd. Cancer Biochemistry BioPhysics, 1974—; mem. editl. bd. Oncology Rsch., 1989—; contbr. articles to profl. jours. Wellcome vis. prof., 1994. With Med. Svc. Corps U.S. Army, 1955-58. Grantee Nat. Cancer Inst., 1969—, Am. Cancer Soc., 1970-75, 83-88. Fellow AAAS, N.Y. Acad. Sci.; mem. Am. Soc. Biol. Chemists, Am. Assn. for Cancer Research, Endocrine Soc., Am. Soc. Photobiol., Soc. Exptl. Biology and Medicine, Am. Cancer Soc. (adv. com. biochemistry and chem. carcinogenesis 1986-89, vice chmn., chmn. adv. com. biochemistry and endocrinology 1990-91). Home: 85 Willowcrest Dr Rochester NY 14618-4337 Office: 601 Elmwood Ave Rochester NY 14642-0001 E-mail: russell_hilf@urmc.rochester.edu.

HILFERTY, BRYAN CAREY, public relations specialist; b. Arlington, Mass., Aug. 10, 1960; s. Walter Gerard and Ruthe (Hughes) H.; m. Shawna LaNaye Patton, Aug. 16, 1990. BA, U. Mass., 1987; MA, Colo. State U., 1996. Commd. 2d lt. U.S. Army, 1984, advanced through grades to lt. col., 2002; asst. prof. English U.S. Mil. Acad., West Point, N.Y., 1996-99; pub. affairs officer U.S. Army, Alaska, 1999—2001, pub. affairs officer 10th Mountain divsn., 2001—. Contbr. articles to profl. jours. Decorated Bronze Star medals (2). Mem. Pub. Rels. Soc. Am., Assn. U.S. Army, VFW, Rotary. Roman Catholic. Avocations: chess, boating. Home: 9066 A Bassett St Fort Drum NY 13603 E-mail: bhilferty@us.army.mil., bryan.hilferty@drum.army.mil.

HILFSTEIN, ERNA, science historian, educator; b. Krakow, Poland; arrived in U.S., 1949, naturalized, 1954; d. Leon and Anna (Schornstein) Kluger; m. Max Hilfstein; children: Leon, Simone Juliana. BA, CCNY, 1967, MA, 1971; PhD, CUNY, 1978. Tchr. secondary schs., N.Y.C., 1968-84, 86-92; collaborator Polish Acad. Scis., 1968-85. Vis. prof. Queens Coll., 1973; affiliate Grad. Sch./Univ. Ctr., CUNY. Author: Starowolski's Biographies of Copernicus, 1980; collaborator English version of Nicholas Copernicus Complete Works, vol. 1, 1972, vol. 2, 1978, vol. 3, 1985, vols. 2 and 3, 2d edit., 1992; co-translator: The Leviathan in the State Theory of Thomas Hobbes: Meaning and Failure of a Political Symbol, 1996; editor: Science and History, 1978, Copernicus and His Successors, 1995, Sebastian Petrycy, A Polish Renaissance Scholar, 1997; contbr. articles and revs. to profl. jours. Recipient Rector's medal, Univ. M. Kopernik, Torun, 1989, medal, Towarzystwo Naukowe Torun, Poland, 1990, Dom Kopernika in Torun medal, 1989, Order of Merit Silver medal, Rep. of Poland, 1991, Scholar of Polish Descent medal, 1989; grantee, NEH, 1984—85. Mem. History Sci. Soc., Polish Inst. Arts and Scis. in Am., CUNY Acad. for the Humanities and Scis., N.Y. Acad. Scis., Kosciuszko Found., United Fedn. Tchrs. (chpt. chmn. 1978-84, 86-92, del. 1980-92), Am. Mus. Nat. History, Libr. Congress,Nat. Commn. Am. Fgn. Policy, New Cracow Friendship Soc. (bd. dirs. 1998—). Home: 1523 Dwight Pl Bronx NY 10465-1121 also: Woodheaven Estate 375 Westwood Dr Hurleyville NY 12747-5506

HILGARTNER, MARGARET WEHR, retired pediatric hematologist, educator; b. Balt., Nov. 6, 1924; d. Andrew Henry and Margaret Elizabeth (Wehr) H.;m. Albert Milton Arky; children: George, Elizabeth, John. AB, Bryn Mawr Coll., 1946; MA, Duke U., 1951, MD, 1955. Diplomate Am. Bd. Pediatrics, Am. Bd. Pediatric Hematology/Oncology. Intern Bellevue Hosp., N.Y., 1955-56; resident in pediatrics N.Y. Hosp.-Cornell Med. Ctr., 1956-58, fellow in hematology/oncology, 1958-61, instr. in pediatrics, 1961-67, physician-in-charge pediatric coagulation, 1965-95, asst. prof., 1967-73, dir. hemophilia comprehensive treatment, 1970-95, assoc. prof., assoc. attending pediatrician outpatient dept., 1973-78, prof., dir. pediatric hematology/oncology div., attending pediatrician, 1978-94, Harold Weill prof. pediatric hematology, 1988-2000; assoc. attending pediatrician N.Y. Hosp., 1974-94; adj. attending physician Sloan-Kettering Cancer Ctr., N.Y., 1979-97; retired, 2000. Bd. dirs., mem. exec. com. N.Y. Blood Ctr., 1989; cons. Bur. Handicapped Children, N.Y., 1971, Factor VIII Inhibitor Study Group, 1974, Ho. Reps. Ways and Means Com., 1977, Senate and Ho. Reps. Health Subcom. on Health, 1978-80, Fgn. and Interstate Commerce Com.-Ho. Reps. Subcom. on Pub. Health and Environment, 1979, N.Y. State Com. on Transfusion, 1979-84, Ad Hoc Com. Rev. Rsch. in Edn., 1981-82; cons. in medicine Englewood (N.J.) Hosp., 1974-86, in pediatric hematology, 1982-; lectr.-in-medicine Mt. Sinai Hosp., N.Y., 1979—; vis. prof. Rochester (Minn.) Hemophilia Ctr. 1979, 1980, Marshfield (Wis.) Clinic, 1979, Oakland Children's Hosp., 1981, Hangchow, Beijing, Kian, Peoples Republic of China, 1981, Johns Hopkins U. 1982, Rochester Strong Meml., 1985, Duke U. 1985; chmn. Gov.'s adv. coun. to N.J. Dept. Health Hemophilia Program, 1973-80; mem. task force Factor VIII-Inhibitors Nat. Heart Lung Inst., 1975-80; mem. adv. com. publ. health #94-63 Health Svcs. Adminstrn., 1976, blood disease and resources Nat. Hear Lung Inst. NIH, 1985-89; chmn. Feiba Study Com., U.S. chpt., 1981-86, pediatric working group World Fedn. Hemophilia, 1982; mem. ad hoc AIDS adv. com. Nat. Heart Lung Blood Inst. NIH, 1985-87. Mem. profl. adv. bd. mag. Baby Talk, 1987—; contbr. numerous articles to profl. jours. Mem. Am. Acad. Pediat. (chmn. sect. program oncology/hematology), Am. Heart Assn., Am. Med. Women's Assn., Am. Pediatric Soc., Am. Soc. Hematology, Assn. Women in Sci. (treas. 1974-76), Harvey Soc., Internat. Soc. Blood Transfusion, Internat. Soc. Thrombosis and Hemostasis, Nat. Hemophilia Found. (bd. dirs. met. chpt. 1965-69, trustee 1968-88, med. dir. met. chpt. 1970-90, mem. med. and sci. bd. 1973-87, v.p. 1979-84, mem. edn. resources project 1979-84), N.Y. Acad. Sci., N.Y. Soc. Study Blood, World Fedn. Hemophilia (chmn. child care com. 1990), Am. Soc. Pediatric Hematology/Oncology, Children's Blood Found. (med. dir 1978—, bd. dirs. 1987—, pres. 1995-96), Cooley's Anemia Found. (bd. dirs. 1987-98). Office: Cornell U Med Coll Dept of Pediatrics 525 E 68th St New York NY 10021-4870 Home: 73 Depeyster Ave Tenafly NJ 07670 E-mail: mah2015@med.cornell.edu.

HILGEMANN, DONALD WILLIAM, medical educator; b. Postville, Iowa, Aug. 20, 1952; married. Student, U. Iowa, 1972; MS in Biology, Univ. Tübingen, Germany, 1977, PhD in Pharmacology & Physiology, 1980. Rsch. and tchg. asst. Dept. Pharmacology U. Tübingen, 1977—80; rsch. assoc. Merrell Internat., Strasbourg, France, 1980—81; asst. rsch. physiologist UCLA Sch. Medicine, 1981—87; asst. clin. prof. nursing UCLA Sch. Nursing, 1982—87; asst. prof. Dept. Physiology U. Tex. Southwestern Med. Ctr., Dallas, 1988—91, assoc. prof., 1991—96, prof. physiology, 1996—. Tchr., lectr. UNISEF, 1992, Univ. Kaiserlautern, 1994; vis. rsch. fellow Oxford (England) U., 1985—88; invited spkr. Kyoto (Japan) U., 1993—94, Northwestern U., Chgo., 1994, U. Konstanz, Germany, 1994, Johns Hopkins U., Balt., 1994, Tokyo Med. Coll., 1994, Univ. Laussane, Switzerland, 1994, U. Pa., Phila., 1994, Oreg. Health Sci. Ctr., Portland, 1995, N.Y. Acad. Scis., Woods Hole, Mass., 1995, Rush Med. Ctr., Chgo., 1995, Swiss Fed. Inst. Tech., Zurich, 1994, Tel Aviv U., 1995. Fellow: Binational Israeli-USa Found.; mem.: Physiol. Soc., Soc. Gen. Physiologists, Soc. Neurosci., Biophys. Soc. (young investigator award 1997), Japan Soc. for Promotion Sci. Office: U Tex Southwestern Med Ctr 5323 Harry Hines Blvd Dallas TX 75390-7208

HILGENBERG, JOHN CHRISTIAN, corporate financial executive, consultant; b. Balt., Sept. 6, 1941; s. Carl R. and Elizabeth (Rianhard) Hilgenberg; m. Evelyn Brantley Handy, Apr. 1, 1971; children: Rodney, Crady. BA, Yale U., 1963; MBA, U. Va., 1965. With internat. lending divsn. Md. Nat. Bank, Balt., 1970-75; v.p., dir. fin. svcs. S.M. Hyman Co., Balt., 1975-78; v.p. fin. Eastmet Corp., Balt., 1978-85. Trustee Harbor Hosp. Ctr., 1975—2002, Harbor Hosp. Found., 2002—; v.p., treas., dir. Sky Alland Rsch. Corp., 1986, 1989—90; pres., bd. dirs. Ski Tech. Holdings, Inc., 1987—89, CADS USA, Inc., 1987—89; pres. Eager St. Group, Inc., Balt., 1991—; cons., investor in early-stage cos.; bd. dirs. Synthecell Corp., pres., 1992—95; bd. dirs. Cyto Pulse Scis., Inc. Lt. USNR, 1965—70. Mem.: Balt. Choral Arts Soc. (dir. 1975—), Bachelors Cotillon, Md. Club, Elkridge Club. Republican. Episcopalian. Home: PO Box 338 Stevenson MD 21153 Office: 6 E Eager St Baltimore MD 21202

HILGENKAMP, KATHRYN DARLINE, exercise and sport psychologist, health educator; b. Denver, Nov. 5, 1952; d. LeRoy C. and Darline L. (Callaway) Thoms; children: Jessica Erin Hoffman, Whitney Jayne Hoffman, Colton James Hilgenkamp, Devin Corinne Hilgenkamp. BS in Edn., U. Nebr., Lincoln, 1977; MS in Edn., Southern Ill. U., Carbondale, 1980; EdD, U. Nebr., Lincoln, 1987. Asst. prof. Creighton U., Omaha, 1990-93; adj. faculty U. Nebr., Omaha, 1994-95; asst. prof. La. Tech. U., Ruston, 1995-99, Coastal Carolina U., Conway, SC, 1999—2002, U. No. Colo., Greeley, Colo., 2002—. Author: Taking Charge of Your Health, 2002. CPR instr. Am. Heart Assn., ARC, Blair, Nebr., 1980-95. Recipient 2nd pl. Student Rsch. award, Soc. Prospective Med., Atlanta, 1987; Enhancement grantee La. Bd. Regents, 1997. Mem.: AAHPERD, APA, Am. Assn. Health Edn. Avocations: running, weightlifting, aerobic dance, golf, volleyball. Office: Cmty Health and Nutrition Box 93 Greeley CO 80639

HILGERS, JOHN JACK WILLIAM, management and transportation consultant; b. Carmel-by-the-Sea, Calif., Nov. 17, 1934; s. Rudolph Joseph and Eleanor Maude (King) H.; m. Sharon Ann Hilgers, Dec. 15, 1968; children; Jon Marc, John Jack William Jr. BA in Psychology, San Jose State U., 1956; BA in Criminology, U. Calif., Berkeley, 1963; MS in Sys. Mgmt., U. So. Calif., 1984; MS in Urban Studies, Old Dominion U., 1995, PhD in Urban Svcs., 1998. Enlisted USMC, 1957, advanced in grades to col., ret., 1988; rsch. asst. Bur. Rsch. Old Dominion U., Norfolk, 1988-90, program mgr. Coll. Bus. and Pub. Adminstrn., 1991-98, assoc. dir. Internat. Maritime Ports and Logistics Inst., 1993—98; exec. asst. Va. Legislature, 1999—. Dir., mem. exec. com. Atlantic Rim Network, Boston, 1995-2001; exec. sec. Maritime Adv. Coun., Norfolk, 1991—; mem. tech. com. Met. Planning Orgn., Hampton Roads, Va., 1996-98; internat. maritime com. chmn. Conf. of World Regions, 1997—. Editor (newsletter) Bullets and Cannonballs, 1993-98, (mag.) Bus. and Econ. Quar., 1992-96. Divsn. dir. United Way, Norfolk, 1996, 97, Virginia Beach Sister City Group, 1995-200o; trustee Old Dominion U., 1998-2002, Old Dominion U. Rsch. Found., 2001--. Recipient Va. Commerce Builder award, 1999, Va. Patrick Henry award, Commonwealth of Va., 2001. Mem. ASPA (exec. com. transp. policy and adminstrn. com. 1997-2001), Rotary (pres. Sunrise Norfolk chpt. 1997-98, asst. gov. Dist. 7600, 2002—, Paul Harris fellow 1996, 2002), Econs. Club (Hampton Rds), Internat. Bus. Coun., Pepper Lovers Club Va. Internat. (dir. 1994-96), Propeller Club U.S. (dir. Port of Norfolk 1996—), Hampton Rds. Fgn. Commerce Club (pres. 1996), Phi Kappa Phi, Phi Alpha Alpha. Avocation: antique and classic automobiles. Home and Office: 2505 Forehand Ln Virginia Beach VA 23454-2744

HILGERT, ARNIE, management and marketing educator; b. Detroit, Feb. 24, 1944; d. Norris Bersford and Romayne Catherine (Kent) Clarke; m. Jeffrey L. Hilgert, Dec. 21, 1964 (div. Dec. 1981); children: Michele Leanne, Tracy Lee. BA, U. Redlands, 1982; MBA, Peter F. Drucker Sch. Mgmt., 1984; MA Ctr. Ednl. Studies, The Claremont Grad. U., 1991, PhD Ctr. Ednl. Studies, 1992. Ptnr. Durawood Shasta Pacific Industries, Chico, Calif., 1971-78; mgr., owner Homefront Home Improvement Stores, Chico, Calif., 1975-78; rsch. assoc. exec. mgmt. program The Claremont (Calif.) Grad. Sch., 1984-85, adminstr. exec. mgmt. program, 1985-89; sponsored rsch. analyst Calif. State U., L.A., 1989-90; assoc. prof. mgmt. and mktg. No. Ariz. U., Yuma, 1992-98, 1998—. Mem. faculty devel. in internat. bus. U. S.C., 1993; mem. faculty devel. in internat. mktg., Thunderbird, 1989; participant Global Learning Day; participant in nat. and internat. profl. confs.; rschr. in multimedia and distance learning, implementation of ADA Act; Peernet reviewer MCB U. Press, Jour. Mgmt. Devel. Mem. editl. bd. Jour. Bus. Adminstrn., 1988—; textbook reviewer McGraw Hill Pubs.; contbr. articles to profl. jours. Participant Rio Colorado Commn., Yuma, 1993—. State of Calif. Grad. fellow, Claremont, 1982-84; Econs. scholar John Randolph Haynes and Dora Haynes Found., 1981, Elizabeth Malpass scholar Zonta Club Redlands, 1980. Mem. Acad. Bus. Adminstrn. (Tchg. Excellence award 1998), Ariz. Distance Learning Assn. (membership chmn. 2002-), Acad. Mgmt., Acad. Internat. Bus., Ctr. for Study of Intellectual Devel., Claremont U. Sch. Womans Scholars. Home: 11843 E Calle Del Cid Yuma AZ 85367-7216 Office: No Ariz U PO Box 6236 Yuma AZ 85366-6236

HILGERT, RAYMOND LEWIS, management and industrial relations educator, consultant, arbitrator; b. St. Louis, July 28, 1930; s. Lewis Francis and Frieda Christine (Keune) H.; m. Bernice Alice Nerl, Apr. 28, 1951; children—Brenda, Diane, Jeffrey. BA, Westminster Coll., Fulton, Mo., 1952; MBA, Washington U., St. Louis, 1961; DBA, Washington U., 1963. Mgmt. positions with Southwestern Bell Telephone Co., 1956-60; mem. faculty Olin Sch. Bus. Washington U., St. Louis, 1963—2001, dir. summer workshop Olin Sch. Bus., 1964-68; dir. mgmt. devel. programs Olin Sch. Bus. Washington U., St. Louis, 1967-84; asst. dean, dir. undergrad. program Olin Sch. Bus. Washington U., St. Louis, 1968-69. Cons.; lectr.; labor arbitrator Author: (with C. Ling and Ed Leonard Jr.) Cases, Incidents and Experiential Exercises in Human Resource Management, 1990, 3d edit., 2000; (with David Dilts) Cases in Collective Bargaining and Industrial Relations: A Decisional Approach, 1969, 10th edit., 2002, Labor Agreement Negotiations, 1983, 6th edit., 2001; (with Ed Leonard Jr.) Supervision: Concepts and Practices of Management, 1972, 8th edit., 2001; (with Philip Lochhaas and James Truesdell) Christian Ethics in the Workplace, 2001; contbr. articles to profl. jours. Mem. adv. coun. St. Louis region SBA, 1983-91. Served to 1st lt. USAF, 1952-56 Named Tchr. of Yr., Washington U. Sch. Bus., 1968, 81, 85, 89. Mem. Acad. Mgmt., Indsl. Rels. Rsch. Assn., Soc. for Human Resource Mgmt. (sr. profl. in human resource mgmt.), Am. Mgmt. Assn. Lutheran. Avocations: sports, movies. Home: 1744 Lynkirk Ln Kirkwood MO 63122-2251 Office: Washington U Olin Sch Bus PO Box 1133 Saint Louis MO 63130-4899

HILKE, JOHN CORYELL, economist; b. Lackawanna, N.Y., Nov. 26, 1950; s. John Lewis and Charlotte May (Coryell) H.; m. Deborah Durkee Smith, May 27, 1973; children: James Coryell, Anne Catherine. BA, Swarthmore Coll., 1973; MA, Cornell U., 1975, PhD, 1978. Vis. lectr. Cornell U., Ithaca, N.Y., 1977-78; staff economist Fed. Trade Commn., Bur. of Econs., Washington, 1978-79, 82—, asst. to the dir., 1979-82, electricity project coord., 1997—. Cons. U.S. Dept. Justice, Washington, 1988; expert witness Fed. Trade Commn., Washington, 1980-81, 89—. Author: U.S. International Competitiveness: Evolution or Revloution, 1988; co-author: Competition in Govt.-Financed Svcs., 1992; contbr., articles. Chmn. bd. trustees Cedar Lane Unitarian Church, Bethesda, Md., 1988-90; co-pres. Cheverly (Md.) Area Schs. PTA, 1985-87; mem. Swarthmore (Pa.) Presdl. Search Com., 1972-73; pres. Unitarian Universalist Affordable Housing Corp., Washington, 1996-97. Recipient Competition Advocacy award, 1989, Francis Walker award, 1994, 98; Fed. Trade Commn. Outstanding scholar, Washington, 1987; Herbert Lehman Fellowship, State of N.Y., 1973-77. Mem. Am. Econ. Assn., Indsl. Orgn. Soc., Phi Kappa Phi. Democrat. Unitarian Universalist. Avocations: skiing, science fiction. Office: Federal Trade Commn 125 S State St Rm 2105 Salt Lake City UT 84138 E-mail: jhilke@ftc.gov.

HILKEMEYER, RENILDA ESTELLA, nurse; b. Martinsburg, Mo., July 29, 1915; d. Henry Gerard and Anna Marie (Bertels) Hilkemeyer. Diploma in nursing, St. Mary's Hosp., St. Louis U., 1936; BS in Nursing Edn., George Peabody Coll. for Tchrs., Nashville, 1947; postgrad., U. Minn., 1950, U. Tex. Sch. Nursing, 1981; D of Pub. Svc. (hon.), St. Louis U., 1988. Staff nurse o.r. St. Mary's Hosp., Jefferson City, Mo., 1936—37; dist. pub. health nurse Mo. Divsn. Health, Jefferson City, 1937—40, 1950—55; asst. dir. nursing Gen. Hosp. No. 1, Kansas City, Mo., 1947—49; asst. exec. sec. Mo. Nurses Assn., Jefferson City, 1949—50; dir. nursing U. Tex. Sys. Cancer Ctr., Houston, 1955—77, asst. to pres. nursing resources, 1977—79, staff asst. to pres., prof. oncology nursing, 1979—84. Mem. grant rev. com. NIH Nat. Cancer Inst., 1979—83, program rev. com., 1975—77, cons., 1982—, NIH Nat. Heart, Blood and Lung Inst., 1983—, Worker's Inst. Safety, Health, 1983—; chmn., mem. scholarship and professorship com. Cancer Soc., 1980—, mem. nursing adv. com., 1963—80, 1985—, profl. edn. com., 1984—, emeritus mem., 1996—;

chmn. nursing adv. com., mem. adminstrv. bd. Renilda Hilkemeyer Child Care Ctr., U. Tex. Med. Ctr., 1969—. Book reviewer Am. Jour. Nursing, 1982; contbr. articles to profl. jours., chapters to books. Pres. Braes Interfaith Ministries, 1991, 1994, 1995, 1998, bd. dirs. emeritus, 2002—. Named Vol. of the Yr., Braes Interfaith Ministries, 1997; recipient Outstanding Profl. Women's award, Tex. Fedn. Houston Profl. Women, 1983, Outstanding Contbns. award, NCI, 1983, Disting. Svc. award, Am. Cancer Soc., 1981, Nurse of the Yr. award, Houston Area League Nursing, 1973, Matrix award, Theta Sigma Phi, Houston, 1963, Disting. Merit award, Internat. Soc. Nurses in Cancer Care, 1986, new child care ctr. named in her honor, U. Tex. Med. Ctr., 1981, 1st Nat. Nursing Leadership award, Am. Cancer Soc., 1989; grantee, HEW, 1974—77, Am. Cancer Soc., 1974—75, Tex. Fedn. Profl. Women's Clubs, 1977—83. Mem.: ANA, Am. Med. Writers Assn. (Houston-Galveston sect. 1983—84), Tex. Nursing Assn. (pres. 1962—64, bd. dirs. 1964—66, 1971—75, Dist. 9 Svc. award 1970, Nurse of Yr. award 1979), Oncology Nursing Soc. (founding mem. 1991, Lifetime Achievement award 2002), Altrusa Club (pres. Houston chpt. 1983—84, emeritus mem. 2002—), Sigma Theta Tau. Achievements include first to in cancer nursing. Home: 3707 Murworth Dr Houston TX 77025-3531

HILKER, WALTER ROBERT, JR., lawyer; b. L.A., Apr. 18, 1921; s. Walter Robert and Alice (Cox) H.; m. Ruth H. Hibbard, Sept. 7, 1943; children: Anne Katherine, Walter Robert III. BS, U. So. Calif., 1942, LLB, 1948. Bar: Calif. 1949. Sole practice, Los Angeles, 1949-55; ptnr. Parker, Milliken, Kohlmeier, Clark & O'Hara, 1955-75; of counsel Pacht, Ross, Warne, Bernhard & Sears, Newport Beach, Calif., 1980-84. Trustee Bella Mabury Trust; bd. dirs. Houchin Found. Served to lt. USNR, 1942-45. Decorated Bronze Star with V. Mem. ABA, Calif. Bar Assn., Orange County Bar Assn. Clubs: Spring Valley Lake Country (Apple Valley, Calif.); Balboa Bay (Newport Beach, Calif.). Republican. Home and Office: 143 Stonecliffe Aisle Irvine CA 92612-3778

HILL, ALAN GORDON, sociologist, educator; b. Greenville, SC, Jan. 25, 1945; s. Arthur G. Hill, Bonta Bush Hill; m. Toyo Murono; 1 child, Arthur. M.Phil., MA, Columbia University, New York, NY, 1967—76; BA, Furman University, Greenville, 1963—67. Chair, Dept. of Sociology Delta College, University Center, MI, 1987—2002; Sociology Instructor Furman University, Greenville, SC, 1979—87. Executive Officer Michigan Sociological Association, MI, 2000—02. Author: (Book) Discovering Society, 1999 (Distinguished Contribution to Instruction, Computers and Sociology Section, American Sociological Assn., 2000). Moderator New Hope Baptist Church, Bay City, MI, 2001—02; Vice President Michigan Region of the American Baptist Churches, E. Lansing, MI, 1996—97; President Delta Chapter of AAUP, University Center, MI, 2002—02. Sergeant Army Medical Service Corps, 1969—75, various. Mem.: Michigan Sociological Association (Past President), Michigan Sociological Association (Executive Officer 2000—02), American Sociological Association (Distinguished Contribution to Instruction (listed above) 2000). Baptist. Home: 3637 Monitor Road Bay City MI 48706-9219 Office: Delta College 1961 Delta Road University Center MI 48710 Personal E-mail: aghill@alpha.delta.edu. Business E-Mail: aghill@alpha.delta.edu.

HILL, ALFRED, lawyer, educator; b. N.Y.C., Nov. 7, 1917; m. Dorothy Turck, Aug. 12, 1960; 1 dau., Amelia. BS, Coll. City N.Y., 1937; LL.B., Bklyn. Law Sch., 1941, LL.D., 1986; S.J. D., Harvard U., 1957. Bar: N.Y. State bar 1943, Ill 1958. With SEC, 1943-52; prof. law So. Meth. U., 1953-56, Northwestern U., 1956-62, Columbia U., 1962-75, Simon H. Rifkind prof. law, 1975-87, Simon H. Rifkind prof. law emeritus, 1988—. Contbr. articles on torts, conflict of laws, fed. cts. constl. law to legal jours. Mem. Am. Law Inst. Home: 79 Sherwood Rd Tenafly NJ 07670-2734 Office: Columbia Law Sch New York NY 10027

HILL, ALICE LORRAINE, history, genealogy and social researcher, educator; b. Moore, Okla., Jan. 15, 1935; d. Robert Edward and Alma Alice (Fraysher) H.; children: Debra Hrboka, Pamela Spangler (dec.), Eric Shiver, Lorraine Styczinski. BS in Bus. and Acctg., Ctrl. State U., 1977; student, U. Okla., 1977-78; postgrad., Calif. Luth. U., 1988; ed. Sch. Edn., UCLA, 1990. Cert. cmty. coll. life instr. acctg., bus. and indsl. mgmt., computer and related techs., and real estate, Calif.; ordained min. Former model, 1990-95; with L.A. Unified Sch. Dist., 1990-95; tchr. mentor K-12 Asuza (Calif.) Pacific U., 2000—; active real estate broker. Founder Los Artistas for creative activities for young people, 1996. Author: America, We Love You (Congl. Record Poem, made into World's 1st Internat. Patriotic song), 1975, Land of Lands (now world's first internat. patriotic song); author: (lyrics) Come Listen to the Music, 1996, Someday John, 1996. Mem. bd. advisors Family Health Rsch., Seattle. Named hon. grad. Patricia Stevens Modeling Sch. (Fla.); recipient scholarship Leadership Enrichment Program, Okla., 1977, Hon. recognition Okla. State Bd. of Regents for Higher Edn., 1977, Presdl. citations for Pres. Ford, 1975, 76, Admired Woman of the Decade award, 1994, Life Time Achievement award, 1995, Most Gold Record award, 1995, Key award for Rsch., Internat. Cultural Diploma of Honor, 1995, Woman of Yr. award, 1995, Internat. Woman of Yr. award Order Internat. Fellowship, 1994, 95, The Alice Lorraine Hill 2003 Poet of Yr. Medallion, The Famous Poets Soc., 2003. Mem. NAFE, NEA, AAUW, Internat. Platform Assn., Internat. Poetry Soc. (disting. mem., named to internat. hall of fame, 1996, named in Best Poets of 20th Century), Ventura County Profl. Women's Networking. Home: 1646 Lime Ave Oxnard CA 93033-6897

HILL, ANITA CARRAWAY, retired state legislator; b. Chatfield, Tex., Aug. 13, 1928; d. Archie Clark and Martha (Butler) Carraway; BA in Journalism, Tex. Woman's U., 1950; m. Harris Hill, Sept. 20, 1952; children: Stephen Victor, Virginia Evelyn. Reporter Garland (Tex.) Daily News, 1950-51; ednl. dir. First Meth. Ch., Garland, 1951-53; chemist Kraft Foods Co., Garland, 1953-56; legis. aide, Tex. Legislature, 1975-77; mem. Tex. Ho. of Reps., 1977-92, mem. mcpl. bond and revenue sharing coms., 1971-74; ret., 1992. Awards chmn. City of Garland Environ. Council; mem. City of Garland Park and Recreation Bd., 1971-77, chmn., 1976-77; life mem. PTA; mem. Dallas County Mental Health Mental Retardation bd. trustees. Named Disting. Alumna, Tex. Woman's U., 1981. Mem. Garland C. of C., Rowlett C. of C., Bus. and Profl. Women's Club (Garland Woman of Year, 1980), AAUW, Tex. Assn. Elected Women. Republican. Methodist.

HILL, BARON P. congressman; b. Seymour, Ind., June 23, 1953; m. Betty Schepman; children: Jennifer, Cara, Elizabeth. BS in History, Furman U., 1975. Fin. analyst Merrill Lynch; mem. U.S. Congress from 9th Ind. dist., 1999—. Mem. Agr., Armed Forces coms., Blue Dog Dems., New Dem. Coalition, Joint Econ. Com., Com. Veterans Affairs. Elected to Ind. Ho. Reps., 1982-90; appointed by Speaker of the House to serve as chmn. House Rules Com.; asst. whip for Dem. Caucus, as chmn. Ind. House Campaign Com. from 1985-89; exec. dir. State Student Assistance Commn., 1992. Democrat. Office: 1204 Longworth Hob Washington DC 20515-1409*

HILL, BEN, broadcast executive; Gen. mgr. Sta. WCAO, Balt.; v.p. Sta. WXYV, Balt., Sta. WPGC-AM and WPGC-FM, Washington; v.p. and gen. mgr. CBS Radio; pres., gen. mgr. WPEC AM/FM Infinity Broadcasting (CBS subs.), Washington. Office: 4200 Parliament Pl Ste 300 Lanham Seabrook MD 20706-1881

HILL, BEVERLEY JANE, physician assistant; b. Balt., May 19, 1938; d. Isaac Corbert Hill and Grace Vivian Bryant. BS in Phys. Edn., Western Md. Coll., Westminster, 1960, MEd, 1968; postgrad., Johns Hospkins Univ., 1972; cert. in physician asst., Essex Cmty. Coll., Balt., 1991. Lic. physician asst. Md., Va., Del., N.C. Tchr. phys. edn. Balt. County Sch. Sys., Towson, Md., 1960—65; tchr. John Carroll Sch., Bel Air, Md., 1965—86, dean of students, 1965—86, dir. of athletics, 1965—86; physician asst. Beebe Gen. Hosp., Lewes, Del., 1991—94, Johns Hopkins Hosp., Balt., 1992, San Carlos (Ariz.) Hosp., Apache Reservation, 1992; physician asst. Indian Health Svcs., Supai Indian Reservation, Grand Canyon, Ariz., 1992; physician asst. St. Agnes Hosp., Balt., 1993—94, EMSA, Ltd., Pax River, Md., 1994; ambulatory care Md. State Penitentiary, 1992—96; physician asst. Ft. Belvoir/Dewitt Army Hosp., 1996—97, Coastal Govt. Svcs., 1994—97, Profl. Occupl. Health, Lanhan, Md., 1997—98, Dept. of Def., Womack Army Med., Ft. Bragg, NC, 1998—, USN Acad., Annapolis, Md., 2001—02. Contbr. articles to profl. jours. Named to, Western Md. Coll. Sports Hall of Fame. Mem.: Phi Theta Kappa (mem. Nat. Deans list). Democrat. Avocations: running, walking, reading, writing.

HILL, BONNIE GUITON, company executive; b. Springfield, Ill., Oct. 30, 1941; d. Henry Frank and Zola Elizabeth (Newman) Brazelton; m. Walter Hill Jr.; 1 child, Nichele Monique. BA, Mills Coll., 1974; MS, Calif. State U., Hayward, 1975; EdD, U. Calif., Berkeley, 1985. Adminstr. asst. to pres.'s spl. asst. Mills Coll., Oakland, Calif., 1970-71, adminstrv. asst. to asst. v.p., 1972-73, student svcs. counselor, adv. to resuming students, 1973-74, asst. dean of students, interim dir. ethnic studies, lectr., 1975-76; exec. dir. Marcus A. Foster Ednl. Inst., Oakland, 1976-79; adminstrv. mgr. Kaiser Aluminum & Chem. Corp., Oakland, 1979-80; v.p., gen. mgr. Kaiser CTR Inc., Oakland, 1980-84; vice chair Postal Rate Commn., Washington, 1985-87; asst. sec. for vocat. and adult edn. Dept. Edn., Washington, 1987-89; sec. State and Consumer Svcs. Agy. State of Calif.; spl. adv. to Pres. for Consumer Affairs, dir. U.S. Office Consumer Affairs, 1989-90; pres., CEO Earth Conservation Corps, Washington, 1990-91; sec. State and Consumer Svcs. Industry, State of Calif., 1991-92; dean McIntire Sch. Commerce U. Va., Charlottesville, 1992-97; v.p. The Times Mirror Co., 1997-2000; pres. B. Hill Enterprises, LLC, 2001—; COO Iconblue, Inc., LA Times, 2001—. Sr. v.p. comm. and pub. affairs L.A. Times, 1998—2001; pres., CEO The Times Mirror Found., 1997—2001; bd. dirs. The Home Depot Co., Hershey Foods Corp., AK Steele Corp., Choice Point Inc., Nat. Grid Group, plc, Albertsons Inc. Office: B Hill Enterprises LLC Ste 600 5670 Wilshire Blvd Los Angeles CA 90036

HILL, BRIAN DONOVAN, lawyer; b. Sanford, Fla., July 27, 1947; s. Herbert Charles and Catherine (Kenny) H.; m. Carol Ponton, Aug. 24, 1978; children: Erin, Chad, Michael, Matthew, Casey. BS, JD, U. Fla. Bar: Fla. 1975, U.S. Dist. Ct. (mid. dist.) Fla. Assoc. Maquire, Voorhis & Wells, Gainesville, Fla., 1974-80, Swann and Haddock, Orlando, Fla., 1980-82; ptnr. Taraska and Hill, Orlando, 1983-86, Hill and Hill, Orlando, 1986-87, Hill & Ponton P.A., Orlando, 1987—. Served to lt. USN, 1969-74. Mem. Phi Beta Kappa, Phi Kappa Phi. Office: Hill & Ponton PA PO Box 2673 Orlando FL 32802-2673 Home: Apt 210 11 Kings Grant Rd Daytona Beach FL 32117-2545

HILL, BRUCE MARVIN, statistician, scientist, educator; b. Chgo., Mar. 13, 1935; s. Samuel and Leah (Berman) H.; m. Linda Ladd, June 18, 1958; children— Alec Michael, Russell Andrew, Gregory Bruce; m. Anne Edith Gardiner Bruce, Aug. 5, 1972. BS in Math., U. Chgo., 1956; MS in Stats., Stanford U., 1958, PhD in Stats., 1961. Mem. faculty U. Mich., Ann Arbor, 1960—, assoc. prof. stats. and probability theory, 1964-70, prof., 1970—. Vis. prof. bus. Harvard U., 1964-65; vis. prof. systems engring. U. Lancaster, U.K., 1968-69; vis. prof. stats. U. London, 1976; vis. prof. econs. U. Utah, 1979; vis. prof. math. U. Milan, U. Rome, 1989. Author: Hill Tail index estimator; editor Jour. Am. Statis. Assn., 1977-83, Jour. Bus. and Econ. Stats., 1982—; contbr. articles to profl. jours., chpts. to books on stats, encys. Grantee NSF, 1962-69, 81-86, 89—, USAF, 1971-73, 87-89. Fellow Am. Statis. Assn. (pres. Ann Arbor chpt. 1986-91), Inst. Math. Stats.; mem. AAUP, Am. Math Assn., Rsch. Club U. Mich., Psi Upsilon, Sigma Chi. Office: U Mich Dept Stats Ann Arbor MI 48109-1027 Home: 1645 Polipoli Rd Kula HI 96790-7524 E-mail: bhill@prodigy.net.

HILL, BRYCE DALE, school administrator; b. Seminole, Okla., Mar. 5, 1930; s. Charles Daniel and Ollie (Nichols) Hill; m. Wilma Dean Carter, Aug. 16, 1956; children: Bryce Anthony, Brent Dale. BS, East Ctrl. State Coll., 1952, M in Tchg., 1957; postgrad., U. Okla., 1959—70; profl. adminstrs. cert., 1969. Tchr. pub. schs., New Lima, Okla., 1952—56; supt. pub. schs., 1956—95; owner New Lima Gas Co., 1958—82. Mem. Seminole County Bd. Health, 1985—95, v.p., 1986—88, chmn., 1988—95; edn. leader com. Okla. Farmers Union, 1990—93; exec. com. Okla. Commn. for Ednl. Leadership, 1993—95; chmn. Seminole County Dem. Ctrl. Com., 1962—64, 1970—95; chmn. bd. dirs. Seminole County chpt. ARC, 1969—90; v.p. bd. dirs. Redland Cmty. Action Program, 1968—71; mem. Seminole County Rural Devel. Coun.; v.p. bd. dirs. Okla. Assn. Acad. Competition, 1991—95. Named to Seminole Jr. Coll. Hall of Fame, 1995. Mem.: NEA, Seminole County Sch. Adminstrs. Assn. (chmn. 1969—70, 1993—95), Seminole County Tchrs. Assn. (pres. 1964—65, 1971—72, 1979—80, 1990—91), Orgn. Rural Okla. Schs. (bd. dirs. 1986—92, pres. 1993—94, Pioneer award 1998), Okla. Assn. Sch. Adminstrs. (exec. com. 1976—78, 1979—81, bd. dirs. 1979—81, 1993—95, Dist. 8 Adminstr. of Yr. 1983, 1994, Lifetime Achievement award 1996), Am. Assn. Sch. Adminstrs., Okla. Edn. Assn. (Friend of Edn. award Zone 6 1996), Okla. Assn. Svc. Impact Schs. (bd. dirs. 1987—95), Seminole Hist. Soc. (v.p. 1971—73, 1974—76), Okla. Ret. Educators Assn., Seminole County Ret. Tchrs. Assn. (pres. 1996—), Legislation Steering Com., Seminole County Schoolmasters Club (pres. 1963—64, 1969—70, 1977—78). Baptist. Home: 32 Sequoyah Blvd Shawnee OK 74801-5570 Personal E-mail: bryce.wilma@charter.net.

HILL, C. THOMAS, JR., radiologist; b. Corinth, Miss., Oct. 23, 1919; s. C. Thomas Hill and Ruby Paris Bryant; widowed. BS, U. Miss., 1951; MD, U. Tenn., Memphis, 1952. Diplomate Am. Bd. Nuc. Medicine, Am. Bd. Radiology. Intern Bapt. Hosp., Knoxville, Tenn., 1952—53; resident Southwestern Med. Sch., Dallas VA Hosp., Baylor U. Hosp., Dallas, 1965—68; radiologist, 1958-96. Capt. USAF. Mem. Radiol. Soc. N.Am., Am. Coll. Radiology, Am. Roentgen Ray Soc.

HILL, CAMILLE CRUNELLE, music educator; b. Chgo., Nov. 1, 1938; d. Lawrence D. and Helen (Doft) Crunelle; m. J. Robert Hill, June 28, 1963; children: Anne, Yvonne. BMus, Northwestern U., 1960, MusM, 1962; BME, Wis. State U. Stevens Point, 1961; PhD, U. Ky., 1996. Instr. Music, French Lindsey Wilson Coll., Columbia, Ky., 1962—66, Elizabethtown C.C., Elizabethtown, Ky., 1966—86, assoc. prof., prof. Music, 1986—. Choir dir. First Presbyn. Ch., Elizabethtown, 1970—88. Chair Program Artists VSA Arts, Elizabethtown, 1985—. Mem.: Music Educators Nat. Conf., Am. Choral Dirs. Assn., Am. Musicol. Soc., Hardin County Arts Coun. Democrat. Office: Elizabeth Cmty Coll 600 College Street Rd Elizabethtown KY 42701

HILL, CAROL KOELLING, library director; BS, Mo. Western State, 1974; MLS, Emporia State U., 1980. Libr. dir. City of Fort Walton Beach, Fla., 1995—. Office: 185 Miracle Strip Pkwy SE Fort Walton Beach FL 32548-6614 E-mail: chill@fwb.org.

HILL, CATHERINE STANTON, freelance artist; BA, UCLA. Creator musical notes posters, 1980-97; illustrator Engring. and Sci. mag., newspapers CALTECH, 1985-96. Author, artist: (comics) Mad Raccoons, 1-7, 1991-97, (book) The Mad Raccoons Collection, 1995; illustrator (book) The Three Palladins, 1977, Beware of the Mouse, 1978, Quest of Excalibur, 1979, The Blue World, 1979; prodn. designer Clash of the Titans, 1979; contbr. (comics) The Dreamery, 1987-90; creator poster Stephen J. Gould lecture, press kit Screamin' Jay Hawkins, 1988, raccoon comic strip appeared in Nickelodean Mag., 1994; paintings Harlan Ellison; caricaturist (book) Martin Scorsese—A Journey, 1991; exhibns. include The Poulsen Galleries, 1998-2000, Tirage Gallery, 1999-2000, Pasadena Hist. Mus., 1999, Glendale Art Assn., 1999-2000. Recipient First prize (2) Glendale Art Assn., 1999. Mem. San Gabriel Art Assn. (1st prize and mem. award 1997), Calif. Art Club, Oil Painters Am., Laguna Plein Air Painters. Avocation: plein air oil painting around california and the southwest.

HILL, CHARLES GRAHAM, JR., chemical engineering educator; b. Elmira, N.Y., July 28, 1937; s. Charles Graham and Ethel Mayburn (Pfleegor) H.; m. Katharine Mertice Koon, July 11, 1964; children: Elizabeth, Deborah, Cynthia. BS, MIT, 1959, MS, 1960, ScD, 1964. Asst. prof. MIT, Cambridge, 1964-65, U. Wis., Madison, 1967-71, assoc. prof., 1971-76, prof. chem. engring., 1976—, John T. and Magdalen L. Sobota prof. chem. engring., 1995—, prof. food sci., 1989—, chmn. dept. chem. engring., 1989-92. Cons. A.D. Little, Cambridge, 1964-65, Joseph Schlitz Brewing Co., Milw., 1973-76, Nat. Bur. Stds., 1979-95. Author: Introduction to Chemical Engineering Kinetics and Reactor Design, 1977; contbr. articles to profl. jours. Capt. U.S. Army, 1965-67. Gen. Motors Nat. scholar, 1955-59; NSF fellow, 1959-62, Ford Found. fellow, 1964-65, Fulbright Sr. fellow, 2000. Fellow AIChE; mem. Am. Chem. Soc., Inst. Food Technologists, Am. Oil Chemists Soc., Sigma Xi, Tau Beta Pi, Phi Lambda Upsilon. Republican. Presbyterian. Office: U Wis Dept Chem Engring 1415 Engineering Dr Madison WI 53706-1607 E-mail: hill@engr.wisc.edu.

HILL, CLINTON, artist; b. Payette, Idaho, Mar. 8, 1922; s. Samuel Edgar and Iva Marie (Horn) H. BS U. Oreg., 1947; postgrad., Bklyn. Mus. Sch., 1949-51, Academie de la Grande Chaumiere, Paris, France, 1951, Instituto d'Arte Statale, Florence, Italy, 1951-52. Prof. Queens Coll., N.Y.C., 1968-87, now prof. emeritus. One-man shows include Marilyn Pearl Gallery, N.Y.C., 10 shows 1979-92, Monclair Mus., N.J., 1981, Galleria Blu, Milan, Italy, 1984, Worcester Mus., Mass., 1992, Andre Zarre Gallery, N.Y.C., 1993-2001; represented in permanent collections Mus. Modern Art, N.Y.C., Met. Mus., N.Y.C., Phila. Mus., Albright Knox Gallery, Buffalo, Nat. Gallery Australia, Canberra, Bklyn. Mus., Phoenix Art Mus., Whitney Mus., N.Y.C., Brit. Mus., London, Fogg Mus., Harvard U., Princeton (N.J.) U. Libr. Rare Books Divsn., Godwin-Ternbach Mus. Queens Coll., N.Y., others. Served to lt. (j.g.) USN, 1943-47. Fulbright grantee India, 1956; Creative Artists Pub. Service grantee, 1975; Nat. Endowment for Arts grantee, 1976, 80 Home: 178 Prince St New York NY 10012-2905

HILL, CLYDE VERNON, JR., prosecutor; b. Oxford, Miss., May 30, 1952; s. Clyde Vernon and Doris Elizabeth Hill; m. Lisa K. Proctor, Aug. 18, 1984; children: Tara C., Ami E. (dec.), Christina K., Amanda G., Lisa Michelle. BS, Miss. State U., 1978; JD, U. Miss., 1983. Bar: Miss. 1983, U.S. Dist. Ct. (no. dist.) Miss. 1983. Asst. dist. atty. 11th Cir. Miss., Clarksdale, 1983-94, 5th Cir. Miss., Grenada, 1995—. Sunday sch. tchr. adult bible study. Mem. Miss. Prosecutors Assn. (bd. dirs. 1995—, v.p. 1999-2000, pres. 2001-02). Baptist. Avocation: farming. Home: 14 Northwoods Dr Grenada MS 38901-9274 Office: Dist Attys office 234 1st St Grenada MS 38901-2602 E-mail: cvhilljr@dixie-net.com.

HILL, CONNIE RAY, JR., physicist; b. Martinsville, Va., Jan. 9, 1950; s. Connie Ray and Doris Ann (Minter) H.; m. Lu-Anne P. Hill, Apr. 23, 1976; children: Christopher J., Patrick E. BS, Coll. William & Mary, 1971, MS, 1973; PhD, U. Ill., 1978. Postdoctoral fellow Northwestern U., Evanston, Ill., 1978-79; asst. prof. Ill. State U., Normal, 1979-81; rsch. engr. Johnson Controls Inc., Milw., 1981-84; scientific assoc. Aluminum Co. of Am., Pitts., 1984-96; prin. sys. engr. Concurrent Techs. Corp., Johnstown, Pa., 1997-2000; sr. mem. engring. staff Lockheed Martin Advanced Tech. Labs., Cherry Hill, NJ, 2000—. Rsch. assoc. Nat. Bur. Stds., Gaithersburg, Md., 1982-83. Co-author chpt. in book: Innovative Applications of Artificial Intelligence, 1989. Mem. IEEE, Sigma Xi. Home: 6108 Forrest Ave Pennsauken NJ 08110-3321 Office: 3 Exec Campus Cherry Hill NJ 08002 E-mail: rhill@atl.lmco.com.

HILL, CYNTHIA MARESSA, ecological planner, environmental scientist; b. Gainesville, Fla., May 8, 1959; d. Richard Allen and Vivian Jean H.; m. Joseph John Maressa, Mar. 16, 2000; 1 child, Joanna Claire. BA in Regional Sci., MA in Regional Sci., U. Pa., 1981, M in Regional Planning, 1992; PhD, Cornell U., 2003. Project coord. Gen. Urban Cons., Phila., 1981; rsch. economist Data Resources, Inc., Lexington, Mass., 1982-83; sr. planner Monmouth County Planning Bd., Freehold, NJ, 1984—86, prin. environtl. planner, 1987-90; environ. planner Wallace Roberts and Todd, Phila., 1990-91; sr. planner Wayne County, Lyons, NY, 2002; prin. Fresh Perspectives Land Use Planning, Palmyra, NY, 2003—. Mem. Local Law Rev. Com., Phelps, N.J., 2000. Contbr. articles to profl. jours. Tech. advisor Assn. N.J. Environtl. Commns., 1989-92. Mellon grantee, Cornell Small Grant Biogecochemistry grantee NSF. Mem. Soc. Of Friends. Home: 111 Floodman Rd Palmyra NY 14522 Office: PO Box 359 224 E Main St Palmyra NY 14522

HILL, DALE STEWART, volunteer; b. Pasadena, Calif., Nov. 13, 1928; d. Frederick Woodward and Dorothy Pierce (Stewart) Walker; m. Robert Hill, Oct. 20, 1951; children: Barry Robert, Allan Stewart, Lorin Frederick. AB, U. Calif., Berkeley, 1949. Registered physical therapist Calif. Staff phys. therapist Orthopedic Hosp., L.A., 1950-51, Alta Bates Hosp., Berkeley, Calif., 1951-53, pvt. practice, Concord, Calif., 1955-61; sec., treas. Hill Rsch. Assocs., Inc., Los Gatos, Calif., 1985—2002. Chair Charter Rev. Com., Santa Clara County, Calif., 1973-75; foreman Grand Jury, Santa Clara County, 1974-75; planning commr. Town of Los Gatos, 1976-82; bd. dirs. Live Oak Adult Day Svcs., Inc., Los Gatos, 1986-98; libr. bd. Rown of Los Gatos, 1996—. Recipient Silver Bowl award Jr. League, San Jose, 1991; named Woman of Achievement San Jose Nercury-News, 1976, Los Gatos Sr. of Distinction, 1999. Mem. LWV (pres. 1971-73, v.p. mgmt. 1981-85, manual series writer 1987-88), AAUW (grantee 1978), Phi Beta Kappa.

HILL, DAVID, broadcast executive; b. Australia; V.p. of Sports Nine Network, Australia, 1977—88; head Eurosport, England, 1988—91, Sky Sports, England, 1991—93; pres. Fox Sports, Los Angeles, 1993—; CEO Fox Sports Network, 1996—; chmn., CEO Fox TV, 1996—. Office: Fox Sports PO Box 900 Beverly Hills CA 90213-0900 also: 575 Amalfi Dr Pacific Palisades CA 90272-4504

HILL, DAVID ALLAN, electrical engineer; b. Cleve., Apr. 21, 1942; s. Martin D. and Geraldine S. (Yoder) H.; m. Elaine C. Dempsey, July 9, 1971. BSEE, Ohio U., 1964, MSEE, 1966; PhD in Elect. Engring., Ohio State U., 1970. Vis. fellow Coop. Inst. for Rsch. Environ. Sci., Boulder, Colo., 1970-71; rsch engr. Inst. for Telecommunication Scis., Boulder, 1971-82; sr. scientist Nat. Inst. Standards and Tech., Boulder, 1982—. Adj. prof. U. Colo., Boulder, 1980—. Editor Geosci. and Remote Sensing Jour., 1980-84, Antennas and Propagation Jour., 1986-89; contbr. over 100 articles to profl. jours., chpts. to books. Recipient award for best paper Electromagnetic Compatability Jour., 1987. Fellow IEEE (chpt. chmn. 1975-76, editor 1986-89); mem. Electromagnetic Soc. (bd. dirs. 1980-86), Internat. Union Radio Sci. (nat. com. 1986-89), Colo. Mountain Club (Boulder), Sierra Club. Office: Nat Inst Standards & Tech 813-02 325 Broadway St Boulder CO 80305-3337 E-mail: dhill@boulder.nist.gov.

HILL, DAVID LAWRENCE, research corporation executive; b. Nov. 11, 1919; s. David Alexander and Mabel Clair (Brown) H.; m. Mary M. Shadow, Dec. 31, 1950 (dec. Jan. 1992); children: David A., Mary C., Robert L., John F., Cynthia A., Sandra E., James A. BS, Calif. Inst. Tech., 1942; PhD (Socony Vacuum Co. fellow), Princeton U., 1951. With U. Chgo. Metall. Lab. and Argonne Nat. Lab., 1942-46, assoc. physicist, group leader, 1944-46; assoc. prof. physics Vanderbilt U., Nashville, 1949-52, assoc. prof., 1952-54; staff mem. Los Alamos (N. Mex.) Sci. Lab., 1954-58, group leader theoretical nuclear physics, 1955-58, mgmt. cons., 1958-60; pres. Phys. Sci. Corp., Fairfield, Conn., 1960-62, Nanosecond Systems, Inc., Fairfield, Conn., 1963-72, Particle Measurements, Inc., Southport, Conn., 1965-81, Harbor Rsch. Corp., Southport, Conn., 1978—. Guest scholar Inst. Theoretical Physics, Copenhagen, summer 1950; cons. theoretical physics U. Calif., Los Alamos (N. Mex.) Sci. Lab., 1952-54; chmn. bd. Integrated Total Systems, Inc., Hingham, Mass, 1968-81; pres. Southport Computers, Inc., Conn., 1973-81, Valutron N.V., Netherlands Antilles, 1980—; pres. Patent Enforcement Fund, Inc., Southport, Conn., 1990—, Inventors' Def. Fund, Inc., 1996—; chmn. bd. dirs. Cassar Hill L.L.C., mgr., 1996—, Panatron Inc., Panama, 1999—, Safriton Inc., Panama, 1999—, Diamotron Inc., Panama, 2000—; lectr. in field; sci. adv. to Vice Presdl. nominee, Senator Estes Kefauver, 1956; incorporator, exec. v.p. dir. Los Alamos Investment Corp., 1956-58; cons. physicist in field. Contbr. articles to profl. jours. Adv. com. on sci. and tech. of Adv. Coun. of Dem. Nat. Com., 1959-61. Fellow Am. Phys. Soc., AAAS; mem. IEEE, Fedn. Am. Scientists (nat. chmn. 1953-54), Sigma Xi. Office: Patent Enforcement Fund PO Box 569 Southport CT 06490-0569 E-mail: dlhpanatron@aol.com.

HILL, DAVID WAYNE, geologist; b. Brenham, Tex., May 20, 1954; s. Charles Bethel Hill and Anita Joyce (Myrow) King; m. Gay Ann Weaver, Aug. 21, 1976; children: Jennifer L., Samantha M. BS, Tex. A&M U., 1976; MS, U. Tex., 1993. Registered profl. engr., Tex. Engr. Dresser Industries, Victoria, Tex., 1976-91; team project mgr., geologist Tex. Natural Resource Conservation Commn., Austin, 1994-2001; sr. engr. Profl. Svc. Industries, Austin, 2001—. Instr. Austin C.C., 1994—. Coord. Martin Luther King Commemorative March, Round Rock, Tex., 1994—. Mem. Nat. Ground Water Assn., Am. Inst. Hydrology (student chpt. v.p. 1992, 93), Ground Water Assn., Nat. Soc. Profl. Engrs., Phi Kappa Phi. Avocations: bridge, youth work. Home: 1104 Saint Williams Ave Round Rock TX 78681-6461

HILL, DEBORA ELIZABETH, writer, journalist, screenwriter; b. San Francisco, July 10, 1961; d. Henry Peter and Madge Lillian (Ridgeway-Aarons) H. BA, Sonoma State U., 1983. Talk show host Rock Jour. Viacom, San

Francisco, 1980-81; interviewer, biographer Harrap Ltd., London, 1986-87; editor North Bay Mag., Cotati, Calif., 1988; guest feature writer Argus Courier, Petaluma, Calif., 1993-95; concept developer BiblioBytes, Hoboken, N.J., 1994-95; feature writer The Econs. Press, 1996-97; film cons., editor United Film Prodns. Internat., 2003—. Assoc. prodr. White Tiger Films, 1995—; concept developer Star Trek: Voyager and Star Trek: Deep Space Nine, 1997—98; mem. MedioCom, 2001—; script cons. Shadowhawk Prodns., Ireland, 2003—. Author: CUTS from a San Francisco Rock Journal, 1982, Punk Retro, 1988, Gale Research-Resourceful Woman, 1994, St. James Guide to Fantasy Writers, 1996, St. James Guide to Famous Gays and Lesbians, 1997; co-author: A Ghost Among Us, 2003; author: (sequel) Jerome's Quest, 2003; co-writer, cons. prodr. The Danger Club, contbr. (anthologies) Between Darkness and Light, 2000, Best Poets of 2000, Eyes of the World, 2001, Poetry's Elite, 2001, Hidden Frontiers, 2002, Celebrations Book Series, 2002—03, Best Poets of 2001, Best Poets of 2002; contbr. anthologies, stories and articles to profl. jours., anthologies. Democrat. Avocations: clothing design, cooking, internet, reading, interior design. Home and Office: Lost Myths Ink 8312 Windmill Farms Dr Cotati CA 94931-4570 E-mail: debhill@att.net.

HILL, DON, state representative; b. Smith Center, Kans., Dec. 28, 1946; m. Robbie Hill Hill; children: Holly, Spencer. Student, Kans. State U., 1965—68; BS, U. Kans., 1971. Pharmacist, CEO Hill's Apothecary, 1972—2002; mem. Kans. Ho. of Reps., 2003—. Chair Kans. Hwy. Adv. Commn., 1998; mem. rev. panel Transp. Econ. Devel., 2000. Drive chair United Way, Flint Hills, 1998; chair Leadership Kans., 1990. With U.S. Army, 1972. Republican. Methodist. Office: 182-W State Capitol 300 SW10th Ave Topeka KS 66612*

HILL, DONALD DEE, management consultant, lecturer, writer; b. Moultrie, Ga. s. Thomas Dee and Vivan Mae (Monk) H. BCE, Ga. Inst. Tech. Registered Ala., Ga. Structural engr. Patchen & Zimmerman Cons. Engrs., Augusta, Ga.; asst. dir. F.S.D. Am. Plywood Assn., Tacoma; mng. dir., CEO ASME Internat. Gas Turbine Inst., Atlanta; lectr. for vis. Asian execs. Kennesaw State U. Lectr. and spkr. in field; spl. cons., lectr. to Czech Republic, 1996; lectr. pilot program, Vietnam, 1997; lectr. advanced mgmt. course for vis. Asian execs. Kennesaw State U. Columnist Convene Mag. Vice pres. Letterman's Club; ruling elder Presbyn. Ch. 1st lt. U.S. Army. Named Eagle of the Acropolis, Palais de Congres, Nice, France; named to Coll. of 17 Gentlemen, Netherlands Congress Bur.; named Ark. Traveler, Gov. of Ark.; recipient R. Tom Sawyer Gas Turbine award ASME, 1996. Mem.: Ga. Tech. Alumni Assn., Meeting Profls. Internat., Am. Soc. Assn. Execs., Kappa Sigma. Avocation: weightlifting. Home and Office: 6870 Lisa Ln Atlanta GA 30338-3952 E-mail: nopain.nogain@att.net.

HILL, DONALD WAIN, education accreditation commission executive; b. Montfort, Wis., June 14, 1924; s. Victor Charles and Emma Grace (Carr) H.; m. Phyllis Kay Hogan, July 2, 1949; children: Leslie Scott Hill Barnett, Lance Howlett Hill, Lawson Wain Hill. BBA, U. Wis., 1949, MBA, 1953. Budget analyst City of Milw., 1950-53; adminstrv. analyst State of Wis., Madison, 1953-54; bus. mgr. U. Wis., Milw., 1954-56; mem. joint staff Coord. Comm. for Higher Edn., Madison, 1956-59; asst. supt. schs. Chgo. Pub. Schs., 1959-66; exec. vice chancellor City Colls. of Chgo., 1966-84; ednl. cons. Hill Assocs., Carlsbad, Calif., 1984-86; asst. dir., sr. accreditation specialist Accreditation Commn. of Career Sch. and Colls. of Tech., Arlington, Va., 1986—. Chmn. fin. com. Ill. Task Force on Edn., Springfield, 1965-66; mem. Ill. Higher Edn. Master Plan Com., Urbana, 1963-64; chmn. facilities com. Task Force to Form U. of Wis.-Milw., 1956; mem. fin. study com. U.S. Office Edn., Washington, 1963. Contbr. articles to profl. jours. Mem. ednl. credentials and credit rev. team Am. Coun. on Edn., Abu Dhabi, 1987; mem. task force on collective bargaining Carnegie Found., N.Y.C., 1975-76. With U.S. Infantry, 1942-46, ETO. Mem. Wis. Acad. Scis., Arts and Letters (higher edn. rep. for Wis. Acad. Rev. 1957-59), Econ. Club Chgo. Methodist. Avocations: golf, tennis, genealogy, travel. Home: 8435 W Tonto Ln Peoria AZ 85382-8802 Office: Accreditation Commn Career Schs and Colls Tech 2101 Wilson Blvd Ste 302 Arlington VA 22201-3062 E-mail: donwhill@aol.com.

HILL, DONNA MARIE, writer, retired librarian; d. Clarence Henry and Emma Charlotte (Wirthlin) Hill. Student, Phillips Gallery Art Sch., 1940—43; BA, George Washington U., 1948; MS, Columbia U., 1952. Code clk. U.S. Embassy, Paris, 1949—51; asst. to librarian NY Pub. Libr., N.Y.C., 1952—59; instr. Hunter Coll., CUNY, N.Y.C., 1970—75, head tchrs. ctrl. lab., 1974—84, asst. prof., 1975—79, assoc. prof., 1980—84, prof. emeritus, 1984—. Established Donna Hill Collection Marriott Libr., U. Utah, Salt Lake City, 1994. Author: First Your Penny, 1985, Murder Uptown, 1992, Shipwreck Season, 1998 (Christopher award, 99); Exhibited in group shows at Paris, Washington, world tour, 1950—51. Recipient Cert. of Distinction, Alumni Assn. Ctrl. H.S., 1984. Mem.: Women's Nat. Book Assn. (membership chmn. N.Y.C. chpt. 1991—93), Am. Recorder Soc. (nat. sec. 1959—61, editor-in-chief 1962—63), Delta Kappa Gamma (Ruth Mack Havens award 1991), Phi Beta Kappa. Mem. Lds Ch. Avocations: opera, Baroque music, recorder playing, drawing, painting.

HILL, DRAPER, editorial cartoonist; b. Boston, July 1, 1935; s. L. Draper and Jean Hutchins (Thompson) H.; m. Sarah Randolph Adams, Apr. 22, 1967; children: Jennifer Randolph, Jonathan Draper. BA magna cum laude, Harvard C., 1957; postgrad, Slade Sch. Fine Arts, Univ. Coll., London, Eng., 1960-63. Reporter and cartoonist Quincy (Mass.) Patriot Ledger, 1957-60; editorial cartoonist Worcester (Mass.) Telegram, 1964-71, Comml. Appeal, Memphis, 1971-76, The Detroit News, 1976-99. Dir. Play of Month Guild, N.Y.C., 1958-82; instr. drawing Worcester Art Sch., 1967-71; lectr. Thomas Nast, Garibaldi, Beerbohm, Gillray, and others. Author: Mr. Gillray, The Caricaturist, 1965, Fashionable Contrasts, 1966, (with James Roper) The Decline and Fall of the Gibbon, 1974, The Satirical Etchings of James Gillray, 1976, (essay) Cartoons & Caricatures in Ency. of Collectibles, 1978, Political Asylum: Editorial Cartoons by Draper Hill, 1985; also catalogs; one-person shows include Art Gallery of Windsor (Ont.), 1985-86, Detroit Hist. Mus., 1996. Mem. Egyptians, Memphis, 1972—76, Witenagemote, Detroit, 1977—, Club of Odd Vols., 1965—2000; mem. adv. bd. Swann Found. for Caricature and Cartoon, N.Y.C., 1980—93, 1998—. Winner Thomas Nast prize for editorial cartooning Landau-in-der-Pfalz, Fed. Republic Germany, 1990. Mem.: Assn. Am. Editl. Cartoonists (2d v.p. 1972—74, 1st v.p. 1974—75, pres. 1975—76, author quar. column History Corner Assn. Notebook 1974—99), Prismatic Club. Home: 368 Washington Rd Grosse Pointe MI 48230-1616

HILL, EDWIN D. trade association administrator; b. Center Township, Pa., Aug. 11, 1937; m. Rosemary Hill; children: Michele Hill, Toni Hill, Edwin Jr. Hill. V.p. 3d Dist. Internat. Brotherhood Elec. Workers, 1994—97, internat. sec., 1997, internat. sec.-treas., 1998, pres., 2001—. With March of Dimes, YMCA, United Way. Office: 1125 15th St NW Washington DC 20005

HILL, ELIZABETH TREZISE, economics educator; b. DuBois, Pa., Mar. 26, 1936; d. William H. and Ethel L. (Lyons) Trezise; m. Richard A. Hill, May 30, 1958 (dec. Sept. 1981); children: Joan H. Smeltzer, David R. BSBA, Pa. State U., University Park, 1958; MA in Econs., U. Del., 1974; PhD in Econs., U. Md., 1985. Instr. in econs. Pa. State U., York, 1976-78; economist Pa. Milrite Coun., Harrisburg, 1982-84; asst. prof. econs. Pa. State U., Mont Alto, 1985—. Mem. Am. Econ. Assn., Ea. Econ. Assn., Pa. Econ. Assn. (bd.dirs. 1989—), Com. on Status of Women in Econs. Profession. Office: Pa State U Mont Alto Campus Mont Alto PA 17237

HILL, ELLEN BROCKETT BROWN, emergency medicine nurse, geriatrics services professional; b. Pitts., Dec. 21, 1944; d. F. Gordon and Muriel Edith (Dunkerley) Brown. Diploma in nursing, St. Francis Gen. Hosp., Pitts., 1969; AA magna cum laude, Butler County Community Coll., Butler, Pa., 1982; BSN, La Roche Coll., Pitts., 1986; postgrad., Slippery Rock (Pa.) U., 1987. Cert. sch. nurse, EMT, pre hosp. trauma technician. Gerontology staff nurse St. Barnabas Free Home, Gibsonia, Pa., 1970-76; head athletic trainer BCCC, Butler, 1981-84; spl. dep. Butler county Sheriff's Dept., 1982—; trauma technician Richland Emergency Med. Svcs., Gibsonia, Pa., 1983—; head athletic trainer Mars (Pa.) Area Sch. Dist., 1984-86, LaRoche Coll., 1983-84; sch. nurse substitute Mars (Pa.) Area Sch. Dist., 1984-98; staff and emergency rehab. nurse Gentiva Health Svcs., Green Tree, Pa., 1986—; gerontology staff nurse Vincentian Home, Pitts., 1992-93. Test adminstr. for nursing assts. in long-term care facilities Pa. state cert., 1990—92; staff rehab. nurse D.T. Watson Rehab. Hosp. for Children and Adults, 1987—93; profl. tractor-trailer driver Storming Eagle Transport, Gibsonia, Pa., 1992—; agy. staff nurse Polk Ctr., Pa., 1997; pit crew chief Travis Hill Racing, 1997—. Disaster health svcs. specialist, shelter mgr., instr. CPR and first aid ARC, 1976—; Sunday sch. tchr. Presbyn. Ch., 1959-70; cub scout leader Boy Scouts Am., 1977-79; leader Girl Scouts U.S., 1971-74; cmty. resource person PTO, 1969-82; women's day program chmn. Gulf Oil Corp. (Mellon Inst.), Pitts., 1967-69; athletic trainer, statistician Am. Legion Baseball, 1985-86; statistician Baseball BCCC, 1981-84. Recipient Thanks for Helping at fires, blood drives, disasters award ARC, 1984. Mem.: Pa. Assn. EMTs, Emergency Nurses Assn., Butler County Hist. Soc., Greater Pitts. Civil War Round Table, Butler County Civil War Roundtable, DAR (Kushkushkee Trail), Valencia Area Hist. Soc., Pa. Sheriffs Assn. (charter), Mars Bowling Assn., St. Francis Gen. Hosp. Alumni Assn., Internat. Arabian Horse Assn., Cmty. Vol. Fire Dept. Valencia Aux., Pa. Arabian Horse Assn. (sec. 1976—77), Butler Horsemen's Assn. (horse show sec. 1972—79, treas. 1972—79), BCCC Alumni Assn., Jacques Cousteau Soc., Traildusters of We. Pa. Snowmobile Club, Butler County Saddle Club (sec., horse show treas.), Friends of the Nat. Parks of Gettysburg, Pa., Phi Theta Kappa (scholar 1982). Avocations: community resource person, neighborhood veterinarian, acupressure and relaxation through massage therapist. Home: 122 Butler Street Ext Valencia PA 16059-1606 E-mail: theladyinwhite@pocketmail.com.

HILL, EMITA BRADY, academic administrator, consultant; b. Balt., Jan. 31, 1936; d. Leo and Lucy McCormick (Jewett) Brady; children: Julie Beck, Christopher, Madeleine Vedel. BA, Cornell U., 1957; MA, Middlebury Coll., 1958; PhD, Harvard U., 1967. Instr. Harvard U., 1961-63; asst. prof. Western Reserve U., 1967-69; from asst. prof. to v.p. Lehman Coll. CUNY, Bronx, N.Y., 1970-91; chancellor, grad. faculty Ind. U., Kokomo, Ind., 1991-99, chancellor emerita, 1999—. Vis. advisor Salzburg Seminar Univs. Project; cons. in field. Trustee Am. U. in Kyrgyzstan; mem. Women's Forum of NY. Mem.: Internat. Assn. Univ. Pres., Phi Beta Kappa. Avocations: music, scuba diving, tennis. E-mail: ehill@indiana.edu.

HILL, ERIK BRYAN, newspaper photographer; b. Eugene, Oreg., Feb. 17, 1957; s. Robert Donald and Dagmara (Grislis) H.; m. Robin Mackey, Aug. 30, 1986; children: Mara, Emma. BA in Internat. Rels., Stanford U., 1979; MS in Journalism, Ohio U., 1987. Photographer, photo editor The Kansas City (Mo.) Star, 1981-84; photographer The Anchorage Daily News, 1984—. Adj. instr. U. Alaska, Anchorage, 1990—. Recipient Pulitzer prize gold medal for pub. svc. Columbia U., 1989, finalist Pulitzer prize for feature photography, 1990. Mem. Nat. Press Photographers Assn. Avocations: political pin collecting, family hikes, travel. Office: Anchorage Daily News 1001 Northway Dr Anchorage AK 99508-2098

HILL, ESTHER DIANNE, business education educator; b. Maysville, Ky., Apr. 14, 1943; d. Frank Hinson and Jean Pepper (Yelton) H. BS, Ea. Ky. State Coll., 1966. Cert. bus. edn., typing and English tchr., Ohio. Tchr. Milton-Union Schs., West Milton, Ohio, 1966-68, Forest Hills Sch. Dist., Cin., 1968-96; tchr. evenings Cin. Tech. Coll., 1977-80; software verifyer South Western Pub. Co., Cin., 1982-83, ret., 1996. Writer Dist. Curriculum, Cin., 1975-96; dist. mem. County Textbook Com., Cin., 1982-96. Mem. NEA, Ohio Edn. Assn., Nat. Bus. Edn. Assn., Ohio Bus. Tchrs. Assn., Forest Hills Tchrs. Assn., Eastern Ky. U. Alumni assn. Republican. Mem. Ch. of Christ. Avocations: embroidery, travel, counted cross stitching, golf, reading. Home: 40 Bonnie Ln Fort Thomas KY 41075-2532 E-mail: dhill@fuse.net.

HILL, EVAN, retired journalism educator, writer; b. Phila., Jan. 20, 1919; s. Louis and Marie Eugenia (Schmeltz) H.; m. Priscilla Anne Fiske, Sept. 21, 1946, children: Lucinda, Peter. BA, Stanford U., 1948; MA, Boston U., 1950. Reporter Sta. KVOS, Bellingham, Wash., 1938-39, Daily Alaska Empire, Juneau, 1940-41; editor Argus-Champion, Newport, N.H., 1948-49; instr. journalism Boston U., 1949-51, asst. prof., 1951-54, assoc. prof., 1954-56, Ohio State U., Columbus, 1956-57; freelance writer, 1957-65; prof. journalism, head dept. U. Conn., Storrs, 1965-83; ret., 1983. Cons. on writing Office Sci. and Tech., Washington, 1972-73, Boston Globe, 1971; dir. The Day, New London, Conn.; trustee The Day Trust, 1979-89; dir. Para Rsch., Gloucester, Mass., 1984-88. Author: (with George Gallup) The Secrets of Long Life, 1960, Beanstalk, 1966, The Connecticut River, 1972; (with John Breen) A Beginner's Guide to Writing (and Thinking) Clearly, 1974, Reporting and Writing the News, 1988; The Primary State, 1976, A Greener Earth, 1977; contbr. articles to mags., including Saturday Evening Post, Reader's Digest, Saturday Rev., N.Y. Times Mag., Redbook, True, Venture, Yankee. Sec. Newport (N.H.) Planning Bd., 1956-65; trustee Richards Libr., Newport, 1954-64; mem. Newport Sch. Bd., 1991-92. Capt. inf. U.S. Army, 1941-48, PTO, ETO. Decorated Purple Heart, Bronze Star. Home: PO Box 566 Newport NH 03773-0566

HILL, FAY GISH, librarian; b. Rensselaer, Ind., Sept. 19, 1944; d. Roy Charles and Vergie (Powell) Gish; m. John Christian Hill, May 20, 1967; 1 child, Christina Gish. BA, Purdue U., 1967; MLS, U. Tex., 1971. Asst. librarian basic reference dept. Tex. A&M U., College Station, 1972, assoc. librarian sci. ref. dept., 1972-74, acting head librarian sci. reference dept., 1975; reference librarian Cen. Iowa Regional Library, Des Moines, 1984—. Bd. dirs. State Historian. Troop leader Girl Scouts U.S., Ames, Iowa, 1983—88; bd. dirs. Friends of Fgn. Wives, Ames, 1982—86, Iowa Questers, 2001—. Mem. ALA, Iowa Libr. Assn., Iowa Libr. Assn. Found. (bd. dirs. 1990-95). Presbyterian. Avocation: collecting antiques. Home: 5604 Thunder Rd Ames IA 50014-9448 Office: Cen Iowa Regional Libr Reference 515 Douglas Ave Ames IA 50010-6215

HILL, GARY D. journalist; b. Green Bay, Wis., Apr. 11, 1952; s. Doc Allen and Helen Bernice (Hunt) H.; m. Minda Joyce Gilbert, Aug. 7, 1976; 1 child, Nathan Gilbert. BA, U. Wis., 1974. Film/video editor Sta. KSTP-TV, Mpls., 1974-76, photographer, 1976-79, weekend assignment editor, 1978-80, assoc. prodr., 1979-82, assignment editor, 1982-85, mng. editor, 1985—. Chairman Ethics Committee Society of Professional Journalists, Indianapolis, IN, 2000—01; Chairman Freedom Of Information Committe Society of Professional Journalists MN Chapter, Minneapolis, MN, 2000—01; Vice President MN Joint Media Committee, Minneapolis, MN, 1995—2001; IRE Broadcast Advisory Committe Investigative Reporters & Editors, Columbia, MO, 2000—01. V.p. Minn. Joint Media Com., 1993—. Mem. Soc. Profl. Journalists (pres. 1991-92, Mark of Excellence winner for investigative reporting 1995), Investigative Reporters and Editors. Office: Sta KSTP-TV 3415 University Ave SE Minneapolis MN 55414-3348

HILL, GEORGE JAMES, physician, educator; b. Cedar Rapids, Iowa, Oct. 7, 1932; s. Gerald Leslie and Essie Mae (Thompson) H.; m. Helene Zimmermann, July 16, 1960; children: James Warren, David Hedgcock, Sarah, Helena Rundall. AB, Yale U., 1953; MD, Harvard U., 1957; MA, Rutgers U., 1999. Intern N.Y. Hosp., 1957-58; fellow and resident in surgery Peter Bent Brigham hosp. and Harvard Med. Sch., 1958-61, 63-66; clin. assoc. NIH, Bethesda, Md., 1961-63; instr. surgery U. Colo., 1966-67, asst. prof., 1967-72, asso. prof., 1972-73; prof. Washington U., 1973-76; prof., chmn. Marshall U., 1976-81; prof., dir. surg. oncology U. of Medicine and Dentistry of N.J.-N.J. Med. Sch., Newark, 1981-96; prof. emeritus U. of Medicine and Dentistry of N.J. - N.J. Med. Sch., Newark, 1997—; Am. Cancer Soc. prof. clin. oncology U. Medicine and Dentistry N.J.-N.J. Med. Sch., Newark, 1989-92; pres. faculty N.J. Med. Sch., Newark, 1991-92; clin. prof. surgery Uniformed Svcs. U. of the Health Scis., Bethesda, Md., 1989—, Mt. Sinai Sch. Medicine, N.Y.C., 1999—; interim pres. Sterling Coll., Craftsbury Common, Vt., 1996; rsch. coord. St. Barnabas Med. Ctr., Livingston, N.J., 1997-99. Adj. prof. history Kean U., Union, N.J., 2000-2001; hon. mem. med. sch. staff St. Barnabas Med. Ctr., 1999—, chmn. clin. cancer edn. com. Nat. Cancer Inst., 1978-80; vis. fellow in molecular biology Princton U., 1988. Author: Leprosy in Five Young Men, 1970, paperback edit., 1979, Outpatient Surgery, 1973, 3d edit., 1988, Clinical Oncology, 1977; contbr. 150 articles to med. jours. Nat. dir.-at-large Am. Cancer Soc., 1989—96, mem. nat. exec. com., 1990—91, hon. life mem., 1996—; pres. Tri-State Area coun. Boy Scouts Am., Huntington, W.Va., 1980—82, v.p. Essex coun., 1983—89, commr., 1998, commr. No. N.J. Coun., 1998—2000, v.p., 2000—, chmn. nat. health careers exploring com., 1987—92; pres. W.Va. divsn. Am. Cancer Soc., 1980—81, pres. N.J. divsn., 1987—89; pres. Am. Assn. Cancer Edn., 1985—86; mem. N.J. State Commn. on Cancer Rsch., 1983—84; trustee Frost Valley YMCA, 1986—, Sterling Coll., Craftsbury Common, Vt., 1990—2002, sec., 1993—96, 1999—2002, emeritus trustee, 2003—; pres. Hill Family Trust, 1989—; vestry Ch. of the Holy Innocents, 1994—96, 2002—. Capt. M.C. USNR, active duty USN, 1990—91, ret., 1992. Named Jerseyan of Week, Newark-Star Ledger, 1987, 1993; recipient Civic Actions medal, Republic South Vietnam, 1972, Lederle Med. Faculty award, 1970, Silver Beaver award, Boy Scouts Am., 1981, Silver Antelope award, 1998, Am. Cancer Soc. Nat. Divisional award, St. George medal, 1992, Gorgas medal, Assn. Mil. Surgeons U.S., 1991, Outstanding Svc. medal, Uniformed Svcs. U. Health Scis., 1992, Meritorious Svc. medal, USN, 1993, Nat. William Spurgeon III award, Boy Scouts Am., 1994, N.J. Disting. Svc. medal, 2001, Damon Runyon fellowship, 1973—76. Mem.: SAR (chpt. sec. 1999—2001, pres. N.J. Soc. 2001—02, nat. trustee 2002—03), AAUP (pres. chpt. 1988—89), ACS (com. on cancer 1987—93), N.J. Med. Club (pres. 1999—2001), Med. Soc. N.J. (chmn. com. cancer control 1985—94, sec. 1995—96), Essex County Med. Soc. (pres. 1995—96), Med. History Soc. N.J. (v.p. 2000—02), Am. Assn. Cancer Rsch., Am. Assn. Cancer Edn. (pres. 1985—86, Edwards medal 1994), Ctrl. Surg. Assn., Soc. Surg. Oncology (exec. coun. 1985—88), Soc. Univ. Surgeons, Acad. Medicine N.J. (pres. 1992—93), Oncology Nursing Soc. (hon.), Soc. of the Cincinnati, Soc. Mayflower Descs. (bd. dirs. NJ state soc. 2002—), Order Founders and Patriots of Am. (dep. gov. N.J. state soc. 2003—), Soc. of Colonial Wars (sec. N.J. state soc. 2003—, sec. 2003—), Soc. Sons of the Revolution, Yale Club (Ctrl. N.J.) (trustee 1986—, pres. 1991—93), Army and Navy Club, Harvard Club (N.Y.C. and Boston), Univ. Club (Denver), Explorers Club, Alpha Omega Alpha, Sigma Xi (chpt. pres. 1986—87). Republican. Episcopalian. Address: 3 Silver Spring Rd West Orange NJ 07052-4317 also: PO Box 313 South Orange NJ 07079-0313 E-mail: ghill@drew.edu.

HILL, GEORGE ROBERT, musicologist, music bibliographer; b. Denver, July 12, 1943; AB in Music with honors, Stanford U., 1965; AM in Libr. Sci., U. Chgo., 1966; PhD in Hist. Musicology, NYU, 1975. Libr. music divsn. N.Y. Pub. Libr., N.Y.C., 1966-70; asst. music libr. NYU, N.Y.C., 1971-72; fine arts libr. U. Calif., Irvine, 1972-73; assoc. prof. music Baruch Coll. CUNY, 1973—. Author: (with others) A Thematic Locator for Mozart's Works as Listed in Kochel's Chronologisch-Thematisches Verzeichnis, 6th edit., 1970, A Preliminary Checklist of Research on the Classic Symphony and Concerto to the Time of Beethoven (excluding Haydn and Mozart), 1970, A Thematic Catalogue of the Instrumental Music of Florian Leopold Gassmann, 1976, Florian Leopold Gassmann, Seven Symphonies, 1981, Joseph Haydn Werke, Floetenuhrstuecke, 1984, A Handbook of Basic Tonal Practice, 1985, Collected Editions, Historical Series & Sets & Monuments of Music: A Bibliography, 1997; contbr. articles, revs. to profl. jours. including The New Grove Dictionary of Music and Musicians. Home: 84 Highgate Ter Bergenfield NJ 07621-3922 E-mail: georgerhill@prodigy.net.

HILL, GORDON CHARLES, III, company executive; b. Springfield, Mass., Sept. 8, 1948; s. Gordon Charles and Sophia Catherine (Samsel) H.; m. Margaret Maria Thibeault, Mar. 20, 1949; children: Catherine Margaret, Gordon Charles, Nicholas John, Matthew David. BSBA, Am. Internat. Coll., Springfield, Mass., 1971. Cert. bldg. svc. exec.; cert. Weight Watchers instr. Mgr. Grace Food Svc., Springfield, 1971-74, Pappys Ent., Balt., 1974-78, account exec. Canteen Corp., Washington/Hartford, 1978-83; account rep. Paul Revere Ins. Co., New Haven, 1983-84; ops. mgr. Premier Maint., Inc., Milford, Conn., 1984-85, dir. ops., 1985-86, v.p. ops., 1986—; regional mgr. Primerica Fin. Svcs., 1993-95; cons./mgr. Key Comms., Guilford and Hamden, Conn., 1993-94; sales mgr. Seaborad, Inc., New Haven, 1995—, mgr. telemktg. ops. Guilford, Conn., 1994—. Author/editor various tng. manuals, orientation manuals. Mem. Guilford (Conn.) 350th Birthday Com., 1988—; mem. Parish Coun., Guilford, 1989—; commr. E div. Guilford Soccer Club, 1990, F div., 1991; commr. Guilford Youth Basketball Midgets, 1991; mem. bus. adv. bd. Milford Mental Health, 1990-91. Recipient Cert. of Merit, Men of Achievement, 1993. Mem. Nat. Recycling Coalition, Bldg. Svc. Contrs. Assn., Bldg. Svc. Contrs. Assn. Internat., Milford C. of C., 3928 Club (pres. 1986-89), Columbus Club (1st v.p. 1987-88), K.C. (grand knight 1988, coun. trustee 1989-91). Roman Catholic. Avocations: stamp and coin collecting, golf, coaching soccer. Home: 199 Church St Guilford CT 06437-2470 Office: Seaboard Inc 24 River St New Haven CT 06513-4317

HILL, GRACE LUCILE GARRISON, education educator, consultant; b. Gastonia, N.C., Sept. 26, 1930; d. William Moffatt and Lillian Tallulah (Tatum) Garrison; m. Leo Howard Hill, July 24, 1954; children: Lillian Lucile, Leo Howard Jr., David Garrison. BA, Erskine Coll., 1952; MA, Furman U., 1966; PhD, U. S.C., 1980. Lic. sch. psychologist, S.C. Tchr. Bible, Clinton (S.C.) Pub. Schs., 1952-53; tchr. English Parker High Sch., Greenville, S.C., 1953-55; elem. tchr. Augusta Circle Sch., Greenville, 1955-57; tchr. homebound children Greenville County Sch. Dist., Greenville, 1961-64, psychologist, 1966-77; adj. prof. grad. studies in edn. Furman U., Greenville, 1977—, U. S.C., Columbia, 1982—; ednl. cons. Ednl. Diagnostic Svcs., Greenville, 1980—. Exec. dir. Camperdown Acad., Greenville, 1986-87; cons. learning disability program Erskine Coll., Due West, S.C., 1978—; Disting. lectr. Erskine Coll., 1999. Contbr. articles to profl. jours. Pres. Lake Forest PTA, Greenville, 1970-71; pres. of Women A.R. Presbyn. Ch., Greenville, 1973-75, adult Bible tchr., 1978—; sec. bd. trustees Erskine Coll., 1982-88; bd. dirs. Children's Bur. S.C., Columbia, 1981-87, YWCA, Greenville, 1984-88; bd. advisors for adoption S.C. Dept. Social Svcs., Columbia, 1987-92. Recipient Order of the Jessamine, Greenville News award, 1994-95, Sullivan award Erskine Coll., 2000. Mem. Am. Edn. Rsch. Assn. (southeastern rep. 1982-84, editor newspaper for SIG group 1982-83), Jean Piaget Soc., Assn. for Supervision and Curriculum Devel., Orton Dyslexia Soc. (pres. Carolinas br. 1984-88), Ea. Ednl. Rsch. Assn., S.C. Psychol. Assn., Order of the Jessamine, 21st Century Learning Initiative, Delta Kappa Gamma. Democrat. Avocations: travel, writing. Home and Office: 28 Montrose Dr Greenville SC 29607-3034 *Where did we get the idea that for children to succeed we must set them up to fail? Poverty, crime, and abuse beget poverty, crime, and abuse--not success and achievement. When will America wake up?*

HILL, GRANT, professional basketball player; b. Dallas, Oct. 5, 1972; s. Calvin and Janet Hill. BA in History, Duke U., 1994. Forward Detroit Pistons, 1994—99, Orlando Magic, Fla., 2000—. Mem. Dream Team III U.S. Olympic Team, 1996. Named Co-Rookie of Yr., 1994. Office: Orlando Magic 8701 Maitland Summit Blvd Orlando FL 32810

HILL, GREGORY PAUL, oil company executive; b. Springfield, Ill, Mar. 2, 1961; s. James Isaac and Bonnie Lee (Ball) H.; m. Sandra Lynne Lozano, May 17, 1986; 1 child, Justin Gregory. BSME, U. Wyo., 1983. Divsn. engring. mgr. Shell Calif. Prodn., Inc., Bakersfield, Calif., 1988-90; strategic planning mgr. Shell Oil Co., Houston, 1991-92; mgr. petroleum engring. Shell Western E&P, Houston, 1992-93; area mgr. LA Basin Calresources, LLC, Bakersfield, 1994-95, v.p. oper., 1996, Aera Energy, LLC, Bakersfield, 1996—97; v.p. planning exec. strategy/affairs Shell Internat., London, 1998; sr. v.p. innovation and breakthrough performance Aera Energy LLC, Bakersfield, 1999, sr. oper. v.p., 1999—2002; CEO, Enterprise/Shell, Shell Internat. E&P, London, 2002—03. Chmn. bd. dir., Terrain Tech., LLC, 1999-2002, prod. dir., Europe, Shell Int. E&P, 2003-, chmn., Enterprise Oil PLC, 2002-2003. Lobbyist Shell Oil Co., Calif., 1987. Mem. Phi Kappa Phi, Pi Tau Sigma, Tau Beta Pi (treas. 1982-83). Republican. Roman Catholic. Avocations: mountaineering, skiing, fishing, hunting, investing. Home: PO Box 4704 Houston TX 77210 Office: Shell Ctr London SE1 7NA England E-mail: gregory.hill@shell.com., gpslhill@aol.com.

HILL, HAROLD NELSON, JR., lawyer; b. Houston, Apr. 26, 1930; s. Harold Nelson and Emolyn Eloise (Geeslin) H.; m. Betty Jane Fell, Aug. 16, 1952; children: Douglas, Nancy. BS in Commerce, Washington and Lee U., Lexington, Va., 1952; PhD, Washington & Lee U., 1981; LL.B., Emory U., 1957, PhD, 1986. Bar: Ga. 1957. Assoc., then partner firm Gambrell, Harlan, Russell, Moye & Richardson, 1957-66; asst. atty. gen. Ga., 1966-68; exec. asst. atty. gen., 1968-72; partner firm Jones, Bird & Howell, 1972-74; assoc. justice Supreme Ct. Ga., 1975-82, chief justice, 1982-86; ptnr. Hurt, Richardson, Garner, Todd & Cadenhead, Atlanta, 1986-92, Judicial Resolutions Inc., Atlanta, 1993-94; of counsel Long, Aldridge & Norman, Atlanta, 1994-95. Served with AUS, 1952-54. Fellow Am. Bar Found.; Mem. Am. Law Inst., State Bar Ga., Lawyers Club Atlanta, Old War Horse Lawyers Club. Methodist.

HILL, HARRY DAVID, city official, human resources professional; b. Whittier, Calif., Oct. 29, 1944; s. Harry Boreman and Winifred Nell (Purvis) Hill; m. Linda Mae Price, Nov. 8, 1969; 1 child, Jon Ryan. AA, Los Angeles Harbor Coll., Wilmington, Calif., 1964; BA in Polit. Sci., UCLA, 1966; M of Pub. Adminstrn. in Human Resources, U. So. Calif., 1972. Personnel aide City of Anaheim, Calif., 1966-67, personnel analyst, 1967-71, sr. personnel analyst, 1971-75, personnel services mgr., 1975-83, asst. human resources dir., 1983-88, asst. labor rels. dir., 1988-94, dir. human resources, 1994—. Chmn. supervisory com. Anaheim Area Credit Union, 1981-89, bd. dirs., 1989-95. Pres. personnel and employee rels. dept. League of Calif. Cities, 2002—03; pres. Leadership Anaheim, 2003—. Mem. So. Calif. Pub. Labor Coun. (treas. 1986-87, pres. 1988), Internat. Pers. Mgmt. Assn. (pres. western region 1983-84), So. Calif. Pers. Mgmt. Assn. (pres. 1978-79), Coop. Pers. Svcs. (bd. dirs. 1987-2001, chmn. bd. 2001—). Democrat. Office: City of Anaheim 200 S Anaheim Blvd Fl 3 Anaheim CA 92805-3820 E-mail: dhill@anaheim.net.

HILL, HENRY ALLEN, physicist, educator; b. Port Arthur, Tex., Nov. 25, 1933; s. Douglas and Florence Hill. BS, U. Houston, 1953; MS, U. Minn., 1956, PhD, 1957; MA (hon.), Wesleyan U., 1966. Research asst. U. Houston, 1952-53; teaching asst. U. Minn., 1953-54, research asst., 1954-57; research assoc. Princeton U., 1957-58, instr., then asst. prof., 1958-64; assoc. prof. Wesleyan U., Middletown, Conn., 1964-66, prof. physics, 1966-74, chmn. dept., 1969-71; prof. physics U. Ariz., Tucson, 1966-95, prof. emeritus, 1995—. Chmn. bd. Zetetic Inst., 1992—; researcher on nuclear physics, relativity, astrophysics, and optics. Contbr. articles to profl. jours. Sloan fellow, 1966-68 Fellow Am. Phys. Soc.; mem. AAAS, Am. Astron. Soc., Optical Soc. Am., Am. Geophys. Union. Office: Zetetic Inst 1665 E 18th St Ste 206 Tucson AZ 85719-6809

HILL, HOWARD DARNELL, educator, university administrator; b. May 4, 1942; s. Howard Jr. and Della Mae (Williams) H.; m. Clemmie Faye Coulter, Dec. 24, 1963; children: Ray Darnell, Edith Renee (dec.). BA in Social Studies, Philander Smith Coll., 1964; MSE in Secondary Sch. Adminstrn., Ark. State U., 1968; PhD in Curriculum and Instrn., Kans. State U., 1973; postdoctoral study in ednl. adminstrn., U. S.C., 1983-85. Secondary sch. tchr. Jonesboro Pub. Sch., Ark., 1964-66; supr. instrn. Marion Sch., Ark., 1966-69; asst. prin. West Memphis (Ark.) Schs., 1969-70; secondary sch. tchr. Tunica Pub. Sch., Miss., 1970-71; asst. prof. edn. U. Houston, 1973-77; assoc. prof. Miss. Valley State U., Itta Bena, 1977-78; prof., chmn., program coord. dept. edn. S.C. State U., Orangeburg, 1978-87; dir. chpt. programs Phi Delta Kappa Hdqs., Bloomington, Ind., 1987-97; dean Sch. Grad. Studies S.C. State U., 1997-98, dir. doctoral program, chair ednl. leadership/counselor edn., 1998—2001; v.p. acad. affairs Claflin U., Orangeburg, SC, 2001—. Cons. Nat. Ednl. Svc., Bloomington, Ind. Contbr. articles to profl. jours. and books. Bush-Hewlett scholar Harvard U., 2002. Mem. ASCD, John Dewey Soc., Am. Assn. Colls. Tchr. Edn., Nat. Coun. Social Studies, Nat. Alliance Black Sch. Educators, Coun. of Grad. Sch. Deans, Assn. Tchr. Educators, Nat. Assn. Secondary Sch. Prins., Orangeburg County C. of C. (v.p. 2001-2002), Orangeburg Rotary Club-Morning (pres. 2001-2002), Phi Delta Kappa. Home: 1186 Pruitt Dr NW Orangeburg SC 29118-4024 Office: Claflin U Ste 9 Tingley Meml Hall Orangeburg SC 29115 E-mail: howard.hill@claflin.edu.

HILL, HULENE DIAN, accountant; b. Salisbury, N.C., Mar. 17, 1948; d. Hulon Clive and Matie Cordelia (Plyler) H.; m. Ed Adkins; 1 child, Daren Steven Starnes. BS in Acctg., U. N.C., Charlotte, 1971. CPA, N.C., PFS. Staff acct. Peat, Marwick Mitchell & Co., Charlotte, 1971-74; sr. tax acct. Arthur Andersen & Co., Charlotte, 1974-76; tax mgr. Ernst & Young (formerly Clarkson, Harden & Gantt), Columbia, 1976-79; ptnr. Deloitte & Touche, Charlotte, 1979-92; v.p. tax Steward Ingram Cooper PLLC, Raleigh, NC, 1992—. Recipient Hon. Mention as Bus. Woman of Yr. Shearson Lehman and Queens Coll., 1986, 89, 90, 91; named Acct. of Yr. Acad. Women Achievers YWCA, 1985. Mem. AICPA, Women Execs. (pres. 1987-88), Univ. N.C. Charlotte Athletic Found. (v.p. 1986-87), U. N.C. Charlotte Alumni Assn. (pres. 1985-86), Beta Alpha Psi (Acct. of Yr. U. N.C. chpt. 1985). Republican. Roman Catholic. Avocations: bridge, travel, reading. Home: 409 W Cameron Ave Chapel Hill NC 27516-2758 Office: PO Box 41168 Raleigh NC 27629-1168

HILL, I. KATHRYN, medical certification, licensing and education consultant; b. Phila., Apr. 6, 1950; d. Joseph Anthony and Irma Lorraine (Walther) Piehs; m. John Patrick McElwain, May 17, 1969 (div. Aug. 1979); children: John Charles, Brian Patrick; m. David Terence Hill, Sept. 27, 1980. BA, Widener Coll., 1979; MEd, Temple U., 1982. Cert. secondary tchr., Pa. Translator, transcriber Sci-Tech, Inc., Phila., 1970-77; tchr. West Chester (Pa.) East High Sch., 1978, Garnet Valley Jr.-Sr. High Sch., Concordville, Pa., 1979; asst. to dir. Nat. Bd. Med. Examiners, Phila., 1980-81, evaluation program asst., 1981-82, evaluation program assoc., 1982-84, sr. program assoc., 1984-85; asst. exec. v.p. Fedn. State Med. Bds., Ft. Worth, 1985-86, asst. exec. v.p., exec. dir. of the examination bd., 1986-94, sr. v.p., exec. dir. examination bd., 1995-96; exec. dir. Nat. Commn. on Cert. of Physician Assts., Atlanta, 1996—2001; ind. cons., 2001—. Editor: FLEX/SPEX Guidelines, 1985, 87, 90, FLEX/SPEX Info. Bull., 1987-94; co-editor Fedn. Exchange, 1986-95; contbr. articles to profl. jours. Mem. Am. Ednl. Rsch. Assn., Nat. Coun. on Measurement in Edn., Am. Soc. of Assn. Execs., Nat. Ctr. for Nonprofit Bds. Lutheran. Office: 7709 Georgetown Chase Roswell GA 30075-3581 E-mail: katehillroswell@cs.com.

HILL, ISABEL THIGPEN, urban planner, filmmaker; b. Montgomery, Ala., Sept. 9, 1951; d. Wiley Croom and Sarah Isabel (Dunn) H.; m. James David Sweeny, Jan. 11, 1992; 1 child, Anna Reese. BA, Hollins Coll., 1973; MA, George Washington U., 1982. Survey worker Va. Historic Landmarks Commn., Richmond, 1973; staff asst. U.S. Ho. Reps., Washington, 1974-76; rsch. specialist NEH, Washington, 1976; historian Historic Am. Engring. Record, Washington, 1977-83; program analyst N.Y. State Coun. Arts, N.Y.C., 1984-85; cmty. planner N.Y.C. Dept. Housing Preservation & Devel., 1985-87; assoc. city planner N.Y.C. Dept. City Planning, 1987-93; exec. dir. Southwest Bklyn. Indsl. Devel. Corp., 1994-95; econ. devel. urban planning cons. Bldg. History Assoc., Bklyn., 1993—; cons. N.Y.C. Landmarks Preservation Commn., 2000—. Bd. Econ. Devel. Assistance Consortium; project advisor Bklyn. Hist. Soc., 1995—; mem. New Day Films. Producer, dir. (film) Made In Brooklyn, 1993. Mcpl. Art Soc. fellow, 1989. Mem. Am. Planning Assn., Nat. Trust Historic Preservation, Women Make Movies, Assn. Independent Video and Filmmakers, Architects, Designers, Planners for Social Responsibility. Office: Building History Assoc 562 4th St Brooklyn NY 11215-3009

HILL, JAMES CLINKSCALES, federal judge; b. Darlington, S.C., Jan. 8, 1924; s. Albert Michael and Alberta (Clinkscales) H.; m. Mary Cornelia Black, June 7, 1946; children: James Clinkscales, Albert Michael. BS in Commerce, U. S.C., 1948; JD, Emory U., 1948. Bar: Ga. 1948, U.S. Supreme Ct. 1969. Assoc. Gambrell, Russell, Killorin & Forbes, Atlanta, 1948—55, ptnr., 1955—63, Hurt, Hill & Richardson, Atlanta, 1963—74; judge U.S. Dist. Ct. (no. dist.) Ga., 1974—76, U.S. Cir. Ct. (5th cir.), Atlanta, 1976—81, U.S. Cir. Ct. (11th cir.), Atlanta, 1981—89; sr. U.S. cir. judge U.S. Ct. Appeals, Atlanta, 1989—. Past chmn. com. on appellate ednl. programs Fed. Jud. Ctr.; former mem. com. on intercir. assignments Jud. Conf. U.S. With USAF, 1943—45. Fellow: ACTL; mem.: ABA, Am. Judicature Soc., Atlanta Bar Assn., State Bar Ga., World Assn. Judges, Am. Law Inst., Am. Bar Found. (life), Old War Horse Lawyers, Lawyers Club Atlanta (life). Republican. Baptist. Office: US Ct Appeals PO Box 52598 Jacksonville FL 32201-2598 also: Elbert P Tuttle US Ct Appeals Bldg 56 Forsyth St NW Atlanta GA 30303 E-mail: JCHretreat@aol.com.*

HILL, JAMES EDWARD, insurance company executive; b. Chgo., Mar. 3, 1926; s. George and Mary Luella (Hutchens) H.; m. Jessie Mae Birmingham, Jan. 29, 1949; children: James R. (dec.), Ellen M. Student, Denver U., 1947; MS in Fin. Svcs., Am. Coll., Bryn Mawr, Pa., 1980. CLU; chartered fin. cons.; cert. fin. planner. Office mgr., purchasing agt., acct. Steve Tojek Co., Milw., 1948-54; office mgr., acct. Oreg. Athletic Equipment Co., Portland, 1954-56; spl. agt. Prudential Ins. Co., Portland, 1956-58, div. mgr., 1958-70; gen. agt. Gt. Am. Res. Ins. Co., Portland, 1970—; v.p. Robert A. Amey Co., Inc., mfrs. reps., 1971-75; pres. Diversified Plans, Inc., 1979-89, v.p., 1989-96, pres., 1996—. V.p. Multnomah County Young Reps., 1957-58; vice chmn. Washington County Parks Adv. Bd., 1978, chmn., 1979-83; local sch. committeeman Beaverton, Oreg. Sch. Dist., 1993 (elected); instr. Life Underwriter Tng. Coun.; mem. task force for curriculum and instrn. Oreg. Sch. Dist. Beaverton dir. Citizens for Pub. Edn. Inc., 1991—; bd. dirs. Christian Heritage Month Assn., 1997-2002; treas. Evergreen Presbyn. Ch., 1993-2001, elder emeritus, 1997—. With U.S. Army, 1944-47. Recipient Edgar M. Kelly award Prudential, 1967. Mem. Oreg. Life Underwriters Assn. (edn. chmn. 1981-82, pres.-elect 1982-83, pres. 1983-84), Portland Life Underwriters Assn. (dir. 1978-80, chmn. edn. com. 1978-80, pres. 1980-81, Am. Soc. C.L.U.s (C.L.U. of Yr. award Portland chpt., instr.), Am. Family Assn. (Oreg. state dir. 1993—). Home and Office: 12980 NW Saltzman Ct Portland OR 97229-4668 E-mail: dpi@afo.net.

HILL, JAMES ROBERT, accountant; b. Marshalltown, Iowa, Jan. 20, 1960; s. James Ralph and Darlene Shirley (Kaufmann) H.; m. Debra Sue Wantz, May 11, 1985; children: Bradley James, Kayla Marie, Erica Kristi. BA in Acct. and Systems Mgmt., Cen. Coll., Pella, Iowa, 1982. Livestock acct. Swift Ind., Marshalltown, Iowa, 1982-83, departmental acct., 1983-86, acctg. supr. St. Joseph, Mo., 1986-88; plant contr. Monfort (formerly Swift Ind.), St. Joseph, 1988-89; acctg. mgr. Jet Stream Plastic Pipe Co., Siloam Springs, Ark., 1990-98; ops./acctg. mgr. Millbrook Distbn. Svcs., Harrison, Ark., 1998-99; v.p. fin. PipeLife Jet Stream, Inc., Siloam Springs, Ark., 1999—. Trustee, mem. fin. com. ACTS Free Meth. Ch., also treas.; cmty. edn. adv. bd. mem.; bd. dirs. United Way of Benton County; chmn. pack com., den leader Boy Scouts Am. Mem. Inst. Mgmt. Accts., Jaycees (treas. Gladbrook, Iowa chpt. 1984, Jaycee of Yr. Gladbrook chpt. 1985, v.p. 1986, state finalist Brownfield award 1983, dist. dir. 1991, pres. Siloam Springs chpt. 1992-93, 94-95, Dist. Dir. of Quarter 1991, Number 5 Dist. Dir. in U.S. 1991-92, Number 1 Local Pres. 2d quarter 1992-93, Internat. senator), Ark. State JCI (senate pres. 1998-99). Avocations: golf, woodworking, photography. Home: 22977 Lawlis Rd Siloam Springs AR 72761-8257 Office: Pipelife Jet Stream Inc PO Box 190 Siloam Springs AR 72761-0190 E-mail: jim.hill@pipelife-jetstream.com., jimhill@cox-internet.com.

HILL, JAMES SCOTT, lawyer; b. Boston, Mar. 21, 1924; s. Benjamin B. and Dorothy (Scott) H.; m. Sally C. Foss, June 28, 1945; children: Richard B., Chessye F., Cynthia C., Michael O. BA magna cum laude, Williams Coll., 1947; JD, Columbia U., 1949. Bar: N.Y. 1949, N.J. 1958. Assoc. Baldwin, Todd & Lefferts, N.Y.C., 1949-50; corp. sec., atty. Johnson & Johnson, N.J., 1950-66; v.p., sec., gen. counsel Celanese Corp., N.Y.C., 1966-74; v.p., gen. counsel, dir. Liggett & Myers, Durham, N.C., 1974-76; v.p. law and govt. affairs CBS Inc., N.Y.C., 1976-78; group pres. law and regulatory affairs Am. Hosp. Supply Corp., Evanston, Ill., 1978-81; of counsel Shanley & Fisher, 1981-88, Smith, Stratton, Wise, Heher & Brennan, Princeton, N.J., 1988—. Judge Princeton (N.J.) Twp., 1959-65 Treas. N.J. Republican Fin. com., 1965-70; trustee John Seward Johnson Sr. Charitable Trusts, Princeton Med. Ctr., N.J. State Aquarium, Trinity Counselling Svc., Princeton, N.J.; chmn. Williams Coll. Devel. Coun.; chmn. Boyden Soc.-Deerfield Acad.; bd. dirs. Friends of Channel 13; mem. exec. com. Friends of the Inst. for Advanced Study, Princeton. Served to 1st lt. USAAF, 1943-46. Fellow Am. Coll. Trust and Estate Counsel (mem. charitable planning and exempt orgn. com.); mem. Assn. Gen. Counsel, Met. Club (Washington), Princeton Club (N.Y.C.), Mid-Ocean Club (Bermuda), Bedens Brook Club (bd. govs. 1995—), Springdale Club, Nassau Club (trustee 1993-96), Jasna Polana Golf Club (Princeton), Gasparilla Club (Boca Grande, Fla.), Chi Psi. Republican. Episcopalian (warden). Home: 155 Lambert Dr Princeton NJ 08540-2306 also: PO Box 1767 Boca Grande FL 33921-1767 Office: 600 College Rd E Princeton NJ 08540-6636

HILL, JAMES STANLEY, computer consulting company executive; b. Merrickville, Ont., Can., July 24, 1914; m. Doris C. Huelster, 1938; children: George, Janice, Mary, Beverly, Richard. With Minn. Life Ins. Co., 1930-69; sr. v.p., 1966-69; pres. Digiplan, Inc., White Bear Lake, Minn., 1969—, Red Oak Press, 1994—. Bd. dirs., chmn. audit com. Hadco Inc., 1981-98; pub. spkr., 1994—. Author: Confessions of an 80 Year Old Boy, 1994, Almost Immortal, 1996. Treas. Minn. State H.S. Math. League, St. Paul Area Coun. of Chs. Found.; bd. dirs. United Hosp., 1972-99. Fellow Soc. Actuaries (bd. govs., v.p.). Home and Office: Digiplan Inc 5011 Lake Ave Apt 205 Saint Paul MN 55110-2655 *To live each day free from guilt, worry and fear, with opportunities to serve and love others and to exercise both mind and body vigorously— with these goals (and it's taken me over 60 years to come even close), the other things (money, recognition, love from others, and appreciation) come automatically. Christ and others have said it better, but the important thing is: It Works.*

HILL, JAMES T. career officer; b. Ohio, Aug. 10, 1946; m. Antoinette Griffin; 2 children. BA, Trinity U., 1968; MA in Personnel Mgmt., Ctrl. Mich. U., 1980; grad., Command and Gen. Staff Coll., Nat. War Coll., U.S. Army Inf. Sch. Commd. 2d lt. U.S. Army, 1968, advanced through grades to gen., 1996, various assignments; bde. comdr. 101st Airborne Divsn., 1989-91, chief of staff, 1991-92; asst. dep. dir. politico-mil. affairs Jt. Chiefs of Staff, 1992—94; asst. divsn. comdr. U.S. Forces, Haiti, 1994; dep. chief of staff ops. Forces Command, Ft. McPherson, Ga., 1995-97; commdg. gen. 25th Inf. Divsn., Schofield Barracks, Hawaii, 1997—99, I Corps and Fort Lewis, 1999—2002; comdr. U.S. Southern Command, Miami, Fla., 2002—. Decorated D.S.M., Silver Star with 2 oak leaf clusters, Def. Superior medal with oak leaf cluster, Bronze Star with 2 oak leaf clusters, Purple Heart. Episcopalian. Avocation: golf.

HILL, J(AMES) TOMILSON, investment banker; b. Westbury, N.Y., May 24, 1948; s. James Tomilson Jr. and Dorothy H. (Kutcher) H.; m. Janine A. Wolf, Feb. 2, 1980; children: Margot Langdon, Astrid Tomilson. BA, Harvard U., 1970, MBA, 1973. Vice pres. mergers and acquisitions 1st Boston Corp., N.Y.C., 1973-79; sr. v.p. Smith Barney, Harris Upham & Co. Inc., N.Y.C., 1979-82; mng. dir., dir. mergers and acquisitions, co-head investment banking div. Shearson Lehman Bros. Inc., N.Y.C., 1982-90; vice-chmn., co-chief exec. officer Lehman Bros., N.Y.C., 1990-93; also bd. dirs. Shearson Lehman Bros. Holdings, Inc., co-pres., co-chief operating officer, 1993; co-chief exec. officer Lehman Bros., 1993, Shearson Lehman Bros., 1993, SLB Asset Mgmt., 1993; vice chmn., mem. investment and mgmt. com. Blackstone Group, N.Y.C., 1993—; pres., CEO Blackstone Alternative Asset Mgmt., 1995—. Bd. dirs. Allied Waste. Contbr. articles to profl. publs. Bd. dirs. Hirshhorn Mus. and Sculpture Garden; vice chmn. Lincoln Ctr. Theater, Milton Acad., Nightingale-Bamford Sch. Mem. Coun. Fgn. Rels. (chmn. investment subcom. of fin. and budget com.), Piping Rock Club, Meadow Brook Club, Links Club, River Club, Knickerbocker Club. Home: 4 E 72nd St New York NY 10021-4144 Office: Blackstone Group 345 Park Ave Ste New York NY 10154-0004

HILL, JERRY DEAN, secondary school educator; b. Stuart, Va., June 27, 1952; s. Walter Doyle and Doris Gracie Hill. AA in Liberal Arts, Bluefield Coll., 1972; BA in Religious Edn., Gardner-Webb U., 1974; MD in Christian Edn., So. Bapt. Theol. Sem., 1978. Educatoral dir. Martinez Bapt. Ch., Augusta, Ga., 1978—80; farmer Lawsonville, NC, 1980—84; tchr. Martinsville (Va.) City Schs., 1984—89; music dir. Bethany Christian Ch., Roanoke, Va., 1986—89; fine and performing arts chair Newport Sch., Kensington, Md., 1989—2001; tchr. Arlington (Va.) County Pub. Schs., 2001—. Mem. accreditation teams Middle States & Assn. Ind. Md. Schs., 1996—2000; mem. profl. devel. com. Assn. Ind. Md. Schs., Md., 1997—2001; liaison Nat. Assn. Music Educators, Reston, Va., 2000. Avocations: piano, photography, travel.

HILL, JIM B. state legislator; b. Nashville, Ark., July 5, 1938; m. Charlotte Hill. Mem. Ark. Ho. Reps., Little Rock, 1993-96, Ark. State Senate, Little Rock, 1997—, chmn. Ark. Legis. Coun. policy making com., mem. adminstrv. rules and regulations com., personnel com., mem. agr., econ. and indsl. devel. com., legis. audit com., legis. audit edn. instns., others, pres., 2003—. Rancher, Nashville, Ark. Democrat. Baptist. Office: Arkansas State Senate 320 State Capitol Bldg Little Rock AR 72201 also: 100 Center Nashville AR 71852*

HILL, JIM TOM, retired consulting firm executive; b. Cushing, Okla., Apr. 27, 1939; s. Wilburn C. and Susie (Ruckman) H.; m. Linda J. Archer, Aug. 30, 1963; children: Sheri, David, Susan. BS in Chemistry, Abilene Christian U., 1961; MS in Biochemistry, U. Tenn., 1964, PhD, 1968. Sr. rsch. scientist E.R. Squibb & Sons, New Brunswick, NJ, 1968-69, Lakeside Labs., Milw., 1969-75; sr. rsch. specialist Monsanto, St. Louis, 1975-78; dir. chemistry Covance, Vienna, Va., 1978-80; mgr. toxicology Phelps Dodge, Washington, 1980-81; dir. sci. affairs Chem. Specialties Mfrs. Assn., Washington, 1981-86, dir. product ingredient rev. program, 1987-97; v.p. Specialty Product Group SRS Internat., Washington, 1997—2003. Contbr. articles to profl. jours. Mem. Am. Coll. Toxicology, Am. Soc. Pharmacology and Exptl. Therapeutics, Environ. Mutagen Soc., Am. Chem. Soc., Soc. Toxicology, Sigma Xi. Home: 2477 Freetown Dr Reston VA 20191-2527 E-mail: jimtomhill@aol.com.

HILL, JIMMIE DALE, retired government official; b. Fort Worth, Tex., Dec. 28, 1933; s. William Haden and Myrtle Maude H.; m. Martha Lea Hoad, May 26, 1956; children: William, Loretta, Carol, Patricia. Student, DelMar Coll., 1955-57, U. Okla., 1957-58, U. Wichita, 1963-64. Enlisted in U.S. Air Force, 1951, advanced through grades to maj., 1974; comptroller for space systems acquisition Los Angeles, 1963-70; adv. CIA, 1970-73; ret., 1974; spl. asst. to undersec. Air Force, Washington, 1974-78; dir. Office of Space Systems, Dept. Air Force, 1978-82; dep. undersec. Air Force Space Systems, 1982-96; dep. dir. Nat. Reconnaissance Office, 1982-96. Scoutmaster Boy Scouts Am., 1971-76. Decorated Legion of Merit; recipient Disting. Civilian Svc. medal Dept. Def., 1974, 76, 87, 96, Presdl. Rank award of Meritorious Exec., 1980, 88, Presdl. Rank of Disting. Exec., 1981, 91, Air Force sr. exec. award, 1982-87, 89, 90, 92, 93, 94, 95, Air Force Exceptional Civilian Svc. award, 1987, 96, Nat. Intelligence Disting. Svc. medal, Ctrl. Intelligence Agy. Disting. Intelligence medal, Disting. Svc. medal NASA, Goddard Meml. Trophy, Nat. Space Club, 1996, Goddard Astronautics award AIAA, 1998. Mem. Air Force Assn. Methodist. Home: 7920 Lewinsville Rd Mc Lean VA 22102-2407 E-mail: jimmiehill@aol.com. *Choose an occupation or profession because you like it, not for recognition and reward. For if you're happy in your work, with loyalty, dedication and hard work, ample recognition and reward will follow.*

HILL, JOHN GLENWOOD, JR., university counsel, lawyer; b. Hartford, Conn., Aug. 2, 1929; John Glenwood and Marion E. (Cullen) H.; m. Barbara Oppel, Nov. 12, 1955; children— John G., Ellen E. B.A., LL.B., U. Conn., 1954, Ph.D., 1972; M.A., Trinity Coll., 1962. Bar: Conn. 1954, U.S. Dist. Ct. Conn. 1956, U.S. Supreme Ct. 1971; Mass. 1977, U.S. Dist. Ct. Mass. 1978, Wis. 1980. Asst. atty. gen., counsel pub. Utilities Commr., State of Conn., 1958-67; gen. counsel U. Conn., Storrs, 1967-76, Boston U., 1976-80, Marquette U., Milw., 1980— ; dir. Colloquium on Anglo Am. Law, London, 1984, 86. Co-author: The Student, The College, The Law, 1972; also articles. Served with USCG, 1954-56. Mem. Nat. Assn. Coll. and Univ. Attys. (exec. bd. 1980-83). Home: 649 W Acacia Rd Glendale WI 53217

HILL, JOHN HOWARD, lawyer; b. Pitts., Aug. 12, 1940; s. David Garrett and Eleanor Campbell (Musser) H. BA, Yale U., 1962, JD, 1965. Bar: Pa. 1965, U.S. Dist. Ct. (we dist.) Pa. 1965, U.S. Ct. Appeals (3d cir.) 1965, U.S. Supreme Ct. 1982. Assoc. Reed, Smith, Shaw & McClay, Pitts., 1965-75, ptnr., 1975-90; of counsel Jackson Lewis LLP, Pitts., 1991—. Bd. dirs. Travelers Aid Soc., Pitts., 1972-99, treas., 1982-87, pres., 1987-90; bd. dirs. Pitts. Opera, Pitts. Symphony Soc. Mem.: ABA, Allegheny County Bar Assn., Pa. Bar Assn., Pa. Soc., Hosp. Assn. Pa., Rolling Rock Club, Duquesne Club, Fox Chapel Golf Club, Phi Gamma Delta. Republican. Presbyterian. Home: 4722 Bayard St Pittsburgh PA 15213-1708 Office: Jackson Lewis LLP One PPG Pl 28th Fl Pittsburgh PA 15222-5414 E-mail: hillj@jacksonlewis.com.

HILL, JOHN WALLACE, special education educator; BA in Elem. Edn. cum laude, Am. U., 1970, MEd in Spl. Edn., 1971, PhD in Edn., 1974. Dir. Learning Disabilities Clinic Meyer Children's Rehab. Inst., U. Nebr. Med. Ctr., Omaha, 1974-87; prof. spl. edn. Coll. of Edn., U. Nebr., Omaha, 1974—, acting chair dept., Regents prof., 1989-95. Adj. prof. Coll. of Pharmacy, U. Nebr. Med. Ctr., 1986-98; lectr. various univs., assns. and confs.; former mem., bd. dirs. Omaha Head Start Program, Child and Family Devel. Corp. Contbr. articles to profl. jours. Recipient Outstanding Tchg. award, U. Nebr. Omaha Alumni, 2002. Fellow Am. Acad. for Cerebral Palsy and Devel. Medicine; mem. Phi Delta Kappa, Sigma Xi. Office: Univ Nebr at Omaha Dept Spl Edn Omaha NE 68182-0001

HILL, JONATHAN DAVID, anthropology researcher, educator, editor; b. Charlotte, NC, Feb. 21, 1954; s. Leland Halsey Hill, Jr. and Dorothy Scheer Hill; m. Lori Elizabeth Millner, Mar. 4, 2000; m. Gabriela Gheorghiu, Feb. 18, 1979 (div. Aug. 0, 1987); children: Rachael Marin Leader, Alexander Cornelius, Charles Millner. BA, U. of Chgo., 1972—76; PhD, Ind. U., 1976—83. Vis. asst. prof. Dept. of Anthropology, U. of Ga., 1983—86; asst. prof. Dept. of Anthropology, So. Ill. U., 1986—89, assoc. prof., 1990—95; vis. assoc. prof. Dept. of Anthropology, UCLA, 1993—94; prof. Dept. of Anthropology, SIUC, 1996—98, prof. and chair, 1999—. Dir. of grad. studies Dept. of Anthropology, SIUC, 1991—96. Author: (monograph) Keepers of the Sacred Chants: The Poetics of Ritual Power in an Amazonian Society; editor: Rethinking History and Myth: Indigenous South American Perspectives on the Past, History, Power, and Identity: Ethnogenesis in the Americas, 1492-1992, Comparative Arawakan Histories: Rethinking Language Family and Culture Area in Amazonia, Identities: Global Studies in Culture and Power, 2001; contbg. editor: Handbook of Latin Am. Studies, Libr. of Congress, Hispanic Divsn., 1986—94; editl. adv. Am. Anthropologist, 1989—93, book reviewer various pubs. in field; contbr. Hon. mem., ethnol. adv. com., intercultural-bilingual edn. Ministerio de Educacion, Caracas, Venezuela, 1981—81; coach SAY Soccer, Carbondale, 1988—91; mem., music com. Ethical Soc. of St. Louis, 1999—2002. NDEA Title VI Fellowship, Portuguese and Latin Am. Studies, Ctr. for Latin Am. Studies, Ind. U., 1977—78, Fulbright-Hays Tchg. Grant, Doctoral Dissertation Abroad Program, U.S. Dept. of Edn., 1980—81, Internat. Doctoral Rsch. Fellowship, Program for L.Am. and the Caribbean, Social Sci. Rsch. Coun. and the Am. Coun. of Learned Societies, 1980—81, Fulbright-Hays Faculty rsch. abroad, U.S. Dept. of Edn., 1984, Postdoctoral Fellowship, Dept. of Anthropology, Smithsonian Instn., Nat. Mus. of Natural History, 1988, Summer Rsch. Stipend, Nat. Endowment for the Humanities, 1998, small grant for rsch., Wenner-Gren Found. for Anthrop. Rsch., 1998, Conf. Grant, 2000. Fellow: Am. Anthrop. Assn. (life); mem.: Soc. for Linguistic Anthropology, Soc. for Cultural Anthropology, Am. Soc. for Ethnohistory, Am. Ethnol. Soc. Independent. American Ethical Union. Achievements include research in human ecology in the Upper Rio Negro Basin, Venezuelan Amazon (1980); field study on musical performances of indigenous Arawakan peoples, Upper Rio Negro, Venezuelan Amazon (1980-1981); field study of Northern Arawakan adaptations to extralocal factors, Venezuelan Amazon (1984, 1985); field study on the social and ecological impact of gold mining among Arawak-Speaking peoples, Colombian Amazon (1989); field study of trickster narratives, musicality, and social constructions of history, Venezuelan Amazon (1998). Avocations: classical music (piano performance), soccer, golf. Home: 801 S Johnson Carbondale IL 62901 Office: Department of Anthropology MC 4502 So Ill U Carbondale IL 62901-4502 Office Fax: 618-453-5037. E-mail: jhill@siu.edu.

HILL, JOSEPH C. lawyer; b. Kingston, N.Y., Sept. 23, 1964; BA, Fordham U., 1986; JD, Columbia U., 1989. Bar: N.Y., Spain. With Uria & Menendez, Madrid, Mayer, Brown & Platt, N.Y.C.; mng. dir., assoc. gen. counsel J.P. Morgan Chase & Co., N.Y.C., 1994—. Mem. Assn. Bar City N.Y. (chair inter-Am. affairs com.), Coun. on Fgn. Rels., Phi Beta Kappa. Office: JP Morgan Chase & Co 270 Park Ave Fl 40 New York NY 10017-2014 E-mail: joe.hill@chase.com.

HILL, JUDITH DEEGAN, lawyer; b. Chgo., Dec. 13, 1939; d. William James and Ida May (Scott) Deegan; children: Colette M., Cristina M. BA, Western Mich. U., 1960; cert., U. Paris, Sorbonne, 1962; JD, Marquette U., 1971; postgrad., Harvard U., 1984. Bar: Wis. 1971, Ill. 1973, Nev. 1976, D.C. 1979. Tchr. Kalamazoo (Mich.) Bd. Edn., 1960-62, Maple Heights (Ohio) Bd. Edn., 1963-64, Shorewood (Wis.) Bd. Edn., 1964-68; corp. atty. Fort Howard Paper Co., Green Bay, Wis., 1971-72; sr. trust adminstr. Continental Ill. Nat. Bank & Trust, Chgo., 1972-76; atty. Morse, Foley & Wadsworth Law Firm, Las Vegas, 1976-77; dep. dist. atty., criminal prosecutor Clark County Atty., Las Vegas, 1977-83; atty. civil and criminal law Edward S. Coleman Profl. Law Corp., Las Vegas, 1983-84; pvt. practice law, 1989-99; ret., 1999. Bd. dirs. YMCA, Highland Park, 1973-75, Planned Parenthood of So. Nev., 1977-78, Nev. Legal Svcs., Carson City, 1980-87, state chmn., 1984-87; bd. dirs. Clark County Legal Svcs., Las Vegas, 1980-87, St. Jude's Ranch for Children, 1999-2001; mem. Star Aux. for Handicapped Children, Las Vegas, 1986-96, Greater Las Vegas Women's League, 1987-88; jud. candidate Las Vegas Mcpl. Ct., 1987, New Symphony Guild, Variety Club Internat., 1992-93; mem. Nat. Conf. for Cmty. and Justice, So. Nev., 1998-2000; mentor in Clark County Sch., 1999-2002. Auto Splties. scholar, St. Joseph, Mich., 1957-60, St. Thomas More scholar Marquette U. Law Sch., Milw., 1968-69; juvenile law internship grantee

Marquette U. Law Sch., 1970; honored as one of first 100 Women Attys. in the State of Nev., Oct. 1999. Mem. Nev. Bar Assn., So. Nev. Assn. Women Attys., Children's Village Club (pres. 1980). Home: 521 Sweeney Ave Las Vegas NV 89104-1436 Fax: 702-384-4167.

HILL, JUDITH SWIGOST, business analyst, information systems engineer; b. Harvey, Ill., Dec. 31, 1942; d. J.W. and M.J. (Kuczaik) Swigost; m. Wallace H. Hill, May 16, 1982; stepchildren: Scott, Amy, Molly, Elizabeth. BA in Theater, U. Ill., 1964; postgrad., Am. U., 1967-69, New Sch. U., N.Y.C., 1977-85. Vol. U.S. Peace Corps, Philippines, 1964-66, recruiter, 1966-67, program mgr. Micronesia, 1968, dir. corr. Washington, 1969; editor, prin. Congl. Monitor, Inc., Washington, 1970-76; legis. analyst Philip Morris, Inc., N.Y.C., 1976-77; tech. analyst, writer Jesco, Inc., N.Y.C., 1978-79; assoc. pub. Thomas Pub. Co., N.Y.C., 1980-84; bus. analyst AGS, Inc. Ind. Cons., N.Y.C., 1984-93; dir. MIS N.Y.C. Sch. Constrn. Authority, 1993-94; ind. cons. in project mgmt. N.Y.C., 1994—. Ind. cons. info. engring. and tech. orgn., N.Y.C., 1987—. golf instr., 2002-. Editor, contbr. Golf for Women newsletter, 1999—; golf instr., 2003-, contbr. articles to profl. jour. Mem. Internat. Women's Writing Guild, Nat. Assn. Returned Peace Corps Vols. Greater N.Y., Nat. Peace Corps. Assn. Avocations: golf, writing, banjo, piano. E-mail: joodgolf@yahoo.com.

HILL, KAREN CAECILIA, education educator; b. LaCrosse, Wis., Apr. 23, 1961; BA, U. Ark., 1984; MEd, U. So. Miss., 1996. Instr. in writing Hartnell Coll., Salinas, Calif., 2000—. Pub. cons. Hill Pub., Marina, Calif. Author: One Bird, 2001. Home: PO Box 279 Marina CA 93933

HILL, KATHLEEN BLICKENSTAFF, lawyer, mental health nurse, nursing educator; b. Greenville, Ohio, Oct. 24, 1950; d. Donald Edward and Mary Ann (Subler) Berger; children: Benjamin Arin, Amanda Marie, Kathryn Megan; m. David M. Hill, Sr., Sept. 27, 2002. BS, Ohio State U., 1972, MS, 1973, sch. nurse cert., 1990; JD, Capital U. Law Sch., 1998. Cert. sch. nurse grades K-12. Cons. cmty. educator S.W. Cmty. Mental Health Ctr., Columbus, 1973-77; patient and cmty. educator Daniel E. Blickenstaff, DDS, Inc., Columbus, 1977-86; staff nurse Riverside Meth. Hosp., Columbus, 1986-90; clin. instr. Columbus (Ohio) State C.C., 1989; from asst. to assoc. prof. Capital U., Columbus, 1989-2000, prof., 2000—01, adj. prof., 2001—; assoc. Porter, Wright, Morris & Arthur LLP, Columbus, 2000—. Mem. cmty. svcs. com. Mid Ohio Dist. Nurses Assn., Columbus, 1990—2001, bd. dirs., 1991—94, mem. legis. com., 2002—. Leader Girl Scouts, Grandview Heights, Ohio, 1989-93; bd. dirs. H.S. PTO, Grandview Heights (Ohio) City Schs., 1990-93, treas. H.S. PTO, 1990-92, co-chair oper. levy, 1991. Mem.: ANA, ABA, Columbus Bar Assn. (health law com.), Ohio State Bar Assn. (health and disability law com.), Ohio Nurses Assn., Am. Health Lawyers Assn., Sigma Theta Tau. Avocations: quilting, sewing, gardening. Home: 1935 Marblecliff Crossing Ct Columbus OH 43204-4968 Office: Porter Wright Morris & Arthur LLP 41 S High St Ste 2900 Columbus OH 43215-6194 E-mail: kblicken@columbus.rr.com., khill@porterwright.com.

HILL, KATIE, contractor; b. N.Y.C., Mar. 21, 1956; d. Peb Grumman and Else Amy Kopf; m. Howard Hill, Oct. 11, 1989. BA in English, Yale Coll., 1978. Freelance copywriter, Phila., 1978—82; sr. copywriter Grey Advt., N.Y.C., 1982—83, McCaffrey & McCall, N.Y.C., 1983—84, Leber Katz Ptnrs., N.Y.C., 1984—86; creative dir. Tracy-Locre Direct, Dallas, 1986—87; freelance creative dir. Katie Hill & Assocs., Oyster Bay, NY, 1988—92; restoration contractor Sands Hill Restoration, LLC, Torrington, Conn., 1992—. Recipient Caples award, John Caples Internat. Awards, 1987. Mem.: Remodeling Contractors Assn. (bd. dirs. 2002—03), Yale Club Conn. Avocations: horseback riding, reading, antiques, collecting books.

HILL, KEITH MAURICE, editor; b. Washington, Dec. 23, 1954; s. Raymond Alexander and Lois (Holmes) H. BS in Zoology, Duke U., 1976; JD, Am. U. Law Sch., 1982. Law clk. Slover & Loftus, Washington, 1980-81; law clk., paralegal Miller, Loewinger & Assocs., Washington, 1982-84; database search asst. CACI, Inc., Washington, 1984-87; cons. Nat. Forum Black Pub. Adminstrs., Washington, 1988; issues, rsch. analyst Associated Builders and Contractors, Washington, 1988; legal editor, labor rels. reporter, individual employment rights and labor arbitration cases Bur. Nat. Affairs, Washington, 1989-93; reporter Medicare Report & Daily Labor Report, 1993-94; editor Payroll Libr. on CD, 1994—. Mem. D.C. Coalition of Black Profl. Orgns. (pres. 1987-89), Concerned Black Men (project northstar and internat. awareness com.), Capital Press Club (2d v.p. 1997-98), Duke U. Black Alumni Connection (v.p. D.C./Mid-Atlantic chpt. 1997-99, acting pres. 1999-2001), BNA Toastmasters (v.p. pub. rels. 1998-2000, dir. mentoring 2001-02, sgt.-at-arms 2002-2003). Democrat. Baptist. Avocations: chess, movies, tv, travel. Home: 5924 Surratts Village Dr Clinton MD 20735-2545 E-mail: kmh1223@aol.com., khill@bna.com.

HILL, KENDERSON, career systems development executive, city councilman; b. Albany, Ga., Nov. 12, 1959; s. Emmitt and Pearlie Mae Hill; m. Tango Roberta Dawkins-Hill, Apr. 3, 1992. BS, Albany State U., 1983; MA, Troy State U., 1990. City councilman City of Albany, Ga., 1994—2002; dir. ind. living Career Sys. Devel. Corp., Albany, Ga., 2001—. Cons. T.R. Hill Internat. Network, Inc., Albany, 1995—. Mentor Boy and Girls Club Albany, 1995. Maj. U.S. Army, 1986—92. Recipient Cert. of Appreciation, Dougherty City H.S., 1996. Mem.: Nat. League Cities, Ga. Mcpl. Assn. (city councilman), Phi Beta Sigma. Baptist. Avocations: tennis, swimming, working out at the gym. Home: 2510 Beachview Dr Albany GA 31705

HILL, KENNETH CLYDE, clergyman; b. Kingsport, Tenn., Mar. 22, 1953; s. Hubert Clyde and Erma Lee (Harless) H.; m. Janet Reynolds, Oct. 15, 1976; children: Matthew Joseph, Timothy Aaron, Lydia Rebekah. BS in Speech, History, East Tenn. State U., 1974; MS in Speech, Ind. State U., 1976; BA in Bibl. Studies, Bapt. Christian Coll., 1986; M Religious Edn., Manahath Sch. Theology, 1989; D in Religious Edn., Andersonville Bapt. Sem., 2001. Ordained to ministry Evang. Meth. Ch., 1982. Pastor Crestwood Bapt. Ch., Ft. Wayne, Ind., 1980-81; pres., chief exec. officer Appalachian Ednl. Communication Corp., Bristol, Tenn., 1981—; pulpit supply various ch. congregations Ind., 1976—82; deacon Evang. Meth. Ch., Kingsport, Tenn., 1982-86, elder, 1986—; chmn. Publs. Bd. of the Evang. Meth. Ch., Kingsport, 1986—; sec. Gen. Conf. Evang. Meth. Ch., Kingsport, 1990—; gen. dir. Siloam Internat., Inc., 1990—96; v.p. Southwest Radio Ch. of the Air, Inc., 1993—; pastor Lakeview Bible Chapel, Kingsport, Tenn., 1993-96, Morrison City Mission, Kingsport, 1999—. Gen. dir. Mission Field Task Force, Santiago, Chile, 1991, 93, 95-96, 98, 2000; bd. dirs. Bancroft Gospel Ministry, Kingsport, 1984—, Manahath Sch. Theology, Hollidaysburg, Pa., 1986-93, 1995-2001, 2002—; chmn. Servant Ministries, Kingsport, 1990-91; mem. Mission Field Task Force, Blantyre, Malawi, 1989. Author: (with Ronald Cooke) Reconstructionism: Is It Scriptural, 1989; (with Keith Walsworth) What's Next? 1993; (with others) Why I Still Believe We Live in the Last Days—Nuclear Proliferation, 1993; (with Joan B. Collins) Constitution in Crisis, 1994; (with Bill Usselton) Constitution Conspiracy, 1994; (with Jim Nicholls) Reflections on the Fairness Doctrine, 1994; (with Jose Holowaty and N.W. Hutchings) International Christian Broadcasting from South America, 1995, Prayers Jabez Did Not Pray, 2002; editor: A Classic Christmas, 1995; prodr. (video) The Temple Mount, 1993, Petra in History and Prophecy, 1993, The Revived Roman Empire, 1993, 25 Messianic Signs, 1993, Prayers Jabez Didn't Pray, 2002; contbr. articles to profl. jours. Disaster vol. ARC, 1986-92; bd. dirs. Radio Reading Svcs. Corp., Kingsport, 1989-90; vol. World Reach, Inc., Honduras, 1986-91. Mem. Delta Sigma Rho, Tau Kappa Alpha. Home: Ste 100 340 Edgemont Ave Bristol TN 37620 Office: Appalachian Ednl Comm Corp PO Box 2061 Bristol TN 37621-2061 E-mail: KCHill@aecc.org.

HILL, KENNETH WAYNE, physicist; b. Winston-Salem, N.C., Apr. 23, 1945; s. Dewey William and Grace Iola (Bryant) H.; m. Mary Elizabeth Clinkscales, Oct. 15, 1966; children: Kenneth Wayne Jr., Lisa Renée. BS, Drexel U., 1968; MS, U. N.C., 1969, PhD, 1974. Staff physicist Oak Ridge (Tenn.) Nat. Labs., 1976-78; prin. rsch. physicist Princeton U., 1978—. Co-author 262 articles for profl. jours. Mem. Am. Phys. Soc. Avocation: piano. Home: 2651 Princeton Pike Lawrenceville NJ 08648-3639 Office: Plasma Physics Lab Princeton U PO Box 451 MS 15 Princeton NJ 08543-0451 E-mail: hill@pppl.gov.

HILL, KENT RICHMOND, federal agency administrator; b. Nampa, Idaho, May 24, 1949; s. Double E. and Helen Louise (Robertson) H.; m. Janice Elaine Hurn, June 12, 1972; children: Jennifer Lynn, Jonathan Kent. BA in History, N.W. Nazarene Coll., 1971; diploma for basic Russian lang., Def. Lang. inst., 1972; postgrad., Georgetown U., 1973-74; MA in Russian and East European Studies, U. Wash., 1976, PhD in History, 1980. Teaching asst. in history N.W. Nazarene Coll., Nampa, Idaho, 1969-71; Russian translator U.S. Army, 1972-74; teaching asst. in history of Christianity U. Wash., Seattle, 1980, asst. prof. history, 1980-85; assoc. prof. history Seattle Pacific U., 1985-86; pres. Inst. on Religion and Democracy, Washington, 1986-92, Ea. Nazarene Coll., Quincy, Mass., 1992—2001; asst. adminr. bur. for Europe and Eurasia USAID, Washington, 2001—. Interviews, speaker, presenter in field. Author: The Puzzle of the Soviet Church: An Inside Look at Christianity and Glasnost, 1989, Turbulent Times for the Soviet Church, 1991, The Soviet Union on the Brink, 1991; contbr. articles to profl. publs. Bd. dirs. Peter Deyneka Russian Ministries, 1991-2001, Keston Coll., 1985-2001; mem. nat. exec. bd. World Without War Coun., Berkeley, Calif., 1986-2001; bd. advisors Inst. on Religion and Democracy, 1984-86, bd. dirs., 1993-2001; mem. ch. bd. 1st Ch. of Nazarene, Seattle, 1980-85; bd. trustees Russian-Am. Christian U., Moscow, 1998-2000; bd. dirs. Quincy Hist. Soc., 1997-2000. Named Alumnus of Yr., N.W. Nazarene Coll., 1988, to Presdl. Leadership list John Templeton Found., 1999; presented with Key to City, Mayor of City of Nampa, 1983; named Prof. of Yr. Seattle Pacific U., 1986; grantee Seattle Pacific U., 1981-82, 82-83, 84, 85, U. Wash., 1979-80; Nat. Def. Fgn. Lang. fellowship, 1976-77, Earhart fellow Internat. Rsch. and Exchs. fellow, 1978; recipient Pushkin award for Outstanding Scholarship, Def. Lang. Inst., 1972. Office: USAID Bur for Europe and Eurasia RRB 1300 Pennsylvania Ave NW Washington DC 20523 Office Fax: 202-216-3057.

HILL, LARKIN PAYNE, real estate company data processing executive; b. Oct. 30, 1954; d. Max Lloyd and Jane Olivia (Evatt) H. Student, Coll. Charleston, 1972-73, U. N.C., 1973. Lic. real estate broker, N.C. Sec., property mgr. Max L. Hill Co., Inc., Charleston, S.C., 1973-75, sec., data processor, 1979-82, v.p. adminstrn., 1982—. Resident mgr. Carolina Apts., Carrboro, N.C., 1975-77; sales assoc., Realtor, Southland Assocs., Chapel Hill, N.C., 1977-78; cons. specifications com. Charleston Trident Multiple Listing Service, 1985. Bd. dirs. Charleston Area Arts Coun., 1992-93; co-chair Beaux Arts Ball, Sch. Arts. Mem. Royal Oak Found., Scottish Soc. Charleston (bd. dirs. 1989-91), Preservation Soc., Charleston Computer Users Group, N.C. Assn. Realtors, Spoleto Festival USA (chmn. auction catalog com. 1990-92). Republican. Methodist. Avocations: reading, crossword puzzles, American Staffordshire Terriers. Home: 7 Riverside Dr Charleston SC 29403-3217 Office: Max L Hill Co Inc 824 Johnnie Dodds Blvd Mount Pleasant SC 29464-3103 E-mail: larkinhill@charleston.net.

HILL, LAURYN, vocalist, actress; b. South Orange, N.J., May 25, 1975; Student, Columbia U. Appeared on TV in serial "As the World Turns"; featured in "Sister Act II; Back in the Habit." Teamed with Prakazrel "Pras" Michel and Wyclef Jean as the Fugees while still in H.S.; trio produced 2 albums: Blunted on Reality, 1994, and The Score, 1996 (17 million copies sold). Solo debut The Miseducation of Lauryn Hill earned 10 Grammy award nominations including Album of the Yr. and Best New Artist; wrote and produced On That Day for gospel artist CeCe Winans; wrote A Rose is Still a Rose for Aretha Franklin album, also directed song's accompanying video, solo album MTV Unplugged N. 2.0, 2002; actress films Sister Act 2: Back in the Habit, 1993, King of the Hill, 1993, Rhyme & Reason, 1997, Hav Plenty, 1997, Restaurant, 1998; television appearances As the World Turns, 1991, Daddy's Girl, 1997. Founder non-profit The Refugee Youth Camp Youth Project. With Fugees received 2 1996 Grammy awards--Best Rap Album for The Score and Best R&B Performance by a Duo or Group With Vocal (Killing Me Softly). Recipient 1999 Grammy awards for Album of Yr., Best New Artist, Best R&B Song, Best R&B Album, Best Female R&B Vocal Performance. Nominated for several awards at 13th Annual Soul Train Music Awards in L.A. Recipient 4 awards (Outstanding New Artist, Outstanding Female Artist, Outstanding Album and NAACP President's award) 30th Annual NAACP Image Awards, Pasadena, Calif., 1999. Other awards include Favorite New Soul/R&B Artist (26th Annual Am. Music Awards), Best New Artist (Danish Grammy Awards), Entertainer of Yr. (Entertainment Weekly), #1 Album of Yr. (Time mag., N.Y. Times), Best R&B Album of 1998 (USA Today), Artist of Yr. (Spin mag.), Artist of Yr. (Details mag.), 3 Rolling Stone Music Awards. Office: Sony Music 550 Madison Ave New York NY 10022-3211

HILL, LAWRENCE SIDNEY, finance educator; b. Gary, Ind., Nov. 10, 1923; m. Evelyn Honig, Mar. 22, 1964; 1 child, Robert J. *His wife, Evelyn Hill, a University of California, Los Angeles, graduate holds Life Credentials in Kindergarten-Primary and General Elementary Education with the Los Angeles Unified School District. Son Robert Jonathan Hill, Esq. BS 1987 University California, Berkeley, J.D. 1990 Loyola Law School, is currently Deputy Public Defender for the County of Los Angeles, California. Prior affiliations: 1995-97, attorney Law Offices of Speiser, Krause, Madole and Cook, 1990-95, Law Office of James H. Barnes, and 1988, Law Office of Charles E. Clark. Also, 1986 intern for Office of Assemblyman Gray Davis, Sacramento, California.* BSE, Purdue U., 1947; MBA, U. So. Calif., 1960, MSIE, 1962, Engr. I.E., 1965, PhD, 1968. Registered profl. engr., Calif. Asst. indsl. engr. USX Corp., Gary, 1947, indsl. engr., 1951-52; indsl. hygiene engr. Ill. Dept. Pub. Health, Chgo., 1948-51; sr. engr. Nat. Safety Coun., Chgo., 1953; sr. indsl. engr. Martin Marietta Co., Balt., 1953-55; group head McDonnell Douglas Co., Santa Monica, Calif., 1955-57; sr. mem. staff Rand Corp., Santa Monica, 1957-71; prof. mgmt. Calif. State U., L.A., 1969—; cons., prin. engr. Ralph M. Parsons Co., Pasadena, Calif., 1973-82; cons., sr. mem. tech. staff TRW Inc., Redondo Beach, Calif., 1982-90; cons., environ. mgr. USN, Long Beach, Calif., 1991-94. Lectr. U. So. Calif., 1964—70; vis. lectr. Ops. Rsch. Soc. Am./Inst. Mgmt. Scis., 1973—95; expert witness in safety, mgmt., 1986—. Contbr. articles to profl. jours., chapters to books. Mem.: Alpha Iota Delta, Alpha Pi Mu. Avocation: sports. Home: 3653 Oceanhill Way Malibu CA 90265-5637

HILL, LEAH AILEEN, law educator, consultant; d. Hector Warren and Robbie Hill; 1 child, Maya Ny-aya Peart-Hill. BA, Bklyn. (N.Y.) Coll., 1982; JD, Rutgers U., 1985. Bar: U.S. Dist. Ct. (so. and ea. dists.) N.Y. 1993, U.S. Supreme Ct. (2d cir.) N.Y. 1987, U.S. Supreme Ct. 1993. Atty. Legal Svcs. N.Y.C., 1985—90; atty. Civil Divsn. The Legal Aid Soc., N.Y.C., 1990—95; acting asst. clin. prof. Sch. Law NYU, 1995—96, supervising atty., 1995—96; assoc. clin. prof. Sch. Law Fordham U., N.Y.C., 1996—. Mem. adv. bd. Violent Crimes Against Women on Campuses Tech. Assistance Program, Sacramento, 1999—2003. Fellow, Reginald Haber Smith Found., 1985. Mem.: ABA (assoc.), Assn. of Am. Law Schs. (assoc.), Assn. of the Bar of the City of N.Y. (assoc.). Office: Fordham University School of Law 33 West 60th Street New York NY 10023

HILL, LEDA KATHERINE, librarian; b. Bklyn., Feb. 16, 1952; d. David and Leda Louise (Jones) H. BA, Bklyn. Coll., 1974, MS in Edn., 1989; MLS, Queens (N.Y.) Coll., 1995. New bus. cood. INAC Corp., Cranford, N.J., 1974-80; paralegal Orgn. Women for Legal Awareness, Inc., East Orange, N.J., 1980-83; tchr. Roselle (N.J.) Bd. Edn., 1983-84; libr., tchr. N.Y.C. Bd. Edn., Bklyn., 1985—. Mem. ALA, Bklyn. Reading Coun., N.Y.C. Sch. Librs. Assn., N.Y. Libr. Assn., Am. Assn. Sch. Librs. Office: Middle School 2 655 Parkside Ave Brooklyn NY 11226-1505

HILL, LEWIS REUBEN, horticulturist, nursery owner, author; b. Greensboro, Vt., July 1, 1924; s. Alvah Aaron and Grace Gibson (Towle) H.; m. Nancy May Davis, May 4, 1969. High sch. grad., Greensboro, Vt. Owner, mgr. Hillcrest Nursery, Greensboro, 1947-82, Vermont Daylilies, Greensboro, 1982-93, Berryhill Nursery, Greensboro, 1993—. Author: Fruits and Berries for the Home Garden, 1977, Pruning Simplified, 1979, Cold Climate Gardening, 1981, Secrets of Plant Propagation, 1985, Yankee Summer, 2000; co-author (with Nancy Hill): Country Living, 1987, Successful Perennial Gardening, 1988, Christmas Trees, 1989, Fetched Up Yankee, 1990, Daylilies, The Perfect Perennial, 1991, Bulbs-Four Seasons of Beautiful Blooms, 1994, Pruning Made Easy, 1997, Lawns, Grasses & Groundcovers, 1995, The Lawn and Garden Owners Manual, 2000, The Flower Gardener's Bible, 2003; (with others) Berries, 1991, Vines, 1992, Wise Garden Encyclopedia, 1997, 1990 edit., Vermont Voices, 1991, others; contbr. numerous articles to gardening publs. Del. State Rep. Conv. twice; various town offices and coms. Recipient Disting. Svc. award for youth work Vt. Edn. Assn., 1967, Gov's Commn. on Children and Youth, Montpelier, Vt., 1970; 4-H citation Nat. Extension Svc., Washington, 1974; cert. of appreciation Ea. Nurserymen's Assn., Montpelier, 1982; Lit. Excellence award Greensboro Libr., 1990, Vt. Horticulture Achievement award Vt. Profl. Horticulturists, 1993, Quill and Trowel award Garden Writers of Am., 1995. Mem. League Vt. Writers, Vt. Profl. Horticulturists (bd. dirs., pres.),Internat. Ribes Assn. Mem. United Ch. Avocations: photography, skiing, motorcycling, nature. Home and Office: Hillcrest Farm 353 Hillcrest Rd Greensboro VT 05841 E-mail: hillnl@vtlink.net. *Nancy and I think having a goal, and always keeping it in mind, is important, whether it is developing a new plant or a book.*

HILL, LORIE ELIZABETH, psychotherapist; b. Buffalo, Oct. 21, 1946; d. Graham and Elizabeth Helen (Salm) H. Student, U. Manchester, Eng., 1966-67; BA, Grinnell Coll., 1968, MA, U. Wis., 1970, Calif. State U., Sonoma, 1974; PhD, Wright Inst., 1980. Instr. English U. Mo., 1970-71; adminstr., supr. Antioch-West and Ctr. for Ind. Living, San Francisco, Berkeley, 1975-77; dir. tng. Ctr. for Edn. and Mental Health, San Francisco, 1977-80, exec. dir., 1980-81; pvt. practice Berkeley and Oakland, Calif., 1976—; instr. master's program in psychology John F. Kennedy U., Orinda, Calif., 1985, 94—. Founder group of psychotherapists against racism; spkr. on cross-cultural psychology; creater Jump Start, a violence prevention and unlearning racism program for youth; trainer for trainers 3rd Internat. Conf. Conflict Resolution, St. Petersburg, Russia; sr. facilitator Color of Fear. Organizer against nuclear war; founding mem. Psychotherapists for Social Responsibility; psychologist Big Bros. and Big Sisters of the East Bay, 1986-88; vol. instr. City of Oakland Youth Skills Devel. Program; active Rainbow Coalition for Jesse Jackson's Presdl. Campaign, Ron Dellums Re-election Com.; campaigner for Clinton-Gore; founder, dir. Providing Alternatives to Violence; creator JumpStart program; co-founder Wellstone Progressive Dem. Club, 2003. Mem. Calif. Psychol. Assn. (chairperson pub. interest divsn. 1997, Helen Margulies Mehr Pub. Svc. award 1996, chair social issues 1996—, Silver Psi award 1999), Wellstone Dem. Renewal Club (co-founder). Democrat-Socialist. Avocations: sports, travel, music, reading. Office: 2955 Shattuck Ave Berkeley CA 94705-1808

HILL, LOUIS ALLEN, JR., former university dean, consultant; b. Okemah, Okla., May 18, 1927; s. Louis Allen and Gladys Adelia (Dietrich) Hill Wise; m. Jeanne Rose Murray, June 14, 1951; children: Dawn, David, Dixon. BA, Okla. State U., 1949, BSC.E., 1954, MSC.E., 1955; PhD, Case Inst. Tech., 1965. Registered profl. engr., Okla., Ariz. Engr. Lee Hendricks Engring., Tulsa, 1955-57, Hudgins, Thompson, Ball & Assocs., Oklahoma City, 1957-58; asst. prof. civil engring. Ariz. State U., 1958-66, assoc. prof., 1966-70, prof., 1970-74, chmn. dept. civil engring., 1974-81; dean Coll. Engring. U. Akron, 1981-88, assoc. v.p. rsch. and grad. studies, 1988. Chmn. Ohio Engring. Dean's Council, 1983-85; trustee Engring. Found. of Ohio, 1985-88; staff engr. Salt River Project, Ariz., 1962; cons. in field. Author: Fundamentals of Structures, 1975, Compendium of Structural Aids, 1975, Structured Programming in Fortran, 1981; contbr. numerous articles to profl. jours.; designer numerous bridges, hwys. Ch. leader-tchr. 1st Bapt. Ch., 1971-88, Scottsdale Presbyn. Ch., 1990—. Served to capt. C.E., U.S. Army, 1945-47, 51-53, The Philippines, Japan. Recipient Disting. award Akron Coun. Engring. and Sci. Socs., 1987, commendation Minorities in Mainstream Tech. Com., 1990, Disting. Svc. award U. Akron Coll. Engring., 1994; named Educator of Yr., Inroads N.E. Ohio, Inc., 1986, Sr. Svc. award Presbytery of Grand Canyon, 2001; Louis A. Hill Jr. award established in his honor Qua Tech., 1987, Mayor Plusquellic proclaimed April 23, 1997 as Dr. Louis A. Hill Day in City of Akron; fellow Continental Oil Co., 1955, faculty fellow NSF, 1963. Fellow ASCE (life); mem. NSPE (sec., profl. engr. in edn. 1986-88), Am. Soc. Enging. Edn. (life, Western Electric Fund award 1967), Sigma Xi, Tau Beta Pi, Omicron Delta Kappa. Republican. Home and Office: 3208 N 81st Pl Scottsdale AZ 85251-5800

HILL, LOWELL DEAN, agricultural marketing educator; b. Delta, Iowa, Apr. 27, 1930; s. Frederick Carl and Harriet Jane (Atwood) H.; m. Betty Elaine Carpenter, Dec. 9, 1951; children: Rebecca Elaine, Brent Howard. BS in Agrl. Edn., Iowa State U., 1951; MS in Agrl. Econs., Mich. State U., 1961, PhD in Agrl. Econs., 1963. Asst. prof., then assoc. prof. dept. agrl. econs. U. Ill., Urbana, 1963-72, prof., 1972-77, L.J. Norton prof. agrl. mktg., 1977-98, L.J. Norton prof. emeritus, 1998—. Cons. Office Tech. Assessment, Washington, 1986-88, South Am. and Europe, 1995, FAO, Rome, 1978-80, U.S. AID, 1983, World Bank, Washington, 1989-90, 92-93, Argentina, Colombia, Chile, 1989-94, U.S. Feed Grains Coun., Venezuela, Japan, Korea, 1990-93, USDA, Russia, 1993-96; mem. adv. com. Fed. Grain Inspection Svc., USDA, 2000-2003. Author: Grain Grades and Standards: Historical Issues, 1990; editor: Role of Government in a Market Economy, 1982, Corn Quality in World Markets, 1985. Cpl. U.S. Army, 1952-54. Fellow East West Ctr.; recipient Quality of Comm. award, 1980, 88, Disting. Policy Contbr. award 1988, Extension Programs award, 1989, Disting. Svc. award USDA, 1989, Internat. Mktg. Support award Am. Soybean Assn., 1989, Faculty award for rsch. excellence, 1991; Univ. scholar, 1992. Fellow: Am. Agrl. Econ. Assn.; mem.: Coun. Agrl. Sci. and Tech. (chmn. 1989—90), Rotary. Office: Univ Ill Mumford Hall 1301 W Gregory Dr Urbana IL 61801-9015 E-mail: l-hill3@uiuc.edu.

HILL, LUTHER LYONS, JR., lawyer; b. Des Moines, Aug. 21, 1922; s. Luther Lyons and Mary (Hippee) H.; m. Sara S. Carpenter, Aug. 12, 1950; children— Luther Lyons III, Mark Lyons. BA, Williams Coll., 1947; LLB, Harvard U., 1950; LLD (hon.), Simpson Coll., 1979. Bar: Iowa 1951. Law clk. to Justice Hugo L. Black U.S. Supreme Ct., 1950-51; assoc., ptnr. Henry & Henry, Des Moines, 1951-69; mem. legal staff Equitable Life Ins. Co. of Iowa, 1952-87, exec. v.p., 1969-87, gen. counsel, 1970-87; of counsel Nyemaster, Goode, McLaughlin, Voigts, Wiest, Hansell O'Brien, Des Moines, 1992—. Counsel, adminstr. Iowa Life and Health Ins. Guaranty Assn. Bd. dirs., past pres. United Comty. Svcs. Greater Des Moines; past trustee, past chmn. Simpson Coll., Indianola, Iowa. Capt. M.I., AUS, WWII, ETO. Mem. ABA, Iowa Bar Assn., Polk County Bar Assn., Assn. Life Ins. Counsel, Des Moines Club, Wakonda Club. Republican. Avocation: walking in the swiss mountains. Home: 2801 Park Ave Des Moines IA 50321-1515 Office: Ste 1600 700 Walnut St Des Moines IA 50309-3929

HILL, MACK C. career officer; b. Tampa, Fla. Commd. officer U.S. Army, advanced through grades to brig. gen.; comdg. gen. Madigan Army Med. Ctr./Western Regional Med. Command, Tacoma, 1998-99; chief Med. Svc. Corps, Office Surgeon Gen. U.S. Army, Falls Church, Va., 1999—. Office: Office Surgeon Gen US Army 6 Skyline Pl 5109 Leesburg Pike Falls Church VA 22041-3208 Address: 549 Riviera Dr Tampa FL 33606-3807

HILL, MARIE See DAVIS, MAGGIE

HILL, MARTHA N. community health nurse; b. Boston, July 14, 1943; d. Paul Lawrence Norton and Margaret M. Hagerty; m. Gary S. Hill, June 18, 1966; children: Paul, Justin. Diploma, Johns Hopkins Hosp., Balt., 1964; BSN, The Johns Hopkins U., 1966, PhD, 1987; MSN, U. Pa., 1977. Instr. Johns Hopkins Hosp. Sch. Nursing, assoc. prof.; nurse specialist in hypertension Hosp. of U. Pa., Phila.; now dean Johns Hopkins Univ. Sch. of Nursing, Baltimore, Md., 2002—. Contbr. articles to profl. jours. Recipient Malcolm Alderfer Schweiker award, 1985, Ruth B. Freeman award 1987; fellow Am. Acad. Nursing, 1989. Mem. ANA (rep. to NIH high blood press coord. com.), Am. Heart Assn. Coun. Cardiovascular Nursing (vice-chmn. 1989-91).

HILL, MAY BRAWLEY, art historian; b. Salisbury, N.C., Dec. 10, 1942; d. Boyden and Marguerite Brawley; m. Frederick David Hill, July 12, 1967; children: Marguerite Boyden, Nathaniel. BA, Salem Coll., 1963; MA, Inst. Fine Arts, NYU, 1967; postgrad., CUNY, 1985. Curator Am. Soc. Art Gallery, N.Y.C., 1968-73. Author: Women: An Historical Survey of Women Artists, 1972, Three American Purists: Mason, Miles, von Wiegand, 1975, Dance Image: A Tribute to Serge Diaghelev, 1979, Fidelia Bridges, American Pre-Raphaelite, 1981, The Woman Sculptor: Malvina Hoffman and Her Contemporaries, 1984, Grez Days: Robert Vonnoh in France, 1987, Joellyn Duesberry, 1988, Edward Gobbi: Representative Works 1953-1993, 1994; Grandmother's Garden: The Old-Fashioned American Garden, 1865-1915, 1995, Furnishing the Old-Fashioned Garden: Three Centuries of American Summerhouses, Dovecotes, Fences, Privies, and Pergolas, 1998. Bd. dirs. Warren (Conn.) Land Trust, 1989—; mem. Friends of Hort., Wave Hill, N.Y.,

1993—. Mem. Hort. Soc. N.Y. (bd. dirs. 1997—), Ft. Ticonderosa Assn., Garden Conservancy Fellows, Century Assn. Avocation: gardening. Home: 184 Brick School Rd Warren CT 06754-1424

HILL, MELODIE ANNE, director; b. Cortez, Colo., May 24, 1959; d. DaleWentworth and Lette Belle (Green) Higman; m. Jeffrey A. Hill, Feb. 16, 1985; children: Kevin Patrick, Virginia Laurel. BA in Edn. & Psychology, U. Denver, 1983; MA in Curriculum, Adams State Coll., 1987; MEd in Spl. Edn. Adminstrn., N.Mex. State U., 2000. Reading specialist Kemper Elem. Sch., Cortez, Colo., 1983-85, sci. specialist, 1985-89; faculty Ctrl. Consol. Sch. Dist., Shiprock, N.Mex., 1989—; asst. prin. spl. edn. Tse Bit Ai Mid. Sch.; reading specialist, math and sci. coord. Montezuma Cortez Sch. Dist. Presenter in field, 1995—. Mem. GoodSamaritan Ctr., Cortez, 1990—. NSF grantee, 1990, Los Alamos Nat. Lab. grantee, 1998; Hornbeck scholar, 1983. Mem. ASCD, AAUW, NEA, N.Mex. CEC. Episcopalian. Avocations: hiking, photography, mountain biking, swimming, writing. Office: Ctrl Consol Sch Dist PO Box 1703 Shiprock NM 87420-0280

HILL, MELVIN JAMES, oil company executive; b. Santa Ana, Calif., May 19, 1919; s. Albert Frederick and Alice Lucile (Moody) H.; m. Daphne G. Langston, Mar. 1, 1947; children: Patricia (Mrs. Michael Michalek), Candace A. AB, U. Cal. at Berkeley, 1941. With Western Gulf Oil Co., Calif., 1941-56, Gulf Research & Devel. Co., Harmarville, Pa., 1956-63; with Gulf Oil Corp., Pitts., 1963-75, v.p., 1971-74, sr. v.p., 1974-75, exec. v.p., 1981-84; ret., 1984; pres. Gulf Energy and Minerals Co.-Internat., Houston, 1975-78, Gulf Exploration & Prodn. Co., Pa., 1978-81. Mem. Am. Petroleum Inst., Am. Assn. Petroleum Geologists, Am. Inst. Profl. Geologists, Geol. Soc. Am., Soc. Exploration Geophysicists, Am. Geophys. Union. Home: 970 Aurora Ave Apt F201 Boulder CO 80302

HILL, MILTON KING, JR., retired lawyer; b. Balt., Nov. 29, 1926; s. Milton King and Mary Fusselbaugh (Hall) H.; m. Agnes Ciotti, June 11, 1949; children: Thomas Michael, Milton King, III, Susan Hill. BS in Bus. and Pub. Adminstrn., U. Md., 1950, JD, 1952. Bar: Md. 1952, U.S. Dist. Ct. Md. 1952, U.S. Ct. Appeals (4th cir.) 1952. Assoc. Smith, Somerville & Case, Balt., 1952-55, ptnr., 1955-90; ret. Mem. faculty Md. Hosp. Ednl. Inst. Served with USAF, 1944-46. Fellow Am. Coll. Trial Lawyers, Internat. Soc. Barristers; mem. Md. State Bar Assn., Md. Bar Assn., Nat. Conf. Commrs. Uniform State Laws (pres. 1981-83, chmn. model punitive damages act drafting com.), Assn. Def. Trial Counsel (pres. 1964-65), Internat. Assn. Ins. Counsel, ABA (ho. of dels. 1981-83), Md. Bar Found., Am. Acad. Hosp. Attys. Clubs: Potapskut Sailing Assn., Wednesday Law. Home: 8810 Walther Blvd Apt 2329 Parkville MD 21234-5762 E-mail: khill2329@comcast.net.

HILL, NICHOLAS SNOWDEN, physician, researcher, educator; b. Troy, N.Y., Dec. 27, 1949; s. Nicholas Snowden IV and Barbarba Charlotte (Seim) H.; m. Sophia Paraskos, Aug. 16, 1975; children: Kyra, Alyssa. AB, Harvard U., 1971; MD, Dartmouth Coll., 1975. Diplomate Am. Bd. Internal Medicine. Asst. prof. medicine Tufts U., Boston, 1982—87; assoc. prof. medicine Brown U., Providence, 1987-94, prof. medicine, 1994—2002, Tufts U., Boston, 2002; chief, pulmonary critical care and sleep divsn. Tufts-New England Med. Ctr., Boston. Contbr. articles to Jour. Applied Physiology; mem. editl. bd. Chronic Respiratory Failure. Recipient Disting. Scholar award, Chest Found., 2002; Parker B. Francis fellow, PFB Found., 1983. Fellow Am. Coll. Chest Physicians; mem. Am. Thoracic Soc., Mass. Thoracic Surgery (councilor Boston chpt. 1983-87), Am. Physiology Soc., Am. Jour. Respiratory Critical Care Medicine (edit. bd.). Achievements include research in respiratory physiology, hypoxia, and respiratory failure; noninvasive ventilation, pulmonary hypertension. Office: Tufts New Engl Med Ctr 750 Washington St No 257 Boston MA 02111

HILL, NILS ARVID, artist, educator; b. New York, Ny, July 7, 1949; s. Frederick Alexander and Edith M. (Meyer) Hill; m. Ivy Dachman, June 19, 1977; m. Judith Gregory (div.); 1 child, Ian Wesley. MFA, Ind. U., 1971—73; BFA, Phila. Coll. of Art, 1967—71. Permanent Certification, Art NY State Edn. Dept., 1991. Tchr. of art BOCES So. Westchester, North White Plains, NY, 1988—. Exhibitions include Tenth Anniversary Exhbn. Noho Gallery, NYC, 1985, exhibitions include 1,2,3 Progressions, 1980, exhibitions include Nine Artists, 1982, one-man shows include Exhibitions, 1981—82, exhibitions include In Search of the Spirit The Gallery at Hastings-on-Hudson, Hastings -on-the Hudson, NY, 1994, exhibitions include Group Exhbn. Waterside Art Studios, Stamford, Conn., 1992, exhibitions include Neighbors, Artists of Westhchester and So. Conn. Krasdale Foods Gallery, White Plains, NY, 1992, exhibitions include Dark Cool and Personal: Four Views Garrison Art Ctr., Garrison, NY, 1992, exhibitions include Neo Geo in Peekskill Paramount Ctr. for the Arts, Peekskill, NY, 1991, exhibitions include Brandreth Studios, Plus Two Old Libr. Art Ctr.., Westport, Conn., 1989, exhibitions include Painting and Scupture Annual The Berkshire Art Mus., Pittsfield, Mass., 1989, exhibitions include Rebirth Pamela Stockwell Gallery, NYC, 1988, exhibitions include Transformations, The No. Westchester Ctr. for the Arts, Goldens Bridge, NY, 1986, exhibitions include The Beautiful Object Phila. Coll. of Art, 1976, exhibitions include The Size Show The Arts Exchange, White Plains, NY, 2001, exhibitions include Invitational Exhibit, 2000, exhibitions include Soho 20 and Friends, A Salon Exhibition Soho 20, NYC, 1998, exhibitions include Abstract Morphology Pace Univ., Pleasantville, NY, 1996, exhibitions include All of Piece Katonah Mus. of Art, Katatonah, NY, 1995, exhibitions include Ossining Area Artists Rye Art Ctr., Rye, NY, 1989, exhibitions include Fantasy in Form Rye Arts Ctr., 1995, one-man shows include exhibitions Noho Gallery, NYC, 1985. Fellow Position of Assoc. Instr., Fine Arts Dept., Ind. U., 1972-1973. Home: 8 1/2 Narragansett Ave Ossining NY 10562 Personal E-mail: arvid@aol, com.

HILL, NORMA LOUISE, librarian; b. Somerville, Mass., Oct. 27; d. Southern G. and Marguerite M. (Smith) Smallwood; m. George Forris Hill, Dec. 30, 1954; children: Gregory Harrison, Jonathan Smallwood. AB, Wheaton Coll., 1952; MS in Libr. Sci., Our Lady of the Lake Coll., 1975; postgrad., Harvard U., 1994. Grad. asst. Our Lady of the Lake Coll., San Antonio, 1974-75; libr. Cmty. Guidance Ctr., San Antonio, 1975; 86th tactical fighter wing 86th Tactical Fighter Wing, Ramstein, Fed. Republic Germany, 1976-79; info. mgmt. specialist Exec. Office of the Pres., Washington, 1980; dept. head Howard County (Md.) Libr., 1980-81, asst. dir., 1981—96, dir., 1996—2001, dir. emeritus, 2001—, cons., 2001—. Del. Gov.'s. Conf. on Libr. and Info. Sci., 1991. Mem. Friends of the Howard County Libr., Howard County Literacy Coalition, 1984, Md. Adv. Coun. on Librs., 1987—88; mem. adv. bd. State Libr. Resource Ctr., 1986—88, mem. network planning and resource sharing task force, 1988—89; mem. adv. bd. Johns Hopkins U. Columbia Ctr., 1994—2001; mem. cmty. rels. coun. Howard County Gen. Hosp., 1995—2001; mem. Leadership Howard County, 1991—2000, Bd. Health Improvement, 1996—99; mem. adv. bd. Healthy Families Howard County, 1998—2001; bd. dirs. Columbia Found., 1992—98, sec., 1994—98; bd. dirs. Howard County Housing Alliance, 1992—93, Equal Bus. Opportunity Commn., 1996—2001; mem. Commn. for Women, 2001—, vice-chmn., 2003—; chair Howard County Gen. Hosp. Aux., 2001—02. Recipient Insp. Gen. Spl. Achievement award USAF, 1977, 78. Mem. Md. Assn. Pub. Libr. Adminstrs., Md. Libr. Assn. (hon. mem., chair nominations com. 1984-85, co-chmn. fed. rels. subcom. 1985-86, 1st v.p., pres.-elect 1986-87, pres. 1987-88, exec. bd. 1988-89, chair awards com. 1991, legis. com. 1997-2001, award 1993), ALA (pub. libr. divsn., nominations com. 1989-90), Pub. Libr. Assn., NAFE, Leadership Howard County, Nat. Coun. of Negro Women, Alpha Kappa Alpha. Democrat. E-mail: no.hill@comcast.net.

HILL, PATRICIA FRANCINE, information services executive; b. Buffalo, Jan. 9, 1955; d. Walter W. and M. Phyllis (Jones) H. BA in Math., BS in Engring., Swarthmore Coll., 1977; MS in Computer Engring., U. Mich., 1980; MBA, Harvard U., 1990. Tech. staff AT&T Bells Labs., Middletown, NJ, 1980-86; sr. systems analyst Internat. MarketNet (IMNET), N.Y.C., 1986, Marine Midland Bank, N.Y.C., 1987-88; sr. bus. cons. Kraft Gen. Foods, Skokie, Ill., 1990—92; dir. support svcs. Hyatt Hotel Corp., Chgo., 1993-94; mng. prin. Oracle Corp., 1995-96; cons. Ameritech, Chgo., 1996—2003; analyst Motorola Corp., Ill., 2003—. Cons. McDonald's Corp., Oakbrook, Ill., 1992-93; lectr. in field. Active various charitable orgns. Mem. Nat. Assn. Negro Bus. and Profl. Women, Nat. Tech. Assn. Democrat. Mem. Ch. of Christ. Avocation: athletics.

HILL, PATRICIA JO, workforce development specialist; b. Muncie, Ind., Oct. 28, 1944; d. Frederic Burnside and Elizabeth Becom (Zaring) Harbottle; widowed; 1 son, Thomas Frederic. BS, Ball State U., 1964, MA, 1978, EdS, 1981. Cert. EMT, nat. pharmacy technician. Instr., head immunology dept. Ball Meml. Hosp., Muncie, 1963-74; tchr. emotionally disturbed Indpls. Pub. Schs., 1974-75, lead tchr. severe/profound mentally retarded, 1979-84, media specialist in spl. edn., 1984-86, tchr. moderately mentally handicapped, 1986-87, tchr. mildly mentally handicapped, 1987-93, cross categorical spl. edn. tchr., 1993-2000; ret.; pharmacy technician Walgreens, Indpls., 2000—01; pvt. contractor Social Security Adminstrn. Ticket-to-Work Program. Seminar presenter Ind. State Prevent Child Abuse Conf., 1998; participant Leadership Series between C. of C. and Inpls. Pub. Schs., Area 15 Spl. Olympics Coach. Black history liaison Ind. Chpt. Prevention Child Abuse; chair Indy PAC, instnl. and profl. devel. com.; vol. first aid team, disaster team ARC; vol. Protect the Promise Coalition; med. vol. Sr. Action Coalition, 2001—; del. Ind. State Rep. Convention, Rep. Leadership conf. for Midwestern States, 1997; staff to elect 10th Dist. Rep. Congresswoman Virginia Blankenbaker, 1998; media rels. Indpls. Americans United for Separation of Ch. and State, 2001—; public rels. Angel Flight, Ctrl. Ind. Wing, Angel Flight Am., 2001—. NSF grant, 1961; Shroyer scholar Mchts. Nat. Bank Muncie, 1972, Indpls. Pub. Schs. scholar, 1981. Mem. Assn. Behavioral Analysts, Coun. Exceptional Children (med. and health problems), Ind. State Tchrs. Assn. (ret. bd. rep., spl. edn. com.), Indpls. Edn. Assn. (exec. bd., sec. 1997-2000), Greater Indpls. Rep. Women,, Indpls. C. of C., Ind. C. of C. (workforce develop com., K-12 com.), Ind. BBB, Internat. Assn. Rehab. Profls. Methodist. Home: 7330 Scarborough Blvd East Dr Indianapolis IN 46256-2053 E-mail: patricia.j.hill@att.net.

HILL, PAUL MARK, clergyman; b. Cin., Aug. 29, 1953; s. Paul Frederick and Helen Faith (Skeen) H.; m. Rebecca Sue Helm, Dec. 29, 1977; children: Aaron Israel Paul, Revkah Lauren Amara, Hadassah Sue Elizabeth. BA in Biology, Asbury Coll., 1975; DivM, Anderson Sch. Theology, 1981; D of Min, Covenant Theol. Sem., 2002. Ordained to ministry Meth. Ch., 1984. Sr. pastor United Meth. Ch., Marion, Ind., 1978—, camp dir., 1990—. Speaker and lectr. in field. Dir. TV show Offer Them Christ, 1986; reprodn. furniture designer and craftsman, 1989. Actor Civic Theater, Logansport, Ind., 1981-82, Peru Civic Theater, 1981-82; coach baseball, basketball, soccer, Marion, Ind., 1986-89; baseball coach, Lafayette, Ind., 1995; organizer, dir. Stockwell Youth Orch., 1990; coach basketball, Lafayette, Ind., 1993-95. Named to Outstanding Young Men of Am., 1988. Avocations: basketball, skiing, wood working, running, baseball. E-mail: mark519@msn.com.

HILL, PEGGY SUE, principal; b. Roswell, N.Mex., Aug. 4, 1953; d. Cecil Vecoe and Edith Augustine (Raney) H. BS, U. Ark., 1978, MEd, 1982; EdS, 1994. Cert. elem. prin., tchr. music and libr. Music tchr., K-6 Springdale (Ark.) Schs., 1978-83, elem. prin., 1983-98, tech. coord., 1998—, coord. for curriculum, instrn., assessment and tech. Named Outstanding Young Educator Springdale Jaycees, 1983, Prin. of Ark. Exemplary Sch., Ark. Dept. Edn., 1989-90, 91-92, 93-94; recipient nat. award for teaching of econs. Joint Coun. Econ. Edn., 1990, 91, 92, 94. Mem. ASCD, Internat. Reading Assn., Ark. Assn. Edn. Administrs., Ark. Assn. Elem. Sch. Prins., (presenter conf. 1990), Phi Delta kappa (Outstanding Administr. award 1991). Office: Springdale Schs PO Box 8 Springdale AR 72765-0008

HILL, PHILIP, retired lawyer; b. East Saint Louis, Ill., Mar. 13, 1917; s. Nehemiah William and Lulu Myrtle (Johnson) H.; m. Betty Jean Stone, July 4, 1942; children: William Stone, Thomas Chapman, Nancy Layton, Mary Anne. AB in Chemistry, U. Ill., 1937; PhD in Chemistry, Ohio State U., 1941; JD, John Marshall Law Sch., Chgo., 1968. Bar: Ill. 1968, U.S. Patent Office 1969, U.S. Ct. Appeals (fed. cir.) 1982. With Standard Oil Co. Ind., 1941-78, patent atty., 1969-73, dir. petroleum and corp. patents and licensing, 1973-78; ptnr. Hill & Hill, Lansing, Ill., 1978-86; pvt. practice law Philip Hill, P.C., 1987-96; ret., 1996. Cons. Univ. Patents, Inc., Norwalk, Conn., 1980-89; treas. Am. Waste Reduction Corp., 1992-96. Contbr. articles to profl. jours.; patentee in field. Mem.: Am. Chem. Soc., Am. Intellectual Property Law Assn., Ill. State Bar Assn., AAAS, ABA, Kiwanis (Lansing, pres. 1959, 84), Sigma Xi, Phi Beta Kappa. Methodist. Home: 17946 Chicago Ave Lansing IL 60438-2261 Office: PO Box 187 Lansing IL 60438-0187

HILL, PHILIP BONNER, lawyer; b. Charleston, W.Va., May 1, 1931; AB, Princeton U., 1952; LLB, W.Va. U., 1957. Bar: W.Va. 1957, Iowa 1965. Assoc. Dayton, Campbell & Love, Charleston, W.Va., 1957-61; ptnr. Porter, Hill, Thomas, Williams & Hubbard, Charleston, 1961-65; v.p. Thomas & Hill, Charleston, 1961-65; assoc. counsel Equitable Life Ins. Co. of Iowa, Des Moines, 1965-68, counsel, 1968-75; ptnr. Riemenschneider, Hanes & Hill, Des Moines, 1975-79, Austin & Gaudineer, Des Moines, 1979-82, Snyder & Hassig, Sistersville and New Martinsville, W.Va., 1982-96, of counsel, 1997-99, Bowles Rice McDavid Graff & Love, PLLC, Martinsburg, W.Va., 2000—. Mem. staff W.Va. Law Rev., 1955-57; contbr. articles to profl. jours. Lt. USNR, 1952-54. Fellow W.Va. Bar Found.; mem. ABA (exec. coun. young lawyers sect. 1966-67), W.Va. State Bar (chmn. jr. bar sect. 1961-62, bd. govs. 1989-92), W.Va. Bar Assn. (pres. 1998-99), Iowa State Bar Assn., Assn. Life Ins. Counsel, Am. Land Title Assn., Am. Judicature Soc., Phi Delta Phi. Office: Bowles Rice McDavid Graff & Love PLLC PO Drawer 1419 101 S Queen St Martinsburg WV 25402-1419

HILL, RAYMOND JOSEPH, packaging company executive; b. Chanute, Kans., May 4, 1935; s. Raymond Joseph and Emma Leona (Arthurs) Hill; m. Bettie Anne Handshumaker, Mar. 2, 1957; children: David, Dianne, Todd, Scott, Jennifer. A in Engring., Coffeyville (Kans.) Coll., 1955; MBA, U. Denver, 1977. Field engr. Phillips Petroleum Co., Bartlesville, Okla., 1957—59; design engr. Thiokol Chem. Corp., Brigham City, Utah, 1959—60; tech. supr. Hercules Chem. Corp., Salt Lake City, 1960—68; project mgr. aerospace div. Ball Corp., Boulder, Colo., 1968—70, plant mgr. and v.p. mfg. metal container div. Findlay, Ohio and Denver, Colo., 1970—78, pres. agrl. systems div. Westminster, Colo., 1978—85, 1990—93; exec. v.p. food plastics N.Am.; pres. Chesnee Assocs., Inc., Internat. Cons., 1993—97; exec. v.p. The PopStraw Co., also bd. dirs.; bd. dirs. Navaho Agrl. Products Industries, United Energy Devel., Packaging Adv. Coun., Flex Packing Assn., The Hallmark Group, Packaging Ptnrs., Classic Signatures, Inc., PopStraw Co.; mem. policy adv. com. to Office of U.S. Trade Rep., 1980—. Mem.: Irrigation Assn., Soc. Tool Engrs., Nat. Food Processors Assn., Am. Ordnance Assn., Rotary. Republican. Episcopalian. Home: 889 Turnbridge Cir Naperville IL 60540-8342 Office: Chesnee Assocs Inc 2010 E Algonquin Rd Ste 210 Schaumburg IL 60173-4168

HILL, RICHARD A. advertising executive; b. Detroit; Student, Mich. State U.; MS in Mktg., Wayne State U. With J. Walter Thompson, Young & Rubicam; media supr. Buick/GMC Truck divsn., assoc. media dir. McCann-Erickson, Troy, Mich., 1970-75, sr. account exec. Buick account, 1975-77, v.p. media, mktg. dir. Detroit, 1977-79, account supr. multi-products group, 1979-81, account supr. Buick, 1981-86, sr. v.p., mgmt. rep., 1986-91, dep. mgr., chmn. mgmt. bd., 1991-93, exec. v.p., gen. mgr., 1993-97, dir. profl. devel., 1997—, also exec. v.p., 1993—. Avocation: golf. Office: McCann-Erickson 755 W Big Beaver Rd Ste 2500 Troy MI 48084-0230

HILL, RICHARD EARL, academic administrator; b. Clintonville, Wis., Mar. 30, 1929; s. Lyle Earl and Gladness Josephine (Love) H.; m. Marilyn Jean Thompson, June 5, 1951; children: Mark R., Kenneth L., Richard Earl, Joy A., Sarah J. BA, Carroll Coll., Waukesha, Wis., 1951, L.H.D., 1974; M.Div., McCormick Theol. Sem., 1956. Ordained to ministry Presbyterian Ch., 1956; pastor chs. in Wis., 1955-62; pastor Frame Meml. Presbyn. Ch., Stevens Point, Wis.; also univ. pastor U. Wis., Stevens Point, 1962-69; asst. to pres. Carroll Coll., 1969-74; pres. Huron (S.D.) Coll., 1974-77, Lakeland Coll., Sheboygan, Wis., 1977-89, pres. emeritus, 1991—, chancellor, 1989-91. Pres. S.D. Fedn. Pvt. Colls., 1977; exec. com. Colls. Mid-Am., 1975-77; mem. 6th Congl. Dist. Acad. Selection Com., 1978-89; v.p. Wis. Found. Ind. Colls., 1983-85, pres., 1985-86. Mem. Am. Assn. Colls., Council Advancement and Support Small Colls., Council Advancement and Support Edn., Wis. Assn. Ind. Colls. and Univs. (pres. 1980-83), Am. Mgmt. Assn., Sheboygan Econ. Club (pres. 1985), Pi Kappa Delta, Pi Gamma Mu. Clubs: Rotary. Address: 23033 Westchester Blvd Apt C-404 Port Charlotte FL 33980

HILL, RICHARD WARREN, lawyer; b. Orange, N.J., Sept. 10, 1941; s. Warren and Grace Elizabeth (Kerr) Hill; m. Valerie Loy, Aug. 7, 1964. A.B., Colgate U., 1963; J.D., Rutgers U., 1966. Bar: U.S. Dist. Ct. N.J. 1966, U.S. Ct. Appeals (3d cir.) 1967, N.J. 1966. Law clk. to judge U.S. Circuit Ct., 1966-67; assoc. McCarter & English, Newark, 1967-71; asst. U.S. atty. Dist. N.J., 1971-75, U.S. bankruptcy judge, 1975-84; ptnr. McCarter & English, Newark, 1984— . Mem. ABA, N.J. Bar Assn., Assn. Fed. Bar N.J. Office: Four Gateway Center McCarter & English 100 Mulberry St Newark NJ 07102-4004

HILL, RICK ALLAN, former congressman; b. Grand Rapids, Minn., Dec. 30, 1946; m. Betti Christie, June 10, 1983; children: Todd, Corey, Mike. BA in Econs. and Polit. Sci., St. Cloud State U., 1968. Surety bonding businessman, owner InsureWest, 1968-90; real estate and investment ptnr., 1983—; committeeman State Rep. Party, 1990-94; legis. liaison to Gov. Marc Racicot, Mont., 1993; mem. 105th-106th Congress from Mont. dist. U.S. Ho. Reps., Washington, 1997-2001, mem. banking and fin. svcs. com., mem. resources com., mem. small bus. com. Fin. chair State Rep. Party, 1989-91, state chair, 1991-92. Bd. dirs. Mont. Sci. and Tech. Alliance, 1992. Republican.*

HILL, ROBERT F. lawyer; b. Clarinda, Iowa, Mar. 5, 1945; s. Gordon and Irma M. Hill; m. Laura L. Hill; children: Kristine, Lisa, Catherine. BA, U. Nebr., 1967; JD, U. Colo., 1970. Bar: Calif. 1971, DC 1971, Colo. 1975, U.S. Supreme Ct. 1975. Law clk. to Hon. Warren J. Ferguson U.S. Dist. Ct., L.A., Calif., 1970-71; assoc. Covington & Burling, Washington, 1971-74; staff atty. Neighborhood Legal Svcs. Prog., Washington, 1973; vis. assoc. prof. law U. Colo., Boulder, 1974-75; 1st asst. atty. gen. Antitrust Sect., State of Colo., Denver, 1975-78; founding ptnr. Hill & Robbins, P.C., Denver, 1978—. Co-editor-in-chief: U. Colo. Law Rev., 1969—70. Mem. com. conduct U.S. Dist. Ct., 1998—, chmn., 2002—; founding mem. bd. dirs. Project Safeguard, 1981—83; pres. bd. dirs. Tech. Assistance Ctr., 1984—85; bd. dirs. Colo. Common Cause, 1994—99, L.Am. Rsch. and Svc. Agy., 1994—99; co-founder, co-chmn. bd. dirs. Invest in Kids, 1996—; bd. dirs. Ocean Journey, Colo., 1997—, chmn., 2002—03. Recipient Dunklee award; Storke scholar. Fellow: Colo. Bar Found., Am. Bar Found., Am. Coll. Trial Lawyers; mem.: ABA, Colo. Lawyers Com. (chmn. bd. dirs. 1985—87), Denver Bar Assn., Colo. Bar Assn. (Hoagland award Pro Bono Svc. 1997), Order of Coif. Home: 700 High St Denver CO 80218-3698 Office: Hill & Robbins PC 1441 18th St Ste 100 Denver CO 80202-5932 E-mail: RobertHill@HillandRobbins.com.

HILL, ROBERT FOLWELL, JR., information systems specialist; b. High Point, N.C., July 24, 1946; s. Robert Folwell Sr. and Antilee (Dinkins) H.; Cynthia Hightower, Mar. 5, 1971 (div. Dec. 1977); 1 child, Robert Folwell III; m. Linda Kay Frier Balfour, June 7, 1978. BS in Computer Sci., N.C. State U., 1971. Supr. quality control Mac Panel Computer Tape Co., High Point, N.C., 1965-68; computer programmer U. N.C., Wilmington, 1972-74, programmer, analyst Gen. Adminstrn. Chapel Hill, 1974-79, dir. info. systems Gen. Adminstrn., 1979—. Pres. Triangle chpt. Nat. Found. for Ileitis and Colitis Rsch., Triangle Park, N.C., 1983, treas., 1984, v.p., 1985-88; pres. Crohn's and Colitis Found. Am., 1989-91, v.p. membership, 1991-99; spl. registrar Orange County Bd. Elections, Hillsborough, N.C., 1984; mem. exec. com., mem.-at-large N.C. Vol. Health Agys., 1990, sec., 1991; bd. mem. Combined Health Appeal of N.C., 1991-95, treas. 1993-95. Recipient Mary Ann Mobley Vol. Leadership award, 1996. Mem. Data Processing Mgmt. Assn., N.C. Assn. Instnl. Rsch., State Employees Assn. N.C., Coll. and Univ. Sys. Exch., Nat. Assn. Stock Car Auto Racing, Toastmasters Internat. (v.p. edn.). Democrat. Avocation: auto racing. Home: 5917 Willow Oak Dr Mebane NC 27302-9279 Office: U NC Gen Adminstrn PO Box 2688 Chapel Hill NC 27515-2688 E-mail: rhilljr@mindspring.com.

HILL, RONALD CHARLES, surgeon, educator; b. Parkersburg, W.Va., Sept. 4, 1948; s. Lloyd E. and Margaret (Pepper) H.; m. Lenora Jane Rexrode, June 12, 1971; children: Jeffrey, Mandy. BA, W.Va. U., 1970, MD, 1974. Diplomate Diplomate Am. Bd. Surgery, Am. Bd. Thoracic Surgery. Intern dept. of surgery Duke U. Med. Ctr., Durham, N.C., 1974-75; resident in surgery Duke U., Durham, N.C., 1974-85, rsch. assoc., 1976-79, tchg. scholar, 1984-85; asst. prof. surgery W.Va. U., Morgantown, 1985-90, assoc. prof., 1990-96, prof. surgery, 1996—, clin. prof. surgery Sch. Osteopathic Medicine, 1999—. Cons. VA Med. Ctr., Clarksburg, W.Va., 1985—; dir. surg. rsch. dept. surgery W.Va. U., 1986—88, student coord. dept. surgery, 1986—97; mem. adh hoc com. merit rev. bd. for cardiovasc. studies VA, Washington, 1988—90; mem. Surg. Edn. and Self-Assessment Program '99 Com., Surg. Edn. and Self-Assessment Program #11, Surg. Edn. and Self-Assessment Program #12; chmn. instnl. rev. bd. Protection Human Subjects, 1994—, program chmn. dept. surgery, 1998—2003. Contbr., co-contbr. numerous book chpts. and articles to profl. publs. Mem.-at-large adminstrv. bd. Drummond Chapel United Meth. Ch., Morgantown, 1987—89, 1993—95, fin. com., 1994—96, lay del. to ann. conf., 1995—97, chmn. coun. on evangelism, 1999—2001. Recipient Lange Med. Book award, 1971, 1973, 1974, Roche Med. award, 1972, Merck Med. Book award, 1974, Sowers award, Founders Soc. Duke U., 1992. Fellow ACS (coun. W.Va. chpt. 1999-2001, sec.-treas. 2001-02, 2d v.p. 2002-03, 1st v.p. 2003—, chmn. com. on applicants dist. 1 W.Va.), Southeastern Surg. Congress, Assn. Acad. Surgery, Sabiston Soc., Am. Coll. Cardiology, Am. Coll. Chest Physicians, So. Thoracic Surg. Assn. (program chmn. 1995-96, coun. 1999-2000), Soc. Thoracic Surgeons; mem. Am. Heart Assn., (v.p., pres. elect, pres. W. Va. affiliate 1994-96), Soc. Univ. Surgeons, Am. Assn. Thoracic Surgery, Internat. Surg. Soc., Assn. Programs Dirs. in Surgery, Assn. Surg. Edn., So. Surg. Assn., W.Va. Med. Assn., Mended Hearts, Lakeview Country Club, Pines Country Club, Phi Beta Kappa, Alpha Omega Alpha, Alpha Epsilon Delta, Profl. Assn. Diving Instrs. Soc. (cert. master scuba diver). Republican. Avocations: fishing, photography, scuba diving, shell collecting. Home: 10 Flegal St Morgantown WV 26505-2240 Office: WVa U Med Ctr Dept of Surgery Medical Center Dr Morgantown WV 26506 E-mail: rhill@hsc.wvu.edu.

HILL, RONALD CLAIR, anesthesiologist; b. Salt Lake City, Feb. 11, 1953; AA in Humanities/Spanish, BS in Zoology, Brigham Young U., 1976, MS in Zoology, Physiology, 1980; MD, Tulane U., 1983. Diplomate Am. Bd. Anesthesiology. Intern, then resident in anesthesiology Brooke Army Med. Ctr., Ft. Sam Houston, Tex., 1983-87; pvt. practice Lincoln (Nebr.) Anesthesiology Group; mem. staff St. Elizabeth's Regional Med. Ctr., Lincoln, Nebr. Surg. Ctr., Lincoln, Urology Surg. Ctr., Lincoln. Mem. AMA, Am. Soc. Anesthesiologists, Internat. Anesthesia Rsch. Soc., So. Med. Soc., Soc. Pediat. Anesthesiologists, Soc. Ambulatory Anesthesiologists. Office: Lincoln Anesthesiology Group 575 S 70th St Lincoln NE 68510

HILL, RONALD GUY, SR., non-profit organization consultant; b. Andrews, N.C., Aug. 18, 1934; s. H. Guy and Martha Floriede (Henson) H.; m. Shirley Hendrix, Nov. 15, 1955; children: Ronald Guy Jr., Rebecca, William Felix. BS, U. Nebr., Omaha, 1969; postgrad., Indsl. Coll. Armed Forces, Washington, 1970. Enlisted U.S. Army, 1952, advanced through grades to capt.; comdg. officer 198th Pers. Svc. Co. and 61st Army Band, Fed. Republic Germany, 1967-69; dir. entertainment divsn. U.S. and free world forces, Vietnam, 1969-70; procurement officer Joint Mil. Svcs., Gunter AFB, Ala., 1970-71; exec. Chief Staff Mil. Ops., Washington, 1971-73; ret., 1973; active duty Operation Desert Storm, 1991; county mgr. Cherokee County, Murphy, N.C., 1974-81; mgr. Saudi Corp., Taif, Saudi Arabia, 1981-85; dir. John C. Campbell Folk Sch., Brasstown, N.C., 1985-91; founding dir. Allison's Wells Sch. Arts & Crafts and Small Bus. Incubator for Artists, 1991-96. Founder orphanage, Fed. Republic Germany, 1968, Cherokee County Hist. Mus., 1977; founder, builder 12 community ctrs., Cherokee County, 1976, former mem. bd. dirs. Nat. Assn. Counties; bd. dirs. Western N.C. Assoc. Communities, Smoky Mountain Host N.C., Cherokee County Arts Coun., Western N.C. Tomorrow, Appalachian Consortium, So. Appalachian Highlands Conservancy, Mountain Outdoor Recreation Alliance, SE Tourism Soc.; past mem. Southwestern N.C. Planning and Econ. Devel. Commn.; bd. dirs. John C. Campbell Folk Sch.; also numerous other orgns. Decorated Legion of Merit, Bronze Star; Bravery Gold medal (Greece), Presdl. citation (Republic of Korea), Gallantry Cross (Republic of Vietnam); recipient numerous other medals, badges, letters of appreciation and commendation. Mem. Cerkokee County C. of C., Am. Craft Coun., N.C. Arts Advs., Artists and Blacksmiths Assn. N.Am., Tenn. Artist-Craftsmen's Assn., N.Am. Folk Music and Dance Alliance, Cherokee County Hist. Soc. (past bd. dirs.), Am. Legion, VFW, Ret. Officers Assn., Soc. 3d Inf. Div. U.S.A., Masons

(32 degree), Shriners, SAR. Democrat. Methodist. Avocations: blacksmithing, collecting pottery and antiques, wood carving, genealogy. Address: 2127 Duncan Bridge Rd Sautee Nacoochee GA 30571-3614 E-mail: ronhill@alltelnet.

HILL, RUTH FOELL, language consultant; b. Houston, Sept. 13, 1931; d. Ernest William and Florence Margaret (Kane) Foell; children: Linden Ruth, Andrea Grace. Student, Principia Coll., 1950; BA, U. Calif., Berkeley, 1952; postgrad., San Diego State, 1955, Cen. Piedmont, 1981. Cert. tchr., Calif. Owner, dir. Art Gallery of Chapel Hill (N.C.), 1966-75; ecumenical bd. Campus Ministry, Charlotte; with referral svc. Charlotte (N.C.) Bed and Breakfast Registry, 1980-90; lang. cons. Berlitz Internat., Raleigh, N.C., 1988-91; ESL tchr. Albemarle Elem. Sch., 2000—. Cert. cons. Performax Internat.; rep. UN Decade for Women Conf., NGO Forum, Nairobi, Kenya, 1985, Women and Global Security Conf., 1986; rep. emerging issues forum N.C. State U., 1987-93; presenter Southeastern Women's Studies Conf. Contbr. poetry to Nat. Libr. of Poetry Internat. Hall of Fame. Bd. dirs., chmn. natural resources com. LWV; coord. USIA grant region 6, Internat. Exch. Network; mem. N.C. Leadership Forum, N.C. Citizens Assembly, 1989; chmn. Week of Edn. Pub. Forum on Energy, Union Concerned Scientists, 1990 93; bd. dirs. Nat. Women's Conf. Commn., 1994—; mem. edn. subcom. Mayor's Internat. Cabinet, 1995; mem. Congress House Spkr.'s Citizen Task Force, 1995—; mem. Rep. Platform Com. and Nat. Presdl. Task Force, 1999, Rep. Inner Cir., 1995; mem. edn. com. Charlotte/Mecklenberg Historic Properties, 1986-88; mem. groundwater subcom. Mecklenburg County Commrs., 1987, So. Summit Queen's Coll., 2002. Named Outstanding Athlete Women's Athletic Assn., Woman of the Yr., Am. Biog. Inst., 1994, Internat. Poetry Hall of Fame, 1998; Hewlett Found. scholar. Mem. AAUW (v.p. membership com., bd. dirs.), Ams. for Legal Reform (adv. bd.), Am. Farm Land Trust, UN Assn. U.S.A. (chpt. pres. 1991-93, co-chair UN Day Queens Coll. 1992, N.C. divsn. sec. 1993-94, UN50 chair 1995, So. Summit Queens Coll. 2002), Am. Biog. Inst. Rsch. Assn. (nominated to bd. govs.), Am. Biog. Inst. (apptd. adv. bd.), Carolina Coun. on World Affairs, Chapel Hill-Carrboro Sch. Art Guild (pres.), Midwest Acad., World Wide Women in Environment, N.Y. Acad. Sci. Republican. Christian Scientist. Avocations: travel, environmental issues, international exchange networking. Office: PO Box 220802 Charlotte NC 28222-0802 E-mail: rhill37901@aol.com.

HILL, SHARON A. language educator; b. Arkansas City, Kans., Oct. 28, 1948; d. J. R. and Elene Marie Yarbrough; m. Larry George Hill, May 30, 1985 (dec. July 14, 1999); 1 child, Molly Marie. AA, Cowley Coll., Ark. City, Kans., 1968; BS, Kans. State U., Manhattan, 1970, PhD, 1994; MEd Wichita State U., Kans., 1974. Tchr. speech/English/theatre Wellington Jr. and Sr. H.S., Kans., 1970—75, Arkansas City H.S., Kans., 1975—80; instr. speech/English Cowley Coll., Arkansas City, 1980—97; assoc. prof. English Northwestern Okla. State U., Alva, 1997—. Folio reviewer Okla. Commn. on Tchr. Preparation, Okla. City, 1999—. Lay reader and Eucharistic minister Sacred Heart Cath. Ch., Alva, Okla., 2002. Recipient Nat. Master Tchr. award, Nat. Inst. for Staff Devel., Austin, Tex., 1992. Mem.: Okla. Coun. Tchrs. of English, Nat. Film and History Assn., Phi Delta Kappa. Office: Northwestern Okl State Univ 709 Oklahoma Blvd Alva OK 73717 E-mail: sahill@aloosu.edu.

HILL, STAN WAYNE, video producer; b. Marion, Ill., Dec. 30, 1945; s. Clayal Clint and Okie Magdalene (Rodgers) H.; divorced; children: Amanda C., Kirstan C. BS in Communications, So. Ill. U., 1967; M in Religious Edn., So. Bapt. Thol. Sem., 1969. Producer talk show Sta. WJCL-TV, Savannah, Ga., 1971-72, producer news, 1977-78; pres. Video Media Prodns., Statesboro, Ga., 1975-78; freelance producer Birmingham, Ala., 1978-83; video producer, website mgr. Woman's Missionary Union So. Bapt. Conv., Birmingham, 1983—2001. Mgr. 9 Web sites and 3 e-commerce sites. Exec. prodr. (documentary video) "One Common Need", 1996 (Bronze Telly award 1996, Silver Angel award 1996, Silver medal Houston Internat Film Festival 1996); prodr., dir., writer (video program) Christian Women's Job Corps, 1998 (Silver Angel award 1998, Communicator award 1998); prodr., dir. over 750 shows, sports events; writer, prodr. over 100 ednl. videos. Mem. Media Communicator's Assn. (regional v.p. 1986-88, chpt. pres. 1989-90), Assn. of Ind. Video and Filmmakers, Religion Communicators Coun., Bapt. Communicators Assn., Assn. Internet Profls., Internat. Webmasters Assn. Baptist. Avocations: victorian architecture, science fiction. E-mail: stanlines@att.net.

HILL, STEPHEN L., JR., lawyer, former prosecutor; m. Marianne Matteson; 2 children. BS in Polit. Sci., Southwest Mo. State U., 1981; JD, U. Mo., 1986; postgrad., London U. Staff U.S. Congressman Ike Skelton, 4th dist Mo., 1982; trial atty. Smith, Gill, Fisher & Butts, Kansas City, 1986-94; U.S. atty. Western Dist. Mo., Kansas City, 1993—2001; partner Blackwell Sanders Peper Martin, LLP, Kansas City, Mo., 2001—. Office: Blackwell Sanders Peper Martin LLP Two Pershing Sq 2300 Main St Ste 1000 Kansas City MO 64108 Office Fax: 816-983-8080. E-mail: shill@bspmlaw.com.

HILL, SUSAN SLOAN, safety engineer; b. Quincy, Mass., June 1, 1952; d. Ralph Arnold and Grace Elenore (Sloan) Crosby; m. William Loyd Hill, Dec. 16, 1973 (div. July 1982); m. William Joseph Graham, Sept. 10, 1983 (div. Feb. 1985). AS in Gen. Engring., Motlow State C.C., Tullahoma, Tenn., 1976; BS in Indsl. Engring., Tenn. Technol. U., 1978. Intern, safety engr. Intern Tng. Ctr., U.S. Army, Red River Army Depot, Tex., 1978-79, Field Safety Activity, Charlestown, Ind., 1979, sys. safety engr. Comm.-Electronics Command Ft. Monmouth, N.J., 1979-84, gen. engr., 1984-85; chief sys. safety Arnold Air Force Sta., USAF, Tullahoma, 1985-91; medically ret.; ind. cons. sys. safety, 1991—. Founder Fibromyalgia Support Group; leader Arthritis Found. Support Group; active Arthritis Found. Recipient 5 letters of appreciation, U.S. Army, letter of appreciation, Arthritis Found. Mem. NAFE, Assn. Fed. Safety and Health Profls. (regional v.p. 1980-84), Soc. Women Engrs., Nat. Safety Mgmt. Soc., Am. Soc. Safety Engrs., Sys. Safety Soc., Order Engr. Republican. Episcopalian. Avocations: reading, gardening, walking, cooking, golf. Home and Office: 1307 Bel-Aire Dr Tullahoma TN 37388

HILL, TABITHA KIMBERLY, science educator; b. Feb. 11, 1968; BA in Sociology, U. Md., 1989, BS in Microbiology, 1993; postgrad. in Biomed. Scis., Hood Coll., 1994-99. Instr. sci. Butler Sch., Darnestown, Md., 1994-96, Montgomery County Pub. Schs., Rockville, Md., 1997—. Mem. Montgomery County Young Reps., 1995-99. Mem. AAAS, AAUW, Am. Assn. Microbiology. Republican. Lutheran. Avocations: traveling, boating. Office: Montgomery County Pub Schs Parkland Middle Sch Rockville MD 20906 E-mail: tabhill1@aol.com., tabitha_hill@fc.mcps.k12.md.us.

HILL, TERRELL LESLIE, chemist, biophysicist; b. Oakland, Calif., Dec. 19, 1917; s. George Leslie and Ollie (Moreland) H.; m. Laura Etta Gano, Sept. 23, 1942; children: Julie Lisbeth Eden, Carolyn Jo (Mrs. Gary Lineburg), Ernest Evan. AB, U. Calif. at Berkeley, 1939, PhD, 1942; postgrad., Harvard U., 1940. Instr. chemistry Western Res. U., 1942-44; rsch. assoc. radiation lab. U. Calif. at Berkeley, 1944-45; rsch. assoc. chemistry, then asst. prof. chemistry U. Rochester, 1945-49; chemist U.S. Naval Med. Rsch. Inst., 1949-57; prof. chemistry U. Oreg., 1957-67, U. Calif. at Santa Cruz, 1967-71, adj. prof., 1977-89, prof. emeritus, 1989—, vice chancellor for scis., div. natural scis., 1968-69; research chemist NIH, Bethesda, Md., 1971-88, scientist emeritus, 1988—. Mem. biophysics study sect. USPHS, 1954-57; chemistry panel NSF, 1961-64 Author: Statistical Mechanics, 1956, 87, Statistical Thermodynamics, 1960, 86, Thermodynamics of Small Systems, vol. I, 1963, 94, 2002, vol. II, 1964, 94, 2002, Matter and Equilibrium, 1965, Thermodynamics for Chemists and Biologists, 1968, Free Energy Transduction in Biology, 1977, Cooperativity Theory in Biochemistry, 1985, Linear Aggregation Theory in Cell Biology, 1987, Free Energy Transduction and Biochemical Cycle Kinetics, 1989, also rsch. papers. Guggenheim fellow Yale, 1952-53; recipient Arthur S. Flemming award U.S. Govt., 1954; Distinguished Civilian Service award U.S. Navy, 1955; award Washington Acad. Scis., 1956; Disting. Service award USPHS, 1981; Disting. Service award U. Oreg., 1983; Sloan Found. fellow, 1958-62 Mem Nat. Acad. Scis., Am. Chem. Soc. (Kendall award 1969), Biophys. Soc., NAACP, ACLU, Phi Beta Kappa. Home: 3400 Paul Sweet Rd Apt C220 Santa Cruz CA 95065

HILL, THOMAS ALLEN, lawyer; b. Salem, Ohio, Mar. 29, 1958; s. Charles Spencer and Dorothy Jane (Allen) H. BA magna cum laude, Hiram Coll., 1980; JD, George Washington U., 1984. Bar: Ohio 1984, Pa. 1987, D.C. 1988, U.S. Supreme Ct. 1989, Tex. 1990, Okla. 1991. Legis. intern Office of Hon. John Conyers, Jr., Washington, 1979; asst. to dean campus Life for Housing, conf. dir. Hiram (Ohio) Coll., 1980-81; corp. counsel Capital Oil & Gas Inc., Austintown, Ohio, 1984-93; gen. counsel, sec. North Coast Energy, Inc., Cleve., 1987-2001, Trinity Oil & Gas, Inc. subs. North Coast Energy Inc., Warren, Ohio, 1990-93; gen. counsel Eric Petroleum Corp., Canfield, Ohio, 2001—. Mem. mini-task force on notices of violation Ohio Div. Oil and Gas, Columbus, 1988-90; part-time fin. analyst Primerica Fin. Svcs., Inc., 1997-2000; corp. sec. Peake Energy, Inc., Ravenswood, W.Va., 2000-01. Mem. ABA, Ohio Bar Assn., Mahoning County Bar Assn., Pa. Bar Assn., Okla. Bar Assn., D.C. Bar Assn., State Bar Tex., Trumbull County Bar Assn., Ohio Oil and Gas Assn., Christian Legal Soc., Energy Bar Assn., Ohio Land Title Assn., Ohio Geneal. Soc., Mahoning Valley Hist. Soc., Austintown Hist. Soc., Gen. Soc., War of 1812, SAR, Order of Arrow, Kappa Delta Pi, Pi Gamma Mu. Republican. Avocations: local history, study of amaranth. Home: 4841 Westchester Dr Apt 102 Youngstown OH 44515-2548 Office: Eric Petroleum Corp 4206 1/2 Boardman-Canfield Canfield OH 44406 *Motto: I Peter 1: 23-25.*

HILL, THOMAS CLARK, lawyer; b. Prestonsburg, Ky., July 17, 1946; s. Lon Clay and Corinne (Allen) H.; m. Barbarie Friedly, June 13, 1968; children: Jason L., Duncan L. BA, Case Western Reserve U., 1968; JD, U. Chgo., 1973. Bar: Ohio 1973, U.S. Supreme Ct. 1976. Assoc. atty. Taft, Stettinius & Hollister LLP, Cin., 1973-81, ptnr., 1981—. Author: Monthly Meetings in North America: A Quaker Index, 4th edit., 1998. Trustee, treas. Wilmington (Ohio) Coll., 1982-94, 99—, sec., 2002—; treas. Ams. sect. Friends World Commn. for Consultation, 1990-95, presiding clk., 1995-99, interim com., presiding clk., London, 2000—; trustee Wilmington Yearly Meeting of Friends (Quakers), 1986-98, Friends United Meeting, 1999—, presiding clk. trustees, 2002—. Mem. ABA, Ohio State Bar Assn., Cin. Bar Assn., Friends Hist. Assn. (bd. dirs. 1994-95). Republican. Mem. Soc. Of Friends. Avocation: Quaker history. Office: 425 Walnut St Ste 1800 Cincinnati OH 45202-3923 E-mail: hill@taftlaw.com.

HILL, THOMAS QUINTON, communication specialist, graphic designer; b. Talladega, Ala., June 27, 1959; s. Sandy and Maude Verdell (Griggs) H. Student, San Francisco Art Inst., 1978-79, Acad. of Art, San Francisco, 1993-94; BS in Bus. Mgmt., U. Phoenix, 1997; MA in Orgnl. Devel., U. San Francisco, 2001. Comms. coord. Sedgwick, San Francisco, 1990-92; comm. cons. Sedgwick Noble Lowndes, San Francisco, 1992-97; prin. Graphic Details Design, San Francisco, 1993—; sr. comm. analyst Kaiser Permanente, Oakland, Calif., 1997-99; sr. comm. cons. Bank of Am., 1999-2000; sr. comm. specialist Nat. Semiconductor Corp., 2000—. Creative cons. Sedgwick Proposal Com., San Francisco, 1996-97; design cons. Francisco Med. Soc., San Francisco, 1993—; part-time instr. Graphic Arts Inst., San Francisco, 1998. Vol. Alzheimer's Svcs. Orgn., Berkeley, Calif., 1994, Leukemia Soc. Am., San Francisco, 1994, United Way, San Francisco, 1994—; mem. bd. dirs. Calif. divsn. Am. Cancer Soc., Off the Leash arts orgn, 2000—. Recipient Award of Appreciation, Leukemia Soc. Am., 1994, Pinnacle of Success award Am. Assn. Med. Soc. Execs., 1995. Mem. Internat. Assn. Bus. Communicators (chpt. pres. 1998, exec. bd. 2000—, judge blue ribbon panel 1998, Cert. Appreciation 1997), Am. Inst. Graphic Arts (outreach com. 1993—), Commonwealth Club of Calif., Coun. Comm. Mgmt. Avocations: health and fitness, music, theater, films. Office: Nat Semiconductor 1130 Kifer Rd San Francisco CA 94086

HILL, THOMAS WILLIAM, JR., lawyer, educator; b. N.Y.C., Dec. 25, 1924; s. Thomas William Sr. and Marion (Bond) H.; m. Elizabeth Rowe, June 18, 1949; children: Gretchen P., Catharine B., Thomas William III. BS, U. Pa., 1948; MBA, NYU, 1950; JD, Columbia U., 1953. Bar: N.Y. 1953, D.C. 1954, U.S. Supreme Ct. 1958, Fla. 1989; CPA N.Y. Sr. tax acct. Hurdman & Cranstoun, 1949-50; asst. U.S. atty. So. Dist. N.Y., 1953-54; assoc. Cahill, Gordon, Reindel & Ohl, 1954-58; sr. ptnr. Spear & Hill, 1958-75; ptnr. Sidley & Austin, 1981-86; pres. Belco Petroleum Co., N.Y.C., 1962-63; legal adviser Sultanate of Oman, 1972-76. Adj. prof. law U. Miami, 1986-97. Contbr. articles to profl. jours. Vice chmn., pres., trustee Internat. Coll., Beirut, Lebanon, 1978-91. 1st lt. AUS, 1943-46. Decorated Bronze Star, Purple Heart, Medal of Oman (Sultanate of Oman), Order of Homayun (Iran). Mem. ABA, Assn. of Bar of City of N.Y., IBA, Racquet and Tennis Club (N.Y.C.), Mayacoo Golf Club, Taconic Golf Club, Phi Delta Phi, Kappa Sigma. Home: 1967 Breakers Pointe Way West Palm Beach FL 33411-5119 E-mail: twhilljr@aol.com.

HILL, TYRONE, professional basketball player; b. Cin., Mar. 19, 1968; BA in Comm. Arts, Xavier U., 1986-90. Forward Golden State Warriors, San Francisco, 1990-93, Cleve. Cavaliers, 1993-97, Milw. Bucks, 1997-99, Philadelphia 76ers, 1999—2001, Cleveland Cavaliers, 2001—. Active NBA Stay In Sch. Program. All-time leading rebounder, scorer Xavier U.; leader Cleve. Cavaliers field-goal percentage, 1993-94; named to NBA All-Star Game Eastern Conf., 1995. Avocation: music. Office: Cleveland Cavaliers Gund Arena One Center Court Cleveland OH 44115

HILL, VIRGIL LUSK, JR., academic administrator, naval officer; b. Shelby, N.C., Apr. 2, 1938; s. Virgil Lusk and Ellen (Dilling) H.; m. Mary Kimberly Jordan, Jan. 11, 1964; children: James S., Katherine E. BS in Naval Sci., U.S. Naval Acad., 1961. Commd. ensign USN, 1961, advanced through grades to rear adm. (upper half), 1989; served on USS Thomas Jefferson, Groton, Conn., 1968-70; material officer COMSUBRON 18, Charleston, S.C., 1970-73; exec. officer USS L. Mendel Rivers, Charleston, 1973-75; comdg. officer USS Hammerhead, Norfolk, Va., 1976-80; dir. spl. projects Office Chief Naval Ops., Washington, 1980-83; comdr. Submarine Devel. Squadron 12, Groton, 1983-85; dir. attack submarine divsn. Office of Chief Naval Ops., Washington, 1985-87; comdr. Submarine Group 5, San Diego, 1987-88; supt. U.S. Naval Acad., Annapolis, Md., 1988-91; comdr. operational test and evaluation forces USN, Norfolk, 1991-93; pres. Valley Forge (Pa.) Mil. Acad. and Coll., 1993-2000; sr. fellow Villanova U., 2002—. Bd. dirs. Greater Main Line br. ARC, Southeastern Pa. chpt. Decorated Distinguished Svc. medal with gold star, Legion of Merit with 3 gold stars, Meritorious Service medal with 3 gold stars, Navy Commendation medal with 1 gold star; recipient Admiral David Glasgow Farragut award Naval Order of U.S. 1996, Robert Morris award Boy Scouts Am., 1996, Order of Magna Charta, 1996. Mem. Assn. Mil. Colls. and Schs. of the U.S. (former pres.), United Svcs. Orgn. of Phila. (bd. dirs.), Assn. Ind. Colls. and Univs. Pa. (bd. dirs.), Nat. Assn. Ind. Colls. and Univs. (pub. rels. commn.), Pa. Assn. Colls. and Univs., Pa. Assn. Ind. Schs., Nat. Assn. Ind. Schs., U.S. Naval Inst., Naval Order of the U.S., Mil. Order of Fgn. Wars, U.S. Navy League, Naval Submarine League, World Affairs Coun. of Phila., Sunday Breakfast Club of Phila., Penn Club of Phila., Union League of Phila. (bd. dirs.), St. David's Golf Club (Wayne, Pa.), others. E-mail: virgilhill@aol.com.

HILL, WALLACE HARRY, sports television consultant; b. Chgo., Oct. 14, 1935; s. Wallace George and Evelyn Teresa (O'Connor) H.; m. Mary Helen Du Beau, Oct. 21, 1956 (div. Jan. 1970); children: Scott, Amy, Molly, Betsi; m. Judith Ellen Swigost, May 16, 1982 BA in Comm., Am. U., 1960. TV prodn. mgr. NBC Sports, N.Y.C., 1973-92; pvt. practice sports TV cons. N.Y.C., 1992—. Mem. broadcast adv. bd. NBA, N.Y.C., 1992-98. Prodr. (film) Skills That Last A Lifetime, 1972 (Silver award), In Search of Spring, 1973 (Silver award), Internat. Film & TV Festival N.Y. With U.S. Army, 1954-56. Mem. Internat. TV Assn. Avocation: golfer. Home and Office: 5602 Rutherford Ct North Port FL 34287

HILL, WALTER A. agricultural sciences educator, researcher; b. New Brunswick, N.J., Aug. 9, 1946; s. Henry Solomon and Tessie Paisley H.; m. Jill Karen Harris; children: Shaka W.T., Askia A.H., Osei J.E. BA in Chemistry, Lake Forest Coll., 1968; MAT in Chemistry, U. Chgo., 1970; MS in Soil Chemistry, U. Ariz., 1973; PhD in Agronomy, U. Ill., 1978. From asst. prof. to assoc. prof. dept. agrl. scis. Tuskegee (Ala.) U., 1978-84, adminstr. USDA Cooperative Extension Program, 1987-91, prof. dept. agrl. scis., 1984—, rsch. dir. USDA Cooperative State Rsch. Program, 1986—, dir. G.W. Carver Agrl. Experiment Sta., 1986—, dean Sch. Agriculture and Home Economics, 1987—. Bd. dirs. Agrl. Satellite Corp., 1990-93; chair 1890 Coun. Deans and Dirs., 1992—, Profl. Agrl. Workers Conf., 1988—, Internat. Symposium Sweetpotato Tech. for 21st Century, 1991; co-dir. Nat. Sweetpotato Info. Ctr., 1991—; dir. NASA Ctr. Food Prodn., Processing and Waste Mgmt. for CELSS, 1991—, So. Food Systems Edn. Consortium; mem. various coms. Nat. Rsch. Coun.; mem. adv. bd. NSF, 1992—; USAID sci. liaison Asian Vegetable Rsch. and Devel. Ctr., Taiwan, 1989—; mem. agrl. biotech. rsch. adv. com. USDA, 1992—; vis. sci. NASA Kennedy Space Ctr., 1987, Internat. Inst. Tropical Agriculture, Nigeria, 1985, Dept Agronomy Purdue U., summer 1981. Founder Tuskegee Horizons Mag./Jour., 1990—; editor Sweetpotato Technology for the 21st Century, 1993; contbr. numerous articles, book, book chpts., procs., abstracts; patentee in field. Trustee Lake Forest Coll., Ill., 1989—; vol. Cub Scouts Am., Tuskegee, 1990—; mem. PTA, Washington Chapel A.M.E. Recipient Outstanding Rsch. and Teaching award Ala. Soil & Water Conservation Soc., 1992, Futurist in Sci. and Tech. award Black Enterprise Mag., 1990, Faculty award execellence in sci. & tech. White House Initiative on HBCU, 1988, Disting. Alumni Svc. citation Lake Forest Coll., 1986; named Exec. of Yr. by Profl. Secs. Internat., 1991, Danforth assoc. for excellence in undergrad. teaching Danforth Found., 1980; Kellogg fellow, 1988; USDA grantee, NASA grantee, U.S. Dept. Edn. grantee, USAID grantee, others. Fellow Am. Soc. Agronomy (Outstanding Minority Educator award 1990); mem. Am. Soc. Gravitational & Space Biology, Am. Soc. Horticultural Sci., Crop Sci. Soc. Am. (strategic planning com. 1993), Internat. Soil Sci. Soc., Internat. Soc. Tropical Root Crops (Plucknett Outstanding Rsch. Paper award 1983), Internat. Soc. Horticultural Sci., Soil Sci. Soc. Am., Assn. Rsch. Dirs. (chair elect 1992—), Phi Beta Kappa, Sigma Xi, Gamma Sigma Delta. Office: Tuskegee Univ Carver Agrl Expt Sta Campbell Hall Rm 100 Tuskegee Institute AL 36088

HILL, WILLIAM A(LEXANDER), judge; b. Carmel, Calif., Aug. 21, 1946; s. R. William and Ruth M. (McDonald) H.; m. Diane K. Hartman, Apr. 25, 1981; children: Erin, Georgia. BS, U. N.D., 1968, JD, 1971; cert., Hastings Coll. Law Civ. Advocacy, 1977; grad. in fed. evidence, U. Mich. Law Sch., 1981. Bar: N.D. 1971, Minn. 1974, U.S. Dist. Ct. N.D. 1971, U.S. Tax Ct. 1973, U.S. Ct. Appeals (8th cir.) 1973. Dep. sec. of state State of N.D., 1971-72; law clk. to judge U.S. Dist. Ct. N.D., 1972-74; ptnr. Pancratz Law Firm, Fargo, N.D., 1974-83; magistrate U.S. Dist. Ct., N.D., 1975-83; judge U.S. Bankruptcy Ct., 1983—. Mem. 8th cir. bankruptcy appellate panel, 1996—; part-time magistrate U.S. Dist. Ct. N.D., 1975-83; active N.D. Supreme Ct. Joint Procedures Com. Commr., 1978-83. Mem. exec. bd. dirs. No. Lights coun. Boy Scouts Am., 1993-98; bd. dirs. Fargo Moorhead Symphony, 1995-2001, Heritage Hjemkomst Ctr., Moorhead, Minn.; chmn. Gethemane Episcopal Found., Fargo, 1981-83; pres. Plains Art Mus., Moorhead, 1982. Office: US Bankruptcy Ct Quentin N Burdick US Courthouse 655 1st Ave N Ste 350 Fargo ND 58102-4952 E-mail: hill@ndb.uscourts.gov.

HILL, WILLIAM U. state supreme court chief justice; Atty. gen., Cheyenne, Wyo., 1995—98; justice Wyo. Supreme Ct., Cheyenne, 1998—2002, chief justice, 2002—. Office: Wyoming Supreme Court 2301 Capitol Ave Cheyenne WY 82001-3656

HILL, WILLIAM VICTOR, II, retired army officer, secondary school educator; b. Carlisle, Pa., Dec. 14, 1936; s. William Victor and Frances Ellen (Swanson) H.; m. Doris Ann Cox, Nov. 11, 1961; children: William Victor III, David C., Stephanie C. Hill Trede. BBA, Tex. A&M U., 1959; MPA, U. Mo., Kansas City, 1972; diploma, Command and Gen. Staff Coll., 1969, Air War Coll., 1982. Lic. realtor. Commd. 2d lt. U.S. Army, 1959, advanced through grades to col.; tank bn. comdr. 2d Bn., 13th Armor, Ft. Knox, Ky., 1976-78; prof. mil. sci. Sam Houston State U., Huntsville, Tex., 1979-81; insp. gen. 5th U.S. Army, Ft. Sam Houston, Tex., 1982-85; ret. U.S. Army, 1986; dir. army Jr. Res. Officers Tng. Corps South San Antonio (Tex.) Ind. Sch. Dist., 1988-97; sr. Army instr. South San Antonio H.S., 1988-97, ret., 1997. Author army materials. City Coun. apptd. mem. San Antonio Conv. Ctr. Contract Rev. Com., 1998-99; asst. crew leader Cenusus, 2000; stewardship com. United Way; ethics cons. San Antonio Ethics Com. Decorated Legion of Merit, Bronze Star medal, Combat Inf. badge, Airborne-Ranger, Silver medal Order of St. George, others. Mem. U.S. Armor Assn. Avocations: fishing, conservation activities. Home: 3208 Bent Bow Dr San Antonio TX 78209-3518 E-mail: billhillII@aol.com.

HILLABRANDT, LARRY LEE, service industry executive; b. Apr. 5, 1947; s. Ronald Edward and Marion Alice (Smith) H.; m. Beverly Ann Johnson, Jan. 25, 1969; 1 son, Larry Lee. BS, Purdue U., 1969, MS, 1971. With Mobil Chem. Co., various locations, 1971-84, fin. analyst Jacksonville, Ill., 1973, sr. systems analyst Macedon, N.Y., 1973-74, fin. analyst, 1974, plant controller Frankfort, Ill., 1974-77, distbn. supt. NE region, 1979-80; div. gen. mgr. Belleville, Ont., Can., 1980-84; bus./fin. mgr. George Heisel Corp., Rochester, N.Y., 1984-85; pres. ZIP, Inc., Rochester, N.Y., 1985-97, prin., owner. Steering com. Mendon Found. Linear Pk. Bd. dirs. Mendon Found. Mem. Purdue Alumni Assn., Krannert Grad. Sch. Alumni Assn., Zeta Psi Alumni Assn. Club: Lima Gun. Home: 53 Stoney Lonesome Rd Honeoye Falls NY 14472 E-mail: csscorp@frontiernet.net., tinytoo@netzero.net.

HILLARD, CAROLE, former lieutenant governor; b. Deadwood, S.D., Aug. 14, 1936; m. John M. Hillard (dec.); children: David, Sue Ellen, Todd, Eddie, Lornell. BA in Edn., Univ. of Ariz., 1957; MA in Edn., S.D. State Univ., 1982; MA in Polit. Sci., Univ. of S.D., 1984. State rep. State of S.D., 34th dist., 1991-95; lt. gov. State of S.D., 1995—2003. Dir. Mich. Nat. Bank., Black Hills Regional Eye Inst., YMCA; mem. exec. bd. Nat. Crime Prevention Coun. Active Rapid City Common Coun., Rapid City C. of C., S.D. Bd. of Charities and Corrections, McGruff Crime Prevention Coun. (exec. bd.), S.D. Corrections Commn., Cmty. Care Ctr., S.D. Children's Home Soc., S.D. Assurance Alliance, Nat. Child Protection Partnership, First United Methodist Ch. (exec. bd.), Rapid City Econ. Devel. Partnership, F.L.A.G.S. Found.; mem. exec. bd. Bog Bros./Big Sisters. Recipient Pub. Svc. award, 1987, Gov.'s Outstanding Citizen award, 1988, George award Rapid City C. of C., 1994; named Outstanding Chirperson, United Way, 1986, S.D. Guardian Small Bus., 1994. Mem. LWV, Women's Network, Mt. Rushmore Soc., Indian-White Coun., Toastmasters, Ninety-niners, Rapid City Fine Arts Coun. Republican. Methodist. Avocations: flying (lic. pvt. pilot), snow skiing, scuba diving, reading. Home: PO Box 8187 Rapid City SD 57709*

HILLBERG, MARYLOU ELIN, lawyer; b. Chgo., Nov. 6, 1950; d. Harold Andrew Hillberg and Eunice Elin (Anderson) Peterson; m. Andrew Charles Lennox, Aug. 6, 1983; children: Elin Elizabeth Lennox, David Andrew Lennox. BFA, San Francisco Art Inst., 1973; JD, U. Calif., San Francisco, 1979. Bar: Calif. 1979, U.S. Dist. Ct. (no. dist.) Calif. 1979. Dep. dist. atty. Sonoma County, Santa Rosa, Calif., 1980; sole practice Santa Rosa, 1981—. Asst. prof. Sonoma State U., Rohnert Park, Calif., 1982—; mem. United Christian Ch., mem. cmty. adv. coun., 1992—, chair, 1994-95; co-founder Redwood Empire Appellate Lawyers, 1998—. Chmn. bd. dirs. Sonoma County Drug Abuse Alternatives Ctr., Santa Rosa, 1983-84; bd. dirs. ACLU, Santa Rosa, 1982-84; mem. adv. coun. Sonoma County Cmty., 1992—. Mem. Sonoma County Women in Law (chairperson 1983-84), Calif. Pub. Defenders Assn., Criminal Appellate Def. Counsel, Calif. Atty. Criminal Justice. Democrat. Office: PO Box 1879 Sebastopol CA 95473 E-mail: hillberg@sonic.net.

HILLE, BERTIL, physiology educator; b. New Haven, Oct. 10, 1940; s. C. Einar and Kirsti (Ore) H.; m. Merrill Burr, Nov. 21, 1964; children: Erik D., J. Trygve. BS, Yale U., 1962; PhD, Rockefeller U., 1967. H.H. Whitney fellow Cambridge U., 1967-68; asst. prof. U. Wash., Seattle, 1968-71, assoc. prof., 1971-74, prof. physiology, 1974—. Vis. prof. U. Saarland, Hamburg, Germany, 1975-76. Author: Ion Channels of Excitable Membranes, 3d edit., 2001; mem. edit. bd.: Jour. Gen. Physiology, 1971—, Am. Jour. Physiology, 1984—87, Jour. Neurosci., 1984—87, Neuron, 1987—, Curr. Opinion Neurobiol., 1990—99, Procs. of NAS, 1996—99; contbr. articles to profl. jours. Recipient Alexander von Humboldt Sr. Scientist award, 1975, Bristol-Myers Squibb award, 1990, (with Dr. Clay Armstrong) Louisa Gross Horowitz prize for biology or biochemistry Columbia U., 1996, (with Drs. Clay Armstrong and Roderick MacKinnon) Albert Lasker Basic Med. Rsch. award, 1999; co-recipient Gairdner Found. 2001 Internat. award, 2001. Mem. NAS, Biophys. Soc. (K.S. Cole award 1975), Am. Acad. Arts and Sci., Inst. of Medicine, Soc. Neurosci. Home: 10630 Lakeside Ave NE Seattle WA 98125-6934 Office: U Wash Box 357290 Seattle WA 98195-7290 E-mail: hille@u.washington.edu.

HILLE, ROBERT ARTHUR, healthcare executive; b. Hartford, Conn., June 19, 1931; s. Henry Oscar and Mary (Zelanski) H.; m. Barbara White, Nov. 20, 1954; children: Richard, Marilyn, David, Thomas, Catherine. BS in Edn. and Biology with honors, U. Conn., 1954; MS in Healthcare Adminstrn., Baylor U.,

1969. Commd. 2d lt. U.S. Army, 1954, advanced through grades to col., ret., 1978, various positions in healthcare, 1954-69; adminstr. U.S. Army Hosp., Ft. Benjamin Harrison, Ind., 1969-71, Seoul, Korea, 1971-72; dep. dir., asst. prof. grad. program Baylor U., Waco, Tex., 1972-74; chief patient adminstrn. Office Surgeon Gen., Washington, 1974-77; assoc. dir. med. staff Baylor U. Med. Ctr., Dallas, 1978-79; adminstr. Reynolds Army Hosp., Ft. Sill, Okla., 1977-78; assoc. exec. dir. Baylor U. Med. Ctr., Dallas, 1979-80, sr. v.p., 1980-84, exec. v.p., COO, 1984-95, internal cons., 1995-96; retired. Adj. instr. health svcs. adminstrn. Washington U., St. Louis, 1981-96; adj. prof. U. Ala., Birmingham, 1981-95; mem. edn. com. Dallas-Ft. Worth Hosp. Coun., 1981-88, trustee, 1989-90; trustee Baylor Inst. Rehab., 1982-87, chmn., 1984-85; bd. dirs., assoc. dir. Tex. Cmty. Bank; trustee Baylor Ctr. Restorative Care, 1990, Helicopter Ambulance Svc. North Tex., 1987-96, chmn., 1994-95, sec. bd. dirs. Transplant Inst. S.W. Active Our Lady of the Lake Cath. Ch.; mem. long range planning com. Heath, Tex., 1995-96; mem. Planning and Zoning Commn., Heath, Tex., 1997—, chmn., 1998-. Decorated Legion of Merit. Fellow ACHE; mem. Am. Hosp. Assn., Tex. Hosp. Assn. (mem. ho. of dels. 1984-85, chmn. dist. V 1984-85), Fed. Health Care Execs. Inst., KC (4th degree).

HILLE, ROBERT JOHN, lawyer, trust officer; b. St. Louis, July 20, 1953; s. Robert E. and Virginia (Curry) H.; m. Carol A. Fukuchi, May 30, 1982; children: Jessica, Stephanie. BS, U. Tulsa, 1976; JD, Washington U., St. Louis, 1983. Bar: Mo. 1983. Assoc. Mathis and Long, P.C., St. Louis, 1983-84; ptnr. Anderson, Preuss and Bachman, St. Louis, 1984-86; pvt. practice St. Louis, 1986-88; ptnr. Brackman, Hille and Freed, P.C., St. Louis, 1988-94; trust officer Bank Am., St. Louis, 1994-99; sr. v.p. SunTrust Bank, Orlando, 1999—; v.p. fin, capital svcs. Asset Mgmt. Advisors, Orlando, Fla., 2002—. Mem. Mo. Bar Assn., Ctrl. Fla. Estate Planning Coun. Office: Asset Mgmt Advisors 200 S Orange Ave Orlando FL 32801 E-mail: robert.hille@suntrust.com.

HILLEARY, VAN, former congressman, lawyer; b. Rhea County, Tenn., June 20, 1959; m. Meredith Hilleary. BS in Bus. Adminstrn., U. Tenn., 1981; JD, Samford U., 1990. With SSM Industries, Inc., 1984-86, dir. planning and bus. devel., 1992—; mem. U.S. Congress from 4th Tenn. dist., 1995—2002; mem. fin. svcs. com; mem. edn. and the workforce com.; mem. armed svcs. com. 106th Congress from 4th Tenn. dist.; atty. Sonnenschein, Nash & Rosenthal. With USAF, 1981-1982; with USAFR, 1982—; served in Persian Gulf. Decorated 2 U.S. Air medals, Nat. Svc. medal, Kuwaiti Liberation medal. Mem. Am. Legion, Sigma Chi. Republican. Presbyterian.

HILLEL, DANIEL, soil physics and hydrology educator, researcher, consultant; b. L.A., Sept. 13, 1930; s. Morris Jacob and Sarah Frances (Fromberg) Bugeslov; m. Michal Artzy; children: Adi, Ron, Sari, Ori, Shira. BS, U. Ga., 1950; MS, Rutgers U., 1951; PhD, Hebrew U., Jerusalem, 1958; postgrad., U. Calif., Berkeley, 1960-61; DSc honoris causa, U. Guelph, 1992. Founding mem. Kibbutz Sdeh-Boker, Negev Region, Israel, 1952-56; advisor land devel. Govt. of Burma, Rangoon, 1957-58; head soil tech. Agrl. Rsch. Orgn., Bet Dagan, Israel, 1959-65; head soil and water scis. Hebrew U., Rehovot, Israel, 1966-76; prof. soil physics and hydrology U. Mass., Amherst, 1977—; DSc (hon.) Ohio State U., 1995. Vis. scientist Japan Soc. for Promotion Sci., Tottori and Fukuoka, 1972, 82, 90; nat. lectr. Sigma Xi, 1987-89; cons. agrl. applications Internat. Atomic Energy Agy., Vienna, 1971-72, environ. dept. The World Bank, Washington, 1987-90, FAO of UN, Rome, 1995, Govt. of Jordan, Amman, 1995; v.p. soil physics com. Internat. Soil Sci. Soc., The Hague, Netherlands, 1964-68, 82-86. Author: Computer Simulation of Soil-Water Dynamics, 1977, Fundamentals and Applications of Soil Physics, 1980, Negev: Land, Water and Life in a Desert Environment, 1982, Out of the Earth: Civilization and the Life of the Soil, 1991, The Rivers of Eden: Water for Peace in the Middle East, 1994, Environmental Soil Physics, 1998; co-author: The Global Harvest—Potential Impacts of the Greenhouse Effect on Agriculture, 1998; contbr. over 200 articles to profl. jours.; patentee in field. Recipient Chancellor's medal U. Mass., 1982; John Simon Guggenheim Meml. Found. fellow, 1993. Fellow AAAS, Am. Soc. Agronomy, Soil Sci. Soc. Am. (chmn. soil physics div. 1988-89, disting. svc. award 1995); mem. Am. Geophys. Union. Office: Ctr for Environ Studies PO Box 585 37105 Karkur Israel

HILLEMAN, MAURICE RALPH, virus research scientist; b. Miles City, Mont., Aug. 30, 1919; s. Robert A. and Edith (Matson) H.; m. Lorraine Witmer, Aug. 3, 1963; children: Jeryl Lynn, Kirsten Jeanne. BS, Mont. State U., 1941; PhD, U. Chgo., 1944; DSc (hon.), Mont. State U., 1966, U. Md., 1968, Washington and Jefferson Coll., 1992; D hon. causa (hon.), U. Leuven, 1984. Asst. bacteriologist U. Chgo., 1942-44; rsch. assoc. virus labs. E.R. Squibb & Sons, 1944-47, chief virus dept., 1947-48; chief research and diagnostic sects. virus and rickettsial diseases Army Med. Service Grad. Sch., Walter Reed Army Med. Ctr., 1948-56, asst. chief lab. affairs, 1953-56; chief dept. respiratory disease rsch. Walter Reed Army Inst. Rsch., Washington, 1956-57; dir. virus and cell biol. rsch. Merck Inst. Therapeutic Rsch., Merck & Co. Inc., 1957-66, exec. dir., 1966-71, v.p., 1971-78, sr. v.p., 1978-84; dir. Merck Inst., 1984-2000; dir. Merck Inst. for Vaccinology, 2001—; dir. virus and cell biology rsch., v.p. Merck, Sharp & Dohme Rsch. Labs., 1970-78, sr. v.p., 1978-84. Vis. investigator Hosp. of Rockefeller Inst. for Med. Rsch., 1951; vis. prof. bacteriology U. Md., 1953-57; adj. prof. virology pediatrics Sch. Medicine U. Pa., 1968—; cons. Children's Hosp. of Phila., 1968—; mem. coun. divsn. biol. scis. Pritzker Sch. Medicine, 1977-95; John Herr Musser lectr. Musser-Burch Soc., Tulane U. Sch. Medicine, 1969, 19th Graugnard lectr., 1978; mem., spl. cons. panel respiratory and related viruses USPHS, 1960-64; mem. Nat. Cancer Inst. primate study group, 1964-70; mem. coun. analysis and projection Am. Cancer Soc., 1971-76; mem. expert adv. panel on virus diseases WHO, 1952—; bd. dirs. W. Alton Jones Cell Sci. Ctr., Lake Placid, N.Y., 1980-82, Am. Liver Found. (hon.), 1986—, Am. Type Culture Collect, 1992-95, Nat. Found. Infectious Diseases, 1987—, Nat. Cancer Inst. Bd. Sci. Counselors, 1990-95, Bd. Sci. Counselors Paul Erlich Found. (Frankfurt, Germany), 1993—; bd. dirs. Jos. J. Stokes Rsch. Inst. U. Pa.; mem. overseas med. rsch. labs. com. Dept. Def., 1980; mem. virology dept. rev. com. Am. Type Culture Collection, 1980; mem. Ad Hoc Vaccine Subcom. AIDS Program NIH, 1991, AIDS Rsch. and Devel. Vaccine Working Group, 1992—, panel 1995—, Panel Internat. Task Force NIH Strategic Plan, 1992; mem. vaccine design and evaln. group, NIAID, NIH, 1995—; trustee Internat. Vaccine Inst., Korea; mem. program evaluation task force NIH Office AIDS Rsch., 1996-97; mem. adv. bd. Civilian R&D Found., 2001—; mem. com. to review CDC anthrax vaccine safety and efficacy rsch. program Inst. Medicine, 2000-02. Mem. editl. bd. AIDS Rsch. and Human Retroviruses, 1995—, Internat. Jour. Cancer, 1964-71, Inst. Sci. Information, 1968-70, Am. Jour. Epidemiology, 1969-75, Infection and Immunity, 1970-76, Excerpta Medica, 1971—, Proc. Soc. Exptl. Biology and Medicine, 1976—, Jour. Antiviral Research, 1980—, Vaccine, 1983, Virus Genes, 1986, Vaccine Research, 1990; contbr. some 500 articles to sci., profl., med. jours. Decorated by King Hassan II of Morocco, 1997; Phi Kappa Phi fellow, 1941-42, Koessler fellow, 1943-44; recipient Howard Taylor Ricketts prize, 1945, 83, Disting. Civilian Svc. award Sec. Def., 1957, Walter Reed Army Med. Incentive award, 1960, Dean M. McCann award, 1970, Procter award, 1971, Lasker Med. Rsch. award, 1983; Achievement award Indsl. Research Inst., 1975, Joseph E. Smadel award, 1984, Alumni medal, U. Chgo., 1987, Albert B. Sabin medal, 1988, Nat. Medal Sci., Pres. of U.S., 1988, San Marino award, 1989, Robert Koch Gold medal, 1989, Spl. Lifetime Achievement award Children's Vaccine Initiative of WHO, 1996, Albert B. Sabin Found. gold medal, Lifetime Achievement award 1997, Maxwell Finland award Nat. Fedn. Infectious Disease, 1998, Tower of Hope award, 2002, Prince Mahidol award King of Thailand, 2002. Fellow Am. Acad. Microbiology; mem. NAS, Am. Acad. Arts and Scis., Inst. of Medicine of Nat. Acad. Sci., Am. Philos. Soc., Am. Soc. Microbiology, Soc. Exptl. Biology and Medicine (mem. editl. and publs. com. 1977—), Tissue Culture Assn. (mem. coun. 1977—), Am. Assn. Immunologists, Am. Assn. Cancer Rsch., Infectious Diseases Soc., Permanent sect. Microbiol. Standardization Internat. Assn. Microbiol. Soc.s., Internat. Vaccine Inst. (UN bd. trustees 1995—), Russian Acad. Biotechnology (hon. fgn. mem.), L'Academie Nationale de Pharmacie (fgn. corr.). Office: Merck Inst for Vaccinology WP53C 350 West Point PA 19486 E-mail: maurice_hilleman@merck.com. *Once the problem is defined and the facts are known, decision and action are little more than the implementation of the obvious.*

HILLENBRAND, GARY F. chemist, educator; b. Evansville, Ind., Feb. 7, 1945; m. Sharon L. Hillenbrand, June 26, 1965; children: Andrew, Gina. BA in Chemistry, U. Evansville, 1967; PhD in Chemistry, Clemson (S.C.) U., 1982. Chemist Eli Lilly Co., Indpls., 1967-75; chemist, rsch. fellow Mead Corp., Dayton, Ohio, 1981-93. Adj. prof. Sinclair C.C., Dayton, 1995—2001; adj. asst. prof. U. Cin., 2001—02; adj. prof. USI, 2002, Vincennes U., 2002—03; assoc. prof. Oakland City U., 2003. Contbr. articles to profl. publs.; patentee in field. Avocation: wood working. Home: 102 W Mulberry St Fort Branch IN 47648-9649

HILLENBRAND, SHEA MATTHEW, baseball player; b. Mesa, Ariz., July 27, 1975; Attended, Mesa C.C., 1994—96. Profl. baseball player Boston Red Sox, 2001—. Lectr. Polaroid Clinic, Fenway Park. Avocation: weightlifting. Office: Boston Red Sox Fenway Pk 4 Yawkey Way Boston MA 02215

HILLENMEYER, HENRY REILING, JR., restaurant company executive; b. Temple, Tex., Nov. 13, 1943; s. Henry Reiling and Lucy Carolyn (Taylor) H.; m. Sallie Long Sigler, Oct. 30, 1976; children: Henry Reiling, Edward Ferriday, Taylor Jennings, Morgan Andrew, Hunter Taverner. BA, Yale U., 1965. Trainee Kanawha Valley Bank, Charleston, W.Va., 1965-67, asst. sec., 1967-68; v.p. CBM, Inc., Cleve., 1968-70, pres., 1970-72, chmn., dir., 1972-74; pres., dir. Ireland's Restaurants, Inc., Nashville, 1974-78; exec. v.p. Womco, Inc., Nashville, 1978-82; pres., dir. So. Hospitality Corp., Nashville, 1983-89, chmn., pres., dir., 1989-94; chmn., CEO, dir. Skillsearch Corp., Nashville, 1995-99, Cooker Restaurant Corp., 1999—. Bd. dirs. Jr. Achievement, Nashville, 1985—, chmn., 1991-92, 97-99; bd. dirs. Tenn. Spl. Olympics, Nashville, 1986-90; trustee Harding Acad., Nashville, 1985-90; nat. assoc. Boys Clubs of Am., N.Y.C., 1986-90. Mem. World Pres. Orgn., Chief Exec.'s Orgn., Belle Meade Country Club, Scroll and Key Soc., Fence Club, Yale Club of Middle Tenn. (pres. 1983-88). Republican. Episcopalian. Home: 8 Foxhall Close Nashville TN 37215-1808 Office: Cooker Restaurant Corporation 2609 W End Ave Nashville TN 37203 E-mail: hhillenmeyer@the-cooker.com.

HILLER, ARTHUR, motion picture director; b. Edmonton, Alta., Can., Nov. 22, 1923; Ed., U. Toronto and U. B.C., Alta., Toronto and B.C.; F.V.Ch.C., Victoria Coll., Glasgow, 1967; MA in Psychology; LHD, London Inst. Applied Research, 1973; DFA (hon.), U. Victoria, 1995; LLD, U. Toronto, 1995. Dir. TV prodns. Matinee Theatre, Playhouse 90, Alfred Hitchcock Presents, Route 66, Naked City; dir. films Americanization of Emily, 1965, Out of Towners, 1970, Love Story, 1970, Plaza Suite, 1971, Hospital, 1971, Man of La Mancha, 1972, The Man in the Glass Booth, 1975, Silver Streak, 1976, The In-Laws, 1979, Making Love, 1982, Teachers, 1984, Outrageous Fortune, 1987, The Babe, 1992. Decorated comdr. Internat. Order Sursam Corda; doctor laureate Imperial Order Constantine Brussels, 1972; recipient Can. radio awards, 1951, 52, awards for edn. by radio Ohio U., 1952, 53; best dir. nomination Nat. Acad. TV Arts and Scis., 1962; best dir. nomination Acad. Motion Picture Arts and Scis., 1970; Golden Globe award for best dir., 1970; Dir.'s award nomination Dirs. Guild Am., 1970; Best Dir. award N.Y. Fgn. Press, 1970; Jean Hersholt Humanitarian award Acad. Motion Picture Arts and Scis., 2002. Mem. Directors' Guild of Am. (pres. 1988-92), Acad. Motion Picture Arts and Scis. (pres. 1993-97), Nat. Film Preservation Bd. of Libr. Congress. Office: Golden Quill 8899 Beverly Blvd Ste 702 Los Angeles CA 90048-2431

HILLER, JACOB MOSES, research scientist; b. N.Y.C., Dec. 12, 1939; s. Nathan and Ilse (Katzman) H.; m. Deborah Tamar Posen, May 2, 1965; children: Simona, Sarah, Rachel. BS, CCNY, 1961; MS, NYU, 1967, PhD, 1970. Rsch. asst. U.S. Antarctic Rsch. Program, Washington, 1964-65; asst. rsch. scientist NYU, N.Y.C., 1966-69, NYU Med. Ctr., 1970-73, assoc. rsch. scientist, 1973-74; rsch. asst. prof. NYU Sch. Medicine, 1974-80, rsch. assoc. prof., 1980—2002, rsch. prof., 2002—. Mem. rsch. rev. com. Nat. Inst. Drug Abuse, Bethesda, Md., 1992; spkr. Gordon Rsch. Conf., 1977, 83. Author: (book chpt.) Basic Neurochemistry, 1995; mem. editl. adv. bd. Life Sciences, 1984-93; reviewer numerous sci. jours.; contbr. rsch. articles to sci. jours. Mem. bd. edn. Adolph Schreiber Hebrew Acad. of Rockland, Suffern, N.Y., 1980-88; v.p. Cmty. Synagogue of Monsey, N.Y., 1985-87; vice chmn. bd. dirs. Hatzoloh EMS Ambulance Corps of Rockland County, N.Y., 2001--. Recipient medal for Antarctic svc. U.S. Congress, 1965; rsch. grantee Nat. Inst. Aging, 1990-93, Nat. Inst. on Drug Abuse, 1996-97. Mem. AAAS, Internat. Narcotics Rsch. Conf., Am. Soc. for Microbiology, N.Y. Acad. Sci. Democrat. Jewish. Avocations: fishing, skiing, gardening, reading. Home: 17 Carlton Rd Monsey NY 10952-2519 Office: NYU Med Ctr 550 1st Ave New York NY 10016-6402

HILLER, NEIL HOWARD, lawyer; b. Detroit, Jan. 21, 1950; s. Leo and Rita Dorothy Hiller; m. Peggy Lee Abrams, Aug. 27, 1972; children: Evan, Kimberly. BA, U. Mich., 1971; JD cum laude, Wayne State U., 1974. Bar: Ariz. 1974, U.S. Dist. Ct. Ariz. 1975, U.S. Tax Ct. 1984. Atty. Burch & Cracchiolo, Phoenix, 1975-78, Lane & Smith, Ltd., Phoenix, 1978-79; shareholder Ehmann & Hiller, P.C., Phoenix, 1979—. Pres., v.p., treas. Jewish Fedn. Greater Phoenix, 1994-99. Office: Ehmann & Hiller PC 2525 E Camelback Rd Ste 720 Phoenix AZ 85016-4229 E-mail: hiller@ehpclaw.com.

HILLER, SUSAN, artist; Lectr. Slade Sch. Art, Univ. Coll., London, 1980-91; prof. art and design U. Ulster, Belfast, No. Ireland, 1991-98. Resident Karoly Found., Vence, France, 1968, Ministry Fine Arts, Morocco, 1969; contract tchg. and lectr. Royal Coll. Art, Ealing Poly., Goddard Coll., Vt., 1972—78; artist-in-residence U. Sussex, Brighton, England, 1975; lectr. II Maidstone (Kent, Eng.) Coll. Art, 1975—80; disting. vis. prof. dept. art Calif. State U., Long Beach, 1988; vis. art coun. chmn. dept. fine art UCLA, 1991, vis. prof., 92; vis. lectr. numerous instns. and colls. including N.S. Coll. Art and Design, Kunst Akademi, Oslo, Sch. Visual Arts, N.Y.C., Power Inst. Sydney (Australia) Coll. Arts, Leeds (Eng.) U., U. London, Calif. Inst. Arts, U. Plymouth, Brighton U., Ruskin Sch. Fine Art, Bath Acad. Fine Art, Ctrl. Sch. Art and Design, Glasgow Coll. Art, Royal Coll. Art, Rotterdam Art Acad., Byam Show Sch. Art; external examiner dept. art U. Lodnon Goldsmith's Coll., 1984—88, 1993—96, Stourbridge Coll. Art and Tech., St. Martin's Sch. Art, London Inst., 1993—96, U. Northumbria, Newcastle, England, 1993—96; dept. art and design Gwent Coll. Higher Edn., Newport, South Glamorgan Coll. Higher Edn., Cardiff, Wales, 1987—91; external examiner dept. painting Wimbledon Sch. Art, London, 1997—99; examiner dept. printmaking and electronic imaging Royal Coll. Art, London, 1997—2000; mem. visual arts panel Greater Lodnon Arts Assn., 1976—80; mem. visual art panel Arts Coun. Eng., 1997—99; guest curator Brit. Coun.-Franklin Furnace Gallery, N.Y.C., 1981. One-woman shows include Gimpel Fils, London, 1980, 1982, 1983, 1994, 1995, Roslyn Oxley Gallery, Sydney, 1982, Exptl. Art Found., Adelaide, Australia, 1982, 1998, Andre Emmeich Gallery, Zurich, Switzerland, Vivienne Esders Galerie, Paris, 1984, Orchard Gallery, Londonderry, No. Ireland, 1984, Inst. Contemporary Art, London, 1986, Pat Hearn Gallery, N.Y.C., 1987, 1989, 1991, 1992, Univ. Mus., Calif. State U., Long Beach, 1988, Pierre Birtschansky Galerie, Paris, 1989, Mappin Mus. and Art Gallery, Sheffield, Eng., 1990, 1991, Nicole Klagsburn Gallery, N.Y.C., 1991, Foksal Gallery, Warsaw, 1997, Oriel Gallery, Cardiff, 1997, Projektgalerie, Leipzig, Germany, 1998, Ctr. Contemporary Photography, Melbourne, Australia, 1998, Inst. Contemporary Photography, 1998, Inst. Contemporary Art, Phila., 1998, Berry Bouse, London, 1998, Henie Onstad Kusntctr., Oslo, 1999, exhibited in group shows at Entwistle Gallery, London, 1994, Tate Gallery, Liverpool, Eng., 1996, exhibited in group shows, 1995, 1997, Inst. Contemporary Art, Boston, Mus. Women, Washington, Mus. Modern Art, N.Y.C., 1999, Represented in permanent collections Tate Gallery, Arts Coun. Gt. Britain, Victoria and Albert Mus., Tokyo Met. Mus. Photography, Nat. Gallery Art South Australia, Adelaide, Leeds City Mus. and Art Gallery, Imperial War Mus., London; author (with David Coxhead): Dreams: Visions of the Night, 1981, revised, 1989, 1991, 1994, 1996. Recipient visual artist's award, Gulbenkian Found., 1976, 1977; travel fellow, Visual Arts Bd., Australia, 1982, Guggenheim fellow in visual art practice, 1998, hon. fellow, Dartington Coll. Arts, 1998, grantee, Greater London Arts Assn., 1981, NEA, 1982. Studio: 83 Loudoun Rd London NW8 OD6 England E-mail: aceposible@aol.com.

HILLERMAN, TONY, writer, former journalism educator; b. Sacred Heart, Okla., May 27, 1925; s. August Alfred and Lucy Mary (Grove) Hillerman; m. Marie Elizabeth Unzner, Aug. 16, 1948; children: Anne, Janet Hillerman Grado, Anthony Jr., Monica Hillerman Atwell, Steven, Daniel. Student, Okla. State U., 1942-43; BA, U. Okla., 1948; MA in English, U. N.Mex., 1965, LittD (hon.), 1990, Ariz. State U., 1991. Police reporter Borger (Tex.) News-Herald, 1948; reporter, city editor constn. Morning Press, Lawton, Okla., 1949-50; polit. reporter UP, Oklahoma City, 1950-52, bur. mgr. Santa Fe, 1952-54; reporter, then city editor and editor The New Mexican, Santa Fe, 1954-62; prof. journalism U. N.Mex., Albuquerque, 1965-87, asst. to pres., 1963-65, 81-84. Author: (novels) The Blessing Way, 1970, The Fly on the Wall, 1971, The Boy Who Made Dragonfly, 1972, Dance Hall of the Dead, 1973 (Edgar Allen Poe award, 1973), Listening Woman, 1986, People of Darkness, 1986, The Dark Wind, 1986, The Ghostway, 1986, Skinwalkers, 1986 (Anthony award, 1987), A Thief of Time, 1988 (Macavity award Mystery Readers Internat., 1988, Dept. Interior award, 1990), Talking God, 1988 (Media award Am. Anthrop. Assn., 1990), The Joe Leaphorn Mysteries, Coyote Waits, 1990, Sacred Clowns, 1993, Finding Moon, 1995, The Fallen Man, 1996, The First Eagle, 1998, Hunting Badger, 1998, The Wailing Wind, 2002, (non-fiction) The Great Taos Bank Robbery, 1996, New Mexico, 1996, Rio Grande, 1996, The Spell of New Mexico, 1996, Indian Country, 1996, The Best of the West, 1996, The Oxford Book of American Detective Stories, 1996, Seldom Disappointed, 2001; contbr. articles, audio recs.; editor: The Mysterious West, 1994. With inf. U.S. Army, 1943—45, ETO. Decorated Bronze Star, Silver Star, Purple Heart; recipient Golden Spur award, Western Writers Am., 1987, Spl. Friend of Dineh award, Navajo Tribal Coun., 1987, Grand Prix de Littérature Policière award, France, 1992, Amb. award, Ctr. for the Indian, 1992. Mem.: Internat. Crime Writers Assn., Mystery Writers Am. (pres. 1988, Grand Master award 1991). Democrat. Roman Catholic. Avocation: trout fishing.

HILLERT, GLORIA BONNIN, anatomist, educator; b. Brownton, Minn., Jan. 25, 1930; d. Edward Henry and Lydia Magdalene (Luebker) Bonnin; m. Richard Hillert, Aug. 20, 1960; children: Kathryn, Virginia, Jonathan. BS, Valparaiso (Ind.) U., 1953; MA, U. Mich., 1958. Instr. Springfield (Ill.) Jr. Coll., 1953-57; teaching asst. U. Mich., Ann Arbor, 1957-58; instr., dept. head St. John's Coll., Winfield, Kans., 1958-59; asst. prof. Concordia Coll., River Forest, Ill., 1959-63; vis. instr. Wright Jr. Coll., Chgo., 1974-76, Ill. Benedictine Coll., Lisle, 1977-78, Rosary Coll., River Forest, 1976-81; prof. anatomy and physiology Triton Coll., River Grove, 1982-92, prof. emeritus, 1992—; vis. asst. prof. Concordia U., 1993—. Vis. instr. Wheaton (Ill.) Coll., 1988; advisor Springfield Jr. Coll. Sci. Club, 1953-57, Concordia Coll. Cultural Group, 1959-62; program dir. Triton Coll. Sci. Lectr. Series, 1983-87; participant Internat. Educators Workshop in Amazonia, 1993. Dem. campaign asst., Maywood, Ill., 1972, 88; vol. Mental Health Orgn., Chgo., 1969-73, Earthwatch, St. Croix, 1987, Costa Rica, 1989, Internat. Med. Care Team, Guatemala, 1995, Earthwatch End of Dinosaurs, 1997. Mem. AAUW, Ill. Assn. Community Coll. Biol. Tchrs., Nat. Assn. Biol. Tchrs. Lutheran. Avocation: traveling. Home: 1620 Clay Ct Melrose Park IL 60160-2419 Office: Triton Coll 2000 N 5th Ave River Grove IL 60171-1907

HILLERT, RICHARD WALTER, composer, educator, author; b. Granton, Wis., Mar. 14, 1923; s. Richard Henry and Amelia Matilde (Trimberger) H.; m. Gloria Rose Bonnin, Aug. 20, 1960; children: Kathryn, Virginia, Jonathan. BS in Edn., Concordia U., 1951; MusM, Northwestern U., Evanston, Ill., 1955, MusD, 1968; DHL (hon.), Concordia U., Nebr., 2000; LittD (hon.), Concordia Sem., St. Louis, 2001; D in Sacred Music (hon.), Valparaiso U., 2002. Tchr., dir. music Bethlehem Luth. Ch., St. Louis, 1951-53, Trinity Luth. Ch., Wausau, Wis., 1953-59; prof. music Concordia U., River Forest, Ill., 1959-91, disting. prof. music, 1987, prof. emeritus, 1991—. Music editor: Inter Lutheran Commission on Worship, 1966-78, Lutheran Church-Missouri Synod, 1968-69, Chrismas Annual, 1985-89; assoc. editor Ch. Music, 1966-81; contbr. articles to profl. jours.; composer: Sonata for Violin and Piano, 1953, Sonata for Flute and Piano, 1954, Symphony in Three Movements, 1955, Prelude and Toccata for Organ, 1956, Alternations Number One for 7 Instruments, 1966, Divertimento for 5 Instruments, 1967, Angus Dei for 3 Choirs and Percussion, 1974, Partita for Organ: Picardy, 1978, Divertimento Number Two for 11 Players, 1983, Evening Prayer for Cantor, Congregation, and Organ, 1984, The Pillars for Wind Symphony, 1989, Fantasia on The Nunc Dimittis for Chamber Orch., 1990, Sine Nomini for Symphonic Band, 1995, Suite for Strings, 1996, Sonata for Flute and Harpsichord, 1997, Seven Psalms of Grace for Baritone Solo, Choirs and Orch., 1998. Recipient 1st prize Internat. Soc. Contemporary Music, 1961-62. Mem. Assn. Luth. Ch. Musicians (life), Pi Kappa Lambda, Sigma Alpha Iota. Avocations: traveling, american popular music before 1950, political and music biography. Home: 1620 Clay Ct Melrose Park IL 60160-2419 E-mail: richard@richardhillert.com.

HILLERY, MARY JANE LARATO, columnist, producer, television host, reserve army officer; b. Boston, Sept. 15, 1931; d. Donato and Porzia (Avellis) Larato; m. Thomas H. Hillery, Feb. 25, 1961; 1 son, Thomas H. Assoc. Sci. (scholar), Northea. U., 1950; BS, U. Mass. Harvard Extension, 1962; grad., Command and Gen. Staff Coll., 1982. Sales agt., linguist Pan Am. Airways, Boston, 1955-61; interpreter Internat. Conf. Fire Chiefs, Boston, 1966; tchr. Spanish YWCA, Natick, Mass., 1966-67; cmty. rels. cons., adv. bd. dirs., lectr. for migrant edn. project divsn., Mass. Dept. Cmty. Affairs, Boston, 1967-69; editor-in-chief Sudbury (Mass.) Citizen, 1967-76; assoc. editor The Beacon, 1976-79, contbg. editor, 1979-83; area editl. adviser Beacon Pub. Co., Acton, Mass., 1970-80, editor, 1976-80; columnist Town Crier, 1987—; contbg. editor Towne Talk, 1975-79, Citizens' Forum, 1975-81; editor Spl. Forces Ann. History, 1989-90; dir. pub. affairs Mass. Dept. Environ Quality Engring., 1981-83; prodr., host TV interview show For the Record, 1985—. Pub. affairs officer Fed. Emergency Mgmt. Agy., 1995—; women vets. spkr. State House Mass. ofcl. Vets. Day observances, ceremonies, 1999. Editor Hansconian, 1983-85. Mem. Bus. Adv. Com., 1972-77, Sudbury Sch. Com., 1976-77; mem. Meml. Day Celebration Com., 1972—, master of ceremonies, 1973—, parade marshal, 1997, 2003; chmn. Sudbury WWII Commemorativ e Cmty., 1992-96; chmn. Sudbury Korean War 50th Anniversary Commemorative Com., 2000—; mem. Sudbury Town Report, 1967-72, 85-88, chmn., 1969-72; chmn. Sudbury Vets. Adv. Com., 1986-92; panelist Internat. Women's Year Symposium, 1975, Women in Politics, 1987, Women in Mil., 1987; mem. congl. 5th dist. Mass. nomination bd. West Point, apptd. mil. aide-de-camp to Mass. Gov. Wm. Weld, 1992—; Veterans' agt. Town of Sudbury, 1992—. With USN, 1950-54; lt. col. USAR; Persian Gulf, 1991-92; liaison officer U.S. Mil. Acad. West Point, 1976-89, 93—; pub. affairs officer 94th USAR Command, 1982-83, Office of Sec. of Def., The Pentagon, Washington, 1989-93; dir. pub. rels. Mission One, Employer Support Guard and Res., Dept. of Def.; parade marshall Sudbury Meml. Day Parade, 2003. Decorated Meritorious Svc. medal, 1985, Joint Svc. Achievement medal, 1991, Nat. Def. medal-Bronze Star, 1991, Outstanding Svc. award Sec. Def. Pub. Affairs, 1992, Joint Meritorious unit award, 1992, Def. Superior Svc. medal, 1993, Employer Support Guard and Res. Mission One award, 1999; named Editor of Yr., Beacon Pub. Co., 1970; recipient medal of appreciation Internat. Order DeMolay, 1969, cert. of appreciation U.S. Def. Civil Preparedness Agy., 1975, Mass. Bicentennial Commn., 1976, Appreciation award U.S. Mil. Acad., 1976-86, citations Mass. State Senate, 1979, 82, Newswriting award Media Contest Air Force Sys. Command, 1984, Outstanding Svc. award Sec. Def. Pub. Affairs, 1991, Cmty. Citizen award Citizen of Yr., Sudbury Grange, 1996, Cmty. Svc. award DAR, 2000, George Washington Honor medal Bay State chpt. Freedoms Found. at Valley Forge, 1998. Mem. LWV (dir. 1964-68), Nat. Editl. Assn., Nat. Newspaper Assn., Nat. Press Club, Rotary Internat. (mem. Sudbury chpt. scholarship chmn. 1993—, bd. dirs. 1994-95, 96-97, 97—, pub. rels. chmn. 1995-97, assoc. editor The Bull., 1996-97, Found. chmn. 1997-99, pres.-elect 2000-01, pres. 2001—), New Eng. Press Assn., Internat. Platform Assn. (Silver Bowl award for poetry 1997), Bus. and Profl. Women's Club (Sudbury 1st v.p. 1973, pres. 1973-76, parliamentarian 1978-88, 90-92, legis. chair 1990-92, state bylaws com. 1977-78, 79-81, 86-88, state legis. chmn. 1979-81, 86-88, state polit. action com. chmn. 1988-89, Woman of Yr. 1979, Woman of Achievement 1982), Nat. League Am. Pen Women (exec. bd. Boston 1974-76, 78-88, pres. Boston br. 1976-78, 94-98, 2000—, state exec. bd. 1994-1998, publicity chmn. 1979-80, chmn. bylaws com. 1979-80, 86-88, parliamentarian 1978-80, 82-88, auditor 1980-82, 84-88, 1st v.p. 1988-92, nat. editor Achievements, The Pen Woman 1992-94, nat. protocol chairperson 1998, nat. scholarship chmn. 1998—, nat. 4th v.p. 2000-02, nat. 3d v.p. 2002—), Res. Officers Assn. (life, dept. sec. 1978-79, dept. army v.p. 1992-95, pres. Boston chpt. 1986-88, dept. pres.-elect 1995-96, dept. pres. 1996-97, army v.p. 1995-96, army coun. rep. 1989-92, 1999—, budget com., 1990-91, dept. publicity chmn. 1988-92, editor Advisor 1991-95, Outstanding Svc. award 1978-79, co-chair Nat. Conv. 1995-98), Spl. Forces Assn. (Green Berets, asst. to chmn. nat. conv. 1999-2000), Am. Legion (post comdr. 2000-01, exec. bd. 1996—, chaplain 1996-2000, 2002-, vet. svc. officer 2001—), Korean War Vets. Mass. (life), Omega Sigma. Home: 66 Willow Rd Sudbury MA 01776-2663

HILLERY, SUSIE MOORE, retired elementary school educator; b. Lunenburg County, VA, Feb. 25, 1928; d. William Edward and Sarah Anderson Moore; m. Herbert Vincent Hillery, June 17, 1956 (div. Jan. 1969); children:

Vincent, Nathan. BA, Lynchburg Coll., 1950; MA, U. Ky., 1955; student, Lexington Sem., Ky.; student, U. Va., U. Tex. Youth min. Christian Ch. Disciples of Christ, Clarksville, Tenn., 1950—52; tchr. religious edn. Martinsville (Va.) Pub. Sch., 1952—53; elem. sch. tchr. Lynchburg (Va.) Pub. Schs., 1953—54, Austin (Tex.) Pub. Schs., 1956—58, 1964—69, Henrico County Pub. Schs., Richmond, Va., 1969—91; youth min. Colonial Christian Ch., Richmond, 1983—86; pastor/min. Christian Ch., Gordonsville, Va., 1993—98, Bella Grove Christian Ch., Louisa, Va., 1998—2000; vol. chaplain Henrico Drs. Hosp., Richmond, 1999—. Rep. Interfaith Coun., 1993—; with Ch. Women United, 1998—.

HILLERY, THOMAS HUNGIVILLE, journalist, financial consultant; b. Boston, Dec. 15, 1962; BA, Clark U., 1985; Magistri in Artibus Liberalibus, Harvard U., 1997. Accredited assessor # 666, Mass. Promotions dept. WCRB-FM, Waltham, Mass., 1990-92; journalist Dorchester News, Boston, 1992—. Author: "Make Advertising Work! Use Demographics, Psychographics and Purchasing Data." Bd. assessors Town of Sudbury, 1987-96; trustee Hillery Charitable Trust; mem. Boston (Mass.) com. fgn. rels. Thomas H. Hillery fellowship. Mem. Internat. Assn. Assessing Officers, Mass. Assn. Assessing Officers, U.S. Libr. Congress, Jonas Clark Fellows, Clark U. Alumni Coun., Clark Legacy Soc., Harvard Club Boston, Harvard Investment Assn., Nat. Press Club, Nat. Trust for Hist. Preservation, Internat. Platform Assn., New Eng. Hist. Geneaol. Soc., Sons Union Vets. Civil War, KC, Masons (past master Charles A. Welch Lodge, past high priest Houghton Royal Arch, Grand Royal Arch chpt. exemplification degree team 1992-93, dist. dep. grand treas. 1992-93), Scottish Rite, Order Eastern Star, Shriners, Mil. Order Loyal Legion U.S., Sons of Am. Legion Post 191 (chaplain, sgt. of artillery, color guard), Ancient and Honorable Artillery Co. (Hillery pedigree registered Coll. of Arms London, armorial bearings granted, pub. rels. officer), Freedom's Found. at Valley Forge (Bay State chpt.). Home: 66 Willow Rd Sudbury MA 01776-2663 Office: 299 Savin Hill Ave Ste 1 Boston MA 02125-1055 E-mail: tomhillery02125@cs.com.

HILLESTAD, CHARLES ANDREW, lawyer; b. McCurtain, Okla., Aug. 30, 1945; s. Carl Oliver and Aileen Hanna (Sweeney) H.; m. Ann Ramsey Robertson, Oct. 13, 1973. BS, U. Oreg., 1967; JD, U. Mich., 1972. Bar: Colo. 1972, U.S. Dist. Ct. Colo. 1972, U.S. Ct. Appeals (10th cir.) 1972, Oreg. 1993; lic. real estate broker, Colo. Law clk. to presiding justice Colo. Supreme Ct., Denver, 1972-73; ptnr. DeMuth & Kemp, Denver, 1973-83, Cornwell & Blakey, Denver, 1983-90, Scheid & Horlbeck, Denver, 1990-93, Gablehouse & Epel, Denver, 1993-94; pvt. practice Cannon Beach, Oreg., 1994—. Co-developer award winning Queen Anne Inn, Capitol Hill Mansion and Cheyenne Canyon Inn Hotels (4-diamond award AAA); mem. ad hoc com. Denver Real Estate Atty. Specialists. Author: Preventive Law for Innkeepers, co-author: Annual Surveys of Real Estate Law for Colorado Bar Association; contbr. articles to profl. jours.; assoc. editor Inn Times. Past coun. mem. Denver Art Mus.; past chmn. Rocky Mountain chpt. Sierra Club; past v.p., bd. dirs. Seaside C. of C.; past bd. dirs. Hist. Denver, Inc. Staff sgt. U.S. Army, 1968-70. Recipient Colo. Co. of Yr. award Colo. Bus. Mag., Award of Honor Denver Ptnrship., Newsmaker of Yr. and Outstanding Achievement awards Am. Assn. Hist. Inns, Tourism Person of Yr. award Denver Conv. and Visitor's Bur., Rocky Mountain Spectacular Inn award B&B Rocky Mountains Assn., Best Inns of Yr. awards County Inns Mag. and Adventure Rd. Mag., Best of Denver award Westward newspaper. Mem. ABA, Colo. Bar Assn., Oreg. Bar Assn., Denver Bar Assn., Colo. Lawyers for the Arts, POETS, Astoria C. of C., Seaside C. of C., Cannon Beach C. of C. Avocations: photography, art collecting, historic and environmental preservation, history and architecture reading, rafting. Office: PO Box 1065 1347 S Hemlock Cannon Beach OR 97110

HILLEY, JOSEPH HENRY, lawyer; b. Birmingham, Ala., June 29, 1956; s. Howard Guy and Ruby Josephine Hilley; m. Joy Elaine Fitzgerald, Aug. 11, 1984. BA, Asbury Coll., 1978; MDiv, Asbury Theol. Sem., 1984; JD, Cumberland Sch. Law, 1988. Bar: Ala. 1988, Ga. 1988, U.S. Dist. Ct. (no. dist.) Ala. 1988, U.S. Tax Ct. 1988, U.S. Ct. Appeals (11th cir.) 1993, U.S. Supreme Ct. 1995. Sports photographer World Wide News Svc., 1978-84; law clk. Gen. Counsel to Sec. of Def., Washington, 1987; assoc. Redden, Mills and Clark, Birmingham, Ala., 1988-96; pvt. practice, 1996-98; assoc. Carr Allison Pugh Howard Oliver & Sisson, Birmingham, Ala., 1998-00. Coord. capital campaign Asbury Coll., Wilmore, Ky., 1989-91. Author: (screenplays) Wake Up, 1994, Union Town, 1995, Coldwater, 1999, Fourth Generation, 2003; assoc. editor Cumberland Law Rev., 1986-88. Mem. Pinnelas County Dem. Exec. Com., St. Petersburg, Fla., 1984; trustee Woodlawn United Meth. Ch., Birmingham, 1988; co-founder, former chmn. bd. dirs. Children of the World, Inc. Mem. ABA, Ala. Bar Assn., Ga. Bar Assn., Birmingham Bar Assn., Baldwin County Bar Assn., Mobile Bar Assn. Anglican. Avocations: sports, theatre, writing.

HILL-FESSENDEN, ANNE LYNN, multi-faceted food and beverage consultant; b. Uniontown, Pa., Sept. 3, 1944; d. Robert Benjamin and Katherine Rebecca (Reynolds) Rankin; m. Howard Harry Hill, Aug. 23, 1964 (div. Dec. 1979); children: Jennifer Leigh, Carolyn Jeanne; m. Thomas A. Fessenden, Apr. 29, 1990. BS, U. Md., 1966. Elem. tchr. Prince George's County Bd. Edn., Upper Marlboro, Md., 1966-68; food svc. mgr. Bloomingdales, White Flint, Md., 1976-78; dist. mgr. ice cream parlors/restaurants Drug Fair, Inc., Alexandria, Va., 1978-80; dir. quality assurance and product devel. Marriott Internat., Washington, 1980-88, sr. dir. corp. procurement, 1988-90, sr. v.p. food and beverage, 1990-97; pres. ALH & Assocs., Germantown, Md., 1997—. Bd. dirs. Balt. Internat. Culinary Coll.; founding mem. ISUS Foodsvc. Consultancy. Mem. NAFE, DAR, AAUW, Soc. for Advancment of Foodservice Rsch., Internat. Dairy/Deli/Baking Assn., Internat. Assn. Women Chefs and Restaurateurs, Nat. Assn. Convenience Stores, Inst. Food Techs., Roundtable for Women in Foodservice (Pacesetter award 1986), Restaurant Assn. Md., Rsch. Chefs Assn. (founding). Republican. Presbyterian. Avocations: gourmet cooking, needlework, wreathmaking, ceramics, furniture refinishing. Office: ALH & Assocs 21525 Davis Mill Rd Germantown MD 20876-4419 E-mail: frfess@aol.com.

HILL-FOSTER, IALINE, retired secondary school educator; b. Houston, Apr. 13, 1936; d. Charlie B. and Alice Bernice Burch; m. James Willie Foster. BA, Dallas Bapt. Coll., 1975. Educator Dallas Ind. Sch. Dist., 1970—96. He Called Our Name, 2001 (Editor's Choice Award, 2002); author: Keep Looking Li'l Girl, 2001 (Internat. Poet of Merit Award, 2001). Recipient Outstanding Svc. and Dedication award, Disabled Am. Veterans, 2001. Mem.: AARP, Internat. Soc. of Poets (Disting. Mem. Award 2001), Parent Tchr. Assn. (life Outstanding Vol. Svc. Award). Avocation: reading, gardening, cooking, writing, collecting antiques. Office: Peaches' Place PO Box 398693 Dallas TX 75339

HILLGREN, SONJA DOROTHY, journalist; b. Sioux Falls, S.D., May 17, 1948; d. Ralph Oliver and Priscilla Adaline (Mannes) Hillgren; m. Ralph Lee Hill (dec.). BJ, U. Mo., 1970, MA, 1972; postgrad. (Nieman fellow), Harvard U., 1982-83. Washington corr. Ohio-Washington News Svc., 1972-73; reporter UPI, Annapolis, Md., 1974-76, reporter, editor Washington, 1976-78, farm editor, 1978-88; Washington corr. Knight-Ridder, Washington, 1988-90; Washington editor Farm Jour., 1990-95, editor, 1995—, sr. v.p., 2000—. Exec.-in-residence U. Mo., 1997; mem. campaign steering com. U. Mo. Sch. Journalism, 2003—. Chair bd. dirs. Nat. Press Bldg. Corp., 1997; bd. dirs. Winrock Internat., Philabundance, 2000—; mem. capital campaign com. U. Mo. Sch. Journalism, 2003—. Named Old Master, Purdue U., 1992, Agrl. Communicator of Yr., Nat. Agri-Mktg. Assn., 1996; recipient J.R. Russell award, Newspaper Farm Editors Am., 1985, Reuben Brigham award, Agrl. Comms. in Edn., 1988, Oscar in Agr. for Excellence in Agrl. Reporting, U. Ill., 1998, Recognition of Excellence in Print Media award, Ill. Soybean Assn., 2002, Prodr. Comms. award, United Soybean Bd. Prodr., 2003; Woodrow Wilson vis. fellow, 1993—94. Mem.: AAUW, Coun. on Fgn. Rels., Farm Found., Nat. Agri-Mktg. Assn., Am. Agrl. Editors' Assn., Am. Soc. of Mag. Editors, Investigative Reporters and Editors, Soc. Profl. Journalists, N.Am. Assn. Agrl. Journalists (pres. 1987—88), Congl. Country Club, Nat. Press Club (bd. govs. 1991—96, chair 1993—94, v.p. 1995, pres. 1996), Alpha Zeta, Pi Beta Phi (Carolyn Helman Lichtenberg Crest award 1999). Lutheran. Avocations: sports, reading. Home: 315 S 18th St Philadelphia PA 19103-6619 Office: Farm Jour 1818 Market St Fl 31 Philadelphia PA 19103-3654 E-mail: SHillgren@farmjournal.com.

HILLIARD, ANDREA LEIGH, writer; b. Columbus, Ohio, Feb. 23, 1973; d. Robert Matthew and Maryanne Feeney; m. Jason William Hilliard, July 20, 1996; children: Maxwell Robert, Quinn Michael. Telemarketer, auditor TruGreen-Chemlawn, Westerville, Ohio, 1989, customer svc. adminstr., 1989—94, bus. analyst Memphis, 1994—96, office mgr. Florence, Ky., 1996—97, customer svc. adminstr. Columbus, Ohio, 1997—98, ops. asst. Westerville, 1998—99. Author: Tales of the Eventide and Other Dark Matter, 2003, Patterns of Life, 2003, (poetry) Suburban Fall - The Best Poems and Poets of 2003. Home: 317 Kenbrook Dr Columbus OH 43085

HILLIARD, DAVID CRAIG, lawyer, educator; b. Framingham, Mass., May 22, 1937; s. Walter David and Dorothy (Shortiss) H.; m. Celia Schmid, Feb. 16, 1974. BS, Tufts U., 1959; JD, U. Chgo., 1962. Bar: Ill. 1962, U.S. Supreme Ct. 1966. Mng. ptnr. Pattishall, McAuliffe, Newbury, Hilliard & Geraldson, Chgo., 1983—2002, sr. ptnr., 2003—. Adj. prof. law Northwestern U., 1971—, chmn. Symposium Intellectual Property Law and the Corp. Client, 1987—; lectr. in advanced trademark law and info. regulation U. Chgo. Law Sch., 1999—. Author: Unfair Competition and Unfair Trade Practices, 1985, Trademarks, 1987, Trademarks and Unfair Competition, 1994, 5th edit., 2002, Trademarks and Unfair Competition Deskbook, 2001, 2d edit., 2003; editor-in-chief Chgo. Bar Record, 1978-81. Trustee Art Inst. Chgo., 1980—, vice-chmn., 1998-2000, exec. com., 1994-2000, chmn. sustaining fellows, 1981-85, chmn. adv. com. dept. architecture, 1981—, pres. aux. bd., 1977-79, chmn. exhbns. com., 1993—, chmn. bd. govs. of the sch., 1997-2000; trustee Newberry Libr., 1983—, exec. com., 1987—; trustee Robert Allerton Trust, 2002—; pres. Lawyers Trust Fund Ill., 1985-88; vis. com. DePaul U. Law Sch., U. Chgo. Sch. of Law, chmn., 1987-88, Northwestern U. Assocs., 1985—; profl. adv. bd. Atty. Gen. Ill., 1982-84; mem. Ill. Commn. on Rights of Women, 1983-85; bd. dirs. Ill. Inst. Continuing Legal Edn., 1980-82; pres. Planned Parenthood Assn. Chgo., 1975-77. Lt. JAGC, USN, 1962-66. Recipient Maurice Weigle award, 1974, Chgo. Coun. Lawyers award for jud. reform, 1983. Fellow Am. Coll. Trial Lawyers (chmn. courageous adv. com. 1995-97); mem. ABA (chmn. trademark divsn. 1986-87, mem. coun. 1991-95, intellectual property law sect.), Ill. Bar Assn., Chgo. Bar Assn. (pres. 1982-83, founding chmn. young lawyers sect. 1971-72), Internat. Trademark Assn. (bd. dirs. 1989-91, ADR panel of neutrals 1994—), Arts Club, Chgo. Club, Econ. Club, Grolier Club, Lawyers Club, Legal Club (pres. 1989-90), Univ. Club, Casino, Wayfarers Club (pres. 1994-95). Home: 1320 N State Pkwy Chicago IL 60610-2118 Office: Pattishall McAuliffe Newbury Hilliard & Geraldson 311 S Wacker Dr Ste 5000 Chicago IL 60606-6631 E-mail: dhilliard@pattishall.com.

HILLIARD, EARL FREDERICK, congressman, lawyer; b. Apr. 9, 1942; s. Mary Franklin Hilliard; m. Iola H. Hilliard, June 9, 1967; children: Alesia, Earl F. BA, Morehouse Coll., 1964; JD, Howard U., 1967; MBA, Atlanta U., 1970. Rsch. asst. Howard U., 1965-67; instr. Miles Coll., 1967-68; asst. to pres. Ala. State U., 1968-70; ptnr. Hilliard, Jackson, Little & Stansel, Birmingham, 1974-78; pvt. practice Birmingham; pres. Am. Trust Life Ins. Co.; mem. Ala. Ho. of Reps., 1974-80, chmn. Black legis. caucus, 1975; mem. Ala. Senate, 1980-93, U.S. Congress from 7th Ala. dist., 1993—2002; ptnr. Hillard, Smith & Hunt, Birmingham, 2003—. Reginald Herber Smith Comty. Lawyer fellow, 1970-71. Mem. NAACP (life), Nat. Bar Assn. (life), Ala. Black Lawyers Assn., Morehouse Coll. Alumni Assn. (life), Alpha Phi Alpha (life). Democrat. Baptist. Home: 1625 Castleberry Way Birmingham AL 35214-4867 Office: Hilliard Smith & Hunt PO Box 12445 Birmingham AL 35202-2445

HILLIARD, KIRK LOVELAND, osteopathic physician, educator; b. Phila., Mar. 9, 1941; s. Kirk Loveland and Lillian Adele (Hinkle) H.; m. Janet Louise Moyer, Aug. 29, 1970; children: Marian Lynn, Stephen Matthew, Allison Day. AB, Haverford Coll., 1963; DO, Phila. Coll. Osteo. Medicine, 1967. Diplomate Am. Coll. Osteo. Internists, Internal Medicine and Med. Diseases of Chest. Intern Doctors' Hosp., Columbus, Ohio, 1967-68, resident, 1970-72, sr. attending, 1977—, dir. respiratory svcs., 1978-97; fellow Hahnemann Hosp., Phila., 1972-74; pvt. practice Columbus, 1974-95; part time practice pulmonary medicine, 1996-2000. Asst. prof. Ohio U., Athens, 1979-88, assoc. prof., 1988—; med. dir. CP Home Care, Columbus, 1986-97, Am. Home Patient, 1997-2000; acting dir. Med. Edn. Doctors Hosp., Columbus, Ohio, 1991-92; bd. trustees Doctors Hosp., 1995, program dir. internal medicine, 1994-95; v.p. med. edn. Doctors Hosp., 1995—. Capt. M.C., U.S. Army, 1968-70, Vietnam. Fellow Am. Coll. Osteo. Internists; mem. Am. Osteo. Assn., Assn. Osteo. Dirs. Med. Edn., Am. Lung Assn., Assn. Hosp. Med. Edn., Inst. for Nat. Health Policy and Rsch., Am. Legion, Masons, Shriners. Avocations: hunting, fishing, scuba diving, horseracing. Office: Doctors Hosp 1087 Dennison Ave Columbus OH 43201-3496 E-mail: khilliard@doctorshospital.org.

HILLIARD, LANDON, banker; b. Norfolk, Va., Apr. 13, 1939; s. Landon and Irene (Bernard) H.; m. Mary Warfield Eichert, May 28, 1960 (div. Nov. 1980); children: Landon, IV., David Shelburne; m. Mary Cary Myers, Dec. 6, 1980; children: Harrison Carter; stepchildren: Mary Cary Morrison, R. Hamilton Morrison BA in Econs., U. Va., 1962. V.p. Morgan Guaranty Trust Co. of N.Y., N.Y.C., 1962-74; ptnr. Brown Bros. Harriman & Co., N.Y.C., 1974—. Bd. dirs. Owens-Corning, Toledo, Norfolk So. Corp., Western World Ins. Co., Ins., Franklin Lakes; mem. trustee Provident Loan Soc., N.Y.C., 1975—, chmn., 1992—. Mem. Econ. Club of N.Y. (sec. 1988—), Nat. Golf Links of Am. (Southampton, N.Y.), The Links, Downtown Assn., Racquet and Tennis Club, Piping Rock Club (Locust Valley, N.Y.), Meadow Brook Club (Jericho, N.Y.). Avocations: skiing; golf. Office: Brown Bros Harriman & Co 59 Wall St New York NY 10005-2808

HILLIARD, LIL, sales executive; b. Montgomery, Ala, Sept. 30, 1955; d. Louis C. and Laura M. Brewington; (div. Feb. 1, 1992); 1 child, Jeremiah Brewington. AA, So. Jr. Coll., 1974; student, Ala. State U. Sales rep. Lucky Heart Cosmetics, Memphis, Vulcan Svc., Birmingham, Ala. Avon rep., 1998-2001. Sec. Gibbs Village Cmty. Ctr., Montgomery, Ala., 1996-97; pres. Levi Watkins Libr. Club Ala. State U., 1999-2000. Recipient Golden Poet award, Poetry Guild, Calif., 1990. Mem. Custom Clothier Assn., Xperte Profl. Orgn. Democrat. Home: 2001 Terminal Rd Apt B Montgomery AL 36108-3136

HILLIARD, SAM BOWERS, geography educator; b. Hart County, Ga., Dec. 21, 1930; s. Asa Farris and Flora Elizabeth (Bowers) H.; m. Joyce Collier, June 4, 1955; children— Steven Glen, Anita Joy. AB, U. Ga., 1960, MA, 1962; MS, U. Wis., 1963, PhD, 1966. Electrician Savannal River Valley plant Dupont Co., Aiken, S.C., 1954-59; teaching asst. U. Wis., 1961-65, instr., 1965-67; asst. prof. geography So. Ill. U., 1967-71; prof. La. State U., Baton Rouge, 1971-82, alumni prof., ret., 1983-93, chmn. dept. geography, 1976-79, 85-86, dir. Sch. Geosci., 1977-79. Columnist The Hartwell Sun newspaper; historian Hart County. Author: Hog Meat and Hoecake: Food Supply in the Old South, 1972, An Atlas of Antebellum Southern Agriculture, 1984; co-author: Louisiana: Its Land and People, rev. edit., 1987, The South Revisited: Forty Years of Change, 1992, Vignettes of Hart, vol. 1, 2001, vol. 2, 2002, A Century of Rural Education: Hart County, 1860-1960, A Calling of Churches: Sketches of Hart County Churches, 2003; contbr. articles to profl. jours. County historian, 1998. Served with U.S. Navy, 1950-54. Mem. Nat. Geog. Soc., Agrl. History Assn.

HILLIER, FREDERICK STANTON, industrial engineer, educator; b. Aberdeen, Wash., Mar. 4, 1936; s. Alfred James Hillier and Bertha Sigurbjorg Jonasson; m. Ann Hardy Lester; children: David Alfred, Mark Stanton, John Kenneth. BS in Indsl. Engring., Stanford U., Calif., 1954—58, MS in Indsl. Engring., 1958—59, PhD in Indsl. Engring., 1958—61. Vis. asst. prof., indsl. engring. and adminstrn. Cornell U., Ithaca, NY, 1962—63; asst. prof., indsl. engring. Stanford U., Calif., 1961—64, assoc. prof., indsl. engring., 1964—67, assoc. prof., ops. rsch., 1967—68, prof., ops. rsch., 1968—96, assoc. chmn., dept. ops. rsch., 1977—88, prof. of ops. rsch., emeritus, 1996—; vis. prof., indsl. adminstrn. Carnegie-Mellon U., Pitt., 1969—70; guest prof., prodn. mgmt. inst. Nat. Tech. U. Denmark, Lyngby, 1976—77; Erskine fellow, Dept. Ops. Rsch. U. Canterbury, Christchurch, New Zealand, 1989; Arthur Andersen vis. fellow, judge Inst. Mgmt. Studies U. Cambridge, England, 1995—96, disting. academic visitor, Queens' Coll., 1995—96. Treas. Ops. Rsch. Soc. Am., Balt., 1974—76; v.p. for meetings Inst. of Mgmt. Scis., Providence, 1981—84, co-gen. chmn., internat. meeting, Balt., 1989; cons. Am. Coll. Testing, Iowa City, 1990—99; cons. editor Kluwer Acad. Publishers, Norwell, Mass., 1993—. Co-author: (book) Introduction to Operations Research, Introduction to Management Science, Introduction to Mathematical Programming, Introduction to Stochastic Models in Operations Research, Queueing Tables and Graphs, The Evaluation of Risky Interrelated Investments. Pres. Coun. of Chs. of Santa Clara County, San Jose, Calif., 1973—76; chmn. Commn. on Investment Responsibility of Stanford U., Calif., 1977—79, Commn. on Investment for Stanford U., Calif., 1986—88. Grantee, Office of Naval Rsch., 1964—91, NSF, 1965—85. Mem.: Math. Programming Soc., Inst. of Indsl. Engring., Inst. of Ops. Rsch. and Mgmt. Scis. Home: 915 Cottrell Way Stanford CA 94305-1057 Office: Stanford Univ Mgmt Sci and Engring Stanford CA 94305-4026 Home Fax: 603-687-0647. E-mail: fhillier@stanford.edu.

HILLIER, JAMES, technology management executive, researcher; b. Brantford, Ont., Can., Aug. 22, 1915; came to U.S., 1940; s. James Sr. and Ethel Anne (Cooke) H.; m. Florence Marjory Bell, Oct. 24, 1936 (dec. 1992); children: James Robert, William Wynship (dec.). BA, U. Toronto, 1937, MA, 1938, PhD, 1941, DSc (hon.), 1978, N.J. Inst. Tech., 1981; LLD (hon.), Wilfrid Laurier U., 2002. Rsch. asst. Banting Inst. U. Toronto Med. Sch., 1938-40; head electron microscope rsch. RCA Labs., Camden and Princeton, N.J., 1940-53; adminstrv. engr. corp. rsch. and engring. RCA Corp., Princeton, 1954-55, chief engr. comml. electronic products Camden, 1955-57, gen. mgr. labs. Princeton, 1957-58, v.p. labs., 1958-68, v.p. corp. rsch. and engring. N.Y.C., 1968-69, exec. v.p. rsch. and engring., 1969-76, exec. v.p., sr. scientist, 1976-77, ret., 1977; dir. corp. rsch. Westinghouse Air Brake Co., Pitts. and Alexandria, Va., 1953-54. Mem. higher edn. study com. Gov.'s Office, State of N.J., 1963-64; mem. commerce tech. adv. bd. U.S. Dept. Commerce, Washington, 1964-70; chmn. adv. coun. dept. elect. engring. Princeton U., 1963-65; mem. adv. coun. Coll. Engring., Cornell U., Ithaca, N.Y., 1966-99; mem. joint consultative com. U.S. AID/Egyptian Acad. Sci. Rsch. and Tech., Cairo, 1978-84. Co-author: Electron Optics and the Electron Microscope, 1945; co-contbr.: Medical Physics, 1944, vol. II, 1950, Colloidal Chemistry, vol. VI, 1946; contbr. Ency. Britannica, 1948. Pres., founder James Hillier Found., Inc., 1996—. Decorated officer Order of Can; inducted into Nat. Inventors Hall of Fame, 1980, N.J. Inventors Hall of Fame, 1992; recipient James Loudon Gold medal U. Toronto, 1937, Albert Lasker award APHA, 1960, Commonwealth award, 1980, Presdl. award Microbeam Analysis Soc., 1989; mem. Can. Sci. and Engring. Hall of Fame, 02. Fellow AAAS (chmn. nomination com. sect. M 1965), IEEE (David Sarnoff award 1967, Founders medal 1981), Am. Phys. Soc. (mem. at large, governing bd. 1964-65); mem. Microscope Soc. Am. (pres. 1944, Disting. Scientist award 1977), Indsl. Rsch. Inst. (bd. dirs. 1960-65, pres. 1964, Inst. medal 1975), Nat. Inventors Hall of Fame Found., Inc. (bd. dirs. 1992—, Lifetime Achievement award 2002), Nat. Acad. Engring. (coun. 1971), Rotary (bd. dirs. 1988-91), Nassau Club, Sigma Xi. Achievements include 41 patents in field; co-design of first successful electron microscope in North America; of first commercially available electron microscope in North America; discovery of principle of Stigmator for correcting astigmatism of electron microscope objective lenses; invention of electron microprobe microanalyser; first to picture tobacco mosaic virus, bacterial viruses and ultra-thin section of a single bacterium. Home: 22 Arreton Rd Princeton NJ 08540-1402

HILLIER, J(AMES) ROBERT, architect; b. Toronto, Ont., Can., July 24, 1937; came to U.S., 1941, naturalized, 1961; s. James and Florence (Bell) H.; m. Barbara Ann Weinstein, Apr. 7, 1986; 1 child, Jordan Rebecca Hillier; children by previous marriage-Kimberly (dec.), James Baldwin. BA, Princeton U., 1959, MFA, 1961; MBA (hon.), Bryant Coll., 1992. Project designer J. Labatut, Princeton, N.J., 1961-62; project mgr. Fulmer & Bowers, Princeton, 1961-66; prin. J. Robert Hillier, Princeton, 1966-72; pres. The Hillier Group, Princeton, 1972-87, chmn. bd., 1987—. Adj. faculty mem. Sch. Arch. Princeton U. Prin. works include Bryant Coll. campus, Smithfield, R.I., 1969, Peddie Campus Bldgs., 1970—, Rutgers U. Athletic Center, Piscataway, N.J., 1977, Butler Hosp, Providence, 1978, N.J. State Justice Complex, Trenton, 1985, Harbor Island Design, Tampa, Fla., 1981, Beneficial Corp. Complex, 1982, Merritt Tower, 1985, Wharton Sch. Exec. Ctr., 1986, N.J. Aquarium, 1991, Am. Home Products Corp. Headquarters, 1992, Sprint World Hqrs., 1997, Glaxo Smith Kline Hdqrs., 1998, Capital One Corp. Hdqrs., 2002. Trustee Peddie Sch., Hightstown, N.J., 1981—, McCarter Theatre, Princeton, 1983-89, Bryant Coll., Smithfield, R.I., 1993-96, Edison Coll. Found., Milton Hershey Sch.; bd. overseers N.J. Inst. Tech. Recipient over 250 design awards from archtl. assns., 1966—; Architect of Yr. award N.J. Contractors Assn., 1976, 87, 92, 97, Disting. Svc. award Internat. Assn. Conf. Ctrs., 1988, Award of Excellence N.J. Bus. and Industry Assn., 1988, N.J. Entrepreneur of Yr., 1989, Community Svc. Human Rels. award, 1992, Da Vinci award Profl. Svc. Mgmt. Assn., 2002. Fellow AIA (v.p. N.J. chpt. 1974); mem. Nat. Coun. Archtl. Registration Bds., Princeton Quadrangle Club, Nassau Club, Princeton Club, Lookaway Golf Club. Avocations: running, swimming, golf. Home: 2846 River Rd New Hope PA 18938-9527 Office: The Hillier Group 500 Alexander Rd Princeton NJ 08540-6002 E-mail: jrhillier@hillier.com.

HILLIER, WYNSHIP WEST, systems engineer; b. Norwood, Mass., June 13, 1968; s. William Wynship and Jacquelyn (West) Hillier. BA, U. Calif., Santa Cruz, 1994; MS, Stanford U., Calif., 1997. Software engr. Century Analysis, Inc., Pacheco, Calif., 1995—96, sys. analyst, 1996; prin. Kalchas, Inc., South Bend, Ind., Pitts. and San Francisco, 1997—. Cons. South Bend Med. Found., 1996—97; dir. East End Food Coop Fed. Credit Union, Pitts., 2001—02. Recipient Dean's Undergrad. Rsch. award, Natural Scis. divsn. U. Calif.-Santa Cruz, 1994. Mem.: Soc. for Bayesian Analysts, Inst. for Ops. Rsch. and the Mgmt. Scis., The Commonwealth Club (sci. and tech. com. 2002—). Achievements include development of nonparametric method of estimating probability densities using a Bayesian network. Office: Kalchas Inc 3380 20th St #202 San Francisco CA 94610-1959

HILLINGER, CHARLES, journalist, writer; b. Evanston, Ill., Apr. 1, 1926; s. William Agidious H. and Caroline Bruning; m. Arliene Otis, June 22, 1948; children: Brad, Tori. BS in Polit. Sci., UCLA, 1951; degree (hon.), Marymount Coll., Rancho Palos Verdes, 1997. Circulation mgr., columnist Park Ridge (Ill.) Advocate, 1938-41; copy boy, libr., feature writer Chgo. Tribune, 1941-43; reporter, feature writer, syndicated columnist L.A. Times, 1946-92, ret., 1992. Author: California Islands, 1957, Bel-Air Country Club, A Living Legend, 1993, Charles Hillinger's America, 1996, Charles Hillinger's Channel Islands, 1998, Hillinger's California, 1997, California Characters, 2002, (audiobooks) Charles Hillinger's America, 1999, California Characters, 2001, California, 2003. Mem. adv. bd. Santa Cruz Is. Found., Santa Barbara, Calif., 1992—; treas. 8-Ball Welfare Found. Greater L.A. Press Club, 1992—. With USN, 1943-46. Mem. Greater L.A. Press Club (sec. 1978-88, v.p. 1988-90, pres. 1990-92), Dutch Treat Club W. Avocations: tennis, golf, hearts. Home: 3131 Dianora Dr Rancho Palos Verdes CA 90275 E-mail: chxlat@aol.com.

HILLIS, JOHN DAVID, television news executive, producer, writer; b. Washington, Dec. 28, 1952; s. Willard E. and Holly M. Hillis; m. Catherine H. McQuaig, Nov. 21, 1975; children: Faith Courteney, David Esten, Elizabeth Nicole. AB in Journalism, U. Ga., 1975. Film editor Sta. WSB-TV, Atlanta, 1973-74, asst. producer, 1974-76, news producer, 1976; exec. news producer Sta. KOTV-TV, Tulsa, 1976-79; news producer Sta. WRAL-TV, Raleigh, N.C., 1979-80, Cable News Network, Inc., Atlanta, 1980-81, exec. producer, Newswatch, 1981-83, exec. producer, 1983-84, spl. events producer, 1984; news dir. Cablevision Systems Corp., Woodbury, N.Y., 1984-86; gen. mgr. Rainbow News 12 Co., Woodbury, 1986-89; pres., CEO Allnewsco, Inc., Washington, 1989—, Newschannel 8 Cable Svc., Springfield, Va., 1991—. Contbr. articles to profl. jours. Mem. strategic com. Greater Washington Bd. of Trade; bd. dirs. Va. Cmty. Found. Recipient Radio Newscast award Ga. AP Broadcasters, 1973, TV Newscast award Okla. AP Broadcasters, 1978, TV Series award News Acad. Cable Programming, 1985, Washington Region Emmy award, 1997, Cable Ace awards, 1996, 97, 98, Cmty. Spirit award NCTA, 1999, Scripps-Howard award, 1999. Mem. NATAS (Bd. of Govs. award Washington chpt.), Soc. Profl. Journalists (disting. svc. award 1998), Radio TV News Dirs. Assn., Nat. Press Club, Assn. Regional News Channels (founder, chmn. 1993), Nat. Cable T.V. Assn. (satellite network com.). Methodist. Office: Newschannel 8 7600 Boston Blvd # D Springfield VA 22153-3136

HILLIS, ROBERT GREGORY, investment executive; b. Meadville, Pa., Sept. 9, 1959; s. Robert Ellsworth Hillis and Nancy Marie (Bish) Johnson; m. Akleema Ali, June 16, 1984; children: Donna Marie, Nicole Marie. BS with honors, Pa. State U., 1981; grad., Securities Industry Inst./U.Pa, 1995. Student intern U.S. Securities and Exch. Commn., Arlington, Va., 1981; compliance examiner Rauscher Pierce Refsnes, Inc., Dallas, 1982-83, investment broker, asst. br. mgr., 1983-86, investment broker, 1988-90, Banc Texas Securities, Inc.,

Dallas, 1983, Tucker Anthony & R.L. Day, Inc., Dallas, 1986-88; v.p., asst. br. mgr. Kemper Securities, Inc., Dallas, 1990-94, v.p., mgr. tng. and devel. Chgo., 1994; sr. v.p., dir. tng. and devel. H.J. Meyers & Co., Inc., Dallas, 1994-98; dir. edn. and devel., regional sales mgr. Tex. Josephthal and Co., Inc., Dallas, 1998-2000; pres. Josephthal & Co. Ins. Agy. of Tex., Inc., Dallas, 1999-2000; chief learning mgr. Penson Fin., Svcs., Inc., Dallas, 2001—02; v.p., chief learning and comm. officer Penson Fin. Svcs., Inc., Dallas, 2002—. Republican. Presbyterian. Avocations: gourmet cooking, fitness, travel. Home: 11024 Creekmere Dr Dallas TX 75218-1950 Office: 1700 Pacific Ave Ste 1400 Dallas TX 75201 E-mail: bhillis@penson.com.

HILLIS, STEPHEN KENDALL, secondary education educator; b. Hillsboro, Oreg., Jan. 5, 1942; s. Earnest Howard Hillis and Phyllis Noreen (Bagley) Gortner; m. Sharon Ione Arbogast, Aug. 5, 1967; children: Jeff Wise, Teryl Dorothy, Tonya Noreen. BA, Pacific U., 1965. Cert. Std. Oreg. Dept. Edn. H.s. tchr., Eagle Grove, Iowa, 1967-73, Madras, Oreg., 1973—2002; ret., 2002. Mem. consumer adv. coun. Oreg. Atty. Gen., 1998—. Precinct com. Jefferson County Dems., Madras, 1978-89, 2000—, chair precinct com. 1988-91, 2003—, vice chair, 2001-2003; bd. dirs. Jefferson County Libr., 2000—; bd. dirs. Area Cmty. Action Team, 2002—, Oreg. Cmty. Found., 2003—; ctrl. Oreg. leadership team Oreg. Cmty. Found. With USAR, 1959—65. Mem. ASCD, NEA (human civil rights com. 1990-96, bd. dirs. 1993-2000), Oreg. Edn. Assn. (bd. dirs. 1983-2000, v.p. 1988-93). Democrat. Home: 375 NE Chestnut St Madras OR 97741-1910 Office: 509J Sch Dist 390 S Tenth St Madras OR 97741 E-mail: shillis@crestviewcable.com.

HILLIS, WILLIAM DANIEL, biology educator; b. Paris, Ark., June 12, 1933; s. Charles Raymond Hillis and Carra Elizabeth (Daniel) Coffee; m. Argye Idell Briggs, Dec. 23, 1952; children: William Daniel Jr., David Mark, Argye Elizabeth Trupe. BS, Baylor U., 1953; MD, Johns Hopkins U., 1957. Lic. in medicine and surgery, Md., Tex. Asst. prof. pathobiology Johns Hopkins U. and Sch. Hygiene and Pub. Health, Balt., 1965-68, assoc. prof., 1968-72; asst. prof. Johns Hopkins U. Sch. Medicine, Balt., 1972-76, assoc. prof., 1976-82; prof., chmn. dept. biology Baylor U., Waco, Tex., 1982-85, Cornelia Marshall Smith prof. biology, 1985-98, disting. prof. biology, 1995—, exec. v.p., 1985-89, v.p. student affairs, 1989-98. Cons. Nat. Cancer Inst., Bethesda, Md., 1965-68, Nat. Heart and Lung Inst., Bethesda, 1977-82; dir. Health Professions Rsch. Tng. Program, Balt., 1979-82, Out-Patient Clin. Rsch. Ctr., Balt., 1975-82. Contbr. articles to profl. jours. Pres. Bapt. Home Md., Balt., 1972-81; Md. rep. exec. com. So. Bapt. Conv., NAshville, 1977-82; bd. dirs. Food for Hungry, Glendale, Calif., 1972-82, Caritas, Waco, Tex., chair, 1989-95. Col. USAF, 1960-65, USAFR, 1965-85. Recipient Louis Livingston Seaman award Assn. Mil. Surgeons U.S., 1978, Disting. Alumnus award Baylor U., 1998; named Outstanding Prof. Baylor U., 1985. Mem. Am. Assn. Immunologists, Soc. for Exptl. Biology and Medicine, Am. Soc. for Microbiology, N.Y. Acad. Sci., McLennan County Med. Soc., Waco C. of C. (bd. dirs. 1987), Johns Hopkins Soc. of Scholars, Mortar Bd., Phi Beta Kappa, Alpha Omega Alpha, Omicron Delta Kappa. Clubs: Brazos (Waco); Johns Hopkins (Balt.). Democrat. Avocations: vocal music, drama, gardening, carpentry, philately. Home: 3640 Alta Vista Dr Waco TX 76706-3741 Office: Baylor Univ PO Box 97388 Waco TX 76798-7388

HILLIS-DINEEN, MADALYN, marketing professional, astrologer, writer; b. Bklyn, NY, June 23, 1951; d. Arthur and Agatha (Bartoletti) Botterio; m. Daniel Patrick Hillis, Sept. 6, 1971 (div. Aug. 1984); children: Mark Christopher, Katharine Zoe; m. Douglas W. Dineen, Sept. 29, 1996. BS, St. John's U., 1972. Fin. analyst Nat. Bank N.Am., NYC, 1972-75; asst. dir. N.Y. State Chiropractic Assn., NYC, 1975; vol. Nat. Coun. for Geocosmic Rsch., Ramsey, NJ, 1979-90, exec. dir., 1990-94; mktg. dir. Astrolabe, Inc., Brewster, Mass., 1994—. Cons. Astrascope Corp., Melrose, Mass., 1991-93; cons., mgr. astrology product Malhotra and Assoc., Cranbury, NJ, 1992-93. Co-author: Astrology for Women: Roles and Relationships, 1997; editor Urania, 1986-87; author, editor Nat. Coun. for Geocosmic Rsch. Memberletter, 1986-94; author Nat. Coun. for Geocosmic Rsch. Jour., 1991; monthly columnist Horoscope Guide, 1991-92; contbg. author: (mag.) Cape Women, 1998-2000, Your Birthday Sign in Time, 2002; feature author www.stariq.com, 1999-2001. Pres. Village Sch. Parent Guild, Ridgewood, NJ, 1987-89; troop leader Girl Scouts US, 1991-94; dir. yearbook Ramsey Jr. Football Assn., 1991-93. Recipient Regulus award for cmty. svc. United Astrology Congress, 1995. Mem. Astrological Soc. Princeton, Assn. for Astrological Networking, Nat. Coun. Geocosmic Rsch., B.P.W. Lower Cape Cod (pres. 2001-02). Office: Astrolabe Inc PO Box 1750 Brewster MA 02631-7750 E-mail: madalyn@alabe.com.

HILLJE, BARBARA BROWN, lawyer; b. Carlisle, Pa., Dec. 18, 1942; d. R. Morrison and Gladys M. (Lauver) Brown; m. John W. Hillje, Mar. 23, 1968. AB, Vassar Coll., 1964; BS in Edn., Ind. U. Pa., 1965; MA, Temple U., 1971, ABD, 1977; JD, Villanova U., 1984. Bar: Pa. 1984, U.S. Dist. Ct. (ea. dist.) Pa. 1984, N.J. 1985, U.S. Dist. Ct. N.J. 1985, U.S. Supreme Ct. 1990. English tchr. Council Rock Sr. High Sch., Newtown, Pa., 1965-68; assoc. Harry J. Agzigian and Assocs., Levittown, Pa., 1985-87; pvt. practice Langhorne, Pa., 1987—. Contbr. articles to profl. journals. Bd. dirs., pres. bd. Children of Aging Parents, Levittown, 1985-93; mem. facility ethics com. Statesman Health & Rehab. Ctr., Levittown, Pa., 1996—; bd. dirs. D'Youville Manor, 2001—. Recipient Women Helping Women award Soroptimists of Indian Rock, Inc., 1995; named Woman of Yr., Lower Bucks AAUW, 1985, Neshaminy BPW, 1987, Legal Humanitarian of Yr., Bucks County United Way, 1994, Consumer Connection award, 1996. Mem. AAUW (bd. dirs. 1978—, legis. cons. Pa. divsn. 1990-92), Middletown-Newtown LWV (bd. dirs. 1983-89, citizen campaign watch adv. panel 1992, 94, 96), Pa. Bar Assn., Nat. Acad. Elder Law Attys., Older Women's League (legis. chair 1984-94, Women of Worth award 1993). Office: 506 Corporate Dr W Langhorne PA 19047-8011

HILLMAN, ALAN L. internist, educator, researcher; b. NYC, July 12, 1956; s. Herman David and Edith (Geilich) H.; m. Janice Kubo, July 9, 1983; children: Jennifer, Abigail. BA cum laude, Cornell U., 1978, MD, 1981; MBA, U. Pa., 1986. Intern in internal medicine N.Y. Hosp., 1981-82, asst. resident in internal medicine, 1982-84; dir. clin. programs Hosps. of U. of Pa., Phila., 1986-90, med. dir. Health Pass, 1987-90; assoc. dir. med. group U. Pa., Phila., 1987-90, sr. scholar clin. epidemiology, 1990—, dir. Ctr. for Health Policy, 1990-98, mem. comprehensive cancer ctr., 1992; assoc. prof. health care Wharton Sch., U. Pa., Phila., 1993—96, prof. health care mgmt., 1996—; assoc. prof. medicine Sch. of Medicine, U. Pa., Phila., 1993—96, prof. medicine, 1996—; assoc. dean health svcs. rsch. U. Pa., Phila., 1995-98. Asst. instr. dept. medicine NY Hosp.-Cornell Med. Ctr., 1981-84; asst. prof. medicine and health care mgmt. Sch. Medicine and Wharton Sch., U. Pa., Phila., 1986-93, assoc. prof., 1993-99, prof., 1999—; mem. Inst. for Human Gene Therapy, U. Pa. Med. Ctr., Phila., 1995-96; discharge planning com. Hosp. of U. Pa., 1986-88, drug use effects com., 1990-91; admissions and awards com. health care mgmt. dept. Wharton Sch., 1990-92; exec. com. Leonard Davis Inst. Health Econs., 1990—, sr. fellow, 1984—; co-dir. Health of the Pub. program Sch. Medicine, 1991-92; com. on jud. ethics U. Pa., 1993-99; ctr. for bioethics adv. com., faculty senate Sch. Medicine, 1994-2000, master's program in med. ethics adv. com. Coll. Arts and Scis., 1995-99, com. on health svcs. rsch. Sch. Medicine, 1995-99, com. on multiculturalism in rsch. Inst. on Aging, 1995-99, info. sys. strategic planning steering com. Sch. Medicine, 1996; cons. Solvay Pharms., Marietta, Ga., U. Mo. Sch. Medicine, Columbia, 1994, UNISYS Corp., Blue Bell, Pa., 1993, Prudential Ins. Co., Atlanta, 1993-96, PACC Bd. of Dirs., Clackamas, Oreg., 1993, Gate Pharms., Kulpsville, Pa., 1994-95, Exogen Co., Princeton, N.J., 1994-96, Forest Labs., N.Y.C., 1994-96, VidaMed Corp., Palo Alto, Calif., 1993-95, Health Industry Mfrs. Assn., Washington, 1993-99, Proctor & Gamble, Morris Plains, N.J., 1993, Syntex, 1993-99, Eli Lilly Corp., Indpls., 1993-95, Amgen, Thousand Oaks, 1993—, Rhone-Poulenc Rorer, Antony Cedex, France, 1992—, Abbott Labs., Abbott Park, Ill., 1991-99, others. Contbr. numerous articles to profl. jours. and newspapers. Recipient Article of the Year award Assn. for Health Svcs. Rsch., 1990, Young Investigator's award, 1993. Fellow ACP, Am. Bd. Internal Medicine; mem. Internat. Soc. Tech. Assessment in Health Care, Soc. Gen. Internal Medicine, Phila. Coll. Physicians, Internat. Soc. for Pharm. Outcome Rsch., Am. Fedn. for Clin. Rsch., Assn. for Health Svcs. Rsch., Physicians for Social Responsibility, Soc. Gen. Internal Medicine, Am. Soc. for Clin. Investigation, Alpha Omega Alpha, Gamma Beta Sigma. Office: U Pa Sch Medicine Dvsn Gen Internal Med 423 Guardian Dr Philadelphia PA 19104-4209

HILLMAN, BRUCE JAY, radiologist, researcher, consultant, educator; b. Miami, Apr. 16, 1947; s. Henry and Mildred (Semel) H.; 1 child, Aaron Gartner. BA, Princeton U., 1969; MD, U. Rochester, 1973. Diplomate Am. Bd. Radiology. Med. intern George Washington U. Med. Ctr., Washington, 1973-74; radiology resident Peter Bent Brigham Hosp., Boston, 1974-78; NIH clin. rsch. fellow Harvard U., Boston, 1975-78; asst. prof. U. Ariz., Tucson, 1978-81, assoc. prof., 1981-85; Pew Health Policy fellow Rand Corp., Santa Monica, Calif., 1984-85; prof. radiology, vice-chmn. radiology dept. U. Ariz., 1985-92; prof. radiology and health evaluation scis. U. Va., Charlottesville, 1992—, chmn. radiology dept., 1992—2003. Sr. scholar Va. Health Policy Ctr., Charlottesville, 1992-2000; cons. Rand Corp., Santa Monica, 1985—, United Mine Workers of Am. Health and Retirement Funds, Washington, 1989-1995; pres. U. Radiology Devel. Corp., Charlottesville, 1996-; chmn. Am. Coll. Radiology Imaging Network-NCI Clin. Trials Cooperative Group, 1999-. Author: Imaging and Hypertension, 1981; contbr. more than 140 articles to profl. jours., 47 chpts. to books, revs., and editls.; editor-in-chief Investigative Radiology, 1989-94, Academic Radiology, 1994-97, Am. Coll. Radiology, 2003-. Mem. Princeton Schs. Commn., Charlottesville, 1993—. Recipient 4 major fellowships, 29 honorary or named lectures. Fellow Am. Coll. Radiology; mem. Soc. Uroradiology (pres. 1994), Soc. Health Svcs. Rsch. in Radiology (pres. 1995-1997), Assn. Univ. Radiologists (pres. 1997), Soc. Chmn. Acad. Radiology Depts. (councillor 1994-96), Acad. Radiology Rsch. (exec. com. 1995—), Ea. Radiol. Soc. (pres. 1994), bd. chancellors Am. Coll. Radiology, 1997-. Avocations: golf, fly fishing, reading, digital photography. Office: Univ Va Health Sci Ctr Dept Radiology PO Box 170 Charlottesville VA 22902-0170

HILLMAN, CAROL BARBARA, communications executive, consultant; b. Sept. 6, 1940; d. Joseph Hoppenfeld and Elsa (Spiegel) Hoppenfeld Resika; m. Howard D. Hillman, May 25, 1969. BA with honors, U. Wis., 1961; postgrad., U. Lyon, France, 1961-62; MA, Cornell U., 1966. Asst. editor Holt Rinehart & Winston Pubs., 1965-66; staff assoc. pub. rels. Ea. Airlines, N.Y.C., 1966-74; pub. affairs mgr. Squibb Corp., N.Y.C., 1974-75; asst. dir. corp. pub. rels. Burlington Industries, N.Y.C., 1975-77, dir. corp. pub. rels., 1977-80, v.p. pub. rels., 1980-82; v.p. corp. comms. Norton Co., Worcester, Mass., 1982-89, sr. cons., 1989-90; nat. dir. pub. rels. and comms. Deloitte & Touche, Wilton, Conn., 1990-91; v.p. univ. rels. Boston U., 1991-95; prin. Hillman & Kersey Strategic Comms., 1995-2000, CB Hillman & Assocs., 2000—. Mem. pub. affairs coun. Machinery & Allied Products Inst., 1982-89; mem. dep. policy com., agenda com. Mass. Bus. Roundtable, 1982-89; trustee Mass. Econ. Stabilization Trust, 1986-2003; bd. dirs. Commonwealth Corp. Mem. Cornell Coun., Ithaca, 1981—85, pub. rels. com., 1981—88; mem. adv. coun. Coll. Human Ecology, Cornell U., Ithaca, 1982—84; mem. bd. visitors coll. letter sci. U. Wis., 1996—99; mem. adv. bd. Ct. Apptd. Spl. Advocates, Worcester, 1983—87; bd. dirs. Planned Parenthood League Mass., 1986—90, pub. affairs com., 1991—2002; trustee Quinsigamond C.C., Worcester, 1987—98; mem. exec. com. Save America's Treasures: Preserving Eleanor Roosevelt's Home at Val-Kill, 2000—; voting mem. Wis. Union Trustees, U. Wis., Madison, 1982—, trustee, 1990—; mem. Clark U. Assocs., Worcester, 1983—89. Fulbright scholar, U. Lyon, 1961—62, Cornell grad. fellow, 1962—63. Mem. Internat. Women's Forum, Mass. Women's Forum, Arthur Page Soc., The Wisemen, Phi Beta Kappa, Mortar Bd., Phi Kappa Phi. Home: 299 Belknap Rd Framingham MA 01701-4716 Office: CB Hillman & Assocs 299 Belknap Rd Framingham MA 01701-4716 E-mail: chillman96@aol.com.

HILLMAN, CAROLE DOROTHY, education educator, educator; b. Chgo., Nov. 24; d. Thomas James and Dorothy Marianne (Fritz) H.; m. Leo Frank Obriecht, Aug. 28, 1953 (dec. May 1983). BEd, Chgo. State U., 1953; MEd, U. Ill., 1959; EdD, No. Ill. U., 1985, postgrad., 1986. Learning ctr. coord. and dir. Sch. Dist. 161, Flossmoor, Ill., 1960-79; 6th grade tchr. Hollister (Mo.) Elem. Sch., 1979-80; asst. prof. edn. Coll. of the Ozarks, Pt. Lookout, Mo., 1980-82; assoc. prin., gifted coord., computer coord., libr. Butler Sch. Dist. 53, Oak Brook, Ill., 1982-95; assoc. prof. edn., dir. elem. edn. Elmhurst (Ill.) Coll., 1995—. Pvt. practice ednl. cons., Downers Grove, Ill., 1982—; spokesperson Valley Pub. Co., Appleton, Wis., 1993—. Author: Bold Beginning in Early Childhood, 1976, Learning Center/Organization an2 Implementation, 1977, Early Math Tapes, 1978, Critical Thinking Skills, 1984; appeared in film Beyond the Book, 1975 (award State of Ill.); writer Chgo. Tribune. Recipient Hon. Mention award for media program State of Ill. Bd. Edn., 1989, award for outstanding media program in U.S., Ednl. Facility Ctr., 1974. Mem. ASCD (bd. dirs. 1994-95, chair Ill. state elem. conf. 1995), Phi Delta Kappa, Kappa Delta Pi (pres. Tau Nu chpt. 1993-95, chair state 3d ann. elem. IASCD conf., editor Record). Avocations: collecting antiques, oil painting, stewarding dog shows, writing. Home: 10604 Golf Rd Orland Park IL 60462-7421 Office: Elmhurst Coll Elmhurst IL 60126

HILLMAN, DOUGLAS WOODRUFF, retired judge; b. Grand Rapids, Mich., Feb. 15, 1922; s. Lemuel Serrell and Dorothy (Woodruff) H.; m. Sally Jones, Sept. 13, 1944; children: Drusilla W., Clayton D. (dec.). Student, Phillips Exeter Acad., 1941; AB, U. Mich., 1946, LL.B., 1948. Bar: Mich. 1948, U.S. Supreme Ct. 1967. Assoc. Lilly, Luyendyk & Snyder, Grand Rapids, 1948-53; partner Luyendyk, Hainer, Hillman, Karr & Dutcher, Grand Rapids, 1953-65, Hillman, Baxter & Hammond, 1965-79; U.S. dist. judge Western Dist. Mich., Grand Rapids, 1979—, chief judge, 1986-91, sr. judge, 1991—2002; ret., 2002. Instr. Nat. Inst. Trial Adv., Boulder, Colo; dir. Fed. Judges Assn.; mem. jud. conf. com. on Adminstrn. of Magistrate Judges Sys., 1993-99; chair 6th Circuit Standing Com. on Jud. Conf. Planning; mem. exec. com. ABA jud. adminstrn. divsn. Nat. Conf. Fed. Trial Judges, 1995-98. Co-author articles in legal publs. Chmn. Grand Rapids Human Relations Commn., 1963-66; chmn. bd. trustees Fountain St. Ch., 1970-72; pres. Family Service Assn., 1967. Served as pilot USAAF, 1943-45. Decorated Air medal DFC; named One of 25 Most Respected Judges, Mich. Laywers Weekly, Grand Rapids Med. Hall Fame, 2001; recipient Ann. Civil Liberties award, ACLU, 1970, Disting. ALumni award, Ctrl. High Sch., 1986, Raymond Fox Advocacy award, 1989, Champion of Justice award, State Bar Mich., 1990, Profl. & Cmty. Svc. award, Young Lawyers Sect., 1996, Svc. to Profession award, Fed. Bar Assn., 1991; grantee Paul Harris fellow, Rotary Internat. Fellow Am. Bar Found.; mem. ABA, Mich. Bar Assn. (chmn. client security fund), Grand Rapids Bar Assn. (pres. 1963), Am. Coll. Trial Lawyers (Mich. chmn. 1979, com. on teaching trial and appellate adv.), 6th Circuit Jud. Conf. (life), Internat. Acad. Trial Lawyers, Fedn. Ins. Counsel, Internat. Assn. Ins. Counsel, Internat. Soc. Barristers (pres 1977-78, chair annual Hillman Trial Adv. Seminar 1982—), M Club of U. Mich. (com. visitors U. Mich. Law Sch.), Univ. Club (Grand Rapids), Torch Club. Home: 10743 Lost Valley Rd Montague MI 49437

HILLMAN, HENRY L. investment company executive; b. Pitts., Dec. 25, 1918; s. J.H. (Jr.) and Juliet Cummins (Lea) H.; m. Elsie Mead Hilliard, May 12, 1945; children: Lea, Audrey, Henry, William. AB, Princeton U., 1941. Chmn. bd. Hillman Co. Emeritus mem. exec. com. Allegheny Conf. on Cmty. Devel.; chmn. Hillman Found., Inc.; trustee emeritus Carnegie Inst. Lt. USNR, 1942—45. Mem.: Duquesne (Pitts.), Pitts. Golf, Fox Chapel Golf, Rolling Rock (Ligionier, Pa.) (hon. gov.), Laurel Valley Golf (Ligionier, Pa.), Links (N.Y.C.). Home: Morewood Heights Pittsburgh PA 15213 Office: Hillman Co 330 Grant St Pittsburgh PA 15219-2202

HILLMAN, HOWARD BUDROW, author, editor, publisher, consultant; b. Hollywood, Calif, Dec. 8, 1934; s. Donald Edward and Rebecca (Budrow) H. BA, Calif. State U.-Long Beach, 1959; MBA, Harvard U., 1961. Pres. Nat. Acad. Sports, N.Y.C., 1961, Howard Hillman Co., N.Y.C., 1966—; editor, pub. Howard Hillman Publs., N.Y.C., 1982—; pres. Customer Satisfaction Inst., N.Y.C., 1986—; editor, pub. Quality Digest, N.Y.C., 1987—. V.p. Am. Film Theatre, N.Y.C., 1972-74; internat. lectr. and cons. in field Author: Hillman's Insiders Guide to New York Restaurants, 1969, The Ins and Outs of Living in New York, 1970, New York at a Glance, 1971, San Francisco at a Glance, 1971, Chicago at a Glance, 1971, Hawaii at a Glance, 1972, Washington at a Glance, 1972, Boston at a Glance, 1972, Florida at a Glance, 1972, The Complete New Yorker, 1972, The Art of Winning Foundation Grants, 1975, The Art of Winning Government Grants, 1977, The Diner's Guide to Wine, 1978, The Book of World Cuisines, 1979, The Art of Winning Corporate Grants, 1980, The Art of Writing Business Reports and Proposals, 1980, The Cook's Book, 1981, Kitchen Science, 1981, Great Peasant Dishes of the World, 1983, The Gourmet Guide to Beer, 1983, The Art of Dining Out, 1984, The Macmillan Complete Computer Buyer's Checklist, 1984, The Computer Log, 1985, Avoiding Computer Nightmares, 1985, Public Domain Software on File for the Apple, 1985, Hillman's Restaurant Ratings, 1986, Public Domain Software on File for the IBM, 1986, New Kitchen Science, 1989, The Educated Palate, 1991, Quality Digest, 1992, The Art of Satisfying Customers, 1993, Quality Consensus, 1994, The CSI Critique Book, 1995, The Art and Psychology of Pleasing Diners, 1996, Hillman Travel Wonders of the World, 1998, Hillman Wonders, 2000, New Kitchen Science, 2002; contbr. articles to various mags., newspapers and jours.; guest radio, TV talk shows. Served with U.S. Army, 1954-56. Mem.: Harvard (N.Y.). Episcopalian. Home and Office: 220 E 63rd St New York NY 10021-7660

HILLMAN, LEON, electrical engineer; b. N.Y.C., July 31, 1921; s. Harry and Jennie (Gartenberg) H.; m. Rita Katchen, July 18, 1948; children: David, Deborah. BEE, NYU, 1950. Registered profl. engr., N.J. Radio engr. Communication Devel. Co., Newark, 1940-42; head elec. sect. U.S. Army Engring. Lab., Ft. Monmouth, n.J., 1942-45; rsch. assoc. Elec. Engring. Dept., NYU, N.Y.C., 1946-51; v.p., chief engr. Prodn. Rsch. Corp., Thornwood, N.Y., 1951-56; pres. Automation Dynamics Corp., Northvale, N.J., 1957-71, ADCO Aerospace Inc., Closter, N.J., 1971—. Electronics cons. Johnson Controls, Milw., 1949-69; lectr. in field. Contbr. articles to profl. jours. Chmn. United Jewish Appeal, Englewood, N.J., 1960, Demarest, N.J., 1978. Sgt. USAAF, 1945-46. Named Hon. Citizen, State of Md., 1957. Mem. IEEE, Am. Phys. Soc., Sigma Xi, Eta Kappa Nu. Achievements include patents for meteorological instruments, industrial controls and water sterilization; design of instruments used in space flight and lunar landing; invention of electronic controlled water treatment system.

HILLMAN, LIN (LINDA LOU HILLMAN), nursing administrator; b. Hillsboro, Wis., July 1, 1948; d. Laurence Jones and Carole Louise (Sonnenberg) Anderson; children: Chad Anthony, Liza Lin. ADN in Tech. Nursing, Western Wis. Tech. Coll., 1984; BSN, Viterbo Coll., 1990. RN, Wis. Staff nurse ob-gyn., med. surg. nurse Tomah (Wis.) Meml. Hosp., 1984-85; staff nurse respiratory care Vets. Affairs Med. Ctr., Tomah, 1985-90, head nurse, 1990, instr. nursing edn., 1990-93, assoc. chief nursing svc./edn., 1993-94, assoc. chief nursing, 1994-99, specialty clinics bus. devel. program mgr., 1999—2000, patient safety nurse, 2000—03. Avocations: horticulture, bicycling, oil painting. Home: PO Box 922 Tomah WI 54660 Office: Vets Adminstrn Med Ctr Tomah WI 54660

HILLMAN, SANDRA SCHWARTZ, public relations executive, marketing professional; b. Chester, Pa., 1941; m. Robert S. Hillman, Apr. 1964; children: Pamela Hillman Loeb, Allison Buchalter. BA, Pa. State U., 1962. Assoc. editor McFadden-Bartell Pub., N.Y.C., 1963-64; pub. rels. account exec. Edward M. Meyers & Assocs., N.Y.C., 1964-66; info. officer Nat. Tchr. Corps, U.S. Office Edn., Washington, 1966-68, Balt. Dept. Housing and Cmty. Devel., 1968-71; prin., CEO Trahan, Burden & Charles, Inc., 1984—. Mktg., pub. rels. cons. to cities of Pitts., San Diego, Buffalo, Niagara Falls, N.Y., N.Y.C., Miami, Milw., Curacao, Netherlands Antilles, Charleston, Chattahooga, Edinburg; mem. bd. Gov.'s Tourism Task Force; presenter, lectr. in field. Bd. dirs. Balt. Symphony Orch., World Trade Ctr. Inst., Balt. City Found., Boy Scouts Am., Md. Film Commn., The Nat. Aquarium, Jr. League Cmty. Coun., Urban League; pres. Balt. Ctr. for Performing Arts, 1976-92. Recipient Lifetime Achievement award Balt. Pub. Rels. Soc., 1996. Fellow Pa. State U. (Disting. 1991); mem. Gov.'s World Trade Ctr. Inst. (mem. bd., coms.), Md. C. of C. (strategic planning com.), Children's Theater Assn. Office: Trahan Burden & Charles 1030 N Charles St Baltimore MD 21201-5442

HILLMAN, WILLIAM CHERNICK, federal bankruptcy judge, educator; b. Providence, R.I., Oct. 15, 1935; s. Harold S. and Anne (Chernick) H.; m. Edith Boren, June 22, 1958 (div. 1982) ; children: Harold S. II, Daniel C.A. JD cum laude, Boston U., 1957, LLM, 1968. Bar: R.I. 1957, U.S. Supreme Ct. 1965, Mass. 1990. Ptnr. Strauss, Factor, Hillman & Lopes (and predecessors), Providence, 1957—91; U.S. bankruptcy judge U.S. Bankruptcy Ct., Boston, 1991—99, chief judge, 1999—2002. Judge of probate Town of Barrington and West Greenwich, R.I., 1975-91; program chmn. Practicing Law Inst., N.Y.C., 1978—, chmn. Banking Law Inst., N.Y.C., 1983-88, R.I. Law Inst., Providence, 1982-86; adj. prof. law Suffolk U., 1996-98, Northeastern U., 1998—. Author: Commercial Loan Documentation, 1986, 3d edit., 1990, Secured Transactions Law and Documentation, 1986, Documenting Secured Transactions: Problem Avoidance and Effective Drafting, 1987, 10th edit., 1997, Personal Bankruptcy, 1993, 2d edit., 1995; co-author: (with Margaret M. Crouch) Bankruptcy Deskbook, 3d edit., 2000; editor Letters of Credit: Current Thinking in America, 1987; contbr. articles to profl. jours. Capt. U.S. Army, 1958. Mem. ABA, Am. Coll. Bankruptcy, Boston Bar Assn., R.I. Bar Assn., Nat. Conf. Commrs. on Uniform State Laws (life, commr. 1969—), Scribes. Office: US Bankruptcy Ct 10 Causeway St Rm 1101 Boston MA 02222-1009

HILLMER, MARGARET PATRICIA, library director; b. Cirencester, Gloucestershire, Eng., Mar. 17, 1936; came to U.S., 1960; naturalized, 1973; d. John Albert and Margaret Evelyn (Richardson) Hall; m. Max Lorraine Hillmer, Mar. 24, 1962; children: Felicity Margaret, Jennifer Anne. ALAM, London Acad. Music Dram. Art, London, 1955; AB magna cum laude, Heidelberg Coll., 1976; AM in Libr. Sci., U. Mich., 1977. Cert. libr. Ohio. Speech and ballet tchr., Cirencester, 1955-58; governess, 1959-60; ballet instr., choreographer Heidelberg Coll., Tiffin, Ohio, 1969-73, adminstrv. asst. pub. rels. Water Quality Lab., 1978-79; head reference dept. Tiffin-Seneca Pub. Libr., 1979-80, libr. dir., 1980—. Contbr. articles to profl. publs. Chair Take Our Daughters to Work Day, 1993-2000; bd. dirs. Tiffin-Seneca Teen Ctr., 1992—; mem. Tiffin City Schs. Bd. Edn., 1991—, pres., 1995-96; mem. Seneca County Dept. Human Svcs. Bd., 1984-91, pres., 1987-89. Recipient Liberty Bell award Seneca County Bar Assn., 1990, People's Law Sch. award Ohio Acad. Trial Lawyers, 1993, Athena award Tiffin Area C. of C., 1999. Mem. ALA, AAUW, LWV (pres. Tiffin chpt. 1980-82, chair internat. rels. Ohio 1975-76), Ohio Libr. Assn. (legislation com. 1985-89, chair legis. network 1989-93, chair awards and honors com. 1995-96, seminar spkr. 1985—), Pub. Libr. Assn., Freedom to Read Assn., Tiffin Rotary Club (pres. 2001-02), Beta Phi Mu. Democrat. Episcopalian. Avocations: reading, theater, classical music. Home: 25 Southview Pl Tiffin OH 44883-3312 Office: Tiffin-Seneca Pub Libr 77 Jefferson St Tiffin OH 44883-2339 E-mail: hillmepa@oplin.org.

HILLOCKS, GEORGE, JR., English educator, researcher, consultant; b. Cleve., June 15, 1934; s. George and Ina Ternan Hillocks; m. Jo Anne Bruce, 1957 (div. 1998); children: Marjorie Anne, George McInnes. BA, Coll. of Wooster, 1956; MA, Case Western Res. U., 1958; diploma in English Studies, U. Edinburgh, 1959; PhD, Case Western Res. U., 1970. English tchr. Euclid (Ohio) Pub. Schs., 1956-58, 59-65; English instr. Bowling Green (Ohio) State U., 1965-70, asst. prof. English, 1970-71; asst. prof. Edn. U. Chgo., 1971-75, assoc. prof. Edn., 1975-85, prof. Edn. and English, 1985—2003. Dir. MA program in tchg. English U. Chgo., 1971-2002; vis. Thomas R. Watson disting. prof. U. Louisville, 2000. Author: Research on Written Composition: New Directions for Teaching, 1986, Teaching Writing as Reflective Practice, 1995 (David H. Russel award 1997), Ways of Thinking, Ways of Teaching, 1999, The Testing Trap: How Statewide Writing Assessments Control Learning, Choice: Outstanding Academic Work, 2002; co-author: The Dynamics of English Instruction, 1971. Fellowship Ctr. for Advanced Study in Behavioral Scis., 2000—. Fellow Nat. Conf. on Rsch. on Lang. and Literacy (pres. 2000—); mem. Nat. Acad. Edn., Nat. Coun. of Tchrs. of English (chair Assembly for Rsch. 1986), Am. Ednl. Rsch. Assn. Avocations: reading, writing, bagpipes. Home: 2012 W 110th St Chicago IL 60643 Office: U Chgo 5835 S Kimbark Ave Chicago IL 60637-1635 E-mail: g-hillocks@uchicago.edu.

HILLOOWALA, RUMY A. retired anatomist and anthropologist; b. Surat, India, Dec. 20, 1935; arrived in U.S., 1960; m. Julianne S Stauffer, June 26, 1965; children: Franak, Yasmin. DDS, U. of Bombay, 1959; PhD, U. of Ala., 1969; MS, Howard U., 1965. Prodr.: (videotapes) Michelangelo's Madonna and Son: The Human Form, 1995, (videotape) Michelangelo's Apollo and Pathos: The Human Form, 1999. Home: 1505 Woodland Drive Morgantown WV 26505 Office: West Virginia University HSN None Morgantown WV 26506 Home Fax: 304-293-8159; Office Fax: 304-293-8159. E-mail: rhilloowala@hsc.wvu.edu.

HILLS, ALAN, performing company executive; Grad., Wright State U. Arranger, handling co. tours rock Ballet Blue Suede Shoes; bus. mgr. Lord of the Dance prodn. at Beau Rivage Resort and Casino, Biloxi, Miss.; former gen. mgr. Cleve./San Jose Ballet; exec. dir. Cin. Ballet, 2001—. Office: Cin Ballet 1555 Central Pkwy Cincinnati OH 45214 Office Fax: 513-621-4844.

HILLS, AUSTIN EDWARD, vineyard executive; b. San Francisco, Oct. 13, 1934; s. Leslie William and Ethel (Lee) H.; m. Erika Michaela Brunar, May 20, 1978; children: Austin, Justin. AB, Stanford U., 1957; MBA, Columbia U., 1959. Chmn. bd. dirs. Hills Bros. Coffee, Inc., San Francisco, 1976, Grgich Hills Cellar, Rutherford, Calif., 1977—. Pres. Hills Vineyards, Inc., Rutherford, 1975-97; pres. Pacific Coast Coffee Assn., San Francisco, 1975-76, Hills Vineyard, Inc., 1999—. Pres. San Francisco Soc. for Prevention of Cruelty to Animals, 1972-78, No. Calif. Soc. for Prevention of Cruelty to Animals, 1972-78. With Air N.G. Mem. Am. Soc. Enologists. Libertarian. Office: 490 Post St Ste 1049 San Francisco CA 94102-1301 E-mail: hillsa@pacbell.net.

HILLS, CARLA ANDERSON, lawyer, former federal official; b. Los Angeles, Jan. 3, 1934; d. Carl H. and Edith (Hume) Anderson; m. Roderick Maltman Hills, Sept. 27, 1958; children: Laura Hume, Roderick Maltman, Megan Elizabeth, Alison Macbeth. AB cum laude, Stanford U., 1955; student, St. Hilda's Coll., Oxford (Eng.) U., 1954; LLB, Yale U., 1958; hon. degrees, Pepperdine U., 1975, Washington U., 1977, Mills Coll., 1977, Lake Forest Coll., 1978, Williams Coll., 1981, Notre Dame U., 1993, Wabash Coll., 1997. Bar: Calif. 1959, DC 1974, US Supreme Ct. 1965. Asst. US atty. civil divsn., LA, 1958-61; ptnr. Munger, Tolles, Hills & Rickershauser, LA, 1962-74; asst. atty. gen. civil divsn. Justice Dept., Washington, 1974-75; sec. HUD, 1975-77; ptnr. Latham, Watkins & Hills, Washington, 1978-86, Weil, Gotshal & Manges, Washington, 1986-88; US trade rep. Exec. Office of the Pres., 1989-93; chmn., CEO Hills & Co. Internat. Cons., 1993—. Chair Nat. Com. for US-China Rels.; bd. dir. Inst. for Internat. Econ., CSIS, Asia Soc., Am. Internat. Group, AOL-Time Warner, Lucent Tech., Inc., Chevron Texaco Corp., TCW Group, Inc.; mem. adv. bd. Calif. Coun. on Criminal Justice, 1969—71; adj. prof. Sch. Law UCLA, 1972; mem. corrections task force LA County Sub-Regional; mem. standing com. discipline US Dist. Ct. for Ctrl. Calif., 1970—73; mem. Adminstrv. Conf. US, 1972—74; bd. councillors U. So. Calif. Law Ctr., 1972—74; mem. at large exec. com. Yale Law Sch., 1973—78; mem. exec. com. law and free soc. State Bar Calif., 1973; trustee Pomona Coll., 1974—79; mem. com. on Law Sch. Yale U. Coun.; mem. Sloan Commn. on Govt. and Higher Edn., 1977—79, Internat. Found. for Cultural Cooperation and Devel., 1977—89, Am. Com. on East-West Accord, 1977—79, Trilateral Commn., 1977—82; mem. adv. com. Princeton U., Woodrow Wilson Sch. of Pub. and Internat. Affairs, 1977—80; mem. Fed. Acctg. Std. Adv. Coun., 1978—80; Gordon Grand fellow Yale U., 1978; trustee Brookings Instn., 1985, Am. Productivity and Quality Ctr., 1988; coun. mem. Calif. Gov. Coun. Econ. Policy Adv., 1993—98, Coun. Fgn. Rels., 1993—; mem. Trilateral Commn., 1993—; vice-chair bd. dir. Inter-Am. Dialogue, 1999—; vice chair Coun. Fgn. Rels., 2001—. Co-author: Federal Civil Practice, 1961; co-author, editor: Antitrust Adviser, 1971; 3d edit., 1985; contbg. editor: Legal Times, 1978-88; mem. editorial bd. Nat. Law Jour., 1978-88. Trustee U. So. Calif., 1977-79, Norton Simon Mus. Art, Pasadena, Calif., 1976-80; trustee Urban Inst., 1978-89, chmn., 1983-89; co-chmn. Alliance to Save Energy, 1977-89; vice chmn. adv. coun. on legal policy Am. Enterprise Inst., 1977-84; bd. visitors, exec. com. Stanford U. Law Sch., 1978-81; bd. dir. Am. Coun. for Capital Formation, 1978-82; mem. exec. com. Inst. for Internat. Econ., 1993—; mem. adv. com. MIT-Harvard U. Joint Ctr. for Urban Studies, 1978-82. Fellow Am. Bar Found.; mem. Am.'s Soc. (bd. dir.), LA Women Lawyers Assn. (pres. 1964), ABA (chair publ. com. antitrust sect. 1972-74, council 1974, 77-84, chair 1982-83), Fed. Bar Assn. (pres. LA chpt. 1963), LA County Bar Assn. (fed. rules and practice com. 1963-72, chair issues and survey 1963-72, chair sub-com. revision local rules for fed. cts. 1966-72, jud. qualifications com. 1971-72), Am. Law Inst., Am.-China Soc. (bd. dir. 1995—), Am. Soc. (bd. trustees), Asia Soc. (bd. trustees), Yale of So. Calif. Club (bd. dir. 1972-74), Yale Club. Clubs: Yale of So. Calif. (dir. 1972-74); Yale (Washington). Office: Hills & Co 901 15th St NW Ste 400 Washington DC 20005

HILLS, FREDERIC WHEELER, editor, publishing company executive; b. East Orange, N.J., Nov. 26, 1934; s. Frederic Wheeler and Mildred Chambers (Hood) H.; m. Patricia Schulze, Jan. 17, 1958 (div. Dec. 1973); children: Christina, Bradford; m. Kathleen Matthews, Apr. 21, 1980; children: Gregory, Teddy. BA, Columbia U., 1956; MA, Stanford U., 1959. Editor F.W. Dodge Corp., San Francisco, 1959-60, N.Y.C., 1960-61; editor McGraw-Hill Book Co., N.Y.C., 1961-68, editor-in-chief Coll. divsn., 1968-72, editor-in-chief Gen. Books divsn., 1972—79; mem. editorial bd. Simon & Schuster Book Co., N.Y.C., 1979—, v.p., 1981—. With AUS, 1958. Mem. PEN, Assn. Am. Pubs., Shelter Island Yacht Club, N.Y. Athletic Club. Home: 218 Monterey Ave Pelham NY 10803-2310 also: PO Box 1061 Shelter Island Heights NY 11965-1061 Office: Simon & Schuster Book Co 1230 Ave of the Americas New York NY 10020-1586 E-mail: fred.hills@simonandschuster.com.

HILLS, JOHN F. design educator; b. Bronx, N.Y., June 5, 1947; s. John Francis Hills Sr. and Esther Margaret Casson; m. Lynn Robin Stockhamer, Oct. 5, 2001; 1 child, Tamar. BA, Cath. U. Am., 1969; MA in Edn., Seton Hall U., 1996. State Tchrs. Cert. N.J. Adj. prof. Bloomfield Coll., NJ, 1996—97; instr. Union County Coll., Elizabeth, NJ, 1998, Essex County Coll., Newark, 1999—2003, prof., 2003—. Adj. prof. Seton Hall U., South Orange, NJ, 1996—99; set carpenter NBC Scenic Studio, 1987—89; set designer Print Ads, 1982—87.

HILLS, JOHN MERRILL, educational administrator, consultant, former public policy research center executive; b. Wethersfield, Conn., May 6, 1944; s. Merrill Clarke and Elizabeth (Tarrant) H.; m. Irene Jeanne Lavallee, Oct. 7, 1974 (div.); children: John M. Jr., Sara Clarke. Student, U. Hartford, 1963; BBA, Nichols Coll., 1969; postgrad., U. Md., 1976. Salesman Peter A Frasse and Co., Inc., Hartford, Conn., 1963-64; dir. alumni relations, asst. dir. admissions Nichols Coll., Dudley, Mass., 1969-72; regional dir. Georgetown U., Washington, 1972-74; dir. devel. cen. adminstrn. U. Md., College Park, 1974-77; v.p. Roanoke Coll., Salem, Va., 1977-86, The Brookings Instn., Washington, 1986-98; pres. JMH Assocs., 1998—. Pres. J.M.H. Assocs., Washington, 1979—; cons. Am. Assn. Univ. Cons., Inc., Washington, 1975-77; mgmt., pub. relations and fund raising cons. Trustee, mem. exec. com. Nichols Coll., Dudley, Mass., 1993-2000, Higher Edn. Roundtable, Lamplighters; judge U.S. Steel Alumni Award, Pitts., 1979-86; bd. dirs. Mill Mountain Theater, Roanoke, 1983-86, Roanoke ARC, 1984-86, Roanoke Valley C. of C., 1983-86; mem. adv. bd. Phoenix Soc. Georgetown U. Sch. Law.; mem. Little Theater of Alexandria. With U.S. Army, 1965-67, N.G. Recipient Alumni Achievement award Nichols Coll., 1991; named one of Outstanding Young Men Am., U.S. Jaycees, 1980, Outstanding Nat. Advisor, Pi Lambda Phi, Conn., 1983, 86. Mem. Nat. Soc. Fund Raiser Execs., Coun. for Advancement and Support of Edn. (faculty chmn.), Alexandria Sportsman's Club (mem. exec. com.), Hunting Hills Club, Jefferson Club (Roanoke), Met. Club Washington, Paul Hill Choral Soc. (mem. corp. bd.). Roman Catholic. Avocations: sailing, jogging. Home (Summer): 17 Josephine St Rehoboth Beach DE 19971-2017 Office: JmH Associates 1626 S St NW Washington DC 20009

HILLS, REGINA J. journalist; b. Sault Sainte Marie, Mich., Dec. 24, 1953; d. Marvin Dan and Ardithanne (Tilly) H.; m. Vincent C. Stricherz, Feb. 25, 1984 BA, U. Nebr., 1976. Reporter UPI, Lincoln, Nebr., 1976-80, state editor, bur. mgr., 1981-82, New Orleans, 1982-84, Indpls., 1985-87; asst. city editor Seattle Post-Intelligencer, 1987-99, online prodr., 1999—2001, mng. prodr., 2001—. Panelist TV interview show Face Nebr., 1978-81; vis. lectr. U. Nebr., Lincoln, 1978, 79, 80; columnist weekly feature Capitol News, Nebr. Press Assn., 1981-82 Recipient Outstanding Coverage awards UPI, 1980, 82 Mem. U. Nebr. Alumni Assn., Zeta Tau Alpha. Office: Seattle Post Intelligencer 101 Elliott Ave W Ste 200 Seattle WA 98119-4295

HILLS, RODERICK M. lawyer, business executive, former government official; b. Seattle, Mar. 9, 1931; s. Kenneth Maltman and Sarah B. (Love) H.; m. Carla Helen Anderson, Sept. 27, 1958; children: Laura, Roderick Jr., Megan, Allison. BA in History, Stanford U., 1952, LLB, 1955. Bar: Calif. 1957, U.S. Supreme Ct. 1960, D.C. 1977. Law clk. to Justice Stanley F. Reed U.S. Supreme Ct., 1955-57; assoc. Musick, Peeler & Garrett, L.A., 1957-62; ptnr. Munger, Tolles & Hills, L.A., 1962-75; chmn. Republic Corp., L.A., 1971-75; counsel to Pres. U.S., 1975; chmn. SEC, 1975-77; chmn., CEO Peabody Coal Co., St. Louis and Washington, 1977-79; ptnr. Latham, Watkins & Hills, Washington, 1978-82; chmn. Sears World Trade, Inc., Washington, 1982-84; chmn., mng. dir. The Manchester Group, Ltd. (renamed Hills Enterprises, Ltd.), Washington, 1984—; mng. ptnr. Donovan, Leisure, Rogovin, Huge & Schiller, Washington, 1989-92; chmn. internat. practice group Shea & Gould, Washington, 1992-94; ptnr. Mudge Rose Guthrie Alexander & Ferdon, Washington, 1994-95, Hills & Stern, Washington, 1995—. Vis. prof. law Harvard U., 1969—70; lectr. law Stanford U., 1960—69; disting. faculty fellow in internat. fin. Yale U. Sch. Mgmt., 1986—89; bd. dirs., vice chmn. Oak Industries, 1990—2000, Feg. Mogul Corp., 1977—2003, chmn., 1996; bd. dirs. Regional Market Makers, Chiquita Brands Internat.; chmn. Hills Governance Program, CSIS, 2001—. Bd. editors, comment editor: Stanford Law Rev, 1953-55. Trustee Com. Econ. Devel., 1978—; dir. U.S.-ASEAN Bus. Coun., Inc., 1982—, chmn., 1986-90, vice chmn., 1990—; mem. Bretton Woods Com. Fellow Am. Bar Found.; mem. ABA, U.S. Supreme Ct. Bar Assn., L.A. County Bar Assn., State Bar Calif., Order of Coif, Chancery Club, Chevy Chase Club, Phi Delta Phi. Republican. Episcopalian. Avocations: tennis, golf, history. Home: 3125 Chain Bridge Rd NW Washington DC 20016-3411 Office: Hills Enterprises Ltd 1200 19th St NW Washington DC 20036-2412

HILLS, RUSTY, state official; BA in Telecom., Mich. State U.; M in Govt. and Internat. Studies, U. Notre Dame. Dir. comm. Rep. Mich. chmn. Spencer Abraham, Mich. Gov. John Engler, Lansing, dir. pub. affairs, 1995—. Bd. dirs. Mich. chpt. Cath. Campaign Am.; chmn. Mich. Reps; chmn. Mich. Dem. Party, 2000-. Mem. Mayo Smith Soc. Democrat. Office: Mich Rep State Com 2121 E Grand River Ave Lansing MI 48912-3231

HILLSTEAD, RICHARD AVERILL, product development executive; b. Miami, Fla., Apr. 7, 1953; s. Robert Averill and Mattie Lee Hillstead; m. Christine Anne O'Brien, June 24, 1989; children: Shanti Dawn Hall, Katherine Averill. AA, Miami-Dade Jr. Coll., 1976; BS in Profl. Mgmt., Nova Southeastern U., Ft. Lauderdale, Fla., 1990, MBA, 1992; postgrad., Southwest U., Kenner, La. Engring. prototype lab. mgr. Panelfold Inc., Miami, 1985-87; product devel. engr. Cordis Corp., Miami, 1987-88, sr. rsch. engr., 1989-91, mktg. mgr., 1991-93; dir. new techs. Novoste Corp., Norcross, Ga., 1993-98; v.p. rsch. The Innovation Factory, Duluth, Ga., 1999—; pres., CEO. partner-swanted.net, 1999—. Expert witness in field of interventional cardiology products. Contbr. chapters to books, articles to profl. jours.; patentee 33 US and 42 internat. patents in interventional cardiology. Vol. Gwinnett County chpt. Am. Heart Assn., 1994—. Mem. Am. Heart Assn. (coun. on clin. cardiology 1987—, radiology coun. 1987—), Am. Stroke Assn. Avocations: golf, fishing, boating, music. Office: The Innovation Factory 2750 Premiere Pky Ste 200 Duluth GA 30097 E-mail: rhillstead@innofactory.com., rick@partnerswanted.net.

HILLSTROM, THOMAS PETER, engineering executive; b. Lakewood, Ohio, Apr. 20, 1943; s. Harry Edward and Mary Pauline (Mauss) H.; m. Jean Elizabeth Greenfield; children: Edward, Mary. BS in Mech. Engring., Northwestern U., Evanston, 1966; MBA, Northwestern U., Chgo., 1977. Design engr. Internat. Harvester, Hinsdale, Ill., 1966-74, project engr., 1974-78, product safety engr., 1978-82; mgr. engring. Fire Apparatus Div., FMC, Tipton, Ind., 1982-85; mgr. contract engring. FMC Naval Systems Div., Mpls., 1985-87, program mgr., 1987-90, mgr. eplty. engring., 1990-91; program mgr. United Def., L.P., Mpls., 1985—. Patentee in field. Mem. Soc. Automotive Engrs., Am. Soc. Agrl. Engrs., System Safety Soc., Boy Scouts Am. Order of the Arrow. Republican. Home: 17955 39th Pl North Plymouth MN 55446 Office: United Def LP 4800 E River Rd Minneapolis MN 55421-1402

HILLYARD, IRA WILLIAM, pharmacologist, educator; b. Richmond, Utah, Mar. 23, 1924; s. Neal Jacobsen and Lucille (Duce) H.; m. Venice Lenore Williams, July 10, 1945 (dec.); children: Christine, Kevin, Eric; m. Norma Larsen, May 1, 1970. BS, Idaho State U., 1949; MS, U. Nebr., 1951; PhD, St. Louis U., 1957. Pharmacologist Mead Johnson Co., Evansville, Ind., 1957-59; sr. pharmacologist, sect. leader Warner-Lambert Research Inst., Morris Plains, N.J., 1959-69; assoc. prof. pharmacology Idaho State U. Coll. Pharmacy, Pocatello, 1969-73, 77-79, dean, 1979-87, prof. pharmacology, 1979-91, prof. emeritus, 1991—. Dir. pharmacology and toxicology ICN Pharms., Irvine, Calif., 1973-77, cons., 1977-80; cons. Pennwalt Pharm. Co., Rochester, N.Y., 1978-83 Contbr. articles to profl. jours. Served with USN, 1943-45, 51-53. Decorated Purple Heart. Fellow Am. Found. Pharm. Edn.; mem. Western Pharmacology Soc., Am. Assn. Colls. Pharmacy, Am. Soc. Pharmacology and Exptl. Therapeutics, N.Y. Acad. Scis., Sigma Xi, Rho Chi, Phi Delta Chi. Lodges: Rotary. Home: 594 S 800 W Mapleton UT 84664-4313 *I firmly believe that we make individual contributions to the welfare and progress of mankind only if every action is based on truth. If we remain honest and open-minded in our approach, truth will always be recognized and those challenging decisions which must precede every action, will be correctly made even though each decision may not always be agreeable to us or to others. In the end, however, if truth prevails, progress will be made because we will all recognize the correctness of what is said or done.*

HILLYARD, LYLE WILLIAM, state legislator, lawyer; b. Logan, Utah, Sept. 25, 1940; s. Alma Lowell and Lucille (Rosenbaum) H.; m. Alice Thorpe, June 24, 1964; children: Carrie, Lisa, Holly, Todd, Matthew. BS, Utah State U., 1965; JD, U. Utah, 1967. Bar: Utah 1967, U.S. Supreme Ct. 1977. Pres. Hillyard, Anderson & Olsen, Logan, 1967—; mem. Utah Senate, Dist. 25, Salt Lake City, 1985—. Rep. chmn. Cache County, Logan, 1970-76; Utah State Rep., 1981-84; pres. Cache County C. of C., 1977. Named one of Outstanding Young Men of Am., Utah Jaycees, 1972; recipient Disting. Svc. award, Logan Jaycees, 1972, Merit award Cache Valley coun. Boy Scouts Am., 1981. Mem. ABA, Utah State Bar Assn., Cache County Bar Assn., Assn. Trial Lawyers Am., Am. Bd. Trial Advocates. Clubs: Big Blue (Logan). Lodges: Kiwanis. Mem. Lds Ch. Office: Hillyard Anderson & Olsen 175 E 1st N Logan UT 84321-4601

HILLYER, GEORGE V. microbiologist, educator, medical researcher; b. San Juan, PR, Dec. 8, 1943; s. William V. and Ruth L. Hillyer; m. Josefina G. Gomez-Piza, June 15, 1968; children: George Jr., Julian. PhD, Univ. of Chgo., Chgo., IL, 1967—72. Prof. of pathology & lab med UPR Sch. of Medicine, San Juan, PR, 1987—; chancellor UPR Rio Piedras Campus, Rio Piedras, PR. Cons. NIH, Bethesda, Md.; secretary-treasurer Am Soc Trop Med Hyg, Chgo., 2003—. Author over 200 scientific articles 7 reviews. Mem. Soc. of the Sigma Xi, Rsch. Triangle Park, NC, 1997—99. Mem.: Am Soc Trop Med Hyg. (coun. mem. 1983—86). Roman Catholic. Avocations: travel, birdwatching, swimming. Home: 254 Himalaya St Monterrey Urb San Juan PR 00926 Office: Univ PR Med Sci Campus Puerto Rico Med Center San Juan PR 00936-5067 Personal E-mail: ghillyer@rcm.upr.edu. E-mail: ghillyer@rcm.upr.edu.

HILPERT, DALE W. retail shoe company executive; BS, U. Wyo., 1966; MBA, U. Denver, 1970. With Dayton Hudson Corp., Mpls., 1970-76, Cook United, Inc., Cleve., 1976-78, May Dept. Stores, St. Louis, 1978-80, Volume Shoe Corp., Topeka, Kans., 1980-92, chief fin. officer, sr. v.p., 1980-81, exec. v.p., 1981-82, now chmn., chief exec. officer, dir., 1982-92; pres., COO Venator Group Inc., N.Y.C., 1995-90, pres., CEO, 1999-2000, chmn., CEO, 2000—. Office: Venator 233 Broadway New York NY 10279-0001

HILPERT, EDWARD THEODORE, JR., lawyer; b. Frazee, Minn., Apr. 29, 1928; s. Edward Theodore Sr. and Hulda Gertrude (Wilder) H.; m. Susan Hazelton, May 5, 1973. AB, U. Wash., 1954, JD, 1956. Bar: Wash. 1956, U.S. Dist. Ct. (we. dist.) Wash. 1956, U.S. Tax Ct. 1959, U.S. Ct. Appeals (9th cir.) 1959, U.S. Supreme Ct. 1970. Law clk. to Hon. George H. Boldt U.S. Dist. Ct. (we. dist.) Wash., Tacoma, 1956-58; assoc. Ferguson & Burdell, Seattle, 1958-63, ptnr., 1963-91; sr. ptnr. Schwabe, Williamson, Ferguson & Burdell, Seattle, 1992—. Exec. com. 9th cir. Jud. Conf., San Francisco, 1987-90. Judge pro tem Seattle Mcpl. Ct., 1971-80. Capt. USAR, 1946-49, 50-52, Korea. Mem. ABA, Mensa, The Rainer Club, Seattle Tennis Club, Broadmoor Golf Club, Sea Pines Country Club. Republican. Lutheran. Home: 10405 - 192nd Ave NE Redmond WA 98053 Office: Schwabe Williamson Ferguson & Burdell US Bank Ctr 1420 5th Ave Ste 3010 Seattle WA 98101-2393

HILSABECK, LARRY L. education educator; b. Eldora, Iowa, Sept. 27, 1942; s. Howard Valerian Hilsabeck and Katherine Mary Kramer; m. Joann Linda Peek, Nov. 27, 1963; children: Lori Ann, Jamie Lee, Larry Lee II. AA, Fullerton C.C., 1963; BS, U. Calif., Fullerton, 1968. Cert. tchr. Calif. Head football coach, tchr. North H.S., Riverside, Calif., 1968-75, 83-88, Corona (Calif.) H.S., 1976-82, Centennial H.S., Corona, 1989-94, Don Lugo H.S., Chino, Calif., 1995—. Mem. Calif. Interscholastic Fedn. Football adv. bd., Norwalk, Calif. Author: (computer software) Football Scouting Program for Small Computers, 1979, Computer Programs for Baseball, Basketball, and Track, 1979; inventor in field. Mem. Riverside Jr. Tackle Football Bd., Calif., 1972-75, Anaheim Pop Warner Football Bd., Calif., 1961-65. Named Coach of Yr. Riverside Press Enterprise Newspaper, 1969, Head Football Coach-All Stars, Riverside County Coaches Assn., 1972, others. Mem. So. Calif. Football Coaches Assn., Football Coaches Profl. Growth Assn. Avocations: hist. rsch., computer programming, football consulting. E-mail: lhilsab420@aol.com.

HILSENRATH, JOEL ALAN, computer scientist, entreprenuer; b. Bklyn., Apr. 18, 1965; s. Daniel Wallace and Lee Betty (Batch) H. Cert. computer tech., Manhattan Career Inst., N.Y.C., 1988. Asst. dir. registry Grand Lodge Free and Accepted Masons, N.Y.C., 1988-90, database adminstr., 1991; pres. Xoanon Enterprises, Bklyn., 1991—, Quixtar IBO, 1999—. Mem. Wildlife Conservation Soc., Midwood Civic Action Coun. (v.p. 2001—), N.Y. Amateur Computer Club, Bklyn. Mus. of Art, Masons. Democrat. Jewish. Avocations: Shakespeare, Dr. Who, Star Trek, bowling. Home: 945 E 15th St Brooklyn NY 11230-3703 Office: Xoanon Enterprises PO Box 300679 Brooklyn NY 11230-0679 E-mail: xe11230@hotmail.com.

HILSINGER, RAYMOND L., JR., otolaryngologist; b. Cin., Aug. 24, 1936; BA, Dartmouth Coll., 1958; MD, U. Cin., 1964. Diplomate Am. Bd. Otolaryngology, 1971 (guest examiner 1991, 92, 97); lic. physician, Ariz., Calif., Pa. Rotating intern Phila. Gen. Hosp., 1964-65; resident in gen. surgery Hahnemann Med. Coll. and Hosp., Phila., 1965-66; resident in otolaryngology Eye and Ear Hosp., U. Pitts., 1966-69; with dept. head and neck surgery Kaiser Permanente Med. Ctr., Oakland, Calif., 1971—2001, dir. otolaryngology-head and neck surgery, resident program, 1972-2001, courtesy staff San Francisco, 1976—, chief dept. head and neck surgery Oakland, 1985—, Richmond, Calif., 2000—. Courtesy staff Childrens Hosp., Alta Bates Med. Ctr.; chief dept., head and neck surgery Kaiser Permanente Med Ctr., Richmond, 2000—; profl. competence examiner Med. Bd. Calif., 1996; presenter and spkr. in field. Contbr. articles to med. jours. Coach youth baseball, basketball and soccer leagues, 1990-2000; spkr. on health and safety Orinda Unified Sch. Dist., 1990—. Maj. USAF, 1969-71. Fellow ACS, Am. Soc. for Head and Neck Surgery, Am. Laryngol., Rhinol. and Otol. Soc., Am. Acad. Otolaryngology-Head and Neck Surgery (Honor award 1986); mem. AMA, Soc. of Univ. Otolaryngologists-Head and Neck Surgeons, Assn. of Acad. Depts. of Otolaryngology-Head and Neck Surgery, Pan Am. Assn. Otorhinolaryngology-Head and Neck Surgery, Am. Coun. Otolaryngology, Pacific Coast Oto-Ophthalmol. Soc. (pres. 1997-99, chmn. continuing med. edn. com. 1997-98), No. Calif. Kaiser Permanente Head and Neck Surgery Soc. (pres. 1975-76), Alameda-Contra Costa County Med. Assn., Calif. Med. Assn., Soc. Kaiser Permanente Otolaryngology Rsch., Am. Bronchoesophagological Assn. Office: Kaiser Permanente Med Ctr Dept Head and Neck Surgery 280 W Macarthur Blvd Oakland CA 94611-5693 E-mail: Raymond.hilsinger@kp.org.

HILSMAN, ROGER, government educator; b. Waco, Tex., Nov. 23, 1919; s. Roger and Emma (Prendergast) H.; m. Eleanor Willis Hoyt, June 22, 1946; children— Hoyt R., Amy, Asby, Sarah. BS, U.S. Mil. Acad., 1943; MA, Yale U., 1950, PhD, 1951. Commd. 2d lt. U.S. Army, 1943, advanced through grades to maj., 1951; with (Merrill's Marauders), Burma, 1944; comdg. officer (OSS guerrilla group in), Burma, 1944-45; asst. chief Far East intelligence operations, Hdqrs. OSS, Washington, 1945-46; spl. asst. to exec. officer CIA, 1946-47; planning officer NATO affairs, Joint Am. Mil. Adv. Group, London, Eng., 1950-52; internat. politics br. Hdqrs. U.S. European Command, 1952-53; resigned, 1953; research fellow Center Internat. Studies, Princeton, 1953-54, research asst., 1954-55; research assoc., lectr. Woodrow Wilson Sch.; lectr. internat. relations Columbia, 1958; research asso. Washington Center Fgn. Policy Research, lectr. internat. affairs Sch. Advanced Internat. Studies, Johns Hopkins, 1957-61. Chief fgn. affairs div., legislative reference service Library Congress, 1956-58, dep. dir. for research, 1958-61; dir. bur. intelligence and research State Dept., 1961-63; asst. sec. state Far Eastern affairs, 1963-64; prof. govt. Columbia U., 1964-89, prof. emeritus, 1990—; lectr. Nat. War Coll., Air U., Army War Coll., Indsl. Coll. Armed Forces.; Fulbright Disting. lectr., India, 1985; USMC Found. chair mil. affairs, 1991. Author: Strategic Intelligence and National Decisions, 1956, To Move a Nation, 1967, The Politics of Policy Making in Defense and Foreign Affairs, 1971, The Crouching Future: International Politics and U.S. Foreign Policy— A Forecast, 1975, To Govern America, 1979, The Politics of Governing America, 1985, The Politics of Policy Making: Conceptual Models and Bureaucratic Politics, 1987, 90, 92, American Guerrilla: My War Behind Japanese Lines, 1990, George Bush vs Saddam Hussein: Military Success! Political Failure?, 1992, The Cuban Missle Crisis, The Struggle Over Policy, 1996, From Nuclear Military Strategy to a World Without War, A History and Proposal, 1999; co-author: Military Policy and National Security, 1956, Alliance Policy in the Cold War, 1959, NATO and American Security, 1959, Foreign Policy in the Sixties, 1965, The Superpowers and Revolution, 1986, Nuclear Strategy and Arms Control, 1986. Rockefeller fellow, 1958.

HILT, MARY LOUISE, artist; b. Muskegon, Mich., May 17, 1947; d. Jack Lyle and Martha Campbell (Van Epps) H.; m. Randolph Allen Austill, March 3, 2000. Student, Milw. Inst. Design and Art, 1966—68. Art tchr. for spl. needs adults Kelliher Ctr., Arlington, Mass., 1994-96. One-woman shows include Harvard Law Sch., Cambridge, 1987, Armenian Genocide Collection, Mass. State House, Boston, 1995, Armenian Libr. and Mus. Am., Watertown, Mass., 1995-96, 99; two-person show Fruenthal Ctr. for Performing Arts, Muskegon, 1989; exhibited in group shows at Bravos Gallery, Georgetown, Mass., 1987, 90-92, 94, 96, 2002, Nat. Arts Club, NYC, 1997, Fed. Res. Bank, Boston, 1998, Art and Cultural Ctr., Fallbrook, Calif., 2000, others. Mem.: Copley Soc. Boston. Episcopalian. Office: Hilt Studio 116 Beech St Belmont MA 02478-1812

HILT, MEREDITH DYKSTRA, foundation administrator; b. Ill., Apr. 10, 1973; d. David and Linda Dykstra; m. Marc Hilt, May 25, 1997; 1 child, Kathryn. BA, Miami U., Oxford, Ohio, 1994. Program coord. Conservation Found., Naperville, Ill., 1994—96; devel. dir. YWCA DuPage Ctr., Glen Ellyn, Ill., 1996—2001; exec. dir. Tellabs Found., Naperville, 2001—. Presbyterian. Office: Tellabs Found 1415 West Diehl Rd MS 10 Naperville IL 60515 E-mail: meredith.hilt@tellabs.com.

HILT, THOMAS HARRY, minister; b. Phila., May 19, 1947; s. Francis Joseph and Alice Elizabeth (Flanagan) H.; m. Carolyn Louise Poulsen, Aug. 23, 1969; 1 child, Tamara Leah. BA, Tusculum Coll., Greeneville, Tenn., 1969; grad., Missionary Tng. Sch., Long Beach, Calif., 1974; M Ministry, Internat. Sem., Plymouth, Fla., 1983, D Ministry, 1984; PhD, Carolina U. of Theology, 1992. Ordained min. of Gospel, Okinawa, Japan, 1979. Mem. staff Christians in Action, Long Beach, 1974-77, missionary Okinawa, Japan, 1977-79; founder Christians in Action Evang. Ch., Guam, 1979-81; founder, dir. Micronesian Evang. Mission, Barrigada, Guam, 1981—; founder, adminstr. Evang. Christian Acad., Chalan Pago, Guam, 1982—; sr. pastor Ch. of the Cross, Sarasota, Fla., 2001—02; pres. SonHaven Ministries Internat., Sarasota, 2001—; founder, adminstr. SonHaven Prep. Acad., Sarasota, 2002—. Founder, dir. Family Counseling Ministries, 1990—; mem. Nat. Bible Week-Guam Com., 1988-92; advisor Guam chpt. Women's Aglow Fellowship Internat., 1987-90; chaplain Guam Fire Dept., 1992-2000; chmn. bd. Guam Critical Incident Stress Mgmt. team, 1997-2000. Mem. Guam Gov.'s Social Svcs. Adv. Bd., 1981-83; mem. standards of licensing com. child welfare task force Guam Dept. Pub. Health and Social Svcs., 1982-83; mem. Blue Ribbon Commn. on Edn., 1991-93. With U.S. Army, 1970-73. Recipient award Ancient Order of Chamorri, 1983, 1st place award Guam Press Club, 1985. Fellow Am. Acad. Experts in Traumatic Stress; mem. Am. Acad. Experts in Traumatic Stress, Guam Ministerial Assn. (sec.-treas. 1980-81, pres. 1983-84, 86-88, v.p. 1991-92), Bible Soc. Micronesia

(pres. bd. dirs. 1989-90, v.p. bd. 1991-92, 99-2000). Home: 5351 Avant Ave Sarasota FL 34235 Office: Po Box 50517 Sarasota FL 34232-0304 *It has been my experience that God does not grant us special favors, but rather special grace.*

HILTON, ANDREW CARSON, investor, management consultant, former manufacturing company executive; b. D'Lo, Miss., Nov. 20, 1928; s. A.C. and Pearl (Walters) H. BA, U. Md., 1952; MA, George Washington U., 1953; PhD, Western Res. U., 1956. Former research asso. Personnel Research Inst., Western Res. U.; cons. Psychol. Corp., N.Y.C.; dir. personnel relations Raytheon Co.; then dir. personnel Internat. Tel.& Tel. Corp.; sr. v.p. adminstrn. Coltec Industries Inc., N.Y.C., 1963-83, exec. v.p., 1983-91, vice chmn., 1991-94, also bd. dirs.; vice chmn. Coltec Industries Inc, 1991-94; proprietor Hilton Mgmt. Enterprises, 1994—. Contbr. articles to profl. jours. Mem. APA, N.Y. Acad. Scis. Clubs: University (N.Y.C.), Aspetuck Valley Country Club, Weston, Conn. Office: Hilton Mgmt Enterprises Inc 147 E 48th St New York NY 10017-1223

HILTON, BARRON, hotel executive; b. Dallas, 1927; s. Conrad Hilton. Founder, pres. San Diego Chargers, Am. Football League, until 1966; v.p. Hilton Hotels Corp., Beverly Hills, Calif., 1954, pres., chief exec. officer, 1966—, chmn., 1979—, also dir.; chmn. Hilton Equipment Corp, Beverly Hills, Calif. Mem. gen. adminstrv. bd. Mfrs. Hanover Trust Co., N.Y.C. Office: Hilton Hotels Corp 9336 Civic Center Dr Beverly Hills CA 90210-3604*

HILTON, JAMES GORTON, pharmacologist; b. Balt., Sept. 21, 1923; s. George Edward and Ethel Alberta (Schaefer) H.; m. Elizabeth Earline Lindsay, Sept. 21, 1946; children: James Lindsay, William Edward. BS in Chemistry, Va. Poly. Inst., Blacksburg, 1947; MS in Pharmacology, U. Tenn., 1952, PhD, 1954. Teaching fellow dept. pharmacology U. Tenn., Memphis, 1950-53; asst. prof. to assoc. prof. pharmacology U. Miss., Oxford and Jackson, 1953-58; assoc. prof. pharmacology Marquette U., Milw., 1959-61; assoc. prof. U. Tex., Galveston, 1961-63, prof. dept. pharmacology, 1963-92, acting chmn. dept. pharmacology and toxicology, 1979-82; chief div. pharmacology Shriners Burn Inst., Galveston, 1976-90; prof., chmn. pharmacology St. Georges U., Grenada, W.I., 1990. Contbr. in field. Served with USNR, 1941-46. Fellow Am. Heart Assn.; mem. Am. Physiol. Soc., Am. Soc. Pharmacology and Exptl. Therapeutics, Internat. Soc. Burn Injuries, Peruvian Pharmacology Soc., Am. Burn Assn. Clubs: Masons. Episcopalian. Home: Apt 1106 3404 American Dr Lago Vista TX 78645-6500

HILTON, JOHN DAVID, business owner, infosystems specialist; b. Glastonbury, Conn., Apr. 20, 1958; s. John Chadwick and Carol Marion (Bickerstaffe) H. BS in Econs., Norwich U., 1980; BA in Geography, Fla. Atlantic U., 1983, MA in Econs., 1984. Instr. Vt. Coll., Montpelier, 1984; programmer Input-Output Computer Svcs., Waltham, Mass., 1984-86; systems analyst PSI, Internat., Inc., Fairfax, Va., 1986-87; project leader Vanguard Techs. Corp., Falls Church, Va., 1987-88; software engr. Synetics Corp., Wakefield, Mass., 1988-89; software specialist PSI, Internat., Inc., Fairfax, 1989-94; applications designer Starter Corp., New Haven, 1995-97; software and database designer The Wiremold Co., West Hartford, Conn., 1997—. Owner, pres. JDH Assocs., Glastonbury, 1988—. 1st lt. USAF, 1980-81. Mem. Am. Econ. Assn., Nat. Assn. Accts. (bd. dirs. 1989-91), Appalachian Mountain Club. Republcian. Episcopalian. Avocations: golf, skiing, sea kayaking, flying. Office: JDH Assocs 240 Cedar Ridge Dr Glastonbury CT 06033-1836 E-mail: JDHAssociates@msn.com.

HILTON, JOSEPH D. state agency administrator; b. Hudson, N.Y., May 10, 1948; s. Paul S. and Laura P. Hilton; m. Judith M. Manhey, Jan. 17, 1970; children: Rebecca Heeps, Amy, Sarah. BS in Econs., Siena Coll., 1970; MS in Pub. Svc., Russell Sage Coll., 1981. Dir. mcpl. rsch. N.Y. State Comptr. Office, Albany, 1979-98, sr. mgr., 1998—. Mem. Task Force Property Assessment, Albany, 1996-97, project leader succession planning and career devel., 2000-01. Capt. N.Y. Army N.G., 1972-77. Avocations: motorcycling, swimming, golf. Home: 18 Indian Maiden Pass Altamont NY 12009 Office: NY State Office Comptr 110 State St Albany NY 12236

HILTON, PETER JOHN, mathematician, educator; b. London, Apr. 7, 1923; s. Mortimer and Elizabeth (Freedman) H.; m. Margaret Mostyn, Sept. 14, 1949; children: Nicholas, Timothy. MA, Oxford (Eng.) U., Eng., 1948; PhD, Oxford (Eng.) U., 1950, Cambridge (Eng.) U., Eng., 1952; HHD (hon.), No. Mich. U., 1977; DSc (hon.), Meml. U. Nfld., Can., 1983, U. Autonoma Barcelona, Spain, 1989. Lectr. Manchester U., Eng., 1948-52, sr. lectr., 1956-58; lectr. Cambridge U., 1952-55; Mason prof. pure math. Birmingham U., Eng., 1958-62; prof. math. Cornell U., 1962-71, U. Wash., 1971-73; Beaumont prof. Case Western Res. U., 1973-82; disting. prof. SUNY, Binghamton, 1982-93, emeritus, 1993—; disting. prof. U. Ctrl. Fla., Orlando, 1993—. Guest prof. Swiss Fed. Inst. Tech., Zurich, 1966—67, Zurich, 1981—82, Zurich, 1988—89, Courant Inst. Math. Scis., NYU, 1967—68, Ohio State U., 1977, U. Autonoma, Barcelona, 1989, U. Lausanne, 1996; Erskine fellow U. Canterbury, 2001, 02; Mahler lectr. Australian Math. Soc., 1997; vis. fellow Battelle Seattle Rsch. Ctr., 1970—71, fellow, 1971—; co-chmn. Cambridge Conf. on Sch. Math., 1965; chmn. com. applied math. tng. NRC, 1977—; chmn. U.S. Commn. on Math. Instrn., 1979—80; sec. Internat. Commn. Math. Instrn., 1979—82; vis. Erskine fellow U. Canterbury, New Zealand, 2001, 02. Author: Homotopy Theory, 1953, (with S. Wylie) Homology Theory, 1960, Homotopy Theory and Duality, 1966, (with H.B. Griffiths) Classical Mathematics, 1970, General Cohomology Theory and K-Theory, 1971, (with U. Stammbach) Course in Homological Algebra, 1971, 2d edit., 1997, Le Langage des Categories, 1973, (with Y.C. Wu) Course in Modern Algebra, 1974, (with G. Mislin and J. Roitberg) Localization of Nilpotent Groups and Spaces, 1975 (with J. Pedersen) Fear No More, 1982, Nilpotente Gruppen und Nilpotente Räume, 1984, (with J. Pedersen) Build Your Own Polyhedra, 1987, (with J. Pedersen) College Preparatory Mathematics, 1992, (with D. Holton and J. Pedersen) Mathematical Reflections, 1997, (with D. Holton and J. Pedersen) Mathematical Vistas, 2002; editor: Ergebnisse der Mathematik, 1964—, Ill. Jour. Math., 1962-68, Jour. Pure and Applied Algebra, 1970-75, Topics in Modern Topology, 1968, Miscellanea Mathematica, 1991; contbr. articles to profl. jours. Recipient Silver medal U. Helsinki, Finland, 1975, Centenary medal John Carroll U., 1985. Mem. Am. Math. Soc., Math. Assn. Am. (1st v.p. 1978-80), Can. Math. Soc., Math Soc. Belgium (hon.), London Math. Soc., Cambridge Philos. Soc., Brazilian Acad. Scis. (hon.). Home: 29 Murray St Binghamton NY 13905-4504 Office: SUNY Dept Math Scis Binghamton NY 13902-6000 E-mail: marge@math.binghamton.edu.

HILTON, STANLEY GOUMAS, lawyer, educator, writer; b. San Francisco, June 16, 1949; s. Loucas Stylianos and Effie (Glafkides) Goumas; m. Raquel Estrella Villalba, Feb. 25, 1996; children: Loucas, Angelika, Karmen (triplets). BA with honors, U. Chgo., 1971; JD, Duke U., 1975; MBA, Harvard U., 1979. Bar: Calif. 1975, U.S. Dist. Ct. Calif. 1975, U.S. Ct. Appeals (9th cir.) 1983, U.S. Supreme Ct. 1985. Libr. asst. Duke U. Libr., Durham, N.C., 1972-75, Harvard U. Libr., Cambridge, Mass., 1977-79; minority counsel U.S. Senator Bob Dole, Washington, 1979-80; adminstrv. asst. Calif. State Senate, Sacramento, 1980-81; pvt. practice San Francisco, 1981—; CEO Froggg, Inc., 1999—, San Francisco Landlords Union, 1999—. Adj. assoc. prof. Golden Gate U., San Francisco, 1991—; profl. spkr.; polit. writer; pres. Fair Play In the Middle East Com., 2002—; tutor Harvard U., 1978—79. Author: Bob Dole: American Political Phoenix, 1988, Senator for Sale, 1995, Glass Houses, 1998 (Best writer 1998), To Pay or Not to Pay, 2003. Pres. Com. to Stick With Candlestick Park, San Francisco, 1992-96, Value Added Tax Now, San Francisco, 1994—, Save the 4th Amendment, San Francisco, 1995—; pres., CEO Animalism, Inc., San Francisco Landlord's Union, 2001—; CEO Fountain of Youth; alt. mem. San Mateo County Dem. Ctrl. Com., 2002—; Dem. candidate for Gov. Calif. spl. recall election, 2003. Mem. Calif. State Bar, Abolish the Fed. Res. Bank Assn. (pres. 1999—), Hellenic Law Soc., Bechtel Toastmasters Club (pres.), Rhinoceros Toastmasters Club. Democrat. Avocations: philately, photography, classical music, ancient greek and roman history. Office: 580 California St Ste 500 San Francisco CA 94104-1000

HILTON, THEODORE CRAIG, computer scientist, Internet company executive; b. Oakland, Calif., June 14, 1949; s. Theodore Caldwell and Maxine (Donnelly) Hilton; m. Peggy Estes, May 21, 1990; children: Christopher, Kelly, Clark, Lisa, Trey, Veronique. BS in Internat. Rels., Occidental Coll., 1972; BS, Calif. Inst. Tech., 1972; MS in Computer Sci., N.Y. Inst. Tech., 1980. Ptnr., founder Ctrl. Data Corp., L.A., 1971—, CEO, 1988—; engr. RSK, L.A., 1972-73; prof. Lake (Fla.) Coll., 1981-85, dept. chmn., 1983-85; prin. rsch. invest. U.S. Dept. Def., L.A., 1985-88; chmn. Access LLC, 1996—; chmn., CEO E-City Corp., 1996—; chmn. WEB Holdings Corp., 1998. Creator computer sys. E-City, 1956, Broadcast Mgmt. Sys., 1972, ICSS, 1974, EBook, 1993, Quality Assurance Sys., 1994, Nat. Curriculum Clearinghouse Sys., 2002; U.S. presenter SOLE Internat. Conv., 1991; CALS presenter, 95; adv. bd. Accurate Rsch. Corp., 2000; bd. dirs. TBS S.A., Carolina Access LLC, S.E. Data Comms. Author: (book) Web Databases & PHP3, 1999, Web Databases & PHP3, Japanese edit., 2000, Web Databases & PHP3, Polish/Russian edits.., 2002, Data-Base Development, 1999, Web Databse, 2000; contbr. articles to profl. jours. Named SC Bus. Man of Yr., 1999, Wall St. Businessman of Yr., 2000, NC Businessman of Yr., 2001—02; recipient Congl. medal Distinction, 2001. Mem.: IEEE, N.Y. Acad. Scis., Data Processing Mgmt. Assn., Logistics Engrs. Soc., Am. Mgmt. Assn., IEEE Computer Soc., Rotary (Paul Harris fellow). Achievements include patents for for autonomous network smart labels; for filterable digital advertising; for internet databse management system; on image system and public network exchange system; others. Office: Cen Data Corp 145 N Church St Ste 402 Spartanburg SC 29306-5163 E-mail: chilton@upstate.net.

HILTS, EARL T. lawyer, government official, educator; b. Ilion, N.Y., Mar. 31, 1946; stepson Leon Thomas and Gertrude Annette (Daly) Butler; m. Mae Hwa Kim, Apr. 13, 1973; children: Troy Alan, Kimberly Michelle. BS, St. Lawrence U., 1967; JD, Albany Law Sch., 1970. Bar: N.Y. 1972. Gen. atty.-advisor Dept. Army Watervliet Arsenal, N.Y., 1978-80, supervisory atty.-advisor, 1980-99; ret., 1999; pvt. practice, 1999—. Adj. prof. Schnectady C.C., 1985—, St. Rose Coll., 1999—. Catechism instr. St. Mary's Ch., 1990-92; pee wee football coach, wrestling coach Shenendehowa Sch., 1983-87; little league coach West Crescent Halfmoon Baseball League, 1980-90. Capt. JAGC, U.S. Army, 1972-76. Scholar St. Lawrence U., 1963-67, Albany Law Sch., 1967-70. Mem. N.Y. State Bar Assn., Am. Legion, Pi Mu Epsilon. Republican. Roman Catholic. Home and Office: 28 Oakwood Blvd Clifton Park NY 12065-7413

HILTS, RUTH, artist; b. Sparks, Nev., Dec. 4, 1923; d. William and Nellie Elisa (DeGoosh) Gonzales; m. Robert Norton Hilts, Sept. 28, 1942; children: Robert Norton, Jr., Deirdre Lynne. BA, U. Nev., 1962. Grad. teaching asst. dept. English U. Nev., Reno, 1962-63, editor-interviewer dept. oral history, 1967-74; profl. artist Reno, 1975—. One-man shows include Gov.'s Mansion, Carson City, Nev., 1982, Sierra Nev. Mus. Art, 1987—88, Nev. Gallery, Reno, 1990, River Gallery, 1995, 1998, Red Mountain Gallery at Truckee Meadows C.C., 1995, Nev. Legis. Bldg., Carson City, 1997, Heritage Bank, Reno, 2001, Nev. State Libr. & Archives Gallery, Carson City, 2003, exhibited in group shows at Watercolor West XIV, Riverside, Calif., 1982, Nev. Mus. Art Biennial, Reno, Las Vegas, 1990, 1996, Sierra Nev. Coll., Tahoe, 1992—93, Stremmel Gallery, Reno, 1992—94, River Gallery, 1993—94, Sierra Arts Found. Gallery, Reno, 1994, 1995, 1998, 1999, Represented in permanent collections Nev. Mus. Art, Reno, Tournament Players Club Summerlin, Las Vegas, Eureka (Nev.) Opera Ho.; contbr. art to publs. Nev. Mag., 1988, Encore, 1995, 98, 2003, Neon, 1995, 97. Mem. Nev. Mus. Art, Sierra Arts Found. (grantee for excellence 1995), Georgia O'Keeffe Mus., Nat. Mus. Women in the Arts (charter mem.), Phi Kappa Phi. Avocation: reading. Home and Office: 1895 Wren St Reno NV 89509-2334

HILTY, DONALD M, psychiatrist, educator; s. Marvin S and Mary L Hilty; 1 child, Sarah E. M.D., U. of Cin., Cin., Ohio, 1987—91; B.S., Bowling Green State U., Bowling Green, Ohio, 1983—87. Board Certification Am. Bd. of Psychiatry and Neurology, 1996, License Calif., 1992. Assoc. prof. of clin. psychiatry U. of Calif., Davis, Sacramento, Calif., 2002—, asst. prof. of clin. psychiatry, 1995—2001. Med. dir. Sacramento County Mental Health Treatment Ctr., Sacramento, 2000—; dir., telepsychiatry U. of Calif., Davis, Sacramento, 1995—. Editorial board (publishing) Textbook of Psychiatry (Nat. Leadership Award, US Congress, 2002); author: (continuing medical education) Study Guide to the Textbook of Psychiatry. Mem. Am. Psychiat. Assn. Com. on Info. Tech., Washington, 1998—2003; vol. spkr. Nat. Alliance for the Mentally Ill-Sacramento, Sacramento, Calif., 1998—2003; officer Ctrl. Calif. Psychiat. Soc., Sacramento, Calif., 1995—2003. Grantee Telemedicine Rsch., U. of Calif., Davis Health Sys., 1998, Health Services Rsch., U. of Calif., Davis Dept. of Psychiatry, 2000-01. Mem.: Assn. For Academic Psychiatry (treas., sec. 2001—03), Am. Psychiat. Assn. Avocations: running, golf, reading, travel. Office: U Calif Davis 2230 Stockton Blvd Sacramento CA 95817 Office Fax: 916-734-3384. Personal E-mail: dmhilty@ucdavis.edu. E-mail: dmhilty@ucdavis.edu.

HILTY, JAMES WALTER, historian, educator, media consultant; b. Columbus, Ohio, May 22, 1939; s. Robert Burns and Henrietta Isabel Hilty; m. Shirley Brown, Jan. 1963 (dissolved June 1975); children: Carolyn Marland, Robert; m. Kathleen Griffin Hilty, Oct. 19, 1979; 1 child, Maura. BS, Ohio State U., 1965, MA in Edn., 1966, MA in History, 1967; PhD in History, U. Mo., 1973. Prof. history Temple U., Phila., 1970—, assoc. dean Grad. Sch., 1978—80, acting dean Grad. Sch., 1980—81, asst. v.p. acad. affairs, 1982—82, dir. planning, 1982—85, asst. to pres., 1985—88, chair dept. history, 1988—94. Trustee Atwater Kent Mus., Phila., 1985—2002; cons. NBC News, N.Y.C., 1993, A&E Biography, N.Y.C., 2002. Author: JFK: Idealist Without Illusions, 1976, Robert Kennedy: Brother Protector, 1998; contbr. articles to profl. jours. Pres. Ogontz Vol. Fire Co., Montgomery County, 1980—85; bd. mem. Fire Adv. Bd., Montgomery County, Pa., 1979—94, ARC, Phila., 1985—95. With USMC, 1958—62, PTO. Recipient Disting. Tchg. award, Lindback Found., 2001. Mem.: Orgn. Am. Historians. Democrat. Avocations: golf, gardening. Office: History Dept 11th and Berks Sts Philadelphia PA 19122

HILTZ, ARNOLD AUBREY, former chemist; b. P.E.I., Canada, July 31, 1924; came to the U.S., 1953; s. Aubrey Claremont and Fannie Mae (Bryanton) H.; m. Margery Jane Beer, July 17, 1946; children: Sharon Lynne, Deborah Jane. BS in Chemistry, Acadia U., Wolfville, Nova Scotia, 1947; PhD in Phys. Chemistry, McGill U., Montreal, Quebec, Canada, 1952. Ordained deacon Episc. ch., 1976, ordained priest, 1976. Rsch. scientific officer Def. Rsch. Bd. Canada, Quebec City, Canada, 1951-53; rsch. chemist Am. Viscose Corp., Phila., 1953-59, group leader, 1959-60, Avisun Corp., Phila., 1960-65; rsch. chemist Borden Chem. Co., Phila., 1965-66; sr. scientist Gen. Electric Co., Phila., 1966-79, mgr. materials applications, 1979-91. Tutor math. and sci. Rose Tree Media (Pa.) Sch. Dist., 1958-74. Contbr. articles to profl. jours.; patentee in field. Docent Phila. Mus. of Art, 1988—; sch. dir. Rose Tree Media Sch. Dist., 1969-74; bd. dirs., treas. Middletown (Pa.) Free Libr., 1964-69; bd. dirs. Sheepscot Island Co., MacMahan Island, Maine, 1983-85; treas. Hebrides Home Owners Assn., 2003—. Recipient Silver medal Gov.-Gen. Can. 1942, The Defense Medal (Can.), The Canadian Vol. Svc. medal, Claspto CVSM, The War medal 1939-45, Gen. Svc. badge, Canadian Overseas medal 1945, Frank J. Sensebrenner fellow McGill U., 1949-51, inventor's medal GE 1984. Mem.: Am. Chem. Soc. (sci. lectr. 1958—, chem. abstractor 1958—79), Hebrides Home Owners Assn. (bd. dirs., pres. 1999—2001). Republican. Episcopalian. Avocations: art appreciation, music appreciation, reading, gardening, golf. Home: 40 Regency Park Dr #607 Halifax NS Canada B3S 1L4 E-mail: aandmhiltz@aol.com.

HILTZ, STARR ROXANNE, sociologist, educator, computer scientist, writer, lecturer, consultant; b. Little Rock, Sept. 7, 1942; d. John Donald and Mildred V. (Koons) Smyers; m. Murray Turoff, 1985; children: Jonathan David, Katherine Amanda. AB, Vassar Coll., 1963; MA, Columbia U., 1964, PhD, 1969. Prof. sociology Upsala Coll., 1969-85; info. sys. N.J. Inst. Tech., 1985-93, disting. prof. computer sci., 1993—; pres. Computerized Conferencing, Inc., 1998—. Cons. social impacts of computer systems. Author: Creating Community Services for Widows, 1976, (with M. Turoff) The Network Nation, 1978, 2d edit., 1993, (with E. Kerr) Computer-Mediated Communication, 1982, Online Communities, 1984, The Virtual Classroom, 1994, (with L. Harasim, L. Teles and M. Turoff) Learning Networks, 1995. Recipient N.J. Woman of the Millennium for Ednl. Tech., 2000. Mem.: Assn. for Info. Sys., Assn. Computing Machinery. Unitarian Universalist. Home: 19 Meadowbrook Rd Randolph NJ 07869-3808 Office: NJ Inst Tech Info Systems Newark NJ 07102

HILWIG, JOSEPH MICHAEL, electric company director; b. LaPlata, Md., Nov. 10, 1947; s. Gerald Joseph and Florence A. Hilwig; children: Joseph Michael Jr., Jeffery David. Course, Dale Carnegie & Assocs., Waldorf, Md., 1977. Master elec. lic., Md., Prince George's County, Charles County, St. Mary's County, Calvert County. Lineman So. Md. Electric Coop., Hughesville, 1966-85, gen. foreman, 1985-86, engring. supr., 1986-87, meter foreman, 1987-94, asst. meter and load mgmt. supt., 1994-95, meter ops. dir., 1995—. Chmn. lineman's apprentice, chmn. load mgmt. com. So. Md. Electric Coop.; mem., treas. Charles County Elec. Bd., LaPlata, 1990—. Dir. Charles County Fair Bd., Spring Hill, Md., 1988—. Mem. Waldorf Rotary (pres. 1991-92, Chmn. of Yr. 1987-88, Rotarian of Yr. 1988-89, Disting. Svc. citation 1996). Avocations: 3rd dan tae kwan do, tennis, boating, fishing, skiing. Home: 15830 Wilson Rd Newburg MD 20664 Office: So Md Elec Coop PO Box 1937 Hughesville MD 20637-1937 Fax: 301-274-9288. E-mail: hilwijos@smeco.com.

HIMEL, HARVEY NORMAN, medical educator; b. N.Y.C., Apr. 30, 1954; s. Sanford Zygmunt and Sonja (Geldzahler) H.; m. Beth Fisher, Sept. 8, 1984; 1 child, Samuel Fisher. BA, Yale U., 1975; MD, NYU, 1979; MPH, Harvard U., 1984. Diplomate in surgery and critical care medicine Am. Bd. Surgery, in plastic surgery and surgery of the hand Am. Bd. Plastic Surgery. Intern N.Y. Med. Coll., Valhalla, 1979-80; resident in surgery Boston U. Med. Ctr., 1980-86; rsch. fellow divsn. plastic surgery Mass. Gen. Hosp., Boston, 1986-87; resident plastic surgery U. So. Calif. Med. Ctr., L.A., 1988-90; asst. prof. U. Va., Charlottesville, 1990-96, Cornell U. Med. Ctr., N.Y., 1997—. Dir. DeCamp Burn Ctr. U. Va., Charlottesville, 1990-96, Hyperbaric Medicine Svc., N.Y. Hosp.-Cornell Med. Ctr.; attending surgeon N.Y. Hosp. Burn Ctr., 1997—; vis. scientist lab developmental biology and anomalies Nat. Inst. Dental Rsch. NIH, Bethesda, Md., 1987-88. Mem. editl. bd. Advances in Plastic and Reconstructive Surgery, 1995-98, Key Issues in Plastic and Cosmetic Surgery, 1999—. Fellow ACS; mem. AMA, Internat. Soc. Burn Injuries, Undersea and Hyperbaric Medicine Soc., Am. Burn Assn., Wound Healing Soc., Am. Soc. Plastic Reconstructive Surgeons. Office: NYH-CUMC Dept Surgery 525 E 68th St New York NY 10021-4870 E-mail: hnhimel@med.cornell.edu.

HIMELES, MARTIN STANLEY, JR., lawyer; b. Balt., Mar. 13, 1956; s. Martin Stanley and Betty Jean (Applebaum) H.; m. Paula Kilimnik, Aug. 26, 1984. BA summa cum laude, Yale U., 1978; JD magna cum laude, Harvard U., 1981. Bar: N.Y. 1982, U.S. Dist. Ct. (so. and ea. dists.) N.Y. 1982, U.S. Ct. Appeals (4th cir.) 1982, U.S. Dist. Ct. Md. 1986, Md. 1989, U.S. Ct. Appeals (8th cir.) 1999, U.S. Supreme Ct. 2003. Law clk. to judge U.S. Ct. Appeals (4th cir.), Balt., 1981-82; assoc. Parker, Auspitz, Neesemann & Delehanty P.C., N.Y.C., 1982-86; asst. U.S. atty. U.S. Atty's. Office, Balt., 1986-90; ptnr. Zuckerman Spaeder LLP, Balt., 1990—. Fellow: Am. Coll. Trial Lawyers; mem.: Balt. Jewish Coun. (mem. bd. govs.), Levindale Hebrew Geriatric Ctr and Hosp. (mem. bd. govs.), Fed. Bar Assn. (past pres. Md. chpt.), The Associated Jewish Comty. Fedn. of Balt. (bd. dirs., mem. investment com.), Am. Jewish Com. (1st v.p. Md. chpt.), Phi Beta Kappa. Democrat. Office: 100 E Pratt St Ste 2440 Baltimore MD 21202-1031 E-mail: mhimeles@zuckerman.com.

HIMELFARB, RICHARD JAY, investment firm executive; b. Balt., Feb. 3, 1942; s. Jacob and Jennie (Willen) H.; m. Margaret Conn, Sept. 7, 1969; children: Elizabeth Jayne, Michael Ross. BA, Johns Hopkins U., 1962; LLB, Yale U., 1965. Bar: Md., 1965. Employed, then ptnr. Saul Ewing LLC (formerly Weinberg & Green), Balt., 1967-83; sr. exec. v.p. Legg Mason, Inc., Balt., 1983—, also bd. dirs. With Center Stage, Inc., Balt., 1984-2002, Balt. Goodwill Industries, 1984-93, Kennedy Krieger Inst., 1993—, Bryn Mawr Sch., 1991-94; mem. bd. visitors U. Md., Balt., 1990-96, chmn., 1996-2000; chmn. U. Md. Balt. Found., 2000—; bd. visitors Inst. of Human Virology, 1997—; bd. dirs. Balt. Devel. Corp., 1997—. Capt. U.S. Army, 1965—67. Mem. Phi Beta Kappa. Home: 116 Taplow Rd Baltimore MD 21212-3312 Office: Legg Mason Inc 100 Light St Baltimore MD 21202-1099

HIMELFARB, STEPHEN ROY, lawyer; b. Washington, Feb. 19, 1954; s. Jordan Sheldon and Marion (Soloman) H.; m. Anne Patricia Spille, June 26, 1983; children: Kara Michelle, Bradley Richard. BSBA, Am. U., 1976; JD, George Mason U., 1980. Bar: D.C. 1982, Md. 1982, Va. 1988, U.S. Dist. Ct. D.C. 1982, U.S. Dist. Ct. Md. 1982, U.S. Ct. Appeals (D.C. and 4th cirs.) 1982, U.S. Dist. Ct. (ea. dist.) Va. 1988, U.S. Tax Ct. 1990, U.S. Bankruptcy Ct. (ea. div.) Va. 1988, U.S. Supreme Ct. 1985. From v.p. to pres. ECA Bus. Comm. Network, Washington, 1982-85; ptnr. Himelfarb & Podryhula, Washington, 1984-93, Speights & Micheel, Washington, 1986-88, Sheeskin, Hillman & Lazar, PC, Rockville, Md., 1989-90, Ahmad & Himelfarb, PC, Rockville, Md., 1993-95; pvt. practice Bethesda, Md., 1995—. V.p. Video Shack Inc., Woodbridge, Va., 1984-95. Mem. ABA, Md. State Bar Assn., Va. Bar Assn., Assn. Trial Lawyers Am., Phi Delta Phi. Democrat. Jewish. Avocations: electronics, coin-op/americana collecting, model trains, radio control models. Home: 1214 Winter Hunt Rd Mc Lean VA 22102-2434 Office: 4701 Sangamore Rd Ste S-225 Bethesda MD 20816-2508

HIMES, BARBARA ALISON (SYDNEY KENDALL), writer; b. Cincinnati, OH, June 19, 1954; d. Albert Kendall Himes, Ruth Mary Himes., University of Cincinnati, Cincinnati, Ohio, 1973—75. Author: (Novel) A Turn for DeWurst, 2000. Mem.: Society of Children's Book Writers and Illustrators. Avocation: acting, ballroom dancing, drawing, poetry writing, playgoing, reading, jewelry design, philosophy .

HIMES, DIANE ADELE, buyer, fundraiser, actress, lobbyist; b. San Francisco, Aug. 11, 1942; d. L. John and Mary Louise (Young) H. BA, San Francisco State U., 1964. Rep. west coast home furnishings Allied Stores, nationwide; gift buyer Jordan Marsh, Miami; buyer The Broadway Stores; west coast sales mgr. Xmas divsn. Vincent Lippe Corp., L.A.; midwest sales mgr. Vincent-Lippe Chgo. Actress Nine 'O Clock Players, 1995, short film The Traveling Companion, 1998. Statewide co-chair Californians Against Initiative No On #102, 1988; founding co-chair Life AIDS Lobby, 1985—88; mem. Beverly Hills rent control bd., 1984; co-chair Californians Against Proposition #64, 1986; co-chmn. Mcpl. Elections Com., L.A.; co-chmn. bd. dirs. L.A. Women's Shakespeare Group, 1992—94. Named Woman of Yr. of L.A., ACLU, 1987, Christopher Street West, 1988. Avocations: acting, appearing in short films.

HIMES, GEORGE ELLIOTT, pathologist; b. Huntington, W.Va., Jan. 5, 1922; s. Connell Bradley and Elizabeth (Skeans) H.; m. Rita T. Wasniewski (dec. July 1993); children: Rita Ann Brust, Susan Ruth Burger, George Elliott Jr., Brent Lee; m. Barbara A. Cunningham, Dec. 21, 1994. Student, U. Cin., 1939-42; DO, Chgo. Coll. Osteo. Medicine, 1942-45. Intern Lamb Mem. Hosp., Denver, 1945-46; resident pathology Chgo. Osteo Hosp., 1946-48; asst. prof. pathology Chgo. Coll. Osteo Med., 1948-56; asst. lab. dir. Chgo. Osteo Hosp., 1948-51; dir. of labs Flint (Mich.) Osteo Hosp., 1951-87, dir. of labs and nuclear med., 1957-80, dir. sch. med. tech., 1975-85; assoc. prof. pathology Coll. Osteo Med., Des Moines, 1968-89; adj. prof. pathology Coll. Osteo. Medicine Mich. State U., East Lansing, Mich., 1974-84, clin. prof. pathology Coll. Osteo. Medicine; mem. adv. coun. on diabetes Genesys Regional Med. Ctr., 2003, mem. Type II diabetes. Mem. radiation, chem. & biol. safety com. Mich. State U., 1978—; mem. Am. Osteo. Bd. Pathology, 1959-68, Am. Osteo. Bd. Nuclear Medicine, 1974-84. Bd. dirs. ARC, Flint, 1963-74, United Way, 1964-72; pres. Flint Civitan Club, 1954. Mem. AMA, AAAS, Am. Osteo. Coll. Pathologists (past pres. and sec.-treas. 1954-72), Am. Osteo. Assn., Am. Assn. Blood Banks, Mich. Osteopathic Assn., Coll. Am. Pathologists, Am. Soc. Clin. Pathologists, Soc. Nuclear Medicine, Mich. Soc. Pathologists, Genesee Country Osteo. Assn., Nat. Assn. Photoshop Profls., Flint Golf Club (past pres.). Avocations: golf, stamps, computing sciences. Home and Office: 444 Luce Ave Flushing MI 48433-1411

HIMES, JOHN HARTER, medical researcher, educator; b. Salt Lake City, July 25, 1947; s. Ellvert Hiram and Mildred Anna (Harter) H.; children: Rachel Anne, Matthew Hiram, Sarah Elizabeth; m. LaVell Gold. BS, Ariz. State U., 1971; PhD, U. Tex., 1975; MPH, Harvard U., 1982. Rsch., sr. scientist Fels Rsch. Inst., Yellow Springs, Ohio, 1976-79; Fels asst. prof. Wright State U. Sch. Medicine, Dayton, Ohio, 1977-79; sr. analyst, project dir. Abt Assocs., Cambridge, Mass., 1979-82; assoc. prof. CUNY, Bklyn., 1982-87; from assoc. prof. to prof. U. Minn. Sch. Pub. Health, Mpls., 1992—, dir. nutrition coord. ctr., 1995—. Expert com physical status WHO, Geneva, Switzerland, 1991-94, expert adv. panel nutrition, 1994—; mem. tech. working groups Ctrs. for Disease Control, Washington and Atlanta, 1988-97. Author: Parent-specific Adjustment for Assessment of Recumbent Length & Stature, 1981, Anthropo-

metric Assessment of Nutritional Status, 1991; contbr. articles to profl. jours. Recipient Nathalie Masse Meml. prize Internat. Children's Ctr., Paris, 1979. Fellow Human Biology Coun.; mem. APHA, N.Am. Assn. Study Obesity, Internat. Assn. Human Auxology, Pan Am. Health Orgn. (tech. adv. nutrition 1994—2000, Nat. Ctr. Health Stats. (tech. working group 1994-97), Am. Soc. Nutritional Scis., Soc. for Study Human Biology, Sigma Xi, Phi Kappa Phi, Delta Omega. E-mail: himes@epi.umn.edu.

HIMES, KENNETH ALAN, retired marketing executive; b. Phila., Nov. 2, 1937; s. Kenneth Elwood and Thelma Frances (Dieffenbacher) H.; m. Diane Margaret Zurinsky, Sept. 14, 1959; children: Christine Ann Himes Daly, Susan Leigh. BS in Bus., Lycoming Coll., 1959. With Woolrich (Pa.) Inc., 1959-90, sales rep., 1960-85, sr. v.p. mktg., 1985-90. Founder, sec. Woolrich Vol. Fire Co., 1960; trustee Lycoming Coll., 1987-95, Williamsport Hosp. and med. Ctr., 1988-95; fire commr. Bluffton Twp., 1995-2003; co-chmn. Fire Commn., 1997-98. Named Outstanding Alumnus Lycoming Coll., 1987. Mem. Nat. Assn. Men's and Boys' Apparel, Somerset Hills Jaycees, Masons, Rotary, Sigma Pi (treas. 1957). Republican. Methodist. Avocations: golf, travel, fishing. Office: Woolrich Inc Mill St Woolrich PA 17779

HIMLE, JOSEPH ALAN, social sciences educator; b. Sioux Falls, S.D., July 28, 1961; s. David Paul and Ilga Kramins Himle; m. Lisa Marie Gembrowski, Dec. 29, 1984; children: Lauren Michelle, Jennifer Marie. BA, U. of Mich., 1983, MSW, 1984, PhD, 1995. LCSW Mich., 1986. Caseworker Family Svc. of Genessee County, Flint, Mich., 1985—86; clin. social worker U. of Mich. Dept. of Psychiatry, 1986—95, asst. clin. prof., 1995—. Edit. bd. Rsch. on Social Work Practice; author: (book) Shy Bladder Syndrome; contbr. Rsch. chair Internat. Paruresis Assn., Balt., 2000—03. Recipient Tchr. of the Yr., U. of Mich. Dept. of Psychiatry, 1997, 2001. Lutheran. Avocations: golf, skiing. Office: University of Michigan - Psychiatry 1500 E Medical Center Dr Ann Arbor MI 48109-0118 Home Fax: 734-936-7868; Office Fax: 734-936-7868. Personal E-mail: himlej@umich.edu. E-mail: himlej@umich.edu.

HIMMELBERG, CHARLES JOHN, III, mathematics educator, researcher; b. North Kansas City, Mo., Nov. 12, 1931; s. Charles John and Magdalene Caroline (Batliner) H.; m. Mary Patricia Hennessy, Jan. 27, 1962; children: Charles, Ann, Mary, Joseph, Patrick. BS, Rockhurst Coll., 1952; MS, U. Notre Dame, 1954, PhD, 1957. Assoc. analyst Midwest Rsch. Inst., Kansas City, Mo., 1957-59; asst. prof. math. U. Kans., Lawrence, 1959-65, assoc. prof., 1965-68, prof., 1968—, chmn. dept. math., 1978-99. Mem. editorial bd. Rocky Mountain Jour. Math, 1972-88; contbr. articles to profl. jours. Mem. Am. Math. Soc., Math. Assn. Am. Roman Catholic. Office: U Kans Dept Math Lawrence KS 66045-7523 E-mail: himmelberg@math.ukans.edu.

HIMMELBERG, ROBERT FRANKLIN, historian, educator; b. Kansas City, Mo., July 16, 1934; s. Alexander Franklin and Genevieve Fay (Leonard) H.; m. Josephine Ann Boone, Dec. 27, 1958; children: Thomas A., Robert A., Juliana Ruth. BA, Rockhurst Coll., 1956; MA, Creighton U., 1958; PhD, Pa. State U., 1963. Instr. Am. history Fordham U., Bronx, N.Y., 1961-63, asst. prof., 1963-68, assoc. prof., 1968-77, prof., 1977—, chmn. dept., 1969-72, pres. faculty senate, 1989-92, dean Grad. Sch. Arts and Scis., 1993-2000. Hoover Presdl. Library fellow, 1984 85, grantee, 1993. Author: The Origins of the National Recovery Administration: Business, Government and the Trade Association Issue, 1921-1933, 1976, revised edit., 1994; editor: Business and Government in America Since 1870, 1994; co-editor: Historians and Race: Autobiography and the Writing of History, 1996, The Great Depression and the New Deal, 2000; contbr. articles to profl. jours. Am. Philos. Soc. grantee, 1978. Mem.: Orgn. Am. Historians, Republican. Roman Catholic. Office: Fordham Univ Dept History Bronx NY 10458 E-mail: himmelberg@fordham.edu.

HIMMELBLAU, DAVID MAUTNER, chemical engineer; b. Chgo., Aug. 29, 1923; s. David and Roda (Mautner) H.; m. Betty H. Hartman, Sept. 1, 1948; children: Andrew, Margaret Ann. BS, MIT, 1947; MBA, Northwestern U., 1950; PhD, U. Wash., 1957. Cost engr. Internat. Harvester Co., Chgo., 1946-47; cost analyst Simpson Logging Co., Seattle, 1952-53; mgr. Excel Battery Co., Seattle, 1953-54; teaching asst., instr. U. Wash., Seattle, 1955-57; successively asst. prof., asso. prof., prof. chem. engring. U. Tex., Austin, 1957—, chmn. dept., 1973-77. Pres. RAMAD Corp.; Univ. Fed. Credit Union, 1964-68; exec officer CACHE Corp. of Mass., 1984-2000. Author: Basic Principles and Calculations in Chemical Engineering, 1962, 7th edit., 2003, Process Analysis and Simulation, 1968, Process Analysis by Statistical Methods, 1970, Applied Nonlinear Programming, 1974, Optimization of Chemical Processes, 1989, 2d edit., 2000; contbr. articles to profl. jours. Served with U.S. Army, 1943-46, 51-52. Grantee, NSF, 1953—94, NATO Sci. Com., 1969. Mem. Am. Inst. Chem. Engrs. (dir. 1973-76), Am. Chem. Soc., Am. Math. Soc., Ops. Research Soc. Am., Soc. Indsl. and Applied Mathematics, Sigma Xi, Delta Mu Delta. Clubs: Headliners (Austin). Home: 4609 Ridge Oak Dr Austin TX 78731-5211 Office: Univ Texas Coll Engring Austin TX 78712 E-mail: himmelblau@che.utexas.edu.

HIMMELFARB, JOHN DAVID, artist; b. Chgo., June 3, 1946; s. Samuel and Eleanor (Gorecki) H.; m. Mary Louise Day. AB, Harvard U., 1968; MA, Grad. Sch. Edn., 1970. One-man shows: Ill. Arts Council, Chgo., 1974, Graphics I&II, Boston, 1974, Ill. Center, Chgo., 1975, U. Nebr., Omaha, 1976, Dorothy Rosenthal Gallery, Chgo., 1976, Ill. State Mus., Springfield, 1978, Albrecht Mus. Art, St. Joseph, Mo., 1978, Ball State U., 1978, 89, Sheldon Meml. Art Gallery, 1978, Ill. Wesleyan U., 1979, Terry Dintenfass Inc., N.Y.C., 1979, 83, 86, 89, 91, Gallery 72, Omaha, 1979, 83, 85, 87, 90, 92, 94, 96, 99, 2001, Fountain Gallery, Portland, Oreg., 1980, Hull Gallery, Washington, 1980, Barbara Balkin Gallery, Chgo., 1982, Area X Gallery, N.Y.C., 1985, Brody's Gallery, Washington, 1985, 90, Sioux City Art Ctr., 1985, 2000, Davenport Mus., 1986, John Nichols, N.Y.C., 1986, Blanden Art Mus., 1987, Evanston Art Ctr., 1987, 96, Fundacio Josep Artigas, Barcelona, Spain, 1989, Kalamazoo Inst. Arts, 1989, Miami U. Art Mus., 1990, Ark. Art Ctr., 1990, Madison Art Ctr., 1990, Huntington Mus. Art, 1990, Cissie Peltz Gallery, 1991, Anchor Graphics, 1992, U. No. Iowa, 1993, Gallery 1756, Chgo., 1995, Chgo. Cultural Ctr., 1995, Spaightwood Gallery, Madison, Wis., 1996, 99, Jean Albano Gallery, Chgo. 1996, 98, 2000, 2002, William Havu Gallery, Denver, 2002, Ind. U. N.W., 2002, others; group shows include: Minn. Mus. Art, Total Mus. Contemporary Art, Seoul, Korea, Bklyn. Mus., Indpls. Mus. Art, Art Inst. Chgo., Walker Art Ctr., Nat. Mus. Am. Art; represented in permanent collections: Art Inst. Chgo., Indpls. Mus. Art, Nat. Mus. Am. Art, Fogg Mus. Art, Cleve. Mus. Art, Mpls. Inst. Art, Portland Mus. Art, Ill. State Mus., Bklyn. Mus., Balt. Mus. Art, Des Moines Art Center, High Mus. Art, Atlanta, Toledo Mus. Art, Univs. Wis., Minn., Oreg., Iowa, Total Mus. of Contemporary Art, Seoul, Korea, Brit. Mus., others. NEA fellow in painting, 1982, in drawing, 1985; Ill. Arts Council fellow, 1986, 2003, Pollock-Krasner fellow, 2002. Studio: 2400 S Oakley Ave Chicago IL 60608-4902

HIMMELFARB, MILTON, editor, educator; b. Bklyn., Oct. 21, 1918; s. Max and Bertha (Lerner) H.; m. Judith Siskind, Nov. 26, 1950; children: Martha, Edward, Miriam, Anne, Sarah, Naomi, Dan. BA, CCNY, 1938, MS, 1939; B.Hebrew Lit., Jewish Theol. Sem. Coll., 1939; diplôme, U. Paris, 1939; postgrad., Columbia U., 1942-47. Dir. information and research Am. Jewish Com., N.Y.C., 1955-86; editor Am. Jewish Year Book, N.Y.C., 1959-86; contbg. editor Commentary mag., N.Y.C., 1960-86. Vis. prof. Jewish Theol. Sem., N.Y.C., 1967-68, 71-72; vis. lectr. Yale, 1971; vis. prof. Reconstructionist Rabbinical Coll., Phila., 1972-73. Author: The Jews of Modernity, 1973. Mem. U.S. Holocaust Meml. Coun., 1986-89.

HIMMELHOCH, JONATHAN M. psychiatrist, educator; b. Detroit, July 25, 1938; s. Akiba Joseph and Sarah Jane Himmelhoch; m. Judith Elaine Sugarmann, Feb. 1, 1963; children: Naomi Ann, Leah Ruth, Rachel Elizabeth, Darah Lynn. BA in Russian History and Lit., Harvard U., 1960, MD, 1964. Asst. prof. psychiatry Yale Med. Sch., 1969—73, asst. prof. psychopharmacology, 1969—73; tenured assoc. prof. psychiatry U. Pitts. Med. Sch. and Med. Ctr., 1973—78, tenured prof. psychiatry, 1978—2001, prof. emeritus, 2001—. Contbr. chapters to books, articles to profl. jours. Capt. USAR, 1966—72. Grantee in field, 1975—93. Fellow: APA, Am. Acad. Experts in Traumatic Stress, Am. Coll. Forensic Examiners. Democrat. Jewish. Achievements include research in parvate; defined moods of bipolar illness. Avocation: Russian and classical literature. Home: 109 Wilmar Dr Pittsburgh PA 15238 Office: 1382 Old Freeport Rd Pittsburgh PA 15238

HIMMELMANN, WILLIAM CHARLES, municipal official; b. Bklyn., Nov. 9, 1938; s. Charles and Eleanor Vivian (Martin) H.; m. Audrey S. Dezendorf, Sept. 19, 1959 (div. July 1979); children: John William, Katherine Jean. Student, Queens Coll., 1957-58, Xavier Labor Inst., Cornell U., George Meany Inst., U. Colo., Colo. State U., Rocky Mountain Labor Sch. Splicer's helper, frame, repair and test desk technician N.Y. Telephone Co., 1956-69; comm. svc. and test desk technician Mountain Bell, 1969-72; pres. Comm. Workers Am., Denver, 1972-77, Denver Area Labor Fedn., 1977-92; coun. mem. Dist. 7 Denver City Coun., 1995-99; rsch. asst. Denver City Coun., 1999-2000. Steward, chief steward, v.p. local # 7777 Comms. Workers of Am., 1969-72, internal organizer, steward, legis. chmn. local # 1101, 1957-64; del. United Telephone Orgns. Founder, bd. dirs. Citizens Appreciate Police, Inc., Denver, 1978—; hon. life bd. dirs. Mile High United Way, Denver; mem. city issues com. Denver LWV, 1981—. With USAR, 1956-64. Mem. Minoru Yasui Cmty. Vol. Assn. (pres. bd. dirs.). Democrat. Episcopalian. Avocations: model railroading, home decorating, collecting, dating. Home: 571 S Emerson St Denver CO 80209-4336

HIMMELREICH, DAVID BAKER, lawyer; b. Reading, Pa., Feb. 11, 1954; s. Lester Leon and Jane (Baker) H. AB in Econs., Lafayette U., 1976; JD, U. Pitts., 1979. Bar: Pa. 1980, U.S. Tax Ct. 1980. Sr. atty. Ayco Corp., Albany (N.Y) and Stamford (Conn.), 1979-84; sr. cons. Peat Marwick Main & co., N.Y.C., 1984-86; ptnr. Hynes, Himmelreich, Glennon & Co., Stamford, 1986—. Bd. dirs. Project Return, Westport, Conn., 1986—; dir. Alcohol and Drug Dependency Coun. of Conn., Westport. Republican. Lutheran. Home: 190 Gregory Blvd Norwalk CT 06855-2620 Office: Hynes Himmelreich Box 4004 Darien CT 06820-4004 Address: 30 Old Kings Highway South Darien CT 06820

HIMMELRIGHT, ROBERT JOHN, JR., rubber company executive; b. Canton, Ohio, Mar. 29, 1926; s. Robert John and Katherine Dewees (Nusly) H.; m. Suzanne Hadley, Mar. 11, 1950; children: Robert John III, Christina S., George H., Anne D. BA, U. N.Mex., 1951; LLD (hon.), Kenyon Coll., 1987. With Teledyne Monarch Rubber Co., Hartville, Ohio, 1950-84, asst. to pres., then v.p., 1955-62, pres., 1963-84; chmn. Monarch South Seas Ltd., Delray Beach, Fla., 1984—. Alt. del. Rep. Nat. Conv., 1972, 76; trustee Kenyon Coll., Gambier, Ohio. With USNR, 1944-46, 50-51. Lutheran. Home and Office: 200 N Ocean Blvd Delray Beach FL 33483-7126 E-mail: redhjr@aol.com.

HIMMELSTRAND, J. ULF I. sociology educator, writer; b. Tirupattur, India, Aug. 26, 1924; arrived in Sweden, 1935; s. John Sebastian and Elsa (Nygren) H.; m. Karin Birgitta Hagberg, Dec. 3, 1949; children: Jonas, Annika, Nina. BA, U. Uppsala, Sweden, 1948, Fil.lic., 1955, DSc, 1960. Rockefeller postdoctoral fellow U. Calif., Berkeley, 1960-61, U. Chgo., 1960-61, Columbia U., 1960-61; docent in sociology U. Uppsala, 1960-69, prof. sociology, 1969-89, prof. emeritus, 1989—; vis. prof. sociology U. Nairobi, Kenya, 1987-91; prof. sociology U. Ibadan, Nigeria, 1964-67; fellow Ctr. for Advanced Behaviorial Sci., Palo Alto, Calif., 1968-69. Author (in Swedish): The Civil War Nigeria-Biafra, 1969; editor, co-author Africa Reports on the Nigerian Crisis, 1978, Beyond Welfare Capitalism, 1981, Interfaces in Economic and Social Analysis, 1992, co-editor, co-author African Perspectives on Development, 1994, Normativity, Rationality, Materiality and Emotionality in Sociological Analysis-A 50-Year Perspective, 1997, How to Become and Remain a Marxicizing Sociologist, 1998, Three Faces in Russian Sociology[0097]Surviving Intellectually in A Totalitarian Society, 2000, The Twinkling of An Eye-Memoirs, 2000, (in Swedish) Image & Life: Collection of Poems, 2003, columnist (newspaper) Dagens Nyheter, Stockholm, 1988—90, local newspapers, Härnösand and Uppsala, 1994—, writer, commentator Aftonbladet, 1992—95; contbr. articles to profl. jours. Chmn. Swedish Sociol. Assn., 1972-74; v.p. Internat. Sociol. Assn., 1974-78, pres., 1978-82; v.p. Internat. Social Sci. Coun., Paris, 1981-86. Grantee Bank of Sweden Tercentenary Found., Swedish Coun. for Humanities and Social Scis., 1955-86. Mem. Internat. Sociol. Assn. (life), Swedish Sociol. Assn., Soc. for Advancement of Socio-Econs. Mem. Swedish Social Dem. Party. Avocations: reading and writing poetry, classical music, long distance bicycling. Home: Hamnesplanaden 4B S-753 19 Uppsala Sweden Office: Inst Sociology PO Box 821 S-75108 Uppsala Sweden E-mail: ulf.himmelstrand@soc.uu.se.

HIMMS-HAGEN, JEAN MARGARET, biochemist, educator; b. Oxford, Eng., Dec. 18, 1933; d. Frederick Hubert and Margaret Mary (Deadman) Himms; m. Paul Hagen, Sept. 29, 1956; children: Anna, Nina. BSc, U. London, 1955; PhD, Oxford U., 1958. Postdoctoral fellow Harvard U., 1958-59; asst. prof. physiology U. Man., 1959-64; assoc. prof. biochemistry Queen's U., 1964-67, U. Ottawa, 1967-71, prof., 1971-99, acting chmn. dept., 1975-77, 87, chmn. dept., 1977-82, prof. emeritus, 1999—. Mem. coun. Med. Rsch. Coun., 1970-75; mem. Exec. Med. Rsch. Coun., 1970-73, mem. grants coms., 1969-75, chmn. metabolism grants com., 1972-75. Assoc. editor Can. Jour. Biochemistry, 1967-71, Can. Jour. Physiology and Pharmacology, 1971-75, Am. Jour. Physiology, 1979-89, 92—; mem. editl. bd. proc. Soc. Exptl. Biology and Medicine, 1984-90, Obesity Rsch., 1993—; contbr. over 150 articles and revs. to sci. jours., chpts. to books. Recipient research grants Med. Research Council, 1960-2001, career award, 1968-77, Bond award Am. Oil Chemists Soc., 1972 Fellow Royal Soc. Can.; mem. Can. Biochem. Soc. (Ayerst award 1973), Am. Soc. Nutritional Scis., Biochem. Soc. U.K., Soc. for Exptl. Biology and Medicine (coun. 1991-94), N.Am. Assn. Study of Obesity (coun. 1995-98), Am. Physiol. Soc., Am. Soc. Pharmacology and Exptl. Therapeutics. Home: 507-420 MacKay St Ottawa ON Canada K1M 2C4 Office: U Ottawa Dept Biochemistry 451 Smyth Rd Ottawa ON Canada K1H 8M5 E-mail: jhagen@uottawa.ca.

HIMPSEL, FRANZ JOSEF, physicist, educator; b. Rosenheim, Germany, 1949; arrived in U.S., 1977; Diploma in physics, U. Munich, 1973, PhD in Physics, 1977. With IBM Rsch., Yorktown Heights, NY, 1977-95, 1st level mgr., 1982-85, 2nd level mgr., 1985-95; prof. physics U. Wis., Madison, 1995—, co-dir. sci. Synchrotron Radiation Ctr., 1997—2002, Ednor M. Rowe prof. physics, 2000—. Co-author (et al.): (jours.) Exptl. Energy Band Dispersions and Exch. Splittings for Ni, 1979, Micros. Structure of the Si02/Si Interface, 1988; co-author: (with J.E. Ortega) Quantum Well States as Mediators of Magnetic Coupling in Superlattices, 1992; co-author: (et al.) Magnetic Nanostructures, 1998; author: Angle-resolved Measurements of the Photoemission of Electrons in the Study of Solids, 1983. Fellow: Am. Vacuum Soc. (Peter Mark award 1985), Am. Phys. Soc.; mem.: German Phys. Soc., NY Acad. Sciences. Office: Univ Wis Dept Physics 1150 University Ave Madison WI 53706-1390 Fax: 608-265-2334. E-mail: fhimpsel@facstaff.wisc.edu.

HINCHEY, BRUCE ALAN, environmental engineering company executive, state legislator; b. Kansas City, Mo., Jan. 24, 1949; s. Charles Emmet and Eddie Lee (Scott) H.; m. Karen Adele McLaughlin, Nov. 27, 1969 (div. Nov. 1983); children: Scott Alan, Traci Denise, Amanda Lee, Richard Austin; m. Karen Robitaille, Apr. 10, 1993. Student, U. Mo., Rolla, 1967-71. Source testing crew chief Ecology Audits, Inc., Dallas, 1971-76, lab. mgr. Casper, Wyo., 1976-78, mgr. ops. Dallas, 1978-79; v.p. Kumpe & Assoc. Engrs., Casper, 1979-81; pres. Western Environ. Svcs. and Testing, Inc., Casper, 1981—2002, Hawk Industries, Inc., 1993 2000; mem. Wyo. Senate, Dist. 27, Cheyenne, 1998-; pres. Petroleum Assn. Wyo., Casper, 2002—. Pres. Mining Assocs. Wyo., Cheyenne, 1986-87. Mem. Wyo. State Ho. of Reps., Cheyenne, 1989-99, spkr. of house, mgmt. coun., rules com., energy coun., select water com., sel. edn. com., active Natrona County Rep. precinct, Casper, 1986—, Am. Legis. Exch. Coun., 1989; chair Natrona County Rep. Party, 1988-89; mem. appropriations com. Wyo. Senate, 1999—. Mem. Am. Inst. Mining Engrs., Nat. Fedn. Ind. Bus. (Guardian award), Air Pollution Control Assn., Casper C. of C., Rotary, Shriners, Masons. Methodist. Office: Petroleum Assn Wyo 951 Werner Ct Ste 100 Casper WY 82601

HINCHEY, JOHN WILLIAM, lawyer; b. Knoxville, Tenn., June 18, 1941; s. Roy William and Ruth (Ownby) H.; m. Sherie Paulette Archer, May 12, 1968; children: Paul William, Meredith Marie, John Oliver. AB, Emory U., 1964, LLB, 1965; LLM, Harvard U., 1966; MLitt., Oxford U., 1980. Bar: Ga. 1965, U.S. Dist. Ct. (no., mid. and so. dists.) Ga. 1968, U.S. Ct. Appeals (11th cir.) 1968, U.S. Supreme Ct. 1970. Asst. atty. gen. State of Ga., Atlanta, 1968-72; ptnr. McConaughey & Hinchey, Decatur, Ga., 1972-76, Phillips & Mozley, Atlanta, 1976-84, Phillips, Hinchey & Reid, Atlanta, 1984-92, King and Spalding, Atlanta, 1992—. Contbr. articles to profl. jours. Mem.: ABA (chair Forum on Constrn. Industry), Nat. Constrn.Dispute Resolution Com., CPR Inst., Alternative Dispute Resolution Counsel, Chartered Inst. Arbitrators, London Ct. Internat. Arbitration, Atlanta Bar Assn. (chair constrn. law sect. 1999—2000), Ga. Bar Assn., Am. Arbitration Assn., Am. Coll. Constitution Lawyers (bd. govs. 2001—), Druid Hills Golf Club. Republican. Methodist. Office: King & Spalding LLP 191 Peachtree St SW Atlanta GA 30303-1763 E-mail: jhinchey@kslaw.com.

HINCHEY, MAURICE D. congressman; b. N.Y.C., Oct. 27, 1938; s. Maurice D. and Rose (Bonack) H.; m. Ilene Marder; children: Maurice Scott, Josef L., Michelle R. BA, SUNY, New Paltz, 1968, MA, 1970. Mem. N.Y. State Assembly, 1974-93, U.S. Congress from 22d N.Y. dist., 1993—; mem. appropriations com., agr. subcom., interior subcom., joint econ. com. Chmn. N.E. Task Force Food & Farm Policy & Assembly Environ. Conserv. Comm., Higher Ednl. Rules & Racing & Wagering Comm., Joint Legis. Comm. Solid Waste Mgmt., Interstate Coun. on Migrant Edu., N.Y. Urban Cultural Parks Adv. Coun.; bd. visitors, house minority legions whip U.S. Mil. Acad. Author: (with others) Organized Crime and the Solid Waste Industry, 1986; N.Y. City Water Supply, A History, 1988. Hudson River Greenway Coun.; bd. dirs. Children's Rehab. Ctr., WAMC Nat. Pub. Radio. Recipient of Legislator of the Yr. award, Environ Planning Lobby, 1975, 1979, N.Y. State Bar Assn. Environ award, 1989. Mem. Saugerties Dem. Club (founding mem.), N.Y. State Dem. Commn. (vice-chmn.). Democrat. Roman Catholic. Office: US Ho of Reps 2431 Rayburn Hob Washington DC 20515-3222*

HINCKLEY, DAVID MALCOLM, journalist, editor, critic; b. Hartford, Conn., Nov. 23, 1948; s. Malcolm Slate and Evelyn Gladys (Nason) H.; m. Francis McCarthy, May 24, 1986; children: Marcia, Kip, Ric, Nell. BA, Drew U., 1970. Writer, editor Morristown (N.J.) Record, 1972-80; writer, editor, critic-at-large N.Y. Daily News, N.Y.C., 1980—. Judge Ralph J. Gleason Book Awards, N.Y.C., 1990—. Author: The Rolling Stones: Black & White Blues, 1995. Office: NY Daily News 450 W 33rd St Fl 3 New York NY 10001-2681

HINCKLEY, DEBORAH CLARK, language services professional; b. Cin., Sept. 16, 1947; d. Timothy Dwight and Helen Marilyn (Clark) H.; m. Richard Austin Beaumont, Feb. 26, 1993. BA cum laude, Brown U., 1969; postgrad., Sorbonne U., Paris, 1970-71. Instr. English Lang. Studies, Ltd., Paris, 1969-71; self-employed instr. English Paris, 1971-73; instr. French and English Cincilingua, Cin., 1973-76; tchr., trainer, dir. Nat. Inst. of Langs., N.Y.C., 1976-84; pres. inlingua Lang. Ctrs., Ridgewood and Summit, N.J., 1984—. Pres. inlingua Americas' Nat. Commn., 1987-93, 96—, inlingua Internat. Commn., 1992-93; bd. dirs. inlingua Internat., 1993-96. Mem. ASTD, Sietar. Office: inlingua Lang Ctr 171 E Ridgewood Ave Ridgewood NJ 07450-3824

HINCKLEY, GORDON B. religious organization administrator; b. Salt Lake City, June 23, 1910; s. Bryant S. and Ada (Bitner) H.; m. Marjorie Pay, Apr. 29, 1937; children: Kathleen Hinckley Barnes, Richard G., Virginia Hinckley Pearce, Clark B., Jane Hinckley Dudley. Ordained 15th pres., prophet LDS Ch., 1995. Asst. Coun. of Twelve Apostles LDS Ch., Salt Lake City, 1958-61, mem. Coun., 1961-81, mem. Quorum Twelve Apostles, 1961—95, counselor in 1st presidency, 1981-81, 2d counselor in 1st presidency, 1982-85, 1st counselor in 1st presidency, 1985-95, pres. of ch., 1995—. Proselyting mission Brit. Isles LDS Ch. Named One of most admired men in world 2d consecutive yr., ann. survey Ams., 2001. Mem. Lds Ch. Office: First Presidency LDS Ch 47 E South Temple Salt Lake City UT 84150-9701 Address: LDS Ch Office of Pres 47 E South Temple Salt Lake City UT 84150

HINCKLEY, GREGORY KEITH, software industry executive; b. San Francisco, Oct. 3, 1946; s. Homer Clair and Josephine F. (Gerrick) H. BS in Math. and Physics, Claremont Men's Coll., 1968; MS in Applied Physics, U. Calif., San Diego, 1970; MBA, Harvard U., 1972. CPA, Ill. Second v.p. Continental Bank, Chgo., 1972—78; dir. fin ITEL Corp., San Francisco, 1978—79; group contr. Raychem Corp., Menlo Park, Calif., 1979—83; v.p. fin., CFO Bio-Rad Labs., Richmond, Calif., 1983—89; sr. v.p. fin., CFO Crowley Maritime Corp., San Francisco, 1989—91; sr. v.p., CFO VLSI Tech. Inc., 1992—97; pres., COO Mentor Graphics Corp., Wilsonville, Oreg., 1997—. Bd. dirs. OEC Med. Systems, Inc., Salt Lake City, Amkor Tech., West Chester, Pa., Oreg. Mus. Sci. and Industry, Portland. Bd. dirs. Portland Opera. Fulbright fellow, Eng., 1968. Mem. AICPAs. Home: 2417 SW 16th Ave Portland OR 97201-2308

HINCKLEY, ROBERT CRAIG, lawyer, media company executive; b. New Orleans, Sept. 5, 1947; s. Marsden Donald and Doris Camille (Engelhardt) H. BS, U.S. Naval Acad., 1969; JD, Tulane U., 1976. Bar: La. 1976, Calif. 1977. Commd. Navigator, anti-submarine warfare officer USS Brinkley Bass, Long Beach, Calif., 1969-71; aide to dir. naval intelligence Pentagon, Washington, 1971-73; spl. asst. U.S. atty., legal officer Naval Air Sta., Alameda, Calif., 1976-79; with Lillick McHose & Charles, San Francisco, 1979-81, Jones, Walker, Waechter, Poitevent, Carrere & Denegre, New Orleans, 1981; v.p., gen. counsel, sec. NEC Electronics, Inc., Mountain View, Calif., 1981-87; sr. v.p., CFO Spectra Physics, San Jose, Calif., 1988-90; v.p. strategic programs, COO Xilinx, Inc., San Jose, 1991—99; bd. dirs. Lexar Media, 2003--. Bd. dirs. San Jose (Calif.) Symph., 1995. Mem. Assn. Publicly Traded Cos. (bd. dirs. 1995—99), Xandex, Inc., Lexar Media, Inc. Home: 79 Crescent Drive Palo Alto CA 94301

HINCKLEY, TED C. historian, educator, writer; b. NYC, Oct. 4, 1925; s. Theodore Charles and Eunice Marguerite (Platt) H.; m. Caryl Fay Chesmore, June 17, 1948; children: Susan Platt Hinckley Koester, Deborah Christine Hinckley Brooks. BA in Bus. Adminstrn., Claremont McKenna Coll., Claremont, Calif., 1950; BS in History, N.W. Mo. State U., Maryville, 1951; MA in Edn., U. Mo., Kansas City, 1953; PhD in History, Ind. U., 1961. Jr. exec. Chesmore Seed Co., St. Joseph, Mo., 1950; tchr. history Barstow Sch., Kansas City, Mo., 1951-53; asst. to pres. Claremont McKenna Coll., 1953-55; headmaster St. Katharine's Sch., Davenport, Iowa, 1955-57; tchg. asst. Ind. U., Bloomington, 1957-59; prof. history San Jose State U., Calif., 1959-90, adj. prof. Western Wash. U., Bellingham, 1991—. Lectr. Fulbright Assocs., Yogyakarta, Indonesia, 1994—95; PACE lectr. USS Boxer, 1997, USS A. Lincoln, 1998, USS Leyte Gulf, 1999, USS Nicholas, 2001; ACCL lectr. SS Grande Mariner, 2001; AP reader Hist., 2000—. Author: John G. Brady, 1982, The Canoe Rocks, 1995, War, Wings. . .1945, 1996, The Americanization of Alaska, 1972; mem. editl. bd. Pacific N.W. Quar., 1974-93, Alaska History, 1984-2000, Jour. of the West, 1977—. Mem. Calif. Hist. Preservation Commn., Sacramento, 1980—85; assoc. Danforth Found., St. Louis, 1962; playwright Four Women, Webb Sch., Knoxville, 2001; elder Saratoga Presbyn. Ch., Calif., 1968—70. With USN, 1943—46, 2d lt. USAR, 1950—53, ensign USNR, 1953—56. Huntington Libr. summer fellow, 1971, Alaska Hist. Commn. fellow 1983-84; grantee Am. Philos. Soc., 1962, 66. Mem.: Fulbright Assn., Alaska Hist. Soc., Western Hist. Assn. (coun. 1987—90), Am. Hist. Assn., Phi Beta Kappa. Christian. Avocations: play writing, gardening, carpentry. Home: 950 Chesley Park Dr Sedro Woolley WA 98284-9565 E-mail: hinckley@cc.wwu.edu.

HIND, HARRY WILLIAM, pharmaceutical company executive; b. Berkeley, Calif., June 2, 1915; s. Harry Wyndham and B.J. (O'Connor) H.; m. Diana Vernon Miesse, Dec. 12, 1940; children: Leslie Vernon Hind Daniels, Gregory William. BS, U. Calif., Berkeley, 1939; LLD, U. Calif.-Berkeley, 1968; DSc (hon.), U. Scis. Phila., 1982. Founder Barnes-Hind Pharms., Inc., Sunnyvale, Calif., 1939—. Pres. Hind Health Care, Inc. Contbr. articles to profl. jours.; designer ph meter and developer of ophthalmic solutions. Mem. chancellor's assocs. U. Calif.; trustee emeritus U. Calif.-San Francisco Found. Recipient Ebert award for pharm. research, 1948, Eye Research Found. award, 1958, Helmholtz Ophthalmology award for research, 1968, Carbert award for sight conservation, 1973, Alumnus of Yr. award U. Calif. Sch. Pharmacy, 1965, Disting. Service award U. Calif. Proctor Found., 1985, Commendation by Resolution State of Calif., 1987, Pharmaceutical Achievements commendation State of Calif. Assembly, Hon. Recognition award Contact Lens Mfrs. Assn., 1990. Fellow AAAS; mem. Am. Pharm. Assn., Am. Optometric Assn. (Man of Yr. award Pharmacist's Planning Svc. 1987), Contact Lens Soc. Am. (Hall of Fame 1989), Am. Assn. Pharm. Scientists, Am. Chem. Soc., Calif. Pharm. Assn., N.Y. Acad. Scis., Los Altos Country Club, Sigma Xi, Rho Chi, Phi Delta Chi.

HINDEN, BARRY HARRIS, lawyer; b. Bklyn., Sept. 21, 1943; s. Richard A. and Freda (Zucker) H.; m. Marilyn Hausner, July 19, 1970; children: Stephen M., Traci M. BA, Calif. State U., 1970; JD, Southwestern U., L.A., 1974. Bar: Calif. 1974, U.S. Ct. Appeals 1974. Pvt. practice law, L.A., 1974-78; sr. ptnr. Sobo & Hinden, Beverly Hills, Calif., 1978-88, Hinden, Rodich & Grueskin, L.A., 1988-90, Hinden & Grueskin, L.A., 1989-96, Hinden, Glauber, Grueskin & Aguirre, L.A., 1996-97, Hinden, Grueskin & Rondeau, L.A., 1997—. Adj. prof. Southwestern U. Sch. Law, 2002; lectr. CompPro Seminars, L.A., 1992-95, Westwood Seminars, Encino, Calif., 1992, Coalition of Medicare Providers, L.A., 1992, Calif. Soc. Indsl. Medicine, Calif. Applicants' Attys. Assn., Lorman Seminars; adj. prof. Calif. Poly. U., 1996—. Author: Surviving the Storm of Reform, 1993, How to Prepare Your Client for Trial, Medical Control: Advanced Worker's Compensation in California, 1997, Workers Compensation in California, 1998, How to Litigate the Post Termination Claim: Indentifying the Collateral Issues to Workers Compensation, Handling a Workers Compenstaion Case Bench Book, 2000, others. Judge pro tem Workers Compensation Appeals Bd., Santa Monica, Calif., L.A., 1989-95; adminstrv. asst. Calif. Polit. Forum, 1968; vol. Beverly Hills Edn. Found., 1988-95; coach Beverly Hills Little League, Am. Youth Soccer Orgn.; scoutmaster Boy Scouts Am., 1962-65, 73-76, cubmaster, 1982-85; baseball & football coach U.S. Army Dependents, 1962-65; bd. dirs., v.p. Nat. Kidney Assn., Westside Jewish Cmty. Ctr., 1980-88, Temple Emanuel, Beverly Hills, 1989-92, also pres. brotherhood, 1990-92; vol. L.A. Mission, 1993-95, Lokrantz Sch. for Retarded, 1969-70; mem. L.A. Mid City Redevel. P.A.C. Served in U.S. Army, 1962-65, Germany. Mem. Calif. Applicants Atty. Assn. (edn. chair 1992-93, bd. govs.), L.A. County Bar Assn. (lectr.), L.A. Trial Lawyers Assn., Consumer Attys. of Calif., L.A. Lawyers Club, Mid City C. of C. Democrat. Avocations: cross-country skiing, golf, travel, jogging, baseball card collecting. Office: Hinden Grueskin & Rondeau 4661 W Pico Blvd Los Angeles CA 90019-4237 also: 81-840 Ave 46th Indio CA

HINDEN, STANLEY JAY, newspaper editor; b. N.Y.C., Jan. 27, 1927; s. Edward I. and Rose (Kroshinsky) H.; m. Sara Leopold, May 24, 1953; children: Alan, Lawrence, Pamela. BA, Syracuse U., 1950. Successively reporter, polit. editor, editor editorial pages, nat. corr. Washington Newsday, Garden City, N.Y., 1952-71; successively exec. editor, editor Nat. Jour., Washington, 1971-73; editl. page features editor, editor Dist., Md. and Va. weekly sects., fin. reporter, columnist Washington Post, 1973-96, fin. writer column Washington Investing. Author: How to Retire Happy, 2001; contbr. polit. column. Inside Politics, Newsday, 1955-65, Retirement Jour. column Washington Post, 1996—. Served with AUS, 1945-46. Home: Apt 630 3310 N Leisure World Blvd Silver Spring MD 20906-5664 Office: 1150 15th St NW Washington DC 20071-0001 E-mail: hindens@washpost.com.

HINDERAKER, IVAN, political science educator; b. Hendricks, Minn., Apr. 29, 1916; s. Theodore and Clara (Hanson) H.; m. Evelyn Birkholz, June 7, 1941; 1 child, Mark. BA, St. Olaf Coll., 1938; MA, U. Minn., 1942, PhD, 1949. Mem. faculty UCLA, 1948—, prof. polit. sci., 1956—, chmn. dept., 1960-62; vice chancellor acad. affairs U. Calif.-Irvine, 1962-64; chancellor U. Calif.-Riverside, 1964-79, chancellor emeritus, 1979—. Mem. Minn. Ho. of Reps., 1941-43; mem. Calif. Transp. Commn., 1978-84, chmn., 1982. Served to 1st lt. USAAF, 1943-46. Home: 943 Goldenrod Ave Corona Del Mar CA 92625-1504

HINDERLITER, RICHARD GLENN, electrical engineer; b. Tulsa, Apr. 9, 1936; s. Robert Verl and Aileen (Burton) H.; m. Leila Ratzlaff, June 8, 1958; children: Daniel Scott, Susan Paige, Alison Ann, Matthew Glenn. BSEE with honors, U. Kans., 1958; MSEE, NYU, 1960, PhD in Ops. Rsch., 1973. Staff mem. Bell Labs., Murray Hill, NJ, 1958-62; dept. head Bell Labs., Holmdel, NJ, 1962-72, Whippany, NJ, 1972-82; divsn. mgr. AT&T, N.Y.C., 1982-83, Bellcore, Morristown, NJ, 1984-91. Contbr. articles to Internat. Conf. on Communications, Computer Mag., Internat. Symposium on Subscriber Loops, Internat. Teletraffic Conf. Chmn. Zoning Bd. of Adjustment, Chatham Twp., N.J., 1992-99; scoutmaster Boy Scouts Am., Kansas City, Mo., Chatham Twp., Red Bank, N.J., Wichita, Kans., 1958—; v.p. Stonebrooke Estates Howeowners Assn. Recipient Silver Beaver award Morris-Sussex coun. Boy Scouts Am., 1988, Eagle Scout Hall of Fame, 1998, Outstanding Vol. award with spl. recognition Vols. of Morris County; James E. West fellow Boy Scouts Am. Fellow AAAS; mem. IEEE (sr.), N.Y. Acad. Scis., Inst. for Ops. Rsch. and the Mgmt. Scis., Meth. Friday Niters Fellowship Soc. (pres.), Methodist Inquirers Fellowship (pres.), Kiwanis (treas. Chatham, pres. North Kansas City, Mo. chpt., George F. Hixon fellow), Tau Beta Pi, Sigma Tau (v.p.), Theta Tau (vice regent), Eta Kappa Nu (pres.), Alpha Phi Omega, Pi Mu Epsilon, Sigma Pi Sigma. Methodist. Achievements include application of ops. rsch. techniques to large software systems. E-mail: hondolite@prodigy.net.

HINDI, NITHAM M. finance educator, department chairman; b. Amman, Jordan, Sept. 6, 1959; s. Mohammad and Latifa Hindi; m. Sawsan Siam Siam, Aug. 18, 1992; children: Haneen, Basel, Osamah. D in Bus. Adminstrn., Miss. State U., 1991. Asst. prof. acctg. Shippensburg (Pa.) U., 1994—97; prof. acctg. Emporia (Ky.) State U., 1997—. Contbr. articles. Mem.: Inst. Mgmt. Accountants (v.p., pres. local chpt. 1992—2003, dir. manscripts 2001—03, mem. regional ops. com. 1997—98, Outstanding IMA Mem. 1995—96, cert. mgmt. acct.). Home: 1128 W 18th St Emporia KS 66801 Office: Emporia State Univ 1200 Commercial St Campus Box 4057 Emporia KS 66801 Office Fax: 620-341-6346. E-mail: hindinit@emporia.edu.

HINDIN, SEYMOUR, lawyer; b. N.Y.C. s. Joseph S. and Sara L. (Altman) H.; m. Vera (dec. Mar. 1987); children: Steven D., Joel S. BA, NYU, 1939, JD, 1941. Bar: U.S. Dist. Ct. (so. dist.) N.Y. 1947, U.S. Dist. Ct. (ea. dist.) N.Y. 1959, U.S. Supreme Ct. 1961, U.S. Ct. Appeals (2d dist.) 1980. Atty. pvt. practice, N.Y.C., 1943—. Mem. Environ. Conservation Adv. Bd., Port Jefferson, NY, 1975—90; arbitrator U.S. Dist. Ct. Ea. Dist. N.Y., 1985, Dist. Ct. Suffolk County, 1985, Nassau County, 1985—90; adult edn. instr. Earl L. Vandermeulen H.S., Port Jefferson, 1975—86, Miller Place, 1983—85. Mem. Score-Counselor to Am. Small Bus., 1988. Recipient Ten Yr. award for Svc. Small Bus. Cmty., 1998, Gold Mem. award SCORE, 1999. Mem. Suffolk County Bar Assn. (Golden Anniversary Award of Practice of Law 1993), Knights of Pythias (Cosmopolitan Lodge chancellor comdr. 1946). Home: 105 E Gate Rd Port Jefferson NY 11777

HINDLE, MARGUERITA CECELIA, textile chemist, consultant; b. Providence, Nov. 26, 1928; d. Joseph and Elsie Cecelia (Johnson) Lombardo; m. Robinson J. Hindle, June 17, 1950. BS in Chemistry, U. R.I., 1949, DSc, 1993. Textile chemist Kenyon (R.I.) Industries, 1950-88, lab. dir., 1960-88, R&D dir., 1968-88, v.p. R&D/tech., 1978-88; ind. textile cons., 1988—. Mem. textile adv. com. U. Mass., Dartmouth, 1979—; mem. textile adv. bd. U. R.I., Kingston, 1991—; environ. com. chair Am. Textile Mgrs. Inst., Washington. Mem. Am. Assn. Textile Chemists and Colorists (nat. pres. 1987-88). Home and Office: TCE Consulting Svcs 15 Belle Rose Dr Westerly RI 02891-3917

HINDLE, PAULA ALICE, nursing administrator; b. Cambridge, Mass., Feb. 26, 1952; d. Edward Adam and Geraldine Ann (Donahue) H. BSN, Fitchburg State Coll., 1974; MSN, Duke U., 1980; MBA, Simmons Coll., 1988. Staff nurse Mt. Auburn Hosp., Cambridge, Mass., 1974-75, U. Hosp., Boston, 1975-77, head nurse, 1977-79; staff nurse Duke U. Med. Ctr., Durham, N.C., 1979-80, clin. instr., 1980-81, area mgr., 1981; nurse leader, clin. dir. New Eng. Med. Ctr., Boston, 1981-87; cons. Ctr. for Nursing Case Mgmt., Boston, 1984-87; v.p. nursing Faulkner Hosp., Boston, 1987-94; v.p. nursing and support svcs. Alexandria (Va.) Hosp., 1994-97; v.p. for patient care, chief nurse exec. Loyola U. Med. Ctr., Maywood, Ill., 1997—. Mem. adv. com. Regis Coll. Nursing, 1993; mem. planning and resource com. Simmons Coll., 1993-94; mem. affiliate faculty George Mason U., 1994-95. Active Am. Heart Assn. Mem. Am. Orgn. Nurse Execs., Va. Orgn. Nurse Execs., Mass. Orgn. Nurse Execs. (treas. 1991-93), Humane Soc., Simmons Coll. Grad. Sch. Mgmt. Alumni Assn. (bd. dirs. 1991-93, pres. 1992-93), Sigma Theta Tau. Democrat. Roman Catholic. Avocations: ballroom dancing, reading, theatre, music. Home: 1123 Mistwood Ln Downers Grove IL 60515-1284 Office: Loyola U Med Ctr 2160 S 1st Ave Maywood IL 60153-3304

HINDMAN, LARRIE C. lawyer; b. Meservey, Iowa, Mar. 30, 1937; s. Marvin C. and Fredona E. (Lemke) H.; m. Jeannie Carol Richey, June 18, 1961; children: Bryant C., Derek Cory. BS, Iowa State U., 1959; JD, U. Iowa, 1962. Bar: Mo. 1963, Kans. 1975. Ptnr. Stinson Morrison & Hecker LLP, Kansas City, Mo., 1962-2000. Contbr. legal articles to profl. jours. Mem.: Am. Land Title Assn. (lender counsel), Am. Coll. Real Estate Lawyers, Club at Porto Cima. Home: 67 Grand Cove Dr Sunrise Beach MO 65079-9217 Office: Stinson Morrison & Hecker LLP 2600 Grand Blvd Ste 1200 Kansas City MO 64108-4606

HINDO, WALID AFRAM, radiology educator, researcher; b. Baghdad, Iraq, Oct. 4, 1940; arrived in U.S., 1966, naturalized, 1976; s. Afram Paul and Laila Farid (Meshaka) H.; m. Fawzia Hanna Batti, Apr. 20, 1965; children: Happy, Rana, Patricia, Heather, Brian MB, ChB, Baghdad U., 1964. Diplomate Am. Bd. Radiology. Instr. radiology Rush Med. Coll, Chgo., 1971-72; asst. prof. Northwestern U., Chgo., 1972-75; assoc. prof. medicine and radiology Chgo. Med. Sch., 1975-80, prof., chmn. dept. radiology, 1980-90, prof. dept. radiology, 1990—, dir. radiology rsch. program, 1990-94; cons. UtiliMed, Northbrook, Ill., 1994—96; pres. Northbrook Inst. for Rsch. and Devel., 1992—. Dir. radiology rsch. program VA Med. Ctr., North Chicago, Ill., 1990-94; cons. Ill. Cancer Coun. Contbr. articles on cancer treatment, imaging and managed care to profl. jours. Bd. dirs. Lake County div. Am. Cancer Soc., Ill., 1975-80. Served to lt. M.C., Iraq; Army, 1965-66 Recipient Golden Apple award, The Chgo. Med. Sch., 1994; named Prof. of Yr., Chgo. Med. Sch., 1981, 82, 83, 85, 86. Mem. Radiology Soc. North Am., Am. Soc. Acad. Radiologists. Republican. Roman Catholic. Office: Northbrook Inst for R&D Ste 117 1955 Raymond Dr Northbrook IL 60062-6732

HINDS, C. ROBERT (BOB), retired writer; children: Karen Hinds Foster, Cynthia Hinds Wehmer, Kelly Andrew, Sandra Lynn. BS in Agr., U. Mo., 1953; grad., Reich Sch. Auctionnering, 1958. Field supr. Vets. Agr., Willow Springs, Mo., 1947—51; agr. cons. Export Corp., Japan, Taiwan, Bolivia, Germany, 1972—77. Spkr. in field; bd. dirs. Nat. Hampshire Swine Reg., Peoria, Ill.; pres. Prodrs. Creamery, Cabool, Mo., 1955—57. Author: College the Easy Way, 1998, Ozark Pioneer, 1999, Ozark Laughter, 1999, Train Your Own Stock Dog, 1999, Double Your Church Attendance, 1999, Arthritis, 1999, Computer Short Cuts, 1999, Solving the Mysteries of Dating, 1999, Ozark Attractions, 2000, Ozark Recipes, 2002. Recipient Disting. Svc. resolution, Mo. Stat Legis., 1982. Mem.: Lions Club, Gamma Sigma Delta. Avocations: fishing, hunting. Home: PO Box 100 Willow Springs MO 65793

HINDS, EDWARD DEE, insurance and investment professional financial planner; b. Madera, Calif., May 13, 1949; s. Edward Dee Jr. and Donna (Parker) H.; m. Olga P. Hinds; children: Sarah, Stephen, Rebekah. Grad., Life Underwriting Tng. Coun. CLU; ChFC; registered fin. cons.; fellow Life Underwriter Tng. Coun. Sr. acct. agt. Allstate, Lemoore, Calif., 1983-90; gen. agt. various, Paso Robles, Calif, 1990—; gen. ptnr. Edward D. Hinds, Ins. and Fortress Fin. Strategies, Paso Robles, 1990—, Edward D. Hinds, Ins., 1995—; founder, gen. ptnr. Fortress Fin. Strategies, A Registered Investment Adviser, 1995-97; founder, gen. mgr. Hinds Fin. Group, LLC, 1998—. Benefits cons. U-Haul Dealers, Cen. Calif., 1992—, KOA, Calif., 1997. Mem.: Nat. Assn. Alternative Benefit Cons., Million Dollar Roundtable, Nat. Assn. Health Underwriters, Nat. Assn. Ins. and Fin. Advisors, Soc. Fin. Profls.

HINDS, GLESTER SAMUEL, financial consultant; b. N.Y.C., July 4, 1951; s. Glester Samuel and Kathryne Elizabeth (Ellison) H. BBA, Bernard M. Baruch Coll., 1973; MBA in Fin., Columbia U., 1975. Cert. Stock broker, ins. broker, financier, notary pub. Staff acct. Peat Marwick Mitchell, N.Y.C., 1975-77; fin. analyst Citicorp, N.Y.C., 1977-79; sr. fin. analyst Am. Express, N.Y.C., 1979-80; owner, cons. Hinds Fin. Svcs., Long Island, N.Y., 1980-87; owner, founder, pres. Emerald Advt. Co., 1985—; program specialist Calif. FTB, Manhasset, N.Y., 1987-2000; founder, dir., pres. New Alliance Inc., 1999—; founder, dir. Worldstar Enterprises, Inc., 1999—. Dir., ptnr. D.H. Holdings, Inc.; cons. Am. Entrepreneur's Assn., L.A., 1980-89, Mildred Burke Prodns., 1982-84, Worldwide Diamonds Assn., 1983-85, Acad. Fin. Aid Matching Svcs., 1983-87; licensee Creative Capital Pubs., Inc., 1983; with Mail Order Assocs., Inc., 1984—; holder minority interest Carlton Blues Football Team, Australia. Editor: Financial Newsletter the H-Club, 1978-82; actor: On Camera TV Acting, 1986; contbr. articles to profl. jours., to Passport For Travel newsletter. Funder U.S. Olympic Com. Team Ptnr. Program, 1999; mem. Presdl. Nat. Steering Com., Rep. Presdl. Task Force; founder Heritage Found., Washington, 1981, Ronald Reagan Rep. Ctr., 1989; founding mem. FDR Meml. Constrn. Project, 1996; mem. chmn.'s com. U.S. Senatorial Bus. Adv. Bd., 1981, 82; mem. Nassau-Suffolk Neighborhood Network; mem. Jim Valvano Found. for Cancer Rsch., Am. Heart Assn., The Children's Charity Fund, N.Y. Sportscene Children's Found. Recipient Edward M. Paster Meml. award, Sigma Alpha award, Beta Gamma Sigma award, Beta Alpha Psi award, Bernard M. Baruch Coll., 1973, Distinction award Am. Express, 1993, 97, Humanitarian Gold Record of Achievement ABI, 1994, Leader in sci. award, 1995, Presdl. Seal of Honor, 1996, Internat. Man of the Yr. award in Sci., 1993, Internat. Cultural Diploma of Honor Am. Biog. Inst., 1994, name permanently enshrined on Nat. Rep. Victory Monument, Ronald Reagan Rep. Ctr., Rep. medal of merit, 1995, task force cert. of merit; named Toronto Sports Club Athlete of Yr., 1987, Nat. Wrestling Hall of Fame, 1991. Mem. Am. Mgmt. Assn., USA Amateur Athletes, Interval Internat., Am. Mus. Natural History (assoc.), Am. Soc. Notaries (life), U.S. Olympic Soc. (life), N.Y. Pub. Interest Rsch. Group, 24K Club, USA Wrestling, Franklin Mint Collectors Soc., Pro-Wrestling Hall of Fame (fhmn. until 1994), U.S. Tennis Assn., Nat. Amateur Wrestling Hall of Fame (ptnr., fundraiser), Insiders Money Club, Internat. Platform Assn., Am. Cancer Soc., Am. Inst. Cancer Rsch., Troy Aikman Found., Carter Ctr., Environ. Def. Fund, Internat. Soc. Financiers (cert. 1985), Coram Civic Assn. (acting pres.), Oxford Club (life), Carlton Blues Football Team (Australia). Methodist. Home: 1021 Andrew St Cuthbert GA 39840

HINDS, LEONARD DALE, education educator, research scientist; b. Detroit, Mich., Jan. 6, 1966; s. David Lee and Lillian Adriana Hinds; life ptnr. George E. Barker. BA, Univ. Mich., Ann Harbor, Mich., 1989; PhD, Emory Univ., Altanta, Ga., 1995. Vis. asst. prof. Emory Univ., Atlanta, 1996; asst. prof. Ind. Univ., Bloomington, Ind., 1996—2003. Author: Narrative Transformations, 2002. Mem.: Modern Language Assn. (reg. del. 2000—02). Home: 4410 West Craig Dr Bloomington IN 47404 Office: Ind Univ Dept of French and Italian Bloomington IN 47405

HINE, JONATHAN TRUMBULL, JR., educator, translator; b. Norfolk, Va., Aug. 3, 1947; s. Jonathan Trumbull Hine and Carrie Louise Curtis; m. Carol Ann Snyder, Dec. 29, 1970; 1 child, Daniel Edward. BS in Italian, U.S. Naval Acad., Annapolis, Md., 1969; MPA, U. Okla., 1982; PhD, U. Va., 2000. Cert. rsch. adminstr. Commd. ensign USN, 1965, advanced through grades to lt. comdr., 1976, ret., 1989; profl. translator, 1961—; rsch. analyst U.S. Naval War Coll., Newport, R.I., 1988-89; adminstr. physics dept. U. Va., Charlottesville, 1989-95, assoc. dir. housing, 1995-2000. Owner Scriptor Svcs LLC, Charlottesville, 1984—. Translator: Fundamentals of Naval Strategy, 1990; contbr. articles and book revs. to mags. and profl. jours. Vet. scouter Boy Scouts Am., Italy, R.I., Va., 1986—. Decorated Navy Commendation medal, 1982, 86, 89; recipient Cross of St. George, Episcopal Ch., 1988. Mem.: Am. Translation Studies Assn., U.S. Naval Inst., Soc. Tech. Comm., Am. Evaluation Assn., Soc. Rsch. Adminstrs., Am. Translators Assn. (accreditation). Episcopalian. Avocation: bicycling. Office: Scriptor Svcs LLC PO Box 4623 Charlottesville VA 22905-4623 Business E-Mail: hine@scriptorservices.com.

HINE, ROBERT VAN NORDEN, JR., historian, educator; b. Los Angeles, Apr. 26, 1921; s. Robert Van Norden and Elizabeth (Bates) H.; m. Shirley M. McChord, June 24, 1949; 1 child, Allison. BA, Pomona Coll., 1948; MA, Yale U., 1949, PhD, 1952. From instr. history to prof. emeritus U. Calif., Riverside, 1954—90, prof. emeritus, 1990—, prof. recalled Irvine, 1990—. Author: California's Utopian Colonies, 1953, California's Utopian Colonies, rev. edit., 1983, Edward Kern and American Expansion, 1962, Edward Kern and American Expansion, rev. edit., In the Shadow of Fremont, 1982, Bartlett's West: Drawing the Mexican Boundary, 1968, The American Frontier: Readings and Documents, 1972, The American West: A New Interpretive History, 1973; author: (with John Mack Faragher) The American West: A New Interpretive History, 3d edit., 2000 (Wrangler award Cowboy and Western Heritage Mus., Caughey award, Western Hist. Assn.); author: Community on the American Frontier: Separate But Not Alone, 1980, California Utopianism: Contemplations of Eden, 1981; editor: William Andrew Spalding, Los Angeles Newspaperman, 1961, Soldier in the West: Letters of Theodore Talbot, 1972, Josiah Royce: West As Community in Writing Western History, 1991, Josiah Royce: From Grass Valley to Harvard, 1992 (Commonwealth Club award, 1992), Second Sight, 1993 (N.Y. Times Notable Book of 1993); contbr. articles to profl. jours. Recipient Harbison award for disting. teaching Danforth Found., 1968, Wagner Meml. award Calif. Hist. Soc., 1986; Huntington Libr. fellow, 1953, 60, Guggenheim fellow, 1958, 68, Nat. Endowment for Humanities sr. fellow, 1977, Calif. Coun. for Promotion of History award, 1994. Mem. Western History Assn. (life, hon. 1990, Award of Merit 1996), Orgn. Am. Historians, Phi Beta Kappa. Home: 19191 Harvard Ave # 317 Irvine CA 92612-4670 E-mail: rvhine@uci.edu.

HINER, ELIZABETH ELLEN, pharmacist; b. Balt., Aug. 11, 1943; d. Samuel Joseph and Zola Mae (Hedrick) Bracken; m. William O. Hiner (div.); children: Christine Ellen, Oliver Joseph; m. Ray Danforth Crossley, Aug. 3, 1985. BS in Pharmacy, W.Va. U., 1966; postgrad., Johns Hopkins U., 1984-87; cert. in pub. health pharmacy, Royal Soc. Health, London, 1996; PharmD (hon.), 2002. Registered pharmacist, W.Va., Md., Va. Staff pharmacist U. Va. Hosp., Charlottesville, 1965-66; pharmacy supr. Andrew Rader Army Health Clinic, Ft. Meyer, Va., 1977; pharmacist NIH, Bethesda, Md., 1977-78; consumer safety officer Bur. Biologics FDA, Bethesda, 1978-80, freedom of info. officer, 1980-81, biologics adverse reaction coord., 1981-84, sr. regulatory officer divsn. bacterial products, 1984-92, dir. health promotion fed.-state rels. Rockville, Md., 1992—. Mem., chair pharmacy adv. com. USPHS, Rockville, 1991—; ad hoc mem. Bur. Voluntary Compliance, Nat. Assn. Bds. of Pharmacy, Chgo., 1993-98; mem. faculty Food and Drug Law Inst., 1996-97. Contbr. articles to sci. jours. Mem. parent adv. bd. Beaver Coll., Glenside, Pa., 1993-2000; mem. Olney (Md.) Women's League, 1986—. Capt. USPHS, 1978—. Recipient Cert. of Recognition, Nat. Assn. Bds. of Pharmacy, 1993, 94, 95, 96, 98, 99. Mem. Am. Pharm. Assn., Am. Soc. Health Sys. Pharmacists, Commd. Officers Assn., Lambda Kappa Sigma Alumni. Avocation: sailing.

HINER, LESLIE DAVIS, lawyer, consultant; b. Canton, Ohio, Sept. 30, 1957; d. Wendell Hughes and Margaret Alvina (Klebaum) Davis; m. Ward Christopher Hiner, July 23, 1983; children: Elaine Margaret, Travis Davis. BA, Coll. Wooster, 1980; JD, U. Akron, 1985. Bar: Ind. 1985. Intern Legis. Svcs. Agy., Indpls., 1984; assoc. Ecklund, Frutkin & Grant, Indpls., 1985-87; co-owner, v.p., gen. counsel Hiner Van & Storage, Kokomo, Ind., 1987-91; assoc. Russell McIntrye Jessup Hilligoss & Raquet, Kokomo, Ind., 1991-91; Ind. senate majority atty., 1993-94; pvt. practice, 1994-95; gen. counsel, elections dep. Ind. Sec. of State, 1995-97; pvt. practice, session atty. Rep. caucus Ind. Ho. of Reps., Indpls., 1997-2000, policy dir., caucus atty. Rep. caucus, 2000—. Mem. adj. faculty U. Indpls., 1986—87, 1992—93. Bd. dirs. Montessori Children's Home, 1989—90, cmty. affairs com. chmn., 1990; mem. Altrusa Cmty. Affairs Com., 1989—91; mem. sch. bd. Irvington Cmty. Sch. (Pub. Charter Sch.), 2002—; chair Irvington Cmty. Sch. (Pub. Charter Sch.), 2003—; campaign chair Johnson for State Senate Re-election Com., 1990; campaign mgr. Kenley for State Senate, 1992; mem. fin. com. Howard County Reps., 1991; mem. bd. dirs. Irvington Cmty. Charter Sch., 2002—; mem. devel. adv. com. Ctr. on Philanrophy I.U. Charter Sch. Bd., 2003—; chair Irvington Cmty. Charter Sch., 2003—; bd. dirs. United Way, Howard County, 1990, exec. com., 1990, allocations coun., 1987—91, vice chmn., 1989, chmn., 1990, past chmn., 1991, campaign vol., 1988, 1989; atty. Legal Aid, Kokomo, 1987—91; vol. Bona Vista Rehab. Ctr., Capital Campaign Col., 1991; mem. Indpls. Symphonic Choir. Named Howard County Woman of the Yr. in Bus. Industry, 1991. Mem.: Indpls. Bar Assn. (women in law divsn., govt. practice divsn.), Federalist Soc. (bd. dirs. lawyers divsn. Indpls. chpt. 1994—), Ind. State Bar Assn. (women in law com. 2003—, improvements in the judicial system com. 2003—), Brebeuf Jesuit Mother's Assn., U. Akron Sch. Law Alumni Assn. (life), Richard D. Lugar Excellence Pub. Svc. Series Alumna, Greater Indpls. Rep. Women's Club (life). Lutheran. Avocations: piano, reading, needlepoint, tennis, singing. Office: Ind Ho of Reps Statehouse 200 W Washington St Indianapolis IN 46204 E-mail: lhiner@iga.state.in.us.

HINERFELD, LEE ANN, veterinarian; b. San Francisco, Apr. 24, 1955; d. Norman Martin and Ruth Jean (Gordon) H. BA, Vassar Coll., 1977; DVM, Tufts U., 1986; MS, U. Wyo., 1987. Lic. Conn., Mass. Sr. rsch. technician U. Mass. Med. Ctr., Worcester, 1977-80; small animal clinician, assoc. vet. Mt. Pleasant Hosp. for Animals, Newtown, Conn., 1987, Shakespeare Vet. Hosp., Stratford, Conn., 1988-90, New London (Conn.) Vet. Hosp., 1990-2000; vet. Critter Care: House Call and Acupuncture Veterinary Med. Practice, 2000—. Fellow Conn. Acad. Vet. Practice, Am. Vet. Med. Assn., Conn. Vet. Med. Assn., Am. Acad. Veterinary Acupuncture; mem. Defenders of Wildlife, Population Comm. Internat., Natural Resources Def. Coun., Technoserve, Environ. Def., The Carter Ctr., New Forests Project. Avocations: jogging, skiing, hiking, cooking, photography.

HINERFELD, NORMAN MARTIN, manufacturing company executive; b. N.Y.C., May 17, 1929; s. Benjamin B. and Anne (Blitz) H.; m. Ruth Jean Gordon, Dec. 25, 1952; children— Lee Ann, Thomas Benjamin, Joshua Gordon. AB, Harvard U., 1951, MBA, 1953. Security underwriter, underwriting dept. Goldman Sachs & Co., 1953; asst. to pres. Julius Kayser & Co., 1955-56, Catalina, Inc., 1956-57, v.p. mfg., 1957-64, sr. v.p., 1964-67; v.p. Kayser-Roth Corp., 1967—74, exec. v.p., 1967-74, mem. exec. com., 1972—85, pres., COO, 1974-76, dir., 1958-85, chmn. exec. com., 1976-85; chmn., CEO Wingspread Corp., 1985—88; chmn. Pandora Industries, Inc., N.Y.C., 1988—, Tica Industries, Inc., N.Y.C., 1990—; chmn., CEO The Delta Group, 1993—. Sec.-treas. Thermacon Industries Inc., New Hyde Park, N.Y., 1989—; chmn. ehomecare-.com Home Healthcare Sys., Inc., 1999—; bd. dirs. Supermarkets Gen. Corp.; chmn. council Ctr. for Study Democratic Instns.; mem. U.S.A.-BIAC to OECD, 1978—; mem. exec. com. Dist. Export-Council U.S. Dept. Commerce, 1978—; mem. adv. council on Japan-U.S. Econ. Relations, 1980—; adjucator Mass Tort Life Ins. Settlement, 1999-2001. Author: (with D. Moross) Automation-Challenge to Management, 1953; patentee self-programmed automatic machinery. Bd. overseers NYU Sch. Bus., 1984-88; chmn. Metro N.Y.-Bus. Execs. for Nat. Security, 1990—, mem. exec. com., 1992—; chmn. fin. com. Animal Med. Ctr., N.Y.C., 1999—. 1st lt. U.S. Army, 1953-55. Mem. Am. Arbitration Assn. (chmn. bd. 1984-90, exec. com., bd. dirs. 1969—), Am. Apparel Mfrs. Assn. (bd. dirs., past pres., mem. exec. com.), Internat. Apparel Fedn. (past pres.), Nat. Knitted Sportswear Assn. (exec. com., bd. dirs.), U.S. C. of C. (chmn. export policy com. 1979-89). Home: 11 Oak Ln Larchmont NY 10538-3917 Office: Thermacon Industries Inc 1983 Marcus Ave New Hyde Park NY 11042-1016 E-mail: Norcomp@aol.com.

HINERFELD, ROBERT ELLIOT, lawyer; b. N.Y.C., May 29, 1934; s. Benjamin B. and Anne (Blitz) H.; m. Susan Hope Slocum, June 27, 1957; children: Daniel Slocum, Matthew Ben. AB, Harvard U., 1956, JD, 1959. Bar: Calif. 1960. Asst. U.S. atty So. Dist. Calif., 1960-62; assoc. Leonard Horwin, Beverly Hills, Calif., 1962-66; mem. Simon, Sheridan, Murphy, Thornton & Hinerfeld, Los Angeles, 1967-74, Murphy, Thornton, Hinerfeld & Cahill, 1975-83, Murphy, Thornton, Hinerfeld & Elson, 1983-85, Manatt, Phelps & Phillips LLP, 1985-2000, sr. of counsel, 2000—; arbitrator bus. panel Los Angeles Superior Ct., 1979-82; assoc. ind. counsel (diGenova), 1993-95. Judge pro tempore Beverly Hills Municipal Court, 1967-74; clin. lectr. U. So. Calif. Law Center, 1980-81, guest lectr., 1993-96; expert witness, 1987—, legal affairs on-air guest spkr. sta. KCRW-FM, Santa Monica, Calif., 1998-99. Contbr. articles to profl. jours. Trustee Westland Sch., Los Angeles, 1970-75, Pacific Hills Sch., 1971-72. Fellow Am. Bar Found. (life); mem. ABA, Fed. Bar Assn., Assn. Profl. Responsibility Lawyers, Ctr. for Profl. Responsibility, Los Angeles County Bar Assn. (spl. com. jud. evaluation 1978-82, arbitration com. 1981-83, settlement officer 2d appellate dist. appellate case settlement project 1996—, spl. com. on appellate evaluation 1996-1999), Beverly Hills Bar Assn., State Bar Calif. (mem. com. on criminal law and procedure, chmn. spl. com. revision fed. criminal code, mem. disciplinary investigation panel dist. 7 1977-80, hearing referee State Bar Ct. 1981-83, referee rev. dept. 1984-87, exec. com. litigation sect. 1983-85, civil litigation adv. group 1985-88, mem. Jud. Nominees Evaluation Commn. 2000—), Am. Arbitration Assn. (arbitrator comml. panel 1966—), Calif. Acad. Appellate Lawyers (membership com. 1983-88, 2d v.p. 1985-87, 1st v.p. 1987-88, pres. 1988-89), Harvard Club So. Calif. (dir. 1974-83, sec. 1978-80, mem. prize book com. 1992-94), Harvard Club N.Y.C. Home and Office: 371 24th St Santa Monica CA 90402-2517

HINERFELD, RUTH G. civic organization executive; b. Boston, Sept. 18, 1930; m. Norman Hinerfeld, children: Lee, Thomas, Joshua AB, Vassar Coll., 1951; grad., Program in Bus. Adminstrn., Harvard-Radcliffe Coll., 1952. With

LWV, 1954—, UN observer, 1969-72, chairperson internat. relations com., 1972-76, 1st v.p. in charge legis. activities, 1976-78, pres., 1978-82. Dir. LWV Overseas Edn. Fund, 1975-76, trustee, 1975-86; chairperson LWV Edn. Fund, 1978-82; mem. White House Adv. Com. for Trade Negotiations, 1975-82; sec. UN Assn. of U.S., 1975-78, vice chmn., 1983—, bd. govs., 1975—, mem. econ. policy coun., 1976-93; bd. dirs. Overseas Devel. Coun. 1974-2000; trustee Inst. of Internat. Edn., 1997—; mem. U.S. del. auspices of Nat. Com. on U.S.-China Rels. and Chinese People's Inst. Fgn. Affairs, 1978. Mem. coun. Nat. Mcpl. League, 1977-80, 83-86; del.-at-large Internat. Women's Yr. Conf., Houston, 1977; mem. exec. com. Leadership Conf. on Civil Rights, 1978-82; trustee Citizens Rsch. Found., 1978-2000; mem. Nat. Petroleum Coun., 1979-82; mem. U.S. del. to World Conf. on UN Decade for Women, 1980; mem. adv. com. Nat. Inst. for Citizen Edn. in the Law, 1981-91; mem. North South Roundtable, 1978-88; mem. nat. gov. bd. Common Cause, 1984-90; vice chmn. U.S. com. UNICEF, 1986-90, treas., 1990-91; mem. vis. com. Harvard U. Bus. Sch., 1984-90; mem. Bretton Woods Com.; bd. dirs. Com. for Modern Cts., 1993-96. Recipient Disting. Citizen award Nat. Mcpl. League, 1978; Outstanding Mother award Nat. Mother's Day Com., 1981; Aspen Inst. Presdl. fellow, 1981 Mem. Council on Fgn. Relations, Phi Beta Kappa. Office: 11 Oak Ln Larchmont NY 10538-3917

HINES, ANDREW HAMPTON, JR., utilities executive; b. Lake City, Fla., Jan. 28, 1923; s. Andrew Hampton and Louise Dixie (Howland) H.; m. Ann Groover, June 28, 1947' children: Andrew Hampton III, Elizabeth Renee, John Bradford, Daniel Howland. BME with high honors, U. Fla., 1947; degree (hon.), Stetson U., 1987, U. South Fla., 1989, Rollins Coll., 1989, Fla. So. Coll., 1994. Registered profl. engr., Fla. With R&D depts. GE, 1947-51; pres. Fla. Power Corp., 1972-82; chmn. bd. Fla. Progress Corp., St. Petersburg, 1982-91, Precise Power Corp., Bradenton, Fla., 1990-97. Cons. Triangle Cons. Group; bd. dirs. Templeton Mut. Funds, Franklin Mutual Series Funds; past chmn. N.Am. Electric Reliability Coun.; exec.-in-residence Eckerd Coll., 1990-2001. Trustee Asbury Theol. Sem.; bd. dirs. Fla. Coun. Econ. Edn., U. Fla. Found., Sunday sch. tchr. Christian Missionary Alliance Ch.; chmn. Pinellas County Cmty. Reuse Orgn., 1994-97; chmn. No Casinos in Fla., Inc., 1994-1998. 2d lt. USAAF, 1943-45. Decorated Air medal, Prisoner of War medal. Fellow ASME; mem. U.S. Energy Assn., Blue Key, St. Petersburg Yacht Club, Sigma Tau, Phi Kappa Phi, Tau Beta Pi, Beta Gamma Sigma. E-mail: ahh@tampabay.rr.com. *You cannot out give God. If you cast your bread upon the waters it will come back buttered.*

HINES, ANGUS IRVING, JR., petroleum marketing executive; b. Suffolk, Va., Aug. 7, 1923; s. Angus Irving and Lois E. (Howell) H.; m. Genevieve Hopkins McCollum, Nov. 24, 1949 (div. 1977); children: Ann Russell Hines Mauer, Marilyn N. Hines Stulb, A. McCollum, Angus Irving III. Pres. Angus I. Hines, Inc., Suffolk, 1945—; Angus Hines, Inc., Svc. Gas Co., Inc. Served with U.S. Maritime Service, 1943-45; ETO. Mem. Va. Petroleum Jobbers Assn. (past pres.), Rotary (past pres.), Quiet Birdmen. Methodist. Office: Angus I Hines Inc PO Box 1080 1426 Holland Rd Suffolk VA 23439-1080

HINES, CHARLES A. academic administrator; BS, Howard U.; grad., FBI Nat. Acad. Commd. officer U.S. Army, advanced through grades to maj. general; numerous command staff assignments including dir. Organizational Effectiveness/Curriculum, U.S. Army War Coll.; dir. Women in the Army Policy Rev. Group U.S. Army War Coll.; ret. U.S. Army, 1992; pres. Prairie View A&M U., 1994—. Adj. prof. U. Md.; est. Ctr. for Study and Prevention of Juv. Crime and Delinquency, Prairie View A&M U., est. privatized housing, others. Dir. of Protection and Health Svc., Smithsonian Instn., 1992-94; apptd. chmn. of Gov.'s Mil. Strategic Planning Comm., Gov. of Tex. Inducted into Nat. Boys and Girls Club Hall of Fame, 1992; selected Outstanding Black Man, So. Christian Leadership Conf., 1994. Mem. Alpha Phi Alpha. Office: PO Box 188 Prairie View TX 77446-0188

HINES, EDWARD FRANCIS, JR., lawyer; b. Norfolk, Va, Sept. 5, 1945; s. Edward Francis and Jeanne Miriam (Caulfield) H.; m. Elaine Geneva Carroll, Aug. 21, 1971; children: Jonathan Edward, Carolyn Adele. AB, Boston Coll., 1966; JD, Harvard U., 1969. Bar: Mass. 1969. Assoc. Choate Hall & Stewart, Boston, 1969-77, ptnr., 1977-2001, Hines & Corley LLC, Lexington, Mass., 2001—. Bd. dirs. Boston Med. Ctr., 1996—, Boston Med. Ctr. Ins. Co., Cayman Islands, 2003—, Chase Corp. (AMEX), 2003—; trustee Merrimac Fund Complex, 1996—. Trustee, treas. World Heart Fedn., Geneva, 2003—; trustee Social Law Libr., 1993—98; bd. dirs. Cath. Charities, 2002—, Assoc. Industries Mass., 1990—, chmn., 1996—98; bd. dirs. Am. Heart Assn., Dallas, 1984—86, 1991—2000, chmn., 1998—99; bd. dirs. Mass. Taxpayers Found., 1987—, Carroll Ctr. for the Blind, 1983—89, 1990—96, chmn., 1994—96. With USAR, 1969—75. Recipient Boston Coll. High Sch. St. Ignatius award, 1998, Gold Heart award, Am. Heart Assn., 2003. Fellow: Am. Coll. Trust and Estate Counsel; mem.: Mass. CLE (pres. 1985—87), Accion Internat. (bd. dirs. 1999—), Supreme Jud. Ct. Hist. Soc. (trustee 1989—96), Am. Coll. Greece (Athens bd. dirs., vice chmn. 1988—97), Boston Bar Found. (pres. 1995—97), Boston Bar Assn. (pres. 1988—89), Boston Coll. Club, North Andover Country Club. Office: Hines & Corley LLC Ste 3200 55 Hayden Ave Lexington MA 02421 E-mail: efh@hinesandcorley.com.

HINES, GEORGE LAWRENCE, surgeon; b. Bklyn., June 10, 1946; s. Frank and Ruth (Katzman) H.; m. Helene Anne Reitman, Aug. 23, 1969; children: Brian, Jennifer. BA, MD, Boston U., 1969. Diplomate Am. Bd. Gen. Surgery, Am. Bd. Thoracic Surgery, Am. Bd. Gen. Vascular Surgery. Intern Maimonides Med. Ctr., Bklyn., 1969-70; resident Sinai Hosp., Detroit, 1970-71; to chief resident L.I. Jewish Med. Ctr., N.Y.C., 1971-74; cardiothoracic resident NYU Med. Ctr., N.Y.C., 1974-76; attending physician Winthrop U. Hosp., Mineola, N.Y., 1976—; pvt. practice Mineola; chief div. vascular surgery Winthrop U. Hosp., Mineola, N.Y., 1995—. Maj. U.S. Army Res., 1970-79. Fellow ACS; mem. Am. Assn. for Thoracic Surgery, Soc. Thoracic Surgeons, Soc. for Vascular Surgery. Democrat. Jewish. Avocations: jogging, piano. Office: Winthrop Cardiothoracic Vascular Surgery Group 120 Mineola Blvd Mineola NY 11501-4073

HINES, JUDITH ALBERGOTTI, social worker, management consultant; b. Orangeburg, S.C., July 29, 1939; d. James McAlpin and Maude Ramsey (Dew) Albergotti; m. Hans J. Heller, July 14, 1963 (div. 1979); children: Lucas Heller, Nina Heller; m. Paul Garry Hines, June 2, 1979; stepchildren: Erin, Tara, Gael. BS, U. N.C., 1961; MSW, Columbia U., 1963. Social worker Columbia Presbyn. Med. Ctr., NY, 1963-65, Kennedy Child Study Ctr., N.Y.C., 1965-67; dir. social svc. Operation Head Start, Charleston, S.C., 1967-68; program dir., cons. St. John's Mission Ctr., Charleston, 1968-76; faculty assoc. Coll. Charleston, 1976-78; CEO, Charleston County Mental Retardation Bd., 1976—78; exec. dir. Oak Grove Residential Treatment Ctr., Charleston, 1978-79; dir. Evaluation and Devel. Coun. on Accreditation of Svcs. to Families and Children, N.Y.C., 1980-96; co-dir. Ctr. for Hope, Darien, Conn., 1992, Coun. on Accreditation, CEO, 1996-98; prin. Cons. Firm Hines Group, 1999—2002. Sr. prin. Acton Burnell/CACI for U.S. State Dept. Intercountry Adoption Regulations Project. Editor: Standards for Agency Management and Service Delivery, 1982—97. Trustee Marvelwood Sch., Cornwall, Conn., 1985—90; vice-chmn. S.C. Human Affairs commn., Columbia, 1974—77; mem. Gov.'s Commn. on Children State of S.C., 1979; bd. dirs. Ctr. for Hope, Darien, Conn., 1995—2000. Named Disting. Alumna, U. N.C., 1987. Mem.: Order of Golden Fleece. Democrat. Roman Catholic. Avocations: gardening, sailing. Office: Hines Group 17 Trachelle Ln Charleston SC 29407-3774 E-mail: judysgardn@aol.com.

HINES, N. WILLIAM, dean, law educator, administrator; b. 1936; AB, Baker U., 1958; LLB, U. Kans., 1961; LLD, Baker U., 1999. Bar: Kans. 1961, Iowa 1965. Law clk. U.S. Ct. Appeals 10th cir., 1961-62; tchg. fellow Harvard U., 1961-62; asst. prof. law U. Iowa, 1962-65, assoc. prof., 1965-67, prof., 1967-73, disting. prof., 1973—, dean, 1976—. Vis. prof. Stanford U., 1974—75. Editor (notes and comments): Kans. Law Rev. Fellow, Harvard U., 1961—62. Fellow: Iowa State Bar Found., ABA Found.; mem.: Assn. Am. Law Schs. (exec. com. 2002—), Environ. Law Inst. (assoc.), Order of Coif, Jo. Co. Her. Trust (founder, pres.). Office: U Iowa Coll Law Iowa City IA 52242-0001

HINES, PATRICIA, social worker, educator; b. Watertown, N.Y., Nov. 4, 1947; d. Arthur and Bella (O'Neil) H. BS, SUNY, Oswego, 1969; MSW, SUNY, Buffalo, 1975; MPA, Fairleigh Dickinson U., 1982. Cert. Dr. Thomas Gordon Parent Effectiveness Trainer. Supr. social work Ocean County Bd. Social Svcs., Toms River, N.J., 1973-77, adminstrv. supr. social work, 1977-83, dep. dir., 1983-96; exec. dir. Ocean First Found., Toms River, 1996—. Social work cons. Ocean County Vis. Homemaker Svc., Inc., Toms River, 1975-80, Cmty. Meml. Hosp., Toms River, 1978-79, Manchester Manor, Bartley Manor Convalescent Ctr., Barnegat Nursing Facility, Burnt Tavern Convalescent Ctr., Logan Manor, Medicenter, Keswick Pines, Green Acres Manor,Imperial Care Center. Chmn. Ocean County Title XX Coalition, 1977-82; bd. dirs. Ocean County Family Planning Program, Toms River, 1969-73, Mental Health Bd., 1983-84; mem. exec. bd. United Way, 1983-96; mem. Aging Network Svc., 1992—. Mem. NASW (nat. register clin. social workers), Acad. Cert. Social Workers (diplomate clin. social work). Home: 13 Bay Harbor Blvd Brick NJ 08723-7303 Office: Bldg 1 1027 Hooper Ave Toms River NJ 08753-8320

HINES, PRESTON HARRIS, state supreme court justice; b. Atlanta, Sept. 6, 1943; AB in Polit. Sci., Emory U., 1965, JD, 1968. Bar: Ga. 1968, U.S. Dist. Ct. Ga. 1973. Law clk. Civil Ct. Fulton County, 1968-69; pvt. practice Marietta, Ga., 1969-74; judge State Ct. of Cobb County, 1974-82, Superior Ct. of Ga., 1982—95; justice Ga. Supreme Ct., 1995—. Chmn. attys. divsn. Cobb County United Appeal, 1972; participant Leadership Ga., 1975, Leadership Atlanta, 1978-79; pres. YMCA Cobb County, 1976; co-treas. Cobb Landmarks Soc., 1976-77; former bd. dirs. Cobb County Emergency Aid Assn., Cobb-Marietta Girls Club, Ga. chpt. Leukemia Soc. Am., Cobb County Children's Ctr., Met. Atlanta Red Cross, First Presbyn. Day Kindergarten; mem. cmty. adv. com. Marietta-Cobb County LWV; bd. dirs. Kennesaw Coll. Found.; trustee Cobb Cmty. Symphony. Named Outstanding Young Man of Yr., Ga. Jaycees, 1975, Boss of Yr., Cobb County Legal Secs. Assn., 1975-76, 83-84. Mem. ABA, State Bar Ga. (chmn. Law Day com. 1975, mem. exec. com. younger lawyers sec. 1974-76), Cobb Jud. Cir. (sec. 1972-73, chmn. Law Day com. 1972), Joseph Henry Lumpkin Inn of Ct. Ga., Atlanta Lawyers Club, Kiwanis (bd. dirs. Marietta chpt., chmn. Key Club com., past chmn. spiritual aims com., past pres.), Cobb County C. of C., Sigma Alpha Epsilon (Atlanta and Marietta chpts.). Office: Supreme Court 244 Washington St Atlanta GA 30334*

HINES, THOMAS SPIGHT, historian, educator, architecture critic; b. Oxford, Miss., Oct. 28, 1936; s. Thomas S. and Polly M. Hines; children: Tracy Odessa, Taylor Spight. BA, U. Miss., 1958; PhD, U. Wis., 1971. Prof. history and architecture UCLA, 1968—. Vis. prof. Sch. Architecture and Am. studies program U. Tex., Austin, 1974-75; Fulbright prof. Am. studies U. Exeter, Eng., 1984-85. Author: Burnham of Chicago: Architect and Planner, 1974, Richard Neutra and the Search for Modern Architecture: A Biography and History, 1982, The Architecture of Richard Neutra: From International Style to California Modern, 1982, William Faulkner and the Tangible Past: The Architecture of Yoknapatawpha, 1996, Irving Gill and the Architecture of Reform, 2000; hist. advisor, co-author film Frank Lloyd Wright, 1985; hist. advisor Robert Moses: Urban Planner for WGBH, 1988; contbr. chpts. to books, articles to profl. jours. 1st lt. U.S. Army, 1960—63. Recipient John H. Dunning prize Am. Hist. Assn., 1976; NEH fellow, 1978-79; Fulbright fellow, 1984-85; Guggenheim fellow, 1987-88; Getty scholar, 1996-97. Mem.: Am. Acad. Arts and Scis. Democrat. Episcopalian. Office: UCLA Dept Architecture Perloff Hall 405 Hilgard Ave Los Angeles CA 90095-9000

HINES, VIRGINIA LEE, poet, writer; b. Evansville, Ind., May 25, 1927; d. Edgar Lee H. and Lora Belle McKenney; widowed; children: Susan Lora Heftel, Lee David Heftel. BA, Roosevelt U., 1952; postgrad., Depaul U., 1952—55, Rochester Inst. Tech., 1966—75, Beth Israel Nursing Sch., 1980. LPN, N.Y. Tchr. Chgo. Pub. Schs.; freelance writer Rochester, NY. Contbr. poetry to various pubs. Mem. AAUW, Nat. Writers Union, Am. Acad. Am. Poets, New Eng. Poets Club, N.Y. Poetry Forum. Democrat. Unitarian Universalist. Avocations: painting, photography. Home: 20 San Mateo Rd Rochester NY 14624

HINES, VONCILE, special education educator; b. Detroit, Dec. 1, 1945; d. Raymond and Cleo (Smith) H. AA, Highland Park Community Coll., 1967; BEd, Wayne State U., 1971, MEd, 1975; MA, U. Detroit, 1978. Tchr. primary unit Detroit Bd. Edn., 1971-79, spl. educator, 1979-94; self-employed ednl. rsch. edn. co-creations. Tchr. trainee Feuerstein's Instrumental Enrichment, 1988—; cons. Queen's Community Workers, Detroit, 1977—; evaluator Teen Profl. Parenting Project, New Detroit Inc., 1986-87; guest educator, critic "Express Yourself", Sta. WQBH 1400 AM, 1989; advisor to home sch. educators. Author: I Chose Planet Earth, 1988; inventor in field. Recipient cert. of merit State of Mich., 1978, 88, cert. of appreciation Queen's Cmty. Workers, 1980, Wayne County Bd. Commrs., 1988, award of recognition Detroit City Coun., 1984, 88. Mem. Assn. for Children and Adults with Learning Disabilities, Assn. Supervision and Curriculum Devel., Nat. Thinking Skills Network, NAFE, Nat. Council Negro Women (presenter 1987), Met. Detroit Alliance of Black Sch. Educators. Democrat. Avocation: travel.

HINES, WILLIAM EUGENE, banker; b. N.Y.C., July 5, 1914; s. William J. and Alice M. (Callahan) H.; m. Dorothy H. Moore, June 4, 1949; children—Alice M., Dorothy H., Margaret M., William J., Elizabeth A., Robert J. Student, Columbia; grad., Rutgers U. Grad. Sch. Banking, 1948. With Bankers Trust Co., N.Y.C., 1950—, asst. v.p., 1958-63, v.p., 1963—. Instr. Am. Inst. Banking, 1948-64, Am. Youth Hostels, 1954-65, former chmn., now dir. Chmn. planning bd. Village of Quogue, N.Y., 1991—; trustee Quogue Libr., 1995—, treas., 2001—. Mem. N.Y. Soc. Security Analysts, Accts. Club N.Y.C., Nat. Assn. Mental Health (nat. treas., dir. 1966, nat. trustee), Quogue (N.Y.) Assn. (pres. 1994-96, trustee 1992—), Shinnecock Yacht Club (commodore 1974-76, treas. 1980-94). Office: PO Box 5035 21 Quaquanantuck Ln Quogue NY 11959

HINESLEY, GAIL ANN, social sciences educator; b. Sacramento, Sept. 5, 1952; d. Edwin Duncan and Elva Lois (Perryman) McDonald; m. Ted Wilson Hinesley, July 16, 1988; children: Kelsey Robin, Janelle Lynn; m. Geoffrey John Fallon (div.); 1 child, Sheana Rochelle Fallon Hinesley. BA in psychology, U. Calif., Berkeley, 1974; MS in psychology, I. Ill., Urbana, 1986; post grad., U. Colo., Boulder, 2003—. Instr. USAF Acad., Colo. Springs, 1985—88, asst. prof., 1991—92; instr. Pk. Coll., Davis - Monthan AFB, Ariz., 1993—94; exec. dir. Youth Ctr., Hot Springs, SD, 1995—96; assessment coord. Nat. Coll., Rapid City, 1995—96; owner Hinesley Custom Prodns., Edgemont, SD, 1996—2000; asst. prof. Chadron State Coll., Nebr., 2001—. Rsch. dir. USAF Acad., 1991—92. Pres. Edgemont City Coun., 1999, Edgemont C. of C., 1998. Major USAF, 1979—97. Recipient Small Town Leadership award, Wal - Mart, 1999. Mem.: Am. Psycholog. Assn., Am. Psycholog. Soc. Avocation: cattle rancher. Office: Chadron State Coll 1000 Main St Chadron NE 69337

HING, BARBARA LIM, elementary school educator, assistant principal; b. Jan. 06; arrived in U.S., 1973; d. Amado K. H. and Bee-chu Tan Lim; m. Y. Ray Hing, Oct. 11, 1975; children: Abigail Hing Wen, Byron Lim, Colleen Lim. BA, Maryknoll Coll., Quezon City, The Philippines, 1971; MA, Ea. Mich. U., 1975; prin. cert., Cleve. State U., 1994. Cert. tchr. Ohio, Ill., adminstr. Ohio, Ill. Instr. St. Claire Coll., Windsor, Canada, 1975; substitute tchr. Shawnee Local Schs., Lima, Ohio, 1980-84, Solon (Ohio) City Schs., 1984-86; tchr. Cleve. Pub. Schs., 1986-95, title I tchr., 1995—2000; asst. prin. Buhrer Elem. Sch., Cleve., 2003—. Contbr. strategic planning com. Solon Schs., 1989—91; chairperson Fundraising Com., Cleve., 1995—98, Attendance Com., Cleve., 1995—. Author: (book) Joy the Spider, 1975; writer, editor, pub.: Harvey Rice Attendance Newsletter, 1996—99, Harvey Rice Newsletter, 1999—. Mem., supporter Heritage Found., Washington, 1991—, Cmty. Action Team, 1993—94, Concord Coalition, Washington, 1996; chairperson scholarship com. Solon Acad. Boosters Club, 1995—97; sustaining mem. Rep. Nat. Com., Washington, 1994—. Named Outstanding Leader, Health Den, Mentor, Ohio, 1999; recipient Outstanding award, Charities of Choice, Cleve., 1995—97. Mem.: Orgn. Chinese Ams. Greater Cleve. (supporter, v.p. 1998—2003, bd. dirs. 1999—, Outstanding Citizen award 1999, 2002), Chinese Womens Club Cleve. (founder, treas. 1999—2001).

HINGLE, PAT, actor; b. Miami, Fla., July 19, 1924; s. Clarence M. and Marvin (Patterson) H.; m. Julia Wright, Oct. 25, 1979; children— Jody, Billy, Molly. BFA, U. Tex., 1949; PhD (hon.), Otterbein Coll., 1974. Numerous acting roles on stage, screen and TV, including End as a Man, 1953, On the Waterfront, 1953, The Long Grey Line, 1954, Festival, 1954, Cat on a Hot Tin Roof, 1955, 83, 93, Girls of Summer, 1956, The Strange One, 1956, Dakr at the Top of the Stairs, 1957, No Down Pavement, 1957, J.B., 1958, The Deadly Game, 1960, Macbeth, 1961, Troilus and Cressida, 1961, Strange Interlude, 1963, Blues for Mr. Charlie, 1964, A Girl Could Get Lucky, 1964, Invitation to a Gunfighter, 1964, The Glass Menagerie, 1965, The Odd Couple, 1966, Nevada Smith, 1966, Johnny No-Trump, 1967, Hang 'Em High, 1968, The Price, 1968, Bloody Mama, 1969, Child's Play, 1970, Norwood, 1970, Wusa, 1970, The Selling of the President, 1972, That Championship Season, 1973, Super Cops, 1973, Hazel's People, 1973, Running Wild, 1973, The Lady from the Sea, 1976, Independence, 1976, The Gauntlet, 1977, Norma Rae, 1979, When You Comin' Back, Red Ryder, 1979, Thomas A. Edison, Reflections of a Genius, 1978, A Life, 1980, Running Brave, 1982, Sudden Impact, 1983, Falcon and the Snowman, 1984, Brewster's Millions, 1985, Blue Skies, 1988, Rescue of Jessica McClure, 1989, Batman, 1989, The Kennedys of Massachusetts, 1989, The Grifters, 1990, Moon for the Misbegotten, 1990, The Habitation of Dragons, 1991, Gunsmoke III, 1991, Batman Returns, 1992, Citizen Cohn, 1992, Simple Justice, 1992, Will and Bart Show, 1992, Cheers, 1993, In the Heat of the Night, 1993, Lightnin' Jack, 1994, The Quick and the Dead, 1994, Friendly Suit, 1994, One Christmas, 1994, Batman Forever, 1995, Truman, 1995, Wings, 1996, Larger Than Life, 1996, Bastard Out of Carolina, 1996, A Thousand Acres, 1996, Batman and Robin, 1997, The Shining, 1997, 1776, 1997-98, Touched By an Angel, 1999, Morning, 2000, The Angel Doll, 2000, Road to Redemption, 2000, The Runaway, 2000, Our Town, 2002. Served with USNR, 1942-46, 51-52.

HINICH, MELVIN JAY, government and economics educator; b. Pitts., Apr. 29, 1939; s. Joseph and Sara (Rubinstein) Hinich; m. Sonje Gregg, Sept. 14, 1966; 1 child, Amy Sara. BS, Carnegie Inst. Tech., 1959, MS in Math, 1960; PhD in Statistics, Stanford, 1963. Asst. prof. indsl. adminstrn. Carnegie Inst. Tech., 1963-68; assoc. prof. indsl. adminstrn., statistics, 1968-70; prof. statistics, polit. economy Carnegie Mellon U., 1970-73; prof. econs. dept. Va. Poly. Inst. and State U., Blacksburg, 1973-82; prof. govt. and econs. U. Tex., Austin, 1982—, Frank Erwin prof. govt., 1984-86, Mike Hogg prof. govt. and econs., 1986—, with Applied Rsch. Labs., 1985—. Fairchild disting. scholar Calif. Inst. Tech. Inc., Pasadena, 1975-76; cons. Teledyne-Isotopes, Inc., Internat. Research & Tech., Inc., FDA, Air Pollution Control-Allegheny County Health Dept., U.S. Naval Coastal Systems Center, Tracor Applied Scis., Inst. Macroeconomics, Fed. Res. Bank of Mpls.; cons. task force on regulatory reform U.S. Senate Govt. Ops. Com., NATO Saclant Research Ctr., La Spezia, Italy, devel. program UN. Author: Introduction to Continuous Probability, 1969, Consumer Protection Legislation and the U.S. Food Industry, 1980, The Spatial Theory of Voting: An Introduction, 1984, Advances in the Spatial Theory of Voting, 1990, Political Economy: Institutions, Competition and Representation, 1993, Ideology and the Theory of Political Choice, 1994, Analytical Politics, 1997, Empirical Studies in Comparative Politics, 1998; assoc. editor: Macroeconomic Dynamics; contbr. articles to profl. jours. Fellow: Am. Statis. Assn., Pub. Choice Soc. (pres. 1992—94), Inst. Math. Stats.; mem.: Sigma Xi. Home: 3902 Cresthill Dr Austin TX 78731-3808 Office: U Tex Burdine Hall Austin TX 78712-1087

HINING, MICHAEL LYNN, music educator, conductor; b. St. Petersburg, Fla., May 5, 1962; s. Verdus L. and Kathryn R. Hining. MusB, No. Ill. U., 1985, MusM, 1987, cert. in Performing, 1989. Musician Rockford (Ill.) Symphony, 1982—94, Elgin (Ill.) Symphony, 1986—98; co-founder Ill. Valley Youth Symphony, La Salle, Ill., 1987—92, condr.; founder The Violin and Viola Studio, Oak Park, Ill., 1987—, tchr., 1987—. Founder The Windy City String Ensemble, Oak Park, Ill., 1994—, condr., 1994—; vis. prof. violin and viola Ill. Wesleyan U., Bloomington, 1999—. Composer: Rhapsody on Themes of Rachmoninoff, 2002 (award, 2002), Elegy on Palestian and Hebrew Themes, 2003; condr. Windy City String Ensemble, Carnegie Hall, N.Y., 2003. Mem. campaign com. Michelle Harton for Sch. Bd., Oak Park, 2003; fund raiser Cmty. Response Aids Care, Oak Park, 1998, Amity Sch. Childes Aid, Oak Park, 2000, Oak Park (Ill.) Animal Care League, 2000. Named Outstanding Tchr., Musicians Union, 1999; recipient Gold medal, Sydney (Australia) Internat. Music Festival, 1999, Bloomfield award, Ea. Music Festival, 1981. Mem.: Oak Park (Ill.) Area Arts Coun., Am. String Tchrs. Assn. (tchr. 1998—), Suzuki Assn. Am. (tchr. 1998—, mem. outstanding outreach group 2000). Avocations: animal rights, dogs. Office: Sch Music Ill Wesleyan Univ PO Box 2900 Bloomington IL 61702-2900

HINKELMAN, RUTH AMIDON, insurance company executive; b. Streator, Ill., June 4, 1949; d. Olin Arthur and Marjorie Annabeth (Wright) Amidon; m. Allen Joseph Hinkelman, Jr., Oct. 28, 1972; children: Anne Elizabeth, Allen Joseph III. AB in Econs., U. Ill., 1971. Underwriter Kemper Ins. Group, Chgo., 1971-75; acct. exec. Near North Ins. Agy., Chgo., 1975-76; underwriter Gen. Cologne Reinsurance Corp., Chgo., 1976-78, asst. sec., 1978-79, asst. v.p., 1979-83, 2nd v.p., 1983-87, v.p., 1987—. Home: 133 Linden Ave Wilmette IL 60091-2838 Office: Gen Colongne Reinsurance Corp 1 N Wacker Dr Ste 1700 Chicago IL 60606 E-mail: rhinkelm@gcr.com.

HINKLE, BARTON LESLIE, retired electronics company executive; b. Miami Beach, Fla., Nov. 2, 1925; s. Frank Leslie and Kathryn Barton (Paddock) H.; m. Christine Smith, Aug. 22, 1949 (dec. Aug. 1955); m. Sabrena Sanford, Apr. 4, 1959; children— Karen, Douglas, Jean, Maria, Elizabeth. BS in Chem. Engring, Purdue U., 1949; MS, Inst. Textile Tech., 1951; PhD, Ga. Inst. Tech., 1953. Research asst. Ga. Inst. Tech. Exptl. Sta., Atlanta, 1951-53; research engr. E.I. duPont de Nemours & Co., Inc., Richmond, Va., 1953-55, research supr., 1955-57, tech. supt., 1957-61, mfg. supt., 1961-62, asst. plant mgr., 1962-64, plant supt., 1964-69, product mgr. Wilmington, Del., 1969-71, lab. mgr., 1971-75, adminstrv. and planning asst., 1976-77, personnel mgr., 1977-84; v.p. human resources Electromagnetic Scis., Inc., Norcross, Ga., 1984-87, cons. human resources, 1987—. Patentee in field aerosol electrification, viscous polymers, cellophane. Sr. warden, vestryman St. Davids Episcopal Ch., 1975-78. Served with AUS, 1944-46, ETO. Republican. Home: 9399 Colvincrest Dr Mechanicsville VA 23116 2909 E-mail: blhink@comcast.net.

HINKLE, BETTY RUTH, educational administrator; b. Atchison, Kans., Mar. 18, 1930; d. Arch W. and Ruth (Baker) Hunt; m. Charles L. Hinkle, Dec. 25, 1950 (div.); children: Karl, Eric. BA, U. Corpus Christi, 1950; MS, Baylor U., 1956; MA, U. North Colo., 1972, EdD, 1979. Cert. tchr., Tex., Mass., Colo.; cert. adminstr., Colo. Tchr. Alice (Tex.) Ind. Sch. Dist., 1950, Waco (Tex.) Ind. Sch. Dist., 1951-52, 53-58, Hawaii Pub. Schs., Oahu, 1952-53, Newton Pub. Schs., Newtonville, Mass., 1962-63, Colorado Springs (Colo.) Pub. Schs., 1966-78; cons., exec. dir. spl. project unit Colo. State Dept. Edn., Denver, 1978-92, asst. commr., 1995, ret., 1995, rep. fed. rels. Office Commr. Edn., 1995-96, ret., 1996. Pvt. cons., 1997-2001; pres. BH Cons., Colorado Springs, 1997-2001; mem. cabinet Colo. Dept. Edn., mem. Quality Coun., fed. liaison rep. to chief state sch. officers, Washington, chmn. 1996, alt. foreman Denver Grand Jury, 1983. Vol. for Colo. Mountain Reclamation Projects, 2001—. Recipient Dept. Edn. Specialists award Colo. Assn. Sch. Execs., 1979, Employee Yr. award Colo. Dept. Edn,. 1986, Fed. Ednl. Program Adminstrv. Coun. ann. award for Distinctive Svc. to Colo. Children, 1988. Mem. ASCD, Am. Assn. Sch. Adminstrs., Colo. Assn. Sch. Execs. (coord. coun. 1976-79, v.p. dept. edn. specialists 1974-75, pres. 1975-76), Colo. Assn. Sch. Execs., Phi Delta Kappa. Home: 1011 N 18th St Colorado Springs CO 80904-2852 E-mail: betty.hinkle@worldnet.att.net.

HINKLE, CHARLES FREDERICK, lawyer, clergyman, educator; b. Oregon City, Oreg., July 6, 1942; s. William Ralph and Ruth Barbara (Holcomb) H. BA, Stanford U., 1964; MDiv, Union Theol. Sem., N.Y.C., 1968; JD, Yale U., 1971. Bar: Oreg. 1971; ordained to ministry United Ch. of Christ, 1974. Instr. English, Morehouse Coll., Atlanta, 1966-67; assoc. Stoel Rives LLP (formerly Stoel, Rives, Boley, Jones & Grey), Portland, Oreg., 1971-77, ptnr., 1977—. Adj. prof. Lewis and Clark Law Sch., Portland, 1978-2001; bd. govs. Oreg. State Bar, 1992-95. Oreg. pres. ACLU, Portland, 1976-80, nat. bd. dirs., 1979-85; bd. dirs. Kendall Cmty. Ctr., 1987-93, Youth Progress Assn., 1994-98, Portland Baroque Orch., 1999-2000; mem. pub. affairs com. Am. Cancer Soc., 1994-99; mem. Oreg. Gov.'s Task Force on Youth Suicide, 1996. Recipient Elliott Human Rights award Oreg. Edn. Assn., 1984, E.B. MacNaughton award ACLU Oreg., 1987, Wayne Morse award Dem. Com. Oreg., 1994, Tom McCall Freedom of Info. award Women in Comm., 1996, Civil Rights award Met. Human Rights Commn., 1996, Pub. Svc. award Oreg. State Bar, 1997. Fellow Am. Bar Found.; mem. ABA (ho. of dels. 1998-2000), FBA, Multnomah County Bar Assn., City

Club Portland (pres. 1987-88). Democrat. Home: 14079 SE Fairoaks Way Milwaukie OR 97267-1017 Office: Stoel Rives 900 SW 5th Ave Ste 2600 Portland OR 97204-1268 E-mail: cfhinkle@stoel.com.

HINKLE, DOUGLAS PADDOCK, retired languages educator; b. Stamford, Conn., June 9, 1923; s. Frank Leslie and Kathryn B. Paddock Hinkle; m. Rose-Marie Hecker, Apr. 14, 1966; children: Anthony Barton, Monica Kathryn. BA, U. Va., 1952, MA, 1954. Lic. law enforcement officer, Ohio. Tchr. English Va. Pub. Schs., Nelson County, 1948-49; dir. binat. ctr. U.S. Info. Svc., La Paz, Bolivia, 1955-57, Caracas, Venezuela, 1958; asst. prof. Spanish and French Sweet Briar Coll., Amherst, Va., 1958-62, Southwestern U., Memphis, 1962-63; coll. editor modern langs. D.C. Heath & Co., Boston, 1963-65; assoc. prof. modern langs. Ea. Ky. U., Richmond, 1965-67; sr. lectr. modern langs. Ohio U., Athens, 1967-93, prof. emeritus modern langs., 1994—; forensic artist LETN-TV, Dallas, 1990-91. Program evaluator NEH, Washington, 1975-78. Author: (books) Faces of Crime, 1989, Mug Shots, 1990, (book of poetry) Poetry Is You, 1977, (slideshow/video program) Remembering Faces, 1990; mem. editl. bd. NAMES, 1968-74; contbr. numerous articles to profl. jours. Chmn. drug abuse com. Kiwanis Club, Athens, Ohio, 1983-87; cert. aux. Athens Police Dept., 1982-87, forensic artist, 1981-87; bd. dirs. Cen. Va. Crime Clinic, Richmond, 1994-97. Cpl. U.S. Army, 1943-46. Recipient Caballero, Order of Condor award Republic of Bolivia, 1957, Citizenship award Athens Bar Assn., 1983. Mem. Portrait Soc. Am., Am. Soc. Marine Artists, Ctrl. Va. Crime Clinic (bd. dirs. 1995-98), Va. Mus. Fine Arts, Fraternal Order of Police (hon. permanent mem.), Raven Soc., Phi Beta Kappa. Republican. Roman Catholic. Avocations: painting, writing, historical linguistics, marksmanship. Home: 9305 Cason Rd Glen Allen VA 23060-3513 E-mail: dphrmh@cs.com.

HINKLE, JANET, project leader; b. Groton, Conn., Mar. 26, 1958; d. David Randall and Muriel (Nelson) Hinkle; m. Richard Alden Wilcox, Oct. 1, 1983 (div. Mar. 1991); 1 child, Lillian Marie Hinkle. AA in Fashion Design cum laude, Endicott Jr. Coll. for Women, Beverly, Mass., 1978; BA in Psychology, Conn. Coll., 1981. Project leader Sonalysts, Inc., Waterford, Conn., 1983—. Corporator Lawrence and Meml. Hosp., New London, Conn., 1995—, mem. cmty. rels. com., 1998—, mem. planned giving com., 1999—; mem. gift. com. adv. Cmty. Found., New London, 1998—. Named to Outstanding Young Women of Am., 1997. Mem. AAUW, Thames Club, Mystic Seaport Mus. Republican. Avocations: training horses, ballet dancing, rollerblading, skiing, painting. Home: 221 Elm St Stonington CT 06378-1165 Office: Sonalysts Inc 215 Parkway N Waterford CT 06385-1209 E-mail: jlhinkle@sonalysts.com.

HINKLE, MINERVA HERNANDEZ, airport terminal executive; b. Dallas, Oct. 18, 1959; d. Tony and Otalia (Ayala) H.; m. Jeffrey W. Hinkle, May 31, 1997. B of Criminal Justice, So. Meth. U., 1982, MPA, 1986. Intern, housing dept. City of Dallas, 1982-84, agenda coordinator, budget & rsch., 1984-85, coun. asst. mayor and coun. office, 1985, adminstrv. asst. city mgr. office, 1985-86, 88-89, field rep. Office Minority Bus. Opportunity, 1989-90, budget analyst pub. works, 1990; from adminstr. minority bus. enterprise to interim asst. v.p. Dallas Area Rapid Transit, 1990-98; asst. v.p. minority affairs Ctr. Operating Co., Dallas, 1998—2002; asst. v.p. small and emerging bus. dept. Dallas/Ft. Worth Internat. Airport, 2002—. Mem. So. Meth. U. Alumni Assn. Republican. Methodist. Avocations: piano, bicycling. Office: Dallas/Ft Worth Internat Airport PO Box 619428 DFW Airport TX 75261-9428

HINKLE, MURIEL RUTH NELSON, naval warfare analysis company executive; b. Bayonne, N.J., Mar. 17, 1929; d. Andrew and Florence Martha Ida (Nuber) Nelson; m. David Randall Hinkle, June 5, 1954; children: Valerie Nelson, Janet Lee, Sally Ann. Student, Md. Coll. for Women, 1947-49; BA, U. Md., 1951. Mgr. Wildacres Thoroughbred Horse Farm, Waterford, Conn., 1960-70; illustrator naval warfare predictions/computer simulated naval engagements Analysis & Tech., Inc., North Stonington, Conn., 1970-73; pres. Sonalysts, Inc., Waterford, Conn., 1973-88, 94-98, CEO, 1973-2001, pres., CEO emerita, 2001—; also founder, past dir. Command Engring. & Tech. Svcs. Co.; pres., CEO, chmn. Stonington Farms Inc. (now Mystic Valley Hunt Club), 1983. Adv. bd. Conn. Nat. Bank, 1988-92; chmn., CEO Angiers Assocs., 1989-96, S.I. Devel. Corp., 1989-2001; cons. Def. Nuclear Agy. for Tactical Nuclear Effects in anti-submarine warfare, 1974-75; spl. edn. substitute tchr. Waterford Pub. Schs., 1968-74. Co-author: Scope of Acoustic Communications Systems in Naval Tactical Warfare, 1974, Non-Acoustic Anti Submarine Warfare, 1974, Nuclear Weapons Effects in Anti Submarine Warfare, 1974, Measures of Effectiveness, Naval Tactical Communications, 1975, Destroyer ASW Barrier, 1977. Bd. trustees Thames Sci. Ctr., 1979-82. Recipient commendation for svcs. to submarine force Comdr. Submarine Squadron Ten, 1973, SBA New Eng. Contractor of Yr. award, 1986, SBA Adminstr.'s award for excellence, 1985, 86, bus. assoc. of yr. award Naval Inst., 1999, Disting. Cmty. Svc. award Mitchell Coll., 2001, William Crawford Disting. Svc. award C. of C., 2002. Mem. Am. Horse Shows Assn., Nat. Audubon Soc., Submarine Devel. Group Two Wives Club (pres. 1968), Sigma Kappa (pres. Senesk chpt. 1987-89), Navy Wives Club. Republican. Baptist. Home: 9 Cove Rd Stonington CT 06378-2304 Office: Sonalysts Inc PO Box 280 215 Parkway N Waterford CT 06385-1209

HINKLE, RICHARD ALLEN, JR., internist; b. Conway, Ark., May 7, 1950; s. Richard Allen and Hazel Janice (Wells) H.; m. Jane Ann Jamell, Feb. 14, 1982; 1 child, Jay Preston. BA, Hendrix Coll., 1971; MD, U. Ark., 1975. Diplomate Am. Bd. Internal Medicine, Am. Bd. Forensic Medicine. Pvt. practice Sparks Med. Found., Ft. Smith, Ark., 1979—. Mem. ACP, Alpha Omega Alpha. Methodist. Office: Sparks Med Found 1501 S Waldron Rd Fort Smith AR 72903-2574 E-mail: rhinkle@sparks.org.

HINKLE, WADE P. political scientist; b. Alexandria, Va., Feb. 28, 1955; s. Charles Wade and Emily (Trevillian) H.; m. Katherine Lynn Rhyne, Aug. 14, 1977 (div. Oct. 21, 1995); m. Mary Denise Lamorte, Aug. 22, 1998. BA, U. Va., 1977, MA, 1980; PhD, U. Md., 1990. Assoc. dir. United Way, Charlottesville, Va., 1977-79; presdl. mgmt. intern Dept. Def., Arlington, Va., 1980-82; ops. rsch. analyst Office of Sec. Def., Arlington, 1982-91, dir. policy planning, 1991-94; rsch. staff mem. Inst. Def. Analysis, Alexandria, 1994—. Adj. prof. U. Md., College Park, 1989-93, George Mason U., Fairfax, Va., 2000—; adj. faculty George C. Marshall Ctr. European Security Studies, Garmisch, Germany, 1994-2002; instr. CIA, 1998-2000; vis. faculty Cornell U., Ithaca, N.Y., 1999-2000, Air War Coll., Montgomery, Ala., 2001; spkr. in field. Contbr. articles to profl. jours. Bd. dirs. Louisa County Intergrity Coun., Va., 1978-79, Nelson County, 1978-79. MacArthur fellow U. Md., 1989-90. Mem. Mil. Ops. Rsch. Soc., Pa. R.R. Tech. & Hist. Soc., U.S. Naval Inst., Air Force Assn., Assn. U.S. Army, Phi Kappa Phi. Episcopal. Avocations: railroads, historical wargames, typography. Home: 4200 Cordell St Annandale VA 22003 Office: Inst Def Analyses 4850 Mark Center Dr Alexandria VA 22311 E-mail: whinkle@ida.org.

HINKLEY, EVERETT DAVID, JR., physicist, business executive; b. Augusta, Maine, Nov. 19, 1936; s. Everett David and Julina Margaret Hinkley; m. Christine Marie, June 18, 1960; children: Anne, Mark, Kristin, David. Student, Rensselaer Poly. Inst., 1954-56; BS in Engring. Physics, Washington U., St. Louis, 1958; MS in Physics, Northwestern U., 1961, PhD in Physics, 1963. Mem. rsch. staff Gen. Telephone Labs., Northlake, Ill., 1958-59; rsch.-teaching assoc. Northwestern U., Evanston, Ill., 1960-63; mem. tech. staff MIT Lincoln Lab., Lexington, Mass., 1963-76; v.p. Laser Analytics, Inc., Lexington, 1976-77; sect. mgr., program mgr., sr. rsch. scientist Calif. Inst. Tech. Jet Propulsion Lab., Pasadena, 1976-86; chief electronics scientist Lockheed Aero. Rsch. Lab., Valencia, Calif., 1986-87; chief scientist Hughes Aircraft Co., El Segundo, Calif., 1987-89; chief scientist, global change initiative TRW Space & Tech. Group, Redondo Beach, Calif., 1989-92; v.p., chief scientist Bainbridge Tech. Group, Ltd., L.A., 1992-93; sr. scientist, mgr. Sci. and Tech. Corp., 1993—. Sr. rsch. fellow Ctr. for Internat. Rels., UCLA, 1991-94, mem. physics dept. adv. coun., 1993-95, chmn. atmospheric scis. adv. coun., 1991-98; mem. space systems and tech. adv. com. NASA, 1991-94. Author, editor: Laser Monitoring of the Atmosphere, 1976; contbr. articles to tech. jours., chpts. to books. Mem. Pasadena Lung Assn., 1980—86. Fellow Optical Soc. Am. (co-chmn. Conf. on Lasers and Electro-Optics 1986); mem. IEEE (sr., chmn. aerospace policy com. 1993-96, co-chmn. spaceborne photonics conf. 1991, co-chmn. combined optical-microwave earth and atmospheric sensing conf. 1993), IEEE Lasers and Electro-Optics Soc. (sec.-treas. 1987-89, bd. govs. 1987—), Washington U. Alumni Coun., Sigma Xi, Tau Beta Pi. Avocations: racquetball, music.

HINKLEY, NANCY EMILY ENGSTROM, foundation administrator, educator; b. St. Louis, Jan. 3, 1934; d. Sigfrid E. and Ida C. (Stenstrom) Engstrom; children: Karen Elizabeth, Christine Marie, Catherine Andrea. BA, Augustana Coll., 1955; MA, U. Fla., 1956; EdD, N.C. State U., 1975. Adult edn. specialist Nationwide Long Term Care Edn. Ctr., Raleigh, N.C., 1975-77, dir., 1977-78; owner, pres. Aging and Long Term Care Ednl. and Cons. Svcs., Raleigh, 1978-82; dir. edn. Beverly Found., South Pasadena, Calif., 1983-84; dir. tng. and mgmt. devel. Care Enterprises, Anaheim, Calif., 1984-87; pres. The Hillhaven Found., Tacoma, 1987-93; dir. employment & tng. divsn. Kitsap Cmty. Resources, 1997-99; pres. AJM Assocs., 1993—. Bd. dirs. Tacoma Community Coll. Found.; mem. editorial bd. Nursing Homes, 1988—; mem. editorial bd. Aspen Rsch. Pub. Group, 1989-93. Author: (with others) A Time and Place for Sharing: A Practical Guide for Developing Intergenerational Programs, 1984; mem. editorial bd. Jour. Univ. Programs, 1988-93; contbr. articles to profl. jours. Vol. Big Bros./Big Sisters, Tacoma, 1989-90; bd. dirs. Jessie Dyslin Boy's Ranch, Tacoma, 1988-90. Mem. ASTD, Am. Med. Dirs. Assn. (assoc.), Am. Assn. Homes for the Aging (assoc.), Am. Coll. Health Care Adminstrs. (assoc.), Am. Soc. on Aging, Gerontol. Soc. Am., Phi Kappa Phi, Phi Alpha Theta, Alpha Kappa Delta, Alpha Psi Omega, Sigma Phi Omega. Home and Office: PO Box 64190 Tacoma WA 98464-0190

HINMAN, ALAN RICHARD, public health administrator, epidemiologist; b. New Orleans, Mar. 23, 1937; s. E. Harold and Katharine Ellen (Fradenburgh) H.; m. Donna Virgene Graham, Dec. 21, 1959 (div. 1962); m. Lucy Winkler Householder, May 30, 1965; children: Johanna Mary, Katharine Emily. BA, Cornell U., 1957; MD, Western Res. U., 1961; MPH, Harvard U., 1969. Intern Cleve. Met. Hosp., 1961—62, resident in internal medicine, 1962—64, chief resident, 1964-65; with USPHS, 1965-70, 77-96; advanced through grades to asst. surgeon gen., 1988; epidemic intelligence svc. officer Ctr. for Disease Control, Calif. State Dept. Health, 1965-66; regional evaluation officer malaria eradication program Ctrs. for Disease Control, Atlanta, 1966-67, San Salvador, El Salvador, El Salvador, 1967-68, asst. chief viral diseases br. epidemiology program Atlanta, 1969-70; dir. Bur. Epidemiology, N.Y. State Dept. Health, Albany, 1970-71, asst. commr. epidemiology and preventive health svcs., 1971-75; asst. commr., dir. Bur. Preventive and Med. Svcs., Tenn. Dept. Pub. Health, Nashville, 1975-77; dir. divsn. immunization Ctr. for Prevention Svcs., Ctrs. for Disease Control, Atlanta, 1977-88; coord. nat. vaccine program Office of Asst. Sec. for Health, 1987-90; asst. surgeon gen. USPHS, 1988-96; dir. Nat. Ctr. for Prevention Svcs. Ctrs. for Disease Control, 1988-95; sr. advisor to dir. Ctrs. for Disease Control and Prevention, 1995-96; coord. CDC World Bank collaboration on immunizations Task Force Child Survival and Devel., Atlanta, 1996-2000, sr. cons. pub. health programs, 1996—; prin. investigator All Kids Count, Atlanta, 2000—; coord. PARTNERS TB ctrl. program, Atlanta, 2001—02. Adj. asst. prof. preventive and cmty. medicine Albany Med. Coll., Union U., 1970-75; adj. asst. prof. pub. health Rensselaer Poly Inst., 1971-75; assoc. clin. prof. dept. preventive medicine Vanderbilt U., 1975-77; clin. asst. prof. dept. cmty. medicine Divsn. Healthcare Svcs., U. Tenn., 1975-77; clin. asst. prof. dept. family and cmty. health Meharry Med. Coll., 1975-77; clin. assoc. prof. dept. preventive medicine-cmty. health Emory U. Sch. Medicine, Atlanta, 1978-90; vis. prof. Case Western Res. U. Sch. Medicine, 1984; adj. prof. Emory U. Sch. Pub. Health, 1990—; vis. lectr. Shanghai 1st Med. Coll., 1981; sr. cons. for pub. health programs, The Task Force for Child Survival and Devel., 1996—. Contbr. over 300 articles to profl. jours. Decorated D.S.M.; recipient Indian Health Svc. Dir. Spl. Excellence award, 1992. Fellow ACP, APHA (mem. gov. coun. 1975-77, mem. program devel. bd. 1984-86, mem. nominating com. 1984-86, chair 1985-86, chair-elect epidemiology sect. 1985-87, chair sect. 1987-89, past chair 1989-91, mem. exec. bd. 1991-95, spkr. governing coun. 1995—), Am. Acad. Pediat., Am. Coll. Epidemiology (mem. exec. bd. 1990-94, v.p. 1991-92, pres. 1992-93), Am. Coll. Preventive Medicine (regent 1974-75, 77-81, v.p. for pub. health 1975-76); mem. AMA, Am. Epidemiol. Soc., Am. Soc. Tropical Medicine and Hygiene, Am. Venereal Disease Assn. (bd. dirs. 1972-75, sec.-treas. 1975-77), Assn. Tchrs. Preventive Medicine, Infectious Diseases Soc. Am., Internat. Epidemiol. Assn., Physicians for Social Responsibility, Soc. Epidemiol. Rsch., Soc. Med. Decision Making. Home: 2194 Creek Park Rd Decatur GA 30033-2714 E-mail: ahinman@taskforce.org.

HINMAN, EVE CAISON, retired academic administrator; b. Charleston, S.C., May 17, 1951; d. Robert Lee Jr. and Ella Louise (Cross) Caison; m. William DeLeon Thrasher, June 9, 1972 (div. 1997); 1 child, Beverly Ann Thrasher Varner; m. Charles Steven Hinman, Feb. 27, 1998. Student, Francis Marion Coll., 1974-78, Trident Tech. Coll., 1990-91. Adminstrv. asst. to dean, acad. v.p. Francis Marion Coll., Florence, S.C., 1973-78; bus. mgr. dept. neurology Med. U. S.C., Charleston, 1978—2001; ret., 2001; part-time fiscal analyst Med. U. S.C., 2001—02; tech. support team mem. Universal Data Solutions, Charleston, SC, 2002—. Pianist, asst. choir dir. Friendship United Meth. Ch., Cross, S.C., 1988-96, chairperson worship com., 1993. Mem. Assn. Am. Med. Colls. (group on bus. affairs), Southeastern Bluegrass Assn. Avocations: bluegrass guitar and bass, singing and performing. E-mail: hinmane@universaldata.net.

HINMAN, FRANK, JR., urologist, educator; b. San Francisco, Oct. 2, 1915; s. Frank and Mittie (Fitzpatrick) H.; m. Marion Modesta Eaves, Dec. 3, 1948. AB with great distinction, Stanford U., 1937; MD, Johns Hopkins U., 1941. Diplomate Am. Bd. Urology (trustee 1979-85). Intern Johns Hopkins Hosp., 1941-42; resident Cin. Gen. Hosp., 1942-44, U. Calif. Hosp., 1945-47; pvt. practice San Francisco, 1947-85; assoc. clin. prof. urology U. Calif., San Francisco, 1954-62, clin. prof., 1962—; urologist-in-chief Children's Hosp., 1957-85. Adv. council Nat. Inst. Arthritis, Diabetes, Digestive and Kidney Diseases, 1983-86 Lt. USNR, 1944-46. Named Disting. Alumnus, Johns Hopkins U., 1995. Fellow ACS (regent 1972-80, vice-chmn. 1978-79, v.p. 1982-83), Royal Coll. Surgeons (hon., Eng.); mem. Am. Urol. Assn. (hon.), Am. Assn. Genito-Urinary Surgeons (hon., pres. 1981, Keyes medalist 1998), Clin. Soc. Genito-Urinary Surgeons (pres. 1979), Internat. Soc. Urol. (pres. Am. sect. 1980-84), Am. Assn. Clin. Urologists, Am. Fedn. Clin. Research, Soc. Pediatric Urology (founding mem., pres. 1971), Soc. Univ. Urologists (founding mem., pres. 1973), Am. Acad. Pediatrics (pres. urology sect. 1986), Urodynamics Soc. (founding mem., pres. 1980-82), Genito Urinary Reconstructive Soc. (founding mem.), Pan Pacific Surg. Assn. (v.p. 1980-83), Internat. Continence Soc., Brit. Assn. Urologic Surgeons (hon.) (St. Paul Medalist 1991), Soc. Française d'Urologie, Australasian Soc. Urologic Surgeons (hon.), Phi Beta Kappa, Alpha Omega Alpha. Clubs: Bohemian, St. Francis Yacht, San Francisco Yacht. Home: 1000 Francisco St San Francisco CA 94109-1127 Office: U Calif Med Ctr San Francisco CA 94143-0738 E-mail: fhinman@urol.ucsf.edu. *Devoting two afternooons each week to research, teaching and other academic pursuits, uninterrupted by surgery and clinical practice, can result in advances.*

HINMAN, HARVEY DEFOREST, lawyer; b. May 7, 1940; s. George Lyon and Barbara H.; m. Margaret (Snyder), June 23, 1962; children: George, Sarah, Marguerite. BA, Brown U., 1962; JD, Cornell U., 1965. Bar: Calif., 1966. Assoc. Pillsbury, Madison, and Sutro, San Francisco, 1965—72, ptnr., 1973—93; v.p., gen. counsel Chevron Texaco Corp., San Francisco, 1993—2002. Bd. dir. Legal Aid Soc., San Francisco. Bd. dir., sec. Holbrook Palmer Park Found., 1977—86; trustee Castillija Sch., 1988—89; bd. gov. Filoli Ctr., 1988—, pres., 1994—95; bd. dir. Phillips Brooks Sch., 1978—84, pres., 1983—84. Fellow: Am. Bar Found.; mem.: ABA, San Francisco Bar Assn. Office: 50 Fremont St San Francisco CA 94105

HINNANT, CLARENCE HENRY, III, health care executive; b. Richmond, Va., June 7, 1938; s. Clarence Henry Jr. and Billie Louise (Chewning) H.; m. Barbara Ann Livingston, June 10, 1966 (div. Feb. 1971); children: C.H. IV, W.W. Tuck. BS, Va. Poly. Inst. and State U., 1961; BS magna cum laude, Med. Coll. Va., 1981. Math. tchr. Hopewell (Va.) H.S., 1961-64; staff mem. Harper & Row Pub., N.Y.C., 1964-67; stockbroker Merrill Lynch & Co., Richmond, Va., 1967-71; pres. Lancaster Corp., White Stone, Va., 1971-81; v.p., treas. Westminster Canterbury, Lynchburg, Va., 1981-89; pres. Westminster Canterbury of Blue Ridge, Charlottesville, Va., 1989—. Faculty Am. Coll. Healthcare Adminstrn., Washington, 1982-84; bd. dirs. Workforce Investment. Contbr. articles to profl. jours. Rep. del. to State Conv., Richmond, 1973; pres., bd. dirs. Westminster Canterbury Blue Ridge Found.; bd. dirs. United Way, Workforce Investment. Fellow Am. Coll. Healthcare Adminstrs.; mem. Va. Assn. Non-Profit Homes for Aging (bd. dirs. 1983-84), S.R., Country Club of Va. (Richmond), Keswick Club, Rotary. Republican. Episcopalian. Avocations: golf, sailing. Home: 407 Key West Dr Charlottesville VA 22911-8423 Office: Westminster Canterbury Blue Ridge 250 Pantops Mountain Rd Charlottesville VA 22911-8694 E-mail: hinnant3@hotmail.com.

HINNANT, JERRY HERBERT, surgeon; b. Dallas, Feb. 27, 1934; MD, U. Tex. SW, 1957. Diplomate Am. Bd. Surgery. Intern VA Hosp., Dallas, 1957-58, resident in gen. surgery, 1958-59, Meth. Hosp., Dallas, 1959-60; chief resident in gen. surgery St. Paul Hosp., 1960-61; pvt. practice Dallas; chmn. dept. surgery Irving Cmty. Hosp., 1976; mem. staff Charleton Meth. Hosp.; mem. active and tchg. staff, chief gen. surgery Meth. Med. Ctr., Dallas, 1978—92; staff Med. Ctr. Lancaster, 1978—. Participant numerous surg. missions, L.Am., Russia. Founding trustee Canterbury Episcopal. Sch., Los Barrios Unidos Clinic. Fellow Am. Coll. Surgeons; mem. Dallas Soc. Gen. Surgeons, John Paul North Surgical Soc., Am. Soc. Gen. Surgeons, Dallas County Med. Soc., Tex. Med. Assn. Home: 909 Brook Valley Ln Dallas TX 75232-1625 Office: Surg 800 N Bishop Ave Ste 4 Dallas TX 75208-4203 Fax: (214) 942-6154.

HINNERS, R. GORDON, language educator; b. St. Charles, Ill., Sept. 26, 1955; s. R. Gordon and Jane (Elam) Hinners; m. Rebecca Keeter; children: Wyatt Keeter, Silas Keeter. BA in History, U. N.C. Asheville, 1988; MA in Spanish, U. Wis., 1995. Tchr. Asheville H.S., 1988—93; asst. prof. Spanish Mars Hill Coll., Mars Hill, NC, 1995—, dir. Internat. Edn., 1999—. Musician Ralph Blizard & New Sawhorse Ramblers, Bloundville, Tenn., 1982—; dancer, musician Green Grass Cloggers, Asheville. Musician (rec.): Fox Chase, 2000, Southern Rambler, 1994, Blizard Train, 1988. Office: Mars Hill College 100 Athletic St Mars Hill NC 28754

HINNRICHS-DAHMS, HOLLY BETH, middle school educator; b. Milw., Oct. 31, 1945; d. Helmut Ferdinand and Rae W. (Beebe) Hinnrichs; m. Raymond H. Dahms, June 11, 1983 (dec. Oct. 1983). Student, U. Wis., Milw., 1964, 66, 79—, Chapman Coll., 1965-67, Intenrat. Coll. Copenhagen, summer 1968, Temple U., summer 1970; BA, Alverno Coll., 1971; postgrad., Marylhurst Coll., 1972, Chapman Coll., World Campus Afloat, summer 1973, 74, Inst. Shipboard Edn., 1978, 79, 94. V.p. Hinnrichs Inc., Germantown, Wis., 1964-72, tchr. Germantown Recreation Dept., 1965; coach Milw. Recreation Dept., 1966-67; rep. for wis. Chapman Coll., Orange, Calif., 1967; clk. Stein Drug Co., Menomonee Falls, Wis., 1967-72; tchr. Milwa. Area Cath. Sch., 1967-72, 83, 90-91, 96—, Germantown Schs., St. Lawrence Sch., 1991-92; asst. mgr. Original Cookie Co. (Mother Hubbard's) Cookie Store, Northridge Mall, Milw., 1977-84, Sav-U Warehouse Deli, 1984-85, mgr. office, 1985-90; with Pilgrim Message Ctr., 1987—. Substitute tchr. Cath. schs. Milw. area, 1975-80, 83-89, 90, 92—, St. Rose Sch., 1989-90; tchr. Indian Cmty. Sch., Milw., 1971-72, 88, 94-2000, Martin Luther King Sch., 1973-74, Crossroads Acad., Milw., 1974-75, Harambee Cmty. Sch., 1980-83; tutor Brookfield (Wis.) Learning Ctr., 1986-87; Midwest rep. World Explorer Cruises, 1978-82; mem. replacement crew Hallmark Cards, 1997-98; with U.S. Census, 2000. Mem Wis. Math. Coun., Nat. Coun. Tchrs. Math., Internat. Inst. Milw. Friends of Mus., U.S. Lighthouse Soc., Great Lakes Lighthouse Soc., Miniss Kitigan Drum (Milw. chpt.), Golden Rule, Order Eastern Star, Hostelling Internat., Alpha Theta Epsilon. Christian Scientist. Home: N88w15041 Cleveland Ave # 3 Menomonee Falls WI 53051-2239 E-mail: hhinnrichsdahms@yahoo.com.

HINOJOSA, FEDERICO GUSTAVO, JR., judge; b. Edinburg, Tex., Apr. 16, 1947; s. Federico Gustavo and Zulema (Trevino) H.; m. Yolanda Silva, 1970 (div. 1977); children: Cynthia, Zelda Cassandra; m. Magdalena Garza, Oct. 30, 1992. BA, Pan Am. U., 1969; JD, U. Houston, 1977. Bar: Tex. 1977, U.S. Dist. Ct. (so. dist.) Tex. 1977, U.S. Ct. Appeals (5th cir.) 1980, U.S. Supreme Ct. 1980. Assoc. Clark, Lowes & Carrithers, Houston, 1977-79; ptnr. Clark & Hinojosa, Houston, 1979-81; child support atty. Tex. Dept. Human Resources, McAllen, 1981-83; asst. dist. atty. Hidalgo County, Edinburg, 1983-84; assoc. Atlas & Hall, McAllen, 1984-87; ptnr. Lewis, Pettitt & Hinojosa, McAllen, 1987-91; justice Tex. Ct. Appeals for 13th Dist., Corpus Christi, 1991—. Sgt. USAF, 1970-74. Mem. State Bar Tex., Mexican-Am. Bar Tex., Mexican-Am. Bar Assn. Coastal Bend (dir. 1993-94), Hidalgo County Bar Assn. (dir. 1986-90). Democrat. Office: 13th Ct Appeals 100 E Cano St Edinburg TX 78539-4548 E-mail: fghinojosa@courts.state.tx.us.

HINOJOSA, RICARDO H. federal judge; b. 1950; BA, U. Tex., 1972; JD, Harvard U., 1975. Judge U.S. Dist. Ct. (so. dist.) Tex.; law clk. Tex. Supreme Ct., 1975-76; assoc. Ewers & Toothaker, McAllen, Tex., 1976-79, ptnr., 1979-83; judge U.S. Dist. Ct. (so. dist.) Tex., McAllen, 1983—. Office: US Dist Ct So Dist Tex 1701 W Bus Hwy 83 Ste 1028 Mcallen TX 78501

HINOJOSA, RUBEN, congressman; b. Edcouch, Tex., Aug. 20, 1940; m. Martha Lopez; 5 children. BBA, U. Tex., Austin, 1962; MBA, U. Tex.-Pan Am., 1980. Pres., CFO H & H Foods; mem. U.S. Congress from 15th Tex. dist., 1997—; mem. edn. and workforce com., fin. svcs. com., resources com. Mem. Tex. State Bd. Edn, 1974-84.; Tex. Higher Edn. Named Hispanic Man of the Yr. Rio Grande Valley, 1994; recipient Lifetime Achivement award Hispanic Bus. Mag. Democrat. Office: 2463 Rayburn House Washington DC 20515-4315*

HINOJOSA-SMITH, ROLAND, language educator, writer; b. Mercedes, Tex., Jan. 21, 1929; s. Manuel Guzman and Carrie Effie (Smith) H.; children: Clarissa Elizabeth, Karen Louise, Robert Huddleston. BS, U. Tex., 1953; AM, N.Mex. Highlands U., 1963; PhD, U. Ill., 1969. Chmn. dept. modern langs. Tex. A&I U., Kingsville, 1970-74, dean Coll. Arts and Scis., 1974-76, v.p. acad. affairs, 1976-77; prof. English U. Minn., Mpls., 1977-81; Ellen Clayton Garwood prof. English U. Tex., Austin, 1985—, Mari Sabusawa Michener chair, 1989-93, dir. Tex. Ctr. for Writers, 1989-93, prof. dept. Spanish and Portuguese, 1993—. USIA cons., Panama, Mexico, Iraq, France; lectr. in field. Author: Estampas del Valle, 1973 (Quinto Sol 1973), Klail City, 1976 (Casa de las Americas 1976), Korean Love Songs, 1978, The Valley, 1983, Dear Rafe, 1985, Partners in Crime, 1985, Fair Gentlemen of Belken County, 1986, Klail City, 1987, Becky and Her Friends, 1990, Los Amigos de Becky, 1991, Korea Liebes Lieder, 1992, The Useless Servants, 1993, Ask a Policeman, 1998; guest editor Am. Short Fiction, 1993-94. Illini (U. Ill.) Comback Guest, 1996. Named Disting. Alumnus, U. Ill., 1998, U. Tex.-Brownsville, 1998, Celebrity Author, Scott Foresman, 1999—2001, Disting. Vis. Prof., U. Kans., summer, 1994, Marshal, U. Tex., 1995—2001; recipient Outstanding Latino faculty mem., Hispanic Caucus Am. Assn. Higher Edn., Disting. Achievement award, U. Ill., 1998; fellow, Ford Found., 1979. Fellow Soc. Spanish and Spanish Am. Studies, The Hispanic Soc. (assoc.); mem. MLA, Academia Real de la Lengua. Democrat. Roman Catholic. Home: 1800 E Stassney Ln Apt 802 Austin TX 78744-2749 Office: U Tex Dept English Austin TX 78712 E-mail: rorro@mail.utexas.edu.

HINRICHS, STEPHEN ERNEST, education educator, consultant; b. Maplewood, NJ, Mar. 7, 1918; s. Louis Ernets and Vera McEnery Hinrichs; m. Mary Grace Eames, Aug. 21, 1985; m. Nancy Litchfield Chapman, May 7, 1944 (dec. Dec. 1973); children: Victoria, Christian, Katherine, Deborah. BA, Yale U., 1940; MA, Harvard U., 1947. Instr. North Shore CDS, Winnetka, Ill., 1946—48; chmn. hist. dept. John Burroughs Sch., St. Louis, 1948—63; dir. Alamoosook Island Camp, Bucksport, Maine, 1956—68; headmaster The Harley Sch., Rochester, NY, 1963—77; exec. dir. NY State Assn. of Ind. Schools, 1977—86; pres. Designs Unlimited, 1986—. Sec. Samoset Village Assn., Rockport, Maine, 1996—; pres. Rockport Libr. Commn., Rockport, Maine, 2001—; mem. Rockport Bldg. Commn., Rockport, Maine, 1998—. 1st lt. U.S. Army, 1941—45, ETO. Mem.: Mid-Coast Forum on Fgn. Rels. Avocations: sailing, writing, golf. Home: 39 Village Way Rockport ME 04856 Office: Designs Unlimited Ltd 39 Village Way Rockport ME 04856

HINRICHS, TODD AARON, securities executive; b. Windom, Minn., July 8, 1969; s. Theodore Lynn and Shirley Ann (Hughes) H.; m. Sonja Anne Warinner, June 26, 1999. AB, U. Chgo., 1993. V.p. Kemper Securities, Chgo., 1992-97; v.p., sr. analyst ABN-AMRO Inc., Chgo., 1997—. Adv. bd. One team One Bank rep. ABN-AMRO, 1999; adv. asset divestiture Govt. of N.S., Halifax, 1999. Contbr. articles to profl. jours. Presbyterian. Avocations: travel, running, biking, gardening, playing piano. Office: ABN-AMRO Inc 208 S Lasalle St Lbby 2D Chicago IL 60604-1004

HINSCH, JAMES ERWIN, retired chemical engineer; b. Pontiac, Mich., Oct. 18, 1937; s. Erwin James and Viola Hinsch; m. Beverly A. Corner, Aug. 16, 1958; children: Kathryn, Debra Renauer, James E. Hinsch, Jr., Robert G. BS in Chem. Engring., U. Detroit, 1960; M in Chem. Engring., Wayne State U., 1963. Rsch. scientist Ford Motor Co., Dearborn, Mich., 1957—71, rsch. dir. Mt. Clemens, Mich., 1972—80, mfg. mgr., 1980—83, ops. mgr., 1985—86, mfg. mgr. Milan, Mich., 1983—85; lab. mgr. Du Pont, Troy, Mich., 1986—89, supply chain mgr., 1990—93; ops. mgr. Akzo Nobel Coatings, Pontiac, Mich., 1993—97, dir. technolgy Troy, Mich., 1997—2001; ret., 2002. Mem. fin. com. Sch. Bd., Livonia, Mich., 1968—69. Mem.: Am. Chem. Soc. Achievements include patents for electron beam curing of coatings. Home: 19030 Shay Ct Livonia MI 48152 Personal E-mail: jhinsch@prodigy.net.

HINSHAW, ADA SUE, dean, nursing educator; b. Arkansas City, Kans., May 20, 1939; d. Oscar A. and Georgia Ruth (Tucker) Cox; children: Cynthia Lynn, Scott Allen Lewis. BS, U. Kans., 1961; MSN, Yale U., 1963; MA, U. Ariz., 1973, PhD, 1975; DSc (hon.), U. Md., 1988, Med. Coll. of Ohio, 1988, Marquette U., 1990, U. Nebr., 1992; D Sci. (hon.), Mount Sinai Med. Ctr. Instr. Sch. Nursing U. Kans., 1963-66; asst. prof. U. Calif., San Francisco, 1966-71; prof. U. Ariz., Tucson, 1975-87; dir. nursing rsch. U. Med. Ctr., Tucson, 1975-87; dir. Nat. Inst. Nursing Rsch. Pub. Health Svc., Dept. Health and Human Svcs., NIH, Washington, 1987—; now dean Sch. Nursing U. Mich., Ann Arbor. Contbd. articles to profl. jours. Recipient Kay Schilter award U. Kans., 1961, Lucille Petry Leone award Nat. League for Nursing, 1971, Wolanin Geriatric Nursing Rsch. award U. Ariz., 1978, Alumni of the Yr award Sch. Nursing U. Kans., 1981, Disting. Alumni award Sch. Nursing Yale U., 1981, Alumni Achievement award U. Ariz., 1990, Disting. citation Kans. Alumni Assn., 1992, Health Leader of the Yr. award PHS, 1993, Centennial award Columbia Sch. Nursing, 1993. Mem. ANA (Nurse Scientist of the Yr. award 1985), Coun. on Nursing Rschrs. (Nurse Scientist of the Yr. award 1985), Md. Nurses Assn., Western Soc. for Rsch. in Nursing, Am. Acad. Nursing, Nat. Acad. Practice, Inst. Medicine, Sigma Xi, Sigma Theta Tau (Beta Mu Chpt. award of Excellence in Nursing Edn., 1980, Elizabeth McWilliams Miller award, 1987), Alpha Chi Omega. Avocations: hiking, camping, bicycling. Office: U Mich Sch Nursing 400 N Ingalls St Ann Arbor MI 48109-2003

HINSHAW, CHESTER JOHN, lawyer; b. Sacramento, Mar. 10, 1941; s. Chester Edward and Gertrude Lorraine (Miller) H.; m. Karen Forbes Breakey, Feb. 19, 1977. AB, Stanford U., 1963; JD, U. Calif., Berkeley, 1966. Bar: Calif. 1966, U.S. Dist. Ct. (no. dist.) Calif. 1967, U.S. Ct. Appeals (9th cir.) 1967, N.Y. 1968, U.S. Dist. Ct. (so. dist.) N.Y. 1972, U.S. Dist. Ct. (ea. dist.) N.Y. 1974, U.S. Ct. Appeals (2d cir.) 1974, U.S. Dist. Ct. (no. dist.) N.Y. 1980, U.S. Dist. Ct. (ea. dist.) Mich. 1982, U.S. Dist. Ct. (no. dist.) Tex. 1983, Tex. 1984, U.S. Ct. Appeals (5th cir.) 1984, U.S Supreme Ct. 1991. Assoc. Chadbourne & Parke, N.Y.C., 1967-74, ptnr., 1974-83, Jones, Day, Reavis & Pogue, Dallas, 1983-99. Lectr. U. Calif. Berkeley, 1966. Mem. ABA, Tex. Bar Assn., Calif. Bar Assn. Home: 5510 Park Ln Dallas TX 75220-2158

HINSHAW, EDWARD BANKS, retired broadcasting company executive; b. Aurora, Ill., Feb. 27, 1940; s. Lorenzo M. and Emily (Roach) H.; m. Victoria Leone Biggers, Jan. 16, 1965; children: Eric, Brian. Student, Harvard Coll., 1958-59, U. Minn., 1959-62. Announcer Sta. KSTP-Radio-TV, Mpls., 1959-64; announcer Voice of America, Washington, 1964-65; reporter, anchorman Jour. Broadcast Group, Inc. (formerly Sta. WTMJ, Inc.), Milw., 1965-70, editorialist, 1970-74, editorial dir., 1974—, mgr. public affairs, 1979-90, mgr. pers. and editorial affairs, 1990-94, v.p. human resources, 1994—2002. Instr. broadcast journalism U. Wis., Whitewater, 1976, 79, 86. Trustee Nat. First Amendment Congress, 1980-83; chair Wis First Amendment Congress, 1985; bd. chair Milw. Urban League, 1987; bd. dirs. Children's Outing Assn., 1987-90, Ko Thi Dance Co., 1992-99, pres., 1994-96; bd. dirs. Richard and Ethel Herzfeld Found., 1997—, Pabst Theater, 2002—, N.E. Milw. Indsl. Devel. Corp. Recipient DuPont-Columbia Citation in Broadcast Journalism, 1978; Abe Lincoln Merit award So. Baptist Radio-TV Commn., 1978; NCCJ Gold Media Medallion, 1977; named to Wis. Broadcasters Hall of Fame, 2002. Mem.: Milw. Press Club (bd. dirs. 1990—95, pres.-elect 1992, pres. 1993, past pres. 1994, Knight of the Golden Quill, Hall of Fame 2002), Wis. Broadcasters Assn. Found. (treas. 2000), Nat. Broadcast Editl. Assn. (pres. 1980—81), Sigma Delta Chi (Disting. Svc. award 1977, Excellence in Journalism award 1988, Freedom of Info. award 1994). E-mail: hinshaw@wi.rr.com.

HINSHAW, ERNEST THEODORE, JR., private investor, former Olympics executive, former finance company executive; b. San Rafael, Calif., Aug. 26, 1928; s. Ernest Theodore and Ina (Johnson) H.; m. Nell Marie Schildmeyer, June 24, 1952; children: Marc Christopher, Lisa Anne, Jennifer, Amy Lynn. AB, Stanford U., 1951, MBA, 1957. Staff asst. to pres. Capital Research and Mgmt. Co., Los Angeles, 1957-58, dir. planning, 1967-68; fin. analyst Capital Research Co., Los Angeles, N.Y.C., 1958-68, v.p., 1962-71, mgr. N.Y.C. office, 1962-66; dir., exec. v.p. Am. Funds Service Co., Los Angeles, 1968-69, pres., 1969-72, chmn. bd., 1972-82; dir. pres. Capital Data Systems, Inc., Los Angeles, 1971-73, chmn., 1973-79; v.p. Capital Group, Inc., Los Angeles, 1973-83; sr. v.p. Growth Fund Am., 1973-74, pres., 1974-76, chmn. bd., 1976-82, dir., 1974-96; sr. v.p. Income Fund Am., 1973-74, pres., dir., 1974-76, chmn. bd., 1976-82, dir., 1974-96; commr. yachting 1984 Olympic games Los Angeles Olympic Organizing Com., 1980-84. Dir. Capital Research & Mgmt. Co., 1972-83; mem. guest faculty Northwestern U. Transp. Center, 1965-66; mem. ops. com. Investment Co. Inst., 1970-74 Bd. dirs. Newport Harbor Nautical Mus., 1989-92, Girl Scout Coun. Orange County, 1993—, chair fin. com., 1996-97, treas., 1998—; trustee Friends of Girl Scouts Trust; mem. investment com. Hoag Hosp. Found., 1992-97. Served to 1st lt. USMC, 1951-53. Mem. Soc. Airline Analysts (sec. 1965-66), Los Angeles Soc. Fin. Analysts, N.Y. Soc. Security Analysts, Am. Statis. Assn., Town Hall Calif., Nat. Kite Class (pres. 1968-69), Lido 14 Internat. Class Assn. (pres. 1978-79), Assn. Orange Coast Yacht Clubs (commodore 1976), So. Calif. Yachting Assn. (commodore 1979), B.O.A.T., Inc. (dir. 1977-81), Pacific Coast Yachting Assn. (dir. 1979-80), U.S. Yacht Racing Union (dir. 1980-81), U.S. Sailing Ctr. Long Beach, Calif. (adv. coun. mem.). Clubs: Wall Street (N.Y.C.); University (Los Angeles); Lido Isle Yacht (Newport Beach, Calif.) (commodore 1973); Stanford U. Sailing (trustee 1984-96); St. Francis Yacht (San Francisco); Ft. Worth Boat. Democrat. Home: 729 Via Lido Soud Newport Beach CA 92663-5530

HINSHAW, JUANITA, electric distributor executive; CFO Graybar Elec., St. Louis, 2000—, sr. v.p., 2000—. Bd. dirs. Ipsco Inc. Office: Graybar Electric PO Box 7231 Saint Louis MO 63177

HINSHAW, MARK LARSON, architect, urban planner; b. Glendale, Calif., Aug. 17, 1947; s. Lerner Brady and Alice Elaine (Larson) H.; m. Caryl Ann Kunsemuller, Dec. 21, 1968 (div. 1982); 1 child, Erica; m. Marilyn Kay Smith, June 18, 1983 (div. 1997); children: Lindsay, Christopher. BArch magna cum laude, U. Okla., 1970; M Urban Planning, CUNY, 1972. Registered architect, Wash. Sr. planner Planning Dept., Anchorage, 1976-77; project planner TRA, Seattle, 1977-82; urban designer City of Bellevue, Wash., 1982-90; ind. cons., 1991-97; dir. urban design LMN Architects, Seattle, 1997—. Architect-in-the-sch. Seattle Sch. Dist., 1979. Columnist on architecture, urban design: Seattle Times, 1993—; author: Citistate Seattle: Shaping a Modern Metropolis, 1999 ; contbr. articles to profl. jours. and books, articles to Landscape Arch. mag. Mem. Urban Beautification Commn., Anchorage, 1975, Design Jury, Hemet (Calif.) Civic Ctr. Competition, Seattle Design Commn., 1990-91; mem. Downtown Seattle Design Rev. Bd., 1996—. 1st lt. USAF, 1972-76. NEA grantee, 1975; recipient merit award for Hist. Preservation, City Seattle, 1983. Fellow AIA (pres. Seattle chpt. 1992-93), Am. Inst. Cert. Planners (mem. nat. bd. 1994-98); mem. Am. Planning Assn. (sec. Wash. chpt. 1982, v.p. 1983-85, pres. 1987-89). Office: 801 2nd Ave Fl 5 Seattle WA 98104-1576 E-mail: mhinshaw@lmnarchitects.com.

HINSHAW, MARK WALDO, psychiatrist, educator; b. St. Louis, Oct. 23, 1938; s. James Waldo and Martha Meredith (Shepard) H.; m. Candace Ann Ward; children: Elizabeth, Sarah. AB, Dartmouth Coll., 1960; MD, U. Mo., 1965. Diplomate Nat. Bd. Med. Examiners; diplomate in psychiatry and in child and adolescent psychiatry Am. Bd. Psychiatry and Neurology. Resident in psychiatry and child-adolescent psychiatry U. Mich., Ann Arbor, 1966-70, chief resident Children's Psychiat. Hosp., 1969-70; chief dept. neuropsychiatry Ireland Army Hosp., Ft. Knox, Ky., 1971-72; asst. prof. dept psychiatry Mich. State U., East Lansing, 1972-75, assoc. prof., 1975-90, clin. prof., 1990—, assoc. dir. psychiatry residency program, 1982-90, asst. chmn. in charge of Grand Rapids divsn., 1986-90; pvt. practice, Grand Rapids, 1972—. Dir. med. student psychiat. edn. Grand Rapids Med. Edn. Ctr., 1972—80; dir. child psychiat. tng. Mich. State U., Grand Rapids, 1976—80; med. dir. Psychiat. Consultation Svcs., Grand Rapids, 1976—98, Aurora Behavioral Health Sys., Grand Rapids, 1997—98; cons. to numerous sch. sys. and cmty. agys., Grand Rapids, 1972—; cons. Mich. Dept. Mental Health, 1984—94; examiner, sr. examiner in gen. and child-adolescent psychiatry Am. Bd. Psychiatry and Neurology, 1979—2003. Contbr. articles to profl. jours., including Med. Aspects of Human Sexuality, Advances in Neurology, Jour. Psychiat. Edn. Maj. M.C. U.S. Army, 1970—72. Daniel Webster nat. scholar Dartmouth Coll., 1956. Fellow: Am. Acad. Child and Adolescent Psychiatry (life), Am. Psychiat. Assn. (life; disting.); mem.: Mich. Coun. Child and Adolescent Psychiatry (pres. 1985—87), Alpha Omega Alpha. Avocations: travel, antiques, cultural arts, golf. Home: 7622 Lime Hollow Dr SE Grand Rapids MI 49546-7441 Office: 1000 Parchment Dr SE Grand Rapids MI 49546-3663

HINSHAW, STEPHEN P. education educator; b. Columbus, Ohio, Dec. 1, 1952; s. Virgil Goodman Hinshaw, Jr. and Alene Pryor Hinshaw; m. Kelly M. Campbell, July 22, 2001; children: Evan R. Neukomm children: Jeffrey W., John W. Neukomm. BA summa cum laude, Harvard U., 1974; PhD, U. of Calif., LA, 1983. Licensure Bd. of Psychology, Calif., 1984. Prof. Dept. of Psychology, U. of Calif., Berkeley, 1990 ; asst. prof. Dept. of Psychology, UCLA. Prin. investigator U. of Calif., Berkeley, 1990—2003. Author: (book) The Years of Silence are Past: My Father's Life with Bipolar Disorder, Attention Deficits and Hyperactivity in Children; contbr. over 130 articles to profl. jours. Recipient Detur prize, Harvard U., 1974, Disting. Tchg. award, U. of Calif., Berkeley, 2001; John Harvard scholarship, Harvard U., 1972, 1973, Nat. Merit scholarship, 1970. Fellow: Am. Psychol. Soc.; mem.: Profl. Group on Attention and Related Disorders (pres. 1996—2000), Internat. Soc. for Rsch. in Child and Adolescent Psychopathology (pres. 1999—2001), APA (pres., divsn. 53 2000—02). Achievements include contributor to multimodal treatment study of children with ADHD. Avocations: basketball, hiking. Office: Dept of Psychology U of Calif Tolman Hall #1650 Berkeley CA 94720-1650 Office Fax: 510-643-5336. E-mail: hinshaw@socrates.berkeley.edu.

HINSON, GALE MITCHELL, social worker; b. Bklyn., June 29, 1951; d. Albert Lee and Doris (Purdie) Mitchell; m. Lawrence Hinson, Aug. 31, 1975; 1 child, Terrence. Assocs degree in Community Svcs., SUNY, Farmingdale, 1972; BSW, Adelphi U., 1984, MSW, 1986. Cert. social worker II, N.Y.; cert. criminal justice specialist. Mem. staff Nassau Univ. Med. Ctr., E. Meadow, NY; forensic mental health specialist, clin. supr. Nassau County Correctional Ctr., East Meadow, 1987, psychiat. social worker I, 1987—. Crisis counselor Project Liberty. Mem. Ryan White Title I HIV Health Svcs. Planning Council, Nassau and Suffok Counties; commr.'s rep. multicultural adv. com.; mem. Christian Edn.; trustee bd. mem. Naomi Temple AME Zion Ch., Roosevelt, NY. Mem.: NASW, Nat. Assn. Forensic Social Workers. Home: 6 Brown Ave Hempstead NY 11550-6907 Office: Nassau Univ Med Ctr 2201 Hempstead Tpke East Meadow NY 11554

HINSON, GRADY MAURICE, music educator; b. Marianna, Fla., Dec. 4, 1930; s. Bartlett Abner Hinson, Willie Beatrice Hinson; m. Margaret Hume, June 16, 1952; children: Jane Leslie Enoch, Susan Elizabeth Jordan. BA, U. Fla., 1952; MMus, U. Mich., 1955, DMA, 1957. Instr. piano U. Mich., Ann Arbor, 1955—57; prof. piano So. Bapt. Theol. Sem., Louisville, 1957—96, sr. prof. piano, 1996—. Vis. prof. piano Drake U., Des Moines, 1984. Author: Guide to the Pianist's Repertoire, 1973, Guide to the Pianist's Repertoire, 3d edit., 2000, The Piano in Chamber Ensemble, 1978, Music for Piano and Orchestra, 1981; author: (enlarged edit.), 1993; editor: Am. Music Tchr., 1984—88. 1st lt. U.S. Army, 1952—54. Recipient Liszt medal, Hungarian Govt., 1986, Honor, N.Y. Music Tchrs. Assn., 1999. Mem.: Ky. Music Tchrs. Assn. (pres. 1963—65), Music Tchrs. Nat. Assn. (cert. master tchr., so. divsn. pres. 1966—68), Am. Liszt Soc. (jour. editor 1977—87, adv. coun. 1975—, Medal 1984). Democrat. Avocation: Avocations: tennis, gardening, travel. Home: 6907 Windham Pkwy Prospect KY 40059-8864 Office: So Bapt Theol Sem 2825 Lexington Rd Louisville KY 40280

HINSON, JACK ALLSBROOK, research toxicologist, educator; b. Mullins, S.C., Aug. 18, 1944; s. Layton Liston and Will (Allsbrook) H.; m. Joanne Edwards Kidd; children: Edward Thomas, Richard William. BS, Coll. of Charleston, 1966; MS, U. S.C., 1968; PhD, Vanderbilt U., 1972. Postdoctoral fellow Nat. Inst. of Health, Bethesda, Md., 1972-75, sr. staff fellow, 1975-80; rsch. toxicologist Nat. Ctr. Toxicological Rsch., Jefferson, Ark., 1980-90, chief biochem. mechanisms br., 1989-90; adj. prof. U. Ark. Med. Sci., Little Rock, 1980-90, prof., dir. div. toxicology. Dir. interdisciplinary toxicology program, occupl. and environ. health program U. Ark. Med. Sci., 1990-95; chmn. Ark. Toxicology Symposium, 1992—; adj. assoc. prof. U. Tenn. Ctr. for Health Scis., Memphis, 1982-90; vis. fellow Middlesex Hops. Med. Sch., London, 1982; vis. prof. U. Leiden, The Netherlands, 1986. Editor Drug Metabolism Revs., 1997—, mem. editl. bd., 1995-97; mem. editl. bd. Toxicology and Applied Pharmacology, 1980-89, 96—, Jour. Toxicology and Environ. Health, 1991—; contbr. chpts. to books and articles to profl. jours. Mem. Soc. Toxicology (pres. South Ctrl. chpt. 1990-92), Am. Soc. Pharmacology and Exptl. Therapeutics, Internat. Soc. for Study of Xenobiotics, Am. Indsl. Hygiene Assn. Episcopalian. Home: 8 Piedmont Ln Little Rock AR 72223-2232 Office: U Ark Med Sci Divsn Toxicology 4301 W Markham St # 638 Little Rock AR 72205-7101 E-mail: HinsonJackA@exchange.uams.edu.

HINSON, ROBERT C. career officer; BS in Edn., U. Tenn., 1970; student, Squadron Officer Sch., 1977; MA in Humanities and Edn., Ark. State U., 1977; student, Air Command and Staff Coll., 1982, Nat. War Coll., 1989, Harvard U. Commd. 2d lt. USAF, 1971, advanced through grades to lt. gen., 1998; adminstrv. specialist 379th Aeromed. Airlift Wing, Scott AFB, Ill., 1970-71; officer trainee Officer Tng. Sch., Lackland AFB, Tex., 1971; B-52 co-pilot, aircraft comdr. and instr. pilot 97th Bombardment Wing, Blytheville AFB, Ark., 1973-77; air staff tng. officer Sec. Air Force Personnel Coun., Pentagon, Washington, 1977-78; pilot, instr. pilot and flight evaluator 529th Bomb Squadron, Plattsburgh AFB, N.Y., 1979-82; various assignments Plattsburgh AFB, N.Y., 1986-88, 1982-86; chief strategic nuc. policy br., joint staff and J-5 Pentagon, Washington, 1989-91, exec. officer strategic plans and policy directorate, 1989-91; comdr. 99th Ops. and Maintenance Group, Ellsworth AFB, S.D., 1991-93; wing comdr. 99th Tactics and Tng. Wing, Ellsworth AFB, S.D., 1991-93; dep. dir. plans and programs Hdqs. Air Combat Command, Langley AFB, Va., 1993-94; dir. ops. Hdqs. Air Force Space Command, Peterson AFB, Colo., 1997-2000, comdr., 28th Bomb Wing and installation comdr. Ellsworth AFB, S.D., 1994-95, comdr., 45th Space Wing and dir., Ea. Range Patrick AFB, Fla., 1995-97, dir. ops. Peterson AFB, Colo., 1997-99; comdr. 14th Air Force and component comdr. U.S. Air Force Space Ops., U.S. Space Command, Vandenberg AFB, Calif., 1999-2000; dep. comdr. in chief, promoted to lt. gen. U.S. Strategic Command, Offutt AFB, Nebr., 2000—. Decorated Legion of Merit. Office: USSTRATCOM/J001 901 SAC Blvd Ste 2A Offutt A F B NE 68113-6001

HINSON, ROBERT WILLIAM, advertising executive, consultant; b. Neptune, N.J., Nov. 30, 1944; s. Herbert William and Bernice (Stadelhofer) H. AB in Econs. and Sociology, Boston Coll., 1966. Media planner Benton & Bowles, Inc., N.Y.C., 1968-70; v.p., assoc. media dir. SSC&B: Lintas Worldwide, N.Y.C., 1970-74, sr. v.p., dir. media ops., 1976-80; v.p., assoc. media dir. Foote Cone & Belding, Inc., L.A., 1974-76; exec. v.p., chmn. mgmt. com., chmn. ops. com., dir. media svcs. Rosenfeld, Sirowitz & Lawson, Inc., N.Y.C., 1980-85, exec. v.p., dir. mktg. and media svcs., chief adminstrv. officer, 1986-87; pres., chief exec. officer Hinson and Assocs., Inc., N.Y.C., 1987-91. Cons. in field, 1991 . Author: Media Leverage, 1985. Media dir. Tuesday Team, Reagan-Bush '84 campaign, 1984; sustaining mem. Rep. Nat. Com.; mem. Ronald Reagan Presdl. Libr. Found., Monmouth County (N.J.) Rep. Orgn.; bd. dirs. Monmouth (N.J.) Symphony Orch.; mem. nat. campaign com. Boston Coll. Mem. NATAS, Internat. Assn. TV, Arts and Scis., Internat. Radio and TV Soc., Media Dirs. Industry Coun., Am. Assn. Advt. Agys. (media policy com. 1980-87), Am. Rsch. Found. (media com. coun. 1983-86), Boston Coll. Alumni Assn., Wagner Soc. N.Y., Monmouth County Hist. Soc., Alliance Francaise of Monmouth County (N.J.), Alliance Francaise of Ft. Lauderdale, Nature Conservancy, Nat. Trust for Hist. Preservation, Vieux Carre Property Owners Assn., N.Y. Athletic Club, Deal (N.J.) Golf and Country Club, Allenhurst (N.J.) Beach Club, Coral Ridge (Fla.) Country Club. Roman Catholic. Home: PO Box 182 Allenhurst NJ 07711-0182 also: 133 N Pompano Beach Blvd Pompano Beach FL 33062-5728 also: 921 Chartres St New Orleans LA 70116-3227

HINSVARK, DON GEORGE, social services agency professional; b. Helena, Mont., Mar. 27, 1934; s. Almer Burton and Carmen Christine Hinsvark; m. Jacqueline Rica Sarfati, July 10, 1958; children: Jon Felix, Timothy Joel, Michael David, Symone Hinsvark Sass. BA, U. So. Calif., 1956; MA in Tchg. and Counseling, San Diego State U., 1967; postgrad., sch. adminstrn. cert., U. La Verne, 1984-86; Cert. Career Counseling/Legal Asst., U. Calif.-San Diego, 1994. Cert. tchr. gen. elem. and jr. high edn., sch. adminstrn., sch. counselor, Calif. Tchr. San Diego (Calif.) City Schs., 1962-65, dist. counselor, 1965-85, dist. counselor team leader, 1985-91, chmn. sch. attendance rev. bd., 1992; career counselor Dyasayd Consultation, San Diego, 1993; program supr. Voices for Children, San Diego, 1994-99. Mem. San Diego Commn. on Children, Youth and Families, 1994-99, adv. bd. San Diego State U. Sch. Social Work, 1993-95; adv. bd., instr. U. La Verne (Calif.), Edn. Dept., 1984-88; presenter in field. Joint author: Crisis Team Handbook, 1988; contbr. articles to profl. jours. Coach Age Group Swim Team, Coronado, Calif., 1962, Pop Warner Football, Coronado, 1970-71; coach and mgr. Little League Baseball, Coronado, 1970-75, Sr. Little League Baseball, Coronado, 1976-77. Lt. USN, 1956-61, Atlantic and Pacific; capt. USNR; commdg. officer Res. Naval Spl. Warfare Staff unit, 1980-82, 84-86. Recipient NROTC scholarship USN, 1952-56; scholar Nat. Def. Edn. Inst., U.S. Govt. 1966, 68. Mem. Calif. Sch. Social Workers Assn. (pres. San Diego chpt. 1972, state area rep. 1979), San Diego City Student Svcs. Assn. (pres. 1983-84, 86-87), Calif. Sch. Counselors Assn. (area rep. 1982-83, 92-93, Area Counselor of Yr. 1992), Calif. Assn. for Counseling and Devel. (pres. San Diego chpt. 1992-93), Kiwanis (v.p., sec. San Diego chpt. 1987, Educator of Yr. 1991), Am. Counseling Assn. Avocations: swimming, nordic skiing, reading, travel. Home: # 807 1830 Avenida del Mundo Coronado CA 92118-3020

HINTERBUCHNER, L. P. neurologist; b. Zlatá Baňa, Slovak Republic, Dec. 10, 1922; arrived in U.S., 1951; s. Frantisek and Margita Hinterbuchner; m. Catherine Nicolaides, Dec. 10, 1955. MD, Komensky U., Bratislava, Slovak Republic, 1947; postgrad., N.Y. Postgrad. Med. Sch., N.Y.C., 1952—53. Instr. neurology Health Sci. Ctr., SUNY, Bklyn., 1956—61, clin. asst. prof. neurology, 1961—67, clin. prof. neurology, 1967—95, clin. prof. neurology emeritus, 1995—; vis. prof. neurology N.Y. Coll. Osteo. Medicine, Westbury, NY, 1977—84; adj. prof. N.Y. Med. Coll., Valhalla, 1983—97. Dir. dept. psychiatry and neurology Kingsbrook Jewish Med. Ctr., Bklyn., 1961—66; chmn. dept. neurology Bklyn. Hosp. Med. Ctr., 1971—85, cons. in neurology, 1991—96. V.p. Slovak World Congress, Pasadena, Calif., 1996—2001; mem. exec. com. Slovak League of Am., Passaic, NJ, 1997—. Recipient Ellis Island Medal of Honor, Nat. Ethnic Coalition, N.Y.C., 2000. Fellow: N.Y. Acad. Sci.; mem.: AMA (life), Med. Soc. County of Kings (pres. 1994, chmn. bd. trustees), Am. Acad. Neurology (sr.). Office: 10 Polly Park Rd Rye NY 10580

HINTHORN, MICKY TERZAGIAN, volunteer, retired; b. Jersey City, N.J., July 5, 1924; d. Bedros H. and Aznive (Hynelian) Terzagian; m. Wayne L. Hinthorn, Aug. 11, 1957. BS in Occupational Therapy, U. So. Calif., 1953; MBA, Notre Dame de Namur U., Belmont, Calif., 1984. Registered occupational therapist. Gen. office worker Drake Secretarial Coll., Jersey City, 1941-42; sec., expediter Western Electric Co., Kearny, N.J., 1943-45; sec. div. edn. CBS, NYC, 1945-46; sec. to v.p. sales Simon and Schuster, Inc., NYC, 1947-51; gen. office worker in Sch. of Edn. U. So. Calif., L.A., 1951-52; occupational therapist Palo Alto (Calif.) Clinic, 1954-55; chief occupational therapist Children's Health Coun., Palo Alto, 1954-56; sec. to chief mil. engr. Lenkurt Electric Co., San Carlos, Calif., 1956-58; sr. sec. re-entry program Bank of Am., Redwood City, Calif., 1979-80; ret., 1980. Organizer occupational therapy dept. Children's Health Coun., Palo Alto, Calif., 1954, chief 1954-56. Author, editor numerous newsletters and orgns.' papers. Charter mem., membership chair U. So. Calif. Pres. Cir., San Francisco, 1978-80; treas. North Peninsula chpt. San Francisco Opera Guild, San Mateo, Calif., 1979; vol. pub. info. chair re-election San Mateo County Supr., Redwood City, Calif., 1978; founder, charter pres. Friends of Belmont (Calif.) Libr., 1974-75; mem. Coastside Fireworks Com., 1989-94, chair corp. sponsorship, 1992-93. Recipient Hon. Mem., Friends of San Francisco Pub. Libr., 1974, 1990-1995, Assoc. Mem. Half Moon Bay Coastside Chamber Comm. (chair Bus. Edn. scholarships 1992, 93), Recognition Award 1993. Mem. AAUW (pres. San Mateo br. 1976-77, Half Moon Bay br. chair local scholarships 1992, mem. Half Moon Bay scholarship com. 1999, 2000, historian 1992-94, corr. sec. 1995-97, name grant honoree Edn. Found. Jodi Gordon Endowment 1991-92, mem. Half Moon Bay-AAUW edn. found. com. 1999-2003), U. So. Calif. Alumni Assn. (life), Notre Dame de Namur U. Alumni Assn., Friends of Filoli, Friends of Half Moon Bay Libr., Half Moon Bay Coastside C. of C. (chair bus. edn. scholarship 1992-94, Recognition award 1993), Coastside Women's Club (scholarship com. 1999-2003, mem. com. for scholarships and charities 2003—). Avocations: photography, walking, reading, writing, attending performing arts events. Home: PO Box 176 Half Moon Bay CA 94019-0176

HINTIKKA, JAAKKO, philosopher, educator; b. Helsinginpitäjä, Finland, Jan. 12, 1929; s. Toivo Juho and Lempi J. (Salmi) H.; m. Merrill Bristow Provence, Feb. 11, 1978 (dec.); m. Ghita Holmström, Dec. 19, 1987. Grad. in Philosophy, U. Helsinki, Finland, 1952; postgrad., Harvard U., 1954; PhD, U. Helsinki, Finland, 1956; Doctorate (hon.), U. Liège, 1984, Jagiellonian U., 1995, Uppsala U., 2000, U. Oulu, 2001, U. Turku, 2003. Jr. fellow Soc. Fellows, Harvard U., 1956-59; prof. philosophy U. Helsinki, 1959-70; research prof. Acad. Finland, 1970-81; prof. philosophy Fla. State U., Tallahassee, 1978-90, McKenzie prof., 1986-90, also prof. computer sci., 1986-90; prof. Boston U., 1990—. Vis. prof. Brown U., 1962, U. Calif., Berkeley, 1963, Hebrew U. Jerusalem, 1974; part-time prof. philosophy Stanford U., 1964-82, Immanuel Kant lectr., 1985; John Locke lectr. Oxford (Eng.) U., 1964; fellow Center for Advanced Study in Behavioral Scis., 1970-71; Hägerström lectr. U. Uppsala, 1983; co-chair Am. organizing com. Twentieth World Congress Philos., 1998. Author: Knowledge and Belief, 1962, Models for Modalities, 1969, Tieto on valtaa, 1969, Logic, Language-Games and Information, 1973, Time and Necessity, 1973, Knowledge and the Known, 1974, (with U. Remes) The Method of Analysis, 1974, The Intentions of Intentionality, 1975, The Semantics of Questions and the Questions of Semantics, 1976, Aristotle on Modality and Determinism, 1977, The Game of Language, 1983, (with J. Kulas) Anaphora and Definite Descriptions, 1985, (with Merrill B. Hintikka) Investigating Wittgenstein, 1986, (with Martin Kusch) Kieli ja maailma, 1988, (with Merrill B. Hintikka) The Logic of Epistemology, 1989, Intentionnalite et mondes possibles, 1989, (with James Bachman) What If? Toward Excellence in Reasoning, 1990, (with Gabriel Sandu) On the Methodology of Linguistics, 1991, Eseje Logiczno-Filozoficzne, 1992, Fondements d'une theorie du langage, 1994, The Principles of Mathematics Revisited, 1996, Ludwig Wittgenstein: Half-truths and One-and-a-Half Truths, 1996, Lingua Universalis vs. Calculus Ratiocinator, 1996, Language, Truth and Logic in Mathematics, 1997, Paradigms for Language Theory, 1997, El Viaje Filosófico más Largo, 1998, Inquiry as Inquiry, 1999, On Goedel, 2000, On Wittgenstein, 2000, Filosofian Koyhyys ja Rikkaus, 2001; contbr. over 300 articles to profl. jours.; editor-in-chief: Internat. Jour. Synthese, 1965-76, 82-2002; editor: Synthese Libr., 1965-2002 Acta Philosophica Fennica, 1973-79, Synthese Lang. Libr., 1976-84, (with Patrick Suppes) Aspects of Inductive Logic, 1966, Philosophy of Mathematics, 1969, (with Donald Davidson) Words and Objections, 1969, (with Patrick Suppes) Information and Inference, 1970, (with others) Approaches to Natural Language, 1973, Rudolf Carnap, Logical Empiricist, 1976, (with others) Essays on Wittgenstein in Honor of G.H. von Wright, 1976, (with Robert Butts) Procs. 5th Internat. Congress Logic, Methodology and Philosophy of Science (4 vols.), 1977, (with Lucia Vaina) Cognitive Constraints on Communication, 1984, (with S. Knuuttila) The Logic of Being, 1986, (with Leila Haaparanta) Frege Synthesized, 1987, Aspects of Metaphor, 1994, From Dedekind to Gödel, 1995. Decorated comdr. Order of the Lion of Finland, 1st class, 1987; recipient Wihuri Internat. prize, 1976, E.J. Nyström prize Soc. Scientiarum Fennica, 1988, Suomen Kulttuurirahasto grand prize, 1989; Guggenheim fellow, 1979-80 Mem. Assn. Symbolic Logic (v.p. 1968-70), Internat. Inst. Philosophy (v.p. 1993-96, pres. 1999-2002), Internat. Union History and Philosophy Sci. (v.p. 1971-75, pres. 1975), Finnish Acad. Sci. and Letters (coun. 1972-79), Philosophy of Sci. Assn. (governing bd. 1970-72), Societas Scientiarum Fennica, Internat. Fedn. Philos. Socs. (governing bd. 1978-88, 93-98, v.p. 1993-98), Am. Philos. Assn. (v.p. Pacific divsn. 1974-75, pres. 1975-76), Am. Acad. Arts and Scis., Norwegian Acad. Sci., C.S. Peirce

Soc. (pres. 1997), Russian Acad. of Scis. (fgn. mem.), Hungarian Acad. Scis., Phi Beta Kappa (hon.). Home: 38 Flint Dr Marlborough MA 01752-6701 Office: Boston U Dept Philosophy Boston MA 02215-4701 also: U Helsinki Inst Philosophy PO Box 9 FIN 00014 Helsinki Finland

HINTON, DAVID OWEN, retired electrical engineer; b. Guilford County, N.C., May 12, 1938; s. George Owen Hinton and Barbara Elizabeth (Greeson) Wilder; m. Thelma Marie Arrington, Jan. 26, 1963; 1 child, David Scott. BSEE, N.C. State U., 1965. Electronics officer USN Destroyer, Norfolk, Va., 1965-67; naval flight officer Patrol Squadron 23, Brunswick, Maine, 1967-70; aircraft maintenance officer USN Rsch. Lab., Patuxent River, Md., 1970-72; project officer Health Effects Rsch. Lab. U.S. EPA, Research Triangle Park, N.C., 1972-79, dep. dir. Human Exposure & Field Rsch. Divsn., 1992; dir. Quality Assurance and Tech. Support Divsn., Research Triangle Park, N.C., 1993-95; ret., 1995. Mem. Air Sampling Instruments Com., Cin., 1976-84; chmn. Electronics Tech. Adv. Com., Durham, N.C., 1981-85. Author: (with others) Air Sampling Instruments for Evaluation of Atmospheric Contaminants, 1983; contbr. papers, articles to profl. jours. Capt. USPHS, 1977-95, ret. Recipient Nat. Def. medal USN, 1972, Commendation medal USPHS, 1986, Bronze medal U.S. EPA, 1988. Mem. Am. Conf. Govt. Indsl. Hygienists, Soc. Am. Inventors, Commd. Officers Assn. (sec., treas. 1988), Navy Res. Assn. (life), Res. Officers Assn. (life). Achievements include patents in field. Home: 8616 Bluff Pointe Ct Raleigh NC 27615-4192 E-mail: david_h_27615@yahoo.com.

HINTON, JAMES FORREST, JR., lawyer; b. Gadsden, Ala., Nov. 19, 1951; s. James Forrest Sr. and Juanita Grey (Weems) H. BA, Vanderbilt U., 1974; JD, U. Ala., 1977. Bar: Ala. 1977, D.C. 1979, U.S. Dist. Ct. (so. dist.) Ala. 1979, U.S. Ct. Appeals (5th cir.) 1980, U.S. Ct. Appeals (11th cir.) 1981, La. 1982, U.S. Dist. Ct. (ea. and mid. dists.) La. 1982, U.S. Dist. Ct. (no. dist.) Ala 1982, U.S. Supreme Ct. 1982, U.S. Dist. Ct. (we. dist.) La. 1983, U.S. Dist. Ct. (no. dist.) Ohio 1983, U.S. Ct. Appeals (D.C. cir.) 1984, U.S. Ct. Appeals (fed. cir.) 1985, U.S. Dist. Ct. (so. dist.) Tex. 1987, U.S. Dist. Ct. (no. dist.) Tex. 1991, Tex. 1992, Tenn. 1992, U.S. Dist. Ct. (ea. and we. dists.) Ark. 1992, U.S. Ct. Appeals (6th and 8th cirs.) 1992, U.S. Dist. Ct. (ea. and we. dists.) Tex. 1993, U.S. Dist. Ct. (mid. dist.) Ala. 1993, U.S. Dist. Ct. (ea. and mid. dist.) Tenn. 1994, U.S. Dist. Ct., Colo. 2000. Law clk. to chief judge U.S. Dist. Ct. (so. dist.) Ala., Mobile, 1977-79; ptnr. Darby, Myrick & Hinton, Mobile, 1979-82; dir. McGlinchey Stafford Lang, New Orleans, 1982-93; ptnr. Adams & Reese, New Orleans, 1993-97; shareholder Berkowitz, Lefkovits, Isom & Kushner, Birmingham, 1997—2003, Baker, Donelson, Bearman, Caldwell & Berkowitz, 2003—. Contbr. articles to profl. jours. Mem. ABA (antitrust, intellectual property, litigation sects.), FBA, La. Assn. Def. Counsel, Order of Coif, Phi Beta Kappa. Office: Baker Donelson Bearman Caldwell & Berkowitz PC 420 20th St N Ste 1600 Birmingham AL 35203-5200 E-mail: fhinton@bakerdonelson.com.

HINTON, JULIANA GUILLORY, biologist, educator; b. Lake Charles, La., Sept. 9, 1943; d. Julian Guth and Molly Hennigan Guillory; children: Michael Alan Hinton, John David Hinton. BS in Biology Edn., McNeese State U., 1970; MEd in Biology Edn., McNeese State Coll., 1976; PhD in Curriculum and Instrn., La. State U., 2000. Instr. biology LaGrange HS, Lake Charles, La., 1969—71, Barbe HS, 1971—79; vis. lectr. McNeese State Coll., Lake Charles, 1984—89, instr., 0190—1999, asst. prof., 1999—. Com. chmn. Mayor's Commn. Women, Lake Charles, 1984—86. Named Outstanding Sci. Tchr. of Yr., La. Acad. Scis., 1976. Mem.: La. Acad. Scis., Nat. Assn. Biology Tchrs., Women in Engring. Programs and Advs. Network, McNeese Orgn. for Sci. and Tech., Assn. Southeastern Biologists, Delta Kappa Gamma. Methodist. Home: 2838 Walden Dr Lake Charles LA 70607 Office: Mcneese State U Ryan St PO Box 92000 Lake Charles LA 70609-2000 Office Fax: (337)475-5677. Business E-Mail: jhinton@mail.mcneese.edu.

HINTON, KAROLYN KAY, retired elementary school educator; b. Fairview, Okla., Mar. 9, 1945; d. Albert Lowell Woods and Jewel Deloria Bromlow-Woods; m. Patricia Jeanne Woods. AA, Frank Phillips Coll., 1965; BS, West Tex. State U., 1968; MEd, West Tex. A&M. Cert. profl. certification in English, Speech Tex. State Bd. Edn., provisional certification in Spanish. Tchr. Friona (Tex.) Ind. Sch. Dist., 1967—2000. Tchr. GED classes, Friona. Contbr. poetry. Mem.: OES (Worthy Matron 1968—). Democrat. Baptist. Avocation: needlework, painting, writing.

HINTON, NORMAN WAYNE, retired information services executive; b. Maysville, Ky., Mar. 8, 1944; s. Eugene Fay and Julia Lafelle (Dalton) H.; m. Juanita Ann Smith, Nov. 16, 1968; children: Janis Renee Proctor, Brian Wayne. BA in Bus. Adminstrn., Centre Coll. Ky., 1966. Notary public, 1999—; ordained elder. Programmer, systems analyst Union Cen. Life Ins., Cin., 1966-70, Electronic Data Systems Corp., Dallas, 1970-99; ret., 1999; realtor Century 21 Park One Realtors, Allen, Tex., 1999—. Bd. dirs. Christian Ednl. Ministries. Bd. dirs. S.E. La. chpt. ARC, New Orleans, 1991-92, Orleans Svc. Ctr., 1990-92; chmn. emergency svcs. commn. Info. and Referral Ctr. of Collin County, 1994-97, vice chmn., 1995-96, chmn., 1996-97; mem. Tulane U. Coll. Bus. Adv. Bd., New Orleans, 1989-92; mem. Dallas-Ft. Worth Ch. coun. Ch. of God Internat., 1994-96, treas., 1995, pres., 1996; bd. dirs. Christian Ednl. Ministries, 2000—; chmn., bd. dirs. Christian Ednl. Ministries Festival Assn., 1999-2002. Fellow Life Office Mgmt. Assn., Am. Mgmt. Assn.; mem. Assn. Ky. Cols., Rotary Club of Allen (bd. dirs. 2002—, chmn. program com. 2002-03, chmn. internat. com., 2003—), Sigma Alpha Epsilon. Avocations: quarterhorses, golf, travel. E-mail: waynehinton@realtor.com.

HINTON, PAULA WEEMS, lawyer; b. Gadsden, Ala., Dec. 5, 1954; d. James Forrest and Juanita (Weems) H.; m. Steven D. Lawrence, Mar. 31, 1984; 1 child, David Hinton Lawrence. BA, U. Ala., 1976, MPA, JD, U. Ala., 1979. Bar: Ala. 1979, Tex. 1982, U.S. Dist. Ct. (so. dist.) Ala. 1980, U.S. Dist. Ct. (so. dist.) Tex. 1981, U.S. Dist. Ct. (no. dist.) Tex. 1988, U.S. Dist. Ct. (ea. and we. dists.) Tex. 1989, U.S. Dist. Ct. (no. and mid. dists.) Ala. 1993, U.S. Ct. Appeals (5th and 11th cirs.) 1981, U.S. Supreme Ct. Law clk. to magistrate U.S. Dist. Ct. Ala., Mobile, 1979-80; assoc. Vinson & Elkins, LLP, Houston, 1981-88; ptnr. Akin Gump Strauss Hauer & Feld, L.L.P., Houston, 1989—2001, Vinson & Elkins, Houston, 2001—. Mem. Supreme Ct. Gender Bias Reform Implementation Com., 1998—, co-chair, 2000—, chmn., 2002-. Bd. dirs. Planned Parenthood Houston and S.E. Tex., Inc., 2000—. Rotary fellow U. Sevilla, Spain, 1980-81. Mem.: ABA (mem. ligation sect., internat. law sect., antitrust and bus. litigation sect., women andthe law sect., alternate dispute resolution sect.), ATLA, Tex. Bar Found. (nominating co-chair 2002, co-chmn. nominating com. 2002), London Ct. of Internat. Arbitration, Internat. Bar Assn., Houston Bar Assn., Greater Houston Partnerships, Exec. Women's Partnership (steering com. 2002, Ma'at Justice award 2001), U. Houston Law Found. (adv. bd.), Houston Bar Found. (bd. dirs. 1994—96, chmn. 1996—97, bd. dirs. 2002—), State Bar Tex. (chair women in the profession com. 1996—98, mem. disciplinary rules of profl. conduct com. 2000—01, bd. dir. 2002—, mem. litigation sect., internat. law sect., antitrust and bus. litigation sect., alternative dispute resolution sect., women and law sect.). Office: Vinson and Elkins LLP 2300 First City Tower 1001 Fannin St Houston TX 77002-6760 Office Fax: 713-615-5543. Business E-Mail: phinton@velaw.com.

HINTZ, CHARLES B. finance company executive; BS, Purdue U., 1971; MS, U. So. Calif., 1976; MBA, U. Pa., 1978. Corp. treasury staff Chevron Corp., 1978-82; group v.p., dir. strategic planning The Northern Trust Co., 1982-84; v.p., corp. treas. Anderson Clayton & Co., 1984-86; mng. dir., treas. Morgan Stanley Group; mng. dir., CFO Lehman Bros. Holdings Inc., N.Y.C.; CFO PlusFunds.com, N.Y.C., 2000—. Alumni dir. Purdue U. Krannert Sch. Lt. comdr. USNR. Mem. Treasury Mgmt. Assn. (bd. dirs.), Fin. Execs. Inst., Nat. Investor rels. Inst. Office: PlusFundscom 5th Fl 440 9th Ave New York NY 10001*

HINTZEN, ERICH HEINZ, lawyer; b. Grosse Pointe, Mich., June 9, 1960; s. Heinz and Hanna Hintzen; m. Valerie L. Parker; children: Andrew P., Emma L. AB, U. Mich., 1983; JD, U. Minn., 1989. Bar: Tex. 1989, Mich. 1990, U.S. Dist. Ct. (we. dist.) Mich. 1991, U.S. Ct. Appeals (6th cir.) 1991, U.S. Dist. Ct. (ea. dist.) Mich. 1992, U.S. Dist. Ct. (ea. dist.) Tex. 1995, U.S. Dist. Ct. (we. dist.) Tex. 1995, U.S. Ct. Appeals (5th cir.) 1995, U.S. Supreme Ct. 1996, U.S. Dist. Ct. (no. dist.) Tex. 1997, U.S. Dist. Ct. (so. dist.) Tex. 1998. Briefing atty. to Justice C.L. Ray Tex. Supreme Ct., Austin, 1989-90; assoc. Miller, Canfield, Paddock & Stone, PLC, Detroit, 1990-95, 96-98, Parkers Parks & Rosenthal, LLP, Austin, 1995-96; prin. Miller Canfield Paddock & Stone, PLC, Troy, Mich., 1998—. Office: Miller Canfield Paddock & Stone PLC 840 W Long Lake Rd Ste 200 Troy MI 48098-6358

HINZ, CARL FREDERICK, JR., physician, educator; b. Cleve., Apr. 9, 1927; s. Carl Frederick and Marie (Jones) H.; m. Joan Herndon, June 5, 1953; children— Elizabeth, Richard, Catherine, Gretchen. BS, Western Res. U., 1948, MD, 1951. Faculty dept. medicine Western Res. U. Sch. Medicine, Cleve., 1953-67, asst. prof., 1961-67, research asso. div. research in med. edn., 1964-67; prof., asso. dean U. Conn. Sch. Medicine, 1967-92, acting head dept. medicine, 1979-80, emeritus, 1992—. Mem. Conn. Med. Exam. Bd., 1976-80 Chmn. bd. dirs. blood svcs. Conn. region ARC, 1993-95, chair coun. of chairs North Atlantic area, 1995-98. Markle scholar, 1959-64; scholar-in-residence Inst. Medicine, Nat. Acad. Sci., 1987-88. Fellow ACP; mem. Am. Soc. Clin. Investigation, Am. Assn. Immunologists, Am. Soc. Hematology, Central Soc. Clin. Research, Am. Fedn. Clin. Research, Conn. Med. Soc., Hartford County Med. Assn. (dir. 1976-92, pres. 1986-87), Conn. Lung Assn. (pres. 1979-81) Home: 11 Highwood Dr Avon CT 06001-2411

HINZ, THEODORE VINCENT, architect; b. June 5, 1933; s. Theodore V. and Lillian (Adolph) H.; m. Louise R. Symmons; 1 child, Linda. BArch, Pratt Inst., 1956. Registered arch., N.Y., N.J., Va., Md., Conn., Ill. Draftsman, designer Muller & Ash Archs., N.Y.C., 1956-59; designer Urban, Brayton & Burrows, N.Y.C., 1959; designer, project arch. Goldstone & Dearborn, N.Y.C., 1959-66, assoc., 1966-70; ptnr. Goldstone, Dearborn & Hinz, N.Y.C., 1970-73, Goldstone & Hinz, N.Y.C., 1973—. Capt. C.E., U.S. Army, 1956-57. Recipient cert. Merit for Excellence in Design for Greenacre Park, 1972, Good Neighbor award Volvo Hdqs. N.J. Mfg. Assn., 1973, Bus. Friend of Arts award, 1988, Lumen citation Illumination Engring. Soc., 1990, Spl. Recognition award Concrete Industry Bd., 1993, Build N.Y. award Gen. Bldg. Contractors of N.Y., 1993. Mem. AIA, N.Y. Soc. Archs., N.Y. State Assn. Archs., Constrn. Specifications Inst., Bayside Hist. Soc. (trustee 1975-77, 81-83, v.p. 1977-79, pres. 1979-81), Queens Hist. Soc. (trustee 1980-87). Office: Goldstone & Hinz Architects PC 104 E 40th St Rm 803 New York NY 10016-1838

HINZE, VICKI KAY, writer, educator; b. Denver, Mar. 10, 1954; d. Victor Harry Sampson and Edna Mae Martin-Sampson; m. Lloyd H. Hinze, July 3, 1976; children: Raymond, Michael, Kristen. Undergrad., Miss. Gulf Coast Jr. Coll., 1973; undergrad in bus., Our Lady Holy Cross Coll., 1975; MBA in Creative Writing, LaSalle U., New Orleans, 1996; PhD in Philosophy, Theocentric Bus. and Ethics, Am. Coll., 1999. Lectr. in field. Author: Mind Reader, 1993 (Five Star Gold award Heartland Critiques), Maybe This Time, 1996 (Five Star Gold award Gothic Jour., Laurel Leaf award), Beyond the Misty Shore, 1996, Festival, 1997, Upon a Mystic Tide, 1997, Shades of Gray, 1998 (Top Pick award Romantic Times, Best Contemporary Suspence Novel of the Yr. Romantic Times), Duplicity, 1999 (Golden Quill award, Top Pick award Romantic Times), Acts of Honor, 1999 (Laurel Leaf award of excellence, Maggie award of excellence, Silver Star award Romance Communications, Gold Medal award Romantic Times, Top Pick award Romantic Times), All Due Respect, 2000 (Daphne de Maurier award, RT Book Club Top Pick award), Lady Liberty, 2002 (Daphne de Maurier award, Romantic Times Gold medal and Top Pick awards, Best Romantic Intrigue, 2003), (anthology) Seeing Fireworks!, 1998, A Message From Cupid, 1999, All-About Writing to Sell, 2001; contbr. articles to profl. jours. Recipient SARA award for svc. and faithful support romance genre, 2000. Mem.: Novelists Inc., Authors Guild, Mystery Writers Am., Romance Writers Am. (cons., com. mem., Nat. Svc. award 1995). Avocations: reading, home remodeling, painting. Office: PO Box 235 Niceville FL 32588

HIPFEL, STEVEN J. lawyer; Grad., U.S. Army Command and Gen. Staff Coll., 1998; LLM in Environ. Law, George Washington U., 2000. Head internat. environ. law br. Internat. and Operational Law Divsn. Office of Judge Advocate Gen. of Navy, Pentagon, 1997—99; acting ocean affairs asst. Under Sec. of Def. for Policy, Pentagon, 1998; environ. counsel to commdr. Navy Region S.W., 2000—03, chief naval ops. environ. coun., 2003—. Contbr. ; article submissions editor: Environ. Lawyer, 1999—2000, bd. editors: Free Speech Yearbook, 1997—2000. Address: 6035 Wilmington Dr Burke VA 22015

HIPP, KENNETH BYRON, lawyer; b. Charlotte, N.C., Aug. 4, 1945; s. Junius B. and Jeanne Carol (Gwaltney) H.; m. Ann Winfield Birmingham, Sept. 23, 1966; children: Kenneth Byron Jr., Andrew Clay. AB, Duke U., 1967; JD with high honors, U. N.C., Chapel Hill, 1971. Bar: N.C. 1971, Hawaii 1987, U.S. Dist. Ct. (no. dist.) Tex. 1978, U.S. Dist. Ct. Hawaii 1987, U.S. Ct. Appeals (2d, 4th and 5th cirs.) 1972, U.S. Ct. Appeals (9th cir.) 1976, U.S. Ct. Appeals (10th cir.) 1977, U.S. Supreme Ct. 1993. Assoc. Micronesian Claims Com., Saipan, Northern Mariana Islands, 1973-74; regional dir. Micronesian Claims Co., Palau, Western Caroline Islands, 1974-76; atty. enforcement litigation NLRB, Washington, 1971-73, 76-77, supr. atty. enforcement litigation, 1977, dep. asst. gen. counsel spl. litigation, 1977-78, dep. asst. gen. counsel appellate litigation, 1978-86, dep. asst. gen. counsel contempt litigation, 1986-87; ptnr. Goodsill Anderson Quinn & Stifel, Honolulu, 1987-95; mem. Nat. Mediation Bd., Washington, 1995-98, chmn., 1996-97; ptnr. Marr Hipp Jones & Pepper, Honolulu, 1998—; mediator, mem. Hawaii Appellate Conf. Program, 1999—. Bar examiner State of Hawaii, 1988-92; vis. assoc. prof. Law Sch., Boston Coll., 1983-84; adj. prof. Law Sch., Cath. U. Am., 1978-79, Law Ctr., Georgetown U., Washington, 1984-87; adj. prof. Grad. Sch. Bus. U. Hawaii, 1989-94. Mem. Hawaii State Bar Assn. (chair labor and employment law sect. 1990-91), Order of Coif. Presbyterian. Home: 314 Poipu Dr Honolulu HI 96825-2125 Office: Marr Hipp Jones Pepper Ste 1550 1001 Bishop St Pauahi Tower Honolulu HI 96813 E-mail: khipp@marrhipp.com.

HIPP, WILLIAM HAYNE, broadcast executive; b. Greenville, S.C., Mar. 11, 1940; s. Francis Moffett and Mary Matilda (Looper) H.; m. Anna Kate Reid, June 14, 1963; children: Mary Henigan, Francis Reid, Anna Hayne. BA, Washington and Lee U., 1962; MBA, U. Pa., 1965. With Met. Life Ins. Co., 1965-69; v.p. Liberty Life Ins. Co., Greenville, S.C., 1969-74, exec. v.p., 1977-79, chmn. bd. dirs., 1979—; chief exec. officer Liberty Corp., Greenville, 1979—, also bd. dirs. Bd. dirs. Wachovia Corp., SCANA Corp., S.C. Rsch. Authority, Trustee, vice-chmn. Nat. Urban League, 1979-89; trustee Com. Econ. Devel., N.Y., 1988—, Episcopal H.S., Alexandria, Va., 1982-88; chmn. Greenville Urban League, 1978, Greenville YMCA, 1979; trustee Greenville County Sch. Sys., 1975-76, Washington and Lee U., Lexington, Va., 1985-95, Greenville C. of C., 1985; trustee, chmn. Alliance for Quality Edn., 1986—, Greenville Hosp. Sys., 1989-95; bd. dirs. Am. Coun. Life Ins., 1995—, S.C. State Devel. Bd., 1980-85, and others. Mem. Greenville C. of C. (chmn. 1985). Office: Liberty Corp PO Box 789 2000 Wade Hampton Blvd Greenville SC 29615-1037

HIPPE, ANNE ELAINE, nursing educator; b. Lincoln, Nebr., Mar. 23, 1951; d. Thomas Dean and Arlene (Foreman-Elliott) Buffington; children: Kim, Debbie, Rob, Jenney, Eric, Bryce; m. Robert Hippe, July 4, 1986. Diploma, Nebr. Meth. Hosp., 1974; postgrad., Chadron State Coll.; BSN with distinction, Bishop Clarkson Coll., Omaha, 1991; MSN, U. Nebr. Med. Ctr., 1997. RN, Nebr. RN ICU, CCU St. Elizabeth Community Health Ctr., Lincoln, 1974-75, RN labor and delivery, 1975-77; RN pediatrics Bryan Meml. Hosp., Lincoln, 1979, RN PAR/OR, 1979-82; RN ICU Regional West Med. Ctr., Scottsbluff, Nebr., 1982; instr. Western Nebr. C.C., Scottsbluff, 1982—, divsn. chair for health occupations, 1994—. Active St. Agnes Parish, Scottsbluff, Nebr., 1999. Democrat. Roman Catholic. Avocations: music, needlework, computers. Home: 1018 E 35th St Scottsbluff NE 69361-4535 Office: Western Nebr Community Coll 1601 E 27th St Scottsbluff NE 69361-1899 E-mail: ahippe@wncc.net.

HIPPEAU, ERIC, book publishing executive; b. Paris, Aug. 16, 1951; came to U.S., 1986; Student, Sorbonne Univ., Paris. V.p. computer publs. IDG, N.Y.C.; pub. IDG Info World; pub. Computer World Ziff-Davis, N.Y.C., 1989—90, exec. v.p., 1990—91, pres., COO, 1991, chmn., CEO, 1991—93, Ziff Comms. Co., N.Y.C., 1993—2000; pres., exec. mng. dir. Softbank Intl. Ventures, 2000—. Office: Ziff-Davis Inc 28 E 28th St New York NY 10016-7900

HIPPEE, WILLIAM H., JR., lawyer; b. Des Moines, 1946; BS, U. Pa., 1968; JD, Stanford U., 1972. Bar: Minn. 1972. Ptnr. Dorsey & Whitney LLP, Mpls. Office: Dorsey & Whitney LLP 50 South 6th St Ste 1500 Minneapolis MN 55402-1498

HIPPLE, WALTER JOHN, English language educator; b. Chgo., Mar. 14, 1921; s. Walter John and Emilie (Scheu) H.; m. Anne Ruth Poier, Nov. 27, 1962; children: Heidi Kristina, Ethan John; m. Kay F. Moomaw. BA, U. Chgo., 1947, MA, 1948, PhD, 1954; postdoctoral, U. London, 1957, Cambridge (Eng.) U., 1961-62; LittD, Shimer Coll., 1977. Lectr. Roosevelt U., Chgo., 1948; instr. U. Chgo., 1948-50, U. Ark., 1951-52; asst. prof. U. Fla., Gainesville, 1952-56; assoc. prof. Cornell Coll., Mt. Vernon, Iowa, 1957-61; prof. U. Pacific, Calif., 1962, Idaho State U., 1963, U. So. Calif., 1963; prof., chmn. dept. humanities Ind. State U., Terre Haute, 1963-72; dean Shimer Coll., Mt. Carroll, Ill., 1972-76; acad. v.p. West Chester (Pa.) State Coll., 1976-77; prof. philosophy West Chester (Pa.) U., 1977-91, assoc. to pres., 1977-79, dir. honors, 1979-91, prof. emeritus, 1991; prof. English Heilongjiang (People's Republic of China) U., Harbin, 1991-92. Chmn. Com. on Humanities in Secondary Schs. Ind., 1965-69; prof. univs. and insts. in Peoples Republic of China, 1986-92; guest prof. U. Autonomous Region Caribbean Coast Nicaragua, 1997, U. Guyana, 2001. Author: The Beautiful, the Sublime and the Picturesque in Eighteenth Century British Aesthetic Theory, 1957; editor, author introduction: Alexander Gerard, An Essay on Taste, 1963; contbr. articles to profl. jours. With U.S. Army, 1943-45. Guggenheim fellow, 1961-62. Home: 328 S Darlington St West Chester PA 19382-3341

HIPPS, KERRY W(AYNE), chemistry educator, research scientist; b. El Paso, Tex., Mar. 16, 1948; s. Manson J. and Amaline (Nabhan) H.; m. Ursula Mazur, July 12, 1979; children: Autumn, Lorry. BS, U. Tex., El Paso, 1970; PhD, Wash. State U., 1976. Lectr. U. Mich., Ann Arbor, 1976-78; asst. prof. Wash. State U., Pullman, 1978-81, assoc. prof., 1981-84, prof. chemistry, 1984—, prof. material sci., 1991—. Lectr. 68th Disting. Faculty Conf., Wash. State U. Co-author: Tunneling Spectroscopy, 1982; contbr. over 110 artciles to sci. publs. Named Tchr. of Yr., Wash. State Tchrs. Assn., 1987; Alfred P. Sloan Found. fellow, 1982, NSF energy-related postdoctoral fellow, 1976; grantee NSF, 1979—, Petroleum Rsch. Fund, 1981—. Mem. Am. Chem. Soc. (chmn. N.W. regional chpt. 1983), Am. Phys. Soc., Materials Rsch. Soc., Sigma Xi, Phi Lambda Upsilon (faculty advisor 1979-86). Achievements include the development of inelastic electron tunneling spectroscopy of electronic transitions; exited state metal complex structure determination through vibronic structure analysis; observation of resonant tunneling in M-I-M diodes and in the STM, spectroscopy of buried interfaces, scanning tunneling microscopy studies of molecular and sub-molecular conductivity; organizer physical chemistry on the nanometer scale; development of sub-molecular imaging of electron transfer processes in molecules, single molecule electronic spectroscopy. Office: Wash State U Dept Chemistry Pullman WA 99164-0001 E-mail: HIPPS@wsu.edu.

HIRAHARA, PATTI, public relations executive; b. Lynwood, Calif., May 10, 1955; d. Frank C. and Mary K. Hirahara; m. Terry K. Takeda, Sept. 1995. AA, Cypress Coll., 1975; BA, Calif. State U., Fullerton, 1977. Pub. affairs dir. United TV, L.A., 1977-80; v.p. Asian Internat. Broadcasting Co., L.A., 1980-81; mktg. cons. Disneyland, Anaheim, Calif., 1982; pub. rels. agt. Japan External Trade Orgn., L.A., 1982-86, 87-92; owner, pres. Prodns. By Hirahara, Anaheim, 1982—. Comml. photographer Hirahara Photography, Anaheim, 1977-83; publicist Tokyo Met. Govt., 1981, World Trade Week So. Calif., 1997, 98, 99; advisor State Colo. Trade Mission to Japan, 1986, State Ariz. Trade/Investment Mission to Japan, 1987, County Riverside, Calif. for Japanese trade, investment, tourism, 1986-88; coord. JETRO's Bus. Study Series, L.A., 1988; advisor Japan External Trade Orgn., 1987-88, TV Prodr./Host: Images, 1980, Expressions, 1994. Mem. reader panel Golf for Women Mag. Bd. dirs. Nisei Week Japanese Festival, L.A., 1980-81; mem. Anaheim H.S. 20 Yr. Reunion Com., 1993. Nat. scholar Seventeen Mag. Youth Adv. Coun., 1973; named Orange County Nisei Queen, Suburban Optimist Club, Buena Park, Calif., 1974, nat. semi-finalist Outstanding Working Women Competition Glamour Mag., 1975; recipient svc. award Suburban Optimist Club of Buena Park, 1975. Mem. NAFE, Soc. Profl. Journalists (bd. dirs. 1980-81), World Trade Ctr. Assn. Orange County, Japanese Am. Citizens League, Am. Women in Radio and TV (bd. dirs. So. Calif. chpt. 1980-82, vice-chair western conf. 1981), So. Calif. Golf Assn., Pub. Rels. Soc. Am. (Orange County chpt. 1990), Adelaide Price Elem. Sch. (30 yr. reunion chair 1997), Suburban Optimist Club of Buena Park (bd. dirs. 1993-96, chairperson 30th Anniversary Celebration 1996, Optimist of Yr. 1995-96), Alpha Gamma Sigma.

HIRAI, CRAIG KAZUO, lawyer; b. Honolulu, Jan. 3, 1949; s. Ralph and Tamie (Matsuo) H.; m. Linda Kuulei Goto, Oct. 12, 1980; children: Susan, Midori. BS, U. So. Calif., 1970; MS, MBA, U. Pa., 1971, 72; JD, U. Calif., Hastings, 1978; LLM in Taxation, NYU, 1979. Bar: Hawaii 1978, U.S. Dist. Ct. Hawaii, 1978, U.S. Tax Ct. 1979, U.S. Ct. Appeals (9th cir.) 1982; CPA, Hawaii, lic. real estate broker, Hawaii. Assoc. Fong & Miho, Honolulu, 1980-82; from assoc. to dir. Torkildson, Katz, Fonseca, Jaffe, Moore & Hetherington, Honolulu, 1982—. Mem. 1st taxation dist. Hawaii Bd. of Taxation Rev., 1988-92; chmn., vice chmn., mem. Hawaii Rental Housing Trust Fund Commn., 1992-98. Deacon Ctrl. Union Ch., Honolulu, 1988-92, trustee, 1992-95; chmn., mem. Hawaii Rental Housing Trust Fund Adv. Commn., 1998-2001; dir. Housing and Cmty. Devel. Corp. Hawaii, 1998-2000; chmn. Hawaii Tax Rev. Commn., 2001-03. Mem. ABA, AICPA, Hawaii Bar Assn., Hawaii Soc. CPAs (chmn. tax com. 1986-87, vice chmn., then chmn. ethics com. 1994-95, 99—), Hawaii Assn. Realtors (chmn. taxation/fin. subcom. 1988-2001, vice chmn. legis. com. 1992-93, 96-99). Democrat. Home: 802 Puuikena Dr Honolulu HI 96821-2500 Office: Torkildson Katz et al 700 Bishop St Fl 15 Honolulu HI 96813-4187 E-mail: ckh@torkildson.com.

HIRAI, DENITSU, surgeon; b. Yokkaichi, Mie, Japan, July 27, 1943; came to U.S. 1969; s. Denyomu and Shizuo (Tanaka) H.; m. Fumiko Hada, June 14, 1969; 1 child, R. Lisa. MD, U. Tokyo, 1968; MBA, U. So. Calif., 2003. Diplomate Am. Bd. Surgery, Am. Bd. Quality Assurance and Utilization Rev. Physicians, Am. Bd. Surg. Critical Care; cert. nutrition support physician; cert. wound care specialist. Intern and residency Waterbury (Conn.) Hosp., 1969-74; fellow Mt. Sinai Hosp., 1974-75; asst. chief surgery VA Med. Ctr., Lincoln, Nebr., 1975-80, chief surgery, 1981-2000; asst. clin. prof. surgery Creighton U., Omaha, 1982-84, assoc. prof. surgery, 1984-2000; clin. instr. U. Nebr., Omaha, 1986-88, clin. asst. prof. surgery, 1988-2000; assoc. prof. clin. surgery, mem. surgery staff Sch. Medicine U. So. Calif., L.A., 2000—. Author: Brain Ticklers (Japanese), 1983. Fellow ACS, Am. Coll. Critical Care Medicine; mem. AAAS, AMA, ACS, Am. Soc. Parenteral and Enteral Nutrition, Soc. Am. Gastrointestinal Endoscopic Surgeons, Southwestern Surg. Congress, Soc. Critical Care Medicine, Assn. VA Surgeons. Avocations: photography, braille transcription, karate (okinawa koburyu nidan). Office: LAOPC 351 E Temple St Los Angeles CA 90012

HIRANO, ASAO, neuropathologist; b. Tomioka, Gunma, Japan, Nov. 26, 1926; s. Yoshiro and Miyoe Hirano; m. Keiko Okubo, May 23, 1959; children— Michio, Ikuo, Yoko, Shigeo MD, Kyoto U., 1952. Chief resident neurology Montefiore Hosp., Bronx, 1957-58; vis. scientist NIH, 1959-65; head div. neuropathology Montefiore Med. Ctr., Bronx, 1965—, Harry M. Zimmerman prof. neuropathology, 1995—; prof. pathology Albert Einstein Coll. Medicine, 1971—, prof. neurosci., 1974—. Vis. prof. Kansai Med. U., Osaka, Japan, 1985, Nippon Med. Sch., Tokyo, 1993. Author: Atlas of Neuropathology, 2d rev. edit., 1974, A Guide to Neuropathology, 1981, Metastatic Tumors of the Nervous Systems, 1982, Color Atlas of Neuropathology, 1988; editor: Neuropsychiatric Disorders in the Elderly, 1983, Patholoy of the Myelinated Axon, 1985, Amyotrophic Lateral Sclerosis, Progress and Perspectives in Basic Research and Clinical Application, 1995; mem. internat. editl. bd. Sec. 5 Excerpta Medica, 1976—; mem. editl. com. Neurol. Medicine, 1978—; mem. adv. bd. Jour. Neuropathology and Exptl. Neurology, 1971-81, mem. editl. bd., 1981-84; mem. editl. bd. Progress in Computerized Tomography, 1978—, Annals of Neurology, 1983-89, Acta Neuropathologica, 1991—, Amyotrophic Lateral Sclerosis and Other Motor Neuron Disorders, 1999—, Amyotrophyic Lateral Sclerosis and Other Motor Neuron Diseases, 1999—; mem. cons. editor Human Cell; mem. adv. bd. Clin. Neuropathology, 1982—, Neuropathology and Applied Neurobiology, 1983—; hon. editor Brain Tumor Pathology, 1993—, Neuropathology, 1994—; mem., neuropathology cons. Surg. Neurology, 1996—; mem. internat. adv. bd. Med. Electron Microscopy, 1997—; mem.,

cons. editor Human Cell. Recipient Billings Silver medal AMA, 1959, Key to Osaka City, Japan, 1977, Royal Coll. Lectr. award Can. Assn. Neuropathologists, Royal Coll. Physicians and Surgeons Can., 1980, 1st Jack Prichard Meml. Lectr. award Queen's U., Belfast, 1981, 1st Endowment Lectr. of Neuropathology in memory of Mrs. Rajan Bharati and 150th Yr. Celebration of Madras Med. Coll., 1984, Commendation award Hon. Ben Blaz, 1992, Plaque, U.S. Ho. Reps., 1992, Order of Rising Sun, Gold Rays with Rosette, Govt. of Japan, 2001. Mem.: World Fedn. Neurology (rsch. com. 1978), Brit. Neuropathol. Soc. (assoc. 1982—2000), Japanese Soc. Neuropathology, Internat. Soc. Neuropathology, Am. Soc. Cell Biology, Assn. for Rsch. in Nervous and Mental Diseases, Am. Assn. Neuropathologists (pres. 1977—78, Weil award 1968, award for meritorious contbn. to neuropathology 1995), Australian and New Zealand Soc. Neuropathology (hon.), Western Pacific Neurol. Soc. (hon.), Am. Neurol. Assn. (hon.), Japanese Soc. Neurosurgery (sr.), Am. Acad. Neurology (sr.). Office: Montefiore Med Ctr 111 E 210th St Bronx NY 10467-2401

HIRANO, SHIGERU, surgeon, researcher; b. Kurume, Fukuoka, Japan, Nov. 30, 1964; s. Minoru and Nobuko Hirano; m. Chika Saito, May 29, 1964. MD, PhD, Kyoto U., Japan, 1998. Lic. med. dr. Ministry of Health, Japan. Resident Kyoto U. Hosp., 1990—91; med. staff Tenri Hosp., Japan, 1991—94, Kyoto U. Hosp., 1994—98; lectr. Kyoto U., 1998—; rsch. assoc. U. of Wis., Madison, 2001—. Contbr. articles to profl. jours. Mem.: Am. Bronchoesophagological Assn. (corr.), Am. Acad. of Otolaryngology Head and Neck Surgery (corr.). Achievements include research in brain function for speech and hearing, tissue engineering for voice. Avocations: singing, travel, tennis. Office: U Wis Dept Surgery K4/789 CSC 600 Highland Ave Madison WI 53792 Office Fax: 608-263-7652. E-mail: hirano@surgery.wisc.edu.

HIRES, WILLIAM LELAND, psychologist, consultant; b. South Orange, N.J., July 5, 1918; s. Harrison Streeter and Christine B. (Leland) H.; m. Karen Reynolds Perrott, July 12, 1975; 1 child, Jennifer Leland. BS, Haverford Coll., 1949; PhD, U. Pa., 1972. Asst. to dean of admissions, asst. dir of scholarships U. Pa., 1952-55; supr. psychol. svcs., spl. classes, asst. supt. Office Supt. Chester County (Pa.) Schs., 1956-59; assoc. prof. West Chester Coll., 1960-61; adminstrv. asst. Office of Pres., asst. to sec. U. Pa., 1961-64; assoc. Edward N. Hay & Assocs., 1964-65; asst. supt. pub. schs. Chester County, 1966-68, pvt. cons., 1968-75; dir. diagnostic and consultative svc. Chester County Intermediate Unit, 1975-76, pvt. practice psychology, 1976-78; dir. pupil svcs. Upper Darby (Pa.) Sch. Dist., 1978-81; dean acad. studies Curtis Inst. Music, Phila., 1981-86; ptnr. Hires Assocs., Phila., 1987—. With USMC, 1942—46, with U.S. Army, 1941—42, to lt. col. USAR, 1950—52, col. hon. Pa. Army N.G. ret. Mem. AAAS, APA, Soc. of Cin. (bd. dirs.), Welcome Soc., Hist. Soc. Pa., 1st Troop Phila. City Cavalry (hon.), Soc. Colonial Wars Pa. (hon. gov.), Phila. Club, Franklin Inn Club, Merion Cricket Club, The Rabbit.

HIROHATA, DEREK KAZUYOSHI, air force officer, lawyer; b. Dos Palos, Calif., June 26, 1963; s. Vincent Yoshinobu and Gertrude Sumiko (Kimura) H. BA in Polit. Sci., Calif. State U., Fresno, 1987; grad., Italian Mil. Jump Sch., 1989, USAFE Command & Control Sch., 1990, Brit. Army Jump Sch., 1990; MA in Aerospace Sci., Embry riddle U., Carbondale, 1992; JD, So. Ill. U., Carbondale, 1996. Bar: Calif. 1997, U.S. Ct. Appeals (armed forces) 1997, U.S. Ct. Criminal Appeals (air force) 1997. Commd. 2d lt. USAF, 1987, advanced through grades to maj., 1999, ground launched cruise missile launch control officer, 1988-90; emergency actions officer 501 Tactical Missile Wing, RAF Greenham Common, U.K., 1989-90, chief force mgmt. 513 Svcs. Squadron, RAF Mildenhall, U.K., 1990-92; billeting & food svc. coord., laison officer Air Fete, Eng.; treaty inspector escort Conventional Forces Europe; USAFR, 1993—; 932 SVS ops. officer, 1993-97; dep. JAG, USAF, 1997-2000, high rep. Brcko (Bosnia) law revision commn., 2000—; staff judge adv. Iraq Survey Group, Baghdad, 2003—. Legal counsel Office High Rep. Bosnia, North, Brcko Law Revision Commn., USAF JAG Mission, 1999-00. Contbr. to poetry anthologies Am. Poetry Soc., 1993, Poets Pen Quarterly, 1993, Memories Anthology, 1994, Delta. Coord. peer support network Sch. Law So. Ill. U., Carbondale, founder, capt. trial advocacy competition team, 1994-95; mem. Jessup Internat. Moot Ct. team. Mem. ABA, ATLA (founder So. Ill. U.-Carbondale chpt.), Calif. State Bar Assn. Am. Psychology and Law Soc., Christian Legal Soc., Internat. Law Soc., So. Ill. U.-Carbondale Student Bar Assn., So. Ill. U.-Carbondale Law & Medicine Soc., Air and Space Smithsonian, Officers' Christian Fellowship, Airforce Assn., Air Force Edn. Soc., U.S. Capitol Hist. Soc., Calif. State U.-Fresno Alumni Orgn., West Coast Karate Assn., Assn. Air Force Missileers (assoc.), Sigma Nu (alumni advisor So. Ill. U.-Carbondale chpt., dist. comdr., div. comdr. Far West), Fed. Bar Assn., State Bar Calif., Lawyer-Pilots Bar Assn., Ground Launched Cruise Missile Hist. Found., Judge Adv. Assn. Republican. Methodist. Avocations: Karate, flying, scuba diving, sky diving, photography. Home: 1625 Open Field Loop Brandon FL 33510- E-mail: ninjaderek@aol.com.

HIRONO, MAZIE KEIKO, lieutenant governor; b. Fukushima, Japan, Nov. 3, 1947; arrived in U.S., 1955, naturalized, 1959; d. Laura Chie (Sato) H. BA, U. Hawaii, 1970; JD, Georgetown U., 1978. Dep. atty. gen., Honolulu, 1978-80; Shim, Tam, Kirimitsu & Naito, 1984-88; mem. Hawaii Ho. of Reps., Honolulu, 1980-94; lt. gov., 1994—. Chair Hawaii Policy Group, Nat. Commn. on Tchg. and Ams. Future, Govs. Task Force on Sci. and Tech. Bd. dirs. Nuuanu YMCA, Honolulu, 1982-84, Moiliili Cmty. Ctr., Honolulu, 1984; dep. chair Dem. Nat. Com., 1997. Mem. U.S. Supreme Ct. Bar, Hawaii Bar Assn., Phi Beta Kappa. Democrat. Office: State Capitol Lt Govs Office PO Box 3226 Honolulu HI 96801-3226 also: Office of Lt Gov State Capital 5th Fl Honolulu HI 96813 E-mail: ltgov@exec.state.hi.us.

HIRONS, WILLIAM BEACOM, retired chemical company executive; b. Wilmington, Del., Mar. 28, 1922; s. John Wilbur and Bernie Mae (Walls) H.; m. Eleanor R. Russell, July 21, 1945 (dec. July 1994); children: Molly, Allen; m. Marjorie M. Wright, Aug. 5, 1995. BA, Dartmouth Coll., 1946, MBA, 1947; grad., Goldey Beacom Coll., 1940. Bus. analyst, then mgr. bus. analysis E.I. DuPont DeNemours, Wilmington, 1947-59; treas. DuPont subsidiary, The Hague, The Netherlands, 1959-62; control supt. Nylon Plant, Martinsville, Va., 1962-64; mgr. European bus. analysis DuPont, Geneva, 1964-69, mng. dir. U.K. subsidiary London, 1969-79, asst. dir. Europe Wilmington, 1979-83; ret. Chmn. Sarasota Meml. Healthcare Found., 1999-2001. 1st lt. U.S. Army Air Force, 1943-45. Avocations: tennis, golf. Home: 375 Macewen Dr Osprey FL 34229-9281

HIROSE, AKIRA, physics educator, researcher; b. Kijimadaira, Nagano, Japan, Aug. 16, 1941; came to Can., 1971; s. Genji and Katsuyo (Yamada) H.; m. Kimiko Yamamoto, Feb. 4, 1969; children: Tadashi, Kyoko. B Engring., Yokohama (Japan) Nat. U., 1965, M Engring., 1967; PhD, U. Tenn., 1969; DSc, U. Sask., 1994. Mem. rsch. sect. Oak Ridge (Tenn.) Nat. Lab., 1969-71; rsch. scientist U. Sask., Saskatoon, Can., 1971-77, assoc. prof., 1977-79, prof. physics, 1979—. Corr. Plasma Phys. Controlled Fusion, 1984—; chmn. Internat. Conf. on Plasma Sci., Saskatoon, 1986; vis. prof. FOM Inst. Plasma fysica, The Netherlands, 1989, Tokyo Met. Inst. Tech., 1996; disting. fgn. rschr. Japan Atomic Energy Rsch. Inst., 1995. Author: Introduction to Wave Phenomena, 1985; contbr. numerous articles to profl. jours. Recipient IEEE Merit award Nuclear and Plasma Scis. Soc., 1993, Disting. Rschr.'s award U. Sask., 1995, Plasma Sci. and Applications award IEEE Nuclear Plasma Sci. Soc., 1998, Can. Rsch. Chair, 2001; Fulbright scholar, 1967; Nat. Sci. Engring. Rsch. Coun. grantee, 1977; Japan Soc. Promotion Sci. rsch. fellow, 1984. Fellow: IEEE (assoc. editor Trans. Plasma Sci. 1983—), Acad. Sci. Royal Soc. Can., Am. Phys. Soc.; mem.: Can. Assn. Physicists (chmn. divsn. plasma physics 1981—82, 1994—95, divsn. assoc. editor Phys. Rev. Letter 1999—2002), European Acad. Sci. Home: 2914 East View Saskatoon SK Canada S7J 3H9 Office: U Sask Dept Physics & Engring Phys Saskatoon SK Canada S7N 5E2 E-mail: akira.hirose@usask.ca.

HIROSE, HITOSHI, medical doctor, cardiovascular surgeon; b. Narita City, Chiba, Japan, Dec. 8, 1965; s. Kohsen Hirose and Kin (Kobayashi) H.; m Rika Akiyama, Apr. 4, 1992. MD, Nagasaki Univ. Sch. Medicine, Nagasaki, Japan, 1990. Cert. Japanese Bd. Surgery 2001. Surg. resident St. Luke's Roosevelt Hosp. Ctr., N.Y., NY, 1992—95, vascular surgery rsch. fellow, 1995—96; faculty mem. Nagasaki U. Hosp., Nagasaki, Japan, 1997—98; staff surgeon Shin-Tokyo Hosp., Matsudo City, Japan, 1998—2000; chief cardiovasc. surgery Kobari Gen. Hosp., Noda City, Japan, 2000—02; clin. assoc. dept. cardiothoracic surgery Cleve. Clinic Found., 2002—. Mem. editl. bd. Heart Surgery Forum, Med. Sci. Monitor, Jour. Am. Coll. Angiology; contbr. articles to profl. jours. Fellow ACP, Am. Coll. Angiology, Internat. Coll. Surgeons, Internat. Coll. Angiology, Internat. Coll. Thoracic Surgery, Am. Chest Physician; mem. Internat. Surg. Soc., Internat. Soc. Artificial Organs, Asian Soc. Thoracic Surgeons, European Soc. Cardiothoracic Surgery, Soc. Thoracic Surgeons, Internat. Cardiovascular Soc. Home: 2300 Overlook Rd # 312 Cleveland OH 44106 Office: Cleve Clinic Found Dept Thoracic and Cardiovasc Surg 9500 Euclid Ave F25 Cleveland OH 44195 Home Fax: 216-707-9445.

HIROSE, TERUO TERRY, surgeon, educator; b. Tokyo, Jan. 20, 1926; s. Yohei and Seiko (Ogushi) H.; m. Tomiko Kodama, June 1, 1976; 1 son, George Philamore. BS, Tokyo Coll., Japan, 1944; MD, Chiba U., Japan, 1948, PhD, 1958. Diplomate Am. Bd. Surgery, Am. Bd. Thoracic Surgery. Intern Chiba U. Hosp., Japan, 1948-49, resident in surgery, 1949-52; practice medicine specializing in surgery Chiba, Japan, 1952-53; resident in surgery Am. Hosp., Chgo., 1954; resident in thoracic surgery Hahnemann Med. Coll., Phila., 1955-56; chief of surgery Tsushimi Hosp., Hagi, Japan, 1958-59; tchg. fellow surgery NY Med. Coll., NYC, 1959-60; research fellow advanced cardiovascular surgery Hahnemann Hosp., Phila., 1959; asst. prof. surgery Chiba U., Japan, 1959; instr. NY Med. Coll., NYC, 1961-62, resident in thoracic surgery, 1961-62; sr. attending surgeon St. Barnabas Hosp., NYC, 1965-81; pvt. practice NYC, 1965-89, 1965-89; chief vascular surgery Union Hosp., Bronx, NY, 1966-67; attending surgeon Flower and Fifth Ave Hosp., NYC, 1973-80; clin. prof. surgery NY Med. Coll., NY, 1974-89; dir. cardiovasc. lab. St. Barnabas Hosp., NYC, 1975-84; attending surgeon Jewish Hosp. Med. Center, Bklyn., 1976-80, St. Vincent Hosp., NYC, 1976-88, Mamonides Hosp., Bklyn., 1976-78, Passaic Gen. Hosp., 1977-88, Westchester County Hosp., NY, 1977-78, Yonkers Profl. Hosp., NY, 1978-79, Westchester Sq. Hosp., 1978-84, Yonkers Gen. Hosp., Yonkers, NY, 1980-89, St. Joseph Hosp., Yonkers, NY, 1980-89; dir. KPMG Health Care, Japan, 1997—2001; chmn., prof. dept. head, health care admin. Shumei U., Tokyo, 1999; chmn., pres. Japanese Assn. for Healthcare Adminstrs., 2002—. Author: (in Japanese) A Chaos of American Medicine, 1987, Japanese Doctor, 1987, Where American Medicine Is Going, 1988, Major Surgery Without Blood Transfusion, 1990, Problems and Solutions of American Medicine, 1991, Warning for Modern Medical Science (New Medical Ethics), 1992, Comparative Studies of Medical System in the World, 1992, The Changing Face of Geriatrics, 1994, Monologue of Japanese American Physician, 1995, Environmental Medicine, 1998, Japan! Do Not Follow American Health Care System, 1998, Quality of Life in Modern Medicine, 1998, Medicine About Life and Death, 1998, 99, Why AIDS Can Not Be Conquered, 1999, Mechanism of Human Body, 2000, Comparison of Healthcare Systems Between U.S.A. and Japan, 2000, Medicine of Death, 2000, Lifestyle Related Medicine and Cutting Edge Technique, 2001, Alternative Medicine, 2001, Thanatology, 2000, Protect Japanese Health Care System By Health Care Reform, 2002, Basic and Practice of Health Care Administration, 2002, Better Understanding of Physician and Hospital, 2003; author 10 med. monographs, 1968-80; editor Japanese Med. Planner Ltd.; contbr. over 900 articles to profl. jours. Recipient Hektoen Bronze medal AMA, 1965, Gold medal, 1971. Fellow: NY Acad. Medicine, Internat. Coll. Surgeons, Am. Coll. Cardiology, Am. Coll. Chest Physicians, Am. Coll. Angiology; mem.: Japanese Assn. Health Care Admnis. (chmn., pres.), Japan PEN Club, Am. Writers Assn., Am. Fedn. Clin. Rsch., Am. Geriatric Soc., Internat. Cardiovasc. Soc., Pan Pacific Surg. Assn., NY Soc. Thoracic Surgery, Am. Assn. Thoracic Surgery. Achievements include invention of single pass low prime oxygenator; pioneer aortocoronary direct bypass surgery, open heart surgery without blood transfusion. *One should respect another's religion or creed and offer assistance regardless of whether or not one is in agreement with the other's belief, provided that belief harms no other.*

HIRSCH, ANN ULLMAN, retired academic administrator; b. N.Y.C., Feb. 12, 1929; d. Julian S. and Louise (Levien) Ullman; m. James E. Galton, Aug. 22, 1948 (div. 1962); children: Beth, Jean; m. David I. Hirsch, Mar. 22, 1963; stepchildren: Peter, Amanda. BS, NYU, 1950; postgrad., Queens Coll., Flushing, N.Y., 1955-57. Music tchr. Herricks (N.Y.) Sch., 1950-52, East Meadow (N.Y.) Pub. Schs., 1952-53; exec. dir. Ea. Suffolk Sch. Music, Riverhead/Southampton, N.Y., 1977 88. Self-employed piano tchr., N.Y., 1950-95; dir. music edn. Unitarian Sunday Sch., Freeport, N.Y., 1956-63; singer Oratorio Socs., Levittown and Bridgehampton, N.Y., 1950-85, L.I. Philharm. Chorus, Westbury, N.Y., 1989—; violinist Sound Symphony, Shoreham, Wading River, N.Y., 1980—, orch. pianist, 1980—. Author: Basic Guide to the Teaching of Piano, 1974. Mem. Arts in Edn. Task Force, BOCES, Westhampton, NY, 1977—87; planning mem., panelist Nat. Guild Cmty. Schs. of the Arts, 1980—88; tchr. Literacy Vols. Am., Riverhead, Mastic, NY, 1988—91; bd. mem. LI Masterworks Chorus, Commack, NY, 1992—2000. Named East End Woman of Yr. in Edn., East End Mag., Suffolk County, N.Y., 1979. Mem.: LWV, Southampton Twp. Wildfowl Assn., Bay Area Friends of the Fine Arts, Westhampton Beach Hist. Soc., Peconic Land Trust. Avocations: reading, sewing, walking, golfing, photography. Home: PO Box 304 Remsenburg NY 11960-0304

HIRSCH, ARTHUR (BUZZ HIRSCH), film producer, educator; b. Evanston, Ill., July 26, 1944; s. Arthur R. and Ruth (Hammond) H.; 1 child. BA, Washington U., St. Louis, 1968; MA, Columbia Coll., 1983; MFA, UCLA, 1983. Writer, dir. ind. films, Chgo., 1972—; prodr. ind. films L.A., N.Y.C., 1980—; prof. of film, dir. film prodn. program Washington U., St. Louis, 1994—. Pres. Hirsch/Stovall Entertainment, L.A., 1985—. Writer, dir. (film) Matinee, 1972 (7 internat. film festival awards); prodr. (film) Silkwood, 1983. Nominee 5 Academy awards Academy Motion Picture Art & Scis., 1984, 5 Golden Globe awards Fgn. Press Assn., 1984. Mem. AAUP, U. Film and Video Assn. Episcopalian. Avocations: sculpture, anthropology, travel, reading, writing. Office: Washington U One Brookings Dr Saint Louis MO 63130

HIRSCH, BARRY, lawyer; b. N.Y.C., Mar. 19, 1933; s. Emanuel M. and Minnie (Levenson) H.; m. Myra Seiden, June 13, 1963; children: Victor Terry II, Neil Charles Seiden, Nancy Elizabeth. BSBA, U. Mo., 1954; JD, U. Mich., 1959; LL.M., N.Y. U., 1964. Bar: N.Y. bar 1960, Assoc., then partner firm Seligson & Morris, N.Y.C., 1960-69; v.p., sec., gen. counsel dir. B.T.B. Corp., 1969-71; v.p., sec., gen. counsel Loews Corp. (and subsidiaries), 1971-86, sr. v.p., sec., gen. counsel, 1986—. Bds. dirs. Neuberger and Berman Funds. Served to 1st lt. AUS, 1954-56. Mem. ABA, Assn. of Bar of City of N.Y., N.Y. State Bar Assn., Zeta Beta Tau, Phi Delta Phi. Home: 1010 5th Ave New York NY 10028-0130 Office: Loews Corp 667 Madison Ave Fl 8 New York NY 10021-8087 E-mail: bhirsch@loews.com.

HIRSCH, BARRY T. economist, educator; b. Nov. 28, 1949; PhD, U. Va., 1977. Instr. U. Va., Charlottesville, 1975—75; asst. prof. U. N.C., Greensboro, 1976—79, assoc. prof., 1979—83, prof., 1983—90, Fla. State U., Tallahassee, 1990—99, disting. rsch. prof., 1999; E.M. Stevens disting. prof. Trinity U., San Antonio, 2000—. Vis. assoc. prof. U. Ky., Lexington, 1981—82; rsch. assoc. Pepper Inst. Aging and Pub. Policy, 1993—99; dist. rsch. prof. Fla. State U., Tallahassee, 1999. Mem.: Econometric Soc., So. Econ. Assn., Soc. Labor Economists, Am. Econ. Assn. Office: Trinity Univ One Trinity Pl San Antonio TX 78212 Office Fax: 210-999-7255. E-mail: bhirsch@trinity.edu.

HIRSCH, BETTE G(ROSS), college administrator, foreign language educator; b. N.Y.C., May 5, 1942; d. Alfred E. and Gladys (Natburn) Gross; m. Edward Raden Silverblatt, Aug. 16, 1964 (div. Feb. 1975); children: Julia Nadine, Adam Edward; m. Joseph Ira Hirsch, Jan. 21, 1978; stepchildren: Hillary, Michelle, Michael. BA with honors, U. Rochester, 1964; MA, Case Western Res. U., 1967, PhD, 1971. Instr. and head French dept. Cabrillo Coll., Aptos, Calif., 1973-90, 2003—, divsn. chair fgn. langs. and comms. divsn., 1990-95, interim dir. student devel., 1995-96, dean of instrn., transfer and distance edn., 1996—2003. Mem. steering com. Santa Cruz County Fgn. Lang. Educators Assn., 1981-86; mem. liaison com. fgn. langs. Articulation Coun. Calif., 1982-84, sec., 1983-84, chmn., 1984-85; workshop presenter, 1982—; vis. prof. French Mills Coll., Oakland, Calif., 1983; mem. fgn. lang. model curriculum stds. adv. com. State Calif., 1984; instr. San Jose (Calif.) State U., summers 1984, 85; reader Ednl. Testing Svc. Advanced Placement French Examination, 1988, 89; peer reviewer for div. edn. programs, NEH, Washington, 1990, 91, 93; grant evaluator, NEH, 1995; mem. fgn. lang. adv. bd. The Coll. Bd., N.Y.C., 1986-91. Author: The Maxims in the Novels of Duclos, 1973; co-author (with Chantal Thompson) Ensuite, 1989, 93, 98, 2003, Moments Litteraires, 1992 (with Chantal Thompson and Elaine Phillips) Mais Oui! workbook, lab. manual, video manual, 1996, 2000; contbr. revs. and articles to profl. jours. Pres. Loma Vista Elem. Sch. PTA, Palo Alto, Calif., 1978-79; bd. dirs. United Way Stanford, Palo Alto, 1985-90, mem. allocations com., 1988, bd. dirs. Cabrillo Music Festival, 1996—, sec., 1998, v.p., 2000-2002; bd. dirs. Cmty. TV of Santa Cruz County, 1997-99, vice chair, 1997-98. Grantee NEH, 1980-81, USIA, 1992; Govt. of France scholar, 1982, 2003. Mem.: MLA (mem. adv. com. on fgn. langs. and lits. 1995—2000, chair 1999—2000, com. on info. tech. 2001—, chair 2003—), Assn. Depts. Fgn. Langs. (exec. com. 1985—88, pres. 1988), Assn. Calif. C.C. Adminstrs. Democrat. Jewish. Avocations: traveling, reading, antique collecting, gourmet eating and cooking. Home: 4149 Georgia Ave Palo Alto CA 94306-3813 Office: Cabrillo College 6500 Soquel Dr Aptos CA 95003-3194 E-mail: behirsch@cabrillo.edu. *Treat life like a work of art in progress. Strive for the creative, the exceptional. Do it all with style.*

HIRSCH, CARL HERBERT, retired manufacturing company executive; b. Pontiac, Mich., Aug. 24, 1934; s. Robert Reynolds and Charlotte (Zeiss) H.; m. Anne Louise Dearing, June 27, 1959; children: Jeffrey Todd, Gregory Scott. BS in Mech. Engring., U. Mich., 1957; M in Indsl. Engring., U. Toledo, 1962, MBA, 1967; grad. Advanced Mgmt. Program, Harvard U., 1974. Registered profl. engr., Mich. Product engr. Babcock & Wilcox Co., Barberton, Ohio, 1959-60, Dana Corp., Toledo, 1960-67, mfg. mgr. Perfect Cir. divsn., 1967-69, pres. C.A. Danaven subs. Valencia, Venezuela, 1969-72, v.p. L.Am. Dana Internat. divsn. Toledo, 1972-73, v.p., gen. mgr. Spicer Clutch divsn. Ft. Wayne, Ind., 1973-75, Spicer Universal Joint divsn. Toledo, 1975-76, group v.p., 1977-78, exec. v.p. vehicular, 1979-80, v.p. corp. planning, 1980-85, sr. v.p., 1985-91, exec. v.p., 1991-95; pres. Dana Internat., Toledo, 1996-98; ret., 1998. Instr. Earlham Coll., 1967-69, U. Toledo, 1962-65; mem. Mfg. Alliance for Productivity and Innovation, Global Bus. Coun.; industry adv. com. Coll. Engring., U. Mich.; adv. com. Ctr. Internat. Bus. Edn. U. Mich.; bd. dirs. Brazeway Corp., Adrian, Mich., IBH corp., Caracas, Venezuela. Bd. dirs. ATA Found., World Trade Ctr., Toledo, Toledo Area coun. Boy Scouts Am., N.W. Ohio Jr. Achievement, Child Abuse Prevention Ctr., Toledo Zool. Soc., Maumee Valley Country Day Sch., Sta. WGTE-PBS. Lt. USN, 1957-59. Mem. Nat. Mgmt. Assn., Sigma Alpha Epsilon. Presbyterian. Home: 19 Oyster Landing Ln Hilton Head Island SC 29928

HIRSCH, DANIEL OREN, nonprofit nuclear policy organization executive; b. Oakland, Calif., Feb. 12, 1950; s. Werner Zvi and Hilde Esther Hirsch. BA, Harvard U., 1968—72. Pres. Com. to Bridge the Gap, LA, 1972—; lectr. UCLA, 1975—83, U. Calif., Santa Cruz, 1983—89, 2000; dir. Adlai Stevenson Program on Nuc. Policy, U. Calif., Santa Cruz, 1984—89; energy and environment fellow Fedn. Am. Scientists, Washington, 1989—89. Co-chair Santa Susana Field Lab. Adv. Panel, LA, 1992—; nuc. policy cons. Govtl. and Non-governmental Organizations, 1986—. Contbr. articles to jour. Expert witness Congl., Legislative, and agy. nuc. hearings, 1980—2002. Recipient Environ. Leadership Award, Calif. League Conservation Voters, 1999, Jack Jennings Meml. Award, So. Calif. Fedn. Scientists, 1997. Achievements include research in Nuclear Waste And Reactor Safety Issues, Approaches To Reducing Risks Of Nuclear Terrorism And Proliferation. Avocations: hiking, organic gardening. Office: Committee to Bridge the Gap 1637 Butler Ave Ste 203 Los Angeles CA 90025

HIRSCH, EDWARD MARK, poet, English language educator, foundation administrator; b. Chgo, Jan. 20, 1950; s. Kurt and Irma (Ginsburg) H.; m. Janet Landay, May 29, 1977. BA, Grinnell Coll., 1972; PhD, U. Pa., 1978. Asst. prof. Wayne State U., Detroit, 1978-82, assoc. prof., 1982-85, U. Houston, 1985-87, prof. English, 1987—; pres. John Simon Guggenheim Meml. Found., 2003—. Author: (poems) For the Sleepwalkers, 1981 (Lavan Younger Poets award 1985), Wild Gratitude, 1986 (Nat. Book Critics Cir. award), The Night Parade, 1989, Earthly Measures, 1994, On Love, 1998, How to Read a Poem and Fall in Love with Poetry, 1999, Responsive Reading, 1999, The Demon and the Angel: Searching for the Source of Artistic Inspiration, 2002, Lay Back the Darkness, 2003; editor: Transforming Vision: Writers on Art, 1994. Nat. Endowments for Arts Creative Writing fellow, 1982, Guggenheim fellow, 1985; recipient Tex. Inst. of Arts and Letters award, 1987, Lit. award Am. Acad. Arts Letters, 1998; recipient Prix de Rome, 1988, Lyndhurst prize, 1994-96; MacArthur fellow, 1998. Office: John Simon Guggenheim Meml Found 90 Park Ave New York NY 10016

HIRSCH, ERIC DONALD, JR., English language educator, educational reformer; b. Memphis, Mar. 22, 1928; s. Eric Donald and Leah (Aschaffenburg) H.; m. Mary Monteith Pope, June 15, 1958; children: Eric, John, Frederick, Elizabeth. BA, Cornell U., 1950; MA, Yale U., 1955, PhD (Fulbright fellow), 1957; LittD (hon.), Williams Coll., 1989, Rhodes Coll., 1993, Rollins Coll., 1994, Marietta Coll., 1997. Instr. Yale, 1956-61, asst. prof. English, 1961-64, assoc. prof., 1964-66; prof. U. Va., Charlottesville, 1966—, chmn. dept. English, 1968-71, 81-83, dir. composition, 1971—, Kenan prof. English, 1973—, Linden Kent prof. English, 1989-94, Univ. prof. edn. and humanities, 1994; founder, pres. Core Knowledge Found., Charlottesville, 1986—. Bd. dirs. U. Press; lectr. in field; supervising com. English Inst., 1972-74; mem. nat. adv. coun. N.Y. Regent's Competency Tests in Writing, 1979; advisor Nat. Coun. Ednl. Rsch., 1983; bd. dirs. Founds. Literacy Project, 1985—; pres. Cultural Literacy Found., 1987, Core Knowledge Found., 1990; dir. Albert Shanker Inst., 1997—. Author: Wordsworth and Schelling: A Typological Study of Romanticism, 1960, Innocence and Experience: An Introduction to Blake, 1964 (Explicator award), Validity in Interpretation, 1967, The Aims of Interpretation, 1976, The Philosophy of Composition, 1977, Cultural Literacy: What Every American Needs to Know, 1987; co-author: A Dictionary of Cultural Literacy, 1988; editor: A First Dictionary of Cultural Literacy, 1989, The Core Knowledge Series, Book I: What First Graders Need to Know, 1991, Book II: What Second Graders Need to Know, 1991, Book III: What Third Graders Need to Know, 1992, Book IV: What Fourth Graders Need to Know, 1992, Book V: What Fifth Graders Need to Know, 1993, Book VI: What Sixth Graders Need to Know, 1993, The Schools We Need and Why We Don't Have Them, 1996; mem. adv. bd. Jour. Basic Writing, Blake Studies, Critical Inquiry, Genre New Lit. History, Lit. in Performance; contbr. articles to profl. jours. Pres. Coalition for Core Curriculum, 1989—. Served with USNR, 1950-52. Recipient Fordham award 2003; Morse fellow, 1961-62, Guggenheim fellow, 1964-65, sr. fellow NEH, 1971, 80-81, fellow Center for Humanities Wesleyan U., 1973, fellow Council Humanities Princeton U., 1976, fellow Center for Advanced Study in Behavioral Scis., 1980-81, fellow Humanities Research Ctr., Australian Nat. U., 1982; Bateson lectr. Oxford U., 1983 Fellow Internat. Acad. Edn. in Royal Acad. Sci. Lit. and Arts (Brussels); mem. Am. Acad. Arts and Scis. (supervisory com. 1981-86), MLA, Byron Soc., Am. Fedn. Tchrs. (Biennial Quest award 1997). Home: 2006 Pine Top Rd Charlottesville VA 22903-1233 E-mail: edh9k@virginia.edu.

HIRSCH, GEORGE AARON, publishing executive; b. N.Y.C., June 21, 1934; s. George J. and Sylvia (Epstein) H.; m. Shay Yandell Scrivner; children: David Aaron, William George; stepchildren: Ian Gregory Scrivner, Sean Gabriel Scrivner. AB magna cum laude, Princeton U., 1956; MBA, Harvard U., 1962. With Time-Life Internat., 1962-67; founding pub., pres. New York Mag., N.Y.C., 1967-71; chmn., pres., CEO New Times Comm. Corp., N.Y.C., 1973-79; founding pub. New Times mag., N.Y.C., 1973-79, The Runner Mag., N.Y.C., 1978-87; v.p., pub. Runner's World Mag., 1987—2000, worldwide pub., 2000—02, worldwide pub. emeritus, 2003—; group pub. Rodale Active Network, 1987—97; pub. dir. Men's Health mag., 1987—2002; dir. internat. mags. Rodale Press, 1995—2002. Host "The Runner's Corner", ESPN Sports Ctr., 1983—84; TV sports commentator Olympic Games, 1984, 88, 92; bd. dirs. Motor Press-Rodale, Stuttgart, Germany, Mondadori-Rodale, Milan. A founder N.Y.C. Marathon, 1976; hon. mem. exec. com. alumni coun. Princeton U.; Dem. candidate for 15th Congl. Dist., N.Y., 1986; del. Dem. Nat. Conv., 1988. With USNR, 1957-60. Mem. Mag. Pubs. Assn. (chmn. internat. com.), Century Assn. Club. Office: Runner's World 733 3rd Ave Fl 15 New York NY 10017-3204 E-mail: george.hirsch@rodale.com.

HIRSCH, GILAH YELIN, artist, writer; b. Montreal, Quebec, Can., Aug. 24, 1944; came to US, 1963; d. Ezra and Shulamis (Borodensky) Y. BA, U. Calif., Berkeley, 1967; MFA, UCLA, 1970. Prof. of art Calif. State U., Dominguez Hills, L.A., 1973—. Adj. prof. Internat. Coll., Guild of Tutors, LA, 1980-87, Union Grad. Sch., Cin., 1990. Founding mem. Santa Monica (Calif.) Art Bank, 1983-85; bd. dir. Dorland Mountain Colony, Temecula, Calif., 1984-88. Recipient Disting. Artist award Calif. State U., 1985, Found. Rsch. award,

1988-89, 97-98; grantee Nat. Endowment for the Arts, 1985; Dorland Mountain Colony fellow, 1981-84, Banff Ctr. for the Arts fellow, Can., 1985, MacDowell Colony fellow, NH, 1987, Dorland Mountain Arts Colony fellow, 2003; named artist-in-residence RIM Inst., Payson, Ariz., 1989-90, Tamarind Inst. Lithography, Albuquerque, 1973, Rockefeller Bellagio Ctr., Italy, 1992, Tyrone Guthrie Ctr. for Arts, Annamahkerrig, Ireland, 1993, Creative Rsch. award Sally Canova Rsch. Scholarship and Creative Activities awards program, 1997-99, 2003; Class Found. grant, 2003. Office: Calif State Univ Dominguez Hills 1000 E Victoria St Carson CA 90747-0001 E-mail: gilah@linkline.com.

HIRSCH, GORDON, British literature educator; b. Norwich, N.Y., May 15, 1943; m. Louella Elizabeth Edwards, Mar. 30, 1972. BA, Cornell U., 1965; MA, U. Calif., Berkeley, 1967, PhD, 1971. Prof. English, U. Minn., Mpls., 1970—, dir. honors div. Coll. Liberal Arts, 1989—2001. Co-editor: Dr. Jekyll and Mr. Hyde After 100 Years, 1988; contbr. articles to profl. jours. Office: U Minn English Dept 207 Church St SE Minneapolis MN 55455-0134

HIRSCH, HARVEY STUART, psychiatrist; b. N.Y.C., Nov. 3, 1950; s. Leoanrd Samuel and Roberta Joan (Dreyer) H.; m. Linda Karen Green, Sept. 27, 1981; children: Daniel, Carly. BA, Columbia U., 1972; MD, Mt. Sinai Med. Sch., N.Y.C., 1976. Diplomate Am. Bd. Psychiatry and Neurology, Nat. Bd. Med. Examiners, 1976. Intern Mt. Sinai Hosp., N.Y.C., 1976, attending physician, 1979—; clin. instr. Mt. Sinai Med. Sch., N.Y.C., 1979—; resident Mt. Sinai Hosp., N.Y.C., 1977-79, chief resident, 1979—. Recipient Ams. Top Psychiatrists, Consumers Rsch. Coun. of Am., Wash., D.C., 2003. Mem. Am. Psychiat. Assn., Cum Laude Soc., Le Club (N.Y.C.), Phi Beta Kappa. Avocations: tennis champion, swimming champion. Office: 1185 Park Ave New York NY 10128-1308

HIRSCH, HORST EBERHARD, business consultant; b. Woelsendorf, Fed. Republic Germany, July 26, 1933; came to U.S., 1984; s. Albert and Emilie (Eberhardt) H.; m. Helga G. Gruber, May 2, 1961; children: Manon K., Fabiane M., Erin A. Diploma in chemistry, Tech. U. Karlsruhe, Fed. Republic Germany, 1959, D in Chem. Tech., 1961. Postdoctoral fellow NRC of Can., 1961-62; research and devel. engr., mgr. Cominco Ltd., Trail, B.C., Can., 1962-84; pres., CEO Cominco Electronic Materials Inc., Spokane, Wash., 1984-88; pres. Johnson Matthey Electronics N.Am., Spokane, 1989-91, MSM (Metals and Semiconductor Materials), 1991—; vis. exec. IESC (Internat. Exec. Svc. Corps), 1992, field assoc., 1993—; co-founder, CM, HT Metals LLC, 2001—. Mem. bd. mgmt. B.C. Rsch. Coun., Vancouver, 1980-84; senate U. B.C., Vancouver, 1981-85; mem. adv. com. Wash. Tech. Ctr., 1992-94. Contbr. articles on chemistry and metallurgy to profl. pubs., chpts. to books; patentee in field. Recipient Excellence in Innovation award Fed. Govt. Can., 1985. Mem. Soc. German Mining and Metall. Engrs. Lutheran. Avocations: reading, skiing, swimming, golfing. E-mail: zollegeg@aol.com.

HIRSCH, JEFFREY ALLAN, lawyer; b. Chgo., June 14, 1950; m. Lennie Sue Henderson, June 16, 1979; children: Lea, Ashley. BSBA, U. Fla., 1972, JD with honors, 1975. Bar: Fla. 1975, U.S. Dist. Ct. (so. and mid. dists.) Fla. 1975. Assoc. Swann & Glass, Coral Gables, Fla., 1975-76, Glass, Schultz, Weinstein & Moss, Coral Gables, 1976-80; ptnr. Holland & Knight, Ft. Lauderdale, Fla., 1980-93; prin. shareholder Greenberg, Traurig, P.A., Ft. Lauderdale, Fla., 1993—. Exec. dir. Govtl. Research Ctr., Gainesville, Fla., 1975. Active Leadership Broward, Ft. Lauderdale, 1986—, Leadership Fla., 1994—. Mem. ABA, Fla. Bar Assn., Broward County Bar Assn. Avocations: reading, travel. Office: Greenberg Traurig PA 401 E Las Olas Blvd Ste 2000 Fort Lauderdale FL 33301-2278 E-mail: hirschj@gtlaw.com.

HIRSCH, JEROME S. lawyer; BA in Econs., SUNY, Binghamton, 1970; JD, Fordham U., 1974. Bar: N.Y. Assoc. Skadden, Arps, Slate, Meagher & Flom, N.Y.C., 1974-81, ptnr., 1982—. Mem. ABA, N.Y. State Bar Assn., Assn. of Bar of City of N.Y. Office: Skadden Arps Slate Meagher & Flom 4 Times Sq New York NY 10036-6595

HIRSCH, JUDD, actor; b. N.Y.C., Mar. 15, 1935; s. Joseph Sidney and Sally (Kitzis) H.; m. Bonni Chalkin, Dec. 24, 1992. BS in Physics, CCNY, 1960. Broadway appearances in Barefoot in the Park, 1966, Knock Knock, 1976 (Drama Desk award for best featured actor), Chapter Two, 1977-78, Talley's Folly, 1980 (Tony nomination), I'm Not Rappaport, 1985-86, (Tony award for best actor in play 1986, Outer Critics Circle award, 1986), Conversations with My Father, 1992 (Tony award for best actor in play 1992, Outer Critics Circle award, 1992), A Thousand Clowns, 1996, Art, 1998, I'm Not Rappaport, 2002; off-Broadway appearances in On the Necessity of Being Polygamous, 1963, Scuba Duba, 1967-69, King of the United States, 1972, Mystery Play, 1972, Hot L Baltimore, 1973, Prodigal, 1973, Knock Knock, 1975, Talley's Folly, 1979 (Obie award), The Seagull, 1983, I'm Not Rappaport, 1985, Below the Belt, 1996; regional appearences include Theater for Living Arts, Phila., 1969-70, Line of Least Existence, Harry Noon and Night, The Recruiting Officer, Annenberg Ctr., Phila., 1971, Hough in Blazes, 1971, Conversations with My Father, Seattle Repertory, 1991, L.A., 1993, Scarborough, Eng., 1994, London, 1995, Death of a Salesman, Chapel Hill, N.C., 1994, Robbers, Long Wharf Theater, 1995, Death of a Salesman Manitoba Theatre Ctr., Winnipeg and Royal Alexandra Theatre, Toronto, 1997, Art, London, 1999, 2001; stock and tour appearances in A Thousand Clowns, Threepenny Opera, Fantastiks, Woodstock, N.Y., 1964, Peterpat, Houston and Ft. Worth, 1970, Harvey, Chgo., 1971, And Miss Reardon Drinks a Little, Palm Beach, Fla., 1972, I'm Not Rappaport, nat. tour, 1986-87, Art, nat. tour, 1999-2000; TV appearances include The Keegans, 1975, Medical Story, 1975, Delvecchio series, 1976-77, Rhoda, 1977, Taxi series, 1978-83 (Emmy award for best actor in a comedy series, 1981, 1983), Noel Edmunds Saturday Road Show, 1990 (Eng.), Dear John series (Golden Globe award 1988), 1988-92, George and Leo, 1997; TV movies include The Law, 1974, Fear on Trial, 1975, The Legend of Valentino, 1975, The Halloween That Almost Wasn't, 1979, Sooner or Later, 1979, Marriage Is Alive and Well, 1980, First Steps, 1985, Brotherly Love, 1985, The Great Escape-Untold Story, 1988, She Said No, 1990, Betrayal of Trust, 1993, Color of Justice, 1997, Rocky Marciano, 1999; films include King of the Gypsies, 1978, Ordinary People (nominated Acad. Award), 1980, Without a Trace, 1983, Teachers, 1984, The Goodbye People, 1984, Running on Empty, 1988, Independence Day, 1996, Man On the Moon, 1999, A Beautiful Mind, 2001; dir. Squaring the Circle, 1962, Not Enough Rope, 1973, Talley's Folly, 1981, Art, 2000-01. Mem. Acad. Motion Picture Arts and Scis., Acad. TV Arts and Scis., Screen Actors Guild, Actors Equity Assn., AFTRA, SSDC. Office: care J Wolfe Provident Fin Mgmt 10345 W Olympic Blvd Los Angeles CA 90064-2548

HIRSCH, JULES, physician, scientist; b. N.Y.C., Apr. 6, 1927; Student, Rutgers U., 1943—45; MD, U. Tex., 1948; DSc (hon.), SUNY, 1988. Intern pathology and medicine Duke Hosp., NC, 1948—50; from asst. resident to resident coll. medicine SUNY, Syracuse, 1950—52; asst. prof., assoc. physician Rockefeller U., N.Y.C., 1954—60, assoc. prof., physician, 1960—67, prof., sr. physician, 1967—. Sherman Fairchild prof. Rockefeller U., 1988—98, emeritus, 1998—; sr. physician Rockefeller U. Hosp., 1967—, physician-in-chief, 1992—96, emeritus, 1996—. Recipient Robert H. Herman award, 1994, McCollum award, 1984. Fellow: ACP, Royal Coll. Physicians Edinburgh; mem.: Harvey Soc., Am. Fedn. Clin. Rsch., Assn. Am. Physicians, Am. Soc. Clin. Nutrition, Am. Soc. Clin. Investigation, Inst. of Medicine of NAS, AAAS, Assn. for Patient Oriented Rsch. (founding mem.). Achievements include research in obesity, human behavior, internal medicine, biochemistry and physiology of lipids, lipid metabolism and nutrition. Office: Rockefeller U 1230 York Ave New York NY 10021-6399 E-mail: hirsch@mail.rockefeller.edu.

HIRSCH, JUNE SCHAUT, priest; b. Green Bay, Wis., Sept. 30, 1925; d. Clifford Charles and Eleanor Josephine (Arts) Schaut; m. Marshall E. Gilette, Jan. 23, 1946 (div. 1974); children: Ronald Leigh Gilette, Patrick Allen Gilette, Vicki Jeanne Baumann; m. Hubert L. Hirsch, Nov. 7, 1975 (dec. Mar. 2002). Student, St. Mary's Sch. Nursing, Rochester, Minn., 1973—75, U. Wis., Sheboygan, 1974-75. Cert. med. asst. Med. asst. James W. Faulkner, M.D., Phoenix, 1953-56; med. office mgr. Edward E. Houfek, M.D., Sheboygan, 1956-75; med. office cons. Profl. Mgmt. Inc., Milw., 1975-77; office mgr., adminstrv. asst. Schroeder & Holt Archs. Ltd., Milw., 1977-90; vol. chaplain St. Camillus Health Ctr., Milw., 1991—, Children's Hosp. and Froedent Meml. Hosp., Milw., 1991-95; staff chaplain Froedert Meml. Hosp., 1995—. Instr. med. asst. program Lake Shore Tech., 1975—76. Mem.: Lake Shore Med. Assts. (mem. exec. bd. 1959—75), Am. Assn. Med. Assts. (nat. trustee 1963—66), Wis. Soc. Med. Assts. (life; mem. exec. bd. 1975—89), Nat. Assn. Cath. Chaplains (cert.). Republican. Roman Catholic. Home: 10200 W Bluemound Rd Apt 918 Milwaukee WI 53226-4372 Office: Froedtert Meml Luth Hosp 9200 W Wisconsin Ave Milwaukee WI 53226-3522

HIRSCH, LARRY JOSEPH, retired retail executive, lawyer; b. Boston, July 1, 1938; s. Samuel and Anne (Rossman) H.; m. Kay Pollock, Mar. 16, 1974. BA, Syracuse U., 1962; JD, Suffolk U., Boston, 1968; grad. gemologist, Gem Inst. Am., Los Angeles, 1981. Bar: Mass. 1968, R.I. 1968, Fla. 1970. Mgr. Vality Dept. Store, Groton, Conn., 1962—63; asst. area dir. Am. Jewish Com., Miami, Fla., 1968—69; asst. city atty. City of Miami, Fla., 1969—71; atty Feuer & Feuer, Miami, Fla., 1971—74, Turano & Turano, Westerly, RI, 1974—78; asst. town solicitor Town of Westerly, RI, 1975—76; pres. Westerly Jewelry Co. Inc., Westerly, RI, 1978—2000; ret., 2000—; atty., 1974—. Mem. adv. bd. Fleet Bank, Westerly, 1984-90; chmn. adv. group Westerly Edn. Endowment Fund, 2000-01, dir., 2001—; bd. dirs. Washington Trust Bancorp, Inc., 1994—. Pres. Chariho-Westerly Animal Rescue League, 1976—2001; incorporator Cmty. Hosp. of Westerly, 1985—, bd. govs., 1995—2002, v.p., 1999—2002, trustee, 1984—94, mem. fin. com., 1984—2001, mem. human resources com., 1998—2000; trustee Ctr. for the Arts, Westerly, 1984; v.p. Westerly Heart Assn., 1986; incorporator Westerly Pub. Libr., 1997—; mem. site planning group West H.S., 1998—2000, mem. student handbook com., 1999—2000; mem. Dante Italian Heritage Soc., 1999—; pres. Local Devel. Corp., 1998—; v.p. Stand Up for Animals, 2002—; dir. Chariho-Westerly Animal Rescue League, 2001—; v.p. Congregation Sharon Zedek, 1993—; bd. dirs. Am. Heart Assn., Westerly, 1986—93; mem. Charter Revision Com. Westerly, 1985—89; bd. dirs., v.p. Joint Devel. Task Force, Westerly, 1988—, v.p., 1994—99, dir., 2001—, pres., 1999—2000; bd. dirs. Animal Rescue League of So. R.I., 1988—94; mem. adv. coun. Westerly Integrated Social Svcs. Program, 1996, chmn., 1997—2000; mem.salary rev. and benefits coms. Westerly Fire Dist., 1996—2002. With U.S. Army, 1958—60. Larry Hirsch Day named in his honor, Town of Westerly, 1980; recipient Someone Spl. award, Channel 26 WTWS TV, New London, Conn., 1987, Sam Walton Bus. Leadership award Westerly-Pawcatuck C. of C., 2000, named Columbus Citizen of Yr., Golden Key Club, Westerly, 1989, Citizen of Yr., Westerly-Pawcatuck C. of C., 2000. Mem.: Gemological Inst. Am., Am. Gem Soc. (cert. gemologist, L.A. 1986), New Eng. Appraisers Assn., Nat. Assn. Jewelry Appraisers, Westerly Track Club (pres. 1976, bd. dirs. 1976—95), Elks (Larry Hirsch Run 1980—), Fraternal Order of Police (assoc.; scholar com.). Avocations: long distance running, humane treatment of animals. E-mail: hirsch@riconnect.com.

HIRSCH, LAURENCE ELIOT, construction executive, mortgage banker; b. N.Y.C., Dec. 19, 1945; s. S. Richard and Lillian (Avenet) H.; m. Susan Judith Creskoff, Dec. 23, 1967; children: Daria Lee, Bradford Richard. BS in Econs., U. Pa., 1968; JD cum laude, Villanova U., 1971. Bar: Pa. 1972, Tex. 1973. Assoc. Wolf, Block, Schorr & Solis Cohen, Phila., 1971-73, Bracewell & Patterson, Houston, 1973-76, ptnr., 1976-78; pres. Southdown, Inc., Houston, 1977-85, CEO, 1984-85; pres. Centex Corp., Dallas, 1985-88, CEO, 1988—, also chmn. bd. dirs., 1991—; chmn. Centex Constrn. Products, Inc., Dallas, 1994—. Bd. dirs. Belo Corp., Luminex Corp., dir. Heidelberger Zement, A.G.; trustee U. Pa. Mem. bd. cons. Villanova U. Law Sch. With USAR, 1968—75. Office: Centex Corp PO Box 199000 Dallas TX 75219-9000 also: 2728 N Harwood St Dallas TX 75201-1593 E-mail: lhirsch@centex.com.

HIRSCH, LAWRENCE LEONARD, physician, retired educator; b. Chgo., Aug. 20, 1922; m. Donna Lee Sturm; children: Robert, Edward, Sharon. BS, U. Ill., 1943; MD, U. Ill., Chgo., 1950. Diplomate: Am. Bd. Family Practice. Intern. Ill. Masonic Med. Ctr., Chgo., 1950-51; practice medicine specializing in family medicine Chgo., 1951-70; dir. ambulatory care Ill. Masonic Med. Ctr., Chgo., 1970-71, dir. family practice residency program, 1971-75; prof., chmn. dept. family medicine Chgo. Med. Sch., 1975-89, prof. emeritus, 1989—. Mem. med. licensing bd. State of Ill., 1982-94, chmn., 1988-94, hosp. licensing bd., 1994—; bd. dirs. Ill. Coun. for continuing Med. Edn., 1981-85, pres., 1986-87; cons. recombinant DNA Abbott Labs., 1980-87; lectr. in field; staff pres. Ill. Masonic Med. Ctr., 1970. Book rev. editor: Soc. of Tchrs. Family Medicine, 1979-89; book reviewer: Jour. AMA, 1969— ; contbr. articles to profl. jours. Bd. dirs. Mid-Am. chpt. ARC, Chgo., 1978-88; nat. pres. Alpha Phi Omega, Kansas City, Mo., 1974-78; exec. com. Chgo. Found. Med. Care and PSRO, 1977-84, Ill. State Inter-Ins. Exchange, 1975— ; bd. dirs. Crescent Counties Found. for Med. Care, 1985-91; commr. Northbrook (Ill.) Park Dist., 1987-91, pres., 1990—; mem. Village of Northbrook Planning Commn., 1987-89. Served with U.S. Army, 1943-46. Recipient Silver Beaver award Boy Scouts Am., 1963; recipient Silver Antelope award Boy Scouts Am., 1967, Disting. Eagle award Boy Scouts Am., 1969, Brotherhood award Lakeview Interfaith Council, 1968, Physician Speaker award AMA, 1981; inducted into City of Chgo. Sr. Citizens Hall of Fame, 1991. Fellow AAAS, Am. Acad. Family Physicians (mem. congress of dels.); mem. Chgo. Med. Soc. (pres. 1979, Pub. Svc. award 1990), Ill. Acad. Family Physicians (pres. 1977), Assn. Depts. Family Medicine (exec. com.), Masons, Shriners, Kiwanis (dir. local club). Democrat. Unitarian Universalist. Office: 1324 Coventry Ln Northbrook IL 60062-4339

HIRSCH, LOIS CELESTE, retired librarian; b. Seattle, July 30, 1929; d. Albert Chester and Susan Milliken (Osborne) Heidenreich; m. Julius Hirsch, June 19, 1952; children: Steven Allan, David Stewart, Mark Edward. BS, Northwestern U., 1951; MLS, Rosary Coll., 1967. Libr. Sch. Dist. #68, Skokie, Ill., 1967—;, 1967-94. Mem. NEA, Ill. Edn. Assn. (treas. 1990—), Ill. Computing Educators, No. Ill. Apple Users Group, Ill. Quilters Guild, Dulcimer Soc. No. Ill. (pres. 1990—), Chgo. Zither Club. Avocations: tournament bridge, sewing, spinning, miniatures, zither. Home: 7453 Lowell Ave Skokie IL 60076-3829

HIRSCH, MARTIN, dentist; m. Noreen Hirsch; 2 children. BS, CUNY, 1968; DMD, U. Pa., 1972; splty. in prosthondontics, U. Iowa, 1975; splty. in maxillofacial prosthetics, U. Chgo., 1976. Dental extern The Coatsville (Pa.) Hosp., 1971-72; dental intern Mt. Sinai Hosp., N.Y.C., 1972-73; resident VA Hosp., Iowa City, 1973-75, U. Chgo. Hosp. and Clinics, 1975-76; asst. prof. dept. otolaryngology Abraham Lincoln Sch. of Medicine U. Ill. Med. Ctr., Chgo., 1976-77; dir. maxillofacial prosthetics clinic Ctr. for Craniofacial Anamolies U. Ill. Med. Ctr., Chgo., 1976-77; asst. prof. U. Ill. Coll. Dentistry, Chgo., 1977-93; staff dept. dentistry U. Ill. Hosp. Med. Ctr., Chgo, 1979-83; staff dept. surgery dental section Cuneo Hosp., Chgo., 1979-87, Cabrini Hosp., Chgo., 1979-92; staff dept. dentistry Ill. Masonic Med. Ctr., Chgo., 1979—, mem. head and neck treatment ctr., 1981—; sr. staff Columbus Hosp. dept. surgery dental sect., Chgo., 1979-98; pvt. practice gen., cosmetic and prosthetic dentistry Chgo., 1979—; attending Cath. Health Ptnrs., Chgo., 1998-2001, Resurrection Health Care St. Joseph's Hosp., 2001—. Adj. instr. U. Chgo. Hosps. and Clinics, 1975—76; spkr. dental confs., symposiums, seminars; presenter to lay audiences on radio and TV. Spkr. Am. Cancer Soc., Chgo., 1981—87, chmn. profl. edn. com., 1981—85, mem. oral cancer com., 1982—86. Mem.: ADA, Chgo. Dental Soc., Ill. Dental Soc. Avocations: swimming, reading. Office: 2800 N Sheridan Rd Chicago IL 60657-6156

HIRSCH, MARTIN STANLEY, physician, researcher, educator; b. Cortland, N.Y., Apr. 16, 1939; s. Hans and Grete (Lipper) H.; m. Corinne Becker, Oct. 18, 1964; children: Tera Gretchen, Michael Edward. AB, Hamilton Coll., 1960; MD, Johns Hopkins U., 1964; MA, Harvard U., 1990. Diplomate Am. Bd. Internal Medicine, Am. Bd. Internal Medicine and Infectious Diseases. Intern in medicine U. Chgo. Clinics and Hosp., 1964-65, resident in medicine, 1965-66; fellow in virology Ctr. for Disease Control, Atlanta, 1966-68; fellow Nat. Inst. for Med. Rsch., London, 1968-69; fellow in infectious diseases Harvard U., Boston, 1969-71, asst. prof., 1971-76, assoc. prof., 1976-88, prof. medicine, 1988—; assoc. physician MGH, Boston, 1981-87; physician Mass. Gen. Hosp., Boston, 1988—. Mem. sci. adv. bd. AM Found. for AIDS Rsch., 1987—; chmn. AIDS program adv. com. NIH, Bethesda, Md., 1989-92. Contbr. 138 chpts. to books, more than 225 articles to profl. jours.; editor-in-chief: Jour. of Infectious Diseases, 2002—. Surgeon USPHS, 1966-68. Fellow Infectious Disease Soc. Am.; mem. Am. Soc. Clin. Investigation, Am. Soc. Virology, Assn. Am. Physicians, Phi Beta Kappa, Alpha Omega Alpha. Achievements include first isolation of HIV-1 from genital secretions, central nervous system and blood monocytes; pioneering treatment of human Herpes virus and HIV infections with agents used singly or in combination. Office: Mass Gen Hosp Infectious Disease Unit 65 Landsdowne St Cambridge MA 02139

HIRSCH, MICHAEL LEE, mayor; b. Mar. 22, 1957; s. Ronald Raymond and Rosemary Hirsch; Carol Jane Moczygemba, Sept. 5, 1987. BA, U. Wis., Milw., 1980, MA, 1984; PhD, U. Tex., 1990. Lectr. U. Wis., Milw., 1986-88; instr. Lawrence U., Appleton, Wis., 1988-90; vis. asst. prof. St. Norbert Coll., DePere, Wis., 1990-92; assoc. prof. sociology Ctrl. Meth. Coll., Fayette, Mo., 1992-98, prof., 1999—, Barker-Oakes disting. prof. social scis., 1998—. Facilitator City Vote Electoral Democracy Conf., 1997. Contbr. chpts. to books, articles to profl. jours.; presenter papers in field. Mem. City Coun., Fayette, 1994-98, mayor of Fayette, 1998—; bd. dirs. Fox Valley Fair Housing Coun., Appleton, 1990-92, Sr. Ctr., Fayette, 1994-99; mem. ethics bd. Lenoir Retirement Cmty., Columbia, Mo., 1992-99; mem. Fayette Area Heritage Assn.; mem. Soc. for Better Fayette Cmty.; mem. Fayette Area Betterment Group; mem. Howard County Tourism Coun., Mid-Mo. Solid Waste Dist. Recipient Congl. citation, 1994. Mem. Am. Sociol. Assn., Soc. for Study of Symbolic Interaction, Midwest Sociol. Soc., Soc. Study Applied Sociology, Mo. Sociol. Assn. Avocations: reading, weight lifting, travel, community service, running. Home: 200 N Vine St Fayette MO 65248-1180 Office: Ctrl Meth Coll 411 Central Methodist Sq Fayette MO 65248-1129 E-mail: mhirsch@cmc2.cmc.edu.

HIRSCH, MILTON, lawyer; b. Chgo., Sept. 10, 1952; s. Charles Ira and Beverly Ruth (Kelner) H.; m. Ilene Lonnie Schreer, Feb. 16, 1986. BA, U. Calif., San Diego, 1974; MS, DePaul U., 1979; JD, Georgetown U., 1982. Bar: Fla. 1982, U.S. Dist. Ct. (so., mid. dists.) Fla. 1983, U.S. Dist. Ct. (no. dist.) Fla. 1985, U.S. Ct. Appeals (5th and 11th cirs.) 1983, U.S. Tax Ct. 1983, U.S. Ct. Claims 1983, U.S. Supreme Ct. 1988. Acct. Arthur Young & Co., CPAs, Chgo., 1977-79; asst. state atty. Office State Atty., Miami, Fla., 1982-84; assoc. Finley, Kumble, Wagner, Heine, Underberg, Manley et al, Miami, 1985-87; pvt. practice, Miami, 1987—. Adj. prof. Nova U. Law Sch., Ft. Lauderdale, Fla., 1988, 94, 95. Author: Florida Criminal Trial Procedure; contbg. editor Jour. Nat. Assn. Criminal Def. Attys., 1987—; contbr. articles to profl. jours. Mem. ABA (litigation sect.), Nat. Assn. Criminal Def. Lawyers, Fla. Bar Assn.), Fla. Criminal Def. Attys. Assn. (former pres., Presdl. award for Disting. Svc. 1987-88). Office: Ste 1200 9130 S Dadeland Blvd Miami FL 33156-7848

HIRSCH, PAUL J. orthopedist, surgeon, medical executive, educator, editor; b. Bklyn., Oct. 12, 1937; s. Morris M. and Dorothy (Wolitzer) H.; 1 child, Jeremy S. BA in English, Roanoke Coll., 1957; MD, U. Va., 1961. Diplomate Am. Bd. Orthopedic Surgery. Intern NYU-Bellevue Med. Ctr., N.Y.C., 1961-62, resident, 1964-68; chief orthop. surgery Raritan Valley Hosp., Green Brook, N.J., 1969-71; pvt. practice orthop. surgery Bridgewater, N.J., 1971—; clin. prof. orthop. surgery Seton Hall Sch. Grad. Med. Edn. Vice chmn., bd. dirs. MIIX Group, Inc.; pres., med. dir. InterMedix, Lawrenceville, N.J.; emeritus staff, orthop. svc. Somerset (N.J.) Med. Ctr.; courtesy staff Robert Wood Johnson U. Hosp., New Brunswick, N.J.; clin. asst. prof. orthop surgery Rutgers Med. Sch., 1971-79; clin. instr. orthop. surgery NYU-Bellevue Med. Ctr., 1969-79; clin. assoc. prof. orthop. surgery N.J. Med. Sch., 1980—; clin. prof. orthop. surgery Seton Hall Sch. Postgrad. Medicine; chmn., bd. trustees Jour. Bone and Joint Surgery, 1999; mem. practicing physicians adv. group Nat. Com. Quality Assurance, 1996-98. Chmn. publs. com. Jour. Med. Soc. N.J., 1980-85; contbr. articles, editor profl. jours.,; mem. editl. bd. N.J. Medicine; editor-in-chief N.J. Medicine. Chmn. N.J. Com. for Quality Orthop. Care; trustee Rutgers Prep. Sch., pres. bd. trustees, 1983—86; trustee Raritan Valley C.C., 1986—; bd. dirs. N.J. Med. Polit. Action Com., 1983—; bd. trustees Orthop. Rsch. and Edn. Found., 1989—94. Mem.: N.J. State Med. Underwriters, Inc. (bd. dirs. 1990—99, vice chmn. bd. dirs. 1991—99), Med. Inter-Ins. Exch. N.J. (bd. govs. 1987—90), Ind. Sch. Chmn. Assn., N.J. Assn. Med. Splty. Socs. (pres. 1979—80, dir. 1981—85), N.J. Hosp. Assn. (trustee 1986—89), N.J. Health Scis. Group (treas. 1982—83), Internat. Soc. Orthop. Surgery and Traumatology, Am. Trauma Soc. (pres. ctrl. Jersey unit 1977—81), Acad. Medicine of N.J. (chmn. orthop. sect. 1975—78, trustee 1978—91, pres.-elect 1982—83, pres. 1983—84), Somerset County Med. Soc. (bd. trustees), Med. Soc. N.J. (chmn. orthop. sect. 1977—78, ho. of dels. 1976—, treas. 1982—86, 2d v.p. 1986—87, 1st v.p. 1987—88, pres.-elect 1988—89, pres. 1989—90, trustee 1982—91), N.J. Orthop. Soc. (pres. 1979—80), Ea. Orthop. Assn. (trustee 1981—84), Am. Coll. Physician Execs., Am. Acad. Orthop. Surgeons (bd. councilors 1982—88), Am. Orthop. Assn., AMA, ACS. Office: Green Knoll Profl Park #720 US Hwy 202-206 Bridgewater NJ 08807-1746

HIRSCH, PHILIP FRANCIS, pharmacologist, educator; b. Stockton, Calif., June 24, 1925; s. Harold and Elsa (Frohman) H.; m. Eugenia Isaeff, Sept. 21, 1956; children— Steven, Lisa, Kenny, Nancy. BS in Chemistry, U. Calif., Berkeley, 1950, PhD in Physiology, 1954. Lectr. physiology U. Calif., Berkeley, 1954-55; instr. pharmacology Sch. Dental Medicine, Harvard U., Boston, 1955-57, asso. in pharmacology, 1957-63, asst. prof. pharmacology, 1964; physiologist Lawrence Livermore Lab., 1964-66; asso. prof. pharmacology Sch. Medicine, U. N.C., Chapel Hill, 1966-70, prof., 1970-92; dir. dental research ctr. U. N.C., 1975-83, prof. dental ecology Sch. of Dentistry, 1988-92, prof. emeritus, 1992—. Mem. gen. medicine B study sect. NIH, 1974-78, clin. scis. study section, 1981-85. Contbr. articles to profl. jours. Bd. dirs. YMCA, Chapel Hill, 1981-83. Served with AUS, 1943-46. Mem. AAAS, Am. Soc. for Bone and Mineral Rsch., Endocrine Soc., Am. Soc. Pharmacology and Exptl. Therapeutics, Internat. Bone and Mineral Soc., Sigma Xi. Home: 135 Carolina Meadows Villa Chapel Hill NC 27517-8512 Office: U NC Dental Rsch Ctr Chapel Hill NC 27599-7455 E-mail: pfhirsch@med.unc.edu.

HIRSCH, RAYMOND ROBERT, chemical company executive, lawyer; b. St. Louis, Mar. 20, 1936; s. Raymond Winton and Olive Frances (Gordon) H.; m. Joanne Therese Dennis, Jan. 30, 1960; children: Amy Elizabeth, Thomas Christopher, Timothy Joseph, Mary Patricia. LL.B., St. Louis U., 1959. Bar: Mo. 1959. With Treasury Dept., 1960-62, Petrolite Corp., St. Louis, 1962—, sec., 1971—, v.p., gen. counsel, 1973-82, sr. v.p., gen. counsel, 1982-92; of counsel Guilfoil, Petzall & Shoemake, St. Louis, 1992-2000. Mem. Pub. Defender Commn., Mo. Mcpl. judge City of Bridgeton, Mo., 1970-73; mem. City of Des Peres Planning and Zoning Commn., 1974-78; mem. bd. edn. Spl. Sch. Dist. St. Louis County, 1981-83; mem. Mo. Air N.G., 1959-60; trustee Childhaven. Mem. ABA, Am. Soc. Corp. Secs., Mo. Bar Assn., Bar Assn. St. Louis, Mo. Athletic Club. Roman Catholic. Home: 3 W Walinca Walk Saint Louis MO 63105-2007 Office: Guilfoil Petzall & Shoemake 100 S 4th St Saint Louis MO 63102-1800 E-mail: r.r.hirsch@worldnet.att.net.

HIRSCH, RICHARD ARTHUR, retired mechanical engineer; b. N.Y.C., Jan. 2, 1925; s. Melvin Mordecai and Gertrude Matilda (Schwarz) H.; m. Carol Walter Sampson, June 18; children: Andrew Sampson, Patricia Ann. BAE, Rensselaer Poly. Inst., Troy, N.Y., 1945; MS in Applied Math., Brown U., Providence, 1950. Structural engr. Republic Aviation Corp., Farmingdale, N.Y., 1946-47; devel. engr. Swank, Inc., Attleboro, Mass., 1947-48; vibrations engr. Boeing Vertol, Morton, Pa., 1950-52; chief structures engr. AAI Corp., Balt., 1952-60; asst. tech. dir. Martin Marietta Corp., Balt., 1960-68; assoc. prof. U.S. Naval Acad., Annapolis, Md., 1968-82; prog. mgr. AAI Corp., Balt., 1982-93. Chair projects com. United Engring. Found., 1999. Contbr. articles to profl. jours. With USN, 1943-46. Fellow ASME (v.p. 1984-88, bd. govs. 1990-92); mem. NSPE, United Engring. Found. (chair projects com. 1998-2001). Home: 8220 Marcie Dr Baltimore MD 21208-1944 E-mail: hirschr@asme.org.

HIRSCH, RICHARD GARY, lawyer; b. L.A., June 15, 1940; s. Charles and Sylvia (Leopold) H.; m. Claire Renee Recsei, Mar. 25, 1967; 1 child, Nicole Denise. BA, UCLA, 1961; JD, U. Calif., Berkeley, 1965. Bar: Calif. 1967, U.S. Dist. Ct. (ctrl. dist.) Calif. 1967, U.S. Supreme Ct. 1972, U.S. Ct. Appeals (9th cir.) 1989, U.S. Dist. Ct. (ea. dist.) Calif. 1991. Dep. dist. atty. L.A. Dist. Atty.'s Office, 1967-71; ptnr. Nasatir, Hirsch & Podberesky, Santa Monica, Calif., 1971—. Commr. Calif. Coun. Criminal Justice, 1977-81; mem. Spl. Com. on Cts. in the Media/Judicial Coun. Calif., 1979. Co-author: California Criminal Law Proceedings/Practice, 5 edits. Pres. bd. trustees Santa Monica Mus. Art, 1984-91; chmn. Greek Theatre Adv. Com., L.A., 1976-79; mem. L.A. Olympic Organizing Com., 1981-84; bd. dirs. Ocean Park Cmty. Ctr., 1995—, bd. chair, 1997-2001. Recipient Spl. Merit Resolution, L.A. City Coun., 1984, Criminal Def. Atty. of Yr. award Century City Bar Assn., 1996. Lifetime achievement and crim. courts bar assoc., 2003. Fellow Am. Bd. Criminal Lawyers (bd. dirs., v.p. 1998-2000, pres.-elect 2001, pres. 2002); mem. Calif. Attys. Criminal Justice (pres. 1987, bd. trustees), Criminal Cts. Bar Assn. (pres. 1981, Spl. Merit award

1988), L.A. County Bar Assn. (Criminal Def. Atty. of Yr. 1999), Santa Monica C. of C. (bd. dirs. 1995-97). Avocations: cooking, reading, community service. Office: Nasatir Hirsch Podberesky & Genego 2115 Main St Santa Monica CA 90405-2215

HIRSCH, ROBERT ALLEN, lawyer; b. Phila., July 1, 1946; s. Leon Sidney and Harriet Roselyn (Benson) H.; BS, Pa. State U., 1968; JD, U. Akron (Ohio), 1974; m. Victoria Ingold, Apr. 23, 1977; 1 child, Courtney Benson. Claims rep. State Farm Ins. Co., Springfield, Pa., 1968-69; claims mgr. Ins. Placement Facility Pa. and Del., Phila., 1970-71; Bar: D.C. 1974; atty. Bur. Enforcement, ICC, 1974-79; assoc. gen. counsel Am. Trucking Assns., Inc., Washington, 1979-87; gen. counsel, dir. govt. affairs Nat. Pvt. Trucking Assn., Washington, 1987-88; gen. counsel, dir. regulatory affairs Nat. Pvt. Truck Coun., Washington, 1988-91; sec., gen. counsel Pvt. Fleet Mgmt. Inst., 1990—; sr. assoc., office mgr. Krukowski & Costello, P.C., Washington, 1991—. Co-author: Drug Testing Handbook for the Trucking Industry. Mem. Hazardous Materials Adv. Coun. Served with USAR, 1969-76. Mem. ABA, Nat. Transp. Indsl. Rels. Assn., Assn. Transp. Practitioners, Va. Bar Assn., D.C. Bar Assn., Transp. Lawyers Assn. (chmn. fed. agy. practice com.), Phi Alpha Delta. Democrat. Home: 3323 Parkside Ter Fairfax VA 22031-2715 Office: 2011 Pennsylvania Ave NW Washington DC 20006-1813

HIRSCH, ROBERT LOUIS, energy executive; b. Evanston, Ill., Mar. 6, 1935; s. Louis Aaron and Dorothy Jean (Block) H.; m. Evelyn Podhouser, Feb. 1, 1959 (div. 2000); children— Allen, Lauri, Scott. BS, U. Ill., 1958, PhD, 1964; MS, U. Mich., 1959. Research engr. Atomics Internat., 1959-60; physicist, later dir. ITT Indsl. Labs., Fort Wayne, Ind., 1964-68; sr. physicist controlled thermonuclear research AEC (now Dept. Energy), Washington, 1968-72; div. dir., 1972—76; asst. adminstr. solar, geothermal and advanced energy sys. ERDA (presdl. appointment), 1976-77; dep. mgr. sci. and tech. dept. Exxon Corp., 1977; gen. mgr. exploratory petroleum research Exxon Research and Engring. Co., 1977-80, mgr. Synthetic Fuels Research Lab., 1980-83; v.p., mgr. rsch. and tech. svcs. dept. Arco Oil and Gas Co., Dallas, 1983-91; chief exec. officer ARCO Power Techs., Inc., 1986-91; v.p. Washington office Electric Power Rsch. Ins., 1991-94; cons. in tech. and mgmt., 1994—; exec. advisor Advanced Power Technologies, Washington, 1997—2001; pres. The Energy Tech. Collaborative, Inc., 1995-97; sr. energy analyst Rand, 2001—02; chmn. bd. on energy and environ. sys. NRC, 1996—2003; sr. energy program adv. SAIC, 2003—. Mem. bds. Annapolis Ctr. and Fusion Power Assocs.; participant in Atlantic Coun. Studies; mem. LDRD Bd. Lawrence Livermore Nat. Lab., 1993-95; mem. U.S.-USSR Joint Commn. on Peaceful Uses of Atomic Energy, 1970s; chmn. U.S. del. U.S.-USSR Joint Fusion Power Coord. Com., 1970s; mem. Internat. Fusion Rsch. Coun., 1970s, Dept. Energy Rsch. adv. bd., 1980s; vice chmn. com. on sci., engring. and tech. Fed. Coord. Coun. for Sci. Engring. and Tech., 1976; adv. bd. Princeton Plasma Physics Lab., 1980s, Oak Ridge Nat. Lab., 1993-97; rsch. coord. coun. Gas Rsch. Inst., 1980s. Contbr. articles to profl. jours; patentee in field. Elected nat. assoc. Nat. Acads., 2001. Recipient Meritorious award William Jump Found., 1971, Disting. Service award AEC, 1974, spl. achievement award Fusion Power Assocs., 1982, spl. Achievement award ERDA, 1976, 77, commendation NASA, 1982, merit award U. Mich. Engring. Alumni Soc., 1997; AEC Spl. fellow, 1960-63 Fellow AAAS; mem. Am. Nuclear Soc. (chmn. fusion tech. group, dir. 1975-76, 78-79, outstanding tech. achievement award 1983), Tau Beta Pi (U. Ill. Alumni Honor award), Phi Epsilon Pi. Home and Office: 122 Princess St Alexandria VA 22314 E-mail: rlhirsch@comcast.net.

HIRSCH, ROSEANN CONTE, publisher; b. N.Y.C., Feb. 5, 1941; d. Frank and Anna (Burzycki) Conte; m. Barry Jay Hirsch, Oct. 1, 1967; children: Brian Christopher, Nicholas Benjamin, Jonathan Alexander. Student, Boston U., 1958-61. Editorial asst. Grolier, Inc., 1962-64; editor Ideal Pub. Corp., N.Y.C., 1968-74; editorial dir. Sterling's Mags., Inc., N.Y.C., 1975-78, Hearst Spl. Publs., Hearst Corp., N.Y.C., 1978-84; v.p. Ultra Communications, Inc., N.Y.C., 1984-89; pub., pres. Dream Guys, Inc., N.Y.C., 1986-93; pres. Lamppost Press, Inc., N.Y.C., 1989-. Author: Super Working Mom's Handbook, 1986; editor: Young & Married Mag., 1976-77, 100 Greatest American Women, Good Housekeeping's Moms Who Work; contbr. articles to various mags. Home and Office: Lamppost Press Inc 710 Park Ave # 19B New York NY 10021-4944

HIRSCH, STEVEN A. lawyer; b. Ariz., 1955; BA with distinction, U. Ariz., 1977, JD with high distinction, 1980. Bar: Ariz. 1980; cert. real estate specialist State Bar Ariz. Law clerk to Hon. James D. Hathaway Ariz. Ct. Appeals Divsn. 2, 1980-81; ptnr. Bryan Cave, Phoenix, Ariz. Editorial bd. Ariz. Bar Jour., 1986-89. Fellow Ariz. Bar Found. (bd. dirs. 1989-97, pres. 1995); mem. ABA (del. and dist. rep. young lawyers divsn. assembly 1990-92), Maricopa County Bar Assn. (bd. dirs. 1987-88), Order of Coif. Office: Bryan Cave 2 N Central Ave Ste 2200 Phoenix AZ 85004-4406

HIRSCH, WERNER ZVI, economist, educator; b. Linz, Germany, June 10, 1920; arrived in US, 1946, naturalized, 1955; s. Waldemar and Toni (Morgenstern) H.; m. Hilde E. Zwirn, Oct. 30, 1945; children: Daniel, Joel, Ilona. BS with highest honors, U. Calif., Berkeley, 1947, PhD, 1949. Instr. econs. U. Calif., 1949-51; econ. affairs officer UN, 1951-52; economist Brookings Instn., Washington, 1952-53; asst. rsch. dir. St. Louis Met. Survey, 1956-57; prof. econs. Washington U., St. Louis, 1953-63, dir. Inst. of Urban and Regional Studies; economist Resources for Future, Inc., Washington, 1958-59; dir. Inst. Govt. and Pub. Affairs UCLA, 1963-73, prof. econs., 1963—; mem. senate acad. coun. U. Calif., 1985-87, 89-91. Mem. acad. senate faculty welfare com. U. Calif., 1984—96; exec. bd. acad. senate UCLA, 1996—99, chair u. faculty welfare com., 1985—87, 1989—91, mem. restructure task force, 1993—95, long-range planning com., 1995—98; scholar in residence Rockefeller Study Ctr., 1978; cons. Rand Corp., 1958—98; U.S. Senate Com. on Pub. Works, 1972; Calif. Senate Select Com. on Structure and Adminstrn. Pub. Edn., 73; Joint Econ. Com. of Congress, 1975—76; OECD, 1977—80; mem. com. to improve productivity of Govt. Com. Econ. Devel., 1975—76; chmn. LA City Productivity Adv. Com., 1982—85; active Transit Rsch. Panel of NRC, 1993—96; mem. Internat. Steering Com., Glion Colloquium on Challenges Facing Higher Edn., 1997—. Author: Introduction to Modern Statistics, 1957, Analysis of the Rising Costs of Education, 1959, Urban Life and Form, 1963, Elements of Regional Accounts, 1964, Regional Accounts for Public Decisions, 1966, Inventing Education for the Future, 1967, The Economics of State and Local Government, 1970, Regional Information for Government Planning, 1971, Fiscal Crisis of America's Central Cities, 1971, Program Budgeting for Primary and Secondary Public Education, 1972, Governing Urban America in the 1970s, 1973, Urban Economic Analysis, 1973, Local Government Program Budgeting: Theory and Practice, 1974, Recent Experiences with National Planning in the United Kingdom, 1977, Law and Economics: An Introductory Analysis, 1979, 2d rev. edit., 1988, 3rd rev. edit., 1999, Higher Education of Women: Essays in Honor of Rosemary Park, 1978, Social Experimentation and Economic Policy, 1981, The Economics of Municipal Labor Markets, 1983, Urban Economics, 1984, Economist's Role in Government at Risk, 1989, Public Finance and Expenditures Under Federalism, 1990, Privatizing Government Services, 1991, Renting, 2000, Challenges Facing Higher Education at the Millennium, 1999, Governance in Higher Education, 2001, As the Walls of Academia are Tumbling Down, 2002; mem. editl. bd. Pakistani Jour. Applied Econs., 1980—, Internat. Rev. Law and Econs., 1985-88, Urban Affairs Quar., 1991-94. Pres. Am. Friends of Wilton Pk., 1983—85; mem. Friends of Graphic Arts, 1974—79; trustee U. Art Mus., Berkeley, 1991—; bd. dirs. Calif. Coun. Environ./Econ. Balance, 1974—, Calif. Found. on Economy, 1979—89, U. Calif. Retirement Sys., 1986—94; mem. exec. com. Wilstein Inst., 1993—; mem. bd. govs. Edmund G. Brown Inst., 1981—86; mem. UCLA Bldg. Authority, 1984—87, UCLA Com. on Planning and Budget, 1995—; mem. exec. com. regional bd. Anti-Defamation League, 1986—; gov. U. Calif. Faculty Ctr., 1992—94; bd. dirs. Assoc. Students UCLA, 2000—. Mem. Am. Econ. Assn., Am. Farm Econs. Assn., Internat. Biograph. Ctr. (mem. adv. coun. 1997—), Western Regional Sci. Assn. (bd. dirs., pres. 1978-80), Law and Econs. Assn., Soc. for Advancement of Socio-Econs., Town Hall West (pres. 1978-79), L.A. World Affairs Coun., Phi Beta Kappa, Sigma Xi. Home: 11601 Bellagio Rd Los Angeles CA 90049-2112 Office: U Calif Dept Econs Los Angeles CA 90095-1477

HIRSCHAUER, DAVID R. physician; b. Des Moines, Oct. 17, 1961; s. Richard E. and Betty J. Hirschauer; children: Jonathan David, Elizabeth Anne. BS in Biology, S.D. State U., Brookings, 1984; DO, U. Osteo. Med./Health Scis., Des Moines, 1988. Diplomate Am. Osteo. Bd. Anesthesia, Pain Mgmt. Shareholder, ptnr. Pinellas Med. Anesthesia Assocs., St. Petersburg, Fla., 1992-94; chmn. dept. pain mgmt. The Bonati Inst., Hudson, Fla., 1995—. Mem. adv. bd. Nat. Med. Underwriting Risk Group, L.A., 1998—, Nutrition Superstores Inc., West Palm Beach, Fla., 1998—, Med. Rsch. Industries, West Palm Beach, 1998—. Mem. Rep. Senatorial Inner Cir., Washington, 1998. Comdr. USN Res., 1988—. Mem. Am. Osteo. Assn., Am. Osteo. Coll. Anesthesiologists. Methodist. Avocations: sports, weight training, automobiles. Office: The Bonati Inst 7315 Hudson Ave Hudson FL 34667-1158

HIRSCHBERG, BESSE BRYNA, social worker; b. N.Y.C., Aug. 12; d. Sigmund and Lottie (Popick) H. BA, Hunter Coll.; postgrad. various including, Columbia U., Fordham U., Yale, U., Rutgers U., L.I. U., Cornell U., 1952-72. Cert. social worker, tchr., N.Y. Various to social worker and supr. social svc. caseworkers N.Y. City Dept. Social Svcs., 1965-76; cons. Community Svcs. and Resources, N.Y.C., 1976—. Participant TV dramatizations and progs. in field; lectr./cons. in field. Recipient Personal citation Bronx Borough Pres., 1965, Outstanding Profl. Woman of Yr., Dist. I N.Y. State Bus. and Profl. Clubs, 1981 and special recognition in 2002. Mem. Am. Soc. Psychodrama and Group Therapy, North Am. Assn. Alcoholism Progs., N.Y. League of Bus. and Profl. Women (pres., other offices), others.

HIRSCHBERG, JOSEPH GUSTAV, educator, physicist; b. Chgo., Apr. 13, 1921; s. Joseph Gustav and Lillian H.; m. Ginette Henriette Tetard, Apr. 26, 1947 (dec. Aug. 1992); children— Dorothy Jean Pixomatis, Joseph Gerald, Anne Marie Tumarkin, Lynn Susan Sontag; m. Judith Wladimira Mintz, Apr. 2, 1996. AB, Dartmouth, 1943; MS, U. Wis., 1951, PhD, 1952. Research asso. U. Wis., 1953-57; head optical group, also research physicist Plasma Physics Lab., Princeton, 1958-65; professeur d'Echange U. Paris, France, 1963; prof. physics U. Miami, Fla., 1965-86, chmn. dept., 1965-72, dir. optical physics lab., 1968—, prof. emeritus physics, 1986—. Contractor Langley Rsch. Ctr., NASA, 1966-69; vis. rsch. physicist Princeton (N.J.) U., 1976; leader solar eclipse expdns., Mex., 1970, Can., 1972, Kenya, 1973; vis. astronomer Sacramento (N.Mex.) Peak Obs., 1977; vis. scientist Inst. de Pathologie Cellulaire, Paris, 1980, Chercheur d'Echange, Mus. d'Histoire Naturel, Paris, 1983, Chercher d'Echange, Hopital Henri Mondor, Creteil, France, 1985, Princeton U., 1986-89; vis. sr. scientist Max Planck Inst. for Biophys. Chemistry, Göttingen, Germany, 1996, 97. Co-discoverer telluric sodium absorption in solar radiation; inventor optical spectroscopic devices, infrared turbidity meter, Brillouin laser ocean probe, non-linear optical interference microscope, microfluorospectrometers, x-ray microscopy, solar and tidal energy systems, compact triangular interferometer. Served to capt. USAAF, 1943-47. Fellow Am. Phys. Soc., Optical Soc. Am., European Acad. Scis., Arts and Letters, Papanicolaou Cancer Research Inst.; mem. AAAS, Am. Soc. Photobiology, Fla. Acad. Scis., Phi Beta Kappa, Sigma Xi, Sigma Pi Sigma, Omega Delta Kappa. Home: 1046 Alfonso Ave Miami FL 33146-3302 E-mail: hirschberg@phyvax.ir.miami.edu.

HIRSCHBERG, RUTH, retired social worker; b. Berlin, June 5, 1925; came to U.S., 1936; d. Fritz W. and Zerline (Zempelburg) Ackermann; m. Erich Hirschberg, June 3, 1945; children: Michael, Judy Hirschberg Atwood, Robert. BA, CUNY, 1946; MSW, Adelphi U., 1960. Lic. social worker, N.Y., Conn.; CTRS. Sr. med. social worker Columbia-Presbyn. Hosp., N.Y.C., 1962-82; social work cons. Vis. Nurse Assn., Stamford, Conn., 1982-90; ret., 1990. Mem. Acad. Cert. Social Workers, LWV (v.p. fin., chmn. voter svc. Greenwich, Conn. 1986-90). Democrat. Jewish. Avocations: music, theatre, bridge, community vol. work. Home: 107 Putnam Park Greenwich CT 06830-5777

HIRSCHBERG, VERA HILDA, writer; b. N.Y.C., Sept. 19, 1929; d. Bernard and Minnie (Margolis) Lieberman; m. Peter Hirschberg, Aug. 21, 1949; children: Karen Hirschberg Reses, Paul. BA, Hunter Coll., 1950. Staff writer Pacific Stars and Stripes, Tokyo, 1956-64; corr. Newsweek, Guatemala, 1964-65; transp. staff writer N.Y. Jour. Commerce, Washington, 1969-70; transp. editor Nat. Jour. Mag., Washington, 1970-72; dir. women's programs, presdl. speechwriter The White House, Washington, 1972-74; dir. tech. transfer HUD, Washington, 1974-75; dep. spl. asst. to Sec. Pub. Affairs Dept. Treasury, Washington, 1975-77; press. sec. U.S. Sen. William Roth, Jr., Washington, Jan. to Dec. 1977; editorial cons. various govt. and non-govt. clients, 1977-78; pub. affairs dir. White House Conf. on Libr. and Info. Svcs., Washington, 1978-80; sr. writer, adminstr.'s speechwriter NASA, Washington, 1980-92; cons. in field., 1992—. Author numerous newspaper and mag. articles. Recipient Outstanding Svc. citation The White House, 1973, Meritorious Svc. award Dept. Treasury, 1977, Exceptional Performance award NASA, 1982, Exceptional Svc. medal, 1988. Mem. Exec. Women in Govt. (founding mem. 1973), Zionist Orgn. Am. Republican. Jewish. Avocations: gourmet cooking, foreign travel, reading, museums, art collecting.

HIRSCHFELD, ARLENE F. civic worker, homemaker; b. Denver, Apr. 6, 1944; d. Hyman and Gertrude (Schwartz) Friedman; m. A. Barry Hirschfeld, Dec. 17, 1966; 2 children. Student, U. Mich., 1962-64; BA, U. Denver, 1966. English tchr. Abraham Lincoln High Sch., Denver, 1966-70. Pres. Jr. League of Denver, 1986-87, v.p. ways and means, 1985-86, v.p. mktg., 1982-83, chmn. Colo. Cache cookbook mktg. com., 1978-79, chair holiday mart, 1981, 85-87, participant in Nat. Jr. League Mktg. Conf.; trustee Graland Country Day Sch., 1988-97, bd. sec., 1990-95, chmn. edn. com., 1989-95, pres. parent coun., 1982-83, auction chmn., 1980, 81; bd. dirs. Allied Jewish Fedn., 1988-96, 98—, women's campaign chair, 1993; bd. dirs. Allied Jewis Fedn. Colo., 1999-03, bd. chair 1999-2001; co-chmn. collector's choice event Denver Art Mus., 1989, 94, trustee, 1995—, co-chair mktg. com.; co-chair ann. dinner Inst. Internat. Edn., 1997; co-chmn. benefit luncheon Pub. Edn. and Bus. Coalition, 1990, mini grants selection com., 1985-87; mem. bd. Minoru Yasui Comty. Vol. award, 1986-87; mem. Greater Denver C. of C. Leadership Denver, class of 1987-88; bd. dirs. Women's Found. Colo., 1992-97, hon. trustees coun., 1997—, annual event co-chair, 2001; bd. dirs. Anti-Defamation League, 1996—, Colo. Spl. Olympics Coun. Advisors, 1995-98, Mizel Ctr. for Art, Film and Culture, 1996—; trustee Rose Cmty Found., 2000—, Mile High coun. Girl Scouts U.S, 1998—; mem. dean's coun. Harvard Div. Sch., 1992—; mem. nat. leadership com. Harvard Women's Studies in Religion Program, 1994—; exec. com. Children's Diabetes Found., Denver, 1993—; Rose Cmty. Found. mem. Jewish life commn.; appointee to exec. endemic bd. Gov. Roy Roman, 1989-99, residence bd. Gov. Bill Owens, 1999—; gov. appointee mem. Colo. Women's Econ. Devel. Coun., 1989-99. Named Humanitarian of Yr., Nat. Jewish Ctr., 1988, Sustainer of Yr., Jr. League, 1992, Collectors Choice honoree, Denver Art Mus., 2002, Outstanding Vol. Fundraiser, Nat. Philanthropy Day in Colo., 2003; recipient Colo. Chpt. award, Nat. Women's Mus. of the Arts, 1991, Alumni Cmty. Svc. award, U. Denver Founder's Day, Woman of Distinction award, Rocky Mountain News and Hyatt Beaver Creek, 1993, Colo. I Have A Dream Found. award, 1992, Vol. award, Denver br. AAUW, Golda Meir award, Allied Jewish Fedn. Colo., 1999, Intermountain Jewish News Feature, 1999, Martin Luther King Bus. Social Responsibility award, 2002, Mizel Mus. Cmty. Cultural Enrichment award, 2001, Rex Morgan award, Sci. and Cultural Facilities Dist., 2002. Mem. Colo. Women's Forum. Avocations: aerobics, snow and water skiing, golf. Office: 5200 Smith Rd Denver CO 80216-4525

HIRSCHFELD, ELIE, real estate developer; b. Tel Aviv, Dec. 17, 1949; came to U.S., 1950; s. Abraham Hirschfeld and Zipora Teicher; m. Marcia Riklis, Feb. 14, 1980 (div. Feb. 1995); children: Daniella, David; m. Susan T. Aronson, May 18, 1996; children: Benjamin, Jonathan, Matthew. BA, Brown U., 1971; JD, NYU, 1974. Lawyer Milbank, Tweek, Hadley & McCloy, N.Y.C., 1974-76; pres. Hirschfeld Properties LLC, N.Y.C., 1976—. Gov. Young Real Estate Assoc., N.Y.C., 1980-85; Tony awards voter Theater League, N.Y.C., 1996—; mem. NYU real estate round table, 1980-90; trustee St. Lukes-Roosevelt Hosp., 1983—, L.I. U., 1986-91, Brown U., 1992—, Beth Israel Hosp., N.Y.C., 2001--, N.Y. Eye and Ear Hosp., N.Y.C., 2001--; regent L.I. Coll. Hosp., 1998—; bd. dirs. Jewish Nat. Fund, 1980-90, Weizmann Inst. Sci., 1988—. Jewish. Avocations: art collecting, skiing, marathons, triathalons. Home: 1067 5th Ave New York NY 10128-0101 Office: 5 E 59th St Rm 700 New York NY 10022-1027

HIRSCHFELD, MICHAEL, lawyer; b. Bronx, N.Y., July 4, 1950; s. Lawrence John and Ida (Miller) H.; m. Heidi P. Greenspan, June 17, 1973; children: Adam Lawrence, Philip Richard. BEE summa cum laude, CCNY, 1972; JD cum laude, U. Pa., 1975; LLM in Taxation, NYU, 1980. Bar: N.Y. 1976, U.S. Dist. Ct. (so. and ea. dists.) N.Y. 1976, U.S. Tax Ct. 1978. Assoc. Shearman and Sterling, N.Y.C., 1975-80, Roberts and Holland, N.Y.C., 1980-83, Carro, Spanbock, Kaster and Cuiffo, N.Y.C., 1983-85, ptnr., 1985-88, Winstown & Strawn, N.Y.C., 1988-98, Dechert LLP, N.Y.C., 1998—. Lectr. NYU, Assn. of Bar of City of New York, Fundamentals of Internat. Taxables, 2001-03, ABA, ALI-ABA, PLI, Syracuse U., U. Tex., Tulane U., Georgetown U.; chmn. NYU Inst. Real Estate Taxation; co-chmn. 49th, 50th, 52d, 53d and 54th ann. Fed. Income Taxation Confs.; 11th-23d ann. NYU Confs. on Fed. Taxation of Real Estate Taxations: mem. nat. edn. bd., Business Entities (RIA publ.) Real Estate Tax Digest, Jour. of Internat. Tax, Tax. Mgmt. Real Estate Jour.; mem. adv. bd. Tax Mgmt. Real Estate, Inst. Fed. Tax. Co-author: Real Estate Limited Partnerships, 3rd edit., 1991; bd. editors Real Estate Tax Digest, BNA Tax Mgmt.; editl. adv. bd. NYU Real Estate Adv. Bd. Mem.: Am. Coll. Tax Counsel, Internat. Tax Assn., Assn. of Bar of City of N.Y. (mem. com. on taxation of bus. entities), N.Y. State Bar Assn. (exec. com. 1987—97, lectr., co-chmn. coms. on income from real property tax sect. 1988—91, co-chmn. com. on preferences and minimum tax 1991—92, co-chmn. com. on individuals 1992—93, co-chmn. com. U.S. activities of fgn. taxpayers 1993—96, co-chmn. com. on real property 1996—98, co-chmn. tax accts. 1997—98, com. on internat. mems.), Am. Law Inst. (lectr.), ABA (tax sect. vice chmn. ACRS depreciation recapture subcom. 1983—85, task force pres.'s tax reform proposals minimum tax subcom. 1985—86, chmn. syndications subcom. 1985—87, chmn. real estate tax problems com. 1989—91, co-chmn. govt. subcom. 1992—94, vice chmn. gov. submission com. 1992—95, chmn. govt. subcom. 1994—97, coun. 1997—2000, coun. dir. tax sect. internat. com. 1997—2000, vice chmn. individual income taxpayers com. 2000—02, vice chair com. ops. 2001—, lectr. taxaction sect., chair 911 task force). Avocation: music (drum). Office: Dechert LLP 30 Rockefeller Plz Fl 22 New York NY 10112-2200 Fax: (212) 698-3599. E-mail: michael.hirschfeld@dechert.com.

HIRSCHFIELD, ALAN JAMES, entrepreneur; BS, U. Okla.; MBA, Harvard U. V.p. Allen & Co., Inc., 1959-67; v.p. fin., dir. Warner Bros. Seven Arts, Inc., 1967-68; with Am. Diversified Enterprises, Inc., 1968-73; pres., CEO Columbia Pictures Industries, N.Y.C., 1973-78; vice chmn., COO 20th Century-Fox Film Corp., L.A., 1979-81, chmn. bd., CEO, 1981-85; cons., investor entertainment industries, L.A., 1985-89; mng. dir. Wertheim Schroder & Co., L.A., 1990-92. Co-CEO, co-chair Data Broadcasting Corp., 1990-2000; bd. dirs. Cantel Med. Corp., Interactive Data Corp.; dir. JNET Inc., 1998—, Carmike Cinemas, Inc., Wiltel Comms. V.p. bd. dirs. Cure for Lymphoma Found., 1998; bd. dirs. Nat. Mus. Am. Indian George Gustav Heye Ctr., 1997—; trustee Grand Teton Music Festival, 1998—, Dana Farber Cancer Inst, 2001. Office: PO Box 7443 Jackson WY 83002-7443

HIRSCHFIELD, JIM, artist, educator; b. Pitts., Mar. 7, 1951; BFA, Kansas City Art Inst., 1976; MFA, U. Oreg., 1978. Vis. lectr. U. Oreg., Eugene, 1978; vis. artist U. Wash., Seattle, 1984; cons. Seattle Arts Commn., 1982-84, King County Arts Commn., Seattle, 1988-98; full prof. U. N.C., Chapel Hill, 1988—. Vis. asst. prof. U. Nev., Reno, 1986; vis. lectr. Ohio State U., Columbus, 1987. Solo exhbns. include Factory of Visual Art, Seattle, 1980, and/or, Seattle, 1980, 80 Langton St., San Francisco, 1982, U. Wash., Seattle, 1983, Northwest Artists Workshop 1983, Mattress Factory, Pitts., 1985, A.R.C. Raw Space, Chgo., 1986, Nev. Art Mus., Reno, 1986, Sierra Nevada Coll., 1986, Ohio State U., 1987, U. Hawaii, 1987, U. Nev.-Reno, 1987, U. Calif.-Santa Cruz, 1988, Henry Art Gallery, Seattle, 1989, Seattle Art Mus., 1989, N.C. Art Mus., Raleigh, 1989, Wake Forest U., Winston-Salem, 1990, Nexus Contemporary Arts Ctr., Atlanta, 1991, Sarratt Gallery, Nashville, 1991, Walker's Point Ctr. for Arts, Milw., Kala Inst., Berkeley, Calif., 1992, ACME Arts, Columbus, 1994, SPACES, Cleve., 1994, Asheville (N.C.) Art Mus., 1994, Southeastern Ctr. for Contemporary Art, Winston-Salem, 1994; group shows include and/or, Seattle, 1976, 80, U. Oreg. Art Mus., 1978, Museo Carillo Gil, Mexico City, 1980, Farm project, Arlington,1981Whitcom Mus. History and Art, Bellingham, 1982, Artquke, Portland, 1984, San Francisco Mus. Modern Art, 1985, Brockton (Mass.) Art Mus., 1986, King County Arts Commn., Mercer Island, Wash., 1988, Atlanta Coll. Art, 1990, Weatherspoon Gallery, Greensboro, N.C., 1990,Bath House, Atlanta, 1991 Ackland Art Mus., Sculpture Work, Knoxville, Chapel Hill, 1992, Fayerweather Gallery, U. Victoria 1992, Duke U., Durham, Snug Harbor Galley, N.Y., Painted Bride Gallery, Phila., 1996, . N.C., Wilmington, 2000, Tampa Art Mus., 2001, Contemporary Art Nus., Raleigh, 2002; commns. include Seattle Arts Commn. Rainier Sq., 1981, Passage Point Parks, 1978,Tampa/Pierce Civic Arts Com., 1982, Wash. Arts Com. 1983, Internat.Sculpture Conf., 1983, Pub. Art Study, 1984, Wash. Arts Commn., 1984, Connemara Found., 1986, Mass. Coun. on the Arts, 1986, Duke Med. Ctr., 1989, 90, 93, Pub.Art Works, San Rafael, 1991, City of Atlanta Detention Ctr., 1994, South Reg. Libr., Charlotte, 1996, Broward Club Street Cafe, Ft. Lauderdale, 1996, N.C. Zoo, 1996, Doernbecher Chidlren's Hosp., Portland, Oreg., 1996, N.C. Sch. for the Arts, Winston-Salem, 1997, Hope and Healing Ctr., Memphis, 1998, Mid. Tenn. State U., Murfreesboro, 1999, Fla. Atlantic U., Boca Raton, 1999, Bellevue Comm. Coll., 2000, TF Green Airport, RI, 2000, Transit Stations, FL, 2000, Anchorage Jail, AK, 2000, Grand Ave Overpass, AZ, 2000; Houston Airport System, 2002, others; co-author: (public art studies) Artwork/Network, 1984, Public Art Master Plan for the Kingdome, 1988; contbr. articles to profl. jours. Bd. dirs. Ctr. on Contemporary Art, Seattle, 1984-88; pub. art commr. Chapel Hill Arts Commn., 1994-97. Nat. Endowment for Arts/Rockefeller Found. grantee, 1986, Pollock Krasner Found., 1987, King County Art Commn., 1988, Art Matters Inc., 1988, Artist Trust, 1989, Seattle Arts Commn. via Allied Arts Found., 1989, N.C. Art Coun., 1995; fellow Nat. Endowment for the Arts, 1980 1989, 90, Inst. Art and Humanities, 1990, 93, Phillip and Ruth Hettleman Prize for Artistic Excellence, 1993, N.C. Art Coun., 1991, 96, 2000; recipient award in visual arts Graham Found., 1990. Office: Univ of North Carolina Dept Art Hanes Art Ctr Cb 3405 Chapel Hill NC 27599-0001 E-mail: jhirschf@email.unc.edu.

HIRSCHHORN, BERNARD, educator, historian, researcher, writer; b. N.Y.C., Aug. 23, 1922; s. Benjamin and Pauline (Schechner) H. BSS cum laude, City Coll. N.Y., 1943; MA in History, Columbia U., 1944, MPhil in History, 1978, PhD in History, 1981. Licensed tchr., chmn. Bd. Examiners of Bd. Edn. N.Y. High sch. social studies tchr. Bd. Edn., N.Y.C., 1952-65, high sch. chmn., 1965-91; rschr., writer N.Y.C., 1991—. Adj. asst. prof. history Bd. Higher Edn., N.Y.C., 1947-76; dir. N.Y.C. Coun. on Economic Edn., 1980's; asst. examiner Bd. Examiners of City of N.Y., 1965-1980s; assoc. Seminar on The City Columbia U., 1976—. Author: The Perilous Presidency, 1979, Words and Issues: From 'Slivers' to Missiles (N.Y. Times paperback), 1985, Democracy Reformed: Richard Spencer Childs and His Fight For Better Government, 1997; co-author: The Encyclopedia of New York City, 1995, Dictionary of American Biography, 1995, Walt Whitman: An Encyclopedia, 1998, A Global Encyclopedia of Historical Writing, 1998, Scribner's Encyclopedia of American Lives, 1999, American National Biography, 1999, Encyclopedia of the American Civil War, 2000, Historical Dictionary of the Gilded Age, 2003, Encyclopedia-USA, vol. 29, 2003; bibliographer Richard Spencer Childs, The Urban History Newsletter, 1996, 1997; editor (guest): Urban History (Mag. History issue), 1990; reviewer Social Education, The New American Poverty, 1985, Boston's Wayward Children: Social Services for Homeless Children, 1830-1930 (Mag. History issue), 1990, Good-Bye Machiavelli: Government and American Life (History issue), 1998, The History Teacher, The Great Depression, 1999, The History Teacher, The House of Rothschild: Money's Prophet 1798-1848, 2000, White House Studies, FDR and His Enemies, 2002, White House Studies, The Kennedys and Cuba: The Declassified Documentary History, 2003; contbr. articles to profl. jours. and newspapers. Pvt. U.S. Army, 1946-47. Named one of Outstanding Intellectuals of the 21st Century, Internat. Biog. Ctr., Eng., 2002; recipient NEH award, Harvard U., 1983, Tufts U., 1984, Brandeis U., 1985, Brown U., 1986, Princeton U., 1987, St. Andrews (Scotland) U., 1987; Fulbright scholar, Institut d'Etudes Politiques, Paris, 1963, English-Speaking Union scholar, Oxford (Eng.) U., 1982. Mem.: Pen American Ctr., New Eng. Historical Assn., Nat. Civic League, Soc. Historians of the Gilded Age and Progressive Era, Urban History Assn., Org. Am. Historians, Nat. Coun. History Edn. Democrat. Jewish. Avocations: attending cultural events (including films), nature walks, beach walking, swimming. Home: 301 E 21st St New York NY 10010-6534

HIRSCHHORN, ERIC LEONARD, lawyer; b. N.Y.C., Apr. 28, 1946; m. Leah Wortham, Oct. 31, 1981; children: Alexander, Elizabeth, Anne. BA, U. Chgo., 1965; JD, Columbia U., 1968. Bar: N.Y. 1968, U.S. Supreme Ct. 1972, D.C. 1973. Reginald Heber Smith Community Lawyer fellow MFY Legal Svcs., N.Y.C., 1968-71; counsel Dem. Study Group N.Y. State Assembly, Albany, 1971; legis asst. to Rep. Bella Abzug, U.S. Ho. of Reps., Washington,

1971-73; assoc. Cadwalader, Wickersham & Taft, N.Y.C., 1973-75; chief counsel subcom. on govt. info. and individual rights U.S. Ho. of Reps., Washington, 1975-77; dep. assoc. dir. internat. affairs & trade U.S. Office Mgmt. & Budget, Washington, 1977-80; dep. asst. sec. for export adminstrn. U.S. Dept. Commerce, Washington, 1980-81; ptnr. Winston & Strawn (formerly Bishop, Cook, Purcell & Reynolds), Washington, 1981—. Exec. sec. Industry Coalition on Tech. Transfer, Washington, 1986—. Author: The Export Control and Embargo Handbook, 2000; contbr. articles to profl. jours. Mem. Assn. Bar City N.Y., Thurgood Marshall Am. Inn of Ct., ABA Ctr. on Profl. Responsibility, D.C. Bar (legal ethics com. 1997-98, 99—; vice-chmn. 2001-03, chmn. 2003—). Office: Winston & Strawn 1400 L St NW Washington DC 20005-3508

HIRSCHHORN, JOEL STEPHEN, engineer; b. N.Y.C., Sept. 8, 1939; s. Leon and Blanche H.; m. Jacqueline M. Rams; children: Terri, Lesa. B of Engring., Poly Inst. Bklyn., 1961; MS, Poly. Inst. Bklyn., 1962; PhD, Rensselaer Poly Inst., 1965. Rsch. metallurgist Pratt & Whitley Aircraft, North HAven, Conn., 1962-63; prof. U. Wis., Madison, 1965-78; sr. assoc. Congl. Office of Tech. Assessment, Washington, 1978-90; pres. Hirschhorn & Assocs. Inc., Wheaton, Md., 1990-99; dir. natural resources policy studies divsn. Nat. Govs. Assn., 1999—. Cons. in field. Author: Introduction to Powder Metallurgy, 1969, Technology and Steel Industry Competitiveness, 1980, Serious Reduction of Hazardous Waste, 1986 (with others) Prosperity Without Pollution, 1990, (1 chpt.) The Greening of American Business, 1992, Environmental Strategies Handbook, 1994, Sprawl Kills, 2003; editor Remediation: The Jour. of Environ. Cleanup Costs, Techs. and Techniques; contbr. articles to profl. jours. Recipient Engring. News-Rec. award McGraw Hill, 1990, Environ. award Clean Water Fund, 1988, Citizens Clearinghouse for Hazardous Waste, 1989. Mem.: NSPE. Achievements include 2 patents on powder metallurgy alloys; pioneer in pollution prevention and waste reduction. Home: 3231 Coquelin Ter Chevy Chase MD 20815-4840

HIRSCHHORN, KURT, pediatrics educator; b. Vienna, May 18, 1926; arrived in U.S., 1940, naturalized, 1945; s. Emanuel and Helen (Mayberger) Hirschhorn; m. Rochelle Reibman, Dec. 20, 1952; children: Melanie D., Lisa R., Joel N. Student, U. Pitts., 1944; BA, NYU, 1950, MD, 1954, MS (Bergquist fellow), 1958. Intern Bellevue Hosp., N.Y.C., 1954—55, resident, 1955—56; fellow NYU, 1956—57, U. Upsala, Sweden, 1957—58; instr. NYU Sch. Medicine, 1956—58, asst. prof., 1958—63, assoc. prof., 1963—66; Arthur J. and Nellie Z. Cohen prof. genetics and pediat. Mt. Sinai Sch. Medicine, CUNY, 1966—76, Herbert H. Lehman prof., chmn. pediat., 1977—95, prof. pediat., human genetics and medicine, 1995—. Adj. prof. biology NYU, 1966—74; established investigator Am. Heart Assn., 1960—65; career scientist N.Y.C. Health Rsch. Coun., 1965—75. Author numerous sci. publs.; editor (with Harry Harris): Advances in Human Genetics, 1969—95; mem. editl. bd.: 16 sci. jours. Mem. coun. Village Cmty. Sch., 1968—73, chmn., 1972—73. Served with U.S. Army, 1944—47. Recipient Rudolph Virchow medal, 1974, Alumni Achievement award, NYU Sch. Medicine, 1982, Jacobi medal, Mt. Sinai Med. Ctr., 1993, William Allan award, Am. Soc. Human Genetics, 1995, J. Lester Gabrilove award for significant contbns. to medicine, Mt. Sinai Sch. Medicine, 2001. Fellow: AAAS, N.Y. Acad. Medicine, Am. Acad. Pediat.; mem.: Am. Cancer Soc. (coun. 1989—92), Am. Soc. Pediatric Chmn. (coun. 1983—86), Environ. Mutagen Soc. (coun. 1969—76), Genetics Soc. Am., Harvey Soc. (v.p. 1979—80, pres. 1980—81, coun. 1981—84), Am. Assn. Immunologists, Am. Soc. Human Genetics (pres. 1969, dir. 1964—65, 1968—71, Human Genetics Edn. Excellence award 2002), Am. Pediatric Soc., Am. Assn. Physicians, Am. Soc. Clin. Investigation, Am. Coll. Med. Genetics, Inst. Medicine of NAS, Pediatric Travel Club, Alpha Omega Alpha, Sigma Xi, Phi Beta Kappa. Home: 29 Washington Sq W New York NY 10011-9180 Office: Mt Sinai Sch Medicine 1 Gustave L Levy Pl New York NY 10029-6500 E-mail: kurt.hirschhorn@mssm.edu.

HIRSCHHORN, ROCHELLE, genetics educator; b. Bklyn., Mar. 19, 1932; d. Hyman and Anna Reibman; m. Kurt Hirschhorn; children: Melanie D., Lisa R., Joel N. BA, Barnard Coll., 1953; MD, NYU, 1957. Intern NYU-Bellevue Med. Divsn., N.Y.C., 1958—59; rsch. fellow, teaching asst. NYU Sch. Medicine, N.Y.C., 1963—65, assoc. rsch. scientist, 1965—66, instr. medicine, 1966—69, asst. prof. medicine, 1969—74, assoc. prof. medicine, 1974—79, prof. medicine, 1979—95, head divsn. med. genetics, 1984—, prof. medicine and cell biology, 1996—. Hon. fellow Galton Lab. Human Genetics & Biometry Univ. Coll., London, 1971—72; assoc. attending physician in medicine Beffevue Hosp., N.Y.C., 1969—80, Univ. Hosp., NYU Sch. Medicine, 1974—81; attending physician Bellevue Hosp., 1980—, Univ. Hosp., 1981—; mem. numerous coms. & study sects. NIH, 1973—; vis. prof. Harvard U., 1995, U. Calif., San Francisco, 1995. Trustee AIDS Med. Found./AMFAR; judge Westinghouse Nat. Sci. Talent Search; founding mem. Village Cmty. Sch.; senator NYU Senate, mem. pediatrics search com., 1987—89, human subjects instl. rev. bd., 1989—94, co-dir. second year med. genetics course, 1989—93, NYU appts. and promotions com., 1995—2002. Named Disting. Alumna, Barnard Coll. Fellow: Hero Arthritis Found., Am. Coll. Med. Genetics (founder), AAAS, Am. Coll. Rheumatology; mem.: Harvey Soc. (coun. 1989—92), Soc. for Inherited Metabolic Diseases, Peripatetic Soc., Interurban Clin. Club (pres. 1987—88), Am. Soc. Human Genetics (cert. 1987), Am. Assn. Immunologists, Assn. Am. Physicians, Am. Soc. for Clin. Investigation, Inst. Medicine, NAS, Alpha Omega Alpha (councillor Delta of N.Y. 1982—2002). Achievements include elucidation of pathophysiologic mechanisms, delineation of molecular and biochemical defects of genetic disorders including adenosine deaminase and glycogen storage disease type II. Office: NYU Med Ctr 550 1st Ave CD612 New York NY 10016-6402 Business E-Mail: hirscr01@med.nyu.edu.

HIRSCHL, SIMON, pathologist; b. Zagreb, Yugoslavia, Nov. 22, 1935; s. Ludwig and Hilda Hirschl; m. Mirna Kriznic, Apr. 27, 1961; children: Cynthia, Sandra, Melissa, Diane. MD, U. Zagreb, 1961. Resident Albert Einstein Coll. Medicine, Bronx, 1963—67, Columbia U., N.Y.C., 1966; pathologist Hosp. for Joint Diseases, N.Y.C., 1967-69, Flower and Fifth Ave Hosp., N.Y.C., 1969-77; assoc. prof. pathology N.Y. Med. Coll., Valhalla, N.Y., 1969-78; dir. pathology lab. Lourdes Hosp., Binghamton, N.Y., 1977-90; clin. prof. pathology SUNY, Syracuse, N.Y., 1978-90; dir. pathology Mather Meml. Hosp., Port. Jefferson, NY, 1990—2000, pathologist Port Jefferson, NY, 2000—; dir. pathology St. Charles Hosp., Port Jefferson, NY, 1990—2000, pathologist, 2000—. Cons. dir. MDS, Inc., Toronto, Ont., Can., 1979-90. Fellow Coll. Am. Pathologists. Office: St Charles Hosp 200 Belle Terre Rd Port Jefferson NY 11777-0214

HIRSCHMAN, ALBERT OTTO, political economist, educator; b. Berlin, Apr. 7, 1915; s. Carl and Hedwig (Marcuse) H.; m. Sarah Chapiro, June 22, 1941; children: Catherine Jane, Elisabeth Nicole (dec. 1999). Student, U. Sorbonne, Paris, Hautes Etudes Commerciales, London Sch. Econs., 1933-36; D in Econs. Sci., U. Trieste, 1938; hon. degree, Rutgers U., 1978, U. So. Calif., 1986, U. Turin, Italy, 1987, New Sch. for Social Rsch., 1988, Free U. of Berlin, 1988, U. Paris, 1989, U. Buenos Aires, 1989, U. Campinas, Brazil, 1990, Georgetown U., 1990, Yale U., 1990, U. Trier, Germany, 1990, Santander, Spain, 1992, U. Coimbra, Portugal, 1993, U. Paris, Nanterre, France, 1993, Williams Coll., 1993, U. Naples, 1998, U. Complutense, Madrid, 2001, Harvard U., 2002; hon. (hon.), European U. Inst., Florence, 2002. Rockefeller fellow U. Calif., Berkeley, Calif., 1941-433; Economist Fed. Res. Bd., Washington, 1946-52; fin. adviser Nat. Planning Bd., Bogotá, Colombia, 1952-54; pvt. econ. cons. Bogotá, Colombia, 1954-56; research prof. econs. Yale U., 1956-58; prof. internat. econ. relations Columbia U., 1958-64; prof. polit. economy Harvard U., 1964-74, Littauer prof. polit. economy, 1967-74; prof. Inst. for Advanced Study, Princeton, 1974-85, prof. emeritus, 1985—, chair in econs., 2000. Fellow Ctr. Advanced Study Behavioral Scis., 1968-69; mem. Inst. for Advanced Study, 1972-73; fellow Wissenschaftskolleg zu Berlin, 1990-91. Author: National Power and the Structure of Foreign Trade, 1945, The Strategy of Economic Development, 1958, Journeys Toward Progress: Studies of Economic Policy-Making in Latin America, 1963, Devlopment Projects Observed, 1967, 2d edit., 1995, Exit, Voice, and Loyalty: Responses to Decline in Firms, Organizations and States, 1970, A Bias for Hope: Essays on Development and Latin America, 1971, The Passions and the Interests: Political Arguments for Capitalism Before Its Triumph, 1977, Essays in Trespassing: Economics to Politics and Beyond, 1981, Shifting Involvements: Private Interest and Public Action, 1982, Getting Ahead Collectively: Grassroots Experiences in Latin America, 1984, Rival Views of Market Society and Other Recent Essays, 1986, 2nd edit., 1992, The Rhetoric of Reaction: Perversity, Futility, Jeopardy, 1991, A Propensity to Self-Subversion, 1995, Crossing Boundaries: Selected Writings, 1998, paperback edit. 2001; editor Latin Am. Issues-Essays and Comments, 1961; contbr. articles to profl. jours. Served with AUS, 1943-45. Decorated Orden de San Carlos (Colombia), Nacional de Cruzecro do Sul, Brazil; recipient Frank E. Seidman Disting. award in polit. economy, 1980, Talcott Parsons prize for social sci., 1983, Kalman Silvert prize L.Am. Studies Assn., 1986, 1st prize for social sci. articles Fritz Thyssen Found., 1992, Toynbee prize, 1998. Fellow Am. Econ. Assn.; mem. NAS, Council Fgn. Relations, Am. Acad. Arts and Scis., Am. Philos. Soc. (Thomas Jefferson medal 1998); fgn. mem. Brit. Acad., Accademia Nazionale dei Lincei (Rome), Acad. Scis. Berlin-Brandenburg. Address: Inst for Advanced Study Princeton NJ 08540

HIRSCHMAN, CHARLES, JR., sociologist, educator; b. Atlanta, Nov. 29, 1943; s. Charles Sr. and Mary Gertrude (Mullee) H.; m. Josephine Knight, Jan. 29, 1968; children: Andrew Charles, Sarah Lynn. BA, Miami U., Oxford, Ohio, 1965; MS, U. Wis., 1969, PhD, 1972. Vol. Peace Corps, Malaysia, 1965-67; prof. Duke U., Durham, N.C., 1972-81, Cornell U., Ithaca, N.Y., 1981-87, U. Wash., Seattle, 1987—, chair dept. sociology, 1995-98, Boeing internat. prof., 1999—. Cons. Ford Found., Malaysia, 1974-75; chair social scis. and population study sect. NIH, Washington, 1987-91; vis. scholar Russell Sage Found., 1998-99. Author: Ethnic and Social Stratification in Peninsula Malaysia, 1975; editor: The Handbook of International Migration: The American Experience, 1999; contbr. articles to profl. jours. Fellow Ctr. Advanced Study in the Bahavioral Scis., Stanford, Calif., 1993-94. Fellow AAAS (chair-elect sect. K on social, econs. and polit. scis. 2003—), Am. Acad. for Arts and Scis.; mem. Assn. for Asian Studies (bd. dirs. 1987-90), Population Assn Am. (bd. dirs. 1992-94, v.p. 1997). Office: U Wash Dept Sociology PO Box 353340 Seattle WA 98195-3340 E-mail: charles@u.washington.edu.

HIRSCHMAN, SHERMAN JOSEPH, lawyer, accountant, educator; b. Detroit, May 11, 1935; s. Samuel and Anna (Maxmen) H.; m. Audrey Hecker, 1959; children: Samuel, Shari. BS, Wayne State U., 1956, JD, 1959, LLM, 1968; D in Bus. Adminstrn., Nova Southeastern U., 1996. Bar: Mich. 1959, Fla. 1983; CPA, Mich., Fla.; cert. tax lawyer, Fla. Pvt. practice, Mich., 1959—; instr. Davenport U., 1971—. Adj. instr. Ctrl. Mich. U., 1997—, Fla. Metro U., 2001—. With USAR, 1959-62. Mem. Mich. Bar Assn., Fla. Bar Assn., Am. Arbitration Assn., Am. Assn. CPA Attys. Office: 340 Woodlake Wynde Oldsmar FL 34677-2190 E-mail: rgwh2oa@aol.com.

HIRSCHMANN, EDWIN A. historian, educator; b. Balt., Sept. 3, 1932; s. Joseph R. and Ruth (Rosen) Hirschmann; m. Del Greenblatt, Dec. 27, 2001. BA, Johns Hopkins U., Balt., 1954; MA, Pa. State U., 1968, U. Wis., 1968, PhD, 1972. Prof. history Towson U., Md., 1969—2002, coord. Asian studies, 1973—83, 1999—2002. Mem.: AAUP (pres. Md. conf. 1993—95), Assn. of Asian Studies (pres. Mid-Atlantic 1988—89). Home: 5715 Ridgedale Rd Baltimore MD 21209 Office: Towson Univ Dept History Towson MD 21252-0001

HIRSCHOWITZ, BASIL ISAAC, physician; b. Bethal, South Africa, May 29, 1925; came to U.S., 1953, naturalized, 1961; s. Morris and Dorothy (Drieband) H.; m. Barbara L. Burns, July 6, 1958; children: David E., Karen, Edward A., Vanessa. BSc, Witwatersrand U., Johannesburg, 1943, MB.BCh, 1947, MD, 1954. Intern, resident Johannesburg Gen. Hosp., 1948-50; house physician Postgrad. Med. Sch., London, Eng., 1950; registrar Central Middlesex Hosp., London, 1951-53; instr., asst. prof. U. Mich., 1953-56; asst. prof. Temple U., 1957-59; assoc. prof. medicine U. Ala. Med. Center, Birmingham, 1959-64; prof. medicine U. Ala. Med. Ctr., 1964-95, emeritus prof., 1995; prof. physiology U. Ala. Med. Center, 1970—; Disting. faculty lectr. U. Ala., 1988; chmn. faculty coun. U. Ala. Sch. Medicine, 1989-90; dir. div. gastroenterology U. Ala. Hosp. and Clinics, 1959-87; chmn. exec. com. U. Ala. Hosp., 1986-88. Named to, Ala. Acad. Honor, 1991, Ala. Health Care Hall of Fame, 2002; recipient Charles F. Kettering prize, GM Cancer Found., 1987, Seale Harris award, So. Med. Assn., 1992, Markowitz award, Am. Soc. Surg. Rsch., 1999, Pioneer in Endoscopy award, Soc. Am. Gastrointestinal Surgeons, 2003. Master ACP (Laureate award 1989); fellow AAAS, Assn. Am. Physicians, Royal Coll. Physicians (Edinburgh), Royal Coll. Physicians (London), Royal Soc. Medicine (hon.), Royal Philatelic Soc., (London); mem. AMA, South African, Brit., Ala. Med. Assns., Med. Rsch. Soc. Gt. Britain, Am. Fedn. Clin. Rsch., So. Soc. Clin. Investigation, Am. Physiol. Soc., Biophys. Soc., Am. Gastroent. Assn. (Friedenwald medal 1992), Am. Soc. Gastro-Intestinal Endoscopy (Schindler medal 1974, Disting. lectr. 1994), Am. Coll. Gastroenterology (Disting. Sci. Achievement award 1982), Brit. Soc. Gastro-Intestinal Endoscopy (hon.), Brit. Soc. Gastroenterology (Hurst lectr. 1966, Founders lectr. 1988, Astra internat. lectr. 1997), Italian Soc. Gastroenterology corr.), William Beaumont Soc. (Eddy Palmer award for contbns. to endoscopy 1976), Soc. Exptl. Biology and Medicine, Sigma Xi, Alpha Omega Alpha. Office: U Ala Med Ctr Birmingham AL 35294-0001 E-mail: bih@uab.edu.

HIRSCHSON, LINDA BENJAMIN, lawyer; b. N.Y.C., Jan. 21, 1941; d. Philip David and Ruth (Levy) Benjamin; m. Albert M. Hirschson, Dec. 22, 1963; children: Jay Philip, Pamela Ellen. AB, Barnard Coll., 1962; JD, Columbia U., 1965; LLM in Taxation, NYU, 1973. Bar: N.Y. 1965, U.S. Tax Ct. 1975, U.S. Dist. Ct. (so. and ea. dists. N.Y. 1976. Assoc. Kaye, Scholer, et. al., N.Y.C., 1965-70; tchg. fellow NYU Law Sch., N.Y.C., 1970-73; assoc. prof. Hofstra Law Sch., Hempstead, N.Y., 1974-77; assoc. Gilbert Segall and Young, N.Y.C., 1977-79, ptnr., 1979-93, Katten, Muchin & Zavis, N.Y.C., 1994-96, Parson & Brown, N.Y.C., 1996-98; shareholder Greenberg Traurig, N.Y.C., 1998—. Contbg. editor Rev. of Taxation/Individual jour., 1982-89, editor-in-chief, 1976-79, (book chpt.) Estate and Gift Tax After ERTA, 1982; chmn. CLE Satellite Network, Current Estate Planning, 1990. Treas. Friends of Joffrey Ballet, N.Y. chpt., 1988-91; treas., bd. dirs. Barnard Bus. and Profl. Women, N.Y.C., 1982-86; trustee The Calhoun Sch., N.Y.C., 1986-92; mem. EPTL Adv. Com. to N.Y. State Legislature, 1990-94, 97—, advisor, 1997. Named Outstanding Alumna The Calhoun Sch., 1985. Fellow Am. Coll. Trust and Estate Counsel (chmn. transfer tax com. 1998-01, mem. real property probate and trust sect. 2001—, regent 2003); mem. ABA (chmn. marital deduction com. real property, probate and trust sect. 1996—), N.Y. State Bar Assn. (chmn. taxation com. of tax sect. 1986-89, chair trusts and estates law sect. 1996), Assn. Bar City N.Y. (com. on trusts, estates and surrogate's ct. 2001--, chmn. Mortimer Hess lectr. com. 1992-94, estate and gift tax com. 1989-92, trustee, bd. dirs. Assn. Bar City N.Y. Fund), UJA Fedn. (honoree trusts and estates group). Avocations: skiing, tennis, jogging. Home: 501 E 79th St New York NY 10021-0735 Office: Greenberg Traurig 200 Park Ave Fl 14 New York NY 10166-1400 E-mail: hirschsonl@gt.law.com.

HIRSCHY, GORDON HAROLD, real estate broker, auctioneer; b. Sturgis, Mich., Jan. 28, 1942; s. Harold L. and Clara L. (Roy) H.; m. Alice Ann Grossman, Aug. 8, 1964 (dec. 1983); m. Sarah Lee Gerber, Nov. 20, 1994; children: Daniel, Benjamin, Matthew, Kurtt, Lori, Hannah, Nichole, Caitlyn, Sarah, Josh. BS in Gen. Agriculture, Purdue U., 1964; degree in auctioneering sci. and mgmt., Am. Acad. Auctioneers, 1990. FIC, LUTCF. State nitrogen engr., constrn. supr. Smith-Douglass Fertilizer Co., Indpls., 1965-67; asst. mgr. LaGrange County (Ind.) Farm Bur. Corp., 1967-72; county office mgr., agt. LaGrange County Farm Bur. Ins., 1972-80; owner, operator Community Ins. Svcs., Inc., LaGrange, 1980-88; ins. agt. Ins. Market Place, Inc., LaGrange, 1988-89; dist. rep. Modern Woodmen of Am., Inc., Rock Island, Ill., 1989-91; auctioneer Century 21 Fairfield Real Estate, Fort Wayne, Ind., 1999, Hirschy Real Estate & Auctioneering, 1999—. Named one of Outstanding Young Men Am., 1972, Rookie of Yr. Mich. Football Ofcls. Assn., 1988. Mem. N.E. Ind. Assn. Life Underwriters (pres. 1983, Mem. of Yr. 1982), Ind. Life and Health Ins. Leaders Club (exec. dir., sec. 1978-91), Nat. Auctioneers Assn., Ind. Auctioneers Assn., Nat. Assn. Realtors, Ind. Assn. Realtors, Am. Soc. Farm Equipment Appraisers, Gideons Internat., Ind./Mich. Football Ofcls. Athletic Assns. Republican. United Methodist. Avocations: football officiating, auctioneering. Office: 6110 Bluffton Rd Ste 110 Fort Wayne IN 46809 E-mail: hrareal@hotmail.com.

HIRSH, ALLAN THURMAN, JR., publishing executive; b. Cumberland, Md., Aug. 19, 1920; s. Allan Thurman and Ellinor Goldsmith (Ottenheimer) H.; m. Eleanor R. Rosenthal, June 17, 1944; children: Helene, Allan III, Eleanor. BS in Econs., Johns Hopkins U., 1941. CPA, Md. Acct. Burke Landsberg Gerber, Balt., 1941-42; pres. Ottenheimer Pubs., Inc, Balt., 1946-89, chmn. bd., 1989—; v.p. Allan Pubs., Inc., Balt., 1980—, Creative Horizons (formerly Ottenheimer Creations Inc.), Balt., 1994—, Thurman House, Hong Kong, 1994—. Bd. dirs. Balt. Hebrew Congregation, 1960-63, 83-86; assoc. Jewish Charities, Balt., 1972-79; pres. Forest Park H.S. PTA, 1968, Balt. City Coll. PTA, 1971; bd. dirs. Hebrew Burial and Social Service Soc., 1946—, pres. 1972-79; bd. dirs. 11 Slade Apt. Corp., 1985-88, 98—, pres., 1987-88, treas., 1998-2002, bd. dirs. With USN, 1942-46. Mem.: Suburban (Balt.) (dir. 1974-79, v.p. 1976-79); Presidents (West Palm Beach, Fla.). Democrat. Jewish. Home: Apt 710 11 Slade Ave Baltimore MD 21208 E-mail: allanhirsh@aol.com.

HIRSH, BERNARD, supply company executive, consultant; b. Seguin, Tex., July 18, 1916; s. Samuel and Sarah (Marks) H.; m. Johanna Charlotte Cristol, Feb. 14, 1941 (dec. Jan. 1977); children: Richard, Robert, Terry, Cristy; m. Beatrice Castelle, Feb. 11, 1978. BA, LLB, JD, U. Tex., 1939. Bar: Tex. 1939. Claims rep. Handley Claim Svc., Dallas, 1939-41; spl. agt. War Food Adminstrn., U.S. Govt., Dallas, 1941-44; pres. Milliners Supply Co., Dallas, 1945-82, chmn. bd., 1982—2000, cons., 2000—. Dir. Forestwood Nat. Bank, 1980—86. Pres. Temple Emanu-El Brotherhood, Dallas, 1960-62, Temple Emanu-El, Dallas, 1970-72, Nat. Fedn. Temple Brotherhoods, N.Y.C., 1974-76; chancellor Jewish Chautauqua Soc., N.Y., 1970-72. Mem. Dallas Bar Assn., State Bar Tex. Avocations: travel, reading. Office: 10716 Grand Cypress Ave Las Vegas NV 89134-5308

HIRSH, CRISTY J. principal; b. Dallas, Oct. 3, 1952; d. Bernard and Johanna (Cristol) H. BS in Early Childhood and Elem. Edn., Boston U., 1974; MS in Spl. Edn., U. Tex., Dallas, 1978; MEd in Counseling and Student Svcs., U. North Tex., 1991. Cert. counselor, sch. counselor; lic. profl. counselor, Tex.; cert. tchr., Tex., Mass.; cert. prin., Tex. Dir., learning specialist Specialized Learning, Dallas, 1981-93; counselor, mem. adj. faculty Eastfield Coll., Mesquite, Tex., 1992-95; counselor Grapevine (Tex.)-Colleyville Ind. Sch. Dist., 1995-2000, alternative sch. prin., 2000—. Mem. adj. faculty Richland Coll., Dallas, 1991—92. Mem. ACA, ASCD, Am. Sch. Counselor Assn., Coun. for Exceptional Children, Coun. for Children with Behavior Disorders, Tex. Assn. for Alternative Edn., Pi Lambda Theta, Phi Delta Kappa. Avocations: travel, theater, film, cooking, reading. Office: VISTA Alternative Campus 3051 Ira E Woods Ave Grapevine TX 76051-3817

HIRSH, ROBERT JOEL, lawyer; b. Shamokin, Pa., May 18, 1935; s. David and Rose (Coplansky) H.; children: Christine, Jonathan, Thomas. BS, U. Ariz., 1960, LLB, 1964. Bar: Ariz. 1964, U.S. Dist. Ct. Ariz. 1964, U.S. Ct. Appeals (9th cir.) 1968, U.S. Supreme Ct. 1971; cert. criminal specialist, State Bar of Ariz. Ptnr. firm Messing Hirsh & Franklin, Tucson, 1969-72, Hirsh & Hooker, Tucson, 1972-73, Hirsh, Shiner & Walker, Tucson, 1973-77, Hirsh & Bayles, Tucson, 1977-82, Hirsh & Fines, P.C., Tucson, 1982-84, Hirsh, Sherick & Murphy, P.C., 1985-90, Hirsh & Sherick, P.C., 1990-91, Hirsh, Davis, Walker & Piccarreta, P.C., 1991-95, Hirsh, Davis & Piccarreta, P.C., 1995-97, Hirsh, Bjorgaard & Rogers, PLC, 1998—2003, Hirsh & Rogers PLC, 2003—. Mem. ABA, State Bar Ariz, Ariz. Attys. for Criminal Justice (founder, pres. 1990), 9th Cir. Jud. Conf. (del. 1986-88), Ariz. Supreme Ct. Commn. on Cts. (task force mem.), Pima County Bar Assn., Ariz. State Bar Assn., Nat. Assn. Criminal Def. Lawyers, Calif. Attys. for Criminal Justice, Am. Bd. Criminal Lawyers, Am. Coll. Trial Lawyers. Office: 177 N Church Ave Ste 700 Tucson AZ 85701-1119 E-mail: rhirsh@hbrlaw.com.

HIRSH, THEODORE WILLIAM, lawyer; b. Gary, Ind., Nov. 16, 1934; s. Phillip and Libby (Krieger) H.; m. Beatrice Elaine Given, Aug. 28, 1955; children: Robert, Margo, Elizabeth, Irwin. AB, Ind. U., 1954, JD, 1957. Bar: Ind. 1957, Ill. 1958, Md. 1965. Atty. Montgomery Ward & Co., Chgo., 1958; pvt. practice Gary, 1958-60; trial lawyer, chief counsel IRS, Chgo., 1960-65; ptnr. Venable, Baetjer & Howard, Balt., 1965-76, Miles & Stockbridge, Balt., 1978-86; prin. Sussman & Hirsh, P.A., Balt., 1976-78; ptnr. Melnicove, Kaufman, Weiner, Smouse & Garbis, P.A., Balt., 1986-89, Miles & Stockbridge, Balt., 1989-96; with Law Offices of Peter G. Angelos, P.C., Balt., 1996-99, Ballard, Spahr, Andrews & Ingersoll, LLP, Balt., 1999—. Office: Ballard Spahr Andrews & Ingersoll LLP 300 E Lombard St Ste 1800 Baltimore MD 21202-6739 E-mail: hirsht@ballardspahr.com., twhirsh@aol.com.

HIRSHFIELD, PEARL, artist; b. Chgo., July 5, 1922; d. Louis and Anna (Nissenson) Belly; m. Hyman J. Hirshfield, Dec. 17, 1944; children: Leslie, Laura, Deborah, Jo-Anne. BA, Sch. of Art Inst., Chgo., 1979; AA, Herzl Jr. Coll., 1944; student, Northwestern U. Curator Midwest Artists for Peace, Chgo., 1967; co-curator art works Peace March, 1982; organizer Midwest Arts Festival, Chgo.; presenter Nat. Sculpture Conf., Cin., 1987, Found. Auschwitz, Brussels, 1997. Author: Conspiracy The Artist as Witness, 1972; film coordinator, Peace Prodns., 1983; creator, organizer Godine Press Art Portfolio, 1972; contbr. articles to jours. and newsletters; art exhibits include Nat. Sculpture Conf./Works by Women, Cin., 1987, Am. Internat. Archs. Hdqrs., San Francisco, 1987, Peace Mus., Chgo., 1988, 93, Holocaust Meml. Mus., Skokie, Ill., 1988, Internat. Conf. Ctr., Hiroshima, Japan, 1989, Archi-Center Gallery, Chgo., 1989, Lafayette Mus. Art, Ind., 1990, Franklin Furnace Mus., N.Y., 1991, Palais de Congres, Montreaux, Switzerland, 1992, Arthur Woods Gallery, Embach, Switzerland, 1992, Met. Mus. & Art Ctr., Coral Gables, Fla., Aurora U. Gallery, Ill., 1994, Northern Illinois Art Mus., Chicago, 1996, Nat. Mus. of Women in the Arts, Washington DC, 1996, Orange Ctr. for Contemporary Art, Santa Ana, Calif, 1997, Woman Made Gallery, Chgo., 1999, others; Witness and Legacy: Contemporary Art About the Holocaust, Minn. Mus. of Am. Art, St. Paul, 1995, Columbus Mus. of Art, Ohio, 1995, Finegood Gallery of Art, West Hills, Calif., 1996, Aurora Public Art Commission, Ill, 1997, Blaffer Gallery, Houston, 1997, Knoxville Mus. Art, 1998, Tampa Bay Holocaust Mus., 1998, N.J. State Mus., Trenton, 1999, Oklahoma City Art Mus., 1999, Telfair Mus., Savannah, Ga., 1999, DeCordova Art Mus., Lincoln, Mass., 2000, Huntsville Mus. Art, Ala., 2000, Tucson Art Mus., 2000-01, South Bend Reg. Mus. Art, 2001, Frye Mus., Seattle, 2001-02; installation "Shadows of Auschwitz" on three year loan to Fla. Holocaust Mus., 2002-; Ill. Women Artists: The New Millenium, Ill. State Mus., Chgo., 1999, Nat. Mus. of Women in the Arts, 1999, Lakeview Mus. Arts & Scis., Ill, 2000, So. Ill. State U., 2000, So. Ill. Art Gallery, 2000, The Galleries, Ill. State U., 2000, Rockford Art Mus., 2001, Parkland Art Gallery, 2001, Quincy Art Ctr., 2001; permanent pub. collections include Flaxman Libr., Sch. of Art Inst. Chgo., The Peace Mus., Chgo. Organizer, Peace Ctr., Evanston, 1958, bd. mem., 1958-60; co-chmn., organizer, Peace Walk, 1982; coord. Peace March, N.Y.C., 1982; mem. planning com., Art for a Nuclear Freeze, Chgo., 1983; cons. Art in Chgo., Mus. Contemporary Art, Chgo., 1997; mem. com. Paul Robeson 100th Birthday, Chgo., 1997. Recipient prize Whirlpool Found. Sculpture Competition, 1986, Nat. Holocaust Memorial Competition finalist, 1988, visual arts award Citizens Alert Bill of Rights, 1991, Task Force Against Police Brutality, 1993, Best 3 Dimensional Art award Baer Competition, 1998, Ill. Arts Coun. Visual Arts award, 1993; scholar Columbia Coll., 1940; grantee Ill. Art Coun. tech. assistance grant, 1983, Sculpture grant, 1984, Puffin Found., 1996; fellow Ill. Arts Coun., 1986. Mem. AAUW, Nat. Mus. Women in Arts (charter), Chgo. Artists' Coalition, Women's Caucus for Art, Physicians for Social Responsibility. Home and Office: 1333 Ridge Ave Evanston IL 60201-4131

HIRSHFIELD, STUART, lawyer; b. N.Y.C., Dec. 31, 1941; s. William Louis and Anne (Frank) H.; m. Susanne Drucker, Jan. 22, 1967; children: Matthew S., Edward R. BA, Syracuse U., 1963, JD, 1966. Bar: N.Y. 1966, U.S. Dist. Ct. (so. and ea. dists.) N.Y. 1968, U.S. Ct. Appeals (2nd cir.) 1968. Assoc. Krauss & Krauss, N.Y.C., 1966-67; atty. N.Y. Cen. RR, N.Y.C., 1967-69; assoc. Blum, Haimoff, Gersen, Lipson & Szabad, N.Y.C., 1969; atty. CIT Fin., N.Y.C., 1970-72; assoc. Shea & Gould, N.Y.C., 1972-77, ptnr., 1977-88; ptnr., chmn. bankruptcy practice group Dewey Ballantine, N.Y.C., 1988—2003; ptnr., head NY bankruptcy practice group Ropes & Gray LLP, NYC, 2003—. Bd. dirs. 565 Tenants Corp. Contbr. Asset Based Financing--A Transactional Guide, 1985. Assn. atty. Allenwood Civic Assn., Great Neck, N.Y., 1984; bd. visitors Syracuse U. Coll. Law, 1990—, exec. com., 1991-96. With USAR, 1966-72. Fellow Am. Coll. Bankruptcy (2d cir. admissions com. 1994-2001, chair 1998-2001, bd. regents 1998-2001, bd. dirs. 2002—), Am. Bar Found.; mem. ABA (com. on bankruptcy 1983—), N.Y. Bar Assn., Assn. Bar City N.Y. (corp. reogn. com. 1975-78, 82-85), Assn. Comml. Fin. Attys. (dir. 1980-93), Am. Coll. Bankruptcy Found. (bd. dirs. 2002—), Rockefeller Ctr. Club. Office: Ropes & Gray LLP 45 Rockefeller Plaza New York NY 10111

HIRSHON, JACK THOMAS, lawyer; b. LA, July 25, 1931; s. Jack W. Hirshon and Dorothy Sanborn; m. Patricia Lee Boldt, Mar. 30, 1957; children: David, Susan, Lori, Thomas. BS, UCLA, 1955; LLB, Golden Gate Coll., 1962. Bar: Calif. 1963. Ins. adjuster, claim mgr. United Pacific Ins. Co., San Francisco, 1962-63; pvt. practice law Santa Clara County, 1963—2000, Tahoe City, Calif., 2000—. Planning commr. City of Cupertino, Calif., 1964-72. 1st lt. U.S. Army, 1955-57. Mem. Consumer Attys. Calif., Tahoe Truckee Bar Assn., Sunnyvale Bar Assn. (pres.), Kiwanis. Democrat. Roman Catholic. Avocations: golf, skiing, running, football, gemology. Office: 210 Grove St PO Box 5126 Tahoe City CA 96145 E-mail: jhirshon@aol.com.

HIRSHON, ROBERT EDWARD, lawyer; b. Portland, Maine, Apr. 2, 1948; s. Selvin and Gladys (Wein) H.; m. Roberta Lynn Miller, Aug. 16, 1969; children: Todd, Sara, Jason, Miriam. BA, U. Mich., 1970, JD, 1973. Bar: Maine 1973, U.S. Dist. Ct. Maine 1973, U.S. Ct. Appeals (1st cir.) 1977, U.S. Supreme Ct. 2000. Shareholder Drummond, Woodsum & MacMahon P.A., Portland, 1973—. Adj. prof. law U. Maine Law Sch. Contbr. articles to profl. jours. Chairperson Breakwater Sch Bd., Portland, 1978-85; mem. Zoning Bd. Appeals, Cape Elizabeth, Maine, 1983-90. Mem. ABA (mem. Ho. of Dels. 1992—, chair standing com. lawyers pub. svc. responsibility 1990-93, chair steering com. pro bono ctr. 1991-96, chair torts and ins. practice sect. 1996-97, chair standing com. on membership 1997-2000, pres. 2001-02), Maine Bar Assn. (pres. 1986, chair continuing legal edn. com. 1975-83), Cumberland County Bar Assn., Maine Bar Found. (pres. 1990). Avocations: reading, tennis, skiing. Home: 9628 NW Arborview Dr Portland OR 97229 Office: Tonkon Torp LLP 1600 Pioneer Tower 888 SW Fifth Ave Portland OR 97204

HIRSHON, SHELDON IRA, lawyer; b. Bklyn., Mar. 27, 1947; s. Jay and Jeanne (Benk) H.; m. Claudia Glenn Barasch; children: Ariel, Yaniv, Jessica. BS, NYU, 1968, JD, 1972, LLM, 1978. Bar: N.Y. 1972. Assoc. Graubard, Moskovitz, McGoldrick, Dannett & Horowitz, N.Y.C., 1972-76, Windels, Marx, Davies & Ives, N.Y.C., 1976-78, Krause, Hirsch & Gross, N.Y.C., 1978-80; assoc., ptnr. Stroock & Stroock & Lavan, N.Y.C., 1980-87; ptnr. Proskauer, Rose, Goetz & Mendelsohn, N.Y.C., 1987—. Mem. ABA, N.Y. Bar Assn., Assn. Bar City N.Y. Office: Proskauer Rose LLP 1585 Broadway Fl 27 New York NY 10036-8299

HIRSHOWITZ, MELVIN STEPHEN, lawyer; b. N.Y.C., Dec. 11, 1938; s. Samuel Albert and Lillian Rose (Minkow) H.; m. Susan Bonnie Brezel, June 19, 1983; children: Lauren Allison, Emily Sara. BA with hons., Cornell U., 1960; LLB cum laude, Harvard U., 1963; MA in Biology, CUNY, 1977. Bar: N.Y. 1963, N.J. 1987, U.S. Dist. Ct. (so. dist.) N.Y. 1969, (ea. dist.) N.Y. 1977, N.J. 1993, U.S. Ct. Appeals (2d cir.) 1978, U.S. Supreme Ct. 1994. Assoc. atty. SEC, N.Y.C., 1963-65; sole practitioner Melvin Hirshowitz Law Office, N.Y.C., 1966-76, 87--; of counsel Hyman Bravin Law Offices, N.Y.C., 1976-87. Author: (manual) Proof of an Over the Counter Manipulation, 1964. Vice chmn. N.Y. Libertarian Party, 1970-72, candidate for surrogate ct. judge and ct. of appeals judge. Mem. N.Y. County Lawyers Assn. (com. on profl. ethics 1986-92, com. fed. legislation 1986-88), Assn. of Bar of City of N.Y. (com. on the civil ct. 1986-89), N.Y. State Bar Assn., Harvard Club of N.Y.C., Phi Beta Kappa, Pi Delta Epsilon. Republican. Jewish. Avocations: bird watching, art, tennis. Office: 630 3rd Ave New York NY 10017-6705 E-mail: mshlawoffices@aol.com.

HIRSH-PASEK, KATHRYN ANN, psychology educator; b. Williamsport, Pa., Mar. 10, 1953; d. Morton and Joan (Cramer) Hirsh; m. Jeffrey Ivan Pasek, Aug. 17, 1975; children: Joshua, Benjamin, Michael. Student, Manchester Coll., Oxford, Eng., 1973—74; BS in Psychology-Music summa cum laude, U. Pitts., 1975; PhD in Human Devel.-Psycholinguistics, U. Pa., 1981. Asst. prof. psychiatry Med. Coll. N.J., Rutgers U., Newark, 1981—85; asst. prof. psychology, dir. Infant Speech Perception Lab., Swarthmore (Pa.) Coll., 1982—84; asst. prof., dir. Infant Lang. and Perception Lab. Haverford (Pa.) Coll., 1984—87; assoc. prof., infant lang. and perception lab. Temple U., Phila., 1987—96, prof. psychology, 1997—. Pres. Spl. Things Distbg. Co., Inc., Ardmore, Pa., 1983—98; cons. Head Start and Get Set program, Sch. Dist. Phila., 1989; cons. on reading Katzenbach Sch. for Deaf, West Trenton, NJ, 1981—85; cons. on lang. comprehension in pygmy chimpanzee Yerkes Primate Ctr., Atlanta, 1989; cons. Elec. Schoolhouse, Brilliant Beginnings; ad hoc reviewer Jour. Child Lang., Devel. Psychology, Child Devel., Jour. Ednl. Psychology, Jour. Applied Psychology, Freeman Press; presenter papers at profl. meetings; assoc. editor Child Development, 2001—. Co-editor: 6 books, including How Babies Talk, 2000 and Einstein Never Used Flashcards, 2003; editl. bd. Infancy; contbr. articles to profl. jours.; composer, lyricist, performer (children's music cassettes) Jumpin' in a Puddle, 1987, Staying Up, 1988, Hugs and Kisses, 1990, Around the World, 1991, Making a Difference for K.I.D.S., 1993, An Ethical Start With Pasek, 2002. Condr. workshops for cmty. groups in psychology, music and edn.; bd. dirs. Kaiserman br. Jewish Cmty. Ctr., 1988—91; mem. exec. bd. young leadership coun. Fedn. Jewish Agys., 1980—84. Named Wexner fellow, 1991—93; recipient Psychol. Roundtable award, 1991; grantee NIH, 1979—80, 1982—84, 1989—, Pew Meml. Trust, 1985—87, Spencer Found., 1986—89, Temple U., 1988—90, NSF, 1996—. Fellow: APA, Am. Psychol. Soc. (Great Tchr. award 1999); mem.: Piaget Soc. (ad hoc reviewer), Omicron Delta Kappa, Pi Lambda Theta, Sigma Xi.

HIRSHSON, STANLEY PHILIP, history educator; b. Bklyn., June 8, 1928; s. Morris M. and Rose (Gallant) H.; m. Claire Shibin, Nov. 21, 1965; 1 son, Mark Robert; m. Janet N. Feldman, Mar. 4, 1974; 1 son, Scott Garad. AB, Rutgers U., 1950; MA, Columbia U., 1951, PhD, 1959. Lectr. history Seton Hall U., South Orange, N.J., 1957-59; asst. prof. Paterson (N.J.) State Coll. (now William Paterson Coll.), 1959-62; asso. prof. Queens Coll., City U. N.Y., Flushing, 1963-66, prof., 1966—. Author: General Patton; A Soldier's Life, 2002, The White Tecumseh: A Biography of General William T. Sherman, 1997, The Lion of the Lord, A Biography of Brigham Young, 1969, Grenville M. Dodge, Soldier, Politician, Railroad Pioneer, 1967, Farewell to the Bloody Shirt, Northern Republicans and the Southern Negro, 1962, My History Is Holy, A Biography of Mary Baker Eddy. Served with AUS, 1946-47, 53-55. Am. Coun. Learned Socs. fellow, 1962-63, Guggenheim fellow, 1966-67, Rockefeller Found. fellow, 1981-82, Andrew W. Mellon fellow Huntington Libr., 1993. Home: 59 Wilson Pl Closter NJ 07624-2321 Office: Queens Coll Dept History Flushing NY 11367

HIRSHTAL, EDITH, concert pianist, educator, chamber musician; b. Bregenz, Austria, May 31, 1950; d. Izak and Sabina (Silbershein) Hirschthal; 1 child, Jessica Elise. B of Music, Temple U., 1973, M of Music, 1975; artist diploma, Peabody Conservatory, 1983; studied with Leon Fleisher, studied with Adele Marcus, studied with Harvey Wedeen. Adj. faculty mem. Temple U., Phila., 1973-83, Bryn Mawr (Pa.) Conservatory, 1980-83; pianist, mem. faculty Downeast Summer Chamber Inst., 1983, Dobbs Ferry Chamber Inst., 1984; prof. piano Calif. State U., Long Beach, 1984—. Collaborations with Phila. Opera Co., Sequoia Quartet, Joanne Faletta, Mostovoy Concerto Soloists, Stephanie Chase, Jonathan Mack, Antoinette Perry, Peter Marsh, Michael Carson, Dudley Moore. Musician: (compact discs) Impromptu, Despite the Odds; performed at Weill Recital Hall, N.Y.C., Carnegie Hall, Lincoln Ctr., Alice Tully Hall, co-prodr., music supr. (documentary) The Phoenix Effect. Recipient Galica prize Paderewski Found., Phila., 1970. Democrat. Jewish. Office: Calif State U Dept Music 1250 N Bellflower Blvd Long Beach CA 90840-0006

HIRST, HESTON STILLINGS, former insurance company executive; b. Concord, N.H., Nov. 8, 1915; s. Edgar Clarkson and Mary Walker (Stillings) H.; m. Ruth Elizabeth Galway, Sept. 9, 1939; children— Ann, Edgar, George. AB, Dartmouth Coll., 1936, postgrad., 1937. Chem. engr. Factory Mut. Engring. Corp., 1937-44; chief engr. Blackstone Mut. Ins. Co., 1945-49, sec., asst. treas., 1949-52, v.p., sec., 1952-65, exec. v.p., 1965-68; sr. v.p. engring.-underwriting MFB Mut. Ins. Co., Providence, 1968-72; sr. v.p., sec. corp. affairs Allendale Mut. Ins. Co., Johnston, R.I., 1972-81; ret., 1981. Sr. v.p., sec. corp. affairs Affiliated FM Ins. Co., Appalachian Ins. Co., New Providence Corp. Mem. Republican Town Com., Barrington, R.I., 1952-76, Com. on Appropriations, Barrington, 1961-70, town moderator, Barrington, 1970-76. Mem. Am. Chem. Soc., Soc. Fire Protection Engrs., Providence Engring. Soc., Dartmouth Soc. Engrs., Univ. Club (Providence). Republican. Unitarian Universalist.

HIRST, PAUL HEYWOOD, retired education educator; b. Huddersfield, Yorkshire, Eng., Nov. 10, 1927; s. Herbert and Winifred (Michelbacher) H. BA in Math., Cambridge U., 1948, MA, 1951, Oxford U., 1955; DEd (hon.), Coun. Nat. Academic Awards, Eng., 1992; DPhil (hon.), Cheltenham and Glouchester Coll. Higher Edn., 2000; D. Litt. (hon.), U. Huddersfield, 2002. postgrad. cert. in edn., Cambridge U., 1952; academic diploma in edn., U. London, 1954. H.S. tchr. in Math. various schs., Eng., 1948-55; lectr., tutor, Dept. Edn. Oxford U., 1955-59; lectr. in Philosophy of Edn. U. London Inst. Edn., 1959-65; prof. Edn. U. London Kings Coll., 1965-71; prof. Edn., fellow Wolfson Coll., Cambridge U., 1971-88, emeritus prof. Edn., emeritus fellow, 1988—. Vis. prof. U. London Inst. Edn., 1991—, U. B.C., 1964, 67, U. Malawi, 1969, U. Edmonton, Alta., 1988, Sydney, 1988; mem. govt. inquiry into edn. of ethnic minority children, 1981-85; dir. govt. rsch. project on tchr. tng., 1982-86; mem., chmn. Univs. Coun. for the Edn. of Tchrs., 1970-88. Author: Knowledge and the Curriculum, 1974, Moral Education in a Secular Society, 1974, (with R.S. Peters) The Logic of Education, 1970; editor, contbr.; Educational Theory and Its Foundation Disciplines, 1983; co-editor, contbr.: Philosophy of Education: The Analytic Tradition, 1998; mem. editl. bd. Jour. Philosophy Edn., 1968—, Brit. Jour. Tchr. Edn., 1980—, McGill Jour. Edn., 1984—. De Carle lectr. U. Otago (New Zealand), 1976; Fink lectr. U. Melbourne, 1976. Mem. Royal Norwegian Soc. Scis. and Letters (overseas), Philosophy of Edn. Soc. (honorary v.p.), Royal Inst. Philosophy Coun., Athenaeum. Avocation: music (especially opera). Home: Flat 3 6 Royal Crescent Brighton BN2 1AL England

HIRST, PETER CHRISTOPHER, consulting actuary; b. Nairobi, Kenya, Aug. 22, 1943; s. Harold Rupert and Maureen (Doherty) H.; m. Audrey Kennett, July 27, 1968; children: Philippa Anne, Sara Elizabeth. BA, Balliol Coll., Oxford U., 1965, MA, 1969. Supr. group pension dept. Imperial Life of Can., Toronto, Ont., 1967-70; cons. actuary Peat Marwick & Partners, Toronto, 1970-74; asst. v.p., sr. cons. actuary Johnson & Higgins, Willis, Faber, Toronto, 1974-76; founder, actuary Hirst Cons. Ltd., Toronto, 1976-80; pres., actuary Tillinghast, Nelson & Warren, Inc., Toronto, 1980-86; co-founder, pres. Actrex Ptnrs. Ltd., 1986-93; exec. v.p. Buck Consultants Ltd., Toronto, 1993—, now sr. exec. v.p. Hon. faculty Centre for Continuing Studies in Employee Benefits, Humber Coll., bd. dirs. Contbr. articles on pensions and actuarial topics to profl. jours. Fellow Can. Inst. Actuaries (past pres.), Inst. Actuaries; mem. Soc. Actuaries (assoc.), Conf. Consulting Actuaries (bd. dirs.), Internat. Assn. Actuaries, Internat. Assn. Cons. Actuaries, Can. Pension & Benefits Inst. (past pres.), Assn. Can. Pension Mgmt., Human Resources Profl. Assn. Ont. Toronto (bd. dirs.). Clubs: Bd. Trade of Met. Toronto, Canadian, Mississaugua Golf and Country. Home: 19 Chisholm St Oakville ON Canada L6K 3W2 Office: Buck Consultants Ltd Box 15 Ste 1500 95 Wellington St W Toronto ON Canada M5J 2N7

HIRT, JANET ROSE, law educator, law librarian; b. Meadville, Pa., Mar. 14, 1942; d. Ira George and Gladys Gertrude (McLaren) H. AB in English, Eastern Coll., St. Davids, Pa., 1964; MA in English, Allegheny Coll., Meadville, Pa., 1969; MA in Counseling, Villanova (Pa.) U., 1973, JD, 1987; MS in Info. Sci., Drexel U., Phila., 1977; postgrad., Oxford U., 1970, Sussex U., 1977. Bar: Pa. 1987, U.S. Dist. Ct. (ea. dist.) Pa. 1988, U.S. Ct. Appeals (3d cir.) 1988), U.S. Ct. Appeals (D.C. cir.) 1989; cert. tchr., Pa. Copy editor Am. Bapt. Bd. Publs., Valley Forge, Pa., 1964; tchr. English Springfield High Sch., Pa., 1964-73, 76-85, guidance counselor, 1973-75; evening and weekend supr. reader svcs., reference librarian Villanova U. Sch. Law, 1985; legal rschr. Schnader, Harrison, Segal & Lewis, Phila., 1986-87; reference rsch. libr. Widener U. Sch. Law, Wilmington, Del., 1987-89, assoc. dir. Law Libr. Wilmington and Harrisburg, Pa., 1989-95; dir. Law Libr., assoc. prof. law U. Orlando, Fla., 1995-96; libr., lectr. law Vanderbilt U., Nashvile, 1997—. Liaison Coun. on Internat. Edn., Springfield H.S. and Bexhill (Eng.) Grammar Sch.; cons. acad. law libr. evaluation for schs. seeking ABA approval; rschr. small law firms. Contbg. editor An Internet Guide for Tennessee Lawyers, 1998. Mem. ABA (bus. law sect., tax sect., sect. on legal edn.), ALA (Am. Coll. and Rsch. Librs. Divsn.), Godort Roundtable, Libr. Adminstrn. and Mgmt. Assn., Nat. Coun. Tchrs. English (life), Am. Assn. Law Librs. (acad. librs. spl. interest sect., editor newsletter 1994-96, mem. standing com. on copyright 1989-91, adv. com. indexing periodical lit. 2003—), Pa. Bar Assn. (unauthorized practice of law com. 1994—. local ct. rules com. 1989-91, com. on professionalism 1998—), Greater Phila. Law Libr. Assn. (newsletter prodr. 1990-91, mem. planning com. (copyright inst. 1992), exec. bd. 1989-91), S.E. Assn. Law Librs. (placement com. 2000-02, membership com. 2002—, local arrangements ann. meeting 1999, 2002). Home: 3818 West End Ave Nashville TN 37205 Office: Alyne Queener Massey Law Libr Vanderbilt U Nashville TN 37203 E-mail: janet.hirt@law.vanderbilt.edu.

HIRT, JOAN B. education educator; b. Huntington, N.Y., Feb. 20, 1951; d. Warren G. and Ruth T. Hirt. BA in Russian Studies, Bucknell U., 1972; MAEd, U. Md., 1979; PhD, U. Ariz., 1992. Assoc. dir. housing and dining svcs. Humboldt State U., Arcata, Calif., 1979-88; assoc. dean students U. Ariz., Tucson, 1988-92; assoc. prof. higher edn. and student affairs Va. Tech. U., Blacksburg, 1994—. Cons. in edn.; corp. cons. Contbr. chpts. to books, articles to profl. jours. Mem. Am. Coll. Pers. Assn. (bd. dirs. CxII 1996-99), Assn. for Study of Higher Edn., Nat. Assn. Student Pers., Am. Coll. Pers. Assn. Office: ELPS 0302-Va Tech U 307 W Eggleston Hall Blacksburg VA 24061

HIRTH, JOHN PRICE, metallurgical engineering educator; b. Cin., Dec. 16, 1930; s. John Willard and Betty Ann (Price) H.; m. Martha Joan Davis, Nov. 28, 1953; children: John Marcus, Laura Ellen, James Gregory, Christina Louise. B. Metall. Engring., Ohio State U., 1953; MS, Carnegie-Mellon U., 1953, PhD, 1957; DSc (hon.), Ohio State U., 1995. Asst. prof. metall. engring. Carnegie-Mellon U., Pitts., 1958-61; Mershon prof. Ohio State U., 1961-67; vis. prof. Stanford, 1967-68; prof. Ohio State U., Columbus, 1967-88, Wash. State U., Pullman, 1988—. Aizen vis. prof. Nat. U. Mex., Mexico City, 1976; cons. in field; bd. overseers Acad. for Contemporary Problems, 1971-76. Author: Condensation and Evaporation, 1964, Theory of Dislocations, 1968, 82; editor: Scripta Metallurgica, 1974-94. Served with USAF, 1953-55. Fulbright fellow Bristol U., Eng., 1957-58 Fellow TMS (Hardy medal 1960, Mehl medal 1980, Mathewson medal 1982), Am. Soc. Engring. Edn. (McGraw award 1967), Am. Soc. Metals (Stoughton award 1964, Campbell lectr. 1972, White award 1989, Gold medal 1994, Sauveur Achievement award 1998); mem. NAS, NAE, ASME (Nadai medal 1999), Norwegian Acad. Scis. and Letters, AIME (hon.), Sigma Xi. Home: 114 E Ramsey Canyon Rd Hereford AZ 85615-9614 E-mail: jphmdh@theriver.com.

HIRZEL, CHARLES K. retired architect; b. Phila., Oct. 14, 1906; s. Carl Henry and Clara (Koch) H.; m. Helen E. Vogt, Dec. 5, 1936. BArch, U. Pa., 1927, MArch, 1930. Registered profl. arch., N.Y., N.J. Draftsman, renderer George E. Crane, 1926; draftsman Cherry and Matz, 1927-28; draftsman, designer, renderer, constrn. inspector Vahan Hagopian, N.Y.C., 1929, 31-33, 46-56; draftsman Georgina Pope Yeatman, 1929-30, Austin Co., N.Y.C., 1930, 1940; draftsman, designer R.H. Macy & Co., N.Y.C., 1930-31; comml. artist Senff and Lang, 1932-33; draftsman M.V. Liddell, 1934-35; draftsman, designer L.I. Lighting Co., Mineola, N.Y., 1940-45; draftsman, designer, constrn. inspector Francis Keally FAIA, N.Y.C., 1940, 1957—70, 1976—77; draftsman Spence and Rigolo, 1945 46, Myron R. Dassett, 1950-68; cons. architect Luth. Ch. Am., 1957, 1960—74; mng. assoc. Morris Ketchum, Jr., FAIA & Assoc., 1970; draftsman Meier-Marus, L.I., 1977, 1979, 1981, George A. Bielich, 1971; designer, draftsman Giorgio Cavaglieri, FAIA, N.Y.C., 1978-79; draftsman, designer P.H. Tuan, N.Y.C., 1980, 82. Prin. works include modernization Christian Sci. Reading Rm. and Office, N.Y.C., addition St. James Episcopal Ch., Fordham, N.Y., alterations Collegiate Sch., N.Y.C., site plan and 1st unit St. John Greek Orthodox Ch., Tenafly, N.J.; contbr. articles to profl. jours. Bd. dirs. Luth. Social Svcs., N.Y.C., 1956-84; bd. dirs. Covenant Luth. Ch., Ridgewood, N.Y., organist, choir dir., 1936-42; mem., sec. commn. on ch. architecture Luth. Ch. in Am.; mem. fin. and pers. com. Luth. Com. Svcs. and antecedents. Mem. AIA (chmn. com. N.Y. chpt.), NY Soc. Architects (profl. practices-ethics com., bldg. code com.), Nat. Trust Hist. Preservation. Avocations: gardening, church choir, travel. Home: 1100 Ponce de Leon Blvd 102 N Clearwater FL 11756

HISADA, MICHIE, physician, epidemiologist; MD, Keio U., Tokyo, 1988; MPH, Harvard U., 1993, ScD, 1998; PhD, Keio U., 2000. Diplomate Japan, 1988. Investigator Nat. Cancer Inst., Rockville, Md., 1998—. Office: Nat Cancer Inst 6120 Exe Blvd EPS 8008 Rockville MD 20852 Office Fax: 301-402-0817.

HISCOCK, RICHARD CARSON, marine safety investigator; b. Washington, Dec. 18, 1944; s. Earle Francis and Alice Morgan (Carson) H.; m. Nancy Lynn Schafer, Oct. 12, 1968 (div. Jan. 1986); m. Virginia Murray Brierley, July 6, 1996. Student, Am. U., 1964-66. Fisherman F/V Benjo, Chatham, Mass., 1977-78; asst. harbormaster Town of Chatham, 1977—87; exec. dir. U.S. Lifesaving Mfrs. Assn., North Chatham, Mass., 1984-86; investigator Marine Safety Cons., Fairhaven, Mass., 1987-91; pres. ERE Assoc. Ltd., Waitsfield, Vt., 1991—2002. Instr. hypothermia, cold water survival, emergency rescue equipment and fishing vessel safety, 1979—; mem. Comm. Fishing Industry Vessel Adv. Com., 1991-98; mem. Cape Cod Coastal Zone Mgmt. Adv. Com., 1977-92, chmn., 1986-91; mem. Barnstable County Coastal Resources Com., 1992-93; mem., chmn. Chatham Waterways Adv. Com., 1983-87; founder, bd. dirs. Marine Safety Found., Inc., Mass., 1993, v.p., 1999—; mem. Chatham Fin. Com., 1993-95; mem. Chatham Bylaw Rev. Com., 1995-97; industry advisor USCG Fishing Vessel Casualty Task Force, 1999. Contbr. articles to profl. jours. Recipient Pub. Svc. Commendation, USCG, 1984, Cert. of Merit, USCG, 1998, Meritorious Team Commendation, USCG, 1999. Mem. Soc. Naval Architects and Marine Engrs., U.S. Marines Safety Assn., Mass. and Vt. Soc. Mayflower Descendents. Achievements include drafting a bill to establish crew licensing, inspection and additional safety requirements of certain fishing industry vessels; rsch. on comml. fishing, uninspected vessel safety, fishing vessel safety and hypothermia. Home: 2257 E Warren Rd Waitsfield VT 05673 E-mail: rch@gmavt.net.

HISE, MARK ALLEN, dentist; b. Chgo., Jan. 17, 1950; s. Clyde and Rose T. (Partipilo) Hise. AA, Mt. San Antonio Coll., Walnut, Calif., 1972; BA with highest honors, U. Calif., Riverside, 1974; MS, U. Utah, 1978; DDS, UCLA, 1983. Instr. sci. NW Acad., Houston, 1978-79; chmn. curriculum med. coll. prep program UCLA, 1980-85; instr. dentistry Coll. of Redwoods, Eureka, Calif., 1983; pvt. practice Arcata, Calif., 1983—2001, Scotia, Calif., 2002—. Participant numerous radio and TV appearances; spkr. in field. Editor: Preparing for the MCAT, 1983—85; contbr. articles to profl. jours. Named Best Dentist on North Coast, Times-Std. Newspaper, 2002; recipient awards for underwater photography; fellow, NIH, 1975—79; Henry Carter scholar, U. Calif., 1973, Regents scholar, 1973, Calif. State scholar, 1973, 1974. Mem.: ADA, AAAS, Nat. Soc. Med. Rsch., Acad. Gen. Dentistry, Calif. Dental Assn., North Coast Scuba Club. Roman Catholic. Avocation: underwater photography. Office: PO Box 68 Scotia CA 95565

HISE, RICHARD TODD, marketing professional, educator, consultant; b. Washington, D.C., July 10, 1937; s. Theodore Richard and Lenor Mary (Parry) H.; m. Carol Lee Zeigler, Dec. 20, 1964; children: Richard William (dec.), Amy Caroline, Emily Carol. BA, Gettysburg Coll., 1959; MBA, U. Md., 1961, DBA, 1970. Instr. Elizabethtown (Pa.) Coll., 1962-64, Mich. State U., East Lansing, 1964-65, U. Md., College Park, 1965-70; assoc. prof., prof., head bus. adminstrn. Shippensburg (Pa.) State Coll., 1970-74; assoc. prof., dir. MBA program Va. Commonwealth U., Richmond, 1974-77; prof., holder Foley's professorship in retailing and mktg. Tex. A&M U., College Station, 1977—. Cons. IBM, Color Tile, Harley Davidson, Hotel Sofitel, Rosewood Properties, Mary Kay Cosmetics, Fleetwood Enterprises, OI Corp. Author: Quantitative Techniques for Marketing Decisions, 1973, Product/Service Strategy, 1977, Basic Marketing: Concepts and Decisions, 1979, Effective Salesmanship, 1980, Cases in Marketing Strategy, 1984, Basic Marketing: Concepts, Decisions, and Strategies, 1986, Millennial Marketing: Strategies for Success in the 21st Century and Beyond, 2001; contbr. more than 75 articles to profl. jours. including Jour. Mktg., Jour. Advt., Jour. Advt. Rsch., Jour. Global Mktg., Jour. Product Innovation Mgmt., Jour. Tchg. Internat. Bus., Mgmt. Acctg., Jour. Retailing, Jour. Acad. Mktg. Sci., among others. Sustaining mem. Rep. Nat. Com., 2001. Mem. Am. Mktg. Assn., Acad. Internat. Bus., Internat. Mgmt. Devel. Assn., Am. Legion, Pi Lambda Sigma, Beta Gamma Sigma, Phi Kappa Phi. Republican. Baptist. Avocations: international travel, impressionism art. Home: 1107 Merry Oaks Dr College Station TX 77840 Office: Tex A&M U Dept Mktg College Station TX 77843 E-mail: dick-hise@tamu.edu.

HISERT, GEORGE A. lawyer; b. Schenectady, N.Y., Sept. 18, 1944; BS summa cum laude, MS, Brown U., 1966; JD cum laude, U. Chgo., 1970. Bar: Calif. 1971. Law clk. to Hon. Sterry R. Waterman U.S. Ct. Appeals (2nd cir.), 1970-71; ptnr. McCutchen, Doyle, Brown & Enersen, San Francisco, 1977-93, Brobeck, Phleger & Harrison, San Francisco, 1993—2003; now ptnr. Bingham McCutchen LLP. Mem. editl. bd. Chgo. Law Rev., 1969-70; ABA sect. on bus. law liaison to UCC Permanent Editl. Bd. Mem. ABA (subcom. letter of credit, subcom. secured trans. of uniform comml. code com. bus. law sect., subcom. on syndications and loan participations of comml fin. svc. com., bus. law sect.), Internat. Bar Assn. (banking law com., bus. law sect.), State Bar Calif. (uniform comml. code com. bus. law sect., vice-chair 1992-93, chair 1993-94), Am. Coll.Comml. Fin. Lawyers, Order of Coif, Sigma Xi. Office: Bingham McCutchen LLP Three Embarcadero Ctr San Francisco CA 94111 E-mail: george.hisert@bingham.com.

HISEY, LYDIA VEE, educational administrator; b. Memphis, Tex., July 10, 1951; d. Murray Wayne Latimer and Jane Kathryn (Grimsley) Webster; m. Gregory Lynn Hisey, Oct. 4, 1975; children: Kathryn Elizabeth, Jennifer Kay, Anna Elaine. BS in Edn., Tex. Tech U., 1974, MEd, 1990. Cert. tchr., mid-mgmt., Tex.x. Tchr. phys. edn. Lubbock (Tex.) Ind. Sch. Dist., 1975-79, tchr., 1982-91, asst. prin., 1991-95, prin., 1995-2000, assoc. H.S. prin., 2000. Recipient Way-To-Go award Lubbock Ind. Sch. Dist., 1989, Impact II grantee, 1991. Mem. Tex. Assn. Secondary Sch. Prins., Tex. Elem. Prins. and Suprs. Assn., Lubbock Elem. Prins. and Suprs. Assn. (v.p. 1997-98, pres. 1998-99), Delta Kappa Gamma, Phi Delta Kappa. Baptist. Avocation: gardening. Home: 4417 87th St Lubbock TX 79424-4231 E-mail: veehisey@lubbock.k12.tx.us.

HISKES, DOLORES G. educator; b. Chgo. d. Leslie R. and Dagmar (Brown) Grant; m. John R. Hiskes; children: Robin Caproni, Grant. Student, U. Ill., Chgo. Tutoring programs cons.; presenter in field. Author, illustrator: Phonics Pathways, Pyramid, The Short-Vowel Dictionary; developer ednl. games: The Train Game, Blendit!, Wordworks. Mem. Assn. Am. Educators, Assn. Ednl. Therapists, Calif. Assn. of Res. Specilaists, Orton Dyslexia Soc., Learning Disabilities Assn., Nat. Right to Read Found., The Calif. Reading Assn., Pubs. Mktg. Assn., Calif. Watercolor Soc., Commonwealth Club of Calif., Bay Area Ind. Pubs. Assn. Avocations: watercolors, travel, reading, exercise. Office: Dorbooks PO Box 2588 Livermore CA 94551-2588 E-mail: dor@dorbooks.com.

HISLE, LINDA BETH See FRYE, LINDA BETH

HISS, ROLAND GRAHAM, physician, medical educator; b. Newark, Oct. 9, 1932; s. George Crosby and Adrianne (Graham) H.; m. Margaret Barringer McGrath, Aug. 23, 1957; children: John Barringer, Meredith Graham Brown. BS, U. Mich., 1955, MD, 1957. Diplomate Am. Bd. Internal Medicine. Intern in medicine Phila. Gen. Hosp., 1957-58; resident in medicine U. Mich. Hosp., Ann Arbor, 1961-64; fellow hematology Simpson Meml. Inst., Ann Arbor, 1964-66; faculty medicine U. Mich. Med. Sch., Ann Arbor, 1966—, chmn. dept. med. edn., 1982—; coordinator edn. Mich. Diabetes Research and Tng. Ctr., Ann Arbor, 1977—. Contbr. 60 articles to profl. jours. Served to capt. USAF, 1958-61. Recipient Teaching award Kaiser Permanente Found. and U. Mich., 1976. Fellow ACP; mem. Am. Diabetes Assn., AMA, Mich. State Med. Soc. Home: 3551 Chatham Way Ann Arbor MI 48105-2827 Office: U Mich Med Sch Towsley Ctr Box 0201 G-1103 Ann Arbor MI 48109-0201 E-mail: redhiss@umich.edu.

HITCH, DAVID CHARLES, pediatric surgeon; b. Raleigh, N.C., Oct. 6, 1941; s. Joseph Martin and Helen Frances (Goss) H.; m. Melanie Audrey Snell, Sept. 2, 1972; children: Charles Joseph, Kathryn Elizabeth Frances. BA, U. N.C., 1963; MD, Duke U., 1966. Cert. in surgery, specialty in pediat. surgery; recert. Intern U. Va. Med. Ctr., Charlottesville, 1966-67, resident, 1967-72, Childrens Hosp., Toronto, Ont., Can., 1973-75; rsch. fellow U. Va. Med. Ctr., Charlottesville, 1968-69; staff U. Va. Hosp., 1972-73, Colo. Gen. Hosp., 1975-78, Okla. Childrens Meml. Hosp., 1978-82, Univ. Hosp. SUNY, Syracuse, 1982—89; with Dayton Childrens Med. Ctr., Ohio, 1989—, Miami Valley Hosp., 1989—, Kettering Meml. Hosp., 1989—. Instr. U. Va., 1972; asst. prof. surgery U. Colo., 1975—78, U. Okla., 1978—81, clin. asst. prof., 1981—82; assoc. prof. surgery, chief divsn. pediat. surgery SUNY, Syracuse, 1982—87, clin. assoc. prof., 1998; assoc. clin. prof. Wright State U., Dayton, 1989—92,

clin. prof., 1992—, assoc. program dir. surgery, 1993—; cons. investigator Okla. Med. Rsch. Found., 1981—82, U. Hosp., Syracuse, 1982—88. Contbr. articles to profl. jours. Bd. dirs. Ronald McDonald House, Dayton. Mem. AMA (Ohio chpt.), ACS, Am. Acad. Pediats., Am. Pediat. Surg. Assn., Can. Assn. Pediat. Surgeons, Phi Beta Kappa. Episcopalian. Office: Pediat Surgeons Dayton One Children Plz Dayton OH 45404-1815

HITCHCOCK, BION EARL, lawyer; b. Muscatine, Iowa, Oct. 9, 1942; s. Stewart Edward and Arlene Ruth (Eichelberger) H. BSEE, Iowa State U., 1965; JD, U. Iowa, 1968. Bar: Iowa 1968, Okla. 1968, U.S. Ct. Customs and Patent Appeals 1973, U.S. Ct. Appeals (fed. cir.) 1982. Atty. Phillips Petroleum Co., Bartlesville, Okla., 1968-69, 73-76; mgr. licensing Phillips Petroleum Co. Europe-Africa, Brussels, 1977-80; sr. patent counsel Phillips Petroleum Co., Bartlesville, 1980-84, assoc. gen. patent counsel, 1984-2000; asst. gen. counsel intellectual property Chevron Phillips Chem. Co., LP, Houston, 2000—02; pvt. practice Sugar Land, Tex., 2002—. Bd. dirs. Bartlesville Symphony Orch., 1973-77, 80-91, pres., 1975-77, 82-84; bd. dirs. Bartlesville Allied Arts and Humanities Coun., 1976-77, 80-86, 1st v.p., 1982-83; mem. Govt. and Fin. Goals for Bartlesville Com., 1974-75; bd. dirs. Bartlesville Cmty. Concert Assn., 1982-90, Okla. Assn. Symphony Orchs., 1983-88. Lt. JAGC, USN, 1969-73. Mem. ABA, Okla. Bar Assn. (dir. patent trademark and copyright sect. 1980-86, sec. 1982-83, vice chmn. 1983-84, chmn. 1984-85), Iowa Bar Assn., Washington County Bar Assn. (pres. 1981-82), Am. Intellectual Property Law Assn., Am. Judicature Soc., Fed. Cir. Bar Assn., Licensing Execs. Soc., Eta Kappa Nu. Home: 1227 Misty Lake Ct Sugar Land TX 77478-5613 Office: 1227 Misty Lake Ct Sugar Land TX 77478-5613

HITCHCOCK, CANDIA POST, psychologist; b. Amityville, N.Y. d. John E.H. and Marie (Calhoun) Post; children: Steven, Heather, Danielle, Mitchell. BA, Adelphi U., 1965; MA, UCLA, 1966, U. Mo., 1989; PhD in Psychology, Ohio State U., 1993; postgrad., U. Wash. Intern Palo Alto VA Med. Ctr.; postdoctoral fellow U. Wash. Sch. Medicine; neuropsychologist MetroHealth Med. Ctr./Case Western Res. U. Sch. Medicine, Cleve., 2002—. Contbr. articles to profl. jours. Fellow Am. Bd. Profl. Psychology Rehab., Am. Bd. Profl. Neuropsychology; mem. APA, Congress Rehab. Medicine, Nat. Acad. Neuropsychology, Kappa Delta Pi, Phi Alpha Theta. Office: MetroHealth Med Ctr Dept Phys Medicine and Rehab 2500 MetroHealth Dr Cleveland OH 44109-1998 E-mail: chitchcock@metrohealth.org.

HITCHCOCK, FRITZ, automotive company executive; CEO, owner Hitchcock Automotive Resources, City of Industry, CA, 1980—. Office: Hitchcock Automotive Resour 17340 Gale Ave La Puente CA 91748-1512*

HITCHCOCK, JOANNA, publisher; b. London; BA, Oxford (Eng.) U., 1960, MA in Modern History, 1965. Asst. publicity dept. Oxford U. Press, London, 1962-66; asst. promotion mgr. Princeton (N.J.) Univ. Press, 1966-68, advt. and exhibits mgr., 1968-69, staff editor, 1970-72, mng. editor, 1972-80, exec. editor, 1980-84, asst. dir., 1985-87, exec. editor for humanities, 1988-92; dir. U. of Tex. Press, Austin, 1992—. Mem. Princeton U. Libr. Coun., 1986-95; adv. com. Tex. Book Festival, 1996-. Mem. Am. Assn. Univ. Presses (bd. dirs. 1984-87, chair equal opportunities com. 1985-86, ann. program planning com. 1986-87, pres. 1997-98, past pres. 1998-99). Home: 1507 Preston Ave Austin TX 78703-1903 Office: Univ of Texas Press PO Box 7819 Austin TX 78713-7819

HITCHCOCK, KEN, professional hockey coach; b. Edmonton, Alta., Can., Dec. 17, 1951; m. Nancy; children: Emily, Alex, Noah. Student, U. Alta., Edmonton, Can. Head coach Kamloops Blazers, 1984-90; asst. coach Phila. Flyers, 1990-93; head coach Kalamazoo Wings, 1993-94; coach All-Star Games IHL, 1993-94, 94-95; coach Dallas Stars, 1996—. Named Coach of Yr. Minor Hockey, 1982-83, Alta. Minor Hockey Assn., 1983-84, WHL, 1986-87, 89-90, top coach Canadian Major Jr. Hockey, 1989-90. Office: Dallas Stars 211 Cowboys Pkwy Irving TX 75063-5931

HITCHCOCK, LILLIAN DOROTHY STAW, educator, actress, artist; b. Detroit, Dec. 19, 1922; d. Charles Stawowczyk And Mary Waligora; m. Richard Elmer Hitchcock, June 28, 1952; children: Charles, Harriet, Roger, Stephen. BA in Edn., Wayne State U., 1946, MA in Interpretative Speech, 1952; postgrad., U. Wis., 1948; cert. in art, Inst. for Am. Univs., Avignon, France, 1981; cert. in French, Cath. U. Paris, 1983; postgrad., Inst. for Am. Univs., Aix-en-Provence, France, 1991. Speech and English tchr. Lakeview High Sch., St. Claire Shores, Mich., 1947-49; speech and journalism tchr. Mercy Coll., Detroit, 1949-52; substitute tchr. in speech and English Birmingham (Mich.) Pub. Schs., 1960-88; speech and English tchr. Bloomfield Hills (Mich.) Pub. Schs., Detroit Pub. Schs., 1960-70; tchr. French, Montessori Sch., Bloomfield Hills, 1988—. Performer, dir. Civic Theatre, Wayne State U., Cath. Theatre, Detroit, 1943-46; chmn. Detroit Theatre Olympiade for World Cmty. Theatre, 1979; mem. St. Dunstan's Theatre, Bloomfield Hills; docent Cranbrook Mus. Modern Art, Bloomfield Hills, 1988—; adj. instr. speech Oakland C.C., Mich., 1998; performer Mercy Theatre, Greece, 2002. Performer Festival Original One-Act Plays, Ann Arbor, Mich., 1994, 98, Detroit film yard movie Loopholes, 1998, Rock n' Roll Lystristrata, U. Detroit-Mercy Theatre Co., 2002. Del. People to People-Health Care, China, 1984. Mem. AAUW (bd. dirs. children's theatre Birmingham 1960-80), UN rep. and del. 1970-73), Tuesday Musicale. Mem. Internat. Platform Assn. (1st Place and Silver Bowl award 1994), Birmingham Cultural coun. Roman Catholic. Home: 6140 Westmoor Rd Bloomfield Hills MI 48301-1355

HITCHCOCK, VERNON THOMAS, farmer, lawyer; b. Selma, Ind., Feb. 21, 1919; s. Lucian Elmer and Loda Alice (King) H.; m. Betty Kathryn Orr, May 24, 1949; children: Brenda, Linda, Nancy, Debra, Randolph. BS in Agr., Purdue U., 1940; JD, Stanford U., 1953. Bar: Calif. 1954, U.S. Supreme Ct. 1961. Pilot Southwest Airways, San Francisco, 1946, TWA, Kansas City, Mo., 1947-51; pvt. practice Healdsburg, Calif., 1954-55; dep. atty. gen. State of Calif., Sacramento, 1956; dep. county counsel Sonoma County, Santa Rosa, Calif., 1957-65; exec. dir. Libyan Aviation Co., Tripoli, 1966-67; legal counsel Sonoma County Schs., 1967-82; farm mgr. Selma, Ind., 1975—. Originator Freedom Under Law program. Author: The Airline to Infinity, Diary of a Pilot, The Mildura March. Active Am. Security Coun., 1965-95; trumpeter New Horizons Band, Santa Rosa. Served to comdr. USNR, 1941-79. Mem.: Odd Fellows, Nat. Space Soc., Naval Order U.S., Res. Officers Assn., Quiet Birdmen, Commonwealth Club San Francisco. Republican. Episcopalian. Avocations: music, amateur radio.

HITCHCOCK, WALTER ANSON, educational consultant, retired educational administrator; b. Shelton, Wash., Dec. 9, 1918; s. Paul H. and Hazel (Boyington) H.; m. Helen Nadine Rainbolt, Mar. 13, 1944; children: Paul H., Walter Anson, Larry W. BABA, Wash. State U., 1940, BEd, 1941, MA in Edn., 1948; postgrad., U. Okla., 1943-44, summer 1946; EdD, Wash. State U., 1966. Tchr. bus. subjects Omak (Wash.) Sr. High Sch., 1941-42; counselor Weatherwax Sr. High Sch., Aberdeen, Wash., 1946-47; prin. Wilbur (Wash.) High Sch., 1947-49; supt. schs. Nespelem, Wash., 1949-50, Wilbur, 1950-55, Moxee, Wash., 1955-59, West Valley schs., Spokane, 1959-66, Kennewick schs., 1966-69; dep. supt. Spokane city schs., 1969-72, supt., 1972-80; assoc. Interpacific Investors Services, 1980-85. Mem. adv. com. on tchr. edn. Ea. Wash. State U., 1959-63, ednl. imperatives com., 1984-86; adminstrv. adv. com. State Sch. Supt., mem. spl. edn. com., 1976-79; mem. Wash. State Ednl. TV Adv. Com., 1972-74; mem. spl. edn. adv. com. Cen. Wash. State U., 1975-79. Mem. Tri-Cities United Cmty. Svcs., 1967-69, v.p., 1968; active Benton-Franklin Govtl. Conf., 1968-69; bd. dirs. Expo 74, 1972-75, United Way, Spokane County, 1972-79, Inland Empire Red Cross, Inland Empire Coun. Boy Scouts Am., Spokane Area Youth Com., OK Boys Ranch sponsored by Olympia Kiwanis, 1993-94; panel mem. Eastern Wash. Area Agy. on Aging, 1984-85. Served with AUS, 1942-45. Mem. Am. Assn. Sch. Adminstrs. (mem. SASA-AASA rels. com. 1971-74), NEA, Wash. Edn. Assn. (bd. dirs. dept. adminstrn. and supervision 1968-69), Inland Empire Edn. Assn. (pres. 1972-73), N.W. Regional Sch. Adminstrs. (chmn.), Yakima Valley Sch. Adminstrs. (chmn.), Spokane Area Supts. Assn. (pres.), Lincoln-Adams Bi-County Activities Assn. (pres.), Wash. Assn. Sch. Adminstrs. (pres. 1969-70, mem. exec. com.), Wash. State Sch. Retirees Assn. (del. 1986-99, 2001—, mem. fin. com. 1994—, chmn. 1996-97, 99—, actuarial study com. 1998-2000, facility need com. 1999-2000), Thurston County Sch. Retirees Assn. (bd. dirs. 1986-95, 97, 99-2002, found. com. 1996-2002), Phi Kappa Phi, Alpha Kappa Psi, Phi Delta Kappa, Sigma Phi Epsilon. Presbyterian. (trustee 1957-59, ruling elder). Clubs: Lion, Wilbur Commercial (pres. 1952-54), Kiwanis (trustee 1961-63, 67-69, 72-76). E-mail: whitchcock@juno.com.

HITCHENS, WILLIAM RANDOLPH (RANDY HITCHENS), health care executive; b. Logansport, Ind. s. William T. and Alberta J. Hitchens; m. Katherine J. Hitchens, Oct. 8, 1977; children: Cyrena, Chase, Carin. BS in Pharmacy, Purdue U., 1976; MBA, Ind. U., 1983. Pharmacist, mgr. Revco Drug, Ft. Wayne, Ind., 1977-83; assoc. product mgr. Boehringer Mannheim, Indpls., 1983, account mgr., 1984, product mgr., 1984-87, group mktg. mgr., 1987-90, sr. group product mgr., 1990-92, regional bus. mgr., 1992-94, nat. accounts managed care, 1994-97, dir. corp. partnership, 1997-98; corp. accts. dir. Roche, Indpls., 1998, nat. dir. corp. accounts, 1998—. Ofcl. U.S. Swimming, 1996-2002. Mem. Acad. Managed Care Pharmacists (legis. com. 1997-98, strategic mtkg. com. 1999). Presbyterian. Avocations: running, travel. Office: Roche 9115 Hague Rd Indianapolis IN 46256-1045

HITCHINS, KEITH ARNOLD, historian, educator; b. Schenectady, N.Y., Apr. 2, 1931; s. Henry Arnold Hitchins and Lillian Mary Turrian. AB, Union Coll., 1952; AM, Harvard U., 1953, PhD, 1964; D (hon.), U. Cluj, Romania, 1991, U. Sibiu, 1993, U. Alba Iulia, 2001. Instr., asst. prof. History Wake Forest U., Winston-Salem, NC, 1958—65; asst. prof. History Rice U., Houston, 1965—67; assoc. prof., prof. History U. Ill., Urbana-Champaign, 1967—. Author: Rumanian Nat. Movement in Transylvania 1780-1849, 1969, Orthodoxy and Nationality, 1977, Rumania 1866-1947, 1994, The Romanians, 1774-1866, 1996, A Nation Discovered, 1999, A Nation Affirmed, 1999; editor: Jour. of Kurdish Studies, 1995—; cons.: Caucasian Studies, —. Recipient Nat. Order for Merit, Pres. Romania, 2000. Mem.: Romanian Acad. (hon.). Home: 117 W Delaware Ave Urbana IL 61801 Office: Univ Illinois Dept History 309 Gregory Hall 810 S Wright St Urbana IL 61801

HITE, DAVID L. lawyer; b. Thornville, Ohio, Apr. 30, 1916; s. Frank C. Hite and Mary Pannabaker; m. Maxine Witherbee, July 15, 1943; 1 child, Diane. BS, Kent Sate U., 1938; JD, Capital U., 1946. Neuropsychiat. fellow Psychology Ct. Neuropsychiat. Inst., Hartford, Conn., 1939; pvt. practice Utica and Newark, Ohio, 1946—. Capt. OSS, 1942-46. Mem. ABA (pub. utilities sect., small trusts and estate com., adminstrn. and distbrn. of estates com.), Ohio Bar Ass., Cleve. Bar Assn., Licking Bar Assn. Office: Hite & Hite 964 N 21st St Ste D Newark OH 43055-7230 E-mail: hite@nextek.net.

HITE, PAMELA RENE, emergency medicine physician; b. Greene County, Iowa, Nov. 5, 1957; m. Blaine Grenell, May 17, 1986; children: Joshua, Jeremy. BS in Zoology, U. Iowa, 1982; MD, U. Iowa Coll. Medicine, 1988. Diplomate Am. Bd. Emergency Medicine. Intern U. Calif., San Francisco, 1988-89; resident in emergency medicine Maricopa Med. Ctr., Phoenix, 1989-92; assoc. dir. U. Kans. Med. Ctr., 1992—. Bd. dirs. Kans. U. Physicians, Inc., 1994—; bd. med. control EMS Wyandotte County, 1995—; adv. bd. Kans. Bd. Healing Arts, 1999—. Fellow Am. Coll. Emergency Physicians; mem. Am. Coll. Emergency Physicians (sec. Kans. chpt. 1994-96, v.p. 1996-98, pres. 1999-2001), Am. Assn. Women Emergency Physicians, Med. Soc. Johnson and Wyandote Counties, Kans. Med. Soc. Office: U Kans Med Ctr G 535 Bell Meml Hosp 3901 Rainbow Blvd Kansas City KS 66160-0001

HITE, ROBERT GRIFFITH, lawyer; b. San Antonio, Nov. 24, 1932; s. Raymond Griffith and Violet (Peck) H.; m. Gay Ann Bickham, Aug. 25, 1971; m. Carol Jean Peterson, June 5, 1953 (div. Aug. 1971); children: R. David, Kevin L., Brent R. B.S., U. Utah, 1960, J.D., 1966. Bar: Hawaii 1966. Ptnr., Goodsill Anderson Quinn & Stifel, Honolulu, 1966— . Editor-in-chief Utah Law Rev., 1965-66. Fellow Am. Coll. Trust and Estates Counsel (Hawaii state chmn. 1983-88); mem. Hawaii State Bar Assn., Hawaii Estate Planning Council (exec. com. 1978-79, 81-82, pres. 1987). Home: 92-1539 Aliinui Dr Apt F Kapolei HI 96707-2224 Office: Goodsill Anderson Quinn & Stifel 1099 Alakea St Ste 1800 Honolulu HI 96813-4512

HITES, RONALD ATLEE, environmental science educator, chemist; b. Jackson, Mich., Sept. 19, 1942; s. Wilbert T. and Evelyn J.H.; m. Bonnie Rae Carlson, Dec. 26, 1964; children: Veronica, Karin, David. BA in Chemistry, Oakland U., 1964; PhD in Analytical Chemistry, MIT, 1968. NAS fellow Agrl. Rsch., Peoria, Ill., 1968-69; mem. rsch. staff, dept. chemistry MIT, Cambridge, 1969-72, asst. prof. chem. engring., 1972-76, assoc. prof., 1976-79; prof. Ind. U., Bloomington, 1979-89, Disting. prof. pub. and environ. affairs and chemistry, 1989—, dir. Environ. Sci. Rsch. Ctr., 2001—. Cons. EPA, 1974—. Assoc. editor Environ. Sci. Tech., 1990—; mem. editorial bd. Chemosphere, 1979-99; contbr. articles to prof. jours. Grantee NSF, 1974—, EPA, 1974—, Dept. Energy, 1977-95. Fellow AAAS; mem. Am. Chem. Soc. (award in environ. sci. 1991), Am. Soc. for Mass Spectrometry (pres. 1988-90, mem. editl. bd. 1990-96), Soc. Environ. Toxicol. Chemistry (bd. dirs. 1997-2000, Founders award 1993), Sigma Xi. Office: Ind U Sch Pub and Environ Affairs 410H Bloomington IN 47405 E-mail: Hitesr@indiana.edu.

HITLIN, DAVID GEORGE, physicist, educator; b. Bklyn., Apr. 15, 1942; s. Maxwell and Martha (Lipetz) H.; m. Joan R. Abramowitz, 1966 (div. 1981); m. Abigail R. Gumbiner, 1982 (div. 1998); m. Martha Mann Slagerman, 2000. BA, Columbia U., 1963, MA, 1965, PhD, 1968. Instr. Columbia U., N.Y.C., 1967-69; research assoc. Stanford (Calif.) Linear Accelerator Ctr., 1969-72, asst. prof., 1975-79, mem. program com., 1980-82; asst. prof. Stanford U., 1972-75; assoc. prof. physics Calif. Inst. Tech., Pasadena, 1979-85, prof., 1985—. Mem. adv. panel U.S. Dept. Energy Univ. Programs, 1983; mem. program com. Fermi Nat. Accelerator Lab., Batavia, Ill.; 1983—87, Newman Lab., Cornell U., Ithaca, NY, 1986—88; mem. rev. com. U. Chgo., Argonne Nat. Lab., 1985—87; chmn. Stanford Linear Accelerator Ctr. Users Orgn., 1990—93; mem. program com. Brookhaven Nat. Lab., Upton, NY, 1992—95; spokesman BABAR Collaboration, 1994—2000; mem. high energy physics adv. panel DOE/NSF, 2001—; mem. Univs. Rsch. Assn. Fermilab Bd. Overseers, 2003—. Contbr. numerous articles to profl. jours. Fellow Am. Phys. Soc. Achievements include research in elementary particle physics. Office: Calif Inst Tech Dept Physics 356-48 Lauritsen Pasadena CA 91125-0001 E-mail: hitlin@hep.caltech.edu.

HITT, DAVID HAMILTON, SR., retired hospital executive; b. Tuscaloosa, Ala., May 14, 1925; m. Lola McKinney, Mar. 12, 1999 (dec.); children: David Hamilton, Kathryn Ann. BS, MS in Commerce and Bus. Adminstrn, U. Ala.; MHA, U. Minn., 1952. Hosp. adminstr. U. Ala. Hosp., 1947-50; various positions, including chief exec. officer Baylor U. Med. Center, 1952-79; sr. v.p. James A. Hamilton Assocs. (hosp. consultants), Dallas, 1979-84; pres., chief exec. officer Meth. Hosps. of Dallas, 1984-96, also bd. dirs., pres. emeritus; bd. dir. Am. Rubber Tech. Inc., Jacksonville, Fla. Dir. emeritus Bapt. Med. Ctr., Jacksonville, Fla., Dallas Meth. Hosps. Found.; pres. Dallas Hosp. Coun., 1959; mem. adminstrv. bd. Coun. Tchg. Hosps. of Assn. Am. Med. Colls., 1972-79; assoc. clin. prof. Washington U., St. Louis, 1961-96; adj. assoc. prof. Trinity U., San Antonio, 1964-96. Contbr. numerous articles to profl. jours. Mem. exec. bd. council Boy Scouts Am.; v.p. Community Council Greater Dallas. Recipient Earl M. Collier award Distinguished Hosp. Adminstrn. Tex., 1973, Dean Conley award, Silver Beaver award Boy Scouts Am. Fellow Am. Coll. Healthcare Execs. (Gold medal award for excellence in healthcare mgmt. 1990, past regent, editl. bd. Frontiers Health Svcs. Mgmt. 1991-93); mem. Am. Hosp. Assn. (Citation for Meritorious Svc. 1987, Disting. Svc. award 1992, trustee, past chmn. coun. financing), Tex. Hosp. Assn. (trustee, treas., v.p., pres., chmn. ho. of dels. 1967), Am. Protestant Hosp. Assn. (past trustee), Alumni Assn. U. Minn. Program Hosp. Adminstrn. (past pres.), Marine Corps Assn., Exch. Club East Dallas (pres. 1957), Masons, Shriners, Rotary (Dallas) (bd. dirs., dist. Ethics Bus. award 1993). Home: 7231 Twin Tree Ln Dallas TX 75214-1941

HITT, JOHN CHARLES, academic administrator; b. Houston, Dec. 7, 1940; s. John Charles and Mary W. (Green) H.; m. Martha Ann Halsted, Dec. 23, 1961; children: John Charles, Sharon Aileen. AB cum laude, Austin Coll., 1962; MS (Danforth fellow, NSF fellow), Tulane U., 1964, PhD (Danforth fellow, NSF fellow), 1966. Cert. psychologist, Tex. Asst. prof. psychology Tulane U., 1966-69; assoc. prof. psychology Tex. Christian U., Ft. Worth, 1969-77, assoc. dean of univ., 1972-77; v.p. Tex. Christian U. Research Found., 1974-77; dean Grad Sch. Tex. Christian U., 1975-77; v.p. acad. affairs Bradley U., Peoria, Ill., 1977-87, provost, 1981-87; v.p. acad. affairs, prof. psychology U. Maine, Orono, 1987-92, interim pres., 1991-92; pres. U. Cen. Fla., Orlando, 1992—. Bd. dirs. Space Coast Devel. Commn., Orlando Regional Health Care Sys.; bd. trustees EDUCOM, 1993—; adv. bd. World Trade Ctr., 1993-94, Orlando Sci. Ctr., 1992—; bd. dirs. Seminar on Acad. Computing, 1984-88, chmn. bd. dirs., 1986-87; chair task force distance learning State U. Sys. of Fla., 1993; pres.'s commn. NCAA, 1993—; nat. adv. bd. Ctr. for the Study of Sports in Soc., 1994—. Mem. bd. co-editors Psychological Research, 1973-77; editl. bd. TQM in Edn., 1993—; editl. adv. bd. Met. Univs., 1993—; contbr. articles in psychology and neurosci. to profl. jours. Chmn. com. on social scis. Austin Coll. 125th Anniversary Commn., 1973-77; charter mem. Austin Coll. Bd. Edn. Visitors, 1976-80; Tex. Christian U. rep. Leadership Ft. Worth, 1973-74; program chmn. Forum Ft. Worth, 1976-77; mem. Tarrant County United Way Budget Com., 1975-77, Forward Ft. Worth, 1976-77, Econ. Devel. Commn. Mid-Fla., Found. Orange County Pub. Schs., Fla. Info. Resource Network; chmn. loaned exec. program Heart of Ill. United Way, 1979, chmn. edn. unit, 1980, bd. dirs. 1983-87; bd. dirs. Greater Peoria YMCA, 1980-84, SunBank, 1992—, mem. community adv. council St. Francis Med. Ctr., Peoria, 1984-87; bd. dirs. Inst. Phys. Medicine and Rehab., Peoria, 1981-87, pres. bd. dirs., 1986-87, Heart of Fla. United Way, 1993—; v.p. Penobscot Valley United Way, Bangor, Maine, 1989-92; trustee Bangor YWCA, 1991-92; vestry St. John's Episcopal Ch., Bangor, 1990-91. Mem. APA, AAAS, Psychonomic Soc., Soc. for Neurosci., Am. Assn. Higher Edn., Peoria Area C. of C. (bd. dirs. 1986-87), Greater Orlando C. of C., Winter Park C. of C., Fla. Assn. of Colls. and Univs. (bd. dirs.), Sigma Xi, Alpha Chi, Psi Chi, Phi Kappa Phi, Beta Gamma Sigma, Omicron Delta Kappa. Home: 1000 Central Florida Blvd Orlando FL 32826-2404 Office: U Ctrl Fla PO Box 160002 Orlando FL 32816-0002

HITT, LEO N. lawyer, educator; b. Pitts., Oct. 20, 1955; s. Joe Stephen and Laurene (Lally) H.; m. Mary Elizabeth Wolf, Jan. 26, 1985; children: Nancy Anne, Elizabeth Lea. BA summa cum laude, U. Pitts., 1977, JD cum laude, 1980; LLM in Taxation, N.Y.U., 1983. Bar: Pa. 1980, U.S. Dist. Ct. (we. dist.) Pa. 1983, U.S. Tax Ct. 1981, U.S. Ct. Fed. Claims, 1997. Atty., tax sr. Kenneth Leventhal & Co., N.Y.C., 1980-81; atty., tax counsel Touche Ross & Co., Pitts., 1981-83; assoc. Reed Smith LLP, Pitts., 1983-88, ptnr., 1989—. Adj. prof. tax. grad. sch. Robert Morris Coll., Pitts., 1983—, tax grad. sch., law sch. Duquesne U., Pitts., 1987—, sch. law U. Pitts., 1988—; seminar speaker various profl. orgns., Pitts., 1983—. Comments editor: U. Pitts. Law Review, 1979-80. Mem. Allegheny County Bar Assn., Pitts. Internat. Tax Soc., Allegheny Tax Soc., Pitts. Tax Club. Democrat. Roman Catholic. Avocations: alpine skiing, opera, gourmet cooking. Home: 4209 Summervale Dr Murrysville PA 15668-3515 Office: Reed Smith LLP 435 6th Ave Pittsburgh PA 15219-1886 E-mail: LHitt@ReedSmith.com.

HITT, MARY FRANCES LYSTER, environmentalist, deacon; b. Garfield, Utah, Dec. 22, 1924; d. Arthur Frederick and Marion Aurilla Morrill (Brown) Lyster; m. Mortimer G. Hitt, June 2, 1947 (dec. June 1994); children: Monica Louise, Mary Victoria, Jeremy Arthur Curtis, Geoffrey Christopher Ambrose. AB, MacMurray Coll., 1945; BS in Edn., Kans. State U., 1954; MA, U. Ill., 1946. Ordained deacon, 1995. Asst. city editor Jacksonville (Ill.) Journal, 1945-46; asst. in English U. Ill., Urbana, 1946-48; manuscript editor AMA, Chgo., 1948-51; tchr. North Shore schs., Glen Cove, N.Y., 1966-68, Pawtucket (R.I.) Sch., 1969-70, Cen. Falls (R.I.) Sch., 1969-71; asst. mgr. Cathedral House Bookstore, Providence, 1971-72, mgr., 1972-82; with computer forwarding U.S. Postal Svc., Providence, 1980-91; environ. chair Episcopal Diocese of R.I., Providence, 1991—. Com. chair Christian Social Rels., Providence, 1991-96, sec., 1993-2001; mem. Ecumenical commn., 1999—. Columnist: The Ecolumn, 1991—. Bd. dirs. Childhood Lead Action Project, Providence, 1993—; rep. Environ. Coun. R.I., 1991—, v.p. for development, membership, 1999-2002; mem. R.I. Earth Day Com., 1995—, sec., 2003—; mem. edn. com. Mayor's Lead Task Force, 1998—. Episcopal. Avocations: reading, walking, travel. Home: 11 Beaufort St Providence RI 02908-4406 E-mail: MIhitt@aol.com.

HITTINGER, WILLIAM CHARLES, electronics company executive; b. Bethlehem, Pa., Nov. 10, 1922; s. John Tilghman and Pearl (Heimbach) H.; m. Elizabeth Herman, July 9, 1944; children— Patricia, William, David, Nancy. BS with honors in Metall. Engring, Lehigh U., 1944, D.Engring. (hon.), 1973. Engr. Western Electric Co., 1946-52; prodn. mgr. Semiconductor div. Nat. Union Radio Corp., 1952-54; exec. dir. Bell Telephone Labs., 1954-66; pres. Bellcomm Inc., Washington, 1966-68, Gen. Instrument Corp., N.Y.C., 1968-70; v.p., gen. mgr. RCA Corp., Somerville, NJ., 1970-72, exec. v.p. N.Y.C., 1972-86. Bd. dirs. UNC Inc., Annapolis, Md., Stabler Cos., Inc., Harrisburg, Pa., Biotechnica Internat. Inc., RCA Corp., Thomas & Betts, Recognition Equipment, Allen Bradley, Am. Fletcher Corp., Bethlehem Steel. Bd. dirs. Bethlehem Fgn. Policy Assn., 1960-62, Nat. Action Council for Minorities in Engring., Inc.; trustee, interim pres. Lehigh U., 1997. Served to capt. AUS, 1943-46. Named hon. citizen Bethlehem, 1966 Fellow IEEE, Royal Acad. Arts; mem. Nat. Acad. Engring., Omicron Delta Kappa, Phi Gamma Delta, Sigma Xi, Tau Beta Pi. Home and Office: 52 Pippins Way Morristown NJ 07960-6984

HITTLE, LARRY GLENN, lawyer, electrical engineer; b. Seattle, Apr. 5, 1933; s. Oliver Glenn and Ruth Pauline (Stryker) H.; m. Betty Ann Davis, Jan. 30, 1954; children: Vanessa Ann Hittle Jordan, Gretchen Lynn. BSEE, Wash. State U., 1954; JD, Lewis & Clark Coll., 1968. Bar; Oreg. 1968, U.S. Dist. Ct. Oreg. 1968, U.S. Ct. Appeals (9th cir.) 1990; registered profl. engr., Wash. Flight test instrument engr. Douglas Aircraft Co., Santa Monica, Calif., 1954; elec. engr. Boeing Airplane Co., Seattle, 1956-57; engr. Lewis County Pub. Utility Dist. #1, Chehalis, Wash., 1957-64; contract engr. Bonneville Power Adminstrn., Portland, Oreg., 1964-67, head power contracts, 1967-72; spl. asst. regional solicitor U.S. Dept. of Interior, Portland, 1972-78; asst. gen. counsel Bonneville Power Adminstrn., Portland, 1978-81; ptnr. Lindsay, Hort, Neil & Weigler, Portland, 1981-90, Ater Wynne Hewitt, Dodson & Skeritt, Portland, 1990-93, 96—; pvt. practice Portland, 1993-95; of counsel Ater Wynne LLP, Portland, 1996—. Served with U.S. Army, 1954-56. Mem. ABA, Oreg. Bar Assn., Multnomah County Bar Assn., Multnomah Club. Democrat. E-mail: lgh@aterwynne.com.

HITTLE, RICHARD HOWARD, corporate executive, international affairs consultant; b. Columbus, Nebr., Apr. 30, 1923; s. Arthur Howard and Frieda Margaret (Poppe) H.; m. Catherine Louise Dethlefsen, May 11, 1951; children: Ann-Louise, Thomas Woodford, Bradley Arthur. Student, Cambridge (Eng.) U., 1945; BS, U. Denver, 1950, LLB, 1951; MBA, Harvard U., 1955. With Conoco Inc., 1955-87, mgr. internat. acquisitions, 1964-75; pres. Continental Overseas Oil Co., N.Y.C. also Stamford, Conn., 1969-75; gen. mgr., v.p. internat. govt. affairs Conoco, Inc., Stamford, 1975-83, Wilmington, Del., 1983-87. Bd. govs. Dorset Field Club; bd. advisors Merck Forest and Farmland Ctr., Rupert, Vt. Mem. Dorset Nursing Assn. (bd. trustees), Harvard Club (N.Y.C.), Stanwich Club, Dorset Field Club (Vt.), Met. Club (Washington), Dorset Field Club (bd. dirs.), Merck Forest and Farmland Ctr. (bd. advisors). Clubs: Harvard (N.Y.C.); Stanwich (Greenwich, Conn.); Dorset Field. (Vt.); Metropolitan (Washington). Republican. Lutheran. Home: PO Box 325 Dorset VT 05251-0325 Office: PO Box 469 Old Greenwich CT 06870-0469 E-mail: rhkh@adelphia.net.

HITTNER, DAVID, federal judge; b. Schenectady, N.Y., July 10, 1939; s. George and Sophie (Moskowitz) H.; children: Miriam, Susan, George. BS, NYU, 1961, JD, 1964. Bar: N.Y. 1964, Tex. 1967. Pvt. practice, Houston, 1967-78; judge Tex. 133d Dist. Ct., Houston, 1978-86, U.S. Dist. Ct. (so. dist.) Tex., Houston, 1986—. Author 2 books; contbr. articles to profl. jours. Mem. Nat. coun. Boy Scouts Am. Capt. inf., paratrooper U.S. Army, 1965-66. Recipient Silver Beaver award Boy Scouts Am., 1974, Silver Antelope award Boy Scouts Am., 1988, Samuel E. Gates award Am. Coll. Trial Lawyers. Mem. ABA (Merit award), State Bar Tex. (Outstanding Lawyer in Tex. award), Houston Bar Assn. (Pres.'s and Dirs.' award), Am. Law Inst., Masons (33d degree), Order of Coif (hon.). Office: US Courthouse 515 Rusk St Ste 8509 Houston TX 77002-2603

HITTNER, JAMES BRYANT, psychologist, educator; b. Boston, Nov. 25, 1965; s. Kenneth M. and Renee E. Hittner; m. Rhonda Swickert Hittner, May 6, 2001. BS in Psychology, Ohio State U., 1987; MA in Clin. and Sch. Psychology, Hofstra U., 1989, PhD in Clin. and Sch. Psychology, 1993. Lic. clin. psychologist RI, cert. sch. psychologist NY. Adj. instr. psychology Hofstra U., Hempstead, NY, 1989—93; applied behavior specialist P.L.U.S. Group Homes, Merrick, NY, 1990; adj. instr. psychology Nassau C.C., Garden City,

NY, 1991—93, St. John's U., Queens, NY, 1992; postdoctoral rsch. fellow Brown U. Sch. Medicine, Providence, 1993—95; asst. prof. psychology Coll. of Charleston, SC, 1995—2000, assoc. prof. psychology, 2000—. Instnl. rev. bd. mem. Coll. of Charleston, Charleston, SC, 1996—2002, chair instnl. rev. bd., 1998—2000; substance abuse cons. Coll. of Charleston Coalition on Combatting Underage Drinking, 1999—2003; presenter confs. in field. Contbr. numerous articles to profl. jours.; co-editor: A Guidebook of Statistical Software for the Social and Behavioral Sciences, 1998; exec. editor: The Jour. of Psychology, 2001—, mem. editl. bd.:, 1999—2001, ad hoc reviewer: jours. in field. Rsch. adv. bd. mem. Lowcountry Children's Ctr., Charleston, 1996—2000. Recipient Sharon Chauncey Fellowship award, Brown U. Ctr. for Alcohol and Addiction Studies, 1995; grantee for alcoholism treatment rsch., NIH, 1995—97, curriculum infusion grantee, Network for Dissemination of Curriculum Infusion, 1997. Avocations: reading, travel, music, weightlifting, theater. Office: Coll of Charleston Dept Psychology 66 George St Charleston SC 29424 Fax: 843-953-7151. E-mail: hittnerj@cofc.edu.

HITZ, DUANE EVERETT, brokerage executive; b. St. Paul, Nov. 24, 1939; s. Bernard R. and Marcella M (Kruel) H.; m. Theresa A. Bieza, June 30, 1962; children: Amy, Michelle, Duane, Junior. BA, U. Minn., 1962. Asst. underwriter St. Paul Fire & Marine Ins. Co., 1957-63; exec. v.p. E.W. Blanch Co., Mpls., 1963-82; pres. G.L. Hodson & Son, Inc., St. Paul, 1982-85, exec. v.p. New Hyde Park, N.Y., 1985-87; pres. Hitz and Assocs., Inc., Mpls., 1988-89; sr. v.p. E.W. Blanch Co., Mpls., 1989-91. Capt. Minn. N.G., 1957-68. Mem. Soc. CPCU (cert., bd. dirs. Minn. chpt. 1980-83), Internat. Ins. Seminars. E-mail: dhitz10@yahoo.com.

HITZ, FREDERICK PORTER, public and international affairs educator; b. Washington, Oct. 14, 1939; s. Frederick Porter and Elizabeth (Hume) H.; m. Mary Buford Bocock, Sept. 7, 1963; 1 child, Eliza. AB, Princeton U., 1961; JD, Harvard U., 1964. Bar: Mass. 1965, Va. 1966, D.C. 1976, U.S. Supreme Ct. 1988. Asst. lectr., law dept. U. IFE, Ibadan, Nigeria, 1964-65; fgn. svc. officer U.S. Dept. State, Abidjan, Ivory Coast, 1967-73, congl. rels. officer Washington, 1974-75; dep. asst. sec. legis. affairs U.S. Dept. Def., Washington, 1975-77; mem. energy policy and planning staff Exec. Office of Pres., Washington, 1977; dir. congl. affairs U.S. Dept. Energy, Washington, 1977-78; legis. counsel CIA, Washington, 1978-81; ptnr. Schwabe, Williamson & Wyatt, Washington, 1982-90; inspector gen. CIA, Washington, 1990-98; lectr. in pub. and internat. affairs Woodrow Wilson Sch., Princeton U., 1998—, Weinberg prof. of pub. policy, 1999—, sr. fellow Butler Coll., 2000—. Mem. Coun. Fgn. Rels., 2003—. Co-author: Report to ABA Standing Com. on Law and Nat. Security: Oversight and Accountability of U.S. Intelligence Agencies: An Evaluation, 1985. Trustee Potomac Sch., McLean, Va., 1989-95, chmn. bd. trustees, 1992-94; vestry St. Paul's Ch., Alexandria. Mem. ABA, Wash. Nat. Cathedral, Protestant Episcopal Cathedral Found., Deer Isle Yacht Club (Maine), Met. Club (Washington, bd. govs. 1994-99, sec. 1995-96, pres. 1998-99), Ivy Club (Princeton, N.J., grad. bd. 2001-). Democrat. Episcopalian. Avocations: sailing, skiing, squash. Office: Princeton U Woodrow Wilson Sch Ctr Internat Studies Princeton NJ 08540

HITZMAN, DONALD OLIVER, microbiologist; b. Milw., Dec. 2, 1926; s. Walter John and Irene (Smith) H.; m. Mary Elizabeth Neumann, Aug. 20, 1952; children: Murray W., Daniel C. AB, Carleton Coll., Northfield, Minn., 1948; MS, U. Ill., 1950, PhD, 1954. Resident microbiologist Texaco Co., Long Beach, Calif., 1951; sr. rsch. assoc. Phillips Petroleum Co., Bartlesville, Okla., 1954-85; v.p. rsch. Geo-Microbial Tech., Inc., Ochelata, Okla., 1985—. Contbr. articles to sci. publs. With USAAF, 1944-45. Fulbright scholar, Australia, 1951. Mem. Soc. Microbiology, Soc. Indsl. Microbiology, Am. Chem. Soc. Republican. Episcopalian. Achievements include over 60 patents; numerous fgn. patents. Office: Geo-Microbial Tech East Main St Ochelata OK 74051 E-mail: gmtgeochem@aol.com.

HIXON, ANDREA KAYE, healthcare quality specialist; b. Clifton Forge, Va., Jan. 15, 1955; d. Leon Malcolm and Mary Ruth (Bowyer) Whitmer; m. Charles L. Hixon Jr., Sept. 11, 1976. ADN, Frederick (Md.) Community Coll, 1974; BSN, George Mason U., Fairfax, Va., 1981; MS, U. Md., Balt., 1986. Cert. profl. for healthcare quality, 1993. With VA Med. Ctr., Martinsburg, W.Va., 1974—82, nursing home adminstr., 1982—86; quality assurance coord. nursing James A. Haley VA Hosp., Tampa, Fla., 1987-93; coord. med. ctr. CQI Program, Fla., 1993—2002. Examiner Malcolm Baldrige Nat. Quality Program; appraiser ANA Magnet Nursing Svcs. Program. Mem. Nat. Assn. for Healthcare Quality. Home: 1641 Schalamar Creek Dr Lakeland FL 33801

HIXON, DONALD L. librarian, musician; b. Columbus, Ohio, Aug. 9, 1942; s. Nellie E. Hixon, Elbert Hixon; life ptnr. Don A. Hennessee. MSLS, UCLA, 1967; BA in Music, Calif. State U., 1967; MA in Music, Calif. State U., Long Beach, 1968. Fine arts bibliographer, cataloger U. Calif., Irvine, 1968—92; monographic cataloger Palm Springs Pub. Libr., Palm Springs, 1995—2002; ref. libr. Palm Desert (Calif.) Pub. Libr., 2002—. Series adviser, Bio-Bibliographies in Music Greenwood Pub. Group, Westport, Conn., 1984—2002, series adviser, Music Ref. Collection, 1984—2002. Author: Gian Carlo Menotti: A Bio-Bibliography, 2000, Women in Music, 2d. edit., 1993, Thea Musgrave: A Bio-Bibliography, 1984, Verdi in San Francisco, 1980, (Book) Nineteenth-Century American Drama, 1977. Bd. dirs. Parents, Friends, and Families of Lesbians and Gays, Palm Springs, 1994—99. Mem.: Music Tchrs. Nat. Assn., Palm Springs Hist. Site Found. (exec. asst. 2001—02), Music Tchrs. of the Desert (bd. dirs. 1997—, treas. 1997—), Calif. Assn. Profl. Musicians (dist. coord. 2000—). Home: 76922 Tricia Ln Palm Desert CA 92211-7143 Personal E-mail: dhixondon@yahoo.com.

HIXSON, ELMER L. retired engineering educator; Prof. emeritus dept. elec. engrng. U. Tex., Austin. Recipient Fellow Mems. award Am. Soc. Engrng. Educators, 1992. Fellow Acoustical Soc. Am.; mem. IEEE (life), Inst. for Noise Control Engrng. (founding mem.). Office: U Tex Dept Elec & Computer Engrng Austin TX 78712 E-mail: ehixson@mail.utexas.edu.

HIXSON, NATHAN HANKS, retired military officer; b. Breezewood, Pa., Dec. 15, 1913; s. Ernest Amos Hixson and Jennie Augusta Hanks; m. Mary Frances Williamson, Mar. 5, 1948; children: Glenn Williamson, Pauline Frances. AB, Temple U., 1935; MBA, U. Pa., 1952; grad., U.S. Army War Coll., 1962. Asst. credit mgr. Julius Garfinkel & Co., Washington, 1937-41, 1945-47; commd. 2nd lt. U.S. Army, 1941—43, advanced through grades to col., 1960, ret., 1969, battery comdr., 1942—45, chief machine records unit, 1947-48, chief various brs. Washington, 1948-69, served in Korea, 1962—63, comdt. Adjutant Gen.'s Sch., 1966-69. Instr. George Washington U., Washington, 1958-61, Maryland U., Taegu, Republic of Korea, 1963-64. Scout master Boy Scouts Am., Ft. McPherson, 1947; coord. charitable fund raising U.S. Army War Coll., 1962. Decorated D.S.M., Bronze Star with oak leaf cluster; Disting. Svc. award, Republic of China. Republican. Methodist. Avocations: music, stamp collecting, gardening, walking, conservation. Home: Apt B116 733 Plantation Estates Dr Matthews NC 28105-9106

HIXSON, STANLEY G. speech, language and computer technology educator; b. Chgo., Nov. 25, 1947; s. George Samuel and Alice Elizabeth (Domino) H.; m. Alice Jean Ray, May 25, 1975; children: Polly Alice, Jay Stanley, Christa Renee, Michael Wayne. BA, William Jewell Coll., Liberty, Mo., 1969; MS, Cen. Mich. U., 1986; postgrad., U. Kans. Dir. comm. and retail mktg. Successful Living, Inc., Mpls., 1975-78; pres. LightShine Comm., Shawnee Mission, Kans., 1979-91; editor-in-chief Successful Living, Inc., Mpls.; pub. affairs specialist U.S. Army C.E., Kansas City, Mo., 1983-84; instr. leadership, speech and lang. U.S. Army Command and Gen. Staff Coll., Ft. Leavenworth, Kans., 1984-91; sr. tng. instr. total quality leadership Naval Supply Sys. Command, Washington, 1991-92; dir. quality and process improvement Bur. of Naval Pers., Washington, 1992-94; pres. Great Ideas! in Edn., Alexandria, Va., 1994—. Adj. prof. William Jewell Coll., 1989-90; presenter computer tech., leadership, mktg. and mgmt. seminars, 1973—. Author: Research and Study Skills, 1989, Implementing Total Quality Leadership in the U.S. Navy, 1992, Professional Graphics Presentations, 1995, Intermediate and Advanced Relational Database Management Using MS Access, 1996; co-author: Effective Staff Communications, 1985, 89, Visions and Revisions, 1981, Total Quality Leadership: Customers, Teams and Tools, 1992; editor: An Application of Multiple Intelligences Theory in an Elementary Music Classroom, 1998. With USAF, 1969-73. Recipient Achievement cert. Dept. Army, 1988, Outstanding Svc. award Successful Living, Inc., 1979, 81-82, 84. Mem. Fed. Info. Coun., Washington Deming Study Group, Navy Total Quality Leadership Advocates Network, Genealogy Club (Loudon County, Va.), Assn. Philippe Du Trieux, Alpha Phi Omega (life). Home: 5211 Leeward Ln Kingstowne VA 22315-3944

HIXSON, WENDELL MARK, lawyer; b. Oklahoma City, Dec. 6, 1966; s. Wendell Dee and Mary Theresa (Landgraf) H.; m. Shaa Marie Green, June 22, 1996. BA, Conception Sem. Coll., 1989; JD, U. Okla., 1992. Bar: Okla. 1992, U.S. Dist. Ct. (we. dist.) Okla. 1992, U.S. Dist. Ct. (ea. and no. dists.) 1993, U.S. Ct. Appeals (10th cir.) 1993, U.S. Supreme Ct. 1995. Assoc. Stan Chatman, P.C., Yukon, Okla., 1992-94, Bill James, Yukon and Oklahoma City, 1994-96; pvt. practice Yukon, 1996—. Spl. mcpl. judge, Oklahoma City, 1997—2002; juvenile defender, City of Yukon, 1994—; indigent defender Okla. Indigent Def. Sys., Norman, 1994—. Mem. troop com. Boy Scouts Am., Oklahoma, 1992-97. Fellow Okla. Bar Found.; mem. U.S. Supreme Ct. Hist. Soc., Okla. Criminal Def. Lawyers Assn., Cath. Lawyers Guild of Archdiocese of Oklahoma City, Okla. Bar Assn. (chmn. 2003, litigation sect., sec. 1998-99, 2001, treas. 2000-01, family law sect., mem., vice chmn. criminal law com., 2002, mem. rules of profl. conduct com., del. ho. of dels. 1996, 97, 98, alternate del. 1999-2002, mem. strategic planning com., mem. legal ethics com. 2003--, Outstanding Young Lawyer 1998), Canadian County Bar Assn. (pres. 1997-98), mem. Legal Ethics Com. Republican. Roman Catholic. Office: 800 W Main Yukon OK 73099-1040 E-mail: ykn66law@prodigy.net.

HJALAGER, ANNE-METTE, management consultant; b. Terndrup, Denmark, Sept. 15, 1955; d. Borge and Anne Marie H.; m. Bue Beck, May 27, 1989; children: Alexandra, Leonora. BA in Bus. Econs., The Aarhus Sch. of Bus., Denmark, 1980, MA in Architecture, 1981; PhD, Aalborg U., Denmark, 1986. Rsch. asst. Local Govt.'s Rsch. Inst., Denmark, 1981-84; rschr./cons. Nellemann, Consulting Planners, Denmark, 1984-91; mng. dir. Advance/1, Denmark, 1991-97, 97-99; assoc. rsch. prof. The Aarhus Sch. of Bus., Denmark, 1997-99. Mem. high level group on tourism and employment, European Union, 1998-99; mem. com. for reformation of the Denmark planning system, 1999-2000; mem. funding bd. for Danish tourism, 2000—. Contbr. over 35 articles to profl. jours. Mem. Regional Sci. Assn., Assn. of Danish Town Planners. Office: Advance/1 Science Park Gustav Wiedsved 10 Aarhus 8000 Denmark

HJELMÉR, PATRICK, investment banker; b. Uppsala, Sweden, Dec. 5, 1962; s. Gustav and Charlotte Simone (Baumann) H.; m. Claudia Emerita Schmidt, Sept. 12, 1992; children: Philip Jr, Anna-Giorgia. B of Econs. and Bus. Adminstrn., Uppsala U., 1985, MBA. Trainee Landesbank Schleswig-Holstein, Kiel, Germany, 1985; equity analyst, equities fund mgr. Union Bank of Switzerland, Zurich, 1986-90; equity analyst BZ Bank Zurich Ltd., 1990-92; equity sales mgr. Enskilda Securities and Alfred Berg, London, 1992-93; dir. FNS Securities Ltd., London, 1994-96; co-founder, bd. dirs., group head of sales, head Swiss br. ABG Sundal Collier, Stockholm, Oslo, London, Zurich, 1997—. Summer trainee Svenska Handelsbanken, Stockholm, 1981-84. Served as sgt. Swedish Marines, 1983-84. GH Nation grantee for studies and work abroad Uppsala U., 1985; recipient scholarship German/Swedish C. of C. Avocations: tennis, golf, alpine sports, kynologics (especially italian spinone gundogs). Home: Fallacher 14 CH-8126 Zumikon Switzerland Office: Schipfe 2 CH-8007 Zurich Switzerland

HJELMFELT, DAVID CHARLES, lawyer; b. Chgo., Nov. 25, 1940; s. Allen T. and Doris (Hauber) H.; m. Kendall L. Lawrence, Aug. 17, 1969; children: Trevor Christian, Rebecca Kirstan. AB cum laude, Kans. State U., Manhattan, 1962; LLB, Duke U., 1965; MTh, Christian Life Sch. Theology, 2003. Bar: Kans. 1965, Colo. 1965, D.C. 1973, U.S. Supreme Ct. 1978, U.S. Ct. Appeals (D.C. cir.) 1973, U.S. Ct. Appeals (5th and 11th cirs.) 1981, U.S. Ct. Appeals (10th cir.) 1982. Vis. prof. Sch. Law U. Okla., Norman, 1970-71; staff atty. U.S. AEC, Albuquerque, 1971-73; ptnr. Goldberg, Fieldman & Hjelmfelt, Washington, Colo., 1973-78; sole practice Fort Collins, Colo., 1978-81; ptnr. Hjelmfelt & Larson, Fort Collins, Colo., 1981-90; sole practice Fort Collins, Denver, Colo., 1990-95, Denver, 1995—. Author: Antitrust and Regulated Industries, 1985, Executive's Guide to Marketing, Sales & Advertising Law, 1990; contbr. articles to profl. jours. Mem. coun. liberal edn. Kans. State U.; bd. dirs. Heritage Christian Sch., 1988; bd. dirs. Christian Conciliation Svc., Fort Collins. Lt. JAGC USNR, 1965-68. Mem. ABA (essential facilities monograph com. antitrust sect.), Colo. Bar Assn., Rep. Sen. Inside Circle Club. Office: 1212 Raintree Dr G-137 Fort Collins CO 80526

HJELMSTAD, WILLIAM DAVID, lawyer; b. Apr. 4, 1954; s. Alvin Gordon and A. Thecla (Walz) H.; m. Jenny M. Dube, Nov. 27, 1993; children: Jennifer Ashley, Allison Caitlin. AA in Social Sci., Casper Coll., 1974; BS in Psychology, U. Wyo., 1976, JD, 1979. Bar: Wyo. 1979, U.S. Dist. Ct. Wyo. 1979. Dept. county pros. atty. Hot Springs County, Thermopolis, Wyo., 1979-80; asst. pub. defender Natrona County, Casper, Wyo., 1980-82; sole practice Casper, Wyo., 1981—. Mem. ATLA, ABA (mem. family law com. 1983-84, adoption com. 1983-84), Wyo. State Bar Assn. (mem. alcohol and substance abuse com., lawyers assistance com. 1988-95, computer and technical com. 1997—, bench-bar rels. com. 2002—), Natrona County Bar Assn., Wyo. Trial Lawyers Assn., Assn. Conflict Resolution, Am. Judicature Soc., Acad. Family Mediators, U. Wyo. Alumni Assn., Casper Coll. Alumni Assn., Wyo. Cowboy Shootout Com., Elks, Kiwanis. Office: 416 S Beech St Casper WY 82601-2808

HJERPE, EDWARD ALFRED, III, finance and banking executive; b. Worcester, Mass., Jan. 25, 1959; s. Edward Alfred Jr. and Nancy Ann (O'Connor) H.; m. Macrina Groody, Aug. 17, 1985; children: Christine G., Edward A. IV, Catherine Ann. BA in Econs. and Bus., St. Anselm Coll., 1981; MA in Econs., U. Notre Dame, 1984, PhD in Econs., 1985. Industry economist Commodity Futures Trading Commn., Washington, 1985-86; fin. economist Fed. Home Loan Bank Bd., Washington, 1986-88; v.p., chief economist Fed. Home Loan Bank, Boston, 1988-89, sr. v.p., 1989-92, exec. v.p., CFO, 1992-97; sr. v.p., treas., CFO First Fed. Am. Bancorp, Inc., Fall River, Mass., 1997—98, exec. v.p., COO, CFO Swansea, Mass., 1998—. Bd. dirs. Dentaquest Ventures, 2003—. Contbr. articles to profl. jours. Bd. trustees St. Anselm Coll., 1992—, chmn. fin. com., mem. exec. com.; chmn. fin. com. Medway Town, 1995-98; bd. trustees Roger Williams Med. Ctr., Providence, 2000—; bd. dirs. United Way Fall River, Mass, 2001—. Recipient A. Schmitt Dissertation fellowship. Mem. Am. Econ. Assn., Omicron Delta Epsilon, Delta Epsilon Sigma, Pi Gamma Mu. Roman Catholic. Home: One Great Rd Barrington RI 02806-1579 Office: First Fed Savs Bank Am One First Park Swansea MA 02777

HJORT, HOWARD WARREN, consultant, economist; b. Plentywood, Mont., Dec. 20, 1931; BS, Mont. State U., 1958, MS, 1959; postgrad., N.C. State U. Staff economist Office of Sec. Agr., Washington, 1963-65, spl. asst. to under sec., 1965; dir. staff for program planning and analysis Office of Sec., 1965-69; planning and mgmt. adviser with Ford Found., India, 1969-72, dir. Office of Econs., Policy Analysis and Budget, 1977-81; co-founder Schnittker Assocs. (agrl. cons.), Washington, 1972-77; ptnr. EPI (McLean), Va., 1981-84; dir. policy analysis div. FAO, Rome, 1984-90, dir. liaison office for N.Am. Washington, 1990-91, dep. dir. gen. Rome, 1992-97; cons., 1998—. Office: 1910 Franklin Ave Mc Lean VA 22101-5307 E-mail: howardhjort@aol.com.

HJORTSBERG, WILLIAM REINHOLD, writer; b. N.Y.C., Feb. 23, 1941; s. Helge Reinhold and Anna Ida (Welti) H.; m. Marian Souidee Renken, June 2, 1962 (div. 1982); children— Lorca Isabel, Max William.; m. Sharon Leroy, July 21, 1982 (div. 1985). BA, Dartmouth Coll., 1962; postgrad., Yale U., 1962-63, Stanford U., 1967-68. Ind. author, screenwriter, 1969—. Adj. prof. media and theatre arts Mont. State U., 1991—. Author: Alp, 1969, Gray Matters, 1971, Symbiography, 1973, Toro! Toro! Toro!, 1974, Falling Angel, 1978, Tales & Fables, 1985, Nevermore, 1994, films: Thunder and Lightning, 1977, Legend, 1986, Angel Heart, 1987; co-author TV film: Georgia Peaches, 1980; contbg. editor Rocky Mountain Mag., 1979; contbr. fiction to Realist, Playboy, Cornell Rev., Penthouse, Oui, Sports Illustrated; contbr. criticism to N.Y. Times Book Rev. Recipient Playboy Editorial award, 1971, 78; Wallace Stegner fellow, 1967-68; Nat. Endowment Arts grantee, 1976. Mem. Authors Guild, Writers Guild Am. Avocations: fly fishing, skiing, collecting modern first editions, art, antique toys. Home: 2586 Boulder Rd Mc Leod MT 59052 Office: care Harold Matson Co Ste 714 276 Fifth Ave New York NY 10001

HLAD, GREGORY MICHAEL, psychometrist, institutional test administrator, career assessment and testing manager; b. McKeesport, Pa., Feb. 14, 1947; s. Michael Gregory Jr. and Helen Delores (Harman) H.; m. Carol Ann Huzinec, July 15, 1972; 1 child, Kristen. BEd, U. Miami, Coral Gables, 1969; MEd, Calif. (Pa.) State U., 1974. Cert. tchr., Fla., Pa.; cert. work evaluator; cert. occupational specialist. Tchr. Wilkinsburg (Pa.) Sch. Dist., 1969—79; asst. prof. Pasco-Hernando Community Coll., New Port Richey, Fla., 1979—83; occupl. specialist Pasco-Pvt. Industry Coun., Fla., 1983—93; assessment coord. Workforce Devel. Authority, Ocala, Fla., 1993—96, Pasco-Hernando C.C., New Port Richey, Fla., 1996—, career testing ctr. mgr., 1996—. Cons. Xerox Ednl. div. New Haven, 1977-79, Pasco-Hernando Community Coll., 1983—, mem. learning lab. adv. com., 1985-86; v.p. Ednl./Psychol. Assessments Inc. Mem. budget adv. com. Safety Harbor (Fla.), 1986-87. Recipient Cert. of Appreciation Dept. of Corrections, 1982, Appreciation of Service award Boy Scouts Am., 1986. Mem. Nat. Assn. Psychometrists, Nat. Assn. Workforce Profls. Avocations: jogging, sports car racing, home computers. Home: 1070 Misty Hollow Ln Tarpon Springs FL 34688 Office: Pasco-Hernado Cmty Coll 10230 Ridge Rd New Port Richey FL 34654 E-mail: gregh6783@aol.com., hladg@phcc.edu.

HLATKY, MARK ANDREW, cardiologist, medical researcher; b. Windber, Pa., June 4, 1950; s. George Andrew and Rose Annette (Gonnella) H.; m. Donna Marie Alvarado, May 12, 1984; 1 child, Nicholas Michael. BS, MIT, 1972; MD, U. Pa., 1976. Diplomate Am. Bd. Internal Medicine, Am. Bd. Cardiovasc. Disease; lic. physician, Calif. Intern, resident U. Ariz., Tucson, 1976-79; Robert Wood Johnson clin. scholar U. Calif., San Francisco, 1979-81; fellow in cardiology Duke U., Durham, N.C., 1981-83, asst. prof. medicine, 1983-89; assoc. prof. health rsch. and policy, assoc. prof. medicine Stanford (Calif.) U., 1989-96, prof. health rsch. and policy, prof. medicine, 1996—. Attending physician, cardiovasc. medicine svc. Stanford U. Med. Ctr., 1989—; mem. Health Care Tech. Study sect. NIH, Rockville, Md., 1992-96. Contbr. over 160 articles to profl. jours. Sloan scholar, 1972. Fellow Am. Coll. Cardiology; mem. Am. Heart Assn. (fellow coun. on clin. cardiology), Am. Fedn. Clin. Rsch., Internat. Soc. for Tech. Assessment in Health Care, Phi Beta Kappa. Achievements include research in outcomes after coronary surgery, coronary angioplasty, acute myocardial infarction, and cardiac arrhythmias. Home: 168 Rinconada Ave Palo Alto CA 94301-3725 Office: Stanford U Sch Medicine HRP Redwood Bldg Rm 150 Stanford CA 94305 E-mail: hlatky@stanford.edu.

HLAVACEK, ROY GEORGE, publishing executive, magazine editor; b. Chgo., Sept. 17, 1937; s. George Louis and Lillian Barbara (Vasovic) H.; m. Nancy Elaine Wroblaski, Aug. 3, 1963; children: Carrie Lee Felix, Alexander Michael. BS, U. Ill., 1960; MBA, U. Chgo., 1969. Project engr. Research and Devel. Center, Swift & Co., Chgo., 1960-65; v.p., editor, pub. Food Processing mag., Foods of Tomorrow mag. Food Publs. div. Putman Pub. Co., Chgo., 1965-92; v.p., group pub. Food Group, Delta Comms. Inc., Chgo., 1992-2001; v.p. comms. Inst. Food Technologists, 2001—. Adv. com. dept. food sci. U. Ill., Urbana-Champaign, 1988-93. Patentee in field. Commr. Oak Park (Ill.) Landmarks Commn., 1972-79, chmn., 1976-79; treas. Oak Park Bicentennial Commn., 1973-76, Ernest Hemingway Found. of Oak Park, 1983-2000. Mem. ASME, Food Processing Machinery and Supplies Assn. (dir. 1987-91), Inst. Food Technologists (councilor 1975-81, chmn. Chgo. sect.), Pi Tau Sigma, Sigma Tau. Home: 904 Forest Ave Oak Park IL 60302-1310 Office: Inst Food Technologists 525 W Van Buren Chicago IL 60607 E-mail: rghlavacek@ift.org.

HLAVAY, JAY ALAN, financial analyst; b. Pitts., Sept. 30, 1956; s. Joseph and Margaret Marie (Danjou) H.; m. Cayce Avril Martin, Sept. 26, 1992; children: Joseph Martin, Christopher Jay. Student, Rutgers U., 1979; BS in Geology magna cum laude, U. Pitts., 1983, MBA, 1989. Geologist RSC Energy Corp., New Philadelphia, Ohio, 1983-85; dist. geologist Carless Resources Inc., New Philadelphia, 1985-89; gen. mgr. What on Earth, Pitts., 1989-90; prin. OPUS Energy Cons. Svcs., Coraopolis, Pa., 1990-92; exploration fin. analyst Union Pacific Resources, Ft. Worth, 1991-92, Austin chalk analyst, 1992-93, contr. Gulf of Mexico/Other Profit Ctr., 1993-95, contr. Gulf Coast Profit Ctr., 1996, project mgr. fin. ops., 1996-97, mgr. compensation, people dept., 1997-98, fin. advisor, 1998—2000, Food Lion, LLC, Salisbury, NC, 2000—02, mgr. strategic and bus. analysis, 2002—. Navy ROTC scholar, 1974; recipient Appreciation award Tuscarawas Valley Desk and Derrick Club, 1985, 86, 87; recipient West Allegheny Sch. Dist. Disting. Alumni award, 1988. Mem. Am. Assn. Petroleum Geologists (co-chmn. fin. com. S.W. sect. ann. conv. 1993), Sigma Gamma Epsilon. Home: 104 Longboat Rd Mooresville NC 28117 Office: Food Lion Inc 2110 Executive Dr PO Box 1330 Salisbury NC 28145-1330

HLOBIK, LAWRENCE S. agricultural products executive; With fertilizer, chem., and agribus. industries, 27 yrs.; pres. AgriBusiness Group J.R. Simplot Co., Boise, 1998—2002, CEO, 2002—. Office: JR Simplot Co PO Box 27 Boise ID 83707 also: JR Simplot Co 999 Main St Ste 1300 Boise ID 83702*

HLOUSEK, JOYCE B(ERNADETTE), school system administrator; b. Chgo., Sept. 7, 1949; d. Theodore P. and Helen J. (Pietrzak) Brewer. BSEE, DePaul U., Chgo., 1971, MA, 1976; EdD, Vanderbilt U., 1993. Cert. in elem. edn., learning disabilities, gen. adminstrn., Ill. Tchr., asst. prin. Chgo. Pub. Schs., 1970-71; tchr. Community Consol. Sch. Dist. 54, Schaumburg Twp., Ill., 1971-73, learning disabilities specialist, 1973-80, 1980-85, dir. program assessment, 1985-96, adminstr., 1996—. Instr. Ill. Adminstrv. Acd., North Cook Region, Ill., 1989-92; due process hearing officer Ill. State Bd. Edn., 1976-84. Author: The Missing Piece of Change, 1993, Understanding Your Child's Test Scores, 1982, (series) Action Mathematics, 1976; feature writer Chgo. Daily Herald and Chgo. Tribune, 1996—. Sec. Community Communicators, Schaumburg Twp., 1978-81; bd. dirs., edn. Strays Halfway House; electee Parish Religious Edn. Bd., 1997. Named Outstanding Educator, Schaumburg Jaycees, 1974. Mem. ASCD, Am. Assn. Sch. Adminstrs., Ill. Assn. for Supervision and Curriculum Devel., Inst. for Ednl. Rsch. (bd. editorial advisors), Phi Delta Kappa. Office: Schaumburg Twp Cmty Consol Sch Dist 54 Lakeview Sch 524 E Schaumburg Rd Schaumburg IL 60194-3510

HLOZEK, CAROLE DIANE QUAST, business executive; b. Dallas, Apr. 17, 1959; d. Robert E. and Bonnie (Wootton) Quast. BS, BBA, Tex. A&M U., 1982. CPA, Tex. Internal auditor Brown & Root Inc., Houston, 1982-84; asst. contr. Wilson Supply Co., Houston, 1984-86; sr. acctg. supr. Hydro Conduit Corp., Houston, 1986-87; fin. analyst Am. Capital, Houston, 1989-94; dir. adminstrn. Am. Gen. Securities, Inc., Houston, 1994-98; CFO 1st Fin. Group Am., Houston, 1998-2000; contr. Clearworks, 2000-01; dir. Ornate Holdings Inc., Houston, 2001—02; full time cons., 2002—. Chmn. bd. dirs. On Our Own Inc., 1987-91; mentor CPA's Helping Schs.; treas. Sampson Elem. PTO, 2002-. Mem. Mensa, Houston Livestock Show and Rodeo. Home: 13527 Greenwood Manor Cypress TX 77429-4840

HO, ALEX WING-KEUNG, statistician; b. Hong Kong, Feb. 16, 1956; came to U.S., 1980; s. Tak-Kam and Sam-mui (Tong) H. BSc, U. Alta., Edmonton, Can., 1979; MA, SUNY, Buffalo, 1988, MS in Social and Preventive Medicine, 2002. Tchg. asst. SUNY, Buffalo, 1981-86, adminstrv. asst., 1986-87, head/supr. Ridge Lea Libr., 1987-89, statis. cons., 1988—, statistician, 1989—. Statis. cons. various pharm. cos., 1992—; presenter in field. Ad hoc jour. reviewer Jour. Periodontology, 1994; abstract reviewer Jour. Dental Hygiene, Jour. Periodontology; contbr. articles to profl. jours. Adminstr. St. Joseph's Coll., U. Alta., 1982-83. Recipient Cmty. Svc. awards Univ. Height Cmty., Buffalo, 1984, 85, Clin. Rsch. award Am. Acad. Periodontoloty, 1998. Mem. Am. Assn. Dental Rsch., Internat. Assn. Dental Rsch., Am. Assn. Pub. Health Dentistry, Am. Statis. Assn. (sec./treas. Buffalo-Niagara chpt. 1996), Biometrics Soc., Soc. for Epidemiologic Rsch. Avocations: tennis, fishing, computing, reading, soccer. Home: 45 Hillsboro Rd Buffalo NY 14225-1625 E-mail: alexho@acsu.buffalo.edu.

HO, CHIH-MING, physicist, educator; b. Chung King, China, Aug. 16, 1945; arrived in U.S., 1968; s. Shao-Nan and I-Chu Ho; m. Shirley T.S. Ho, Mar. 4, 1972; 1 child, Dean. BSME, Nat. Taiwan U., 1967; PhD, Johns Hopkins U., 1974. Assoc. rsch. scientist Johns Hopkins U., Balt., 1974-75; asst. prof. U. So. Calif., L.A., 1976-81, assoc. prof., 1981-85, prof., 1985-91; assoc. vice-chancellor for rsch. UCLA, 2001—, prof., 1991—, Ben Rich-Lockheed Martin prof., 1996—. Dir. Ctr. for Micro Sys., 1993—2000; cons. Flow Industries, Kent, 1982, Dynamics Tech., Torrance, Calif., 1977, Rockwell Internat., Canoga Park, Calif., 1980—83; dir. Inst. for Cell Mimetic Space Exploration, 2002—. Contbr. articles to profl. jours.; patentee in field. Fellow AIAA, Am.

Phys. Soc.; mem. Nat. Acad. Engring., Academia Sinica, Phi Beta Kappa. Achievements include research in micro-electro-mechanical systems, biomedical engineering, turbulence, aerodynamics, noise.

HO, CHING, surgeon; b. Canton, China, 1929; MB BS, U. Hong Kong, 1953. Diplomate Am. Bd. Surgery. Intern St. Vincents Hosp., Erie, 1955-56, resident, 1956-60, St. Boniface Hosp., Winnipeg, Man., Can., 1961; fellow cardiovascular surgery U. Man. Hosp., 1960-61; mem. staff Houston N.W., 1979; pvt. practice Houston, 1979; mem. staff Cypress Fairbanks Med. Ctrs., Tex., 1983. Fellow ACS, Internat. Coll. Surgeons, Royal Coll. Surgeons Can. Office: 17070 Red Oak Dr Ste 209 Houston TX 77090-2615

HO, CHU EU, civil engineer; b. Singapore, Aug. 26, 1959; s. Ching Yu and Mei Foon (Lim) H.; m. Pee She Patsy Chen; children: Ivan, Vivianne. BCE with honors, Nat. U. Singapore, 1984; MSc, U. London, 1985; DIC, Imperial Coll. London, 1985; postgrad., MIT, 1999—. Reg. profl. engr., Singapore. Civil engr. Housing Devel. Bd., Singapore, 1984; assoc. Ove Arup & Ptnrs., Singapore, 1986-95; gen. mgr. Presscrete Engring., Singapore, 1995-99; grad. tchg. asst. MIT, 1999—. Mem. examining panel Profl. Engrs. Bd., Singapore, 1996—. Recipient Lee Found. award, 1984. Mem. ASCE (mem. protem com. 1996—), Inst. Engrs. Singapore. E-mail: chueuho@mit.edu.

HO, DAVID D. research physician, virologist; b. Taichung, Taiwan, Nov. 3, 1952; arrived in U.S., 1964; s. Paul and Sonia Ho; m. Susan Kuo Ho; children: Kathryn, Jonathan, Jaclyn. Student, MIT; BS summa cum laude, Calif. Inst. Tech., 1974; MD, Harvard, 1978. Resident internal medicine UCLA Sch. Medicine, 1981, chief resident, 1982; clin. and rsch. fellow Infectious Disease Unit Mass. Gen. Hosp., 1982—85; rsch. fellow medicine Harvard U., 1982—85; physician, rsch. scientist divsn. infectious diseases, dept. medicine Cedars-Sinai Med. Ctr., 1986—90; dir. Ctr. for AIDS Rsch. NYU, 1994—96, prof. medicine and microbiology, co-dir., 1990—96; dir. Diamond AIDS Rsch. Ctr., N.Y.C., 1990—. Assoc. prof. medicine in residents UCLA, 1986—89, assoc. prof., 1989. Contbr. articles to profl. jours. Named 1996 Man of Yr., Time Mag.; recipient Mayor's award (N.Y.C.) for Excellence in Sci. and Tech., Sci. award, Chinese Am. Med. Soc. Fellow: AAAS (Ernst Jung prize in medicine); mem.: NIH vaccine working group, Com. of 100 (Chinese Am. leadership orgn.), AmFAR (bd. dirs. sci. bd.). Office: Aaron Diamond AIDS Rsch Ctr 455 1st Ave Fl 7 New York NY 10016-9121

HO, DAVID KIM HONG, educator; b. Honolulu, Mar. 5, 1948; s. Raymond T.Y. and Ellen T.Y. (Fong) H.; m. Joan Yee, July 6, 1968 (div. Apr. 1982); 1 child, Michael J.; m. Patricia Ann McAndrews, June 25, 1983. BS in Indsl. Engring., U. So. Calif., 1970; MBA, Butler U., 1976; MS in Acctg., U. Wis., Whitewater, 1981. Cert. fellow in prodn. and inventory mgmt. Indsl. engr. FMC Corp., L.A., 1970-73, mgr. prodn. planning and inventory control Indpls., 1973-77; materials mgr. Butler Mfg. Co., Ft. Atkinson, Wis., 1977-81, systems mgr. Kansas City, Mo., 1981-82; dir. materials and systems Behlen Mfg. Co., Columbus, Nebr., 1982-84, v.p. operations, bd. dirs., 1984-86; mgr. corp. materials Lozier Corp., Omaha, 1986-90, plant mgr., 1990-91; v.p. mfg. Heatilator Inc., Mt. Pleasant, Iowa, 1991-93; prof. profl. studies Bellevue (Nebr.) U., 1993—. Instr. Met. C.C., Omaha, 1989—, Iowa Wesleyan Coll., Mt. Pleasant, 1991—92; cons., evaluator The Higher Learning Commn. of the North Ctrl. Assn., Chgo., 2001—; evaluator Assn. of Collegiate Bus. Sch. Programs, Overland Pk., Kans., bd. dirs. Mem.: Inst. Supply Mgmt., Am. Prodn. and Inventory Control Soc. Home: 11729 Fisher House Rd Bellevue NE 68123-1112 Office: Met CC PO 3777-Soc 121 Omaha NE 68103-0777 E-mail: dho@metropo.mccneb.edu.

HO, DOMINIC KC, electrical engineering educator; b. Hong Kong, July 28, 1965; Keng Wai Ho and Po Mei Chan. BSc in Engring., Chinese U. Hong Kong, 1983-88, PhD in Electronic Engring., 1988-91. Rsch. assoc. Royal Mil. Coll. Can., Kingston, Ont., 1991-94; mem. sci. staff Nortel Networks (formerly BNR), Montreal, 1995-96; assoc. prof. U. Saskatchewan, Saskatoon, Can., 1996-97; asst. prof. U. Mo., Columbia, 1997—2003, assoc. prof., 2003—. Cons. Nortel Networks, Montreal, 1996—. Contbr. articles to profl. jours.; patentee in field. Mem. IEEE (sr.). Avocation: reading. Office: U Mo Dept Elec and Computer Engring Columbia MO 65211-0001 E-mail: hod@missouri.edu.

HO, HON HING, biology educator; b. Hong Kong, May 3, 1939; BS in Botany and Zoology, U. Hong Kong, 1962, BS in Botany, 1963; PhD in Botany, U. Western Ont., London, Can., 1966. Teaching asst. U. Western Ont., 1964-66, postdoctoral rsch. fellow, 1966-67; asst. prof. botany and bacteriology Ohio Wesleyan U., Del., 1967-68; from asst. prof. to prof. biology SUNY, New Paltz, 1968—, chmn. dept. biology, 1991—. Vis. rsch. assoc. U. Calif., Riverside, 1975; vis. prof. Nanjing (China) Agr. U., 1982, 92-93, Academia Sinica, Taipei, Taiwan, 1989-91, 97-99, Chinese Acad. Tropical Agrl. Sci., 1998, 2003. Contbr. numerous articles to profl. jours. Recipient Spl. Cert., Nat. Edn. Coun. China, 1992; Can. Commonwealth scholar, 1963-66, SUNY faculty scholar, 1990-93; SUNY Rsch. Found. faculty fellow, 1969, 70, 77; grantee SUNY Rsch. Found., 1969-70, 77-78, Whitehall Found., 1986-89, Nat. Rsch. Coun. China, 1989-91, Nat. Geog. Soc., 1991-93. Mem. Am. Phytopathological Soc., Mycological Soc. Am., Mycological Soc. China, Internat. Soc. Plant Pathology (mem. com. 1993—). Home: 11 Bonticou View Dr New Paltz NY 12561-1004 Office: SUNY Biology Dept 75 S Manheim Blvd Ste 1 New Paltz NY 12561-2499 E-mail: hoh@newpaltz.edu.

HO, HWA-SHAN, engineering executive, civil engineer, consultant, drilling engineer; b. Hualien, Taiwan, Sept. 10, 1941; arrived in U.S.A., 1964; s. Tung-Mu and Mien (Lin) H.; m. Rita Ying-Huei Chia, Aug. 24, 1969 (dec. Dec. 1993); m. Lily Hai You; children: Yvonne Y.F., Isaac Y.J., Yvette Y.F.; mem. Lily Hai You. BSCE, Nat. Taiwan U., 1963; MS in Engring., Brown U., 1966, PhD in Engring., 1969. Assoc. in rsch. Brown U., Providence, R.I., 1968-69; asst. prof. civil engring. Univ. So. Calif., L.A., 1969-74; sr. engring. technologist Ralph M. Parsons Co., Pasadena, Calif., 1974-76; assoc. prof. civil engring. U. Utah, Salt Lake City, 1976-81; sr. rsch. specialist Exxon Production Rsch. Co., Houston, 1981-84; cons. scientist Sperry-Sun Drilling Svcs., Houston, 1984-92; pres. Tapong RTI, Inc., Spring-Klein, Tex., 1992—. Cons. Diamant Boart Stratabit, Brussels, 1991-95, Geothermal Energy Rsch. & Devel. Co., Tokyo, 1994-96. Mem. Orgn. of Chinese Americans, Houston, 1990—, Chinese Profl. Club (officer 1993), Houston, 1992-94. 2nd lt. USAF, 1963-64, Taiwan. Mem. ASCE, Soc. Petroleum Engrs. Achievements include 10 U.S. patents on directional drilling tech.; first to use software program to correct error in MWD Survey due to drillstring deformations enabling elimination of gyro wireline re-survey; first to devel. comprehensive rock-bit interaction model in drilling trajectory prediction; first to propose designed PDC Bits with specific walk tendencies and anti-walk bits; first to study the effect of drillstring stiffness in torque-drag monitoring calculations; first to propose "compliance-based" torque-drag monitoring; improved self-consistent forward stepping algorithm in trajectory prediction; first to infer formation dip and strike from directional drilling data; rsch. on a new gen. variational method to solve boundary value problems in linear sys. with interfaces, multiple connectivities. Home: 5411 Mineral Creek Ct Spring TX 77379-8869 Office: TAPONG RTI INC PO Box 11170 Spring TX 77391-1170 E-mail: HwashanHo@aol.com.

HO, JOHN WING-SHING, biochemistry educator, researcher; b. Hong Kong, Sept. 10, 1954; came to U.S., 1979; s. Tak-Kam and Sam-Mui (Tong) H. BS in Biochemistry, U. Alberta, Can., 1979; MA in Chemistry, SUNY, Buffalo, 1982, PhD in Chemistry, 1985. Teaching asst. dept. chemistry SUNY, Buffalo, 1979-82, rsch. asst. dept. chemistry, 1982-85; chemistry lectr. Millard Fillmore Coll., SUNY, Buffalo, 1985; postdoctoral fellow SUNY, Buffalo, 1985-87; rsch. assoc. dept. chemistry U. Utah, Salt Lake City, 1987-88, rsch. faculty Ctr. for Human Toxicology, 1988—. Vis. prof. dept. applied biology and chem. tech. Hong Kong Poly., 1992; lectr. dept. biochemistry Chinese U. of Hong Kong, 1994—; spkr. seminars and confs., 1983—. Reviewer Jour. Chromatography (Biomedical Applications), 1990—; contbr. articles to profl. jours. IBR fellow Inst. Basic Rsch., 1986-88; recipient traineeship Health and Human Svcs., 1985-86. Fellow Am. Inst. Chemists; mem. AAAS, Am. Chem. Soc., N.Y. Acad. Scis., U.S. Tennis Assn.

HO, KALON KL, internist, researcher; MD, Harvard U., 1987, MS, 1995. Diplomate Am. Bd. Internal Medicine, Cardiovasc. Diseases, Interventional Cardiology. Med. resident Brigham and Women's Hosp., Boston, 1987-90; fellow in cardiology Beth Israel Hosp., Boston, 1990-95, assoc. medicine, 1995—; instr. Harvard U. Med. Sch., Boston, 1994—2002, asst. prof., 2002—. Fellow: ACP, Soc. for Cardiovascular Angiography and Interventions, Am. Coll. Cardiology. Office: Beth Israel Deaconess Med Ctr Med Ctr 330 Brookline Ave Boston MA 02215-5400

HO, KWOK YUEN, data processing executive; b. China, Dec. 27, 1950; married; 3 children. BSEE, Cheng Kung U., Taiwan, 1974. With Control Data, Hong Kong, Data Products, Hong Kong, Nat. Semiconductor, Hong Kong, Philips, Hong Kong, Wongs, Hong Kong; pres., co-founder ATI Technologies, Inc., Toronto, 1985—, CEO, chmn. bd., 1993—. Named Entrepreneur of the Yr., Ernst & Young, 1998. Office: ATI Technologies Inc 33 Commerce Valley Dr E Markham ON Canada L3T 7N6 Fax: (905) 882-2620.

HO, LOW-TONE, physician, researcher, educator; b. Chousan, Chekiang, China, May 1, 1947; s. Tzen and Jo-Hsiu (Yen) H.; m. Shu-Hsia Tu, Nov. 12, 1973; children: Pei-Ling, Pei-Shuan, Ming-Han. MD, Nat. Def. Med. Ctr., Taipei, Taiwan, 1971. Med. diplomate; lic. physician, Taiwan, U.S. Resident Vets. Gen. Hosp., Taipei, 1971-75, attending physician, 1975—, chief endocrine function unit, 1982-85, chief divsn. endocrinology and metabolism, 1985-94, chmn. dept. med. rsch. and edn., 1994—. Prof. medicine Nat. Def. Med. Ctr., Taipei, 1986—, prof. nuclear medicine, 1991—; prof. medicine Nat. Yang-Ming U., Taipei, 1986—, prof. physiology, 1988—, dean Faculty Medicine, 1999—; prof. biomed. sci. Nat. Tsing-Hua U., Taipei, 1991—; prof. Grad. Inst. Clin. Medicine, NYMU, 1995—, prof. and dean, NYMU Sch. of Med., 1999—. Contbr. articles to profl. jours. Col. Taiwan Nt. Def. Med. Ctr., 1971-89. Recipient Outstanding Rsch. Accomplishment award Nt. Sci. Coun., 1989-91; faculty fellow U. Mich., Ann Arbor, 1977-79; Nat. Health grantee, 1983-86. Mem. Diabetes Assn. China (exec. bd. 1988—), Endocrine Soc. China (exec. bd. 1988—), Soc. Lipid and Atherosclerosis China (exec. bd. 1994—). Avocations: chess, bridge, philosophy, computer, golf. Office: Vets Gen Hosp Shipai Rd Sect 2 # 201 Taipei 112 Taiwan

HO, MATTHEW R, physician; b. Los Angeles, Calif., July 12, 1970; s. Frances and John A Ho; m. Candice C Chaya, Dec. 15, 1996. MD, Loma Linda, 1992—96. Emergency Medicine CA, 2000. Physician Kaiser Permanente, Baldwin Park, Calif., 1999—. Personal E-mail: ho4acan@aol.com.

HO, REGINALD CHI SHING, medical educator; b. Hong Kong, Mar. 30, 1932; came to U.S., 1940; s. Chow and Elizabeth (Wong) Ho; m. Sharilyn Dang, Nov. 14, 1964; children: Mark, Reginald, Gianna Masca, Timothy. Student, St. Louis U., 1954, MD, 1959. Diplomate Nat. Bd. Med. Examiners, Am. Bd. Internal Medicine. Rotating intern U. Cin. Hosps., 1959-60, resident in internal medicine, 1960-62; fellow in hematology and oncology Barnes Hosp./Washington U., St. Louis, 1962-63; attending physician in oncology, hematology and internal medicine Queen's Med. Ctr., 1962—; instr. in medicine Sch. Medicine U. Hawaii, Honolulu, 1967-69, asst. clin. prof. medicine, 1969-72, assoc. clin. prof., 1972-77, clin. prof., 1977—; attending physician dept. hematology and oncology Straub Clinic and Hosp., Honolulu, 1973—. Mem. tech. rev. com. Regional Med. Program Hawaii, 1970-71, long range planning com. 1971; prin. investigator Hawaii Community Clin. Oncology Program, Honolulu, 1983-86; adj. prof. clin. sci. Cancer Rsch. Ctr. Hawaii, 1989—, mem. various coms. Contbr. articles to med. jours. Bd. dirs. Cath. Svcs. for Families, 1987-91. Mem. AMA, ACP, Am. Cancer Soc. (divsn. del. 1982-93, del. dir. 1983-92, exec. com. 1989—, chair med. and sci. exec. com. 1991-92, past officer dir. 1994—, v.p. 1991-92, pres. 1992-93, immediate past pres. 1993-94, Clin fellow 1962, bd. dirs. Hawaii divsn. 1968—, v.p. 1970-71, chmn. exec. com. 1971-73, v.p. 1973-75, pres. 1976-77, chmn. bd. dirs. 1977-78, hon. life mem. 1989—, bd. dirs. Honolulu chpt. 1980-86, bd. dirs. Oahu unit 1966-71, chair svc. and rehab. com. 1967-71), Hawaii Med. Assn. (Hawaii cancer commn. 1980-85, chair cancer com. 1981-90), Honolulu County Med. Assn. (del. to Hawaii Med. Assn. 1969-72, alt. del. 1972-74, bd. govs. 1972), Exptl. Med. Care Rev. Orgn. (exec. com., chair ambulatory care edn. audit com. 1972), Alpha Omega Alpha. Roman Catholic. Avocation: tennis. Office: Straub Clinic Hosp 888 S King St Honolulu HI 96813-3083

HO, ROBERT EN MING, neurosurgeon, educator; b. Honolulu, Nov. 13, 1942; s. Donald Tet En Ho and Violette (Weeks) Gould; m. Edie Olsen, June 27, 1964; children: Lisa, Amy. BS cum laude, Mich. State. U., 1964; MD, Wayne State U., 1968. Diplomate Am. Bd. Neurol. Surgery. Surg. intern Detroit Gen. Hosp., 1968-69, surg. resident, 1969-70, neurosurg. resident, 1972-76; microsurg. fellow Neurochirurgische Universtatskilinik, Zurich, Switzerland, 1976; instr. dept. neurosurgery Wayne State U., Detroit, 1977-79; dir. dept. neurosurgery Gertrude Levin Pain Clinic, 1977-80; asst. prof., 1979-84; chief neurosurg. svcs. Health Care Inst., 1979-84; clin. asst. prof., 1984—. Founder, dir. Microneurosurg. Lab., 1977-89, dir. spine and spine reconstruction dept. neurosurgery med. sch., 1992-97; dir. neuroscis. intensive care unit Harper Hosp., Detroit, 1980-84, spine and spine reconstruction fellowship Wayne State Med. Sch., 1992-97; mem. audit com. Detroit Gen. Hosp., 1977-80, mem. med. device com., 1977-80, mem. credentials com, 1978-84; sec., treas. Detroit Neurosurg. Acad. Program Com., 1978-84; mem. emergency room com. Harper Hosp., 1980-84, neuroscis. intensive care unit com., 1980-84; dir. Oakland-Macomb PPO; chief neurol. sect. William Beaumont Hosp., Troy, Mich., mem. adv. bd., 1986-90; chmn. adv. com. traumatic brain injury/spinal cord injury, State Mich., 1993-96; presenter of numerous exhibits, profl. papers; organizer numerous med. meetings; lectr. in field. Contbr. articles to profl. jours. Served with U.S. Army, 1970-72, Vietnam. Recipient Intern of Yr. award Detroit Gen. Hosp., 1969. Mem. AMA, ACS, Congress Neurol. Surgeons, Detroit Neurosurg. Acad., Mich. Assn. Neurol. Surgeons (sec.-treas. 1979-82, v.p. 1982-84, pres. 1984-86, bd. dirs. 1986-90), Mich. State Med. Soc., Oakland County Med. Soc., Wayne County Med. Soc., Internat. Coll. Surgeons (U.S. sect.), Am. Assn. Neurol Surgeons (spinal disorders sec. 1981-2002, cerebrovascular surgery sect.). Office: 15520 19 Mile Rd Ste 450 Clinton Township MI 48038-6332 Office Fax: 810-263-3819.

HO, STUART TSE KONG, health facility administrator; b. Manila, Nov. 18, 1935; came to U.S., 1936; s. Chinn and Betty (Ching) H.; children: Peter, Cecily; m. Elizabeth Clancey, 2001. BA, Claremont (Calif.) McKenna, 1957; JD, U. Mich., 1963. Bar: Hawaii. Asst. sec. to chmn. bd. Capital Investment of Hawaii, Honolulu, 1965—2003; pres., CEO Rehab. Hosp. Pacific, Honolulu, 2003—. Bd. dirs. Aloha Airgroup, Inc., Honolulu. Representative Hawaii Ho. of Reps., Honolulu, 1966-70, majority fl. leader, 1968-70; del. Constnl. Conv. of 1968, Honolulu, 1968; regent U. Hawaii, Honolulu, 1971-74. 1st lt. U.S. Army, 1958-60, ETO. Democrat. Office: Rehab Hospital of the Pacific 226 N Kaukini St Honolulu HI 96817

HO, THOMAS INN MIN, computer scientist, educator; b. Honolulu, Oct. 17, 1948; s. Herbert Low Seu and Rose (Lee) H.; m. Laura Loh; children: Brian Koon Leong, Tabitha En Hui. BS, Purdue U., 1970, MS, 1971, PhD, 1974. Asst. prof. computer sci., mgmt. Purdue U., West Lafayette, Ind., 1975-78, assoc. prof., 1978-84, prof., 1984-90, head computer tech., 1978-88; exec. dir. Intelenet Commn., Indpls., 1986-88; dir. Info. Networking Inst. Carnegie Mellon U., Pitts., 1990-92; sr. fellow info. systems and computer sci. Nat. U. Singapore, 1993-94; chairperson, prof. computer tech. Ind. U. Purdue U., Indpls., 1995—. Cons. in field. Author: (with J.L. Whitten and L.D. Bentley) Systems Analysis and Design Methods, 1986; contbr. articles to profl. jours. NSF fellow, 1970-72 Mem. Am. Soc. Engring. Edn., Assn. Info. Sys., Internat. Soc. Office: Ind U Purdue U Indpls Dept Computer Tech 723 W Michigan St Indianapolis IN 46202-5191

HO, WEIFAN LEE, merchandise executive; Student, Middlebury Coll.; BA, CCNY, 1972. Furniture buyer Gimbels East, N.Y.C., 1972-86; sr. buyer Carson Pirie Scott, Chgo., 1986-89; buyer Bloomingdales, N.Y.C., 1989-92; divsnl. mgr. Conran's-Habitat, N.Y.C., 1992-93; buyer Abraham and Straus/Jordan Marsh, N.Y.C., 1994, Macy's East, N.Y.C., 1995—. Mem.: WITHIT. Office: Macy's East 151 W 34th St New York NY 10001-2180

HO, YHI-MIN, university dean, economics educator; b. Nanking, China, Nov. 18, 1934; came to U.S., 1958, naturalized, 1972; s. Yung-Tung and Hsing-In H.; m. Shu-Fen Ma, Nov. 23, 1962; Andrew M., Katherine. BA in Econs., Nat. Taiwan U., 1955; MS in Econs., Utah State U., 1961; PhD in Econs., Vanderbilt U., 1965. Mem. managerial staff mktg. div. Chinese Petroleum Corp., 1955-58; asst. prof. U. So. Miss., 1963-65, U. Houston, 1965-66, Tulane U., New Orleans, 1966-70; chmn. dept. econs. and bus. adminstrn. U. St. Thomas, Houston, 1970—, acting dean Cameron Sch. Bus., 1978-80, dean, 1980—, Cullen Found. chair in econs., 1989—. Author: Agricultural Development of Taiwan, 1903-1960, 1966; contbr. articles to profl. jours. Mem. adb. bd. Vols. for Arts; mem. adminstrv. bd. Houston-Taipei Soc., Inc., 1978—; trustee Meml. Hosp. Sys., Houston, 1987-97, Meml. Found. Bd., 1997-99; bd. dirs. Meml. Hermann Affiliated Svcs., Inc., 1999—, Houston Works USA, 1999—. Ford scholar, 1960-61; Rockefeller fellow, 1961-63; NSF grantee, 1973-75 Mem. Am. Econ. Assn., So. Econ. Assn. Office: U St Thomas 3800 Montrose Blvd Houston TX 77006-4626 E-mail: yhiminho@stthom.edu.

HO, YIK HONG, colon and rectal surgeon; b. Singapore, Apr. 21, 1956; s. Peng Yoke Ho and Mei Yiu (Lucy) Fung; m. Chui Wah Ludmilla Tung, Sept. 13, 1984; 1 child, Elaine Jo-Lan. MBBS with honors, U. Queensland, 1980, MD, 2001. Intern Princess Alexandra Hosp., Brisbane, Australia, 1980-81, resident, 1981-82; med. officer Sai Ying Pun Hosp./Tang Shiu Kin Hosp., Hong Kong, 1982-83; registrar U. Surg. Unit Queen Mary Hosp., Tung Wah Hosp., Hong Kong, 1983-89; sr. registrar Singapore Gen. Hosp., 1989-93, cons., 1993-98, dir. Pelvic Floor Lab., 1996—2002, sr. cons., 1998—2002; vis. staff sr. cons. surg. oncology Nat. Cancer Centre, 1999—2002; clin. sr. lectr. Nat. U. Singapore, 2001—02; prof., head discipline of surgery Sch. Medicine James Cook U., 2002—. Rsch. fellow U. Hosp U. Nottingham, England, 1989; part-time clin. lectr. Nat. U. Singapore, 1990—2001; dep. chmn. Electronics Med. Records Workgroup Singapore Gen. Hosp., 1994—2002. Mem. editl. rev. com. Annals of Acad. of Medicine, 1994-2002, mem. editl. com., 2000-2002; mem. editl. com. Singapore Gen. Hosp. Procs., 1995-99, assoc. editor, 1995-98, editor, 1999-2002; mem. editl. bd. Internat. Surgery, 2002—; contbr. articles to profl. jours. Scholarship Australian Kidney Found., 1977. Fellow Royal Australasian Coll. Surgeons, Royal Coll. Surgeons (Edinburgh), Royal Coll Physicians and Surgeons (Glasgow), Internat. Coll. Surgeons (Singapore sect. com. mem. 1994-96, 98-99, treas. 97-99, sec. 1999, pres. 2000-2002, world additional gov. 1999-2000, additional v.p. 2001—); mem. Singapore Soc. Continence (v.p. 1993-2002), Biomed. Rsch. and Exptl. Therapeutics Soc. Singapore (hon. sec. 1993-95, pres. 1995-97), Internat. Soc. Surgery (nat. rep. 1999-2002), Am. Soc. Colon-Rectal Surgeons (mem. internat. adv. com. 2000). Avocations: fitness, computer, photography, swimming, tai-chi. Office: James Cook U Dept Surgery Sch Medicine Townsville, Queensland 4811 Australia

HOADLEY, JOHN FRANK, health policy analyst, educator; b. Hartford, Conn., Jan. 8, 1951; s. Frank T. Hoadley and Margaret Walker; m. Beth Carol Fuchs. BA, Bucknell U., 1972; PhD, U. N.C., 1979. Asst. prof. polit. sci. Duke U., Durham, N.C., 1979-85; legis. asst. U.S. Ho. Reps., Washington, 1984-86; sr. rsch. assoc. Nat. Health Policy Forum, Washington, 1986-91; prin. policy analyst Physician Payment Rev. Commn., Washington, 1991-98; dir. Divsn. Health Financing Policy HHS, Washington, 1998—2002; rsch. prof. Georgetown U. Health Policy Inst., Washington, 2002—. Author: (book) Origins of American Political Parties, 1789-1803, 1986. Congl. fellow Am. Polit. Sci. Assn., 1983-84, others.

HOAG, DAVID GARRATT, aerospace engineer; b. Boston, Oct. 11, 1925; s. Alden Bomer and Helen Lucy (Garratt) H.; m. Grace Edward Griffith, May 10, 1952; children— Rebecca Wilder, Peter Griffith, Jeffrey Taber, Nicholas Alden, Lucy Seymour. BS, MIT, 1946, MS, 1950. Staff engr. instrumentation lab. MIT, Cambridge, 1946-57; tech. dir. Polaris Missile Guidance, 1957-61; tech. dir., program mgr. Apollo Spacecraft Guidance, 1961-72; advanced system dept. head C.S. Draper Lab., Inc., Cambridge, 1972-86. Recipient Pub. Svc. award NASA, 1969, Spl. award Royal Inst. Navigation, Britain, 1970, Laurels, Aviation Week, 1970. Fellow AIAA (Louis W. Hill Space Transp. award 1972, chmn. New Eng. sect. 1979-80); mem. Nat. Acad. Engring., Inst. Navigation (Thurlow award 1969, pres. 1978-79), Internat. Acad. Astronautics (assoc. editor ACTA Astronautica 1973-79) Home: 116 Winthrop St Medway MA 02053-2310

HOAG, PAUL STERLING, architect; b. Spokane, Aug. 7, 1913; s. Percival Doane and Emma Imogen (Rusk) H.; m. Nancy Jean Lawrence, Oct. 21, 1967. Student, Washington State Coll., Pullman, 1930-31, Stanford U., 1932-33. Lic. architect, Calif., Colo., Tex., Wash. Gen. mgr. Hoag X-Ray Co., Spokane, 1933-42; designer various war industry cos., 1942-45; architect apprentice Richard Neutra, L.A., 1945-46, Paul Robinson Hunter and others, L.A., 1946-48; prin. Paul Sterling Hoag, L.A., 1948-87, Crane Island, Wash., 1987—97. Intr. advanced design So. Calif. Inst. Architecture; entire body of archtl. design drawings placed in archives U. Calif. Art History Dept. Prin. works include Falcon Plastics Factory, Oxnard, Calif. (top plant of 1970 award Modern Mfg.), Old Ranch Country Club, Seal Beach, Calif., Huntington Harbor (Calif.) Beach Club, Happy Valley Sch., Ojai, Calif., Adobe Hotel, Yachats, Oreg., Sterling Holloway residence, Laguna Beach, Calif., Beatrice Wood studio and residence, Ojai; author: (novel) Life of Antonio Vivaldi, 1994-98; monthly columnist The Listener, L.A. Architect; contbr. articles to profl. jours. and newspapers. Architect mem. Bel-Air Archtl. Com., L.A., 1982-88, San Vicente Design Rev. Bd., 1980-86; design cons. San Juan County (Wash.) for Eastsound town redesign, 1990-94. Fellow AIA. *The most exciting discovery of my professional life was Carl Jung's revelatory concept of "archaic memories" because it enabled me to understand how intuitive design makes it possible to create building forms and interior spaces which are free of fashion and therefore timelessly meaningful, my constant goal.* Died Nov. 2, 2002.

HOAGLAND, ALBERT SMILEY, electrical engineer, researcher; b. Berkeley, Calif., Sept. 13, 1926; s. Dennis Robert and Jessie Agnes (Smiley) H.; m. Janine Maryse Simart, May 23, 1950; children: Catherine, Nicole, Richard. BS, U. Calif.-Berkeley, 1947, MS, 1948, PhD, 1954. Registered profl. engr., Calif. Asst. prof. elec. engring. U. Calif.-Berkeley, 1954-56; sr. engr. IBM, San Jose, Calif., 1956-59; mgr. engring sci. San Jose Research Lab., 1959-62; sr. tech. cons. IBM World Trade, The Hague, Holland, 1962-64; mgr. engring. sci. IBM Research Ctr., N.Y.C., 1964-68, dir. tech. planning Research Div., 1968-71; corporate program coordinator IBM, Boulder, Colo., 1971-76; mgr. exploratory magnetic rec. San Jose Research Lab., 1976-82; tech. adv. Gen. Products Div., 1982-84; acting dir. Ctr. for Magnetic Recording Research, U. Calif. San Diego, 1983-84; prof. elec. engring., dir. Inst. Info. Storage Tech. Santa Clara U., Calif., 1984—. Lectr. computer design U. Calif. Berkeley, 1948-54, 56-62; adj. prof. U. Calif. San Diego, 1986; cons. State Calif., 1955-56, IBM, 1954-56, also numerous cons. in data storage industry, 1984—; chmn. Nat. Computer Conf. Bd., 1976-78; adj. prof. Harvey Mudd Coll. Author: Digital Magnetic Recording, 1963, 2d edit., 1991, reprinted, 1998; contbr. articles on magnetic rec. and info. storage tech. to profl. publs.; patentee in field. Chmn. adv. com. The Magnetic Rec. Conf., 1993—; trustee Charles Babbage Inst.; regent Inst. Info. Mgmt., 1985—92; dir. Magnetic Disk Heritage Ctr., 2001—. With USNR, 1943—46. Recipient outstanding paper award IEEE, 1957 Fellow IEEE (dir. 1974-77, Centennial medal 1984, 3d Millenium medal 2000), Am. Fedn. Info. Processing Socs. (dir. 1969-78, pres. 1978-80); mem. IEEE Computer Soc. (pres. 1971-73), Rsch. Soc. Am. (pres. Sequoia chpt. 1962-63), Phi Beta Kappa, Sigma Xi, Eta Kappa Nu, Tau Beta Pi. Clubs: Golden Bear. Home: 13834 Upper Hill Dr Saratoga CA 95070-5334 Office: Santa Clara U Inst Info Storage Tech Santa Clara CA 95053-0001 Personal E-mail: a.hoagland@attbi.com. Business E-mail: ahoagland@scu.edu.

HOAGLAND, DONALD WRIGHT, lawyer; b. NYC, Aug. 16, 1921; s. Webster Comley and Irene (Wright) H.; m. Mary Tiedeman, May 14, 1949; children— Peter M., Mary C., Sara H., Ann W. BA, Yale U., 1942; LLB, Columbia U., 1948. Bar: N.Y. 1948, Colo. 1951. Assoc. firm Winthrop, Stimson, Putnam & Roberts, N.Y.C., 1948-51; ptnr. Davis, Graham & Stubbs, Denver, 1951-63, 66-87, of counsel, 1987—; with AID, 1964-66, asst. adminstr. devel. finance and pvt. enterprise, 1965-66, cons., 1967-75. Lectr. U. Denver Sch. Law, 1971-75; chmn. bd. Bi-Nat. Devel. Corp., 1968-70; dir. Centennial Fund, Inc., 2d Centennial Fund, Inc., Gryphon Fund, Inc., 1959-63; mem. Colo. Supreme Ct. Grievance Com., 1992-98. Mem. Denver Planning Bd., 1955-61, 67-70, chmn., 1959-61; bd. dirs., v.p. Denver Art Mus., 1959-63, 72-76, 79-82; bd. dirs. Colo. Urban League, 1960-63, 66-72, chmn. bd., 1968-72; adv. bd. Vols. Tech. Assistance vice-chmn. bd. Denver chpt. ARC, 1959-61; bd. dirs. Legal Aid Soc. Colo., 1972-84, pres., 1975-79; trustee Phillips Exeter Acad., 1960-67, Colo. Rocky Mountain Sch., 1981-84, Am. U., Washington, 1982-85; chmn. bd. dirs. Legal Aid Found., Colo., 1983-87; bd. dirs. Colo. Bus. Coalition for Health, 1988-89, Colo. Found. for Edнl. Excellence, 1998—; exec. dir. Ctr.

for Health Ethics and Policy U. Colo., Denver, 1987-91; chmn. Colo. Health Data Commn., 1986-88, Gov. Romer's panel health advisors, 1992-94, Social Sci. Found. Denver U., 1995—; chmn. Caring for Colo. Found., 1999-2002, Colo. Pub. Health and Edn. Rsch. Adv. Com., 2002—; pres. Colo. Found. Pub. Health and Environment, 1995-98; ethics com. Nat. Jewish Med. and Rsch. Ctr., 1993—. With USNR, 1943-45. Decorated Air medal with oak leaf cluster. Mem. ABA, Colo. Bar Assn., Denver Bar Assn. Home: 355 Garfield St Denver CO 80206-4509 Office: Davis Graham & Stubbs 1550 17th St Ste 500 Denver CO 80202 E-mail: donald.hoagland@dgslaw.com.

HOAGLAND, EDWARD, author; b. NYC, Dec. 21, 1932; s. Warren Eugene and Helen Kelley (Morley) H.; m. Amy J. Ferrara, 1960 (div. 1964); m. Marion Magid, Mar. 28, 1968, (dec. 1993); 1 child, Molly. AB, Harvard U., 1954. Mem. faculty New Sch. for Social Research, N.Y.C., 1963-64, Rutgers (N.J.) U., 1966, Sarah Lawrence Coll., Bronxville, N.Y., 1967, 71, CUNY, 1967, 68, U. Iowa, 1978, 82, Columbia U., 1980, 81. With Bennington Coll., Vt., 1987—, Brown U., 1988, U. Calif., Davis, 1990, 92, Beloit Coll., 1995. Author: Cat Man, 1956, The Circle Home, 1960, The Peacock's Tail, 1965; Notes from the Century Before: A Journal from British Columbia, 1969, The Courage of Turtles, 1971, Walking the Dead Diamond River, 1973, The Moose on the Wall: Field Notes from the Vermont Wilderness, 1974, Red Wolves and Black Bears, 1976, African Calliope: A Journey to the Sudan, 1979, The Edward Hoagland Reader, 1979, The Tugman's Passage, 1982, City Tales, 1986, Seven Rivers West, 1986, Heart's Desire, 1988, The Final Fate of the Alligators, 1992, Balancing Acts, 1992, Tigers & Ice, 1999, Compass Points, 2001, Hoagland on Nature, 2003; gen. editor: Penguin Nature Library, 1985—; contbr. nature and cityscape editorials N.Y. Times, 1979-89. Served with U.S. Army, 1955-57. Houghton Mifflin Lit. fellow, 1954, AAAL traveling fellow, 1964, Guggenheim fellow, 1964, 75; recipient Longview Found. award 1961, O. Henry award, 1971, Lit. Citation, Brandeis U. Creative Arts Awards Commn., 1972, N.Y. State Coun. on Arts award, 1972, Harold D. Vursell award AAAL, 1981, NEA award, 1982, Literary Lion award N.Y. Pub. Libr., 1988, 1996, Nat. Mag. award, 1989, Lannan Literary award, 1993, Lit. Lights award Boston Pub. Libr., 1995. Mem. AAAL Home: PO Box 51 Barton VT 05822-0051 Office: care Pantheon Books New York NY

HOAGLAND, JIMMIE LEE, newspaper editor; b. Rock Hill, S.C., Jan. 22, 1940; s. Lee Roy and Edith Irene (Sullivan) H.; m. Jane Stanton Hitchcock, July 14, 1995; children: Laura Lee, Lily Hue, Lee Clayton. AB in Journalism, U. S.C., 1961; student, U. Aix-en-Provence, France, 1961-62, Columbia U., 1968-69. Reporter Evening Herald, Rock Hill, 1960; copy editor N.Y. Times Internat. Edit., Paris, France, 1964-66; reporter Washington Post, 1966-69, Africa corr., 1969-72, Middle East corr., 1972-75, Paris corr., 1975-77, fgn. editor, 1979-81, asst. mng. editor, 1981-86, assoc. editor, chief fgn. corr., 1986—. Author: South Africa: Civilizations in Conflict, 1972. Ford Found. fellow Columbia U., 1968-69; recipient Pulitzer prize internat. report, 1970; Overseas Press Club award internat. reporting, 1977; Pulitzer prize for commentary, 1991; Eugene Meyer Career Achievement award, 1994. Mem. Council on Fgn. Relations, Phi Beta Kappa, Pi Kappa Alpha. Office: Washington Post 1150 15th St NW Washington DC 20071-0002

HOAGLAND, KARL KING, JR., lawyer; b. St. Louis, Aug. 21, 1933; s. Karl King and Mary Edna (Parsons) H.; m. Sylvia Anne Naranick, July 13, 1957; children: Elisabeth Parsons, Sarah Stewart, Karl King III, Alison T. BS in Econs., U. Pa., 1955; LLB, U. Ill., 1958. Bar: Ill. 1958, U.S. Dist. Ct. (so. dist.) Ill. 1958. V.p., gen. counsel, sec. Jefferson Smurfit Corp., St. Louis, 1960-92, Container Corp. Am., St. Louis, 1986-92; of counsel Hoagland, Fitzgerald, Smith & Pranaitis, Alton, Ill., 1987—. Chmn. bd. dirs. Millers' Mut. Ins. Assn. Ill., 1989-92. Asst. editor: U. Ill. Law Forum, 1957-58. Trustee, treas. Monticello Coll. Found., 1965—. 1st lt. USAF, 1958-60. Mem. Ill. Bar Assn., Madison County Bar Assn., Alton-Wood River Bar Assn., Lockhaven Country Club, Mo. Athletic Club, Crystal Lake Club, Orcas Tennis Club, Order of the Coif, Beta Gamma Sigma. Episcopalian. Avocations: tennis, skiing, hunting, fishing, golf. Home (Summer): PO Box 1454 Eastsound WA 98245 Home (Winter): PO Box 130 Alton IL 62002 Mailing: 91 Hawthorne Dr Alton IL 62002

HOAGLAND, MAHLON, biochemist, educator; b. Boston, Oct. 5, 1921; s. Hudson and Anna (Plummer) H.; m. Olley Virginia Jones, Jan. 10, 1961; children from previous marriage: Judith, Mahlon, Robin. Student, Williams Coll., 1940-41, Harvard U., 1941-43, MD, 1948; Sc.D. (hon.), Worcester Poly. Inst., 1973, U. Mass., 1984. From rsch. fellow to asst. prof. medicine Med. Sch. Harvard U. at Mass. Gen. Hosp., 1948-60; assoc. prof. bacteriology and immunology Med. Sch. Harvard U., 1960-67; prof. biochemistry, chmn. dept. Med. Sch. Dartmouth, 1967-70; pres., sci. dir. Worcester Found. for Biomed. Rsch., Shrewsbury, Mass., 1970-85, pres. emeritus, 1985—. Rsch. assoc. Carlsberg Labs., Copenhagen, 1951-52, Cavendish Labs., Cambridge, Eng., 1957-58; cancer rsch. scholar Am. Cancer Soc., 1953-58; founder, spokesman Del. for Basic Biomed. Rsch., 1978-85. Author 5 books, 65 articles to profl. publs. Recipient Franklin medal, 1976; 2 book awards Am. Med. Writers Assn., 1982, 96. Fellow Am. Acad. Arts and Scis.; mem. NAS. Achievements include discovery of mechanism of amino acid activation and (with P.C. Zamecnik) transfer ribonucleic acid. Home: Academy Rd Thetford VT 05074

HOAGLAND, PORTER, JR., electrical and mechanical engineer, consultant; b. N.Y.C., Sept. 8, 1925; s. Porter and Marjorie Bruce (Stewart) H.; m. Cornelia Elizabeth Register, June 30, 1951; children: Porter III, Matthew Register. BS, Yale U., 1950. Registered profl. engr., Conn. Asst. dir. engring. Wilcolator Co., Elizabeth, N.J., 1950-55; chmn. bd., pres., founder Hoagland Instrument Co., Red Bank, N.J., 1956-72; pres. Hoagland Engring. Corp., West Mystic, Conn., 1973—. Cons. elec., electronic, mech. product design. Patentee in field. With USNR, 1944-46. Mem. IEEE, Holland Soc. N.Y., Yale Sci. and Engring. Assn., Nat. Soc. Profl. Engrs. (Conn. br.), ACEC of Conn. Home: 25 Main St Noank CT 06340-5775 Office: PO Box 174 West Mystic CT 06388-0174 E-mail: hoaglandengineering@rcn.com.

HOAGLAND, SAMUEL ALBERT, lawyer, pharmacist; b. Mt. Home, Idaho, Aug. 19, 1953; s. Charles Leroy and Glenna Lorraine (Gridley) H.; m. Karen Ann Mengel, Nov. 20, 1976; children: Hiliary Anne, Heidi Lynne, Holly Kaye. BS in Pharmacy, Idaho State U., 1976; JD, U. Idaho, 1982. Bar: Idaho 1982, U.S. Dist. Ct. Idaho 1982, U.S. CT. Appeals (9th cir.) 1984. Lectr. clin. pharmacy Idaho State U., Pocatello, 1976-78, lectr. pharmacy law, 1985-86, dean's adv. council Coll. Pharmacy, 1987-92; hosp. pharmacist Mercy Med. Ctr., Nampa, Idaho, 1978-79; retail pharmacist Thrifty Corp., Moscow, Idaho, 1980-82; assoc. Dial, Looze & May, Pocatello, 1982-89, Prescott & Foster, Boise, Idaho, 1989-90; gen. counsel Design Innovations and Rsch. Corp., 1991-95; pvt. practice, 1990—2001; assoc. Hoagland, Dominick & Hicks, PLLC, 2001. Chmn. malpractice panel Idaho Bd. Medicine, Boise, 1983-92, adminstrv. hearing officer, 1989-92; adj. assoc. prof. pharmacy law Idaho State U., 2002--. Contbr. to law publs. Bd. dirs. Cathedral Pines Camp, Ketchum, Idaho. Mem. Idaho State Bar Assn., Idaho Pharm. Assn., Idaho Trial Lawyers Assn., Boise Bar Assn., Capital Pharm. Assn., Am. Pharm. Assn., Idaho Soc. Hosp. Pharmacists (bd. dirs.), Am. Soc. Pharmacy Law, Flying Doctors Am. (Atlanta) (bd. dirs.). Home: 11901 W Mesquite Dr Boise ID 83713-0813 Office: 1471 Shoreline Dr Ste 100 Boise ID 83702-9104

HOAGLIN, DAVID CASTER, statistician, researcher; b. Charleston, W.Va., Mar. 4, 1944; s. Raymond Isaac and Martha Jean (Caster) Hoaglin; m. Dianne L. Mendenhall, July 20, 1968; 1 child, Christopher David. BS, Duke U., 1966; PhD, Princeton U., 1971. Instr. in stats. Harvard U., Cambridge, Mass., 1970—71, asst. prof. stats., 1971—72, lectr. on stats., 1972—77, rsch. assoc. in stats., 1977—94; sr. rsch. assoc. Nat. Bur. Econ. Rsch., Cambridge, Mass., 1972—75; sr. analyst Abt Assocs. Inc., Cambridge, Mass., 1977—78, sr. scientist, 1978—2001, prin. scientist, 2001—; core biostatistician, Harvard Anesthesia Ctr. Mass. Gen. Hosp., Boston, 1983—88. Cons. Nat. Inst. Child Health and Human Devel., Bethesda, Md., 1975—; cons., divsn. rsch. resources NIH, Bethesda, Md., 1977—80; mem., program adv. subcommittee Nat. Inst. on Deafness and Other Communication Disorders, Bethesda, Md., 1993—96. Co-author: Applications, Basics, and Computing of Exploratory Data Analysis, 1981, Data for Decisions: Information Strategies for Policymakers, 1982; co-editor, co-author (monograph) Understanding Robust and Exploratory Data Analysis, 1983, (monograph) Exploring Data Tables, Trends, and Shapes, 1985, (monograph) Fundamentals of Exploratory Analysis of Variance, 1991; co-editor: Perspectives on Contemporary Statistics, 1992; co-author: (monograph) How to Detect and Handle Outliers, 1993. Treas. First Parish of Sudbury, Sudbury, Mass., 1979—80. Fellow: AAAS (electorate nominating com., sect. u 2000—03), Am. Statis. Assn. (v.p. 1996—98, Founders award 1994); mem.: Math. Assn. Am. (editl. bd. Am. Math. Monthly 1996—2001), Soc. for Indsl. and Applied Math., Inst. of Math. Stats., Internat. Statis. Inst., Phi Beta Kappa. Avocations: ham radio, bicycling, hiking. Home: 73 Hickory Rd Sudbury MA 01776-2928 Office: Abt Assocs Inc 55 Wheeler St Cambridge MA 02138 Office Fax: 617-349-2605. E-mail: dave_hoaglin@abtassoc.com.

HOAGLUND, SUSAN ELIZABETH, music educator; b. Worcester, Mass., Apr. 16, 1957; d. Robert Holdsworth and Janesse Audrey Hoaglund. BM, Boston U., 1980; diploma, Goethe Inst., Munich, Germany, 1986; MA, U. Pa., 1995. Violin and viola tchr. Stadtische Musikschule, Dusseldorf, Germany, 1980-84; tchr., head dormitory St. Paul's Sch., Concord, N.H., 1984-94; violin and viola tchr. Settlement Music Sch., Phila., 1994-98; head performing arts dept., music tchr. The Shipley Sch., Bryn Mawr, Pa., 1996—. Adj. prof. music Chestnut Hill Coll., Phila., 1997—; various adminstrv. jobs Boston U., Tanglewood Inst., 1982-92; site dir. Ctr. for Talented Youth, Johns Hopkins U., Balt., summers 1994-69, creative writing tchr., 1995-96. Adminstrv. asst. vol. Bath Festival Phila., 1994-2000; sponsor Save the Children, 1998—; mem. Phila. Reads, 2000—; mem. Save the Bay, 1984—. Mem. Pa. Music Educators Assn., Music Educators Nat. Assn. Episcopalian. Avocations: playing in handbell choir, travel, reading, writing, tutoring children in reading. Home: 12-B St Albans Ave Newtown Square PA 19073 Office: The Shipley Sch 814 Yarrow St Bryn Mawr PA 19010

HOAK, MICHAEL SHANE, historian; b. Harrisonburg, Va., June 18, 1975; s. Jerry Wayne and Brenda Ann Hoak; m. Allison Curran. BA, James Madison U., 1997; MA in History, Coll. William and Mary, 2000, postgrad. Instr. Coll. William and Mary, Williamsburg, Va., 1999—2001; policy analyst Legis. Strategies Group, Washington, 2000—02; dir. legis. Strategic Health Solutions, Washington, 2002—. Cons. Nat. Park Svc., Shenandoah, Va., 1999; hist. cons. Colonial Nat. Park, Yorktown, Va., 1998. Mem.: Am. Hist. Assn., Orgn. Am. Historians. Avocations: golf, reading, hiking. Office: Strategic Health Solutions 1001 Pennsylvania Ave Washington DC

HOANG, DUC VAN, theoretical pathologist, educator; b. Hanoi, Vietnam, Feb. 17, 1926; came to U.S. 1975, naturalized 1981; s. Duoc Van and Nguyen Thi (Tham) H.; m. Mau Ngo Thi Vu, 7 children. MD, Hanoi U. Sch. Medicine, Vietnam, 1952; DSc, Open Internat. U., Sri Lanka, 1989. Dean Sch. Medicine Army of the Republic of Vietnam, Saigon, 1959-63; dean Minh-Duc U. Sch. Medicine, Saigon, 1970-71; clin. prof. theoretical pathology U. So. Calif. Sch. Medicine, L.A., 1978—. Adj. prof. Emperor's Coll. Traditional Oriental Medicine, Santa Monica, Calif., 1988-91; initiator of attitudinal immunology. Author: Towards an Integrated Humanization of Medicine, 1957; The Man Who Weights the Soul, 1959; Eastern Medicine, A New Direction?, 1970; also short stories; author introdn. to work of Marie Noël, Vietnamese transl. of La Rose Rouge; translator: Pestis, introduction to the work of Albert Camus, Vietnamese translation of La Peste; editor: The East (co-founder); jour. Les Cahiers de l'Asie du Sud-Est. Founder, past pres. Movement for Fedn. Countries S.E. Asia; co-founder, past v.p. Movement for Restoration Cultures and Religions of Orient; mem. The Noetic Inst., 1988—. Internat. Found. for Homeopathy, 1987; founder, pres. Intercontinental Found. for Electro-Magnetic Resonance Rsch., 1989 ; coord. Unity and Diversity World Health Coun., 1992—. Named hon. dean The Open Internat. U. of Complementary Medicines, Sri Lanka, 1989; Unity-and-Diversity World Coun. fellow, 1990—. Mem. AAUP, Assn. Clin. Scientists, Am. Com. for Integration Eastern and Western Medicine (founder), Assn. Unitive Medicine (founder, pres.), U. So. Calif. Faculty Member Club (L.A.). Roman Catholic. Home: 3630 Barry Ave Los Angeles CA 90066-3202 E-mail: hoangvduc@yahoo.com.

HOANG, HUNG MANH, technology advisor; b. Hanoi, Vietnam, July 6, 1954; came to U.S., 1975; s. Frank Dinhue and Dianne (Nguyen) H.; m. Candice Kim Truong, Apr. 6, 1986; 1 child, Judy Anh. BSME, Tex. A&M U., 1982; postgrad., Sch. Engring. and Logistics, 1987; MS in Software Engring., Monmouth Coll., 1988. Mech./electronics engr. Dept. Army, Texarkana, Tex., 1984-88, Ft. Monmouth, N.J., 1984-88; programmer/analyst Computer Scis. Corp., Houston, 1988-89; engr. specialist McDonnell Douglas Space Systems Co., Houston, 1989-91; info. sys. analyst Texaco Inc., Houston, 1991-95; consulting database adminstr. Brown and Root Inc., Houston, 1995-96; software engr. Landmark Graphics Corp., Houston, 1996—97; staff Engr./DBA Honeywell Internat., 1997—99; advisor Aspen Tech., Houston, 1999—. Sec. gen. Phat Quang Temple, South Houston, 1984; com. mem. Vietnamese-Am. Space Tech. Assn., Houston, 1991; pres. Vietnamese-Am. Student Assn., Tex. A&M U., College Station, 1981-83, spring 1983. Mem. IEEE, Assn. Computing Machinery, Phi Theta Kappa. Home: 8210 Creek Glen Dr Sugar Land TX 77478-4747 Office: Aspen Tech Inc 1293 Eldridge Pkwy Houston TX 77077

HOANG, LOC BAO, electrical engineer; b. Saigon, Vietnam, Feb. 26, 1964; came to U.S., 1980; s. Chau Van Hoang and Quy Thi Bui; m. Tracy Phuong-Nga Doan, Dec. 7, 1990; children: Kimberly Bao, Christopher Dang-Khoa. BSEE, U. Calif., Berkeley, 1988; MSEE, San Jose State U., 1993. Design engr. Xicor, Inc., Milpitas, Calif., 1989-90; sr. design engr. Nat. Semiconductor Corp., Santa Clara, Calif., 1991-93, Silicon Storage Tech., Inc., Sunnyvale, Calif., 1993-94; design mgr. Winbond Memory Lab., San Jose, Calif., 1994-97; dir. design Winbond Electronics Corp. Amer., San Jose, Calif., 1997—. Presenter Internat. Symposium on VLSI Tech., 1993. Mem. IEEE. Achievements include patent for Row Decoder and Driver with Switched-Bias Bulk Regions; semiconductor mem. device with dataline undershoot detection and reduced read access time, electrically byte selectable and byte alterable mem. arrays, flash cell having self-timed programming, memory device and method of operation, semiconductor memory device with reduced read disturbance, semiconductor memory array with buried drain lines and method therefore, semiconductor memory array partitioned into memory blocks and sub-blocks and method of addressing, and other patents; patent pending for notable findings of methods and design techniques to improve performance and/or reliability of non-volatile semiconductor memories. Office: Winbond Electronics Corp Am 2727 N 1st St San Jose CA 95134-2029 E-mail: locbaohoang@yahoo.com.

HOANG, THU-ANH, diagnostic radiologist; b. Dalat, Vietnam, Oct. 22, 1956; MD, U Iowa Coll. Med., 1983. Diplomate Am. Bd. of Radiology. Intern Strong Meml. Genesee Hosp., Rochester, N.Y., 1983-84; resident in diagnostic radiology Allegheny Gen. Hosp., Pitts., 1985-89; fellow U. Calif. Irvine Med. Ctr., Orange, 1989-90; fellow in neuroradiology Loma Linda (Calif.) U. Med. Ctr., 1991-93; chief neuroradiology Jerry L. Pettis Vets. Meml. Hosp., Loma Linda, 1993-98; staff radiologist Lima (Ohio) Meml. Hosp., 1999-2000, Good Samaritan Hosp., L.A., 2000—01, Cedars-Sinai Med. Ctr., L.A., 2001—. Asst. prof. radiologist, Loma Linda, CA, 1992-98. Mem. Am. Coll. Radiology, Radiol. Soc. N. Am. Address: 1272 Stonewood Ct San Pedro CA 90732 E-mail: thuanh.hoang@attbi.net.

HOAR, FREDERICK M. public relations executive; With Miller/Shandwick, 1989—; pres. Miller/Shandwick West, L.A., 1992-98; chmn. Miller/Shandwick Technologies, Boston, 1998—.

HOAR, JERE RICHMOND, journalism educator, writer; b. Dyersburg, Tenn., Oct. 23, 1929; s. Eldon Jesse and Lula Mae Zimmerman (Parks) H.; m. Betty Jane Smith, May 12, 1954 (div. Sept. 1977); children: Lu Ann Smith, Thomas Jonathan, Benjamin Jere. BS, Auburn U., 1951; MA, U. Miss., Oxford, 1954; PhD, U. Iowa, 1960. Bar: Miss. 1971. Reporter Troy (Ala.) Messenger, 1947-49, Troy Herald; news editor The Oxford (Miss.) Eagle, 1953-54, Jour. So. Commerce, Oxford, 1953-54; editor Iowa Pub. Mag., Iowa City, 1954-56; grad. asst. U. Iowa, Iowa City, 1954-56; asst. prof. journalism U. Miss., University, 1956-59, assoc. prof. journalism, 1959-67, prof. journalism, 1967-86, emeritus prof. journalism, 1986—. Preceptorship in law Freeland & Gafford Law Offices, Oxford, 1966-67, 69-71; lawyer, Oxford, 1971—; prof. journalism Ctr. for Cooperative Study in Britains, King's Coll., London, summer 1988, 90; advisor Miss. Poll; reference person Miss. Press; expert witness in field. Author: Comprehensive Construction Planning, 1975, Body Parts, 1997, The Hit, 2003; editor: Erosion Control, 1962, Mississippi Newspapers and the Law, 1965, 69; co-editor: Lawyer in the Classroom Directory, 1978, Media Law Handbook, 1981; author of short stories; contbr. articles to profl. jours. Local in polit. campaigns. With USAF, 1951-53. Recipient first place internat. lit. competition Writers Unlimited, Pascagoula, Miss., 1973, Kansas Arts Coun./KQ award, 1989-90, Ione Burden Novel award Deep South Writers Competition, U. Southwestern La., 1994, William Faulkner Prize Pirate's Alley, 1994, Silver Em for Contbns. to Journalism, Miss. Scholastic and the Dept. Journalism, University, 1995; Fulbright grantee Costa Rica. Mem. ABA (governing com. forum on comm. law), Assn. for Edn. in Journalism and Mass Comm. (chair tchg. com. law divsn.), Miss. Bar Assn., Sigma Delta Chi, Kappa Tau Alpha. Republican. Methodist. Avocations: reading, raising and training English setters, shooting, riding. Home: 71 County Road 215 Oxford MS 38655-8858 E-mail: jrhoar@watervalley.net.

HOAR, WILLIAM PATRICK, editor, author; b. Haverhill, Mass., Nov. 7, 1945; s. John Patrick and Helen Rose (Powers) H.; m. Louisa Miller, July 29, 1978; children: Meredith Miller Hoar, Emily Erin Hoar. AB, Bowdoin Coll., 1967. Contbg. editor Am. Opinion, Belmont, Mass., 1971-85; assoc. editor The Rev. of the News, Belmont, 1971-85; exec. editor, v.p. Conservative Digest, Washington, 1985-89, World Networks, 1989-91; Washington corr. Southern Africa Spl. Dispatch, 1990-91, Newslink Africa, 1990-91; exec. dir. Second Decade Found., 1991—; Washington editor, sr. v.p. World News Digest, Silver Spring, Md., 1991-94. Consulting editor Conservative Review, 1993-97; Washington editor New American, 1992—; mng. editor CD Publs., Silver Spring, 1996-99; editor-in-chief United Comm. Group, Rockville, Md., 1999—. Author: Architects of Conspiracy: An Intriguing History, 1984 (updated Japanese edit. 1991), Our Corrupt Congress, 1992, Handouts and Pickpockets, 1996: editor various jours. including Regions in Transition, 1990, Counter-Terrorism, 1997; contbr. articles to profl. jours. Mem. Bel Pre Civic Assn., Silver Spring, Md., 1985—. Staff sgt. U.S. Army, 1968-70. Decorated Army Commendation medal. Mem. White House Corres. Assn., Congl. Periodical Press Gallery, Soc. Profl. Journalists, Am. Legion, Nat. Press Club, Am. Running Assn., Internat. Policy Forum (bd. govs.), Chi Psi. Home: 2916 Bluff Point Ln Silver Spring MD 20906-3043 Office: United Comm Group 11300 Rockville Pike Ste 1100 Rockville MD 20852-3012 E-mail: wphoar@aol.com., whoar@ucg.com.

HOAR, WILLIAM STEWART, zoologist, educator; b. Moncton, N.B., Can., Aug. 31, 1913; s. George W. and Nina (Steeves) H.; m. Margaret MacKenzie, Aug. 13, 1941; children: Stewart George, David Innes, Kenzie Margaret, Melanie Frances. BA hon., U. N.B., 1934, D.Sc. (hon.), 1965; MA, U. Western Ont., 1936, D.Sc. (hon.), 1978; PhD, Boston U., 1939; D.Sc. (hon.), Meml. U. Nfld., 1967, St. Francis Xavier U., 1976, LL.D. (hon.), Simon Fraser U., 1980, Toronto U., 1981, Mt. Allison U., 1998. Asst. prof. biology U. N.B., 1939-42, prof. zoology, 1943-45; research assoc. U. Toronto, 1942-43; prof. zoology and fisheries U. B.C., Vancouver, 1945-64, head dept. zoology, 1964-71, prof., 1971-79, prof. emeritus, 1979—. Research scientist Fisheries Research Bd. Can., 1935-57 Author: General and Comparative Physiology, 3d edit., 1983; sr. editor 14 vol. treatise on fish physiology; contbr. articles to profl. jours. Decorated Order of Can.; recipient Flavelle medal, 1965, Fry medal, 1974, Shinkishi Hatai medal Pacific Sci. Assn., 1991. Fellow Royal Soc. Can., Canadian, U.S. socs. zoology and physiology. Home: 3561 W 27th Ave Vancouver BC Canada V6S 1P9

HOARD, HEIDI MARIE, lawyer; b. Mt. Clemens, Mich., Feb. 8, 1951; d. Duane Jay and Elizabeth Hoard; m. John B. Lunseth II, Jan. 11, 1980; children: John B. III, Steven J. BA, Macalester Coll., 1972; JD cum laude, U. Minn., 1976. Bar: Minn. 1976, U.S. Dist. Ct. Minn. 1976. Assoc. Faegre & Benson, Mpls., 1976-83, ptnr., 1984-93; sr. legal counsel Medtronic, Inc., 1993-95; v.p., gen. counsel, corp. sec. The Musicland Group, Minnetonka, 1995—. Mem. State Bd. Women in the Legal Profession Task Force, State Bd. Legal Cert., 1986-88, pres. Tel-Law, Bar Assn. Com., Mpls., 1978-80; bd. dirs. Fund for Legal Aid Soc. Mem. Minn. Region G, Law Enforcement Assistance Assn. Com., 1971-72; vol. aide U.S. Senate Nursing Home Investigation and Hearing, Mpls., 1971-72; student dir. Legal Aid Clinic, U. Minn., Mpls., 1975-76. Mem. Am. Soc. Corp. Secs. (bd. dirs. Minn. sect.), Am. Corp. Counsel Assn., Minn. Bar Assn., Phi Beta Kappa. Democrat. Office: Musicland Group 10400 Yellow Circle Dr Hopkins MN 55343

HOARE-TEMPLE, PIERS HOWARD, building maintenance executive; b. London, Mar. 5, 1946; s. Euan Temple and Margot Carol Blaut Temple Hoare; m. Jane Evelyn Montague Browne, Aug. 19, 1978; 1 child, Guy Arthur Anthony. Salesman Va. Oak Tannery, Luray, 1965-67; barrister The English Bar, London, 1972-87; chmn. bd., majority shareholder Blaut Verwaltung & Grundstücks GmbH & Co., Neu Isenburg, Germany, 1987—, Heritage Restoration Ltd., Jersey, Channel Islands, 1991—, Heritage Restoration GmbH, Dusseldorf, Germany, 1992—; owner Reisebüro Engels, Friedberg, Germany, 1987-94. Cons. Riverside (Great Stour Ltd.), Canterbury, Eng., 1994, dir. Canterbury Leisure Devel. Ltd., 1993—. Mem. mgmt. com., trustee Hearing Rsch. Trust, London, 1988—; chmn. Richmond Legal Advice Svc., London, 1973—. Lt. comdr. Naval Res. Decorated Reserve Decoration, Her Majesty the Queen, 1985. Mem. Criminal Bar Assn., Conservative Lawyers Assn., Pres.'s Res. Officers' Assn. (com. mem.), Naval Club London (counselor bd.), Old Pauline Club (com. mem.). Ch. of Eng. Avocations: travel, wining and dining, swimming, socializing. Office: Blaut Verwaltung und Grundstucks GMBh & Co Dornhofstrasse 89 Neu Isenburg 63263 Germany

HOART, GLADYS GALLAGHER, English language educator; b. N.Y.C., June 27, 1914; d. Martin and Edna (Parker) Gallagher; m. Francis Xavier Hoart, June 25, 1939; children: Robert, Helen, Andrew. AB cum laude, NYU, 1967, MA, 1970; MA in Liberal Studies, New Sch. for Social Rsch., 1975. Cert. mem. N.Y. Stock Exchange. Adj. prof. English Nassau C.C., Garden City, N.Y., 1970—. Dir. Career Seminars for Teenage Girls, Flushing, N.Y., 1963-64; tutor Black Studies Program, Manhasset, N.Y., 1968-69. Pres., co-founder Broadway Homeowners' Assn., Flushing, N.Y., 1964-65; committeewoman Dem. Party, Manhasset, N.Y., 1970; organizer Parkchester (N.Y.) Golden Age Club, 1953; trustee Dalcroze Sch. of Music, 1998—, treas., 2001. Mem. AAUW, Alliance Floor Brokers, Musicians Club (bd. dirs. 1993—, v.p. 2001). Roman Catholic. Avocations: architecture, equitation, gardening, music.

HOBACK, RONALD DEAN, retired engineer; b. Palmer, Nebr., Mar. 22, 1935; s. James Burt and Mazie May (Cargill) H.; m. Ann Louise Horner, Nov. 17, 1956; children: Alan Dean, Laura Ann, Larry Evan. BS in Agriculture, Univ. Nebr., 1956, BSME, 1974. Registered profl. engr. emeritus, Nebr. Tchr. Dewitt (Nebr.) Pub. Schs., 1956-58, Burwell (Nebr.) Pub. Schs., 1958-60; salesman John Hancock Life Ins. Co., Lincoln, Nebr., 1960-62, Strata Oil Co., Ralston, Nebr., 1962-63; draftsman Gordon & Morgan Machine Co., Lincoln, 1963-66; engr. Goodyear Tire & Rubber Co., Lincoln, 1966-81, Gates Rubber Co., Elizabethtown, Ky., 1981—97. Inventor, patentee method and assembly for making a power transmission belt, belt drive and belts and pulleys, flexible matrix for forming a toothed belt, belt drive of improved configuration. Mem.: Lions. Republican. Southern Baptist. Avocation: golf. Home: 2257 Westwood Dr Crete NE 68333-9440

HOBART, BILLIE, education educator, consultant; b. Pitts., Apr. 19, 1935; d. Harold James Billingsley and Rose Stephanie (Sladack) Green; m. W.C.H. Hobart, July 20, 1957 (div. 1967); 1 child, Rawson W. BA in English, U. Calif., Berkeley, 1967, EdD, 1992; MA in Psychology, Sonoma State U., 1972. Cert. tchr. Calif., Irlen screener 2003. Asst. prof. Coll. Marin, Kentfield, Calif., 1969-78; freelance cons., writer, 1969—; asst. prof. Contra Costa Coll., San Pablo, Calif., 1986-99, Santa Rosa (Calif.) Jr. Coll., 1999—. Author: (cookbook) Natural Sweet Tooth, 1974, (non-fiction) Expansion, 1972, Purposeful Self: Coherent Self, 1979, 2002, (non-fiction) Talking to Dead People, 1996, On the Subject of Prayer, 2000, (biography) Captain Granville Perry Swift, California Pioneer and Sonoma Bear, 1999, (fiction) Last Days of Gifted Light, 2000, Timethinner, 2001, Getting to Start, 2001, Clearing to Core, 2002; contbr. articles to profl. jours. Served with WAC, 1953-55. Mem. No. Calif. Coll. Reading Tchrs. Assn. (pres. 1996-98), Mensa, Commonwealth Club San Francisco, Phi Delta Kappa. Home and Office: PO Box 1542 Sonoma CA 95476-1542

HOBART, THOMAS D. lawyer; b. Lake City, Iowa, Jan. 1, 1947; s. Francis W. and Blanche E. Hobart; m. Jeri W. Hobart, July 17, 1971; children: Thomas Wilson, Jaye States. BA in Polit. Scis. and Psychology, U. Iowa, 1969, JD, 1974. Bar: Iowa 1974, U.S. Dist. Ct. (no. and so. dists.) Iowa 1974. Assoc. atty.

Meardon, Sueppel & Downer, Iowa City, 1974-77, mem., 1978—. Bd. dirs., v.p. Sys. Unlimited, Iowa City, 1994—98. Fellow: Iowa Acad. Trial Lawyers; mem.: Order of Coif, Johnson County Bar Assn. (pres. 1993—94). Democrat. Home: 1205 Seymour Ave Iowa City IA 52240 Office: Meardon Sueppel and Downer 122 S Linn St Iowa City IA 52240 E-mail: TomH@meardonlaw.com.

HOBART, THOMAS YALE, JR., union president; b. Buffalo, Dec. 26, 1936; s. Thomas Yale and Anne Rita (Guastaterro) H.; m. Dorothy A., Aug. 10, 1963; children: Elizabeth Anne Rottner, Catherine Marie, Thomas Yale III. BS in Edn., SUNY, Buffalo, 1960; MS in Edn., Canisius Coll., Buffalo, 1964. Cert. tchr., N.Y. Tchr., guidance counselor Buffalo Bd. Edn., 1959-71; co-founder, pres. N.Y. State United Tchrs., Albany, 1972—; v.p. Am. Fedn. Tchrs., Washington, N.Y. State AFL-CIO, Albany. Pres. Buffalo Tchrs. Fedn., 1969; mem. Tchr. Edn. and Cert. Bd., 1973; vice chmn. N.Y. State Employment Tng. Coun., 1979; vice chmn. Job Tng. and Partnership Coun., 1983; co-chair Task Force on Career Pathways, 1991; v.p. Tchr. Edn. Conf. Bd., Commrs. Task Force on Edn. and Cert., 1975; chair Pub. Employee Benefit Fund, 1975-91; mem. Gov.'s Task Force on Taylor Law, 1974, Gov.'s Task Force on Financing of Elem., Sec. and Continuing Edn., 1975; v.p. N.Y. State Adv. Coun. on Vocat. Edn., 1977-1982; mem. Regents and Gov.'s Task Force on Equity and Excellence in Edn., 1978; mem. State Plan Com. for Vocat. Edn., 1979; mem. adv. bd. Northeast Lab.; co-founder, co-chair N.Y. State Labor-Religion Conf.; co-chair Task Force on Tchg. Profession; commr. N.Y. State Gov.'s Conf. on Libr. and Info. Svcs., 1990, Child Labor Law Edn. Fund; del. World Confedn. Orgns. Tchg. Profession, Internat. Fedn. Free Tchr. Unions, Edn. Internat., state and nat. AFL-CIO, Jewish Labor Coun., Coun. Profl. Employees, AFL-CIO, Pub. Employment Dept. AFL-CIO, Edn. Internat., Coalition of Black Trade Unions; mem. adv. coun. Cornell Sch. Labor/Mgmt. Rels., St. Joseph's Guild, Am. Labor Coun., Jewish Labor Comm. Chair, bd. dirs. United Way N.Y., 1999-2001, Albany, 1999-01; bd. trustees, United Way Am.; charter mem. Martin Luther King Commn.; bd. dirs. Welfare Rsch. Inst.; mem. adv. bd. N.Y. State Occupational Disease Diagnostic Ctr. Network Study; mem. N.Y. State Svc. Coun., ARC, 1996-99; pres. N.Y. State Tchrs. Assn., 1971-73; chair Am. Labor Ctr., 2002—. Staff sgt. U.S. Army, 1960-68. Mem.: NEA (bd. dirs.), Buffalo Ski Club, Transit Valley Country Club, Shaker Ridge Country Club, Ft. Orange Club. Democrat. Roman Catholic. Home: 157 Bassett Rd Amherst NY 14221-2641 Office: NY State United Tchrs 159 Wolf Rd # Albany NY 12205-1106 E-mail: thobart@nysutmail.com.

HOBAUGH, CHARLES O. astronaut; b. Bar Harbor, Maine, Nov. 5, 1961; s. Jimmie and Virginia Hobaugh; m. Corinna Lynn Leaman; 4 children. BSc in Aerospace Engring., U.S. Naval Acad., 1984. Commd. 2d lt. USN, 1984; advanced through grades to maj. USMC, various assignments, 1984—87, with marine attack squadron, 1987—91; student Naval Test Pilot Sch., 1991—92; project officer, 1992—94; instr. Naval Test Pilot Sch., 1994—96; astronaut NASA, Houston, 1996—. Astronaut mission to Internat. Space Sta., 2001. Decorated Strike/Flight Air medal USN, Combat Action ribbon. Mem.: U.S. Naval Acad. Alumni Assn. Avocations: weightlifting, volleyball, boating, water skiing, snow skiing. Office: Astronaut Office CB NASA Johnson Space Center Houston TX 77058

HOBBINS, ROBERT LEO, lawyer; b. Des Moines, June 5, 1948; s. Leo Michael and Margaret Ellen Hobbins; m. Carmela Theresa Tursi, Dec. 27, 1974; children: Brian, Patrick, Edward. BA magna cum laude, Creighton U., 1970; JD, NYU, 1973. Bar: Minn. 1973. Assoc. Dorsey & Whitney, Mpls., 1973-78, ptnr., 1979. Adj. faculty U. St. Thomas Sch. Law, 2002—. Root-Tilden scholar. Mem. ABA (labor sect., EEO law com.), Minn. State Bar Assn., Hennepin County Bar Assn., Creighton U. Alumni Assn. (v.p. 1994). Office: Dorsey & Whitney 50 S 6th St Ste 1500 Minneapolis MN 55402-4502 E-mail: hobbins.robert@dorseylaw.com.

HOBBINS, WILLIAM T. career officer; BS in Bus. Fin., U. Col., 1969; grad., Squadron Officer Sch., Maxwell AFB, Ala., 1976; MA in Bus. Adminstr., Troy State U., 1977; grad., Armed Forces Staff Coll., Norfolk, Va., 1981, Air War Coll., Maxwell AFB, 1985; grad. Jt. Flag Officer Warfighting, Maxwell AFB, 1997; grad., Joint Force Air Cmdrs., 1999; postgrad., Syracuse U., 2000. Cert. command pilot. Commd. 2d. lt. USAF, 1969, advanced through grades to Lt. Gen., 2001; pilot trng. Laredo AFB, Tex., 1970-70; instr. pilot 3389th Pilot Training Squadron, Keesler AFB, Miss., 1970-73; instr. pilot, class commander 29th Flying Trng. Wing, Craig AFB, Ala., 1973-74; At-28 fight pilot/chief 1131st Spl. Activity Squadron, Udorn Royal Thai AFB, Thailand, 1974-75; chief 29th Flying Tng. Wing, Craig AFB, Ala., 1975-77; flight comdr., instr. pilot, opers. officer 7th Tactical Fighter Squadron, 49th Tactical Fighter Wing, Holloman AFB, N.Mex., 1977-80; F-15 ops. monitor, chief weapons sys. br., program element monitor Hdrs. USAF, Washington, 1981-84; chief wing inspections 33rd. Tactical Fighter Wing, Eglin AFB, Fla., 1985-87; dep. comdr. opers. 12th Flying Trng. Wing, Randolph AFB, Tex., 1987-88; vice commander, then commdr. Air Forces Iceland, Keflavik Naval Air Sta, Iceland, 1988-90; vice comdr., then comdr. 405th Tactical Tng. Wing, Luke AFB, Ariz., 1990-91; vice comdr. 58th Fighter Wing, Luke AFB, Ariz., 1991-92; J-3 US forces Yokota Air Base, Japan, 1992-94; comdr. 18th Wing, Kadena AFB, Japan, 1994-96; dir. plans and policy (J-5) U.S. Atlantic Command, Norfolk, Va., 1996-98; dir. ops. Hdqs. USAF in Europe, Ramstein Air Base, Germany, 1998-2000. Nat. security leadership course, Syracuse U., 2000. Decorated Disting. Svc. Medal, Def. Superior Svc. medal with oak leaf cluster, Legion of Merit, Meritorious Svc. medal with four oak leaf clusters, Joint Svc. Commendation medal Air Force Commendatin medal with oak leaf cluster, Ord. of the Rising Sun with Gold Rays; recipient Khmer Aviation citation, Air Force Assn. citation. Office: HQ USAF/XI 1800 Air Force Pentagon Washington DC 20330-1800

HOBBS, C. FREDRIC, artist, filmmaker, author; b. Phila., Dec. 30, 1931; s. Robert Frederic and Gertrude (Madison) H.; children: Leslie Newbold, Mary Alison. Grad., Menlo Sch.; BA, Cornell U., 1953; grad., Academia de San Fernando de Bellas Artes, Madrid, 1955-56. Pres. Fredric Hobbs Films, Inc., 1975; chmn., chief exec. officer Virginia City (Nev.) Restoration Corp., 1978-85. Writer, dir., producer 4 feature films, (TV series) Taiwan, The Other China, 1988-90, (TV/multimedia series) Fastfuture, 2000—; author: The Richest Place on Earth, 1978, Eat Your House: Art Eco Guide to Self Sufficiency, 1980, The Spirit of the Monterey Coast, 1990, and others; also articles.; one-man shows include, Calif. Palace Legion of Honor, San Francisco, 1958, Mus. Sci. and Industry, Los Angeles, 1976, San Francisco Mus. Modern Art, 1980-81, Sierra Nevada Mus. Art, 1984; maj. mus. exhbns. include Concurso Internat. Palacio de la Virreina, Barcelona, Spain (17 countries), Art USA, Madison Sq. Garden, N.Y., Pa. Acad. Fine Arts., Phila, Internat. Drawing Competition II, Nat. Fine Arts Collection, Smithsonian Inst., Washington, Drawings USA 63" II Biennial, St. Paul Art Ctr., Minn., Ann. Sculpture-Painting Exhbns., SFAI, San Francisco Mus. Art, III and V Invitationals, Finch Coll. Mus. Art., N.Y.C., Gallery Modern Art., N.Y.C., Nat. Gallery Art, Washington, Reed Coll., Portland, Oreg., U. Pacific, Stockton, Calif., San Diego Mus. Art., Mills Coll., Oakland, Calif., Touring Am. Mus., Ebert Gallery, 1994, 95, 97, others; permanent collections include Mus. Modern Art, N.Y.C., Met. Mus. Art, N.Y.C., Spencer Meml. Ch., N.Y.C., Calif. Palace Legion of Honor, Finch Coll. Mus. Art, St. Paul Art Gallery, San Francisco Mus. Modern Art, Fine Arts Mus. San Francisco, Sierra Nevada Mus. Art, Reno, Stanford (Calif.) U. Mus. Art., San Francisco State Coll., U. Calif. Media Ctr., San Jose (Calif.) Mus. Art., Oakland (Calif.) Mus. Art., Johnson Mus., Cornell U., others; galleries include Twentieth Century West Galleries, N.Y.C., Braunstein Gallery, San Francisco, Heritage Gallery, L.A.; represented by Ebert Gallery, San Francisco. 1st lt. USAF, 1953-55. Mem. Film Arts Found. Democrat. Episcopalian. Home and Office: The Madison Hobbs Studio PO Box 223759 Carmel CA 93922 *To create a work of art is an act of faith in the human spirit and in God. Art must always transcend materialist values and monuments to success. It is often the work of fools and children yet it is the ultimate reality.*

HOBBS, CASWELL O., III, lawyer; b. Sherman, Tex., Aug. 25, 1941; s. Caswell Owen II and Marie Elizabeth (Bloomfield) H.; m. Anne Louise Simpson, June 7, 1968; children: Elizabeth Ellen, Emily Jane. BS, U. Kans., 1963; LLB, U. Pa., 1966. Bar: D.C. 1967, U.S. Ct. Appeals (4th cir.) 1975, U.S. Supreme Ct. 1972. Asst. to chmn., dir. Office of Policy Planning and Evaluation, FTC, Washington, 1970-73; assoc. Morgan Lewis & Bockius, Washington, 1973-76, ptnr., 1976—, chmn. Washington office mgmt. com., 1987-89, mem. governing bd., 1989-92, 95-99; lectr. Conf. Bd., ABA. Author: Antitrust Strategies for Mergers, Acquisitions, Joint Ventures and Strategic Alliances, 2000; contbr. articles to profl. jours. Trustee Legal Aid Soc. D.C., 1982-92, pres., 1989-91, pres. coun., 1991—. Served to capt. JAGC, USAR, 1966-72. Fellow ABA (chair antitrust sect. 1994-95, officer 1991-96, co-chair task force on competition policy 1993, mem. commn. to study the FTC, 1988); mem. Am. Law Inst. E-mail: cohobbs@morganlewis.com. Office: Morgan Lewis & Bockius 1800 M St NW Lbby 6 Washington DC 20036-5828

HOBBS, DAVID ELLIS, mechanical engineer; BA in Engring. Sci., Dartmouth Coll., 1963; BSME, Case Inst. Tech., 1964; MSME, Rensselaer Poly. Inst., 1967, PhD in Mech. Engring., 1983. With turbine component design group Pratt & Whitney, East Hartford, Conn., 1964-67, with turbine analysis and tech. devel. group, 1967-77, with compressor analysis and tech. devel. group, 1977-94; gas turbine design sys. cons. FTS Cons., Inc., East Hartford, Conn., 1995-2000, TurboVision Cons. Group, Miami, Fla., 1995—. Contbr. articles to profl. jours. Recipient Horner citation United Technologies Corp., 1993. Fellow AIAA (assoc., chmn. Conn. sect. 2001-02); mem. ASME (gas turbine turbomachinery com., axial compressor panel, Gas Turbine award 1988). Home: 20 Bayberry Trl South Windsor CT 06074-3809 E-mail: dehobbs@cox.net.

HOBBS, EDWARD CRAIG, religious studies educator; b. Richmond, Ind., Oct. 10, 1926; s. Vernon Daniel Hobbs and Benona Klare Heath; m. Violet April VanOstran, June 17, 1950; 1 child, Kevin David. PhB, U. Chgo., 1946, PhD, 1952. Asst. prof. New Testament So. Meth. U., Dallas, 1952—58; prof. of theology and hermeneutics Grad. Theol. Union, Berkeley, Calif., 1958—81; lectr. medicine U. of Calif., Sch. of Medicine, San Francisco, 1959—81; prof. of religion Wellesley (Mass.) Coll., 1981—; vis. prof. of New Testament Harvard U., Cambridge, Mass., 1982—83. Author: (book) The Book of the Judges of Israel, 1950, Hermeneutical Cartography, 1990; editor and co-author (book) A Stubborn Faith, 1956, co-author and co-editor Gospel Studies, 1974; contbr. Mem.: Studiorum Novi Testamenti Societas, Soc. of Bibl. Lit. (v.p. and pres. 1955—57). Episcopalian. Avocations: wine tasting, wine judging. Home: 32 Upson Rd Wellesley MA 02482 Office: Wellesley Coll 106 Central St Wellesley MA 02481 E-mail: ehobbs@wellesley.edu.

HOBBS, GARY G, music educator; b. Portland, Oreg., Nov. 7, 1948; s. Lawrence Nordstrom and Johanna Marie Hobbs; m. Marcia B Brown, Apr. 23, 1952; 1 child, Britta Marie. AA, Mt. Hood C.C., 1969—71. Profl. musician-(drums) Stan Kenton Orch., Los Angeles, Calif., 1975—77; band dir. Prairie H.S., Battle Ground, Wash., 1995—97; drummer Woody Herman Orch., Miami, 2001, Bud Shank Band, Port Townsend, Wash., 1998—, Tom Grant Band, Portland, Oreg., 1980—, Gary Hobbs Bands, Vancouver, 1982—; clinician performing artist Yamaha Drum Co., Buana Park, Calif., 1980—, Zildjian Cymbal Co., Norwell, Mass., 1975—; drumset instrn. U. Of Oreg., 1997—, Whitman U., Walla Walla, Wash., 1996—2000. Musician: (albums) (record) Stan Kenton Orchestra:, Jim Widner Big Band: Rides Again, Mike Vax Big Band: I Remember You, Mike Vax Big Band: Live On The Road, Tom Grant: You Hardly Know Me, Tom Grant: Tom Grant, Tom Grant: Big Fun, Dan Siegel: Night Ride, Dan Siegel: Reflections, Richard Cole: The Forgotten, Gary Hobbs: Low Flight Through Valhalla, Stan Kenton Orchestra: Journey To Capricorn, Stan Kenton Orchestra: Live In Europe, Stan Kenton Orchestra:Live In Cologne, Stan Kenton Orchestra: Artistry In Symphonic Jazz, Dave Frishberg: Quality Time, Nancy King and Glen Moore: Cliff Dance, Jim Widner Big Band: Yesterdays And Today, Jim Widner Big Band: Body And Soul. Lutheran. Avocations: running, bicycling, cars. Office: 200 W37th St Vancouver WA 98660 E-mail: tubmanbeat@hotmail.com.

HOBBS, GREGORY JAMES, JR., state supreme court justice; b. Gainesville, Fla., Dec. 15, 1944; s. Gregory J. Hobbs and Mary Ann (Rhodes) Frakes; m. Barbara Louise Hay, June 17, 1967; children: Daniel Gregory, Emily Mary Hobbs Wright. BA, U. Notre Dame, 1966; JD, U. Calif., Berkeley, 1971. Bar: Colo. 1971, Calif. 1972. Law clk. to Judge William E. Doyle 10th U.S. Cir. Ct. Appeals, Denver, 1971-72; assoc. Cooper, White & Cooper, San Francisco, 1972-73; enforcement atty. U.S. EPA, Denver, 1973-75; asst. atty. gen. State of Colo. Atty. Gen.'s Office, Denver, 1975-79; ptnr. Davis, Graham & Stubbs, Denver, 1979-92; shareholder Hobbs, Trout & Raley, P.C., Denver, 1992-96; justice Colo. Supreme Ct., Denver, 1996—. Counsel No. Colo. Water Conservancy, Loveland, Colo., 1979-96. Contbr. articles to profl. jours. Vol. Peace Corps-S.Am., Colombia, 1967-68; vice chair Colo. Air Quality Control Com., Denver, 1982-87; mem. ranch com. Philmont Scout Ranch, Boy Scouts Am., Cimarron, N.Mex., 1988-98; co-chair Eating Disorder Family Support Group, Denver, 1992—. Recipient award of merit Denver Area Coun. Boy Scouts, 1993, Pres. award Nat. Water Resources Assn., Washington, 1995. Fellow Am. Bar Found.; mem. ABA, Colo. Bar Assn., Denver Bar Assn. Avocations: backpacking, fishing, writing poetry. Office: Colo Supreme Ct 2 E 14th Ave Denver CO 80203-2115*

HOBBS, GUY STEPHEN, financial executive; b. Lynwood, Calif., Feb. 23, 1955; s. Franklin Dean and Bette Jane (Little) H.; m. Laura Elena Lopez, Jan. 6, 1984; 1 child, Mariah Amanda. BA, U. Calif., Santa Barbara, 1976; MBA, U. Nev., 1978. Sr. rsch. assoc. Ctr. for Bus. and Econ. Rsch., Las Vegas, Nev., 1978-80; pvt. practice mgmt. cons. Las Vegas, 1979-82; mgmt. analyst Clark County, Las Vegas, 1980-81, sr. mgmt. analyst, 1981-82, dir. budget and fin. planning, 1982-84, comptroller, dir. fin., chief fin. officer, 1984-96; pres. Hobbs, Ong & Assocs., Inc., 1996—. Lectr. in mgmt. Coll. Bus. and Econs., U. Nev., Las Vegas, 1977-88; pres. Pacific Blue Ent., 1991—; mem. Interim Legis. Com. Infrastructure Fin., 1993-94; mem. Interim Legis. Com. Studying Laws Relating to the Distbn. of Taxes in Nev., 1995-96, 97—; mem. fiscal rev. com. Henderson State Coll., 2001, County Mgrs.'s orgnl. rev. com., 2001; chmn. Gov.'s Task Force on Tax Policy in Nev., 2001-02. Author publs. in field. Instr. Las Vegas Baseball Acad., 1998—2001; mem. exec. bd. Miss Nev. USA and Miss Nev. Teen USA, 1996—2002; head coach Silver State Girls Soccer League, 1998—2001; pres. U.S. Youth Soccer-Nev., 2003—; exec. prodr. WUSA exhbn. game between San Diego Spirit and San Jose Cyber Rays, 2002, WUSA exhbn. game between Boston Breakers and San Jose Cyber Rays, 2003; exec. producer Las Vegas Soccer spectacular. Mem. Am. Soc. Pub. Adminstrn. (Pub. Adminstr. of Yr. 1987), Govt. Fin. Officers Assn. (Fin. Reporting Achievement award 1984-95, Disting. Budget Presentation, award 1993-96), Nev. Taxpayers Assn. Republican. Avocations: sports, photography, travel. Office: Hobbs Ong & Assocs Inc 3900 Paradise Rd Ste 152 Las Vegas NV 89109-0928

HOBBS, HELEN T.B. librarian; (parents Am. citizens); m. Lawrence Deighton Hobbs, Aug. 2, 1970; children: Laureen, Deighton, Ayana, Helena. BS in Polit. Sci., Hunter Coll., Bronx, N.Y., 1970; MS in Edn., Queens (N.Y.) Coll., 1976, MLS, 1995. Tchr. jr. high sch. I.S. 55, Brooklyn, N.Y., 1971-76, JHS 194, Queens, 1979; tchr. computer sci. various Cath. schs., Queens, 1982; sch. libr., media specialist Harry Daniels Primary Sch., Roosevelt, N.Y., 1994-96, Far Rockaway H.S., Queens, 1996-97, Benjamin Cardozo H.S., Bayside, Queens, 1997—. Quilting exhbns. include numerous librs., Queens Hist. Soc., 1996—, Quilter's Heritige Celebration, Lancaster, Pa., 1996—. Active PTA Magnetech 231, Queens, 2000—. Mem. Ebony Quilters S.E. Queens (historian griot 1996—). Avocations: quilting, writing, reading. Office: Benjamin Cardozo HS 5700 223 St Queens NY 11364 E-mail: hhcardozo@yahoo.com.

HOBBS, HORTON HOLCOMBE, III, biology educator; b. Gainesville, Fla., Dec. 17, 1944; s. Horton Holcombe Jr. and Georgia Cates (Blount) H.; m. Susan Claire Krantz, Oct. 12, 1967; children: Heather H. Killion, Horton Holcombe IV. BA, U. Richmond, 1967; MS, Miss. State U., 1969; PhD, Ind. U., 1973. Instr. Christopher Newport Coll., Newport News, Va., 1973-75; asst. prof. George Mason U., Fairfax, Va., 1975-76; prof. biology Wittenberg U., Springfield, Ohio, 1976—. Com. mem. Nongame Wildlife Tech. Adv. Com., Columbus, Ohio, 1989-95; trustee Island Cave Rsch. Ctr., 1987—. Author: The Crayfishes and Shrimp of Wisconsin, 1988; life scis. editor: Nat. Speleological Soc. Bull., Huntsville, Ala., 1985-96; contbr. more than 180 articles to profl. jours. Campaign co-chair County Park Dist., Springfield, 1980. Fellow Nat. Speleological Soc. (bd. govs. 1985-88, hon. life mem.), The Explorers Club, Ohio Acad. Sci.; mem. Crustacean Soc. (coun. mem. 1980-83), Biol. Soc. Wash. (exec. coun. 1976-77), Am. Cave Conservation Assn. (bd. dirs. 1993—), Karst Waters Inst. (bd. dirs. 1999—), Cave Conservancy of the Virginias (bd. dirs. 1988—). Achievements include development of Ohio's Cave Protection Law; participation in International Speleological Expeditions to Costa Rica. Office: Wittenberg U Dept Biol Springfield OH 45501 E-mail: hhobbs@wittenberg.edu.

HOBBS, J. TIMOTHY, SR., lawyer; b. Yakima, Wash., Sept. 23, 1941; s. Leonard M. and Virginia (Snider) H.; m. Barbara J. Hatfield, June 14, 1964; children: Amy Elizabeth, J. Timothy Jr. BA in Polit. Sci., U. Wash., 1964; JD, Am. U., 1968. Bar: D.C. 1969, U.S. Ct. Supreme Ct. 1973, U.S. Ct. Appeals Fed. Crct. 1982, U.S. Ct. Appeals (11th cir.) 1986, U.S. Ct. Appeals (5th cir.) 1989, U.S. Ct. Appeals (6th cir.) 1996. Assoc. Mason Fenwick & Lawrence, Washington, 1969-76, ptnr., 1977-82, sr. ptnr., 1982-91; ptnr., head intellectual property dept. Dykema Gossett, 1991-99; ptnr. Wiley, Rein & Fielding, Washington, 1999—. Author chpt. on copyright law, West's Federal Practice Manual, 1983. Pres. Arlington Outdoor Edn. Assn., 1990-92. Mem. D.C. Bar (chmn. trademark com. 1982-84), Internat. Trademark Assn. Forums (speaker 1988), Washington Golf and Country Club. Home: 6135 Lee Hwy Arlington VA 22205-2134 Office: Wiley Rein & Fielding 1776 K St NW Washington DC 20006-2304

HOBBS, JAMES BEVERLY, business administration educator, writer; b. Topeka, Sept. 9, 1930; s. Kenneth Beverly and Ida (Burkholder) H.; m. Peggy Genevieve Whitney, Nov. 2, 1957; children: David Beverly, Nancy Ruth. AB, Harvard U., 1952; MBA, U. Kans., 1957; DBA, Ind. U., 1962. Fin. analyst Hotpoint divsn. GE, Chgo., 1957-60; asst. prof. mgmt. and acctg. Kans. State U., 1962-66, assoc. dean, 1964-66; assoc. prof. mgmt. and acctg. Lehigh U., 1966-70, prof., 1970-79, Frank L. Magee Disting. prof. bus. adminstrn., 1979-91, Frank L. Magee Disting. prof. bus. adminstrn. emeritus, 1991—, chmn. dept. mgmt., fin., mktg. and law, 1970-75, chmn. dept. mgmt., fin. and mktg., 1982-83, dir. MBA program, 1986-89, co-chmn. mgmt. dept., 1989-90, assoc. dean Coll. Bus. and Econ., 1993, assoc. dean Coll. Arts and Scis., 1993-95, chmn. art and architecture dept., 1996, assoc. dean emeritus Coll. Arts & Scis., 1999—. Vis. prof. acctg. U. Canterbury, New Zealand, 1976, Mich. Technol. U., 1975; vis. prof. mgmt. U. Edinburgh, Scotland, 1984, Ecole Superieure Commerce de Poitiers, France, 1990. Acad. Ednl. Devel., Bishkek, Kyrghystan, 1999; participant mission to Ulan Bator, Mongolia, UN Devel. Program, 1992; participant missions to Ternopil, Ukraine, Vladivostok, Russia, Bratislava, Slovak Republic and Kishnev, Moldova, Internat. Exec. Svc. Corps, 1993, 95, 97, 98, mission to Skopje, Macedonia, U.S. Energy Assn., 1997; acad. cons. Author: Financial Accounting, 1984, Corp. Staying Power, 1987, Homophones & Homographs, 1999. Served as naval aviation cadet USN, 1952, as regtl. sgt. maj. U.S. Army, 1953-54, Korea. Mem. Mensa, Phi Beta Kappa, Phi Kappa Phi, Beta Gamma Sigma, Beta Alpha Psi, Sigma Iota Epsilon, Omicron Delta Epsilon, Omicron Delta Kappa, Delta Mu Delta, Phi Beta Delta. Unitarian Universalist. Home: 1915 Black River Rd Bethlehem PA 18015-8920 E-mail: jbh1@lehigh.edu.

HOBBS, JERRY DEAN, county manager; b. Roseboro, N.C., Jan. 4, 1946; s. Cecil Wright and Virgie Mae Hobbs; m. Mary Margaret Kelly; children: Christopher Neal, Mary Katherine. BSBA, Campbell U., 1968. Tchr., coach Sampson County Bd. Edn., Clinton, N.C., 1968-77; fin. officer Sampson County, Clinton, 1977-86, county mgr., 1986—. Named County Leader of the Yr. Ea. Ctr. Regional Devel., 1997. Mem. Internat. City Mgrs. Assn. Home: 312 W Main St Clinton NC 28328-4437 Office: 435 Rowan Rd Clinton NC 28328-4729 E-mail: jerryh@intrstar.net.

HOBBS, LEWIS MANKIN, astronomer; b. Upper Darby, Pa., May 16, 1937; s. Lewis Samuel and Evangeline Elizabeth (Goss) H.; m. Jo Ann Faith Hagele June 16, 1962; children: John, Michael, Dara. B of Engring. Physics, Cornell U., 1960; MS, U. Wis., 1962, PhD in Physics, 1966. Jr. astronomer Lick Obs., U. Calif., Santa Cruz, 1965-66; faculty U. Chgo., 1966—, prof. astronomy and astrophysics, 1976—2003, prof. emeritus, 2003; dir. Yerkes Obs. Williams Bay, Wis., 1974-82. Bd. dirs. Assn. Univs. for Rsch. in Astronomy, Washington, 1974-85; mem. Space Telescope Inst. Coun., 1982-87; astronomy com. of bd. trustees Univs. Rsch. Assn., Inc., Washington, 1979-83, chmn., 1979-81; bd. govs. Astrophys. Rsch. Consortium, Inc., Seattle, 1984-91; mem. Users Com. for Hubble Space Telescope, NASA, 1990-94; mem. telescope allocation com. Nat. Optical Astronomy Obs., 1998-2000. Contbr. articles to profl. jours. Bd. dirs. Mil. Symphony Assn. of Walworth County, 1972-88. Alfred P. Sloan scholar, 1955-60. Mem.: Internat. Astron. Union, Am. Phys. Soc., Am. Astron. Soc. Office: U Chgo Yerkes Observatory Williams Bay WI 53191

HOBBS, MARCUS EDWIN, chemistry educator; b. Chadbourn, N.C., Aug. 11, 1909; s. Julius Charles and Maude Elizabeth (Player) H.; m. Sarah Ferguson Blanchard, July 3, 1937; children: Sarah Lillian, Joan Elizabeth. AB, Duke U., 1932, MA, 1934, PhD, 1936. Indsl. rsch. fellow tobacco Duke, 1931-33, instr. chemistry, 1936, asst. prof., 1942, assoc. prof., 1945, prof., 1950—, univ. disting. svc. prof. emeritus, 1978—, chmn. dept. chemistry, 1951-54; dean Duke (Grad. Sch. Arts and Scis.), 1954-58, dean of univ., 1958-64, vice provost 1960-64, provost, 1969-71, charge spl. courses in chemistry of explosives 1941-42. Research assoc. Nat. Def. Rsch. Com., George Washington U., 1942-45; civilian cons. Nat. Def. Rsch. Com., George Washington U. (divsn. 2) 1942-44, Nat. Def. Rsch. Com., George Washington U. (divsn. 3), 1943-45 adviser Office Ordnance Rsch., 1951-61, chief scientist, acting, 1951-52; Dir. N.C. Blue Cross and Blue Shield, Inc., 1967-81, chmn. exec. com., 1978-81 mem. adv. coun. Army Rsch. Office, 1970-76; mem. adv. com. jr. sci. and humanities symposia Dept. Army, 1974-77, adviser, 1980-85 ; mem. NSF adv. panel U.S.-Japan Coop. Svc. Program, 1963-65; adv. com. utilization R & D USDR, 1964-70; mem. N.C. Bd. Sci. and Tech., 1963-75; chmn. exec. com. Rsch. Triangle Inst., 1958-68, 71-98. Contbr. articles to profl. jours. Recipient Army-Navy Certificate of Merit for sci. work with OSRD during World War II 1945; Outstanding Civilian Svc. medal Dept. Army, 1959; Cigar Industry Rsch award, 1959, Univ. medal for Disting. Meritous Svc. Duke U., 1989, Archie K Davis award, 1999. Fellow AAAS; mem. Am. Chem. Soc. (chmn. N.C. sect. 1946), AAUP, Rotary (pres. Durham 1978-79), Phi Beta Kappa, Sigma Xi, Phi Lambda Upsilon, Sigma Pi Sigma, Sigma Chi. Home: 2701 Pickett Rd Apt 4009 Durham NC 27705-5652

HOBBS, MICHAEL EDWIN, broadcasting company executive; b. Washington, Nov. 26, 1940; s. Robert Boyd and Barbara Alberta (Davis) H.; m. Ann Reed, Sept. 16, 1989. AB cum laude, Dartmouth Coll., 1962; JD, Harvard U., 1965. Bar: Mass. 1966. Staff counsel, asst. to gen. mgr. Sta. WGBH Edn. Found., Boston, 1966-67; exec. asst. ednl. TV stas. Nat. Assn. Ednl. Broadcasters, Washington, 1967-70; sec. PBS, Washington, 1970-87, gen. counsel 1970-71, dir. adminstrn., 1970-73, v.p., 1973-76, sr. v.p., 1976-87, sr. v.p. fo policy and planning, 1987-91; sr. fellow Hartford Gunn Inst., Alexandria, Va. 1991—. Mem. Alexandria Rep. City Com., 1997—, chmn. 1998-2000; bd. dirs Old Town Civic Assn., 2001—. Mem. ABA (intellectual property law sect.), Mass. Bar Assn., Nat. Acad. TV Arts and Scis., George Town Club, Phi Beta Kappa. Home and Office: Hartford Gunn Inst 419 Cameron St Alexandria VA 22314-3221

HOBBS, NEDDA MARIE, pediatrician; b. Cambridge, Mass., July 21, 1956; d. J. David and Rose-Marie (Delgrego) H. BS, MIT, 1978; MD, U. Mass., 1982. Diplomate Am. Bd. Pediatrics; bd. cert. Neurodevel. Disabilities. Resident in pediatrics Children's Hosp. of Phila., 1982-86; fellow devel. disabilities R.I. Hosp., Providence, 1986-88; chief of pediatrics Lakeville (Mass.) Hosp. 1988-91; pediatrician coordinated care svc. Children's Hosp., Boston, 1991-94, co-dir. coordinated care svc., 1994—, pediatrician, myelodysplasia program 1992—. Fellow Am. Acad. Pediatrics, Soc. Devel. Pediatrics; mem. Mass. Med. Soc., Soc. Mayflower Descs. (life), Phi Beta Kappa. Avocations: swimming, sewing, gourmet cooking, photography, music. Office: Children's Hosp 300 Longwood Ave Boston MA 02115-5737

HOBBS, ROBERT ELLICE, JR., artist; b. Richmond, Va., Nov. 28, 1955; s. Robert Ellice Hobbs Sr., Dorothy Mae Evans; AS, U. Hawaii, 1983. Illustrator U.S. Naval War Coll., Newport, RI, 1987—96; digital artist, animator Ctrs. for Disease Control, Atlanta, 1997—. With USN, 1973—77. Named Illustrators of the Future, L. Ron Hubbard Found., 1986. Mem.: Assn. Sci. Fiction Artists. Home and Office: 614 St Marlowe Dr Lawrenceville GA 30044-7368 E-mail: bobhobz@bellsouth.net.

HOBBS, TRUMAN MCGILL, federal judge; b. Selma, Ala., Feb. 8, 1921; s. Sam F. and Sarah Ellen (Greene) H.; m. Joyce Cummings, July 9, 1949; children— Emilie C. Reid, Frances John Rose, Dexter Cummings, Truman McGill. AB, U. N.C., 1942; LL.B., Yale U., 1948. Bar: Ala. 1948. Practiced in Montgomery, 1951-80; law clk. U.S. Supreme Ct., 1948-49; ptnr. Hobbs, Copeland, Franco & Screws, 1951-80; U.S. dist. judge Montgomery, 1980 ; now sr. judge. Chmn. Ala. Unemployment Appeal Bd., 1952-58 Pres. United Appeal Montgomery; pres. Montgomery County Tb Assn.; v.p. Ala. Com. for Better Schs.; Chmn. Montgomery County Exec. Democratic Com., 1970. Served to lt. USNR, 1942-46, ETO, PTO. Decorated Bronze Star medal. Fellow Am. Coll. Trial Lawyers; mem. Internat. Acad. Trial Lawyers, Ala. Plaintiffs Lawyers Assn. (past pres.), Ala. Bar Assn. (pres. 1970-71), Montgomery County Bar Assn. (past pres.) Home: 2301 Fernway Dr Montgomery AL 36111-1603

HOBBS, WALTER CLARENCE, retired educator; b. Richmond Hill, N.Y., Dec. 15, 1932; s. Clarence Wellington and Ella Marie (Schmidt) H.; m. June Florence Anderson, Mar. 16, 1957; 1 child, Eric E. BA, U. Buffalo, 1961; MA, SUNY, Buffalo, 1963, PhD, 1968, JD, 1976; LLD (hon.), Houghton Coll., 1988. Dir. instnl. rsch. SUNY, Buffalo, 1963-70, mem. faculty, 1969-93, emeritus, 1993—. Vis. prof. Trinity Evang. Div. Sch., Deerfield, Ill., 1987, 89; lectr., manuscript reviewer in field. Editor: Government Regulation of Higher Education, 1978, Understanding Academic Law, 1982, Jour. Higher Edn. Mgmt., 1992-94; contbr. articles to profl. publs., chpts. to books. Tchr., officer Randall Bapt. Ch., Williamsville, NY, 1960—97, Eastbrook Ch., Milw., 1997—; sec. Patkai Ministries, Inc., U.S. and India, 1963—; pres. Coalition for Common Ground, Buffalo, 1993—95; bd. dirs. Coun. Chss. Buffalo and Erie County, NY, 1993—96. Mem. Am. Assn. for Higher Edn., Assn. for Study of Higher Edn. (legal counsel 1987-2000, Spl. Merit award 1993), Gospel and Our Culture Network. Democrat. Home: 623 Lake Bluff Rd Thiensville WI 53092-1286

HOBBY, WILLIAM PETTUS, broadcast executive, retired; b. Houston, Jan. 19, 1932; s. William Pettus and Oveta (Culp) H.; m. Diana Poteat Stallings, Sept. 11, 1954; children: Laura Poteat Beckworth, Paul William, Andrew Purefoy, Katherine Pettus Gibson. BA, Rice U., 1953. Pres. H & C Communications, Inc., 1979-83, chmn. bd., chief exec. officer, 1983-96; lt. gov. Tex., 1973-91; chancellor Univ. of Houston Sys., 1995-97. Sid Richardson prof. Lyndon B. Johnson Sch. Pub. Affairs, U. Tex., Austin, 1990-97; Radoslav Tsanoff prof. Rice U., Houston, 1991—. Served to lt. (j.g.) USNR, 1953-57. Office: Hobby Comm LLC 2131 San Felipe Houston TX 77019-5620

HOBDELL, MARTIN HOWARD, dental educator, researcher; b. Harrow, United Kingdom, Aug. 26, 1938; s. Howard George and Mabel Phyllis Hobdell; m. Helen Constance Mary Keegan, June 26, 1987. B in dental surgery, The Royal London Hosp. Med. Coll., 1961—61, PhD, 1970. Dean Faculty of Dentistry, U. of the Western Cape, South Africa, 1992—97; prof. and chair of dept., dental pub. health and hygiene U. of Tex. Health Sci. Ctr. at Houston Dental Br., 1998—. Reader in dental anatomy King's Coll. London, 1970—71; prof. of stomatolgy Ministry of Health, Faculty of Medicine, U. of Eduardo Mondlane, Mozambique, 1976—79; reader in oral health U. of London, 1980—82; hon. cons. dental surgeon Tower Hamlets Health Authority, London, 1980—82; prof. and chair cmty., preventive dentistry U. of Dublin, Trinity Coll., 1983—92; head WHO Collaborating Ctr. for Oral Health, South Africa, 1993—97; fellow Trinity Coll., Dublin, 1987. Author: (book) Assisting Dental Education and Dental Public Health in Developing Countries, The Planning and Development of Educational Programs for Personnel in Oral Health, Planning and Managing District Dental Services; contbr. chapters to books. Elected hon. sec. Fedn. Dentaire Internat Pub. Health Sect., Ferney-Voltaire, 1994—2003; elected mem. Fedn. Dentaire Internat., 2002—; editor Commonwealth Dental Assn., London, 1996—2003; advisor WHO, Geneva and Brazzaville, 1981—2002; mem. Fluoridation Com. Nat. Dept. of Health, Pretoria, South Africa, 1994—97, Nat. Commn. on Higher Edn. Reference Panel, Pretoria, South Africa, 1995—96; bd. mem. then chair Appropriate Health Resources and Technologies Action Group, London, 1979—83, Health Policy Coord. Unit, Johannesburg, 1994—97. Recipient Hon. fellowship, Acad. of Dentistry Internat., 2002; Planning grant, Nat. Inst. for Dental and Cranio-facial Rsch., 2002—, grant, Permanent Fund for Children Tex. Dept. of Health, 2000—01. Mem.: Health Volunteers Overseas, Brit. Assn. for the Study of Cmty. Dentistry, Brit. Dental Assn., Am. Assn. for Pub. Health Dentistry, Am. Dental Edn. Assn., Internat. Assn. for Dental Rsch. (past pres. irish divsn. 1985—86), ADA (assoc.). Office: University of Tex Dental Branch 6516 MD Anderson Blvd Houston TX 77030 Personal E-mail: martin.h.hobdell@uth.tmc.edu.

HOBELMAN, CARL DONALD, lawyer; b. Hackensack, N.J., Dec. 26, 1931; s. Alfred Charles and Marion (Gerrish) H.; m. Grace Palumbo, Apr. 25, 1964 BCE, Cornell U., 1954; JD, Harvard U., 1959. Bar: N.Y. 1960, U.S. Supreme Ct. 1975, D.C. 1980, Calif. 1993. Assoc. LeBoeuf, Lamb, Greene & MacRae, N.Y.C., 1959-64, ptnr. L.A., N.Y.C., Washington, 1965-94, of counsel Washington, 1995—2001. Contbr. articles on energy-related topics to profl. jours. Served to 1st lt. U.S. Army, 1954-56 Mem. Energy Bar Assn. (pres. 1980-81), D.C. Bar Assn., Met. Club (Washington), Univ. Club (N.Y.C.). Avocations: travel, philately. Office: LeBoeuf Lamb Greene & MacRae 1875 Connecticut Ave NW Washington DC 20009-5728

HOBERG, MICHAEL DEAN, management analyst, educator; b. Pipestone, Minnesota, Feb. 27, 1955; s. Dennis Edwin and Beverly Ann (Voss) H.; 1 child, Heather; m. Janet Lee (Freeman). BS in Pk. Adminstrn., Calif. State U., Sacramento, 1977; MPA, Calif. State U., Turlock, Ca., 1982; PhD in Pub. Adminstrn., Greenwich Univ., 1993; post grad. in computer info. sys. and project mgmt., U. Calif., Berkeley, 1996—2003. Cert. govt. fin. mgr., project mgmt. profl., Internat. Pers. Mgmt. Assn. Pk. ranger Nat. Pk. Svc., State of Calif., and San Joaquin County, Calif., 1977-82; pk. svc. specialist San Joaquin County, Stockton, Calif., 1983-86, mgmt. analyst, 1986—. Adj. instr. Delta Coll., Stockton, Calif., 1987-90; dir. Hoberg Mgmt. and Consulting, Stockton, Calif., 1987—. Fencing Champion foil, No. Calif. Intercollegiate Athletic Conf., 1977; 9th Place award USFA Nat. Championships, 1988; High Jump champion, City of Stockton, 1971-73; inducted into Sacramento C. of C. Athletic Hall of Fame, 1977. Mem.: Mensa, Am. Planning Assn., Project Mgmt. Inst. Democrat. Home: 2209 Meadow Ave Stockton CA 95207-1428 Office: San Joaquin County PO Box 1810 Stockton CA 95201 E-mail: hoberg2@aol.com.

HOBERMAN, MARY ANN, author; b. Stamford, Conn., Aug. 12, 1930; d. Milton and Dorothy (Miller) Freedman; m. Norman Hoberman, Feb. 4, 1951; children: Diane, Perry, Charles, Meg. BA, Smith Coll., 1951; MA, Yale U., 1984. With advt. dept. Gimbel's Dept. Store, N.Y.C., 1951-52; newspaper reporter Harrisburg, Pa., 1952; editor N.Y. Graphic Soc., Greenwich, Conn., 1963-64. Poetry cons.; lectr. in field; program coord. C.G. Jung Ctr., N.Y.C., 1981; adj. prof. Fairfield (Conn.) U., 1980-83; instr. Yale U., New Haven, 1989; founder, mem. The Pocket People, 1968-75; founder, performer Women's Voices, 1983-93. Author: All My Shoes Come in Two's, 1957, How Do I Go?, 1958, Hello and Good-by, 1959, What Jim Knew, 1963, Not Enough Beds for the Babies, 1965, A Little Book of Little Beasts, The Raucous Auk, 1973, The Looking Book, 1973, Nuts to You and Nuts to Me, 1974, I Like Old Clothes, 1976, Bugs, 1976, A House Is a House for Me, 1978, Yellow Butter, Purple Jelly, Red Jam, Black Bread, 1981, The Cozy Book, 1982, Mr. and Mrs. Muddle, 1988, A Fine Fat Pig and Other Animal Poems, 1991, Fathers, Mothers, Sisters, Brothers, 1991; editor: My Song is Beautiful, 1994, The Cozy Book, 1995, The Seven Silly Eaters, 1997, One of Each, 1997, Miss Mary Mack, 1998, The Llama Who Had No Pajama, 1998, And to Think that We Thought We Would Never Be Friends, 1999, The Cozy Book, 1999, The Eensy Weensy Spider, 2000, the Two Sillies, 2000, Michael Finnegan, 2001, It's Simple, Said Simon, 2001, You Read to Me, 2001, The Looking Book, 2002, The Marvelous Mouse Man, 2002, Right Outside My Window, 2002, Bill Grogan's Goat, 2002. Bd. dirs. Greenwich Libr., 1988-91, Literacy Vols., 1997—. Recipient Nat. Book award, 1984, Poetry for Children award Nat. Coun. Tchrs. of English, 2003. Mem. Authors Guild. Avocations: dancing, gardening, hiking, tennis. Home: 98 Hunting Ridge Rd Greenwich CT 06831-3134

HOBERMAN, STUART A. lawyer; b. New York, Nov. 21, 1946; BBA, Baruch Coll., N.Y., 1969; JD, Bklyn. Law Sch., 1972; LLM, N.Y. Univ., 1973. Bar: N.Y., 1973, N.J., 1977, Pa., 1979, U.S. Supreme Ct., 1976. Assoc. Windels and Marx, N.Y.C., 1973-77, Wilentz, Goldman, and Spitzer, Woodbridge, NJ, 1977-80, ptnr., 1980—. Trustee, Emmanuel Cancer Found., Kenilworth, N.J., 1983-90; trustee, Cancer Care of NJ, 1999—. Mem.: N.J. State Bar Assn. (bank law sect. chmn. 1986—87, corp. and bus. law sect. chmn. 1988—90, chmn. exec. com. of gen. coun. 1990—92, trustee 1990—94, trustee N.J. State Bar Found. 1992—, treas. 1995—96, trustee 1997—2001, pres. 1999—2001, first v.p. 2003—). Office: Wilentz Goldman & Spitzer PO Box 10 90 Woodbridge Ctr Dr Ste 900 Woodbridge NJ 07095-1142

HOBEROCK, LAWRENCE LINDEN, mechanical engineer, educator; b. Wichita, Kans., Oct. 21, 1939; s. Lawrence H. and Teresa B. (Gornick) H.; m. Judith L. Anderson, June 6, 1964; children: Michael Jo, Barbara T., Timmothy M. BSME, U. Mo., Rolla, 1961, MSME, 1963; PhD, Purdue U., 1966. Registered profl. engr., Tex., Okla. Asst. prof., then assoc. prof. U. Tex., Austin, 1968-78; rsch. assoc. Amoco Prodn. Co., Tulsa, 1978-81, rsch. supr., 1981-85; v.p. rsch. Derrick Mfg. Corp., Buffalo, 1985-86; pvt. practice engring. cons. Buffalo, 1986-87; prof., head mech. and aero. engring. Okla. State U., Stillwater, 1987—. Cons. Amoco Prodn. Co., 1977-78, 88, Shell Devel. Co., Houston, 1989-91, Conoco, Ponca City, Okla., 1990, Cagle Oilfield Svcs., Tulsa, 1990. Contbr. articles to profl. publs. Capt. U.S. Army, 1966-68. Fellow ASME (dedicated svc. award, chair dynamic sys., v.p. sys. and design, assoc. editor); mem. AIAA, IEEE, IEEE Control Sys. Soc., Soc. Petroleum Engrs. (assoc. editor), Am. Soc. Engring. Edn. Avocations: carpentry, bird watching, wines, upland bird hunting. Office: Okla State U Sch Mech and Aero Engring 218 En Stillwater OK 74078-5016

HOBGOOD, E(ARL) WADE, college chancellor; b. Wilson, N.C., June 28, 1953; s. Max Earl and Mary (Carpenter) H.; m. Dianne Bland, Apr. 24, 1977; children: Courtney, Heather. BFA, E. Carolina U., 1975, MFA, 1977; postgrad., Am. Inst. for Philanthropic, Studies, 1995, Harvard U., 1997, Sashakawa Fellowship/AACSCU, 1998. Asst. prof. art Ark. State U., Jonesboro, 1977-78; design dir. and asst./assoc. prof. art Western Carolina U., Cullowhee, N.C., 1978-84; chmn., assoc. to full prof. art and design Winthrop U., Rock Hill, S.C., 1984-88, acting chmn. dept. music, 1991-92, assoc. dean and prof. Coll. Visual and Performing Arts, 1988-92; dean Coll. of Fine Arts, Stephen F. Austin State U., Nacogdoches, Tex., 1992-93; dean Coll. of Arts, Calif. State U., Long Beach, 1993-2000; chancellor N.C. Sch. of the Arts, Winston-Salem, 2000—. Sr. evaluator Nat. Assn. Schs. of Art and Design, 1987-99; bd. dirs. Rancho Los Cerritos Found., 1996-2000; presenter Global Arts Conf., New Zealand, 1999; mem. cultural planning com. City of Long Beach, 1996-2000; evaluator/cons. Arts Edn. Partnership Grants, Ky. Arts Coun., 1992; evaluator/panelist Challenge grants, NEA, 1991, correspondent/cons. Arts Edn. Rsch. Briefing, 1991; mem. bd. advisors First Wachovia Bank, 2003—. Bd. dirs. Winston-Salem Alliance, 2001--, Davidson Coll. Friends of the Arts, Brenner Children's Hosp., 2002--, Forsyth County Tourism Devel. Authority, 2002--, So. Arts Fedn., 2002—, Winston-Salem Symphony, 2002—; mem. Mayor's Task Force on Smithsonian, City of Long Beach, 1996-2000; chair bd. dirs. Kenan Inst. for the Arts, 2000—. Mem. Winston-Salem/Forsyth C. of C. (bd. dirs. 2001—). Office: NC Sch of the Arts PO Box 12189 Winston Salem NC 27117-2189 E-mail: wh@ncarts.edu.

HOBLIN, PHILIP J., JR., securities lawyer; b. S.I., N.Y., July 31, 1929; s. Philip J. and Mary A. (Brown) H.; m. Eileen P. Killilea, Jan. 10, 1959; children: Philip, Monica, Michael. BS, Fordham U., 1951, LLD, 1957. Bar: N.Y. 1957. Regional atty. Bache & Co., N.Y.C., 1958-63; exec. v.p. Shearson Lehman Hutton, Inc., 1963-89; co-chmn. Inst. Fin. Law Ctr., N.Y.C., 1972-92; chief exec. officer Buttonwood Securities, 1989-90; of counsel Jenkens Gilchrist Parker Chapin, N.Y.C., 1990—. Adj. prof. law Fordham U., 1986-96; mem. Joint Industry Com. Securities Protection, 1969; mem. bd. arbitration N.Y. Stock Exch., 1977-89; chmn. arbitration com. Chgo. Bd. Options Exchange, 1977-78, mem. conduct com., 1979-80; mem. exec. and nat. arbitration coms. Nat. Assn. Securities Dealers, 1984-85, also mem. bus. conduct com. dist. 12, 1974-77; mem. Securities Industry Conf. on Arbitration, 1977—. Author: Securities Arbitration: Procedures, Strategies and Cases, 1988, 2d edit., 1991, Compliance and Business Procedures Manual, also law rev. articles. Served as spl. agt. USAF, 1951-53; col. (ret.). Mem. ABA, Security Industry Assn. (pres. compliance divsn. 1970-72, compliance divsn. award 1995), Am. Legion Res. Officers Assn. (v.p. air N.Y. state chpt. 1973-74, 87-88, pub. rels. sec. judge adv. gen. N.Y.C. chpt., pres. N.Y. state chpt. 1988-89), VFW, Air Force Assn., Assn. Former OSI Agts., Respect for Law Alliance (former dir.), Ret. Officers Assn., Constn. Island Assn. (treas.), KC, Elks. Home: 499 N Broadway White Plains NY 10603-3235 Office: Jennings Gilchrist Parker Chapin 405 Lexington Ave New York NY 10174-0002

HOBLIT, GREGORY, film director, television executive; b. Abilene, Tex. m. Debrah Farentino; 1 child, Sophie. Bachelors, Masters, UCLA. Dir. (TV series): Hill Street Blues, 1981 (Emmy awards Outstanding Drama Series, 1981, 82, 83, 84, nominated 1985, 86), L.A. Law, 1986 (nominated Emmy award Outstanding Drama Series, 1986), NYPD Blue, 1993 (DGA award Outstanding Directorial Achievement in Dramatic Shows-Night, pilot episode, 1993, TV Prodr. of Yr. award 1994, Emmy award Outstanding Drama Series, 1995); dir.: (TV movie) Roe vs. Wade (Emmy award, 1994), 1989, (movies) Primal Fear, 1996, Fallen, 1998, Frequency, 2000, Hart's War, 2002; assoc. prodr. (TV) Dr. Strange, 1978, Bay City Blues, (exec.) 1983, Hooperman (Emmy award, outstanding directing in a comedy series 1988), 1987, Cop Rock (co-exec.), 1990, Civil Wars, 1991; supervising prodr. (TV series) Paris, 1979; prodr. (TV movies): Vampire, 1979. Office: c/o DGA 7920 W Sunset Blvd Los Angeles CA 90046-3300 and: Abilene Pictures 335 N Maple Dr Beverly Hills CA 90210-3857 Office: c/o David Wirtschafter William Morris Agy 151 El Camino Dr Beverly Hills CA 90212*

HOBSON, BURTON HAROLD, publishing company executive; b. Galesburg, Ill., Apr. 16, 1933; s. Burt and Geneva (Sornberger) H.; m. Maxine C. Meyer, Aug. 9, 1953; children: Alice L., Andrew J., Mark R. BA, U. Chgo., 1953; LHD honoris causa, Johnson & Wales U., 2002. Mgr. collector's coin dept. Marshall Field & Co., Chgo., 1953-61; sales mgr. Sterling Pub. Co., Inc., N.Y.C., 1961-66, v.p. sales, 1966-72, exec. v.p., 1972-79, pres., 1979-95, chmn., 1995—2003, dir., 1966—2003; pres. Pub. Adv. Svc., 2003—. Author: (with Fred Reinfeld) Manual for Coin Collectors and Investors, 1963, Picture Book of Ancient Coins, 1963, U.S. Commemorative Coins and Stamps, 1964, Catalogue of the World's Most Popular Coins, 1965, What You Should Know about Coins and Coin Collecting, 1965, Hidden Values in Coins, 1965, International Guide to Coin Collecting, 1966, Coins You Can Collect, 1966, Coin Identifier, 1966, Coin Collecting As a Hobby, 1967, (with Robert Obojski) Illustrated Encyclopedia of World Coins, 1970, Catalogue of Scandinavian Coins, 1970, Historic Gold Coins of the World, 1971, Coin Collecting for Beginners, 1970, Stamp Collecting for Beginners, 1970, Coins and Coin Collecting, 1971; editor: The Benenson Restaurant Guide, 1985; pub. Gastronome mag., 1993—. Recipient Robert Friedberg award for numismatic lit., 1972 Mem. Am. Numismatic Soc., Confrérie des Chevaliers du Tastevin, Confrérie de la Chaine des Rôtisseurs (nat. pres.), Culinary Inst. Am. (trustee), Am. Acad. Chefs (hon. trustee), Univ. Club of N.Y., Delta Upsilon. Home: 600 Harbor Blvd Unit 833 Weehawken NJ 07086-6748 E-mail: burtonhh@msn.com.

HOBSON, CALVIN J., III, state legislator, real estate firm executive; b. Tucson, Mar. 30, 1945; s. Calvin J. II and Wardena (Webb) H.; m. Elaine Hobson; children: Jack, Aubrey, Matt. BA, postgrad., U. Okla.; grad. with highest honors, Air War Coll., 1993. Pres. Glenwood, Inc.; mem. Okla. Ho. of Reps., 1978-90, Okla. State Senate, 1990—, pres. pro tempore. Mayor, Lexington, Okla., 1976. Served with Okla. Air N.G., ret. Mem. Lexington C. of C., Noble C. of C., Norman C. of C., Am. Legion. Democrat. Methodist. Office: State Capitol Bldg 2300 N Lincoln Blvd Oklahoma City OK 73105-4805 also: PO Box 1067 Lexington OK 73051-1067 E-mail: hobson@lsb.state.ok.us.*

HOBSON, DAVID LEE, congressman, lawyer; b. Oct. 17, 1936; m. Carolyn Alexander; children: Susan Marie, Lynn Martha, Douglas Lee. BA, Ohio Wesleyan U., 1958; JD, Ohio State Coll. Law, 1963; hon. degree, Ctrl. State U., Wittenberg U. Former resident counsel Kissell Co., Springfield, Ohio; former atty. Union Ctrl. Life Ins. Co., Cin.; mem. Ohio Senate, 1982-90, majority whip, 1986-88, pres. pro tem, 1988-90; mem. U.S. Congress from 7th Ohio dist., Washington, 1991—; mem. house appropriations com., def. subcom., VA, HUD and Ind. Agys. subcom., chmn. mil constrn. subcom. House coms. appropriations, budget, standards of ofcl. conduct. Former trustee Wilberforce U., Ohio, Urbana U.; trustee Ohio Wesleyan; bd. dirs. Ohio. Mem. ABA, AMVETS, Ky. Bar Assn., Ohio Bar Assn., Springfield Bd. Realtors, Springfield Area C. of C. (past bd. dirs.), Non-Commissioned Officers Assn., Masons (32 degrees), Am. Legion, VFW, Moose, Elks, Rotary, Shrine Club. Republican. Home: # 200 5 W North St # 200 Springfield OH 45504-2544 Office: US Ho of Reps 2346 Rayburn Hob Washington DC 20515-3507*

HOBSON, FRED COLBY, JR., English educator, author; b. Winston-Salem, Apr. 23, 1943; s. Fred Colby and Miriam Brevard (Tuttle) Hobson; m. Linda V. Whitney, June 17, 1967 (div. 1977); 1 child, Jane Gregory. AB, U. N.C., 1965, PhD, 1972; MA, Duke U., 1967. Editl. writer Winston-Salem Jour. and Sentinel, 1969—70; asst. prof. English U. Ala., Tuscaloosa, 1972—75, assoc. prof., 1975—79, prof., 1980—86; prof. English La. State U., Baton Rouge, 1987—; co-editor Southern Rev., 1987—89; Lineberger prof. humanities U. N.C., 1989—. Vis. prof. Am. studies U. Hull, England, 1982; cons. NEH, 1979—83. Author: Serpent in Eden: H.L. Mencken and the South, 1974, Tell About the South: The Southern Rage to Explain (Jules F. Landry award, 1983), The Southern Writer in the Postmodern World, 1992, Mencken: A Life, 1994, But Now I See: The White Southern Racial Conversion Narrative, 1999; editor: South-Watching: Selected Essays of Gerald W. Johnson, 1983; co-editor: Literature at the Barricades: The American Writer in the 1930's, 1982, H.L. Mencken's Thirty-Five Years of Newspaper Work, 1995, The Literature of the American South, 1998; editor: South to the Future, 2001, Absalom, Absalom: Selected Essays, 2003; contbr. Co-recipient Pulitzer Prize in Journalism, 1970; recipient Nat. Humanities fellowship, 1992—93; NEH fellow, 1976—77, 1992—93. Mem.: MLA, Mencken Soc., Soc. for Study of So. Lit. Democrat. Office: Univ NC Chapel Hill Dept English Cb # 3520 Chapel Hill NC 27599-0001 E-mail: fhobson@email.unc.edu.

HOBSON, GEORGE DONALD, retired geophysicist; b. Hamilton, Ont., Can., Jan. 8, 1923; s. Robert Charles and Agnes Hamilton (Mathieson) H.; m. Arletta Louise Russell, May 21, 1948; children: Robert, Linda, Douglas, Donna. BA, McMaster U., 1946, DSc (hon.), 1991; MA, Toronto U., 1948. Registered profl. geophysicist, Can. Party chief, ptnr. Heiland Exploration Can. Ltd., Calgary, Alta., 1948-55; geophysicist Can. Fina Oil Co., Calgary, 1955-56; chief geophysicist Merrill Petroleums Ltd., Calgary, 1956-57; geophysicist Pacific Petroleums Ltd., Calgary, 1957-58; chief seismic sect. Geol. Survey Can., Ottawa, Ont., 1958-69, chief geophysics div., 1969-71; dir. Polar Shelf Project, Ottawa, 1972-88, sr. advisor, 1988-90; rsch. assoc. Nunavut Rsch. Inst., Iqaluit, NWT, Can., 1997—. Author or co-author over 200 articles in field. Recipient No. Sci. award and Centennial medal Dept. Indian and No. Affairs, Can., 1991, Ind. Achievement award Am. Soc. Mech. Engrs., Massey Medal, 1991, Royal Can. Geog. Soc., Queen Elizabeth Goldn Jubilee medal 2002. Fellow Exploration Geophysicists India, Royal Can. Geog. Soc. (bd. govs. 1987-94, Massey medal 1991, Camsell award 1998, The Queen's Golden Jubilee Medal), Arctic Inst. N.Am. (bd. govs. 1984-91); mem. Sci. Inst. N.W. Territory (bd. govs. 1990-93), Soc. Exploration Geophysicists (v.p. 1968), Assn. Profl. Engrs., Geologists, Geophysicists Alta., Can. Soc. Exploration Geophysicists. Mem. United Ch. Can. Avocations: genealogy, barbershop singing. Home: PO Box 161 5428 Long Island Rd Manotick ON Canada K4M 1A3

HOBSON, ROBERT WAYNE, II, surgeon; b. DeKalb, Ill., Dec. 21, 1939; s. Robert Wayne and Jean Helen (Sampson) H.; m. Joan Patricia Souza, Dec. 5, 1985; children: Lisa, Wayne, Laura, Matthew. BS in Chemistry, George Washington U., 1959, MD, 1963. Diplomate Am. Bd. Surgery; cert. of spl. qualification in gen.-vascular surgery. Intern Tripler Gen. Hosp., Honolulu, 1963-64; resident gen. surgery Walter Reed Gen. Hosp., Washington, 1967-71, fellow peripheral vascular surgery, 1972-73; group surgeon 3rd Spl. Forces Group, Ft. Bragg, N.C., 1964-65; surgeon Detachment C-3 5th Spl. Forces Group, Republic of Vietnam, 1965-66; chief exptl. surgery, dept. dir. Divsn. Surgery Walter Reed Inst. Rsch., Washington, 1971-75; asst. chief peripheral vascular surgery svc. Walter Reed Army Med. Ctr., Washington, 1973-75; chief surg. svc. East Orange VA Med. Ctr., N.J., 1975-83; chief sect. vascular surgery Univ. Medicine and Dentistry of N.J., Newark, 1978-86, assoc. prof. surgery, 1975-79, prof. surgery, 1980-86; James Utley prof. surgery, chmn. dept. surgery Boston U. Sch. Medicine, 1986-88; surgeon-in-chief Univ. Hosp. Boston U. Med. Ctr., 1986-88; prof. surgery, physiology U. Medicine and Dentistry of N.J., Newark, 1988—, dir. vascular surgery, 1988—2003; dir. Dept. Surgery St. Michael's Med. Ctr., Newark, 1989 2003. Editl. cons. Jour. AMA, 1982 ; mem. editl. bd. Jour. Surg. Rsch., 1983-88, Jour. Vascular Surgery, 1989-99, Stroke: Clinical Updates, 1990—, International J Angiol, 1992—, Vascular Surgery, 1995—, Stroke, 2003—; contbr. articles to profl. jours. Served to col. M.C., U.S. Army, 1963-75. Recipient Franklin Metcalfe award for surg. rsch. U.S. Army Med. Dept., 1969-70, Acad. award in Vascular Disease NHLBI, NIH, 1995-2000; decorated Bronze Star, Air Medal, Medal of Honor (RVN), Cross of Gallantry, Airborne (all Republic of Vietnam); NIH grantee, 1979-82, 95—, other rsch. project grants. Fellow ACS (sec. N.J. chpt. 1998, pres. 2001-2002), Am. Surg. Assn., Stroke Coun. (exec. com. 1987-89, 95—2002, program chmn. internat. stroke conf., 2000, 01), Am. Heart Assn.; mem. Am. Assn. for Vascular Surgery (pres.-elect 1999, pres. 2000), Soc. Vascular Surgery (treas. 1989-93), Ea. Vascular Soc. (pres. 1996), Am. Venous Forum (pres. 1997), Assn. Program Dirs. in Vascular Surg. (pres. 1998-2000), Soc. Univ. Surgeons, Assn. VA Surgeons (v.p. 1983), Southeastern Surg. Congress, Am. Fedn. Clin. Rsch., Chesapeake Vascular Soc., Assn. Mil. Surgeons, Assn. Acad. Surgery (pres.-elect 1980, pres. 1981), Assn. Surg. Edn., Soc. Med. Cons. to Armed Forces, Assn. Internat. Vascular Surgeons, Soc. Surgeons of N.J., Vascular Soc. N.J. (pres. 1981). Republican. Office: U Medicine and Dentistry NJ Sect Vascular Surgery ADMC Bldg 6 Rm 620 30 Bergen St Newark NJ 07107 E-mail: hobsonrw@umdnj.edu.

HOBURG, JAMES FREDERICK, electrical engineering educator; b. Pitts., Dec. 30, 1946; s. William Lawrence and Virginia (Stewart) H.; m. Margaret Jean Ryan, Mar. 4, 1978 BS, Drexel U., 1969; SM, MIT, 1971, PhD in Elec. Engring., 1975. Instr. MIT, Cambridge, Mass., 1973-75; asst. prof. elec. engring. Carnegie-Mellon U., Pitts., 1975-80, assoc. prof. elec. engring., 1980-84, prof. elec. and computer engring., 1984—, assoc. head, dept. elec. and computer engring., 1985-91. Cons. to rsch. and devel. orgns. Contbr. articles to profl. jours. Recipient teaching award MIT, 1972, Ryan award for Excellence in Undergrad. Edn., Carnegie-Mellon U., 1980; named Outstanding Prof. in Elec. Engring. Dept., Carnegie-Mellon U., 1977, 80, 84, 90, 95. Fellow IEEE; mem. Electrostatics Soc. Am., Am. Soc. Engr. Edn., Sigma Xi, Tau Beta Pi, Eta Kappa Nu Avocations: long distance running, walking, mountaineering. Home: 1000 Oak Creek Ln Baden PA 15005-2856 Office: Carnegie-Mellon U Dept Elec and Computer Engring Schenley Park Pittsburgh PA 15213-3830

HOCH, DAVID ALLEN, athletic director; b. Northampton, Pa., July 26, 1946; s. Sterling Palmer and Evelyn Mae (McCallister) H.; m. Diane Duffy, June 18, 1977; children: Matthew David, Jennifer Lynn. AB in German, Grove City (Pa.) Coll., 1968; MEd in Phys. Edn., The Coll. N.J., 1972; EdD in Phys. Edn., Temple U., 1989. Tchr., coach Washington Twp. H.S., Sewell, N.J., 1968-71, Upper Dublin H.S., Ft. Washington, Pa., 1972-78, Ramsey (N.J.) H.S., 1978-79, Germantown Acad., Ft. Washington, 1981-89; instr., coach Pa. State U., Altoona, 1979-80; instr. phys. edn., basketball coach U. Pitts., Bradford, 1989-93; athletic dir. Eastern Tech. H.S., Balt. County, 1994—2003, Loch Raven H.S., Balt. County, 2003—. Presenter in field. Mem. editl. adv. bd. Athletic Bus. mag., pub. com. NFHS Coaches Quar., 2002—; contbr. articles to profl. jours., chpts. in books. Mem. AAHPERD, NEA, Nat. H.S. Athletic Coaches Assn. (Regional Athletic Dir. of Yr. award 1999), Nat. Interscholastic Athletic Adminstrs. Assn. (state award of merit for Md. 2002), Nat. Fedn. Coaches Assn. (Md. state dir. 2000—),, N.Am. Soc. for Sports Mgmt., Md. State Athletic Dirs. Assn. (v.p. 1999-2003, pres. 2003, Athletic Dir. of Yr. 2000), Md. Assn. for Health, Phys. Edn., Recreation and Dance (v.p. athletics, 2000-01, pres. 2003—), Md. State Coaches Assn. (pres. 2002-03, newsletter editor and membershiup dir. 2001—). Presbyterian. Avocations: running, marathons, gardening, photography. Home: 1207 Peachtree Rd Fallston MD 21047-1804 Office: Loch Raven HS 1212 Cowpens Ave Towson MD 21286 E-mail: dhoch@bcps.org.

HOCH, EDWARD DENTINGER, writer; b. Rochester, N.Y., Feb. 22, 1930; s. Earl George and Alice Mary (Dentinger) Hoch; m. Patricia Ann McMahon, June 5, 1957. Student, U. Rochester, 1947-49. Rsch. asst. Rochester (N.Y.) Pub. Libr., 1949-50; circulation asst. Pocket Books, N.Y.C., 1952-54; pub. rels. writer Hutchins Advt. Co., Rochester, 1954-68. Author: (novels) The Shattered Raven, 1969, The Judges of Hades, 1971, The Transvection Machine, 1971, The Spy and the Thief, 1972, City of Brass, 1972, Fellowship of the Hand, 1973,

The Frankenstein Factory, 1975, The Thefts of Nick Velvet, 1978, The Monkey's clue and the Stolen Sapphire, 1978, The Quests of Simon Ark, 1984, Leopold's Way, 1985, The Night My Friend, 1991, Diagnosis: Impossible, 1996, The Ripper of Storyville, 1997, The Velvet Touch, 2000, The Night People, 2001, The Old Spies Club, 2001, The Iron Angel, 2003; editor Dear Dead Days, 1972, All But Impossible, 1981, Murder Most Sacred, 1989, (book) The Best Detective Stories of the Year, 1976—81, Year's Best Mystery and Suspense Stories, 1982—95, Twelve American Detective Stories, 1997. Trustee Rochester Pub. Libr., 1981—98. With U.S. Army, 1950—52. Mem.: Crime Writers Assn. (Eng.), Authors Guild, Sci. Fiction Writers Am., Mystery Writers Am., Inc. (dir., pres. 1982, Edgar award 1967, Edgar scroll 1980, Grand Master 2001). Roman Catholic. Home and Office: 2941 Lake Ave Rochester NY 14612-5529 E-mail: ehoch-rochester@worldnet.att.net. *After publishing over 875 short stories and 50 books, I have to admit that I write primarily to entertain. But I've yet to decide whether it's more to entertain the reader or myself.*

HOCH, FREDERIC LOUIS, medical educator; b. Vienna, Apr. 14, 1920; came to U.S., 1922, naturalized, 1928; s. Samuel and Dore (Glinert) H.; m. Martha Louise Ludwig, Apr. 8, 1961. BS, CCNY, 1939; MD, N.Y. U., 1943; MS, M.I.T., 1951. Intern Michael Reese Hosp., Chgo., 1943; resident in pathology Tufts Med. Sch., Boston, 1947; research asso. in biology MIT, 1948-51; research fellow in biochemistry Mass. Gen. Hosp., Boston, 1951-53; research asso., asst. prof. medicine Harvard Med. Sch., Boston, 1953-66; jr. asso., sr. asso. medicine Peter Brent Brigham Hosp., Boston, 1953-66; asso. prof. internal medicine and biol. chemistry U. Mich. Med. Sch., Ann Arbor, 1967-77, prof. internal medicine and biol. chemistry, 1977-86, prof. emeritus internal medicine, biol. chemistry, 1987—. Author: Energy Transformations in Mammals: Regulatory Mechanisms, 1971. Served to capt. M.C. U.S. Army, 1944-46. Fellow Baruch Found., 1948, NIH, 1949-51, Jane Coffin Childs Found., 1951-53, Howard Hughes Med. Inst., 1957-64. Mem. AAAS, Am. Chem. Soc., Biochem. Soc. (London), Am. Soc. Biol. Chem. Molecular Biology, Phi Beta Kappa, Sigma Xi. E-mail: fredhoch@umich.edu.

HOCH, GARY W. lawyer; b. Duluth, Minn., Jan. 14, 1943; s. Roland J. and Virginia H.; m. Marilyn Turnquist, June 13, 1970; children: Ryan M., Nicole S., Carrie L. BA in Polit. Sci., U. Minn., 1965, JD, 1968. Bar: Minn. 1968, U.S. Dist. Ct. Minn. 1968, U.S. Ct. Appeals (8th cir.). Ptnr. Meagher & Geer PLLP, Mpls. Mem. ABA, Am. Coll. Trial Lawyers, Am. Bd. Trial Advs., Minn. Bar Assn., Internat. Soc. Barristers. Office: Meagher & Geer 4200 Multifoods Tower 33 S 6th St Minneapolis MN 55402-3788 E-mail: ghoch@meagher.com.

HOCH, IVO, former library director; b. Slany, Czech Republic, Aug. 14, 1950; s. Antonín Hoch and Helena (Šlapáková) Hochová; m. Eva Šelová, June 20, 1975; 1 child, Dana. PhD, Charles U., Prague, Czech Republic, 1979. Libr. Czech Nat. Libr., Prague, 1969-71; info. specialist Teplotechna, 1971-90; libr. dir. CAFL, Prague, 1990—2001; libr. analysis specialist Nat. Libr. Czech Republic, Prague, 2002—. Contbr. articles to profl. jours. Mem. IAALD, Sdružení knihovníku a inf. pracovníku. Avocations: cultural activities, travel. E-mail: ivo.hoch@nkp.cz.

HOCH, ORION LINDEL, corporate executive; b. Canonsburg, Pa., Dec. 21, 1928; s. Orion L.F. and Ann Marie (McNulty) H.; m. Jane Lee Ogan, June 12, 1952 (dec. (1978); children: Andrea, Brenda, John; m. Catherine Nan Richardson, Sept. 12, 1980. BS, Carnegie Mellon U., 1952; MS, UCLA, 1954; PhD, Stanford U., 1957. With Hughes Aircraft Co., Culver City, Calif., 1952-54; with Stanford Electronics Labs., 1954-57; sr. engr., dept. mgr., divsn. v.p., divsn. pres. Litton Electron Devices div., San Carlos, Calif., 1957-68; group exec. Litton Components divsn., 1968-70; v.p. Litton Industries, Inc., Beverly Hills, Calif., 1970, sr. v.p., 1971-74, pres., 1982-88, chief exec. officer, 1986-93, chmn., 1988-94, chmn. emeritus, 1994—, also dir.; pres. Intersil, Inc., Cupertino, Calif., 1974-82; chmn. exec. com. Western Atlas, Inc., Beverly Hills, Calif., 1994-98. Trustee Carnegie-Mellon U. Served with AUS, 1946-48. Mem. IEEE, Sigma Xi, Tau Beta Pi, Phi Kappa Phi.

HOCH, PEGGY MARIE, computer scientist; b. Balt., Dec. 2, 1959; d. Stanley Elijah Hoch, Jr. and Nancy Irene (Bishop) Austin; 1 child, Kiana Mariah Shurkin. AA, Catonsville (Md.) Community, Coll., 1982; BS, Towson State U., 1987; MS, Johns Hopkins U., 1989. Lab. technician McCormick & Co., Hunt Valley, Md., 1980-84; computer scientist U.S. Army Concepts Analysis, Bethesda, Md., 1985-88; sr. assoc. programmer IBM Corp., Rockville, Md., 1989-91; sys. analyst Nat. Oceanic and Atmospheric Adminstrn., Silver Spring, Md., 1991—. Author: (software) Design CDRLs for IBM/FAA, 1991, Design CDRLs for NOAA, 1994. Recipient Nat. Computer Sci. award U.S. Achievement Acad., 1987, Computer Sci. award Towson (Md.) State U., Chemistry award Catonsville Community Coll., 1980. Mem. AIAA, Am. Assn. Artificial Intelligence, Johns Hopkins U. Alumni Assn. Avocations: gourmet cooking, chess, reading, movies, walking. Home: 10551 Twin Rivers Rd Apt D2 Columbia MD 21044-2120 Office: Nat Weather Svc 1325 E West Hwy Silver Spring MD 20910-3280 E-mail: peggy.hoch@noaa.gov.

HOCH, RAND, lawyer, mediator; b. Everett, Wash., Apr. 2, 1955; s. Harold S. and Thelma (Frisch) H. AB in Am. Govt., Georgetown U., 1977; JD, Stetson U., 1985. Bar: Fla. 1985, U.S. Dist. Ct. (mid., so. dists.) Fla. 1986, U.S. Ct. Appeals (11th cir.) 1986, D.C. 1989. Adminstrv. aide Henry M. Jackson for Pres. Com., Washington, 1974-76; rsch. dir. Coun. Active Ind. Oil and Gas Producers, Washington, 1977; polit. cons. New South Communications, Washington and Fla., 1977-82; asst. to regional coord. North Shore Coun. on Alcoholism, Mass., 1978; exec. dir. Fund for A New Direction, Washington and West Palm Beach, Fla., 1979-91; real estate salesman Adams Cameron/Realty World, Ormond Beach, Fla., 1980-81; real estate broker South 1st Realty Inc., Ormond Beach, 1981-82; rsch. asst. Stetson U. Coll. of Law, St. Petersburg, Fla., 1983—85; law clk. real estate and constrn. De Santis, Cook, Gaskill & Silverman, North Palm Beach, Fla., 1984; labor, election and ERISA atty. Kaplan, Sicking & Bloom P.A., West Palm Beach, 1985-88; workers' compensation atty. Law Offices of Gerald Rosenthal P.A., West Palm Beach, 1989-91; gen. master div. worker's compensation Fla. Dept. Labor & Employment Security, 1991-92; judge compensation claims State of Fla., Daytona Beach, 1992-96; pvt. practice The Law & Mediation Offices of Rand Hoch, West Palm Beach, Fla., 1996—. Cons. in field. Contbr. articles to profl. jours. Mem. Dem. Exec. Com., Volusia County Fla., 1980-82, Pinellas County, Fla., 1983, Palm Beach County, 1989-92, 96—, chair, 1990, vice-chair, 1989-90; del. Fla. Dem. Conv., 1981, 83, 85, 87, 89, 91, 97, 99, 2001; alt. del. Dem. Nat. Conv., 1988, 2000; bd. dirs. ACLU, Palm Beach and Martin Counties, 1985-87, Fla. Consumer Fedn., 1987-89, Fla. Task Force, 1987-89, Nat. Gay & Lesbian Task Force, 1989-92, Palm Beach County Human Rights Coun., Inc., 1990-92, 2002—, Compass, Inc., 2002-03, Ctrl. Fla. Friends of 440, 1995-96; mem. exec. com. Lesbian and Gay Dems. of Am., 1988-92; regional coord. Dukakis for Pres., Fla., 1987-88; pres. Palm Beach County Human Rights Coun., 1987-92; chmn. pro tem employment practices rev. com. City West Palm Beach, 1990-91; mem. ethics ordinance adv. com. Palm Beach County, 1991-92; mem. Young Friends of Bob Graham, 1989-92, Leadership 2000, 1990-92, Young Friends of the Kravis Ctr., 1996—, Young Friends of the Norton Mus., 2001-03; mem. adv. bd. Volusia County Elections, 1993-94; bus. com. for culture Palm Beach County Cultural Coun., 1998—; trustee Fla. Stage, 2002—, sec., 2002—; bd. dirs. Lambda Legal Def. and Edn. Fund, 2003—. Recipient Am. Jurisprudence Book awards, 1983, 84, Fred C. Fantz award, 1985, Hank Godley Meml. award Met. Bus. Orgn. of South Fla., 1992, Spectrum Lifetime Achievement award Greater Orlando Gay & Lesbian Cmty. Ctr., 1994, Compass Pub. Svc. award, 2003; named Charles A. Dana scholar, 1983-85. Mem. ABA (young lawyers divsn. 1985-91, labor and employment law sect. 1986-92, mem. sect. on individual rights and responsibilities 1990-92, 2002-2003, campaign ethics com. 1987-92), Fla. Bar Assn. (labor and employment law sect. 1989-93, workers compensation law sect. 1988--, equal opportunities law sect. 1999--, mem. editl. bd. Fla. Bar News and Fla. Bar Jour. 1995-01), D.C. Bar Assn., Acad. Trial Lawyers Am., Assn. Bipartisan Cons., Fla. Acad. Trial Lawyers, Am. Mediation Assn. (nat. bd. accredited mediators 1993—), Internat. Assn. Lesbian and Gay Judges (bd. dirs. 1993-95, v.p. 1995-97), Nat. Gay and Lesbian Lawyers Assn., Nat. Lesbian and Gay Bar Assn., Fla. Conf. Judges of Compensation Claims (pres. 1994-95, mem. exec. com. 1995-96), Volusia County Bar Assn. (mem. jud. evaluation rev. com. 1994), Palm Beach County Bar Assn. (alt. dispute resolution com. 1997—, workers compensation com. 1997—), Internat. Wine and Food Soc. (Boca Raton chpt.), Phi Alpha Delta, Lambda Legal Def. and Edn. Fund. Jewish. Avocation: political button collecting. Office: 400 N Flagler Dr Apt 1402 West Palm Beach FL 33401-4315 E-mail: rand-hoch@usa.net.

HÖCHBAUER, TOBIAS FRANZ WOLFGANG, physicist, researcher; b. Mallersdorf, Bavaria, Germany, Dec. 1, 1969; s. Karl and Agnes Höchbauer. MSc, U. Augburg, Bavaria, Germany, 1997; PhD. in Physics, Philipps U., Marburg, Germany, 2001. Rschr. in Materials Sci. Los Alamos (N. Mex.) Nat. Lab., 1997—2001, postdoctoral fellow, 2001—. Contbr. over 20 articles to internat. profl. jours. Home: 1002 Don Juan Santa Fe NM 87501 Office: Los Alamos Nat Lab Ms G-755 Los Alamos NM 87545 Business E-Mail: hoechbauer@lanl.gov.

HOCHBAUM, MARTIN, trade association administrator; b. N.Y.C., Nov. 7, 1941; s. Issie and Lena H.; m. Victoria Eiger, June 15, 1982; children: Eden, Lee, David. BA, NYU, 1963; MA, Bklyn. Coll., 1968; PhD, CUNY, 1974. Nat. affairs dir. Am. Jewish Congress, N.Y.C., 1972-97; mng. dir. Diamond Dealers Club, N.Y.C., 1997—. Dir. Ctr. Applied Rsch., N.Y.C., 1975-85. Editor: Poor Jews, 1974; contbr. op-eds to newspapers. Avocations: jogging, reading. Home: 89 Essex Ave Montclair NJ 07042-4124 Office: Diamond Dealers Club 580 5th Ave Fl 10 New York NY 10036-4781 E-mail: mhochbaum@ddcny.com.

HOCHBERG, BAYARD ZABDIAL, lawyer; b. N.Y.C., May 16, 1932; s. Abraham and Sonia (Pincus) Hochberg; m. Arlene Beethoven, Feb. 15, 1953; children: Ronny Mark, Randy Jean, Elizabeth Joyce. BA, CCNY, 1953; LLB, U. Va., 1958, JD, 1958. Bar: Md. 1958, Va. 1958. Law bailiff to Hon. Joseph Allen Supreme Bench Balt., 1958-59; asso. law office Paul Berman, Esq., Balt., 1959-68; ptnr. Levin, Hochberg & Chiarello, Balt., 1968-82; sr. ptnr. Hochberg, Chiarello & Costello, Balt., 1983-2000, Hochberg, Costello & Baron, Balt., 2001—02, of counsel, 2002—. Mem. editl. bd. Va. Law Rev., 1956—58; editor: Law Weekly DICTA. Served to maj. USAR, 1953—75. Fellow: Md. Bar Found., Am. Coll. Trial Lawyers; mem.: ATLA, ABA (Md. del. standing com. state legis. 1970—73, mem. tort and ins. practice sect. 1979—2002), Md. Trial Lawyers Assn. (co-chmn. com. legis. 1970—72, bd. govs. 1970—76, v.p. Balt. 1975, mem. Amicus brief com. 1979—81), Balt. County Bar Assn. (mem. family law com.), Balt. Bar Assn. (chmn. legis. com. 1968—69, bd. govs. 1969—70, mem. jud. adminstrn. com. 1980—86, mem. family law com. 1985—88), Md. Bar Assn. (chmn. ins., negligence and workmens compensation section 1973, mem. exec. bd., mem. state-city medicolegal com. 1979—91, chmn. 1983—86, mem. ct. appeals rules com. 1993—2002), Cavalier King Charles Spaniel Club (v.p. 1998—2001), Order of Coif (bd. dirs. 1993—2001). Home: 1978 Shadybrook Trail Charlottesville VA 22911 Office: 528 E Joppa Rd Baltimore MD 21286-5403

HOCHBERG, EDWARD S. insurance executive; b. Phila., Jan. 17; s. Richard Barry and Alice Jane Wofsy; m. Deborah Sharon Steinaltz, Dec. 26, 1992; children: Amanda, Jeffrey, Alice Jane Wofsy. BS in Econs., U. Pa., 1989. Audit mgr. Deloitte & Touche, Phila., 1989-94; dir. fin. PMA Reins. Corp., Phila., 1994-96, v.p. fin., 1996-98, sr. v.p. fin. products, 1998—. Treas. Congregation Beth El, Cherry Hill, N.J., 1999—, bd. trustees, 1996—. Mem. AICPA, Pa. Inst. CPAs, Am. Inst. CPCUs, Soc. Ins. Fin. Mgmt., Life Mgmt. Inst. Jewish. Avocations: swimming, golf, travel, running. Office: PMA Reins Corp Mellon Bank Ctr 1735 Market St Philadelphia PA 19103-7501

HOCHBERG, MARK STEFAN, professional society administrator, cardiac surgeon; b. Providence, Nov. 26, 1947; s. Robert and Gertrude (Meth) H.; m. Faith Shapiro, June 6, 1976; children: Alyssa T., Asher R. BA, Brown U., 1969; MD, Harvard U., 1973; MD (Honoris Causa), Chongqing Sch. Med. Sci., China, 1987. Diplomate Am. Bd. Thoracic Surgery, Am. Bd. Surgery. Chief resident cardiothoracic surgery Mass. Gen. Hosp., Boston, 1980; clin. fellow in surgery Harvard Med. Sch., Boston, 1980; attending cardiac surgeon Newark Beth Israel Med. Ctr., 1981-93, dir. cardiac surgery, 1988-93; cons. cardiac surgeon Overlook Hosp., Summit, N.J., 1983-93; asst. prof. surgery U. Medicine and Dentistry of N.J., Newark, 1981-87, assoc. prof. surgery, 1987-93; spl. asst. to pres., vis. prof. surgery George Washington U., Washington, 1993-94, dean of univ. affairs, prof. surgery, 1994-95; sr. scholar Assn. Acad. Health Ctrs., 1995-96; pres. Healthcare Found. N.J., Roseland, NJ, 1996—2002; CEO Coll. Physicians Phila., 2003—. Chmn. grant rev. com. N.J. affiliate Am. Heart Assn., New Brunswick, 1986-88, also bd. dirs.; mem. com. on med. affairs Corp. of Brown U., Providence, 1987-2002. V.p. Temple B'nai Jeshurun, Short Hills, 1988-92; trustee Coun. N.J. Grantmakers, 1997-2002, pres. 2000-02; mem. vis. com. Northeastern U. Sch. of Law. Lt. comdr. USPHS, 1975-77. Fellow ACS, Am. Coun. Edn.; diplomate Am. Bd. Surgery, Am. bd. Thoracic Surgery; mem. Soc. Thoracic Surgery, Am. Assn. Thoracic Surgery, Alpha Omega Alpha. Office: Coll Phy Phila 19 S Twenty Second St Philadelphia PA 19103-3097

HOCHBERG, RONALD MARK, lawyer; b. Bklyn., Apr. 3, 1955; s. Fred S. and Adele (Gunsberg) H.; m. Sharon A. Berg, Aug. 11, 1985; children: Rachel, Sarah. BA, Rutgers U., 1977; JD, Bklyn. Law Sch., 1980; LLM, U. Miami, 1982. Assoc. Klatsky & Klatsky, Red Bank, N.J., 1980-81, Fuerst, Singer & Yusem, Somerville, N.J., 1982-83, Law Offices of Steven Schanker, Melville, N.Y., 1983-86; ptnr. Schanker & Hochberg, Attys., Huntington, N.Y., 1986—. Frequent lectr. on estate planning; instr. Adelphi U., 1984-93. Columnist Financial World Mag., 1993-97; contbr. articles to profl. publs. Mem. ABA, N.Y. State Bar Assn., Estate and Tax Planning Coun. Avocations: skiing, sailing. Office: Schanker & Hochberg 27 W Neck Rd PO Box 1905 Huntington NY 11743-2618 E-mail: mark@schankerhochberg.com.

HOCHBERG, STEPHEN HUGH, retired human resources specialist; b. N.Y.C. s. Joseph George H. and Bernice (Chapman) Epstein; m. Shielagh R. Shusta. BA in Anthropology cum laude, Queens Coll., 1966; MA in Liberal Studies, New Sch. Social Rsch., 1970; M in Pub. Adminstrn. with honors, John Jay Coll., 1980. Caseworker Human Resources Adminstrn., N.Y.C., 1966-70; student counselor Bklyn. Coll., 1970-74; student personnel adv. Touro Coll., N.Y.C., 1974-80; dep. project dir. Nat. Ctr. Pub. Productivity John Jay Coll., N.Y.C., 1980-85; tng. mgr. Citicorp, N.Y.C., 1985-92, Bd. Elections City of N.Y., N.Y.C., 1993—2002; ret., 2002. Editor, pub.: newsletter Tally Sheet; contbr. articles to profl. jours. Bd. dirs. Windsor Pl. Condominiums, Bklyn., 2001—. With U.S. Army, 1958—61. Recipient Pi Alpha award, Am. Soc. Pub. Adminstrn., 1980. Mem.: ASTD (lamplighter mem. N.Y. chpt. 1985—), Poets Against the War. Democrat. Avocations: tennis, creative writing, poetry, short stories. Home: 113 Prospect Park SW Apt 12 Brooklyn NY 11218-1285 E-mail: stopspin@earthlink.net.

HOCHBERG, VICTOR I. retired neurologist; b. Newark, Dec. 3, 1931; BS, Rutgers U., 1953; MD, Boston U., 1963. Diplomate Am. Bd. Neurology and Psychiatry. Intern U. Hosp., Boston, 1963-64; resident Mt. Sinai Hosp., N.Y.C., 1964-66, U. Hosp., Boston, 1966-67; neurologist Hollywood, Fla., 1967—; chief of staff Meml. Regional Hosp., Hollywood, Fla., 1993-96. Adv. bd. Myasthenia Gravis Found. Fellow ACP, Am. Acad. Neurology. Office: Neurological Consultants 4925 Sheridan St Ste 200 Hollywood FL 33021-2829

HOCHFELD, WILLIAM SIDNEY, construction executive, consultant; b. Bklyn., May 10, 1933; s. Louis and Sadie Hochfeld; m. Joyce Oster Hochfeld, Dec. 10, 1955; children: Elise Gayle, Marla Beth, Eric David. Cert., Rantoul (Ill.) Sch. Meteorology, 1952, Cert., 1955, Inst. Design and Constrn., Bklyn., 1956—57, Pohs Inst. Real Estate, Jamaica, NY, 1964—65. Lic. real estate sales NY. Exec. adminstr. Goodrich Bldg. Corp., N.Y.C., 1968—71; cons., owner's rep. 1410 Bedford Ave. Corp., Bklyn., 1971—75; v.p./constrn. analyst Nat. Westminster Bank USA, N.Y.C., 1975—85; constrn. cons. William Cons. Svcs., Oceanside, NY, 1985—92; archtl. cons. D.E. Leibowitz, Architects, N.Y.C., 1992—96; developers cons. Temple Beth Torah, Melville, NY, 1996—98; arch./cons. D.E. Leibowitz/ LiRo, N.Y.C., NY, 2000—. Mem. exec. com., bd. dirs. 1410 Bedford Ave. Corp., Bklyn., 1971—75; bd. dirs., mem. real estate com. Nat. WestBank USA, N.Y.C., 1975—85; bd. dirs., mem. exec. com. Temple Beth Torah, Melville, 1996—98. Author, editor Architects Prison Surveys & Investigations (Fin., 1995); author: (book of poetry) The Arc, Family History. S/Sgt. USAF, 1952—56, U.S., Japan, Korea. Named Ky. Col., 1967. Mem.: Mortgage Bankers Assn., Odd Fellows. Achievements include design of acousti-shell ceiling tile (w. Barry Oster); General & specific designs; interior design innovations & new products; worked on WTC, prisons (Riker's Island, Manhattan, Bronx), sch. cons. authority renovations, Sperry Rand Bldg; listed with father Louis & brother Stanley on Military Wall of Honor, East Meadow, LI, NY. Avocations: history, carpentry, genealogy, theatre, puzzles.

HOCHHALTER, GORDON RAY, advertising communications executive; b. Jerome, Idaho, Oct. 3, 1946; s. Ralph R. and Evelyn (McClellan) H. BA, Brigham Young U., 1972. Asst. promotion supr. Armstrong World Industries, Lancaster, Pa., 1972-74, promotion supr., 1974-76, sr. promotion supr., 1976; asst. advt. mgr. R.R. Donnelley & Sons Co., Chgo., 1976-79, asst. mgr. advt., sales promotion, 1979-81, advt. mgr., 1981-84, group mgr. mktg. com., creative devel., 1984-86, dir. mktg. com., creative dir., 1986-91; v.p., gen. mgr., creative dir. Mobium Corp. Design & Comm., Chgo., 1991-96, v.p., creative dir. design and conceptual devel., 1996-97; chief creative officer Mobium Creative Group, Chgo., 1998-99, mng. ptnr./creativity, strategy, technology, 2000—. V.p., creative cons. Caviale Fashions, NYC, 1987—; mem. internet adv. bd. B2B Works. Author: Strategies for a New Age of Bus. Comm., 1998, New Media in a New Age of Bus. Comm., 1998, Creative Leverage in a New Age of Bus. Comm., 1999, Hugging Your Customers in the Face of Bus. Comm. Change, 2002, Leveraging the Paradigm Shifts that are Changing Bus. Comm., 2001, Increasing Your Brandwidth in the Face of Bus. Comm. Change, 2002, Interactivating Your Messages in the Face of Bus. Comm. Change, 2002, others; monthly columnist Integrated Mktg. and Promotion Mag.; contbr. to profl. jour. and Libr. of Congress; Bd. dir. Lit. Chgo., 2000-01, Design Indus. Found. Fighting AIDS/Chgo., 2003. Bd. dirs. Literacy Chgo., 2000—01. Recipient London Internat. Advt. awards, 1987, One Show, Type Dirs. Club, Clio awrds, Art Dirs. Club awards, Andy awards, Addy awards, Internat. Advt. Festival AIGA awards, ProCom awards, Ace awards, Chgo. Tower awards, 1987-2003, Am. Bus. Media CEBA awards, 2002, Am. Bus. Press Objective and Results award, 1992, Cresta Internat. Advt. award, 1993, Sawyer award Bus. Mktg. Mag., 1993, Marcom High-Tech. Advt. award, 1994-96, Pinnacle award, 1994, Icon award Bus. Week Mag., 1994-95, 98-2000, Creativity, 2000. Mem. Am. Ctr. for Design, Am. Advt. Fedn., Chgo. Advt. Fedn., Bus. Mktg. Assn.(bd. dir. Chgo. chpt. 1998-2000), NY Art Dir. Club. Office: Mobium Creative Group The Merchandise Mart 200 World Trade Ctr Ste 2000 Chicago IL 60654 E-mail: ghochhalter@mobium.com.

HOCHHEIMER, FRANK LEO, brokerage executive; b. N.Y.C., Sept. 27, 1943; s. Arthur A. and Alice Hochheimer; m. Beverly Widman, Dec. 24, 1967; 1 child, Martin. BA in Math., Queens Coll., 1965; MA in Math., Hofstra U., 1966; MA in Econometrics, New Sch. Social Rsch., 1973. Instr., chmn. math dept. N.Y. Inst. Tech., 1966-74; mgr. S. Bauer & Sons, N.Y.C., 1974-75; analyst Merrill Lynch, N.Y.C., 1974-75, computer specialist, commodity div., 1976-78, mgr., tech. analysis, 1978-79, v.p., dir. rsch.; v.p., dir. Futures Info. Svcs., N.Y.C., 1983-85, v.p., mgr. global securities data and pricing svc., 1985-90; v.p., mgr. CMO dept. Merrill Lynch Mortgage Capital, N.Y.C., 1990-95; v.p., mgr. Merrill Lynch Ops. Sys. and Telecomm., N.Y.C., 1995-2001; dir., dept. mgr. Merrill Lynch Global Markets and Investment Banking Divsn., N.Y.C., 2001—03; vendor data mgr. Am. Internat. Group, N.Y.C., 2003—. Contrbr. articles to profl. jours. Mem. Am Econs. Assn., Nat. Assn. Bus. Economists, Market Technicians Assn., Futures Industry Assn. (former dir., teas. rsch. div.), Securities Industry Assn. (data mgmt. divsn.).

HOCHHEISER, MARILYN, author, actress; b. LA, Sept. 3, 1935; d. Froman Jackson and Ann Nemerofsky; m. Sidney Ralph Hochheiser, Feb. 28, 1959 (dec. Sept. 1995); children: Glenda, Sharon, Steven. LVN, L.A. Trade Tech., 1959; cert. writing instr., Calif. Luth. Coll., Thousand Oaks, 1979. ordained to ministry, Glory House Ministries (Full Gospel), 1990. Instr. creative writing Simi Valley (Calif.) Adult Edn., 1976-89; editor poetry Ventura (Calif.) County Woman, 1985-87; minister Glory House Ministries, Simi Valley, 1992—; actress Am. Broadcasting Network, Hollywood, Calif., 1996—2002. Freelance writing cons., 1975—; prodr., moderator videos Inglewood, Calif., 1999-2000. Founder, moderator Simi Poetry Series, 1975-96; author: A View Through The Thicket, 1977; contbg. poet (anthology) So Luminois the Wildflowers, 2003; editor Verve mag., 1989-99; lyricist Call Me Eddie, 2001; author numerous poems. Recipient 1st place Ark. Benton County Sesquicentennial, 1986, 2d place Chgo. Libr. Poetry, 1993. Mem.: First Stage, Poets and Writers, Nat. League Am. Pen Women (Woman of Achievement award 1992—94, Disting. Svc. award 1994). Avocations: yoga, movies, plays, grandchildren, nature. Home: 5406 E Los Angeles Ave Simi Valley CA 93063

HOCHLERIN, DIANE, pediatrician, educator; b. N.Y.C., Feb. 4, 1942; d. William J. and Bertha Hochlerin. BS, U. City of N.Y., 1958; MD, Med. Coll. Pa., 1966. Diplomate Am. Bd. Pediats. Intern Albert Einstein Hosp., Phila., 1966-67; resident Phila. Gen. Hosp., 1967-69; attending pediatrician St. Luke's Roosevelt Hosp., N.Y.C., 1969—; clin. assoc. prof. pediats. Columbia U., N.Y.C., 1969—; asst. attending physician Cath. Med. Ctr., N.Y.C., 1993-99. Faculty advisor Adelphi U., N.Y.C., 1994. Fellow Am. Acad. Pediats.; mem. N.Y. State Med. Soc., County Med. Soc. Office: 241 Central Park W New York NY 10024-4530

HOCHMAN, KENNETH GEORGE, lawyer; b. Mt. Vernon, N.Y., Nov. 12, 1947; s. Benjamin S. and Lillian (Gilbert) H.; m. Carol K. Hochman, Apr. 8, 1979; children: Brian Paul, Lisa Erin. BA, SUNY, Buffalo, 1969; JD, Columbia U., 1972. Bar: Ohio 1973, Fla. 1977, N.Y. 1979. Assoc. Jones, Day, Reavis & Pogue, Cleve., 1972-79, ptnr., 1980—. Trustee Katharine Kenyon Lippitt Found., Cleve., 1988, Kenridge Fund, Cleve., 1989, Bolton Found., Cleve., 1990, Elisha-Bolton Found., Cleve., 1993. Trustee United Way of Cleve., 2002—. Harlan Fiske Stone scholar Columbia U., 1971, 72. Fellow Am. Coll. Trusts and Estate Counsel; mem. Phi Beta Kappa, Oakwood Club (Cleve.) (trustee 1997, officer 2000). Office: Jones Day Reavis & Pogue 901 Lakeside Ave E Cleveland OH 44114-1190

HOCHMAN, STANLEY RICHARD, journalist; b. N.Y.C. s. Isadore and Rose Hochman; m. Gloria Selma Honickman, Oct. 30, 1960; 1 child, Anndee Elyn. BA, NYU, 1948, MEd, 1950. Sportswriter Brownsville (Tex.) Herald, 1953-54, Corpus Christi (Tex.) Caller, 1954-55, Waco (Tex) Tribune, 1955-58, San Bernardino (Calif.) Sun, 1968-59; columnist Phila. Daily News, 1959—. Author: King of Swing, 1983, Clown Prince of Baseball, 1995. Named Pa. Sportswriter of Yr., Nat. Sportswriters Assn., 1967, 83, 85, 87, Best Column award Keystone Awards, 1978, Nat Fleischer award Boxing Writers Assn., N.Y. 1991. Home: 44 Trent Rd Wynnewood PA 19096 Office: 400 N Broad St Philadelphia PA 19130-4015

HOCHMAN, STEPHEN ALLEN, lawyer; b. N.Y.C., June 25, 1935; s. Henry and Ida Hochman; m. Gloria Cole, June 16, 1957; children: Glen, Susan, Lisa. BA, Cornell U., 1957, JD with distinction, 1959. Bar: N.Y. 1960, U.S. Supreme Ct. 1963, U.S. Dist. Ct. (so. dist.) N.Y. 1963. Assoc. Proskauer Rose Goetz & Mendelsohn, N.Y.C., 1960-64; ptnr. Feldman, Kramer, Bam & Nessen, N.Y.C., 1964-66, Kramer, Nessen & Hochman, 1966-68, Kramer, Levin, Nessen Kamin & Frankel, N.Y.C., 1968-86, Friedman, Wittenstein & Hochman N.Y.C., 1986—. Chmn. ALI/ABA Ann. Program on Corp. Acquisitions 1985—, Program on Arbitration, Mediation and ADR, 1993—; mediator U.S. Dist. Ct. (so. and eas. dists.) N.Y., U.S. Bankryptcy Ct. (so. dist.) N.Y., N.Y. State Supreme Ct., N.Y. Stock Exch., NASD mediator, arbitrator; mediator trainer of mediators in N.Y. State Supreme Ct., also Spl. Master Appellate divsn., 1st dept. Contbr. articles to profl. jours. Trustee, sec. Beth Israel Med. Ctr., N.Y.C., 1982—, Jewish Communal Fund N.Y., N.Y.C., 1982—; mem. N.Y. State Adv. Commn. on Substance Abuse, 1977-83; trustee State Communities Aid Assn., N.Y. State, 1976—. 1st lt. USAR, 1959-60. Mem. ABA (former chair arbitration com. sect. dispute resolution, co-chair large/complex case sub-com.), Assn. of Bar of City of N.Y., Am. Arbitration Assn., Am. Law Inst., Order of Coif, Phi Kappa Phi. Home: 303 West St White Plains NY 10605-5304 Office: Friedman Wittenstein & Hochman 101 E 52nd St New York NY 10022-6018 E-mail: shochman@prodigy.net.

HOCHREITER, JOHN ALLEN, computer company owner, firefighter; b. Buffalo, Mar. 5, 1949; s. Robert Allen and Dorothy Eileen (Scully) H.; m. Shelley Cunningham, July 30, 1977; children: Sean Scully, Mark Andrew. BA, Niagara U., 1971; MEd, Boston Coll., Chestnut Hill, Mass., 1975. Mid. sch. tchr. sci. St. Rose of Lima Sch., Buffalo, 1971-73; mgr., dir. Snowflake Ventures, Ellicottsville, N.Y., 1973-74; itinerant tchr. for blind and visually impaired Buffalo Pub. Schs., 1975-77, itinerant tchr. coord., 1977-79; dept. mgr. Computac, Inc., West Lebanon, N.H., 1979-87, exec. v.p., 1987-92, pres., CEO

1992—. Bd. dirs. Mascoma Savs. Bank, Lebanon, N.H. Baseball coach Babe Ruth League, 1993-2001; mem. Hanover (N.H.) Improvement Soc., 1996—, bd. dirs., 1997-99, v.p. bd. dirs., 1999—; chmn. Dresden Sch. Bd., Hanover, 1988-89, Hanover Sch. Bd., 1987; lt. Hanover Dept.-Etna Sta., 1983—; mem. Hanover Adv. Bd. of Assessors, 2003—. Recipient Hanover Vol. Svc. award, 2001. Mem. Conn. and Passumpsic Rivers R.R. Assn.,Hanover Firefighters ASsn. (pres. 2002—), Hanover Country Club, Rotary (pres. 1996, presdl. citation 1996, Paul Harris fellow 1998), Montcalm Golf Club. Republican. Roman Catholic. Avocation: golf. Fax: 603-298-6189. E-mail: john@computac.com.

HOCHREITER, JOSEPH CHRISTIAN, JR., engineering company executive; b. Bristol, Pa., Jan. 29, 1955; s. Joseph Christian and Mary Claire (Boyer) H.; m. Eileen Grace Wachtman, Aug. 31, 1984; children: Erich, Kristen. BA, Temple U., 1978; postgrad., Drexel U., 1983-85. Cert. ground water prof. Hydrologic tech. U.S. Geological Survey, Trenton, N.J., 1973-78, hydrologist, 1979-87; hydrologic mgr. Environ. Resources Mgt., Inc., Princeton, N.J., 1987-90, br. mgr., 1990-92, principal, 1991-92; v.p. Blasland, Bouck & Lee, Cranbury, N.J., 1992—. Lectr. Pa. State U., Trevose, Pa., 1980-84. Author and co-author numerous reports, papers in related field; editl. bd Jour. Ground Water, Columbus, Ohio, 1989-93. Founder Bucks County Homeless Shelter, Levittown, Pa., 1985; bd. dirs. ARC, Langhorne, Pa., 1985-91, Human Growth Ctr., Holland, Pa., 1987-92, 96-2000, pres. bd. dirs., 2001—; mem. fin. com. LBCCC Welcoming the Strangr program, 2001-02; recording engr. Youth Orch. of Bucks County, 1999—. Recipient Adult Vol. award Bucks County Courier Times, 1987. Mem. Am. Geophysical Union, Nat. Ground Water Assn. (mem. fellowship com. 1995), Assn. Ground Water Scientists and Engrs., N.J. Acad. Sci., Geol. Assn. N.J. Home: 252 Hollow Branch Ln Yardley PA 19067-5791 Office: BBL Inc Ste 106 100 Four Falls Corporate Ctr West Conshohocken PA 19428 E-mail: jjh@bbl-inc.com.

HOCHSCHILD, ADAM, writer, commentator, journalist; b. N.Y.C., Oct. 5, 1942; s. Harold K. and Mary (Marquand) H.; m. Arlie Russell, June 26, 1965; children: David, Gabriel. AB cum laude (hon. nat. scholar 1960-61), Harvard U., 1963. Reporter San Francisco Chronicle, 1965-66; writer, editor Ramparts mag., 1967-68, 73-74; commentator Nat. Pub. Radio, 1982-83. Regents lectr. U. Calif.-Santa Cruz, 1987; lectr. Grad. Sch. Journalism U. Calif., Berkeley, 1992, 95, 97—; Fulbright lectr., India, 1997-98. Author: Half the Way Home: A Memoir of Father and Son, 1986 (Notable Book of Yr. ALA and N.Y. Times Book Rev.), The Mirror at Midnight: A South African Journey, 1990, The Unquiet Ghost: Russians Remember Stalin, 1994 (Notable Book of Yr. N.Y. Times Book Rev. and Libr. Jour., Madeline Dane Ross award Overseas Press Club Am., Gold medal Soc. Am. Travel Writers), Finding the Trapdoor: Essays, Portraits, Travels, 1997 (PEN/Spielvogel-Diamonstein award for the Art of the Essay), King Leopold's Ghost: A Story of Greed, Terror and Heroism in Colonial Africa, 1998 (finalist Nat. Book Critics Circle award, Mark Lynton History prize, Gold medal Calif. Book awards, Lionel Gelber prize, Duff Cooper prize); freelance writer nat. mags.; co-founder, editor : Mother Jones mag., 1974—81, commentator: Pub. Interest Radio, 1987—88, included in: Best American Essays, 2001. Recipient Cert. of Excellence, Overseas Press Club, N.Y.C., 1981, Spann prize Eugene V. Debs Found., 1984, Thomas Storke Internat. Journalism award World Affairs Coun. No. Calif., 1987, award for mag. reporting Soc. Profl. Journalists, 1999. Mem. PEN, Nat. Writers Union, Nat. Book Critics Circle. Home: 84 Seward St San Francisco CA 94114-2337

HOCHSCHILD, CARROLL SHEPHERD, computer company and medical equipment executive, educator; b. Whittier, Calif., Mar. 31, 1935; d. Vernon Vero and Effie Corinne (Hollingsworth) Shepherd; m. Richard Hochschild, July 25, 1959; children: Christopher Paul, Stephen Shepherd. BA in Internat. Rels., Pomona Coll., 1956; Teaching credential, U. Calif., Berkeley, 1957; MBA, Pepperdine U., 1985; cert. in fitness instrn., U. Calif., Irvine, 1988. Cert. elem. tchr., Calif. Elem. tchr. Oakland (Calif.) Pub. Schs., 1957-58, San Lorenzo (Calif.) Pub. Schs., 1958-59, Pasadena (Calif.) Pub. Schs., 1959-60, Huntington Beach (Calif.) Pub. Schs., 1961-63, 67-68; adminstrv. asst. Microwave Instruments, Corona del Mar, Calif., 1968-74; co-owner Hoch Co., Corona del Mar, 1978—. Rep. Calif. Tchrs. Assn., Huntington Beach, 1962-63. Mem. Alta Bahia com. Orange County Philharm., 2002. Mem. AAUW, P.E.O. (projects chmn. 1990-92, corr. sec. 1992-94, 98-99, 99-2003, chpt. pres. 1994-95), NAFE, ASTD (Orange County chpt.), Internat. Dance-Exercise Assn., Assistance League Newport-Mesa, Orange County Philharm. Soc. (assoc., Alta Bahia chpt.), Toastmistress (corr. sec. 1983), Jr. Ebell Club (fine arts chmn. Newport Beach 1966-67). Republican.

HOCHSCHILD, RICHARD, medical instruments executive, researcher; b. Berlin, Aug. 28, 1928; came to U.S., 1939; s. Paul and Ann Ida (Schosstag) H.; m. Carroll Corinne Shepherd, July 25, 1959; children: Christopher Paul, Stephen Shepherd. BA in Physics, Johns Hopkins U., 1950; MA in Physics, U. Calif., Berkeley, 1957. Tech. adv. U.S. Atomic Energy Commn., N.Y.C., 1951-53, chief 300 area Hanford, Wash., 1953-54; pres. Metrol, Inc., Pasadena, Calif., 1957-60, Microwave Instruments Co., Corona del Mar, Calif., 1962-74; chief exec. officer Hoch Co., Corona del Mar, 1975—. Developer H-SCAN computerized med., physiol. and psychol. testing and measuring instruments; specialist in biomarkers of aging; pioneer devel. eddy current and microwave methods of nondestructive testing, automated instrumentation for biol. age testing. Patentee and author in field. Avocations: long distance running, down hill skiing, aerobics. Office: Hoch Co 2915 Pebble Dr Corona Del Mar CA 92625-1518

HOCHSCHWENDER, HERMAN KARL, international consultant; b. Heidelberg, Federal Republic Germany, Mar. 1, 1920; came to U.S., 1930, naturalized, 1935; s. Karl G. and Maria (Recken) H.; m. Janet Elliott (div. 1961); children: Lynn Anne Hochschwender McGowin, Herman Karl Jr., Irene Hochschwender Harris, James E.; m. Mary Koger, July 3, 1965; 1 child, J. Michael. BS, Yale U., 1941; postgrad., Harvard U. Asst. indsl. rels. mgr. Sargent and Co., New Haven, 1943-45; mgr. corp. planning Firestone Tire and Rubber Co., Akron, Ohio, 1945-56; pres. Mohawk Rubber Co., N.Y.C., 1959; founder, pres. Hochschwender and Assocs., Akron, 1959-72, Smithers Sci. Svcs., Inc., Akron, 1972-90, bd. dirs., 1972-96, chmn. bd., 1996—. Lectr. in field. Contbr. articles to profl. jours. Vice chmn. bd. trustees Akron Gen. Med. Ctr. Inducted into Tire Ind. Hall of Fame, 1994. Mem. ASTM, Am. Coun. Ind. Labs., Union Internat. des Laboratoires Independents (pres. 1987-93, bd. govs.), Soc. Automotive Engrs., Am. Assn. Lab. Accreditation, Yale U. Alumni Assn. Clubs: Akron City (trustee); Portage Country (Akron), Yale (N.Y.C.), Naples Yacht, Royal Poinciana Golf. Lodges: Rotary. Address: Smithers Sci Svcs 425 W Market St Akron OH 44303-2044

HOCHSCHWENDER, KARL ALBERT, international trade and government relations consultant; b. Mannheim, Germany, Feb. 1, 1927; came to U.S., 1931, naturalized, 1938; s. Karl Georg and Maria Irma (Recken) H.; m. Lilli Bettinger, July 4, 1964 (dec. 1999). BA, Yale U., 1947, MA, 1949, PhD, 1962. Instr. polit. sci. Fla. State U., Tallahassee, 1949-51; assoc. Mott of Washington & Assocs., Washington, 1954-58; rsch. analyst U.S. Govt., Washington, 1959-60; asst. to mgmt. Am. Hoechst Corp., Bridgewater, N.J., 1961-63, mgr. govt. rels., 1963-68, dir. pub. rels., 1968-72, dir. pub. affairs, 1972-83; prin. Palatine Assocs., Princeton, N.J., 1983—. Mem. roster of tech. specialists Office of Spl. Rep. for Trade Negotiations, Exec. Office Pres., 1964-67. Trustee United Fund Somerset Valley, N.J., 1969-75; mem. Princeton Site Plan Rev. Adv. Bd., 1992-99, vice chmn., 1994-99. Recipient Leonard D. White Meml. award Am. Polit. Sci. Assn., 1963; fellow Yale U., 1952-54. Mem. Am. Assn. Exporters and Importers (bd. dirs. 1963-2000, v.p. 1967-83, pres. 1983, chmn. 1983-85), Chem. Comm. Assn. (bd. dirs. 1976-80), Soc. Plastics Industry (chmn. food, drug and cosmetics packaging material com. 1972-76), Yale Club N.Y.C. Office: Palatine Assocs PO Box 1466 Princeton NJ 08542-1466

HOCHSTEIN, ERIC CAMERON, software executive; b. N.Y.C., May 9, 1956; s. Morton Herbert and Rolaine Hochstein; m. Linda Marcus, June 4, 1983; children: Matthew Lewis, Claudia Elise, Jeffrey Marcus. BA in Govt., Oberlin Coll., 1978; MBA in Mktg., Georgetown U., 1984. Legis. asst. to Congressman Andrew Maguire U.S. Ho. of Reps., Washington, 1978-79; to Senator Carl Levin, U.S. Senate, Washington, 1979-81; mgmt. cons. Arthur D. Little, Inc., Washington, 1984-85, Partridge Group, Washington, 1986; ind. cons. Washington, 1981-83; product mgr. new product devel. Bell Atlantic, Washington, 1987-89; mgr. market rsch. and strategy Computer Consoles, Inc., Rochester, N.Y., 1989-91; sr. mgr. strategic mktg. Network Applications Systems divsn. Nortel Networks, Rochester, 1991-94; dir. new bus. devel. Ameritech, Hoffman Estates, Ill., 1994-96; sr. mgr. bus. devel. and strategic planning Switching Sys. divsn. Rockwell Internat., Chgo., 1996-97; dir. mktg. and strategic planning Electronic Commerce divsn. Rockwell Internat., Chgo., 1997-98; practice mgr. strategic svcs. BroadVision Inc., Itasca, Ill., 1999—2001; practice dir. bus. devel., ind. mgmt. cons. Highstone Assocs., 2001—. Bd. dirs. Com. Internat. Human Rights Community, Washington, 1981; bd. dirs. Ill. and Mich. Canal Corridor Assn.; organizer, cons. Le Fante for Senate, Jersey City, 1982. Georgetown U. fellow, 1982-84. Mem. Am. Mktg. Assn., Strategic Planning Assn., Soc. Competitive Intelligence Profls., Interactive Svcs. Assn., Beta Gamma Sigma. Avocations: scuba diving, tennis, softball, golf. E-mail: echoch@aol.com.

HOCHSTEIN, MARTIN ALAN, endocrinologist; b. Bklyn., Mar. 24, 1943; s. Isaac Leib and Ann Hochstein; m. Rachel Hochstein, June 15, 1969; children: David, Rosalyn. BA, Yeshiva U., 1964; MD, U. Louisville, 1969. Straight med. intern Maimonides Med. Ctr., Bklyn., 1966-70, med. resident, 1970-71; 2nd yr. med. resident Albert Einstein Coll. Medicine, Bronx, 1971-72; asst. chief med., lt. comdr. USPHS Hosp., Staten Island, N.Y., 1972-74; fellow John's Hopkins Sch. Medicine, Balt., 1974-75; dir. medicine Bergen Pines County Hosp., Paramus, N.J., 1976-81; clin. assoc. prof. medicine U. Medicine and Dentistry N.J., Newark, 1976—; pvt. practice endocrinology and metabolism Paramus, 1981—. Author: (with others) The Practice of Medicine: A Self-Assessment Guide, 1976. Fellow ACP, Am. Assn. Clin. Endocrinology, N.J. Acad. Medicine; mem. The Endocrine Soc., Johns Hopkins Med. and Surg. Assn. Jewish. Avocations: scuba diving, cycling, swimming. Office: One Sears Dr Paramus NJ 07652

HOCHSTRASSER, DONALD LEE, cultural anthropologist, community health and public administration educator; b. Taylorsville, Ky., June 10, 1927; s. Emil John and Mary E. (Schad) H.; m. Marie Emlen, Apr. 9, 1960; 1 child, Letitia Cope; stepchildren— Eloise Q. Hatch, Laura A. Hatch. B.A., U. Ky., 1952, M.A., 1955; postgrad. (univ. fellow) Northwestern U., 1955-56; Ph.D. in Anthropology, U. Oreg., 1963; M.P.H., U. Calif.-Berkeley, 1969. Research asst. dept. rural sociology U. Ky., Lexington, 1954-55, instr. dept. anthropology, 1956-57, 1959-60, instr. dept. community medicine, 1961-63, asst. prof., 1963-66, assoc. prof., 1966-73, prof., 1973-80, assoc. dir. Ctr. Developmental Change, 1970-73, prof. community health Coll. Allied Health, prof. anthropology Coll. of Arts and Scis., prof. pub. adminstrn. Grad. Ctr. Pub. Adminstrn., 1980-93, prof. emeritus dept. health svcs., 1993—; teaching fellow dept. anthropology U. Oreg., Eugene, 1957-58, instr., 1958-59, NSF research fellow, 1960-61; USPHS spl. research fellow Sch. Pub. Health, U. Calif.-Berkeley, 1968-69; chmn. state family planning rev. com. Ky. State Comprehensive Health Planning Council, 1972-74; mem. state family planning task force Council Health Services, Ky. State Dept. Human Resources, 1974-78; cons., adv. numerous orgns.; vis. scholar dept. adminstrv. and social health scis. Sch. Pub. Health, U. Calif.-Berkeley, 1979; dir. Bluegrass Regional Birth Planning Council, Inc., Lexington, 1978-81, Lexington Planned Parenthood, Inc., 1982-89; mem. adv. coun. Ctr. of Creative Living/Adult Care Program of Lexington-Fayette County Health Dept., 1989. Mem. Union of Concerned Scientists, Am. Farmland Trust, Wilderness Soc. Served with USN, 1946-47. Grantee pub. health, family planning, sickle cell anemia, Tb control and occupational health-risk factors. Fellow Am. Anthrop. Assn., Soc. Applied Anthropology; mem. Soc. Med. Anthropology (founding), Am. Pub. Health Assn. (founding mem. population sect.), Assn. Tchrs. Preventive Medicine, AAAS, AAUP, Phi Beta Kappa, Sigma Xi, Alpha Kappa Delta, Delta Omega. Democrat. Clubs: Univ. Faculty, Alumni. Contbr. numerous articles to profl. publs. Home: 953 Holly Springs Dr Lexington KY 40504-3119 Office: Univ Ky Med Ctr 208A Annex 2 Lexington KY 40536-0001

HOCHSTRASSER, JOHN MICHAEL, environmental engineer, industrial hygienist; b. Cin., July 19, 1938; s. Alvin Louis and Helen Augusta (Furst) H.; m. Wilma Ruth Reckman, Feb. 27, 1960; children: Ronald, Jennifer, Caroline. BSME, U. Cin., 1963, MS in Environ. Engring., 1972, PhD in Environ. Health, 1976. Registered profl. engr., Ohio, Ill., N.J., Ky.; diplomate of environ. engring. Am. Acad. Environ. Engrs.; qualified environ. profl. Inst. Profl. Environ. Practice; cert. indsl. hygienist Am. Bd. Indsl. Hygiene; registered occupational hygienist, Can. Reliability and safety engr. GE Co., Evendale, Ohio, 1963-72; dir. environ. affairs G.D. Searle & Co., Skokie, Ill., 1975-78; dir. indsl. hygiene Tenneco Chem., Inc., Piscataway, NJ, 1978-83; project dir. Roy F. Weston, Inc., West Chester, Pa., 1983-85; dir. health and safety CH2M Hill, Inc., Parsippany, NJ, 1985-89; tech. dir. First Environ., Inc., Riverdale, NJ, 1989-92; dir. environ. health and safety Tastemaker, Cin., 1992-97, Am. Tool Cos., Inc., Wilmington, Ohio, 1998—2002, EHS Engring., Union, Ky., 2002—. Mem. ACGIH, NSPE, Am. Indsl. Hygiene Assn. (bd. dir. 1987-90, chair ethics com. 1992-93), Am. Soc. Safety Engr., Am. Acad. Indsl. Hygiene (councilor 1995-98), Am. Acad. Environ. Engr. (chair indsl. hygiene com. 1995—), Air and Waste Mgmt. Assn., Water Environment Fedn., System Safety Soc., Soc. for Risk Analysis. Achievements include research on the use of fault tree analysis to solve environmental problems; research of short circuit flow in cyclone dust collectors; established occupational exposure limits for estrogen dusts and availability requirements for incinerators. Home: 11317 Longden Way Union KY 41091-8004

HOCK, FREDERICK WYETH, lawyer; b. Newark, July 10, 1924; s. Herbert Hummel and Carol (Wyeth) H.; m. Alfheld Catherine Larsen, Mar. 4, 1945; children: Carolyn, Sandra, Rhonda; m. Ellen Barbara Weidner, June 28, 1975. AA, Princeton U., 1944; BA, Rutgers U., 1948, LLB, 1950, JD, 1968. Bar: N.J. 1949. Assoc. Stevenson, Willette & McDermott, 1949-51; pvt. practice, 1951-65; ptnr. Hock & Sharkey, East Orange, N.J., 1965-79; sr. ptnr. Hock Silverlieb & Kramer, Livingston, N.J., 1979-93, Gulkin, Hock & Lehr, 1994-2000, Hock Graziano & Koprowski, 2000—. Acting judge East Orange Mcpl. Ct., 1954-57; mem. adv. bd. Maplewood Bank and Trust Co., Livingston, 1987-91, Summit Trust Co., 1991-98. Chmn. Juvenile Conf. Com., 1958-62; trustee Cmty. Day Nursery of the Oranges & Maplewood, 1962-75, pres. 1973-75; trustee founders Endowment Fund, 1954-87, House of Good Shepherd, 1970-90, Nu Beta Found., 1970-91; bd. dirs. Essex County chpt. ARC, 1987-91; post adv. VFW post 5445, 1955-90. With USMC, 1942-46. Mem. ABA, N.J. Bar Assn., Northwestern N.J. Estate Planning Coun. (dir. 1988-90), No. N.J. Estate Planning Coun., Marina Bay Club (trustee 2000—). Office: 155 Pompton Ave Ste 206 Verona NJ 07044

HOCK, LISABETH MARIE, language educator; b. Seattle, June 17, 1963; d. Eugene Arnold Hock and Rometta Mary Achenbach. BA in German with distinction, U. Kans., 1987, MA in Germanic Lang. and Lit., 1991; PhD in Germanic Lang. and Lit., Washington U., 1998. Vis. asst. prof. German Coll. Wooster, Ohio, 1998—2001; asst. prof. German Wayne State U., Detroit, 2001—. Author: Replicas of a Female Prometheus: The Textual Personae of Bettina von Arnim, 2001. Fulbright scholar, Humboldt U., Berlin, 1988—89. Mem.: MLA, Women in German, German Studies Assn., Am. Assn. Tchrs. German. Office: Wayne State U German and Slavic Studies 443 Manoogian Hall 906 W Warren Ave Detroit MI 48202

HOCK, MORTON, entertainment advertising executive; b. N.Y.C., June 24, 1929; s. Louis and Grace Dora (Solomon) H.; m. Anita Zagerman, Nov. 8, 1959; children— Jennifer, Jonathan With Blaine Thompson Co., N.Y.C.; acct. supr. David Merrick Productions, 1954-60; advt. mgr. Paramount Pictures, N.Y.C., 1960-63, v.p., 1967-71; dir. advt. United Artists Corp., N.Y.C., 1963-67; exec. v.p. Charles Schlaifer & Co., Inc., N.Y.C., 1972-83; exec. v.p. entertainment div. DDB Needham Worldwide, N.Y.C., 1983—. Mgmt. supr. Universal Pictures Account, United Artists Theatres Account, Gramercy Pictures Account. Contbr. articles to Variety. Mem. adv. com., bd. dirs. Will Rogers Found., 1983— . Named Showman of Yr. Nat. Assn. Theatre Owners; recipient Nat. Screen Svc. award for best theatre trailer. Mem. Acad. Motion Picture Arts and Scis. (bd. dirs.), Motion Picture Pioneers. Clubs: Variety of N.Y. (pres. 1979-80); Friars (admission com.). Lodges: B'nai Brith (trustee cinema unit 1980—). Avocations: sports; music; reading; travel.

HOCKEIMER, HENRY ERIC, business executive; b. Winzig, Germany, Apr. 3, 1920; came to U.S., 1946, naturalized, 1951; s. Erich and Gertrude (Masur) H.; m. Margaret Feeny, May 26, 1956; children: Ellen Patricia, Henry Eric. Student, RCA Insts., 1946-47; electronics and bus. mgmt., N.Y.U., 1948-51. With Philco-Ford Corp., Phila., 1947—, gen. mgr. communications and tech. services div., 1962-63, corp. v.p., 1963-72; v.p., gen. mgr. refrigeration products div. Connorsville, Ind., 1972-75; pres. Ford Aerospace & Communications Corp., Dearborn, Mich., 1975-85; v.p. Ford Motor Co., 1981-85; cons. USIA, Washington, 1985, dep. dir. TV and film service, 1986-87, asst. dir., 1987-88, assoc. dir. for mgmt., 1988-91, cons., 1991—; commr. RIAS, 1991—; mem. exec. adv. bd. Casals Assocs., 2002—. Mem. Engring. Soc. Detroit, Smithsonian, Univ. Club Washington, Washington Arts Soc. E-mail: hhockeimer@aol.com.

HOCKENBERG, HARLAN DAVID, lawyer; b. Des Moines, July 1, 1927; s. Leonard C. and Estyre M. (Zalk) H.; m. Dorothy A. Arkin, June 3, 1953; children: Marni Lynn, Thomas Leonard, Edward Arkin. BA, U. Iowa, 1949, JD, 1952. Bar: Iowa 1952. Assoc. Abramson & Myers, Des Moines, 1952-58, Abramson, Myers & Hockenberg, Des Moines, 1958-64; sr. ptnr. Davis, Hockenberg, Wine, Brown, Koehn & Shors, Des Moines, 1964-95; shareholder, dir. Sullivan & Ward, P.C., Des Moines, 1995—. Bd. dirs. West Des Moines State Bank, Rep. Jewish Coalition, Smoother Sailing Found. Mem. bd. editors U. Iowa Law Review. Mem. Citizens for Ind. Cts., Internat. Rels. and Nat. Security Adv. Coun., Rep. Nat. Com., 1978; chmn. Coun. Jewish Fedns., Small Cities Com., 1970-71; mem. exec. com. Am. Israel Pub. Affairs Com.; pres. Wilkie House, Inc., Des Moines, 1965-66, Des Moines Jewish Welfare Fedn., 1973-74; mem. Presdl. Commn. on White House Fellowships, 1988-92; mem. Holocaust Meml. Coun., 2003—; mem. ins. devel. bd. Iowa Dept. Econ. Devel. With USNR, 1945-46. Mem. Iowa State Bar Assn. (past chair professionalism com.), Des Moines C. of C. (pres. 1986, chmn. bur. econ. devel. 1979, 80, bd. dirs. 1986, chmn. Metro Forum), Des Moines Club, Pioneer Club, Delta Sigma Rho, Omicron Delta Kappa, Phi Epsilon Pi. Home: 2880 Grand Ave Des Moines IA 50312-4274 Office: Sullivan & Ward PC 801 Grand Ave Ste 3500 Des Moines IA 50309-8005 E-mail: bhockenberg@sullivan-ward.com.

HOCKER, JOHN ROBERT, technical operations executive; b. Elwood, Ind., Aug. 11, 1935; s. Joseph Eugene and Helen Margaret (Benedict) H.; m. Barbara Siemers, Aug. 11, 1962; children: Constance Lynn, Guy Albert. BS in Engring., U.S. Mil. Acad., 1957; MS in Applied Math., U. Freiburg, Germany, 1965; M of Mil. Arts and Sci., U.S. Army Command and Gen. Staff Coll., 1971; student, French War Coll., Paris, 1976-78. Commd. 2d lt. U.S. Army, 1957, advanced through ranks to Col., 1978, co-comdr. 1st Calvary divsn., 1966-67; assoc. prof. dept. math. U.S. Mil. Acad., West Point, NY, 1967-70; insp. Infantry Airborne/Spl Units for Mil Equipment Delivery Team, Phnom Penh, Cambodia, 1971-72; comdr. 2d bn. 325th airborne infantry 82d airborne divsn. U.S. Army, Fort Bragg, NC, 1972-75; joint exercise dir. Orgn. of Joint Chief of Staff, Washington, 1975-76; policy dir. Hdqrs. U.S. European Command, Stuttgart, Germany, 1978-80; spl. asst. to Supreme Allied Comdr. Supreme Hdqrs. Allied Powers Europe, Belgium, 1980-82; chief of staff Def. Mobilization Systems Planning Activity, Washington, 1982-84; ret. U.S. Army, 1984; dir. bus. devel. Info. Systems Group Martin Marietta, Bethesda, Md., 1984-91, dir. tech. ops., 1991-95; dir. engring. edn. Lockheed Martin Corp., 1995; exec. dir. Nat. Sci. and Tech. Medals Found., Washington, 1995—. Decorated Bronze Star, Def. Superior Svc. Medal; recipient Sec. of Army Outstanding Civil Svc. medal, 2002; Olmsted Found. scholar, 1963. Mem. Assn. Fund Raising Profls., Internat. Congress of Dist. Awards. Avocations: travel, golf. Home: 6112 Goldtree Way Bethesda MD 20817-5839 Office: Nat Sci and Tech Medals Found 1818 N St NW Ste 600 Washington DC 20036-2476 E-mail: nstmf@aecc.org.

HOCKERSMITH, CHARLES EDWIN, information technology educator; b. Chambersburg, Pa., Nov. 12, 1947; s. Charles Samuel and Marietta Maxine (Potter) H.; m. Nancy Nickles, Nov. 21, 1970; children: Michael Charles, Alexander Nickles. BSEd, Shippensburg U., 1973; MLS, Syracuse U., 1998. Humanities librarian Christiana H.S., Newark, Del., 1973-78; librarian Newark H.S., 1978-80; libr. dir. Cecil C.C., North East, Md., 1980-95; ops. officer Del. NG, Wilmington, 1995-99; tech. instr. Newark H.S., 1999—2002; libr. Kirk Mid. Sch., Newark, Del., 2002—. Adj. prof. U. Del., 1998—. Dir. 1st State Symphonic Band, Chesapeake Brass Band, 287th Army Band; pres. Christina Bd. Edn., 1994-97. With U.S. Army, 1965-68, with Del. N.G., 1978—. Mem. ALA, Libr. Info. Tech. Assn., Assn. Internet Profls., Internat. Webmasters Assn. Methodist. Home and Office: 1 Andries Rd Newark DE 19711-5616 E-mail: ed@hockersmithdesigns.com.

HOCKETT, CHRISTOPHER BURCH, lawyer; b. Hutchinson, Kans., Sept. 6, 1959; s. George Rundell and Shirley Hockett. BA, William & Mary, 1981; JD, U. Va., 1985. Bar: Calif. 1985, U.S. Dist. Ct. (no. dist.) Calif. 1985, U.S. Dist. Ct. (cen.dist.) Calif. 1988, U.S. Dist. Ct. Colo. 1997, U.S. Ct. Appeals (9th cir.) 1988, U.S. Ct. Appeals (10th cir.) 1996, U.S. Ct. Appeals (fed. cir.) 2000. Assoc. McCutchen, Doyle, Brown, & Enersen, San Francisco, 1985-92, ptnr., 1992—. Editl. chair The Antitrust Source on-line mag., www.antitrustsource-.com. Author: (chpt.) State Antitrust Law Handbook, 1990, 2nd edit., 1999; assoc. editor Antitrust Mag., 1990-91. Bd. dirs. San Francisco Neighborhood Legal Assistance Found., 1992-99, Bay Area Legal Aid, 1999—. Mem. ABA (council sect. of antitrust law, 1998-2001, vice chairperson antitrust law civil practice and procedure com. 1991-95, chairperson 1995-98, mem. task force on civil justice reform 1992-93), No. Calif. Assn. Bus. Trial Lawyers, Bar Assn. San Francisco, Wildlife Conservation Soc. (bd. advisors), Barristers Club. Avocations: running, golf. Office: Bingham McCutchen LLP 3 Embarcadero Ctr Ste 1800 San Francisco CA 94111-4074 E-mail: chris.hockett@bingham.com.

HOCKETT, SHERI LYNN, radiologist; b. Cleburne, Tex., Apr. 20, 1953; d. Dale and Rosamond (Prater) Hockett; m. David Alexander Campbell, Apr. 22, 1978; children: Courtney Michelle, Jonathan David. BA, So. Meth. U., 1974; MD, Southwestern Med. Sch., 1978. Diplomate Am. Bd. Radiology. Resident diagnostic radiology St. Paul Hosp., Dallas, 1978-81, chief resident, 1980-81, fellow, 1981-82; chmn. dept. radiology Baylor Med. Ctr., Garland, Tex., 1992-96. Mem. AMA, Am. Assn. Women Radiologists, Am. Coll. Radiology, Radiol. Soc. N.Am., Tex. Radiol. Soc., Dallas-Ft. Worth Radiol. Soc. Office: 2300 Marie Curie Dr Garland TX 75042-5706

HOCKFIELD, SUSAN, medical educator; d. Thomas and Elizabeth Byrne; m. Thomas Byrne; 1 child, Elizabeth Byrne. BA in Biology, U Rochester, 1973; PhD in Anatomy & Neuroscience, Georgetown U, 1979; MA (hon.), Yale U, 1994. PhD Anatomy and Neuroscience Georgetown U Schs. of Med. and Dentistry, Thesis rsch. Supervised by Dr. S. Gobel NIDR, NIH State of Md., Washington, 1975—79; NIH Post-Doc Fellow Dept. of Anatomy and Neuroscience Program, U of Calif. Sponsored by Drs. A. Basbaum and H.S. Ralston, San Francisco, 1979—80; jr. staff invesigator Cold Spring Harbor Lab, Cold Spring Harbor, NY, 1980—82, sr. staff investigator, 1982—85; asst. prof. Sect. of Neurobiology Yale U Sch. of Med., New Haven, 1985—89, assoc. prof. (term) Sect. of Neurobiology, 1989—91, assoc. prof. (tenure) Sect. of Neurobiology, 1991—94, prof. Dept. of Neurobiology, 1994—; Dean Grad. Sch. of Arts and Sci. Yale U, 1998—2002, Provost, 2003—. Mem. Nat. Adv. Neurological Disorders and Stroke Council (NIH), 2002—; mem. at large AAAS, Sect. on Neuroscience, 2000—; bd. trustees Cold Spring Harbor Lab., Cold Spring Harbor, NY, 1998—; Brain Cancer Adv. Panel James S. McDonnell Found., 1997—2002; bd. dir. Haskins Lab., 1988—2002; U Adv. Council Yale-New Haven Tchrs. Inst., 1998—2002; elected mem. of the bd. Council of Grad. Sch., 2002; neuroscience adv. bd. Astra Pharmaceuticals, 1997—99; program dir. Summer Neurobiology Program Cold Spring Harbor Lab., Cold Harbor Springs, NY, 1985—97; councilor Soc. for Neuroscience, 1992—96; sci. adv. bd. Hereditary Disease Found., 1991—95, 1996—2000; mem. NIH Study Section (Visual Sci. B), 1988—92; chair Gordon Plasticity, 1997; participant Molecular Cloing of Eukaryotic Genes Cold Spring Harbor Lab. Course, Cold Harbor Springs, 1985; participant, mem. of bd. several orgns., studies and soc. Contbr. articles, J. Neuroscience 22, 7536-7547, Cancer Res. 61, 7056-7059, chapters to books, book. Recipient PHS Post-doctoral Rsch. Award, NIH, 1980, Grass Traveling Sci. Award, Soc. for Neuroscience, 1987, Charles Judson Herrick Award, Am. Assoc. of Anatomists, 1987, William Edward Gilbert Prof. of Neurobiology, Yale U, 2001; grantee Esther A. and Joseph Klingenstein Fellowship in the Neurosciences, Ester A. and Joseph Klinenstein Fellowship, 1985, can Brain Specific Matrix Mediate Glioma Invasion?, Molecular cytoarchitecture of ctrl visual areas, Monoclonal antibodies to neural tissue: LM and EM study., Indentification of major cells classes in embryonic mammalian CNS., numerous grants and fellowships including the Sloan Found., Office for naval Rsch., McKnight Found., The Klingenstein

Found. Mem.: FASEB, Soc. for Devel., Am. Assoc. of Anatomists (Charles Judson Herrick Award 1987), Soc. for Neuroscience (Grass Traveling Scientist 1987), Am Assn. for Advancement of Sci. (assoc.; mem.-at-large, Section on Neuroscience 2000—). Achievements include three patents in field of neuroscience. Home: 35 Hillhouse Ave 06511 Office: Yale U One Hillhouse Ave New Haven CT 06511

HOCKING, MARIAN RUTH, women's health nurse; b. Detroit, Aug. 31, 1934; d. John Frederick and Clara Elizabeth (Numbers) Johnson; m. Wilbert Joseph Hocking, June 19, 1954; children: David, James, Debra, Timothy, Thomas, John. ADN, Grand Rapids (Mich.) Jr. Coll., 1975; student, Wayne State U. Cert. inpatient obstet. care, cert. in fetal monitoring. Receptionist dental office, Royal Oak, Mich., 1955-56; nurse's aide Ctrl. Mich. Cmty. Hosp., Mt. Pleasant, 1959-66; nurse FDF Hosp., Grand Rapids, 1966-75; from staff nurse to asst. coord. Met. Hosp., Grand Rapids, 1975-94; nurse No. Mich. Hosp., 1988-99; ret., 1999; relief nurse Dr. Joseph Sypniewski, DO, Petoskey, Mich., 1999; relief supr. Meadowbrook Med. Care Facility, Bellaire, Mich., 1999—. Home: 4512 Chessie Ln Central Lake MI 49622-9724

HOCKINGS, PAUL EDWARD, anthropologist, editor; b. Hertford, Eng., Feb. 23, 1935; came to U.S., 1960; s. Arthur and Mary Frances Hockings; m. Amelia Reyes, June 30, 1964; m. Joan Lee Hockings, Aug. 24, 1998. BA, U. Sydney, 1957; MA, U. Toronto, 1960; PhD, U. Calif., Berkeley, 1965. Asst. prof. UCLA, 1965-69; rsch. dir. M-G-M Studios, Culver City, Calif., 1969; from assoc. prof. to prof. emeritus U. Ill., Chgo., 1970—2002. Adj. curator Field Mus., Chgo., 1995—. Author: Badaga-English Dictionary, 1992, Kindreds of the Earth, 1999; editor: Principles of Visual Anthropology, 1995; editor-in-chief Visual Anthropology, 1991—; editor: Encyclopedia of World Cultures, 1987-94, Encyclopedia of Modern Asia, 1999-2002. Fellow Royal Anthropol. Inst.; mem. Am. Anthropol. Assn. (life mem.), Soc. for Visual Anthropology. Avocation: mountain hiking. E-mail: visualanthro@yahoo.com.

HOCKMUTH, JOSEPH FRANK, physicist, psychotherapist; b. Buffalo, N.Y., Mar. 6, 1942; s. Joseph Frank and Gertrude Marie (Merkley) H.; m. Sharon Louise Van Deusen Tiernan, June 30, 1965 (div.); children: Joseph Fess, Catherine Marie; m. Katherine Nancy Genco, June 1, 1991 (div.); m. Holly Lynn Knapp, Oct. 14, 2000. BS in Physics, Calif. State U., 1965; MA in Psychology, Norwich U., 1992. Cert. substance abuse counselor, Ariz. Bd. Behavioral Health Examiners; cert. coll. instr., Ariz. State Bd.; cert. profl. counselor. Rsch. engr. Westinghouse Astroelectronics, Newbury Park, Calif., 1965-66, Lockheed Missile & Space Co., Sunnyvale, Calif., 1966-69, sr. rsch. engr., 1972-78; radiation effects engr. IRT Corp., San Diego, 1969-72, staff scientist, 1984-87; addictions counselor Charter Hosp., Glendale, Ariz., 1992-93; prin. staff engr. Motorola Govt. Sys. & Tech. Group, Scottsdale, Ariz., 1978-84; tech. staff engr. Motorola GSTG, Scottsdale, Ariz., 1987—, divsn. cons. for radiation effects, 1987—; psychotherapist Fountain Hills, Ariz., 1992—. Contbr. Awakenings mag., 1992—. Funds coord. United Way, Scottsdale, 1988-90; class sponsor Wounded Knee (Wyo.) Tribal Elem. Sch., 1992—. Sgt. Calif. NG, 1960-68. Fellow Am. Counseling Assn., Ariz. Counselors Assn., Noetic Scis. Inst.; mem. ASTM (com. 1985—), IEEE (ofcl. tech. paper reviewer 1993). Roman Catholic. Avocations: guitar, piano, fishing, camping, american indian culture studies. Home: 15024 E Windyhill Rd Fountain Hills AZ 85268-1323 Office: Motorola GSTG 8201 E Mcdowell Rd # H2550 Scottsdale AZ 85257-3893

HOCKNEY, DAVID, artist; b. Bradford, Yorkshire, Eng., July 9, 1937; s. Kenneth and Laura H. Attended, Bradford Coll. Art, 1953-57, Royal Coll. Art, London, 1959-62; D (hon.), U. Aberdeen, 1988; hon. degree, Royal Coll. Art, London, 1992. Lectr. U. Iowa, 1964, U. Colo., 1965, U. Calif. Berkeley, 1967, UCLA, 1966, hon. chair of drawing, 1980. One-man shows include Kasmin Gallery, 1963-89, Mus. Modern Art, N.Y.C., 1964, 68, Stedelijk Mus., Amsterdam, Netherlands, 1966, Whitechapel Gallery, London, 1970, Andre Emmerich Gallery, N.Y.C., 1972-96, Musee des Arts Decoratifs, Paris, 1974, Museo Tamayo, Mexico City, 1984, L.A. Louver, Calif., 1986, 89—, Nishimura Gallery, Tokyo, 1986, 89, 90, 94, Met. Mus. Art, 1988, L.A. County Mus. Art, 1988, 96, Tate Gallery, London, 1988, 92, Royal Acad. Arts, London, 1995, Hamburger Kunsthalle, 1995, Nat. Mus. Am. Art, Washington, 1997, 98, Mus. Ludwig, Cologne, 1997, MFA, Boston, 1998, Centre Georges Pompidou, Paris, 1999, Musee Picasso, Paris, 1999, Mus. Contemporary Art, L.A., 2001, Kunst-Und Ausstellung Halle, Bonn, 2001, La. Mus Mod. Art, Copenhagen, 2001, Annely Juda Fine Art, London, 1997, 99., 2003, Nat. Portrait Gallery, London, 2003, others; designer: Rake's Progress, Glyndebourne, Eng., 1975; sets for Magic Flute, Glyndebourne, 1978, Parade Triple Bill, Stravinsky Triple Bill, Met. Opera House, 1980-81, Tristan und Isolde, Los Angeles Music Ctr. Opera, 1987; Turandot, Lyric Opera, Chgo., 1992—, San Francisco Opera, 1993, Die Frau Ohne Schatten, Covent Garden, London, 1992, L.A. Music Ctr.Opera, 1993; author: David Hockney by David Hockney, 1976, David Hockney: Travels with Pen, Pencil and Ink, 1978, Paper Pools, 1980, David Hockney Photographs, 1982, Cameraworks, 1983, David Hockney: A Retrospective, 1988, Hockney Paints the Stage, 1983, That's the Way I See It, 1993, David Hockney's Dog Days, 1998, Hockney on Art, 1999, Secret Knowledge: Rediscovering the Lost Techniques of the Old Masters, 2001; illustrator: Six Fairy Tales of the Brothers Grimm, 1969, The Blue Guitar, 1977, Hockney's Alphabet, 1991. Recipient Guinness award and 1st prize for etching, 1961, Gold medal Royal Coll. Art, 1962, Graphic prize Paris Biennale, 1963, 1st prize 8th Internat. Exhbn. Drawings Lugano, Italy, 1964, 1st prize John Moores Exhbn. Liverpool, Eng., 1967, German award of Excellence 1983, 1st prize Internat. Ctr. of Photography, N.Y., 1985, Kodak photography book award for Cameraworks, 1984, Praemium Imperiale Japan Art Assn., 1989, 5th Ann. Gov. Calif. Visual Arts award, 1994; named Companion of Honour, Her Majesty, the Queen of Eng., 1997. Office: 7508 Santa Monica Blvd Los Angeles CA 90046-6407

HOCUTT, MAX OLIVER, philosophy educator; b. Berry, Ala., July 3, 1936; s. Harry Juell and Edith Pauline (Skelton) H.; m. Dorothy Lois Etheredge, Nov. 22, 1957; children— James Max, Cassandra Diane. BA with honors in philosophy (honors scholar), Tulane U., 1957, MA, 1958; PhD (So. Fellowships Career Teaching fellow), Yale, 1960. Instr. U. South Fla., Tampa, 1960-62, asst. prof., chmn. dept. philosophy, 1962-65; asso. prof. U. Ala., 1965-70, prof., 1970—2001, chmn. dept., 1978-91. Vis. fellow Princeton U., 1979, St. Andrews U., 1987; bd. dirs. ACLU, University, 1969 Author: The Elements of Logical Analysis and Inference, 1979, First Philosophy, 1980, Grounded Ethics, 2000; editor: Behavior and Philosophy, 1992-96; contbr. articles to profl. jours. Mem. Ala. Philos. Soc. (pres. 1967), So. Soc. Philosophy and Psychology, Am. Philos. Assn., Phi Beta Kappa. Home: 5510 Golden Pond Ave Northport AL 35473-1529 Office: U Ala Dept Philosophy Tuscaloosa AL 35487-0001

HODAKIEVIC, JAMES JOSEPH, retired secondary education educator; b. Cleve., Aug. 21, 1947; s. Joseph Edward and Genevieve Sophie (Chodakowski) H.; m. Johanna Rita Dolphin, Feb. 15, 1969; children: Peter James, Bethany Nanette. BS in Edn., Bowling Green State U., 1969, MEd, 1972; postgrad., Kent State U., 1980-82. Cert. edn., Ohio. Driver edn. tchr. Lakota Local Schs., Kansas, Ohio, 1969; tchr., coach Western Res. H.S., Warren, Ohio, 1969-71; instr., football coach Bowling Green (Ohio) State U., 1971-72; tchr., head football coach West Holmes H.S., Millersburg, Ohio, 1972-75, Defiance (Ohio) H.S., 1975—79; tchr. Bedford (Ohio) H.S., 1979—2002, head football coach, 1982—. Guest lectr. Bowling Green State U. Athletics, 1975-77; staff dir. Ozzie Newsome Football Camp, Cleve., 1987; spkr. Youngstown (Ohio) State U. Athletics, 1994; staff Ohio State Summer Football Camp, 1997, Pa. State Summer Football Camp, 1997, 2000. Recipient Dr. Lee Tressel Meml. Coaching award Cleve. Touchdown Club, 1994; named Coach of Yr., Coshocton (Ohio) Tribune, 1974, Greater Cleve. Conf., 1993, Lake Erie League Erie Divsn., 1998, 99, 2001, NFL H.S. Coach of the Yr. finalist, 2000. Mem. Nat. Fedn. Interscholastic Coach, Am. Football Coaches Assn. (assoc.), Ohio H.S. Football Coaches Assn., Greater Cleve. Football Coaches Assn. (pres., league dir., Golden Deeds award 1997). Avocation: golf. Home: 907 School Ave Cuyahoga Falls OH 44221-4113 Office: Bedford City Schs Bedford HS 481 Northfield Rd Bedford OH 44146-2201

HODEL, MARY ANNE, library director; b. St. Louis, Aug. 12; d. William George and Florence Marie (Betz) H.; children: Courtney Hodel Denham, Christian Hodel Denham. BA, U. Wis., 1972; MLS, Catholic U., 1973. Project libr. TRACOR-JITCO, Rockville, Md., 1973-74; from project mgr. to database mgr. Nat. Resources Libr. U.S. Dept. of Interior, Washington, 1974-77; cataloger USAF Base Libr., Ramstein, Germany, 1977-79; from project libr. to automation libr. Law Libr. Georgetown U., Washington, 1984-85, automation libr. Law Libr., 1985-91; chief state libr. resource ctr. Enoch Pratt Free Libr., Balt., 1991-95; dir. Ann Arbor (Mich.) Dist. Libr., 1995—2001, Orange County (Fla.) Libr. System, 2002—. Network coord. Coun. Md. Librs., 1991-95; mem. Sailor Implementation group, 1992-95, grants and devel. task force liaison, 1993-95; v.p. Mich. Libr. Consortium, 1998-99, bd. pres., 1999-2000, bd. dirs. Mem. exec. com. Ann Arbor Hands On Mus., 1998—2001. Recipient Libr. of Yr. award Libr. Jour., 1997-98. Mem.: ILAMA, ALA, ALA (Libr. of Yr. award 1997—98), Law Librs. Soc. Washington (program coord. 1989, 1990, chair innovative interfaces users workshop 1989, pres. acad. spl. interest sect. 1988—89, rec. sec. 1989—91), Md. Libr. Assn. (del. to ALA legis. day 1992, co-chair tech. interest group 1994, conf. planning com. 1993, 1994, program coord. 1994), Md. Assn. Profl. Libr. Adminstrs., Pub. Libr. Assn. (sys. sect. v.p./pres.-elect 1994—95, pres. 1995—, chair Leonard Wertheimer award com. 2000—01), Mich. Libr. Consortium (v.p. 1999, pres. 1999—2000), Am. Assn. Law Librs. (program coord. ann. meeting 1987, chair innovative interfaces users com. 1988—89, editor innovative interfaces users com. 1989), Mich. Libr. Assn. (chair pub. libr. divsn. 2001—). Avocations: travel, photography. Home: 9152 Pinnacle Cir Windermere FL 34786 Office: 101 Central Orlando FL 32801

HODES, RICHARD J. immunologist, researcher; Grad., Yale U.; MD, Harvard U. Diplomate Am. Bd. Internal Medicine. Clin. investigator Nat. Cancer Inst. NIH, Bethesda, Md., dep. chief, acting chief immunology br. Nat. Cancer Inst., dir. Nat. Inst. Aging, 1993—. Program coord. U.S.-Japan Coop. Cancer Rsch. Program, 1982—; mem. sci. adv. bd. Cancer Rsch. Inst., 1992—; mem. The Dana Alliance for Brain Initiatives, 1995—. Editor scholarly jours. including Jour. Exptl. Medicine and Therapeutic Immunology; contbr. numerous rsch. papers to profl. publs. Fellow AAAS. Office: Nat Inst on Aging 31 Center Dr Bldg 31 Rm 5c35 Bethesda MD 20892-0001

HODES, ROBERT BERNARD, lawyer; b. Bklyn., Aug. 25, 1925; s. James and Florence (Cohen) H.; m. Florence R. Rosenberg, Dec. 22, 1946 (div. Nov. 1984); 1 child, Paul; m. Cecilia Mendez, Dec. 18, 1984; children: James, Maria Paz. AB, Dartmouth Coll., 1946; LLB, Harvard U., 1949. Bar: N.Y. Supreme Ct. 1950, U.S. Dist. Ct. (so. dist.) N.Y. 1951, U.S. Tax Ct. 1955, U.S. Claims Ct. 1957, U.S. Ct. Appeals (2d cir.) 1959. Assoc. Willkie Farr & Gallagher, N.Y.C., 1949-56, ptnr., 1956-95, co-chmn., 1982-95, counsel, 1995—. Bd. dirs. K&F Industries, Inc., LCH Investments N.V., Loral Space & Telecomm., Ltd., Mueller Industries, Inc., Space Systems/Loral Inc., RV1 Guaranty Co., Ltd., Restructured Capital Holdings, Ltd. Active Cremer Found., Beaver Dam Sanctuary, Inc., Nat. Philanthropic Trust. Home: 860 United Nations Plz New York NY 10017-1810 Office: Willkie Farr & Gallagher Equitable Ctr 787 7th Ave New York NY 10019-6099

HODES, SCOTT, lawyer; b. Chgo., Aug. 14, 1937; s. Barnet and Eleanor (Cramer) H.; m. Maria Bechily, 1982; children— Brian Kenneth, Valery Jane, Anthony Scott. AB, U. Chgo., 1956; JD, U. Mich., 1959; LLM, Northwestern U., 1962. Bar: Ill. 1959, D.C. 1962, N.Y. 1981. Assoc. Arvey, Hodes, Costello & Burman, Chgo., 1959-61, ptnr., 1965-91, Ross & Hardies, Chgo., 1992—. Bd. dirs. First Investors Life Ins. Co. NY, Richardson Electronics, Ltd., State Ill. Savs. and Loan Bd., Expressions of Culture, Inc. Author: The Law of Art and Antiques, 1966, What Every Artist and Collector Should Know About the Law, 1974; Assoc. news editor: Fed. Bar News, 1963-70; co-editor: Conf. Mut. Funds, 1966, Legal Rights in the Art and Collectors' World, 1986; Contbr. articles to profl. jours. Chmn. Philippine Exch. Nurses award com., 1966; nat. chmn. Lawbooks U.S.A., 1962-73; chmn. Mut. Funds and Investment Mgmt. Conf., 1966-75; co-chmn. Chgo. World Friendship Day, 1967; mem. Ill. Arts Coun., 1973-75; Committeeman Ill. 9th Dist. Dem. Com., 1970-82; bd. dirs. Michael Reese Hosp. Rsch. Inst., 1965-73, Found. of Fed. Bar Assn., 1970—, United Cerebral Palsy Chgo., 1976-84; governing bd. Chgo. Symphony Soc., 1978-1999; governing mem. Art Inst. Chgo., 1980—; com. on internat. investment and tech. Dept. State, 1980-83; bd. dirs. Chgo. Neighborhood Theatre Found., 1980-92, Harold Washington Found., 1988-2000; exec. com. Anti Defamation League, 1990-98; chmn. Mayor's Task Force on Neighborhood Land Use, 1986-88; chmn. Navy Pier Devel. Authority, 1988-89; mem. Ill. Atty. Gen. adv. com., 1991-95; spl. counsel Art in Embassies Program, Dept. State, 1992-94; co-chmn. Private Enterprise Rev. and Adv. Bd., Ill., 1992-94; pres. Lawyers Creative Arts, 2000—; dir. Mex. Fine Arts Ctr. Mus., 2003—. Capt. JAGC, AUS, 1962-64. Decorated Army Commendation medal; named one of Chicago's ten outstanding young men Jr. Assn. Commerce and Industry, 1968, Chgo. Artist's award for Support of Visual Arts, 1996, Disting. Svc. award Lawyer's for the Creative Arts, 1997. 02169408, Fed. Bar Assn. (chmn. council financing 1966-71, chmn. younger lawyers div. 1963-64, nat. council 1965—, Distinguished Service award 1971, 75, 86, Earl Kintner award for Outstanding Service, 1998), Ill. Bar Assn., Chgo. Bar Assn., Chgo. Art Inst. (life), Chgo. Hist. Soc. (life), Judge Adv. Gens. Assn. (life), Zeta Beta Tau, Tau Epsilon Rho. Clubs: Standard, Econ. (Chgo.), Mid-Day. Lodges: Masons (32 degree). Jewish. Home: 1540 N Lake Shore Dr Chicago IL 60610-6684 Office: Ross & Hardies 150 N Michigan Ave Ste 2500 Chicago IL 60601-7567 E-mail: scott.hodes@rosshardies.com.

HODESS, ARTHUR BART, cardiologist; b. N.Y.C., Jan. 15, 1950; s. Samuel and Dora (Rosenkrantz) H.; m. Carol Yasuna, Aug. 31, 1969 (div. May 1985); children: Joshua David, Jeremy Scott; m. S. Christina Ellsworth, Dec. 23, 1987; children: Jonathan Ellsworth, Jason Dorian, Jordan Gottier. BA, Boston U., 1970; MD, Columbia U., 1974. Intern Hosp. of U. Pa., Phila., 1974-75, resident in medicine, 1975-77, fellow in cardiology, 1977-79; asst. instr. dept. medicine Hosp. U. of Pa., Phila., 1974-79; instr. physiology, dept. animal biology U. Pa., Sch. Veterinary Medicine, Phila., 1977-78; clin. assoc. dept. medicine U. Pa., Phila., 1979-81; attending cardiologist Brandywine Hosp., Coatesville, Pa., 1979—, dir. critical care, 1989—, chief of cardiology, 1990—, chmn. dept. medicine, 1991-95; pres. Brandywine Valley Cardiovascular Assocs., Thorndale, Pa., 1991—. Contbr. articles to profl. jours. V.p. Chestnut Hollow Homeowners Assn., West Chester, Pa., 1990-94, bd. dirs. 1995; bd. dirs. Beth Israel Congregation, Chester County, 1991-96. Fellow Clin. Coun. Cardiology Am. Heart Assn. Fellow: ACP, Am. Heart Assn., Am. Coll. Chest Physicians, Am. Coll. Cardiology; mem.: Soc. Critical Care Medicine, Cardiac Electrophysiology Soc., Am. Soc. Echocardiography. Office: Brandywine Valley Cardio 3025 Zinn Rd Thorndale PA 19372-1131

HODGE, BOBBY LYNN, mechanical engineer, manufacturing executive; b. Yadkinville, N.C., Oct. 14, 1956; s. Robert Henry and Betty Jean (Martin) H.; m. Robin Mayhue Renegar, June 8, 1979; children: Andrew, Adam. AAS with honors, Forsyth Tech. Inst., Winston-Salem, N.C., 1976; BS in Engring. Tech., U. N.C., Charlotte, 1978. Design engr. Clark/Gravely Corp., Clemmons, N.C., 1978-79, project engr., 1979-80; design engr. Ingersoll-Rand, Davidson, N.C., 1980-83, devel. engr., 1983-85; sr. applications engr. INA Bearing Co., Ft. Mill, S.C., 1985-87, automotive driveline engring. group, 1987-88, mgr. automotive applications engring., 1988-89, dir. automotive applications engring., 1989-96, dir. automotive engring., 1996-99; v.p. engring./product devel. The Setco Group, Cin., 1999—. Internat. spkr. on design and application of anti-friction bearings. Contbr. articles to profl. jours.; inventor, 9 patents in field. Mem. adv. coun. U. N.C.-Charlotte Coll. Engring. Mem. ASME, SAE, Soc. Mfg. Engrs., Soc. Tribologists and Lubrication Engrs., Am. Soc. Metals. Republican. Baptist. Avocations: golf, hunting, woodworking. Home: 1518 Jolee Dr Hebron KY 41048-9514 Office: The Setco Group 5880 Hillside Ave Cincinnati OH 45233-1599 E-mail: bhodge@setcousa.com., hodge1518@aol.com. *One of the most important tasks anyone can undertake is to establish a vision for their life. Without a vision there can not be direction. Without direction, any success or achievement comes merely by accident.*

HODGE, DAVID R. social science researcher; s. Bernard Hodge and Helen Pollock. MSW, N.Mex Highlands U., Las Vegas, 1998; MCS, Regent Coll., Vancouver, BC, 1998; PhD, Washington U., St. Louis, 2003. Rene Sand scholar Washngton U., St. Louis, 2003; postdoctoral fellow Ctr Rsch on Religion and Urban Civic Soc., U. Pa., Phila., 2003—. Contbr. articles to profl. jours. and Encyclopedia of Social Measurement, chapters to books.

HODGE, GLENN ROY, retired postmaster; b. Billings, Mont., May 5, 1947; s. Roy William and Helen Maxine (Sarbo) H.; m. Kay Lorraine Waller, Nov. 30, 1968; children: Theresa Kay, Alan Roy, Sheila Yvonne. Student, Rocky Mountain Coll., 1967-68, Ea. Mont. Coll., 1968. With U.S. Postal Svc., Billings, 1968-92, postmaster Cut Bank, Mont., 1978-81, Livingston, Mont., 1981-90, ret., 1992. Mem. Employer Support N.G. Res., Washington, 1982—, Park County Emergency Med. Assn., Livingston, 1983-90; instr. Cardio-Pulmonary Recusitation, Livingston, 1983-90; pres. Park County Rural Fire Dist., Livingston, 1986-87; mem. Chester Vol. Fire Dept. and Ambulance, 1990-92. Mem. Nat. League of Postmasters (pres. 1984-85), Lions. Baptist. Avocations: white water rafting, fishing, golf, camping. Home: # 1A 405 Park Dr N Great Falls MT 59401-2356 E-mail: pakawigle@bresnan.net.

HODGE, JAMES EDWARD, lawyer; b. Alexander City, Ala., Sept. 24, 1936; s. William H. and Nellie (Greene) H.; m. Nancy Bates, Aug. 24, 1963; children: Stephanie Lynne, Christopher Murray, Timothy James, Michael Bates. BA, Stetson U., 1958; JD, U. Fla., 1963. Bar: Fla. 1963, U.S. Dist. Ct. (mid. dist.) Fla. 1963, U.S. Ct. Appeals (5th cir.) 1963, U.S. Supreme Ct. 1972, U.S. Ct. Appeals (11th cir.) 1981. Ptnr. Jones, Foerster & Hodge, Jacksonville, Fla., 1966-74, Foerster & Hodge, Jacksonville, 1974-82, Milne, Hodge & Milne, Jacksonville, 1982-85; pvt. practice Jacksonville, 1985-86; ptnr. Blackwell, Walker, Fascell & Hoehl, Jacksonville, 1986-87; chmn. Bus. Acquisitions, Inc., Jacksonville, 1988-91; pvt. practice Jacksonville, Fla., 1991—. Gen. counsel Gov. Fla. 1981-82. Pres. Cerebral Palsy Jacksonville, 1972; bd. dirs. Little League Baseball, Jacksonville, 1976-81, The Bolles Sch. Dads Assn., Jacksonville, 1978-82; bd. dirs. Jacksonville Port Authority, 1980-86, chmn., 1986-88; bd. dirs. The Bolles Sch. Dads Assn. Named one of Outstanding Young Men Am., 1968. Mem. ABA, Fla. Bar, Jacksonville Bar Assn. (bd. govs. 1972-73), Stetson U. Alumni Assn. (pres. 1968), Rotary (pres. West Jacksonville club 1979-80, The Robert T. Shircliff Svc. award 1988), Phi Delta Phi, Omicron Delta Kappa. Episcopalian. Avocations: tennis, reading biographies, spectator sports, walking, travel. Office: PO Box 27055 Jacksonville FL 32205-0055

HODGE, JAMES LEE, German language educator; b. Harrisburg, Pa., Sept. 18, 1935; s. Earl Henry and Catherine Margaret (Ferber) M.; m. Janice Ellen Dunn, June 21, 1958; children: Geoffrey Lee, Stephen Charles. AB, Tufts U., 1957; A.M., Pa. State U., 1960, PhD, 1961. Grad. asst. Pa. State U., 1957-60; instr. German Bowdoin Coll., Brunswick, Maine, 1961-63, asst. prof., 1963-68, asso. prof., 1968-74, prof., 1974—, George Taylor Files prof. modern langs., 1977, chmn. dept. German, 1974—93, 1999—2002. Mem. IIE Fulbright Screening Com., 1973, 91. Author: Portable German Tutor, 1970; editor: (with Buehne and Pinto) Helen Adolf Festschrift, 1968; editor: (with T. Beebee and S. Cerf) The Speech of Richard von Weizsacker on May 8, 1985; editorial staff German Quar, 1976-83; contbr. articles to profl. jours. and reference works. Cubmaster Pine Tree council Boy Scouts Am., Brunswick, 1974. NDEA grantee, 1966-67; Bowdoin Mellon grantee, 1977, 84 Mem. AAUP, Am. Assn. Tchrs. German, MLA. Independent. Home: 37 Meadowbrook Rd Brunswick ME 04011-3421 Office: Bowdoin Coll Dept German Brunswick ME 04011 E-mail: jhodge@bowdoin.edu.

HODGE, KATHLEEN O'CONNELL, academic administrator; b. Balt., Dec. 26, 1948; d. William Walsh and Loretto Marie (Wittek) O'Connell; m. Vern Milton Hodge, Apr. 8, 1972; children: Shea, Ryan. BS, Calif. State U., Fullerton, 1971, MS, 1975; EdD, U. So. Calif., 2002; postgrad., U. Calif., Irvine, 1977-84. Cert. marriage and family therapist. Counselor Saddleback Coll., Mission Viejo, Calif., 1975-87, prof. of psychology, speech, 1975—2002, dean of continuing edn., cmty. svcs., dean emeritus inst., 1987-95, vice chancellor, 1995—, acting chancellor, 1998-99. Accreditation liaison officer Saddleback Coll., 1986; mem. adv. bd. Nat. Issues Forum, Calif., 1985, 87, Saddleback Coll. Community Services, 1984, Access and Aspirations U. Calif., Irvine, 1979. Author: (workbook) Assessment of Life Learning, 1978; editor emeritus: Flavors in Time Anthology of Literature, 1992. Mem. Calif. Community Coll. Counselors Assn. (region coord. 1987), Calif. Tchrs. Assn., Am. Assn. Women Community and Jr. Colls., Assn. Marriage Family Therapists, C.C. Educators of Older Adults (pres. 1990-92). Democrat. Roman Catholic. Avocations: skiing, reading, political advocacy. Home: 4011 Calle Juno San Clemente CA 92673-2616 Office: South Orange County C C Dist 28000 Marguerite Pky Mission Viejo CA 92692-3635

HODGE, MARK LOUIS, music educator, conductor; b. Buffalo, Apr. 9, 1967; s. William Louis and Marjorie Francis Hodge; m. Rachelle Rene Reed, May 26, 1990; children: Hayden Lucas, Hailey Rene. BA in Music Edn., U. Ariz., 1994. Cert. tchr. Ariz., 1994. Band dir. Barry Goldwater H.S., Phoenix, 1994—2001; band dir., orch. dir. Ironwood Ridge H.S., Oro Valley, 2001—. State marching festival coord. Ariz. Band and Orch. Directors Assn., 1997—2001. Dir.(assoc conductor): Casas Orch. Staff sgt. USAF, 1986—90. Decorated Good Conduct medal. Mem.: Ariz. Music Educators Assn. (v.p. H.S. activities 2003—), Music Educator Nat. Conf. Conservative. Avocation: music. Office: Ironwood Ridge High Sch 2475 W Naranja Dr Oro Valley AZ 85742 Home Fax: 520-696-3999 Office Fax: 520-696-3999. Personal E-mail: mhodge@amphi.com. E-mail: mhodge@amphi.com.

HODGE, PATRICIA ANDREA, archivist, consultant; b. Pitts. d. James Cormack and Isabel (McAuley) H. Student, McGill U., 1957; BA in English Carlow (Mt. Mercy) Coll., 1957; MA in English, Duquesne U., 1964; MSLS, Villanova U., 1972; postgrad., NYU, 1966-67, U. Colo., 1966-67; advanced cert. archival adminstrn./mgmt., U. Pitts., 1991. Elem., secondary sch. tchr. Pitts.; assoc. prof. Carlow Coll., chair. dept. English, 1967-70, coord. libr. svcs. 1972-75; co-dir. hosp. wide edn. dept. Holy Cross Hosp., Ft. Lauderdale, Fla. 1976; libr. dir. Trinity Coll., Burlington, Vt., 1976-82; dir. libr. Caldwell (N.J.) Coll., 1983-89; dir. archives Sisters of Mercy, Pitts., 1989—. Archives cons mgmt./adminstrn., 1990—; exec. bd. mem./treas. Women's Nat. Book Assn. 1977-80, co-founder Pitts. chpt., 1976; trustee Pitts. Regional Libr. Ctr. 1972-76. Book reviewer Review for Religious, 1975, 77, 83, 92. Bd. dirs Essex-Hudson Regional Libr. Cooperative, Burlington, 1980-82; vol. Western Pa. Hist. Soc., Pitts., 1983. Newspaper fellow, 1960. Mem. Archivists Congregations Women Religious (exec. dir. 1993-97, newsletter editor 1994-97, bd mem. 1999-2002), Soc. Am. Archivists, Mid-Atlantic Regional Archives Conf Avocations: writing, editing, travel, music, art. Office: Sisters of Mercy of the Am 3333 5th Ave Pittsburgh PA 15213-3109

HODGE, PATRICIA MARIE CASCIO, nurse practitioner in psychiatry; b Bklyn., Nov. 1, 1955; d. Vincent J. and Mary (Farrell) Cascio; children: George E. IV, Kristen Lenore. AAS in Nursing with Distinction, Suffolk County C.C. 1981; BS in Cmty. Health with distinction, St. Joseph's Coll., 1987; postgrad. Inst. Pastoral Formation, Rockville Centre, N.Y.; MS Nurse Practitioner in Psychiatry, Stony Brook U., 1997. Cert. health counseling; cert. clin. specialist in adult psychiat. mental health nursing, chem. addictions registered nurse. Day nursing supr. Sisters of St. Joseph, Maria Regina Convent, Brentwood, N.Y. 1986-90; psychiat. nurse mental health div. Cath. Charities, Diocese Rockville Centre (N.Y.), 1990—. Mem. Network of N.Y. Clin. Specialists in Psychiatric/Mental Health Nursing, The Nurse Practitioner Assn. of Long Island, Sigma Theta Tau Internat. E-mail: phodge111@aol.com.

HODGE, PAUL WILLIAM, astronomer, educator; b. Seattle, Nov. 8, 1934; s Paul Hartman and Frances H.; m. Ann Uran, June 14, 1962; children: Gordon Erik, Sandra. BS, Yale U., 1956; PhD, Harvard U., 1960. Lectr. Harvard 1960-61; asst. prof. astronomy U. Calif. at Berkeley, 1961-65; asso. prof. U Wash., Seattle, 1965-69, prof. astronomy, 1969—, chmn. Astronomy dept 1987-91; fellow Mt. Wilson, Palomar Obs., Calif. Inst. Tech., Pasadena 1960-61; physicist Smithsonian Astrophys. Obs., Cambridge, Mass., 1956-74 Author: Solar System Astrophysics, 1964, Galaxies and Cosmology, 1966, The Large Magellanic Cloud, 1967, Concepts of the Universe, 1969, Galaxies, 1972 Concepts of Contemporary Astronomy, 1974, The Small Magellanic Cloud 1977, An Atlas of the Andromeda Galaxy, 1981, Interplanetary Dust, 1982, The Universe of Galaxies, 1985, Galaxies, 1986, The Andromeda Galaxy, 1992 Meteorite Craters and Impact Structures of the World, 1994, An Atlas of Local Group Galaxies, 1999, Higher Than Everest: An Adventurer's Guide to the Solar System, 2001, Galaxies and the Cosmic Frontier, 2003; editor: The Astron. Jour., 1984—. Mem. Am. Astron. Soc. (v.p. 1990-93), Internat. Astron. Union, Astron. Soc. Pacific (v.p. 1974-75), Korean Astron. Soc., Euro-asian Astron. Soc. (hon.). Office: U Wash Dept Astronomy Box 351580 Seattle WA 98195-1580

HODGE, PHILIP GIBSON, JR., mechanical and aerospace engineering educator; b. New Haven, Nov. 9, 1920; s. Philip Gibson and Muriel (Miller) H.; m. Thea Drell, Jan. 3, 1943; children: Susan E., Philip T., Elizabeth M. AB

Antioch Coll., 1943; PhD, Brown U., 1949. Rsch. asst. Brown U., 1947-49, asso., 1949; asst. prof. math. UCLA, 1949-53; assoc. prof. applied mechanics Poly. Inst. Bklyn., 1953-56, prof., 1956-57; prof. mechanics Ill. Inst. Tech., 1957-71, U. Minn., Mpls., 1971-91, prof. emeritus, 1991—. Russell Severance Springer vis. prof. U. Calif., 1976; vis. prof. emeritus Stanford U., 1993—; sec. U.S. nat. com. Theoretical and Applied Mechanics, 1982-2000. Author: 5 books, the most recent being Limit Analysis of Rotationally Symmetric Plates and Shells, 1963, Continuum Mechanics, 1971; also numerous rsch. articles in profl. jour.; tech. editor Jour. Applied Mechanics, 1971-76. Recipient Disting. Service award Am. Acad. Mechanics, 1984; Karman medal ASCE, 1985. NSF sr. postdoctoral fellow, 1963 Mem. NAE, ASME (hon., Worcester Reed Warner medal 1975, ASME medal 1987, Daniel C. Drucker medal 2000), Internat. Union Theoretical and Applied Mechanics (del. 1982-2000, asst. treas. 1984-92, mem. at large 2000—). Home: 580 Arastradero Rd Apt 701 Palo Alto CA 94306-3948 E-mail: phodge1@stanford.edu.

HODGE, ROBERT JOSEPH, retail executive; b. St. Louis, July 5, 1937; s. Joseph Edward and Alberta Marie (Oehler) H.; m. Carmen Maria Villalobos, Sept. 1, 1960; children: Ralph, Robert, Carmen. BS in Indsl. Relations, St. Louis U., 1959. Meat dept. merchandiser Kroger Co., Cleve., 1972-74, corp. v.p. deli/bakery Cin., 1981-83, v.p. Atlanta div., 1983-85, meat merchandiser, 1977-80, v.p. gateway region, 1985-87; v.p. meat ops. Ralph's Grocery Co., Los Angeles, 1974-77; gen. mgr. Super X Drug, Melbourne, Fla., 1980-81; sr. v.p. Dillon Co., Hutchinson, Kans., 1987-89; sr. v.p. merchandising, manufacturing Kroger Co., Cin., 1989-92, pres. Cin./Dayton mktg. area, 1992—. Sgt. U.S. Army, res., 1959-66. Avocations: golf, skiing. Home: 614 Watchcove Ct Cincinnati OH 45230-3777 Office: Kroger Co 150 Tri County Pkwy Cincinnati OH 45246-3246

HODGE, VERNE ANTONIO, retired chief judge; b. St. Thomas, V.I., Nov. 16, 1933; s. John Wesley Hodge and Idalia Victoria Stout; children: Verne Jr., Bridget, Teresa. BS magna cum laude, Hampton U., 1956; JD cum laude, Howard U., 1969. Bar: V.I. 1969, D.C. 1969, U.S. Ct. Appeals (3d cir.) 1970, U.S. Supreme Ct. 1973. Internal auditor, internal revenue agt. V.I. Govt., 1958-61; pub. accountant, comptroller Mannassah Busline, Inc., St. Thomas, 1961-65; bus. mgr., personnel dir. V.I. Dept. Pub. Works, 1965-66; private practice law V.I., 1969-73; atty. gen., 1973-76; chief judge V.I. Territorial Ct., St. Thomas, 1976-99, ret., 1999. Past chmn. Eastern region Nat. Assn. Attys. Gen.; Mem. V.I. Indsl. Incentive Bd., 1963-64, V.I. Bd. Elections, 1964-66 Author: The Need for Constitutional Courts in U.S. Territories, 1968, The Mirror Theory and Its Effects, 1969. Served to 1st lt., inf. U.S. Army, 1956-58. Recipient Am. Jurisprudence awards in state, local and fed. taxation, 1968-69, certificate in advanced income tax law Internal Revenue Service, 1960, award of merit 9th Inf. Div. U.S. Army, 1958 Mem. Am. Judges Assn., Am., Nat., V.I. bar assns. Democrat. Lutheran. *Nothing is so complicated that it cannot be simplified by hard work.*

HODGELL, MURLIN RAY, university dean; b. Mankato, Kans., Jan. 6, 1924; s. Ray Darius and Lora Henrietta (Overman) H.; m. Billie RoJean Seward, July 20, 1947; children— Janet, Kristen, Kevin. BS, Kans. State U., 1949; MS, U. Ill., 1952; M.R.P., Cornell U., 1956, PhD, 1959. Licensed architect, engr. and planner. Prof. U. Ill., 1950-54, Kans. State U., 1957-63; chmn. dept. city and regional planning Rutgers U., 1963-64; dir. Sch. Architecture, U. Nebr., 1964-69; dean Coll. Environ. Design, U. Okla., 1969—, dean emeritus; prin. Hodgell Assocs. in Architecture, Engring. and Planning. City planning dir., Manhattan, Kans., 1957-58, planning commr., 1959-63; dir. Kans. State U. Center Community Devel., 1959-63 Author: Contemporary Farmhouses, 1956, Forgotten Millions, 1959, Zoning, 1957. Trustee Weigal Found., Leonard Bailey Found. Served to lt. (j.g.) USNR, 1943-45. Named Kan. Outstanding Young Man of Yr. Kans. Jr. C. of C., 1959, Man of Yr. Manhattan, Kans., 1960; recipient citation distinguished community service Lane-Bryant Found., 1960 Fellow AIA, ASCE; mem. Am. Inst. Cert. Planners, Am. Soc. Planning Ofcls., Assn. Collegiate Schs. Architecture, Asso. Schs. Constrn. Home: 5800 Highland Hills Ln Colleyville TX 76034-5734

HODGEN, MAURICE DENZIL, management consultant, retired education educator; b. Timaru, New Zealand, Aug. 7, 1929; s. William Arnold and Lindsey Frances (Neill) H.; m. Rhona Brandstater, June 20, 1951; children: Philip Denzil, Victoria Anne. Student, Avondale Coll., Cooranbong, Australia, 1948-50; BS, Pacific Union Coll., 1953; MA, Columbia U., 1956, Ed.D., 1958. Asst. prof. La Sierra Coll., Riverside, Calif., 1958-64; lectr. Solusi Coll., Bulawayo, Zimbabwe, 1964-66; dir. tchr. edn. Helderberg Coll., Somerset W., S. Africa, 1966-68; assoc. prof. Sch. Edn., Loma Linda U., Calif., 1968—72, prof., 1972—84, dean Grad. Sch., 1978—87, coop. faculty, 1985—88; adminstr. fin. devel. Claremont (Calif.) Grad. U., 1987-93; mgmt. cons., 1999—. Exec. dir. Cmty. Found. of Riverside County, 1993-99. Served with U.S. Army, 1953-55.

HODGES, ANN, actress, singer, dancer; b. Elizabethtown, Ky., June 24; d. Henry Lavely and Margaret Rhodes (Lewis) H.; m. Richard Angleine; 1 child, Michael Christian Angleine; m. Barry C. Tuttle, Sept. 16, 1969 (div. 1972). Cert., registered yoga alliance tchr.; ordained min. Congl. Ch. Practical Theology. Yoga instr., Tampa, St. Petersburg, Safety Harbor, Clearwater, Fla., Under the Live Oak, Casa Bella Vista. Pvt. instr. Yoga, Fla. Appeared in (Broadway shows) No Strings, The Rothchilds, Heathen, (off-Broadway shows) The Boys From Syracuse, There Goes The Old Ballgame, Bella, (TV shows) The Jackie Gleason Show, The Steve Allen Show, The Ed Sullivan Show, Bell Telephone Hour, Ellery Queen, Omnibus, The Vic Damone Show, The Big Record, (TV spls.) Once Upon A Mattress, The G.M. Spectacular, The Esso Spectacular, (motion pictures) The Cardinal, The New Life Style, Oldsmobile, (plays) Applause, The Best Little Whorehouse in Texas, Gypsy,(leading roles in plays) Hello Dolly!, Sugar Babies, Chicago, Can Can, Sweet Charity, Mame, Damn Yankees, See How They Run, Catch Me If You Can., Legends!, I Ought to Be in Pictures, How the Other Half Loves, Pajama Tops, The Last of the Red Hot Lovers, Pal Joey, Cole Porter Reveiw, Gone with the Wind (role of Belle Watling in American Premiere Production), The Greenwich Village Scandals of 1923; also many commls., voice overs and indsls.; performer numerous charities including Am. Cancer Soc., Am. Heart Assn., Handicapped, Abused Wives and Children; star performer Gasparilla Coronation, 1991, guest performer Fla. Orch. at Clearwater Jazz Festival. Yoga instr. Safety Harbor Spa, Don CeSar, Harbour Island Athletic Club, Casa Bella Vista. Named the Queen of Mus. Theatre by the Press, one of Tampa Bay's top achievers. Mem.: Suncoast Yoga Tchrs. Assn. (past pres., bd. dirs.). Avocations: yoga, swimming, horse back riding, piano playing, embroidery.

HODGES, CARROLL BROADUS, retired army officer; b. Tulsa, Okla., Jan. 3, 1914; m. Harriet Eloise; children: Keith, Howard. BA, Okla. Bapt. U., Shawnee, 1935; MS, U. Okla., 1936; postgrad., Duke U., 1937-38, U. Edinburgh, Scotland, 1938-39; PhD, U. Munich, Germany, 1948; LLD (hon.), Chosun U., Korea, 1973; ScD (hon.), Chung-Ang U., Korea, 1974. Instr./dean of men Anatolia Coll., Salonika, Greece, 1939-40; asst. to pres./instr. Judson Coll., Marion, Ala., 1940-41; commd. 2d lt. U.S. Army, 1942, advanced through grades to col., instr. OCS, U. Fla., 1942-43, adminstr. Economic Divsn., Mil. Govt. Hdqs., U.S. Forces Frankfort, Germany, 1945-46, ops. officer U.S. Army/USAF CIC Munich, 1947-50, chief pers. rsch. U.S. Army Rsch. & Devel. Command Washington, 1951-56, asst. chief, staff pers., Hdqs. UN Command/U.S. Forces Japan Tokyo, 1956-60, chief Pers. Mgmt. & Systems Devel. Group, R&D Command Washington, 1960-62, dir. pers. tng. & adminstrn., U.S. Combat Devels. Command Ft. Belvoir, Va., 1962-64, chief of staff, Korea Mil. Adv. Group Seoul, 1964-69, ret., 1969; mgmt. cons. Kelly & Assocs., Ft. Pierce, Fla., 1969-72; dir. Am.-Korean Found., Seoul, 1972-79. Internat. rels. advisor to comdr. U.S. Forces, Seoul, 1979-85. Mem. exec. com. USO Coun. of Korea; dir. Korean-Am. Assn.; com. chmn. Seoul Internat. Rotary Club; spl. mem. Am. C. of C., Korea Advisor to Pres., Korea Vet.'s Assn.; dep. dir. Open Heart Surgery program, Korea; advisor Pearl S. Buck Found. for Amerasian Children. Awarded Legion of Merit medals, 1962, 1964; apptd. Am. spl. advisor to Japanese Olympic Planning Com., 1957-60; awarded prime min.'s citation as one of 50 Ams. making the most significant contributions to U.S.-Korea rels. during past 100 yrs.; recipient Korea Presdl. medal for disting. svc. to veterans of Korea and Vietnam; apptd. hon. col., U.S. Army Mil. Adv. Group, upon 100th anniversary of U.S.-Korea rels.; featured in book A Degree of Difference, 1983, as one of 10 most disting. grads. of Okla. Bapt. U. since its founding in 1912; honored by erection of bronze statue by Girls' Comml. H.S. for major contributions to Korea-wide edn.; nominated by Hdqs. U.S. Forces Command, for the Assn. of the U.S. Army's Exceptional Svc. award for contributions to the Command's mission, the cmty. and U.S.-Korea rels., 1994. Mem. Assn. of the U.S. Army. Home: 972 Fostoria Dr Melbourne FL 32940-1512 Fax: 321-253-6014. E-mail: chodges4@cfl.rr.com.

HODGES, DAVID ALBERT, electrical engineering educator; b. Hackensack, N.J., Aug. 25, 1937; s. Albert R. and Katherine (Rogers) H.; m. Susan Spongberg, June 5, 1965; children: Jennifer, Alan. B.E.E., Cornell U., 1960; MS, U. Calif., Berkeley, 1961, PhD in Elec. Engring, 1966. Mem. tech. staff Bell Telephone Labs., Murray Hill, N.J., 1966-69, head system elements research dept. Holmdel, N.J., 1969-70; asso. prof. dept. elec. engring. and computer scis U. Calif., Berkeley, 1970-74, prof., 1974-98, chmn. dept., 1989-90, dean Coll. Engring., 1990-96, prof. Grad. Sch., 1998—. Contbr. articles to profl. jours.; patentee in field. Fellow AAAS, IEEE.; mem. NAE. Office: Univ Calif Coll Engring 516 Cory Hl Berkeley CA 94720-0001

HODGES, DEWEY HARPER, aerospace engineer, educator; b. Clarksville, Tenn., May 18, 1948; s. Plummer Maxwell Sr. and Etha Maude (Harper) H.; m. Margaret Elin Jones, Aug. 14, 1971; children: Timothy, Jonathan, David, Philip, Benjamin. BS in Aerospace Engring., U. Tenn., 1969; MS in Aero. and Astronautical Engring., Stanford U., 1970, PhD in Aero. & Astronautical Engring., 1973. Rsch. scientist U.S. Army Aeroflight Dynamics Directorate, Ames Rsch. Ctr., Moffett Field, Calif., 1970-80, sr. rsch. scientist, theoretical group leader, 1980-86; prof. aerospace engring. Ga. Inst. Tech., Atlanta, 1986—. Instr. No. Calif. Bible Coll., San Jose, 1974-86; lectr. Stanford U., 1980-86; guest rsch. scientist DLR Inst. Structural Mechanics, Braunschweig, Fed. Republic of Germany, 1984. Contbr. more than 230 articles to profl. jours. and conf. procs.; co-patentee hingeless helicopter rotor with improved stability, 1976, real time missle guidance system, 1995. Elder Christian Cmty. Ch., San Jose, 1980-86, Mt. Paran Ch., Atlanta, 1992-94, Chalcedon Presbyn. Ch., Cumming, Ga., 2003—. Fellow AIAA; mem. ASCE, ASME, Am. Helicopter Soc., Am. Acad. Mechanics, Sigma Xi, Tau Beta Pi, Pi Tau Sigma. Republican. Presbyterian. Home: 1172 Branch Water Ct Atlanta GA 30338-4026 Office: Ga Inst Tech Sch Aerospace Engring Atlanta GA 30332-0001 E-mail: dewey.hodges@ae.gatech.edu. *We know about the wise men who sought the Lord Jesus at His birth. I believe that wise men still seek Him and that His promise of abundant life to those who follow Him is still being fulfilled today.*

HODGES, ELIZABETH SWANSON, educational consultant, tutor; b. Anoka, Minn., Apr. 7, 1924; d. Henry Otto and Louise Isabel (Holiday) Swanson; m. Allen Hodges, June 27, 1944; children: Nancy Elizabeth, Susan Kathleen, Jane Ellen, Sara Louise. BA cum laude, Regis Coll., Denver, 1966; postgrad., U. No. Colo., 1966-79, Valdosta State U., 1979-81. Cert. secondary edn., hosp./homebound, learning disabilities, Colo., Ga., Ariz. Vol. emergency St. Anthony's Hosp., Denver, 1960-64; v.p., tutor St. Elizabeth's Adult Tutorial, Denver, 1964-69; hosp./homebound tchr. Liberty County Sch. System, Hinesville, Ga., 1979-87; ednl. tutor Colo. River Indian Tribes, Parker, Ariz., 1986-87; vol. Twin Cities Community Hosp., Templeton, Calif., 1987-89, Guardian Ad Litem Cir. Ct. 5th Dist. Fla., 1992—. Munroe Regional Med. Ctr., Ocala, Fla., 1991-92; cons., tutor Sylvan Learning Ctr., Ocala, 1990—. Vol. tutor Blessed Trinity Sch., Ocala, 1996—. Democrat. Roman Catholic. Avocations: swimming, reading, sewing, piano, gardening. Home and Office: 101 Clyde Morris Blvd #221 Ormond Beach FL 32174

HODGES, FREDERICK MANSFIELD, historian; b. San Francisco, Dec. 7, 1961; s. Jack David and Carolyn Clewley H. BA, U. Calif., Berkeley, 1991; DPhil, Oxford U., 2000. Postdoctoral rsch. scholar Yale U., New Haven, 2001—02. Scholar Magdalen Coll. Author: Sweet Dreams: A Pediatrician's Secrets for Baby's Good Night's Sleep, 2000; editor: Male and Female Circumcision: Medical, Legal, and Ethical Considerations in Pediatric Practice, 1999, What Your Doctor May Not Tell You about Circumcision, 2002; co-author: Sexual Mutilations: A Human Tragedy, 1997. McKinnon scholar Magdalen Coll., Oxford, 1999-2000. Home: PO Box 5815 Berkeley CA 94705-0815 E-mail: frederick.hodges@cal.berkeley.edu.

HODGES, JIM, former governor; b. Nov. 19, 1956; married; 2 children: Luke, Sam. BBA, U. S.C., 1979, JD, 1982. Rep. Dist. 45 (Lancaster County) S.C. House of Reps., 1986—97, chmn. house judiciary com., 1992-94, chmn. joint com. judicial screening, 1993-94, minority leader of house, 1995-98; gov. State of S.C., 1999—2003. Sec., gen. counsel The Springs Co. Named. Legislator of Yr., S.C. C. of C., 1993; recipient Compleat Lawyer Silver medallion U. S.C. Sch. of Law, 1994. Mem. Phi Beta Kappa. Democrat.*

HODGES, JOT HOLIVER, JR., retired lawyer, business executive; b. Archer City, Tex., Nov. 16, 1932; s. Jot Holiver and Lola Mae (Hurd) H.; m. Virginia Cordray Pardue, June 11, 1955; children: Deborah, Jot, Darlene. BS, BBA, Sam Houston State U., 1954; JD, U. Tex., 1957. Bar: Tex. 1958, U.S. Dist. Ct. (so. dist.) Tex. 1958, U.S. Ct. Appeals (5th cir.) 1958. Asst. atty. gen. State of Tex., Austin, 1958-60; chmn. bd. Presidio Devel. Corp., Missouri City, Tex., 1971. Organizer, founder 3 banks, several corps. and ltd. partnerships; residential and comml. real estate developer. Contbr. articles to legal, med., pharm., and hosp. jours. Capt. U.S. Army. Mem. Houston Club, Quail Valley Country Club. Home: 3527 Thunderbird St Missouri City TX 77459-2445 Office: 3660 Hampton Dr Ste 200 Missouri City TX 77459-3044

HODGES, KENNETH STUART, financial consultant; b. Bronx, N.Y., Nov. 2, 1955; s. Arthur Stuart and Arlene Marilyn (Hemme) H.; m. Diane Jean Lama, Aug. 20, 1977; children: Jonathan Stuart, Erika Jean. BBA, Iona Coll., 1977; MS in Adminstrn., Western Conn. State U., 1987. CPA, Conn. Staff acct. Coopers and Lybrand CPAs, Stamford, Conn., 1977-79; sr. acct. U.S. Surg. Corp., Norwalk, Conn., 1979-80; supr. accts. receivable Howmet Turbine Components, Greenwich, Conn., 1980-84; mgr. acctg. Guinness Import Co., Stamford, 1985-86; contr. Fujitsu Imaging Systems Am., Danbury, Conn., 1986-90; dir. fin. Ultimate Data Systems, Wilton, Conn., 1990-91; contr. Prentice Hall Legal & Fin. Svcs., N.Y.C., 1991-93, Mal Dunn Assoc. Inc., Croton Falls, N.Y., 1994-95, The Patterson Club, Inc., Fairfield, Conn., 1995-97; v.p., CFO Shared Techs. Comms., Hartford, Conn., 1997-99; CFO Discount Trophy & Co., Vernon, Conn., 1999-2000; fin. cons. Parson Group, N.Y.C., 2000—. Mem. Am. Inst. CPAs, Conn. Soc. CPAs. Republican. Avocations: golf, tennis, boating, swimming, cycling. Office: Parson Group LLC 70 E 55th St 5th Fl New York NY 10022 E-mail: k.s.hodges@att.net.

HODGES, LOUIS WENDELL, religion educator; b. Eupora, Miss., Jan. 24, 1933; s. John Calvin and Lorene (Phillips) H.; m. Helen Elizabeth Davis, June 6, 1954; children: John David, George Kenneth. BA, Millsaps Coll., 1954; BD, Duke U., 1957, PhD, 1960. Ordained to ministry Meth. Ch., 1958. Asst. prof. religion Washington and Lee U., Lexington, Va., 1960-64, assoc. prof., 1964-67, prof., 1967-87, Fletcher Otey Thomas prof. Bible, 1987-97, Knight prof. ethics in journalism, 1997—. Vis. prof. U. Va., 1967-71; vis. disting. prof. applied and profl. ethics Ohio U., 1990. Co-author: The Christian and His Decisions, 1969; editor Social Responsibility: Bus., Journalism, Law, Medicine, 1974-98, Ethics in Journalism, 1998—; mem. editl bd. Jour. Mass. Media Ethics 1988—, Newspaper Rsch. Jour., Media Ethics; prodr., anchor TV program series, 1984. Chmn. Coun. on Human Rels., Lexington, 1965-68; mem. Va. adv. com. U.S. Commn. on Civil Rights, Richmond, 1968-74; founder, pres. Rockbridge Area Housing Corp., Lexington, 1968-74; 1st v.p. bd. dirs. Lexington-Rockbridge United Fund, 1972. Gurney Harris Kearns fellow Duke U., 1958-60, Univ. Ctr. in Va. fellow, 1965-66, The Hastings Ctr. fellow, 1985-99, Fulbright lectr. journalism, India, 1995-96; named to Va. Comms. Hall of Fame, 2003. Mem. Assn. for Edn. in Journalism and Mass Comm., Soc. Profl. Journalists (mem. nat. ethics com.), Orgn. News Ombudsmen. Democrat. Home: 688 Still House Dr Lexington VA 24450-6319 Office: Washington and Lee U Dept Journalism Lexington VA 24450 E-mail: lhodges@wlu.edu.

HODGES, MARGARET MOORE, author, educator; b. Indpls., July 26, 1911; d. Arthur Carlisle and Anna Marie (Mason) Moore; m. Fletcher Hodges, Jr., Sept. 10, 1932; children: Fletcher III, Arthur Carlisle, John Andrews. AB with honors, Vassar Coll., 1932; MLS; Carnegie Libr. Staff scholar, Carnegie Inst. Tech., 1958. Lectr. U. Pitts. Grad. Sch. Library and Info. Services, 1964-68, asst. prof., 1968-72, assoc. prof., 1972-75, prof., 1975-77, emeritus, 1977— (Children's libr., radio and TV storyteller) Carnegie Library Pitts., 1953—64, (story specialist) Pitts. Pub. Schs., 1964—68, (storyteller) WQED Schs. Svcs. Dept NIT network., 1965—; author: (juvenile books) One Little Drum, 1958, What's for Lunch Charley?, 1961, Club Against Keats, 1962, Tell It Again, 1963, Secret in the Woods, 1963, Wave, 1964, Hatching of Joshua Cobb, 1967, Constellation, a Shakespeare Anthology, 1968, Sing Out, Charley!, 1968, Lady Queen Anne, 1969, Making of Joshua Cobb, 1971, Gorgon's Head, 1972, Hopkins of the Mayflower, 1972, Fire Bringer, 1972, Persephone and the Springtime, 1973, Baldur and the Mistletoe, 1974, Freewheeling of Joshua Cobb, 1974, Knight Prisoner, The Tale of Sir Thomas Malory and His King Arthur, 1976, The High Riders, 1980, The Little Humpbacked Horse, 1980, The Avenger, 1982, If You Had a Horse, 1984, Saint George and the Dragon, 1984, Making a Difference, 1989, The Voice of the Great Bell, 1989, The Arrow and the Lamp, 1989, The Kitchen Knight, 1990, Buried Moon, 1990, Brother Francis and the Friendly Beasts, 1991, Saint Jerome and the Lion, 1991, Hauntings, 1991, Don Quixote and Sancho Panza, 1992, Of Swords and Sorcerers, 1993, St. Patrick and and the Peddler, 1993, The Hero of Bremen, 1993, Hidden in Sand, 1994, Gulliver in Lilliput, 1995, Comus, 1996, Molly Limbo, 1996; co-editor: Elva S. Smith's The History of Children's Literature, 1980, The True Tale of Johnny Appleseed, 1997, Silent Night, the Song and Its Story, 1997, Up the Chimney, 1998, Joan of Arc, the Lily Maid, 1999, The Boy Who Drew Cats, 2002, The Legend of St. Christopher, 2002. Mem. ALA (Newbery-Caldecott com. 1960), Pa. Library Assn., Am. Assn. Library Schs., Pitts. Bibliophiles, Zonta Internat., Distinguished Daus. Pa. Republican. Episcopalian. Home: Longwood at Oakmont 48 Garden Ct Verona PA 15147-3852 Office: U Pitts Bellefield Ave Pittsburgh PA 15260

HODGES, MITCHELL, computer executive; b. Fayetteville, N.C., Mar. 10, 1959; s. Eddie Jr. and Phyliss Marie (Dill) H.; Ilene Michelle Cohen; m. Aug. 16, 1986. BS in Philosophy, Randolph-Macon Coll., 1981; MS in Info. Systems, Nova U., 1992. Applications engr. Anderson Jacobson, Inc., Gaithersburg, Md., 1983-85; sr. product engr. Baxter Sys./Compucare, 1985-89; PC coord. Racal-Datacom, Sunrise, Fla., 1988-92; mgr. global electronic messaging W.R. Grace & Co., Boca Raton, Fla., 1992-95; mgr. engring. Delta Tech., Inc., Atlanta, 1995—. Mem. Alpha Psi Omega (chpt. pres. 1980-81), Theta Chi (chpt. chaplan 1979-80), Omnicron Delta Kappa. Republican. Home: 976 Oakleigh Manor Ct Powder Springs GA 30127-4941

HODGES, NORMAN, retired district judge; b. Silver City, N. Mex., Aug. 5, 1925; s. Joseph William and Eva Irene H.; m. Tressie Lee Murdock Weiland, Oct. 5, 1963; 1 stepchild, William V. Weiland. BA, U. N. Mex., 1947, BS, 1948, LLB, 1951, JD, 1968. Bar: N. Mex. 1951, U.S. Dist. Ct. N. Mex. 1952, U.S. Ct. Mil. Appeals 1960, U.S. Supreme Ct. 1960. Ptnr. Hodges, Hodges & Hodges, Attorneys, Silver City, 1951-52; assoc. H. Veale Payne, Lordsburg, N. Mex., 1952-56; dist. attorney Grant, Luna, Hidalgo Counties, Silver City, 1957-63; dist. judge 6th Judicial Dist., Silver City, 1963-86, retired, 1986—. Mem. N. Mex. Supreme Ct. Children's Ct. Rules com., Albuquerque, 1970-73. Capt. USN, 1942-99. Recipient Judge of Yr. award N. Mex. State Bar Assn., Albuquerque, 1982. Mem. Retired Officers Assn., Copper Crest Country Club (bd. dirs. 1965-69), Elks Club, Sigma Chi (pres. 1944). Democrat. Protestant. Avocations: books, southwestern america. Home: PO Box 390 Silver City NM 88062-0390

HODGES, RALPH B. state supreme court justice; b. Anadarko, Okla., Aug. 4, 1930; s. Dewey E. and Pearl R. (Hodges) H.; m. Janelle H.; children: Shari, Mark, Randy. BA, Okla. Baptist U.; LL.B., U. Okla. Atty. Bryan County, Okla., 1956-58; judge Okla. Dist. Ct., 1959-65; justice Okla. Supreme Ct., Oklahoma City, 1965—, chief justice, 1977—78, 1993—94. Office: Okla Supreme Ct State Capital Bldg Rm 200 Oklahoma City OK 73105*

HODGES, SHARON GREEN, editor, consultant, writer; b. Miami, Fla., Aug. 16, 1944; d. Charles Purrington and Ruth Mary (Hall) Green; m. William Clark Hodges, June 22, 1966; children: Michael David, Matthew Ryan. BA, U. Miss., 1966; postgrad., San Diego State U., 1969, Fla. Atlantic U., 1988—90. Writer, Deerfield Beach, Fla., 1980—84; tchr. Deerfield Beach H.S., 1988—90; rsch. asst. Fla. Atlantic U., Boca Raton, 1989—90; writer The Apelian-DuBois Group, Boca Raton, 1997—98; editl. dir. Clover Devel. Strategies, Inc., Boca Raton, 1998—2000, Backbone Celebrity Classic, Miami Lakes, Fla., 2001—02; editor-in-chief The BACKBONE Chronicles, 2002 . Editl. cons. Horses and the Handicapped, Boca Raton, 1982—85, Boy Scouts Am., Miami Lakes, 1984—, Broward County Schs., Ft. Lauderdale, Fla., 1986—90, Aid to Victims of Domestic Abuse, Inc., Delray Beach, Fla., 1994—97, Jr. Achievement South Fla., Inc., Pompano Beach, 1996—98, Broward Sheriff's Office, Ft. Lauderdale, 1997—99, Patrons of the Arts of the Vatican Mus., Vatican City, 1999, South Fla. Forensic Assn., Ft. Lauderdale, 1999. Designer, editor: newsletter The Scouter, 1997—2000 (award of excellence Fla. Printing Assn., 1998), author, designer, project dir.: Champions of Free Enterprise, 1996—98, author, designer: Student Handbook, 1998, author, designer, project dir.: A Place of Our Own, 1999, A Call to Greatness, 2000, As Far as the Eye Can See, 2001, A Matter of Importance, 2001, A Mission of Love, 2002, The Samaritan Fund, 2000 (Best Booklet, Fla. Printing Assn., 2000), The Disciple Fund, 2000 (Judges' award Fla. Printing Assn., 2000). Mem. Boy Scouts of America's James E. West Soc., 2003—; mem. exec. com., mem. at large South Fla. Coun.-Boy Scouts Am., 1998—2002; chmn. Learning Disabilities Early Identification Program Broward County Schs., Ft. Lauderdale, 1976—77; co-founder Second Chance Club, North Ridge Med. Ctr., Ft. Lauderdale, 1977; adult leader South Fla. Coun. Boy Scouts Am., Miami Lakes, 1979—94; treas., pres. Middle Sch. Band Parents Assn., Deerfield Beach, 1984—85; pres. Friends of the Libr., Deerfield Beach, 1984—86; sec. High Sch. Band Parents Assn., Deerfield Beach, 1987—89, pres., 1987—90; chmn. Libr. Adv. Bd., Deerfield Beach, 1988—89; prin. mem. textbook evaluation com. Broward County Schs., Ft. Lauderdale, 1988—89; pub. rels. Poinciana Women's Rep. Club of Fla. Fedn. Rep. Women, Boca Raton, 1994—98; exec. bd. mem. South Fla. Coun. Boy Scouts Am., Miami Lakes, 1985—; adv. bd. mem. Broward County Schs., Ft. Lauderdale, 1996—98; mem. campaign com. City Mayoral Election, Boca Raton, 1997, Gubernatorial Election, Boca Raton, 1997; v.p. South Fla. Coun. Boy Scouts Am., Miami Lakes, 1997—2000, Board of Trustees, 2000—; South Fla. Council, BSA Honoree Eagle Class of 2002 - 2003, 2003. Named to Soc. Golden Eagles, South Fla. Coun., Boy Scouts Am., Miami Lakes, 2000—; recipient Spl. Commendation, City of Deerfield Beach, 1982, Award of Merit, South Fla. Coun. Boy Scouts Am., Miami Lakes, 1982, Spl. Commendation, United Way Broward County, Ft. Lauderdale, 1988, Outstanding Vol. award, Broward County Schs., Ft. Lauderdale, 1989, Silver Beaver award, Boy Scouts Am., Irving, Tex., 1994, Commendation, Broward Sheriff's Office, Ft. Lauderdale, 1997, Pres. award for best mktg. strategy, Boy Scouts Am., Irving, 1998, Good Turn award, South Fla. Coun. Boy Scouts Am., Miami Lakes, 2002, U Scholar, Dean's List, Panhellenic Council, U Miss., Pres. List, Coll., of Edn. Dean's Adv. Bd., U Boca Raton. Mem.: Alpha Omicron Sorority (life; v.p. 1962—66). Republican. Roman Catholic. Avocations: reading, sports, travel.

HODGES, STANLEY M. physician, educator; b. Lakeland, Fla., Aug. 24, 1952; s. Julian Eugene and Jacqueline B. (Highlands) H.; m. Deborah Teresa Pearce, Aug. 11, 1953; children: Lisa Marie, Allison Lynn. BS, BA, Troy State U., Phoenix City, Ala., 1981; MD, Mercer U., Macon, Ga., 1992. Diplomate Am. Bd. Internal Medicine; registered technologist radiology and nuclear medicine. Radiologic technologist Halifax Hosp., Daytona Beach, Fla., 1971-73; nuclear medicine technologist U. Ala., Birmingham, 1973-75, 76-79; chief technologist nuclear medicine St. Francis Hosp., Columbus, Ga., 1979-81; chief technologist radiology Dept. Americus (Ga.) Hosp., 1981-84; chief technologist radiology Clark Holder Clinic, LaGrange, Ga., 1984-86; emergency rm. physician Carraway Meth. Med. Ctr., Birmingham, 1991-92; pvt. practice Ellijay, Ga., 1995—2001; hospitalist Global Med. Svcs. Hosp., 2001—, Johnson City Med. Ctr., 2001—. Adv. bd. Gilmer County Health Dept., Ellijay, 1996-2000; assoc. prof. Mercer U. Sch. Medicine, 1995-2001; dir. respiratory dept. North Ga. Med. Ctr., Ellijay, 1996—; clinician physician asst. outpatient skills Emory U.; preceptor East Tenn. State U. Sch. Nurse Practitioners, East Tenn. State U. Sch. Medicine. Mem. ACP. Baptist. Avocations: target shooting, fishing, computers, boating, music. Office: Johnson City Med Ctr State Franklin Rd Johnson City TN 37604 Home: 405 Lambeth Dr Johnson City TN 37601-1041

HODGES, VERNON WRAY, mechanical engineer; b. Roanoke, Va., Dec. 26, 1929; s. Charlie Wayne and Kathleen Mae (Williams) Hodges; m. Lorraine Patricia Smart, Apr. 1, 1955 (div. 1966); children: Vernon Wray Jr.(dec.),

Gregory Elmer, Michelle Lynn; m. Linda Lou Wall, Feb. 3, 1967 (dec. Apr. 1997); children: Kenneth Wray, Kelly Diane; m. Emily Louise Tinsley, Aug. 19, 2000; children: John Keith Tinsley, Karen Denise Tinsley. BS in Mech. Engring., Va. Poly. Inst. and State U., 1951; MS in Systems Mgmt., U. So. Calif., 1979. Registered profl. engr., Kans., Wash., Calif. Commd. 2d lt. USAF, 1951, advanced through grades to major, 1964, ret., 1965; flight test engr. Boeing Co., Wichita, Kans., 1966-71, sr. engr. Seattle, 1971-76; systems test engr. Rockwell Internat., Edwards AFB, Calif., 1976-77, sr. engr. El Segundo, Calif., 1981—84, Palmdale, Calif., 1984—90, Hughes Helicopters, Inc., Culver City, Calif., 1977-81, Computer Scis. Corp., Edwards AFB, 1990-93. Comml. pilot, 1953—; asst. prof. air sci. Boston U., 1958—61. Active Rep. Party, Sacramento, 1977—, Rep. Nat. Com., Washington, 1977—; elder, deacon Presbyn. Ch. USA, Lancaster, 1981—. Recipient Letters of Commendation, USAF. Mem. ASME, NSPE (sec. 1972-75), Air Force Assn., Masons (50 yr. mem.), Shriners, Elks. Home: 2731 W Avenue J-8 Lancaster CA 93536-5832 E-mail: vernh@aol.com.

HODGES-ROBINSON, CHETTINA M. nursing administrator; b. Roosevelt, N.Y., Mar. 12, 1963; d. Clifford and Janice (Revis) Hodges-Jones; m. Darrell K. Robinson, Mar. 17, 1991. BSN, NYU, 1986; postgrad., C.W. Post U. Cert. med.-surg. nurse basic life support and advanced cardiac life support. Staff nurse NYU Med. ctr., N.Y.C., 1986-87, Christ Hosp., Jersey City, 1986-87; cardiothoracic recovery rm. and post-anesthesia nurse, staff nurse Lenox Hill Hosp., N.Y.C., 1987-94; asst. nurse mgr. critical care/intensive/coronary care unit Good Samaritan Hosp., West Islip, L.I., N.Y., 1994—; staff nurse cardiovasc. ICU U. Hosp. at Stony Brook, N.Y., 1995—; field nurse Staff Builders, Medford, N.Y., 1995—; asst. head nurse, sub-acute, rehab. unit Jewish Home and Hosp., Bronx, NY, 1996—2003; staff nurse North Shore Univ. Hosp., Manhasset, Long Island, NY, 2003—. Mem. Luth. Ch. of the Good Shepherd, Roosevelt, N.Y. Mem. ANA, N.Y. State Nurses Assn., N.J. Nurses Assn., Black Nurses Assn. (L.I. chpt.), Zeta Alpha Beta (bd. election Suffolk County inspector). Home: 119 S 28th St Wyandanch NY 11798-2813 E-mail: Chettina@msn.com.

HODGKIN, JOHN E. pulmonologist; b. Portland, Oreg., Aug. 22, 1939; s. Williard E. and Dorothy (Rigsby) H.; m. Jeanie Walker, Sept. 6, 1980; children: Steve, Kathryn, Carolyn, Jonathan, Jamie. BS, Walla Walla Coll., 1960; MD, Loma Linda U., 1964. Fellow in pulmonology Mayo Clinic, Rochester, Minn., 1970-72; chief pulmonary sect. Loma Linda (Calif.) U., 1974-80; clin. prof. medicine U. Calif., Davis, 1983—. Med. dir. respiratory care St. Helena Hosp., Deer Park, Calif., 1983—, med. dir. pulmonary rehab., 1983—, med. dir. ctr. for health promotion, 1983-96, asst. to pres., 1994—, med. dir. smoking cessation program, 2003—; med. dir. Adventist Health No. Calif., Roseville, Calif., 1995-98, Calif. Med. Found., 1995-98; med. dir. pulmonary rehab., Redbud Hosp., Clearlake, Calif., 2003. Editor: Chronic Obstructive Pulmonary Disease: Current Concepts in Diagnosis and Comprehensive Care, 1979, Respiratory Care: A Guide to Clinical Practice, 1977, 4th rev. edit. 1997, Pulmonary Rehabilitation: Guidelines to Success, 1984, 3rd rev. edit., 2000, Lung Sounds: A Practical Guide, 1988, 2d rev. edit., 1996. Decorated bronze star U.S. Army, 1968. Fellow Am. Assn. Cardiovas. & Pulmonary Rehab. (pres. 1995-96), Am. Coll. Chest Physicians, Am. Coll. Physicians, Am. Thoracic Soc., Nat. Assn. Med. Direction of Respiratory Care, Am. Assn. Respiratory Care (bd. med. advisors). Avocations: tennis, softball, skiing. Home: 1330 Crestmont Dr Angwin CA 94508-9634 Office: Saint Helena Hosp Lloyd Bldg Ste 502 Deer Park CA 94576 E-mail: drjohn@napanet.net.

HODGKINS, DOUGLAS WENDELL, music educator; b. Winchester, Mass., Apr. 18, 1965; s. Wendell W. and JoAnn M. Hodgkins; m. Pamela Jean Dalton. MusB in Edn., U. Mass., 1987. Music tchr. Bishop Fenwick HS, Peabody, Mass., 1989—91, Sharon (Mass.) HS, 1991—92, Sandwich (Mass.) HS and Oak Ridge Elem. Sch., 1992—97, Lynnfield (Mass.) HS, 1997—. Organist Christ Meth. Ch., Malden, Mass., 1989—2001, choir dir., 1989—2001; organist Ctr. Congl. Ch., Lynnfield, 2001—, choir dir., 2001—. Mem.: Am. Choral Dirs. Assn., Mass. Music Educators Assn., Music Educators Nat. Conf. Avocations: baseball, basketball, football. Office: Lynnfield High School 275 Essex Street Lynnfield MA 01940

HODGKINS, FRANCIS IRVING (BUTCH HODGKINS), county official; BS with honors in Civil Engring., Calif. State U., Sacramento, 1972. Licensed civil engr. Mem. staff County of Sacramento, Calif., 1965-89, engr. tech., 1965-68; pvt. prac. Sacramento, 1972-74; chief engr. Sacramento Co. Sanitation Dist., 1974-89; Dep. dir. pub. works Sacramento County (Calif.), 1989-93; exec. dir. Flood Ctrl. Agy. Sacramento Area, 1993—. Mem. Calif. Flood Plain Mgrs. Assn. Office: Flood Ctrl Agy Sacramento Area 1007 7th St Fl 7 Sacramento CA 95814-3407

HODGKINS, W. GRANT, supply chain improvements manager, consultant; b. Ft. Worth, Apr. 5, 1962; s. Chris Hulen and Renee (Early) H.; m. Barbara J. Bryan, Oct. 1, 1988 (div. Dec. 17, 1998). BA, Tex. Christian U., 1984. Validation scientist analytical chemistry Alcon Labs., Inc., Ft. Worth, 1985-92, software quality engr. corp. quality assurance, 1992-93, software quality mgr. corp. quality assurance, 1993-99, internal cons., change agt., supply chain mgr., 1999—. Contbr. articles to profl. jours. Mem. Am. Soc. Quality (cert. software quality engr.), Assn. Software Engring. Excellence, Software Engring. Inst., Project Mgmt. Inst. Episcopalian. Avocations: art collecting, hiking, mountain biking, travel, gourmet cooking. Home: 6200 Sea Meadow Dr Fort Worth TX 76132 Office: Alcon Labs Inc 6201 S Freeway AM4 Fort Worth TX 76134 E-mail: Grant@Grant-Hodgkins.com., Grant.Hodgkins@Alconlabs.com.

HODGKINS, WILLIAM F. career officer; BS in Secondary Edn., Auburn U., 1970, M in Edn. Adminstrn., 1973; grad., Squadron Officer Sch., 1974, USAF Fighter Weapons Sch., 1982, Air Command and Staff Coll., 1983, Can. Forces Command and Staff Coll., 1986; student, Air War Coll., 1995; student program for execs., Carnegie-Mellon U., 1997. Commd. 2d lt. USAF, 1974, advanced through grades to brig. gen., 1998; F-15 aircraft comdr., instr. pilot 33rd Tactical Fighter Wing, Eglin AFB, Fla., 1982, standardization and evaluation pilot, 1982, unit weapons and tactics officer, 1982; instr. pilot, wing weapons and tactics officer 18th Tactical Fighter Wing, Kadena AFB, Japan, 1983-85; air ops. joint staff officer various weapons programs Can. Forces Nat. Def. Hdqs., Ottawa, Ont., 1986-88; chief weapons and tactics div. 1st Tactical Fighter Wing, Langley AFB, Va., 1988-89; chief spl. programs div., dep. chief staff ops. Hdqs. Tactical Air Command, Langley AFB, 1989-92; dep. chief staff ops. Hdqs. 17th Air Force, Sembach Air Base, Germany, 1992-93; comdr. 32d Fighter Group, Soesterberg Air Base, The Netherlands, 1993-94; chief war plans and mobilization div., various positions Hdqs. USAF, the Pentagon, Washington, 1995-97; dir. ops. J-3 US Forces Japan, Yokota Air Base, 1997-98; dep. comdr. Can. N.Am. Aerospace Def. Command Region, Winnipeg, 1998—. Decorated Legion of Merit, Def. Superior Svc. medal. Office: CAN/DCR Aircom Hq Box 17000 Station Forces Winnipeg Manitoba Canada R35 3Y5

HODGKINSON, GRETA, dancer; b. Providence, R.I. Grad., Nat. Ballet Sch., 1990. Mem. Nat. Ballet of Can., Toronto, Canada, 1990—96, prin. dancer, 1996—. Dancer (ballets) Swan Lake, 1999, Romeo and Juliet, The Merry Widow, The Sleeping Beauty, The Taming of the Shrew, La Bayadère, Giselle, Manon, The Four Seasons, Herman Schmerman Pas de Deux, Sphinx, the Rubies Variation; internat. guest artist Can., U.S., Europe, Australia. Office: Walter Carsen Ctr Nat Ballet of Canada 470 Queens Quay West Toronto ON Canada M5V 3K4

HODGKINSON, WILLIAM JAMES, publishing executive; b. July 31, 1939; s. William James and Augusta Anne (Botka) H.; m. Virginia Evelyn Humphreys, Sept. 7, 1963; 1 child, Elizabeth Anne. AB, Bucknell U., 1961; MBA, Columbia U., 1963. Mktg. rsch. analyst Singer Co., N.Y.C., 1963-66; asst. adminstrn. writing paper divsn. Am. Paper Inst., N.Y.C., 1966-67; market rsch. mgr. Diners Club, N.Y.C., 1967-68; with Dun & Bradstreet Cos., Inc., 1968-92, mgmt. cons. William E. Hill Co. divsn., 1971-73, mgr. fin. svcs. group Donnelly Mktg. divsn. Stamford, Conn., 1973-86, v.p., 1987-92; COO Career Sys., Inc., Fairfield, Conn., 1993-97; pres. Marketview Pub. Corp., Fairfield, 1997—. Contbr. articles to profl. jours. Bd. dirs. Bklyn. Pub. Libr. br., 1974-79, Enlightenment Together, Inc., 1971-76; rsch. coord. Presdl. Task Force on Improving Small Bus., 1969-70; v.p., trustee Montessori Sch. Bklyn., 1975-79; trustee Greens Farms Congl. Ch., 1983-85; co-chmn. Save Fairfield Com., 1984—; bd. deacons Episc. ch., 1971-78, pres., 1977-78. With U.S. Army, 1963. Recipient Brotherhood award Bucknell U., 1960; grantee Columbia U., 1962-63. Mem. Bank Mktg. Assn., Am. Mktg. Assn., Direct Mail Mktg. Assn., Princeton Club (N.Y.C.), Phi Lambda Theta. Home: 4454 Black Rock Tpke Fairfield CT 06430-1807

HODGMAN, VICKI JEAN, retired school system administrator; b. Joliet, Ill., May 22, 1933; d. Joseph and Mary (Desman) Mikolic; divorced; children: Michael James, Tudy Magnuson, Kathy Lynn. BEd, Ill. State U., 1954, MEd, 1970; postgrad., Okla. State U., 1969, U. Bridgeport, 1972, U. Hawaii, 1982, No. Ill. U., 1978, 79, 80, Nat. Coll., 1983, 86, U. Utah, 1984, U. Ill., 1988, U. Ljubljana, Slovenia, 1999. Cert. tchr., Ill., Md. Tchr. Will County (Ill.) Pub. Schs., Joliet, Rockdale and Lockport, 1954-55, 58-68, Balt. County (Md.) Pub. Schs., Sparrow's Point, 1955-56, McLean County (Ill.) Pub. Schs., Heyworth, 1957; tchr. spl. edn. So. Will County Coop. for Spl. Edn., 1969-79, supr., coordinator, 1979-93. Sec. Pulse-Chicagoland Spl. Edn. Suprs., 1983-85, proctor, Midwestern U., 2003. Vol. Youth with a Mission, Gospel Outreach, 1985; treas. Women's Ch. Council, Rockdale, Ill., 1966-67, Band Parents Assn., Rockdale, 1966-67; election judge, 1996-2002; active Will County PTA; vol. tutor, 1999-2002; vol. Joliet Hist. Soc. Mus., 2003—. Sys. Edn. grant, 1969, Nat. Def. Edn. grantee, 1982-83. Mem. Coun. Exceptional Children, Ill. Coun. Exceptional Children (bd. dirs. 1991-92), Ill. Coun. Children with Behavior Disorders (pres.-elect 1988, pres. 1989, bd. dirs. 1986-87), Will County Reading Assn., Will County Coun. for Exceptional Children, Coun. Behavior Disorders, Divsn. Learning Disabilities (del. to China 1994), Ill. Alliance for Exceptional Children and Adults, ASCD, Am. Assn. Ret. Persons, Ret. Tchrs. Assn., Ill. Ret. Tchrs. Assn., Nat. Home Gardening Club, Heritage Quilters Guild (sec. 1988, treas. 1989), Joliet Area Garden Club, Ill. Garden Club. Republican. Roman Catholic. Avocations: sewing, quilting, world travelling. Home: 310 S Reedwood Dr Joliet IL 60436-1461

HODGSON, DOROTHY L. social studies educator; b. Mar. 10, 1962; m. Richard A. Schroeder; children: Luke Schroeder, Toby Schroeder. BA in English Lit., U. Va., 1983; PhD in Anthropology, U. Mich. Asst. prof. anthropology Rutgers U., New Brunswick, NJ, 1995—2001, assoc. prof. anthropology, 2001—. Grad. program dir. anthropology Rutgers U., 2002—; program co-chair Assn. for Feminist Anthropology; mrm. steering com. Women's Caucus of the African Studies Assn., 1998—; mem. adv. bd. Women Africa and Dispora Series U. Wis. Press, 2002—; editl. com. Social Text, 1996—2001. Author: Once Intrepid Warriors: Gender, Ethnicity and the Cultural Politics of Maasai Development.; editor: Comparative Perspectives on the Indigenous Rights Movement in Africa and the Americas, Gendered Modernities: Ethnographic Perspectives, Wicked Women and the Reconfiguration of Gender in Africa, Rethinking Pastoralism in Africa: Gender, Culture and the Myth of the Patriarchal Pastoralist. Recipient Fulbright-Hays Doctoral Dissertation Abroad award, U.S. Dept. of Edn., 1991—92, Anne U. White award, Assn. Am. Geographers, 1999—2000; fellow Jacob K. Javits fellow, U.S. Dept. Edn., 1988—91, Internat. Doctoral Rsch. Fellowship, Social Sci. Rsch. Coun.- Am. Coun. Learned Socs., 1991—93, Richard Carley Hunt Meml. postdoctoral fellow, Wenner Gren Found., 1996—98, Am. Philos. Soc., 1999—2000, Ctr. Advanced Study Behavioral Sciences, 2001—02, Rutgers U., 2001; grantee, NSF, 1991. Mem.: West African Rsch. Assn., African Studies Assn. (bd. dirs. 1997—2000), Am. Anthrop. Assn.

HODGSON, ERNEST, toxicology educator; b. Durham, Eng., July 26, 1932; arrived in U.S., 1955; s. Ernest Victor and Emily (Moses) H.; m. Mary Kathleen Devlin, Dec. 21, 1957 (dec.); children: Mary Elizabeth, Audrey Catherine, Patricia Emily Devlin, Ernest Victor Felix. B.Sc. with honors, Kings Coll. U. Durham, Eng., 1955; PhD, Oreg. State U., 1959. Rsch. fellow Oreg. State U., Corvallis, 1955-59, U. Wis., Madison, 1959-61; asst. prof. N.C. State U., Raleigh, 1961-63, assoc. prof., 1963-65, prof. toxicology, 1965—, William Neal Reynolds prof., 1977—, chmn. toxicology dept., 1982-97, Disting. Alumni Rsch. prof., 1987-90. Mem. adv. panel U.S. EPA, Washington, 1982-85; mem. toxicology study sect. NIH, Washington, 1985-89, mem. NIEHS study sect., 1992-96, chmn. 1994-96; pres. Toxicology Comm., Raleigh, 1982—; vis. scientist U. Wash., Seattle, 1975. Author, editor: Introduction to Biochemical Toxicology, 1980, 3d edit., 2000, Modern Toxicology, 1987, 2d edit., 1997, Dictionary of Toxicology; editor: Reviews in Biochemical Toxicology, 1979—, Reviews in Environmental Toxicology, 1984—, Jour. Biochemical and Molecular Toxicology; mem. editorial bd. Chemico-Biol. Interactions; contbr. articles to profl. jours. Chmn. policy rev. com. Gov.'s Waste Mgmt. Bd., Raleigh, 1984. Grantee NIH, 1962—, U.S. Army, 2000—. Mem. AAAS, Soc. Toxicology (edn. com. 1984—, Edn. award 1984, Merit award 1994, pres. mechanisms sect. 1991-92, pres. N.C. chpt. 1984-85), Am. Soc. Pharmacology (drug metabolism com. 1981-84), Am. Chem. Soc. (Burdick and Jackson Internat. award in pesticide chemistry, Sterling Hendricks award USDA, 1997), Internat. Soc. Study Xenobiotics (coun. 1986-89, sec.-elect 1990-92, sec. 1992-94, pres.-elect 1996-97, pres. 1998-99), Sigma Xi (chpt. pres. 1974). Democrat. Avocations: history, writing, travel. Office: NC State U Dept Toxicology PO Box 7633 Raleigh NC 27695-0001 E-mail: ernest_hodgson@ncsu.edu.

HODGSON, JANE ELIZABETH, obstetrician and gynecologist, consultant; b. Crookston, Minn., Jan. 23, 1915; d. Herbert and Adelaide (Marin) H.; m. Frank Walter Quattlebaum, Feb. 22, 1940; children: Gretchen, Nancy. BS, Carleton Coll., 1934, DSc (hon.), 1994; MD, U. Minn., 1939, MS in Ob-Gyn., 1947. Diplomate Am. Bd. Ob.-Gyn. Fellow Mayo Clinic, Rochester, Minn., 1941-44; pvt. practice in ob-gyn. St. Paul, 1947-72; med. dir. Preterm Clinic, Washington, 1972-74; med. dir. fertility control clinic St. Paul Ramsey Med. Ctr., 1974-79; med. dir. Planned Parenthood Minn., St. Paul, 1980-82, Midwest Health Ctr. Women, Mpls., 1981-83, Women's Health Ctr., Duluth, Minn., 1981-84, mem. staff, 1986—, also bd. dirs.; ostetrician/gynecologist Project Hope, Grenada, West Indies, 1984; vis. prof. ob-gyn. project hope Zheijiang Med. Sch., Hangzhou, People's Republic of China, 1985-86; clin. assoc. prof. ob-gyn. U. Minn., Mpls., 1986—. Vis. med. educator Project Hope, Cairo, 1979-80; vis. prof. dept. ob-gyn. U. Calif., San Francisco, 1983. Editor: Abortion & Sterilization, 1981; contbr. numerous articles to profl. jours. Bd. dirs. Genesis II Women, Mpls., 1988—, Pro Choice Resources, Mpls., 1991—, Wellstone Alliance, Mpls., 1992—, Ctr. for Reproductive Law and Policy, N.Y.C., 1995—. Recipient Ann. Humanitarian award Nat. Abortion Fedn., 1981, Woman Physician of Yr. award Med. Women Minn. Med. Assn., 1983, Ann. Jane Hodgson Reproductive Freedom award Nat. Abortion Rights Action League, 1989, Hanah G. Solomon award Nat. Coun. Jewish Women, 1990, Margaret Sanger award Planned Parenthood Fedn. of Am., 1995, Harold Swanberg award Am. Med. Writer's Assn., 1996. Fellow Am. Coll. Ob-Gyn. (founding); mem. Am. Med. Women's Assn. (E. Blackwell award 1992, Reproductive Health award 1994), Minn. Ob-Gyn. Soc. (pres. 1967), Minn. Med. Assn. (So. Minn. Med. award 1952), Minn. Women's Polit. Caucus (16th Ann. Founding Feminist award 1988), Mayo Clinic Alumni Assn. Home and Office: 211 2nd St NW Apt 1405 Rochester MN 55901-2895

HODGSON, PAUL EDMUND, surgeon, department chairman; b. Milw., Dec. 14, 1921; s. Howard Edmund and Ethel Marie (Niemi) H.; m. Barbara Jean Osborne, Apr. 22, 1945; children: Ann, Paul. BS summa cum laude, Beloit Coll., 1943; MD cum laude, U. Mich., 1945. Diplomate: Am. Bd. Surgery. Intern U. Mich. Hosp., 1945-46, resident in surgery, 1948-52; mem. faculty dept. surgery U. Mich., 1952-62, assoc. prof., 1956-62; prof. surgery U. Nebr. Coll. Medicine, Omaha, 1962-88, prof. emeritus, 1988—, asst. dean for curriculum, 1966-72, chmn. dept. surgery, 1972-84. Trustee Beloit Coll., 1977-80 Served to capt. M.C. U.S. Army, 1946-48. Mem. A.C.S., Frederick A. Coller Surg. Soc., Soc. Univ. Surgeons, Central Surg. Assn., Soc. Surgery Alimentary Tract, Am. Assn. Surgery Trauma, Western Surg. Assn., Am. Surg. Assn. Presbyterian. Office: U Nebr Med Ctr 600 S 42nd St Omaha NE 68198-3280

HODGSON, PETER JOHN, author, composer, lecturer; b. Birmingham, Eng., Apr. 6, 1929; came to U.S., 1965, naturalized, 1974; s. Eric Christopher and Dorothy (Price) H.; m. Mary Thatcher, 1958; 1 son, Michael. MusB, U. London, 1964; MusM, Royal Coll. Music, 1965; PhD in Music (Univ. fellow), U. Colo., 1970. Resident music master Univ. Sch., Victoria, B.C., Can., 1952-55; mem. faculty, adminstr. Mt. Royal Coll., Calgary, Alta., Can., 1955-65; mem. faculty Banff (Alta.) Sch. Fine Arts, 1960-66; mem. faculty, adminstr. Sch. of Music, Ball State U., Muncie, Ind., 1968-78; dean New Eng. Conservatory of Music, 1978-83; prof. music, chmn. dept. music Tex. Christian U., Ft. Worth, 1983-87; dean faculty Principia Coll., Elsah, Ill., 1987-94, prof. music, 1987-96; ind. scholar, 1996—. Author: Music of Herbert Howells, 1971, Toward an Understanding of Renaissance Musical Structure, 1972, Benjamin Britten: A Composer Resource Manual, 1996; composer: 39 pieces for piano and/or organ, 1996, 10 vocal solos, 1996-98. Served with Brit. Army, 1947-49. Recipient award Brit. Council, 1964 Home: 13894 Hemlock Dr Penn Valley CA 95946

HODGSON, RICHARD, electronics company executive; b. Anyox, B.C., Can., Jan. 7, 1917; s. Arthur R. and Mabel (Malmstrom) H.; m. Geraldine Coursen Reed, Nov. 26, 1945; children: Philip, Morgan, Brooke, Peter. AB in Engring, Stanford U., 1937; MBA, Harvard U., 1939. With Radiation Lab., Mass. Inst. Tech., 1942-45; head engr. mgmt. div. Brookhaven Nat. Lab., AEC, 1946; dir. TV Paramount Pictures, 1947-50; pres., dir. Chromatic TV Labs., 1950-56; exec. v.p. Fairchild Camera & Instrument Corp., Syosset, L.I., 1955-62, pres., dir., 1962-68; corp. sr. v.p., group mgr. ITT Corp., 1968-80; dir. McCowan Assocs. Inc., N.Y.C., 1980-98. Expert cons. to U.S. sec. war, 1943-45; bd. dirs. Intel Corp., I-Stat Corp., Inc., IBIS Tech. Corp., Accent Color Sci. Inc. Mem. IEEE (sr.), Tau Beta Pi. Home: New Canaan, Conn. Died Mar. 4, 2000.

HODGSON, THOMAS RICHARD, retired healthcare company executive; b. Lakewood, Ohio, Dec. 17, 1941; s. Thomas Julian and Dallas Louise (Livesay) H.; m. Susan Jane Cawrse, Aug. 10, 1963; children: Michael, Laura, Anne. BSChemE, Purdue U., 1963, DEng. (hon.), 1993; MSE, U. Mich., 1964; MBA, Harvard U., 1969. Devel. engr. E.I. Dupont, 1964; assoc. Booz-Allen & Hamilton, 1969-72; with Abbott Labs., North Chicago, Ill., 1972—, gen. mgr. Faultless div., 1976-78, v.p. gen. mgr. hosp. div., 1978-80, pres. hosp. div., 1980-83, group v.p., pres. Abbott Internat. Ltd., 1983-84; also bd. dirs. Abbott Internat. Ltd.; exec. v.p. parent co., pres. Abbott Internat. Inc. Abbott Labs., North Chicago, Ill., 1985-90, pres., chief oper. officer Abbott Park, 1990-99. Mem. engring. vis. com. Purdue U., 1996—; bd. dirs. St. Paul Cos. Mem. Lake Forest (Ill.) Bd. Edn., 1986-90; trustee and mem. exec. com. Rush-Presbyn. St. Luke's Med. Ctr. Chgo., 1992—; overseer Harvard Bus. Sch. Club Chgo., 1993—. Baker scholar; NSF fellow; recipient Disting. Engring. Alumni award Purdue U., 1985 Mem. Chgo. Coun. Fgn. Rels., Econ. Club, Knollwood Club, Shoreacres Club, Chgo. Club, Phi Eta Sigma, Tau Beta Pi. Home: 1015 Ashley Rd Lake Forest IL 60045-3379 Office: Abbott Labs 225 E Deerpath Ste 222 Lake Forest IL

HODGSON, W(ALTER) JOHN (BARRY HODGSON), surgeon; b. Middlesborough, England, Sept. 17, 1939; came to U.S., 1975; s. Walter Aggett and Constance Lillian (Nelson) H.; m. Jean C. Morgan, Apr. 20, 1967; children: Sean, Russell, Miranda. MB, BS, Charing Cross Med. Sch., London, 1964; M of Surgery, London U., 1976. Rotating intern, resident London U., 1964-75; surgeon Bronx (N.Y.) VA Med. Ctr., 1975-78, asst. chief surg. service, 1977-82; pvt. practice specializing in surgery Mt. Sinai Hosp., N.Y.C., 1978-81; chief gastro-intestinal surgery Westchester Med. Ctr., Valhalla, N.Y., 1981-94; dept. surg. Montefiore Med. Ctr. and Einstein Hosp., Bronx, NY, 1997—; prof. surgery N.Y. Med. Coll., Valhalla, 1987-98, course organizer for laparoscopic surgery, 1990-92, prof. cell biol. and anatomy, 1993—; clin. prof. surgery NYU, 1995—; prof. surgery Albert Einstein Coll. Medicine, 1998—. Contbr. articles to profl. jours.; editor: Liver Tumors: Multidisciplinary Management, 1987; inventor cavitron surg. technique for livor tumor surgery. Organizer, coach Larchmont Jr. Soccer League, 1977; mem. Larchmont Rep. Com., 1985. Cavitron Co. grantee, 1978, Cavitron Lasersonics grantee, 1987, Ethicon grantee, 1999. Fellow ACS, Am. Coll. Gastroenterology; mem. N.Y. Sur. Soc. for Acad. Surgery, Am. Assn. Clin. Anatomists, Am. Soc. Colon & Rectal Surgery, Soc. Am. Gastroendoscopic Surgery. Clubs: Larchmont Yacht. Episcopalian. Avocations: sailing, hill walking, skiing. Office: Montefiore Med Park Dept Surgery 1575 Blondell Ave Dept Surgery Bronx NY 10461-2660 E-mail: wjb.hodgson@verizon.net.

HODINAR, MICHAEL, lawyer, publishing company executive; b. Prague, Czechoslovakia, Dec. 25, 1954; came to U.S., 1969; s. Adolf and Dagmar H.; m. Bernadette Callerame, Nov. 10, 1979. BA, Columbia U., 1977, MIA, 1981; JD, N.Y. Law Sch., 1983. Bar: N.J. 1984, N.Y. 1985, Conn. 1985, U.S. Dist. Ct. N.J. 1984, U.S. Dist. Ct. (ea. dist.) N.Y. 1985, U.S. Dist. Ct. (so. dist.) N.Y. 1986. Pvt. practice, Paramus, N.J., 1984-92, Pelham Bay, N.Y., 1985—, 1985—; pres., pub. VonPalisaden Publs., Inc., Paramus, 1986-92; pvt. practice Hillsdale, N.J., 1992—. Fin. cons. N.Y., N.J., Conn. Bus. editor Jour. Internat. Affairs, 1979-80. John Jay Nat. scholar, 1973, Solomon scholar, 1981. Mem. ABA, N.J. Bar Assn., N.Y. State Bar Assn., Columbia U. Sailing Club, Blue Key Soc., Phi Gamma Delta. Democrat. Roman Catholic. Avocations: tennis, sailing, skiing, travel. Home and Office: 60 Saddlewood Dr Hillsdale NJ 07642-1336

HODKINSON, SYDNEY PHILLIP, composer, educator; b. Winnipeg, Man., Can., Jan. 17, 1934; s. Ernest and Irene (Pilgrim) H.; m. Elizabeth Jane Deischer, July 22, 1955; children: Mark, Scott, Grant. MusB, U. Rochester, 1957, MusM, 1958; D of Mus. Arts, U. Mich., 1968. Mem. faculty U. Va., 1958-63, Ohio U., Athens, 1963-66, U. Mich., Ann Arbor, 1968-73; prof. composition, chair conducting and ensembles Eastman Sch. Music, Rochester, N.Y., 1973-98. Artist-in-residence, Mpls.-St.Paul, 1970-72; Meadows chair composition So. Meth. U., Dallas, 1984-86; vis. prof. composition U. Western Ont., London, Can., 1990, Aspen Music Festival, 1998—, Ind. U., 2002, Duke U., 2003. Composer numerous works for brass, woodwinds, strings and percussion, 1958—, also for orch., chorus, stage, opera, wind and chamber ensembles; artist various recs. Guggenheim fellow, 1978-79; grantee U. Va., 1961, Ohio U., 1964, Can. Coun., 1966, 69, 77-78, Danforth Found., 1966-68, U. Mich., 1969, 70-73, Ford Found., 1976, Nat. Endowment for Arts, 1975-76, 78, 83-84, 90-91, Martha Baird Rockefeller Found., 1976. Mem. Broadcast Music Inc., Am. Composers Alliance, Am. Music Ctr., Phi Mu Alpha Sinfonia. Home: 2589 John Anderson Dr Ormond Beach FL 32176-2417

HODNICAK, VICTORIA CHRISTINE, pediatric nurse; b. Detroit, Dec. 29, 1960; d. Roderick Lewis and Beverly Caroline (Backus) Turner; m. Mark Michael Hodnicak, Sept. 20, 1986; children: (twins) Christopher Alan and Matthew Lewis (dec.). ADN, Henry Ford C.C., Dearborn, Mich., 1982. RN, Mich., Tenn. Charge nurse, surg. nurse Harper Grace Hosp., Detroit, 1982-86; neonatal nurse St. John Hosp., Detroit, 1986; home care nurse, coord. med. mgmt. Bloomfield Nursing Svcs., Clawson, Mich., 1986-88; coord. pediat. endocrine growth study So. Health Sys., Memphis, 1988-92; nurse specialist, growth study coord. U. Tenn. Med. Group/St. Jude Children's Rsch. Hosp., Memphis, 1992-98; care coord., educator Pediat. Svcs. Am., Memphis, 1998-99; edn. coord. of nursing Meth. Alliance Healthcare, Memphis, 2001—02, clin. nurse educator, developer home care nurse tng. program, 2002—. Home care pediat. nurse Personal Pediat. Nursing Profls., Pontiac, Mich., 1987-88; staff nurse Nancy Kissick's Profl. Nursing Svc., Mt. Clemens, Mich., 1988; website cons. Family Pathfinder Resource Ctr. of Tenn.; parent advisor TIPS; mem. Project DOCC. Inventor Growth Hormone new dose form, 1991, Hydrocortisone dose and stress dosing card, 1990; contbr. articles to profl. jours.; inventor equipment cart for vent. patients. Mem. tng. com. Ctr. for Devel. Disabilities, 2000—. Mem. Pediat. Endocrinology Nursing Soc. (membership com. 1992), Endocrine Nursing Soc., Human Growth Found., Neurofibromatosis Found., Turner Syndrome Soc., MAGIC Found., Alexander Graham Bell Assn. for Deaf, Project DOCC. Lutheran. Avocations: crafts, doll collecting, travel. E-mail: vnumber1survivor@aol.com.

HODNIK, DAVID F. retail company executive; b. 1947; Grad., Western Ill. U., 1970. Sr. auditor Paul Pettengill & Co., 1969-72; with Ace Hardware Corp., Hinsdale, Ill., 1972—, acct., 1972-74, mgr. acctg., 1974-76, controller, 1976-80, v.p., treas., 1980-82; v.p. fin., treas. ACE Hardware Corp., Oak Brook, Ill., 1982-88, sr. v.p., 1988-90, exec. v.p., 1990-93, exec. v.p., COO, 1993-95, pres., COO, 1995-96, pres., CEO, 1996—. Office: ACE Hardware Corp 2200 Kensington Ct Oak Brook IL 60523-2100

HODOUS, ROBERT POWER, lawyer; b. Zanesville, Ohio, July 29, 1945; s. Robert Frank and Nancy Aurelia (Power) H.; m. Susan Cottrell Birkhead, Feb. 1, 1969; children: Robert Everett, Shannon Alycia. BA, Miami U., Oxford, Ohio, 1967; JD, U. Va., Charlottesville, 1970. Bar: Va. 1970. Assoc. firm McGuire, Woods & Battle, Charlottesville, 1970-71; asst. trust officer Nat. Bank & Trust Co., Charlottesville, 1971-72, trust officer, 1972-75, sec., 1975-79, Jefferson Bankshares, Inc. (formerly NB Corp.), Charlottesville, 1979-91, v.p., sec., 1985-91, sr. v.p., sec., 1987-91; asst. to pres. Jefferson Nat. Bank,

Charlottesville, 1987-91; pvt. practice law Charlottesville, 1991-92; mem. firm Payne & Hodous, L.L.P., Charlottesville, 1992—. Author: Let's Really Change Taxes, 1998. Chmn. profl. div. Thomas Jefferson Area United Way, 1973, vice-chmn., 1978-79, campaign chmn., 1979-80, v.p. planning, 1981, pres., 1983; bd. dirs. Central Va. chpt. ARC, 1972-78, treas., 1972-75, chmn., 1975-77; commr. Charlottesville Redevel. and Housing Authority, 1974-78; mem. Region X Community Mental Health and Retardation Services Bd., 1973-79, chmn., 1974-76, mem. exec. com., 1976-78; v.p. Soccer Orgn. of Charlottesville-Albemarle, 1985-86, pres., 1986-88; co-pres. Greenbier Sch. PTA, 1985-86; chmn. recreation precinct Charlottesville City Dem. Com., 1971, Rep. com., 1992—; chmn. City Rep. Com., 2000—; bd. dirs. Charlottesville-Albemarle Community Found., 1987-2000, chmn. devel. com., 1991-93, mem. exec. and fin. coms., 1991-2000, chmn. fin. com., 1997-2000; mem. governing bd. Charlottesville Area Legis. Action Coalition, 2002--. Mem.: Charlottesville C. of C. (govt. affairs com. 1996—, co-chair 2002—), Computer Law Assn., Va. Bankers Assn. (com. drafted Va. Trust Subs. Act 1973, trust com. 1974—77, legal affairs com. 1986—91, large bank legis. coord. 1987—91), Va. State Bar, Charlottesville-Albemarle Bar Assn., Va. Bar Assn., Fairview Club (Charlottesville) (pres. 1974—75). Roman Catholic. Home: 1309 Lester Dr Charlottesville VA 22901-3143 Office: 412 E Jefferson St Charlottesville VA 22902-5109 *To me success is indicated by feelings of personal peace and satisfaction, not by external possessions. My goals are to do my best in contributing to the success of endeavors in which I become involved and to remember that the people involved in activities are the most important part of the activities. I feel my family is my most important endeavor. I hope never to become so involved in activities that I cannot enjoy my family, my surroundings and people I meet, or that I cannot spend the time necessary to do well those activities in which I am involved.*

HODSON, ROY GOODE, JR., retired logistician; b. Enon, Ala., July 22, 1927; s. Roy Goode and Ilda Fern (Jinks) H.; m. Mildred Bernice Parlier, Dec. 3, 1966 (dec. July 1992); children: Joan Hodson Bash, Scott Daniel, Jayne Clymer. Student, San Diego Jr. Coll., 1947-49, San Diego Vocational, 1947-49, San Diego State Coll., 1949-50. Security officer US Naval CB Ctr. (Civil Service), Port Hueneme, Calif., 1950-52; logistician Gen. Dynamics, San Diego, 1952-64, GTE Govt. Systems, Inc., Mt. View, Calif., 1964-89. Bd. dirs. San Jose Civic Light Opera Assn., 1988-95; advisor San Jose Children's Musical Theater, 1995 2002. With U.S. Army, 1945-47. Recipient Bravo award Silhoutte mag., 1988, Ginny award, 1989. Mem.: Wildlife Land Trust, Cornell Lab. of Ornithology, Nat. Audubon Soc., Archaeol. Inst. Am., Am. Indian Relief Coun., Am. Indian Edn. Found., Am. Birding Assn., Limestone County Hist. Soc., Humane Soc. Limestone County, Ind. Sheriffs Assn., Nat. Humane Edn. Soc., Spiceland Hist. and Tourism Soc., Nat. Pks. and Conservation Assn., Am. Philatelic Soc., Internat. Platform Assn., Internat. Freelance Photographers Orgn., Nature Conservancy, Nat. Svc. Found., Easter Seals Found., Nat. Arbor Day Found., Am. Legion, Humane Soc. U.S., Am. Film Inst., Am. Assn. Ret. Persons, AMVETS, Athens C. of C., Am. Image Press Club. Democrat. Mem. Church of Christ. Avocations: photography, lapidary, geneaology, music. Home: 17266 Seven Mile Post Rd Athens AL 35611-8457

HOE, RICHARD MARCH, insurance and securities consultant, writer; b. Plainfield, N.J., June 16, 1939; s. Arthur James Hoe and Marjorie (Vandergrift) Beeson; m. Lynne Hovell, Sept. 26, 1964; children: Joshua Blake, Susan Brooke, Seth Jamieson. Student, Pace U., 1964-67, U. Tenn., 1976. CLU. Asst. to controller, fleet mgr., asst. purchasing agt. Hoe & Co. Inc., Bronx, NY, 1964—66; pres. OJS Mfg. Co., Bklyn., 1966-68, Fresh Impressions Inc., N.Y.C., 1968; agt. Fidelity Mut. Life, N.Y.C., 1968—72; asst. mgr. Fin. Life, N.Y.C., 1972—73; brokerage mgr. Am. Life N.Y., N.Y.C., 1973—75; exec. Provident Life & Accident Ins. Co., Chattanooga, 1975—78; mgr. Jefferson Standard, Tulsa, Okla., 1978—81; pres. Hoe & Co. Inc., Tulsa, 1981—93; fin. planner, designer, cons. Tulsa, 1978—99; specialist Am. Citizens Fin. Svcs., Tulsa, 1989—99; exec. v.p. Summit Fin. Group, Tulsa, 2000—. Lectr. project bus. Tulsa Pub. Schs., 1983, 85, cons., 1984-86; lectr. in field; founder employee and exec. benefit plans, residual split-dollar, money purchase flexible spending plans, pvt. sector social security alternative portable plans, satellite split-dollar, satellite supplemental pensions, lifetime income nontaxable retirement plans, balanced funding plans. Author: Love in Pasadena, 1996; columnist (monthly) Broker World, 1985-86, 87-88, Probe, Life Assn. News, Life Insurance Selling, 2000—; contbr. articles to profl. jours., novelist. Chmn. fund raising Grimes Elem. Sch., Tulsa Pub. Schs., 1984-87; mem. gifted and talented com. Tulsa Pub. Schs., 1982; bd. dirs. Nat. ALS Found., N.Y.C., 1971-82. Fellow: Life Underwriter Tng. Coun. (moderator 1979—86); mem.: Tulsa Estate Planning Fourm, Reach Across Divs., Nat. Okla. Multiple Sclerosis Soc. Republican. Episcopalian. Avocations: writing, chess, bicycling, jazz. Home: 5843 E 50th St Tulsa OK 74135-6885 Office: Summit Fin Group 1350 S Boulder Ave Ste 300 Tulsa OK 74119-3203

HOECKER, THOMAS RALPH, lawyer; b. Chicago Heights, Ill., Dec. 14, 1950; s. William H. and Norma M. (Wynkoop) H.; m. V. Sue Thornton, Aug. 28, 1971; children: Elizabeth T., Ellen T. BS, No. Ill. U., 1972; JD, U. Ill., 1975. Bar: Ill. 1975, Ariz. 1985. Assoc. Davis and Morgan, Peoria, Ill., 1975-80, ptnr., 1980-84; assoc. Snell and Wilmer, Phoenix, 1984-86, ptnr., 1987—. Mem. steering com. Western Pension Conf., Phoenix, 1986-92, pres., 1991-92. Fellow Am. Coll. Employee Benefits Coun. (charter), Ariz. Bar Found.; mem. ABA (chair tax sect. employee benefits com. 2002-03, co-chair legis. and adminstrv. subcom. of labor sect. employee benefits com. 1994-96), Ariz. Bar Assn., Ill. Bar Assn., Marciopa County Bar Assn., (mem. investment com. 1988-94). Avocation: fly fishing. Office: Snell Wilmer 1 Arizona Ctr Phoenix AZ 85004

HOEFFEL, JOSEPH M. congressman, lawyer; b. Phila., Sept. 3, 1950; m. Francesca Montori; children: Mary, Jake. BS, Boston U., 1972; JD, Temple U., 1988. Lawyer Murphy, Oliver, Caiola & Gowen, Norristown, Pa.; mem. 108th congress from PA 13th dist., 1999—; mem. budget com., 1999—; mem. internat. relations com., sci. com., 1999—. Mem. Pa. Ho. of Reps., 1976-84; dem. candidate U.S. House 13th dist., 1984, 86, 96; Montgomery County commr., Pa., 1992-98; chmn. Pa. Leadership Coun.; Montgomery County chmn. Clinton-Gore Campaign, 1992. Served with USAR. Democrat. Office: Ho of Reps 426 Cannon HOB Washington DC 20515-0001*

HOEFLE, PAUL RYAN, lawyer; b. Aurora, Ill., July 25, 1956; s. Ronald Anthony and Shirley Ann Hoefle; m. Mary Beth Wredling, June 25, 1983; children: Mary Elyse, Mitchell, Matthew. BS in Fin. summa cum laude, U. Ill., 1978; JD, U. Mich., 1981. Bar: Wis., U.S. Dist. Ct. (ea. and we. dists.) Wis. Assoc. Frisch, Dudek & Slattery, Milw., 1981-86, shareholder, 1986-88, Slattery, Hausman & Hoefle, Waukesha, Wis., 1988-98; shareholder, mng. ptnr. Bode, Carroll, McCoy, Hoefle & Mihal, Waukesha, 1998—2001; ptnr. Laufenberg & Hoefle, SC, Milw., 2002—. Bd. dirs. Wildlife in Need, Oconomowoc, Wis., 1998-2000. Mem. State Bar Wis., Milw. Bar Assn., Waukesha Bar Assn., Wis. Acad. Trial Lawyers (bd. dirs. 1988—, exec. com. 1997—), Waukesha Rotary Club. Avocations: outdoor activities, children's activities. Office: Laufenberg & Hoefle SC 115 S 84th St Ste 330 Milwaukee WI 53214 Office Fax: 414-778-1770. E-mail: prh@lauflaw.com.

HOEFLE, RONALD ANTHONY, civil engineer; b. Freeport, Ill., Apr. 24, 1929; s. Everett G. and Mary Pauline (Brubaker) H.; m. Shirley Ann Stegeman, June 12, 1954; children: Jo Ellen, Paul R., Julie Lynn. BSCE, U. Ill., 1951. Registered profl. engr., Ill.; registered structural engr. Engr. Dravo Corp., Pitts., 1951-55, Walter E. Deuchler Assocs., Aurora, Ill., 1955-77, prin., 1977—. Elder, Westminster Presbyn. Ch., Aurora. Capt. USAF, 1951-53. Fellow ASCE; mem. Ill. Soc. Profl. Engrs. (pres. 1987-88), Am. Acad. Environ. Engrs. (diplomate), Rotary Club of Aurora (pres. 1989-90). Achievements include design of storm-water detention system to minimize flooding. Home: 145 S Edgelawn Dr Aurora IL 60506-4509

HOEFLER, ERIC ALEXANDER, language educator; b. Petersburg, Va., Jan. 21, 1973; s. George and Diane Hoefler. BA, Mary Washington Coll., 1995. Cert. tchr. English Va. Bi-cultural curriculum developer Chinle Schs., Chinle, Ariz., 1995—96; tchr. Woodbridge (Va.) Sr. H.S., 1997—; asst. coord. Ctr. Fine & Performing Arts, Woodbridge, 1998—; tech. liaison, cons. No. Va. Writing Project, Fairfax, Va., 2001—. Mentor Commonwealth Challenge Va., Virginia Beach, 2001—02. Office: Woodbridge Sr HS 3001 Old Bridge Rd Woodbridge VA 22192 Business E-Mail: hoefella@pwcs.edu.

HOEFLICH, CHARLES HITSCHLER, banker; b. Phila., Apr. 4, 1914; s. Llewellyn Ashbridge and Mary Ann (Osterheldt) H. BS in Econs., U. Pa., 1936; cert. in banking, Rutgers U., 1949; cert. in bank mktg., Northwestern U., 1955; LLD, Okla. Christian U., 1972. V.p. Phila. Nat. Bank, 1951-62; pres. Union Nat. Bank & Trust Co., Souderton, Pa., 1962-76, chmn. bd. dirs., 1976-84, chmn. exec. com., 1984-86; chmn. Univest Corp. Pa., Souderton, 1973-86, chmn. emeritus, 1986—. Mem. Rep. presdl. task force, 1981-97. Sec.-treas. Intercollegiate Studies Inst., Wilmington, Del., 1955—; trustee Okla. Christian U., Oklahoma City, 1974—; founder Penn Found. for Mental Health, 1965—, now dir. emeritus. Recipient Presdl. citation USAAF, 1946, Citizen of Yr. award Fed. Bar Assn., 1960, Lifetime Achievement award Intercoll. Studies Inst., 2000. Mem. Bank Mktg. Assn. (pres. 1964-65), Am. Bankers Assn.(recipient Eisenhower Commn., 2002), Union League Club (Phila.), Indian Valley Country Club (Telford, Pa.), Pres.'s Club, Heritage Found., Intercollegiate Studies Inst. Republican. Avocations: collecting americana antiques and art, painting, horticulture. Office: Univest Corp Pa Main And Broad St Souderton PA 18964 Fax: 215-7212433.

HOEFLIN, RONALD KENT, philosopher, writer; b. Richmond Heights, Mo., Feb. 23, 1944; s. William Eugene and Mary Elizabeth (Dell) Hoeflin. Student, Calif. Inst. Tech., 1962-63, U. Calif., Berkeley, 1966-67, U. N.C., 1970-71; BA, U. Minn., 1968, Shimer Coll., 1974; MLS, Ind. U., 1970; MA, New Sch. Social Rsch., 1979, PhD, 1987. With various librs., 1969-85; publisher, editor Triple Nine Soc., N.Y.C., 1979-81, 85-89; publisher, editor, founder Top One Percent Soc., N.Y.C., 1989—, One-in-a-Thousand Soc., N.Y.C., 1992—. Designer (intelligence test) Mega Test, 1985, Titan Test, 1990, Ultra Test, 1995, Hoeflin Power Test, 1996; author: To Unscrew the Inscrutable: A Theory of Categories and Unifying Paradigm for Philosophy, 2003. Mem.: Am. Philos. Assn. (Fifth Ann. Rockefeller prize 1988), Prometheus Soc. (founder 1982), Mega Soc. (founder 1982), Mensa. Office: PO Box 539 New York NY 10101-0539

HOEFT, MARJORIE CLAIRE, librarian; b. Vancouver, B.C., Can., Feb. 26, 1938; came to U.S., 1947; d. Leonard Neil and Jessie R. R. (McKinnon) Osgood; m. Robert Dean Hoeft, Dec. 19, 1959; children: Melissa Kathryn, Eric Von. BA, U. Oreg., 1960, MA, 1964. Tchr., libr. Creswell (Oreg.) High Sch., 1961; tchr. Agana (Guam) High Sch., 1961-63; cataloging libr. Umatilla County Library, Pendleton, Oreg., 1965, Blue Mountain Community Coll., Pendleton, 1966— . Mem. Alpha Psi Omega, Phi Beta Kappa. Republican. Avocations: travel, study, reading, sewing, hiking. Home: 1374 SW 37th St Pendleton OR 97801-3650 Office: Blue Mountain C C 2411 NW Carden Ave Pendleton OR 97801-1292

HOEFT, ROBERT GENE, agriculture educator; b. David City, Nebr., May 21, 1944; s. Otto O. Hoeft and Lula (Barlean) Pleskac; m. Nancy A. Bussen, Sept. 1, 1990; children: Jeffrey, Angela. BS, U. Nebr., 1965, MS, 1967; PhD, U. Wis., 1972. Asst. prof. S.D. State U., Rapid City, 1972-73, U. Ill., Urbana, 1973-77, assoc. prof., 1977-81, prof., 1981—. Author: Modern Corn Production, 1986, Modern Corn & Soybean Production, 2000; editor Jour. Prodn. Agr., 1986-92. Recipient Funk award U. Ill., 1990, Robert E. Wagner award Potash and Phosphate Inst., 1998. Fellow Soil Sci. Soc. Am., Am. Soc. Agronomy (pres. 2002-03, CIBA-Geigy award 1978, Agronomic Extension award, grantee 1988, Agronomic Achievement award-soils 1995, Werner Nelson award for diagnosis of yield limiting factors 1996); mem. Coun. for Sci. and Tech. Office: U Ill 1102 S Goodwin Ave Urbana IL 61801-4730

HOEG, DONALD FRANCIS, chemist, consultant, former research and development executive; b. Bklyn., Aug. 2, 1931; s. Harry Herman and Charlotte (Bourke) H.; m. Patricia Catherine Fogarty, Aug. 30, 1952; children— Thomas Edward, Robert Francis, Donald John, Mary Beth, Susan Catherine. BS in Chemistry summa cum laude, St. John's U., N.Y., 1953; PhD in Chemistry, Ill. Inst. Tech., 1957. Fellow in chemistry and chem. engring. Armour Research Found., 1953-54; grad. research asst. Ill. Inst. Tech., 1954-56; research chemist W.R. Grace & Co., 1956-58, sr. research chemist, 1958-61; group leader addition polymer chemistry Roy C. Ingersoll Research Center, Borg-Warner Corp., Des Plaines, Ill., 1961-64, mgr. polymer chemistry, 1964-66, assoc. dir., head chem. research dept., 1966-75, dir., 1975-88; pres. DFH Assocs., 1988—. Former mem. solid state scis. adv. bd. NAS; bd. overseers Lewis Coll. Scis. and Letters of Ill. Inst. Tech., 1980-91; bd. dirs. Ill. Inst. Tech. Alumni, 1979-82, Mt. Prospect Combined Appeal, 1963-65 Bd. editors: Research Mgmt. Mag, 1979-82; contbr. numerous articles tech. publs., chpts. in books; patentee in field. TaPing Lin scholar, 1955-56; AEC asst., 1954; Armour Research Found. fellow, 1953-54; Ill. Inst. Tech. Achievement award, 1983 Mem. Am. Chem. Soc., AAAS, N.Y. Acad. Scis., Dirs. Indsl. Research, Am. Mgmt. Assn. (v.p. council 1984-88), Research Dirs. Assn. Chgo. (pres. 1977-78), Indsl. Research Inst. (bd. dirs. 1986-88), Sigma Xi. E-mail: dfh1931@aol.com. *I've counseled myself that all ideas and concepts, no matter how seemingly difficult, are products of man's mind, and, therefore fundamentally understandable.*

HOEHN, ELMER LOUIS, lawyer, state and federal agency administrator, educator, consultant; b. Memphis, Ind., Dec. 19, 1915; s. Louis and Agnes (Goss) H.; m. Frances Cory, June 10, 1943; children: Kathleen Gillmore, G. Patrick. BS, Canterbury Coll., 1936, Northwestern U., 1937; JD, U. Louisville, 1940. Bar: Ky. 1940, D.C. 1969, U.S. Supreme Ct. 1969, U.S. Ct. Appeals 1970, Ind. 1981. Prof. bus. and law Jeffersonville High Sch., Ind., 1937-41, Ind. U., 1940-41; with legal and personnel div. Am. Barge Lines, 1942-44; realtor Ind., 1949—; apptd. dir. by Gov. Ind. Oil and Gas, 1949-53; apptd. adminstr. by Pres. U.S. Oil Import Adminstrn., 1965-69; sec.-treas. Am. Assn. Oil Well Drilling Contractors, 1956-60; exec. sec. Ind. Oil Producers and Land Owners Assn., 1953-64; pvt. practice law Washington, 1969-91, Indiana, 1981—. ADR civil mediator, Ind., 1993; gov.'s rep. Interstate Oil & Gas Compact Commn., 1949—53, 1961—65; apptd. commr. by gov. Ohio River Greenway Devel. Commn., 1994; cons. petroleum, natural resources, energy and environment; chmn. Clark County Redevel. Commn., 1996—, Charlestown Ammo INAAP Reuse Authority, 1997—. Mem. Ind. Gen. Assembly, 1945- 49, minority floor leader, 1947, chief clk., 1949, Democratic chmn., Clark County, Ind., 1945-52; Ind. del. Dem. Nat. Conv., 1964, chmn. 8th Congl. Dist., 1952-58; mem. Ind. Dem. Exec. Com., 1952-58, Ind. and Midwest campaign mgr., LBJ campaign for president, 1960. Named Hon. Citizen, Ind. and Ky., Citoyen Honneur, Soufflenheim, France, Ambassador, Clark County, Ind., Disting. Benefactor, Clark Meml. Hosp. Interfaith Ctr.; recipient Humanitarian award, ARC, 2003, Chancellor's Medallion award, IUS, 2003, Helping Hand award, Haven House Svcs., Lewis & Clark Bicentennial Commemoration, Falls of the Ohio, 2003—. Mem. ABA, Fed. Bar Assn., Ky. Bar Assn. (Disting. sr. counselor 1990), D.C. Bar Assn., Ind. Bar Assn. (Disting. Sr. Counselor 1990), Coop. Oil and Gas Assns. (liason com. Washington 1969-91), Am. Inn of Ct., Univ. Club, Sigma Delta Kappa. Clubs: Nat. Lawyers, Nat. Press (Washington); Ind. Legislators (Indpls.); Filson (Louisville), Elks Country (Jeffersonville). Roman Catholic. Home: 2105 Utica Pike Jeffersonville IN 47130-5005

HOEHN, MARGARET MAIER, neurologist; b. San Francisco, Nov. 24, 1930; d. Peter Paul and Eva Till Maier; children: Robert Anthony Till, Margaret Eve Maier Hanan. BA, U. Sask., Saskatoon, Can., 1950; MD, U. B.C., Vancouver, Can., 1954; postgrad., U. B.C. and Nat. Hosp. Neurol. Diseases, London, 1954—60. Asst. in neurology Boston U., 1961-62; asst. prof. Columbia U., N.Y.C., 1963-70; clin. prof. U. Colo., Denver, 1970—, dir. Parkinson's disease and movement disorder clinic, 1984—. Clin. rschr. Parkinson's Disease and other movement disorders; cons. in clin. rsch., lectr. in field. Contbr. over 100 articles to profl. jours.; developer Hoehn and Yahr Scale as a measure of severity of Parkinson's disease. Fellow ACP, Royal Coll. Physicians Can., Am. Acad. Neurology; mem. Am. Neurol. Assn., Movement Disorder Soc., Colo. Soc. Clin. Neurology, Alpha Omega Alpha. Avocations: travel, bridge, swimming, reading, theater. Office: 3851 S Xanthia St Denver CO 80237-1602

HOEHN, RICHARD ALBERT, association executive, clergyman; b. Butler, Pa., Oct. 12, 1936; s. Clarence Albert and Mary Catherine (Rieger) Hoehn; m. Carole Lee Zimmerman, Oct. 26, 1991; children: Christine Joyce, Thomas Albert, Karen Elizabeth, Benjamin Douglass, Kristin Nicole Sizemore. BA, Capital U., 1958; BD, Trinity Luth. Sem., Columbus, Ohio, 1962; MA, U. Chgo., 1970, PhD, 1972. Ordained to ministry Evang. Luth. Ch. in Am. Pastor Good Shepherd Luth. Ch., Brunswick, Maine, 1962-65; prof. ch. in society Brite Div. Sch., Tex. Christian U., Ft. Worth, 1970-88; regional organizer Bread for the World, Washington, 1988-91; dir. Bread for the World Inst., Washington, 1991—2001, dir. spl. programs, 2001—. Author: Up from Apathy, 1983; contbr. articles to profl. jours., ann. reports on world hunger. Recipient rsch. awards Tex. Christian U. Found.; Lily Found. postdoctoral fellow, 1976; Fulbright tchg. fellow, 1986; grantee Ford Found., W.K. Kellogg Found., MacArthur Found., Rockefeller Found., others. Mem. Soc. Christian Ethics. Democrat. Home: 2007 Wooded Way Adelphi MD 20783-1348 Office: Bread for the World Inst 50 F St NW # 500 Washington DC 20001-1530 E-mail: rhoehn@bread.org., zimhoe@att.net.

HOEHN, ROBERT J. plastic surgeon, educator; b. East St. Louis, Ill., 1929; children: Robert Anthony Till, Margaret Eve, David Ivan, Daniel Vincent; m. Nancy Ruth Vincent. MD, Washington U., St. Louis, 1956. Diplomate Am. Bd. Plastic Surgery. Intern Vancouver (B.C., Can.) Gen. Hosp., 1956-57; resident in internal medicine, 1957-58; resident McGill U., Montreal, Que., Can., 1960-61; assoc. prof. plastic surgery U. Colo., Denver, 1970—78, Columbia U., N.Y., 1965—70; resident in gen. surgery Boston City Hosp., 1961-62; fellow in orthopaedic surgery, 1962; fellow in transplantation immunology Westminster Hosp., London, 1962-63; resident in plastic surgery N.Y. Hosp.-Cornell, 1963-65; clin. prof. plastic surgery U. Colo., 1978—2002; with Aurora Presbyn. Hosp., 1978—2002, Aurora Regional Med. Ctr., 1978—2002, Denver Children's Hosp., 1978—2002, Porter Meml. Hosp., 1978—2002, Swedish Hosp., 1978—2002; pvt. practice; ret., 2002. Fellow ACS; mem. AAPS, Am. Soc. Plastic Surgeons, Plastic Surgery Rsch. Coun. Home: 2601 S Quebec St Villa 3 Denver CO 80231-6039

HOEKSTRA, PETER, congressman, manufacturing executive; b. Groningen, The Netherlands, Oct. 30, 1953; m. Diane M. Johnson; children: Erin, Allison, Bryan. BA, Hope Coll., 1975; MBA, U. Mich., 1977. Furniture exec. Herman Miller, Inc., 1977-92, project mgr., product mgr., dir. product mgmt., dir. dealer mktg., v.p. dealer mktg., 1988-92, v.p. product mgmt., 1992-93; mem. U.S. Congress from 2d Mich. dist., 1993—, mem. edn. and the workforce com., chmn. select edn. subcom. edn. and the workforce com., 2001, mem. select com. on intelligence, 2001, mem. com. on transp. and infrastructure, mem. subcom. on C.G. and maritime transp., mem. subcom. on hwys., transit and pipelines. Chmn. edn. and the workforce ctr. subcom. on oversight and investigations. Contbr. to project devel. Equa Chair, recognized as outstanding product of 1980s by Time Mag. Republican. Office: US Ho of Reps Office Of Ho Mems 2234 Rayburn House Office Bldg Washington DC 20515-2202 E-mail: tellhoek@mail.house.gov.*

HOEKWATER, JAMES WARREN, treasurer; b. Grand Rapids, Mich., Nov. 4, 1946; s. William Harold and Sena (Hoeksema) H.; m. Roberta Joyce Paczala, July 12, 1975; children: William Paczala, Elizabeth Veronica. BA, Mich. State U., 1970. CPA, Mich. With Touche Ross & Co., Detroit, 1970-77; v.p., controller Great Lakes div. Nat. Steel Corp., Detroit, 1977-83; treas. Nat. Steel Corp., Pitts., 1983-89, v.p., 1987-89; corp. contr. ITT Rayonier Inc., Stamford, Conn., 1989-94; treas. Acme Metals Inc., Riverdale, Ill., 1994—2002; cons., 2002—. Mem. AICPA. Republican. Episcopalian. Home: 6420 Lane Ct Hinsdale IL 60521-5354 Office: Acme Metals Inc 13500 S Perry Ave Riverdale IL 60827-1148

HOEL, LESTER A. civil engineering educator; b. Bklyn., Feb. 26, 1935; s. Johannes and Julia (Michelsen) Hoel; m. Unni Sonja Blegen, Jan. 24, 1959; children: Julie Britt Bryan, Sonja Leslie, Lisa Hoel Rafael. B.C.E., City Coll., N.Y., 1957; MS in Civil Engring, Bklyn. Poly. Inst., 1960; D.Eng., U. Calif. at Berkeley, 1963. Registered profl engr, Calif, Pa, Va. Asst. prof. engring. San Diego State Coll., 1962-64; Fulbright research scholar Inst. Transport Economy, Oslo, 1964-65; prin. engr. Wilbur Smith & Assoc., San Francisco, 1965-66; faculty Carnegie-Mellon U., Pitts., 1966-74, prof. civil engring., 1970-74; assoc. dir. Transp. Research Inst., 1966-74; Hamilton prof. dept. civil engring. U. Va., 1974-99, chmn. dept., 1974-89, L.A. Lacy Disting. prof., 1999—; dir. Ctr. Transportation Stud., 2002—. Author: (book) Traffic and Highway Engineering, 3d edit., 2002; editor: Public Transportation, 1979, Public Transportation, rev 2d ed, 1992; mem. editl. bd.: transp. jours.; contbr. technical papers, books and articles. Recipient Alumni Award in Civil Eng, Col City NY, 1957, Stanley W Gustafson Leadership Award, Hwy Users Fedn, 1989, S S Steinberg Educ Award, Am Rd and Transp Builders, 1991, Disting. Faculty award, Coun. Univ. Transp. Ctrs., 2002, Jack H. Dillard Best Paper award, Va. Transp. Rsch. Coun., 2003; grantee Fulbright Travel, 1964—65. Fellow: ASCE (Huber Research Prize 1976, Frank Masters Award 1990, James Laurie Prize 1999), Inst Transp Engrs (Wilbur S Smith Dinsting Educator Award 2001), Nat Acad Eng; mem.: Am Soc Eng Educ, Transp Research Bd (chmn exec comt 1986, chmn comt tranps profl needs, truck weight study, Pyke Johnson Award 1977), Tau Beta Pi, Chi Epsilon, Sigma Xi. Home: 1340 Sunset Cir Charlottesville VA 22901 E-mail: LAH@virginia.edu.

HOELL, KATHY, disability rights advocate; b. Brattleboro, Vt., Apr. 8, 1955; d. Irene Ruth and David Allen Dearborn; m. Perry E. Hoell, June 11, 1976; 1 child, Graham. RN, Holyoke Hosp. Sch. Nursing, 1976; B in Behaviorial Sci., U. N.H., 1989; MPA, U. Nebr., 1998. Rsch. health sci. specialist VA Hosp., Omaha, 1998—2000; disability rights adv. Statewide Indep. Living Coun., Lincoln, Nebr., 1999—. Bd. dirs. Nebr. Advocacy Svcs.; mem. Nat. Coun. Independent Living. Mem.: Am. Soc. Pub. Adminstrn. Home and Office: 7301 Sarpy Ave Bellevue NE 68147-1456 E-mail: khoell@cox.net.

HOENIGSWALD, HENRY MAX, linguist, educator; b. Breslau, Germany, Apr. 17, 1915; s. Richard and Gertrud (Grunwald) H.; m. Gabriele Schoepflich, Dec. 26, 1944, (dec. 2001); children: Frances Gertrude, Susan Ann. Student, U. Munich, 1932-33, U. Zurich, 1933-34, U. Padua, 1934-36; DLitt, U. Florence, 1936, Perfezionamento, 1937; LHD (hon.), Swarthmore Coll., 1981, U. Pa., 1988, MA (hon.), 1971. Staff mem. Istituto Studi Etruschi, Florence, 1936-38; lectr., rsch. asst., instr. Yale U., 1939-42, 44-45. Lectr., instr. Hartford Sem. Found., 1942-43, 45-46; lectr. Hunter Coll., 1942-43, 46; lectr. charge Army specialized tng. U. Pa., Phila., 1943-44, assoc. prof., 1948-59, prof. linguistics, 1959-85, prof. emeritus, 1985—, chmn. dept. linguistics, 1963-70, co-chmn., 1978-79, cn. Caldwell Prize com., 1989-91; P-4 Fgn. Service Inst., Dept. State, 1946-47; assoc. prof. U. Tex., 1947-48; sr. linguist Deccan Coll., India, 1955; Fulbright lectr., Kiel, 1968, Oxford U., 1976-77; corp. vis. com. fgn. lits. and linguistics MIT, 1968-74; chmn. overseers com. to visit dept. linguistics Harvard U., 1978-84; vis. assoc. prof. U. Mich., 1946, 52, Princeton U., 1959-60; vis. assoc. prof. Georgetown U., 1952-53, 54, Collitz prof., 1955; vis. prof. Yale U., 1961-62, U. Mich., 1968; mem. Seminar, Columbia U., 1965—; vis. staff mem., Leuven, 1986; fellow St. John's Coll., Oxford U., 1976-77; del. Comparative Linguistics Internat. Rsch. and Exchs. Bd., 1986; cons. Etymological Dictionary of Old High German, 1980—; Poultney lectr. Johns Hopkins U., 1991; co-promotor, Leuven, 1992; mem. acad. com. Yarmouk U., 1997. Author: Spoken Hindustani, 1946-47, Language Change and Linguistic Reconstruction, 1960, Studies in Formal Historical Linguistics, 1973; editor: Am. Oriental Series, 1954-58, The European Background of American Linguistics, 1979, (with L. Wiener) Biological Metaphor and Cladistic Classification, 1987, (with M.R. Key) General and American Ethnolinguistics, 1989; assoc. editor Indian Jour. Linguistics, 1977—; cons. editor Jour. History of Ideas, 1978—; adv. bd. Lang. and Style, 1968—, Jour. Indo-European Studies, 1973—, Diachronica, 1984-94, Lynx, 1988—; csr. internat. adviser, cons. editor Internat. Ency. Linguistics, 1986-91, 2d edit., 2000—; editl. cons. Biographical Dictionary of Western Linguistics, 1994—. Am. Council Learned Socs. fellow, 1942-43, 44, Guggenheim fellow, 1950-51, Newberry Library fellow, 1956, NSF and Center Advanced Study Behavioral Scis. fellow, 1962-63, Faculty fellow Modern Langs. Coll. House, 1990-91; Festschrift in his honor, 1987. Fellow British Acad. (corr.), Am. Acad. Arts and Scis.; mem. NAS, Am. Philos. Soc. (rsch. com. 1978-84, libr. com. 1984-94, chmn. 1988-94, membership com. class IV 1984-90, chmn. 1987-90, exec. com. 1988-94, publs. com. 1994—, Henry Allen Moe prize 1991), N.Y. Acad. Scis., Linguistic Soc. Am. (pres. 1958), Am. Oriental Soc. (editor 1954-58, pres. 1966-67), Philol. Soc. (London), Linguistic Soc. India, Linguistics Assn. Gt. Britain, Internat. Soc. Hist. Linguistics, Indogermanische Gesellschaft, Am. Philol. Assn., Classical Assn. Atlantic States, Henry Sweet Soc., Studienkreis Geschichte der Sprachwissenschaft, Deutsch-polnische Gesellschaft der U. Wroclaw/Breslau, N.Am. Assn. History of Lang. Scis., Fulbright Assn., Internat. Soc. Friends of Wroclaw U., Fedn. Am. Scientists. Office: U Pa 618 Williams Hall Philadelphia PA 19104-6305 Home: 3300 Darby Rd # 3107 Haverford PA 19041-1069 E-mail: henryh@babel.ling.upenn.edu.

HOEPFNER, KARLA JEAN, designer, artist; b. Bridgeton, N.J., Nov. 24, 1958; d. Victor Robert and Thelma J. Hoepfner. Student, U. Md., 1977-78; BFA cum laude, Va. Commonwealth U., 1983; postgrad., Sch. Visual Arts, N.Y.C., 1993, Empire State Coll., 1994-95; MFA, Pratt Inst., 2000. Designer Fortress, Phila., 1985-88, Total Concept Inc., N.Y.C., 1989-92; mgr. Archetype Gallery, N.Y.C., 1994-96; self employed painter N.Y.C., 1992—. Art cons. Viart Corp., N.Y.C., 2000—01. One-woman shows include Steuben West Gallery, N.Y.C., 2000, exhibited in group shows at Cabell Libr., Richmond, Va., 1980, Montauk Club, Bklyn., 1993, Empire State Coll., N.Y.C., 1995, Hammerstein Ballroom, 2000, The Puck Bldg., 2000, OSP Gallery, Boston, 2002, Creative Arts Workshop, New Haven, Conn., White Columns Gallery, N.Y.C., 2003, Dorsky Gallery, 2004. Mem.: Phi Kappa Phi. Avocations: philosophy, metaphysics. Home: 121 8th Ave Brooklyn NY 11215-1709

HOEPRICH, PAUL DANIEL, physician educator; b. Alliance, Ohio, Jan. 3, 1924; s. Michael and Katharina (Wagner) H.; m. Muriel Lucy Blackwell, July 11, 1948; children: Martha Sue Kennedy, Paul Daniel Jr., Thomas Eric, Kurt Lincoln. Student, Harvard Coll.; MD, Harvard Med. Sch., 1947. Diplomate Am. Bd. Internal Medicine. Instr. medicine Johns Hopkins Sch. Medicine, Balt., 1956; instr. epidemiology Johns Hopkins Sch. Hygiene & Pub. Health, Balt., 1956; asst., assoc. prof. medicine U. Utah Coll Medicine, Salt Lake City, 1957-67, asst., assoc. prof. pathology, 1959-67; prof. medicine U. Calif. Sch. Medicine, Davis, 1967-91, emeritus, 1991—, prof. pathology, 1968-86, chief infectious and immunlogic diseases, 1967-80, chief med. mycology, 1986-91. Cons. physician in field. Editor, author: The Fluids of Parenteral Body Cavities, 1959, Infectious Diseases, Edits. 1-5, 1972-94; editor The Infectious Diseases Newsletter, 1985-90; contbr. chpts. to books and articles to med. and scientific jours. Capt. U.S. Army M.C., 1950-53. Recipient Soma Weiss award Harvard Med. Sch., 1947, Disting. Faculty award U. Calif. Davis Med. Ctr., 1986; Fogarty sr. fellow NIH, 1976. Fellow ACP, Infectious Disease Soc. Am. (founding); mem. AAAS, Am. Soc. Clin. Investigation, Assn. Am. Physicians.

HOERING, HELEN G. elementary educator; b. Liberty, N.Y., Mar. 27, 1946; d. Lewis J. and Charlotte (Huggler) Gerow Sr.; m. Rudolf O. Hoering, Dec. 23, 1968; children: Otto, Katrina. BS, SUNY, Oneonta, 1968; MSEd, SUNY, 1971. Elem. tchr. Liberty Cen. Sch. at WSS, Liberty, N.Y. Mem. N.Y. State Reading Assn., Sullivan County Reading Coun., Alpha Delta Kappa (past pres.). Home: RR 1 Box 543 Jeffersonville NY 12748-9706

HOERNEMAN, CALVIN A., JR., economics educator; b. Youngstown, Ohio, Sept. 30, 1940; s. Calvin A. and Lucille A. (Leiss) H.; m. Cheryl L. Morand, Aug. 10, 1973; children: David, Jennifer, Christina. BA, Bethany Coll., 1962; MA, Mich. State U., 1964, postgrad., Cambridge U. Mem. faculty, Delta Coll., University Center, Mich., 1966—, prof. econs., 1976—; cons. Prentice-Hall, Acad. Press, Goodyear Pub., Random House Pub., Forbes Econ. Survey Panel; econ. expert witness; mem. Forbes mag. Econ. Survey Panel. Author: Poverty, Wealth and Income Distribution, 1969; co-author: "Caper" Principles of Economics Software Study Guide; contbr. articles to various publs. Recipient Recognition award AAUP, 1972, Bergstein award Delta Coll. Grad. Class, 1972, Competition for Excellence award IBM and the League for Innovation, 1988. Mem. AAUP, Am. Econ. Assn., Midwest Econ. Assn., Nat. Assn. Forensic Economists. Home: 5712 Lamplighter Ln Midland MI 48642-3137 Office: Delta Coll Dept Econs University Center MI 48710-0001

HOERNER, ROBERT JACK, lawyer; b. Fairfield, Iowa, Oct. 12, 1931; s. John Andrew and Margaret Louise (Simmons) Hoerner; m. Judith Chandler, Apr. 21, 1954 (div. Feb. 1975); children: John Andrew II, Timothy Chandler, Blayne Marie Hoerner Murray, Michelle Margaret Hoerner Smith; m. Mary Paolano, June 3, 1989. BA, Cornell Coll., 1953; JD, U. Mich., 1958. Bar: Ohio 1960, US Supreme Ct 1964, US Ct Appeals (6th cir) 1972, US Ct Appeals (fed cir) 1990. Law clk. to hon. Chief Justice Earl Warren U.S. Supreme Ct, Washington, 1958-59; assoc. Jones, Day, Reavis & Pogue, Cleve., 1959-63, 65-66; chief evaluation sect. antitrust divsn. Dept. Justice, Washington, 1963-65; ptnr. Jones, Day, Reavis & Pogue, Cleve., 1967-93. Contbr. articles to profl jours; editor (editor-in-chief): (journal) Mich Law Rev. Trustee New Orgn Visual Arts, Cleveland, Ohio, 1976—80, 1987—90. With Counter Intelligence Corps U.S. Army, 1953—55. Mem.: ABA (antitrust sect, patent sect), Cleve. Intellectual Property Law Assn., Greater Cleve. Bar Assn., Ohio Bar Assn., Leland Mich. Country Club, Order of Coif, Phi Beta Kappa. Democrat. Home: 360 Darbys Run Bay Village OH 44140-2968 Office: Jones Day Reavis & Pogue 901 Lakeside Ave E Ste N-335 Cleveland OH 44114-1190 Business E-Mail: rjhoerner@jonesday.com.

HOERTH, KENNETH D. music educator; b. Eureka, SD, Sept. 16, 1948; s. Waiter E. and Elizabeth Hoerth; m. Debora M. Krueger, June 9, 1978; children: Victoria, Kayla, Chris. BS Composite music, Valley City State U, Valley City, ND, 1971. Dir. Streeter HS, Streeter, ND, 1971—73, Hosmer HS, Hosmer, SD, 1973—76, Lakota HS, Lakota, ND, 1976—. Musician Aristocrats (prof. dance band), Devils Lake, ND, 1985—, Shriners Band, Grand Forks, ND, 2000—. Mem. Elks, Devil's Lake, ND, 1985—, Masons, Grand Forks, ND, 2000—, Shriners, Grand Forks, ND, 2000—. Recipient 30 yr., Music Ed. Nat. Conf., 2001, Citation of Excellence award, ND chpt. Nat. Band Assn., 2003. Mem.: Lakota Ed. Assoc., NEA, Am. Choral Dir. Assoc. Democrat. Lutheran. Achievements include first to Lakota Music program deemed 100 best places to live in Am. for music ed. Avocations: umpiring, softball, walking, bicycling, performing. Home: 618 W2 Box 131 Lakota ND 58344-0131 Office: Lakota High School E Ave at Main Lakota ND 58344-0131

HOESLY, EILEEN M. academic administrator, educator; b. Portland, Oreg., Jan. 16, 1947; d. Ferdinand J. Hoesly and Nancy Jane Whitmore; m. Heracles J. Petropakis, June 5, 1975; children: Janeka Petropakis, Christina Petropakis. BA, Portland State U., 1969, MBA, 1974, postgrad., 1985—86. Video program adminstr. Ctrl. Tex. Coll., Athens, Greece, 1976—83; lectr. U. Md., Athens, Greece, 1974—90; mktg. asst. AT&T, Pacific N.W. Bell, Portland, Oreg., 1974; prof. fin., mgmt. U. LaVerne, Athens, Greece, 1977—, CFO, 1995—. Acct. Uniwest Inc., Portland, Oreg., 1969—72; mgmt. cons. Eli Lilly, Athens, Greece, 1980—83; vis. prof. Imperial Coll., London, 1995—96, U. LaVerne, Calif., 1990—91; pres. bd. edn. Am. Cmty. Schs., Athens, Greece, 1999—. Mem.: AAUP. Home: 15409 SE Oatfield Rd Milwaukie OR 97267 Office: Univ LaVerne P Tsaldari Athens Greece

HOESSLE, CHARLES HERMAN, zoo director; b. St. Louis, Mar. 20, 1931; m. Marilyn Mueller, Jan. 5, 1952; children: Maureen, Kirk, Tracy, Bradley. AA, Harris Tchrs. Coll., 1951; student, Am. Assn. Zool. Parks and Aquariums Zoo Mgmt. Sch., 1976-77; LLD (hon.), Maryville Coll., 1986, St. Louis U., 1990, U. Mo., St. Louis, 1994. Reptile keeper St. Louis Zoo, 1963, asst. curator, 1964, curator reptiles and curator edn., 1968-69, gen. curator and dep. dir., 1969-82, dir., 1982—2002, dir. emeritus, 2002—. Adj. prof. dept. biology St. Louis U., 1973-74, 81-82, 83; owner, operator Exotic Pet Shop, St. Louis; host St. Louis Zoo Show, 1968-78 Chmn. Reptile Study Merit Badge counselors, St. Louis; mem. adv. bd. Mo. Coalition for Environment, 1997; state chmn. UN Day, 1982; mem. St. Louis County Counts; bd. dirs. Harris-Stowe State Coll. Found., City Mus.; mem. Bd. Regents Harris-Stowe State Coll. Recipient Disting. Alumnus award Harris-Stowe State Coll., 1987. Mem. Internat. Union Dirs. Zool. Gardens, Am. Zoo and Aquarium Assn. (bd. dirs. 1977-79, 85-87, v.p. 1988, pres. 1990-91, past pres. 1991-92, rep. to species survival commn. Internat. Union for Conservation Nature and Natural Resources), St. Louis Naturalists Club, St. Louis Ctr. for Internat. Rels. (bd. dirs. 1993—), St. Louis Mus. Collaborative (pres. 1993), Animal Protective Assn. (bd. dirs.), Internat. Friendship Alliance St. Louis County (chmn. cultural com.), Explorers, St. Louis Herpetological Society, Hawthorne Soc., St. Louis Rotary Club, St Louis Ambassadors Club (bd. dir.). Home: 10814 Forest Circle Dr Saint Louis MO 63128-2007 Office: St Louis Zoo Forest Park Saint Louis MO 63110-1380

HOEVEN, JOHN, governor; b. Bismarck, N.D., Mar. 13, 1957; m. Mical (Mikey); children: Marcela, Jack. B in history and econ., Dartmouth Coll., 1979; MBA, J.L. Kelloge Grad. Sch. Mngmt., Northwestern U., 1981. Exec. v.p. First Western Bank, Minot, N.D., 1986-93; pres. and CEO Bank of N.D. (BND), 1993-2000; gov. N.D., 2000—. Econ. adv. N.D. Univ.; trustee Bismarck State Coll.; regent Minot State U. Cmty. chair Mo. Slope Areawide Campaign, 1998; chair Minot Chamber Commerce AFB Retention com., Minot Area Devel. Corp.; dir. Minot Kiwanis Club, Souris Valley Humane Soc, State Fair Adv. com.; mem. bd. dirs. First Western Bank and Trust, N.D. Bankers Assn., State Bank Bd., N.D. Small Bus. Investment Co., Prairie Pub. Broadcasting, N.D. Econ. Devel. Assn., Bismarck YMCA, Harold Schafer Leadership Ctr. Republican. Roman Catholic. Office: Gov Office 600 E Blvd Ave Bismarck ND 58505-0001*

HOEXTER, CORINNE ROSENFELDER KATZ, author, editor; b. Scranton, Pa., Nov. 3, 1927; d. Edward David and Aimee Helen (Rosenfelder) Katz; m. Rolf Hoexter, Dec. 25, 1955; children: Vivien, Michael Frederic. BA in English with high honors, Wellesley Coll., 1949; MA, U. Chgo., 1950. Promotion asst. Expt. Internat. Living, Putney, Vt., 1950-51; editl. asst. Parents mag., 1951-53; assoc. editor Mag. Mgmt., Inc., 1953-54; from assoc. editor to mng. editor Pines Pub. Inc., N.Y.C., 1954—57; picture editor J.J. Little & Ives, N.Y.C., 1957—59; mng. editor Portfolio and Art News Ann., 1959-60; exec. editor Asia mag. of Asia Soc., 1978-84; editor travel sect. N.Y. Times, 1984-85; freelance writer-editor, 1985—. Author: From Canton to California, The Epic of Chinese Immigration, 1976, Black Crusader: Frederick Douglass, 1970; co-author: A Nation Conceived and Dedicated, 1970; contbr. to N.Y. Times and other periodicals. Trustee Flat Rock Book Nature Assn., 1973-78; mem. adv. coun. Chamber Orch. Palisades, 1993-2000; active Asian Cinevision, Chinese Am. planning Coun., Sta. WNYC, N.Y.C.; mem. Mus. Modern Art, Met. Mus. Art, Whitney Mus. Am. Art, Friends N.Y. Pub. Libr., Friends Carnegie Hall, Friends Orch. St. Lukes, Marlboro Music, Chamber Music Am., South St. Seaport. Fulbright fellow U. Bologna (Italy), 1953. Mem. LOWV, NOW, Authors Guild, Am. Soc. Journalists and Authors, Assn. Preservation of Cape Cod, N.Y. Zool. Soc., Common Cause, Mass. Audubon Soc., Amnesty Internat., Chatham Yacht Club (Mass.), Wellesley Club Englewood, Wellesley Club N.Y.C., Phi Beta Kappa. Home and Office: 67 Spring Ln Englewood NJ 07631-3009

HOEY, RITA, public relations executive; b. Chgo., Nov. 4, 1950; d. Louis D. and Edith M. (Finnemann) Hoey; m. Joseph John Dragonette, Sept. 4, 1982 (dec.). BA in English and History, No. Ill. U., 1972. Asst. dir. Nat. Assn. Housing and Human Devel., Chgo., 1975; pub. rels. account exec. Weber Cohn & Riley, Chgo., 1975-76; publicity coord. U.S. Gypsum Co., Chgo., 1976-77; with Daniel J. Edelman, Inc., Chgo., 1977-84, sr. v.p., 1981-84; exec. v.p. Dragonette, Inc., Chgo., 1984-91, pres., 1991-99, GCI Dragonette, Chgo., 1999—. Mem. Pub. Rels. Soc. Am. Home: Ste 2200 680 North Lake Shore Dr Chicago IL 60611 Office: GCI Dragonette 205 W Wacker Dr Ste 2200 Chicago IL 60606-1215

HOFBAUER, MICHELE PACE, illustrator, writer; b. Bridgeport, Conn., May 19, 1953; d. Michael F. and Theresa A. Pace; m. John Alfred Hofbauer, July 22, 1978; 1 child, Michael. BS in Spl. Edn., So. Conn. State U., 1975, MS in Spl. Edn., 1982. Spl. edn. tchr. Chalk Hill Mid. Sch., Monroe, Conn., 1976—83; freelance illustrator, author Trumbull, Conn., 1984—; assoc. pub. Green Bark Press, Inc., Bridgeport, 1996—. Edn. cons. Monroe Bd. Edn., 1984—85; spkr., lectr. in field. Author, illustrator: children's book All the Letters, 1993, Couldn't We Make A Difference, 2000, illustrator: children's book The Bug and the Slug in the Rug, 1995. Mem. first day book selection com. Bridgeport Edn. Fund., 2001. Mem.: Conn. Classic Artists, Nat. League Am. Pen Women (v.p. Fairfield County chpt.). Republican. Roman Catholic. Home: 111 Williams Rd Bridgeport CT 06611

HOFELDT, JOHN W. lawyer; b. Elkhart Lake, Wis., Sept. 6, 1920; s. Johann Heinrich and Matilda A. (Kuester) H.; m. Marion Ruth Meyer, Nov. 27, 1943; children: Nancy R. Hofeldt Werley, William A., Mark R. Ph.B., U. Wis.-Madison, 1943, LL.B. (editor Law Rev. 1946-47), 1947. Bar: Wis. 1947, Ill. 1948. Since practiced in, Chgo.; ptnr. Haight & Hofeldt (and predecessors), 1955—89; ret., 1989. Lectr. John Marshall Grad. Sch., Chgo., 1971-91. Mem. Ill. Sch. Dist. 194 Bd. Edn., 1964-72. Served with USN, 1943-46. Mem. Am., Wis., Ill. bar assns., Patent Law Assn. Chgo. Clubs: Masons (Chgo.), Shriners (Chgo.), Union League (Chgo.). Republican. Home: 5555 Tancho Dr Madison WI 53718-1920

HOFER, INGRID, artist, educator; b. N.Y.C., Aug. 25, 1926; d. William D. and Martha G. Kassul; m. Peter H. Hofer, Mar. 10, 1951; 1 child, Mark A. BFA, Meisterschule für Mode, Hamburg, Germany, 1949; postgrad., Traphagen Sch. Design, N.Y.C., 1949-51. Instr. Acad. Arts Trailside Mus., N.J., 1968-70, Grosse Pointe War Meml., Mich., 1974-78, Countryside Arts, Arlington Heights, Ill., 1981-93, Toledo Arts Club/Lourdes Coll., 1983-93, McCormick (S.C.) Arts Coun., 1994—. Represented in permanent collections Fairleigh Dickinson U., N.J., First Nat. Bank, Barrington, Ill., Good Shepherd Hosp., Ill., Lumus Co., N.J., Dana Corp., Ohio, others; exhbns. include Nat. Juried Shows, 1972-99, Union League, Chgo., 1981, Winter Sojourn, Toledo, 1987, Women Alive Ohio, 1986, 87, 89, Women on Paper, Anderson, S.C., 1996, The Arnold Gallery, Aiken, S.C., 1997, 98, Aiken Ctr. Arts, 2001-2002, USCA Etherredge Art Gallery, 2002, 2003. Vol. John De La Howe Sch., McCormick, 1963-99, others. Fellow Am. Artist Profl. League; mem. Catharine Lorillard Wolfeart, N.J. Inst. Art, S.C. Inst. Art, Ga. Inst. Art, Ala. Inst. Art, Gertrude Herbert Inst. Art. Home: 209 Old Ferry Rd Mc Cormick SC 29835-3409

HOFER, MYRON A(RMS), psychiatrist, researcher; b. N.Y.C., Dec. 20, 1931; s. Philip and Frances Louise (Heckscher) H.; m. Lynne Hofer, June 12, 1954; children: Timothy Philip, Adeline Van Nostrand; Andrew Paul. AB, Harvard U., 1954, MD, 1958. Diplomate Am. Bd. Psychiatry and Neurology. Resident in medicine Mass. Gen. Hosp., Boston, 1958-60; rsch. assoc. N.Y. Hosp. - Cornell, N.Y.C., 1960-62, NIMH, Bethesda, Md., 1962-64; resident in psychiatry N.Y. State Psychiat. Inst., N.Y.C., 1964-66; asst. prof. to prof. psychiatry & neurosci. Albert Einstein Coll. Medicine, Bronx, N.Y., 1966-84; prof. psychiatry Coll. Physicians and Surgeons Columbia U., N.Y.C., 1984-2000, Sackler Inst. prof., dir. Sackler Inst. for Devel. Psychobiology, 2000—. Dir., Dept. Devel. Psychobiology, N.Y. State Psychiatric Inst., 1984-2000; Thomas William Salmon lectr., 1996. Author: Roots of Human Behavior, 1981; editor jours. Psychosomatic Medicine, 1972-99, Devel. Psychobiology, 1981—, Behavioral Neurosci., 1993-97, Perinatal Devel., 1987. Mem. nat. adv. bd. Healthy Steps for Young Children Program, The Commonwealth Fund, 1996-2002. Lt. comdr. USPHS, 1962-64, Washington. Recipient Rsch. Scientist award, NIMH, Bethesda, 1977-2003, Merit award, 1986-96. Mem. Am. Psychosomatic Soc. (pres. 1982-83), Internat. Soc. Devel. Psychobiology (pres. 1980-81), Psychiatric Rsch. Soc., Acad. Behavior Medicine Rsch., Century Club. Avocations: sailing, gardening, reading, photography, drawings and prints. Office: NY State Psychiat Inst 1051 Riverside Dr Unit 40 New York NY 10032-2603

HOFER, ROY ELLIS, lawyer; b. Cin., Oct. 10, 1935; s. Eric Walter and Elsie Katherine (Ellis) H.; m. Suzanne Elizabeth Sturtz, June 6, 1956 (div. 1974); m. Cynthia Ann Corson, June 5, 1981; children: Kimberly, Tracy, Eric. BChemE, Purdue U., 1957; JD, Georgetown U., 1961. Patent examiner U.S. Patent & Trademark Office, Washington, 1957-59; patent agt. Exxon Corp., Washington, 1959-61; ptnr. Brinks Hofer Gilson & Lione, Chgo., 1961—, pres., 1995-99. Adv. com. No. Dist. Ill., 1991-95. Contbr. articles to profl. jours. Bd. dirs. Chgo. Lung Assn., 1982-83, Ctr. for Conflict Resolution, 1983-88, 90-91, pres., 1991-97; bd. dirs. Union League Club Chgo., 1984-88, Boys and Girls Club, Chgo., 1985-89, Ill. Inst. CLE, Chgo., 1986-88. Mem. ABA (dir. litigation sect. 1982-87), Fed. Cir. Bar Assn. (pres. 1993-94), Chgo. Bar Assn. (pres. 1988-89), Intellectual Property Law Assn. Chgo., Am. Intellectual Property Law Assn., Legal Club Chgo., Phi Eta Sigma, Tau Beta Pi, Omega Chi Epsilon. Republican. Office: Brinks Hofer Gilson & Lione Ste 3600 455 N Cityfront Plaza Dr Chicago IL 60611-5599

HOFER, STEPHEN ROBERT, lawyer; b. Anderson, Ind., July 25, 1950; s. Robert E. and Maxine (Hert) H.; m. Cheryl A. Stiles, Aug. 27, 1994; children: Victoria Sloane, Morgan BrynRose. AB, Ind. U., 1976; JD, Northwestern U., 1980. Bar: Calif. 1980, U.S. Dist. Ct. (ctrl. dist.) Calif. 1980, U.S. Ct. Appeals (9th cir.) 1980, U.S. Dist. Ct. (ea., no., and so. dists.) Calif. 1982, U.S. Supreme Ct. 1995. Mng. editor Daily Herald-Tel., Bloomington, Ind., 1972-74; asst. city editor Miami Herald, Ft. Lauderdale, Fla., 1976-77; atty. Gibson Dunn & Crutcher, L.A., 1980-84; venue press chief L.A. Olympic Organizing Com., 1983-84; v.p., gen. counsel Am. Golf Corp., Santa Monica, Calif., 1984-92; of counsel Bailey & Marzano, Santa Monica, 1992-98; ptnr., chair corp. and transactional dept. Bailey & Ptnrs., Santa Monica, 1998—. Instr. law U. So. Calif., L.A., 1983-84, lectr. aviation law Calif. State U., L.A. Sec., bd. dirs. Mus. of Flying, Santa Monica, 1986-89; bd. dirs. L.A. Philharmonic Assn., 1992-95, Santa Monica Symphony Assn., 1999-2000; pres. L.A. Philharmonic Bus. and Profl. Assn., 1992-95. Mem.: SAR, Sons of Union Vets. of Civil War, Jamestown Soc. Democrat. Avocations: symphonic music and jazz, mountain climbing, travel, genealogy, photography. Office: Bailey & Ptnrs 2d Fl 2828 Don Douglas Loop N Santa Monica CA 90405-2959 E-mail: SHofer@baileypartners.com.

HOFEREK, MARY JUDITH, information systems specialist, educator; b. East Orange, N.J., Nov. 1, 1943; d. George William and Jessie (Rucki) H. BA, Trenton State Coll., 1965; MA, U. Mich., 1969; PhD, U. Wis., 1978; MS, Am. U., 2000. Sys. analyst Fed. Govt., Kansas City (Mo.), Washington, 1984-88; sr. sys. engr. CDSI, Rockville, Md., 1988-90; sr. database adminstr. IBM/Loral/Lockheed Martin, Reston, Va., 1990-2001; program dir. computer sys. mgmt. U. Md., U. Coll., College Park, 2001—. Adj. prof. U. Md. Univ. Coll., College Park, 1988—2001. Author: Going Forth: Leadership Issues for Women in Sport, 1978, Build It For the Real World: A Database Workbook, 2001; co-editor: Women and Leadership, 1978; contbr. articles to profl. jours. Mem. Women's Polit. Caucus, Washington, Polish Am. Arts Assn., Washington. Mem.: IEEE. Avocation: tennis. Home: 218 Rabbitt Rd Gaithersburg MD 20878-1135

HOFERT, JACK, consulting company executive, lawyer; b. Phila., Apr. 6, 1930; s. David and Beatrice (Schatz) H.; m. Marilyn Tukeman, Sept. 4, 1960; children: Dina, Bruce. BS, UCLA, 1952, MBA, 1954, JD, 1957. Bar: Calif. 1957; CPA, Calif. Tax supr. Peat, Marwick Mitchell & Co., L.A., 1959-62, tax mgr., 1974-77; v.p. fin. Pacific Theaters Corp., L.A., 1962-68; freelance cons. L.A., 1969-74; tax mgr. Lewis Homes, Upland, Calif., 1977-80; pres. Di-Bru, Inc., L.A., 1981-87, Scolyn, Inc., L.A., 1988-95; bus. cons., 1995—. Dir. Valley Fed. Savs. and Loan Assn., 1989-92. Mem. UCLA Law Rev., 1956-57; contbr. articles to tax, fin. mags. Served with USN, 1948-49. Avocation: tennis. Home and Office: 2479 Roscomare Rd Los Angeles CA 90077-1812 E-mail: jhofert90077@yahoo.com.

HOFF, BENJAMIN LLOYD, writer, scriptwriter; b. Portland, Oreg., Nov. 27, 1946; s. Lloyd Henry and Clementine Catlin (Elmer) Hoff; m. Deborah Alysoun Pratt, May 1, 1993; 1 child, Joel Orion Newman. BA Asian Art, The Evergreen State Coll., Olympia, Wash., 1972—73; BFA Graphic Design, Pacific NW Coll. of Art, Portland, Oreg., 1966—68; BArch, The Univ. of Oreg., Eugene, Oreg., 1965—66; miscellaneous credits Three years, various colleges. The Tao of Pooh was the subject of a question in a TV Guide crossword puzzle, and both it and The Te of Piglet were the subjects of a question on the television quiz program Jeopardy. The Am. Booksellers Asso. newsletter, Bookselling This Week, ranked Benjamin Hoff in fourth place, tied with Thomas Moore, in their list of New York Times bestselling paperback authors of 1994 (for sales in 1993). For years, The Tao of Pooh and The Te of Piglet have been popular HS and coll. texts for classes in a variety of subjects including philosophy, bus., sci., lit., and world culture. Author: (book) The Tao of Pooh, 1982, The Singing Creek Where the Willows Grow: the Mystical Nature of Opal Whiteley, 1986, 1988, The Te of Piglet, 1992, The Singing Creek Where the Willows Grow: the Mystical Nature of Opal Whiteley, 1995. Recipient Am. Book Award for "The Singing Creek Where the Willows Grow", Book-of-the-Month Club, 1988. The first two titles became internat. bestsellers and were publ. in eighteen fgn. lang. The Tao of Pooh was on The New York Times bestseller list for 49 weeks and The Te of Piglet for 59 weeks. Both books were selections of the Book-of-the-Month Club and the Quality Paperback Book Club.

HOFF, CHARLES WORTHINGTON, III, banker; b. Balt., Mar. 1, 1934; s. Charles Worthington Jr and Sarah Durant (Yearley) Hoff; m. Margaret Elizabeth Ober, Sept. 7, 1967; children: Zoe Carey, Alexandra Yearley, Juliana Macgill, Margaret Frazier, Charles Worthington IV. BS in Bus., Johns Hopkins U., 1961; postgrad., Stonier Sch. Banking, 1964-66. With First Nat. Bank Md., Balt., 1955-77, div. v.p., 1968-77; exec. v.p. Farmers & Mechanics Nat. Bank, Frederick, 1977-81, pres., 1981-93, chmn., 1993—2001, also bd. dirs.; ret, 2001. Bd dirs F & M Bancorp, pres, 1983—93, chmn., 1993—2001, chmn. emeritus, 1991—; bd dirs Frederick Brick Works. Bd dirs Children's Aid and Family Serv Soc Baltimore, 1972—77, mem exec comt, fin comt, 1974—76; pres Oriole Advs, Inc, 1963, treas, 1964—65; mem exec comt, mem fin comt, trustee Hood Col, 1985—97, chmn fin comts, trustee emeritus, 1997—; trustee Frederick Mem Hosp, 1983—89, Community Found Frederick County Md, 1987—92. Mem.: Frederick County CofC (bd dirs 1980—82), Md Bankers Asn (bd dirs 1988—90, vpres 1992—93, pres-elect 1993—94, pres 1994—95), Am Inst Banking, Am Bankers Asn (coun, vpres Md 1983, educ, policy and develop coun 1990—93, bd dirs 1995—98), Club 18, Frederick Cotillion Club, Bryce Resort Country Club (Bayse, Va), Cap and Gown Club (Princeton, NJ), Holly Hills Country Club, Rotary. Democrat. Methodist. Home: 231 E Church St Frederick MD 21701-5405 Personal E-mail: mrchair@aol.com.

HOFF, GERHARDT MICHAEL, lawyer, insurance company executive; b. Vienna, June 12, 1930; came to U.S., 1951, naturalized, 1955; s. Erich Theodor and Vilma (Frank) Klockenhoff; m. Lisa Decristoforo, June 1, 1970; children: Michael, Elisabeth, Anne-Christine. Student, U. Munich Law Sch., Germany, 1948-51, Columbia U., 1951-52; LL.B., NYU, 1958; LL.M. in Taxation, Emory U., 1982; C.L.U., 1961. Bar: Mass. 1959, D.C. 1968, Ga. 1984. With Mass. Mut. Life Ins. Co. and Variable Annuity Life Ins. Co., 1958-67; v.p. Variable Annuity Life Ins. Co. Am., Washington, 1967-68; mem. staff fin. services group ITT Corp., 1968-69; pres. ITT Hamilton Life Ins. Co., also ITT Variable Annuity Ins. Co., St. Louis, 1970-72, Sun Life Ins. Co. Am., Balt., 1972-78, 81-83, chief exec. officer, 1972-83; pres. Sun Life Group Am., Inc., Atlanta, 1978-83. Chmn. law practice Bus. Planning Corp. Am., Atlanta, 1983—; founder (with Lisa Hoff) Cities in Color, Inc., 1985—. Served with AUS, 1955-57. Decorated Commendation ribbon with pendant. Mem. Am. Soc. C.L.U.'s, ABA Clubs: Capital City (Atlanta). Presbyterian. Office: 12 Braemore Dr NW Atlanta GA 30328-4845 E-mail: gmhoff2@aol.com. *We'll get along better with others if we recognize their right to be hard or easy on themselves, depending on their own choice of priorities.*

HOFF, JOHN SCOTT, lawyer; b. Des Moines, Jan. 2, 1946; s. John Richard and Valetta R. (Scott) H.; m. Susan Murial Felver, June 21, 1972 (div. 1975); m. Shirley Jo Ward, June 21, 1975; children: Jennifer Jo, John Baron. BSBA, Drake U., 1967; MBA, Calif. State U., Fullerton, 1971; postgrad., Oxford (Eng.) U., 1973; JD, Southwestern U., L.A., 1975; MA in Mil. History, Am. Mil. U., 1995. Bar: Iowa 1976, U.S. Ct. Claims 1976, U.S. Ct. Customs and Patent Appeals 1976, U.S. Ct. Mil. Appeals 1976, Ill. 1977, U.S. Dist. Ct. (no. dist.) Ill. 1977, U.S. Ct. Appeals (7th cir.) 1979, Calif. 1980, U.S. Supreme Ct. 1982, Nebr. 1983, D.C. 1983, Wis. 1984, U.S. Dist. Ct. (so. dist.) Iowa 1987, U.S. Ct. Appeals (9th and 10th cirs.) 1988, U.S. Dist. Ct. Ariz. 1990, U.S. Ct. Appeals (6th cir.) 1990, Mich. 1991, U.S. Ct. Appeals (8th cir.) 1991, N.Y. 1995, Minn. 1996, U.S. Dist. Ct. (cen. dist.) Ill. 1996; CPCU; chartered cost analyst; FAA comml. pilot; cert. art. flt. instr. instrument and mult-eng ratings Staff atty. FAA Hdqrs., Washington, 1975-76; assoc. Lord, Bissell & Brook, Chgo., 1976-81; ptnr. Lapin, Hoff, Slaw & Laffey, Chgo., 1981-92, John Scott Hoff & Assocs., P.C., Chgo., 1992—. Real estate broker Ill. Dept. Profl Regulation, Springfield, 1980— Contbr. articles to profl. jours. Col. USAF 1967—98. Decorated Legion of Merit. Mem. ABA, Aviation Ins. Assn. (dir 1988-1990, v.p. 1990-92, pres. 1992-94), Air Force Assn. (v.p., pres. 1980-93) Internat. Soc. Air Safety Investigation (v.p.), Nat. Aero. Assn., Gen. Aviation Pilots' Assn., Res. Officers Assn., Ret. Officers Assn., Chgo. Bar Assn. Lawyers-Pilots Bar Assn., NTSB Bar Assn., Aircraft Owners and Pilots Assn. Exptl. Aircraft Assn., Nat. Assn. Flight Instrs., Aero. Club Chgo. Republican Presbyterian. Avocations: flying, military history. Office: John S Hoff 20 S Clark St Ste 2210 Chicago IL 60603-1816 E-mail: jsh@aviationattorney.com.

HOFF, JULIAN THEODORE, physician, educator; b. Boise, Idaho, Sept. 22 1936; s. Harvey Orval and Helen Marie (Boraas) H.; m. Diane Shanks, June 3 1962; children— Paul, Allison, Julia. BA, Stanford U., Calif., 1958; MD Cornell U., N.Y.C., 1962. Diplomate Am. Bd. Neurol. Surgery. Intern N.Y. Hosp., N.Y.C., 1962-63, resident in surgery, 1963-64, resident in neurosurgery 1966-70; asst. prof. neurosurgery U. Calif., San Francisco, assoc. prof neurosurgery, 1974-78, prof. neurosurgery, 1978-81, U. Mich., Ann Arbor 1981—, head sect. neurosurgery, 1981—. Sec. Am. Bd. Neurol-Surgery 1987-91, chmn., 1991-92; mem. bd. sci. councillors Nat. Inst. Neurol. Disease and Stroke-NIH, 1993-97, nat. adv. coun., 1999—. Editor: Practice of Neurosurgery, 1979-85; Current Surgical Management of Neurological Diseases

1980; Neurosurgery: Diagnostic and Management Principles, 1992, Mild to Moderate Head Injury, 1989; co-editor: Neurosurgery: Scientific Basis of Clinical Practice, 1985, 3rd edit., 1999; contbr. articles to profl. jours. Served to capt. US Army, 1964-66. Recipient Tchr.-Investigator award, NIH, 1972—77, Javits Neurosci. Investigator award, 1985—99, Macy Faculty scholar, London, 1979. Fellow: ACS (2d v.p.-elect 1998—99); mem.: Soc. Neurol. Surgeons (pres. 1999—2000, Grass prize 2001), Cen. Neurosurg. Soc. (pres. 1985—86), Am. Acad. Neurosurgeons (treas. 1989—92, sec. 1992—, pres. 1996—), Congress Neurol. Surgeons (v.p. 1982—83, Honored Guest 2003), Am. Surg. Assn., Am. Assn. Neurol. Surgeons (v.p. 1991—93, pres. 1993—94, Cushing medal 2001), Inst. Medicine NAS. Republican. Presbyterian. Home: 2120 Wallingford Rd Ann Arbor MI 48104-4563 Office: U Mich Hosp TC 2128 Ann Arbor MI 48109

HOFF, PETER SLOAT, academic administrator; m. Dianne L. Balzer; children: Marc, Jay, Lara. BA in English with honors, U. Wis., 1966; MA in English and Humanities, Stanford U., 1968, PhD in English and Humanities, 1970. Prof., faculty devel. leader U. Wis., 1970—87, adminstr.; acad. vice chancellor Ind. U. S.E., 1987—90, Univ. Sys. of Ga., 1990—93, Calif. State U., 1993—97; pres. U. Maine, Orono, 1997—. Contbr. articles on nineteenth and twentieth century Brit. fiction. Player French horn in orchs. Mich., Wis., Ind., Ga., Calif., Maine. Mem. Phi Kappa Phi, Phi Beta Kappa. Office: U Maine 200 Alumni Hall Pres Office Orono ME 04469-0001

HOFF, RENO R. academic administrator; b. 1937; BS, Western Baptist Bible Coll.; MS, Oreg. Coll. Edn.; LLD (hon.), Western Baptist Coll. Bus. mgr. Western Baptist Coll., chair, bus. mgmt. dept., prof., v.p. admin., 1991—97, exec. v.p. & provost, 1998—99, pres., 1999—. Office: Western Baptist Coll 5000 Deer Park Dr SE Salem OR 97301

HOFF, SAMUEL BOYER, political science educator; b. Williamsport, Pa., June 7, 1957; s. Samuel Romberger and J. Mattie (Schultz) H.; m. Phyllis Rose Oliveto, Aug. 16, 1986. BA in Polit. Sci., Susquehanna U., 1979; MA in Polit. Sci., Am. U., 1981, SUNY, Stony Brook, 1983, PhD in Polit. Sci., 1987. Instr. SUNY, Stony Brook, 1982-86, asst. prof. Geneseo, 1987-88; asst. prof. dept. history and polit. sci. Del. State U., Dover, 1989-92, assoc. prof. dept. history and polit. sci., 1992-96, prof., 1996-99, George Washington disting. prof., 1999—, ROTC dir., 1993-99, chair dept. history and polit. sci., 2000—. Adj. instr. dept. social sci. N.Y. Inst. Tech., Old Westbury, N.Y., 1986; adj. asst. prof. Wittenberg U., Springfield, Ohio, 1987; vis. asst. prof. dept. govt. and politics Ohio Wesleyan U., Delaware, 1986-87; vis. asst. prof. Wichita (Kans.) State U., 1988-89; congl. intern U.S. Rep. Allen Ertel, Washington, 1978; mem. canvass staff Clean Water Action Project, Washington, 1980; rsch. asst. subcom. on human resources U.S. Ho. of Reps., Washington, 1980; asst. Senator Jacob Javits, Stony Brook, 1983-85. Contbr. articles to profl. jours. Committeeman Suffolk County Dems., L.I., 1984-86; presdl. candidate Dem. Party, 1988, Ind. Party, 1992, 96, 2000. Freedoms Found. scholar, 1990, 94, 2003; USMA-ROTC Mil. History fellow, 1994; Nat. Security Law fellow, 1995, Carnegie Coun. fellow, 1997, faculty fellow ExxonMobil, 2002-04. Mem. Am. Polit. Sci. Assn., Acad. Polit. Sci., Nat. Social Sci. Assn., Northeastern Polit. Sci. Assn., Midwest Polit. Sci. Assn., Western Polit. Sci. Assn., So. Polit. Sci. Assn., Social Sci. History Assn., Western Social Sci. Assn., Nat. Capital Area Polit. Sci. Assn., Pa. Polit. Sci. Assn., N.Y. Polit. Sci. Assn. Lutheran. Avocations: sports, antique collector, musician. Home: 813 Maple Pky Dover DE 19901-4238 Office: Del State Univ Dept History Polit Sci Dover DE 19901 E-mail: shoff@dsc.edu

HOFF, THEODORE FRANCIS, neurological surgeon; b. Parsons, Kans., Apr. 12, 1927; s. Theodore P. and Celeste (Pabst) H.; m. Barbara Fowler, Oct. 4, 1959; 1 child, Christopher. BA, U. Kans., 1948, MD, 1952; MS in Neurosci., McGill U., 1954. Diplomate Am. Bd. Neurological Surgery. Pvt. practice in neurol. surgery, Orlando, Fla., 1958—. With USN, 1944-46. Fellow ACS (sr.); mem. Fla. Neurosurg. Soc., Congress of Neurol. Surgeons, Am. Assn. Neurol. Surgery. Home and Office: 1315 S Orange Ave Ste 1A Orlando FL 32806-2145

HOFF, TIMOTHY, law educator, priest; b. Freeport, Ill., Feb. 27, 1941; s. Howard Vincent and Zillah (Morgan) H.; m. Virginia Nevill; children: Brian Charles, Morgan Witherspoon; stepchildren: Guy Baker, Katherine Baker. Student, U. London, 1961—62; AB, Tulane U., 1963, JD, 1966; LLM, Harvard U., 1970. Bar: Fla. 1967, Ala. 1973, U.S. Dist. Ct. (mid. dist.) Fla. 1967; ordained priest Episcopal Ch. Assoc. Williams, Parker, Harrison, Dietz & Getzen, Sarasota, Fla., 1968-69; asst. legal editor The Fla. Bar, 1969; asst. prof. U. Ala., 1970-73, assoc. prof., 1973-75, prof. law, 1975-93, Gordon Rosen prof., 1993—2002, prof. emeritus, 2002—. Cons. Ala. Law Inst.; reporter Ala. Adminstrv. Procedure Act, 1977—. Author: Alabama Limitations of Actions, 1984, 2d edit., 1992, Forms for Civil Trial Practice, 1991; contbr. articles to profl. jours. V.p., founding dir. Hospice of West Ala.; founding dir. Cmty. Soup Bowl, Inc.; Episc. priest assoc. Canterbury Chapel U. Ala.; rector St. Michael's Episc. Ch., Fayette, Ala., 1988-96, 2003—. Recipient Hist. Preservation Svc. award, 1976. Mem. ACLU, AAUP, Maritime Law Assn. U.S., Coun. on Religion and Law, Episc. Soc. for Ministry in Higher Edn., Univ. Club, Phi Beta Kappa, Order of Coif, Omicron Delta Kappa, Eta Sigma Phi. Democrat. Home: 2601 Lakewood Cir Tuscaloosa AL 35405-2727 Office: U Ala Law Sch 101 Paul W Bryant Dr E PO Box 870382 Tuscaloosa AL 35487-0382 E-mail: thoff@law.ua.edu.

HOFFA, HARLAN EDWARD, retired university dean, art educator; b. Kalamazoo, June 23, 1925; s. Leolan William and Pearl (Foster) H.; m. Marian Perko, Aug. 10, 1946 (div. 1971); children: Kathryn Jane, Thomas Scott; m. Suzanne Aldridge Dudley, Sept. 11, 1971. BS, Wayne U., 1948, MEd, 1949; EdD, Pa. State U., 1959. Tchr. Evanston (Ill.) Pub. Schs., 1949-51; instr. art edn. Ohio State U., 1951-53; asst. prof. art State U. Coll. at Buffalo, 1953-59; assoc. prof. fine arts and edn. head dept. Boston U., 1959-65; art edn. specialist U.S. Office Edn., 1964-67; prof. edn. and fine arts, chmn. art edn. program Ind. U., 1967-70; prof., head dept. art edn. Pa. State U., 1970-76, head div. art and music edn., 1976-79, acting dir. Sch. Visual Arts, 1979-80, 84 85, assoc. dean for research and grad. studies Coll. Art and Architecture, 1985-90, ret., 1990, prof. emeritus, 1990—. Assoc. dir. Ctr. Policy Studies in the Arts, 1989; Fulbright sr. lectr./researcher, Helsinki, Finland, Jan.-Jun., 1987. With AUS, 1943-45. Mem. Nat. Art Edn. Assn. (pres. 1971-73) Home: 1343 Penrose Cir State College PA 16803-3255

HOFFA, JAMES P. labor union administrator; b. Detroit, May 19, 1941; m. Virginia Harris; children: David, Geoffrey. Degree in Econs., Mich. State U., 1963; JD, U. Mich., 1966. s. James R. Hoffa. Teamster laborer Internat. Brotherhood Teamsters, Detroit and, Alaska, 1960's, atty., 1968-93, exec. asst. to pres. Mich. Joint Coun. 43, 1993-98, gen. pres., 1999—. Office: Internat Brotherhood Teamsters Office of the Gen Pres 25 Louisiana Ave NW Washington DC 20001-2130

HOFFA, THOMAS EDWARD, lawyer; b. Marshalltown, Iowa, Sept. 20, 1935; s. Harvey Edward and Janette (Nason) H. BS, Iowa State U., 1958; JD, John Marshall Law Sch., 1972. Bar: Ill. 1972, U.S. Dist. Ct. (no. dist.) Ill. 1972 (Gen. Bar), U.S. Tax Ct. 1976, U.S. Dist. Ct. (no. dist.) Ill. 1983 (Trial Bar), U.S. Ct. Appeals (7th cir.) 1987. Sole practice, Chgo., 1972—. With USAF, 1958-60. Mem. ABA, Assn. Trial Lawyers Am., Ill. State Bar Assn., Chgo. Bar Assn. Republican. Presbyterian. Office: 30 W Chicago Ave Ste 1320 Chicago IL 60610-4339

HOFFACKER, CHARLES EDWARD, minister, writer; b. Philadelphia, Pa., Oct. 16, 1953; s. Carl Theil and Anne Niblett Hoffacker; m. Cynthia Ann Guthrie, Jan. 8, 1983; 1 child, Sophia. BA, St. John's Coll., 1975; MDiv, Nashotah House, 1982; cert. in core curriculum, Coll. Preachers, Washington, 1992; Ch. Devel. Inst., U. of South, 1996. Ordained deacon Episcopal Diocese of Colo., 1982, ordained priest Episcopal Diocese of Chgo., 1982. Episcopal chaplain No. Ill. U., DeKalb, Ill., 1982—86; interim priest-in-charge St. Jude's Episc. Ch., Rochelle, Ill., 1985—86; rector St. Peter's Episc. Ch., Akron, Ohio, 1986—92, St. Paul's Episc. Ch., Port Huron, Mich., 1992—; dean Blue Water Convocation, Port Huron, Mich., 1993—. Dean's adv. bd. Huron Coll., London, 2002—; pastors adv. com. bridge Builders Counseling, Inc., Port Huron, 2000—; adj. faculty St. Clair County CC, Port Huron, 1998—; reader Gen. Ordination Exam., 1998—; dep. gen. conv. of the episc. ch. Diocese of Ea. Mich., Saginaw, Mich., 1997—. Author: A Matter of Life and Death: Preaching at Funerals, 2003; contbr. email publication SermonWriter, sermon website Worship That Works, columns in newspapers. Episc. Avocations: reading, writing, dog walking. Home: 2737 Military Street Port Huron MI 48060 Office: St Paul's Episcopal Church 3201 Gratiot Avenue Port Huron MI 48060

HOFFENBERG, MARVIN, retired political science educator, consultant; b. Buffalo, July 7, 1914; s. Harry and Jennie Pearl (Weiss) H.; m. Betty Eising Stern, July 20, 1947; children— David A., Peter H. Student, St. Bonaventure Coll., 1934-35; B.Sc., Ohio State U., 1939, MA, 1940, postgrad., 1941. Asst. chief div. interindustry econs. Bur. Labor Statistics, Dept. Labor, 1941-52; cons. U.S. Mut. Security Agy., Europe, 1952, Statistik Sentralbyra, Govt. of Norway, Oslo, 1955; dir. research, econ. cons. dept. deVegh & Co., 1956-58; economist RAND Corp., 1952-56; staff economist Com. Econ. Devel., 1958-60; project chmn. Johns Hopkins U., 1960-63; dir. cost analysis dept. Aerospace Corp., 1963-65; Research economist Inst. Govt. and Pub. Affairs, UCLA, 1965-67, prof.-in-residence polit. sci., 1967-85, prof. emeritus, 1985—; dir. M.P.A. program, co-chmn. Interdepartmental Program in Comprehensive Health Planning UCLA, 1974-76. Author: (with Kenneth J. Arrow) A Time Series Analysis of Inter-Industry Demand, 1959; editor: (with Levine, Hardt and Kaplan) Mathematics and Computers in Soviet Economics, 1967; contbr. articles to profl. jours., chpts. to books Mem. bd. advisers Sidney Stern Meml. Trust; bd. dirs. L.A. chpt. Am. Jewish Com.; foreman L.A. County Grand Jury, 1990-91; commr. L.A. County Economy and Efficiency Commn., 1991-92. C.C. Stillman scholar; Littauer fellow Harvard U., 1946; recipient Disting. service award Coll. Adminstrv. Scis., Ohio State U., 1971 Fellow: AAAS (life). Jewish. Home: 1365 Marinette Rd Pacific Palisades CA 90272 E-mail: hoffen@ucla.edu.

HOFFENBLUM, ALLAN ERNEST, political consultant; b. Vallejo, Calif., Aug. 10, 1940; s. Albert A. and Pearl Estelle (Clarke) H. BA, U. So. Calif., 1962. Mem. staff L.A. County Rep. Com., 1967-71; staff dir. Rep. Assembly Caucus Calif. legislature, Sacramento, 1973-75; polit. dir. Rep. Party of Calif., L.A., 1977-78; owner Allan Hoffenblum & Assocs., L.A., 1979—. Pub. Calif. Target Book, 1994—. Capt. USAF, 1962-67, Vietnam. Decorated Bronze Star medal. Mem.: Am. Assn. Polit. Cons. Jewish. Office: 9000 W Sunset Blvd Ste 707 West Hollywood CA 90069-5807 E-mail: targetbook@aol.com.

HOFFER, ALMA JEANNE, nursing educator; b. Dalhart, Tex., Sept. 15, 1932; d. James A. and Mildred (Zimlich) Koehler; m. John L. Hoffer, Oct. 7, 1954; children: John Jr., James Leo, Joseph V., Jerome P. BS, Bradley U., 1970; MA, W. Va. Coll. Grad. Study Inst., 1975; EdD, Ball State U., 1981, MA, 1986. Reg. Nurse. Staff nurse St Joseph Hosp., South Bend, Ind., 1958-59, Holy Cross Cen. Sch., St Joseph Hosp., South Bend, 1959-63; sch. nurse South Bend Sch. Corp., 1970-72; faculty staff Morris Harvey Coll., Charleston, W.Va., W.Va. Inst. Tech., Montgomery, 1975-76; asst. prof. Ball State U., Ind., 1976-77, Ind. U.-Purdue U., Ft. Wayne, 1977-81; assoc. prof. U. Akron, Ohio, 1981-83, 91 95, asst. dean, grad. edn., 1983-90, assoc. prof., 1991-93; prof., chair Dept. of Nursing St. Francis Coll., Fort Wayne, Ind., 1993-95; prin. investigator rsch. project Well Begun is Well Done Children's Med. Ctr. Women's Bd. Akron, 1995-96; coord. parish nurse St. Hilary Ch., 2001— Trustee Akron Child Guidance, 1983-88, 89-95, chair planning com., 1988; nursing Blick Clin., Akron, 1988; rsch. cons. St. Joseph Hosp., Ohio, 1989; cons. Health Sense, 1996-98; rschr., presenter in field. Contbg. author: Family Health Promotion Theories and Assessment, 1989, Nursing Connections, 1992. Task force mem. Gov. Celeste's Employee Assistance Program for State U. Campuses, Ohio, 1983-84, del. People to People Citizen Amb. Program to Europe, 1988; mem. health and wellness com., coord. St. Hilary Parish. Mem. ANA, Nat. League for Nursing, Midwest Nursing Rsch. Soc., Transcultural Nursing Soc. (chair certification and recertification com. 2000—, Leininger Leadership award 2002), Portage Country Club, Cleve. Country Club, Sigma Theta Tau. Republican. Roman Catholic. Avocations: tennis, golf, skiing. bus. Office: PO Box 794 Bath OH 44210-0794 E-mail: ajhoffer@earthlink.net., ajh1@uakron.edu.

HOFFER, DAVID PAUL, investment banker, lawyer; b. Boston, Aug. 23, 1968; s. Axel and Anita Panenka H.; m. Deborah Rogell, Oct. 13, 1991. AB, Harvard U., 1991, JD, MBA, Harvard U., 1996. Bar: Mass., Washington. Pres., COO TreeAge Software, Inc., Williamstown, Mass., 1985—; assoc. mediator Endispute, Inc., Cambridge, Mass., Washington, 1991-92; atty. Mundt & MacGregor, Seattle, 1996-97, Perkins Coie LLP, Seattle, 1998-99; COO, gen. counsel Iconomy.com., Inc., Cambridge, 1999-2000; COO Beachfire, Inc., Boston, 2000—01; mng. dir. RCW Mirus, Inc., Boston, 2002—. Bd. dir. Ninevah Found., Harvard/Radcliffe Hillel, Cambridge, 1992-96. Office: RCW Mirus Inc 100 Franklin St Boston MA 02110

HOFFER, DEBRA HUMES, educational association administrator; Exec. dir. Louisville Ballet, 1991—99; pres. Jr. Achievement Kentuckania Inc., 2000—. Office: Louisville Ballet PO Box 24403 Louisville KY 40224-4403

HOFFER, GEORGE E. economist, educator; b. Richmond, Va., May 12, 1942; s. Hans Maurice and Margaret (Schmuckler) Hoffer; m. Betty Evans, Aug. 26, 1970; children: Michael, Meghan. BS, U. Richmond, Va., 1964; MS, Va. Tech., Blacksburg, 1967; PhD, U. Va., Charlottesville, 1972. Asst. prof. econs. U. Va., Charlottesville, 1969—70; from asst. prof. to prof. Va. Commonwealth U., Richmond, 1970—. Cons. to Am. Automotive Industry and Insurers. Recipient numerous tchg. and rsch awards, 1975—. Achievements include most cited academic on various topics concerning the auto industry. Avocation: collecting model cars, planes,trucks etc. . Office: Va Commonwealth Univ Box 844000 Richmond VA 23284

HOFFER, JAMES BRIAN, physicist, consultant; b. Madera, Calif., Aug. 2, 1956; s. Robert C. and Jane A. (Rylander) H.; m. Florina Bojeri, Aug. 20, 1983. BS in Physics and Math., Pacific Union Coll., 1977; MS in Physics, Mich. State U., 1979, PhD in Physics, 1983. Vis. scientist Los Alamos (N.Mex.) Nat. Lab., 1981; instr. Mich. State U., East Lansing, 1983, rsch. assoc., nat. superconducting cyclotron lab., 1983; rsch. assoc., lab. for atmospheric and space physics U. Colo., Boulder, 1983-85; asst. scientist Applied Rsch. Corp., Landover, Md., 1985-86; pres. Hoffer and Assocs., Darnestown, Md., 1986-98, HofTek, Inc., Darnestown, 1998—. Mem. tech. adv. com. Aviation Week, 1990-91. Author: Utilizing VAX/UMS Utilities and DCL, 1989; contbr. articles to sci. jours. Appointee Consumer Affairs Adv. Com., Montgomery County, Md., 1988-95; sci. fair judge, Fairfax, Va., 1989. Mem. Am. Astron. Soc., Sigma Pi Sigma. Achievements include development of technique to reduce computer time required for planetary ring model, of technique to reduce computer time required for modeling of gravitational interactions between pairs of binary stars. Home and Office: 15413 Deep Bottom Rd Darnestown MD 20874-3630

HOFFER, MICHAEL E. otolaryngologist, naval officer; b. Key West, Fla., Aug. 13, 1962; m. Deborah L. Pfeiffer, Apr. 23, 1988; children: Kyle P., Ali N. BS, Stanford U., 1984, MD, U. Calif., San Diego, 1988. Diplomate Am. Bd. Otolaryngology, Nat. Bd. Med. Examiners. Intern in gen. surgery Hosp. of U. Pa., Phila., 1988-89, resident in otorhinolaryngology, 1989-93; fellow in otology and neurotology Fla. Otologic ctr., 1993-94; commd. officer USN, 1995; dir. dept. of def. Spatial Orientation Ctr. Naval Med. Ctr., San Diego, 1995-97; dir. Dept. Def. Spatial Orientation Ctr., 1997—. Instr. U. Pa. Sch. Medcine, 1989-92, instr. level II, 1992-93, lectr. B dept. otorhinolaryngology, head and neck surgery, 1993—; clin. asst. prof. dept. surgery Uniformed Svcs. U. Health Scis., Bethesda, Md., 1995—; presenter in field, 1985—. Contbr. articles and abstracts to med. jours., including Circulation, Laryngoscope, Ear, Nose and Throat Jour., Otolaryngology-Head and Neck Surgery, Skull Base Surgery, Archives Otolaryngology-Head and Neck Surgery, Am. Jour. Rhinology, also chpts. to books. Various rsch. grants, 1994—. Fellow Am. Acad. Otolaryngology-Head and Neck Surgery, Am. Laryngol., Rhinol. and Otol. Soc., Am. Coll. Surgeons; mem. Assn. for Rsch. in Otolaryngology, Propser Meniere's Soc., Soc. Unit. Otolaryngologists. Home: 11675 Timberlake Dr San Diego CA 92131-2326 Office: Naval Med Ctr Dept Otolaryngology San Diego CA 92134-5000 E-mail: mehoffer@nmcsd.med.navy.mil.

HOFFER, PHILIP CRAIG, information technology manager, consultant; b. Ft. Collins, CO, Oct. 6, 1961; s. Roger Milton Hoffer, Connie Ann Hoffer; m. Cheryl Ann Avery; children: Megan L., Rachel M., David A. M.B.A, University of Dallas, Irving, TX, 1987—91; BS, Purdue University, West Lafayette, IN, 1980—85; D.M, Colorado Technical University, Colorado Springs, CO, 2001—Cur. Sr. Manager, Global Advanced Technology J. D. Edwards, Denver, 1997—Cur.; Manager Arthur Anderson LLP, Denver, 1995—97; Sr. Consultant AT & T, Denver, 1994—97, Coopers & Lybrand LLP, Dallas, 1991—94; Sr. Programmer/ Analyst Texas Oil & Gas, Dallas, 1989—91; Technical Account Manager Cap Gemini, Dallas, 1985—89. Mem.: Acadamey of Managment, American Management Association, Society for Organizational Learning. Office: J D Edwards One Technology Way Denver CO 80237 Office Fax: (720) 294-9839. Business E-Mail: philip_hoffer@jdedwards.com.

HOFFER, ROY, forensic electrical engineer, fire and explosion analyst; b. Lancaster, Pa., 1956; BS in Physics magna cum laude, Millersville U., 1979; MSEE, U. Pa., 1981. Lic. profl. engr., Pa. Lighting, ballast and switching power supply design engr. Armstrong World Industries, Lancaster, Pa., 1981-86; variable speed motor dr./switching power supply design engr. York (Pa.) Internat. Corp., 1986-91; supr. instrument engring./design engr. Instrument divsn. High Voltage Engring. Corp., Boston, 1991-93; tech. rep., applications engr. Consulting Engrs., Lancaster, 1993; mfg. and instrument calibration engr. Warner-Lambert Co., Morris Plains, NJ, 1994—96. Forensic elec., mech., vehicle, mfg. and safety engr., expert witness fire and explosion origin and cause analysis, accident analysis, elec. and electronic design cons. Hoffer Engring., Lancaster, 1994—; alumni writing mentor U. Pa. Mem. Leadership Lancaster, 1992; com. mem., vol. Redeemer Luth Ch., Lancaster, 1986—2000, bd. dirs., 1992—2000. Recipient Sojourners award USAR, 1976; Ashton fellow, 1979-81. Mem. Nat. Fire Protection Assn., Internat. Fire Marshalls Assn., Internat. Assn. Arson Investigators, Pa. Assn. Arson Investigators, Nat. Assn. Fire Invetigators, Lancaster Sci. Alliance (bd. dirs., treas.), Mentor Net. Achievements include 27 patents for slow acting photocell lamp dimming control, power ltd. fluorescent lighting system, variable speed single and 3 phase AC motor drive systems and motor controls. Office: 453 Haverhill Rd Lancaster PA 17601-3519 E-mail: royhoffer@aol.com.

HOFFERT, MARTIN IRVING, applied science educator; b. Bklyn., July 1, 1938; s. Solomon and Ceil (Hyman) H.; m. Linda Epstein, Sept. 4, 1960; 1 child, Eric; m. 2d, Iris E. Fierst, Jan. 29, 1965. BS in Aero. Engring., U. Mich., 1960, MS in Astronautics, 1964; PhD in Astronautics, Poly. Inst. Bklyn., 1967; MA in Liberal Studies, New Sch. for Social Research, 1969. Sr. scientist Gen. Applied Sci. Labs., Westbury, N.Y., 1962-67; research scientist NYU, 1967-68; sr. research scientist Advanced Tech. Labs., Westbury, 1968-69; mem. research staff Riverside Research Inst., N.Y.C., 1969-72; sr. research assoc. Goodard Inst. for Space Studies NASA, N.Y.C., 1972-74; sr. research scientist NYU, 1974-76, assoc. prof. applied sci., 1976-83, prof. applied sci., 1983-94, prof. physics, 1995—, chmn. applied sci., 1984-91. Mgmt. ops. working group in planetary atmosphere NASA, Washington, 1986-90; bilateral coop. working group VIII U.S. Del. Joint U.S.-USSR Commn., 1986-92; cons. Exxon Rsch. & Engring., Annandale, N.J., 1986-95, Lawrence Livermore Nat. Lab., 1990—. Contbr. over 65 articles to profl. jour. and chpts. to books. Fellow AAAS; mem. AAIA, Am. Geophys. Union, Am. Metereol. Soc., Aspen Global Change Inst. (adv. bd.). Democrat. Jewish. Avocations: bicycling, hiking, boating. Home: 12 Oak Dr Great Neck Long Island NY 11021 Office: NYU Dept Physics New York NY 10003 E-mail: marty.hoffert@nyu.edu.

HOFFERT, PAUL WASHINGTON, surgeon; b. N.Y.C., Feb. 22, 1923; s. Charles and Rose (Isaacs) H.; m. Rosolyn Sheiman, Apr. 20, 1947; children: Marvin Jay, Renee Beth, Deborah Susan. AB with honors, Columbia U., 1942; MD cum laude, Yale U., 1945. Diplomate Am. Bd. Surgery, Am. Bd. Abdominal Surgery. Intern New Haven (Conn.) Hosp., 1945-46; fellow radiology Hosp. U. Pa., 1948-49; resident surgery VA Hosp., Bronx, NY, 1949-53; pvt. practice medicine specializing in gen./vascular surgery Yonkers, NY, 1953—. Attending surgeon Yonkers Gen. Hosp., 1953—, chief of surgery, 1987—; sr. gen. and vascular surgeon St. Joseph's Hosp., 1953—; assoc. vascular surgeon Montefiore Hosp., 1965—; asst. prof. surgery Albert Einstein Coll., 1955—. Contbr. articles to profl. jours. Capt. U.S. Army Med. Corps, 1946-48. Fellow Am. Coll. Surgeons (pres. Westchester, N.Y. chpt.), Am. Coll. Angiology, N.Y. Acad. Medicine, Westchester Acad. Medicine (charter), Clin. Soc. N.Y. Diabetes Assn.; mem. N.Y. Surgical Soc., N.Y. Soc. Cardiovascular Surgery, Zionist Orgn. Am. (life, past pres. Lincoln Park, Yonkers region), Phi Beta Kappa, alpha Omega Alpha, Phi Delta Epsilon, Masons. Home: 26 Indian Cove Rd Mamaroneck NY 10543-4439

HOFFHEIMER, DANIEL JOSEPH, lawyer; b. Cin., Dec. 28, 1950; s. Harry Max and Charlotte (O'Brien) Hoffheimer; m. Elizabeth Lee Hoffheimer; children: Rebecca, Rachel, Leah. Grad., Phillips Exeter Acad., 1969; AB cum laude, Harvard Coll., 1973; JD, U. Va., 1976. Bar: Ohio 1976, U.S. Dist. Ct. (so. dist.) Ohio 1976, U.S. Ct. Appeals (6th cir.) 1977, U.S. Ct. Appeals (D.C. and fed. cir.) 1986, U.S. Ct. Internat. Trade 1986, U.S. Tax Ct. 1992, U.S. Supreme Ct. 1980, cert.: (Specialist Estate Planning Trust and Probate Law). Assoc. Taft, Stettinius & Hollister, Cin., 1976-84, ptnr., 1984—. Lectr. law Coll. Law, U. Cin., 1981-83; trustee Judges Hogan & Porter Meml. Trust; mem. adv. bd. Ohio Dist. Ct. Rev. Editor-in-chief U. Va. Jour. Internat. Law, 1975-76; co-author: Practitioners' Handbook Ohio First District Court Appeals, 1984, 2d edit., 1991, Federal Practice Manual, U.S. 6th Circuit Court of Appeals, 1999, Manual on Labor Law, 1988; mem. editl. bd. Probate Law Jour. Ohio, 2000—; contbr. articles to profl. jours. Mem. Cin. Symphony Bus. Rels. Com., 1977-86, Cin. Composers Guild, 1988-93, Ohio Supreme Ct. Com. Racial Fairness, 1993-2000; trustee Underground R.R. Freedom Mus., 1995—; mem. adv. bd. Consumer Protection, Cin., 1978-80, Hoxworth Blood Ctr. Univ. Cin. Hosp., 1994-99; mem. bd. Hebrew Union Coll. Jewish Inst. Religion, 1994—, WGUC-FM Pub. Radio, 1988—, vice chmn., 1993-96, chmn., 1996-98; trustee Cin. Chamber Orch., 1977-80, Seven Hills Sch., Cin., 1980-86, Internat. Visitors Ctr., Cin., 1980-84, Friends Coll. Conservatory of Music, Cin., 1985-86, Cin. Symphony Orch., 1988-94, 96—, sec., 1996-99, vice chair 1999-2000, chair, 2001—, Children's Psychiat. Ctr., Cin., 1986-89, treas., 1987-89; vice chmn. Jewish Hosp., Cin., 1989-92; Leadership Cin., 1989-90; sec., trustee Cin. Symphony Musicians Pension Fund, 1989-99, Jewish Cmty. Rels. Coun., 1990-98, v.p., 1996-98; sec. Nat. Conf. Commn. Justice, 1992-99, treas. 1999-2000, trustee emeritus, 2000—; counsel Cin. AIDS Commn., 1991—, Cin. Inst. Fine Arts Govt. Affairs Com., 1993-94, B'nai B'rith Nat. Coun. Legacy Devel., 1996-97; trustee Nat. Underground R.R. Freedom Ctr., 1995-. Named Outstanding Young Man, U.S. Jaycees, 1984, 98. Life fellow Am. Bar Found., Ohio Bar Found.; fellow Am. Coll. Trust and Estate Counsel; mem. ABA, Internat. Bar Assn., Internat. Trade Bar Assn., Internat. Arbitration Assn. (comml. arbitrator 1991-95), Fed. Bar Assn. (treas. 1984, sec. 1985, v.p. 1986-87, pres. 1987-88), Ohio State Bar Assn. (bd. govs. Est. Pl. Trust and Probate Law sect. 1996—), Cin. Bar Assn. (trustee 1988-93, v.p. 1990-91, pres. 1992-93, chair Cin. Acad. Leadership for Lawyers 1998-2000), Harvard Club of Cin. (bd. dirs. 1980-88, v.p. 1983-86, pres. 1986-87). Democrat. Avocations: music, tennis, chinese and japanese art. Home: 1 Forest Hill Dr Cincinnati OH 45208-1953 Office: 425 Walnut St Ste 1800 Cincinnati OH 45202-3923 E-mail: hoffheimer@taftlaw.com. *The elusive meaning and joy of life is really at our fingertips: to make life better for others.*

HOFFHEIMER, MINETTE GOLDSMITH, community service volunteer; b. Cin., May 1, 1927; d. Philip Hess and Cecile (Crager) Goldsmith; m. Arthur Hoffheimer Jr., June 16, 1948; children: Craig R., Roger Steven, James Martin, Mark Todd. Student, Conn. Coll. for Women, New London, 1945-48. Editor, prodr. (book in braille) Lilias Yoga and You, 1974, (poems) Marjorie's Book, 1974; editor: Lilias Yoga and Your Life, 1981; contbr. short story: (anthology) Cincinnati Short Story Winners, 1985. Trustee, sec. Cin. chpt. Nat. Coun. Jewish Women, 1966-73, chmn. and developer Large Type Program of Aid to Visually Handicapped, 1964-75, chmn. Angel Ball, 1968, on Angel Ball com. 1964-69, treas. thrift shop, 1965-67, auditor, mem. budget, ways and means, survey and evaluation coms., 1971; trustee Clovernook Home and Sch. for Blind, Cin., 1980-87; founder, 1st pres. Clovernook Assocs., Cin., 1981-85; trustee, chmn. edn. com., Boca Raton (Fla.) Mus. Art, 1996—; program developer, tchr. of Yoga to Blind, Cin., 1973-87 Named Vol. of Yr. Clovernook Home and Sch. for Blind, 1976, Woman of Yr. Cin. Enquirer, 1983. Mem. Brandeis, Nat. Braille Assn. (After 4000 hours svc. award 1971, 30 yr. cert. svc. 2001), Cin. Yoga Tchrs. Assn., Life Long Learning Soc. Fla. Atlantic U., Friends of Boca Raton Mus. Art., others. E-mail: mghno1@aol.com.

HOFFINGER, ADAM STEVEN, lawyer; b. N.Y.C., Oct. 22, 1956; s. Jack S. and Bernice Claire (Green) H.; m. Elizabeth Katherine Ramage, Aug. 4, 1985; children: Katherine, William, Margaret. BA, Trinity Coll., Hartford, Conn., 1978; JD, Fordham U., 1982. Bar: N.Y. 1983, D.C. 1992, U.S. Supreme Ct.

1992, U.S. Dist. Ct. (so. dist.) N.Y. 1983, U.S. Dist. Ct. (ea. dist.) N.Y. 1983, U.S. Ct. Appeals (2d cir.) 1986, U.S. Ct. Appeals (D.C. cir.) 1990, U.S. Dist. Ct. Md. 1996. Assoc. Anderson, Russell, Kill & Olick, N.Y.C., 1982-85; asst. U.S. Atty. So. Dist. N.Y., N.Y.C., 1985-90; prin. Schwalb, Donnenfeld, Bray & Silbert, Washington, 1990—. Editor Fordham Urban Law Jour., 1981, 82. Bd. dirs. N.Y. Ave. Found., Washington, 1993—. Mem. ABA (white collar crime com.). Democrat. Jewish. Office: Piper Rudnick 1200 19th St NW Fl 7 Washington DC 20036-2430

HOFFLEIT, ELLEN DORRIT, astronomer; b. Florence, Ala., Mar. 12, 1907; d. Fred and Kate (Sanio) H. AB, Radcliffe Coll., 1928, MA, 1932, PhD, 1938; DSc (hon.), Smith Coll., 1984, Ctrl. Conn. State U., 1998. From research asst. to astronomer Harvard Coll. Obs., 1929-56; mathematician Ballistic Research Labs., Aberdeen Proving Ground, Md., 1943-48; tech. expert, 1948-62; lectr. Wellesley Coll., 1955-56; mem. faculty Yale U., 1956—, sr. research astronomer, 1974—. Dir. Maria Mitchell Obs., Nantucket, Mass., 1957—78; mem. Hayden Planetarium Com., N.Y.C., 1975—90; editor Meteoritical Soc., 1958—68. Author: Some Firsts in Astronomical Photography, 1950, Yale Bright Star Catalogue, 4th edit., 1982, Astronomy at Yale, 1701-1968, 1992, (autobiography) Misfortunes as Blessings in Disguise, 2002; also rsch. papers. Recipient Caroline Wilby prize Radcliffe Coll., 1938, Grad. Soc. medal, 1964, cert. appreciation War Dept., 1946, alumnae recognition award Radcliffe Coll., 1983, George van Biesbroeck award U. Ariz., 1988, Glover award Dickinson U., 1995, Maria Mitchell Women in Sci. award, 1997; asteroid Dorrit named in her honor, 1987, Anni Mirabiles Symposium in hon. of 90th birthday Yale U., 1999; inducted into Conn. Women's Hall of Fame, 1998. Fellow AAAS, Meteoritical Soc.; mem. Internat. Astron. Union, Am. Astron. Soc. (Annenberg award 1993), Am. Geophys. Union, Astron. Soc. New Haven (hon.), Am. Assn. Variable Star Observers (hon., William Tyler Olcott Disting. Svc. award 2002), Am. Def. Preparedness Assn., N.Y. Acad. Scis., Conn. Acad. Arts and Scis., Nantucket Maria Mitchell Assn. (hon.), Nantucket Hist. Soc., Yale Peabody Mus. Assocs., Astron. Soc. Pacific, Phi Beta Kappa, Sigma Xi, Harvard Club of So. Conn. E-mail: hoffleit@astro.yale.edu. *The guiding motto of my life has been: Work for the work's sake and it will become a part of you. Work for the sake of worldly gain and you sell your soul to the Devil: Love for research and boundless perseverance have enabled me to achieve, not all that I might have wished, but far more than I would ever have dared to expect on the basis of mediocre high school grades.*

HOFFLUND, PAUL, lawyer; b. San Diego, Mar. 27, 1928; s. John Leslie and Ethel Frances (Cline) H.; m. Anne Marie Thalman, Feb. 15, 1958; children: Mark, Sylvia. BA, Princeton (N.J.) U., 1950; JD, George Washington U., 1956. Bar: D.C. 1956, U.S. Dist. Ct. D.C. 1956, U.S. Ct. Appeals (D.C. cir.) 1956, Calif. 1957, U.S. Dist. Ct. (so. dist.) Calif. 1957, U.S. Ct. Mil. Appeals 1957, U.S. Ct. Claims 1958, U.S. Ct. Appeals (9th cir.) 1960, U.S. Supreme Ct. 1964, U.S. Tax Ct. 1989. Assoc. Wencke, Carlson & Kuykendall, San Diego, 1961-62; ptnr. Carlson, Kuykendall & Hofflund, San Diego, 1963-65, Carlson & Hofflund, San Diego, 1965-72; Christian Sci. practitioner San Diego, 1972-84; arbitrator Mcpl. Cts. and Superior Ct. of Calif., San Diego, 1984-99; pvt. practice San Diego, 1985—. Adj. prof. law Nat. U. Sch. Law, San Diego, 1985-94; judge pro tem Mcpl. Ct. South Bay Jud. Dist., 1990-99; disciplinary counsel to U.S. Tax Ct., 1989—; asst. U.S. atty. U.S. Dept. of Justice, L.A., 1959-60, asst. U.S. atty. in charge, San Diego, 1960-61, spl. hearing officer, San Diego, 1962-68; asst. corp. counsel Govt. of D.C., 1957-59. Author: (chpt. in book) Handbook on Criminal Procedure in the U.S. District Court, 1967; contbr. articles to profl. jours. Treas. Princeton Club of San Diego; v.p. Community Concert Assn., San Diego; pres. Sunland Home Found., San Diego, Trust for Christian Sci. Orgn., San Diego; chmn. bd. 8th Ch. of Christ, Scientist, San Diego. With USN, 1950-53, comdr. JAGC, USNR, 1953-72, ret. Mem. ABA, San Diego County Bar Assn., World Affairs Coun., Phi Delta Phi. Democrat. Avocations: theater, classical music, bridge, fine art, biblical study. Home and Office: 6146 Syracuse Ln San Diego CA 92122-3301 *Decisions should be based on divine direction rather than human determination. Pray first; then act. A life devoid of spirituality lacks dimension. The steps of a good man are ordered by the lord: And he delighteth in his way.*

HOFFMAN, ALAN CRAIG, lawyer, consultant; b. Chgo., Oct. 1, 1944; s. Morris Joseph and Marie E. Hoffman; m. Pamela Hoffman. BA, Carthage Coll., 1968; JD, John Marshall Law Sch., 1973. Bar: Fla. 1973, Ill. 1973, U.S. Dist. Ct. (no. dist.) Ill. 1974, U.S. Dist. Ct. (mid. dist.) Fla. 1981, U.S. Ct. Appeals (7th cir.) 1975, U.S. Ct. Appeals (5th and 11th cirs.) 1981, U.S. Supreme Ct. 1977. Staff atty. Cook County Legal Assistance Found., Brookfield, Ill., 1973-74, Patient Legal Svcs., Chgo., 1974; pvt. practice law Chgo., 1973—, River Grove, Ill., 1973-86, Oak Brook, Ill., 1980-87, Hinsdale, Ill., 1987-93; with assocs., 1980—. Spl. asst. atty. gen. Ill. Criminal Justice Divsn., Chgo., 1977—79, Ill. Condemnation Divsn., Chgo., 1980—87; pres. Almar, Ltd., 1986—91; v.p. Marach, Ltd., 1986—89, Hoffman Realty, 1978—; pres., dir. North Shore Greenview Bldg. Corp., 1978—2002; asst. prof. Lewis U., 1974—79; vis. profl. Coll. Law Paraprofl. Ctr., 1974—76, adj. prof., 1979—80; adj. prof. law Health Law Inst. Loyola U., Chgo., 2000—; assoc. prof. No. Ill. U., 1979—80; v.p. Adv. Svc., Inc.; cons. Med-Legal Cases, 1982—. Author (with F. Lane and D. Birnbaum): Lane's Medical Litigation Guide, 1981; contbr. Mem. Oak Park Twp. (Ill.) Mental Health Bd., 1975—80, v.p., 1975, chmn. program com., 1975—77, pres., 1978; mem. governing bd. Women In Need Growing Stronger, 1993—96; bd. govs. Jewish Fedn. Chgo., Coun. for Elderly, 1995—98; co-chair Rainbow House Bread and Roses Ann. Fundraiser, 1997—98. Fellow: Am. Coll. Legal Medicine (editl. bd. med. and legal textbook com. 1987—, textbook update com. 1988, program com. 1988—, legal com. 1988—, profl. devel. com. 1990—98, student awards com. 1992—, moot ct. competition com. 1992—98, co-chair com. violence and abuse in the family 1993); mem.: ATLA, ABA (civil procedure and evidence com. 1993—, comml. tort com. 1993—), Chgo. Acad. Law and Medicine, West Suburban Bar Assn., DuPage Bar Assn., Chgo. Bar Assn., Ill. State Bar Assn. (vice chmn. standing com. on mentally disabled 1975—77, chmn. 1977—78), Fla. Bar Assn. (health law com. 1983—84, out-of-state practitioner com. 1988—91), Ill. Trial Lawyers Assn. (profl. negligence com. 1982), Am. Soc. Law and Medicine, Mensa, Phi Alpha Delta.

HOFFMAN, ALAN JAY, lawyer; b. Phila., Aug. 31, 1948; s. Heinz Julius and Sylvia (Wise) H.; children: Jennifer, Lauren, Allison. BBA, Temple U., 1970; JD, Villanova U., 1973. Bar: Pa. 1973, U.S. Dist. Ct. (ea. dist.) Pa. 1973, U.S. Dist. Ct. Del. 1973, U.S. Ct. Appeals (3rd cir.) 1973, Del. 1977, U.S. Supreme Ct. 1984, D.C. 1990. Asst. U.S. atty. U.S. Dept. Justice, Wilmington, Del., 1973-78; ptnr. Dilworth, Paxson, Kalish & Kauffman, Phila., 1979-92, mem. exec. mgmt. com., 1989-90, chmn. new bus. com., 1990-91; ptnr. Blank, Rome, Comisky and McCauley, Phila., 1992—, mem. exec. mgmt. com., 1998—, co-chmn. atty. recruiting com., adminstrv. ptnr. in charge Wilmington, Del., chmn. litigation and dispute resolution dept., 1996—. Lectr. Widener Del. Law Sch., Wilmington, 1974, Mealy's Conf. on Toxic Torts, 1999—, Mealy's Conf. on MTBE pollution, 2000. Contbg. co-editor Villanova Law Rev., 1972-73; contbr. articles to profl. jours. Bd. dirs. Men's Club Temple Adath Israel, Merion, Pa., 1993-94; pres. Villanova Law Sch. Inn of Ct., 1999—. Recipient Atty. Gen.'s Spl. Commendation U.S. Dept. Justice, Washington, 1977. Fellow Am. Bar Found.; mem. ATLA, ABA, Pa. Bar Assn., Fed. Bar Assn., Phila. Bar Assn., Del. Bar Assn., Del. Trial Lawyers Assn., Pa. Trial Lawyers Assn., White Manor Country Club (pres. 1993—, 1st v.p. 1990-93, bd. dirs. 1988-90, admissions chmn. 1989—), J. Willard O'Brien Villanova Law Sch. Inn of Ct. (pres. 1999—). Avocation: golf. Office: Blank Rome Comisky & McCauley One Logan Sq Philadelphia PA 19103-6998

HOFFMAN, ALAN JEROME, mathematician, educator; b. N.Y.C., May 30, 1924; s. Jesse and Muriel (Schrager) H.; m. Esther Atkins Walker, May 30, 1947 (dec. July 1988); children: Eleanor, Elizabeth Hoffman Perry; m. Elinor Klausner Hershaft, Sept. 2, 1990. AB, Columbia U., 1947, PhD, 1950; DSc (hon.), Technion U., 1986. Mem. Inst. Advanced Study, Princeton, N.J., 1950-51; mathematician Nat. Bur. Standards, Washington, 1951-56; sci. liaison officer Office Naval Research, London, 1956-57; cons. Gen. Electric Co., N.Y.C., 1957-61; rsch. staff mem. IBM Rsch. Ctr., Yorktown Heights, NY, 1961—2002, fellow, 1978—2002, fellow emeritus, 2002—. Vis. prof. Technion, Haifa, Israel, 1965, Stanford U., 1980-91, Rutgers U., 1990-96, Ga. Inst. Tech., 1992-93; adj. prof. CUNY, 1965-76, Yale U., 1976-85; Phi Beta Kappa lectr., 1989-90; mem. Inst. Ops. Rsch. and Mgmt. Scis. With U.S. Army, 1943-46, ETO, PTO. Recipient von Neumann prize Ops. Rsch. Soc. and Inst. Mgmt. Sci., 1992, Founder's award Math. Programming Soc., 2000. Fellow Inst. for Ops. Rsch. and Mgmt. Sci., N.Y. Acad. Sci., Am. Acad. Arts and Scis.; mem. NAS, Am. Math. Soc. (coun. 1982-84). Office: IBM TJ Watson Rsch Ctr PO Box 218 Yorktown Heights NY 10598-0218

HOFFMAN, ALBERT ADAM, JR., retired structural engineer, educator; b. Chgo., Mar. 2, 1928; s. Albert Adam and Marie Catherine (Cremer)H. BS in Civil Engring., Ill. Inst. Tech., 1950; MS in Civil Engring., U. Calif., Berkeley, 1952; MBA, St. Louis U., 1960. Lic. structural engr., Ill. Structural engr. DeLeuw Cather, Chgo., 1954-56, Dunlap and Esgar, Chgo., 1956-58; asst. prof. civil engring. St. Louis U., 1958-61; tchr. Purdue U., Lafayette, Ind., 1961-63; sales engr. Bethlehem Steel Corp., Chgo., 1963-83; tchr. Gordon Tech. High Sch., Chgo., 1983—99. Author: Letters to Paul, 2100. Mem. adv. bd. Chgo. Park Dist., 1973-78; mem. sch. bd. St. Timothy Parish, Chgo., 1975-78; volleyball coach Loyola Acad., Willmette, Ill., 1990-93; vol. docent Chgo. Hist. Soc., 1996—. 1st lt. C.E. U.S. Army, 1952-54. Mem. ASCE (dir., program chmn. 1972-80), Ill. Soc. Structural Engrs. (dir. 1968-82), Ill. Inst. Tech. Alumni Assn. (v.p. 1968-75). Republican. Roman Catholic. Home: Resurrection Retirement Cmty 7260 W Peterson Ave E-125 Chicago IL 60631

HOFFMAN, ALFRED JOHN, retired mutual fund executive; b. Amarillo, Tex., Apr. 16, 1917; s. Kurt John and Mabel (Beven) H.; m. Falice Mae Pittinger, Jan. 5, 1946 (dec. Feb. 1990); children: Peter Kurt (dec.), Susan Terry, John; m. Frances Ward, Sept. 15, 1990.. JD, U. Mo., 1942. Atty. Prudential Ins. Co. Am., 1946-50, Kansas City Fire & Marine Ins. Co., 1950-59; CEO, founder Jones & Babson, Inc., Kansas City, 1959-85, vice chmn., 1985-93; pres., dir. Babson and UMB Mut. Funds, 1959-85, dir., 1985-93. Naval aviator USN, 1942-46. Mem. ABA, Mo. Bar Assn., Kansas City Golf Assn. (past pres., bd. dirs.), Kansas City Golf Found. (founder, chmn., bd. dirs.), Kansas City Srs. Golf Assn. (past pres., bd. dirs.), U.S. Golf Assn. (com.), Western Golf Assn. (past dir.). Home and Office: 6701 High Dr Shawnee Mission KS 66208-2260

HOFFMAN, ALICIA CORO, retired federal executive; b. Havana, Cuba, Mar. 28, 1937; d. Daniel P. and Alicia G. (Mignagaray) Camacho; m. Carlos J. Coro, May 1958 (dec. 1983); children: Alicia Biciocchi, Carlos M. Coro, Christina Kunowsky; m. Kenneth M. Hoffman, Mar. 1997. Tchg. diploma, U. Havana, 1961; MEd, U. Md., 1972. Tchr., supr. Montgomery County Pub. Schs., Rockville, Md., 1966-71; edn. spcialist U.S. Dept. Edn., Washington, 1971-80, dir. Horace Mann Learning Ctr., 1980-85, dep. asst. sec., acting asst. sec., Office for Civil Rights, 1985-87, dir. bilingual edn., 1987-88, dir. sch. improvement, 1988-96, sr. advisor, 1996-97; ret., 1997. Bd. dirs. Montgomery Pub. TV, 1984-94. Recipient Presdl. Meritorious Rank award, U.S. Sr. Exec. Svc., 1992, Hispanic Achievement award in Edn., Hispanic Orgns., 1992, named Hispanic Woman of Yr., 1986. Mem. Nat. Asns. Cuban Am. Educators (bd. dirs. 1992-98), Nat. Assn. Cuban Am. Women (advisor 1980-88). Roman Catholic. Home: 909 Parsons Dr Madison MD 21648-1103

HOFFMAN, ALLAN SACHS, chemical engineer, educator; b. Chgo., Oct. 27, 1932; s. Saul A. and Frances E. (Sachs) H.; m. Susan Carol Freeman, July 29, 1962; children: David, Lisa. BSChemE, MIT, 1953, MSChemE, 1955, ScD-ChemE, 1957. Instr. chem. engring. MIT, Cambridge, 1954-56, asst. prof., 1958-60, assoc. prof., 1965-70; research engr. Calif. Research Corp., Richmond, 1960-63; asso. dir. research Amicon Corp., Cambridge, 1963-65; prof. bioengring. and chem. engring. U. Wash., Seattle, 1970—; asst. dir. Center for Bioengring., 1973-83. Cons. to various govtl., indsl. and acad. orgns., 1958—; UN adviser to Mexican govt., 1973-74. Author: (with W. Burlant) Block and Graft Copolymers, 1960; author numerous articles and book chpts. on chem. engring. and biomaterials; patentee in field. Kimberly Clark fellow, 1954-55, Visking fellow, 1955-56, Fulbright fellow, 1957-58, Battelle fellow, 1970-72; Festschrift in honor of 60th birthday 8 issues of Jour. Biomaterials Sci., Polymer Edn., 1993. 94. Mem. Am. Chem. Soc., Am. Inst. Chem. Engrs., Am. Soc. for Artificial Internal Organs, Internat. Soc. Artificial Internal Organs (trustee, bd. dirs. 1987-1990), Soc. for Biomaterials (pres. 1983-84, Clemson award for biomaterial sci. lit., 1985, Founder's award, 2000), Controlled Release Soc. (Excellence in Guiding Grad. Rsch. award 1989, 98), Japan Biomaterials Soc. (Biomaterials Sci. prize 1990, Symposium in honor of 70th birthday 2002). Home: 10616 Riviera Pl NE Seattle WA 98125-6938 Office: U Wash Mail Box 352255 Seattle WA 98195-2255 E-mail: hoffman@u.washington.edu.

HOFFMAN, AMY, publishing executive; Publisher Computer Reseller News, Jericho, NY. Office: CMP Media Inc 600 Community Dr Manhasset NY 11030-3875

HOFFMAN, ANDREW JOHN, environmental management educator; b. Easton, Pa., Oct. 18, 1961; s. Joseph Henry and Kathryn Marie (Hylind) H. BSChemE, U. Mass., 1983; SM in Environ. Engring., MIT, 1991, PhD in Mgmt. and Environ. Engring., 1995. Engr.-in-tng., Mass. Compliance engr. EPA, Boston, 1984-86; environ. engring. cons. Metcalf and Eddy, Inc., Wakefield, Mass., 1986-87; constrn. mgr. T&T Constrn. and Design, Inc., Ridgefield, Conn., 1987-90; policy analyst Amoco Oil Co., Chgo., 1993; vis. asst. prof. Kellogg Sch. Mgmt., Evanston, Ill., 1995-97; asst. prof. mgmt. Boston U. Sch. Mgmt., 1997—. Organizer, facilitator Sr. Level Dialogue on Climate Change, 1997, 98; sr. advisor The Canopy Inst.; svc. advisor Cath. Charities. Author: From Heresy to Dogma: An Institutional History of Corporate Environmentalism, 1997, Competitive Environmental Strategy, 2000; editor: Global Climate Change, 1998, Organizations, Policy and the Natural Environment, 2002; mem. editl. bd. Orgns. and Environ. Project leader, vol. City Yr., Boston and Chgo., 1992—; project mgr., vol. Boston Cares, 1997—; staff supporter Rosie's Place Homeless Shelter, Boston, 1997—; lector St. Paul's Ch., Cambridge, Mass., 1998—. Environ. Coun. postdoctoral fellow Northwestern U., 1995. Mem. Acad. Mgmt., Soc. Environ. Journalists, Com. for Nat. Inst. for Environ., Tau Beta Pi. Avocations: classical music, golf, motorcycle touring, carpentry. Office: Boston U Sch Mgmt 595 Commonwealth Ave Boston MA 02215-1704 Fax: 617-353-5244. E-mail: ahoffman@bu.edu.

HOFFMAN, BARBARA A. state legislator; b. Mar. 8, 1940; d. Sidney Wolf and Eve (Simonoff) Marks; m. Donald Edwin Hoffman, 1960; children: Alan Samuel, Michael Stuart, Carolyn Mara. BS, Towson State U., 1960; MLA, Johns Hopkins U., 1966; DHL (hon.), Towson U.; D of Pub. Svc. (hon.), U. Md. Baltimore County, U. Md., Balt., U. Md./Univ. Coll. Secondary sch. tchr., Balt., 1960-63; supr. student tchrs. Morgan U., Balt., 1968-73; exec. dir. Md. Dem. Com., 1979-84; mem. Dist. 42 Md. Senate, Annapolis, 1983—, chair budget and tax com. Mem. Edn. Commn. of the States; bd. dirs. U. Md. Med. Sys., Balt. Mus. Art, Living Classrooms Found. Recipient numerous awards and honors. Democrat. Jewish. Office: Md Senate 733 W 40th St Ste 105 Baltimore MD 21211-2113 Home: 2905 W Strathmore Ave Baltimore MD 21209-3810 E-mail: barbara_hoffman@senate.state.md.us.

HOFFMAN, BARBARA JO, health and physical education educator, athletic director; b. Dayton, Ohio, Aug. 10, 1952; d. Harold Lee and Virginia May (Dafler) H. BA, Otterbein Coll., 1974; MEd, Ashland Coll., 1987. Cert. Athletic Adminstr. Tchr. Harrison Hills City Sch., Hopedale, Ohio, 1974—; coach volleyball, track, basketball Cadiz HS, Ohio, 1974-85, athletic dir., 1996—2003. Key advisor Ohio FHA/HERO, Columbus, 1990-96, mentor advisor, 1992. Recipient Golden Apple Achiever award Ashland Oil, Inc., 1989, Ohio Home Econs. Tchr. of Yr. award, 1991, Vocat. Home Econs. Program award, 1990, Pacesetter award, 1992, 93, 96, 97. Mem. NEA, AAHPERD, Nat. Interscholastic Athletic Adminstrs. Assn., Ea. Ohio Interscholastic Athletic Adminstrs. Assn. Republican. Methodist. Home: 647 Kerr Ave Cadiz OH 43907-1022 Office: Harrison Ctrl HS 440 E Market St Cadiz OH 43907-1244 E-mail: bhoffman@clover.net.

HOFFMAN, BARRY PAUL, lawyer; b. Phila., May 29, 1941; s. Samuel and Hilda (Cohn) H.; m. Mary Ann Schrock, May 18, 1978; children: Elizabeth Barron, Hayley Rebecca. BA, Pa. State U., 1963; JD, George Washington U., 1968. Bar: Pa. 1972, Mich. 1983. Asst. U.S. Senator Wayne Morse, Oreg., Washington; spl. agt. FBI, Washington; asst. dist. atty. Phila. Dist. Atty.'s Office; exec. v.p., gen. counsel Valassis Communications, Inc., Livonia, Mich., also bd. dirs. 1st lt. U.S. Army, 1963-65, Korea. Home: 49933 Standish Ct Plymouth MI 48170-2882 Office: Valassis Communications Inc 19975 Victor Pkwy Livonia MI 48152-7001 E-mail: hoffmanb@valassis.com.

HOFFMAN, BRENDA JOYCE, gastroenterology educator; b. Madisonville, Ky., Sept. 4, 1957; d. John Willis and Lavada Fae (Baxter) H. BS, Murray State U., 1979; MD, U. Ky., 1983. Diplomate Am. Soc. Gastroenterology and Internal Medicine. Resident Med. U. S.C., Charleston, 1983-86, chief med. resident, 1986-87, gastroent./internal medicine fellow, 1987-89, therapeutic fellow, 1989-90, clin. instr. medicine, 1990-91, asst. prof. medicine, 1991-95, assoc. prof. medicine, 1995-2000, prof. medicine, 2001—, chief endosonography, clin. dir., 1993—. Contbr. articles to profl. jours. Fellow ACP, Am. Coll. Gastroenterology; mem. Am. Gastroent. Assn., Am. Soc. Gastroenterology Examiners. Avocations: soccer, sailing, reading. Office: Med U SC 171 Ashley Ave Charleston SC 29425-0001

HOFFMAN, CARL H. lawyer; b. St. Louis, May 28, 1936; s. Carl Henry and Anna Marie (Remlinger) H.; m. Pamela L. Polk, May 8, 1971 (div. Novl 1982); children: Kurt M., Jennifer K. BS, St. Louis U., 1958; postgrad., U. Mex., Mexico City, 1958, U. Nev., 1960—61, Tex. Technol. Coll., 1961—62; JD, Washington U., St. Louis, 1966. Bar: Mo. 1966, Fla. 1969, U.S. Supreme Ct. 1970; cert. civil trial adv. Nat. Bd. Trial Advocacy. Pilot Eastern Airlines, Inc., Miami, Fla.; assoc. Spencer & Taylor, Miami, Fla., 1969—70; pvt. practice atty. Miami, 1970—80; ptnr. Hoffman & Hertzig, P.A., Coral Gables, Fla., 1980—. Capt. USAF, 1958-63. Mem. AIAA, ABA, ATLA, SAE Internat., Fla. Bar (cert. civil trial lawyer, cert. bus. litigation lawyer, chmn. aviation law com. 1997-98), Fla. Acad. Trial Lawyers, Am. Jurisprudence Soc., Greater Miami C. of C. (trustee). Office: Hoffman & Hertzig PA 901 Ponce De Leon Blvd Ste 500 Coral Gables FL 33134-3073 E-mail: hoffhertz@att.net.

HOFFMAN, CHARLES FENNO, III, architect; b. Greenwich, Conn., May 28, 1958; s. Harrison Baldwin Wright and Louise Elkins (Sinkler) H.; m. Pia Christina Ossorio, Dec. 27, 1980; children: Wilhelmina C. L., Frederic W. S., Henry F., C. Fenno IV. BA in Environ. Design, U. Pa., 1983; MArch, U. Colo., 1986. Designer Fenno Hoffman & Assocs., Boulder, Colo., 1983—; pvt. practice designer Boulder, 1985; assoc. William Zmistowski Assoc. Architects, 1987, Pellecchia-Olson Architects, Boulder, 1989—; prin. Fenno Hoffman Architects PC, Boulder, Colo., 1991—. Cons. Summit Habitats, Inc., 1984—, design cons. The Denver Partnership, 1985, Downtown Denver, Inc., 1985; guest critic U. Colo., 1990—, guest lectr., 1991-92, 94, 95, 96, 97, design instr., 1995—; comml. cons. and design, comm. and software facilities, shopping malls, large scale, mixed use devel., urban renewal projects, corp. facilities, 1997—. Prin. works include Ca'Venier Mus. for Venice Bienalle, 1985, Cleveland Pl. Connection, Denver, 1985 (1st prize, 1985), hist. renovated house, Boulder, 1986, 3 Gates 3 Squares, Denver, 1986, Geneva Ave. House, 1992, Jarrow Sch. master plan, 1994, numerous residential, multi-family and corp. projects, 1991—, Northeast Classroom, 1995, US Navy and Marine Corps. Facilities Assessments, 1996, Golden Run Town Plan, 1999, Erie Performing Arts Ctr., 2000, Civic Ctr., Erie, Colo., 2000, Lucent Techs. Pub. Safety Sys., Chgo., 2001, Intrado Corp World Hdqs., 2001; author: Urban Transit Facility, A Monorail for Downtown Denver, 1985. Bd. dirs. Jarrow Sch., Dairy Ctr. for the Arts. Mem. Am. Inst. Architects (nat. com. on design; Design award Colo. chpt.), Architects & Planners of Boulder, Congress for New Urbanism. Democrat. Episcopalian. Avocations: drawing, skiing, bicycling, computers. Office: 505 Geneva Ave Boulder CO 80302-7139

HOFFMAN, CHERI, social services administrator; b. Suffern, N.Y., Nov. 6, 1973; d. J.C. and Judith C. Hoffman. BS in Child Devel., Syracuse U., 1995; M in Marriage and Family Therapy, Trevecca Nazarene U., Nashville, 1999. Cert. grant specialist Nat. Grant Writer's Assn., 2000. Dir. of edn. Mercy Ministries of Am., Nashville, 1996—99; dir. of devel. Rocketown of Mid. Tenn., Nashville, 2000—01; program dir., Bounty Hunter Coalition Rocketown Youth Svcs., Nashville, 2002—. Ghostwriter (biographical vignettes) Mercy Moves Mountains. Vol. ARC, Nashville, Tenn., 2001—02. Mem.: Future Bus. Leaders of Am. Profl. Divsn. (life). Conservative. Avocations: travel, reading, writing. Office: Rocketown Youth Svcs 401 6th Ave S Nashville TN 37203 Personal E-mail: cherihoffman@rocketown.org.

HOFFMAN, DANIEL (DANIEL GERARD HOFFMAN), literature educator, poet; b. N.Y.C., Apr. 3, 1923; s. Daniel and Frances (Beck) H.; m. Elizabeth McFarland, May 22, 1948; children: Kate, Macfarlane. BA, Columbia U., 1947, MA, 1949, PhD, 1956. Instr. English Columbia U., 1952-56; vis. prof. Am. Lit. Faculté des Lettres, Dijon, France, 1956-57; asst. prof. to prof. English Swarthmore Coll., 1957-66; prof. English U. Pa., 1966-83, poet-in-residence, 1978-93, Felix E. Schelling prof. English lit., 1983-93, prof. emeritus, 1993—. Fellow Ind. U. Sch. Letters, 1959; George Elliston lectr. poetry U. Cin., 1964; lectr. 6th Internat. Sch. Yeats Studies, Sligo, Ireland, 1965; poetry cons. Libr. of Congress, 1973-74, hon. cons. in Am. letters, 1974-77; poet-in-residence Cathedral Ch. of St. John the Divine, 1988-99; vis. prof. English, King's Coll. London, 1991-92. Author: (poetry) An Armada of Thirty Whales, 1954, A Little Geste and Other Poems, 1960, The City of Satisfactions, 1963, Striking the Stones, 1968, Broken Laws, 1970, The Center of Attention, 1974, Able Was I Ere I Saw Elba, 1977, Brotherly Love, 1981, Hang-Gliding from Helicon, 1988, Middens of the Tribe, 1995, Darkening Water, 2002, Beyond Silence: Selected Shorter Poems, 2003; (poetry transl.) A Play of Mirrors by Ruth Domino, 2002; (criticism) Paul Bunyan: Last of the Frontier Demigods, 1952, The Poetry of Stephen Crane, 1957, Form and Fable in American Fiction, 1961, Barbarous Knowledge, 1967, Poe Poe Poe Poe Poe Poe Poe, 1972, Faulkner's Country Matters, 1989, Words to Create a World, 1993; (memoir) Zone of the Interior, 2000; editor: The Red Badge of Courage, 1957, American Poetry and Poetics, 1962, Ezra Pound and William Carlos Williams, 1983; editor, contbr.: (criticism) Harvard Guide to Contemporary American Writing, 1979. Served to 1st lt. USAAF, 1943-46. Decorated Legion of Merit; recipient U. Chgo. Folklore prize, 1949, Poetry Center Introductions prize, 1951, Yale Series of Younger Poets award, 1954, Ansley prize, 1957, Lit. award Athenaeum of Phila., 1963, 83, medal for excellence Columbia U., 1964, Nat. Inst. Arts and Letters award in poetry, 1967, meml. medal Hungarian PEN, 1980, Hazlett Meml. award for lit., 1984, Paterson Poetry prize, 1989, Aiken Taylor Prize for Modern Am. Poetry, 2003; poetry grantee Ingram Merrill Found., 1971-72; fellow Am. Council Learned Socs., 1961-62, 66-67, NEH, 1975-76, Guggenheim Meml. Found., 1983-84. Mem. MLA, Assn. Literary Scholars and Critics, Acad. Am. Poets (chancellor 1973-97, chancellor emeritus 1997—), Authors Guild (council). Clubs: Century (N.Y.C.); Franklin Inn (Phila.).

HOFFMAN, DANIEL STEVEN, lawyer, law educator; b. N.Y.C., May 4, 1931; s. Lawrence Hoffman and Juliette (Marbes) Ostrov; m. Beverly Mae Swenson, Dec. 4, 1954; children: Lisa Hoffman Ciancio, Tracy Hoffman Cockriel, Robin Hoffman Black. BA, U. Colo., 1951; LLB, U. Denver, 1958. Bar: Colo. 1958. Assoc., then ptnr. Fugate, Mitchem, Hoffman, Denver, 1951—55; mgr. of safety City and County of Denver, 1963—65; ptnr. Kripke, Hoffman, Carrigan, Denver, 1965—70, Hoffman, McDermott, Hoffman, Denver, 1970—78; of counsel Hoffman & McDermott, Denver, 1978—84; mem. Holme Roberts & Owen, LLC, Denver, 1984—94; dean Coll. Law, U. Denver, 1978—84, dean emeritus, prof. emeritus, 1984—; ptnr. McKenna & Cuneo LLP, Denver, 1994—2000, Hoffman Reilly Pozner & Williamson LLP, 2000—. Chmn., mem. Merit Screening Com. for Bankruptcy Judges, Denver, 1979—84; chmn. subcom. Dist. Atty.'s Crime Adv. Commn., Denver, 1984—; chmn. Senator Wirth's jud. nomination rev. com., Cong. DeGette's jud. nomination rev. com. Contbr. chpts. to books Mem. Rocky Mountain region Anti Defamation League, Denver, 1985; bd. dirs. Colo. chpt. Am. Jewish Com. 1985, Legal Ctr., Denver, 1985—; mem. adv. com. Samaritan Shelter, Denver, 1985; chmn. Rocky Flats Blue Ribbon Citizens Com., Denver, 1980-83; mem. bd. visitors J. Reuben Clark Law Sch. Brigham Young U., 1986-88. With USAF 1951-55. Recipient Am. Jewish Com. Nat. Judge Learned Hand award, 1993 Humanitarian award Rocky Mountain chpt. Anti-Defamation League, 1984 Alumni of Yr. award U. Denver Coll. Law, 1997, Lifetime Achievement award Colo. Trial Lawyers Assn., 2001. Fellow: Am. Bar Found., Colo. Bar Found. Am. Coll. Trial Lawyers (state chmn. 1975—76), Internat. Soc. Barristers; mem.: Am. Judicature Soc. (bd. dirs. 1977—81), Assn. Trial Lawyers Am. (nat. com. mem. 1962—63), Colo. Trial Lawyers Assn. (pres. 1961—62, Lifetime Achievement award 2001), Colo. Bar. Assn. (pres. 1976—77, Young Lawyer of Yr. award 1965), Order of Coif (hon.). Democrat. Jewish. Avocation: platform tennis. Office: Hoffman Reilly Pozner & Williamson LLP Kittredge Bldg 511 16th St Ste 700 Denver CO 80202-4248 E-mail: dhoffman@hrpwlaw.com.

HOFFMAN, DARLEANE CHRISTIAN, chemistry educator; b. Terril, Iowa, Nov. 8, 1926; d. Carl Benjamin and Elverna (Kuhlman) Christian; m. Marvin Morrison Hoffman, Dec. 26, 1951; children: Maureane R., Daryl K. BS in Chemistry, Iowa State U., 1948, PhD in Nuclear Chemistry, 1951; D (hon.), U. Bern, Switzerland, 2001; PhD (hon.), Clark U., 2000. Chemist Oak Ridge (Tenn.) Nat. Lab., 1952—53; staff radiochemistry group Los Alamos (N.Mex.) Sci. Lab., 1953—71, assoc. leader chemistry-nuclear group, 1971—79, leader chem.-nuclear divsn., 1979—82, leader isotope and nuclear chem. divsn., 1982-84; prof. chemistry U. Calif., Berkeley, 1984—91, prof. emeritus, 1991—93, prof. grad. sch., 1993—; faculty sr. scientist Lawrence Berkeley Lab., 1984—; dir.'s fellow Los Alamos Nat. Lab., 1990—; dir. G.T. Seaborg Inst. for Transactinium Sci., 1991—96. Spkr. in field; subcom. on nuclear and radiochemistry NAS-NRC, 1978—81, chmn. subcom. on nuclear and radiochemistry, 1982—84, bd. on radioactive waste mgmt., 1994—99; titular mem. commn. on radiochem. and nuclear techniques Internat. Union of Pure and Applied Chem., 1983—87, sec., 1985—87, chmn., 1987—91, assoc., 1991—93; organizer of symposiums in field ; com. mem. Internat. Symposium on Nuclear and Radiochemistry, 1988; organizing com. Actinides, 1993, nat. adv. com., 2001; planning panel Workshop on Tng. Requirements for Chemists in Nuclear Medicine, Nuclear Industry, and Related Fields, 1998; radionuclide migration peer rev. com., Las Vegas, 1986—87; steering com. Advanced Steady State Neutron Source, 1986—90; steering com., panelist Workshop on Opportunities and Challenges in Rsch. with Transplutonium Elements, Washington, 1983; energy rsch. adv. bd. cold fusion panel Dept. Energy, 1989—90, nuclear energy rsch. adv. com, 2000—01; separations subpanel of separations tech. and transmutation systems panel NAS, 1992—94; steeering com. Accel. Transmutation Waste Roadmapping Study, 1999; subcom. NERAC, 2000—01; mem. NAS-NRC Russian-Am. Commn., 2001—02; Welch Found. lectr. Tex. univs., 2000. Author: The Transuranium People, 2000; contbr. articles to profl. jours. Named Disting. Lectr., Inst. Phys. Rsch and Tech., Ames Lab., 1998, Welch Found. lectr., 2000; named to Women in Tech. Internat. Hall of Fame, 2000; recipient Alumni Citation of Merit, Coll. Scis. and Humanities, Iowa State U., 1978, Disting. Achievement award, Iowa State U., 1986, Berkeley citation, U. Calif., 1996, U.S. Nat. Medal Sci., 1997, Leonard A. Ford Lectureship, Mankato State U., 1998, Frontiers Sci. award, Soc. Cosmetic Chemists, 1998; fellow, Guggenheim Found., 1978—79; Sr. postdoc.fellow, NSF, 1964—65. Fellow: AAAS (coun. mem. 1995—97), Am. Acad. Arts and Scis., Am. Phys. Soc., Am. Inst. Chemists (pres. N.Mex. chpt. 1976—78); mem.: Radiochem. Soc. (Lifetime Achievement award 2003), Norwegian Acad. Sci. & Letters, Am. Chem. Soc. (John Dustin Clark award 1976, Nuc. Chemistry award 1983, Francis P. Garvan-John M. Olin medal 1990, Priestley medal 2000, Mosher award 2001), Alpha Chi Sigma (Hall of Fame 2002), Sigma Delta Epsilon, Pi Mu Epsilon, Iota Sigma Pi, Phi Kappa Phi, Sigma Xi Rsch. Soc. (Procter prize for sci. achievement 2003). Methodist. Home: 2277 Manzanita Dr Oakland CA 94611-1135 Office: Lawrence Berkeley Nat Lab MS70 R0319 NSD Berkeley CA 94720

HOFFMAN, DARNAY ROBERT, management consultant; b. N.Y.C., Nov. 25, 1947; s. Bill and Toni (Darnay) H.; m. Jennifer Lea Sheppard, Aug. 20, 1984; children by previous marriage: Brandon, Brett; m. Sydney Biddle Barrows, May 14, 1994. BA, SUNY, 1977; MBA, CUNY, 1980; JD, Yeshiva U., 1982. Bar: N.Y. 1995, U.S. Dist. Ct. (so., ea., we. and no. dists.) N.Y. 1995, U.S. Ct. Appeals (fed. cir.) 1995, U.S. Tax Ct. 1995, U.S. Ct. Internat. Trade 1995, U.S. Dist. Ct. Colo. 2000, U.S. Dist. Ct. (no. dist.) Ga. 2000, U.S. Ct. Appeals (fed. cir.). Pres., mgmt. cons. Darnay Hoffman Assocs., Inc., 1969—; mgmt. cons. Hoffman Rsch. Group Inc., N.Y.C., 1977—; rsch. assoc. Baruch Coll., 1977-79. Bd. dirs. Hobton Realty Corp.; dir. Nat. Conf. Law Historians Am., 1987—. Author: Murder in the Wilderness, 1989, Allen Contact, 1989, (pamphlet) Products in Decline, 1980. Mem. ABA, ATLA, Am. Mgmt. Assn., Am. Mktg. Assn., Acad. Mgmt. Scis., Nat. Assn. Criminal Def. Attys., N.Y. State Bar Assn., N.Y. County Lawyers Assn., Assn. Bar of City of N.Y., N.Y. State Trial Lawyers Assn., Player's, Beta Gamma Sigma, Alpha Delta Sigma.

HOFFMAN, DAVID ALAN, lawyer; b. Balt., Jan. 3, 1947; s. Edward Joseph H. and Pauline (Narva) Jacobs; m. Marjorie Fox, Sept. 7, 1968 (div. 1978); m. Elisabeth Lawson Andrews, Sept. 27, 1980; children: Jessica, Jacob, Lily. AB summa cum laude, Princeton U., 1970; MA, Cornell U., 1974; JD magna cum laude, Harvard U., 1984. Bar: Mass. 1985, U.S. Dist. Ct. Mas. 1985, U.S. Ct. Appeals (1st cir.) 1985, U.S. Ct. Appeals (5th cir.) 1990, U.S. Supreme Ct. 1989. Instr. legal methods Harvard Law Sch., Cambridge, Mass., 1982-83, research asst., 1984; clk. 1st Cir. Ct. of Appeals, Boston, 1984-85; assoc. Hill & Barlow, Boston, 1985-92, mem., 1992—2002, The New Law Ctr., LLC, Boston, 2002—03, Boston Law Collaborative, LLC, 2003—. Adj. prof. law Harvard Law Sch., 1997-99, Northeastern U., 1994-96; staff atty. Civil Liberties Union Mass., 1988-89; mem. Supreme Judicial Ct. Standing Com. on Dispute Resolution, 1994-2002; mediator and arbitrator Mass. Office Dispute Resolution, Am. Arbitration Assn., Ctr. for Pub. Resources, Pvt. Adjudication Ctr. Co-author: Massachusetts Alternative Dispute Resolution, 1994; mem. editl. bd. Mass. Law Rev., 1987-89; contbr. articles to profl. jours. Bd. dirs. Walden Ctr. for Peace and Justice, Concord, Mass., 1987-89. Recipient Kennedy Prize for Best Thesis in English Dept., Princeton U., 1970. Mem. ABA (coun. mem. sect. individual rights and responsibilities, 1991-94, chmn.-elect sect. dispute resolution), ACLU, Mass. Bar Assn. (commn. on the bicentennial the constitution 1986-88, chmn. individual rights and responsibilities sect. 1988-90), Boston Bar Assn. (chmn. ADR com. 1993-95), Nat. Lawyers Guild, Soc. Profls. in Dispute Rsolution (pres. N.E. chpt. 1998-2000) Office: Boston Law Collaborative 99 Summer St Ste 1600 Boston MA 02110-2606

HOFFMAN, DONALD ALFRED, lawyer; b. Milw., May 4, 1936; s. Harry Gustav and Emily Frances (Schwartz) H.; m. Louise Hardie Chapman, June 8, 1963; children: Donald Hardie, Richard Rainey. BBA, U. Wis., 1958, JD, 1968. Bar: La. 1969, U.S. Supreme Ct. 1972, U.S. Ct. Appeals (5th cir.) 1973, U.S. Dist. Ct. (ea., mid. and we. dists.) La. Assoc. Lemle & Kelleher, New Orleans, 1968-73; ptnr. Lemle, Kelleher, Kohlmeyer, Matthews & Schumacher, New Orleans, 1973-75, McGlinchey, Stafford, Mintz & Hoffman, New Orleans, 1975-78; city atty. City of New Orleans, 1978-79; dir. Carmouche, Gray & Hoffman, New Orleans, 1979-82; sr. dir. Hoffman, Siegel, Seydel, Bienvenu & Centola, New Orleans, 1982—. Fellow Am. Bar Found., La. Bar Found.; mem. Am. Bd. Trial Advocates (sec.-treas. La. chpt.), French-Am. C. of C. (chmn. La. chpt.). Presbyterian. Home: 1524 4th St New Orleans LA 70130-5918 Office: Hoffman Siegel Seydel Bienvenu & Centola 650 Poydras St New Orleans LA 70130-6121

HOFFMAN, DONALD DAVID, cognitive and computer science educator; b. San Antonio, Dec. 29, 1955; s. David Pollock and Loretta Virginia (Shoemaker) H.; m. Geralyn Mary Souza, Dec. 13, 1986; 1 child from previous marriage, Melissa Louise. BA, UCLA, 1978; PhD, MIT, 1983. MTS and project engr. Hughes Aircraft Co., El Segundo, Calif., 1978-83, rsch. scientist MIT Artificial Intelligence Lab, Cambridge, Mass., 1983; asst. prof. U. Calif., Irvine, 1983-86, assoc. prof., 1986-90, prof., 1990—. Cons. Fairchild Lab. for Artificial Intelligence, Palo Alto, Calif., 1984; panelist MIT Corp. vis. com., Cambridge, 1985, NSF, Washington, 1988; conf. host IEEE Conf. on Visual Motion, Irvine, 1989; conf. host Office of Naval Rsch. Conf. on Vision, Laguna Beach, Calif., 1992; vis. prof. Zentrum für Interdisziplinäre Forschung, Bielefeld, Germany, 1995-96. Author: Visual Intelligence, 1998; co-author: Observer Mechanics, 1989; mem. editl. bd. Cognition, 1991-2002, Psychol. Rev., 1995-96; contbr. articles to profl. jours. Vol. tchr. Turtle Rock Elem. Sch., Irvine, 1988-90. Recipient Distinguished Scientific award, Am. Psychol. Assn., 1989, Troland Rsch. award U.S. Nat. Acad. Scis., 1994; grantee NSF, 1984, 87, 2001. Mem. Vision Sci. Soc., Am. Psychol. Soc. Avocations: running, swimming, racket sports, ice skating. Office: U Calif Dept Cognitive Sci Irvine CA 92697-0001 E-mail: ddhoff@uci.edu.

HOFFMAN, DONALD M. lawyer; b. Los Angeles, Aug. 27, 1935; s. Henry Maurice and Viola Gertrude (Rothe) H. BS, UCLA, 1957, LL.B., 1960. Bar: Calif. 1961. Pvt. practice, L.A. County, 1961—; ptnr. firm Greenwald, Hoffman, Meyer & Montes, 1964—. Pres. L.A. Estate Planning Council. Served to 2d lt. U.S. Army. Mem. Am., Los Angeles County bar assns., Phi Alpha Delta, Beta Gamma Sigma. Clubs: Jonathan. Home: 3520 St Elizabeth Rd Glendale CA 91206-1226 Office: 500 N Brand Blvd Ste 920 Glendale CA 91203-1923

HOFFMAN, DONALD RICHARD, pathologist, educator; b. Boston, Aug. 25, 1943; s. William Maurice and Laura (Rodman) H.; m. Valeria Anne Mossey, Oct. 24, 1971; children: Anthony Horatio, Maria Lauren, Avram Joseph. AB, Harvard, 1965; PhD, Calif. Inst. Technology, 1970. Asst. prof. pediatrics U. So. Calif. Sch. Medicine, L.A., 1971-75; assoc. prof. pathology Creighton U. Sch. Medicine, Omaha, 1975-77, East Carolina U. Sch. Medicine, Greenville, N.C., 1977-82, prof. pathology and lab. medicine, 1982—. Mem. adv. com. on allergenic products, HHS, FDA, Rockville, Md., 1990-94. Mem. editorial bd. Jour. Allergy Clin. Immunology, 1988-93, Immunochemistry, 1974-77; contbr. articles to profl. jours. Fellow Am. Acad. Allergy and Immunology; mem. Am. Assn. Immunologists, Protein Soc., N.Y. Acad. Scis., AAAS. Achievements include research isolation of insect venom allergens. Office: Brody Sch Medicine East Carolina U Dept Pathology/Lab Medicine Greenville NC 27858 E-mail: hoffmand@mail.ecu.edu.

HOFFMAN, DUSTIN LEE, actor; b. L.A., Aug. 8, 1937; s. Harry Hoffman; m. Anne Byrne, May 4, 1969 (div.); children: Karina, Jenna; m. Lisa Gottsegen, Oct. 21, 1980; children: Jacob, Rebecca, Max, Alexandra. Student, Santa Monica City Coll., Pasadena Playhouse. Stage debut: Sarah Lawrence Coll. prodn. of Yes Is for a Very Young Man; Broadway debut: A Cook for Mr. General, 1961; appeared in Endgame, The Quare Fellow, In The Jungle of Cities, A Country Scandal, The Dumbwaiter, The Room, Waiting for Godot, Picnic on the Battlefield, Dirty Hands, The Cocktail Party, All Theatre Company of Boston, Three Men on a Horse, 1964, Harry, Noon and Night, 1965, The Journey of the Fifth Horse (Obie award 1966), 1966, Fragments, 1966, Eh? (Drama Desk award 1967, Verna Rice award 1967, Theatre World award 1967), 1966, Jimmy Shine, 1968, Death of a Salesman, 1984, The Merchant of Venice, 1989; recorded: Death of a Salesman on Caedmon Records (Drama Desk award 1984); appeared in films: The Tiger Makes Out, 1967, The Graduate, 1967 (Acad. award nomination), Midnight Cowboy, 1969 (Acad. award nomination), John and Mary, 1969, Madigan's Millions, 1970, Little Big Man, 1970, Who is Harry Kellerman and Why Is He Saying Those Terrible Things About Me?, 1971, Straw Dogs, 1971, Alfredo, Alfredo, 1973, Papillion, 1973, Lenny, 1974 (Acad. award nomination), All the President's Men, 1976, Marathon Man, 1976, Straight Time, 1978, Agatha, 1979, Kramer vs. Kramer, 1979 (Acad. award for Best Actor, N.Y. Film Critics award), Tootsie, 1982 (Acad. award nomination, Golden Globe award), Ishtar, 1987, Rainman, 1988 (Acad. award for Best Actor), Family Business, 1990, Dick Tracy, 1990, Billy Bathgate, 1991, Hook, 1991, Hero, 1992, Outbreak, 1995, Sleepers, 1996, American Buffalo, 1996, Sphere, 1997, Mad City, 1997, Wag the Dog, 1998, The Messenger: the Story of Joan of Arc, 1999, Being John Malkovich, 1999, Tuesday (voice), 2001, Moonlight Mile, 2002, Confidence, 2003; starred in TV prodn. of Death of a Salesman, 1985 (Emmy award nomination 1986). Recipient Golden Globe award, 1989; decorated officer Order of Arts and Letters (France), 1995, Golden Globe lifetime achievement award, 1997. Office: Ste 222 11661 San Vicente Blvd Los Angeles CA 90049-5110*

HOFFMAN, E. LESLIE, lawyer; b. Charleston, W. Va., Aug. 8, 1947; s. E. Leslie and Mary Jane (Lively) H.; m. Susan Sandy, Sept. 9, 1967 (div. 1983); children: Melissa North, Marc Clayton. BA Polit. Sci., West Va. U., 1969, JD, 1972. Bar: W.Va. 1972, U.S. Dist. Ct. (no. and so. dists.) W.Va. 1972, U.S. Ct. Appeals (4th crct.) 1973, U.S. Ct. Appeals (9th crct.) 1984. Asst. atty. gen. State W. Va., Charleston, 1972-76; asst. U.S. Atty. so. dist. W. Va., Charleston, 1976-81; asst. dir. atty, gen's. advocacy inst. U.S. Dept. Justice, Washington, 1982, trial atty. fraud sect., 1983-86; dep. sect. chief fraud sect. U.S Dept. Justice, Washington, 1987-88; counsel Pettit & Martin, Washington, 1988-90, ptnr., 1991-95, Piper Marbury Rudnick & Wolfe, Washington, 1995—2002, Jackson & Kelly PLLC, Washington, 2002—. Mem. ABA. Democrat. Episcopalian. Office: Jackson & Kelly PLLC 2401 Pennsylvania Ave NW Washington DC 20037

HOFFMAN, ELMER, surgeon; b. Balt., Sept. 5, 1921; MD, Johns Hopkins U., 1944. Diplomate Am. Bd. Surgery. Intern Sinai Hosp., Balt., 1944-45, resident in gen. surgery, 1945-52, resident in pathology, 1948; mem. staff Greater Balt. Med. Ctr., 1952-94, Harbor Hosp., 1952-94, Johns Hopkins U., Balt., 1954-94, N.W. Hosp. Ctr., 1972-94, chief surg. surgeon, 1983-94, emeritus, 1994—; asst. prof. surgery emeritus Johns Hopkins Sch. Medicine. Cons. quality assurance N.W. Hosp. Ctr., U.S. Govt., 1994—; staff Sinai Hosp., 1952-94. Fellow ACS, Am. Geriatric Soc., Southeastern Surg. Congress; mem. Soc. Am. Gastrointestinal Endoscopic Surgeons. Home: 41 River Oaks Cir Baltimore MD 21208-6358 Fax: 410-484-0595.

HOFFMAN, FAITH LOUISE, social worker; b. Buffalo, June 7, 1944; d. William George Hoffman, Louise Caroline Hoffman; children: Donald Louis, Louis William, Christopher Robert. BS magna cum laude, Medaille Coll., 1983—87; MSW, SUNY, Buffalo, 1991—93. LCSW 1993. Case mgr. N.Y. Crime Victim's Assistance Program, Buffalo, 1987—88; dir. domestic violence program YWCA of Tonawanda's, 1988—90; dir. family support program Concerned Ecumenical Ministry, Buffalo, 1990—92; social worker Dept. Veteran's Affairs Med. Ctr., Buffalo, 1993—95, women veteran's program mgr., 1995—. Dir., founder Hopegivers, Buffalo, 1991—; dir. VA Domestic Violence Program, Buffalo, 1995—; field faculty SUNY, Buffalo, 1996—; domestic violence cons. Erie County Dept. Health, Buffalo, 2000—02; spkr. in field. Named cmty. hero, torchbearer Western N.Y. Olympic Torch Relay, Atlanta Olympic Com., 1996—96; recipient Svc. to Mankind award, Sertoma Greater Buffalo, 1998—98, ann. leadership award, YWCA Western N.Y., 2001—01, Joan A. Levine award, Woman Focus, 2002, Fed. Woman of Yr. award, Buffalo (N.Y.) Fed. Exec. Bd., 2003. Office: VA Western NY Healthcare Sys 3495 Bailey Ave Buffalo NY 14215

HOFFMAN, FRED L. human resources professional; b. Wauseon, Ohio, Mar. 13, 1953; s. Lowell Max and Annabell (Whitmire) H.; m. Diane Patricia Pope, Sept. 19, 1975; Brandon C. BSBA, Bowling Green U., 1975. Asst. mgr. indsl. rels. Colonial Press div. Sheller-Globe Corp., Clinton, Mass., 1975-76, dir. human resources Leece-Neville div. Gainesville, Ga., 1976-88; v.p. human resources, staff ops. Golder Assocs., Atlanta, 1988—. Bd. dirs. Hoffman-Rettig Foods, Inc., Maquoketa, Iowa, Golder Assocs. Inc., Atlanta. Guest columnist BG News, 1971-75. State dir. pub. rels. Ohio League of Coll. Reps., Columbus, 1974, 75; lt. col. aide-de-camp gov.'s staff Gov. Joe Frank Harris, Atlanta, 1983-91. Recipient disting. svc. award Bowling Green State U., 1975. Mem. Atlanta C. of C., Soc. Human Resources Mgmt., Antaen Soc. (pres. 1974-75), Pres.'s Club Bowling Green State U., Omicron Delta Kappa, Phi Delta Theta. Home: 235 Parian Run Duluth GA 30097-2418 Office: Golder Assocs Corp 3730 Chamblee Tucker Rd Atlanta GA 30341-4414

HOFFMAN, FREDERICK WILLIAM, automotive executive; b. Detroit, May 18, 1951; s. Frederick W. Hoffman and Elizabeth C. Filipovich. AA, Henry Ford C.C., 1971; BA, U. Mich., 1973; JD, Detroit Coll. Law, 1995. Reporter, editor Times Herald Newspapers, Dearborn, Mich., 1967-70; editor Dearborn Guide Newspapers, 1970-77; city ofcl., deputy mayor City of Dearborn, 1977-82; with commerce dept. State of Mich., Lansing, 1985-88; dir. state rels. Daimler Chrysler Corp., Auburn Hills, Mich., 1988—. Dir. Oakland Bus. Round Table, Pontiac, Mich.; pres. Automation Alley, Pontiac. Pres. Dearborn Facilities & Svcs. for Retarded, 1972-98. Mem. Nat. Assn. PACs, Mich. C. of C. (dir.). Democrat. Roman Catholic. Avocations: Hummel collector, travel, writing. Home: 3180 Quail Ridge Cir Rochester Hills MI 48309 Office: Daimler Chrysler Corp CIMS 485-09-95 1000 Chrysler Dr Auburn Hills MI 48326-2760 E-mail: fwh4@dcx.com.

HOFFMAN, GEORGE BERNARD, estate planner; b. St. Louis, Dec. 11, 1942; s. George Bernard and Ethel Eva (Drobina) H.; m. Peggy Ke Bei, Apr. 25, 1997. AA, Mt. San Antonio Coll., Walnut, Calif., 1966; BA, Calif. State Coll., L.A., 1971; MBA, Calif. State U., L.A., 1974; JD, Western State U., 1998; postgrad., Abraham Lincoln U., 2001. Cert. estate planner, paralegal. Pers. specialist Alpha Beta Mkts., La Habra, Calif., 1965-69, mgr., 1969-79; dir. mktg. Auburn Cord Dusenberg of Calif., L.A., 1979-81; prin. Bertcourt Securities Corp., Upland, Calif., 1981-88; gen. mgr. Penita Investment Ltd., Hong Kong, 1988-92; owner George B. Hoffman Estate Planning, Newport Beach, Calif., 1992—. With U.S. Army, 1966-68; Vietnam. Decorated Army Commendation medal, Air medal. Mem. ABA, VFW, Am. Legion, Calif. Advs. for Nursing Home Reform. Democrat. Roman Catholic. Avocations: golf, sailing, travel. Office: 5000 Birch St Newport Beach CA 92660-2127 E-mail: retirement_plan@msn.com.

HOFFMAN, GLENN JERRALD, retired agricultural and biological engineering educator, consultant; b. Delaware, Ohio, Oct. 16, 1939; s. Herbert L. and Wilma (Lavender) H.; m. Marna Luisa Hunter; children: Kimberly, Karen, Sheryl. BS in agrl. engring., MS, Ohio State U., 1963; PhD, N.C. State U., 1967. Rsch. agrl. engr. USDA Rsch. Svc., Riverside, Calif., 1966-84, rsch. leader Fresno, Calif., 1984-89; dept. head U. Nebr., Lincoln, 1989—2003; ret., 2003. Consultant World Bank, Pakistan, 1996, Turkey, 1997, Assn. Regional Consortia, Argentina, 1997, China Agrl. Union, 1998. Lead editor: (monograph) Management of Farm Irrigation Systems, 1990; patentee in field; contbr. 168 articles to profl. jours.; developer models for predicting crop salt tolerance and determining leaching requirement for controlling soil salinity. Disting. alumnus Ohio State U., 1995. Fellow: Am. Soc. Agrl. Engrs. (pres.'s citation 1994, Hancor Soil and Water Engring. award 1999, Massey Ferguson Ednl. award 2003); mem.: Am. Soc. for Engring. Edn., Soil Sci. Soc. Am., Internat. Com. on Irrigation and Drainage. Avocations: bridge, golf. Office: U Nebr 223 L W Chase Hall Lincoln NE 68583

HOFFMAN, GLORIA LEVY, communications executive; b. Norfolk, Va., Feb. 8, 1933; d. Maxwell Lewis and Jessie (Mashbitz) Levy; m. Frank Katz Hoffman (dec.); children: Daniel L., L. Stephen, Victoria Anne, Jonathan M. (dec.). BA in Speech and Radio, U. Wis., 1954. Pres. Creative Concepts in Comm., Ltd., Kansas City, Mo., 1984—, Peoplehood Products, Kansas City, 1987—. Author: I Belong to Me!: A Trip Thru Our Own Feelings, 1984, rev. edit., 1989, (catalog) Peoplehood-by-Mail, 1990; creator: The Super Sluggers, 1989, Captain Slug Slugs Drugs, 1990, Clown Around With Clancy, 1991, Sammy Slugger Slugs Drugs, 1993, rev. edit., 1993, I Slug Drugs apparel and buttons, 1993, Project Play-It-SAFE, 1994; creator, developer The Toddle Tent, 1996. Promotional and pub. rels. dir. Menorah Med. Ctr., Trans-Menorahs, Brandeis Books Drives; vol. Nelson Gallery Art, Kansas City Art Inst., Young Woman's Philharm., Children's Mercy Hosp. Recipient Commemorative Medal of Honor Hallmark, 1987; honored by Health Net Sr. Excel in its Sta. KMBZ-TV Amazing People series, 1999, Squires South Express, 2000. Jewish. Home and Office: 212 E 130th Ter Kansas City MO 64145-1376 E-mail: hshoffman@home.com.

HOFFMAN, HOWARD STANLEY, experimental psychologist, educator; b. N.Y.C., May 23, 1925; s. Melvin Leo and Henrietta (Rosenthal) H.; m. Alice Marie Cruikshank, June 7, 1961; children: Randall, Gwendolyn, Russell, Franklin, Daniel, Martha. BA, New Sch. for Social Research, N.Y.C., 1952; MA, Bklyn. Coll., 1953; PhD, U. Conn., 1957. Rsch. fellow in auditory perception U. Conn., 1953-56, instr. dept. stats., 1956-57; asst. to prof. psychology Pa. State U., 1957-70; prof. psychology Bryn Mawr Coll., 1970-92, prof. emeritus, 1992—. Bd. editors: Jour. Exptl. Analysis Behavior, 1966-69, Jour. Exptl. Psychology, Animal Behavior Processes, 1974-84; reviewer: Jour. Comparative and Physiol. Psychology. Served with AUS, 1943-45. Fellow AAAS, Am. Psychol. Assn., Am. Psychol. Soc.; mem. Eastern Psychol. Assn., AAUP, Sigma Xi, Phi Kappa Phi, Psi Chi. Home: 3300 Darby Rd Apt 3211 Haverford PA 19041-1070 Office: Bryn Mawr Coll Dept Psychology Bryn Mawr PA 19010 E-mail: hshoffman@comcast.net.

HOFFMAN, IRA ELIOT, lawyer; b. Highland Park, Mich., Jan. 3, 1952; s. Maxwell Mordecai and Leah (Silverman) Hoffman; m. Ruth Felsen, Aug. 19, 1975 (div. 1981); 1 child, Daniel Gideon; m. Meredith Lippman, Dec. 17, 1988; 1 child, Lauren Samantha. BA, U. Mich., 1973; MSc in Econs., London Sch. Econs., 1975; JD cum laude, U. Miami, 1983. Bar: Fla. 1983, U.S. Ct. Appeals (D.C. cir.) 1984, D.C. 1985, Md. 1991, U.S. Ct. Appeals (10th and 4th cirs.) 1992, U.S. Dist. Ct. D.C. 1992, U.S. Dist. Ct. Md. 1992, U.S. Ct. Appeals (fed. cir.) 1994, U.S. Ct. Fed. Claims 1998, U.S. Ct. Appeals (11th cir.) 2001, U.S. Dist. Ct. (so. dist.) Fla. 2001. Tchr. London Sch. Econs., 1975-77; rsch. assoc. Shiloah Ctr. Mid. East Studies, Tel Aviv U., 1978-80; staff atty. FTC, Washington, 1983; law clk. U.S. Ct. Appeals (D.C. cir.), Washington, 1983-84; assoc. Fried, Frank, Harris, Shriver & Jacobson, Washington, 1984-86, 87-88; counsel Ministry of Def. Mission to the U.S., Govt. of Israel, N.Y.C., 1986-87; counsel to vice chmn. U.S. Internat. Trade Commn., Washington, 1988-89; assoc. Howrey & Simon, Washington, 1989-91; pres. Israel Housing Investors, Inc., Rockville, Md., 1990-92; v.p. H.P.F. Prefab Constrn., Ltd., Givatayim, Israel, 1991-92; of counsel Savage & Schwartzman, Balt., 1992-94, McAleese & Assocs., P.C., McLean, Va., 1995-98, Grayson & Kubli, P.C., McLean, 1998—2001; pres. Smart Planet, LLC, Rockville, Md., 1998—2000; v.p. Grayson, Kubli & Hoffman, P.C., McLean, 2002—. Translator: (book) The Emergency of Pan-Arabism in Egypt, 1980; contbr. articles to profl. jours. Spl. counsel Nat. Sudden Infant Death Syndrome Found., Landover, Md., 1984—86; hon. counsel to chmn. Nat. Holocaust Meml. Coun., Washington, 1985. Mem.: ABA. Jewish. Avocations: travel, sports, history. E-mail: hoffman@graysonlaw.net.

HOFFMAN, IRWIN, orchestra conductor; b. N.Y.C., Nov. 26, 1924; s. Harry and Augusta (Cohen) H.; m. Esther Glazer, Feb. 21, 1946 (div. 1990); children: Joel H., Gary, Toby, Deborah; m. Maria Lourdes Lobo, 1990. Student, Juilliard Sch. Music, 1942-43, 45-48; MusD (hon.), U. Tampa, 1984. Dir. music Orquesta Sinfonica de Chile, 1994-97. Condr. Phila. Orch. at Robin Hood Dell, summer 1942, Bronx (N.Y.) Symphony, 1948-52, Yonkers (N.Y.) Philharm., 1950-52, Westchester (N.Y.) Chamber Orch., 1950-52, for Martha Graham Dance Co., 1949-50; condr., mus. dir. Vancouver (B.C., Can.) Symphony Orch., 1952-64; assoc. condr. Chgo. Symphony Orch., 1964-68, acting music dir., 1968-69, condr., 1969-70, prin. condr. Grant Park, Chgo., 1965-73; permanent condr. Belgian Radio and TV Symphony Orch., 1973-76; music dir. Fla. Orch., 1968-87, music dir. laureate, 1987-95; music dir. Flagstaff (Ariz.) Festival of Arts, 1983-95; condr. St. Louis Little Symphony, summers 1959-64, lectr., condr., U. B.C., State Coll. Wash., 1958, guest condr. Toronto, Vancouver, Chgo., Israel Philharm., 1960, Dallas Symphony, 1962, Brazil, 1962, 78, St. Louis Symphony Orch., 1963, Miami and Tampa symphonies, 1967, protege of Serge Koussevitzky, Tanglewood, 1948-50, guest condr. BBC Symphony, Manchester, Eng., 1968, Brussels (Belgium), Radio Orch., 1968, Strasbourg (France) Radio Orch., 1968, BBC Welsh, 1969-82, BBC Scottish, 1971-82, BBC No. Orch., 1971-82, Orch. Nat., France, 1970, Orch. Philharmonique, France, 1970, Orch. Nat., Peru, 1970, Philharmonia Orch., Eng., 1971, Chgo., Vancouver symphonies, 1971, N.J., Denver, Costa Rica, 1977-78, Chgo., 1977, Montevideo (Uruguay) Nat., 1979, Buffalo symphonies, 1980-81, New Orleans Philharm., 1981, Winnipeg Symphony, 1985, Pitts. Symphony, 1986, Colorado Springs Symphony, 1989, Kitchener-Waterloo Symphony, 1989, music dir. Nat. Symphony Orch. of Costa Rica, 1987-2001; guest condr. Israel Chamber Orch., 1990, Jalapa Symphony, Mex., 1990, Phoenix Symphony, 1991, UNAM Mex., 1991, Orch. Symphonique Francaise, 1991, Orquesta Sinfonica, Caracas, 1992, 93, 94, Orquesta Sinfonica De Chile, 1992, 93, 94, music dir. 1995-97; guest condr. Orquesta Sinfonica de San Luis, Argentina, 1994, Orquesta de Sodre, Montevideo, Uruguay, 1994, Orquesta de Concepcion, Chile, 1995, Orquesta Sinfonica de Buenos Aires, 1996, 98, Taipei Symphony Orch., 1997, 98, 99, 2000, Orquesta Sinfonica de Bogotá, 1998, 99, Fla. Orch., 1999, Nat. Symphony Guatemala, 1998, Orquestra Sinfonica Panama, 1999; music dir. Orquesia Sinfonica-De Bogota, Colombia, 2000—; composer two string quartets, violin sonata, Orquesta Filarmónica of Bogotá, Columbia, 1997, 98, others; collector autography music manuscripts, mus. memorabilia. Served with AUS, 1943-45. Juilliard fellow, 1948. Home and Office: Apdo 818-1260 Plaza Colonial Escazu San José Costa Rica

HOFFMAN, JAMES EVAN, investment banker; b. Skokie, Ill., Sept. 12, 1967; s. Howard Barry and Sharon Sandra (Goldman) H.; m. Dina Lynn Burland, June 9, 1996; 1 child, Mark David. BBA, U. Mich., 1989; MBA, Harvard U., 1993. Fin. analyst Credit Suisse First Boston, N.Y.C., 1989-91, assoc. Chgo., 1993-97, v.p., 1997-99, dir. Robert W. Baird, 1999—2002, mng. dir., 2003—. Mem. fin. divsn. Jewish United Fund, Chgo., 1997—. Mem. Young Execs. Club. Avocations: golf, tennis, theater. Office: Robert W Baird 227 W Monroe St Ste 2100 Chicago IL 60606-5016

HOFFMAN, JAMES PAUL, lawyer, hypnotist; b. Waterloo, Iowa, Sept. 7, 1943; s. James A. and Luella M. (Prokosch) H.; 1 child, Tiffany K. B.A., U. No. Iowa, 1965, J.D. U. Iowa, 1967. Bar: Iowa 1967, U.S. Dist. Ct. (no. dist.) Iowa 1981, U.S. Dist. Ct. (so. dist.) Iowa 1968, U.S. Dist. Ct. (so. dist.) Ill, U.S. Tax Ct. 1971, U.S. Ct. Appeals (8th cir.) 1970, U.S. Supreme Ct. 1974. Sr. mem. James P. Hoffman, Law Offices, Keokuk, Iowa, 1967— ; chmn. bd. Iowa Inst. Hypnosis. Fellow Am. Inst. Hypnosis; mem. ABA, Iowa Bar Assn., Lee County

Bar Assn., Assn. Trial Lawyers Am., Ill. Trial Lawyers Assn., Iowa Trial Lawyers Assn. Democrat. Roman Catholic. Author: The Iowa Trial Lawyers and the Use of Hypnosis, 1980. Home and Office: PO Box 1087 Middle Rd Keokuk IA 52632-1087

HOFFMAN, JAY C. state legislator; b. Nov. 6, 1961; m. Laurie Hoffman; children: Emily, Katelyn. Grad., Ill. State U., 1983; JD, St. Louis U., 1986. Bar: Ill. 1986. Mem. from Dist. 112, Ill. Ho. of Reps., Dem. floor leader. Mem. exec. fin. inst., jud. criminal com., welfare reform task force Ill. H. of Reps. Dem Cand. for U.S. House, 20th district, I.L., 1996 Named Outstanding Legislator of Yr., Ill. State Atty. Assn., 1994. Address: 7 Driftwood Ln Collinsville IL 62234-5279 Also: 2099 M Stratton Bldg Springfield IL 62706-0001*

HOFFMAN, JENNIFER ANNE, vascular technician, director; b. Bklyn., Aug. 29, 1971; d. Louis Frank Marchese and Carol Maryann Sclafani; m. Brian David Hoffman, Sept. 24, 2000. BS, SUNY, Bklyn., 1997. Registered vascular technologist, cert. EMT N.Y. Office mgr. Maimonides Med. Ctr.., Bklyn., 1996—98, clin. vascular specialist, 1998—99; tech. coord. St. Luke's-Roosevelt Hosp. Ctr., N.Y.C., 1999—2001, tech. dir., 2001—. Instr. SUNY Health Sci. Ctr., Bklyn., 1998—99; vascular ultrasound tng. dept. radiology St. Luke's-Roosevelt Hosp. Ctr., N.Y.C., 2001—. Contbr. articles to profl. jours.; spkr. in field. Recipient Musical Achievement award, N.Y. State Bd. Edn., 1989, Am. Venous Found. Beiersdorf-Jobst Rsch. fellowship, 1999. Mem.: Soc. Vascular Tech., Am. Registry Diagnostic Med. Sonographers. Avocations: flute, saxophone, poetry, travel. Office: St Luke's-Roosevelt Hosp Ctr 1090 Amsterdam Ave New York NY 10025 Office Fax: 212-523-4946. Personal E-mail: vascsono@aol.com.

HOFFMAN, JERRY IRWIN, retired dental educator; b. Chgo., Nov. 20, 1935; s. Irwin and Luba Hoffman; m. Sharon Lynn Seaman, Aug. 25, 1963; children: Steven Abram, Rachel Irene. Student, DePaul U., 1953-56; BS in Biology and Chemistry, Roosevelt U., 1956; DDS, Loyola U., Chgo., 1960; M of Health Care Adminstrn., Baylor U., 1972. Certificate, General Practice Residency, U.S. Army, 1978. Commd. officer U.S. Army, 1960 (served to 1962, returned 1964), advanced through grades to col., 1978, hdqrs. rep. local dental tng. confs. Europe, 1965-67; cons. to Comdg. Gen. U.S. Army Med. Research and Devel. Command, Washington, 1972-76; cons. Office of Surgeon Gen. U.S. Army, Washington, 1972-76, liaison rep. to Nat. Adv. Council and Oral Biology and Medicine Study Sessions of the Nat. Inst. Dental Research and NIH, 1973-76, resident in Gen. Practice Residency, 1976-78; comdg. officer U.S. Army Dental Activity, Fort Monmouth, N.J., 1979-82; ret., 1982; pvt. practice dentistry, 1962-64; assoc. prof. operative dentistry Loyola U. Sch. Dentistry, Maywood, Ill., 1982-93, dir. gen. practice residency, 1982-85, coordinator extramural dental resources, 1983-85, assoc. dean for clin. affairs, 1985-93; dir. sci. programs Chgo. Dental Soc., 1993—2002, ret., 2002. Staff dentist Silas B. Hayes Army Hosp., Fort Ord, Calif., 1976-79, Patterson Army Hosp., Ft. Monmouth, 1979-82; lectr., presenter seminars in field. Contbr. articles to profl. jours. Decorated Legion of Merit, Meritorious Svc. Medal with oak leaf cluster. Fellow: Am. Coll. Dentists, Internat. Coll. Dentists, Odontographic Soc.; master: Acad. Gen. Dentistry; mem. ADA, Ill. Dental Soc., Chgo. Dental Soc., Am. Assn. Dental Schs., Am. Soc. Assn. Execs., Assn. Healthcare Execs., Profl. Conv. Mgmt. Assn., Omicron Kappa Upsilon.

HOFFMAN, JETHA L. piano and vocal teacher, musician; b. New Orleans, Oct. 2, 1948; d. Jether Anthony and Dorothy Carmen (Adriani) Hübsch; m. James Tyre Dennis, Oct. 6, 1965 (div. Jan. 1972); 1 child, James Tyre Dennis; m. Gary William Hoffman, Oct. 2, 1988. Grad. h.s., New Orleans, 1966. Performer, soloist, entertainer, concert pianist, 1962—; prof. accompanist all opera and theatre, New Orleans; piano tchr., vocal tchr. New Orleans, Cathedral City, Calif., 1994—; performed in numerous bands, 1967—. Piano/vocals, entertainer Pete Fountain Enterprises, New Orleans, 1979-86, performed throughout U.S. Composer piano solos; arranger and editor for piano, vocals. Recipient numerous awards and trophies. Mem. Music Tchrs. Nat. Assn., Calif. Assn. Profl. Music Tchrs. Roman Catholic. Home: 68590 Tachevah Dr Cathedral City CA 92234-3879 Fax: 760-325-1220.

HOFFMAN, JOEL ELIHU, lawyer; b. N.Y.C., Sept. 23, 1937; s. Samuel S. and Flora (Pasachoff) H.; m. Sandra Joyce Stone, June 3, 1962 (div. June 1985); children: Susanna Beth, Alexander Laurence, Jeremy Andrew; m. Katherine Louise Joss, Feb. 15, 1986. BA, NYU, 1957; LLB, Yale U., 1960. Bar: N.Y. 1960, D.C. 1963. Trial atty. antitrust div. U.S. Dept. Justice, Washington, 1960-63; assoc. Wald, Harkrader and Ross, Washington, 1963-68, ptnr., 1968-85, Sutherland, Asbill and Brennan, Washington, 1985-99, of counsel, 1999—. Adj. prof. law Franklin Pierce Law Sch., 1997—, Law Sch. George Mason U., 1998—. Mem. editorial adv. bd. Food Drug and Cosmetic Law Jour., 1981-89; contbr. articles to profl. jours. Mem. ABA (chmn. food and drug com. adminstrv. law sect. 1976-82, 95-99, vice chmn. consumer product regulation com. 1976—, coun. mem. 1973-76). Office: Sutherland Asbill & Brennan 1275 Pennsylvania Ave NW Washington DC 20004-2415

HOFFMAN, JOEL HARVEY, composer, educator; b. Vancouver, BC, Canada, Sept. 27, 1953; came to U.S., 1964; s Irwin and Esther Beatrice (Glazer) H.; m. Dorotea Vittoria Vismara, Dec. 30, 1988. MusB summa cum laude, U. Wales, Cardiff, 1974; MusM, Juilliard Sch. Music, 1976, D of Mus. Arts, 1978. Prof. composition Coll./Conservatory Music U. Cin., 1978—. Mem. faculty U. Cin.; artistic dir. Music 03 festival; resident composer MacDowell Colony Yaddo, Rockefeller Found., Camargo Found., Hindemith Found.; new music advisor Buffalo Philharm., 1991-92; composer-in-residence Nat. Chamber Orch., 1993-94. Composer: Sonata for Cello and Piano, 1982, Chamber Symphony, 1983, Double Concerto, 1984, Duo for viola and piano, 1984, Between Ten, 1985, Violin Concerto, 1986, The Hancock Trio, 1987, Fantasia Fiorentina for violin and piano, 1988, Crossing Points for string orch., 1990, Partenze for violin solo, 1990, Cubist Blues for piano trio, 1991, Music in Blue in Green for orch., 1991, Each for Himself/90? for piano solo, 1991, Metasmo for percussion trio, 1992, String Quartet No. 2, 1993, Self-Portrait with Mozart, 1994, Music for chamber orch., 1994, ChiaSsO for orch., 1995, L'Immensita dell'Attimo for voice and piano, 1995, The Music Within the Words, Part I for flute, oboe, cello and piano, 1996, Part II for viola, cello, harp and piano, 1996, Portogruaro Sextet for clarinet, horn, string trio, piano, 1996, l'Chaim Chantata, 1996, Stone Soup for violin and narrator, 1996, Millennium Dances for Orchestra, 1997, Self-Portrait with Gebirtig, 1998, Krakow Variations for viola sola, 1999, Reyzele, A Portrait for chamber ensemble, 1999, The Smile for orch., 2001, Gebirtig Speaks, for clarinet, string trio and piano, 2001, Round Midnight variation for piano, 2001, Self-Portrait with JS for string trio, 2001, The Memory Game, opera in three acts 2002, to listen, to hear, 2003, coast to coast, 2003; (recs.) Duo for Viola and Piano, CRI, 1991, Partenze for violin solo, Koch Internat., 1992, Music for Two Oboes, Centaur, 1995, Fantasy Pieces, Gasparo, 1996, Tum-Balalayke EMA Records, 1996;Cubist Blues, Gasparo, 2002; pianist in various recitals and solo concerts, Italy, France, Great Britain, US; pianist and arranger Trio Gebirtig. Artistic dir. Music 03 Festival. Recipient award Am. Acad.-Inst. Arts and Letters, 1987, commn. Nat. Endowment for the Arts, 1986, 91, Fromm Found., 1980, 82, Am. Harp Soc., 1982, Am. Music Ctr., 1991, Cin. Symphony Orch., 1993, Shanghai String Quartet, 1993, Nat. Chamber Orch., 1993; Ohio Arts Coun. fellow, 1983, 87, 91, 94, 96. Mem. ASCAP, Am. Music Ctr., Gruppo Aperto Musica Oggi, Coll. Music Soc., Composers Forum, Cin. Chamber Music Soc., U. Cin. Faculty Jewish Coun. (past pres.). Avocations: chinese, italian cooking. Office: U Cin Coll Conservatory Music Cincinnati OH 45221-0001 Fax: 513 556-0202. E-mail: joel.hoffman@uc.edu.

HOFFMAN, JOHN DOUGLAS, lawyer, mediator; b. Easton, Pa., Jan. 9, 1939; s. John Douglas and Margaret Shirley (Kummer) H.; m. Lynne Ellen Campbell, Feb. 4, 1967; children: Alison, Mark. BA magna cum laude, Yale U., 1960, LLB, 1964. Bar: N.Y. 1965, Calif. 1967, U.S. Ct. Appeals (2d cir.) 1966, U.S Ct. Appeals (9th cir.) 1967, U.S. Ct. Appeals (D.C. cir.) 1975, U.S. Ct. Appeals (fed. cir.) 1998, U.S. Dist. Ct. (so. and ea. dist.) N.Y. 1966, U.S. Dist. Ct. (no. dist.) Calif. 1967, U.S. Supreme Ct. 1972. Assoc. Cleary, Gottlieb, Steen & Hamilton, N.Y.C., 1964-67, Cooley, Godward, Castro, Huddleson & Tatum, San Francisco, 1967-71; exec. dir., atty. Sierra Club Legal Def. Fund, Inc., San Francisco, 1972-77, trustee, 1978—; mem. Ellman, Burke, Hoffman & Johnson, San Francisco, 1978—2003. Woodrow Wilson fellow, 1960; Fulbright scholar Free U. Berlin, 1960-61. Mem. ABA, San Francisco Bar Assn. Home and Office: 14 Lincoln Ave Mill Valley CA 94941-1124 E-mail: jdhoffman@attbi.com.

HOFFMAN, JOHN ERNEST, JR., retired lawyer; b. N.Y.C., May 1, 1934; s. John E. and Effe K. (Dooling) H.; m. Jean Wheeler, Aug. 13, 1955; children: Jean E., John E., Katherine P., Carolyn W., Christine D. AB cum laude, Princeton U., 1955; JD, Harvard U., 1960. Bar: N.Y. 196l, U.S. Dist. Ct. (so. and ea. dists.) N.Y. 1963, U.S. Ct. Appeals (2d cir.) 1963, U.S. Supreme Ct. 1964, U.S. Ct. Appeals (3d cir.) 1974, U.S. Ct. Appeals (l0th cir.) 1975, U.S. Ct. Appeals (6th cir.) 1986, U.S. Dist. Ct. (no. dist.) N.Y. 1989, U.S. Ct. Appeals (4th cir.) 1989. Assoc. Shearman & Sterling, 1960-68, ptnr., 1968-92, ret., 1992. Co-author: American Hostages in Iran: The Conduct of a Crisis, 1985. Trustee Monadnock United Way, Monadnock Conservancy, Soc. for the Protection of N.H. Forests, Monodnock Cmty. Found.; pres. Apple Hill Ctr. for Chamber Music; vice-chair Monadnock Cmty. Found.; bd. chair Giving Monadnock. 1st lt. U.S. Army, 1955-57. Fellow Am. Coll. Trial Lawyers. Congregationalist. Home: Seward Mt Farm Bowlder Rd PO Box 187 East Sullivan NH 03445-0187

HOFFMAN, JOHN FLETCHER, lawyer; b. N.Y.C., May 22, 1946; s. George Fletcher and Helen (Gilbert) H.; m. Coralie Tallman, June 29, 1969; children: Julie Gilbert, William Delano. BS, St. Lawrence U., 1969; JD, Washington and Lee U., 1975. Bar: N.Y. 1976, U.S. Dist. Ct. (so. dist.) N.Y. 1976, U.S. Dist. Ct. (ea. dist.) N.Y. 1978, U.S. Supreme Ct. 1980, U.S. Ct. Appeals (2d cir.) 1982, U.S. Dist. Ct. (no. dist.) Tex. 1988, U.S. Ct. Appeals (11th cir.) 1991, U.S. Ct. Appeals (fed. cir.) 1999. Assoc. Cadwalader, Wickersham & Taft, N.Y.C., 1975-83, ptnr., 1983-94; v.p., assoc. gen. counsel Schering-Plough Corp., Kenilworth, N.J., 1995—. Trustee First Unitarian Congl. Soc. Bklyn., 1980-83; v.p. fin. Unitarian Universalist Congregation of Monmouth County, 2002—; trustee, treas. Bklyn. Children's Mus., 1985-95. Mem. ABA, Order of Coif, Omicron Delta Kappa. Office: Schering Plough Corp 2000 Galloping Hill Rd Kenilworth NJ 07033-1320

HOFFMAN, JOHN R. mediator, arbitrator; b. Rochester, Minn., Nov. 23, 1940; s. John Ralph and Helen Gertrude (Romens) H.; m. Carol Jean Hoffmann, May 9, 1964; children: Stephen John Raymond, Melinda Carol. BA in History, U. Minn., 1964; JD, William Mitchell Coll. of Law, 1968. Bar: Minn. 1968, Wis. 1984. Assoc. Mordaunt Walstad Cousineau & McGuire, Mpls., 1968-70, Murnane, Murnane Battis De Lambert & Conlin, St. Paul, 1970-76; ptnr. Murnane Conlin, White Brandt & Hoffman, St. Paul, 1976-92; pvt. practice mediation and arbitration John R. Hoffman & Assocs., Mpls., 1992—. Fax: (612) 338-8087. E-mail: jchoff@visi.com.

HOFFMAN, JOHN RALEIGH, physicist; b. Evansville, Ind., July 7, 1926; s. John Henry and Ruth Margaret (Bryant) H.; m. Phyllis Christine Reindel, July 5, 1950; children: John Russell, Gary Paul. BS, U. Richmond (Va.), 1949; MS, U. Fla., 1951, PhD, 1954. Research asst. U. Fla., 1950-54; research scientist Sandia Corp., Albuquerque, 1954-57; project supr. Kaman Nuclear Co., Colorado Springs, 1957-68; v.p. Kaman Scis. Corp., Colorado Springs, 1968-86, sr. v.p., 1986-90, exec. v.p., 1990-92; gen. mgr. Kaman Instrumentation Corp., 1989-90; ret. Kaman Scis Corp., 1992; tech. and mgmt. cons., 1992—. Bd. dirs. Red Spot Paint and Varnish Co., 1993—; mem. nominating commn. Colo. Supreme Ct., 1998—. Served with USNR, 1944-46. Mem. Am. Phys. Soc., IEEE. Republican. Presbyterian. Home and Office: 5020 Lyda Ln Colorado Springs CO 80904-1008 E-mail: JRaleighHo@aol.com.

HOFFMAN, JOSEPH FREDERICK, physiology educator; b. Oklahoma City, Mar. 7, 1925; s. Henry Raymond and Rena Virginia (Crossman) H.; m. Elena Citkowitz. BS, U. Okla., 1947, MS, 1948; MA, Princeton U., 1951, PhD, 1952. Lectr., rsch. asst. Princeton (N.J.) U., 1952-56; physiologist, sec. Nat. Heart Inst., Bethesda, Md., 1957-65; prof. physiology Yale U. Sch. Med., New Haven, 1965-74, chmn. dept. physiology, 1973-79, Eugene Higgins prof. cellular and molecular physiology, 1974—. Fellow AAAS, Am. Acad. Arts and Scis.; mem. NAS, Biophys. Soc. (pres. 1985-86), Soc. Gen. Physiologists (pres. 1975-76), Am. Physiol. Soc., Argentine Soc. Physiol Sci. (hon.). Office: Yale U Dept Cellular & Molec Phys 333 Cedar St New Haven CT 06520-8026 E-mail: joseph.hoffman@yale.edu.

HOFFMAN, JUDY GREENBLATT, preschool director; b. Chgo., June 12, 1932; d. Edward Abraham and Clara (Morrill) Greenblatt; m. Morton Hoffman, Mar. 16, 1950 (div. Jan. 1983); children: Michael, Alan, Clare. BA summa cum laude, Met. State Coll., Denver, 1972; MA, U. No. Colo., 1976, MA in Spl. Edn. Moderate Needs, 1996. Cert. tchr., Colo. Pre-sch. dir. B.M.H. Synagogue, Denver, 1968-70, Temple Emanuel, Denver, 1970-85, Congregation Rodef Shalom, Denver, 1985-88; tchr. Denver Pub. Schs., 1988—. Bilingual tchr. adults in amnesty edn. Denver Pub. Schs., 1989-90. Author: I Live in Israel, 1979, Joseph and Me, 1980 (Gamoran award), (with others) American Spectrum Single Volume Encyclopedia, 1991. Coord. Douglas Mountain Therapeutic Riding Ctr. for Handicapped, Golden, Colo., 1985—; dir. Mountain Ranch Summer Day Camp for Denver Pub. Schs., 1989-91. Mem. Nat. Assn. Temple Educators. Democrat. Avocations: riding, writing, music. E-mail: jhoff3@earthlink.net.

HOFFMAN, JULIEN IVOR ELLIS, pediatric cardiologist, educator; b. Salisbury, South Rhodesia, July 26, 1925; arrived in U.S., 1957, naturalized, 1967. s. Bernard Isaac and Minrose (Bermant) H.; m. Kathleen (Lewis), 1986; children: Anna, Daniel. BS, U. Witwaterstrand, Johannesburg, South Africa, 1944, BSc (hon.), 1945, MB, BCh, 1949; MD, 1970. Intern, resident internal medicine, South Africa, 1950-56; research asst., postgrad. Med. Sch., London, 1956-57; fellow pediatric cardiology Boston Children's Hosp., Boston, 1957-59; fellow Cardiovasc. Rsch. Inst., San Francisco, 1959-60; asst. prof. pediat., internal medicine Albert Einstein Coll., N.Y.C., 1962-66; assoc. prof. pediat. U. Calif., San Francisco, 1966-70, prof., 1970-94, prof. physiology, 1981-88, prof. emeritus, 1994. Sr. mem. Cardiovasc. Rsch. Inst., U. Calif., San Francisco, 1966— ; mem. bd. examiners, sub-bd. pediatric cardiology Am. Bd. Pediat., 1973-78, sub-bd. pediat. intensive care, 1985-87; chmn. Louis Katz Award Com., Basic Sci. Coun., Am. Heart Assn., 1973-74; George Brown Meml. Lectr., Am. Heart Assn., 1977; George Alexander Gibson Meml. Lectr. Royal Coll. Physicians (Edinburgh), 1978; Lilly lectr. Royal Coll. Physicians (London), 1981; Isaac Starr lectr. Cardiac Systems Dynamics Soc., Eng., 1982; John Keith Lectr., 1985; Disting. Physiology Lectr. Am. Coll. Chest Physicians, 1985; Nadas Lectr. Am. Heart Assn., 1987; 1st Donald C. Fyler Lectr. Children's Hosp., Boston, 1990; First MacDonald Dick Lectr. U. Mich., Ann Arbor. Recipient Bayer Cardiovasc. Mentor Award, 1989. Fellow Royal Coll. Physicians; mem. World Congress Pediat. Cardiology and Cardiac Surgery (hon. joint pres. Paris, 1993); MacDonald Dick Lectr. U. Mich., Anabor, 2003; Am. Physiol. Soc., Am. Pediatric Soc., Soc. Pediatric Rsch. Achievements: extensive rsch. into congenital heart disease and coronary blood flow. Home: 925 Tiburon Blvd Belvedere Tiburon CA 94920-1525 Office: U Calif Med Ctr 1331 M Dept Pediat San Francisco CA 94143 E-mail: jhoffman@pedcard.ucsf.edu.

HOFFMAN, KARLA LEIGH, mathematician, educator; b. Paterson, N.J., Feb. 14, 1948; d. Abe and Bertha (Guthaim) Rakoff; m. Allan Stuart Hoffman, Dec. 26, 1971; 1 child, Matthew Douglas. BA, Rutgers U., 1969; MBA, George Washington U., 1971, DSc in Ops. Rsch., 1975. Ops. rsch. analyst IRS, Washington, 1970-72; rsch. asst. George Washington U., 1972-75, assoc. professional lectr., 1978-85; NSF postdoctoral rsch. fellow NAS, Washington, 1975-76; assoc. prof. sys. engrng. dept. George Mason U., Fairfax, Va., 1985-86, assoc. prof. ops. rsch. and applied stats., 1986-89, prof. ops. rsch., 1990—, disting. prof., 1989, interim dept. chmn., 1996-97, chmn., 1997-98, chmn. sys. engrng. and ops. rsch., 1998—2000. Mathematician Nat. Bur. Stds., Washington, 1976—84; vis. assoc. prof. ops. rsch. U. Md., 1982; mng. ptnr. Optimization Software Assocs.; cons. Govt. Agys., Airline, Telecomm. and Def. Industries. Contbr. Recipient Applied Rsch. award, Nat. Inst. Stds. and Tech., 1984, Silver medal, U.S. Dept. Commerce, 1984, Disting. Prof. award, 1989. Fellow: Inst. Ops. Rsch. and Mgmt. Sci. (treas. 1995—96, exec. com. 1995—99, pres. 1998); mem.: Math. Programming Soc. (editor newsletter 1979—82, chmn. com. algorithms 1982—85, coun. 1985—88, exec. com., chmn. membership com. 1988—89), Ops. Rsch. Soc. Am. (sec.-treas. Computer Sci. Tech. sect. 1979—80, vis. profl. lectr. 1980—, vice chmn. sect. 1981, chmn. sect. 1982, chmn. tech. sect. com. 1983—86, coun. 1985—88, chmn. Lanchester Prize com. 1989, treas. 1993—94). Home: 6921 Clifton Rd Clifton VA 20124-1525

HOFFMAN, KENNETH MYRON, mathematician, educator; b. Long Beach, Calif., Nov. 30, 1930; s. Myron Grant and Madge (Harrison) H.; children: Donna, Laura, Robert; m. Alicia C. Coro, Mar. 1997. AA, John Muir Coll., 1950; AB, Occidental Coll., 1952; MA, UCLA, 1954, PhD, 1956. Instr. math. MIT, Cambridge, 1956-59, asst. prof., 1959-61, assoc. prof., 1961-63, prof., 1963-96, prof. emeritus, 1996—, chmn. pure math., 1968-69; chmn. Commn. on Edn., 1969-71, head dept. math., 1971-79; exec. dir. Commn. on Resources for Math. Sci., NRC, 1981-85, Math. Scis. Edn. Bd. NRC, Washington, 1989-91; assoc. exec. officer for edn. NRC, Washington, 1991-94; pres. MSTE.NET, Madison, Md., 1996—. Chmn. adv. com. NSF Sci. and Engring. Edn. Directorate, 1984-85; cons. Math. Scis. Edn. Bd. NRC, 1985-89; head, Office Govtl. and Pub. Affairs, Joint Policy Bd. for Math., 1984-89; chmn. Md. Math. & Sci. Coalition, 1996—; pres. Nat. Alliance State Sci. and Math. Coalitions, 1997-2002, sr. counsel, 2002–. Author: (with Ray Kunze) Linear Algebra, 1961, Fundamentals of Banach Algebras, 1962, Banach Spaces of Analytic Functions, 1962, Analysis in Euclidean Space, 1975; Contbr. (with Ray Kunze) articles to profl. jours. Mailing. Fellow Alfred P. Sloan Found., 1964-66 Fellow AAAS (coun.); mem. Am. Math. Soc. (past mem. coun.), Math. Assn. Am., Nat. Coun. Tchrs. Math., Phi Beta Kappa. Office: MSTE net 909 Parsons Dr Madison MD 21648 E-mail: ken@mste.net.

HOFFMAN, LARRY J. lawyer; b. N.Y.C., Aug. 20, 1930; s. Max and Pauline (Epstein) H.; m. Deborah E. Alexander, Oct. 2, 1954; children: Lisa, Ken, Heidi, Mark. AA, U. Fla.; JD, U. Miami. Bar: Fla. 1954. Chmn. Greenberg, Traurig, PA, Miami, 1968—; also bd. dirs. Greenberg, Traurig, Hoffman, Lipoff, Rosen & Quentel, PA, Miami. Mem. ABA, Fla. Bar Assn., Dade County Bar Assn. Avocations: music, art, tennis, computers, photography. Office: Greenberg Traurig 1221 Brickell Ave Miami FL 33131-3224 E-mail: hoffmanl@gtlaw.com.

HOFFMAN, LINDA M. chemist, educator; b. N.Y.C., Dec. 18, 1939, d. Theodore and Esther (Schaeffer) Weiss; m. Robert G. Hoffman, Feb. 2, 1958; 1 child, Samuel A. BS in Chemistry, Queens Coll., 1959; MS, NYU, 1967, PhD in Organic Chemistry, 1970. Rsch. assoc. Kingsbrook Jewish Med. Ctr., N.Y.C., 1973-77; asst. prof. Baruch Coll., CUNY, N.Y.C., 1977-79, assoc. prof., 1979-82, prof., 1982—, chair dept. natural scis., 1995-98. Reviewer grant proposals NIH. Contbr. articles on Tay-Sachs disease and glycosphingolipids to profl. jours. Mem. edn. com. UN Internat. Sch., N.Y.C., 1981-84; bd. dirs. Forest Hills Gardens Corp., 1993-2000. Recipient Moore award Am. Soc. Neuropathologists, 1981, 84, Founders Day award NYU, 1971, 112th Precinct Cmty. Coun. award, 1993; postdoctoral fellow Sloan Kettering Inst. Cancer Rsch., N.Y.C., 1972-73. Mem. AAAS, Am. Chem. Soc., Sigma Xi. Office: Baruch Coll Dept Natural Scis One Bernard Baruch Way New York NY 10010-5518 E-mail: linda_hoffman@baruch.cuny.edu.

HOFFMAN, LINDA R. social services administrator; b. New Haven, July 23, 1940; d. Bernard Harry and Sylvia (Paul) Rosenfield; m. Peter A. Hoffman, Sept. 25, 1965; 1 child, Tracie Hoffman Cohen. BA, Russell Sage Coll., 1962; MSW, U. Mo., 1968. Cert.,social worker, N.Y. Case worker Conn. Dept. Welfare, New Haven, 1962-63, N.Y.C. Bur. Child Welfare, N.Y.C., 1963-65, supr., 1965-66; asst. to commr. program planning N.Y.C. Dept. Social Svcs., N.Y.C., 1968-70; spl. asst. to commr. N.Y.C. Spl. Svc. for Children, N.Y.C., 1972-79; pres. N.Y. Found. Sr. Citizens, N.Y.C., 1979—. Cons., USIA, Teheran, Iran, summer 1975; adj. prof., mem. dean's adv. coun. Columbia Sch. Social Work. Mem. Cmty. Bd. # 8, N.Y.C., 1982—; bd. dirs. YWCA/N.Y.C. Acad. Women Achievers, 1995—, bd. dir., Grosvenor Neighborhood House, 2003; mem. Women's Forum, 1998—. Recipient, Presdl. Recognition award for Community Svc., 1983, East Manhattan C. of C., award for Disting. Civic Svc., 1990, The Mcpl. Art Soc. of N.Y. award, 1997; named to Columbia U. Sch. Social Work Hall of Fame, 2000. Mem. Nat. Assn. Social Workers (cert.), Women's City Club of N.Y. Avocations: boating, fishing, and thoroughbred race horses. Office: NY Found Sr Citizens Ste 1416 11 Park Pl Rm 1416 New York NY 10007-2801

HOFFMAN, LOU, public relations executive, educator, writer; Pvt. practice Hoffman Agy., 1987—. Spkr., writer of pub. rels. in field. Contbr. columns in newspapers including MC mag.; appeared in BusinessWeek, The Wall Street Jour., other pub. rels. trade mags. Office: Hoffman Agy 10 S 3d St 5th Fl San Jose CA 95113

HOFFMAN, MADELYN KAY, psychoanalyst, social worker; b. Waco, Tex., Jan. 28, 1948; d. Nathan and Evelyn (Giniger) H.; married; 1 child. AB in Psychology, Rutgers U., 1970; MSW, Yeshiva U., 1973; grad. in psychoanalysis, Nat. Psychol. Assn. Psychoanalysis, 1991. With Henry St. Settlement Mental Health Clinic, NYC, 1971-72; social work intern Albert Einstein Med. Ctr., Jacobi Hosp., Bronx, NY, 1972-73; social worker Cornell Med. Ctr., The NY Hosp., NYC, 1973-77; coord. social work internship program Ctrl. Westchester Mental Health Clinic, White Plains, NY, 1977-84, Dep. Coord. Day Treatment Ctr., 1978-79; faculty advisor Adelphi Univ. Sch. Social Work, LI, NY, 1986-87; pvt, practice, NYC, 1986—. Mem. Assocs. For Lives In Transition; mem. Internat. Dyslexia Assn., Children and Adults with ADD, specialist in treatment of bereavement, med. social work, trauma and adults with attention deficit disorder or dyslexia. Contbr. articles to profl. jours.; appeared as specialist on nat. TV and radio programs. Office: 2 W 86th St New York NY 10024-3666

HOFFMAN, MARGARET MAY, writer; b. Danville, Va. d. Julian and Marjorie Hoffman. BA, U. N.C., Greensboro, 1971; MA, George Mason U., 1995. Writing instr. Ga. State U., Ga. Inst. Tech., Dekalb CC, Atlanta, 1975—79, Greensboro Ctr. Creative Arts, 1984—90, Writers Ctr., Bethesda, Md., 1991—93. Spkr. NC Humanities Coun., Greensboro, 2002. Author: Blackbeard: A Tale of Villainy and Murder in Colonial America, 1998, Dead in the Water, 2003; contbr. articles to profl. jours. Mem.: N.C. Writers Network.

HOFFMAN, MARILYN KAY, psychologist; d. Vernon C. and Moyne L. Hoffman; m. Robert J. Jewett, Sept. 3, 1993. Postgrad., U. Colo., Denver, 2002—. Human resources coord. Alfalfa's/Wild Oats Markets, Denver, 1993—94; rsch. mgr. Strategic Programs, Inc., Denver, 2000—02; project mgr. Level 3 Comm., Inc., Broomfield, Colo., 2002—03, human resources coord., 2003—. Mem.: Soc. Human Resource Mgmt., Acad. Mgmt., Soc. Indsl. Orgnl. Psychology, Golden Key. Home: 4589 N Alcott St Denver CO 80211 Office: Level 3 Communications Inc 1025 El Dorado Blvd Broomfield CO 80021

HOFFMAN, MARK LESLIE, lawyer, film maker; b. Cleve., Jan. 12, 1952; s. Nathan Norman and Sally (Coleman) H. B.A. with spl. honors, George Washington U., 1973; J.D., Case Western Res. U., 1976, Ph.D., 1978. Bar: Ohio 1976, D.C. 1978, U.S. Dist. Ct. (no. dist.) Ohio 1976, U.S. Tax Ct. 1979, U.S. Ct. Appeals (6th cir.) 1981, U.S. Supreme Ct. 1981. Ptnr. Hoffman & Foote, Shaker Heights, Ohio, 1976— ; pres. Advocate Films, Inc. Shaker Heights, 1978— ; acting judge Cleveland Heights Mcpl. Ct., Ohio, 1983— . Mem. Assn. Trial Lawyers Am., Ohio State Bar Assn., Greater Cleve. Bar Assn., Ohio Acad. Trial Lawyers, Cleve. Acad. Trial Lawyers. Office: Hoffman & Foote 20133 Farnsleigh Rd Cleveland OH 44122-3613

HOFFMAN, MARK PETER, animal scientist; b. West Reading, Pa., Feb. 4, 1941; s. Mark Webber and Pearl Matilda (Troutman) Hoffman; m. Lorraine Carolyn Johnson, Aug. 24, 1969; children: Kourtney Katherine, Royelle Marka. BS, Delaware Valley Coll., Doylestown, Pa., 1963; MS, Iowa State U., 1967, PhD, 1969. Asst. prof. animal sci. Iowa State U., Ames, 1969-75, assoc. prof. animal sci., 1975-80, prof. animal sci., 1980—. Author: (manuals) Basic Principles of Animal Nutrition, 1972-75, Reproductive Physiology of Livestock, 1978-79, Food Animal Science, 1998-2003; co-author: (manuals) Introduction to Animal Science, 1975-76, Beef Cattle Production, 1984-96. Recipient Purebred Seedstock Producer award, Nat. Swine Improvement Fedn., 1981, Iowa Pork Producers Assn., 1981. Mem. Am. Soc. Animal Sci. (Animal Mgmt.

award 1989), Am. Dairy Sci. Assn., Am. Registry of Profl. Animal Scientists, Coun. for Agrl. Sci. and Tech., Am. Inst. Biol. Sci., AAAS. Republican. Lutheran. Home: 55432 265th St Ames IA 50010-9321 Office: Iowa State U 301 Kildee Ames IA 50011

HOFFMAN, MARTIN LEON, psychology educator; b. Bayonne, N.J., Mar. 20, 1924; s. Nathan D. and Ann E. (Goldberg) H.; m. Lois Norma Wladis, June 24, 1951 (div 1981); children: Amy, Jill; m. Elizabeth Ann Mercer, June 4, 1989. BSEE, Purdue U., 1945; MS in Psychology, U. Mich., 1948, PhD in Social Psychology, 1951. Asst. prof. Purdue U., Lafayette, Ind., 1949-53; sr. rsch. assoc. Merrill-Palmer Inst., Detroit, 1953-65; prof. U. Mich., Ann Arbor, 1965-85; prof. psychology NYU, 1985—. Editor: (series) Social and Emotional Development; co-editor: Review of Child Development Research, Vol. 1, 1964, Vol. 2, 1966 (Book of Yr. award Child Study Assn.); editor: Merrill-Palmer Quar., 1955-80, 80—; contbr. numerous articles to profl. jours. Ens. USN 1943-46. Founds. Fund for Psychiatry grantee, 1953-55, NIMH grantee 1957-70. Fellow APA (assoc. editor Devel. Psychology jour. 1980-82, editor Psychol. Rev. 1982-88), AAAS, Am. Psychol. Soc.; mem. AAUP, Soc. Rsch. in Child Devel. Office: NYU FAS Dept Psychology 6 Washington Pl Dept New York NY 10003-6634

HOFFMAN, MARVIN KENNETH, political science educator; b. Phillipsburg, N.J., May 2, 1945; s. Frank Elven and Ethel Florence (Niece) H.; m. Pamela Waller, May 19, 1984; children: Rebeccah, Jessica. BA, Rutgers U., 1967; MA, U. Ga., 1969, PhD, 1971. Fire dept. planner City of Charlotte, N.C., 1978-79; city mgr. Town of Boone, N.C., 1979-84; county mgr. Chatham County, Pittsboro, N.C., 1984-89; cons. Emergency Response Planning & Mgmt., Cary, N.C., 1989-90; prof. polit. sci. Appalachian State U., Boone, N.C., 1970-78, 90—, dir. master pub. adminstrn. program, 1990—. Part time cons. Emergency Response Planning and Mgmt., Cary, 1990—; vis. prof. U. Gdansk, Poland, 1996-97. Capt., asst. chief, then chief Boone Fire Dept. Office: Appalachian State U Dept Polit Sci Boone NC 28608-0001 E-mail: hoffmanmk@appstate.edu.

HOFFMAN, MARY CATHERINE, retired nurse, anesthetist; b. Winamac, Ind., July 14, 1923; d. Harmon William Whitney and Dessie Maude (Neely) H. RN, Meth. Hosp., Indpls., 1945; cert. obstet. analgesia and anesthesia, Johns Hopkins Hosp., 1949; grad., Cleve. Sch. Anesthesia, 1952. Staff nurse Meth. Hosp., 1945-49; rsch. asst., then staff anesthetist Johns Hopkins Hosp., 1949-62; staff anesthetist Meth. Hosp., 1962-64, U. Chgo. Hosps., 1964-66; chief nurse anesthetist Paris (Ill.) Cmty. Hosp., 1966-80; staff anesthetist Hendricks County Hosp., Danville, Ind., Ball Meml. Hosp., Muncie, Ind., 1981-86. Mem. Am. Assn. Nurse Anesthetists, Am. Heart Assn., Ind. Fedn. Bus. and Profl. Women's Clubs (Ill. dist. chmn. 1977-78, state found. chmn. 1978-79, Found. award 1979). Republican. Presbyterian. Home: 1700 N Maddox Dr Muncie IN 47304-2674

HOFFMAN, MATHEW, lawyer; b. Bklyn., Mar. 9, 1954; s. S. David and Naomi B. (Brosterman) H.; m. Bracha Hoffman; children: Ari, Gavriel, Shelhevet, Miri, Shira, Tova, Elisheva. BA, U. Mich., 1974; JD, Columbia U., 1977. Bar: N.Y. 1978, U.S. Dist. Ct. (so. and ea. dists.) N.Y. 1978, U.S. Ct. Appeals (2d and 7th cirs.) 1980, U.S. Dist. Ct. (we. dist.) Mich., 2003; ordained rabbi, 1988. Atty. Proskauer, Rose, N.Y.C., 1978-80, Gordon, Hurwitz, N.Y.C., 1980-85; ptnr. Koether, Harris & Hoffman, N.Y.C., 1985-89, Keck Mahin & Cate, N.Y.C., 1989-94, Rosen & Reade, N.Y.C., 1994-96; ptnr., head of litigation Todtman, Nachamie, Spizz & Johns, P.C., N.Y.C., 1997—. Contbr. articles to profl. jours. Mem. Jewish Flame (trustee 1979—). Home: 62 Rosehill Ave New Rochelle NY 10804-3615 Office: Todtman Nachamie Spizz & Johns PC 425 Park Ave New York NY 10022-3506 E-mail: mhoffman@tnsj-law.com.

HOFFMAN, MICHAEL JEROME, humanities educator, educator; b. Phila., Mar. 13, 1939; s. Nathan P. and Sara (Perlman) H.; m. Margaret Boegeman, Dec. 27, 1988; children by previous marriage: Cynthia, Matthew. BA, U. Pa., 1959, MA, 1960, PhD, 1963. Instr. Washington Coll., Chestertown, Md., 1962-64; asst. prof. U. Pa., Phila., 1964-67; from asst. prof. to prof. U. Calif., Davis, 1967—2001, asst. vice chancellor acad. affairs, 1976-83, chmn. English dept., 1984-89, dir. Davis Humanities Inst., 1987-91, coord. writing programs, 1991-94, undergrad. coord., 1994-95, grad. advisor, 1995-98, dir. honors program, 1992-99. Chmn. joint projects steering com. U. Calif.-Calif. State U., 1976-87; chmn. adv. bd. Calif. Acad. Partnership Program, 1985-87; dir. Calif. Humanities Project, 1985-91. Author: The Development of Abstractionism in the Writings of Gertrude Stein, 1965, The Buddy System, 1971, The Subversive Vision, 1972, Gertrude Stein, 1976, Critical Essays on Gertrude Stein, 1986, Essentials of the Theory of Fiction, 1988, rev. edit., 1996, Critical Essays on American Modernism, 1992. With USAR, 1957-61. Nat. Def. Edn. Act fellow U.S. Govt., 1959-62. Mem. Modern Lang. Assn. (Am. lit. group). Democrat. Jewish. Avocation: tennis. Home: 4417 San Marino Dr Davis CA 95616-5012 Office: U Calif Dept English Davis CA 95616

HOFFMAN, MICHAEL LINSAY, economist; b. Salisbury, NC, June 13, 1915; s. Edwin Michael and Mary (Lidsay) H.; m. Catherine Hughes, Sept. 3, 1936; 1 child, Peter Lindsay. AB, Oberlin (Ohio) Coll., 1935; PhD, U. Chgo., 1941. Instr. Oberlin Coll., 1936-39; fgn. corr. NY Times, 1945—57; various positions The World Bank, Washington, 1957—75. Mem. Cosmos. Democrat. Congregationalist. Avocation: birding. Home: Vineyard Haven, Mass. Died June 29, 2001.

HOFFMAN, MICHAEL WILLIAM, lawyer, accountant; b. Bowling Green, Ohio, Feb. 5, 1955; s. Oscar William and Marie Louise Hoffman; m. Lynne Ellen Steele, Aug. 31, 1975; children: Megan, Jessica, Kristine, Robert. BA in Acctg. summa cum laude, Bowling Green State U., 1976; JD, U. Toledo, 1981. Bar: Ohio 1981, Ga. 1983; CPA, Ga., Ohio. Acct. Ernst & Whinney, Toledo, 1976—81; acct., ptnr. Touche Ross & Co., Atlanta, 1981—86; v.p. Profl. Svcs. Network Inc., Atlanta, 1986; assoc. Chamberlain, Hrdlicka, White, Johnson & Williams, Atlanta, 1986—89; ptnr. Somers & Altenbach, Atlanta, 1989—91; chmn., CEO Hoffman & Assocs., Attys. at Law, LLC, Atlanta, 1991—. Organizing dir. Paces Bank & Trust Co., Atlanta; spkr. in field. Author: RIA's U.S.A. News for the Inbound Investor, 1983. Treas. Friendship Force Internat., 1984; mem. troop com. Boy Scouts Am. Recipient Leadership award Boy Scouts Am., Eagle Scout, 1986. Mem.: AICPA, ABA, Estate Planning Coun. of North Ga., Ga. Soc. CPAs (chmn. Tax Forum Com. 1990—92, chmn. Estate Gift & Trust Sect. 1997—2000, v.p. mgmt. com. 2000—01, bd. dirs. 2000—01, Disting. Chair award 1998—99), Am. Assn. Atty.-CPA, State Bar Ga. (fiduciary law sect., tax sect.), Bowling Green State U.-Atlanta Alumni Atty. CPA Assn. (parents adv. coun. 1999—), Atlanta Country Club (bd. dirs. 1998—2001). Republican. Roman Catholic. Avocations: golf, tennis, hiking, camping, reading, fishing. Home: 535 Willow Knoll Dr Marietta GA 30067-4647 Office: 6075 Lake Forrest Dr NW Ste 200 Atlanta GA 30328-3845 E-mail: hoff_law@bellsouth.net.

HOFFMAN, MITCHEL SCOTT, gynecologic oncologist, educator; b. West Palm Beach, Fla., Dec. 21, 1956; m. Sylvia Orrantia, Sept. 11, 1982; children: David Benjamin, Emily Ann. BS in Biology, Emory U., 1978; MD, U. South Fla. Diplomate Am. Bd. Obstetrics and Gynecology; lic. physician, Fla. Resident ob-gyn. Tampa (Fla.) Gen. Hosp., 1981-85; fellow in gynecologic oncology U. South Fla., Tampa, 1985-87, prof. divsn. gynecologic oncology, 1991—, dir. divsn. and fellowship program gynecologic oncology, 2000—, dir. med. student edn. in ob-gyn., 1987-2000; physician H. Lee Moffitt Cancer Ctr., Tampa. Examiner Am. Bd. Ob-Gyn.; lectr. in field. Editl. bd. Gynecologic Oncology, 1991—; contbr. more than 170 articles and abstracts to profl. jours., chpts. to books. Fellow ACOG, ACS; mem. South Atlantic Assn. Obstetricians and gynecologists, Soc. Pelvic Surgeons, Soc. Gynecologic Oncologists. Office: 4 Columbia Dr Ste 500 Tampa FL 33606-3589

HOFFMAN, MURRAY STANLEY, internist, cardiologist, educator; b. Denver, Apr. 15, 1924; s. Harry and Rose (Tokarsky) H.; m. Eleanor Cynara Reeves, Dec. 23, 1962; children: Eric, Rachel, Hugh. BA, U. Denver, 1944; MD, U. Colo., 1947; MS, U. Minn., 1953. Diplomate Am. Bd. Internal Medicine, Am. Bd. Cardiovascular Disease. Intern Cin. Gen. Hosp., 1947-48, resident, 1948-49; fellow Mayo Found., Rochester, Minn., 1949-51; mem. attending staff Univ. Hosp./Colo. Health Scis. Ctr., Denver, 1993—, assoc. clin. prof. medicine, 1993-97, clin. prof. medicine, 1997—. Fellow Am. Coll. Cardiology (trustee 1972-77), Coun. on Clin. Cardiology, Am. Heart Assn.; mem. AMA, Nat. Mayo Clinic Alumni Assn. (pres. 1970-72), Colo. Heart Assn. (pres. 1968-69). Home: 501 S Harrison Ln Denver CO 80209-3516 Office: U Colo Health Scis Ctr Campus Box B120 4200 E 9th Ave Denver CO 80262-0001 E-mail: mshoffman@earthlink.net.

HOFFMAN, NANCY E. lawyer; b. NYC, Mar. 19, 1944; d. Jack and Catherine (Wertheim) H.; m. Thomas G. Spagnoletti. BS in Indsl. and Labor Rels., Cornell U., 1966; MA in Am. History, N.Y.U., 1968; JD, St. John's U., 1973. Bar: NY 1974, US Dist. Ct. (so. and ea. dists.) NY 1975, US Dist. Ct. (we. and no. dists.) NY 1984, US Supreme Ct. 1975, US Ct. Appeals (2d cir.) 1975. Asst. corp. counsel NY Dept. Law, 1973-75; assoc. Plunkett & Jaffee, 1978-79; assoc. counsel Office Gen. Counsel NY State United Tchr., 1975-78, 79-84; asst. atty. gen. State of NY, Albany, 1984-85; dep. counsel div. legal affairs NY State Dept. Social Svc., 1985-86, first asst. counsel for fair hearings, 1986-89; gen. counsel Civil Svc. Employees Assn., Inc., 1989— . Recipient Disting. Svc. award Am. Arbitration Assn., 1997. Mem. ABA (labor/employment law sect., com. mem., com. on state and local govt. bargaining, commn. on racial and ethnic diversity), NY State Bar Assn. (labor/employment law sect., future directions com., govt. bargaining com.ethics com.), Women's Bar Assn. State of NY. Office: Civil Svc Employees Assn 143 Washington Ave Albany NY 12210-2303 E-mail: hoffman@cseainc.org.

HOFFMAN, NANCY YANES, medical author, patient educator, writer, editor, health care consultant, lecturer; b. Boston, July 2, 1930; d. William Phillip and Edith Sara (Bernstein) Yanes; m. Marvin J. Hoffman; children: William Yanes, Holly Hoffman Brookstein, Jennifer Yanes. Student, Conn. Coll., 1946-48; BS with high distinction, U. Rochester, 1950, MS, 1968. Med. writer, lectr., editor, educator, healthcare and bioethical comm. cons., Rochester, NY, 1970—; asst. prof. English St. John Fisher Coll., Rochester, 1969-79, assoc. prof., 1979-86; dir. Am. Guardian Life Ins. Co., Jenkintown, Pa., 1979-85; pub. relations cons. Ochsner Med. Insts., New Orleans, 1978-82; pres. NYH Healthcare Comm. Group, Rochester, 1985—. Spl. clin. investigator Walter Reed Army Med. Ctr., Washington, 1983—85; vis. prof. med humanities U. New Eng. Med. Sch., 1985; mem. breast cancer detection awareness task force Am. Cancer Soc., Syracuse, NY, 1986—; mem. adv. bd. Rochester Health Commn.; guest prof. St. Catherine's Coll., Oxford U., 1996; lectr. on health care comm., United States, France, South Africa, Spain, Australia, New Zealand, Austria, Norway, Mexico, Hong Kong, Greece, Netherlands, Lithuania, others; seminar leader. Author: (book) Change of Heart: The Bypass Experience, 1985, Genetics for the Non-Geneticist Physician, 2001; co-author: Breast Cancer: A Practical Guide to Diagnosis, 1995; columnist: AMA, 1972—85; contbr. articles to profl. and popular jours. Bd. dirs. Lifeline (Suicide Hot Line), 1997—, Monroe Cmty. Hosp., 1998—, mem. palliative care adv. bd.; dir. Dr. Marvin and Nancy Yanes Hoffman Merit Scholarship Fund U. Rochester. Named Instr. of Excellence, N.Y. State English Coun., 1982; scholar, NEH, 1978. Mem.: MLA, AAAS, Am. Acad. Physician and Patient, Am. Culture Assn., Nat. Coun. Tchrs. English, Am. Heart Assn., Women in Comm., Soc. Tech. Comm., Soc. Diabetes Educators, Coun. Am. Diabetes, Am. Diabetes Assn. (profl. sect.), N.Y. Acad. Scis., Authors Guild, Internat. Sci. Writers Assn., Am. Soc. Journalists and Authors, Nat. Assn. Sci. Writers, Am. Med. Writers Assn., Phi Beta Kappa. Home and Office: 16 San Rafael Dr Rochester NY 14618-3702 E-mail: nywriter@rochester.rr.com.

HOFFMAN, NANNETTE HERTZ SCHWEIG, artist, poet, educator; b. Long Beach, N.Y., Aug. 18, 1929; d. Saul Clifford and Miriam Kendi (Ehrenreich) Hertz; m. Noel Asher Schweig, June 18, 1950 (div. July 1971); children: Graham Manfred Schweig, Gwendolyn Amelie Schweig Seidlitz; m. Edwin Young Hoffman, Mar. 11, 1977; 1 child, Mirella Kendra Hoffman. BA in Lit., Hofstra U./Columbia U., 1950; MA, Georgetown U., 1973; also art studies, N.Y.C. and The Netherlands, 1947-57. Pvt. tchr. studio art, Washington and Reston, Va., 1960—. Tchr. poetry writing and art. pub. and pvt. schs., 1963—; tchg. asst. Shakespeare class Georgetown U., Washington, 1972; lectr. art Nat. Gallery, Washington, 1973-83, Washington Women's Club, 1977; theater critic Georgetowner newspaper, Washington, 1976; TV program prodr. on original poetry Artsights and Insights, Jones Cable, Reston, 1987-2001; creative arts counsellor, 1984—. Exhibited in more than 20 solo shows, 1960—, including U.S. GEol. Survey, Reston, Va., 1992, Reston Art Gallery, 1988, Dupont Theater, Washington, 1968; group shows at League Reston Artists, 1984—; portrait commns.; author, illustrator: The Palette and The Pen, 1992, The Image and the Leaf, 2001; illustrator: The Friendship Tree, 1977, The Lavender Box, 1999. Tchr., vol. enrichment in art and writing Ben Murch Sch., Washington, 1963. Recipient various awards for art and poetry, including 1st prize poetry award Arcadia Press, 1984. Mem. League Reston Atists (pres. 1986-87), Ellicott Poets Group (founder). Jewish. Avocations: doll making, crafts, piano studies. Home: 205 Erin Leigh Cir Newport News VA 23602-8360

HOFFMAN, NATHANIEL A. lawyer; b. Cin., Mar. 4, 1949; s. Ralph H. and Betty (Goldfarb) H.; m. Sara Naomi Fishman, Aug. 3, 1980; children: Joshua, Rebecca, Esther, David. BA, Yale U., 1971; JD, U. Mich., 1975. Bar: Calif. 1975, Wis. 1983. Assoc. McDonough, Holland & Allen, Sacramento, 1975-78, Herz, Levin, Teper, Sumner & Croysdale, Milw., 1982-85; ptnr. Michael, Best & Friedrich, Milw., 1985—. Atty. N.Y.C. Pub. Devel. Corp., 1980-82. Mem. ABA, State Bar Wis., Milw. Bar Assn., State Bar Calif. Home: 3258 N 51st Blvd Milwaukee WI 53216-3236 Office: Michael Best & Friedrich 100 E Wisconsin Ave Ste 3300 Milwaukee WI 53202-4108 E-mail: nahoffman@mbf-law.com.

HOFFMAN, NEIL JAMES, academic administrator; b. Buffalo, Sept. 2, 1938; s. Frederick Charles and Isabella Dias (Murchie) Hoffman; m. Sue Ellen Jeffery, Dec. 30, 1960; children: Kim, Amy, Lisa. BS, SUNY, Buffalo, 1960, MS, 1967; PhD (hon.), Otis Coll. Art & Design, 2000. Chmn. unified arts dept. Grand Island Pub. Schs., NY, 1968—69; assoc. dean, assoc. prof. Rochester Inst. Tech. Coll. Fine and Applied Art, NY, 1969—74; dir. program in artisanry Boston U., 1974—79; dean, chief adminstrv. officer Otis Art Inst., Parsons Sch. Design, L.A., 1979—83; pres. Sch. Art Inst. Chgo., 1983—85, Calif. Coll. Arts and Crafts, Oakland, 1985—93, Otis Coll. Art and Design, L.A., 1993—2000, Hoffman Cons., 2000—. Cons. to higher edn. instn. and non profit orgns. Chmn. evaluation teams Western Assn. Schs. and Colls., 1982—; chmn. cultural planning process City of Oakland, 1986—91. Mem.: Phi Delta Kappa. Avocation: photography. E-mail: neilsuehoffman@qwest.net.

HOFFMAN, OSCAR ALLEN, retired forest products company executive; b. Newark, Feb. 4, 1920; s. Ernest Benjamin and Edith Marie (Myers) H.; m. Carolyn Ruth Layman, May 10, 1947 (div.); children: Peter Miles, Jared Mark; m. Geri McReynolds, Aug. 21, 1956. AB, Drew U., 1943; MS, Syracuse U., 1945; PhD, Stanford U., 1948; postgrad., U.S. Naval War Coll., 1953. Sect. leader MIT-Naval Ops. rsch. group, Washington, 1948-54; mgr. ops. rsch. AMF, Greenwich, Conn., 1954-58; v.p., spl. asst. to pres. Champion Internat. Corp., Stamford, Conn., 1958-85; commr. fin. City of Stamford, 1978—82. Chief ops. research Turkish Gen. Staff, Ankara, summer 1956 Episcopalian. Home: 1546 Georgetowne Ln Sarasota FL 34232-2014 E-mail: ohoff1546@aol.com.

HOFFMAN, PAUL JEROME, psychologist, statistician; b. San Francisco, June 25, 1923; s. Louis and Bessie (Brodofsky) H.; m. Elaine Stroll, Mar. 18, 1944; children: Valerie, Elizabeth, Jonathan. BA in Exptl. Psychology, Stanford U., 1949, PhD in Psychology and Statistics, 1954. Diplomate Am. Coll. Forensic Examiners, Am. Bd. Psychol. Specialties; lic. psychologist, Oreg., Calif. Asst. prof. Wash. State U., Pullman, 1953-57, U. Oreg., Eugene, 1957-60, adj. prof., 1967-76; prin. Paul J. Hoffman Assocs., San Carlos, Calif., 1985—; pres. Magic7 Software Co., Los Altos, Calif., 1985-98, Paul J. Hoffman Psychometrics, Inc., Los Altos, Calif., 1978-83. Cons. Am. Airlines, Dallas, 1990, 91, Nat. Heart, Lung and Blood Inst. NIH, Bethesda, Md., 1978, Am. Assn. State Psychol. Bds. Nat. Exam. Com., N.Y.C., 1972-78; prof. dept. adminstrv. sci. U.S. Naval Postgrad. Sch., Monterey, Calif., 1981-84; consulting psychologist Hewlett Packard Co., Palo Alto, Calif., 1981-83; vis. disting. prof. psychology U. Hawaii, Honolulu, 1978; testing cons. Nat. Bd. Med. Examiners and Am. Bd. Internal Medicine, Phila., 1971-72; pres., founder Oreg. Rsch. Inst., Eugene, 1960-77. Author: (with others) Decision Processes, 1954, Formal Representation of Human Judgement, 1968, Computer Aided Decision Analysis, 1993, Expert Evidence: A Practitioner's Guide to Law, Science and the FJC Manual, 1997; contbr. 53 articles to profl. jours. Chair fgn. policy Dem. Ctrl. Com., Oreg., 1960-72; advisor Sen. Wayne Morse, Oreg., 1964-70; chmn. Bob Straub for Gov. Com., Oreg., 1974. Lt. USAF, 1942-46. Grantee NIH, 1958-77, NSF, 1961-63. Fellow AAAS, APA, Psychonomic Soc., Psychometric Soc., Human Factors Soc.; mem. Am. Statis. Assn., Oreg. Psychol. Assn. (pres. 1962-63), Oreg. Inventors Coun., Am. Coll. Forensic Examiners. Achievements include copyrights for expert systems software, consensus building software. Home: 1120 Royal Ln San Carlos CA 94070-4277 E-mail: paul.hoffman@mindspring.com.

HOFFMAN, PAUL SHAFER, lawyer; b. Harrisburg, Pa., Dec. 12, 1933; s. Paul and Lucy Rose (Shafer) H.; m. Patricia Ann Rudisill, 1958; children: Eric, Kathryn, Julia, Margot. AB in Physics, Gettysburg Coll., 1957; JD, Harvard U., 1962. Bar: N.Y 1963, U.S. Patent Office 1963, U.S. Dist. Ct. (so. dist.) N.Y. 1977, U.S. Ct. Appeals (2d cir.) 1977, U.S. Supreme Ct. 1977. Assoc. Kenyon & Kenyon, N.Y.C., 1962-63; application analyst IBM-ASDD, Yorktown, N.Y., 1963-66; dir. tech. research Matthew Bender Co., N.Y.C., 1966-68; v.p. Bowne and Co., Inc., N.Y.C., 1968-77; sole practice Croton-on-Hudson, N.Y., 1977—. Mem. Croton Sch. Bd., 1972-75, pres., 1974-75; trustee Village Croton-on-Hudson, 1977-81, acting village justice, 1991—; bd. dirs. Croton Caring Com., Inc., 1982—. Served to cpl. U.S. Army, 1952-54. Mem. N.Y. State Bar Assn. (assoc. editor-in-chief N.Y. State Bar jour. 1991-98), Westchester County Bar Assn., Computer Law Assn. (bd. dirs. 1984-94, 96-2001). Clubs: Harvard (N.Y.C.). Lodges: Masons. Republican. Lutheran. Office: 139 Grand St Croton On Hudson NY 10520-2306

HOFFMAN, PENELOPE JOAN (PENNY HOFFMAN), adult nurse practitioner, administrator; b. Grand Rapids, Mich., Jan. 31, 1947; Diploma, Butterworth Hosp. Sch. Nursing, Grand Rapids, Mich., 1968; BSN, Mich. State U., 1972; MS in Edn., SUNY, Albany, 1978; MSN, U. Conn., 1995. Cert. in nursing adminstrn., adult nurse practitioner. Field tchr., pub. health nursing supr. Kent County Health Dept., Grand Rapids, 1972-74; pub. health staff nurse Greene County Pub. Health Nursing Svc., Cairo, N.Y.; staff nurse Vis. Nurse Assn. Albany, 1975-78; staff devel. coord. Washtenaw County Health Dept. and Vis. Nurse Assn., Ann Arbor, Mich., 1978-85; home care and hospice adminstr. United Hosp., Port Chester, N.Y., 1985-93; clin. supr., dir. patient care, quality assurance coord. Vis. Nurse and Cmty. Care, Inc., Vernon, Conn., 1993-98; nurse practitioner Cons. Rheumatologists, Hartford, Conn., 1996-98, Advanced Practice Nursing Assocs., Rocky Hill, Conn., 1998-99; nurse practitioner, continence mgmt. Manchester (Conn.) Meml. Hosp., 1999—2001; clin. coord., nurse practitioner Borgess Vis. Nurse and Hospice Svcs., Kalamazoo, 2001—. Mem.: ANA, Sigma Theta Tau. Office: Borgess Vis Nurses 348 N Burdick Kalamazoo MI 49007

HOFFMAN, PHILIP GUTHRIE, former university president; b. Kobe, Japan, Aug. 6, 1915; s. Benjamin Philip and Florence (Guthrie) H. (Am. citizens); m. Mary Elizabeth Harding, Aug. 31, 1939; children: Philip Guthrie, Mary Victoria Hoffman Cobb, Ruth Ann Hoffman Cabler, Jeanne Hoffman Camp. Student, George Washington U., 1936-37; AB, Pacific Union Coll., 1938; MA, U. So. Calif., 1942; PhD, Ohio State U., 1948; H.H.D. (hon.), Jacksonville U.; LL.D. (hon.), U. Americas, U. Akron; L.H.D. (hon.), Pikeville Coll., Marshall U., U. Houston, 1987; D.L. (hon.), Kyung Hee U., Korea; D.H.C. (hon.), Autonomous U., Guadalajara (Mex.); Litt.D. (hon.), U. St. Thomas, 1979. Credit mgr. Harding Sanitarium, Worthington, Ohio, 1938-40; instr. history Ohio State U. Columbus, 1946-49; asst. prof. history U. Ala., Tuscaloosa, 1949-51, assoc. prof., 1951-53, dir. arts and scis. extension services, 1949-53; dean, assoc. prof. history gen. extension div. Oreg. System Higher Edn., Portland, 1953-55; prof. history Portland State Coll., Oreg., 1955-57, dean faculty, 1955-57; v.p., dean faculties, prof. history U. Houston, 1957-61, pres., 1961-79, pres. emeritus, 1979—. Cons. Mitchell Energy and Devel. Corp., Houston, 1980-81; pres. Tex. Med. Ctr. Inc., Houston, 1981-85; dir. Fed. Res. Bank Dallas Mem. Nat. Commn. on Accrediting; mem. Am. Council on Edn., Coll. Entrance Exam. Bd. Lt. (j.g.) USNR, 1943-45. Recipient Centennial Achievement award Ohio State U., 1970, Merit award U. So. Calif., 1975. Mem. Tex. Hist. Assn., Gulf Hist. Assn., Am. Hist. Assn., Assn. Tex. Coll. and Univs. (pres.), Assn. Urban Univs. (pres. 1965-66), Nat. Assn. State Univs. and Land-Grant Colls. (dir. 1971-75), So. Univ. Conf. (pres. 1976-77), Phi Kappa Phi, Phi Alpha Theta (nat. pres. 1952-54), Omicron Delta Kappa Clubs: Petroleum (Houston), Torch (Houston); Houston; River Oaks (Houston). Lodges: Rotary. Home: 2929 Buffalo Speedway Unit 2208 Houston TX 77098-1711

HOFFMAN, PHILIP SEYMOUR, actor; b. Fairport, N.Y., July 23, 1967; Grad., NYU, Tisch Sch. Drama. Actor: (TV series) Law & Order, 1990; (films) Triple Bogey on a Par Five Hole, 1991, My New Gun, 1992, Leap of Faith, 1992, Scent of a Woman, 1992, Szuler, 1992, My Boyfriend's Back, 1993, Money for Nothing, 1993, Joey Breaker, 1993, The Getaway, 1994; (TV films) The Yearling, 1994; (films) When a Man Loves a Woman, 1994, Nobody's Fool, 1994, The Fifteen Minute Hamlet, 1995, Hard Eight, 1997, Twister, 1996, Boogie Nights, 1997, Montana, 1998, Next Stop Wonderland, 1998, The Big Lebowski, 1998, Happiness, 1998, Patch Adams, 1998, Culture, 1998, Flawless, 1999, Magnolia, 1999, The Talented Mr. Ripley, 1999, State and Main, 2000, Almost Famous, 2000, Forest Hills Bob, 2001, Love Liza, 2002, Punch-Drunk Love, 2002, Red Dragon, 2002, 25th Hour, 2002. Office: Paradigm Talent Agy # 2500 10100 Santa Monica Los Angeles CA 90067-4003*

HOFFMAN, PHILIP THOMAS, university educator; children: Jane, Anna. AB, Harvard Univ., 1969; MA, UC Berkeley, 1971; PhD, Yale U., 1979. Prof. history and social sci. Calif. Inst. Tech., Pasadena, 1980—. Author: Priceless Markets, 2001; contbr. articles to profl. jours. Fellow, John Simon Guggenheim Found., 2001. Office: Calif Inst Tech Hss 228- 7 Pasadena CA 91125 E-mail: pth@hss.caltech.edu.

HOFFMAN, RANDY MICHAEL, automotive executive; b. Bklyn., Sept. 9, 1965; s. Sheldon and Lois (Wolff) H., m. Randi Marie Rosenson, Oct. 18, 1987. Grad. high sch., North Miami Beach, Fla. Store mgr. Club 2000 Ltd., North Miami Beach, 1981—83, Chess King, Inc., Hialeah, Fla., 1983—84; dist. sales mgr. The Electronic Concept, Inc., Miami, 1984—85; wholesale retail distbr. Impulse Distbrs., Inc., North Miami Beach, 1985—; owner Blue Ribbon Food Svc., Inc., Oakland Park, Fla., 1986—88; bus. mgr. Maroone Chevrolet, Pembroke Pines, Fla., 1988—93; sr. dir. sales tng., fin. and ins. Ed Morse Automotive Group, 1994—. Mem. Distributive Edn. Clubs Am. (pres. 1982-83, treas. 1981-82), Assn. Fin. and Ins. Profls. Democrat. Jewish. Avocations: coin collecting, photography, spectator sports. Office: Impulse Distbrs Inc PO Box 820283 South Florida FL 33082-0283 E-mail: rhoff10337@aol.com., randy_hoffman@edmorse.com.

HOFFMAN, RICHARD BRUCE, lawyer; b. Columbus, Ohio, June 8, 1947; s. Marion Keith and Ruth Eileen (McLear) Hoffman; m. Sandra Kay Schenkel, July 26, 1975; children: Kipp Hunter, Tyler Blake. BS in Gen. Engring., U. Ill., 1970; JD, DePaul U., 1973; LLM, John Marshall Sch. of Law, 1981. Bar: Ill. 1973, U.S. Dist. Ct. (no. dist.) Ill. 1973, U.S. Patent and Trademark Office 1973, U.S. Ct. Appeals (7th cir.) 1979, U.S. Ct. Appeals (fed. and 9th cirs.) 1982. Assoc. McCaleb, Lucas & Brugman, Chgo., 1973-76, ptnr., 1976-84, Tilton, Fallon, Lungmus & Chestnut, Chgo., 1984-2001, Marshall, Gerstein & Borun LLP, Chgo., 2001—. Mem.: ABA, Intellectual Property Law Assn. Chgo., Internat. Trademark Assn., Am. Intellectual Property Law Assn., Chgo. Bar Assn., Ill. Bar Assn., Union League-Chgo., Lawyers Club Chgo. Office: Marshall Gerstein & Borun 6300 Sears Tower 233 S Wacker Dr Chicago IL 60606-6402 E-mail: rhoffman@marshallip.com.

HOFFMAN, RICHARD GEORGE, psychologist; b. Benton Harbor, Mich., Oct. 6, 1949; s. Robert Fredrick and Kathleen Elyce (Watts) H.; m. Julia Ann May, Dec. 18, 1970; children: Leslie Margaret, Michael Charles, Angela Lynn, Jennifer Elizabeth. BS with honors, Mich. State U., 1971; MA in Psychology, Long Island U., 1974, PhD in Clin. Psychology, 1980. Lic. con. psychologst. Instr. pediat. U. Va., Charlottesville, 1977—80; asst. prof. pediat. and family medicine U. Kans., Wichita, 1980—84; asst. prof. behavioral sci. U. Minn., Duluth, 1984—90, dir. neuropsychology lab., 1986—, co-dir. hypothermia and water safety lab., 1987, assoc. prof. behavioral sci., 1990—, co-dir. neurobehavioral toxicology lab., 1990—, asst. dean for med. edn. and curriculum, 1997—2002; assoc. dean for med. edn. and curriculum U. Minn., Duluth, 2002—; vis. sr. fellow in human clin. neuropsychology U. Okla. Health Scis. Ctr., 1995—96. Assoc. dir. Child Evaluation Ctr., Wichita, 1981-82; dir. adminstrn. Comprehensive Epilepsy Clinic, Wichita, 1983-84; cons. psycholo-

gist U. Assocs., P.A., Duluth, 1984—. Contbr. articles to profl. jour. Pres. Home and Sch. Assn., St. Michael's Sch., Duluth, 1986. Grantee Rsch. grantee, NIH, 1985, USCG, 1986, Sch. Medicine U. Kans., 1984, U. Minn., 1984, U.S. Army Med. Rsch. Command, 1988—, Naval Med. Rsch. Command, 1988, Gt. Lakes Protection Fund, 1991—93, Agy. for Toxic Substances and Disease Registry, 1992—95, 1995—. Fellow Am. Psychol. Soc., Am. Assn. Applied and Preventive Psychology; mem. APA, Nat. Acad. Neuropsychologists. Democrat. Roman Catholic. Avocations: bicycling, hiking. Home: 219 Occidental Blvd Duluth MN 55804-1365 Office: U Minn Dept Behavioral Scis Duluth MN 55812 E-mail: rhoffman@d.umn.edu.

HOFFMAN, RICHARD M. lawyer; b. N.Y.C., Oct. 22, 1942; s. Simon and Pearl (Lancet) H.; children— Mark, Michael Grad., CCNY, 1964; LL.B., Bklyn. Law Sch., 1967. Bar: N.Y. 1968. Law clk. to U.S. Dist. Judge U.S. Dist. Ct. (ea. dist.) N.Y., N.Y.C., 1967-69; assoc. Kramer, Lowenstein, Nessen & Kamin, N.Y.C., 1969-73; various positions legal dept. Gen. Instrument Corp., N.Y.C., 1973-81, v.p., gen. counsel, 1981-86, v.p. gen. counsel, sec., 1986-91; pvt. practice, N.Y.C., 1991-94; sr. v.p., gen. counsel Coltec Industries Inc., N.Y.C., 1994-95; of counsel Rubin, Baum, Levin, Constant & Friedman, N.Y.C., 1995-99; ptnr. Friedman Kaplan Seiler & Adelman and predecessor firm, N.Y.C., 1999—. Mem. ABA, Am. Corp. Counsel Assn., N.Y.C. Bar Assn. (com. corp. law depts. 1981-84). Home: 60 Brite Ave Scarsdale NY 10583-2328

HOFFMAN, RICHARD WILLIAM, banker; b. Rice Lake, Wis., Feb. 8, 1918; s. William A. and Anna (Amundson) H.; m. June M. Weink, June 27, 1948; children: William H., Stephen C. BA, U. Wis., 1939; MBA, 1954; postgrad., Grad. Sch. Banking, U. Wis., 1952, BAI Sch. for Bank Auditors and Comptrollers, 1957; grad. certificate, Am. Inst. Banking, 1960. With First Wis. Nat. Bank Milw., 1939-83, asst. v.p., asst. comptroller, 1959-63, v.p., comptroller, 1963-70, 1st v.p., 1970-83, v.p. First Wis. Corp., 1965-83; instr. Duke U., 1943-45, Army Finance Sch., Ft. Benjamin Harrison, 1945, Am. Inst. Banking, 1946-62, U. Wis., 1946-62, BAI Sch. Bank Adminstrn., 1956-77. Mem. Polit. Edn. and Action League, 1962-68; adv. com. Pub. Expenditure Survey Wis., 1963-83; asso. div. chmn. Milw. County United Fund, 1960-63; mem. Milw. Am. Revolution Bicentennial Commn., 1975-76; exec. v.p. army fin. K.I.T., 1979—. Served to maj., Finance Corps AUS, 1941-46. Mem. Am. Inst. C.P.A.s, Am. Legion, Fin. Execs. Inst., Nat. Alumni Assn. Bank Adminstrn. Inst., Res. Officers Assn., Wis. Econ. Devel. Assn., Soc. Ret. U.S. Army Fin. Officers, Ala. Soc. CPA's, Beta Alpha Psi, Beta Gamma Sigma. Clubs: Wisconsin Alumni. Home: 6499 Eastwood Glen Dr Montgomery AL 36117-4713

HOFFMAN, ROBERT JOSEPH, artist, art educator; b. Gary, Ind., Oct. 26, 1930; s. Sherman Francis and Josephine (Hitchens) H.; m. Wilma Lynnette Hoffman, Aug. 29, 1952; children: James, Barbara, Laura. Grad., Tolleston H.S., 1949, Artist landscapes and seascapes. Recipient Best of Show award Washington Park Art Fair, Michigan City, Ind., 1982, Merit award Hoosier Salon, Indpls., 1989, Outstanding Pastel award Ind. Healing Arts, Nashville, 1998, award of excellence Chesterton (Ind.) Women's Club, 1999. Mem. Oil Painters Am., Brown County Art Guild, Artists and Craftsmen Porter County, Hoosier Salon. Home: 2106 E 73rd Ave Merrillville IN 46410-4815

HOFFMAN, ROBERT PAUL, medical educator; b. Akron, Ohio, May 19, 1956; s. Wilbur and Margaret (Pahle) H.; m. Lynn Martha Vesey, Oct. 26, 1985; children: Carolyn Ruth, Rebecca Ann, Timothy Robert. BSChemE, U. Akron, 1978; MD, Ohio State U., 1981. Diplomate Am. Bd. Pediat., Am. Bd. Pediat. Endocrinology. From intern to resident Children's Hosp. Med. Ctr., Akron, Ohio, 1981-84; pediat. endocrine fellow Children's Hosp. of Pitts., 1984-87; asst. prof. U. Fla., Jacksonville, 1987-89; from assoc. to asst. prof. U. Iowa, Iowa City, 1989-96, assoc. prof., 1996-2000, Ohio State U., Columbus, 2001—. Contbr. articles to profl. jours. Deacon Bethany Bapt., Iowa City, 1994-99. Rsch. grantee Juvenile Diabetes Found., 1995-97, 99-2001, Genertech Found. for Growth and Devel., 1996-2000. Mem. Am. Diabetes Assn. (bd. dirs. 1990-96, pres. Iowa affiliate 1995-96, bd. dirs. Great Plains affiliate 1996-97, Clin. Rsch. award 1991-94, rsch. grantee 2001—). Republican. Baptist. Avocations: cleveland indians, tennis, golf, softball, hiking. Office: Columbus Children's Hosp 700 Children's Dr Columbus OH 43205 E-mail: Hoffmanr@pediatrics.ohio-state.edu.

HOFFMAN, RONALD, historical institute administrator, educator; b. Balt., Feb. 10, 1941; s. Emanuel and Ethel (Lubin) H.; m. Sandra Zalma Rudman, Aug. 28, 1965; children: Maia, Barak. AA, Balt. C.C., 1963; BA, George Peabody Coll., 1964; MA, U. Wis., 1965, PhD, 1969. Asst. prof. history U. Md., College Park, 1969—74, assoc. prof., 1974—92, prof., 1992—95; dir. Omohundro Inst. Early Am. History and Culture, Williamsburg, Va., 1992—; prof. Coll. William and Mary, Williamsburg, 1993—. Cons. Office Sec. Def., Washington, 1975—; symposia dir. U.S. Capitol Hist. Soc., Washington, 1977-93. Author: A Spirit of Dissension, 1973, Princes of Ireland, Planters of Maryland: A Carroll Saga, 1500-1782, 2000, (winner Libr. Va. Book Literary award non-fiction, So. Hist. Assn. Frank L. and Harriet C. Owsley award for disting. book in So. history, Md. Hist. Soc. book prize 2002); co-author: The Pursuit of Liberty: A History of the American People, 1983; editor: Dear Papa, Dear Charley: The Papers of Charles Carroll of Carrollton, 3 vols.; co-editor: Diplomacy and Revolution, 1971, Sovereign States in an Age of Uncertainty, 1982, Slavery and Freedom in the Age of the American Revolution, 1983, Arms and Independence: The Military Character of the American Revolution, 1983, An Uncivil War: The Southern Backcountry during the American Revolution, 1985, Peace and Peacemakers: The Treaty of 1783, 1985, The Economy of Early America: The Revolutionary Period, 1763-1790, 1989, We Shall Overcome: Martin Luther King, Jr., and the Black Freedom Struggle, 1990, To Form a More Perfect Union: The Critical Ideas of the Constitution, 1992, Religion in a Revolutionary Age, 1994, Of Consuming Interests: The Style of Life in the Eighteenth Century, 1994, The Transforming Hand of Revolution, 1996, Launching the Extended Republic: The Federalist Era, 1996, The Bill of Rights: Government Proscribed, 1997, Native Americans and the New Republic, 1999; contbr. articles to hist. publs. 3d class petty officer USNR, 1959-61. Fellow Ford Found., 1967, Eleutherian Mills-Hagley Found., 1978; grantee NEH, 1977, Nat. Hist. Publs. and Records Commn., 1979—. Mem. Am. Hist. Assn., Orgn. Am. Historians, Assn. Documentary Editing, So. Hist. Assn., Va. Hist. Soc., Md. Hist. Soc. Democrat. Jewish. Home: 201 Palace Green St Williamsburg VA 23185-4238 Office: Omohundro Inst Early Am History and Culture PO Box 8781 Williamsburg VA 23187-8781 E-mail: ieahc1@wm.edu.

HOFFMAN, RONALD BRUCE, biophysicist, life scientist, consultant; b. Balt., Mar. 29, 1939; s. Marvin Lionel and Edna Mildred (Fillman) H.; m. Carolyn Jean Phillips, July 6, 1969; children: Christine B., David A., Matthew T. BS in Physics, U. Md., 1962; MA in Psychology, U. Houston, 1971, PhD in Biophys. Sci., 1974. Cert. human factors engring. profl. Assoc. engr. Douglas Aircraft Co., Inc., Santa Monica, Calif., 1962-64; aerospace engr. NASA Johnson Space Ctr., Houston, 1964-67, 68; sr. rsch. analyst Northrop Svcs., Inc., Houston, 1974; NRC-NASA rsch. assoc. NRC, Washington, 1975-77; rsch. scientist, mgr. life scis. GE/MATSCO, Houston and Moffett Field, Calif., 1977-80; site mgr. Tech. Inc., Washington, 1980-82; sr. project mgr. GE, Washington, 1982-85; mgr. biotech. Advanced Tech. Inc., Reston, Va., 1985-87; lead scientist MITRE Corp., McLean, Va., 1987-95, sr. human factors engr., 1995-96; lead human factors engr. Mitretek Systems (formerly with MITRE Corp.), McLean, 1996—2001; sr. rsch. psychologist Sci. Applications Internat. Corp., McLean, 2001—. Co-investigator Apollo-Soyuz Test Project exptl. team NASA, Houston, 1974-75; mem. govt. industry adv. group for man systems integrated standards, Houston, 1988; life sci. cons. Mitsui and Co., Ltd., Biosystems Internat., Tokyo, 1985-86. Fellow AIAA (assoc., USAF space ops. workshop Colorado Springs, Colo. 1984-85, chmn. life scis. and sys. tech. com. 1989-91, chmn. human factors engring. working group 1991-96, dep. group dir. space and missiles group 1993-96), Aerospace Med. Assn., Aerospace Human Factors Assn.; mem. Soc. for Neurosci., Human Factors and Ergonomics Soc. (pres. Potomac chpt. 1997), Southwestern Psychology Assn., Am. Soc. Gravitational and Space Biology, Sigma Xi (rsch. fellow 1974), Phi Kappa Phi. Avocations: photography, scuba diving. Office: SAIC Transp Rsch Divsn 6300 Georgetown Pike Mc Lean VA 22101-2296 E-mail: ronald.b.hoffman@saic.com.

HOFFMAN, S. DAVID, lawyer, engineer, educator, artist; b. N.Y.C., June 16, 1922; s. Joseph and Ida Hoffman; m. Naomi Barbara Brosterman, June 30, 1946; children: Mathew E., Robert Adam. BE in Elec. Engring., Yale U., 1945; JD, St. John's U., N.Y.C., 1955. Bar: N.Y. 1955, U.S. Supreme Ct. 1960, U.S. Ct. Mil. Appeals 1961, U.S. Patent Office 1964, Ill. 1981. Engr. Western Electric Co., N.Y.C., Newark, 1946-49; head elec. engring. Am. Nat. Stds. Inst., N.Y.C., 1949-66, resident legal counsel, 1955-66, dir. contracts and cert., 1955-66; v.p., gen. counsel Underwriters Labs. Inc., Northbrook, Ill., 1966-88, cons. counsel to the pres., 1988-90; arbitrator Lake and Cook County (Ill.) Cts., 1989—. Sec. U.S. nat. com. Internat. Electrotech. Commn., 1955-66; vol., cons. multimedia resource Highland Park (Ill.) H.S., 1990—; adj. prof. divsn. of indsl. and systems engring. dept. mech. engring. U. Ill., Chgo., 1974-92; vol. Internet tutor Highland Park Libr., 1996—; mgr. tech. activities Nat. Bur. Stds. for U.S. Consumer Products Safety Commn., 1970-71. Contbr. numerous articles to profl. jours. Mem. indsl. adv. bd. U. Ill., Chgo., 1974-95; commr. City of Highland Park (Ill.) Telecomms. Commn., 1998-2000; on-line instr. Sr. Net, 1998—; lic. amatuer radio operator, 1981—; mem. U.S. Navy-Marine Military Affiliate Radio Svc., 1991—. With USNR, 1942-46, 50-52, ret. comdr. JAG Corp. Recipient Achievement award U.S. Pres. Commn. on Exec. Interchange, 1973-74, Merit awards Am. Nat. Stds. Inst., Joint award ASTM-Stds. Engring. Soc., 1980, Margaret Dana award ASTM. Fellow IEEE (life), Stds. Engring. Soc. (Leo B. Moore medal 1980). E-mail: dhoffman49@attbi.com.

HOFFMAN, SCOTT LEE, lawyer; b. Marion, Ohio, Sept. 4, 1957; s. Max E. and Sue A. (Coffey) H.; m. Margo L. Mills, Aug. 12, 1979; children: Kelsey Elizabeth, Evan Andrew Thomas. BA in Polit. Sci., Ohio No. U., 1979; JD cum laude, Syracuse U., 1982. Bar: N.Y. 1983, D.C. 1988, Ohio 1996, U.S. Ct. Appeals (D.C. cir.) 1988, U.S. Supreme Ct. 1988. Mng. ptnr. project fin. group Nixon, Hargrave, Devans & Doyle, Washington and N.Y.C., 1982-96; ptnr. Evans, Evans & Hoffman L.L.P., Richwood, Ohio, 1996—. Lectr. practicing Law Inst., N.Y.C., 1985-87. Author: Project Financing, 1987, The Law and Business of International Project Finance, 1998, 2d edit., 2001; contbr. articles to profl. jours. Bd. dirs. United Meth. Children's Home, Epworth Preschool and Daycare, Inc., 1996-2002. Mem. ABA, N.Y. State Bar Assn., D.C. Bar Assn., Ohio Bar Assn., Rotary, Theta Chi, Omicron Delta Kappa. Home: 1320 Chaucer Ct Marion OH 43302-8707 Office: Evans Evans & Hoffman LLP 15 W Ottawa St Richwood OH 43344-1138

HOFFMAN, SHARON LYNN, adult education educator; b. Chgo. d. David P. and Florence Seaman; m. Jerry Irwin Hoffman, Aug. 25, 1963; children: Steven Abram, Rachel Irene. BA, Ind. U., 1961; M Adult Edn., Nat.-Louis Univ., 1992. High sch. English tchr. Chgo. Pub. Schs., 1961-64; tchr. Dept. of Def. Schs., Braconne, France, 1964-66; tchr. ESL Russian Inst., Garmisch, Fed. Republic Germany, 1966, 67; tchr. adult edn. Monterey Peninsula Unified Schs., Ft. Ord, Calif., 1977-79; tchr. ESL MAECOM, Monmouth County, N.J., 1979-80; lectr., tchr. adult edn. Truman Coll./Temple Shalom, Chgo.; tchr. homebound Fairfax County Pub. Schs., Fairfax, Va., 1976; entry operator Standard Rate & Data, Wilmette, Ill., 1986-87; rsch. editor, spl. projects editor Marquis Who's Who, Wilmette, 1987-92; mem. adj. faculty Nat.-Louis U., Evanston and Wheeling, Ill., 1993-99, tutor coord., then coord. learning specialist, 1993-99; pres. Cultural Transitions, Highland Park, Ill., 1992—. Mem.: TESOL, ASTD, Nat. Coun. Tchrs. English. Home and Office: 2270 Highmoor Rd Highland Park IL 60035-1702 E-mail: culturaltrans1@aol.com.

HOFFMAN, STANLEY MARC, editor, composer; b. Cleve., 1959; BMus in Music Composition cum laude, Boston Conservatory of Music, 1981; MMus in Music Composition, New Eng. Conservatory of Music, 1984; PhD in Music Composition/Theory, Brandeis U., 1993. Engraver Scores Internat., Boston, 1990-98; chief editor ECS Pub., Boston, 1998—. Vocalist Temple B'nai Torah High Holiday Choir, 1997—; condr. Temple Israel High Holidays Choir, Swampscott, Mass., 1988-96, Temple Emmanuel Choir, Newton, Mass., winter 1983. Composer: There Is a Flower (oboe and piano), 1980, rev., 2000, Three Short Piano Pieces, 1980, Two-part Invention (piano), 1980, The Man in the Street (cello), 1981, Romance for Orchestra (in C minor), 1982, Rondino (wind quintet), 1983, Little Sea Nocturne (orch.), 1982, String Sextet (2 violins, 2 violas, 2 cellos), 1984, rev. 2000, Cycles (piano), 1985, Thirteen Ways of Looking at a Blackbird (BMI award 1984-85, mezzo soprano, string quartet), 1984, rev., 1993, Of All the Souls that Stand Create (baritone, piano), 1985, rev., 1993, Anim Zemiros (acapella choir), 1985, rev., 1993, String Quartet, 1987, rev., 1993, Poem and Lamentations (violin, piano), 1987, Piano Piece, 1986, Hymn of Glory (violas, cellos), 1988, rev., 1994, Rain (a cappella choir), 1988, rev., 1993, Nocturne for Nine Players (2 flutes, oboe, clarinet, bassoon, 2 horns, harp, percussion), 1992, Veshameru (cantor, choir, organ), 1993, Moulded Clay-Chiselled Rock (instrument in C, piano), 1994, Bagatelle (bassoon or bass trombone), 1994, A Song Without Words (horn), 1994, A Psalm Beyond the Silences (choir, piano), 1994, Lord of the World (a cappella choir, 1994, A Pacific Prelude (brass quintet), 1995; There Is a Name (children's choir, guitar) 1995, Trio in One Movement (clarinet, viola, cello), 1995, Psalm 23 (a cappella choir), 1998, Psalm 1 (a cappella choir), 1998, Psalm 121 (a cappella choir), 1998, The Writing of Autumn (choir, piano), 1999, Psalm 130 (a cappella choir), 1999, Psalm 146 (a cappella choir), 1999, Three Miniatures (a cappella treble choir), 1999, Intermezzo, Organ, 1999, Psalm 67 (choir, organ), 1999, She Gave Him All Her Heart, 2000, Psalm 117 (a cappella male, treble or mixed choir), 2000, A Lovely Summer Night (alto saxophone and piano), 2000, Behold, God Is My Salvation (choir, organ), 2001, Yih'yu l'ratzon (May the words of the mouth) (a cappella), 2001, A Prayer for Chanukah, (choir, piano), 2001, Grant Us Peace (a cappella choir), 2002, FantasyPiece (cello, bass), 2001. Office: ECS Pub Co 138 Ipswich St Boston MA 02215-3534

HOFFMAN, STEVEN ARLIE, musician; b. Milw., Wis., Oct. 10, 1965; s. Arlyn Karl and Joyce Mae Hoffman. MusB, Lawrence U., Conservatory of Music, 1989; MusM, U. of SD, 1997; MusD, U. of Mich., 2000. Dir. of music St. Stephen's Luth. Ch., Monona, Wis., 1989—93; dir. of music, youth and edn. Zion Luth. Ch., Laramie, Wyo., 1993—96; kantor Concordia Luth. Ch., Vermaillion, SD, 1996—97; elem. sch. music tchr. Emmanuel Luth. Ch. and Sch., Dearborn, Mich., 1997—2000, kantor, 1997—2000, King of Glory Luth. Ch., Cheyenne, Wyo., 2000—, St. Andrew's Luth. Ch., Laramie, Wyo., 2000—; u. organist/organist-in-residence U. of Wyo., Laramie, Wyo., 2000—. Founder/pres. Am. Pipe Organ Project, Cheyenne, Wyo., 2002—; pres./ ceo Hoffman Enterprises, Cheyenne, Wyo., 2002—; founder King's Concert Series, Cheyenne, Wyo., 2002—. Author: (book) Toward Christomusicology; organist performances include U. of Wyo. Youth dir. King of Glory Luth. Ch., Cheyenne, Wyo., 2000, instr. of Christian edn., 2000. Mem.: Organ Hist. Soc., Am. Guild of Organists. Lutheran Church-Missouri Synod. Achievements include research in relationship between Lutheran theology and church music in the reformation. Avocations: travel, hiking, photography, bowling, cooking. Home: 8806 Yellowstone Rd Cheyenne WY 82009 Office: King of Glory Lutheran Church 8806 Yellowstone Rd Cheyenne WY 82009 Office Fax: 307-632-0609. Personal E-mail: lutherankantor@bresnan.net. E-mail: pipeorganproject@bresnan.net.

HOFFMAN, STEVEN JAMES, historian, educator; b. Ft. Belvoir, Va., Oct. 28, 1959; m. Margaret A. Waterman. BA, Ga. State U., 1985, M of Heritage Preservation, 1987; PHD, Carnegie Mellon U., 1993. Adj. asst. prof. Bentley Coll., Waltham, Mass., 1993-95; lectr. in history Bradford (Mass.) Coll., 1993-95; asst. prof. S.E. Mo. State U., Cape Girardeau, 1995—2001, assoc. prof., 2001—. Contbr. articles, book revs. to profl. jours. Mem. Am. Assn. for History and Computing (bd. mem. 1999—), Midwest Assn. for the Recognition and Recording of Ethnic Heritage (sec. 1997—). Office: SE Mo State U Dept History 1 University Plz Cape Girardeau MO 63701-4799 E-mail: shoffman@semo.edu.

HOFFMAN, SUE ELLEN, elementary education educator; b. Dayton, Ohio, Aug. 23, 1945; d. Cyril Vernon and Sarah Ellen (Sherer) Stephan; m. Lawrence Wayne Hoffman, Oct. 28, 1967. BS in Edn., U. Dayton, 1967; postgrad., Loyola Coll., 1977, Ea. Mich. U., 1980; MEd, Wright State U., 1988. Cert. reading specialist and elem. tchr., Ohio. 5th grade tchr. St. Anthony Sch., Dayton, Ohio, 1967-68, West Huntsville (Ala.) Elem. Sch., 1968-71; 6th grade tchr. Ranchland Hills Pub. Sch., El Paso, Tex., 1973-74; 3rd grade tchr. Emerson Pub. Sch., Westerville, Ohio, 1976, St. Joan of Arc Sch., Aberdeen, Md., 1976-78, Our Lady of Good Counsel, Plymouth, Mich., 1979-80; 5th grade tchr. St. Helen Sch., Dayton, 1980—2002; ret., 2002. Selected for membership Kappa Delta Pi, 1988. Mem. Internat. Reading Assn., Ohio Internat. Reading Assn., Dayton Area Internat. Reading Assn., Nat. Cath. Edn. Assn. Roman Catholic. Home: 2174 Green Springs Dr Kettering OH 45440-1120

HOFFMAN, THOMAS EDWARD, dermatologist; b. L.A., Oct. 14, 1944; s. David Maurice and Ann (Corday) H.; m. Donna Madsen, 1973 (div. 1977); m. Linda L., Feb. 20, 1979; children: David, Jay. AB, U. So. Calif., 1966; MD, Tulane U., 1970. Intern U. So. Calif. USC Med. Ctr., 1970-71; residency dermatology Stanford (Calif.) U., 1973-76, fellow dermatopathology, 1973-74; dermatologist pvt. practice, Menlo Park, Calif., 1976—. Clin. assoc. prof. Stanford (Calif.) U., 1981-97, clin. prof. dermatology, 1997. With USPHS, 1971-73. Recipient Achievement award Tulane U., 1970. Fellow Am. Coll. Physicians, Am. Acad. Dermatology, Am. Soc. Dermatopathology, Am. Soc. Dermatologic Surgery, Am. Soc. Laser Medicine & Surgery, San Francisco Dermatologic Soc. (pres. 2000—). Avocations: tennis, skiing. Office: Menlo Dermatology Med Group 888 Oak Grove Ave Menlo Park CA 94025-4432

HOFFMAN, THOMAS PAUL, realtor, educator; b. Anderson, Ind., Jan. 30, 1939; s. Paul Edward and Thelma Kathleen Hoffman; m. Rebecca JoAnne Fitzpatrick, Sept. 4, 1964; children: Shellie Dawn Crow, Hollie Jeanne Pavlica. BS in Edn., Ball State U., 1966, MA, 1967; PhD, U. Okla., 1978. Lic. brokers Tex. Real Estate Commn., 1980. Prof. Speech West Tex. A & M U., Canyon, 1967—68; prof. English Midwestern State U., Wichita Falls, Tex., 1968—. Lectr. in field. Editor: (military newspaper) Five Star Review, (poetry anthology) Of Time, Truth and Trivia, Through a Knothole Darkly, A Crazy Quilt. Vice-chmn. bd. dirs. Taft Counseling Ctr., Wichita Falls, 2001—02. With U.S. Army, 1961—64. Decorated Sec. of the Army Commendatin medal U.S. Army. Mem.: Tex. Assn. Coll. Tchrs. (state pres. 1997—99, Acievement of Excellence award 1999). Roman Catholic. Avocations: travel, reading, public speaking. Home: 1521 Celia Dr Wichita Falls TX 76302 Office: Midwestern State Univ 3410 Taft Blvd Wichita Falls TX 76308 Personal E-mail: hoffmanproperties@prodigy.net. E-mail: tom.hoffman@mwsu.edu.

HOFFMAN, VALERIE JANE, lawyer; b. Lowville, N.Y., Oct. 27, 1953; d. Russell Francis and Jane Marie (Fowler) H. Student, U. Edinburgh, Scotland, 1973-74, BA summa cum laude, Union Coll., 1975; JD, Boston Coll., 1978. Bar: Ill. 1978, U.S. Dist. Ct. (no. dist.) Ill. 1978, U.S. Ct. Appeals (3rd cir.) 1981, U.S. Ct. Appeals (7th cir.) 1983. Assoc. Seyfarth Shaw, Chgo., 1978—87, ptnr., 1987—. Adj. prof. Columbia Coll., 1985. Contbr. articles to legal publs. Dir. Remains Theatre, Chgo., 1981-95, pres., 1991-93, v.p., 1991-95; dir. The Nat. Conf. for Cmty. and Justice, Chgo. Region, 1993—, nat. trustee, 1995—; trustee bd. advisors Union Coll., 1996-99, trustee, 1999—, trustee, Grad. Coll. Union U., 2003—; dir. AIDS Found. of Chgo., 1997—, sec., 1999—. Mem. ABA, Chgo. Bar Assn., Law Club Chgo., Univ. Club Chgo. (bd. dirs. 1984-87), Phi Beta Kappa. Office: Seyfarth Shaw 55 E Monroe St Ste 4400 Chicago IL 60603-5713

HOFFMAN, W. MICHAEL, philosophy educator, administrator; b. Huntington, W.Va., Feb. 23, 1943; s. Claude Michael Hoffman and Josephine Snow Letton; m. A. Bliss Hoffman. AB, Transylvania Coll., 1965; MA, U. Mass., 1968, PhD, 1972. Asst. prof. philosophy Hiram (Ohio) Coll., 1969-74; assoc. prof., prof. philosophy, dept. chair Bentley Coll., Waltham, Mass., 1974-91, prof. philosophy, exec. dir. Ctr. for Bus. Ethics, 1976—. Cons. numerous cos. and univs.; expert witness and spkr. in bus. ethics; bd. dirs. Bus. & Soc. Rev., 1998—. Co-editor: The Work Ethic in Business, 1981, Ethics and the Management of Computer Technology, 1982, Business Ethics: Readings and Cases in Corporate Morality, 1984, 90, 95, 01, Corporate Governance and Institutionalizing Ethics, 1984, Ethics and the Multinational Enterprise, 1986, Emerging Global Business Ethics, 1994, others; co-author: The Ethical Edge, 1995, Ethics Matters, 2000; contbr. numerous articles to profl. jours. Fellowship Nat. Def. Edn. Act, 1966-69; Coun. for Philos. Studies grant, 1970, 74, Matchette Found. grant, 1972, grant NEH, 1976-77, G.E. Found., 1990-92, others. Mem. Acad. of Mgmt., Assn. of Practical and Profl. Ethics, European Bus. Ethics Network, Internat. Soc. of Bus., Econs., and Ethics, Internat. Soc. for Environtl. Ethics, Italian Bus. Ethics Network, Soc. for Bus. Ethics, Ethics Officer Assn. (bd. dirs.). Office: Bentley Coll Ctr for Bus Ethics 175 Forest St Waltham MA 02452-4705 E-mail: mhoffman@bentley.edu.

HOFFMAN, WAYNE MELVIN, retired airline official; b. Chgo., Mar. 9, 1923; s. Carl A. and Martha (Tamillo) H.; m. Laura Majewski, Jan. 26, 1946; children— Philip, Karen, Kristin. BA cum laude, U. Ill., 1943, JD with high honors, 1947. Bar: Ill. bar 1947, N.Y. bar 1958. Atty. I.C. R.R., 1948-52; with N.Y.C. R.R. Co., 1952-57, exec. asst. to pres., 1958-60, v.p. freight sales, 1960-61, v.p. sales, 1961-62, exec. v.p., 1962-67; chmn. bd. N.Y. Central Trans. Co., 1960-67, Flying Tiger Line, Inc. and Tiger Internat., Inc., 1967-86. Trustee McCallum Theatre, Palm Desert, Calif., Eisenhower Med. Ctr., Rancho Mirage, Calif. Served to capt. inf. AUS, World War II. Decorated Silver Star, Bronze Star with oak leaf cluster, Purple Heart with oak leaf cluster; Fourragere (Belgium). Mem. Bohemian Club (San Francisco), Vintage Club (Indian Wells), Phi Beta Kappa. Home: 74-435 Palo Verde Dr Indian Wells CA 92210-7367 Office: 2450 Montecito Rd Ramona CA 92065-1644

HOFFMAN, WILLIAM KENNETH, retired obstetrician, gynecologist; b. Milw., Jan. 18, 1924; s. William Richard and Marian (Riegler) H.; m. Peggy Folsom, July 28, 1952; children: Janet Susan, Ann Elizabeth. Student, U. Wis., 1942-43, U. Pa., 1943-44, postgrad., 1954-55; MD, Marquette U., 1947. Diplomate Am. Bd. Ob-Gyn. Intern Columbia Hosp., 1947-48, resident ob-gyn., 1948-49, mem. staff, 1949-91; ret., 1991. Preceptor R.E. McDonald, MD, Milw., 1949-50; resident in ob-gyn U. Chgo., 1950-51; practice medicine specializing in ob-gyn, Milw., 1955-74; mem. staff, Columbia Hosp.; dir. health service U. Wis.-Milw., 1974-91, cons. Sch. Nursing, 1976-77, clin. assoc. prof., 1979-91, vice chmn., mem. instl. rev. bd., 1976-91, mem. instl. safety and health com., 1981-91, chmn., 1984-88. Recipient Spaights Plaza award U. Wis.-Milw., 1998. Fellow Am. Coll. Ob-Gyn.; mem. Am. Coll. Health Assn., Am. Coll. Sports Medicine, Royal Soc. Medicine, Am. Cancer Soc. (bd. dirs. Wis. divsn. 1983-88, pub. edn. com. Milw. divsn.). Home: 2023 E Trolley Ct Boise ID 83712-8445

HOFFMANN, CHARLES WESLEY, retired foreign language educator; b. Sioux City, Iowa, Nov. 25, 1929; s. John Wesley and Gertrude J. (Giessen) H.; m. Barbara Brandel Frank, Aug. 11, 1954; children: Eric Gregory, Karla Jennifer. BA, Oberlin Coll., 1951; MA, U. Ill., 1952, PhD, 1956. Fulbright fellow U. Munich, Germany, 1953-55; Instr. German UCLA, 1956-58, asst. prof., 1958-64; assoc. prof. Ohio State U., 1964-66, prof., 1966—92, chmn. dept. German, 1969-77, 86-87. Author: Opposition Poetry in Nazi Germany, 1962, Survey of Research Tool Needs in German Language and Literature, 1978; also: articles on 20th Century German lit; adv. editor: Dimension, 1968-74. Recipient Disting. Teaching award UCLA, 1962, Lou Nemzer award for def. acad. freedom, 1982, Exemplary Faculty award Ohio State U., 1991; Fulbright grantee Germany, 1953-55, 1981. Mem. MLA, Am. Assn. Tchrs. German, ACLU, AAUP (pres. Ohio State U. 1984-86). Home: 291 Mccoy Ave Worthington OH 43085-3748 Office: Dieter Cunz Hall Columbus OH 43210

HOFFMANN, CHRISTOPH LUDWIG, lawyer; b. Elsterwerda, Germany, Oct. 9, 1944; came to U.S., 1965; s. Gunther and Ruth (Hornschuh) H.; m. Susan Magnuson, June 18, 1983. Student, Freie U. Berlin, 1964-65; BA, U. Wis., 1966; JD, Harvard U., 1969. Bar: Mass. 1969, R.I. 1977. Assoc. Bingham, Dana & Gould, Boston, 1969-76; asst. gen. counsel Textron Inc., Providence, 1976-83; v.p., gen. counsel, sec. Pneumo Corp., Boston, 1983-85; sr. v.p., gen. counsel, sec. Pneumo Abex Corp., Boston, 1985-91; v.p., sec., gen. counsel Raytheon Co., Lexington, Mass., 1991-94, sr. v.p. law, human resources and corp. adminstrn., sec., 1994-95, exec. v.p. law and corp. adminstrn., sec., 1995-98; ltd. ptnr. Carlisle 1999, L.P., 1998—. Bd. dirs. Assoc. Industries Mass., 1994, Med. Web Techs., Inc., 2001—; chmn., trustee Deaconess Glover Hosp., 1994—; mem. adv. bd. eLaw Forum Corp., 1999—. Mem. ABA, New Eng. Legal Found. (bd. dirs. 1991-98), Mass. Bar Assn., R.I. Bar Assn., Assn. Gen. Counsel.

HOFFMANN, DONALD, architectural historian; b. Springfield, Ill., June 24, 1933; s. George C. and Ines (Catron) H.; m. Theresa Cecelia McGrath, Apr. 12, 1958; children— George, Alan, Eric, Michael, Valerie. Student, U. Chgo., 1949-53, U. Kansas City, Mo., 1958. Mem. staff Kansas City (Mo.) Star,

1956-90, art critic, 1965-90. Mem. journalism adv. com. Fulbright Scholarship Program, 1968-70. Editor: The Meanings of Architecture-Buildings and Writings by John Wellborn Root, 1967; author: The Architecture of John Wellborn Root, 1973, Frank Lloyd Wright's Fallingwater, 1978, 2d rev. edit., 1993, Frank Lloyd Wright's Robie House, 1984, Frank Lloyd Wright: Architecture and Nature, 1986, Frank Lloyd Wright's Hollyhock House, 1992, Understanding Frank Lloyd Wright's Architecture, 1995, Frank Lloyd Wright's Dana House, 1996, Frank Lloyd Wright, Louis Sullivan and the Skyscraper, 1998, Frank Lloyd Wright's House on Kentuck Knob, 2000; asst. editor Jour. Soc. Archtl. Historians, 1970-72; contbr. articles to profl. jours. Younger Humanist fellow NEH, 1970-71; Art Critic's fellow-grantee Nat. Endowment for Arts, 1974. Mem. Soc. Archtl. Historians (bd. dirs. 1968-70), Art Inst. Chgo. (life) Home: 6441 Holmes St Kansas City MO 64131-1110

HOFFMANN, ELINOR R. lawyer; b. N.Y.C., Apr. 18, 1954; BA magna cum laude, NYU, 1974, LLM in Antitrust and Trade Regulation, 1984; JD cum laude, Bklyn. Law Sch., 1977. Bar: N.Y. 1978, U.S. Dist. Ct. (so. and ea. dists.) N.Y. 1978, U.S. Supreme Ct. 1982, U.S. Ct. Appeals (2nd cir.) 1991, U.S. Ct. Appeals (5th cir.) 1994, U.S. Tax Ct. 1996. Ptnr. Coudert Bros. LLP, N.Y.C., 1986—; mediator U.S. Dist. Ct. (so. dist.) N.Y., 1994—. Mng. editor Bklyn. Law Rev., 1976-77; contbr. articles to profl. jours. Mem. ABA, Internat. Bar Assn., N.Y. State Bar Assn., Assn. Bar City NY, Phi Beta Kappa. Office: Coudert Bros LLP 1114 Avenue Of The Americas New York NY 10036-7710 E-mail: hoffmanne@coudert.com.

HOFFMANN, FRANCES PORTER, librarian, development coordinator; b. Louisville, Dec. 27, 1927; d. Robert Hugh and Frances (Pfeffer) Porter; m. John F. Hoffmann, Sept. 14, 1948; children: Frances H. Stains, Amy H. Aird. BA in History, Trinity U., San Antonio, 1949; MSLS, Our Lady of the Lake U., San Antonio, 1978. Office mgr. acad. libr. St. Mary's U., San Antonio, 1975-77, library assoc., 1977-79, tech. svcs. librarian, 1979-84; coord. tech. svcs. & automated systems Palo Alto Coll., San Antonio, 1986-90, spl. project librarian, 1990-95; devel. coord. I Care San Antonio, 1995—. 1st v.p. Nueces County Pharm. Assn. Auxiliary, Corpus Christi, Tex., 1965; chaplain Tom Brown Middle Sch. PTA, Corpus Christi, 1966; troop leader Girl Scouts of Am., Corpus Christi, 1960-65; docent San Antonio Mus. Assn., 1968-69; v.p. Tech. Svcs. Int. Group, 1992-93; pres. Coun. Rsch. Acad. Librs., 1993-94; devel. coord. I Care San Antonio, 1998. Mem. ALA, Nat. Soc. Daughters of the Am. Revolution, San Antonio Genealogical & Hist. Soc. Presbyterian. Avocations: genealogical research, collecting pre-1950 fashion jewelry, needlework, family activities, travel.

HOFFMANN, GREGG J. journalist, author, publisher; b. Oak Park, Ill, Feb. 23, 1949; s. Robert and Jeanine (Casper) H.; m. Pauline Ehlen, July 20, 1974. BA in Journalism, U. Wis., 1973; MA in Comm., U. Wis., Milw., 1985. Assoc. editor Burlington Std. Press, Wis., 1973-76; owner, operator M & T Comm., Whitefish Bay, Wis., 1976—; columnist OnMilwaukee.com, Milw., 2000—, Wispolitics.com, Wis., 2002—. Milw. corr. USA Today, Baseball Weekly, The Sporting News On-Line, 1998-2001; sr. lectr. U. Wis., Milw., 1987—; bd. dir., v.p. media rels. Internat. Soc. Gen. Semantics, Concord, Calif.; trustee Inst. Gen. Semantics, Englewood, NJ, 1991—; cons. in field. Author: The American Challenge, 1979, Media Maps and Myths, 1993, What You Can Do to Help the Hungry Feed Themselves, 1994, Mapping the Media, 1997, Down in the Valley; The History of Milwaukee County Stadium, 1999, pub. The Brew Crew Rev.; contbr. articles to profl. jour. Recipient Enterpise Reporting award Wis. Newspaper Assn., 1973-74, Freedom Found. Honor medal, 1980, Top Journalism award Am. Planning Assn., 1980, Irving Lee award Inst. Gen. Semantics, 1997, Milw. Idea Cmtys. and Cultures grant; Sanford Berman fellow Internat. Soc. Gen. Semantics, 1989; fellow Environ. Jounalism Inst./Knight Ctr. at Mich. State U. Mem. Midwest Soc. Gen. Semantics (founder), Assn. Educators Mass Communication, Soc. Profl. Journalists, Milw. Press Club, Soc. Environ. Journalists, Pro Basketball Writers Assn., Milw. Media Connection (founder). Avocations: trout fishing, golf, hiking, reading. Home and Office: 4842 N Shoreland Ave Milwaukee WI 53217-5821 E-mail: gregghoff@aol.com.

HOFFMANN, INGE SCHNEIER, psychologist, educator; b. Vienna, Jan. 16, 1929; came to U.S., 1940; d. Josef Michael Schneier and Szerena Susan Löffelholz; m. Stanley Harry Hoffmann, Oct. 6, 1963. BA, Bard Coll., 1950; MA, Harvard U., 1953. Lic. clin. psychologist, Mass. Lectr., asst. to dir. Social Sci. Found. U. Denver, 1953-54; rsch. assoc., assoc. dir. rsch. AIR, Inc., 1954-56; rsch. assoc. Ctr. for Internat. Studies, MIT, 1956-59; lectr. Harvard Coll., 1970-76; lectr. psychology, dept. psychiatry Harvard U. Med. Sch., Cambridge Hosp., 1976—. Faculty assoc. Currier House, Harvard U., 1970—; affiliate Ctr. for European Studies, Harvard U., 1994—. Co-author: Coercive Persuasion, 1961, DeGaulle, Artiste de la Politique, 1973; contbr. articles to profl. jours.; patentee design of art fabrics. Active in mediating Palestinian-Israeli conflict, 1976—. Recipient painting awards Mus. of Modern Art, others; Bard scholar Schepp Found., N.Y., 1947, 48, 49, 50; Radcliffe Inst. scholar Harvard U., 1970, 71, 72. Mem. Cambridge Art Assn., Harvard U. Shop Club, Boston Psychoanalytic Inst. (friend, collaborator 1972-89), Internat. Soc. Polit. Psychology (founding mem. 1997). Avocations: lieder singing, painting. Office: 91 Washington Ave Cambridge MA 02140-2716

HOFFMANN, JAMES VERNON, JR., social studies educator, writer; b. Elmhurst, Ill., Feb. 21, 1964; s. Linda Jean Emmering, James Vernon Hoffmann, Sr.; m. Debbie Lynn Dombrow; children: Nancey Lynn, Destinie Lee;1 child, Devinne Jean. MS, No. Ill. U., 1990. Lic. tchr. Calif., cert. cross-cultural lang. and develop. Calif., lic. tchr. Ill. H.s. tchr. Indian Prairie CUSD #204, Naperville, Ill., 1986—95; jr. high tchr. Franklin-McKinley Sch. Dist., San Jose, Calif., 1997—98, 6th gr. self-contained tchr., 1998—99; educator Manteca Unified Sch. Dist., Manteca, Calif., 1999—. Mentor tchr. Indian Prairie CUSD #204, Naperville, Ill., 1994—95; disciplinary team mem. Franklin-McKinley Sch. Dist., San Jose, 1997—98. Dir.: (films) The Fourth Amendment, 1995 (used by Aurora Police Dept. in schs. program, 1994); author: (book) Art of Teaching, 1996, (short stories) DMZ Diary, 1996, (plays) Moving Day, 1997, (book) 22: Silicon Valley in 8 Acts, 1999. City coun. candidate, Manteca, 2000. Scholar Ruth Coleman, Ea. Ill. U., 1985. Mem.: Ill. Educators Assn., Calif. Educators Assn., Indian Prairie Educators Assn., Franklin-McKinley Educators Assn., Manteca Educators Assn. Liberal. Avocations: history, writing. Home: 125 / Crom St #242 Manteca CA 95337 Office: Calla High School 130 S Austin Rd Monteca CA 95336 Home Fax: 209-239-8837. Personal E-mail: d3jhoffmann@aol.com.

HOFFMANN, JOAN CAROL, retired academic dean; b. Cedarburg, Wis., Feb. 20, 1934; d. Frank Ernst and Althea Wilhelmina (Behm) H. Nursing diploma, Michael Reese Hosp., 1955; BS in Zoology, U. Wis., Madison, 1959; PhD in Physiology, U. Ill., Chgo., 1965. RN, Wis., Ariz. Sci. instr. Michael Reese Hosp., Chgo., 1959-62; USPHS trainee U. Ill., Chgo., 1962-64; NSF postdoctoral fellow Coll. de France, Paris, 1964-65; asst. prof. U. Rochester, N.Y., 1965-70; assoc. prof., prof. U. Hawaii, Honolulu, 1970-83; dean of students U. Mass. Med. Sch., Worcester, 1983-94; ret., 1994. Chmn. anatomy U. Hawaii, 1973-80. Contbr. articles to sci. jours. NIH rsch. grantee, 1966-75. Mem. Endocrine Soc., Soc. for Study of Reprodn., Am. Assn. Anatomists, Women in Endocrinology (sec. 1978-79, pres. 1987-88), Am. Coun. Edn. (bd. dirs., Mass. chpt., network identification program 1993-94), Phi Beta Kappa, Sigma Xi. Avocations: gardening, needlework, wood turning, reading. Home: 77618 Malone Cir Palm Desert CA 92211-0419

HOFFMANN, JON ARNOLD, retired aeronautical engineer, educator; b. Wausau, Wis., Jan. 13, 1942; s. Arnold D. and Rita J. (Haas) H.; m. Carol R. Frye. BSME, U. Wis., 1964, MSME, 1966. Register profl. engr., Calif. Rsch. engr. Trane Co., 1966—68; prof. aerospace engring. Calif. Poly. State U., San Luis Obispo, 1968—2001, prof. emeritus, 2002. Research engr. Stanford U. NSF Program, 1970; research fellow Ames Research Ctr. Ctr. NASA/ASEE, 1974-75; tech. cons. NASA/AMES Research Ctr., 1977; design engr. Cal/ Poly ERDA contract, 1976-77; prin. investigator NASA-ARC Cooperative Agreement, 1983. Contbr. articles to profl. jours. Grantee NASA, NSF. Home: 1044 Via Chula Robles Arroyo Grande CA 93420-4915

HOFFMANN, KATHRYN ANN, humanities educator; b. Rockville Centre, N.Y., Oct. 26, 1954; d. Manfred and Catherine (Nanko) H.; m. Brook Ellis, Nov. 25, 1987. BA summa cum laude, SUNY Buffalo, 1975; MA, The Johns Hopkins U., 1979, PhD, 1981. Asst. prof. French lit. and lang. U. Wis., Madison, 1981-88, U. Hawaii-Manoa, Honolulu, 1992-97, assoc. prof., 1997—2001, prof., 2001—; mng. ptnr. Yuval Design Partnership, Chgo., 1988-92. Author: Society of Pleasures: Interdisciplinary Readings in Pleasure in Power during the Reign of Louis XIV, 1997 (Aldo and Jeanne Scaglione prize for French and Francophone Studies 1998); assoc. editor Substance, 1982-87; transl. Masturbation: The History of a Great Terror, 2001; contbr. articles to profl. jours.; designer clothing accessories. Recipient Regents' medal for excellence in tchg., 1998; fellow, Inst. Rsch. in Humanities, 1984—85, Am. Coun. Learned Socs., 1984—85, Camargo Found., 1998; grantee, NEH Endowment Fund, 1993, 1995. Mem.: MLA (Aldo and Jeanne Scaglione prize for French and Francophone studies 1998), History of Sci. Soc., Soc. for Interdisciplinary Study Social Imagery, Soc. for Interdisciplinary French 17th Century Studies (exec. com. 1994—96), N.Am. Soc. for 17th Century French Lit., Am. Soc. for 18th Century Studies, Internat. Soc. for the Study of European Ideas, Phi Beta Kappa. Home: Apt M12 217 Prospect St Honolulu HI 96813-1778 Office: U Hawaii Manoa Langs & Lits Europe Ams 1890 East West Rd Rm 483 Honolulu HI 96822-2318

HOFFMANN, KENNETH MICHAEL, music educator; s. George Edward Hoffman and Alice Mae Hoffmann; m. Deborah Sue Shaw, June 10, 1989; children: Zachary Michael, Emily Elizabeth, Joseph Samuel. BA music, Ohio U., Athens, Ohio, 1981—85; MS edu., U. Dayton, Dayton, Ohio, 1985—98. Cert. teaching Ohio. Band dir. No. Local Schools, Thornville, Ohio, 1988—93; band dir./tchr. Cedar Cliff local schools, Cedarville, Ohio, 1993—. Recipient Tchr. Yr., Miami Valley serc, 1998, Howard L. Post, Greene county schools, 2002. Home: 3538 Winchester Ct Cedarville OH 45314-9500 Office: Cedarville High School 248 North Main Street Cedarville OH 45314 Home Fax: 937-766-5211. E-mail: cc_khoffmann@mveca.org.

HOFFMANN, LEONARD A, church administrator, director; b. St. Louis, Mo., Apr. 5, 1949; s. Leonard C and Joyce E Hoffmann; m. Cathy Susan Kleist, Mar. 24, 1972; 1 child, Bethany Terese. D in ministry, Luther Northwestern Sem., 1993. Cons. Walsh and Assoc., Kairos, Baldwin, Wis., 1995—99; v.p. Luth. Social Svcs., Natick, Mass., 1999—. Sr. pastor Gethsemane Luth. Ch., Baldwin, Wis., 1991—94. Contbr. articles. Bd. LSSNE Found., Natick, Mass., 2001. Mem.: Assn. of Luth. Devel. Execs. D-Conservative. Lutheran. Avocations: travel, politics. Office: Lutheran Social Svcs New England 624 Congdon St W Middletown CT 06457

HOFFMANN, LOUIS GERHARD, immunologist, educator; b. Bloemendaal, Netherlands, July 12, 1932; arrived in U.S., 1950; s. Gerhard Hendrik and Louise Gertrude (Tobi) Hoffmann; m. Georgianna Grace Stracke, Nov. 4, 1955; children: Julianna Tobi, Eugenie Claire. BA with honors, distinction, Wesleyan U., 1953; MSc in Hygiene, Johns Hopkins U., 1958, ScD, 1960. Diplomate Am. Bd. Sexology. NSF postdoctoral fellow U. Calif., Berkeley, 1960-62; from instr. to asst. prof. microbiology Johns Hopkins U., Balt., 1962-64; asst. prof. U. Iowa, Iowa City, 1964-67, assoc. prof., 1967-74, prof., 1974-96; ret., 1997; pvt. practice sex therapy team, 1978—. Contbr. articles to profl. jours. Mem. Dem. Ctrl. Com., Johnson County, Iowa, 1966—76. Fellow, NIH, 1962—63; grantee, 1964—67, 1980—83, NSF, 1968—74, Iowa Heart Assn., 1969—72, 1977—79, Damon Runyon Meml. Fund, 1972—74. Home: 4 Timberwick Rd Santa Fe NM 87508 E-mail: annilou2@earthlink.net.

HOFFMANN, MANFRED WALTER, consulting company executive; b. Bklyn., Apr. 21, 1938; s. Hermann Karl and Emilie (Talmon) H.; m. Barbara Ann Kenvin, Aug. 5, 1961; children: Lisa Joy, Lauren Kimberly, Kurt William. BS, Cornell U., 1960; MEd, Temple U., 1972, PhD, 1977. With Sun Oil Co., 1967-71, mgr. mktg. devel., 1971-72, mgr. tng., 1973-77, dir. orgn. and mgmt. devel., 1977-79; dir. human resources and adminstrn. Sun Prodn. Co., Dallas, 1979-83; dir. world wide human resources Sun Exploration & Prodn. Co., 1983-90; pres. Gyroscopic Mgmt. Inc., 1989—. Lectr. Grad. Sch., U. Tex., Dallas, 1979-2000. Pres. PTA, bd. mem. Beechwood Sch., 1975-77; cons. exec. com. Orgns. Industrialization Congress Am., 1975-79; bd. dirs. Job Opportunity for Youth, 1980-81; bd. dirs. Dallas SER, 1986—. Served with USMCR, 1956-62. Mem. Am. Soc. Tng. and Devel., Am. Soc. Pers. Adminstrn., Dallas C. of C., Tex. Assn. Bus. Republican. Episcopalian. Home: 3979 Bay Ln Anacortes WA 98221-1115

HOFFMANN, MARTIN RICHARD, lawyer; b. Stockbridge, Mass., Apr. 20, 1932; m. Margaret Ann McCabe; children: Heidi H. Slye, William, Bern. AB, Princeton U., 1954; LLB, U. Va., 1961. Bar: D.C. 1961. Law clk. U.S. Ct. Appeals (4th cir.), 1961-62; asst. U.S. atty. Washington, 1962-65; minority counsel com. on judiciary Ho. of Reps., Washington, 1965-67; legal counsel to Senator C. Percy, U.S. Senate, Washington, 1967-69; asst. gen. counsel Univ. Computing Co., Dallas, 1969-71; gen. counsel AEC, Washington, 1971-73; spl. asst. to sec. and dep. sec. def. Washington, 1973-74; gen. counsel Dept. Def., Washington, 1974-75; sec. Dept. Army, Washington, 1975-77; mng. ptnr. Gardner, Carton & Douglas, Washington, 1977—89; v.p., gen. counsel, sec. Digital Equipment Corp., Maynard, Mass., 1989-93; of counsel Skadden, Arps, Slate, Meagher & Flom, Washington, 1996-2000. Sr. vis. fellow Ctr. for Policy, Tech. and Indsl. Devel., MIT, Cambridge, 1993-95; bd. dirs. Castle Energy, Phila., Sea Change Corp., Maynard, Mass., Mitretek Systems, Inc., Falls ch., Va.; chmn. Beamhit LLC, Columbia, Md. Maj. USAR, 1954-73. Mem. Met. Club. Home: 1546 Hampton Hill Cir Mc Lean VA 22101

HOFFMANN, PETER CONRAD WERNER, history educator; b. Dresden, Germany, Aug. 13, 1930; came to Can., 1970; s. Wilhelm and Elfriede Frances (Müller) H.; m. Helga Luise Hobelsberger, July 22, 1959. Student, U. Stuttgart, 1953-54, U. Tübingen, 1954-55, U. Zurich, 1955, Northwestern U., 1955-56; PhD, U. Munich, 1961. William Kingsford prof. history McGill U., Montreal, Que., Can. Author: Die diplomatischen Beziehungen zwischen Württemberg und Bayern im Krimkrieg und bis zum Beginn der Italienischen Krise (1853-1858), 1963, Widerstand, Staatsstreich, Attentat: Der Kampf der Opposition gegen Hitler, 1969, Die Sicherheit des Diktators: Hitlers Leibwachen, Schutzmassnahmen, Residenzen, Hauptquartiere, 1975, The History of the German Resistance 1933-1945, 1977, Hitler's Personal Security, 1979, Widerstand gegen Hitler, 1979, La résistance allemande contre Hitler, 1984, German Resistance to Hitler, 1988, Claus Schenk Graf von Stauffenberg und seine Brüder, 1992, Tedeschi contro il nazismo: La Resistenza in Germania, 1994, Stauffenberg: A Family History, 1905-1944, 1995, Stauffenberg und der 20. Juli 1944, 1998. Mem.: German Studies Assn., Royal Soc. Can., Can. Hist. Assn., Wurttembergischer Geschichts-und Altertumsverein, Deutsche Schillergesellschaft, Can. Com. History of 2d World War, Sigma Alpha Epsilon. Home: 4332 Montrose Ave Montreal QC Canada H3Y 2A9 E-mail: peter.hoffmann@mcgill.ca.

HOFFMANN, ROALD, chemist, educator; b. Zloczow, Poland, July 18, 1937; arrived in U.S., 1949, naturalized, 1955; s. Hillel and Clara (Rosen) Safran, Paul Hoffmann (Stepfather); m. Eva Börjesson, Apr. 30, 1960; children: Hillel Jan, Ingrid Helena. BA, Columbia U., 1958; MA, Harvard U., 1960, PhD, 1962; D Tech. (hon.), Royal Inst. Tech., Stockholm, 1977; D.Sc. (hon.), Yale U., 1980, Columbia U., 1982, Hartford U., 1982, CUNY, 1983, U. P.R., 1983, U. Uruguay, 1984, U. La Plata, 1984, SUNY, Binghamton, 1985, Colgate U., 1985, Lehigh U., 1989, Carleton Coll., 1989, Ben Gurion U. of the Negev, 1989, U. Md., 1990, U. Athens, 1991, U. Thessaloniki, Greece, 1991, U. Ariz., 1991, U. Cen. Fla., 1991, Bar Ilan U., 1991, U. St. Petersburg, Russia, 1991, U. Barcelona, 1992, Ohio State U., 1993; others. Jr. fellow Soc. Fellows Harvard U., 1962—65; assoc. prof. Cornell U., Ithaca, NY, 1965—68, prof., 1968—74, John A. Newman prof. phys. sci., 1974—96, F.T. Rhodes prof. humane letters, 1996—. Author (with R.B. Woodward): Conservation of Orbital Symmetry, 1970; author: Solids and Surfaces, 1988; author: (with V. Torrence) Chemistry Imagined, 1993; author: (poetry) The Metamict State, 1987, Gaps and Verges, 1990, (non-fiction) Soliton, 2002, (poetry) Memory Effects, 1999, The Same and Not the Same, 1995; author: (with S. Leibowitz Schmidt) Old Wine, New Flasks, 1997; author: (drama, with C. Djerassi) Oxygen, 2000; author: Soliton, 2002, Catalista, 2002. Recipient award in pure chemistry, Am. Chem. Soc., 1969, Arthur C. Cope award, 1973, Fresenius award, Phi Lambda Upsilon, 1969, Harrison Howe award, Rochester sect. Am. Chem. Soc., 1970, ann. award, Internat. Acad. Quantum Molecular Scis., 1970, Pauling award, 1974, Nobel prize in Chemistry, 1981, inorganic chemistry award, Am. Chem. Soc., 1982, Nat. medal of Sci., 1983, Priestley medal, 1990, Centennial medal, Harvard U., 1994, Jawarharlal Nehru Birth Centenary award, 1998. Mem.: NAS (award in chem. scis. 1986), Finnish Acad. Arts and Letters, Royal Swedish Acad. Scis., Indian Nat. Sci. Acad., Royal Soc. (fgn. mem.), Internat. Acad. Quantum Molecular Scis., Russian Acad. Scis. (N.N. Semenov Gold medal), Am. Acad. Arts and Scis. Office: Cornell U Dept Chemistry Ithaca NY 14853 E-mail: rh34@cornell.edu.

HOFFMANN, ROBERT SHAW, museum administrator, educator; b. Evanston, Ill., Mar. 2, 1929; s. Robert Charles and Dorothy Elizabeth (Shaw) H.; m. Sally Ann Monson, June 17, 1951; children: Karl Robert, John Frederick, David Randolf, Brenna Elizabeth. BS, Utah State U., 1950; MA, U. Calif., Berkeley, 1954, PhD, 1955; DS (hon.), Utah State U., 1988. From instr. to prof. U. Mont., Missoula, 1955-68; prof., curator U. Kans., Lawrence, 1968-86, Summerfield Disting. prof., 1982; dir. Nat. Mus. Natural History, Washington, 1986-87; asst. sec. for rsch. Smithsonian Instn., Washington, 1988-92, asst. sec. sci., 1992-94, provost, 1994-95; acting dir. Nat. Air & Space Mus., Washington, 1995-96; sr. scientist Nat. Mus. Natural History, Washington, 1996—2003. Gis. fellow Nat. Mus. Natural History, Washington, 1975-76; mem. U.S. Nat. Com. for INQUA, NAS, 1970-82, sec.-treas., 1972-74, vice chmn., 1974-77, chmn., 1977-82, mem. adv. com. on USSR and Ea. Europe, 1970-75, mem. com. on Yellowstone Grizzlies, 1973-74, mem. ad hoc com. discussion group on US-USSR sci. policies, 1973; mem. mountain habitats com. Internat. Union for Conservation of Nature and Natural Resources, 1971—; mem. organizing com. First Internat. Theriological Congress, Moscow, 1974, mem. presidium, 1974-78; mem. Insectivore group, 1987—, Lagomorph Group, 1990—, Species Survival Commn.; mem. Soviet Union and Ea. Europe area com. Coun. Internat. Exch. Scholars, 1985-90; co-chair high latitude directorate U.S. Nat. Com. for Man and Biosphere, 1989-92; mem. com. on monographs and classification Systematics Agenda 2000, 1991; mem. adv. com. Internat. Sci. Found., 1992-94, chair biology III panel, 1993-94; mem. biodiversity working group of China Coun. for Internat. Cooperation in Environment and Devel., 1997—; co-chair planning com. Smithsonian-Am. Inst. Biol. Sci. "Challenges for the New Millenium" conf.; cons. Faisalabad U., Pakistan, 1971—; adviser Inst. Arctic and Alpine Rsch., Boulder, Colo., 1980—, Quaternary Rsch. Ctr., Seattle, 1981—, and numerous others; rsch. assoc. Mus., Tex. Tech U., 1998—. Co-author: Mammals in Kansas, 1981, Mammals of the Northern Great Plains, 1983; coord., contbr. Mammal Species of the World, 1982, 93; also articles. NAS fellow, 1963-64; NSF grantee, 1957-87, and numerous other grants; recipient 30 Yr. medal U.S.-USSR Interacad. Exch., 1989. Fellow AAAS; mem. Internat. Coun. Mus. (mem. exec. coun. 1995-98, mem. ethics com. 1998-00, U.S. Nat. Com. (bd. dirs. 1990-01), Am. Assn. Mus., Am. Assn. Quarternary Rsch., Am. Soc. Mammalogists (bd. dirs., chmn. com. internat. rels. 1964-68, 72-78, 1st v.p. 1973-78, pres. 1981-82), Brit. Mammal Soc., Ecol. Soc. Am., Internat. Assn. Ecology, Internat. Mountain Soc., Soc. Systematic Biology (pres. 1988-89), Xerces Soc. (bd. dirs.), Acta Zoologica Sinica (editl. bd. 1990—), Acta Theriologica Sinica (editl. bd. 1993—), Russian Acad. Natural Scis. (fgn.), All-Union Theriological Soc. (hon.), Sigma Xi, Phi Kappa Phi, Phi Sigma. Avocations: birdwatching, hiking, skiing, traveling. Office: NMNH Divsn Mammals Smithsonian Instn Mrc 108 Washington DC 20560 E-mail: hoffmann.robert@nmnh.si.edu.

HOFFMANN, THOMAS RUSSELL, business management educator; b. Milw., Sept. 10, 1933; s. Alfred C. and Florence M. (Morlock) H.; m. Lorna G. Gruenzel, Aug. 31, 1957; 1 child, Timothy Jay. BS, U. Wis., 1955, MS, 1956, PhD, 1959. Engring. trainee Allis-Chalmers Mfg. Co., 1956-59; asst. prof. U. Wis. Sch. Commerce, 1959-63; mem. faculty U. Minn. Sch. Mgmt., Mpls., 1963-99, prof., 1965-99, chmn. dept. mgmt. scis., 1969-78; dir. West Bank Computer Center, 1971-87. Cons. to industry. Author: Production Management and Manufacturing Systems, 2 edit., 1967-71, (with others) Fortran 77: A Structured, Disciplined Style, 1978, 83, 88, Production and Inventory Management, 1983, 2d edit., 1991, Production and Operations Management, 1989; editor-in-chief Jour. Ops. Mgmt., 1993-95; contbr. articles to profl. jours. Chmn. long range planning com. Luth. Ch., 1971, pres., 1974, 89, treas., 1977-82, 93-98. Mem. Am. Prodn. and Inventory Control Soc. (pres. Twin Cities chpt., 1970-71, internat. pres. 1998). Home: 4501 Sedum Ln Edina MN 55435-4051 Office: U Minn Carlson Sch Mgmt Minneapolis MN 55455 E-mail: thoffmann@csom.umn.edu.

HOFFMEISTER, DONALD FREDERICK, zoologist, educator; b. San Bernardino, Calif., Mar. 21, 1916; s. Percival George and Julia Bell (Hillgartner) H.; m. Helen E. Kaatz, Aug. 11, 1938; m. 2d Florence Williamson, Aug. 15, 1995; children: James Ronald, Robert George. AB, U. Calif.-Berkeley, 1938, MA, 1940, PhD, 1944; ScD (hon.), MacMurray Coll., Jacksonville, Ill., 2000. Research, curatorial asst. Museum Vertebrate Zoology, U. Calif.-Berkeley, 1941-44, teaching asst. zoology, 1943-44; assoc. curator modern vertebrates Mus. Natural History, U. Kans., 1944-46, asst. prof. zoology, 1944-46; dir. Mus. Natural History, U. Ill., 1946-84, dir. emeritus, 1984—, mem. faculty univ., 1946—, prof. zoology, 1959-84, prof. emeritus, 1984—; research assoc. Mus. No. Ariz., 1969—. Author: Mammals, 1955, 1963, Fieldbook of Illinois Mammals, 1957, Zoo Animals, 1967, Mammals of Grand Canyon, 1971, Mammals of Ariz., 1986, Mammals of Illinois, 1989; also articles, reports. Fellow Ariz.-Nev. Acad. Sci.; mem. Am. Soc. Mammalogists (hon., sec. 1946-52, v.p. 1961-64, pres. 1964-66, Hartley H.T. Jackson award 1987), Midwest Mus. Conf. (hon., exec. v.p. 1962-63, pres. 1963-64), Am. Assn. Mus. (coun. 1973-76), Assn. Sci. Mus. Dirs. Home: 20 Fields E Champaign IL 61822-6129 Office: U Ill Mus Natural History Urbana IL 61801

HOFFMEISTER, JANA MARIE, cardiologist; MD, SUNY Upstate Med. Ctr., Syracuse, 1976. Diplomate Am. Bd. Internal Medicine, Am. Bd. Cardiovascular Diseases. Intern Albany (N.Y.) Med. Ctr., 1976-78, resident, 1978-80, fellow div. cardiology, 1981-83, Emory U., Atlanta, 1984; fellow coronary angioplasty and interventional cardiology Emory U. Hosp., 1985-86. Presenter numerous cardiology confs. Contbr. numerous articles to profl. jours. Mem. ACP, AMA, Cardiac Soc. Upstate N.Y., N.Y. State Soc. Internal Medicine, Am. Soc. Cardiovascular Intervention. Home: PO Box 11049 Albany NY 12211-1632

HOFFMEYER, WILLIAM FREDERICK, lawyer, educator; b. York, Pa., Dec. 20, 1936; s. Frederick W. and Mary B. (Stremmel) H.; m. Betty J. Hoffmeyer, Feb. 6, 1960 (div.); 1 child, Louise C.; m. Karen L. Semmelman, 1985. AB, Franklin and Marshall Coll., 1958; JD, Dickinson Sch. Law, 1961. Bar: Pa. 1962, U.S. Dist Ct. (mid. dist.) Pa. 1981, U.S. Supreme Ct. 1983. Pvt. practice law, 1962-81; sr. ptnr. Hoffmeyer & Semmelman, 1982—. Adj. prof. real estate law York Coll. Pa., 1980-92, real estate law, paral legal program Pa. State U., 1978-2000. Autor: Abstractor's Bible, 1981, Pennsylvania Real Estate Installment Sales Contract Manual, 1981, Real Estate Settlement Procedures, 1982, Contracts of Sale, 1984, How to Plot a Deed Description, 1985; author, lectr., moderator and course planner numerous Pa. Bar Inst. CLE Programs. Recipient Disting. Svc. award Gen. Alumni Assn. Dickinson Sch. Law, 1993, Pa. Bar medal, 1997. Mem. ABA, Pa. Bar Assn. (co-chmn. unauthorized practice of law com.), York County Bar Assn. (chmn. continuing legal edn. com. 1992-96), Am. Coll. Real Estate Lawyers, Lions (past pres. East York club), York Area C. of C. (chair small bus. support network 1997-99), Masons, Shriners (past pres. York County). Address: 30 N George St York PA 17401-1214

HOFFNER, MARILYN, university administrator; b. N.Y.C., Nov. 16, 1929; d. Daniel and Elsie (Schulz) H.; m. Albert Greenberg, May 29, 1949; children: Doren Roe, Peter Cooper. BFA, Cooper Union. Art dir. Printers' Ink mag., N.Y.C., 1953-63, Print Mag., N.Y.C., 1960-62; corp. art dir. Vision, Inc., L.Am., 1963-75, 92-95; dir. alumni rels. and devel. Cooper Union, 1974-96, exec. dir. instnl. advancement, 1996-99, cons., 1999-2001; pres. Alumni Assn., 1999-2001. Project dir. Nat. Graphic Design Archives, 1990-97; bd. dirs. Art Dirs. Club N.Y., 1973-75, 79-82, exec. sec., 1973-75, exec. treas., 1979-82. Contbg. editor Print mag., Art Direction, Graphis mag.; designer mags., advt., books and exhbns. Mem. Citizens Adv. Cultural Arts Com. Dutchess County, 1978-80. Recipient Gold medal Art Dirs. Club, 1979, N.Y. State Coun. of the Arts award, 1995; named Alumnus of the Yr., Cooper Union, 1968. Mem. Cooper Union Alumni Assn. (editor-in-chief 1971-74, 1st v.p. 1974-75), Coun. Advancement and Support of Edn., Type Dirs. Club (numerous awards), Nat. Arts Club (Exhbn. com.). Home: 51 5th Ave New York NY 10003-4320 E-mail: cu1948@aol.com.

HOFFORD, JAMES LOVEDAY, Christian evangelist, columnist, poet; b. Columbus, Ohio, Oct. 3, 1928; s. Harry Raymond and Charlotte (Loveday) H.; m. Roxanne Herrick, Jan. 29, 1955 (div. 1964); children: William, Dana, Paul; m. Ellen Gale Reed, Apr. 16, 1966; children: Gregg, Adam. BS in Pub. Comm., Boston U., 1952; MA in Speech, U. Mich., 1955; grad. Ecumenical Inst., Boston U. Sch. Theology, 1962; PhD in Edn., Syracuse U., 1970. Lic. to preach, United Meth. Ch., 1960. Editor sales promotion publs. Detroit Steel Products Co., 1952-53; instr., speech and English U. Toledo, 1954-57; tchg. asst. dept. radio-TV Northwestern U., Evanston, Ill., 1957-58; field entertainment dir., spl. svcs. AUS, Augsburg, Germany, 1958-60; dir. pub. rels. Mass. Coun. Churches, Boston, 1961-65; prof. speech and English Boston State Coll., 1964-82; supr. student tching. Syracuse (N.Y.) U. Sch. of Speech, 1967-69; prof. speech and English Bunker Hill C.C., Boston, 1982-89; ordained elder Valley Bible Chapel, Hillsborough, N.H., 1991-96. Pres. Mass. Speech Comm. Assn., Boston, 1979-81; founder Ctr. Continuing Christian Edn., Washington, N.H., 1978-88. Author: Sidewalk America: Poems of the Race Age, 1964, 2d edit. 1969, Speech for Teachers in Training, 1967, revised 1978, A Study of Communication Within Intimacy, 1973, Memories Green, 1995, Born Again-Slowly (memoirs), 2003; columnist Boston Sunday Herald, Springfield Union, Christian Century, 1961-65, N.H. Week in Review, 1992-97; numerous articles syndicated by New Eng. Press Assn., Nat. Newspaper Assn.; columnist Good News; appearances on radio and TV in Ohio, Chgo. and Boston; prodr. (radio) Healing in Christ, 1982; prodr., dir. cmty. and coll. plays and programs, including original multimedia passion play The Good News, N.H., 1985, 95, Ukraine, 1994. Toured Ctrl. Am. for 1965 food relief; created fund-raising concept Diet Dollars for Ch. World Svc., 1963; Rep. nominee U.S. Congress 11th Dist., Mass., 1966; dir. comm. Robertson for Pres. primary, N.H., 1987-88; Ukraine mission with Eastern European Outreach, 1993-2000; coord. Kosovo Kids Clothing Drive, 2001; active in pub. svc. in Washington, N.H., including svc. as town auditor, vol. fireman, CD dir., moderator of Congl. Ch. Capt. USAFR, 1959-68. Republican. Evangelical. Avocations: photography, poetry readings. Fax: 603-495-0103.

HOFFSIS, GLEN F. dean; B in Animal Sci., Ohio State U., 1962, DVM, 1966, M in Internal Medicine, 1969. Bd. cert. Am. Coll. Vet. Internal Medicine. Intern vet. medicine Colo. State U., 1967; dir. Ohio State U.'s Vet. Hosp., Columbus, 1991; mem. faculty Ohio State U., Columbus, 1970—, head sect. food animal medicine and surgery dept. vet. clin. scis., 1970—91; dean Ohio State U. Coll. Vet. Medicine, Columbus, 1995—. Food cons. FDA; past chmn. FDA Ctr. for Vet. Medicine Adv. Com. Mem.: Ohio Vet. Med. Assn. (mem. biologics and pharm. com.), Am. Assn. Bovine Practitioners (past pres., Award of Excellence), Nat. Milk Prodrs. Fedn., Am. Vet. Med. Assn. (joint liaison com.). Office: Ohio State U 1900 Coffey Rd Columbus OH 43210

HOFKIN, ANN GINSBURGH, photographer, poet; b. Holyoke, Mass., Dec. 20, 1943; d. Albert and Fruma (Winer) G.; m. Michael Gary Hofkin, June 30, 1966; children: Daniel, Benjamin. AB, Mt. Holyoke Coll., 1965; MSS, Bryn Mawr Coll., 1967. One-woman shows include Unicorn Galleries, Mpls., 1980, Warm Gallery, Mpls., 19882-85, 87-88, 90, 96, 98, St. Mary's Coll., Winona, Minn., 1986, U. Wis., Meml. Union, 1993, Bladin Found., 1990, Phipps Ctr. for the Arts, Wis., 1994, So. Light Gallery, Tex., 1994-95, MC Gallery, Mpls., 1986, 89, 91-92, 94, 97, Bethany Luth. Coll., Minn., 1999, Hoyt Inst. Fine Arts, 1999, Pietra di Luna Gallery, Fla., 2000; group shows include Gallery Triangle, Washington, 1996, Pindar Gallery, N.Y., 1987, Phinney Ctr., Seattle, 1987, Print Club, Phila., 1988, U. Minn., 1988, Plains Art Mus., 1988, U. Minn., 1989, Durango Arts Ctr., Colo., 1989, Northfield Arts Guild, Minn., 1982, 90, Mich. Friends of Photography, 1992, Jewish Cmty. Ctr., Houston, 1990, 92, Hennepin History Mus., 1992, LaGrange (Ga.) Coll., 1992, Chautauqua Art Assn., N.Y., 1992, Edn. Testing Svc., N.J., 1992, Slocumb Galleries, Tenn., 1993, Barrett House Galleries, N.Y., Erector Sq. Gallery, Conn., 1993, McPherson Coll., Ks., 1993, Middle (Tenn.) State U., 1993, Sioux City Art Ctr., Iowa, 1987, 89, 93, Mpls. Coll. Art and Design, 1987, 89, 94, Lubbock (Tex.) Fine Arts Ctr., 1995, Shoestring Gallery, N.Y., 1993, 94, 95, Phila. Art Alliance, 1995, Murray (Ky.) State U., 1996, Ctrl. Mo. State U., 1996, Stephen Austin State U. Tex., 1996, Houston Ctr. for Photography, 1995, 96, Perry House Galleries, Va., 1996, 97, U. S.D., Vermilion, 1994, 97, Nebr. Wesleyan U., 1997, U. No. Iowa, 1997, ekliktikos gallery, Washnigton, 1997, Chuck Levitan Gallery, N.Y., 1997-98; group exhibitions: Mpls. Inst. Arts, 85, 86, 2000, Minnesota State Fair, 1986-93, 95-97, 99-2000, U. Wisconsin, Green Bay, 1988, 94, 98, Coll. St. Catherine, MN, 1997, 99, Mpls., Jewish Community, Ctr., 1997, 99, Phipps Ctr. For the Arts, WI, 98, 99, Bausch & Lomb, Rochester, NY, 1998, Texas Nat., 1998, 2000, Savannah COll. of Art & Design, 1998, St. John'sU., MN, 1999, Pentimenti Gallery, PA, 2000, Euro Galleries, MN, 2000, GOCAIA Gallery, AZ, 2000, San Diego Art Inst., CA, 2000, Wellington B Gray Gallery, NC, 2001. Home: 1422 Tamarack Dr Long Lake MN 55356

HOFKIN, GERALD ALAN, gastroenterologist; b. Balt., July 4, 1936; m. Phyllis Hofkin, Aug. 23, 1959; children: Leah, Stephen, Karen. AB, MA, Johns Hopkins U., 1957, MBA, 2003; MD, U. Md., 1961. Diplomate Am. Bd. Internal Medicine, Am. Bd. Gastroenterology. Intern U. Md. Hosp., Balt., 1961, resident in medicine, 1962-63, 64-65, Sinai Hosp., Balt., 1963-64, 65-66; resident in gastroenterology Letterman Hosp., San Francisco, 1966-67; pvt. practice Balt., 1969-91; staff Sinai Hosp., Balt., 1991-99; part-time pvt. practice Woodholme Gastroenterology Assocs., Balt., 1999—. Chmn. med. exec. com. Sinai Hosp. Med. Staff, Balt., 1989, pres., 1992-93. Contbr. articles to profl. jours. Maj. U.S. Army, 1966-69. Decorated Army Commendation medal; named Disting. Physician, Sinai Hosp., 1992. Fellow ACP, Am. Coll. Gastroenterology; mem. Am. Soc. Gastroenterol. Endoscopy, Md. Soc. Gastrointesinal Endoscopy (pres. 1995-97), Balt. Amateur Radio Club (v.p. 1978-79), Balt. Radio Amateur TV Soc., Alpha Omega Alpha. Avocations: amateur radio, computers, bridge. Office: Woodholme Gastroenterology Assoc 1838 Greene Tree Rd Baltimore MD 21208-6391 E-mail: ghofkin@pol.net.

HOFMANN, ALAN FREDERICK, biomedical researcher, educator; b. Balt., May 17, 1931; s. Joseph Enoch and Nelda Rosina (Durr) Hofmann; m. Marta Gertrud Pettersson, Aug. 15, 1959 (div. 1976); children: Anthea Karin, Cecilia Rae; m. Helga Katharina Aicher, Nov. 3, 1978. BA with honors, Johns Hopkins U., 1951, MD with honors, 1955; PhD, U. Lund, Sweden, 1965; MD (hon.), U. Bologna, Italy, 1988. Intern, resident dept. medicine Columbia Presbyn. Med. Ctr., N.Y.C., 1955-57; clin. assoc. clin. ctr. Nat. Heart Inst., NIH, Bethesda, Md., 1957-59; postdoctoral fellow, dept. physiol. chemistry U. Lund, Sweden, 1959-62; asst. physician Hosp. Rockefeller U., N.Y.C., 1962-64, assoc. physician, 1964-66; outpatient physician N.Y. Hosp., N.Y.C., 1963-64; cons. in medicine, assoc. dir. gastroenterology unit Mayo Clinic, Rochester, Minn., 1966-77; prof. medicine, attending physician Med. Ctr. U. Calif., San Diego, 1977-98, emeritus prof., 1998—. Asst. prof. dept. medicine Rockefeller U., N.Y.C., 1964—66; assoc. prof. medicine and biochemistry U. Minn. Mayo Grad. Sch., 1966—69, assoc. prof. medicine and physiology, 1969—70, prof., 1970—73, Mayo Med. Sch., 1973—77; cons. physiology Mayo Clinic, Rochester, 1975—77; adj. prof. pharmacy U. Calif., San Francisco, 1986—94; vis. prof. U. Mich., Ann Arbor, 1980—85. Contbr. articles to profl. jours., chapters to books. Co-recipient Eppinger prize, Falk Found., 1976; recipient Travel award, Wellcome Trust, 1961—63, NSF, 1964, Sr. Scientist award, Humboldt Found., Fed. Rep. Germany, 1976, 1991, Disting. Achievement award, Modern Medicine mag., 1978, Chancellor's Rsch. Excellence award, U. Calif., 1986, Disting. Alumnus award, Mayo Found., 2001; Sr. fellow, NIH, 1986. Fellow: AAAS, Royal Soc. Medicine, Royal Coll. Physicians (hon.); mem.: Am. Gastroent. Assn. (chmn. biliary diseases coun. 1991—92, Disting. Achievement award 1970, co-winner Beaumont prize 1979, Fridenwald medal 1994), Am. Physiol. Soc. (Horace Davenport medal 1996), Am. Liver Found. (chmn. sci. adv. bd. 1986—91), Serbian Soc. Medicine (hon.), Royal Flemish Acad. Medicine (hon.; fgn. corr. mem.), Chilean Soc. Gastroenterology (hon.), Soc. Gastrointestinal Radiology (hon.), Swedish Soc. Gastroenterology (hon.), Gastroent. Soc. Australia (hon.), Brit. Soc. Gastroenterology (hon.), German Soc. Digestive and Metabolic Disease (hon. Siegfried Thannhauser medal 1996), Assn. Am. Physicians, Am. Soc. Clin. Investigation, Am. Assn. Study Liver Disease (pres. 1984, numerous coms., Disting. Achievement award 1997), Sigma Xi, Phi Beta Kappa, Omicron Delta Kappa, Alpha Omega Alpha. Achievements include patents for solvent for direct dissolution of cholesterol gallstones; breath test for pancreatic exocrine function; bile acid replacement therapy. Home: 5870 Cactus Way La Jolla CA 92037-7069 E-mail: ahofmann@ucsd.edu., hofmannaf@cs.com.

HOFMANN, FRIEDER KARL, biotechnologist, consultant; b. Eppstein, Hessen, Germany, June 15, 1949; came to U.S., 1984; s. Friedrich Karl and Anna Johannette (Heist) H.; m. Sigrid Marianne Thomae, Sept. 5, 1975. MS, J.W. Goethe U., Frankfurt, Germany, 1977, PhD, 1981. Staff scientist, asst. prof. J.W. Goethe U., Frankfurt, 1977-81; sci. mgr. Brunswick Corp., Eschborn, Germany, 1982-84; tech. dir. Biotechnetics, San Diego, 1984-90; pres. ProCon Internat., Vista, Calif., 1990—, Ctr. for Continuous Edn., Vista, Calif., 1992—. Author: (with others) Scale-Up and Downstream Processing of rDNA Products, 1991, GMP Production of Monoclonal Antibodies, 1991; contbr. over 40 articles to profl. jours. Recipient Senckenberg prize Senckenberg Rsch. Soc., Frankfurt, 1977; Kirkpatrick Chem. Engring. Achievement Honor award Chem. Engring., 1989, Parenteral Drug Assn. Jour. award Parenteral Drug Assn., Pa., 1985. Mem. AIChE, Am. Chem. Soc., Tissue Culture Assn., European Soc. for Animal Cell Tech. Achievements include 6 patents for bioreactor and membrane technology; invention and development of tester for membrane filters, of first scalable membrane based animal cell reactor; first integration of upstream and downstream processes in bioreactor system; invention of formulation and procedure to grow animal cells in protein-free nutrient. Office: ProCon Internat 1773 Kings Rd Vista CA 92084-3640

HOFMANN, GEORGE W. artist, educator; b. Jamaica, N.Y., May 22, 1938; s. George Hofmann and Margarete Vogl; 1 child, David E. Student, Akademie d.Bildenden Kuenste, Nuremberg, Germany, 1958—61. Instr. Pratt Inst., Bklyn., 1967—68; prof. Hunter Coll., CUNY, 1967—2002. Dir. Francis J. Greenburger Found., N.Y.C., NY, 1986—88. Painting, After Tiepolo (Purchase, Institute of History and Art, Albany, NY, 2001). Judge N.Y. Found. for Arts, N.Y.C., 1995—2002. Fellow Visual Arts, NEA, 1976.

HOFMANN, JOHN RICHARD, JR., retired lawyer; b. Oakland, Calif., June 24, 1922; s. John Richard and Esther (Starkweather) H.; m. Mary Macdonough, Feb. 6, 1954; children: John Richard III, Gretchen Hofmann, Sarah Worthington Hack, John Macdonough Alexander. AB, U. Calif., Berkeley, 1943; JD, Harvard U., 1949. Bar: Calif. 1950. Assoc. Pillsbury, Madison & Sutro, San Francisco, 1949-58, ptnr., 1959-92, of counsel, 1992-96, ret., 1996—; exec. v.p. MPC Ins., Ltd., 1988-96. City atty. City of Belvedere (Calif.), 1957-58. Mem. Calif. Bar Assn. Office: Pillsbury Winthrop LLP PO Box 7880 San Francisco CA 94120-7880

HOFMANN, PAUL BERNARD, healthcare consultant; b. Portland, Oreg., July 6, 1941; s. Max and Consuelo Theresa (Bley) H.; m. Lois Bernstein, June 28, 1969; children: Julie, Jason. BS, U. Calif., Berkeley, 1963, MPH, 1965, DPH, 1994. Research assoc. in hosp. adminstrn. Lab. of Computer Sci., Mass. Gen. Hosp., Boston, 1966-68, asst. dir., 1968-69; asst. adminstr. San Antonio Community Hosp., Upland, Calif., 1969-70, assoc. adminstr., 1970-72; dep. dir. Stanford (Calif.) U. Hosp., 1972-74, dir., 1974-77; exec. dir. Emory U. Hosp., Atlanta, 1978-87; exec. v.p., chief ops. officer Alta Bates Corp., Emeryville, Calif., 1987-91, cons., 1991-92, Alexander & Alexander, San Francisco, 1992-94; disting. vis. scholar Stanford (Calif.) U. Ctr. for Biomed. Ethics, 1993-97; sr. fellow Stanford (Calif.) U. Hosp., 1993-94; sr. cons. strategic healthcare practice Alexander & Alexander Cons. Group, San Francisco, 1994-97; sr. v.p. strategic healthcare practice Aon Cons., San Francisco, 1997-99; pres. The Hofmann Healthcare Group, San Francisco, 2000-01; with Provenance Health Ptnrs., Moraga, Calif., 2001—. Instr. computer applications Harvard U., 1968-69; lectr. hosp. adminstrn. UCLA, 1970-72, Stanford U. Med. Sch., 1972-77; assoc. prof. Emory U. Sch. Medicine, Atlanta, 1978-87. Author: The Development and Application of Ethical Criteria for Use in Making Programmatic Resource Allocation Decisions in Hospitals, 1994; co-editor: Managing Ethically: A Guide for Executives, 2001; contbr. articles to profl. jours. Served with U.S. Army, 1959. Fellow Am. Coll. Hosp. Adminstrs. (recipient Robert S. Hudgens meml. award 1976); mem. Am. Hosp. Assn., U. Calif. Alumni Assn.

HOFMANN, POLLY A. physiologist, science educator; b. Dixon, Ill., July 8, 1960; married; 1 child. BS in Biology, U. Ill., 1982; PhD in Physiology, U. Pitts., 1987. Postdoctoral fellow dept. physiology U. Wis., Madison, Wis., 1987; asst. prof. dept. physiology and biophysics U. Tenn., Memphis, 1991—97, assoc. prof. dept. physiology, 1997—. Mem. prof. search com. Dept. Physiology and Biophysics, U. Tenn., 1991—92, grad. program tng. com., 1992—93, 1993—; student progress and promotions com. biomed. sci. Coll. of Medicine, U. Tenn., 1992—96; chmn. search com. Dept. Preventive Medicine, U. Tenn., 1993—94; Alma and Hal Reagan fellowship seletion com. Coll. Grad. Health Scis., U. Tenn., 1994—; mem. conflict resolution coun. of student mistreatment program Coll. of Medicine, U. Tenn., 1995—. Ad hoc reviewer Am. Jour. Physiology, Jour. Pharmacology and Exptl. Therapeutics; contbr. articles to profl. jours. Recipient Dave McClain Rsch. award, Am. Heart Assn., 1988, Established Investigator award, 1995; fellow predoctoral fellow, NIH, 1983—87, postdoctoral fellow, 1989—92, Am. Heart Assn., 1988—89; grantee, NIH, 1992—, Am. Heart Assn., 1992—93. Mem.: Internat. Soc. Heart Rsch. (Upjohn Young Investigator award 1990), Biophys. Soc., Am. Physiol. Soc. (career opportunities in physiology com. 1995—), Sigma Xi. Office: U Tenn 894 Union Ave Ste 426 Memphis TN 38163-0001

HOFMANN, STEFAN GEORG, psychologist, researcher; b. Bietigheim, Germany, Dec. 15, 1964; arrived in U.S., 1993; s. Walter and Gisela (Tauchmann) Hofmann. BS, Gymnasium Ellental, Bietigheim, 1988; MS, U. Marburg, Germany, 1990, PhD, 1993. Lic. psychologist Mass. Asst. prof. U. Dresden, Germany, 1993-94; rsch. scientist SUNY, Albany, 1994-96; rsch. asst. prof. Boston U., 1996-99, asst. prof., 1999—, dir. social phobia treatment program, 1999—. Asst. dir. Ctr. for Anxiety Disorders, Boston, 1996—. Contbr. Recipient Young Investigator award, Nat. Alliance for Rsch. on Schizophrenia and Depression, 1997, 2000, 1st award, NIMH, 1998. Avocations: science, music, art, cooking. Office: Boston U Dept Psychology 648 Beacon St 6th Fl Boston MA 02215-2013 E-mail: shofmann@bu.edu.

HOFMANN, THEO, biochemist, educator; b. Zurich, Switzerland, Feb. 20, 1924; emigrated to Can., 1964, naturalized, 1969; s. Edwin and Hedwig (Moos) H.; m. Doris Topham Forbes, July 15, 1953; children: Martin Ian, Tony David, Peter Adrian. Diploma chem. engring., Swiss Fed. Inst. Tech., Zurich, 1947, Dr. Sc. Tech., 1950. Research asst. U. Aberdeen, Scotland, 1950-52; sci. officer Hannah Dairy Research Inst., Ayr, Scotland, 1952-56; lectr. Sheffield (Eng.) U., 1956-64; prof. biochemistry U. Toronto, Ont., Can., 1964-89, emeritus prof. biochemistry, 1989—. Vis. assoc. prof. U. Wash., 1962-63; vis. scientist Commonwealth Sci. and Indsl. Research Orgn., Sydney, Australia, 1971-72; vis. prof. divsn. natural scis. U. Calif.-Santa Cruz, 1981; vis. prof. physical chemistry, U. Lund, Sweden, 1987. Asso. editor: Can. Jour. Biochemistry, 1968-71; Contbr. numerous articles to profl. jours. Med. Rsch. Coun. (Can.) grantee, 1964-94. Mem. Can. Soc. Biochemistry and Molecular and Cellular Biology, Am. Soc. Biochemistry and Molecular Biology, Biochem. Soc. Achievements include rsch. in function and evolution of enzymes. Home: 199 Arnold Ave Thornhill ON Canada L4J 1C1 Office: U Toronto Dept Biochemistry Toronto ON Canada M5S 1A8 E-mail: theo@hera.med.utoronto.ca.

HOFMANN, WOLF K, internist, researcher; children: Konstantin E, Franziska A. MD, U. of Jena and Frankfurt, 1994; PhD, U. of Jena and Franfurt, 1999. Bd. Certification Internal Medicine Hessen, 2002. Attending U. Hosp., Frankfurt/Main, Germany, 2002—02; post doc. Cedars Sinai Med. Ctr., 1999—2001. Dir., genomics program, 2002—. Avocation: music. Office: Cedars Sinai Medical Center 8700 Beverly Blvd D5005 Los Angeles CA 90048

HOFRICHTER, DAVID ALAN, management consultant; b. Lakewood, Ohio, July 10, 1948; s. David Christian and Virginia Amelia (Rickley) H.; m. Carol Ann Rybak, May 15, 1971; children: Kristin Ann., Matthew David. BA, Baldwin-Wallace Coll., 1970; MA, Duquesne U., 1972, PhD, 1976. Assoc. Hay Group, Inc., Pitts., 1977—78, prin., 1978—80, dir. orgn. and manpower svc., 1980—81, gen. mgr. Cin., 1981—89, ptnr., gen. mgr., 1983—85, v.p., gen. mgr., 1985—86, sr. v.p., gen. mgr. Chgo., 1986—89, v.p., regional mgr., 1989—90, v.p., mng. dir., 1990—94, v.p., mng. dir. global account mgmt. and midwest ops., 1994-98; sr. v.p., mng. dir. U.S. Bus. Devel., 1998—99, global mng. dir. e-bus., 1999; ptnr. in charge midwest consulting Pricewaterhouse Coopers, Chgo., 1999—2001, ptnr., nat. practice dir., 2001—02; nat. practice dir., prin. Buck Cons. (a Mellon Cons. Co.), 2002—03; mng. dir. Mellon Human Resource and Investor Solutions Mellon Fin. Corp., 2003—. Ptnrs. mgmt. com. Hay Group, Inc., 1990—, bd. dirs.; bd. dirs. Nat. Health Care Practice, Chgo.; lectr. Hay Compensation Confs.; spkr. Conf. Bd. Fortune Mag. Conf., 1996. Author: Executive Compensation in Health Care, 1986, Selecting People Who Can Implement Strategy, 1989, Reinforcing Organizational and Individual Competencies Through Compensation, 1992, Broad Banding: Fit or Fad, 1993, The Changing Nature of Work and Organization, 1993, People, Performance, and Pay, 1996, Secrets of the Rich and Famous, 1999, How to Survive the Invasion of the E-People, 2000, People, Competencies and Performance, 2001, Dreaming About Performance, 2001, Managing Compensation in Uncertain Times: A Total Performance System, 2002. Named Top 25 Cons. in World, Consuting Mag., 2003. Mem. Am. Psychol. Assn., Am. Soc. Cons. Mgmt. Engrs., Fin. Planning Assn. for City Chgo., Pa. Psychol. Assn., Nat. Register Health Svc. Providers in Psychology, Chgo. Exec. Club, Ruth Lake Country Club (Hindsdale, Ill., officer), Oak Brook (Ill.) Polo Club. Republican. Roman Catholic. Avocations: golf, swimming, flying, tennis, shooting. Home: 60 Derby Ct Oak Brook IL 60523-2650 Office: Buck Cons (Mellon) One N Dearborn St Chicago IL 60602 E-mail: dhofrichte@aol.co.

HOFSOMMER, DONOVAN LOWELL, history educator; b. Ft. Dodge, Iowa, Apr. 10, 1938; s. Vernie George and Helma J. (Schager) H.; m. Sandra Louise Rusch, June 13, 1965; children: Kathryn Anne, Kristine Beret, Knute Lars. BA, U. Northern Iowa, 1960, MA, 1966; PhD, Okla. State U., 1973. Tchr. Fairfield (Iowa) High Sch., 1961-65; instr. U. Northern Iowa, Cedar Falls, 1965-66, Lea Coll., Albert Lea, Minn., 1966-70; teaching asst. Okla. State U., Stillwater, 1970-73; assoc. prof. and dept. head Wayland Coll., Plainview, Tex., 1973-81; corp. historian So. Pacific Co., San Francisco, 1981-85; hist. cons. Burlington No. Inc., Seattle, 1985-87; vis. prof. U. Mont., Missula, 1986-87; exec. dir. ctr. Western studies Augustana Coll., Sioux Falls, S.D., 1987-89; prof. history St. Cloud (Minn.) State U., 1989—. Cons. Dyanelectron and Dynarail, Pueblo, Colo., 1979-81, Grand Trunk Corp., Detroit, 1988-95; mem. editl. bd. annals of Iowa, Iowa City, 1975-94, R.R. history, Akron, Ohio, 1975—. Author: Prairie Oasis, 1975, Katy Northwest, 1976, Southern Pacific 1901-1985, 1986; co-author: History of Great Northern Railway, 1988, Quanah Route, 1991, Grand Trunk Corp., 1995; editor: Lexington Group Transport History, 1975—; mem. editl. bd. Annals of Iowa, Iowa City, 1975-92, R.R. History, Akron, Ohio, 1975—. With U.S. Army, 1960-66. Mem. Okla. Hist. Soc. (Wright Heritage award 1979), Ry. and Locomotive Hist. Soc. (Book award 1988, Sr. Achievement award 1995), Western History Assn., Orgn. Am. Historians, State Hist. Soc. Iowa, Am. Assn. for State and Local History. Presbyterian. Home: 1803 13th Ave SE Saint Cloud MN 56304-2231 Office: St Cloud State U Dept History Saint Cloud MN 56301

HOFSTEAD, JAMES WARNER, laundry machinery company executive, lawyer; b. Jackson, Tenn., Feb. 3, 1913; s. Harry Oliver and Agnes Lucile (Blackard) H.; m. Ellen Frances Bowers, Dec. 27, 1940 (dec.); 1 child, Eda Lucile. AB, Vanderbilt U., 1935, LLB, 1938. Bar: Tenn. Pvt. practice law; v.p., bd. dirs. United Tel. Co., Nashville, 1969—, emeritus; ret.; pres., bd. dirs. Wishy Washy, Inc., Nashville, 1946—, Wishy Sales Inc., Nashville, 1959—, pres. emeritus. Capt. USMC, 1942-45. Mem. SAR (nat. committeeman, state pres. emeritus, nat. trustee), SCV, Vanderbilt Bar Assn. (pres. emeritus), So. Srs. Golf Assn., Soc. of Cincinnati, English Spkg. Union (chmn.), Soc. Colonial Wars (past gov. Tenn., past dep. gov. gen.), Nashville C. of C., Belle Meade Country Club, 200 Club, Exch. Club, Eccentric Club (London), Gasparilla 48 Club, Cumberland Club (charter), Sigma Chi. Home: 504 Elmington # 406 Nashville TN 37205 Office: 3729 Charlotte Pike Nashville TN 37209-3734

HOFSTRA, WARREN RAYMOND, historian, educator; b. New York, NY, May 12, 1947; s. Raymond Hofstra and Myrtle Florence Anderson; m. Mary Theresa DiGiorgio, June 3, 1979; children: Andrew Raymond, Kate Eileen. BA, Wash. U., 1965—69; MA, Boston U., 1971—74; PhD, U. of Va., 1977—85. Asst. prof. of history Shenandoah U., Winchester, Va., 1985—90, assoc. prof. of history, 1990—95, Stewart Bell Prof. of History, 1995—, dir. of cmty. history project, 1986—. Author: (boo) The Planting of New Virginia: Shenandoah Valley Landscapes, 1700-1800, (book) A Separate Place: The Formation of Clarke County, Virginia; editor: George Washington and the Virginia Backcountry; editor: (coeditor) After the Backcountry: Rural Life in the Great Valley of Virginia, 1800-1900, Virginia Reconsidered: New Histories of the Old Dominion; mem. editl. bd. The Papers of George Wash., 2003. Rev. bd. Va. Dept. of Hist. Resources, 1999; chmn. rev. bd. Va. Dept. of Hist., Richmond, Va., 2003—; Mellon fellow Va. Hist. Soc. Fellow Rsch. fellowship, Nat. Endowment for the Humanities, 1995, Mednick fellowship, Found. for Ind. Colleges, 1991, Rsch. fellowship, Mus. of Early So. Decorative Arts, 1991, Resident fellowship, Va. Found. for the Humanities and Pub. Policy, 1988. Mem.: So. Hist. Assn., Orgn. of Am. Historians, Am. Hist. Assn. Democrat-. Protestant. Achievements include founder and director of Community History Project of Shenandoah University. Avocations: furniture making, outdoor sports, reading. Home: 506 West Leicester Winchester VA 22602 Office: Shenandoah University 1460 University Dr Winchester VA 22601 Home Fax: 546-665-4644; Office Fax: 540-665-4644. E-mail: whofstra@su.edu.

HOGAN, BRIAN JOSEPH, editor; b. Aberdeen, S.D., Apr. 11, 1943; s. Arthur James and Magdalena (Frison) H.; m. Jamie Isabelle Schwingel, June 21, 1987. BS in Aerospace and Mech. Engring., U. Ariz., 1965, BS in Geophysics-Geochemistry, 1968; MS in Journalism, U. Utah, 1972. Rsch. asst. U. Va. Rsch. Labs for Engring. Scis., Charlottesville, 1965-66; exploration geophysicist Anaconda Co., Tucson, 1968-71; assoc. editor Benwill Pub. Co., Brookline, Mass., 1973-74; asst. editor Design News, Boston, 1974-75, midwest editor Chgo., 1975-87, sr. editor Newton, Mass., 1987-89, mng. editor, 1989-97; chief editor Mfg. Engring.-Soc. Mfg. Engrs., Dearborn, Mich. Author stage plays The Young O'Neil, 1983, Awakening, 1984. Precinct worker Cook County Rep. Com., Oak Park, Ill., 1986-87; interpreter Frank Lloyd Wright Home and Studio Found., Oak Park, 1981-87. Recipient numerous awards Am. Soc. Bus. Press Editors, Soc. Tech. Communication, Aviation Space Writers Assn. Mem. Am. Soc. Bus. Press Editors, Am. Hist. Print Collectors Soc. Republican. Roman Catholic. Avocations: photography, print collecting, cycling, hiking. Office: Mfg Engring 1 SME Dr PO Box 930 Dearborn MI 48121-0930 E-mail: hogabri@sme.org.

HOGAN, CLARENCE LESTER, retired electronics executive; b. Great Falls, Mont., Feb. 8, 1920; s. Clarence Lester and Bessie (Young) H.; m. Audrey Biery Peters, Oct. 13, 1946; 1 child, Cheryl Lea. BSChemE, Mont. State U., 1942, Dr. Engring. (hon.), 1967; MS in Physics, Lehigh U., 1947, PhD in Physics, 1950, D in Engring. (hon.), 1971; AM (hon.), Harvard U., 1954; Doctorate (hon.), Mont. State U., 1968; D in Sci. (hon.), Worcester Poly. U., 1969. Rsch. chem. engr. Anaconda Copper Mining Co., 1942-43; instr. physics Lehigh U., 1946-50; mem. tech. staff Bell Labs., Murray Hill, N.J., 1950-51, sub-dept. head, 1951-53; assoc. prof. Harvard U., Cambridge, Mass., 1953-57, Gordon McKay prof., 1957-58; gen. mgr. semi-conductor products divsn. Motorola, Inc., Phoenix, 1958-60, v.p., 1960-66, exec. v.p., dir., 1966-68; pres., CEO Fairchild Semicondr. (formerly Fairchild Instruments), Mt. View, Calif., 1968—74, vice chmn. bd. dirs., 1974-85. Gen. chmn. Internat. Conf. on Magnetism and Magnetic Materials, 1959, 60; mem. materials adv. bd. Dept. Def., 1957-59; mem. adv. coun. dept. electrical engring. Princeton U.; mem. adv. bd. sch. engring. U. Calif., Berkeley, 1974—, adv. bd. dept. chem. engring. Mont. State U., 1988—; mem. nat. adv. bd. Desert Rsch. Inst., 1976-80; mem. vis. com. dept. electric engring. and computer sci. MIT, 1975-85; mem. adv. coun. div. electrical engring. Stanford U., 1976-86; mem. sci. and ednl. adv. com. Lawrence Berkeley Lab., 1978-84; mem. Pres.'s Export Coun., 1976-80; mem. adv. panel to tech. adv. bd. U.S. Congress, 1976-80. Patentee in field; inventor microwave gyrator, circulator, isolator. Chmn. Commn. Found. Santa Clara County, Calif., 1983-85; mem. vis. com. Lehigh U., 1966-71, trustee, 1971-80, also life trustee; trustee Western Electronic Edn. Fund; mem. governing bd. Maricopa County Jr. Coll.; bd. regents U. Santa Clara. Lt. (j.g.) USNR, 1942-46. Recipient Community Svc. award NCCJ, 1978, Medal of Merit Am. Electronics Assn., 1978, Berkeley Citation U. Calif., 1980; named Bay Area Bus. Man of Yr. San Jose State U., 1978, One of 10 Greatest Innovators in Past 50 Yrs. Electronics Mag., 1980. Fellow AAAS, IEEE (Frederick Philips gold medal 1976, Edison silver medal Cleve. Soc. 1978, Pioneering medal for microwave theory and tech. 1993), Inst. Elec. Engrs. (hon.); mem. NAE, Am. Phys. Soc., Menlo Country Club, Masons, Sigma Xi, Tau Beta Pi, Phi Kappa Phi, Eta Kappa Nu, Kappa Sigma. Democrat. Baptist. Avocations: woodworking, computer programming. Home: 36 Barry Ln Atherton CA 94027-4023

HOGAN, CURTIS JULE, union executive, industrial relations consultant; b. Greeley, Kans., July 25, 1926; s. Charles Leo and Anna Malene (Rousselle) H.; m. Lois Jean Ecord, Apr. 23, 1955; children: Christopher James, Michael Sean, Patrick Marshall, Kathleen Marie, Kerry Joseph. BS in Indsl. Rels., Rockhurst Coll., 1950; postgrad., Georgetown U., 1955, U. Tehran, Iran, 1955-57. With Gt. Lakes Pipeline Co., Kansas City, Mo., 1950-55; with Internat. Fedn. Petroleum and Chem. Workers, Denver, 1955-85, gen. sec., 1973-85; pres. Internat. Labor Rels. Svcs., Inc., 1976—. Cons. in field; lectr. Rockhurst Coll., Kansas City, 1951-52. Contbr. articles to profl. publs. Served with U.S. Army, 1945-46. Mem. Internat. Indsl. Rels. Assn., Indsl. Rels. Rsch. Assn., Oil Chem. and Atomic Workers Internat. Union. Office: Internat Fed Petroleum Chem Workers 435 S Newport Way Denver CO 80224-1321

HOGAN, DONNA HELEN, school librarian, educator; b. Dallas, Apr. 21, 1937; d. Donald William Ross and Lillian Ethel Andrews; m. Jerry Don Hogan, June 11, 1960 (div. Jan. 29, 1986); children: Laura, Leslie, Donald. BA, U. Tulsa, 1959; MLIS, U. Okla., Norman, 1990. Cert. secondary edn. tchg. Okla., 1965. Tchr. French, Eng. Midwest City Pub. Schs., Okla., 1965—67; tchr. French Lexington Pub. Sch., Okla., 1971—72; owner Hogan's Carpets, Purcell, Okla., 1976—86; staff asst. Bilingual Edn. Multifunctional Resource Ctr., U. Okla., Norman, 1987—90; libr. Met. Libr. Sys., Oklahoma City, 1990—93, U. Ala. Librs., Tuscaloosa, 1993—98; asst. dir. pub. svcs. U. Tex. at San Antonio Libr., 1998—. Guest spkr., libr. U. Ala., Tuscaloosa, 1994—97; 2d v.p. Oklahoma Libr. Assn., Oklahoma City, 1975—93; com. chair Ala. Libr. Assn., Birmingham, 1993—98. Contbr. articles to profl. jours. Treas. Norman Cmty. Choral Soc., Norman, 1981—90; pres. Tuscaloosa Cmty. Choral Soc., 1993—98; trustee, chair Pioneer Multi-County Libr. Bd., Norman, 1975—83; pres. Friends of Librs. in Okla., Oklahoma City, 1980—82. Recipient Scholarship, Oklahoma Libr. Assn., 1988. Mem.: AAUW (Past Pres., Purcell Branch), ALA (com. chair New Mems. Roundtable 1990—2000, pres.'s program chair Reference and User Svcs. Assn. 1992—, chair mgrs. 1998—2000), Am. Soc. Engring. Edn. (mem. engring. libr. divsn.), San Antonio Choral Soc., Beta Phi Mu. Methodist. Avocations: travel, hiking, homemaking arts. Office: U Tex San Antonio Libr 6900 N Loop 1604 West San Antonio TX 78249 Office Fax: 210-458-4884. Business E-Mail: dhogan@utsa.edu.

HOGAN, EDWARD ROBERT, financial services executive; b. Yonkers, N.Y., Mar. 21, 1939; s. John J. and Blanche (Corradi) H.; m. Linda Carroll, Sept. 25, 1959 (div. Oct. 1975); children: Linda Hogan Benya, Edward R. Jr., Barbara Hogan Comblo; m. Sandra Lesperance, Sept. 17, 1993. Dist. mgr. New Eng. Life, Thornwood, N.Y., 1962-64; pres. Profl. Employment Svcs., Scarsdale, N.Y., 1964-66, Royal Transport & Distbn. Inc., Yonkers, N.Y., 1966-71; v.p. Fin. Ins. Group, N.Y.C., 1971-74, Franklin United Life Ins. Co., Garden City, N.Y., 1974-79; sr. v.p. Adv. Svcs. Corp., White Plains, N.Y., 1979-83; pres. Faculty Svcs. Corp., Wappingers Falls, N.Y., 1983—, FSC Adminstrv. Svcs. Corp., Wappingers Falls, N.Y., 1986—. Registered prin. Cadaret, Grant & Co., Inc., Syracuse, N.Y., 1989—. Pres. Yonkers Young Rep. Orgn., 1960-64; v.p. Westchester County Young Reps., White Plains, 1961-63; candidate 1st Assembly Dist. State Assembly, Yonkers, 1962; Westchester County campaign dir. U.S. Sen. James L. Buckley, 1968. With USN, 1957-59. Mem. Nat. Tax Shelter Annuity Assn. Avocations: boating, flying, skiing. Office: Faculty Svcs Corp PO Box 1635 Wappingers Falls NY 12590-8635

HOGAN, ELWOOD, lawyer; b. Augusta, Ga., Mar. 4, 1929; s. William Elwood and Geneva Isabell H.; m. Myrtle Elizabeth McCall, June 15, 1957; children: Martha Elizabeth Ondrejca, Darrell William Hogan. BBA, U. Ga., 1954; JD, Stetson U., 1958. Bar: Fla. 1958, U.S. Ct. Appeals (6th circuit) Fla. 1958, U.S. Dist. Ct. Fla. 1959, U.S. Ct. Appeals (11th circuit) 1959, U.S. Tax Ct. 1965, U.S. Supreme Ct. 1973; cert. circuit ct. mediator. Assoc. Wolfe & Bonner Attys., Clearwater, Fla., 1958-63; ptnr. Wolfe, Bonner & Hogan, Clearwater, 1964-75; pres. Bonner & Hogan P.A., Clearwater, 1985—99, McFarland, Gould, Lyons, Sullivan, Perenich & Hogan, P.A., Clearwater, 2000—. Prosecutor Mcpl. Ct., Clearwater, 1966-68, judge, 1968-74; bd. trustees Morton Plant Hosp., Clearwater, 1981-86, chmn., 1984-86; pres. Fla. Mcpl. Judges Assn., 1972; Fla. Circuit Ct. mediator. Vice chmn. Clearwater Hist. Com., 1974; mem. Clearwater Hist. Soc.; past mem. adv. bd. Clearwater (Fla.) Salvation Army; deacon Calvary Bapt. Ch., 1958—; founder The Presential Prayer Team, 2001; past bd. dirs. Girls Clubs Pinellas County, Inc. Recipient Businessman of Yr. award, Fla. Rep. Com. Bus. Adv. Coun., 2003. Mem. ABA, Fla. Acad. Profl. Mediators, Kiwanis Club (dist. gov. Fla. dist. 1979-80), Clearwater Bar Assn. (pres. 1972-73), Phi Alpha Delta (life). Avocations: swimming, tennis, fishing. Office: McFarland Gould Lyons Sullivan Perenich & Hogan 311 S Missouri Ave Clearwater FL 33756-5833 E-mail: ehogan@mglsplaw.com.

HOGAN, HOWARD, statistician, educator; s. Ollen and Mary Hogan; m. Christine Brim; children: Tara, Brenna. BA, Pomona Coll., 1971; Cert. in Econs., Stockholm U., 1972; MPA, Princeton U., 1974, MA, PhD, Princeton U., 1976. Chief decennial statis. methods and programming divsn. U.S. Census Bur., Washington, 1998—2001, chief econ. statis. methods and programming divsn., 2002—. Professorial lectr. dept. stats. George Washington U., Washington. Fellow: Am. Statis. Assn. Office: ESMPD US Census Bureau Washington DC 20233

HOGAN, ILONA MODLY, lawyer; b. Erlangen, Fed. Republic of Germany, Nov. 23, 1947; arrived in U.S., 1951, naturalized, 1960; d. Stephen Bela and Gunda Pauline (Gastiger) Modly; m. Lawrence J. Hogan, Mar. 16, 1974; children: Matthew Lawrence, Michael Alexander, Patrick Nicholas, Timothy Stefan. Student, Marymount Coll., 1965-67; AB in Internat. Affairs, George Washington U., 1969; JD, Georgetown U., 1974. Bar: D.C. 1975, Md. 1975. Intern and clk. AID, 1965-69; adminstrv. and legis. asst. to mem. Ho. of Reps., 1969-72; editor Legis. Digest, Ho. of Reps., Washington, 1972-73; asso. and law clk. firm Trammell, Rand, Nathan and Lincoln, Washington, 1972-74; mng. ptnr. firm Hogan and Hogan, Washington and Md., 1974-93; of counsel Venable, Baetjer, Howard & Civiletti, Washington, 1989-91; pres. Amcom Inc., 1978—; of counsel Salisbury & McLister, Frederick, Md., 1993-2001; global mgr. Bechtel Telecom., 2001—. Mem. Prince George's Bd. Libr. Trustees, Md., 1976—78, Prince George's County Econ. Devel. Adv. Com., 1979—82; v.p. St. John's Sch. Bd., 1987—88, pres., 1989; treas. U. Md. Bd. Regents, 1988—95; trustee St. James Sch., 1989—90; mem. Lawyers Steering com. for Reagan-Bush, 1980; nat. vice-chmn. Assn. Execs. for Reagan-Bush, 1984; mem. bus. and industry adv. com. 50th Am. Presdl. Inaugural, 1985; mem. Md. steering com. Bush for Pres., 1988; mem. Presdl. Personnel Adv. Com., 1989, Gov.'s Higher Edn. Transition Team, 1988; elected mem. County Commrs. Frederick County, 1994—2001; Frederick County co-chair Bush-Cheney Campaign, 2000; bd. advisors Frostburg State U., 2001—03; trustee Frederick C.C. Found., 2001—03, Md. Higher Edn. Commn., 2003—. Mem.: ABA, D.C. Bar, Md. Bar Assn. Republican. Roman Catholic. Home: 5614 New Design Rd Frederick MD 21703-8306 Office: 5275 Westview Dr Frederick MD 21703-8306 E-mail: ilonahogan@aol.com., imhogan@bechtel.com.

HOGAN, JAMES CARROLL, JR., public health administrator, research biologist; b. Milledgeville, Ga., Jan. 3, 1939; s. James C. and Leanna (Johnson) H.; m. Izola Stinson, Nov. 29, 1959; children: Pamela Renita, Gregory Karl, Jeffrey Darryl. BS, Albany State Coll., 1961; MS, Atlanta U., 1968; PhD, Brown U., 1972; postdoc. fellow, Yale U. Biology Dept., 1972-73. Rsch. assoc. Yale U. Sch. Medicine, New Haven, 1973-76; asst. prof. anatomy Howard U. Sch. Medicine, Washington, 1976-78; assoc. prof. U. Conn., Storrs, 1978-83; dir. minority student affairs U. Conn. Health Ctr., Farmington, 1983-87; chief clin. chemistry and hematology Conn. Dept. Health Svcs., Hartford, 1991—95, chief, dir. biochemistry and environ. chemistry, 1997—. Mem. Cmty. Svcs. Commn. and Bd. of Edn., 1994—, North Haven, Conn., 1989—; bd. dirs. Greater New Haven State Tchrs. Coll., 1989—, A Better Chance, Glastonbury, Conn., 1990—, Hartford (Conn.) Alliance for Sci. and Math. Edn., adv. com. Math. Connections. Contbr. articles to Jour. Ultrastructural Rsch., Jour. Protozoology, Jour. Embryology and Exptl. Morphology, Jour. Cell Biology, Jour. Nat. Tech. Assn., Jour. Pediatrics. Founder, pres. North Haven Assn. Black Citizens, 1988—, Chpt. Nat. Tech. Assn., 1990; coord. Martin Luther King Jr. annual luncheon Dept. Pub. Health, Conn., 1988—; active Dem. Town Com., North Haven, 1989—; com. chmn. Greater New Haven chpt. NAACP; mem. Bd. Edn., North Haven, 1993—. Josiah Macy Found. fellow, Marine Biol. Labs., 1978-80, Ford Found. postdoctoral fellow Marine Biol. Labs., 1980-81; vis. faculty fellow Yale U., 1984—. Mem. NAACP (life), Am. Pub. Health Assn., Conn. Pub. Health Assn., Conn. Acad. Sci. and Engring., New Eng. Pub. Health Assn., Am. Chem. Soc., Am. Soc. Cell Biology (Conn. chpt. pres.), Nat. Tech. Assn. (bd. dirs. Conn. chpt.), N.Y. Acad. Scis., Planetary Soc., Morehouse Coll. Nat. Alumni Assn. (life), Immanuel Bapt. Ch. Mens Club (pres. 1998—), Sigma Xi, Omega Psi Phi. Baptist. Achievements include first confirmation of Antigenic variation in Trypanosomes using the electron microscope, first confirmation of cytoplasmic markers in sex cells of killifishes using the electron microscope. Home: 51 Pool Rd PO Box 146 North Haven CT 06473-0146 E-mail: james.hogan@po.state.ct.us.

HOGAN, JEREMY ROBERT, photojournalist; b. Porterville, Calif., Sept. 3, 1972; s. Jerry Wayne Hogan and Kathleen Marie Dodd. BS in Journalism, San Jose State U., 1997. Staff photographer Bloomington (Ind.) Herald-Times, 1997—. Recipient Photo of the Yr. award Hoosier State Press Assn., 1998. Mem. Nat. Press Photographers Assn., Ind. Press Photographers Assn. Avocations: traveling, writing, reading, astrophotography, bicycling. Office: 1900 S Walnut St Bloomington IN 47401-7720 E-mail: Hoganj8@aol.com.

HOGAN, JOHN DONALD, retired college dean, finance educator; b. Binghamton, N.Y., July 16, 1927; s. John D. and Edith J. (Hennessy) H.; m. Anna Craig, Nov. 26, 1976; children: Thomas P., James E. AB, Syracuse U., 1949, MA, 1950, PhD, 1952. Registered prin. Nat. Assn. Securities Dealers. Prof. econs., chmn. dept. Bates Coll., Lewiston, Maine, 1953-58; dir. edn. fin. research State of N.Y., 1959, chief mcpl. fin., 1960; staff economist, dir. research Northwestern Mut. Life Ins. Co., Milw., 1960-68; v.p. Nationwide Ins. Cos., Columbus, Ohio, 1968-76; dean Sch. Bus. Adminstrn. Central Mich. U., Mt. Pleasant, 1976-79; v.p. Am. Productivity Ctr., Houston, 1979-80; pres., chmn., chief exec. officer Variable Annuity Life Ins. Co., Houston, 1980-83; sr. v.p. Am. Gen. Corp., Houston, 1983-86; dean, prof. fin. Coll. Commerce U. Ill., Champaign, 1986-91; dean, prof. fin. and econs. Coll. Bus. Adminstrn. Ga. State U., Atlanta, 1991-97, prof. fin. and econs., 1998—2001, dean and prof. emeritus, 2002—. Bd. dirs. Sinfonia da Camera, Champaign, Ga. Coun. on Econ. Edn., Pvt. Industry Coun., World Trade Ctr., Atlanta; vis. prof. fin. Poznan (Poland) U. Econs., Caucasus Sch. Bus., Tbilisi, Georgia; cons. in field. Author: American Social Legislation, 1965, U.S. Balance of Payments and Capital Flows, 1967, School Revenue Studies, 1959, Fiscal Capacity of the State of Maine, 1958, American Social Legislation, 1973; editor: Dimensions of Productivity Research (2 vols.), 1981; contbr. articles to jours., abstracts to profl. meetings. Bd. dirs. Goodwill Industries, Columbus, 1972-76, chmn. capital fund drive, 1974-75; mem. Houston Com. on Fgn. Rels., 1980—, Chgo. Coun. on Fgn. Rels., 1986—, Chgo. com., 1987—. Served with U.S. Army, 1944-46, ETO; capt. (ret.) USAR. Maxwell fellow Syracuse U., 1950-52; recipient Best Article award Jur. Risk and Ins., Alumni Appreciation award U. Ill., 1991, 1964, Medal of Merit Poznan U., Poland, 1999; Maxwell Centennial lectr. Maxwell Grad. Sch., Syracuse U., 1970. Mem.: Inst. Rsch. in Econs. of Taxation (dir. 1984—), Nat. Tax Assn. (dir. 1981—85, treas., exec. com. 1988—2001), Nat. Assn. Bus. Economists, Inst. Mgmt. Scis., Am. Econ. Assn., Acad. Mgmt., Columbus C. of C. (chmn. econ. policy com. 1972—76), World Trade Club (Atlanta, bd. dirs. 1993—99), Columbus Athletic Club, Heritage Club (Houston), Commerce Club (Atlanta), Lincolnshire Fields Country Club (Champaign), Univ. Club (Chgo.), Beta Gamma Sigma, Phi Kappa Phi. Office: Ga State U Coll Bus Adminstrn 3892 Byrnwyck Pl NE Atlanta GA 30319

HOGAN, JOHN PAUL, chemistry researcher, consultant; b. Lowes, Kentucky, Aug. 7, 1919; s. Charles F. and Alma (Wyman) H.; m. Glenda M. (Moultrie), 1943; children: E. Fay, Hogan Sweney, Kenneth B., Susan G., Hogan Lair. Attended, U. Redlands, 1940-41; BS in Chemistry and physics, Murray State U., 1942, ScD (hon.), 1971. Tchr. Mayfield High Sch., Ky., 1942-43; physics instr. Okla. State U., Stillwater, 1943-44; rsch. chemist Phillips Petroleum Co., Bartlesville, Okla., 1944-48, group leader, 1948-60, polymer sci. sect. mgr., 1960-77, polymer sci. sr. research assoc., 1977-85, cons., 1985-86, Bartlesville, Okla., 1986—. Chmn. N.E. Okla. sect. Am. Chem. Soc., 1970. Patentee in field; contbg. chapters to books. Recipient Creative Invention Award, Am. Chem. Soc., 1969; Pioneer Chemists Award, 1972; Perkin medal, Soc. Chem. Industry, 1987; Heros in Chemistry Award Am. Chem. Soc., 1998; named Disting. Alumnus, Murray State U., 1972; Inventor of Yr., Okla. Bar Assn. Copyright and Patent Sect., 1976; Polymeric Materials Man of Yr., Soc. Plastics Engr., 1981; Paul Harris fellow Rotary Found., 2000; named to Hon. Order of Ky. Col., 1972; inductee Nat. Inventor Hall of Fame, 2001, Okla. Inventors Hall of Fame, 2002. Fellow Am. Inst. Chemists. Republican. Baptist. Avocations: Ch. work, fly fishing, chess, gardening. Home: 1049 S E Greystone Ave Bartlesville OK 74006-5010

HOGAN, JOHN PAUL, consumer products company executive; b. Mpls., Jan. 13, 1947; s. Bernard Edward and Jeannette Margaret (McGraw) Hogan; m. Marcia Ellen Newcomb, July 11, 1970. AB cum laude, St. Louis U., 1969; MA in Art, U. Iowa, 1988, MFA in Art, 1990. Founder Tecton-Fabricator, Williamsburg, Iowa, 1975—. Exhibitions include Des Moines Art Ctr. Achievements include patents for various structural systems, ranging from toy blocks to the original modular space station, employing a space shuttle as the delivery system. Home: PO Box 809 Williamsburg IA 52361-0809 Office: Tecton-Fabricator 600 Elm St Williamsburg IA 52361-0809

HOGAN, KATIE J. English educator, women's studies researcher; d. Andrew J. and Norma (Bennett) Hogan; life ptnr. BBA, Western Case State U., 1983; MA, Northeastern U., 1987; PhD, Rutgers U., New Brunswick, 1997. Adj. instr., tchg. asst. English & Women's Studies Rutgers U., New Brunswick, NJ, 1991—97; assoc. prof. English LaGuardia Cmty. Coll./City U. N.Y., Long Island City, 1997—. Panel mem. City U. N.Y. Rsch. Found. Women's Studies Panel, N.Y.C., 1999—. Editor: (book) Gendered Epidemic, 1998; author: Women Take Care: Gender Race, 2001. Faculty mem. Student Ctr. for Women, LaGuardia CCI CUNY, 2000—. Recipient PSC-CUNY rsch. awards, Rsch. Found., CUNY, 1999, 2002. Mem.: Mid-Atlantic Pop Culture Assn. (panel chair 2003), Nat. Women's Studies Assn. Democrat. Avocations: yoga, hiking, puzzles, films, playing with dog.

HOGAN, KEMPF, lawyer; b. East Grand Rapids, Mich., May 11, 1939; s. Romain Grammel and Helen Maude (Kempf) H.; BBA, U. Mich., 1961; MBA with distinction, 1965; JD, 1966; postgrad. Harvard U., 1962. Security analyst Comerica Bank-Detroit, 1961-62; tax analyst Standard Oil Co. of N.J., N.Y.C., 1964; admitted to Mich. bar, 1967; assoc. firm Poole Littell & Sutherland, Detroit, 1967-71, partner, 1971-76; partner firm Butzel, Long, Gust, Klein & Van Zile, P.C., 1976-81, stockholder, 1982—; former mem. trust and trust investment com. Mich. Nat. Bank Detroit. Bd. dirs., founders jr. council Detroit Inst. Arts, 1971-78, mem. adv. bd., 1979—, patron and benefactor; active Friends of U. Mich. Mus. Art; friend Birmingham-Bloomfield Art Assn., Cranbrook Acad. Art Mus., Detroit Artists Market, Inc.; bd. dirs. Meadow Brook Art Gallery Oakland U.; bd. dirs., v.p. Friends of Modern Art Detroit Inst. Arts; past bd. dirs. The Children's Center, Planned Parenthood League, Inc., Readings for the Blind, Inc. Mem. State Bar Mich., Am., Detroit Bar Assn., Oakland County Bar, Am. Judicature Soc., Phi Kappa Phi, Beta Gamma Sigma, Beta Alpha Psi, Beta Theta Pi, Phi Delta Phi. Presbyterian. Clubs: Harvard (Detroit); Bloomfield Hills Country. Home: Piety Hill Place # 307 600 W Brown St Birmingham MI 48009 Office: 32270 Telegraph Rd Ste 200 Franklin MI 48025-2457

HOGAN, KENNETH JAMES, lawyer; b. Chgo., Apr. 22, 1970; s. James Kenneth and Marlene Ann (Beaman) H.; m. Melanie Sue Niles; 1 child, Maximillian Seamus. BA, U. Ill., Urbana, 1992; JD, U. Ill., Champaign, 1995. Bar: Ill. 1995, U.S. Dist. Ct. (no. dist.) Ill. 1995. Legal advisor, hearing officer dept. adminstrv. hearings Office of Ill. Sec. of State, Joliet, Ill., 1996-98; staff atty. rsch. dept. Appellate Ct. of Ill. 3d Dist., Ottawa, Ill., 1998-99, appellate law clk. Justice Kent Slater Macomb, Ill., 1999-2001; asst. pub. guardian Office of Cook County Pub. Guardian, Chgo., 2001—03; assoc. Stellato & Schwartz, Ltd., Chgo., 2003—. Asst. to committeeman Orland Twp. Rep. Orgn., Orland Park, Ill., 1996-98; chmn. Ind. Leadership 2000, Orland Park, 1997. Republican. Roman Catholic. Home: 425 Sherwood Rd #2 La Grange Park IL 60526 Office: Stellato & Schwartz Ltd 120 N LaSalle St Ste 3400 Chicago IL 60602 E-mail: khogan@stellatoschwartz.com.

HOGAN, MARTHA A. academic administrator, educator; d. Forrest R. and Eleanor Foster; m. James W. Hogan, Feb. 28, 1970; children: Bryan, Kevin. BS, Iowa State U., 1970; MS, U. of Tex., 1978. Faculty math. Tyler Jr. Coll., Tex., 1982—87, dir. computer learning svcs., 1987—92; grad. asst. U. of Ga., Athens, 1993—95; is/lan support mgr. Richland Coll., Dallas, 1997—2000, dean edn. and adminstrv. tech., 2000—. Chair, vice chair of bd. First Christian Ch., Allen, Tex., 2002—03; bd. mem. working connections faculty devel. inst. Educator to Educator, Nat. Workforce Ctr. for Emerging Technologies, Bellevue, Wash., 2002—03. Avocations: digital photography, travel, reading, gardening. Personal E-mail: mahogan@att.net.

HOGAN, MARY BETH, medical educator; b. Elizabeth, N.J., Sept. 10, 1963; BS, John Carroll U., 1985; MD, U. Cin., 1989. Resident pediat. Ohio State U., Columbus, 1989-92; fellow allergy and immunology Northwestern U., Chgo., 1992-94, asst. prof., 1994—2001, assoc. prof., 2001—; asst. prof. W.Va. U., Morgantown, 1995—2001. Contbr. chpts. to books and articles to profl. jours. Fellow Am. Acad. Pediat., Am. Acad. Allergy, Asthma and Immunology; mem. Am. Coll. Allergy, Asthma and Immunology. Office: WVa U Sch Medicine PO Box 9214 Morgantown WV 26506-9214

HOGAN, MICHAEL RAY, life science executive; b. Newark, Ohio, Apr. 21, 1953; s. Raymond Carl and Mary Adele (Whalen) H.; m. Martha Ann Gorman, July 24, 1976; children: Colleen Michael, Patrick Gorman, Mary Kate, Andrei Sean. BA, Loyola U., Chgo., 1978; M in Mgmt. with distinction, Northwestern U., 1980. Cert. FLMI, HIA. Assoc. McKinsey & Co., Inc., Chgo., 1980-81, engagement mgr., 1982-83; sr. v.p., treas. FBS Ins. Co., Mpls., 1984-85; group v.p., gen. mgr. Gen. Am. Life Ins. Co., St. Louis, 1986, v.p., 1987-89, exec. v.p., 1990-95; pres., CEO Cova Corp., St. Louis, 1995-96; corp. v.p., controller Monsanto Co., St. Louis, 1996-99; v.p., CFO, CAO Sigma-Aldrich Corp., 1999—. Cons. Swedish Trade Commn., Chgo., 1978, Lee Wards Creative Crafts Co., Elgin, Ill., 1979; chmn. Consultec, Inc., Atlanta, 1990-95, Cova Fin. Life Ins. Co., Oakbrook Terrace, 1995; chmn., CEO Genelco, Inc., St. Louis, 1990-95; mem. adv. bd. Integrated Hlth Svcs. Managed Care, Owings Mills, Md., 1994-2002; pres. GenCare Hlth Sys., Inc., 1990-95; bd. dirs. Allegiant Bancorporation, 2001—. Contb. articles to profl. jours. Active Experience St. Louis, 1986; mem. Leadership Ctr. of Greater St. Louis, 1987-95, bd. dirs., 1988-95, v.p. comms., 1989-90, pres., 1991-92; bd. dirs. Focus St. Louis, Inc., 1996-2002; treas., 1996-98; bd. dirs. Combined Health Appeal of Greater St. Louis, 1992-97, v.p. programs, 1992-94, pres., 1995-96; bd. dirs. St. Louis Coll. Pharmacy, 1995-2000, Wyman Ctr., 1997-2000, Combined Health Appeal of Am., 1997-98, United Way of Greater St. Louis, 1997—, vice-chmn., 1997-99, Small World Adoption Found., 1998—, pres., 2000—; mem. adv. bd. Washington U. Olin Sch. Nat. Coun., 2002—, Scholar F.C. Austin Found., 1978-80, Phi Gamma Nu, 1980; recipient Nat. Vol. of Yr. award Combined Health Appeal of Am., 1996, Person of Yr. award Juvenile Diabetes Assn. St. Louis chpt., 1998, Gala Honoree, 1998, Health Citizen of Yr. award Combined Health Appeal Greater St. Louis, 1998, Corp. Leadership Divsn. award United Way Gtr. St. Louis, 1993, 95, Employee Divsn. award, 1997, 98. Mem. Beta Gamma Sigma, Greenbriar Hills Country Club. Roman Catholic. Avocations: reading, family, golf, travel. Home: 9368 Robyn Hills Dr Saint Louis MO 63127-1316

HOGAN, NEVILLE JOHN, mechanical engineering educator, consultant; b. Dublin, Feb. 11, 1949; came to U.S., 1970; s. Walter Henry and Edna Constance (Liller) H.; m. Sara Jane Seiden; children: Alexandra, Brian, Amanda, Victoria. Diploma in engring. with honors, Coll. of Tech., Dublin, 1970; MS in Mech. Engring., MIT, 1973, mech. engring. degree, 1976, PhD in Mech. Engring., 1977; D (hon.), Tech. U. Delft, 1997. Product devel. and design engr. Donnelly Mirrors Ltd., Nass, Ireland, 1977 78; prof. MIT, Cambridge, 1978—; dir. Newman Lab., 1992—. Cons. in phys. systems modeling, design and control and in biomed. engring. Contbr. numerous articles to profl. jours. TRW Found. fellow, Whitaker Health Scis. Fund fellow. Mem. AAAS, ASME, Sigma Xi.

HOGAN, ROBERT HENRY, trust company executive, investment strategist; b. N.Y.C., Apr. 12, 1926; s. Frederick Avertus and Carrie (Cronhardt) H.; m. Katherine Ann Wilkes, Feb. 9, 1957; children: Robert Wilkes, Mary Katherine, Margaret Ann, John William. Student, CCNY, 1943-44. Field rep. Moral Re-Armament, Inc., various locations, 1947-65, dir. N.Y.C., 1965-68; portfolio mgr. U.S. Trust Co., N.Y.C., 1969-72, asst. sec., 1972-78, asst. v.p., 1978-82, v.p., 1982-85, sr. v.p., 1985-2000. Mem. hon. bd. dirs. Uncommon Friends Found., Ft. Myers, Fla. M/sgt. U.S. Army, 1944-46, ETO. Mem. Assn. Investment Mgmt. and Rsch., N.Y. Soc. Security Analysts. Republican. Episcopalian. Avocations: philately, antiquarian books, fishing.

HOGAN, ROXANNE ARNOLD, nursing consultant, risk management consultant, educator; b. Connellsville, Pa; d. Tyree Franklin Sr. and Reva Gayle (Thieler) A.; m. Patrick B. Hogan. AAS, Gloucester County Coll., 1983; BSN, Widener U., 1989. Lic. health care risk mgmt.; RN Fla., cert. operating rm. nurse. Staff devel. instr., nursing supr., cardiac care nurse Meth. Hosp., Phila., 1982-89; emergency nurse Underwood Meml. Hosp., Woodbury, NJ, 1988-89; critical care nurse Jupiter Hosp., Fla., 1989—92; emergency clin. nurse III Indian River Meml. Hosp., Vero Beach, Fla., 1990-92; EMT/paramedic instr. Indian River CC, Ft. Pierce, Fla., 1990-92; emergency asst. nurse mgr. Holmes Regional Med. Ctr., Melbourne, Fla., 1992-94; post anesthesia clin. nurse III Indian River Meml. Hosp., Vero Beach, Fla., 1994-98; surg. dir. The Rosato Plastic Surgery Ctr., Vero Beach, Fla., 1998-99; nurse mgr. pre-admissions IV Team and Ambulatory Surgery Ctr. Indian River Meml. Hosp., Vero Beach, Fla., 1999—2001; nurse mgr. spl. procedures GI Lab. IV Team and Ambulatory Surgery Ctr., Vero Beach, Fla., 1999—2001, nurse mgr. ambulatory infusion team, 1999—2001; pres. Treasure Coast Cons., Inc., 2001—02; risk mgmt. coord. HCA/St. Lucie Med. Ctr., Port St. Lucie, Fla., 2002—03; claims med. specialist S.E. Fla. Nationwide Ins., 2003—. Mem.: Fla. Soc. Healthcare Risk Mgmt., Am. Soc. Healthcare Risk Mgmt., Am. Assn. Legal Nurse Cons. (South Fla. Chpt.), Assn. of Operating Room Nurses (Platinum Coast Chpt.), Eta Beta Chpt., Sigma Theta Tau. Home: 5346 NW Rugby Dr Port Saint Lucie FL 34983-3384

HOGAN, STEVEN L. lawyer; b. Los Angeles, Aug. 31, 1953; s. Kenneth Carlton Hogan and Ninon Michelle Kingsley; m. Debra Karen Garshfield, June 27, 1975; children: Rebecca Sarah, Cheryl Lee. AB magna cum laude, UCLA, 1975; JD, U. So. Calif., 1978. Bar: Calif. 1978, U.S. Ct. Appeals (9th cir.) 1979,U.S. Dist. Ct. (cen. dist.) Calif. 1979, U.S. Supreme Ct. 2000, U.S. Ct. Appeals (3d cir.) 2002, U.S. Dist. Ct. (so. dist., ea. dist., no. dist.) Calif. 1985. Assoc. Anderson, McPharlin & Conners, L.A., 1978-80; ptnr. Bryan Cave, L.A., 1980-95; shareholder Lurie, Zepeda, Schmalz & Hogan, Beverly Hills, CA, 1995—. Mem. Los Angeles County Bar Assn., Order of Coif, Phi Beta Kappa, Phi Gamma Mu. Office: Lurie Zepeda Schmalz & Hogan 9107 Wilshire Blvd Ste 800 Beverly Hills CA 90210-5533 E-mail: shogan@lurie-zepeda.com.

HOGAN, SUSAN COX, association executive; b. Wheeling, W.Va., Dec. 9, 1949; d. Michael Cresap and Beatrice (Emblen) Cox; m. David Proctor Nelson, July 18, 1969 (div. 1973); 1 child, Michael David; m. William N. Hogan, Jr., Jan. 3, 1986; 6 stepchildren. Student, W.Va. U., 1967-69. Music dir. Bach Soc., Half Moon Bay, Calif., 1975-78; exec. dir. Wheeling Symphony Soc., W. Va., 1979 87; vol. U.S. Peace Corps, Benin, West Africa, 1987-91; exec. dir. YWCA of Wheeling, 1991—; exec. dir. Wheeling Symphony Orch Wheeling, W. Va. Bd. dirs. Homeless Coalition, 1991—, Soup Kitchen of Greater Wheeling, 1991—, United Way Friends, 1993—, Victorian Wheeling Soc. 1993—; active Family Resource Network, Drug & Alcohol Coun. Mem. Returned Peace Corps Vols., Rotary. Democrat. Avocations: reading, art, music. Office: Wheeling Symphony Orch 1025 Main St Ste 811 Wheeling WV 26003-2724

HOGAN, THOMAS FRANCIS, federal judge; b. Washington, May 31, 1938; s. Bartholomew W. and Grace (Gloninger) H.; m. Martha Lou Wyrick, July 16, 1966; 1 son, Thomas Garth. AB, Georgetown U., 1960, JD, 1966; postgrad., George Washington U., 1960-62. Bar: Md. 1966, U.S. Dist. Ct. D.C. 1967, D.C. 1967, U.S. Ct. Appeals (D.C. cir.) 1972, U.S. Dist. Ct. Md. 1973, U.S. Supreme Ct. 1973. Law clk. to presiding judge U.S. Dist. Ct. D.C., 1966-67; counsel Nat. Commn. on Reform of Fed. Criminal Laws, Washington, 1967-68; ptnr. McCarthy & Wharton, Rockville, Md., 1968-75, Kenary, Tietz & Hogan, Rockville, 1975-81, Furey, Doolan, Abell & Hogan, Chevy Chase, Md., 1981-82; judge U.S. Dist. Ct. D.C., Washington, 1982—. Asst. prof. Potomac Sch. Law, Washington, 1977-79; adj. prof. law Georgetown Law Ctr., 1985—; mem. U.S. Jud. Conf., 2001—, mem. specialties com., 2001—. Pub. mem. Officer Evaluation Bd. U.S. Fgn. Service, 1973; chmn. Christ Child Inst. for Disturbed Children, 1975; bd. dirs. Providence Hosp., Washington, 1984-86. Recipient cert. recognition and appreciation for vol. services Montgomery

County Govt., 1976; recipient cert. appreciation Christ Child Soc., 1976; St. Thomas More fellow Georgetown U. Law Ctr., 1965-66 Mem. ABA (Md. chmn. Drug Abuse Edn. Program, Young Lawyers sect. 1970-73, mem. Litigation sect.), Bar Assn. D.C. (mem. com. on D.C. cts.), Md. State Bar Assn. (Litigatin sect.), Montgomery County Bar Assn. (chmn. legal ethics com. 1973-74, lawyer referral service com. 1974-75, adminstrn. justice com. 1979-82, bd. govs. 1977-78), Nat. Inst. for Trial Advocacy Assocs., Def. Research Inst., Md. Assn. Def. Trial Counsel, Md. Trial Lawyers Assn., Georgetown U. Alumni Assn., Smithsonian Assocs., John Carroll Soc., Knights of Malta. Clubs: Barristers, Chevy Chase, Lawyers.

HOGAN, THOMAS HARLAN, publisher; b. Summit, N.J., July 8, 1944; s. Thomas John and Dorothy Ester (Bakker) H.; m. Mary Suzanne Howarth, Aug. 3, 1968; children: Thomas, Kathleen, Deborah. BA, LeMoyne Coll., 1966. Salesman Auerbach Pubs., Phila., 1968-69; mktg. mgr. IEEE, N.Y.C., 1969-70, BioSciences Info. Services, Phila., 1971-73; v.p. Data Courier Inc., Louisville, 1973-77; pres. Plexus Pub. Co., Medford, N.J., 1977—, Info. Today, Inc., Medford, 1980—. Co-author: Online Searching: A Primer, 1984, Proceedings of the National Online Meeting, 1980—; editor articles Information Today. Mem. Am. Soc. Info. Sci. Tech. (pres. 1998-99, Watson Davis award 2002), Assn. Info. and Dissemination Ctrs. (pres. 1998-99). Democrat. Roman Catholic. Avocations: golf, sailing, skiing. Home: 3 Durwood Ct Medford NJ 08055-9123 Office: Info Today Inc 143 Old Marlton Pike Medford NJ 08055-8750 E-mail: hoganiti@aol.com.

HOGAN, THOMAS VICTOR, insurance company executive; b. Jay, Okla., Feb. 1, 1936; s. Thomas Victor and Eula Mae (Cating) H.; m. Patsy Lynn Weir, June 12, 1955; children: Terry Michael, Jeffrey Robert. MS in Fin. Services, The Am. Coll., 1986. CLU, chartered fin. cons. Agent Northwestern Nat. Life, Wichita, Kans., 1955-61, field supr. Dallas, 1961-64, dist. mgr. Houston, 1964-67, mktg. mgr. St. Louis, 1967-72, supt. of agys. Mpls., 1972-75, br. mgr. Dallas, 1975-83; pres. Metroplex Fin. Services, Dallas, 1983-96, also bd. dirs.; v.p., mgr. employee benefits and fin. svcs. Roach Howard Smith & Hunter, Dallas, 1996—. Contbr. articles to profl. jours., tape series. Loan exec. United Way Mpls., 1973; treas. Royal Oaks Bapt. Ch., Dallas, 1979-87; bd. dirs. Carrollton Parks and Recreation Dept., 1993-99, chmn., 1996-98. Merit scholar Phillips U., 1954. Mem. Nat. Assn. Ins. and Fin. Advisors (found. bd. dirs. 1994-99, chmn. 1997-99), Am. Soc. Fin. Svc. Professions (pres. 1986, bd. dirs. 1983-89), Gen. Agts. and Mgrs. Assn. (bd. dirs. 1980-83), Dallas Estate Planning Coun. Republican. Avocations: golf, fishing, travel. Office: Roach Howard Smith & Hunter 9330 Lbj Fwy Ste 1500 Dallas TX 75243-3449 Home: 6073 Dory Way Tavares FL 32778-9219

HOGAN, WILLIAM JEPHTHA, JR., financial consultant; b. Atlanta, June 1, 1949; s. William Jephtha and Mary Frances (Cundy) H.; m. Janet Riley, Nov. 5, 1983; children: William Riley, Claire Frances, Elizabeth Knox, Eloise Bennett, Robert Jephtha. BA, Oglethorpe U., 1972. CFP, CIMA. Asst. to region mgr. Pepsi-Cola Co., Chgo., 1979-80, dist. mgr. Wichita, Kans., 1980-83; fin. cons. Robinson-Humphrey Co., Atlanta, 1983-92; investment exec. PaineWebber, Atlanta, 1992-94; 1st v.p. investments Smith Barney, Atlanta, 1994—. Chair pres.'s adv. coun. Oglethorpe U. Recipient Talmage award Oglethorpe U., 1990, Alumni Svc. award The Westminster Schs., Atlanta, 1997. Mem. Oglethorpe U. Nat. Alumni Assn. (pres. 1988-90), Rotary (pres. Vinings, Ga.1994-95). Episcopalian. Avocations: jogging, golf, tennis, coaching children's sports teams. Office: Smith Barney 3333 Peachtree Rd NE Atlanta GA 30326-1070 Business E-Mail: jep.hogan@smithbarney.com.

HOGANSON, SUSAN COOK, non-profit organization executive; b. Providence, R.I., Apr. 5, 1947; d. Richard Foster and Betty Heneman Cook; m. John A. Hoganson, Nov. 25, 1978. AB, Hollins Coll., 1969; MEd, Boston U., 1973; postgrad., Stanford U., 2002. Mgr. trainee, v.p., mgr. The Bank of Calif., San Francisco, 1980-88; v.p. to sr. v.p. The Boston Co., San Francisco, 1988-90; v.p. Union Bank of Switzerland, San Francisco, 1991-93; exec. dir., CEO Enterprise for H.S. Students, San Francisco, 1995—. Bd. dirs. United Way of Bay Area, San Francisco, 1997—2001, No. Calif. Presbyn. Homes and Svcs., San Francisco, 1994—97; pres. The Modern Art Coun. of San Francisco, Mus. Modern Art, 1998—2000, Jr. League of San Francisco, Inc., 1991—92; trustee Hamlin Sch., San Francisco, 2000—; mem. Leadership San Francisco, 2000. Recipient Vol. Merit award United Way of Bay Area, 1996; fellow Ctr. for Social Innovation, Stanford U., 2002. Office: Enterprise for HS Students 200 Pine St Ste 600 San Francisco CA 94104

HOGBERG, CARL GUSTAV, retired steel company executive; b. Escanaba, Mich., July 19, 1913; s. Claus Emil and Anna C. (Franson) H.; m. June Loraine Evans, June 10, 1935 (dec. Aug. 1991); children: David K., Janet H. (Mrs. Nicholas A. Matwiyoff). BS in Meall. Engring., Mich. Coll. Mining and Tech., 1935; DEng (hon.), Mich. Tech. U., 1968. Blast-furnace apprentice South Chgo. works Carnegie-Ill. Steel Corp., 1935, various operating positions blast-furnace dept., 1935-39, sec. blast-furnace and coke-oven com., 1939-41; asst. chmn. blast-furnace com. U.S. Steel Corp., Pitts., 1942-54; asst. to v.p. Mich. Limestone divsn., Detroit, 1955, asst. v.p., 1956, v.p., 1957-60, pres., 1960-63, v.p. raw materials svc., parent co., 1964; pres. Orinoco Mining Co. subs., Caracas, Venezuela, 1965-70; v.p. internat. U.S. Steel Corp., 1970-73. Contbr. tech. articles to trade publs. Mem. AIME (J.E. Johnson, Jr. award 1945), Assn. Iron and Steel Inst., Ea. Western States Blast Furnace and Coke Assns. Home: 263 Norman Dr Cranberry Township PA 16066-4205

HOGE, FRANZ JOSEPH, accounting firm executive; b. N.Y.C., Apr. 2, 1944; s. Albert and Sophie (Hutter) H.; m. Margaret Ann Hoefling, Oct. 11, 1969; children: Joanne Curoe, Susan Glennon, Daniel. BBA, CCNY, 1966. CPA, N.Y., Ohio. Staff acct. Coopers and Lybrand, N.Y.C., 1968-70, in-charge acct., 1970-73, mgr., 1973-77, ptnr., 1977-80, mng. ptnr. Dayton, Ohio, 1980-97, Ohio unit leader, 1993-97, middle market industry leader, 1993-97; ret., 1997. Chmn. bus. adv. bd. Wright State U., 1986-2001, Dayton Pub. Schs.; chmn. bd. The Fund for Dayton Urban Children and Schs., 1997-2003; bd. dirs. Nat. Ctr. Indsl. Competitiveness, Premier Health Ptnrs., Athenaeum of Ohio; chmn. bd. Good Samaritan Hosp., 1989-99, chmn. Montgomery County Human Svc. Levy Coun., 2001—. Co-author two audit and acctg. guides, 1978, 79. Bd. dirs. Dayton Mus. Natural History, pres. 1983-90, Dayton Opera Assn., pres. 1983-92, Maria Joseph Living Care Ctr., chmn. 1984-95; chmn. bd. dirs. NCCJ, 1999-2002, chmn., Kettering Children's Choir; v.p. Assn. for Corp. Growth, Hipple Cancer Rsch. Ctr., Dayton, 1981-87, Big Bros./Big Sisters Found., Dayton, 1983-87, Dayton Performing Arts Fund, 1983-87; bd. dirs. Wright State U. Found., 1996-2001 Mem. AICPA, Ohio Soc. CPAs, N.Y. State Soc. CPAs, Moraine Country Club. Republican. Roman Catholic. Home: 939 Laurelwood Rd Dayton OH 45419-1228 Office: PriceWaterhouseCoopers 2080 Kettering Tower Dayton OH 45423-2080

HOGE, MEDORA DAVIDSON, dance educator; b. Merriam, Kans., July 2, 1930; d. John Archibald and Mabel Adelaide Davidson; m. Daniel Howe Hoge, Jr., Feb. 6, 1971 (div. June 14, 1984); m. Harry Lee Lydick, June 21, 1953 (div. Nov. 5, 1965); children: Harry Lee Lydick, Jr., Robin Louis Lydick. Grad. h.s., Merriam, 1948. Instr. ballet, tap, jazz, gymnastics, ballroom dance, low-impact aerobics Davidson Dance Studio, Prairie Village, Kans., 1950—89; dance instr. N.A.D.A.A. city chpts., St. Paul, St. Louis, Omaha, Tulsa, Dallas, 1957—59; jazz dance instr. nat. faculty Nat. Assn. Dance and Affiliated Artists, Inc., L.A., Dallas, Chgo., 1957—59; choreographer outdoor mus. shows Johnson County (Kans.) Pks. and Recreation, 1971—73; choreographer Kansas City (Mo.) Royals Banquet shows, 1972—74; tchr. ballet, tap, gymnastics Visitation Parochial Sch., Kansas City, Mo., 1989—91; former owner, instr. ballet, tap, jazz, gymnastics, low-impact aerobics Davidson Dance Studio, Ottawa, Kans., 1991—99; tchr. low-impact aerobics Albuquerque Sr. Ctrs., 1999—2000; tchr. modern dance and children's drama Carnegie Cultural Ctr., Ottawa, 2000—02, tchr. piano, 2002—03, instr. Kindermusik Internat., 2002—03. Dance therapist activity dept. Psychiat. Receiving Ctr., Western Mo. Mental Health Ctr., Kansas City, 1969—; taped 65 half-hour ballet class lessons for children Medora and Me, 1970—71; taped 65 half-hour interviews for women The Feminine Touch, 1970—71; dir. Picnic A.C.T. Ottawa!, Ottawa Cmty. Theatre, 1997; writer, dir. 3 plays Fine Arts Singles, Johnson County, Kans., 1990—91; dir. Show Boat Baldwin Cmty. Theater, Baldwin City, Kans., 1999; formed Crackerjack Children's Theatre, Ottawa, 2001; writer, dir. Coventown A.C.T. Ottawa!, Ottawa, 2001, dir. An Old Time Radio Show, 02, dir. Playboy of the Western World, 02; dir. Crackerjack Children's Theatre Christmas Reader's Theatre, 2001, Nunsense 2003, Baldwin City Cmty. Theatre, 2003, Another Old Time Radio Show, Ottawa Cmty. Theatre, 2003, Bye, Bye, Bye Birdie, Baldwin City Cmty. Theatre, 2003. Actor: (plays) Gypsy, 1973, Lady Audley's Secret, 1976, The Farsighted Dragon and the Nearsighted Knight, 1985, Night of January 16th, 1994, Greater Tuna, 1996, The Tempest, 1998, Nunsense, 1999; (plays) Diamonds to Die For, 2000, Cabaret, A Black Tie Affair, 2001. Vol. dance therapist Johnson County Mental Health Ctr., Overland Park, Kans., 1967—69. Avocations: gardening, painting, sewing, reading. Home: 1103 S Main St Ottawa KS 66067-3523 E-mail: medorad@sbcglobal.net.

HOGE, MICHAEL ALAN, psychologist; b. Lima, Ohio, Dec. 20, 1954; s. Ned William and Marilyn (Henkener) H.; m. Nancy Anderson, June 4, 1988; children: Christopher, Connor. BA summa cum laude, Kent State U., 1977, MA in Clin. Psychology, 1981, PhD in Clin. Psychology, 1984. Lic. psychologist, Conn. Psycholgy intern, dept. psychology Kent (Ohio) State Univ., 1980-81; psycholgy intern Columbiana County Mental Health Counseling Ctr., Lisbon, Ohio, 1981-82; psycholgy intern, Counseling and Group Resources Ctr. Kent (Ohio) State Univ., 1982-83; psychology fellow VA Med. Ctr., West Haven, Conn., 1983-84; instr. Yale Univ. Sch. Medicine, New Haven, 1984-85; asst. dir. Hill Mental Health Clinc, Conn. Mental Health Ctr., New Haven, 1984-85; asst. prof. psychology in psychiatry Yale U. Sch. Medicine, New Haven, 1985-91, assoc. prof., 1991—; dir. psychol. svcs. div. inpatient and partial hosp. Conn. Mental Health Ctr., New Haven, 1985-87, exec. dir. day hosp., 1987-90, dir. managed care system and asst. dir. edn. and tng., 1990-94, mem. exec. com. med. staff, 1989-94, acting v.p., 1990; dir. managed behavioral health svcs. devel. dept. psychiatry Yale U., 1995—2002, CEO behavioral health, 2002—; dir. behavioral health svcs. Conn. Mental Health Ctr., 2002—. Lectr., cons. and presenter in field. Contbr. reviews, chpts. to books and articles to profl. jours. Mem. Am. Assn. for Partial Hospitalization (bd. dirs. 1987-89, chair rsch. com. 1987-89, cons. rsch. com. 1989-93, chair continuing edn. com. 1987-89, pub. com. 1987-89, regional rep. for Conn. 1985-87), Partial Hospitalization Assn. Conn. (chair legis. and fin. com. 1985-86, v.p. 1985-86, pres. 1986-87), Am. Psychol. Assn., Consortium for Edn. in Groups and Orgns. (cons. 1988), Conn. Psychol. Assn., Nat. Alliance for the Mentally Ill, Catchment Area Coun., Am. Coll. Mental Health Adminstrs. (bd. dirs. 2002—), Acad. Behavioral Health Consortium (v.p. 2000), Phi Beta Kappa, and others. Office: Yale Univ Sch Medicine 25 Park St Fl 6 New Haven CT 06519-1110 E-mail: michael.hoge@yale.edu.

HOGE, WARREN M. newspaper and magazine correspondent, editor; b. N.Y.C., Apr. 13, 1941; s. James F. Hoge and Virginia (McClamroch) Barber; m. Olivia Larisch, Nov. 21, 1981; 1 child, Nicholas; stepchildren: Christina, Tatjana. BA, Yale U., 1963; postgrad., George Washington U., 1964-65. Reporter Washington Star, 1964-66; bur. chief N.Y. Post, Washington, 1966-69, city editor, asst. mng. editor N.Y.C., 1970-75; dep. met. editor N.Y. Times, N.Y.C., 1976-78, fgn. corr. Rio de Janeiro, Brazil, 1979-83, fgn. editor N.Y.C., 1984-87, asst. mng. editor, 1987-90; asst. mng. editor and editor N.Y. Times Mag., N.Y.C., 1991-92, asst. mng. editor for culture, style, book rev., and recruitment of writers, 1993-96; chief London Bur., N.Y. Times, 1996—. Baptist. Home: 4 Cheltenham Terr London SW3 4RD England Office: NY Times 66 Buckingham Gate London SW1E 6AU England

HOGEN-ESCH, THIEO E. chemistry educator; b. Terneuzen, The Netherlands, Feb. 22, 1936; came to U.S., 1968; s. Jan Jogen-Esch and Elisabeth Wietje Roelofs; m. Chryl E. McCafferty, Nov. 19, 1966 (div. 1991); children: John, Thomas, Christopher. BSc, Leiden State U., The Netherlands, 1958, MSc, 1961, PhD, 1967. Adv. technologist Shell, Rotterdam, The Netherlands, 1966-68; postdoctoral SUNY, Syracuse, 1968-70; asst. prof. chemistry U. Fla., Gainesville, 1970-75, assoc. prof. chemistry, 1975-79, prof. chemistry, 1979-88, U. So. Calif., L.A., 1988—. Vis. prof., U. Bordeaux, France, 1991. Editor: Recent Advances in Anionic Polymerization, 1987; contbr. 200 articles to profl. chem. and polymer jours.; mem. editl. bd., Polymer Internat., 1997—, Designed Monomers and Polymers, 1997—. Fellow Japanese Soc. Advancement of Sci.; mem. AAAS, Am. Chem. Soc.

HOGENKAMP, HENRICUS PETRUS CORNELIS, biochemistry researcher, biochemistry educator; b. Doesburg, Gelderland, The Netherlands, Dec. 20, 1925; came to U.S., 1958; s. Johannes Hermanus and Maria Margaretha J. (Abeln) H.; m. Lieke Ter Haar, Apr. 25, 1953; children: Harry Peter, Derk John, Margaret Angelina. BSA, U. B.C., Vancouver, 1957, MSc, 1958; PhD, U. Calif., Berkeley, 1961. Rsch. biochemist U. Calif., Berkeley, 1961—62; assoc. scientist Fisheries Rsch. Bd. Can., Vancouver, 1962—63; asst. prof. U. Iowa, Iowa City, 1963—67, assoc. prof., 1967—71, prof., 1971—76; prof., head dept. biochemistry U. Minn., Mpls., 1976—92, prof. dept. biochemistry, 1992—2002, prof. emeritus, 2002. Vis. prof. Australian Nat. U., Canberra, Australia, 1966-67, Philipps U., Marburg, Fed. Republic of Germany, 1986-87, 1988, 1990; guest scientist U. Calif. Los Alamos (N.Mex) Sci. Lab., 1974-75. Sgt. Royal Netherlands Army, 1946-50, Indonesia. Recipient Alexander von Humboldt-Stiftung award Philipps U.-Fachbereich Microbiology, Marburg, Fed. Republic of Germany, 1986-87; named to Minn. Acad. Medicine,Mpls., 1980--; Guggenheim fellow U. Iowa, Iowa City, 1974-75. Mem. Am. Chem. Soc., Am. Soc. Biochemistry and Molecular Biology (mem. pub. affairs com. 1986-91), Assn. Med. Sch. Depts. Biochemistry, Internat. Union Biochemists (chmn. U.S. nominating com. 1988). Home: 2211 Marion Rd Saint Paul MN 55113-3805 Office: U Minn BMBB Dept Ste 6-155 321 Church St SE Minneapolis MN 55455

HOGENSEN, MARGARET HINER, librarian, consultant; b. Ottawa, Kans., Oct. 11, 1920; d. Hebron Henry and Nellie Evelyn (Godard) Hiner; widowed. BA, U. Wichita, 1942; BS in Library Sci., U. Denver, 1945. Circulation librarian Boise (Idaho) Pub. Library, 1945-49, Pomona (Calif.) Pub. Library, 1950-51; reference librarian WFIL-TV, Phila., 1963-69; rsch. dir. Concept Films, Washington, 1969-72; ind. researcher, cons. Greenbelt, Md., 1973-80. Bd. dirs. Greenbelt Homes, Inc., 1977-93, 98-2000, 2003—, pres., 1983-88, treas. 1998-2000; past mem. bd. dirs. Greenbelt Consumer Coop., Nat. Coop. Bus. Assn.; pres. Ea. Coop. Housing Orgn., 1992-95. Mem. Nat. Assn. Housing Coops (bd. dirs. 1986-87, 1990-94). Democrat. Christian Scientist. Avocation: travel. Home: PO Box 218 Greenbelt MD 20768-0218

HOGG, DAVID CLARENCE, physicist; b. Vanguard, Sask., Can., Sept. 5, 1921; came to U.S., 1953, naturalized, 1964; s. Francis Sandison and Frances Katherine (Gadsby) H.; m. Jean E. MacMillan, Feb. 15, 1947; children— David Randal, Rebecca Jean. BSc, U. Western Ont. (Can.), London, 1949; MSc, McGill U., Montreal, Que., Can., 1951, PhD, 1953. With Bell Telephone Labs., 1953-77, head atmospheric physics research, 1966-72, head antenna and propagation research, 1972-77; chief environ. radiometry wave propagation lab. Environ. Research Lab., NOAA, Boulder, Colo., 1977-83, chief radio meteorology, 1983-86; lectr., adj. prof. U. Colo., Boulder, 1984—, lectr. ECE dept, 1989—; sr. scientist Colo. Inst. Research Environ. Scis., U. Colo., Boulder, 1986-89. Research, numerous publs. on microwaves, optics, satellite communications and remote sensing; patentee microwave antennas; composer vocal, choral, strings and piano classical music. Served with Can. Army, 1940-45. Recipient Silver medal U.S. Dept. Commerce, 1983, Composer's award Colo. Music Educators Assn., 1992. Fellow IEEE (founder Jersey Coast sect., Disting. Achievement award 1984); mem. NAE, Union Radio Scientifique Internat., Am. Music Ctr. Episcopalian. Home: 4978 Carter Ct Boulder CO 80301-3895

HOGG, JAMES HENRY, JR., retired education educator; b. Pleasantville, Pa., Aug. 15, 1926; s. James Henry and Carrie Ethel (Swan) H.; m. Elizabeth Beatrice George, Sept. 8, 1945 (dec. Feb. 1988); children: Carolyn Elizabeth, James Henry III; m. Reva Rowene Heffernan, Jan. 1, 1992. BA, Houghton Coll., 1951; MA, Allegheny Coll., 1961; EdD, Pa. State U., 1971. Cert. secondary tchr., Pa. Tchr. English and social studies Meadville (Pa.) Sr. H.S., 1962-67; instr. in secondary edn. Pa. State U., University Park, 1968-71, asst. prof., 1971-77, assoc. prof., 1977-91; ret., 1991. Trustee Houghton Coll., 1964-67; Pa. State Adv. Bd., Mid. States Assn. Colls. and Schs., 1984-91 (chmn. evaluation teams, 1983-91). Contbr. articles to profl. jours. Councilman Cooperstown Borough, 1993-98, 2000—. With U.S. Army, 1944-46, ETO. Named participant in 2d Inst. Am History Pa. State U., 1966, Assn. Tchr. Educators LaureATE, 1989; recipient cert. of appreciation U.S. House Reps. Page Sch., 1985. Mem. Nat. Assn. Tchr. Educators, Pa. Assn. Tchr. Educators, Phi Delta Kappa, Alpha Tau. Republican. Methodist. Avocations: hunting, fishing, bowling, chess. Home: 148 Lakeview Dr Cooperstown PA 16317

HOGG, KAREN SUE, telecommunications and information systems executive; b. Bay City, Tex., Jan. 12, 1952; d. Ernest Bascom Hogg and Allene (Bishop) Watson; m. Wesley Ray Tucker, Mar. 10, 1989. BS in Indsl. Engring., Tex. Tech. U., 1974; MBA, Washington U., 1982. Profl. engr. Tex. Computer ops. supr. Southwestern Bell, Houston, 1974-75, St. Louis, 1975-76, from mgr. installation to staff mgr., 1976-83; prin. cons. AT&T Internat., Basking Ridge, N.J., 1983-85; nat. sales mgr. AT&T Network Sys., Morristown, N.J., 1986; mgr. telecom. Goldman Sachs & Co., N.Y.C., 1986-90, v.p. info. tech., 1990-2000. Mem. indsl. adv. bd. Tex. Tech U., Lubbock, 1980-86, mem. dean's coun. Coll. Engring., 1998-2000, dean's coun., sec. 1999-2000. Judge YWCA Tribute to Women, Knoxville, Tenn., 1992; trustee Burgdorf Cultural Commn., 1997—2001. Named Disting. Engr., Tex. Tech. U., 1994. Mem.: Alpha Pi Mu, Inst. Indsl. Engrs., Acad. Indsl. Engring. (sec.-treas. 1994, vice chmn. 1995, chmn. 1996, pres. 2000—02), Maplewood Club (trustee 1994—96), Maplewood Strollers (treas. 1996—98, prodn. dir. 1998, v.p. 1999, trustee, pres. 2000—02), Phi Kappa Phi, Tau Beta Pi, Beta Gamma Sigma. Republican. Methodist. Avocations: theater, singing, dancing, needlecraft, reading.

HOGG, ROBERT VINCENT, JR., mathematical statistician, educator; b. Hannibal, Mo., Nov. 8, 1924; s. Robert Vincent and Isabelle Frances (Storrs) H.; m. Carolyn Joan Ladd, June 23, 1956 (dec. June 1990); children: Mary Carolyn, Barbara Jean, Allen Ladd, Robert Mason; m. Ann Burke, Oct. 15, 1994. BA, U. Ill., 1947; MS, U. Iowa, 1948, PhD, 1950. Asst. prof. math. U. Iowa, Iowa City, 1950-56, assoc. prof., 1956-62, prof., 1962-65, chmn. dept. stats., prof. stats., 1965-83, 92-93, Hanson prof. mfg. productivity, 1993-95, prof. emeritus, 2001—. Co-author: Introduction to Mathematical Statistics, 1959, 5th edit., 1995, Finite Mathematics and Calculus, 1974, Probability and Statistical Inference, 1977, 6th edit., 2000, Applied Statistics for Engineers and Physical Scientists, 1987, 2d edit., 1992; assoc. editor Am. Stats., 1971-74; contbr. articles to profl. jours. Vestryman local Episc. ch., 1958-60, 66-68, 91-92, 2001—. With USNR, 1943-46. Grantee NIH, 1966-68, 75-78, NSF, 1969-74; Disting. Alumni Award, U. Iowa, 2003. Fellow Inst. Math. Stats. (program sec., bd. bd. 1968-74), Am. Statis. Assn. (pres. Iowa sect. 1962-63, coun. 1965-66, 73-74, vis. lectr. 1965-68, 77-85, chmn. tng. sect. 1973, assoc. editor jour. 1978-80, pres.-elect 1987, pres. 1988, past pres. 1989, Founders award 1991, Noether award 2001); mem. Math. Assn. Am. (pres. Iowa sect. 1964-65, 95-96, bd. govs. 1971-74, visa. lectr. 1976-81, Outstanding Tchg. award 1993), Internat. Statis. Inst., Rotary (pres. Iowa City 1984-85), Sigma Xi (pres. Iowa dist. chpt. 1970-71), Pi Kappa Alpha. Home: 30130 Trails End Buena Vista CO 81211 Office: U Iowa Dept Statis Acturial Sci Iowa City IA 52242 E-mail: bhogg@starband.net.

HOGGARD, LARA GULDMAR, conductor, educator; b. Kingston, Okla., Feb. 9, 1915; s. Calvin Peter and Eva Lillian (Smith) H.; m. Mildred Mae Teeter, Sept. 11, 1943; 1 dau., Susan. BA, Southea. Tchrs. Coll., 1934; MA, Columbia U., 1940, EdD, 1947. Supr. music Durant (Okla.) Pub. Schs., 1934-39; dir. choral activities, opera and oratorio U. Okla., 1940-43; assoc. founder, prin. instr. Waring Summer Choral Workshops, 1948-52; co-editor Shawnee Press, Del. Water Gap, Pa., 1946-52; dir. music and music edn. rsch. Indian Springs Sch., Ala. Edn. Found., Birmingham, 1955-60; founder Nat. Young Artist Competition, Midland-Odessa, 1962—; William Rand Kenan prof. music U. N.C., Chapel Hill, 1967-80, founder Carolina Choir, 1967—; founder N.C. Collegiate Choral Festival, 1969—; Fuller E. Callaway prof. music Columbus Coll., U. Ga., 1981-82. Condr. NBC-USN Navy Hour, 1945, assoc. condr. Waring's Pennsylvanians, 1946—52, condr., dir. (nat. touring concert group) Civic Music and Nat. Concert Artists Corp., Festival of Song, 1952—53; dir.: N.C. Summer Insts. in Choral Art, 1953—83; founder, condr., musical dir. Midland-Odessa (Tex.) Symphony Orch. and Chorale, 1962—67, condr. numerous music festivals, Am., Europe, artistic dir., prin. condr. Festival of Three Cities, Vienna-Budapest-Prague, 1973, Internat. Jugendmuskfest in Wien, 1973, 1974, guest lectr. and condr. univs. and conservatories in Am. and Europe, condr. several musical premieres, including Behold the Glory (Talmage Dean) with Louisville Orch., 1964, Light in the Wilderness (Dave Brubeck), Chapel Hill, 1968, new edit. Ein deutsches Requiem (Brahms) with N.C. Symphony, 1986, numerous others; author: Improving Music Reading, 1947, Exploring Music, 1967; editor: an oratorio Light in the Wilderness (Dave Brubeck), 1968; composer, arranger, editor 37 choral publs.; editor: new English transl. and corr. orch. score and parts Ein deutsches Requiem (Brahms), 1983—89; composer: Le Jongleur, 1951. Served to lt. (j.g.) USN, 1943-45, PTO. Recipient award for outstanding svc. to music in Ala., Ala. Fine Arts Festival, 1958, citation for outstanding svc. to fine arts in Tex., Tex. Senate and Gov., West Texan award, 1967, Tanner award U. N.C., 1972, Ten Best Profs. award, 1978, Order Long Leaf Pine Gov. N.C., 1980, Disting. Alumnus award Southeastern Okla. State U., 1981, Lara G. Hoggard endowed professorship named in his honor U. N.C., 1993. Mem. Music Educators Nat. Conf. (life; Master Builder), Am. Choral Dirs. Assn. (life, award for contbn. to music in N.C. 1976, citation for contbn. to music in Am., divsn. 5, 1986, award for excellence and lifelong commitment So. divsn. 1998), AAUP, N.C. Music Educators Assn. (hon. life), N.C. Lit. Soc. (life), Rotary, Phi Mu Alpha Sinfonia (nat. hon. life). Democrat. Presbyterian. *Creativity within the individual is our best weapon against total conformity and robotism. The arts challenge and elevate both the intellect and the spirit. Sensitivity and respect for the true, the good and the beautiful, stand in defiance of three attitudes which must not prevail, if civilization is to survive: bigotry, arrogant ignorance, and acceptance or approval of mediocrity.*

HOGLANDER, HARRY R. legislative staff member; m. Judith Hoglander. JD Suffolk U. Law Sch. Bar: Fla. Mem. Nat. Mediation Bd., 2002—; legis. specialist office of Congressman John Tierney, Mass.; capt. Trans World Airline; master chmn. Twa Master Exec. Coun.; named, Aviation Labor rep. US Bi-Lateral Negotiating Team. Retired, Lieutenanct Colonel USAF, dir of plans Mass. Air Nat. Guard, 102nd Air Wing. Office: 1301 K St NW Washington DC 20005-7011*

HOGLEN, JEWEL PAMELA, retired secondary school educator; b. Columbia, Miss., Sept. 22, 1919; d. Irvin Armstrong Blackburn and Inez Geraldine Dickens; m. Hubert J. Hoglen, Nov. 4, 1944; 1 child, Pamela J. BS, La. State Normal (now Northwestern State U. of La.), 1941; MA in Edn., Washington U., 1953. Cert. home economist, family & consumer scis. Home economist H.S., Kentwood, La., 1941—42; chmn. home economy Ward & Hanley Jr. H.S., U. City, Mo., 1947—69, Parkway N. H.S., Chesterfield, Mo., 1972—78; asst. prof. Meramec C.C., Kirkwood, Mo., 1972—75, ret., 1975. Vice chmn. profl. sect. Am. Home Econs. Assn., 1987—89; pres. Home Econs. Coun., St. Louis, 1964—65. Louis IX art mus. group Art Mus., St. Louis, 1978—. Recipient Disting. Svc. to the Profession award, Am. Home Econ. Assn., 1991—93, 50 Yrs. of Svc. award, Am. Home Econs. Assn., 1998. Mem.: AAUW, Mo. Home Econs. Assn. (pres. 1968—69, 1969—70, chmn. home economists in homemaking section, Cert. for Outstanding Contbn. & Svc. to the Profession 1985, 50 Years Dedication & Svc. to Home Econs. Profession award 1998), Am. Assn. Home (history & archives com., sec. to leader in leadership mtg.), Coll. Club of St. Louis (chmn. Centennial birthday celebration 2000, pres. 2001—03). Republican. Protestant. Avocations: tailoring, reading, horse back riding, travel. Home: 1009 Dougherty Ferry Rd Kirkwood MO 63122

HOGLUND, FORREST EUGENE, petroleum company executive, retired; b. Lawrence, Kans., July 1, 1933; s. Roy A. and Edna M. (McMichael) H.; m. Sally Sue Roney, June 19, 1956; children— Kelly M., Shelly L., Kristan K. BS in Mech. Engring, U. Kans., 1956. Registered profl. engr., Tex. With Exxon Corp., 1957-1977; v.p. ops. Exxon Corp. (Middle East), N.Y.C., 1973-75, v.p. gas, 1976-77; pres., chief oper. officer Tex. Oil and Gas, Dallas, 1977-83, pres., chief exec. officer, 1983-87; dir. USX Corp., Pitts., 1986-87; chmn., CEO EOG Resources, Houston, 1987—99, Arctic Resources, Houston. Former chmn. bd. visitors Univ. Cancer Found.--M.D. Anderson; former chmn. Houston Mus. Natural Sci. With C.E., U.S. Army, 1957-58. Mem. Am. Petroleum Inst., AIME, Soc. Petroleum Engrs., Ind. Petroleum Assn. Am., Tex. Ind. Producers and Royalty Assn., Petroleum Club, Dallas Country Club, River Oaks Country Club, Tau Beta Pi, Pi Tau Sigma, Sigma Tau, Omicron Delta Kappa. Office: Hoglund Interests 333 Clay St Ste 1325 Houston TX 77002-4005

HOGLUND, JOHN ANDREW, lawyer; b. Cleve., July 19, 1945; s. Paul Franklin and Louise (Anderson) H.; m. Patricia Olwell, May 27, 1972; children: Britt Hannah, Maeve Olwell, Marc Paul-Joseph. BA, Augustana Coll., 1967; JD, George Washington U., 1972. Bar: Wash. 1973, U.S. Dist. Ct. (we. dist.) Wash. 1973, U.S. Ct. Appeals (9th cir.) 1973. Law clk. Wash. State Supreme Ct.,

1973-74; assoc. Mooney, Cullen & Holm, Olympia, 1973-75; ptnr. Cullen, Holm, Hoglund & Foster, Olympia, 1975-81; pvt. practice Olympia, 1981—2003; of counsel Graham, Lundberg & Peschel, Olympia, 2003—; pres. Hoglund Group Internat., 1987—. Adj. prof. law sch. U. Puget Sound, Tacoma, Wash., 1989-90, trustee, 1984-92. Co-author: SKYCYL Practicing Law Manual, 1986-95, WSBA Book Automobile Negligence Law, 1988. Vice chmn. Group Health Coop., Olympia, 1978, Thurston County Dem. Cen. Com., Olympia, 1980; chmn. bd. dirs. S.W. Wash. Health Sys. Agy., 1979; alumni bd. dirs. George Washington U. Nat. Law Ctr., 1994-97, emeritus mem., 1997—. With U.S. Army, 1967-69. Named Boss of Yr. Thurston County Legal Secs. Assn., 1985. Mem. ABA, Thurston County Bar Assn. (trustee 1988-90, Svc. awards 1987, 90), ATLA, Wash. State Trial Lawyers Assn. (pres. 1983-84, Brandeis award 1980), Wash. State Trial Lawyers Found. (pres. 1985-87), Wash. State Bar Assn. (chmn. UPL com. 1979, CPR com., pub. rels. com., chmn. Lawyer Protection Fund com. 1999), Nat. Law Ctr. George Washington U. (alumni bd. 1994-2000), Kiwanis (Disting. Pres. award 1980).

HOGNESS, JOHN RUSTEN, physician, academic administrator; b. Oakland, Calif., June 27, 1922; s. Thorfin R. and Phoebe (Swenson) Hogness. Student, Haverford Coll., 1939—42, DSc (hon.), 1973; BS, U. Chgo., 1943, MD, 1946; DSc (hon.), Med. Coll. Ohio at Toledo, 1972; LLD, George Washington U., 1973; DLitt, Thomas Jefferson U., 1980. Diplomate Am. Bd. Internal Medicine. Intern Presbyn. Hosp., N.Y.C., 1946—47, asst. resident, 1949—50; chief resident King County Hosp., Seattle, 1950—51; asst. U. Wash. Sch. Medicine, 1950—52, Am. Heart Assn. research fellow, 1951—52, mem. faculty, 1954—64, prof. medicine, 1964—71, med. dir. univ. hosp., 1958—63, dean, chmn. bd. health scis., 1964—69, exec. v.p., 1969—70; dir. Health Scis. Ctr., 1970—71; pres. Inst. Medicine, Nat. Acad. Scis., 1971—74; prof. medicine George Washington U., 1972—74; pres. U. Wash., Seattle, 1974—79, pres. emeritus, 1979—, prof. medicine, 1974—79; pres. Assn. Acad. Health Ctrs., 1979—88. Disting. professorial lectr. dept. medicine Georgetown U., 1983—88, prof. U. Wash. Sch. Pub. Health, 1989—92; provost Hahnemann U., 1992—93; commr.'s adv. com. on exempt orgns. IRS, 1969—71; adv. com. for environ. scis. NSF, 1970—71; adv. com. to dir. NIH, 1970—71; mem. Nat. Cancer Adv. Bd., 1972—76, Nat. Sci. Bd., 1976—82; selection com. for Rockefeller pub. svc. awards Princeton U., 1976—82; chmn. med. injury compensation study steering com. Inst. Medicine NAS, chmn. com. to evaluate the artificial heart, 1990—91; council for biol. scis. U. Chgo. Pritzker Sch. Medicine, 1977—89; chmn. adv. panel on cost-effectiveness of med. techs. Office Tech. Assessment, U.S. Congress, 1978—80; chmn. study sect. for health care tech. assessment Nat. Ctr. for Health Svcs. Rsch. and Health Care Tech. Assessment, 1985—88; pres. Sun Valley Forum on Nat. Health, 1986—94; dir. Inst. for Health Policy Edn. and Rsch., U. Tex. Health Sci. Ctr., Houston, 1988; council health care tech. HEW; adv. panel for study fin. grad. med. edn. Dept. Health and Human Svcs., 1980—87. Contbr. articles to profl. jours. Trustee Case Western Res. U., 1972—73. With U.S. Army, 1947—49. Recipient Disting. Svc. award, Med. Alumni Assn. U. Chgo., 1966, Profl. Achievement award, Alumni Assn. U. Chgo., 1973, Convocation medal, Am. Coll. Cardiology, 1973, Cartwright medal, Columbia U. Coll. Physicians and Surgeons, 1978, Carel C. Koch Meml. award, Am. Acad. Optometry, 1986; scholar Centennial scholar, Johns Hopkins U., 1976. Master: ACP (regent 1987—2000); fellow: AAAS, Am. Acad. Arts and Scis. (v.p. 2001—); mem.: Assn. Am. Med. Colls., Assn. Am. Physicians, Inst. Medicine NAS, Assn. Am. Med. Colls. (chmn.-elect coun. of deans 1968—69, exec. coun.), Assn. Am. Physicians, Inst. Medicine NAS, Alpha Omega Alpha, Alpha Omega Alpha.

HO-GONZALEZ, WILLIAM, lawyer; b. N.Y.C., Mar. 27, 1957; s. Jack Ho and Iluminada Gonzalez; m. Elizabeth Perez, June 8, 1985. BA, Columbia U., 1979; JD, Harvard U., 1982. Bar: N.Y. 1983, D.C. 1985, Va. 1985. Aeronautical atty. FAA, U.S. Dept. Transp., Washington, 1983-87; asst. U.S. atty. U.S. Atty.'s Office for D.C., Washington, 1987-92; spl. counsel immigration-related unfair employment practices Civil Rights divsn. U.S. Dept. Justice, Washington, 1992-96; sr. trial atty. criminal sect., civil rights divsn. U.S. Dept. Justice, Washington, 1996-98, spl. counsel office of atty. personnel mgmt., 1998—2001, sr. trial atty. criminal sect., civil rights divsn., 2001—02, sr. trial atty., alien smuggling task force, 2002—03, sr. litig. counsel domestic security sect. criminal div., 2003—. Mem. nat. adv. bd. Inst. for Puerto Rican Policy, Inc., 1985-91; mem. cmty. coun. WAMU-FM, 1997-99; mem. unauthorized practice of law com. Va. State Bar, 1999-2002. Mem. D.C. Cir. Task Force on Gender, Race and Ethnic Bias, Washington, 1993-94, Va. Commn. on Women and Minorities in Legal Profession, 1995-98; mem. bus. adv. coun. Campagna Ctr. Mem. Nat. Hispanic Bar Assn., Asian Pacific Am. Bar Assn., Hispanic Bar Assn. Commonwealth of Va. (founding, v.p. 1995-96, mem. bd. govs. 1996-97, 99-2000, pres. 1998-99). Office: Dept Justice Criminal Divsn 1301 New York Ave NW Washington DC 20530-0001

HOGSETT, JOSEPH H. political organization worker, former state official; b. Nov. 2, 1956; Law clk. Judge James H. Dixon Monroe Cir. Ct.; atty. Bingham, Summers, Welsh & Spillman, 1981—87; dep. sec. state Ind., 1987—88; sec. state State of Ind., 1989—94; chmn. Ind. Dem. Party, Indpls., 2003—. Candidate U.S. Senator, Ind., 1992, U.S. Ho. Reps. 2d dist., Ind., 1994.*

HOGSHIRE, EDWARD LEIGH, judge; b. Norfolk, Va., Apr. 14, 1943; S. Russell Blake and Margaret Maria (Johnston) H.; m. Diane Hoyle Austin, June 12, 1992; children by previous marriage: Edward Carlisle, Charles Kent; stepchildren: Jason Austin, Jennie Austin Pitts, Benjamin Austin. BA in English; JD, U. Va. Bar: Va. 1970, D.C. 1972. Law clk. to Hon. Albert V. Bryan, Sr. U.S. Ct. Appeals (4th cir.), 1970-71; staff atty. Coun. of Better Bus. Burs., Washington, 1971-72; dir. Student Legal Svcs., Charlottesville, Va., 1972-73; assoc. Lowe & Gordon, Ltd., 1973-76; ptnr. Paxson, Smith, Boyd, Gilliam & Gouldman, 1976-82, Buck, Hogshire & Tereskerz, Ltd., Charlottesville, 1982-98; judge Charlottesville Cir. Ct., 1998—, chief judge, 2000—02. Lectr. in law U. Va. Sch. Law, 1980-98; dir. criminal practice clinic, 1987-98; mem. professionalism course faculty Va. State Bar, 2000-03. Chmn. Criminal Justice Adv. Coun., Charlottesville, 1975-76; pres. Charlottesville/Albemarle Mental Health Assn., 1981-83. Served as 1st lt. U.S. Army, 1965-67. Recipient Scribner-Garnett award, Charlottesville/Albemarie Mental Health Assn., 1981, Cert. of Merit Criminal Justice Adv. Coun., Thomas Jefferson Planning Dist. Com., 1978. Mem. Va. Bar Assn. (statewide coord. inmate assistance project 1977-79, Citation for Significant Svc.). Episcopalian. Office: Cir Ct City Charlottesville 315 E High St Charlottesville VA 22902-5118

HOGUE, BOB, state senator; b. Whittier, Calif., Sept. 7, 1953; m. Elaine Hogue; children: Jessica, Becky, Jeff, Amanda. BS in Bus., U. So. Calif., 1975. CPA, Hawaii. Acct. Price Waterhouse and Co.; instr. U. Hawaii, U. No. Iowa, Columbia Sch. Broadcasting; Rep. senator dist. 24 Hawaii State Senate. Mem. commerce, consumer protection, housing, health and human svcs., edn. and agr. coms. Hawaii State Senate. Sportscaster KHON-TV, Honolulu, KCRA-TV, Sacramento, KWWL-TV, Waterloo, Iowa, KTIV-TV, Sioux City, KFBB-TV, Great Falls, Mont.; columnist MidWeek; play-by-play announcer U. Iowa, U. Hawaii, HPU. Coach Kailua Basketball Assn., Kailua Am. Little League; vol. Am. Heart Assn., Am. Cancer Soc., Hawaii Arthritic Found. Office: Hawaii State Senate State Capitol Rm 204 415 S Beretania St Honolulu HI 96813 Fax: 808 587-7220. E-mail: senhogue@Capitol.hawaii.gov.*

HOGUE, DALE CURTIS, SR., lawyer; b. St. Louis, Feb. 11, 1942; s. William Curtis Hogue and Juanita Estel Bean; m. Alice Jeam Smith, 1963 (div. 1964); m. Carolyn Frances Jones, Oct. 24, 1965; children: Dale Curtis Jr., Sean Cyril Raymond, Stuart Ridgely. Student, U.S. Naval Acad., 1961; BS in Engring. Sci., Washington U., St. Louis, 1964; JD, Georgetown U., 1972. Bar: Va. 1972, D.C. 1973, N.C. 1990. Ptnr. Hogue, Rhodes & Boss, Washington, 1972-74, Cross, Murphy & Smith, Washington, 1974-77, Hogue, Crothers & Bernard, Washington, 1977-79; corp. sec., gen. counsel ADI, Las Vegas, Nev., 1979-81; pvt. practice Washington, 1981-88, Charlotte, N.C., 1988-89; atty. IBM, Charlotte, 1989-90; assoc. Pennie & Edmonds, Washington, 1990-92; ptnr. Mason, Fenwick & Lawrence (merged with Popham Haik Schnobrich & Kaufman 1994), Washington, 1992-95, Marks & Murase LLP, Washington, 1995-98, Kilpatrick & Cody, Washington, 1996-98, Coudert Bros., Washington, 1998-99, Antonelli, Terry, Stout & Kraus, LLP, Arlington, Va., 1999—2001, Wouble Carlyle Sandridge Rice PLLC, McLean, 2002—. Sec. Nat. Motor Vehicle Safety Adv. Coun., Dept. Transp., Washington, 1971-77. Author: (with others) Association of University Technology Managers Manual, 1992, 94, Minority opinion reporter Alexandria Va. Charter Rev. Commn. Capt. USAF, 1964-68, Vietnam. Mem. Am. Intellectual Property Law Assn., Licensing Execs. Soc. Republican. Episcopalian. Avocations: flying, golfing, sailing. Office: Womble Carlyle Sandridge & Rice 4th Fl 8065 Leesburg Pike Tysons Corner VA 22182-2738 Fax: 703-918-2262. E-mail: dhogue@wcsr.com.

HOGUE, JAMES LARRY, retired academic administrator, business executive; b. Phila., Dec. 14, 1941; s. Coyt Leon and Bobbye Brantley H.; m. Sandra Gilbreath, July 10, 1969; children: Laura Hogue Butler, Lisa Marie. AA, East Ctrl. C.C., 1961; BS, Delta State U., 1963; MS, U. So. Miss., 1969. Tchr. English and speech Biloxi (Miss.) Pub. Schs., 1963-64; pub. rels. dir. Copiah-Lincoln C.C., Wesson, Miss., 1964-67, Vocat. Tech. Edn., Jackson, Miss., 1967-69, Miss. Dept. Edn., Jackson, 1969-79, Entergy Corp., Jackson, 1979-96; v.p. devel. & alumni rels. East Ctrl. C.C., Decatur, Miss., 1996-2001. Cons. in field. Alderman City of Flowood, Miss., 1989-2001; pres. Capital Optimists, Jackson, 1990-91; dist. gov. Ala.-Miss. Optimists, 1991-92. Named Outstanding Young Man, Jackson, 1976, Alumnus of Yr., East Ctrl. C.C., 1990. Mem. Nat. Soc. Fund Raising Execs., Pub. Rels. Assn. Miss. (pres. 1976), Coun. Advancement & Support Edn., Coun. Resource Devel., Flowood Exch. Club. Independent. Methodist. Avocations: travel, nature, reading, photography, politics. Fax: 601-992-1229. E-mail: olmpian61@msn.com.

HOGUE, TERRY GLYNN, lawyer; b. Merced, Calif., Sept. 23, 1944; s. Glynn Dale and Lillian LaVonne (Carter) H.; m. Joanne Laura Sharples, Oct. 3, 1969; children: Morgan Taylor, Whitney Shannon. BA, U. Calif., Fresno, 1966, postgrad., 1967; JD, U. Calif., San Francisco, 1972. Bar: Calif. 1972, Idaho 1975, U.S. Dist. Ct. (cen. dist.) Calif. 1973, U.S. Dist. Ct. Idaho 1975, U.S. Supreme Ct. 1976. Assoc. Reid, Babbage & Coil, Riverside, Calif., 1972-75; pvt. practice, Hailey, Idaho, 1975-77; ptnr. Campion & Hogue, Hailey, 1977-80, Hogue & Speck, Hailey and Ketchum, Idaho, 1980-82, Hogue, Speck & Aanestad, Hailey and Ketchum, 1982-97, Hogue & Dunlap, L.L.P., Hailey and Ketchum, 1998 . Bd. dirs. Blaine County Med. Ctr., Hailey, 1975-91. Sgt. U.S. Army, 1969-71. Mem. ABA, Calif. Bar Assn., Idaho Bar Assn. (hearing panel of profl. conduct bd. 1991-97, chmn. profl. conduct bd. 1994-95), 5th Jud. Dist. Bar Assn. (magistrate com. 1991-93, ethics com. 1991-93), Idaho Trial Lawyers Assn. (bd. dirs. 1982-93, treas. 1985-86, sec. 1986-87, v.p. 1988-89, pres. 1989-90), Assn. Trial Lawyers Am. (sec. coun. of pres. 1989-90, Atla Weideman Wisocki award 1990), Am. Inns. of Ct. (charter Master Bench chpt.), Hailey C. of C. (bd. dirs. 1975-83), Rotary. Home: PO Box 1259 500 Onyx Dr Ketchum ID 83340-1259 Office: Hogue & Dunlap LLP PO Box 460 Hailey ID 83333-0460 also: PO Box 538 Ketchum ID 83340-0538

HOGWOOD, CHRISTOPHER JARVIS HALEY, music educator; b. Nottingham, Eng., Sept. 10, 1941; s. Haley Evelyn and Marion Constance (Higgott) Hogwood. BA, Cambridge (Eng.) U., 1964, MA, 1969; postgrad., Charles U., Prague, Czechoslovakia, 1964-65; DMus (hon.), Keele (Eng.) U., 1991. Founding mem. Early Music Consort London, 1965—76; dir. Acad. Ancient Music, London, 1973—; music faculty Cambridge U., 1975—, hon. prof. music, 2002. Artistic dir. Handel & Haydn Soc., Boston, 1986—2001, condr. laureate, 2001—; hon. prof. music Keele U., 1986—90; dir. music St. Paul Chamber Orch., 1987—92, prin. guest condr., 1992—98; internat. prof. early music performance Royal Acad. Music, London, 1992—; vis. prof. dept. music King's Coll., London, 1992—96; artistic dir. Summer Mozart Festival Nat. Symphony Orch. USA, 1993—2001; assoc. dir. Beethoven Academie, Antwerp, 1998—2002; prin. guest condr. Kammerochester Basel, 2000—, Orquesta Ciudad de Granada, 2001—, Orch. Sinfonica di Milano Giuseppe Verdi, 2003—. Author: (book) Music at Court, 1977, The Trio Sonata, 1979, Haydn's Visits to England, 1980, Handel, 1984; editor: Music in Eighteenth Century England, 1983, Holmes' Life of Mozart, 1991, The Keyboard in Baroque Europe, 2003. Decorated Comdr. of the Brit. Empire; named Freeman, Worshipful Co. Musicians, London, 1989, Chistopher Hogwood Historically Informed Performance Fellowship in his honor, Handel & Hadyn Soc.; recipient Wilson Cobbett medal, Worshipful Co. Musicians, London, 1986, Disting. Musician award, Inc. Soc. Musicians, 1997, Martinu medal, Bohuslav Martinu Found., Prague, 1999; Hon. fellow, Jesus Coll., Cambridge, 1989—, Pembroke Coll., Cambridge, 1992—. Home and Office: 10 Brookside Cambridge CB2 1JE England

HOHENDAHL, PETER UWE, German language and literature educator; b. Hamburg, Fed. Republic Germany, Mar. 17, 1936; came to U.S., 1964; s. Wilhelm and Emilie (Uelschen) H.; m. Iky Maria Zoetelief, July 2, 1965; children: Deborah, Gwendolyn. Student, U. Bern, Switzerland, 1955, U. Hamburg, 1955-57, 59-63, PhD, 1964; postgrad., U. Goettingen, Fed. Republic Germany, 1958. Asst. prof. Pa. State U., 1965-68; assoc. prof. Washington U., St. Louis, 1968-69, prof., 1970-77, head dept., 1972-77; prof. comparative and German lit. Cornell U., Ithaca, N.Y., 1977—, chmn. dept. German, 1981-86, Schurman prof. German and Comparative lit., 1985—, dir. Inst. for German Cultural Studies, 1992—. Merton vis. prof. Berlin U., 1976; disting. vis. prof. Ohio State U., 1987; supr. Studien zur Literatur des 19, Jahrhunderts, 1993, sr. fellow Am. Inst. Contemporary German Studies, Washington, 2000, corr. fellow Inst. Germanic Studies, U. London-Sch. Advanced Study, London, 2001--; Passagen, Festschrift fuer Peter Uwe Hohendahl zum 65. Geburtstag Weidler Buchverlag, Berlin, Germany, 2001. Author: Literaturkritik und Oeffentlichkeit, 1974, Der Europaeische Roman der Empfindsamkeit, 1977, The Institution of Criticism, 1982, Literarische Kultur im Zeitalter des Liberalismus, 1985, A History of German Literary Criticism, 1988, Building a National Literature, 1989, Reappraisals: Shifting Alignments in Postwar Critical Theory, 1991, Heinrich Heine and the Occident: Multiple Identities, Multiple Receptions, 1991, Geschichte, Opposition, Subversion, Studien zur Literatur des 19, Jahrhunderts, 1993, Prismatic Thought: Theodor W. Adorno, 1995, (with R.A. Berman, K. Kenkel and A. Strum) Oeffentlichkeit: Geschichte eines kritischen Begriffs, 2000, others; mem. editl. bd. Studies in 20th Century Lit., 1979—, German Quar., 1983-88. Fellow Harvard U., 1964-65, fellow Ctr. for Interdisciplinary Rsch., Bielefeld, 1981, 87, Guggenheim Found., 1983-84. Mem. MLA, Am. Assn. Tchrs. German, N.Am. Heine Soc. (exec. coun. 1982—, pres. 1986-90), Zeitschrift fuer Germanistik (bd. dirs. 1990—). Home: 81 Genung Rd Ithaca NY 14850-9602 Office: Cornell U Dept of German Studies Ithaca NY 14853 E-mail: puh1@cornell.edu.

HOHMAN, A. J., JR., lawyer; b. San Antonio, Dec. 19, 1934; s. A.J. and Helen (Stehling) H.; m. Mary C. Leonard, Aug. 30, 1958; children: Kristin Marie, Jonathan David. BA in Econs., LLB, St. Mary's U., San Antonio, 1959. Bar: Tex. 1961, U.S. Dist. Ct. (we. and so. dists.) Tex. 1970, U.S. Ct. Appeals (5th cir.) 1971; U.S. Supreme Ct. 1974. Asst. dist. atty. Bexar County, San Antonio, 1961-64; ptnr. Hohman, Georges & Gehring, San Antonio, 1964-93. Editor: Barrister News, 1958-59. Bd. dirs. St. Peter's and St. Joseph's Ch.'s Home, San Antonio, 1974-2003, 92-96, pres., 1980-81, 86-87; pres. Ursuline Acad., San Antonio, 1982-84, bd. dirs., 1984-87. 1st lt. U.S. Army, 1959-61. Fellow Am. Bd. Trial Advocates (pres. San Antonio chpt. 1983-84); mem. Tex. Trial Lawyers Assn. (assoc. dir. 1981-88), San Antonio Trial Lawyers Assn. (pres. 1980), Am. Trial Lawyers Assn. (1975-93). Democrat. Roman Catholic. Avocations: travel, all outdoor activities, reading. Office: Hohman Georges & Gehring 4940 Broadway Ste 101 San Antonio TX 78209 Fax: 210-223-1496.

HOHMANN, JOHN G. neurobiologist; s. John A. and Maxine M. Hohmann; children: Brett, Brendon, Shay. BSc, Western Wash. U., 1995; PhD, u. Wash., 2000. Mgr. W. Bates and Son, Chertsey, England, 1977—80; bus. owner LaConner (Wash.) Landing, 1981—91; logistics coord. Outward Bound, Anacortes, Wash., 1994—95; neurobiologist Primal, Inc., Seattle, 2001—. Contbr. chapters to books, articles to profl. jours. Adult literacy tutor Literacy Coun., London, 1977—81; vol. fireman Hope Island Fire Dept., LaConner, 1989—91; gun control adv. Handgun Control, Washington, 1995—. Huckabay fellow, U. Wash., 1999. Mem.: Faculty Undergrad. Neurosci., Soc. for Neurosci., Skagit Alpine Club, Phi Kappa Phi. Democrat. Achievements include development of galanin transgenic mice as model for Alzheimer's Disease; characterized galanin knock out mice phenotypes; first characterization of GPCR receptor superfamily expression profile. Office: Primal Inc 1124 Columbia St #650 Seattle WA 98104

HOHN, DAVID, physician; b. Tucson, 1942; BS cum laude, U. Ill., 1964, MD, 1970. Intern Rush-Presbyn. St. Luke's Hosp., Chgo., 1970—71; resident in gen. surgery U. Calif., San Francisco, 1971—78, asst. prof. surgery, 1978—84, assoc. prof. surgery, 1984—87, U. Tex. Med. Sch., M.D. Anderson Cancer Ctr., 1987—90; prof. surgery U. Tex. Med. Sch., 1990—97; v.p. patient care M.D. Anderson Cancer Ctr.-U. Tex., Houston, 1993—97; pres., CEO Roswell Park Cancer Inst., 1997—. Mem.: Soc. of Surg. Oncology, Surg. Infection Soc., Surg. Infection Soc., Am. Assn. for Cancer Rsch., Am. Soc. for Clin. Oncology, Am. Fedn. for Clin. Rsch., Am. Coll. Physician Execs., Assn. for Acad. Surgery. Office: Roswell Park Cancer Inst Elm And Carlton St Buffalo NY 14263-0001

HOHN, HARRY GEORGE, retired insurance company executive, lawyer; b. N.Y.C., Mar. 1, 1932; s. Harry George and Violia (Meehan) H.; m. Janet Jean LaRosa, June 19, 1954; children: Cynthia, Jennifer, Nancy, Patricia. BS, NYU, 1953, LLM, 1959; JD, Fordham U., 1956. Bar: N.Y. 1956, U.S. Supreme Ct. 1976. With N.Y. Life Ins. Co., N.Y.C., 1956-2000, sr. v.p., gen. counsel, 1977-82, exec. v.p., gen. counsel, 1982-83, exec. v.p., 1983-86, CEO, 1990-97, also chmn. bd. dirs., past vice chmn. bd. dirs., 1997—, ret. chmn., CEO, 1997. Bd. dirs. Life and Health Ins. Med. Rsch. Fund, Million Dollar Roundtable Found.; chmn. bd. dirs. Life Ins. Coun. N.Y.; past chmn. Am. Coun. Life Ins.; mem. internat. adv. bd. Credit Comml. de France; trustee Mainstay Funds. Editor: Fordham Law Rev, 1955-56. Trustee Am. Coll., Com. Econ. Devel.; trustee emeritus Found. Ind. Higher Edn.; chmn., bd. trustees Nat. AIDS Fund; bd. govs. United Way of Tri-State; mem. adv. bd. North Fork Environ. Coun., Bowery Mission; chmn. bd. advisors Resurrection Sch. in Harlem, N.Y.C.. Fellow Am. Bar Found. (life); mem. Assn. Life Ins. Counsel (bd. govs.), Bus. Roundtable. Republican. Roman Catholic. Office: NY Life Ins Co 51 Madison Ave New York NY 10010-5077

HOHNER, KENNETH DWAYNE, retired fodder company executive; b. St. John, Kans., June 24, 1934; s. Courtney Clinton and Mildred Lucile (Forrester) H.; m. Sherry Eloi Anice Edens, Feb. 14, 1961; children: Katrina, Melissa, Steven, Michael. BS in Geol. Engring., U. Kans., 1957. Geophysicist Mobil Oil Corp., New Orleans, Anchorage, Denver, 1957-72; sr. geophysicist Amerada Hess Corp., Houston, 1972-75, ARAMCO, London, 1975-79; far east area geophysicist Hamilton Bros., Denver, 1979-83; owner Hohner Poultry Farm, Erie, Colo., 1979-94; pres. Hohner Custom Feed, Inc., Erie, Colo., 1982-94. Mem. Soc. Exploration Geophysicists. Home: 1201 W Thornton Pkwy Lot 390 Denver CO 80260-5424

HOHNHORST, JOHN CHARLES, judge; b. Jerome, Idaho, Dec. 25, 1952; m. Raelene Casper; children: Jennifer, Rachel, John. BS in Polit. Sci./Pub. Adminstrn., U. Idaho, 1975, JD cum laude, 1978. Bar: Idaho 1978, U.S. Dist. Ct. Idaho 1978, U.S. Ct. Appeals (9th cir.) 1980, U.S. Ct. Claims 1983, U.S. Supreme Ct. 1987. Adminstrv. asst. to Sen. John M. Barker Idaho State Senate, 1975; ptnr. Hepworth, Lezamiz & Hohnhorst, Twin Falls, Idaho, 1978—2001; dist. judge 5th Jud. Dist. Ct., Twin Falls County, Idaho, 2001—. Contbr. articles to profl. jours. Mem. planning & zoning commn. City of Twin Falls 1987-90. Mem. ABA, ATLA, Idaho State Bar (commr. 1990-93, pres. 1993), Am. Coll. Trial Lawyers, Idaho Trial Lawyers Assn. (regional dir. 1985-86), 5th Dist. Bar Assn. (treas. 1987-88, v.p. 1988-89, pres. 1989-90), Am. Acad. Appellate Lawyers, Greater Twin Falls C. of C. (chmn. magic valley leadership program 1988-89, bd. dirs. 1989-92), Phi Kappa Tau (Beta Gamma chpt., Phi award 1988). Office: Theron Ward Jud Bldg 427 Shoshoe St N PO Box 126 427 Twin Falls ID 83303-0126

HOIBY, LEE, composer, concert pianist; b. Madison, Wis., Feb. 17, 1926; s. Henry Bjorn and Violet Ethel (Smith) H. MusB, U. Wis., 1947; MA, Mills Coll., Oakland, Calif., 1952; cert., Curtis Inst., Phila., 1952; DFA (hon.), Simpson Coll., Indianola, Iowa, 1985. Composer (operas) The Scarf, 1955, Piano Concerto 1, 1957, A Month in the Country, 1964, Summer and Smoke, 1970, Something New for the Zoo, 1979, The Italian Lesson, 1980, The Tempest, 1985, This Is the Rill Speaking, 1992, (ballet) After Eden, 1967, (cantatas) Hymn of the Nativity, 1960, For You O Democracy, 1993, (oratorio) Galileo Galilei, 1975, Piano Concerto 2, 1979, (baritone and orch.) The Tides of Sleep, 1960, I Have A Dream, 1988, Serenade for Violin and Orch., 1987, Flute Concerto, 1994, (opera) Romeo and Juliet, 2003, also chamber, choral, vocal, theatre music. Recipient Am. Acad. Arts and Letters award, 1957; fellow Fulbright Found., 1952, Guggenheim Found., 1958, Nat. Endowment for the Arts, 1980, Rockefeller Found. grantee, 1979. Mem. ASCAP, Am. Guild Organists (hon.) Home: 9807 County Hwy 28 Long Eddy NY 12760

HOIM, TERJE, mathematician, educator; b. Tartu, Estonia, July 30, 1971; d. Ants and Saima Haljaste; m. Kurmet Hoim, May 29, 1993. BSc in Math. cum laude, MSc in Math. cum laude, U. Tartu, 1995; MA in Math., PhD in Pure Math., Kent (Ohio) State U., 2000. Asst. prof. math. Trinity Coll., Hartford, Conn., 2000—. Contbr. articles to profl. jours. Recipient Ann. Internat. Academic Excellence awards, Phi Beta Delta, 1997, 1998, 1999, 2000; grantee, Soros Open Soc. Inst., 2001. Mem.: Math. Assn. of Am., Assn. Women in Math., Am. Math. Soc. Achievements include research in operation theory and geometry of Banach spaces. Avocations: sports, travel, music. Office: Trinity Coll 300 Summit St MCEC 227 Hartford CT 06106 E-mail: terje.hoim@trincoll.edu.

HOINES, DAVID ALAN, lawyer; b. St. Paul, Minn., Oct. 18, 1946; s. Arnold H. and Patricia (Olson) H.; m. Bonnie K. Smith, June 4, 1983. BA, Calif. State U., San Jose, 1969; JD, Santa Clara U., 1972; LLM in Taxation, Boston U., 1973. Bar: Fla. 1975, Calif. 1975, N.Y. 1999, U.S. Dist. Ct. (so. dist.) Fla. 1975, U.S. Dist. Ct. (no. dist.) Calif. 1980, U.S. Dist. Ct. (mid. dist.) Fla. 1984, U.S. Dist. Ct. (ctrl. dist.) Calif. 1990, U.S. Ct. Claims 1980, U.S. Tax Ct. 1975, U.S. Ct. Appeals (fed. cir.) 1990, U.S. Ct. Appeals (4th cir.) 1985, U.S. Ct. Appeals (5th cir.) 1978, U.S. Ct. Appeals (9th cir.) 1980, U.S. Ct. Appeals (11th cir.) 1981, U.S. Supreme Ct. 1980; cert. civil trial lawyer. Pvt. practice, Ft. Lauderdale, Fla., 1975—. Adj. instr. Nova U. Ctr. for Study of Law, 1977. Author: Taxman and the Textbook, The Ripon Forum, 1972. Mem. ABA, ATLA., Broward County Bar Assn., Fla. Bar Assn., Calif. Bar Assn., State Bar of N.Y., Hundred Club of Broward County, Tau Delta Phi. Avocations: ocean diving (free and scuba), snowskiing, boating, reading. Office: 1290 E Oakland Park Blvd Fort Lauderdale FL 33334-4443 E-mail: dahfl@aol.com.

HOIVIK, THOMAS HARRY, military educator, international consultant; b. Mpls., June 6, 1941; s. Tony Horace and Helen Lenea (Carlsen) H.; m. Judith Lisa Kohn; children: Todd, Gregory. BA, U. Minn., 1963; grad. with distinction, Naval Test Pilot Sch., 1969; MS with distinction, Naval Postgrad. Sch., 1973; grad. with distinction, Naval War Coll., 1976; MA, Salve Regina U., 1988. Cert. exptl. test pilot, air transport pilot, jet aircraft, helicopter, glider single and multi-engine. Commd. ensign USN, 1963, advanced through grades to capt., 1963-91; test pilot Naval Air Test Ctr., Patuxent River, Md., 1968-71; program mgr. H-53 aircraft Naval Air Systems Command, Washington, 1976-78; comdg. officer Helicopter Mine Countermeasure Squadron 14, Norfolk, Va., 1978-80; dir. U.S. Naval Test Pilot Sch., Patuxent River, 1980-82; fed. exec. fellow Ctr. for Strategic and Internat. Studies, Washington, 1982-83; chair tactical analysis Naval Postgrad. Sch., Monterey, Calif., 1983-85; comdg. officer Naval Air Sta., Willow Grove, Pa., 1985-87; chair applied systems analysis Naval Postgrad. Sch., Monterey, 1987-91, prof. acquisition mgmt. and ops. rsch., 1991—; ret. capt. USN, 1991; dir. test and evaluation sr. level curriculum Defense Acquisition U., 1993—. Mem. U.S. Congrl. Study Group on Nat. Strategy, Washington, 1982-83, World Economy, 1982-83; cons. U.S., Internat. Govt. Orgns., 1990—; founder, pres. Lysonics Rsch. Internat., 1993, Inst. for In-Flight Rsch., 1996; flight demonstration pilot Paris Internat. Air Show, 1967 Contbr. articles to profl. jours. Bd. dirs. Vocat. Edn. Bd., Montgomery County, Pa., 1985-87, Congrl. Svc. Acad. Appointment Bd., Phila., 1985-87; youth leader, counselor YMCA, St. Paul, 1955-61. Recipient Legion of Merit Pres. of U.S., 1987, Outstanding Youth Leadership award YMCA, 1960; established U.S. Helicopter Speed Record, 1966. Mem. AIAA, Soc. of Exptl. Test Pilots, Internat. Test and Evaluation Assn. (Internat. Test and Evaluation Cross award 1997), Nat. Contract Mgmt. Assn., Ops. Rsch. Soc. Am., Mil. Ops. Rsch. Soc., U. Minn. "M" Club, Disable Am. Vets, Sigma Alpha Epsilon. Avocations: tennis, music composition. Office: Naval Postgrad Sch Monterey CA 93943

HOJNOWSKI, JULES AUSTIN, entrepreneur; b. Elmira, N.Y., Nov. 3, 1959; d. Richard Glenn and Audrey Marie Hovencamp; m. Michael Q. Hojnowski, Sept. 4, 1994. BS, Elmira Coll., 1985, MS, 2001. Profl. spinner of exotic fibers, 2000—. Author (contributor): (books, web sites) Mark Twain's in-law's - the Langdons. Mem.: So. Atlantic MLA (corr.; spkr.), Elmira, Mark Twain Soc. (assoc.; student asst. 1982—2000), Mark Twain Boyhood Assn. (assoc.), Mark Twain Found (corr.), Mark Twain Soc.; pres. 1976—77). Home: 1690 Trumansburg Rd Ithaca NY 14850-9213 Personal E-mail: jah@twcny.rr.com.

HOJO, LAWRENCE MATTHEW, JR., legislative director; b. North Charleroi, Pa., Apr. 20, 1954; s. Lawrence Matthew and Rose Anna (Cole) H. BA in English and Journalism, Ind. U. Pa., 1976, MPA, 1984. Reporter, photographer Pioneer Newspapers, Monongahela, Pa., 1976-77; feature writer Punxsutawney (Pa.) Spirit, 1977-78; reporter Kittanning (Pa.) Leader-Times, 1978-79, Indiana (Pa.) Gazette, 1979-88; legis. asst. U.S. Rep. Joel Hefley, Washington, 1988-94, legis. dir., 1994—. Recipient hon. mention, Coll. and Univ. Pub. Rels. Assn., 1984. Fellow Brit. Interplanetary Soc.; mem. Am. Polit. Sci. Assn. (fellow 1987-88), Am. Mensa, Friends of Taliesin. Lutheran. Avocations: reading, travel, hiking, fine dining, ballroom dancing. Office: Office US Rep Joel Hefley 2230 Rayburn HOB Washington DC 20515-0001

HOKANA, GREGORY HOWARD, engineering executive; b. Burbank, Calif., 1944; s. Howard Leslie and Helen Lorraine H.; m. Eileen Marie Youell, 1967; children: Kristen Marie, Kenneth Gregory. BS in Physics, UCLA, 1966. Design engr. Raytheon Co., Oxnard, Calif., 1967-74; staff engr. Bunker Ramo Corp., Westlake Village, Calif., 1974-84; mgr. analog engring. AIL Systems, Inc., Westlake Village, 1984-91; mgr. product devel. Am. Nucleonics Corp., Westlake Village, 1991-93; tech. mgr. Litton Data Sys., Agoura Hills, Calif., 1994-2000; sr. tech. staff Litton Guidance and Control Sys., Woodland Hills, Calif., 2000—01; tech.mgr. Northrop Grumman Nav. Systems Divsn., Woodland Hills, 2001—. Mem. IEEE, Assn. Old Crows. Democrat. Methodist. Avocations: golf, swimming, photography. Office: Northrop Grumman Navigation Systems Divsn 21240 Burbank Blvd Woodland Hills CA Business E-Mail: greg.hokana@ngc.com. E-mail: ghokana@ix.netcom.com.

HOKE, GEORGE PEABODY, lawyer; b. St. Paul, Mar. 18, 1913; s. George Edward and Carolyn Grahfs (Peabody) H.; m. Carolyn Elizabeth Glass, May 25, 1940 (div. 1963); children— Carolyn G., George G. Jared Peabody. A.B. cum laude, Dartmouth Coll., 1935; J.D., Yale U., 1938. Bar: Minn. 1939, U.S. Dist. Ct. Minn. 1940, U.S. Dist. Ct. (so. dist.) Iowa 1965, U.S. Tax Ct. 1945, U.S. Ct. Appeals (8th cir.) 1970. Ptnr., Snyder Gale Hoke, Richard & Janes, Minneapolis, 1943-57, Wheeler, Fredriksen, Hoke & Larson, Minneapolis, 1957-61; sr. ptnr. Hoke, Roehrdenz, Bigelow & Chamberlain, Mpls., 1975-86; central U.S. counsel Inter-provincial Pipe Line Co., Can., 1950-54; sec. and chmn. bd. Velie Ryan, Inc., Rochester, Minn., 1940-70, trustee Shattuck Sch., Faribault, Minn. 1940-70. Vestryman St. David's Episc. Ch., Hopkins, Minn., 1940-65, St. Paul's Episc. Ch., Mpls., 1985—; chmn. Henn County Civil Def., Mpls. and Wayzata, 1942-45; campaign sec. Republican State Central Com. Minn., St. Paul, 1944-48; campaign chmn., 1948; mem. Minn. Rep. Central Com., 1940-48. Served to lt. j.g., USN, 1942-1943. Mem. Am. Law Inst. (life mem., mem. joint com. A.B.A./Am. Law Inst. 1940-50), ABA (Minn. state dir. jr. bar. conf. 1945-55), Hennepin County Bar Assn. (chmn. tax sect. and jr. bar sec. 1945-55), Minn. State Bar Assn., Am. Judicature Soc. (state dir. 1960), Phi Delta Phi (province pres. 1940-70), Beta Theta Pi. Republican. Episcopalian. Clubs: Minneapolis, Mory's Assn. (New Haven). Home and Office: PO Box 102 Marine On Saint Croix MN 55047-0102

HOKE, JUDY ANN, physical education educator; b. Mesa, Ariz., May 3, 1951; d. Jewell Juett and Margaret Lucille (Gibson) H. BA, Ariz. State U., 1973, MS, 1976. Cert. tchr. Ariz. Tchr., coach womens Tennis Tempe (Ariz.) Union High Sch. Dist., 1973—, chmn. Phys. Edn., 1978—. Former co-chmn. sch. improvement com.; chmn. East Valley Women's Tennis Region. Mem. First Christian Ch., Phoenix Zoo. Named Outstanding Secondary Phys. Edn. Tchr. Yr. State of Ariz., 1991. Mem. NEA, AAHPERD, Ariz. Alliance Health Phys. Edn. Recreation and Dance, Tempe Secondary Edn. Assn., Women's Internat. Tennis Assn., U.S. Tennis Assn. Republican. Avocation: reading. Office: Marcos de Niza High Sch 6000 S Lakeshore Dr Tempe AZ 85283-3049

HOKE, SHEILA WILDER, retired librarian; b. Greensboro, N.C. d. Herbert Bruce Wilder and Virginia Dare (Caylor) Wilder-Dell; m. Robert Edward Hoke, Nov. 22, 1958 (dec.); children: Raymond Fellow, Philip Wilder. Student, Montclair Coll., 1948; BA in History, U. Kans., 1950, postgrad., 1951, BS in Edn., 1952; postgrad., JOhn Hopkins U., 1955; MLS, U. Wis., 1955; MS in Edn., Southwestern Okla. State U., 1977; postgrad., Johns Hopkins U., Montclair State Coll. Tchr. history Fredonia (Kans.) High Sch., 1952-54; student asst. U. Wis., Madison, 1954-55; children's libr. BR Enoch Pratt Libr., Balt., 1955-58; libr. dir. U.S. Army Spl. Svcs., Bavaria, Fed. Republic Germany, 1958-59; libr. U.S. Army Dependent Schs., Straubing, Fed. Republic Germany, 1959-60; cataloger Southwestern Okla. State U. Libr., Weatherford, 1963-69, libr. dir., 1969-93; ret., 1993. Mem. spl. projects com. Okla. Dept. Edn., 1974, adv. com. Okla. State Regents Libr., 1975-77. Mem. Okla. State Regents for Higher Edn. Libr. Networking, 1989-93; mem. sr. citizens choir 1st Bapt. Ch., Weatherford; vol. with children Agape Med. Clinic; reading tutor to 1st grade student Weatherford Pub. Schs.; vol. helper for home-bound; active sr. citizens groups. Mem. AAUW (pres., state bd. dirs. 1980, Weatherford br. 1981-83), Nat. Assn. Ret. Fed. Employees, Okla. Libr. Assn. (chmn. tech. svcs. divsn. 1969-70, chmn. coll. and univ. divsn. 1972-73, chmn. adminstrs. workshop 1973, chmn. libr. edn. divsn. 1975-76, chmn. recruitment com. 1978, archives com. 1980), Okla. Ret. Tchrs. Assn., Weatherford C. of C. (edn. com. 1974-75, cert. meritorious achievement from Gov. Nigh 1985), Custer County Hist. Soc., western Okla. Hist. Soc., Higher Edn. Alumni Coun. Okla., Delta Kappa Gamma (pres. Lambda chpt. 1980-82), Phi Alpha theta, Kappa Kappa Iota (pres. Lambda chpt. 1984-85). Republican. Baptist. E-mail: shoke@itlnet.net.

HOKENSON, DAVID LEONARD, secondary school educator; b. Mpls., Nov. 9, 1950; s. Raymond Leonard and Barbara Jean (Hooker) H.; m. Cynthia Jane Luehmann, July 28, 1979. BA, St. Olaf Coll., 1972; postgrad., U. Minn., 1977, 78, 82. Lic. secondary sch. social studies and history tchr., Minn. Social studies tchr. Preston (Minn.)-Fountain Pub. Schs., 1972-93, Fillmore Ctrl. H.S., Harmony, Minn., 1993-95; Fillmore Ctrl. Mid. Sch., Preston, Minn., 1995—. Mem. team evaluation State Dept. Edn., St. Paul, 1981, 83, 91, 98. Mem. Nat. Trust for Hist. Preservation; treas. Preston-Fountain Edn. Assn., 1987—93, negotiator, 1993—94; treas. Edn. Minn. Fillmore Ctrl., 1994—; mem. evaluation team North Ctrl. Accreditation Assn., 1994; participant Project 120, 1995; mem. Minn. Hist. Soc.; precinct chair Dem.-Farmer-Labor Party, Preston, 1990—; pres. Christ Luth. Ch., 2001—02. Recipient scholarship Minn. Inst. for Advancement of Teaching, St. Paul, 1992, 97. Mem. Nat. Geog. Soc., Am. Scandinavian Found., Am.-Swedish Inst., Smithsonian Instn., Minn. Hist. Soc., Libr. of Congress. Office: Fillmore Ctrl Schs PO Box 50 Preston MN 55965-0050 E-mail: david.hokenson@isd2198.k12,mn.us., d.hokenson@mchsi.com.

HOKENSTAD, MERL CLIFFORD, JR., social work educator; b. Norfolk, Nebr., July 21, 1936; s. Merl Clifford and Flora Diane (Christian) H.; m. Dorothy Jean Tarrell, June 24, 1962; children: Alene Ann, Laura Rae, Marta Lynn. BA summa cum laude, Augustana Coll., 1958; Rotary Found. fellow, Durham (Eng.) U., 1958-59; MSW., Columbia U., 1962; PhD, Brandeis U., 1969, Inst. Ednl. Mgmt., Harvard U., 1977. With Lower East Side Neighborhood Assn., N.Y.C., 1962-64; community planning assoc. United Community Services, Sioux Falls, S.D., 1964-66; instr. Augustana Coll., Sioux Falls, 1964-66; research assoc. Ford Found. Project on Community Planning for Elderly, Brandeis U., Waltham, Mass., 1966-67; prof., dir. Sch. Social Work, Western Mich. U., Kalamazoo, 1968-74; prof., dean Sch. Applied Social Scis., Case Western Res. U., Cleve., 1974-83, Ralph and Dorothy Schmitt prof., 1983—, chmn. PhD program, 1990-94; prof. internat. health Sch. of Medicine, 1994—. Vis. prof. Inst. Sociology, Stockholm U., 1978, Fulbright lectr., 1980; vis. prof. Nat. Inst. Social Work, London, 1981, Sch. Social Work, Stockholm U., 1982-86, Eotvos Lorand U., Budapest, Hungary, 1992, 95, 96, London Sch. Econs., 1994; Fulbright rsch. scholar Inst. Applied Social Rsch., Oslo, 1989; fellow U. Canterbury, Christchurch, New Zealand, 1994; mem. UN tech. com. World Assembly on Aging, 2000-02; mem. U.S. delegation UN World Assembly on Aging, 2002. Author: Participation in Teaching and Learning: An Idea Book for Social Work Educators; editor: Meeting Human Needs: An International Annual, Vol. V, Linking Health Care and Social Services: International Perspectives; editor-in-chief Internat. Social Work Jour., 1985-87; co-editor: Profiles in Internat. Social Work, 1992, Issues in International Social Work, 1997, Models of International Exchange, 2003; (internat. issue) Jour. Gerontol. Social Work, 1988, Jour. Sociology and Social Welfare, 1990, Jour. Social Policy and Administration, 1993, Jour. Aging Internat., 1994, Jour. Applied Social Scis., 1996; contbr. articles to profl. jours., chpts. to books. Mem. alcohol tng. rev. com. Nat. Inst. Alcoholism and Alcohol Abuse, 1974-78; workshop leader Am. Assn. State Colls. and Univs., 1974; chmn. U.S. com. XVIII Internat. Congress Schs. Social Work, 1976; chmn. Kalamazoo County Cmty. Mental Health Svcs. Bd., 1971, vice chmn., 1972; mem. edn. and tng. task force Mich. Office Drug Abuse and Alcoholism, 1972-73; mem. Mich. Assn. Mental Health Bds., 1972; bd. dirs. Cleve. United Way Svcs., 1982-84, del. assembly, 1974-82, mem. periodic rev. oversight com., 1982, mem. leadership devel. com., 1978, cmty. resources com., 1988—; bd. dirs. Kalamazoo United Way, 1968-72; trustee Cleve. Internat. Program for Youth Workers and Social Workers, chmn. program com., 1985-87; mem. program devel. com. Cleve. Center on Alcoholism, 1976; trustee Alcoholism Services Cleve., Inc., 1977-86, v.p., 1982-85; trustee Cmty. Info./Vol. Action Ctr., 1982-88, chmn. leadership devel. com., 1984-86, chmn. unmet needs com., 1986-88, exec. com., 1985-88, v.p., 1986-88; exec. com. Western Reserve Geriatric Edn. Ctr., 1995—; mem. adv. com. Coun. for Internat. Exch. Scholars, 1991-93, Fedn. for Cmty. Planning Coun. on Older Persons, 1991—, chmn. caregiver support program initiative, 1995-96; mem. adv. coun. Cuyahoga County Dept. Sr. and Adult Svcs., 1998—, chair, 2001—; mem. task force of social transition in Soviet Union, U.S. State Dept. Bur. Human Rights and Humanitarian Affairs; mem. UN NGO Com. on Aging, 1996—; co-chmn. U.S. Com. for Internat. Yr. of Older Persons, 1999. Named Outstanding Alumnus, Augustana Coll., 1980, Ohio Soc. Worker of the Yr., 1992; Fulbright Research fellow; NIMH trainee, 1960-62; Vocat. Rehab. trainee, 1966; Gerontology trainee, 1967; Rotary Found. fellow, 1958-59; recipient Golden Achievement Award, Golden Age Ctr., 2003. Mem. NASW (internat. com. 1989-93, chmn. 1992-93, Found. Pioneer 2003—), Acad. Cert. Social Workers, Internat. Assn. Schs. Social Work (exec. bd. 1978-92, 98—, treas. 1978-86, v.p. N.Am. 1988-92, membership sec. 1996-2000), Internat. Coun. on Social Welfare (dir. U.S. com. 1982-92), Coun. on Social Work Edn. (del. 1972-75, 77-83, chmn. ann. program meeting 1973, chmn. com. on nat. legis. and adminstrv. policy 1975-79, nominating com. 1978-81, internat. com. 1980-86, 96—, chmn. com. 1982-84, dir. 1979-82, exec. com. 1986-89, pres. 1986-89, Lifetime Achievement award 2002), Nat. Conf. on Social Welfare (bd. dirs. 1978-80, chmn. sect. V program com. 1977-78), World Future Soc. (area coord. 1972-74), Fulbright Assn. (v.p. N.E. Ohio chpt. 1990-91), Nat. Coun. on Aging (bd. dirs. 1991-97, internat. com. 1991-97, pub. policy com. 1992-97), NASW Found. Pioneer, 2003-. Democrat. Episcopalian. Home: 2917 Weymouth Rd Cleveland OH 44120-2234 Office: Case Western Res U 10900 Euclid Ave Cleveland OH 44106-1712 E-mail: mch2@po.cwru.edu.

HOKIN, LOWELL EDWARD, biochemist, educator; b. Chgo., Sept. 20, 1924; s. Oscar E. and Helen (Manfield) H.; m. Mabel Neaverson, Dec. 1, 1952 (div. Dec. 1973); children: Linda Ann, Catherine Esther (dec.), Samuel Arthur; m. Barbara M. Gallagher, Mar. 23, 1978 (div. July 1998); 1 child, Ian Oscar. Student, U. Chgo., 1942-43, Dartmouth Coll., 1943-44, U. Louisville Sch. Medicine, 1944-46, U. Ill. Sch. Medicine, 1946-47; MD, U. Louisville, 1948; PhD, U. Sheffield, Eng., 1952. Postdoctoral fellow dept. biochemistry McGill U., 1952-54, faculty, 1954-57, asst. prof., 1955-57; mem. faculty U. Wis., Madison, 1957—, prof. physiol. chemistry, 1961-68, prof. pharmacology, 1968-99, prof., chmn. pharmacology, 1968-93, prof. emeritus, 1999—. Contbr. numerous articles to tech. jours., chpts. to numerous books on phosphoinositides, biol. transport, the pancreas, the brain and lithium in manic-depression. With USNR, 1943-45. Mem. AAAS, Am. Soc. Biochemistry and Molecular Biology, Biochem. Soc. (U.K.), Am. Soc. Pharmacology and Exptl. Therapeutics, N.Y. Acad. Scis. Achievements include discovery of phosphoinositide signaling system. Home: 4021C Monona Dr Monona WI 53716 Office: U Wis Med Sch Dept Pharm 1300 University Ave Madison WI 53706-1510 E-mail: lehokin@facstaff.wisc.edu.

HOLABIRD, JOHN AUGUR, JR., retired architect; b. Chgo., May 9, 1920; s. John Augur and Dorothy (Hackett) H.; m. Donna Katharine Smith, Nov. 25, 1942 (div. 1969); children: Jean, Katharine, Polly, Lisa (dec.); m. Marcia Stefanie Fergestad, June 28, 1969 (dec. Mar. 1994); children: Ann, Lynn; m. Janet Nothhelfer Connor, May 7, 1996. BA, Harvard U., 1942, MArch, 1948. Archtl. designer Holabird & Root, Chgo., 1948-49, 55-64, assoc. firm, 1964-70, ptnr., 1970-87. Tchr. drama Francis Parker Sch., Chgo., 1949-55; stage designer NBC-TV, 1955 Major: archtl. works include Francis Parker Sch, Chgo., Ravinia Stage and Restaurant, Highland Park, Ill., 1970, Bell Telephone Labs, Naperville, Ill., 1975, Canal Bldg, Chgo., 1974. Pres. Park West Community Assn., 1962; dir. Lincoln Park Conservation Assn., 1960-64, Corlands, 1979-85; mem. Chgo. Commn. on Historic and Archtl. Landmarks, 1981-85; bd. dirs. Lincoln Park Community Conservation, 1964; trustee Francis Parker Sch., Ravinia Festival Assn., Ill. Inst. Tech., 1980-86. Served with U.S. Army, 1942-45. Decorated Silver Star, Bronze Star; Fourragère (Belgium); Order of William (The Netherlands). Fellow AIA (pres. Chgo. chpt. 1977-78); mem. Tavern Club, Harvard Club (dir. 1974-78), Phi Beta Kappa. Democrat. Home: 200 E Pearson St Apt 3W Chicago IL 60611-2352 Office: Holabird & Root 300 W Adams St Chicago IL 60606-5101

HOLADAY, SUSAN G. editor; b. Batavia, N.Y., Nov. 2, 1938; d. Norman and Sada Jule (Jacobson) Goldberg.; m. William C. Holaday, Dec. 25, 1968 (dec. Feb. 1977). BA, Syracuse U., 1960; MA, U. Chgo., 1963. Editor Foodservice East and predecessor publ., 1975—. Co-chair Navy Yard Neighborhood Assn., Charlestown, Mass., 1998—; mem. Area A-1 Police Neighborhood Adv. Coun., Boston, 1993—. Avocations: reading, walking, houseplants, photography. E-mail: fdsvceast@aol.com.

HOLAHAN, JOHN MICHAEL, music educator, researcher; b. Medina, N.Y., Oct. 1, 1956; s. Eugene Francis and Virginia Marie Holahan; m. Cathy Jean Zack, Aug. 12, 1995. BA in Music and Psychology, MFA in Music Pedagogy, SUNY, Buffalo, 1979; PhD in Music Edn. Rsch., Temple U., 1983. Cert. music edn. N.Y. Asst. prof. music edn. Temple U., Phila., 1983—86; rsch. data analyst dept. psychiatry VA Med. Ctr., U. Pa., Phila., 1987—88; dir. data mgmt. Yale U. Sch. Medicine, Ctr. Study of Learning and Attention, New Haven, 1988—. Prin., 2d trumpet, concert mgr., bd. dirs. Civic Orch. New Haven, 1989—; prin., asst. prin., 2d trumpet Hamden Symphony Orch., 1990—; adj. assoc. prof. music edn. Hartt Sch., U. Hartford, West Hartford, Conn., 1999—; instr. grad. liberal studies program Wesleyan U., Middletown, Conn., 1999; adj. assoc. Ctrl. Conn. State U., New Britain, 2000. Contbr. chapters to books, articles to profl. jours. Fellow Russell Conwell U. fellow, Temple U., 1980—82. Mem.: Soc. Music Perception and Cognition, Soc. Rsch. Music Edn. Home: 108 Mattabasset Dr Durham CT 06422 Personal E-mail: jholahan1@comcast.net.

HOLAND, PAMELA KRISIDA, professional organizer; b. Dallas, Jan. 22, 1940; d. John Lowery and Mary Elizabeth Vines; children: David, Deborah, DiAnn, Brian, Michael. Investment brokers various firms, Mpls., 1982—85, Dallas, 1982—85; legal asst. Dallas, 1986—96; pvt. practice profl. organizer, 1996—. State senator, ND, 1974. Mem.: Nat. Study Group on Chronic Disorganization, Nat. Assn. Profl. Organizers, Dallas Ft. Worth Assn. Profl. Orgns. (founder-leader 2000—). E-mail: unclutter@aol.com.

HOLBERG, EVA MARIA, volunteer; b. Stralsund, Germany, Apr. 22, 1931; came to U.S., 1957, naturalized, 1962; d. Hans Herbert and Helene Wilhelmine (Engelhardt) Thieshen; m. Dieter E. Holberg, May 28, 1955; children: Marion (dec.), Astrid. Student, Free U., West Berlin, 1952-55. Mgr. Pathways to Music, Mt. St. Mary's Coll., L.A., 1972-74; pres., mgr. Palisades Symphony, Pacific Palisades, Calif., 1974—; pres. Theatre Palisades, 1979-81, 82-83, v.p., 1983—, bd. dirs., chmn. ways and means, 1981—. Active mem. westside jr. com. L.A. Philharmon., 1971—, bd. dirs., 1972-85, pres., 1975-77, chmn. seasonal ticket sales, 1977-83, chmn. Bus. to Hollywood Bowl, 1972—, coord. affiliates for youth programs and season tickets, 1979-81; cultural rep. Palisades Cmty. Coun., 1976. Named Citizen of Yr. Pacific Palisades, 1981. Mem. Am. Symphony League. Home: 1081 Palisair Pl Pacific Palisades CA 90272-2459 Office: Box PO Box 214 Pacific Palisades CA 90272-0214

HOLBERT, CAROLYN D. education educator, writer; d. Joe S. and Willa Mae Holbert; 1 child, Adrianna. BA in comparative lit., Berea Coll., 1968—73; MA in english, U. of N.Mex, 1988—91, PhD, 1991—98. Social worker SC. Dept. of Social Services, Spartanburg, SC, 1980—88; English instr. U. of N.Mex, 1993—99; asst. prof. of English Matanuska-Susitna Coll., Palmer, Alaska, 1999—. Judge Willow Libr. Poetry Contest, Alaska, 2000—; mem., adv. bd. Bachelor of Liberal Studies Program, Anchorage, 2000—; area coord. for Alaska SW/Tex. Popular Culture Assn., Albuquerque, 2001—, Film and History League, Okla. Pres. Mat-Su Info, Wasilla, Alaska, 2001—02; sec. to the bd. Mat-su Info, 2000—01. Mem.: ACCFT, AAUW, NCTE, AAUP, Phi Kappa Phi. Office: Matanuska-Susitna Coll/UAA PO Box 2889 Palmer AK 99645 Office Fax: 907-745-9711. E-mail: pfcdh@matsu.alaska.edu.

HOLBERTON, PHILIP VAUGHAN, entrepreneur, educator, professional speaker; b. N.Y.C., Sept. 29, 1942; s. Robert Maynard and Charlotte Metcalf (Stone) H.; m. Gale Russell, May 16, 1970 (div. 1980); children: Matthew Russell, Alexandra; m. Anne Meigs Blodget, June 6, 1987; 1 child, Philip Vaughan Jr., Tod. AB in Acctg., Franklin and Marshall Coll., Lancaster, Pa., 1964. CPA, N.Y. Auditor Hurdman and Cranstoun CPAs, N.Y.C., 1964-72; mgr. audit svcs. Peat Marwick CPAs, N.Y.C., 1975-79; investment profl. McDonald & Co., N.Y.C., 1972-75; asst. contr. Becton Dickinson & Co., Franklin Lakes, N.J., 1979-81, group contr. Paramus, N.J., 1981-85; v.p. fin. Gen. Cinema Theatres, Chestnut Hill, Mass., 1985-91; v.p. fin. and adminstrn., CFO, Cambridge, Neuroscience, Inc., Cambridge, Mass., 1991-95; founder Holberton Group, Inc., Lincoln, Mass., 1995—. Outside dir. Mgmt. Decision Lab., NYU, 1981-84; adj. faculty Northeastern U., Brandeis U., Babson Coll.; bd. dirs. Barbour Stockwell, Inc. Chmn. strategic planning panel United Way of Bergen County, Paramus, 1983-85; dir. Poppenhusen Inst., College Point, N.Y., 1981-83; sr. warden St. Anne's in the Fields, Lincoln, Mass., 1994-96. Mem. AICPA, Fin. Execs. Inst. (pres. bd. dirs. Boston chpt. 1995-96), Nat. Spkrs. Assn., New Eng. Spkrs. Assn. (bd. dirs.). Office: Holberton Group Inc PO Box 254 Lincoln MA 01773-0254 E-mail: pholberton@holberton.com.

HOLBIK, KAREL, economics educator; b. Czech Republic, Sept. 9, 1920; came to U.S., 1948, naturalized, 1952; s. Karel and Catherine (Krouzel) H.; m. Olga Rehackova, Sept. 10, 1956; 1 son, Thomas. JD, Charles U., Prague, 1947; MBA, U. Detroit, 1949; PhD, U. Wis., 1956. Researcher Bank of Am., San Francisco, 1951-53; teaching asst. in banking U. Wis., 1953-55; asst. prof. econs. Lafayette Coll., Easton, Pa., 1955-58; prof. econs. Boston U., 1958-86, prof. econs. emeritus, 1986—. Cons. U.S. Naval War Coll., Newport, R.I., 1963-64, lectr., 1964-73; vis. prof. U. Brussels, 1969-70; vis. faculty Harvard U., 1981-98; chief sect. for devel. fin. instns. UN, 1976-80; Fulbright sr. scholar U. Tunis, 1983-84; internat. fin. cons., 1986—. Author: Italy in International Cooperation, 1959, Postwar Trade in Divided Germany, 1964, The United States, The Soviet Union and the Third World, 1968, West German Foreign Aid 1956-1966, 1968, American-East European Trade, 1969, Contemporary American Economic Problems, 1970, Trade and Industrialization in the Central American Common Market, 1972, Monetary Policy in Twelve Industrial Countries, 1973, Industrialization and Employment in Puerto Rico, 1975; others. Mem. Am. Econ. Assn., Am. Fin. Assn. Home: 313 Country Club Rd Newton MA 02459-3148 *It appears that America, more than any other country, challenges human capabilities and permits individual dreams to come true.*

HOLBROOK, DONALD BENSON, lawyer; b. Salt Lake City, Jan. 4, 1925; s. Robert Sweeten and Kinnie Benson H.; m. Bety J. Gilchrist, Apr. 23, 1947; children: Mark, Thomas, Gregory, Mary. Student, Colo. Coll., U. Utah; JD, U. Utah, 1952, PhD (hon.), 1990; PhD (hon.), HHD (hon.), Utah Valley C.C., 1990; DFA (hon.), 1990; DHL (hon.), Salt Lake City C.C. Bar: Utah 1953. Pres. Jones Waldo, Holbrook and McDonough, Salt Lake City, 1973-89; of counsel, 1995—. Exec. v.p., legal officer Am. Stores Co., 1990-95; bd. dirs. Blue Cross/Blue Shield Utah, The Regence Group; commr. Utah Bar, 1983-87; bd. advs. Mountain Bell, 1974-84. Editor in chief: Utah Law Rev., 1951-52. Bd. dirs. Utah Ass. UN, 1963-64; bd. dirs., exec. com. Utah Coop. Assn., 1962-83, vice chmn., 1970-73, chmn., 1974-82, 83-85; chmn. Utah Partnership for Ednl. and Econ. devel., 1987-95; pres. and chmn. bd. Ballet West, 1982-84; bd. dirs. Utah Dem. Party, exec. sec., 1955-65, exec. com., 1956-65; chmn. antitrust and monopoly subcom. Western States Dem. Conf., 1962-66; campaign mgr. Gov. Calvin L. Rampton, 1964-68; candidate for U.S. Senate, 1964; commr. Western Interstate Commn. on Higher Edn., 1978-83, chmn., 1982. Recipient Disting. Alumni award U. Utah, 1985, Resolution of Appreciation Utah Ste Bd. Regents, 1990, Light of Learning award Utah State Bd. Edn., 1994; named Lawyer of Yr. Utah State Bar, 1990. Fellow Internat. Acad. Trial Lawyers, Am. Bar Found.; mem. U. Utah Coll. Law Alumni Assn. (pres. 1957), ABA (gen. chmn. Rocky Mountain region 1962, Utha chmn., mem. com. sect. corp., banking, bus. law 1962-95), Utah Bar Assn. (bd. commrs. 1982-87, chmn. com. World Peace Through Law 1964, pres. 1964-65), Order of the Coif (award for contbns. to law, scholarship and cmty. svc. 1968), Salt Lake City Country Club, Beta Theta Phi, Phi Kappa Phi, Delta Theta Phi (disting. alumni award 1967). Home: 1752 Laurelhurst Dr Salt Lake City UT 84108-3310

HOLBROOK, JAMES RUSSELL, law educator; b. Kansas City, Mo., Sept. 24, 1944; s. Newell James and Martha Inez Holbrook; m. Meghan Zanolli, Feb. 12, 1983. Student, MIT, 1962-63; BA, Grinnell (Iowa) Coll., 1966; MA, Ind. U., 1968; JD, U. Utah, 1974. Bar: (Utah) 1974, Utah (U.S. Dist. Ct.) 1974, (U.S. Ct. Appeals (10th cir.)) 1977, (U.S. Supreme Ct.) 1980. Law clk. to chief judge U.S. Dist. Ct. Utah, Salt Lake City, 1973—75; pvt. practice Salt Lake City, 1975—78; asst. U.S. Atty. Dist. Utah, 1978—80; ptnr. Giauque & Williams, Salt Lake City, 1980—82; staff counsel Intermountain Power Agy., Murray, Utah, 1982—83; ptnr. Callister Nebeker & McCullough, Salt Lake City, 1983—2002, of counsel, 2002—. Vis. clin. prof. S.J. Quinney Coll. of Law U. Utah, 2002—; mem. alt. dispute resolution subcom. U.S. Dist. Ct. Utah, 1991—, mem. conduct com., 1997—; mem. alt. dispute resolution com. Utah Jud. Coun., 1993—. Editor (articles): Jour. Contemporary Law, 1973—74. Mem. exhbns. coun. Utah Mus. Fine Arts, Salt Lake City, 1986—92, pres., 1988—90; bd. govs. Salt Lake Found., Salt Lake City, 1987—92, ex-officio, 1992—; bd. dirs. Hansen Planetarium, Salt Lake City, 1997—2000, pres., 1998—2000; bd. dirs. Utah Mus. Natural History, Salt Lake City, 1996—2000, v.p., 1997—99; bd. dirs. Internat. Visitors Utah Coun., Salt Lake City, 1984—96, pres., 1992—93. With U.S. Army, 1968—70, Vietnam. Decorated Bronze Star, Army Commendation medal; recipient Billings Excellence in Tchg. award, 2000, Billings award for Outstanding Dispute Resolution Svc., 2002; fellow NSF, 1966—68, Woodrow Wilson Found., 1966. Fellow: Am. Bar Found.; mem.: ABA, Sutherland Inn of Ct. (master of the bench 1984—95, emeritus 1995—2001), Am. Arbitration Assn. (bd. dirs. N.Y.C. 1996—), Fed. Bar Assn. (pres. Utah chpt. 1984—85, Disting. Svc. award 1995), Alta Club, Phi Beta Kappa. Democrat. Avocations:, skiing. Home: 775 Hilltop Rd Salt Lake City UT 84103-3311 Office: Callister Nebeker & McCullough 10 E South Temple Ste 900 Salt Lake City UT 84133-1115 E-mail: jimholbrook@cnmlaw.com.

HOLBROOK, JAY MACK, publishing company executive; b. Chesterfield, Idaho, Jan. 12, 1937; s. Lawrence E. and Mary Marjorie Holbrook; m. DeLene Clark, Dec. 20, 1962; children: Jalene, Lanae, Marinda, Danelle. BS, Utah State U., 1961; MA, Georgetown U., 1967, U. Wis., 1970. Contract adminstr. Dept. Navy, Washington, 1962-66; instr., asst. prof. Edgewood Coll., 1969, Brigham Young U., 1970-71, Utah State U., 1971-72, Nichols Coll., 1972-74, Cen. N.E., 1979-83, Mt. Wachusett Community Coll., 1979-80; pub. Holbrook Rsch. Inst., Oxford, Mass., 1975—, Archive Pub., Oxford, 1990—. Sr. trainer Applicon, Burlington, Mass., 1983-84, Apollo, Chelmsford, Mass., 1984-85; bd. dirs. Holbrook Rentals, Oxford, Micro Tech Supply, Oxford, Archive Pub., Oxford. Author numerous publs. on Mass. vital records, census and demographic reconstrn. of colonial New Eng. Mem. Oxford Fin. Com., 1989-96, pers. bd., 1999—, cable adv. com., 1999--. Home and Office: 4 Mayfair Cir Oxford MA 01540-2722 E-mail: jmholbrook@att.net.

HOLBROOK, MEGHAN ZANOLLI, fundraiser, public relations specialist, political organization chairman; b. N.Y.C., Oct. 12, 1949; m. James R. Holbrook. BS in English and Edn., U. Tenn., 1971, postgrad., 1978-83. Dir. ancillary svcs. Ridgeview Psychiat. Hosp., Oak Ridge, Tenn., 1971-83; therapist The Children's Ctr., Salt Lake City, 1985-86; mgr. corp. contbns. Sundance Inst. and Film Festival, Salt Lake City, 1989-91; fund raising and pub. rels. cons. Salt Lake City, 1992—. Fundraiser congl. campaign Wayne Owens, 1986, bus. liaison, 1986-88; fin. dir. gubernatorial campaign Ted Wilson, 1988, mayoral campaign Deedee Corradini, 1991; campaign mgr. gubernatorial campaign Stewart Hanson, 1991-92; del. Dem. Nat. Conv., 1996; chair Utah State Dem. Party, 1996—; mem. bd. dirs. Sundance Inst., 1989—, Inst. at Deer Valley, 1995—; mem. Utah Air Travel Commn., 1996—; mem. pres.'s adv. com. on arts Kennedy Ctr., Washington, 1996—. Mem. Assn. State Dem. Chairs (exec. com. 1998—). Home: 775 Hilltop Rd Salt Lake City UT 84103 3311 Office: 455 S 300 E Ste 102 Salt Lake City UT 84111-3222*

HOLBROOK, STEPHEN EUGENE, printing executive; b. Warsaw, Ind., Sept. 15, 1952; s. Harold Eugene and Phyllis Jean (Grable) H.; m. Debra Jane Orr, Jan. 10, 1981; children: Chad Ryan, Kelly Nicole, Ryan Stephen. BS, Ind. U., 1974; MBA, Keller Grad. Sch., Chgo., 1998. Store mgr. Firestone Tire & Rubber Co., Akron, Ohio, 1974—78; customer svc. mgr. Donnite Corp., Plymouth, Ind., 1978—79; customer svc. rep. R.R. Donnelley & Sons, Warsaw, Ind., 1979—83, customer svc. supr., 1995—2000, 2001—03, customer care account mgr., 2003—, customer svc./dist. svc. supr. Dwight, Ill., 1983—94, human resources supr., 1994—95, regional procurement mgr. Downers Grove, Ill., 2000—01. Leader new product start-up R.R. Donnelley & Sons, Dwight, Ill., 1983-86, mem. joint mfg./sales team, Chgo., 1985-87, quality cons. bindery, Dwight, Ill. 1984-89. Vol. Am. Cancer Soc., Warsaw, Ind., 1997, Am. Heart and Lung Assn.; coach Warsaw Little League, bd. dirs., 1996—99, fin. chairperson, 1999; cons. Jr. Achievement, Ft. Wayne, Ind.; bd. dirs. Jr. Achievement of No. Ind., 2003—; charter mem. Warsaw Cmty. Found. Pub. Edn., Inc.; coach Shorewood (Ill.) Soccer League, 1988—93, Troy Youth Baseball, Shorewood, 1990—94, Troy All-Stars, 1994, Warsaw Youth Travel Roller Hockey Team, 1996—97; mem. Dirs. Club Wagon Wheel Playhouse Theatre; program dir. Warsaw Youth Roller Hockey League, 1999—2000; v.p. Jr. Achievement of No. Ind., 2003—. Mem. Ind. U. Alumni Assn. (life), Ind. U. Varsity Club, Assn. for Quality and Participation, Hoosiers for Higher Edn., Kiwanis (bd. dirs. Warsaw club 1993—, Dir. of Yr. 1993), Masons, Shriners, Scottish Rite. Avocations: travel, clowning, youth activities, stock car racing. Home: 842 Lydia Dr Warsaw IN 46582-1949

HOLBROOK, THOMAS ALDREDGE, state legislator; b. St. Louis, Nov. 23, 1949; Ill. state rep. Dist. 113, 1995—. Office: 9200 W Main St Ste 4 Belleville IL 62223-1710*

HOLBROOKE, RICHARD CHARLES ALBERT, ambassador, government official, investment banker, author; b. N.Y.C., Apr. 24, 1941; s. Dan and Trudi (Moos) H.; children: David Dan, Anthony Andrew. BA, Brown U., 1962; postgrad., Princeton, 1969-70. Joined Fgn. Service, 1962; served in Vietnam, 1963-66; mem. White House staff, 1966-67; assigned State Dept.; staff Paris (France) peace talks on Vietnam, 1968-69; dir. Peace Corps, Morocco, 1970-72; mng. editor Fgn. Policy mag., 1972-77; cons. Commn. Orgn. Govt. for Conduct of Fgn., 1974-75; contbg. editor Newsweek Internat., 1976; asst. sec. for East Asian and Pacific affairs Dept. State, Washington, 1977-81; v.p. Public Strategies, Washington, 1981-85; sr. advisor Lehman Bros., 1981-84, mng. dir., 1985-93; U.S. amb. Federal Republic of Germany, 1993-94; asst. sec. state European and Can. affairs Dept. State, Washington, 1994-96; vice chmn. Credit Suisse First Boston, N.Y.C., 1996-99; U.S. amb. to U.N. N.Y.C., 1999—2001; vice chmn. Perseus LLC, N.Y.C., 2001—; pres. Global Bus. Coalition on HIV/AIDS, 2001—. Chief negotiator Dayton Peace Accords, Bosnia, 1995; spl. presdl. emissary to Cyprus; mem. Trilateral Commn. Author: vol. The Pentagon Papers, 1967, To End a War, 1998; contbr. numerous articles to N.Y. Times, Washington Post, Wall St. Jour., Atlantic, other mags. and jours. Bd. dirs. Internat. Rescue Com.; chmn. Refugees Internat. Mem. Am. Acad. Berlin, Coun. Fgn. Rels., Inst. Strategic Studies. Office: Coun Fgn Rels 58 E 68th St New York NY 10021

HOLBROW, CHARLES HOWARD, physicist, educator; b. Melrose, Mass., Sept. 23, 1935; s. Frederick and Florence Louisa (Gile) H.; m. Mary Louise Ross, June 17, 1956; children: Gwendolyn J., Elizabeth M., Alice J., Katherine A., Martha R. BA, U. Wis., Madison, 1955; AM, Columbia U., N.Y.C., 1957; MS, U. Wis., Madison, 1960; cert. Russian Inst., Columbia U., 1957; PhD, U. Wis., Madison, 1963. Asst. prof. Haverford Coll., 1962-65; research investigator U. Pa., 1965-66; assoc. editor Physics Today, N.Y.C., 1967; assoc. prof. Colgate U., Hamilton, N.Y., 1967-72, prof., 1972-86, Charles A. Dana prof. physics, 1986—, chmn. dept. physics and astronomy, 1978-81, 82-84, dir. div. natural scis. and math., 1985-88, Charles A. Dana prof. physics emeritus, 2003. Vis. assoc. Calif. Inst. Tech., 1975—76, 2002; vis. physicist Brookhaven Nat. Lab., 1980—81; vis. prof. MIT, 1982, 1988—89; guest scientist SUNY, Stony Brook, 1983—93; guest sci. investigator GSI Darmstadt, Germany, 1994—95; vis. rsch. scholar Harvard U., 1995; guest prof. U. Vienna, 2001—02. Named acad. intern, Am. Coun. Edn., 1972—73; NSF coop. fellow, 1959—60, NSF rsch. grantee, 1981—82. Fellow: Am. Phys. Soc.; mem.: AAUP, History of Sci. Soc., Am. Assn. Physics Tchrs. (pres. elect 2002, pres. 2003). E-mail: cholbrow@mail.colgate.edu.

HOLCEPL, JAMES ROBERT, sales professional; b. Cleve., Sept. 23, 1947; s. Robert J. and Julia M. Holcepl; m. Julie M. Holcepl, Sept. 18, 1971; children: Christopher J., Andrew J. AA, Cuyahoga C.C., Cleve., 1971; BA, Baldwin-Wallace Coll., 1979; MBA, Cleve. State U., 1999. Trade/text buyer Metro Campus Book Ctr./Cuyahoga C.C., Cleve., 1974—77; dist. sales mgr. Bantam Books, Inc., N.Y.C., 1977—81, regional sales mgr., 1981—90; divsn. sales mgr. Bantam-Doubleday-Dell, N.Y.C., 1990—92, retail chain sales mgr., 1992—99; ea. region sales mgr. McGraw-Hill Prof. Book Group, N.Y.C., 1999—, nat. field sales mgr., 2000—; sales mgr., assoc. dir. U. Press. Fla., 2001. Pres. of church consistory Ch. of the Redeemer UCC, Westlake, Ohio, 1995-96. Tech. sgt. Ohio ANG/USAF, 1967-76. Mem. Sales and Mktg. Execs. of Cleve., U.S. Power Squadron (chmn. elective courses 1995-97, Jim Crane Meml. Elective Course award 1997-98), Beta Gamma Sigma. Methodist. Avocations: musician/banjo and guitar, collecting old musical instruments.

HOLCH, GREGORY JOHN, children's book editor, author; b. Tokyo, Nov. 19, 1952; (parents Am. citizens); s. Arthur Everett and Ellen Constance (O'Keefe) H.; m. Rhonda Lyn Brauer, Sept. 7, 1989; children: Jillian Brauer, Justin Brauer. BA in English, Manhattanville Coll., 1974; MA in Am. Civilization, NYU, 1984. Editl. asst. Globe Comm., Greenwich, Conn., 1977-78, Random House Student Book Clubs, N.Y.C., 1978-80, Bantam Books, N.Y.C., 1981-83; assoc. editor Scholastic, N.Y.C., 1983-85, editor, 1985-94, sr. editor, 1994—. Guest editor Mademoiselle mag., 1974. Author: (novel) The Things with Wings, 1998; co-author: Jungle Jokes, 1979; author short stories; contbr. photographs in mags. Mem. Soc. Children's Book Writers and Illustrators, Am. Radio Relay League (life). Avocations: amateur extra class ham radio, photography. Office: Scholastic Inc 555 Broadway New York NY 10012-3919

HOLCOMB, CARAMINE KELLAM, volunteer worker; b. Painter, Va., Jan. 23, 1941; d. Emerson Polk and Amine (Cosby) Kellam; m. Isaac Somers White, Nov. 25, 1961 (div. 1975); children: Kellam White Griffin, Caramine White, Virginia Somers White; m. Harry Sherman Holcomb III, May 12, 1979 (div. Mar. 2001). AA, St. Mary's Coll., Raleigh, 1960; Cert., Richmond Bus. Coll., Va., 1961. Bd. dirs. Kellam Energy, Inc., Belle Haven, Va., 1980—, Auto Plus, Inc., Belle Haven, 1980-89, Shore Stop, Inc., Belle Haven, 1981-89. Contbr. articles to profl. jours. Trustee Northampton-Accomack Meml. Hosp., Nassawadox, Va., 1986-98, v.p. aux., 1986-88, pres., 1988-90, sec. bd. trustees, 1989-91, vice chmn., 1991-94, chair, 1994-96; bd. dirs. Ea. Shore Hist. Soc., Onancock, Va., 1987-92, Shore Life Svcs., 1998—; bd. dirs. Eastern Shore C.C. Found., 1998—, v.p. Found. bd., 2001-03, pres., 2003—; bd. dirs. Med. Soc. Va. Alliance, Richmond, 1984-94, v.p., 1989-91, pres., 1992-93; treas. E. Polk Kellam Found., 1991—; mem. session Belle Haven Presbyn. Ch., 1999-2002, Shore Meml. Bd. Trustees, 2003-. Mem. AMA Alliance Bd. (ERF com. 1994, AMA ERF com. chmn. 1994-95, field dir. 1995-98, bylaws chmn. 1999-2000), Med. Soc. Va. Trust, Garden Club Ea. Shore (pres. 1973-75, Garden Week chmn. 2001—02). Avocations: travel, reading, flower arranging. Home: PO Box 38 Franktown VA 23354-0038

HOLCOMB, CONSTANCE L. sales and marketing management executive; b. St. Paul, Oct. 28, 1942; d. John E. Holcomb and Lucille A. (Westerdahl) Hope; m. Walter D. Serwatka, May 1991. BS, U. Minn., 1965; MA in Intercultural Edn., U. of the Americas, Puebla, Mex., 1975. Rsch. analyst U.S. Dept. Def., Washington, 1965-66; br. gen. mgr. Berlitz Lang. Schs., Mexico City, 1966-68; pres., gen. mgr. Centro Linguistico, Puebla, 1968-72; gen. mgr., prof. Lang. Ctr. Am. Sch. Found., Puebla, 1972-74; assoc. prof., dir. lang. programs U. of the Americas, Puebla, 1974-76; prof., dean faculty of langs. Nat. Autonomous U. Mex., Mexico City, 1976-78; dir. sales & mktg. Longman Pub. Co., N.Y.C., 1978-80, dir. internat. sales & mktg., 1980-84; mng. dir. ESL Pub. Div. McGraw-Hill Book Co., N.Y.C., 1984-85; dir. mktg. mgmt. McGraw-Hill Tng. Systems and Book Co., N.Y.C., 1985-86; dir. mktg. electronic bus. McGraw-Hill Book Co., N.Y.C., 1986-87; info. industry mgmt. cons., career mgmt. cons., ind. contractor, N.Y.C., 1987-91; mktg. cons. Sarasota, Fla., 1991—. V.p. MexTESOL, Mexico City, 1977-78. Editor: English Teaching in Mexico, 1975; pub.: Rubens to Rhubarb, The Ringling Museum of Art, 1995, Baroque, Basil and Thyme, The Ringling Museum of Art, 1997, Ringling, the Art Museum, The Ringling Museum of Art, 2002; contbr. articles to profl. jours. Bd. trustees, devel. com. mem. John and Mable Ringling Mus., 1993-99; bd. dirs. Safe Place and Rape Crisis Ctr., Sarasota, 1995-2002; bd. dirs. Friends of Selby Pub. Libr., 1997-99. Mem. Assn. Am. Pubs. (com. chmn. internat. div. 1980-84, exec. com. 1980-84), Info. Industry Assn., Nat. Assn. Women Cons., Am. Soc. Profl. and Exec. Women. Office: 3555 Mistletoe Ln Longboat Key FL 34228-4103

HOLCOMB, DONALD FRANK, physicist, academic administrator; b. Chesterton, Ind., Nov. 8, 1925; s. Roger L. and Ethel (Frank) H.; m. Barbara Page, Aug. 26, 1950; children: Douglas Page, Jane D., Nancy M. AB, DePauw U., 1949; MS, U. Ill., 1950, PhD, 1954. Instr. U. Ill., 1954; mem. faculty Cornell U., 1954—, prof. physics, 1962—, dir. lab. atomic and solid state physics, 1964-68, chmn. dept. physics, 1969-74, 82-86, trustee, 1976-81. Cons. Corning Glass Research Lab., 1959-64, Central Inst. Indsl. Research, Oslo, Norway, 1962 Contbr. profl. jours. Served with USNR, 1944-46. Sr. vis. fellow NATO, 1962; Guggenheim fellow, 1968-69; Sci. Research Council sr. fellow, 1978 Fellow Am. Phys. Soc., AAAS; mem. Am. Assn. Physics Tchrs. (pres. 1987, Oersted medal 1996), Sigma Xi. Presbyterian. Achievements include spl. rsch. solid state physics, chem. physics, coll. physics course devel. Home: 385 Savage Farm Dr Ithaca NY 14850-6505

HOLCOMB, GRANT, III, museum director; b. San Bernardino, Calif., Sept. 30, 1944; BA, UCLA, 1967; MA, U. Del., 1970, PhD, 1972. Asst. prof. Mt. Holyoke Coll., South Hadley, Mass., 1972-80, SUNY, Stony Brook, 1980-81; curator San Diego Mus. Art, 1981-83; assoc. dir. Timken Art Mus., San Diego, 1983-85; dir. Meml. Art Gallery, Rochester, N.Y., 1985—. Author: (exhibit catalogue) John Sloan, The Gloucester Years, 1980, Wake of the Ferry, 1984; editor: Voices in the Gallery: Writers on Art, 2001; contbr. articles to profl. jours. Bd. dirs. BOA edits., 1991—, Conv. Vis. Bur., 1990—, Friends of Ganondagan, 1994—. Kress fellow Nat. Gallery Art, 1972; Am. Council Learned Socs. grantee, 1980. Mem.: Arts Cultural Coun. Rochester, Aesthetic Edn. Inst. (bd. dirs. 1985—), Arts and Cultural Coun. of Greater Rochester (bd. dirs. 1985—), Assn. Art Mus. Dirs. Office: Meml Art Gallery 500 University Ave Rochester NY 14607-1414

HOLCOMB, HOMER SIMMONS See GARRETT, LEE

HOLCOMB, LEE, federal agency administrator; BS, UCLA; MS, Calif. Inst. Tech.; SM, MIT. Sr. engr. Jet Propulsion Lab.; dir. info. tech. strategy NASA, Washington, chief info. officer, 1997—. Recipient Sloan fellowship. Office: NASA Hdqrs Mail Code A 300 E St SW Washington DC 20546

HOLCOMB, LYLE DONALD, JR., retired lawyer; b. Miami, Fla., Feb. 3, 1929; s. Lyle Donald and Hazel Irene (Watson) H.; m. Barbara Jean Roth, July 12, 1952; children: Susan Holcomb Davis, Scott H. (deceased), Douglas J., Mark E. BA, U. Mich., 1951; JD, U. Fla., 1954. Bar: U.S. Ct. Appeals (5th and 11th cirs.) 1981, U.S. Supreme Ct. 1966. Ptnr. Holcomb & Holcomb, Miami, 1955-72; assoc. Copeland, Therrel, Baisden & Peterson, Miami Beach, Fla., 1972-75; ptnr. Therrel, Baisden, Stanton, Wood & Setlin, Miami Beach, Fla., 1976-85, Therrel, Baisden & Meyer Weiss, Miami Beach, Fla., 1985-93; pvt. practice Tallahassee, Fla., 1993-95. Organizing pres. So. Fla. Migrant Legal Svcs. Program (now Fla. Rural Legal Svcs.), 1966-68. Mem. exec. coun. So. Fla. coun. Boy Scouts Am., 1958-93; past pres., past counselor Miami chpt. Huguenot Soc. Fla. Served with USNR, 1947-53. Recipient Silver Beaver award So. Fla. coun. Boy Scouts Am., 1966. Fellow Am. Coll. Trust and Estate Counsel, 1980-94, Acad. Fla. Probate and Trust Litigation Attys., 1980-95; mem. Dade County Bar Assn. (dir. 1960-71, sec. 1963-71), Miami Beach Bar Assn. (pres. 1980), Estate Planning Coun. Greater Miami, Soc. Mayflower Descs. (past pres. Miami club, past counselor soc.), SAR (past pres. Miami chpt.), Univ. Yacht Club. Republican. Mem. United Ch. of Christ. Home: 3538 Killarney Plaza Dr Tallahassee FL 32309-3491 E-mail: lholcomb23@aol.com.

HOLCOMB, MICHELLE K. elementary education educator; b. Indpls., Mar. 20, 1971; d. James M. and Barbara B. Klene; m. Eric J. Holcomb, Dec. 23, 1993. BS cum laude, St. Mary of the Woods, 1999. Cert. elem. edn., Ind., reading recovery. Dep. dir. NATO Preschool, Lisbon, Portugal, 1994-97; tchr. Vincennes (Ind.) Cmty. Sch. Corp., 1998—. Mem. adv. bd. Heart to Heart, Vincennes, 1999-2000; Ct. Appointed Spl. Adv., Vincennes, 1998—. Named Outstanding Future Educator, Ind. Colls. for Tchr. Edn., 1998. Mem. Nat. Coun. Tchrs. Math., Nat. Rep. Women, Fortnightly Club, Kappa Delta Pi, Psi Iota Xi. Republican. Avocations: gardening, art history, reading, writing, aerobics. Office: Vincennes Cmty Sch Corp 300 N 6th St Vincennes IN 47591 Home: 2550 Grandview Dr Vincennes IN 47591-5024 E-mail: holcomb@vincennes.net.

HOLCOMB, MILDRED GENEVA COMRIE, elementary education educator; b. New London, Conn., Sept. 22, 1941; d. Wendell Silas and Florence Marjorie (Gallup) Comrie; m. Michael Alan Holcomb, Dec. 22, 1973. BS, Ea. Nazarene Coll., 1963; MA, U. Conn., 1968; MS, U. Houston, Clear Lake, Tex., 1983; EdD, Nova S.E. U., 2002. Cert. elem. edn. tchr., Tex. Tchr. 2d grade Ledyard (Conn.) Sch. Dist., 1963-68; tchr. 1st and 2d grades Mt. Vernon (Ohio) Sch. Dist., 1968-72; tchr. 4th grade Sheldon Ind. Sch. Dist., Houston, 1972-75; tchr. K-2d Pasadena (Tex.) Ind. Sch. Dist., 1976-83; tchr. kindergarten and 1st grade Sheldon Ind. Sch. Dist., Houston, 1985—. Vol. Nixon polit. campaign, Houston, 1972; organist Open Fellowship Ch. of the Nazarene, Houston, 1987-88, Broadway Ch. of the Nazarene, Houston, 1988-89, Pasadena Ch. of the Nazarene, 1980-81, Crosby Ch. of the Nazarene, 1994—; v.p. Pasadena Ind. Sch. Dist. PTO, 1979-80; pres. Parkway Elem. Sch. PTO, Houston, 1993-94; founder Parkside C.H.A.T.S. miniworkshops, 1990—. Named Tchr. of Yr., Parkway Elem. Sch., 1990-91. Mem. Assn. Tchrs. and Profl. Educators, Sheldon Educators Assn. Republican. Avocations: organ, reading, photography, gardening, travel.

HOLCOMB, RICHARD DENNIS, lawyer; BA in Polit. Sci., Hampden Sydney Coll. Va., 1976; JD, U. Richmond, 1979. Chief staff U.S. Reps. John Linder, D. French Slaughter, Jr., Craig T. James, 1989-94; commr. Va. Dept. of Motor Vehicles, Richmond, 1994—2001; gen. counsel, sr. v.p. law and regulatory affairs Am. Trucking Assns., Alexandria, Va., 2001—. Office: Am Trucking Assns 2200 Mill Rd Alexandria VA 22314-4677

HOLCOMB, RITA, landscaper; b. Bonham, Tex., Aug. 29, 1948; d. Guy M. and Marie (Moore) Ownby; m. Darrell Holcomb, July 29, 1972; 1 child, Stuart. A in Fine Arts, Grayson County Coll., Denison, Tex., 1974, A in Bus. Adminstrn., 1991. Owner Holcomb Miniatures, Sherman, Tex., 1980-90; sales Breathco/Mediserv, Sherman, 1990-94; owner Plants on the Move, Sherman, 1994—. Pres. bd. dirs. Red River Hist. Mus., Sherman, 1997, Sherman Cmty. Players Theater Guild, 1989; mem. Sherman City Coun., 1999—2000; bd. mem. Texoma Coun. Govts., 1999—2000; co-chair Conv. and Visitors Coun., 2002; bd. dirs. LWV Sherman/Grayson County, Tex., 2001—02, Grayson County Tri-County Nutrition, 1998—2003, Sherman Preservation League, 1995—97, 2000—01. Avocations: theater, miniatures, Tae Kwan Do, genealogy.

HOLCOMB, SARA NEES, museum director, artist; b. Middleton, Wis., Nov. 8, 1955; d. Paul Oliver and Helen Patricia N.; m. Harmon R. Holcomb III, Aug. 8, 1981. BS in Art History, U. Wis., 1981. Store mgr. Very Finest, Madison, Wis., 1979-81; artist Holcomb Pottery, Lexington, Ky., 1981-95; dir. Arts in Action, Inc., Lexington, 1996-98; also bd. dirs., 1998—; exec. dir. Lexington Children's Mus., 1998—. Cons. Ky. Arts Coun., Frankfort, 1998—. Mem. adv. bd. Ky. Art and Craft Found., Louisville, 1992—; mem. program com. Humanitarium, Lexington, 1998—; mem. Gov.'s Coun. Early Childhood Devel., 1999; spkr. Ky. I Am Your Child, 1998, Speak Out Lexington, 1999; mem. Grad. Leadership Lexington Class of 2002. Mem. Lexington Arts and Cultural Coun., Ky. Guild Artists and Craftsmen (bd. dirs. 1988-92), C. of C. Home: 360 S Broadway Park Lexington KY 40504-2609 Office: Lexington Children's Mus 440 W Short St Lexington KY 40507-1200

HOLCOMBE, ALFRED ROBERT, JR., museum curator; b. Macon, Ga, May 8, 1945; s. Alfred Robert and Elizabeth Claire Holcombe; m. Jane Elizabeth Holcombe, Aug. 12, 1978. BS in Edn., Ga. So. Coll., 1968; MA in Maritime History, East Carolina U., 1993. Curator, naval historian Port Columbus Civil War Naval Ctr., Ga., 1973—. Cons. US Army Corps of Engr., Savannah, Ga., 1980—, SC State Mus., Columbia, 1994, Ga. Dept. Natural Resources, 1989; cons., mem. adv. bd. Apalachicola (Fla.) Maritime Mus., 1996. Author: (with others) Confederate Navy: Ships, Men, and Organization, 1997, American Civil War: A Handbook of Literature and Research, 1996; contbr. more than 20 articles to profl. jour. Kennedy Libr. Found. Hemingway Rsch. grantee JFK Libr. Found., 1997; recipient Jefferson Davis award for excellence in history United Daus. Confederacy, 1988. Mem. N.Am. Soc. for Oceanic History, Hist. Naval Ships Assn. (Henry A. Vadnais award 1999), Internat. Naval Rsch. Orgn., Co. Mil. Historians, Soc. Civil War Historians. Methodist. Avocations: model boat building, reading, snorkeling. Home: PO Box 804 Columbus GA 31902-0804 Office: Port Columbus Civil War Naval Ctr PO Box 1022 Columbus GA 31902-1022

HOLCOMBE, JOSEPH STEVEN, academic administrator, educator; b. Charlotte, N.C., Oct. 2, 1950; s. Joseph and Lois Inez Holcombe; m. Suzanne Camille Keller, June 24, 1972; 1 child, Allison Camille. BS in Indsl. Mgmt., Clemson U., 1972; MBA, Clemson-Furman U., 1979; MS in Indsl. Mgmt., Clemson U., 1991. Mgr. comml. tufted plans Bigelow-Sanford, Inc., Greenville, SC, 1972—88; indsl. engr. Asten, Inc., Clinton, SC, 1993—2000; prodn. mgr. Tungsten, Inc., Travelers Rest, SC, 2000—01; asst. dir. of faculty svcs. So. Wesleyan U., Central, SC, 2002—. Mem. adj. faculty Furman U., Greenville, SC, 1991—93; adj. prof. So. Wesleyan U., Central, 2002—; vis. instr. Clemson U., 1991—93. Vol. builder Habitat for Humanity, Greer, SC, 2000—; learn-to-swim instr. Upstate S.C. chpt.ARC, Greenville, 2001—02, first aid/cardiopulmonary instr., 1999—, mem. first aid/safety com., 2001—; Sunday sch. tchr. Brushy Creek Bapt. Ch., Taylors, SC, 1990—; deacon Brushy Creek Bapt., Taylors, SC, 1990—2002. Named New Vol. of the Yr. Runner-up, Upstate S.C. chpt. of the ARC, 2001. Mem.: Am. Prodn. and Inventory Control Soc. (assoc.; cert. prodn. and inventory mgmt. 1992, cert. integrated resource mgmt. 1995, Instr. of the Yr. Indsl. Crescent chpt. 2001). Conservative. Southern Baptist. Avocations: jogging, reading historical fiction, travel. Office: So Wesleyan U 907 Wesleyan Dr Central SC 29630 E-mail: sholcombe@swu.edu.

HOLCOMBE, RANDALL GREGORY, economics educator; b. Bridgeport, Conn., June 4, 1950; s. Lynn Montanye Holcombe and Gloria Gabriel (Rita) Ledbetter; m. Lora Hunt Pritchett, June 18, 1983. BS, U. Fla., 1972; MA, Va. Poly. Inst. and State U., 1974, PhD, 1976. Asst. prof. Tex. A&M U., College Station, 1975-77; prof. Auburn (Ala.) U., 1977-88, Fla. State U., Tallahassee, 1988 . Mem. rsch. adv. coun. James Madison Inst., Tallahassee, 1987—, chmn., 1991—; mem. editl. bd. Rev. Austrian Econs., 1987-97, Pub. Fin. Rev., 1995—, Quar. Rev. Austrian Econs., 1998—; adj. scholar Ludwig Von Mises Inst., 1982—; mem. Fla. Gov.'s Coun. Econ. Advisors, 2000—. Author: Public Finance and the Political Process, 1983, An Economic Analysis of Democracy, 1985, Public Sector Economics, 1988, Economic Models and Methodology, 1989, The Economic Foundations of Government, 1994, Public Policy and the Quality of Life, 1995, Public Finance: Government Revenues and Expenditures in the United States Economy, 1996, (with R. Sobel) Growth and Variability in State Tax Revenue, 1997, Writing Off Ideas, 2000, From Liberty to Democracy: The Transformation of American Government, 2002; contbr. articles to profl. jours. Scaife Found. fellow, 1972-73, H.B. Earhart Found. fellow, 1973-75; research grantee Earhart Found., 1979-80, 83, 89, 90, 98. Mem. Am. Econ. Assn., Pub. Choice Soc., So. Econ. Assn., Western Econ. Assn. Home: 3514 Limerick Dr Tallahassee FL 32309-3139 Office: Fla State U Dept Econs Tallahassee FL 32306

HOLCOMBE, THOMAS CHARLES, technology executive; b. Birmingham, Ala., Jan. 21, 1948; s. William Collis and Bernell (Johnson) H.; children: Tiffany, Sonya; m. Meryl Schwartz, July 31, 1994; stepchildren: Miriam, Gary. BSChemE, Va. Polytechnic Inst., 1970; MBA in mgmt., Pace U., 1979, D of profl. studies, 1991. Registered profl. engr., N.J. Product coord. Procter & Gamble Co., Cin., 1970-74; assoc. dir. tech. Union Carbide Corp., Tarrytown, N.Y., 1974-89; pres. Hanover Rsch. Corp. and Dehydro-Tech Corp., Somerville, N.J., 1989-97; pres., CEO EnviRes LLC, Somerville, N.J., 1994-2000; pres. Am. Biotherm Co., LLC, Somerville, 1997-99; mgr. new ventures Engelhard Corp., 2000—. Patentee in field; contbr. articles to profl. jours. Mem.: AIChE, Soc. Automotive Engrs. Avocations: tennis, guitar, scuba diving. Home: 200 Beekman Ln Hillsborough NJ 08844 Office: Engelhard 101 Wood Ave Iselin NJ 08830-5340 E-mail: thomas.holcombe@engelhard.com.

HOLCOMBE, TROY LEON, marine geologist; b. Roxton, Tex., Mar. 8, 1940; s. Horace Cleveland and Nellie Estelle (Jenkins) H.; m. Janis Eileen O'Neal, Aug. 21, 1971; children: Leigh Harold, Virginia Luce, Terry Estelle. BA, Hardin-Simmons U., 1961; AM, U. Mo., 1964; PhD, Columbia U., 1972. Research oceanographer U.S. Naval Oceanographic Office, Chesapeake Beach, Md., 1968-75; head geology br. Naval Ocean Research and Devel. Activity, Nat. Space Tech. Labs., Miss., 1975-84; dep. chief Marine Geology and Geophysics div. Nat. Geophys. Data Ctr., NOAA, Boulder, Colo., 1984—99; rsch. assoc. Coop. Inst. Rsch. Environ. Scis., U. Colo., 1999—2002; rsch. scientist dept. oceanography Tex. A&M U., College Station, 2002—. Author: Bathymetric Charts of the Great Lakes; mem. editl. bd.: Internat. Bathymetric Charts of Guld Mex./Caribbean, 1986—, Western Indian Ocean, 1989—, Ctrl. Ea. Atlantic, 1990—, Mediterranean, 1999—; contbr. articles to profl. jours. Mem. Am. Assn. Petroleum Geologists, Geol. Soc. Am., Internat. Assn. Great Lakes Rsch. Democrat. Baptist. Home: 415 Chimney Hill Dr College Station TX 77840-1833 Office: Tex A&M U Dept Oceanography College Station TX 77843

HOLDAR, ROBERT MARTIN, chemist; b. Ozark, Ark., Feb. 10, 1949; s. Luther and Francess Ethyl (Briscoe) H.; m. Barbara Jean Sobczak, Jan. 5, 1985; children: Luther Edward, William Thomas, Frank King, Samuel Robert. BS in Chemistry, U. Ark., 1976; MS in Chemistry, Tex. A&M U., 1979; MBA, U. Dallas, 1996. Chemist Parkem Indsl. Svcs., LaPorte, Tex., 1979-80, Mohawk Labs div. NCH Corp., Irving, Tex., 1980—. Patentee in field. Chmn. Zoning Bd. Adjustments, Irving, 1991-95; mem. Local Emergency Planning Commn., Dallas, 1991-93; mem. bd. amortizations and appeals City of Irving, 1994; Grand Awards Judge, INTEL 49th Internat. Sci. Fair, 1998; bd. advisors The North Hills Sch., trustee, 2000-02. With USAF, 1968-73. W.K. Noyce scholar U. Ark., 1975. Mem. Am. Chem. Soc., Nat. Assn. Corrosion Engrs., Am. Soc. Lubrication Engrs. (chmn. North Tex. sect. 1982-83), Irving Rep. Club (editor 1989-92, 94-97, treas. 1992-94), Irving Noon Toastmasters (pres. 1983, Accomplished Toastmaster award 1986). Avocations: snow skiing, scuba, gardening. Home: 2816 Brockbank Dr Irving TX 75062-4523 Office: NCH Corp Mohawk Labs 2730 Carl Rd Irving TX 75062-6405

HOLDCRAFT, JANET RULON, academic administrator; b. Bridgeton, N.J., Sept. 30, 1940; d. Mulford M. and Sarah Hansel (Dilks) Rulon; m. E. Larry Holdcraft, Feb. 21, 1964 (wid. Sept. 1979); children: Larry B., Jodi Holdcraft Coates. BA, Glassboro State, 1962, MA, 1968; EdD, Seton Hall U., 1994. Tchr. fourth grade Glassboro (N.J.) Bd. Edn., 1962-67, tchr. devel. reading grade 7, 1967-68, tchr. corrective reading, grades 6-8, 1968-75, coord. Right-to-Read, 1975-77, tchr. compensatory edn. reading, 1977-80, Title I reading tchr. grades 7-8, 1980-84, BSI/lang. arts tchr., grades 7-8, 1984-93, tchr. GED adult evening sch., 1988-89, head tchr., dir. student activities, 1988-93, asst. supt. curriculum and personnel, 1995—. Prin. BSI Spl. Edn. program Glassboro Bd. Edn., summers 1991-93; prin. alt. evening h.s. Supr. Adult Cmty. Sch., Glassboro, 1993-94; dir. curriculum and instrn., Pennsville Sch. dist., N.J., 1994-95. Asst. leader Holly Shores chpt. Girl Scouts USA, Franklinville, NJ, 1979—82; mem. Mothers Football Club Delsea Regional High Sch., Franklinville, 1979—80; mem. Glassboro Mcpl. Alliance, 1995—, chair, 1995—97; mem. Gloucester County Curriculum Consortium, 1995—, treas., 1999—; mem. Ladies Rep. Club, Franklinville, 1980—83; mem. adminstrv. coun., budget com., pantry com., bd. dirs. Bright Promises Nursery Sch. Franklinville United Meth. Ch.; mem. adv. bd. so. region N.J. Statewide Systemic Initiative, 1999—. Co-dir. reading grant U.S. Office of Edn., 1978-80; recognized by Gov.'s Tchrs. Recognition Program, State of N.J., 1988; recipient Elizabeth M. Bozarth scholarship N.J. Alpha Zeta, 1990. Mem. ASCD, AASA, N.J. Assn. Sch. Adminstrs., Reading Coun. of So. N.J. (bd. dirs.), N.J. Assn. Supervision and Curriculum (so. region bd. dirs.), Rotary Club Glassboro/Clayton/Elk Twp.,

Delta Kappa Gamma (chpt. 1st v.p. 1990-92, rec. sec. 1988-90), N.J. Coun. Edn., Kappa Delta Pi. Methodist. Avocations: golf, reading, collecting salt and pepper shakers, the beach. Home: 589 Judy Ave Franklinville NJ 08322-3913 Office: Glassboro Pub Schs Glassboro NJ 08028

HOLDEN, BOB, governor; b. Kansas City, Mo. m. Lori Hauser; children: Robert, John. BS in Polit. Sci., Southwest Mo. State; Degree Kennedy Sch. Govt. for Public Execs. and Flemming Fellow Leadership Inst., Harvard U. Former adminstrv. asst./liaison U.S. Congressman Richard Gephardt, St. Louis; mem. Mo. Ho. of Reps., 1983-89; state treas. State of Mo., Jefferson City, 1993—2000, gov., 2001—. Chmn. gen. approations com.; co-sponsor Excellence in Edn. Act; mem. Bd. Fund Commrs., Mo. State Employees Retirement System, Mo. Bus. Coun., Mo. Rural Opportunities Coun.; past chmn. Mo. Housing Devel. Commn. Dean Am. Legion Mo. Boy's State Legislative Sch.; mem. Holden Scholarship Fund, Leadership St. Louis; former mem. Confluence's Edn. Implementation, Tower Grove Hgts. Neighborhood Assn., Save the Children's Program; mem. Mo. Coun. Econ. Edn., Coun. State Govts.; vice-chair Mo. Cultural Trust. Mem. Nat. Assn. State Treas. (legis. chair). Democrat. Office: Office Governor MO Capital Bldg Rm 216 Jefferson City MO 65101*

HOLDEN, FREDERICK DOUGLASS, JR., lawyer; b. Stockton, Calif., Nov. 21, 1949; s. Frederick Douglass and Sarah Frances (Young) H.; m. Patricia Brierton, June 25, 1988; children: Elizabeth, Andrew. BA, U. Calif., Santa Barbara, 1971; JD, U. Calif., Davis, 1974. Bar: Calif. 1974, U.S. Dist. Ct. (no., cen., ea. and so. dists.) Calif. 1974, U.S. Ct. Appeals (9th cir.) 1974, D.C. 1996, U.S. Dist. Ct. D.C. 1996, U.S. Supreme Ct. 2001. Assoc. Brobeck, Phleger & Harrison LLP, San Francisco, 1974-81, ptnr., 1981—2003; co-chair bench-bar liaison com. U.S. Bankruptcy Ct. No. Dist. Calif., 2002—03; ptnr. Orrick, Herrington & Sutcliffe, LLP, 2003—. Mem. faculty Practising Law Inst., 1990; spkr. Nat. Conf. Bankruptcy Judges, 1987, 91, Banking Law Inst., 1986, Calif. Continuing Legal Edn. of Bar, Calif., 1983-85, Calif. State Bar, 1993; bd. dirs. Bay Area Bankruptcy Forum. Mng. editor U. Calif. Davis Law Rev., 1974. Fellow Am. Coll. Bankruptcy; mem. ABA (bus. bankruptcy com., spkr. 1991, 95), Calif. Bar Assn. (commendation 1983), San Francisco Bar Assn. (cert. appreciation 1985, 88, 90, 95, vice chair 2003—), Turnaround Mgmt. Assn. (dir., sec. 1994-96), Am. Bankruptcy Inst., San Francisco Yacht Club, Sigma Pi (pres. 1970). Democrat. Avocations: triathlons, skiing, sailing. Home: 140 Bella Vista Ave Belvedere CA 94920-2466 Office: Orrick Herrington & Sutcliffe LLP Old Fed Res Bank Bldg 400 Sansome St San Francisco CA 94111 E-mail: fholden@orrick.com.

HOLDEN, RAYMOND THOMAS, physician, educator; b. Washington, Apr. 11, 1904; s. Raymond Thomas and Celeste Selma (Moritz) H.; m. Mary Lightle, Oct. 9, 1958; 1 dau., Mary Elliott. Student, U. Notre Dame, 1922-24; MD, Georgetown U., 1928, D.Sc. (hon.), 1980. Diplomate: Am. Bd. Obstetrics and Gynecology. Intern Providence Hosp., Washington, 1928-29, assoc., then attending obstetrician and gynecologist, 1932-56, cons., 1956-60; resident Columbia Hosp. for Women, Washington, 1929-30, asst., asso., attending staff, 1933, chief med. staff, 1952-54, 62-64, acting adminstr., 1958-59; preceptorship Dr. R.Y. Sullivan Georgetown U. Sch. Medicine, 1930-32; assoc., attending obstetrics and gynecology D.C. Gen Hosp., 1932-47; asst., assoc., also attending obstetrics and gynecology Georgetown U. Hosp., 1933—; from clin. instr. to clin. prof. obstetrics and gynecology Georgetown U. Sch. Medicine, 1933-85, assoc. chmn. dept. ob/gyn, 1977-85, emeritus clin. prof., 1985—; cons. obstetrics and gynecology U.S. Naval Hosp., Bethesda, Md., 1948-68. Bd. dirs., exec. com. Tb Assn. D.C., 1947-49; bd. dirs., exec. com. D.C. divsn. Am. Cancer Soc., 1950-56; mem. Health Facilities Planning Coun., Washington, 1964-70; bd. dirs. D.C. chpt. ARC, mem. exec. com., 1975-86; trustee Columbia Hosp. for Women. Served to capt., M.C. USNR, 1942-46; rear adm. Res. Fellow ACS, Am. Coll. Obstetricians and Gynecologists; mem. AMA (D.C. mem. Ho. Dels. 1952-68, chmn. com. on human reproduction 1964-68, trustee 1968-77, vice chmn. 1974-75, chmn. 1975-77, Disting. Svc. award 1987), D.C. Med. Soc. (chmn. exec. bd. 1951-52, pres. 1946-47), Washington Gynecology Soc. (sec. 1950-54, pres. 1956), So. Med. Assn., Assn. Profs. Gynecology and Obstetrics, Am. Legion, Alpha Omega Alpha. Clubs: Fifty Year of Am. Medicine (pres. 1979-80), Chevy Chase, Metropolitan. Home: 5120 Watson St NW Washington DC 20016-5340

HOLDEN, REBECCA LYNN, artist; b. Monterey, Calif., Nov. 29, 1952; d. Derrel Wayne and Zella Fay (Reed) Holden; m. Mark Stuart Bales, June 3, 1971 (div. Nov. 1983); children: Shelly Dawn Bales(dec.), Matthew Gregory Bales. BA, U. Ark., 1995. Potter/owner Rebecca Holden Studio, Searcy, Ark., 1984-94; artist/owner Rebecca Holden's Red Lick Mountain Studio, Clarksville, Ark., 1994-00; owner Old Carriage House Gallery and Studio, Jasper, Ark., 2000—. Established Old Carriage House Gallery and Studio, Jasper, Ark., 2000. Potter, sculptor, artist specializing in natural art forms. Recipient Art scholarship Susan Jones Rand Foun., 1992, 93. E-mail: carriage@jasper.yournet.com.

HOLDEN, ROBERT WATSON, radiologist, educator, university dean; b. Brazil, Ind., Mar. 31, 1936; s. John William and Naomi Ellen (Watson) H.; m. Miriam Ann Bognanno, June 20, 1964; children: Anne, Robert II, Jennifer. BS in Pharmacy, Purdue U., 1958; MD, Ind. U., 1963. Diplomate Am. Bd. Radiology. Intern L.A. County Gen. Hosp., 1963-64; resident radiology Vanderbilt U., Nashville, 1970-73; asst. prof. Ind. U. Sch. Medicine, Indpls., 1973-77, assoc. prof., 1977-82, prof., 1982—, prof., chmn. dept. radiology, 1991-95, dean, 1996—2000; ret., 2000. Chief vascular and interventional radiology Wishard Meml. Hosp., Indpls., 1973-79, chief radiology, 1977-91; counselor NIH, 1990-94. Contbr. over 100 articles to profl. jours. Chmn. bldg. com. 1st United Meth. Ch., Mooresville, 1988-95. Capt. U.S. Army, 1964-66. Recipient Gold medal Assn. Univ. Radiologists, 1999, Gold medal Am. Roentgen Ray Soc., 2000; named Disting. Alumnus, Purdue U. Sch. Phharmacy, 1992. Fellow Soc. Cardiovascular and Interventional Radiology, Am. Coll. Radiology (counselor), Radiologic Soc. N.Am. (counselor), Ind. Roentgen Soc. (past pres.). Republican. Avocations: forestry, agriculture, tennis. Office: Ind U Sch Medicine fH 302 1120 South Dr Rm 302 Indianapolis IN 46202-5135

HOLDEN, TIM, congressman, protective official; b. St. Clair, Pa., Mar. 5, 1957; s. Joseph F. and Catherine Siney H.; m. Gwen Kieres. BA in Sociology, Bloomsburg State Coll., 1980. Ins. broker/real estate agent; probation officer Schuylkill County, Pa.; sgt.-at-arms Pa. Ho. of Reps.; sheriff Schuylkill County, Pa., 1985-93; mem. U.S. Congress from 17th Pa. dist., Washington, 1993—; mem. agr. com., transp. and infrastructure com.; mem. Blue Dog Coallition. Democrat. Roman Catholic. Office: US Ho of Reps 2417 Rayburn Ho Office Bldg Washington DC 20515-0001*

HOLDEN, WILLIAM HOYT, JR., lawyer; b. Chgo. s. William Hoyt and Bernice Elizabeth (McKenzie) H.; m. Mary Ann Kula, June 23, 1954 (div. June 1982); children: William, Christopher, Sarah, Peter. BS, U. Ill., 1954; JD, U. Md., Balt., 1965. Bar: Md. 1965, U.S. Supreme Ct. 1969. Assoc. Weinberg and Green, Balt., 1965-72, ptnr., 1973-83; sr. v.p. CRI, Inc., Rockville, Md., 1983-85; sr. advisor Legg Mason Wood Walker, Inc., Balt., 1985-86; pvt. practice Bethesda, Md., 1987—. Pres., bd. dirs. Am. Franchise Cons., Inc., Bethesda, 1987—, Mid-Atlantic Title Closing, Inc. Capt. USNR, 1977, ret., 1982. Mem. Order of Coif, Rotary. Republican. E-mail: wholden1@cox.net.

HOLDEN, WILLIAM WILLARD, insurance executive; b. Akron, Ohio, Oct. 5, 1958; s. Joseph McCullem and Lettitia (Roderick) H.; m. Kim Homan, Aug. 31, 1985; 1 child, Jennifer Catharine. BA, Colgate U., 1981. Crime ins. trainee Chubb & Son, Inc., N.Y.C., 1981-82, exec. protection dept. mgr. San Jose, Calif., 1982-85, Woodland Hills, Calif., 1986-91; sr. v.p., mgr. Fin. Svcs. Group, Inc., Rollins, Hudig, Hall, Aon Fin. Svcs. Group, L.A., 1991-2000; tng. analyst Chubb & Son, Inc., Warren, N.J., 1985-86; exec. v.p. USI of So. Calif. Ins. Svcs., Sherman Oaks, 2000—. Co-author manual: Chubb Claims Made Training, 1985; contbr. articles to Colgate alumni mag. Mgr., coach Campbell (Calif.) Little League, 1983-85; coach Simi Valley Girls Softball, 1995-2003; pres. Le Parc Homeowners Assn., Simi Valley, Calif., 1987-89; mem. Community Assn. Inst., L.A., 1986—; bd. dirs. Friends of the Vols. for L.A. Unified Sch. Dist., 2001—, chmn., 2001-03. Mem. Profl. Liability Underwriting Soc. (L.A. steering com.), Forum for Corp. Dirs. Republican. Avocations: golf, reading, running, swimming, skiing. Office: USI of So Calif Ins Svcs Inc 14140 Ventura Blvd 3d Fl Sherman Oaks CA 91423 E-mail: william.holden@usi.biz.

HOLDER, ANGELA RODDEY, lawyer, educator; b. Rock Hill, S.C., Mar. 13, 1938; d. John T. and Angela M. (Fisher) Roddey; 1 child, John Thomas Roddey Holder. Student, Radcliffe Coll., 1955-56; BA, Newcomb Coll., 1958; postgrad., Faculty of Law-King's Coll., London, 1957-58; JD, Tulane U., 1960; LLM, Yale U., 1975. Bar: La. 1961, S.C. 1960, Conn. 1981. Counsel Roddey, Sumwalt & Carpenter, Rock Hill, S.C., 1960-91; atty. criminal div. New Orleans Legal Aid Bur., 1961-62; counsel York County Family Ct., S.C., 1962-64; asst. prof. polit. sci. Winthrop Coll., Rock Hill, 1964-74; research assoc. Yale U. Law Sch., 1975-77, exec. dir. program in law, sci. and medicine, 1976-77; lectr. dept. pediatrics Yale U. Sch. Medicine, 1975-77, asst. clin. prof. pediatrics and law, 1977-79, assoc. clin. prof., 1979-83, clin. prof., 1983-2001; prof. practice of med. ethics Duke Univ. Med. Ctr., Durham, N.C., 2001—. Trustee Am. Bd. Pediatrics, 2003—; mem. com. on pediat. palliative care Inst. of Medicine, 2001—02, mem. com. on clin. rsch. with children, 2002—. Author: The Meaning of the Constitution, 1968, 2d edit., 1987, 3d edit., 1997, Medical Malpractice Law, 1975, 2d edit. 1978, Legal Issues in Pediatrics and Adolescent Medicine, 1977, 2d edit., 1985, 3d edit., 1997; contbg. editor: Prism mag.; contbg. editor., AMA; mem. editorial bd.: IRB, 1976=2000, Medicine and HealthCare, 1978-2000, Jour. Philosophy and Medicine; contbr. articles to profl. jours. Mem. Rock Hill Sch. Bd., 1967—68; chmn. bd. dirs. Family Planning Clinic, 1970—73; bd. trustees Ednl. Commn. for Fgn. Med. Grads., 1990—97, exec. com., 1997; bd. dirs. Conn. Planned Parenthood, 1993—99, exec. com., 1996—99; mem. lawyers' rev. group Health Care Task Force, The White House, 1993; bd. trustees Cushing/Whitney Med. Libr. at Yale U., 1996—2001; ethics com. Leeway AIDS Hospice, New Haven, 1996—2001; alumnae bd. visitors Nat. Cathedral Sch., Washington, 2000—; cons. Artificial Reproductive Techs. Com., Ct. Ho. of Reps.; bd. dirs. Am. Bd. Pediatrics, 2003—. Mem. ABA, S.C. Bar Assn. (medico-legal com. 1973—), La. Bar Assn., New Haven County Bar Assn., Am. Soc. Law and Medicine (treas. 1981-83, sec. 1983-85, pres. 1986-88, bd. dirs. 1977-91). Democrat. Episcopalian. Home: 3408 Hope Valley Rd Durham NC 27707 Office: Ctr for Study of Med Ethics and Humanities Duke U Med Ctr Box 3040 108 Seeley G Mudd Bldg Durham NC 27710 E-mail: angela.holder@duke.edu.

HOLDER, CALVIN BERESFORD, history educator; b. Barbados, Sept. 28, 1946; s. Clifford Beresford and Beryl Leotta (Smith) H.; divorced; children: Aisha Margaret, Oshun Doris. AB, CCNY, 1970; AM, Harvard U., 1971, PhD, 1976. Prof. history Coll. of S.I., CUNY, N.Y., 1975—. Office: Coll SI CUNY Dept History 2800 Victory Blvd Staten Island NY 10314

HOLDER, DONALD, lighting designer; b. Y; Grad., Yale Sch. of Drama. Lighting designer (Broadway) The Lion King (Tony, Drama Desk, Outer Critics Cir. awards), Juan Darien (Tony, Drama Desk nominations), Hughie (Am. Theatre Wing nomination), Eastern Standard, Holiday, Solitary Confinement, (Off-Broadway) Most Fabulous Story Ever Told, Sight Unseen, Three Days of Rain, All My Sons, Communicating Doors, Caucasian Chalk Circle (Drama Desk nomination), Spunk, Avenue K, Fit to be Tied, From Above, Richard II/III, Titus Andronicus, The Green Bird (Am. Theater Wing nomination), The Changeling, Jeffrey, Maiden's Prayer, Pterodactyls, many others, (include Operas) Salome, (regional therater includes) Hartford Stage, Long Wharf, Mark Taper Forum, La Jolla Playhouse, American Repertory Theatre, Center Stage, many others, (archtl. lighting includes) Sony Plaza, Swiss Ctr. in N.Y., Jitney, 2000. Recipient Tony award for Lion King lighting design. Office: c/o Second Stage Theatre Box 1807 Ansonia Station New York NY 10023

HOLDER, GERALD D., JR., dean; b. L.A., July 29, 1950; s. Gerald D. Sr. and Pauline Ruth Holder; m. Diane Holder; children: Nancy, Elizabeth, Jonathan. BA in Chemistry, Kalamazoo Coll., 1972; BSE in Chem. Engring., U. Mich., 1973, MSE in Chem. Engring., 1974, PhD in Chem. Engring., 1976. Asst. prof. Columbia U., N.Y.C., 1976-79, U. Pitts., 1979-82, assoc. prof., 1982-86, prof., 1986-87, chmn., 1987-95, assoc. dean for rsch., 1995-96, dean engring., 1996-98, USX dean engring., 1998—. Bd. dir. Pitts. Tissue Engring. Initiative, Southwestern Pa. Indsl. Resource Ctr., Coun. for Chem. Rsch. Contbr. articles to profl. jours. Oak Ridge Associated Univs. fellow U. Pitts., 1986—. Mem. AIChE, Am. Soc. for Engring. Edn., Am. Chem. Soc., Soc. for Petroleum Engrs., Pitts. Athletic Assn., Pitts. Golf Club. Home: 4760 Bayard St Pittsburgh PA 15213 Office: U Pitts 240 Benedum Hall O'Hara and Thackeray Sts Pittsburgh PA 15261 E-mail: holder@engrng.pitt.edu.

HOLDER, HAROLD DOUGLAS, SR., investor, brokerage house executive, hotel executive; b. Anniston, Ala., June 25, 1931; s. William Chester and Lucile (Kadle) H.; m. Anna Maria Yaccarino, 1996; children: Debra Holder Carnaroli, Harold Douglas Jr., Charlie Kadle. Student, Anniston Bus. Coll., 1949, Jacksonville State U., 1954-57, Druitt Sch. Speech, 1962. Dept. mgr. Sears, Roebuck & Co., Anniston, 1954-57, merchandising mgr. Atlanta, 1957-59, dir. coll. recruiting, 1959-61, dir. exec. devel. program, 1961, asst. personnel dir., 1962-63, store mgr. Cocoa, Fla., 1965-67, Ocala, Fla., 1963-65, opers. zone mgr. Atlanta, 1967-68, asst. gen. mgr. mdse., 1968-69, sales promotion mgr. So. area, 1968; pres., bd. dirs. Cunningham Drug Stores, Inc., Detroit, 1969-70; v.p. Interstate Stores, 1971; pres., bd. dirs. Rahall Communications Corp., 1971-73; chmn. bd., chief exec. officer, dir. Am. Agronomics Corp., 1973-86; pres. Harold Holder Leasing; mng. dir. The Holder Group, Inc., 1987—. CEO, bd. dirs. Cutler Mfg. Corp., 1989-2000, Atlas Aircraft Corp., 1987-2000; mem. exec. com., bd. dirs. Coastland Corp., Fla., 1979-84; pres., bd. dirs. Golden Harvest, Inc., 1976-88; bd. dirs., treas. Dome Products, Inc., 1989-2000; CEO Casino Mgmt. Svcs. Internat., 1999—; chmn., CEO Holder Hospitality Group, Inc.; CEO Silver Club Hotel Casino, El Capital Resort Casino, Sharkey's Nugget Casino, Sundance Casino, Model "T" Resort Casino, Charlie Holder's Casino, Fernley Truck-Inn and Casino. Author: Don't Shoot, I'm Only a Trainee, 1975. Chmn., bd. dirs. Miracle, Inc., Brevard County; chmn. United Appeal, Ocala, Fla., 1964, Cocoa, Fla., 1966; bd. dirs. United Way Hillsborough County (Fla.); chmn. Heart Fund Drive, Ocala, 1964, Marion (Fla.) Com. of 100; bd. dirs. So. Coll. Placement Assn., Am. Acad. Achievement; bd. dirs. Marion chpt. ARC, Opera Arts Assn.; exec. com. Share, U. Fla.; bd. trustees U. Tampa; chmn. bd. trustees, trustee emeritus Eckerd Coll. With USMC, 1950-53. Named Harold D. Holder chair of Internat. Bus. and Fin., Eckerd Coll.; recipient Disting. Svc. award, Marion County 4-H Club, 1965, Golden Plate award, 1983, Champion of Higher Edn. award, 1982, Fla. NAACP Humanitarian award, 1984. Mem.: Young Pres. Orgn. (past chmn. Fla. chpt.), C. of C. (chmn. beautification com., retail bus. com.), Chief Execs. Forum, Omicron Delta Kappa. Episcopalian. Office: Holder Hospitality Group 1040 Victorian Ave Sparks NV 89431-4923

HOLDER, HOLLY IRENE, lawyer; b. Albuquerque, May 16, 1952; d. Howard George and Dorothy Evelyn (Doll) Holzum; m. William B. Holder Jr., June 4, 1974; 1 child, Eric James. BA with honors, U. Colo., 1974; JD with honors, U. Denver, 1980. Bar: Colo. 1980, U.S. Ct. Appeals (10th cir.) 1980. Chemist Indsl. Labs., Denver, 1974-76; law clk. to presiding justice Colo. Supreme Ct., Denver, 1979; assoc. Calkins, Kramer, Grimshaw and Harring, Denver, 1980-82, 84-88, McKenna, Conner & Cuneo, Denver, 1988-90, Saunders, Snyder, Ross & Dickson, Denver, 1990-93; pvt. practice Denver, from 1993. Mem. adv. com. Regional Coun. Govts. Water Resources Mgmt., 1984—; chmn. Chatfield Basin Assn., Denver, 1987, Chatfield Basin Master Plan Task Force, Denver, 1986—. Recipient Disting. Svc. award Denver Regional Coun. Govts., 1987, 2000. Mem. Colo. Bar Assn., Denver Bar Assn., Mensa, Denver Rotary. Republican. Avocations: golf, reading, book-collecting. Home: Littleton, Colo. Died 2001.

HOLDER, HOWARD RANDOLPH, SR., broadcasting company executive; b. Moline, Ill., Nov. 14, 1916; s. James William and Charlotte (Brega) H.; m. Clementi Lacey-Baker, Feb. 21, 1942; children: Janice Clementi Black, Susan Charlotte Holder, Marjory Estelle Holder, Howard Randolph Jr. BA, Augustana Coll., 1939. With radio stas. WHBF, Rock Island, Ill., 1939-41, WOC, Davenport, Iowa, 1945-47, WINN, Louisville, 1947, WRFC, Athens, Ga., 1948-56; pres. Clarke Broadcasting Corp., 1956-91, chmn., from 1991, WGAU and WNGC, Athens, from 1956, KVML and KZSQ, Sonora, Calif., from 1987, KJMQ, Atwater, Calif., from 1995, KTFN and KLOQ, Merced, Calif., from 1996. Mem. adv. bd. U. Ga. Coll. Journalism and Mass Comm., 1973-78, sec., 1973-74; pres. Mid-West Ga. Broadcasting, Inc., 1965-68; bd. dirs. AP Broadcasters, Inc., 1983-91, C&S Nat. Bank (now Bank of Am.), 1965-68. Author: Escape to Russia, 1995. Chmn. adv. bd. Salvation Army, 1962-63, life mem., 1952—; chmn. Athens Parks and Recreatoin Bd., 1952-62; chmn. Cherokee dist. Boy Scouts Am., 1966-67, bd. N.E. Ga. Eagle Scout Assn., 1989; mem. adv. bd. Clarke County Juvenile Ct., 1960-72, Athens-Clarke ARC, 1950-70; chmn. region IV Ga. divsn. Am. Cancer Soc., 1968; bd. dirs. Athens Crime Prevention Com., 1960-70; mem. Georgians for Safer Hwys., 1970; trustee Ga. Rotary Student Fund, Inc., 1969-90, trustee emeritus, 1990—; mem. Model Cities Policy Bd., 1970-71, Ga. Criminal Justice Coord. Com.; mem. Ga. Productivity Bd., 1984-85, hon. chmn. N.E. Ga. March of Dimes, 1996, 97, Walk Am., 1997; mem. bicentennial alumni activities com. U. Ga., 1982; co-pres. Friends U. Ga. Mus. Art, 1973-75; state bd. advisors Ga. Mus. Art, 1984—, life mem., 1997—; sec. adv. bd. Henry W. Grady Coll. Journalism and Mass Comm., U. Ga. adv. coun., 1990-92; mem. adv. group views for the nineties U. Ga., 1989-92; mem. fine arts task force, adv. com. for evaluation v.p. for svcs., U. Ga., 1989; mem. adv. com. Ga. Commn. for Nat. Bicentennial, 1976; bd. dirs. Rec. for the Blind, 1977-83, Athens Symphony, 1981-85, Quality Growth Task Force N.E. Ga., 1989-91; mem. Ga. Gov.'s Jail/Prison Overcrowding Com., 1982; mem. svcs. adv. coun. UGA, 1990—; mem. WWII Commemorative Com., 1993-95; trustee Clementi and Randolph Holder Girl Scout Trust, 1997—; bd. dirs. Lyndon House Arts Ctr. Found., 1995-97. With AUS, 1941-46, ETO, maj. USAR ret.; hon. adm. Navy Supply Corps, 1997; col. R.I. Militia, 1997. Decorated Bronze Star with valor in battle insignia; named Boss of Yr., Athens Jr. C. ofC., 1959, Broadcaster-Citizen of Yr., Ga. Assn. Broadcasters, 1962, Ga. Assn. Broadcasters Hall of Fame, 1993, Employer of Yr., Bus. and Profl. Women's Club, 1969, Athens Citizen of Yr., Rotary Club, 1971, Athens Woman's Club, 1971; recipient Silver Beaver award Boy Scouts Am., 1973, James E. West Fellowship award, Inspiration award Athens Cmty. Coun. on Aging, 1990, Advt. Silver medal Am. Advt. Fedn., Liberty Bell award Athens Bar Assn., 1977, Robert Stolz medaille, 1973, Nat. DAR medal of Hon., 1983, Cert. of Merit United Daus. of the Confederacy, 1983, Disting. Citizen award Ga. Dept. Labor, 1994, George Washington Patriotic Achievement award Soc. of Cin. in the State of Ga., 1996, Outstanding Ga. Citizen Sec. of State, 1997, Gov.'s Outstanding Svc. award, 1997, Key to City, Athens/Clarke County, 1997, Disting. Eagle award and Regent for life Nat. Eagle Scout Assn.; Paul Harris fellow, 1978, Will Watt fellow, 1984, Hue Thomas fellow, 1989, James E. West fellow, 1999; H. Randolph Holder Day proclaimed by the City of Athens, 1989, 98; named hon. admiral Navy Supply Corps, 1998, Key to Athens/Clarke, 1998, hon. col. R.I. Militia, 1998, NSCS Goodwill Ambassador award, 1999. Mem. Res. Officers Assn. (life, pres. Athens chpt. 1962), Am. Ex-Prisoners War (life), Ga. Assn. Broadcaster (pres. 1961), Athens Area C. of C. (pres. 1970), Ga. AP Broadcasters (pres. 1963), Augustana Coll. Alumni Assn. (bd. dirs. 1973-76, Outstanding Achievement award 1973), Golden Quill, Gridiron, Sigma Delta Chi, Alpha Psi Omega, Alpha Delta Sigma, Gamma Kappa (Ga. Pioneer Broadcaster of Yr. award 1971, 91, Lamplighter award 1993), Phi Omega Phi (pres. 1938-39), Touchdown Club (pres. Athens club 1963-64), Rotary (pres. Athens club 1957-58, govt. dist. 692 1969-70, Rotary internat. pub. rels. com. 1987-90, W. Lee Arrandale Vocat. Excellence award 1992). Home: Athens, Ga. Died May 6, 2002.

HOLDER, KATHLEEN, elementary education educator; b. Peoria, Ill., Jan. 19, 1942; d. Clifford B. and Margaret Anne (Bowker) Bourne; m. James Sherman Holder, Dec. 29, 1962; children: Laurie Lynn, Cheryl Anne. BS, Bradley U., 1965; MEd, Regents Coll., 1981; postgrad., SUNY, Cortland, 1990-91. Cert. elem. tchr., Ky., N.Y., Ga., Ill., Calif., tchr. birth-6 yrs., Am. Montessori Soc. Tchr. St. Philomena Sch., Peoria, Ill., 1962-63, Garfield Sch., Danville, Ill., 1964-67, St. David's Sch., Willow Grove, Pa., 1972-74, St. Austin Sch., Mpls., 1974-75, Knoxville (Tenn.) City Schs., 1977-79, Chenango Forks (N.Y.) Schs., 1985-92, Fayette County Schs., Lexington, Ky., 1992-96, Glynn County Schs., Brunswick, Ga., 1996-98; substitute tchr. Cedar Rapids, Iowa, 1999—; 1st grade tchr. Van Buren, Cedar Rapids, 1999-2000; presch. tchr. Clovis Unified, 2000—. Team coord. sci. impact project SUNY, Cortland, 1987-90, presenter tchrs. teaching tchrs., 1988, sci. insvc. workshops for tchrs. Fayette County Schs., 1994-96; team coord. Broome Tioga Boces Coop. Regional Curriculum Devel. Project. Author: Science Curriculum Resource Guide K-3, 1989. Grantee Hoyt Found., 1988, Family and Children's Svcs., 2001. Mem. Nat. Assn. for Edn. of Young Child, Calif. Assn. for Edn. of Young Child, Fresno Assn. for Edn. of Young Child, Calif. Reading Assn., Nat. Reading Assn., Knoxville Reading Assn. (treas. 1978-79), Delta Zeta (Sec. 1977-79, Rose of Honor 1979), Sigma Alpha Iota. Lutheran. Avocations: singing, gardening, cooking, reading. Home: 29 Laurel Ave 1st flr Binghamton NY 13905 E-mail: kathybourne1@aol.com.

HOLDER, LEE, human services administrator; b. Upland, Calif., Jan. 19, 1932; s. Lee Newcomer and Mattie Beatrice (Richards) Holder; m. Charlotte Rosa LaVars, Feb. 15, 1954; children: Lee Kurt, Liese Anne, Lawrence Keith, Lon Karl, Laurie Kristin. BS, U. Calif., Berkeley, 1953, MPH, 1958; postgrad., U. Wyo., 1961-63; PhD, U. Mich., 1968. With Oakland (Calif.) City Health Dept., 1956-57; dir. health edn. Monterey County (Calif.) Health Dept., 1958-59; asst. dir. health edn. Wyo. Health Dept., 1959-63; dir. cmty. action studies project Nat. Commn. Cmty. Health Svcs.; assoc. pub. health adminstrn. Johns Hopkins, 1963-66; assoc. prof. U. N.C., Sch. Pub. Health; dir. Planning and Evaluation Regional Med. Program N.C., 1968-71; dean coll. allied health professions, prof. cmty. medicine U. Tenn., Memphis, 1972-82; prof. health edn., adj. prof. health adminstrn. U. Okla., Oklahoma City, 1982-96, prof. emeritus, dean emeritus; pres. Allied Health Internat., Inc., 1998—. Adj. prof. polit. sci. Memphis State U., 1972—82; cons. in health planning, Toledo, Idaho Falls, Idaho, Franklin, NC; cons. Gov.'s Task Force Health, W.Va.; chmn. coordinating com. Memphis Area Vocat. Tech. Edn., 1973—74; chmn. Area-Wide Coun. Aging, 1974—76; manpower cons. Nat. Assn. Ptnrs. Ams., Caracas, Venezuela, 1976—82, Jordanian Royal Med. Svcs., Amman, 1977, U. Riyadh, 1980—86; mem. Health Sys. Agy. Contbr. articles to profl. jours. Chmn. Cmty. Planning Coun. Okla. Health Careers Coun., 1992—95; pres. Okla. Civic Music Assn., 1996—98, 2000; bd. dirs., 1st v.p. Okla. Alliance Aging, 1996—2002, pres., 2000—02; bd. dirs. Areawide Aging Agy., 1997—, Okla. Town Hall, 2000—, Okla. Coun. Aging, 1999—, chmn., 2002—. Fellow: Am. Soc. Allied Health Professions (pres. 1979—80, dir., mem. editl. bd. Jour. Allied Health 1973—80), Royal Soc. Health, Soc. Pub. Health Educators, Am. Pub. Health Assn.; mem.: SAR, VFW, Res. Officers Assn., Coun. Ednl. Instns. (chmn. 1976), Kiwanis (bd. dirs. 1998—2000), Am. Legion, Odd Fellow Club, Mil. Order World Wars, Alpha Eta (pres. 1978, 1992—93, sec.-treas. 1994—), Delta Omega, Phi Kappa Phi. Home: 8674 N May Ave Oklahoma City OK 73120-4469 Office: 801 NE 13th St Oklahoma City OK 73104-5005 E-mail: lee-holder@ouhsc.edu.

HOLDER, LONNIE EDWARD, engineering administrator, design engineer; b. Ft. Campbell, Ky., Jan. 29, 1956; s. William L. Dennison; m. Sonnie Holder, Dec. 29, 1976; children: Corwin Christopher, Shannara Kim. AS in Electronics, Yuba Coll., 1979; BS in Physics, U. Mo., 1982; MBA, Webster U., 1993. Registered patent agent U.S. Patent and Trademark Office. Laser system engr. Naval Weapons Ctr., China Lake, Calif., 1982-84; design engr. McDonnell Douglas Astronautics, St. Louis, 1984, quality assurance engr., 1985-86; field engr. McDonnell Douglas Korea, Inc., Changwon, 1987-88; sr. engr. McDonnell Douglas Electronic Systems, St. Louis, 1988-90; project mgr. McDonnell Douglas Aerospace, St. Louis, 1991-93; engring. sect. mgr. Hydro-Gear Ltd. Partnership, Sullivan, Ill., 1994-97, engring. mgr., 1997—2001, intellectual property mgr., 2001—. Served to sgt. USAF, 1975-79. Mem. Soc. Automotive Engrs. Republican. Achievements include research in bound state of helium near aluminum; development of first 100 watt diode pumped rod laser; 3 patents for electro-mechanical bypass for hydrostatic transmission. Home: 18 Chad Ave Sullivan IL 61951-9483 Office: Hydro-Gear 1411 S Hamilton St Sullivan IL 61951-2264 E-mail: lholder1@one-eleven.net., lholder@hydro-gear.com.

HOLDER, NEVILLE LEWIS, chemist; b. St. Joseph, Barbados, May 28, 1940; came to U.S., 1968, permanent resident, 1982; s. Cardon Elliot and Viola (Brathwaite) Tudor; m. Hyacinth Isoline Swaby, Sept. 4, 1965; children: Louis, Nadine, Nicole. BS with honors, U. West Indies, 1965, MS, 1969; PhD, U. Waterloo, 1973; MS, Temple U., 2002. Chemist Gillette Rsch. Inst., Rockville, Md., 1968-69, rsch. chemist, 1973-78; assoc. sr. investigator SmithKline Beecham Pharms., King of Prussia, Pa., 1978-92; sr. rsch. scientist Rhone-Poulenc Rorer Pharms., Collegeville, Pa., 1992-98; rsch. fellow Aventis Pharms. (formerly Rhone-Poulenc Rorer Pharms.), Bridgewater, 1998—2002; principal sci. Aventis Pharms., Bridgewater, NJ, 2003—. Mem. editl. bd. Jour. Organic Chemistry, Carbohydrate Chemistry; contbr. numerous articles to profl. jours.; patentee in field. Mem. com. Boy Scouts Am., Cherry Hill, N.J., 1980-90. Recipient Barbadian Am. Alliance Accomplishment award, 1991; grad. scholar U. W.I., 1968-68, Ministry Edn. Bursary, Barbados Govt., 1961-64. Mem. Am. Chem. Soc., Nat. Orgn. Profl. Advancement Black

Chemists & Chem. Engrs. (facilities chair Sci. Bowl Del. Valley chpt. 1990-98, scholarship & edn. coms. 1995—, v.p. 1996, v.p. Delaware Valley chpt. 1997-98, pres. Del. Valley chpt. 1998—, Corp. Liason award 1991), Phila. Organic Chemist Club, Toastmasters Internat. (charter, sergeant at arms 1990-91, treas. 1991-92, v.p. membership 1992, Compotent Toastmaster award 1989, Able Toastmaster award 1997). Episcopalian. Achievements include research in isolation and structure elucidation of natural products from the Jamaican cedar plant, synthesis of carbohydrate enones and their photochemical transformation to branched-chain monosaccharides, organic synthesis of drug substances, intermediates, isomers and potential impurities, chromatographic isolation and structure elucidation of impurities and decomposition products of drug substances and their synthetic intermediates, application of preparative HPLC using chiral and achiral stationary phases. E-mail: Neville.Holder@Aventis.com; home email: holder@quixnet.net. Home: 13 Clemson Rd Cherry Hill NJ 08034-1213 Office: Aventis Pharms Rte 202-206 PO Box 6800 Bridgewater NJ 08807-0800 E-mail: Neville.Holder@Aventis.com.

HOLDHUSEN, J. DAVID, music educator; b. Worthington, Minn., May 30, 1974; s. John B. and Linda L. Holdhusen; m. Deedra J. Halverson, July 29, 1995; 1 child, Annika Ruth. BA, Gustavus Adolphus Coll., 1992—96; MusM, Northwestern U., 1997—98. Type 10 Spl. Tchg. Ill. Asst. choir dir. Menomonie H.S., Wis., 1996—97; dir. of vocal music Lake Zurich H.S., Ill., 1998—. Musician: (choirs) performed in several venues including St. Patrick's Cathedral (Dublin), Mall of American and Walt Disney World. Mem.: NEA, Am. Choral Directors Assn., Ill. Music Edn. Assn. (co-chair dist. 7 2002), Pi Kappa Lambda. Avocations: sports, travel, fine arts. Office: Lake Zurich High School 300 Church St Lake Zurich IL 60047 Office Fax: 847-438-5989. E-mail: david.holdhusen@lz95.org.

HOLDING, LEWIS R. banker; b. 1927; married BS, U. N.C.; MBA, Harvard U. With First Citizens Bank & Trust Co., Raleigh, N.C., 1953—, former pres., chmn., dir., CEO, 1979—. Served with USAF, 1952-53. Office: First Citizens Banc Shares Inc PO Box 29549 Raleigh NC 27626-0549 also: 1st Citizens Bancshares Inc 20 E Martin St Raleigh NC 27601-1842*

HOLDING, R(OBERT) E(ARL), oil company executive; Pres. Sinclair Oil Corp., Salt Lake City, 1976—, bd. dirs., now CEO. Office: Sinclair Oil Corp PO Box 30825 Salt Lake City UT 84130*

HOLDITCH, WILLIAM KENNETH, American literature educator; b. Ecru, Miss., Sept. 18, 1933; s. Sidney Wiliamson and Dora Faye (Dickerson) H. BA with honors, Southwestern at Memphis, 1955; MA in English, U. Miss., 1957, PhD in English, 1961. Instr. Am. lit. U. Miss., Oxford, 1957-59; asst. prof. U. New Orleans, 1964-69, assoc. prof., 1969-78, prof., 1978-90, rsch. prof., 1990-96, rsch. prof. emeritus, 1996—. Bd. dirs. Tennessee Williams Festival, New Orleans, 1986-97, v.p., 1987—. Author numerous essays and short stories; co-author: Tennesee Williams and the South, 2002, Galatoire's: Tales of a Bistro, 2003; editor: In Old New Orleans, 1983, The Tennessee Williams Journal, 1989—; co-editor: (with Mel Gussow) Two Tennessee Williams Volumes, Library of America; adv. editor: South Central Journal, 1990-93. Pres. Friends of U. New Orleans Libr., 1990-94; founder, bd. dirs. Pirate's Alley Faulkner Soc.; advisor Clarksdale Tennessee Wiliams Festival, 1992—. Named La. U. Tchr. of Yr., Amoco, 1980; recipient LIfetime Achievement award, La. Endowment Humanities, 2001. Mem. MLA, South Cen. MLA. Avocations: walking, reading, collecting glass. Home: 732 Frenchmen St New Orleans LA 70116-1614 Office Fax: 504-948-7821. E-mail: kholditch@cox.net.

HOLDMAN, BETTIE, retired elementary school educator; b. Somerset, Ky., Dec. 16, 1939; d. Thomas Edward and Vada Lou Van Hoozer; m. William R. Holdman, July 8, 1962; 1 child, Marvin L. AA, Enterprise (Ala.) State Jr. Coll., 1973; BS magna cum laude, Troy State U., 1976; MEdn., U. So. Miss., 1980. Cert. tchr. K-12, spl. edn. Ala. Tchr. Enterprise City Schs., 1975—2001; ret., 2001. Coord. Spl. Olympics Enterprise City Schs., 1996—2000. Named Coach of Yr., Ala. State Spl. Olympics, 1999. Mem.: NEA, Ala. Edn. Assn., Enterprise Edn. Assn. (sec. 1996—2001), Enterprise Civitan Club (sec. 1983—86, edn. mgr. 1995—97), Order Eastern Star (worthy matron 1976—77). Home: 65 Private Rd 1508 Enterprise AL 36330 E-mail: bholdman@entercomp.com.

HOLDORF, HARRY HULBERT, health services administrator; b. Jamestown, N.Y., May 1, 1958; s. John A. and Louise Holdorf; m. Cynthia L. Baron, Aug. 28, 1982; children: Christopher, Nicholas. AS in Radiol. Tech., Union County Coll.; BA in Environ. Scis., Stockton State Coll.; MPA, Kean U.; PhD in Health Svcs. Adminstrn., Southwest U. Lic. radiologic technologist Am. Registry Radiologic Technoligsts N.J., N.Y., med. sonographer Am. Registry Diagnostic Med. Sonographers. Radiol. technologist Elizabeth (N.J.) Gen. Med. Ctr., 1983-86, St. Barnabas Med. Ctr., N.J., 1986-87; splty. technologist Dover (N.J.) Hosp., 1987-88; staff ultrasonagrapher Overlook (N.J.) Hosp., 1988, Elizabeth Gen. Med. Ctr., 1988-89, coord. ultrasound program, 1989-92, mem. faculty sch. radiol. scis., 1988-97, dir. ultrasound program, 1992-97, mgr. radiology, 1997-2000; quality assurance coord., mgr. med. imaging svcs. Irvington (N.J.) Gen. Hosp., 2001—. Cons. Schs. Med. Imagery and Med. Scis. Muhlenberg Regional Med. Ctr., 2000—03, adminstrv. dir. med. imaging svcs. Schs. Med. Imagery and Med. Scis., 2001—03; program dir. diagnostic med. sonography program Schs. Nursing, Med. Imaging and Therapeutic Scis., 2003—; site visitor Joint Rev. Com. on Edn. in Diagnostic Med. Sonography. Mem. Am. Soc. Diagnostic Med. Sonographers, Am. Soc. Radiol. Technologists, Am. Soc. Notaries, N.E. Assn. Allied Health Educators, Am. Inst. Ultrasound in Medicine, Pi Alpha Alpha. Home: 532 Woodland Ave Mountainside NJ 07092-2524 Office: Schs of Nursing Med Imaging and Therapeutic Scis Park Ave and Randolph Rd Plainfield NJ 07062 E-mail: hholdorf@solarishs.org.

HOLDRIDGE, BARBARA, book publisher; b. N.Y.C., July 26, 1929; d. Herbert L. and Bertha (Gold) Cohen; m. Lawrence B. Holdridge, Oct. 9, 1959; 2 children. AB, Hunter Coll., 1950. Asst. editor Liveright Pub. Corp., N.Y.C., 1950-52; co-founder Caedmon Records, Inc., N.Y.C., 1952, partner, 1952-60, pres., 1960-62, treas., 1962-70, pres., 1970-75; founder Stemmer House Pubs. Inc., Owings Mills, Md., 1975, pres., 1975—. Co-founder, v.p. Shakespeare Rec. So., Inc., N.Y.C., 1960-70, Theatre Rec. Soc., Inc., N.Y.C., 1964-70; founder BEDE Prodns., 1984; co-founder History Rec. Soc., Inc., N.Y.C., 1964, pres., 1964-70; lectr. on Ammi Phillips, 1959--; lectr. on book pub., 1992—; adj. prof. writing media Loyola Coll., Balt., 1987-91. Author: Ammi Phillips, 1968, Aubrey Beardsley Designs from the Age of Chivalry, 1983, Chinese Cut-Out Designs of Costumes, 1989; articles on Am. paintings. Named to Hunter Coll. Hall of Fame, 1972, Nat. Women's Hall of Fame, 2002; recipient Am. Shakespeare Festival award, 1962, N.Y.C. cert. of appreciation, 1972, Lifetime Achievement award, Audio Pubs. Assn., 2001. Mem. 14 West Hamilton Street Club, Phi Beta Kappa Assn. of Greater Balt. (bd. dirs.). Office: 2627 Caves Rd Owings Mills MD 21117-2919 E-mail: stemmerhouse@comcast.net.

HOLDSCLAW, CHAMIQUE SHAUNTA, professional basketball player; b. Flushing, N.Y., Aug. 9, 1977; Grad., U. Tenn., 1999. Basketball player Washington Mystics, 1999—. Named Sports Illustrated and Sporting News Nat. Women's Player of Yr., 1999, Naismith finalist, AP Women's Basketball Player of Yr., 1997—98, 1998—99, N.Y.C. Player of Yr., Rawlings/WBCA Player of Yr., Player of Yr., Columbus, Ohio Touchdown Club, 1995; named one of 12 female athletes selected as inspirational role models, Women's Sports and Fitness mag., 1998; named to Kodak 25th Anniversary Team, Women's Basketball Jour., Street & Smith All-Am., three-time, USA Today All-Am.; recipient Sullivan award, Gold medal, 1998 World Championships, 1997 World Qualifying Tournament, 1995 Olympic Festival, USA Basketball Player of Yr. award, 1997, ESPY's for Female Athlete of Yr. award, second consecutive Women's Basketball Player of Yr. award, 1999, Naismith award, Atlanta's Tip-Off Club, 1995, Gold medal, U.S. Olympic Team, 2000. Office: Washington Mystics MCI Center 601 F St NW Washington DC 20004-1605

HOLDSWORTH, JANET NOTT, women's health nurse; b. Evanston, Ill., Dec. 25, 1941; d. William Alfred and Elizabeth Inez (Kelly) Nott; children: James William, Kelly Elizaveth, John David. BSN with high distinction, U. Iowa, 1963; M of Nursing, U. Wash., 1966. RN, Colo. Staff nurse U. Colo. Hosp., Denver, 1963-64, Presbyn. Hosp., Denver, 1964-65, Grand Canyon Hosp., Ariz., 1965; asst. prof. U. Colo. Sch. Nursing, Denver, 1966-71; counseling nurse Boulder PolyDrug Treatment Ctr., Boulder, 1971-77; pvt. duty nurse Nurses' Offcl. Registry, Denver, 1973-82; cons. nurse, tchr. parenting and child devel. Teenage Parent Program, Boulder Valley Schs., Boulder, 1980-88; bd. dirs., treas. Nott's Travel, Aurora, Colo., 1980—; nurse Rocky Mountain Surgery Ctr., 1996—. Instr., nursing coord. ARC, Boulder, 1979-90, instr., nursing tng. specialist, 1980-82. Mem. adv. bd. Boulder County Lamaze Inc., 1980-88; mem. adv. com. Child Find and Parent-Family, Boulder, 1981-89; del. Rep. County State Congl. Convs., 1972-96, sec. 17th Dist. Senatorial Com., Boulder, 1982-92; vol. Mile High ARC, 1980; vol. chmn. Mesa Sch. PTO, Boulder, 1982-92, bd. dirs., 1982-95, v.p., 1983-95; elder Presbyn. Ch. Mem. ANA, Colo. Nurses Assn. (bd. dirs. 1975-76, human rights com. 1981-83, dist. pres. 1974-76), Coun. Intracultural Nurses, Sigma Theta Tau, Alpha Lambda Delta. Republican. Home: 1550 Findlay Way Boulder CO 80305-6922 Office: Rocky Mountain Surgery Ctr 1630 30th St # 153 Boulder CO 80301-1014

HOLE, RICHARD DOUGLAS, lawyer; b. Auburn, N.Y., Aug. 23, 1949; s. Robert B. and Barbara (Swift) H.; m. Deborah Elizabeth Muldoon, Jan. 8, 1972; children: Emily, Brian, Jeffrey. BA, Hamilton Coll., 1971; JD, Syracuse (N.Y.) U., 1975. Bar: N.Y. 1976, U.S. Dist. Ct. (no. dist.) N.Y. 1976, U.S. Dist. Ct. (we. dist.) N.Y. 1980. Assoc. Bond, Schoeneck & King, Syracuse, 1976—83, ptnr., 1984—. Pres. N.Y. Employee Benefits Conf., Rochester, 1987-88. Pres. Fayetteville-Manlius (N.Y.) Little League, Inc., 1988-93; pres. Eye Rsch. Inst. of Ctrl. N.Y., Syracuse, 1988-93; bd. dirs. Cystic Fibrosis Found., Syracuse, 1988-93; pres., bd. trustees United Ch. of Fayetteville, 1990-95, 98—; bd. dirs. Syracuse Symphony, 1995-2001; pres. Ctrl. N.Y. Alumni Coun. Hamilton Coll., 1999—. Mem.: Nat. Assn. Coll. and Univ. Attys., Onondaga County Bar Assn., NY State Bar Assn. Republican. Presbyterian. Office: Bond Schoeneck & King 18th Fl One Lincoln Ctr Syracuse NY 13202

HOLEC, ANITA KATHRYN VAN TASSEL, civic worker; b. Rahway, N.J., Nov. 11, 1947; d. Edward T. and Irene Eleanor (Barna) Van Tassel; m. Sidney W. Holec, Oct. 26, 1968. BS, U. Houston, 1969. Stockbroker Drexel Burnham Lambert, Inc., Miami, Fla., 1976-78, Merrill Lynch, Venice, Fla., 1979-80; fin. cons. Shearson Lehman Bros., Venice, 1981-87; owner, mgr. Closet Stretchers, Venice, 1987-89. Bd. dirs. Safe Place and Rape Crisis Ctr., Sarasota, 1987-99, Womens Resource Ctr., Sarasota, 1981-86, 90-94, Friends Venice Libr., 1992-94, New Coll. Libr., 1991-94; mem. Leadership Sarasota, 1991-95, Jr. League of Sarasota, 1982—, Argus Found., 1982—, Planned Parenthood S.W. and Ctrl. Fla., 2001—. Mem.: Chautauqua Women's Club. Avocations: reading, feminism. Mailing: PO Box 1049 Osprey FL 34229 E-mail: ansidco@aol.com.

HOLECHEK, JERRY, agricultural studies educator; b. Lebannon, Oreg., Mar. 6, 1948; s. Harry Alois and Patsy Lee Holechek. BS, Oreg. State U., 1971, PhD in Animal Sci., 1980; MS, Mont. State U., 1976. Prof. N.Mex. State U., Las Cruces, N.Mex., 1979—. Natural resources cons. Sustainable Environ. Solutions, Kansas City, Mo., 2002—. Author: Range Management: Principles and Practices, 2001, Natural Resources: Ecology Economics and Policy, 2003. Recipient Outstanding Achievement award, Soc. for Range Mgmt., 1998. Office: Dept Animal and Range Sci N Mex State Univ Las Cruces NM 88003 Home: 2328 Terrace Ct Las Cruces NM 88001

HOLEMAN, GEORGE ROBERT, health physicist, consultant; b. Danville, Ky., Dec. 23, 1937; s. Ernest R. and Rosa Mae (Tuggle) H.; m. Pamela Reed, Sept. 5, 1959 (div. June 1984); children: David R., Heather L. Holeman; m. Penny Hope Hausser, Jan. 11, 1997; 1 child, William Pieper Holeman. BA, Centre Coll. of Ky., 1960; AM, Harvard U., 1961. Health physicist Knolls Atomic Power Lab. GE, Schenectady, N.Y., 1961-63; health physicist Yale U., New Haven, 1963-71, dir. health physics div., 1971-86, lectr. pub. health, 1963-85, lectr. epidemiology, 1985-97, dir. radiation safety dept., 1986-94; team leader pers. monitoring Brookhaven Nat. Lab., Upton, N.Y., 1994-99, group leader pers. monitoring, 1999, mem. instnl. rev. bd., mem. radioactive drug rsch. com., 1996-99. Pres. JAG, Inc., 1970-79, Radiation Consulting Svcs., Inc., 1979-85, Holeman Cons., Inc., 1985—; mem. working group Am. Nat. Standards Inst., 1993-96; attending health physicist VA Med. Ctr., West Haven, 1976-97; dir. Radionuclide Lab., Yale U. Cancer Ctr., 1974-77; cons. Environ. Evaluation Group, State of N.Mex., 1979-89; mem. ind. risk assessment team Gov.'s Office State of Conn., 1980-90; cons. N.Y. State Energy Rsch. and Devel. Authority, 1993-2002. Duke U., 1998, Brookhaven Nat. Lab., 2000—. Contbr. 2 book chpts. and 26 articles to profl. jours. Bd. dirs. Conn. Hazardous Waste Mgmt. Svc., 1983-97, vice chmn., 1983-97, acting chmn. and CEO, 1990-91, 95-96. AEC health physics fellow, Harvard U., 1960-61, Brookhaven Nat. Lab., Upton, L.I., 1961; WHO fellow, Sweden, Fed. Rep. Germany, U.K., 1985; del. IRPA Congress, Health Physics Soc., West Berlin, 1983. Fellow APHA (governing coun. 1988-89), Am. Acad. Health Physics (diplomate, bd. dirs. 1988-90), Nat. Coun. on Radiation Protection (chair sci. com. 1985-90); mem. Am. Assn. Physicists in Medicine (chair radiation protection com. 1980-85, mem. sci. coun. 1980-85, mem. radiation protection com. 1993-99), Health Physics Soc. (sec. 1980-82, bd. dirs. 1980-83). Avocation: house restoration. E-mail: ghol899852@aol.com.

HOLEMAN, LORA WHITE, music educator; b. Oklahoma City, Jan. 11, 1964; d. Marvin E. and Lora Edith White; m. Gerald E. Holeman, Jr., July 25, 1999. MusB in Edn., U. Ctrl. Okla., 1987, MusM in Edn., 1990. K-12 License Okla. State Dept. of Edn., 1987. Instr. piano, voice, Oklahoma City, 1982—90; instr. music Jefferson State Coll., Birmingham, Ala., 1991—94. Ind. voice & piano instr., Oklahoma City, 1982—90; adj. instr. music Birmingham-So. Coll., Ala., 1990—94. Founder, pres. BIG Options, Oklahoma City, 2003—. Mem.: Ctrl. Okla. Music Tchrs. Assn., Okla. Music Tchrs. Assn., Music Tchrs. Nat. Assn., Music Educator's Nat. Conf., Nat. Assn. Advance Fat Acceptance (founder chpt.). Avocations: medical arts, cats. Office: BIG Options PO Box 30094 Oklahoma City OK 73140 Office Fax: 405-732-3586. E-mail: big options4u@aol.com.

HOLEMAN, RUSSELL KENT, civil engineer; b. Lexington, Mo., Oct. 23, 1957; s. E.G. and Joyce Lynette (Bredehoeft) H.; m. Linda Lea Cameron, May 23, 1981; children: Jared Tyler, Chelsea Paige. BSCE, Tex. Tech. U., 1979. Registered profl. engr., Tex. Civil engr. U.S. Army Facilities Engrs., Fort Hood, Tex., 1979-81, U.S. Army Corps Engrs., Fort Hood, Tex., 1981-83, chief, office engring., 1983-85, chief, contract adminstrn. Amarillo, Tex., 1985-87, area engr., 1987-95, dir. mil. project mgmt. Tulsa, 1995—2000, asst. chief engring. and constrn., 2000—02, chief hydrology, 2002—. Facilitator U.S. Army, Ctr. for Army Leadership, Ft. Leavenworth, Kans., 1989-2001. Co-developer: (software) Construction Office Contract Administrator, 1983-86. Pres. Tex. Panhandle Fed. Exec. Assn., 1994; v.p. Prince of Peace Luth. Ch., Amarillo, 1988; major acct. exec. govt. sector, United Way, Amarillo, 1991, vice chmn., 1992, chmn., 1993, vice chmn. Tulsa combined fed. campaign, 1997; asst. scoutmaster Boy Scouts Am., 1996—, vice chmn. outer limits com., 1997—, venturing tng. chmn., 2002—, advisor Boy Scout Explorer Post 2001, 1998—. Recipient Engr. of Yr., Tulsa Dist., 1990, Leadership award Tulsa Dist., 1993, Comdr.'s award for civilian svc., 1998, Venturing Leadership award Boy Scouts Am., 1999. Mem. NSPE, Tex. Soc. Profl. Engrs., Tex. Panhandle Fed. Exec. Assn. (sec., treas. 1991-92, v.p. 1992-93, pres. 1993-94). Avocations: softball, snow skiing, backpacking, camping.

HOLEN, NORMAN DEAN, art educator, artist; b. Cavalier, N.D., Sept. 16, 1937; s. Alvin C. and Norma H. Holen; m. Ilene Gronaas, Sept. 3, 1960; children: Peter John, Alisa Ilene. BA, Concordia Coll., 1959; MFA, State U. Iowa, 1962; postgrad., U. Minn., 1972. Instr. Northwestern Coll., Orange City, Iowa, 1962-63, Concordia Coll., Moorhead, Minn., 1963-64; prof. Augsburg Coll., Mpls., 1964—2002, ret., 2002. Contbr. articles to profl. jours. including The Artists mag., Pottery Making Illustrated, Clay Times, The Am. Artist; commns. including Kirchbak Gardens, Richfield, Minn., King Olav, Oslo, Norway, Augsburg Coll., Mpls., King Herald V, Norway. Mem. Artist Equity Assn. (chpt. pres., nat. exec. bd. 1974-75, v.p. Minn. chpt. 1973-74), Soc. Minn. Sculptors, Nat. Sculpture Soc. (Bronze Medal, 1980, Joel Meisner award, 1983), Allied Artists of Am. (Rachel L. Armour award, 1980, 82, In Memorium award, 1983). Republican. Lutheran. Avocations: playing classical guitar, inventing tools and splints for my physically challenged students. Home: 7332 12th Ave S Minneapolis MN 55423-3343

HOLFELD, DONALD RAE, railroad consultant; b. Lestock, Sask., Can., Apr. 10, 1947; came to the U.S., 1994; s. Alexander R. and Edith (Schwab) H.; m. Patricia Elizabeth Sewell, July 16, 1994. BS, U. Alta., 1973. Registered prof. engr. Assn. Profl. Engrs. B.C. Maintenance engr. CN Rail, Kamloops, B.C., 1977-80, track and roadway engr., 1980-81, planning engr. Montreal, 1981-82, track rsch. engr., 1982-83, sys. engr. tech., 1983-89, sys. dir. ops. tng., 1989-94; dir. tng. and engring. Zeta-Tech. Assocs., Inc., Cherry Hill, N.J., 1994—. Aux. prof. McGill U., Montreal, 1988-94; lectr. in field. Inventor in field. Recipient Golden Spike awards Internat. Rwy. Tng. Assn., 1989-94. Mem. ASTD, Am. Rlwy. Engring. and Maintenance of Way Assn. Avocations: singing, jogging, travelling, reading, cooking. Office: Zeta-Tech Assocs Inc 900 Kings Hwy N Ste 208 Cherry Hill NJ 08034-1516 E-mail: donandpattie@netzero.net, holfeld@zetatech.com.

HOLFELDER, LAWRENCE ANDREW, pediatrician, allergist; b. Bklyn., June 7, 1939; MD, Albany Med. Coll., 1965. Diplomate Am. Bd. Pediats., Am. Bd. Allergy and Immunology. Intern St. Vincent's Med. Ctr., N.Y.C., 1965-66, resident, 1966-68, fellow in allergy and immunology, 1972, U. Chgo. Hosps., 1970-71; now pvt. practice Tampa, Fla. Mem. staff St. Joseph's Hosp., Tampa; clin. prof. medicine and pediats. in allergy U. So. Fla. Mem. Am. Acad. Allergy and Immunology. Office: Harrelson Med Arts Bldg 3709 W Hamilton Ave Ste 1 Tampa FL 33614-4015

HOLFORTY, PEARL MARTHA, accountant; b. Detroit, Oct. 31, 1928; d. Johannes and Martha Mary (Francoys) Kramer; m. Clifford W. Holforty, Mar. 27, 1948; children: Kathleen Diane, David Alan(dec.), Wendy Lauren, Michael Todd. Student, Mich. State U., 1945-47; BS, Wayne State U., 1970, MBA, 1973. Contr. Sta. WPON, Pontiac, Mich., 1958-60; bus. mgr. Holforty, Widrig & O'Neill Assocs., Inc., Troy, Mich., 1960-69; staff acct. Plante & Moran, CPAs, Southfield, Mich., 1970-77, ptnr., 1977-91; founder, chair, pres., CEO Liberty BIDCO Investment Corp., 1988—. Part-time faculty Wayne State U., 1974-77; mem. small bus. adv. coun. Fed. Res. Bank Chgo., 1985-87; del. White House Conf. on Small Bus., 1986. Past chair Met. Detroit YMCA; former mem. Gov.'s Entrepreneurial and Small Bus. Com.; former mem. employability skills task force State of Mich.; former trustee Mich. Accountancy Found.; former treas. Wayne County Intermediate Sch. Dist.-Found. for Excellence; past bd. dirs. United Way of S.E. Mich., United Am. Healthcare Corp., Auto Club Trust (bd. dirs.); past treas. Mich. Women's Found. Recipient Edward G. Erickson award, 1970, Elijah Watts Sells award, 1971, Headliners award Wayne State U., 1983, Corp. Leadership award Wayne State U., 1998; Phi Gamma Mu scholar, 1970; named Woman Advocate of Yr. SBA Mich., 1986. Mem. AICPA, Nat. Assn. Accts. (pres. chpt. 1979), Mich. Assn. CPAs, Nat. Assn. Women Bus. Owners (chpt. pres. 1986-87), Women's Econ. Club (pres. 1989-90), Beta Gamma. Presbyterian. Home and Office: 28721 Hidden Trl Farmington Hills MI 48331-2982 E-mail: pholforty@lbico.com.

HOLGERS-AWANA, RITA MARIE, electrodiagnosis specialist; b. Chgo., Nov. 24, 1933; d. Joseph Theodore and Kathleen (Cooney) Konecny; m. Alan Miles Holgers, Aug. 8, 1960 (div. Sept. 1986); children: Dale, Ross; m. Benedict E.C. Awana, June 13, 1989 (dec. Feb. 1995). BS, N.Am. U., 1984, M of Nutripathic Sci., D of Nutripathy, N.Am. U., 1988, PhD in Nutritional Philosophy, 1990. Nutritional cons. Vitality Testing, Phoenix, 1982-84, pres., CEO Glendale, Ariz., 1984-86, Zac Engring. Inc., Lombard, Ill., 1986-2000; credentials coord. Prin. Health Care, Oakbrook Terrace, Ill., 1995-98; ptnr. Age-Less Group, Lombard, 2001—. Spkr. women's coffee break group Harvard Ave. Free Evangelical Ch., 1997-98; spkr. Dowser's Club, 1997-98, spkr. in field; cons. Ubid, Inc., 1999—; presenter 3d Whole Life Expo, Chgo., 1999, Health, Beauty and Fitness Expo, Coll. of DuPage, Glen Ellyn, Ill., 2001; bd. dirs. Global Deactivation of Radiation. Author: Me and My Non-Disease, 1983, Radiation, The Hidden Enemy, 1995; invention electronic water filter unit. Pres., v.p. S.W. Herbal Edn. Assn., Phoenix, 1984-85; sec. Better Breathers Club, Chula Vista, Calif., 1992-93, Concerned Citizens, Biggsville, Ill., 1975; co-founder, charter mem. Exec. Women's Coun., Moline, Ill., 1974; cub scout den leader Boy Scouts Am., Eldridge, Iowa, 1973; treas. food coop., Asuncion, Paraguay, 1958. With U.S. Fgn. Svc., 1956-61. Recipient Internat. Championship Golf Trophy, U.S. Dept. of State, 1959, Championship Golf trophy Hend-Co-Hills, 1974, 75, 77, Tai Chi Black Belt, Shingumatsu Martial Arts, 1993; named Woman of the Year, Internat. Biog. Ctr., Cambridge, Eng., 1998. Mem. Nat. Health Fedn., The Am. Dowsers Soc. (v.p. 1999), Anti-Aging Acad., 2001, Computrek Computer Club, N.Am. Dowser's Club. Mem. Unity Ch. Avocations: golf, bowling, knitting, computer, martial arts. Home and Office: Apt E 239 S Westmore Ave Lombard IL 60148-3066 E-mail: docradrita@aol.com.

HOLIDAY, EDITH ELIZABETH, former presidential adviser, cabinet secretary; b. Middletown, Ohio, Feb. 14, 1952; d. Harry Jr. and Kathlyn (Watson) H.; m. Terrence B. Adamson, June 8, 1985; children: Kathlyn Holiday Adamson, Elizabeth Holiday Adamson; 1 stepchild, Terrence Morgan Adamson. Student, Miami U., Oxford, Ohio, 1970-71; BS with honors, U. Fla., 1974, JD, 1977. Bar: Fla. 1977, D.C. 1978, Ga. 1984. Assoc. Read Smith Shaw & McClay, Washington, 1977-83, Dow Lohnes & Albertson, Atlanta, 1983-84; exec. dir. Commn. on Exec. Legis. and Jud. Salaries, Washington, 1984-85; spl. counsel polit. action com. Fund for Am. Future, Washington, 1985-87; dir. ops. George Bush for Pres., Inc., Washington, 1987-88; chief counsel, nat. fin. and ops. dir. Bush-Quayle 88, Washington, 1988; with legal svcs. staff George Bush for Pres. Compliance Com., Washington, 1988; asst. sec. for pub. affairs and pub. liaison, counselor to sec. Departmental Offices, U.S. Dept. Treasury, Washington, 1988; gen. counsel U.S. Dept. Treasury, Washington, 1989-90; asst. to U.S. pres., sec. of cabinet Washington, 1990-93. Legis. asst. to U.S. Sen. Nicholas F. Brady, Washington, 1982—83; bd. dirs. Amerada Hess Corp., H.J. Heinz Co., Beverly Enterprises, Inc., Franklin Templeton Group Funds, RTI Internat. Metals, Inc., Canadian Nat. Railway Co.; oper. trustee TWE Holdings I, II, III Trusts, 2002—. Recipient Alexander Hamilton award Sec. of Treasury, 1991, spl. citation John Marshall Bar Assn. Mem. Phi Delta Phi, Kappa Tau Alpha. Republican.

HOLIFIELD, LEONARD CLEVE, security firm executive, educator; b. Johnstown, Pa., Jan. 5, 1960; s. Cleveland and Ruth Holifield; m. Ena Herminia Faulkner, May 22, 1996; 1 child, Cameron Seth. PhD in Martial Sci.(hon.), Am. Coll. Martial Sci., 2002. Cert. advanced exec. protection Exec. Security Internat. Chief combatives instr. US Army, NC, 1988—97, advanced through grades to E6 staff sgt., 1996; chief instr./owner/founder Sikaron Karate Fedn., Montgomery, Ala., 1980—; exec. security officer / cert. protection specialist, dep. marshal Ala. Supreme Ct., Montgomery, 2000—. Dean homeland security Am. Coll. Martial Sci., 2003. Author: Close Quarter Combat, 1997; video artist : Close Quarter Fighting Series, 1994. Exec. v.p. World Martial Arts Hall Fame, Cleve., 1991—2002. Recipient Authorship award, Soldiers Mag., 1990, Army Trainers Mag., 1997, 1994, Grandmaster of the Yr. award, Wa No Michi-Ryu Kai Internat., 1998, Meritorious Svc. Award (U.S Army JROTC), 1995, Spl. Recognition award, U.S. Congress, 1991, award of excellence, U.S. Army, 1995, more than 200 Letters of Commendation. Mem.: World Martial Arts Hall of Fame (exec. v.p. 1995—2002, Instr. of the Yr. 1998, Head Founder of the Yr. award 1999, Exec. Valor award 1997), Phi Theta Kappa (life). Achievements include first to close-engagement-target-acquisition. Avocations: classical music, exercise, martial arts, classic movies, self improvement. Office: Alabama Supreme Court 300 Dexter Ave Montgomery AL 36104-3741 Home Fax: 334-356-3087; Office Fax: 334-356-3087. Personal E-mail: HolifieldCPS@aol.com.

HOLIFIELD, PEARL KAM (KAM HOLIFIELD, MOMI KAM HOLIFIELD), poet; b. Honolulu, Dec. 13, 1916; d. Albert Tin Kam and Helen Wo Soon Lyau; m. Harold Desmond Holifield, 1947; children: Wallace Grant, Harry. BA, U. Hawaii, 1944; MA, U. Calif., Berkeley, 1945; postgrad., U. Wash., 1946—47. Univ. libr. U. Hawaii, Honolulu, 1945—46; children's libr. N.Y. Pub. Library, N.Y.C., 1948—80; haiku poet N.Y.C., 1978—. Author: Workshop Poems, 1989. Mem.: Spring St. Haiku Workshop, Haiku Soc. Am. Avocations: gardening, singing, hula.

HOLIK, BOBBY, hockey player; b. Jihlava, Czech Republic, Jan. 1, 1971; Left wing Hartford Whalers, 1989—92, N.J. Devils, 1992—2002; with N.Y. Rangers, 2002—. Player World Championships, 1991. Recipient Bronze medal, Czech Nat. Jr. Team, World Championships, 1990. Office: New York Rangers Madison Square Garden 2 Penn Plaza New York NY 10121

HOLINGER, RICHARD, secondary school educator, writer; b. Chgo., Mar. 20, 1949; m. Tia Rush. BA, Harwick Coll., 1971; MA, Washington U., St. Louis, 1975; PhD, U. Ill., Chgo., 1993. Tchr. Marmion Acad., Aurora, Ill., 1979—. Editl. cons., Geneva. Grantee, Ill. Arts Coun., 1983. Home: 335 Colonial Cir Geneva IL 60134 Office: Marmion Acad 1000 Butterfield Rd Aurora IL 60504 Business E-Mail: rholinger@marmion.org.

HOLK, GEORGE BERTWELL, accountant; b. Florence, Ala., Jan. 17, 1951; s. George Littleton and Martha Evelyn (Ticer) H.; m. Minerva Ratliff, Aug. 30, 1980; children: Eric Thomas, Nathan Scott. BS in Math., Auburn. U., 1973; MBA in Acctg., Seattle U., 1997. CPA, Wash.; lic. airline transport pilot. Commd. ensign USN, 1973, advanced through grades to commdr., 1988; command ctr. contr. U.S. Transp. Command, Scott AFB, Ill., 1988-91; air ops. officer USS Nimitz CVN68 USN, Bremerton, Wash., 1991-95; staff acct. Allen, Nelson, Turner & Co., Bremerton, 1997, Sterling Clay Couch, III, CPA, Bellevue, Wash., 1998; asst. state auditor Wash. State Auditor'sOffice, 1998—. Cubmaster, scoutmaster Boy Scouts Am., Silverdale, Wash., 1993—; youth baseball coach Silverdale Pee Wees, 1996-97. Mem. Wash. Soc. CPAs, Beta Gamma Sigma. Avocations: golf, flying, sports. Home and Office: 8571 Payne Ln NW Bremerton WA 98311-8000

HOLL, DAVID RUSSELL, construction executive; b. Portland, Oreg., Apr. 21, 1949; s. David LaVerne and Miriam Mason Holl; m. Christine Brumbaugh (div.); children: Robyn, Carole, Russell. BA, Bridgewater (Va.) Coll., 1973. Fabrication technician Kanneer Co., Harrisonburg, Va., 1977—83; draftsman Vistawall Arch Products, Terrell, Tex., 1983—89; project mgr. Harmon Contract, Balt., 1989—95, Svc. Glass, 1995—97, Spear Window & Glass, 1997—2000, Zephyr, 2000—. Mem. Ch. Of The Brethren. Avocation: choral singing. Home: 5809 B Bartonsville Rd Frederick MD 21704

HOLL, JOHN WILLIAM, engineering educator; b. Danville, Ill., Feb. 20, 1928; s. William Benjamin and Anna Marie (Waldo) H.; m. Antoinette Fillhouer, Aug. 20, 1950; children— Jessica, Vanessa, Melissa, Cassandra, Alyssa, Nathan, Zachary. BS in M.E, U. Ill., 1949, MS in M.E, 1951; PhD in M.E, Pa. State U., 1958, B of Music, 1996. Rsch. asst. in mech. engring. Engring. Experiment Sta. U. Ill., Urbana, 1949-51; rsch. assoc. Applied Rsch. Lab. Pa. State U., 1951-54, 56-58, asst. prof. engring. rsch., 1958-59, asso. prof. aerospace engring., 1963-67, prof., 1967-91, prof. emeritus, 1991—. Asso. prof. mech. engring. U. Nebr., Lincoln, 1959-63; cons. in field Mem. Lincoln Symphony Orch., 1960-63; mem. Nittany Valley Symphony Orch., State College, Pa., 1969—, State Coll. Mcpl. Band, 1977— ; Trustee Unitarian Ch., Lincoln, 1961-62. Served with U.S. Army, 1955-56. Fellow ASME (R.T. Knapp award 1970, 91, Melville medal 1970, Centennial medallion 1980, dedicated service award 1985); assoc. fellow AIAA; mem. Internat. Clarinet Assn., Golden Key Nat. Honor Soc., Sigma Xi, Phi Mu Alpha Sinfonia, Pi Kappa Lambda. Home: 1108 Mayberry Ln State College PA 16801-6952 Office: Pa State U Aerospace Engring 227 Hammond Bldg University Park PA 16802

HOLL, WALTER JOHN, architect, interior designer; b. Richardton, N.D., May 14, 1922; s. John and Rose Mary Holl; m. Eleanor Mary Triervieler, Jan. 23, 1943; children: Mark Walter (dec. 2001), Michael John, Randolph Gregory, Linda Michelle, Timothy James, John Walter. Student, Internat. Corr. Schs., 1946-47, 59; student in interior design, U. Nebr., 1976; student, student in photography, Clarke Coll., 1981. Licensed arch., Calif., interior designer, Ill.; cert. Nat. Coun. for Interior Design Qualifications. Steel detailer, estimator E.J. Voggenthaler Co., Dubuque, Iowa, 1941-42; engr., also methods developer Marinship Corp., Sausalito, Calif., 1942-44; ptnr. Holl & Everly, Dubuque, Iowa, 1946-47; prin. Holl Designing Co., also W. Holl & Assocs., Dubuque, San Francisco, 1947-87, Walter J. Holl, Arch., Burlingame, Calif., 1987, 89, San Diego, Calif., 1989—. Cons. Clarke Coll. Art Students, Dubuque, 1953-61; commd. arch., interior designer, constructor renovations and hist. preservation Dubuque County Courthouse, 1978-85; mem. convoy USCG Ofcl. Presdl. Security Patrol, 1979; oral exam commr. Calif. Bd. Archtl. Examiners, 1994-96; cert. mem. Calif. State Office Emergency Svc.; participant The Brit. Coun.-Archs. Study Tour, Belfast, No. Ireland, 1995; juror Nat. Coun. for Interior Design Qualification, 1996, 98. Chmn. Dubuque Housing Rehab. Commn., 1976-77. With AUS, 1944-46, ETO. Decorated 2 bronze stars; recipient Nat. Bldg. Design awards, 1968, 69, 73, 94. Mem. AIA (bd. dirs. 1993-99, pres.-elect north county sect. San Diego chpt. 1995, pres. 1996, bldg. codes and stds. com. San Diego chpt. 1998-99), USCG Aux. (comdr. 1975-78), Am. Soc. Interior Designers (profl.), Am. Arbitration Assn. (panel arbitrators), Inst. Bus. Designers (profl. Chgo. chpt.), Dubuque Golf and Country Club (bldg. commn. 1953-54), Julien Dubuque Yacht Club (commodore 1974-75), Mchts. and Mfrs. Club (Chgo.). Roman Catholic. Achievements include patent for castered pallet. Home and Office: 20261 Gaines Ct Bend OR 97702-2747

HOLLADAY, CARL R. New Testament educator; b. Huntingdon, Tenn., Oct. 18, 1943; s. Ben R. and Inus R. Holladay; m. Donna H. Holladay, Aug. 28, 1964; children: John Krister, Ben Hardeman, Andrew Patrick. BA, Abilene Christian U., 1965, MDiv, 1969; ThM, Princeton Theol. Sem., 1970; PhD, U. Cambridge, Eng., 1975. Asst. prof. New Testament, Yale Div. Sch., New Haven, 1975-78, assoc. prof. New Testament, 1978-80, Candler Sch. Theology, Emory U., Atlanta, 1980-90, prof. New Testament, 1990—2002, Charles Howard Candler prof. New Testament, 2002—, assoc. dean, 1983-91, dean faculty and acad. affairs, 1992-94. Author: Theios Aner in Hellenistic Judaism, 1977, First Letter of Paul to the Corinthians, 1979, (with J. Hayes) Biblical Exegesis, 1982, Fragments From Hellenistic Jewish Authors, 4 vols., 1983-96. Exec. dir. Christian Scholarship Found., Atlanta, 1983—; pres. North Ga. chpt. Fulbright Assn., Atlanta, 1998-99, 2000-01. Fulbright Sr. scholar, 1994-95; recipient Henry T. Luce Fellow in Theology award Assn. Theol. Schs., 1999-2000. Home: 668 Clifton Rd NE Atlanta GA 30307-1789 Office: Emory Univ Candler Sch Theology Atlanta GA 30322-0001

HOLLADAY, MARTIN JOHN, editor; b. San Andreas, Calif., Mar. 23, 1955; s. William Lee Holladay and Jean Mary Grosbach; m. Marie Anne Manning, July 8, 1989; children: Moses Mohandas, Noah Nehemiah. Student, Yale Coll., 1972-74. Assoc. editor Jour. Light Constrn., Williston, Vt., 1999—2002; editor Energy Design Update, Sheffield, Vt., 2002—. Plowshares activist Atlantic Life Cmty., Whiteman AFB, 1985; mem. sch. bd. Millers Run Sch., Wheelock, Vt., 1997—. Office: Energy Design Update PO Box 153 Sheffield VT 05866

HOLLADAY, WILHELMINA COLE, interior design and museum executive; b. Elmira, N.Y., Oct. 10, 1922; d. Chauncy E. and Claire Elizabeth (Strong) Cole; m. Wallace Fitzhugh Holladay, Sept. 27, 1946; children: Wallace Fitzhugh, Scott Cole. BA, Elmira Coll., 1944; postgrad. art history, U. Paris, 1953-54, U. Va., 1960-61; PhD (hon.), Moore Coll. Art, 1988, Mt. Vernon Coll., 1988, Elmira Coll., 1989. Exec. sec. Howard Ludington, Rochester, N.Y., 1944-45, Chinese Embassy, Washington, 1945-48; staff Nat. Gallery of Art, Washington, 1957-59; dir. interior design div. Holladay Corp., Washington, 1970-95. Dir. Adams Nat. Bank, 1978-86, chmn., 1978-86; founder, chmn., bd. dirs., creator art collection by women (Renaissance through contemp.), Nat. Mus. Women in Arts, 1982—. Founder archival libr. of periodicals, books, exhbn. catalogs on women's art for rsch. purposes; bd. dirs. Am. Field Svc., 1964-80, Internat. Student House, 1973—, Leeds Castle Found.; mem. coun. Friends of Folger Shakespeare Libr., 1978-82; mem. world svc. coun. YWCA; trustee Corcoran Gallery of Art, 1980-90; mem. Mayor's Blue Ribbon Com. Decorated Order of Merit (Norway); named Woman of Achievement, Washington Ednl. TV Assn., 1984, Woman of Distinction, Coun. Ind. Colls., 1987, Birmingham So. Coll., 1991, Washingtonian of Yr., Washingtonian Mag., 1987, Hon. Citizen, State of Tex., laureate, Washington Bus. Hall of Fame, Hon. Athenian, Mayor of Athens, 2002; named to Nat. Women's Hall of Fame, 1996; recipient Horizon's Theatre award, 1987, Thomas Jefferson award, Am. Soc. Interior Designers, Disting. Woman's award, Northwood Inst., 1987, Disting. Achievement award, Nat. League Am. Pen Women, 1988, Women Achievers award, Internat. Alliance, 1991, Woman That Makes a Difference award, Internat. Women's Forum, 1991, Women First award, YWCA, 1993, Key to City of Kansas City, Fellow award for disting. svc. to arts, New Orleans Mus. Art, 1997, Disting. Washingtonian award in lit. and the arts, Univ. Club Washington, 1998, Gold medal honor award, Nat. Inst. Social Scis., 2000, honors, Women's Caucus for Art, 2001, Leadership award, Pine Manor Coll. Mem. Am. Assn. Mus., Am. Fedn. Art, Women's Caucus for Arts, Mus. Modern Art, Art Librs. N.Am., Archives Am. Art, Arttable, Smithson Soc., Internat. Women's Forum, Nat. Women's Econ. Alliance (bd. dirs. 1984—, Soaring Eagle award 1988). Episcopalian. Home: 3215 R St NW Washington DC 20007-2941 Office: Nat Mus Women Arts 1250 New York Ave NW Washington DC 20005-3970 *You haven't failed until you quit trying.*

HOLLADAY-HICKS, SYLVIA A. humanities educator; b. Lanett, Ala., Jan. 14, 1936; d. Edward David and Florence Mae Holladay; m. Thomas E. Hicks Sr., Jan. 18, 1942. BS in English Edn., Auburn U., 1958, MA in English, 1961; ArtsD in English, Carnegie-Mellon U., 1983. Cert. profl. auctioneer Fla., specialist in tchg. English in two-yr. colls. Instr. English Auburn U., Ala., 1958—61; tchr. English Land O' Lakes Jr. H.S., Fla., 1962; adminstr. and prof. St. Petersburg Jr. Coll., Fla., 1962—98, adj. prof. English, 1999—2001, Hillsborough C.C., Brandon, Fla., 2000—; co-owner Premier Auctions Inc. Cons. Fla. Dept. of Edn., Tallahassee, 1968—2002; cons. ETS and ACT various colls. and univs., 1965—. Author: (textbook) Developing Style: An Extension of Personality, 1972 (SCETC Cowan Award for Excellence in tchg., 1982), Options in Rhetoric, 1982 (TETYC Best Article of Yr. award, 1984), The Bedford Guide for College Writers, 6th edit., 2002 (Nat. Tchg. Excellence award, 1985); contbr. articles and poems to profl. jours., chpts. to books, encycopedia and Internet. Recipient Vol. of Yr. award, Crosstown Cmty. Ch., 2002. Mem.: AARP, MLA (mem. com. on tchg. as a profession 1995—98, mem. exec. com. and newsletter editor 1968—92), Nat. Assn. Women Execs., Bus. and Tech. Assn., Fla. Assn. C.C.'s, Fla. Assn. Depts. English (pres. 1987—90), Coll. English Assn. (exec. com. 1976—78), Assn. Depts. English (exec. com. 1988—91), Two-Yr. Coll. Assn. (Best Article of Yr. award 1984), Coll. Composition and Comm. (exec. bd. various coms. 1968—96), World Future Soc., Fla. Auctioneers Assn., Delta Kappa Gamma. Baptist. Avocations: travel, writing, music. Home: 819 Hilltop Dr Brandon FL 33511-5915 Home Fax: 813-681-8540. Personal E-mail: sill11697@aol.com.

HOLLAND, BETH, actress; b. N.Y.C. d. Samson and Florence (Liebman) Hollander; m. Louis L. Friedman, Aug. 28, 1953; children: Ellen Lynn, Cathy Jayne. Pvt. studies in acting, voice tng. Arts funding cons. N.Y. State Senate, 1974-89. Appeared in various roles on TV, film and theatre, also comedy video Your Favorite Jokes, 1988. Bd. dirs. Fla. Opera Soc. Recipient Carbonell performance award Theatre League of South Fla., 1996. Mem. AFTRA (pres. N.Y. chpt. 1989-91, bd. dirs., trustee Health and Retirement Funds, past treas.), SAG, English Speaking Union, N.Y. TV Acad. (past bd. dirs.), Actors Equity Assn., Twelfth Night Club (bd. dirs.), Episcopal Actors Guild (mem. coun.), Players Club (libr. bd.), Lambs Club, Tower Club, Friars Club. Avocations: travel, politics, arts. Home: 4300 N Ocean Blvd Fort Lauderdale FL 33308-5944

HOLLAND, BRIAN JOSEPH, corporate financial executive; s. Michael Francis and Louise Grace Holland. BA, Vanderbilt U., Nashville, 1985—89, MBA, 1990—92. Equity analyst First Albany Corp., N.Y.C., 1992—94; sr. portfolio mgr. Bankers Trust N.Y./Deutsche Bank, N.Y.C., 1994—99; rsch. dir. Boyd Watterson Asset Mgmt., Cleve., 2000—. Mem. Cleve. Soc. Security Analysts, 2001—, AIMR. Bd. mem. Easter Seals, Cleve., 2001—03; ptnr. Playhouse Partners, Cleve., 2002—. Mem.: AIMR, Cleve. Soc. Securty Analysts, Cleve. 20/30 Club (assoc.), Cleve. Athletic Club (assoc.). Democrat. Methodist. Avocations: running, travel, tennis, golf. Home: 598 S Court St Medina OH 44256 Office: Boyd Watterson Asset Mgmt 1801 E 9th St Ste 1400 Cleveland OH 44114 E-mail: bholland@boydwatterson.com.

HOLLAND, BURT S. statistics educator, consultant; b. Bklyn., Dec. 4, 1945; s. Samuel J. and Bernice S. (Sanders) H.; m. Margaret Robin Mondros, Mar. 15, 1975; children: Irene, Andrew, Benjamin. BA, Binghamton (N.Y.) U., 1966; MS, N.C. State U., 1968, PhD, 1970. Asst. prof. stats. Temple U., Phila., 1970-76, assoc. prof., 1976-91, prof., 1991—, chairperson Dept. Stats., 1991-96. Cons. in field; chairperson Collegial Assembly Temple U. Sch. Bus & Mgmt., 1989-90; reviewer in field. Contbr. articles to profl. jours. Grad. trainee grantee Nat. Sci. Found., 1966-69; Regent's Coll. scholar N.Y. State Dept. Edn., 1962-66. Fellow Am. Stats. Assn.; mem. Biometric Soc., Inst. Math. Stats. Achievements include development of new procedures for simultaneous inference.

HOLLAND, CHARLES EDWARD, medical products corporate executive; b. Pottstown, Pa., Aug. 31, 1940; s. Charles Edward and Ethel Viola (Ludwig) H.; m. Linda Beth VandeBerg, Nov. 20, 1982 Student, Messiah Coll., 1962-63; BS in Biology and Chemistry, Albright Coll., 1966; PhD in Zoology, Rutgers U., 1974. Clin. lab. technician Reading Hosp., West Reading, Pa., 1962-66; rsch. assoc. dept. biochemistry St. Louis U. Sch. Medicine, 1972-75; rsch. assoc. dept. pharmacology and surgery U. Ill.Med. Ctr., Chgo., 1975-77; clin. project mgr. Am. Critical Care (Am. Hosp. Supply), McGraw Park, Ill., 1977-81; asst./assoc. dir. clin. rsch. Glaxo Inc., Research Triangle Park, N.C., 1981-84, dir. planning and project mgmt., 1984-86, dir. human resources, 1986-87, dir. strategic planning, 1987-88, dir. dermatology bus. expansion, 1988-89, dir. dermatology bus. and product devel., 1989-91, group dir. dermatology bus. and product devel., 1991-95; pres. XPharm, Inc., Chgo., 1996—; sr. dir. licensing and tech. alliances Searle, Skokie, Ill., 1996-2000; sr. dir. bus. devel. Elan Pharms., San Diego, 2000—02; v.p. corp. devel. Therapeutics Inc., La Jolla, Calif., 2002—. Bd. trustees Glaxo Bus. Sch., 1986-89, chmn. 1986-88. Contbr. articles to profl. jours. USPH fellow Rutgers U., 1966-71; grad. teaching fellow Rutgers U., 1971-72; NIH fellow St. Louis U. Sch. Medicine, 1973-75, U. Ill., 1975-77. Mem. Project Mgmt. Inst. (editor newsletter 1986-87), Nat. Psoriasis Found., Soc. Investigative Dermatology, Am. Acad. Dermatology, Lic. Exec. Soc., Am. Cont. Dermatology Soc., Chgo. Biotech. Network (founder), Sigma Xi. Avocations: travel, nature, hiking, fishing. Office: 4180 La Jolla Village Dr La Jolla CA 92037 E-mail: cholland@therapeuticsinc.com.

HOLLAND, CHARLES R. military officer; BS in Aero. Engring., USAF Acad., 1968; grad., Squadron Officer Sch., 1974, Air Command and Staff Coll., 1975; MS in Bus. Mgmt., Troy State U., 1976; nat. security mgmt. course, 1982; grad., Indsl. Coll. of Armed Forces, 1986; program for sr. ofcls. in nat. security, Harvard U., 1990. Commd. 2d lt. USAF, 1968, advanced through grades to gen., 1997; air ops. staff officer directorate of airlift Hdqs. U.S. Air Forces in Europe, Ramstein Air Base, West Germany, 1974-76; joint tng. exercise plans officer Mil. Airlift Ctr. Europe, Ramstein Air Base, 1976-77; chief space shuttle flight ops. br., exec. to comdr. L.A. Air Force Sta., 1979-83; comdr. 21st Tactical Airlift Squadron, Clark Air Base, The Philippines, 1983-85; dep. chief airlift and tng. divsn., mil. dep. acquisition Office of Asst. Sec. of Air Force, Washington, 1986-87, chief airlift and tng. divsn., mil. dep. acquisition, 1987-88; vice comdr., comdr. 1550th Combat Crew Tng. Wing, Kirtland AFB, N.Mex., 1988-91; comdr. 1st Spl. Ops. Wing, Hurlburt Field, Fla., 1991-93; dep. comdg. gen. Joint Spl. Ops. Command, Ft. Bragg, N.C., 1993-95; comdr. Spl. Ops. Command, Pacific, Camp H.M. Smith, Hawaii, 1995-97, Air Force Spl. Ops. Command, Hurlbert Field, 1997-99; vice comdr. Hdqs. U.S. Air Forces in Europe, Ramstein Air Base, Germany, 1999—2000; comdr. U.S. Spec. Ops. Command, MacDill AFB, Fla., 2000—. Decorated Def. Superior Svc. medal with 2 oak leaf clusters, Legion of Merit with oak leaf cluster, D.F.C., Meritorious Svc. medal with 2 oak leaf clusters.*

HOLLAND, CHRISTIE ANNA, biochemist, virologist; b. Newport News, Va., Aug. 25, 1950; d. Charles Everett and Helen (Bailey) Holland; 1 child, Helen. BS, U. Richmond, 1972; PhD, U. Tenn., 1977. Postdoctoral fellow Worcester Found. for Exptl. Biology, Shrewsbury, Mass., 1977-79, Ctr. for Cancer Rsch.-MIT, Cambridge, Mass., 1979-84; asst. prof. dept. radiation oncology U. Mass. Med. Ctr., Worcester, 1985-90, assoc. prof., 1990-91; dir. Ctr. for Virology, Immunology and Infectious Diseases Children's Nat. Med. Ctr., Washington, 1991—; assoc. prof. pediats., microbiology and biochemistry George Washington U. Med. Ctr., Washington, 1991-95, prof. pediats., assoc. prof. microbiology and biochemistry, 1995—. Mem.: AAAS, Am. Soc. Pediats., Am. Soc. Virology, Am. Soc. Cell Biology, Internat. Soc. Exptl. Hematology. Home: 9105 Goshen Valley Dr Gaithersburg MD 20882-1447 Office: Childrens Nat Med Ctr 111 Michigan Ave NW Washington DC 20010-2916 E-mail: chhollan@cnmc.org.

HOLLAND, DAVID THURSTON, former editor; b. Phila., May 26, 1923; s. Rupert Sargent and Margaret Currier (Lyon) H. BA, Harvard, 1944, MA, 1946. Vice consul U.S. Fgn. Svc., Budapest, Hungary, 1945; teaching fellow Harvard U., Cambridge, Mass., 1946-49; coll. traveler Oxford U. Press, N.Y.C., 1953-54; asst. editor Harcourt Brace, N.Y.C., 1955-59; asst. editor Ency. Internat. Grolier Inc., N.Y.C., 1959-62, assoc. editor Ency. Americana, 1962-65, sr. editor, 1965-85; exec. editor, 1985; editor in chief Ency. Americana Grolier Inc., Danbury, Conn., 1985-91; ret., 1991. Democrat. Episcopalian.

HOLLAND, GARY NORMAN, ophthalmologist, educator; b. Long Beach, Calif., July 30, 1953; s. Richard L. and Edith (Hewson) H. MD, UCLA, 1979. Diplomate Am. Bd. Ophthalmology, Nat. Bd. Med. Examiners; lic. MD, Calif., Ga. Intern in internal medicine UCLA, 1979-80; resident in ophthalmology Jules Stein Eye Inst., L.A., 1980-83; fellowship in uveitis rsch. Proctor Found. U. Calif. San Francisco, 1983-84; cornea fellowship Emory U. Med. Sch., Atlanta, 1984-85; prof. ophthalmology Jules Stein Eye Inst. UCLA, 1985—. Assoc. editor Am. Jour. Ophthalmology, 1993—. Mem. Am. Uveitis Soc. Office: UCLA 100 Stein Plz Los Angeles CA 90095-7003

HOLLAND, GENE GRIGSBY (SCOTTIE HOLLAND), artist; b. Hazard, Ky., June 30, 1928; d. Edward and Virginia Lee (Watson) Grigsby; m. George William Holland, Sept. 22, 1950; 3 children. BA, U. So. Fla., 1968; pupil of, Ruth Allison, Talequah, Okla., 1947-48, Ralph Smith, Washington, 1977, Clint Carter, Atlanta, 1977, R. Jordan, Winter Park, Fla., 1979, Cedric Baldwin Egeli Workshop, Charleston, S.C., 1984. Various clerical and secretarial positions, 1948-52; news reporter, photographer Bryan (Tex.) Daily News, 1952; clk. Fogarty Bros. Moving and Transfer, Tampa and Miami, Fla., 1954-57; tchr. elem. schs., Hillsborough County, Fla., 1968-72; salesperson, assoc. real estate, 1984-2000; owner, operator antique store, 1982-87. One-woman and group shows include Tampa Woman's Clubhouse, 1973, Cor Jesu, Tampa, 1973, Bank, Monks Corner, S.C., 1977, Summerville Artists Guild, 1977-78, Apopka (Fla.) Art and Foilage Festival, 1980, 81, 82, Fla. Fedn. Women's Clubs, 1980, 81, 82; numerous group shows, latest being Island Gifts, Tampa, 1980-82, Brandon (Fla.) Station, 1980-81, Holland Originals, Orlando, Fla.; represented in permanent and pvt. collections. Vol. ARC, Tampa, 1965-69, United Fund Campaign, 1975-76; pres. Mango (Fla.) Elem. Sch. PTA, 1966-67; pres. Tampa Civic Assn., 1974-75; vol. Easter Seal Fund Campaign, 1962-63; art chmn. Apopka Art & Foilage Festival, 1990; deaconness Ctrl. Christian Ch. Orlando, 1992-94, chmn. bible study, 1993-94; deaconness First Christian Ch. Tampa, 1996-99. Recipient numerous art awards, 1978-82. Mem. AARP (parlimentarian Apopka chpt.), Internat. Soc. Artists, Coun. Arts & Scis. for Cen. Fla., Fedn. Women's Clubs (pres. Tampa Civic 1974-75), Meth. Women's Soc. (sec. 1976-77), Nat. Trust Hist. PReservation, Nat. Hist. Soc., Fla. Geneal. and Hist. Soc., Am. Guild Flower Arrangers, The Nat. Grigsby Family Soc. (assoc. sec. 1991-92, corp. sect. 1992-96, dir. 1995-97, 99-2001, S.W. chpt. dir. 1997-2000), Internat. Inner Wheel Club (past chmn. dist. 696, pres. Tampa 1972-73), Friday Morning Musicale Club (1st v.p. bd. incorporators Tampa 1974-75, bd. dirs.), Gen. Fedn. of Fla. Clubs Apopka Woman's Club (pres. 1981-82, bd. dir. 1983-85, Woman of Yr. 1991-92), Apopka Tennis Over 50's Group Club (pres. 1988-90), Federated Garden Club Plant City Fla. (conservation chmn.), South Bay Geneal. Soc., Tampa PC User Group, Computer Club Inc. of Sun City Ctrs., Lexington Geneal. Assn. Home: 231 Mooring Ln Lexington SC 29072-9106

HOLLAND, HAROLD MERVIN, urologist; b. Easton, Pa., Jan. 30, 1922; s. Ben and Leah Holland; m. Renee Holland, Apr. 2, 1967. AB, Lafayette Coll., 1943; MD, NYU, 1946. Bd. cert. in urology, 1957. Asst clin. prof. surgery (urology) U. So. Calif., 1960--. Lt. (j.g.) USN, 1947-49. Mem. Am. Coll. Surgeons, Internat. Coll. Surgeons, Am. Urol. Assn., Am. Bd. Urology. Avocations: golf, swimming. Office: 2080 Century Park E Los Angeles CA 90067-2001

HOLLAND, HENRY NORMAN, marketing and management consultant; b. Norfolk, Va., Oct. 13, 1947; s. Henry Norman and Edith Leigh (O'Bryan) H.; m. Linda Diane Eggerking, June 1, 1968 (div. 1983); 1 child, Steven Frederick; m. Jane Elizabeth Bond, Dec. 27, 1983. BA, Chaminade Coll., 1972; MBA, U. Hawaii, 1977. Lic. ins. broker, Calif. Mgr. Chevron USA, Honolulu, 1965-75; dealer Dillingham Chevron, Honolulu, 1975-82; gen. mgr. Barcat Enterprises, San Francisco, 1982-85; counselor E.K. Williams of San Francisco, 1985; gen. mgr. Woodside (Calif.) Oil Co., 1985-88; cons. Holland Bus. Mgmt., San Francisco, 1989—. Dir. Chevron Fed. Credit Union, Honolulu, 1971-75. Author: Make Yours Service, tng. seminars, newsletter, safety programs; contbr. articles to profl. jours. Loaned mgr. United Way, Honolulu, 1972; nation chief YMCA Indian Guides, Kailua, Hawaii, 1976-79. With U.S. Army, 1967-69, Vietnam. Mem. English Speaking Union, Met. League San Francisco Symphony, Golden Gate Nat. Parks Assn., Nat. Trust for Historic Preservation, San Francisco Mus. Soc., Chevron Adv. Coun., Nat. Assn. Enrolled Agts., Calif. Assn. Enrolled Agts., Sovereign Order of Saint John of Jerusalem Knights Hospitaller, VFW. Republican. Presbyterian. Avocations: travel, sports, bridge, cooking, reading. E-mail: henryhollandhbm@cs.com.

HOLLAND, JAMES R. real estate corporation executive; b. St. Louis, Feb. 20, 1944; s. Randolph and Thelma (Robinson) H.; m. Helen M. Devine, Feb. 18, 1972; children: Danielle, James Randolph, Eric Marc. Student, Principia Coll., 1962-64; BFA, Ohio U., 1966; postgrad., U. Mo. Sch. Journalism, 1966. Photog. intern Nat. Geog. Soc., Washington, 1966, contract photographer for mag., 1967-68; film prodr. Christian Sci. Ctr., Boston, 1969-74; real estate developer, pres. Brownstone Properties, Inc., Boston, 1975-77; real estate broker Street & Co., Inc., Boston, 1978-82; pres. A Bit of Boston Real Estate, Inc., Boston, 1982—. Author: The Amazon, 1971, Mr. Pops-Arthur Fiedler, 1972, Tanglewood (foreward Michael Tilson Thomas), 1973; illustrator-photographer Continental and Colonial Currency of Colonial America; contbr. Photojournalism-Principles and Practice (Clifton Edom), 2d edit., 1980; articles, photographs contbd. to nat., internat. newspapers, mags., encys., video games, numerous textbooks; writer documentary film scripts appearing on NBC, ABC, CBS, PBS, BBC, Travel Channel; prodr. limited edit. karate video tapes Twinkle Toes Videos; photographs and films in permanent collections Truman Libr., JFK Libr., Boston Pub. Libr., Ohio, Mo. univs., others. Active Neighborhood Assn. Back Bay, 1972—, Boston Home and Property Owners Assn.; assoc. Boston Pub. Libr.; lifetime Friend of Beverly Hills (Calif.) Pub. Libr., Dickerson Park Zoo, Mus. Ozarks History; 10th Anniversary com. Boston U.'s Photographic Resource Ctr., Samuel Fletcher and Angeline Drury Soc., Drury U.; sponsor Babe Ruth Baseball League Team, 1992—; league sponsor Back Bay, Beacon Hill and North End Little League Teams, 1999—. Recipient World Press Competition award, 1967, Newsweek/Bolex documentary film awrad, 1969, Indsl. Photography Film Competition award, 1970, Internat. Film and TV Festival of N.Y. bronze medal, 1971; named AAU Nat. Karate Champion, 1989; ranked 6th nationally in weapon's forms Reeves Sport Karate Ratings, 1989. Mem. Am. Soc. Mag. Photographers, Nat. Press Photographers (awards 1966, 67, 68), N.Am. Sport Karate Assn. (various awards), The Samuel Fletcher and Angeline Drury Soc. Home: 208 Commonwealth Ave Boston MA 02116-2534 Office: A Bit of Boston Real Estate Inc 5 Brimmer St Boston MA 02108-1001

HOLLAND, JAMES TULLEY, retired plastic products company executive; b. Pikeville, Ky., May 24, 1940; s. Thomas Joseph and Mary Alta (Tulley) Holland; m. Susan Ellen Joy; children: James Christopher, Kathleen Holland Wiesel. BA in Econs., U. Va., 1962; MBA, Am. U., 1969. With br. banking ops. United Va. Bank, Alexandria, 1965-67; with Booz Allen & Hamilton, Washington, 1967-76; treas., chief fin. officer O'Sullivan Corp., Winchester, Va., 1976-84, exec. v.p., COO, 1984-86, pres., COO, 1986—95, CEO, 1995-98, ret., 1998, also bd. dirs. Bd. dirs. Va. Nat. Bank-Winchester Region, adv. bd. Liberty Mut. Ins. Co., bd. of dirs. Valley Health Systems, Shenandoah Meml. Hosp. pres. bd. of dir. Winchester Country Club. Trustee Glass Glen Burnie Found. Capt. U.S. Army, 1963—65. Mem. Winchester Country Club, Farmington Country Club (Charlottesville, Va.), Belle Haven Country Club (Alexandria). Roman Catholic. Avocations: golfing, reading, writing. Home: 261 Merrifield Ln Winchester VA 22602-2306 E-mail: jimholland@adelphia.net.

HOLLAND, JEFFREY R. religious organization administrator; b. St. George, Utah, Dec. 3, 1940; s. Frank D. and Alice (Bentley) H.; m. Patricia Terry, June 7, 1963; children: Matthew, Mary, David. BS, Brigham Young U., 1965, MA, 1966; PhD, Yale U., 1973. Dean religious instrn. Brigham Young U., 1974-76; commr. Latter Day Saints Ch. Ednl. System, 1976-80; pres. Brigham Young U., 1980-89; gen. authority, mem. 1st Quorum of the 70 LDS Ch., 1989-94; Apostle Quorum of the Twelve, 1994—. Dir. Deseret News Pub. Co., Key Bank of Utah,

Key Bancshares of Utah, Inc. Mem. Am. Assn. Presidents of Ind. Colls. and Univs. (past pres.), Nat. Assn. Ind. Colls. and Univs. (former bd. dirs.), Am. Council Edn., Phi Kappa Phi. Office: LDS Church 50 E South Temple Salt Lake City UT 84150-0001

HOLLAND, JIMMIE C. psychiatrist, educator; b. Forney, Tex., Apr. 9, 1928; m. James F. Holland; 5 children. BA, Baylor U., 1948, MD, 1952. Diplomate Am. Bd. Psychiatry, Am. Bd. Neurology. Instr. to prof. SUNY, Buffalo, 1956-73; assoc. prof., assoc. attending physician to asst. dir. cons.-liaison psychiatry Albert Einstein Coll. Medicine and Montefiore Med. Ctr., Bronx, N.Y., 1973-77; chair dept. psychiatry and behavioral Scis., Wayne E. Chapman prof. in psychiat. oncology Meml. Sloan Kettering Cancer Ctr., N.Y.C., 1977—. Prof. dept. psychiatry Cornell U. Med. Coll., N.Y.C., 1977—; asst. attending physician to dir. dept. psychiatry E.J. Meyer Meml. Hosp./Erie County Med. Ctr., Buffalo, 1956-73; cons. NIMH-USSR joint schizophrenia study Psychiat. Rsch. Inst., Moscow, 1972-73, NIMH, Rockville, Md., 1973-75; chmn. psychiatry com. Cancer and Leukemia Group B Clin. Trials, Brookline, Mass., 1976-2001. Editor: Handbook of Psycho-oncology: Psychological Care of the Patient with Cancer, 1989, Psychooncology, 1998; co-editor Jour. Psycho-oncology; author, co-author: The Human Side of Cancer, 258 jour. articles, book chpts., monographs. Bd. dirs. Cancer Care, Inc., 1979-81. Recipient Disting. Alumna award Baylor U., Waco, Tex., 1982; Am. Cancer Soc. Medal of Honor, 1994 Fellow Inst. Medicine, Am. Coll. Psychiatrists, Am. Psychiat. Assn., Acad. Psychosomatic Medicine (founding pres.), Internat. Psycho-Oncology Soc., Am. Psychosocial Oncology Soc., Am. Psychosomatic Soc., Soc. for Liaison Psychiatry (Spl. citation 1989), Am. Soc. Clin. Oncology. Office: Meml Sloan-Kettering Cancer Ctr 1275 York Ave New York NY 10021-6094 E-mail: hollandj@mskcc.org.

HOLLAND, JOHN BEN, clothing manufacturing company executive; b. Scottsville, Ky., Mar. 26, 1932; s. Elbridge Winfred and Lou May (Whitney) H.; m. Margaret Irene Pecor, Jan. 31, 1954; children: John Sandra, Robert. BS in Acctg., Bowling Green U., 1959. With Union Underwear Co., Inc., Bowling Green, Ky., 1961—2001, v.p. adminstrn., 1972-74, vice chmn., 1975, chmn., chief exec. officer, 1976-96; ret., 1996; cons., 1996—99; pres., CEO Fruit of the Loom, Inc., 2002—. Bd. dirs. Dollar Gen. Corp., Farmers Nat. Bank. Bd. dirs. Ky. Coun. Econ. Edn., Louisville, 1981-90, Ky. Advocates for Higher Edn. Inc., 1985-93, Ky. C. of C., 1987-88, Camping World Inc., 1985-97, Associated Industries of Ky., Ireland-Am. Econ. Adv. Bd., Tech. Corp. Inc.; chmn. corp. coun. Western Ky. U., devel. steering com., 1985-96; vice-chmn. West Point Pepperial, Inc., 1989-92; chmn. Intermodal Transp. Authority, 1998-2000. Mem. Bowling Green-Warren County C. of C. (bd. dirs. 1981-85), Am. Arbitration Assn. (panel 1985-93). Office: Fruit of the Loom Inc PO Box 90015 Bowling Green KY 42102-9015

HOLLAND, JOHN MADISON, retired family practice physician; b. Holden, W.Va., Oct. 7, 1927; s. Ophia I. and Lou V. (Elliott) H.; m. Mary Louise Bourne, Sept. 2, 1950; children— David, Stephen, Nancy BS, Eastern Ky. State U., Richmond, 1949; MD, U. Louisville, 1952. Diplomate Am. Bd. Family Practice, Am. Bd. Hospice and Palliative Medicine. Intern St. Joseph Infirmary, Louisville, 1952-53; gen. practice family medicine Physicians Group, Springfield, Ill., 1955-80; med. dir. St. John's Hosp., Springfield, 1971-94, St. John's Hospice, 1995—; clin. prof. family practice So. Ill. U., Springfield, 1978—; ret., 1995. Served to capt. USAF, 1953-55 Mem. Am. Acad. Family Physicians, Am. Acad. Hospice/Palliative Medicine. Baptist. Home: 2131 Lindsay Rd Springfield IL 62704-3242 E-mail: dochol170@aol.com.

HOLLAND, KATHLEEN, political science educator; b. Burbank, Calif., Feb. 25, 1960; f. Robert and Lenore Gates; m. David Holland, Sept. 18, 1982. B, Calif. State U., 1990, M, 1993. Instr. L.A. Piece Coll., Woodland Hills, Calif., 1996—, Glendale (Calif.) C.C., 1999—, L.A. Trade Tech., 1999—. Author: Instructor's Manual for Democracy Under Pressure, 2001. Mem. exec. bd. AFT Guild, Local 1521, L.A., 2000-01. Mem. Am. Polit. Sci. Assn., Faculty Assn. Calif.'s Cmty. Colls. (com. mem. 2000-01). Democrat. Roman Catholic. Office: LA Pierce Coll 6201 Winnetka Ave Woodland Hills CA 91371-0002 Fax: 818-710-8944. E-mail: kdholland@earthlink.net.

HOLLAND, KEN, sports team executive; b. Vernon, B.C., Can. m. Cindy Holland; children: Brad, Julie, Rachel, Greg. Hockey player Medicine Hat, 1974-75, Toronto Maple Leafs, 1975-80, Hartford, 1980-83, Detroit Red Wings, 1983-84, Springfield, amateur scouting dir., asst. gen. mgr., gen. mgr., 1987—. Named to Binghamton Hall of Fame, 1998. Office: c/o Detroit Red Wings 600 Civic Center Dr Detroit MI 48226-4408

HOLLAND, LESLIE ANN, special education educator; b. Oak Lawn, Ill., Sept. 26, 1969; d. Ronald Leo and Rosemary Seymour; m. Brian Michael Holland, Dec. 31, 1999. AA, Moraine Valley C.C., Palos Hills, Ill., 1991; BS in Edn., Ea. Ill. U., 1995. Day camp site dir. Southwest Spl. Recreation Assn., Alsip, Ill., 1996—2000, spl. edn. dept. chair Momence, Ill., 1996—; tchr., spl. edn. dept. Sylvan Learning Ctr., Tinley Park, Ill., 2001—; chair, spl. edn. dept. Momence H.S., 1996—. Home: 14600 W Aston Way Lockport IL 60441 Office: Momence Unit Sch Dist # 1 101 N Franklin Momence IL 60954

HOLLAND, LYMAN FAITH, JR., lawyer; b. Mobile, Ala., June 17, 1931; s. Lyman Faith and Louise (Wisdom) H.; m. Leannah Louise Platt, Mar. 6, 1954; children: Lyman Faith III, Laura. BS in Bus. Adminstrn, U. Ala., 1953, LLB, 1957. Bar: Ala. 1957, U.S. Supreme Ct. 1992. Assoc. Hand, Arendall & Bedsole, Mobile, 1957-62; ptnr. Hand, Arendall, Bedsole, Greaves & Johnston, 1963-94, mem., 1995, Hand Arendall LLC, 1996—. Mem. Mobile Hist. Devel. Com., 1965-69, v.p., 1967-68; bd. dirs. Mobile Azalea Trail, Inc., 1963-68, chmn. bd., 1963-65; bd. dirs. Mobile Mental Health Ctr., 1969-76, v.p., 1972, pres., chmn. bd., 1973; bd. dirs. Mobile chpt. ARC, 1969-89, 91-97, vice chmn., 1975-77, exec. vice chmn., 1978-80, chmn., 1980-82, life bd. dirs. emeritus, 1997—; bd. dirs. Deep South coun. Girl Scouts U.S., 1965-71, Gordan Smith Ctr. Inc., 1973, Bay Area Coun. on Alcoholism, 1973-76, Cmty. Chest Coun. of Mobile County, Inc., 1976-81; bd. dirs. Greater Mobile Mental Health-Mental Retardation Bd., Inc., 1975-81, pres., 1975-77; mem. exec. com. Mobile Estate Planning Coun., 1988-97, pres., 1994-95. 1st lt. USAF, 1953-55; lt. col. USAF ret. Mem.: ABA, Ala. Law Found., Ala. Law Inst. (coun. 1978—), Am. Coll. Trust and Estate Counsel Found., Am. Coll. Trust and Estate Counsel, Am. Counsel Assn., Mobile County Bar Assn., Ala. State Bar (chmn. sect. corp., banking and bus. law 1978—80), Camellia Club of Mobile, Bienville Club, Country Club of Mobile, Athleston Club (Mobile), Lions, Phi Delta Phi, Phi Kappa Alpha. Baptist (deacon, ch. trustee 1968-73, chmn. trustees 1971-73). Home: 3606 Provident Ct Mobile AL 36608-1534 Office: Hand Arendall LLC PO Box 123 Mobile AL 36601-0123 E-mail: lymanh@handarendall.com.

HOLLAND, MARK ROBERT, research scientist; b. Kalamazoo, Feb. 18, 1959; s. Robert J. and Kathryn F. (Mortellaro) H.; m. Marion U. Dokey, June 4, 1982; children: Tara, Cassandra. BA in Physics, Kalamazoo Coll., 1981; MA in Physics, Washington U., St. Louis, 1983, PhD of Physics, 1989. Lead engr. McDonnell-Douglas Corp., St. Louis, 1989-90; rsch. scientist Washington U., St. Louis, 1990—. Mem. IEEE, Am. Soc. Echocardiography, Acoustical Soc. Am., Am. Inst. Ultrasound in Medicine, Am. Assn. Physicists in Medicine (liaison with Am. Soc. Echocardiography 1998—, pres. Missouri River Valley chpt. 2003). Office: Washington Univ 1 Brookings Dr Saint Louis MO 63130-4899 E-mail: mrh@wuphys.wustl.edu.

HOLLAND, MARVIN ARTHUR, lawyer; b. Bklyn., Oct. 5, 1930; s. Leo and Rose (Auslander) H.; m. Barbara Lee Birnstein, Dec. 16, 1971 (div. 1979). B.A., Lafayette Coll., 1951; J.D., Cornell Law Sch., 1954. Bar: N.Y. 1955, U.S. Dist. Ct. (ea. and so. dists.) N.Y. 1960. Assoc., then ptnr. Holland & Radoyevich, Smithtown, N.Y., 1956-67, sole practice, Smithtown, 1967-69, 75-79; ptnr. Holland, Greshin & Sloan, Smithtown, 1969-75, Holland & Zinker, Smithtown, 1978— ; lectr. Practising Law Inst., N.Y.C., 1981, Suffolk Acad. Law, Ronkonkoma, N.Y., 1978—, Am. Acad. Matrimonial Attys., Chgo., 1981-83, Nassau County Acad. Law, Mineola, N.Y., 1982-83. Contbr. bankruptcy entry to Money Ency., 1984; also articles. Mem. B'nai B'rith Anti-defamation League, N.Y.C., 1974—, Nat. Law Com. Served with U.S. Army, 1954-56. Mem. Suffolk County Bar Assn. (bd. dirs. 1974-77), N.Y. State Bar Assn., Bankruptcy Bar Assn., Nassau County Bar Assn. Jewish. Office: Holland & Zinker 12 Bank Ave Smithtown NY 11787-2704 also: US District Court 75 Clinton St Brooklyn NY 11201-4201 Home: # 1C 62 Pierrepont St Brooklyn NY 11201-2452

HOLLAND, MICHAEL FRANCIS, investment company executive; b. Cleve., July 8, 1944; s. Joseph Thomas and Mary Louise H.; m. Louise Grace, Aug. 20, 1966; children: Brian, Thomas, Joseph, Daniel, John, Michael Jr. AB, Harvard U., 1966; MBA, Columbia U., 1968. With Morgan Guaranty Trust Co., N.Y.C., 1968-80, investment mgr., 1972-80, v.p., 1975-80; sr. v.p. investments Reliance Group, Inc., also Reliance Ins. Co., N.Y.C., 1980-83; pres. Holland & Co., Inc., 1983-84; pres., chief exec. officer First Boston Asset Mgmt. Corp., 1984-89; chmn., CEO Salomon Bros. Asset Mgmt., Inc., 1989-92; vice chmn. Oppenheimer & Co. Inc., 1992-94; dir., chmn. bd. dirs., chief exec. officer Global Growth and Income Fund, Inc., 1986-89; dir. The China Fund, Inc., 1992—; gen. ptnr. The Blackstone Group, 1994-95; chmn. Holland & Co. L.L.C., 1995—. Dir. The Latin Am. Investment Fund, Inc., 1990-92. Panelist: Wall Street Week with Louis Rukeyser, 1990—. Vice chmn. Harvard Coll. Fund Assoc. Program, 1998—; mem. com. on univ. resource, com. on faculty selection Harvard U.; trustee Vanguard Charitable Endowment Program, 1997—; mem. bd. fin. Town of New Canaan, Conn., 1997—; trustee Harvard Club N.Y.C. Found., 2001—. Mem. Harvard Club of N.Y.C. (bd. mgrs. 1998-2001). Clubs: Racquet & Tennis; Country of New Canaan, Winter (New Canaan); Harvard of Fairfield County. Home: 1 Greenley Rd New Canaan CT 06840-3513 Office: Holland & Co LLC 375 Park Ave Ste 1903 New York NY 10152-1994

HOLLAND, MICHAEL JAMES, computer services administrator; b. N.Y.C., Nov. 20, 1950; s. Robert Frederick and Virginia June (Wilcox) H.; Anita Garay, Jan. 5, 1981 (Aug. 1989); 1 child, Melanie. BA in Comparative Lit., Bklyn. Coll., 1972. Enlisted USN, 1975, advanced to CPO, 1989; field med. technician 3rd Marine Divsn., Okinawa, Japan, 1976-77, 1st Marine Divsn., Camp Pendleton, Calif., 1978-79; clin. supr. Naval Hosp. Subic Bay, Philippines, 1979-81; dept. head Tng. Ctr. USMCR, Johnson City, Tenn., 1981-84; clin. supr. No. Tng. Area, Okinawa, 1984-85, 3rd Marine Air Wing, Camp Pendleton, 1985-88; cons. Naval Regional Med. Command, San Diego, 1988-90; system analyst Naval Med. Info. Mgmt. Ctr. Detachment, San Diego, 1990-92; computer svcs. adminstr. U.S. Naval Hosp., Guam, 1993-95; ret., 1995; svc. rep. SBC Calif., 1997—. Mem. Fleet Res. Assn., Comm. Workers Am., Nat. City C. of C. (com. 1989-91).

HOLLAND, NICHOLAS V., III, music educator; b. Chapel Hill, N.C., June 21, 1967; s. Jacqueline Martin Holland and Nicholas V. Holland, Jr.; m. Karen Lynn Rogowski; 1 child, Nicholas IV. BMus, East Carolina U., 1991, MMus, 1993; postgrad. in Music Edn., U. N.C., Greensboro, 1997—2000. Dir. bands, instr. percussion Ea. N.Mex. U., Portales; percussionist The N.C. Symphony, Raleigh, 1994—95; grad. asst. conductor U. N.C., Greensboro, 1997—2000; assoc. dir. bands U. Memphis, 2000—. Mem.: West Tenn. Band and Orch. Assn., Coll. Band Dirs. Nat. Assn., Music Educators Nat. Conf., Percussive Arts Soc., Phi Mu Alpha Sinfonia, Alpha Phi Omega (hon.), Sigma Alpha Iota (hon. Friend of the Arts award 1996), Tau Beta Sigma (hon.), Kappa Kappa Psi (hon.). Home: 7107 Anisettee Dr Cordova TN 38018 Office: Univ Memphis CFA 116 Memphis TN 38152 Home Fax: 901-678-5546; Office Fax: 901-678-5546. Business E-Mail: nholland@memphis.edu.

HOLLAND, NORMAN NORWOOD, literary critic; b. N.Y.C., Sept. 19, 1927; s. Norman Norwood and Harriette (Breder) H.; m. Jane Kelley, Dec. 17, 1954; children: Kelley, John. BS, MIT, 1947; LLB, Harvard U., 1950, PhD, 1956; cert. in psychoanalysis, Boston Psychoanalytic Inst. From instr. to assoc. prof. MIT, Cambridge, 1955-66; McNulty prof. English SUNY, Buffalo, 1966-83; assoc. prof. U. Paris, 1971-72, 85; Marston-Milbauer eminent scholar U. Fla., Gainesville, 1983—. Cons. various pubs., 1960—, Pres's. Coun. on Obscenity, 1971, Can. Coun., 1980. Author: The First Modern Comedies 1959, The Shakespearean Imagination, 1964, Psychoanalysis and Shakespeare, 1966, The Dynamics of Literary Response, 1968, Poems in Persons: An Introduction to the Psychoanalysis of Literature, 1973, rev. edit., 2000, 5 Readers Reading, 1975, Laughing: A Psychology of Humor, 1982, The I, 1985, The Brain of Robert Frost: A Cognitive Approach to Literature, 1988, Holland's Guide to Psychoanalytic Psychology and Literature-and-Psychology, 1990, The Critical I, 1992, Death in a Delphi Seminar, 1995. Am. Couns. Learned Socs. fellow, 1974-75, Guggenheim Found. fellow, 1979-80. Mem. Am. Acad. Psychoanalysis (sci. assoc.), Boston Psychoanalytic Soc., Modern Lang. Assn. (div. exec. com. 1975-81). Democrat. Avocation: movies. Office: U Fla Dept English Gainesville FL 32611

HOLLAND, PATRICIA CHRISTINE, music educator, musician; b. Ann Arbor, Mich., Apr. 19, 1957; d. William Franklin Jewell, III and Joan Lorey Jewell; m. Daniel Olin Holland, June 26, 1982. BA, U. Mich., 1979; AMusD U. Mich., 1993; MusM, Mich. State U., 1990. Prin. bassoon Jackson (Mich.) Symphony Orch., 1981—94; prof. music U. Wis., Stevens Point, 1994—. Bassoon instr. Hillsdale (Mich.) Coll., 1988—94; adj. instr. Jackson (Mich.) C.C., 1993—94; aux. bassoon Grand Rapids (Mich.) Symphony Orch., 1989—94; prin. bassoon Fox Valley Symphony Orch., Appleton, Wis., 1999—; contra bassoon Peninsula Music Festival, Fish Creek, Wis., 1999—. Contbr. articles to profl. jours. Mem.: Coll. Music Soc., Am. Fedn. Musicians, Internat. Double Reed Soc., Phi Kappa Phi, Pi Kappa Lambda. Office: Univ Wis Stevens Point Stevens Point WI 54481

HOLLAND, PETER MARC, ophthalmologist; b. N.Y.C., Apr. 7, 1944; s. George and Estelle (Alpert) H.; m. Merle Lumish, May 26, 1968; children: Matthew David, John Michael. BA, Clark U., 1965; MD, N.Y. Med. Coll., 1969. Diplomate Nat. Bd. Med. Examiners, Am. Bd. Ophthalmology. Med. intern Montefiore Hosp. & Med. Ctr., Bronx, NY, 1969—70; resident in ophthalmology Duke U. Eye Ctr., Durham, NC, 1972—75; fellow in diseases and surgery of retina and vitreous Mass. Eye and Ear Infirmary, Harvard Med. Sch., Boston, 1975—76; asst. prof. dept. ophthalmology George Washington U. Med. Ctr., Washington, 1976—77; clin. asst. prof. Baylor Coll. Medicine, Houston, 1977-90, clin. assoc. prof. dept. ophthalmology, 1990—; ophthalmologist Bayshore Eye Assocs., Pasadena, Tex., 1977—. Clin. assoc. prof. Dept. Ophthalmology U. Tex. Med. Br. Galveston, 1996—; cons. space shuttle flights #1 and #2, NASA, Houston, 1978-81; chmn. inst. rev. com. Bayshore Med. Ctr., Pasadena, 1984-93; mem. com. for appointment and promotion Baylor Coll. Medicine, Dept. Ophthalmology, Houston, 1988-92. Contbr. articles to profl. jours. Lt. comdr. USPHS, 1970-72. Mem. Houston Ophthalmologic Soc. (pres. elect 1993-94, pres. 1994-95, exec. com. 1983-86, 93-95), Tex. Med. Assn., Tex. Ophthalmologic Assn. (chmn. Diabetes 2000 com. 1993-94), Harris County Med. Soc., Am. Acad. Ophthalmology, Am. Diabetes Assn., Alpha Omega Alpha. Office: Bayshore Eye Assocs 3320 Plainview St Pasadena TX 77504-1906

HOLLAND, RANDY JAMES, state supreme court justice; b. Elizabeth, N.J., Jan. 27, 1947; s. James Charles and Virginia (Wilson) H.; m. Ilona E. Holland, June 24, 1972 BA in Econs., Swarthmore Coll., 1969; JD cum laude, U. Pa., 1972; LLM, U. Va., 1998; Doctorate (hon.), Widener U. Sch. Law, 2001. Bar: Del. 1972. Ptnr. Dunlap, Holland & Rich and predecessors, Georgetown, Del., 1972-80, Morris, Nichols, Arsht & Tunnell, Georgetown, Del., 1980-86; justice Supreme Ct. Del., Georgetown, 1986—. Mem. Del. Bar Examiners, 1978-86; mem. Gov.'s Jud. Nominating Commn., 1978-86, sec., 1982-85, chmn., 1985-86; mem. Del. Supreme Ct. Consol. Com., 1985-86; pres. Terry-Carey Inn of Ct., 1991-94; v.p. Am. Inns of Ct., 1996-2000, pres., 2000—; co-chair Racial and Ethnic Task Force, 1995—; adj. prof. Widener U. Sch. Law, 1991—, U. Pa. Sch. Law, 1993-94, U. Iowa Sch. Law, 1997—, Vanderbilt Law Sch., 2000—; co-chair Del. Cts. Planning Com., 1996; chair nat. jud. adv. com. fed. Office of Child Support Enforcement; Jud. Ethics Adv. Commn., 1994—; del. Code Jud. Conduct Rev. Commn., 1991-94; del. Ban Bench Media Conf., 1990—. Mem. editL. bd. Del. Lawyer Mag., 1981-85; contbr. chpt. Del. Appellate Handbook, 1985—. Pres. adminstrv. bd. Ave. United Meth. Ch., Milford, Del. Bar Found.; hon. chmn. History of the Del. Bar in 20th Century, 1992—. Recipient Henry C. Loughlin prize for legal ethics U. Pa. 1972, St. Thomas More award, 1999, Alumni award of merit U. Pa. Sch. Law, 2002; named Judge of the Yr. Nat. Child Support Enforcement Assn., 1992. Mem. ABA (standing com. on lawyer competence, nat. jud. coll. adv. commn. model rules jud. disclosure enforcement 1996, appellate judge's conf. exec. com. 2001—, chmn. joint com. on lawyer regulation 2002—), Am. Judicature Soc. (nat. trustee 1992—, ctr. for jud. ethics, 1994, chair 1997-, Herbert Harley Award 2003.), Am. Inns of Ct. Found. (trustee 1992—, nat. trustee 1996—, v.p. 1996-2000, nat. pres. 2000—), Am. Law Inst., Del. Bar Found., Am. Law Inst. Republican. Avocations: gardening, swimming, cycling. Office: Del Supreme Ct 34 The Cir Georgetown DE 19947-1500

HOLLAND, RICHARD A. statistician; s. Myron L. and Elizabeth M. Holland; m. Joan M. Probst, Oct. 16, 1971 (div. June 1987). BS, U. Mo., 1972, MS, 1975. Statis. analyst Mo. Dept. Mental Health, St. Louis, 1975—88, Monsanto Corp., St. Louis, 1989—90; sys. analyst Stuart, Maue, Mitchell and James, St. Louis, 1990—2001. Instr. U. Mo., St. Louis, 1988. Contbr. articles. With U.S. Army, 1965—68, Vietnam. Mem.: Math. Assn. Am., Am. Statis. Assn., Alpha Sigma Lambda. Avocation: skydiving.

HOLLAND, ROBERT CAMPBELL, anatomist, educator; b. Bushnell, Ill., Aug. 16, 1923; s. Harvey Howard and Lois Sarah (Campbell) H.; m. Hilda P. Burgi, Sept. 26, 1946 (dec. 1980); children: Jonathan Robert, Heather, Judith Ashley. BS, U. Wis., 1948, MS, 1949, PhD, 1955. Instr. Dental Sch. Northwestern U., 1949-51; asst. prof. anatomy Sch. Medicine U. N.D., 1955-60; assoc. prof. Sch. Medicine U. Ark., 1960-66; prof. chmn. dept. anatomy Mahidol U., Bangkok, 1966-76; prof., chmn. dept. anatomy Morehouse Sch. Medicine, Atlanta, 1976-90, prof. emeritus dept. anatomy, 1990—. Mem. staff Rockefeller Found., 1966-76; vis. prof. UCLA Sch. Medicine, 1976. Author research pubs. on the brain. With M.C., U.S. Army, 1943-46. Postdoctoral fellow Wis. Alumni Rsch. Found., 1951-54, Nat. Found. for Infantile Paralysis, UCLA Sch. Medicine, 1957-58; NIH grantee, 1959-88. Mem. Am. Assn. Anatomists, Am. Acad. Neurology, Soc. Exptl. Biology and Medicine, Soc. Neurosci., Sigma Xi

HOLLAND, ROBERT CARL, economist; b. Tekamah, Nebr., Apr. 7, 1925; s. Carl Luther and Gretchen (Thompson) H.; m. DeEtte Harriet Hedlund, Sept. 7, 1947; children: Joan DeEtte Holland Geltz, Nancy Gretchen Holland Kerr, Timothy Robert. Student, U. Nebr., 1942-43, 46; BS in Fin., U. Pa., 1948, MA in Econs., 1949, PhD in Econs., 1959. Instr. money and banking U. Pa., 1948-49; with Fed. Res. Bank Chgo., 1949-61, v.p., 1959-61; with bd. govs. Fed. Res. System, 1961-76; mem. bd. govs. FRS, 1973-76, sec. of bd., 1968-71, exec. dir., 1971-73, sec. to fed. open market com., 1966-73; pres. Com. for Econ. Devel., Washington, 1976-90, sr. econ. cons., 1990-96. Sr. fellow, bd. dirs. SEI Ctr. for Advanced Studies in Mgmt., U. Pa., 1990—; sr. fellow dept. Legal Studies, U. Pa., 1992—. With AUS, 1943-45. Mem. Am. Econ. Assn., Nat. Acad. Pub. Adminstrn., Internat. Soc. of Bus. Econs. and Ethics, Cosmos Club, Kenwood Country Club (Bethesda, Md.), Beta Theta Pi. Home: 5508 Cromwell Dr Bethesda MD 20816-2006 Fax: 301-229-5205. E-mail: r.c.holland@worldnet.att.net.

HOLLAND, ROBERT DALE, retired judge; b. Sayre, Okla., June 10, 1928; s. Claude Henry and Alva Mae (Joyce) H.; children: Arlene, Burton Dale, Rhonda Jo. Student, Tex. A&M, 1946, Internat. Corr. Schs., 1963, 65, 67-68; PhD of Sociology (hon.), Scholars U., 1975. Safety, security, loss prevention officer Copper Queen Br. Phelps Dodge Corp., Bisbee, Ariz., 1946-85; probation officer Cochise County, Bisbee, 1986—87; safety dir., loss prevention dir. Spray Sys. Environ., Phoenix, 1987-93; city magistrate City of Bisbee, 1989-93; pres., owner Copper City Cons., Bisbee, 1989—. Referee & hearing officer Cochise County Juvenile Ct., 1969-78; juvenile ct. judge pro tem, 1990-93; justice ct. judge pro tem, 1991-93; bd. dirs. Southern Ariz. Safety Coun., Tucson, 1986-91. Councilman City of Bisbee, 1973-82; chmn. relief com. Salvation Army, 1980—; chmn., vice chmn. bd. dirs. Copper Queen Hosp. Corp., Bisbee, Ariz. With USMC, 1947-52. Mem. Ariz. Dept. Health Svcs. (state health planning and coord. com. 1973-76, region VI health planning bd. 1973-78, treas. regional govt. orgn. 1973-78, water quality com. 1974), Am. Mining Congress (ad-hoc com. 1980), Perfect Ashlar Lodge F&AM (master 1964, 50 yr.life mem.), Masons (Scottish Rite). Democrat. Avocations: gun collecting, reading, church work. Home and Office: PO Box 5427 206 Black Knob View Bisbee AZ 85603-5427

HOLLAND, ROBERT DEBNAM, SR., investment company executive; b. Norfolk, Va., Mar. 5, 1922; s. Ralph Frederick and Erma Gwendoly (Debnam) H.; m. Frances Lee Hodges, Dec. 26, 1943 (div. June 1984); children: Robert Debnam Jr., Elizabet Lee, William Peyton; m. Anne-Marie Lamb, Aug. 10, 1984. BA, U.S. Merchant Marine Acad., 1943, Centre Coll., Danville, Ky., 1949; postgrad., U. Va., 1950. Salesman IBM Corp., 1952-56, Burroughs Corp., 1956-61, mgr. indsl. mktg., 1961-65; v.p. fin., pres. CIER, Inc., Washington, 1965-67; CEO Computer Leasing Co., 1967-74; asst. adminstr. Small Bus. Adminstrn., 1975-76; pres. Photomatrics Corp., L.A., 1985-88; mng. ptnr. Transnat. Corp., Washington, 1975-85, Las Vegas, 1988—. Bus. adv. U. Nev., Las Vegas, 1989—; treas., bd. dirsn. Internat. Label Co., Las Vegas, 1992—; chmn. exec. com. Network Recovery Sys., San Ramon, Calif., 1994—. Lt. comdr. USNR, 1942-55. Mem. AIM, Inst. Automation Rsch., Am. Mgmt. Assn., Sigma Chi, Omicron Delta Kappa, Phi Kappa Delta. Democrat. Episcopalian. Home: 855 Palmer Ave Winter Park FL 32789 E-mail: rd-am-holland@att.net.

HOLLAND, ROBERT JAMES, retired lawyer; b. Dayton, Ohio, Jan. 8, 1936; s. John Edward and Alma Naomi (Himes) Holland; m. Barbara Jane Drake, Aug. 27, 1960; children: Robert Jr., Duncan, Wendolyn, Justin. BA, Yale U., 1958; JD, Ohio State U., 1963. Bar: Ohio 1963, U.S. Supreme Ct. 1972. Assoc. Chester & Rose, Columbus, Ohio, 1963—67; gen. counsel Banc Ohio Corp., Columbus, 1967—71; city atty. City of Upper Arlington, Ohio, 1976—86; ptnr. Bodiker & Holland, Columbus, 1971—97; pres. Mid-Ohio Regional Planning Commn., Columbus, 1970—71, gen. counsel, 1971—85; gen. counsel, bd. dirs. Servinat, Inc., N.Y.C., 1976—2001; ret., 2001. Founder, bd. dirs. 1st Cmty. Bank. Co-author: (book) Ohio Taxation: Truth in Lending, 1969. Bd. dirs. Wellington Sch., Columbus, 1979—89; pres., bd. dirs. Ctrl. Ohio Transit Authority, Columbus, 1971—74. Served to lt. USNR, 1958—60. Named to Ten Outstanding Men, Columbus Jaycees, 1970. Mem.: ABA, Columbus Bar Assn. (chmn. law insts. com. 1968—70, chmn. unauthorized practice 1973—74, mem. ethics com. 1973—77), Ohio State Bar Assn., Internat. Food and Wine Soc., Union League (Chgo.), Scioto Club, Athletic Club. Home: 907 Cheyenne Ct Box 3007 Ketchum ID 83340

HOLLAND, SAMUEL STINSON, music educator, writer, musician; b. Louisville, Sept. 24, 1952; s. De Witte Talmadge and Mary Stinson Holland; m. Bethany S. Conway, Nov. 18, 1991; children: Kristen Elizabeth, Benjamin Austin, Elias Clark Conway. MusB, U. Tex., 1975; profl. cert., New Sch. for Music Study, Princeton, N.J., 1977; MusM, U. Houston, 1979; PhD, U. Okla., 1996. Nat. cert. tchr. music. Dir. New Sch. for Music Study, Princeton, 1979—87, asst. prof. U. Ky., Lexington, 1987—91; prof. So. Meth. U., Dallas, 1991—. Adj. instr. Westminster Choir Coll., Princeton, 1982—87. Co-editor: Celebrate Composers Series, 2002—; co-author: (piano method) The Music Tree, 2000; author: Teaching Toward Tomorrow, 1993. Mem.: European Piano Tchrs. Assn., Music Tchrs. Nat. Assn. Achievements include research in keyboard pedagogy and music education.

HOLLANDER, ADRIAN WILLOUGHBY, accounting services company executive; b. Sumter, S.C., Oct. 12, 1941; s. Willard Fisher and Mildred Hanna (Willoughby) H.; m. Eleanor Busby Smith, May 26, 1963; children: Richard, David, Robert. BS, Iowa State U., 1963. CPA; cert. info. system auditor; cert. internal auditor; cert. bank auditor; cert. fin. svcs. auditor. Mem. audit and cons. staff Arthur Andersen and Co., Chgo., 1965-71; auditor Beverly Bancorporation, Chgo., 1971-73; v.p. Cullinane Corp., Chgo., 1973-78; auditor Cen. Nat. Bank in Chgo., 1978-79; pres. EDP Audit Assocs., Inc., Summit, Ill., 1980, Complus, Inc., Hickory Hills, Ill., 1982-87, Chgo., 1987—. Cons., owner EDP Audit Service, Chgo., 1979—. Contbr. articles to profl. jours. Trustee St. Paul's Union Ch., Chgo., 1973-75; bd. dirs. Beverly Improvement Assn., Chgo., 1972-88; council of dels. Beverly Area Planning Assn., Chgo., 1980-85; del. Chgo. Agenda for Pub. Edn., 1983-87. Served to 1st lt. U.S. Army, 1963-65. Mem. AICPA, Ill. CPA Soc. (sec. Chgo. South chpt. 1991-92, treas. 1992-93, v.p. 1993-94, sr. v.p. 1994-95, pres. 1995-96, del. 1996-97), Info. Systems Audit and Control Assn., Nat. Assn. Fin. Svcs. Auditors, Inst. Internal Auditors, Chgo. Beverly Ridge Lions Club (pres. 1992-93). Republican. Avocations: fishing, camping, scouting. Home: 9360 S Pleasant Ave Chicago IL 60620-5644 Office: Complus Inc 9500 S Vanderpoel Ave Chicago IL 60643-1228

HOLLANDER, ANNE, writer; b. Cleve., Oct. 16, 1930; d. Arthur and Jean Hill (Bassett) Loesser; m. John Hollander, June 15, 1953 (div. 1977); children: Martha, Elizabeth; m. Thomas Nagel, June 26, 1979. BA, Barnard Coll., 1952. Author: Seeing Through Clothes, 1978, Moving Pictures, 1989, Sex and Suits, 1994, Feeding the Eye, 1999, Fabric of Vision, 2002. Guggenheim fellow, 1975. Fellow N.Y. Inst. for the Humanities (interim dir. 1995-96); mem. Costume Soc. Am., College Art Assn., PEN Am. Ctr. (pres. 1995-96), Century Assn.

HOLLANDER, BRUCE LEE, lawyer, business executive; b. Queens, N.Y., Aug. 16, 1943; s. I. Gerard and Argate (Polmer) H.; m. Beverly Ann Olund, Apr. 28, 1967; children— Aaron Gerard, Adam Robert. Student Cornell U., 1961-62; B.S. in Psychology, U. Miami, 1970; J.D. cum laude, 1973. Bar: Fla. 1973, U.S. Dist. Ct. (mid. and so. dists.) Fla. 1973, U.S. Ct. Appeals (5th cir.) 1973. Assoc. Snyder, Young, Stern & Tannenbaum, Miami, Fla., 1973-76; ptnr. Garlick, Cohn, Darrow & Hollander, Hollywood, Fla., 1976-82, Hollander & Assocs., P.A., Hollywood, 1982— ; lectr. in field; mem. adv. bd. Broward Bank, 1982, mem. elect, 1983; pres. Automated Title Services, Hollywood, Automated Credit Svcs., Hollywood. Contbr. articles to Mortgage Notes, Fla. Bar Jour. Bd. dirs. Broward County chpt. ARC, Fla., 1979-81. Mem. ABA, Broward County Bar Assn., Fla. Bar (rep. 17th jud. cir. for real property, probate and trust law sect. 1978—, exec. council real property, probate and trust law sect. 1979-83, chmn. 2d mortgage law subcom. 1979-83, also corp., banking and bus. law sect. and econs. and mgmt. law practice sect.), Nat. Second Mortgage Assn., Nat. Consumer Fin. Assn. (home equity sect.), Nat. Assn. Mortgage Brokers, Fla. Assn. Mortgage Brokers (bd. dirs. Gold Coast chpt.), Soc. Wig and Robe, Soc. Bar and Gavel (justice, honor council), Sports Car Club Am. (S.E. divisional champion 1968, 76-77, 86), Delta Theta Phi, Phi Kappa Phi. Jewish. Office: Hollander & Assocs PA 1940 Harrison St Hollywood FL 33020-5082

HOLLANDER, DANIEL, gastroenterologist, medical educator; b. Mar. 3, 1939; Student, UCLA, to 1960; MD, Baylor U., 1964. Diplomate Am. Bd. Internal Medicine, Am. Bd. Gastroenterology. Intern Phila. Gen. Hosp., 1964-65; resident in internal medicine Med. Ctr., U. Kans., Kansas City, 1965-67; NIH rsch. fellow in gastroenterology U. Wash., Seattle, 1967-69; asst. prof. medicine Albany (N.Y.) Med. Coll., Union U., 1971-73, assoc. prof., 1973; assoc. prof. medicine, head div. gastroenterology Wayne State U., Detroit, 1973-77, prof. medicine, head div. gastroenterology, 1977—94, U. Calif., Irvine, 1978-94, prof. physiology and biophysics, 1981-94, assoc. dean for rsch. and program devel. Coll. Medicine, 1984-85, assoc. dean for acad. affairs, 1985-89, sr. assoc. dean for clin. affairs, 1989-91, chief gastroenterology Irvine Med. Ctr., 1979-94; exec. dean Sch. of Medicine U. Kans., Kansas City, 1994—96; chief med. officer Sierra Pacific Network, San Francisco, 1996-98; prof. medicine U. Calif., San Francisco, 1996-98; pres., CEO Harbor-UCLA Rsch. and Edn. Inst., 1998-2001; prof. medicine UCLA, 1998—, dir. inflammatory bowel disease grants broad med. rsch. program for Eli and Edythe L. Broad Found., 2001—. Attending physician, attending gastroenterologist Albany Med. Ctr. Hosp., 1971-73; chief gastroenterology svc., attending physician Harper Hosp., Detroit, 1973-78; cons. in gastroenterology Children's, Detroit Gen. and VA hosps., 1973-78; chief gastroenterology VA Med. Ctr., Long Beach, Calif., 1978-80; chmn. Gastrointestinal Gerontology Rsch. Group, 1988-89; vis. scientist dept. molecular medicine U. Auckland, New Zealand, 1990-91; vis. prof., invited speaker numerous other univs., profl. meetings, confs. Author: (with G. Gitnick, N. Kaplowitz, I.M. Samloff, L.J. Schoenfield) Principles and Practice of Gastroenterology and Hepatology, 1988, (with A. Tarnawski) Gastic Cytoprotection—A Clinician's Guide, 1989, (with Porro G. Bianchi) Treatment of Digestive Disease with Sucralfate, 1989; mem. editl. bd., reviewer Can. Jour. Gastroenterology; contbr. numerous articles, revs. to profl. jours., book chpt. With USAF, 1969-71. Calif. Heart Assn. rsch. fellow, 1960; Fogarty Sr. Internat. fellow Oxford (Eng.) U., 1984-85; grantee NIH, Nat. Inst. on Aging, Nat. Insts. Arthritis, Metabolism and Digestive Diseases, Skillman Found., VA, Goldsmith Found., Internat. Pharm. Products. Mem. ACP (A. Blaine traveling scholar 1973), Am. Fedn. for Clin. Rsch. (pres. Midwestern sect. 1979-80), Am. Gastroent. Assn., Am. Physiol. Soc., Am. Soc. for Clin. Investigation, Orange County Gastroenterology Assn. (pres. 1986-87), Brit. Soc. Gastroenterology, European Assn. Gastroenterology, Western Assn. Physicians, Western Gut Club (pres. 1981-82), Alpha Omega Alpha. Office: The Eli and Edythe L Broad Found 10900 Wilshire Blvd 12th Fl Los Angeles CA 90024-6532 E-mail: dhollander@broadmedical.org.

HOLLANDER, FRANK, lawyer; b. York, Pa. B in Bus. Adminstrn. magna cum laude, U. Fla., 1984, JD, 1987. Bar: Fla. 1988, U.S. Ct. Appeals (11th cir.) 1989, U.S. Dist. Ct. (so. dist.) Fla. 1993, U.S. Supreme Ct. 1997. Prosecutor Fla. State Atty. Janet Reno, Miami, 1987; atty., pres. Law Offices Frank L. Hollander, Miami, 1988—. Mem.: ATLA, ABA, Nat. Assn. Criminal Def. Lawyers, Acad. Fla. Trial Lawyers, Fed. Bar Assn. Office: 200 S Biscayne Blvd 51st Fl Miami FL 33131-2340 E-mail: fhollander@attyatlaw.org.

HOLLANDER, GERALD MARTIN, physician; b. N.Y.C., June 28, 1947; s. Emanuel and Miriam Hollander; m. Barbara Sarah Hollander, Jan. 26, 1975; children: Aviva, Shani, Nahva. BS, CCNY; MD, SUNY, Bklyn. Resident in medicine Brookdale Hosp. Med. Ctr., Bklyn., 1973-75, fellow in cardiology, 1976-78; dir. cardiac ICU Maimonides Med. Ctr, Bklyn., 1978—, dir. cardiology, 1994-99, dir. clin. cardiology, 1999—; assoc. prof. clin. medicine SUNY Health Sci. Ctr., Bklyn., 1994—. Contbr. articles to profl. jours. Bd. dirs. Hebrew Acad. of Long Beach, N.Y., 1986—. Fellow Am. Coll. Cardiology, Am. Coll. Physicians, Am. Coll. Chest Physicians; mem. Phi Beta Kappa. Office: Maimonides Med Ctr 4802 10th Ave Brooklyn NY 11219-2844

HOLLANDER, HERBERT I. consulting engineer; b. N.Y.C., July 23, 1924; s. Jacob and Saide (Sporer) H.; m. Evelyn V. Schovajsa, Sept. 4, l949; children: Keith R., Janice G. BME, CCNY, l955; MBA, Bernard Baruch Coll., l963. Registered profl. engr., Conn., Fla., N.Y., Ohio, Maine, Va.; diplomate Am. Acad. Environ Engrs. Dist. mgr. Detroit Stoker Co.-Div. United Indsl. Corp., N.Y.C., l948-65; regional mgr. Riley Stoker Co., Worcester, Mass., 1965-69; prin. cons. Roy F. Weston Inc., West Chester, Pa., l969-72, Gilbert Assocs., Inc., Reading, Pa., l972-80; v.p. STV/Sanders & Thomas, Pottstown, Pa., 1980-88; prin. Hollander Assocs., Wyomissing, Pa., 1988—. Presenter in field. Contbr. to Standard Handbook of Environmental Engineering; compiler, editor: ASTM Thesaurus on Resource Recovery Terminology; contbr. articles on indsl. and mcpl. waste-residue mgmt., fuel preparation and utilization, energy conversion, and power generation systems to confs., seminars and profl. jours. Mem. spring Twp. (Pa.) Zoning Bd., l982-85. Fellow ASME (founding, past chmn. solid waste processing div., rsch. com. on indsl. and mcpl. wastes, Disting. medal of achievement 1990); mem. ASTM (founding mem. com. on resource recovery, com. on hazardous waste disposal, cert. of merit 1983, Frank W. Reinhart award 1984), Air and Waste Mgmt. Assn., Solid Waste Assn. N.Am., Am. Acad. Environ. Engrs. (former trustee). Avocations: photography, golf. Home and Office: 1605 Sherwood Rd Reading PA 19610-1127 Fax: 610-678-2877.

HOLLANDER, HOWARD ROBERT, software engineering executive; b. N.Y.C., Oct. 1, 1952; s. Maxwell and Rhoda (Scheller) H.; m. Linda Robin Pike, May 24, 1975; children: Aileen Dara, Jonathan Lee. BEE, NYU, 1973; MS in Engring. Mgmt., Northeastern U., 1975. Software engr. GTE Sylvania Co., Boston, 1974-75, sr. engr. Ogden, Utah, 1975-78; specialist engr. Boeing Aerospace Co., Ogden, 1978-82; engring. mgr. GE Aerospace Co., Syracuse, N.Y., 1982-93; sr. engring. mgr. Martin Marietta Corp., Syracuse, 1993-95; engring. mgr. Lockheed Martin Corp., Syracuse, 1995—. Cons. U. Utah, Salt Lake City, 1980-82, Minimax Systems, Syracuse, 1982—, Eastern Communications, N.Y.C., 1983-86, The Combined Sch., 1989-96; bd. dirs. LMN Pike Co., Syracuse. Contbr. articles to tech. publs. Mem. Leadership Greater Syracuse, 2001, bd. dirs., 2003—, Combined Sch. Syracuse, 1987—96; treas. Congregation Brith Sholem, Ogden, 1980—82; bd. dirs. Temple Beth El, Syracuse, 1985—, treas., 1990—91, pres. men's club, 1991—94, 1995—96, v.p., 1996—97. Named. hon. Ky. col., 1987. Mem. Mensa, Tech. Alliance of Ctrl. N.Y. (bd. dirs. 1996—, editor Technologist 1997-98, v.p. 2003-), Eta Kappa Nu. Avocations: skiing, running, bicycling. Office: Lockheed Martin PO Box 4840 Syracuse NY 13221-4840 E-mail: hollander@juno.com.

HOLLANDER, IRWIN JOEL, pathologist, educator; b. Bayonne, N.J., May 29, 1949; s. Max Leo and Miriam Hilda (Berger) H.; m. Aileen Rhonda Sosnow, June 2l, l970; children: Lori, Sheri, Eric. BS, Pa. State U., 1970; MD, Thomas Jefferson U., 1972. Diplomate Am. Bd. Internal Medicine, Am. Bd. Pathology. Intern in medicine Mt. Sinai Hosp., N.Y.C., 1972—73; resident in pathology Hosp. of U. Pa., Phila., 1973—75; resident in medicine Thomas Jefferson. U. Hosp., Phila., 1975—77, resident in pathology, 1977—79; assoc. pathologist Grand View Hosp., Sellersville, Pa., 1979—81, dir. labs., 1981—. Adj. clin. assoc. prof. pathology Thomas Jefferson U., 1994—. Fellow ACP, Coll. Am. Pathologists; mem. Bucks County Med. Soc. (pres. 1989). Office: Grand View Hosp 700 Lawn Ave Sellersville PA 18960-1576

HOLLANDER, JOHN, humanities educator, poet; b. NYC, Oct. 28, 1929; s. Franklin and Muriel (Kornfeld) H.; m. Anne Helen Loesser, June 15, 1953 (div. 1977); children: Martha, Elizabeth.; m. Natalie Charkow, Dec. 15, 1981. AB, Columbia U., 1950, AM, 1952; PhD, Ind. U., 1959; DLitt (hon.), Marietta Coll., 1982; LHD (hon.), Ind. U., 1990; DFA (hon.), Maine Coll. of Art, 1993; DHL (hon.), CUNY, 2001; DHL (hon.), New Sch. U., 2003. Jr. fellow Soc. Fellows, Harvard, 1954-57; lectr. English Conn. Coll., New London, 1957-59; instr. English Yale, 1959-61; asst. prof. English, fellow Ezra Stiles Coll., 1961-64, assoc. prof., 1964-66; prof. Hunter Coll., CUNY, 1966—77; prof. English Yale U., New Haven, 1977—, A. Bartlett Giamatti prof., 1987—, Sterling prof., 1995—2002, prof. emeritus, 2002. Vis. prof. Linguistic Inst., Inc. U., 1964; faculty Salzburg Seminar in Am. Studies, 1965; Christian Gauss seminarian Princeton U., 1962; Clark lectr. Trinity Coll., Cambridge, Eng., 2000. Author: A Crackling of Thorns, 1958, The Untuning of the Sky, 1961, Movie-Going and Other Poems, 1962, Various Owls, 1963, Visions from the Ramble, 1965, The Quest of the Gole, 1966, Types of Shape, 1968, 2d edit., 1991, Images of Voice, 1970, The Night Mirror, 1971, Town and Country Matters, 1972, The Head of the Bed, 1973, Tales Told of the Fathers, 1975, Vision and Resonance, 1975, Reflections on Espionage, 1976, 2d edit., 1999, Spectral Emanations, 1978, In Place, 1978, Blue Wine, 1979, The Figure of Echo, 1981, Rhyme's Reason, 1981, 2d edit., 1989, 3rd edit., 2000, Powers of Thirteen, 1983, (with Saul Steinberg) Dal Vero, 1983, In Time and Place, 1986, Some Fugitives Take Cover, 1988, Harp Lake, 1988, Melodious Guile, 1988, Tesserae, 1993, Selected Poetry, 1993, The Gazer's Spirit, 1995, The Work of Poetry, 1997, The Poetry of Everyday Life, 1998, Figurehead and Other Poems, 1999, Picture Window, 1993; editor: Poems of Ben Jonson, 1961, (with Harold Bloom) The Wind and the Rain, 1961, (with Anthony Hecht) Jiggery-Pokery, 1966, Poems of Our Moment, 1968, Modern Poetry: Essays in Criticism, 1968, American Short Stories Since 1945, 1968, (with Frank Kermode) The Oxford Anthology of English Literature, 1973, (with Reuben A. Brower and Helen Vendler) For I.A. Richards: Essays in His Honor, 1973, (with Irving Howe and David Bromwich) Literature as Experience, 1979, The Essential Rossetti, 1990, Animal Poems, 1994, Garden Poems, 1996, Committed to Memory, 1997, Marriage Poems, 1997, War Poems, 1999, Sonnets, 2001, (with Joanna Weber) A Gallery of Poems, 2001; contbg. editor: Harper's mag, 1969-71; mem. editorial bd. Raritan, 1981—, Art and Lit., 1985—, Lit., 1989—; assoc. for poetry Partisan Review, 1959-65; mem. poetry bd. Wesleyan U. Press, 1959-62; author numerous poems. Recipient Yale Younger Poets award, 1958, Poetry Chap Book award, 1962, award in lit. Nat. Inst. Arts and Letters, 1963, Levinson prize, 1974, Bollingen prize, 1983, Mina P. Shaughnessy award, 1963, Melville Cane award, 1990, Ambassador Book award, 1994, Gov.'s Arts award State of Conn., 1997, Robert Penn Warren-Cleanth Brooks award, 1998; Overseas fellow Churchill Coll., Cambridge (Eng.) U., 1967-68, sr. fellow NEH, 1973-74, Guggenheim fellow, 1979-80, MacArthur Found. fellow, 1990-95. Mem.: Am. Acad. Arts and Scis., Am. Acad. Arts and Letters (sec. 2000—03), Am. Assn. Lit. Scholars and Writers (pres. 2000—01), Century Assn. (N.Y.C.), Phi Beta Kappa. Office: Yale U Dept English PO Box 208302 New Haven CT 06520-8302 E-mail: john.hollander@yale.edu.

HOLLANDER, LAWRENCE JAY, marketing executive; b. Chgo., Feb. 15, 1940; s. Harry and Ann Blanche Hollander; m. Sallie Sue Mines, June 21, 1964 (div. Aug. 1999); children: Marla, Amy, Rebecca. BSBA, Roosevelt U., 1963. Dir. Far East ops. Indsl. & Sci. Conf. Mgmt., Chgo., 1972-77; dir. mktg. Far East ops. Clapp & Poliak, Inc., N.Y.C., 1978-81; pres. Expoconsul Internat. Inc., Princeton, N.J., 1981-95, El Mktg., Inc., Princeton, 1987-94, Ctr. for Tech. Concepts, Inc., Princeton, 1988-92, Expoconsul Mktg. Group, Inc., Princeton, 1992-94; dir. corp. fin. J.S. Holdings Group, Inc., Bay Head, N.J., 1996; shareholder, investment banker J.S. Securities, Inc., Bayhead, N.J., 1995-96; pres. Entrepreneurial Mgmt. Group, Inc., Princeton, N.J., 1996—. Bd. dirs. Congregation Beth Chaim, West Windsor, N.J., 1984, Jewish Cmty. Ctr., of Delaware Valley, Ewing, N.J., 1987-96, v.p. 1990-92, pres. 1993-94; bd. dirs. Jewish Fedn. Mercer and Buck Counties, N.J., Pa., 1988-95, v.p., 1989-90; mem. planning bd. West Windsor Twp., N.J., 1997—2002. Mem.: Rotary Club of the Princeton Corridor (charter mem. 1986—, sec. 1990—91, sgt.-at-arms 1991—92, bd. dirs. 1992—93, 1996—, sgt.-at-arms 1997—98, v.p. 2001—02, pres.-elect 2002—03, pres. 2003—). Republican. Jewish. Avocations: weight-lifting, walking, tennis. Office: Entrepreneurial Mgmt Grp Inc 4 Thorngate Ct Princeton NJ 08540

HOLLANDER, MICHAEL FREDERIC, communications executive; b. N.Y.C., Dec. 27, 1946; s. Harold Martin and Irma Jeanne (Rabinoff) H.; m. Sandra Gail Horwitz, July 3, 1983; 1 child, Sharon Elizabeth. AA, Solano Coll., 1974. Enlisted USN, 1966, resigned, 1974; instr. engring. Litton Systems, Van Nuys, Calif., 1974-79, prin. engr., 1979-84; dir. product info. William Esty Co., Los Angeles, 1984-87; editor Racing Info. Systems, Redondo Beach, Calif., 1976—; dir. product info. Chiat/Day Advt., Venice, Calif., 1987-95; mgr. info. resources Pacific Comm. Group, 1997—; editor-at-large MotoRacing, 1998—. Author: The Complete Datsun Guide, 1979, The New Mazda Guide, 1983. Recipient Drag Racing All-Star Team Media award, 1995; named one of 10 most influential journalists in motor sport Racer Mag., 1996. Mem. Am. Auto Racing Writers and Broadcasters Assn. (gen. v.p. 1986, western v.p. 1984-86, 97—, STP award 1975), Motor Press Guild, Soc. Automotive Historians, Am. Racing Press Assn., Datsun Owners Clubs Assn. (nat. chmn. 1977-79), Soc. Profl. Journalists, Sigma Delta Chi. Republican. Jewish. Home and Office: 2314 Harriman Ln # A Redondo Beach CA 90278-4426

HOLLANDER, MILTON BERNARD, corporate executive; b. Bayonne, N.J., Nov. 29, 1928; s. Harry and Lena (Hutner) H.; m. Betty Ruth Grodberg, June 8, 1952; children— Eva Lynn, J. Steven, Aaron Phillip, Joel Daniel. BS, Purdue U., 1951; MS, MIT, 1953; PhD, Columbia U., 1959. Dir. engring. ctr. Am. Machine & Foundry Co., Springdale, Conn., 1956-67; v.p. tech. Am.-Standard, Inc., N.Y.C., 1967-72; chmn. bd. Gulf & Western Invention Devel. Corp., N.Y.C., 1974-85; v.p. sci. and tech. Gulf & Western Industries, Inc., N.Y.C., 1972-85; ret., 1985; exec. v.p. Tech. Mgmt. Inc., Stamford, Conn., 1985—; chmn. bd., chief exec. officer Newport Electronics Inc., Stamford, 1989—; pres. Analog & Numeric Devices, Inc., Stamford, 1990—. Cons. electronics lab. Columbia U., 1955-57; dir., tech. cons. Omega Engring. Inc., Stamford, Conn. Author tech. papers temperature measurement, metal cutting, instrumentation; patentee in field. Bd. dirs. Conn. Tech. Inst. Served with C.E. AUS, 1946-48, Korea. Recipient Outstanding Alumnus award Purdue U., 1972, Outstanding Mech. Engring. award, Purdue U., 1991; rsch. fellow MIT 1952-53; duPont rsch. fellow Columbia U., 1955-57; rsch. fellow Am. Soc. Tool and Mfg. Engrs., 1954-55; named Outstanding Young Man Am., 1965. Mem. ASME, Am. Welding Soc., Indsl. Research Inst. (bd. dirs.), Instrument Soc. Am., Soc. Mfg. Engrs., Sigma Xi. Office: Newport Electronics 1 Omega Dr PO Box 4047 Stamford CT 06907-0047

HOLLANDER, RACHELLE D. b. Balt., July 4, 1944; d. Martin and Irene Snyder Diener; m. Charles Hollander, Mar. 2, 1969; children: Kathryn Ariel, Johanna Rose Sood. PhD, U. of Md., 1975. Program dir. U.S. Nat. Sci. Found., Arlington, Va., 1976—. Chair, 4s ad hoc com. on ethics and pub. policy Soc. for Social Studies of Sci., Baton Rouge; chair Sect. X, Am. Assn. for Advancement Sci., Washington, 2001—. Author: (article in sci. and engring. ethics) Social Genomics, 2002, (entry) Internat. Ency. on Social and Behavioral Sci., 2001, (book chpt.) Ethics of Research, 1999; editor (and author): Acceptable Evidence: Science and Values in Risk Management, 1991; editl. bd. Sci. and Engring. Ethics, London, Eng., 1994—. Bd. mem. Waverly Improvement Assn, Balt., 2001—. Mem.: Assn. for Practical and Prof. Ethics, Am. Philos. Assn. Avocations: reading mystery novels, walking, swimming. Office: US Nat Sci Found 4201 Wilson Blvd Rm 995 Arlington VA 22230 Home Fax: 703-292-9068. E-mail: rholland@nsf.gov.

HOLLANDER, ROBERT B., JR., Romance languages educator; b. N.Y.C., July 31, 1933; s. Robert B. and Laurene (McGookey) H.; m. Jean Haberman, Apr. 23, 1964; children: Cornelia Vanness, Robert B. III. AB, Princeton U., 1955; PhD, Columbia U., 1962. Tchr. Latin and English, Collegiate Sch., N.Y.C., 1955-57; instr. English Columbia U., N.Y.C., 1958-62; mem. faculty dept. Romance langs. Princeton (N.J.) U., 1962—, prof. European lit., 1974—, chmn. comparative lit., 1994-98. Mem. Nat. Coun. on Humanities, 1974-80, 87-92, vice chmn., 1978-80; mem. N.J. Com. for Humanities, 1980-86; dir. Dartmouth Dante Project, 1982—, Princeton Dante Project, 1997—; v.p. Assn. Internat. Studi de Lingua et Lett. Italiana, 1985-94; trustee La Scuola d'Italia, N.Y.C., 1986-92, Collegiate Sch., 1990-96, vice pres. bd., 1994-96, pres. bd., 98-2001. Author: Allegory in Dante's Commedia, 1969, Boccaccio's Two Venuses, 1977, Studies in Dante, 1980, Il Virgilio dantesco, 1983, Boccaccio's Last Fiction: Il Corbaccio, 1988, Dante's Epistle to Cangrande, 1993, Boccaccio's Dante and the Shaping Force of Satire, 1997, Dante Alighieri, 2000, Dante, 2001; editor and translator: (with T. Hampton and M. Frankel) Amorosa Visione, 1986; co-editor: L'Esposittione di Bernardino Daniello da Lucca sopra la Comedia di Dante, 1989, (with Jean Hollander) Dante Alighieri, Inferno, 2000, Purgatorio, 2003. Trustee Nat. Humanities Ctr., 1981—, chmn. bd. trustees, 1988-91. Guggenheim fellow, 1970-71; NEH fellow, 1974-75, 82-83; recipient Gold medal of the City of Florence for work on behalf of Dante, 1988, Bronze medal of the City of Tours, 1993, John Witherspoon award in the Humanities, Com. for the Humanities, N.J., 1988, Internat. Nicola Zingarelli prize for Dantean philology and criticism, 1999; named Disting. Alumnus, Collegiate Sch., 2003; hon. citizen Certaldo, Italy, 1997. Mem. Dante Soc. Am. (mem. council 1976-85, pres. 1980-85), Am. Boccaccio Assn. Clubs: Cosmos (Washington). Republican. Office: Princeton U Dept French and Italian E Pyne Princeton NJ 08544-0001

HOLLANDER, SAMUEL, economist, educator; b. London, Apr. 6, 1937; s. Jacob and Rachel-Leah (Bornstein) H.; m. Perlette Kéroub, July 20, 1959; children: Frances, Isaac. BSc in Econs, London Sch. Econs., 1959; MA, Princeton U., 1961, PhD, 1963; LLD, McMaster U., 1999. Asst. in instrn. Princeton U., 1962-63; asst. prof. econs. U. Toronto, Ont., Can., 1963-66, assoc. prof., 1966-70, prof., 1970-84, univ. prof., 1984-98, univ. prof. emeritus, 1998—; rsch. dir. U. Nice (CNRS), France, 1999—2000; prof. Ben Gurion U., Israel, 2000—. Author: The Sources of Increased Efficiency, 1965, The Economics of Adam Smith, 1973, The Economics of David Ricardo, 1979, The Economics of J.S. Mill, 1985, Classical Economics, 1987, Ricardo: The 'New View'-Collected Essays I, 1995, The Economics of Thomas Robert Malthus, 1997, The Literature of Political Economy-Collected Essays II, 1998, John Stuart Mill on Economic Theory and Method-Collected Essays III, 2000. Decorated officer Order of Can.; Guggenheim fellow, 1968-69, Killam sr. fellow, 1973-75, Connaught sr. fellow, 1984-85. Fellow Royal Soc. Can. Jewish. Home: 2 Rehov Sapir 89066 Arad Israel E-mail: sholland@bgumail.bgu.ac.il.

HOLLANDER, SIDNEY, computer systems engineer; b. Boston, Mar. 23, 1949; s. Morris and Edith (Feldman) H.; m. Betty Sandra Groppel, Feb. 24, 1973 (dec.). BSEE, Rensselaer Poly. Inst., 1970, MEE, 1971. Commd. 2d lt. USAF, 1971, project mgr. satellite control facility, 1974-78, resigned, 1978; project engr. The Aerospace Corp., 1978—. Program systems engr. UNISYS Def. Systems, Sunnyvale, 1987-88. Lt. col. USAFR, ret. 1994. Mem. IEEE (sr. mem., chmn. Santa Clara Valley sect. 1989-90), Silicon Valley Engring. Coun. (bd. dirs. 1989-91, K-12 outreach chmn. 1990-91), San Francisco Bay Wildlife Soc. (bd. dirs. 1990-2000, pres. 1995-2000). Democrat. Unitarian-Universalist. Office: Aerospace Corp 2350 E El Segundo Blvd El Segundo CA 90245-4691 Home: PO Box 4034 Redondo Beach CA 90277-1737

HOLLANDER, TOBY EDWARD, education educator; b. Queens, N.Y., June 21, 1931; s. David and Eve (Shroot) H.; m. Harriet Goldberg, June 14, 1953; children: Marc, Deborah. BS cum laude, NYU, 1952, MBA, 1953; PhD, U. Pitts., 1960. Instr. econs. U. Pitts., 1957-58; asst. prof. Duquesne U., 1958-59; prof. Baruch Coll., CUNY, 1963-67, dean, 1967-69, vice chancellor, 1969-71; dep. commr. higher edn. N.Y. State Edn. Dept., 1971-77; chancellor N.J. Dept. Higher Edn., Trenton, 1977-90; prof. Rutgers U., 1990—. Author books in field; contbr. articles to profl. jours. Served with U.S. Army, 1953-55. Mem. State Higher Edn. Exec. Officers Assn. (pres. 1977-78). Home: 889 Lawrenceville Rd Princeton NJ 08540-4317 Office: Rutgers U Sch Bus 180 University Ave Newark NJ 07102-1818 E-mail: hollande@infionline.net.

HOLLANS, IRBY NOAH, JR., retired association executive; b. Christiansburg, Va., Nov. 3, 1930; s. Irby Noah and Annie May (Lester) H.; m. Frances Jo Cox, June 21, 1957; children: Susan Frances, Carol Leigh, Irby Neil. BS in Gen. Bus. Adminstrn., Va. Poly. Inst. and State U., 1953. Mgr. promotion Sta. WRVA-Radio, Richmond, Va., 1956-64, editor bus. news, 1956-64; dir. travel devel. Va. State C. of C., 1964-70, asst. exec. dir., 1970-72; exec. dir. Optical Labs. Assn., Washington, 1972-96. Instr. bus. Va. Commonwealth U., Richmond, 1965-71 Mem. Dulles (Va.) Internat. Airport Devel. Commn., 1968-76; mem. Va. Nat. Capital Airports Acquisition Study Commn., 1968-76; bd. dirs. Va. Thanksgiving Festival Inc., 1965-70, Keep Va. Beautiful, Inc., 1965-73, Central Va. Ednl. TV, 1970-72, Va. Travel Coordinating Com., 1964-72. Served to maj. USAF, 1953-72, Korea. Recipient Service award Va. Profl. Photographers Assn., 1966; Nat. award Profl. Photographers Assn. Am., 1970 Mem. Am. Soc. Assn. Execs. (cert.), Va. Pub. Rels. Conf., Nat. Assn. Wholesaler-Distbrs.-Pros Group, Am. Nat. Stds. Inst. (med. devices stds. mgmt. bd. 1973-80), Washington Soc. Assn. Execs., Va. C. of C., Vienna (Va.) Photog. Soc. (pres. 1990-92), Greater Washington Coun. Camera Clubs (exec. v.p. 1988-93), Rotary Internat. (exec. dir. 1996—). Home and Office: 5339 Cristfield Ct Fairfax VA 22032-3809 E-mail: ihollans@earthlink.net.

HÖLLDOBLER, BERTHOLD KARL, zoologist, educator; b. Erling-Andechs, Germany, June 25, 1936; came to U.S., 1973; s. Karl and Maria (Russmann) H.; m. Friederike Probst, Feb. 9, 1980; children: Jakob, Stefan, Sebastian. Dr. rer. nat., U. Wurzburg, 1965; Dr. habil., U. Frankfurt a.M., 1969; D (hon.), U. Konstanz, 2000. Prof. zoology U. Frankfurt a.M., 1971-72; prof. biology Harvard U., Cambridge, Mass., 1973-90, Alexander Agassiz prof. zoology, 1982-90; prof. U. Wurzburg, Germany, 1989—. Adj. prof. U. Ariz., Tucson; rsch. assoc. Harvard U.; Andrew D. White prof. at large Cornell U., 2002—. Author: (with Edward O. Wilson) The Ants, 1990 (Pulitzer Prize for gen. non-fiction 1991), (with E.O. Wilson) Journey to the Arts, (Shortlisted for the Rhone-Poulenc Sci. Book prize, 1995, Phi Beta Kappa prize, 1995). John Simon Guggenheim fellow, 1980; recipient Sr. Scientist award Alexander von Humboldt Found., 1986-87, Gottfried Wilhelm Leibniz prize, 1989, Phi Beta Kappa prize (with E.O. Wilson) 1995, Karl Ritter von Frisch medal and Sci. prize, German Zool. Soc., 1996, Körber-prize for European Sci., 1996, Benjamin Franklin, Wilhelm v. Humboldt Prize of the German Amer. Acad. Coun. (GAAC), 1999, Werner Heisenberg medal Alexander v. Humboldt Found. Fellow AAAS, Am. Animal Behavior Soc.; mem. Nat. Acad. of Sci. (fgn. mem.), Am. Acad. Sci., German Acad. der Naturforscher Leopoldina, Bayerische Acad. der Wissenschaften, Acad. Europaea, Berlin-Brandenburgische Acad., Am. Philos. Soc. (fgn. mem.), Bundesverdienstkrenz (Nat. Merit medal Germany 2000). Office: Biozentrum Am Hubland D-97074 Würzburg Germany

HOLLE, REGINALD HENRY, retired bishop; b. Burton, Tex., Nov. 21, 1925; s. Alfred W. and Lena (Nolte) H.; m. Marla C. Christianson, June 16, 1949; children: Todd, Joan. BA, Capital U., 1946, DD (hon.), 1979; MDiv, Trinity Luth. Sem., 1949; D of Ministry, Ohio Consortium Religious Stdy, 1977; DD (hon.), Wittenberg U., 1989. Ordained minister Evang. Luth. Ch. Am., then bishop. Assoc. pastor Zion Luth. Ch., Sandusky, Ohio, 1949-51; sr. pastor Salem Meml. Luth. Ch., Detroit, 1951-72, Parma Luth. Ch., Cleve., 1973-78; bishop Mich. dist. Am. Luth. Ch., Detroit, 1978-87; bishop NW Lower Mich. Synod Evang. Luth. Ch., Lansing, 1988-95. Bd. dirs. Augsburg Fortress Pub. House, Wittenberg U. Author: Planning for Funerals, 1978; contbr. to Augsburg Sermon Series. Bd. dirs. Ronald McDonald House Ctrl. Mich., 1995—, Planned Giving Luth. Social Svcs. Mich., 1995—. Recipient Pub. Svc. citation Harper Woods City Coun., 1976, Recognition for Community Svc., Detroit Pub. Schs., 1974.

HOLLEB, DORIS B. urban planner, economist; b. N.Y.C., Oct. 26, 1922; m. Marshall M. Holleb, Oct. 15, 1944; children: Alan, Gordon, Paul. BA magna cum laude, Hunter Coll., 1942; MA, Harvard U., 1947; postgrad., U. Chgo., 1959-60, 65-66. Economist Fed. Res. Bd., Washington, 1943—44; freelance journalist, 1945-63; econs. cons. Chgo. Dept. City Planning, 1963-64; rsch. assoc. Ctr. Urban Studies U. Chgo., 1966-78, sr. rsch. assoc., 1978-88; dir. Met. Inst., 1973-84, professorial lectr., 1979—. Chmn., Francis W. Parker Sch. Ednl.

Coun., 1963-80; cons., 1980-92; bd. dirs. Adlai E. Stevenson Inst., 1972-79; mem. adv. coun. Ctr. for the Study Democratic Inst., 1975-79; bd. dirs. Inter. Am. Found., 1979-84, Pacific Basin Inst., 1981-98; mem. nat. adv. com. White House Conf. on Balanced Nat. Growth and Econ. Devel., 1978; mem. Northea. Ill. Planning Commn., 1973-77; mem. Chgo. Met. Area Transp. Coun., 1980-84; mem. adv. coun. to Nat. Ctr. Rsch. on Vocat. Edn., Dept. Edn., 1979-82, Dept. State adv. com. internat. investment, tech. and devel., 1979-81; commr. Chgo. Plan Commn., 1986—; bd. dirs. Internat. Ctr. for Rsch. on Women, 1985-91, Nat. Coun. on Humanities, 1998-2003. Author: Social and Economic Information for Urban Planning, 1968, Colleges and the Urban Poor, 1972; contbr. articles to profl. jours.; v.p. editl. bd. Ill. Issues, 1977-2001. Fellow: Phi Beta Kappa Soc. (bd. dirs.).

HOLLEB, MARSHALL MAYNARD, lawyer; b. Chgo., Dec. 25, 1916; s. A. Paul and Sara (Zaretsky) H.; m. Doris Bernstein, Oct. 15, 1944; children: Alan R., Gordon P., Paul D. BA, U. Wis., 1937; MBA, Harvard U., 1939; IA, 1941, JD, 1942. Bar: Ill. 1947, U.S. Supreme Ct. 1960. Assoc. Levenson, Becker & Peebles, Chgo., 1947-51; ptnr. Yates & Holleb, Chgo., 1952-59, Holleb, Gerstein & Glass, Chgo., 1960-81; sr. ptnr. Holleb & Coff, Chgo., 1982-2000; sr. counsel Wildman, Harrold, Allen & Dixon, 2000—. Chmn. bd. dirs. Urban Assocs. Chgo., Inc. Contbr. articles to profl. jours.; profiled on PBS-TV program Chicago Stories, 2001. Trustee Acorn Fund, 1971-95; life trustee Hull House Assn., pres., 1980-82; trustee emeritus nat. Bldg. Mus., Chgo. Inst. Psychoanalysis; overseer Harvard Bus. Sch. Club Chgo.; founder, life trustee, gen. legal counsel Mus. Contemporary Art Chgo.; mem. adv. bd. Landmarks Preservation Coun., Fair Housing Ctr. Home Investments Fund, Citizens Sch. Com.; mem. vis. coms. Oriental Inst. and Visual Arts U. Chgo.; bd. dirs. Intenat. Visitors Ctr., Mostly Music, Inc., Chgo. Fund. on Aging and Disability; mem. Ill. Internat. Trade and Port Promotion Adv. Com., 1982, Chgo.'s Future Project Com. of Trust, Inc., 1982, Pacific Basing Inst.; mem. nat. adv. bd. on internat. edn. programs U.S. Dept. Edn., 1981, City Chgo. Local Cultural Devel. Commn.; pres. Chgo. Theater Preservation Group Ltd., sec., bd. dirs. Arts Club Chgo.; bd. dirs. Chgo. Maritime Soc.; me. industry sector adv. com. on svcs. for trade policy matters U.S. Dept. Commerce, 1995-98; mem. nat. adv. com. and del. White House Conf. on Aging, 1971, 81; mem. Ill. Coun. Aging, 1961-81, chmn., 1973-81; panel mem. Ill. Statewide Comprehensive Outdoor Recreation Plan; mem. weatherization adv. com. Ill. Dept. Bus. and Econ. Devel., 1975—; mem. Ill. appeal bd. SSS, 1966-73; cons. Vt. rsch. project HUD. 1st lt. U.S. Army, Philippines and Japan, 1943-46. Recipient Humanitarian of Yr. Henry Booth House award Hull House Assn., 1979; Am. Heritage award Am. Jewish Com., 1986, Arts award Mostly Music Inc., 1986, City Brightener award Bright New City Chgo., 1987. Mem. ABA, Ill. Bar Assn., Chgo. Bar Assn., Fed. Bar Assn., Am. Soc. Internat. Law, Am. Arbitration Assn. (nat. panel), Am. Inst. Planners, Nat. Assn. Housign and Redevel. Ofcls., Urban Land Inst., Harvard Law Soc. Ill. (bd. dirs.), Arts Club, Univ. Club, Bryn Mawr Country Club, Execs. Club (Chgo.), Lambda Alpha. Democrat. Office: 225 W Wacker Dr Ste 3000 Chicago IL 60606-1229

HOLLEMAN, JOHN L. priest; b. Mobile, Ala., Sept. 15, 1940; s. Joseph Eugene and Audrey Gunn Holleman. BS in Math., Tulane U., 1962, MA in Philosophy, 1971; MDiv, Gen. Theol. Sem., N.Y.C., 1968; BLitt in Theology, Christ Ch. Coll., Oxford, Eng., 1974; STL in Theology, Gregorian U., Rome, 1982. Ordained Episc. Ch., 1969, Roman Cath. Ch., 1981. With various parishes Episcopal Ch. USA, 1968—78; tchr. math. and chemistry St. Ignatius Coll. Prep., Chgo., 1978—80; with various parishes Archdiocese of New Orleans, 1982—86, 1988—92; with Immaculate Conception Ch/Chgo. Archdiocese, 1986—88; prodn. mgr., pres. Hospitality TV Network, New Orleans, 1995—2000; with Christ the King Ch. Archdiocese of Mobile, Andalusia, Ala., 2000—. Lt j.g. USN, 1962—64. Mem.: Rotary.

HOLLEMAN, SANDY LEE, religious organization administrator; d. Guy Lee and Gustine (Kirby-Sheets) Luna; m. Allen Craig Holleman. Cert., Eastfield Coll., 1979. With Annuity Bd. So. Bapt. Conv., Dallas, 1958—, mgr. personnel, 1983-85, dir. human resources, 1985-91, v.p. human resources, 1991-99; ret., 1999—. Mem.: Soc. Human Resource Mgmt., Dallas Soc. Human Resource Mgmt., Am. Mgmt. Soc. (dir. salary surveys local chpt. 1986—, v.p. chpt. svcs. 1987—), Am. Mus. Miniature Arts, Book End Rev. Club, Daus of Nile, Order of Ea. Star, Diversity Club Dallas (program chmn. 1976, v.p. 1977). Baptist. Avocations: needlepoint, genealogy, decorating, doll collecting.

HOLLEMAN, VERNON DAUGHTY, physician, internist; b. Brownwood, Tex., Oct. 1, 1931; s. Vernon Edgar and Olene Nollie (Reece) H.; m. Shirley Eyvonne Roberts, April 26, 1961; children: Richard, Joel, Douglas. BA in Chemistry and Biology, Howard Payne Coll., Brownwood, 1953; MD, Baylor U., 1958. Mem. med. staff Santa Fe Meml. Hosp, 1962-83; pres. med. staff Santa Fe Meml. Hosp., 1979-83; mem. med. staff Scott and White Hosp., 1962—; asst. chief physician Santa Fe Employees Hosp. Assn., 1962-85, med. dir., 1985—; intern Scott and White Clinic and Hosp., Temple, Tex., 1958-59, resident in internal medicine, 1959-62; dir. div. gen. internal medicine Santa Fe Ctr., Temple, Tex., 1985—; assoc. prof. internal medicine Tex. A&M Coll. Medicine, Temple, 1982—. Adj. faculty clinician Ohio Coll. of Podiatric Medicine, Cleveland, 1982-86; med. dir. Consol. Assns. Railroad Employees, 1997—. Illustrator: Aesculapian, 1957, So. Bapt. Student Union Projects, 1954-58; illustrator ltd. edit. lithographs Baylor U. Lettermans Assn., 1994; contbr. photography to books, including Colorados Biggest Bucks and Bulls, Boone and Crocket Books, Awesome Antlers, Records of North American Mule Deer; author: articles on health, preventive medicine, and numerous others. Bd. dirs Santa Fe Meml. Found.; hon. chmn. physicians adv. bd. Tex. Nat. Rep. Congl. Com. Art Instrn., Inc. scholar, 1952; recipient Centennial award Santa Fe Meml. Found., 1991. Mem. AAAS, Nat. Assn. Ret. and Vet. Railway Employees (hon. life), AMA, ACP, Am. Coll. Phys. Execs., Am. Soc. Internal Medicine, Tex. Med. Assn. (Vernon D. Holleman-Lewis M. Rampy Scott and White Centennial chair gerontology 1999), Tex. Med. Found., Am. Heart Assn. (cardiopulmonary coun.), Am. Assn. Ry. Physicians, World Med. Assn., Tex. Diabetes and Endocrine Soc., N.Y. Acad. Scis., So. Med. Assn. (life), Am. Coll. Occupl. Medicine, Am. Pain Soc., Am. Acad. Pain Mgmt. (diplomate), Internat. Soc. Phys. Activity in Prevention of Osteoporosis (charter), Boone and Crockett Club, Tex. Taxidermy Assn., Nat. Safari Club (life), Alpha Chi, Phi Chi. Baptist. Avocations: medical history, art, hunting, photography, conservation. Office: Scott and White Clinic 600 S 25th St Temple TX 76504-5227

HOLLENBAUGH, H(ENRY) RITCHEY, lawyer; b. Shelby, Ohio, Nov. 12, 1947; m. Diane Robinson Nov. 21, 1973 (div. 1989); children: Chad Ritchey, Katie Paige; m. Rebecca U., Aug. 8, 1995. BA, Kent State U., 1969; JD, Capital U., 1973. Bar: Ohio 1973, U.S. Dist. Ct. (so. dist.) Ohio 1974, U.S. Ct. Appeals (6th cir.) 1976, U.S. Supreme Ct. 1978. Investigator Ohio Civil Rights Com., Columbus, Ohio, 1969-72; legal intern City Atty.'s Office, Columbus, Ohio, 1972-73, asst. city prosecutor, 1973-75, sr. asst. city atty., 1975-76; ptnr. Hunter, Hollenbaugh & Theodotou, Columbus, Ohio, 1976-85, Delligatti, Hollenbaugh, Briscoe & Milless, Columbus, Ohio, 1985-91, Climaco Seminatore Delligatti & Hollenbaugh, Columbus, 1991-93, Delligatti, Hollenbaugh & Briscoe, Columbus, 1993-95, Draper, Hollenbaugh, Briscoe, Yashko & Carmany, 1996-99, Carlile Patchen & Murphy, Columbus, 1999—. Mem. Ohio Pub. Defender Commn., 1988-94; chmn. Franklin County Pub. Defender Commn., 1986-92. Treas. The Gov's. Com., 1987-96, Friends With Celeste, Friends of Gov's. Residence, 1987 92, Participation 2000, 1987-91, Ohio Legal Assistance Found., 1998—. Fellow ABA Found. (chair commn. on advt. 1993-97, ho. of dels. 1993—, chair nat. conf. lawyers and reps. of media 2000—); mem. Ohio State Bar Assn. (bd. govs. 1989-94, pres. 1992-93), Columbus Bar Assn. (pres. 1987-88), Nat. Conf. Bar Pres., Nat. Assn. Criminal Def. Lawyers, Capital Club. Democrat. Methodist. Avocations: golf, politics. Home: 8549 Glenalmond Ct Dublin OH 43017-9737 Office: Carlile Patchen & Murphy 336 E Broad St Columbus OH 43215-3202 E-mail: HRH@CPMLAW.com.

HOLLENBECK, DOROTHY ROSE, principal; b. Yakima, Wash., May 8, 1941; d. George Milford and Blance Mary (McCarthy) Hollenbeck; m. Thomas M. Chambers, Aug. 14, 1971; adopted children: David Chambers, Monique Chambers, Christopher Chambers, George Chambers, Elizabeth Chambers. BS in Speech and Lang. Therapy, Marquette U., 1964; MA in Spl. Edn., San Francisco State U., 1969; cert. instr. develop. therapy, U. Ga., 1982. Speech pathologist Mpls. Pub. Schs., 1964-65, Milbrae (Calif.) Sch. Dist., 1964-65; reading specialist Dept. of Def., Landstuhl, Germany, 1970-71; tchr. children with extreme learning problems Portland (Oreg.) Pub. Schs., 1971-80, dept. chmn. spl. edn., 1980-84, program specialist program devel., 1984-86, diagnostic specialist assessment program spl. edn., 1986-94; speech and lang. pathologist, spl. edn. tchr. Chinacum (Wash.) Sch. Dist., 1995-2000, prin., 2000—. Instr. Portland State U., 1982, 83. Author: (book) PEACHES (Pre-School Educational Adaptation for Children Who are Handicapped), 1978. Dept. Rehab. fellow, HEW, 1969. Mem.: NEA, Nat. Coun. Exceptional Children (presenter nat. conv. 1984), Oreg. Edn. Assn., Am. Speech and Hearing Assn. (cert. in clin. competence), Costeau Soc., Common Cause. Democrat. Roman Catholic. Home: 505 Garfield St Port Townsend WA 98368-4405 Office: Chinacum Pub Schs PO Box 278 Chimacum WA 98325-0278 Personal E-mail: dhollenbeck@cablespeed.com.

HOLLENBECK, KAREN FERN, foundation consultant; b. Snover, Mich., Mar. 30, 1943; d. Glenn Lee and Ada Gertrude (Robinson) Roberts; m. Marvin Allan Hollenbeck, June 18, 1966. AA, Kellogg Community Coll., 1980; BSBA, Nazareth Coll., 1987. Dir. fellowships W.K. Kellogg Found., Battle Creek, Mich., 1979-85, asst. v.p. adminstrn., 1985-88, v.p. adminstrn., 1988—98; cons., 1999—. Bd. dirs. Cutting Edge Designs, Denver, 1993-96. Editor: Marco Messenger, 1999—. Bd. dirs. Arc Ministries, Allegan, Mich., 1982—, Vol. Bur., Battle Creek, 1984-86, ARC, Calhoun County, Mich., 1985-96, Emerging Young Leaders, 1996 2000; pres. com. Marco Presbyn. Ch., 2002—; trustee Ind. Wesleyan U., 2001—. Recipient Outstanding Young Women of Am. award. Mem. NAFE, Am. Mgmt. Assn., Soc. Human Resources Mgmt. Avocations: knitting, music, drama activities. Home and Office: 741 S Collier Blvd Apt 312 Marco Island FL 34145-6007

HOLLENBERG, HARVARD, lawyer, writer; b. NYC, Dec. 14, 1938; s. William Gustave and Harriet Grace (Renault) Von Höllenberg. BA, NYU, 1960; MA in Polit. Sci., Victoria U., Wellington, New Zealand, 1962; JD, Harvard U., 1965. Bar: N.Y. 1967, U.S. Dist. Ct. (so. and ea. dists.) N.Y. 1993. Sr. atty. Supreme Ct. Mental Hygiene Legal Svc., N.Y.C., 1965-70; chief counsel, staff dir. N.Y. State Commn. to Evaluate the Drug Laws, N.Y.C., Albany, N.Y., 1970-76; asst. state atty. gen. litigation N.Y. State Dept. Law, N.Y.C., 1976-78; spl. counsel to speaker N.Y. State Assembly, N.Y.C., Albany, 1978-83; dep. pub. advocate N.J. Dept. Pub. Advocate, 1983-85; gen. counsel N.Y.C. Dept. Mental Hygiene, 1985-88; pvt. practice NYC, 1988—. Author: Employing the Rehabilitated Addict, 1972, Drug Abuse Prevention, 1973, How People Overseas Deal with Drugs, 1974, A Law of Vengeance, 1993, The Vinyard Diamonds, 1994; contbr. frequent articles to Nat. Law Jour., N.Y. Times, Atlanta Constn., St. Louis Post-Dispatch, Phila. Inquirer, Chgo. Tribune, Manchester (N.H.) Union Leader; regular monthly food and travel columnist World's Fare in Newsday. Vol., Met. Opera Guild, N.Y.C. Fulbright scholar Inst. for Internat. Edn., New Zealand, 1960-62, Felix Frankfurter scholar Harvard Law Sch., 1962-65. Mem. N.Y. State Bar Assn., Assn. of Bar of City of N.Y., N.Y. County Bar Assn., Phi Beta Kappa. Democrat. Jewish.

HOLLENBERG, PAUL FREDERICK, pharmacology educator; b. Phila., Sept. 18, 1942; s. Frederick Henry and Catherine (Dentzer) H.; m. Emily Elizabeth Vanootighem, May 6, 1967; children: Kathryn Mary, David Paul. BS in Chemistry, Wittenberg U., 1964; MS in Biochemistry, U. Mich., 1966, PhD in Biochemistry, 1969. Postdoctoral fellow U. Mich., Ann Arbor, 1969, U. Ill., Urbana, 1969-72; asst. prof. Northwestern U., Chgo., 1972-81, assoc. prof., 1981-84, prof. pathology and molecular biology, 1984-87; prof. pharmacology, chmn. dept. Wayne State U. Sch. Medicine, Detroit, 1987-94, U. Mich. Med. Sch., Ann Arbor, 1994—. Mem. pharmacology test com. Nat. Bd. Med. Examiners; mem. Chem. Pathology Study Sect. NIH, 1987-91. Co-founder, assoc. editor Chem. Rsch. in Toxicology, 1988—; assoc. editor Jour. Pharmacology and Exptl. Therapeutics; mem. editl. bd. Drug Metabolism and Disposition, British Jour. Pharmacology. Schweppe Found. research fellow, 1974-77; NIH research grantee, 1974—. Mem. Am. Chem. Soc., Am. Soc. Biochemists and Molecular Biologists, Am. Soc. Pharmacology and Exptl. Therapeutics (sec./treas. 1998-99, pres.-elect 2001-02, pres. 2002-)), Am. Assn. for Cancer Rsch., Soc. Toxicology, Internat. Soc. for Study of Xenobiotics. Avocations: reading, running, golf. Home: 1968 Woodlily Ct Ann Arbor MI 48103-9728 Office: Univ Mich 2301 MSRB III Sch Medicine 1150 W Medical Center Dr Ann Arbor MI 48109-0632 E-mail: phollen@umich.edu.

HOLLENDER, LARS GÖSTA, dental educator; b. Veinge, Sweden, Oct. 22, 1933; arrived in U.S., 1984; s. Gunnar Yngve and Astrid Margareta (Andersson) H.; m. Gunnel Charlotta Bergdahl, May 19, 1956 (div. 1975); children: Peter, Marie, Lena, Stefan; m. Sheridan Ellen Houston, Apr. 8, 1989; 1 child, Ashley Ellen. DDS, Sch. Dentistry, Malmö, Sweden, 1958, PhD, 1964. Diplomate Am. Bd. Oral and Maxillofacial Radiology. Assoc. prof. Sch. Dentistry, Malmö, 1964-68, prof., chair Göteborg, Sweden, 1969-87; prof., dir. U. Wash. Sch. Dentistry, Seattle, 1988—. Sec. gen. Internat. Assn. Dentomaxillofacial Radiology, 1974-85; vis. prof. UCLA Sch. Dentistry, 1980-82, U. Wash. Sch. Dentistry, 1984-87; sec./treas. Am. Bd. Oral and Maxillofacial Radiology, 1992-94, pres., 1995, councillor, 1996—. Editor-in-chief Odontologist Revy, 1964-69; contbr. over 100 chpts. to books and articles to profl. jours. Recipient Rsch. prize South Swedish Dental Soc., 1964, Rsch. prize Swedish Dental Assn., 1965, Elander Rsch. prize Gothenburg Dental Soc., 1976. Fellow Am. Acad. Oral and Maxillofacial Radiology (pres. 1997-98); mem. ADA (mem. review com. for OMFR commn. on dental accreditation 1999—), Internat. Assn. Dental and Maxillofacial Radiology (hon.), Australian Maxillofacial Radiology Soc. (hon.), Wash. State Dental Assn., King County Dental Assn. Avocations: reading, golf, cooking, travel, music. Office: Univ Wash Sch Dentistry PO Box 356370 Seattle WA 98195-6370 E-mail: larsholl@u.washington.edu.

HOLLENSHEAD, ROBERT EARL, retired judge; b. St. Louis, July 24, 1940; s. Earl Finley and Marguerite Louise (Milburn) H.; m. Lily Gee, Apr. 24, 1999; children by previous marriage: Cynthia Estelle, David Hugh. BA, U. Mich., 1963, JD, 1966. Bar: Mich. 1967, U.S. Dist. Ct. (ea. dist.) Mich. 1967, U.S. Dist. Ct. (ea. dist.) Mich. 1972. Law clk., assoc. Langs, Molyneau & Armstrong, Detroit, 1966-67; assoc. firm Strommel Sharp Walsh O'Sullivan Beauchamp & Edson, Port Huron, Mich., 1971-72; adminstrv. law judge Mich. Pub. Svc. Commn., Lansing, 1972-99; hearing officer Mich. Office Retirement Svcs., 2003—. Adj. prof. Cooley Law Sch., Lansing, 1977; faculty advisor Nat. Jud. Coll., 1982, 90. Mem. Mich. Utility Consumer Participation Bd., 2000-03. Capt. JAGC, U.S. Army, 1967-71. Mem. State Bar Mich. (coun. adminstrv. law sect. 1976-84, pub. utility law com., adminstrv. law judges com.), Mich. Assn. Adminstrv. Law Judges (v.p. 1975-76, pres.-elect 1991, pres. 1992-93), Nat. Assn. Regulatory Utility Commrs. (staff subcom. on adminstrv. law judges 1984-89), Phi Alpha Delta. Home: 6068 Columbia St Haslett MI 48840-8224

HOLLER, ADLAI CORNWELL, JR., minister; b. Orangeburg, S.C., Mar. 21, 1925; s. Adlai Cornwell and Miriam (Fair) H.; m. Elizabeth Cobb, June 4, 1949; children: Suzanne Elizabeth, Adlai Stephen, Stephanie Elwood. AB, Wofford Coll., 1947; MDiv, Duke U., 1952; D of Ministry, Columbia Sem., 1987. Lic. marriage and family therapist, profl. counselor; nat. bd. cert. counselor. Mil. pilot USAAF, 1943-46; chaplain USAF, various cities, 1952-82; minister of counseling Bethany United Meth. Ch., Summerville, S.C., 1982-87; pres. Pyramid Counseling Svcs., Inc., Summerville, S.C., 1992—. Bd. dirs. Medicine and Ministry Conf., Kanuga, N.C., 1983-92; dir. Charleston (S.C.) Dist. Pastoral Counseling Ctr., 1987—; mem. Bd. Ordained Ministry, Columbia, 1980-88. Author: Ministry to Flying Students, 1957, Training Laity for Counseling, 1987. Mem. ACA, Am. Assn. for Marriage and Family Therapy (clin. mem., approved supervisor), Daedalians, DAV, Rotary. Methodist. Avocations: antique automobiles, travel. Home: 112 Old Dominion Dr Charleston SC 29418-3012 Office: Pyramid Counseling Svcs Inc 204 Trestlewood Dr Summerville SC 29483-1824

HOLLER, MANFRED JOSEPH, economics educator; b. Munich, July 25, 1946; s. Joseph and Rosalie Holler; m. Barbara Klose Ullman, Nov. 18, 1995; 1 child, Michael. Diploma, U. Munich, 1971, PhD, 1975, Dr. rer. pol. habil., 1983. Asst. prof. U. Munich, 1974-85; assoc. prof. U. Aarhus, Denmark, 1986-91; prof. econs. U. Hamburg, Germany, 1991—. Founding editor: European Jour. of Polit. Economy, Homo Oeconomicus; editor volumes for sci. jours. Mem. Internat. Acad. Sci. (dir. edn.), European Acad. Standardization (pres.), Gesellschaft Integrierte Studien (bd. dirs.). Office: Inst Econs U Hamburg Von-Melle-Park 5 20146 Hamburg Germany E-mail: holler@econ.uni-hamburg.de.

HOLLERBACH, PAULA ELIZABETH, demographer, researcher; b. Elizabeth, NJ, Jan. 14, 1945; d. George Henry and Norma (Pierron) Hollerbach; 1 child, Erik Glen Hass. BA in Sociology cum laude, Cornell U., 1966; MA in Sociology, Duke U., 1968, PhD in Sociology, 1971; postgrad., Columbia U., 1991. Lectr. sociology Duke U., Durham, N.C., 1970-71; asst. prof. sociology Queens Coll. CUNY, Flushing, 1971-76, assoc. prof. sociology, 1976-78; assoc. The Population Coun., N.Y.C., 1978-90; adj. prof. sociology Hunter Coll. CUNY, N.Y.C., 1991; rsch. officer Family Health Internat., Arlington, Va., 1992-95; sr. rsch. and evaluation officer Acad. for Ednl. Devel., Washington, 1995—. Evaluation advisor Catalyst Consortium, 2001—; sr. assoc. cons. Sociomed. Resource Assocs., Westport, Conn., 1995. Author: (with S. Diaz-Briquets) Fertility Determinants in Cuba, 1983. Grantee Ford Found., N.Y.C., 1987, Nat. Inst. Child Health and Human Devel., Washington, 1984-85, Rockefeller Found., N.Y.C., 1984-85; fellow NIH Tng. Grant, Duke U., Durham, 1966-69. Mem. Population Assn. Am. (bd. dirs. 1988-90). Democrat. Avocation: reading. Office: Acad for Ednl Devel 1825 Connecticut Ave NW Washington DC 20009-5708 Fax: 202-884-8879. E-mail: Phollerb@aed.org.

HOLLERMAN, CHARLES EDWARD, retired pediatrician; b. Turtle Creek, Pa., Apr. 22, 1929; s. Harry R. and Lena F. H.; m. Catharine, Aug. 22, 1953; children: James, Karen, Jeffrey, Pamela. BS in Chemistry, Allegheny Coll., 1951; MD, Cornell U., 1955; student, U.S. Navy Sch. Aviation Medicine, 1957. Lic. pediatrician Pa. Intern York County (Pa.) Hosp., 1955-56; pvt. practice Cochranton, Pa., 1959-60; resident in pediat. Children's Hosp., Buffalo, 1960—62; fellow in clin. nephrology SUNY, 1962-65, instr. pediatrics, 1965-66; from asst. prof. to prof. pediat. Georgetown U., 1966—75; prof. pediat. U. S.D., Vermillion, 1976—82, asst. dean clin. services; acting dean, exec. dean U. S.D. Sch. Medicine, 1977-79, dean, 1979-82, v.p. health affairs, 1979-82; chmn. dept. pediatrics Mercy Hosp., Pitts., 1982-86, v.p. med. affairs, 1985-92; chief divsn. Pediat. Nephrology Mercy Childrens Med. Ctr., Pitts., 2000—; v.p. med. affairs St. Joseph's Mercy Hosps., Clinton Twp., Mich., 1992-95; regional v.p. physician and clin. integration Mercy Health Ptnrs. Southwest Ohio, Cin., 1995-99. Author: Pediatric Nephrology-Medical Outline Series, 1979; contbr. in field. Served with USN, 1956-59. Fellow Am. Coll. Physician Execs. (cert. physician exec.); mem. AMA, Am. Acad. Pediats., Phi Beta Kappa (cert. pediatrician, pediat. nephrologist, med. mgr.). Home: 4550 Nature Trail Dr Allison Park PA 15101-1131

HOLLEY, CYRUS HELMER, management consulting service executive; b. Chgo., June 14, 1936; s. Cyrus Howell and Elizabeth Fay (Helmer) H.; m. Shirley Marquitta Cannon, Aug. 31, 1957; children— Barrett Cannon, Russell William BS in Chem. Engring., Tex. A&M U., 1957; LLD (hon.), Bloomfield (N.J.) Coll., 1998. Registered profl. engr. Vice pres. indsl. chems. BASF Wyandotte Corp., Parsippany, N.J., 1976-79; sr. v.p. minerals & chem. div. Engelhard Corp., Edison, N.J., 1979-81, v.p., exec. v.p., 1981-83, v.p., pres., chief operating officer metals div., 1983-84, sr. v.p., pres. chem. div., 1984-85, exec. v.p., chief operating officer, 1985-91; pres. Mgmt. Cons. Svcs., 1991—. CEO Oakmont Enterprises, Inc., 1993—; bd. dirs. Kerns Oil & Gas. Contbr. articles to profl. jours. Trustee Bloomfield (N.J.) Coll., 1988-97, trustee emeritus, 1997—; dir. Nat. Assn. Ptnrs. in Edn., 1990-95, 99-02, Tex. Assn. Ptnrs. in Edn., 1991-99, 2001-03, N.J. Assn. Ptnrs. in Edn., 1991-99, Tex. Bus. & Edn. Coalition, 1992-96; chair Ind. Coll. Fund. N.J., 1990-92; bd. dirs. Tex. Ind. Coll. Fund, 1998-2001. Mem. AIChE. Republican. Presbyterian. Avocations: reading; golf; music. Office: Mgmt Cons Svcs 120 Oakmont Dr Trophy Club TX 76262

HOLLEY, IRVING BRINTON, JR., historian, educator; b. Hartford, Conn., Feb. 8, 1919; s. Irving B. and Mary L. (Sharp) H.; m. Janet Carlson, Oct. 9, 1945; children: Janet Turner Holley Wegner, Jean Carlson Holley Schmidt, Susan Sharp Holley. BA cum laude, Amherst Coll., 1940; MA (Brooker scholar), Yale U., 1942, PhD, 1947; student, Oxford U., summer, 1937. Instr. dept. history Duke U., Durham, N.C., 1947-51, asst. prof., 1952-54, asso. prof., 1955-61, prof., 1962-89, prof. emeritus, 1989—; vis. prof. U.S. Mil. Acad., 1974-75, Nat. Def. U., 1978-79; cons. to Army Research Office, 1963-73; mem. U.S. Commn. on Mil. History, 1974—. Occasional lectr. Army War Coll., USAF Acad., Inf. Sch., Air War Coll., Command and Gen. Staff Coll.; chmn. adv. com. on history Sec. Air Force, 1970-79; mem. adv. com. on history NASA, 1974-81 Author: Ideas and Weapons, 1953, Buying Aircraft, 1964, Development of Aircraft Gun Turrets in the AAF, 1917-1944, Evolution of the Liaison Type Airplane, 1917-1944, 1946, An Enduring Challenge: The Problem of Air Force Doctrine, 1974, General John M. Palmer, Citizen Soldiers, and the Army of a Democracy, 1982; contbr. articles on mil. history to scholarly publs.; editor: The Transfer of Ideas: Historical Essays, 1968, editorial adviser various jours. Trustee Air Force Hist. Found., 1973—. With USAAF, 1942—47, capt. USAAF, 1947—81, reserves, maj. gen. USAAF, 1981, reserves. Decorated D.S.M., Legion of Merit; recipient Outstanding Civilian Service to the Army medal, 1975, Exceptional Civilian Service to the Air Force medal., 1979 Fellow AIAA (assoc.); mem. Am. Hist. Assn., Soc. History of Tech., Soc. Mil. History, Phi Delta Theta. Episcopalian. Home: 2701 Pickett Rd Apt 3028 Durham NC 27705-5651 Office: Duke Univ Dept History Durham NC 27708 E-mail: ibholley@duke.edu.

HOLLEY, PAMELA SPENCER, retired librarian; b. Mpls., July 31, 1944; d. Boyd Edgar Gustafson, Jane Lenore Gustafson; m. Richard Howard Holley; m. Arthur Snow Spencer (dec. Oct. 24, 1996). BS Biology and Secondary Edn., Longwood Coll., 1965; MS, Coll. William and Mary, 1970; MLS, U. Md., 1973. Cert. libr. Va., 1973. Tchr. sci. Stephen Foster Intermediate/Fairfax County Pub. Schs., Alexandria, Va., 1965—72; libr. Lake Braddock Secondary Sch., Burke, 1973—75, Mount Vernon H.S., Alexandria, 1975—86; media specialist Area I Office, 1986—87; libr. Thomas Jefferson H.S. for Sci. and Tech., 1987—94; libr. program specialist Chapel Sq. Ctr., Annandale, 1994—96; coord. librs. FCPS, 1996—98; ret., 1998. Chair film series com. Virginia Beach Pub. Libr. Friends Bd., Va., 2000—, v.p., 2002—; mem. editl. adv. bd. Voice of Youth Advocates Mag., Lanham, 2000—; chair adv. com. Am. Econoclad Svcs., Topeka, 1988—95; host, co-host Cable 21 Ednl. Channel, Annandale, 1992—97; editl. adv. bd. Booklist Mag., Chgo., 1988—90; bd. dirs. Libr. Friends, v.p., 2002—03. Author: What Do Young Adults Read Next? (continuing series), 1993; editor: VOYA Book of Lists, 2002; author: (audiobooks) It Is!, 2002—, Column, VOYA, 2002—. Mem.: ALA (councilor 1995—99, bd. dirs. divsn. young adult libr. svcs. assn. 1990—93), Beta Phi Mu. Episcopalian. Avocations: kayaking, exercise, travel, reading, needlepoint. Home: PO Box 9 Assawoman VA 23302 Home Fax: 757-824-0428.

HOLLEY, ROBERT WILLIAM, sales executive, minister; b. Phila., Pa., Dec. 11, 1948; s. Robert John and Grace Mildred Holley(Stepmother), Evelyn Holly and Charles Hague Mavian(Stepfather); m. Patricia Ruth Meluzio, Dec. 26, 1970; 1 child, Jephthah David. BS in Bible, Phila. Coll. Bible, 1974; MDiv, Bibl. Sch. Theology, Hatfield, Pa., 1977; STM, Bibl. Theol. Sem., Hatfield, Pa., 1978. Saint Stephen's Course in Orthodox Theology Antiochian Orthodox Christian Archdiocese N.Am., 1999. Author: (book) How Do I Choose the Right Partner for Life?, 2003. Mem. com. on marriage and family Antiochian Orthodox Christian Archiocese, 2000—. Staff sgt. USAF, 1967—70, Viet Nam. Republican. Avocations: writing, language study, bible study. Home: 431 Portola Ave LaHabra CA 90631-5463 Office: McCrometer Incorporated 3255 W Stetson Ave Hemet CA 92545-7799 Home Fax: 1-562-691-8394. Personal E-mail: bobh@mccrometer.com. E-mail: bobh@mccrometer.com.

HOLLEY, STEVEN LYON, lawyer; b. Ft. Wayne, Ind., Apr. 5, 1958; s. Wesley Lewis and Cornelia Alice (Reeder) H. BA in History/Polit. Sci., Ind. U., 1980; JD, NYU, 1983. Bar: N.Y. 1984, U.S. Dist. Ct. (so. and ea. dist.) N.Y. 1985, U.S. Dist. Ct. (no. dist.) N.Y. 1988. Law clk. Hon. Jose' A. Cabranes, Hartford, Conn., 1983-84; assoc. Sullivan & Cromwell, N.Y.C., 1984-90, ptnr., 1991—. Mem. Assn. Bar City of N.Y. (sec. com. on profl. and jud. ethics 1988-90). Democrat. Home: 832 Broadway New York NY 10003-4813 Office: Sullivan & Cromwell 125 Broad St Fl 34 New York NY 10004-2498 E-mail: holleys@sullcrom.com.

HOLLEY, TAMMY DANNETTE FENNELL, critical care nurse; b. Rockmart, Ga., Mar. 29, 1967; d. Ira Eugene and Barbara Ann (Sprayberry) Fennell; m. Jonathan Olin Holley, Dec. 23, 1989; children: Jonathan Olin Adam, Jacob Emery Aaron ASN, Floyd Coll., Rome, Ga., 1987. Cert. ACLS. Med.-surg./telemetry unit nurse Paulding Meml. Med. Ctr., Dallas, Ga., 1986-88; staff nurse, relief charge nurse CCU, Floyd Med. Ctr., Rome, Ga., 1988—94, CCU

charge nurse, utilization rev. nurse, 1994-99, case mgmt. utilization rev. nurse, 1999—2001, cert. profl. utilization rev. nurse, 2001—. Home: 930 Lowery Rd Rockmart GA 30153-3416 E-mail: tholley@floydmed.org.

HOLLI, MELVIN GEORGE, history educator; b. Ishpeming, Mich., Feb. 22, 1933; s. Walfred and Sylvia (Erickson) H.; m. Betsy Biggar, Aug. 12, 1961; children: Susan, Steven. Student, Suomi Coll., 1952-54; BA, North Mich. U., 1957; MA, U. Mich., 1958, PhD, 1969. Curator manuscripts Bentley Libr., U. Mich., Ann Arbor, 1962-64; asst. prof., assoc. prof. history U. Ill., Chgo., 1965, prof., 1975—, chmn. dept., 1991-94. Fulbright prof. U. Finland, 1978, 89-90. Author: Reform in Detroit, 1969, Detroit, 1975, Ethnic Chicago, 1981, 3d edit., 1995 (nonfiction prize Soc. Midland Authors 1985, Best book award Ill. Polit. Sci. Assn. 1985), Bashing Chicago Traditions, 1989, Restoration: Chicago Elects a New Daley, 1991, The Mayors: The Chicago Political Tradition, 1995, The American Mayor: The Best and Worst Big City Leaders, 1999; (with Paul M. Green) From Mid Century to Millennium: A View From Chicago's City Hall, 1999, (with F. Beuttler and R. Remini) The University of Illinois at Chicago: A Pictorial History, 2000, The Wizard of Washington: Emil Hurja Franklin Roosevelt and the Birth of Public Opinion Polling, 2002; bd. editors Urban Affairs Quar., 1992-95; editor: U. Ill. Press Ethnic History in Chicago book series. Bd. dirs. Scandinavian Ctr., North Park Univ., Chgo., 1997—. Woodrow Wilson fellow, 1957-58; recipient Disting. Alumni award No. Mich. U., 1985. Mem. Am. Hist. Assn., Orgn. Am. Historians, Swedish Am. Hist. Soc. (mag. bd. 1990-93), Soc. Midland Authors (bd. dirs. 1989-93, 94—), Finnish-Am. Soc. of the Midwest (bd. dirs.). Home: 1311 Ashland Ave River Forest IL 60305-1029 Office: Dept History U Ill Chicago IL 60607-7109 E-mail: mholli@uic.edu.

HOLLIDAY, CHARLES O., JR., chemical company executive; b. Nashville, Tenn., Mar. 9, 1948; s. Charles O. Sr. and Ann (Hunter) H.; m. Ann Blair, June 27, 1970; children: Scot, Chad. BS in Indsl. Engring., U. Tenn., 1970; DSc (hon.), Washington Coll., Chesterton, Md., 1988. Registered profl. engr., Tenn. Engr. DuPont, Nashville, 1970-72, mfg. supr., 1972-74, Wilmington, Del., 1974-77, various mfg. assignments in fibers dept. Charleston, S.C., Martinsville, Va., Seaford, Del., 1978-84, corp. plans mgr. Wilmington, 1984-86, global bus. dir. Nomex, 1986-87, global bus. dir. Kevlar, 1987-88, dir. mktg. chems. & pigments, 1988-90, v.p., then pres. Asia Pacific Tokyo, 1990-92, sr. v.p., 1992-95, chmn. Asia Pacific, 1995, exec. v.p., mem. office chief exec., 1995-97, CEO, 1998—, chmn., 1999—. Vice chmn. John F. Kennedy Ctr. Performing Arts; active Alliance Global Sustainability, Del. Bus./Pub. Edn. Coun., U. Tenn., Winterthur Mus. Mem. World Bus. Coun. Sustainable Devel. (vice chmn.), Asia Pacific Coun., Bus. Coun., Bus. Roundtable, Catalyst, Del. Bus. Roundtable, Japan Am. Soc. Del., Pioneer Hi-Bred Internat. Inc., Singapore-U.S. Bus. Coun., Soc. Chem. Industry, Inst. Indsl. Engrs. (sr.) Office: E I Du Pont de Nemours 1007 Market St Wilmington DE 19801-1227

HOLLIDAY, PATRICIA RUTH MCKENZIE, evangelist; b. Jacksonville, Fla., Nov. 17, 1935; d. Robert Irving and Leona Adele (Bell) McKenzie; m. Jan. 20, 1965; children: Connie, Katheryn, Alexander. Student, Massey Bus. Coll., 1969, Luther Rice Sem., 1976; DD, Southeastern Theol. Sem., 1986, ThD, 1989, PhD, 1992. Sec. Delta Drug Corp., Jacksonville, 1965—; pres. Microfilm Ctr., Jacksonville, 1974—, Miracle Outreach Ministry, Jacksonville, 1974—; pastor Miracle World Outreach, Jacksonville; prof. Southeastern Theol. Sem., Jacksonville, 1992—; with Internat. Evang. Miracle Outreach, 2000—. Author: Holliday for the King, 1978, Be Free, 1979, Only Believe, 1980, Born Anew, 1981, The Walking Dead, 1982, Anointing Power, 1982, Signs, Wonders and Reactions, 1984, Dealing with Heresies, 1986, Marriage Answers, 1992, Solitary Satanist, 1993, Entertaining Angels of Light, 1993, The Plan: Ascended Masters, 1994, The New World Aftershock, 1994, Can. Women Preach?, 1995, New Creations, 1995, From Curses to Blessings Vols. 1, 2 & 3, 1995, Angel Fire, 1995, Can Witches Be Saved, 1996, Spirit of Idolatry, 1996, Is Halloween Pagan?, 1996, Gods of the Stars, Astrology, 1997, Gifts of the Holy Spirit, 1997, Baptism of the Holy Spirit, 1997, Deliverance Manuals, Vols. 1, 2 & 3, 1997, Spiritual Welfare Army, 1997, Spiritual Warfare - Weapons, 1997, Healing & Miracles, 1998, The Spiritual Armor of God, 1998, Children of the New Age, 1998, Prayer Warriors, 1998, Battling Territorial Spirits, 1998, New Age Inner Healing, 1999, Demons Tremble, 1999, Transference of Spirits, 1999, Experiencing Jesus, 2001, Witch Doctor and the Man-Fourth Generational Witch Doctor Finds Christ, 2001, Satan's Romper Room, 2002, Never, Never Land, 2003, The Fallen Prince, 2003, others; columnist Christian Courier. Sec. Four Found., Inc.; Rep. candidate Fla. Ho. of Reps., 1972; mem. Fla. Rep. Com., 1976-80; lobbyist Fla. Legislature, 1978-80; hostess Pat Holliday TV Show, Jacksonville. Mem. Minutewomen of Fla. Club (founder) Univ. Women Club, Ponte Vedra Women's Club. Home: 9252 San Jose Blvd Apt 2804 Jacksonville FL 32257-9205 E-mail: mominK1@hotmail.com., holliday_pat@hotmail.com.

HOLLIDAY, PETER OSBORNE, JR., dentist; b. Macon, Ga., July 9, 1921; s. Peter Osborne and Martha Elizabeth (Riley) H.; m. Mary Lucille Dozier, Nov. 12, 1949; children: Peter III, Lucy, Lindsay, Mary. DDS, Emory U., 1945; postgrad., U. Mich., 1947-48. Pvt. practice dentistry, Macon, 1947—. Mem. Gov. Carter's Dental Adv. Com., Atlanta, 1972. Head dental div. United Givers Fund, Macon, 1956; mem. bicycle com. Macon-Bibb County Planning & Zoning Commn., 1995—. With USNR Dental Corps, 1945-47, China. Fellow Am. Coll. Dentists, Internat. Coll. Dentists (dep. regent for Ga. 1983-85); mem. ADA (alt. del. 1978), Ga. Dental Assn. (sec.-treas. 1971-76, v.p. 1977, pres. 1978-79), Ga. Acad. Dental Practice (charter), Hinman Dental Soc., Ctrl. Dist. Dental Soc. (pres. 1963, Dentist of Yr. 1962), Pierre Fauchard Acad., League of Am. Wheelmen, So. Bicycle League. Democrat. Unitarian Universalist. Home: 744 Forest Hill Rd Macon GA 31210-4202 Office: Holliday Dental Assocs 360 Spring St Macon GA 31201-6789

HOLLIDAY, POLLY DEAN, actress; b. Jasper, Ala., July 2, 1937; d. Ernest Sullivan and Velma Mabell (Cain) H. B. Music Edn., Ala. State Women's Coll. (now U. Montevallo), 1959; postgrad., Fla. State U., 1960; D.H.L. hon., Mt. St. Mary's Coll., 1982. Tchr. music Sarasota (Fla.) public schs., 1961. Appeared with Asolo Theatre Repertory Co., Sarasota, 1962-72; appeared in Off-Broadway, Wedding Band, 1972; Quarrel of Sparrows, 1993, The Time of the Cuckoo, 2000, Chaucer in Rome, 2001, A Few Stout Individuals, 2002, Broadway shows All Over Town, 1975, Arsenic and Old Lace, 1986-87, Cat on a Hot Tin Roof, 1990 (Tony nomination), Picnic, 1994; appeared in plays The Glass Menagerie, Tyrone Guthrie Theatre, Mpls., 1988; appeared as Flo on CBS-TV series Alice, 1976-80 (4 Emmy nominations), Flo, 1981 (Emmy nomination); appeared in CBS-TV series The Client, 1995-96, Golden Girls, 1986, Amazing Stories, 1986, Home Improvement, 1993, 94; appeared in TV movies You Can't Take It With You, 1981, The Shadyhill Kidnapping, 1981, All the Way Home, 1981, Missing Children, 1982, A Gift of Love, 1983; PBS Wonderworks series Konrad, 1985, (TV movies) Triumph of the Heart, 1991; appeared in feature films All The Pres.'s Men, 1975, The One and Only, 1977, Gremlins, 1984, Moon Over Parador, 1987, Mrs. Doubtfire, 1993, Mr. Wrong, 1996, The Parent Trap, 1998. Recipient Golden Globe award for best supporting actress on TV series, 1978, 79 Episcopalian.

HOLLIDAY, ROBERT KELVIN, corrections officer, retired state senator, former newspaper executive, educator; b. Logan, W.Va., Feb. 11, 1933; s. James Kelvin and Helen Kathleen (Harris) Holliday; children: Kelvin Edward, Kathleen Holliday Eddy, Stephen Kerr, Robert L., Jeffrey, Tracey, Brandon. BA, W.Va. U. Tech., 1954; MA, Marshall U., 1955. Co-owner, editor Montgomery (W.Va.) Herald, 1955—85; co-owner, editor The Fayette Tribune, 1955—85, Fayette Tribune, 1955—85, Meadow River Post, Rainelle, W.Va., 1966—85; with W.Va. Divsn. Corrections, 2001—03. Mem. W.Va. Ho. of Dels., 1963-68, W.Va. Senate, 1968-72, 80-94; adj. polit. sci. instr. W.Va. U. Inst. Tech., 1994, 99, 2000, 02, W.Va. State Coll., 1997-98, Bluefield State Coll., 1996, Greenbrier C.C., 1995, Glenville State Coll., 1997. Author: Tests of Faith, 1966, About Montgomery, 1956, Our Chat, 1956, A Portrait of Fayette, 1960, Politics in Fayette County, 1958. Mem. W.Va. State Dem. Exec. Com., 1978-80; pres. Fayette Needy Assn., 1960-68; elder Presbyn. Ch. With U.S. Army. Recipient Gov.'s Living Dream award Martin Luther King Jr., 1988, Outstanding Leadership award W.Va. NAACP, 1988, award Kanawha-Fayette Cmty. Svc., Inc., 1985-2002; named Outstanding Legislator, W.Va. Trial Lawyers Assn., 1988, 92. Mem.: Rehab Assn. (Structural Barriers award 1988), W. Va. Edn. Assn. (Pearl S. Buck award 1982), W. Va. Mental Health Assn. (past dir.), New Rivers Nat. River (founder), Shriners, Masons (32 degree), Pi Sigma Alpha. Presbyterian.

HOLLIDAY, THOMAS EDGAR, lawyer; b. Ft. Hood, Tex., July 3, 1948; s. William Lamont and Eileen (Fiebig) H.; m. Linda Loudon, May 7, 1988; children: Devon M., Trey S. BA, Stanford U., 1971; JD, U. So. Calif., 1974. Bar: Calif. 1974. Assoc. Gibson, Dunn & Crutcher LLP, L.A., 1974-81; ptnr. Gibson, Dunn & Crutcher, L.A., 1981—. Editor: (book, desk edition) Antitrust and Trade Regulations. Trustee S.W. Mus., L.A., 1981-98, bd. pres., 1995-97; trustee Found. for People, L.A., 1985-90, Clarkson U., 2000—; mem. L.A. Police Dept. Meml. Found. Bd. Fellow Am. Coll. Trial Lawyers; mem. Fed. Bar Assn. (exec. com. L.A. chpt. 1990, pres. 1998). Avocation: collecting southwestern art. Office: Gibson Dunn & Crutcher LLP 333 S Grand Ave Ste 4400 Los Angeles CA 90071-3197

HOLLIE, GLADYS MIRIAM, nurse; b. Coupland, Tex., Nov. 2, 1932; d. John Charles and Cora Rebecca (Atkinson) H.; m. Simon Jackson Davis, Oct. 25, 1956 (div. 1961); 1 child, Harold Gene Holli Johnson. AD, McClennen Community Coll., Waco, Tex., 1980. Vocat. nurse St. Paul Hosp., Dallas, 1955-58, Tex. Children's Hosp., Dallas, 1958-60, Long Beach (Calif.) VA Med. Ctr., 1960-77, VA Med. Ctr., Waco, 1977-82, RN Fresno, Calif., 1982-95, ret., 1995. Vol. Am. Cancer Soc., Fresno, 1991, YWCA, Fresno, 1991, Ch. Women United. Mem. AARP, Order Ea. Star (asst. matron 1983—). Democrat. Mem. African Methodist Episcopal Ch. Avocations: reading, sewing, history, travel.

HOLLIEN, HARRY FRANCIS, speech and communications scientist, educator; b. Brockton, Mass., July 16, 1926; s. Henry Gregory and Alice Bernice (Coolidge) H.; m. Patricia Ann Milanowski, Aug. 26, 1969; children: Karen Ann, Kevin Amory, Keith Alan, Brian Christopher, Stephanie Ann, Christine Ann. BS, Boston U., 1949, MEd, 1951; MA, U. Iowa, 1953, PhD, 1955. Asst. prof. Baylor U., 1955-58, U. Wichita, 1958-62; assoc. prof. speech U. Fla., Gainesville, 1962-68, prof., 1968-98, prof. linguistics, 1976-98, prof. criminal justice, 1979-98, assoc. dir. comm. scis. lab., 1962—65, dir. comm. scis. lab., 1968—75, dir. Inst. Advanced Study Comm. Processes, 1975—84; prof. emeritus, rsch. scientist Inst. Advanced Study of Communication Processes, 1998—, assoc. dir. linguistics, 1989-91; founding dir. Inst. Advanced Studies Comm. Processes U. Fla, 1984—98. Vis. prof. Inst. Telecomm. and Acoustics, Wroclaw Tech. U., Poland, 1974; adj. prof. Juilliard Sch. Music, N.Y.C., 1973-84; rsch. assoc. Gould Rsch. Lab., 1958; vis. sci. Speech Transmission Lab., Royal Inst. Tech., Stockholm, 1970; prof. U. Trier, Germany, 1987; fencing coach U. Iowa, 1953-55; mem. comm. sci. study sect. NIH, 1963-67; mem. neurobiology merit rev. bd. VA, 1969-74; pres. Hollien Assocs., 1966—; cons. in field. Author: Current Issues in Phonetic Sciences, 1978, Acoustics of Crime, 1990, Forensic Voice Identification, 2002; assoc. editor Jour. Speech and Hearing Rsch., 1967-69, Jour. Voice, 1987—; editor The Phonetician, 1975-92; mem. edtl. bd. Jour. Comm. Disorders, 1980-91, Jour. Rsch. in Singing, 1980-83, Jour. Phonetics, 1982-85, Studia Phonetica Posnan, 1985—, Speech, Language and the Law, 1993-2002. Chmn. bd. Unitarian Fellowship, Waco, Tex., 1956-58; chmn. bd. Wild Animal Retirement Village, 1981-90. Served with USN, 1944-46; with USNR, 1946-75. Recipient Garcia/Sandoz prize Internat. Assn. Logopedics and Phoniatrics, 1971, Gould award Wm. and Harrett Gould Found., 1975, Gutzmann medal Union European Phoniatrists, 1980; NIH career fellow, 1965-70, Fulbright scholar, 1987. Fellow AAAS, Am. Speech and Hearing Assn., Acoustical Soc. Am., Internat. Soc. Phonetic Scis. (pres. 1989-98, sec.-gen. 1975-89, exec. v.p. 1983-89, Kay Elemetrics prize 1987, S. Smith prize 1991, Soc. Honors 1998, hon. pres. 1999—), Am. Acad. Forensic Sci. (John R. Hunt award 1988), Inst. Acoustics; mem. SAR (pres. local chpt. 2001-03, regional v.p. 2000—, state rec. sec. 2001-03, Patriot medal, 2003), Am. Assn. Phonetic Scis. (pres. 1973-75, editor 1976-79, exec. com. 1979-82), Japan Soc. Phonetic Scis. (hon. v.p. 1989-97), World Congress Phoneticians (permanent coun.), Voice Found. (sci. bd., merit awards 1981, 93), Internat. Assn. Forensic Phonetics, Mayflower Descs. (gov. local chpt. 2002—, capt. state soc. 1999-2002), Order Found. Patriots, Sigma Xi. Republican. Achievements include patent for apparatus using radiation sensitive switch for signalling and recording data. Home: 229 SW 43rd Ter Gainesville FL 32607-2270 Office: U Fla Inst Advanced Study Comm Processes 46 Dauer Hall Gainesville FL 32611 E-mail: Hollien@Grove.ufl.edu.

HOLLIEN, PATRICIA ANN, small business owner, scientist; b. N.Y.C., May 11, 1938; d. Leon and Sophia (Biernacki) Milanowski; m. Harry Hollien, Aug. 26, 1969; children: Brian, Stephanie, Christine. AA, Sante Fe Jr. Coll., 1969; ScD (hon), Marian Coll., 1983; student, U. Fla., 1977—. Rsch. asst. Marineland Rsch. Labs., 1965-69; co-owner, exec. v.p. Hollien Assocs., 1969—; owner, dir. Forensic Comm. Assocs., Gainesville, Fla., 1981—, The Eden Group, Gainesville, 1995-97. Vis. assoc. Royal Inst. Spl. Transmission Lab., Stockholm, 1970, Wroclaw Tech. U., Poland, 1974; asst. in research Inst. Advanced Study Communication Scis. U. Fla., 1977-83, assoc. in research, 1983—; adj. asst. prof. Communication Sci. Lab., N.Y., 1982—. Co-author: Current Issues in the Phonetic Sciences, 1979; editor The Phonetician, 1991-98; contbr. articles to profl. jours. Treas. Soc. Son's of the Am. Revolution, 2001—; bd. dirs. Ann. Retirement Village, Waldo, Fla., 1981—93. Fellow Am. Acad. Forensic Scis., Internat. Soc. Phonetic Scis. (coun. reps. 1983—, Honors of the Assn. for 1995, 1997); mem. Am. Assn. Phonetic Scis., Acad. Forensic Application of the Comm. Sci., Internat. Assn. Forensic Phonetics (sec. gen. 7th ann. congress 1995). Home: 229 SW 43d Ter Gainesville FL 32607-2270 Office: Forensic Comm Assocs PO Box 12323 Gainesville FL 32604-0323 E-mail: fca@forcomm.com.

HOLLINBECK, ETHEL LINDELL, sculptor; b. Kewanee, Ill., Feb. 1, 1910; d. Gustav (Lindstrom) and Hilda Louise (Gustafson) Lindell; m. Richard Oftebro Hollinbeck, Mar. 27, 1928; children: Marilyn, David, Richard Jr. Grad., Mpls. Sch. of Arts, 1948. Exhibited in group shows at Met. Mus., N.Y.C., Walker, Mpls. on Com., Minn. First Outdoor Sculpture Show, Woman's Club of Mpls., Swedish Mus. of Art, St. Paul Gallery of Arts, Mpls. Inst. of Arts; works include many portraits. Recipient many awards. Mem. Soc. of Minn. Sculptors, Profl. Artists' Equity Assn. Home: 3330 Edinborough Way Apt 1407 Edina MN 55435-5955

HOLLINGER, MORTON, business owner; b. Port Chester, N.Y. s. Max and Anna Hollinger; m. Myrna Rachel Hollinger, Mar. 30, 1958; children: Nancy Samson, Steven. BA, Syracuse U., 1949; studied with William Arrowsmith, prin. oboist, Met. Opera; studied painting with Louis Di Valentin. Pres. M.H. Pierce & Co., Stamford, Conn., 1958—. Oboist Westchester Symphony, White Plains, N.Y., 1982-85, Bronx (N.Y.) Symphony, 1986-89. Author: Paintings of Morton Hollinger, 1998. Pres. Jr. C. of C., Port Chester, N.Y., 1957. Recipient Stamford Mus. award for oil painting, 1968, Windsor-Newton award for oil painting, 1990. Mem. Stamford Art Assn. Avocations: clarinet, oboe, english horn, painting. Home: 11 Ledge Terr Stamford CT 06905

HOLLINGS, ERNEST FREDERICK, senator; b. Charleston, S.C., Jan. 1, 1922; s. Adolph G. and Wilhlemine D. (Meyer) H.; m. Rita Louise Liddy, Aug. 21, 1971; children by previous marriage— Michael Milhous, Helen Hayne, Patricia Salley, Ernest Frederick III. BA, The Citadel, 1942, LL.D. (hon.), 1960; LL.B., U. S.C., 1947, LLD (hon.), 1980. Bar: S.C. 1947, U.S. Supreme Ct. 1952, U.S. Ct. Appeals (D.C.) 1989. Mem. S.C. Ho. of Reps., 1948-54, speaker pro tem, 1951-54; lt. gov. of S.C., 1955-59, gov., 1959-63; practiced in Charleston, SC, 1963-66; U.S. senator from S.C., 1966—; chmn. Senate commerce, sci. and transp. com., 1987—95, 2001—; sr. mem. Senate appropriations comm., 1971—; chmn. commerce, justice, state, judiciary and related agencies subcoms.; sr. mem. Senate com. on the budget, 1974—; chmn. Senate com. on the budget, 1980—81. Mem. Hoover Commn. on Intelligence Activities, 1954—55, Pres.'s Adv. Commn. on Intergovtl. Rels., 1959—63, Pres.'s Adv. Commn. on Federalism, 1981; chmn. Legis. Coun., 1955—59, Regional Adv. Coun. on Nuclear Energy; mem. adv. com. Nat. River and Harbors Congress; del. Law of Sea Conf.; mem. Senate Dem. Policy Com., Senate Dem. Tech. and omms. om. Author: The Case Against Hunger: A Demand for a National Policy, 1970. Served to capt. U.S. Army, 1942-45, ETO, NATOUSA. Recipient Founders award S.C. Com. for Tech. Edn., 1963, Nat. Vet. award, 1968, Friend of Edn. award S.C. Edn. Assn., 1974, Neptune award Am. Oceanic Orgn., 1978, James Woodruff award Assn. U.S. Army, 1980, Nat. Future award Am. Space Found., 1984, S.C. Disting. Pub. Svc. award, 1983, Consumer Fedn. of Am. Disting. Pub. Svc. award 1985, Govt. Social Responsibility award Martin Luther King Jr. Ctr., 1986, Golden Bulldog award Watchdogs of the Treasury, 1988, Outstanding Leadership award Nat. Assn. Black-owned Broadcasters, 1988, Disting. Health Svcs. award, 1988, The Sound Dollar award, 1988-90, Hall of Leaders award Nat. Travel Industry, 1990, Disting. Svc. award Nat. Assn. Ind. Colls. and U., 1990, Nat. Security Indsl. Assn., 1990, Congl. award Nat. Coalition for Cancer Rsch., 1992, Sgt. Jasper Freedom award S.C. C. of C., 1992, No. 1 Govtl. Friend of Tourism, SE Tourism Soc., 1993, Spl. Health Recognition award N.H. Assn. Cmty. Health Ctrs., 1994; named one of Ten Outstanding Young Men U.S. Jr. C. of C., 1954, and numerous other awards. Mem. ABA, Charleston County Bar Assn., S.C. Bar Assn., Assn. Citadel Men, Hibernian Soc., Am. Legion, Univ. S.C. Law Fedn., St. Andrews Soc. Lodges: Elks, Masons. Democrat. Lutheran. Office: US Senate 125 Russell Senate Bldg Washington DC 20510-0001*

HOLLINGSWORTH, ABNER THOMAS, university dean; b. Wilmington, Del., Mar. 19, 1939; s. Abner and Dorothy Elizabeth (Dunn) H.; m. Jacqueline Manning, Mar. 19, 1966; 1 child, Alexander Thomas. BSin BA, U. Del., Newark, 1964; MBA, Mich. State U., 1966, PhD, 1969. Asst. prof. mgmt. So. Ill. U., Carbondale, 1969-71, Fla. Atlantic U., 1971-73; assoc. prof. mgmt. U. S.C., 1973-77, prof. mgmt., 1977-80, U. Petroleum and Minerals, Dhahran, Saudi Arabia, 1980-82; prof. mgmt., chmn. mgmt. dept. U. N.C., Asheville, 1983-87; dean Sch. Bus. Adminstrn. Monmouth Coll., 1987-88, prof. mgmt., 1988; prof. mgmt. and dir. Bus. Rsch. Inst. St. John's U., 1988-90; prof. mgmt. and dean Sch. Bus. Fla. Inst. Tech., Melbourne, 1990—. Cons. in field; conductor numerous tng. programs. Author: (with Richard Hodgetts) Readings in Basic Management, 1975, (with H. H. hand) A Practical Approach to the Management of Small Business, 1979, Readings in Small business Management, 1979, Supervisory Behavior, 1974, (with R. Howell and R. Hodgetts) A Reader, Study Guide in Basic Management, 1979, others; assoc. editor Jur. Bus. Rsch., 1984-87; editorial bd. Jour. Mgmt., 1977-79, book reviewer for Acad. Press, Bus. Pubs., Inc., Wiley/Hamilton, many others; contbr. articles to profl. jours. Bd. dirs. Holmes Regional Med. Ctr. & Health First, Inc., Melbourne, Jr. Achievement of Ea. Ctrl. Fla., United Way. Rsch. grantee, Inst. Pub. Utilities, Mich. State U., 1967, Fla. Atlantic U., 1972, U. S.C., 1975, Social Security Adminstrn., 1977, others. Avocations: scuba diving, sailing, reading. Office: Fla Inst Tech Sch Bus 150 W University Blvd Melbourne FL 32901-6982 E-mail: aholling@fit.edu.

HOLLINGSWORTH, BOBBY G. career officer; BS in Elec. Engring., La. State Univ. Flight line officer Marine Attack Squadron 331, Beaufort, S.C.; embarkation officer Marine Attack Squadron 223, Chu Lai, South Vietnam; landing signal officer Marine Aircraft Group 12, Chu Lai, South Vietnam; asst. divsn. air officer 3rd Marine Divsn., Phu Bai, South Vietnam; combat tactics instr. Marine Training Squadron 103, Yuma, Ariz.; asst. ops. officer Marine Fighter Squadron 112, Dallas; exec. officer Marine Aircraft Group 42, Alameda, Calif.; commander Marine Attack Squadron 133, Alameda, Calif.; asst. chief of staff 4th Marine Aircraft Wing, New Orleans; chief of staff II Marine Expeditionary Brigade, Camp Lejeune, N.C.; commanding gen. Marine Corps Res. Support Command, Kans. City, Mo., Fourth Force Svc. Support Group, New Orleans; deputy commander Jt. Task Force, Saudi Arabia; vice commander Marine Forces Pacific, Camp Smith, Hawaii; exec. dir. Nat. Com. Employer Support of Guard and Res., 1999—. Advisor to Asst. Sec. Def. for Res. Affairs U.S. Armed Forces. Decorated Legion of Merit, Distinguished Flying Cross, Def. Meritorious Svc. medal, Air Medal with numeral 5, Combat Action Ribbon, Presdl. Unit Citation with Bronze Star, Meritorious Unit Commendation, Select Marine Corps. Res. medal with Silver Star, Nat. Def. Medal with Bronze star, Armed Forces Expiditionary medal, Vietnam Svc. medal with two Bronze Stars, Navy and Marine Corps Overseas Svc. Ribbon with two Bronze Stars, Armed Forces Res. medal with hourglass Device, Rep. of Vietnam Unit Citation, Rep. Vietnam Campaing medal with 1960 Deivce. Office: U S Marine Corps Forces Pacific Camp H M Smith HI 96861

HOLLINGSWORTH, BRENDA JACKSON, employment consultant; b. Roxboro, N.C., Aug. 12, 1958; d. John Vanstory and Effie Clayton Jackson; children: Brandy Effie, William (Denzel). BS, St. Augustine's Coll., Raleigh, N.C., 1981. Income maintenance caseworker Social Svcs., Durham, N.C., 1987-89, fraud investigator Roxboro, 1990-92; youth counselor Job Tng. Partnership Act, Roxboro, 1992-94; employment cons. Employment Security Commn., Roxboro, 1997—. Avocations: volleyball, writing poetry, aerobics. Home: 95 Gatesworth Rd Roxboro NC 27573

HOLLINGSWORTH, DAVID SOUTHERLAND, chemical company executive; b. Wilmington, Del. BS in Chem. Engring., Lehigh U., 1948. Chem. engr. research ctr. Hercules Inc., Wilmington, chem. engr. lab. Kalamazoo, Mich., tech. rep. sales office New Orleans and Wilmington, 1953-61, asst. sales mgr. paper chems. Wilmington, 1961-63, sales mgr. specialty chems., 1963-65, mgr. specialty paper chems. pine and paper chem. dept., 1965-67, dir. sales paper chems., 1967-72, from dir. mktg. to asst. gen. mgr., 1972-74, gen. mgr. new enterprise dept., 1974-75, gen. mgr. food and fragrance devel. dept., 1975-78, dir. worldwide bus. ctr. organics, 1978-79, v.p. planning, 1979-82, group v.p. water-soluable polymers, 1982-83, also bd. dirs., divisional v.p. mktg., 1983-84; pres. Hercules Specialty Chems. Co., Wilmington, 1984-86, vice chmn., 1986; chmn., chief exec. officer Hercules Inc., Wilmington, 1987-90. Bd. dirs. Del. Trust Co. Trustee Grand Opera House Inc.; bd. dirs. Med. Ctr. Del., Del. Symphony. Recipient Nat. medal Tech. U.S. Dept. Commerce Tech. Adminstrn., 1991. Mem. Chem. Mfrs. Assn. (bd. dirs.), Conf. Bd. Clubs: Hercules Country. Office: Hercules Inc 1313 N Market St Fl 2 Wilmington DE 19894-0003

HOLLINGSWORTH, DENNIS, state senator; m. Natalie Hollingsworth; 1 child. Student, Calif. Poly. State Univ., San Luis Obispo, Cornell U. Bus. owner; mem. dist. 66, Calif. State Senate, dist. 36, Calif. State Assembly, 2002—. Chair Am. Legis. Exch.Coun., Calif. Pub. Sector; leader Senate Calif. Taxpayer Protection Caucus; inc. legis. dir. Riverside County Farm Bur. Mem.: Quail Unltd. (past chair Calif. orgn.). Democrat. Mailing: State Capitol Rm 2048 Sacramento CA 95814 Office: 1870 Cordell Ct Ste 107 El Cajon CA 92020*

HOLLINGSWORTH, GARY MAYES, sales executive, marketing professional; b. Mexico, Mo., June 1, 1944; s. Allan Dee and Mabel Etta (Mayes) H.; m. Theresa Ann LaRoche, June 30, 1984; children: Lisa Marie, Allan Dee, Sarah Elizabeth. BS, Truman State U., 1972; MA, Webster U., St. Louis, 1982. CPA, Mo. Staff announcer Sta. KXEO-KWWR-FM, Mexico, 1962-64, news dir., 1964-65, program dir., account exec., 1969-72; sr. acct. KPMG Peat, Marwick, St. Louis, 1972-75; audit mgr. T.G. Bancshares Co., St. Louis, 1975-76; group contr. Wetterau Inc., St. Louis, 1976-80; chief fin. officer Gen. Grocer Co., St. Louis, 1980-84; v.p., sec., bd. dirs. Dana Brown Pvt. Brands, Inc., St. Louis, 1984-92; exec. v.p., gen. mgr. Private Brands Coffee & Tea Co., St. Louis, 1992-93; nat. sales mgr. store brands Chock Full O' Nuts Corp., N.Y.C., 1993-96; exec. v.p. Inlink Comm., St. Louis, 1996-2000; v.p. store brands and alternate channels Sara Lee Coffee & Tea, Harrison, NY, 2000—03; sr. v.p., gen. mgr. Heartland Fragrance & Herb Co., Springfield, Mo., 2003—. Mem. adj. faculty Maryville U., St. Louis, 1982-83, The Dive Shop of St. Louis, 1990—; bd. dirs. Phythe Group, Ltd., St. Louis. Mem. Zoning Bd. of Adjustment, Olivette, Mo., 1992-97; city clk. City of Olivette, Mo., 1997, Olivette, mem. city coun., 1997-99; mem. devel. bd. PARA QUAD, Inc., 1990-93; pres., trustee Bon Aire Subdivsn., 1990. Capt. U.S. Army. Mem. AICPA, Mo. Soc. CPAs, Fin. Exec. Inst. (bd. dirs. St. Louis chpt. 1988-94, pres. 1993-94), Profl. Assn. Dive Instrs. (cert.), Clayton Jaycees (pres. 1979), M.C. Investment Club (pres. 1991-92), Masons. Methodist. Avocations: scuba diving, reading, golf. Home: 14 Bon Aire Dr Olivette MO 63132-4301

HOLLINGSWORTH, JACK WARING, mathematics and computer science educator; b. South Haven, Kans., Mar. 3, 1924; s. Virgil Braxton and Ethel (Waring) H.; m. Nancy Lee Harris, Sept. 14, 1950; children: Joel, Priscilla, Seth (dec.). BS in Engring. Physics, U. Kans., 1948, BA, 1949; MS, U. Wis., 1951, PhD, 1954. Teaching asst. U. Kans., 1947-49, U. Wis., 1949-50, computing asst., 1950-54; gen. sci. aide U.S. Naval Ordnance Lab., 1950; mathematician Gen. Electric Co., 1954-57; mem. faculty Rensselaer Poly. Inst., 1957-79, prof. math., 1961-79, supr. computer lab., 1957-70, chmn. interdisciplinary com. computer sci., 1967-73; prof. Sch. Computer Sci. and Tech./Rochester Inst. Tech., N.Y., N.Y., 1979-86, dir., 1980-82; prof. math. Rochester Inst. Tech., 1986-96, prof. emeritus, 1996—. Mem. Bd. Coop. Ednl. Services, Saratoga-Warren Counties, 1970-79 Served to 1st lt. USAAF, 1943-45. Decorated D.F.C., Air medal with 4 oak leaf clusters, Purple Heart; Jack Hollingsworth Prize in Computer Sci. established in his honor Rennselaer Poly. Inst. Mem. Assn. Computing Machinery (treas. spl. interest group of univ. computing centers

1964-70), Am. Math. Soc., Soc. Indsl. and Applied Math., Math. Assn. Am., Sigma Xi, Tau Beta Pi, Omicron Delta Kappa, Kappa Eta Kappa. Mem. Reformed Ch. (elder). Home: 55 Crestview Dr Pittsford NY 14534-2242

HOLLINGSWORTH, JOHN ALEXANDER, retired science and mathematics educator, writer, consultant; b. Owego, N.Y., Sept. 25, 1925; s. John Alexander Sr. and Florence Eve (Haley) W.; m. Winifred Louise Stoelting Hollingsworth. BS in Agr., N.C. A&T State U., 1950, MS in Adult Edn., 1985; MS in Biology, N.C. Ctrl. U., 1960; postgrad., Cornell U., 1962-63. Staff sgt. U.S. Army, 1943-46, advanced through grades to capt., 1949-57; tchr. sci. Fayetteville (N.C.) City Schs., 1959-73, coord. sci., 1968-83, coord. math., 1973-83; cons., author, artist Cherokee Village, Ark., 1985—. Dir. Emergency Sch. Assistance Act Pilot Project, Fayetteville, 1972-80; grants writer Title I and Emergency Sch. Assistance Act Pilot Project, Fayetteville, 1972-80. Co-author: (booklet) The Improvement of High School Research Through the Research Participation Program, 1968. Active Ecology Action/Common Ground, Willits, Calif.; active, charter mem. Nat. Mus. of the Am. Indian. Mem. NEA (life), Nat. Ret. Tchrs. Assn., N.C. Sci. Tchrs. Assn. (state pres. 1971-73), N.C. Assn. Educators (pres. Fayetteville unit 1970-71), N.C. Ret. Sch. Pers., N.C. Ret. Govtl. Employees Assn., Inst. Noetic Scis., Nat. Assn. Black Vets. (life). Avocations: watercolor painting, genealogy, gardening. Home: 61 Otalco Dr Cherokee Village AR 72529

HOLLINGSWORTH, JOHN ARTHUR, business educator; b. Martins Ferry, Ohio, Oct. 12, 1952; s. William Arvine and Lillian Theo (Dean) H. AAB in Retail Mktg. cum laude, Belmont Tech. Col., 1975; BSBA in Helth and Hosp. Admin., Wheeling Jesuit U., 1979, MBA, 1984; PhD in Bus. Admin., U. Miss., 1993. Cert. secondary edn. tchr., Ohio. Computer operator Stone & Thomas Co., Wheeling, W. Va., 1971-76; mgr. carpet dept. L.S. Good & Co., Wheeling, 1976-78; store mgr. Rite Aid Corp., Harrisburg, Pa., 1978-79; lectr. Belmont Tech. Col., St. Clairsville, Ohio, 1981-83; rsch. and teaching asst. U. Miss., Oxford, 1984-88; bus. admin. instr. St. John's U., N.Y.C., 1989-94; asst. prof. bus. dept. Coll. Staten Island/CUNY, 1994-98; asst. prof. mgmt. info. sys. No. State U., Aberdeen, S.D., 1998—. Statis. cons. Reidenbach, Grubbs & Assoc., Jackson, Miss., 1986-87; session chair and discussant Internat. Bus. Schs. User Group, Omaha, Nebr., 1990. Poll election judge, Shadyside, Ohio, 1975-80. Selected for Group Projects Abroad to Turkey, Fulbright Program and Am. Forum Global Edn., N.Y.C., 1996. Mem. Inst. Mgmt. Sci., Acad. Mgmt., Assn. Info. Sys., Info. Resources Mgmt. Assn., Nat. Decision Scis. Inst. (session chair, discussant 1993-95, selected for New Faculty Consortium, 1993). Republican. Avocations: travel, photography, ethnography. Office: No State Univ Box 682 1200 S Jay St Aberdeen SD 57401-7155 E-mail: hollingj@northern.edu.

HOLLINGSWORTH, MARGARET CAMILLE, financial services administrator, consultant; b. Washington, Feb. 20, 1929; d. Harvey Alvin and Margaret Estelle (Head) Jacob; m. Robert Edgar Hollingsworth, July 14, 1960 (div. July 1980); children: William Lee, Robert Edgar Hollingsworth Jr., Barbara Camille, Bradford Damion; m. James Aldo Boland, Sept. 12, 1998 (dec. Aug. 1999). AA, Va. Intermont Coll., 1949. Bookkeeper Fred A. Smith Real Estate, Washington, 1949-53; adminstrv. mgr. Airtronic, Inc., Bethesda, Md., 1953-61; pers. adminstr. Sears Roebuck, Washington, 1973-74; adminstrv. mgr., communication mgr. Garvin GuyButler Corp., San Francisco, 1980-88, exec. sec., pers. mgr., 1989-95, adminstrv. cons., ret., 1996; adminstrv. cons., Concord, Calif. Assoc. Robert Hollingsworth Nuclear Cons., Walnut Creek, Calif., 1975-79. Bd. dirs. Civic Arts, Walnut Creek, 1975-2001. Recipient Spl. Recognition award AEC, 1974. Mem.: Rancho Bernardo Joslyn Ctr., San Diego Mus. Art, San Diego Natural Hist. Mus., Oaks North Country Club, Oaks North Travel Club, Beta Sigma Phi (pres. 1954). Democrat. Presbyterian. Avocations: travel, art appreciation, investments, hiking, reading. Home: 17758 Caminito Balata San Diego CA 92128 E-mail: mcb100501@aol.com.

HOLLINGSWORTH, MARTHA LYNETTE, secondary school educator; b. Waco, Tex., Oct. 9, 1951; d. Willie Frederick and Georgia Cuddell (Bryant); m. Roy David Hollingsworth, Dec. 31, 1971; children: Richard Avery, Justin Brian. AA, McLennan C.C., 1972; BBA, Baylor U., 1974, MS in Edn. Adminstrn., 1992. Tchr. Connally Ind. Sch. Dist., Waco, 1974—. With Adult Edn. Night Sch., 1974—78; chair Area III leadership conf. Vocat. Office Careers Clubs Tex., Waco, 1985—. Active Lakeview Little League Booster Club, 1985—; mem. PTA. Mem.: Assn. Tex. Profl. Educators (v.p. local chpt. 1988—90), Vocat. Office Edn. Tchrs. Assn. Tex., Tex. Future Farmers Am. (hon.), Future Homemakers Am. Area VIII (hon.), Delta Kappa Gamma. Baptist. Office: Connally Vocat Dept 715 N Rita St Waco TX 76705-1140

HOLLINGSWORTH, SAMUEL HAWKINS, JR., bassist; b. Birmingham, Ala., June 29, 1922; s. Samuel Hawkins and Bennie Louise (Brown) H.; m. Patricia Ann Patton, Apr. 1, 1957 (div. 1967); children: Priscilla P., Samuel Hawkins III; m. Elizabeth Mary Malezi, Dec. 31, 1974. Student, Juilliard Sch. Music, N.Y.C., 1940-42, George Peabody Coll. Tchrs., Nashville, 1953-54. Prin. bassist Nashville Symphony, 1946-65, Chamber Symphony of Phila., 1966-68, Dallas Symphony, 1968-70, Pitts. Symphony, 1970-92, prin. emeritus, 1992-95; retired, 1995. Mem. governing bd. dirs. Nashville Symphony Orch., 1960-63; chmn. Dallas Symphony Orth Players, 1969-70. Home: 1111 Pinewood Dr Pittsburgh PA 15243-1809

HOLLINGTON, RICHARD RINGS, JR., lawyer; b. Findlay, Ohio, Nov. 12, 1932; s. Richard Rings and Annett (Kirk) H.; m. Sally Stecher, Apr. 4, 1959; children: Florence A., Julie A., Richard R. III. Peter S. BA, Williams Coll., 1954; JD, Harvard U., 1957. Bar: Ohio 1957. Ptnr. Marshman, Hornbeck & Hollington, Cleve., 1958-67, McDonald, Hopkins, Hardy & Hollington, Cleve., 1967-69; law dir. City of Cleve., 1971-72; sr. ptnr. Baker & Hostetler, Cleve., 1969-71, 73—. Lead bd. dirs. Sky Fin. Group; mem. FDIC Advisory Com. on Banking Policy, 2002-, mem. Ohio Banking Comm., 2001—. Mem. Ohio Gen. Assembly, 1967-70, Cuyahoga County Rep. Ctrl. Com., 1962-66; exec. com. Ohio Rep. Fin. Com., 1971-98, Cuyahoga County Rep. Orgn., 1968-98, Geauga County Rep. Orgn., 1998—; trustee Cleve. State U., 1970-73, Greater Cleve. Hosp. Assn., 1976-82, Cleve. Mus. Natural History, 1969-81, Cleve. Zool. Soc., 1970-99, N. E. Ohio Regional Sewer Dist., 1972-73, Cuyahoga County Hosp. Found., 1968-73, Cleve. 500 Found., 1990-95, U. Findlay, 1991—, others; bd. commrs. grievance and discipline Ohio Supreme Ct., 1993-95. Mem. ABA, Ohio Bar Assn., Greater Cleve. Bar Assn., Sixth Cir. Jud. Conf. (life), Eighth Dist. Ohio Jud. Conf. (life), Ct. Nisi Prius, Union Club (Cleve.), The Country Club (Pepper Pike), Pepper Pike Club, Roaring Gap (N.C.) Club, Rolling Rock (Pa.) Club. Home: 13792 County Line Rd Chagrin Falls OH 44022-4008 Office: Baker & Hostetler 3200 National City Ctr 1900 E 9th St Ste 3200 Cleveland OH 44114-3475

HOLLINGWORTH, BEVERLY A. state legislator; b. Haverhill, Mass., Oct. 18, 1935; m. William P. Gilligan, 1978; children: David, Mary Beth. Therese, Kimberly. Student, U. N.H. Mem. N.H. Ho. of Reps., Concord, 1980-90; mem. Dist. 23 N.H. Senate, Concord, 1991—, pres., 1999-00; owner, mgr. Hollingworth Motor Ct., Hampton Beach, N.H. Chmn. appropriations com.; mem. ways and means com., mem. judiciary com., mem. fin. exec. com., mem. joint adminstrv. peals com. Active United Way, Heart Fund, ARC, Lane Meml. Friends Libr. Mem. Hampton Beach (N.H.) C. of C. Democrat. Roman Catholic. Office: Room 120 State House Concord NH 03301

HOLLINS, MITCHELL LESLIE, lawyer; b. N.Y.C., Mar. 11, 1947; s. Milton and Alma (Bell) H.; m. Nancy Kirchheimer, Mar. 27, 1977 (div. 1999); children: Herbert K. II, Dorothy Ann, Betsy Ann Mizell; m. Jan C. Philipsborn, Oct. 24, 1999; 1 child. BA, Case Western Res. U., 1967; JD, NYU, 1971. Bar: Ill. 1971, U.S. Dist. Ct. (no. dist.) Ill. 1971. Assoc. Sonnenschein Nath & Rosenthal, Chgo., 1971-78, ptnr., 1978—. Asst. sec., dir. Jr. Achievement Chgo., 1980—; bd. dirs. Young Men's Jewish Coun., 1973-75; bd. dirs. young people's div. Jewish United Fund Met. Chgo., 1972-76; bd. dirs. Med. Rsch. Inst. Coun. Mem. exec. com., 1979-92, sec., 1981-82, gen. counsel, 1983-86, vice chmn., 1987-92, chmn. jr. bd., 1978-79. Editor NYU Jour. Internat. Law and Politics, 1970-71. Asst. sec., dir. Jr. Achievement Chgo., 1980—; bd. dirs. Young Men's Jewish Coun., 1973-75; bd. dirs. young people's divsn. Jewish United Fund Met. Chgo., 1972-76; bd. dirs. Med. Rsch. Inst. Coun., mem. exec. com., 1979-92, sec., 1981-82, gen. counsel, 1983-86, vice chmn., 1987-92, chmn. jr. bd., 1978-79. Mem. ABA, Am. Coll. Investment Counsel, Chgo. Bar Assn., Standard Club, Lake Shore Country Club (mem. bd. govs. 1984-92, sec. 1985-92), Lawyers Club. Republican. Home: 265 Wentworth Ave Glencoe IL 60022-1931 Office: Sonnenschein Nath & Rosenthal 8000 Sears Tower Chicago IL 60606

HOLLINSHEAD, ARIEL CAHILL, research oncologist, educator; b. Allentown, Pa., Aug. 24, 1929; d. Earl Darnell and Gertrude Loretta (Cahill) H.; m. Montgomery K. Hyun, June 12, 1957; children: William C., Christopher C. Student, Swarthmore Coll., 1947-48; AB, Ohio U., 1951, DSc (hon.), 1977; MA, George Washington U., 1955, PhD, 1957. Asst. prof., fellow in virology Baylor U. Med. Ctr., 1958-59; asst. prof. pharmacology George Washington Med. Ctr., 1959-61, asst. prof. medicine, 1961-64, assoc. prof. medicine, head lab. virus and cancer rsch., 1964-73, prof., dir. lab. virus and cancer rsch., 1974-89; on sabbatical leave 1990, prof. medicine emeritus, 1991—; rschr. H2 Virus and Cancer Rsch., 1991—. Clin. rschr. trials in oncology and virology; cons. to biotech. cos. and FDA panel; panelist FDA and NIH. Contbr. over 270 articles on active immunotherapy and immunochemotherapy of cancer and virus diseases to sci. jours. Bd. dirs. Nat. Women's Econ. Alliance, Ohio U., Med. Coll. Pa.,1980—, Women's Inst., 1995-97. Named Med. Woman of Yr., Joint Bd. Am. Med. Colls., 1975-76, Bicentennial Honor award Joint Bd. Am. Med. Colls., 1976, one of Outstanding Woman of Am., 1987, Outstanding Alumnus of Yr., Ohio U., 1990; recipient Cert. merit Med. Coll. Pa., 1975-76, Marion Spencer Fay Med. Woman of Year award Med. Coll. Pa.; decorated Star of Europe, 1980. Fellow AAAS (med. sci. com. 1993-96, 99—), Washington Acad. Sci. N.Y. Acad. Scis.; mem. Grad. Women in Sci. (nat. pres. 1985-86, bd. dirs. 1986-92, nat. liaison to Washington, 1992—), Internat. Soc. Preventive Oncology, Nat. Soc. Exptl. Biology and Medicine (Disting. Scientist award 1985, Disting. Scientist emeritus award for Outstanding Career in Tchg. and Rsch. in Medicine 1996, past pres. Greater Washington chpt.), Am. Soc. Microbiology, Am. Assn. Cancer Research, Am. Assn. Immunologists, Women in Cancer Rsch., Vet. Females Am., Clin. Immunology Soc., Internat. Soc. Antiviral Research, Am. Soc. Clin. Oncology, Internat. Assn. Study Lung Cancer, Internat. Union Against Cancer, Am. Med. Writers Assn., Phi Beta Kappa (alumnus 1990). Clubs: Kenwood Country, Blue Ridge Mountain Country, Washington Forum (pres. 1987, 91). Achievements include being first to purify, develop and test cancer gene products, including peptides and to study activities; first to invent field called proteomics; peptides were studied and identified for the ability to induce long-lasting cell-mediated immunity; developed proteomics technology and pioneered clinical testing and monitoring epitope activity during clinical trials; patentee in field. Home: 3637 Van Ness St NW Washington DC 20008-3130 *The Latin phrase "Carpe diem", meaning seize the day, or, guard the moment: my first discovery for effective viral disease treatment was the use of purine, pyrimidine and sulfur-containing analogues, one of which was used to attenuate virulent polioviruses; another discovery was the first non virion antigen to block virus-induced animal tumors; my first discovery for effective cancer immunotherapy was the separation and identification of active peptides from cell membranes and the first proof of their efficacy in tumor prevention in animals and in man. Phase I, II or III clinical trials were conducted with individual tumor-related peptides selected for nineteen forms of human cancer. I discovered that little pieces of these active proteins (called epitopes) not only were useful for monitoring tumor progression U.S. patent received but were the oncogene products for even better polyvalent therapies in the future. With Dr. T.H.M. Stewart, established the first identification of induced dormancy in human lung cancer patients in USA and Canada receiving our vaccines and, greater than 12 year survival free of lung cancer.*

HOLLINSHEAD, EARL DARNELL, JR., lawyer; b. Pitts., Aug. 1, 1927; s. Earl Darnell and Gertrude (Cahill) H.; m. Sylvia Antion, June 29, 1957; children: Barbara, Kim, Earl III, Susan. AB, Ohio U., 1948; LLB, U. Pitts., 1951. Bar: Pa. 1952, U.S. Ct. Mil. Appeals 1954, U.S. Dist. Ct. (we. dist.) Pa. 1955, U.S. Supreme Ct. 1956, U.S. Ct. Appeals (3d cir.) 1959, U.S. Dist. Ct. (ea. dist.) Ohio 1978. Sole practice, Pitts., 1955-70; ptnr. Hollinshead and Mendelson, Pitts., 1970-89, Hollinshead, Mendelson, Bresnahan & Nixon, P.C., Pitts., 1990-97; sole practitioner Pitts., 1997—. Mem. Pitts. Estate Planning Council. Contbr. articles to profl. jours. Served to lt. USNR, 1951-55. Fellow Pa. Bar Found. (life); mem. Pa. Bar Assn. (chmn. real property divsn. 1983-85, real property, probate and trust sects. 1985-86), Allegheny County Bar Assn. (chmn. real property sect. 1975-76), Pa. Bar Inst. (lectr., planner, bd. dirs. 1988-94), Am. Coll. Real Estate Lawyers. Home: 2535 Windgate Rd Bethel Park PA 15102-2730 Office: Regional Enterprise Tower 425 Sixth Ave Ste 2490 Pittsburgh PA 15219-1819

HOLLIS, BRUCE WARREN, experimental nutritionist, industrial consultant; b. May 29, 1951; s. Warren Eugene and Evelyn Katherine (Jabbusch) H.; m. Betsy Eberle Yount, Aug. 16, 1980. BS, Ohio State U., 1973, MS, 1976; PhD, U. Guelph, Ont., 1979. Postdoctoral fellow Case We. Res. U., Cleve., 1979-82, asst. prof. nutrition, 1982-86; assoc. prof. pediatrics Med. U. S.C., Charleston, 1986-94, assoc. prof. biochemistry and molecular biology, 1989-94, dir. gen. clin. rsch. ctr. lab., 1990-95, prof. pediatrics, biochemistry and molecular biology, 1994—. Med. rschr., indsl. cons. Contbr. chpts. in books, articles to sci. jours. Recipient NIH awards, 1980, 82, Disting. Alumni award Ohio State U., 1996. Mem. Endocrine Soc., Am. Soc. Bone and Mineral Rsch., Am. Inst. Nutrition (Mead Johnson Nutritionals award 1991), Sigma Xi. Republican. Home: 906 Kushiwah Cr Ct Charleston SC 29412-4938 Office: Med Univ SC Dept Pediatrics Charleston SC 29425 E-mail: hollisb@musc.edu.

HOLLIS, CHARLES EUGENE, JR., savings and loan association executive; b. Daytona Beach, Fla., Sept. 14, 1948; s. Charles Eugene and Betty Lou (Beech) H.; m. Carol Repass, Mar. 20, 1971 (div. Nov. 1993); children: Stephanie Dyane, Charles Preston, Robin Jene. AA, Dayton Beach Jr. Coll., 1968; BA, U. South Fla., 1972. CPA Fla. Asst. Deloitte Haskins & Sells, Tampa, Fla., 1972—73, sr. asst., 1973—75, sr., 1975—78, mgr., 1978—82; audit mgr. Jack Eckerd Corp., Clearwater, Fla., 1982—85; v.p. fin., contr. Freedom Savs. and Loan Assn., Tampa, 1985—87, sr. v.p., CFO, treas., 1987—88, exec. v.p., 1988—89, CenTrust Fed., Miami, Fla., 1990; supervisory fin. instn. specialist Resolution Trust Corp., Atlanta, 1990—95; exec. v.p. Beech Mgmt. Group, Inc., 1996—2000; portfolio mgr. GMAC Comml. Mortgage Corp., 2000—. Chmn. fin. and taxation com. Fla. League Cities, Tallahassee, 1979—81; mem. fin. com. Nat. League Cities, Washington, 1980—86; code enforcement bd. City of Temple Terrace, 1986—91; trustee Univ. Community Hosp., 1987—91; charter mem., treas. Northeast Sertoma, 1989—90; City councilman City of Temple Terrace, Fla., 1976—86, vice mayor, 1981—82; treas. Christ Our Redeemer Luth. Ch., 1984—86, pres., 1987—88; treas. Fla. Synod-Evangelical Luth. Ch. in Am., 1988—92. Recipient Disting. Service award, U. South Fla. Coll. Bus., 1972, Outstanding Alumnus award, Beta Alpha Psi, 1983. Mem.: Tampa C. of C. (Leadership Tampa 1987—88), Fin. Mgrs. Soc., Fla. Soc. CPAs, Am. Inst. CPAs, Beta Alpha Psi. Republican. Home and Office: 985 Gardendale Dr Columbia SC 29210-4906

HOLLIS, CHARLES HATFIELD, lawyer; b. Washington, Feb. 27, 1956; s. Charles Bernard and Mary Rebecca (Hatfield) H.; m. Catherine Anne Gleason, Sept. 1, 1979; children: Mary Catherine, Charles Joseph. BSBA, U. Md., 1978; JD, U. Ga., 1981. Bar: Ga. 1981, La. 1981, U.S. Dist. Ct. (ca. dist.) La. 1981, U.S. Supreme Ct. 1981, U.S. Ct. Appeals (5th cir.) 1982, U.S. Ct. Appeals (11th cir.) 1984, U.S. Dist. Ct. (mid. dist.) La. 1985, U.S. Dist. Ct. (we. dist.) La. 1988. Assoc. The Kullman Firm, New Orleans, 1981-86, ptnr., 1986—. Mem. ABA, New Orleans Bar Assn., Beta Gamma Sigma. Republican. Avocations: hunting, golf. Home: 3756 Lake Charles Dr Gretna LA 70056-8350 Office: The Kullman Firm 1600 Energy Ctr 1100 Poydras St New Orleans LA 70163-1101

HOLLIS, DONALD ROGER, management consultant; b. Warren, Ohio, Mar. 4, 1936; s. Louis and Lena (Succo) Hollis; m. Marilyn G. Morganti, Aug. 23, 1958; children: Roger, Russel Kirk, Gregory, Heather. BS, Kent State U., 1959. Regional mgr. Glidden Corp., San Francisco, 1959-65, dir. mgmt. info. svcs. Cleve., 1965-68; dir. mgmt. info. services SCM Corp., N.Y.C., 1968-71; v.p. Chase Manhattan Bank, N.Y.C., 1971-81; sr. v.p. First Chgo. Corp., 1981-85, exec. v.p., 1986-95, head sys., data processing, cash mgmt. and security products and quality programs, 1986-95; pres., CEO DRH Strategic Cons., Chgo., 1995—. Bd. dirs. S2 Corp., Quickstream, E.K.I., Optipay. Trustee Ill. Inst. Tech. Office: 20 S Clark St Ste 620 Chicago IL 60603-1803 E-mail: don_hollis@bankone.com.

HOLLIS, JAN MICHAEL, astrophysicist, scientific computer analyst; b. Martinsburg, W.Va., June 5, 1941; s. Delbert Irvin and Betty (Collier) H.; m. Carol Ann Getz, Feb. 1, 1964 (div. Oct. 1993); children: David Collier, Mary Morgan; m. Joan Ellen Isensee, Nov. 8, 1995. AB in Math., Duke U., 1963; MA in Astronomy, U. Va., 1972, PhD in Astronomy, 1976. Submarine officer USN, 1963-69; sci. computer analyst Nat. Radio Astronomy Obs., Tucson, 1973-79; space telescope data mgr. NASA, Greenbelt, Md., 1979-82, head sci. ops. br., 1982-88, asst. chief earth and space data computing divsn., 1988—. Mem. Internat. Halley Watch Sci. Working Group, NASA, Greenbelt, 1981, mem. Hubble Space Telescope Image Processing Sci. Working Group, 1990. Contbr. over 80 articles to profl. jours. Trustee Glenelg (Md.) United Meth. Ch., 1997-99, 2003—. Lt. USN, 1963-69. Recipient Exceptional Sci. Achievement medal NASA, 1990. Fellow Royal Astron. Soc.; mem. Am. Astron. Soc. (Van Biesbroeck Award com. 1997-2001), Internat. Astron. Union. Democrat. Avocations: astronomy, model trains, tennis, hiking, peanut butter fudge. Office: NASA Goddard Space Flight Ctr Code 930 Greenbelt MD 20771-0001 E-mail: jan.m.hollis@nasa.gov.

HOLLIS, JANICE DENISE, publishing executive, minister; b. Hazelhurst, Ga., Dec. 13, 1964; d. Moses and Janie Hollis. DDiv(hon.), World Christianship Theol. Sem., 2002. Ordained minister. Pub. Hollis Pub. Network, Phila., 1996—; asst. pastor Olivet Bapt. Ch., Phila., 2001—. Author: Life is Positively Astounding, 2002, The Warrior Within, 2002, Personal Management: It Matters, 2003; singer: (music recording) You Stole My Heart, 1988. Founder Progress Believes Ministries, 2003—; vol. Phila. Cares, 2001—02. Named to Sisters in Bus., Phila. Bus. News Jour., 1999. Mem.: Women's Alliance Exclusive Assn. (pres. 1988—2002). Baptist. Avocations: lecturing, sailing, rock climbing, singing, writing.

HOLLIS, JESSICA LEXIE, literature educator; b. Birmingham, Ala., June 30, 1968; d. Jesse and Mamie Lee Hollis; m. Anthony Carl Brusate, Sept. 22, 1997. PhD in English Lit., U. of Ky., 1997—. Instr. English U. of Ala., Tuscaloosa, 1995—96, U. of Ky., Lexington, 1997—2003. Editor: (acad. jour.) disClosure; a journal of social theory. Participant Coalition to Prevent the War in Iraq, Cin., 2003, A.N.S.W.E.R., 2003, Moveon.Org, 2003; mem. PETA. Recipient Haggin fellowship, U. Ky. Opportunity fellowship. Mem.: AAUW, MLA (assoc.), Physicians Com. for Responsible Medicine, Am. Soc. for Eighteenth-Century Studies (assoc.). Green Party. Office: U Ky 1215 Patterson Office Tower Lexington KY 40506 Office Fax: 323-257-1073.

HOLLIS, JULIA ANN ROSHTO, critical care, medical, and surgical nurse; b. Monroe, La., June 25, 1945; d. Joseph Edward Roshto and Eleanor Coverdale Larsen; m. William Davis Hollis, Mar. 2, 1964; children: David Terrel, Julia Allison. BSN, N.E. La. U., 1976. RN, La., Ala., Miss.; cert. BCLS, ACLS. Staff nurse to head nurse E.A. Conway Hosp., Monroe, 1977-84; staff nurse, charge nurse ICU, critical care North Monroe Community Hosp., Monroe, 1984-87; staff nurse neurotrama surg. ICU U. South Ala. Med. Ctr., Mobile, 1988-89; staff nurse, charge nurse Norrell Health Care, Mobile, 1990—, Medforce Internat., New Orleans; owner Resource Mgmt., 1997. Mem. AACN, AAUW, Ala. Nurses Assn., Met. Writer's Guild. Home: 5073 Dawes Lane Ext Theodore AL 36582-9627

HOLLIS, KATHERINE MARY, information scientist, consultant; d. Albert George and Rosalyn Mary Duren; m. David Martin Hollis, Aug. 25, 1990; children: Kent David Miller, Jason Randolph Miller;children: Brittany Frances, David Christopher. MS in Nat. Security Strategy, Nat. War College, 1999; B in Polit. Sci., U. Minn., 1983. Dir. resource mgmt. installation support modules program Program Exec. Office - STD. Mgmt. Info. Sys., Ft. Belvoir, Va., 1989—93; program mgr. electronic commerce/electronic data interchange Def. Info. Sys. Agy., Falls Church, Va., 1993—96, spl. asst. to the dep., pub. key infrastructure program mgmt. office, 1999—2000; dep. dir. electronic processes initiatives coun. task force Office of the Deputy Sec. of Def., Rosslyn, Va., 1996—98; deputy dir. dept. def. Y2K office Office of the Sec. of Def., Crystal City, Va., 1998—99; dir. global info. assurance solutions Electronic Data Sys., Herndon, Va., 2000—. Adv. com. Fed. Electronic Commerce Coalition, Falls Church, Va., 1999—; chair smart card integrated process team Def. Info. Sys. Agy., 1999—2000; spkr. in field. Vol. educator Prince William County Schools, Manassas, Va., 2001. Recipient Commanders award, Dept. of the Army, Dept. of Def., 1989, Federal 100 award, Federal Computer News, 1998. Avocations: archaeology, Egyptology, travel, writing. Office: Electronic Data Sys 13600 EDS Dr (A2S-D49) Herndon VA 20171

HOLLIS, MARY FERN CAUDILL, nurse educator, music educator, writer; b. Augusta, Ga., Mar. 13, 1942; d. Robert Paul and Fern (Alderton) Caudill; children: Harry N. III (dec.), Mary Melissa, H. Newcombe IV. B in Music Edn., U. Louisville, 1964; AS in Nursing, Tenn. State U., 1980; postgrad., Nashville Tech. Inst., 1987. RN, Tenn. Staff nurse oncology and med.-surg. units St. Thomas Hosp., Nashville, 1981-82; dir. nursing Home Health Svcs. of Tenn., 1985; staff oncology nurse Alive Hospice, Nashville, 1982-83; scheduling coord. HCA Parkview Med. Ctr., Nashville, 1987-88; nurse, staff relief coord. Partners Home Health, Nashville, 1989-90; nursing supr. Kimberly Quality Care Staffing, Nashville, 1991-92; RN coord. on call MedPartners Nursing Svc. of Mid. Tenn., Nashville, 1994-95. Profl. concert vocal soloist; tchr. piano, music edn., music theory, voice, 1962—; vocal soloist Nashville Symphony Chorus and Orch., 1974. Author: Out of My Suffering: Reflections of a Hospice Nurse, 1984. Mem. Music Tchrs. Nat. Assn., Tenn. Music Tchrs. Assn., Nashville Area Music Tchrs. Assn., Am. Coll. Musicians, Nat. Guild Piano Tchrs., Sigma Alpha Iota, Gamma Phi Beta.

HOLLIS, MARY FRANCES, aerospace educator; b. Indpls., Sept. 18, 1931; d. Lucian Albert and Clara Frances Coleman; divorced; 1 child, Booker Albert Hollis. BS, Butler U., 1952, MS, 1962; postgrad., Stanford U., 1975, San Francisco State U., 1980-81. Cert. elem. tchr., Ind., Calif. Kindergarten tchr. Lockerbie Nursery Sch., Indpls., 1952, Indpls. Pub. Schs., 1952-69; tchr. K-6 San Mateo (Calif.) City Sch. Dist., 1969-91; summer sch. prin. San Mateo City Sch. dist., Foster City, Calif., 1983-91; aerospace educator, 1982—. Bd. dirs. Coun. of Math./Sci. Educators of San Mateo County, Belmont, Calif.; resident mgr. Lesley Found., Park Twrs., 1999—. Editor: San Mateo County Math./Sci. Coun. quarterly newsletter, 1988-90. Bd. dirs. Arts Coun. of San Mateo County, 1986-91, Mid-Peninsula chpt. ACLU, San Mateo, 1990—, Unitarian-Universalist Ch. San Mateo, 1996-98; bd. dirs. Peninsula Funeral and Meml. Planning Soc., 1996-2000, co-pres., 1998-99; office mgr. Roger Winston Campaign for San Mateo Union H.S. Dist. Bd. Trustees, 1993; mem. adv. com. USAF-Pacific Liaison Region-CAP, 1988-94; sr. peer counselor San Mateo County Mental Health, 1996—. Recipient Life Down to Earth award NASA, Moffet Field, Mt. View, Calif., 1985-86, Earl Sams Tchr. of Yr. award Calif. Assn. Aerospace Educators, 1989, award of merit Am. Legion, San Bruno, Calif., 1989, citation Air Force Assn., Mountain View, Calif., 1991, Aviation Summer Sch. cert. of appreciation Am. Legion Dept. Calif. Aerospace Commn., 1994. Mem. NEA (life), AAUW (bd. dirs. San Carlos chpt. 1993-95), NAACP (life), Am. Bus. Women's Assn. (rec. sec. Foster City chpt. 1985), World Aerospace Edn. Orgn. Democrat. Unitarian-Universalist. Avocations: reading, travel, music-jazz, rhythm and blues, swimming, aerospace/aviation. Office: PO Box 625 Belmont CA 94002-0625 E-mail: mfrances@pacbell.net.

HOLLIS, NICHOLAS EVERETT, trade association executive; b. Randolph, Vt., May 11, 1944; s. Everett Loftus and Marion Armstrong (Jennings) H.; m. Sue Eleanor Headlee, Aug. 21, 1966 (div. Mar. 1979); m. Ruth Patricia Griffith, Mar. 26, 1983; 1 child, Nathaniel Randolph. BA in History with hons., DePauw U., Greencastle, Ind., 1966; MA in Internat. Econs., Johns Hopkins U., 1968; Hon. Degree in Internat. Law, City of London Coll., 1965. Tchr. D.C. Pub. Schs., 1968-69; fgn. trade exec. U.S. C. of C., Washington, 1969-72; v.p. internat. Nat. Assn. Mfrs., N.Y.C., Washington, 1972-75; CEO Ind. Ctr. for Trade Negotiations, Geneva, Washington, 1975-76; dep. coord. U.S. Dept. State/AID, Washington, 1977-78; pres. Global Projects, Inc., Washington, 1979-80; exec. dir. Agri-Energy Roundtable, Washington, 1980—. Lectr. in field; condr. workshops in field; spkr. various sci. and internat. confs. Editor Agri-Energy RT, 1980-87; contbr. articles to profl. jours. Mem. Nat. Adv. Coun. Vocat. Edn., 1972-73; pres. Agribus. Coun., Washington, 1987—; mem. pvt. sector adv. com. House Com. on Hunger, Washington, 1985-90; spokesman/negotiation UN World Food Coun., Paris, 1985; spkr., negotiator UNIDO African Mins. Conf., Harare, Zimbabwe, 1989; spkr. Pres.'s Com. on USAID Mgmt., Washington, 1992; spkr., panel chmn. DOJ-Econ. Crime

Summit, St. Louis, 1998; founder US-EC Businessmen's Conf., 1972—, US-Arab Bus. Roundtable, 1978-81; co-founder US-USSR Trade and Econ. Coun., 1973; admiral Cherry River Navy, 1999—; judge, reviewer Dept. Edn. Civic Edn. grant proposals, 2002. Named European Parliament/Young Leader, EC, Brussels, 1974; recipient World Food Security award Bd. Dirs. Agri-Energy, 1988, Gulf Peace award Govt. Oman, 1989. Mem. Am. Soc. Assn. Execs. (internat. com. 1974-76), Assn. of Export Mgmt. Cos. (advisor 1972-74). Congregationalist. Avocations: skiing, hiking, golf, chess, reading. Home: 3312 Porter St NW Washington DC 20008 Office: Agribusiness Coun (ABC) 1312 18th St NW #300 Washington DC 20036 E-mail: info@agribusinesscouncil.org.

HOLLIS, REGINALD, archbishop; b. Eng., July 18, 1932; emigrated to Can., 1954; s. Jesse Farndon and Edith Ellen (Lee) H.; m. Marcia Crombie, Sept. 7, 1957; children— Martin, Hilda, Aidan. BA, Cambridge U., Eng., 1954; MA, Cambridge U., 1958; BD, McGill U., Montreal, 1956; DD (hon.), U. South, 1977, Montreal Diocesan Theol. Coll., 1975. Ordained to ministry Anglican Ch. as deacon, 1956, as priest, 1956. Chaplain Montreal Diocesan Theol. Coll.; also chaplain to Anglican students McGill U., 1956-60; asst. St. Matthias Parish, Westmount, Que., 1960-63; incumbent St. Barnabas Ch., Roxboro, Que., 1963-66, rector, 1966-71, Christ Ch., Beaurepaire, Que., 1971-74; dir. parish and diocesan services Diocese Montreal, 1974-75, bishop, 1975-90; archbishop of Montreal Met. of the Ecclesiastical Province of Can., 1989-90; asst. bishop Diocese of Ctrl. Fla., Orlando, 1990-94; episc. dir. Anglican Fellowship of Prayer, 1990-94; rector St. Paul's Ch., New Smyrna Beach, Fla., 1994-97; ret., 1997. Author: Abiding in Christ, 1987. Anglican. Home: 1175 Newport Ave Ste 303 Victoria BC Canada V8S 5E6

HOLLIS, ROBBIE SMAGULA, marketing communications executive; b. Dover, Del., Oct. 15, 1957; d. Thomas David and Billie Jo (Talkington) Smagula; m. Mark Steven Dennis, May 26, 1979 (div. May 1982); 1 child, Gregory Steven; m. Stuart D. B. Hollis, Nov. 18, 1989; children: Hanna Joellen, Rachael Nicole. BS in Marine Biology, Tex. A&M U., 1978. Tech. writer Tex. Trans. Inst., College Station, Tex., 1978-80; documentation coord. Genentech, Inc., South San Francisco, Calif., 1980-82; sr. tech. writer Cen. & South West Svcs., Inc., Dallas, 1982-88; sales promotion mgr. Computer Assocs. (formerly UCCEL Corp.), Dallas, 1984-88; with corp. comm. J. Driscoll & Assocs., Dallas, 1988—89; mgr. mktg. comm. ANTRIM Corp., Plano, Tex., 1989—94; mgr. Hogan Corp. Comms., Dallas, 1994-96; comms. ministry First Presbyn. Ch., McKinney, Tex., 2000—02; instrnl. aide Anna (Tex.) Elem., 2002—03, tchr., 2003—. Mem. Soc. Tech. Communication (Best of Show and Excellence Achievement award 1985, 86), Internat. Assn. Bus. Communicators, NAFE.

HOLLIS, SHEILA SLOCUM, lawyer; b. Denver, July 15, 1948; d. Theodore Doremus and Emily M. (Caplis) Slocum (dec.); m. John Hollis; 1 child, Windsong Emily Lanford. BS in Journalism with honors, BS in Gen. Studies cum laude, U. Colo., 1971; JD, U. Denver, 1973. Bar: Colo. 1974, D.C. 1975, U.S. Supreme Ct. 1980. Trial atty. Fed. Power Commn., Washington, 1974-75; assoc. firm Wilner & Scheiner, Washington, 1975-77; dir. office enforcement Fed. Energy Regulatory Commn., Washington, 1977-80; pvt. practice, 1980—; ptnr. Vinson & Elkins, Washington, 1987-92; sr. ptnr. Metzger, Hollis, Gordon & Alprin, Washington, 1992-97; mem. exec. com., mng. ptnr. D.C. Duane Morris LLP, Washington, 1997—2003. Professorial lectr. in energy law George Washington U., 1980—2000; bd. dirs. U.S. Energy Assn. Co-author: Energy Decision Making, 1983, Energy Law and Policy, 1989; mem. editl. bd. Oil and Gas Reporter, Pub. Utility Fortnightly; contbr. articles to profl. publs. Established and developed enforcement program Fed. Energy Regulatory Commn.; mem. adv. bd. Pub. Utility Ctr. N.Mex. State U., 1986—94; mem. adv. bd. N.Am. Energy Stds. Bd., 1998—; pres. Women's Coun. Energy and Environment, 1997—2003; bd. dirs. Found. for Vets. Health Care., Wyo. State Soc. U. Denver scholar, 1972-73. Fellow: ABA (chair coord. group energy law 1989—92, mem. ho. dels. 1992—2001, chair coord. group energy law 1995—97, chair standing com. environ. law 1997—2000, mem. bd. editors ABA Jour. 2000—, immediate past chair sect. environ., energy and resources 2001—02, standing com. on fed. judiciary 2002—); mem.: U.S. Energy Assn. (bd. dirs.), John Carroll Soc., Women's Bar Assn. D.C., D.C. Bar Assn., Colo. Bar Assn., Internat. Legal Edn. Ctr. (trustee), Oil and Gas Ednl. Inst., Energy Bar Assn. (pres. 1991—92), Am. Law Inst., Internat. Bar Assn., Comml. Bar of Eng. and Wales (hon.), Sir Thomas More Soc. (pres.), Cosmos Club, Nat. Press Club. Roman Catholic. Office: DuaneMorris LLP 1667 K St NW Ste 700 Washington DC 20006-1608 E-mail: sshollis@duanemorris.com.

HOLLIS, SUSAN TOWER, history educator; b. Boston, Mar. 17, 1939; d. James Wilson and Dorothy Parsons (Moore) Tower; m. Allen Hollis, Nov. 10, 1962 (div. Feb. 1975); children: Deborah Durfee, Harrison. AB, Smith Coll., 1962; PhD, Harvard U., 1982. Cert. C.C. instr. history and humanities. Asst. prof. Scripps Coll., Claremont, Calif., 1988-91; prof. Coll. of Undergrad. Studies The Union Inst., L.A., 1991-93; dean of the college and prof. humanities Sierra Nev. Coll.-Lake Tahoe, Incline Village, Nev., 1993-95; ind. scholar, cons. Reno, 1995-96; ctr. dir., assoc. dean Ctrl. N.Y. Ctr. Empire State Coll. of SUNY, Syracuse, 1996-99; assoc. prof. SUNY Empire State Coll., Rochester, N.Y., 1999—, coord. western region MA in Liberal Studies program, 2000—. Convener hist. studies Empire State Coll. of SUNY, 2000—, co-chair acad. policies an learning programs com., 2003—. Author: The Ancient Egyptian "Tale of Two Brothers", 1990; editor: Hymns, Prayers and Songs: Anthology of Ancient Egyptian Lyrics & Poetry (by John L. Foster), 1996; co-editor: Feminist Theory and the Study of Folklore, 1993; contbr. Music vol. Open Readings, Belmont, Mass., 1982—88; vol. Sierra Club, 1988—; problem capt. Odyssey of the Mind, Nev., 1994—95, judge, 1997—98; crew chief Tahoe Rim trail, 1994—96; active Masterworks Chorale, NY, 1996—99. Mem.: N.Y. State Network for Women Leaders in Higher Edn. (assoc. coord. 1999—2000, bd. dirs. 1997—, coord. 2000—03), N.Y. Acad. Scis., Egyptological Soc. N.Y., Soc. Bibl. Lit. (co-chair Egyptology and Ancient Israel group 1995—96, chair Egyptology and Ancient Israel group 1996—2003, convenor Ancient Near East Consortium 1998—), Soc. for Study Egyptian Antiquities, Internat. Assn. Egyptologists, Am. Rsch. Ctr. Egypt, Am. Oriental Soc., Am. Folklore Soc., Am. Assn. Higher Edn., Am. Acad. Religion, Incline Village/Crystal Bay C. of C. (sec., bd. dirs. 1994—95), Ka-na-wa-ke Canoe Club (bd. dirs. 1998—2000), Adirondack Mountain Club, Appalachian Mountain Club (co-leader 1987—88). Democrat. Home: 7 New Wickham Dr Penfield NY 14526-2703 Office: Empire State Coll of SUNY 1475 Winton Rd N Rochester NY 14609-5803 E-mail: susan.hollis@esc.edu.

HOLLIS, TIMOTHY MARTIN, bank executive; b. Marietta, Ga., Nov. 13, 1962; s. Milton Joel and Mary Syvila (Skanner) H. BSBA in Mgmt., Shorter Coll., 1986. Desk supr. front desk Wyndham Hotel Co., Atlanta, 1986-87; personal banker C&S/Sovran Corp., Atlanta, 1987-90, sr. personal banker, 1990-91; asst. br. mgr., banking officer NationsBank of Ga., N.A., Atlanta, 1991-92, banking ctr. mgr., 1992-95; sales mgr. Wachovia Bank, NA (formerly First Union Nat. Bank Ga.), Atlanta, 1995—97; fin. specialist AVP, 1997—. Treas., mktg. chairperson, fin. com., bd. trustees Choral Guild of Atlanta, 1991; mem. Buckhead Young Reps., Atlanta, 1989-92; bd. dirs. Artcare, Inc., Atlanta, 1991-94; docent, vol., mem. Friends of Zoo Atlanta; mem. steering com. First Night Atlanta, 1993-99, 1994 class Atlanta Midtown Leadership Program, Atlanta Midtown Alliance, 1992—, Human Rights Campaign Fund, 1992—, GAPAC, 1993-95; mem. adv. bd. Atlanta Exec. Network, 1993-96, Joining Hearts, Inc., 1994-99; steering com. Aids Walk Atlanta, 1995-97; bd. dirs. Positive Impact, 1996-97, Pets are Lovin Support, Inc., 1997-99; co-chair Young Profls. of Atlanta Exec. Network, 1996-98; conf. chair First Night Internat., 1998—; bd. dirs. AIDS Treatment Initiatives, 1997—, pres., 1998—. Mem. Atlanta Track Club (vol.). Methodist. Avocations: running, singing, working-out, volunteering. Home: 28 Finch Trail NE Atlanta GA 30308-2418 Office: Wachovia Bank NA 1605 Monroe Dr NE Atlanta GA 30324-5003 E-mail: tim.hollis@wachovia.com.

HOLLIS, WILLIAM FREDERICK, information scientist; b. Cleve., May 25, 1954; s. Raymond Frederick and Elizabeth (Meyer) H.; m. Jo Anne Kohlenberg, June 25, 1977; children: George Anthony, Dawn Elizabeth. BS, Bowling Green State U., 1976; MLS, Kent State U., 1979, EdD, 1992. Cert. chemisty/physics educator Ohio. Info. specialist B.F. Goodrich Rsch. & Devel. Ctr., Brecksville, Ohio, 1979-82; instr. libr. and info. sci. Coll. Wooster (Ohio), 1982-84; sr. info. specialist GenCorp Rsch., Akron, 1984, acting head tech. info., 1985, head tech. info ctr., 1986—2002; cons. polymer sci. and tech. Polymer Networking.com, 2003—. Instr. sci. & tech. Stark Tech. Coll., Canton, Ohio, 1983-84. Elder United Ch. of Christ, Suffield, Ohio, 1986-89. Mem. Am. Chem. Soc., Am. Inst. Physics, Am. Soc. Info. Sci., Assn. Ednl. Communications & Tech. Home and Office: 1880 Hamden Ln Stow OH 44224-6035

HOLLIS-SAWYER, LISA ANN, psychologist, gerontologist, researcher; d. Dale Eugene and Patricia Ann Hollis; m. Thomas Paul Sawyer, Aug. 9, 1997; 1 child, Joshua Thomas Sawyer. PhD in Indsl. Gerontol. Psychology, U. of Akron, 1996. Asst. prof. of psychology and gerontology, gerontology program coord. Northeastern Ill. U., Chgo., 1998—. Editor (author): (book) Intersections of aging: Readings in Social Gerontology, 2000; author: (coll. textbook and instr.'s guide) Exercises in Psychological Testing Laboratory Manual, 2002, (book chpt.) Social Inequities, Health, and Healthcare Delivery, vol. XX; contbr. articles to profl. jours. Acad. advisor Met. Family Svcs. - Seniorcare Adv. Coun., Chgo., 2000—02. Recipient Found. Faculty Rsch. and Scholarly Project grant, Northeastern Ill. U. Mem.: Gerontol. Soc. of Am. (assoc.), Sigma Phi Omega (life 3 Faculty Excellence awards). Avocations: travel, photography, writing children's books, volunteering, painting. Office: Northeastern Ill U 5500 N Saint Louis Ave Chicago IL 60625 E-mail: l-hollissawyer@neiu.edu.

HOLLISTER, ALAN SCUDDER, clinical pharmacologist, internist; b. Balt., Feb. 28, 1947; m. Susan Blair, Aug. 29, 1970; children: Rebecca, Nathan. BA in Chemistry, Swarthmore Coll., 1970; PhD in Pharmacology, U. N.C., 1976, MD, 1977. Diplomate Am. Bd. Internal Medicine. Fellow in neuropharmacology U. NC, Chapel Hill, 1977; intern then resident dept. medicine Shands Tchg. Hosp. U. Fla., Gainesville, 1977-80; postdoctoral fellow divsn. clin. pharmacology Vanderbilt U., Nashville, 1980—83, asst. prof. dept. medicine divsn. clin. pharmacology, 1983-90; assoc. prof. medicine and pharmacology U. Colo. Health Scis. Ctr., Denver, 1990-98, dir. human physiology lab. clin. rsch. ctr., mem. faculty senate, 1991-98; dep. dir. dept. clin. pharmacology Bayer Corp., 1998—2000, dir., sr. clin. rsch. physician, 2000—01; sr. dir. Sanofi-Synthelabo, 2001—03; dir. clin. pharm. unit GlaxoSmithKline, 2003—. Clin. assoc. physician, 1983-85; cons. Tenn. Bd. Med. Examiners, Nashville, 1986-90. Contbr. over 175 articles to profl. jours., abstracts and chpts. to books. Bd. mgrs. Unitarian-Universalist Ch., Nashville, 1984-85, Golden, Colo., 1991-95. Charles A. Dana scholar Guilford Coll., 1967; Pharm. Mfrs. Assn. Rsch. fellow, 1974-75, Burroughs Wellcome, 1982-83; grantee NIH, Am. Cancer Soc., 1980-81, Nat. Heart, Lung and Blood Inst., 1983-91, Sandoz, Inc., 1985-87, E.R. Squibb and Sons, 1987, 89-90, VA, 1991-92. Fellow: ACP, Coun. for High Blood Pressure Rsch.; mem.: Am. Soc. for Clin. Pharmacology and Therapeutics, Am. Fedn. Med. Rsch. (councillor 1986—89), Am. Heart Assn., Am. Soc. Pharmacology and Therapeutics.

HOLLISTER, ARTHUR CLAIR, JR., epidemiologist, public health officer; b. New Orleans, May 9, 1918; s. Arthur Clair Hollister and Cora Preston Odom; m. Olivia Ewing, Aug. 2, 1942; children: Arthur III, Olivia Corinna. BS, Tulane U., 1938, MD, 1941; MPH, Johns Hopkins U., 1948. Diplomate Am. Bd. Preventive Medicine and Pub. Health. Intern So. Bapt. Hosp., New Orleans, 1941-42; pub. health med. officer Calif. State Dept. Health, Berkeley, Sacramento, 1946-48, med. epidemiologist, 1946-83; cons. Ctr. Disease Control and NIH, Atlanta, Washington, Calif., 1950-70; lectr. U. Calif. Sch. Pub. Health, Berkeley, L.A., 1950-65; cons. epidemiologist Contra Costa County Social Svcs., Martinez, Calif., 1992—. Mem., chair health com. Adv. Coun. on Aging, Martinez, 1986—, chair longterm care com., 1992—; mem. health svcs. study sect. NIH, Bethesda, Md., 1968-73; mem. workgroup Calif. Coun. Longterm Care Integration, 2001—. Contbr. scientific reports and articles to profl. jours., including Am. Jour. Pub. Health, Calif. Med. Jour., Am. Jour. Epidemiology. Mem. City of Pleasant Hill (Calif.) Commn. on Aging, 1987-92; vestry and choir mem., St. Stephen's Episc. Ch., Orinda, Calif., 1960—. Maj., USAAF, 1942-46. Fellow APHA, Am. Coll. Preventive Medicine; mem. Am. Epidemiol. Soc. (various offices 1952—), Ret. Pub. Employees Assn., Gray Panthers, U. Calif.-Berkeley Faculty Club, Delta Omega, Kappa Sigma, Alpha Kappa Kappa. Democrat. Avocations: classical and popular piano, jazz, railroads, classic cars. Home and Office: 14 Boies Ct Pleasant Hill CA 94523 E-mail: magikcats@earthlink.net.

HOLLISTER, CLIFTON DAVID, social work educator; b. Roseau, Minn., Oct. 29, 1938; s. Clifton Day and Elvera Margaret Hollister; m. Georgiana Gillespie, June 14, 1964; children: Patrick, Jonathan, Martha. BA cum laude, Hamline U., St. Paul, Minn., 1960; MSW, U. Mich., Ann Arbor, 1962, PhD, 1966. Lic. ind. social worker, Minn. Asst. prof. sch. social welfare U. Wis., Milw., 1966-69, U. Calif., Berkeley, 1969-71; assoc. prof. U. Minn., Duluth, 1971-79; prof. social work U. Minn., Twin Cities, 1980—, dir. sch. social work, 1983-91. External examiner Chinese U. Hong Kong., 1979-98; bd. dirs. Family and Children's Svcs., Mpls., 1985-91; assoc. sec. gen. Inter-Univ. Consortium Internat. Social Devel., Columbia, Mo., 1991—; pres. Minn. Conf. Social Work Edn., 1992-94; adj. prof. Humphrey Inst. Pub. Affairs, U. Minn., Mpls., 1999—. Co-author (book): Distance Learning: Principles for Effective Design, Delivery and Evaluation, 2001; contbr. articles to profl. jours. Bd. dirs. St. Jean's Sch., Duluth, 1974-78, Twin Cities Internat. Project for Youth Leaders and Social Workers, 1981-88. Recipient Disting. Alumni award U. Mich. Sch. Social Work Alumni Soc., 1986, Founders award Inter-Univ. Consortium for Internat. Social Devel., Washington, 1992. Mem. Nat. Assn. Social Workers (Lifetime achievement award Minn. chpt. 2001), Coun. Social Work Edn., Assn. Cmty. Orgn. and Social Work Administrn. Home: 2707 Lake Court Cir Mounds View MN 55112 Office: U Minn Sch Social Work 1404 Gortner Ave Saint Paul MN 55108 E-mail: dhollist@che.umn.edu.

HOLLISTER, DEAN, publishing company executive; b. Allentown, Pa., July 16, 1948; s. Charles and Mary-Jane (Marsteller) Hollister; m. Sylvia Reubens, Sept. 11, 1976; children: Peter, Daniel. BA, Washington and Lee U., 1970; MPhil, Columbia U., 1976. With Reed Reference Pub., New Providence, NJ, 1976—; now v.p. database production Reed Elsevier-New Providence, 1993—. Republican. Lutheran. Office: Reed Elsevier-New Providence 121 Chanlon Rd New Providence NJ 07974-1541

HOLLISTER, NANCY, state legislator; Lt. gov. State of Ohio, 1995-98, rep. Ho. of Reps., 1999—. Office: State House 77 S High St Columbus OH 43266-0001

HOLLISTER, ROBINSON GILL, JR., economics educator; b. Newark, Oct. 11, 1934; s. Robinson Gill and Jean Ackerman Hollister; m. Valerie Dutton, Oct. 10, 1964; children: Arusha Alexandra, Matissa Nicole. BA, Amherst Coll., 1956; PhD, Stanford U., 1965. Asst. prof. Williams Coll., Williamstown, Mass., 1962-64; rschr. Orgn. for Econ. Cooperation and Devel., Paris, 1964-65; dir. rsch. and planning Office Econ. Opportunity, Washington, 1966-67; assoc. prof. econs. U. Wis., Madison, 1967-70; prof. econs. Swarthmore (Pa.) Coll., 1971—. Chair com. on youth employment programs NAS, Washington, 1983-85; rsch. adv. com. Pub./Pvt. Ventures, Phila., 1988—; internat. expert Prime Mins. Planning Unit, Govt. Malaysia, Kuala Lumpur, 1979-80; cons. labor markets in Near East, U.S. Agy. for Internat. Devel., Washington, 1992-93. Co-author: Labour Market Policy and Unemployment, 1991, Labor Markets in Near East, 1994; co-author, editor: The National Supported Work Demonstration, 1984, Youth Employment and Training Programs, 1985. Bd. dirs. Chester (Pa.) Cmty. Improvement Project, 1990—. Fulbright scholar U.S. Govt., London, 1962, resident scholar Rockefeller Found., Bellagio, Italy, 1992, vis. scholar Russell Sage Found., N.Y.C., 1992-93. Mem. Am. Econ. Assn., Assn. for Pub. Policy and Mgmt., Econometrics Soc. Avocations: tennis, swimming, skiing. Home: 1 Whittier Pl Swarthmore PA 19081 Office: Swarthmore Coll Dept Econs 500 College Ave Swarthmore PA 19081 E-mail: rhollis1@swarthmore.edu.

HOLLISTER, WILLIAM GRAY, psychiatrist; b. Lincoln, Nebr., July 21, 1915; s. Vernon Leo and Lela Gretchen (Pilcher) H.; m. Frances Flora Scudder, Mar. 23, 1940; children— David W., Robert Michael, Alan Scudder, Frances Virginia. AB in Anthropology, U. Nebr., 1937, BS in Psychology, 1940, MD, 1941; M.P.H. (Rockefeller fellow), Johns Hopkins U., 1947; postgrad., Washington Psychoanalytic Inst., 1958-65. Diplomate Am. Bd. Psychiatry and Neurology, Am. Bd. Preventive Medicine. Intern Grady Hosp., Atlanta, 1941-42; resident in psychiatry Bishop Clarkson Meml. Hosp., Omaha, 1942-43, USPHS Hosp., Fort Worth, 1947-49; supr. venereal disease control Miss. Bd. Health, Jackson, 1943-46; psychiat. cons. Region IV USPHS, Atlanta, 1949-56; nat. sch. mental health cons. NIMH, Bethesda, Md., 1956-61, chief br. community research and services, 1962-65; prof. psychiatry, dir. comty. psychiatry U. N.C., Chapel Hill, 1965-86, prof. emeritus, 1988—. Cons. in occupational psychiatry IBM, Research Triangle Park, N.C., 1965-85; nat. mental health chmn. Nat. Congress PTA, 1958-62, 65-69 Author: Experiences in Rural Mental Health, 1974, Alternative Services in Community Mental Health: Programs and Processes, 1985; (with E. M. Bower) Behavior Science Frontiers of Education, 1967; composer, librettist (opera) Inca's Chosen Bride, 1997. Served with NIMH, 1943-65. Fellow Am. Psychiat. Assn., Am. Public Health Assn. (Disting. Service medal 1964); mem. AMA. Unitarian Universalist. Home: 750 Weaver Dairy Rd Apt 134 Chapel Hill NC 27514-1481 E-mail: wghfsh@aol.com.

HOLLISTER, WINSTON NED, pathologist; b. Milw., Mar. 23, 1942; s. Harold Arthur and Jeannette Clara (Gastrav) H.; m. Carol Jean Potter, Dec. 7, 1963 (div. May 1978); children: Timothy Carl, David Andrew; m. Margaret Ravenel Papen, Oct. 29, 1988; children: Charles Davis, Margaret Ravenel. BS in Physics, U. Wis., 1964; MD, Med. Coll. Wis., 1971. Diplomate Am. Bd. Internal Medicine, Am. Bd. Pathology. Staff pathologist St. Joseph's Hosp., Milw., 1976—; pres., CEO Franciscan Shared Lab, Wauwatosa, Wis., 1988-90; med. dir., chmn. bd. dirs. Med. Sci. Labs., Wauwatosa, 1989—2003. Cons. in field. Contbr. articles to profl. jours. Vestry mem. St. Paul's Episcopal Ch., Milw., 1978-83. Lt. USN, 1964-67. Recipient Houghton & Houghton award Med. Soc. Wis., 1971. Fellow Coll. Am. Pathologists (clin. practice com. 1984-87); mem. ACP, Am. Pathology Found. (pres. 1994—), River Tennis Club (bd. dirs., pres. 1978-98), The Milw. Club, Univ. Club Milw. Republican. Episcopalian. Avocations: sailing, skiing, tennis, travel, music. Home: 9949 N Valley Hill Dr Mequon WI 53092-5350 Office: Med Sci Labs 11020 W Plank Ct Wauwatosa WI 53226-3279

HOLLMAN, BARBARA CAROL, psychoanalyst, psychotherapist, consultant; b. N.Y.C., July 18, 1941; d. Samuel and Lillian (Verlin) Malkin; 1 child, Lee Jeffrey. BA, CUNY, 1964; MA, NYU, 1965; MSW, Adelphi U., 1985; postgrad., Manhattan Inst. Psychoanalysis, N.Y.C., 1995. Cert. social worker, N.Y. Tchr. Syosset (N.Y.) Schs., 1966-70; social work technician Variety Pre Schooler's Workshop, Syosset, 1976-83; psychotherapist Cen. Nassau Guidance, Hicksville, N.Y., 1985-86, Melillo Ctr. for Mental Health, Glen Cove, NY, 1987—2001; pvt. practice, Hicksville, 1985—, Teaneck, N.J., 1995—. Speaker in field. Contbr. articles to profl. jours. Bd. dirs. The Family Exch. Ctr., 1978-83; parent mem. Com. on Handicapped, 1982-83. Fellow Soc. Clin. Social Workers; mem. NASW, Acad. Cert. Social Workers. Office: 175 Cedar Ln Teaneck NJ 07666-4315 E-mail: Bhollman2000@aol.com.

HOLL-MATTHEWS, DEE LYNN, career counselor, psychotherapist, nutrition coach; b. Lima, Ohio, Mar. 8, 1949; d. James Adam Holl and Eileen (Gross) Parker; m. Geoff Matthews, Dec. 1998; children: Jeffrey Holl, Jennifer Holl Flowers. BA, U. Houston, 1985; MA, Amber U., 1993. Lic. profl. counselor; cert. natural health profl. Human resources generalist Omniplan, Houston, 1986-87; plant pers. mgr. Digital Equipment, Greenville, S.C., 1987-90, sr. human resources cons. Dallas, 1990-93; cons. Drake, Beam, Morin, Dallas, 1993-95; sr. human resources mgr. Stream Internat., Dallas, 1995; site mgr., career counselor, profl. coach CDS/Mobil Oil, Dallas, 1995-2000; corp. human resources mgr. Bi-Lo LLC. Personal devel. and success coach; conf. spkr. Visions, Dallas, 1995. Vol. counselor AIDS Interfaith Coun., Dallas, 1994. Recipient plaque Johnson Space Ctr., 1984. Mem. ACA, ASTD, IACMP (Internatl. Assn. of Career Mgmt. Profls.), (pres.-elect, conf. spkr. Dallas 1996), Internat. Coach Fedn. Office: Career Devel Svcs Mobil Pl 3000 Pegasus Park Dr Dallas TX 75247-6204

HOLLOMAN, MARILYN LEONA DAVIS, nurse non profit administrator, health products executive; b. Bklyn., Oct. 6, 1952; d. Leon Courbourne and Gwendolyn Omega (Crichlow) Davis; m. Theodore Albert Holloman, July 30, 1971 (div. Apr. 1975); children: Tedette Ann (dec.), Amina Omega Suedi. AAS in Nursing, Queensboro C.C., Bayside, N.Y., 1973; FNP, U. Miami, 1980. Founder, pres., CEO Women and Children 1st Inc., Miami, 1992—; v.p. Omega Health Network, inc., 2000—01. Allocations panel mem. United Way, Dade County, Fla., 1989-96; mem. at large Switchboard of Miami, 1992, treas., 1993-94, sec., 1994-95; fellow Common Ground Kellogg Found./U. Miami, 1993-95; primary cand. 1996 (Fla. House Rep., Dist 101). Author: Melody's of Life, 1982; editor Health Plan Baby Book, 1985; editor, pub. Legislative Update Women and Children 1st Inc., 1994—. Former pres. Dem. Black Caucus-Dade County chpt., 1991-92; Dem. candidate Fla. Ho. Reps., 1996; mem. Planned Giving Coun. of Dade County, 1994-95. Mem.: ANA (cert. specialist family nurse practitioner), Miami Parliamentary Law Unit (pres. 1993—95, v.p. 1995—97), Nat. Assn. Parliamentarians, Fla. Nurses Assn. (legis. dist. coord. 1984—99). Democrat. Achievements include patents pending for 9-11 Omega Buddysack/InjurEvac. Avocations: drama, reading, dance, travel. Home and Office: 114 SW Peacock Blvd #201 Port Saint Lucie FL 34986

HOLLOMON, CAROL HOWELL, social worker; b. Dallas, Jan. 23, 1942; d. Sam J. and Anne (Barrentine) Howell; children: Michael R. II, Lana C. BS, Memphis State U., 1964; BSN, George Mason U., 1985; MSW, U. Ill., 1990. RN, Va., D.C., Ill.; lic. clin. social worker, Ill., Colo. Psychiat. nurse Psychiat. Inst. of D.C., Washington, 1985-88, Carle Pavilion Hosp., Champaign, Ill., 1988-89; child welfare specialist Ill. Dept. of Children and Family Svcs., Urbana, 1990-91; program mgr. residential treatment facility Onaraga (Ill.) Acad., 1991-92; coord. men's program Alternatives to Family Violence, Denver, 1992—97, exec. dir. Northglenn, Colo., 1997—. Mem. Colo. Legis. Subcom. on Battered Woman Syndrome, 1994-95; presenter in field. Chmn.17th Jud. Dist. Domestic Violence Task Force; past urban chmn. Colo. Coalition Against Domestic Violence, 2000-02; mem. DV task force Colo. Dept. Human Svcs. Metro Denver Fatality Rev. Bd.; mem. Colo. Mental Health Profls. Amb. Program. Mem. NOW. Office: Alternatives to Family Violence PO Box 385 Commerce City CO 80037-8

HOLLON, JOHN O(AKS), lawyer; b. Taunton, Mass., Sept. 8, 1968; s. Alva A. Jr. and Laura B. Hollon; m. Julia L. Kincaid, Aug. 15, 1992; children: Elizabeth D., John O. Jr. BA, Vanderbilt U., 1991; JD, U. Ky., 1994. Bar: Ky. 1994, U.S. Dist. Ct. (we. and ea. dists.) Ky. 1995, Fla. 1997, U.S. Ct. Appeals (6th cir.) 1997, U.S. Dist. Ct. (mid. dist.) Fla. 1998, U.S. Ct. Appeals (11th cir.) 1999. Lawyer Hollon, Hollon & Collins, Hazard, Ky., 1994-95, Clark, Ward & Cave, Lexington, Ky., 1995-97, Sams & Hollon, Jacksonville, Fla., 1997—. Class agt. Woodberry Forest (Va.) Sch., 1987-93. Mem. ABA, Ky. Bar Assn., Fla. Bar. Avocations: golf, jogging, reading. Office: Sams & Hollon 7835 Bayberry Rd Jacksonville FL 32256-6845

HOLLORAN, THOMAS EDWARD, business educator; b. Mpls., Sept. 27, 1929; s. Edward Francis and Florence G. (Loftus) H.; m. Patricia M. Holloran, June 26, 1954; children: Mary Patricia Harley, Anne Florence. BS, U. Minn., 1951, JD, 1955. Bar: Minn. 1955, Fed. 1955. Ptnr. Wheeler and Fredrikson, Mpls., 1955-67; exec. v.p. Medtronic, Inc., Mpls., 1967-73, pres., 1973-75; chmn., chief exec. officer Inter-Regional Fin. Group, Inc. (renamed Dain Rauscher Corp), Mpls., 1976-85; prof. U. of St. Thomas, St. Paul, 1985—2002, prof. emeritus, 2002—. Bd. dirs. Flexsteel Industries, Inc., Dubuque, Iowa, Ctr. for Diagnostic Imaging, Mpls.; dir. emeritus Medtronic, Inc. Spl. judge Mcpl. Ct. of Shorewood, Excelsior, Tonka Bay, Greenwood and Deephaven, Minn., 1961-65; Mayor, City of Shorewood, 1971-74; chmn. Urban Coalition, Mpls., 1977-78, City of Mpls. Task Force on Tech., 1983-84; mem. Mpls.-St. Paul Met. Airports Commn., 1974-82, vice chmn., 1976-82, chmn., 1989-91; bd. trustees Coll. St. Scholastica, 1971-81, chmn., 1979-81; trustee Coll. St. Thomas, 1979-88, U. Minn. Found., 1983-85, Bush Found., 1982—, chmn. 1991-96; trustee Mpls. Art Inst., 1986-93, Mpls. Children's Health Ctr., 1983-84; pres. Upper M.W. Coun., Mpls., 1978-80; bd. dirs. InterStudy, Excelsior., 1975-85, Minn. Press Coun., 1982-87, mem. corp. bd. Cath. Archdiocese Mpls. and St. Paul, 1990—. With USN, 1952-54, Korea. Mem. ABA, Minn. State Bar Assn. Roman Catholic.

HOLLOWAY, CHARLES ARTHUR, public and private management educator; b. Whittier, Calif., May 28, 1936; s. Heber H. and Theodosia S. (Stephens) H.; m. Christina Ahlm, July 11, 1959; children: Deborah, Susan, Stuart. BSEE with honors, U. Calif., Berkeley, 1959; MS, UCLA, 1963, PhD in Bus. Administrn. with distinction, 1969. Sr. engr. Bechtel Corp., San Francisco, 1964-65; teaching fellow UCLA, 1965-66; asst. prof. to prof. Stanford (Calif.) U., 1968—, Herbert Hoover prof. pub. and pvt. mgmt., 1980-91, assoc. dean acad. affairs Grad. Sch. Bus., 1980-87, 90-91, Kleiner Perkins Caufield and

Byers prof. mgt., 1991—. Bd. dirs. Axicon, Escalate Corp., SRI Internat.; co-chair Stanford Ctr. for Entrepreneurial Studies, 1995-. Author: Decision Making Under Uncertainty: Models and Choices, 1979, Perpetual Enterprise Machine: Seven Keys to Corporate Renewal, 1994. Bd. dirs. Save Redwoods League. With USN, 1959-63. Fellow Ford Found., 1966-68 Mem. Inst. Mgmt. Sci., Ops. Rsch. Soc. Am., Stanford Integrated Mfg. Assn. (co-chair 1991-95). Home: 730 Santa Maria Ave Palo Alto CA 94305-8438 Office: Stanford U Grad Sch Bus Stanford CA 94305 E-mail: holloway_chuck@gsb.stanford.edu.

HOLLOWAY, CHARLES EDWARD, language educator; b. Delhi, La., Sept. 3, 1959; s. Charles Adrian and Norma Ernestine Holloway; m. Sandra Carol Wood, Aug. 2, 1988. BBA, N.E. La. U., 1982; MA, La. State U., 1990, PhD, 1993. Prof. Spanish, U. La., Monroe, 1989—. Author: Dialect Death: The Case of Brule Spanish, 1997; contbr. articles to profl. jours. Mem.: Linguistic Soc. of the S.W., La. Fgn. Lang. Tchrs. Assn. (exec. bd. 1993—2001), Am. Assn. Tchrs. Spanish and Portuguese (pres. Antonio Margil chpt. 1998—99, Outstanding Univ. Prof. of Yr. 2001), U. La. Monroe Faculty Senate (sec./exec. coun. 1999—2000).

HOLLOWAY, CHRISTOPHER MATTHEW, brokerage house executive; b. Portsmouth, Va., Jan. 23, 1973; s. Marc Vincent and Mabel Lurlene H.; m. Susan Janrae Spears Holloway, June 26, 1999. BS in Bus. Adminstrn., Old Dominion U., Norfolk, Va., 1995, MBA, 1998. Regis. Series 4 NASD Options Prin., Series 7 Rep. N.Y. Stock Exchange, Series 24 NASD Gen. Securities Prin., Series 55 OTC Equity Trader, Series 63 NASD Uniform State Law, Series 65 NASD Regis. Investment Adv., Series 27 Fin. and Ops. Prin., Series 53 MSRB Prin. Trend analyst The Finance Co., Norfolk, Va., 1993-96; fin. analyst TFC Enterprises, Inc., Norfolk, Va., 1996-98; v.p. of ops. and compliance Investors Security Co., Inc., Suffolk, Va., 1998—. Dir. Investors Security Co., Inc., Suffolk, Va., 1998—; ops. mgr. Old Dominion Investors Trust, Inc., Mutual Fund, Suffolk, Va., 1998—. Recipient 6 All Am. Scholar awards, U.S. Achievement Acad., 1991-95; named Outstanding Jr. Phi Kappa Phi, Norfolk, Va., 1994, Univ. Scholar Old Dominion U., Norfolk, Va., 1995, Outstanding Mgmt. Acctg. Student of Yr., Inst. of Mgmt. Acctg./Old Dominion U. Mgmt., Norfolk, Va., 1998. Mem. Inst. Mgmt. Accts., Golden Key Nat. Hon. Soc., Beta Gamma Sigma, Phi Kappa Phi. Republican. Mem. Christian and Missionary Alliance. Avocations: coin collecting, travel, auto enthusiast, antique collecting. Office: Investors Security Co Inc 110 Bank St Suffolk VA 23434-4544 Fax: 757-925-4353. E-mail: cholloway@investorssecurity.com.

HOLLOWAY, DIANE ELAINE, psychological consultant, psychotherapist, writer; b. Tulsa, Oct. 19, 1937; d. Lawrence Lynn and Helen May (Six) Hatcher; m. 1961; children: Brian, Kathleen; m. 2d, Bob Cheney, 1980. BS, Tex. Woman's U., 1972, MA, 1974, PhD, 1979. Lic. psychotherapist, Tex. Brit. rep. Study Abroad, Inc., London, 1957-59; psychologist Presbyn. Hosp., Dallas, 1970-75, dir. psychol. svcs., assoc. dir. continuing edn. psychiatry, 1976-78; mental health/mental retardation cons. Drug Rehab. and Law Enforcement Offices, Dallas County, 1975-77; psychotherapist in pvt. practice Dallas, 1978-89; assoc. Pain Therapy Assn., Dallas, 1979-81, pres. Security & Mgmt. Sys., Dallas, 1979-81, Mental Health Profl. Group, Dallas, 1980-89; drug coord. Dallas Office of Mayor, 1989-92; vis. prof. various univs., 1993—. Author: Before You Say I Quit, 1990, The Mind of Oswald, 2000, Dallas and the Jack Ruby Trial, 2001, Analyzing Leaders, Presidents and Terrorists, 2002; contbr. newsletter, articles to profl. jours.; editor internet sites. Hogg Found. grantee, Southwestern Med. Sch., 1972-73. Mem. APA, Am. Med. Writers Assn., Internat. Assn. Chiefs of Police, Archaeol. Inst. Am., Soc. Police and Criminal Psychology, Mensa. Office: 20402 N 150th Dr Sun City West AZ 85375-5765

HOLLOWAY, DONALD PHILLIP, lawyer; b. Akron, Ohio, Feb. 18, 1928; s. Harold Shane and Dorothy Gayle (Ryder) H. BS in Commerce, Ohio U., Athens, 1950; JD, U. Akron, 1955; MA, Kent State U., 1962. Bar: Ohio 1955. Title examiner Bankers Guarantee Title & Trust Co., Akron, 1950-54; acct. Robinson Clay Product Co., Akron, 1955-60; libr. Akron-Summit Pub. Libr., 1962-69, head fine arts and music divsn., 1969-71, sr. libr., 1972-82; pvt. practice Akron, 1982—. Payroll treas. Akron Symphony Orch., 1957-61; treas. Friends Libr. Akron and Summit County, 1970-72. Mem. ABA, ALA, Ohio Bar Assn., Akron Bar Assn., Ohio Libr. Assn., Nat. Trust Hist. Preservation, Music Libr. Assn., Soc. Archtl. Historians, Coll. Art Assn., Art Librs. N.Am., Akron City Club, North Coast Soc. Republican. Episcopalian. Avocations: art and architecture, music, travel. Home: 293 Delaware Pl Akron OH 44303-1275

HOLLOWAY, EDWARD OLIN, human services manager; b. Rochester, N.Y., July 3, 1944; s. Charles Robert and Chrystal Gertrude (Darling) Holloway; m. Hama Elizabeth Farris, Dec. 23, 1967. AA, Palm Beach Jr. Coll., Lake Worth, Fla., 1964; BA, Lenoir Rhyne Coll., 1967; MS in Pub. Health, U. N.C., 1975. From sanitarian I to sanitarian supr. I Palm Beach County Health Dept., West Palm Beach, Fla., 1969-73; from emergency med. svcs. coord. to exec. dir. dist. IX Health Planning Coun., Inc., West Palm Beach, 1975-89; sr. health and human svcs. planner bd. county commrs. Palm Beach County Dept. Cmty. Svcs., West Palm Beach, 1989—2000. Mem. faculty Pub. Health Physician Residency Program, 1990—2002, apptd. spl. advisor, 2002—; mem. accreditation five yrs. U. Miami, 1999; mem. steering com. Fla. Atlantic U. Inst. Govt., 1992—2000, vice chmn., 1994—99, apptd. spl. adv., 2000—. Chmn. dist. 9 adv. coun. Dept. Health and Rehab. Svcs., West Palm Beach, 1990—92; pres. Fla. Assn. Health Planning Agys., Inc., 1984—89; mem. planning unit steering com. Leadership Palm Beach County, 1991; mem. Palm Beach County data collection com. Health and Human Svcs. Planning Assn., 1992—98; mem. Interagy. Planning Group, 1994—2000; mem. sch. adv. com. Palm Beach Gardens Cmty. HS, 1994—, vice chair, 2000—, mem. membership safety com., 2000—, mem. budget com., 2001—; appointee for customer svc. West Palm Beach VA Med. Ctr., 1997—; mem. Palm Beach County Partnership for Aging program United Way, 1998—; apptd. ex officio mem., spl. advisor Palm Beach County Citizens Adv. Com. on Health and Human Svc., 2000—; vol. State of Fla. Dept. Health, 2000—, vol. staff, chair planning implementing and evaluation needed health and human svc. sys. improvements Guiding Principles and Ops. Comm., 2002; vol. mem team to evaluate quality of care and customer svc. provided at local VA Med. Ctr.. Fed. Insp. Gen.'s Office, 2002. With U.S. Army, 1967—69, Vietnam. Decorated Bronze Star, Purple Heart, Army Commendation medal, Cross of Gallantry (Vietnam); nominee Fla. as 1 of 500 nationally to serve on Rep. Presdl. Roundtable, U.S. Senate, 2001; recipient Outstanding Svc. award, Fla. Assn. Health Planning Agys., 1989, Outstanding Achievement award, Bd. County Commrs., Palm Beach County Citizens Adv. Com. on Health and Human Svcs., 1995, 10 Yrs. Svc. award, 1989—99, Letters of Commendation, CDC, 1980, State of Fla., Lawton Chiles, 1998, Cert. of Merit, Rep. Nat. Com., 2001, Eisenhower Commn. in recognition of exemplary svc. to related polit. party and country, 2002, Cert. Appreciation, Americans Disabled for Life Meml., 2003; grantee State Fla. Dept. Transp. planning grantee, Regional Emergency Med. Svcs., 1975. Mem.: APHA, ASPA (chpt. 102 coun. 1989—98), Nat. Environ. Health Assn., Am. Coll. Grad. Med. Edn., U. N.C. Sch. Pub. Health Alumni Assn. (bd. dirs. 1994—2001). Republican. Lutheran. Avocations: reading, target and skeet shooting, machairology. Home and Office: 104 Vision Ct Palm Beach Gardens FL 33418-3859 Home Fax: 561-622-8495.

HOLLOWAY, ERNEST LEON, university president; b. Boley, Okla., Sept. 12, 1930; m. Jan. 19, 1957; children: Ernest L., Reginald, Norman. BS, Langston U., 1952; MS, Okla. State U., 1955; EdD, U. Okla., 1970. Tchr., prin. Boley H.S., 1952-62; with Langston U., 1963—, profl. sci. higher edn., 1978—, v.p. adminstrn., 1975-77, acting pres., 1977-78, pres., 1979—. Cons. in field. Elected to Okla. Afro-Am. Hall of Fame, 1987, Okla. Educators Hall of Fame, 1996; inducted into Okla. Higher Edn. Hall of Fame, 1999, Okla. State U. Alumni Assn.'s Hall of Fame, 2001; recipient Thurgood Marshall Schoolarship Fund Edn. award, 2002, Lifetime Achievement award, U. Okla. Mem. Okla. Higher Edn. Alumni Coun., Nat. Assn. State Univs. and Land-Grant Colls., Nat. Assn. Equal Opportunity in Higher Edn., Langston U. Alumni Assn., Alpha Phi Alpha, Phi Delta Kappa, The Lions Club, Imperial Coun. of Shriners. Office: Langston U PO Box 907 Langston OK 73050-0907 E-mail: elholloway@lunet.edu.

HOLLOWAY, GORDON ARTHUR, lawyer; b. Wichita, Kans., July 27, 1938; s. George Arthur and Margurite (Bondurant) H.; m. Carol H. Criss, Sept. 1, 1960; children: Gregory Arthur, Suzanne Criss, Garrett Austin. BBA, U. Tex., 1960, JD, 1963. Bar: Tex. 1963, Colo. 1993. Assoc. McGregor, Sewell, Junell & Riggs, Houston, 1963-71; ptnr. Sewell and Riggs, Houston, 1971-93, Holloway & Rowley, 1994—. Staff sgt. Air N.G., 1964-71. Mem. Am. Bd. Trial Advocates (diplomate), Nat. Assn. Railroad Trial Counsel, Internat. Assn. Defense Counsel, Tex. Bd. Legal Specialization (cert. personal injury, civil trial law, qualified atty.-mediator), Houston Club, Intertel. Office: Holloway & Rowley P C 1415 Louisiana St Ste 2550 Houston TX 77002-7378 E-mail: gordonholloway@swbell.net.

HOLLOWAY, JACQUELINE, county commissioner; b. Knoxville, Tenn., Mar. 16, 1935; d. Clyde Herbert and Ernestine Cooper; m. George Rudolph Holloway, July 21, 1951; children: Lynda, George Jr., Michelle, Cheryl, Ingrid. AA in Bus., Cooper Inst., Knoxville, 1961; cert., U. Tenn. Ctr. Govt. Tng., 1990. Cert. pub. adminstr. U. Tenn. Biol. technician Oak Ridge (Tenn.) Nat. Lab., 1963-96; county commr. Anderson County, Clinton, Tenn., 1990—. Chmn. Families First Coun., 1997—; vice chair Am.'s Promise, 1999—; bd. dirs. Anderson County Health Coun., 2000—, chmn., 2002, Quality Childcare Initiative, TNCEP; v.p. CORRE, 2000—03, United Way Anderson County; mem. Anderson County Headstart Policy Coun.; mem. exec. com. Anderson County Dems.; pres. Dem. Women, Tenn., 1996—98; v.p. Dem. Fedn., Tenn., 1996—2003. Mem. Tenn. County Commn. Assn. (bd. dirs. 1991-2000), Tenn. County Svcs. Assn. Methodist. Home and Office: 102 Artesia Dr Oak Ridge TN 37830-7817 E-mail: G32284@aol.com.

HOLLOWAY, JAMES LEMUEL, III, foundation executive, retired naval officer; b. Charleston, S.C., Feb. 23, 1922; s. James Lemuel and Jean Gordon (Hagood) H.; m. Dabney Hix Rawlings, Dec. 14, 1942; children: Lucy Dabney Lyon, Jane Meredith. BSEE, Naval Acad., Annapolis, 1942. Cert. naval aviator, naval nuclear reactor operator. Commd. ensign USN, 1942, served in destroyers, 1942-45, carrier jet fighter pilot, 1951—53; comdr. jet squadron USS Valley Forge Lebanon Landings Quemon-Matsu Def., 1958-59; comdr. 1st nuclear carrier Enterprise USN, Vietnam, 1965-67, advanced through grades to adm., 1973; comdr. carrier striking force U.S. 6th fleet, Ea. Mediterranean, 1970; comdr. U.S. 7th fleet USN, Vietnam, 1971-73, vice chief naval ops., 1973-74, mem. Joint Chiefs of Staff, Dept. Def., 1974-78, chief naval ops., 1974-78, ret., 1978; pres. Coun. Am.-Flag Ship Operators, Washington, 1981-88, Naval Hist. Found., Washington, 1982-98, chmn., 1998—. Def. and fgn. policy cons. Paine Weber, Inc., 1980-88; chmn. Dept. of Def. Spl. Rev. Group investigating Iranian hostage rescue, 1981; exec. dir. Presdl. Task Force on Combatting Terrorism, 1985; spl. envoy V.P. Bush to Middle East, 1986; commr. Predl. Blue Ribbon Commn. on Def. Mgmt., 1985, congl. Commn. on Mcht. Marine and Def., 1987 88, Presdl. Commn. on Long Term Integrated Strategy, 1987-88; U.S. rep. to South Pacific Commn., 1990-94. Tech. advisor: (film) Top Gun, 1985; contbr. articles to mags. Trustee St. James Sch., Md., 1962—, pres., 1989—, chmn. 1996, chmn. emeritus, 2001; bd. dirs. Olmsted Found., Washington, 1978-2000; mem. bd. advisors The Citadel, 1981-86; chmn. adv. bd. U.S. Naval Acad., 1983-91; chmn. Hist. Annapolis Found., Inc., 1986-96, chmn. emeritus, 1996—; pres., chmn. Naval Acad. Found., 1994-2001, chmn. emeritus, 2001—; trustee George Marshall Found., 1988-96; dir. Atlantic Coun., 1987-96; bd. visitors and govs. St. John's Coll., 1995, Bd. Mariners Mus., Newport News, Va., 1995-97, dir. emeritus. Decorated Bronze Star, Air medals (3), Legion of Merit (2), DFC, Def. DSM with 2 oak leaf cluster, Navy DSM with 4 oak leaf clusters, Order of Rising Sun (Japan), Grand Cross (Fed. republic Germany), Legion of Honor (France), Rank of Commandeur, 31 others; recipient Triennial Modern Patriot award SAR, 1994, Disting. Pub. Svc. award Navy League, 1996, Disting. Patriot award SAR, 1999, Disting. Grad. award U.S. Naval Acad., 1999, 2000; elected Nat. Wrestling Hall of Fame, 1998; named to Naval Aviation Hall of Fame, 2003. Mem. Assn. Naval Aviation (pres. 1982-91, chmn. 1991-96), Met. Club (Washington gov. 1988—, pres. 1992), Golden Eagles, Brook Club (N.Y.C.), N.Y. Yacht Club (N.Y.C.), Md. Club (Balt.), Annapolis Yacht Club, Soc. Cin., Alfalfa Club (Washington). Republican. Episcopalian. Avocation: sailing. E-mail: xcocvan65@aol.com.

HOLLOWAY, JOHN THOMAS, physicist, consultant; b. Cape Girardeau, Mo., June 19, 1922; s. Herbert Henry and Addie Mae (Cahill) H.; m. Kay Vickers, Nov. 11, 1965; children: Linda, Kim (dec. Jan. 1999). AB, Millikin U., Decatur, Ill., 1943; PhD, Iowa State U., 1957. With nuclear physics br. Office Naval Research, Washington, 1946-53, head br., 1951-52; research asst. Ames Lab., AEC, Iowa, 1954-57; with Office Dir. Def. Research and Engring., Washington, 1958-61; dep. dir. Office of Sci. Dir. Def. Research and Engring., 1959-61; with NASA, 1961-68, dep. dir. grants and research contracts, 1961-67, chief advanced programs and tech., space applications div., 1967-68; dir. Nat. Hwy. Safety Research Center, Dept. Transp., 1968-69; v.p. research Ins. Inst. Hwy. Safety, 1969-72; asso. dir. ops. Interdisciplinary Communications Program, Smithsonian Instn., 1972-77, program mgr. internat. program population analysis, 1972-77, research and devel. cons. in hwy. safety, biomed. electronics, energy conservation, 1977-78; sr. staff officer bd. on radioactive waste mgmt. Nat. Acad. Scis.-NRC, 1978-85; cons. on radioactive waste mgmt., hwy. safety, 1985—. Mem. conf. com. Nat. Conf. Advancement Research, 1971-75 Author papers in field; adviser documentary films. Served with USNR, 1944-46. Mem. Am. Phys. Soc., Sigma Xi. Clubs: Cosmos (Washington); Army-Navy Country (Arlington, Va.). Home: 2220 Cathedral Ave NW Washington DC 20008-1504

HOLLOWAY, KIMBERLEY MICHELE, freelance/self-employed writer, communications executive, language educator; b. Knoxville, Tenn., Aug. 19, 1958; d. Bobby Howard and Gwendolyn Warwick Holloway; children: Jennifer Leigh Mongold, Stephanie Michele Kidd. BS in Secondary Edn. & English, Tenn. Tech. U., 1980; MA in English, East Tenn. State U., 1998. Tchr. Tri-Cities Christian Schs., Blountville, Tenn., 1985—87; freelance writer, 1997—; assoc. dir. comm., lectr. English King Coll., Bristol, Tenn., 2002—. Employee Ltd. Svc., Eastman, Kingsport, Tenn., 1994—96; grad. asst. English. dept. East Tenn. State U., Johnson City, Tenn., 1996—97, adj. instr., 1997—; lectr. in English King Coll., Bristol, Tenn., 1998—. Author: The Encyclopedia of Multiculturalism, 1998, The Sixties in America, 1999, Masterplots: Poetry Supplement, 1998, St. James Encyclopedia of Popular Culture, 1999, African American Encyclopedia, 2000, The Supreme Court, Encyclopedia of Appalachia, Encyclopedia of Great Athletes, Revised, 2001, Masterplots II: Poetry Supplement, 2002, Great Events of the Twentieth Century, 2002; editor: From a Race of Storytellers: Essays on the Ballad Novels of Sharyn McCrumb, 2003; contbr., chapters to books. Prodr. ch. bull. Heritage Bapt. Ch., Johnson City, Tenn., 1989—95. Recipient George Allen Outstanding Graduate award, East Tenn. State U., 1998. Mem.: Appalachian Writers Assn. (program chmn. 2000—01, pres. 2001—02, officer-at-large 2002—03). Republican. Baptist. Avocations: reading, writing, bicycling. E-mail: kimhkidd@aol.com., khollawa@king.edu.

HOLLOWAY, M(ARY) KATHARINE, research scientist, chemist; BS in Chemistry summa cum laude, U. Southern Miss., 1979; MA in Organic Chemistry, U. Tex., Austin, 1982, PhD in Organic Chemistry, 1985. Sr. rsch. chemist molecular sys. dept. Merck & Co., 1985-90, rsch. fellow molecular design and diversity, 1990-96, sr. rsch. fellow molecular design and diversity, 1996—. Recipient Inventor of Yr. award Intellectual Property Owners, 1997. Mem. ACS (sec. computers in chemistry divsn. 1992-95, co-editor newsletter 1992, mem. membership com. 1990-95, vice chair Quantitative Structure-Activity Relationships Gordon Conf. 1999, Award for Creative Invention 1999). Achievements include patents for HIV protease inhibitors useful in the treatment of AIDS, 1995, 97 (2), HIV protease inhibitors useful in the treatment of AIDS, and their preparation, 1996, treatment of Alzheimer's disease with 5-(tetradecyloxy)-2-furan carboxylic acid, 1997, method of finding transcription activators of the NER steroid hormone receptor, 1997. Home: 171 Forest Trail Dr Lansdale PA 19446-6416 E-mail: kate_holloway@merck.com.

HOLLOWAY, PAUL FAYETTE, retired aerospace executive; b. Hampton, Va., June 7, 1938; s. Eldridge Manning and Minnie Powell H.; m. Barbara Jane Menetch, June 23, 1956; children: Paul Manning (dec.), Eric Scott. BS, Va. Poly. Inst. and State U., 1960; postgrad., U. Va., 1961, Coll. William and Mary, 1962-63; grad. advanced mgmt. program, Harvard U., 1988; PhD (hon.), Old Dominion U., 1994. With NASA Langley Rsch. Ctr., Hampton, Va., 1960-97, aerospace technologist, 1960-69, space shuttle task group, 1969, chief space sys. divsn., 1972-75; acting dep. assoc. adminstr. Office Aeronautics and Space Tech., 1977, dir. for space, 1975-85, dep. dir., 1985-91, dir., 1991-96, acting dep. adminstr., 1992-93, ret., 1997. Cons. in field. Mem. editl. bd. Jour Spacecraft and Rockets, 1972-77, editor in chief, 1978-80; contbr. articles to profl. jours. Mem. Poquoson (Va.) Planning Commn.; v.p. local PTA; mem. coll. bd. Thomas Nelson C.C., 1997-2001. Recipient Outstanding Leadership medal NASA, 1980, Exceptional Svc. medal, 1981; Presdl. Rank award for meritorious exec., 1981, Presdl. Rank award for disting. exec., 1987, 93, Equal Opportunity medal, 1992, Disting. Svc. medal, 1992; named Peninsula Engr. of Yr., Peninsula Engrs. Club, 1996; elected to Va. Tech. Acad. Engring. Excellence, 2002. Fellow AIAA (v.p. publs. 1991-94), Am. Astronautical Soc.; mem. Internat. Acad. Astronautics, Sigma Gamma Tau. Methodist. Home: 16 N Westover Dr Poquoson VA 23662-1424 E-mail: pholloway@erols.com.

HOLLOWAY, PAUL HOWARD, materials science educator; b. Marion, Ind., Oct. 31, 1943; s. Charles D. and Pauline (Poe) H.; m. Bette Lorraine Zubrod, Jan. 10, 1943; children: Michael, Brian, Kimberly. BS, Fla. State U., 1965, MS, 1966; PhD, Rensselaer Poly. Inst., Troy, N.Y., 1972. Metallurgist Gen. Electric Co., Schenectady, 1966-69; staff mem. Sandia Nat. Lab., Albuquerque, 1972-78; assoc. prof. dept. materials sci. and engring. U. Fla., Gainesville, 1978-81, prof. dept. materials sci. and engring., 1981—, rsch. prof., 1997-99, Disting. prof., 2000—. Dir. MICROFABRITECH, Gainesville; statewide coord. Advanced Microelectronics and Materials Program, Tampa, 1988—91; Ellis D. Verink endowed prof. U. Fla., 1999, disting. prof., 2000. Editor: Compound Semiconductor Growth, Processing Devices, 1988, Characterizatin of Metals and Alloys, 1993, Handbook of Compound Semiconductors, 1995, Critical Revs. in Solid State and Materials Scis.; contbr. chpts. to books, articles to profl. jours. Mem., chmn. Alachua County 4-H Adv. Coun., Gainesville, 1986-88, 95—; mem Alachua County Extension Office Adv. Coun., Gainesville, 1986-91. Named Tchr. of Yr., Coll. Engring. U. Fla., Gainesville, 1988; recipient Muller award, U. Wis., Milw., 1988. Fellow: ASM Internat., Am. Vacuum Soc. (hon.; pres. 1987, Albert Nerken award 1999); mem.: TMS, ASTM (vice chmn. 1983—86), Alpha Sigma Mu. Office: U Fla Dept Materials Sci Gainesville FL 32611

HOLLOWAY, RALPH LESLIE, anthropology educator; b. Phila., Feb. 6, 1935; s. Ralph L. and Marguerite (Grugan) H. BS in Geology, U. N.Mex., Albuquerque, 1959; PhD in Anthropology, U. Calif., Berkeley, 1964. Asst. prof. anthropology Columbia U., N.Y.C., 1964-69, assoc. prof., 1969-73, prof., 1973—. Editor: Primate Aggression, Territoriality and Xenophobia: A Comparative Perspective, 1974; contbr. numerous articles to profl. jours. Recipient Ctr. for Rsch. into the Anthropol. Found. Tech., Ind. U. annual award for outstanding rsch. Ctr. for Rsch. into Anthropologic. Found. of Tech., 2002, Craft award, 2002; Guggenheim Found. fellow, 1974; NSF grantee, 1984 Fellow AAAS, N.Y. Acad. Sci.; mem. Am. Anthrop. Assn., Am. Assn. Phys. Anthropologists, Soc. for Neurosci., Sigma Xi, Phi Beta Kappa. Office: Columbia U Dept Anthropology New York NY 10027 E-mail: rlh2@columbia.edu.

HOLLOWAY, RICHARD LAWRENCE, marriage-family therapist, college official; b. Buffalo, May 18, 1949; s. Robert Lee and Aurelia (Muresan) H.; m. Julie Ann Sianko, Sept. 26, 1987; children: Evan Richard, Kendall Marie. AB in Speech and Theater, Heidelberg Coll., Tiffin, Ohio, 1971; MS in Instrnl. Des. Devel. and Evaluation, Syracuse U., 1974, PhD in Instrnl. Des. Devel. and Evaluation, 1976; postgrad. in marriage and family therapy, Baylor Coll. Medicine, 1987-90. Asst. prof. ednl. measurement Coll. Pharmacy U. Minn., Mpls., 1977-78, asst. prof. family medicine Sch. Medicine, 1978-82, assoc. prof., 1982-84; assoc. prof., head com. resources Minn. Ext. Svc., St. Paul, 1985-86; prof. Baylor Coll. Medicine, Houston, 1986-91, prof., rsch. dir., 1991-92; prof., assoc. dean student affairs, vice chair, divsn. chief Med. Coll. Wis., Milw., 1992—, assoc. dean for student affairs, 1996—. Vis. prof. Syracuse (N.Y.) U., 1981. TV host Campus Closeup, One Step Ahead, Mpls., 1984-86; contbr. chpts. to books, articles to profl. jours.; mem. edit. rev. bd. Am. Family Physician, 1994—. Bd. dirs. Milw. Ave. Homeowners Assn., Mpls., 1976-83. Recipient E.B. Knight Jour. award NACTA, 1977, Standing Ovation award Med. Coll. Wis. students, 2000; vis. scholar U. Mich., 1983. Mem. APA, Am. Assn. Marriage and Family Therapy, Am. Ednl. Rsch. Assn. (Recognition award 1985), Soc. Tchrs. Family Medicine (bd. dirs. 1989-95, pres. 1993-94, Recognition award 1982). Democrat. E-mail: holloway@mcw.edu.

HOLLOWAY, ROBERT CHARLES, orchestrator, arranger, composer; b. Balt. s. George Albert and Edna Mildred (Smith); m. Leslee R. Seymour, June 4, 1960; children: Bruce, Collin, Christy, Heather, Deven, Duana. Arranger, orchestrator Alvin Ailey Dance Co., 1987; pres. Chelsea Music Svc., Inc., N.Y.C., 1990-92. V.p. St. Croix Records. Arranger, orchestrator for ABC-TV, CBS Radio, NBC Tonight Show, Radio City Music Hall, Children's TV Workshop Sesame Street, USN Band, Boston Pops Orch., PS Classics, San Antonio Symphony, Denver Symphony, Pacific N.W. Ballet; orchestrator Le Ballet de Coeurs commd. by San Francisco Ballet, (film) Edith Piaf: Her Story...Her Songs; (Broadway musicals) Odyssey, Barnum, Peter Pan, Dancin', Sophisticated Ladies, On Your Toes, Jerome Robbins Broadway; (performers) Skitch Henderson, Enrique Madriguera, Richard Hayman, Tommy Tune, Betty Carter, Eddie Fisher, Caterina Valente, Connie Francis, Raquel Bitton, Philip Chaffin, Vt. Jazz Ensemble; composer: Prelude, Busybody, Southern Suite, Improvisations in Jazz, Celebration. Mem. ASCAP, Am. Soc. Music Arrangers, Am. Fedn. Musicians. Avocation: boxing. Home: 1079 Forest Rd Alstead NH 03602 E-mail: bobholloway@cheshire.net.

HOLLOWAY, ROBERT ROSS, archaeologist, educator; b. Newton, Mass., Aug. 15, 1934; s. Charles Thomas and Mildred Evelyn (Guthrie) H.; m. Nancy Jane Degenhardt, May 21, 1960; children: Anne Lovelace Studholme, Susannah Porter Hollers. AB summa cum laude, Amherst Coll., 1956; AM, U. Pa., 1957; MA, PhD, Princeton U., 1960; LHD (hon.), Amherst Coll., 1976; MA (hon.), Brown U., 1967; D honoris causa, U. Louvain, Belgium, 1997. Asst. prof. U. N.C., Chapel Hill, 1963-64; mem. faculty Brown U., Providence, 1964—, prof. archaeology, 1970—; dir. Ctr. for Archaeology and Art, 1978—87, 1994—2001. Cons. curator ancient art Mus. Art, RISD, 1971—; del. Centro Internat. di Studi Numis., Naples, Italy, 1973—, pres., 1980-86. Author: The Thirteen Months Coinage of Hieronymos of Syracuse, 1969, Satrianum, 1970, Buccino, 1973, A View of Greek Art, 1973, Influence and Styles in the Late Archaic and Early Classical Greek Sculpture of Sicily and Magna Graecia, 1978, Italy and the Aegean, 1981, The Archeology of Ancient Sicily, 1990, The Archeology of Early Rome and Latium, 1994, Catalogue of Ancient Greek Coins Museum Art, 1998; co-author: Terina, 1983, Ustica I, 1995, Ustica II,2001; editor catalogue of classical collection Mus. Art, RISD, 1965. Grantee, Am. Philos. Soc., 1962; NEH rsch. grantee, 1972, 80, 82, 83, sr. fellow, 1977; Am. Coun. Learned Soc. fellow, 1969, Gold medal Archaeol. Inst. Am., 1995. Fellow Am. Numis. Soc., Royal Numis. Soc., Am. Acad. Rome; mem. Assn. Field Archaeology (pres. 1975-77), Archaeol. Inst. Am., Royal Belgian Numis. Soc. (hon.), Nat. Inst. Etruscan and Italic Studies (Italy; hon.), Inst. Prehist. Studies (Florence, Italy), German Archaeol. Inst. (corr.), Soc. Art Historians (Rome; corr.), Soc. War of 1812 (Md., Conn.), Soc. Colonial Wars (Md., R.I.), Bristol Yacht Club, Providence Art Club, Phi Beta Kappa. Home: 185 Elmgrove Ave Providence RI 02906-4240

HOLLOWAY, ROBERT WESTER, radiochemist; b. Morrilton, Ark., Jan. 3, 1945; s. Otho and Bessie Vance (Woolverton) H.; m. Mary Ella Hamel, Dec. 31, 1970; children: David, Jason. BS, Harding Coll., 1967; postgrad., U. Okla., 1968; PhD, U. Ark., 1977. Asst. prof. U. Ark., Pine Bluff, 1976-79; research chemist DuPont Corp., Aiken, S.C., 1979-81; supervisory chemist EPA, Las Vegas, 1981-94; pres. Nev. Tech. Assocs., Inc., 1994—. Contbr. articles to profl. jours. Served to capt. USAF, 1967-72. Mem. Am. Chem. Soc., Health Physics Soc., Toastmasters, Optimists. Republican. Avocation: sailing. Office: Nev Tech Assocs Inc PO Box 90748 Henderson NV 89009-0748 E-mail: holloway3@aol.com.

HOLLOWAY, SHARON KAY SOSSAMON, vocational/secondary school educator; b. Ft. Smith, Feb. 26, 1958; d. Floyd Clinton and Ruth Ann (Clemons) Sossamon; m. David Arthur Holloway, Dec. 27, 1985 (div. Aug. 1995). BS in Bus. Edn., N.E. State U., Tahlequah, Okla., 1980, MS, 1987. Cert. tchr. vocat. bus., Okla. Tchr. vocat. bus. Pawhuska Pub. Schs., Okla., 1982—2001, Sapulpa Pub. Schs., 2001—02, Pawhuska Pub. Schs., 2002—. Cons. tchr. Pawhuska Pub. Schs., 1992-93, computer tchr. community edn. program, 1988—. Recipient Tandy Tech. award for Outstanding Tchr., 1994. Mem. Nat. Bus. Assn., Am. Vocat. Assn., Okla. Bus. Assn., Pawhuska Edn. Assn., Delta Zeta Alumnae. Democrat. Baptist. Avocations: reading, crocheting, computers, computer games. Home: 316 E 14th St 1377 Pawhuska OK 74056-2214 Office: Pawhuska Pub Schs 621 E 15th St Pawhuska OK 74056-1843

HOLLOWAY, SYBIL LYMORISE, psychologist, writer; b. New York, NY, Apr. 16, 1967; d. Thomas Carvin and Bannie Lymorise Holloway. BA, Smith Coll., Northampton, Mass., 1989; MA, Ind. Univ. of PA, Ind., Pa., 1991, PhD, 1994. Lic. psychologist Pa. Coun. intern Univ. of Calif., Santa Barbara, Calif., 1993—94; psychol. coun., asst. prof. Bloomsburg Univ., Bloomsburg, Pa., 1999—. Bd. of dir. Smith club of Long Is., Long Is., NY, 1998—99. Recipient Fin. Aid Success Story, Nat. Assoc. of Student Fin. Aid Admin./Wash., D.C., 2000, Vol. Svc. Award, Alice Paul House/Ind., Pa., 1992, Alumnae Scholarship, Smith Coll./Northampton, Mass., 1989; fellow IUP Found. Fellowship, Ind. Univ. of Pa./Ind., Pa., 1989. Mem.: Pennwriters, Pa. Coll. Pers. Assoc., Nat. Acad. Adv. Assoc., Assoc. for Women in Psychol., Pa. Psychol. Assoc., Am. Psychological Assoc. Avocations: writing, reading, tap, TV watching, stamp collecting. Home: 915 country Club Dr, Apt 6 Bloomsburg PA 17815 Office: Bloomsburg Univ 400 E 2nd St (240 SSC) Bloomsburg PA 17815

HOLLOWAY, WILLIAM JIMMERSON, retired educator; b. Smithfield, Va., May 6, 1917; s. Arnett Jimmerson and Lucy Pernell (White) H.; m. Julia Naomi Edmundson, June 17, 1944; children: Wendell, Arnett, Lynn. BS with honors, Hampton Inst., 1940; MA, U. Mich., 1946; Ed.D., U. Ill., 1961; postgrad., Harvard U., 1950. Prin. Union Sch., Hampton, Va., 1946-47; dean students Savannah State Coll., 1947-55; prin. Ligon High Sch., Raleigh, N.C., 1956-57; counselor N.C. Central U., Durham, 1959-61; supt. Va. State Sch., Hampton, 1961-65; edn. program officer U.S. Office Edn. Washington, 1965-70; vice provost Ohio State U., Columbus, 1970-78, prof. edn., 1970-82, prof. emeritus, 1982—; dir. Nigerian edn. program, Ohio State U., 1980-82; pres. Internat. Ednl. and Service Inst., Inc., Raleigh, N.C., 1981-88; disting. prof. edn. St. Augustine's Coll., Raleigh, 1983-87. Author: The Education of Blacks in Virginia Before the Civil War, 1619-1860, 1993, The Odyssey of a North American Educator, 2001; mem. editl. bd. The Negro Educational Review, 1972, editor-in-chief, 1995; editor-in-chief emeritus, 1999; chief cons. Insight Enterprises African Am. Disability Program, 1998. Trustee Freedoms Found., 1974, St. Augustines Coll., 1968-77. Recipient Freedoms Found. medal, 1954, Superior Accomplishment award HEW, 1968, Disting. Alumni award Hampton Inst., 1970, award Nat. Press Inst., 1972, Outstanding Citizen award Ohio Gen. Assembly, 1978, Outstanding Achievement award Ohio State U., 1978, Disting. Service award Ohio State U., 1984, Community Leadership award Capital U., 1978, Nat. Disting. Service award United Negro Coll. Fund, 1979, Excellence in Internat. Edn. award Govt. of Nigeria, Disting. Career award Negro Ednl. Rev., 1984, Outstanding Achievement award U. Mich., 1987, Negro Ednl. Rev. Golden Anniversary Disting. Svc. award, 2000; Harvard Far Eastern Studies fellow, 1956, Disting. Svc. award Insight Enterprises Emmet H. Scott, 1998.; named to Ohio State U. Coll. Edn. Hall of Fame, 2002. Mem. Am. Assn. Higher Edn., Am. Personnel and Guidance Assn., Alpha Kappa Delta, Phi Delta Kappa, Kappa Delta Pi. Democrat. Presbyterian (elder). Clubs: Lions (pres. 1975); Cosmos (Washington). Avocations: duplicate bridge, saltwater fishing. Home: 3618 Littledale Rd Ste 213 Kensington MD 20895 *As an educator I have worked to develop sensitivity to the needs, hopes, and aspirations of all people, particularly those at the bottom of the socio-economic ladder. With youth and adults I have labored to kindle sparks of brotherhood leading to harmony. I feel that our survival on this planet is linked with our capacity to use cultural differences in creative and constructive ways.*

HOLLOWAY, WILLIAM JUDSON, JR., federal judge; b. 1923; AB, U. Okla., 1947; LLB, Harvard U., 1950; LLD (hon.), Oklahoma City U. Ptnr. Holloway & Holloway, Oklahoma City, 1950—51; atty. Dept. Justice, Washington, 1951—52; assoc., ptnr. Crowe and Dunlevy, Oklahoma City, 1952—68; judge U.S. Ct. Appeals (10th cir.), Oklahoma City, 1968—84, chief judge, 1984—91, sr. judge, 1992—. Mem.: FBA, ABA, Oklahoma County Bar Assn., Okla. Bar Assn. Office: US Ct Appeals 10th Cir PO Box 1767 Oklahoma City OK 73101-1767

HOLLRAH, DAVID, lawyer; b. Norman, Okla., June 8, 1948; s. Victor and Dorothy E. (Friedland) H.; children: Kendall, Lauren. Student U. Heidelberg, Ger., 1969; B.A., U. Tex., 1970; postgrad. U. Tuebingen, Fed. Republic Germany, 1970-71; J.D., Harvard U., 1974. Bar: N.Y. 1975, Tex. 1977. Assoc. firm Briger & Assocs., N.Y.C., 1974-76, firm Butler & Binion, Houston, 1976-81; mng. ptnr. firm Hollrah, Lange & Thoma, Houston, 1981-92; dir. Morris, Lendais, Hollrah & Brown, Houston, 1992—. Editor-in-chief Harvard Internat. Law Jour., 1974. Mem. State Bar Tex., ABA. Lutheran. Home: 4417 Acacia St Bellaire TX 77401-4301

HOLLYER, A(RTHUR) RENE, lawyer; b. Wycoff, N.J., July 28, 1938; s. Richard W. and Florence (Vervaet) H.; m. Lauraine Dennis, Apr. 8, 1978; children: James Richard, Jennifer Ashley. BA, Williams Coll., 1961; MPA, Woodrow Wilson Sch., Princeton, 1963; LLB, Columbia U., 1966. Bar: N.J. 1966, U.S. Dist. Ct. N.J. 1966, N.Y. 1968, U.S. Dist. Ct. (so. and ea. dists.) N.Y. 1969, U.S. Ct. Appeals (3rd cir.) 1970, U.S. Ct. Appeals (2d cir.) 1971, D.C. 1972, U.S. Supreme Ct. 1974. Law sec. to judge chancery divsn. N.J. Superior Ct., Newark, 1966-67; assoc. Olwine, Connelly, Chase, O'Donnell & Weyher, N.Y.C., 1968-70, 72-74; asst. U.S. atty. Dist. N.J., 1970-71; ptnr. Hollyer, Brady, Smith & Hines, L.L.P. and predecessor firms, N.Y.C., 1974—. Mem.: Assn. of Bar of City of N.Y. (profl. discipline com. 1990—92, 1995—98, 2001—, chmn. complaint mediation panel 1991—92, ethics com. 1992—95, profl. responsibility com. 1998—2001), N.Y. State Bar Assn. (chair spl. com. on procedures for judicial discipline 2001—). Home: 50 Hamilton Rd Glen Ridge NJ 07028-1109 Office: Hollyer Brady Smith & Hines LLP 551 5th Ave New York NY 10176-0001 E-mail: arh-esq@worldnet.att.net.

HOLLYFIELD, JOHN SCOGGINS, lawyer; b. Harlingen, Tex., Aug. 20, 1939; m. Penny Pounds, Dec. 27, 1962; children: Jon Scott, Courtney. Bar: Tex. 1968. Assoc. Fulbright & Jaworski, Houston, 1968—75, ptnr., 1975—2001, of counsel, 2001—. Lt. USNR, 1961-65. Recipient Pres.'s award Houston Bar Assn., 1986. Mem. ABA (coun. real property sect. 1986-93, sec. 1993-94, vice chair real property divsn. 1994-96, chair elect 1996-97, chair 1997-98, ho. of dels. 1999—), Am. Coll. Real Estate Lawyers (pres. 1990-91), Anglo-Am. Real Property Inst. (chair 2001). Office: Fulbright & Jaworski LLP 1301 Mckinney St Houston TX 77010-3095 E-mail: jhollyfield@fulbright.com.

HOLM, BRUCE ALLEN, academic administrator, researcher; b. Waterloo, Iowa, Jan. 20, 1959; s. Howard Laverne and Bernita Clara Holm; m. Allison Leslie Wishner, June 10, 1989; children: Alexander Nathan, Christopher Isaac. BS in biochemistry, U. of Iowa, Iowa City, IA, 1977—81; MS in biophysics, Unviersity of Rochester Sch. of Medicine, 1982—83; PhD, U. of Rochester Sch. of Medicine, 1982—86. Perinatology fellow Children's Hosp., Buffalo, 1988—89; assoc. prof. of pediat. SUNY at Buffalo, 1991—95, sr. assoc. dean of medicine, 1993—98, prof. of pediat., ob/gyn, and pharmacology, 1996—, sr. assoc. v.p. of health sciences, 1998—2002, sr. vice provost, 2002—. Sci. dir. ONY, Inc., Amherst, NY, 1988—; cons. Forest Pharmaceuticals, New York, 2000—; dir. STAR Ctr. for Therapy Discovery, Buffalo, 2001—. Editor: (book series) Clinics in Perinatology, (book) Acute Lung Injury. Bd. mem. CUBRC, Buffalo, 1999—2002; pres. Health Care Industries Assn., Buffalo, 1999—2002; bd. mem. Women & Children's Health Rsch. Found., Buffalo, 1993—2002. Recipient Tech./Discovery award, Health Care Industries Assn., 1998, 2000, Merit Scholar, U. of Iowa, 1977, Harold C. Hodge award, U. of Rochester, 1987, Alpha Omega Alpha Med. Honor Soc., U. at Buffalo, 1997, George Thorn award, 1999, Chancellor's Award for Rsch. in Scinece and Medicine, SUNY, 2001, Chancellor's Award for Entrepreneurial Activity, State Unviersity of NY, 2002; grantee Rsch. of Diseases in Infants and Newborns, Nat. Instituties of Health, 1991-2005; Predoctoral fellowship, NIH, 1982—87, Rsch. Career Devel. award, NIH: Heart, Lung and Blood Inst., 1991—96, Genomics and Proteomics, Howard Hughes Med. Inst., 1999—2003, Microbial Pathogenesis Ctr., Lucille P. Markey Charitable Trust, 1996—2001. Mem.: AAAS, NY Acad. of Sci., Am. Physiol. Soc., Am. Thoracic Soc., Perintal Rsch. Soc. D-Liberal. Lutheran. Achievements include patents for lung surfactant replacements drugs; research in molecular therapies in inflammatory lung disease; treatments for congenital anomalies in newborn infants; first to surfactant deficiencies in lung disease. Home: 1425 Clover St Rochester NY 14610 Office: State University of New York at Buffalo 562 Capen Hall Buffalo NY 14260 Office Fax: 716-645-3685. E-mail: baholm@buffalo.edu.

HOLM, CELESTE, actress; b. N.Y.C., Apr. 29, 1919; d. Theodor and Jean (Parke) H.; m. Wesley Addy, May 22, 1966; children: Theodor Holm Nelson, Daniel Schuyler Dunning. Ed., Univ. Sch. for Girls, Chgo., Lycee Victor Durui, Paris, Francis W. Parker Sch., Chgo., Adelphi Acad., Bklyn.; DHL (hon.), Centenary Coll., 1980, Northwood U., 1981; AA (hon.), Middle Ga. Coll., 1982; ArtsD (hon.), Ea. Mich. U., 1984; DHL (hon.), Kean Coll. of N.J., 1984, Felician Coll., 1985, Jersey City State Coll., 1986; DFA (hon.), Monmouth Coll., 1987; D Liberal Arts (hon.), Fairleigh Dickinson U., 1988; D Pub. Svc. (hon.), Ea. Ill. U., 1989; DFA (hon.), Seton Hall U., 1990. Appeared in Broadway shows Gloriana, 1938, The Time of Your Life, 1939, Another Sun, 1940, Return of the Vagabond, 1940, Eight O'Clock Tuesday, 1941, My Fair Ladies, 1941, Papa Is All, 1941-42, All the Comforts of Home, 1942, The Damask Cheek, 1942-43, Oklahoma!, 1943-44, 48, Bloomer Girl, 1944-45, She Stoops to Conquer, 1949, Affairs of State, 1950-51, Anna Christie, 1952, The King and I, 1952, His and Hers, 1954, Interlock, 1958, Third Best Sport, 1958, Invitation to a March, 1960-61, Mame, 1967, Candida, 1970, Habeas Corpus, 1975-76, The Utter Glory of Morrissey Hall, 1979, I Hate Hamlet, 1991; appeared in films Three Little Girls in Blue, 1946, Gentleman's Agreement, 1947 (Acad. Award for Best Supporting Actress), Carnival in Costa Rica, 1947, The Snake Pit, 1948, Road House, 1948, Chicken Every Sunday, 1948, Come to the Stable, 1949 (Acad. Award nomination for Best Supporting Actress), Everybody Does It, 1949, Champagne for Caesar, 1950, All About Eve, 1950 (Acad. Award nomination for Best Supporting Actress), The Tender Trap, 1955, High Society, 1956, Bachelor Flat, 1961, Doctor, You've Got to be Kidding, 1966, Tom Sawyer, 1972, Three Men and a Baby, 1987, Still Breathing, 1996; other stage appearances include (tours) Hamlet, 1937, The Women, 1937-38, Back to Methuselah, 1957, Finishing Touches, 1974, Light Up the Sky, 1975, (one-woman show) Paris Was Yesterday, 1978, (other prodns.) A Month in the Country, 1963, Madly in Love, 1964, Night of the Iguana, 1964, Captain Brassbound's Conversion, 1966, Mame (nat. tour), 1967-68 (Sarah Siddons award), Hay Fever, 1979-83, Lady in the Dark (Eng.), 1981, The Trojan Women, 1985, The Road to Mecca, 1989, Love Letters, 1990, 94, The Cocktail Hour, 1990, 94, Allegro, 1994, 50th Anniversary of The Glass Menagerie, Chgo., 1994, Don Juan in Hell, Irish Rep., N.Y.C., 2000; numerous supper club appearances, N.Y.C., Chgo., San Francisco, Washington, L.A., 1943-59, (London cabaret debut) Pizza on the Park, 2003; U.S.O. entertainer, ETO, 1945; 21,000 mile tour of U.S. Army bases, 1949; TV appearances include (spls. & TV movies) Cinderella, 1965, The Shady Hill Kidnapping, 1979, Backstairs at the White House, 1979 (Emmy nomination), Nora's Christmas Gift, 1989, Polly, 1989, Polly, One Mo' Time, 1990; regular roles (series) Archie Bunker's Place, 1980-81, Falcon Crest, 1985, Loving, 1986 (Emmy nomination), 91-92, Christine Cromwell, 1989-90, Promised Land, CBS-TV, 1997-99, PBS Great Performances Talking With..., 1994; guest starring roles on Trapper John, M.D., The F.B.I., Disney's Wide World of Color, The Streets of San Francisco, Columbo, Medical Center, Captains and the Kings, Spencer For Hire, Magnum P.I., The Underground Man, Fantasy Island, The Love Boat; radio interviewer People at the UN, 1963-65; toured with theatre-in-concert program Interplay, 1963-74; appeared in The Cole Porter 100th Birthday Celebration, Carnegie Hall, 1991. Past mem. gov. bd. U.S. Com. for UNICEF; mem. Nat. Mental Health Assn., 1965—, chmn., 1969-70; v.p. Arts and Bus. Coun.; mem. Nat. Arts Coun., 1982-88; chmn. bd. dirs. N.J. Film Commn., 1983—; bd. dirs. Mayor's Midtown Com., 1975—, Actor's Fund Am., 1988—; pres. bd. Creative Arts Rehab. Ctr., 1978—; mem. nat. vis. coun. for health scis. faculties Columbia U., N.Y.C., 1989—; mem. adv. bd. N.J. Sch. for the Arts, 1989—, adv. coun. UN Assn. of N.Y.C., 1992—; chmn. Stage South Supporting Players, S.C. State Theatre, 1977, Arts Horizons, 1995—. Decorated Dame King Olav of Norway; recipient Brotherhood award Nat. Conf. Christians & Jews, 1952, Disting. Svc. award United Jewish Appeal, 1953, Award of Merit, 1954, Achievement award Israel Bonds, 1958, Award of Appreciation March of Dimes, 1959, Hadassah, 1960, Nat. Assn. for Retarded Children award, 1961, Disting. Alumni award Francis W. Parker Sch., 1964, U.S. Com. for World Fedn. of Mental Health award, 1965, Performer of Yr. award Variety Clubs Am., 1966, Edward Strecker Meml. Medal for outstanding contbns. to mental health movement, rehab. of mentally disabled, 1971, Woman of Yr. award Anti-Defamation League, 1972, Golden Needle award Am. Home Sewing Coun., 1972, Woman of Yr. award N.Y. Variety Club, 1973, Woman of Yr. nomination Ladies Home Jour., 1975, Spirit of Am. award VFW, 1976, Woman of Yr. award Westchester Fedn. Women's Clubs, 1977, Woman of Yr. award Creative Arts Rehab. Ctr., 1977, Disting. Woman award Northwood Inst., 1977, Golden Scroll award Mayor's Midtown Citizens Com., 1979, Achievement in Arts award Northwood Inst./IASTA, 1979, Actor's Studio award, 1980, Mental Health Assn. Greater Chgo. award, 1982, Zonta Internat. Humanitarian award, 1984, Compostella award, 1984, Town Hall Friend of the Arts award, 1985, Humanitarian award Creative Arts Rehab. Ctr., 1988, Internat. Platform award, 1989, The Coalition of Arts Therapy Assn. Cert. Appreciation, 1990, Edwin Forrest award for Outstanding Contbn. to Theatre, Walnut St. Theatre, Phila., 1991, The Cardinal's Com of Laity Cardinal's award, 1991, The Ellis Island Medal of Honor, 1992, Gold medal Holland Soc. N.Y., 1994, Dorothea Dix award Mental Illness Found., 1995, Silver Circle award, 1999; named to The Theatre Hall of Fame, 1992, Grandparent of Yr., 1997, Utah Shakespeare Festivals Imperial Order, 2000; rsch. scholar in semiotics, Claremont Grad. Sch., Calif., 1988-89.

HOLM, ERIK, foundation director, political scientist, economist; b. Hobro, Denmark, Dec. 6, 1933; s. Carl and Ane Margrethe (Nielsen) H.; m. Ank Kortleven, Apr. 16, 1960 (dec. 1984); children: Irene, Jacob, Carl-Erik, Marianne. MA in Econs., U. Copenhagen, 1961, PhD in Polit. Sci., 1992. Economist Ctrl. Statis. Office, Copenhagen, 1961-65, Internat. Monetary Fund, Washington, 1965-69; sr. economist Ministry of Econ. Affairs, Copenhagen, 1969-72; personal adviser to Prime Min. Copenhagen, 1972-82; prin. advisor Directorate Gen. II, European Commn., Brussels, 1982-87; vis. scholar U. Calif., Berkeley, 1987-89; dir. Eleni Nakou Found., London, 1989—. Author: Money and International Politics, 1991, Union Eller Nation, 1992, Europe, A Political Culture?, 1994, The European Anarchy: Europe's Hard Road into High Politics, 2001. Mem.: Acad. Polit. Sci., Royal Inst. Internat. Affairs. Home: Wiedeweltsgade 27 2100 Copenhagen Denmark E-mail: erholm@attglobal.net.

HOLM, SIR IAN, actor; b. Sept. 12, 1931; s. James Harvey and Jean (Wilson) Cuthbert; m. Lynn Mary Shaw, 1955 (div. 1965); m. Sophie Baker, 1982 (div. 1986); m. Penelope Wilton, 1991 (div. 2001). Student, Royal Acad. Dramatic Art, 1950-53; LittD (hon.), U. Sussex, 1999. Actor with Shakespeare Mem. Theatre, 1954-55; in repertory, 1956; toured in Titus Andronicus, 1957; numerous roles Royal Shakespeare Co. including Henry V, Romeo and Richard III, 1958-67; plays include Moonlight, 1993, Landscape, 1994, King Lear, 1997 (Evening Std. award for Best Actor, Olivier award Best Actor and Critics Cir. award, 1998); film appearances include Young Winston, Alien, Chariots of Fire (named Best Supporting Actor, Cannes Film Festival, 1981, Brit. Acad. Film and TV Arts, 1982, Acad. Award nomination Best Supporting Actor, 1982), Greystoke, Brazil, Dance With A Stranger, 1985, Wetherby, 1985, Dreamchild, 1985, Another Woman, 1988, Henry V, 1990, Hamlet, 1990, Kafka, 1991, The Naked Lunch, 1992, Blue Ice, 1992, Hour of The Pig, 1993, The Madness of King George, 1994, Lochness, 1994, Mary Shelley's Frankenstein, 1995, Big Night, 1995, Night Falls on Manhattan, 1995, The 5th Element, 1996, A Life Less Ordinary, 1996, The Sweet Hereafter, 1996 (Genie Best Actor award), Existenz, 1998, Simon Magus, 1998, The Match, 1998, Esther Kahn, 1999, Joe Gould's Secret, 1999, Beautiful Joe, 1999, Lord of the Rings, 2000, From Hell, 2000; others; TV appearances include The Lost Boys (Best Actor award Royal TV Soc., 1979), Strike, 1981, (miniseries) Game, Set and Match, 1988, The Last Romantics, 1991, (series) The Borrowers, 1992-93, others; TV appearances include Landscape, BBC, 1995, King Lear, BBC, 1997, Alice Through the Looking Glass, Channel 4, 1998, The Last of the Blonde Bombshells, 2000, The Emperor's New clothes, 2000. Awarded Knighthood by Queen of Eng.; recipient Tony award for Best Supporting Actor, 1967, Evening Std. award, 1967, 93, 97, Genie award, 1997, Olivier award, 1998.

HOLM, JOHN ALEXANDER, linguist, educator; b. Jackson, Mich., May 16, 1943; s. James P. and Leah (Reisbig) H. BA in English, U. Mich., 1965; MA in Tchg. English as a Fgn. Lang., Columbia U., 1968; PhD in Linguistics, U. London, 1978. Tchr. English U. Los Andes, Bogotá, Colombia, 1965-66; tchr. English and German Detroit Inst. of Tech., 1971-73; tchr. of English Kollegium Sarnen, Switzerland, 1973-75; lectr. in linguistics Coll. of the Bahamas, Nassau, 1978-80; prof. English Hunter Coll., CUNY, 1980-98; prof. linguistics Grad. Ctr., CUNY, 1989-98; chair English linguistics U. Coimbra, Portugal, 1998—, dir. grad. program descriptive linguistics, 2002—. Editor: (with F. Byrne) Atlantic Meets Pacific, 1993; editor: Central American English, 1983; author: (with A. Shilling) Dictionary of Bahamian English, 1982, Pidgins and Creoles, 1988-89 (2 volumes), Introduction to Pidgins and Creoles, 2000, Languages in Contact: The Partial Restructuring of Vernaculars, 2003; bd. editors Jour. of Pidgin and Creole Langs. Fulbright scholar U. Coimbra, Portugal, 1993-94, U. London, 1986-87, Excellence in scholarship Hunter Coll., 1988; rsch. grantee NEH, 1973-84; travel grantee U. Papua New Guinea, 1989, Brazilian Linguistics Assn., 1999, Linguistic Soc. So. Africa, 2000, Inst. Cervantes de Manila, 2000, U. Copenhagen, 2001, U. Puerto Rico, 2001, U. de la Reunion, 2002; Woodrow Wilson fellow, 1967-68. Mem. Soc. for Pidgin and Creole Linguistics (pres. 1993-95), Am. Speech, Creole Lang. Libr. (bd. editors). Avocations: travel, languages. Office: Grupo Estudos Anglo Am U Coimbra Faculdade Letras 3004-530 Coimbra Portugal E-mail: jholm@mail.telepac.pt.

HOLM, JOY ALICE, psychology educator, goldsmith, artist, art educator; b. Chgo., May 21, 1929; d. Alvin Herbert and Willette Eugenia (Miller) Holm. BFA, U. Ill., 1952; MS in Art Edn. Inst. Design, Ill. Inst. Tech., 1956; PhD in Edn., U. Minn., 1967. Tchr. art, Eng. West Chgo. H.S., 1952-54; instr., tchr. art J.S. Morton H.S. & Jr. Coll., Cicero, Ill., 1954-65; asst. prof. art & design Mankato (Minn.) State U., 1965-66; asst. prof. art Ill. State U., Normal, 1966-69; assoc. prof. art & design So. Ill. U., Edwardsville, 1969-71; assoc. prof. art, art edn. Winona (Minn.) State U., 1971-75; assoc. prof., chmn. dept. art St. Mary's Coll. of Notre Dame, Ind., 1975-76; assoc. prof. art & design, secondary, continuing edn. U. Wis., Eau Claire, 1976-78; assoc. prof. art & design Sch. Art & Design Kent (Ohio) State U., 1978-80; lectr. Jungian studies C.G. Jung Inst., Chgo., 1980-82; adj. assoc. prof. art edn. Sch. Art and Design, Sch. Edn. U. Ill., Chgo., 1981-82; lectr. U. Calif. Ext., Santa Cruz, 1983—; adj. prof. art edn., design San Jose (Calif.) State U., 1983-84; owner bus. designer-goldsmith Oak Park, Ill., 1980-82, Carmel, Calif., 1982-87, Atelier XII, Winona, 1988—. Curriculum cons. North Ctrl. Assn. Accreditation Team State of Ill., Edwardsville, 1970; regional cons. Supt. Pub. Instrn., Springfield, Ill., 1970; juror exhbns.; panelist, spkr., presenter confs., meetings. Contbr., cons. Alternative Medicine: A Definitive Guide, 1994; contbg. author: Living Science, 2002; contbr. articles to profl. jours; one-woman shows: J. Sterling Morton H.S. & Jr. Coll., 1963, Russell Art Gallery, Bloomington, 1968, Owatonna (Minn.) Art Ctr., 1980, 86; exhbns. include La Grange (Ill.) Art League (Best of Show, 1st Place award prints), 1963, 64, Minn. Mus. Art, 1974, 75, Craft & Folk Art Mus., L.A., 1978, The Gallery Kent State U., 1978, 79, Saenger Nat. Small Sculpture and Jewelry Exhibit, 1978, Diamonds Internat., N.Y., 1978, Inst. Design Alumni, 1988, Internat. Biographical Ctr. Congress Exhbn., Edinburgh, Scotland, 1994, others. Fellow World Lit. Acad.; mem. AAUP, Nat. Art Edn. Assn. (rep. Wis. Women's Caucus Houston Conf. 1978, higher edn. divsn. 1961—), Am. Assn. Higher Edn., Coll. Art Assn., Soc. N.Am. Goldsmiths, Gemological Inst. Am., C.G. Jung Inst. (Chgo.), Hon. Soc. Illustrators (hon.), Internat. Soc. Study of Subtle Energies and Energy Medicine, Inst. Noetic Scis., Alpha Lambda Delta (hon.), Phi Kappa Phi (hon.). Methodist. Office: Atelier XII PO Box 183 Winona MN 55987-0183

HOLM, VANJA ADELE, developmental pediatrician, educator; b. Kiruna, Sweden, Oct. 5, 1928; came to U.S, 1955. d. C.V. Hjalmar and Elma Adele (Nystrom) H.; m. Carl Holm, June 15, 1952; children: Ingrid Adele, Erik Carl Anders. Med. Kand., Karolinska Inst., Stockholm, 1950, MD, 1955. Intern Swedish Hosp., Seattle, 1955-56; resident in pediatrics U. Wash. Sch. Medicine, Seattle, 1956, 62-64, fellow in devel. pediatrics, 1964-65, instr. pediatrics, 1965-69, asst. prof. pediatrics, 1969-81, assoc. prof. pediatrics, 1981-96, prof. emeritus, 1996—. Attending pediatrician Children's Orthopedic Hosp., Univ. Hosp. Editor: Early Intervention: A Team Approach, 1978 (Am. Med. Writers award 1979), The Prader Willi Syndrome, 1981; contbr. some 60 articles to profl. jours. Fellow Am. Acad. Pediatrics, Am. Acad. Cerebral Palsy and Devel. Medicine, Am. Assn. Mental Retardation; mem. Soc. Devel. Pediatrics, Wash. State Med. Assn. (Aesculapius award 1979), Soc. Behavioral Pediatrics. Democrat. Office: U Wash CHDD PO Box 357920 Seattle WA 98195-7920

HOLMAN, ARTHUR STEARNS, artist; b. Bartlesville, Okla., Oct. 25, 1926; s. Newton Davis and Barbara (Hendry) H. BFA, U. N.Mex., 1951; postgrad., Hans Hofmann Sch., 1951, Calif. Sch. Fine Arts, San Francisco, 1953. One-man shows include Esther Robles Gallery, L.A., 1960, David Cole Gallery, San Francisco, 1962, 80, De Young Mus., San Francisco, 1963, San Francisco Mus., 1963, Gumps Gallery, San Francisco, 1964-66, 69, 87, Marin Civic Ctr. Gallery, 1970, 95, William Sawyer Gallery, San Francisco, 1971, 73, 74, 76, John Bolles Gallery, Santa Rosa, Calif., 1982, Braunstein, Quay Gallery, San Francisco, 1992, The Art Foundry, Sacramento, Calif., 2003; exhibited in group shows at San Francisco Mus., 1960-76, Downey Mus., L.A., 1961, 50 Calif. Artists, Whitney Mus., N.Y.C., Walker Art Ctr., Albright-Knox Gallery, Des Moines Art Ctr., 1962, U. N.C. Annual, 1965, Smithsonian Instn., Washington, 1977, Coll. of Marin, 1983, Hall of Flowers, San Francisco, 1985, 86, 20th Century Landscape Drawings, De Young Mus., San Francisco, 1989, Jan Holloway Gallery, San Francisco, 1989, Bolinas (Calif.) Mus., 1997, San Francisco Art Inst., 2001; represented in permanent collections, San Francisco Mus., Oakland Mus., Mills Coll., Stanford U., Eureka Coll., Achenbach Found., San Francisco. With USAAF, 1945-46. Address: PO Box 72 Lagunitas CA 94938-0072

HOLMAN, BILL, composer; b. Calif. Student, U. Colo., 1944—45, UCLA, 1947, Westlake Coll. Music, 1948—50. Mem. Lighthouse All Stars, 1950—51, Conte Candoli, 1955, Shelley Manne, 1955, Shorty Rogers, 1957. Recs. include Kenton Presents: The Bill Holman Octet, 1954, The Fabulous Bill Holman, 1957, In a Jazz Orbit, 1958, Jive for Five, 1958, Bill Holman's Great Big Band, 1960, The Bill Holman Band, 1988, A View From the Side (Grammy award for Best Instrumental Composition, 1996), Brilliant Corners, 1997, composer for various artists including Count Basie, Louis Bellson, Natalie Cole, Maynard Ferguson, Woody Herman, Stan Kanton, Peggy Lee, Carmen McRae, Diane Schuur, Sarah Vaughn, Joe Williams, Doc Severinsen, others. Named Best Arranger, Jazz Times Readers Poll, 1990, 1995, 1998, 1999, Arranger of Yr., Downbeat Readers' Poll and Critics Poll, 1998, 1999; recipient Grammy award for Best Instrumental Arrangement, 1987, 1997.

HOLMAN, BUD GEORGE, lawyer; b. N.Y.C., June 30, 1929; s. Harry and Fannie Abrams (Bass) H.; m. Kathleen Barbara McLean, Sept. 1, 1961; children: Jennifer Jean, Wayne George. BBA, CCNY, 1950; LLB, Yale U., 1956. Bar: N.Y. 1956, Conn. 1979, D.C. 1982. Law sec. to judge N.Y. Ct. Appeals, 1956-58; practice in N.Y.C., 1958—; ptnr. Kelley Drye & Warren (and predecessor firms), 1965—. Pres., chmn. bd. dirs. Sixty Sutton Corp., 1969-97; lectr. Practising Law Inst., Wage Price Inst., Young Pres. Orgn. Editor: The Bar, 1949-50, Yale Law Jour., 1955-56. Trustee U.S. Naval Acad. Found., 1978-85; bd. dirs. USO Met. N.Y. Mem. Naval Res. Assn. (pres. 3d naval dist. chpts. 1973-75, mem. nat. adv. coun. 1975-94), Am. Arbitration Assn. (bd. dirs., mem. exec. com.), Navy League (bd. dirs. coun. N.Y. chpt. 1979-99), Yale U. Law Sch. Assn. (mem. exec. com. 1987-90, 93-96, bd. dirs.), Yale Law Sch. Assn. N.Y.C. (bd. dirs.), Met. Club, Yale Club, Beta Gamma Sigma. Democrat. Presbyterian. Home: 350 Park Ave Box 978 Mattituck NY 11952 Office: Kelley Drye & Warren LLP 101 Park Ave New York NY 10178-0002 E-mail: bholman@kelleydrye.com., holmanbg@aol.com.

HOLMAN, C. RAY, medical products executive; BSBA, U. Mo., 1964; postgrad., Harvard U., 1978, 91. CPA. Sr. acct. Price Waterhouse & Co., 1966-68, audit mgr., 1969-76; asst. contr., fin. planning and control Mallinckrodt Med. Inc., 1976-77, v.p., contr., 1977-82, v.p. fin. administrn., treas., contr., 1978-79, v.p. fin., treas., CEO, 1979-82, group v.p. fin. and corp. devel., CFO, 1982-83, group v.p. hosp. and lab. products group, 1983-85, group v.p. med. products group, 1985-88, pres., 1988-90, pres., CEO, 1990-92, Mallinckrodt Inc., 1992-94, chmn., pres., CEO, 1994-95, chmn., CEO, 1995—. Bd. dirs. Laclede Gas Co., NationsBank, Barnes Hosp. 1st lt. U.S. Army, 1966-68. Office: Mallinckrodt Inc PO Box 5840 675 McDonnell Blvd Saint Louis MO 63134

HOLMAN, CHARLES MILLIGAN, urologist; b. Atlanta, Dec. 19, 1944; BA in Biology, EMory U., 1967, MD, 1971. Diplomate Am. Bd. Urology. Intern Vanderbilt U., Nashville, 1971-72; resident Emory U., Atlanta, 1972-73, 73-76; urologist pvt. practice, Biloxi, Miss., 1976—. Bd. dirs. Biloxi Regional Med. Ctr.. Maj. USAF, 1976-78. Mem. Am. Urologists Assn. Avocations: fishing, hunting. Office: Gulf South Urology 147 Reynoir St Ste 306 Biloxi MS 39530

HOLMAN, DAVID CALVIN, independent television and film producer and director; b. Mercedes, Tex., May 22, 1937; s. Cecil C. and Carolyn (Young) H. Student, Pan Am. Coll., 1955-57, U. Tex., 1957-60, 62-64. Dir. Sta. KTBC-TV, Austin, Tex., 1962-64; producer Norman, Craig, Kummel, Inc., N.Y.C.,

1964-67; unit mgr. ABC, N.Y.C., 1968-71, prodn. exec., 1971-74; prodn. exec. sports/1984 Olympics Hollywood, Calif., 1982-84; assoc. producer The Muppet Show Henson Assocs., N.Y.C., 1975-79, producer The Muppets, 1977-79; assoc. producer Ira Barmak Prodns., Hollywood, 1980-81; unit mgr. Trans-Am. Video, Inc., Hollywood, 1981-82; dir. tape prodn. Columbia Pictures TV, Hollywood, 1984-88; v.p. prodn. ops. Columbia Tristar TV, Culver City, Calif., 1988—2000; v.p. Worldwide Sales High Definition Stock Shots, 2001—. Guest lectr. U. Tex., Austin, 1987, So. Ill. U., Carbondale, 1987, ex-students assn. of U. Tex., L.A., 1987, 90. Contbr. City to City column Boston Sunday Urbanite, 1969; singer, dancer (off-Broadway prodn.) Ernest In Love, 1965. Served with U.S. Army, 1960-62. Recipient Merit award Tex. Soc. Profl. Engrs., 1963; named an Outstanding Young Men in Am. U.S. Jaycees, 1970. Mem. Nat. Acad. TV Arts and Scis. (Emmy award 1985), Ex-Students Assn. U. Tex. at Austin (life). Republican. Methodist. Avocations: singing, ballroom dancing, creative writing. Home: 53600 Eisenhower Dr La Quinta CA 92253-3566

HOLMAN, DONALD REID, retired lawyer; b. Astoria, Oreg., Jan. 30, 1930; s. Donald Reuben and Hattie Laveda (Card) H.; m. Susan Muncy Morris, Aug. 31, 1956; children: Donald Reid, Laura Morris Holman O'Brien, Douglas Edward. BA, U. Wash.-Seattle, 1951, JD, 1958; postgrad., U. Oreg.-Eugene, 1955-57. Bar: Oreg. Assoc. Miller Nash LLP, Portland, 1958-63, ptnr., 1963-93, mng. ptnr., 1987-90, sr. counsel, 1994-2001, ret., 2001. Lt. (j.g.) USN, 1951-55; capt. JAGC USNR, 1977-90, ret. Fellow Am. Bar Found.; mem. Order of Coif, Multnomah Athletic club (trustee 1983-85, v.p. 1985-86), Waverley Country Club, Phi Delta Phi. Republican. Avocations: tennis, golf, squash. Home: 8040 SW Broadmoor Ter Portland OR 97225-2121 E-mail: holmor@comcast.net.

HOLMAN, FREDERICK JOHN, landscape architect; b. Syracuse, N.Y., Feb. 18, 1947; s. Harvey John and Rena Mae (Kenyon) H.; m. Karen Elise Visconti, July 11, 1970. AAS, Paul Smiths (N.Y.) Coll., 1967; B Landscape Architecture, SUNY, Syracuse, 1970; BA, Syracuse U., 1970. Registered landscape architect, N.Y., Mass. Planner Urban Renewal Agy., Schenectady, N.Y., 1970-71, N.Y. Bur. of Planning, Schenectady, 1971-72; landscape technician Saratoga Assocs., Saratoga Springs, N.Y., 1972-75; prin. L.A. Partnership, Saratoga Springs, 1975-81, Frederick J. Holman Assocs., Saratoga Springs, 1981-83, Rochester, N.Y., 1986-89, Buffalo, 1989-95, Cumberland, R.I., 1995—; sr. assoc. Reimann Buechner Partnership, Syracuse, 1983-86; landscape arch. Providence Parks Dept., 1996—. Guest critic SUNY, Syracuse, 1985, U.R.I., 2000-03; guest critic, lectr. SUNY, Buffalo, 1989-94; lectr. Fedn. Garden Club, N.Y., 1985-86; guest lectr. Buffalo State Coll., 1993. Illustrator, tech. editor: Reforestation of Arid Lands, 1977, 2d edit., 1986, 3d edit., 1988, (manual) Understanding Soil Conservation Techniques, 1991. Pres. Saratoga Springs Preservation Found., 1979-83; chmn. Saratoga Springs Planning Bd., 1980-83; chair Cumberland Design Rev. Commn., 2001—, mem. Cumberland Visioning Com., 2002—; bd. dirs. Buffalo Friends of Olmsted Parks, 1991-93, greenways com., 1993-95; mem. Vision R.I. steering com., 1997-2000; Main st. design com. Providence Southside Broad St., 1997-2001; mem. Southside Design Review Com., Providence, 1999—; chair Cumberland Design Rev. Commn., 2001—. Mem. Am. Soc. Landscape Architects (N.Y. upstate chpt. pres. 1985-89, trustee 1991-95, Svc. award 1989, R.I. chpt. exec. com. 1996-2000), N.Y. State Coun. Landscape Architects (pres. 1989-92, bd. dirs. 1994-95), N.Y. Planning Fed., Rotary (bd. dirs. Williamsville, N.Y. chpt. 1992-94, horizon & waterfront commn., waterfront design and architecture com. 1993-95). Avocation: wood-carving. E-mail: fholman186@cox.net.

HOLMAN, HALSTED REID, medical educator, physician; b. Cleve., Jan. 17, 1925; s. Emile Frederic and Ann Peril (Purdy) H.; m. Barbara Marie Lucas, June 26, 1949 (div. July 9, 1982); children: Michael, Andrea, Alison; m. Diana Barbara Dutton, Aug. 10, 1985; 1 child, Geoffrey. Student, Stanford U., 1942-43, UCLA, 1943-44; MD, Yale U., 1949. Med. resident Montefiore Hosp., N.Y.C., 1952-55; staff physician Rockefeller Inst., N.Y.C., 1955-60; prof. medicine Stanford (Calif.) U., 1960—, chmn. dept. medicine, 1960-71, co-chief, divsn. family and community medicine, 1987-2001, dir. clin. scholar program, 1969-97, dir. Multipurpose Arthritis Ctr., 1977-97, co-chief, divsn. immunology and rheumatology, 1997-2000, dir. Stanford Program for Mgmt. of Chronic Disease, 1997—. Pres. Midpeninsula Health Svc., Palo Alto, Calif., 1975-80; mem. adv. bd. Calif Health Facilities Commn., Sacramento, 1978-81, Office Tech. Assessment, U.S. Congress, 1979-81, Inst. Advancement of Health, N.Y.C., 1982-90; Guggenhime prof. medicine, 1960—. Author 2 books; assoc. editor Arthritis and Rheumatism, 1995-2000; contbr. articles to profl. jours. Recipient Bauer Meml. award, Arthritis and Rheumatism Found., N.Y., 1964. Master: Am. Coll. Rheumatology (Presdl. Gold medal 2001); fellow: AAAS (coun. 1974—79), ACP (Laureate award no. Calif. chpt. 1994); mem.: Improving Chronic Illness Care-R.W. Johnson Found. (Vision award 2001), Arthritis Found. (Hero Overcoming Arthritis 1998, Engalitcheff award 1999, McGuire Educator award 2000), Western Assn. Physicians (pres. 1966), Am. Soc. Clin. Investigation (pres. 1970), Assn. Am. Physicians. Democrat. Home: 747 Dolores St Stanford CA 94305-8427 Office: Stanford U Divsn Immunol and Rheumatol 1000 Welch Rd Ste 203 Palo Alto CA 94304-1808 E-mail: Holman@Stanford.edu.

HOLMAN, HARLAND EUGENE, retired motion picture company executive; b. Waupaca, Wis., Oct. 4, 1914; s. Clair R. and Elizabeth (Anderson) H.; m. Evelyn June Hooper, Dec. 24, 1940; children: John H., June Elizabeth (Mrs. Jon D. Huss), Catherine Ellen (Mrs. John F. Chavez). BA, U. Wis., 1936. C.P.A., Wis., Calif. Auditor Gen. Mills, Inc., 1936-42; v.p. finance Aviation Maintence Corp., Van Nuys, Calif., 1946-48; studio mgr., COO Warner Bros. Pictures, Inc., 1948-70; v.p. fin., treas. A.J. Industries, Inc., L.A., 1970-92, ret., 1992. Served to lt. comdr. USNR, 1942-46; rear adm. Res. Decorated commendation USMC; recipient Civilian commendation Vice Pres. U.S., 1967; Minuteman award Treasury Dept., 1967 Mem. AICPA, Calif. Soc. CPAs, Navy league, Phi Beta Kappa. Presbyterian (elder). Home: 5011 Hayvenhurst Ave Encino CA 91436-1114

HOLMAN, JAMES, allergist, immunologist; b. Jacksonville, Tex., Aug. 13, 1921; MD, U. Tex. Southwest, 1945. Diplomate Am. Bd. Allergy and Immunology. Intern Parkland Meml. Hosp., Dallas, 1945-46; resident in allergy U. Va., Charlottesville, 1947-48; fellow in medicine U. Tex. Southwest, Dallas, 1946-47, 48-50; with Presbyn. Hosp., Dallas, 1966—. Asst. clin. prof. pharmacology U. Tex. Southwest Med. Sch., 1950-83, clin. assoc. prof. internal medicine, 1981-88. Fellow Am. Acad. Allergy, Asthma and Immunology, Am. Coll. Allergy, Asthma and Immunology, Am. Coll. Clin. Pharmacology and Chemotherapy. Office: Presbyn Prof Bldg 8210 Walnut Hill Ln Ste 818 Dallas TX 75231-4421

HOLMAN, JAMES LEWIS, financial and management consultant; b. Chgo., Oct. 27, 1926; s. James Louis and Lillian Marie (Walton) H.; m. Elizabeth Ann Owens, June 18, 1948 (div. 1982); children: Craig Stewart, Tracy Lynn, Mark Andrew, Bonnie Gwen (dec.); m. Geraldine Ann Wilson, Dec. 26, 1982. BS in Econs. and Mgmt., U. Ill., Urbana, 1950, postgrad., 1950; postgrad. Northwestern U., 1954-55. Traveling auditor, then statistician, asst. controller parent buying dept. Sears, Roebuck & Co., Chgo., 1951-54; asst. to sec.-treas. Hanover Securities Co., Chgo., 1954-65; asst. to controller chem. ops. div. Montgomery Ward & Co. Inc., Chgo., 1966-68; controller Henrotin Hosp., Chgo., 1968; bus. mgr. Julian, Dye, Javid, Hunter & Najafi, Associated, Chgo., 1969-81, cons. 1981-84; vol. cons., adminstrv. asst. Fiji Sch. Medicine, Suva, 1984-86, cons., 1987-89; vol. bus. cons. U.S. Peace Corps, Honduras, 1989, cons., 1989—; cons., dir., sec.-treas. Comprehensive Resources Ltd., Glenview (Ill.), Wheaton (Ill.) and Walnut Creek, Calif., 1982; bd. dirs., sec.-treas. Medtran, Inc., 1980-83; sec. James C. Valenta, P.C., 1979-82; sponsored project adminstr. Northwestern U., Evanston, Ill., 1984. Sec., B.R. Ryall YMCA, Glen Ellyn, Ill., 1974-76, bd. dirs., 1968-78; trustee Gary Meml. United Meth. Ch., Wheaton, 1961-69, 74-77; bd. dirs. Goodwill Industries Chgo., 1978-79, DuPage (Ill.) Symphony, 1954-58, treas., 1955-58. Served with USN, 1944-46. Baha'i. Mem. Kiwanis (bd. dirs. Chgo. 1956-60, bd. dirs. youth found. 1957-60, pres. 1958-60). Home and Office: 1571 Burr Oak Ct Wheaton IL 60187-2709

HOLMAN, JOHN CLARKE, lawyer; b. Milw., Apr. 19, 1938; s. John Abner and Myrtle Vivian (Salter) H.; m. Jeanne Riba, Sept. 2, 1960 (div.1971); children: Lee Anne, Melaney Anne; m. Anne Elizabeth Wooster, Apr. 28, 1973; 1 child, Elizabeth Anne. BS, U. Wis., 1961; JD, Am. U., 1965; postgrad., Holborn Coll. Law, London, 1965-67. Bar: U.S. Dist. Ct. D.C. 1966, U.S. Ct. Appeals (D.C. and fed. cirs.) 1968, U.S. Supreme Ct. 1972. Examiner U.S. Patent Office, Washington, 1961-65; expert intellectual property Marks & Clerk, London, England, 1965-67; ptnr. Holman & Stern, Washington, 1967-77; pres. Holman & Stern, Chartered, Washington, 1977-89; ptnr. Fleit Jacobson Cohn Price Holman & Stern, Washington, 1989-92, Jacobson Holman PLLC, Washington, 1992—. Author: U.S. Patent Law, 1971. Mem. ABA, Licensing Execs. Soc., Assn. Internat. Patent Law Attys., Am. Inst. Mining Engrs., Internat. Fed. Indsl. Property Attys., Interam. Assn. Indsl. Property, Am. Intellectual Patent Law Assn., Internat. Assn. Protection Indsl. Property, U.S. Trademark Assn., Am. Soc. for Metals. Republican. Episcopalian. Office: 400 7th St NW Ste 600 Washington DC 20004-2232 Fax: 202-393-5350. E-mail: JHOLMAN@JHIP.com.

HOLMAN, JOHN FOSTER, investment banker; b. Chgo., Dec. 11, 1946; s. William Judson and Evelyn Mae (Foster) H.; m. Paula Susan Anderson, Aug. 1, 1970 (div. Oct. 1978). BS, Ariz. State U., 1969, MBA, 1971, JD, 1975; Cert. Fin. Planner, Coll. for Fin. Planning, 1991. Bar: Ariz. 1975; cert. Fin. Planner Coll. for Fin. Planning, 1975, registered investment advisor, lic. fed. securities, cert. Investment Mgmt. Analyst Wharton Sch. Bus. U. Pa., 2002. Congl. legis. intern, 1971; trial atty. Johnson, Tucker, Jessen & Dake, Phoenix, 1975-78, Holman, Meador and Hergott, Phoenix, 1978-80; nat. mktg. dir. Franchise Fin. Corp. Am., Phoenix, 1980-87; mng. dir. Fin. Resource Group, Sausalito, Calif., 1987-89; pres. Holman Internat. Group, Phoenix, 1990-2000; CEO, Internat. Salvage Corp., 1992—; pres. Fin. Freedom Assocs., Ltd., Phoenix, 1992—; v.p. retail and instnl. mktg. McKee Securities, 1993-94; mktg. dir. McKinley Capital Mktg., 1994—; mng. dir. Systematic Fin. Mgmt., 1996—; nat. mktg. dir. Microtherm Energy Deuras, 1999—; regional mktg. dir. Ashfield & Co., San Francisco, 2000—. Prin. John F. Holman P.C., 1981—. Founder Am. Wellness Assn., 1989—; mem. camp com. YMCA, Phoenix, 1968—; life mem. Rep. Senatorial Inner Circle, 1984—, Senatorial Commn., 1991; mem. Rep. Presdl. Task Force, 1989—; elder Presbyn. Ch., 1970—; mem. Ariz. Acad. Town Halls, 1969—. Capt. U.S. Army, 1968-76. Recipient Presdl. Order of Merit, 1991. Mem. Fed. Bar Assn., State Bar Ariz., Sales and Mktg. Execs. Phoenix, Ariz. State U. Alumni Assn. (bd. dirs. 1975-81), Internat. Platform Assn., World Record Setting Am. Transcontinental Relay Team, Mt. Kenya Safari Club, Capitol Hill Club, Delta Sigma Pi, Pi Sigma Epsilon. Home and Office: 3500 E Lincoln Dr Phoenix AZ 85018-1010 Address: 853 Ocean Ave Point Richmond CA 94801-3735 also: 853 Ocean Ave Point Richmond CA 94801-3735

HOLMAN, J(OHN) LEONARD, retired manufacturing corporation executive; b. Moose Jaw, Sask., Can., Aug. 30, 1929, s. Charles Claude and Lillian Kathleen (Haw) H.; m. Julia Pauline Benfield, July 18, 1953; children: Nancy Jane, Sally Joan. BS in Civil Engring., U. Alta., 1953. Pres. Consolidated Concrete Ltd., Calgary, Alta., Can., 1969-72; dir., pres. BACM Industries Ltd., Calgary, 1972-76; exec. v.p. Genstar Corp., Calgary, 1976-79, San Francisco, 1980-87, dir. several subs. cos.; pres., chief exec. officer CBR Cement Corp., San Mateo, Calif., 1986-88, chmn. bd., 1988-89, ret., 1990. Bd. dirs., officer several nat. trade assns. Mem. Assn. Profl. Engr. Alta. (life), Calgary Exhbn. and Stampede (hon. life., dir.), Calgary Golf and Country Club, Bernardo Heights Country Club. Home: 111 Country Club Estates 111-5555 Elbow Dr SW Calgary AB Canada T2V 1H7 E-mail: johnlholman@shaw.ca.

HOLMAN, JOSEPH FREDERICK, retired lawyer; b. Farmington, Maine, Aug. 15, 1925; s. Currier Carleton and Rosa (Skillings) H.; m. Brenda Hart, June 24, 1977. AB, Bowdoin Coll., 1947; LLB, Boston U., 1950. Bar: Maine 1951, U.S. Dist. Ct. Maine 1963, U.S. Supreme Ct. 1963. Pvt. practice, Farmington, 1951—2002; atty. Franklin County, Farmington, 1953-58. Pres., Farmington Pub. Libr., 1998—; assessor, Farmington Village Corp., 1980—. Sen. State of Maine, 1970; mem. Maine State Claims Comm., 1990-2001. Mem. ABA, Maine Bar Assn. (exec. com. 1963-71, pres. 1971-72), Franklin County Bar Assn. (pres. 1993). Republican. Avocations: hunting, fly fishing. Home: 129 Orchard St Farmington ME 04938-5925

HOLMAN, KAREN MARIE ANDERSON, purchasing agent; b. Anchorage, Sept. 6, 1962; d. Joseph Willie and Rose Millicent (Watson) Anderson; m. Robert L. Holman Jr., Nov. 27, 1982. AA in Bus. Adminstrn., Anchorage Community Coll., 1984; BA in Orgnl. Adminstrn., Alaska Pacific U., 1991; postgrad., Concord U., 2003—. Cert. purchasing mgr.; accredited purchasing practitioner. masters cert. gov. contracting, George Washington U. 1996. Sr. office clk. Bur. of the Census, Anchorage, 1980; premium audit clk. Providence Wash. Ins., Anchorage, 1981-82; info. systems clk. G.A Ltd., Anchorage, 1982-83; purchasing agt. State of Alaska, Anchorage, 1984-89, U. Alaska, Anchorage, 1989-92, ATU Telecommunications, 1992—97; purchasing sys. mgr. Am. Airlines, Ft. Worth, 1999—2002, sr. commodity mgr., 1997—, 2002—; co-woner Holman & Assocs. real estate rentals, 1984—. Del. Dem. Group State Caucuses, Anchorage, 1989; state dir. pub. rels. Alaska Ecclesiastical Jurisdiction; bd. dirs. Alaska Women's Resource Ctr., 1989-91, chmn. bd., 1999-2001, 1st v.p., 2002-03; chair bd. dirs. Greater Ft. Worth Chpt. Sickle Cell Disease Assn., Ft. Worth, 2003—. Mem. Nat. Assn. Purchasing Mgmt. Home: 7601 Meadowlark Dr Fort Worth TX 76133-7939

HOLMAN, KERMIT LAYTON, chemical engineer; b. Morris, Minn., Nov. 16, 1935; s. Melvin Martinous and Jennie Ethel (Erickson) H.; m. Audrey Mae Redwing, Nov. 21, 1959; children: Erik, Jennifer, Peter. Student, St. Olaf Coll., 1953-54; BS, U. N.D., 1957; MS, U. Idaho, 1961; PhD, Iowa State U., 1964. Tape devel. engr. 3M Co., St. Paul, 1957-60; sr. chem. engr. Dow Chem. Co., Golden, Colo., 1964-65; mem. faculty dept. chem. engring. N.Mex. State U., Las Cruces, 1965-76, prof., 1976—; prof., chmn. dept. chem. engring. U. Idaho, Moscow, 1976-81; tech. assoc. Weyerhaeuser, Tacoma, 1981-85, sr. engring. specialist, 1985-97, engring. advisor, 1997-2001; ret., 2001. Chmn. Forest products Divsn., 1996-97; cons. in field. Mem. Am. Inst. Chem. Engrs., Sigma Xi, Tau Beta Pi. Independent. Lutheran. Home: 31619 37th Ave SW Federal Way WA 98023-4008 E-mail: holman_ka@msn.com.

HOLMAN, LARRY DEAN, health care administrator; b. Lincoln, Nebr., Nov. 1, 1940; s. Clarence Woodford and Ethel Elizabeth (Remmenga) H.; m. Setsuko Umekawa, Dec. 5, 1960 (div. Aug. 1978); children: Lori Akiko, Yuko Donna; m. Debbie Joan Berkowitz, Dec. 8, 1980; children: Andrew Joseph, Jodi Michelle, Matthew Jacob. AA, Palomar Community Coll., San Marcos, Calif., 1971, C.C. of Phila., 1999; BS, George Washington U., 1974; MBA, LaSalle U., 1989, MS, 1990. Enlisted USN, 1958, advanced through grades to lt. comdr., ret., 1982, hosp. corpsman, 1958-71; with USN Med. Service Corps, 1971-82; purchasing dir. St. Francis Country House, Darby, Pa., 1982-85; bus. mgr. Stapeley Hall, Phila., 1985-86; bus., program mgr. Seaman's Ch. Inst., Phila., 1986-87; buyer Grad. Hosp., Phila., 1988-89, Grad. Health System, Phila., 1989; purchasing agt. Shriners Hosps., Phila., 1989-91; purchasing mgr. Jeanes Hosp., Phila., 1991-98; Y2K project site coord. Temple U. Health Sys., Phila., 1998-2000; asst. dir. purchasing Temple U., Phila., 2000—. Mem.: AMVETS, VFW (life), Nat. Assn. of Purchasing Mgrs., Jewish War Vets. U.S. (comdr. Post 706, nat. dep. adjutant, legis. chmn. Phila. County Coun., rep. on bd. dirs. East Boro's Housing Corp.), Vets. Vietnam War, Naval. Res. Assn., Ret. Officers Assn., Vietnam Era Seabees, Navy Seabee Vets. Am., Fleet Res. Assn., Non-Commd. Officers Assn., Am. Assn. Navy Hosp. Corps, Am. Soc. Mil. Compts., Assn. Mil. Surgeons U.S., Navy League U.S. (life), Vietnam Vets. Am. (life), Am. Legion. Jewish. Avocations: reading, counseling. Home: 6746 Souder St Philadelphia PA 19149-2208 Office: Temple U 1601 N Broad St Philadelphia PA 19122-6099 E-mail: lholman@prodigy.net.

HOLMAN, MARGARET ALICE, writer; d. Lenn Carlyle Holman and Miriam Elizabeth Macpherson-Holman; m. Ronald Emil N/A, Mar. 8, 1982 (div. Dec. 15, 1983); m. Christopher Vern N/A, June 8, 1984 (div. May 4, 1985); m. Marc L. Schwebke; children: Brandon Lee Peterson, Kristen Elaine Ricketts. Student, Blue Mountain C.C., Pendleton, Oreg., 1992, Ea. Oreg. U., La Grande, 1998. Author (poet): (poetry from manuscript) Only Today (Editor's Choice Award, 2002), (poetry anthology/collabor. coll. book) Waves of Wonder, (poetry anthology/collabor. coll. cd) The Sounds Of Poetry, (poetry anthology/collabor. coll. book) The Best Poems and Poets Of 2002; author: (poet) Theatre of the Mind. Optical courier Lion's Club Eye Bank, La Grande, Oreg., 1996; sec. safety com. Red Lion Inn, Pendleton, Oreg., 1992. Achievements include writing of a book (poetry) about my life dealing with and over-coming every conceivable kind of abuse; hoping that it could help someone else find the courage to break the cycle.

HOLMAN, MARGARET MEZOFF, fundraising consultant; b. Pitts., Mar. 6, 1951; d. Earl Robert and Margaret Joan (Miller) Mezoff; m. Richard L. Holman, Nov. 3, 1973. BA in Journalism, U. Nebr., 1973. Dir. community rels. Monterey (Calif.) Peninsula Hosp., 1978-81; assoc. dir. devel. Barnard Coll., N.Y.C., 1982-83; acting dir. devel. CARE, Inc., N.Y.C., 1983-84; dir. devel. Am. Acad. Dramatic Arts, N.Y.C., 1984-86; sr. v.p. devel. and mktg. ASPCA, N.Y.C., 1986-91; pres. Holman Consulting, Inc., N.Y.C., 1991—. Mem.: Women in Devel. N.Y. (pres. 1990—93), Assn. Fundraising Exec. Office: Holman Cons Inc 575 Lexington Ave Ste 400 New York NY 10022

HOLMAN, PAUL DAVID, plastic surgeon; b. Waynesboro, Va., Mar. 13, 1943; s. Wallace D. and Rosalie S. Holman. BA, U. Va., 1965; MD, Jefferson Med. Coll., 1968. Intern, George Washington U. Hosp., Washington, 1968-69, resident in gen. surgery, 1969-70, 72-74; resident in plastic surgery Phoenix Plastic Surgery Residency, 1974-76; practice medicine specializing in plastic surgery, Phoenix, 1977—; mem. staff Good Samaritan Hosp., Phoenix, St. Joseph's Hosp., Phoenix, Phoenix Children's Hosp. Served to lt. comdr. USNR, 1970-72. Diplomate Am. Bd. Surgery, Am. Bd. Plastic Surgery. Mem. AMA, ACS, Am. Soc. Plastic Surgeons, Phi Beta Kappa. Office: 2111 E Highland Ave Ste 105 Phoenix AZ 85016-4755

HOLMAN, RALPH THEODORE, biochemistry and nutrition educator; b. Mpls., Mar. 4, 1918; s. Alfred Theodore and May Carlia Anna (Nilson) Holman; m. Karla Calais, Mar. 26, 1943; 1 child, Nils Teodore. AA, Bethel Jr. Coll., 1937; BS, U. Minn., 1939; MS, Rutgers U., 1941; PhD, U. Minn., 1944. Instr., div. of biochemistry U. Minn., Mpls., 1944-46; NRC-Nat. Acad. Scis. fellow Med. Nobel Inst., Stockholm, Sweden, 1946-47; Am. Scandinavian Found. fellow U. Uppsala, Sweden, 1947; assoc. prof. biochemistry and nutrition Tex. A&M U., College Station, 1948-51; assoc. prof. biochemistry Hormel Inst., U. Minn., Austin, 1951-56, prof., 1956-88, exec. dir., 1975-85, emeritus prof., 1988—; also adj. prof. of biochemistry Mayo Med. Sch., Rochester, Minn., 1977—. Mem. nutrition study sect. NIH, 1959-63; pres., organizer Golden Jubilee Internat. Congress on Essential Fatty Acids and Prostaglandins, 1980; mem. adv. bd. Deul. Conf. on Lipids, 1960-86; Sinclair Meml. lectr. Third Internat. Congress on Essential Fatty Acids and Eicasanoids, Adelaide, 1992. Founding editor Progress in Lipid Research, 1951—; editor Lipids, 1974-85; mem. editl. bd. Jour. Nutrition, 1962-66; contbr. 400 publs. on nutritional biochemistry of lipids; initiated omega 3 and omega 6 nomenclature for essential fatty acids, 1963; current rsch. on essentiality of omega 3 fatty acids. Pres. Mower County Coun. Churches., Austin, 1953-57; mem. Hormel Found., Austin, 1979-86. Recipient Fachini award Italian Oil Chemists, Milan; named Disting. Alumnus Bethel Coll., 1998. Fellow Am. Inst. Nutrition (Borden award 1966); mem. NAS, Am. Chem. Soc., Am. Oil Chemists Soc. (pres. 1974-75, Lipid Chemistry award 1979, Baldwin Disting. Svc. award 2001), Am. Soc. Biol. Chemists, Am. Orchid Soc. (rsch. com. 1980-85), Am. Heart Assn. (bd. dirs. Minn. affiliate 1991-93). Democrat. Congregationalist. Achievements include original research on essential nature of omega 3 polyunsaturated fatty acids. Home: 1403 2nd Ave SW Austin MN 55912-1609 Office: U Minn Hormel Inst 801 16th Ave NE Austin MN 55912-3679 E-mail: rtholman@maroon.tc.umn.edu.

HOLMAN, SANDY LYNNE, writer, consultant; BA in psychology, U. Calif., Davis; MA in sch. counseling, Calif. State U., Sacramento. Founder and dir. The Culture C.O.-O.P., Davis, Calif. Author: (childrens books) Grandpa, Is Everything Black Bad? (Blackboard Childrens Book of the Yr. award, 2002, Writer's Digest, Skipping Stones), We All Have a Heritage. Recipient Human Rels. Commn. award, City of Davis.

HOLMAN, WILLIAM BAKER, surgeon, coroner; b. Norwalk, Ohio, Mar. 22, 1925; s. Merlin Earl and Rowena (Baker) Holman; m. Jane Elizabeth Henderson, June 24, 1951; children: Craig W., Mark E., John S. BS, Capital U., 1946; MD, Jefferson Med. Coll., 1950. Intern St. Luke's Hosp., Cleve., 1950—51, resident in gen. surgery, 1951—52, 1955—57; practice medicine specializing in surgery Norwalk, 1957—92; coroner Huron County, Norwalk, 1962—95, health commr., 1985—95; asst. clin. prof. surgery Med. Coll. Ohio at Toledo, 1984—92. Mem. Norwalk City Sch. Bd. Edn., 1962—78, pres., 1964, 1967—71, 1978; mem. exec. com. Huron County Rep. Com., Norwalk, 1980; bd. dirs. REMSNO, Toledo, 1974—92, Norwalk Profl. Colony, 1983—92, Fisher-Titus Med. Ctr., 1977—82, chmn., 1982; bd. dirs. Norwalk Area Health Svcs., Inc., 1987—92, 1994—. Served to 1st lt. U.S. Army, 1952—54. Fellow: ACS; mem.: AMA, Nat. Assn. Med. Examiners, Ohio State Coroners Assn., Huron County Med. Soc. (pres. 1978), Ohio State Med. Assn. Lutheran. Avocations: boating, photography, stamp collecting, gun collecting. Home: 39 Warren Dr Norwalk OH 44857-2447

HOLMBERG, ALBERT WILLIAM, JR., retired publishing company executive; b. Orange, N.J., Sept. 18, 1923; s. Albert William and Margaret (Flanagan) H.; m. Dorothy McCollum, Oct. 27, 1945 (div. Apr. 1972); children— Jeanne (Mrs. Fletcher J. Johnson, Jr.), Margaret D. (Mrs. Roy D. Duckworth III), Ellen T.; m. Ruth Sulzberger Golden, May 26, 1972. BS in Bus. Adminstrn, Lehigh U., 1947. With N.Y. Times, 1947-70, circulation mgr., 1964-70; pres. Chattanooga Times Co., 1970-99. Served to 1st lt. USAAF, World War II. Mem.: Mountain City Club (Chattanooga). Home: 1108 Cumberland Rd Chattanooga TN 37419-1006 Office: TIPRCO LLC PO Box 951 100 E 10th St Chattanooga TN 37401-0951

HOLMBERG, BRANTON KIETH, management consultant; b. Tacoma, Mar. 6, 1936; s. Victor August and Ann Irene (Warren) H.; BA, Central Wash. U., 1962, MEd, 1964; EdD, U. Idaho, 1970; m. Margaret Ann Nelson, Sept. 17, 1960; children: James Michael, Ann Marie, Nelson John. Asst. prof. Pacific Lutheran U., 1964-70; assoc. prof. Cen. Wash. U., Ellensburg, 1970-76, asso. dir. Orgn. Devel. Ctr., 1972-73; PhD program dir. U.S. Internat. U., McChord AFB, 1977-78; pres. Holmberg Assoc., mgmt. and orgn. devel. cons., Bellingham, 1975—, Northpoint Corp., geriatric care ctrs., Bellingham, 1978-84, Northwest Horticulture, Inc., 1979-90, Internat. Highpoint Corp., 1983-91, Advanced Laundry Svc., 1984-88, assoc. dean Northwest Indian Coll., 1993-94; dean Northwest Indian Coll., Tacoma campus, 1994-95. Mem. Ellensburg Criminal Law and Justice Planning Com., 1972-73. Served with USAF, 1954-58. U. Idaho fellow, 1968. Mem. Am. Psychol. Assn., Am. Mgmt. Assn., Am. Personnel and Guidance Assn., Internat. Assn. Quality Circles, Internat. Registry Orgn. Devel. Cons., Acad. Mgmt., AAUP, Orgn. Devel. Network, Phi Delta Kappa. Home: 14115 Goodrich Dr NW Gig Harbor WA 98329-8634

HOLME, JOHN CHARLES, JR., lawyer; b. N.Y.C., Aug. 3, 1940; s. John Charles and Anne Robinson (Mackey) H.; m. Diane Louise Stover, July 24, 1965; children: Christopher Scott, Jennifer Anne. Student Washington Coll., 1958-60; BA, U. Vt., 1962; LLB, Cornell U., 1965. Bar: N.Y. 1966, U.S. Dist. Ct. (we. dist.) N.Y. 1966, Ohio 1974, U.S. Dist. Ct. (no. dist.) Ohio 1974, U.S. Ct. Appeals 1979, Vt. 1982, U.S. Dist. Ct. Vt. 1983. Assoc. Dutcher, Witt, Sidoti & Considine, Rochester, 1966-69; assoc. Antell Harris, Githler & Calleri, Rochester, 1968-69; trust adminstr. Marine Midland Bank, Rochester, 1969-70, asst. trust officer, 1970-73, trust officer, 1973-74; staff atty. Advocates for Basic Legal Equality, Toledo, 1974-82; assoc. William E. Dakin, Jr., Chester, Vt., 1982-83; v.p., sec. Dakin & Holme, P.C., Chester, 1984-90; atty. pvt. practice, Chester, Vt., 1990-97, Springfield, Vt., 1997—. Mem. ABA, Am. Inn of Ct. (sec.-treas. 1994—), Vt. Bar Assn., Vt. Bar Found. (bd. dirs. 1995—, pres. 1996-97), Vt. Trial Lawyers Assn. (bd. govs. 1987—, treas. 1995—), Assn. Trial Lawyers Am., Rotary (Chester pres. 1997—). Democrat. Mem. United Ch. of Christ. Home: PO Box 474 Chester VT 05143-0474

HOLME, RICHARD PHILLIPS, lawyer; b. Denver, Nov. 6, 1941; s. Peter Hagner Jr. and Lena (Phillips) H.; m. Barbara June Friel, July 17, 1944; children: Daniel Friel, Robert Muir. BA, Williams Coll., Williamstown, Mass., 1963; JD, U. Colo., 1966. Bar: Colo. 1966, U.S. Dist. Ct. Colo. 1966, U.S. Ct. Claims 1990, U.S. Ct. Appeals (10th cir.) 1966, U.S. Ct. Appeals (1st cir.) 1980, U.S. Dist. Ct. D.C. 1988, U.S. Ct. Appeals (D.C. cir.) 1988, U.S. Ct. Appeals (4th cir.) 1989, U.S. Ct. Appeals (fed. cir.) 1995, U.S. Supreme Ct. 1975. Assoc. Davis, Graham & Stubbs, Denver, 1966-68, ptnr., 1972-87, 91—, mng. ptnr., D.C. office Washington, 1987-91; dep. Denver Dist. Atty., 1969-71. Grievance com. Colo. Supreme Ct., Denver, 1979-85, civil rules com., 1994—, civil justice com., 1998—. Fellow Am. Bar Found., Am. Coll. Trial Lawyers (Colo. state chair 1994-96); mem. ABA, ABA Found., Colo. Bar Found., Colo. Bar

Assn. (bd. govs. 1974-76, 85-87, 95-99, 2001-2003), Denver Bar Assn. (trustee 1977-80, 1st v.p. 1997-98), Order of Coif. Republican. Presbyterian. Home: 3944 S Depew Way Denver CO 80235-3105

HOLME, THOMAS A. chemistry educator, researcher; b. Green Bay, Wis., July 18, 1961; s. Walter C. and Ruth A. Holme; m. Ann C. Blankendaal, May 4, 1985; children: Kurtis, Ella. BS, Loras Coll., 1983; PhD, Rice U., 1987. Fulbright lectr. U. Zambia, Lusaka, 1989-90; asst. prof. U. S.D., Vermillion, 1990-94; assoc. prof. U. Wis., Milw., 1994—2002, prof., 2002—. Vis. prof. Ajou U., Suwon, Kyonggi-do, Republic of Korea, 2000. Editor: Users Newsletter for Chemistry in Context, 1998; featured guest WTMJ-TV News, Live at 11; assoc. editor Chemistry Encyclopedia; contbr. articles to profl. jours.; . Inductee Hall of Fame, Loras Players Theatre Co., 1997; Fulbright scholar Coun. for Internat. Exch. of Scholars, 1989. Mem. Am. Chem. Soc. (councilor 2000—, Helen Free award for Pub. Outreach 1999, dir. Exams Inst. 2002--), Nat. Sci. Tchrs. Assn., Sigma Xi. Avocations: baseball, bike riding. Home: 1628 N 50th Pl Milwaukee WI 53208 Office: U Wis-Milw Chemistry Dept PO Box 431 Milwaukee WI 53201 Office Fax: (414) 229-5530. E-mail: tholme@uwm.edu.

HOLMEN, REYNOLD ALGOTT EMANUEL, chemist; b. Essex, Iowa, Oct. 23, 1916; s. John Algott and Clara Amelia (Christensen) H.; m. Betty Jane Heginbottom, June 20, 1942 (dec. 1990); children: Karen C., John R., Robert C.; m. Johnnie Mae Leak, Nov. 20, 1993 (dec. 2000). AB, Augustana Coll., Ill., 1936; MS, U. Mich., 1937, PhD, 1949. Rsch. chemist DuPont Co., Phila., also Flint, Mich., 1937-46; sr. rsch. chemist ctrl. rsch. dept. 3M Co., St. Paul, 1948-55, sect. mgr. tech. info. and patient liaison, 1955-57, sect. mgr. inorganic sect., 1957-62, organic scouting mgr., 1959-62, mgr. R&D Lab., Reflective Product divsn., 1962-71, lab. mgr. R&D spl. enterprises dept., 1971-82; v.p. R&D KEMSERCH, Inc., Onamia, Minn., 1984-96. Author: Kasimir Fajans: The Man and His Work, 1990. With med. corps. U.S. Army, 1941. Rackham scholar U. Mich., 1936-37; named to Wisdom Hall of Fame. Mem. Am. Chem. Soc., Phi Lambda Upsilon, Sigma Gamma Epsilon. Lutheran. Achievements include 20 U.S. patents; development of first catalytic dehydration of lactic acid to acrylic acid, first catalytic dehydrochlorination of alpha-chloropronic acid to acrylic acid, (with other) first sealed polycellular cube-corner retroreflective sheet, first conterfeit-resistant driver's license adopted by a state, development of first binary packaging film from two disparate solid films joined sans adhesive, improved authenicatable document construction. Home: 2225 Lilac Ln White Bear Lake MN 55110-3824 E-mail: reholmen@aol.com.

HOLMER, ALAN FREEMAN, trade association executive, lawyer; b. N.Y.C., July 24, 1949; s. A. Freeman and Marcia K. (Wright) H.; m. Joan Mary Ozark, June 30, 1973; children— Scott, Joy AB, Princeton U., 1971; JD, Georgetown U., 1978. Bar: D.C., Oreg. Adminstrv. asst. Senator Bob Packwood, Washington, 1972-78; assoc. Steptoe & Johnson, Washington, 1978-81; dep. asst. to pres. for intergovtl. affairs The White House, Washington, 1981-83; dep. asst. sec. for import adminstrn. Dept. Commerce, Washington, 1983-85; gen. counsel Office of U.S. Trade Rep., Washington, 1985-87; amb. Dep. U.S. Trade Rep., Washington, 1987-89; ptnr. Sidley & Austin, Washington, 1989-96; pres., CEO, Pharm. Rsch. and Mfrs. Am., Washington, 1996—. Adj. prof. Georgetown U. Law Ctr., Washington, 1990; amb. and chmn. U.S. del. to Bonn Econ. Conf., 1990. Author: (with Judith H. Bello) The Antidumping and Countervailing Duty Laws: Key Legal and Policy Issues, 1987, Guide to the U.S.-Canada Free-Trade Agreement, 1990; contbr. numerous articles to profl. jours. Mem. Svcs. Policy Adv. Com., 1991-94; mem. adv. coun. Korea Econ. Inst. Am., 1992-96; trustee Met. D.C. chpt. Cystic Fibrosis Found., 1984-96, pres., 1991-94); bd. dirs. Coun. on Family Health, 1996—, Friends of the Nat. Libr. of Medicine, 1996—, Nat. Health Coun., 1999—. Recipient Disting. Cmty. Svc. award, Princeton Club Washington, 1992, Marriott Lifetime Achievement award, Arthritis Found., 2001. Mem. Internat. Fedn. of Pharm. Mfrs. (mem. coun. 1996—), Coun. Fgn. Rels.. Republican. Office: Pharm Rsch and Mfrs Am 1100 15th St NW Washington DC 20005-1707

HOLMES, ALBERT WILLIAM, JR., physician; b. Chgo., Feb. 3, 1932; s. Albert William and Eleanor Muir H.; m. Lois Ann Geiger, Sept. 4, 1954; children: Nancy, William, Elizabeth, Robert. Student, U. Chgo., 1947-49; BA, Knox Coll., 1952; MD, Western Res. U., 1956. Diplomate Am. Bd. Internal Medicine. Intern Presbyn. Hosp., Chgo., 1956-57; resident Presbyn.-St. Luke's Hosp., Chgo., 1957-59, 61-62; instr. U. Ill., Chgo., 1961-62, asst. prof., 1963-65, assoc. prof., 1966-68, prof. medicine, 1968-70; prof. medicine and microbiology Rush Med. Coll., Chgo., 1971-75; dir. sect. hepatology Rush-Presbyn.-St. Luke's Med. Center, Chgo., 1966-75, asso. chmn. dept. medicine, 1972-75, acting v.p. research affairs, 1973-74; prof., chmn. dept. internal medicine Tex. Tech U., Lubbock, 1975-83, prof. medicine, 1983-85; prof., chmn. dept. medicine U. Ill., Peoria, 1985-89; prof. medicine U. Calif., San Francisco, 1990-96, prof. emeritus medicine, 1996—; chief medicine Valley Med. Ctr., 1990-96. Contbr. articles in field to profl. jours. Served with U.S. Army, 1959-61. Recipient Alumni Achievement award Knox Coll., 1976; NIH spl. fellow, 1963-66 Fellow ACP; mem. Am. Assn. Study Liver Diseases, Ctrl. Soc. Clin. Rsch., Alpha Omega Alpha. Presbyterian. Home: 1137 W Escalon Ave Fresno CA 93711-2018 Office: U Med Ctr Dept Med Fresno CA 93702 E-mail: bi2332@msn.com.

HOLMES, ANN HITCHCOCK, journalist; b. El Paso, Apr. 25, 1922; d. Frederick E. and Joy (Crutchfield) H. Student, Whitworth Coll., 1940, So. Coll. Fine Arts, 1944. With Houston Chronicle, 1942—, fine arts editor, 1948-89, critic-at-large, 1989-98. Author: Presence, The Transco Tower, 1985, Joy Unconfined—Robert Joy in Houston: A Portrait of Fifty Years, 1986, Alley Theater: Four Decades in Three Stages, 1986. Mem. Houston Mcpl. Art Commn., 1965-74; mem. fine arts adv. coun. U. Tex., Austin, 1967—; bd. dirs. Rice Design Alliance, Houston, 1988-91, Alliance Francaise, Houston, 1989-93, Bus. Arts Fund, Houston, 1993-96. Recipient Ogden Reid Found. award for study of arts in Europe, 1953; Guggenheim fellow, 1960-61; recipient Ford Found. award, 1965, John G. Flowers award archtl. writing Tex. Soc. Architects, 1972, 74, 77, 80 Mem. Am. Theater Critics Assn. (exec. com. 1975—, co-chmn. 1987-88) Home and Office: 10807 Beinhorn Rd Houston TX 77024-3008 E-mail: ann.holmes@chron.com.

HOLMES, ANNA-MARIE, ballerina, ballet mistress; b. Mission City, B.C., Can., Apr. 17, 1942; arrived in U.S., 1981; d. George Henry and Maxine Marie (Botterill) Ellerbeck; m. David Holmes; 1 child, Lian-Marie. Diploma, Royal Conservatory of Music. Lectr. in field. Dancer (ballets) Swan Lake, Cinderella, Romeo and Juliet, Sleeping Beauty, Bayadere, Laurencia, Paquita, Graduation Ball, Les Sylphides, Prince Igor, Giselle, Nutcracker, Firebird, Raymonda, Kirov Ballet, Leningrad, 1963, (films) Tour En L'Air, Ballet Adagio, Don Juan, Chinese Nightingale, numerous appearances on European N.Am. TV, Don Quixote, 1989—; co-dir.: (ballets) Massimo Opera Theatre, 1993; prodr.(film documentation): Kirov Vagonova Tchg. Sys.; choreographer Swan Lake, Tokyo, 1991, Norwegion Nat. Ballet, 1998, Sleeping Beauty Act III, Boston Ballet, 1991, Giselle, 1991, Sleeping Beauty, Boston Ballet, 1993, 1996, Tokyo, 1996, Le Corsaire, Boston Ballet, Am. Ballet Theatre, 1998, Great Performances, 1999, Met. Opera House, N.Y.C., 1999, Don Quixote, Boston Ballet, 2000. Recipient Emmy award, 2000. Office: Carnegie House 100 W 57th St Ste 11-O New York NY 10019 E-mail: Aellerbeck@aol.com.

HOLMES, BARBARAANN KRAJKOSKI, secondary education educator; b. Evansville, Ind., Mar. 21, 1946; d. Frank Joseph and Estella Marie (DeWeese) Krajkoski; m. David Leo Holmes, Aug. 21, 1971; 1 child, Susan Ann Sky. BS, Ind. State U., 1968, MS, 1969, specialist cert., 1976; postgrad., U. Nev., 1976-78. Acad. counselor Ind. State U., 1968-69, halls dir., 1969-73; dir. residence halls U. Utah, 1973-76; sales assoc. Fidelity Realty, Las Vegas, Nev., 1977-82; cert. analyst Nev. Dept. Edn., 1981-82; tchr. Clark County Sch. Dist., 1982-87, computer cons., adminstrv. specialist, instrnl. mgmt. sys., 1987-91, chair computer conf., 1990-92, adminstrv. specialist K-6, 1990-93; dean of student summer sch. site adminstr. Eldorado H.S., 1991-96; asst. prin. Garrett Mid. Sch., Boulder City, Nev., 1997-1999, So. Nev. Vocat. Tech. Ctr. Magnet H.S., 1999—. Mem. leadership design team Clark County Sch. Dist., 1996—98, 2001—. Named Outstanding Sr. Class Woman, Ind. State U., 1969; recipient Dir.'s award U. Utah Residence Halls, 1973, Outstanding Tchr. award, 1984, Dist. Excellence in Edn. award, 1984, 86, 87, 88. Mem. AAUW, Am. Assn. Women Deans, Adminstrs. and Counselors, Am. Pers. and Guidance Assn., Nat. Assn. Sch. Adminstrs. (Clark County sch. adminstrv. sec., 2002—), Clark County Assn. Secondary Sch. Prin. (sec. 2003—), Am. Coll. Pers. Assn., Alumnae Assn. Chi Omega (treas. Terre Haute chpt. 1971-73, pres., bd. officer Las Vegas 1977-81, state rush info. chair, 1997—), Clark County Panhellenic Alumnae Assn. (pres. 1978-79), Computer Using Educators So. Nev. (sec. 1983-86, pres.-elect 1986-87, pres. 1987-88, state chmn. 1988-89, conf. chmn. 1989-92, sec. 1994-96, Hall of Fame 1995), Job.'s Daus. Club (guardian sec. 1995-99, dir. music 1999-2001, Supreme Dep. 2001—), Order Eastern Star (worthy matron 2003—), Phi Delta Kappa (Action award 1990-96, newspaper editor 1992-93). Achievements include developing personal awareness program U. Utah, 1973-76. Home: 1227 Kover Ct Henderson NV 89015-9017 Office: So Nev Vocat Tech Magnet HS 5710 Mountain Vista St Las Vegas NV 89120-2310

HOLMES, BERT OTIS E., JR., retired editor; b. Milan, Tenn., Sept. 20, 1921; s. Otis E. and Mary (Lassiter) H.; m. Marian Bush, June 10, 1942 (dec. Nov. 1964); m. Helen Hankins, July 24, 1965; children: Bert Otis E., Richard Bush; children: Chris, David. AA, Magnolia A. and M. Jr. Coll., 1940; BS, So. Meth. U., 1942. Successively copy reader, makeup editor, state editor, city staff reporter, city editor Dallas Times Herald, 1946-56, news editor, 1956-60, asst. mng. editor, 1960-64, exec. editor, 1964-65, assoc. editor, 1965-90. Pres. Family Svc. Agy., 1963-68, Tex. United Community Svcs., 1970-72, Sr. Citizens of Greater Dallas, 1995-96; bd. dirs. Dallas United Fund, Dallas Community Coun. With AUS, 1942-46, PTO. Mem. Dallas Assembly, Sigma Delta Chi, Dallas Press Club (pres. 1957, 78-79) Methodist. Home: 4515 W Lawther Dr Dallas TX 75214-1935

HOLMES, BROOX GARRETT, lawyer; b. Mobile, Ala., Nov. 15, 1932; s. Williams Coghlan and Philomene (Boogaerts) H.; m. Laura Claire Hays, Feb. 21, 1955 (dec. 2000); children: Broox Garrett, Dupree Hays, Williams Coghlan II. BA, U. Ala., 1954, JD, 1960. Bar: Ala. 1960. Since practiced in, Mobile; mem. firm Armbrect Jackson LLP, 1960—. Trustee St. Paul's Episcopal Sch., chmn. bd., 1980-83. Capt. USMCR, 1954-58. Fellow Am. Coll. Trial Lawyers (state chmn. 1991-92), Am. Bar Found.; mem. ABA, Ala. State Bar (bd. commrs. 1987-93, chmn. litigation sect. 1991, pres. 1994-95), Ala. Bar Found., Mobile Bar Assn. (exec. com. 1987-93), Nat. Assn. R.R. Trial Counsel, Internat. Assn. Def. Counsel, Am. Law Inst., Ala. Law Inst., Ala. Def. Lawyers (pres. 1977-78, named one of Best Lawyers in Am. bus. and personal injury litigation), Mobile Country Club (pres. 1983-84), Mobile Touchdown Club, Athelstan Club, Delta Kappa Epsilon, Phi Delta Phi. Episcopalian. Home: 609 Fairfax Rd E Mobile AL 36608-2939 Office: Armbrecht Jackson LLP PO Box 290 Mobile AL 36601-0290

HOLMES, CAROLYN COGGIN, museum director; b. Raleigh, N.C., Jan. 6, 1939; d. Robert Clifton and Nola (Henley) Coggin; m. David Lynn Holmes; children: Henley Madden, Catesby Coggin. BA, Wake Forest U., 1961; MAT, Duke U., 1962. Tchr. of French Needham Broughton Sr. High Sch., Raleigh, N.C., 1961-64, Washington-Lee R. High Sch., Arlington, Va., 1964-66; asst. prof. East Carolina U., Greenville, 1966-67, Campbell Coll., Buie's Creek, N.C., 1967-68; tchr. of French Tidewater Acad., Wakefield, Va., 1968-74; restoration contractor, cons. Smithfield, Va., 1972-75; exec. dir. Ash Lawn-Highland (home of James Monroe), Charlottesville, Va., 1975—. Cons. on restoration, Charlottesville, 1972—. Commr. Isle of Wight (Va.) Planning Com., 1973-77. Mem. Am. Assn. Museums, Va. Assn. Museums (sec., coun. mem. 1985-89), Va. Assn. Presdl. Houses and Museums (sec., treas., pres. 1984—), Nat. Trust for Hist. Preservation, Assn. Presdl. Homes and Museums (pres.). Democrat. Episcopalian. Avocations: music, antiques, swimming, travel. Office: Ash Lawn-Highland 1000 James Monroe Pky Charlottesville VA 22902-9806

HOLMES, CLAIRE COLEMAN, real estate broker; b. Ruston, La., Sept. 14, 1931; d. Eusel Monroe and Mabel Claire (Cahoon) Coleman; m. Major Joe Holmes, Dec. 20, 1951; children: George David, Claire Anne de Noble, William Gray. BA cum laude, U. Ark., 1952. Tchr. Pulaski (Ark.) County Spl. Sch. Dist., 1952-53, Pine Bluff (Ark.) Sch. Dist., 1953-55; real estate salesman Sullivant-Cross Realty, Pine Bluff, 1979-83; legal sec. Joe Holmes, Atty., Pine Bluff, 1985-91; real estate broker C & J, Inc., Pine Bluff, 1985—. Mem. DAR, Soc. Mayflower Descendants, Jr. League, Pine Bluff Duplicate Bridge Club, Am. Contract Bridge League, Nat. Audubon Soc., Three Rivers Audubon Soc. Avocations: bridge, swimming. Home: 22 S Pines Dr Pine Bluff AR 71601 Office: C & J Inc 22 Southern Pines Dr Pine Bluff AR 71603-6934

HOLMES, DALE ARTHUR, optics scientist; b. Biwabik, Minn., Dec. 31, 1937; s. Arthur Emil Holmes and Saima Amanda Luoma; m. Joan Christine Cawthon, May 4, 1962 (dissolved July 1996); children: Kevin, Camille. BEE, Purdue U, 1960; MS, Carnegie Inst. Tech., 1961, PhD, 1965; MS, U Rochester, 1969. Asst. prof. EE Carnegie Inst. Tech., Pitts., 1965—66; officer USAF Weapons Lab, Albuquerque, 1966—74; optical engr. Boeing, Canoga Park, Calif., 1974—2003. Contbr. articles. Capt. USAF, 1966—74. Decorated R&D award USAF. Republican. Christian. Achievements include patents in field. Avocations: pistol shooting, fishing. Home: 27904 Doubletree Way Castaic CA 91384

HOLMES, DALLAS SCOTT, judge, educator; b. L.A., Dec. 2, 1940; s. Donald Cherry and Hazel (Scott) H.; m. Patricia McMichael, Aug. 21, 1965; children: Mark Scott, Tobin John. AB cum laude, Pomona Coll., 1962; MS, London Sch. Econs., 1964; JD, U. Calif., Berkeley, 1967. Bar: Calif. 1968. Assoc. Best, Best & Krieger, Riverside, Calif., 1968-74, ptnr., 1974-96; mem. Calif. Jud. Coun., 1995-96; adj. prof. Hastings Coll. Law U. Calif., San Francisco, 1990; exec. asst. to Assembly majority fl. leader, Calif. State Legislature, Sacramento, 1969-70; asst. adj. prof. Grad. Sch. Mgmt., U. Calif.-Riverside, 1977-88; lectr. UCLA Extension, 1987—; Superior Ct. judge, 1996—; chair Riverside Superior Ct. Jury Com., 1997-2003; chair Calif. jud. coun. task force jury sys. improvements, 1998-2003; mem. bd. trustees, U. Calif., Riverside Found., 1983-; city atty. City of Corona, Calif., 1976-96; lectr. local govt. and univ. extension groups. Pres., Pomona Coll. Alumni Coun., 1973-74, Century Club, Riverside, 1974-76, Citizens Univ. Com., 1983-85, Downtown Riverside Assn., 1987-88; chmn. legal affairs com. Assn. Calif. Water Agys., 1985-91. Mem. bd. govs. State Bar Calif., 1990-93, v.p. 1992-93. Named Man of Yr., Riverside Press-Enterprise, 1962, Young Man of Yr., Riverside Jr. C. of C., 1972. Mem. Riverside County Bar Assn. (pres. 1982), Calif. State Bar Assn. (exec. com. pub. law sect. 1983-86), Am. Judicature Soc. Republican. Presbyterian. Contbr. articles on mass transit, assessment of farmland in Calif., exclusionary zoning and environ. law to profl. jours.; author proposed tort reform initiative for Calif. physicians. Office: Riverside Superior Ct 4050 Main St Riverside CA 92501-3702

HOLMES, DAVID JAMES, elementary school educator; b. Lock Haven, Pa., Sept. 8, 1947; s. Edward James and Jean Elizabeth (Taylor) H.; m. Sandra Ann Melchert, Jan. 15, 1995. BS in Edn., Lock Haven State Coll., 1969; MEd, Kutztown U., 1992. Cert. elem. and comprehensive social studies tchr., elem. prin., Pa. Elem. tchr. Tri-Valley Sch. Dist., Valley View, Pa., 1972—; ret., 2002. Adv. bd. TLC Day Care Ctr., Valley View, 1974-81; presenter in field. Mem. coun. Trinity Luth. Ch., Valley View, 1988-91, ch. sch. tchr., 1988-96; active St. Peter Luth. Ch., Mechanicsburg, Pa., 1998—. Recipient Gift of Time Tribute Am. Family Inst., 1993. Mem. Train Collectors Assn., Phi Delta Kappa (treas. Wilkes U. chpt. 1995—, Educator of Yr. 2003). Democrat. Avocations: toy trains, tennis. Home: 418 Clemens Dr Dillsburg PA 17019-1321

HOLMES, DAVID LEO, recreation and leisure educator; b. Hammond, Ind., Jan. 4, 1943; s. Leo Victor and Hannah Marget (Robertson) H.; m. Barbara Ann Krajkoski, Mar. 21, 1971; 1 child, Susan Ann Sky. AA, Vincennes U., 1967; BS, Ind. State U., 1969, MS, 1970; PhD, U. Utah, 1976. Tchr., dir. sch. recreation and outdoor edn. Rockville (Ind.) Jr. Ctr., Ind. State Dept. Corrections, 1970-72; instr. Nat. Outdoor Leadership Sch., Washington, Conn., 1972; teaching fellow U. Utah, Salt Lake City, 1973-76; from asst. to prof. program coord. sport and leisure dept. U. Nev., Las Vegas, 1976-91, prof. dept. leisure studies, 1991—. Adj. asst. prof. dept. recreation Ind. State U., Terre Haute, 1972-73; lectr. in field. Contbr. more than 125 articles to profl. jours.; author 5 monographs; editor 6 jours. Active State Comprehensive Outdoor Recreation Planning Com., Nev., 1988; planning team Clark Country Nev. Sch. Dist., 1987-88; adv. bd. Clark Country Nev. Parks and Recreation, 1979-88, vice-chmn., 1984. Officer USMCR, Desert Storm, 1990-91. Recipient Pacemaker award, Faculty Citation Vincennes U., 1990, Spl. Pres. award Nat. Assn. Country Parks & Recreation Officials, 1986; named Outstanding Alumni U. Utah, 1987; recipient Spl. Recognition award Ind. State U., 1987, Hon. Mem. Wings, Blue Parachute Team, # 1 USAF Acad., 1982; grantee various institutions. Mem. AAHPERD (life, Cmty. Svc. award 1987), Nev. Recreation and Park Soc. (Excellence award 1995), Am. Assn. for Leisure and Recreation (bd. dirs. 1981-82, v.p. recreation S.W. dist. 1981), Nev. Parks and Recreation Soc., Nev. State Parks Coop. Assn. (bd. dirs. 1991-92, 93-94), Nev. Assn. for Health, Phys. Edn. and Recreation (pres. 1979-80, Profl. of Yr. 1983-84), Armed Forces Recreation Soc. (v.p. 1998), U. Nev. Alumni Assn. (Prof. Worthy of Recognition 1995, Boyd award for svc. 2001). Methodist. Avocations: running, weightraining. Home: 1227 Kover Ct Henderson NV 89015-9017 Office: U Las Vegas Leisure Studies Program Dept Tourism/Conv Adminstrn 4505 S Maryland Pky Las Vegas NV 89154-9900 E-mail: dholmes@ccmail.nevada.

HOLMES, DAVID LYNN, religion educator; BA in English, Mich. State U.; MA in English, Columbia U.; MA, PhD in Religion, Princeton U.; postgrad., Columbia U., Union Theol. Sem., N.Y.C., Duke U. Div. Sch.; DHL (hon.), Lycoming Coll., 2000. Prof. religion Coll. of William and Mary, Williamsburg, Va., 1965—. Instr. Carnegie-Mellon U.; vis. prof. U. Va. Author: A Brief History of the Episcopal Church, 1993, Devereux Jarratt: An Autobiography, 1995, A Nation Mourns, 1999, James Monroe and the Religion of the Founding Fathers, 2002, others; ch. revs. editor: Anglican and Episcopal History; contbr. articles to profl. jours. Exec. bd. dirs. Coun. for America's First Freedom. Mem. Am. Soc. Ch. History (mem. exec. coun.), Hist. Soc. Episcopal Ch. (exec. bd. dirs.), Ptnrs. for Sacred Places, Episcopal Guild of Scholars, Bishop James Madison Soc., Phi Beta Kappa. Democrat. Episcopalian. Office: Coll William and Mary Dept Religion Sir Christopher Wren Bldg Williamsburg VA 23187-8795 E-mail: dlholm@wm.edu.

HOLMES, DAVID RICHARD, JR., cardiologist; b. Oak Park, Illinois, Nov. 21, 1945; s. David R. and Ethel B. H.; m. Virginia Mary (Zuchlke); children: David, Joshua, Nathaniel, and Jessica. BA, Princeton Univ., 1963-67; MD, Marquette Univ., 1967-71. Intern Va. Mason Hosp., Seattle, 1971-72; fellow internal med., cardiology Mayo Clinic, Rochester, Minn., 1972-76, physician, 1978—, dir. cardiac catheterization lab., dir. ACC/SVS renal and iliac stenting project, 2001—. Pres., Soc. for Cardiac Angiography and Interventions, Breckenridge, Colo., 1995-96. Capt., USN, 1976-78. Recipient Internal Med. Achievement Award, Mayo Graduate Sch., 1974; Transcatheter Therapeutics Career Achievement Award, Washington Cardiology Ctr., 1995. Fellow Am. Coll. Cardiology (cardiac catheterization com. 1991-96, edn. program com., co-dir. interventional symposium 1999-00, chmn. procedures tng. work 1999-, co-chair, ACC ann. sci. sessions 2003, pres.-elect Minn. ACC chpt. 2003); Soc. Cardiac Angiography and Interventions; mem. Minn. Soc. Internal Med.; Am. Heart Assn.; cardiac adv. cmty.; Sigma Xi; Alph Omega Alpha Honor Soc.; inaugral mem. Interventional Andreas Gruentzig Soc.

HOLMES, DWIGHT ELLIS, architect; b. Ashville, N.C., Nov. 8, 1938; s. John Dwight and Leymon (Butler) H.; m. Mary Rose Speer; children— Sheryl, John, Scott BS in Architecture, Ga. Inst. Tech., 1960; B.Arch., N.C. State U., 1962. Registered architect, Fla. Architect Mark Hampton, Architect, Tampa, Fla., 1961-72; architect Rowe Holmes Assocs. Architects, Inc., Tampa, Fla., 1972-84, The Design Arts Group, Inc., Tampa, 1984-85, Rowe Holmes Hammer Russell Architects, Inc., Tampa, 1986-92, Holmes, Hepner & Assocs. Architects, Tampa, 1992—. Contbr. articles to profl. jours. Mem. State of Fla. Smart Schs. Clearinghouse, 1997—. Recipient numerous awards Am. Assn. Sch. Adminstrs., Am. Plywood Assn., Archtl. Record, Council Ednl. Facilities Planners, Fla. Concrete and Products Assn., Inc., Fla. Growers' Assn., Hillsborough County Planning Commn., Owens Corning Co., Fla. Solar Energy Ctr., Hillsborough County Hist. Preservation Bd., State of Fla. Fellow AIA (medal of honor Fla. Central chpt. 1980, award of honor Fla./Caribbean region 1982, numerous other awards) Clubs: University, Tampa Yacht and Country. Republican. Roman Catholic. Home: 5800 S Gordon Ave Tampa FL 33611-4768 Office: Holmes Hepner & Assocs Architects 100 W Kennedy Blvd Tampa FL 33602-5180 E-mail: holmes@holmeshepner.com.

HOLMES, EDWARD W. dean, physician, medical educator; b. Winona, Miss., Jan. 25, 1941; s. Edward and Mary (Hart) H.; m. Judith L. Swain, Jan. 25, 1980. BS, Washington and Lee U., 1963; MD, U. Pa., 1967. Intern Hosp. of U. Pa., 1967-68; resident in medicine Duke U. Med. Ctr., Durham, N.C.; prof. medicine and biochemistry Duke U., Durham, N.C., 1974-91; investigator Howard Hughes Med. Inst., 1974-87; prof., chmn. dept. medicine U. Pa., Phila., 1991-97; assoc. dean for rsch. Stanford U. Sch. Medicine, 1997-2000; dean Duke U. Sch. Medicine, Durham; vice chancellor academic affairs Duke U. Med. Ctr., Durham; vice chancellor health scis., dean U. Calif. Sch. Medicine, La Jolla, 2000—. Reviewer in molecular medicine. With USPHS, 1968-70. Grantee NIH. Mem. Am. Soc. Clin. Investigation, Assn. Am. Physicians. Office: Univ Calif Sch Medicine 1313 Basic Sci Bldg 9500 Gilman Dr La Jolla CA 92093-0602

HOLMES, EVERLENA MCDONALD, health science administrator, consultant, retired dean; b. Eufaula, Ala., Feb. 15, 1934; d. Oscar Lee and Carrie Belle McDonald; children: Rufus James Jr., Parvin Holmes Porsche, Gregory Warren. BS, Ky. State U., 1957; MEd, U. Houston, 1974; EdD, Va. Tech. U., 1981. Registered health info. adminstr. Chair, dept. health info. sci. Ea. Ky. U., Richmond, 1975—79; assoc. dean, Coll. Allied Health Profns. Tenn. State U., Nashville, 1982—84; dir., Helath Info. Adminstrn. George Washington U., Washington, 1984—86; dean, Sch. Health Scis. Hunter Coll., CUNY, N.Y.C., 1986—96; dean, Sch. Health Scis. and Human Performance East Stroudsburg (Pa.) U., 1996—98; dean, Coll. Allied Health Charles Drew U., L.A., 1998—2001; cons. Holmes and Assocs., Chattanooga, 2001—. Cons. developing health sci. program Project Hope, Mex., Barbados, West Indies, 1974—75; cons. evaluating health sci. program Am. Assn. State Colls. and Univs., Washington, 1984; cons. developing health sci. edn. 10 colls. and univs., various states, 1970s and 80s; cons. HEW Grant Rev. Com., NIH, VA, USPHS, HHS, 1970s and 80s. Contbr. articles to profl. jours. Mem. health and edn. brain trust Nat. Congl. Black Caucus, Washington, 1974—; program dir. Macon County/Tuskegee Model Cities Assn., Ala., 1970—73; campaign mgr. for Link Turner Freeholders' Election for Essex County, N.J., 1976. Recipient Disting. Svc. award, U. Medicine and Dentistry of N.J., 1987, Eminent Scholar award, Norfolk (Va.) State U., 1982. Mem.: NAACP, Am. Assn. Health Info. Mgmt., Nat. Soc. Allied Health Profns. (treas. 1978—81, pres. 1982—83, Outstanding Leadership award 1984), Nat. Coun. Negro Women, Phi Kappa Phi, Phi Delta Kappa. Democrat. African Methodist Episcopal. Avocation: international travel. Home and Office: Holmes & Assocs 512 Kilmer St Chattanooga TN 37404

HOLMES, FRANCIS WILLIAM, plant pathologist, educator; b. Yonkers, N.Y., May 21, 1929; m. Helen M. Bequaert, June 7, 1953; children: Peter, Sarah, Joseph. AB in Botany and Zoology, Oberlin Coll., 1950; PhD in Plant Pathology, Cornell U., 1954. Asst. prof. shade tree labs. U. Mass., Amherst, 1954-61, assoc. prof., 1961-70, prof., 1970-91, dir. shade tree labs., 1973-88, extension prof., 1988-91, prof. emeritus, 1991—; pvt. practice Amherst, 1991-2000. NSF sr. postdoctoral fellow U. Utrecht, Baarn, Netherlands, 1962—63; lectr. U. Novi Sad, U. Belgrad, U. Sarajevo, 1971; sr. fellow Agrl. U., Wageningen, Netherlands, 1984—85; guest investigator New Zealand Forest Rsch. Inst., 1986. Incorporator, treas. Amherst Human Rels. Coun., 1968—70; active Boy Scouts Am., 1942—70; libr. New Eng. Quaker Rsch. Libr., 1965—85. Recipient Pub. Svc. award, Nat. Arbor Day Found., 1980, Environ. Merit award, EPA, 1980; grantee, Am. Philos. Soc., 1984—85; Fulbright travel grant, Netherlands, 1962—63, 1970—71, Internat. Agrarisch Centrum Wageningen fellow, 1985. Mem.: Assn. for Women in Arboriculture, Internat. Soc. Arboriculture (treas. New Eng. chpt. 1979—84, membership sec. 1985—96, chair rsch. com. 1979—93, Author award 1980, Award of Merit 1993, hon. life), Internat. Soc. Plant Pathology, Can. Phytopath. Soc., Am. Phytopath. Soc., Royal Dutch Bot. Soc. (corr.), Mass. Arborists Assn. (hon.), Mass. Tree Wardens and Foresters Assn. (hon.; advisor, Disting. Svc. award 1986, George E. Stone award 1991). Mem. Soc. Of Friends.

HOLMES, FREDERIC LAWRENCE, science historian; b. Cin., Feb. 6, 1932; m. Harriet Holmes, 1959; (dec. 2000), 3 children. BS, MIT, 1954; MA, Harvard U., 1958, PhD, 1962. Asst. prof. history of sci. MIT, 1962-64; asst. prof. to assoc. prof. Yale U., New Haven, 1964-72, prof., chmn. sect. history of medicine, 1979—2003, master Jonathan Edwards Coll., 1982-87; prof. history of sci., chmn. dept. history of medicine and sci. U. Western Ont., 1972-79; Dept. of Hist. of Med. Yale U Schl Med, New Haven, 1979—2003. Author: Claude Bernard and Animal Chemistry, 1974, Lavoisier and the Chemistry of Life,

1985, Eighteenth Century Chemistry as an Investigative Enterprise, 1989, Hans Krebs: The Formation of a Scientific Life, 1991, Hans Krebs: Architect of Intermediary Metabolism, 1993, Antoine Lavoisier-The Next Crucial Year: or the Souras of His Quantitative Method in Chemistry, 1998, Meselson, Stahl, and the Replication of DNA: A History of the Most Beautiful Experience in Biology, 2001; contbr. articles to profl. jours. Rsch. grantee NIH, 1963-67, NSF, 1968-70, 1988-2003, Can. Coun., 1973-74 Mem. History of Sci. Soc. (pres. 1981-83), Am. Assn. History Medicine, Can. Soc. Hist. and Philos. Sci. Died Mar. 27, 2003.

HOLMES, GARY LEE, medical/surgical nurse; b. Garden City, Kans., Aug. 30, 1951; s. Vern Lynn and Phyllis Ann (Vincent) H.; m. Margaret Emily Holmes, Jan. 10, 1973; children: Gary Lee Jr., Andrew Martin. BSN, Spalding U., 1985. RN, Ky., 1985, Ind., 1992; BCLS instr. CPR. Staff nurse burn unit Humana Hosp. U. Louisville (Ky.), 1985-86, staff nurse Humana Hosp. U. Louisville, 1986—87; staff nurse emergency rm. Humana Hosp. U. Louisville (Ky.), 1987-88, staff nurse, 1989-92; staff nurse, telemetry Humana Hosp. Audubon, Louisville, 1992; infusion therapy, med.-surg. RN Kimberly Quality Care, Jeffersonville, Ind., 1992-93; med.-surg. nurse Hillcreek Manor Nursing Home and Rehab. Ctr., 1993—95; night shift supr. Hillcreek Manor Nursing Home Rehab. Facility, 1997—; nurse Prime Stat and Star Med. Health Profls., 1997—; with Tri County Bapt. Hosp., La Grange, Norton S.W. Hosp., Louisville; traveling nurse O'Grady-Peyton Internat., Inc., 2000; nurse tele-med.-surg. unit VA Med. Ctr., Louisville, 2000; nurse Norton Suburban Hosp., Louisville, 2001—; with Mercy Health Ctr. Manhattan, Kans.; nurse Med-Pro Staffing Solutions/Jewish Hosp., 2002—. With USN, 1969-85. Mem. Spalding U. Nursing Students. Home: 5418 Ripple Ln Louisville KY 40218-4224

HOLMES, GENTA HAWKINS, diplomat; b. Anadarko, Okla., Sept. 3, 1940; BA, U. So. Calif., 1962. Jr. officer U.S. Embassy, Abidjan, Ivory Coast, 1964-66; with office spl. assistance to Sec. of State for Refugee Affairs, 1966-68; spl. asst., youth officer U.S. Embassy, Paris, 1968-71; with N.Y. regional office OEO, 1972-73; with office devel. fin., econ. bur. U.S. Dept. State, 1973-74; chief econ. and commercial sect. U.S. Embassy, Bahamas, 1974-77; congl. fellow Am. Polit. Sci. Assn., 1977-78; with bur. congl. rels. U.S. Dept. State, 1978-79; asst. adminstr. legis. affairs AID, 1979-82; mem. 25th Exec. Seminar in Nat. and Internat. Affairs, 1982-83; mem. bd. examiners, 1983-84; dep. chief of mission U.S. Embassy, Lilongwe, Malawi, 1984-86, Port-au-Prince, Haiti, 1986-88, Pretoria, South Africa, 1988-90; U.S. amb. to Namibia, 1990-92; dir. gen. fgn. svc., dir. pers. U.S. Dept. State, Washington, 1992-95; diplomat in residence U. Calif., Davis, 1995-97; U.S. amb. to Australia, 1997—2000. Office: US Embassy 15106 Oak Meadow Rd Penn Valley CA 95946

HOLMES, HARRY DADISMAN, health facility administrator; b. Houston, Aug. 8, 1944; s. Harry Newton and Ruth Eleanor (Dadisman) H.; children: Hillary Hunt, Ashley Elizabeth. BA, Rice U., 1966; MA, La. State U., 1968; PhD, U. Mo., 1973. Asst. prof. urban devel. U. Tenn., Knoxville, 1973—76; asst. to exec. v.p. Tex. Med. Ctr., Inc., Houston, 1976—80; dir. govt. affairs, orgnl. liaison U. Tex. System Cancer Ctr., Houston, 1980—90; asst. to pres. U. Tex. Sys. Cancer Ctr., Houston, 1981—90; v.p. govt. rels. U. Tex. M.D. Anderson Cancer Ctr., Houston, 1990—. Mem. Cancer Ctrs. Adminstrs. Forum, 1994—; mem. select com. on pub. issues Greater Houston Hosp. Coun., 1983-94; mem. exec. adv. bd. White, Petrov and McHone, 1987-95; mem. pub. rels. adv. coun. Tex. Med. Ctr., 1985—; chair South Tex. Legis Conf., 1985, 87; founder Biotech. Assn., 1986; mem. exec. com. Nat. Comprehensive Cancer Networks, 1998—. Mem. adminstrv. bd. St. Luke's Meth. Ch.; mem. Mayor's Task Force on Pvt. Sector Initiatives for Houston, 1981-82, Houston C.C. Found. Bd., 1992—, Greater Houston Partnership State and Fed. Com., 1989—; mem. U. Tex. Tex./Mex. Border Health Task Force, 1989—, exec. com., 1989—; pres. Houston Higher Edn. Fin. Corp., 1989—, Houston Health Facilities Corp., 2000—, Houston Indsl. Devel. Corp., 2000—; mem. Rice U. Fund Coun., 1991-94, Nat. Cancer Ctrs. Task Force, 1991—; mem. steering com. Tex. Colorectal Cancer Plan; mem. exec. bd. Leadership Houston, 1983-86, Houston Ctr. for Humanities, 1983-86; mem. govt. rels. com. Greater Houston Hosp. Coun., 1985-95; mem. com. Instnl. Task Force on Oncology in Chile, 1986-87; exec. com. Instnl. Strategic Planning Com., 1986-95; divsn. chmn. United Way of Houston, 1983; com. to evaluate the status of minority and women faculty, faculty adminstrs. and adminstrv. staff U. Tex., M.D. Anderson Cancer Ctr., 1990. White fellow U. Mo., 1972. Mem. Am. Assn. Cancer Insts. (mem. govt. rels. com. 1998—, chair 1999-2000), Houston C. of C. (co-chmn. govt. rels. com. 1982-83), Rice U. Alumni Assn. (exec. bd., chmn. publs. com. 1982-83), Phi Alpha Theta. Office: U Tex MD Anderson Cancer Ctr 1515 Holcombe Blvd Houston TX 77030-4009 Home: 3302 W Dallas St Houston TX 77019-3805

HOLMES, HENRY, literary agent, book publicist, writer and editor; AS in Broadcast Journalism, Grahm Coll., 1961; Cert. in Leadership, Dale Carnegie, 1962; postgrad. in non-fiction writing, Famous Writers Sch., Westport, Conn., 1966-69; hon. degree, Grahm Coll., 1970. Prodr. news/sports Report on Sports WHDH-TV-Radio (CBS); asst. pub. rels. dir. Doherty, Clifford, Steers & Shenfield, Inc., N.Y.C., 1962-64, Boston; sports dir. WCEE-TV (CBS), Rockford, Ill.; news dir. WRLH-TV (NBC), Hanover, N.H.; media comms./mktg. Boston Red Sox, 1961-62, 73-75; sports dir. WRLM-FM, Providence; mktg. profl. Zayre Corp., Natick, Mass., 1984-86; mktg./sales promotion McGraw Hill Corp., Heightstown, N.J., Castle Harlan, Inc., N.Y.C.; project coord. Addison Wesley Publ. Co., Reading, Mass. Broadcast instr. Career Acad., Boston; advt. instr. Fisher Coll., Fall River, Mass., 1976; announcer Avco Pro Golf Classic, 1969; (with Bruce Martin) Voice of Detroit Red Wings and Detroit Lions; speaker in field. Writer : (documentaries); prodr.: (JFK assasination spl.), 1963; narrator : (Election Capsule '68); (Best in Sports Interviews), 1961; (Pro Football Hall of Famer Elroy Hirsch), 1970; anchor (Heartbeats in Sports Headlines pre-game sports features) WSAR-AM; lit. agt., book publicist Short Rage - An autobiographical look at Heightism in Am., 2002, Leading by Heart - Through the World of Quantum Civics, 2003. Fundraiser Jerry Lewis Telethon, Rockford, United Cerebral Palsy, Rockford, Internat. Club for Physically Handicapped, Rockford, (Ill.), Beloit (Wis.) Jaycees, WBEL Community Charity Drive, Beloit. With USN, 1956-58. Avocations: nonfiction writing, general research, interviewing, current events, professional and college sports. Home and Office: PO Box 433 Swansea MA 02777-0433

HOLMES, HENRY ALLEN, government official; b. Bucharest, Romania, Jan. 31, 1933; (parents Am. citizens); s. Julius Cecil and Henrietta (Allen) H.; m. Marilyn Janet Strauss, July 25, 1959; children: Katherine Anne, Gerald Allen. AB, Princeton U., 1954; Woodrow Wilson fellow, U. Paris, 1958. Intelligence rsch. analyst Dept. State, Cameroon, 1958-59, commd. fgn. svc. officer, 1959, assigned to Am. Embassy, 1959—61, Rome, 1963-67, counselor polit. affairs Am. embassy Paris, 1970-74, sr. exec. Seminar in Fgn. Policy Washington, 1974-75; assigned as dir. Office NATO and Atlantic polit. mil. aff. Bur. European Affairs, Washington, 1975-77; dep. chief mission U.S. Embassy Dept. State, Rome, 1977-79, prin. dep. asst. sec. state for European and Can. affairs Washington, 1979-82, amb. Am. embassy Portugal, 1982-85, asst. sec. Bur. Politico Mil. Affairs Washington, 1985-89, amb. at large for burdensharing, 1989-93, asst. sec. def. for spl. ops. and low-intensity conflict, 1993-99; adj. prof. Georgetown U., 2000—. Served as capt. USMC, 1954-57. Mem. Am. Fgn. Svc. Assn., Coun. Fgn. Rels., Am. Acad. Diplomacy, Washington Inst. Fgn. Affairs, Metro Club (Washington). Episcopalian. E-mail: hallenholmes@aol.com.

HOLMES, JACK EDWARD, political science educator; b. Wichita, May 16, 1941; s. Herbert Paul and Marguerite Elizabeth (Duerr) H.; m. Linda Sue Pacheco, Dec. 28, 1996; stepchildren: Valerie, Cynthia, Jacqueline, Elizabeth. BA, Knox Coll., 1963; MA, U. Denver, 1967, PhD in Internat. Studies, 1972. Asst. prof. Hope Coll., Holland, Mich., 1969-72; dist. asst. Congressman Don Brotzman, Denver, 1973-75; asst. prof. Hope Coll., Holland, 1975-76, assoc. prof., 1976-87, prof., 1987—. Chmn. polit. sci. dept. Hope Coll., 1988-95, 99—. Author: Mood/Interest Theory of American Foreign Policy, 1985; co-author: American Government Essentials and Perspectives, 1991, 94, 98. Campaign chmn. Ottawa County Reps., Holland, 1978, 82-96, chmn., 1997-2002, Ottawa County Bush for Pres, 2000; del. Rep. Nat. Conv., 2000; chmn. 2d Congl. Dist. Rep. Party, 2003—. Capt. U.S. Army, 1967-69. Named to Mich. Model UN Hall of Fame. Mem. Internat. Studies Assn., Am. Polit. Sci. Assn., Holy Cross Wilderness Def. Fund. Presbyterian. Avocations: backpacking, fishing. Home: 10 N 160th Ave Holland MI 49424-6203 Office: Hope Coll 210 Lubbers Hall Holland MI 49422-9000 E-mail: holmes@hope.edu.

HOLMES, JAMES HILL, III, lawyer; b. Birmingham, Ala., Sept. 10, 1935; s. Houston Eccleston and Celia Lindsey (Wearn) Holmes; m. Julia (Judy) Ryman, Aug. 17, 1963; children: James H. IV, Randell Ryman, Tucker Malone. BBA, So. Meth. U., 1957, LLB, 1959. Bar: Tex. 1959, U.S. Ct. Mil. Appeals 1960, U.S. Dist. Ct. (no. dist.) Tex. 1963, U.S. Dist. Ct. (ea. dist.) Tex. 1966, U.S. Dist. Ct. (we. dist.) Tex. 1979, U.S. Ct. Appeals (5th and 11th cirs.) 1981, U.S. Supreme Ct. 1974. Ptnr. Burford & Ryburn, Dallas, 1962—. Mock trial participant Tex. Nurses Assn., 1978—86; spkr. State Bar Tex. Profl. Devel. Program, 1987—2002; co-chair adv. com. professionalism Supreme Ct. Tex., 1989—90. Contbr. articles to profl. jours. Past mem. University Park (Tex.) Bd. Adjustment; chmn. University Park (Tex.) Planning and Zoning Commn., 1988—94; numerous other offices in civic orgns.; city councilman City of University Park, 1994—2000; mayor pro tem City of Univ. Pk., 1998—2000, 2002—; past dir. Child Guidance Clinic; past bd. dirs. Park Cities Town North YMCA; trustee Tex. Ctr. Legal Ethics & Professionalism, 2001—; past dir., past pres. All Sports Assn., Dallas, 1977; pres. Univ. Pk. Cmty. League, 1987—88; vice chmn. adminstrv. Tex. Ctr. Legal Ethics and Professionalism, 2001—. With USAF, 1959—62. Recipient Presdl. Citation, State Bar of Tex., 1995, Judge Sam Williams Local Bar Leadership award, 2001, Professionalism award, Coll. of the State Bar Tex., 1999, Morris Harrell Professionalism award, Dallas Bar Assn. and Tex. Ctr. for Ethics and Professionalism, 2000, Lola Wright Found. award, 2002. Fellow: Tex. Bar Found., Am. Coll. Trial Lawyers; mem.: Patrick E. Higginbotham Am. Inn of Ct. (master 1989—95), Am. Bd. Trial Advocates (pres. Dallas chpt. 2000), Tex. Bar Assn., Dallas Bar Assn. (numerous coms.), Def. Rsch. Inst. (state chmn. 1994), Internat. Assn. Def. Counsel, Assn. Def. Trial Attys., Tex. Assn. Def. Counsel (pres. 1992—93, Founder's award 1997), Dallas Assn. Def. Counsel (chmn. 1975), ABA, Blue Key, Phi Delta Theta, Phi Alpha Delta. Episcopalian. Avocations: jogging, spectator sports, outdoors. Home: 3804 Lovers Ln Dallas TX 75225-7101 Office: Burford & Ryburn LLP 3100 Lincoln Pla 500 N Akard St Ste 3100 Dallas TX 75201-6697

HOLMES, JAMES M. social studies educator, educator; b. Cleveland, Jan. 3, 1938; m. Patricia Hutton; children: Elizabeth, John, Michael. BA, Wabash Coll., 1959; MA, U. Chgo., 1963, PhD, 1967. Asst. prof. Purdue U., Lafayette, Ind., 1964—67; vis. prof. U. SC, Columbia, SC, 1973, Monash U., Melborne, Australia, 1974, U. Calif., Santa Barbara, 1976—77; dist. vis. prof. Az. State U., Tempe, 1978; vis. prof. Wayne State U., Detroit, 1978—79, U. Manitoba, Winnipeg, Canada, 1979—80; prof. of econ. SUNY, Buffalo, 1967—. Editorial bd. Jour. of Macroeconomics, 1979—. Contbr. articles various profl. jours. Commentator TV and Newspapers, Buffalo, 1980—; Leader Boy Scouts of Am., Buffalo, 1991—99; coach Am. Soccer League, Amherst, NY, 1997—. Mem.: Am. Stat. Assn., Royal Econ. Soc., Am. Econ. Assn. Achievements include discovery of the effect of taxes on liquidity preference, The Holmes-Smyth Effect; a new non-parametric test for causality in a non-experimental science. Avocations: horseback riding, sailing, bicycling, camping, kayaking. Home: 23 Carriage Hill West Buffalo NY 14221 Office: SUNY Econ Dept 431 Fronczak Hall Buffalo NY 14260-1520 E-mail: ecoholme@buffalo.edu.

HOLMES, JEAN LOUISE, real estate investor, Holocaust scholar, educator; b. Butler, Mo., Dec. 9, 1943; d. Victor Julius and Helen Emilia (Knapheide) Witte; m. Eugene Philmore Carter Jr., Aug. 21, 1965 (div. Aug. 1992); children: Kristin, Lance; m. Reed M. Holmes, Jan. 26, 1993. AA, Graceland Coll., Lamoni, Iowa, 1963; BA, Iowa State U., 1965; postgrad., U. Paris, 1965, Tufts U., 1973; MA in Judaic Studies magna cum laude, Hebrew Coll., Brookline, Mass., 1989; postgrad., Ratisbonne Ctr. of Judaic Studies, Jerusalem, 1993-95, Hebrew U./Yad Vashem, 1992, 95, Yad Vashem/Poland, 1998. Lic. bldg. constrn. supr., Mass. Tchr. French, Iowa, Mass., 1966-69; tchg. English lang. and lit., 1966-67; real estate broker Carter Realty, Pepperell, Mass., 1975—; pres., mgr. Viewpax Mondiale, Independence, Mo., 1982—; pres. Keshet Hashalom, Jerusalem, 1989—. Clk. Ctrl. Middlesex Multiple Listing Svc., Concord, Mass., 1980-81, v.p., 1982, pres., 1983; lectr. Remembering for the Future II, Berlin, 1994, Internat. Holocaust Scholars Conf., Mpls., 1996; dir., adj. prof. student intercultural travel to Israel, Jordan, Egypt, Park U., Mo., Graceland U., 1982—. Co-author: The Forerunners, 2003. Mem. adv. bd. Peace Ctr., Independence, 1989-91; mem. interfaith rels. com. RLDS/Cmty. of Christ, Independence, 2000—; dir. Maine Friendship House, Tel Aviv, Israel; exec. com. Nat. Christian Leadership Conf. for Israel, 2001—. Recipient Friendship award Israel Ministry of Tourism, Jerusalem, 1992. Avocations: photography, archaeology, adventure travel, literature. Home: PO Box 680 Pepperell MA 01463-0680 Office: Holmes Mgmt 125 Littleton Rd Apt 9 Ayer MA 01432-1733 E-mail: jeanreed@mindspring.com.

HOLMES, JENANNE NELSON, lawyer; b. Evanston, Ill.; d. Oscar William and Anne L. (Moll) Nelson. B.S. magna cum laude, U. So. Calif., 1967, J.D., 1976. Admitted to D.C. bar, 1977, Calif. bar, 1983; sec., corp. officer Sta. KUPD-AM-FM, Phoenix, 1959-61; media dir. West, Weir & Bartel, Los Angeles, 1962-65; assoc. media dir. Eisaman, Johns & Laws, Los Angeles, 1966-68; media supr. Ogilvy & Mathers, N.Y.C., 1968-69; v.p. media and mktg. services Smith-Gent Advt. Co., N.Y.C., 1969-71; media supr. The Media Dept., N.Y.C., 1971-72; v.p. media Perkal Advt. Co., Los Angeles, 1972-74; research asst. U. So. Calif. Law Center, 1975-76; atty. advisor FCC, Washington, 1977-80; gen. atty. U.S. Dept. Energy, 1980-88; supervisory hearing officer USDA Farmers Home Adminstrn., Memphis, 1988—; pro bono atty. Friends of Animals, N.Y.C. Mem. ABA, Calif. Bar Assn., D.C. Bar Assn., Fed. Bar Assn., Los Angeles Advt. Women, U. So. Calif. Alumni, Presbyterian. Mensa, Cactus and Succulent Soc., Sierra Club, North Shore Animal League, Phi Beta Kappa, Beta Gamma Sigma. Office: Farmers Home Adminstrn Nat Appeals Staff 7777 Walnut Grove Rd Memphis TN 38120-2130

HOLMES, JENNIFER SMITH, political scientist, educator; b. Edina, Minn., Aug. 15, 1971; d. Theodore Gerald and Carolyn April Smith; 1 child. BA in Polit. Sci., U. Chgo., 1993; PhD in Polit. Sci., U. Minn., 1998. Vis. asst. prof. govt. and politics U. Tex. at Dallas, Richardson, 1998—2000, asst. prof. govt. and politics and polit. economy, 2000—. Author: (book) Terrorism and Democratic Stability, 2001, New Approaches to Comparative Politics: Insights from Political Theory, 2003; contbr. articles to profl. jours. Mem. Dallas Com. on Fgn. Rels., 2000. Mem.: Southwestern Polit. Sci. Assn., Asociacion de Colombianistas, Latin Am. Studies Assn., So. Polit. Sci. Assn., Am. Polit. Sci. Assn. Democrat. Office: Univ Tex at Dallas GR 31 PO Box 830688 Richardson TX 75083-0688 Office Fax: 972-883-2735. E-mail: jholmes@utdallas.edu.

HOLMES, JERRY DELL, retired chemist; b. Mt. Vernon, Tex., Nov. 30, 1935; s. W. L. and Amie E. (Marshall) Holmes; m. Margaret L. King, June 22, 1957; children: Lisa, Melinda, Jerry D. Jr., James. BS, E. Tex. State U., 1956; PhD, U. Tex., 1962; postgrad., Harvard U., 1991. Chemist Am. Oil Co., Texas City, Tex., 1956-60; from chemist to sr. chemist Tex. Eastman Co., Longview, 1963-74, div. dir., 1974-80, dir. R&D, 1982-84; staff asst. R&D chem. divsn. Eastman Kodak Co., Kingsport, Tenn., 1980-82, dir. devel. chems. divsn., 1984-88, acting dir. R&D, 1988, assoc. dir. research, chem. divsn., 1988-89, dir. rsch. chem. divsn., 1989-90; v.p. rsch. Eastman Chem. Co., Kingsport, 1990-95, v.p. R&D, 1995-97; ret., 1997. Lectr. in field R&D; bd. dirs. Reilly Industries, Inc. Contbr. articles to profl. jours. Presbyterian. Achievements include patents in field. E-mail: jdholmes@chartertn.net.

HOLMES, JOHN LEONARD, chemistry educator; b. London, Nov. 29, 1931; came to Can., 1958; s. Leonard Thomas and Jessie Ethel (Doble) H.; m. Una Jane Watts, Dec. 12, 1958 (div. 1993). children: Susan P., Jonathan B.; m. Sheila Jean Robertson, Apr. 13, 1994; stepchildren: John Fergus, Isobel Clare. BSc, London U., 1954, PhD, 1957, DSc, 1983. Postdoctoral fellow NRC, Ottawa, Can., 1958-60; I.C.I. fellow Edinburgh U., Scotland, 1960-61, lectr., 1961-62; asst. prof. U. Ottawa, 1962-65, assoc. prof., 1965-73, prof., 1973-97, emeritus prof., 1997—. Nuffield vis. prof. U. Ghana, 1971, Overbeek vis. prof. U. Utrecht, The Netherlands, 1979, Disting. vis. scholar U. Adelaide, Australia, 1984; vis. fellow Australian Nat. U., Canberra, 1993, 2000; internat. sci. exchange fellow U. Bern, 1993. Editor Organic Mass Spectrometry jour., 1976-93, European Mass Spectrometry jour., 1994-2001; contbr. over 280 articles to profl. jours. Recipient Barringer Rsch. award Can. Spectroscopy Soc., 1980, Herzberg award Can. Spectroscopy Soc., 1990, F.P. Lossing award Can. Mass Spectrometry Soc., 2000. Fellow Chem. Inst. Can. (medal 1989), Royal Soc. Can.; mem. Am. Soc. Mass Spectrometry, Brit. Soc. Mass Spectrometry (life), Internat. Yacht Racing Union (judge 1986-99), Can. Yachting Assn., Royal Yachting Assn. Clubs: Britannia Yacht (Ottawa). Home: 121 Buell St Unit 58 Ottawa ON Canada K1Z 7E7 Office: U Ottawa Chem Dept Ottawa ON Canada K1N 6N5

HOLMES, JOHN RICHARD, physicist, educator; b. Chula Vista, Calif., Sept. 24, 1917; s. Robert and Mary Elizabeth (Burns) H.; m. Louise Murphy, 1951 (dec. Oct. 1989); children: Susan Diana, Ronald John, Sandra Kathleen. AB in Physics, U. Calif., Berkeley, 1938, MA, 1941, PhD, 1942. With radiation lab. U. Calif., 1942-45; mem. faculty physics U. So. Calif., Los Angeles, 1945-63, prof., 1954-63, chmn. dept. physics, 1956-62; prof. U. Hawaii, Honolulu, 1963—, chmn. physics dept., 1963-72, emeritus prof. physics, 1989—. Fulbright lectr. U. Madrid, 1962-63; cons. Autonetics Corp., Anaheim, Calif., Douglas Aircraft, Santa Monica, Calif., Electro-Optical Sys., Pasadena, Calif.; lectr. Edwards AFB, Loyola U., L.A.; UNESCO cons., Argentina, 1970 Mem. internat. adv. bd. Optica Pura y Aplicada, Madrid Whiting fellow in physics U. Calif., Berkeley, 1938. Fellow Am. Phys. Soc., Optical Soc. Am.; mem. AAAS. Home: 820 N Delaware St # 210 San Mateo CA 94401-1538

HOLMES, KATHERINE NOELLE, actor; b. Toledo, Ohio, Dec. 18, 1978; d. Martin and Kathy Holmes. Actress, 1997—. Actor: (films) The Ice Storm, 1997, Disturbing Behavior, 1998, Go!, 1999, Teaching Mrs. Tingle, 1999, Wonder Boys, 2000, The Gift, 2000; (TV series) Dawson's Creek, 1998. Office: c/o BWR Pub Rels 9100 Wilshire Blvd West Tower 6th Fl Beverly Hills CA 90210

HOLMES, KING KENNARD, medical educator; b. St. Paul, Sept. 1, 1937; AB, Harvard Coll., 1959; MD, Cornell U., 1963; PhD in Microbiology, U. Hawaii, 1967. Diplomate Am. Bd. Internal Medicine, infectious diseases. Resident U. Wash., Seattle, 1967-68, chief resident, 1968-69, from instr. to assoc. prof. medicine, 1969-78, vice chmn. dept. medicine, 1984-89, prof. medicine, 1978—, dir. Ctr. AIDS and Sexually Transmitted Diseases, 1989—. Head divsn. pulmonary diseases USPHS Hosp., Seattle, 1969-70, asst. chief dept. medicine, 1969-83, head divsn. infectious diseases, 1970-83; dir. Sexually Transmitted Disease Clinic, Harborview Med. Ctr., 1972-79, chief med., 1984-89; mem. numerous adv. coms. Nat. Inst. Allergy & Infectious Diseases, NIH, USPHS, WHO, NAS; prin. investigator NIH, Nat. Cancer Inst., Nat. Inst. Allergy & Infectious Diseases, Nat. Inst. Child Health & Human Devel., Ctrs. Disease Control, 1983—. With USN, 1965-67. Recipient Squibb award Infectious Disease Soc. Am., 1978, Thomas Parran award Am. Veneral Disease Assn., 1983. Fellow ACP, Royal Coll. Physicians Eng.; mem. AMA, Inst. Medicine-NAS, Assn. Am. Physicians, Am. Epidemiol. Soc., Am. Fedn. Clin. Rsch. Office: U Wash Str AIDS & STDs Harborview Med Ctr 325 9th Ave MS# 359931 Seattle WA 98104-2420 Fax: 206-731-3694.*

HOLMES, LARRY, JR., retired professional boxer; b. Cuthbert, Ga., Nov. 3, 1949; s. John and Flossie Holmes; children: Listy, Lisa. Ed. public schs. Formerly worked in car wash, quarry, rug mill, foundry; profl. boxer, 1973—. Heavyweight champion World Boxing Council, 1978-83, Internat. Boxing Fedn., 1983-85. Achievements include winning 19 of 22 amateur fights. Undefeated for a record 13 years. Office: Larry Holmes Enterprises 704 Alpha Bldg Easton PA 18042

HOLMES, LARRY WAYNE, artist, educator; b. Kansas City, Kans., Nov. 12, 1942; s. Victor Debs and Vickey Margaret (Denk) H.; m. Maureen Ann Cook, Aug. 27, 1967 (dec. Dec. 1968); m. Kathleen Teodecki, June 12, 1972; 1 child, Phoebe Jeanette. BFA, Pittsburg (Kans.) State U., 1964, MS, 1965; MFA, Cranbrook Acad. Art, Bloomfield Hills, Mich., 1973. Tchr. art Shawnee Mission Sch. Dist., Overland Park, Kans., 1965-68, Center Sch. Dist., Kansas City, Mo., 1969-71; instr. painting U. Del., Newark, 1973—, prof. art, chmn. dept., 1983-92. Artist-in-residence Yaddo Artists Colony, Saratoga Springs, N.Y., 1981; vis. lectr. art U. Wolverhampton, Eng., 1989. One-man shows include Littlejohn-Smith Gallery, N.Y.C., 1989, Littlejohn/Sternau Gallery, N.Y.C., 1992, Hoyt Inst. Fine Arts, New Castle, Pa., 1996, Jack Meier Gallery, Houston, 1996, 98, 2000, Pitts. State U. Art Gallery, 2001; exhibited in group shows Sherry French Gallery, N.Y.C., 1996; represented in permanent collections City of Parsons, Kans., Akin, Gump & Strauss, Washington, McDonald's Corp., Wilmington Trust Corp. Office: U Del Art Dept Newark DE 19716 E-mail: lholmes@udel.edu.

HOLMES, LOIS REHDER, composer, piano and voice educator; b. Canton, Ill., Jan. 8, 1927; d. John and Elizabeth Mary Grace (Staton) Kleinsteiber; div.; 1 child, Jessica Regina. BA in Sociology, Ill. Wesleyan U., 1949, MusB in Voice, Organ & Piano, 1950; MS in Reading, Western Ill. U., 1981. Cert. tchr., Ill. Libr. worker Withers Pub. Libr., Bloomington, Ill., 1950-51; music tchr. Toledo (Ill.) Schs., 1951-52; music and art librarian Hutchinson (Kans) Pub. Libr., 1952-53; pvt. practice piano & voice tchr. various cities, Ill., 1955—. Tchr. 1st & 2d grades South Fulton Sch., Havana, Ill., 1972-81. Composer: Musical Notions, 1991, Seascape, 1993, Divertimento, 1995, Bittersweet, 1996, Buglers at Sunrise, 1997, Dream Catcher, 1998, Fourteen New Christmas Carols for the 21st Century, 1999, The Abandoned Lighthouse, 2001, Do Daisies Dream, 2003, Petals On the Pond, 2003, Dragon Mist, 2003, Giselle, The Gypsy, 2003, others. Organist/choir dir. Ctrl. Christian Ch., Havana, 1974-79; vol. March of Dimes, Chgo., 1997—, Amnesty Internat. USA, Chgo., 1993—. Mem. Nat. Guild Piano Tchrs. (adjudicator internat. piano composition contest 1996—), Phi Kappa Phi. Home: 321 Mary Alice Rd Rantoul IL 61866-2832

HOLMES, LOUIS IRA, physician assistant, educator, photojournalist; b. L.A., July 16, 1943; s. Louis Issac and Mabel Jane (Walsh) H.; m. Krystal Ladda Premchaona, Nov. 16, 1991 (separated); children: Jonathan Joseph, Kimberly Ellen, Louis Boon. AA, El Camino Coll., Torrance, Calif., 1972; cert. physician asst., U. So. Calif., 1978. Cert. Nat. Commn. Cert. Physician Assts.; cert. ACLS. Resident in surgery Norwalk Hosp.-Yale U. Sch. Medicine, 1980; nursing staff emergency dept. South Bay Dist. Hosp., Redondo Beach, Calif., 1970-75; nursing staff trauma and surg. intensive care Harbor Gen. Hosp.-UCLA Med. Ctr., Torrance, 1976-77; physician asst. Gen. Med. Corp., L.A., 1979; physician asst., divsn. thoracic surgery City of Hope Med. Ctr., Duarte, Calif., 1980-81; sr. physcian asst. thoracic and cardiovascular surgery Bert Meyer MD, et al, L.A., 1981-91; sr. physician asst. cardiothoracic surgery, instr. postgrad. cardiothoracic surgery residency program Cedars-Sinai Med. Ctr., L.A., 1991-95; asst. prof. clin. surgery and family medicine U. So. Calif., L.A., 1995—, phys. asst. in cardiothoracic surgery, 1995—. Vis. surg. instr., China; examiner Nat. Commn. on Cert. of Physician Assts., 1981—92; mem. program planning com. Masters Degree program in Health Sci. for Physician Assts., Calif. State U., Dominguez Hill, 1991—95; adj. faculty physician asst. program U. So. Calif., 1982—90, mem. adv. com., 1983—84, mem. long-range planning com., 1988—90, spkr., cons., expert witness in field; contbr. numerous color photographic images The Green Berets: Weapons and Equipment (Hans Halberstadt), 1989; bd. dirs. TV Parade Mag., 1991—2001. Contbr. articles to profl. jours. and chpts. to books; mem. editl. bd. Clinician Reviews, 1990-96, Physician Asst. Jour., 1987-90; med. tech. advisor, appeared in (feature film) City of Angles, TV program on History Channel. Instr. ACLS, Am. Heart Assn., 1980-96. With Spl. Forces, U.S. Army, 1964-70; with Calif. Army N.G., 1976-83, U.S. Army Res., 1984-91. Recipient 21 mil. decorations, including awards from U.S., Vietnam, Thailand, Outstanding Svc. award Physician Asst. Jour., 1989. Fellow Soc. Critical Care Medicine (bd. dirs. Calif. chpt. 1995), Am. Acad. Physician Assts. (ho. of dels. 1982-87, vice chair surg. coun. 1985-87, conf. planning com. 1986-88, vets. caucus chair 1986-88, advisor to bd. dirs. 1989-91), Calif. Acad. Physician Assts. (chmn. govt. affairs 1984-86, pres. 1985, Presdl. Leadership award 1986, 88), Am. Assn. Surgeons Assts. (v.p. 1988), Assn. Physician Assts. Cardiovascular Surgery (pres. 1989-91), Mil. Order World Wars, Mil. Surgeons of the U.S., VFW, Spl. Forces Assn., Spl. Ops. Assn. Republican. Buddhist. Avocations: photo journalism, running, military history. Office: Cardiothoracic Surgeons Inc 50 Bellefontaine St Ste 403 Pasadena CA 91105 Home: 24 Country Ridge Rd Pomona CA 91766-4815

HOLMES, LU ANN, interior designer, sales representative; b. Richmond, Ky., Aug. 10, 1956; d. Ernest Lee and Clara Adelaine (Showalter) H. BA with high distinction, U. Ky., 1979; MBA, U. Pitts., 1986. Designer Garrison Brewer Co., Marietta, Ohio, 1979-82; sr. designer Thomas Interior Systems, Chgo., 1982-83; design mgr. Franklin Interiors, Pitts., 1983-85, account rep., 1985-88, account mgr., 1989-94; sr. territory mgr. Haworth, Pitts. and Cin., 1994—. Mem. Jr.

League Pitts., 1984—; vol. North Hills Affordable Housing, Art of the Eye, Phillipi Project, Pitts. Zoo Centennial Celebration, Children's Home of Pitts., ATP Tennis, Cin.; mem. No. Ky. Leadership Class 2003. Recipient Am. Soc. Interior Designers Medalist award, 1997, Haworth Pinnacle award, 1996; named to Pittsburgh's Fifty Finest by Cystic Fibrosis Found., Ky. Col., 2003. Mem. AIA (affiliate), Internat. Facilities Mgrs. Assn., Internat. Interior Design Assn., Am. Soc. Interior Designers (membership chmn. 1986-88, bd. dirs. 1986-94, Presdl. citation 1986, chpt. pres. 1993, nat. bd. dirs. 1994-96, industry adv. coun. co-chair 1995-98), Ky. Cols. Avocations: tennis, reading, international travel. Home: 1029 Rose Cir Park Hills KY 41011-1924

HOLMES, MELVIN ALMONT, insurance company executive; b. West New York, N.J., Jan. 2, 1919; s. Edward L. and Sarah J. (Brown) H.; m. Clare G. White, May 30, 1943; children: Clare Ann, Karen, Joan, Patricia, Catherine, Donald, Jacqueline. Student in bus. adminstrn., NYU; L.H.D. (hon.), Coll. of Ins., 1976. C.P.C.U., 1955. With Frank B. Hall & Co., Inc., Briarcliff Manor, N.Y., 1937-84, asst. mgr. liability dept., 1945-52, asst. v.p., 1952-56, v.p., 1956-68, chief exec. officer, pres., 1968-73, vice chmn., 1973-79, cons., dir., 1979-84. Chmn. bd. trustees Coll. of Ins., 1974-76 Hon. trustee Valley Hosp., Ridgewood, N.J. Served to capt. C.E., U.S. Army, 1941-46. Recipient Good Scout award Boy Scouts Am., 1975; Free Enterprise award Ins. Fedn. N.Y., 1975 Mem. Nat. Assn. Ins. Brokers (past pres.), Ins. Soc. N.Y., Soc. C.P.C.U.s (Eugene A. Toale Meml. award 1976), Ins. Inst. Am., Am. Inst. Property and Liability Underwriters Inc. (past trustee), Ins. Fedn. N.Y. (past pres.) Clubs: Tequesta Country. Home: 605 Universe Blvd Apt T100 Juno Beach FL 33408-2449

HOLMES, MICHAEL GENE, lawyer; b. Longview, Wash., Jan. 14, 1937; s. Robert A. and Esther S. Holmes; children: Helen, Peyton Robert. AB in Econs., Stanford U., 1958, JD, 1960. Bar: Oreg. 1961, U.S. Dist. Ct. Oreg. 1961, U.S. Ct. Appeals (9th cir.) 1961, Temp. Emergency Ct. Appeals 1976, U.S. Supreme Ct. 1976. Assoc. Spears, Lubersky, Bledsoe, Anderson, Young & Hilliard, Portland, 1961-67, ptnr., 1967-90, Lane Powell Spears Lubersky, Portland, 1990-95, of counsel, 1995. Mem. Oreg. Joint Com. of Bar, Press & Broadcasters, 1982-85, sec., 1983-84, chmn. 1985. Author Survey of Oregon Defamation and Privacy Law, ann., 1982-95. Trustee Med. Rsch. Found. Oreg., Portland, 1985-94, exec. com., 1986-94; hon. trustee Oreg. Health Scis. Found., 1995—; trustee Portland Civic Theatre, 1962-66. Mem. Oreg. Bar Assn., Phi Beta Kappa.

HOLMES, MICHAEL L. career officer; m. Viola Holmes; children: Jared, Justin, Michael Jason. Diploma in Math., Pembroke State U., 1972. Commd. ensign USN, 1973, advanced through ranks to rear adm.; various assignments to aircraft comdr. Patrol Squadron 24, Jacksonville; comdr. Patrol Wings, U.S. Pacific Fleet, Pearl Harbor, Hawaii. Office: PSC 817 Box 2 Fpo AE 09622-0002 E-mail: mlholmes@aol.com.

HOLMES, MIRIAM H. publisher; b. Bavaria, Germany, June 2, 1951; came to U.S., 1952; d. Max J. and Mala (Rosenwasser) H.; m. Stephen H. Gelb, June 25, 1995. BA, Queens Coll., 1972; JD, Yeshiva U., 1987. Bar: N.Y. 1988. Pres. Holmes & Meier Pub., N.Y.C., 1990—. Mem. Assn. Jewish Book Coun. (exec. com.), Pubs. Mktg. Assn. Office: East Bldg 160 Broadway New York NY 10038-4201

HOLMES, NANCY ELIZABETH, pediatrician; b. St. Louis, Aug. 3, 1950; d. David Reed and Phyllis Anne (Hunger) Holmes; m. Arthur Erwin Kramer, May 15, 1976; children: Melanie Elizabeth Kramer, Carl Edward Kramer. BA in Psychology, U. Kans., 1972; MD, U. Mo., 1976. Diplomate Am. Acad. Pediatrics. Intern., resident in pediatrics St. Louis Children's Hosp., Washington U., St. Louis, 1976-81; pediatrician Ctrl. Pediatrics, St. Louis, 1981—. Sch. physician Sch. Dist. Clayton, Mo., 1985—92; assoc. prof. clin. pediats. Washington U., St. Louis, 1993—2000, assoc. prof., 2000—; cons. 1st Congregational Preschool, Clayton, 1984—86, Jewish Hosp. Daycare Ctr., St. Louis, 1993—97, Flynn Park EArly Edn. Ctr., University City, Mo., 1994—; cmty. outpatient experience Preceptor Hosp., St. Louis Children's Hosp., 1991—93, 1994—; mem. med. exec. com. St. Louis Children's Hosp., 1992—94. Vol. reading tutor Flynn Park Sch., University City, 1992—98, cub scout leader, 1993—98; mem. com. Troop 493 Boy Scouts Am., 2000—; elder Trinity Presbyn. Ch., University City, 1989—92, 1996—2001; bd. dirs. Children's Hosp. Care Group. Fellow Am. Acad. Pediatrics; mem. AMA, Mo. State Med. Assn., St. Louis Metro. Med. Soc, St. Louis Pediatric Soc. Presbyterian. Avocations: reading, gardening, photography, travel. Office: Ctrl Pediatrics Inc 8888 Ladue Rd Ste 130 Saint Louis MO 63124-2056

HOLMES, PAUL KINLOCH, III, former prosecutor; b. Newport, Ark., Nov. 10, 1951; s. Paul K. Jr. and Virginia (Harrison) H.; m. Katherine Hewitt, July 28, 1978; children: Christopher, Stephen. BA, Westminster Coll., 1973; JD, U. Ark., Fayetteville, 1978. Bar: Ark. 1978. Ptnr. Warner & Smith Attys. at Law, Ft. Smith, Ark., 1978-93; U.S. atty. Western Dist. Ark., Ft. Smith, Ark., 1993—2001.

HOLMES, PAUL LUTHER, political scientist, educational consultant; b. Rock Island, Ill., Mar. 7, 1919; s. Bernt Gunnar and Amanda Sophia (Swenson) H.; m. Ardis Ann Grunditz, Nov. 1, 1946; children: Mary Ann, David Stephen. BA, U. Minn., 1940; MA, Stanford U., 1949, George Washington U., 1964; EdD, Stanford U., 1968. Career officer USN, 1941-64, ret. at capt.; adminstr. Laney Coll., Oakland, Calif., 1965-70; dean Contra Costa Coll., San Pablo, Calif., 1970-71; pres. Coll. Alameda (Calif.), 1971-75, prof. polit. sci., 1975-80; dir. doctoral studies program Nova U., No. Calif., 1975-80. Cons. higher edn. Gig Harbor, Wash., 1981—; regent Calif. Luth. U., 1973-76. Decorated with medals. Mem. Stanford U. Alumni Assn., Rotary, Phi Delta Kappa. Lutheran.

HOLMES, PRIEST, football player; b. Fort Smith, Ark., Oct. 7, 1973; children: De'Andre, Jekovan. Postgrad in sport mgmt., Univ. Texas. Running back Kans. City Chiefs, 2001—, Balt. Ravens, 1997—2001; winner Super Bowl 35, 2001. Spokesperson Md. Dept. Edn. Gear Up Program; contbr. Dr. Ben Carson Scholarship Fund; spkr. Ray Kroc youth achievement awards McDonald's Corp.; spokesperson McDonald House Charities; mem. Fellowship Christian Athletes; spkr. Youth Explosion, 2000; contbr. Children's Miracle Net.; spkr. Urban Youth Min. Office: 1 Arrowhead Dr Kansas City MO 64129

HOLMES, RANDALL KENT, microbiology educator, physician, university administrator; b. Muskegon, Mich., Nov. 7, 1940; s. Scott Travis and Helen Marie (Rosell) H.; m. Kathryn Louise Voelker, June 16, 1962; children: Rebecca Kathryn, Elisabeth Marie. AB, Harvard U., 1962; MD, PhD in Microbiology, NYU, 1968. Diplomate Am. Bd. Internal Medicine, Am. Bd. Infectious Diseases. Intern, then resident Beth Israel Hosp., Boston, 1968-70; research assoc. NIH, Bethesda, Md., 1970-72; instr. medicine U. Tex. Southwestern Med. Sch., Dallas, 1972-73, asst. prof., 1973-75, assoc. prof., 1975-76; prof., chmn. microbiology and immunology Uniformed Services U. Health Scis., Bethesda, 1976-95, assoc. dean for acad. affairs, 1984-93, acting chmn. biochemistry, 1993-95; prof., chmn. microbiology U. Colo. Sch. Medicine, Denver, 1995—. Adv. com. vaccines and related biol. products Nat. Ctr. for Drugs and Biologics, Bethesda, 1983-87; cholera panel NIH, 1987-92, bacteriology and mycology 1 study sect., 1993-95, microbiology and infectious disease rsch. com., 2000-03, chair, 2003—; chair VA-DOD Rsch. Program on Mechs. of Emerging Pathogens Rev. Panel, 1997; steering com. postdoc. rsch. assoc. program in infectious diseases and pub. health microbiology ASM/Nat. Ctr. for Infectious Disease, 1993-95, chair, 1996-2002. Contbr. articles to profl. jours. Served to surgeon USPHS, 1968-70. Recipient Research Career Devel. award NIH, 1975-76. Fellow ACP, Infectious Diseases Soc. Am.; mem. Am. Acad. Microbiology (bd. govs. 1992-95, com. on awards 1995-2001, chair 2002—), Am. Soc. for Clin. Investigation, Am. Soc. for Microbiology (editl. bd. Infection and Immunity 1978-86, Microbiol. Revs. 1983-88), Nat. Bd. Med. Examiners (mem. microbiology test com. 1984-86, chair 1987-93, mem. U.S. med. licensing exam. step I com. 1990-92, mem. U.S. med. licensing exam. composite com. 1992-95), Coun. Acad. Socs. of Assn. Am. Med. Colls., Phi Beta Kappa, Alpha Omega Alpha. Republican. Avocations: reading, hiking, camping, swimming. Office: U Colo Health Scis Ctr Dept Microbiology PO Box B175 Denver CO 80262-0001

HOLMES, RICHARD ALBERT, software engineer, consultant; b. Santa Barbara, Calif., May 7, 1958; m. Janet M. Dunbar; children: Brian D., Kevin M. AA in Music summa cum laude, City Coll. San Francisco, 1987; BS in Computer Sci. summa cum laude, Nat. U., 1991; postgrad., Stanford U., 1993—. Ind. software cons., San Francisco, 1986-88; software quality assurance contractor Oxford & Assocs., Mountain View, Calif., 1988-89; microkernel diagnostics engr. Apple Computer, Cupertino, Calif., 1990-93, file system engr., 1994-96; operating sys. engr. Hewlett Packard, Cupertino, Calif., 1996-99; staff engr. Veritas, Mountain View, Calif., 1999—2001; mgr. Amberlight Acad. Music, Colleyville, Tex., 2001—, CCSF tchr. & faculty scholar, 1986, 87, Alpha Gamma Sigma scholar, 1987. Mem. IEEE, Assn. for Computing Machinery, Alpha Gamma Sigma (treas. 1986-87). Avocations: playing classical guitar, gem & mineral collecting, computer music and sound generation, music improvisation and composition.

HOLMES, RICHARD BROOKS, mathematical physicist; b. Milw., Jan. 7, 1959; s. Emerson Brooks Holmes and Nancy Anne Schaffter; m. Sandra Lynn Wong, June 27, 1998. BS, Calif. Inst. Tech., 1981; MS, Stanford (Calif.) U., 1983. Sr. sys. analyst Comptek Rsch., Vallejo, Calif., 1982-83; staff scientist Western Rsch., Arlington, Va., 1983-85; sr. scientist AVCO Everett (Mass.) Rsch. Lab., 1985-88; prin. rsch. scientist North East Rsch. Assocs., Woburn, Mass., 1988-90; sr. mem. tech. staff Rocketdyne divsn. Rockwell Internat., Canoga Park, Calif., 1990-95; sr. staff scientist Lockheed Martin Rsch. Labs., Palo Alto, Calif., 1995-98; pres. Nutronics, Inc., Carson City, Nev., 1998—, Gen. Nutronics, Inc., Milpitas, Calif., 2001—. Cons. North East Rsch. Assocs., 1990. Contbr. Matched Asymptotic Expansions, 1988; contbr. articles to Phys. Rev. Letters, Phys. Rev., Jour. of the Optical Soc. Am. and IEEE Jour. of Quantum Electronics. Mem. No. Calif. Scholarship Founds., Oakland, 1977; mem. Wilderness Soc., Washington, 1989. Stanford fellow Stanford U., 1982; fellow MIT, 1990; recipient Presdl. Medal of Merit, 1992. Mem. AAAS, SPIE (conf. organizer 1995—), Am. Phys. Soc., Optical Soc. Am. Achievements include patents for means for photonic communication, computation, and distortion compensation; discovery of spin-two phonons. Office: Gen Nutronics Inc 230 Caribbean Drive Sunnyvale CA 94089

HOLMES, RICHARD DALE, history consultant; b. Sandown, N.H., Sept. 6, 1945; s. John B. Jr. and Marjorie A. (Andrews) H.; m. Carol A. Martineau, Dec. 19, 1970; children: John B. III, Leah K. BEd, Keene (N.H.) State Coll., 1968; MA, Rivier Coll., Nashua, N.H., 1980. Cert. tchr., N.H. Tchr. social studies Pelham (N.H.) Meml. Sch., 1968-2000, chmn. dept., 1975-2000. Hist. cons., rschr. Sandown Mus., 1980-88, Chester (N.H.) Hist. Soc., 1989—. Author: View from Meeting House Hill, 1988, Derry, 1995, Chester Revisited, 1997. Pres. Old Meeting House Assn., Sandown, 1987—; dir. Derry Mus., 2001—; mem. Derry Hist. Dist. Commn., 1988—, chmn. 1998—. With U.S. Army, 1969-71, Vietnam. Decorated Cross of Gallantry with palm, Civic Action medal 1st class (Vietnam). Mem.: NEA, Derry Hist. Soc., Sandown Hist. Assn. (hist. cons., rschr. 1980—88, pres. 1986—87), N.H. Hist. Soc., Pelham Edn. Assn. (v.p. 1976—77), N.H. Guide Dog Users Assn., Nat. Fedn. Blind. Congregationalist. Avocations: collecting books, public speaking, research. Home: 33 Hillside Ave Derry NH 03038-2215 Office: Town Hall 48 E Broadway Derry NH 03038 Fax: 603-432-6131. E-mail: rholmes33@comcast.net.

HOLMES, ROBERT ALEXANDER, state legislator; b. Shepherstown, W.Va., July 13, 1943; s. Clarence and Priscilla H.; div.; children: Donna Lee Vaughn, Darlene Marie Jackson, Robert A., Jr. BS in Polit. Sci., Shepherd Coll., 1964; MA in Pub. Law and Govt., Columbia U., 1966, PhD in Polit. Sci., 1969. Dir. summer studies program Harvard-Yale-Columbia, 1968-69; assoc. prof. So. Univ., 1969-70; dir. SEEK CUNY, 1970-71; prof. Atlanta U., 1971—, dir. Ctr. Studies Pub. Policy, 1989—; mem. Ga. Ho. of Reps., Atlanta, 1974—, chmn. edn. com., mem. appropriations, rules coms. Bd. dirs. Capital City Bank and Trust; past pres. Rsch. Atlanta, Inc. Author, co-author over 25 monographs and books; contbr. over 70 articles to profl. jours. Chmn. bd. dirs. JOMANDI Theater Co., Sickle Cell Found., Metro-Atlanta YMCA; pres. S. Fulton Running Ptnrs. Named Outstanding Young Man of Yr., Atlanta Jaycees, Layman of Yr., Metro Atlanta YMCA, Vol. of Yr., S.W. Atlanta YMCA, Legis. of Yr., Am. Assn. Adult Educators, Ga. Environ. Coun., Lobbying Network Hall of Fame, Atlanta NAACP; recipient Legis. Svcs. award Ga. Mcpl. Assn., Tchg. Excellence award Amoco Found., Torchbearer award Sickle Cell Found., Cmty. Svc. award Fannie Lou Hamer. Fellow Joint Ctr. Polit. Studies (adj.); mem. Nat. Conf. Black Polit. Scientists (pres. 1973-74), Assn. Social Behavioral Scientists (pres. 1976-77), (Am. Polit. Sci. Assn. (exec. com. 2000-02). Office: State Capitol Rm 226 Atlanta GA 30334 also: PO Box 110009 Atlanta GA 30311-0909 also: Clark-Atlanta U So Ctr Studies Pub Policy 223 James P Brawley Dr Atlanta GA 30314 E-mail: bholmes@cau.edu.

HOLMES, ROBERT EUGENE, legislative staff member, journalist; b. Shelbyville, Ind., June 5, 1928; s. Eugene Lowell and Sarah Lucinda (Hughes) H.; m. Retha Carolyn Richey, June 27, 1955 (div. Sept. 1966); children: Enid Adair Offley, William Houstoun (dec.), Holly Ann Holmes. BA in Polit. Sci., DePauw U., 1950; MA in Journalism, Ind. U., 1953; MA in Communs. and Urban Affairs, Stanford U., 1976. Staff reporter Elkhart, Ind. Truth, 1954-57; city editor, investigative editor Press-Enterprise, Riverside, Calif., 1957-70; sr. cons. Calif. State Senate Dem. Caucus, Sacramento, 1971-74, dep. dir., 1978-79; press sec. Lt. Gov. of Calif., Sacramento, 1975-77; project dir. Border Area Devel. Study, U.S. Econ. Devel. Adminstrn., Sacramento, 1978; staff dep. dir. Calif. Senator Robert Presley, Sacramento, 1979-83; chief cons. Joint Legis. Ethics Com., Calif. Legislature, Sacramento, 1981-82; staff dir. Joint Com. on Prison Constrn. and Ops., Calif. Legislature, Sacramento, 1983-94. Rsch. cons. Calif. Rsch. Bur., Calif. State Libr., Sacramento, 1991-92; cons. Calif. Hist. State Capitol Commn., 1995-96. Author, editor rschr. legis. reports; contbg. editor creative writing quar. Noah's Hotel, Inverness, Calif., 1991—; editor/pub. sports newsletter weekly Big Red Ramblings, 1997-2001; contbr. articles to mags., short stories, 1961—. Pres., Golden Bear Dem. Club, Sacramento, 1972-74; media dir. Lt. Gov. Campaign, Sacramento and L.A., 1974. Sgt. USMC, 1952-53. Recipient Silver Gavel award ABA, 1969, 1st Place media award Calif. State Bar Assn., 1968, 1st Place award Calif. Newspaper Pubs. Assn. Best Series, 1969, 70, 71; Am. Polit. Sci. Assn. Ford Found. fellow Stanford U., 1970, Jack Anderson award for excellence in journalism Calif. Correctional Peace Officers Assn., 1993. Mem. NAACP, ACLU, Calif. Writers Club, Common Cause. Democrat. Avocations: bicycling, tennis, world travel, short story writing. Home: 416 Florin Rd Sacramento CA 95831-2007

HOLMES, ROBERT M. minister, counselor, educator; b. Mitchell, S. Dak., May 4, 1925; s. Merrill Jacob and Carrie Rowena (McFadon) Holmes; m. Pauline Leigh Mudge, Aug. 31, 1951; children: Stephen Merrill, Tim Edmund, Krys Leigh. BA, Illinois Wesleyan U, Bloomington, Ill, 1948; MDiv, Garrett Evangelical Sem., Evanston, Ill, 1951; MA, Northwestern U, Evanston, Ill, 1956; ThD, Pacific Sch./ Rel., Berkeley, Calif., 1965. Min. to mil. pers. First Meth. Ch., Rapid City, SD, 1951—53; pastor United Meth. Ch., Canyon Lake, Rapid City, SD, 1953—61; chaplain, asst. prof Rocky Mountain Coll., Billings, Mont., 1965—81; pastor St. Paul's United Meth. Ch., Helena, Mont., 1981—88; instr., part time Pacific Sch. of Religion, Stockton, Calif., 1962—64. Chaplain (vol) Helena Police Dept., Helena, Mont., 1986—, Sherrif Dept., Lewis and Clark County, Helena, Mont., 1986—; preacher Nat. Protestant Hour, Atlanta, 1986, Atlanta, 2002. Author: (book) The Academic Mysteryhouse", 1970, (book of sermons) Why Jesus Never Had Ulcers, 1986. Lt. (JG) USN, 1943—46, Pacific. Recipient Angel Award, Religion in Media, for Protestant Hour Series, 1986—87, Francis Asbury Award, United Meth. Ch. (higher ed.), 1999. Home: 822 Breckenridge Helena MT 59601

HOLMES, ROSCETTE YVONNE LEWIS, organizational development and training consultant; b. Portland, Oreg., Dec. 1, 1944; d. Roscoe Warfield and Burnadine (Langston) Lewis; m. Johnny Mason Holmes, Jr., July 28, 1971; children: Roderick Earl, Andriette Yvonne. BS, Tex. So. U., 1965, MS, 1970, EdD, 1991; postgrad., U. Houston, 1979. Cert. in adminstrn. and supervision; cert. family, civil and adolescent mediator. With Houston Ind. Sch. Dist., 1965-96, sch. tchr. E.O. Smith Jr. H.S., 1965-69, tchr. biology, coord. sch. sci. fair Madison Sr. H.S., 1970-74, mem. sci. content team Emergency Sch. Aid Act, 1974-76, staff. devel. specialist for tchr. tng., 1976-78, instrnl. specialist for sci. Area I, 1978-81, asst. prin. Hogg Mid. Sch., 1981-84, dir. chpt. I, 1984-90, asst. prin. Fleming Fine Arts Mid. Sch., 1990-96; owner, pres., CEO (tng. and orgnl. devel. consulting firm) Roscette's Diversified Svcs. and Assocs., Houston, 1996—; dir. field experiences, dir. student tchg. Tex. So. U., 1998—. Cons. Prairie View, Tchr. Corp, Peace Corps, 1976-78; cons. Ednl. Leadership Inst., Prescription Learning Inc.; endl. cons. North Forest Ind. Sch. Dist.; mem. Tex. adv. coun. Dept. Human Resources Adv. Bd., Tex., vice chair Tex. Adv. Coun. Social Work Cert. NSF grantee, 1968-70. Mem. ASCD, Houston Profl. Adminstrs., Experiment in Internat. Living, Top Ladies of Distinction Inc., Delta Sigma Theta (voter registration, Sch. After Sch. Project, hypertension screening, v.p., dean of probates 1967, v.p. 1980-81, pres. Suburban Houston-Ft. Bend Alumnae chpt. 1981-83, nat. membership intake trainer, nat. scholarship and standards com. 1997-2001), Phi Delta Kappa. Democrat. Episcopalian. Address: RDS & Assocs Orgnl Devel and Tng Cons 7919 Oakington Dr Ste D Houston TX 77071-2018 E-mail: rdsa@houston.rr.com.

HOLMES, SUSAN G. educator; b. Kansas City, Mo., Mar. 7, 1955; d. Burton E. and Gloria A. (Spencer) H. BA, U. Kans., Lawrence, 1980. Cert. music therapy, education. Tchr. Dade County Schs., Miami, Fla.; music therapist, tchr. ESOL Miami, Fla.; tchr., music therapist The Palace Retirement Cmty.; tchr. ESOL Miami-Palmetto (Fla.) Adult Edn. Ctr., Korean cmty., Miami, Fla.; instr. writing lab. Miami Dade C.C., Miami, Fla. Tchr. ESOL to newly-arrived immigrants. Recipient Honor for TV series CBS News. Mem. Nat. Orgn. for Exec. Women. Avocations: writing, music composition.

HOLMES, SUZANNE MCRAE, nursing supervisor; b. Birmingham, Ala., June 23, 1952; d. Paul Bickman and Mabel E. (Tyler) McRae; m. Bryan Thomas Holmes, Jan. 14, 1989; 1 child, Meredith Rae. ADN, Jefferson State Coll., Birmingham, 1988. RN, Ala.; cert. BCLS instr.; cert. asthma educator, Am. Lung Assn.; ACLS. Staff nurse burn unit The Children's Hosp., Birmingham, 1988-89; staff nurse dept. medicine The Kirklin Clinic at U. Ala.-Birmingham, 1989-90, head nurse gen. medicine clinic, 1990-91, head nurse allergy clinic, 1991—. Facilitator and spkr. on nursing at asthma workshops Aventis Pharms., Collegeville, Pa., 1994—; mem. faculty Genecom, N.Y.C., 1994—; operator 1-800 Allergy Info. Svc., 1991—92. Editor Allergy Update, 1991-92. Leader Girl Scouts Am. Mem. Am. Coll. Allergy and Immunology, Am. Acad. Allergy, Asthma and Immunology,mem. Am. Lung Assn. (cert. asthma educator), Asthma and Allergy Found. Am. (charter bd. dirs. Ala. chpt.), Assn. Asthma Educators. Methodist. Avocations: baking, sewing, gardening. Office: The Kirklin Clinic Allergy Clinic 4th Fl 2000 6th Ave S Birmingham AL 35233-2110

HOLMES, SVEN ERIK, federal judge, educator; b. Grand Junction, Colo., Feb. 13, 1951; s. Clifford Newton and Ruth (Bradley) H.; m. Lois Romano, Oct. 31, 1983; children: Kristen Elizabeth Romano, Virginia Morgan Romano. AB, Harvard U., 1973; JD, U. Va., 1980; LLM, Georgetown U., 1987. Bar: Okla. 1980, D.C. 1985, U.S. Dist. Ct. D.C. 1985, U.S. Dist. Ct. (no., ea. and we. dists.) Okla. 1985, U.S. Ct. Appeals (10th and D.C. cirs.) 1985, U.S. Tax Ct. 1985, U.S. Ct. Claims 1985, U.S. Supreme Ct., 1994. Campaign coord. David L. Boren for Gov., Oklahoma City, 1975; adminstrv. asst. to gov. State of Okla., Oklahoma City, 1975-77; law clk. to judge U.S. Dist. Ct. (no. dist.) Okla., Tulsa, 1980-81; assoc. Doerner, Stuart, Saunders, Daniel & Anderson, Tulsa, 1981-83; exec. dir. Dems. for "80's", Washington, 1983-85; from assoc. to ptnr. Williams & Connolly, Washington, 1985-87, 89-95; designated liaison staff mem. Senate Select Com. on Secret Mil. Assistance to Iran, Washington, 1987; gen. counsel, staff dir. Senate Select Com. on Intelligence, Washington, 1987-89; U.S. dist. judge U.S. Dist. Ct.for No. Dist. Okla., Tulsa, 1995—. V.p. Balt. Orioles, 1989-93; adj. prof. constl. law U. Tulsa Sch. Law. Mem. Okla. Bar Assn., D.C. Bar Assn. Lutheran. Avocations: reading, tennis. Office: US Dist Ct 411 US Courthouse 333 W 4th St Tulsa OK 74103-3839

HOLMES, THOMAS J. economist, educator; b. Abington, Pa., Nov. 16, 1959; married. PhD, Northwestern U., 1985. Economist Fed. Res. Bank Mpls., 1993—95; prof. U. Minn., Mpls., 1995—. Asst. prof. U. Wis., Madison. Office: Univ Minn Dept Econ 1035 Heller Hall 271 19th Ave S Minneapolis MN 55455

HOLMES MARTIN, NORMA ANNE, electronic and computer consultant, web site designer, writer; b. Long Branch, NJ, May 19, 1948; d. George Washington Holmes and Lillian Dove Wall; m. Jimmie Lee Martin (dec. June 21, 1990); children: Karen Martin, Cynthia Bridges. Bookkeeping cert., Cert. Edn. Tng. Assn., Little Silver, New Jersey, 1978—78; Electronic Technician Class B Cert., Intco Telecom., Asbury Park, New Jersey, 1978—79; ASE refrigerant and recovery certification, ASE, automotive services edn., 1995—95; VCR Repair Technician Diploma, PCDI, Profl. Career Devel. Inst., Norcross, Georgia, 1996—97; Digital Electronic Systems, Computer Sci., Brookdale C.C., Lincroft, New Jersey, 1975—80; Electrician trades helper elec., Port Authority of NY and NJ., La Guardia Airport, 1980—80; Automotive Auto Parts Counterperson cert., Advance Auto Parts Stores, 3020 Jefferson Davis Highway, Richmond Virginia, 1988—88; Automotive Asst. Store Mgr. Cert., Advance Auto Parts Stores, 3020 Jefferson Davis Highway, Richmond, Virginia, 1988—89. Cert. Automotive Master Parts Specialist, AC Delco Corp. 1992, Michelin Tire Specialist 1996, Electronic Technician Class B 1979, VCR Repair Technician 1997, Cert. Edn. Tng. Assn N.J., 1978, MVAC 1995. Electronic tester ASE Atlantic Semi-Conductor, Asbury Park, NJ, 1967—69; hotwalker Monmouth Pk. Race Track, James Bowes Bond, trainer, NJ, 1975—80; electronic technician class b Intco Telecom., Asbury Park, 1978—80; electrician trades helper Port Authority of NY and NJ, 1980—82; cable tv sales rep., ind. contractor Ultracom Telco Cablevision, NJ, 1983—84; sales rep., ind. contractor Harte Hanks Cable TV, NJ, 1984—86; electronic technician, bench technician United Telecontrol Electronics, Asbury Park, NJ, 1986—88; sales, auto parts counterperson, asst. store mgr. Advance Auto Parts Stores, Richmond, Va., 1988—90; draftsperson Continental Cablevision, Mechanicsville, Va., 1990; electromechanical technician on donations Goodwill Industries, Richmond, Va., 1990—90; auto parts counterperson and svc. writer Western Auto Stores, Richmond and Norfolk, Va., 1992—92; pres. Norma Martin a Home Electronics Cons., Richmond, Va., 1992—93; parts counterperson and warehouse receiving VASCO, Va. Automotive Svc. Corp., Richmond, Va., 1993—97; website designer, marketer Norma Holmes Martin A Name Worth Remembering, Richmond, Va., 1999—2002, pres. electronic and computer cons., 2001—02, broadcaster, writer, talk show host and co-producer wale 990 am, 2001—01; broadcaster, talk show host, talk jockey, prodr., writer, TJ Norma Holmes Martin Show, A Name Worth Remembering, Richmond, Va., 2001—02. Composer: For A Love That's Killing Me Each Day, 1993; author: (book) Ghostwriters Your Name is Not Important, Just Your Number, 2000, LBC #001 Hanging Over My Head Like a Dark Cloud, 1998, Norma #9's Lucky Number Strategies-Getting Back to Basics, 1995, (literary work, nonfiction manuscript) My Heart is heavy, 2001, (literary work,science-fiction manuscript) Carrier Frequency, 2001; contbr. collection of non-fiction literary works; composer: (song lyrics and melodies) Collection NAHM1994, 5 parts, 1994, (song lyrics) Collection of 1994, 5 parts, 1994; author: (manuscript fiction, and instruct manual) Collection 2000, Psychological Rape, and Brachet, an art worth learning, 2000, instructional booklets and cassettes. Vol. electrician and overall helper Richmond Habitat for Humanities, Richmond, 1999—2002; vol. seamstress Hosp. Hospitality Ho. of Richmond, 1999—2002; automotive mechanic The LDS Ch., Richmond, 1999; campaign hdqs. vol. Dem. Party for Dwight C. Jones, Richmond, 1997. Recipient Editor Choice award, The Nat. Libr. of Poetry, 1995,1996,1997, Inducted in the Internat. Poetry Hall of Fame, 1997, 20th Century Award for Achievement in Humanity and Applied Sci., Internat. Biog. Ctr., Cambridge Eng., 1998. Mem.: Va. Orgn. of Composers and Lyricists, Internat. Soc. of Poets (life), The LDS Ch. (life; relief soc. tchr. 1998—99, relief soc. pres. 1999—99). Lds, Endowed Sister Of The Church Of Jesus Christ Of Latter Day Saints. Avocations: antiques, writing, board games, movie memorabilia, travel. Home: 2000 Riverside Dr, 9H Richmond VA 23225 Office: A Name Worth Remembering 1915 Powell Road Richmond VA 23224 Personal E-mail: norma@nahm.tv. Business E-Mail: norma@nahm.tv.

HOLMGREN, JANET L, college president; b. Chgo., Dec. 1, 1948; d. Kenneth William and Virginia Ann (Rensink) H.; m. Gordon A. McKay, Sept. 7, 1968 (div. 1990); children: Elizabeth Jane, Ellen Katherine. BA in English summa cum laude, Oakland U., Rochester, Mich., 1968; MA in Linguistics, Princeton U., 1971, PhD in Linguistics, 1974. Asst. prof. English studies Federal City Coll. (now U. D.C.), Washington, 1972-76; asst. prof. English U. Md., College Park, 1976-82, asst. to chancellor, 1982-88; assoc. provost Princeton (N.J.) U., 1988-90, vice-provost, 1990-91; pres. Mills Coll., Oakland, Calif., 1991—. Mem. external adv. bd. English dept. Princeton U. Bay Area Biosci. Ctr. Author: (with Spencer Cosmos) The Story of English: Study Guide

and Reader, 1986, Narration and Discourse in American Realistic Fiction, 1982; contbr. articles to profl. jours. Faculty rsch. grantee U. Md., 1978; fellow NEH, 1978, Princeton U., 1968-69, 70-72, NSF, 1969-70; recipient summer study aid Linguistic Soc. Am., Ohio State U., 1970. Mem. Assn. Ind. Caif. Colls. and Univs. (exec. com.), Nat. Assn. Ind. Colls. and Univs., Am. Coun. on Education (chair office of women in higher edn.), Calif. Acad. Sci. (coun.). Democrat. Episcopal. Avocations: traveling, swimming, reading. Office: Mills Coll Office Pres 5000 Macarthur Blvd Oakland CA 94613-1301

HOLMGREN, MIKE, professional football coach; b. San Francisco, June 15, 1948; m. Kathy Holmgren; children: Gretchen, Emily, Jenny and Calla (twins). BS in Bus. Fin., U. So. Calif., 1970. Coach Lincoln High Sch., San Francisco, 1971-72, Sacred Heart High Sch., 1972-74, Oakgrove High Sch., 1975-80; quarterbacks coach, offensive coord. San Francisco State U., 1981-82; quarterbacks coach Brigham Young U., 1982-85, San Francisco 49ers, 1985-89, offensive coord., 1989-92; head coach Green Bay Packers, 1992-98, Seattle Seahawks, 1999—. Office: Seattle Seahawks Kingdome 11220 NE 53rd St Kirkland WA 98033-7595

HOLMGREN, MYRON ROGER, social sciences educator; b. Willmar, Minn., Mar. 19, 1933; s. Alfred and Cleora Victora (Scott) H.; m. Ellen Mary Shaheen, June 9, 1957; children: Brian, Mary Jo Haas. BA, Mankato State U., 1958; MA, No. Colo. State U., 1959. Instr. Grinnell (Iowa) H.S., 1959-62, Joliet (Ill.) Jr. Coll., 1962-66; instr., fin. advisor Am. Express Fin. Advisors, Joliet, 1966-72; instr. Benedictine Coll., Atchison, Kans., 1973, Moraine Valley C.C., Palos Hills, Ill., 1974-75, Minooka (Ill.) H.S., 1974-93, dept. chmn., 1984-87, dir., coach Scholastic Bowl Team, 1976-93. Local dir. Exrox Award in Humanities, 1988=93; chmn. philosophy and goals North Ctrl. Accreditation, 1987-88. Author: Profitable Pricing Techniques, 1973; contbr. articles to profl. jours. Block chmn. March of Dimes, Am. Cancer Soc., 1989, 92-93; treas. bd. dirs. The Family Counseling Agy. of Will and Grundy Counties, 1996-99. Asian Found. grant, 1962. Mem. Internat. Platform Assn. Republican. Episcopalian. Avocations: reading, writing, travel, gourmet cooking, market analysis. Home: 1314 Douglas St Joliet IL 60435-5814

HOLMQUEST, DONALD LEE, physician, astronaut, lawyer; b. Dallas, Apr. 7, 1939; s. Sidney Browder and Lillie Mae (Waite) H.; m. Ann Nixon James, Oct. 24, 1972. BS in Elec. Engring., So. Meth. U., 1962; MD, Baylor U., 1967, PhD in Physiology, 1968; JD, U. Houston, 1980. Student engr. Ling-Temco-Vought, Dallas, 1958-61; electronics engr. Tex. Instruments, Inc., Dallas, 1962; intern Meth. Hosp., Houston, 1967-68; pilot tng. USAF, Williams AFB, Ariz., 1968-69; scientist-astronaut NASA, Houston, 1967-73; research assoc. MIT, 1968-70; asst. prof. radiology and physiology Baylor Coll. Medicine, 1970-73; dir. nuclear medicine Eisenhower Med. Ctr., Palm Desert, Calif., 1973-74; assoc. dean medicine, assoc. prof. Tex. A&M U., College Station, 1974-76; dir. nuclear medicine Navasota (Tex.) Med. Ctr., 1976-84, Med. Arts Hosp., Houston, 1977-85; ptnr. Wood Lucksinger & Epstein, Houston, 1980-91, Holmquest & Assocs., Houston, 1991—; v.p. legal affairs N.Am. Med. Mgmt., Inc., Nashville, 1995-96; practice leader profl. svcs. group McKesson Info. Solutions, San Francisco, 2002—. Asst. prof. internal medicine Baylor Coll. Medicine, Houston, 1999—. Contbr. articles to med. jours. Mem. Soc. Nuclear Medicine, Am. Coll. Nuclear Physicians, Tex. Bar Assn., Am. Fighter Pilots Assn., Sigma Xi, Alpha Omega Alpha, Sigma Tau. Home and Office: 229 Princeton Rd Menlo Park CA 94025-5217

HOLMQUIST, DARREL VERNON, geotechnical engineer; b. Worcester, Mass., Aug. 8, 1947; s. Vernon Henry and Virginia (Simpson) H. BS in Civil Engring. with honors, U. Tex., 1974, MS in Civil Engring., 1976. Registered profl. engr., Colo. Rsch. asst. U. Tex., Austin, 1973-76; project engr. CTL/Thompson Inc., Denver, 1976-78, project mgr., 1978-84, v.p., 1984-95, pres., 1995—2001, sr. prin. cons., 2001—. Mem. steering com. Rocky Mountain Asphalt User/Prodr. Group, 1991-96; rsch. com. Colo. Transp. Inst., 1992-95; com. mem. Transp. Rsch. Bd., Washington, 1990—. Author: Engineering and Design Manual for Disposal of Excess Spoil, 1982; contbr. articles to profl. jours. Mem. tech. adv. com. Jefferson County Expansive Soils Task Force, 1994-96; pres. Suburban Met. Dist., Denver, 1987—. With USNR, 1966-72. Named New Prin. of the Yr., Cons. Engrs. Coun. Colo., 1989; recipient Preston Millar award Am. Coun. Ind. Labs., 1990, Appreciation award City of Denver, 1994. Fellow Am. Cons. Engrs. Coun. (pres. nat. dir. 1991-96, Orley Phillips award 2000); mem. Am. Cons. Engrs. Coun. Colo. (Pres.'s award 1996), Am. Coun. Ind. Labs. (com. chair), Am. Arbitration Assn. (mediation com. 1995—), Phi Kappa Phi, Tau Beta Pi, Chi Epsilon. Avocations: scuba diving, woodworking, flying. Office: CTL/Thompson Inc 1971 W 12th Ave Denver CO 80204-3436

HOLMQUIST, JEFFERY R. retail executive; b. Park Ridge, Ill., June 12, 1961; s. Gene Edward and Virginia Lucille Holmquist; m. Lisa Sena, Mar. 21, 1987; children: Benjamin, Christine. BS in Accountancy, BS in Orgnl. Behavior, U. Ill., 1985; postgrad., U. Chgo., 2000—. Sys. analyst Sears Roebuck and Co., Chgo., 1985—, sr. sys. programmer, 1990, sys. cons. Hoffman Estates, Ill., 1991-92, quality mgr., 1993-94, strategic initiative mgr., 1995-97, strategic initiative dir., 1997—2000, dir. volunteerism, 1998, integration mgr., 2000—. Bd. dirs. Vol. Ctr., Barrington, Ill., 1999—2002. Mem.: Mensa. Avocations: travel, Tae Kwon Do. E-mail: jeffrholmquist@juno.com.

HOLMSTEAD, JEFFREY RALPH, federal agency administrator; b. American Fork, Utah, June 20, 1960; s. R. Kay and Mary L. (Gillison) H.; m. Elizabeth Tisdel, Aug. 17, 1985; children: Emily Kay, Eric Noble, Elizabeth Anne, Eli Jeffrey. BA, Brigham Young U., 1984; JD, Yale U., 1987. Bar: Pa. 1988, D.C. 1998. Jud. clk. to Hon. Douglas H. Ginsburg D.C. Cir. Ct. Appeals, Washington, 1987-88; assoc. Davis Polk & Wardwell, Washington, 1988-89; asst. counsel to Pres. of U.S. The White House, Washington, 1989-90, assoc. counsel, 1990-93; assoc. Latham & Watkins, Washington, 1993-95, ptnr., 1996—2001; asst. adminr. air and radiation EPA, Washington, 2001—. Republican. Mem. Lds Ch. Office: EPA Air and Radiation 1200 Pennsylvania Ave NW MC 6101A Washington DC 20460 Office Fax: 202-501-0986.

HOLNESS, GORDON VICTOR RIX, engineering executive, mechanical engineer; b. London, Sept. 6, 1939; came to U.S., 1969; s. Ernest Arthur and Ivy A. (Rix) H.; m. Susan F. Sage (dec.); m. Audrey A. Bezz, Apr. 18, 1984. Cert., Croydon Tech. Coll., Surrey, Eng., 1962; diploma in environ. engring., Nat. Coll., London, 1964. Registered profl. engr. Mich., Minn., Tex., Conn., Calif., Kans., Colo., Fla., Ariz., N.Y., D.C., Ala., N.C., Ky., Ohio, Mo., Tenn., Ill., Ont., Can. Design engr. West Sussex County Coun., Chichester, Sussex, Eng., 1956-59, C. McKechnie Jarvis & Ptnrs., London, 1959-64, Barlow Leslie & Ptnrs., Croydon, 1964; sr. engr. R. J. Tamblyn & Ptnrs., Toronto, Ont., Can., 1964-66; asst. chief engr. Giffels Assocs., Windsor, Ont., Can., 1966-69; from asst. chief engr. to chmn. and CEO, bd. dirs. Albert Kahn Assocs. Inc., Detroit, 1969—2001, also bd. dirs.; ret. chmn. emeritus, 2001. Contbr. articles to profl. jours. Bd. dirs. YMCA, Mt. Clemens, Mich., 1980-82; commr. Grosse Pointe Shores Planning Commn. Fellow ASHRAE (chmn. energy mgmt. com. 1987, chmn. govt. affairs com. 1989, bd. dirs. 2002); mem. NSPE, Am. Cons. Engrs. Coun., Chartered Inst. Bldg. Svcs. of Eng., Engring. Soc. Detroit, Mich. Soc. Profl. Engrs. (v.p. 1986, fellow 1998), Detroit Econ. Club (bd. dirs.). Republican. Presbyterian. Avocations: golf, tennis, racquetball, chess, sailing. Home: 55 S Edgewood Dr Grosse Pointe Shores MI 48236-1226 Office: Albert Kahn Assocs Inc 7430 2nd Ave Ste 800 Detroit MI 48202-2798 E-mail: gholness@comcast.net.

HOLONYAK, NICK, JR., electrical engineering educator; b. Zeigler, Ill., Nov. 3, 1928; s. Nick and Anna (Rosoha) Holonyak. BS, U. Ill., 1950, MS, 1951, PhD (Tex. Instruments fellow), 1954; DSc (hon.), Northwestern U., 1992; DEng. (hon.), Notre Dame U., 1994. Tech. staff Bell Telephone Labs., Murray Hill, NJ, 1954—55; physicist, unit mgr., mgr. advanced semiconductor lab. Gen. Electric Co., Syracuse, NY, 1957—63; prof. elec. engring. and materials research lab. U. Ill., Urbana, 1963—, John Bardeen chair prof. elec. & computer engring. & physics, 1993—; mem. Center Advanced Study, 1977—. Author (with others): Semiconductor Controlled Rectifiers, 1964, Physical Properties of Semiconductors, 1989. With U.S. Army, 1955—57. Recipient Cordiner award GE, 1962, John Scott medal, City of Phila., 1975, GaAs Conf. award with Welker medal, 1976, Monie A. Ferst award, Sigma Xi, 1988, Nat. Medal Sci., NSF, 1990, Indsl. Application Sci., NAS, 1993, Centennial medal, ASEE, 1993, 50th Ann. award, Am. Elec. Assn, 1993, Japan prize, 1995, Internat. Global Energy prize, 2003. Fellow: AAAS, IEEE (life Morris Liebmann award 1973, Jack A. Morton award 1981, Edison medal 1989, medal of honor 2003, Third Millennium medal), Internat. Engring. Consortium, Am. Phys. Soc., Am. Acad. Arts and Scis., Am. Phys. Soc., Optical Soc. Am. (Charles H. Townes award 1992, Frederic Ives medal 2001); mem.: NAS (Indsl. Application of Sci. award 1993), NAE, Math. Assn. Am., Electrochem. Soc., Ioffe Inst. (hon.), Russian Acad. Scis. (fgn. mem.), Minerals, Metals and Materials Soc. (John Bardeen award 1995), Ioffe Inst. (hon. 1992), Math. Assn. Am., Electrochem. Soc. (Solid State Sci. and Tech. award 1983), Tau Beta Pi (Outstanding Alumnus award 1999), Eta Kappa Nu (eminent mem. 1998, Karapetoff Eminent Mems. award 1994, eminent mem. 1998). Home: 2212 Fletcher St Urbana IL 61801-6915 Office: U Ill Dept Elec/Computer Engring 1406 W Green St Urbana IL 61801-2918

HOLQUIST, JAMES MICHAEL, Russian and comparative literature educator; b. Rockford, Ill., Dec. 20, 1935; s. Leonard and Billye Alverta (Appleby) H.; m. Lydia Landis, July 30, 1960 (div. Dec. 1972); children: Peter Isaac, Benjamin Michael, Joshua Appleby; m. Katerina Clark, Apr. 15, 1974 (div. May 1999); children: Nicholas Manning, Sebastian; m. Elise Snyder, Nov. 6, 1999. BA with highest honors, U. Ill., 1963; PhD, Yale U., 1968; PhD honoris causa, U. Stockholm, Sweden, 2001. Asst. prof. Yale U., New Haven, 1968-72, assoc. prof., 1972-75; assoc. prof., dept. chmn. U. Tex., Austin, 1976-78, prof., 1978-80; prof. Slavic langs. and lit. dept., chmn. Ind. U., Bloomington, 1981-85; prof. comparative lit., dir. lit. major Yale U., 1986-91, chmn. coun. on Russian and East European studies, 1992-98, chmn. dept. comparative lit., 1998—2003, Northrop Frye prof. lit. theory, 2000. Christian Gauss lectr. Princeton U., 1991; NEH exchangee Soviet Acad. Scis., 1983; mem. exec. com. and editl. bd. PMLA. Author: (with Kernan and Brooks) Man and His Fictions, 1973, Dostoevsky and the Novel, 1977, reprinted, 1986; editor: (co-translator) The Dialogic Imagination: Four Essays by M.M. Bakhtin, 1981, (with Katerina Clark) Mikhail Bakhtin, 1984, Dialogism: The World of Mikhail Bakhtin, 1990, 2d edit., 2003, Philosophy of the Act, 1993; editor-in-chief: Tex. Slavic Studies, 1980; co-editor: Ind. Soviet Studies, 1982; editorial bd.: Yearbook of Comparative and Gen. Lit., 1982, Slavic Rev., 1983. Served with U.S. Army, 1958-61. Rockefeller Humanities fellow, 1983; vis. scholar Phi Beta Kappa, 1984-85; grantee NEH, 1979. Morse fellow Yale U., 1970. Mem. MLA, Am. Assn. Advancement of Slavic Studies, Internat. Bakhtin Soc. (newsletter editor 1982—), Internat. Dostoevsky Soc., Am. Assn. Tchrs. Slavic and East European Langs., Grotesque Club, Mory's Assocs., Elizabethean Club. Democrat. Home: 180 Linden St Apt H3 New Haven CT 06511-2459 E-mail: michael.holquist@yale.edu.

HOLROYD, MICHAEL, author; b. London, Aug. 27, 1935; s. Basil and Ulla (Hall) H.; m. Margaret Drabble. Author: Lytton Strachey, 1968, 2d edit., 1994 (filmed as Carrington), Augustus John, 1975, 2d edit., 1996, Bernard Shaw, 1988-93, abridged edit., 1997, Basil Street Blues, 1999, Works on Paper, 2002. Mem. PEN (pres. Eng. chpt. 1986-88), Soc. Authors (chmn. 1973-74), Arts Coun. of Eng. (chmn. lit. panel 1992-95), Royal Soc. of Lit. (chmn. 1998-2001, pres. 2003-). Office: care Lescher & Lescher Ltd 47 E 19th St New York NY 10003-1323

HOLSCHER, ROBERT F. airport terminal executive; With Kenton County Airport Bd, Hebron, Ky., 1961—; dir. avaiation Cincinnati-N. Kentucky Internat. Airport, 1975—. Office: Kenton County Airport Bd PO Box 752000 Cincinnati OH 45275-2000*

HOLSCHUH, JOHN DAVID, federal judge; b. Ironton, Ohio, Oct. 12, 1926; s. Edward A. and Helen (Ebert) H.; m. Carol Eloise Stouder, May 25, 1952; 1 child, John David Jr. BA, Miami U., 1948; JD, U. Cin., 1951. Bar: Ohio 1951, U.S. Dist. Ct. (so. dist.) Ohio 1952, U.S. Ct. Appeals (6th cir.) 1953, U.S. Supreme Ct. 1956. Atty. McNamara & McNamara, Columbus, Ohio, 1951-52, 54; law clk. to Hon. Mell. G. Underwood U.S. Dist. Ct., Columbus, 1952-54; ptnr. Alexander, Ebinger, Holschuh, Fisher & McAlister, Columbus, Ohio, 1954-80; judge U.S. Dist. Ct. (so. dist.) Ohio, 1980—, chief judge, 1990-96. Adj. prof. law Ohio State U. Coll. Law, 1970; mem. com. on codes of conduct Jud. Conf. U.S., 1985-90. Pres. bd. dirs. Neighborhood House, Columbus, 1969-70; active United Way of Franklin County, Columbus. Fellow Am. Coll. Trial Lawyers; mem. Order of Coif, Phi Beta Kappa, Omicron Delta Kappa. Home and Office: US Dist Ct 109 US Courthouse 85 Marconi Blvd Rm 109 Columbus OH 43215-2823

HOLSCHUH, JOHN DAVID, JR., lawyer; b. Columbus, Ohio, Dec. 21, 1955; s. John D. and Carol Elouise (Stouder) H.; m. Wendy G. Ellis, Sept. 22, 1984; children: Heather Elyse, John David III, Jacob Alexander. BS, Miami U., Oxford, Ohio, 1977; JD, U. Cin., 1980. Bar: Ohio 1980, U.S. Dist. Ct. (so. dist.) Ohio 1980, U.S. Ct. Appeals (6th cir.) 1986, U.S. Supreme Ct. 1986, U.S. Dist. Ct. (ea. dist.) Ky. 1987, Ky. 1991. Assoc. Santen, Shaffer & Hughes, Cin., 1980-87, ptnr., 1987-89, Santen & Hughes, Cin., 1989—. Pros. atty. City of Loveland, Ohio, 1987-92, magistrate, 1992—; magistrate Village of Fairfax, Ohio, 1999—; mem. faculty Nat. Inst. Trial Advocacy, 1990, 91, 96; participant Pretrial Civil Litigation Skills Workshop, 1991. Author: Medical Malpractice, 1986, Tort Reform Pleading, 1987, Civil Procedure, 1986, rev. edit., 1989, Damages for Plaintiff and Defense Attorneys in Ohio, 1990, 2d edit., 1991, Tort Reform Update, 1990. Recipient merit award Ohio Legal Ctr. Inst., 1986. Mem.: ATLA, Order of Barristers, Potter Stewart Inns of Ct. (emeritus mem.), Cin. Bar Found. (trustee 2001—), Cin. Bar Assn. (chmn. common pleas ct. 1991—93, trustee 1995—, co-chmn. bench-bar conf. 1997—98, sec. 1999—2000, v.p. 2000—01, pres.-elect 2001—02, pres. 2002—03), Hamilton County Trial Lawyers (pres. 1990—92), Ohio State Bar Assn., Ohio Acad. Trial Lawyers (trustee 1991—95, 1998—2000), Am. Bd. Trial Advs., 6th Cir. Jud. Conf. (life; del. 1983—88). Avocations: sports, travel. Office: Santen & Hughes 312 Walnut St Ste 3100 Cincinnati OH 45202-4044

HOLSEN, JAMES NOBLE, JR., retired chemical engineer; b. Palo Alto, Calif., June 20, 1924; s. James N. and Esther (Giltrud) H.; m. Nancy Schwankhaus, Feb. 24, 1950 (div.); children— James Noble III, David Edwards; m. Margot Meyer Best, Nov. 11, 1977; stepchildren— Victoria, Christopher, John BS, Princeton U., 1948; D.Sc., Washington U., St. Louis, 1954. Registered profl. engr., Mo. Chem. engr. Olin Mathieson Chem. Corp., 1954-55; asst. prof. chem. engring. Washington U., 1955-58, assoc. prof., 1958-61, prof., 1961-73; prof. chem. engring. U. Mo.-Rolla, 1973-74, vis. prof. engring. mgmt., 1974-75; program mgr. McDonnell Douglas Corp., St. Louis, 1977-92; ret., 1992. Cons. chem. engring. and aerospace scis.; vis. prof. engring. Kabul U., Afghanistan, 1963-64, 69-73; mem. U.S. Engring. Team, Kabul, 1963-64, 69-73 Served with AUS, 1942-46 Fellow AIAA (assoc.); mem. Am. Inst. Chem. Engrs. (chmn. St. Louis sect. 1962), Am. Chem. Soc., Am. Soc. Engring. Edn., AAAS, Ethical Soc. Sigma Xi, Tau Beta Pi Clubs: Princeton Quadrangle. Achievements include research on gas phase reaction kinetics, gaseous transport properties, materials processing in space, satellite components and structure, thermodynamics. Active in environmental affairs with St. Louis Audubon Soc. Home: 419 E Argonne Dr Kirkwood MO 63122-4523 E-mail: jholsen@mindspring.com.

HOLSGROVE, GARETH JOHN, medical association administrator; b. London, Jan. 27, 1946; s. Howard Ernest and Margaret Adelaide (Gadau) H.; m. Linda Susan Barnes, Aug. 19, 1970; children: Claire Louise Ann, Gareth Paul Rhys. B in Edn., Sussex U., Brighton, U.K., 1969; MSc, Salford U., 1979; PhD, U. East Anglia, 1987. Cert. tcrh., tchr. deaf, paediatric audiologist. Housemaster Mary Hare Grammar Sch., Newbury, England, 1973—75; tchr. partial-hearing unit County Avon, Bath, England, 1975-76; ednl. audiologist Thomasson Sch., Bolton, England, 1976-79; sr. adv. tchr. Hertfordshire Co. Coun., Hertford, England, 1979-90; dir. med. edn. St. Bartholomew's Med. Sch., London, 1990-96, United Arab Emirates U., Al-Ain, 1996—98; cons. Cambridge Med. Edn. Cons., St. Neots, 1998—2002; academic dean Coll. Osteopaths, London, 1998-2000; head of postgrad. ednl. svcs. Royal Coll. Psychiatrists, 2002—. Ednl. cons. Royal Coll. Gen. Practitioners, London, 1991-95, Aga Khan U., Karachi, Pakistan, 1997—, Coll. Physicians and Surgeons Pakistan, 1999—; cons. med. edn. Australian Govt., Canberra, 1995-96; nat. facilitator curriculum change, Nat. Health Svc. Exec., Leeds, U.K., 1993-96. Contbr. Author: (books) Teaching Medicine in General Practice, 1997, The Certification and Recertification of Doctors, 1994. Recipient 1st prize Nat. Film and Video Competition, Round Table, U.K., 1986; certificate Ednl. Merit, Brit. Med. Assn., 1992, 94. Mem.: Rotary Internat. Avocations: cooking, photography, travel, music. E-mail: gholsgrove@rcpsych.ac.uk.

HOLSINGER, ADENA SEGUINE, music educator, community volunteer; b. Fostoria, Ohio, Aug. 8, 1926; d. Richard and Della Mable (Fry) Seguine; m. John Calvin Holsinger; 1 child, Coradella Elizabeth. BS in Edn., Ind. Wesleyan U., 1948. Cert. tchr., Ohio. Tchr. Canyonville (Oreg.) Christian Acad., 1948-50; music tchr. Ctrl. Bible Coll., Springfield, Mo., 1951—55, 1976—77; tchr. Bowling Green (Ohio) H.S., 1956-58; pvt. practice Costa Mesa, Calif., 1961—71, Springfield, Mo., 1971—. Pres., treas. Evangl. U. Aux., Springfield, 1984—. Mem.: DAR (vice regent 1994—96, regent 2001—02), Springfield Area Music Tchrs. Assn. (treas.), Springfield Piano Tchrs. Forum (pres. 1989, sec. 1999), Nat. Fedn. Music Clubs (dist. coord. 1989—91), Mo. Fedn. Music Clubs (state treas. 1980—87, state sec. 1987—89, regional v.p. 1991—99), Springfield Christian Women's Club (project advisor 1996—, treas.). Republican.

HOLSINGER, JAMES WILSON, JR., physician; b. Kansas City, Kans., May 11, 1939; s. James Wilson and Ruth Leona (Reitz) H.; m. Barbara Jenn Craig, Dec. 28, 1963; children: Anna Elizabeth, Martha Ruth, Sarah Frances, Rachel Catherine. Student, Duke U., 1957-60, MD, 1964, PhD, 1968; MS, U. S.C., 1981; BA, U. Ky., 1997; DS (hon.), Pikeville Coll., 1996. Intern Duke U. Hosp., Durham, N.C., 1964, resident in surgery, 1965, fellow in thoracic surgery, 1966, fellow in anatomy, 1966-68; resident in surgery U. Fla., Gainesville, 1968-70, fellow in cardiology, 1970-72; with VA, 1969-94; chief of staff VA Med. Ctr., Augusta, Ga., 1978-81, dir. Richmond, Va., 1981-90, Lexington, Ky., 1993-94; chief med. dir. Dept. Vets. Affairs, Washington, 1990-93, under sec. health, 1992-93; prof. medicine and anatomy Med. Coll. Ga., Augusta, 1978-81; prof. med. and health admin. Med. Coll. of Va., Richmond, 1981-93; asst. v.p. health scis. VA Commonwealth U., Richmond, 1985-90; chancellor U. Ky. Med. Ctr., Lexington, 1994—2003, chancellor emeritus, 2003—; prof. medicine, surgery and anatomy U. Ky. Coll. Medicine, 1994—; profl. health care adminstrn. U. Ky. Coll. Allied Health Profls., 1994—; sr. v.p. U. Ky., Lexington, 2001—03, Wethington Chair health sci., 2001—. Mem. com. evangelism N. Ga. conf. United Meth. Ch., 1980-81, com. 80, World Meth. Coun., 1981—, bd. discipleship Va. conf., 1982-86, lay mem., 1984-93, assoc. dist. lay leader, 1983-84, dist. lay leader, 1984-86, conf. lay leader, 1986-92, conf. chmn. health and welfare ministries, Ky., 1996-2000, Ky. conf. lay mem., 1996-00, del. gen. conf., 1988, 92, 96, 2000, del. S.E. jurisdictional conf., 1988, 92, 96, 2000; exec. com. World Meth. Coun., 1986—, treas., 1993—, gen coun. on ministries United Meth. Ch., 1988-2000, Gen. Bd. Pubs., 1992-96, bd. dirs. United Meth. Pub. House, 1996-2000, jud. council, 2000—; commr. Joint Commn. on the Accreditation of Healthcare Orgns., 1996-2002. Author, editor med. and religious books; contbr. articles to med, and religious publs. Major gen. M.C., USAR, 1989-92. Fell. ACP, Am. Coll. Cardiology, Am. Coll. Healthcare Execs. (Gold Medal Awd. 1993). Mem. Am. Assn. Anatomists, Am. Heart Assn. (fellow clin. coun.), Soc. Med. Administrs., Internat. Brotherhood Magicians (order of Merlin), Ret. Officers Assn. (bd. dirs. 1998-2000). Republican. Office: U Ky Office of Chancellor Emeritus Chandler Med Ctr B-301 Ky Clinic Ctr Lexington KY 40536-0001 E-mail: jwh@email.uky.edu.

HOLST, ARTHUR MATTHEW, government affairs executive; b. Phila., May 26, 1957; s. Norman Richard and Mary Louise (Rheaume) H. BBA, Temple U., 1979, MPA, 1987, PhD, 1999. Fin. aid counselor Temple U., Phila., 1979-80, Drexel U., Phila., 1980-81; dir. fin. aid Airco - Computer Learning Ctr., Phila., 1981-84, Phila. Coll. Performing Arts (now U. of Arts), 1984-85; fin. aid cons. Temple U., Phila., 1985—; fin. aid adminstr. Episc. Hosp. Sch. Nursing, Phila., 1988-91; chief staff Office Councilman Joseph C. Vignola, Phila., 1991-96; exec. dir. Betsy Ross House, Phila., 1996=99; govt. affairs mgr. Phila. Water Dept., 1996—. Adj. faculty dept. English and polit. sci. Temple U., Phila., 1987—, Widener U. Mem. scholarship com. City of Phila., 1992-00; mem. Mayor's Scholarship Com., 1992-00; treas. Old City Spl. Svcs. Dist., 1999—2002, v.p. 2002-. Recipient Fulbright scholarship, Ukraine, 2001—. Mem. Am. Soc. Pub. Adminstrn. (v.p. 1993-94, pres. 1995-96). Democrat. Roman Catholic. Home: 234 N 34d St #103 Philadelphia PA 19106-1951 Office: Phila Water Dept 1101 Market St Philadelphia PA 19107-2934 E-mail: arthur.holst@phila.gov.

HOLST, RUTH MARY, medical librarian; b. Fond du Lac, Wis., Sept. 22, 1947; d. Delmar and Marie (Daun) H.; m. Robert Peter Thiel, May 7, 1977; 1 child, Alexandra. BS, U. Wis., 1970, MS, 1973. Med. libr. Columbia Hosp., Milw., 1970-82, dir. libr. svcs., 1983—2002; assoc. dir. nat. network libr. medicine U. Ill., Chgo., 2002—. Adj. asst. prof. U. Wis. Milw. Sch. Libr. and Info. Sci., 1981-90; dir. women's health Columbia Hosp., 1988-91, mgr. coordinated care, 1994-98; biomed. libr. rev. com. Nat. Libr. Medicine, Bethesda, Md., 1996-2000. Editor: Hospital Library Managament, 1983; mem. libr. adv. bd. New Eng. Jour. Medicine; contbr. articles to profl. jours. Bd. dirs. Friends of Golda Meir Libr., Milw., 1985-89. Grantee Nat. Libr. Medicine, 1990. Fellow Med. Libr. Assn. (bd. dirs. 2001—, sec., 2002—, editor The Med. Libr. Assn. Guide to Managing Health Care Librs. 2000); mem. Coun. Wis. Librs. (bd. dirs. 1993-97), Spl. Librs. Assn., Columbia History of Medicine Club (sec.), Acad. Health Info. Profls., Milw. Acad. Medicine. Avocations: reading, cooking, singing. Office: Univ Ill at Chgo Libr Health Scis 1750 W Polk St Chicago IL 60612

HOLSTE, JAMES CLIFTON, chemical engineering educator; b. Colby, Kansas, Feb. 8, 1945; s. Clifton John and Irene Ellen (Luedders) H.; m. Cathleen Ann Haring, June 21, 1969; children: Rachel Suzanne, Jill Cathleen. BS, Concordia Tchr.'s Coll., 1966; PhD, Iowa State U., 1973. Profl. engr., Tex. Rsch. assoc. Nat. Bur. Standards, Boulder, Colo., 1973-75; from engring. rsch. assoc. to assoc. dean engring. Tex. A&M, Coll. Sta., 1975—; asst. dir. rsch. Tex. Engring. Exp. Sta., 1995—97. Cons. Precision Measurement, Duncanville, Tex., 1984-90, Shell Devel., Houston, 1978-82, OPC Engring., Houston, 1981-83, Precision Machine Products, Dallas, 1981-84. Bd. dirs., sec. Concordia Univ. Sys., St. Louis, 1992-2001. Recipient alumnus of yr. award Concordia Coll., 1994. Mem. AAAS, AIChE, Am. Physical Soc., Am. Chem. Soc., Am. Soc. Engring. Edn. Lutheran. Avocations: music, softball. Patentee in field. Home: 3025 Hummingbird Cir Bryan TX 77807-3224 Office: Tex A&M U Chem Engring Dept 3122 TAMU 337 Zachry Engring Ctr College Station TX 77843-3122 E-mail: j-holste@tamu.edu.

HOLSTEAD, JOHN BURNHAM, retired lawyer; b. Dallas, Mar. 5, 1938; s. J.B. and Maurice (Cook) H.; m. Marilyn Morris, Nov. 23, 1963; children: Will, Rand, Scott. BA, La. Tech. U., 1959; LL.B., U. Tex.-Austin, 1962. Bar: Tex., U.S. Dist. Ct. Tex. 1965, U.S. Ct. Appeals (5th cir.), U.S. Ct. Appeals (10th cir.), U.S. Supreme Ct. 1974. Briefing clk. Tex. Sup. Ct., 1962-63; assoc. Vinson & Elkins, Houston, 1965-72, ptnr., 1972; ret., 2001. Mem. bd. advisors Biology of Info. Ctr., Baylor Coll. Medicine; spkr. on civil litigation and bus. disputes. Bd. dirs., trustee Goodwill Industries Houston, Inc. Named Centennial Outstanding Alumni, La. Tech. U., 1998. Fellow Internat. Soc. Barristers, Houston Bar Found., Tex. Bar Found.; mem. ABA, Tex. Bar Assn., Houston Bar Assn., River Oaks Country Club. Episcopalian. Office: Vinson & Elkins 3200 First City Tower 1001 Fannin St Ste 3300 Houston TX 77002-6706 E-mail: jholstead@velaw.com.

HOLSTEIN, JOHN CHARLES, former state supreme court judge; b. Springfield, Mo., Jan. 10, 1945; s. Clyde E. Jr. and Wanda R. (Polson) H.; m. Mary Frances Brummell, Mar. 26, 1967; children: Robin Diane Camacho, Mary Katherine Link, Erin Elizabeth Lary. BA, S.W. Mo. State Coll., 1967; JD, U. Mo., 1970; LLM, U. Va., 1995. Bar: Mo. 1970. Atty. Moore & Brill, West Plains, Mo., 1970-75; probate judge Howell County, West Plains, 1975-78, assoc. cir. judge, 1978-82; cir. judge 37th Jud. Cir., West Plains, 1982-87; judge so. dist. Mo. Ct. Appeals, Springfield, 1987-88, chief judge so. dist., 1988-89; judge Supreme Ct. Mo., Jefferson City, 1989—2002, chief justice, 1995-97; shareholder Thomson & Kilroy, P.C., Springfield, 2002—. Instr. bus. law S.W. Mo. State Coll., 1976-77, pub. sch. law S.W. Bapt. U., 1999-2000. Lt. col. USAR, 1969-87. Office: Shugart Thomson & Kilroy PC 901 St Louis St Ste 1200 Springfield MO 65806*

HOLSTEIN, WILLIAM KURT, business administration educator; b. Stamford, Conn., Nov. 19, 1936; s. Kurt Edward and Doris Christiana (Werner) H.; m. Audrey Louise Bedford, Aug. 15, 1959; children: Kurt Edward II, William Kurt Jr., Catherine Louise. BChE, Rensselaer Poly. Inst., Troy, N.Y., 1958; MS in Indsl. Mgmt., Purdue U., 1959, PhD in Econs., 1964. Instr., then asst. prof. indsl. mgmt. Purdue U., 1959-64; asst. prof., then assoc. prof. Harvard U. Grad. Sch. Bus. Adminstrn., 1964-72; prof. SUNY, Albany, 1972-99, disting. svc. prof., 1991-99, dean sch. of bus., 1972-81, 86-87, exec. dir. Inst. for Study of Info. Sci., 1988-96; dir. Ctr. for Pvt. Enterprise Devel., Budapest, Hungary, 1991-93; D. Hollins Ryan prof. bus. adminstrn. Coll. William and Mary, Williamsburg, Va., 1999—; prof. Grad. Sch. Bus. Adminstrn., Zurich, 1996—. Dir. exec. devel. programs in Singapore, Taiwan, Argentina, Switzerland, Eng. and Ctrl. Am., 1969—, cons. to industry and govt.; vis. prof. IMEDE, Lausanne, Switzerland, 1983-85. Co-author: Production Planning and Control, 1963, Casebooks in Production Management, 1968, BASIC: Concepts and Applications, 1987; author articles in field. Trustee Upsala Coll., 1969-72; mem. accreditation com., editorial adv. com., visitation teams Am. Assembly of Collegiate Schs. of Bus., 1972-81; mem. exec. com. Middle Atlantic Assn. Schs. Bus. Adminstrn., 1976-81, pres., 1980; bd. dirs. Albany Symphony Orch., 1976-99, Seagle Music Colony, 1998—; bd. dirs., treas., v.p. adminstrn. Parsons Child and Family Center, Albany, 1977-94, pres., 1989-92; chmn. Metro 2000 Project, 1979; mem. com. on computer-aided mfg. Nat. Acad. Scis., 1980-83. Mem. Inst. Mgmt. Scis., Am. Prodn. and Inventory Control Soc. (hon.), Delta Sigma Pi, Beta Gamma Sigma. Lutheran. Home: 3104 Parkside Ln Williamsburg VA 23185-7696 Office: Coll William and Mary Sch Bus Adminstrn Williamsburg VA 23187-8795 E-mail: William.Holstein@business.wm.edu.

HOLSTI, KALEVI JACQUE, political scientist, educator; b. Geneva, Apr. 25, 1935; s. Rudolf Woldemar and Liisa Anniki (Franssila) H.; children: Liisa, Matthew, Karina. BA, Stanford U., 1956, MA, 1958, PhD, 1961. Mem. faculty U. B.C., Vancouver, 1961—, U. Killam prof. polit. sci. Vis. prof. McGill U., Montreal, 1972-72, Kyoto (Japan) U., 1977, Hebrew U., Jerusalem, 1978, Internat. U. Japan, 1988, 92, 94; vis. fellow Australian Nat. U., 1983; cons. in field. Author: International Politics: A Framework for Analysis, 7th edit., 1994, Why Nations Realign, 1982, The Dividing Discipline: Hegemony and Pluralism in International Theory, 1985, Peace and War: International Order and Armed Conflict, 1648-1989, 1991, Change in the International System: Essays on the Theory and Practice of International Relations, 1991, The State, War, and the State of War, 1996; editor: Internat. Studies Quar., 1970-75; co-editor: Can. Jour. Polit. Sci., 1978-81. Recipient Killam Rsch. prize, 1992; Fulbright scholar, 1959-60; Can. Coun. leave fellow, 1967, 72, 78, Can. Coun. Killam Rsch. fellow, 1987-89; named Univ. Killiam Prof., 1997. Fellow Royal Soc. Can.; mem. Internat. Studies Assn. (pres. 1986-87), Can. Polit. Sci. Assn. (pres. 1984-85). Office: U BC Dept Polit Sci Vancouver BC Canada V6T 1Z1 E-mail: holsti@interchange.ubc.ca.

HOLSTI, OLE RUDOLF, political scientist, educator; b. Geneva, Aug. 7, 1933; came to U.S., 1940, naturalized, 1954; s. Rudolf Waldemar and Liisa (Franssila) H.; m. Ann Wood, Sept. 20, 1953; children: Eric Lynn, Maija. BA with highest honors, Stanford U., 1954, PhD, 1962; MAT, Wesleyan U., Middletown, Conn., 1956. Instr., asst. prof. polit. sci., research coordinator Stanford U., 1962-67; assoc. prof. U. B.C., Vancouver, Can., 1967-71, prof., 1971-74; George V. Allen prof. polit. sci. Duke U., 1974—, chmn. dept. polit. sci., 1977-83; prof. Dept. Polit. Sci. U. Calif., Davis, 1978-79. Mem. adv. com. on hist. diplomatic documentation U.S. Dept. State, 1983-86; mem. oversight com. NSF, 1981-84; co-dir. Triangle Univs. Security Sem. Duke U., 1983-98. Co-author: Content Analysis: Handbook with Application for the Study of Internat. Crisis, 1963; author (with D.J. Finlay and R. R Fagan): Enemies in Politics, 1967; author: Analysis of Communication Content: Development in Scientific Theories and Computer Techniques, 1969, Content Analysis for Social Sciences and Humanities, 1969; co-author: International Crises, 1972; author: Crisis Escalation War, 1972, Unity and Disintegration in International Alliances: Comparative Studies, 1973, Change in the International System, 1980, American Leadership in World Affairs: The Vietnam and Breakdown of Consensus, 1984, Pub. Opinion and Am. Fgn. Policy, 1996—2004; co-author: Political Science Annual, 1975, Thought and Action in Foreign Policy, 1975, The Behavior of Nations, 1976, World Politics, 1976, Diplomacy, 1979, Challenges to America, 1979, Containment, 1986, Behavior, Society and Nuclear War, 1989, Soviet-American Relations after the Cold War, 1991, Explaining the History of American Foreign Relations, 1991, 2003—, Psychological Dimensions of War, 1991, Diplomacy, Force and Leadership, 1993; contbg. author numerous books including The United States and Human Rights, 2000; co-prodr.: American Democracy Promotion, 2000; co-author: Pondering Postinternationalism, 2000, The New International Studies Classroom, 2000; co-prodr.: Eagle Rules?: Foreign Policy and American Primacy in the 21st Century, 2001; co-author: Soldiers and Civilians: The Civil-Military Gap and American National Security, 2001, Millennial Reflections on International Studies, 2002, Encyclopedia of US Foreign Relations, 1997—; assoc editor Western Polit. Quar., 1970—79, Jour. Conflict Resolution, 1967—72, bd. editors Computer Studies in the Humanities and Verbal Behavior, 1968—76, Am. Jour. Polit. Sci, 1975—80, Internat. Interaction assoc., Am. Review of Politics, editor then bd. editors Internat. Studies Quar., 1970—, Jour. Politics, 1991—, Internat. Studies Perspectives, 1999—, adv. bd. Univ. Press Am., 1976—, corr. editor Running Jour, —, corr. Racing South, —; contbr. Served with AUS, 1956-58. Recipient Nevitt Sanford award, 1988, Disting. Tchrs. award Howard Johnson, 1990, Runner of Yr. award CGTC, 1985, Alumni Disting. Undergrad. Tchg. award, 1995, All-Am. award U.S. Masters Track & Field, 2000, 02; GE Found. Owen D. Young fellow, 1960-61, Haynes Found. Rsch. fellow, 1961-62, Can. Coun. Leave fellow, 1970-71, Ctr. Advanced Study in Behavioral Sci. fellow, 1972-73, Ford Found. Faculty Rsch. fellow, 1972-73, Guggenheim fellow, 1981-82, Pew Faculty fellow Harvard U., 1990; grantee Can. Coun. Rsch., 1969, NSF, 1975-77, 79-81, 83-85, 88-90, 92-95, 96-98; mem. Nat. Champion Cross Country Team (men 50-59), 1985, 88, champion, 1988; champion Tar Heel Running Tour, 1987, champion, Triple Crown Race, 1992-93; named Runner Yr., 1993, Carolina Godiva Track Club. Mem. Internat. Studies Assn. (pres. west region 1969-70, south region 1975-77, nat. pres. 1979-80, Tchr.-Scholar award Internat. Studies Assn. 2000), Internat. Soc. Polit. Psychology (coun. 1990-92, v.p. 1993-95, Nev. H. Sanford award 1988), Internat. Peace Sci. Soc. (pres. so. sect. 1975-76), Am. Polit. Sci. Assn. (coun. 1982-84, adminstrn. com. 1982-85, Disting. Lifetime Achievement award 1999), Can. Polit. Sci. Assn., Western Polit. Sci. Assn. (exec. coun. 1971-74), USA Track and Field (N.C. Racewalk chair 1999-2002), Phi Beta Kappa, Duke Master Runners Club, Carolina Godiva Track Club (Runner of Yr. award 1985, 93), Fleet Feet Running Club. Home: 608 Croom Ct Chapel Hill NC 27514-6706 Office: Duke U Dept Polit Sci PO Box 90204 Durham NC 27708-0204 E-mail: holsti@duke.edu.

HOLSTON, A. FRANK, retired broadcaster, communications educator; b. Balt., Feb. 25; s. Arthur F. Sr. and Sara A. Holston; m. Marianne B. Holston, Dec. 27, 1953; children: William Carroll, Sara Anne, Jeanne Marie. BS, U. Ala., 1951; MA, Mich. State U., 1962. Radio and TV broadcaster, sports dir., Balt., 1944-72; announcer ABC-TV, ESPN, N.Y.,Conn., 1974-88; prof. comm. C.C. Balt., 1956-88; ret., 1988. Chmn. faculty senate exec. com., Balt., 1969—70; gen. mgr. Liberty Campus, Balt., 1968—69, WBJC-FM, 1968—69; pres., bd. dirs. Shearwater, Inc., 1996—98; track ofcl. U.S. Naval Acad., 1998—; spkr. in field. Bd. dirs. Annapolis (Md.) Bur. Recreation, 1993—, Broadcast Edn. Assn., Washington, 1985-89, Ecumedia, Balt., 1975-76; v.p. Rep. Ctrl. Com., 1991-97, pres., 1995-97; chmn. '51 reunion U. Ala., 2001; pres. Feddayes, Boumi Temple Shrine, 1967-68. With USN, 1945, USNR. Ford Found. scholar, Northwestern U., 1958, News Am. fellow, Syracuse U., 1960. Mem.: Shriners (v.p. Annapolis club 2003—). Presbyterian. Home: 2B1 Spa Creek Landing Annapolis MD 21403

HOLT, BARBARA LYNN, school nurse practitioner; b. Louisville, Ky., Sept. 29, 1965; d. Robert Earl Katzman and Sherri Anne Toebbe; m. Mark Stephen Holt, July 14, 1983; children: Jason Michael, Corey Stephen, Emily Mae. LPN, Charlotte VO Tech. Nurse St. Joseph Hosp., Port Charlotte, Fla.; sch. nurse Charlotte County Sch. Bd., Port Charlotte, Fla.; sick child daycare Charlotte County, Port Charlotte, Fla.; office nurse Joseph S. Chirillo Jr., MD, Englewood, Fla.; agy. nurse Staff Masters, Port Charlotte, Fla. CPR instr. Charlotte County Schools, Port Charlotte, Fla. Home: 23380 Patera Ave Port Charlotte FL 33980

HOLT, BERTHA MERRILL, state legislator; b. Eufaula, Ala., Aug. 16, 1916; d. William Hoadley and Bertha Harden (Moore) Merrill; m. Winfield Clary Holt, Mar. 14, 1942; children: Harriet Wharton Holt Whitley, William Merrill, Winfield Jefferson. AB, Agnes Scott Coll., 1938; postgrad., U. N.C. Law Sch., 1939-40; LLB, U. Ala., 1941; grad., Sch. Creative Leadership, Greensboro, N.C., 1992. Bar: Ala. 1941. With Treasury Dept., Washington, 1941-42, Dept. Interior, Washington, 1942-43. Mem. N.C. Ho. of Reps. from 22d Dist., 1975-80, 25th Dist., 1980-94, chmn. select com. govtl. ethics, 1979-80, chmn. constl. amendments com., 1981, 83, mem. joint commn. govtl. ops., 1982-88, chmn. appropriation com. justice and pub. safety, 1985-88, co-chair House appropriation sub-com. transp., 1991-92, co-chair appropriation sub-com. Justice and Pub. Safety, 1993-94. Pres., Democratic Women of Alamance, 1962, chmn. hdqrs., 1964, 68; mem. N.C. Dem. Exec. Com., 1964-75, 95—; pres. Episcopal Ch. Women, 1968; mem. coun. N.C. Episcopal Diocese, 1972-74, 84-87, 95-98; chmn. budget com. 1987; chmn. fin. dept., 1973-75, parish grant com., 1973-80, mem. standing com., 1975-78; mem. Episcopal Diocese Ecclesiastical Ct., 1998—; chmn. Alamance County Social Svcs. Bd., 1970; mem. N.C. Bd. Sci. and Tech., 1979-83; chair Legis. Women's Caucus, 1991-94; past bd. dirs. Hospice N.C.; bd. dirs. State Coun. Social Legis., pres. SCSL 1996-97, State Conf. Social Work, N.C. Epilepsy Assn., N.C. Pub. Sch. Forum, 1989, U. N.C. Sch. Pub. Health Adv. Bd., Salvation Army Alamance County, N.C., Nursing Found., 1989, Epilepsy Found., 1989; bd. Alternatives for Status Offenders Burlington, N.C., Sch. Pub. Health Adv. Bd.; bd. dirs. N.C. ACLU, Partnership For Children (N.C.), 1993-98. Recipient Outstanding Alumna award Agnes Scott Coll., 1978, Legis. award for svc. to elderly Non-Profit Rest Home Assn., 1985, health, 1986, ARC, 1987, Faith Active in Pub. Affairs award N.C. Coun. of Chs., 1987, Ellen B. Winston award State Coun. For Social Legis., 1989, N.C. Disting. Women's award in gov., 1991, Disting. Svc. award Alamance County, 1992, Chi Omega award Women in Leadership, 1st ann. Hallie Ruth Allen Dem. Women award Alamance County, 1992, Disting. Svc. award Chi Omega, 1996, Svc. award Triennial Conv., Episcopal Ch. Women of U.S., 1997, Outstanding Alumna award U. N.C.-Chapel Hill, 1998, Gwyneth B. Davis award N.C. Assn. Women Attys., 1998, Outstanding Svc. award N.C. Assn. Women Attys., 1998, Disting. Alumna award U. N.C.-Chapel Hill, 1999, numerous others; named One of 5 Distinguished Women of N.C. (Govt.), 1991. Mem. AAUW, NOW, N.C. Women's Forums, Law Alumni Assn. U. N.C. Chapel Hill (bd. dirs. 1978-81, 1994-99), N.C. Bar Assn. (bd. dirs. sr. lawyers sect.), English Speaking Union, N.C. Hist. Soc., Soc. Wine Educators, Les Amis du Vin, Pi Beta Phi, Phi Kappa Gamma, Delta Kappa Gamma, Phi Theta Kappa, Century Club. Address: PO Box 1111 Burlington NC 27216-1111 E-mail: bholt@netpath.net.

HOLT, CAROLYN MARIE, youth employment and training specialist, secondary school educator; b. Aberdeen, Wash., Jan. 15, 1947; d. Robert Duncan and Margaret F. (Nelson) Allan; m. John A. Holt, Sept. 17, 1967; children: John II, Robert, Frank, Jacob. AA, Grays Harbor Coll., Aberdeen, 1985; BA, Evergreen State Coll., 1990, M in Tchg., 1993. Cert. tchr., Wash. Mgr. ICRAN Svcs., Shelton, Wash., 1979—; mgr., tchr. Holt Piano Studios, Grayland, Wash., 1979-98; sub. tchr. Ocosta Sch. Dist., Westport, Wash., Hoquiam (Wash.) Sch. Dist., 1993-95, Aberdeen Sch. Dist., 1993-95; employment and tng. specialist ESD113 Youth Programs, Olympia, Wash., 1995—; user support facilitator, trainer Pacific Mountain Workforce Devel., Lacey, Wash., 2001—. Bd. dirs., profl. adv. bd. dirs. Evergreen Coll., 1991-98; bd. dirs. Ocosta Sch. Dist., Westport, 1987-89; leader, advisor Boy Scouts Am., 1979-97.. Fellow James Madison Found., 1992; recipient Cmty. Svc. award VFW, 1984. Mem. Nat. Coun. History Educators, Music Tchrs. Assn. (audition chmn.). Mem. Lds Ch. Avocations: community band, gardening, geneaology, writing, reading.

HOLT, CHARLES ASBURY, economics educator; b. Richmond, Va., Oct. 2, 1948; s. Charles Asbury and Josephene (Hannah) H.; children: Abbi Anne, Sarah Holliday. BA, Washington and Lee U., 1970; MS, Carnegie-Mellon U., 1974, PhD, 1977. Asst. prof. econs. U. Minn.-Mpls., 1976-82, assoc. prof., 1982-83, U. Va., Charlottesville, 1983-90, prof., 1990—, Bankard prof. econs., 1996—2002, dir. undergrad. studies in econs., 1984-86, dir. grad. studies, 1989-92, chmn. dept. econs., 1996-99, A. Willis Robertson prof. of political econ., 2002—. Cons. FTC, Washington, 1982-92; vis. scholar U. Barcelona, 1986-88, Stanford (Calif.) U., 1996, Calif. Inst. Tech., 1999, Ga. State U., 2000; bd. dirs. Thomas Jefferson Ctr. Polit. Econ., 1993-96. Author: Experimental Economics, 1993; editor Exptl. Econs., 1997—; assoc. editor Internat. Jour. Game Theory, Econ. Theory, 1995—; contbr. chpt. to book and articles to profl. jours. Served to E4 USNR, 1971-73. Recipient Savage Dissertation award NBER-NSF, 1977, Henderson Dissertation award Carnegie-Mellon U., 1977; NSF grantee, 1980—, U.S.-Spain Joint Com. Post Doctoral Rsch. grantee, 1987. Mem. Am. Econ. Assn., So. Econ. Assn. (1st v.p. 1994, pres. elect 2001), Western Econ. Assn., Altantic Econ. Assn., Econ. Sci. Assn. (pres. 1991-93). Home: 795 Madison Ave Charlottesville VA 22903-2121 Office: U Va Dept Econ Rouss Hall # 114 Charlottesville VA 22903-3288

HOLT, CHARLES WILLIAM, JR., lawyer, mediator; b. Dallas, Aug. 8, 1951; s. Charles William Sr. and Oleta Ruth (Leonard) H.; m. Claudia Capeau, Dec. 2, 1978; 1 child, Auston Charles. BS, East Tex. State U., 1973; JD, So. Meth. U., 1977. Bar: Tex. 1977, U.S. Dist. Ct. (fed. dist.) 1978. Assoc. Ralph M. Hall Law Office, Rockwall, Tex., 1977-89; pvt. practice Rockwall, 1990—. Chmn. Rockwall Firefighter Support Com., 1996-99. Mem.: Rockwall Bar Assn. (pres. 1986—87), State Bar Tex., Rockwall Area C. of C. (bd. dirs. 1982—84, 1997—), Rockwall Noon Club, Rotary Internat. Methodist. Avocations: video production, camping, outdoors, arts. Office: 500 Turtle Cove Blvd Ste 140 Rockwall TX 75087-5300 Business E-Mail: holt@charlesholt.com.

HOLT, DONALD A. agronomist, consultant, retired academic administrator; b. Minooka, Ill., Jan. 29, 1932; s. Cecil Bell and Helen (Eickoff) H.; m. Marilyn Louise Jones, Sept. 6, 1953; children: Kathryn A. Holt Stichnoth, Steven Paul, Jeffrey David, William Edwin. BS in Agrl. Sci., MS in Agronomy, U. Ill.; PhD in Agronomy, Purdue U. Farmer, Minooka, Ill., 1956-63; instr., asst. prof., assoc. prof. then prof. agronomy Purdue U., West Lafayette, Ind., 1964-82; prof., head dept. agronomy U. Ill., Urbana-Champaign, Ill., 1982-83, dir. Ill. Agr. Expt. Sta., assoc. dean Coll. Agr., 1983-96, sr. assoc. dean Coll. Agr., cons. environ. sci., 1996-2002; ret., 2002; interim dir. Nat. Soybean Rsch. Lab., 2003—03. Cons. Deere and Co., Ottumwa, Iowa, 1978, NASA, Houston, 1979, Control Data Corp., Mpls., 1978-79, EPA, Corvallis, Oreg., 1981-90. Town Bd. commr., Otterbein, Ind., 1972-76. Fellow AAAS, Am. Soc. Agronomy (pres. 1988), Crop Sci. Soc. Am.; mem. Agrl. Rsch. Inst. (pres. 1991), Am. Forage and Grassland Coun., Ill. Forage and Grassland Coun., Gamma Sigma Delta (internat. pres. 1974-76). Republican. United Methodist. Home: 1801 Moraine Dr Champaign IL 61822-5261 Office: U Ill 170 N5RC 1101 W Peabody Dr Urbana IL 61801-4723 E-mail: d-holt@uiuc.edu.

HOLT, EDWIN JOSEPH, psychology educator; b. Shreveport, La. s. James S. and Sammie L. (Draper) H.; m. Essie Williams; children: Lisa Michelle, Rachelle Justine. BA, Cen. State U., Wilberforce, Ohio, 1958; MS, Ind. U., 1962; EdD, U. Ark., 1972; postgrad., U. Tenn., 1976. Cert. lic. profl., La. Tchr. Caddo Parish Sch. System, Shreveport, 1959-67, guidance counselor, 1967-68, asst. prin., 1968-71, prin., 1971-74, dir. spl. services, 1974-80, asst. supt., 1980-90; now assoc. prof. psychology La. State U., Shreveport, 1990-2000; clin. mgr., therapist Success Insite, Bossier City, LA, 2000—. Adj. asst. prof. La. State U., Baton Rouge, 1972, N.E. La. U., Monroe, 1973, La. Tech. U., Ruston, 1974, Grambling (La.) State U., 1974-84. Vice-pres. N.W. La. United Way, 1987; dir. Summer Youth Program, Trinity Bapt. Ch., 1980-90; active Shreveport Clean Cmty. Commn., 1981-85, Shreveport Youth Enrichment Program, 1986-90, La. Parental Involvement Task Force, 1987, Shreveport Task Force on Housing, 1984, Caddo Cmty. Coun. of Parents and Educators, 1984-90; bd. dirs. Am. Heart Assn., 1991-92, Norwella Coun. Boy Scouts Am., 1983-87; fin. chmn. Carver br. YMCA Bd. Mgmt., 1983-88; cultural arts chmn. Caddo Dist. PTA Bd. Mgrs., 1981-90; chmn. bd. trustees Trinity Bapt. Ch. Nat. Sci. Found. fellow, So. Fund fellow, NDEA fellow; recipient Nat. Council of Negro Women's award, 1984, 85, Nat. Univ. Women's Council award, 1984, 85. Mem. NEA, ACA, La. Edn. Assn., Am. Assn. Sch. Adminstrs., Nat. Alliance Black Sch. Educators, Caddo Assn. Educators, Kappa Delta Pi, Sigma Pi Phi (pres. 1997-2000). Avocations: bowling, swimming, jogging, reading. Home: 208 Plano St Shreveport LA 71103-2057 Office: Success Insite 1504 Barksdale Blvd Bossier City LA 71111-4602

HOLT, GERALD WAYNE, retired counseling administrator; b. Woodbury, Tenn., July 17, 1935; s. Slaughter L. and Pearl (Simmons) H.; m. May Jane Neeley, Aug. 28, 1955; children: Lucinda Jane, Cheryl Kay, Beth Ann. BS, Ball State U., 1957, MA, 1959, postgrad., 1960-61. Tchr. social studies Union City (Ind.) schs., 1957-60, Storer Jr. High Sch., Muncie, Ind., 1960-69; asst. prin. Storer Middle Sch., Muncie, 1969-78; prin. Franklin Middle Sch., Muncie, 1978-79; Christian edn. dir. Glad Tidings Ch., Muncie, 1975-78, 81-84; tchr. social studies Storer Middle Sch., Muncie, 1979-88; Christian edn. dir. Calvary Christian Ctr., Muncie, 1985-87; guidance dir. Northside Middle Sch., Muncie, 1988-99; in car driving instr. Driving Acad., 1997—2003. Bd. dirs. Sch. Employees Credit Union, Muncie, 1987-94; treas. Glad Tidings Ch., Muncie, 1961-72, trustee, 1974-83; trustee Calvary Christian Ctr., Muncie, 1984-88, 90-98. Mem. Ind. Retired Tchrs. Assn., Muncie Tchrs. Assn., Am. Assn. Counseling and Guidance, Elem. Sch. Guidance and Counseling, NEA, Ind. Tchrs. Assn., Assn. for Supervision and Curriculum Devel., Phi Delta Kappa. Assemblies of God. Avocations: golf, bowling, photography, collecting political buttons. Office: 1120 W Yale Ave Muncie IN 47304-1559 E-mail: gwh1120@aol.com.

HOLT, GLEN EDWARD, library administrator; b. Abilene, Kans., Sept. 14, 1939; s. John Wesley and Helen Laverne (Schrader) H.; m. Leslie Edmonds, Jan. 29, 1994; children from previous marriage: Kris, Karen, Gordon. BA, Baker U., 1960; MA, U. Chgo., 1965, PhD, 1975. From instr. to asst. prof. Wash. U., St. Louis, 1968-82; dir. honors div. Coll. Liberal Arts, U. Minn., 1982-87; exec. dir. St. Louis Pub. Libr., 1987—. Cons. Chgo. Hist. Soc., 1976-79, Mo. Hist. Soc., St. Louis, 1979-87, Buffalo-Erie County Pub. Libr., 1997-98; mem. Online Computer Libr. Ctr. Pub. Libr. Adv. Com., 1991-95. Co-editor: St. Louis, 1975; co-author: Chicago, A Guide to the Neighborhoods, 1979. Recipient Cmty. Svc. award Commerce Bank, 2001; named Woodrow Wilson Found. fellow, 1963-64, Danforth fellow, 1963-68. Mem. Am. Libr. Assn., Pub. Libr. Assn. (Charlie Robinson award 2001), Spl. Librs. Assn. (St. Louis com. on fgn. rels.), Mo. Athletic Club. Avocations: photography, collecting paperweights, books and midwestern art. Home: 4954 Lindell Blvd Apt 4W Saint Louis MO 63108-1520 Office: St Louis Pub Libr 1301 Olive St Saint Louis MO 63103-2389 E-mail: gholt@spl.lib.mo.us.

HOLT, HOMER ANTHONY, JR., urologist, educator; b. Ashland, Ky., July 6, 1938; s. Homer A. Holt, m. Virginia Cayce, Nov. 22, 1962; children: Kathryn Holt Kerpestein, Kimberly Holt Cochran, Homer A. III. BA, Vanderbilt U., 1960; MD, U. Louisville, 1965. Diplomate Am. Bd. Urology. Straight surg. intern U. Louisville Sch. Medicine, 1965-66, resident in gen. surgery, 1966-68, resident in urology, 1969-72, chief resident in urology, 1971-72, clin. prof. surgery (urology), 1972—; pvt. practice, Louisville, 1972—. Cons. dept. surgery (urology) VA Med. Ctr., Louisville; mem. active staff Norton Healthcare Sys.; mem. courtesy staff Kosair Children's Hosp., Bapt. Hosp. East; pres. med. staff Meth. Evang. Hosp., 1989-90. Contbr. articles to med. jours. Capt. M.C., USAF, 1967-69. Fellow ACS (com. on applicants for Ky. 1982-98, chmn. com. 1988-98); mem. Am. Urol. Assn., Southeastern Sect. Am. Urol. Assn., Am. Lithotripsy Soc., Ky. Med. Assn., Ky. Urol. Assn. (pres. 1979-80), Jefferson County Med. Soc. (editor bull. 1978-79, treas. found. bd. 1984-86). Office: Gray Street Med Bldg 210 E Gray St Ste 1000 Louisville KY 40202-3906 Home: 5808 Brittany Woods Cir Louisville KY 40222-5908

HOLT, ISABEL RAE, radio program producer; b. Vineland, N.J., Oct. 5, 1946; d. Frederick Rae and Isabella A. (Foley) Steinborn; m. Robert Eugene Darby, Aug. 13, 1977 (div. 1995); children: Rachel Elisabeth Darby, Nora Odette Darby. BA in Primary Edn., Rowan U (formerly Glassboro State Coll.), 1968; postgrad., Pierce Coll., 1991-93. Dir., coord. Washington Area Free U., 1972-74; prodr. music program Sta. WGTB Georgetown U., Washington, 1972-74; prodr. music program Sta. WMGM, Atlantic City, N.J., 1974, Sta. KJAZ, Alameda, Calif., 1974-76, Sta. KPFA, Berkeley, Calif., 1974-76, Sta. KCRW, Santa Monica, Calif., 1977-88, Sta. KPCC, Pasadena, Calif., 1989-93. Concert prodr.; interviewer radio programs, 1980—; prodr. tapes for dressage/equestrian free-style riders, 1994—, riding instr., trainer, 1999—; instr. Spl. Olympics, Boise, 1999. Mem. ACLU, Amnesty Internat., Childreach, Sierra Club. Democrat. Roman Catholic. Office: 1519 N 23rd St Boise ID 83702-0409

HOLT, JAMES FRANKLIN, retired numerical analyst, scientific programmer analyst; b. Alexander, Ark., Aug. 24, 1927; s. Edward Warbritton and Etta Turner (Ludi) H.; m. Gloria Anne Gaishin, May 5, 1963; children: Gregory James, Elizabeth Diana, Debora Anne. BA in Math., UCLA, 1953. With Pacific Mutual Ins. Corp., L.A., 1953-54; assoc. engr. Lockheed Aircraft Corp., Burbank, Calif., 1954-58; mem. tech. staff Space Tech. Labs., El Segundo, Calif., 1958-61, Aerospace Corp., El Segundo, 1961-91. Author: (play) To Play's the Thing, 1963 (French Grand Prix award); author: Anthony Bacon a.k.a. William Shakespeare, 1994, Order Out of Chaos: Chaos, Fractals, and the Mandelbrot Set Explained, 2003; internat. expert zeros of arbitrary functions, eigenvalues, non linear boundary value problems, differential algebraic equations, chaos theory, numerical integration methods; papers in field. Mem. Univ. Recreation Assn. UCLA (pres. 1952-53), UCLA Student Exec. Council, Young Reps., L.A., 1960-66. Cpl. USAF, 1945-48. Mem. Aerospace Profl. Staff Assn. (1st v.p. 1985-87), Shakespeare Authorship Roundtable, Alliance of L.A. Playwrights. Avocations: chess, research on chaos, fractals, mandelbrot set, shakespeare authorship and identity of jack the ripper, bowling, writing, 8th air force chess champion 1948 (undefeated). Home: 3534 Mandeville Canyon Rd Los Angeles CA 90049-1022

HOLT, JOHN MANLY, retired corporate lawyer; b. Chgo., July 15, 1925; s. Newton Ormand and Annie Marie (Hoover) H.; m. Barbara Lenfesty, Dec. 23, 1950; children: Mark B., Susan Holt Braun, Brent D. AB, DePauw U., 1950; JD, Ind. U., Indpls., 1956. Bar: Ind., D.C., U.S. Supreme Ct. Indsl. engr. Eli Lilly & Co., Indpls., 1952-54, pers. rep., 1954-55, supr., 1955-56, atty., 1956-64, asst. counsel, 1964-69, sr. counsel, 1969-77, sec., gen. counsel Pharm. divsn., 1977-87; ret., 1987. Cons. Nat. Commn. on Marijuana & Drug Abuse, Washington, 1971-73; trustee Food and Drug Law Inst., Washington, 1976-87; chmn. adv. com. Ind. divsn. Addiction Svcs., 1976-82; mem. Ind. Prescription Abuse Study Comm., 1988. Mem. bd. visitors Ind. U. Sch. Law, Indpls., 1991-2001, vice chmn. 1997-98, chmn. 1999-2000; mem. Pepper Com., City/County Govt., Indpls., 1989, Tax Adjustment Bd. of Marion County, Indpls., 1989-94; bd. dirs. Indpls. Park Found., 1992-20013; dir. Ctrl. Ind. Coun. on Aging, 1994-98, vice chair 1997-99. Served with U.S. Army, 1943-46, 1950-52. Named Sagamore of the Wabash by Gov. of Ind., 1988; recipient Spirit of Philanthropy award Ind. U./Purdue U., 1991, Hine medal for svc. to Ind. U./Purdue U., 2002, Order of Constantine, Internat. Sigma Chi, 1989, Disting. Alumni Svc. award Ind. U. Sch. Law, Indpls., 1992. Mem. Ind. Bar Assn., Indpls. Bar Assn., Svc. Club Indpls. (pres. 1999-2000), Columbia Club Indpls., Ind. U. Sch. Law-Indpls. Alumni Assn. (dir. 1968-71, 1988-2001, v.p. 1997, pres. 1998), Sigma Chi (pres. Indpls. alumni chpt. 1964, chmn., 1985-96, chmn. emeritus 1997-2003), Phi Delta Phi. Republican. Presbyterian. Avocations: photography, biking, gardening, travel, fishing. Home: 3421 Bay Road North Dr Indianapolis IN 46240-2970

HOLT, LEON CONRAD, JR., lawyer, business executive; b. Reading, Pa., June 19, 1925; s. Leon Conrad and Elizabeth (Bright) H.; m. June M. Weidner, June 30, 1947; children: Deborah Holt Weil, Richard W. BS cum laude in Metall. Engring, Lehigh U., 1948; JD, U. Pa., 1951. Bar: N.Y. 1952. With firm Mudge, Stern Williams & Tucker (attys.), N.Y.C., 1951-53; atty. Am. Oil Co. (and predecessor co.), N.Y.C., 1953-57; gen. atty. Air Products & Chems., Inc., Allentown, Pa., 1957-61, v.p., 1961-76, v.p. adminstrn., 1976-78, gen. counsel, 1961-78, vice chmn. bd., chief adminstrv. officer, 1978-90, also dir., mem. exec., finance, pub. policy coms. Bd. dirs. VF Corp., exec. fin. and audit coms., 1983-98. Vice chmn. Lehigh Centennial Fund, 1964-65; chmn. Allentown Bd. Ethics, 1970-74; bd. dirs. Lehigh County United Fund, 1971-83, mem. exec. com., 1971-74, campaign chmn., 1972; bd. dirs. Allentown YMCA, 1965-69, trustee, 1972-79; trustee Allentown Art Mus., pres., 1988-92; mem. Allentown Sch. Dist. Authority, 1978-86; trustee Mfrs. Alliance for Productivity and Innovation, 1981-91; mem. adv. bd. Inst. Law and Econs., U. Pa., bd. overseers Law Sch., 1985-94; trustee Dorothy Rider-Pool Health Care Trust, 1982-96, chmn., 1990-96, Rider-Pool Found., Com. Econ. Devel.; dir. Pa. chpt. Nature Conservancy, Pocono Lake Preserve, Pennsylvanians for Modern Cts.; co-chmn. Partnership for Cmty. Health, 1991-94. Lt. (j.g.) USNR, 1943-46. Mem. ABA, Pa. Soc., Assn. Bar NYC, Allentown C. of C. (gov. 1965-68), Tunkhan-

nock Creek Assn. (pres.), Alpha Tau Omega, Lehigh Country Club (bd. govs. 1970-77). Republican. Episcopalian. Home: 3003 Parkway Blvd Allentown PA 18104-5384 Office: 1611 Pond Rd Ste 300 Allentown PA 18104-2258

HOLT, LESTER, commentator; married. Grad., Calif. State U. Reporter WCBS-TV, N.Y.C., 1981—82, reporter, weekend anchor, 1983—86, KCBS-TV, L.A., 1982—83; anchor evening news WBBM-TV, Chgo., 1986—2000; co-anchor CBS News 48 Hours; lead anchor daytime news and breaking news coverage MSNBC; co-anchor NBC Weekend Today, 2003—. Office: Weekend Today NBC News 30 Rockefeller Plz New York NY 10112*

HOLT, MARJORIE SEWELL, lawyer, retired congresswoman; b. Birmingham, Ala., Sept. 17, 1920; d. Edward Rol and Juanita (Felts) Sewell; m. Duncan McKay Holt, Dec. 26, 1946; children: Rachel Holt Tschantre, Edward Sewell, Victoria. Grad., Jacksonville Jr. Coll., 1945; JD, U. Fla., 1949. Bar: Fla. 1949, Md. 1962. Pvt. practice, Annapolis, Md., 1962; clk. Anne Arundel County Circuit Ct., 1966-72; mem. 93d-99th Congresses from 4th Dist. of Md., 1973 86; armed services com., vice-chair Office Tech. Assessment, 1977; chair Republican Study com., 1975-76; of counsel Smith, Somerville & Case, Balt., 1986-90. Supr. elections Anne Arundel County, 1963-65; del. Rep. Nat. Conv., 1968, 76, 80, 84, 88; mem. Pres.'s Commn. on Arms Control and Disarmament; mem. ind. commn. USAR; bd. dirs. Annapolis Fed. Savs. Bank; adv. bd. Crestar; co-chair George W. Bush Presdl. campaign, Md., 2000. Co-author: Case Against The Reckless Congress, 1976, Can You Afford This House, 1978. Bd. dirs. Md. Sch. for the Blind, Hist. Annapolis Found. Recipient Disting. Alumna award U. Fla., 1975, Trustees award U. Fla. Coll. Law, 1984, Alumnae Outstanding Achievement award, 1997. Mem. ABA, Md. Bar Assn., Anne Arundel Bar Assn., Phi Kappa Phi, Phi Delta Delta. Presbyterian (elder 1959).

HOLT, MAVIS MURIAL, parents group executive; b. Sturgis, S.D., Apr. 30, 1932; d. Walter Raleigh and Mabel Henrietta (Krauser) Egnew; m. Howard Ray, Dec. 7, 1951; children: David Ray, Roberta Grace, Timothy Mark, Elizabeth Linda. Cert. in counseling, family issues, Multnomah Sch. of Bible, Portland, Oreg.; cert. youth at risk program, Portland State Coll.; student, North Portland Bible Coll., Long Ridge Writers Group, 1993—, Stratford Career Inst., 1999—. Mgr. The Press, Portland, 1970-71; with McDonald's Corp., Portland, 1970s; exec. dir., founder PAPYAC-Peers and Parents, Inc., Portland, 1991-97. Chairperson Neighbor Watch, Portland; block home chmn., Portland; neighborhood treas., vice chair Mill Park Neighborhood Assn., Portland, land use chair, 1993-98; vice chairperson adv. bd. David Douglas H.S., Portland; activist Neighborhood Involvement, Mill Park, City of Portland, 1985—; mem. Mid County Caring Cmty., David Douglas H.S., 1998; worker various polit. campaigns, 1995-98; mem. Gresham/East Portland C. of C., 2003—. Named Neighbor of Yr., Mid County Memo, Portland, 1994, Citizen of Month, 1997; recipient Neighborhood Plan award Mill Park Neighborhood Assn., 1995, Gateway Opportunity award City of Portland, 2000, Gift cert. Portland Environ. Bur., 2000, cert. of appreciation Mid County Caring Cmty., 2000; grantee Mill Park Nature Scape, Portland Park Bur., 1997, 2000, Howard Holt Neighborhood Park Mill Park Neighborhood Assn. grantee, 2003, use of van grantee City of Portland, 2003. Avocations: gardening, hiking, walking, local park development. Home and Office: 1235 SE 115th Ave Portland OR 97216-3567

HOLT, MICHAEL BARTHOLOMEW, lawyer; b. Jersey City, July 10, 1956; s. William A. and Grace (Donohue) H.; m. Mary Patricia Butler, Aug. 14, 1982; children: Melissa Aislynn, Scott Michael, Eric Michael. BA magna cum laude, Providence Coll., 1978; JD, Seton Hall U., 1982. Bar: N.J. 1982, U.S. Dist. Ct. N.J. 1982, U.S. Dist. Ct. (ea. and so. dists.) N.Y. 1985, U.S. Ct. Appeals (3d cir.) 1985, U.S. Supreme Ct. 1986, N.Y. 1990. Assoc. Keane, Brady & Hanlon, Jersey City, 1982-84, Waters, McPherson, McNeill P.A., Secaucus, N.J., 1984-87; ptnr. O'Halloran, Holt and Assocs., Bayonne, N.J., 1987-89, Carroll & Holt, Secaucus, 1989-91; pvt. practice Secaucus, 1991-95; corp. counsel NYK Lines (N.Am.) Inc., Secaucus, 1995—. Mem. N.Y. State Bar Assn. (corp. counsel com.). Home: 26 Oak Crest Pl Nutley NJ 07110-1516 Office: NYK Line Inc 300 Lighting Way Secaucus NJ 07094-3679 E-mail: mholt81176@aol.com.

HOLT, MICHAEL KENNETH, management and finance educator, consultant, city councilman; b. Jackson, Tenn., Apr. 13, 1961; s. Kenneth Hurvey and Dorothy (Price) Holt; m. Carol Lynn Walls, Aug. 13, 1983; 1 child, Mitchell Harris;1 child, Marleigh Allison. BS, Union U., 1983; MS, La. State U., 1985; postgrad. U. Memphis, 2001—. CPM. Broker First Nat. Bank of Commerce, New Orleans, 1985—86; mgr. Invest at Jackson (Tenn.) Nat. Bank, 1986—87; stock broker Merrill Lynch, Jackson, Tenn., 1987—89; prof. Union U., Jackson, Tenn., 1989—, chmn. supervisory com., 2002—. Chmn. bd. Leaders Credit Union, Jackson, Tenn., 1996-99; dir. Ctr. Bus. and Econ. Devel., 1999—; cons. Best Home Ctr., Jackson, Tenn., 1994-97, mem. regional planning commn., 1996-2001; cons. Quaker Oats, Jackson, 1991, Memphis Cablevision, Memphis, 1990; nominee bd. dirs. Fed. Res. Bank St Louis, 1997 Editor: Jour. Industry and Commerce, 1993-94, Update, 1990—; contbr. articles to profl. jours. City councilman Jackson, Tenn., 1999-2003. Recipient Instrnl. Innovation award Union U., 1995. Office: Union U 1050 Union University Dr Jackson TN 38305-3697 E-mail: kholt@uu.edu.

HOLT, MILDRED FRANCES, educator; b. Lorain, Ohio, July 30, 1932; d. William Henry and Rachel (Pierce) Daniels; B.S., U. Md., 1962, M.Ed., 1967, Ph.D., 1977; m. Maurice Lee Holt, Sept. 11, 1949 (dec.); children— Claudia, Frances, William, Rudi. Tchr. spl. edn. St. Mary's (Md.) County Public Schs., 1962-64, coordinator Felix Johnson Spl. Edn. Center, 1964-66; demonstration tchr. spl. edn. U. Md., College Park, summer 1970, instr. spl. edn. dept. Coll. Edn., 1969-73; supr. spl. edn. Calvert and St. Mary's (Md.) Counties, 1968-69; asso. prof. spl. edn. W. Liberty (W.Va.) State Coll., 1973-75; asst. prof. Eastern Ill. U., Charleston, 1975-77; supr. spl. edn. Warren County Public Schs., Front Royal, Va., 1977-85; spl. edn. tchr. Dallas Ind. Sch. Dist., 1985— . Mem. NEA, Warren County Edn. Assn., Council Exceptional Children, Assn. for Gifted, Assn. Supervision and Curriculum Devel., Va. Edn. Assn., Va. Council Exceptional Children, Blue Ridge Orgn. Gifted and Talented, Assn. Children with Learning Disabilities, Nat. Assn. Gifted Children, Phi Theta Kappa, Kappa Delta Pi. Contbr. articles to profl. jours.; author: Reach Guidebook, 1979. Home: 2916 Sidney Dr Mesquite TX 75150-2253 E-mail: mholt@texas.net.

HOLT, NATALIE FRANCES, physician; b. Wayne, N.J., Dec. 13, 1973; d. William Francis and Carmela Ann Holt. BA, Harvard U., 1995; MD, Yale U., 2001; MPH, Johns Hopkins U., 2003. Intern Mayo Grad. Sch. Medicine, Rochester, Minn., 2001—02; gen. preventive medicine resident Johns Hopkins Bloomberg Sch. Pub. Health, Balt., 2002—. On Call sect. editor: Jour. AMA. Mem.: APHA, AMA, Am. Coll. Preventive Medicine, Delta Omega, Phi Beta Kappa. Home: 655 North Monroe St Ridgewood NJ 07450 Personal E-mail: natalie.holt@post.harvard.edu.

HOLT, PAT MAYO, journalist; b. Gatesville, Tex., Sept. 5, 1920; s. Paschal Duff Holt and Katherine Victoria Mayo; m. LaVerne Bryson, June 18, 1941 (dec. Nov. 2000); children: Philip Gordon, Michael Mayo. BA, BJ, U. Tex., 1940; MS in Journalism, Columbia U., 1941. Reporter Melbourne (Australia) Herald, 1941, Providence Jour.-Bull., R.I., 1942-43; assoc. editor Congrl. Quar., Washington, 1946-49; staff writer Reporter mag., Washington, N.Y.C., 1949-50; profl. staff Senate Fgn. Rels. Com., Washington, 1950-77; contbr. Christian Sci. Monitor, Washington, Boston, 1977—. Am. participant U.S. Info. Agy., Latin Am., 1979, South Asia, 1984; vis. lectr. U. Tex., Austin, 1980, 84; professorial lectr. Georgetown U., Washington, 1981, cons., 1989-90, U. Ky., Lexington, 1981-82 Author: Colombia Today and Tomorrow, 1964, U.S. Policy in Foreign Affairs, 1971, Secret Intelligence and Public Policy, 1995; co-author: Invitation to Struggle, 1980, 84, 88, 92. With U.S. Army, 1943-46. Fellow Inst. Current World Affairs Latin Am., 1961-62. Mem. Coun. on Fgn. Rels. Home and Office: 900 N Taylor St Apt 1423 Arlington VA 22203

HOLT, PETER M. sports team executive; Pres., CEO Holt Co. of Ohio, San Antonio; chmn. bd. San Antonio Spurs. Office: San Antonio Spurs 100 Montana St San Antonio TX 78203-1031

HOLT, PETER ROBERT BACON, geophysicist; b. La Colle, Que., Can., June 8, 1933; s. Charles Robert and Ruth Anita (Bombard) H. AS, Plattsburg Bus. Inst., 1954; D in Optical Sci., Royal Coll. Sci., Toronto, Ont., Can., 1960. Owner Tec-Books Ltd., Ellenburg Center, N.Y., 1960-69; seismologist Associes Omni-Lambda Assocs. Ltd., Ellenburg Center, N.Y., 1970—, also bd. dirs. Bd. dirs. Tec-Books Ltd., Ellenburg Center, N.Y., Adirondack Gospel Group Inc., North Bangor, N.Y. Author: Mandaische Grammatik, 1957, Calculs seismologiques, 1956, Analiz Mathemacheskii, 1957, Koptische Grammatik, 1958. Jewish Orthodox. Avocation: long/medium/short/ultra-high wave-length radio-frequency monitoring. Office: Associes Omni-Lambda Assocs Ltd West Hill Rd Chateaugay NY 12915-0103

HOLT, PETER ROLF, physician, educator; b. Berlin, Sept. 8, 1930; s. Arthur and Ruth H.; m. Joyce Weil, May 15, 1979; children: Rachel Janna, Shawn David, Tamara Naomi. BSc, U. London, 1949, MB, BS with honors, 1954. Intern London Hosp., 1954-55; asst. resident in medicine St. Luke's Hosp. Center, N.Y.C., 1957-59; tng. fellow in medicine Mass. Gen. Hosp., Boston, 1959-61; chief gastroenterology med. Service St. Luke's Hosp. Center, N.Y.C., 1961-96, attending physician, 1971—, Presbyn. Hosp., N.Y.C., 1988; chief gastroenterology St. Luke's-Roosevelt Hosp. Ctr., N.Y.C., 1996-2000; sr. scientist Inst. for Cancer Prevention, N.Y.C., 2000—. Adj. sr. scientist Strang Cancer Ctr., NY, 2000—; rsch. collaborator Brookhaven Nat. Lab., Upton, NY, 1973—79; mem. faculty dept. medicine Coll. Physicians and Surgeons Columbia U., N.Y.C., 1961—, prof., 1975—2000, prof. emeritus, 2000—, mem. Bio-engring. Inst., 1975—2000, Inst. Human Nutrition, 1978—2000, Comprehensive Cancer Ctr.; mem. 12th work group on clin. rsch. Nat. Commn. on Digestive Disease, 1977—79; mem. nat. sci. adv. com., nat. rev. com. Nat. Found. for Ileitis and Colitis, 1976—88, also chmn. rsch. tng. awards com.; vis. investigator Meml. Sloan-Kettering Cancer Ctr., 1988—89; vis. assoc. physician Rockefeller U., 2001—; Trevor Howell lectr. Brit. Geriat. Soc., 1992; Dorothy Ewerson lectr. U. Pisa, 1999. Author, contbr. chpts. to books, articles to med. jours. Served to maj. Brit. Royal Army M.C., 1955-57. Recipient William H. Rorer award in Gastroenterology, 1965, Jannsen Lifetime Achievement award in Digestive Diseases, 2002, Internat. Solvay Nutrition award, 2002; NIH grantee. Fellow: ACP (gov.'s com. 1978—81); mem.: AAAS, Am. Gastroenterology Assn. (pres. 1971), Orgn. Mondiale de Gastro-Enterologie (chair nominating com. 1990—94, nomenclature com. and rsch. com.), Harvey Soc., Gerontol. Soc. Am., N.Y. Acad. Sci., Am. Soc. Cancer Rsch., Am. Soc. Clin. Nutrition, Am. Soc. Clin. Investigation, Am. Physiol. Soc., Am. Fedn. Clin. Rsch., Am. Assn. Study of Liver Diseases, Intersoc. Com. Clin. Investigation in Digestive Disease (chmn. 1975—79), N.Y. Gastroenterol. Assn. (chmn. com. rsch. 1973—74, chmn. com. on aging 1982—86, chmn. admissions com. 1985—86, ethics com. 1997—2000, manpower and tng. com. 2001—). Office: Inst for Cancer Prevention 390 Fifth Ave New York NY 10018-

HOLT, PHILETUS HAVENS, IV, lawyer, consultant; b. Akron, Ohio, Aug. 12, 1936; s. Philetus Havens and Ottilia Dolina (Nichols) H.; B.A., Yale U., 1958, LL.B., 1961; m. Kathy Ann Kuryla, Dec. 2, 1978; children— Elizabeth Hopkins, Stephen. Admitted to Conn. bar, 1962; asso. Durey & Pierson, Stamford, Conn., 1962-64; dep. counsel, dir. downtown projects New Haven Redevel. Agy., 1964-69; partner Cogen Holt & Assos., cons., New Haven, 1969-76; spl. asst. to pres. Yale-New Haven Med. Center, 1976— ; acting pres., 1978-79; partner Holt Wexler & Crawford, New Haven, 1976— ; trustee Conn. Savs. Bank, New Haven, 1971— ; asso. fellow Jonathan Edwards Coll., Yale U., 1968. Bd. dirs. Shubert Performing Arts Ctr., New Haven Preservation Trust. Clubs: New Haven Yacht, New Haven Lawn, Mory's Assn. Home: 39 Wooster Pl New Haven CT 06511-6932 Office: 900 Chapel St New Haven CT 06510-2802

HOLT, ROBERT DONALD, columnist, auditor; b. Mantoa, N.J., July 11, 1954; s. Robert Lewis and Eleanore Geitz Holt. Student, Rowan Coll., 1976. Auditor Sony Corp., Pitman, NJ, 1995—2002; freelance columnist Courier-Post, Cherry Hill, NJ, 1999—2002, Gloucester County Times, Woodbury, NJ, 2001—02, Phila. Inquirer, 2000, Press Atlantic City, 2001—02. Author: Views From the Cheap Seats, 2002. Active Pen-in-Hand Writers, Sewell, NJ, 1998—2002. Avocations: reading, writing, running, weightlifting, travel. Home: 301 Coventry Ct Mantua NJ 08051

HOLT, ROBERT EZEL, data processing executive; b. Red Bay, Ala., May 8, 1957; s. Robert E. Sr. and Ruby (Weathers) H.; m. Elizabeth Ann Simmons, May 19, 1978; children: Robert E. III, James Michael. AA, N.E. Community Coll., 1977; BS, Miss. State U., 1980. Operator, programmer Watkins, Ward & Stafford, CPA, West Point, Miss., 1978-81; computer programmer Gen. Tire Corp., Inc., Columbus, Ohio, 1981-83; programmer, analyst Arvin Industries, Inc., Starkville, Miss., 1983-84; analyst, data processing mgr. Data Systems Mgmt., Inc., Columbus, Miss., 1984—. Data processing cons., West Point, 1983. Deacon, chmn. Calvary Bapt. Ch., West Point, 1990-91; mem. West Point Follies, 1991. Recipient Deacon Cert., Calvary Bapt. Ch., West Point, 1986. Democrat. Baptist. Avocations: golf, hunting, fishing, gardening. Home: 1190 Lone Oak Park West Point MS 39773-9792 Office: Data Systems Mgmt Inc Ste 300 200 6th St N Columbus MS 39703 E-mail: reh9773@lycos.com.

HOLT, ROBERT THEODORE, political scientist, dean, educator; b. Caledonia, Minn., July 26, 1928; s. Oscar Martin and Olga Linnea (Mattson) H.; m. Shirley J. Russell, Dec. 14, 1957; children: Susan Jane, Ann Carol, Sharon Linnea. AB magna cum laude, Hamline U., 1950; MPA, Princeton U., 1952, PhD, 1957. Instr. dept. polit. sci. U. Minn., Mpls., 1956-57, asst. prof., 1957-60, assoc. prof., 1960-64, prof., 1964-2001, prof. emeritus, 2001—, chmn. dept., 1978-81, dir. Ctr. for Comparative Studies in Tech. Devel. and Social Change, 1967-80, dir. rsch. devel. Coll. Liberal Arts, 1975-78, dean Grad. Sch., 1982-91, chair rsch. exec. coun., 1988-91, interim dean Coll. Liberal Arts, 1996, prof. emeritus, 2001. Bd. dirs. Coun. Grad. Schs., 1984-90, chair, 1989-90; mem. Assembly Social and Behavioral Scis., NAS, 1972-75. Author: Radio Free Europe, 1958, (with F.W. Van de Velde) Strategic Psychological Operations, 1960, The Soviet Union: Paradox and Change, 1962, (with J.E. Turner) The Political Basis of Economic Development, 1966, The Methodology of Comparative Research, 1970, Political Parties in Action, 1971, (with Turner and Chase) American Government in Comparative Perspective, 1979 With U.S. Army, 1953-55. Fellow Ctr. for Advanced Studies in Behavioral Scis., 1961-62. Mem. Am. Polit. Sci. Assn., Internat. Studies Assn., Mid West Polit Sci. Assn., Assn of Grad. Schs. (exec. com. 1985-88, chair grad. student fin. assistance com. 1986-91), 39er's Club. Episcopalian. Office: U Minn Polict Sci Dept 1414 Social Sci Tower 267 19th Ave S Minneapolis MN 55455-0499

HOLT, ROCHELLE LYNN, writer, lecturer; b. Chgo., Mar. 17, 1946; d. Russell and Olga G. (Kochick) H. BA in English, U. Ill., 1967; MFA in English, U. Iowa, 1970; PhD in English and Psychology, Columbia Pacific U., 1980. Educator, writer-in-residence (8 states), 1970—. Author: Anais Nin: An Understanding of her Art, 1997, (criticism) SCARS, 1998, Wound, 2001, The Weight of Rain, 2003; co-author (with Olga G. Holt): (novels) Three Southwest Mysteries, 1996, With Promises to Keep, 2003; co-author: (with Va Love Long) Infamous in Our Prime, 1998; columnist S.W. Fla. Poetry Newsletter, 2001—; author: (poetry) Caution: Child at Play, 2000, Whispering Secrets, 2002. Grantee NEA, Birmingham, Ala., 1976-77, Fla. Humanities Coun., 1997, 1999, Puffin Found., 2000, 2002.

HOLT, RUSH DEW, congressman, physics educator, researcher, consultant; b. Weston, W.Va., Oct. 15, 1948; s. Rush Dew and Helen (Froelich) H.; m. Margaret Lancefield, 1985. BA, Carleton Coll., 1970; MS, NYU, 1975, PhD, 1981. Am. Phys. Soc. Congl. fellow U.S. Congress, Washington, 1982-83; vis. scientist High Altitude Obs., Boulder, Colo., 1984; asst. prof. physics dept. Swarthmore (Pa.) Coll., 1980-88; sci. analyst U.S. Dept. State, 1987-89; asst. dir. Plasma Physics Lab. Princeton (N.J.) U., 1989-98; mem. U.S. Congress from 12th N.J. dist., 1999—; intelligence com., budget com., edn. and workforce com., former mem. resources com. Patentee in field. Mem. Am. Phys. Soc., Am. Assn. Physics Tchrs., AAAS, Sigma Xi. Democrat. Achievements include being a five time winner on "Jeopardy". Office: Ho of Reps 1019 Longworth Hob Washington DC 20515-0001 : 50 Washington Rd Princeton Junction NJ 08550*

HOLT, SIDNEY CLARK, journalist; b. St. Louis, Sept. 7, 1955; s. Noel Clark and Rosalee (Powell) H.; m. Jill Brodsky, Nov. 16, 1991; children: Elizabeth Summers, Victoria Edmunds. BA, Columbia U., 1979. Editor Simon & Schuster Inc., N.Y.C., 1979-84; asst. editor Rolling Stone, N.Y.C., 1984-85, assoc. editor, 1985-87, sr. editor, 1987-89, asst. mng. editor, 1989-90, mng. editor, 1990-97; editl. dir. US mag., N.Y.C., 1995-97; v.p. Wenner Media, Inc., N.Y.C., 1996-97; exec. v.p., editor-in-chief Ad Week Mags., N.Y.C., 1998—. Editor: The Rolling Stone Interviews: The 1980s, 1989. Bd. dirs. Fedn. Protestant Welfare Agys., N.Y.C., 1994—. Mem. Am. Soc. Mag. Editors, Columbia Club N.Y. Democrat. Methodist. Home: 200 E 66th St New York NY 10021 Office: AdWeek Magsne 770 Broadway New York NY 10003 E-mail: sholt@adweek.com.

HOLT, STEPHEN S. astrophysicist; b. N.Y.C., May 17, 1940; s. Aaron J. and Faye E. (Schwartz) Holtz; m. Carol Ann Weissman, June 3, 1961; children: Peter David, Eric Lawrence, Laura Kimberly. BS, NYU, 1961, PhD in Physics, 1966. Instr. physics NYU, 1964—66; astrophysicist Goddard Space Flight Center, Greenbelt, Md., 1966-2000; chief high energy astrophysics NASA Hdqrs., 1980-81; dir. Lab. for High Energy Astrophysics Goddard Space Flight Ctr., Greenbelt, Md., 1983-90, dir. space scis., 1990-2000; prof. Physics Olin Coll., Needham, Mass., 2000—; prof., dir. natural scis. Babson Coll., Wellesley, Mass., 2000—. Lectr. physics U. Md., 1967-87, adj. prof. astronomy, 1988—. Contbr. articles to profl. jours. Recipient medal for exceptional sci. achievement NASA, 1977, 80, medal for outstanding leadership, 1991, 2000, Presdl. meritorious exec. award, 1992, John C. Lindsay Meml. award outstanding scientific achievement, 1993, NASA Disting. Svc. medal, 2000. Fellow AAAS, Am. Phys. Soc. (chair divsn. exec. com.); mem. Am. Astron. Soc. (chair div.), COSPAR (chair div.), Sigma Xi, Tau Beta Pi, Sigma Pi Sigma. Home: 77 Pond Ave Apt 1202 Brookline MA 02445-7115 Office: 1735 Great Plain Ave Needham MA 02492-1245 E-mail: steve.holt@olin.edu. *The most important intrinsic requisites for success in experimental science are probably imagination and diligence. Very few individuals possess these in sufficient quantities to dominate the extrinsic variables which shape their careers in research, however. I consider myself fortunate to have been able to capitalize on whatever talent I possess by having my research interests aligned with funding priorities, and by being blessed with the cooperation of unselfish and stimulating colleagues.*

HOLT, THADDEUS, yer; b. Birmingham, Ala., Nov. 26, 1929; s. Thad and Sarah Ames (Oliver) H.; m. Waring Inge, Dec. 1, 1956; children— Sarah, Harrison. B.A., U. of South, 1951; M.A., Yale U., 1952; B.A. (Rhodes Scholar), Oxford U., 1954; LL.B., Harvard U., 1956. Bar: Ala. 1956, D.C. 1959, U.S. Supreme Ct. 1960, N.Y. 1969, Pa. 1985. Assoc. Cabaniss & Johnston, Birmingham, 1956-58; assoc. Covington & Burling, Washington, 1958-65; dep. undersec. Dept. Army, Washington, 1965-67; pres. Leacock Pennebaker Inc., NYC, 1968-69; sec. Corp. for Pub. Broadcasting, N.Y.C. and Washington, 1970-71; ptnr. Breed, Abbott & Morgan, Washington and N.Y.C., 1972-86; sole practice, Washington, Carlisle, Pa., 1986— . Decorated for Disting. civilian service U.S. Army, 1967. Mem. Am. Law Inst., Am. Soc. for Legal History, Washington Inst. for Fgn. Affairs. Reformed Episcopalian. Clubs: Metropolitan (Washington); River (NYC) Contbr. articles to N.Y. Times Book Rev., other magazines. Office: 910 16th St NW Washington DC 20006-2903 also: 1818 N St NW Ste 600 Washington DC 20036-2476

HOLT, WILLIAM E. lawyer; b. Phila., Aug. 31, 1945; BBA, U. Iowa, 1967, JD with distinction, 1970. Bar: Iowa 1970, Wash. 1971. Law clk. to Hon. William T. Beeks U.S. Dist. Ct. (we. dist.) Wash., 1970-71; mem., chmn. Gordon, Thomas, Honeywell, Malanca, Peterson & Daheim, Tacoma, 1999, 2000. Adj. prof. U. Puget Sound Law Sch., 1974-75. Note editor Iowa Law Rev., 1969-70. Mem. ABA, Wash. State Bar Assn. (exec. com. real property, probate and trust sect. 1987-89), Phi Delta Phi. Office: Gordon Thomas Honeywell Malanca Peterson & Daheim PO Box 1157 Ste 2200 Tacoma WA 98401-1157 E-mail: wholt@gth-law.com.

HOLT, WILLIAM HENRY, physicist, researcher; b. San Antonio, Aug. 5, 1939; s. Joseph Marion and Mildred Louise (Ragsdale) H.; m. Margaret Ann Harrell, June 21, 1963; children: Benjamin, Andrew. BS cum laude, St. Mary's U., San Antonio, 1960; MA, U. Tex., 1962, PhD, 1967. Postdoctoral fellow, lectr. U. Man., Winnipeg, Can., 1966-69; rsch. physicist Naval Surface Warfare Ctr., Dahlgren, Va., 1969—. Patentee; contbr. articles and papers to numerous sci. jours. and revs. Past tchr. Sunday sch. St. Matthias United Meth. Ch., Fredericksburg, Va.; past co-chmn. edn., past lay leader, mem. pastor-parish rels. com., past chmn. coun. on ministries. Mem. Am. Phys. Soc., Can. Assn. Physicists, Materials Rsch. Soc., Sigma Xi, Sigma Pi Sigma. Lions. Office: Naval Surface Warfare Ctr Dahlgren VA 22448-5100

HOLTAN, MERRIE SUE, communications educator; b. Rushford, Minn., Nov. 19, 1948; d. Elvin Stanley Dubbs and Elberta Dorothy Eggen; m. Philip E. Holtan; children: Elise M., Mark P., Johanna M. BS in Speech/Comms., U. Minn., 1970; MA in Speech/Comms., N.D. State U., 1989; postgrad. in creative writing, Moorhead State U. Youth dir. Luth. Parishes, St. Paul, Minn., 1970-73; part-time h.s. tchr. Guadalajara, Mex., 1973-81; freelance writer, 1981—; area woman's editor Area Woman Mag., Fargo, N.D., 1984—; instr. Concordia Coll., Moorhead, Minn., 1989—; comms. dir. FM Family YMCA, Fargo, 1986-89. Devel. trainer global awareness Great Plains Software/Microsoft, Fargo, 1998—2000; newsletter editor speech comms. dept. Concordia Coll., 1997—. Editor: Cookbook of Champions, 1992 (Nat. award, 1993); contbr. numerous articles to profl. jours. and newspapers; author: (video and biography) Power and Stride: The Nancy Burggraf Story (Screening and Spl. award at Fargo Film Festival., 2003). Named YWCA Woman of Yr., 1993; recipient Personality Profile Writing award N.D. Presswomen, 1997-99; winner 2 nat. writing awards Nat. Presswomen, 2003. Mem.: Nat. Press Women. Democrat. Lutheran. Avocations: aerobics, gardening, reading, sports psychology, women's sports. Home: 16 N Terrace Fargo ND 58102-3816 Office: Concordia Coll 901 8th St S Moorhead MN 56562-0001

HOLTBY, KENNETH FRASER, retired manufacturing executive; b. Escanaba, Mich., May 18, 1922; s. David William and Nina Kate (Hemenway) H.; m. Bettie Roberts, June 11, 1943; children— Michael Earle, Tracy Linda Buren, Jeffrey Thomas, Kristen Ann Buren, Matt Fraser BSME, Calif. Inst. Tech., 1947; SM in Indsl. Mgmt., MIT, 1961. Aerodynamicist Boeing Co., Seattle, 1947, various mgmt. positions, 1953-82, sr. v.p., 1982-87; ret. Found. mem. Pacific Sci. Ctr., Seattle, 1974—. Served to lt. USAF, 1943-46. Fellow: AIAA (hon. Aircraft Design award 1984, Laureate Bagnou prize), Brit. Royal Aero. Soc.; mem.: U.S. Nat. Acad. Engring., NRC. Avocations: tennis; skiing; sailing. Address: 6346 So Chinook Dr Clinton WA 98236

HOLTE, DEBRA LEAH, investment executive, financial analyst; b. Madison, Wis. d. Daniel Kenneth and Marian Anne Reitan. BA, Concordia Coll., Moorhead, Minn., 1973. Chartered Fin. Analyst, Cert. Divorce Planner. Capital markets specialist 1st Bank Mpls., 1981-83; v.p. Allison-Williams Co., Mpls., 1983-86; exec. v.p. Hamil & Holte Inc., Denver, 1986-93; pres. Holte & Assocs., Denver, Taos, N.Mex., 1993—. Active Denver Jr. League, Western Pension Com., 1986—; bd. dirs. Denver Children's Home, 1987—, treas., 1987-91, chmn. fin. com., 1987-91, v.p., 1990—, chmn. nominating com., 1991—, pres.-elect, 1994-95, bd. pres., 1995—; adv. bd. Luth. Social Svcs., 1987; co-chair U.S. Ski Team Fundraiser; bd. dirs. Minn. Vocat. Edn. Fin., Mpls., 1984-86; bd. dirs. Colo. Ballet, 1988-93, chair nominating com., 1991-93, v.p., 1992-93, chmn. bd., 1993; mem. Fin. Analyst Nat. Task Force in Bondholder Rights, 1988-90; bd. dirs. Ctrl. City Opera Guild, 1994-95, Western Chamber Ballet, 1994-96, Taos Humane Soc., 1997—; social co-chmn. The Arapahoe Fox Hunt, 1993-94; bd. dirs., mem. steering com. Denver Dumb Friends League, 2001—. Mem. Fin. Analysts Fedn., Denver Soc. Security Analysts (bd. dirs. 1990-97, chair ethics and bylaws com. 1987—, chair edn. com. 1988, chair membership com. 1989, rec. sec. 1990, sec. 1991, treas. 1992, program chair 1993, pres. 1994-95, dir. 1995-96).

HOLTER, ARLEN ROLF, cardiothoracic surgeon; b. Sullivan's Island, SC, Feb. 1, 1946; s. Arne and Helen (Soderberg) H.; m. Elizabeth Ann Reid, Nov. 9, 1974; children: Matthew Arlen, Peter Reid, Andrew Douglas. BS, Stanford U., 1968; MS, U. Ill., Chgo., 1971, MD, 1973. Diplomate Am. Bd. Thoracic Surgery, Am. Bd. Surgery. Intern Mass. Gen. Hosp., Boston, 1973-74, resident in surgery, 1974-78; sr. registrar in cardiac surgery South Hampton Chest Hosp., 1978; resident in cardiac surgery Yale U., New Haven, 1978-80; pvt. practice Mpls., 1980—. Instr. surgery Yale U., 1979-80. Contbr. articles to profl. jours. Recipient Franklin McLean rsch. award U. Chgo., 1973. Fellow: ACS; mem.: Mpls. Acad. Medicine, Am. Heart Assn., Soc. Thoracic Surgeons, US Triathlon Assn. (Iron Man finisher). Lutheran. Avocations: skiing, photography, triathlons. Office: Cardiac Surg Assocs Ste 258 2356 University Ave W Saint Paul MN 55112

HOLTER, JOHN WILLIAM, medical instrument manufacturing company executive; b. Chgo., Apr. 1, 1916; s. Charles Robert and Favian (Erskine) H. Grad., Spring Garden (Pa.) Inst., 1938; D.Sc., U. Sheffield (Eng.), 1976. Rsch. technician Socony-Vacuum Oil co., 1946-50; Yale & Towne, 1950-56; founder Holter Co., Bridgeport, Pa., 1956; owner, 1956-67; tech. cons., dir. Extracorporeal Med. Spltys., Inc., King of Prussia, Pa., 1967-77; co-founder Holter-Hausner Internat., 1977—. V.p. Montgomery County chpt. for Retarded Children, 1960-66; pub. rels. chmn. Metric assn. U.S., 1969. Served with AUS, 1941-45. Recipient A.C.S. award, 1957; named Man of Yr., Norristown, Bridgeport (Pa.) V.F.W., 1958. Mem. Soc. for Rsch. into Hydrocephalus and Spina bifida (hon.), Internat. Soc. Pediat. Neurosurgeons (hon.), European Soc. Pediatric Neurosurgery (assoc.). Achievements include invention of valve for controlling hydrocephalus; research on artificial heart; patentee med., mech. and yacht devices. Office: PO Box 100 Bridgeport PA 19405-0100

HOLTER, PATRA JO, artist, art education consultant; b. Ashland, wis., Mar. 6, 1936; d. Cap and Sigrid (Gadda) H. BS, U. Wis., 1958; MA, U. Calif., Berkeley, 1962; student, Nat. Acad. Art and U. Oslo, 1963; cert. in adminstrn., Fairfield U., 1983; postgrad., New Sch. Social Rsch., UCLA, U. Colo., Pratt Inst. Cert. tchr., N.Y., Wis., adminstr., N.Y. Art tchr. Herricks Jr. H.S., New Hyde Park, N.Y., 1958-60; assoc. art U. Calif., Berkeley, 1961-62; adult art tchr. U. Calif. Alumni Camp, Pinecrest, summer 1961; elem. art tchr. Ctrl. Sch., Mamaroneck, N.Y., 1964, Edgewood Sch., Scarsdale, 1971-82; elem. and jr. H.S. art tchr. Quaker Ridge Sch., Scarsdale, N.Y., 1964-70; art tchr. Scarsdale Sr. H.S., 1982-84, chmn. art dept., 1984-93; dist. visual arts supr. Scarsdale Sch. Sys., 1989-93. Art tchr. workshops, curriculum developer, cons. in field, liaison Scarsdale; visual arts coord. Lincoln Ctr. Inst., N.Y.C., 1978-80; liaison art tchr. Westchester Coun. for Arts, Scarsdale, 1970's. Author, artist: Photography Without a Camera, 1972, reprinted 1980; contbr. articles, photographs to profl. publs.; group and solo exhbns. include Wis. Salon of Art, Madison, 1958, Worth Ryder Gallery, Berkeley, 1962, Am. Embassy, Oslo, 1963, Mount Mercy Coll. Gallery, Cedar Rapids, Iowa, 1988, Silvermine Galleries, 1994-2000, Waveny Carriage Barn, New Canaan, 1995-97, Washburn (Wis.) Hist. Mus. and Cultural Ctr., 1995-2000, Northland Coll., Ashland, 1996-99, Meridian Internat. Ctr., Washington, 1997, Tweed Mus. Art, Duluth, Minn., 1997-99, Ct. Graphic Arts Ctr., Norwalk, 1997-98, Wis. Arts Bd. Internat., Madison, 1999, Manhattan Borough Pres.'s Gallery, N.Y.C., 2001. Fulbright scholar, Norway, 1962-63, ext., summer 1963; recipient Exemplary Media award N.Y. Regents Adv. Coun., 1968; Scarsdale Sch. Sys. grantee, 1972. Mem., midwest rep. Fulbright Arts Task Force; mem. Fulbright Assn., Norwegian Fulbright Assn., Silvermine Guild of Art, N.Y. State United Tchrs. Assn., Am. Fedn. Tchrs., Nat. Mus. Women in Arts, N.Y. State Ret. Tchrs., Ashland Hist. Soc., Ashland Alliance for Sustainability, Chequamegon Bay Area Arts Coun., New Canaan Soc. for Arts, Wilton Garden Club, Nat. Coun. State Garden Clubs, Kappa Delta. Avocations: travel, horticulture, antiques.

HOLTHAUSEN, MARTHA ANNE, interior designer, painter; b. Columbus, Ohio, Oct. 28, 1934; d. Clyde Aloysius and Olive Letitia (Marlowe) Gloeckner; m. Don Trudeau Allensworth, Aug. 14, 1960 (div. 1976); 1 child, Karen Ayn; m. Ernest Arthur Holthausen, Dec. 9, 1989. BFA cum laude, Ohio State U., 1956; postgrad., Baldwin-Wallace Coll., 1959, Mt. Vernon Coll., Washington, 1980, 81. Fashion illustrator The Marston Co., San Diego, 1956-57, The Higbee Co., Cleve., 1957-58; instr. art Lakewood (Ohio) Pub. Schs., 1958-60; tchr. Princes Georges County (Md.) Pub. Schs., 1960; account exec. Stansbury Design, Inc., Prince Georges County, Md., 1975-76; interior designer Berwin Interiors, Bethesda, Md., 1977-79, W. & J. Sloane, Inc., Washington, 1980-84; pres., interior designer Martha Allensworth Interior Design, Inc., Falls Church, Va., 1984—. Guest artist-in-residence Nat. Park Svc., Yosemite Nat. Park, Calif., summer 1988, 89, 91, 95. Watercolor and oil paintings in pvt. collections. Bd. dirs. C. of C. Herndon, Va., 1985-86; v.p. Montgomery County (Md.) Art Assn., 1962-63. Mem. AAUW, Vienna (Va.) Arts Soc. Presbyterian. Avocations: gardening, bicycling. Office: Martha Allensworth Interior Design Inc Plaza America Dr No 732 Reston VA 20190-4700

HOLTKAMP, JAMES ARNOLD, lawyer, educator; b. Albuquerque, Apr. 4, 1949; s. Clarence Jules and Karyl Irene (Roberts) H.; m. Marianne Coltrin, Dec. 28, 1973; children: Ariane, Brent William, Rachel, Allison, David Roberts. BA, Brigham Young U., 1972; JD, George Washington U., 1975. Bar: Utah 1976, U.S. Dist. Ct. Utah 1977, U.S. Ct. Appeals (10th cir.) 1979, Colo. 1995. Mem. staff U.S. Senate Watergate Com., Washington, 1974; atty.-advisor Dept. Transp., Washington, 1975; atty. Dept. Interior, Washington, 1975-77; assoc. Van Cott, Bagley, Cornwall & McCarthy, Salt Lake City, 1977-81, ptnr., 1981-89, Davis, Graham & Stubbs, Salt Lake City, 1989-92, Stoel Rives, Salt Lake City, 1992-97, LeBoeuf, Lamb, Greene & MacRae, Salt Lake City, 1997—2003, Holland & Hart, Salt Lake City, 2003—. Adj. prof., Law Sch. Brigham Young U., Provo, Utah, 1979—2002; adj. prof. Coll. Law U. Utah, 1995—. Co-author: Utah Environmental and Land Use Permits and Approvals Manual, 1981; contbr. articles to legal jours. Missionary LDS Ch., 1968-70; active Gt. Salt Lake coun. Boy Scouts Am., 1977—; trustee Coalition for Utah's Future, 1996-2001. Mem. ABA (vice-chmn. air quality commn. 1985-89), Utah State Bar (chmn. energy and natural resources sect. 1984-85, chmn. pub. utilities law com. 1990-93, energy and natural resources sect., Lawyer of Yr. award 1981, Disting. Svc. award 2002), Utah Mining Assn. (bd. dirs. 1999—), Rocky Mtn. Mineral Law Found. (trustee 1999-2002, sec. 2002--), Utah Petroleum Assn., George Washington Law Assn. (nat. bd. dirs. 1999—). Home: 7990 Deer Creek Rd Salt Lake City UT 84121-5752 Office: Holland & Hart 60 E South Temple Ste 2000 Salt Lake City UT 84111-1031

HOLTKAMP, SUSAN CHARLOTTE, elementary education educator; b. Houston, Feb. 23, 1957; d. Clarence Jules and Karyl Irene (Roberts) H. BS in Early Childhood Edn., Brigham Young U., Provo, Utah, 1979, MEd, 1982. Cert. tchr. Utah, ESL endorsement U. Utah, 2002. 2d grade tchr. Nebo Sch. Dist., Spanish Fork, Utah, 1979-84, kindergarten tchr., 1984-85; tchr. 2d grade DODDS, Mannheim, Fed. Republic Germany, 1985-86; tchr. 3d grade Jordan Sch. Dist., Salt Lake City, 1987-92, tchr. 5th grade, 1992—2002, tchr. 6th grade, 2002—. Mem. NEA, JEA, Utah Edn. Assn., ASCD.

HOLTMEIER, ROBERT J. accountant; b. Cin., Apr. 17, 1924; s. Elmer J. and Hilda M. Holtmeier; m. Anna Marie Holtmeier, Sept. 4, 1948; 1 child, Teresa Ann. MBA, U. Cin., 1978. CPA, Ohio. Contr., asst. treas. Aluminum Industries, Cin., 1947-59; v.p. fin. Merry Mfg. Co., Cin., 1958-69, Denby Ltd., Cin., 1969-74; sec., treas. Porter Precision Products, Cin., 1974-86; owner Robert J. Holtmeier CPA, Cin., 1986—. Author: Business Forecasting in Today's World, 1955. Sgt. USAF, 1942-46, ETO. Mem. Ohio Soc. CPAs. Avocations: golf, painting in oil, model building.

HOLTON, GERALD, physicist, science historian; b. Berlin, May 23, 1922; s. Emanuel and Regina (Rossmann) H.; m. Nina Rossfort, Sept. 12, 1947; children: Thomas, Stephan. Nat. certificate elec. engring., Sch. Tech., Oxford, Eng., 1940; BA, Wesleyan U., 1941, MA, 1942, D.H.L. (hon.), 1981; MA, Harvard U., 1946, PhD, 1948; D.Sc. (hon.), Grinnell Coll., 1967, Kenyon Coll., 1977, Bates Coll., 1979; LL.D. (hon.), Duke U., 1981. Instr. Wesleyan U., 1941-42, Brown U., 1942-43; staff, officers radar course and OSRD Harvard, 1943-45, various faculty positions, 1947—; rsch. prof. Harvard-Leningrad U., 1962; vis. mem. Inst. Advanced Study, Princeton, 1964; fellow Center Advanced Study in Behavioral Scis., Stanford, 1975-76. Vis. prof. MIT, 1976-94; Herbert Spencer lectr. Oxford U., 1979; Rothschild lectr. Harvard U., 1997; Jefferson lectr. in humanities, 1981; John Simon Guggenheim fellow, 1980-81; mem. com. scholarly comm. with People's Republic of China, NAS, 1967-72, mem. com. conduct of sci., NAS, 1989-91, mem. office on pub. understanding sci., NAS, 1995-2001; mem. U.S. Nat. Commn. on UNESCO, 1975-80, U.S. Nat. Commn. of IUHPS, 1982-89, Coun. of Scholars, Libr. of Congress, 1980-95, U.S. Nat. Commn. on Excellence in Edn., 1981-83; mem. adv. com. for sci. and engring. edn. NSF, 1985-93, chair, 1986-89; mem. selection bd. Albert Einstein Peace Prize, 1980—; mem. German Am. Acad. Coun. Kuratorium, 1997-2000; mem. com. interdisciplinary rsch. NAS, 2003—. Author: Introduction to Concepts and Theories in Physical Science, 1952, 2d edit., 1985, (with D.H.D. Roller) Foundations of Modern Physical Science, 1958, Science and the Modern Mind, 1958, Science and Culture, 1965, (with others) The Project Physics Course, 1970, 75, 81, The 20th Century Sciences: Studies in Intellectual Biography, 1971, Thematic Origins of Scientific Thought: Kepler to Einstein, 1973, 2d edit., 1988, The Scientific Imagination: Case Studies, 1978, 98, (with others) Limits of Scientific Inquiry, 1979, Albert Einstein, Historical and Cultural Perspectives, 1982, 97, The Advancement of Science and Its Burdens, 1986, 98, Science and Anti-Science, 1993, Einstein, History and Other Passions, 1996, (with Gerhard Sonnert) Gender Differences in Science Careers: The Project Access Study, 1995, Who Succeeds in Science? The Gender Dimension, 1995, (with Stephen Brush) Physics, The Human Adventure, 2001, (with Gerhard Sonnert) Ivory Bridges: Connecting Science and Society, 2002, (with David Cassidy and James Rutherford) Understanding Physics, 2002; editor-in-chief Daedalus, 1957-61; mem. editl. com., editl. adv. bd. The Collected Papers of Albert Einstein, 1980—; contbr. articles to profl. jours. Recipient J.D. Bernal prize Soc. Social Studies Sci., 1989, Joseph Priestley medal Dickinson Coll., 1994. Fellow AAAS (bd. dirs. 1967-71), Am. Philos. Soc., Am. Acad. Arts and Sci. (editor 1957-63, exec. bd. 1970-78, coun. 1991-95), Am. Phys. Soc. (chmn. divsn. history of physics 1992-93), Internat. Acad. History of Sci. (v.p. 1981-89), Deutsche Acad. Naturforscher-Leopoldina, Internat. Acad. Philosophy of Sci.; mem. Am. Inst. Physics (governing bd. 1968-74, Andrew Gemant award 1989), Am. Assn. Physics Tchrs. (Robert A. Millikan medal 1967, Oersted medal 1979), History Sci. Soc. (pres. 1983-84, George Sarton meml. lectr. 1962, George Sarton medal 1989, Joseph H. Hazen Edn. prize 1998). Office: Harvard U Jefferson Phys Lab Cambridge MA 02138 E-mail: holton@physics.harvard.edu.

HOLTON, GRACE HOLLAND, accountant; b. Durham, N.C., Sept. 14, 1957; d. Samuel Melanchthon and B. Margaret (Umberger) Holton. BS in Math., Univ. N.C., Greensboro, 1978; MBA, Univ. N.C., Chapel Hill, 1984; M.Acctg. Sci., U. Ill., 1993. CPA N.C., cert. mgmt. acct. Indsl. engr. Burlington Industries, Inc., Mayodan, N.C., 1978-79, plant indsl. engr. Stoneville, N.C., 1979-80; methods indsl. engr. Blue Cross and Blue Shield of N.C., Durham, 1980-82; fin. analyst R.J. Reynolds, Inc., Winston-Salem, N.C., 1984-85; accounting cons. Ryder Truck Rental, Inc., Miami, Fla., 1985-88; contr. Ryder Jacobs (divsn. Ryder Distbn. Resources), Jessup, Md., 1988-90; grad. asst. in acctg. U. Ill., Urbana, 1990-93; contr. Salem NationaLease, Winston-Salem, N.C., 1993-94; fin. officer Chapel Hill-Carrboro City Schs., 1994-99; mgr. benefits and payroll Ryder Pub. Transp. Svcs., Cin., 1999-2000; exec. dir. budget and evaluation Charlotte-Mecklenburg Schs., 2000—02. Scholar KPMG-Peat Marwick scholar, 1991—92. Mem.: AICPA, N.C. Soc. CPA, Inst. Mgmt. Accts. Democrat. Methodist.

HOLTON, J(ERRY) THOMAS, concrete company executive; b. Middletown, Ohio, June 7, 1932; s. Joseph Walton and Elizabeth (Fagaly) H.; m. Annie Lou Dearborn, Sept. 26, 1958; children: Elizabeth, Luanne, Ruth, Catherine, J. Thomas Jr. BSE, Princeton U., 1954; MBA, Harvard U., 1959. V.p. Sherman Concrete Pipe Co., Birmingham, Ala., 1959-66, pres., 1966-74, Sherman Industries, Birmingham, 1974-84; pres., chmn. Sherman Internat. Corp., Birmingham, 1984—. Bd. dirs. Fed. Res. Bank Atlanta, Robin-Morton Corp., KSA, Inc., Sciotoville, Ohio, The Shaw Group Ltd., Halifax, N.S., Stockham Valve & Fittings Co. Inc. Pres. coun. U. Ala. Birmingham, 1984-92; mem. exec. bd. Boy Scouts Am., Birmingham, 1985—; chmn., Salvation Army, Birmingham; elder Briarwood Presbyn. Ch., Birmingham, 1968—. Lt. comdr. Civil Engring. Corp. USN, 1954-57. Mem. Birmingham Country Club, Shoal Creek, The Club, Summit Club. Home: 10 Ridge Dr Birmingham AL 35213-3632 Office: Sherman International Inc 402 Office Park Dr Ste 100 Birmingham AL 35223-2435 E-mail: jtholton@aol.com.

HOLTON, RAYMOND WILLIAM, botanist, educator; b. Riverside, Calif., Apr. 30, 1929; s. Homer Hopkins and H. Charlotte (Hall) H.; children: Betsey Diane, Nancy Joann, William Louis, Thomas Raymond. BA, Pomona Coll., 1951; MS, U. Mich., 1954, PhD, 1958. Instr. botany U. Mich.-Flint Coll., 1957-59, asst. prof., 1959-61; research asso. U. Tex., 1961-62, USPHS trainee, 1962-63; asst. prof. botany U. Tenn., 1963-64, assoc. prof., acting head botany, 1964-65, prof., head botany, 1965-72, 73-85, prof. botany, 1985-96, prof. emeritus, 1997—, co-dir., 1984-86, acting dir. biology consortium, 1992-93. Sr. Fulbright lectr. dept. botany U. Durham, Eng., 1972-73; vis. prof. U. Groningen, The Netherlands, 1987, 94. Mem. Bot. Soc. Am., Am. Soc. Plant Physiologists, Phycol. Soc. Am., Internat., Brit. phycol. socs., AAAS. Achievements include phylogenetic and biochemical research on algae, particularly cyanobacteria and fresh water rhodophyta. Home: 118 Greenbrier Dr Knoxville TN 37919-4165 Office: U Tenn Dept Botany 437 Hesler Biology Bldg Knoxville TN 37996-0001

HOLTON, WALTER CLINTON, JR., lawyer; b. Winston-Salem, N.C. s. Walter Clinton and Mabel (Hartsfield) H.; m. Lynne Rowley. BA in Polit. Sci., U. N.C., 1977; JD, Wake Forest U., 1984. Bar: N.C. 1984, U.S. Dist. Ct. (mid. dist.) N.C. 1986, U.S. Ct. Appeals (4th cir.) 1990, U.S. Supreme Ct., 1996. Asst. dist. atty. Office 21st Jud. Dist. Atty., Winston-Salem, 1985-87; assoc. White & Crumpler, Winston-Salem, 1987-88; pvt. practice Winston-Salem, 1989; ptnr. Holton & Menefee, Winston-Salem, 1989-92, Tisdale, Holton & Menefee, PA, Winston-Salem, 1992-94; U.S. atty. Office U.S. Atty. Mid. Dist. N.C., Greensboro, N.C., 1994-2001; pvt. practice Grace Holton Tisdale & Clifton PA, Winston-Salem, 2001—. Democrat. Office: Grace Holton Tisdale & Clifton 301 N Main St Ste 100 Winston Salem NC 27101 Fax: (336) 721-1176. E-mail: wholton@ghtclaw.com.

HOLTON, WILLIAM, artist; b. Knoxville, Tenn., 1966; Student, U. Ariz., 1987—88; BFA, Atlanta Coll. Art, 1991. Intern Rolling Stone Press, Atlanta, 1989; asst. Atlanta Arts Festival, 1991. One-man shows include Anthony Ardavin Gallery, Atlanta, TVUUC Gallery, Knoxville, 1999, two-person shows include, Anthony Ardavin Gallery, 1995, 1997, 1999, exhibited in group shows, 1993, Atlanta Coll. Art Gallery, 1993, Southeastern Ctr. Contemporary Art, Winston-Salem, 1997, Zoe Gallery, Louisville, 1998, 1999; contbg. artist Drawing, Space, Form and Expression, 1988. Recipient Merit award, Magic City Arts Festival, 1991, Best of Show award, ARTFEST, 1994; grantee Regional Visual Arts fellow, Southeastern Arts Fedn., Nat. Endowment Arts, 1996.

HOLTON, WILLIAM COFFEEN, electrical engineering executive; b. Washington, July 24, 1930; s. William B. and Esther (Coffeen) H.; m. Mary Schaeffer, Aug. 5, 1953; children: Elizabeth Ashe, William Andrew, Sarah Anne. BS in Physics, U. N.C., 1952; PhD in Physics, U. Ill., 1960. Tech. staff corp. rsch. lab. Tex. Instruments, Dallas, 1960-65, mgr. quantum electronics, 1965-72, dir. advanced components lab., 1972-78, dir. R & D semicondr. group, 1978-82, mgr. strategic planning, 1982-83; dir. Semiconductor Rsch. Corp., Research Triangle Park, N.C., 1984-88, sr. dir., 1989-90, v.p., 1990-95; prof. N.C. State U., Raleigh, 1996—. Lt. (j.g.) USN, 1952-54. Union Carbide fellow, 1959; recipient Dept. of Energy award, 1997. Fellow IEEE (mem. awards bd. 1999—, Phillips award 1998), Am. Phys. Soc., Electron. Device Soc. of IEEE (governing bd. 1975-98, chmn. internat. electron device meeting 1975); mem. Phi Beta Kappa, Phi Eta Sigma. Presbyterian. Home: 601 Brookview Dr Chapel Hill NC 27514-1401 Office: NC State Univ Box 8617 234B Engring Grad Rsch Ctr Raleigh NC 27695-8617 E-mail: holton@eos.ncsu.edu.

HOLTSCHNEIDER, DENNIS H. university official, priest; b. Detroit, Jan. 14, 1962; BA, Niagara U., 1984; MDiv, ThM, Mary Immaculate Sem., Northampton, Pa., 1989; EdD, Harvard U., 1997. Ordained priest Roman Cath. Ch., 1989. Assoc. dean, asst. prof. St. John's U., N.Y.C., 1996-99; exec. v.p., COO, Niagara U., Niagara Falls, N.Y., 2000—. Mem. N.Y. Acad. Pub. Edn. (life). Office: Niagara U Office Exec VP Niagara Falls NY 14109 E-mail: dhh@niagara.edu.

HOLTZ, GILBERT JOSEPH, steel company executive; b. N.Y.C., Jan. 23, 1924; s. Al S. and Carrie (Schindler) H.; m. Carla Kahn, July 18, 1848; children: Steven J., Robert A. Student, NYU, 1940-42. V.p. Hanger Svc. Co., Yonkers, N.Y., 1946-48; owner Economy Sales Co., Yonkers, 1948-50; v.p. Belvedere Space Saving Products, Inc., 1951-72; pres. Walnut Metal Industries, Inc., Yonkers, 1955-72, Belvedere Home Products Inc. (formerly 411 Walnut St. Corp.), 1962—, Holtz Realty Corp., 1962—, Walnut Assn. Inc., 1961—, Belvedere Internat. Ltd., 1970—. Patentee in field. Ward leader 2d Ward Republican County Com., Yonkers. Served with AUS, 1943-46. Decorated Bronze Star; recipient Conspicuous Svc. Cross, N.Y. State. Mem. Rotary. Home: 182 Tibbetts Rd Yonkers NY 10705-2646 Office: 937 Saw Mill River Rd Yonkers NY 10710-3230

HOLTZ, GLENN EDWARD, band instrument manufacturing executive; b. Detroit, Jan. 15, 1938; s. Edward Christian and Evelyn Adele (Priehs) Foutz H.; m. Mary Eleanor Russell, Nov. 25, 1981; children by previous marriage: Robert, Kimberly, Rene, Letitia, Kimberly, Pamela. B in Music Edn., U. Mich., 1960, M in Music Edn., 1964; cons. motivation student, Pers. Dynamics, Mpls., 1980. Music tchr. Middleville H.S., Mich., 1960-62; dist. mgr. Selmer Co., Elkhart, Ind., 1965-74, sales mgr., 1974-76; pres. Knapp Mus. Co., Grand Rapids, Mich., 1976-80; v.p. mktg. sales Gemeinhardt/CBS, Elkhart, 1981-83; pres., CEO Gemeinhardt Co., Inc., 1983—; v.p. CBS, 1983. Pres., bd. dirs., trustee Vandercook Coll. Mus.; chmn. Internat. Found. for Music Rsch., 2000—. Dist. gov. Lions Internat., Jackson, Lansing, Battle Creek, Mich., 1970-71; pres. Middleville Bd. Edn., 1964-66; bd. dirs., treas. Midwest Band and Orch.; mem. bd. music Ind. Coun., pres. Music Industry Conf.; chmn. Internat. Found. Music Rsch. Recipient Disting. award Lions Internat., Mich., 1971. Mem. Nat. Assn. Band Instrument Mfrs. (pres. 1986-88), Am. Music Conf. (bd. dirs. 1987—, past pres. nat. Fla. ind. coun.), Nat. Assn. Music Merchants (bd. dirs., Disting. Music Industry award), Music Industry Conf. Bd. (pres. 1998-2000, Music Industry Hall of Fame award 2002). Republican. Office: G Holtz Corp 120 W Lexington Elkhart IN 46516

HOLTZ, ITSHAK, artist; b. Skernevice, Poland, Dec. 14, 1925; came to U.S., 1950; s. Arie and Lisa (Golup) H.; m. Gertrude Ruth Beck, June 29, 1928; children: Aliza, Arie. Student, Jerusalem Art Acad., 1946-48, N.Y. Art Student's League, 1950-52, N.Y. Nat. Acad. Design, 1953-54; Diploma of Merit, U. De Le Art, Italy, 1982. Group shows include NAD, Allied Artists, Audubon Artists, Internat. Art Show; one-man shows include Theodore Herzel Inst., Yeshiva U. Mus., N.Y.C.; represented in numerous pvt. collections in U.S., Can., Israel, Australia and Europe. Recipicient gold medal Internat. Parliament for Safety and Peace, 1983, Oscar d'Italia, 1985. Mem. Students League of N.Y. (life), Arts Interaction N.Y. (Bd. Dirs. award 1989), Artists Equity N.Y. (Best in Show and Grumbacher Silver medal 1991). Home: 66 Fort Washington Ave Apt 36 New York NY 10032-4711 Studio: 118 E 28th St New York NY 10016-8413

HOLTZ, KLAUS ERICH, computer engineer; b. Hamburg, Germany, June 29, 1938; Degree in elec. engring., Ingenieurschule Hamburg, 1961. Pres. Autosophy, San Francisco. Contbr. numerous articles to profl. publs. Achievements include 6 patents on data compression; invention of self-learning brain-like autosopher, a new information theory. Office: 602 Macon St Ste 305 San Francisco CA 94108-3804 E-mail: holtzk@autosophy.com.

HOLTZ, LAURENCE, artisan, photographer; b. Spangler, Pa., Jan. 9, 1949; s. Paul Omer and Helen Zita (McCombie) H.; m. Priscilla Suzanne Adsit, May 17, 1981; 1 child, Samara Adsit. BA, LaSalle Coll., Phila., 1974. Hand weaver, Hardwick, Vt., 1987—. Contbr. Vt. Arts Coun. Spl. Exhbn., Montpelier, Vt., fall 2000. Exhibited at Wood Gallery and Arts Ctr., Vt. Coll., Montpelier; contbr. short story and poetry to Coldspot, 1998; contbr. poetry to Exit 1, 2003. Mem. Ctrl. Vt. Regional Planning Commn., Montpelier, 1982, Plainfield (Vt.) Planning Commn., 1982; vol. Vt. Dept. Corrections Northeast Regional Correctional Facility, St. Johnsbury, 1998-2002; mem. Reparative Probation Bd., Barre Office, 1998-2000. Mem. New England Antiquities Rsch. Assocs., Vt. Weaver's Guild, Hardwick Area Writer's Group, Handweavers Guild Am., Alliance for Prison Justice (workshop panelist 2002). Zen Buddhist. Avocations: instrumental music, creative writing. Office: PO Box 51 Hardwick VT 05843-0051

HOLTZ, SARA, consultant; b. L.A., Aug. 7, 1951; BA, Yale U., 1972; JD, Harvard U., 1975. Bar: D.C. 1975, Calif. 1982. Assoc. Brownstein, Zeidman & Schomer, Washington, 1975-77; dep. asst. dir. FTC, Washington, 1977-82; divsn. counsel Clorox Co., Oakland, Calif., 1982-90; v.p., dep. gen. counsel Nestle U.S.A., Inc., San Francisco, 1990-94; prin. Client Focus, 1996—. Mem. Am. Corp. Counsel Assn. (bd. dirs. 1986-95, chmn. 1994-95). Office: 5320 Olive Tree Ct Granite Bay CA 95746-9484

HOLTZ-BORDERS, KAREN LYNN, police officer; b. Glendale, Calif., Mar. 10, 1960; d. Denison Lee and Diane Arlyce (Shapiro) Baldwin; m. Steven Henry Holtz, June 1, 1985 (div. Jan. 1992); children: Ashley Holtz, Stacey Holtz. AS, Coll. of the Desert, 1985; BS, U. Redlands, 1992. Police officer Palm Springs (Calif.) Police Dept., 1982—, explorer advisor, 1985-89, detective, 1989-94, field tng. officer, 1994-96, domestic violence detective, 1996—2002, field tng. officer, 2002—. Co-host Time-Warner Crimewatch TV show; host Code 3 Desert Beat TV Show. Recipient Outstanding Cmty. Svc. award Domestic Violence Program, Palm Springs Police Dept., 1997, Medal of Valor, Am. Legion, 1989, Women Helping Women award, Soroptimists, 2001—02. Republican. Roman Catholic. Avocations: ice skating, reading, bicycling. Office: Palm Springs Police Dept 200 S Civic Dr Palm Springs CA 92262-7201 Personal E-mail: cobranodv@aol.com. Business E-Mail: karenb@ci.palm-springs.ca.us.

HOLTZCLAW, DIANE SMITH, elementary education educator; b. Buffalo, May 26, 1936; d. John Nelson and Beatrice M. (Salisbury) Smith; m. John Victor Holtzclaw, June 27, 1959; children: Kathryn Diane, John Bryan. BS in Edn. magna cum laude, SUNY, Brockport, 1957, MS with honors, 1961; postgrad., SUNY, Buffalo, 1960-65, Canisus Coll., 1979, Nazareth Coll., 1981-82. Tchr. Greece Cen. Sch., Rochester, N.Y., 1957-60; supr. SUNY, Brockport, 1960-64, assoc. prof. edn., 1960-64; dir. Early Childhood Ctr., Fairport, N.Y., 1968-80; tchr. Fairport Cen. Schs., 1971—; ednl. cons. in field; specialist child devel. Ch. music dir., Rochester, N.Y., 1983—; pres. bd. dirs. Downtown Day Care Ctr., Rochester, 1974-83; mem. exec. bd. Rochester Theatre Organ Soc., 1988—. Mem. Fairport Edn. Assn. (exec. bd. 1982-83, del. 1983), N.Y. State United Tchrs., AAUW (exec. bd. 1973-74, 77-79, 83-84, pres. Fairport br. 1971-73), Internat. Platform Assn., Kappa Delta Pi. Home: 1455 Ayrault Rd Fairport NY 14450-9301 Office: Fairport Cen Schs 38 W Church St Fairport NY 14450-2130

HOLTZLANDER, STEPHANIE FRANCO, lawyer; b. Indpls., Aug. 14, 1968; d. James Michael and Mary Josephine (Spahn) F.; m. Mark Adam Holtzlander, Dec. 30, 1995; children: Adam Joseph, Benjamin David, Marya Irene. BA, Ind. U., 1990; JD, M, Drake U., 1993. Bar: Ind. 1993, US Dist. Ct. (no. and so. dist.) Ind. 1993. Litig. assco. Price & Barker, Indpls., 1993-96, Bose, McKinney & Evans, Indpls., 1996—. Contbr. articles to profl. jour. Vol. Jr. League Indpls., 1995-96. Recipient AmJur award Am. Jurisprudence, Inc., 1991-92. Mem. ABA, Ind. Bar Assn., Indpls. Bar Assn., Def. Rsch. Inst. Roman Catholic. Avocations: gourmet cooking, entertaining, reading, tennis. Office: Bose McKinney & Evans 2700 First Indiana Plaza 135 N Pennsylvania St Indianapolis IN 46204-2400 E-mail: sholtzlander@boselaw.com.

HOLTZMAN, DAVID H. technologist, security and privacy expert; b. Pitts., Pa., Sept. 30, 1956; s. Stanley E. and Shirley (Fischman) H.; children: Lauren, Samara, Benjamin, Alexandra, Rebecca. BA in Philosophy, U. Pitts., Pa., 1979; grad. Russian Studies, Def. Lang. Inst., Monterey, Calif., 1981; BS in Computer Sci., U. Md., Catonsville, 1987. Software designer BTG, Tysons Corner, Va., 1987-90, program mgr., 1991-92; sys. arch. TRW, McLean, Va., 1990-91; sr. assoc. Booz-Allen & Hamilton, McLean, Va., 1992-94; chief scientist internet info. tech. group IBM, Falls Ch., Va., 1994-96; chief tech. officer NSI, Herndon, Va., 1997-2000; CEO, chmn. Opion, Inc., 2000—01. Adj. assoc. prof. mktg. KOGOD Sch. Bus. Am. U., Washington; bd. dir. Nanotech. Bus. Alliance; pres. Global POV; mem. Forum-21. Designer software sys. Minerva, 1993, Shared Domain Name Registry System, 1998; Flashpoint columnist CSO mag., fellow, Amazon.com. With USN, 1983-87. Named One of 8 Who Made a Difference on the Web, Web Week mag., 1997. Avocations: cooking, scuba. E-mail: david@holtzmans.com.

HOLTZMAN, ELIZABETH, lawyer; b. Bklyn., Aug. 11, 1941; d. Sidney and Filia Holtzman. AB magna cum laude, Radcliffe Coll., 1962; JD, Harvard U., 1965; L.D.S., Regis Coll., 1975, Skidmore Coll., 1980, Simmons Coll., 1981, Smith Coll., 1982. Bar: N.Y. 1966. Assoc. Wachtell, Lipton, Rosen, Katz & Kern, N.Y.C., 1965-67; asst. to mayor N.Y.C., 1968-69; assoc. Paul, Weiss, Rifkind, Wharton & Garrison, 1970-72; mem. 93d-96th Congresses from 16th dist., N.Y.; vis. prof. Law Sch. and Grad. Sch. Pub. Adminstrn. NYU, 1981; dist. atty. Kings County, Bklyn., 1982-89; comptr. City of N.Y., 1990-93. Mem. Am. Jewish Comm. on the Holocaust, Nazi and Japanese War Criminal Records Working Group, 1999—; Dem. nominee U.S. Senate, 1980; N.Y. State Dem.

committeewoman, 1970—72; mem. Pres.'s Nat. Commn. on U.S. Observance Internat. Women's Yr., Helsinki Watch Com., 1981—88, Select Com. on Immigration Policy, 1979—80; bd. overseers Harvard U., 1976—82; bd. trustees Radcliffe Coll., Bklyn. Acad. Music Endowment Trust; mem. Lawyers Com. Internat. Human Right, 1981—88. Recipient Nat. Coun. Jewish Women's Faith and Humanity award, YWCA Elizabeth Cutter Morrow award, Maccabean award N.Y. Bd. Rabbis, Alumni recognition award Radcliffe Coll. Alumnae Assn., 1973, N.J. and L.A. ACLU awards for contbns. to def. of Constn. and preservation of civil liberties, 1981, Athena award N.Y.C. Commn. on Status of Women, 1985, Woman of Yr. award N.Y. League Bus. and Profl. Women, 1985, Jan Korzak award 5th Ann. Kent State Holocaust Conf., 1986, Outstanding and Meritorious Svc. award Jewish War Vets. of U.S., 1986, Award of Remembrance Warsaw Ghetto Resistance Orgn., 1987, Gates of Freedom award State of Israel Bonds, 1987; Award of Honor United Jewish Appeal, 1988, Deed of Tzedakah award, 1991. Fellow N.Y. Inst. Humanities; mem. Assn. of Bar of City of N.Y., Nat. Women's Polit. Caucus (Outstanding Svc. award 1987), Phi Beta Kappa. Office: Herrick Feinstein LLP 2 Park Ave New York NY 10016-9302

HOLTZMAN, GARY YALE, retired administrative and financial executive; b. N.Y.C., Aug. 7, 1936; s. Abram and Pearl (Kashetsky) H.; m. Alice A. Lang, Sept. 5, 1958; children: Bruce, Sheri, Michele. BBA, CCNY, 1958. Exec. v.p. control and ops. Jordan Marsh Co., Miami, Fla., 1967-87; sr. v.p. ops. and stores L. Luria & Sons Inc., Miami, 1987-93; exec. dir. Mar Jewish Community Ctr., Greater Miami, Fla., 1993-95; with Social Security Adminstrn.-TSR, 1995—2002; ret., 2002. Bd. advisers Universal Nat. Bank. Bd. dirs. Dade County Safety Coun., Miami, 1978-85, Jewish Cmty. Ctr. Greater Miami, 1983-88, Fla. Bus. Roundtable, 1975-80, Anti-Defamation League of B'nia B'rith, 1983-87; bd. advisers Opportunities Industrialization Ctr., 1982-84; pres. Michael Ann Russell Jewish Cmty. Ctr., 1984-86, bd. dirs., 1980—; life bd. dirs. Temple Beth Torah Adath Yeshurun, 1969-94, Temple B'nai Aviv, 1994-98, Temple Dor Dorim, 1999—; active Jewish Fedn. Broward City and Greater Miami, Miami Jewish Fedn.; com. chmn. United Way of Dade County. Lt. U.S. Army, 1958-59; capt. USAR, 1959-67. Recipient Americanism award Anti-Defamation League, 1983; recipient Adath Yeshurun Man of Yr. award, 1978 Mem. Greater Miami C. of C., Fla. Retail Fedn. Democrat. Home: 2019 Cove Ln Weston FL 33326-2336

HOLTZMAN, JOAN KING, musician, composer; b. Aberdeen, S.D., Aug. 14, 1925; d. James Wilfred and Miriam Hughes (Evans) K.; m. Wayne Harold Holtzman, Aug. 23, 1947; children: Wayne Jr., James, Scott, Karl. B in Music Edn., Northwestern U., 1947; EdMA, Stanford U., 1948. Pres. Jojo's Prodns., Austin, Tex., 1991—. Author: (with Leslie Holtzman) The Fat Rat and This and That, 1997, (with Rosario Ahumada de Diaz) Happy Times with English, 1987; composer, pianist, singer children's cassettes Jo Jo's Songs for Growing Up, 1991, Beasts, Veggies and Sospetigious Things, 1993; composer melodies song book and cassette Symphony for Simple Simon, 1984 (award of excellence Am. Symphony Orch. League, 1984); composer numerous songs. Active Save Children Fedn., 1954—, pres. 1958; vol. Austin Cerebral Palsy Ctr., 1955-59; mem. Pan Am. Round Table, 1958—, sec. 1965-66; co-founder Internat. Hospitality Com. Austin, 1960—, chmn. host families, 1960-62; pres. PTA Austin H.S., 1972, mem. Austin Arts Commn., 1977-83; mem. nat. adv. coun. Nat. Sch. Vol. Program, Washington, 1976-91; mem. adv. com. Austin Ind. Sch. Dist., 1983-91, forming future com., 1982; mem. arts plan task force City of Austin, 1985; docent, gov. mansion, 1983—; nat. class rep. Northwestern U. Sch. Music, 1977-91; mus. vol. Austin State Hosp., 1967-83; sec., bd. dirs. Austin Symphony Orch. Soc., 1966—; state bd. dirs. Very Special Arts - Tex., 1987-91; bd. dirs., chmn. coms. Child and Family Svcs., Austin, 1965-82; bd. dirs. Austin Musical Theatre, 2000-. Named Outstanding Fundraiser Austin Symphony Devel. fund drive, 1981; Festival Favorite New Tex. Choral Music Festival, Austin, 1995, Yellow Rose Tex., Sec. Gov., 1995, Vol. of Yr., 1995. Mem. Women's Symphony League Austin (pres. 1958-59, charter mem., Woman of Yr. award 1991), Austin Jr. League (Vol. Extraordinaire award 1985), Mortar Bd. U. Tex. Austin (Citation award 1976), Playhouse Singers, Settlement Club, Austin Woman's Club, Univ. Ladies Club (pres. 1971-72), Sigma Alpha Iota (charter mem., pres. 1972-73, Rose of Honor award 1976). Office: Jojo's Prodns 3300 Foothill Dr Austin TX 78731-5823 E-mail: wayne.holtzman@mail.utexas.edu.

HOLTZMAN, MARY, engineering company executive; b. Sanford, Fla., Mar. 16, 1948; d. James Emory and Johnie Ruth (Hardy) McElhannon; m. Calvin Douglas Crenshaw, Sept. 1969 (div. July 1977); 1 child, Christa Ashlee Crenshaw; m. Dean Ward Hillegass, Sept. 1978 (div. July 1986); m. Joel Richard Holtzman, Jan. 12, 1990. BFA, U. Ga., 1972. Draftsman, designer Patterson & Dewar Engrs., Decatur, Ga., 1973-84; drafting supr. Mosler/Am. Standard, Norcross, Ga., 1984-86; GIS dept. mgr. Patterson & Dewar Engrs., Decatur, 1986—. Mem. DAR, Lake Jackson Homeowners Assn., Am. Assn. Ret. Persons, U. Ga. Alumni Assn., Peachtree Handspinners Guild, Red Hat Soc. Democrat. Avocations: photography, painting, internet design, reading, travel. Home: 3144 Caintal Ct Decatur GA 30033-1804 Office: Patterson & Dewar Engrs Inc 2685 Milscott Dr Decatur GA 30033-5906 E-mail: maryholtzman@mindsping.com.

HOLTZMAN, MICHAEL, alcohol abuse professional; b. Chgo. s. Bernard and Juanita (Good) H.; m. Elaine Cyr, Apr. 11, 1967; children: Michael (dec.), Jed, Ann. Student, U. Internat. Studies, Rome. V.p. mktg. Container Corp. Am., 1955-62; pres. Blair Graphics, Chgo., 1962-70; co-founder, dir. Indemnified Cap. Invest. Anglo Am. Commodity Invest. Program, Buenos Aires and London, 1970-77, founder, pres. London, 1980-98; ret., 1998. Arbitrator Am. Arbitration Assn., Coral Gables, Fla., 1980—. Trustee Coll. Rome, 1975-95; mem. exec. com. Found. Educative Pro Deo, Rome, 1980-95; chmn. steering com. Ill. Drug Free Program, Chgo., 1995—; sr. mem. Pres. Coun. on Alcohol:Drug Abuse, 1971—; pres. Sr. Corp Ret. Exec. (SBA), Kankakee, Ill., 1998—; pres. Kankakee Symphony, 1998—; presenter high schs. seminars on alcoholism, Ill., 1995—. Capt. infantry, 1952-55. Mem. Am. Arbitration Assn. (sr. arbitrator 1985—), Am. Club (Buenos Aires), Brit. Army and Navy Club (London), Kankakee County Upstairs Bridge Club. Avocations: golf, bridge, trap shooting, gardening. Home: 160 W Dixie Hwy Saint Anne IL 60964-5400

HOLTZMAN, ROBERT ARTHUR, lawyer; b. L.A., July 17, 1929; s. Ruben and Bertha (Dembowsky) H.; m. Barbara Polis, June 26, 1954 (dec. 1985); children: Melinda, Mark, Bradley; m. Liliane Gurwith Endlich, July 6, 1986. BA, UCLA, 1951; LLB, U. So. Calif., 1954. Bar: Calif. 1955, U.S. Dist. Ct. (cen. dist.) Calif. 1955, U.S. Ct. Appeals (9th cir.) 1958. Assoc. Gang, Tyre & Brown, L.A., 1954, Loeb and Loeb, L.A., 1956-63, ptnr., 1964-95; of counsel, 1996—. Judge pro tem Mcpl. Ct. L.A. Jud. Dist.; lectr. Calif. Continuing Edn. of Bar. Contbr. articles to legal publs. With U.S. Army, 1954-56. Mem. ABA (dispute resolution sect., vice-chmn. arbitration com.), Calif. Bar Assn. (chmn. com. on adminstrn. of justice 1984-85), L.A. County Bar Assn., Am. Arbitration Assn. (panel arbitrators 1974—, panel mediators 1992—, arbitrator large complex case program 1993—) Office: Loeb & Loeb LLP 1000 Wilshire Blvd Ste 1800 Los Angeles CA 90017-2475 E-mail: rholtzman@loeb.com.

HOLTZMAN, ROBERT NEIL NEHEMIAH, neurosurgeon, neurologist; b. Bklyn., Aug. 11, 1941; s. Sidney and Filia (Ravitz) H.; children: Maia Merav, Jonathan Nisson, Matthew Isaac. BA, Harvard U., 1964; MD, Columbia U., 1969. Diplomate Am. Bd. Psychiatry and Neurology, Am. Bd. Neurol. Surgery. Rotating intern Harlem Hosp. Ctr., N.Y.C., 1969-70; resident in neurology Neurol. Inst. N.Y., N.Y.C., 1970-72, resident in neurosurgery, 1973-77; resident in gen. surgery Harbor Gen. Hosp., Torrance, Calif., 1972-73; practice medicine specializing in neurosurgery and neurology, N.Y.C., 1977—. Attending in neurosurgery Harlem Hosp., 1999—; attending in neurosurgery Lenox Hill Hosp., 2000; assoc. attending N.Y. Presbyn. Hosp., N.Y.C., 1996; chief of neurosurgery Cabrini Med. Ctr., 1999; assoc. clin. prof. in neurosurgery Coll. Phys. and Surgeons, Columbia U., N.Y.C., 1996; co-dir., co-founder Stonwin Med. Conf., 1983-91; chief of neurosurgery Met. Hosp. Ctr., NY, 2000; dir. neurosurgery Generations Plus, N.Y., 2001. Editor: Surgery of the Diencephalon, 1989, Endovascular Interventional Neuroradiology, 1995; editor, contbr.: The Tethered Spinal Cord, 1985, Surgery of the Spinal Cord: The Potential for Regeneration and Recovery, 1991, Spinal Instability, 1993; contbr. articles to med. jours. Mem.: N.Y. Soc. Neurol. Surgery, N.Y. State Neurosurg. Soc., Am. Assn. Neurol. Surgeons. Democrat. Jewish.

HOLTZMAN, ROBERTA LEE, French and Spanish language educator; b. Detroit, Nov. 24, 1938; d. Paul John and Sophia (Marcus) H. AB cum laude, Wayne State U., 1959, MA, 1973, U. Mich., 1961. Fgn. lang. tchr. Birmingham (Mich.) Sch. Dist., 1959-60, Cass Tech. H.S., Detroit, 1961-64; from instr. to prof. French and Spanish, Schoolcraft Coll., Livonia, Mich., 1964-84, chmn. French and Spanish depts., 1984—. Trustee Cranbrook Music Guild, Edn. Community, Bloomfield Hills, Mich., 1976-78. Fulbright-Hays fellow, Brazil, 1964. Mem. AAUW, NEA, MLA, Nat. Mus. Women in Arts (co-founder 1992), Am. Assn. Tchrs. of Spanish and Portuguese, Am. Assn. Tchrs. of French, Mich. Edn. Assn. Avocations: swimming, book collecting, photography, travel. Office: Schoolcraft Coll 18600 Haggerty Rd Livonia MI 45152-2696 E-mail: rholtzma@schoolcraft.edu.

HOLTZMAN, WAYNE HAROLD, psychologist, educator; b. Chgo., Jan. 16, 1923; s. Harold Hoover and Lillian (Manny) H.; m. Joan King, Aug. 23, 1947; children: Wayne Harold, James K., Scott E., Karl H. BS, Northwestern U., 1944, MS, 1947; PhD, Stanford U., 1950; LHD (hon.), Southwestern U., 1980. Asst. prof. psychology U. Tex., Austin, 1949-53, assoc. prof., 1953-59, prof., 1959—2003, dean Coll. Edn., 1964-70, Hogg prof. psychology and edn., 1964—2003, prof. emeritus, 2003—. Assoc. dir. Hogg Found. Mental Health, 1955-64, pres., 1970-93, spl. counsel, 1993-2003; dir. Social Sci. Rsch. Coun., 1957-63, Centro de Investigationes Sociales, Mex., 1960-70; cons. USAF, sci. adv. bd., 1969-71; basic rsch. com. NRC, 1968-71; behavioral sci. study sect. USPHS, 1957-59, mem. mental health study sect., 1960, chmn. personality and cognition rsch. rev. com., 1968-72; rsch. adv. panel Soc. Security Adminstrn., 1961-62; L.Am. adv. bd. IBM, 1985-89; dir. WHO Collaborating Ctr. in Mental Health for Tex. and Mex., 1993-2003; pres. Austin Project, 2001-03; bd. dirs. Menninger Clinic, The Learning Initiative. Author: (with B.M. Moore) Tomorrow's Parents, 1964, Computer Assisted Instruction Testing and Guidance, 1971, (with R. Diaz-Guerrero and J. Swartz) Personality Development in Two Cultures, 1975, Introduction to Psychology, 1978; (with K.A. Heller and S. Messick) Placing Children in Special Education, 1982, (with T. Bornemann) Mental Health of Immigrants and Refugees, 1990, School of the Future, 1992, Holtzman Inkblot Technique Research Guide, 1999, (with M.R. Rozenweig, Michel Sabourin and David Belanger) History of the International Union of Psychological Science, 2000; editor: Jour. Ednl. Psychology, 1966-72. Trustee Ednl. Testing Service, Princeton, 1972-74, 77-80, 83-86, J.W. and Cornelia Scarborough Found., 1977-82, Ctr. for Applied Linguistics, 1978-80, Salado Inst. Humanities, 1980-85, Population Inst., 1979-85, Menninger Found., 1982—, Population Resource Ctr., 1980—, chmn. bd. dirs.; dir. Sci. Rsch. Assocs., 1975-88; pres., bd. dirs. S.W. Ednl. Devel. Lab., 1974-75; mem. adv. com. computing activities NSF, 1970-73; mem. computer sci. and engring. bd. NAS, 1971-73, chmn. panel on selection and placement of mentally retarded students, 1979-82; chmn. interdisciplinary cluster on social and behavioral devel. Pres.'s Biomed. Research Panel, 1975-76; bd. dirs. Found.'s Fund for Rsch. in Psychiatry, 1973-77, chmn., 1976-77; dir. Conf. of S.W. Found., 1976-84, pres., 1978-79; mem. nat. adv. mental health coun. Alcohol, Drug Abuse, and Mental Health Adminstrn., 1978-81; mem. acad. info. sys. adv. coun. IBM, 1982-85. Lt. (j.g.) USNR, 1944-46. Faculty Rsch. fellow, Social Sci. Rsch. Coun., 1953—54, Ctr. Advanced Study Behavioral Scis., 1962—63. Fellow APA, AAAS; mem. Tex. Psychol. Assn. (pres. 1957), S.W. Psychol. Assn. (pres. 1958), Am. Statis. Assn., InterAm. Soc. Psychology (pres. 1966-67), Am. Ednl. Rsch. Assn., Internat. Union Psychol. Scis. (sec.-gen. 1972-84, pres. 1984-88, exec. com. 1972-92), Philos. Soc. Tex. (pres. 1982-83), Sigma Xi. Methodist. Home: 3300 Foothill Dr Austin TX 78731-5823 E-mail: wayne.holtzman@mail.utexas.edu.

HOLTZMANN, HOWARD MARSHALL, lawyer, judge; b. N.Y.C., Dec. 10, 1921; s. Jacob L. And Lillian (Plotz) H.; m. Anne Fisher, Jan. 14, 1945 (dec. Aug. 1967); children: Susan Holtzmann Richardson, Betsey; m. Carol Ebenstein Van Berg, Dec. 23, 1972 AB, Yale Coll., 1942, JD, 1947; LittD (hon.), St. Bonaventure U., 1952; LLD (hon.), Jewish Theol. Sem., N.Y.C., 1990. Bar: N.Y. 1947. Atty. Colorado Fuel & Iron Corp., Buffalo, N.Y., 1947-49; ptnr. Holtzmann, Wise & Shepard, N.Y.C., 1949-95; judge Iran-U.S. Claims Tribunal, The Hague, Netherlands, 1981-94; arbitrator and dispute resolution cons., 1994—; arbitrator Claims Resolution Tribunal for Dormant Accounts, Zurich, Switzerland, 1998—2002. U.S. del. UN Commn. on Internat. Trade Law, 1975—, Hague Conf. on Pvt. Internat. Law, 1985; advisor U.S.A. Arbitration agreements with USSR, Russian Fedn., China, Hungary, Bulgaria, Czechoslovakia, Poland and German Dem. Republic. Author, editor: A New Look at Legal Aspects of Doing Business with China, 1979; co-author: A Guide to the Unicitral Model Law on International Commercial Arbitration—Legislative History and Commentary, 1988 (cert. of merit Am. Soc. Internat. Law 1991); contbr. chpts. to books and articles to law jours. Mem. governing coun. Downstate Med. Sch. SUNY, Bklyn., 1961-78; trustee St. Bonaventure U., Olean, N.Y., 1968-90, trustee emeritus, 1990—; chmn. bd. Jewish Theol. Sem., N.Y.C., 1983-85, hon. chmn., 1985—; trustee Inst. Internat. Law, Pace U. Sch. Law, 1992—. Mem. ABA (chmn. com. code ethics comml. arbitrators 1973-77), Internat. Coun. for Comml. Arbitration (hon. vice chmn.), Am. Arbitration Assn. (hon. chmn., Gotshal Internat. Arbitration award 1980), Internat. C. of C. (vice chmn. arbitration commn. 1979-2001), Stockholm Arbitration Inst. (adv. bd.), Am. Bar Found., N.Y. County Lawyers Assn., Internat. Law Assn., Am. Fgn. Law Assn. (v.p. 1995—), Internat. Bar Assn., N.Y. State Bar Assn., Assn. of Bar of City of N.Y., Am. Soc. Internat. Law (cert. merit 1991), Soc. Profls. in Dispute Resolution, Indsl. Rels. Rsch. Assn., N.Y. Law Inst., Am. Judicature Soc., Am. Assn. for Internat. Commn. of Jurists. Office: Ste 2000 630 Fifth Ave New York NY 10111-0100

HOLUB, BARBARA ANN, rehabilitation nurse; b. South Euclid, Ohio, Mar. 29, 1961; d. Peter Cyril Anthony Dominic and Kathleen Theresa (Horner) McHale; m. Thomas John Joseph Holub, June 1, 1991; children: Colleen Marie, Ryan Thomas. ASN, Mattatuck C.C., 1985, Assoc. Liberal Arts, 1983. RN, Conn.; cert. rehab. nurse, ins. rehab. specialist. Rehab. nurse Yale New Haven Hosp., 1985-89, Hosp. St. Raphael, New Haven, 1989-96, Grant St. Health and Rehab. Ctr., Bridgeport, Conn., 1996-97, Cedar Ln. Health & Rehab. Ctr., Waterbury, Conn., 1997-99, Mariner Health Care So. Conn., Ansonia, 1999-2000; CNA instr., program coord., staff nurse Care Mgmt. Group, New Haven, 2000—. Mem. Assn. Rehab. Nurses (v.p. 1992-93, pres. 1993-94, bd. dirs. 1995—). Republican. Roman Catholic. Avocations: decorating, crafts, travel, outdoors, financial management. Home and Office: 205 Skokorat Rd Beacon Falls CT 06403-1412

HOLUB, JEANNE HELEN, English language educator; b. Davenport, Iowa, Sept. 6, 1949; d. Ralph L. and Corinne R. (Jansen) Judge; m. Terry L. Holub, Apr. 14, 1973 (div. Dec. 1986); children: Edward, Sarah, Katherine. Bachelor's degree, Marycrest Coll., 1971. Tchg. cert., Iowa. Tchr. Ft. Madison (Iowa) H.S., 1971-73; feature reporter Waterloo (Iowa) Courier, 1973-75; comms. dir. Hawkeye C.C., Waterloo, 1975-77; tchr. Waterloo Cmty. Schs., 1977—; chairperson English dept. West H.S., 2002—. Mem. NEA, Nat. Coun. Tchrs. English, Assn. Supervision and Curriculum Devel., Iowa Coun. Tchrs. English, Iowa Edn. Assn., Waterloo Edn. Assn. (former pres.), Journalism Edn. Assn. Roman Catholic. Avocations: reading, needlepoint. Office: West H S 425 E Ridgeway Ave Waterloo IA 50702-5043

HOLUB, MARTIN, architect; b. Prague, Czechoslovakia, Dec. 11, 1938; arrived in U.S., 1970, naturalized, 1977; s. Jan and Miloslava (Jerabkova) Holub. MS, Czech Tech. U., 1963, Acad. Art, Prague, 1966. Registered arch., N.Y., N.J., Tenn., Fla., Conn. Designer Konstruktiva, Prague, 1963-67; asst. arch. Greater London Coun., 1967-68; sr. designer R. Seifert and Ptnrs., London, 1968-69, Kahn and Jacobs, N.Y.C., 1970-71; prin. Martin Holub Archs. and Planners, N.Y.C., 1971—, br. office Prague, 1990—. Prin. works include Rokeby Apts., Nashville (Design award, 1976), Patricia Lane Ho. (1st prize Am. Soc. Registered Archs. Design Awards probram, 2001), Dominican Chapel, Sparkill, N.Y. (Design award Am. Soc. Registered Archs., 2002). Mem.: AIA, Archtl. League N.Y., Am. Arbitration Assn. Home: 500 E 77th St Apt 1529 New York NY 10162-0019 Office: 116 W 72nd St Fl 16 New York NY 10023-3338

HOLUTIAK-HALLICK, STEPHEN PETER, JR., retired army officer, businessman, educator; b. N.Y.C., May 3, 1945; s. Stephen and Hope (Kukura) H.; m. Ann Marie Bazycki, July 29, 1972; children: Larissa Ann, Christine Michelle, Stephen Michael III. BA in Russian, Penn State U., 1967; MA in Slavic Studies, U. Man., Winnipeg, Can., 1969; AS in Bus. Mgmt., C.C. of Allegheny County, 1977; MBA in Internat. Bus., Mercer U., 1992; cert. in Russian area studies, Pa. State U. With USAR, 1967-95, advanced through grades to lt. col., 1970-71, 85-95; translator, interpretor, mgr. Russian translation dept. Pullman-Swindell, Inc., Pitts., 1972-76; inspector mech. engring. dept. Robert W. Hunt, Co., Pitts., 1977-79; adminstr., procurement svcs. KHD, Humboldt-Wedag, N.Y.C., Montreal, Atlanta, 1979-82, adminstr., project mgmt. svcs., 1982-84, mgr. expediting and sub-contracts adminstrn., 1984-85; staff intelligence officer Forces Command Hdqs., U.S. Army, 1985-90; asst. prof. mil. sci. Clemson (S.C.) U., 1990-92; mem. INF. Treaty inspection team U.S. Army, 1988, inspector gen. 95th Divsn., 1992-95; ret. Adj. instr. Park Coll., Tinker AFB, Okla., 1993-95, Am. Coll., Atlanta, 1997; pres. TATO's Choice, Duluth, Ga., 1995—; cons. doing bus. in former USSR. Author: Slavic Toponymic Atlas of the United States, Vol. 1, Ukrainian, 1982, Dictionary of Ukrainian Surnames in the United States, 1994; mem. editl. bd. Rudnyckiana, 1986-92, chmn., 1993-95; contbr. articles to profl. jours. Organizer St. Andrew's Ukrainian Orthodox Parish, Atlanta; vol. instr. English Tchrs. for Ukraine, 1996-2001; bd. regents St. Sophia Ukrainian Orthodox Seminary. Decorated Army Commendation medal (2), Meritorious Svc. medal (3); recipient Danforth Leadership award, 1963, Wasyl Swystun prize of Ukrainian Studies, U. Man., 1967-68, grad. assistantship, 1968-69, Cert. of Appreciation, DAV, 1985-2002, Am. Soc. Blind, 1985, Eagle Scout Boy Scouts of Am.; Senatorial grantee Pa. State U., 1963-67. Mem. Res. Officers Assn. of U.S., Am. Security Coun. (U.S. Congl. adv. bd.), Atlanta Com. of Internat. Rels., Am. Name Soc. Home: 2755 Kenwood Ct Duluth GA 30096-3683

HOLVECK, JACK, state legislator; b. Marshalltown, Iowa, May 26, 1943; m. Andrea Holveck; children: John, David. BA, William Penn Coll., 1965; MA, U. Iowa, 1972, JD, 1975. Tchr. Iowa StateTng. Sch.; coll. intern U.S. Dept. State, 1965; classroom tchr., 1967-69, 72-73; labor rels. mgr. Polk County, 1977-82; atty., 1983—; mem. Iowa Ho. of Reps., 1982-2000, Iowa State Senate, 2001—. Democrat. Mem. Soc. Of Friends. Home: 2007 SE 4th St Des Moines IA 50315 E-mail: jack_holveck@legis.state.ia.us.

HOLWAY, DAVID, association administrator; b. Cambridge, Mass. ; Former dep. commr. State Dept. Corrections; chmn. Union's Health and Welfare Trust Fund; legis. dir., chief contract negotiator State employees Mass. Nat. Assn. Govt. Employees, pres., 2002—. Office: 159 Burgin Pkwy Quincy MA 02169

HOLWAY, ELLEN TWOMBLY HAY, primary education educator; b. Summit, N.J. d. Allan and Ellen Clark (Twombly) Hay; m. William Crocker Holway III; children: Julie Ellen, Suzanne Clark, Cammy Twombly, Amy Hay, Daniel Hitchcock, Joanna Howland. AB in Psychology cum laude, Colby Coll., 1953; MEd, U. Lowell, 1975; postgrad., U. Mass., Lowell, 1987—, Boston U., 1978, Cen. New Eng. Coll., 1987. Cert. elem. tchr. and prin., perceptually handicapped, gen. supr., supt./asst.supt., Mass.; asst. psychologist, psychometrist, child welfare worker, pub. assistance caseworker, Maine. Asst. psychologist, acting dept. head Pineland Hosp. and Tng. Ctr., 1953-55; elem. tchr., specialist Odenton, Md., 1955-57; primary tchr., prof. devel. team leader Horace Mann, Maynard, Mass., 1972—; elem. asst. prin. Green Meadow Sch., 1994-97, elem. prin., 1997-99; MPS facilitator 21th century initiatives K-12, 1999—2000; freelance edn. adminstrn. cons. K-12, 2000—. Freelance edn. adminstrv. cons. K-12, 2000—; MPS facilitator 21st century initiatives K-12, 1999-2000; mem. adj. faculty dept. bus. and career edn. Boston U. Grad. Sch. Edn.; freelance editor, cons. pilot program liaison D.C. Heath Pub. Co.; developer, coord. Acton-Boxborough Student Activities Fund, numerous others; cons. Technol. R & D Corp.; mem. Mass. Math. Adv. Com., Mass. Sci. Adv. Com.; lead tchr. New Standards Project. Chmn. Acton and Acton-Boxborough Regional Sch. Com., Acton 250th Celebration; mem. MASC Assessment Com.; charter mem., bd. dirs., mem. pub. rels. com. Acton Hist. Soc.; jr. leader, coord. summer camp Girl Scouts U.S.A.; counselor citizenship badge, Eagle advisor Boy Scouts Am., Acton and Maynard; tchr., supr. ch. sch., numerous others. Mem. NEA, ASCD, Am. Ednl. Rsch. Assn., Nat. Sch. Bd. Assn., Nat. Career Edn. Assn (charter), Mass. ASCD, Mass. Assn. Sch. Coms., Mass. Tchrs. Assn., Maynard Edn. Assn., LWV (charter, v..p., chmn. pub. rels.), Yarmouth Hist. Soc. (life), Phi Beta Kappa, Pi Lambda Theta, Pi Gamma Mu. Home: 48 Alcott St Acton MA 01720-5539 Office: Maynard Pub Schs 12 Bancroft St Maynard MA 01754-1702

HOLWELL, PETER, management consultant; b. Mar. 28, 1936; s. Frank and Helen (Howe) H.; m. Jean Patricia Ashman, 1959; 1 son, 1 dau. BSc in Econ., London Sch. Econs. Articled clk. Arthur Andersen & Co., 1958-61, mgmt. cons., 1961-64; head univ. computing O & M unit U. London, 1967-77, sec. for acctg. & adminstrv. computing, 1977-82; clk. of the ct., 1982-85; prin. U. London, 1985-97, dir. sch. exams coun., 1988-97; mgmt. cons. Prince of Wales' Inst. Architecture, 1998-99, Chatham Hist. Dockyard Trust, 1999-2000, Leeds Castle Found., 2001. Mem. U. London Exams and Assessments Coun., 1991-96. Mem. Samuel Courtauld Avd. Bd., 1985—98; chmn. City of East London Family Health Svcs. Authority, 1994—96; trustee Leeds Castle Found., 2001—; mem. N.E. Thames Regional Health Authority, 1990—94; chmn. St. Marks Rsch. Found. and Ednl. Trust, 1995—2000; vice chmn. coun. Wye Coll., U. London, 1995—2000, mem. coun. Sch. Pharmacy, 1996—2001; mem. Edexcel Found. Coun., 1996—97. ACA Ltd. (dir.), 1998—. Home: Hookers Green Bishopsbourne Canterbury Kent CT4 5JB England

HOLYDAY, DOUGLAS CHARLES, city councillor; b. Etobicoke, Ont., Can., July 31, 1942; s. Arthur John and Anne H.; m. Franca Palma Pellizzari, Aug. 16, 1969; children: Stephen, David. Formerly ward 6 councillor Etobicoke City Coun.; past chmn. Etobicoke Bd. Health; mayor City of Etobicoke, 1994-97; councillor City of Toronto, 1997—, chair admin. com. Former pres., owner Holyday Ins. Brokers, Inc., Etobicoke. Founding chair Etobicoke Lakeshore Oldtimers Hockey Tournament; mem. bd. dirs., 1st v.p. mcpl. sect. Can. Nat. Exhbn. Assn. Mem. Kingsway Kiwanis Club (past pres., past chair youth svcs. com., past dir. music festival). Anglican. Avocations: golf, hockey, reading. Office: City Hall 2d Fl 100 Queen St W Toronto ON Canada M5H 2N2

HOLYER, ERNA MARIA, adult education educator, writer, artist; b. Weilheim, Bavaria, Germany, Mar. 15, 1925; d. Mathias and Anna Maria (Goldhofer) Schretter; m. Gene Wallace Holyer, Aug. 24, 1957 (dec. 1999). AA, San Jose Evening Coll., 1964; student, San Mateo Coll., 1965—67, San Jose State U., 1968—69, San Jose City Coll., 1980—81; DLitt, World U., 1984; DFA (hon.) (hon.), The London Inst. Applied Rsch, 1992. Freelance writer under pseudonym Ernie Holyer, 1960—; tchr. creative writing San Jose (Calif.) Met. Adult Edn., 1968—; artist, 1958—. Exhibited in group shows Crown Zellerbach Gallery, San Francisco, 1973, 74, 76, 77; I.B.C. Gallery, San Francisco, 1978 (medal of Congress, 1988, 89, 92, 94, Congress Challenge trophy, 1991), L.A., 1981, Cambridge, Eng., 1992, Cambridge, Mass., 1993, San Jose, Calif., 1993, Edinburgh, 1994, San Francisco, 1996. Author: Rescue at Sunrise, 1965, Steve's Night of Silence, 1966, A Cow for Hansel, 1967, At the Forest's Edge, 1969, Song of Courage, 1970, Lone Brown Gull, 1971, Shoes for Daniel, 1974, The Southern Sea Otter, 1975, Sigi's Fire Helmet, 1975, Reservoir Road Adventure, 1982, Wilderness Journey, Golden Journey, California Journey, 1997, Self-Help for Writers: Winners Show You How, 2002, Dangerous Secrets: A Young Girl's Travails Under the Nazis, 2003; contbr. articles to mags., newspapers and anthologies. Recipient Woman of Achievement Honor cert. San Jose Mercury-News, 1973, 74, 75, Lefoli award for excellence in adult edn. instr. Adult Edn. Senate, 1972, Women of Achievement awards League of Friends of Santa Clara County Commn., San Jose Mercury News, 1987, various art awards. Mem. N.L.A.P.W. Inc., World Univ Roundtable (doctoral). Home and Office: 1314 Rimrock Dr San Jose CA 95120-5611 E-mail: holyere@aol.com.

HOLYFIELD, EVANDER, professional boxer; b. Atlanta, Oct. 19, 1962; Winner unanimous decision vs. Ray Mercer, 1995; defeated Mike Tyson to win WBC Heavyweight Title, 1996; defended title successfully over Lennox Lewis, 1999. Recipient Bronze medal, 1984 Summer Olympics, World Boxing Assn. cruiserweight title, 1986, Internat. Boxing Fedn. cruiserweight title, 1987, World Boxing Coun. cruiserweight title, 1988, Internat. Boxing Fedn. heavyweight championship, 1997, undisputed heavyweight world champion, 1990—92, 1993—94, loss titles to Lennox Lewis, 1999. Office: Main Event 390 Murray Hill Pkwy East Rutherford NJ 07073-2109

HOLZ, GEORGE G., IV, medical educator, research scientist; b. Santa Monica, Calif., May 8, 1953; s. George G. and Mignon M. (Kiproff) Holz. BS, Cornell U., 1975; PhD, U. Ill., 1984. Rsch. fellow Tufts U. Med. Sch., Boston, 1984—89; rsch. assoc. Howard Hughes Med. Inst., Boston, 1990—93; instr. medicine Mass. Gen. Hosp.-Harvard Med. Sch., Boston, 1990—93, asst. prof. medicine, 1994—98; assoc. prof. physiology and neurosci. NYU Med. Sch., N.Y.C., 1998—; rsch. fellow Marine Biology Lab., Woods Hole, Mass., 2000—. Corp. mem. Marine Biol. Lab., Woods Hole, Mass. Mem. All-Sectional Gymnastics Team N.Y., 1971. Recipient Rsch. award, Am. Diabetes Assn., 1996, 2000; grantee rsch. grantee, NIH; scholar N.Y. State Regents scholar, Cornell U., 1971—75. Mem.: AAAS, Am. Diabetes Assn., Soc. Gen. Physiologists, Endocrine Soc., Soc. for Neurosci. Home: PO Box 288 West Falmouth MA 02574-0288 E-mail: holzg01@popmail.med.nyu.edu.

HOLZ, HAROLD A. chemical and plastics manufacturing company executive; b. N.Y.C., June 26, 1925; s. Herman A. and Genevieve (Murphy) H.; m. Joanne Axtell, Oct. 3, 1953; children: Gretchen, Timothy. BS, Stevens Inst. Tech., 1946, ME, 1947. Tech. rep. Union Carbide Corp., N.Y.C., 1947-49, Hartford, Conn., 1949-52, St. Louis, 1952-58, asst. regional mgr. Chgo., 1958-64, regional mgr., 1964-65, acct. exec., 1965-85; v.p. sales, new product devel. Marval Industries, Inc., 1986-97; cons. Old Lyme, Conn., 1997—. Nat. bd. govs. Nat. Plastics Ctr. and Mus., Leominster, Mass., 1995—. Served to lt. (j.g.) USNR, 1943-50. Named to Plastics Hall of Fame, 2000; recipient Stevens Honor award Stevens Tech., Hoboken, NJ, 2001 Mem. The Plastics Acad. (bd. dirs. 1996—, adminstr. Plastics Hall of Fame), Soc. Plastics Engrs. (disting. mem., pres. 1975-76), Plastics Pioneers Assn. (bd. govs. 1981-85, pres. 1993-95), Plastics Inst. Am. (trustee 1995—), Union Carbide Retiree Corps. (pres. Lower Westchester County chpt. 1996-97), Old Guard Club of Stevens Tech. (pres. 2002—). Home: Lyme Regis B-2 14 Ferry Rd Old Lyme CT 06371 Office: 315 Hoyt Ave Mamaroneck NY 10543-1836 Fax: 860-434-9944.

HOLZ, HARRY GEORGE, lawyer; b. Milw., Sept. 13, 1934; s. Harry Carl and Emma Louise (Hinz) H.; m. Nancy L. Heiser, May 12, 1962; children: Pamela Gretchen, Bradley Eric, Erika Lynn. BS, Marquette U., 1956, LLB, 1950, LLM, Northwestern U., 1960. Bar: Wis. 1958, Ill. 1960. Tchg. fellow Northwestern U. Sch. Law, 1958-59; assoc. Sidley & Austin, Chgo., 1960; ptnr. Quarles & Brady, Milw., 1968—2002, of counsel, 2002—. Lectr. law securities regulation U. Wis. Law Sch., 1971—74; adj. prof. Marquette U. Sch. Law, 1976—91; faculty program on antitrust law Wis. State Bar Sems., 1975—82, 1989, 93; bd. dirs., sec. Creative Sharp Presentations Inc.; lectr. PLI 33rd Antitrust Inst.; lectr., spkr. in antitrust field. Bd. visitors Marquette U. Sch. Law, 1990, 93. Capt. C.E. U.S. Army, 1960-67. Fellow: Am. Bar Found.; mem.: ABA (lectr. nat. antitrust program 1997, Robinson-Patman com., corp. counsel com., antitrust litigation com.), Marquette U. Law Alumni Assn. (bd. dirs.), Milw. Bar Assn., Wis. Bar Assn. (chmn. bus. law com. 1978—79, bd. dirs. 1978—83, chair 180 standing rev. com. 2001—, standing com. bus. law), Marquette U. Sch. Law Woolsack Soc. (bd. dirs., past pres.), Western Racquet Club, Phi Delta Phi, Beta Gamma Sigma. Office: Quarles & Brady 411 E Wisconsin Ave Ste 2550 Milwaukee WI 53202-4497

HOLZ, MICHAEL HAROLD, lawyer; b. Dayton, Ohio, Apr. 10, 1942; s. Harold L. and Norma (Montgomery) Holz; m. Tanya Noffsinger, July 22, 1972 (div. Jan. 1983). BA, Wittenberg U., 1964; JD, U. Cin., 1967; MBA, U. Dayton, 1979. Bar: Ohio 1968, U.S. Dist. Ct. 1971, U.S. Tax Ct. 1975. With office of legal assistance Butler County OEO, Hamilton, Ohio, 1968; legal dep. probate Montgomery County, Dayton, 1971—73; asst. pros. atty. Greene County, Xenia, Ohio, 1973; sole practice Dayton, 1974—. Mem. Dayton Jaycees, 1971—78, Montgomery County Dem. Ctrl. Com., 1972—84. Served with U.S. Army, 1968—70, Vietnam. Mem.: ACLU (dir.), Ohio Bar Assn., Dayton Bar Assn. (ethics com. 1985—89, unauthorized practice of law com. 1990—95, bar exam. and qualifications com. 1996—2003), Mensa, Vietnam Vets. Am., Greater Dayton Real Estate Investors Assn., Phi Alpha Delta. Episcopalian. Home: 507 Wilmington Ave Apt 1 Dayton OH 45420-1876

HOLZ, ROBERT KENNETH, retired geography educator; b. Kankakee, Ill., Nov. 3, 1930; s. Harry H. and Margaret (Conway) H.; m. Joyce F. Harpin, May 19, 1951; 1 child, Eric R. BA in Zoology, So. Ill. U., 1958, MA in Geography, 1959; PhD in Geography, Mich. State U., 1963. Asst. prof. U. Tex., Austin, 1962-67, assoc. prof., 1967-72, prof., 1972—, dir. ctr. for Middle Eastern Studies, 1991-99, Eric W. Zimmerman Regents prof., 1991-99, Eric W. Zimmerman Regents prof. emeritus, 1999—; ret., 1999. Cons. in field. Co-author: Mendes I, 1980; author, editor: The Surveillant Science, 2d edit., 1985. Staff sgt. USAF, 1951-55. Recipient Group Achievement award NASA, 1974, Urban Achievement award L.B.J. Sch. Pub. Affairs, 1984. Mem. Assn. Am. Geographers (chmn. remote sensing specialty group 1980-82, chmn. southwest div. 1971-72, medal for outstanding contbns. to remote sensing Remote Sensing Specialty Group 1998), Am. Soc. Photogrammetry, Tex. Assn. Coll. Tchrs., Am. Congress of Surveying and Mapping. Roman Catholic. Avocations: hunting, fishing, squash. Home: 2610 Fiset Dr Austin TX 78731-5614 Office: U Tex Dept Geography Austin TX 78712 E-mail: holzrj@aol.com.

HOLZAPFEL, CHRISTINA MARIE, biologist; b. Balt., Jan. 24, 1942; d. Carl Martin and Ruby (Carlson) Holzapfel; m. William Emmons Bradshaw, May 10, 1971; 1 child, Pilar Antonia Bradshaw. BA, Goucher Coll., 1964; MS, U. Mich., 1968, PhD, 1970; postdoctoral fellow, Harvard U., 1970-71. Grad. research fellow U. Mich., Ann Arbor, 1964-70, lectr., 1970; research asst. Canary Islands, Spain, 1965-66; research fellow Harvard U., Cambridge, Mass., 1970-71; research assoc. U. Oreg., Eugene, 1971—, Tall Timbers Research Sta., Tallahassee, 1977-78, Imperial Coll., Silwood Park, Ascot, U.K., 1986. Contbr. articles to profl. jours. Bd. dirs. Eugene City Planning Com., 1980-81, Eugene Youth Symphony, 1980-84. Fellow Woods Hole Marine Biol. Labs., 1963. Mem. Ecol. Soc. Am., Soc. for Study of Evolution, Roundtable Club (pres. 2002-2003, Sigma Xi. Lutheran. Office: U Oreg Dept Biology Eugene OR 97403 E-mail: holz@darkwing.uoregon.edu.

HOLZBACH, RAYMOND THOMAS, gastroenterologist, author, educator; b. Salem, Ohio, Aug. 19, 1929; s. Raymond T. and Nelle A. (Conroy) H.; m. Lorraine E. Cozza, May 26, 1956; children: Ellen, Mark, James. BS, Georgetown U., 1951; MD, Case Western Res. U., 1955. Diplomate Nat. Bd. Med. Examiners, Am. Bd. Internal Medicine. Intern, asst. resident U. Ill. Research and Edn. Hosps., Chgo., 1955-56; sr. asst. resident medicine Cleve. Met. Gen. Hosp., 1959-60; asst. chief gastroenterology Case Western Res U., 1961-63; physician Gastroenterology Unit U. Hosps. of Cleve., 1961-63; instr. medicine Case Western Res. U. Sch. Medicine, Cleve., 1961-64, clin. instr. medicine, 1964-71; head gastrointestinal research unit, assoc. physician div. medicine St. Luke's Hosp., Cleve., 1967-73, dir. div. gastroenterology, 1970-73; head gastrointestinal research unit dept. medicine Cleve. Clinic Found., 1973—. Vis. prof. numerous instns. including Mayo Med. Sch., 1974, U. Calif., San Diego, 1977, U. Heidelberg, 1978, U. Pa., 1979, U. Zurich, 1980, U. Munich, 1982, U. Minn. Med. Ctr., 1985, med. ctrs., numerous Japanese univs., 1985, 92, Karolinska Inst., 1986, Royal Soc. London, 1987, Pa. State U. Sch. Med., U. Helsinki, RWTH-Aachen, Düsseldorf, Fed. Republic of Germany, U. Groningen, Utrecht, U. Amsterdam, The Netherlands, 1989, U. Perugia, Italy, Va. Commonwealth U.-Med. Coll. Va., Richmond, Christ Ch. Sch. Medicine, U. Otago, New Zealand, SUNY, Buffalo Sch. Medicine, 1990, Pontifical/Cath. U. Chile Sch. Medicine, 1991, Hiroshima U. Sch. Medicine, 1992, Kyoto U. Sch. Medicine, 1992, Sch. Medicine U. Jikei, Tokyo, 1992, Tel Aviv U., Israel Sch. Medicine, 1995, U. Leipzig, Germany, 1996, U. Heidelberg, Germany, 1996; lectr. in field. Mem. editl. bd. Gastroenterology jour., 1984-89; contbr. revs. and articles to med. jours. Served to capt. USAF, 1957-59. Recipient Alexander von Humboldt Found. Spl. Program award, 1978, 82. Fellow ACP; mem. ABA, Am. Gastroent. Assn. (rsch. com. 1976-79), Ctrl. Soc. Clin. Rsch., Am. Assn. for Study of Liver Diseases, AAAS, Am. Soc. Biol. Chemists, Am. Physiol. Assn., Biophys. Soc., Internat. Assn. Study of Liver, Am. Fedn. Clin. Rsch., Midwest Gut Club, Am. Soc. Clin. Nutrition, Ohio State Med. Assn., Sigma Xi. Unitarian Universalist. Home: 39251 Lander Rd Chagrin Falls OH 44022-2146 Office: Cleve Clin Found 9500 Euclid Ave Cleveland OH 44195-0001

HOLZBAUR, ERIKA L. medical educator; BS in Chemistry and History with honors, Coll. William and Mary, 1982; PhD in Biochemistry, Pa. State U., 1987. Rsch. fellow, teaching asst. Dept. Molecular and Cell Biology, Pa. State U., 1982—87, postdoctoral scientist, 1987—88; postdoctoral fellow NIH, 1988—92; asst. prof. Dept. Animal Biology, Sch. Vet. Medicine, U. Pa., Phila., 1992—98; assoc. prof. biochemistry Dept. Animal Biology, Sch. of Vet. Medicine, U. Pa., Phila., 1998—; assoc. prof. physiology Univ. Pa. Sch. Med. Contbr. articles to profl. jours., chapters to books. Recipient Established Investigator award, Am. Heart Assn., 1996; fellow Grad. Sch., Pa. State U., 1984—85, 1985—86, Keith R. Porter Fellowship, 2000. Mem.: U. Pa. Cancer Inst., Pa. Muscle Inst., Am. Soc. Cell Biology, Phi Beta Kappa. Office: U Pa Dept physiology D400 Richards Bldg 3700 Hamilton Walk Philadelphia PA 19104-6085

HOLZER, BARBARA COURSEY, innkeeper, minister, writer, educator; b. L.A., July 17, 1931; d. Clarence Ray and Grace Marion (Davies) Coursey; m. Richard Gray Hall, Aug. 7, 1954 (div. Mar. 1970); children: Jennifer, Wendy, Andrew; m. Duane Harold Holzer, Sept. 1, 1973. AA, Compton Coll., 1950; BA, Long Beach State U., 1952; MA, U. San Francisco, 1982. Cert. tchr., Calif. Kindergarten tchr. L.A. City Schs., Wilmington, 1952-56; 1st grade tchr. Paramount (Calif.) Unified Schs., 1956-59; adult educator Norwalk (Calif.) Adult Schs., 1962-76; bilingual tchr. Lynwood (Calif.) Unified Schs., 1969-94, tchr., adminstr. liaison, 1990-94; Sunday sch. supt. Ocean View Bapt. Ch., San Pedro, Calif., 1980-84; wedding min. Arcata, Calif., 1994—; co-owner Cats Cradle Bed & Breakfast, Arcata, Calif., 1997—. Author: Titeres de Sonidos, 1979; columnist Arcata Eye, 1996—. Pres. Paramount Jr. Woman's club, 1963-64, Paramount Woman's Club, 1967-68, Paramount Faculty Wives Club, 1958, 60, 67, Vox Players, Compton, Calif., 1950; mem. BBB, 2000, Humboldt Conv. and visitors Bur. Recipient Best Actress award Pasadena Playhouse, 1950. Mem. Arcata C. of C., Profl. Assn. of Innkeepers, Internat. Avocations: gourmet cooking, calligraphy, interior design, wedding planning. E-mail: catcradl@humboldt1.com.

HOLZER, HAROLD, public affairs officer, historian, writer; b. Bklyn., Feb. 5, 1949; s. Charles and Rose (Last) H.; m. Edith Spiegel, Feb. 27, 1971; children: Remy, Meg. BA, CUNY, Queens, 1969; diploma (hon.), Lincoln Meml. U., 1988, Lincoln Coll., 1992. Editor Manhattan Tribune, N.Y.C., 1969-73; dir. spl. projects Dept. Civic Affairs, City of N.Y., 1973-75; press sec. to Congresswoman Bella Abzug N.Y.C., 1975-77; communications specialist Sec. of State office, N.Y., 1978; dir. pub. affairs Sta. WNET (PBS), N.Y.C., 1978-84; v.p. pub. affairs Javits Conv. Ctr., N.Y.C., 1984-85; exec. v.p. pub. affairs Urban Devel. Corp., State of N.Y., 1985-92; chief comm. officer Met. Mus. Art, N.Y.C., 1992-96, v.p. comm., 1996-2001, v.p. comm. and mktg., 2001—. Co-author: The Lincoln Image, 1984, Changing the Lincoln Image, 1985, The Confederate Image, 1987, The Lincoln Family Album, 1990, Lincoln on Democracy, 1990, Mine Eyes Have Seen the Glory, 1993, The Union Preserved, 1999, The Lincoln Forum, 1999, The Union Image, 2000; author: The Lincoln-Douglas Debates, 1993, Washington and Lincoln Portrayed, 1993, Dear Mr. Lincoln: Letters to the President, 1993, Witness to War: The Civil War, 1996, The Civil War Era, 1996; The Lincoln Mailbag: America Writes to the President, 1998, Lincoln As I Knew Him, 1999, Abraham Lincoln, The Writer, 2000, Lincoln Seen and Heard, 2000, Prang's Civil War, 2001, State of the Union, 2002; Rediscovering Abraham Lincoln: The Lincoln Forum, 2002. contbr. over 350 articles on Lincoln and the Civil War to popular mags., scholarly jours. and newspapers; contbr. chpts. in books; columnist Antique Trader, 1985-95; contbg. editor: Americana Mag., 1991-93; writer various pamphlets on Abraham Lincoln; contbg. historian various CD-ROMS, TV spls. on C-SPAN, A&E, The History Channel, NBC, ABC, CBS, PBS. Lectr. on Lincoln and Civil War before various hist. groups; co-organizer 4 exhbns. on Lincoln and Civil War; trustee N.Y. State Archives Partnership Trust, 1994—; mem. U.S. Lincoln Bicentennial Commn. (appointed by Pres. Clinton), 2000, co-chmn., 2001--. Recipient Barondess/Lincoln award Civil War Round Table of N.Y., 1984, 91, 94, George Washington medal Freedom Found. Valley Forge, 1988, Writer of Distinction award Internat. Reading Assn., 1989, award Manuscript Soc. Am., 1996, Newman Book award Am. Hist. Print Collectors' Soc., 2000, Nevins-Freeman award, CWRT/Chgo., 2002. Mem. Abraham Lincoln Assn. (bd. dirs. 1988-95, Achievement award 1991), Lincoln Group of N.Y. (v.p. 1979-90, pres. 1990-96, Achievement award 1988, 93), State Coun. for Humanities (bd. dirs. 1991-93), Ulysses S. Grant Assn. (bd. dirs. 1996—), The Lincoln Forum (vice chmn. 1996—). Office: Met Mus of Art 1000 Fifth Ave New York NY 10028-0113 E-mail: harold.holzer@metmuseum.org.

HOLZER, JENNY, artist; b. Gallipolis, Ohio, July 29, 1950; d. Richard Vornholt and Virginia (Beasley) H.; m. Michael Andrew Glier, May 21, 1984; 1 child. Student, Duke U., 1968-70, U. Chgo., 1970-71; BFA, Ohio U., 1973, DA (hon.), 1994; MFA, R.I. Sch. Design, 1977; postgrad., Whitney Mus. Am. Art, 1977; PhD of Art (hon.), Williams Coll., 2000. One-woman shows include Rüdiger Schöttle Gall, Münich, 1980, Barbara Gladstone Gallery, NYC, 1983, 86, 94, Kunsthalle, Basel, Switzerland, 1984, Des Moines Art Ctr., 1986, MIT, Cambridge, 1986, Mus. Contemporary Art, Chgo., 1987, Inst. Contemporary Art, London, 1988, Bklyn. Mus., NYC, 1988, DIA Art Found., NYC, 1989, Guggenheim Mus., NYC, 1989, Am. Pavilion, 44th Biennale, Venice, Italy, 1990, La. Mus., Humlebaek, Denmark, 1991, Albright-Knox Art Gallery, Buffalo, 1991, Walker Art Gallery, Mpls., 1991, Ydessa Hendeles Art Found., Toronto, 1992, Dallas Mus. Art, 1993, Haus der Kunst, Munich, 1993, Bergen Mus. Art, Norway, 1994, Art Tower Mito, Japan, 1994, Williams Coll. Mus. Art, Williamstown, Mass., 1995, Kunstmus. des Kantons Thurgau, Kartouse Ittingen, Warth, Switzerland, 1996, Contemporary Art Mus., Houston, 1997, Cheim & Read, NY, 1997, Yvon Lambert Gallery, Paris, 1998, Inst. Cultural Itau, São Paulo, Brazil, 1998, Centro Cultural Banco do Brasil, Rio de Janeiro, 1999, BALTIC Ctr. Contemporary Art, Gateshead, 2000, Neue Nat. Galeri, Berlin, 2001, Mus. Contemporary Art, Bordeaux, France, 2001, Monterrey, Mex., 2001, Mönahehaus Mus., Goslar, Germany, 2002, Monika Spruth Philomerie Magers, 2002, others; exhibited in group shows at Documenta 7, Kassel, Germany, 1982, Contemporary Arts Ctr., Cin., 1984, Mus. Art Carnegie Inst., Pitts., 1985, Israel Mus., Jerusalem, 1986, Frankfurter Kunstverein, Frankfurt, Germany, 1986, Europa/Amerika Mus. Ludwig, Koln, 1986, Sonsbeck, Arnhem, The Netherlands, 1986, Whitney Mus. Am. Art, NYC, 1989, Mus. Contemporary Art, LA, 1989, Mus. Modern Art, NYC, 1988, 90, 96, Documenta 8, Kassel, 1987, Ctrl. Mus., Utrecht, The Netherlands, 1991, Kunsthalle, Basel, 1992, Guggenheim Mus., Soho, NYC, 1993, 96, Lenbachhaus, Munich, 1994, SITE Santa Fe, 1995, Pompidou Ctr., Paris, 1996, Biennale di Florence, Italy, 1996, Joseph Helman Gallery, NY, 1997, Kunsthalle Wien, Vienna, Austria, 1998, Nat. Gallery Australia, Canberra, 1998, Rhona Hofman Gallery, 1998, Oslo Mus. Contemporary Art, 2000; represented in permanent collections Ujazdowski Castle, Warsaw, Poland, Black Garden, Nordhorn, Germany, Erlauf (Austria) Peace Monument, Guggenheim Mus., Bilbao, Bundestag, Berlin, U. So. Calif., LA, Ludwig Mus., Aachen, Germany, Neue Nat. Galerie, Berlin, Toyota Mclpl. Mus. Art, Hamburg Kunstalie, US Fed. Courthouse, Sacramento, Allentown, Pa., Telenor Hdqr., Norway. Recipient Golden Lion award 44th Venice Biennale, 1990, Skowhegan medal for installation Skowhegen Sch. Painting and Sculpture, N.Y., 1994, Crystal award World Econ. Forum, Cologny-Geneva, Switzerland, 1996, BMW Art car, BMW, Munich, 1999, Kaiserring award City of Goslar, Germany, 2002. Fellow Am. Acad., Berlin, 2000. Avocation: reading. E-mail: studio@jennyholzer.com., gallery@cheimread.com.

HOLZER, LINDA RUTH, education educator; b. Chgo., Ill., Aug. 9, 1963; d. Robert and Ruth Holzer; life ptnr. Peggy Harstvedt. MusB, Northwestern U, 1981—85; MM, U of N. Carolina, 1985—87; MusD, Fla. State U., 1992—95. Artist-in-residence Wake Tech. CC, Raleigh, NC, 1988—90, Catawba Valley CC, Hickory, NC, 1990—92; asst. prof. of music U of Ark., 1995—2001, assoc. prof. of music, 2001—. Musician: (concerto soloist) Rachmaninoff Concerto #2; contbr. articles to profl. jours. Mem.: Internat. Alliance for Women in Music, Chamber Music Am., Coll. Music Soc., Music Teachers Nat. Assn. Office: UALR Music Dept 2801 S University Ave Little Rock AR 72204 E-mail: lrholzer@ualr.edu.

HOLZER, THOMAS LEQUEAR, geologist; b. Lafayette, Ind., June 26, 1944; s. Oswald Alois and Ruth Alice (Lequear) H.; children: Holly Christine, Elizabeth Alice. BSE, Princeton U., 1965; MS, Stanford U., 1966, PhD, 1970. Asst. prof. geology U. Conn., Storrs, 1970-75; adj. environmentalist Griswold & Fuss, Manchester, Conn., 1973-75; research geol. U.S. Geol. Survey, Menlo Park, Calif., 1975-82, rsch. geologist, 1984-88, 93—, dep. asst. dir. rsch. Reston, Va., 1982-84, chief br. engring. seismology and geology, 1989-93; cons. assoc. prof. geology and environ. sci. Stanford U., 1994—. Contbr. numerous articles to profl. jours. Coach Am. Youth Soccer Orgn., Palo Alto, Calif., 1979-82. Recipient Superior Svc. award U.S Geol. Survey, 1981, Outstanding Pub. Svc. award U.S. Geol. Survey, 1991. Fellow: Geol. Soc. Am. (chmn. engring. geology divsn. 1988—89, councilor 1995—97, Disting. Svc. award hydrogeology divsn. 1995, Richard H. James Disting. Lectr. 1998); mem.: Earthquake Engring. Rsch. Inst., Am. Geophys. Union, AAAS, Sigma Xi. Republican. Presbyterian. Avocation: tennis. Home: PO Box 851 Palo Alto CA 94302-0851 Office: US Geol Survey 345 Middlefield Rd Menlo Park CA 94025-3591

HOLZMAN, D. KEITH, management consultant, record company executive, producer, arts consultant; b. N.Y.C., Mar. 22, 1936; s. Jacob Easton and Minnette Cathryn (Sternberger) H.; m. Jo Susan Handelman, Nov. 16, 1971; children: Susanne Carla, Lucas Jon, Rebecca Leigh. BA, Oberlin (Ohio) Coll., 1957; MFA, Boston U., 1959. Asst. to gen. mgr. and stage mgr. N.Y.C. Light Opera, 1959, 62-64; dir. prodn. Elektra Records, N.Y.C., 1964-70; v.p. prodn. and mfg. Elektra/Asylum/Nonesuch Records, Los Angeles, 1970-81, sr. v.p. prodn. and mfg., 1981-84; pres. ROM Records, 1987—2000; producer, arts cons. Treasure Trove, Inc., 1984—2000; mng. dir. Discovery Records, Santa Monica, Calif., 1991-98; prin. Keith Holzman Solutions Unltd., 1998—. Pres. Treasure Trove Inc.; dir. Nonesuch Records, 1980-84; music supr. Witches of Eastwick, Warner Bros., Los Angeles, 1986; bd. dirs. Plumstead Theatre Soc., Los Angeles, 1985—, Early Music Acad., Los Angeles, 1983-86, Assn. Classical Music, N.Y.C., 1983-86. Served with AUS, 1960-62. Mem. Audio Engring. Soc., Early Music Acad. (bd. dirs.) Nat. Acad. Rec. Arts and Scis., Assn. Classical Music (bd. dirs.), Plumstead Theatre Co. (bd. dirs.). Avocation: flying.

HOLZMAN, PHILIP SEIDMAN, psychologist, educator; b. NYC, May 2, 1922; s. Barnet and Natalie (Seidman) H.; m. Hannah Abarbanell, Sept. 18, 1946; children: Natalie Kay, Carl David, Paul Benjamin. BA, CCNY, 1943; PhD, U. Kans., 1952. Diplomate: Am. Bd. Examiners Profl. Psychology. Psychology intern Topeka VA Hosp., 1946-49; psychologist Topeka State Hosp., 1949-51, cons., 1951-58; psychologist Menninger Found., Topeka, 1949-68, dir. research tng., 1963-68; prof. psychiatry and psychology U. Chgo., 1968-77; prof. psychology dept. psychology Harvard U., 1977-92; prof. dept. psychiatry Med. Sch., 1977-92; Esther and Sidney R. Rabb prof. psychology Harvard U., 1984-92, prof. emeritus, 1992; chief Lab. of Psychology McLean Hosp., Belmont, Mass., 1977—; tng. and supervising psychoanalyst Boston Psychoanalytic Soc. and Inst., 1977—. Vis. prof. U. Minn., 1965, U. Kans., 1966, Boston U., 1973, Jefferson Med. Coll., 1981, U. Pa., 1987; Thomas William Salmon lectr. N.Y. Acad. Medicine, 1994; small grants com. NIMH, 1960-64, clin. projects research rev. com., 1964-68, clin. program projects research rev. com., 1970-74, treatment devel. and assessment rev. com., 1982-86; cons. Ill. State Psychiat. Inst., 1970-77; adv. coms. classification of mental disorders WHO. Author: (with others) Cognitive Control, 1959, Psychoanalysis and Psychopathology, 1970, (with Karl Menninger) The Theory of Psychoanalytic Technique, rev. edit, 1973; editor: (with Merton M. Gill) Psychology Versus Metapsychology, 1975; (with Mary Hollis Johnston) Assessing Schizophrenic Thinking, 1979; bd. editors: Psychol. Issues, 1968—, Contemporary Psychology, 1969-76, Bull. of Menninger Clinic, 1961—, Psychoanalysis and Contemporary Thought, Jour. Psychiat. Rsch., 1980-92; assoc. editor Schizophrenia Bulletin, Schizophrenia Rsch., Harvard Review of Psychiatry, Harvard Mental Health Letter; contbr. articles to profl. jours. Mem. Topeka Mayor's Com. on Human Rels., 1963-68; chmn. bd. dirs. Founds.' Fund for Rsch. in Psychiatry; mem. program adv. com. MacArthur Found., sci. adv. bd. NIMH, 1986-92; bd. trustees Menninger Found., 1978—; mem. sci. coun. Nat. Alliance Rsch. Schizophrenia and Depression, 1989—. With AUS, 1943-46. Recipient Career Scientist award NIMH, 1974-77, 92-2002, Stanley Dean award Am. Coll. Psychiatrists, 1984, Lieber prize Nat. Alliance for Rsch. in Schizophrenia and Depression, 1988, Joseph Zubin award Soc. Rsch. in Psychopathology, 1994, Thomas William Salmon medal N.Y. Acad. Medicine, 1994, Townsend Harris medal CCNY, Gold medal for lifetime achievement APA, 1997, William K. Warren award Internat. Congress on Schizophrenia Rsch., 1997, Alexander Gralnick award Am. Psychol. Found., 2002. Fellow APA, AAAS, Am. Acad. Arts and Scis., Am. Coll. Neuropsychopharmacology, Soc. Neurosci.; mem. Am. Psychoanalytic Assn., Boston Psychoanalytic Soc., Am. Psychopath. Assn., Inst. Medicine NAS, Soc. for Rsch. in Psychopathology (pres. 1997-98). Office: Harvard U William James Hall Cambridge MA 02138 also: McLean Hosp Lab Belmont MA 02478 E-mail: psh@wjh.harvard.edu.

HOLZNER, BURKART, sociologist, educator; b. Tilsit, Germany, Apr. 28, 1931; came to U.S., 1957, naturalized, 1965; s. Hans Otto and Brigitte (Prenzel) H.; children by previous marriage: Steven, Daniel, Claire; m. Leslie Salmon-Cox; stepchildren: Sara Ruth Salmon-Cox, Weir Becket Strange. Student, U. Munich, 1949-52, 53-54, U. Wis., 1952-53, postgrad., 1957-59; Diplom Psychologe, U. Bonn, 1957, Dr.Phil., 1958. Grad. asst., acting instr. U. Wis., 1958-60; asst. prof. U. Pitts., 1960-63, assoc. prof., 1963-65, prof., chmn. sociology dept., 1966-80, dir. bd. visitors field staff Learning Research and Devel. Center, 1964-66, 71-78, dir. Univ. Ctr. for Internat. Studies, 1980-2000, prof. Univ. Ctr. for Internat. Studies, 1998—, disting. svc. prof. internat. studies, 1999—2003, also sr. rsch. assoc., prof. emeritus, 2003—. Assoc. sociologist, assoc. dir. Social Sci. Rsch. Inst., U. Hawaii, 1965-66; vis. prof. sociology, dir. Social Rsch. Centre, Chinese U. of Hong Kong, 1969-70, external examiner in sociology, 1995-98; vis. prof. U. Augsburg, 1977, Chinese Acad. Social Scis., Beijing, 1979, 80; cons. Nat. Inst. Edn., Westinghouse Electric Corp.; mem. exec. com. Pa. Coun. for Internat. Edn., 1980-89, chmn., 1980-83, 88-89. Author: Amerikanische und deutsche Psychologie, 1958, Völkerpsychologie, 1960, Reality Construction in Society, rev. edit, 1972, (with John Marx) Knowledge Application: The Knowledge System in Society, 1979; editor: (with Roland Robertson) Identity and Authority, Explorations in the Theory of Society, 1980, (with Jiri Nehnevajsa) Organizing for Social Research, 1981, (with Zdenek Suda) Directions of Change: Modernization Theory, Research and Reality, 1981, (with Andrew Dinniman) Education for International Competence in Pennsylvania, 1988; co-editor Knowledge: Creation, Distribution, Utilization, 1985, Knowledge in Society, 1987-89. Mem. dist. export council U.S. Dept. Commerce. Recipient Philip R.A. May award for internat. svc., 1991; named hon. citizen of Johnstown, Pa., hon. mem. U. Augsburg, 1990. Mem. Am. Sociol. Assn., North Central Sociol. Assn., Pa. Sociol. Assn., Sociol. Rsch. Assn., Sozialwissenschaftlicher Studienkreis für Internationale Probleme, Internat. Soc. for Comparative Study of Civilizations (mem. U.S. coun., v.p. 1977-79), Assn. Internat. Edn. Adminstrs. (exec. com. 1986—, pres. 1990-91, Charles Klasek award for career achievement in internat. edn. 2000, sr. counselor 2001—), World Federalist Assn. Pitts. (pres. 1996-2001). Home: 1700 Grandview Ave Apt 801 Pittsburgh PA 15211-1006 Office: U Pitts Dept Sociology U Ctr Internat Studies 2J26 Power Hall Pittsburgh PA 15260 E-mail: holzner@ucis.pitt.edu.

HOLZRICHTER, JOHN F. physicist; BS in Applied Math. and Engring. Physics, U. Wis., 1964; MS in Physics, Stanford U., 1966, PhD in Physics, 1971. Laser R&D staff NRL, 1971—72; dir. solid state laser program Lawrence Livermore Nat. Lab., Livermore, Calif., 1976—80, 1984—86, dir. inertial fusion program, 1980—84, dir. lab. sci. and tech. office, 1987—. Mem. Army Sci. Bd.; lectr. in field; mem. rev. bd. Coll. of Sci. and Engring. San Francisco State U. Contbr. Fellow, Hertz Found., A.E. Sloan Found., Fulbright fellow, Germany, Stanford fellow. Mem.: IEEE, AAAS, APS, Sigma Xi. Achievements include patents for in field. Office: Univ of California Lawrence Livermore Nat Lab 7000 East Ave PO Box 808 Livermore CA 94550-0808

HOM, DAVID BRIAN, surgeon; b. San Diego, 1956; s. James and Evelyn Hom; m. Lorraine Hom, 1984. BA summa cum laude, U. Calif., San Diego, 1978; MD, UCLA, 1982. Diplomate Am. Bd. Otolaryngology and Facial Plastic and Reconstructive Surgery. Gen. surg. resident U. Calif., Irvine, 1983-84; otolaryngology, head and neck surgery resident U. Mich., Ann Arbor, 1984-88; facial plastic fellow Am. Acad. Facial Plastic Surgery, Birmingham, Ala., 1988-89; asst. prof. dept. otolaryngology, head and neck surgery U. Minn., Mpls., 1989-96, assoc. prof., 1996—. Mem. otolaryngology expert adv. panel U.S. Pharmacopia Conv., Washington, 1994—. Editor: Wound Healing for the Otolaryngologist-Head and Neck Surgeon, 1995; contbr. numerous articles to profl. jours., chpts. to books. Med. cons. NCAA, Mpls., 1996-97. NIH Rsch. grantee, 1996-2002. Fellow ACS, Am. Acad. Otolaryngology, Head and Neck Surgery (Nat. Percy Meml. Rsch. award 1991), Am. Acad. Facial Plastic and Reconstrv. Surgery (chmn. rsch. 1997-2000, Nat. Ben Shuster Rsch. award 1988); mem. AAAS. Avocations: fishing, kayaking. Office: Univ Minn Dept Otolaryngology Box 396 420 Delaware St SE Minneapolis MN 55455

HOM, DORIS SOO, consultant, investment manager; b. N.Y.C., May 22, 1953; d. Frank Edward and Ngook Ho (Tow) S. BA in Math., CCNY, 1977; MS in Stats., Baruch Coll., 1986. Grants adminstr. to coord. field work Rsch. Found., 1980-81; adminstrv. asst. to dean Sch. Social Work, 1981-82; tchr. math. William Alexander Jr. High Sch., Bklyn., 1979; adj. lectr. Hunter Coll., N.Y.C., 1978-79, N.Y.C. Tech. Coll., 1979-80; math tchr. Meridian (Miss.) Pub. High Sch., 1988-98; investment mgr., 1998—. Researcher women's bur. U.S. Dept. Labor. Grantee NSF, 1979-80. Mem. Nat. Assn. Remeidal Devel. Studies in Post Secondary Edn., Inst. Econ. Rsch., Assn. Tchrs. Math. N.Y.C., Coalition Asian Am. Profl. Women, Phi Theta Kappa.

HOMAN, J. MICHAEL, library administrator; b. Portland, Oreg., Aug. 16, 1947; s. Gerald B. and Beverly J. Homan. BA, Lewis and Clark Coll., 1969; MA, U. Chgo., 1971; cert. advanced study, UCLA, 1972. MEDLARS analyst UCLA, 1972-74, head info. svcs., 1974-79, Upjohn Co., Kalamazoo, Mich., 1979-88; asst. univ. libr. scis. U. Calif., Irvine, 1988-94; dir. libs. Mayo Found./Mayo Clinic, Rochester, Minn., 1994—. Author: (book chpts.) Management of Scientific and Technical Libraries, 1986, Introduction to Reference Sources in the Health Sciences, 1984. USPHS fellow U. Chgo., 1969-71, UCLA, 1971-72. Mem. ALA, Med. Libr. Assn. (pres. 2000-01, bd. dirs. 1987-89, editor jour. 1996-2000, mng. editor of books 1990-96), Assn. Acad. Health Sci. Libr. Dirs. (bd. dirs. 1991-94), Spl. Librs. Assn., Am. Med. Informatics Assn., Coalition for Networked Info. (rep.), Assn. Coll. and Rsch. Librs., Libr. Adminstrn. and Mgmt. Assn. Episcopalian. Avocations: music, opera, traveling, reading. Office: Mayo Clinic Mayo Med Libr 200 1st St SW Rochester MN 55905-0002 E-mail: homan@mayo.edu.

HOMAN, KENNETH LEWIS, auditor; b. Bridgeton, N.J., Feb. 8, 1949; s. Lewis and Brenda Homan. BA, Colo. State U., 1971; BS, Edison State Coll., 1981; AS, Camden County Coll., 1984. Cert. mcpl. fin. officer N.J. Dept. Cmty. Affairs. Social worker Cumberland County Bd. Social Svcs., Vineland, N.J., 1972-74; planning coord. Cumberland County Bd. Freeholders, Bridgeton, N.J., 1974-78; staff auditor Bowman & Co., CPA's, Voorhees, N.J., 1979; coord. Morris County Bd. Freeholders, Morristown, N.J., 1979-80; prin. acct. Camden (N.J.) County Bd. Freeholders, 1980-82, asst. comptr., 1982-84, prin. auditor, 1984-96, Camden County Bd. Social Svcs., 1997—. Sec. Somerdale (N.J.) Planning Bd., 1992-2001. Mem. Assn. Govt. Accts. (cert. govt. fin. mgr.), N.J. Govt. Fin. Officers Assn., N.J. County Fin. Officers Assn., N.Y./N.J. Intergovernmental Audit Forum. Home: PO Box 121 Somerdale NJ 08083-0121 Office: Camden County Bd Social Svcs 600 Market St Camden NJ 08102-1249

HOMAN, RALPH WILLIAM, finance company executive; b. Wilkes-Barre, Pa., June 7, 1951; s. Norman Ryan and Adelaide Bernice (Sandy) H.; m. Donna Marie Webb, Jan. 25, 1975. BS in Acctg., Wheeling Coll., 1977; MBA in Mktg., Nat. U., 1986. Paymaster Dravo Corp., Pitts., 1974-75; tax preparer H&R Block, Wheeling, W.Va., 1977; fin. services exec. NCR Credit Corp., Sacramento, 1977-84; leasing exec. CSB Leasing, Sacramento, 1984-85; pres. Convergent Fin. Svcs., Colorado Springs, Colo., 1985—. Bd. dirs. Concord Coalition, Colorado Springs. Cons. Jr. Achievement, 1990—. Co-winner Name the Plane Contest Pacific Southwest Airlines, 1984; recipient Businessperson of Yr. award, Colo. Springs chpt. Future Bus. Leaders Am., 1995, 2000. Mem. The 30/40 Something Social Club (founder, pres. Sedona chpt.), Am. Assn. Boomers (pres. Pikes Peak chpt. 1992-93), Toastmasters (treas. Oak Creek chpt. 1988-89), Kiwanis (sec. 1988-89, founder, chmn. adult soccer league), Concord Coalition (bd. dirs., pres. Colorado Springs chpt.). Avocations: photography, camping, off-road motorcycling, woodworking. Home and Office: Convergent Fin Svcs 29 Mount Hope Dr Twin Lakes CO 81251-9705 E-mail: cfsleasing@aol.com.

HOMAN, RICHARD WARREN, neurologist, academic administrator, medical educator; b. N.Y.C., July 28, 1940; s. H. Frank and Irmgard Homan; m. Katherine Poulos, June 16, 1963; children: Gregory William, Christopher Allen. BA, Colgate U., 1962; MD, SUNY, 1966; MA, U. Tex. Med. Br., 1999-2001. Diplomate Am. Bd. Psychiatry and Neurology, Am. Bd. Clin. Neurophysiology; cert. Nat. Bd. Med. Examiners. Resident in neurology UCLA, 1970; fellow in neurophysiology Albert Einstein Coll. Medicine, Bronx, NY, 1972—74; asst. prof. neurology U. Tex., Southwestern Med. Sch. and Dallas VA Med. Ctr., 1974—82, assoc. prof. neurology, chief neurology svc., 1982—89; prof., chmn. neurology Med. Coll. Ohio, Toledo, 1989—94; chmn. neurology Tex. Tech. U. Health Sci. Ctr., Lubbock, 1994—97, prof. neuropsychiatry and behavioral medicine, pharm. practice, pharm. scis., dir. Ctr. Neuropsychiat. Studies, 1997—99; bioethics cons., 2001—; mem. bioethics faculty Southwestern Med. Sch., Dallas, 2002—. Examiner Am. Bd. Clin. Neurophysiology, 1981-94; cons. Tex. State Bd. Med. Examiners, Austin, 1995-2000. Editor (collected sci. manuscripts) Rational Polypharmacy, 1996; contbr. chpts. to books. Mem. profl. adv. bd. Dallas Epilepsy Found., 1985-87, Epilepsy Found. N.W. Ohio, Toledo, 1989-94; mediator South Plains Ctr. for Dispute Resolution, Lubbock, 1998. Fellow Am. Electroencepalographic Soc., Am. Acad. Neurology; mem. Am. Epilepsy Soc., Phi Beta Kappa. Avocations: scuba diving, playing harp. Home: 1629 Handley Dr Dallas TX 75208 E-mail: rwhoman@sbcglobal.net.

HOMAN, THOMASITA, English language and literature educator; b. Pawnee City, Nebr., Aug. 7, 1938; d. Richard William and Mary Veronica Homan. BA in Edn., Mt. St. Scholastica, 1970; Reading Specialist, Cardinal Stritch Coll., 1973; MA in English, Iowa State U., 1979. Tchr. jr. high sch., Nortonville, Kans., 1969-70; tchr. Title I Atchison, Kans., 1972-77; primary coord., tchr. ACES Elem. Sch., Atchison, 1970-77; dir. campus ministry Benedictine Coll., Atchison, 1987-89, dir. alumni, 1987-89, asst. prof. English, 1979—. Mem. Assoc. Collegiate Press Evaln. Bd.; cons. in field. Poetry editor Benedictines; mem. editl. staff Atchison Benedictine Newsletter, 1983-2001, Threshold, 2001—; contbr. articles to profl. jours. Organizer Women's Day Presentation, 1980-81; mem. Atchison Art Assn., 1996-98. Mem. Phi Kappa Phi. Roman Catholic. Avocations: reading, walking, foreign travel. Home: 801 S 8th St Atchison KS 66002 Office: Benedictine Coll 1020 N 2d St Atchison KS 66002

HOMAYSSI, RUBY LEE, small business owner; b. Jan. 14, 1945; d. Raymond and Elmira (Carter) K. BS in Food & Nutrition, So. U., Baton Rouge, 1967; MA, Pepperdine U., 1981; A.Hosp. Dietetics, Tuskegee Inst., Ala., 1969. Staff dietitian Nat. Naval Med. Ctr., Bethesda, Md., 1969-70; chief clin. nutrition and dietitian dept. Naval Hosp. Chelsea, Mass., 1970-74; chief dietitian, asst. food mgmt. officer Naval Submarine Med. Ctr., Groton, Conn., 1974-78; chief clin. nutrition Naval Hosp. Portsmouth, Va., 1978-83; chief clin. nutrition and dietetics Naval Hosp. Orlando, Fla., 1983-88; pres. Elmira's P.A.N.T.R.Y., Inc., Orlando, 1988—. Adv. bd. Fla. Hosp. Women; bd. dir. Bridgebuilders of Winter Pk.; cons. in field. Contbr. articles to profl. jours. Dir. Vol. Ctr. Seminole County, 1989-91; 3d v.p. Civic Theatre Bd. Ctrl. Fla., Orlando, 1989, 2d v.p., 1990—, pres., 1992-93; 1st v.p. Orlando Opera Co., 1987-88; bd. dirs. Maitland Arts Coun., New Hope For kids, gala chmn., 2002, 2003; pub. edn. chmn. Am. Cancer Soc., Orlando, 1987-90, bd. dirs.; prodn. chmn. March of Dimes, 1988—; bd. dirs. Hospice of Ctrl. Fla.; mem. cmty. advisors bd. TV-24; bd. dirs. Seminole Chamber-Cmty. Rels., 1990-93, Citrus Coun. Girl Scouts; cmty. advisors bd. Symphony Orch. Assocs., 1991-92 Symphony Ball; bd. dir., chmn. Festival of Orchs., Inc., 2001-03; trainer Jr. Achievement, 1993—; chmn. Bridgebuilders, 2000 01; chmn. bd. dirs. Festival of Orchs., 2001-03; mem. Westside Winter Park Neighborhood Devel. Bd., 2000—;bd. dirs. Seminola County Arts Coun., 2003—. Named Woman of the Yr., Am. Bus. Women's Assn., 1987, Women of Achievement in Arts Downtown Exec. Women's Coun., 1989; recipient Angle award, 1989, Ruby Homayssi Day named in her honor City of Longwood, 199;; Paul Harris fellow Rotary, 2000. Mem. AAUW, NAFE, Am. Dietetic Assn., Fla. Dietetic Assn., Am. Bus. Women's Assn. (pres. 1987), Pvt. Industry Coun. of Seminole County (bd. dirs.), Girl Friends Club, Torch Club, Leadership Seminole, Delta Sigma Theta, Orlando Coun. of Christian Bus. Women, Subuuran Rep. Woman (bd.), Femmes de Coeur (pr chair & underwriting chair), Seminole County Rotary Club. Republican. Baptist. Avocations: reading, traveling, stock car racing, sewing. Home: 1409 Pylewood St Casselberry FL 32730-2450

HOMAYUN, TAHIRA, obstetrician/gynecologist; b. Afghanistan, 1943; came to U.S., 1970; MD, Kabul (Afghanistan) U., 1969. Diplomate Am. Bd. Ob-Gyn. Intern Christ Cmty. Hosp., Oak Lawn, Ill., 1970-71; resident in ob-gyn. N.Y. Infirmary, 1971-74; fellow Brookdale Med. Ctr., Bklyn., 1974-75; pvt. practice N.Y.C., 1976—; staff Beth Israel Med. Ctr. South and North, N.Y.C., 1976—. Address: 20 E 74th St New York NY 10021-2654 Fax: (212) 734-6622.

HOMB, SCOTT MICHAEL, rehabilitation services professional; b. Monroe, Wis., Apr. 13, 1951; s. Wesley C. and Dolores L. Homb. MA, U. South Fla., 1972; PhD, Pacific Western U., 1993. Cert. rehab. counselor; cert. med. case mgr.; cert. vocat. evaluation specialist. Area counseling supr. State of Fla., St. Petersburg, 1978-79; dir. rehab. Nat. Rehab. Assocs., St. Petersburg, 1980-85; sr. med. case mgr. State of Fla., St. Petersburg, 1987-96, brain and spinal cord injury program regional mgr., 1996—

HOMBURGER, THOMAS CHARLES, lawyer; b. Buffalo, Sept. 16, 1941; s. Adolf and Charolotte E. (Stern) H.; m. Louise Paula Shemin, June 6, 1965; children: Jennifer Anne, Richard Ephraim, Kathryn Lee. BA, Columbia U., 1963, JD, 1966. Bar: Ill. 1966, U.S. Dist. Ct. (no. dist.) Ill. 1966. Assoc., ptnr. Sonnenschein, Carlin, Nath & Rosenthal, Chgo., 1966—86, Bell, Boyd & Lloyd LLC, Chgo., 1986—. Adj. prof. John Marshall Law Sch., Chgo., 1989—, chmn. real estate, 1986—2001. Contbr. articles to profl. jours. Chmn. Chgo. regional bd. Anti-Defamation League, B'nai Brith, 1986-88; chmn. nat. exec. com. Anti-Defamation League, 2000-2003; pres. Anti-Defamation League Found., 2003—; mem. exec. com. Glencoe (Ill.) Bd. Edn., 1984-89. Mem.: ABA (real property divsn., probate & trust law sect., fin. subcom.), Chgo. Mortgage Attys. Assn. (pres. 1975—77), Am. Coll. Real Estate Lawyers (bd. govs. 2000—03), Chgo. Bar Assn. (chmn. real property law com. 1984—85), Ill. Bar Assn. (real property sect.), Std. Club, Law Club Chgo., Lambda Alpha Internat. Home: 20 East Cedar St Apt 2F Chicago IL 60611-1149 Office: Bell Boyd & Lloyd 70 W Madison St Ste 3300 Chicago IL 60602-4284 E-mail: tc@homburger.cnchost.com., thomburger@bellboyd.com.

HOMER, BARRY WAYNE, lawyer; b. Junction City, Kans., Jan. 13, 1950; BA, U. Kans., 1972; JD, U. Chgo., 1975. Bar: Calif. 1975, U.S. Dist. Ct. (no. dist.) Calif. 1975, U.S. Tax Ct. 1980. Assoc. Brobeck, Phleger & Harrison, San Francisco, 1975-82, ptnr., 1982—2003, Morgen, Lewis & Bockius, LLP, San Francisco, 2003—. Co-author: Attorney's Guide to Pension and Profitsharing Plans, 1985, Compensating the Executive with Stock: Some Planning Possibilities and the Effect of the Parachute Provisions, 1986; contbr. articles to profl. jours. Mem. ABA (employee benefits com. tax sect. 1978—), Western Pension & Benefits Conf. Office: Morgan Lewis & Bockius LLP Spear St Tower 1 Market Plz San Francisco CA 94105-1420

HOMER, FRANCIS XAVIER JAMES, history educator; b. Scranton, Pa., July 30, 1941; s. Frank X. and Mary E. (Lynott) H. AB, U. Scranton, 1964; MA, U. Va., 1966, PhD, 1971. Instr. history U. Va., Charlottesville, 1967, U. Scranton, 1968-70, asst. prof., 1970-76, assoc. prof., 1976-84, prof. history, 1984—, pre-law advisor, 1971—. Co-editor/contbr.: Germany and Europe in the Era of the Two World Wars, 1986; co-editor newsletter Planc Points, 1989—. Trustee Scranton Prep. Sch., 1994-2000. Woodrow Wilson nat. fellow, 1964, NEH summer seminar grantee, 1977, 81. Mem. N.E. Assn. of Pre-Law Advisors (pres. 1986-87, membership dir. 1989—), Pre-Law Advisor Nat. Coun. (newsletter editor 1989—). Democrat. Roman Catholic. Avocations: crime fiction, train travel. Office: Univ of Scranton Dept Of History Scranton PA 18510 E-mail: homerf1@scranton.edu.

HOMER, RAYMOND RODNEY, film producer, director; b. Bronx, N.Y., Dec. 9, 1926; s. Jermone and Dorothy (Schick) H.; m. Anne Marie Hearn, Sept. 27, 1952 (div.); children: Jeffrey John, Mark Norbert, Scott Daniel, Bruce Raymond; m. Nancy Carman Reisner, 1964; m. Beverly June Elam, Oct. 30, 1983; children: Kelly Ray, Casey Wade. BFA in Art, Morgan Sch. Art, 1949. Pres. Creative Color Inc., N.Y.C., 1959-72, Durham Prodns. Inc., N.Y.C., 1972-86, Raymond R. Homer Prodns., N.Y.C., 1986—. Artistic dir. Vandam Theater, N.Y.C., 1988; pres. Trilateral Pictures, 1991-98, Pavilion Pictures, 1998; dir. Western Eagle Humanitarian Found., World Children's Peace Found. Producer films including American Gothic, 1988, The Pawn, 1980, Rip-Off, 1977, Dream City, 1976, Death Rage, 1975, Queen of Diamonds, 1974, The Inheritance, 1973, Swiss Conspiracy, 1972; dir. plays, N.Y. including Six O'Clock Boys, 1986, Two, 1984, One Night Stand, 1982, Sugar Spice and Everything Nice, 2000, Redemption, 2000, Dance in the Sky, 2001. Seaman USN, 1944-46. Mem. Dirs. Guild Am. Republican. Methodist. Avocations: horseback riding, flying, scuba diving. Home: 6128 Coral Pink Cir Woodland Hills CA 91367-7207 E-mail: trilateralfilms@aol.com.

HOMER, WILLIAM INNES, art history educator, art expert, author; b. Merion, Pa., Nov. 8, 1929; s. Austin and Evelyn (Innes) H.; 1 child, Stacy Innes; m. Christine D. Hyer, Aug. 24, 1986. AB, Princeton U., 1951; postgrad., N.Y.U., 1952-53; MA, Harvard U., 1954; PhD, 1961. Instr. dept. art and archeology Princeton, 1955-59, lectr., 1959-61, asst. prof., 1961-64; assoc. prof. history of art Cornell U., 1964-66; prof. U. Del., Newark, 1966-99, chmn. dept. art history, 1966-81, 86-93; dir. index of dissertations and theses in Am. art Archives of Am. Art, Washington; vis. fellow Princeton U., 1972-73; assoc. fellow Center for Advanced Studies, Nat. Gallery of Art, 1980-81. Mem. Del. Arts Council, 1969-70, New Castle County Beautification Bd., 1967-70; adv. screening com. (overseas) Fulbright-Hays Fellowship Awards, 1970-72, chmn., 1971-72; mem. sr. fellowship panel Nat. Endowment for Humanities, 1970; mem. exhbn. com. Del. Art Mus., 1968-73, chmn. accessions com., 1974-78 Author: Seurat and the Science of Painting, 1964, Robert Henri and His Circle, 1969, Alfred Stieglitz and the American Avant-Garde, 1977, The Photographs of Gertrude Käsebier, 1979, Alfred Stieglitz and the Photo-Secession, 1983, Pictorial Photography in Philadelphia, 1984; co-author Albert Pinkham Ryder: Painter of Dreams, 1989, Thomas Eakins, His Life and Art, 1992, The Language of Contemporary Criticism Clarified, 1999, Stieglitz and the Photo-Secession, 1902, 2002; mem. editl. bd. Am. Art Jour., 1970—, Winterthur Portfolio, 1978-80; sr. editor Am Art Rev., 1992—. Mem. adv. com. Am. Studies Inst., Lincoln U., 1967-76; mem. corp. Mus. Am. Art, Ogunquit, Maine, 1958-92; regional adv. com. Archives Am. Art, 1979—; trustee Am. Friends Nat. Portrait Gallery, London, 1995—, Sewell C. Biggs Mus. Am. Art, 1994-97; bd. dirs. Ctr. Advanced Studies in Visual Arts Nat. Gallery Art, 1994-98. Council of Humanities fellow Princeton U., 1962-63; Am. Council Learned Socs. fellow, 1964-65; Guggenheim fellow, 1972-73; Nat. Endowment for Humanities fellow, 1980-81; Ctr. for Advanced Study U. Del. fellow, 1985-86 Fellow Royal Soc. Arts (London), New Pictorialist Soc. (dir. 1981—); mem. Coll. Art Assn. Am., Pictorial Photographers Am., Royal Photog. Soc., Welcome Soc. of Pa., Phi Kappa Phi. Clubs: Princeton (N.Y.C.); Nat. Arts., Cosmos. Home: 200 Jackson Blvd Wilmington DE 19803 Office: U Del Dept Art History Newark DE 19716

HOMOLKA, DANIEL MICHAEL, lawyer; b. Sioux City, Dec. 24, 1954; s. David Lee Homolka and Darlene Fay Vick; m. Rebecca Sue Lokken, Oct. 22, 1977; children: Michael, Kate. BA with honors, U. Minn., 1977; JD, William Mitchell Coll. Law, St. Paul, 1982. Bar: Minn. Atty. Taylor Law Firm, Mpls., 1982-95, Eckman Strandness Egan, Mpls., 1995-97; pres. Daniel M. Homolka, P.A., Mpls., 1997—. Mem. ABA, Am. Trial Lawyers Assn., Minn. Trial Lawyers Assn., Minn. State Bar Assn., Zurah Shrine Horse Patrol (bd. dirs. 1991—). Avocations: reading, exercise, horseback riding. Office: 1820 IDS Center Minneapolis MN 55402 E-mail: Dan@Lommen.com.

HOMSLEY, DENISE LOUISE, music educator; b. Nampa, Idaho, Sept. 9, 1949; d. Lewis Griffith and Eileen Innes Davis; m. Jon Mark Homsley, June 23, 2001; m. David Karl Stoehr, Sept. 12, 1969 (div. Jan. 4, 1982); children: Melissa Dawn (Stoehr) Joseph, Justen David Stoehr Blackburn, Regan Karl Stoehr. BA in Music, Boise State Coll., 1972. Nat. Cert. Tchr. Music Music Tchrs. Nat. Assn., 2003. Music tchr. Ind., Boise, Idaho, 1966—75; owner, operator Stoehr Orchards, Wilder, Idaho, 1982—85; receptionist Farm Bur. Ins., Nampa, Idaho, 1997—99, Ackerley Outdoor Advt., Portland, 1999—2002; music tchr. Denise Homsley Piano Studio, Portland, 1999—. Hotline referral adminstr. Oreg. Music Tchrs. Assn., Portland, 2001—. Children's leader Bible Study Fellowship, Caldwell, Idaho, 1992—99; pianist Happy Valley Bapt. Ch., Portland, 2001—. Mem.: Nat. Fedn. of Music Clubs, Music Tchrs. Nat. Assn. Baptist. Avocations: travel, gourmet food, sewing. Office: Denise Homsley Piano Studio 210 Southeast 94th Ave Portland OR 97216

HON, JOHN WINGSUN, physician; b. Canton, China, Aug. 21, 1947; s. Yuen-Pak and Yuk-Ying (Zhang) Hon. BA, Hunter Coll., 1972; MA, SUNY, Buffalo, 1975; DO, Kirksville Coll. Medicine, 1979. Diplomate Am. Coll. Emergency Physicians; bd. cert. emergency medicine and family practice. Enlisted U.S. Army, 1975, advanced through ranks to capt., 1979; intern, resident Tripler Army Med. Ctr., Honolulu, 1979-80; gen. med. officer U.S. Army Med. Corps, Honolulu, 1979-80; intern Tripler Army Med. Ctr., Honolulu, 1979-80; gen. med. officer U.S. Army Med. Corps, Korea, 1980-81, U.S. Mil. Acad., West Point, 1981-83; attending physician Woodhull Hosp., Bklyn., 1983-86; pvt. practice Woodside, NY, 1983—2002, Elmhurst, NY, 1993—, Flushing, NY, 2002—. Attending physician Bronx Lebanon Hosp., 1987-91, Mt. Sinai Hosp., Queens, 1983—, St. John Hosp., Elmhurst, N.Y., 1992—, N.Y. Hosp. Dept. Medicine, 1996, Elmhurst Hosp., 1999—; clin. asst. prof. family practice N.Y. Coll. Osteo. Medicine, 1994—; clin. asst. prof. family practice N.Y. Med. Coll.. Fellow Am. Coll. Emergency Physicians; mem. Am. Osteo. Assn., N.Y. State Osteo. Med. Soc., Chinese Am. Med. Soc. (life). Avocation: photography. Home: 148 Cat Rock Rd Cos Cob CT 06807-1302 Office: 132-07 41st Rd Flushing NY 11355 also: 86-08 Elmhurst Ave Elmhurst NY 11373

HONAKER, CHARLES RAY, health facility administrator; b. Charleston, W.Va., Jan. 13, 1947; s. Charles Frederick and Avis Linda (McCarthy) H.; m. Sarah Powers, Aug. 30, 1969; children: Charles Erik, Cara Powers, Katherine Powers, Erin Powers. BA, U. Del., 1977; M in Health Sci., Johns Hopkins U., 1981. Cert. nursing home adminstr., healthcare exec.; diplomate Am. Coll. Healthcare Execs. Dir. residential treatment Gov. Bacon Health Ctr.-State of Del., Delaware City, 1975-80; sr. health planner State of W.Va., Charleston, 1980-83; assoc. hosp. adminstr. Pinecrest State Hosp., Beckley, W.Va., 1983-84; nursing home adminstr. Arthur B. Hodges Ctr., Charleston, W.Va., 1984-86, Carondelet Holy Family Ctr., Tucson, 1986-89; hosp. adminstr. Carondelet Holy Cross Hosp., Nogales, Ariz., 1989-96; CEO St. Thomas More Health Sys., Canon City, Colo., 1996—. Bd. mem., v.p. So. Ariz., Am. Cancer Soc., 1989-94; chair, bd. mem. Office of Rural Health, U. Ariz., Tucson, 1990—; chmn. bd. Ariz. Rural Health Assn., Phoenix. Bd. dirs. Sahuarita (Ariz.) Unified Sch. Dist., 1987-91, C. of C., Nogales, 1995, St. Scholastica Acad., Canon City, 1998—, Fremont County, Colo. Econ. Devel. Coun., 1998—. Fellow Am. Acad. Med. Adminstrs., Am. Coll. Health Care Adminstrs.; mem. U.S.-Mex. Border Health Assn., Ariz.-Mex. Commn. (pub. health coms.). Republican. Roman Catholic. Avocations: dog breeding and showing, arabian horse breeding, shooting, hunting, genealogy. Home: PO Box 2136 Canon City CO 81215-2136 Office: St Thomas More Health Sys 1338 Phay Ave Canon City CO 81212-2302

HONAKER, JIMMIE JOE, lawyer, ecologist; b. Oklahoma City, Jan. 21, 1939; s. Joe Jack and Ruby Lee (Bowen) H.; children: Jay Jimmie, Kerri Ruth. BA, Colo. Coll., 1963; MA, U. No. Colo., 1991; JD, U. Wyo., 1966, MS, 1995; postgrad., Utah State U., 1995—. Bar: Colo. 1966, U.S. Dist. Ct. Colo., U.S. Ct. Appeals (10th cir.), Ute Indian Tribal Ct. Utah. Pvt. practice, Longmont, Colo., 1966 91. Incorporator Longmont Boys Baseball, 1969; chmn. Longmont City Charter Commn., 1973; chmn. ch. bd. 1st Christian Ch., Longmont, 1975, 76; chmn. North Boulder County unit Am. Cancer Soc., 1978, 79. Recipient Disting. Svc. award Longmont Centennial Yr., 1971; named Outstanding Young Man, Longmont Jaycees, 1973. Mem.: ABA, Internat. Assn. Landscape Ecology-U.S. Regional Assn., Ecol. Soc. Am., Denver Bar Assn., Colo. Bar Assn. (interprofl. com. 1972—91, environ. law sect. 1999—), Nat. Eagle Scout Assn., Uintah Mountain Club Utah, Colo. Mountain Club, Alpha Tau Omega, Xi Sigma Pi, Alpha Kappa Psi, Phi Alpha Delta. Avocations: private pilot, mountain climbing. Address: Utah State U Box 1320 Logan UT 84322-0199

HONAMAN, J. CRAIG, health facility administrator; b. Montclair, N.J., June 15, 1943; s. Richard Karl and Gloria (McElwain) H.; m. Dee Dee Toerpe, Dec. 31, 1971; children: Justin Craig Jr., Garman Grayson. BS, N.C. State U., 1965; MS, U. Ala., Birmingham, 1971. Sr. v.p. Bapt. Hosp., Pensacola, Fla., 1970-79; exec. v.p. Tallahassee (Fla.) Meml. Hosp., 1979-89; adminstr. Quorum Health Resources/Leesburg (Fla.) Regional Med. Ctr., 1989-91; v.p., adminstrn. home health care Meth. Med. Ctr., Jacksonville, Fla., 1991-92; pres. Kellogg Healthcare, Inc., Jacksonville, 1992-93, KNH Healthcare, Jacksonville, 1993-95; exec. dir. HomeCare Alliance of Ga., Inc., Atlanta, 1994-98; sr. v.p. Haney & Assocs., Atlanta, 1998—; prin. H&H Cons. Ptnrs., LLC, Atlanta, 2001—. Cons. in field, Atlanta, Ga., 1991—. Contbr. articles to profl. jours. Active Boy Scouts Am., ARC, Am. Cancer Soc., Ronald McDonald House. Capt. U.S. Army, 1966-69, Vietnam. Recipient Nat. Golden Hour award MBB Helicopter, 1988. Fellow Am. Coll. Healthcare Execs. (cert. health care mgr.; regent for north Ga.), Rotary. Methodist. Avocations: golf, running. Office: H&H Cons Ptnrs LLC 560 Cambridge Way NE Ste 101 Atlanta GA 30328-1007 E-mail: Careerdir1@aol.com.

HONAN, MICHAEL BENJAMIN, cardiologist; b. Charlottesville, Va., Jan. 24, 1959; s. Bernard Menahem and Roslyn H.; m. Roxanne Renee Travelute, Apr. 30, 1988; children: Rachel Elizabeth, Benjamin Michael. BS, U. Ala., 1978, MD, 1983. Resident Duke U. Med. Ctr., Durham, N.C., 1983-86, cardiology fellow, 1986—89; cardiologist Cardiovascular Assocs., Birmingham, Ala., 1989—, v.p. exec. bd., 2000—. Chmn. cardiology Brookwood Med. Ctr., Birmingham, 1997-98, dir. cardiac catheterization lab., 1997—. Contbr. articles to profl. jours.; prin. investigator numerous clin. trials. Sec., bd. dirs. Temple Emanuel, Birmingham, 1992-97; bd. dirs. Am. Heart Assn., Jefferson & Birmingham, 1990-93, 98—, pres., v.p. med. rels.; sponsor Big Bros./Big Sisters, Birmingham, 1992-96. Fellow Am. Coll. Cardiology (chair edn. com. Ala. chpt. 2000-02, treas. 2003—); mem. AMA, ACP, Med. Assn. State Ala., Jefferson County Med. Soc., Birmingham Cardiovascular Soc. (pres. 1997). Avocations: travel, backpacking, skiing, piano, bible study. Office: Cardiovascular Assocs Ste 510 2022 Brookwood Medical Ctr Dr 510 Birmingham AL 35209-6807

HONAN, RAENA, writer; b. Pawling, N.Y., Oct. 31, 1952; d. Raymond J and Shirley Honan. BA & MPA, Ariz. State, Tempe, AZ. Certificate in Gerontology Ariz. State U., 2003. Dir., elderly services Hopi Tribe, Kykotsmovi, Ariz., 2001—; legislative dir. Sierra Club, Grand Canyon Chpt., Phoenix, Ariz., 1992—97. Mem.: Cactus Wren GOP Women (past officer & chaplain 2001). Episcopalian. Achievements include Author of www.churchontheweb.org. Avocation: second soprano. Home: P O Box 111 Kykotsmovi AZ 86039-0111 Office: Hopi Tribe Office of Elderly Services P O Box 123 Kykotsmovi AZ 86039 Personal E-mail: raena@prodigy.net. E-mail: rhonan@hopi.nsn.us.

HONAN, WILLIAM HOLMES, journalist, writer; b. N.Y.C., May 11, 1930; s. William Francis and Annette (Neudecker) H.; m. Nancy Burton, June 22, 1975; children: Bradley, Daniel, Edith. BA, Oberlin (Ohio) Coll., 1952; MA, U. Va., 1955. Editor The Villager (weekly newspaper), N.Y.C., 1957-60; asst. editor New Yorker mag., 1960-64; freelance writer nat. mags., 1964-68; asso. editor Newsweek, 1969; asst. editor N.Y. Times mag., 1969-70, travel editor, 1970-72, 73-74, arts and leisure editor, 1974-82, culture editor, 1982-88, chief cultural corr., 1988-93, nat. higher edn. corr., 1993—2000, nat. corr., 2000—; mng. editor Saturday Rev., 1972-73. Author: Greenwich Village Guide, 1959, Ted Kennedy: Profile of a Survivor, 1972, Bywater: The Man Who Invented the Pacific War, Brit. edit., 1990, Visions of Infamy: The Untold Story of How Journalist Hector C. Bywater Devised the Plans That Led to Pearl Harbor, 1991, Remember, Japanese edit., 1991, Treasure Hunt: A New York Times Reporter Tracks the Quedlinburg Hoard, 1997, (Play) Zingers, 2001, (pamphlet) Another La Guardia, 1960; compiler, editor: Fire When Ready, Gridley: Great Naval Stories From Manila Bay to Vietnam, 1993; contbr. articles to nat. mags. and profl. jours. Served with AUS, 1956-57. Office: NY Times 229 W 43rd St New York NY 10036-3959 E-mail: honan@NYTimes.com.

HONAN, WILLIAM JOSEPH, III, lawyer; b. Cleve., Jan. 8, 1945; s. William Joseph and Vernice Louise (Bryan) H. B.A., U. N.C., 1966, J.D., 1969. Bar: N.Y. 1970, U.S. Dist. Ct. (so. dist.) N.Y., U.S. Ct. Appeals (2d cir.). Assoc., Haight, Gardner, Poor & Havens, N.Y.C., 1969-76, ptnr., 1976— ; mem. documentary com. Intertanko, Oslo, Norway, 1981— ; dir. Bergen Lind, Inc., N.Y.C., 1984— . Mem. Maritime Law Assn., Assn. Bar City N.Y. Roman Catholic. Club: India House (N.Y.C.). Home: 235 E 22nd St New York NY 10010-4616 Office: Haight Gardner Poor & Havens 195 Broadway Rm 2400 New York NY 10007-3189

HONDA, MICHAEL M. congressman; b. Walnut Creek, Calif., June 27, 1941; m. Jeanne; children: Mark, Michelle. BA in Biol. Sci., BA in Spanish, MA in Edn., San Jose St. Univ. Sci. tchr., Sunnyvale; prin. pub. sch.; mem. Calif. Assembly, 1997—2000, U.S. Ho. Reps. 15th Calif. dist., 2001—. Conducted ednl. rsch. at Stanford; apptd. to San Jose City Planning Com., 1971; mem. San Jose Unified sch. bd., 1981; served on Santa Clara County Bd. Supr.; elected Reg. Whip, vice chair Congl. Asian Pac. Am. Caucus, Transp. com., Sci. com.

Congress, Calif. 15th dist. Mem. edn. com. Calif. Assembly. Served Peace Corps, 1965-67. Named High Tech Legislator Yr., Am. Electronics Assn. Democrat. Office: 1713 Longworth House Office Bldg Washington DC 20515-0515*

HONEA, JOYCE CLAYTON, critical care nurse; b. San Antoino, Oct. 4, 1952; d. Leslie James and Shirley Louis (Steinfeldt) Clayton; m. Bertrand N. Honea III, May 1, 1982; children: Matt Baker, Elissa Baker. BS in Nursing, Loretto Heights Coll., 1976; MS, Cen. Mich. U., 1990. Nursing faculty Front Range C.C., Ft. Collins, Colo., 1990—; family nurse practitioner U. No. Colo., 1999. Mem. ANA (sec. 1985-87).

HONEGGER, FEDERICO, artist; b. Milan, Sept. 11, 1926; s. Carlo and Maria Antonia (Casiraghi) H.; m. Lucia Serafina Carminati, Apr. 30, 1959; children: Carlo, Marco, Andrea, Anna. Baccalaureat, Coll. St. Michel, 1945; law degree, Cath. U., 1952. Textile practice Vereinigte Seidenwebereien AG, Krefeld, Germany, 1950-51; with Gaspare Honegger, Milan, Italy, 1946-59; buying mgr. Carminati Industrie Tessili SpA, Milan, 1960-82. *Mr. Frederico Honegger endeavors to build up a new art project taking direct inspiration from the Bible (Old and New Testaments). The Digital Outlook is the voyage of Self towards the Other by means of Number, from the One and Same (expressions of Self) to the Innumerable and Different (expressions of the Other), (Think about the foliage of a tree scene through an open window). The Kenosis Project (the key work) means emptying of the Self to make room for the Other; animated, however, not by a spirit of conquest or dominion, but by submission and desire to serve.* Author: The Digital Outlook, 1984, (art project) The Ke'nosis Project, 1986 (award), Jacobs Ladder, 1989, The Eye of the Needle, 1992, Portraits, 1992, Cromatic Alphabets, 1993, Constellations, 1993, Adam's Rib, 1994, Metaphysical Alphabets, 1994, The Signs-Number of Image, 1996, The Universe of Fragments, 1996, The Profecy of Ezechiele, 1998, God All in Everybody, 1999, Soul and Body, 1999, El Shadday-The Primary Numbers, 1999, The Background, Place of Dialogue Between Thou (two) and Innumerable, 2000, Your Voice, My Voice, Our Voice: The Wise Men and the Star, 2000, From One to Two and From I to Thou, 2000, Glory, Grace and Liberty, 2001, Equal and One, 2002, Straight and Curved, 2002. Recipient Silver Palette City of Milan, 1979, Top 70 Winner Art '95 N.Y. Internat. Competition, 1995. Mem. Symbolicum Art Group (co-founder). Home and Office: Via Annunciata 23/2 20121 Milan Italy Fax: 0039-02-6590687.

HONEMANN, DANIEL HENRY, lawyer; b. Balt., Oct. 20, 1929; s. Henry Letcher and Maude Elizabeth (Wilson) H.; m. Rose Ann Clark, Mar. 23, 1974; children by previous marriage: Deborah, Dori, Daniel, Donna. AB, Western Md. Coll., Westminster, 1951; JD, U. Md., 1956. Bar: Md. 1956. Practice law, Balt.; partner firm Clapp, Somerville, Honemann & Beach, 1962-85, Whiteford, Taylor & Preston, 1986—; asst. U.S. atty. Dist. Md., 1960-61. Author: (with others) Robert's Rules of Order Newly Revised, 10th edit. Served to 1st lt. inf. AUS, 1951-53. Decorated Bronze Star, Combat Inf. badge. Fellow Am. Coll. Trust and Estate Counsel, Md. Bar Found.; mem. ABA (ho. of dels. 1978-80), Md. Bar Assn. (sec. 1977-84, bd. govs. 1975-84), Balt. Bar Assn. Home: 2318 Harcroft Rd Lutherville Timonium MD 21093-2638 Office: 7 Saint Paul St Ste 1400 Baltimore MD 21202-1654 E-mail: dhonemann@wtplaw.com., dhonemann@comcast.net.

HONER, RICHARD JOSEPH, surgeon; b. Ottawa, Ill., 1953; MD, U. Ill., 1979. Diplomate Am. Bd. Surgery, Am. Bd. Colon and Rectal Surgery. Intern St. Marys Hosp., Grand Rapids, Mich., 1979-80, resident in surgery, 1980-84; fellow in colon and rectal surgery Ferguson Hosp., Grand Rapids, 1984-85; dir. Winter Haven (Fla.) Hosp., 1985—. Office: Gessler Clinic 635 1st St N Winter Haven FL 33881-4191

HONEY, RICHARD CHURCHILL, retired electrical engineer; b. Portland, Oreg., Mar. 9, 1924; s. John Kohnen and Margaret Fargo (Larrison) H.; m. Helen Waugaman, June 8, 1952 (div. Feb. 1980; children: Leslie, Steven, Laura, Janine; m. Jo Anne Kipp, Jan. 11, 1993. BS, Calif. Inst. Tech., 1945; EE, Stanford U., 1950, PhD, 1953. Research asst. Stanford U., 1948-52; sr. research engr. microwave group Stanford Research Inst., 1952-60; tech. program coordinator Electromagnetic Techniques Lab., 1960-64, lab. dir., 1964-70, staff scientist, 1970-89, sr. prin. scientist, 1989—; 86. Dir. ILC Tech.; mem. Army Sci. Bd., 1978-84. Contbr. articles to books, encyc., profl. jours.; patentee in field. Served with USN, 1943-46. Fellow IEEE, Optical Soc. Am.; mem. Optical Soc. No. Calif., Coyote Point Yacht Club, Sigma Xi. Office: SRI Internat 333 Ravenswood Ave Menlo Park CA 94025-3453

HONEY, SANGEET, molecular biologist, research scientist; b. Sirsa, Haryana, India; s. Dharam Pal; married. MSc, Kurukshetra (India) U., 1986; postgrad. degree, Panjab U., Chandigarh, India, 1987; PhD, Postgrad. Inst. Med. Edn. Rsch., 1993. Sr. rsch. fellow Postgrad. Inst. Med. Edn. and Rsch., 1992-95; rsch. assoc. SUNY, Buffalo, 1995-97; postdoctoral fellow Cold Spring Harbor (N.Y.) Lab., 1997-2000; sr. rsch. scientist SUNY, Stony Brook, 2000-01. Contbr. articles to profl. jours., including Jour. Nucleic Acids Rsch., Trace Elements in Exptl. Medicine, Aquatic Toxicology, Molecular and Cellular Biochemistry, others. Cultural sec. Assn. Basic Med. Scientists, Chandigarh, 1989-90. Sr. rsch. fellow Coun. Sci. and Indsl. Rsch., New Delhi, 1992, Young Scientist travel fellow Dept. Sci. and Tech, New Delhi, 1995. Mem. AAAS, Am. Assn. Cancer Rsch., N.Y. Acad. Scis. Office: Cold Spring Harbor Lab 1 Bungtown Rd Cold Spring Harbor NY 11724 Office Fax: 631-632-9717. E-mail: shoney@ms.cc.sunysb.edu.

HONEY, WILLIAM CHIPMAN, lawyer, educator; b. Ferguson, Mo., Apr. 7, 1932; s. Albert Erroll and Helen Elizabeth (Chipman) H.; m. Roberta Alice Mare, July 19, 1955 (div. 1967); children: Craig (dec.), Sarah, Martha, Alice; m. Barbara Ann Blackwell, Apr. 17, 1968 (div. 1985); 1 son, Christopher. Student U. of South, Sewanee, Tenn., 1949-51; JD, Washington U., St. Louis, 1955; postgrad. U. South Fla., 1974, U. Ark., 1975-76. Bar: Mo. 1955, Ark. 1975, Ariz. 1979, Va. 1982, Fla. 1988, Ala. 1989. Sole practice, St. Louis, 1957-70; asst. prof. English, U. P.R., Mayaguez, 1970-74; exec. v.p. Delray Corp., 1974; sole practice, Rogers, Ark., 1975-79, Scottsdale, Ariz., 1979-81; asst. prof. dept. fin. Sch. Bus. Adminstr., Old Dominion U., Norfolk, Va., 1981-85; assoc. prof. Auburn U. Sch. Bus., Montgomery, Ala., 1985—; pvt. practice, St. Petersburg, Fla., 1988, Phoenix, 1989—; of counsel McPhillips, Shinbaum, Gill & Stoner, Attys., 1995—; mem. firms Kerth Thies & Schreiber, Clayton, Mo., Honey and Kehr, Clayton; pres. Video Learning Systems, Inc., 1985—, Soulard Assocs. Inc.; adj. prof., clin. law dir. U. Ark. Law Sch., Fayetteville, 1976-77; adj. prof. English composition Ariz. State U., Tempe, 1979-81; co-developer Spirit of St. Louis Airport and St. Louis Air Park, Chesterfield, Mo., 1960-67; developer Soulard Area Rehab., St. Louis, 1967-70; city atty. City of Rogers, 1975-79; cons. Human Relations Commn. East St. Louis, Ill., Mid-City Community Congress, St. Louis, OHSA Dept. Labor, others; lectr. various orgns. Author: Guide to Law and Business, 1986; pres., pub., editor-in-chief Montgomery Living Mag., 1996—; contbr. articles to profl. jours, stories, poetry to mags. Trustee U. of South, Sewanee, 1957-70; gen. counsel Mansion House Ctr., St. Louis; mem. vestry, ch. sch. supt. Episcopal Ch. Served with U.S. Army, 1955-57. Mem. Va. Bar Assn., Fla. Bar Assn., Ariz. Bar Assn., Ark. Bar Assn., Mo. Bar Assn., Ala. Bar Assn., Beta Theta Pi (pres. U. of South chpt. 1950). Home: 2094 Myrtlewood Dr Montgomery AL 36111-1000

HONEYCUTT, GEORGE LEONARD, photographer, retired; b. High Point, N.C., Jan. 5, 1936; s. Leonard Franklin and Pearl (Reynolds) H.; m. Sandra Spencer, Mar. 29, 1955; children: George Keith, Stephen Kurt, Kevin Spencer. Student, Sch. Modern Photography, N.Y.C., 1954. Photographer Charlotte (N.C.) News, 1959-62; Staff photographer Houston Chronicle, 1963, dir. photography, 1963-97, retired, 1997. Served with AUS, 1955-57. Recipient awards AP, awards UP, awards Headliners; 4-time winner Profl. Football Hall of Fame Mem. Nat. Press Photographers Assn. (named Nat. Newspaper Photographer of Yr. 1962) Methodist. Office: 801 Texas St Houston TX 77002-2904 E-mail: shoneybee1234@aol.com.

HONEYCUTT, VAN B. computer company executive; b. Va., 1945; BS in Bus. Adminstrn., Franklin U.; grad. exec. program, Stanford U., 1984. With Computer Scis. Corp., El Segundo, Calif., 1975—, corp. v.p. and pres., 1987, COO, 1993—, pres. industry svcs. group, 1993—2001, chmn., CEO, 1995—. Office: Computer Scis Corp 2100 E Grand Ave El Segundo CA 90245-5024*

HONEYSTEIN, KARL, lawyer, entertainment company executive; b. N.Y.C., Jan. 10, 1932; s. Herman and Claire (Rosen) H.; m. Buzz Halliday, Sept. 14, 1965 (div. Dec. 1978); 1 child, Gail; m. Shauna Wood Trabert, Jan. 24, 1995. BA, Yale U., 1953; JD, Columbia U., 1959. Bar: N.Y. 1959. Assoc. Greenbaum, Wolff & Ernst, N.Y.C., 1959-62; v.p. Ashley Famous Agy., N.Y.C., 1962-69, Internat. Famous Agy., N.Y.C., 1969-71; exec. v.p. The Sy Fischer Co., N.Y.C. and L.A., 1971-80; exec. v.p., chief operating officer The Taft Entertainment Co., Los Angeles, 1980-88; pres. K.H. Strategy Corp., Los Angeles, 1988—. Dir. Rhythm & Hues, Inc.; lectr. law Bklyn. Law Sch., N.Y.C., 1973-75 Served to lt. j.g. USNR, 1953-56 Fellow Internat. Coun. NATAS; mem. Friars Club, Regency Club.

HONG, CHIA-SWEE, research scientist; b. Chia-Yi, Taiwan, Oct. 17, 1952; came to U.S., 1975; d. Chi-Chao and Tsay (Wu) H.; m. Sai-Pei Ting, Oct. 5, 1978; children: Grace Ting, Gary Ting. BS, Fu-jen U., 1975; MA, CUNY, 1978, PhD, 1980. Project asst. N.Y. State Dept. Health, Albany, 1980-84, rsch. scientist I, 1984-92, rsch. scientist II, 1992-98, rsch. scientist III, 1998—. Instr., advisor SUNY, Albany, 1993-96, asst. prof., 1996—. N.Y. Sea Grant Inst. grantee, 1990, Nat. Inst. Environ. Health and Sci. grantee, 1995. Fellow Marine Environ. Rsch. Inst.; mem. Am. Chem. Soc., Overseas Chinese Environ. Engr. and Scientist Assn. Achievements include UV combine with titanium dioxide could destroy polychlorinated biphenyls and other contaminants; development of methodology for dioxin-like polychlorinated biphenyls analysis. Home: 18 Bittersweet Ln Slingerlands NY 12159-9424 Office: Wadsworth Ctr Labs & Rsch NY State Dept Health Albany NY 12201-0509 E-mail: hongc@wadsworth.org.

HONG, HOWARD VINCENT, library administrator, philosophy educator, editor, translator; b. Wolford, N.D., Oct. 19, 1912; BA, St. Olaf Coll., 1934; postgrad., Wash. State Coll., 1934-35; PhD, U. Minn., 1938; postgrad., U. Copenhagen, 1938-39; D.Litt. (hon.), McGill U., Montreal, 1977; D.D. (hon.), Trinity Sem., Columbus, Ohio, 1983; D.H.L. (hon.), Carleton Coll., 1987; ThD (hon.), U. Copenhagen, 1992. With English dept. Wash. State Coll., 1934-35; with Brit. Mus., 1937; mem. faculty dept. philosophy St. Olaf Coll., Northfield, Minn., 1938-78, asst. prof. philosophy, 1940-42, assoc. prof., 1942-47, prof., 1947-78, chmn. Ford Found. self-study com., 1955-56, dir. Kierkegaard Library, 1972-84, Vis. lectr. U. Minn., 1955; mem. Nat. Lutheran Council Scholarship and Grant Rev. Bd., 1958-66; lectr. Holden Village, Washington, 1963-70; mem. Minn. Colls. Grant Rev. Bd., 1970 Author, editor, contbr.: Integration in the Christian Liberal Arts College, 1956, books most recent This World and the Church, 1955; editor, contbg. author: Christian Faith and the Liberal Arts, 1960; co-editor, translator: (with Edna H. Hong) works by Gregor Malantschuk, numerous works by Soren Kierkegaard, Soren Kierkegaard's Journals and Papers, Vol. I, 1968 (Nat. Book award for transl. 1968), Søren Kierkegaard's Journals and Papers, Vol. II, 1970, Søren Kierkegaard's Journals and Papers, Vol. III-IV, 1975, Søren Kierkegaard's Journals and Papers, V-VII, 1978, The Controversial Kierkegaard (Gregor Malantschuk), 1980, Two Ages (Søren Kierkegaard), 1978, The Sickness unto Death (Søren Kierkegaard), 1980, The Corsaair Affair (Søren Kierkegaard), 1981, Fear and Trembling-Repetition, 1983, Philosophical Fragments-Johannes Climacus, 1985, Either/Or, 1987, Stages on Life's Way, 1988, The Concept of Irony, 1989, For Self-Examination and Judge for Yourself!, 1990, Eighteen Upbuilding Discourses, 1990, Practice in Christianity, 1991, Concluding Unscientific Postscript, 1992, Three Discourses on Imagined Occasions, 1993, Upbuilding Discourses in Various Spirits, 1993, Works of Love, 1995, Without Authority, 1997, Point of View, 1998, The Moment and Late Writings, 1998, The Book on Adler, 1998, The Essential Kierkegaard, 2000; gen. editor Kierkegaard's Writings, 1972—. Field sec. War Prisoners Aid, U.S., Scandinavia, and Germany, 1943-46; sr. rep. Service to Refugees, Luth. World Fedn., Germany and Austria, 1947-49; sr. field officer refugee div. World Council Chs., Germany, 1947-48; curator Kierkegaard House Found., 1999—. Decorated Order of Dannebrog (Denmark), Order of the Three Stars (Latvia); recipient award Minn. Humanities Commn., 1983, Minn. Forest Stewardship award DNR, 2002; fellow Am.-Scandinavian Found.-Denmark, 1938-39, Am. Council Learned Socs., 1952-53, Rockefeller Found., 1959, sr. rsch. fellow Fulbright Commn., 1959-60, 64, sr. fellow NEH, 1970-71; grantee NEH, 1972-73; publ. grantee Carlsberg Found., 1974, 86, 88, editing-translating grantee NEH, 1978-90, 95-98. Home: 5174 E 90 Old Dutch Rd Northfield MN 55057 Office: St Olaf Coll Kierkegaard Libr Northfield MN 55057

HONG, JAE-DONG, industrial engineering educator; b. Daegu, South Korea, Mar. 20, 1954; came to U.S., 1981; s. Hyun-Tae and Kyung-Hee (Kim) H.; m. Bong-Sun Lee, Sept. 25, 1981; children: Thomas, Christina, James. BS, Korea U., Seoul, 1979; MS, Pa. State U., 1985, PhD, 1988. Cert. in inventory mgmt. and prodn. Quality and process engr. Daewoo Heavy Indsl., Anyang, South Korea, 1979-81; from asst. prof. to assoc. prof. indsl. engring. tech. S.C. State U., Orangeburg, 1988-97; prof., Gov.'s disting. prof. S.C. State U. Sch. Engring. Tech. and Scis., Orangeburg, 1997—. Contbr. articles to prof. jours. Named Dist. Prof. by Gov. S.C., 1993. Home: 106 Fox Run Ct Orangeburg SC 29118-9791 Office: SC State U 102 Lewis Lab Orangeburg SC 29117-7722 E-mail: hong@sets.scsu.edu.

HONG, KUHN, nuclear medicine physician; b. Seoul, Republic of Korea, Aug. 27, 1946; s. Tae Joon Hong and Moon Young Ahn; married; children: Timothy, Joseph, David, Sarah. Student, Seoul Nat. U., 1964-66, MD, 1970. Diplomate Am. Bd. Radiology, Am. Bd. Nuclear Radiology, Am. Bd. Nuclear Medicine. Intern Gottlieb Meml. Hosp., Melrose Park, Ill., 1973-74; resident in radiology Mercy Hosp., Chgo., 1974-77; fellow in nuclear medicine Rush Presbyn.-St. Luke Med. Ctr., Chgo., 1977-79; dir. nuclear medicine, dept. radiology Little Co. of Mary Hosp., Evergreen Park, Ill., 1979—. Trustee No. Bapt. Theol. Seminary, Lombard, Ill., 1998—. Mem. AMA, Am. Coll. Radiology, Soc. Nuclear Medicine, Radiol. Soc. N.Am., Chgo. Med. Soc. (coun. 1990, continuing med. edn. com., profl. liability com., com. for internat. med. grads., past pres., v.p., treas., sec. southwest br.), Ill. State Med. Soc. (del. 1996), Christian Med. and Dental Soc. (coun. mem. Chicagoland area 1999—). Avocations: painting, drawing, downhill skiing, Judo, stamp collecting. Office: Little Co of Mary Hosp 2800 W 95th St Evergreen Park IL 60805-2795 E-mail: KuhnHong@aol.com.

HONG, PATRICIA ANNE, nursing educator; b. Honolulu, Apr. 16, 1950; d. Samuel Kyung Sook and Mariko (Kutsunai) H.; m. Michael Grandinetti, June 30, 1979. BSN, U. Md., 1972; MA in Nursing, U. Wash., 1976. CCRN, AACN. Instr. U. Wash., Seattle, 1976-79; office nurse Pulmonary Med. Assoc., Sacramento, 1979-80; mgr., statewide ADN Anchorage C.C., 1983-84; asst. prof. ADN program U. Alaska, Anchorage, 1984-91, assoc. prof., 1991-98, prof., 1998—. Nursing cons. Delaney, Wiles, Hayes, Reitman and Brubaker, Anchorage, 1990-91, Anderson, Holman and Houghton, Tacoma, 1989; mem. policy transition team for human svcs. State of Alaska, 1995, mem. med. care adv. com., 1996—. Contbr. author: Cardiac Care Nursing, 1981. Officer nurse corps USNR, 1972-79; officer USAFR, 1980-99. Recipient YWCA/BP Woman of Achievement award, 1996; named Individual Mobilization Augmentee of Yr., Nurse Corp, ARPC, USAFR, Denver, 1990; USPHS trainee, Seattle, 1974. Mem. AACN, Alaska Nurses Assn. (pres. 1989-93), Sigma Theta Tau. Democrat. Presbyterian. Office: U Alaska 3211 Providence Dr Anchorage AK 99508-4614 E-mail: afpah@uaa.alaska.edu.

HONG, RAN-E, literature educator; b. Seoul, Republic of Korea, May 20, 1960; arrived in U.S., 1996; d. Iel Hong and Hae-Sook Kim; 1 child, Rhee-Soo. BA, Ewha Woman's U., Seoul, 1981, MA, 1983; PhD 3d cycle, U. Paris-Sorbonne, 1987; PhD, Brown U., 2000. Adj. faculty Ewha Woman's U., Seoul, 1987—93, Hongik U., Seoul, 1992—93, Hankook U. Fgn. Studies, Seoul, 1993—95, Konkuk U., Seoul, 1994—96; asst. prof. Rivier Coll., Nashua, NH, 2000—01, Grand Valley State U., Allendale, Mich., 2001—. Author: L'Impossible Social Selon Moliere, 2002; contbr. articles to profl. jours. Mem.: MLA, Assn. Internat. des Etudes Francaises, N.Am. Soc. 17th Century French Lit. Avocations: reading, movies, travel. Home: 3293 Park Ridge Ln NE Grand Rapids MI 49525 Office: Grand Valley State U 1 Campus Dr Allendale MI 49401 E-mail: hongr@gvsu.edu.

HONG, SE JUNE, computer engineer; b. Seoul, Republic of Korea, May 5, 1944; came to U.S., 1965; s. Eo Kil and Oak Soon (Sohn) H.; m. Karen Fay McCully, Aug. 31, 1968; 1 dau., Kessely Corea. BSEE, Seoul Nat. U., 1965; MSEE, U. Ill., 1967, PhDEE, 1969. Staff engr. Sys. Devel. Lab., IBM, Poughkeepsie, NY, 1969-73, adv. engr., 1973-78, sr. engr., 1978; mem. rsch. staff T.J. Watson Rsch. Ctr., IBM, Yorktown Heights, NY, 1978—2002, emeritus, 2002—, mgr., 1981-82, sr. mgr., 1982-91, 92-94, sr. staff office rsch. divsn., v.p. plans and controls, 1991-92. Vis. prof. Korea Advanced Inst. Sci. and Tech., Seoul, 1980, fgn. invited prof., 2003; vis. prof. POSTECH, Pohang, 1999; vis. assoc. prof. U. Ill., 1974-75, adj. prof., 2001—; chmn. standing sci. com. Pacific Rim Internat. Conf. on Artificial Intelligence, 1992-94. Author: Conversational English, 1963; contbr. articles to profl. jours.; patentee in field. Bd. dirs. Mid-Hudson Arts and Sci. Ctr., Poughkeepsie, N.Y., 1972-78, Dutchess County United Way, 1972-74, Dutchess County Family Counseling Svc., 1973-78. Recipient Honorable Mention award for Outstanding Young Elec. Engr. Eta Kappa Nu, 1975, Disting. Service award NY State Jaycees, 1976, Disting. Alumnus award U. Ill., 1989, various awards IBM. Fellow: IEEE (chmn. E. Peori award com. 1991—92, Disting. Visitor 1972—75), Internat. Fedn. of Info. Processing Socs. (U.S. del. tech. com. on artificial intelligence 1990—94, vice chmn. 1992—94); mem.: Korean Scientist and Engrs. in Am., Nat. Acad. Engring. Korea (fgn.), Am. Assn. Artificial Intelligence, Assn. Computing Machinery, U. Ill. Elec. and Computer Engring. Dept. Alumni Assn. (bd. dirs. 1995—2002, v.p. Eastern Region 1999—2002), Sigma Xi. Democrat. Methodist. Home: 1374 Whitehill Rd Yorktown Heights NY 10598-3643 Office: TJ Watson Rsch Ctr IBM PO Box 218 Yorktown Heights NY 10598-0218 E-mail: sjhong@us.ibm.com.

HONG, SEHEE, education and psychology educator; b. Cheongju, Republic of Korea, Nov. 15, 1963; arrived in U.S., 1987; s. Heesik Hong and Junsook Park; m. Nayoung Kim, July 2, 1995; 1 child, Qurie. BA, Seoul Nat. U., 1986; MS, Ill. Inst. Tech., 1990; PhD, Ohio State U., 1998. Tchg./rsch. assoc. dept. psychology Ohio State U., Columbus, 1994-98; asst. prof. dept. edn. U. Calif., Santa Barbara, 1998—, asst. prof. dept. psychology, 1999—. Author: (book) Structural Equation and Modeling: Theories and Applications, 2001. Recipient Jeffrey Tanaka award, Soc. Multivariate Exptl. Psychology, 2002; U. Calif. Regents' jr. faculty fellow U. Calif., 1999. Mem. APA, Internat. Soc. for Study of Individual Differences, Am. Ednl. Rsch. Assn., Soc. Indsl. and Orgnl. Assn., Soc. Personality and Social Psychology. Office: U Calif Dept Edn 552 University Rd Santa Barbara CA 93106

HON GOH, CHAN, dancer; b. Beijing; Student, Goh Ballet Acad., Vancouver. Mem. Nat. Ballet Co., Toronto, Canada, 1988—, prin. dancer, 1994—. Guest artist Royal Danish Ballet, Singapore Dance Theatre, Hong Kong Ballet, Washington Ballet. Odette/Odile (ballets) Swan Lake, title role Giselle, Tatiana Onegin, Nikiya La Bayadère, Katherina The Taming of the Shrew, Juliet Romeo and Juliet, dancer Jewels, Désir, Forgotten Land, Now and Then, La Ronde. Office: Walter Carsen Ctr Nat Ballet of Canada 470 Queens Quay West Toronto ON Canada M5V 3K4

HONGTHONG, SIRIPORN, mathematician, educator; b. Bangkok, Thailand, Jan. 16, 1975; d. Supoj and Somsri Hongthong. BS, King Mongkut Inst. of Tech. Ladkrabang, Bangkok, Thailand, 1990—94; MS, Mahidol U., Bangkok, Thailand, 1994—98, U. of La. at Lafayette, Lafayette, La., 1999—2002. Instr. Math. Dept., King Mongkut Inst. of Tech. Ladkrabang, Ladkrabang, Thailand, 1996—. Recipient Spring Honors Convocation, U. of La. at Lafayette, 2001; scholar, Math. Dept., U. of La. at Lafayette, 1999, Instn. Strengthening Program, Nat. Sci. and Tech. Devel. Agy. and Faculty of Sci., Mahidol U., 1994-1998, Royal Thai Govt., 1997. Mem.: Phi Kappa Phi (Univ. of La. at Lafayette). Avocations: travel, philately. Home: 83 Moo 2 Ladkrabang Bangkok Ladkrabang 10520 Thailand Office: Math Dept University of Louisiana PO Box 41010 Lafayette LA 70504 Office Fax: 337-482-5346. Personal E-mail: sxh1113@hotmail.com. E-mail: siriporn@louisiana.edu.

HONHART, FREDERICK LEWIS, III, academic director; b. San Diego, Oct. 29, 1943; s. Frederick Lewis Jr. and Rossiter (Hyde) H.; m. Barbara Ann Baker, Aug. 27, 1966; children: David Frederick, Stephen Charles. BA, Wayne State U., 1966; MA, Case-Western Res. U., 1968, PhD, 1972. Cert. archivist. Field rep. Ohio Hist. Soc., Columbus, 1972-73; asst. dir. univ. archives & hist. collections Mich. State U., East Lansing, 1974-79, dir., 1979—. Mem. adv. bd. Mich. Nat. Hist. Publs. & Records Commn., Lansing, 1979—; cons. in field. Creator: (microcomputer sys.), MicroMARC:amc, 1986 (Coker prize 1988), MicroMARC for Integrated Format, 1995; contbr. articles to profl. jours. Mem. Internat. Coun. Archives (steering com. sci. and univ. archives sect. 2000-2004), Soc. Am. Archivists, Mich. Archival Assn. (pres. 1984-86), Midwest Archives Conf. (chair program com. 1982, 94, chair Author Awards com. 2001). Avocations: reading, sports, flying. Office: Mich State U 101 Conrad Hall East Lansing MI 48824-1327

HONIG, ARNOLD, physics educator, researcher; b. N.Y.C., Feb. 28, 1928; s. Ralph and Margaret (Gershman) H.; m. Alice Sterling, Oct. 3, 1947 (div. Nov. 1977); children— Lawrence, Madeleine, Jonathan; m. Dolly Komar, Jan. 6, 1979; stepchildren— Arne, Tanya BA, Cornell U., 1948; MS, Columbia U., 1950, PhD, 1953. Research asst. microwave spectroscopy Columbia U., N.Y.C., 1951-53; research physicist solid state physics U. Calif.-Berkeley, 1953-54; research fellow molecular physics Ecole Normale Superieure, Paris, 1954-56; asst. prof. physics Syracuse U., N.Y., 1956-59, assoc. prof., 1959-62, prof., 1962—. Cons. ITT Labs., 1960-63, Gen. Atomics, 1993-96, Oxford Instruments, 1997—; ptnr., owner Sci.-Art Systems Co., N.Y.C., 1968-78; vis. prof. Hebrew U., Jerusalem, 1962; vis. scientist Com. a l'Energie Atomique, Saclay, France, 1965. Contbr. articles to profl. jours.; patentee infrared image transducer, matrix piano keyboard, prodn. spin-polarized fuels, multi-chronal fluorescence microscope, bulk production and usage of hyperpolarized 129 Xenon. Pres. Oran Meml. Park Assn., N.Y., 1981-83 Recipient Glover Meml. award Dickinson Coll., 1966, Chancellor's citation for exceptional acad. achievement, 1999, numerous research grants, NSF, Dept. Energy, others Mem. Am. Phys. Soc., Fedn. Am. Scientists, AAAS Avocations: music, farming. Office: Syracuse U Dept Physics Syracuse NY 13244-0001 E-mail: honig@phy.syr.edu.

HONIG, GEORGE RAYMOND, pediatrician; b. Chgo., May 5, 1936; s. Joseph C. and Raymonds S. (Moses) Honig; m. Karen R. Jacobson, Dec. 18, 1960 (dec.); children: Sharon, Debra, Robert; m. Olga M. Weiss, May 24, 1998. BS in Liberal Arts and Sci., U. Ill., 1959, MD, MS in Pharmacology, U. Ill., 1961; PhD in Biochemistry, George Washington U., 1966. Diplomate Am. Bd. Pediatrics, Nat. Bd. Med. Examiners. Intern Johns Hopkins Hosp., Balt., 1961-62, fellow in pediatrics, 1961-63, asst. resident in pediatrics, 1962-63; rsch. assoc. Nat. Cancer Inst. NIH, 1963-66; fellow in pediatric hematology U. Ill., Chgo., 1966-68, from asst. prof. to assoc. prof. pediat., 1968—74, prof., 1974-75, 1984—, attending physician, 1968-75, dir. pediatric hematology svc., 1972-75, head dept. pediat. Coll. Medicine, 1984—2003; prof. Northwestern U., Chgo., 1975-83. Attending physician, dir. divsn. hematology Children's Meml. Hosp., Chgo., 1975—83. Contbr. articles to profl. jours. Mem.: AAUP, Soc. Pediatric Rsch., Am. Pediatric Soc., Am. Soc. Hematology, Am. Soc. Biochemistry and Molecular Biology, Am. Assn. Cancer Rsch., Am. Acad. Pediat., Alpha Omega Alpha. Office: U Ill Coll Medicine 840 S Wood St Chicago IL 60612-7317

HONIG, PAUL J. pediatrician, educator; BA, Rutgers U., 1961; MD, SUNY, Syracuse, 1965. Diplomate Am. Bd. Pediats., Am. Bd. Dermatology. Pediat. intern Herbert C. Moffitt Hosp.-U. Calif. Med. Ctr., San Francisco, 1965-66; pediat. resident Children's Hosp. Phila., 1966-67, asst. chief resident in pediats., 1969-70; fellow in dermatology Hosp. of the U. Pa., 1976-79; asst. physician Children's Hosp. Phila., 1970-75, from assoc. physician to sr. physician, 1975-81; co-chmn. pediat. liaison program Phila. Child Guidance Clinic, 1973-81; asst. instr. pediats. U. Pa., 1969-70, from instr. to asst. prof. pediats., 1970-78, prof. pediats., 1989—. Cons. in dermatology Bryn Mawr Hosp., 1986. Mem. editl. bd. Pediat. Dermatology, 1986-91; contbr. more than 100 articles to profl. jours. Chief pediats. USAF, 1967-69. Grantee Ctr. for Genetic Skin Disease. Mem. Ambulatory Pediat. Assn., Am. Acad. Pediats. (adv. com. 1975), Am. Acad. Dermatology (task force pediat. dermatology 1989-92, task force on genetics 1990-93, intersoc. liaison coun. chmn. 1994—), Soc. for Pediat. Dermatology (pres. elect 1992-93, pres. 1993-94), Phila. Pediat. Soc., Pa. Acad. Dermatology, Pa. Acad. Pediats., Nat. Bd. Med. Examiners (interpersonal skills rsch. com. 1974). Office: Childrens Hosp of Phila One Childrens Ctr 34th and Civic Ctr Blvd Philadelphia PA 19104 E-mail: honig@email.chop.edu.

HONIG, STEPHEN MICHAEL, lawyer; b. Albany, N.Y., Nov. 10, 1942; s. Morris and Betty (Tash) H.; m. Laura M. Unflat, June 25, 1989; children: Jennifer, Peter, Charles, Matthew. AB, Columbia U., 1963; LLB, Harvard U., 1966. Bar: Mass. 1966, U.S. Dist. Ct. Mass. 1968, U.S. Ct. Appeals (1st cir.) 1967. Atty. Widett & Widett, Boston, 1966-75, Goldstein & Manello PC, Boston, 1976-99, Schnader Harrison Goldstein & Manello, Boston, 2000—02, Duane Morris LLP, Boston, 2003—. Home: 519 Lewis Wharf Boston MA 02110-3914 Office: Duane Morris LLP 470 Atlantic Ave Boston MA 02210

HONIGBERG, CAROL CROSSMAN, lawyer; b. Salina, Kans., Sept. 23, 1955; d. Robert Denfield and Barbara Jane (Eckberg) Crossman; m. Paul Mark Honigberg, Aug. 18, 1979; children: Michael Crossman, Margaret Ann. AB, Duke U., 1977; JD, Vanderbilt U., 1980. Bar: Va. 1980. Assoc. Hazel & Thomas, P.C., Alexandria, Va., 1980-86, propr. Falls Church, Va., 1986-99; ptnr. Reed Smith LLP (formerly Reed, Smith, Hazel & Thomas, LLP), Falls Church, 1999—, sec., 2001—. Columnist Comml. Investment Real Estate. Mem. ABA, CREW Network (pres. No. Va. chpt. 1998-99, nat. del. 2000-01). Office: Reed Smith LLP 3110 Fairview Park Dr Ste 1400 Falls Church VA 22042-4503 E-mail: chonigberg@reedsmith.com.

HONKANEN, JARI OLAVI, telecommunications company executive; b. Uurainen, Finland, June 3, 1964; came to U.S., 1988; s. Eero Olavi and Aino Inkeri (Kuusisto) H. MS, Helsinki U. Tech., Finland, 1989; MBA, So. Meth. U., 1993. From engr. to sr. engr. Ericsson Network Sys., Richardson, Tex., 1988—94; sr. software engr. Sprint, Irving, Tex., 1994-95, DSC Comms. Corp., Plano, Tex., 1995; pres. Odin TeleSys., Inc., Dallas, 1995—2001; v.p. engring. DSPwork, Inc., 2001—. Sgt. Finnish Air Force, 1983-84. Mem. IEEE, Assn. Computing Machinery, Beta Kappa Sigma. Avocations: weight lifting, biking, rollerblading, tennis, travel.

HONMA, KOICHI, pathologist, researcher; b. Shiroishi, Miyagi, Japan, Mar. 28, 1955; s. Tsuneo and Mieko (Isago) Honma; m. Kiyomi Fukuda, Nov. 27, 1986; children: Shiko, Seiji, Shino. BM, Tohoku U. Sch. Medicine, 1979; MD, Dokkyo U. Sch. Medicine, 1986. Instr. Dokkyo U. Sch. Medicine, Tochigi, Japan, 1981-84, asst. prof., 1984-92, assoc. prof., 1992—. Mem. sci. com. No. 9 ILO Conf., Kyoto, 1995—97; organizer internat. workshops on occupl. lung diseases, 1996—. Contbr. Founder, diplomatic counselor London Diplomatic Acad., 2000—. Mem.: European Soc. Pathology, Pulmonary Pathology Soc., Am. Thoracic Soc., European Respiratory Soc., Deutsche Gesellschaft fur Pathologie. Avocations: music, sports. Home: Tomatsuri 3-6-45 Utsunomiya Tochigi 320-0056 Japan Office: Dokkyo U Sch Medicine Dept Pathology Kitakobayashi 880 Mibu Tochigi 321-0293 Japan Fax: 81-28-625-6075. E-mail: honma@dokkyomed.ac.jp.

HONNER SUTHERLAND, B. JOAN, advertising executive; b. N.Y.C., Oct. 23, 1952; d. William John and Mary Patricia (Edwards) H.; m. Donald J. Sutherland, Oct. 3, 1987; children: Chelsea Lauren, Whitney Devon. Student, Endicott Coll., 1970-71. Art dir. Kerrigan Studio, Darien, Conn., 1971-73, Foote Cone and Belding, Phoenix, 1973-77, sr. art dir. Chgo., 1977-81; v.p., assoc. creative dir. J. Walter Thompson, Chgo., 1982-86; v.p., exec. art dir. BBDO Chgo., 1986-91; creative dir. Knautz & Co., Sarasota, Fla., 1992-93; co-owner X-L Advt., Sarasota, Fla., 1993-94; owner Beyond Design of Sarasota, Inc., 1994—; mktg. dir. Nelson Pub. Inc., Nokomis, Fla., 2001—. Cons. J. Walter Thompson, Toronto and San Francisco, 1983-84; owner Fla. Antiques, Geneva, Ill., 1986-90. Introduced Discover card, 1985. Tchr. elem. sch. art; mem. Southside Sch. PTA Bd., Sarasota, 1996-99; spl. projects Pine View Sch., Sarasota, 1999—. Recipient 1st pla. TV local campaign WGN, 6th dist. Addy, 1980, Kemp. Corp. Addy, 1990, Mktg. Flood awards FEMA/NFIP, 1997, 98, 99; Best Internat. TV campaign Pepsi Clio, 1985. Roman Catholic. Avocation: miniatures. Home: 4941 Commonwealth Dr Sarasota FL 34242-1421

HONNOLD, JOHN OTIS, law educator; b. Kansas, Ill., Dec. 5, 1915; s. John Otis and Louretta (Wright) H.; m. Annamarie Kunz, June 26, 1939; children: Heidi Honnold Spencer, Edward. BA, U. Ill., 1936; JD, Harvard U., 1939; LLD (hon.), Capital U., 1991, Pace U., 1997. Bar: N.Y. 1940, Pa. 1953, U.S. Supreme Ct 1953. Atty. firm Wright, Gordon, Zachry & Parlin, N.Y.C., 1939-41, SEC, 1941; chief ct. rev. br. OPA, 1942-46; mem. faculty U. Pa. Law Sch., 1946-69, 74-84, prof. law, 1952-69, 74-84, prof. emeritus, 1984—; Arthur Goodhart prof. sci. of law. U. Cambridge, Eng., 1982-83. Mem. vis. faculty U. Beijing, 1984, U. Hawaii, 1986, U. Fla., 1988; Canterbury vis. fellow, N.Z., 1986; lectr. UN seminar, Moscow, 1990, U. Stockholm, 1990; chief internat. trade law br. UN; sec. UN Commn. on Internat. Trade Law, 1969-74; mem. faculty law sessions Salzburg (Austria) Seminar Am. Studies, 1960, chmn., 1963, 66; chief counsel Miss. Office, Lawyer's Com. for Civil Rights under Law, 1965; U.S. del., mem. drafting com. diplomatic conf. preparing uniform law for internat. sales of goods, The Hague, Holland, 1964; U.S. del UN Commn. Internat. Trade Law, 1969, 77; U.S. del. diplomatic confs. Conv. Carriage of Goods by Sea, Hamburg, 1978, Contracts for Internat. Sale of Goods, Vienna, 1980; gen. reporter 12th Internat. Congress Comparative Law, 1986 Author: (with C. Mooney, S. Harris, C. Reitz) Sales and Secured Financing, 6th edit., 1993, The Life of the Law, 1964, (with others) Commercial Law, 5th edit., 1993, Uniform Law for International Sales under the 1980 UN Convention, 1982, 3rd edit., 1999, 1991, (with others) United Nations Legal Order, 1995; contbr. articles to profl. jours. Guggenheim fellow, 1958; Fulbright sr. research scholar U. Paris, 1958; recipient Theberge award for contbn. to Pvt. Internat. Law, ABA, 1986; Lincoln Laureate, 1992.

HONNOLD, KATHRYN S. real estate agent; b. Pataskala, Ohio, Nov. 10, 1936; d. Harold S. and Stella E. (Slack) Williams; m. Robert I. Honnold, Aug. 18, 1956; children: Jayne, Robin. Student, Franklin U., N.Y. Sch. Modeling. Sales agt. USA-1Real Estate Corp., Pataskala, Ohio, 1978—; adminstrv. asst., office mgr., sec. Monsanto, Columbus, Ohio, 1983-87; coun. mem. Pataskala Village, 1987-98; adminstrv. asst. Bank One, 1988-99; asst. to exec. dir., asst. to pres. United Svcs. for Effective Parenting Ohio, Inc., 2002—. Pres. Pataskala Village Coun., 1990-92, 94, 96; mem. Pataskala Bd. Zoning Appeals Bd., 1997-2000; appointed mem. Licking County Sr. Citizen's Levy Adv. Bd., 1989-; adv. bd. Licking County Econ. Devel. Task Force, 1991-92; active Rep. Ctrl. Com. Licking County, 1998—; model for fashion shows. Named Sec. of Yr., 1987. Mem.: Nat., State and County Real Estate Assocs., Internat. Assn. Adminstrv. Pers. Home: 325 Laurel Ln Pataskala OH 43062-8547 E-mail: bkhonnold@msn.com.

HONOHAN, PATRICK, economist; b. Dublin, Oct. 9, 1949; m. Iseult Lawlor; 1 child, Theo. MA, U. Coll., Dublin, 1971; PhD, London Sch. Econs., 1976. Sr. economist Ctrl. Bank Ireland, Dublin, 1977—84; econ. adviser Office of the Taoiseach (Prime Minister), Dublin, 1981—86; rsch. prof. Econ. and Social Rsch. Inst., Dublin, 1990—98; sr. adviser World Bank, Washington, 1998—. Author: Finance for Growth: Policy Choices in a Volatile World, 2001; editor: Financial Liberalization: How Far, How Fast, 2001. Mem.: Royal Irish Acad. Office: World Bank 1818 H St NW Washington DC 20433 Personal E-mail: phonohan@indigo.ie. Business E-Mail: phonohan@worldbank.org.

HONOLD, LINDA KAYE, political organization executive, human resources development executive; b. Lansing, Mich., Aug. 16, 1956; d. Ervin Charles and Patricia Kathleen (Couzzins) Gaulke; m. Reynolds Keith Honold, dec. 5, 1987; 1 child, Samatha Kaye. BA in Polit. Sci., U. Wis., Eau Claire, 1980; MS in Indsl. Rels., U. Wis., Madison, 1987; PhD in Human and Orgnl. Sys., Fielding Grad. Inst., Santa Barbara, Calif., 1999. Editorial asst. Lake Pub. Co., Libertyville, Ill., 1980-81; econ. devel. rep. Projects With Industry, Menomonie, Wis., 1981-83; exec. dir. Am. Cancer Soc., Eau Claire, 1983-85; career counselor Hmong Assn., Sheboygan, Wis., 1985-87; mem. resource team personal devel. Johnsonville Foods, Sheboygan Falls, Wis., 1987—90; orgnl. devel. cons., 1990—. Author: Developing Employees Who Love to Learn, 2001; co-author: Organizational DNA, 2003; contbr. articles to profl. jours. Sec. Civil Svc. Commn., Sheboygan, 1986-95; del. Dem. Party, San Francisco, 1984, L.A., 2000; chair Wis. State Dem. Party, 2001—. Mem. Am. Soc. Personnel Adminstrs., Am. Soc. Tng. and Devel., Sheboygan County S. of C. (chmn. edn. coun.), Mortar Bd., Altrusa (sec. 1987-90), Sheboygan Svc. Club. Lutheran. Avocations: jogging, reading, sailing. Home: 1633 N Prospect Ave Unit 20B Milwaukee WI 53202-2482 Office: Democratic Party of Wisconsin 222 West Washington Madison WI 53703

HONORE, GERARD MARCEL, endocrinologist, reproductive endocrinologist; b. N.Y.C., June 6, 1957; s. Marcel and Ellen (Stone) H.; m. Erika Klopfer; children: Wolf Lloyd, Jocelyn Isabel. BA, Pomona Coll., Claremont, Calif., 1979; AM, Duke U., 1981, PhD, 1986; MD, Bowman Gray Sch. Medicine, Winston-Salem, 1992. Diplomate Nat. Bd. Med. Examiners; lic. physician, N.C., Tex. Rsch. asst. Duke U., Durham, 1980-86; rsch. assoc. Duke U. Med. Ctr., Durham, 1986-88; asst. Bowman Gray Sch. Medicine, Winston-Salem, 1993-96; asst. prof. medicine U. Tex. Health Sci. Ctr., San Antonio, 1996—. Contbr. articles to profl. jours. Recipient Frank Lock Soc. award Bowman Gray Sch. Medicine, 1996, Frank greiss Rsch. award, 1994; grantee Alza Corp., 1997—, Lifcore Biomed. Inc., 1997—. Fellow ACOG; mem. Am. Phys. Soc., The Endocrine Soc., Am. Soc. for Reproductive Medicine, Soc. for Gynecologic Investigation. Democrat. Avocations: performing and recording music, running, tai chi. Office: 7703 Floyd Curl Dr San Antonio TX 78284-6200

HONOUR, LYNDA CHARMAINE, research scientist, educator, psychotherapist; b. Orange, NJ, Aug. 9, 1949; d. John Henry, Jr. and Evelyn Helena Roberta (Pietrowski) H. BA, Boston U., 1976; MA, Calif. State U., Fullerton, 1985, UCLA, 1989; PhD, U. So. Calif., 1997. Lic. marriage, family and child psychotherapist and psychologist, Calif. Prof. psychology Pepperdine U., Malibu, Calif., 1989 95; pvt. practice mind-body behavioral medicine, including clin. psychoneuroimmunology and psychoneuroendocrinology LaJolla, Calif., 1991—. Clin. and vis. prof. throughout so. Calif., including Calif. Sch. Profl. Psychology, Calif. State U., Long Beach, Calif. State U., Northridge, 1989—; rsch. scientist in neuroendocrinology and neurochemistry in numerous labs including 3 Nobel Prize winning rsch. teams; condr. rsch. Neuropsychiat. Inst., Brain Rsch. Inst., Mental Retardation Rsch. Ctr., UCLA, Tulane U. Med. Sch., V.A. Med. Ctr., New Orleans, Salk Inst. Biol. Studies; rsch. cons. U. Calif. Med. Ctr., Irvine; cons. in rsch. or psychotherapy, 1976—; guest expert on safety issues regarding magnetic imaging Premiere Radio Network, 2001; rsch. scientist in neuroendocrinology and neurochemistry in numerous labs.; condr. rsch. Neuropsychiat. Inst., Brain Rsch. Inst., Mental Retardation Rsch. Ctr., UCLA, Tulane U. Med. Sch., V.A. Med. Ctr., New Orleans, Salk Inst. Biol. Studies; rsch. cons. U. Calif. Med. Ctr., Irvine, Salk Inst., others; cons. Thomson Internat. Pub.; hon. chmn., Bus. Adv. Coun. Nat. Rep. Congl. Com. Contbr. articles to profl. jours. including Hosp. Practice, Peptides, Physiology and Behavior, Pharmacology, Biochemistry and Behavior, others. Hon. chair bus. adv. coun. Nat. Rep. Congl. Com. Rsch. grantee Organon Internat. Rsch. Group, The Netherlands, 1984-88. Mem. AAAS, APA, Am. Psychological Soc., Soc. for Neurosci., Internat. Behavioral Neurosci. Soc., Internat. Brain Rsch. Orgn., Calif. Assn. Marriage and Family Psychotherapists, N.Y. Acad. Scis., Sons and Daus. of Pearl Harbor Survivors, Psi Chi. Roman Catholic. Achievements include identification of a peptide which facilitates and another peptide inhibits learning and memory task performance permanently in a developmental paradigm in mice; and facilitation peptide can permanently reverse induced learning/memory deficit, with implications for mental retardation and other learning/memory deficit treatment; mem. research team which isolated and characterized corticotropic hormone releasing factor; delineated various effects of peptides on behavior including bipolar disorders, endogenous depression, mania and others; research in risks associated with MRI exposure. Avocations: professional musician, artist, mind-related issues, time-space travel involving the unified field theory, metaphysics. Office: PO Box 369 Santa Monica CA 90406-0369

HONSA, VLASTA, retired librarian; b. Žilina, Czechoslovakia, Sept. 1, 1924; came to U.S., 1951; d. František Petr and Marie (Sirkova) Petrova; m. Vladimir Honsa, June 26, 1948; children: Patricia, Eva Honsa-Hogg. BA, Charles U., Prague, 1947; MLS, Ind. U., 1968. Gifts libr. Ind. U. Libr., Bloomington, 1968-70; head reference dept. Clark County Libr., Las Vegas, Nev., 1970-80, asst. adminstr., 1980-94; ret., 1994. Coord. Found. Collection, part of the Found. Ctr.'s Cooperating Collections network, Clark County Libr., 1979-94. Author: Nevada Foundation Directory, 1984, 2d edit., 1989, 3rd edit., 1994. Bd. dirs. So. Nev. Musical Arts Soc., Las Vegas, 1989-92; organized and presented fundraising workshops for cmty. fund raisers sponsored by Las Vegas-Clark County Libr. Dist., 1979-94. Recipient Ind. U. grant-in-aid to conduct rsch. of publs. in cen. Am. univs. and nat. librs., 1970, Champion award Las Vegas-Clark County Libr. Dist., 1985. Mem. ALA, AAUW, Nev. Libr. Assn., Univ. Nevada Las Vegas Faculty Club. Roman Catholic. Avocations: reading, music, arts, travel. Home: 2680 Congress Ave Las Vegas NV 89121-1316 E-mail: honsa@worldnet.att.net.

HONSE, ROBERT W. agricultural company executive; b. 1943; With Farmland Industries Inc., Kansas City, Mo., 1983—, exec. v.p., 1990, CEO, pres., 2000—02.

HOOBLER, ELIZABETH DRESSEL, anthropologist, educator; b. Boston, Aug. 4, 1926; d. William Alvah Taylor and Ruth Sawtell; m. Ralph William Dressel, July 21, 1945 (div. Sept. 17, 1976); children: David, Lee, Diane, Earl; m. Dale Wayne Hoobler, Sept. 28, 1982 (dec. June 19, 1997); stepchildren: Timothy, Tamara, Mary Elisa. BA in Sociology, U. Ill., 1949; MA in Anthropology, U. N.Mex., 1970, PhD in Anthropology, 1986. Program evaluator Cmty. Mental Health Ctr., Las Cruces, N.Mex., 1970—73; instr. N.Mex. State U., Las Cruces, 1974, 1976; lectr. U. Tex., El Paso, 1975—76; instr. dept. anthropology U. N.Mex., Albuquerque, 1988—95, instr. dept. sociology, 1993, instr. dept. pub. adminstrn., 1994—95, rschr. Ctr. on Aging, 1996; ret. Dir., spkr. Good Life Concepts, Albuquerque, 1986—88; spkr. in field. Contbr. articles to jours. Bd. pres. Share Your Care/Elder Daycare, Albuquerque, 1981—83; bd. mem. Music, Musings and Meditation, Albuquerque, 2000—03; active C.A.R.D., Albuquerque, 1995—99. Recipient Dissertation award, NSF, 1980—86. Fellow: Soc. for Applied Anthropology; mem.: Am. Anthropol. Assn., Assn. for Anthropology and Gerontology (Gamma chpt.), Alpha Kappa Delta, Pi Gamma Mu. Avocations: study of consciousness, photography, travel.

HOOCK, EDWARD THOMAS, III, electrician, scoreboard operator; b. St. Louis, June 25, 1966; s. Edward Thomas Hoock, Jr. and Gloria Irene Hoock; m. Angela Dawn Rodriguez, Jan. 8, 1993; 1 child, Katarina Bianca. AA in Comm. Arts, St. Louis C.C., 1986; BA in Media Comm., Webster U., 1989. Messageboard/scoreboard operator St. Louis Arena, 1985—95, intern pub. rels., 1988—89, freelance writer, 1988—95; sports corr. St. Louis Suburban Jours., 1985—87; scoreboard operator St. Louis Cardinals, 1988—93; journeyman wireman IBEW Local #1, St. Louis, 1989—; scoreboard operator Savvis Ctr., St. Louis, 1995—. Baseball Writers' Edgar Wilkes Meml. Journalism scholar, St. Louis Journalism Found., 1986—88. Democrat. Home: 9013 Kickapoo Dr Saint Louis MO 63123

HOOD, ANTOINETTE FOOTE, dermatologist; b. Honolulu, 1941; MD, Vanderbilt U., 1967. Cert. dermatology. Intern Vanderbilt Affiliated Hosps, 1967-68; resident dermatology Harvard U., 1975-76; resident dermatology-pathology Mass. Gen. Hosp., Boston, 1976-78; fellow dermatology Harvard U., 1973-75; exec. dir. American Board of Dermatology, Detroit, 2001—. Office: Henry Ford Health System 1 Ford Place Detroit MI 48202

HOOD, BARBARA W. musician, educator; b. Oskaloosa, Iowa, May 8, 1930; d. Herbert E. and Gladys (Lockwood) Wolf; m. Fred Warren Hood, Sept. 2, 1950; children: Victoria Lynn Simpson, Christina Elizabeth Adair. Student, U Chattanooga, 1948—50; BMus Ga. State U, 1967—70. Dir. Children's Choir First Bapt. Choir, Chattanooga, 1948 50; prof. mem. violinist Chatanooga Symphony, 1948—53; billing clerk Profident Ins. Co., Chattanooga, 1950—51; sec., file clerk TVA, Chattanooga, 1951—53; sec. Highland Jr. H.S., Louisville, 1956—57; pvt. music tchr. Pvt. Practice, Moultrie, Ga., 1958—63; tchr. strings Marietta Sch. Sys., 1967—73; pvt. music tchr. pvt. practice, Marietta, Ga., 1963—67, 1973—76; tchr. music Weatherly Heights Bap. Ch., Huntsville, Ala., 1977—83; dir. youth orch. Huntsville(Ala.) Youth Orch. Assn., 1979—83; music tchr. pvt. practice, Huntsville, 1976—83; violinist Huntsville (Ala.) Symphony Orch., 1976—83; music tchr. Sea Pines Montessori, Hilton Head, SC, 1984—87; musician pvt. practice, Hilton Head, 1983—97; dir. music Winters Chapel United Meth. Ch., Atlanta, 1987—90; sec, EPA, Atlanta, 1988—90; music tchr. Fayette County Pub. Sch., Tyrone, Ga., 1990—96; dir. music Nat. Heights Bapt. Ch., Fayetteville, Ga., 1997—2003; pvt. tchr. strings Pvt. Practice, Fayetteville, 1996—; prof. performing group Ensemble pour deux pvt. practice, Fayetteville, 1997—. Dir. childrens choir First Bapt. Ch., Marietta, 1963—76; vol. music tchr. Happiness Hill Sch. for Spl. Needs, Marietta, 1966; dir. childrens choir Weatherly Heights Bapt. Ch., 1976—83, First Bapt. Ch., 1983—87; vol. music activities Seabrook Nursing Home, Hilton Head, 1986—87; founding mem. Hilton Head Orch., 1984—87, string quartet, 1986—87; vol. string tchr. Sams Sch. for Spl. Needs, Fayetteville, 2003. Composer: Hilton Head Prep, 1986, Sea Pines Montessori, 1986, "Chaconne", 1989, For Wheeler H.S., 1989, "Lament", 1990. Mem.: Nat. Choristers Guild, Music Edn. Nat. Conventioni, Am. String Assn. (assoc.), Ga. Music Edn. Assn. (assoc.). Avocation: composing, arranging. Home: 445 Cornwllis Way Fayetteville GA 30214 Office: Private Studio 445 Cornwallis Way Fayetteville GA 30214

HOOD, DONALD CHARLES, university administrator, psychology educator; b. Merrick, N.Y., June 2, 1942; s. David and Jessie Theresa (Vetter) H.; m. Nancy Ellen Epstein, Nov. 27, 1978. BA, Harpur Coll.-SUNY, Binghamton, 1965; MS, Brown U., 1968, PhD, 1970. Asst. prof. Columbia U., N.Y.C., 1969-73, assoc. prof., 1973-78, prof. psychology, 1978—, James F. Bender prof. psychology, 1990—, v.p. arts & sci., 1982-87, chmn. psychology dept., 1975-78. Contbr. articles to profl. jours. Trustee Smith Coll., 1989—99, vice chair, 1991—99; trustee Harry Guggenheim Found., 1996—; trustee (fellow) Brown U., 2002—. USPHS fellow, 1967-69, N.Y. State Coll. teaching fellow, 1965-67. Fellow: Optical Soc., Soc. Exptl. Psychology; mem.: Ea. Psychol. Assn., Assn. Rsch. Vision and Ophthalmology. Home: 450 Riverside Dr New York NY 10027-6801 Office: 415 Schernerhorn Hall 116th St And Broadway New York NY 10027 E-mail: dch3@columbia.edu.

HOOD, EARL JAMES, lawyer, state legislator; b. Spearfish, S.D., Apr. 28, 1947; s. Earl Kenneth and Florence Lorraine (Castor) m. Judith G. Witzel, June 2, 1968 (div. Sept. 1974); children: Jason, Jared Jon; m. Kathleen Gay Donahue, Sept. 13, 1975; 1 child, Stewart Lee. BS, Black Hills State Coll., 1969; JD, U. S.D., 1972. Mem. S.D. Ho. of Reps., Pierre, 1983-92, speaker pro tem, 1989-90, speaker of the house, 1991-92; pvt. practice Spearfish, 1972—; pres., shareholder, bd. dirs. Hood, Nies & Dardis, P.C., Spearfish, 2000—. City atty. City of Spearfish, 1972-76, 87—; mem. S.D. Code Commn., 1989-92. Chief Spearfish Vol. Fire Dept., 1982—83; pres. Black Hills State Coll. Found. Inc., Spearfish, 1986; mem. S.D. Pvt. Industry Coun., 1993—94, S.D. Quality Govt. Commn., 1993—94; chair Kids Voting, Spearfish, 1993—94, bd. dirs., 1994—95; eagle scout Boy Scouts Am., 1961; del. Rep. Nat. Conv., 1996; chair Workforce Devel. Coun. S.D., 1994—95; bd.d irs. High Plains Heritage Soc., 1999—; bd. dirs. No. Hills. Tng. Ctr. Found., 1999—, pres., 2001—; bd. dirs. West River Econ. Devel. Corp., 1999—2002. Named named S.D. Firefighter of Yr., Keep S.D. Green Assn., 1984, Friend of Edn., S.D. Edn. Assn., 1990; named one of Outstanding Lawyers Am., 2003; recipient Vigil HOnor Order of Arrow, Boy Scouts Am., 1965, Disting. Alumnus award, Black Hills State U., 1990. Mem. S.D. Bar Assn., S.D. Trial Lawyers Assn., Lions, Masons (Spearfish Lodge #18), Order Eastern Star (Queen City chpt #89), Black Hills Scottish Rite, Naja Shrine. Republican. Avocations: reading, travel. Home: PO Box 611 Spearfish SD 57783-0611 Office: Hood Nies & Dardis PC PO Box 759 Spearfish SD 57783-0759

HOOD, EDWARD EXUM, JR., retired electrical manufacturing company executive; b. Boonville, N.C., Sept. 15, 1930; s. Edward Exum and Nellie (Triplett) H.; m. Kay Transou, Dec. 30, 1950; children: Lisa Kay, Molly Ann. MS in Nuclear Engring., N.C. State U., 1953. Registered profl. engr., Ariz. Powerplant design engr. Gen. Electric Co., 1957-62, mgr. supersonic transport engine project, 1962-67, v.p., gen. mgr. comml. engine div., from 1968, v.p., group exec. internat. group, 1972-73, v.p., group exec., power generation group, 1973-77, sr. v.p., sector exec. tech. systems and materials sector, from 1977, vice-chmn. and exec officer, 1979-93, also bd. dirs. Served with USAF, 1952-56. Fellow AIAA; mem. Nat. Acad. Engring., Aerospace Industries Assn. (chmn. 1981) Home: 11674 Lake House Ct North Palm Beach FL 33408-3318 Office: GE PO Box 8300 260 Long Ridge Rd Stamford CT 06927-9100

HOOD, ERNEST ALVA, SR., pharmaceutical company executive; b. East St. Louis, Ill., July 10, 1910; s. Orestes Rastus and Daisy Ernestine (Eslick) H.; m. Taeko Haruta; children: Ernest Jr., Dharathula (Hood) Harris, Daisy. CEO Cophtra Ltd., N.Y.C., 1950—; power maintainer Con Edison, N.Y.C., 1952-72; N.Y. rep. Coastal Pharm. Co. Ltd., Norfolk, Va., Ghana, 1974-76, cons. Bklyn., Ghana, 1976—. Cons. Uchi Ichi Shoji Ltd., Japan, 1946—, Jaiama Tayorma Natural Scrap Exch., Freetown, Sierra Leone, Lome Natural Scrap Exch., Lome, Togo, 1994—, Abua Farms and Industries, Ashanti, 1996—, Buckberra Trading Co., Okyere Bour & Co., Ashanti, Two Worlds Mfg. Co.; advisor Cophtra Ltd. Author: (autobiography) Hoodisan-1910-1994. Bd. dirs., Cen. Bklyn. Coord. Coun. 1st lt. U.S. Army. Recipient Ulchii award, Republic South Korea. Mem. VFW, Vets. Assn. Home: 8025 Hickory Ave Gary IN 46403-2265 Office: Cophtra Ltd 550 Green Ave Brooklyn NY 11216-5710

HOOD, GLENDA E. state agency administrator; m. Charles M. Hood III; 3 children. BA, Rollins Coll.; postgrad., Harvard U., Ga. State U. Commr. City of Orlando, Fla., 1982-92, mayor, 1992—2002; sec. of state Florida, 2003—. Pres. Glenda E. Hood & Assocs., Inc. Vice chmn. mcpl. planning bd. City of Orlando, mem. nominating bd., chmn. task force bd. and commn. restructure; past chmn., founding mem. bd. dirs. Found. Orange County Pub. Schs.; co-chmn. Orlando Fights Back-Coalition for a Drug-Free Cmty.; bd. dirs. U. Ctrl. Fla. Found., Met. Orlando Urban League; past pres. exec. bd. Ctrl. Fla. Coun. of Boy Scouts; bd. overseers Rollins Coll. Crummer Grad. Sch. of Bus.; mem. adv. bd. Valencia C.C., Fla.- Costa Rica Inst.; past co-chmn. United Negro Coll. Fund; pres. Jr. League Orlando-Winter Park, Vol. Svc. Bur.; mem. Orange County Commn. on Children. Named Mcpl. Leader of Yr., Am. City and County Mag., 1992, one of Ten Outstanding Young Americans, U.S. Jaycees, one of Seven Outstanding Youth Floridians, Fla. Jaycees, Woman of Yr., Downtown Orlando Inc., one of Ten People to Watch, Fla. Trend, one of 100 Young Women of Promise, Good Housekeeping; recipient Willie J. Bruton award for cmty. svc. Met. Orlando Urban League, Summit award Women's Resource Ctr., Svc. to Mankind award Leukemia Soc. Am. Ctrl. Fla. chpt. Mem. Nat. League of Cities (past pres.), Fla. League of Cities (past pres.), Fla. C. of C. (past pres.), Greater Orlando C. of C. (past v.p.). Office: Florida Dept of State R A Gray Bldg 500 S Bronough Tallahassee FL 32399-0250*

HOOD, LEROY EDWARD, molecular biologist, educator; b. Missoula, Mont., Oct. 10, 1938; s. Thomas Edward and Myrtle Evylan (Wadsworth) H.; m. Valerie Anne Logan, Dec. 14, 1963; children: Eran William, Marqui Leigh Jennifer. BS, Calif. Inst. Tech., 1960, PhD in Biochemistry, 1968; MD, Johns Hopkins U., 1964. Med. officer USPHS, 1967-70; staff scientist Pub. Health Svc., Bethesda, Md., 1967-70; sr. investigator Nat. Cancer Inst., 1967-70; asst. prof. biology Calif. Inst. Tech., Pasadena, 1970-73, assoc. prof., 1973-75, prof., 1975-92, Bowles prof. biology, 1977-92, chmn. div. biology, 1980-89; Gates prof. molecular biotech., chmn. bd. U. Wash. Sch. Medicine, Seattle, 1992—2000; pres. Instit. for Systems Biology, 2000—. Dir. NSF Sci. and Tech. Ctr. for Molecular Biotech., 1989—2001. Author: (with others) Biochemistry, a Problems Approach, 1974, Molecular Biology of Eukaryotic Cells, 1975, Immunology, 1978, Essential Concepts of Immunology, 1978, The Code of Codes: Scientific and Social Issues in the Human Genome Project, 1992; co-editor: Advances in Immunology, 1987, Genetics: From Genes to Genomics, 1999. Co-recipient, Albert Lasker Basic Medical Research Award, 1987, recipient Scientist of the Year Award, 1993, R&D Magazine, Kyoto Prize, 2002, Lemelson prize MIT, 2003. Mem. NAS, Am. Assn. Immunologists, Am. Assn. Sci., Am. Acad. Arts and Scis., Sigma Xi, Am. Philosophical Soc. Avocations: mountaineering, rockclimbing, photography. Office: Instit for Sytems Biology 1441 34th St Seattle WA 98103

HOOD, LUANN SANDRA, special education educator; b. Bklyn., Jan. 10, 1955; d. Louie A. and Sylvia M. (Hall) Mayo; m. Stephen J. Hood. BA, St. Joseph's Coll., Bklyn., 1976; MS in Edn., Bklyn. Coll., 1979. Cert. tchr. N.K, 1-6, spl. edn., N.Y.C. lic. Edn. counselor adolescents Am. Indian Cmty. House, Inc., N.Y.C., 1977-79; tchr. children with retarded mental devel. Pub. Sch. 273, Bklyn., 1979-83; tchr. early childhood Pub. Sch. 128, Bklyn., 1983-94; tchr. emotionally handicapped Pub. Sch.215, Bklyn., 1994-95; tchr. learning disabled Pub. Sch. 101, Bklyn., 1995-99, tchr. hard of hearing, 1999—. Mem. sch. leadership team, 1997—. Exec. sec. bd. trustees Am. Indian Cmty. House, Inc., N.Y.C., 1980-91. Regents scholar N.Y. State Edn. Dept., 1972; grantee Indian League of the Americas, Inc. 1972-75, Thunderbird Am. Indian Dancers, Inc., 1972-75, Internat. Order of King's Daughters and Sons, 1976. Mem. Coun. for Exceptional Children, N.Y. State Tchrs. of Handicapped. Democrat. Roman Catholic. Avocation: photography.

HOOD, MARY DULLEA, law librarian; b. Fargo, N.D., Jan. 3, 1947; d. Maurice Eugene and Rosemary (Melican) Dullea; m. Michael L. Hood, May 26, 1974; children: David Patrick, Michelle Marie. BA, U. Santa Clara, 1970, JD, 1975; MLS, San Jose State U., 1979. Bar: Calif. 1976. Libr. asst. Law Libr., U. Santa Clara, Calif., 1970-75, reference libr., 1975-78; instr. legal rsch. Paralegal Inst., 1976-84; head pub. svcs. U. Santa Clara, Calif., 1978-87, assoc. dir., 1987—, mem. univ. automation task force, 1986-91, mem. adj. faculty advanced legal rsch. Law Sch., 1998-99, 2001, acting dir., 2001. Mem. Santa Clara CSC, 1976-78. Mem. Am. Assn. Law Librs. (placement com. 2000-02, awards com. 2002—), No. Calif. Assn. Law Librs. (pres. 1982-83), U. Santa Clara Law Sch. Alumni Assn. (treas. 1983-85). Avocations: needlepoint, reading, stained glass. Office: Santa Clara U Law Libr 500 El Camino Real Santa Clara CA 95053-0430 E-mail: mhood@scu.edu.

HOOD, MAUREEN N, medical/surgical nurse, researcher; d. George C and Shirley E Hood. BS, U. of Puget Sound, 1981—85; MS, U. of Md., Sch. of Nursing, 2000—03. RN, Md. Bd. of Nursing, 2000; Registered Technologist, Radiography Am. Registry of Radiologic Technologists, 1990, Registered Technologist, Magnetic Resonance Am. Registry of Radiologic Technologists. Fgn. fisheries observer Nat. Marine Fisheries Svc., Seattle, 1986—87; joint venture rep. ProFish, Seattle, 1987—87; magnetic resonance technologist Tacoma Magnetic Imaging, Tacoma, 1988—94; sr. technologist Mobile Technologies Inc., Seattle Area, 1994—96; rsch. technologist First Hill Diagnostic Imaging, Seattle, 1996; magnetic resonance rsch. coord./nurse Uniformed Services U., Bethesda, Md., 1996—. Chair, external rels., exec. bd. Sect. for Magnetic Resoance Technologists, Berkeley, Calif., 2001—; policy bd. Sect. for Magnetic Resonance Technologists, Berkeley, Calif., 1998—2001; bd. mem. Inst. for Magnetic Resonance Safety, Edn., and Rsch., Los Angeles, Calif., 2002—; associated sciences consortium Radiol. Soc. of N.Am., Oak Brook, Ill., 2001—. Recipient Scholar Athlete of the Quarter, NW Intercollegiate C.C. Athletic Assn., 1988. Mem.: Sect. for Magnetic Resonance Technologists (exec. com. 2001—03), Capital Area Roundtable on Informatics in Nursing, Am. Med. Informatics Assn., Healthcare Info. and Mgmt. Systems Soc., Am. Radiol. Nurses Assn., Eagles Aux., DC Thetas, Kappa Alpha Theta (editor 1984—85). Avocations: soccer, travel, fine arts, fitness. Office: Uniformed Services University 4301 Jones Bridge Rd Bethesda MD 20814-4799 Office Fax: 301-295-2271. E-mail: mhood@usuhs.mil.

HOOD, MICHAEL LEE, psychologist, clinical researcher, educator; b. Springifield, Mo., July 17, 1959; s. Norvell Dennis and Beverly Anne (Vitzthum) H.; m. Rebecca Jane Apone-Hood; children: Rhonda Jo, Jody Sunshine, Robin, Randal Eric. A Gen. Studies, Ind. U.-Purdue U., Indpls., 1991; cert. psychol. testing, U. Ark., 1993; B Gen. Studies, Ind. U., Bloomington, 1996; postgrad., U. Iowa, 1992-93; MA in Psychology magna cum laude, So. Calif. U., 1999, PhD in Psychology magna cum laude, 2002. Dir. Psychol. Rsch. Assocs., Bolivar, Mo., 1991—. Tchr., facilitator Non-Traditional Edn. and Reading Svcs., Ft. Madison, Iowa, 1990-97, dir., pres., 1993-97; cons., assessor Newport, Bell & Oxley, attys., Davenport, Iowa, 1992-93. With U.S. Army, 1977—79. Mem. ASCD, Am. Psychol. Soc., Soc. for Psychol. Study Social Issues, Am. Assn. for Adult and Continuing Edn., Literacy Vols. Am. (cert. tutor and workshop leader), Inc., Am. Edn. Rsch. Assn., Ind. U. Alumni Assn., So. Calif. U. Alumni Assn., People for Ethical Treatment Animals, Toastmasters Internat. (v.p. edn. 2002, pres. 2003), Phi Theta Kappa. Native Am. Religion (Cherokee). Avocations: writing poetry, astronomy, nature walks, horseback riding, playing chess. Office: Psychol Rsch Assocs 1312 E 490th Rd Bolivar MO 65613-8159

HOOD, RONALD CHALMERS, III, historian, writer; b. Florence, Ala., Apr. 2, 1947; s. Ronald Chalmers II and Elizabeth Woods (Craig) H.; m. Lucile O'Connor, Dec. 20, 1969; children: Ronald Chalmers IV, Reed Cathleen. BS, U.S. Naval Acad., 1969; MA, U. Maine, Orono, 1972; PhD, U. Md., 1979. Commd. 2d lt. USMC, 1969, advanced through grades to capt., 1973, resigned, 1982; historian, writer Johns Hopkins U., Balt., 1982—, George Mason U., Fairfax, Va., 1982—, U. Md., College Park, 1982—, Mary Washington Coll., 1999—. Lectr. Smithsonian Instn., Washington, 1988; speaker Conf. on Strategic Studies, Washington, 1985; co-chair Muscle Shoals Revisited Conf. on Future of Tenn. Valley, 1993; theatre and arts critic The Daily Jour. Author: (history monograph) Royal Republicans, 1985; co-author: (mil. history) Military Effectiveness, 1987, Body, Mind, Spirit: 75 Years of Camp Hazen YMCA, 1995; contbr. editorial columns to Washington Post, Richmond Times-Dispatch, Potomac News, articles to profl. jours. Asst. scoutmaster Boy Scouts Am., Woodbridge, Va., 1989—; advisor County Sch. Bd., Prince William County, Va., 1991; instr. ARC, Prince William County, 1982—. Samuel Eliot Morison fellow U. Maine, Orono, 1971-72, Grad. Sch. fellow U. Md., 1975, fellow Am. Philos. Soc., 1998, sr. fellow to France Am. Coun. Learned Societies, 2000-2001. Mem. AAUP, Writers' Ctr., Smithsonian Instn., Nat. Geographic Soc. Avocations: travel, acting, bike riding, aquatic activities, cross-country skiing. Home and Office: 12317 Oakwood Dr Woodbridge VA 22192-1911 Fax: 703-497-9578.

HOOD, SANDRA DALE, librarian; b. Edmond, Okla., Nov. 28, 1949; d. Rufus Gustav and Hope Louvica (Hutton) Farber; m. Frank D. Hood Jr., May 17, 1971; 1 child, Charles Richard. BA, U. Okla., 1971, MLS, 1972; MA in Bicultural Bilingual Studies, U. Tex., San Antonio, 1996. Libr. South Oklahoma City Jr. Coll., 1973, Daus. of Republic of Tex. Libr. at the Alamo, San Antonio, 1980-88; adad. outreach prof., automation and libr. sys. libr. Palo Alto Coll. Learning Resources Ctr., San Antonio, 1988—. Pres. tech. svcs. spl. interest group Coun. Rsch. and Acad. Librs., San Antonio, 1991-92, chmn. circulation and interlibr. loan spl. interest group, 1997—; sec., mem. exec. bd. Timberwood Park Property Owners Assn., San Antonio, 1991-94. Recipient NISOD award, 2003. Mem. ALA, Tex. Libr. Assn. (conf. planning com. 1992-93, 97-98, 2002—), Tex. Accelerated Libr. Leader 1997—, disaster relief com. 2002—), Bexar Libr. Assn. (exec. bd., dir. editor 1988-90), Tex. Jr. Coll. Tchrs. Assn. Democrat. Lutheran. Avocations: travel, reading, computers. Home: 27030 Foggy Meadows St San Antonio TX 78260-1822 Office: Palo Alto Coll Learning Resources Ctr 1400 W Villaret Blvd San Antonio TX 78224-2417

HOOD, THOMAS GREGORY, minister; b. Stamford, Conn., Mar. 26, 1948; s. George E. and Shirley W. (Brundage) H.; m. Esther A. Whitcomb, July 1, 1967; children: Thomas G., Sarah D. BA, Johnson State Coll., 1984; MDiv, Covington Sem., Rossville, Ga., 1986, PhD in Counseling, 1988. Ordained to ministry Fellowship of Christian Assemblies, 1969, Am. Bapt. Chs. in U.S.A., 1984. Asst. pastor Bethel Full Gospel Ch., Barton, Vt., 1968-71; pastor Lyndonville (Vt.) Full Gospel Ch., 1969-71, Sheffield (Vt.) Fed. Ch., 1971-74, Sutton (Vt.) Bapt. Ch., 1972-84, Adams Center (N.Y.) Bapt. Ch., 1984—. Del. Am. Bapt. Conv., N.Y., 1984—. Author: The Lord's Prayer, 1986, A Theology of Victory, 1987, Biblical Principles, 1988; composer religious songs. Mem. Am. Bapt.Mins. Coun. Republican. Home: 13463 US Rt 11 Adams Center NY 13606 *It is impossible to forgive ourselves for our failures if we are unwilling to forgive others theirs. The rule we use to judge others will always reflect back on ourselves.*

HOOD, WILLIAM BOYD, JR., cardiologist, educator; b. Sylacauga, Ala., Mar. 25, 1932; s. William Boyd and Katherine Elizabeth (Anderson) H.; m. Katherine Candace Todd, May 5, 1972; 1 son, Jefferson Boyce. BS summa cum laude, Davidson Coll., 1954; MD, Harvard U., 1958. Intern Peter Bent Brigham Hosp., Boston, 1958-59, resident in internal medicine, 1959-60, 62-63; from asst. prof. to assoc. prof. medicine Harvard U., 1967-71; from assoc. prof. to prof. medicine Boston U., 1971-82; chief cardiology Boston City Hosp., 1973-82; prof. medicine U. Rochester (N.Y.), 1982-98; head cardiology unit Strong Meml. Hosp., Rochester, 1982-98; emeritus prof. medicine U. Rochester, 1998—. Cons. NIH, 1975—, NASA, 1994—; clin. prof. medicine U. Wash. Sch. Medicine, Seattle, 2000—. Mem. editorial bd. New Eng. Jour. Medicine, 1974-81, Circulation, 1980-83, Circulation Research, 1982-89, Jour. Clin. Investigation, 1984-89, Cochrane Collaboration Heart Group, 1997—; contbr. articles, revs. and editorials on cardiovascular physiology to profl. jours., chpts. to books. Served to capt. USAF, 1963-65. Research grantee NIH, 1971-98; grantee Am. Heart Assn., 1971-76. Fellow ACP; mem. Am. Soc. Clin. Investigation, Assn. Am. Physicians, Am. Heart Assn., Am. Physiol. Soc., Assn. Profs. Cardiology (past pres.), N.Y. Cardiol. Soc. (past pres.), Phi Beta Kappa, Alpha Omega Alpha. Achievements include studies on experimental and clinical myocardial ischemia and infarction, and congestive heart failure.

HOOFARD, JANE MAHAN DECKER, retired elementary school educator; b. Grand Junction, Colo., Apr. 29, 1946; d. Nat Don and Bernita Margaret (Williams) Mahan; m. William Edward Hoofard, Mar. 6, 1982; children: Lynna Kay Decker, Keith Dale. BA, Ft. Lewis Coll., 1968. Cert. tchr. Calif. Tchr. 3rd, 6th grades Shasta Lake Union Sch. Dist., Summit City, Calif., 1968-73; tchr., MGM cons., coord., brain drain writer Shasta County Schs., Redding, Calif., 1975-81; tchr. 2nd, 3rd grades Manton (Calif.) Joint Union Sch. Dist., 1987-89; elem. and mid. sch. tchr. Mineral (Calif.) Elem. Sch. Dist., 1989—2001; ret., 2001. Writer, editor, pub.: AAUW. Mem.: Calif. Ret. Tchrs. Assn. (pres. divsn. 9 Glenn/Tehama Counties 2003—). Home: 19389 Hwy 36W Red Bluff CA 96080

HOOG, THOMAS W. public relations executive; Chief of staff Gary Hart, Washington, 1975-80; pres., CEO Hoog & Assocs., 1980-90; chmn. pub. affairs Hill & Knowlton Worldwide, 1990-96; pres., CEO Hill & Knowlton, U.S., 1996—. Bd. dirs. Smithsonian Air & Space Mus., Wolf Trap Found. for Performing Arts, Am. Fedn. of Aging Rsch., New Deal Inc., Up With People. Office: Hill & Knowlton 466 Lexington Ave 3d Flr New York NY 10017-3140

HOOGLAND, ROBERT FREDERICS, lawyer; b. Paterson, N.J., Apr. 3, 1955; s. Robert J. and Lucretia H. BA, U. Fla., 1976; MBA, Rollins Coll., 1977; JD, U. Fla., 1982. Bar: Fla. 1983, U.S. Dist. Ct. (mid. dist.) Fla. 1989; cert. real estate law. Assoc. Giles, Hedrick & Robinson, Orlando, Fla., 1983-89; ptnr. Hoogland & Durket, P.A., Longwood, Fla., 1989-92, Robert F. Hoogland, P.A., Altamonte Springs, Fla., 1992—. Mem. ABA, Fla. Bar Assn., Orange County Bar Assn.,Voile A. Williams Inns of Court, Phi Delta Phi. Republican. Roman Catholic. Avocations: tennis, golf, fishing. Home: 139 Olive Tree Cir Altamonte Springs FL 32714-3240 Office: PO Box 160021 Altamonte Springs FL 32716-0021

HOOGWERF, BYRON JAMES, physician; b. Sioux Falls, S.D., Feb. 8, 1945; s. Henry (dec.) Hoogwerf and Nellie (Verbrugge) Hoogwerf-Christians; m. Judith Anne Barrett, Aug. 16, 1966 (div. 1985); children: Jennifer Anne, Byron James II; m. Heidi Ellen Gaenslen, Dec. 21, 1985; 1 child, Rebecca Alexandra. BA, Calvin Coll., 1967; MD, U. Minn., 1971. Intern Hennepin County Med. Ctr., Mpls., 1971-72, resident internal medicine, 1976-78; fellow, endocrinology Univ. Minn., Mpls., 1978-81, asst. prof., 1981-85; staff physician Cleve. Clinic Found., 1985—, chmn., endocrinology, 1988-91, program dir. internal medicine residency, 1997—. Contbr. chpts. to books and over 100 articles to profl. jours. Bd. dirs. Diabetes Assn. Greater Cleve., 1986-95, pres. bd. dirs., 1992-93; bd. dirs. Camp Ho Mito Koda, Cleve., 1986—. Recipient Tng. grant NIH, U. Minn., 1978-79, Nat. Rsch. Svc. award NIH, U. Minn., 1979-81, Spl. Emphasis Rsch. Career award NIH-Nat. Inst. Aging, U. Minn., 1982-85, NIH Post CABG Trial award, 1987-95, 2000—. Fellow ACP (cert. diabetes edn.), Am. Assn. Clin. Endocrinologists; mem. AAAS, Endocrine Soc., Am. Diabetes Assn. (chmn. publs. com. coun. on nutritional scis. and metabolism 1988-91, profl. practice com. 1992-94, chmn. coun. on nutritional scis. and metabolism 1996-98, bd. dirs. 1998-2001, pub. com. 1998-2002, physicians recognition com. 2002—), Endocrine Soc., Soc. for Clin. Trials. Presbyterian. Home: 2237 Demington Dr Cleveland OH 44106-3320 Office: The Cleveland Clinic Found 9500 Euclid Ave Cleveland OH 44195-0002 E-mail: hoogweb@ccf.org.

HOOK, DONALD DWIGHT, humanities educator, writer; b. Charlotte, N.C., Dec. 16, 1928; s. Dwight Carlisle Hook, Eunice (Fowler) Hook; m. Harriett Gay Blackwell, Aug. 18, 1954; children: Terence Blackwell, Karen Fowler Hook Chase. Student, Washington & Lee U., 1946—48; AB, Emory U., 1950; AM, Duke U., 1958; postgrad., U. N.C., 1957—58; PhD, Brown U., 1961. Prof. Modern Langs. Trinity Coll., Hartford, Conn., 1961—94. Vis. prof. U. Hartford, Ctrl. Conn. State U., St. Joseph Coll., Chadron State U., Nebr., U. R.I. Author: German Phonology, 1967, Conversational German One, 1st edit., 1970, Conversational German One, 2d edit., 1976, Fahrt ins Weiss-Blaue, 1970, Stimmen aus deutschen Landen, 1972, Goals, 1972, Goals, rev. edit., 1977, Intermediate Conversational German, 3d edit., 1973, Madmen of History, 1976; editor: Dictionary of First Names, 1980; translator: Die Grundlagen des klassischen Tanzes, 1980; author: Book of Insults and Irreverent Quotations, 1980, A Guide to Curriculum Development in Foreign Languages, 1981, The Aetna Manual of Style, 1983, (filmstrip) Men of Conquest, Men of Peace: Great German Leaders of History, Parts I and II, 1986, De Gaulle, Savior of France, 1986, Lafayette, 1986; translator: J. Pierpont Morgan, Collector, 1987; author: Death in the Balance: The Debate Over Capital Punishment, 1989, The Plight of the Church Traditionalist: A Last Apology, 1991, Gun Control: The Continuing Debate, 1993, Between Two Worlds: A Cultural History of German-Jewish Writers, 1992, Changes, 1997; editor: Der Weg ins Exil--Erinnerungen eines Rehlingers, 2001; author: Switching Churches: A Layman's Guide to a New Commitment, 2002, Psychograms of Sickness and Death: A Partial Autobiography, 2002, Back Then - Those Were the Days: Recollections of a Boy Growing Up During the Depression, 2003; contbr. over 100 articles to profl. jours. Cpl. USAF, 1950—52, 1st lt. USAF, 1952—55. Roman Catholic. Avocations: travel, gardening, writing. Home: 5 Blue Heron Dr Georgetown DE 19947-9485

HOOK, HAROLD SWANSON, former management consulting executive; b. Kansas City, Mo., Oct. 10, 1931; s. Ralph C. and Ruby (Swanson) H.; m. Joanne T. Hunt, Feb. 19, 1955; children: Karen Anne, Thomas W., Randall T. BS in Bus. Adminstrn., U. Mo., 1953, MA in Acctg., 1954; grad., So. Meth. U. Inst. Ins. Mktng., 1957; postgrad., NYU, 1967-70; LLD (hon.), U. Mo., 1983, Westminster Coll., 1983. CLU, FLMI. Mem. faculty U. Mo. Sch. Bus., 1953-54; asst. to pres. Nat. Fidelity Life Ins. Co., Kansas City, Mo., 1957-60, dir., 1959-66, adminstrv. v.p., 1960-61, exec. v.p., investment com., 1961-62, pres., exec. com., 1962-66; sr. v.p. U.S. Life Ins. Co., N.Y.C., 1966-67, dir., 1967-70, exec. v.p., mem. exec. com., 1967-68, pres., 1968-70, Calif.-Western States Life Ins. Co., Sacramento, 1970-75, chmn., 1975-79, sr. chmn., 1979-91, also bd. dirs.; mem. exec. com. Am. Gen. Corp., Houston, 1975-97, pres., 1975-81, chmn., chief exec. officer, 1978-96, also bd. dirs., chmn., 1996-97. Founder, pres. Main Event Mgmt. Corp., Houston, 1971—; bd. dirs. Duke Energy Corp.,Charlotte, N.C., Sprint Corp., Kansas City, Mo., Cooper Industries, Inc., Houston, Chase Manhattan Corp., N.Y.C., Chase Manhattan Bank, N.Y.C., Chase Bank ofTex., Houston. Founder, mem. Naval War Coll. Found.; trustee, Baylor Coll. Medicine, Houston; coun. overseers Jesse H. Hones Grad. Sch. Adminstrn., Rice U., Houston; pres. nat. exec. bd. Boy Scouts Am., 1988-90, now mem. nat. adv. coun. Boy Scouts Am., mem. adv. bd. Sam Houston Area coun.; past pres. Houston Commerce, bd. dirs., Greater Houston Partnership (formerly Houston C. of C.), Director Emeritus. Recipient Citation of Merit U. Mo. Alumni Assn., 1965, Faculty-Alumni award U. Mo., 1978; Silver Beaver award Boy Scouts Am., 1974, Disting. Eagle Scout award, 1976, Silver Antelope award, 1989, Silver Buffalo award, 1990; Chief Exec. Officer award Fin. World mag., 1979, 82, 84, 86; named Man of Yr., Delta Sigma Pi, 1969, Outstanding Chief Exec. Officer in Multiline Ins. Industry, Wall Street Transcript, 1981-87. Fellow Life Mgmt. Inst.; mem. Mgmt. Exec. Soc., Philos. Soc. Tex., Tex. Assn. Taxpayers (bd. dirs.), Nat. Assn. Life Underwriters, Houston Assn. Life Underwriters, Forum Club (bd. govs. 1983-93), River Oaks Country Club, Petrolum Club, Econ. Club N.Y.C., Eldorado Country Club, Rotary, Beta Gamma Sigma (dirs. table 1976, nat. honoree 1984). Presbyterian. Office: Main Event Mgmt Corp PO Box 3665Pky Houston TX 77253-3665 also: PO Box 3247 Houston TX 77253-3247

HOOK, JERRY B. pharmaceutical consultant; b. Elk City, Okla., Sept. 7, 1937; m. Jacqueline H. Smith; children: Bruce, Marilyn. BS, B in Pharmacy with honors, Wash. State U., Pullman, 1960; MS, U. Iowa, 1964, PhD, 1966; DSc (hon.), John Jay Coll. Criminal Justice, CUNY, 1989. Diplomate Am. Bd. Toxicology. Assoc. prof. pharmacology Mich. State U., East Lansing, 1971-75, prof. of pharmacology, 1975-78, prof. pharmacology and toxicology, 1978-83, dir. ctr. for environ. toxicology, 1980-83; v.p. preclin. R & D Smith Kline & French Labs. Phila., King of Prussia, Pa., 1983-87, v.p. preclin. R & D worldwide, 1987-88, v.p. devel., R & D, 1988-89, SmithKline Beecham Pharms., King of Prussia, 1989-90, sr. v.p., dir. devel. R & D, 1990-93; pres., chief exec. officer Lexin Pharm. Corp., Horsham, Pa., 1993-96; pres., CEO Sparta Pharm., Inc., Horsham, Pa., 1996-98, chmn., pres., CEO, 1998-99. Burroughs-Wellcome vis. prof. U. N.D., 1981; vis. scientist Fed. Am. Soc. for Exptl. Biology Vis. Scientists for Minority Instns. Program, U. P.R. Med. Sch., 1984, Herbert H. Lehman Coll. of City U., 1985, Calif. State U., 1988, Pembroke State U., 1989; mem. adv. com. to bd. sci. counselors Nat. Toxicology Program, 1982-86; chmn. peer rev. panel of experts Nat. Toxology Program; vis. scientist John Jay Coll. Criminal Justice CUNY, 1987, mem. adv. bd. Toxicology Rsch. and Tng. Ctr., 1986-93. Author 225 publs. peer-reviewed lit., 60 book chpts., published symposia, reviews, symposia presentations. Bd. dirs. Montgomery County Community Coll. Found., 1987-89. Fellow Am. Coll. Clin. Pharmacology (hon.); mem. AAAS, Am. Soc. for Pharmacology and Exptl. Therapeutics, Internat. Union of Pharmacology (vice chmn. toxicology sect. 1987-90, chmn. toxicology sect. 1990-94), Internat. Union of Toxicology (1st v.p. 1989-92), Mid-Atlantic Chpt. Soc. of Toxicology, Soc. of Toxicology (councillor 1983-85, v.p. elect 1985-86, v.p. 1986-87, pres. 1987-88, past pres. 1988-89, IUTOX councillor). E-mail: jhook0937@aol.com.

HOOK, JOHN BURNEY, investment company executive; b. Franklin, Ind., Sept. 6, 1928; s. Burney S. and Elsie C. (Hubbard) H.; m. Georgia Delis, Feb. 8, 1958; children— David, Deborah. BS, Ind. U., 1956, MBA, 1957. CPA, Ohio.; cert. fin. analyst. Store mgr. Goodman-Jester, Inc., Franklin, Ind., 1949-50; auditor Ernst & Ernst, Indpls., 1953-56; financial analyst Eli Lilly & Co., Indpls., 1957-59; gen. ptnr. Ball, Burge & Kraus, Cleve., 1966-72; pres., dir. Cuyahoga Mgmt. Corp., 1966-81; mng. ptnr. Hook Ptnrs., Cleve., 1984—96. Mem. AICPA, Am. Inst. CFAs, Union Club (Cleve.), Westwood Country Club, Ironwood Country Club (Palm Desert, Calif.). Republican. Methodist. Home: 435 Bates Dr Bay Village OH 44140 also: 73233 Ribbonwood Palm Desert CA 92260

HOOK, MARTIN LAWRENCE, music educator, director; b. Humansville, Mo., Mar. 6, 1952; s. Kenneth Bruce Hook, Sr. and Velma Irene Hook; m. Sally Beth Batson, Aug. 10, 1973; children: Benjamin Austin, Joseph Michael. MusB in Edn., S.W. Bapt. Coll., 1974; MusM in Performance, U. of Kans., 1976. Cert. K-12 Instrumental/Vocal Music Tchr. Mo., 1974, Vocal Music Tchr. Kans., 1977. Grad. tchg. asst. U. of Kans., Lawrence, Kans., 1974—76; vocal music tchr. Lawrence Pub. Sch., Lawrence, 1977—77, Pratt Pub. Sch., Pratt, Kans., 1977—80, Columbia Pub. Sch., Columbia, Mo., 1980—2000, dir. of music edn., 2000—. Mem. music adv. com. Mo. State H.S. Activities Assn., Columbia, Mo., 1998—2000; mem. assessment com. Mo. Dept. of Elem. & Secondary Edn., Jefferson City, Mo., 1996—2000, mem. fine arts assessment com., 1998—2002. Contbr. Dir. Columbia Choral Ensemble, Columbia, 1990—95; co-dir. Mo. Symphony Soc. Children's Choir, Columbia, 2002—; bd. dor. Maplewood Barn Cmty. Theatre, Columbia, Mo., 1988—94. Recipient Outstanding Extra-Curricular Educator award, Columbia Fund for Academic Excellence, 1988. Mem.: Mo. Choral Directors Assn. (sec. 1992—94, dist. rep. 2000—02, Outstanding Dir. 1997, Oustanding NE Dist. Dir. 2003), Mo. Music Educators Assn. (dist. pres. 1991—94, vocal v.p. 1994—96, president-elect, pres., past pres. 1996—2002, editorial writer 1994—2000), The Nat. Assn. for Music Edn. (nat. assembly mem. 1996—2000). Methodist. Avocations: travel, woodworking, reading, golf. Office: Columbia Public Schools Music Department 1104 N Providence Road Columbia MO 65203 Office Fax: 573-214-3023. Personal E-mail: mhook@columbia.k12.mo.us. E-mail: mhook@columbia.k12.mo.us.

HOOK, RALPH CLIFFORD, JR., business educator; b. Kansas City, Mo., May 2, 1923; s. Ralph Clifford and Ruby (Swanson) H.; m. Joyce Fink, Jan. 20, 1946; children— Ralph Clifford III, John Gregory. BA, U. Mo., 1947, MA, 1948; PhD, U. Tex., 1954. Instr. U. Mo., 1947-48; asst. prof. Tex. A&M U., 1948-51; lectr. U. Tex., 1951-52; co-owner, mgr. Hook Buick Co., also Hook Truck & Tractor Co., Lee's Summit, Mo., 1952-58; assoc. prof. U. Kansas City, 1953-58; dir. Bur. Bus. Research and Services, Ariz. State U., 1958-66, prof. mktg., 1960-68; dean Coll. Bus. Adminstrn., U. Hawaii, 1968-74; prof. mktg. U. Hawaii, 1974-96, prof. mktg. emeritus, 1996—. Vis. Disting. prof. N.E. La. U., 1979; dir. Hook Bros. Corp., Market City Ltd., M.L. Macadamia Ptnrs., ltd. partnerships. Author: (with others) The Management Primer, 1972, Life Style Marketing, 1979, Marketing Service, 1983; contbr. (with others) monograph series Western Bus. Roundup; founder, moderator Western Bus. Roundup radio series, 1958-68. Bd. dirs. Samaritan Counseling Ctr. of Hawaii and Waikiki Health Ctr. 1st lt. F.A., AUS, 1943-46; col. Res. Recipient alumni citation of merit U. Mo. Coll. Bus. and Pub. Adminstrn., 1969; Distinguished Service award Nat. Def. Transp. Assn., 1977, God and Service award United Meth. Ch./Boy Scouts Am., 1986; named to Faculty Hall Fame Ariz. State U. Coll. Bus. Assn., 1977, Hawaii Transp. Hall of Fame, 1986; named Educator of Yr., Western Mktg. Educators' Assn., 1998, Hawaii Bus. Hall of Fame, 2000. Fellow Internat. Coun. for Sml. Bus. (pres. 1963); mem. Am. Mktg. Assn. (v.p. 1965-67, pres. Cen. Ariz. chpt. 1960-61, pres. Honolulu chpt. 1991-92, Wayne A. Lemberg award for disting. svc. 1995), Western Assn. Collegiate Schs. Bus. (pres. 1972-73), Sales and Mktg. Execs. Internat. (life), Nat. Def. Transp. Assn. (life, Hawaii v.p. 1978-82), Newcomen Soc. N.Am. (Hawaii chmn.), Pi Sigma Epsilon (v.p. for edn. programs 1990-94), Mu Kappa Tau (pres. 1996-98), Beta Gamma Sigma, Omicron Delta Kappa, Beta Theta Pi, Delta Sigma Pi (gold coun.) United Methodist. Home: 311 Ohua Ave Apt 1104D Honolulu HI 96815-3636 Office: U Hawaii Coll Bus Adminstrn 2404 Maile Way Bldg C Honolulu HI 96822-2223

HOOK, WILLIAM FRANKLIN, locum tenens radiologist; b. Williston, N.D., May 26, 1935; s. Charles Ellis and Ann (Franklin) H.; m. Margo Joanne Booth, June 21, 1958 (div. Sept. 1968); children: William, Christopher, Paul; m. Merry Jean Schimke, Nov. 26, 1968 (div. 1987); 1 child, Kari Ann; m. Linda Marie Rohrich, Aug. 18, 1988. AB, Stanford U., 1957; MD, Jefferson Med. Coll., 1961. Diplomate Am. Bd. Radiology, Am. Bd. Nuclear Medicine. Staff radiologist O&R Clinic, Bismarck, N.D., 1969-74, dir. nuclear radiology, 1983-98, chmn. dept. radiology, 1990-98; chief dept. radiology Bismarck Hosp., 1970-74; dir. dept. radiology Mandan (N.D.) Hosp., 1974-81; staff radiologist Meth. Hosps., Dallas, 1981-83, Med. Ctr. One, 1984-98; co-dir. Regional MRI Ctr., Bismarck, 1987-92. Asst. clinical prof. U. N.D., 1978—. Author: Common Sense and Modern First Aid, 1967, (CD-Rom) X-Ray Film Reading Made Easy, 2001. Lt. USNR, 1961-64, col. Res. ret.; comdr. USAR hosp., Persian Gulf, 1991-92. Mem.: AMA (Physicians Recognition award 1983—86, 1986—92), 6th Dist. Med. Soc., N.D. State Radiol. Soc., Radiol. Soc. N.Am., Soc. Nuc. Medicine, Am. Coll. Radiology. Lutheran. Avocations: hunting, golf, aviation. Address: PO Box 2424 36636 N Mule Train Carefree AZ 85377 E-mail: wfhook@aol.com.

HOOKER, ALEXANDER CAMPBELL, JR., foreign language educator; b. Detroit, Mar. 24, 1921; s. Alexander Campbell and Harriet Colladay (Gay) H.; m. Frances Root, June 2, 1945; children: Elizabeth Gay, Jean Campbell. AB, Dartmouth Coll., 1942; AM, Harvard U., 1947; postgrad., U. Mex., 1947, Mex. City Coll., 1947-48; DML, Middlebury Coll., 1954. Instr. Cambridge (Mass.) Jr. Coll., 1946-47; tchg. fellow Harvard Coll., Cambridge, 1948-50; instr. Ripon (Wis.) Coll., 1950-55, from asst. to assoc. prof., 1955-62, prof., 1962-83, prof. emeritus, 1983—. Author: La novela de Federico Gamboa, 1967, 71. Mem. Venice Power Squadron. Lt. USNR, 1942-45, ETO, PTO. Ctrl. Am. fellow Associated Colls. Midwest, 1962. Mem. MLA, St. Andrew Soc. Sarasota, Soc. Mayflower Descendants, Rotary (pres. 1978), Dartmouth Club Sarasota. Episcopal. Avocations: tennis, sailing. Home: 416 Maggiore Rd Venice FL 34285

HOOKER, JAMES TODD, manufacturing executive; b. Ashland, Ohio, Dec. 21, 1946; s. Melvin Todd and Harriett (Lutz) H.; m. Sallie Foulkrod Utz, Feb. 22, 1975; 1 child, Stephanie Rae. BSBA magna cum laude, Ashland U., 1973. From advt. mgr. to v.p. gen. mgr. The Gorman-Rupp Co., Mansfield, Ohio, 1974—2003, v.p. gen. mgr. Bellville, Ohio, 2003—. Solicitor United Way, Mansfield; moderator, bd. deacons Presbyn. Ch., 1988-89, elder, mem. Session; chmn. bd. Trustees Richland County Leadership Unltd.; mem. Heritage Found.; plank owner USN Meml. Found.; chmn. bd. Mansfield Richland County Chamber Edn. Found. Decorated Vietnamese Gallantry Cross; named Ohio State Water Ski Champion, 2002. Mem. Omicron Delta Epsilon. Republican. Home: 1090 Trout Dr Mansfield OH 44903-9144 Office: Gorman-Rupp Industries 180 Hines Ave Bellville OH 44813

HOOKER, JOSEPH DAVID, writer, minister; b. Westover Air Force Base, Mass., May 28, 1955; s. Joseph David and Alice Jane Hooker; m. Connie Ann Richmond, Apr. 4, 1973; children: Montana Crago, Heidi Marie Maurer, Josie Ann, Casandra Jo. DD(hon.), Ministry of Salvation. Ordained min. Gen. Assn. Regular Baptists, 1980. Self employed freelance writer, 1979—; youth min. Garrett (Ind.) 1st Bapt. Ch., 1996—. Supr. youth ministry Garrett 1st Bapt. Ch.,

1996—. Contbr. articles to mags. Republican. Baptist. Avocations: fishing, hunting, canoeing, horses, reading. Home: 3673 Cr 1 Kendallville IN 46755 Office: Hooker's Farms 3673 Cr 1 Kendallville IN 46755 Personal E-mail: jdhooker@zwallet.com.

HOOKER, OLIVIA J. psychologist, educator; b. Muskogee, Okla., Feb. 12, 1915; d. Samuel David and Anita Juliette (Stigger) H. BS, Ohio State U., 1937; MA, Columbia U., 1947; PhD, U. Rochester, N.Y., 1962. Cert. sch. psychologist, N.Y. Elem. tchr. Columbus (Ohio) Pub. Schs., 1937-45; clin. psychologist dept. mental hygiene State of N.Y., Albion, 1948-51, Bedford Hills, 1951-57, Rochester, 1955-57, research psychologist dept. mental hygiene Letchworth Village, 1957-61; sch. psychologist Bur. Child Guidance, N.Y.C., 1951-52; psychologist Kennedy Child Studies Ctr., N.Y.C., 1961-64, dir. psychol. svcs., 1964-83; assoc. prof. Fordham U., Bronx, N.Y., 1974-85. Cons. St. Benedicts's Day Care Ctr., N.Y.C., 1976—, Fred S. Keller Sch., Yonkers, N.Y., 1987-99. Trustee Terence Cardinal Cooke Health Svcs. Coun., N.Y.C., 1984-96; mem. adv. bd. Child Life program Westchester County Med. Ctr., Valhalla, N.Y., 1985-99, v.p. White Plains NAACP, 1985-87, White Plains Sr. Pers. Employment Coun., 1987-96; tutor Literacy Vols. Am., 1987 ; bd. dirs. White Plains Child Day Care Assn., 1988-2000, Vis. Nurse Assn. Westchester, 1988-94; chmn. adminstrv. bd. Trinity United Meth. Ch., 1985-87. Served with women's res. USCG, 1945-46. U. Rochester fellow, 1955-56; recipient Women's award Women's History Assn., 1986. Fellow APA (div. on devel. disability), Am. Assn. Mental Retardation. Avocations: creative writing, gardening, music. Office: Fordham U Dept Psychology Bronx NY 10458

HOOKER, RENÉE MICHELLE, perinatal and perianesthesia nurse; b. Kansas City, Mo., June 26, 1965; d. Roland Edward and Loretta Mae (Rathbun) Woods; m. Joel Thomas Hooker, Sept. 17, 1988; children: Andrew, Catherine, Rebekah. BSN, U. Kans., 1987. RN, Tex., Calif.; cert post anesthesia nurse, inpatient obstetric nurse ANCC; cert. ACLS, neonatal resuscitation; cert. BLS instr. Am. Heart Assn. Staff med.-surg. nurse Desert Hosp., Palm Springs, Calif., 1987-88; staff nurse neonatal ICU Santa Rose Children's Hosp., San Antonio, 1988; staff obstetrics nurse, post anesthesia care unit McKenna Meml. Hosp., New Braunfels, Tex., 1988-00, pre-post anesthesia care nurse mgr., 1999; staff nurse St. Joseph Health Ctr. Pain Clinic, Kansas City, Mo., 2001—; clin. nurse educator surg. svcs. Liberty (Mo.) Hosp., 2001—. Mem. Assn. Women's Health, Obstet. and Neonatal Nursing, Tex. Assn. Post Anesthesia Nurses, Am. Soc. Post Anesthesia Nurses. Avocations: reading, cooking, travel, child advocacy.

HOOKER, ROBERT WRIGHT, journalist; b. New Haven, July 11, 1947; s. Charles Wright and Elma (Black) H.; m. Ellen Ann McMackin, Apr. 13, 1974; 1 child, Matthew Wright. BA in History, Davidson (N.C.) Coll., 1969; MA in History, Vanderbilt U., 1971. Reporter St. Petersburg (Fla.) Times, 1971-78, polit. editor, 1978, night city editor, 1979, projects editor, 1979-87, Tampa city editor, 1987, state editor, 1987-90, bus. editor, 1990-96, metropolitan editor, 1996, asst. mng. editor, 1997-2001, dep. mng. editor, 2001—. Bd. dirs. Trend Mag., Inc., St. Petersburg, 1991-97. Author: The Times and Its Times: 1884-1984, 1984. 1st lt. USAR, 1971. Recipient Nat. Edn. Reporting award, Edn. Writers of Am., 1983, Best Investigative Reporting award, Am. Sports Editors Assn., 1983. Home: 2982 60th Ave S Saint Petersburg FL 33712-4524 Office: St Petersburg Times PO Box 1121 Saint Petersburg FL 33731-1121 E-mail: hooker@sptimes.com.

HOOKER, WADE STUART, JR., lawyer; b. Brockton, Mass., Sept. 23, 1941; s. Wade S. and Eleanor T. Hooker; m. Susan M. Levine, May 20, 1984; children: Thomas A., Richard P. BA, Harvard Coll., 1963; LLB, U. Va., 1966. Bar: N.Y. 1969. Assoc. Casey, Lane & Mittendorf, N.Y.C., 1968-77; ptnr. Burlingham Underwood LLP, N.Y.C., 1979—2001; ind. practice, 2002—. Spkr. in field. Contbr. articles to profl. jours. Maxwell fellow Syracuse U., Resident scholar Indian Law Inst., New Delhi, 1966-67. Mem. ABA, Assn. Bar City of N.Y. (chair aeronautics com.), Computer Law Assn., Inc., Internat. Bar Assn., Maritime Law Assn. U.S. (chair com. maritime regulation and promotion 1990-94), Mensa. Office: 211 Central Park W New York NY 10024 E-mail: wadehooker@post.harvard.com.

HOOKS, AUBREY, ambassador; b. Mullins, SC; married; 6 children. AA, Brevard Coll., 1968; BA, U. SC, 1970; MA in econ., U. Mich., 1984. Amb. Dem. Rep. of Congo US Dept. State, Kinshasa, Democratic Republic of Congo, 2001—; sr. sem. 38th class US Govt.; joined Fgn. Svc., 1971; jr. off. trainee Embassy, Tel Aviv, 1971—73, consular officer Warsaw; cultural affairs off. Dept. of State, 1976—78; econ. off. Ankara, Turkey, 1979—83; dir. econ. sec. Embassy Port-au-Prince, Haiti. Office: Embassy USA 310 Ave des Aviateurs B P 697 Kinshasa Democratic Republic of Congo*

HOOLEY, DARLENE, congresswoman; b. Williston, N.D., Apr. 4, 1939; d. Clarence Alvin and Alyce (Rogers) Olsen; m. John Hooley (div.); children: Chad, Erin. BS in Edn., Oreg. State U., 1961, postgrad., 1963-65, Portland State U., 1966-67. Tchr. Woodburn (Oreg.) & Gervais Sch., 1962-65, David Douglas Sch. Dist., Portland, Oreg., 1965-67, St. Mary's Acad., Portland, 1967-69; mem. West Linn (Oreg.) City Coun., 1976-80; state rep. Oreg. State Ho. of Reps., 1980-87; county commr. Clackamas County (Oreg.) Bd., 1987-96; mem. U.S. Congress from 5th dist. Oreg., 1996—; mem. budget com., fin. svcs. com. Vice-chair Oreg. Tourism Alliance, Portland, 1991—. bd. dirs. Pub. Employees Ret. Bd., Portland, 1989—, Cmty. Corrections Bd., Oregon City, 1990—, Providence Med. Ctr., Portland, 1989—; acting chair Oreg. Trail Found. Bd., Oregon City, 1991—; mem. Urban Growth Policy Adv. Com., Portland, 1991—. Named Legislator of the Year Oreg. Libr. Assn., 1985-86, Oreg. Solar Energy Assn., 1985; recipient Spl. Svc. award Clackamas City Coun. for Child Abuse Prevention, 1989. Mem. LWV, Oreg. Women's Polit. Caucus (Women of the Yr. 1988). Democrat. Office: 2430 Rayburn Bldg Washington DC 20515-3705*

HOON, PEGGY ELLEN, lawyer, librarian; b. Charleston, S.C., Aug. 8, 1955; d. Paul William and Betty Leone Amodt; m. Robert Ross Hoon, Aug. 15, 1988; children: Jessica Jo, Paul Christopher. JD, U. of Wash., 1986; BSN, U. of Colo., 1979. Licensed: Wash. 1986. RN Rose Meml. Hosp., Denver, 1979—80, Swedish Hosp., Seattle, 1980—83; assoc. atty. Reed McClure, Seattle, 1986—89, Rosenow, Hale, and Johnson, Seattle, 1989—92; copyright specialist Wash. State U., Pullman, 1995—97; scholarly communication libr. N.C. State U., Raleigh, 1998—. Editor: (book) Guidelines for Educational Use of Copyrighted Material. Chair, govtl. rels. com. N.C. Libr. Assn., Raleigh, 2000—03. Recipient Office of the Provost Quar. Recognition award, N.C. State U., 2001, 2002 Mover and Shaker award, ACRL Libr. Jour., 2002. Mem.: ALA, N.C. Libr. Assn., Wash. State Bar Assn. Office: NC State Univ 2205 Hillsborough St Raleigh NC 27695 Office Fax: 919-513-3553. Personal E-mail: peggy_hoon@ncsu.edu. E-mail: peggy_hoon@ncsu.edu.

HOOPER, ANNE DODGE, pathologist, educator; b. Groton, Mass., July 16, 1926; d. Carroll William and Bertha Sanford (Wiener) Dodge; m. William Dale Hooper, June 17, 1952; children: Elizabeth Anne, Joan Elaine, Caroline Mac. AB, Washington U., St. Louis, 1947, MD, 1952. Diplomate in pathologic anatomy, clin. pathology and forensic pathology Am. Bd. Pathology. Rotating intern Virginia Mason Hosp., Seattle, 1952-53; resident in internal medicine St. Francis Hosp., Hartford, Conn., 1953-54; resident in pathologic anatomy and clin. pathology New Britain (Conn.) Gen. Hosp., 1954-57, Presbyn. Hosp., Phila., 1957-58; resident in forensic pathology Office Med. Examiner, Phila., 1958-60; from pathologist to acting chief lab svc. VA Hosp., Coatesville, Pa., 1960-66; dir. lab. St. Albans (Vt.) Hosp., 1966-69, Kerbs Hosp., St. Albans, 1966-71, Williamson Appalachian Regional Hosp., South Williamson, Ky., 1971-73, Beckley (W.Va.) Appalachian Regional Hosp., 1974-76; asst. prof. pathology W.Va. Sch. Osteo. Medicine, Lewisburg, 1977, assoc. prof. pathology, 1978-97, cons. in pathology, 1997—. Lab. accreditation insp. CAP, 1992—. Am. Osteo. Assn., 1986—99; assoc. med. examiner State of W.Va., 1999—; med. missionary Kijabe Hosp., Kenya, 1998; med. missionary, pathologist Pathologists Overseas at SALFA Lab., Madagascar, 2000; med. missionary with Glens Falls NY Med. Missionary Found., Nueva Santa Rosa, Guatemala, 2001. Contbr. articles to profl. jours. Pres. local elem. sch. PTA, St. Albans, 1967-68; pres. Greenbrier unit Am. Cancer Soc., Lewisburg, 1989-93, bd. dirs. W.Va. div., Charleston, 1987-94, profl. edn. com. W.Va. div., 1982-94; bd. dirs. ARC, Greenbrier County, W.Va., 2002—. Fellow Coll. Am. Pathologists, Am. Acad. Forensic Scis.; mem. AMA, W.Va. Med. Soc., Raleigh County Med. Soc., Am. Soc. Clin. Pathologists, Internat. Acad. Pathologists, Nat. Assn. Med. Examiners, Am. Osteo. Coll. Pathologists (assoc.). Avocation: playing violin and viola. Office: 63 Cedar Knoll Ronceverte WV 24970-9700

HOOPER, DAWN M. accountant; b. Jackson, Miss., May 8, 1972; d. Robert Wayne Moseley and Judy Elizabeth Reed; m. John Edward Hooper, Jr., June 6, 1998; 1 child, Hope Lauren. AA, Hinds C.C., Raymond, Miss., 1992; B Profl. Accountancy, Miss. State U., 1994, M Profl. Accountancy, 1995. Staff auditor DCH Healthcare Authority, Tuscaloosa, Ala., 1995-97, Blue Cross Blue Shield of Miss., Jackson, 1997-98; in-charge acct. Blue Cross Blue Shield of Ala., Birmingham, 1998—. Active in fundraising events. Named Young Careerist of Yr., Tuscaloosa Bus. and Profl. Women's Club, 1996. Mem.: Leadership Devel. Assn., Inst. Mgmt. Accts. Avocations: shopping, walking, bowling, scrapbooking, cross stitch. Home: 121 Greenfield Cir Alabaster AL 35007-3713 Office: Blue Cross Blue Shield Ala 450 Riverchase Pkwy E Birmingham AL 35244-2858

HOOPER, EDWIN BICKFORD, physicist; b. Bremerton, Wash., June 18, 1937; s. E.B. and Elizabeth (Patrick) H.; m. Virginia Hooper, Dec. 28, 1963; children: Edwin, Sarah, William. SB, MIT, 1959, PhD, 1965. Asst. prof. applied sci. Yale U., New Haven, 1966-70; physicist, dep. program leader FE Lawrence Livermore (Calif.) Nat. Lab., 1970—. Adv. com. Fusion Energy Bruning Plasmic Program, 2003—. Contbr. articles to profl. jours. Pres. Danville (Calif.) Assn., 1982-84; pres. Friends Iron Horse Trail, 1984-86; v.p. San Ramon Valley Edn. Found., 1989-90; dir. Leadership, San Ramon Valley, 1990-92; mem. adv. com. East Bay Regional Pk., 2002—. Fellow Am. Phys. Soc. (bd. dirs. div. Plasma Physics 1990-91); mem. AIAA (sr.), AAAS. Office: Lawrence Livermore Nat Lab L-637 Livermore CA 94550-4436

HOOPER, GERRY DON, retired information systems specialist, consultant; b. Durant, Okla., Aug. 11, 1941; s. Carrell and Edith Pauline (Hancock) H.; m. Patricia Ann Reynolds, July 9, 1960; children: Lisa Dawn, Lauri Anne. BS, postgrad., Southeastern Okla. State U., 1963. Cert. tchr. Tex. Tchr. Amarillo (Tex.) Ind. Sch. Dist., 1963-66; systems analyst VA, Austin, Tex., 1966-68, Svc. Bur. Corp., Dallas, 1968; systems rep. IBM, Dallas, 1968-80, adv. industry specialist, 1980-85, sr. mgmt. cons. Atlanta, 1985-99; ret., 1999. Mem. Am. Prodn. and Inventory Control Soc. Baptist. Avocations: skiing, travel, camping, restoring cars.

HOOPER, HENRY OLCOTT, retired academic administrator, physicist; b. Washington, Mar. 9, 1935; s. Olcott Lorin and Eleanor (Drew) H.; m. Donna Faulkingham, June 10, 1956 (div. 1992); children: Deborah, Bruce, Katherine, Michael, Andrew; m. Jeanne Riley Hughes, Mar. 2, 1996. BS in Engring. Physics, U. Maine, 1956; MS in Physics, Brown U., 1959, PhD, 1961. Asst. prof. Brown U., Providence, 1961-64; asst. prof. physics Wayne State U., Detroit, 1964-66, assoc. prof., 1966-70, prof., 1970-73; prof., chmn. dept. physics U. Maine, Orono, 1973-76, dean Grad. Sch., 1977-80, v.p. acad. affairs, 1979-80; assoc. v.p. acad. affairs, dean Grad. Coll. No. Ariz. U., Flagstaff, 1981-97, interim v.p. acad. affairs, 1993-95, assoc. provost rsch. and grad. studies, 1995-96, prof. physics, dir. Bilby Rsch. Ctr., 1997-2000; dir. sci. and math. Learning Ctr., 1998-2000; ret., 2000; pres. John and Sophie Ottens Found., 2001—. Cons. NASA, Huntsville, Ala., 1967-68; mem. rev. panel div. ednl. programs Argonne (Ill.) Nat. Lab., 1982-84; mem. exec. bd. Assoc. Western Univs., 1991-97, chair 1995-96; v.p. Nat. Coun. Univ. Rsch. Adminstrs., 1991-92, pres., 1992-93. Author: College Physical Science, 3d edit., 1974, Physics and the Physical Perspective, 1977, 2d rev. edit., 1980; editor: Conf. Procs. Amorphous Magnetism, 1973. Fellow Am. Phys. Soc.; mem. AAAS, Am. Assn. Physics Tchrs. E-mail: hoh@independence.net.

HOOPER, IAN (JOHN DEREK GLASS), marketing communications executive; b. London, Sept. 8, 1941; came to U.S., 1979; s. John Desmond Glass and Moira Elizabeth (White) H. Student, Coll. Distributive Trades, London, 1960-62, 65-67, Harvard U., 1979. With S. H. Benson, London, 1960-62, 65-67, Nairobi, Kenya, 1962-64; with McCann-Erickson Advt., London, 1967-79; sr. v.p., group account dir. McCann-Erickson, N.Y.C., 1979-85; exec. v.p., mng. dir. McCann Direct, N.Y.C., 1985-90; sr. v.p., worldwide account dir. Young & Rubicam, N.Y.C., 1990-91; sr. v.p., account dir. Brouillard Communications, N.Y.C., 1991-94; sr. v.p., mktg. dir. DeVries Pub. Rels., N.Y.C., 1994-2000, COO, 2000—. Home: 1049 Park Ave New York NY 10028-1061 Office: DeVries Pub Rels 30 E 60th St New York NY 10022-1008 E-mail: ihooper@devries-pr.com.

HOOPER, JAMES WILLIAM, educator; b. Tuscumbia, Ala., June 13, 1937; s. John Albert and Stella (Tompkins) H.; m. Mona Elaine Nading, Dec. 27, 1959; children: Bruce, Stacey, Blaine. BS in Math., Florence (Ala.) State Coll., 1959; MS in Math., Auburn (Ala.) U., 1960; MS in Computer Sci., U. Mo., Rolla, 1971; PhD in Computer Info. Sci., U. Ala., Birmingham, 1979. Instr. math. Florence State Coll., 1960—62; data systems analyst NASA Marshall Space Flight Ctr., Huntsville, Ala., 1962—74, data systems engr., 1974—80; assoc. prof. computer sci. U. Ala., Huntsville, 1980—88, prof. computer sci., 1988—93; dir. Ctr. for Environ., Geotech. and Applied Scis. Marshall U., Huntington, W.Va., 1993—, prof., Arthur and Joan Meyer Weisberg Chair software engring, 1991—, exec. dir. Office Rsch. and Econ. Devel., 1996—98, v.p. rsch., 1998—2001, dean Coll. Info. Tech. and Engring., 1998—2002. Mem., bd. dirs. Marshall U. Rsch. Corp., 1993-, pres., 1996-2001; cons. computer sci. and software engring.; reviewer jours. and funding agys. Author: (with Rowena O. Chester) Software Reuse: Guidelines and Methods, 1991. Elder Jordan Park Ch. of Christ, Huntsville, 1984-93, 26th St. Ch. of Christ, Huntington, 1994—; bd. dirs. Ann. Nat. Conf. on Software Tech., pres., 1993-94; commr. Fire Civil Svc. Commn., City of Huntington, W.Va., 2000—. Recipient Exceptional Svc. medal NASA, 1977; grantee U.S. govt. agys. and several cos., 1983—. Mem. IEEE (Outstanding Educator of Yr., Huntsville sect. 1986-87), IEEE Computer Soc. (pres. Huntsville chpt. 1987-88), Assn. Computing Machinery, Soc. Am. Mil. Engrs., Internat. Assn. Mgmt. Tech., Phi Kappa Phi, Kappa Mu Epsilon, Upsilon Pi Epsilon. Mem. Ch. of Christ. Home: 148 Honeysuckle Ln Huntington WV 25701-4726 Office: Marshall U Huntington WV 25755

HOOPER, JOHN ALLEN, retired banker; b. Danbury, Conn., Dec. 9, 1922; s. Kenneth Malcolm and Grace Lillian (Jardon) H.; m. Susanne Leona Sipperly, Nov. 27, 1948; children: Judith Elaine, John Nash. BBA, U. Mich., 1947, MBA, 1948. With Chase Manhattan Bank, N.Y.C., 1948-85, exec. v.p., 1972-83, sr. v.p., 1964-71, mem. mgmt. com., 1975-85, vice-chmn. bd., 1983-85; chmn. bd., chief exec. officer Bank of the Commonwealth, Detroit, 1971-72. Served with AUS, 1943-46. Decorated Army Commendation medal; named Man of Year, Inst. Human Relations, 1974 Mem. Patterson Club, Wilderness Country Club, Royal Poinciana Golf Club. Home: 100 Tall Pine Ln # 2101 Naples FL 34105

HOOPER, JOHN DAVID, coast guard officer; b. Cleveland Heights, Ohio, Jan. 19, 1954; s. George John and Grace Isabelle (Maloney) H.; m. Patricia Ann Boucher, May 13, 1979; children: Katherine Ann, Robert John, Christopher John. AS in Math., Lorain C.C., 1975; BS in Marine Sci., Mass. Maritime Acad., 1979; MS in Nat. Security Affairs, U.S. Naval War Coll., 1994; MA in Mil. Studies, Am. Mil. U., 1999. Lic. deck watch officer afloat, 2d mate unlimited, USCG. Commd. ens. USCG, 1979, advanced through grades to comdr., 1995, marine safety officer, 1979-80; divsn., deck watch, boarding officer CGC Bibb, New Bedford, Mass., 1980-82; chief planning-marine info. sect. 7th Coast Guard Dist. (Aids to Navigation Br.), Miami, Fla., 1987-90; civilian staff officer fleet ops., deck-navigation inspector Military Sealift Command Atlantic USN, Bayonne, N.J., 1982-87; exec. officer USCG Res. Unit CGC Gallatin, Gov.'s Island, N.Y., 1983-87; exec. officer, commanding officer USCG Res. Unit CGC Dallas, Gov's Island, N.Y., 1990-95; damage control officer USN, Freehold, N.J., 1990-2000; Coast Guard Res. liaison, staff officer Coast Guard Atlantic Area-Cutter Mgmt., Portsmouth, Va., 1995-98; instr. CG liaison USN Tactical Tng. Group, Atlantic Dam Neck, Va., 1998-2000; commandant (G-OPD/QDR) USCG HQ, Office Def. Planning, Washington, 2000—02; CG liaison to joint staff J8 Joint Requirements Office for Chem., Bio., Radiol., Nuc. Def. (CBRN-D), 2002—. Recipient Inductee Naval Order of U.S., 1994. Mem. U.S. Naval Inst., Res. Officers Assn., Naval War Coll. Found., Mass. Maritime Acad. Alumni Assn. Republican. Roman Catholic. Avocations: sailing, tennis. Home: 25 Newbury Rd Howell NJ 07731-2109 Office: J8 Joint Requirements Office for CBRN Crystal Plaza #5 Ste 606 Washington DC 20318-8000

HOOPER, JOSH, screen actor, director, media producer, writer; b. Pa., 1952; s. Henry Lloyd and Mary Katherine H.; m. Cynthia Yeiser; children: Spencer, Mason. BA, Franklin & Marshall Coll., 1974. Tchr. Lower Dauphin Sch. Dist., Hummelstown, Pa., 1974-76, prodn. mgr. Sta. WLYH-TV, Lebanon, Pa., 1976-79; producer PM Mag. Sta. WTVH-TV, Syracuse, N.Y., 1979-80; co-host, producer PM Mag. Sta. WGAL-TV, Lancaster, Pa., 1980-83; pres. Josh Hooper Prodns., Inc., Harrisburg, Pa., 1983-94; actor-dir., pres. A Different Look, L.A., 1983-92; broadcast advt. dir. The Bon Ton, York, Pa., 1992-94; pres., creative dir. Zero Gravity Films, Harrisburg, Pa., 1994—; v.p. creative direction Panoramic Visions, 2000—02. Theater dir., N.Y., Pa., Calif., 1974—; co-host Sta. WITF Auction, Hershey, Pa., 1982, 83, Easter Seals Telethon, Harrisburg, 1983, Children's Miracle Network, Lancaster, 1983; directing fellow Am. Film Inst., L.A., 1988-89; improv comedian L.A. Connection, 1989, Public Nuisance, L.A., 1989-92. Producer, dir. (TV program) Suite 10.15, 1977; exec. producer (TV kids mag.) Thresholds, 1978; actor (play) Waiting for Godot, 1985, The Winter's Tale, 1986 (film) Station to Freedom, 1987, (TV film) Lucy and Desi: Before The Laughter, 1991; dir. (short film) Collared, 1988, The Point, 1989, Bumper to Bumper, 1989. Mem. Common Cause, Washington, 1980-90; chmn. comms. Three Mile Island Pub. Interest Resource Group, Harrisburg, 1982-84; comm. chair Fox Ridge Neighbors, 1985-87; active Ctr. for Def. Info.; charter mem. Franklin and Marshall Coll. Pres.'s Farwest Adv. Coun.; bd. dirs. Children's Playroom Parent Edn. Ctrs.; mem. Envision Capital Region Task Force. Recipient Addy award Am. Advt. Fedn., 1987, Addy award Cen. Pa. Advt. Fedn., 1985, 87, 88, Telly award, 1987, 88, 89, 99, Gold award Creativity '96; Film Grants Panelist NEH, 1990, Vision award, Mobius award, 1997. Mem. Am. Film Inst. Alumni Assn. (past pres.), SAG, Ctrl. Pa. Ad Club (bd. dirs. 1994, 95), Capital Area Assn. for the Edn. Young Children, Success by Six. Democrat. Episcopalian. Avocations: running, swimming, bicycling, boating.

HOOPER, MICHAEL WAYNE, music educator, director; b. Nashville, July 13, 1975; s. Charles Harper and Shirley Ann Hooper. MusB, Pa. State U., 1997; MusM, Johns Hopkins U., 1999. Dir. of music St. Luke's Ch., Falls Ch., Va., 1997—98, Ch. of the Good Shepherd, Perryville, Md., 1998—2000, Prince of Peace Ch., Gaithersburg, Md., 2001—02; music ops. dir. St. Mary's Coll. of Md., St. Mary's City, Md., 2001—; dir. of music Wesley United Meth. Ch., Washington, 2003—. Chair of music com. Ch. of the Good Shepherd, Perryville, 1998—2000. Musician: Annapolis Symphony Orch., River Concert Series Orch., Washington Symphony Orch., Columbia Symphony Orch., Peabody Symphony Orch. Scholar Music scholarship, Pa. State U., 1993—97, Brevard Music Ctr., 1996. Mem.: Johns Hopkins U. Alumni Assn. (assoc.), Percussive Arts Soc. (assoc.), Pa. State U. Alumni Assn. (life), Phi Mu Alpha (life; warden 1995—97). Avocations: freelance performing, bowling, dancing. Office: St Marys College of Maryland 18952 E Fisher Rd Saint Marys City MD 20686-3001 Office Fax: 240-895-4958. E-mail: mwhooper@smcm.edu.

HOOPER, PERRY OLLIE, retired state supreme court judge; b. Birmingham, Ala., Apr. 8, 1925; s. Ernest J. and Mary Lou (Perry) H.; m. Marilyn Yost, May 16, 1953; children: Perry O. Jr., Walter, Conwell, John. BS, U. Ala., 1950, LLB, 1953. Bar: Ala. 1953, U.S. Dist. Ct. (so. dist.) Ala. 1953. Pvt. practice, Montgomery, Ala., 1953-64, 83—; probate judge Montgomery County, Montgomery, 1964-76; cir. ct. judge State of Ala., Montgomery, 1975-83, presiding cir. judge, 1978-83; chief justice Supreme Ct. of Ala., Montgomery, Ala., 1995—2000; retired chief justice Ala. Supreme Ct., Ala., 2001. Mem. Nat. Republican Com., 1972-96. Methodist. Avocations: golf, gardening. Home: 3191 Thomas Ave Montgomery AL 36106-2425 Office: State Supreme Ct 300 Dexter Ave Montgomery AL 36104-3741

HOOPER, ROBERT ALEXANDER, television producer, international educator; b. Annapolis, Md., Apr. 13, 1947; s. P. Alexander and Louise (Hickey) H.; m. Virginia L. Gordon; 1 child, Julie Alexandra. BA in Econs., U. Calif., San Diego, 1969; JD, U. Calif., Davis, 1974; MFA in Motion Picture and TV, UCLA, 1982. Bar: Calif. 1975. Film prodr. Scripps Inst. of Oceanography, La Jolla, Calif., 1978-79, EPA, Washington, 1979-81; ind. film prodr. with ABC-TV and CBC, Del Mar, Calif., 1981-84; tv prodr. Sta. KUAC-TV, Fairbanks, Alaska, 1984-86; asst. prof. comm. Boston U., 1986-87; assoc. prof. comm. Loyola Marymount U., L.A., 1987-98; exec. prodr. KPBS-TV, San Diego, 1997—2001; assoc. prof. Calif. State U., 2000—. Vis. assoc. prof. U. Calif., San Diego, 1993, 96, UCLA, 2000; cons. CBC, Toronto, 1982-83, Radio-TV Malaysia, 1998, Fiji TV, 1996; cons. Asia-Pacific Inst. for Broadcasting Devel., 1998-99, course dir., 1998—; Fulbright sr. scholar comm. program U. Sains Malaysia, Penang, 1989-90, U. South Pacific, Fiji, 1994, U. Indonesia, 2001; tng. adviser Am. Samoa Govt.-Sta. KVZK-TV, 1992—; acad. specialist U. Papua New Guinea, 1995; Eisenhower fellow, Malaysia, 1996; Fulbright sr. scholar U. Indonesia, Jakarta, 2001; Fulbright sr. specialist, Malaysia, 2002-03; spkr. in field. Prodr., dir. (documentaries) Voices From Love Canal, 1978, Decisions at 1000 Fathoms, 1981, Battle at Webber Creek, 1985 (Press Club award), Alaska's Killer Whales, 1989 (Cine Golden Eagle and Silver Apple award); segment prodr. (ABC 20/20) The Deep, 1983; exec. prodr. Nature's Classic, 1998 (Press Club award, four Emmy nominations), Afoot and Afield, 1998, The Impossible Railroad, 1999 (Press Club award, Telly award, Emmy award); op.-editor writer, L.A. Times, San Diego Union-Tribune, 1999. Recipient Hennessy trophy, Internat. Environ. Film Festival, France, 1983. Mem. NATAS, Calif. Bar Assn., Eisenhower Fellows Assn., Fulbright Sr. Specialists Roster, Sigma Delta Chi. Democrat. Avocations: underwater photography, equestrian endurance riding. E-mail: rahooper@hotmail.com.

HOOPER, ROGER FELLOWES, retired architect; b. Southampton, N.Y., Aug. 18, 1917; s. Roger Fellowes and Justine Van Rensselaer (Barber) H.; m. Patricia Bentley, Aug. 10, 1946; children: Judith Bayard Teresi, Rachel Bentley Zingg, Roger Fellowes III. AB, Harvard U., 1939, MArch, 1948. Ptnr. Malone & Hooper, San Francisco, 1949-60; ptnr., pres. Hooper Olmsted & Emmons, San Francisco, 1964-79; chmn. Hooper Olmsted & Hrovat, San Francisco, 1980-94, retired, 1994. Bd. mgr. Marin YMCA, San Rafael, Calif.; bd. dirs., pres. Marin Conservation League, San Rafael. Lt. comdr. USNR, 1941-45, WWII. Mem. AIA.

HOOPER, ROY B. lobbyist, consultant; b. Lawton, Okla., Mar. 19, 1947; s. Roy Basil and Frances (Castle) H.; m. Lawanna Sue James, Aug. 2, 1969; children: Blake, Mark. BS, Cameron U., 1971. Registered lobbyist 1995-. Real estate broker, Lawton, 1968-90; rep. State of Okla., Lawton, 1974-86, senator, 1986-94; ins. broker Lawton, 1966—; dir. managed care Southwestern Med. Ctr., Lawton, 1994-99, HealthBack, Oklahoma City, 1999-2000; adminstr. Okla. State and Edn. Employees Group Ins. Program, 2000—01. Pres. Cameron Former Students Assn., Lawton, 1974, Lawton Crimestoppers Orgn., 1996, S.W. chpt. Am. Heart Assn., 1995-96, Lawton Pub. Sch. Found., 1998; v.p. Lawton Bd. Realtors, 1974, KTRO, Lawton Pub. Schs. Found., Pres.'s Ptnrs. Cameron U., Lawton Crimestoppers/Drugbusters; councilman Ward 2, Lawton, 1972-74. Sgt. USAR, 1968-74. Democrat. Baptist. Avocations: hunting, fishing, golf, horse back riding, gardening. Office: Hooper Cons 1114 Laird Lawton OK 73507

HOOPER, WAYNE NELSON, clergy member; b. Toronto, Ont., Can., May 25, 1944; s. Earl Edward and Ruby Evelyn (Nelson) H.; m. Diane Elizabeth, Aug. 24, 1968; children: Tanya Joy, Craig Nelson. BA, McMaster U., 1967; MDiv, Gordon-Conwell Theol. Sem., 1970. Ordained to ministry Baptist Ch., 1970. Asst. pastor Emmanuel Bapt. Ch., Cambridge, Mass., 1967-68, First Bapt. Ch., Braintree, Mass., 1968-70; pastor Uxbridge (Ont.) Bapt. Ch., Can., 1970-73; founding pastor Credit Valley Bapt. Ch., Mississauga, Ont., Can., 1973-79; sr. pastor First Bapt. Ch., Orillia, Ont., Can., 1979-83, Avenue Rd. Bapt. Ch., Cambridge, Ont., Can., 1986-98; asst. sec. dept. Can. Missions Bapt. Conv. Ont. and Que., 1983-86; sr. pastor First Baptist Ch., Dartmouth, Canada, 1998—2003, Westview Bapt. Ch., London, Canada, 2003—. Contbr. articles to profl. jours. Mem. recruitment com. Bapt. Conv. Ont. and Que., 1973-75, mem. planning com., 1978-80, mem. coun., 1976-82, mem. exec. com., 1977-78; conv. staff rep. Ottawa and N.W. Assns., 1983-86; Bapt. Conv. Ont. and Que. rep. to Inter-Church Regional Planning Assn., 1983-86; mem. Canadian Baptist Ministries Coun., 1995-98. Mem. Can. Bapt. Fedn. (v.p. 1988-91, pres. 1991-94). Baptist. Avocations: sports, boating, stamp collecting, tennis, golf. Home: 67 Parks Edge Crescent London ON Canada N6K 3P5

HOOPER, WILLIAM DALE, surgeon; b. Pullman, Wash., Jan. 28, 1927; MD, Washington U., St. Louis, 1952. Cert. in surgery. Intern Virginia Mason Hosp., Seattle, 1952-53; resident in surgery New Britain Gen. Hosp., 1953-57; chief surg. svcs. VA Med. Ctr., Beckley, W.Va., 1974-77, assoc. chief surg. svcs., 1977-97; ret., 1997. Fellow ACS, Am. Soc. Abdominal Surgeons; mem. AMA. Home: 104 Elmridge Ct Beckley WV 25801-2406

HOOPER, WILLIAM EDWARD, broadcast journalist; b. Tampa, Fla., Mar. 10, 1964; s. Dennis William and Doris Jean (Burkhart) H. Student, U. Tenn., 1984-87; degree cert., Profl. Acad. Broadcasting, Knoxville, Tenn., 1988. Traffic reporter K-Trans, Knoxville, 1987-93; news dir. Sta. WNOX-FM, Knoxville, 1988-90, Sta. WWZZ-FM, Knoxville, 1991-93; news reporter Sta. WKXT-TV, Knoxville, 1993-96; creator, editor Tenn. Online, 1996—; editor Tenn. Star Jour., Pigeon Forge, Tenn., 2002; news anchor WIVK, Knoxville, 2003—. Host, writer Radio Appalachia, Knoxville, 1987-92, Celebrate Knoxville, 1991, WKXT's Tenn. Bicentennial Moments, 1994-46; feature writer Foothills mag., Knoxville, 1993; host, prodr. Viewpoint Talkshow, 1994-96, freelance writing, 1998—. Author: Images of America: Knoxville, 2003; (broadcast reports) Public Access Denied: Tennessee Statute 40-23-116, Appalachian Minorities: Behind the Spinning Wheel; syndicated columnist Banjo Newsletter, 1981; author Looking Back Column, 1997—; guest columnist So. Partisan mag., Appalachian Quar. mag.; feature writer: Tennessee Outdoors mag.; freelance broadcast news reporter S.E. Radio and TV Co.; ednl. cons. Treas. Knoxville Juvenile Diabetes Assn., 1989; trustee Nat. Medal of Honor Mus. of Mil. History, Chattanooga, 1998—; project mgr. The South Found., 1997—; bd. dirs. Tenn. Civil War Preservation Assn., 1998-2000. Recipient Cert. of Appreciation, Knoxville Transit Co., 1993, Cert. of Merit, Tenn. Hist. Commn., So. Journalism award 1996, Tenn. Jefferson Davis Media award 1996, Cert. of Appreciation City of Knoxville, 1996, Robert E. Lee Media award Tenn. divsn. SCV, 1996, Merit award Tenn. Gov., 1996, Cmty. Svc. award Knox County Commn., 1996, Horace V. Wells Cmty. Svc. award East Tenn. Soc. Profl. Journalists, 1996, 1st place Investigative Reporting award, 2001, 1st place Feature Reporting award, 2001, 1st place series/package/project Reporting award, 2001, 2d place Sports Reporting award, 2001, Cert. of Merit, Tenn. Hist. Commn., 1996, 97, 98, 2000, Hist. Preservation award West Tenn. Sons Confederate Nat. Pk., 1997, SCV Comdr.'s award for hist. preservation, 1999, Golden Press Card Investigative Reporting, 1999, Golden Press Card Gen. News Reporting, 1999, Comdr.'s award SCV, 1999, Cert. of Merit, Tenn. Hist. Commn., 1999,, Cert. of Merit, 2001, Pub. Svc. in Journalism award Tenn. Press Assn., 1999, 2001, Cert. of Appreciation Vietnam War Meml. Assn., 1997, Pulitzer Prize nominee Columbia Sch. of Journalism, 1999, 2000, Edward Carmack Journalism award Tenn. Sons. Confed. Vets., 2000, Hist. Preservation award, 2000, Cert. of Appreciation, Native Am. Indian Movement, 2001, Pub. Svc. in Journalism award Tenn. Press Assn., 2001, medal for Disting. Pub. Svc., U.S. Dept. Def., 2001, Tenn. Conservative Union Fairness in Polit. Reporting award, 2001, East Tenn. Hist. Soc. History in Media award, 2001; named Bard Laureate Tenn. Gen. Assembly, 2002, Letter of Commendation, U.K. House of Lords, London, 2002, Cert. of Appreciation, U.T. ROTC, 2002, Gold Press Card award East Tenn. S.P.J., 2002, E. Tenn. SPJ First Pl. Investigative Reporting Award, 2003; E. Tenn. SPJ First Pl. Series/package/Project Writing, 2003; E. Tenn. SPJ First Pl. Feature Reporting Award, 2003; First Pl. Series/package Project Reporting award, 2002; Gen. News Reporting Award, 2002; Feature Reporting Award, 2002; Cert. of Merit, Tenn. Hist. Commn., 2002, Award of Excellence, US Army Accessions Command, 2002. Mem. Soc. Profl. Journalists (1st pl. award for radio feature reporting Atlanta chpt. 1990, Investigative Reporting award Atlanta chpt. 1994, TV-Feature Reporting award 1995, TV Deadline News award 1995, So. Journalist award 1996), East Tenn. Soc. Profl. Journalists (bd. dirs. 2003—, 1st place Investigative Reporting award 1999, 2000, 1st place Gen. News Reporting award 1999, 2000, 2d place Deadline Photography award 1999, Golden Press Card award, 1st place Feature Reporting award 2000, 2d place Series/Package Reporting award), Investigative Reporters and Editors, Masons (historian Knoxville 1990—, Meritorious cert. 1991, 92). Avocations: musician, horseback riding, whitewater caneoing, hunting, archaeology. Office: South Found Inc PO Box 7121 Knoxville TN 37921 E-mail: ed@teneseehistory.com.

HOOPER, WILLIAM LOYD, music educator, university administrator; b. Sedalia, Mo., Sept. 16, 1931; s. George Francis and Mary Evelyn (McNabb) H.; m. Doris Jean Wallace, Aug. 5, 1951; children: William Loyd Jr., Carol Ann. BA, William Jewell Coll., 1953; MA, U. Iowa, 1956; PhD, Vanderbilt U., 1966. Tchr. Essex (Iowa) Pub. Schs., 1953—55, Atalissa (Iowa) Pub. Schs., 1955—56; music prof. S.W. Bapt. Coll., Bolivar, Mo., 1956—60; prof., dean New Orleans Bapt. Sem., 1962—74; head dept. music Newstead Wood Sch. for Girls, London, 1974—79; chief examiner South-East Exams. Bd., Tunbridge Wells, England, 1976—80; dean fine arts S.W. Bapt. U., Bolivar, 1983—89, dir. rsch., planning and assessment, 1989—98; ret. Author: Church Music in Transition, 1963, Music Fundamentals, 1967, Ministry and Musicians, 1983, Fundamentals of Music, 1986; compositions: (cantata) Litany of Praise, (choral collection) Sing Joyfully, (cantata) Jubilee, (cantata) And He Shall Come, and over 60 anthems for church choir. Recipient citation for achievement William Jewell Coll., 1968, 1st place award Delius Composition Competition, 1973, New Times Composition Competition, 1974, Republican. Baptist. Home: 116 W Auburn St Bolivar MO 65613-2412

HOOPES, ROY HARRY, JR., writer; b. Salt Lake City, May 17, 1922; s. Roy Harry and Lydia Clawson Hoopes; m. Cora Barksdale Redd, Sept. 15, 1948; children: Spencer, Thomas, Sallie(dec.). AB in History, George Washington U., 1943, MA in Am. Diplomatic History, 1948. Publs. cons. Dept. Health, Edn. and Welfare, 1967—73; free-lance writer, 1974—85; dir. pub. affairs Washington Coll., Chestertown, Md., 1985—87; Washington bur. chief Modern Maturity mag., 1987—98. Author: The Steel Crisis -- 72 Hours That Shook the Nation, 1962, The Complete Peace Corps Guide, 1962, 1965, 1966, 1968, The Peace Corps Experience, 1968, What a Baseball Manager Does, 1970, What a Pro Football Coach Does, 1972, Cain, 1982, Ralph Ingersoll: A Biography, 1985, The Making of a Mormon Apostle: The Story of Rudger Clawson, 1990, Everything You Need to Know About Building The Custom Home, 1990, The Life and Hard Times of the Late Great Peter Potomac, 1994, When the Stars Went to War, 1995, (novels) Our Man in Washington, 2000, A Watergate Tape, 2002; contbr. numerous articles to mags. and newspapers. Mng. editor Dem. Digest Dem. Nat. Com., Washington, 1956—60. Lt. USNR, 1943—45, PTO. Recipient Edgar award, Mystery Writers Am., N.Y.C., 1983. Mem.: Nat. Press Club. Avocations: photography, Bridge.

HOOPES, TOWNSEND WALTER, retired management consultant, retired federal agency administrator; b. Duluth, Minn., Apr. 28, 1922; s. Henry Townsend and Edna Andrea (Morterud) Hoopes; m. Ann Merrifield, Oct. 17, 1964; 1 child, Andrea stepchildren: Marsha, Cecily, Briggs, Thomas;children from previous marriage: Townsend Walter III, Peter Schmidt. Grad., Phillips Acad., Andover, Mass., 1940; AB in Econs., Yale U., 1944. Editl. writer Buffalo Evening News, 1946; asst. to chmn. com. armed svcs. Ho. of Reps., Washington, 1947-48, asst. to sec. def., 1948-53; student Nat. War Coll., 1950-51; dep. asst. sec. def. internat. security affairs Dept. Def., Washington, 1965-66, prin. dep. asst. sec. def. internat. security affairs, 1966-67, undersec. air force, 1967-69; asst. to pres. Spencer Chem. Co., 1953-55; assoc. J.H. Whitney & Co., 1955-57; ptnr. Cresap, McCormick & Paget, 1958-64, v.p., dir. Washington office, 1969-71; also corporate dir., pres. Assn. Am. Publishers, Washington and N.Y.C., 1973-86; vice chmn. AIDS Therapy Inst., 1995—2001; ret., 2001. Cons. orgn. NSC, 1954, Dept. State, 1957, Dept. Def., 1957; sec. mil. panel spl. studies project Rockefeller Bros. Fund, 1957—58; cons. Pres.'s Com. USIA Abroad, 1960. Co-prodr.: (musical theatrical co.) Hoopes Troupe, 1985—97; author: (book) The Limits of Intervention, 1970, The Devil and John Foster Dulles, 1973, Townsend Hoopes on Arms Control, 1987; co-author: Eye Power, 1979, Driven Patriot: The Life and Times of James Forrestal, 1992, FDR and the Creation of the UN, 1997; contbr. articles to profl. jours. Bd. dirs. Com. Nat. Security, 1978—88, Am. Com. U.S.-Soviet Rels., Washington, 1980—92. With USMC, 1943—46. Named Disting. Internat. Exec., U. Md., 1991; sr. fellow, Woodrow Wilson Internat. Ctr. Scholars, 1971—73, Washington Coll. Mem.: Coun. Fgn. Rels., Fairfield Country Club (Conn.), Cosmos Club (Washington), Chevy Chase Club (Md.), Century Club (N.Y.C.), Yale Club (N.Y.C.).

HOOPIS, HARRY PETER, insurance executive, entrepreneur; b. Providence, May 14, 1947; s. Peter Harry and Angela Rose (Taraborelli) H.; m. Demetra Psilopoulos, Feb. 20, 1972; children: Krina Angela, Peter Harry. BS in Acctg., U. R.I., 1969. CLU; chartered fin. cons. Coll. agt. Northwestern Mut. Life Ins. Co., Kingston, R.I., 1968-69, spl. agt. Providence, 1969-71, dist. agt. Wakefield, R.I., 1971-74, asst. supt. manpower devel. Milw., 1974-77, gen. agt. Evanston, Ill., 1977—. Cons., speaker ins. industry, U.S. and Can., 1977—, Purdue Mgmt. Inst., Lafayette, Ind., 1987-88; pres. Gama Internat., 1996-97. Author: (with others) Sales Focus Workbook, 1985, Fixed Activity Commitment, 1980, Managing Sales Professionals, 1993, Essentials of Management Development, 1999. Named to GAMA Internat. Hall of Fame, 2003. Mem. Nat. Gen. Agts. and Mgrs. Assn. (pres. 1989-90, Yates Meml. award 1988, named Master Agy. Builder, 1983-97, sec., bd. dirs. 1989—), Am. Soc. CLUs, Chgo. Assn. CLUs (bd. dirs. 1978-81), Gama Internat. (pres. 1997). Republican. Avocations: skiing, golf. Office: Hoopis Fin Group 5215 Old Orchard Rd Ste 1200 Skokie IL 60077

HOOPLE, SALLY CROSBY, retired humanities and communications educator; b. Dansville, N.Y., Oct. 23, 1930; d. Thomas Joseph and Lucille Esther (Rex) Crosby; m. Donald G. Hoople, June 3, 1951; children: Nancy, Anne Ralte, Douglas, David. BA, Syracuse U., 1952, MA, 1953, NYU, 1971; PhD, Fordham U., 1984. Tchr. ESL, citizenship Adult Edn., Syracuse, N.Y., 1953-56, Oneida, N.Y., 1956-62; tchr. ESL Cambridge Bus. Sch., N.Y.C., 1962-63; tchr. English White Plains (N.Y.) H.S., 1963-86; prof. humanities and comms. Maine Maritime Acad., Castine, 1986-96; ret., 1996; fgn. expert tchg. history and composition Henan Normal U., Xinxiang, China, 1997-98, China Agrl. U., Beijing, 1999, 2001. Contbr. Dictionary of Literary Biography, 1994, Oxford Companion to Women's Writing in the U.S., 1994, Dictionary of Art, 1996, articles to profl. jours., newletters. Mem. Am. Lit. Soc., NCTE (chair com. pub. doublespeak 1996-99), Melville Soc., MLA, Phi Beta Kappa. Democrat. Episcopalian. Avocations: music, reading, hiking, boating, bicycling, swimming. Home: PO Box 184 Castine ME 04421-0184 E-mail: dgramho@aol.com.

HOOPS, ALAN R. health care company executive; b. 1947; Asst. administr. Long Beach Mem. Hosp., 1973-77; v.p. PacifiCare Health Sys. Inc., Cypress, Calif., 1977-85, sec., from 1982, sr. v.p., 1985-86, COO, exec. v.p., 1986-93, CEO, pres. 1993—2000; chmn. Benu, Inc., San Mateo, Calif., 2000—. Office: Benu Inc 2929 Campus Dr Ste 175 San Mateo CA 94403

HOOPS, WILLIAM JAMES, clergyman; b. Welch, Okla, June 10, 1957; s. Paul Raymond and Bertha Lue (Stillwell) H.; m. Susan Denise Towers, May 12, 1983; 1 child, Robert Paul. BA, Okla. Bapt. U., 1983; MDiv, Golden Gate Sem., 1987. Ordained to ministry So. Bapt. Ch., 1987. Ministerial intern 1st Bapt. Ch., Concord, Calif., 1984-87, pastor Marina, Calif., 1987-91; chaplain USAFR, Lowery AFB, Colo., 1975-76, Kirkland AFB, N.Mex., 1976-79, Tinker AFB, Okla., 1979-84, Mather AFB, Calif., 1984-93, Travis AFB, Calif., 1993-98, Mar. AFB, Calif., 1998-99, Willow Grove Air Res. Sn., 1999—; instnl. min. Fed. Bur. Prisons, Fed. Correctional Instn., Lompoc, Calif., 1991-99; instl. min. Intensive Confinement Ctr., Lompoc, 1996-99; instnl. min. Fed. Correctional Instn., Allenwood, Pa., 1999—. Prodr. (TV documentary) Insights, 1986-87. V.p. Pa. Racing Outreach, 2000—02; pres. Pa./South Jersey Campers on Mission; Bible tchr. First So. Bapt. Ch., Lompoc, 1991—99. Maj. USAFR. Mem.: Pa./South Jersey Campers on Mission (pres. 2001—), Calif. Campers on Mission (pres. 1995—98, v.p. 1998—99), Ctrl. Coast Ministrial Alliance (pres. 1988—89), Pacific Coast Bapt. Assn., Ctrl. Coast Bapt. Assn. (vice moderator 1987—88, dir. evangelism 1988—91), Calif. So. Bapt. Conv. (revival steering com. 1988—90), Res. Officers Assn., Air Force Assn., Lompoc Fed. Correctional Instn. Employees Club (sec. 1991—92). Avocation: recreational vehicle camping. E-mail: chalpain@jdweb.com., whoops@bop.gov.

HOORNBEEK, LYNDA RUTH COUCH, librarian, educator; b. Springfield, Ill., July 12, 1933; d. Willard Lee and Mabel Magdalene (Forberg) Couch; m. Louis Arthur Hoornbeek, Nov. 9, 1957; children— John Arthur, David William, Mark Benjamin. B.A. in Sociology, U. Ill., 1955; M.Ed., Cornell U., 1956; M.L.S., U. So. Calif., Los Angeles, 1973. Cert. tchr. Ill., N.Y. Tchr. elem. sch. North Haven (Conn.) Pub. Schs., 1956-57; library adminstr. Winfield (Ill.) Pub. Library, 1974-77; interim library adminstr. Bloomingdale (Ill.) Pub. Library, 1977-78; ref. librarian Franklin Park (Ill.) Pub. Library, 1978-83; state literacy dir. program Literacy Vols. of Ill., Chgo., 1983—84; research coordinator Ill. Literacy Council, Office of Sec. State, 1984—85; with office libr. outreach svcs. ALA, 1985-86; adult svcs. libr. Glen Ellyn (Ill.) Pub. Libr., 1986-94; ret., 1994. Bd. dirs. YWCA, Pitts., 1957—62; vol. archivist Glen Ellyn Hist. Soc., bd. dirs. 1994—. YWCA fellow 1954; Ford Found. fellow, 1955-56; U. Ill. scholar, 1951-55. Mem. Mortar Bd., Calif. Library Assn., Ill. Library Assn., ALA, AAUW, LWV, Beta Phi Mu, Pi Lambda Theta, Alpha Phi. Congregationalist. Home: 351 N Park Blvd Glen Ellyn IL 60137-5037

HOORNSTRA, EDWARD H. retail company executive; b. Sault Ste Marie, Mich., 1921; married. Pres. Pik-N-Pak Food Stores, 1952-65; pres. Li'l Gen. Stores, 1965-69; with Gen. Host Co., Stamford, Conn., 1968—, v.p. ops., 1968-70, pres., 1970-74, vice chmn., 1974-87; pres. Del-Tem Investments, Clearwater, Fla., 1987—; dir. Gen. Host Corp., Stamford, Conn. Served with U.S. Army, 1940-45. Mem.: Shriners; Masons. Home: 2321 Kent Pl Clearwater FL 33764-7566

HOOSER, HELEN, artist; b. Mannsville, Okla., Oct. 11, 1921; d. Charlie Valentine Woolard and Lelia May Peterman; m. Ernest Hooser, Sept. 21, 1940; children: Patricia Ann Hooser Morgan, Carl Ernest. Student, Murray State Sch. Agr., Tishomingo, Okla., 1939-40, Okla. State U., 1940-41; grad., Famous Artist Corr. Sch., Westport, Conn., 1961. LPN; cert. med. technologist. Nurse, lab. technician Antlers (Okla.) Clinic, 1946-55, Engles Clinic, Durant, Okla., 1959-75; artist, 1975—. Exhibited in solo show at Kerr Mus., Poteau, Okla., 1969, Tex. Tech. Mus., Lubbock, 1970, Okla. Mus. Art, 1971, Peddler's Cart, Albuquerque, 1974, Omni Gallery, Dallas, 1995-99, Anderson Gallery, Oklahoma City, 1975, Gov.'s Gallery, Oklahoma City, 1980, Ariel Gallery, N.Y.C., 1989, Little Louvre Gallery, Denison, Tex., 1998, VanMeter Gallery, Durant, Okla., 1999, others; group shows include Lasting Impressions Gallery, Sherman, Tex., Art Works, Midway Mall, Sherman, Hooser Art Gallery, Durant, Madill (Okla.) Art Show, Soho Art competition, N.Y.C., Norman Wilkes Gallery, Oklahoma City, Ariel GAllery, N.Y.C.; featured in mag. articles. Mem. So. Watercolor Soc. (signature mem.), Okla. Watercolor Assn., Sherman Art League, Durant Creative Arts Guild, Epsilon Sigma Alpha (state pres. 1958-59). Baptist. Avocations: sewing, reading. Home: 1004 W University Blvd Durant OK 74701-3230

HOOTMAN, HARRY EDWARD, retired nuclear engineer, consultant; b. Oak Park, Ill., June 5, 1933; s. Merle Albert and Rachel Edith (Atkinson) H.; m. Linda P. Smith, Nov. 23, 1963; children: David, Holly, John. BS in Chemistry, Mich. Technol. U., 1959, MS in Nuc. Engring., 1962; LLB, LaSalle Ext. U., 1971, MA in English Lit., U. S.C., 1999. Registered profl. engr., S.C. Rsch. assoc. Argonne (Ill.) Nat. Lab., 1959-62; process engr. Savannah River Plant, Aiken, S.C., 1962-65; rsch. assoc. reactor physics group, nuclear engring. div. Savannah River Lab., Aiken, 1965-87; with New Reactor Devel. Group, 1987-92, adv. engr. Planning, Studies and Analysis, 1992-95; ret., 1995; cons. transuranic waste disposal and incineration, radioisotope prodn., separation and shielding; instr. Math. and Engring. Dept. U. S.C., Aiken, 1979-80, 90-94. Author: (book) Index to British Literary Annuals and Giftbooks 1823-1861; Inventor alpha waste incinerator. Bd. dirs. Central Savannah River Area Sci. and Engring. Fair, Inc., Augusta, Ga., 1972-91. Served to sgt. USAF, 1953-57. Mem. Am. Acad. Environ. Engrs., Nat. Soc. Profl. Engrs. (local chmn. 1978-79), Am. Nuclear Soc. (local chmn. 1979-80), Am. Phys. Soc., Sigma Xi. Baptist. Home: 820 Brandy Rd SE Aiken SC 29801-7281

HOOTON, JAMES G. finance company executive; CFO Arthur Andersen, Chgo. Office: Arthur Andersen 33 W Monroe St Chicago IL 60603 Office Fax: (312) 507-6748.

HOOVER, GARY LYNN, banker; b. Tipton, Ind., Oct. 20, 1937; s. Carmel Wayne and Virginia Ruth (Mitchell) H.; m. Virginia Maxine James Monet, May 8, 1965 (div. Apr. 1976); m. Laura E. Grigg, June 25, 1988; children: Devin Page, Melissa Virginia. BS, Purdue U., 1959. Nat. bank examiner Internat. Comptroller of the Currency, Washington, 1962-71; v.p. Am. Fletcher Nat. Bank, Indpls., 1971-81; credit examiner Internat. Farm Credit Adminstrn., Washington, 1981-84; v.p. Nat. Bank for Cooperations, Englewood, Colo., 1984-95. V.p. Hoover Farms, Inc., Tipton, Ind.; pres. Hoover Fin. Assn., LLC, Highlands Ranch, Colo., 1995—; mem. U. Colo. Scholarship Fund, Boulder. Mem. pres. coun. Purdue U., West Lafayette, Ind., 1997—. With U.S. Army, 1961—66. Mem. Ind. Bankers Assn. Colo. Republican. Avocations: reading, travel, cartography. Home: 9057 S Bear Mountain Dr Highlands Ranch CO 80126-2269 Office: Hoover Fin Assocs PO Box 260826 Highlands Ranch CO 80163-0826 Fax: 303-791-0615.

HOOVER, JOHN ELWOOD, former military officer, consultant, author, speaker on US military history; b. Timberville, Va., Apr. 28, 1924; s. Saylor Cornelius and Ruby Mae (Brill) H.; m. Mary Jo Cox, May 17, 1953; children: M. Kathryn, Holly H. Bullock. Student, Bridgewater (Va.) Coll., 1941-43, Amherst (Mass.) Coll., 1943-44; BS, U.S. Mil. Acad., 1947; MA, Georgetown U., 1955; postgrad., Columbia U., 1955-56, U.S. Army Command and Gen. Staff Coll., Ft. Leavenworth, Kans., 1958-59, U.S. Army War Coll., Carlisle Barracks, Pa., 1962-63. Commd. 2d lt. U.S. Army, 1947, advanced through grades to maj. gen., 1971; with 24th Inf. Div., Japan and Korea, 1948-51, 1951-53; faculty dept. social scis. U.S. Mil. Acad., 1955-58; bn. comdr. U.S. Army, Fed. Republic of Germany, 1959-60, Hdqrs. U.S. Army Europe, Fed. Republic of Germany, 1961-62; with Office Asst. Sec. Def. for Internat. Security Affairs, Washington, 1963-66; chief communications plans Hdqrs. Pacific Command, Hawaii, 1966-69, group comdr. Vietnam, 1969-70; exec. officer, then dir. communications systems, then dep. asst. chief staff for communication-electronics Hdqrs. Dept. Army, Washington, 1970-73; dep. comdg. gen. U.S. Army Communications Command, Ft. Huachuca, Ariz., 1973-74; dir. Joint Tactical Communications Office, Office Sec. Def., Ft. Monmouth, N.J., 1974-78; ret., 1978. Cons. command, control, communications and mgmt.; historian emeritus U.S. Army Signal Rgt.; author and speaker on U.S. mil. communications history. Decorated D.S.M., Legion of Merit with oak leaf cluster, Bronze Star with oak leaf cluster, Meritorious Svc. medal, Air medal with oak leaf cluster, Joint Svc. Commendation medal, Army Commendation medal, Armed Forces Honor medal Republic of Vietnam; Staff Svc. medal (Republic of Vietnam); Vietnam Gallantry Cross with palm; Order Mil. Merit (Republic of Korea), Presdl. unit citation, Meritorious unit citation, Republic of Korea Presdl. unit citation. Mem. Assn. Grads. U.S. Mil. Acad., Signal Corps Assn., Mil. Heritage Found., Warner Robins Rotary..

HOOVER, LOLA MAE, retired communications company executive; b. Monticello, Ark., Apr. 1, 1947; d. Victor Arthur and Essie (Humphries) Piper; divorced; 1 child, Larry Wayne. With prodn. dept. AT&T, West Chicago, Ill., 1965-78, 1st level shop mgr., 1978-83, warehouse mgr., 1983-84, office mgr., 1984-86, with Mfg. Resource Planning Project, 1986-87, leader Mfg. Resource Planning project, 1987-88, mgr. script planning and prodn. control, 1988-91, 2d level mgr. custome svcs. and prodn. shop, 1992-96, mem. pres.'s coun., staff mgr. Bedminster, N.J., 1993-94; mfg. mgr. Dallas Works, Mesquite, Tex., 1994-97; ret. AT&T (Lucent Techs.), 1996. Baptist. Home: 207 Briar Ln North Aurora IL 60542-1211

HOOVER, PAUL, poet; b. Harrisonburg, Va., Apr. 30, 1946; s. Robert and Opal (Shinaberry) H.; m. Maxine Chernoff, 1974; children: Koren, Philip, Julian. BA cum laude, Manchester Coll., 1968; MA, U. Ill., 1973. Asst. editor U. Ill. Press, Champaign, 1973-74; prof. English, Columbia Coll., Chgo., 1974—. Co-founder Poetry Ctr., Sch. of Art Inst. of Chgo., 1974, bd. mem. 1974-87, pres. 1975-78; editor OINK!, 1971-85; co-founder, editor New Am. Writing, 1986. Author: Letter to Einstein Beginning Dear Albert, 1979, Somebody Talks a Lot, 1983, Nervous Songs, 1986, Idea, 1987 (Carl Sandburg award Friends of Chgo. Pub. Libr. 1987), Saigon, Illinois, 1988, The Novel: A Poem, 1990; editor: Postmodern American Poetry, 1994, Viridian, 1997 (Georgia prize 1997), Totem and Shadow: New and Selected Poems, 1999, Rehearsal in Black, 2001, Winter (Mirror), 2002, Fables of Representation: Essays, 2003; contbr. to various periodicals including New Yorker, Partisan Rev., New Directions, Sulfur, Chgo. Rev., Triquarterly, Am. Poetry Rev., New Republic; author: (screenplay) Viridian, 1994. Nat. Endowment for Arts fellow, 1980; Ill. Arts Coun. fellow, 1983, 84, 86; recipient Gen. Electric Found. award for Younger Writers, 1984, Jerome J. Shestack award, 2003. Mem. MLA. Office: Columbia Coll Dept of English 600 S Michigan Ave Chicago IL 60605-1900 Home: 369 Molino Ave Mill Valley CA 94941-2767

HOOVER, PEARL ROLLINGS, nurse; b. LeSueur, Minn., Aug. 24, 1924; d. William Earl and Louisa (Schickling) Rollings; m. Roy David Hoover, June 19, 1948 (dec. Mar. 1987); children: Helen Louise, William Robert (dec.). Grad. in nursing, U. Minn., 1945, BS in Nursing, 1947; MS in Health Sci., Calif. State U., Northridge, 1972. Dir. affiliate nursing sch. Mooselake (Minn.) State Hosp., 1948-49; nursing instr. Anchor Hosp., County Hosp., St. Paul, 1949-51; student nurse supr. and instr. Brentwood VA Hosp., L.A., 1951-52; sch. nurse L.A. Unified City Schs., 1963-91, substitute sch. nurse, 1991-96. Camp nurse United First Meth. Ch., winter and summer past 40 yrs.; corr. sec. Reseda Women's Club, 1st v.p.; courtesy chmn. First United Meth. Women. Mem. L.A. Coun. Sch. Nurses, Calif. Sch. Nurses Orgn. Democrat. Methodist. Home: 17851 Lull St Reseda CA 91335-2237

HOOVER, R. DAVID, packaging company executive; b. Straughn, Ind., June 21, 1945; BS, DePauw U., Greencastle, Ind., 1967; MBA, Indiana U., Bloomington, 1970; postgrad mgmt. program, Harvard U., 1988. Corp. fin. analyst Eli Lilly & Co., Indpls.; asst. to treas. Ball Corp., v.p., fin. & admin. agrl. sys. divsn., 1980—85, v.p., fin. & admin. aerospace sys. group, 1985—87, asst. treas., 1987—88, v.p. & treas., 1988—92, sr. v.p. & CFO, 1992—96, exec. v.p. & mem. bd. dirs., 1996—98, vice chmn. & CFO, 1998—2000, COO, 2000—01, CEO & pres., 2001—, chmn., 2002—. Bd. mem. Datum, Inc., Maxon Corp. & Energizer Holdings; mem. bd. dirs. & former chmn. Can Manufacturers Inst. Bd. mem. Nat. Food Processors Assn., Boulder Cmty. Found., DePauw U. Bd. Visitors & Bd. Trustees, Indiana U., Kelley Sch. Bus., Dean's Adv. Coun. Office: 10 Longs Peak Dr Broomfield CO 80021-2510

HOOVER, RICHARD, set designer; Prodn. designer films including: It Takes Two, 1988, Feeling 109, 1988, Torch Song Trilogy, 1988, Bob Roberts, 1992, Storyville, 1992, Dream Lover, 1994, Panther, 1995, Dead Man Walking, 1995, The Blackout, 1997, Apt Pupil, 1998, The Cradle Will Rock, 1999, Payback, 1999; designer TV movies: Family of Spies, 1990, Heat Wave, 1990, Zooman, 1995, (TV series) Twin Peaks, 1990; art dir.: Somewhere Tomorrow, 1983, Checking Out, 1989, Cradle Will Rock, 1999; set decorator: Wisdom, 1986, In the Mood, 1987; visual cons. Ed Wood, 1994; set designer: Sweet Lorraine, 1987, Girl, Interrupted, 1999, Twilight: Los Angeles, 2000, Fail Safe, 2000. Winner 1999 Tony award for best set design for Not About Nightingales, Evening Standard award, London Critics' Cir. award, Drama Desk award, Outer Critics Cir. award. Office: c/o IATSE Local 847 13949 Ventura Blvd Ste 301 Sherman Oaks CA 91423-3570

HOOVER, ROBERT ALLAN, university president; b. Des Moines, May 9, 1941; s. Claude Edward and Anna Doris H.; m. Jeanne Mary Hoover, Feb. 22, 1968; children: Jennifer Jill Jacobs, Suzanne Elizabeth. BS, Ariz. State U., 1967, MA, 1969; PhD, U. Calif., Santa Barbara, 1973. Instr. polit. sci. Utah State U., Logan, 1971-73, asst. prof. polit. sci., 1973-79, assoc. prof. polit. sci., chair polit. sci. dept., 1979-84, prof. polit. sci., 1984-91, dean Coll. Humanities, Arts and Social Scis., 1984-91; v.p. for acad. affairs U. Nev., Reno, 1991-96; pres. U. Idaho, Moscow, 1996—2003, Albertson Coll., Caldwell, 2003—. Author: The Politics of MX: A New Direction in Weapons Procurement?, 1982, The MX Controversy: A Guide to Issues and References, 1982, Arms Control: The Interwar Naval Limitation Agreements, 1980. Bd. dirs. United Way, Reno, 1994-96, Channel 5, Reno, 1991-95, St. Scholastica Acad., Canon City, Colo., 1991-96. Avocations: skiing, jogging, camping. Office: Albertson Coll 2112 Cleveland Blvd Caldwell ID 83605-9990 E-mail: rhoover@albertson.edu.*

HOOVER, ROLAND ARMITAGE, publisher, printer; b. Buffalo, Jan. 14, 1929; s. John Frank and Constance (More) H.; m. Cynthia Lee Adams, July 14, 1962; children: Sarah Adams, Emily Armitage. BS, Yale U., 1949. Mgmt. trainee Cleve. Electric Illuminating Co., 1949-50; graphic designer studio of Hubert Leckie, Washington, 1955-56; supr. tech. reports Atomic Energy div. Allis-Chalmers Mfg. Co., Washington, 1956-63; editor-in-charge Publs. Office, Research and Engring. Support div. Inst. for Def. Analyses, 1963-65; exec. editor Brookings Instn., Washington, 1965-67, dir. publs., 1967-84; univ. printer Yale U., New Haven, 1984-94, pursuivant of arms, 1989—; sr. critic in graphic design Yale Sch. Art, New Haven, 1991-94. Propr. pvt. press, free lance typographer, 1958— Served from ensign to lt. (j.g.) USNR, 1951-53. Fellow

Davenport Coll., Yale U., 1985-94, assoc. fellow, 1994—. Mem. Am. Printing History Assn., Yale Sherlock Holmes Soc., The Typophiles, Elizabethan Club (Yale U.), Sigma Xi, Tau Beta Pi. Democrat. Episcopalian. Home: 5505 Pembroke Ter Bethesda MD 20817-6318 E-mail: hoovercr@erols.com.

HOOVER, THOMAS E. writer; b. Temple, Tex., May 3, 1941; s. Orrin Garnett and Nettie Rose Hoover. BA, U Tex., 1962; PhD Tex. A & M, 1966. Rsch. United Tech. Rsch. Lab., E. Hartford, Conn., 1967—70; sr. v.p. Parsons Brinckerhoff, N.Y.C., 1970—80. Author: Zen Culture, 1977, The Zen Experience, 1980, The Moghul, 1983, Caribbee, 1985, The Samurai Strategy, 1988, Project Daedalus, 1991, Project Cyclops, 1992, Life Blood, 2000, Syndrome, 2003. Democrat. Avocation: playing Indian sitar. Home: 93 Bedford St New York NY 10014

HOPCROFT, JOHN EDWARD, computer scientist; b. Oct. 7, 1939; BS in EE, Seattle U., 1961; MS in EE, Stanford U., 1962, PhD in Elec. Engring., 1964. Asst. prof. Princeton (N.J.) U., 1964-67; assoc. prof. Cornell U., Ithaca, N.Y., 1967-71, prof., 1972-85, Joseph C. Ford prof., 1985—, chmn. computer sci. dept., 1987-92, assoc. dean coll. affairs Coll. Engring., 1992-93, dean Coll Engring., 1994—2001. Vis. prof. Stanford U., Calif., 1970-71; mem. Info. Sci. and Tech. Office Def. Advanced Rsch. Projects Agy. (DARPA) (chair robotics working group); chmn. adv. bd. NSF, 1987-90; mem. computer sci. and telecomm. bd. NAS/NRC, 1988—, adv. com. for David and Lucille Packard Fellowships in Sci. and Tech., 1991—; mem. sci. adv. bd. USAF, Inst. for Def. Analysis, David and Lucille Packard Found., NSF. Co-author: Formal Languages and Their Relation to Automata, 1969, The Design and Analysis of Computer Algorithms, 1974, Introduction to Automata Theory, Language, and Computation, 1979, Data Structures and Algorithms, 1983, Planning, Geometry and Complexity of Robot Motion, 1987. NSF Grad. fellow, 1961-64. Fellow IEEE, AAAS, Am. Acad. Arts and Scis.; mem. NAE (mem. acad. adv. bd. 1992-95), Nat. Sci. Bd., Inst. for Def. Analysis Supercomputing Rsch. Ctr., Assn. Computing Math. (Turing award 1986), Soc. for Indsl. and Applied Math., Ctr. Excellence Space Data and Info. Sci. (interim dir. 1987-88). Office: Cornell U Dept Computer Sci 5144 Upson Hall Ithaca NY 14853-2201

HOPE, HAKON, research scientist; b. Foerde, Norway, Dec. 15, 1930; s. Harald and Gunhild Hope; m. Sally Pearl Margulies Springer, Feb. 1, 1985; children: Erik Jacob, Mollie Liv. Cand. mag., U. of Oslo, Oslo, Norway, 1950—54; Cand. real., U. of Oslo (and Moscow State U., Moscow), Oslo, Norway, 1954—58. Rsch. asst. U. of Oslo, Oslo, 1958—60, u. fellow, 1961—65; postdoctoral fellow U. of Calif., Los Angeles, Calif., 1961—63; asst. prof. U. of Calif., Davis, Davis, Calif., 1965—68, assoc. prof., 1968—73, prof., 1973—92, prof. emeritus, 1993—. Co-editor Acta Crystallographica, 1984—93; vis. prof. The Weizmann Institue of Sci., Rehovot, Israel, 1978—79, U. of Copenhagen, Copenhagen, 1979—79. Author: (journal articles (about 160) Acta Crystallographica, Journal of the American Chemical Society, Inorganic Chemistry, Journal of Applied Crystallography, and others. Recipient Dr. philos, h. c., U. of Oslo, 1994; Fulbright Fellow, Fulbright Found., 1961-1963. Mem.: Am. Crystallographic Assn. Achievements include research in Developed methods for accurate measurement of electron density in crystals; Developed methods for crystallographic study of proteins at cryogenic temperatures; Developed methods for very rapid structure determination by X-ray crystallography. Avocations: languages; computer programming, gardening; skiing. Office: Department of Chemistry UC Davis One Shields Avenue Davis CA 95616 Office Fax: 530-752-8995. E-mail: hhope@ucdavis.edu.

HOPE, HENRY WELCKER, lawyer; b. Chattanooga, Tenn., Sept. 11, 1940; s. William Boyd and Eleanor Kate Roberson Hope; m. Sara Elizabeth Bailey, Aug. 5, 1961; children: Eleanor Anne Rooke, Julia Cathleen Falick. BS, U. Tenn., 1962; JD, George Washington U., 1966. Bar: Va. 1966, Tex. 1966, U.S. Patent Office 1966. Assoc. Fulbright & Jaworski, LLP, Houston, 1966-75, ptnr., 1975—. Bd. dirs. Royal Ten Cate (USA), Inc., Atlanta, BCM Tech., Inc., Houston. Trustee Houston Ballet Found., 1997—, adv. trustee, 2000-01; mem. corp. ptnrs. com. Mus. Fine Arts, Houston, 1997—; mem. adv. bd. dirs. Houston Jr. Forum, 1988-91; mem. adminstrv. bd. Meml. Dr. United Meth., Houston. Fellow TEx. Bar Found., Houston Bar Found. (sustaining life); mem. ABA (com. mem. 1966-85), Tex. Bar Assn. (com. mem. 1966-90), Va. Bar Assn., Licensing Exec. Soc. (various chairs 1975-85), MIT Enterprise Forum of Tex. (bd. dirs. 1989-94), Lakeside Country Club (bd. dirs. 1996-2000, pres. 1998-99). Methodist. Avocations: golf, reading, travel. Office: Fulbright & Jaworski LLP 1301 Mckinney St Ste 5100 Houston TX 77010-3031 E-mail: hhope@fulbright.com.

HOPE, JAMES FRANKLIN, mayor, civil engineer, consultant; b. Toledo, Aug. 2, 1917; s. George Thomas and Alice Mae (Martin) H.; m. Virginia Lee Mountjoy, June 10, 1944; children: James F. Jr., Virginia Lee BeVille. BCE magna cum laude, U. Toledo, 1939. Registered profl. engr., Ohio, Va.; registered profl. surveyor, Ohio. Field engr., asst. supt. Art Metal Constrn. Co., Jamestown, N.Y., 1939-40; asst. to chief engr. Doyle and Russell and Wise Constrn. Co., Richmond, Va., 1940-41; exec. engr. Doyle and Russell, Norfolk, Va., 1941-43; pres. Reid & Hope, Inc. Contractors & Engrs., Suffolk, Va., 1946-83. Bd. dirs. Old Dominion Investors Trust, Inc., 1952—, pres. 1965—; cons. engr. for comml., indsl. and condominium projects, 1984—. Mem. Suffolk City Coun., 1965-78, 90-94; vice mayor City of Suffolk, 1965, mayor, 1966-78, 90-92; exec. com., bd. dirs. Va. Mcpl. League, 1966-78; mem. Bldg. Codes Bd. of Adjustments and Appeals, 1963-90, chmn. 1985-90; mem. Affordable Housing Com., SE Va. Planning Dist. Commn., 1963-78, chair 1967-68, vice chair 1965-66, Hampton Roads Area Com., 1966-82, chair 1978-82, SE Va. Water Authority, 1970-78, vice chair 1975, chair 1976, Jail Study Com.; chmn. Suffolk 1980 Census Com., Southeastern Tidewater Manpower Authority, 1973-78; trustee, chmn. commn. fin., past chmn. Oxford Meth. Ch.; bd. dirs. Old Dominion coun. Boy Scouts Am., and others. Lt. USN, 1943-46, PTO. Recipient Disting. Svc. medal and plaque Cosmopolitan Club, 1973, Disting. Alumni award U. Toledo Coll. Engring., 1983, Gold T award U. Toledo Alumni Assn.; inducted Hall of Fame, Calvin M. Woodward High Sch., 1985; Paul Harris fellowship Rotary, 1996. Mem. NSPE, Soc. Am. Mil. Engrs., Associated Gen. Contractors of Am. (bd. dirs. Va. br., pres. Va. br. 1959, Constrn. Man of Yr. award), Va. Soc. Profl. Engrs. (bd. dirs. Tidewater chpt. 1960-63), Ea. Va. Assn. Contractors, State Registration Bd. for Contractors (past. chmn., past vice chmn.), Va. State C. of C., Suffolk-Nansemond C. of C. (bd. dirs. 1956-57), Lions (pres., bd. dirs. 1961-62, Melvin Jones fellow 1997). Republican. Home: 704 Jones St Suffolk VA 23434-4951

HOPE, JUDITH H. former political organization administrator; b. Warren, Ark., Nov. 2, 1939; d. Carroll Charles and Mayme (Stevens) Hollensworth; m. Thomas A. Twomey, Jr.; children: Leif Erling, Nisse Elizabeth. Student, Gulf Park Coll. for Women, 1956-57, U. Ark., 1957-60, Tobe Coburn Sch., N.Y., 1960-61. Town supr., East Hampton, N.Y., 1974-76, 84-88; appointments officer to N.Y. Gov. Hugh L. Carey, 1976-79; spl. asst. to Gov. for L.I., 1979-81; mem. Dem. Nat. Com., 1989-92; 1st vice chairwoman N.Y. State Dem. Party, 1989-92; mem. exec. com. Dem. Nat. Com., 1997; chairwoman N.Y. State Dem. Party, 1995—2001. Mem. N.Y. Bldg. Codes Coun. Mem. N.Y. State Women's Dem. Leadership Coun., 1990-95; dir. Planned Parenthood of Suffolk County, 1988—; vice chmn. South Fork Nature Conservancy; founding mem. East End Women's Network; mem. N.Y. State Ctr. for Women in Govt., L.I. LWV; founder, chair Elenor Roosevelt Legacy Com., 2000—. Recipient Woman of Yr. award Suffolk County Human Rights Commn., 1986, Woman of Yr. award East Hampton Assn. Univ. Women, 1988, Pres.'s Pub. Svc. award Nature Conservancy, 1988, Environ. Roll of Honor, Group for the South Fork, 1990, Cmty. Svc. award Apple Inst., 1992. Mem. Pi Beta Phi. Home: #9 Two Holes of Water East Hampton NY 11937

HOPE, KARIN, lawyer, legislative staff member; b. Breckenridge, Minn., Mar. 14, 1967; d. George Huntington and Barbara Jesten H. BA in political sci., Bethel Coll., 1989; JD, Georgetown U. Law Ctr., 1994. Bar: Minn., 1994, U.S. Supreme Ct., 1998. Asst. legis. dir. U.S. Senator Dave Durenberger, Washington, 1987-88, 89-91, legis. asst., 1991-94; legis. counsel U.S. Rep. Jim Ramstad, Washington, 1995, legis. dir./counsel, 1996—. Legal and govt. affaris com., Christian Coll. Coalition, Washington, 1992-94. Tutor/Mentor Neighborhood Learning Ctr., Washington, 1994—, alumni bd. dirs., Bethel Coll., St. Paul, 1995-97, 2000—. Citizenship award, Iowa Bar Assn., Osage, Iowa, 1985. Mem. Tax Coalition. Republican. Baptist. Avocations: vocal and instrumental music, theatre. Office: US Rep Jim Ramstad 103 Cannon House Off Bldg Washington DC 20515-0001 E-mail: karin.hopc@mail.house.gov.

HOPE, MARGARET LAUTEN, civic worker; b. NYC; 1 son, Frederick H., III. Privately educated. Ball com. various charity fund raising events. Mem. Jr. League NYC; Everglades Club, Palm Beach, Fla.; Women's Nat. Rep. Club (NYC); St. James Club (London). Address: PO Box 601 Palm Beach FL 33480-0601 Home: 236 Dunbar Rd Palm Beach FL 33480

HOPE, MELISSA B. radio and television correspondent; b. May 14, 1931; d. Nino Bossi and Elisa Penna. BA equivalent, Internat. Sch. Sacred Heart; postgrad., U. N.Mex., 1991—93. Translator of Italian books into English Smithsonian Inst., Washington, 1980; CEO Universe Corp. Internat. Trading, Washington; sr. nat. corr. US/Senate Radio & TV Press Galleries, 2000, Intellectual Property Security, UN, Geneva, 2001; sci. and tech. reporter Washington. Presenter seminars in field; White House corr. Pres. Ronald Reagan, Pres. George H. Bush; radio and TV corr. U.S. Senate; host Md. Talking with Melissa TV 58, host How to Be More and Better. Author: The Kitchen Rumors, Aurora Borealis - Magnetic Journey in Poetry, The Savannah Man. Election officer Fairfax County Electoral Bd., 1999—; active polit. campaigns Rep. Party, 2000—. Recipient Editor's Choice of Excellency in Poetry, Nat. Libr. Poetry, 1998—2000. Mem.: Hostelling Internat., Nat. Press Club. Mem. Lds Ch. Mailing: PO Box 793 Mc Lean VA 22101-0793

HOPE, SAMUEL HOWARD, accreditation organization executive; b. Owensboro, Ky., Nov. 5, 1946; s. James Russell and Lorraine (Jones) H.; m. Judy Bucher, June 24, 1978. B.Mus., Eastman Sch. Music, Rochester, N.Y., 1967; M.Music Arts, Yale U., 1970; pupil of, Nadia Boulanger, France, 1966, 67; LHD Marywood U. (hon.), 2001. Dean, composer-in-residence Atlanta Boy Choir Sch. Music, 1970-73, trustee, 1973—2001; vis. instr. Lee U., Cleveland, Tenn., 1973-74; exec. dir. music alumni, asso. dir. grad. profl. programs Campaign for Yale, Yale U., 1974-75; exec. dir. Nat. Assn. Schs. Music, Nat. Assn. Schs. Art and Design, Reston, Va., 1975—, Joint Commn. on Dance and Theatre Accreditation, 1978-83, Nat. Assn. Schs. Theatre, 1980—, Higher Edn. Arts Data Services, 1981—, Nat. Assn. Schs. Dance, 1981—, Working Group on Arts in Higher Edn., 1982—, Coun. of Arts Accrediting Assns., 1980—, Commn. Cmty. and Precollegiate Arts Schs., 2000—. Chmn. assembly of specialized accrediting bodies Council on Postsecondary Accreditation, 1979-82, bd. dirs., 1992-93; bd. dirs. Council Specialized Accrediting Agys., 1978-81, sec.-treas., 1979-81; mem. com. recognition Council Postsecondary Accreditation, 1984-88; chmn. adminstv. com. Found. Advancement Edn. in Music., 1986-90. Composer Piano Sonata I, 1968, II, 1971; motet Solus Ad Victimam Procedis, Domine, 1970, Blessed Be Thou Lord, 1976, Trio for Oboe, Cello and Piano, 1970, Cantata I, 1973, Cantata II, 1975, Symphonia: Psalm 145, 1982, Toccata: Psalm 117 for Organ, 1993; exec. editor Arts Edn. Policy Rev. mag., 1984—. Chmn. govt. relations com. Nat. Music Council, 1976-79, bd. dirs., 1978-84; mem. exec. com. Am. Soc. Univ. Composers, 1977-83; nat. alumni council Eastman Sch. Music, 1975-78, chmn., 1976-77; bd. dirs. Am. Music Conf., 1978-82; trustee Am. Acad. for Liberal Edn., 1997—. Recipient Composition prize Yale U., 1968, 69, 70, disting. svc. award Yale U., 2000, Ohio U., 2000. Mem. Am. Music Center, Coll. Music Soc., Music Educators Nat. Conf., Am. Inst. Graphic Artists, Music Tchrs. Nat. Assn., Am. Assn. for Theatre in Higher Edn., Am. Alliance for Theatre and Edn. Clubs: Yale (N.Y.C. and Washington). Episcopalian. Home: 10717 Rosehaven St Fairfax VA 22030-2826 Office: 11250 Roger Bacon Dr Ste 21 Reston VA 20190-5248

HOPE, THOMAS WALKER, marketing professional; b. St. Paul, May 19, 1920; s. Joseph Nathaniel and Alma (Ryden) Hope; m. Mabeth Sue Stewart, Apr. 30, 1949; children: Vincent W., Stephen D., Dana R. Student, U. Minn., 1937-39; BA, U. Tex., El Paso, 1942. Mgr. film dept. Gen. Mills, Inc., Mpls., 1945-54; cons. nontheatrical films Eastman Kodak Co., Rochester, NY, 1954-65; market analyst E. K. Co., Rochester, 1965-70; founder, pres. Hope Reports, Inc., Rochester, 1970-87, chmn., CEO, 1987—. Founder, v.p. Coun. Internat. Nontheatrical Events, Washington, 1956—86; cons. Marshall Plan, Govt. of France, Paris, 1952, various corps., 1970—. Author: Hope Reports AV-USA, 1970-72, 1974, (motion picture photography) Ency. of Imaging Sci. and Tech., 2002, (motion picture lenses) Optics Ency., 2003; co-author: Dollars and Sense of Business Films, 1955, Large Screen Presentation Systems, 2000; prodr.: (films) 66 indsl. films and tng. media, (exec.): (TV series) Lone Ranger, 1949; contbr., articles. Mem. Otetiana Coun. Boy Scouts Am., Rochester, 1954—. Capt. Signal Corps U.S. Army, 1942—45, ETO. Decorated Bronze Star, Can. Parachute Wings with silver maple leaf; recipient Silver Beaver award, Boy Scouts Am., 1960. Fellow: Soc. Motion Picture and TV Engrs. (life; gov.); mem.: Internat. TV Assn., Internat. Comm. Industries Assn. (life), Univ. Film and Video Assn. (life; mem. adv. coun. 1970—), Comm. Media Mgmt. Assn. (life; founder), Nat. Coun. Chs. (mem. comm. commn. 1980—91), Phi Kappa Tau (pres. U. Tex. El Paso chpt. 1941—42). Presbyterian. Fax: 585-442-1725. E-mail: hoperport@aol.com.

HOPE, WILLIAM DUANE, zoologist, curator; b. Fort Collins, Colo., June 7, 1935; s. William Earl and Lois Howe (Burnett) H.; m. Colleen Bryan, Dec. 23, 1956 (div.); children: Pam Hope Herbert, Karen Hope Van Zandt, Linda Hope Greene. BS, Colo. State U., 1957, MS, 1960; PhD, U. Calif., Davis, 1965. Systematic zoologist. dept. invertebrate zoology Nat. Mus. Natural History, Smithsonian Instn., Washington, 1964—69, curator, 1969—75, chmn. dept., 1976—81. Contbr. articles to profl. jours. Mem. Am. Assn. Zool. Nomenclature, Am. Micros Soc., Biol. Soc. Washington, Helminthological Soc. Washington, Soc. Nematologists, Soc. Systematic Zoology, Internat. Assn. Meiobenthologists. Democrat. Avocations: hiking, biking, flyfishing, bird watching. Office: Smithsonian Instn Natural History Mus Dept Systematic Biology Rm W212 MRC 163 Washington DC 20013-7012

HOPEN, HERBERT JOHN, horticulture educator; b. Madison, Wis., Jan. 7, 1934; s. Alfred and Amelia (Sveum) H.; m. Joanne C. Emmel, Sept. 12, 1959; children: Timothy, Rachel. BS, U. Wis., 1956, MS, 1959; PhD, Mich. State U., 1962. Asst. prof. U. Minn., Duluth, 1962-64; prof. U. Ill., Urbana, 1965-85, prof., acting head, 1983-85; prof. horticulture U. Wis., Madison, 1985-97, prof. emeritus, 1997, chmn. dept. horticulture, 1985-91. Mem. Am. Soc. for Hort. Sci., Weed Sci. Soc. Am., North Ctrl. Weed Sci. Soc., Ygdrasil, Sigma Xi. Avocations: reading, gardening. Office: U Wis Dept Hort 1575 Linden Dr Madison WI 53706-1514 E-mail: hjhopen@facstaff.wisc.edu.

HOPF, FRANK RUDOLPH, retired dentist; b. N.Y.C., Sept. 1, 1920; s. Rudolph Aldridge and Jennie Victoria (Fusco) Hopf; m. Elsie Hedlund, Sept. 10, 1949; children: Christine, Frank, Victoria, William, Robert. BS, Purdue U., 1942; postgrad., Middlesex U. Sch. Medicine, 1943—44; DDS, NYU, 1953, postgrad., 1957—61; MA, Columbia U., 1953, MPH, 1955. Asst. dir. Bur. Dental Health, NY State Dept. Health, Albany, 1956—57, regional dental dir. White Plains, 1967—90; pvt. practice dentistry specializing in periodontics Rye, NY, 1957—2003; ret., 2003. Rsch. assoc. periodontics NYU Coll. Dentistry, 1958—61; clin. asst. prof. dept. periodontics NJ Coll. Medicine and Dentistry, Jersey City, 1962—67; adj. asst. prof. dept. cmty. dentistry Columbia Sch. Dental and Oral Surgery, N.Y.C., 1971—76; vis. prof. dept. preventive dentistry Pitts. U. Sch. Dentistry, 1967—72. Contbr. articles to profl. publs. Pres. Country Ridge Home Owners Assn., Rye Brook, NY, 1960—62. Served with USNR, 1944—46. Grantee, NIH, 1957. Fellow: APHA, Am. Coll. Dentists, NY Acad. Dentistry, Am. Sch. Health Assn.; mem.: AAAS, ADA, Fedn. Dentaire Internationale, Am. Soc. Dentistry for Children, Westchester Acad. Medicine, North Eastern Soc. Periodontics, Royal Soc. Health, NY State Pub. Health Assn. (pres. 1970—72), Westchester Country Club, Westchester Shore Dental Study Club (pres. 1960—61, Rye, NY), KC (4 deg.). Roman Catholic. Home: 33 Old Field Hill Rd # 7 Southbury CT 06488

HOPFENBECK, GEORGE MARTIN, JR., lawyer; b. N.Y.C., Mar. 1, 1929; s. George Martin and Margaret Spencer (Felt) H.; m. Ruth Elizabeth Allen, June 27, 1953; children: Ann Elizabeth, James Allen. BA, Williams Coll., 1951; JD, Yale U., 1954. Bar: Colo., 1955. Assoc. Davis, Graham & Stubbs and predecessor Lewis, Grant & Davis, Denver, 1954-59, ptnr., 1959-92, of counsel, 1993—. Bd. dirs. Am. Cancer Soc. Inc., Colo. divsn., Denver, 1966-90, chmn., 1975-77; bd. dirs. Colo. Regional Cancer Ctr. Inc., Denver, 1974-81, pres., 1975-77; bd. dirs. Am. Cancer Soc. Inc., Atlanta, 1984-90, Denver Parks and Recreation Found., 1966-75; bd. dirs. Boys and Girls Clubs of Metro Denver, Inc., 1993—, chmn., 1998-2000; mem. Colo. State Pers. Bd., Denver, 1971-75, chmn., 1971-72; mem. Denver Bd. Parks & Recreation, 1961-69; trustee Kent Sch. for Girls, Denver, 1970-73; chmn. campaign com. for Gov. Love, Colo., 1966, campaign com. for McKevitt for Congress, Denver, 1970. Recipient St. George medal Am. Cancer Soc., 1982. Mem. ABA, Colo. Bar Assn., Denver Country Club (bd. dirs. 1967-70, 2002—), University Club (Denver) (bd. dirs. 1973-82). Republican. Episcopalian. Home: 450 Race St Denver CO 80206-4121 Office: 333 Logan St Ste 108 Denver CO 80203-4089

HOPFIELD, JOHN JOSEPH, biophysicist, educator; b. Chgo., July 15, 1933; s. John Joseph and Helen (Staff) H.; children: Alison, Jessica, Natalie; m. Mary Waltham, 1996. AB, Swarthmore Coll., 1954; PhD, Cornell U., 1958; DSc (hon.), Swarthmore Coll., 1992. Mem. tech. staff ATT Bell Labs., 1958-60, 73-89; vis. rsch. physicist Ecole Normale Superieure, Paris, 1960-61; asst. prof., then asso. prof. physics U. Calif. at Berkeley, 1961-64; prof. physics Princeton U., 1964-80, Eugene Higgins prof. physics, 1978-80; Dickinson prof. chemistry and biology Calif. Inst. Tech., Pasadena, 1980-96; Howard Prior prof. molecular biology Princeton (N.J.) U., 1997—. Trustee Battelle Meml. Inst. Guggenheim fellow, 1969, MacArthur Prize fellow, 1983; recipient Michelson-Morley prize, 1988, Wright prize, 1989, Helmholz award Internat. Neural Network Soc., 1999, Neural Net Pioneer award IEEE, 1997., Dirac medal Internat. Ctr. for Theoretical Physics, 2001, Pender award U. Pa., 2002; named Calif. Scientist of Yr., 1991. Fellow Am. Phys. Soc. (Oliver E. Buckley prize 1968, Biol. Physics prize 1985); mem. NAS, Am. Acad. Arts and Scis., Am. Philos. Soc., Phi Beta Kappa, Sigma Xi. Office: Princeton U Dept Molecular Biology Princeton NJ 08544-0001 E-mail: hopfield@princeton.edu.

HOPGOOD, JAMES F. anthropologist, educator; b. Cape Girardeau, Mo., Apr. 18, 1943; s. Finley Marshall and Marjorie Louise (Schneider) H.; m. Esther Berg, Jan. 29, 1966; 1 child, Myka Lynn. BA, U. Mo., 1965, MA, 1969; MPhil, U. Kans., 1971, PhD, 1976. Asst. prof. anthropology No. Ky. U., Highland Heights, 1973-76, assoc. prof., 1976-90, prof., 1990—2003, prof. emeritus, 2003—, chmn. dept. sociology, anthropology and philosophy, 1984-98, mem. exec. com. faculty senate, 1978-80, dir. Mus. of Anthropology, 2003—. Vis. instr. Washburn U., Topeka, 1969; vis. prof. Instituto Tecnologico y de Estudios Superiores de Monterrey, Mex., 1971, U. Monterrey, 1980; profl. assoc. Asian studies devel. program East-West Ctr. and U. Hawaii, summers, 1991, 93, 94. Author: Settlers of Bajavista: Urban Adaptation in a Mexican Squatter Settlement, 1979; editorial bd. Jour. of Third World Studies; contbr. articles, reports to profl. jours. Mem. edn. com. Cin. Mus. Natural History, 1992-94. Jewish Chautauqua Soc. scholar in residence No. Ky. U., 1988-98; recipient Sasakawa fellowship San Diego State U., summer 1996. Fellow Am. Anthrop. Assn. (mem. exec. com. 1996-98—); mem. Ky. Acad. Sci. (bd. gov. 1995-98), Ctrl. States Anthropol. Soc. (pres. 1996-97, mem. exec. bd. 1989-92, 99-01, editor CSAS Bull. 2001—), Sigma Xi, Lambda Alpha. Home: 4918 Corn Row Ct Independence KY 41051-8101 E-mail: hopgood@nku.edu.

HOPKE, PHILIP KARL, chemical engineering educator, atmospheric scientist; b. Sherman, Tex., Mar. 22, 1944; s. George Karl and Dorothy Virginia (Dawson) H.; m. Eleanor Lois Fritz, June 1, 1968; children: Jane Catherine, Frederick Karl. BS, Trinity Coll., 1965; MA, Princeton (N.J.) U., 1967, PhD, 1969. Rsch. assoc. MIT, Cambridge, Mass., 1969-70; asst. prof. SUNY, Fredonia, 1970-74, U. Ill., Urbana, 1974-78, assoc. prof., 1978-82, prof., 1982-89; Robert A Plane prof. Clarkson U., Potsdam, NY, 1989—2001, dean Grad. Sch., 1997-99, Bayard D. Clarkson disting. prof., 2002—, dir. Ctr. for Air Resources Engring. and Sci., 2002—; dir. Ctr. for Air Resources Engring. and Sci., 2002—. Chair grant rev. panel on air chemistry and physics EPA, Washington, 1987-92, clean air sci. adv. com., 1995-2000, chair clean air sci. adv. com., 2000—. Author: Receptor Modeling in Environmental Chemistry, 1985; editor: Radon and It's Decay Products, 1987, Receptor Modeling for Air Quality Management, 1991; editor-in-chief Aerosol Sci. and Tech., 1993-2002; contbr. articles to profl. jours. Mem. Champaign (Ill.) Environ. Adv. Commn., 1977-78; mem., pres. Champaign Community Sch. Bd. of Edn., 1978-81. Grantee U.S. Dept. Energy, EPA, NSF, Ministry of the Enviroment of Ont., N.J. EPA, Calif. Air Resources Bd., N.Y. State ERDA. Mem. Am. Assn. for Aerosol Rsch. (bd. dirs. 1989-94, v.p. 2001-02, pres. 2003-04), Air and Waste Mgmt. Assn. (chair com. 1990-92), Gesellschaft fur Aerosolforschung, Am. Chem. Soc. Achievements include development of multivariate statistical methods for quantitative determination of airborne particle source/receptor relationships; improvement of size measurement methods for ultrafine aerososls; research on physical chemistry of radon and its decay products and homogeneous and heterogeneous nucleation. Office: Clarkson U Ctr for Air Resources Engring& Sci (CARE PO Box 5708 Potsdam NY 13699-5708 E-mail: hopkepk@clarkson.edu.

HOPKINS, SIR ANTHONY (PHILIP), actor; b. Port Talbot, South Wales, U.K., Dec. 31, 1937; s. Richard Arthur and Muriel Annie (Yeates) H.; m. Petronella Barker, 1967 (div. 1972); 1 child, Abigail; m. Jennifer Ann Lynton, Jan. 13, 1973. Student, Welsh Coll. Music and Drama, Cardiff, Wales, 1954-56, Royal Acad. Dramatic Art, London, 1961-63; DLitt (hon.), Wales, 1988; Fellow (hon.), St. David's Coll., Lampeter, Wales, 1992. Ind. stage, screen, TV actor, 1963—. Made London stage debut in Julius Caesar, 1964; mem. Nat. Theatre Co., 1966-73; appeared in Juno and the Paycock, 1966, A Flea in Her Ear, 1966, Three Sisters, 1967, The Dance of Death, 1967, As You Like It, 1967, The Architect and the Emperor of Assyria, 1971, A Woman Killed with Kindness, 1971, Coriolanus, 1971, The Taming of the Shrew, 1972, Macbeth, 1972, Equus (Best Actor award N.Y. Drama Desk, Best Actor award Outer Critics Circle, Best Actor award Am. Authors Celebrities Forum), N.Y.C., 1974-75, (L.A. Drama Critics award), L.A., 1977, The Tempest, L.A., 1979, Old Times, N.Y.C., 1983, The Lonely Road, London, 1985, Pravda, Nat. Theatre, London, 1985-86 (Olivier award 1985, Stage Actor award Variety Club), King Lear, Nat. Theatre, London, 1986-87, Anthony & Cleopatra, Nat. Theatre, London, 1987, M Butterfly, Shaftesbury Theatre, London, 1989, (also dir.) August, 1994; films include (debut) The Lion in Winter, 1968, Hamlet, 1969, The Looking Glass War, 1969, When Eight Bells Toll, 1971, Young Winston, 1972, A Doll's House, 1973, The Girl from Petrovka, 1974, Juggernaut, 1974, A Bridge Too Far, 1977, Audrey Rose, 1977, International Velvet, 1978, Magic, 1978, The Elephant Man, 1980, A Change of Seasons, 1980, The Bounty, 1984 (Film Actor award Variety Club), The Good Father, 1985, 84 Charing Cross Road, 1986 (Best Actor award Moscow Film Festival 1987), The Dawning, 1988, Silence of the Lambs, 1991 (Acad. award for Best Actor 1992, Best Actor award Chgo. Film Critics 1992, Best Actor award Boston Film Critics 1992, Best Actor award N.Y. Film Critics 1992, Film Actor award Variety Club 1992, Best Film Actor award BAFTA 1992), Freejack, 1992, One Man's War (TV movie), 1991, Spotswood/The Efficiency Expert, 1992, Howard's End, 1992, Bram Stoker's Dracula, 1992, Chaplin, 1992, Remains of the Day, 1993 (Acad. award nominee for Best Actor 1994, Best Actor award L.A. Film Critics Assn. 1993, Best Actor award Nat. Soc. film Critics (U.S.A.) 1993, BAFTA UK best film actor award, Guild of Regional Film Writers UK Best Actor award, Variety Club UK Film Actor award 1993, Japan Critics Best Actor in a Fgn. Film award), Shadowlands, 1993 (Best Actor award Nat. Bd. Rev. 1993, Best Actor award L.A. Film Critics Assn. 1993, Best Actor award Nat. Soc. Film Critics (U.S.A.) 1993), the Trial, 1993, The Road to Welville, 1994, Legends of the Fall, 1994, The Innocent, 1993, Nixon, 1995 (Acad. award nominee for Best Actor 1996), August, 1996, Surviving Picasso, 1996, The Edge, 1997, Amistad, 1997, The Mask of Zorro, 1998, Meet Joe Black, 1998, Instinct, 1999, Titus, 1999, Mission Impossible II, 2000, How the Grinch Stole Christmas (voice), Hannibal, 2001, Hearts in Atlantis, 2001, The Devil and Daniel Webster, 2001, Bad Company, 2002, The Human Stain, 2003, Red Dragon, 2002; BBC-TV series War and Peace (Best TV Actor award Soc. Film and TV Arts), 1972; TV shows include A Heritage and Its History, 1968, Vanya, Hearts and Flowers, Three Sisters, The Peasant's Revolt, Dickens, Danton, The Poet Game, Decision to Burn, War and Peace, Cuculus Canorus, Lloyd George, Q.B. VII, 1971, Find Me, A Childhood Friend, Possessions, All Creatures Great and Small, 1975, The Lindbergh Kidnapping Case, 1976 (Emmy award), Victory at Entebbe, 1976, Dark Victory, Mayflower: The Pilgrim's Adventure, 1979, The Bunker, 1980 (Emmy award), Peter and Paul, 1980, Othello, BBC, 1981, Little Eyolf, BBC, 1981, The Hunchback of Notre Dame, 1982, A Married Man, 1984, The Arch of Triumph, CBS, 1984, Hollywood Wives, ABC, 1984, Guilty Conscience, CBS, 1984, Blunt, BBC, 1985, the Tenth Man, CBS, 1988, Across the Lake, BBC, Heartland, BBC, Great Expectations, 1989, Disney Primetime, To Be The Best, 1990, others. Decorated Comdr. of Order of Brit. Empire, 1987, Knights Bachelor, 1993, Comdr. of Order of Arts & Letters, France, 1996. Office: Creative Artists Agy 9830 Wilshire Blvd Beverly Hills CA 90212-1804

HOPKINS, CECILIA ANN, business educator; b. Havre, Mont., Feb. 17, 1922; d. Kost L. and Mary (Manaras) Sofos; m. Henry E. Hopkins, Sept. 7, 1944. BS, Mont. State Coll., 1944; MA, San Francisco State Coll., 1958; postgrad., Stanford U.; PhD, Calif. Western U., 1977. Bus. tchr. Havre (Mont.) H.S., Mateo, Calif., 1942-44; sec. George P. Gorham, Realtor, San Mateo, 1944-45; escrow sec. Fox & Cars, 1945-50; escrow officer Calif. Pacific Title Ins. Co., 1950-57; bus. tchr. Westmoor H.S., Daly City, Calif., 1958-59, Coll. of San Mateo, 1959-63, chmn. real estate-ins. dept., 1963-76, dir. divsn. bus., 1976-86, coord. real estate dept., 1986-91. Cons. to commr. Calif. Divsn. Real Estate, 1963-91, mem. periodic rev. exam. com.; chmn. C.C. Adv. Com., 1971-72, mem. com., 1975-91; projector direction Calif. State Chancellor's Career Awareness Consortium, mem. endowment fund adv. com., c.c. real estate edn. com., state c.c. adv. com.; mem. No. Calif. adv. bd. to Glendale Fed. Savs. and Loan Assn.; mem. bd. advisors San Mateo County Bd. Suprs., 1981-82; mem. real estate edn. and rsch. com. to Calif. Commr. Real Estate, 1983-90; mem. edn., membership, and profl. exch. coms. Am. chpt. Internat. Real Estate Fedn., 1985-92. Co-author: California Real Estate Principles; contbr. articles to profl. jours. Recipient Citizen of Day award KABL, Outstanding Contbns. award Redwood City-San Carlos-Belmont Bd. Realtors, Nat. Real Estate Educators Assn. award emeritus, 1993; named Woman of Achievement, San Mateo-Burlingame br. Soroptimist Internat., 1979. Mem. AAUW, Calif. Assn. Real Estate Tchrs. (state pres. 1964-65, life hon. dir. 1962—, Outstanding Real Estate Educator of Yr. 1978-79), Real Estate Cert. Inst. (Disting. Merit award 1982), Calif. Bus. Edn. Assn. (cert. of commendation 1979), San Francisco State Coll., Guidance and Counseling Alumni, Calif. Real Estate Educators' Assn. (dir. emeritus, hon. dir. 1990), Real Estate Nat. Educators Assn. (award emeritus for outstanding contbns. 1993), San Mateo-Burlingame Bd. Realtors (award emeritus Outstanding Contbrs. to Membership), Alpha Delta, Pi Lambda Theta, Delta Pi Epsilon (nat. dir. interchpt. rels. 1962-65, nat. historian 1966-67, nat. sec. 1968-69), Alpha Gamma Delta. Home: 504 Colgate Way San Mateo CA 94402-3206

HOPKINS, CYNTHIA, composer; Composer: A Simple Heart, Girl Gone, Hazard of Gravity (could you borrow me a hammer), Toast of Tears; actor: numerous film and theater projects; musician: (albums) Gloria Deluxe.

HOPKINS, DONALD J. lawyer; b. Long Beach, Calif., Jan. 9, 1947; m. Ellen Colokathis, Aug. 29, 1970; children: Melanie J., Shannon R., Christopher S. AB, Stanford U., 1968; JD, Harvard U., 1971. Bar: Mass. 1971, Colo. 1974, U.S. Dist. Ct. Colo. 1974. Mem. firm Holme Roberts & Owen LLP, Denver, 1973—. Fellow Am. Coll. Trust and Estate Counsel. Office: Holme Roberts & Owen LLP 1700 Lincoln St Ste 4100 Denver CO 80203-4541

HOPKINS, EDITH ROSE, artist; b. Norwalk, Conn., Oct. 9, 1926; d. Robert Selden and Annette (Moran) Rose; m. Robert N. Pyle, Feb. 11, 1950 (div. Mar. 1983); children: Robert N. Jr., Mark Cammann, Nicholas Ayrault, Sarah Livingston Moore; m. William R. Hopkins, Nov. 3, 1988. BFA, Yale U., 1949. Art tchr. Tower Hill Sch., Wilmington, Del., 1949-50, Annapolis H.S., 1976-80; comml. artist Creative Connections Inc., Gibson Island, Md., 1996—. Bd. dirs. Torpedo Factory Gallery, Alexandria, Va.; judge Md. State Fair, Timonium, 2000. Permanent galleries at Annapolis Marine Art Gallery, River Gallery, Galesville, Md., Saxon Swan Gallery, Lewes, Del. Docent Gugenheim Mus., N.Y.C., 1949, Nat. Gallery, Washington, 1959-65. Recipient numerous art awards. Mem. Md. Fedn. Art, Balt. Watercolor Soc., Annapolis Watercolor Club, Gibson Island Club. Avocations: golf, tennis, bridge. Home: 756 Ticonderoga Ave Severna Park MD 21146 E-mail: edierhop@aol.com.

HOPKINS, GEORGE MATHEWS MARKS, retired patent lawyer, business executive; b. Houston, June 9, 1923; s. C. Allen and Agnes Cary (Marks) H.; m. Betty Miller McLean, Aug. 21, 1954; children: Laura Hopkins Corrigan, Edith Hopkins Collins. Student, Ga. Tech., 1943-44; BSChemE, Ala. Poly. Inst., 1944; LLB, JD, U. Ala., 1949; postgrad., George Washington U., 1949-50. Bar: Ala. 1949, Ga. 1954; registered patent lawyer, U.S.; registered profl. engr., Ga.; Can. qualified deep-sea diver. Instr. math. U. Ala., 1947-49; assoc. A. Yates Dowell, Washington, 1949-50, Edward T. Newton, Atlanta, 1950-62; ptnr. Newton, Hopkins and Ormsby (and predecessor), Atlanta, 1962-87; sr. ptnr. Hunt, Richardson, Garner, Todd & Cadenhead, Atlanta, 1987-91; ptnr. Hopkins & Thomas, 1991-95; ret., 1996; spl. asst. atty. gen., 1978; chmn. bd. Southeastern Carpet Mills, Inc., Chatsworth, Ga., 1962-77, Thomas-Daniel & Assocs., Inc., 1981-85, Ea. Carpet Mills, Inc., 1983-87; CEO, Airamar Chem. Engring., Inc., Doraville, Ga., 1997—. Asst. dir. rsch., legal counsel Auburn (Ala.) Rsch. Found., 1954-55; spl. asst. atty. gen. State of Ga., 1978; chmn. bd. S.E. Carpet Mills, Inc., Chatsworth, Ga., 1962-77, Thomas-Daniel & Assocs., Inc., 1981-85, Ea. Carpet Mills, Inc.; dir. Xepol Inc. Served as lt., navigator, Submarine Service USNR, 1944-46, 50-51. Mem. ABA, Ga. Bar Assn. (chmn. sect. patents 1970-71), Atlanta Bar Assn., Am. Intellectual Property Law Assn., Am. Soc. Profl. Engrs., Submarine Vets. World War II (pres. Ga. chpt. 1977-78), Phi Delta Phi, Sigma Alpha Epsilon, Atlanta Lawyers Club, Phoenix Soc., Cherokee Town and Country Club, AtlantaSoc. Episcopalian.

HOPKINS, GERALD FRANK, trade association administrator; b. La Grande, Oreg., Dec. 6, 1943; s. Albert Benjamin and Phyllis Nadine (Munn) H.; m. Mary Martha Abbott, June 9, 1967; children: Angela, Ann. BS, Ea. Mont. Coll., 1966, MS, 1967; advanced Master's degree, U. So. Calif., 1973; EdD, Calif. Coastal Coll., 2002. Grad. asst. Ea. Mont. Coll., Billings, 1966-67; tchr., adminstr. Elysian Schs., Billings, 1967-69; adminstrv. asst. Internat. Schs., Bangkok, 1969-73; prin. Nashua (Mont.) Pub. Schs., 1973-76, Roundup (Mont.) Pub. Schs., 1976-86; owner, operator Town Pump, Billings, 1986-90; exec. dir. La Grande/Union County C. of C., 1990-92; tchr., supt., adminstr. Huntington (Oreg.) Pub. Schs., 1992—. Project coord. Title I, 1996-97. Author: BJ & Boz, 1989, Humor in the Classroom, 1995; contbr. articles to profl. jours. Bd. dirs. Family Crisis Intervention, Roundup, 1983-86, Sr. Citizens Vol. Program, Roundup, 1983-86, State Reading Assn., Roundup, 1986-88, Continuing Edn. Coun., La Grande, 1990, Oreg. Trail Days., Continuing Counsel Higher Edn.; mem. Coop. Community Exch. Coun., 1983-86, hist. validation com Airport Svc. Coun., La Grande, 1991. Recipient State Disting. Title I. award, Nat. Disting. Title I program, 1996-97, Oreg. Small Sch. Innovation Program, 1997, 99, Internat. Pres. Humanitarian award, 1998, Salute to Success award Oreg. Sch. Bd. Assn., 2000, Oreg. Small Sch. award of excellence, 2001, 02. Mem. Small Bus. Adminstrn., Nat. C. of C., Elem. Adminstrs. Assn. (dir. ea. dist. 1988-90), Lions (internat. officer 1973-95, Outstanding Achievement award 1986, bd. dirs. La. Grande Club, Roundup of Lion Yr. 1977, 78, 79, 2d Internat. Pres.'s Humanitarian award 1978, Melvin Jones award 2002), Ambs. (assoc.) Home: 68068 Hunter Rd Summerville OR 97876-8133

HOPKINS, GROVER PREVATTE, lawyer; b. Jacksonville, Fla., Sept. 2, 1933; s. John Taylor and Capitola (Prevatte) H.; m. Ann Hutchinson, Oct. 16, 1965 (dec.); children: John, George, James, Corbin; m. Connie Jefferys, June 7, 1973. AB, Fla. State U., 1958; JD, U. N.C., 1971. Bar: N.C. 1971, Fla. 1972, D.C. 1981, U.S. Dist. Ct. (ea. dist.) N.C. 1971, U.S. Ct. Appeals (4th cir.) 1974, U.S. Supreme Ct. 1974; cert. mediator N.C. Cts., 1997. Announcer Sta. WTAL, Tallahassee, 1951-54; pub. rels. dir. Inter-Am. U., San German, P.R., 1958-60; pers. mgr. Northridge Knitting Mills, San German, 1960-62; cons. bus and pers. Mayaguez, P.R., Miami, Fla., 1963-69; mem. Weeks & Muse, Tarboro, N.C., 1971-73, Hopkins & Assocs., Tarboro, 1973—. Served with U.S. Army, 1954-57. Mem. Inter-Am. Bar Assn. (sec. gen. 1989-91). Republican. Office: Hopkins & Assocs 212 N Main St Tarboro NC 27886-5008 E-mail: lawyergph@aol.com.

HOPKINS, HENRY TYLER, museum director, art educator; b. Idaho Falls, Idaho, Aug. 14, 1928; s. Talcott Thompson and Zoe (Erbe) Hopkins; children: Victoria Anne, John Thomas, Christopher Tyler. BA, Sch. of Art Inst., Chgo., 1952, MA, 1955; postgrad., UCLA, 1957-60; PhD (hon.), Calif. Coll. Arts and Crafts, 1984, San Francisco Art Inst., 1986. Curator exhbns., publs. Los Angeles County Mus. of Art, 1960-68; lectr. art history UCLA Ext., 1960—68; dir. Fort Worth Art Mus., 1968-74, San Francisco Mus. of Modern Art, 1974-86; chmn. art dept. UCLA, 1991-94, dir. F.S. Wight Gallery, 1991-95, dir. Armand Hammer Mus. Art and Cultural Ctr., 1994-99, prof. art, 1999—2002, prof. emeritus, 2002—. Instr. Tex. Christian U., Ft. Worth, 1968—74; dir. U.S. representation Venice Bienniel, Italy, 1970; dir. art presentation Festival of Two Worlds, Spoleto, Italy, 1970; co-commr. U.S. representation XVI Sao Paulo Biennale, Brazil, 1981; cons. NEA, mem. mus. panel, 1979—84, chmn., 1981; cons., mem. mus. panel NEH, 1976. Contbr. With AUS, 1952—54. Decorated knight Order Leopold II, Belgium; recipient Spl. Internat. award, Art L.A., 1992. Mem.: We. Assn. Art Museums (pres. 1977—78), Am. Assn. Museums, Coll. Art Assn., Assn. Art Mus. Dirs. (pres. 1985—86). Home: 939 1/2 Hilgard Ave Los Angeles CA 90024-3032 Office: UCLA Art Dept 405 Hilgard Ave Los Angeles CA 90095-9000

HOPKINS, HOMER THAWLEY, chemist, researcher, retired chemist; b. Frederica, Del., July 27, 1913; s. Homer Thawley and Lillian Alexander Hopkins, Sr.; m. Victoria Lafferty, Oct. 26, 1940; 1 child, Rebecca. BS, U. Del., 1935; MS, Cornell U., 1939; PhD, U. Md., 1951. Asst. state chemist Bd. Agr., Dover, Del., 1935—37; soil scientist USDA, Washington, 1939—41, Beltsville, Md., 1941—52; chemist FDA, Washington, 1952—76; food scientist NAS, Washington, 1976—77; ret., 1977. Cons. in field; organizer, oper. office fgn. affairs Inst. Applied Agr., U. Md., 1977—82. Contbr. articles to profl. jours. Lt. USN, 1939—42. Republican. Methodist. Avocations: fishing, gardening, reading. Home: Walnut Tree Village 69 Elizabeth Cir Sandy Hook CT 06482

HOPKINS, JAN, journalist, news anchor; b. Warren, Ohio, May 22, 1947; d. Walter Charles and Lois Avelene (Botroff) Reed; m. Walter Hopkins, June 14, 1969 (div. Nov. 1981); m. Richard Trachtman, Nov. 8, 1986. Dir. news Sta. WTCL, Warren, Ohio, 1973-75; reporter, anchor Sta. WERE, Cleve., 1975-77; reporter Sta. WKBN-TV, Youngstown, Ohio, 1977-80; reporter, anchor Sta. WLWT-TV, Cin., 1980-82; assignment editor CBS News, N.Y.C., 1983; reporter, prodr. ABC News, N.Y.C., 1983-84; anchor bus. news CNN, N.Y.C., 1984—. Author: (chapter) Knight Bagehot Guide to Business Journalism, 1990, 2d edit., 2000. Trustee Hiram Coll., 1988—94; adv. bd. Knight Bagehot program journalism Columbia U., N.Y.C., 1994; mem. nat. bd. Girl Scouts USA, 2001—. Recipient Peabody award U. Ga., 1988, Front Page award Newswomen Club N.Y., 1988, Lifetime Achievement award Women's Econ. Roundtable, 2002; Knight Bagehot fellow Columbia U. Sch. Journalism, 1982-83; named to Hall of Excellence Ohio Found. Ind. Colls., 1993, Warren, Ohio, U.S. Disting. Alumni Hall of Fame, 1995. Mem. Econ. Club N.Y. Office: CNN Bus News 5 Penn Plz Fl 20 New York NY 10001-1810 E-mail: jan.hopkins@turner.com.

HOPKINS, JEANNETTE ETHEL, book publisher, editor; b. Camden, N.J., Dec. 7, 1922; d. Carleton Roper and Gladys Eugenia (Hull) H. BA, Vassar Coll., 1944; MS, Columbia Sch. Journalism, 1945. Asst. to Sunday editor New Haven Register, 1945-46; reporter Providence Evening Bull., 1946-50, Oklahoma City Times, 1950-51; sr. editor Beacon Press, Boston, 1951-56, Harcourt Brace, N.Y.C., 1956-64, Harper & Row, N.Y.C., 1964-73; v.p. Met. Applied Res. Ctr., N.Y.C., 1970-72, cons. editor, 1973-80, 89—; dir. Wesleyan Univ. Press, Middletown, Conn., 1980-89. Adj. prof. English Wesleyan U., 1987-89, U. N.H., 1989; propr. Portsmouth Athenaeum, 1991. Author: Books That Will Not Burn, 1952, 14 Journeys to Unitarianism, 1951, (with K.B. Clark) Relevant War Against Poverty, 1968, Legacy: A History of the South Church Endowment, 1995. The Whole Thing: The Author, The Editor, and The Book, 2004. Mem. coun. Inst. Religion in an Age of Sci., 1968-72, 80-82, 88-91; mem. bd. Unitarian UN Office, 1977-80; mem. Commn. on Appraisal, Unitarian Universalist Assn., 1976-78; bd. dirs. ACLU, 1970-79, mem. nat. adv. coun., 1986—; bd. govs. Comty. Ch. N.Y., 1960-66, Unitarian-Universalist Ch., Portsmouth, 1990-93, lay min., 1991-95; trustee South Ch. Endowment Fund, 1996-99; v.p. Unitarian Fellowship for Social Justice, 1958-62. Louise Hart Van Loon fellow, Vassar Coll., 1944; recipient Disting. Alumni award Columbia Sch. Journalism, 1981. Democrat. Unitarian Universalist. Home and Office: 39 Pray St Portsmouth NH 03801-5226

HOPKINS, JEFFREY P. federal judge; b. 1960; JD, Ohio State U., 1985. Law clk. to Hon. Alan E. Norris U.S. Ct. Appeals (6th cir.), 1985-87; assoc. Squire, Sanders & Dempsey, 1987-90; asst. U.S. atty. JPH (so. dist.) Ohio, 1990-96; bankruptcy judge U.S. Dist. Ct. (so. dist.) Ohio, Cin., 1996—. Office: US Bankr Ct So Dist Ohio 221 E 4th Ste 800 Cincinnati OH 45202-4124 Fax: 513-357-5420.

HOPKINS, JEFFREY WILLARD, economist, researcher; b. Ashland, OH, Nov. 24, 1964; s. Willard Ernest Hopkins, Lillian Elaine Hopkins; m. Rebecca Chase Smith; children: Edith, Wesley. BA, Miami University, Oxford, Ohio, 1987; PhD, Ohio State U., 1998. Forestry extensionist U.S. Peace Corps, San Francisco la Union, Guatemala, 1987—90; rsch. Economist Econ. Rsch. Svc., USDA, Washington, 1999—. Contbr. articles to profl. jours., chapters to books. Adv. bd. mem. New Forests Project, Washington, 1991—98; cmty. vol. Cmty. Tax Aid, Washington, 2002—03; panel mem. Columbus Environ. Risk Assessment: Priorities '95, 1994—96. Fellow rsch. fellow, Ohio State Univ., 1991—98, Fgn. Lang. and Area Studies fellow, U.S. Dept. Edn., 1997, found. fellow, Am. Agrl. Econs. Assn., 1998. Mem.: So. Agrl. Econs. Assn., Western Agrl. Econs. Assn., Am. Agrl. Econs. Assn. Personal E-mail: jhopkins@ers.usda.gov.

HOPKINS, JOHN DAVID, lawyer; b. Memphis, Feb. 8, 1938; s. John and Helen (Sweeney) H.; m. Evelyn Harry, June 8, 1963 (div. Feb. 1985); children: John David III, Katharine Jane, Matthew Joseph; m. Laurie Eileen House, June 3, 1987. BA, Vanderbilt U., 1959; LLB, U. Va., 1965. Bar: Ga. 1966, D.C. 1979. From assoc. to ptnr. King & Spalding, Atlanta, 1965-93; exec. v.p., gen. counsel Jefferson-Pilot Corp., Greensboro, NC, 1993—2003. Bd. dirs., mem. exec. com. Rock-Tenn Co., Atlanta, 1989; mem. Guilford Coll. Bd. of Visitors, 1994-2000; bd. dirs. Univ. N.C. at Greensboro Excellence Found., 1995-2003. Bd. dirs. Atlanta Ballet, 1991-93, Greensboro United Arts Coun., 1994-97, Ea. Music Festival, 1998—; mem. alumni coun. U. Va. Law Sch. Alumni Assn., 2000-03; trustee Children's Sch., Inc., Atlanta, 1971-79, 88-89, Nat. Assn. Children's Hosps. and Related Instns., Alexandria, Va., 1973-79. Lt. USN, 1959-62. Mem. Ga. Bar Assn. (chmn. corp. code revision com., corp. and banking sect. 1970-79), D.C. Bar Assn., Greensboro Country Club, Cherokee Town and Country Club (Atlanta), Highlands Country Club N.C., Order of Coif, Omicron Delta Kappa. Episcopalian. Office: 2660 Peachtree Rd NW Unit 25C Atlanta GA 30305 E-mail: jdhopki@yahoo.com.

HOPKINS, JUDITH OWEN, oncologist; b. Norfolk, Va., Sept. 6, 1952; d. Austin and Edythe Owen; m. Marbry Benjamin Hopkins, III; 1 child, Benjamin Owen Hopkins. BS magna cum laude, Westhampton Coll., 1974; D of Medicine, U. Va., 1977. Diplomate Am. Bd. Internal Medicine, Am. Bd. Internal Medicine-Oncology. Resident in internal medicine Bowman Gray Sch. Medicine, N.C. Baptist Hosp., Winston-Salem, 1977-80, oncology fellowship, 1980-82; pvt. practice Winston-Salem, 1984—; clin. asst. prof. medicine Bowman Gray Sch. Medicine, Winston-Salem, 1984-92, asst. prof. medicine, 1982-84, clin. assoc. prof. medicine, 1992—. Contbg. author: Tumors of the Central Nervous System, 1982; contbr. articles to profl. jours and abstracts. Bd. dirs. Hospice of Winston-Salem/Forsyth County, 1988—92, mem. profl. adv. com., 1982—92; preceptor for alt. curriculum Bowman Gray Sch. Medicine, 1988; mem. spkrs. bur. Am. Cancer Soc., 1982—92, chmn. profl. edn. com., 1982—85; trustee U. Richmond, 2000—. Mem. ACP, Am. Soc. Internal Medicine, N.C. Soc. Internal Medicine, N.C. Med. Soc., Forsyth-Davie-Stokes County Med. Soc., Am. Soc. Clin. Oncology, Piedmont Oncology Assn., Southeastern Cancer Control Consortium (co-prin. investigator 1995—), N.C. Oncology Soc. (chmn. clin. practices com. 1991-92), Phi Beta Kappa, Alpha Omega Alpha. Episcopalian. Avocations: athletics, religion, coaching track. Home: 313 Susanna Dr Kernersville NC 27284-2161 Office: 1010 Bethesda Ct Winston Salem NC 27103

HOPKINS, KAREN BROOKS, performing arts executive; b. 1951; d. Howard and Paula Brooks; divorced; 1 child, Matthew. BA in Theater Arts with honors, U. Md., 1973; MFA, George Washington U., 1980. Mem. group sales staff Am. Theater, Washington, 1973; cmty. rels. dir. Qwindo's Windo Dance Trouing Co., Washington, 1975; theater mgr., asst. dir. Chelm Players Touring Co., 1975-76, prodr., 1975-78; theater dir. Jewish Cmty. Ctr. of Greater Washington, 1976-78; devel. dir. The New Playwright's Theatre, Washington, 1978-79; devel. officer Bklyn. Acad. of Music, 1979-81, v.p. planning and devel., 1981-88, exec. v.p., 1988-98, COO and exec. v.p., 1998-99, pres., 1999—. Adj. prof. program for arts adminstrn. Bklyn. Coll., 1980-84. Author: Successful Fundraising for Arts and Cultural Organizations, 1989, 2d edit., 1997. Fundraising cons. art instns., 1979—; chair Performing Arts Ctrs. Consortium, 1994-96, Cultural Instns. Group, 2003; mem. adv. com. Salzburg Seminar-Alberto Vilar Project of Critical Issues for the Classical Performing Arts; ex-officio mem. N.Y.C. Cultural Affairs Adv. Commn., 2003.. Recipient King Olav medal Norwegian Nat. Ballet, 1982, Dramaten medal, 1995. Office: Brooklyn Acad Music 30 Lafayette Ave Brooklyn NY 11217-1430

HOPKINS, KEVIN W, education educator; m. Lori M Hopkins. BA, Greenville Coll., 1983; M, PhD, U. of Ill., 1989. Prof., math. SW Bapt. U., Bolivar, Mo., 1989—. Mem.: Am. Math. Soc., Math. Assn. of Am.

HOPKINS, LARRY MICHAEL, mathematics and computer science educator; b. Ironwood, Mich., June 2, 1941; s. Roy Hargraves and Mildred E. Hopkins; m. Kristin Kay Ehnbom, Aug. 8, 1964. BS in Naval Sci., U.S. Naval Acad., 1963; MS in Math., Mich. State U., 1971; MS in Computer Sci., Mich. Technol. U., 1990. Officer USN, 1963—69; tchg. asst. Mich. State U., East Lansing, 1970—71; instr. math. and computer sci. Gogebic C.C., Ironwood, 1971—; owner, operator Elements Farm, Hurley, Wis., 1975—; owner Elements Software Engring., Hurley, 1999—. Dir. MIS Gogebic C.C., 1984—87, divsn. chmn., 1998—. Bd. dirs. Theatre North, 2002—; mem., sec. Kimball Vol. Fire Dept., 1974—; mem. The Chamber Singers, 1996—. Lt. USN, 1963—69. Decorated Vietnam Svc. Ribbon, ; recipient Presdl. Unit citation, 1968. Mem.: Mich. Coun. Tchrs. of Math., Am. Math. Assn. of 2-Yr. Colls., Math. Assn. Am. Avocations: raising llamas and sheep, acting, choral singing, stained glass, canoeing. Home: 14202 N Park Rd Hurley WI 54534 Office: Gogebic CC E4946Jackson Rd Ironwood MI 49938 E-mail: hopkinsl@gogebic.cc.mi.us., larry@lkhopkins.com.

HOPKINS, LAYNE VICTOR, computer science educator; b. Boone, Iowa, June 5, 1939; s. Wilson Franklin and Lucy Arlene (Stanley) H.; m. Karen Lynn Kloss, Feb. 19, 1960; 1 child, Ranae Lynn. BS, Dakota State U., 1961; MA, U. Utah, 1965; PhD, Pa. State U., 1971. Tchr. math. Springfield (Minn.) Pub. Schs., 1961-64, Bountiful (Utah) Pub. Schs., 1966-67; prof. computer sci. Mankato (Minn.) State U., 1971—. Dir. IBM-Mankato Project, Mankato, 1987—, dir. Clear With Computers-Mankato Project, Mankato, 1994—. Co-author: CAI Basic, 1984. Twp. supr. Mankato Twp., 1988-91; pres. Tech. Plus Ctr., 1998-02. Mem. Inter-Faculty Assn. Avocation: farming. Home: 21052 594th Ave Mankato MN 56001-8543

HOPKINS, LEE BENNETT, writer, educator; b. Scranton, Pa., Apr. 13, 1938; s. Lee Hall and Gertrude (Thomas) H. BA, Kean Coll., 1960; MS, Bank St. Coll., 1964; profl. diploma, Hunter Coll., 1966; LLD (hon.), Kean Coll., 1980. Elem. tchr. Fair Lawn (N.J.) Pub. Schs., 1960-66; lang. arts supr. Bank St. Coll., N.Y.C., 1966-68; curriculum specialist Scholastic, Inc., N.Y.C., 1968-75; pvt. practice author Scarborough, N.Y., 1975—. Cons., vis. prof. various U.S. and Can. colls. and univs.; bd. dirs. Soc. Sch. Librs. Internat.; lit. cons. Random House Achievement Program in Lit.; chmn. Nat. Coun. Tchrs. English poetry award com. Author: Been to Yesterdays: Poems of a Life, 1996 (The Christopher Book award and Golden Kite Honor Book award), numerous children's and junior books, poetry (awards include Nat. Coun. Tchrs. English, Tchrs. Choice award, Pa. Keystone to Reading award, Am. Inst. Graphic Arts award); contbr. articles, texts, and curriculum materials to mags., profl. jours. Recipient Lasting Contbn. to Field Children's Lit. awad U. So. Miss., 1989, Manhattan Coun. Literacy award Internat. Reading Assn., 1983, Ednl. Leadership award Phi Delta Kappa, 1980; named Keystone (Pa.) Author of Yr.; established Lee Bennett Hopkins Poetry award in conjunction with Children's Lit. Coun. Pa. State U., 1993—, Lee Bennett Hopkins Promising Poet award in conjunction with Internat. Reading Assn., 1995—. Avocations: reading, travel. Home and Office: 307 Kemeys Cove Briarcliff Manor NY 10510-2050 E-mail: lbhcove@aol.com.

HOPKINS, LEWIS DEAN, planner, educator; b. Lakewood, Ohio, Feb. 20, 1946; s. W. Dean and Harriet (Painter) H.; m. Susan Brewster Cocker, Aug. 24, 1968; children: Joshua, Nathaniel. BA, U. Pa., 1968, postgrad., 1968-69, M of Regional Planning, 1970, PhD, 1975. Asst. prof. landscape arch. Inst. Environ. Studies/U. Ill., Urbana-Champaign, 1972-79, assoc. prof. landscape arch., urban and regional planning, 1979-84, prof., head dept. urban and regional planning, 1984-97, prof. landscape arch., 1984—. Vis. lectr. dept. town and regional planning U. Sheffield, Eng., 1980; coord. grad. program in landscape arch. U. Ill., 1976-79, chair search com. for head dept. landscape arch., 1985, chair com. to evaluate dir. Inst. Environ. Studies, 1990, com. pub. adminstrn. program, 1990, campus budget strategies com., 1991-94, chancellors strategic planning com., 1993-95, campus senate, 1976-79, 82-84, chair ednl. policy com. 1978-79, senate coun. 1978-79, 82-83, budget com. 1984-86; project dir. Ill. Streams Info. sys., 1981-90; fellow Com. Instnl. Coop. Acad. Leadership Program, 1989-90; external site visit team dept. landscape arch. and environ. planning, Ariz. State U., 1990; rsch. adv. com. Ill.-Ind. Sea Grant Program, 1991—; exec. com. Office of Solid Waste Rsch., 1992-95; Fulbright sr. scholar to Nepal, 1997-98. Co-editor: (with Gill-Chin Lim) Jour. Planning Edn. and Rsch., 1987-91; mem. editl. bd. Jour. Planning Lit., Computers, Environment and Urban sys., Urban and Regional Info. Sys. Assn. Jour., Jour. Planning Edn. and Rsch., others; reviewer: European Jour. Ops. Rsch., Geographical Analysis, Internat. Regional Sci. Rev., Landscape Jour., Mgmt. Sci., Transp. Rsch., others; contbr. articles to profl. jours. Fellow Am. Inst. Cert. Planners; mem. AAUP (pres. campus chpt. 1983-84), Am. Planning Assn. (chair nominating com. Ill. chpt. 1988), Assn. Collegiate Schs. of Planning (regional rep. to exec. bd. 1989-91), Inst. Mgmt. Scis., Regional Sci. Assn., Urban and Regional Inf. Sys. Assn. for Planning Accreditation Bd. (chair site visit teams 1988, 92, 94, team mem. 1995, com. on dual degree programs 1992-93), Planning Accreditation Bd. (chair 1997—). Achievements include research in human and computer problem solving processes for incompletely defined spatial problems; land and water resources management, information, and decision support systems; comprehensive planning processes and institutions. Office: U Ill Urbana-Champaign Dept Urban/Regional Plan 611 E Taft Dr Champaign IL 61820-6921

HOPKINS, MICHAEL PATRICK, gynecologist, oncologist, surgeon; b. Cleve., Nov. 18, 1949; m. Mary Kay Hopkins; children: Brian, Patrick, Maeve. BS, U.S. Mil. Acad., 1971; MEd, Ga. State U., 1975; MD, Case Western Res., 1980. Diplomate Am. Bd. Gynecologic Oncology. Asst. prof. U. Mich. Med. Sch., Ann Arbor, 1986-89; assoc. prof. N.E. Ohio U. Coll. Medicine, Rootstown, 1989-92, prof., 1993—, vice chmn. dept. ob-gyn., 1994-2000; surgeon Gynecologic Oncology of Medicine, Akron, Canton, Ohio, 1989—; chmn., dir. dept. ob-gyn. Akron Gen. Med. Ctr., 1993-2000; dir. dept. ob-gyn. Aultman Hosp., Canton, Ohio, 2000—. Bd. examiner Am. Bd. Ob-Gyn., 1999—, Am. Bd. Ob-Gyn.-Gynecologic Oncology, 2001—. Editor, co-editor Glass's Office Gynecology, 1998; editl. bd. Gynecologic Oncology, 1998—; author 32 chpts. to books; contbr. articles to profl. jours. Officer U.S. Army, 1971-76. Recipient Tchr. of Yr. award Aultman Hosp., 1999-2000. Fellow ACS, ACOG, Soc. Pelvic Surgeon, Am. Gyn. Ob. Soc., Soc. Gynecol. Surgery. Avocation: golfing. Office: Gyn Oncology of NE Ohio Inc 224 W Exchange St #140 Akron OH 44302

HOPKINS, MITCHELL SHADE, music educator; s. Mitchell Daniel and Christine Hopkins. BS in Pub. Sch. Music, Morris Brown Coll., 1958; MA, Columbia U., 1962. Cert. Tchg. and Supervising Music Ohio, 1964. Vocal music tchr. Fulton County Schools, Atlanta, 1958—63, Dayton Pub. Schs., Dayton, Ohio, 1964—92; adjudicator Nat. Guild of Piano Tchrs., Austin, Tex., 1987—. Adjudicator Nat. Guild of Piano Tchrs., Ohio, 1987—, Ga., 1987—, Ind., 1987—, Mich., 1987—, Ohio Jr. Fedn. of Music Clubs, Dayton and Springfield, Ohio, 1987—, Dayton Music Club Scholarships, Dayton, Ohio, 1998—2000. Host (radio program) Honoring a former college music professor, chairman (festival) Music Contest (Excellence in Orgn., 1989), member (guide for music instruction) Course of study. Designer Salem Bend Condominium Assn., Trotwood, Ohio, 1998—2001; best decorated home City of Trotwood, Trotwood, Ohio, 2000. Recipient Tchr. of Yr., Fairburn H.S., Fulton County, Ga., 1963, Excellence in Tchg. Award, Ohio Music Edn. Assn., 1983, Svc. Tchg. Award, Dayton Pub. Schools, Dayton, Ohio, 1993. Mem.: Music Educators Nat. Conf., Am. Coll. Musicians (assoc.; faculty mem. 1987—2002), Nat. Guild of Piano Tchrs. (assoc.), Am. Fedn. Musicians (assoc.), Dayton Music Club (assoc.; bd. dirs.), Alpha Phi Alpha (life). Achievements include first to Introduced hand bells to Dayton Public Schools & organized first bell choir in school system, conducted inservice workshops for teachers to learn bell choir techniques. All schools have bell choirs; development of My choral groups and piano students have maintained superior ratings in music contests; first to Organized an annual art/music festival in the Dayton Public Schools at Residence Park Elementary School. Avocations: gardening, interior decorating,

fishing, cooking, physical fitness. Home: 5502 Nantucket Rd Dayton OH 45426 Office: Am College of Musicians Po Box 1807 Austin TX 78767 Home Fax: 937-837-1173; Office Fax: 937-837-1173.

HOPKINS, NANCY H. biology educator; PhD, Harvard U., 1971. Prof. biology dept. MIT, Cambridge, 1972—; chmn. comm. on women faculty MIT, Sch. of Science; co-chmn. council on faculty diversity MIT. Recipient Laya Wiesner Community Award, 2001, Women's History Month Honoree of NY Academy of Sciences; fellow Amer. Academy of Arts and Sciences. Mem.: Institute of Med., 1999-. Office: MIT E17-341 77 Massachusetts Ave Cambridge MA 02139-4301 E-mail: nhopkins@mit.edu.

HOPKINS, PATRICIA ANN, management consultant; AS in Gen. Studies, Pikes Peak C.C., 1988; BA in Mgmt., So. Nazarene U., 1993; MS in Mgmt., Nat. Louis U., 1995. Jr. programmer, libr. ITT Telec Svcs. Inc., Colorado Springs, Colo., 1980-87; author, authoring asst. Infotec Devel., Colorado Springs, 1987-89; curriculum developer McDonnel Douglas Tng. System, Norman, Okla., 1989-91, instructional designer, 1991-93, Hazelwood, Mo., 1993-94; tng. mgr. Maritz Performance Improvement Co., Fenton, Mo., 1994-98; CEO Planning Connection, L.A., 1999—. Formerly mem. devel. com. Matthew Dickey Boys Club. With USN, 1974—80. Mem.: NAFE, Am. Bus. Womens Assn. (pres. 1995—98, chmn. St. Louis metro area coun. 1998—99). Avocations: billiards, reading, cooking. Office: Planning Connection 3717 S La Brea Ave # 505 Los Angeles CA 90016-5300

HOPKINS, PHILIP JOSEPH, journalist, information technology executive; b. Orange, Calif., Dec. 10, 1954; s. Philip Joseph and Marie Elizabeth Hopkins; m. Susan Lisa Ingman, Oct. 5, 1991; 1 child, Robin Genevieve. BA in Journalism, San Diego State U., 1977; cert. tissue therapist, Ctr. for Decubitis Ulcer Rsch., 1981. Reporter La Jolla (Calif.) Light & Jour., 1973; editl. cons. San Diego Union, 1974; asst. prodr. Southwestern Cable TV, San Diego, 1974; corr. Mission Cable TV, San Diego, 1975; photojournalist UPI, San Diego, 1976; editor Rx Home Care mag., L.A., 1981, Hosp. Info. Mgmt. mag., 1981; editor, assoc. pub. Arcade mag., 1982; mng. editor Personal Computer Age, 1983-84; bur. chief Newsbytes syndicated column, 1985-86; v.p. Humbird Hopkins Inc., 1978-89; writer, editor, rschr. Ind. Rsch. and Info. Svc., 1988-90; writer, analyst Geneva Bus. Rsch., 1990; sci. writer The Cousteau Soc., 1990; pub. cons. U. So. Calif., 1989-90; sr. web devel. mgr. KP-IT Kaiser Permanente, 1991—2002; exec. dir. info. tech. svcs. Pasadena Unified Sch. Dist., 2002—. Co-author: (book) Student's Survival Guide, 1977, 1978. Pres. Ind. Writers So. Calif., 1988. Recipient 1st and 4th pl. award, Nikon, Inc. Photo Contest, 1974, 3d prize, Minolta Camera Co. Creative Photography awards, 1975, Best Feature Photo award, Sigma Delta Chi Mark of Excellence Contest, 1977. Mem.: Project Mgmt. Inst., Computer Press Assn. (life). E-mail: phopkins@pasadena.k12.ca.us.

HOPKINS, RAYMOND FREDERICK, political science educator; b. Cleve., Feb. 15, 1939; s. William Edward Hopkins and Ada Elizabeth (Cornwall) Lewis; m. Carol Lynnette Robinson, June 5, 1962; children— Mark Raymond, Kathryn Carol BA, Ohio Wesleyan U., 1960; postgrad., Yale Divinity Sch., New Haven, 1960-61; MA, Ohio State U., 1963; PhD, Yale U., 1968. Instr. polit. sci. Swarthmore Coll., Pa., 1968-69, assoc. prof., 1973-78, prof., 1978—, chmn. dept. polit. sci., 1983—2984, 1987—91, 2001, dir. pub. policy, 1990—97. Rsch. assoc. Univ. Coll., Dar es Salaam, 1965-66; vis. scholar U. Mich., summer 1968; vis. scholar Weatherhead Ctr. for Internat. Affairs, Harvard U., summer 1969, 73, 98-99; rsch. assoc. Ind. U., 1970-71, U. Nairobi, 1971; vis. scholar Food Policy Rsch. Inst., Stanford U., Calif., 1982-83; vis. fellow Internat. Food Policy Rsch. Inst., Washington, 1984-86; cons. AID, Food and Agr. Orgn., Rome, World Food Programme, Rome, Dept. State, Washington, World Bank, Washington. Author: Political Roles in a New State, 1971, Structures and Process in International Politics, 1973, Global Political Economy of Food, 1979, Global Food Interdependence, 1980; contbr. numerous articles to profl. jours. Mem. property com. bd. mgrs. Swarthmore Coll., 1979-86; chmn. Swarthmore Democratic Com., 1978-82; ruling elder Swarthmore Presbyterian Ch., 1981-86; del. World Food Summit, 1996; pres. Internat. Svc. Cmty. Inc., 1995—. Fellow NDEA, 1961-63, Social Sci. Rsch. Coun., 1969, NEH, 1973, Guggenheim Found., 1974, Woodrow Wilson Internat. Ctr., 1975, Rockefeller Found., 1979, German Marshal Found., 1986, Pew fellow, Harvard, 1993; Fulbright disting. chair Italy, 1995; Yale Internat. Rels. grantee; recipient Heinz endowment, 1982. Mem. AAUP (pres. Swarthmore chpt. 1971-72), Am. Polit. Sci. Assn. (exec. coun.), Internat. Studies Assn., African Studies Assn.. Home: 308 Ogden Ave Swarthmore PA 19081-1413 Office: Swarthmore Coll Dept Polit Sci Swarthmore PA 19081

HOPKINS, ROBERT ARTHUR, retired industrial engineer; b. Youngstown, Ohio, Dec. 14, 1920; s. Arthur George and Margaret Viola (Brush) H.; m. Mary Madelaine Bailey, Apr. 6, 1946; 1 child, Marlaine Hopkins Kaiser. BBA, Case Western Reserve U., 1949; cert. loss control engr., U. Calif., Berkeley, 1969. Ins. agt. Nat. Life and Accident Ins. Co., Lorain, Akron, Ohio, 1951-56, San Mateo, Calif., 1951-56; ins. agt., engr. Am. Hardware Mt. Ins. Co., San Jose, Fresno, Calif., 1956-60; loss control engr. Manhattan Guarantee-Continental Ins. Co., Calif., 1967-77. Organizer Operation Alert DC, Lorain, 1951-52; prin. spkr. DC, Fresno, 1957; active Pleasant Hill (Calif.) Civil Action Com., 1983-85, 2000—; civilian coord. Office Emergency Svcs., Pleasant Hill, 1983-85; advisor, coord. airshows and warbird aircraft, 1980—; chmn. bd. Western Aerospace Mus., Oakland, Calif., 1988; ops. asst. for tower and ops. 50th Anniversary Golden Gate Bridge, San Francisco, 1987; advisor, coord. Travis AFB Air Expo '90, 1990; advisor Air Expo '96, NAS Alameda (Calif.) 50th Anniversary, 1990; advisor NAS Moffett Field Air Show, 1990, 92, Calif. Coast Air Show, Half Moon Bay, 1993-94, Dixon May Fair honoring WWII 50th anniversary, 1995; warbird coord. Port of Oakland Airshow, 1987; warbird advisor/coord. Beale AFB, 1993—; mem. Smithsonian Mus, Smithsonian Air & Space Mus; charter mem. Nat. Mus. of Am. Indian, Am. Air Mus. Britain, Air Force Meml. Found.; life mem. Western Aerospace Mus. Served with USAAC, 1942-46. Recipient Letter of Appreciation Fresno DC, 1957, cert. of appreciation City of Pleasant Hill, 1986, cert. of recognition and spl. citizenship award Calif. State Senate, 1995. Mem.: VFW (life; state civil disaster chmn. Area 5 Calif. 1991), No. Calif. Safety Engrs. Assn. (v.p., pres., chmn. 1974—77), Castle Air Mus. Found., Inc., Am. Air Mus. in Britain, Air Force Assn., Nat. Aero. Assn., Confederate Air Force (mem. staff, leader Pacific wing 1980—, advisor contr. 1990—), Hamilton Field Assn. (dir. ops. Wings of Victory Air Show 1987, coord. 1988, 1989—, asst. to pres. 1989—), Air Force Meml. Found. Kiwanis (chpt. sec.-treas.), Nat. Trust Hist. Preservation, Aero. Club No. Calif. Republican. Roman Catholic. Avocations: fishing, reading, writing, aircraft restoration. Home: 48 Mazie Dr Pleasant Hill CA 94523-3310

HOPKINS, ROBERT ELLIOTT, music educator; b. Greensboro, N.C., Oct. 2, 1931; s. Julian Setzer and Elizabeth Stewart (Daniel) H. MusB, U. Rochester, 1953, MusM, 1954, D Mus. Arts, 1959; postgrad., Acad. for Music, Vienna, Austria, 1959-60. Instr. Mars Hill Coll., 1954-57, 60-63; prof. music Youngstown (Ohio) State U., 1963-93; prof. emeritus, 1993—. Editor: Alexander Reinagle: The Philadelphia Sonatas, 1978; contbr. New Grove Dictionary of Music and Musicians, 1980, 2d edit., 2001, New Grove Dictionary of American Music, 1987, New Grove Dictionary of Opera, 1992. Music dir. various chs., N.C. and Ohio, 1954-81; chmn. Nat. Piano Concerto Competition, Youngstown Symphony Soc., 1986-90. Recipient Disting. Prof. award Youngstown State U., 1990; Fulbright-Hays grantee, 1959-60, rsch. grantee Youngstown State U., 1969-70, 83. Fellow Am. Guild. Organists (dean Youngstown chpt. 1968-69, 73-74, S. Lewis Elmer award 1962, 66); mem. Am. Musicological Soc., Soc. Am. Music. E-mail: dok109@zoominternet.net.

HOPKINS, SAMUEL, retired investment banker; b. Highland, Md., Oct. 18, 1913; s. Samuel Harold and Roberta (Smith) H.; m. Winifred Holt Bloodgood, Oct. 15, 1938 (dec. Oct. 1954); children: Samuel, Henry; m. Anne E. Dankmeyer, Oct. 21, 1955; children: Robert, Frederick. BS, Johns Hopkins U., 1934; LL.B., U. Md., 1938. With Fidelity & Deposit Co. of Md., 1934-69, asst. to treas., 1934-50, asst. treas., 1950-54, sec., 1954-67, v.p., sec., dir., 1967-69; dir., mem. trust com. Equitable Trust Co., Balt., 1954-81; sec., dir. Md. Life Ins. Co., 1963-69; gen. partner Alex, Brown & Sons (investment bankers), Balt., 1970-75, ltd. partner, 1976-87. Bd. dirs. Am. Maritime Cases, Inc. Mem. adv. com. housing for elderly U.S. Housing and Fin. Agy., 1956-60; mem. Balt. Bd. Recreation and Parks, 1965-77, pres., 1965-67, 74-77, v.p., 1968-74; Rep. candidate for Congress, 1952; mem. Md. Ho. of Dels., 1950-54; Rep. candidate for mayor, Balt., 1955; del. Rep. Nat. Conv., 1976; trustee Balt. Mus. Art, Peale Mus., Sheppard and Enoch Pratt Hosp., 1972-89; trustee, v.p. State Colls. Md., 1963-70; mem. Balt. City Planning Commn., 1985-95. Lt. USNR, 1942-45. Mem.: ABA, Chartered Security Analysts, Balt. Security Analysts Soc., Md. Hist. Soc. (treas. 1956—69, pres. 1970—75, chmn. bd. trustees 1988—90). Episcopalian. Home: 45 Warrenton Rd Baltimore MD 21210-2924 E-mail: annehopx@mindsprings.com.

HOPKINS, THEODORE MARK, minister, guidance counselor; b. Vermontville, Mich., Jan. 2, 1926; s. Donald James and Alice (Truman) H.; m. Ruth Ann Allspaw, Oct. 10, 1954; children: Sarah, Phoebe, Martha, Rebekah. BA, Taylor U., 1954; MRE, No. Bapt. Theol. Sem., Lombard, Ill., 1957; BD, No. Bapt. Theol. Sem., 1958; MDiv (converted from BD), 1971. Ordained to ministry Bapt. Ch., 1958; cert. tchr., high sch. counselor. Pastor First Bapt. Ch., Darlington, Wis., 1958-60, Lexington, Ill., 1960-61, Killdeer (N.D.) Bapt. Ch., 1961-65, First Bapt. Ch., Hardin, Mont., 1965-66, Centerville (S.D.)-Wakonda Bapt. Chs., 1966-68, Liberty Union Bapt. Ch., Milan, Mo., 1995—; interim pastor Meml. Bapt. Ch., Chambers, Nebr., 1969-70; bi/voacat. pastor First Bapt. Ch., Mercer, Mo., 1976-78, Blythedale, Mo., 1979-90; guidance counselor public schs., Lineville, Iowa, 1976-88. Pastor-counselor to Am. Bapt. Men Janesville Bapt. Assn., 1959-60, Am. Bapt. Men of Mont., 1965-66; chmn. Christian edn. N.D. Bapt. Conv. 1962-64, leadership edn., 1964-65; rep. N.D. Bapt. Conv. Open Theol. Conf., Greenlake, Wisc. 1964, S.D. Bapt. Conv., 1968; chmn. Fergus Falls, Minn. Child Evangelism Com., 1972-73; dir. music North Grand River Bapt. Assn., 1986-95,, dir. discipleship tng., 1993-95; dir. music North Ctrl. Bapt. Assn., Mo., 1966-99. Sec. Centerville Ambulance Svc., 1967-68; served two terms pres. Lineville Edn. Assn.; vol. Centerville chpts. Alcoholics Anonymous; dir. of music North Grand River (Mo.) Bapt. Assn., 1986-95; vol. SHARE program, 1997—, Nursing Rehab. Ctr., Corydon, 1998—, North Ctrl. Bapt. Assn., Grand Oaks, 1999-2003. With USN, 1944-46, PTO, 1951-52, Korea; with USNR, 1946-51, 52-54. Republican. Avocations: music, walking, photography, reading. Home: 305 E Monroe St Corydon IA 50060-1632 *I have found the greatest satisfaction and happiness in life comes through being of service to others, even when that service is not always appreciated.*

HOPKINS, THOMAS DUVALL, economics educator; b. Spring Valley, Ill., Mar. 10, 1942; s. Joel Willis and Mildred (Duvall) H.; m. Jane Cole Eveleth, Apr. 20, 1968; children: Edward Eveleth, Catherine Chapin Hopkins. BA, Oberlin (Ohio) Coll., 1964; MA, Yale U., 1965, M of Philosophy, 1967, PhD, 1971. Asst. prof. econs. Bowdoin Coll., Brunswick, Maine, 1968-73; cons. Irwin Mgmt. Co., Inc., Columbus, Ind., 1973-75; asst. dir. Coun. on Wage and Price Stability, Washington, 1975-81, acting dir., 1981; dep. adminstr. Office of Mgmt. and Budget, Washington, 1981-84; assoc. prof. U. Md., College Park, 1984-87; assoc. prof. econs. Am. U., Washington, 1987-88; prof. econs., Arthur J. Gosnell prof. Rochester (N.Y.) Inst. Tech., 1988-99, dean coll. of bus., 1999—. Cons. Adminstrv. Conf. U.S., Washington, 1986-88, Office Tech. Assessment, U.S. Congress, 1987-89, Inst. Liberty and Democracy, Lima, Peru, 1986-91, U.S. Regulatory Info. Svc. Ctr., 1990-92, Congl. Budget Office, 1991, U.S. SBA, 1993-95, 2000-02, OECD, Paris, 1994-96; seminar leader Inst. Internat. Edn., Washington, 1987-88; mem. com. on tank vessel design marine bd. NRC, Washington, 1989-91; mem. com. on taxation, fin. and pricing, 1990-93, com. on pub. policy for surface freight transp., 1993-96, com.on fed. role in marine transp. sys., 2003—, Transp. Rsch. Bd., NRC; lectr. U.S. Bus. Sch. in Prague, Czech Republic, 1992-98; pub. mem. U.S. Adminstrv. Conf., Washington, 1994-95; adj. fellow Washington U. Ctr. for Study of Am. Bus., St. Louis, 1996-2000; pres. U.S. Bus. Sch. in Prague, Czech Republic, 1999—; mem. regulatory studies program adv. bd. George Mason Univ. Mercatus Ctr., 1999—. Co-author: Tanker Spills: Prevention by Design, 1991. Mem. coun. Eastman House, Rochester, 1991—. Woodrow Wilson Found. fellow, 1964. Fellow NSF; mem. Am. Econs. Assn., Nat. Economists Club. Office: Rochester Inst Tech 107 Lomb Memorial Dr Rochester NY 14623-5608 E-mail: thopkins@cob.rit.edu.

HOPKINS, THOMAS CHARLES, behavior specialist; b. Camden, N.J., Sept. 03; s. Paul Wallace and Rose Helen H.; m. Patricia Ann, June 24, 1972; children: Anthony, Claudia, Joshua, Jason, Thomas. BS, Kans. State U., 1970; MEd, Nat. Louis U., 1994. Tchr. spl. edn. Gloucester Twp. Pub. Sch., Erial, N.J., 1971-74, Bass River Twp. Pub. Schs., New Gretna, NJ, 1974-78, Tuckerton (N.J.) Pub. Sch., 1978-83, Pasco County Pub. Sch., Dade City, Fla., 1983-92; behavior specialist Passo County Pub. Sch., Hudson, Fla., 1992—. Asst. coach Spring Hill (Fla.) Dixie Baseball, 1995, 97. Mem. Coun. Exceptional Children (membership chair 2000—). Democrat. Roman Catholic. Avocation: gardening. Home: 1136 Berger Ave Spring Hill FL 34608

HOPKINS, TOM, artist; b. Summerside, P.E.I., Can., Dec. 9, 1944; s. Archibald Sherard and Frances May (McCulloch) H.; m. Joan Marshall; children: Jacob, Anna. BFA, Mt. Allison U., 1970; MFA, Concordia U., 1987. Prof. painting and drawing McGill U., 1980-83, Dawson Coll., 1982-87, Concordia U., 1983-98. V.p. Can. Inst. for Psychosynthesis, 1973-78. Exhibited in shows at Mira Godard Gallery, Toronto, U. Toronto Hart House, Equinox Gallery, Vancouver, Lillian Heidenberg Fine Art, N.Y., West Palm Beach, Miami, Art Gallery of N.S., Galerie du Bellefeuille, Montreal, Concordia U. Art Gallery, others; represented in collections at Alcan, Art Gallery of Lethbridge, Alta., Art Gallery of Windsor, Art Gallery of N.S., Mt. Allison U., Royal Bank of Can., Mus. Que., Microsoft Corp., Seattle, Bank N.S., others. Grantee Can. Coun., 1980, 81, 85, Ministry Cultural Affairs Que., 1988, 90. Avocation: music. Office: Studio 999 rue du College # 30 Montreal QC Canada H4C 2S3 E-mail: tom_hopkins@sympatico.ca.

HOPKINSON, SHIRLEY LOIS, library and information science educator; b. Boone, Iowa, Aug. 25, 1924; d. Arthur Perry and Zora (Smith) Hopkinson. Student, Coe Coll., 1942—43; AB cum laude, U. Colo., 1945; BLS, U. Calif., 1949; MA, Claremont Grad. Sch., 1951; EdM, U. Okla., 1952, EdD, 1957. Tchr. pub. sch., Stigler, Okla., 1946—47; tchr. Palo Verde HS., Jr. Coll., Blythe, Calif., 1947—48; asst. libr. Modesto (Calif.) Jr. Coll., 1949—51; tchr., libr. Fresno, Calif., 1951—52, La Mesa, Calif., 1953—55; asst. prof. librarianship, instrnl. materials dir. Chaffey Coll., Ontario, Calif., 1955—59; asst. prof. librarianship San Jose (Calif.) State Coll., 1959—64, assoc. prof., 1964—69, prof., 1969—. Bd. dirs. NDEA Inst. Sch. Librs., summer, 1966; mem. Santa Clara County Civil Svc. Bd. Examiners. Author: Descriptive Cataloging of Library Materials, Instructional Materials for Teaching the Use of the Library; editor: Calif. Sch. Libraries, 1963—64; asst. editor Sch. Libr. Assn. of Calif. Bull., 1961—63, book reviewer profl. jours.; contbr. articles to profl. jours. Honnold Honor scholar, Claremont Grad. Sch., 1945—46. Mem.: LWV (bd. dirs. 1950—51, publs. chmn.), AAUW (dir. 1957—58), NEA, ALA, AAUP, Kappa Delta Pi, Alpha Beta Alpha, Calif. Tchrs. Assn., San Diego County Sch. Librs. Assn. (sec. 1945—55), Sch. Librs. Assn. Calif. (com. mem., treas. No. sect. 1951—52), Audio-Visual Assn. Calif., Calif. Library Assn., Bus. Profl. Women's Club, Alpha Lambda Delta, Phi Beta Kappa (scholar 1944), Delta Kappa Gamma (sec. 1994—96, legis. liaison 1996—2002, corr. sec. 2002—), Phi Kappa Phi (disting. acad. achievement award 1981). Office: 1340 Pomeroy Ave Apt 408 Santa Clara CA 95051-3658

HOPKO, DEREK RICHARD, psychologist, consultant; b. Winnipeg, Manitoba, Can., June 15, 1969;, U.S.1992; s. Richard Allen and Charlotte Mary Hopko; m. Sandra Denise Barbre, Sept. 11, 1998; 1 child, Isaac Richard. BA in Psychology, U. Manitoba, Can., 1994; MA in Psychology, Cleve. State U., 1996; PhD in Clin. Psychology, W.Va. U., 2000. Lic. psychologist Tenn. Therapist Valley Cmty. Mental Health Ctr., Morgantown, W.Va., 1996—98, Chestnut Ridge Hosp., Morgantown, 1998—99; resident U. Tex. Houston Med. Sch., 1999—2000, fellow, 2000—01; asst. prof. U. Tenn., Knoxville, 2001—. Grant cons. Vet. Health Adminstrn., 2002—. Mem. editl. bd.: Jour. Anxiety Disorders, reviewer: Anxiety, Stress and Coping, Behavior Therapy, Cognitive Therapy and Rsch., Ednl. Psychology, Jour. Anxiety Disorders, Jour. Psychopathology and Behavioral Assessment, Perceptual nd Motor Skills, Personality and Individual Differences, Psychological Reports; co-author: The Brief Behavioral Activation Treatment for Depression (BATD): A Comprehensive Patient Guide, 2002; contbr. articles. Grantee, Nat. Inst. Mental Health, 2003—. Mem.: Am. Psychological Assn., Am. Diabetes Assn. (coun. psychology and behavioral medicine), Anxiety Disorders Assn. Am., Assn. Advancement Behavior Therapy. Avocations: golf, hiking, movies, reading. Office: Univ Tenn Dept Psychology 307 Austin Peay Bldg Knoxville TN 37996-0900 Office Fax: 865-974-3330. E-mail: dhopko@utk.edu.

HOPP, ANTHONY JAMES, advertising agency executive; b. Detroit, Jan. 31, 1945; s. William J. and Beverly (Gildea) H.; m. Nancy Jane Dunckel, Nov. 11, 1969; children: Beth, Michael. BA in Advt./Mktg., Mich. State U., 1967, MA in Advt./Psychology, 1968. Asst. account exec. Campbell-Ewald Adv., Warren, Mich., 1968-70; account exec. Lintas Campbell-Ewald, Warren, Mich., 1970-74, account supr., 1974-75, v.p., account supr., 1975-79, sr. v.p., mgmt. supr., 1979-85, group sr. v.p., group mgmt. supr., 1985-88, exec. v.p., account dir., 1988-93, pres., 1993-95, vice chmn., 1995—97, also bd. dirs., chmn. & CEO, 1997—. Bd. dirs. C-E Comm., Warren, Lintas Ams. Recipient Robert E. Healy award Interpublic Group of Cos., 1989. Mem. Adcraft, Hunters Creek, Bloomfield Hills Country Club, Pine Lake Country Club. Avocations: golf, hunting, boating. Office: Lintas-Campbell-Ewald 30400 Van Dyke Ave Warren MI 48093-2368*

HOPP, DANIEL FREDERICK, manufacturing company executive, lawyer; b. Ann Arbor, Mich., Apr. 14, 1947; s. Clayton A. and Monica E. (Williams) H.; m. Maria G. Lopez, Dec. 20, 1968; children: Emily, Daniel, Melissa. BA in English, U. Mich., 1969; JD, Wayne State U., 1973. Bar: Ill. 1974, Mich. 1980. Atty. Mayer, Brown and Platt, Chgo., 1973-79, Whirlpool Corp., Benton Harbor, Mich., 1979-84, asst. sec., 1984-85, sec., asst. gen. counsel, 1985-89, v.p., gen. counsel, sec., 1989-98, sr. v.p., corp. affairs and gen. counsel, 1998—. Past co-chmn. Conf. Bd. Legal Quality Coun. Mem. City of St. Joseph (Mich.) Planning Comm.; bd. dirs. Lakeland Regional Health Sys., Joseph, Mich., St. Joseph Today; mem. Coun. for World Class Cmtys. With U.S. Army, 1969-71. Mem. Am. Soc. Corp. Secs. (past pres., bd. dirs. Chgo. chpt.), Mich. Bar Assn., Ill. Bar Assn., Berrien County Bar Assn., Mich. Mfrs. Assn. (bd. dirs.) Republican. Mem. Ch. of Christ. Avocation: golf. Office: Whirlpool Corp Adminstrv Ctr 2000 N M 63 Benton Harbor MI 49022-2692

HOPP, NANCY SMITH, marketing executive; b. Aurora, Ill., Nov. 1, 1943; d. C. Dudley and Margaret (McWethy) Smith; m. Edward Thompson Reid, July 19, 1963 (div. Feb. 1966); 1 child, Edward Thompson Jr.; m. James C. Hopp, Feb. 4, 1978. Cert. Chgo. Sch. Interior Design, 1965; BA in Social Scis., Aurora U., 1968, MS in Bus. Mgmt., 1982. Dir. pub. rels. Sta. WLXT-TV, Aurora, 1969-70; bookstore mgr. Waubonsee Coll., Sugar Grove, Ill., 1970-79, dir. purchasing, 1979-85, dir. pub. rels., 1984-85; dir. devel. Assn. for Individual Devel., Aurora, 1985-87; dir. pub. rels. Provena Mercy Ctr., Aurora, 1988-95; dir. mktg. Dreyer Med. Clinic, Aurora, 1995—. Ninety for the 90s com. Ill. Dept. Aging, 1989. Editor: Volunteers Make the Difference, 1982; author Pigeon Woods Cookbook; producer (film) Caring Counts; contbr. articles to profl. jours. Bd. dirs. Family Support Ctr., Aurora, 1984-90, Aurora Area United Way, 1990-96, Corridor Group, 1993-94, Assn. Individual Devel., 1996—, Suicide Prevention Svcs., 1998-2000; adv. coun. Mercy Ctr. Health Care, Aurora, 1985-87; moderator New Eng. Congl. Ch., Aurora, 1983; charter mem. bd. dirs. Aurora Cmty. Coordinating Coun., 1985-86; mem. Block Grant Working Com., Aurora, 1987-2000, Kane County Womens Health Coalition, 1999—; bd. dirs., sec. Cities in Schs./Aurora 2000, Inc., 1993-94, A.I.D., 1999—, Paramount Arts Ctr. Endowment Bd., 1999—, Fox Valley Arts Hall of Fame, 2001-. Recipient citation U.S. Dept. HEW, 1969, Christian Svc. award, 1996; named Woman of the Day, Sta. WAIT AM, Chgo., 1974, Optimist of Yr. for Cmty. Svc., 1987, Woman of Distinction, YWCA, 1990. Mem. Women in Mgmt. (Nat. Charlotte Danstrom Woman of Achievement award 1984), Nat. Soc. Fund Raising Execs. (ethics com. Chgo. chpt. 1987), Ill. Assn. Coll. Stores (pres. 1976), Nat. Assn. Ednl. Buyers (com. 1984)), Exch. Club. Republican. Avocations: water-skiing, auto racing, billiards, art, music. Home: 175 S Western Ave Aurora IL 60506-4617 Office: Dreyer Med Clinic 1877 W Downer Pl Aurora IL 60506-7334

HOPPE, DAVID RUTLEDGE, writer, editor; b. Evanston, Ill., Dec. 28, 1950; s. John and Edmar (von Henke) H.; m. Mary Helen Schaaf, June 10, 1983; 1 child. BA, Macalester Coll., 1973; MA, U. Minn., 1976; MFA, Bennington Coll., 1986. From audio-visual dir. to asst. dir. Michigan City (Ind.) Pub. Libr., 1980-88; resource ctr. dir. Ind. Humanities Coun., Indpls., 1988-94; creative dir. 2d Globe, Indpls., 1994-98; dir. Nuvo Cultural Inst., Indpls., 1998—; assoc. editor Nuvo Newsweekly, Indpls., 1998—; radio host Nuvo's X-Press It on the X, 1998—2002. Writer-in-residence Ball State U., Muncie, Ind., 1994; fellow Butler Univ. Writer's Studio, 1994. Editor: Where We Live, 1989, Hard Pieces: Dan Carpenter's Indiana, 1993; contbr. popular publs. Project dir. Wordstruck Festival, Indpls., 1991, 93, Libr. Literacy Program, Michigan City, 1988. Named Libr. of Yr., Ind. Libr. Assn., 1986; recipient award, Ind. Soc. Profl. Journalist's; Time-Life fellow in creative writing, 1986. Home: 6001 Broadway St Indianapolis IN 46220-1807 Office: 811 E Westfield Blvd Indianapolis IN 46220 E-mail: dhoppe@nuvo.net.

HOPPE, JOHN DAVID, political organization worker; b. Baraboo, Wis., Aug. 25, 1951; s. John Andrew and Carol Field Hoppe; m. Karen Davis; children: Katherine, Geoffrey, Gregory. BA, U. Notre Dame, 1973; MA, Johns Hopkins U., 1976. Chief of staff Congressman Jack Kemp, Washington, 1984-88, Sen. Dan Coats, Washington, 1989-92; staff dir. Senate Rep. Conf. Sec., Washington, 1993-94, Senate Rep. Whip, Washington, 1995-96; chief of staff Senate Majority Leader Trent Lott, Washington, 1996—2001, Senate Minority Leader Trent Lott, Washington, 2001—02; vice chmn. Quinn Gillespie and Assocs., 2003—. Republican. Roman Catholic. Avocations: singing, running. Office: US Senate Majority Leader Trent Lott S-230 Washington DC 20510

HOPPE, LEA ANN, elementary education educator; b. Birmingham, Ala., Mar. 20, 1959; d. George Carson and Annie Merle (Carleton) Jones; m. David Thomas Hoppe, Nov. 21, 1983; children: Kathryn Ann, Emily Louise. BS in Edn., Samford U., Birmingham, 1981; MA in Edn., U. Ala., Tuscaloosa, 1986. Cert. tchr., Ala. Reading tutor Pearson's Reading & Math. Ctr., Birmingham, 1979-81; kindergarten tchr. Scottsboro (Ala.) City Schs.-Brownwood, 1981-86; pre-kindergarten tchr., ctr. dir. First Bapt. Learning Ctr., Scottsboro, 1986-89; kindergarten tchr. Covenant Weekday Kindergarten, Huntsville, Ala., 1990-95, Randolph Sch., Huntsville, 1995—. Chmn. bd. dirs. First Bapt. Child Devel. Ctr., Huntsville, 1992-96; conf. leader Samford U., Birmingham, 1993, Farley Elem. Parents Orgn., Huntsville, 1994. Author: (children's activity books) A Child For All Seasons: Volume 1, 1994, Volume 2, 1994. Children's choir dir. First Bapt. Ch., Huntsville, 1991—, children's Sunday Sch. tchr., 1993—. Mem. Nat. Assn. Edn. Young Children, Orgn. Am. Kodaly Educators, Music Educators Nat. Conf., Music Educators Nat. Assn., So. Early Childhood Assn., Ala. Assn. Young Children, Delta Omicron (life), Kappa Delta Pi, Kappa Delta Epsilon, Pi Gamma Mu, Omicron Delta Kappa. Republican. Baptist. Avocations: singing, playing the trombone, children's literature. Home: 2911 Barcody Rd SE Huntsville AL 35801-2218 Office: Randolph Sch 1005 Drake Ave SE Huntsville AL 35802-1099 E-mail: lhoppe@randolphschool.net.

HOPPENSTEIN, ABRAHAM SOLOMON, investment and merchant banker, consultant; b. Benoni, Republic of South Africa, Oct. 9, 1931; came to U.S., 1976; s. Charles and Rachel (Diner) H.; m. Taubene Judith Frank, Jan. 19, 1954; children: Rachelle Schlosberg, Joel, Saul, Deborah Zucker. B in Commerce, Witwatersrand U. Law Sch., Johannesburg, Republic of South Africa, 1951, LLB, 1955. Barrister of Supreme Ct. Republic of South Africa, High Ct. of Swaziland. Chmn., chief exec. officer Abrubhill Investments Ltd. Chartrex Internat. Ltd., Fairdeal Investments (PTY) Ltd., Selcourt Centre Ltd., Selcourt Fin. Corp. Ltd., South Africa; trade commr. South African Embassy, Tel Aviv, Israel, 1975, counsellor polit. affairs Washington, 1976-77, consul gen., 1979-80, South African Consulate Gen., N.Y.C., 1980-86; pres., chmn., CEO Chartrex Internat. Ltd., 1993—; pres., CEO AHI West Side Creek Inc., AHI Equinox Inc. V.p. internat. affairs Allen & Co. Inc., N.Y.C., 1986-92. Contbr. articles to profl. jours. Mem. steering com. Global Econ. Action Inst., N.Y.; mem. exec. com. South African Jewish Bd. Deps., South African Zionist Fedn., 1978-79; trustee Temple Israel, White Plains, N.Y., 1988-90; bd. dirs. Helen Keller Worldwide, 1997-2002. Aspen Inst. for Humanities fellow, 1988. Mem. East Rand Attys. Assn. (chmn. 1969-70), N.Y. C. of C. (hon. mem.), Lions Internat. (hon. mem. 1980), Econ. Club. N.Y., Fgn. Policy Assn., Polo Club of Boca Raton (gov. 1998—, v.p. 1999-2001, pres. 2002—). Avocations: golf, tennis, swimming, photography, travel. Office: Chartrex Internat Ltd PO Box 812373 Boca Raton FL 33481-2373 Fax: 561-999-0588.

HOPPENTHALER, JOHN GUNTHER, writer, educator; b. Bklyn., Oct. 24, 1960; s. John and Maria Hoppenthaler. BS, SUNY, Brockport, 1984; AA, Rockland C.C., Suffern, N.Y., 1985; MFA, Va. Commonwealth U., 1988. Adj. lectr. Rockland C.C., Suffern, 1989—92, Pace U., Bedford, White Plains, NY, 1989—91, W.Va. Wesleyan Coll., Buckhannon, 1991—97, Manhattanville Coll., Purchase, NY, 1997; personal asst. Toni Morrison, Grandview, NY, 1997—. Staff W.Va. Writer's Workshop, Morgantown, 1997—, Catskill Poetry Workshops, Oneonta, NY, 2001; poet-in-residence Chautauqua Inst., 2003. Poetry editor: Kestrel: A Jour. of Lit. and Art, 1997—; author: (poetry) Lives of Water, 2003. Instr., facilitator Kestrel Festival of the Arts, Fairmont, W.Va., 1997—2000. Grantee Individual Artist grant, W.Va. Commn. on the Arts, Charleston, 1998. Mem.: Associated Writing Programs. Avocations: contemporary folk music, food and wine, fishing, baseball, cooking. Home: 17 Van Houten St Haverstraw NY 10927

HOPPER, CAROL, meeting and incentive trip administrator; b. Montreal, Que., Can., Apr. 23, 1952; m. Cedric Heimrath; stepchildren: Natasha, Erik. Student, McGill U., 1972; cert., Canadian Inst. Orgnl. Mgmt., 1991. Asst. Ben Fuller Assocs., 1973-89; show dir. Nat. Ski Industries Assn., Montreal, 1989-91, exec. dir., 1991-96, dir. show svcs., 1997-98; project mgr. Chateau Travel, Carlson Mktg. Group, 1998—2002; project leader Vision 2000 Travel Group, 2002—. Mem. adv. com. sporting goods bus. program Sir Sandford Fleming Coll., 1994-98. Mem. Can. Assn. Exposition mgrs., Jr. League Montreal (bd. dirs., chmn. coms. 1987-92). Avocations: skiing, golf, reading, travel, sports. Home: 302 Perrault Rosemere QC Canada J7A 1B9

HOPPER, DAVID HENRY, religion educator; b. Cranford, N.J., July 31, 1927; s. Orion Cornelius and Julia Margaret (Weitzel) H.; m. Nancy Ann Nelson, June 10, 1967 (div. June 1984); children: Sara Elizabeth, Kathryn Ann, Rachel Suzanne. BA, Yale U., 1950; BD, ThM, Princeton Theol. Sem., 1953, ThD, 1959. Ordained Presbyn. minister, 1961. Asst. prof. Macalester Coll., St. Paul, 1959-67, assoc. prof., 1967-73, James Wallace prof. of religion, 1973—2001, prof. emeritus, 2001—. Author: Tillich: A Theological Portrait, 1967 (N.J. Authors award 1968), A Dissent on Bonhoeffer, 1975, Technology, Theology, and the Idea of Progress, 1991. With USN, 1945-46. Recipient Newberry ACM Faculty fellow, 1992-93, Templeton Found. Sci./Religion Course award, 1996. Mem. Internat. Bonhoeffer Soc., Hist. of Sci. Soc., Kierkegaard Soc. Home: 1787 Lincoln Ave Saint Paul MN 55105-1954

HOPPER, EDWARD WARREN, language educator; b. Macon, Mo., Sept. 12, 1939; s. Louis Edward Hopper and Kathryn Louise Warren; m. Ruth Elizabeth Thompson, May 12, 1984; children: Thomas Warren, Mary Cagle. BA, N. Tex. State U., 1961; MA, U. Mo., 1964, PhD, 1971. Instr. Spanish U. Mo., Columbia, 1966—67, U. N.C., Charlotte, 1967—71, asst. prof., assoc. prof., 1975—. Home: 633 S Union Concord NC 28025 Office: Univ NC Dept Lang University Blvd Charlotte NC 28223 E-mail: ewhopper@email.uncc.edu.

HOPPER, JACK RUDD, chemical engineering educator; b. Highlands, Tex., May 12, 1937; s. Bonnie Preston and Rosa Mae Hopper; m. Marilyn Joyce Spears, May 30, 1958; children: Connie, Bradley. Student, Lee Coll., 1957; BSChemE, Tex. A&M U., 1959; MChemE, U. Del., 1964; PhD, La. State U., 1969. Rsch. engr. Esso Rsch. and Engring., Baytown, Tex., 1959-67; asst. prof. chem. engring. Lamar U., Beaumont, Tex., 1969-72, assoc. prof. chem. engring., 1972-75, prof. chem. engring., 1975—, chair chem. engring. dept., 1974—99, dir. engring. grad. studies, 1989-99, liaison hazardous waste alternatives ctr., 1987-88; dean coll. engring., 1999—; interim dir Gulf Coast Rsch. Ctr., 1993-94, assoc. dir., 1995-97, dir., 1997-99, Tex. Hazardous Waste Rsch. Ctr., 1993—. Cons. J. M. Montgomery, New Orleans, 1991-92, Texaco Chem., Port Arthur, Tex., 1989-90, Star Enterprise, 1990-93, Tex. Internat. Ednl. Consortium, Austin, 1991-93, Mobil Chem., 1993. Mem. editl. bd. Waste Mgmt., 1992-96, co-editor 1996-2001; contbr. articles to profl. pubs. Officer Rotary, South Park, Tex., 1975-80. Recipient Dow Outstanding Faculty award Am. Soc. for Engring. Edn., 1971, Outstanding Alumni award Lee Coll., 1981. Fellow AIChE. Achievements include inventions in field. Office: Lamar U 4400 MLK Pkwy Beaumont TX 77705

HOPPER, KEVIN R. biologist; b. Lexington, Ky., Sept. 21, 1969; s. Carol and Donald Hopper. BS, U. of Ky., 1993, PhD in Evolutionary Biology, 1998. Post-doctoral fellow Ind. State U., Terre Haute, 1998—99; instr. U. of Ky. Lexington C.C., 1999—2002, asst. prof., 2002—. Author (reviewer): (pub. rsch.) The Am. Naturalist, Ecology; author: Animal Behaviour, Oikos; reveiwer: Can. Jour. Zoology, Jour. Insect Behavior; author: Butterfly Count vol./North Am. Butterfly Assn., 2003. Bird count vol. Audubon Soc., Lexington, Ky., 1999—2003; sec. Lexington Traditional Dance Assn., Ky., 1999—2003. Recipient Rsch. Experience for Undergraduates award, NSF, 1993, Best Student Paper Presentation, Ohio Valley Entomol. Assn., 1995; fellow Pre-doctoral fellowship, NSF, 1994—97, Dissertation Yr. Fellowship, U. of Ky., 1997—98, Post-doctoral Fellowship, Ind. State U., 1998—99. Mem.: Ky. Ornithol. Soc. (assoc.). Achievements include research in the ecology and evolution of cannibalism in larval dragonflies. Office: Univ Ky Lexington C C Cooper Dr Lexington KY 40506-0235 Personal E-mail: hopper@uky.edu. E-mail: hopper@uky.edu.

HOPPER, MARGARET SUE, academic administrator, educational diagnostician, consultant; b. New Gulf, Tex., Feb. 8, 1937; d. Thomas Clinton and Margaret Evelyn (McDaniel) Letts; m. Rufus Denman Hopper Jr., Apr. 7, 1955; children: Lloyd Wade, Nancy Marie. BS, Sam Houston State U., 1960, MEd, 1973. Cert. reading specialist, ednl. disgnostician, tchr. of mentally retarded and learning disabled elem. students, elem. edn. tchr. Tchr. Jarrell (Tex.) Ind. Sch. Dist., 1960-67; tchr. Lohn (Tex.) Ind. Sch. Dist., 1967-68, Brady (Tex.) Ind. Sch. Dist., 1968-70, Huntsville (Tex.) Ind. Sch. Dist., 1970-78, spl. edn. tchr., 1978, edn. diagnostician, 1978-80; pre-lab. student tchr. Sam Houston State U., 1971-78; edn. diagnostician Carrollton (Tex.)-Farmers Branch Ind. Sch. Dist., 1980-85, instructional diagnostician, 1985-88, instructional facilitator, 1988-91, edn. diagnostician, 1991-92; pvt. practice as ednl. cons., diagnostician, tchr. appraiser, 1992-94; inclusion specialist, 1994-95; supr. student tchrs. Sam Houston State U., 1995-97. Mem. Bd. Registry-Diagnostician #0522, Houston, 1984-2002. Mem. Tex. Ednl. Diagnosticians Assn., Tex. State Tchrs. Assn., Tex. Ret. Tchrs. Assn. (legis. com. 1995-2002, state leadership tng. team 2003), Alpha Chi. Methodist. Avocation: water sports. Home and Office: PO Box 1536 Huntsville TX 77342-1536

HOPPER, STEPHEN RODGER, hospital administrator; b. Chgo., Aug. 28, 1949; s. Rodger Patterson and Dorothy Ann (Newberg) H.; m. Janet Sue Waddill, June 10, 1972; children: Nathan John, Amanda Sue. BA, Ill. Coll., 1971; MHA, U. Minn., 1974. Adminstrv. resident Rochester (Minn.) Meth. Hosp., 1973-74; dir. support svcs. Jennie Edmundson Hosp., Council Bluffs, Iowa, 1974-78; asst. adminstr. Trinity Meml. Hosp., Cudahy, Wis., 1978-83, sr. v.p. med. svcs., 1983-84; pres., chief exec. officer McDonough Dist. Hosp., Macomb, Ill., 1985—. Bd. dirs. Midamerica Nat. Bank, Canton, Ill. Bd. dirs. Macomb Area Indsl. Devel., 1985—; Medicine Lodge Dist. com. Illowa coun. Boy Scouts Am., 1997-99. Fellow Am. Coll. Healthcare Execs.; mem. Ill. Hosp. Assn. (past pres. region 1-B, bd. dirs. 1992-95, mem. venture corp. bd. 1999—), Macomb C. of C. (bd. dirs. 1990-94), Rotary (pres.-elect Macomb 1995-96, pres. 1996-97, asst. dist. gov. 2000—). Avocations: golf, reading, computers, travel. Home: 112 W Totem Trl Macomb IL 61455-1272 Office: McDonough Dist Hosp 525 E Grant St Macomb IL 61455-3318 E-mail: srhopper@mdh.org.

HOPPER, TERRY N. pharmaceutical executive, consultant, research scientist; b. Memphis, Tenn., Aug. 12, 1954; s. William S. and Marie A. Hopper. BS in Chemistry, Memphis State U., 1977, MS, 1984. Maintenance mechanic J. Strickland & Co., Memphis, 1972—77; sr. analytical rsch. chemist Schering-Plough Corp., Memphis, 1977—89; sr. rsch. assoc., dept. head Mallinckrodt, Inc., St. Louis, 1989—97; quality scis. sr. chemist ALZA Corp., Vacaville, Calif., 1998—2000; assoc. dir. Inhale Therapeutic Sys., San Carlos, Calif., 2000—01; QAC mgr. NaPro Biotherapeutics, Inc., Boulder, Colo., 2002—. Cons. NaPro Biotherapeutics, Inc., Boulder, 2002; presenter in field. Mem.: Am. Soc. for Quality, Am. Assn. of Pharm. Scientists, Math. Assn. of Am., Am. Chem. Soc., The Smithsonian Instn. (assoc.), U.S. Judo Assn. (life), Internat. Magicians Soc. (life). Conservative. Roman Catholic. Achievements include development of novel process for the customer-focused design and justification of analytical methods; Application of Statistical Quality Control techniques in pharmaceutical stability program analytical laboratory performance and operations. Avocations: sports, magic, travel, electronics/computer science. Home: #1912 761 Eldorado Blvd Broomfield CO 80021 Personal E-mail: ttlpkg@earthlink.net.

HOPPING, RICHARD LEE, college president emeritus; b. Dayton, Ohio, July 26, 1928; s. Lavon Lee and Dorothy Marie (Anderson) H.; m. Patricia Louise Vance, June 30, 1951; children: Ronald, Debra, Jerrold. Student, Chaffey Coll., 1947-48, U. Dayton, 1948-49, Sinclair Coll., 1948-49; BS, OD, So. Coll. Optometry, 1952, DOS (hon.), 1972; DSc (hon.), SUNY, 1995. Practice optometry, Dayton, Ohio, 1953-73; pres. So. Calif. Coll. Optometry, Fullerton, 1973-97, pres. emeritus, 1997—. Mem. Nat. Acads. of Practice, 1983—; chmn. Nat. Acad. Practice in Optometry, 1985-89; vice chmn. 13th dist. med. quality rev. com., State of Calif. Bd. Med. Quality Assurance, 1985-93; member St. Jude Hosp. Adv. Bd., 1985—; nat. spokesperson Better Vision Inst., 1988-2000; cons. in field. Contbr. numerous articles on vision and health care to profl. publs. V.p. Orange County (Calif.) coun. Boy Scouts Am., 1977-79, mem. adv. coun., 1979-94; mem. Coun. Assocs. of Red Cross, North Orange County Svc. Ctr., 1978-80; mem. adv. coun. YWCA, North Orange County, 1984-92. Named Optimist of Yr. Dayton View Optimists, 1956; recipient Orange County Retinitis Pigmentosa award of Excellence in field of vision care, 1988, award of Excellence VisionAmerica, 1991, Dirs. Choice award Optical Labs. Assn., 1995, Leo award of Excellence in Global Eye Care Nat. Eye Rsch. Found., 1995, People of Vision award Prevent Blindness Am., 1997. Fellow APHA (Vision Care Disting. Achievement award 1984), Am. Acad. Optometry (chmn. primary care optometry sect. 1973-79, chmn. awards com. 1981-90); mem. Am. Optometric Assn. (pres. 1971-72, chmn. profl. enhancement adv. com. 1982-89, Calif. Optometrist of Yr. 1988, AOA Nat. Optometrist of Yr. 1988, chair industry rels. com. 1989-95, chair nat. ednl. summit conf. 1990-91, chair Nat. Optometric Edn. Summit com. 1991-92, chair centennial adv. com. 1996-98, Scope of Optometric Practice Conf. 1992, Dr. Raymond I. Meyers award 1990, Disting. Svc. award 1993), Calif. Optometric Assn. (hon. life, jud. coun., Optometrist of Yr. 1988, Paul Yarwood Meml. award 1997), Assn. Ind. Calif. Colls. and Univs. (trustee 1973-97), Optometric Ext. Programs Found. (hon. life), Assn. Schs. and Colls. of Optometry (pres. 1983-85), Ohio Optometric Assn. (pres. 1964-65, Ohio Optometrist of Yr. 1962, hon. life), Retinitis Pigmentosa Internat. (adv. exec. com. 1984-88), Dayton Jr. C. of C. (Man of Yr.), Lincoln of Orange County Club (chmn. ethics com. 1988-92, lifetime achievement awd. SCO, 1997).

HOPPING, WILLIAM RUSSELL, hospitality industry consultant and appraiser; b. Balt., May 3, 1947; s. Russell Leroy and Janet Louise (Cloud) H.; m. Catherine Wilson; 1 child, William Alexander. BS in Hotel Adminstrn., Cornell U., 1969; MBA, U. Denver, 1978. Mgr. Sylvania (Ohio) Country Club, 1972-77; sr. cons. Pannell Kerr Forster, Denver, 1978-82; cons. Ginther Wycoff Grp., Denver, 1982-85; pres. W.R. Hopping & Co., Inc., Denver, 1985—. Mem. adv. bd. travel and tourism dept. Arapahoe C.C., 1998. Vol., Big Bros., Inc., Denver, 1990—; chmn. adv. bd. U. Denver Profl. Career Devel. Prog., 1987-88, chmn. task force, Career and Placement Ctr., 1989; mem. City of Littleton Historic Preservation Bd., 2003—. 1st lt. U.S. Army, 1970-72. Mem. Appraisal Inst., Internat. Soc. Hospitality Cons. (pres. 1990-91, chmn. 1991-93, chmn. emeritus, 1993—), Cornell Soc. Hotelmen (pres. Rocky Mountain chpt. 1984-85), Counselors of Real Estate. Avocations: bicycling, skiing. Office: W R Hopping & Co Inc 5773 Shasta Cir Littleton CO 80123-2732

HOPPLE, RICHARD VAN TROMP, JR., internet media executive; b. Cin., Mar. 20, 1947; s. Richard Van Tromp and Marie (Mitchell) H.; m. Patricia Spalt, July 16, 1972; children: Peter Van Tromp, Richard Halstead, Brooks McNeil BS, Northwestern U., 1969. Acct. exec. Dancer-Fitzgerald-Sample, N.Y.C., 1969-72; sr. v.p. Benton & Bowles, Inc., N.Y.C., 1972-85, D'Arcy-Masius-Benton & Bowles, Inc., N.Y.C., 1985-86; with Wells, Rich, Greene Worldwide, N.Y.C., 1986-91, formerly pres. East, then pres. Worldwide; from vice-chmn. to pres. Darcy Masius Benton & Bowles, N.Y.C., 1992-96; CEO Unicast Comm., 1996—. Bd. dirs. (Conn.) Wilton United Way, 1979. Mem. Racquet and Tennis (N.Y.C.), Am. Rivers (bd. dirs.), City Ctr. of N.Y. (bd. dirs.). Office: Unicast Communications Fl 6 160 Varick St New York NY 10013-1220

HOPPS, CARIN VERA, urologist; d. Helga Hedwig Hopps. BA, Northwestern U., 1990; MD, Vanderbilt U. Sch. of Medicine, 1995. Rsch. fellow Max Planck Inst. for Devel. Biology, Tuebingen, Germany, 1990—91; intership residency Med. Coll. Ohio, Urology, Toledo, 1995—2001; fellow, male reproductive medicine and microsurgery Weill Med. Coll. of Cornell U., NYC, 2001—. Recipient Traveling Scholar award, Soc. for Male Reproduction and Urology, 2002, Thomas S. K. Chang Trainee Travel award, Am. Soc. of Andrology, 2003, Traveling Fellowship award, Soc. for the Study of Male Reproduction, 2003; fellow Ferdinand C. Valentine Fellowship award, NY Acad. of Medicine, 2001-2002, Rsch. fellowship, Deutscher Akademischer Austausch Dienst, 1990-1991; scholar, Am. Found. for Urologic Diseases, 2001-2003. Mem.: Am. Soc. of Andrology, Am. Soc. for Reproductive Medicine, Soc. for Male Reproduction and Urology, European Soc. of Human Reproduction and Embryology, Am. Urol. Assn. (assoc.). Achievements include research in investigation of human spermatogenesis. Office: New York Weill Cornell Medical Center 525 East 68th St Starr 900 New York NY 10021 Office Fax: 212-746-0977.

HOPSON, EDWIN SHARP, lawyer; b. Louisville, Apr. 23, 1945; s. Henry Dockins and Martha (Linton) H.; m. Jane Mayo Fitzpatrick, July 20, 1968; children: Edwin Hopson Jr., Martha. BSL, U. Louisville, 1967, JD, 1969; LLM, George Washington U., 1971. Bar: Ky. 1969, Fla. 1969, U.S. Supreme Ct. 1972, U.S. Dist. Ct. (we. dist.) Ky. 1974, U.S. Ct. Appeals (6th cir.) 1977. Atty. Solicitor's Office, U.S. Dept. Labor, Washington, 1969-72; field atty. NLRB, Balt., 1972-74; assoc. Tarrant, Combs, Blackwell & Bullitt, Louisville, 1974-77; ptnr. Tarrant, Combs & Bullitt, Louisville, 1977-80, Wyatt, Tarrant & Combs, L.L.P., Louisville, 1980—. Chair, mem. exec. com. Labor and Employment Practice Group; mem. legal adv. bd. Access Partnership, 2000. Editor: (jour.) Ky. Bench & Bar, 2001—, 1989—91, (chpt.) How Arbitration Works, 1989, 2nd edit., 2001—; contbr. articles. Bd. dirs. Bellewood Presbyn. Children's Home, Louisville, 1988-96, pres., 1991-93; bd. dirs. Louisville Ballet, 1991—, v.p., 1992-93, pres., 1993-94; bd. dirs. Bellewood Children's Found., 1995-2002, pres., 1995-96. Fellow Coll. Labor and Employment Lawyers, Inc.; mem. ABA (co-chmn. pub. of arbitration awards subcom. 2000—, adr. com. of labor and employment sect.), FBA (chpt. pres. 1991-92), Louisville Bar Assn. (co-chmn. labor and employment law sect. 1982-83), Ky. Bar Assn. (co-chmn. labor and employment law sect. 1987-89, mem. ho. of dels. 1996-2002, chair pub. com. 1989-91, 2001—). Republican. Presbyterian. Avocations: flying, various sports, reading. Home: 3003 Lightheart Rd Louisville KY 40222-6138 Office: Wyatt Tarrant & Combs LLP 2600 PNC Plz Louisville KY 40202-2823 E-mail: ehopson@wyattfirm.com.

HOPSON, EVERETT GEORGE, retired lawyer; b. Stillwell, Ill., Sept. 4, 1922; s. Carman Roy and Adella (George) H.; m. Doris May Hutchins, Aug. 15, 1953 (dec.); children: Christine E., Eugene G. AA, Springfield Jr. Coll., 1942; BS, U. Ill., 1947, JD, 1949; MS in Internat. Affairs, George Washington U., 1967; disting. grad., Air War Coll., 1967. Bar: Ill. 1949, U.S. Ct. Mil. Appeals 1957, U.S. Supreme Ct. 1957. Dep. collector U.S. Treasury, IRS, Carlinville, Ill., 1949-51; commd. officer USAF, 1951, advanced to col., judge advocate, 1951-71; spl. asst. to asst. sec. def. Dept. Def., Washington, 1971; sr. atty. U.S. Postal Svc., Washington, 1972-73; dep. chief gen. law divsn. USAF, Washington, 1973-75, chief gen. law divsn., 1975-94, ret., 1994. Trustee USAF JAG Sch. Found. Served with U.S. Army, 1943-46. Decorated Legion of Merit; recipient Presdl. Rank of Meritorious Exec., USAF, 1981, 87, 92, Freedoms Found. award, 1961, 62, 66. Mem. ABA, Ill. Bar Assn. (sr. counsellor 1999), Fed. Bar Assn., Judge Advocates Assn., Am. Inns of Ct., Phi Alpha Delta. Independent. Methodist. Avocations: coin collecting, gardening. Home: 9719 Limoges Dr Fairfax VA 22032-1115 E-mail: eghdmh@aol.com. *Helpful advice and good counsel need to make sense and be reasonable to be effective. In my professional career and in life, I have attempted, with some degree of success, to let common sense prevail and reason rule the land.*

HOPSON, JAMES WARREN, publishing executive; b. St. Louis, May 24, 1946; s. David Warren and Ruth L. (Dierkes) H.; m. Julie Ann Eastlack, Dec. 21, 1968; children: John, Benjamin, Gillian. BJ, U. Mo., 1968; MBA, Harvard U., 1973. Project mgr. Des Moines Register & Tribune, 1973-76, dir. ops., 1976-78, circulation dir., 1978-79; gen. mgr. Corpus Christi (Tex.) Caller Times, 1979-82; pub. Middlesex News, Framingham, Mass., 1982-88; pres. N.E. Group-Harte-Hanks Comms., Framingham, 1984-88; pub. The Press of Atlantic City, N.J., 1989-94; pres. Community Newspaper Co., Boston, 1994-95, Thomson Ctrl. Ohio, Newark, 1995-2000; pub. Wis. State Jour., Madison, Wis., 2000—; v.p. publishing Lee Enterprises, Madison, 2000—. Pres. Vol. Ctr. Atlantic County, 1992—; treas. DeCordova Mus., Lincoln, Mass., 1983-89, dir., 1983-89; sec. Family Health Svc. Ctrl. Ohio, 1997—, treas.; bd. dirs. Audit Bur. of Circulations, 1999—; bd, dirs. Madison Art Ctr., United Way of Dane County. 1st lt. U.S. Army, 1968-73, Vietnam. Mem. New Eng. Newspaper Assn. (chmn. circulation com. 1986-88), Mass. Newspaper Pub. Assn. (dir. 1984-88), Metrowest C. of C. (chmn. 1987-88, dir. audit bur. of circulations 1999—), Greater Madison C. of C. (bd. dirs.) Office: 1901 Fish Hatchery Rd Madison WI 53713-1248

HOPSON, WILLIAM BRIGGS, JR., surgeon; b. Delhi, La., Sept. 20, 1937; m. Patricia Spearman; children: Karen Renee, Mary Kathryn, William Briggs III, James Walter. BS, U. Miss., 1958; MD, U. Tenn. Ctr. for Health Scis., 1961. Diplomate Am. Bd. Surgery. Intern John Gaston Hosp., 1961-62; resident U. Tenn. Hosp., 1962-67; resident in surgery Memphis City Hosps., 1962-67; clin. assoc. prof. surgery U. Miss. Med. Ctr., 1989—; pvt. practice Vicksburg, Miss. Chief of staff River Region Med. Ctr., Vicksburg, Miss.; mem. adv. bd. Bancorp S.; lectr. in field. Contbr. articles to profl. jours. Active YMCA, adminstrv. bd., Sunday Sch. tchr. Crawford St. United Meth. Ch.; bd. dirs. U. Miss. Alumni Bd., pres.; past pres. Cath. Home Sch. Assn.; past mem. Cath. Sch. bd.; campaign mgr. U.S. Senator Thad Cochran, Warren County, Miss., 1974, 76, 80, lt. gov. Brad Dye, Warren County, 1975, 79, 83, 87; pres. Vicksburg Red Carpet Bowl; team physician Warren Ctrl. High Sch., Vicksburg, 1969-99; chmn. bd. trustees Miss Miss. Pageant; bd. dirs. Nat. Assn. Miss Am. State Pageants, 1996, chmn. judges com., 1993-2002; mem. adv. bd. Ameristar Casino, 1997-2002. Fellow ACS, Am. Assn. Surgery of Trauma, Southea. Surgical Congress; mem. AMA, Ea. Assn. Surgery Trauma, Miss. State Med. Assn. (pres.), West Miss. Med. Assn., Am. Trauma Soc., Soc. Clin. Vascular Surgeons, Am. Coll. Sports Medicine, Nat. Assn. Emergency Med. Physicians, So. Med. Assn., Soc. Endo Laproscopic Surgery, Soc. Clin. Surgery, Harwell Wilson Surg. Soc., Vicksburg C. of C. (bd. dirs. 1991-96), Vicksburg Country Club, River Town Club, Gamma Sigma Epsilon, Alpha Epsilon Delta, Delta Kappa Epsilon, Phi Chi. Office: 2100 Hwy 61 N Bypass Vicksburg MS 39183-2825

HOPWOOD, HOWARD HOPPY PERRY, military officer; b. Mountain Top, Ark., Mar. 16, 1944; s. Ira Homer Hopwood and Hallie Mae Dunn; m. Mary M. White, Oct. 8, 1945; children: Rebecca Marie McDonell, James Howard. BS in Religious Edn., So. Christian U., Montgomery, Ala., 1978. Evangelist, deacon, elder church of Christ, 1969. Sr. master sgt. Hdqs. MAC/LGME USAF, Scott AFB, Ill., 1975—79, chief master sgt. Hdqs. USAFE/LGMA Kiserslautern, Germany, 1981—85. With integrated def. sys. The Boeing Co., Oklahoma City, 1985—. Evangelist, deacon, elder ch. of Christ, Melbourne, Fla., Germany, 1975—2003. Decorated Meritorious Svc. Medal with 3 oak leaf clusters, Air Force Commendation Medal with 31oak leaf clusters, Meritorious Svc. Award. Mem.: Am. Legion (life; KS Post 0062). Conservative. Church Of Christ. Avocations: collecting military memorabilia, history, philosphy, writing, photography. Home: 2318 Ripple Creek Ln Edmond OK 73003 Office Fax: 405-739-1485. Personal E-mail: hophopwood@aol.com. E-mail: howard.p.hopwood@boeing.com.

HOPWOOD, VICKI JEANE, medical center official; b. Oskaloosa, Iowa, Dec. 23, 1967; d. Jerry Lynn and Mary Gaynelle (Emerson) Hopwood. AS in Bus. Adminstrn., Abraham Baldwin Coll., Tifton, Ga., 1988, AS in Polit. Sci., 1989; BBA, Ga. Southwestern U., 1992. Med. records clk. Tift Gen. Hosp., Tifton, Ga., 1986-88, data processing clk., 1989-90, utilization rev. clk., 1990-93, transcriptionist, 1993-94; legal sec. Simpson, Gray & Carter, Tifton, 1994; med. staff asst. St. Francis Hosp., Columbus, Ga., 1994-95, S.E. Ga. Regional Med. Ctr., Brunswick, 1995-96, med. staff office mgr., 1996—98, mgr. managed care svcs., 1998—2000, bus. devel. adminstr., 2000—01, pub. rels./mktg. coord., 2001—03, sr. compliance specialist, 2003—. Mem. Nat. Assn. Med. Staff Svcs. (cert. provider credentialing specialist, cert. med. staff coord.), Ga. Assn. Med. Staff Svcs., Ga. Soc. Healthcare Mktg. & Pub. Rels., Health Care Compliance Assn. Office: SE Ga Health Sys 2415 Parkwood Dr Brunswick GA 31520-4722

HORAHAN, EDWARD BERNARD, III, lawyer; b. Drexel Hill, Pa., Dec. 30, 1951; s. Edward Bernard and Ann Veronica (Schneeweis) H.; m. Rebecca Joy Fusco, Mar. 13, 1976; 1 child, Elizabeth Joy. BA, LaSalle Coll., Phila., 1973; JD, Yale U., 1976. Bar: D.C. 1976. Staff atty. office of gen. counsel SEC, Washington, 1976-78; staff atty. office of solicitor, plan benefits security divsn. U.S. Dept. Labor, Washington, 1978-80; assoc. Arter & Hadden, Washington, 1980-84; ptnr. Parker, Chapin, Flattau & Klimpl, Washington, 1984-88, Stroock & Stroock & Lavan, Washington, 1988-93; pvt. practice Law Offices of Edward B. Horahan III, Washington, 1993-96; counsel Groom Law Group, Washington, 1996-2001, Dechert, Washington, 2001—. Mem. ABA. Office: 1775 Eye St NW Washington DC 20006 E-mail: edward.horahan@dechert.com.

HORAK, JAMES ALBERT, materials scientist, nuclear engineer, educator; b. Plainfield, N.J., Oct. 28, 1931; s. John Sr. and Florence Gladys (Newman) H.; m. Diane Judy Herman, July 10, 1954; children: Ralph James, Kendell John, Gregory Eugene. BS in Metall. Engring., U. Ill., 1958; MS in Materials Sci., Northwestern U., 1963, PhD in Materials Sci., 1966. Reg. nuclear engr., Calif. Mem. staff Argonne (Ill.) Nat. Lab., 1958-68, Los Alamos (N.Mex.) Nat. Lab., 1968-69, Sandia Labs., Albuquerque, 1969-74; assoc. prof. nuclear engring. U. N.Mex., Albuquerque, 1969-74, prof., 1974; mem. staff Lockheed-Martin Energy Sys., Oak Ridge, Tenn., 1974-93, group leader, 1993—. With USAF, 1953. Am. Nuclear Soc. fellow, 1979. Home: 304 Calloway Cir Lenoir City TN 37772-5964 Office: Lockheed Martin Energy Sys PO Box 2009 Oak Ridge TN 37831-2009 E-mail: horakja@y-12.gov.

HORAK, JAN-CHRISTOPHER, film studies educator, curator; b. Bad Münstereifel, Fed. Republic Germany, May 1, 1951; came to U.S., 1951; s. Jerome V. and Giselle (Offermanns) H.; m. Martha F. Schirn, May 17, 1988; 1 child, Gianna. BA, U. Del., 1973; MS, Boston U., 1975; PhD, Westfälische Wilhelms-U., Münster, Germany, 1984. Intern Internat. Mus. Photography, Rochester, N.Y., 1975-76, assoc. curator George Eastman House, 1984-87, curator film, 1987-90, sr. curator, 1990-94; asst. prof. film studies U. Rochester, 1985-90, assoc. prof., 1990-93, prof., 1994; dir. Münchner Filmmuseum, Munich, Germany, 1994-98; prof. Hochschule f. Fernsehen u. Film, 1995-98; dir. Archives and Collections Universal Studios, L.A., 1998-00; prof. UCLA, 1999—; curator Hollywood Entertainment Mus., 2000—. Panelist, chmn. film panel N.Y. State Coun. of Arts, N.Y.C., 1986-89; cons. USIA, 1988-90; archivists adv. bd. The Film Found., N.Y.C., 1990-94; v.p., pres. Assn. Moving Image Archivists, 1991-93; exec. com. Internat. Fedn. Film Archives, 1993-95, Kuratorium Junger Deutscher Film, 1995-97. Author: Anti-Nazi Filme der Emigration, 1984, Fluchtpunkt Hollywood, 1986, The Dream Merchants, 1989, Lovers of Cinema: The First American Film Avant-Garde, 1995, Berge, Licht und Traum: Arnold Fanck und der deutsche Bergfilm, 1997, Making Images Move: Photography and Avant-Garde Cinema, 1997; editor: Film und Foto der 20er Jahre, 1979, Helmar Lerski, 1982; founding editor: The Moving Image, 2001—; contbr. Recipient Louis B. Mayer award Mayer Found., Am. Film Inst., 1975; Heinrich Herz Stiftung fellow, 1979-81. Mem.: Internat. Assn. Audio-Visual Media and History, Soc. Exile Studies, Soc. Cinema Studies. Avocations: travel, skiing, swimming. Office: 545 Sierra Vista Ave Pasadena CA 91107 E-mail: c.horak@hollywoodmuseum.com.

HORAN, JOHN DONOHOE, lawyer; b. N.Y.C., Mar. 4, 1948; s. Michael Joseph, Jr. and Anna Patricia (Donohoe) H.; m. Judith R. Levinson, Aug. 8, 1976; children— Michael L., Emily L. B.A., Fordham Coll., 1970; J.D., Rutgers U., 1974. Bar: N.J. 1974, U.S. Dist. Ct. N.J. 1974, U.S. Ct. Appeals (3d cir.) 1980, U.S. Supreme Ct. 1981. Ptnr., Goodman, Stoldt, Breslin & Horan, Hackensack, N.J., 1974-84, Stoldt, Horan & Cino, 1984— . Bd. dirs. Research Fund for Cystic Fibrosis, Inc., 1985— . Mem. Bergen County Bar Assn. (com. on employment discrimination 1979—, founder, chmn. com. environ. law 1983—, chmn. subcom. on hazardous waste litigation 1983—), Trial Attys. N.J., ABA (litigation), N.J. State Bar Assn. (com. on environ. law). Office: Stoldt Horan & Kowal 401 Hackensack Ave Hackensack NJ 07601-6411

HORAN, MARY ANN THERESA, retired medical/surgical nurse; b. Denver, July 4, 1936; d. John Paul and Lucille (Somma) Perito; m. Stephen F. Horan, Sr., Dec. 28, 1957; children: Seanna, Dana, Michelle, Annette, Stephen Jr., Christine, David. BSN, Loretto Heights Coll./St. Anthony Hosp., Denver, 1958; postgrad., Pima C.C., 1982, postgrad., 2003. RN Ala. Staff nurse Med. Ctr. Hosp., Huntsville, Ala., 1978-79, Crestwood Hosp., Huntsville, 1980-81; RN staff nurse St. Joseph Hosp. Eye Surgery, Tucson, 1981—2002; ret., 2002. Sr. assoc. Shaklee, 1996—; pres. Horan Internat. Air Source Distbr., 2001—. Contbr. articles to nursing jours., poetry to lit. jours. Recipient vol. 10 yr. pin, ARC, 10 yr. pin for tchg., St. Pius X. Republican. Roman Catholic. Home: 8311 E 3rd St Tucson AZ 85710-2550 E-mail: mahoran_horanintl@hotmail.com.

HORCHOW, S(AMUEL) ROGER, marketing consultant; b. Cin., July 3, 1928; s. Reuben and Beatrice (Schwartz) H.; m. Carolyn Pfeifer, Dec. 29, 1960; children: Regen Horchow Fearon, Elizabeth Horchow Routman, Sally Horchow McCauley. BA, Yale U., 1950, LHD (hon.), 1999. Buyer Foley's, Houston, 1953-60; v.p. Neiman-Marcus, Dallas, 1960-68, 69-71; pres. Design Research, Cambridge, Mass., 1968-69, Kenton Collection, Dallas, 1971-73; chmn. Horchow Collection, Dallas, 1973-90. Author: Elephants in Your Mailbox, 1979, Living in Style, 1981; prodr. Crazy for You, 1991-95; co-prodr. Kiss Me Kate, 1999. Bd. dirs. Jefferson Award for Pub. Svc., Ctr. for Human Nutrition, Yale Art Galley, Mus. Modern Art, N.Y.C., Com. for Preservation of the White House,, Friends of Art and Preservation of Embassies. Mem. Yale Club (N.Y.C.), Nantucket Yacht Club, Knickerbocker Club. Office: 5722 Chatham Hill Rd Dallas TX 75225-3208

HORD, PAULINE JONES, primary school educator, educator; b. Memphis, Apr. 18, 1907; d. Samuel Anderson and Loretta (Hall) Jones; m. Andrew Frank Hord, Mar. 30, 1940 (div. Oct. 1946). BA, Southwestern Coll., Memphis, 1929; EdD (hon.), Crichton Coll., Memphis, 1991, Rhodes Coll., 1999. Tchr. Memphis City Sch. System, 1929-67; nat. cons. Phonovisual Products, Inc., Bethesda, Md., 1967-77; freelance cons., workshop dir. Memphis, 1978-87; dir. sing spell read and write model Memphis Sch. System, 1987-95. Dir. TV Lit. Program WKNO-TV, Memphis, 1955-60; acting dir. Primary Day Sch., Bethesda, Md., 1960-61; lit. TV Specialist with Peace Corps., Colombia, S. Am., 1963-64; dir. Heads Up Lit. Program, State Correctional Inst., Parchman, Miss., 1986-96. Author: Praying for the President, 2003, The Master Design, 2003. Lit. tchr. Heads Up Lit. Program, Parchman Penetentiary, 1987-92; bd. mem. Second Chance Prison Min., Tenn., Miss., 1988-92. Recipient Leadership Adult Edn. award Ford Found., 1958, Disting. Col. Christian Svc. award Miss. State Penetentiary, Parchman, 1987, Memphis Comml. Appeal award, 1989, 95th Daily Point of Light award, 1990, Person of Vision award Alliance for the Blind and Visually Impaired, 1993, Disting. Alumni award Rhodes Coll., 1998; named one of Outstanding Bus. Women of Yr., Women's Exec. Coun., Memphis, 1959, Sr. Citizen of Yr., Shelby County Coun. on Aging, 1988. Republican. Mem. United Meth. Avocations: reading, creating educational games, leading prayer groups. Home: 475 S Perkins Rd Apt 601 Memphis TN 38117-3926

HORDON, HARRIS EUGENE, economics educator; b. N.Y.C., Dec. 31, 1942; s. Sidney and Betty (Flacks) H.; m. Carole Schulman, July 27, 1969; children: Elana, Robert, Daniel. BA in Econs., Bklyn. Coll., 1963; MA in Econs., NYU, 1965, PhD in Econs., 1968. Instr. econs. Northeastern U., Boston, 1966-69; economist U.S. Dept. of Transp., Washington, 1970-71; chmn. econ. dept., prof. New Jersey City U., 1969—. Fin. cons. in field, 1975—. Author: Introduction to Urban Economics, 1973. Fellowship Brookings Instn., 1970; faculty fellowship Princeton U., 1986. Avocation: boating. Home: 340 East 64th Street Apt 6J New York NY 10021 Office: New Jersey City U 2039 Kennedy Blvd Jersey City NJ 07305-1597 Fax: 212-759-6204. E-mail: hhordon@njcu.edu.

HORE, JOHN EDWARD, commodity futures educator; b. Dec. 13, 1929; s. Ernest and Doris Kathleen (Horton) H.; m. Diana King, May 3, 1958; children: Edward John Bruce, Celia Kathleen Hore Milne, Timothy Frank. BA with honors, King's Coll., Cambridge, Eng., 1952, MA, 1957. Chartered fin. analyst. Asst. sales mgr. Borthwicks, London, 1952-54; security analyst Dominion Securities, Toronto, Ont., Can., 1955-57; asst. mktg. mgr. Rio Algom, Toronto, 1957-61; dir. Bell, Gouinlock & Co., Toronto, 1961-75; v.p., dir. futures Can. Securities Inst., Toronto, 1979-94, seminar leader, 1980-2000. Investment edn. cons., 1995—; cons. Can. Dept. Agr., 1993; founding sec. Can. Nuclear Assn.; past v.p. Brit. Can. Trade Assn.; chmn. 1st Can. Internat. Futures Rsch. Seminar, 1985, also editor Proc., 2 vols., 1986; spkr. Can.-Am. Inst. Conf. on Fin. Svcs. at Detroit-Windsor, 1989, compliance seminar Futures Industry Assn. at Alexandria, Va., 1990; chmn. Can. Futures Conf., 1986; chmn. 3d, 4th, 5th and 6th Can. Internat. Futures Conf. and Rsch. Seminars, 1987, 88, 89, 90, mng. editor Selected Papers 1988-91. Author: Trading on Canadian Futures Markets, 1984, 5th edit., 1993; co-author: Association for Investment Management and Research Standards of Practice Handbook, 1982 (Pres. Reagan Citation 1984); co-editor: Canadian Securities Course, 1980-94. Gov. Montcrest Sch., 1970-73; mem. Commodity Futures Adv. Bd., Ont., 1989-95; apptd. mem. internat. com. Futures Industry Assn., Washington, 1988-91, rowing com. Upper Can. Coll., Toronto, 1982-86; pres. St. George's Soc. Toronto, 1978-80, chmn. edn. com., 1987. With Royal Army Ednl. Corps, 1948-49, Singapore. Mem. Toronto Soc. Fin. Analysts (bd. dirs. 1968-71), Assn. for Investment Mgmt. and Rsch. (formerly Fin. Analysts Fedn., bd. dirs. investment analysis stds. 1974-85, emeritus 1985), Univ. Club Toronto (bd. dirs. 1980-83), Arts and Letters Club Toronto (exec. com. 2000, treas. 2001—), Leander Club (assoc.) (Henley-on-Thames), Hurlingham Club (London), Royal Overseas League (pres. Ont. chpt.), Toronto Round Table (pres. 1999-2001). Anglican. Avocations: historical research, squash, choral music, poetry. Office: 185 Carlton St Toronto ON Canada M5A 2K7 E-mail: johnhore@aol.com.

HORECKER, BERNARD LEONARD, retired biochemistry educator; b. Chgo., Oct. 31, 1914; s. Paul and Bessie (Bornstein) H.; m. Frances Goldstein, July 12, 1936; children: Doris Colgate, Marilyn Diamond Schnell, Linda Lally. BS, U. Chgo., 1936, PhD, 1939; Laureate honoris causa in Biol. Scis., U. Urbino (Italy), 1982. Rsch. assoc. chemistry U. Chgo., 1939-40; examiner U.S. Civil Svc. Commn., 1940-41; biochemist USPHS, NIH, Bethesda, Md., 1941-59; chief lab. of biochemistry and metabolism Nat. Inst. Arthritis and Metabolic Disease, 1956-59; professorial lectr. enzyme chemistry George Washington U., 1950-57; guest rsch.-worker Pasteur Inst., Paris, 1957-58; prof. microbiology, chmn. dept. NYU Coll. Medicine, 1959-63; prof. molecular biology, chmn. dept. Albert Einstein Coll. Medicine, 1963-72, assoc. dean for sci. affairs, 1971-72; mem. Roche Inst. Molecular Biology, Nutley, N.J., 1972-84, head Lab. Molecular Enzymology, 1977-84; adj. prof. Cornell U. Med. Coll., 1972-84, prof. biochemistry, 1984-89, prof. emeritus biochemistry, 1989, dean Grad. Sch. Med. Sci., 1984-92. Vis. prof. Albert Einstein Coll. Medicine, 1972-84; vis. prof. biochemistry U. Calif., 1954, U. Parana, Brazil, 1960, 63; vis. lectr. U. Ill., 1956; Ciba lectr. Rutgers U., 1962; Phillips lectr. Haverford Coll., 1965; vis. prof. Kyoto (Japan) U., 1967; vis. prof. biochemistry and molecular biology Cornell U., 1965; vis. prof. U. Ferrara, Italy; Reilly lectr. Notre Dame U., 1969; vis. lectr. U. Rotterdam, 1970; prof. honoris causa Fed. U. Parana, Curitiba, Brazil, 1981— ; mem. sci. adv. bd. Roche Inst. Molecular Biology, Nutley, N.J., 1967-72, chmn., 1971-72; dir. Academic Press, Inc., 1968-73; mem. Research Career Award com. Nat. Inst. Gen. Med. Scis., 1966-70; mem. personnel com. Am. Cancer Soc., 1968-72, mem. sci. adv. com. for biochemistry and chem. carcinogenesis, 1974-78, mem. Council for Research and Clin. Investigation Awards, 1984-88; mem. biology div. adv. com. Oak Ridge Nat. Lab., 1976-80; mem. Med. Scientist Tng. Program Sect. NIH, 1970-72. Editor Biochem. and Biophys. Rsch. Communications, 1959-89, Current Topics in Cellular Regulation, 1969-89, Archives Biochemistry and Biophysics, 1960-68; chmn. editorial bd. Archives of Biochemistry and Biophysics, 1968-84; contbr. articles to sci. publs. Recipient Paul Lewis Labs. award in enzyme chemistry, 1952, Superior Accomplishment award Fed. Security Agy., 1952, Rockefeller Pub. Svc. award, 1957, Hillebrand prize Am. Chem. Soc., 1954, Award in Biol. Scis., Washington Acad. Scis., 1954, Fulbright Travel award, 1963; Commonwealth Fund fellow, 1967. Fellow AAAS, Am. Acad. Arts and Scis.; mem. NAS, Am. Chem. Soc. (vice chmn. div. biol. chemistry 1975-76, chmn. 1976-77), Biochem. Soc. (Eng.), Swiss Biochem. Soc. (hon. mem.), Spanish Biochem. Soc., hon. mem.), Japanese Biochem. Soc. (hon. mem.), Hellenic Biochem. and Biophys. Soc. (hon. mem.), Am. Soc. Biol. Chemists (pres. 1967-68, chmn. editorial com. 1962-63, Merck award 1981), Virchow-Pirquet Med. Soc. (Neuburg medal 1981), Harvey Soc. (v.p. 1969-70, pres. 1970-71), Brazilian Acad. Sci. (hon.), PanAm. Assn. Biochem. Socs. (vice chmn. 1971, chmn. 1972, mem. exec. com. 1971-78), Indian Nat. Acad. Sci., Argentine Acad. Sci. (corr.), Phi Beta Kappa, Sigma Xi. Home: 16517 Cypress Villa Ln Fort Myers FL 33908-7609 E-mail: blhorecker@aol.com.

HORENSTEIN, MARCELO GABRIEL, pathologist, educator; b. Mendoza, Argentina, June 27, 1965; s. Mario Luis Horenstein and Maria Cristina Melean; m. Veronica Maria Diaz-Peralta; 1 child, Sofia. MD, Nat. U. Cuyo, Mendoza, Argentina, 1990. Diplomate Am. Bd. Pathology, 1998, Am. Bd. Dermatology, 1999, cert. in anatomic and clin. pathology Am. Bd. Pathology, 1998, in dermatopathology Am. Bd. Pathology, 1999. Pathology resident Cornell U., N.Y.C., 1992—96; oncologic pathology fellow Meml. Sloan-Kettering Cancer Ctr., N.Y.C., 1996—97; dermatopathology fellow Duke U., Durham, NC, 1997—98; asst. prof. U. South Ala., Mobile, 1998—2003, assoc. prof., 2003—, dermatopathology dir., 1998—. Dermatopathology dir. U. South Ala., Mobile, 1998—. Contbr. articles to profl. jours. Recipient Binford-Dammin award, Binford-Dammin Soc. Infectious Pathologists, 1994. Fellow: Am. Soc. Dermatopathology, Coll. Am. Pathologists; mem.: U.S. & Can. Acad. Pathology, Soc. Investigative Dermatology, Am. Acad. Dermatology. Office: Univ South Ala 2451 Fillingim St Mobile AL 36617 Office Fax: 251-741-7884.

HORGAN, SANTIAGO, surgeon; b. Buenos Aires, Sept. 22, 1965; s. Federico Guillermo Horgan and Marta Josefina Benavides; m. Maria Natalia Presas, June 9, 1995. MD, U. Buenos Aires, Argentina, 1989. Diplomate Buenos Aires, Argentina, 1990. Fellow laparoscopic surgery U. of Wash., Seattle, 1995—96, fellow esophageal surgery, 1996—98; chief minimally invasive surgery and robotic surgery U. of Ill., Chgo., 1999—. Recipient Young Surgeon award, Surg. Soc. Alimentary Tract, 2001. Mem.: Assn. Surg. Edn. (assoc.), Internat. Soc. for diseases of the Esophagus (assoc.), Soc. Am. Gastrointestinal Endoscopic Surgeons (assoc. Rsch. Award 1999), Surg. Soc. Alimentary Tract (assoc.). Achievements include research and development of techniques of robotic surgery in U.S; research in surgery for morbid obesity. Office: Univ of Ill at Chgo 840 S Wood St Rm 435 E Chicago IL 60612

HORGAN, SUSAN BEDSOW (SUSAN MERRIL TAYLOR), producer, writer; b. Chgo., Nov. 24, 1947; d. Len and Jane (de Sousa) Bedsow; m. Philip Taylor (div. 1974); m. Patrick Horgan, Oct. 24, 1981; 1 child, James Michael Leonard Noah. BA, U. Calif., Irvine, 1969. Actress stage prodns. including Richard II with Richard Chamberlain/Kennedy Ctr., Ahmanson Theater, Los Angeles Music Ctr., Washington and Los Angeles, 1972; actress Am. Shakespeare Theater, Stratford, Conn., 1973-74, Sherlock Holmes/Broadhurst Theater, N.Y.C., 1974-76; asst. producer One Life to Live, 1976-77, Guiding Light, N.Y.C., 1978-79; assoc. producer As the World Turns, N.Y.C., 1979-80, producer, 1980-83, headwriter, 1984-85; freelance producer, writer, 1987-90; creative cons. internat. soap opera Foreign Affairs Catalyst Prodns., 1990—; supervising producer One Life to Live, 1991-92, assoc. head writer, 1992-94, exec. prodr., 1994-97; freelance writer, producer, 1997—2000; developer projects for prime time networks, cable and features WE3P Prodns., 2000—. Recipient Emmy award nomination for writing Nat. Acad. TV Arts and Scis., 1986, Emmy award for Best Series Drama writing team, 1994. Mem. Writers Guild Am. (com. mem. 1985-86) Democrat. Avocations: cooking, gardening, quilting. Home and Office: The Haunted Ink Bottle 91 Cedar Rd Wilton CT 06897-3628 E-mail: finnwake@aol.com.

HORGER, EDGAR OLIN, III, obstetrics and gynecology educator; b. Eutawville, S.C., May 30, 1937; s. Edgar Olin Jr. and Frances Durant (Jordan) H.; m. Polly Jo Collins, May 29, 1960; children: Edgar Olin IV, David Collins, Patricia Bowen. BS, Furman U., 1959; MD, Med. Coll. S.C., 1962. Intern Med. U. Hosp., Charleston, S.C., 1962-63, resident in ob-gyn, 1963-67; NIH fellow U. Pitts., 1967-68, asst. prof., 1968-69, Med. U. S.C., Charleston, 1969-71, assoc. prof., 1971-76, prof., 1976-90, dir. maternal-fetal medicine, 1973-90; prof. ob-gyn. U. S.C. Sch. Medicine, Columbia, 1990-2001, chmn., 1993-99, disting. prof. emeritus, 2001—. Mem. S.C. Bd. Med. Examiners, 1985-87. Contbr. articles to profl. jours. Adv. bd. Charleston chpt. March of Dimes, 1984-90. Capt. AUS, 1963-66. Recipient Disting. Alumnus award Med. U. S.C., 1995; USPHS fellow, 1967-68. Mem. AMA, S.C. Med. Assn., Am. Coll. Obstetricians and Gynecologists (Outstanding Faculty award dist. IV 1988, vice chmn. S.C. sect. 1993-96, chmn. 1996-98, treas. dist. IV 1997-2000, Outstanding Dist. Svc. award 2001), Coun. Res. Edn. ObGyn, South Ctrl. Ob-Gyn. Soc., South Atlantic Assn. Ob-Gyn. (exec. com. 1983-94, sec. 1987-90, v.p. 1990-91, pres.-elect 1991-92, pres. 1992-93), So. Perinatal Assn. (dir. Mid-Atlantic region 1974-76), Soc. Perinatal Obstetricians (dir. 1977-78), Am. Gynecol. Obstet. Soc., Am. Assn. Ob-Gyn., S.C. Ob-Gyn. Soc. (pres. 1991-92), Columbia Med. Soc., Assn. Profs. Gynecology and Obstetrics (Excellence in Tchg. award 1992), S.C. State Bd. Med. Examiners (bd. dirs. 1985-87), Summit Club, Alpha Omega Alpha. Home: 125 Holliday Rd Columbia SC 29223-3108 Office: U SC Sch Medicine Dept Ob-Gyn 2 Richland Medical Park Dr Columbia SC 29203-6864

HORI, KEIKO, English literature educator; b. Himeji, Hyogo, Japan, Jan. 18, 1954; d. Takeshi Nishiyama and Fumiko Hori; 1 child, Grace. BA summa cum laude, Osaka (Japan) U., 1976, MA, 1978; postgrad., U. N.H., 1979—80, Osaka (Japan) U., 1978—82. Instr. Osaka Kyoiku U., 1981-82, tenured asst. prof., 1982-87, assoc. prof., 1987-2000, prof., 2000—; instr. Osaka U., Toyonaka, Japan, 1988-90, 92-95. Vis. prof. U. Wyo., Laramie, 1986—87; vis. scholar UCLA, 2001—02. Co-author: Imeji to shite no Toshi: Gakusaiteki Toshi Bunkaron, 1996; annotator: (textbook) American Businessman: Lessons from Life, 1994; co-annotator: (textbook) American and English Ideals, 1991. Recipient Kusumoto award, 1976. Mem. Modern Lang. Assn., English Literary Soc. Japan, Japan Assn. English Romanticism, Japan Assn. Coll. English Tchrs. Home: 7-4-1-3 Umamikita Koryo-cho Kitakatsuragi-gun Nara 635-0831 Japan Office: Osaka Kyoiku U 4-698-1 Asahigaoka Kashiwara Osaka 582-8582 Japan

HORI, KIYOAKY, retired anesthesiologist; b. Idaho Falls, Idaho, Nov. 14, 1926; BS, U. Idaho, 1952; MD, U. Oreg., 1956. Diplomate Am. Bd. Anesthesiology. Intern St. Vincents Hosp., Portland, Oreg., 1956-57; resident in anesthesiology Tacoma (Wash.) Gen. Hosp., 1958-60; anesthesiologist Tacoma, 1960-91; ret., 1991. Home: 4102 N 10th St Tacoma WA 98406-4516

HORI, YUKIO, engineering educator, scientific association administrator; b. Tokyo, Aug. 22, 1927; s. Kojiro and Yoshi (Saito) H.; m. Noriko Sunabori, May 15, 1965; children: Gen, Jun, Dan. B.Eng., U. Tokyo, 1951, Dr.Eng., 1960. Instr. U. Tokyo, 1953-55, assoc. prof., 1955-65, prof., 1965-88, emeritus prof., 1988—; exec. dir. Japan Soc. for Promotion of Sci., 1988-94; prof., v.p. Kanazawa Inst. Tech., Tokyo, 1994—. Contbr. articles to profl. jours. Recipient Tokyo Metropolis award, 1984, Purple Ribbon medal, 1993. Mem. ASME, Japan Soc. Mech. Engrs. (pres. 1988-89, awards 1960, 74, 89), Japan Soc. Tribologists (pres. 1990-92, award 1982), Japan Fedn. Engring. Soc. (v.p. 1989-93), Engring. Acad. Japan (v.p. 1993-2000, adviser, 2000—). Avocation: music. Home: Kugayama 3-19-19 Suginami-ku Tokyo 168-0082 Japan Office: Kanazawa Inst Tech Akasaka 2-17-41 Minato-ku Tokyo 107-0052 Japan E-mail: hori@alum.mit.edu.

HORII, NAOMI, editor; b. West Lafayette, Ind., Jan. 12, 1968; d. Yoshiyuki and Nobuko Ruth (Abe) H. BS, U. Colo., 1989; MA, U. Mo., 1993. Editor MYU Pub., Tokyo, 1989-91; tchr., talented and gifted program Boulder, Louisville, Colo., 1994-95; editor Many Mountains Moving, Boulder, 1994—, also bd. dirs.; editor English sect. Rocky Mountain Jiho, 1996—. Vol. Takarazuka Exch. Program, Boulder, 1993—, Nightwalk Women's Safety Program, Boulder, 1987-89. Recipient Anheuser-Busch award, 1997, Boulder Cmty. Action Program award for the arts, 2002; Gary Higa Found. Meml. scholar, 1988; Rocky Mountain Women's Inst. fellow, 1996-97; Colo. Coun. in the Arts fellow for fiction, 2001. Mem. NAFE, Rocky Mountain Book Pub. Assn., Visiones. Avocations: camping, hiking, reading, writing, music. Office: Many Mountains Moving 420 22nd St Boulder CO 80302-7909 E-mail: mmm@mmminc.org.

HORINE, JOHN WILLIAM, aviation educator; b. Richwoods, Mo., Aug. 13, 1929; s. John William and Norma E. (Fox) H.; m. Betty Ruth Lewis, Apr. 28, 1951; children: Jacqueline R., Donna J., Robert W., Karen F., Terri L. BS in Edn., Southeast Mo. State U., 1951; MEd, U. Mo., 1958, EdD, 1961. Tchr. indsl. arts Gideon Jr.-Sr. High Sch., Mo., 1953-59; rsch. asst. U. Mo., Columbia, 1959-61; tchr. indsl. edn. Ctrl. Mo. State U., Warrensburg, 1961-69, chmn. dept. power and transp., 1969-90, prof. dept. power and transp., 1990—2002, prof. aviation, 2002—. Adviser Mo. Aerospace Edn. Assn., 1980—; chmn. Mo. State Aviation Adv. Com., Jefferson City, 1988-92, mem., 1992—. Dir. aerospace edn. Mo. Wing CAP, 1968-92; dep. chief of staff aero. edn. North Ctrl. Region, Civil Air Patrol, 1992—. With U.S. Army, 1951-53, Korea. Recipient Crown Cir. award Nat. Congress Aviation and Space Edn., 1986; regional Adminstr. winner for Excellence in Aviation Edn., FAA, 1987. Mem. AIAA, Am. Indsl. Arts Assn. (life), Am. Vocat. Assn., Am. Assn. Airport Execs., Soc. Mfg. Engrs., Univ. Aviation Assn. (trustee 1979-82), Phi Delta Kappa. Methodist. Office: Cen Mo State Univ Dept Aviation Warrensburg MO 64093

HORINKO, MARIANNE LAMANT, federal agency administrator; BS, U. Md., 1982; JD, Georgetown U., 1986. Staff scientist Nat. Cancer Inst., Bethesda, Md.; atty. Morgan, Lewis, & Bockius, LLP, Washington; atty. advisor, solid wastes & emerg. response EPA, Washington, 1990—93; pres. Clay Assocs., Inc., 1993—2001; asst. adminstr. solid waste and emer. response EPA, 2001—03, acting adminstr., 2003—. Office: EPA Ariel Rios Bldg 1200 Pennsylvania Ave NW Rm 3000 Washington DC 20460*

HORIOKA, CHARLES YUJI, economics educator; b. Boston, Sept. 7, 1956; s. Chimyo and Yasuko (Inoue) H. BA magna cum laude, Harvard Coll., 1977; PhD, Harvard U., 1985. Asst. prof. Kyoto (Japan) U., 1983-85, assoc. prof., 1985-87, Osaka (Japan) U., 1987-97, prof., 1997—. Vis. asst. prof. Stanford (Calif.) U., 1988; vis. assoc. prof. Columbia U., N.Y.C., 1993; vis. prof. U. Tokyo, 2000-01; cons. IMF, 1985; rsch. assoc. Nat. Bur. Econ. Rsch., Cambridge, Mass., 1987—, Ctr. for Japan-U.S. Bus. and Econ. Studies, Leonard N. Stern Sch. Bus. NYU, 1989—; Olin fellow Ctr. for Econ. Policy Rsch., Stanford U., 1988; special guest rsch. officer Inst. Posts and Telecomm. Policy, Ministry of Posts and Telecomm., Tokyo, 1992—2002. Assoc. editor Econ. Studies Quarterly, 1988-94, Internat. Econ. Rev., 1997-98, co-editor, 1998—; assoc. editor Japanese Econ. Rev., 1998—; contbr. articles to profl. jours. Recipient Fulbright-Hays Fellowship U.S. Dept. Edn., 1982-83. Mem. Am. Econ. Assn., Japan Econs. Assn. (Nakahara prize 2001), Royal Econ. Soc., Tokyo Ctr. Econ. Rsch. Avocations: stamp collecting, coin collecting, jogging, swimming. Office: Inst Soc Econ Rsch Osaka U 6-1 Mihogaoka Ibaraki Osaka 567-0047 Japan

HORISBERGER, DON HANS, conductor, musician; b. Millersburg, Ohio, Mar. 2, 1951; s. Hans and Jeannette (Grossniklaus) H. MusB, Capital U., 1973; MusM, Northwestern U., 1974, MusD, 1985. Dir. music 1st Presbyn. Ch., Waukegan, Ill., 1976-88; with Chgo. Symphony Chorus, 1977—, sect. leader, 1984-91, asst. condr., 1990-98, assoc. conductor, 1998—; dir. Waukegan Concert Chorus, 1979-97; organist/choirmaster Ch. of the Holy Spirit, Lake Forest, Ill., 1988—. Lectr. in music Capital U., Columbus, Ohio, 1974-75; asst. to lang. coach Chgo. Symphony Chorus, 1978—. Fulbright-Hayes grantee 1975. Mem. Am. Choral Dirs. Assn. (chair community choruses cen. div. spl. interest 1988-91), Assn. Profl. Vocal Ensembles (chorus Am.). E-mail: DHorisberger@CHSLF.ORG.

HORKEY, WILLIAM RICHARD, retired diversified oil company executive; b. Tulsa, Apr. 22, 1925; s. William Edward and Clara Doris (Rice) H.; m. Barbara Jeanne Williamson, Oct. 18, 1952; children: Elaine Gail, Edward Richard, Ellen Beth. BA, State U. Iowa, 1947; LLB, U. Okla., 1950; grad., Advanced Mgmt. Program, Harvard U., 1962. Bar: Okla. 1950. With Gulf Oil Corp., 1950-51, Skelly Oil Co., 1951-55, Helmerich & Payne, Inc., Tulsa, 1955-90, sec., legal counsel, 1955-64, v.p., 1960-64, exec. v.p., 1964-87, sr. v.p., 1987-90, bd. dirs., 1957-90. Chmn. Grand River Dam Authority, Okla. Ordnance Works Authority, Woolslayer Cos. Inc., EnviroFuels Inc.; bd. dirs. The Great Eastern Shipping Co. London, Asbury Svcs. Inc.; pres. Inverness Village. Bd. dirs. Tulsa United Way, 1978-88; chmn. S.E. Tulsa YMCA, 1970-72; pres. Met. Tulsa YMCA, 1972-73, Tulsa Bus. Health Group 1978-96; chmn. Tulsa chpt. ARC, 1987-88; dir. Tulsa Emergency Med. Authority, 1977-95, chmn., 1981-95; pres. Tulsa Cmty. Found., for Indigent Health Care, 1980—. Mem. ABA, Okla. Bar Assn., Tulsa County Bar Assn., Order of Coif, So. Hills Country Club, Mid-Continent Harvard AMP (Tulsa) (pres. 1969-75), Phi Delta Phi, Phi Delta Theta. Presbyterian (deacon and elder). Home: 5686 S Evanston St Tulsa OK 74105 Office: 5416 S Yale Ave Ste 350 Tulsa OK 74135-6245 E-mail: wci@lcm-wci.com.

HORKOVICH, ROBERT MICHAEL, lawyer; b. Kew Gardens, N.Y., June 11, 1954; s. Andrew Horkovich and Amelia (Rauba) Patti. BA in Econs. and Govt., Fordham U., 1976, JD, 1979. Bar: N.Y. 1980, Md. 1987, U.S. Dist. Ct. (so. and ea. dists.) N.Y. 1980, U.S. Ct. Appeals (2d cir.) 1980, U.S. Ct. Mil. Appeals 1980, U.S. Dist. Ct. Md. 1987, U.S. Ct. Appeals (10th cir.) 1997. Clk. U.S. Senator James L. Buckley, NY, 1975—77; assoc. Skadden, Arps, Slate, Meagher & Flom, N.Y.C., 1979—80, Cadwalader, Wickersham & Taft, N.Y.C., 1984—89; ptnr. Anderson Kill & Olick P.C., N.Y.C., 1989—. Chmn. ins. coverage practice group. Articles editor Fordham Urban Law Jour., 1978-79; editor: The Policyholder Advisor, June 2002; contbr. articles to profl. jours. Served to capt. USAF, 1980-84. Decorated Meritorious Svc. medal, Air Force Commendation medal; named Co. Grade Officer of Yr. 1100 Air Base Wing, 1982, Eagle Scout Boy Scouts Am., 1972; decorated Meritorious Svc. medal. Mem. Pi Sigma Alpha. Roman Catholic. Avocations: impressionist art, scuba diving. Office: Anderson Kill & Olick PC 1251 Avenue Of The Americas New York NY 10020-1104

HORKOWITZ, SYLVESTER PETER, chemist; b. Lansford, Pa., Sept. 7, 1921; s. Simeon and Mary (Leshefka) H.; m. Olga Assaf, Sept. 12, 1964. Student, Kans. State Coll., Pittsburg, 1948-51. Chemist Spencer Chem. Co., Pittsburg, 1946-51, chief chemist Vicksburg, Miss., 1951-56, rsch. mgr. Orange, Tex., 1956-61; v.p. Spencer Chem. Far East, Tokyo, 1961-65; chem. mgr. Far East Gulf Oil Corp., Tokyo, Singapore, Bangkok, 1965-72; cons. chemist New Orleans, 1972—. Cons. chemist New Orleans, 1972—; bd. dirs.; chmn. A-Jin Chem. Co., Pusan, Republic of Korea, 1965-68; adv. bd. Pertamina Gulf, Djakarta, Indonesia, 1969-71; bd. dirs. chmn. Gulf Plastics-Singapore. Contbr. articles to profl. jours. With U.S. Army, 1942-46. Mem. ASTM, Am. Oil Chemists Soc., Soc. Plastics Engrs., Am. Chem. Soc. Republican. Byzantine Catholic Ch. Achievements include patents for ethylene/acrylate co-polymers, deconyl peroxide-free radical polymerization initiator, ammonium nitrate prilling tower process. Home and Office: 5700 Ruth St Metairie LA 70003-2330

HORLICK, GARY NORMAN, lawyer, legal educator; b. Washington, Mar. 12, 1947; s. Reuben S. and Gertrude V. (Cooper) H.; m. Kathryn L. Mann, June 1, 1986. AB, Dartmouth Coll., 1968; BA, MA, Diploma in Internat. Law, Cambridge (Eng.) U., 1970; JD, Yale U., 1973. Bar: Conn. 1974, U.S. Ct. Appeals (D.C. cir.) 1975), D.C. 1977, U.S. Supreme Ct. 1977, U.S. Ct. Internat. Trade 1979, U.S. Ct. Customs and Patent Appeals 1980. Asst. to rep. Ford Found., Santiago, Chile, 1973-74, asst. rep. Bogota, Colombia, 1974-76; assoc. Steptoe & Johnson, Washington, 1976-80; internat. trade counsel U.S. Senate Fin. Com., Washington, 1981; dep. asst. sec. U.S. Dept. Commerce, Washington, 1981-83; ptnr. O'Melveny & Myers, Washington, 1983—2002, Wilmer, Cutler & Pickering, Washington, 2002—. Lectr. law Yale U., New Haven, 1983-86, 2001—, World Trade Inst., U. Berne, 2000—; adj. prof. Georgetown U. Law Ctr., Washington, 1986—, World Trade Inst. U. Rome; lectr. various orgns.; adv. com. U.S. Ct. Internat. Trade, 1993-97; mem. permanent group of experts World Trade Orgn., 1996-2001, chmn., 1996-97. Author: WTO and NAFTA Rules and Dispute Resolution, 2003. Mem. ABA (chmn. standing com. on customs law 1993), Coun. Fgn. Rels., Internat. Law Assn. (mem. exec. coun. Am. br. 1983—), Internat. Bar Assn. (vice chmn. antitrust and trade law 1987-89), D.C. Bar Assn. (chmn. internat. divsn. 1984-85), Am. Soc. of Internat. Law (exec. coun. 1998-99). Office: Wilmer Cutler & Pickering 2455 M St NW Washington DC 20037- E-mail: gary.horlick@wilmer.com

HORMATS, ROBERT DAVID, investment banker; b. Balt., Apr. 13, 1943; s. Saul and Ruth H. BA, Tufts U., 1965, MA, 1966, MA in Law and Diplomacy, 1967, PhD, 1970. Research asst. Fletcher Sch. of Law and Diplomacy, 1968-69; research asso. Univ. Coll., Dar-es-Salaam, Tanzania, 1967-68; staff mem. internat. econ. affairs Nat. Security Council, 1969-73, sr. staff mem., 1974-77; sr. dep. asst. sec. for econ. and bus. affairs Dept. State, 1977-79; ambassador and dep. U.S. trade rep., 1979-81; asst. sec. state for econ. and bus. affairs, 1981-82; v.p. Goldman, Sachs and Co., 1982, mng. dir., 1998—; vice chmn. Goldman

Sachs (Internat.), 1987—. Guest scholar Brookings Instn., 1973-74; vis. lectr. Princeton U., 1983, 03; mem. internat. capital markets com. N.Y. Stock Exch.; bd. dirs. U.S. Russia Investment Fund, Engelhard Hanovia, Inc., Human Genome Scis., Inc.; mem. internat. adv. bd. Toyota Motor Corp. Author: Making U.S. International Economic Policy, 1984, Reforming the International Monetary System, 1987, Am. Albatross: The Foreign Debt Dilemma, 1988, The Global Economy: America's Role in the Decade Ahead, 1989, International Business in the 21st Century, 1999, The Foreign Policy of the Internet, 2000, The Changing Spectrum in Asia, 2003, Abraham Lincoln and the Global Economy, 2003; mem. editorial bd. Fgn. Policy mag., Internat. Economy mag. Bd. overseers Tufts U.; bd. dirs. Coun. on Fgn. Rels.; mem. dean's adv. coun. John F. Kennedy Sch. of Govt., Harvard U.; mem. internat. adv. coun. Ecole dés Hautes Etudes Commercial, Montreal. Decorated Legion of Honor (France); Shell Oil Co. fellow, 1967-68; Council on Fgn. Relations fellow, 1973-74; Recipient Arthur Flemming award, 1978 Mem. Econ. Club of N.Y. (bd. dirs.), Internat. Longevity Inst. (bd. dirs.), US-ASEAN Bus. Coun. (bd. dirs.). Home: 55 E End Ave Apt 8A New York NY 10028-7935 Office: Goldman Sachs & Co 85 Broad St New York NY 10004-2456 E-mail: robert.hormats@gs.com.

HORN, ANDREW WARREN, lawyer; b. Apr. 19, 1946; s. George H. and Belle (Collin) H.; m. Melinda Fink; children: Lee Shawn, Ruth Belle. BBA in Acctg., U. Miami, 1968, JD, 1971. Bar: Fla. 1971, Colo. 1990, U.S. Dist. Ct. (so. dist.) Fla. 1972, U.S. Tax Ct. 1974. Ptnr. Gillman & Horn P.A., Miami, Fla., 1973-74; pvt. practice Miami, 1974—. Active civic coun. Children's Hosp., Miami, Dade County, Fla., 1994—, Blue Ribbon Aviation Panel-Miami-Dade County, Fla., 2000. Recipient Am. Jurisprudence award Lawyers Coop. Pub. Co., 1970. Mem. ABA, ATLA, Fla. Bar, Acad. Fla. Trial Lawyers. E-mail: lawofficehorn@msn.com.

HORN, BERNARD, English language educator, writer, translator; b. Bklyn., Mar. 6, 1944; s. Harry and Bella (Shell) H.; m. Linda L. Watson, Aug. 24, 1980; children: Gabriella Klein, Hedya Klein, Rebecca. BSChemE, MIT, 1965; PhD in English, U. Conn., 1977. Rsch. engr. Shell Oil Co., Deer Park, Tex., 1965-66; English prof. No. Essex C.C., Haverhill, Mass., 1971-84, Framingham (Mass.) State Coll., 1984 , Haifa Univ. Israel, 2000. Cons., tech. writer Cybermation, Medford, Mass., 1983-84, Computervision, Bedford, Mass., 1989-91, InCon text Enterprises, Harvard, Mass., 1995-96; presenter in field. Author: Facing the Fires: Conversations with A.B. Yehoshua, 1997; contbr. articles to profl. jours.; author numerous poems; translater of Israeli poetry. Fellow NEH, 1978-79, 80, 85, 90, 95. Mem. MLA (exec. com. divsn. lit. and religion), Assn. for Jewish Studies, Nat. Assn. Profs. Hebrew. Democrat. Jewish. Home: 1195 Concord St Framingham MA 01701-4517 E-mail: bhorn@frc.mass.edu.

HORN, BRENDA SUE, lawyer; b. Beech Grove, Ind., Apr. 22, 1949; d. Donald Eugene Horn and Barbara Joyce (Waggoner) Christie. AB with distinction, Ind. U., 1971; MS, Purdue U., 1975; JD summa cum laude, Ind. U., 1981. Bar: Ind. 1981, U.S. Dist. Ct. (so. dist.) Ind. 1981. Assoc. Ice Miller, Indpls., 1981-87, ptnr., 1988—. Assoc. editor Ind. Law Rev., 1980-81. Bd. dirs. Ballet Internationale, 1995—, treas., 1996-2000; pres. Greenleaf Cmty. Ctr., 1992-93, 96-99, v.p., 1991, sec., 1990; bd. dirs., v.p. Cmty. Alliance for the Far East Side, 1997-98, hon. dir. 1998-2003; bd. dirs. Big Sisters of Ctrl. Ind., 1995-98, hon. dir., 1998—2002; bd. dirs. Indiana Edn. Svcs. Authority, 1996—, Cmty. Orgns. Legal Assistance Project, 2000—, treas., 2001-2003, pres. 2003-Named among Influential Women in Indpls., Ind. Lawyer and Indpls. Bus. Jour., 1998; Disting. fellow Indpls. Bar Fond. Mem. ABA (com. on tax exempt fin.), Am. Coll. Bond Counsel (bd. dirs., v.p. 1995-98, pres. 1998-2001), Ind. Bar Assn., Indpls. Bar Assn. (bd. mgrs. 1992), Ind. Mcpl. Lawyers Assn., Nat. Assn. Bond Lawyers, Skyline Club (bd. dirs.), Phi Beta Kappa. Office: Ice Miller One American Sq Box 82001 Indianapolis IN 46282 E-mail: horn@icemiller.com.

HORN, CARL, III, federal judge; b. 1951; BA with honors, U. Va., 1973; JD, U. S.C., 1976. Bar: N.C. 1976. Assoc. Grier, Parker, Poe, Thompson, Bernstein, Gage & Preston, Charlotte, N.C., 1976-79; legal counsel, instr. Wheaton Coll., 1979-82; spl. asst. civil rights divsn. U.S. Dept. Justice, Charlotte, 1982-83, chief asst. U.S. atty. for western dist. N.C., 1987-93; ptnr. Horn & Conrad and predecessor, Charlotte, 1984-87; U.S. magistrate judge for western dist. N.C., U.S. Magistrate Ct., Charlotte, 1993—2003. Author: Fourth Circuit Criminal Handbook, 1994—, Horn's Federal Criminal Jury Instructions for the Fourth Circuit, 1997, LawyerLife: Finding a Life and a Higher Calling in the Practice of Law, 2003; editor: Michie's Fourth Circuit Criminal Reporter, 1995—; Federal Civil Practice in the Fourth Circuit, 1997, Law for Physicians, 1999, LawyerLife: Balancing Life and a Career in Law, 2003; editor: The Battle for Morality in Pluralistic America, 1985; contbr. articles to law jours. Office: 401 W Trade St Ste 238 Charlotte NC 28202-1619

HORN, CHARLES M. lawyer; b. Boston, Sept. 28, 1951; s. Garfield Henry and Alexandra (Matz) H.; m. Jane Charlotte Luxton, May 29, 1976; children: Andrew L., Caroline C. AB magna cum laude, Harvard Coll., 1973; JD, Cornell Law Sch., 1976. Bar: D.C. 1976, U.S. Dist. Ct. D.C. 1977, U.S. Ct. Appeals (D.C. cir.) 1977, U.S. Supreme Ct. 1980. Atty. U.S. Securities and Exchange Commn., Washington, 1976-82, br. chief divsn. enforcement, 1982-83; asst. dir. securities and corp. practices Office Comptroller of Currency, Washington, 1983-86, dir. securities and corp. practices, 1986-89; ptnr. Stroock & Stroock & Lavan, Washington, 1989-92, Mayer, Brown & Platt, Washington, 1992—2002, Mayer, Brown, Rowe & Maw LLP, Washington, 2003—. Mem. faculty Am. Bankers Assn. Nat. Grad. Compliance Sch., 1991-92, 94, Fed. Fin. Instns. Exam. Coun. (programs off-balance-sheet risk, Trust Exams. Sch.); lectr. in field. Edit. adv. bd. Bank Acctg. and Fin., 1993—; contbr. articles to profl. jours. Mem. ABA (banking law com., com. fed. regulation securities), D.C. Bar Assn., Washington Golf and Country Club. Home: 1918 Massachusetts Ave Mc Lean VA 22101-4907 Office: Mayer Brown Rowe & Maw LLP 1909 K St NW Washington DC 20006 E-mail: chorn@mayerbrownrowe.com.

HORN, DANIEL JOSEPH, pharmacist; b. Albany, N.Y., Mar. 10, 1953; s. James F. and Alma M. Horn; m. Annette E.G. Horn, Aug. 24, 1974; children: Joshua G., Zachary Daniel. BS in Pharmacy, SUNY, Buffalo, 1976. Pharmacy mgr. CVS, Olean, N.Y., 1977-95, K Mart, Olean, 1995-98; owner Dan Horn Pharmacy and Health Svcs., Olean, 1998—. Coach Olean Soccer club; cub scout leader Allegheny Highlands Coun. Roman Catholic. Avocations: woodworking, health, nutrition, complementary therapies, marathon running. Office: Dan Horn Pharmacy and Health Svcs 111 E Green St Olean NY 14760-3603 E-mail: Danno@localnet.com.

HORN, DANIEL PAUL, music educator, concert pianist; b. Detroit, Sept. 30, 1956; m. Denise Gamez. Student, Peabody Conservatory of Music, 1974—76; MusB, MusM, Juilliard Sch., 1979, D Musical Arts, 1987. Instr. piano Wheaton Coll. Conservatory of Music, Ill., 1984—87, asst. prof. piano, 1987—92, assoc. prof. piano, 1992—2001, prof. piano, 2001—, keyboard chair, 2002—. Artist faculty Sewanee Summer Music Sch., Sewanee, Tenn., 1991—92, Adamant Music Sch., Adamant, 1994—. Composer: (songs) "Give Thanks to God on High", 1984; musician: (chamber music performances) Chicago Symphony Chamber Music Series, Ravinia Festival, Northwestern University Chamber Festival, Artist Series at Wheaton College, WFMT-FM, (soloist) various Midwestern orchestras, (solo recitalist) American Liszt Society Festival, colleges and universities throughout North America, (recording) Titanic Records, 1998, Centaur Records, 1999, College Avenue Arts Records, 2000; contbr. articles to profl. jours. Artistic advisor Artist Series at Wheaton Coll., 1989—92. Recipient 2d prize (ex [00e6]quo), Chopin Competition, Kosciuszko Found., 1977, Carl M. Roeder Meml. prize, Juilliard Sch., 1979. Mem.: Music Tchrs. Nat. Assn. Anglican. Office: Wheaton Coll Conservatory Music 501 College Ave Wheaton IL 60187 Office Fax: 630-752-5341. Business E-Mail: daniel.p.horn@wheaton.edu.

HORN, DONALD HERBERT, lawyer; b. Bronx, NY, Nov. 22, 1945; s. Herbert H. and Alice (Entwistle) H.; m. Marcia Thomas, Oct. 10, 1971. BA cum laude, Queens Coll., 1966; JD, Harvard U., 1969; postgrad. pub. exec., Carnegie-Mellon U., 1981. Bar: N.Y. 1970, D.C. 1975. Sr. trial atty. Bur. Operating Rights CAB, Washington, 1969-76, atty.-advisor Office Gen. Counsel, 1976-80, assoc. gen. counsel for pricing and entry, 1980-84; dep. asst. gen. counsel for internat. law U.S. Dept. Transp., Washington, 1985-88, asst. gen. counsel for internat. law, 1988—. Chmn. transp. Forest Hills Citizens Assn., Washington, 1983-97. Recipient Sec. Transp. Gold medal award Office Internat. Law, 1995, Sec. Transp. award, 1999, 2001, Williams Trophy, Washington Airports Task Force, 1999, Govt. Tech. Leadership award, 1999, Air-21 award FAA, 2000, Code Share Safety award Sec. Transp., 2000, DOT Bronze medal, 2000, award Sec. Transp., 2001. Mem. Fed. Bar Assn., Harvard U. Law Sch. Assn., Queens Coll. Alumni Assn., Phi Beta Kappa, Omicron Delta Epsilon. Office: US Dept Transp 400 7th St SW Washington DC 20590-0001

HORN, EVERETT BYRON, JR., retired lawyer; b. Newton, Mass., Aug. 18, 1927; s. Everett Byron and Ella Frances (Doody) H.; m. Patricia Ann Reusch, Sept. 10, 1949; children: Everett B. III, John M., Daniel J., Cynthia A. Whetten. AB, Harvard U., 1949; JD, Boston Coll., 1954. Bar: Mass. 1954, U.S. Dist. Ct. Mass. 1955, U.S. Supreme Ct. 1965. Asst. counsel Liberty Mut. Ins. Co., Boston, 1954-63; sr. v.p. and gen. counsel Mass. Indemnity and Life Ins. Co., Hyannis, 1964-75; counsel New Eng. Mut. Life Ins. Co., Boston, 1976-77; ret. v.p. and gen. counsel Boston Mut. Life Ins. Co., Canton, Mass., 1977—. Vice chmn. bd. dirs. Vt. Life and Health Ins. Guaranty Assn.; bd. dirs. Maine Life and Health Ins. Guaranty Assn., R.I. Life and Health Ins. Guaranty Assn., Mass. Life and Health Ins. Guaranty Assn., Boston Mut. Mgmt. Corp., Life Ins. Co. of Boston and N.Y., Life Ins. Assn. Mass. (exec. com.). Pres. Seaside Park Taxpayers Assn., West Hyannis Port, Mass. 1961-64. Served as cpl. USAAF, 1945-46. Mem. ABA (vice chmn. life ins. law com. ins. law sect. 1985-89), Mass. Bar Assn., Barnstable County Bar Assn., Norfolk County Bar Assn., Assn. Life Ins. Counsel, Soc. Corp. Ins. Litigators, Hyannis Yacht Club, Harvard Club. Republican. Roman Catholic. Avocation: sailing. Home: 500 Ocean St Apt 120 Hyannis MA 02601-4759

HORN, FLORA LEOLA, retired administrative assistant; b. Putman, Tex., May 20, 1926; d. James Erasmos and Clara Maud (Davenport) Foller; m. Charles Edward Helm, Sr. (div.); children: Leola Florence Helm, Charles Edward, Jr. Helm, Barbara Ann Helm, Carol Elaine Helm, Beverly Sue Helm, Rodney Johnson Helm; m. Hoy Merie Duhon (dec.). Diploma in Writing, Long Ridge Writers Group, 2003. Contbr. poems in books. Active Bapt. Buckneer Home, Dallas. Named Silver leader, Comdrs. Club, 2001; recipient Golden award, World Poetry, 1986, award merit cert., 1987, cert. Appreciation, Marine Corps League, 1995, Good Work award, B.B.Q. Luncheon Fundraiser, 1997. Mem.: VFW Laides Aux. (life; chaplain 1991—2002, chmn. Nat. Children's Home 1999—2002, cert. Appreciation 1989 93), Nat. Children's Home (Rapid, Mich.) (life), Med. Ctr. Hosp. (Conroe, Tex.) (life), Women of the Moose (chaplain 1999—, Novice award 1977—99, Internat. Co-worker of Yr. award 2003). Avocations: writing, art, Bingo, shuffleboard, poetry. Home: PO Box 5436 1720 Thomas St Titusville FL 32780

HORN, HENRY EYSTER, retired minister; b. N.Y.C., May 30, 1913; s. William M. Horn and Marguerite Eyster Jacobs; m. Catherine Hedwig Stainken, June 9, 1939; children: Jean L., Henry S., David J., Charles M., William M., Marguerite E., Richard D., Eleanor A., Michael J., Andrew G. AB with honors, Cornell U., 1933; BD, MST, Luth. Sem., Phila., 1938; DD (hon.), Muhlenberg Coll., 1965; LLD (hon.), Valparaiso U., 1983. Ordained minister, 1936. Pastor Immanuel Luth. Ch., Phila., 1938-43; pres. Marion (Va.) Coll., 1943-49; pastor Luth. Ch. of the Resurrection, Augusta, Ga., 1949-53, Univ. Luth. Ch., Cambridge, Mass., 1953-78, pastor emeritus, 1978—. Lectr. Phila. Luth. Sem., 1981-84, Luther Sem., St. Paul, 1984-86; protestant chaplain Bryn Mawr (Pa.) Coll., 1980-81; chair ch. music com. United Luth. Ch., Phila., 1946-62, mem. bd. deaconess, 1948-62; mem. bd. theol. edn. Luth. Ch. in Am., N.Y.C., 1962-72, chair commn. on liturgy and hymnal, 1964-74. Author: O Sing Unto the Lord, 1956, 62, Christian in Modern Style, 1968, Worship in Crisis, 1972, Lutherans in Campus Ministry, 1972, Models of Ministry, 1989, Thoughts from the Fountainside, 1992. Organizer Friends of the Libr., Augusta, Ga., 1951; active Cambridge Camping Assn., 1950s, Cambridge Econ. Opportunity Com., Cambridge Family Svc. Bd., Cambridge Hosp. Bd., Cambridge Mental Health, Inc., Cambridge Cmty. Svcs., 1960-72; pres. Cambridge Mental Health Assn.; chair Cambridge Somerville Welfare Bd. Recipient Silver Beaver award Boy Scouts Am., Roanoke (Va.) Coun., 1948, Gold medal award for ret. clergymen Religious Heritage of Am., 1990, Christus Lux Mundi award Luther Sem., 2001. Mem. Boston Ministers' Club, Cambridge Club, United Ministry at Harvard (2-time pres.). Democrat. Avocations: nature, reading, compiling notebooks of quotations, family. Home: 47-1 Trowbridge St Cambridge MA 02138

HORN, HOWARD M. labor union administrator, consultant; b. Bklyn., July 31, 1938; s. Moris Norman and Yetta Horn; m. Carol Evelyn Solomon (dec.); m. Lois Bonnie Pfeffer, Nov. 10, 1997; 1 stepchild, Ronald. Post grad. student, Harvard U., 1966. Exec. v.p. Meat Cutters N.Am. Local 627, N.Y.C., 1964—81, UFCW (United Food and Commerecial Workers) Local 50, N.Y.C., 1982—90, UFCW Local 342/50, Mineola, NY, 1991—97, cons., 1997—98. Columnist: On The Truck, 1964—90. Drug counselor N.Y. Ctrl. Labor Coun., Manhattan, 1979—89, referal com., 1975—89; county com. mem. Flushing Dem. Club, NY, 1988—. Pvt. U.S. Army, 1961—63. Avocations: phongraph records, history, travel.

HORN, JANET, physician; b. Oak Ridge, Aug. 10, 1950; d. Harry and Molly (Rich) Horn; m. Alan R. Yuspeh, June 8, 1975. BA magna cum laude, Vanderbilt U., 1972; MS in Physiology and Biophysics, Georgetown U., 1973; MD, George Washington U., 1978. Diplomate Am. Bd. Internal Medicine, also sub-bd. Infectious Diseases, Am. Bd. Med. Examiners. Intern George Washington U. Hosp., Washington, 1978-79, resident in obstetrics and gynecology, 1979-81; resident in internal medicine Georgetown U., Washington, 1981-83; fellow in infectious diseases Johns Hopkins Hosp., Balt., 1983-85; mem. med. staff Georgetown U. Hosp., also Sibley Meml. Hosp., Washington, 1985-86, Johns Hopkins Hosp., 1986—, Sinai Hosp. of Balt., 1989—, Greater Balt. Med. Ctr., 1990—, St. Joseph's Hosp., 1990—. Asst. prof. medicine Johns Hopkins U. Sch. Medicine, 1986-95, assoc. prof., 1995—. Mem. editorial bd. Johns Hopkins Med. Grand Rounds, Am. Jour. Gynecologic Health; contbr. articles to profl. jours., chpts. to books. Bd. dirs. Chesapeake AIDS Found., 1989-92; chair AIDS Coordinating and Adv. Coun. to Mayor, Balt., 1988-92. Recipient Pearl M. Stetler Found. Rsch. award Johns Hopkins U., 1987, Merck Found. Clinician Scientist Rsch. award Johns Hopkins U., 1988. Mem. AAAS, ACP, Am. Soc. for Microbiology, Infectious Diseases Soc. Am., Johns Hopkins Med. and Surg. Assn., Phi Beta Kappa, Alpha Omega Alpha. Office: 1821 Sulgrave Ave Baltimore MD 21209

HORN, JASON G. English educator; s. John Elmo Horn and Mary Elizabeth Ramsey; m. Sharon Diana Luker, June 21, 1987; children: Diana Elizabeth, Sara Jayne, Grace Lynn. A degree, Colo. Mountain Coll., 1982—85; B in english, Ft. Lewis Coll., 1985—88; PhD in english, U. of Colo. at Boulder, 1988—94. Instr. in English U. of Colo. at Boulder, 1990—94, U. of No. Colo., 1992—97; assoc. prof. of English Gordon Coll., Barnesville, Ga., 1997—. Chair of the divsn. of humanities Gordon Coll., Barnesville, Ga., 1998—2001. Author: (book) Mark Twain and William James: Crafting a Free Self, (reference book) Mark Twain: A Descriptive Guide to Biographical Sources, American Literary History: An Annotated Guide; contbr. articles to jours., also encyclopedia entries. Vol. Habitat for Humanity, Barnesville, Ga., 1998—2003; lector St. Ann's Cath. Ch., Barnesville, Ga., 1998—2003. Recipient Conf. fellow, Spiritual Frontiers 2000: Beliefs and Values in the Lit. West, 2000. Mem.: South Atlantic MLA, Mark Twain Cir., William James Soc. (editl. bd. mem. 2000—03). Independent-Republican. Catholic. Achievements include Literary historical study of the documents linking Mark Twain's writings to the psychological work of William James. Avocations: guitar, bluegrass music, drums. Home: 333 Freeman Rd Barnesville GA 30204 Office: Gordon College 419 College Ave Barnesville GA 30204 Personal E-mail: j_horn@gdn.edu.

HORN, JOYCE ELAINE, music educator; d. Alfred Irving Sette and Elma Louise Robertson; 1 child, Camilla Jeanne VandenBerg. MusB, Grand Rapids Bapt. Coll.; MusM, Western Mich. U, 1972. Assoc. prof. music Cornerstone U, Grand Rapids, Mich., 1962—. Republican. Baptist. Avocations: reading, studying Charles Dickens, A.J. Cronin, accompanying. Home: 7355 Casade Terrace Dr SE Grand Rapids MI 49546

HORN, LEE SHAWN, sports analyst; b. Miami, Fla., Feb. 21, 1977; s. Andrew Warren and Melinda F. (Fink) H. Grad. h.s., Miami, 1995. Ind. filmmaker, Miami, 1993—; newsroom worker ABC, Miami, 1996; v.p. Fla. Internat. U., 1999; pres. Sports Ltd. Edits. & Memorabilia, 1996—; v.p. Fla. Internat. U., 1999. Asst. head coach football team Gulliver Prep., 1997-; asst. dir. Super Bowl halftime show, 1999. Vol. Atlanta Com. Olympic Games, 1996; chmn. Ted Wendricks Def. End of Yr. award. Mem. U. Miami Diamond Darlings, Miami Touchdown Club (bd. dirs.). Democrat. Avocations: football, skiing, fishing, traveling.

HORN, LOIS BURLEY, pianist, educator; b. Syracuse, N.Y., Sept. 8, 1928; d. Helen (Smith) Burley; m. Allen F. Horn, July 24, 1954; children: Allen III, Lawrence, Lisa. MusB magna cum laude, Syracuse U., 1950; MusM, Mich. State U., 1952; pvt. studies with Eugene List, Rochester, N.Y., 1969-74; pvt. studies with Leon Fleisher, Balt., 1975-76. Faculty Mich. State U., 1950-53; resident instr. St. Katherine's Sch., Davenport, Iowa, 1953-54; pianist, instr. various colls., Mfss., 1954-55; ind. tchr., clinician Manlius, N.Y., 1955-93; pianist, lectr. Cazenovia (N.Y.) Coll., 1967-82; pianist Two Musicians, N.Y., 1982-93. Clinician, adjudicator various music tchr. orgns., 1975—. Contbr. articles to profl. jours.; performer Lincoln Ctr., N.Y.C., 1987. Organist, choir dir. various chs., 1948-62; pianist Univ. United Meth. Ch., 1956—. Recipient Onondaga County Regrant award N.Y. State Coun. on Arts; grantee Musician Performance Trust Fund. Mem. AFL-CIO, Cen. N.Y. Assn. Music Tchrs. (pres. 1971-73, bd. dirs.), Music Tchrs. Nat. Assn. (cert. Master Tchr., bd. dirs.), N.Y. Fedn. Music Clubs (pres. 1989-91), chmn., v.p. scholarship and awards com. 1979-94, bd. dirs.), Civic Morning Mus. (bd. dirs. 1961-78, Crouse award for keyboard excellence 1977), Beaufort Area Music Tchrs. (founder 1993, pres. 1993-97, chair Monster Concerts 1998, 2000), Haus Musik (founder 1997, pres. 1997-2003), Sigma Alpha Iota (bd. dirs. undergrad. awards com. 1987-90, Sword of Honor 1960, Rose of Honor 1966, Ring of Excellence 1987). Home and Office: 2255 Plantation Dr Beaufort SC 29902-5221

HORN, MYRON KAY, consulting petroleum geologist, author, educator; b. Miami, Fla., Jan. 28, 1930; s. Harry I. and Sykes K. (Kaplan) H.; m. Barbara DeCasseres Rothschild, Apr. 9, 1955; children: Lisa, Marc, Nina. BS, U. Colo., 1952; MS, U. Houston, 1958; PhD, Rice U., 1964. Sr. research geologist Pure Oil Co., Crystal Lake, Ill., 1960-64; group leader geophys. research Cities Service Co., Tulsa, 1964-65, mgr. geol. research, 1965-70, dir. exploration and prodn. rsch., 1970-83, dir. applied rsch. and tech. ops., 1983-1987; ret., 1987; pvt. practice cons., 1987—. Mem. U.S. sci. adv. com. Joint Oceanographic Inst., 1983-87; editor Circum-Pacific Meeting, Am. Assn. Petroleum Geologists, Singapore, 1986, lectr., China and Hungary, Japan, 1986-90, Saudi Arabia, 1993. Contbr. articles to profl. jours. Served to lt. (j.g.) U.S. Navy, 1952-55 Mem. Am. Assn. Petroleum Geologists (hon.; editor 1979-83, exec. com., disting. service award 1986). Home: 5919 S Gary Pl Tulsa OK 74105-7427 E-mail: m.horn@sbcglobal.net.

HORN, PAUL ERVIN, minister; b. Grinnell, Iowa, Mar. 24, 1919; s. Harry Edgar and Florence Henrietta (Bump) H.; m. Elvis Devlin, Dec. 21, 1940; children: Sandra, Eileen, Cynthia, Larry. BA, San Jose State U., 1942; MDiv, Berkeley Bapt. Div. Sch., 1945; PhD, Calif. Grad. Sch. Theology, 1973. Ordained to ministry Conservative Bapt. Assn. Am., 1945. Pastor Elmhurst Bapt. Ch., Oakland, Calif., 1945-55, Bell Bapt. Ch., Cudahy, Calif., 1955-66, 1st Bapt. Ch., Montclair, Calif., 1966-77, Calvary Bapt. Ch., Hemet, Calif., 1977-83, 1st Bapt. Ch., Wrightwood, Calif., 1984-90; pastor emeritus Valley Bapt. Ch., 1995—. Bd. dirs. Conservative Bapt. Assn. So. Calif., Anaheim, 1956-88, pres., 1959-60, min. at large, 1990-99; bd. dirs. Conservative Bapt. Home Mission Soc., Wheaton, Ill., 1960-66; parliamentarian Conservative Bapt. Assn. Am., Wheaton, 1950-85, v.p. western chpt., 1967-74. Mem. Conservative Bapt. Fgn. Mission Soc. (sec. 1988-91). Republican. Avocation: photography. Address: PO Box 1422 Yucaipa CA 92399-1422 E-mail: phorn92399@aol.com.

HORN, RALPH, bank executive; b. Corinth, Miss., Feb. 16, 1941; BS, Miss. State U., 1963; Mgmt. degree, Harvard U., 1992. Mgmt. trainee 1st Tenn. Bank N.A., Memphis, 1963, mgr. bank's bond divsn., 1976; pres., COO, dir. 1st Tenn. Nat. Corp., Memphis, 1991; vice chmn., dir. 1st Tenn. Bank N.A. (subs. 1st Tenn. Nat. Corp.), 1991—2002, CEO, 1994—2002, chmn. bd. dirs., 1996—. Past bd. dirs., past chmn. bd. Mcpl. Securities Rulemaking Bd. Mem. adv. bd. Anthony Commn. Tax Reform. Mem.: Dealer Bank Assn. (past chmn. fed. affairs com., past bd. dirs.), Tenn. Bankers Assn. (past bd. dirs.), Fin. Svcs. Roundtable (past bd. dirs.), Regional Mcpl. Securities Assn. (co-founder, past co-chmn.), Pub. Securities Assn. Office: 1st Tennessee Nat Corp PO Box 84 Memphis TN 38101-0084

HORN, ROBERT F. lawyer; b. Phila., Jan. 9, 1959; s. Albert B. and Helen K. (Earley) H. BS in Edn., West Chester (Pa.) U., 1982; JD, Widener U., 1996. Bar: Pa., N.J.; assoc. in claims. Realtor Carr Real Estate Co., Drexel Hill, Pa., 1986-89; classroom tchr. Gloucester Twp. Sch. Dist., Blackwood, N.J., 1982-88; sr. claim rep. Allstate Claim Office, Exton, Pa., 1988-90, claim support mgr., 1990-91; paralegal Allstate Staff Counsel, Phila., 1991-93, legal unit mgr., 1994-96, trial atty., 1996—2001; assoc. White and Williams LLP, Phila., 2001—. Pres. Wynnwood Condominium Assn., Wilmington, Del., 1998. Pres. Pine St. Condominium Assn. Mem. Phila. Bar Assn., Brehon Law Soc., Cath. Philopatrian Lit. Inst., Men of Malvern. Democrat. Office: White and Williams LLP 1800 One Liberty Pl Philadelphia PA 19103 E-mail: Bobhorn@acninc.net.

HORN, RUSSELL EUGENE, engineering executive, consultant; b. Yoe, Pa., May 4, 1912; s. Eugene M. and Charlotte (Snyder) H.; m. Eleanor B. Baird, Jan. 12, 1934; children: Russell Eugene, Ralph Elliot, Rosalind Emily (Mrs. Lee Kunkel), Robert Errol. BS, Pa. State U., 1933. Foreman Pa. Dept. Hwys. dist. office, York, Pa., 1933-35; draftsman, supr., designer C.S. Buchart, architect, 1935-41; exec. v.p., chief engr. Buchart Engring., 1945-59, pres., chief engr., 1959-61, Buchart-Horn, Inc., 1961-72, chmn. bd. dirs., 1972-2000. Pres. PACE Resources, inc., 1970-87, chmn. bd. dirs. 1970-2001, bd. dirs.; chmn. AAA White Rose Motor Club, 1975-78. Bd. dirs. Auto Club So. Pa.; bd. dirs. emeritus Retirement Homes of Meth. Ch., 1978—. Col. AUS, 1940-45. Mem. NSPE, Soc. Am. Mil. Engrs., Pa. Soc. Profl. Engrs. (pres. Lincoln chpt. 1961), Pa. Assn. Cons. Engrs. (pres. 1965, bd. dirs. 1966), Pa. Hwy Info. Assn. (bd. dirs.), Am. Soc. Hwy. Engrs. (nat. pres. 1962), Tech. Socs. Coun. Southeastern Pa. (chmn. 1963), Engring. Soc. York, Profl. Engrs. Pvt. Practice, Am. Concrete Inst., Assn. Pa. Constructors Assn. Hwy Ofcls. N. Atlantic States, Assn. U.S. Army Res. Officers Assn., ASCE, VFW, Cons. Engrs. Coun., Am. Legion, Pa. State U. Alumni Club (York County), Univ. Club, Lake Club, Exch. Club (Golden Deeds award 1979), Mt. Nittany Soc. Pa. State U., Masons (32 deg., Order of the Double Eagle award 1983, Legion of Freedom award 1986, outstanding engring. alumnus 1987), York County Agrl. Soc. (life), Moose Home: 1270 Brockie Dr York PA 17403-4448 Office: Pace Resources Inc 40 S Richland Ave York PA 17404-3470

HORN, RUSSELL EUGENE, JR., business executive; b. York, Pa., Sept. 15, 1934; s. Russell Eugene and A. Eleanor (Baird) Horn; m. Franziska Kathe Kastner (dec. 1995); children: Silvia S. Kastner, Russell E. III, Monika K., Ursula F., John D.; m. Lilli Maria Funk, 2002. Sgt. 1st class U.S. Army Security Agy., 1952-62; sales trainee, sales rep. Print-O-Stat, Inc., York, Pa., 1962-63, mgr., 1970-73, exec. v.p., 1976-77, pres., 1977-96, mgr. Towson, Md., 1963-70, v.p., 1973-76; office of pres. PACE Resources, Inc., York, 1987-96, pres., CEO, 1996—2001, chmn., pres., CEO, 2001—. Bd. dirs. Buchart-Horn, Inc., others; mem. adv. bd. Dauphin Deposit Bank-York Region, 1984-98; also officer, advisor, exec. various corps. Active various edn1., charitable activities. Mem. York Area C. of C. Home: 995 Detwiler Dr York PA 17404 Office: PACE Resources Inc 40 S Richland Ave York PA 17404-3470

HORN, SABRINA, public relations executive; b. Charleston, W.Va., Aug. 3, 1961; d. Dr. Christian Frederick and Christa (Winkler) H. BA, William Smith Coll., 1983; MS, Boston U., 1984. Sr. acct. exec. Edelman Pub. Rels., San Francisco, 1984—90; sr. acct. exec. Blanc & Otus; founder, pres. & CEO Horn Group, 1991—. Office: Horn Group 621 Howard St San Francisco CA 94105

HORN, SHIRLEY, vocalist, pianist; b. Washington; 1 dau., Rainy. Student, Howard U. Albums include Cat on a Hot Fiddle, 1959, Embers And Ashes, 1960, Live at the Village Vanguard, 1961, Loads of Love, 1963, Shirley Horn with Horns, 1963, Travelin' Light, 1965, For Love of Ivy, 1968, A Dandy in Aspic, 1968, Where Are You Going?, 1972, A Lazy Afternoon, 1979, All Night Long, 1982, Violets For Your Ears, 1983, The Sentimental Touch (titled Songbirds in U.S.), 1985, I Thought About You, 1987, Softly, 1988, Close Enough for Love, 1988, Tune in Tomorrow, 1990, You Won't Forget Me, 1991,

Dedicated to You-Tribute to Sarah Vaughan with Carmen McRae, 1991, Here's to Life, 1992 (Grammy nomination, Best Jazz Vocal for "Light Out of Darkness", 1994), Violets for Furs, 1994, I Love You Paris, 1994, All Night Long, 1994, (with Charles Ables, Billy Hart) At Northsea, 1996, Jazz Round Midnight, 1998 (Grammy). Office: Verve Records 1755 Broadway Fl 3D New York NY 10019-3743

HORN, STEPHEN, lawyer; b. N.Y.C., Sept. 12, 1946; s. Leonard and Gladys H.; m. Kerry Corcoran, Oct. 9, 1977. B.S. in Indsl. Engring., Rutgers, 1968; J.D. cum laude, Seton Hall Sch., 1973. Bar: D.C. 1974, U.S. Dist. Ct. D.C. 1979, U.S. Ct. Appeals (D.C. cir.) 1979, Md. 1982. Trial atty. Dept. Justice, Washington, 1973-78; ptnr. Horn & Conroy, 1979-83, Schmeltzer, Aptaker & Sheppard, P.C., 1983— . Editor-in-chief Jour. Seton Hall Law Rev., 1972-73. Contbr. articles to profl. publs. Served to 1st lt. inf., U.S. Army, 1968-70, Vietnam. Recipient Spl. Achievement award U.S. Dept. Justice, 1976. Mem. ABA (chmn. com. 1981-85). Republican. Jewish. Office: Schmeltzer Aptaker & Sheppard PC 2600 Virginia Ave NW Ste 1000 Washington DC 20037-1922

HORN, STEPHEN, congressman, political science educator; b. San Juan Bautista, Calif., May 31, 1931; s. John Stephen and Isabelle (McCaffrey) H.; m. Nini Moore, Sept. 4, 1954; children: Marcia Karen, John Stephen. AB with great distinction, Stanford, 1953, postgrad., 1953-54, 55-56, PhD in Polit. Sci, 1958; M in Pub Adminstrn., Harvard, 1955. Congl. fellow, 1958-59; adminstrv. asst. to sec. labor James P. Mitchell, 1959-60; legislative asst. to U.S. Senator Thomas H. Kuchel, 1960-66; sr. fellow The Brookings Instn., 1966-69; dean grad. studies and research Am. U., 1969-70; pres. Calif. State U., Long Beach, 1970-88, Trustee prof. polit. sci., 1988-93; mem. U.S. Congress from 38th Calif. dist., 1993—2003; mem. govt. reform com., transp. and infrastructure com. Sr. cons., host The Govt. Story on TV, The Election Game (radio series), 1967-69, vice chmn. U.S. Commn. on Civil Rights, 1969-80 (commr. 1980-82); chmn. Urban Studies Fellow Adv. Com., U.S. Dept. HUD, 1969-70; mem. Law Enforcement Ednl. Prog. Adv. Com., U.S. Dept Justice, 1969-70; adv. bd. Nat. Inst. Corrections, 1972-88 (chmn. 1984-87), Author: The Cabinet and Congress, 1960, Unused Power: The Work of the Senate Committee on Appropriations, 1970, (with Edmund Beard) Congressional Ethics: The View from the House, 1975. Active Pres.-elect Nixon's Task Force on Orgn. Exec. Br., 1968, Kutak Found.; vice chmn. Long Beach Area C. of C., 1984-88; co-founder Western U.S. Com. Arts and Scis. for Eisenhower, 1956; chmn. Am. Assn. State Colls. and Univs., 1985-86; mem. Calif. Ednl. Facilities Authority, 1984-93. USAR, 1954-62. Fellow John F. Kennedy Inst. Politics Harvard U., 1966-67. Fellow Nat. Acad. Pub. Adminstrn.; mem. Stanford Assocs., Stanford Alumni Assn. (pres. 1976-77), Phi Beta Kappa, Pi Sigma Alpha. Republican.

HORN, SUSAN DADAKIS, statistics educator; b. Cleve., Aug. 30, 1943; d. James Sophocles and Demeter (Zessis) Dadakis; m. Roger Alan Horn, July 24, 1965; children: Ceres, Corinne, Howard. BA, Cornell U., 1964; MS, Stanford U., 1966, PhD, 1968. Asst. prof. Johns Hopkins U., Balt., 1968-76, assoc. prof., 1976-86, prof. stats. and health svcs. rsch. methods, 1986-92; sr. scientist Intermountain Health Care, Salt Lake City, 1992-95; prof. dept. med. informatics Sch. Medicine U. Utah, Salt Lake City, 1992—; rsch. prof. U. Tex.-Houston Sch. Nursing, 1999—2001. Sr. scientist Inst. for Clin. Outcomes Rsch., Salt Lake City. Fellow Am. Statist. Assn., Assn. for Health Svcs. Rsch.; mem. APHA, Biometric Soc., Assn. for Health Svcs. Research, Sigma Xi, Phi Beta Kappa, Phi Kappa Phi. Presbyterian. Avocations: tennis, swimming. Home: 1793 Fort Douglas Cir Salt Lake City UT 84103-4451 Office: Inst Clin Outcomes 699 E South Temple Salt Lake City UT 84102-1282 E-mail: shorn@isisicor.com.

HORN, VICKIE LYNN, medical and surgical nurse, nursing educator; b. Bloomfield, Iowa, Sept. 7, 1955; d. Paul Nelson and Norcita Janice (Glasgow) Seals; 1 child, Braden Seth. BSN, N.E. Mo. State U., Kirksville, 1977; MS, Coll. St. Francis, Joliet, Ill., 1988. Cert. ACLS. House supr. Burlington (Iowa) Care Ctr.; float staff nurse Burlington Med. Ctr.; operating room nurse clinician Ottumwa (Iowa) Regional Health Ctr., perioperative nurse clinician; writer, house supr. Diamond@PSCIA.net. Mem. Am. Assn. Operating Room Nurses. E-mail: diamond@pcsia.net.

HORN, WADE FREDERICK, federal agency administrator; b. Coral Gables, Fla., Dec. 3, 1954; s. John David and Daisy (Anderson) H.; m. Claudia Blair, Jan. 7, 1977; children: Christiana Watson, Caroline Lindley. BA in Psychology, Am. U., 1975; MA in Clin. Child Psychology, So. Ill. U., 1978, PhD in Clin. Child Psychology, 1981. Rsch. asst. social skills devel. program Carbondale (Ill.) Elem. Schs., 1976-78; behavior analyst, psychol. cons. early childhood program Wabash and Ohio Valley Spl. Edn. Dist., Norris City, Ill., 1978-79; predoctoral intern dept. pediatric psychology Children's Hosp. Nat. Med. Ctr., Washington, 1980-81, postdoctoral clin. psychology fellow behavioral medicine rsch. lab., 1981-82; asst. prof. dept. psychology Mich. State U., East Lansing, 1982-86; vice chairperson dept. pediatric psychology, dir. outpatient psychol. svcs. dept. psychiatry Children's Hosp. Nat. Med. Ctr., Washington, 1987-88; dir. Pediatric Psychology Splty. Clinic, assoc. dir. Psychol. Clinic Mich. State U., East Lansing, 1984-86; attending staff child health care unit St. Lawrence Hosp., Lansing, Mich., 1983-84; assoc. prof. psychiatry, behavioral scis. and child health and devel. Sch. Medicine, George Washington U., 1986-89; mem. presdl. transition team Office of Pres. Elect, Washington, 1988-89; commr. Adminstrn. on Children, Youth and Families, 1989—93; chief Children's Bur., Washington, 1989—93; asst. sec. Family Support Dept HHS, Washington, 2001—. Adj. faculty dept. pediatrics Coll. Human Medicine, Mich. State U., East Lansing, 1983-86, Pub. Policy Ibst., Georgetown U., 1993-2001; mem. Nat. Commn. Childhood Disability, 1994-95; mem. U.S. Adv. Bd. on WElfare Educators, 1996-97 Author: (with G. Greenberg) Attention Deficit Disorder: Questions and Answers for Parents, 1991; contbr. articles to profl. jours. Mem. Health Care Adv. Group for George Bush for Pres. campaign, 1987-88. Mem. Am. Psychol. Assn. (divs. clin. psychology and child clin. psychology), Assn. for Advancement Behavior Therapy, Phi Kappa Phi. Republican. Presbyterian. Office: Dept HHS Admin for Children and Families 370 L'Enfant Promenade SW Washington DC 20447

HORNACEK, JEFFREY JOHN, professional basketball player; b. Elmhurst, Ill., May 3, 1963; Student, Iowa State. With Phoenix Suns, 1986—92; guard Phila. 76ers, 1992—94, Utah Jazz, 1994—. Named NBA All-Star, 1992.

HORNADAY, ALINE GRANDIER, publisher, independent scholar; b. San Diego, Sept. 14, 1923; d. Frank and Lydia Landon (Weir) Grandier; m. Quinn Hornaday, Oct. 9, 1965. BA, Union of Experimenting Colls., San Diego, 1977; PhD, U. Calif., San Diego, 1984. Pub. San Diego Daily Transcript, 1952-72, columnist, 1972-74; dir. San Diego Ind. Scholars, 1985-87, 94-95; co-pub. Jour. Unconventional History, Cardiff, Calif., 1989-00. Vis. scholar U. Calif., San Diego, 1984—; speaker at profl. confs. Co-author: The Hornadays, Root and Branch; contbr. articles to profl. jours. and books. Commr. San Diego City Libr. Commn., 1964-70. Mem. San Diego Ind. Scholars, Nat. Coalition Ind. Scholars, Med. Assn. of Pacific, Am. Hist. Assn., Medieval Acad. Am., Nat. Soc. Colonial Dames of Am., Wed. Club (pres. 1964-65). Home and Office: 6435 Avenida Cresta La Jolla CA 92037-6514

HORNADAY, RICHARD H. artist, retired art educator; b. Joplin, Mo., Aug. 15, 1927; s. Beecher Hoyt and Zora Hornaday; m. Margaret Ann Gardner, June 29, 1950 (div. Mar. 1972); m. Ruth Mary Miller, Nov. 26, 1972 (dec. Feb. 2002); 1 child, Emily Jane; m. Jenifer Shevis-Packard, Sept. 28, 2002. BFA, U. Iowa, 1950, MFA, 1952; student, Calif. State U., Chico. Cert. art tchr. elem. and secondary schs., Calif. Art instr. Auburn (Calif.) H.S., 1953-54; art supr. elem. sch. dist., Redding, Calif., 1954-67; instr. drawing and painting Shasta Coll., Redding, 1954-68; prof. grad. studies Calif. State U., Chico, 1968-88, chair dept. art, 1972-80, prof. emeritus, 1988—. Judge No. Calif. Art Assn., Crocker Art Mus., Sacramento, 1959. Exhibited works in solo shows at Ruthermore Gallery, San Francisco, 1959-62, Nordness Gallery, N.Y.C., 1962, Henderson Gallery, Monterey, Calif., 1963, Rosicrucian Mus., San Jose, Calif., 1985, Himovitz Pavillions Gallery, Sacramento, 1992, 50-Yr. Crocker-Kingsley Retrospective, Sacramento, Watercolor Gallery, Berkeley, Calif., 1985, Vagabond Rose Gallery, Chico, Calif.; group shows include Mus. Modern Art, N.Y.C., 1962, St. Louis Art Mus., 1963, San Francisco Mus. Art, 1963, Nat. Watercolor Okla., 1994, Nat. Watercolor Exhbn., Concord, Calif., 1996, Visual Arts Ctr. N.E. Fla., Panama City, 1996, Ariz. Aqueous XI Nat., Tubac, 1997, Ga. XVIII Nat. Watercolor Exhbn., Macon, 1997, Taos Nat. Exhbn. Am. Watercolor III, 1997, Gt. Plains Nat., Ft. Hayes, Kans., 1998, Watercolor USA, Springfield, 1998; works in collections at Shasta Coll., Calif. State U., Chico, Iowa State U., others; subject of articles. Mem. Civic Arts Commn., Redding, 1963-78; judge various county fairs, 1965-72; art cons. Shasta County Supt. Schs., 1964-67, Creative Arts Ctr., Chico, 1974-75, others. Served with USN, 1945-46, PTO. Recipient awards for art. Home: PO Box 7652 Chico CA 95927-7652

HORNAK, ANNA FRANCES, library administrator; b. College Station, Tex., June 3, 1922; d. Josef and Anna (Drozd) H. BA, U. Tex., Austin, 1944; B.L.S., U. Ill., Champaign-Urbana, 1945; Ed.M., U. Houston, 1956. Children's librarian Schenectady Pub. Library, N.Y., 1945-47; children's librarian Pasadena Pub. Library, Calif., 1947-49; supr. Juvenile Div. Houston Pub. Library, 1949-57, asst. dir., 1957-89, ret., 1989. Named Outstanding Woman, YWCA of Houston, 1977; Outstanding Houston Profl. Woman, Fed. Houston Profl. Women, 1982 Avocations: collecting miniature books; collecting Bohemian red glass; restoring antique furniture. Home: 2217 Woodhead St Houston TX 77019-6820

HORNAK, MARK RAYMOND, lawyer; b. Homestead, Pa., Mar. 31, 1956; s. Raymond John and Margaret W. (Somiak) H.; m. Elizabeth Ann Meyer, Jan. 30, 1982; children: Samuel A., Rachel A., Rebecca A., Mary R., Matthew S. BA (cum laude), U. Pitts., 1978, JD (summa cum laude), 1981. Bar: Pa. 1981, W.Va. 1982, U.S. Dist. Ct. (we. dist.) Pa. 1981, U.S. Dist. Ct. (so. dist.) W.Va. 1983, U.S. Dist. Ct. (no. dist.) W.Va. 1991, U.S. Ct. Appeals (3rd and 4th cirs.) 1982, U.S. Supreme Ct. 1996. Law clk. to James M. Sprouse U.S. Ct. Appeals (4th cir.), Charleston, W.Va., 1981-82; assoc. Buchanan Ingersoll, P.C., Pitts., 1982-88, shareholder, 1989—. Adj. prof. law U. Pitts., 1988-92; gen. counsel Sports & Exhbn. Authority Pitts., Allegheny County, 1994—; editor-in-chief U. Pitts. Law Rev., 1981; active Leadership Pitts., 1989. Pres. bd. dirs. Steel Valley Sch. Dist., 1987-89, mem. Allegheny Intermediate Unit, 1987-90; chief Munhall Vol. Fire Co. #4, 1982. Scholar Univ. scholar, U. Pitts., 1981. Mem. ABA, Allegheny County Bar Assn., Am. Law Inst., Am. Bar Found., Acad. of Trial Lawyers, Order of Coif. Home: 2368 Mill Grove Rd Uppr Saint Clair PA 15241-2731 Office: Buchanan Ingersoll PC 301 Grant St Fl 20 Pittsburgh PA 15219-1410 E-mail: hornakmr@bipc.com.

HORNAK, THOMAS, retired electronics company executive; b. Bratislava, Slovakia, Oct. 14, 1924; came to U.S., 1968; s. Stefan and Elisabeth (Meer) H.; m. Vera Lautner, Mar. 15, 1958; 1 child, Thomas MSEE, Tech U., Bratislava, 1947; PhD in Elec. Engring., Tech U., Prague, Czech Republic, 1966. Sect. mgr. Tesla Radio Research Lab., Prague, 1947-61; sci. advisor Computer Research Inst., Prague, 1962-68; mem. tech. staff Hewlett Packard Labs., Palo Alto, Calif., 1968-73, mgr. research dept., 1973-91, prin. engr., 1991-99, ret., 1999. Contbr. articles to profl. jours. Patentee in field Fellow IEEE (assoc. editor Jour. Solid State Cirs. 1986-88, 2001—, chmn. solid state cirs. and tech. com. 1979-81).

HORNBACK, JOSEPH HOPE, mathematics educator; b. Nevada, Mo., Apr. 20, 1910; s. Joseph Thomas and Georgia (Munn) H. AB, Central Coll., 1932; MA, Harvard, 1933; PhD, U. Ill., 1952; postgrad., U. Chgo., 1933-34, 41-42, 46-49. Tchr. math. Calumet City (Ill.) High Sch., 1934-37, U. Chgo. Lab Sch., 1937-42; asst. prof. math. U. Ala., 1952 57, asso. prof., 1957-63, prof., 1963-80, prof. emeritus, 1980—. Vis. scientist to high schs. for Ala. Acad. Sci. Chmn. gen. bd. 1st Christian Ch., Tuscaloosa, Ala., 1974-76; mem. world outreach com. Christian Chs. of Ala., 1973-75. Served as lt. USNR, 1942-46. Mem. Am. Math. Soc., Math. Assn. Am., Masons, Sigma Xi, Phi Kappa Phi.

HORNBECK, HAROLD DOUGLAS, psychotherapist; b. Ashtabula, Ohio, Dec. 12, 1952; s. Harold Garnet and Garnet Jean (Osburn) H. BS, Ohio State U., 1977; MS in Social Adminstrn., Case Western Res. U., 1987. ACSW, LISW, QCSW; diplomate NASW; cert. Cleve. Ctr. for Cognitive Therapy. Child life worker Rainbow Babies and Children's Hosp., Cleve., 1977-85; psychotherapist Cmty. Counseling Ctr., Ashtabula, 1985-88, Riverview Psychiat. Assocs., Ashtabula, 1988-98, UHHS Laurelwood Counseling Ctr., 1988-2000, Hornbeck Associates, Ltd., 2001—. Adj. faculty Ursuline Coll., Pepperpike, Ohio, 1989; clin. dir. Critical Incident Stress Mgmt. Team, Ashtabula, 1993-2001; chmn. Ohio Children's Trust Fund LAB, Ashtabula, 1988-2002; v.p. bd. HIV/AIDS Task Force Ashtabula County, 1989-01, co-pres. 2001—; bd. dirs. Homesafe Shelter for Battered Women, Ashtabula, 1988-92. Camp dir. Matthew Salem Camp for Cystic Fibrosis, Lakewood, Ohio, 1993—2001, bd. trustees, 1993—, v.p., 9396, pres., 1996—2001; bd. trustees Matthew Salem Camping Found., 1993—96, v.p., 1996—; pres.; advisor Jr. Achievement, Ashtabula, 1992—94; group leader HIV/AIDS SuppportGroup, Ashtabula County, Lake County, Geauga County, 1993—; mentor Ashtabula City Schs., 1993; facilitator I Can Cope Am. Cancer Soc., Ashtabula, 1988—; co-chair Ashtabula County HIV/AIDS Task Force, 2001—, Tri County HIV/AIDS Task Force, 2001—; chmn. HIV/AIDS Task Force Ashtabula County, 2001—, Tri County HIV/AIDS Task Force, 2001—; bd. dirs. Early Childhood Intervention Project, Ashtabula, 1988—93, We-Can-Week-End, Columbus, Ohio, 1990—94, Ashtabule County Cmty. Housing Devel. Orgn., Inc., 1996—. Recipient Recognition of Excellence award Ashtabula County Med. Ctr., 1990, Vol. of Yr. award Ashtabula chpt. ARC, 1995, Golden Rule award nomination J.C. Penny, 1999. Mem. NASW, Acad. Cert. Social Workers, Assn. for Care Children's Health, Ohio Soc. for Clin. Social Work (v.p. bd. Cleve. chpt. 1995-96, pres. 1996—, state level sec. 1996-97, state bd. dirs. 1996—), Intenrat. Critical Incident Stress Found. Democrat. Methodist. Avocations: collecting miniatures, restoring furniture, bonsai. Home: 3603 Silvius St Ashtabula OH 44004-4140

HORNBEIN, THOMAS FREDERIC, anesthesiologist; b. St. Louis, Nov. 6, 1930; s. Leonard and Rosalie (Bernstein) Hornbein; m. Gene Schwartz (div. 1968); children: Lia, Lynn, Cari, Andrea, Robert; m. Kathryn Mikesell, Dec. 24, 1971; 1 child, Melissa. BA, U. Colo.; MD, Wash. U. Diplomate Am. Bd. Anesthesiology. Intern King County Hosp., Seattle; resident in anesthesiology Wash. U., St. Louis, USPHS postdoctoral residency, instr. anesthesiology div., 1960—61; asst. prof. U. Wash., Seattle, 1963—67, assoc. prof., 1967—70, prof., 1970—. Vice chmn. dept. anesthesiology U. Wash., Seattle, 1972—74, asst. chmn. rsch., 1974—77, chmn., 1979—93, rsch. affiliate Primate Ctr., 1980. Author: Everest the West Ridge, 1966. Mem. bd. trustees Little Sch., Bellevue, Wash., 1982—89. Served to lt. comdr. USN, 1961—63. Recipient George Norlin award, U. Colo., Denver, 1970, Alumni Centennial Symposium award, 1975, Disting. Tchg. award, U. Wash., 1982. Fellow: AAAS; mem.: Inst. of Medicine, Soc. Acad. Anesthesia Chmn., Assn. Univ. Anesthetists (treas. 1969—72, pres. 1974—75), Am. Soc. Anesthesiologists (Rovenstine lectr. 1989), Am. Physiol. Soc. (editor 1967—73), Alpha Omega Alpha, Phi Beta Kappa. Avocation: mountaineering. Office: U Wash Sch Medicine Dept Anesthesiology PO Box 356540 Seattle WA 98195-6540 E-mail: hornbnt@u.washington.edu.

HORNBERGER, DEBORAH LEE, management consultant; b. Harrisburg, Pa., Nov. 4, 1947; d. Grant T. and Jeanette L. Hornberger. BS, Ohio State U., 1969; MBA, Golden Gate U., 1987. Cert. fin. mktg. profl. Am. Bankers Assn. Buyer, trainee Emporium-Capwell, San Francisco, 1969-76; mgr. Levi Strauss & Co., Inc., San Francisco, 1976-82; dir. mktg. Wells Fargo Bank, San Francisco, 1982-89, mktg. mgr. Charles Schwab & Co., Inc., San Francisco, 1989-92; mgm. cons. Hornberger & Assocs., San Francisco, 1992—. Treas., dir. Ohio State coun. Critical Difference Women, Columbus, 1994-99; mem. leadership and devel. com., mem. campaign com. United Way, Bay Area, Calif., 1987-91; trustee San Francisco Maritime Nat. Pak Assn., 1999—; bd. chair Vision Youth, 2002—. Named Outstanding Dir. Jr. C. of C., 1975-77. Mem. Inst. Mgmt. Cons. (cert., pres. 1996-97), Fin. Instns. Mktg. Assn. (treas. 1994-98). Home: 2035 Filbert St Apt 107 San Francisco CA 94123-3542 Office: Hornberger & Assocs 1966 Lombard St San Francisco CA 94123-2807 Fax: 415-346-9993.

HORNBERGER, GEORGE MILTON, environmental science educator; b. Fountain Springs, Pa., June 22, 1942; s. George Vincent and Olive Mae (Delcamp) H.; m. Joan Marie Zackey, Aug. 28, 1965; children: Rachel Joan, George Zackey. BSCE, Drexel U., 1965, MSCE, 1967; PhD, Stanford U., 1970. Asst. prof. U. Va., Charlottesville, 1970-75, assoc. prof., 1975-84, prof., 1984—, disting. prof., 1991—, Ernest H. Ern prof., 1993—; assoc. dean for sci., 2002—. Vis. fellow Australian Nat. U., Canberra, 1977-78; vis. scientist Inst. Hydrology, Wallingford, Eng., 1980, U.S. Geol. Survey, 1990-91; hon. vis. prof. U. Lancaster (Eng.), 1984-85, Stanford U., 1990-91, U. Colo., 1997-98; mem. bd. Radioactive Waste Mgmt. of NAS, 1986-91, chmn. Commn. on Geoscis., Environment and Resources, 1996-2000; chmn. bd. Earth Scis. and Resources of NAS, 2003—, chmn., 2003—; chmn. adv. com. nuclear waste U.S. Nuclear Regulatory Com., 2001—. Author: Numerical Methods in Subsurface Hydrology, 1971, Elements of Physical Hydrology, 1998; assoc. editor Am. Geophys. Union, 1980-84; N.Am. editor John Wiley & Sons, Eng., 1986-92; editor-in-chief Water Resources Rsch., Am. Geophys. Union, 1993-96. Recipient John Wesley Powell award U.S. Geol. Survey, 1995, First Biennial medal for natural systems Australian Simulation Soc., 1995, Bownocker medal Ohio State U., 1999; elected to NAE, 1996; grantee NSF, Army Rsch. Office, EPA, Nat. Park Svc., NATO, Dept. Energy. Fellow Am. Geophys. Union (Robert E. Horton award hydrology sect. 1993, Excellence in Geophys. Edn. award 1999), Assn. for Women in Sci.; mem. NAE, Geol. Soc. Am., Am. Geophys. Union, Sigma Xi. Home: 308 Farm Ln Charlottesville VA 22902-5324 Office: U Va Dept Environ Sci Clark Hall Charlottesville VA 22903-3188 E-mail: hornberger@virginia.edu.

HORNBERGER, LEE, lawyer; b. Elizabethtown, Pa., Oct. 31, 1946; s. Lee and Peggy (Mann) H. AB, U. Mich., 1966, JD cum laude, 1968; LLM in Labor Law, Wayne State U., 1982. Bar: Mich. 1969, Ohio 1982, U.S. Dist. Ct. (no. dist.) Ohio 1971, U.S. Dist. Ct. (so. dist.) Ohio 1982, U.S. Dist. Ct. (we. and ea. dists.) Mich. 1973, U.S. Dist. Ct. (ea. dist.) Ky., U.S. Ct. Mil. Appeals 1970, U.S. Ct. Appeals (6th cir.) 1972, U.S. Supreme Ct. 1998. Atty. Office of Solicitor, U.S. Dept. Labor, Washington, 1971-75; pvt. practice, Cin., 1982—2002, Traverse City, Mich., 2002—. Adj. prof. law U. Cin., 1985-87, Chase Coll., 1992—; presenter Employment Lawyers Assn., Lake Tahoe, 1990, Cin., 1991, Cin. Bar Assn., 1990-93, 95, 97, Ohio State Bar Assn., Cin., 1991, Nat. Employment Lawyers Assn., Cape Cod, 1991, Advanced Ednl. Seminars, Cin., 1991, 2002, Ohio Employment Lawyers Assn., Columbus, 1991, Ohio Edn. Assn., Cin., 1992, Nat. Edn. Network, Cin., 1993, 94, Ky. Employment Lawyers Assn., 1996, U. Ky., 1996, Vail, Colo., 2003, others. Contbr. articles to profl. jours. including Cleve. Law Rev., Capitol U. Law Rev., Mich. Lawyers Weekly and Ohio Trial. Dem. candidate spl. election, 2nd dist. Ohio for U.S. Congress; vol. Mich. Dept of Civil Rights, and Cmty. Svc.. Capt. U.S. Army, 1969-71, Vietnam. Decorated Bronze Star, U.S. Army. Mem. ABA (labor and employment law sect.), Mich. Bar Assn., Ohio State Bar Assn. (cert. labor and employment law specialist), Nat. Employment Lawyers Assn. (chmn. Cin. chpt. 1987-90, mediator Equal Employment Opportunity Commn.), Mich. Dept. Civil Rights; arbitrator Nat. Arbitration Forum. Avocations: camping, sailing, employment law seminars. Office: Ste 407 310 W Front St Traverse City MI 49684-2279 E-mail: leehornberger@leehornberger.com.

HORNBERGER, ROBERT HOWARD, psychologist; b. Trenton, N.J., Jan. 26, 1933; s. Jennings Howard and Leah Margaret (Lewis) H.; m. Anne Deshon Lyman, June 11, 1958; children: Lynn Diane, Todd Lyman. BA, Amherst Coll., 1954; MA, PhD, U. Iowa, 1957. Instr. to assoc. in med. psychology U. Nebr. Coll. Medicine, Omaha, 1958-62; staff psychologist Nebr. Psychiat. Inst., Omaha, 1958-62; chief psychologist Drs. Young, Wigton & Aita, Omaha, 1962-65; dir. Eastern Maine Guidance Ctr., Bangor, 1965-68; assoc. dir. The Counseling Ctr., Bangor, 1968-69; lectr. in psychology U. Maine, Orono, 1966-69; dir. psychology tng. VA Med. Ctr., Gainesville, Fla., 1969-81; asst. to assoc. adj. prof. U. Fla., Gainesville, 1969-2000; staff psychologist VA Med. Ctr., Gainesville, 1981-2000; ret., 2000. Bd. advisors Fla. Mental Health Inst., Tampa, 1987-95; psychologist pvt. practice, Gainesville, 1976 85, 90 98; dir. endowment fund, The Mountain Retreat & Learning Ctrs., Highlands, N.C., 2002—, dir. SoftRent Corp., Clearwater, Fla., 2001—; pres. Gainesville chpt. UNA-USA, 2003—. Contbr. articles to profl. jours. Founder, 1st pres. Sugarfoot Cmty. Improvement Assn., 1972; pres. Mental Health Assn. Alachua County, Gainesville, 1981, Mental Health Assn. Fla., Tallahassee, 1987, Planned Parenthood Nebr., Omaha, 1963; comdr. Gainesville Power Squadron, 1995-96. Mem. Fla. Psychol. Assn. (pres. north ctrl. Fla. chpt. 1996). Democrat. Unitarian Universalist. Avocations: sailing, bridge, bicycling, travel. Home: 4056 NW 23rd Cir Gainesville FL 32605-2683 E-mail: abhornberger@cs.com.

HORNBOSTEL, PAULA RAND, art historian; b. NYC; d. William and Paula Coudert Rand; m. John Patrick Hornbostel, June 13, 1998; children: Summer Rand, Paula Tracy, Frances Isabele. BA, Harvard Coll., Cambridge, Mass., 1993; MA in art and archaeology, NYU, 2000. Eng. tchr. Cambridge Sch. of Eng., Mestre, Italy, 1993—95; asst. to dir. World Monuments Fund, Venice, Italy, 1993—95; art historian Salander-O'Reilly Galleries, NYC, 1997—. Trustee Lachaise Found., Boston, 2001—. Author exhibition catalogues; contbr. articles to Connoisseurs Quarterly. Office: Salander-OReilly Galleries 20 E 79th St New York NY 10021

HORNBY, DAVID BROCK, federal judge; b. Brandon, Manitoba, Can., Apr. 21, 1944; s. William Ralph Hornby and Retha Patricia (Fox) Sword; m. Helaine Cora Mandel, Oct. 9, 1946; children: Kirstin, Zachary. BA, U. Western Ont., 1965; JD, Harvard U., 1969. Bar: Va. 1973, Maine 1974, U.S. Supreme Ct. 1980. Law clk. U.S. Ct. Appeals, New Orleans, 1969-70; assoc. prof. U. Va. Sch. Law, Charlottesville, 1970-74; ptnr. Perkins, Thompson, Hinckley & Keddy, Portland, Maine, 1974-82; U.S. magistrate Dist. Maine, Portland, 1982-88; assoc. justice Maine Supreme Jud. Ct., Portland, 1988-90; judge U.S. Dist. Ct. Maine, 1990—; chief judge, 1996—2003. Contbr. articles to profl. jours.; editor, officer Harvard Law Rev., 1967-69. Fellow Am. Bar Found.; mem. ABA, Am. Law Inst., Maine State Bar Assn., Maine Bar Found. (bd. trustees 1990-94), Cumberland County Bar Assn. Office: US Dist Ct Edward T Gignoux Courthouse 156 Federal St Portland ME 04101-4152

HORNBY, KENNETH PETER, office technology executive; b. Davenport, Iowa, July 22, 1960; married. Advisor Jr. Achievement, St. Paul, 1983. With U.S. Army, 1985-87. Mem. Twin City Aero Historians (v.p. 1995-98), 2d Cavalry Assn. (life, bd. dirs. 2000), U.S. Cavalry Assn., Am. Air Mus. in Britain, League of WWI Aviation Historians, 1st World War Aviation Hist. Soc., Internat. Plastic Modelers Soc., Am. Legion. Avocations: reading, aviation modeling, historical research, travel, collecting books and militaria.

HORNBY, ROBERT RAY, mechanical engineer; b. La Crosse, Wis., Dec. 2, 1958; s. William James and Nancy Kay Hornby; m. Michal Rae Berrey, Aug. 2, 1980; children: Tabitha Kay, Maria Rae, Felicia Anne, Belinda Jo. BS in Mech. Engring., U. of Wis., Platteville, 1981. Registered profl. engr., Wis. Engring. cons. Geoscan Svcs. Co., Tulsa, Okla., 1983-84; sr. project engr. Howard Rotavator Co., Inc., Muscoda, Wis., 1984; mech. design engr. Rayovac, Portage, Wis., 1984-85; designer Gilman Engring. Co., Janesville, Wis., 1985-86, assoc. mech. design engr., 1986-87; mech. design engr. Giddings Lewis, Janesville, 1987-89, sr. mech. design engr., 1989-92, project mgr., 1992-95; sr. engr. NIMCO Corp., Crystal Lake, Ill., 1995-96; asst. project engr. Lamb Assembly & Test, Rockford, Ill., 1996-97, project engr., 1997—. Edn. chmn. Good Shepherd Luth. Ch., Janesville, 1985-88, religious counselor, 1992—; com. chmn. Explorer post 400 Boy Scouts Am., Janesville, 1985-91, scoutmaster troop 516, Janesville, 1985-95, 99—, asst. scoutmaster, 1995-99, also commr. Koshkonong dist., Janesville. Recipient Scoutmaster award of merit Boy Scouts Am., 1990, Dist. Award of Merit, 1992, Silver Beaver award Boy Scouts Am., Janesville, 1999; named Outstanding Leader Exploring Koshkonong Dist. Boy Scouts Am., Janesville, 1991, 93. Mem. ASME, NSPE, Soc. Mfg. Engrs. Achievements include development of math. model to predict lateral movement of oil well drill bit while drilling; patent applied for modular machine that welds plastic caps to gable top cardboard cartons. Home: 2135 Morningside Dr Janesville WI 53546-1121 Office: Lamb Assembly & Test 2140 12th St Rockford IL 61104-7351

HORNBY-ANDERSON, SARA ANN, metallurgical engineer, marketing professional; b. Plymouth, Devon, Eng., Apr. 17, 1952; came to U.S., 1986; d. Foster John and Joanna May (Duncan) Hornby; m. John Victor Anderson, Sept. 2, 1978 (div. May 1987). BSc in Metallurgy with honors, Sheffield (Eng.) City Poly., 1973, PhD in Indsl. Metallurgy, 1980. Chartered engr. Metallurgist Joseph Lucas Rsch., Solihull, England, 1970, William Lee Malleable, Dronfield, 1972; tech. sales specialist Applied Rsch. Labs, Luton, 1973—74; quality assurance metallurgist Firth Brown Tools, Sheffield, 1974—75, rsch. metallurgist high speed steel, 1975; lectr. Sheffield City Poly., 1975—78; grad. metallurgist, strip devel. metallurgist British Steel Corp., Rotherham, 1978—80; program mgr. Can. Liquid Air, Montreal, Canada, 1980—85; group mktg. mgr. Liquid Air Corp., Countryside, Ill., 1986—90, tech. mgr. Walnut Creek, Calif., 1990—93; bus. devel. mgr.-metals and materials Can. Liquid Air,

Toronto, 1993—97, N.Am. steel tech. mgr., 1995—97; dir. steelmaking tech. Goodfellow Techs. Inc., Mississauga, Canada, 1997, dir. ops., 1997—99; mgr. bus. devel. Stantec Global Techs. Ltd. (formerly Goodfellow Techs. Inc.), 1999—2003; product mgr. steel making/ melting Midrex Techs., Inc., Charlotte, NC, 1999—2003; pres. Global Strategic Solutions, Inc., Charlotte, NC, 2003—. Bd. dirs., chmn. R & D com., mem. publs. com., chmn. promotions and mktg. com. Investment Casting Inst., Dallas; presenter to confs. in field. Contbr. articles to profl. jours.; patentee in field of metallurgy. Mem. AIME, Inst. Metals (young metallurgists com. 1974-80), Sheffield Metall. Soc. Inst. Metals (sec. 1978-80), Am. Foundry Soc., Iron and Steel Soc. (steering com. 1987-91, chmn. topics com. 1988-89, sec. 1992, vice chair 1993, chmn. process tech. divsn. 1994, bd. dirs., strategic planning com. 1995-98, internat. affairs com. 1998—, bd. dirs. ad hoc com. on internat. affairs 1998-99, univ. rels. com.). Avocations: scuba diving, horseback riding, swimming, siamese cats, gardening. E-mail: felady@hotmail.com.

HORNE, AARON, academic administrator; b. Chipley, Fla., Dec. 3, 1941; s. Albert and Laura Eva Horne; m. Myrtle A. Horne, June 1972; children: Ericka Michelle, Aaron Jr. BS, Tenn. State U., 1968; MusM, Roosevelt U., 1972; MFA, D of Musical Arts, U. Iowa, 1976. Asst. prof. Music Fla. A&M U., Tallahassee, 1968—72; lectr. African Am. Studies/Music U. Iowa, Iowa City, 1972—76; prof. Music NE Ill. U., Chgo., 1977—89; asst. vice chancellor Acad. Affairs Bd. Govs. U., Springfield, Ill., 1990—95; interim chair African Am. Studies We. Ill. U., Macomb, 1995—96; acting dir. Ctr. for Inner City Studies, Chgo., 1998—2001; dean Coll. Arts and Scis. Winston-Salem State U., NC, 2001—. Assoc. prof. Music, Artist-in-Residence Tex. So. U., Houston, 1976; lectr. African Am. Studies Northwestern U., Evanston, Ill., 1984—89. Author: Brass Music of Black Composers, 1996, Keyboard Music of Black Composers, 1992, String Music of Black Composers, 1991, Woodwind Music of Black Composers, 1990. With U.S. Army, 1958—61. Recipient Profl. Achievement award, Alpha Phi Alpha, 2002, Outstanding Svc. award, Chess Club of North Shore, 1995. Mem.: Coun. Colls. of Arts and Scis. (program com.), Am. Assn. Higher Edn., Internat. Assn. Jazz Educators (selection com. 1985—86, Outstanding Svc. to Jazz Edn. award 1981). Avocations: reading, travel, golf, chess. Home: 122 Scottsdale Dr Advance NC 27006 Office: Winston-Salem State Univ Winston Salem NC 27110*

HORNE, ALEXANDER DOUGLAS, journalist; b. Warsaw, Nov. 9, 1932; came to U.S., 1940; s. Marcel Allen and Lydia (Bryl) H.; m. Ann Elizabeth Hurd, Aug. 27, 1960; children: Julia A. Patchan, Owen, Elizabeth, Jennifer, Gary, Ellen, Brian. BA, Williams Coll., 1954. Reporter, editor The Berkshire Eagle, Pittsfield, Mass., 1955-56; asst. city editor The Washington Post, 1958-60, asst. magazine editor, 1960-62, asst. world editor, 1962-65, day nat. editor, 1965-69, diplomatic reporter, 1969-70, dep. nat. editor, 1970-71, editor of Outlook, 1971-79, 80-82, asst. foreign editor, 1982-97. Dir., sec. South-North News Svc., Hanover, N.H., 1987-95. Columnist The Magazine Rack, 1961-66; editor: The Wounded Generation: America After Vietnam, 1981. With U.S. Army, 1956—58. E-mail: adhorne@earthlink.net.

HORNE, DOUGLAS A. diversified companies executive; Owner Rep. Newpapers, Knoxville, Tenn., Horne Radio, Knoxville, BoWevil Express Trucking, Horne Properties, Knoxville. Office: Horne Properties Inc Suite 205 412 Executive Tower Dr Knoxville TN 37923

HORNE, GRANT NELSON, public relations consultant; b. Salt Lake City, Jan. 14, 1931; s. Joseph Feramorz and Ida Verene (Nelson) H.; m. Georgia Henry, July 6, 1957 (div. Feb. 1977); 1 child, Mary Corneille Horne Geeslin. BA magna cum laude, Yale U., 1952; MA, U. Utah, 1954. Instr. Gunnery Sch., Washington, Conn., 1955-57, Great Books Found., N.Y.C., 1958-61; dir. pub. relations Edison Electric Inst., N.Y.C., 1961-72; sr. v.p. Underwood Jordan Assocs., N.Y.C., 1972-79; retired v.p. corp. comms. Pacific Gas and Electric Co., San Francisco, 1980-96. Past chmn. Pub. Rels. Seminar. Bd. dirs. Patrons the Vatican Mus.; bd. govs. San Francisco Symphony, Knights of Malta. Mem. Arthur W. Page Soc. (Hall of Fame 1998), Yale Club (N.Y.C.), Villa Taverna Club (San Francisco). Roman Catholic. Avocations: chamber music, classical piano. Office: Pacific Gas & Electric Co 77 Beale St San Francisco CA 94105-1814 E-mail: granthorne@aol.com.

HORNE, JEREMY, consultant, writer, research executive; b. Palo Alto, Calif., Dec. 5, 1944; s. Frank Wescott and Mildred Cooley (Wright) H.; m. Deborah Elizabeth Hepburn, June, 1976 (div. Oct., 1979). AB, Johns Hopkins U., 1967; MS, So. Conn. State U., 1969; PhD, U. Fla., 1988. Instr. La. State U., Baton Rouge, 1984-85; adj. instr. Pima C.C., Tucson, 1985-87; tchr. correctional edn. program Ariz. State Prison, Douglas, 1988-89; curriculum coord. summer youth program Cochise Pvt. Industry Coun., Bisbee, Ariz., 1989; adj. faculty Cochise Coll., Douglas and Sierra Vista, Ariz., 1988-91; tech. writer, editor, task leader Sci. Applications Internat. Corp., Sierra Vista, 1990-93; v.p. Griffin Group Internat., Phoenix, 1992-95, pres., 1995—. Adj. prof. Cen. Ariz. Coll., Coolidge, Ariz.; writer Info. Gate Keepers, Boston, 1992-95; co-dir. Profl. Writers Assn., Tucson, 1995-96; cons., writer, rschr., 1993—; ind. cons. writer for Ariz. and N.C. pub. and pvt. orgns. Author: (textbook) Logic: The Theory of Order, 1989; co-author: (mil. handbook) Design Handbook for Fiber Optic Communications Systems, 1993. Active Nat. Sch. Bds. Assn., 1992-94. Mem. Am. Assn. Adv. of Sci., Bioelectromagnetics Soc. Achievements include rsch. and publs. on natural ordering of logical operators, observing the behavior of those operators and applying that knowlege to discovering innate order in the universe; discovered and publ. that discrete binary space is recursive; devel. and presented at AAAS process ontology of scientific methods; created IEEE-12207-style documentation sys. life cycle, used by RhioCorps at White Sands Missile Range. Home: 205 S Higley Rd Lot 185 Mesa AZ 85206-1323

HORNE, JOHN R. farm equipment company executive; b. Gary, Ind., 1938; Grad., Purdue U., 1960, Bradley U., 1964. Group v.p., gen. mgr. Navistar Internat. Transp. Corp.; pres., COO, now CEO Navistar Internat. Corp., 1995—, also bd. dirs., 1995—; pres., CEO Navistar Internat. Corp. and Internat. Truck & Engine Corp., 1995—; also chmn. bd. dirs. Navistar Internat. Corp. Mem.Soc. Automotive Engrs. (chmn. fin. com.). Office: Internat Truck & Engine Corp 455 N Cityfront Plaza Dr Chicago IL 60611-5503

HORNE, MARILYN, mezzo-soprano; b. Bradford, Pa., Jan. 16, 1934; d. Bentz and Berneice Horne; m. Henry Lewis (div.); 1 child. Ed., U. So. Calif.; MusD (hon.), Rutgers U., 1970, Jersey City State Coll., 1973, Brown U., 1984, Juillard Sch. Music, 1994; DLitt (hon.), St. Peter's Coll.; LHD (hon.), Kean Coll., 1977. Singer: (Operas) (debut) as Hata in The Bartered Bride, 1954, (La Scala debut) Oepidus Rex, 1969, (Met. Opera debut) as Adalgisa in Norma, 1970, (other roles) Rosina in Barber of Seville, Cleonte in The Siege of Corinth, Isabella in L'Italiana in Algieri, Carmen at Met. Opera, 1972—73, Laura in Harvest, Chgo. Lyric Opera, Marie in Wozzeck, San Francisco Opera, (appeared in) Phigenie en Tauride, Semiramide, Samson et Dalila at Met. Opera, 1987, The Ghost of Versailles, 1991, Pelléas et Mélisande, 1995, Venice Festival by invitation of Igor Stravinsky, Am. Opera Soc., N.Y.C., for several seasons, Vancouver Opera, Philharm. Hall, N.Y.C., Paris, Dallas, Houston, Covent Garden, London, roles at La Scala, Italy, Rossini Opera Festival, Pesaro, Italy, Met. Opera, 1987, (recital debuts) Madrid, Dresden, East Berlin, 1987; performer: (at inauguration) of U.S. President Clinton, 1993, ann. recital at Carnegie Hall, European tour with husband for Dept. State, 1963; rec. artist London, Columbia, Deutsche Grammaphon and RCA records, recs. include soundtrack Carmen Jones. Founder Marilyn Horne Found. Named Musician of Yr. Musical Am., 1995; named to Harold C. Schonberg's N.Y. Times' list of 9 All-Time, All-Star Singers in Met. Opera's 100 Years, 1984; recipient Grammy awards, 1964, 1981, 1983, 1994, Handel medallion, 1980, Premio d'Oro, Italian Govt., 1982, Commendatore al merito della Repubblica Italiana, 1983, Gold Merit medal Nat. Soc. Arts and Letters, 1987, Fidelio Gold medal, 1988, George Peabody award, 1989, Silver medal Covent Garden Royal Opera House, 1989, Disting. Dau. of Pa. Silver medal San Francisco Opera, 1990, Nat. Arts medal, 1992. Achievements include Achievements includes having the leading exponent florid vocal style, music of Rossini, Handel, Vivaldi. Office: care Columbia Artists Mgmt Inc Wilford Divsn 165 W 57th St New York NY 10019-2201 also: care Met Opera Assoc Attention: Artistic Dept Lincoln Ctr New York NY 10023 also: BMG Classics/RCA 1540 Broadway New York NY 10036-4039

HORNE, MICHAEL STEWART, lawyer; b. Mpls., May 10, 1938; s. Owen Edward and Adeline (DiGeorgio) H.; m. Martha Brean, Sept. 11, 1965; children: Jennifer, Katherine, Sarah, Owen. BA, U. Minn., 1959; LLB, Harvard U., 1962. Bar: D.C. 1963, U.S. Ct. Appeals (D.C. cir.) 1964, U.S. Supreme Ct. 1968, U.S. Ct. Appeals (6th cir.) 1966, U.S. Ct. Appeals (9th cir.) 1978, U.S. Ct. Appeals (4th cir.) 1979, U.S. Ct. Appeals (5th cir.) 1979, U.S. Ct. Appeals (2d cir.) 1980, U.S. Ct. Appeals (11th cir.) 1983, U.S. Ct. Appeals (8th cir.) 1984, U.S. Ct. Appeals (10th cir.) 1997. Assoc. Covington & Burling, Washington, 1964-71, ptnr., 1971—. Co-author (with T.S. Williamson and A. Herman): The Contingent Workforce, Business and Legal Strategies, 2000. Mem. ABA, D.C. Bar Assn., FCC Bar Assn., Am. Judicature Soc. Democrat. Home: 9008 Levelle Dr Bethesda MD 20815-5608 Office: Covington & Burling 1201 Pennsylvania Ave NW PO Box 7566 Washington DC 20044-7566 E-mail: hornems@earthlink.net., mhorne@cov.com.

HORNE, RALPH ALBERT, environmental chemist; b. Haverhill, Mass., Mar. 10, 1929; s. Ralph Lester and Flora Thelma (Kelly) H. SB, MIT; MS, U. Vt., 1952; MA, Boston U., 1953; PhD, Columbia U., N.Y.C., 1955; JD, Suffolk U. Law Sch., Boston, 1979. Scientific staff Arthur D. Little, Inc., Cambridge, Mass., 1960-69, 72-78; assoc. scientist Woods Hole (Mass.) Oceanographic Instn., 1970-71; prin. scientist JBF Scientific Corp., Burlington, Mass., 1971-72; sr. scientist GCA Tech. Div., Burlington, Mass., 1978-80, Energy & Environ. Engring., Inc., Cambridge, Mass., 1980-85. Cons. U.S. Environ. Protection Agy., U.S. Army Corps. Engrs. Author: Marine Chemistry, 1969, The Chemistry of Our Environment, 1978, 2 novels; editor: Water and Aqueous Solutions, 1971; contbr. more than 100 articles to scholarly jours.; numerous poems, short stories, book reviews. Mem. Bar of Fed. Dist. Ct. for Mass. Achievements include elucidation of the mechanism of electron-exchange reactions in aqueous solutions, and of the structure of liquid water and aqueous solutions and the effect of temperature pressure and solutes on these systems; visionary painter. Address: 9 Wellington St Boston MA 02118-3005

HORNE, WILLIAM MCHENRY, management educator; b. Shreveport, La., Mar. 17, 1921; s. William McHenry and Nora (Kalmbach) H.; m. Joan Spear, Sept. 2, 1950 (div. Oct. 1974); children: Lynellyn D., William McHenry III; m. Alice Hobart, Dec. 28, 1980. BA, DePauw U., 1942; JD, Harvard U., 1949. Bar: Mass. 1949, Ind. 1949, D.C. 1955, Md. 1964. Atty., advisor U.S. Tax Ct., Washington, 1949-50; staff atty. joint com. on taxation U.S. Congress, Washington, 1953-55; assoc. Warner, Stackpole, Stetson & Bradlee, Boston, 1955-57; dir. taxes Olin Mathieson Chem. Corp. (now Olin Corp.), N.Y.C., 1957-64; v.p. Comml. Credit Co., Balt., 1964-70; ptnr. Reed, Smith, Shaw & McClay, Pitts., Washington and Harrisburg (Pa.), 1970-73; sr. v.p., gen. tax counsel Citicorp and Citibank N.A., N.Y.C., 1973-80; lectr. dept. mgmt. and policy Coll. Bus. Adminstrn. U. Ariz., Tucson, 1983-89; vis. prof. DePauw U., 1989-91. Mem. adv. com. to commr. IRS, 1969-70; past mem. tax and acctg. com. N.Y. Clearing House; past chmn. taxation com. Fin. Execs. Inst.; trustee Fin. Execs. Rsch. Found., 1975-79; fin. cons., 1980-91; bd. dirs. Ariz. Coun. Ct. Apptd. Spl. Advocates, pres., 1997-99; speaker in field. Author: Proceedings of New York University Annual Institute on Federal Income Taxation: Offers in Compromise, 1958; also chpts. to books and articles to profl. jours. Lt. USAAC, 1942-46, PTO; maj. JAGC, USAF, 1950-52. Recipient Disting. Alumni award DePauw U., Greencastle, Ind., 1976; Alfred P. Sloan fellow MIT, Cambridge, 1942. Mem. Tax Execs. Inst. (hon., pres., chmn. bd. dirs. 1968-69), Sigma Chi, Phi Beta Kappa. Avocations: hiking, water activities, bicycling, tennis, travelling. Home: 2465 W Tom Watson Dr Tucson AZ 85742-8531 E-mail: wmhorne@comcast.net.

HORN EPSTEIN, PHYLLIS LYNN, lawyer; b. Phila., Sept. 10, 1955; d. Harold and Bernice H. BA, Temple U., 1977, JD, 1980, LLM, 1984. Bar: Pa. 1980, U.S. Dist. Ct. (ea. dist.) Pa., U.S. Ct. Appeals (3rd cir.). Assoc. Blumstein, Block & Vanore, Phila., 1980-81, Epstein, Beller & Shapiro, Phila., 1982-85, ptnr., 1985-86, Epstein, Shapiro & Epstein, Phila., 1986—. Instr. LaSalle Coll., Phila., 1980-82; vice-chmn. Fee Dispute Com., Phila. 1985, chmn., 1986. Co-author: Procedure and Administration: Bender's Federal Tax Service, 1989. Bd. dirs. Phila. chpt. Friends of Bezalel, 1987—. Mem. ABA (tax sect., group editor newsletter 1982-85, editor Tax Commentary newsletter 1985-88, court procedure com. 1984—), Pa. Bar Assn., Phila. Bar Assn., Pa. Trial Lawyers Assn., Hadassah (life). Office: Epstein Shapiro & Epstein 1515 Market St 15th Fl Three Penn Ctr Philadelphia PA 19102 E-mail: jeepsu@aol.com.

HORNER, ALTHEA JANE, psychologist; b. Hartford, Conn., Jan. 13, 1926; d. Louis and Celia (Newmark) Greenwald; children: Martha Horner Hartley, Anne Horner Benck, David, Kenneth. BS in Psychology, U. Chgo., 1952; PhD in Clin. Psychology, U. So. Calif., 1965. Lic. psychologist, N.Y., Calif. Tchr. Pasadena (Calif.) City Coll., 1965-67; from asst. to assoc. prof. Los Angeles Coll. Optometry, 1967-70; supr. Psychology interns Pasadena Child Guidance Clinic, 1969-70; pvt. practice specializing in psychoanalysis and psychoanalytic psychotherapy. N.Y.C., 1970-83; supervising psychologist dept. psychiatry Beth Israel Med. Ctr., N.Y.C., 1972-83, coordinator group therapy tng., 1976-82, clinician in charge Brief Adaptation-Oriented Psychotherapy Research Group, 1982-83; assoc. clin. prof. Mt. Sinai Sch. Medicine, N.Y.C., 1977-91, adj. assoc. prof., 1991—; mem. faculty Nat. Psychol. Assn. for Psychoanalysis, N.Y.C., 1982-83; sr. mem. faculty Wright Inst. Los Angeles Postgrad. Inst., 1983-85; pvt. practice L.A., 1983—; clin. prof. dept. Psychology UCLA, 1985-95. Author: (with others) Treating the Neurotic Patient in Brief Psychotherapy, 1985, Object Relations and the Developing Ego in Therapy, 1979, rev. edit., 1984, Little Big Girl, 1982, Being and Loving, 1978, 3d edit. 1990, Psychology for Living (with G. Forehand), 4th edit., 1977, The Wish for Power and the Fear of Having It, 1989, The Primacy of Structure, 1990, Psychoanalytic Object Relations Therapy, 1991, Working With the Core Relationship Problem in Psychotherapy, 1998, Chrysalis, 1999, Get Over It! Untie Your Relationship Knots and Move On, 2000; mem. editorial bd. Jour. of Humanistic Psychology, 1986—, Jour. of the Am. Acad. of Psychoanalysis; contbr. articles to profl. jours. Mem. APA, Am. Acad. Psychoanalysis (sci. assoc.), So. Calif. Psychoanalytic Soc. and Inst. (hon.). Office: PMB 256 3579 E Foothill Blvd Pasadena CA 91107-3119

HORNER, BOB, broadcast executive; Pres. NBC News, Charlotte. Office: care NBC News 925 Woodridge Center Dr Charlotte NC 28217-1986

HORNER, CARL MATTHEW, chemistry educator; b. Cicero, N.Y., June 4, 1930; s. Oscar Wendell and Gladys Cecilia (Horner) H. BS, LeMoyne Coll., 1952; MS, Syracuse U., 1958, PhD, 1965. Asst. prof. analytical chemistry SUNY-Oneonta, 1958-61, assoc. prof., 1961-64, prof., 1964—97, prof. emeritus, 1998—. Coord. ann. instrumental chemistry workshops, 1986-95. NSF CAUSE grantee, 1979-82; NSF CSIP grantee, 1986-88; Walter B. Ford Found. grantee, 1980, 83. Mem. AAAS, Am. Chem. Soc., N.Y. Acad. Scis. Achievements include research in infrared spectroscopy and laboratory robotics. Avocations: scuba diving, photography. Home: 24 Suncrest Ter Oneonta NY 13820-4632 E-mail: chorner@capital.net.

HORNER, CLIFFORD R. lawyer; b. June 21, 1963; BS in Bus., Calif. Poly., 1986; JD, U. Calif., San Francisco, 1991. Bar: Calif., U.S. Dist. Ct. (no. dist.) Calif., U.S. Ct. Appeals (9th cir.) 1991. Atty. Zankel & McGrane, San Francisco, 1991-95, Morgan, Miller & Blair, Walnut Creek, Calif., 1995—. Chair MM&B Comml. Real Estate Practice Group, 1999—. Author: Approaching An Action Against A Real Estate Broker, 2001; contbg. author: California Eviction Defense Manual, 1998; cons. California Landlord-Tenant Practice, 1998—; guest editor: Contra Costa Lawyer, 1998. Co-chair Contra Costa (Calif.) Legis. Coun., 1998—. Mem. Hastings Alumni Assn. (Contra Costa chpt. pres. 1998—, bd. govs. 2001—), Walnut Creek C. of C. (dir. 1998—, chair civic affairs com. 1997-99), Contra Costa County Bar Assn. (bd. dirs. real estate sect. 1997—). Office: Morgan Miller & Blair 1676 N California Blvd Ste 200 Walnut Creek CA 94596-4157 E-mail: chorner@mmblaw.com.

HORNER, CONSTANCE JOAN, federal agency administrator; b. Summit, NJ, Feb. 24, 1942; d. David Earl and Cecelia (Murphy) McNeely; m. Charles Edward Horner, May 7, 1965; children: David Bayer, Jonathan Purcell. BA in English Lit., U. Pa., 1964; MA in English Lit., U. Chgo., 1967. Dep. asst. dir. policy planning and evaluation ACTION Agy., Washington, 1981-82, acting assoc. dir. domestic & anti-poverty ops., 1982-83, dep. assoc. dir. for VISTA & service-learning, 1982-83; assoc. dir. for econs. & govt. Office of Mgmt. and Budget, Washington, 1983-85; dir. Office of Pers. Mgmt., Washington, 1985-89; deputy sec. HHS, 1989-91; asst. to pres. and dir. presdl. pers. The White House, Washington, 1991-93; mem. U.S. Commn. on Civil Rights, Washington, 1993-98. Commr. The White House Fellows Commn., Washington, 1985-89; guest scholar The Brookings Inst., Washington, 1993—; vis. faculty Princeton (NJ) U., 1994; fellow, lectr. Johns Hopkins U., 1994-95; adv. com. on women in svcs. Dept. of Def.; bd. dirs. Pfizer, Inc., Prudential Fin., Inc., Ingersoll-Rand Co. Ltd. Bd. dirs. Annie E. Casey Found., Baltimore, Md., 1994—. Fellow: Nat. Acad. Pub. Adminstrn.; mem.: Cosmos Club. Republican. Home: 3171 Porter St NW Washington DC 20008-3210 Office: Brookings Inst 1775 Massachusetts Ave NW Washington DC 20036-2103

HORNER, ELAINE EVELYN, secondary education educator; b. Portales, N.Mex., Feb. 26, 1941; d. Carlton James and Clara C. (Roberson) Carmichael; m. Bill G. Horner, Feb. 2, 1959; children: Billy G. Jr., Frances E. Moreau, Aaron J. BA, Ea. N.Mex. U., 1973, MEd, 1978. Tchr. Artesia (N.Mex.) Jr. High Sch., 1973-98, ret., 1998. Recipient Honor of Excellence award Navajo Refining, 1993. Mem. NEA, Nat. Coun. Tchrs. Math., N.Mex. Coun. Tchrs. Math., Artesia Edn. Assn. (v.p. 1987-88), Delta Kappa Gamma (treas. 1988—). Democrat. Baptist. Avocations: reading, golf. Home: 2406 N Haldeman Rd Artesia NM 88210-9435

HORNER, GEORGE MARLIN, retired obstetrician-gynecologist; b. Ainsworth, Nebr., 1921; s. Amos Roy and Abbie (Lambley) H.; m. Peggy Lee Hallsted, Sept. 25, 1944; children: Michael J., Susan L., Douglas A., Nancy A. AB, U. Nebr., 1944, MD, 1946. Diplomate Am. Bd. Ob-Gyn, 1957. Intern Charles T. Miller Hosp., St. Paul, 1946-47; capt. Army Med. Corps, 1947-49; resident in ob.-gyn. U. Nebr. Hosp., 1951-54; assoc. clin. prof. ob.-gyn. U. Colo. Med. Sch., 1954-85; ret., 1985. Mem. Ctrl. Assn. Ob.-Gyn., AMA, Am. Coll. Ob.-Gyn. (sec. dist. VIII 1964-67). Republican.

HORNER, HARRY CHARLES, JR., sales executive, theatrical and film consultant; b. Pitts., Oct. 30, 1937; s. Harry Charles and Sara Marie (Hysong) H.; m. Patricia Ann Hagarty, June 15, 1965 (div. 1981); m. Sharon Kae Wyatt, Dec. 30, 1983; children: Jeffrey Brian, Jennifer Leigh, Mark Gregory. BFA, U. Cin., 1963; postgrad., Xavier U., Cin., 1963-64. Mgr. Retail Credit Co., Atlanta, 1964-68; ops. mgr. Firestone Tire and Rubber Co., L.A., 1968-80; exec. v.p. Romney/Ford Enterprises Inc., Scottsdale, Ariz., 1980-85; sales mgr. Environ. Care Inc., Calabasas, Calif., 1985-93; ops. v.p. Albuquerque (N.Mex.) Grounds Maintenance, Inc., 1993—2002; gen. mgr. and ptnr. Landwork S.W., Phoenix, 2002—. Pres., chief exec. officer The Cons. Group Cos. Ltd., Palm Desert, Calif., 1984—; pres. E. Valley Theatre Co., Chandler, Ariz., 1984-86; ge. mgr., ptnr. Landworks SW. Cons. Ariz. Commn. on Arts, Phoenix, 1983-84. Democrat. Mem. Lds Ch. Avocations: flying, model railroads. Office: Landworks SW 4020 E Washington St Phoenix AZ 85034 also: PO Box 60308 Phoenix AZ 85082 E-mail: hhorner@LandworksWest.com.

HORNER, JAMES, composer; b. 1953; Works include: composer (film scores) Battle Beyond the Stars, 1980, Humanoids from the Deep, 1980, Deadly Blessing, 1981, The Hand, 1981, The Pursuit of D.B. Cooper, 1981, Wolfen, 1981, Star Trek II: The Wrath of Khan, 1982, 48 Hours, 1982, Brainstorm, 1983, Gorky Park, 1983, Something Wicked This Way Comes, 1983, Space Raiders, 1983, Testament, 1983, Uncommon Valor, 1983, The Stone Boy, 1984, (with Chris Young) Barbarian Queen, 1985, Cocoon, 1985, Heaven Help Us, 1985, The Journey of Natty Gann, 1985, Volunteers, 1985, Wizard of the Lost Kingdom, 1985, In Her Own Time, 1985, An American Tail, 1986 (Grammy award nominee for best album of original instrumental score, 1987), The Name of the Rose, 1986, Off Beat, 1986, Where the River Runs Black, 1986, *batteries not included, 1987, P.K. & the Kid, 1987, Project X, 1987, Cocoon: The Return, 1988, Red Heat, 1988, Vibes, 1988, Willow, 1988, The Land Before Time, 1988, Dad, 1989, Field of Dreams, 1989 (Acad. award nominee for best original score, 1989), Glory, 1989 (Grammy award for best album of original instrumental score, 1990), Honey, I Shrunk the Kids, 1989, In Country, 1989, I Love You to Death, 1990, Another 48 Hours, 1990, (with Ernest Troost) Andy Colby's Incredibly Awesome Adventure, 1990, Class Action, 1991, My Heroes Have Always Been Cowboys, 1991, Once Around, 1991, The Rocketeer, 1991, An American Tail: Fievel Goes West, 1991, Patriot Games, 1992, Sneakers, 1992, Thunderheart, 1992, Unlawful Entry, 1992, House of Cards, 1993, Jack the Bear, 1993, Swing Kids, 1993, A Far Off Place, 1993, Once Upon a Forest, 1993, Searching for Bobby Fischer, 1993, The Man Without a Face, 1993, Bopha!, 1993, We're Back!: A Dinosaur's Story, 1993, The Pelican Brief, 1993, The Pagemaster, 1994, Clear and Present Danger, 1994, Legends of the Fall, 1994, Apollo 13, 1995 (Acad. award nominee for best original dramatic score, 1996), Braveheart, 1995 (Acad. award nominee for best original dramatic score, 1996), Casper, 1995, The Devil's Own, 1997, Titanic, 1998 (Oscar and Grammy, 1998), Mighty Joe Young, 1998, The Mask of Zorro, 1998, Deep Impact, 1998, (film songs) (from An American Tail) Somewhere Out There, 1986 (Acad. award nominee for best original song, 1986, Grammy awards for song of yr. and best song written for motion picture, 1987), (from The Land Before Time) If We Hold On Together, 1988, (from An American Tail: Fievel Goest West) Way Out West, 1991, Dreams to Dream, 1991, The Girl I Left Behind, 1991, (film shorts scores) Tummy Trouble, 1989, (TV movie scores) Angel Dusted, 1981, A Few Days in Weasel Creek, 1981, Rascals and Robbers-The Secret Adventures of Tom Sawyer and Huck Finn, 1982, A Piano for Mrs. Cimino, 1982, Between Friends, 1983, Surviving, 1985, Extreme Close-Up, 1990, music adaptor, composer: (film score) The Lady in Red, 1979, music condr., composer The Dresser, 1983, music designer, composer Krull, 1983, music dir., composer Star Trek III: The Search for Spock, 1984, music prodr., composer Commando, 1985, music condr., arranger, composer Aliens, 1986 (Acad. award nominee for best original score, 1986, Grammy award nominee for best instrumental composition, 1986). Office: Gorfaine Schwartz Agy 13245 Riverside Dr Ste 450 Sherman Oaks CA 91423-2172

HORNER, JENNIE LINN, retired educational administrator, nurse; b. Memphis, Tex., Feb. 27, 1932; d. Lester C. and Cecil T. (Knight) Linn; m. Billy A. Gooch, June 4, 1951 (dec.); children: Brenda Michael (dec.), Patricia Lynn Magneson, Robert Allen; m. 2d Donald M. Horner, July 26, 1975. RN, U. Tex., 1955; BS, No. Ariz. U., 1977, MA, 1978, EdD, 1984. Cert. tchr., registered nurse, Ariz., Tex. Indsl. nurse Lipton Tea Co., Galveston, Tex., 1955-56; head nurse U. Tex. Med. Br., Galveston, 1956-58; sch. nurse Wash. Sch. Dist., Phoenix, 1970-77, tchr. middle sch., 1977-80; asst. prin. Murphy Sch. Dist., Phoenix, 1980-82; assoc. prin. middle sch. Madison Sch., Phoenix, 1982-84; lang. arts coordinator Madison Sch. Dist., Phoenix; prin. Dysart Unified Sch. Dist., El Mirage, Ariz., 1984-87, adminstr. for edn1. svcs., 1987-91, ret., 1991. Med. cons. Medahab, Phoenix. Mem. Assn. Supervision and Curriculum Devel., Sch. Nurses Orgn. Ariz. (past pres.), Am. Vocat. Assn., Am. Sch. Health Assn., Nat. Assn. Sch. Nurses, Nat. Assn. Elem. Sch. Prins., Nat. Sch. Health Assn., Ariz. Sch. Health Assn. (bd. dirs.), Ariz. Adminstrs. Assn., Award West, Phi Delta Kappa. Democrat. Home: 186 Rainbow Dr PMB 8648 Livingston TX 77399-1086

HORNER, JOHN ROBERT, paleontologist, researcher; b. Shelby, Mont., June 15, 1946; s. John Henry and Miriam Whitted (Stith) H.; m. Virginia Lee Seacotte, Mar. 30, 1972 (div. 1982); 1 child, Jason James; m. Joann Katherine Raffelson, Oct. 3, 1986 (div. 1994); m. Celeste Claire Roach, Jan. 21, 1995. DSc (hon.), U. Mont., 1986. Rsch. asst. dept. geology Princeton (N.J.) U., 1975-82; curator paleontology Mus. of the Rockies, Mont. State U., Bozeman, 1982—; Regents prof. paleontology Mont. State U., 2001—. Rsch. scientist Am. Mus. Nat. History, N.Y.C., 1980-82. Co-author: Maia: A Dinosaur Grows up, 1985, Digging Dinosaurs, 1988 (N.Y. Acad. Sci. award 1989), Digging Up Tyrannosaurus Rex, 1993, The Complete T-Rex, 1993, Dinosaur Lives, 1997, Dinosaurs Under the Big Sky, 2001; contbr. articles to profl. jours. With USMC, 1966-68; Vietnam. MacArthur fellow, 1986. Achievements include discovery of a new genus of duckbilled dinosaur, Maiasaura; accomplishments include: the theory of endothermic metabolism in dinosaur development, of parental nurture of new-born hatchlings, that Tyrannosaurus rex was a scavenger; excavator of the Egg Mountain cache of dinosaur nests. Home: 310 Hoffman Dr Bozeman MT 59715-5724 Office: Mont State U Mus Of The Rockies Bozeman MT 59717-0001

HORNER, MATINA SOURETIS, retired college president, corporate executive; b. Boston, July 28, 1939; d. Demetre John and Christine (Antonopoulos) Souretis; m. Joseph L. Horner, June 25, 1961; children: Tia Andrea, John, Christopher. AB cum laude, Bryn Mawr Coll., 1961; MS, U. Mich., 1963, PhD,

1968; LLD (hon.), Dickinson Coll., 1973; LLD, Mt. Holyoke Coll., 1973; LLD (hon.), U. Pa., 1975, Smith Coll., 1979, Wheaton Coll., 1979, U. Mich., 1989; LHD (hon.), U. Mass., 1973, Tufts U., 1976, U. Hartford, 1980, U. New Eng., 1987, Bentley Coll., 1989, New Eng. Coll., 1989, Pine Manor Coll., 1989, Am. Coll. Greece, 1990; DLitt (hon.), Claremont U. Ctr. and Grad Sch., 1988, Hellenic Coll., 1990; LHD (hon.), Colby Sawyer Coll., 1991. Teaching fellow U. Mich., Ann Arbor, 1962-66, lectr. motivation personality, 1968-69; lectr. social relations Harvard U., Cambridge, Mass., 1969-70, asst. prof. clin. psychology, 1970-72, assoc. prof. psychology, 1972-89, cons. univ. health svcs., 1971-89; pres. Radcliffe Coll., Cambridge, 1972-89, pres. emerita, 1989—; exec. v.p. TIAA-CREF, NYC, 1989—2003; ret., 2003. Bd. dirs. Neiman Marcus Group, Boston Edison Co.-NSTAR. Co-author: The Challenge of Change, 1983; contbr. psychol. articles on motivation to profl. jours. and chpts. to books. Mem. adv. coun. NSF, 1977-87, chair, 1980-86; bd. trustees Twentieth Century Fund, The Century Found., 1973—, Am. Coll. of Greece, 1983-90, Mass. Eye and Ear Infirmary, 1986-90, Com. for Econ. Devel., 1988—, vice-chmn., 1992-98; bd. trustees Mass. Gen. Hosp., Inst. Health Professions, 1988—, vice chmn., 1994, chair, 1995; bd. dirs. Coun. for Fin. Aid to Edn., 1985-89, Beth Israel Hosp., 1989-95; bd. dirs. Revson Found., 1986-92, chmn., 1992-97; bd. dirs. Women's Rsch. and Edn. Inst., 1979—, chair rsch. com., 1982—; mem. Coun. on Fgn. Rels., 1984—; exec. com. ACE Bus. Higher Edn. Forum, 1984-86; exec. com. New Eng. Colls. Fund, 1980—, 2d v.p., 1984-85, 1st v.p., 1985-88, pres., 1988-89; mem. nat. panel to study declining test scores Coll. Entrance Exam. Bd., 1976-77; exec. com., chair task force Pres.'s Commn. for Nat. Agenda for 1980s, 1979-80; adv. com. Women's Leadership Conf. on Nat. Security, 1982—; exec. com. Coun. on Competitiveness, 1986-89; chair task force on health care Challenge to Leadership Conf., 1987-89; bd. dirs. Greenwall Found., 1997, Fund for City of N.Y., chair, 1997. Recipient Roger Baldwin award Mass. Civil Liberties Union Found., 1982, citation of merit Northeast Region NCCJ, 1982, Career Contbn. award Mass. Psychol. Assn., 1987, Disting. Bostonian award, 1990, Ellis Island medal, 1990. Mem. NOW (nat. corp. adv. bd. of legal def. and edn. fund 1984—), Am. Laryngol. Voice Rsch. and Edn. Found. (pres.), Nat. Inst. Social Scis. (medal for outstanding svc. 1973), Phi Beta Kappa, Phi Delta Kappa, Phi Kappa Phi.

HORNER, RONALD GEORGE, music educator, musician; b. Johnstown, Pa., Mar. 12, 1956; s. Clyde Melvin and Keturah Elizabeth Horner. BS, IN U of Penn., Ind., Pa., 1978; MusM, Duquesne U, Pitts., Pa., 1988, dip. artist, 1992. Cert. profl. instrnl. Pa. Dept. of Ed., 1978. Percussionist Israel Philharm. Orch., Tel-Aviv, Israel, 1978 80; dir. of percussion studies Seton Hill Coll., Greensburg, Pa., 1983—85; sr. lectr. of music Frostburg State U, Frostburg, Md., 1983—; instr. of music U of Pitts., Pitts., 1985—96; percussionist sub. Pitts. Symphony Orch., Pitts., 1989—96; asst. prof. of music Ind. U of Pa., Ind., Pa., 1996—. Music dir. Arion Band of Frostburg, Frostburg, Md., 1995—; condr. Bedford All County Band, Bedford, Pa., 2001; adjudicator Western MD ensemble Festival, Hagerstown, Md., 2002. Instrumentalist soloist (world premier performances) Sonus, 1991, Recitative and Scherzo, 1998, Toccata for Timpani, 2002; arranger: songs Pilgrims Chorus, 1997; author: (music method book) The Tuneful Timpanist, 2000. Mem. Sons of the Am. Rev., Wash., DC, 1998, Nat. Huguenot Soc., Bloomington, Minn., 1998, Soc. of the War of 1812, Phila., 1998. Mem.: Percussive Arts Soc., Phi Mu Alpha Sinfonia, Delta Omicron, Pi Kappa Lambda. Republican. Methodist. Avocations: golf, skiing, classic sports cars. Home: 163 Gilmour Rd Somerset PA 15501 Office: Ind U of Pa Cogswell Hall 422 S 11th St Indiana PA 15705-1049

HORNER, SANDRA MARIE GROCE (SANDY HEART), educator, poet, songwriter, lyricist; b. Dallas; d. Larnell and Lee Ella (Lacy) Groce; divorced; 1 child, Danielle Marie. BA in Sociol./Philosophy with honors, Calif. State U., Dominguez Hills, 1980; postgrad., UCLA, 1978, 82-83, Consumnes River Coll., 1987, Nat. U., 1991, So. Utah U., 1993. Cert. elem. edn. K-8, Nev., K-A Occ. Std.: Bus. and Office Occupations; cert. instr. credential Calif.; cert. lifetime tchg. credential bus., Calif. Prodn. asst., sec. Paramount Pictures Corp., Hollywood, Calif., 1968-74; instr. LA C.C. Dist., 1976-78; tchr. Verbum Dei HS, LA, 1977-79; tchr., dept. chair LA Unified Sch. Dist., Calif., 1975-83; tchr. Sacramento City Unified Sch. Dist., Calif., 1985-87; editor, pub. Multi-Family Publ., Sacramento, 1986-89; tchr. Clark County Sch. Dist., Las Vegas, Nev., 1991—2003. Adj. instr. C.C. So. Nev., Las Vegas, 1988-95; radio broadcast interview Poetry Today with Ken Lerch WRTN 93.5 FM, NYC, 1997. Editor: (books/newsletters) Groce Family Newsletter, 1986; recording contracts Hilltop Records, 1996, 97, AME Record Recording Co., 1997, Hollywood Artists Record Co., 1997; author numerous poems; albums include America, Hill Top Country, Star Route USA, Music of Am. Recipient Nat. History recognition award Soc. History Rsch. and Preservation, 1989, Editor's Choice awards Nat. Libr. of Poetry, 1996; inducted into Internat. Poetry Hall of Fame, 1996. Mem. Internat. Soc. Poets (Disting. Mem.), Internat. Platform Assn. Democrat. Avocations: literature, music, history, art, antiques. Office: PO Box 34325 Las Vegas NV 89133-4325 E-mail: sheart1writer@aol.com.

HORNER, SHIRLEY JAYE, columnist, writing and publishing consultant; d. John and Selma (Sosna) Quentzel; m. Robert George Horner (dec. Nov. 1984); children: Charles Bruce, Neil Brian. BA, NYU, 1946; MA, Columbia U., 1948, MPhil, 1976. Instr. English L.I. U., Bklyn., 1948-49, Seton Hall U., Newark, 1949-51, Queens Coll., L.I., 1953-54, Rutgers U., Newark, 1975-76; prodr. preservation experience programs Middlesex County Cultural and Heritage Commn., North Brunswick, N.J., 1980-81; editor fedn. reports Nat. Fedn. State Humanities Couns., Mpls., 1981-84; columnist, writer About Books The N.Y. Times' N.J. Weekly, N.Y.C., 1979—, reporter tri-state regional planning commn., 1979-82. Lectr. for writing workshops Trenton (N.J.) State Coll., 1984, Seton Hall U., South Orange, N.J., 1990-91, N.J. Libr. Assn., Trenton, 1990-93, N.J. Inst. Tech., Newark, 1997; book review panelist WOR-TV, 1986; moderator, panelist Holocaust Rescuers in Italy Day Program, 1995; NEH-funded lectr. Seton Hall U., 1991; reporter Tri-State Regional Planning Commn., The N.Y. Times N.J. Weekly, N.Y.C., 1979-82; founding bd. dirs. N.J. Ctr. for the Book, 2001—; spkr. in field. Co-editor: Ladies at the Cross-roads, 1978 (AAUW award 1978); editor: Conserving Communities: Urban and Suburban, 1979 (N.J. Inst. Tech. award of excellence 1980), (series of booklets) The Preservation Experience in Middlesex County, 1981 (Middlesex County award of distinction 1981; prodr. (TV program) Political Debate for '79 on Suburban Cable, 1979 (Union County award of achievement 1980); featured author N.J. Literary Hall of Fame Authors Brunch, 1997; contbg. editor: N.J. Encyclopedia, 2001; contbr. articles to profl. jours. Co-chmn. Bicentennial Program for Mountainside, Union County, N.J., 1974-77; del. Union County Rep. Party, Linden, N.J., 1982-88; chmn. evaluation N.J. Com. for Humanities/NEH, New Brunswick, 1979-81; chmn. Union County Planning Bd., 1981-84; mem., publs. advisor N.J. Hist. Commn.; trustee N.J. Lit. Hall of Fame, 1987—, N.J. Ctr. for the Book, Opera at Florham Fairleigh Dickinson U., Madison, N.J., 1992—; mem. historic site com. Soc. Profl. Journalists, 1989; counsellor N.J. Cath. Hist. Records Commn. Recipient 1st Pl. Journalism award N.J. Press Women, 1980, 81, award for saving the life of a child Mountainside, N.J., 1968; inducted into N.J. Literary Hall of Fame, 1987; NEH grantee, 1980, 90. Mem. Nat. Book Critics Cir. (bd. dirs. 1990-93, judge for NBCC awards), Images '95 Com. N.J. Ctr. for Visual Arts, Nat. Arts Club (literary com. 2000), Soc. Profl. Journalists (hist. site com. 1989), First Mogilev Podolier Friends Assn. (pres. 1996). Avocations: hiking, archaeological digs. Office: care NY Times NJ Weekly 1575 Brookside Rd Mountainside NJ 07092-1601 E-mail: sjhorner@comcast.net. *How empty is the life that has not known love. Treasure the memory.*

HORNER, STEPHEN VANDYKE, finance educator; b. Washington, D.C., Aug. 31, 1952; s. Dwight Burton Horner and Opal Ruth Hoffman; m. Susan Gay Mitchell, June 28, 1997; m. Margaret Ann Hadley, Nov. 24, 1973 (div. Jan. 28, 1983); children: Jason Thomas, Kristan Elyse. BA, Emporia State U., 1976, MBA, 1991; postgrad. in PhD program, U. Mo., 1999—. Faculty mgr. Ctrl. Parking Sys., Kansas City, Mo., 1979—81; ops. supr. O'Reilly Mgmt., Emporia, Kans., 1981—85; asst. office mgr. Dolly Madison, Emporia, Kans., 1985—87; computer operator Emporia State Bank, Emporia, Kans., 1988—91; asst. prof. Bethany Coll., Lindsborg, Kans., 1991—99. Dir. Leadership Lindsborg, Lindsborg, Kans., 1996—98. Pres. Leadership Lindsborg, Lindsborg, Kans., 1997—98. Office: Univ Mo 350 Cornell Hall Columbia MO 65211-2600 E-mail: horners@missouri.edu.

HORNICK, KATHERINE JOYCE KAY, artist, small business owner; b. Chelan, Wash., Jan. 2, 1940; d. Donald Dale and Dorothy Eleanor (Tilton) Shipton; m. Dan Lewis Hornick, Apr. 6, 1959; children: Tod A. and Daniel D. Student, Kinman Bus. U., Spokane, 1957-58, Shoreline C.C., Bothell, 1972-74. Owner The Traveling Gallery, Bothell, Wash., 1969-74; juror NW Pastel Soc., Redmond, Wash., 1978; resident artist Qraz Gallery, Seattle, 1968-70; represented by Bainbridge Arts & Crafts, Bainbridge Island, Wash., 1989—, Oceanlake Studio Gallery, Lincoln City, Oreg., 1989-92, Ho. of Wyo. Jade and Art, Casper, 1993, 94, Foothills Gallery, Sheriday, Wyo., 1993, 94, Sticks and Stones Gallery, Seattle, 1993-94, 95-96, The Landing, Bainbridge Island, Wash., 1994; owner, operator Katherine J. Hornick Bus. Svcs., Bainbridge Island, 1990—. Condr. Bainbridge Island Studio Tour, 1988-92, 97; lectr. Community Groups & Sch. Puget Sound Area, 1969-92; tchr. Kay Hornick Studios Bothell, 1972-75; juror Bainbridge Music and Arts Scholarship Award, 2000. Exhibited in group shows Kirsten Gallery, 1995, Amy Burnett Gallery, Bremerton, Seattle Asian Art Mus., 1997-98, Janet Laurel Gallery, 1997-98, Harrison Gallery, Seattle, 2001, Women Painters of Wash., 2001; juried shows include Olympic Coll. Group, 2002, Burten Arms Gallery, 2002; featured artist Bainbridge Gallery, 2000; art work appeared on video Earth Day Celebration, 1996. Recipient Hon. Mention Charles & Emma Frye Museum Seattle, 1988, Dorothy Dolph Jensen Meml. award Women Painters of Washington Annual Juried Show, Honorable Mention, Women Painters Washington Juried Show, 1996, Bainbridge Islands Studio Tour, 1996, Group Show Amy Burnett Gallery, 1996, Group Show Kado Tea Rm., Seattle Asian Art Mus., 1997, Group Show Janet Wacorec Gallery, 1997, Woman Painters of Wash. Juried Group Show, Mercer Island, 1998, Solo Show Checkers Gallery, Poulsbo, Wash., 2000. Mem. Nat. League Am. PEN Women (apptd. auditor Seattle 1994, treas. 1996), Nat. Mus. Women in Arts (chpt.), Nat. Western Art Assn., Bainbridge Arts and Crafts (bd. dirs. 1989-90), Women Painters of Washington (exhbn. chair 1996-97), Surface Design Assn. E-mail: kjhornick@aol.com.

HORNICK, SUSAN FLORENCE STEGMULLER, secondary education educator, fine arts educator, curriculum specialist, artist; b. Aug. 29, 1947; d. August George and Florence Maybell (Meisinger) Stegmuller; m. Jesse Allan Hornick, July 20, 1974. BA, Queens Coll., 1969, MS in Art Edn., 1973; permanent N.Y. State reading cert., Hunter Coll., 1984, advanced cert. ednl. supervn./adminstrn. summa cum laude, 1996. Lic. tchr. fine arts, N.Y.C.; permanent cert. tchr. art, N.Y.; cert. in ednl. adminstrn. and supervision, N.Y.; permanent cert. sch. dist. adminstr., N.Y. Fine arts tchr. Hillcrest H.S., Jamaica, N.Y., 1973-74, Ea. Dist. H.S., Bklyn., 1974-75, Tottenville H.S., S.I., N.Y., 1975-76; fine arts tchr., title 1 reading tchr. Prospect Heights H.S., Bklyn., 1976-78; fine arts tchr. Grover Cleveland H.S., Ridgewood, N.Y., 1978—, dept. coord., 1986-98. Tchr. reading. English and reading improvement through art, Grover Cleveland H.S., 1980—85, tchr. ecol. awareness, 1995—, yearbook advisor, 1979; cooperating tchr., trainer art tchrs. Queens Coll., Flushing, NY, 1991, 2000; tchr. "bridge" ESL and math. Newcomers Summer H.S., Long Island City, NY, 2000, ESL tchr., mem. Saturday lit. program, 2000—01; tchr. visual and literary reading, writing and artistic strategies, 2000—; conceptual facilitator reading, writing and artistic skills with written and visual exemplification, 2000—. Exhbns. include U.S. Capitol, Washington, 1982, 86, 88, U.S. Capitol, Washington, Lever House Exhibit, 1984-97, City Hall, N.Y.C., 1984, Queensborough C.C. Art Gallery, Bayside, N.Y., 1984-94, N.Y.C. Transit Mus., 1987-99, Queens Borough Hall, Kew Gardens, N.Y., 1992, Sotheby's, 1992, Internat. Arrivals bldg. JFK Kennedy Airport (award winning mural by Joanna Kadlubowska, 1992), Queens Theater In the Park, Flushing, N.Y., 1993, 97, Nat. Mus. Am. Indian, Smithsonian Inst., 1992, 93, Mus. of City of N.Y., 1998, Grover Cleveland H.S., Ridgewood, N.Y., 1998-2003, N.Y. Joint Bd. Unite, N.Y.C., 2000-01 Recipient Medal for Superior Performance, N.Y.C. Transit Authority, 1996, Cert. of Appreciation for Outstanding Performance as Art Educator in N.Y.C. Pub. Schs., N.Y.C. Bd. Edn., 1985, Cert. of Recognition for Accomplishments as Outstanding Tchr., Nat. Tchrs. Hall of Fame, 2000. Mem. ASCD, N.Y.C. Art Tchrs. Assn., United Fedn. Tchrs., Hunter Coll. Alumni Assn., Nat. Mus. Women in Arts (charter), Colonial Williamsburg Duke of Gloucester Soc., N.Am. Fishing Club (life). Home: 46-05 Hanford St Douglaston NY 11362

HORNING, MARKUS, marine biologist, educator; b. Braunschweig, Germany, Feb. 14, 1960; came to U.S., 1992; s. Hans M. and Ursula Horning. MS, Freiburg (Germany) U., 1988; PhD summa cum laude, Bielefeld (Germany) U., 1992. Biologist Max-Planck-Inst., Seewiesen, Germany, 1989-92; postdoctoral rsch. physiologist Scripps Instn. Oceanography, San Diego, 1992-96; asst. rsch. scientist Tex. A&M U., Galveston, 1996-98, assoc. rsch. scientist, 1998—, dir. Lab. Applied Biotelemetry and Biotech., 2000—. Assoc. prof. marine scis., U. Alaska, Fairbanks, 1999—; sole propr. Ultramarine Instruments, Galveston, 1997—; scientific program com. 1st World Marine Mammal Sci. Conf., Monaco, 1998. Contbr. articles to profl. jours.; inventor in field; assoc. editor Marine Mammal Sci., 1996-98. Recipient U.S. Antarctica medal, NSF, 1981. Mem. AAAS, Ecol. Soc. Am., Am. Physiol. Soc., Animal Behavior Soc., Soc. Marine Mammalogy, Am. Soc. Photogrammetry and Remote Sensing, N.Y. Acad. Sci. Office: Tex A&M U 5007 Avenue U Galveston TX 77551-5926 E-mail: horningm@tamug.tamu.edu.

HORNING, ROSS CHARLES, JR., historian, educator; b. Watertown, S.D., Oct. 10, 1920; s. Ross Charles and Harriett (Meaghan) H. BA, Augustana Coll., 1948; MA, George Washington U., 1952; PhD (Sanders fellow), 1958; postgrad. Russian, Inst. Langs. and Linguistics, Georgetown U., 1952-53. Instr. Wis. State U., Eau Claire, 1958-59; asst. prof. St. John's U., Collegeville, Minn., 1959-64; assoc. prof. Russian history and internat. affairs Creighton U., Omaha, 1964-68, prof., 1968—. Pres. faculty Creighton U., 1984-86, chmn. athletic bd., Athletic Hall of Fame com., 1987-88, mem. athletic bd., 1992—, mem. pub. honors com., 1984-90, 93-96, 97—. Bd. advisors Red Cloud Indian Sch., Pine Ridge, S.D.; bd. govs. Irish Am. Partnership, Boston. Recipient Disting. Faculty Service award Creighton U., 1982; Fulbright scholar India, summer 1967 Mem. AAAS, Am. Assn. Advancement Slavic Studies, Am. Hist. Assn., Am. Soc. Internat. Law, European Studies Assn., Orgn. Am. Historians, Conf. Slavic and European Studies, Am. Com. for Irish Studies, Midwest Conf. on Asian Affairs, Que. Studies Assn., Joslyn Liberal Arts Soc., S.W. Am. Assn. Advancement Slavic Studies, Western Social Sci. Assn., Am. Fgn. Service Assn., Canadian History Assn., Assn. Canadian Studies in U.S., Assn. Asian Studies, Omaha Symphony Assn., Atlanta Econ. Soc., Assn. Canadienne de Sci. Politique, Internat. Law Assn. (Am. br.), World Peace Through Law Center, Fgn. Service Club (Washington), Asia Soc., Opera-Omaha, Assn. Profl. Baseball Players (life), Fulbright Alumni Assn. (life), Omaha Press Club, Alpha Sigma Nu. Home: 4955 Cuming St Omaha NE 68132-1549

HORNSBY, DAVID MCMILLAN, musician, music educator; b. Fort Worth, Tex., Nov. 14, 1928; s. David Franklin and Anna Estelle Hornsby; m. Lenda Ruth Jones, 1969 (div. 1973); m. Tamara Wilder Dower, 1963 (dec. 1964); 1 child, Michael David. Diploma, Ft. Worth Conservatory, 1945; MusB, Tex. Christian U., 1945—49; MA in Music and Music Edn., Columbia U., 1949—50; postgrad., U. Colo., 1949, postgrad., 1956, postgrad., 1978; studied with, Jeannette Tillett, Ernest von Dohnanyi, Dr. Edwin Hughes, Dr. Howard Waltz. Piano faculty mem. Ft. Worth Conservatory, 1946—49; ann. piano concerts Chautauqua, Boulder, Colo., 1951—63; music tchr. PR Pub. Schools, PR, 1953—55; music instr. Colorado Pub. Schools, 1955—58; piano instr. Pvt. Piano Studio, Boulder, Colo., 1956—78; music dir. Colegio Bolivar, Cali, Colombia, 1978—79; piano instr. Pvt. Piano Studio, San Antonio, 1980—; music dir. San Antonio Acad. of Tex., 1981—84. Condr., Christmas concert Gov. of PR, 1954; concert performance Polytechnic Inst., San German, PR, 1955; ann. judging tours Nat. Guild of Piano Teachers, 1963—; lectr. Music Teacher's Nat. Conv., Denver, 1975. Co-author: (book) Bassetti Primer; author: (books of poetry) River Scattered Forest. Recipient Piano Guild Hall of Fame, Nat. Guild of Piano Teachers, 1971, Margie B. Boswell Prize for Best Alumni Poem, Tex. Christian U., 1952. Mem.: San Antonio Music Teachers Assn., Tex. Music Teachers Assn., Music Teachers Nat. Assn., The Leschetizky Assn., The Bohemians (N.Y. Musicians Club), Phi Mu Alpha Sinfonia (life). Home: 340 Montclair No 102 San Antonio TX 78209 Office: 340 Montclair No 103 San Antonio TX 78209

HORNSTEIN, MARK, financial executive; b. N.Y.C., Dec. 7, 1947; s. Joseph and Anne (Fox) H.; BBA, Pace U., 1969; postgrad. N.Y.U., 1973. Staff acct. Peat, Marwick, Mitchell & Co., N.Y.C., 1969-70; sr. acct. Robert J. Cofini & Co., N.Y.C., 1972-74; asst. v.p. United Va. Factors Corp., N.Y.C., 1974-77; asst. v.p., adminstrv. head mortgage loan div. James Talcott, Inc., N.Y.C., 1977-78; loan adminstrn. officer Aetna Bus. Credit, Inc., East Hartford, Conn., 1978-79; asst. v.p. A.J. Armstrong Co. Inc. (now Bankamerica Bus. Credit, Inc.), N.Y.C., 1979-83; v.p. Leucadia Nat. Corp., N.Y.C., 1983—; treas. Am. Investment Co., St. Louis, 1984—; asst. v.p. Cardiff Equities Corp. (merger Leucadia Nat. Corp.), La Jolla, 1984-86; v.p. Charter Nat. Life Ins. Co., St. Louis, 1985-93, PHLCORP, Inc. (formerly Baldwin United Corp.), Phila., 1987—; sec. Bolivian Power Co., Ltd., LaPaz, Bolivia, 1988-94; v.p. Transp. Capital Corp., N.Y.C., 1992-94, chmn., pres., 1994-96. Served with USNR, 1970-72. Home: 25 Sutton Pl S New York NY 10022-2441 Office: 315 Park Ave S New York NY 10010-3607

HORNUNG, HANS GEORG, aeronautical engineering educator, science facility administrator; b. Jaffa, Israel, Dec. 26, 1934; came to U.S., 1987; s. Friedrich Gottlieb and Helene Wilhelmine (Wagner) H.; m. Gretl Charlotte Frank, Jan. 29, 1960; children: Ingrid, Karl, Lisa, Jenny. BMechE with honors, U. Melbourne, Australia, 1960, M in Engring. Sci. with honors, 1962; PhD in Aeros., U. London, 1965. Rsch. scientist Aero. Rsch. Labs., Melbourne, 1962-67; lectr., sr. lectr. then reader Australian Nat. U., Canberra, 1967-80; dir., mem. senate com. for sci. and tech. Inst. Exptl. Fluid Mechanics (DLR), Göttingen, Germany, 1980-87; dir. Grad. Aero. Labs. and Clarence Johnson prof. aero. Calif. Inst. Tech., Pasadena, 1987—. Mem. fluid dynamics panel Adv. Group. Aerospace R & D, 1983-88; mem. adv. com. Internat. Shock Tube Symposia, 1979-95; chmn. adv. com. von Kármán Inst. for Fluid Dynamics, 1984-85; mem. German del. Internat. Union Theoretical and Applied Mechanics, 1984-87; Lanchester Meml. lectr. Royal Aero. Soc., London, 1988; hon. prof. U. Göttingen; Prandtl mem. lectr. Ges. Angew. Math. and Mech., Vienna, 1988. Mem. editl. adv. bd. Zeitschrift für Flugwissenschaften und Weltraumforschung, 1984-96, Experiments in Fluids jour., 1987—, Physics of Fluids, 1988-91, Ing. Archiv, 1989-96; contbr. numerous articles to profl. jours. Recipient von Karman award and medal for internat. coop. in aero. Internat. Coun. Aero. Scis.; Humboldt fellow Tech. U., Darmstadt, Germany, 1974-75. Fellow Royal Aero. Soc.; mem. Nat. Acad. of Engring.(fgn. assoc.), Sci. mem. of bd. DLR Germany, Australian Inst. Physics, Deutsche Gesellschaft für Luft-und Raumfahrt, Gesellschaft für angewandte Mathematik und Mechanik, Am. Phys. Soc., AIAA, Royal Swedish Acad. Engring. Scis., Ludwig Prandtl Ring German Soc. Aerospace Sci. Achievements include making important contbns. in hypersonic flow theory, exptl. methods and results in real-gas flows, Mach reflection and three-dimensional separation. Office: Calif Inst Tech 1201 E California Blvd Pasadena CA 91125-0001 E-mail: hans@galcit.caltech.edu.

HORNYAK, EUGENE AUGUSTINE, bishop; b. Kucura, Backa, Yugoslavia, Oct. 7, 1919; emigrated to U.S., 1948, naturalized, 1955, emigrated to Eng., 1961; s. Peter and Juliana (Findrik) H. Ph.B., Pontifical U., Rome, 1941, S.T.D., 1947; J.C.B., Gregorian U., Rome, 1947. Ordained priest Roman Catholic Ch. (Byzantine rite), 1945; asst. priest Struthers and Warren, Ohio, 1948-49; adminstr. St. Michael's Ch., Newton Falls, Ohio, 1949-50; prof. moral theology, canon law, liturgy, also spiritual dir. Sts. Cyril and Methodius Byzantine Seminary, Pitts., 1950-55; spiritual dir. St. Basil's Ukrainian Minor Seminary, Stamford, Conn., 1958-61; entered Order St. Basil the Great, Can., 1956-57; master novices, also superior St. Josaphat's Monastery, Glen Cove, L.I., 1961; apptd. titular bishop Hermonthis; also aux. to Cardinal Godfrey (for Ukrainian Catholics in Eng. and Wales), London, 1961-63; bishop-apostolic exarch for Ukrainian Catholics in Eng. and Wales, 1963-87, for Ukrainians in Scotland, 1968-87. Mem. Pontifical Commn. of Ea. Code of Canon Law, Rome, 1977-90; consultor Sacred Congragation for Ea. Cath. Chs., Rome, 1978-94. Home and Office: St Olga's House 14 Newburgh Rd Acton London W3 6DQ England *Our earthly life comes, grows and fades away; it has God's support, it has its aims and its destiny. As a Christian, a monk and a Catholic bishop, I am endeavouring to attain those aims, reach that destiny, and be instrumental in helping and guiding my fellowmen to do likewise, according to the teachings and example of Christ, God incarnate, as faithfully transmitted to us by his Church.*

HORNYAK, ROY ROBERT, music educator, minister; b. St. Joseph, Mo., Nov. 4, 1925; s. Roy and Mildred Gertrude Hornyak; m. Mary Margaret Lewis, Aug. 9, 1953; children: Deborah Margaret Crnkovich, Roy Robert Hornyak, Jr. BA, Ctrl. Meth. Coll., 1948; MusM, Ind. U., 1950; Ensign, USNR, Naval Midshipmens Sch., 1945; MusD Edn., Ind. U., 1964. Prof. music U. of Cin., 1954—86, head music edn. campus ch. ministries, 1967—71, head performance studies campus ch. ministries, 1976—81, assoc. dean campus ch. ministries, 1972—75; coord. of campus ministry Am. Bapt. Churches of Ohio, Granville, Ohio, 1988—97; sr. min. Hyde Pk. Bapt. Ch., Cin., 1999—2002; exec. dir. Ohio Campus Ministries, Columbus, 1989—90; music dir. Simon Winds, Cin., 1981—. Moderator Miami Bapt. Associaton, Cincinnati, Ohio, 1993—96; pres. Am. Bapt. churches of Ohio, Granville, Ohio, 1997—98. Author: Attitudes Toward Contemporary American Music. Chmn. Am. Bapt. Campus Ministry at U. Cin., 1959—86. Lt. comdr. USNR, 1943—71, PTO. Recipient Disting. Alumni award, Ctrl. Meth. Coll., 1976, Newton C. Fedder award, 1995. Mem.: Coll. Band Directors Nat. Assoc., Phi Beta Mu (pres. 1986—88, Mu chpt.), Mil. Order of World Wars (life), Torch Club (pres. 1968—69).

HOROSKO, MARIAN, writer, educator; b. Cleve., Aug. 4, 1927; d. Louis Senko and Marian Catherine (Gromand) H. Student, Cleve. Inst. of Music, 1936-43, Juillard Sch. Music, 1944-45, Sch. Am. Ballet, N.Y.C., 1944-51. Prodr. Alvin Ailey Celebration, 1998; N.Y. corr. Dancer Mag., 2000—. Lectr. Balanchine, Graham, Harkness Ballet; leader Martha Graham seminar, Balanchine seminar. Performer Ballet Russe de Monte Carlo, 1939, Met. Opera Ballet, 1951-54, N.Y.C. Ballet, 1954-62; (films) Eight by Eight, 1949, Prince Who Was A Thief, 1950, Royal Wedding, 1950, American in Paris, 1950; (Broadway plays) Oklahoma, 1945-47, Along Fifth Avenue, 1948, Dance Me A Song, 1949; (staged classics) Buffalo Ballet; film curator: Dance Collection, Lincoln Ctr., 1960's; television and radio prodr. Stas. WNET-TV, WNCN-FM, 1961-77; prodr. George Balanchine Celebration, 1992, Alvin Ailey Celebration, 1998, 100 Years of Am. Dance, 1999; author: Pas De Deux, 1979, Ballet Technique for Male Dancers, 1982, Dancer's Survival Manual, 1987, Martha Graham: Technique and Dance Evolution, 1991, (script writer, narrator laserdisc on Martha Graham), Sleeping Beauty: The Ballet, 1994, Pas de Deux-The Art of Partnering, 1999, Pas de Deux reprint, 2000, Reprint: Martha Graham, 2001; prodr. A Harkness Celebration, 1997, Martha Graham seminar, 1991, Balanchine seminar, 1993, Harkness Celebration, 1997, Harkness...as seen Alvin Ailey seminar, 1998, 100 Years of American Dance, 1999 (Juilliard Sch.); contbr. Dance mag., 1952-99, edn. editor, 1980-99; N.Y. corr. Dancer mag., 1999—; prodr. Alvin Ailey Celebration, 1998, Tribute to Yuriko Japan Society, 2003; contbr. numerous seminars in field. Recipient first Spl. Recognition award MEDART, 1992. Home: 357 W 55th St New York NY 10019-4555 Fax: 212-247-1650.

HOROSZEWICZ, JULIUSZ STANISLAW, oncologist, cancer researcher, laboratory administrator; b. Warsaw, Jan. 4, 1931; came to U.S., 1961; s. Tytus Michal and Stefania (Domanska) H.; children: Nike Joanna, Peter Juliusz. D of Medicine summa cum laude, Acad. of Medicine, Lodz, Poland, 1954, DMSc, 1960. Teaching asst. dept. bacteriology Acad. of Medicine, Lodz, 1950-55, asst. prof., 1955-59, assoc. prof., 1959-61; cancer rsch. scientist Roswell Park Meml. Inst., Buffalo, 1962-64, sr. cancer rsch. scientist, 1964-67, assoc. cancer rsch. scientist, 1967-76, prin. cancer rsch. scientist, 1976-86; assoc. chief oncological urology rsch. N.Y. State Dept. Health, Roswell Park Meml. Inst. Div., Buffalo, 1986-88; dir. exptl. cancer ctr. Millard Fillmore Hosp., Buffalo, 1988-98; dir. UICC-Internat. Union against Cancer, 1988-98. Dir. electron microscopy lab. viral oncology, 1963-66, dir. human fibroblast interferon program Roswell Park Meml. Inst., 1976-82; chmn. Pleuro-Pneumonia Like Organisms subcom. human cancer virus task force Nat. Cancer Inst., Bethesda, Md., 1963-64, mem. Nat. Prostatic Cancer Project working cadre, 1972-74; assoc. rsch. prof. microbiology SUNY, Buffalo, 1966-96; rsch. prof. biology Canisius Coll., Buffalo, 1968-96, Niagara U., Niagara Falls, N.Y., 1968-96; sci. cons. Cytogen Corp., Princeton, N.J., 1990-92, Pacific NW Rsch. Found., Seattle, 1993-97. Mem. editl. bd. The Prostate, 1994—; contbr. more than 100 articles to profl. jours.; patentee on specific monoclonal antibody for diagnosis and treatment of human prostate cancer. Rockefeller Found. fellow, 1961-62; Rsch. grantee Nat. Cancer Inst., 1979-82, Phi Beta Psi, 1987-96; named Citizen of Yr. Am.-Polish Eagle, Buffalo, 1967. Mem. AAAS, Am. Assn. Cancer Rsch., Am. Soc. Microbiology, Polish Soc. for Bacteriology, Am. Cancer Soc., Am. Assn. for Clin. Rsch., N.Y. Acad. Scis., Lodz Sci. Soc. Roman Catholic. Achievements include 4 patents on specific monoclonal antibody for diagnosis and treatment of human prostate cancer. Home: PO Box 62 60 Arrow Dr Barry's Bay ON Canada K0J 1B0

HOROWITZ, ZOLA PHILIP, pharmaceutical company executive; b. Pitts., Oct. 12, 1934; s. Reuben and Jean (Liff) H.; m. Marlene C. Davis, Aug. 24, 1958; children: Bonna Lynn, Reid Alan. BS in Pharmacy, U. Pitts., 1955, MS in Pharmacy, 1959, PhD in Pharmacology, 1960. Researcher Vets. Rsch. Labs., Pitts., 1958-60; sr. rsch. investigator Squibb Inst. Med. Rsch., Princeton, N.J., 1959-64, med. monitor, 1964-66, dir. pharmacology, 1967-72, assoc. rsch. dir., 1972-78, assoc. dir. devel., 1978-82, v.p., 1982-89; v.p. licensing Bristol-Myers Squibb Corp., Princeton, 1990-91, v.p. bus. devel. and planning, 1991-94; cons. to biotech. and pharm. industry, 1994—. Bd. dirs. Diacrin Inc., Charlestown, Mass., Phyton Inc., Ithaca, N.Y., BioCryst Pharm., Birmingham, Ala., Magainin Pharm., Plymouth Meeting, Pa., Synaptic Pharm., Paramus, N.J., Avigen, Alameda, Calif., Dov Pharm., Hackensack, N.J. Editor: Angiotensin Conversion Enzyme Inhibition, 1983. Pres. Princeton Jewish Ctr., 1980-82; mem. East Brunswick (N.J.) Bd. Edn., 1965-69, N.J. Cancer Rsch. Commn., 1989-95. Recipient rsch. award Soc. Biol. Psychiatry, 1965. Fellow Am. Pharm. Assn., Acad. Pharm. Scientists; mem. Am., Brit. Pharmacology Socs. Jewish. E-mail: zolamar@aol.com.

HOROWITZ, ALAN JOEL, civil engineer, educator; b. Bklyn., July 17, 1947; s. Mae and Harold Nathan H.; m. Shirley Maxine Auerbach, Sept. 6, 1970; children: Jonathan, Scott. BS in Engring. magna cum laude, MS in Engring., UCLA, 1970, PhD in Urban Planning, 1974. Registered profl. engr., Wis. Assoc. sr. rsch. scientist Gen. Motors Rsch. Labs., Warren, Mich., 1974-79; prof. civil engring. U. Wis., Milw., 1979—. Proprietor AJH Assocs., Milw., 1987—. Author various software programs; contbr. articles to profl. jours. Charles F. Scott fellow UCLA, 1972; Engring. Dept. scholar, 1969. Mem. AICP, ASCE, Am. Planning Assn., Transp. Rsch. Bd., Regional Sci. Assn. Internat., Inst. Transp. Engrs., Tau Beta Pi. Office: U Wis--Milwaukee PO Box 784 Milwaukee WI 53201 Fax: 414-229-6958. E-mail: ajh@execpc.com., horowitz@uwm.edu.

HOROWITZ, BARRY ALLAN, music company executive; b. N.Y.C., June 21, 1948; s. Henry and Tania (Aisenfeld) H.; m. Maida Barbara Schwartzberg, Oct. 9, 1977 (dec. Oct. 1994); children: Jessica, Jared. BA, Hofstra U., Hempstead, N.Y., 1971. From sales staff to sr. dir. ops. Sam Ash Music Corp., Hicksville, N.Y., 1971-95, v.p. purchasing and merchandising, 1995—. Avocations: running, skiing. Office: Sam Ash Music Corp 278 Duffy Ave Hicksville NY 11801-3605 E-mail: barry@samashmusic.com.

HOROWITZ, BEN, health facility administrator; b. Bklyn., Mar. 19, 1914; s. Saul and Sonia (Meringoff) H.; m. Beverly Lichtman, Feb. 14, 1952; children: Zachary, Jody. BA, Bklyn. Coll., 1940; LLB, St. Lawrence U., 1940; postgrad., New Sch. Social Rsch., 1942. Bar: N.Y. 1941. Dir. N.Y. Fedn. Jewish Philanthropies, 1940-45; assoc., ea. regional dir. City of Hope, 1945-50, nat. exec. sec., 1950-53, exec. dir., 1953-85, gen. v.p., bd. dirs., 1985—, bd. dirs. nat. med. ctr., 1980—. Bd. dirs. Beckman Rsch. Inst., 1980—. Mem. Gov.'s Task Force on Flood Relief, 1969-74; bd. dirs., v.p. Hope for Hearing Found., UCLA, 1972-96; bd. dirs. Forte Found., 1987-92, Ch. Temple Housing Corp., 1988-93, Leo Baeck Temple, 1964-67, 86-89, Westwood Property Owners Assn., 1991—. Recipient Spirit of Life award, 1970, Gallery of Achievement award, 1974, Profl. of Yr. award So. Calif. chpt. Nat. Sco. Fundraisers, 1977; Ben Horowitz chair in rsch. established at City of Hope, 1981; city street named in his honor, 1986. Jewish. Formulated the role of City of Hope as pilot center in medicine, science and humanitarianism, 1959. Office: City of Hope 11645 Wilshire Blvd Los Angeles CA 90025-1708

HOROWITZ, BRUCE, social worker, photographer, musician; b. Phila., Feb. 2, 1949; s. Irving Horowitz and Toby Goldberg; m. Beverly Gold, Sept. 1, 1974; 1 child, Emily Gold. MFA in Photography, SUNY, Rochester, 1974; MSW, Syracuse U., 1993. NASW N.Y. State Dept. Edn., 1994. Youth worker, social worker Convalescent Hosp. for Children/Crestwood Children's Ctr., Rochester, NY, 1971—2002; social worker Hillside Children's Ctr., Rochester, 2002—. Photography, MOMA Open Ends Exhibit Innocence and Experience, exhibitions include Smithsonian Instn., Am. Children Exhibit MOMA; music leader: EDzWOOD band. Sch. based planning team mem. Sch. of the Arts, Rochester, 1993—95. Fellow photography, Nat. Endowment for the Arts, 1975, Creative Artist Pub. Svc., 1976—77, John Simon Guggenheim Meml. Found., 1983. Mem.: NASW. Office: Hillside Childrens Ctr 1158 Monroe Ave Rochester NY 14620 Personal E-mail: brucehorowitz@email.com.

HOROWITZ, CAROLE SPIEGEL, landscape contractor; b. Pitts., Mar. 24, 1940; d. Alvin Duane and Leah (Greenstein) Spiegel; m. Don Roy Horowitz, Jan. 31, 1960; children: Cindy H. Urbach, Thomas Samuel. Student, Carnegie Mellon U., 1958-61. Cert. interior horticulturist, landscape profl. Owner Carole Horowitz Interior Design, Pitts., 1965-72; pres. Plantscape, Inc., Pitts., 1973—. Chmn. U. Pitts. Small Bus. Com., 1986-92; bd. dirs. United Way Allegheny County, Pitts., 1991-94, Jr. Achievment Allegheny County, Pitts., 1985-95, Vocat. Rehab. Ctr., Pitts., 1989-91. Recipient Nat. Landscape award White House and Am. Assn. Nurseryman, 1990, YWCA Entrepreneur Leadership award, 1990; named Entrepreneur of Yr. Ernst & Young & Inc. Mag., 1988, Pitts. Bus. Times Pa.'s Best 50 Women in Bus. award 1997. Mem. Interior Plantscape Assn. (sec., v.p., 1982-85), Associated Landscape Contractor of Am. (cert.), Internat. Facility Mgmt. Assn., Rivers Club, Pitts., Westmoreland Country Club, Export, Pa., Rotary (sec. Downtown Pitts. chpt.). Jewish. Avocations: travel, golf. Office: Plantscape Inc 3101 Liberty Ave Pittsburgh PA 15201-1400 E-mail: ch@plantscape.com.

HOROWITZ, DAVID ALLEN, retired judge, mediator, arbitrator; b. Los Angeles, Aug. 2, 1942; s. George and Rose (Ratner) H.; m. Leslie Carol Halpern, Aug. 17, 1963; children: Deborah Ann, Janna Louise. BA in Econ., U. Calif., Berkeley, 1963; JD, UCLA, 1966. Bar: Calif. 1956, U.S. Dist. Ct. (cen. dist.) Calif. 1967. Pub. defender Los Angeles County, 1966-80, mcpl. judge, 1980-81, judge superior ct., 1981—2002; supervising judge Criminal Div. L.A. Superior Ct., 1988-90; mediation/arbitration pvt. judge L.A., 2002—. Chmn. Prof. Lecture series UCLA, L.A. County Task Force on Ct. Process, 1988-90; vice-chmn. Calif. Jury Instrns. Criminal Com.; mem. 2020 vis. com. Future of the Judiciary. Chair L.A. County Task Force on Drug Abuse, 1986— Recipient Jud. Excellence award Criminal Cts. Bar Assn., 1985. Mem. ABA (supervising judge criminal divsn., exec. com. nat. conf. state trial judges, nat. criminal justice standards 1978-79, chair nat. conf. state trial judges 1996-97, jud. divsn. coun. 1997—, jud. divsn. chmn. 2000-01, jud. divsn. to litigation sec. 1996—), Calif. Judges Assn., Am. Judicature Soc., L.A. County Bar Assn. (pres. barristers 1977-78, bd. trustees 1976-81), Phi Delta Phi. Address: 12508 Milbank St Studio City CA 91604 Office Fax: 818-985-7155. E-mail: dhoncho@earthlink.net.

HOROWITZ, DAVID CHARLES, consumer commentator, newspaper columnist; b. Bronx, N.Y., June 30, 1937; s. Marcus Lazar and Dorothy (Lippman) H.; m. Suzanne E. McCambridge, Aug. 26, 1973; children: Victoria, Amanda. BA, Bradley U., 1959; MS in Journalism, Northwestern U., 1961; CBS fellow, Columbia U., 1962-63; DHL (hon.), Bradley U., 2002. Editor in chief Tazewell County (Ill.) Newpaper, 1956; reporter Peoria (Ill.) Jour. Star, 1957-60, Lerner Newspapers and Chgo. City News Bur., 1959-60; newscaster Sta. KCCI Radio-TV, Des Moines, 1960-62; newswriter-producer ABC Radio Network, N.Y.C., 1963; Far East corr. NBC News, 1963-64; pub. affairs dir. Sta. WMCA, N.Y.C., 1965-66; corr., edn. editor, consumer commentator NBC News, Los Angeles, 1966-92; consumer affairs specialist CBS (KCBS-TV) News, 1993-95; syndicated columnist Creators Syndicate, L.A., 1986-99, eight books syndication, 1999—; creator, host, exec. producer syndicated TV show Fight Back! with David Horowitz, L.A., 1977-92; pres. Fight Back! Found. For Consumer Edn.; syndicated commentator Fight Back! Radio Reports, 1989—, Jones-Media Am., 1997—; syndicated consumer talk show Fight Back! Talk Back! Talk Radio Network, 2000—; commentator Sta. CNBC, 1990-96. Pres. Fight Back! Prodns., 1974—. Author: Fight Back and Don't Get Ripped Off, 1979, Business of Business, 1989, Fight Back! For Your Medical Health, vols. 1-4, 1993, Fight Back at Work, 1994; host, exec. prodr. Best Defense, 1993; exec. prodr. Fight Back at Work, 1994, CBS-TV Spl. Frog Girl: The Jenifer Graham Story (Genesis Animal Rights award 1990). Patron Los Angeles County Art Mus.; bd. dirs. Nat. Broadcast Editorial Conf., Am. Cancer Soc.; bd. advisers Los Angeles Jewish Home for Aged, Calif. div. Am. Cancer Soc.; adv. bd. Am. Heart Assn. Los Angeles County, UCLA Publs.; adv. bd. to Los Angeles County Dist. Atty.; bd. dirs. City of Hope; founder, bd. dirs. Fight Back! Found.; mem. charitable adv. com. City of L.A., 1991—; hon. bd. dirs. Caring Inst., Washington, 2000-; hon. mayor Brentwood Cmty., L.A., 1991-98; mem. consumer adv. com. FCC, Washington, 2003—. With USNR, 1954-62. Recipient Los Angeles City and County citation for pub. svc., 1979, 80, 81, 82, 83, 89, 92, Calif. State Legislature pub. svc. citation, 1980, 81, 82, 83, 91, 92, Spirit of Life award City of Hope, 1979, 1983, Chief U.S. Postal Insp.'s award, 1981, 93, Emmy awards for consumer reporting NATAS, 1974, 76-77, 81-86, 89, 90-95, L.A. Press Club award for consumer reporting, 1991, News Reporting award UPI, 1983, 94, Pub. Svc. award Social Security Adminstrn., 1987, medals N.Y. Internat. Film and TV Festival, 1984-86, Golden Mike award, 1986, 94, Armed Forces TV Network Svcs. award, 1988, Toastmasters Internat. Leadership award, 1991, Community Svc. award SBA, 1991, Excellence in Journalism award Nat. Homecare Assn., 1992, Disting. Alumni award Northwestern U., 1994, Cmty. Svc. award UCLA Ctr. Aging, 1995, AP News Reporting award, 1995, Angel award Excellence in Media, 1998, Golden Halo award Motion Picture Coun. So. Calif., 1998, Quality of Life award Proctor Health Care Found., 1998, Lifetime Achievement award Kern County Law Enforcement Found., 1999, Angel award for Outstanding Internet Website and Pub. Svc., 2002; named to Journalism Hall of Achievement, Northwestern U., 1997, L.A. Press Club Best TV Feature Reporting award, 1997. Mem. ASCAP, AFTRA, SAG, BMI, Am. Assn. Travel Agts. (Travelers Adv. award 1991), Broadcast Music, Inc., Internat. Radio-TV Soc., Radio-TV News Dirs. Assn., The Guardians, Soc. Consumer Affairs Profls., Nat. Futures Assn. (adv. bd.), Child Passenger Safety Assn., Ill. Broadcasters Assn. (Disting. Svc. award 1986), Screen Actors Guild, Newspaper Feature Creator's Assn., Writers Guild Am., Medill Journalism Sch. Alumni Assn. (pres. 1990-98), Friars Club, Overseas Press Am. Club (N.Y.C.), Alpha Epsilon Pi, Sigma Delta Chi, Phi Delta Kappa, Omicron Delta Kappa. Avocations: writing, gardening, theater, collecting serious music, collecting contemporary art. Mailing: PO Box 49915 Los Angeles CA 90049-0915 E-mail: dhorowitz@fightback.com. *Life is full of compromise, but to compromise principle is to give up your self-respect. I don't want anyone to take me for a sucker, and I don't like to see anyone else taken, either. A lot of things are unfair in life. It's tough; that's the way it is. But, by heaven, if you can do something about it, do it.*

HOROWITZ, DON ROY, landscape company executive; b. Pitts., Mar. 12, 1930; s. Samuel and Clara (Aberman) H.; m. Carole Spiegel, Jan. 29, 1960; children— Cindy Urbach, Thomas. BS, U. Pitts., 1952. Editor Pitts. Spectator mag., 1951-52; writer Fairchild Publs., 1952-53; pub. relations dir. Dubin. Feldman & Kahn. Inc., 1955-58; pres. Carlton Advt., Pitts., 1959-71, Corp. Communications Counselors, Pitts., 1962-71, Defensive Instruments, Inc., Tulsa, 1968-74, v.p., 1974-77; pres. Mut. Advt. Agy. Network, Mpls., 1969-70, Homehelp Unlimited, Inc., Pitts., 1969-73, Flashguard, Inc., Pitts., 1971-76, Showrooms-On-Wheels, Inc., 1976-77; v.p. Normda Industries, Inc., San Diego, 1969-72, Ednl. Crime Prevention Programs, Inc., Pitts., 1974-77, Plantscape, Inc., Pitts., 1987—. Bd. dirs., v.p. Lawrenceville Devel. Corp., Pitts.; bd. dirs. Phipps Conservatory, Pitts., treas., 1998-01. Chmn. Plants for Clean Air Coun., Reston, Va., 1988-97. Mem. Associated Landscape Contractors Am. (co-chmn., interior plantscape div. 1988-90, chmn. 1992-93). Clubs: Westmoreland (Pitts.), Rivers (Pitts.), Longboat Key Club (Fla.). Home: 5464 Darlington Rd Pittsburgh PA 15217-1506 Office: 3101 Liberty Ave Pittsburgh PA 15201-1415 E-mail: donh@plantscape.com.

HOROWITZ, DONALD LEONARD, lawyer, educator, researcher, political scientist, arbitrator; b. N.Y.C., June 27, 1939; s. Morris and Yetta (Hibscher) H.; m. Judith Anne Present, Sept. 4, 1960; children: Marshall, Karen, Bruce. AB, Syracuse U., 1959, LLB, 1961; LLM, Harvard U., 1962, AM, 1965, PhD, 1968. Bar: N.Y. 1962, D.C. 1979, U.S. Ct. Appeals (D.C., 6th, 7th and 10th cirs.) 1970, U.S. Supreme Ct. 1969. Law clk. U.S. Dist. Ct. (ea. dist.), Pa., 1965-66; rsch. assoc. Harvard U. Ctr. Internat. Affairs, 1967-69; atty. Dept. Justice, Washington, 1969-71; fellow coun. on Fgn. Rels./Woodrow Wilson Internat. Ctr. Scholars, Washington, 1971-72; rsch. assoc. Brookings Instn., Washington, 1972-75; sr. fellow Rsch. Inst. on Immigration and Ethnic Studies/Smithsonian, Washington, 1975-81; prof. law and polit. sci. Duke U., Durham, N.C., 1980—, Charles S. Murphy Prof., 1988-93, James B. Duke prof., 1994—. Vis. prof. Charles J. Merriam scholar U. Chgo. Law Sch., 1988; vis. fellow Cambridge U., Eng., 1988; Sticerd Disting. visitor London Sch. Econs., 1998-2000, Centennial prof., 2001; vis. scholar Universiti Kebangsaan Malaysia Law Faculty, 1991; Fulbright sr. specialist, 2002; cons. Ford Found., 1977-82; mem. internat. adv. com. Office of the High Rep., Bosnia, 1998-99; McDonald-Currie Meml. lectr. McGill U., Montreal, 1980; mem. Coun. on Role of Cts., 1978-83; Opsahl lectr. Queen's U., Belfast, 2000. Author: The Courts and Social Policy (Nat. Acad. Public Adminstrn. Louis Brownlow prize for best book in pub. adminstrn. 1977), 1977; The Jurocracy: Government Lawyers, Agency Programs and Judicial Decisions, 1977; Coup Theories and Officers' Motives, 1980, Ethnic Groups in Conflict, 1985, A Democratic South Africa? Constitutional Engineering in a Divided Soc., 1991 (Am. Polit. Sci. Assn. Ralph J. Bunche award for best book in ethnic and cultural pluralism, 1992), The Deadly Ethnic Riot, 2001; mem. editl. bd. Ethnicity, 1974-82, Law and Contemporary Problems, 1983-84, 89-2000, Jour. Democracy, 1993—. Guggenheim fellow, 1980-81; Nat. Humanities Ctr. fellow, 1984; Carnegie scholar, 2001-2002. Fellow Am. Acad. Arts and Scis. Office: Duke University School Law Durham NC 27708-0360

HOROWITZ, EDWARD JAY, lawyer; b. Milw., Feb. 13, 1942; s. Aaron and Sue Horowitz; m. Marcia Gold, Apr. 29,1990; children: Amy, Aaron. BA, UCLA, 1963; JD, Harvard U., 1966. Dep. atty. gen. Calif. Dept. Justice, L.A., 1966-69; ptnr. Goldhammer & Horowitz, L.A., 1969-72; sr. atty. Calif. Ct. Appeals, L.A., 1972-76; ptnr. Horvitz, Greines & Horowitz, Encino, Calif., 1976-78; pvt. practice L.A., 1978—. Author: (book) Appellate Practice Handbook, 1982. Fellow Am. Acad. Appellate Lawyers; mem. Calif. Acad. Appellate Lawyers (pres. 1985). Avocations: swimming, backpacking, skiing. Office: 1151 Bienveneda Ave Pacific Palisades CA 90272-2316 E-mail: horowitz@appellatelaw.com.

HOROWITZ, FEDORA COHEN, music educator, pianist; b. Iasi, Romania, Apr. 20, 1936; d. Arnold and Rachel Grimberg Cohen; m. Avraham D. Horowitz, Aug. 21, 1960; 1 child, Talya Horowitz Kupin. MM, Ciprian Porumbescu Conservatory, Bucharest, Romania, 1953—58. Piano tchr. Rubin Acad. of Music, Jerusalem, 1959—69, U. of N.C., 1969—73, U. of Mich., 1973—80; founder & artistic dir. Lyric Chamber Ensemble, Detroit, 1980—97, Mich. Piano Festival, Detroit, 1988—98; artistic dir. Chamber Music for Youth Camp, Detroit, 1991—97; piano tchr. Fla. Atlantic U. TOPS Camp, Boca Raton, 2001—. Permanent soloist/pianist Israel Broadcasting Orch., Jerusalem, 1963—69; soloist/pianist various symphony orchestras, NC, 1970—73, Mich., 1974—97. Author: (short stories) Oddisey, Tenth An. Sylvia Wolens Jewish Heritage Writing Competition (Third Pl. Prize - Stories Category, 2001), Eleventh An. Sylvia Wolens Jewish Heritage Writing Competition (1st Pl. Prize - Stories Category, 2002), Twelfth An. Sylvia Wolens Jewish Heritage Writing Competition (2nd Pl. Prize, Holocaust Category, 2003). Mem.: Music Teachers Assn., Hadassah, MADD, Am. Contract Bridge League. Home: 12601 Via Ravenna Boynton Beach FL 33436 Home Fax: 561-865-2289. Personal E-mail: TheOtherHorowitz@bellsouth.net.

HOROWITZ, FRANCES DEGEN, academic administrator, psychology educator; b. Bronx, NY, May 5, 1932; d. Irving and Elaine (Moinester) Degen; m. Floyd Ross Horowitz, June 23, 1953; children: Jason Degen, Benjamin Meyer Levi. BA, Antioch Coll., 1954; EdM, Goucher Coll., 1954; PhD, U. Iowa, 1959. Tchr. elem. sch., Iowa City, 1954-56; grad. rsch. asst. Iowa Child Welfare Sta., U. Iowa, 1956-59; asst. prof. psychology So. Oreg. Coll., Ashland, 1959-61; asst. prof. home econs. U. Kans., Lawrence, 1961-62, USHPS rsch. fellow, 1962-63, assoc. prof. dept. human devel. and family life, 1964-69, prof. dept. human devel. and family life, psychology, 1969—, chmn. dept., 1969-75, rsch. assoc., 1964-75, assoc. dean, 1975-78, vice chancellor rsch., grad. studies and pub. svc., also dean grad. sch., 1978-91, dir. Infant Rsch. Lab., 1964-91; pres. Grad. Sch. and Univ. Ctr. CUNY, 1991—. Bd. dirs. Feminist Press; guest rsch. assoc. Bur. Child Rsch. U. Kans., and Parsons (Kans.) State Hosp. and Tng. Ctr., summer 1960; vis. prof. dept. psychology Tel Aviv U., 1973—74; guest rschr. dept. pediat. Kaplan Hosp., Rehovot, Israel, 1973—74; vis. lectr. dept. psychology Hebrew U., Jerusalem, 1976, cons. rsch. programs in early edn., 1980—; pres. Ctr. for Rsch., Inc., Lawrence, 1978—91; cons. OAS, 1971, U.S. Office Edn., 1969—73, NIMH, 1979; cons. to early infant stimulation program, Caracas, Venezuela, 76; lectr. infant devel., day care to local and regional cmty. groups, 1966—; adv. com. Carolina Inst. on Early Edn. of the Handicapped, 1978—83; reviewer NSF, 1978—91; mem. U. Kans. del. to Peoples Republic China, 1980; exch. scholar Chinese Acad. Scis., China, 1982; mem. Office Sci. Integrity Rev. Adv. Com. PHS, 1991—93; nominating com. Weizmann Women in Sci. award Am. Com. Weizmann Inst. Sci., 1994; mem. Nat. Task Force Grad. Edn., 1994—; workforce devel. subcom. N.Y.C. Partnership, 1994—; mem. U.S. Nat. Com. for the Internat. Union of Psychol. Sci., 1995—97; mem. overseers' com. to visit dept. psychology Harvard U.; mem., founding adv. bd. Sackler Inst. for Human Brain Devel., 1998—; bd. dirs. Nat. Coun. for Rsch. on Women; adv. coun. Nat. Inst. Child Health and Human Devel., 1999—; chair nat. adv. bd. Office Child Devel., U. Pitts.; lectr. in field. Editor Memoir Essay, 2002; co-editor science watch sect. Am. Psychologist, 1993—; mem. editl. bd. Jour. Devel. Psychology, 1969-75, Early Childhood Edn. Quar., 1974—, Devel. Rev., 1981—, Infant Behaviour and Devel., 1984—, Contemporary Psychology, 1986-1991; contbr. articles to profl. jours.; TV host Women to Women, 1994—. Trustee Antioch Coll., 1987-91, L.I. Univ., 1992—; bd. dirs. Cmty. Children's Ctr., 1965-68, Douglas County Vis. Nurse Assn., 1968-69; mem. workforce devel. subcom., N.Y.C. Partnership; mem. coun. advisors, Nat. Ctr. for Children in Poverty; mem. commn. on women in higher edn. Am. Coun. on Edn. Recipient Trustees award medal Cherry Lawn Sch., Conn., 1971, Outstanding Educator of Am. award, 1973, Disting. Psychologist in Mgmt. award Soc. for Psychologists in Mgmt., 1993, Rebecca Rice Alumni award Antioch Coll., 1996, Sue Rosenberg Zalk award The Feminist Press, 2003; named to Women's Hall of Fame U. Kans., 1974; Ford Found. fellow, 1954, Ctr. for Advanced Studies Behavioral Scis. fellow, Stanford U., 1983-84; Spl. Commendation NYC comptroller's office, 1997, NY Women's Agenda Star award, 2002. Fellow APA (pres. divsn. devel. psychology 1977-78, mem. publs. bd. 1985-91, chief sci. adviser 1989-93, pres. 1991-94, Centennial award 1992), AAAS, N.Y. Acad. Scis.; mem. Soc. Rsch. in Child Devel. (editor monographs 1976-83, pres. 1997-2002), Jewish Cmty. Rels. Coun. (mem. bd. 1999—), Hebrew Free Loan Soc. (mem. bd. 2000—), Am. Assn. on Mental Deficiency, North Ctrl. Accrediting Assn. (bd. commrs. 1977-80), Am. Psychol. Found. (pres. 1991-94), Coun. Rsch. Polic and Grad. Edn. (chair, mem. exec. com.), Assn. Grad. Schs. (mem. exec. com.), N.Y. Women's Forum (bd. dirs. 1995—), Nat. Assn. of State Univs. and Lnd-Grant Colls. (past chair commn. on human resources and social change, bd. dirs. 1999-2002), Sigma Xi, Phi Beta Kappa (hon.). Home: 145 Central Park W Apt 4A New York NY 10023-2004 Office: CUNY Grad Ctr 365 5th Ave New York NY 10016-4309 E-mail: pres@gc.cuny.edu.

HOROWITZ, GEDALE BOB, investment banker; b. N.Y.C., June 13, 1932; s. Abraham and Florence (Bob) H.; m. Barbara Silver, Aug. 17, 1958; children: Ruth Ellen, Seth Robert. AB, Columbia U., 1953, JD, 1955. Bar: N.Y. 1956. With Salomon Bros., N.Y.C., 1955-67, gen. ptnr., 1967-81, mng. dir., 1981-87; exec. v.p., dir. Salomon, Inc., N.Y.C., 1981-97; sr. mng. dir. Salomon Smith Barney, 1997—. Vice chmn. bd. trustees Barnard Coll., 1976—; trustee and vice chmn. L.I. Jewish Hosp., 1982-98, chhmn., 1995-98; dir. Mspl. Assistance Corp., City of N.Y., 1989-94; bd. dirs. Jewish Cmty. Rels. Coun. on N.Y., Inc., 1989-2001, pres., 1998-2001; bd. dirs. Statue of Liberty-Ellis Island Found., Inc., 1999—; chmn. N.Y. State Local Govt. Assistance Corp., 1991-94; trustee, chmn. emeritus, exec. com. mem. North Shore/L.I. Jewish Health Sys., 1998—. Served with U.S. Army, 1956-58. Mem. Bond Market Assn. (chm. 1978-79), Securities Industry Assn. (treas. 19 87, chmn. 1991), Mcpl. Securities Rulemaking Bd. (chmn. 1977-78), Mcpl. Bond Club N.Y. (pres. 1982-83), The Bond Club of N.Y., Inc. (pres. 1994-95). Office: Salomon Smith Barney 388 Greenwich St Fl 39 New York NY 10013-2339

HOROWITZ, HARRY I. podiatrist; b. Astoria, N.Y., Nov. 8, 1915; s. Jacob and Fannie (Singer) H.; m. Sylvia Glaser, Feb. 11, 1940; children: Marc, Susan. *Sylvia G. Horowitz, D.P.M., wife of Harry Horowitz, D.P.M., graduated from St. Petersburg Junior College, 1934, earned the podiatry certificate (Pod.G.) from the First Institute of Podiatry, 1937, doctor of podiatry degree (Pod.D) from Long Island University, 1952, doctor of podiatric medicine degree (D.P.M.) from NY College of Podiatric Medicine, 1967. She practiced podiatric medicine from 1937-75 in Queens County, NYC She was born Sylvia Glaser and resided in St. Petersburg, Florida, 1925-37. She is a 70 year member of the Order of the Eastern Star, St. Petersburg chapter and is a 27th year member of the Sisterhood Temple Bnai Israel, Clearwater, Fla. She is a weaver of tapestries. Her mother was Zena C. Levy and her father was John Glaser.* Student, CCNY, 1932-34; Pod.G, First Inst. Podiatry, N.Y.C., 1937; D in Podiatry, L.I.U., 1946; D.P.M., N.Y. Coll. Podiatric Medicine, 1967; LHD (hon.), 1982. Diplomate Am. Bd. Ambulatory Foot Surgery (hon.). Pvt. practice specializing in podiatry, Astoria, N.Y., 1937-76, Belleair, Fla., 1976-95; ret., 1995. Mem. podiatry practice com. Workmen's Compensation Bd. N.Y. State, 1953-66, chmn. com., 1966-76; dir. Foot Clinics of N.Y., 1970-71; chmn. bd. Suncoast Orthotic Labs., Clearwater, Fla., 1978-83; podiatry panel Dept. Welfare N.Y.C.; arbitrator between Am. Bd. Foot Surgery and Am. Bd. Ambulatory Foot Surgery, 1982; cons. Sch. Podiatric Medicine Barry U., 1988-89. With citizens com. Union Free Sch. Dist. 29, Merrick, N.Y., 1957; mem. library com. dist. 29, 1964; founder Fund for Advancement Podiatry Edn., 1958; hon. pres. Fund for Podiatry Edn. and Rsch., 1963-94, sec., 1963-66; chmn. Task Force on Podiatry, Health and Hosp. Corp., N.Y.C., 1976-78; trustee N.Y. Coll. Podiatric medicine, 1973-74, cons., 1981-84; chmn. Commn. to Study and Evaluate Foot Clinics of N.Y., 1980-81; chmn. ADL, Clearwater Lodge, 1985-87, B'nai Brith, Fla. Vol. tutor North Sch. Pinellas County Schs., Fla., 1987-98. With U.S. maritime Svc., 1943-45. Named Podiatrist of Yr., Queens County Podiatry Soc., 1956, 1971, Podiatry Soc. State N.Y., 1957, 1961, Disting. Practitioner, Nat. Acad. Practice, 1992; recipient, Jour. Podiatry, 1948, testimonial, N.Y. Coll. Podiatric Medicine, 1971, Queens County Podiatry Soc., 1976, Apple from the Tchr. award, Pinellas Classroom Tchrs., 1989, 1990, Cert. of Appreciation, Am. Podiatric Med. Assn., 1990, Centennial award, N.Y. State Podiatric Med. Assn., 1995, Hon. Founder award, Fund for Podiat. Med. Edn., 2001. Mem. APHA (emeritus), ACLU, Am. Podiatric Med. Assn. (exec. coun., trustee 1955-62, award 1963, Disting. Svc. award 1982, Spl. Svc. award 1983), Am. Assn. Hosp. Podiatrists, Fla. Pub. Health Assn. (chmn. podiatric sect. 1983-85), Acad. Podiatry, Physicians for Social Responsibility, Nat. Peace Found., Masons, B'nai B'rith (Outstanding Svc. award 1988). Home: 100 Oakmont Ln Clearwater FL 33756-1984

HOROWITZ, HERBERT EUGENE, retired diplomat; b. Bklyn., July 10, 1930; s. Max and Jean (Pomerantz) Horowitz; m. Lenore Joan Glasser, Jan. 6, 1963; children: Jason, Richard. BA, Bklyn. Coll., 1952; MA, Columbia U., 1964, Fletcher Sch. Law & Diplomacy, 1965; diploma, Nat. War Coll., 1972. Econ. officer Am. Embassy, Taipei, Taiwan, 1957-62; chief China econ. unit U.S. Consulate, Hong Kong, 1965-69; chief comml. and econ. sect. U.S. Liaison Office, Beijing, 1973-75; dir. Office for Rsch. of East Asia Dept. State, Washington, 1975-78; dir. Office East-West Econ. Policy Dept. Treasury, Washington, 1979-80; consul gen. U.S. Consulate Gen., Sydney, Australia, 1981-84; dep. chief of mission U.S. Embassy, Beijing, 1984-86; amb. to Republic of Gambia, 1986-89. Lectr. history China, cons. Mem.: Am. Fgn. Svc. Assn., Dacor-Bacon Ho. Home and Office: 2737 Devonshire Pl NW # 111 Washington DC 20008-3454

HOROWITZ, IRVING LOUIS, publisher, educator; b. N.Y.C., Sept. 25, 1929; s. Louis and Esther (Tepper) H.; m. Ruth Lenore Horowitz, 1950 (div. 1964); children: Carl Frederick, David Dennis; m. Mary Curtis Horowitz, 1979. BSS, CCNY, 1951; MA, Columbia U., 1952; PhD, Buenos Aires U., 1957; fellow, Brandeis U., 1958-59. Asst. prof. sociology Bard Coll., 1960; assoc. prof. social theory Buenos Aires U., 1955-58; chmn. dept. sociology Hobart and William Smith Colls., 1960-63; from assoc. prof. to prof. sociology Washington U., St. Louis, 1963-69; chmn. dept. sociology Livingston Coll., Rutgers U., 1969-73; prof. sociology grad. faculty Rutgers U., 1969—, Hannah Arendt prof. social and polit. theory, 1979—, Bacardi chair Cuban studies, 1992—. Vis. prof. sociology U. Caracas, Venezuela, 1957, Buenos Aires U., 1959, 61, 63, SUNY, Buffalo, 1960, Syracuse U., 1961, U. Rochester, fall 1962, U. Calif., Davis, 1966, U. Wis., Madison, 1967, Stanford U., 1968-69, Am. U., 1972, Queen's U., Can., 1973, Princeton U., 1976, U. Miami, 1992; vis. lectr. London Sch. Econs. and Polit. Sci., 1962; prin. investigator for numerous sci. and rsch. projects; chmn. bd. dirs., editor-in-chief Transaction/Soc. Author: Idea of War and Peace in Contemporary Philosophy, 1957, Philosophy, Science and the Sociology of Knowledge, 1960, Radicalism and the Revolt Against Reason: The Social Theories of Georges Sorel, 2d edit., 1968, The war Game; Studies of the New Civilian Militarists, 1963, Historia y Elementos de la Sociologia del Connocimento, 1963, Professing Sociology: The Life Cycle of a Social Science, 1963, The New Sociology: Essays in Social Science and Social Values in Honor of C. Wright Mills, 1964, Revolution in Brazil: Politics and Society in a Developing Nation, 1964, The Rise and Fall of Project Camelot, 1967, rev. edit., 1976, Three Worlds of Development: The Theory and Practice of International

Stratification, 1966, rev. edit., 1972, Latin American Radicalism: A Documentary Report on Nationalist and Left Movements, 1969, Sociological Self-Images, 1969, The Knowledge Factory: Masses in Latin America, 1970, Cuban Communism, 1970, 11th edit., 2003, Foundations of Political Sociology, 1972, Social Science and Public Policy in the United States, 1977, Dialogues on American Politics, 1979, Taking Lives: Genocide and State Power, 1979, 5th edit., 2001, Beyond Empire and Revolution, 1982, C. Wright Mills: An American Utopian, 1983, Winners and Losers, 1985, Communicating Ideas, 1987, Daydreams and Nightmares, 1990 (winner best biography Nat. Jewish Book Award), The Decomposition of Sociology, 1993, Behemoth: Main Currents in the History and Theory of Political Sociology, 1999, Veblen's Century: A Collective Portrait, 2002. Chmn. bd. Hubert H. Humphrey Inst. Ben Gurion U.; bd. mem. Alexis DeTocqueville Inst., 2003—. Recipient Harold D. Lasswell award Policy Sci. Orgn., Lifetime Achievement award Inter-Univ. Seminar on Armed Forces and Society. Fellow AAAS; founding mem. AAAS Sci and Human Rights Program; mem. AAUP, USIA (bd. advisors), Am. Polit. Sci. Assn., Nat. Assn. Scholars (bd. dirs.), Authors Guild, Ctr. for Study The Presidency, Coun. Fgn. Rels., Internat. Soc. Polit. Psychology (founder), Soc. Internat. Devel., U.S. Gen. Acctg. Office (exec. adv. bd.), U.S. Info. Agy. (exec. adv. bd. Radio and TV Marti), Nat. Assn. Scholars (bd. dirs.), Inst. for a Free Cuba. Achievements include Subject of Festschrift: The Democratic Imagination, 1994. Home: 1247 State Rd # Rt206 Princeton NJ 08540-1619 Office: Rutgers U Transaction Pubs Bldg 4051 New Brunswick NJ 08903 Fax: 732-445-3138. E-mail: ihorowitz@transactionpub.com.

HOROWITZ, JACK, biochemistry educator; b. Vienna, Nov. 25, 1931; came to U.S., 1938; s. Joseph and Florence (Gutterman) H.; m. Carole Ann Sager, June 11, 1961; children— Michael Joseph, Jeffrey Frederick. BS, CCNY, 1952; PhD, Ind. U., 1957. Rsch. assoc. Columbia U., N.Y.C., 1957-61; asst. prof. biochemistry Iowa State U., Ames, 1961-65, assoc. prof. biochemistry, 1965-71, prof. biochemistry, 1971-95, Univ. prof., 1995-2000, Univ. prof. emeritus, 2000—, chmn. dept. biochemistry, 1971-74, chmn. molecular, cellular and devel. biology program, 1977-80. Vis. scholar Rockefeller U., N.Y.C., 1968; vis. prof. Yale U., 1974-75; vis. scientist MIT, 1990-91; program dir. biophysics and biochemistry NSF, 1993-94. Contbr. articles to profl. jours. NSF fellow, 1952-54, 57-59; NIH and NSF grantee, 1961—; recipient faculty citation Iowa State U., 1989. Mem. RNA Soc., Am. Soc. Biochemistry and Molecular Biology, AAAS, Phi Beta Kappa, Sigma Xi, Phi Kappa Phi Jewish. Home: 2014 Country Club Blvd Ames IA 50014-7013 Office: Iowa State U Dept Biochemistry Biophys Ames IA 50011-0001

HOROWITZ, KENNETH A. communications executive, entrepreneur; AB cum laude, Cornell U., 1973. One of original founders Cellular One; lead investor S. Fla. Soccer, L.L.C., Ft. Lauderdale; owner, operator various cellular phone bus. ventures, U.S.; banking, real estate, comm. and tech. entrepreneur. Bd. dirs. pvt. and pub. cos. Achievements include pioneer work in the wireless telephone industry. Office: care Miami Fusion FC 2200 W Commercial Blvd Ste 104 Fort Lauderdale FL 33309-3058 Fax: 954-733-6105.

HOROWITZ, KENNETH P. lawyer; b. N.Y.C. s. Philip and Roslyn Horowitz. BA, SUNY, Brockport, 1977; MA in Internat. Rels., Georgetown U., 1984; JD, Bklyn. Law Sch., 1987. Bar: NY 88, Conn. 88. Mem. firm Goldberg Weprin & Ustin LLP, N.Y.C.; pres. 130 Hicks St Owners Corp., Bklyn., 1987—. Mem. ABA, Assn. Bar of City of N.Y. Home: 123 Pierrepont St Brooklyn NY 11201-2759 Office: Goldberg Weprin & Ustin LLP 1501 Broadway Fl 22 New York NY 10036-5686 E-mail: kphorowitz@gwulaw.com.

HOROWITZ, LEE JERALD, psychologist; b. Cleve., Dec. 24, 1942; s. Carl Lawrence and Gertrude (Stark) H.; m. Sheila Anita Goldstock Bossin, Apr. 4, 1965 (div. June 1985); children: Jordan, Ronna; m. Karen Yetta Feigenbaum, Mar. 28, 1991. BA, John Carroll U., 1967, MA, 1969; PhD, U. Akron, 1975. Lic. psychologist, Ohio. Tchr. St. Stephen's H.S., Cleve., 1967; psychologist Orange Bd. Edn., Pepper Pike, Ohio, 1969-72, Beachwood (Ohio) Bd. Edn., 1972-81; pvt. practice Beachwood, 1969—. Instr. psychology John Carroll U., University Heights, Ohio, 1969-91, Cuyahoga Cmty. Coll., Cleve., 1969-81; mem. scholarship com. Matrix Hair Essentials, Soldon, Ohio, 1981—; spkr., lectr. in field. Radio host talk show Sta. WQRC, Cleve., 1989-92. Mem. APA, Psi Chi. Jewish. Avocations: golf, bowling, coin collecting, raising german shepherds, racketball. Office: 23250 Mercantile Rd Beachwood OH 44122-5928

HOROWITZ, MARY CURTIS See CURTIS, MARY

HOROWITZ, MICHAEL DORY, cardiothoracic surgeon; b. Dec. 1, 1954; BS, U. Miami, 1977, MD, 1981. Diplomate Am. Bd. Surgery, Am. Bd. Thoracic Surgery. Resident in surgery then surgeon U. Miami/Jackson Meml., 1981-86, 88-92; fellow in thoracic and cardiovascular surgery Alton Ochsner Med. Found., New Orleans, 1986-88; asst. prof. surgery U. Miami, 1988-92; med. dir. cardiac surgery Singing River Hosp., Pascogoula, Miss., 1993—. Office: 4211 Hospital St Ste 302 Pascagoula MS 39581-5318

HOROWITZ, MICHAEL M. university educator; b. N.Y.C., Nov. 2, 1933; m. Sylvia Gordon Huntley, Sept. 14, 1955; children: Andrew Jesse, Stephanie Ruth, Daniel Benjamin. BA, Oberlin Coll., 1955; MA, Columbia U., 1956, PhD, 1959. Faculty, SUNY-Binghamton, 1961—, prof. anthropology, 1969—, disting. prof. anthropology, 2002; dir. Inst. for Devel. Anthropology, Binghamton, 1976—; sr. social sci. advisor The World Bank, Washington, 1977—, AID, 1973—, UN, Rome, Geneva, N.Y.C., 1975, 80, 82; advisor U.S. Congress Office Tech. Assessment, 1985—; mem. program adv. com. Overseas Devel. Coun., 1984—; mem. devel. program rsch. com. UN, 1990—. Author: Morne Paysan, 1967; Manga of Niger, 1972; author/editor: Peoples/Cultures Caribbean, 1971; co-editor: Anthropology of Rural Development in West Africa, 1986, Lands at Risk in the Third World, 1987, Anthropology and Devel. in North Africa and the Middle East, 1990, Morne Payson: Peasant Village in Martinque, 1992, Pastoral Women and Change in Africa, the Middle East, and Central Asia, 1992, Les Barrages de la Controverse, 1994, Ethnicity and Socioeconomic Vulnerability in Pakistan, 1995, Environment and Society in the Lower Mekong Basin, 1999. Fulbright Rsch. prof. U. Bergen, Norway, 1966. Fellow Am. Anthropol. Assn., Soc. for Applied Anthropology (exec. bd. 1982-84); mem. Sudan Studies Assn. (exec. bd.), Sigma Xi, Phi Beta Kappa. Address: Inst for Devel Anthropology 99 Collier St Binghamton NY 13901-3421

HOROWITZ, MORRIS A. retired economics educator; b. Newark, Nov. 19, 1919; s. Samuel and Anna (Litwin) H.; m. Jean Ginsburg, July 12, 1941; children— Ruth, Joel. BA in Econs., NYU, 1940; PhD in Econs., Harvard U., 1954. Mem. faculty Northeastern U., Boston, 1956—, prof. econs., chmn. dept., 1959-90, prof. emeritus, 1992—. Vice-chmn. Mass. Joint Labor-Mgmt. Com. for Mcpl. Police and Fire, 1980—; ad hoc labor arbitrator, manpower cons. Home: 1010 Waltham St Apt 341 Lexington MA 02421-8064

HOROWITZ, RAYMOND J. lawyer, director; b. N.Y.C., May 7, 1916; s. Israel S. and Sadye (Freiman) H.; m. Margaret Goldenberg, Sept. 22, 1940; 1 dau., Judith. AB, Columbia U., 1936, LL.B., 1939. Bar: N.Y. 1939. Pvt. practice, N.Y.C., 1939-41; asst. corp. counsel City of N.Y., 1941-43; assoc. Meyer, Wallach & Silverson, N.Y.C., 1943-46; ptnr. McGoldrick, Dannett, Horowitz & Golub and predecessors, N.Y.C., 1946-69; former mem., now of counsel firm Graubard Miller and predecessors, 1969—. Cons. Nat. Housing Agy, 1946-47, Office Housing Expediter, 1947, Temporary State Housing Rent Commn., 1950-51 Author: (with others) Building Regulation in New York City, 1944. Chmn. trustees' vis. com. on Am. paintings and sculpture Met. Mus. Art. Mem. Assn. Bar City N.Y., N.Y. County Lawyers Assn., Phi Beta Kappa. Clubs: Century Assn. Home: 930 Fifth Ave New York NY 10021-2651 Office: Graubard Miller 600 3d Ave New York NY 10016-1901

HOROWITZ, ROSALIND, education educator, researcher; b. St. Paul, Aug. 24, 1946; d. Cantor Louis and Fannie (Hartman) H. BS, U. Minn., 1968, MA, 1973, PhD, 1982; postgrad., Harvard U., 1968, Hebrew U., Jerusalem, 1971. Tchr. English Marshall-Univ. High Sch., Mpls., 1969-70; instr. edn. U. Minn., Mpls., 1970-75, supr. of student tchrs., 1972-75, adminstrv. fellow for assoc. dean Coll. Edn., 1975-81, research coordinator edn. planning and devel. office, 1975-81; affiliate mem. Ctr. for Research in Human Learning, 1979-81; prin. tchr. Hebrew and Judaic studies program Adath Jeshurun Religious Sch., Mpls., 1972-76; asst. prof. reading, edn. Coll. Social and Behavioral Scis. U. Tex., San Antonio, 1981-85, assoc. prof., 1986-95, prof. reading and literacy edn., 1995—, prof. edn. Coll. Soc. and Behavioral Scis., 1995—. Rsch. coord. Coll. Social and Behavioral Scis., 1991-93; lectr. in field; rschr. text processing, text linguistics, discourse analysis; cons. in field; participant Bryn Mawr Summer Inst. for Women in Higher Edn. Adminstrn., 1992; vis. scholar Ont. Inst. Studies in Edn., U. Toronto, Can., 2003, dir. Hillel at U. Tex. San Antonio, 1987—. Contbr. 10 chpts. to books, 60 articles to profl. jours. including Harvard Ednl. Review, Australian Jour. Remedial Edn., Jour. of Reading, The Reading Tchr., Instrnl. Sci., Jour. Reading, The Reading Behavior, Nat. Reading Conf. Yearbook, Ednl. Rschr. and Contemporary Psychology, Nat. Assn. Bilingual Edn. Jour., Lang. Learning, Jour. Adolescent and Adult Reading, Hispanic Jour. Behavioral Scis., Jour. of Reading, Jour. Ednl. Rsch.; editor: Talking Texts: Knowing the World Through Instructional Discourse, 2000; co-editor: Comprehending Oral and Written Language, 1987; spl. editor (text) Studies of Orality and Literacy, 1991; guest editor Jour. of Reading, Classroom Talk about Text, 1994; reviewer: Applied Psycholinguistics Child Development, Jour. Ednl. Psychology, Reading Research Quar., Jour. Reading Behavior, Jour. of Reading, Rsch. in the Tchg. of English, Jour. of Reading; editl. adv. bd. Nat. Reading Conf. Yearbook, 1984—; mem. editl. bd. Discourse Prosesses, Written Comm. Rsch. in Tchg. of English, 1979—, Nat. Reading Conf. Yearbook, 2002-03; acquisition editor AERA, Reading and Literacy; co-author: (chpts.) Beliefs about Text and Instruction with Text, 1994, Composing Social Identity in Written Language, 1995, (with D. Olson) Texts that talk: The special and peculiar nature of classroom discourse, 2003, What Should Teachers Know About Bilingual Learners and the Reading Process? (with A. Cohen), 2002. Mpls. Coun. PTA Scholar, 1964; U. Minn. Nicholson Bookstore Scholar, 1965; HEW-U. Minn. grantee 1966, 67; Harvard U. Scholar, 1968; selected to visit Russia and Ukraine Nat. Security Edn. Program, 1998; Wesley E. Peik scholar, U. Minn., 1979; Doctoral Dissertation Spl. grantee, 1979; U. Tex. rsch. grantee, 1984; Spencer fellow Nat. Acad. grantee, 1984; Spencer fellow Nat. Acad. Edn., 1985-88; Tex. Assn. Gifted and Talented fellow, 1993; Soref Fund grantee Hillel Found., 1998, Leader Fund grantee, 1998; recipient Gender and Equity Recognition award Am. Assn. Colls. Tchr. Edn., 1994, Outstanding Alumni, Gordon M.A. Mork award Coll. Edn. U. Minn., 2002. Mem. Internat. Assn. Applied Linguistics, Nat. Coun. Tchrs. English (Promising Rsch. 1983, Student Govt. award 1995), Am. Assn. Higher Edn., Am. Edn. Rsch. Assn. (sec.-treas. lang. and social processes 1990, pres. chair, chair basic rsch. and reading literacy 1991-94, chair Russian contbns. to literacy learning and human devel., program chair divsn. chair learning and instrn. 1994-95, assoc. chair spl. interest group basic rsch. in reading and literacy 1997-98, chmn. reunion contbns. to literacy and learning), Internat. Reading Assn. (Outstanding Dissertation award 1983), Nat. Reading Conf., Soc. Text and Discourse (exec. bd.), Soc. for Sci. Study of Reading, N.Y. Acad. Scis. (linguistics dir.). Office: U Tex Coll Edn and Human Devel Downtn Campus 501 Durango Blvd DB 3 224 San Antonio TX 78207 E-mail: rhorowitz@utsa.edu.

HOROWITZ, SAMUEL BORIS, biomedical researcher, educational consultant; b. Perth Amboy, N.J., Aug. 26, 1927; s. Sol and Lillian (Levine) H.; m. Joan Hughes, June 15, 1956 (div. 1971); m. Marian Sylvia Herman, May 23, 1973 (div. 1986), 1 child, Ann Julia AB, Hunter Coll., N.Y.C., 1951; PhD, U. Chgo., 1956. Research assoc. Eastern Pa. Psychiat. Inst., Phila., 1958-62; vis. investigator Inst. Physiol. and Med. Biophysics U. Uppsala, Sweden, 1962-63; head lab. A. Einstein Med. Ctr., Phila., 1963-72; chief cellular physiology lab. Mich. Cancer Found., Detroit, 1972-93, chmn. dept. biology, 1975-78, chmn. dept. physiology and biophysics, 1981-93. Contbr. articles to profl. jours. Served with U.S. Army, 1946 47 Fellow AAAS; mem. Am. Assn. Cancer Research, Am. Soc. Cell Biology, Sigma Xi. Home and Office: 4159 Woodland Dr Ann Arbor MI 48103-9775 E-mail: sbg3210@aol.com.

HOROWITZ, SARA, labor organizer; b. N.Y.C., Jan. 13, 1963; BS, Cornell U., 1984; MA, SUNY, Buffalo, 1992; MPA, Harvard U., 1995. Labor organizer Working Today. Grantee, fellow Stern Family Fund. Rockefeller Found., Echoing Green. Office: Working Today PO Box 1261 Old Chelsea Box Sta New York NY 10113

HOROWITZ, SHEL, writer, marketing consultant; b. N.Y.C., Dec. 24, 1956; s. Norman Aaron Horowitz and Gloria Gleich Yoshida; m. D. Dina Friedman, Oct. 9, 1983; children: Alana, Rafael. BA, Antioch Coll., 1977. Cmty. organizer N.Y. Pub. Interest Rsch. Group, Bklyn., 1979-80; dir. Accurate Writing & More, Northampton and Hadley, Mass., 1981—. Cons. numerous cos. and non-profits, 1977—, Ragan Strategic Mktg. Conf., Chgo., 2001, Bay Area Ind. Pubs. Assn., San Rafael, Calif., 2001; spkr. in field. Author: Marketing without Megabucks: How to Sell Anything on a Shoestring, 1993, The Penny-Pinching Hedonist: How to Live Like Royalty with a Peasant's Pocketbook, 1995, Grassroots Marketing: Getting Noticed in a Noisy World, 2000, Principled Profit: Marketing That Puts People First, 2003; co-author: Nuclear Lessons, 1980. Organizer Clamshell Alliance, Providence, 1977; bd. dirs. Homesharing in Hampshire County, Northampton, 1985-90, Valley Trade Connection, 1997-99; mem. Dist. Atty.'s Civil Rights Adv. Bd., Northampton, 1985-90; founder Save the Mountain, Hadley, 1999—. Mem. Pubs. Mktg. Assn. (regional organizer 1998—, spkr. 1998, 2000, 2001, 2002), Nat. Writers Union (regional organizing com. 1983-95, spkr. 1987-97). Jewish. Avocations: social change, travel, reading, cultural activities, hiking. Office: Accurate Writing & More PO Box 1164 Northampton MA 01061

HOROWITZ, STEPHEN PAUL, lawyer; b. L.A., May 23, 1943; s. Julius J. and Maxine (Rubenstein) H.; m. Nancy J. Shapiro, Apr. 4, 1971; children: Lindsey Nicole, Keri Lyn, Deborah Arielle. B.S., UCLA, 1966; J.D., 1970; M. Acctg., U. So. Calif., 1967. Bar: Calif. 1971, U.S. Dist. Ct. 1971, U.S. Ct. Appeals 1972. CPA, Calif. Bookkeeper, various law and acctg. firms, 1963-70; staff acct. Touche, Ross & Co., C.P.A.s, L.A., 1968, 69. Pvt. practice law, L.A., 1971-77; partner firm Horowitz & Horowitz, L.A., 1978-79, prin. firm, 1979—; judge pro tem L.A. Mcpl. Ct.; classroom speaker L.A. County Bar Assn.; arbitrator Better Bus. Bur., L.A. County Bar Assn., Am. Arbitration Assn., L.A. Superior Ct.; ombudsman VA, 1970. Bd. dirs. Vols. Am. Detoxification and Rehab. Center, L.A., 1975-81, treas., 1979, vice chmn., 1980-81; legal adv. chmn., parliamentarian Temple Ramat Zion, Northridge, Calif., 1983-88, v.p., 1988. Served with U.S. Army, 1961 62. Mem. Calif. State Bar, L.A. Trial Lawyers. Jewish. Lodge: Masons. Editorial bd. UCLA-Alaska Law Rev., 1968-70, co-editor-in-chief, 1969-70. Office: 8383 Wilshire Blvd Ste 528 Beverly Hills CA 90211-2404

HOROWITZ, STEVEN F. cardiologist; MD, N.Y. Med. Coll., 1972. Diplomate Am. Bd. Internal Medicine with subspecialty in cardiovasc. disease. Resident medicine Beth Israel Med. Ctr., 1976; fellow medicine Mount Sinai Hosp., N.Y.C., 1978-79; attending physician cardiovasc. disease Beth Israel Med. Ctr., N.Y.C. Clin. prof. medicine and nuc. medicine Albert Einstein Coll. Medicine; dir. cardiology dept. Stamford Hosp., Conn. Home: 250 Rosedale Ave 1st Ave 16th St White Plains NY 10605 Fax: 212-420-4222.

HOROWITZ, WINONA LAURA See RYDER, WINONA

HORR, WILLIAM HENRY, retired lawyer; b. Portsmouth, Ohio, Sept. 23, 1914; s. Charles Chick and Effie (Amberg) H.; m. Marjorie Bell Marshall, Aug. 31, 1940; children— Robert W., Thomas M., Catherine, James C., Elizabeth; m. 2d Wilma Crawford, Mar. 12, 1988. AB, Ohio Wesleyan U., 1936; JD, U. Cin., 1939. Bar: Ohio 1939. Practice in, Portsmouth, 1939-42, 45-99; atty. Skelton, Kahl, Horr, Marshall & Burton, 1939-42, 45-78; spl. agt. FBI, Louisville, Indpls., Newark, 1942-45; substitute judge Mcpl. Ct., Portsmouth, 1955-80, gen. counsel Ohio Wesleyan U., 1966-70. Mem. Portsmouth Bd. Edn., 1947-60; pres. Portsmouth YMCA.; trustee Ohio U. Portsmouth Br., Shawnee State C.C., 1975-80, Ohio Wesleyan U., 1953-68; chmn. bd. Hill View Retirement Ctr., 1973-85. Recipient Disting. Svc. award Portsmouth Jr. C. of C., 1947. Mem. Ohio Bar Assn. (past mem. exec. com.), Portsmouth Bar Assn. (past pres.), Phi Delta Phi, Phi Kappa Psi, Omicron Delta Kappa, Rotary (past pres.). Republican. Methodist. Home: 1732 Hillview Cir Portsmouth OH 45662-2673

HORRELL, JEFFREY LANIER, library administrator; b. Carbondale, Ill., Sept. 19, 1952; s. C. William and Ettelye M. (Hanser) H. BA, Miami U., Oxford, Ohio, 1975; AM in Libr. Sci., U. Mich., 1976, MA, 1978; PhD, Syracuse U., 1995. Libr. intern Nat. Gallery of Art, Washington, 1977; asst. libr. art and architecture U. Mich., Ann Arbor, 1977-80; libr. Sherman Art Libr./Dartmouth Coll. Libr., Hanover, N.H., 1981-86; Coun. Libr. Resources libr. mgmt. intern Syracuse (N.Y.) U. Libr., 1986-87, asst. to univ. libr. for planning, 1987-88, asst. univ. libr. pers., budget and planning, 1988-92; libr. Fine Arts Libr. Harvard Coll. Libr., Cambridge, 1992-98; assoc. libr. Harvard Coll. Collections, Cambridge, 1998—. Pres. ARLIS/NA, 1987. Author: Treasures of the Hood Museum of Art, 1985; contbr. articles to profl. publs. Mem. ALA, Coll. Art Assn., Art Libr. Soc. N.Am. (pres. 1987-88), U. Mich. of Info. Studies Alumni Soc. (pres. 1997-98). Avocations: travel, photography. Office: Harvard Coll Libr Rm 193 Widener Library Cambridge MA 02138 E-mail: horrell@fas.harvard.edu.

HORROCKS, NORMAN, library and information scientist, educator, editor; b. Manchester, Eng., Oct. 18, 1927; s. Edward Henry and Annie (Barnes) Horrocks; m. Sandra Sheriff, Feb. 3, 1967; children: Julie Carol, Carl Scott, Gina Louise, Anne Patricia, Sarah Helen. ALAA, Libr. Assn. Australia, 1957; BA, U. Western Australia, 1960; MLS, U. Pitts., 1964, PhD, 1971. Asst. libr. Manchester Pub. Librs., 1943-45, 50-53; libr. Brit. Coun., Cyprus, 1954-55; tech. libr. State Libr. We. Australia, 1956-61; tchg. fellow U. Pitts., 1963-64, instr., 1964-69, asst. prof., 1969-71; assoc. prof. Sch. Libr. Sci., Dalhousie U., Dartmouth, Canada, 1971-73, prof., 1973-86, dir. sch., 1972-86, dean Faculty Mgmt. Studies, 1983-86, prof. emeritus, 1995—. Vis. lectr. Perth Tech. Coll., 1961—63, U. Hawaii, 1969; ext. lectr. Pa. State Libr., 1966—70; chmn. Overseas Book Ctr., Halifax, 1980—83; mem. adv. bd. sci. and tech. info. Nat. Rsch. Coun. Can., 1980—86; mem. adv. bd. com. bibliog. svcs. Nat. Libr. Can., 1980—86; v.p. editl. Scarecrow Press, Metuchen, NJ, 1986—95; adj. prof. Rutgers U., 1987—95; editl. cons., Lanham, Md., 1995—; mem. promotion and distbn. panel Can. Coun. Editor: N. We. Newsletter, 1952—53, Jour. Edn. Librarianship, 1971—76; assoc. editor: Govt. Publ. Rev., 1973—81; contbr. articles to profl. jours. Bd. visitors Pratt Inst. Rutgers U. With Brit. Army, 1945—48. Recipient Merit award, Atlantic Provinces Libr. Assn., 1979, Disting. Alumnus award, U. Pitts., 1982. Fellow: Chartered Inst. Libr. and Info. Profls., Libr. Assn. (U.K.) (hon.); mem.: ALA (coun. 1972—81, exec. bd. 1977—81, coun. 1983—95, various coms., Lippincott award 1995, Forest Press award), Progressive Librs. Guild, N.J. Libr. Assn. (Disting. Svc. award coll. and univ. sect. 1995), Australian Libr. and Info. Assn., Assn. Am. Libr. Schs. (chmn. editl. bd. 1971—76), Assn. Libr. and Info. Sci. Edn. (pres. 1985—86, v.p., Svc. award 1990, Profl. Contbns. award 1996), N.S. Libr. Assn. (life), Intelligence Corps Assn. (life), Can. Coun. Libr. Schs. (chmn. 1974—76), Halifax Libr. Assn., Can. Libr. Assn. (2d v.p. 1978—80, various coms., Outstanding Svc. to Librarianship award 1995), Am. Inst. Parliamentarians, Am. Soc. Info. Sci. (various coms.), Bibliosmiles, Archons of Colophon (convenor 1992), Beta Phi Mu (pres. 1991—93). Home: 2 Casavechia Ct Dartmouth NS Canada B2X 3G6 Office: PO Box 440 Dartmouth NS Canada B2Y 3Y5 E-mail: Norman.Horrocks@Dal.Ca.

HORSAGER, KENT, brokerage house executive; BS in agrl. econ., U. Minn.; MS in agrl. econ., U. Calif., Davis. Pres. Horsager Trading Co., 1987—; bd. dirs. Mpls. Grain Exch., 1991—, bd. chmn., 1996—99, CEO and pres., 2000—. Oilseed and product mcht. Cargill, Inc., Internat. Oilseed Processing Group; econ. lectr. U. Mainz, Germersheim, Germany; mktg. cons. Superior Farming Co., Germersheim, Germany. Office: Mpls Grain Exch 400 S 4th St Minneapolis MN 55415*

HORSBRUGH, PATRICK, architect, educator, environologist; b. Belfast, No. Ireland, June 21, 1920; came to U.S., 1960; s. Charles Bethune and Marion Rose (McQueen) H. Diploma with honors, Archtl. Assn. Sch. Architecture, 1949; diploma city planning, U. London, 1951. With Raglan, Squire and Ptnrs., London, 1956-57; vis. critic Harvard Grad. Sch. Design, 1956; with depts. architecture, planning and landscape architecture univs. Ill., N.C., 1957-58; dep. dir., then dir. Hamilton-Wentworth (Ont.) Planning Area Bd., 1958-60. Vis. prof. architecture U. Nebr., 1960-65, U. Tex., 1965-67; prof. architecture U. Notre Dame, 1967-84, prof. emeritus, dir. grad program environic studies, 1970-80; founder, chmn. bd. Environic Found. Internat., Inc., 1970-94; cons. environ. and planning issues, ednl. and design practices; adj. prof. dept. architecture Andrews U., Mich. Designer: High Paddington Project, London, 1951; co-designer: New Barbican Com. Project, London, 1954; contbr: Winston Churchill Meml. in the U.S. commemorating the Iron Curtain Speech given in Fulton, Mo.; author: High Buildings in the United Kingdom, 1952, Pittsburgh Perceived, The Form, Features and Feasibilities of the Prodigious City, 1963; editor: The Texas Conference on Our Environmental Crisis, 1966. Co-chmn. Internat. Earth Day, 1978; v.p. Channel Tunnel Assn., 1974-94; mem. Ind. curriculum adv. coun. Ind. Bd. Edn., 1986; Earth trustee Earth Soc. Found. With Royal Arty., 1938-41; with RAF Vol. Res., 1941-46. Bernard Webb fellow Academica Britannica, Rome, 1950; B.Y. Morrison Meml. lectr. U.S. Dept. Agr., 1969. Fellow AIA (regional and urban design com.), Royal Soc. Arts, Royal Geog. Soc., Brit. Interplanetary Soc.; mem. AAAS, Royal Inst. Brit. Architects, Royal Town Planning Inst., Am. Planning Assn., Ancient Monument Soc., Soc. Indsl. Archaeology, Soc. Protection Ancient Bldgs, Georgian Group, Nat. Trust (Gt. Britain), Am. Soc. Landscape Architects (hon.), Am. Soc. Interior Designers (hon.), Irish Georgian soc., Ry. Devel. Soc., Christopher Wren Soc. (founder, London 1995), No. Ireland Partnership. Address: 916 Saint Vincent St South Bend IN 46617-1443

HORSCH, LAWRENCE LEONARD, venture capitalist, corporate revitalization executive; b. Mpls., Dec. 2, 1934; s. Leonard Charles and Cecilia May (Chamberlain) H.; m. Kathleen Joanne Simmer, Aug. 25, 1956; children: Daniel Lawrence, Timothy John, Christopher Girard, Catherine Jessica, Sarah Elisabeth. BA with honors, Coll. St. Thomas, 1957; MBA, Northwestern U., 1958. Investment banker Paine Webber Jackson & Curtis, Mpls., 1961-67; v.p. N.Am. Fin. Corp., Mpls., 1967-71; pres. Eagle Investment Corp., Mpls., 1971-87; chmn., CEO Munsingwear Inc., Mpls., 1987—90; chmn. bd. Eagle Mgmt. & Fin. Corp., Mpls., 1990—. Chmn. bd. dirs. Sci. Med. Life Sys., Maple Grove, Minn., 1971-94; bd. dirs. Boston Sci. Corp., Leuthold Funds, Inc., Gillette Specialty Heatlhcare. 1st lt. USAF, 1959-61. Mem. Fin. Analysts Fedn., Mpls. Rotary, Minikahda Country Club. Home: 1404 Hilltop Rdg Saint Joseph WI 54082-2013 Office: Eagle Mgmt & Fin Corp PO Box 235 Stillwater MN 55082-0235

HORSEMAN, BARBARA ANN, church musician, voice educator; b. Clinton, Iowa, Nov. 29, 1935; d. Ted Rex and Lillian Mae (Bean) Smith; m. William F. Horseman, Dec. 26, 1963; children: Megan, Jill. Diploma, Cottey Jr. Coll. for Women, Nevada, Mo., 1955; MusB, U. Mo., Kansas City, 1957, MusM, 1958, postgrad., 1958-61. Dir. chancel choir Zion United Ch. of Christ, Kansas City, Kans., 1957—, dir. founder 4 handbell choirs, 1989—, founding mem., officer 3-C Circle, 1981-83, mem., past pres. adult fellowship, 1963-93, co-sponsor youth group, 1981-83, dir. jr. and sr. high sch. choirs, 1979-80, supt. Sunday sch., 1986-88. Pvt. tchr. voice and piano, Kansas City, 1963—; pre-school tchr., Kansas City, 1991—; vocal and keyboard tchr. Hill Top Dance Ctr., 1992—99; dir. children's choirs Kansas City Dance Theatre Co., 1992—; vocal, keyboard tchr. Starstruck Dance Studio, Tonganoxie, Kans., 1997—. Pres. Philharm Aux., Kansas City, 1975 76; pres. Creative Experiences, Kansas City, 1983; pres. PTA, 1970-72, bd. dirs., 1973-81, now life mem. Mem. Guild English Handbell Ringers, Choristers Guild, Cottey Coll. Alumnae Assn. (bd. dirs. 1963-75, nat. pres. 1973-74), Mozart Music Club, P.E.O. (pres. Kansas City 1975-77), Mu Sigma Epsilon, Delta Psi Omega, Sigma Alpha Iota. Home: 3233 N 85th Pl Kansas City KS 66109-1024 Office: Zion United Ch of Christ 2711 N 72nd St Kansas City KS 66109-1738 E-mail: Bandbhorseman@aol.com.

HORSEMAN, NELSON DOUGLAS, molecular and cellular physiology educator; b. Dayton, Ohio, Sept. 30, 1951; s. Adrian Douglas and Rachel Lucille (Frady) H.; children: Kyle Douglas, David Nelson. BS, Ea. Ky. U., 1973, MS, 1975; PhD, La. State U., 1978. Lectr. Oakton C.C., Des Plaines, Ill., 1978-80; asst. prof. Marquette U., Milw., 1980-86, assoc. prof., 1986-89, dir. biol. & biomed. rsch., 1987-89; dir. grad. studies U. Cin., 1989-96, assoc. prof., 1989-92, prof. molecular & cellular physiology, 1992—, prof. dept. medicine, 1996—, chmn. dept. molecular cell physiology, 2002—. Contbr. articles to profl. jours. Grantee Rsch. grantee, NIH, 1990—95, 1992—98, 1998—, Shriner's Hosps., 1997—, Charlotte Geyer Found., 2000—02. Mem. AAAS, Am. Soc. Biochem. & Molecular Biology, Am. Soc. Microbiology, Endocrine Soc. Democrat. Avocations: canoeing, motorcycling, bird hunting. Office: U Cin Box 670576 231 Albert Sabin Way Cincinnati OH 45229-2827

HORSEY, DAVID, editorial cartoonist; b. Evansville, Ind., Sept. 13, 1951; m. Nole Ann Ulery; children: Darielle Jean, Daniel Rayden. BA in Comms., U. Wash., 1976; MA in Internat. Rels., U. Kent, Canterbury, Eng., 1986. Formerly govt. reporter, polit. columnist Wash. State Capitol; polit. reporter, columnist, editl. cartoonist Daily Jour.-Am., Bellevue, Wash., 1976-79; editl. cartoonist, columnist, mem. editl. bd. Seattle Post-Intelligencer, 1979—. Syndicated Tribune Media Svcs., 1986-89, 2000—, King Features/N.Am. Syndicate, N.Y.C., 1988-2000; instr. Acad. Realist Art, Seattle, 1998; propr. Horsey-Words and Picturs, Seattle, 1993—. Author: Politics and Other Perversions, 1974, Horsey's Rude Awakenings, 1981, Horsey's Greatest Hits of the '80s, 1989, The Fall of Man, 1994, One Man Show, 1999; co-editor: (anthology) Cartooing AIDS Around the World, 1992; exhibited cartoons at Art Inst. Seattle, 1992, Michael Pierce Gallery, Seattle, 1997, Shoreline C.C., 1999, others. Asst. coach North Ctrl. Little League Baseball, 1992-94; youth coach Woodland Soccer Club, 1989-98; chmn. campaign for excellence St. Benedict Elem. and Mid. Sch., 1991-93, pres. sch. commn., 1993-95. Recipient 1st place Best of the West Journalism Competition, 1995, Environ. Media award, 1995, Global Media award Population Inst., 1991, Berryman award Nat. Press Found., 1998, Pulitzer prize for editl. cartooning, 1999, 2003, numerous others. Mem. Soc. Profl Journalists (12 1st place regional awards, Susan Hutchinson Bosch award 1999), Assn. Am. Editl. Cartoonists (pres.-elect 1999-2000, pres. 2000-01). Office: Seattle Post Intelligencer PO Box 1909 101 Elliott Ave W Ste 200 Seattle WA 98119-4295 E-mail: davidhorsey@seattle-pi.com.*

HORSLEY, JACK EVERETT, lawyer, writer; b. Sioux City, Iowa, Dec. 12, 1915; s. Charles E. and Edith V. (Timms) H.; m. Sallie Kelley, June 12, 1939 (dec.); children: Pamela, Charles Edward; m. Bertha J. Newland, Feb. 24, 1950 (dec.); m. Mary Jane Moran, Jan. 20, 1973; 1 child, Sharon. AB, U. Ill., 1937, LLB, JD, 1939, Med./Legal Doctorate, 2001. Bar: Ill. 1939. Instr. Sch. of the Solder, U. Ill. ROTC, 1934, 68, 89, 98; temp. prof. law NYU, 1974, 90, 99, 2000—03; mem. Harlan Moore Heart Rsch. Found., 1968—, asst. treas., 1996—; mem. lawyers adv. coun. U. Ill. Law Forum, 1992—96, 1999—2001, 2001—03; lectr. Practicing Law Inst., N.Y.C., 1967—73, 1993—94, U. Ill., Champaign, 1974, Ct. Practice Inst., Chgo., 1988—2000, Coll. Law Inst. Continuing Legal Edn., U. Mich., 1967, Bankers' Seminar, 1999, 2000, Banker's Seminar, 2002, 03; vis. lectr. Orange County (Fla.) Med. Soc., 1985, San Diego Med. Soc., 1970, 89, lectr., 96, vis. lectr. U. S.C., 1976, 98, Duquesne Coll., 1970, U. Ill. Law Forum and Student Adv. Com., 1984—96; alumni adv. com. U. Ill. Law Forum, 1991—2001; vis. lectr. trial practice NYU Coll. Law, 1972, 94; vis. lectr. faculty banker seminar Wis. Med. Assn., Lake Geneva, 1997; lectr. med./legal seminars on tour Chgo., Cleve., Pa., Orlando, 1995; chmn. rev. bd. Ill. Supreme Ct. Disciplinary Commn., 1973—76, adv. cons., 1976—2003, chmn. emeritus, 2002—; lectr. Cleve. Hosp., Shelby, NC, 1976; vis. prof. trial practice Fordham Law Sch., N.Y.C., 1989—96; vis. prof. U. Berkeley Coll. Law, 1999, vis. prof, 2002; vis. lectr. John Marshall Sch. Law, Chgo., 1999—2003; vis. lectr. trial practice U. Nebr. Law Sch., 1999—2001, Columbia U., N.Y.C., 1999; vis. lectr. Trial Practice Columbia U., NY, 1999—2002; Trial Laureate Ill. Trial Lawyers Acad., 1996, Laureata-emeritus, 2000. Narrator Poetry Interludes, Sta. WLBH-FM, 1977—91; author: Trial Lawyer's Manual, 1967, Voir Dire Examinations and Opening Statements, Real Estate Foreclosuers, 1968, Current Development in Products Liability Law, 1969, Illinois Civil Practice and Procedure, 1970, 2d edit., 2000, The Medical Expert Witness, 1973, Testifying in Court, 1973, Testifying in Court, 4th edit., 1992, Testifying in Court, supplement 4th edit, 1993, The Doctor and the Law, 1975, The Doctor and Family Law, 1975, The Doctor and Business Law, 1976, The Doctor and Medical Law, 1977, Anatomy of a Medical Malpractice Case, 1984, Anatomy of a Medical Malpractice Case, 2d edit., 1993, Heartstrings of the Mind, 1998, My Brother and I, 1999, Trilogy: The Frivolous Law Suit, 2000, Lincoln the Lawyer, 2002, Lincoln-Circuit Lawyer, 2002, U.S. Civil War, Its Military Personnel, 2d edit., 2002, My Father and I, 2003, (municipals) G.O. of Revenue, 1992, World War II, D-Day, 1994, World War II, D-Day, 2d edit., 1998, (co-founder) Life's Challenges Preparation, 1999, (municipals) World War II Air Mus, Duxford, Eng., 1999, Trial Techniques, 1995, Trial Techniques, 3d edit., 2003, Legal Liability Exposure of Trust Co., 1996, Legal Liability Exposure of Trust Co., 2d edit., 1999, On Trust Dept. Guide-lines and Risks, 1996, On Federal Evidence and Examination, 1995, 1996, 1997, Memories of World War II in the European Theater, 1997, 1999, suppl. on post World War II Reserve officer duties, 2000 (USAF Cross, Def. Disting. Svc. WWII Victory medal, 1945, European Theatre Svc. medal, 1943, Judge Advocate Spl. award, 1944, Spl. Svc. medal Rsch. Officer Assn., 1999, Disting. Svc. award USAF Law Dept., 1950), suppl. on post World War II Reserve officer duties, 2d edit., 2001, addendun to 2d edit., 2003, History of the Bar in East Central Illinois, 1997, Remembrances: An Autobiography, 1998, Remembrances: An Autobiography, 2d edit., 2000, Views of Christianity: Origin of Man, 1999, (pamphlet) A Doctor's Duty: Presciption Care, 1999, Thoughts to Ponder, 2001, Heartstrings of the Mind, 2003; co-author: RN Legally Speaking, 1998, Matthew Bender Forensic Sciences, 1988, Matthew Bender Forensic Sciences, 3d edit., 2003; editor: Fifty Eight Years as Attorney, 1997, Fifty Eight Years as Attorney, 3d update, 2003; legal cons. Mast-Head, 1972—; contbr. Forensic Scis. Texts and Treatises, 1981, Forensic Scis. Texts and Treatises, 2d edit., 1999, Fed. Evidence Rules, 1996, Fed. Evidence Rules, 1998, Fed. Evidence Rules, 2000, Fed. Evidence Rules, 2d term, 2001, Cross-Exam Techniques and Potential Traps, 1996, 2d edit., 2002, Eagle Forum (On Pro-Life), Alton, Ill., 1999, Christianity: The Origin of Man Creationism vs. Darwinism, U. Ill. Law Rev., 2000, Selected Poems, Interludes of Poetry, 2001; cons., reviewer Civil Practice State and Fed. Cts., 1998—2001, Thoughts to Ponder, 2001; author: (pamphlet) Thoughts to Ponder, 2d edit., 2002, Thoughts to Ponder, 3d edit.; reviewer Current Developments in Medical Malpractice Law; editl. cons.: Med. Econ., 1969—. Alt. del. to Rep. Platform Com., 2000; active Senatorial Reelection Com., 1993; mem. exec. com. Ill. Rep. Election Campaign, 1997; founding mem. U.S. Supreme Ct. Hist. Soc.; pres. bd. edn. sch. dist. 100, 1946-48; bd. dirs. Harlan Moore Heart Rsch. Found., 1968-91, hon. dir., 1991—; vol. reader in rec. texts Am. Assn. for Blind, 1970-72, 97-98; chmn. exec. com. U. Ill. Law Forum, 1990-91, chair emeritusm 1998-2003; founding mem. Home for Law Alumni Found., Chgo., 1998-99; pres. Res. Officers Assn. East Cen. Ill., 1988-89, 99-2000, pres. emeritus 2001-2003, chair, bd. dirs., 2000-2002; founder Bertha Newland Horsley award St. John's Coll. Nursing, Springfield, Mary Jane Horsley award trophy Mattoon (Ill.) H.S.; mem. exec. com. Ill. Rep. Election Campaign, 1997. Brig. gen. hon. res., ret., 1997; tournament judge Big Ten Debating Contest, 2001, tech. advisor, 2002; mem. U.S. Supreme Ct. Bar, 1980-99. Recipient Disting. Svc. award U. Ill., 1995. Fellow Am. Coll. Trial Lawyers (co-chair membership comm. 1998, 2000, acting regent 2000-01); mem. ABA, Ill. Bar Assn. (exec. coun. ins. law 1961-63, com. chmn. banking law 1972, lectr. law course for attys. 1962, 64-65, sr. counsellor 1989—, Disting. Svc. award 1982-83), Assn. of Bar of City of N.Y. (non-resident), Coles-Cumberland Bar Assn. (v.p. 1968-2000, pres. 1969-70, pres. emeritus 1971—, chmn. com. jud. inquiry 1976-80, chair meml. com. 1989-2000, mem. exec. com. 1998, sr. counsellor 1989, co-author Forensic Scis. Jour. 1991, 2d edit. 1999, Life-time Achievement award 1999), Am. Arbitration Assn. (nat. panel arbitrators, counsel advisor hearing officers in Ill. 1996-97), U. Ill. Law Alumni Assn. (life mem., pres. 1966-67, Alumni of Month Sept. 1974, exec. com. 1990-91, Sr. Alumni of Month 2001), Ill. Appellate Lawyers Assn. (editl. cons. 2002), Soc. Legal Scribes (chair emeritus 1995-2002), Ill. Def. Counsel Assn. (pres. 1967-88, chair adv. bd. 1989—, pres. emeritus 1998–), Soc. Trial Lawyers (chmn. profl. activities 1960-61, bd. dirs. 1966-67, 88-94), Fed. Ct. Hist. Soc. (co-chmn.), Adelphic Debating Soc. (judge of intramural debating U. Ill. 1999), Assn. Ins. Attys., Internat. Assn. Ins. Counsel, Am. Judicature Soc., Res. Officers Assn. (pres. 1997-98, chair exec. com., pres. emeritus 2002, hon. brig. gen. JAGD 1997), U. Ill. Alumni Assn. (exec. com. 1990-91), Masons (lectr. ceremonial 32 degree Scottish Rite 2000, 03, Sr. Master award 1992), Scabbard and Blade Soc. U. Ill. (pres. 1936, pres. emeritus 1998–, bd. dirs. 1993—), Delta Phi (exec. com. alumni assn. 1960-61, 67-68), Sigma Delta Kappa. Lutheran. Home: 913 N 31st St Mattoon IL 61938-2271 *Engrossment in acquiring material possessions is a secondary pursuit. Seeking intangibles may well bring greater rewards and a more enduring legacy.*

HORSLEY, PAULA ROSALIE, accountant; b. Smithfield, Nebr., Sept. 7, 1924; Student, AIB Bus. Coll., Des Moines, 1942-44, YMCA Coll., Chgo., 1944-47, UCLA Extension, 1974. Acctg. mgr. Montgomery Ward & Co., Denver, 1959-62; acct. Harman & Co., CPAs, Arcadia, Calif., 1962-67; contr., officer G & H Transp., Montebello, Calif., 1967-78; comptroller Frederick Weisman Co., Century City, Calif., 1978-80; CFO, Luth. Shipping, Madang, Papua New Guinea, 1980-82; prin. village bookkeeper, acctg. cons. Moreno Valley, Calif., 1982-94; CFO, Insight Computer Products and Tech., Inc., San Gabriel, Calif., 1988—. Vol. crisis counselor, supr. and instr. Melodyland Hotline, Anaheim, Calif., 1997-79. Home: 1440 Brentwood Way Hemet CA 92545-7774 Office: Insight Computer Products and Techs Inc 171 Hazel Way San Gabriel CA 91776-3236

HORSLEY, RICHARD DAVID, banker; b. 1942; With FDIC, Washington, 1964-66, Ernst and Ernst, N.Y.C., 1966-72; compt. 1st Ala. Bancshares Inc., Montgomery, 1972-77, v.p., compt., 1977-82; vice chmn., exec. fin. officer Regions Fin. Corp., Birmingham, Ala., 1982—, also bd. dirs. Office: Regions Fin Corp 417 20th St N Birmingham AL 35203-3203

HORSLEY, WALLER HOLLADAY, lawyer; b. Richmond, Va., July 2, 1931; s. John Shelton Jr. and Lilian (Holladay) H.; m. Margaret Stuart Cooke, Dec. 3, 1955; children: Margaret Terrell, Stuart W., John Garrett. BA with distinction, U. Va., 1953, LLB, 1959. Bar: Va. 1959, U.S. Dist. Ct. (ea. dist.) Va. 1959, U.S. Tax Ct. 1959, U.S. Ct. Appeals (4th cir.) 1959, U.S. Supreme Ct. 1969. Ptnr. Hunton & Williams, Richmond, 1965-92, Horsley & Horsley, Richmond, 1992—. Lectr. taxation U. Va. Law Sch., 1961-65, 69. Mem. editorial bd. Taxation for Lawyers, 1975-86, Probate Lawyer, 1976-87, Probate Notes, 1976-87, editor, 1986-87; bd. advisors Va. Tax Rev., 1981—; contbr. articles to legal jours. Mem. adv. coun. Sch. Bus., Va. Commonwealth U., 1983-91; sr. warden St. Stephen's Episcopal Ch., 1977-79; gen. conv. dep. Diocese of Va., 1979, 85; pres. Richmond Tennis Patrons Assn., 1969, Va. Silver Star Found., 1985-86; mem. bd. visitors U. Va., 1988-92, The Cmty. Found. (sec. bd. govs. 2000—). With USN, 1953-56; to lt. comdr. USNR, 1956-62. Recipient Algernon Sydney Sullivan award, 1953; named Outstanding Young Man of Yr., Richmond Jr. C. of C., 1965. Fellow Am. Bar Found., Va. Bar Found.; mem. ABA, Va. State Bar (pres. 1982-83), Va. Bar Assn., Am. Coll. Trust and Estate Counsel (pres. 1990), Country Club of Va., Westwood Club, Omicron Delta Kappa, Phi Beta Kappa, Order of Coif. Democrat. Episcopalian. Office: Horsley & Horsley 5012 Monument Ave Richmond VA 23230-3632 E-mail: horsleylaw@aol.com.

HORSMAN, DAVID A. ELLIOTT, writer, financial services executive, educator; b. Calvert County, Md., June 28, 1932; s. Alvin W. and Bessie L. (Elliott) H. Student, U. Chgo.; BA, San Francisco State U., 1964; MA, NYU, 1967, PhD, 1970; MDiv, Episc. Div. Sch., 1984. Fl. dir., stage mgr. WTOP-TV, Washington, 1959-61; TV writer/producer Insight, Nat. Coun. Chs., Washington, 1961-62; English master, dir. studies Searing Sch., N.Y.C., 1965-67; asst. prof. humanities Acad. Aeros., Flushing, N.Y., 1967-68; instr. humanities Rensselaer Poly. Inst., Troy, N.Y., 1969-70; assoc. prof., founder and coord. film sequence U. South Fla., Tampa, 1970-80; headmaster All Hallows Acad., Alexandria, Va., 1985-87; pres. Elliott Horsman & Assocs., 1988-89; fin. cons. Shearson Lehman Hutton, Inc., Balt., 1989-91; investment broker RAF Fin. Corp., Atlanta, 1991-92; exec. Josepthal, Lyon & Ross, Atlanta, 1992-93; v.p. Meyers, Pollock & Robbins, Atlanta, 1992-97; pres. Horsman Bros., Inc., 1998—. Adj. prof. Union Grad. Sch., Yellow Springs, Ohio, 1976—; chmn. bd. of fellows All Hallows Hall, 1998—. Author: The Liturgy as Communication, 1970, Introduction to Structural Description of Liturgical Dromena, 1979, (novel and screenplay) Pilgrims on Strange Strands, 1979. With U.S. Army, 1957-59. Recipient Founders Day award NYU, 1971.

HORSMAN, LENORE LYNDE (ELEANORA LYNDE), soprano, educator, actress; b. Saginaw, Mich., Apr. 21, 1931; d. George Clark and Gwendolyn (Steele) McNabb; m. Reginald Horsman, Sept. 3, 1955; children: John, Janine, Mara. BS in Music and Piano, Ind. U., 1956, MA in Theatre-Opera, 1958. profl. certs. in voice, Villa Schifanoia, Florence, Accademia Musicale Chigiana, Siena, Accademia Di Virgiliana, Mantua, Mozarteum, Salzburg. Tchrs: Tito Gobbi, Ettore Campogalliani. Dir. Mt. Clemens Studio of Music, Mich., 1950; tchr. voice, piano and acting for singers Milw. Conservatory of Music, 1964-65; dir., tchr. pvt. voice studio, 1965—; founder, dir., designer Milw. Opera Theater, 1966; vocal coach dept. opera U. Wis., Madison, 1969-70. Dir., performer Cameo Prodn., Milw., 1974, Opera for Two, Milw., 1975, Mu Phi Epsilon Sch. Music, Chgo., 1976-81; dir., tchr. pvt. voice studio, Chgo., 1976-92; voice coach Theatre X, Milw., 1977; tchr. of acting Northshore Theatre, Milw., 1978-80. More than 33 leading roles in opera, operetta, musicals and plays; performances and concerts in US and Italy. Pres. Wis. Women in the Arts, 1973-76; bd. dir. Internat. Women's Yr. Festival, Milw., 1975. Named Women of the Yr., Milw. Panhellenic Assn., 1975; recipient Career Achievement award, 1978, Singers medal of honor Amici della Lirica, Mantua, Italy, 1981, Palcoscenico Music Vocal Silver Stage award, 1981. Mem. AAUW (v.p. 1999-2000), Nat. Assn. Tchr. Singing, Nat. Opera Assn., Wis. Music Tchr. Assn., Mu Phi Epsilon, Theta Alpha Phi. Avocations: theater, opera, oil painting, writing poetry.

HORST, BRUCE EVERETT, manufacturing company executive; b. Three Rivers, Mich., Feb. 17, 1921; s. Walter and Genevieve (Turner) H.; m. Patricia Kranish, Oct. 4, 1969; children: Michael, Diane, Mark. BS in Bus. and Engring. Adminstrn, Mass. Inst. Tech., 1943. With Barber-Colman Co., Rockford, Ill., 1946-76, pres., 1965-75, vice chmn. bd., 1975-76; pres. Mid-States Screw Corp., 1976—. Bd. dirs. Rockford YMCA, 1964-75, pres., 1965-67. Served to 1st lt. USAAF, 1943-45. Decorated Air medal. Mem. Rotary, Univ. Club (Rockford), Rockford Country Club, Moorings Country Club (Naples), Yacht Club at Lake Geneva (Wis.) Office: Mid-States Screw Corp 1817 18th Ave Rockford IL 61104-7399 Home: 1802 Birchwood Ln Rockford IL 61107 E-mail: msscrewco@aol.com.

HORST, CAROLYN DIANE, accountant; b. Balt., May 20, 1945; d. Norman Kramer and Helen Louise (Gover) Lindner; m. William Earnshaw Horst, Jr., Sept. 7, 1968; children: Michelle L., Cynthia E., Julie A. BS in Acctg. magna cum laude, U. Balt., 1968. Staff acct. J.T. Coughlin, C.P.A., Bel Air, Md., 1968-69; controller GM&W Coal Co., Greencastle, Pa., 1969-77, Crunkleton Elec. Co., Greencastle, 1979-82; acct. pvt. practice, Greencastle, 1982—. Assoc. dir. First Nat. Bank, Greencastle, 1984—, pres. assoc.'s bd., 1986. Pres. Greencastle C. of C., 1984; bd. dirs. Habitat for Humanity, Franklin County, Pa., 2002—. Mem. Nat. Assn. Pub. Accts., Nat. Assn. Tax Practitioners, Jobs Daus. (past Bethel guardian, Bethel 26), Rotary (v.p. Greencaste chpt.). Mem. Christian Ch. (Disciples Of Christ). Avocations: cooking, reading. Home: 13613 Paradise Church Rd Hagerstown MD 21742-2427 Office: Carolyn Horst Acct 32 E Baltimore St Greencastle PA 17225-1202

HORST, DEENA LOUISE, state legislator; b. Sacramento, Feb. 14, 1944; s. Orlo John and Louise Helena (Schultze) Poovey; m. Gordon Lee Horst, 1966; children: Randall, Rebecca. BSE, Emporia State U., 1966, MA, 1972; postgrad., Kans. State U., 1993—. Elem. tchr. Peabody Sch., 1966-68; mid. sch. art tchr., dept. chmn. South Mid. Sch., Unified Sch. Dist. # 305, 1968—; mem. from dist. 69 Kans. State Ho. of Reps., 1995—. Vice chmn. Kans. 2000 com.; chmn. e-govt. com., vice chmn. higher edn. com., chmn. arts and cultural resources joint com. Kans. House of Reps. State and nat. ofcl. U.S. Jaycee Women, 1968-84; sec. Saline County Rep. Ctrl. Com., Kans., 1992-95. Named Outstanding State Pres., U.S. Jaycee Women, 1979-80; co-recipient Master Tchr. award State of Kans., 1991. Mem. C. of C., Phi Alpha, Alpha Theta Rho, Phi Delta Kappa, Epsilon Sigma Alpha (Zone Outstanding Sister award 1990). Republican. Address: 920 S 9th St Salina KS 67401-4806

HORST, PAMELA SUE, medical educator, family physician; b. Hershey, Pa., Jan. 23, 1951; d. Ralph H. and Helen (Fry) H.; m. Thomas H. Dennison, Feb. 6, 1982; 1 child, Elizabeth Dennison. BS, Pa. State U., 1972; MD, Pa. State U., Hershey, 1976. Diplomate Am. Bd. Family Practice, Am. Bd. Hospice & Palliative Medicine (cert). Resident in family practice Shadyside Hosp., Pitts., 1979; family physician North Jefferson Health Svcs., Clayton, N.Y., 1979-82; physician emergency rm. Geisinger Med. Ctr., Philipsburg, Pa., 1982-84; asst. prof. family medicine Albany (N.Y.) Med. Coll., 1984-88; assoc. prof. health sci. ctr. SUNY, Syracuse, 1988—. Med. dir. family practice ctr. St. Joseph's Hosp. Health Ctr., Syracuse, 1989—, assoc. residency dir. family practice residency, Syracuse, 1990—; physician Palliative Care Cons. Svc., 1999—, hospice physician, 2002—; chmn. St. Joseph's Health Alliance, 1995-97, SyraHealth, IPA, 1997-98. Author: (with others) Ambulatory Medicine, 1993, Manual of Family Practice, 1996. Mem. Am. Acad. Family Physicians, Soc. Tchrs. Family Medicine, Am. Assn. of Hospice and Palliative Medicine. Avocations: gardening, reading. Office: St Joseph's Health Ctr Family Practice Residency 301 Prospect Ave Syracuse NY 13203-1899

HORST, SAMUEL LEVI, history educator, researcher, writer; b. Lancaster, Pa., July 18, 1919; s. Elmer Kuhns and Katie (Buckwalter) H.; m. Sarah Elizabeth Good, July 19, 1948 (dec. Aug. 1991); children: Kenneth, Hannah, Sylvia, Barbara, Mary, Carol; m. Mary Ellen Stutzman, Mar. 18, 1995. BA in Social Scis., Goshen Coll., 1949; MA in History, Am. U., 1962; PhD in History, U. Va., 1977. H.s. tchr. Eastern Mennonite H.S., Harrisonburg, Va., 1949-50, 50-51, 54-55, 59-60; tchr. Eastern Mennonite Coll., Harrisonburg, Va., 1962-84, prof. emeritus history, 1984—. Author: Mennonites in the Confederacy, 1967, Education for Manhood, 1987; editor: The Fire of Liberty in their Hearts, 1996; co-editor: Conscience in Crisis, 1979. Mem. Harrisonburg/Rockingham Bicentennial Commn., Harrisonburg/Rockingham Coun. on Human Rels. Grantee NEH, 1979; fellow Johns Hopkins U., 1969, Inst. for Editing of History, Nat. Hist. Publs., 1981. Mem. Va. Hist. Soc., So. Hist. Assn., Peace History Soc., Harrisonburg/Rockingham Hist. Soc., Mennonite Hist. Soc., Shenandoah Valley Mennonite Historians. Home: 857 Old Furnace Rd Harrisonburg VA 22802-6004

HORSTMANN, JAMES DOUGLAS, college official; b. Davenport, Iowa, Oct. 2, 1933; s. Leonard A. and Agnes A. (Erhke) H.; m. Carol H. Griffiths, Sept. 8, 1956; children: Kent, Karen, Diane. BA, Augustana Coll., 1955. C.P.A., Ill., Wis. Staff acct., auditor Arthur Andersen & Co., Chgo., 1955-61; v.p., controller Harry S. Manchester, Inc., Madison, Wis., 1961-65; sr. v.p. fin., treas. H. C. Prange Co., Sheboygan, Wis., 1965-83, also dir.; dir. planned giving Augustana Coll., Rock Island, Ill., 1983-85, v.p. for devel., 1985-93, v.p. planned giving, 1993-98, v.p. emeritus, 1998—; pres. Schonstedt Instrument Co., 1993-95. Chmn. Wis. Mchts. Fedn.; dir. First Wis. Nat. Bank, Fond du Lac. Chmn. Sheboygan County (Wis.) Rep. Party, 1969-70; vice-chmn. Wis. 6th Congl. Dist., 1972-73, Rock Island County Reps., 2000-02; del. Nat. Rep. Conv., 1976; campaign chmn. Sheboygan United Way, 1977, treas., 1973-75, v.p., 1975-78, pres., 1978-79; bd. dirs. Public Expenditure Survey Wis., 1981-83, Rock Island YMCA, 1986-87, Franciscan Health Care Systems, 1988-92, Christ Luth. H.S. Found., 2000-03, Alternatives for the Older Adult, 2001—, Marriage and Family Counseling, 2003—, Thrivent for Lutherans, 2003; v.p. Sheboygan Arts Found., 1973-75; v.p., bd. dirs. Sheboygan Retirement Home, 1977-83; bd. dirs. Franciscan Mental Health Ctr., 1984-94, pres., 1985-88; trustee Friendship Manor, 1993-2003, pres., 2000-02; trustee Jr. Achievement Found., 2003—; trustee Coun. on Children at Risk, 1989—, Franciscan Med. Ctr., 1990-92, Cmty. Found. of the Great River Bend, 2002—, vice chair, 2003; trustee Villa Montessori Sch., 1999—, pres. 2000—; v.p. German Am. Heritage Ctr., 2000—; treas. Vis. Nurse/Homemakers Assn., 2001, Pathway Hospice, 2001. With USN, 1955-57. Named Outstanding Fund Raising Exec. Nat. Soc. Fund Raising Execs., 1992; recipient Outstanding Svc. award Augustana Coll., 1979, Jr. Achievement Free Enterprise Found., 2003. Mem. Am. Heart Assn. (bd. dirs. Quad City chpt. 1999—, pres. 2002-), Am. Cancer Soc. (bd. dirs. Rock Island unit 1992-2001), Wis. Inst. CPAs, Ill. Soc. CPAs, Sheboygan County Assn. CPAs, Fin. Execs. Inst. (dir.), Quad-City Estate Planning Coun., Augustana Hist. Soc. (bd. dirs. 1999—), Augustana Coll. Alumni Assn. (pres. 1970-71), Econ. Club Sheboygan (pres. 1976-77), Kiwanis. Lutheran. Home: 1245 36th Ave Rock Island IL 61201-6022 Office: Augustana Coll 639 38th St Rock Island IL 61201-2210

HORSWILL, C. WEIR, retired obstetrician-gynecologist, photographer; b. Madison, Wis., 1924; MD, U. Wis., 1952. Cert. in ob-gyn. Intern Toledo Hosp., 1952-53; resident U. Wis. Hosp., Madison, 1956-60; hon. staff Madison Meriter Hosp.; clin. assoc. prof. ob-gyn. U. Wis. Med. Sch. Fellow ACOG, ACS; mem. Am. Coll. Sports Medicine, Cen. Assn. Obstetricians and Gynecologists.

HORTA, JOSÉ CARLOS DE OLIVEIRA SOUSA, civil engineering consultant; b. Homoine, Mozambique, Dec. 16, 1935; s. José Maria de Sousa Horta and Maria do Carmo de Oliveira; children: Viriato, Soahanta Vololona, Maria Carmen, José Daniel. Candidate in Civil Engring., U. Liege, Belgium, 1957; DSc in Earth Scis., U. Algiers, Algeria, 1972, cert. in Applied Geophysics, 1973. Polit. adviser Movimento Popular de Libertação de Angola, 1959-61; geotech. and hwy. engr. Ministry Pub. Works, Algiers, 1966-73; acting dir. Civil Engring. Lab., SONATRACH, Beni Mered, Algeria, 1978-80; sr. hwy. and geotech. engr. Louis Berger Internat. Inc., Paris and East Orange, N.J., 1980-91; project mgr., regional rep. DMJM Internat., Washington, 1991-92; civil engring. cons., Lisbon, 1992—; quality lead engr ExxonMobil, Cameroon, 2000—02. Participant internat. confs. on soils, constrn. materials, road design, constrn. and maintenance, including 5th Internat. Conf. on Low-Volume Roads, Raleigh, N.C., 1991, 2d Internat. Conf. on Roads and Road Transport Problems, New Delhi, 1995. Contbr. articles to profl. jours. and confs., including Engring. Geology, Geotechnique. Mem. ASTM, Indian Roads Congress (life). Avocations: gymnastics, swimming, dancing, music, reading. Home: Apt 3F Av Bombeiros Voluntários 42 1495-020 Algés Lisboa Portugal Fax: 351-21-4103515. E-mail: soushort.joyc@mail.telepac.pt.

HORTOBAGYI, GABRIEL N. physician; b. July 22, 1946; MD, U. Nacional de Colombia, Bogota, 1970. Assoc. internist, assoc. prof. medicine U. Tex.-M.D. Anderson Cancer Ctr., Houston, 1980-85, internist, prof. medicine, 1985—, dir. multidisciplinary breast cancer rsch., 1991—, chmn. dept. breast med. oncology, 1992—. Mem. Houston Symphony Chorale, 1974-78; contbg. mem. Houston Grand Opera Guild, 1975—; patron mem. Mus. Fine Arts; mem. med. adv. bd. Cancer Counseling, Inc., 1984—; mem. bd. govs. Tex. Arts Alliance, 1985-88; patron mem. Harris County Dep. Sheriffs Assn., 1986-95; mem. sci. adv. bd. Don Shula Found., Inc., 1991—, League of Women Against Cancer, 1995—; mem. nat. adv. coun. The Chemotherapy Found., 1995—; mem. hon. com. Pink Ribbons project Dancers in Motion for Breast Cancer, 1998. Recipient Cinco del Duca award, Paris, 1995, medal Japanese Coll. Surgeons, Osaka, 1997, Sir Peter Freyer medal Univ. Coll. Clin. Sci. Inst., Galway, Ireland, 1997, Brinker Internat. award for clin. rsch. Susan G. Komen Breast Cancer Found., 1997, medal City of Paris, 1999, Policy and Leadership award Houston Area Health Care Coalition, 1999, Horizon award, 2003, Glenn-Robbins award, 2003; Nylene Eckles fellow, 1977-78. Fellow ACP; mem. Am. Soc. Clin. Oncology (bd. dirs. 2002—), La Sociedad Mexicana de Estudios Oncologicos (hon.), Sociedade Brasileira de Cancerologia (hon.), Sociedad Espanola de Oncologia Medica (hon.), Sociedad Argentina de Oncologia Clinica (hon.), Senologic Hellenic Soc. (hon.), Hyngarian Senologic Soc. (hon.), Nat. Acad. Medicine Argentina (corr. mem.), Nat. Acad. Meidcine Mex. (corr. mem.). Office: U Tex MD Anderson Cancer Ctr 1515 Holcombe Blvd Unit 424 Houston TX 77030-4009 E-mail: ghortoba@mdanderson.org.

HORTON, BARBARA LOUISE, business educator; b. Youngstown, Ohio, Nov. 29, 1937; d. John Paul Jomes and Mary Louise Goodridge; m. William Gibson Foster, Jr., June 30, 1960 (div. Oct. 1973); children: Katherine Morgan Foster Shoemaker, William Gibson Foster V; m. John Calvin Horton, Apr. 1, 1989 (dec.). BS, Carnegie-Mellon U., 1959; MEd, Westminster Coll., 1991; cert. mediation, U. Akron, 1999. Cert. bus. edn. ohio, Pa. Bus. edn. instr. Penn-Ohio Coll., Youngstown, Ohio, ITT Tech. Inst., Youngstown, Butler C.C., New Castle, Pa. Republican. Home: 49 Maple Dr Youngstown OH 44512 Office: Chio Real Estate Hanna Realty Poland OH

HORTON, DAVID HARRISON, writer, educator; b. Mount Clemens, Mich., June 21, 1970; s. David Hubert and Carolyn Horton. MA in Medieval Studies, Western Mich. U., Kalamazoo MI, 1995; MA in Religion, U. Ga., Athens, 1997; MFA in English and Creative Writing, Mills Coll., Oakland CA, 2001. Archaeology Certificate Direction Regionale des Affaires Culturelles de Poitou-Charente, Franc, 1995. Freelance art critic Art papers Mag., Atlanta, 1997—; editor and pub. 20 Mule Press, Oakland, Calif., 2000—; freelance art critic Artweek, San Jose, Calif., 2000—; asst. prof. Patten Coll., Oakland, Calif., 2001—; curator 21 Grand Gallery, Oakland, Calif., 2002—. Author: (poetry collection) Pete Hohhman Days; performance, 100 Nails for Mayakovsky, Notes from the mendoza Line, Pantomimes for Streetcorners, For Which It Stands, We Didn't Run; author: (poetry collection) Pete Hoffman Days. Mem.: Medieval Acad. of Am., Acad. of Am. Poets (corr.). Office: 20 Mule Press PO Box 9136 Oakland CA 94613-0136 Personal E-mail: chasepark@hotmail.com.

HORTON, EDWARD CARL, retired military officer, public administrator; b. Syracuse, N.Y., Sept. 5, 1950; s. Carl and Marjorie Lucille (Clark) H.; m. Chong Sun Kim, Aug. 23, 1980; children: Paul E., David S. BS, U.S. Mil. Acad., 1972; MS in Pers. Mgmt., Troy State U., 1980; MPA, U. Mont., 1983; diploma, U.S. Army War Coll., 1996. Commd. 2d lt. U.S. Army, 1972, advanced through grades to lt. col., 1990; platoon leader, exec. officer Co B, 1-506 Infantry, 101st

Airborne divsn., Ft. Campbell, Ky., 1973-74, scout platoon leader, support platoon leader, 1974-75; detachment comdr. 2d Replacement Detachment, 2d Infantry divsn., Camp Casey, Korea, 1975-76; co. comdr., instr., asst. chief Benning Ranger divsn. U.S. Army Ranger Sch., Ft. Benning, Ga., 1977-80; asst. prof. mil. sci. U. Mont., Missoula, 1980-83; with 193d Infantry Brigade, Ft. Clayton, Panama, 1983-86; staff officer Office Tech. Advisor and Army Initiatives Group, Washington, 1987-90; comdr. 5th Battalion, 87th Infantry, 193d Infantry Brigade, Ft. Davis, Panama, 1990-92, Yakima (Wash.) Tng. Ctr., 1992-94; chief spl. studies, sr. planner Office of Asst. Chief Staff for Installation Mgmt., 1994-97; dist. adminstr. Fla. Dept. of Children and Families, Palm Beach County, 1997-99. Mgmt. cons., 1999-2001; mem. policy com. Cultural and Natural Resources Fed. Adv. Panel, Yakima, Wash., 1992-94; project dir. Census 2000. Mem. Palm Beach County Juvenile Justice Coun., Gov.'s Commn. on Child Welfare Stds. and Tng. Children's Svcs. Coun., Palm Beach County Health and Human Svcs. Planning Assn., Dist. IX Health and Human Svcs. Bd.; mem. regional workforce devel. bd. dirs. WAGES Coalition; mem. sch. health task force Palm Beach Spl. Task Force Sch. Readiness; chmn. Fla. State Employees Charitable Campaign; active United Way; mgr. local cencus office Delray Beach., Fla., 2000; exec. dir. Cmty. Devel. Corp., 2000—. Mem. Assn. U.S. Army, Am. Pub. Human Svcs. Assn., Am. Humane Assn., Internat. City/County Mgmt. Assn., Ellensburg C. of C., Greater Yakima C. of C. (ex officio bd. dirs. 1992-94), Rotary. Home: 10129 Caoba St Palm Beach Gardens FL 33410-5121 E-mail: edh1047@aol.com.

HORTON, FINIS GENE, management services company executive; s. Allie George and Zelda Horton. BA, Ark. Coll., 1974; postgrad., Ark. State U., 1974-75, U. Cen. Ark., 1976. Asst. v.p., cost mgr. Worthen Bank, Little Rock, 1975-81; contr. First Fed. Bank of Morrilton, Ark., 1981-82; bank auditor Superior Fed. Bank, Little Rock, Ft. Smith, Ark., 1982-91; mng. dir. Audit Svcs. Group, Little Rock, 1991-95; pres., owner Corp. Bus. Svcs., Conway, Ark., 1991—. Bd. dirs. Corp. Bus. Svcs. Am. Inc. Mem. Nat. Fin. Assocs., Kiwanis (pres. Little Rock 1978-79, bd. dirs. 1979-81). Avocation: sports. Office: PO Box 1352 Conway AR 72033-1352

HORTON, FRANK ELBA, university official, geography educator; b. Chgo., Aug. 19, 1939; s. Elba Earl and Mae Pauline (Prohaska) H.; m. Nancy Yocom, Aug. 26, 1960; children: Kimberly, Pamela, Amy, Kelly. BA, Western Ill. U., 1963; MS, Northwestern U., 1964, PhD, 1966. Faculty U. Iowa, Iowa City, 1966-75, prof. geography, 1966-75; dir. Inst. Urban and Regional Research, 1968-72, dean advanced studies, 1972-75; v.p. acad. affairs, research So. Ill. U., Carbondale, 1975-80; prof. geography and urban affairs, chancellor U. Wis., Milw., 1980-85; prof. geography, pres. U. Okla., Norman, 1985-88; prof. geography, higher edn. adminstrn., pres. U. Toledo, 1988-98, pres. emeritus, 1999—; prin. Horton & Assocs., Denver, 1999—; interim pres. So. Ill. U., 2000. Mem. commn. on leadership devel. and acad. adminstrn. Am. Coun. on Edn., 1983-85; mem. presdl. adv. com. Assn. on Governing Bds., 1986-98; dir. 1st Wis. Nat. Bank of Milw., 1980-85, Liberty Nat. Bank, Oklahoma City, 1986-89, Trustcorp. Bank, 1989-90; bd. dirs. Interstate Bakeries, GAC Corp. Author, editor: (with B.J.L. Berry) Geographic Perspectives on Urban Systems - With Integrated Readings, 1970, Urban Environmental Management - Planning for Pollution Control, 1974; editor: (with B.J.L. Berry) Geographical Perspectives on Contemporary Urban Problems, 1973; editorial adv. bd.: (with B.J.L. Berry) Transportation, 1971-78. Co-chmn. Goals for Milw. 2000, 1981-85, Greater Milw. Com., 1980; mem. bus. devel. sub-com. Okla. Coun. Sci. and Tech., 1985-88; mem. Harry S. Truman Library Inst., 1985-88, William Rockhill Nelson Trust, 1985-88; bd. govs. Am. Heart Assn., Wis., 1980-85, Ohio Supercomputer Ctr., 1993-97; mem. exec. com. Okla. Acad. State Goals, 1986-88; trustee Toledo Symphony Orch., 1989-96, Toledo Hosp., 1989-97, Pub. Broadcasting Found. Northwest Ohio, 1989-93, Key Bank, 1990-2000, Ohio Aerospace Inst., 1990-97; chair Inter-Univ. Coun. Pres. of Ohio Public Univs., 1992-93; mem. exec. com. Com. of 100, Toledo, 1989-92. Served with AUS, 1957-60. Mem. AAAs (nat. coun. 1976-78), Assn. Governing Bds. (mem. presdl. adv. commn. 1986-95), Assn. Am. Geographers, nat. Assn. State Univs. and Land Grant Colls. (chair urban affairs div. 1983-85, chmn. Coun. of Pres. 1987-88, exec. com. 1983-88), Nat. Hwy. Rsch. Soc., Okla. Coun. on Sci. and Tech., MidAm. State Univs. Assn. (pres. 1987-88), Ohio Supercomputer Ctr. (bd. govs. 1993), Ohio Aerospace Inst. (trustee 1990—), Okla. Acad. State Goals (pres. 1987-88), Okla. State C. of C. and Industry (v.p. 1987-88), Toledo Area C. of C. (vice chmn. bd. dirs. 1991-93). Home: 288 River Ranch Cir Bayfield CO 81122-8774 Office: Horton & Associates 825 E Speer Blvd Ste 300H Denver CO 80218-3719*

HORTON, GRANVILLE EUGENE, occupational medicine physician, retired air force officer; b. Jean, Tex., July 2, 1927; s. James Granville and Etna (Boyle) H.; m. Mildred Helen Veale, June 13, 1953; children: Linda Kay, Kevin Bruce, Carson Scott. BA, Tex. Technol. Coll., 1950; MD, U. Tex., 1954; tng. in radioactive isotope techniques, Oak Ridge Inst. Nuc. Studies, 1958; postgrad., U.S. Air Force Sch. Aerospace Medicine, 1975. Intern Detroit Receiving Hosp., 1954-55; practice medicine, 1955-56, Outlar-Blair Clinic, Wharton, Tex., 1956-72; dir. dept. nuc. medicine Nightingale Hosp., El Campo, Tex., 1973-75; mem. staff Horton Med. Clinic, El Campo, 1972-75; commd. col. U.S. Air Force, 1975; chief aeromed. services Brooks AFB, Tex., 1976-82; ret. USAF, 1982; area med. dir. for San Antonio Concentra Med. Ctrs., 1992—. Part-time rsch. assoc. radioisotope dept. Meth. Hosp., Houston, 1961-66; mem. med. adv. com. and sec. med. staff Caney Valley Meml. Hosp., Wharton, 1956-72; clin. dir. Wharton County TB Assn., 1957-67. Bd. dirs. Wharton County divsn. Am. Cancer Soc., pres., 1960-61; dir. 8th dist. Tex., Citizens Com. for Hoover Report, 1957-58. With USN, 1946-47. Fellow Am. Coll. Angiology (state gov. 1979), Am. Coll. Nuc. Medicine; mem. AMA, AAAS, Am. Nuc. Soc., Am. Coll. Emergency Physicians, Soc. Nuc. Medicine, Tex. Assn. Physicians Nuc. Medicine, Law Enforcement Officers Tex. (assoc.), Tex. Med. Found., Tex. Med. Assn. (ho. of dels. 1959-61), Wharton C. of C. (dir., v.p. 1960-61), El Campo C. of C., Elks Lodge, Phi Chi. Republican. Episcopalian. Home: 15102 Oakmere St San Antonio TX 78232-4623 Office: Concentra Med Ctrs Ste 200 10200 Broadway St San Antonio TX 78217-4434

HORTON, JAMES WRIGHT, retired lawyer; b. Belton, S.C., Dec. 24, 1919; s. John Aiken and Emmae (Tate) H.; m. Eunice Rice, Nov. 20, 1948; children—James Wright, Max Rice, Rex Rice. BA, Furman U., 1942; JD, Harvard U., 1948. Bar: S.C. 1948. Ptnr. Nettles & Horton, Greenville, S.C., 1948-52; ptnr. Rainey, Fant & Horton, Greenville, S.C., 1952-70, Horton, Drawdy, Marchbanks, Ashmore, Chapman & Brown, Greenville, S.C., 1970-78, Horton, Drawdy, Ward & Black, Greenville, S.C., 1978-91; ret., 1997. Pres. United Fund Greenville County, 1959; mem. Greenville County Sch. Trustees, 1964-70, vice chmn., 1969; pres. Greenville Family and Children's Service, 1954-55, 68-70; bd. dirs. Salvation Army, 1969—, treas., 1970-71; bd. dirs. Family and Children's Service, Greenville Mental Health Clinic, 1956-59, Greater Greenville Community Found., 1981. Col. USMCR, ret. Decorated Silver Star. Mem. Greenville County Bar Assn. (pres. 1981) Baptist (deacon 1964-69, 71-72, 86-88). Home: 2 Osceola Dr Greenville SC 29605-3013

HORTON, JEANETTE, municipal government official; b. Paterson, N.J., Dec. 1, 1938; d. David and Mary (Carpenter) Potash; m. Troy Horton, Oct. 31, 1958 (dec. May 1990); m. Christos Prousalis, June 29, 1991. Student, Broward C. C., 1970-72, Barry U., 1982, Fla. Atlantic U., 1983-84, Fla. State U., 1985. Cert. master mcpl. clk. Fla. Bookkeeper Fla. Housewares, Miami, Fla., 1961-65; asst. to comptroller Gulf Stream Press, Miami, 1965-70; comptroller Chrysler Plymouth, Miami, Fla., 1970-75; mcpl. clk., fin. dir. Village of Biscayne Park, Fla., 1975-91, Bal Harbour (Fla.) Village, 1991—. Commr. Cooper City, Fla., 1971-73. Mem. Fla. Assn. City Clks. (scholarship 1985-87, scholarship chmn. 1988-89), Am. Bus. Woman of Yr. award 1985, pres., v.p. 1985-87), Dade/Broward City Clks. and Fin. Dirs. (pres. 1992-93), Fla. City and County Mgrs. Assn., Bus. and Profl. Women (pres. 1981), Internat. Mcpl. Clks. Assn., Pers. Mgmt. Assn., Acad. for Advanced Edn. of Mcpl. Clk. Cert. Lic. Ofcl. Democrat. Roman Catholic. Avocation: reading. Home: 5356 SW 34 Ave Fort Lauderdale FL 33312 Office: Village of Bal Harbour 655 96th St Bal Harbour FL 33154-2428 E-mail: clerk@balharbourflorida.com.

HORTON, JEROME E. state official; b. Pine Bluff, Ark. m. Yvonne Horton; children: Myeshia, Matthew. BA in Fin. and Acctg., Calif. State U., Dominguez Hills; AA, El Camino CC. Coun. mem. Inglewood City Coun., Calif.; state assembly mem. Dist. 51 Calif. State Assembly, 2000—. Mem. Centinela Juvenile Diversion Program. Democrat. Mailing: Rm 2163 PO Box 942849 Sacramento CA 95814 Office: PO Box 6500 1 Manchester Blvd Inglewood CA 90306

HORTON, JONATHAN CHARLES, neuroscientist, neuro-ophthalmologist; b. Edmonton, Alta., Can., Nov. 16, 1954; came to U.S., 1960; s. George Klaus and Pamela (Fairbrother) H.; m. Lidia Mucia, Dec. 22, 1984; children: Nathanael Carroll, Matthew David, Christina Ixmukane. AB in History, Stanford U., 1976; MD, PhD, Harvard U., 1984. Diplomate Am. Bd. Ophthalmology. Med. intern Mass. Gen. Hosp., Boston, 1984-85, neurology resident, 1985-86; ophthalmology resident Georgetown U. Hosp., Washington, 1986-89; neuro-ophthalmology/pediatric ophthalmology fellow U. Calif., San Francisco, 1989-90, prof. ophthalmology, neurology and physiology, 2002—. Contbr. articles to profl. jours. Grantee: N. Calif. Soc. to Prevent Blindness, San Francisco, 1990, Nat. Eye Inst., Washington, 1993. Fellow N. Am. Neuro-Ophthalmology Soc., Am. Acad. Ophthalmology; mem. AAAS, Soc. for Neurosci., Assn. for Rsch. in Vision and Ophthalmology, Cordes Eye Soc., Phi Beta Kappa. Home: 2230 Sheraton Pl San Mateo CA 94402-4015 Office: U C San Francisco Dept Ophthalmology 10 Kirkham St # K301 San Francisco CA 94143-0730 E-mail: horton@itsa.uscf.edu.

HORTON, JOSEPH JULIAN, JR., economics and finance educator; b. Memphis, Tenn., Nov. 7, 1936; s. Joseph Julian and Nina (Williams) H.; m. Linda Anne Langley, May 30, 1964; children: Joseph Julian, Anne Adele, David Douglas. AA, Lon Morris Jr. Coll., 1955; BA, N.Mex. State U., 1958; MA, So. Meth. U., 1965, PhD, 1968; postgrad., Harvard U., 1970-71. Claims examiner Social Security Adminstrn., Kansas City, Mo., 1958-60, claims authorizer, 1960-61; with FDIC, Washington, 1967-71, fin. economist, 1967-69, coord. merger analysis, 1969-71; prof., chmn. dept. econs. and bus. Slippery Rock (Pa.) State Coll., 1971-81; vis. fin. economist Fed. Home Loan Bank Bd., Washington, 1978-79; prof., chmn. commerce divsn. Bellarmine (Ky.) Coll., 1981-82, dean W. Fielding Rubel Sch. Bus., 1982-86; dean Sch. Mgmt. U. Scranton, Pa., 1986-96; prof. Coll. Bus. Adminstrn. U. Ctrl. Ark., Conway, 1996—2001, prof. econ. and fin., 2001—. Asst. prof. George Washington U., Washington, 1968-69, U. Md., College Park, 1969-70; pres. Pa. Conf. Economists, Internat. Acad. Bus. Disciplines, Congress of Polit. Economists, U.S.A. Bd. editors Ea. Econ. Jour.; contbr. articles to profl. jours. Recipient Cokesbury award So. Meth. U., 1965; NSF Grad. fellow, 1964-66, Ford Found. Dissertation fellow, 1966-67, Harvard U. Rsch. fellow, 1970-71, Bank Adminstrn. Inst. Clarence Lichtfeldt fellow, 1981, Burk fellow. Mem. Am. Econ. Assn., Am. Fin. Assn., Internat. Acad. Bus. Disciplines (pres.), N.Am. Econs. and Fin. Assn. (bd. dirs., v.p., pres.), Ea. Econ. Assn. (v.p.). Office: U Cen Ark Dept Econ and Fin Coll Bus Adminstrn Conway AR 72035-0001 E-mail: jhorton@mail.uca.edu.

HORTON, LAWRENCE STANLEY, electrical engineer, apartment developer; b. July 25, 1926; s. Gene Leigh and Retta Florene (Abbott) H.; m. Margaret Ann Cowles, Nov. 26, 1946 (dec. 1964); children: Craig, Lawrence Stanley, Steven J.; m. Julia Ann Butler Wirkkula, Aug. 15, 1965; stepchildren: Charles Wirkkula Horton, Jerry Higginbotham Horton. BSEE, Oreg. State U., 1949. Elec. engr. Mountain States power Co., Calif. Oreg. Power Co., Pacific Power and Light Co., 1948-66; mgr. Ramic Corp., 1966-69; cons. elec. engr. Marquess and Assocs., Medford, Oreg., 1969-85, sec., bd. dirs.; pres., owner Medford Better Housing Assn., 1985—. Ptnr. Tyee Apts., Julia Ann Apts., T'Morrow Apts., Johnston Manor; bd. dirs. People's Bank of Commerce; developer various apt. complexes and retirement cmtys., 1969—, Northwood Apts., Horton Plz., Fountain Plz., Anna Maria Creekside, Terpening Terrace, Tucson Way Retirement; grad. instr. Dale Carnegie course, 1955, 56. Contbr. elec. articles to profl. jours. Bd. dirs. Medford Hist. Commn. Active Medford Planning Commn., Archtl. Rev. Commn., Housing Authority; bd. govs. State of Oreg. Citizens Utility; pres. United Fund, 1963-64. With USN, 1945-46. Named Rogue Valley Profl. Engrs. of Yr., 1969. Mem. IEEE, NSPE, Profl. Engrs. of Oreg., So. Oreg. Rental Owners Assn. (pres.), Rogue Valley Geneol. Soc. (pres.), Medford C. of C. (dir.), Rogue Valley Yacht Club (commodore 1974-75, dir., local fleet capt., champion), Rogue Valley Knife and Fork (past pres.), San Juan 21 Fleet Assn. (western vice commodore, Top Ten San Juan Sailor West Coast 1980), Jackson Toastmasters (founder 1957), Medford Rotary, Kiwanis (life, pres. Crater Golden 1990-91). Republican. Methodist. Office: Medford Better Housing Assn 1118 Spring St Medford OR 97504-6272 E-mail: lhorton25@charter.net., info@hortonplza.com.

HORTON, MARTHA HEIM, retired newspaper editor, writer; b. Oneonta, N.Y., July 3, 1934; d. Ralph Daniel and Anna Leona (Kuhlman) Heim; m. Arrigo Raho, Jan. 22, 1965 (div. Jan. 1970); children: Marianna Raho, John Anthony Raho. BA, Pa. State U., 1956. Promotion asst. McGraw-Hill Pub. Co., N.Y.C., 1956-57; asst. editor The Am. Rev., Bologna, Italy, 1963-64; corr. Mc-Graw Hill World News, Milan, 1965; acct. exec. Spiro Assocs., Phila., 1966-68; pub. rels. mgr. Sonesta Hotels, Boston, 1968-72; dir. pub. rels. Marco Beach Hotel, Marco Island, Fla., 1972-76; dir. pub. rels. and publs. Elmira (N.Y.) Coll., 1976-80; editor-in-chief Chemung Valley Reporter, Horseheads, N.Y., 1989-96; dir. pub. rels. Corning C.C., Corning, NY, 1996-97. Contbr. articles to profl. jours. and mags. Bd. dirs. Arnot Art Mus., Elmira, 1991-2000, N.Y. Press Assn. Recipient Gold Key award Am. Hotel and Motel Assn., 1972, Crystal Prism award Am. Advt. Fedn., 1980. Mem. LWV (dir. devel. N.Y. State bd. 1987-88), AAUW, Torch Club of Emira (pres.). Democrat. Congregationalist. Avocations: travel, gardening, poetry, painting. Home: 412 W Clinton St Elmira NY 14901-2414 E-mail: mhscribe@aol.com.

HORTON, PATRICIA MATHEWS, artist, violist and violinist; b. Bklyn., Mar. 6, 1932; d. Edward Joseph and Margaret (Briggs) Mathews; m. Ernest H. Horton Jr., Mar. 6, 1982; 1 stepchild, Carol Horton Tremblay. Student in viola, William Primrose Master Class, 1980; student, Glendale (Calif.) C.C., 1981—90, Glendale (Calif.) CC., 1993, Glendale (Calif.) C.C., 1999—2002, Art Ctr. Coll. Design, Pasadena, Calif., 1988-93; student in painting composition, Peter Liashkov, L.A., 1993-97. Profl. musician on violin and viola, 1951-86; musician on tour, 1952-57. Played with New Orleans Philharm., 1959-61, U.S. Tour of San Francisco Ballet, 1965, L.A. Civic Light Opera, 1974-80; played L.A. engagements of Bolshoi Ballet Co., 1975, Am. Ballet Theatre, 1974-80, N.Y.C. Opera, 1974-80, Royal Ballet of London, 1978, Alicia Alonzo's Cuban Ballet, 1979, Harlem Ballet, 1984, Deutsche Oper Berlin, 1985, also motion picture and TV soundtrack recs.; one-woman shows include Claremont (Calif.) Sch. Theology, 1997, Pasadena First United Meth. Ch., 1997, 99, La Canada Flintridge Libr., 1999. Active Dem. Nat. Com., Women's Caucus for Art. Mem. Am. Fedn. Musicians (life). Avocations: hiking local mountains, desert and beaches, studying classical guitar.

HORTON, PAUL CHESTER, psychiatrist; b. Cin., Jan. 29, 1942; s. Paul Chester Sr. and Elizabeth Pauline (Rice) H.; m. JoAnn Alice Baker, Aug. 30; children: Paul Andrey, Alexander Robert. BA, U. Minn., 1964; MD, &, 1968. Diplomate Am. Bd. Psychiatry and Neurology. Rotating intern U. Cin., 1969; resident in psychiatry Yale U., New Haven, 1972, staff psychiatrist Guidance Clinic of Camden County, West Collingswood, N.J., 1972-74, Milford (Conn.) Family and Child Guidance Clinic, 1974-77; mem. faculty Sch. Medicine Yale U., New Haven, 1974-76; pvt. practice Meriden, 1974—; cons. psychiatrist Child Guidance Clinic Cen. Conn., Meriden, 1980-94; med. dir., 1994-99. Mem. faculty U. Conn. Sch. Medicine, Farmington, 1978-79; cons. Caring for Children, San Francisco, 1989—; psychiat. cons. Meriden Pub. Schs., 1999—; reviewer Am. Jour. Psychiatry, 1980—, and others. Author: Solace, 1981, Solace, paperback edit. 1983, Solace, Japanese edit., 1985; sr. editor: The Solace Paradigm, 1988; contbr. articles to profl. jours. Big Brother Big Bros. Orgn., Mpls., 1964-68. Lt. comdr. USN, 1972-74. Mem. Am. Psychiat. Assn., Meriden Wallingford Med. Assn., Gridiron Club. Home: 18 Metacomet Dr Meriden CT 06450-3568 Office: 234 Hobart St Meriden CT 06450-4380 E-mail: phortonmd@aol.com.

HORTON, ROBERT CARLTON, geologist; b. Tonopah, Nev., July 25, 1926; s. Frank Elijah and Eathel Margaret (Miller) H.; m. Beverly Jean Burhans, Dec. 5, 1952; children: Debra, Robin, Cindy. BS, U. Nev., 1949, D.Sc. (hon.), 1985, Geol. Engr., 1966. Assoc. dir. Nev. Bur. Mines, Reno, 1956-66; cons. Reno, 1966-76; dir. geology div. Bendix Field Engring Corp. (Grand Junction), Colo., 1976-81; dir. U.S. Bur. Mines, Washington, 1981-87; dir. strategic materials rsch. U. Nev., Reno, 1987-90, assoc. dean MacKay Sch. Mines, 1989-90, assoc. dean emeritus, 1990—. Mem. Nev. Gov.'s Mining Adv. Com., 1966-72. Author: Barite Deposits of Nevada, 1962, Fluorspar Deposits of Nevada, 1963, History of Nevada Mining, 1963. Republican candidate for Congress from Nev., 1958. Served to lt. USNR, 1944-46, 53-56, PTO. Kennecott scholar, 1948; named Engr. of Yr. Reno chpt., NSPE, 1967; recipient Outstanding Alumnus John Mackay medal, Mackay Sch. Mines, 1991. Mem. AIME (subsect. chmn. Reno 1962-63), Soc. Econ. Geologists, Mining and Metall. Soc. Am. Methodist.

HORTON, ROSALYN, underwriter; b. Nashville, July 13, 1946; d. W.D. and Irma Jean (Jackson) Donnell; m. Frederick Lee Horton, Aug. 6, 1965; children: Shane Scott, Sundai Horton Reeder, Shalako Lance. Broadcast Diploma, Elkins Inst., Nashville, 1973. Cert. ins. counselor; cert. profl. ins. woman; cert. profl. ins. agt. Office asst. Rich Printing Co., Nashville, 1973-76; office adminstr. Exhibit 4, Inc., Nashville, 1976-84; corp. sec. Horton Paper Svc., Nashville, 1984—; ocean/hill underwriter Fireman's Fund, Atlanta, 1992—. Mem. Middle Tenn. Cath. Diocese Social Justice Conf., Nashville, 1997—; supporter Muscular Dystrophy Assn., Nashville, 1995—; strategy team leader Tying Nashville Together, 2000—. Recipient T.J. Mims Achievement award, 1999, Achievement award Am. Assn. Mng. Gen. Agts.; named Tenn. Coun. Ins. Woman of Yr., 2001 Mem.: Nat. Assn. Ins. Women (state dir. Tenn. coun. 1999—2000, co-chair nat. conv. 2003, region III Rookie of Yr. 1994, Tenn. State Ins. Woman of Yr. 2001), Nashville Ins. Profls. (pres. bd. dirs. 1995—99), Nashville Claims Assn. (parliamentarian 1998—2000, treas. 2000—01, asst. NAIW region III v.p. 2001—02). Democrat. Roman Catholic. Avocations: gardening, crafts, harley davidson motorcycle trips, reading. Office: Fireman's Fund McGee Marine 11605 Haynes Bridge Rd Ste 200 Alpharetta GA 30004 E-mail: rhorton@ffic.com.

HORTON, SHEARON SMITH, piano educator; b. Clarksville, Tenn., Oct. 13, 1950; d. John Herman and Mabel (Herndon) S.; m. Paul Latham Horton, June 7, 1980. BMus, George Peabody Coll., 1972; M of Music, U. Tex., Austin, 1974. Cert. music tchr. Fine arts faculty St. Stephen's Epsicopal Sch., Austin, Tex., 1974-89; music faculty U. New Orleans, 1994; music studio tchr. Austin and New Orleans, 1974—. Adj. music faculty Tulane U., New Orleans, 1990—; lectr. Baton Rouge Music Tchrs. Assn., 1997; co-chair New Orleans Piano Inst., 1999—; mem faculty, coord. piano pedagogy and class piano La. State U., Baton Rouge, 2001—02. Grantee Nat. Piano Technicians Guild, 1990; recipient Tchr. of Yr. Austin Dist. Music Tchrs. Assn., Winner Baldwin Competition Tchr. of South Ctrl. Region, 1998. Mem. Nat. Fedn. of Music Clubs, New Orleans Music Tchrs. Assn. (pres. 1996-98, v.p. 1994-96), Met. Music Tchrs. Assn. (v.p. 1992-94), La. Music Tchrs. Assn. (v.p. 1999—). Avocations: sailing, gardening. Home: 5800 Cleveland Pl Metairie LA 70003-1000

HORTON, SHIRLEY A. state legislator, former mayor; BS in Acctg., San Diego State U. Pres. Grasser/Tate Real Estate Co., Calif.; planning commr. City of Chula Vista, Calif., 1985-91, councilwoman, 1991-94, mayor, 1994—2002; mem. Calif. Ho. of Reps., 2003—. Past govt. svc. positions include: bd. del. San Diego Assn. Govts.; Met. Transit Devel. Bd. alternate, mem. Otay Valley (Calif.) Regional Park Policy com., mem. San Diego Interagy. Water Quality panel, mem. South County Econ. Devel. Coun., mem. Interagy. Water Task Force, mgm. Gang Issues com., mem. Bayfront subcom., mem. Appropriate Techs. subcom. Mem. San Diego County Assessment Appeals bd., 1982-86, pres. South San Diego Bay Cities Bd. Realtors, 1987, mem. Scripps Meml. Hosp. Cmty. Adv. Bd., 1990-91, mem. South Bay YMCA Support Campaign com., 1990. Recipient San Diego Women Who Mean Bus. award, 1997. Mem. Calif. Assn. Realtors (regional v.p. 1989, dir. 1980-90), Chula Vista C. of C. (econ. devel. com. 1984-85). Office: PO Box 942849 Sacramento CA 94249*

HORTON, THELMA WHITE, educational administrator, author; b. Blyesville, Ark., Feb. 7, 1949; d. William Soloman and Corrine (Carrigans) White; m. Charles D. Horton, May 20, 1970 (div. 1991); children: Corrine Daniel Horton, Tiffany Louise, Charles William. Student, Fla. Internat. U.; BSW, Boise State U., 1975; D (hon.), World U. Team tchr. Dade County Pub. Schs., Parks and Recreation Coll., North Miami, 1979—80; lead tchr. gifted edn. Dade County Elem. Schs., Miami Dade C.C., Miami, 1980—; owner, dir. Hi School Day Care and Learning Ctr., Cutler Ridge, Fla., 1981—; reading tchr. Miami Dade CC, 1981—83. Lead tchr. gifted Naranja Elem. Sch.; owner Charisma, Fla.; tutor English, Perrine, Fla., 1982—; with Comet Lab, 1996-97; cons. WESTAT Rsch., Barr Industries, Perrine, 1981—, The Rand Co., Student Travel Svc. student placement; adj. prof. Wardstone Coll.; temp. Dade County Pub. Schs.; alternative edn. tchr. 5th grade Peskoe Elem. Sch.; advocate African-Am. voices; tchr. liberal arts Ward Stone Coll.; adminstr. R.E.S.S. program for implementation of the Met. Test/Archdiocese of Miami; creator of The Horton Chart for Math. Author: Have Your Cake and Eat it Too, The Black C, Reciprocal Reading, African Curriculum Integration for Intermediate Education in the Classroom, Reciprocal Reading 1996-97, Epinions.com., Ms. T. Tuttle's 2nd Grade Class T.E.A.M., The Reading Quagmire: ERIC, (database) Lessonpro. Active Boy Scouts Am., PTSA, ARC; mem. usher bd. Martin Meml. Meth. Ch.; st. capt. Neighborhood Crime Watch; advocate for Nat. Tchr. Cert., 1995-96; vol. The Horton Chart Eisenhower Nat. Clearinghouse; advocate African Am. Voices. Recipient Equity and Excellence award Magnet Innovative Programs; Comet Lab. Tchr. of Yr., 1996; Cmty. Svc. award JESCA orgn. Mem. ACLU, The Exec. Female, Children's Advocates (pres. 1975-83), United Tchrs. Dade County, Alumni Assn. Boise State U., Inst. Children's Lit., Miami C. of C., Fla. Assn. for the Gifted, Kappa Delta Pi. Home: 15905 SW 105th Ct Miami FL 33157-1571 Office: 13990 SW 264th St Homestead FL 33032-7402

HORTON, THOMAS EDWARD, JR., mechanical engineering educator; b. Houston, Jan. 12, 1935; s. Thomas Edward and Minnie Tolula (Sloan) H.; m. Bobbie Jean Newcomb, June 8, 1963; children— Holly Anne, Thomas Edward. BS, U. Tex., 1957, PhD, 1964; MS (Caterpillar rsch. fellow), Stanford U., 1958. Jr. mech. engr. Shell Devel. Co., Houston, 1957-58; tchg. asst., rsch. asst., rsch. scientist U. Tex., Austin, 1959-62; rsch. engr. Jet Propulsion Lab. Calif. Inst. Tech., Pasadena, 1962, sr. rsch. engr., 1963-66; asso. prof. mech. engring., rsch. engr. U. Miss., 1966-71, prof., rsch. engr., 1971-94, emeritus prof., 1994—. Dir. U.S. Army Laser Sci. Lab., Redstone Arsenal, Ala., 1975-76, Reiton Corp. of Houston; cons. Army Research Office, Jet Propulsion Lab., Marathon Oil Co., Shell Devel. Co., Exxon, Chevron, Mobil, Texaco. Contbr. articles to profl. jours.; patentee in field. Fellow AIAA (assoc.; mem. tech. coms.); mem. ASME (life; mem. tech. coms.), Am. Phys. Soc., Am. Soc. Engring. Edn. (research award Southeastern sect. 1971), Sigma Xi (pres. local chpt.), Tau Beta Pi (student adviser), Pi Tau Sigma, Phi Eta Sigma. Republican. Methodist. Home: 209 Saint Andrews Cir Oxford MS 38655-2518

HORTON, THOMAS MARK, futures and options trader, commodity consultant; b. San Angelo, Tex., Dec. 14, 1952; s. Lee Bascom and Mary Jane (Nash) H.; m. Shannon Green, July 18, 1987 (div. Sept. 1990); m. Cindy Neely, Feb. 17, 1995; 3 stepsons. BS, Tex. A&M U., 1975. Self employed rancher, San Angelo, 1976; v.p. Rolling Plains Prodn. Credit Assn., Childress, Tex., 1976-79, Western Prodn. Credit Co., Guymon, Okla., 1979-80, Agrow Credit Corp., Amarillo, Tex., 1980; account exec. Procom Co., Inc., Chgo., 1981; ptnr. Hennessey & Assocs., Chgo., 1981-85; account exec. Linnco Futures, Inc., Chgo., 1985; pres., futures cons., advisor commodities Horton Futures Advisory, Inc., Amarillo, 1985—; ptnr. Green-Horton & Assocs., Amarillo, 1987-89. Fin. cons. Procom Co., Inc., 1981, Shearson-Lehman-Hutton, Amarillo, 1989-90, Merrill Lynch, Pierce, Fenner & Smith, Amarillo, 1990-97, Prudential Securities, 1997-99, Rosenthal-Collins Group, 1999—; tech. analyst, ptnr. Hales Cattle Letter, 1989—. Mem. Civic Ctr. for Performing Arts, Chgo., 1983-85, Newberry Libr., Chgo., 1984-85, Lone Star Ballet, Amarillo, 1986-88, Panhandle Plains Hist. Mus., 1991-93; patron Amarillo Symphony, 1988-89, 98—. Served to 1st lt. U.S. Army, 1975-76. Mem. Chgo. Mercantile Exch., Chgo. Rice & Cotton Exch., Nat. Futures Assn., Trout Unltd., Ducks Unltd., Exec. Club. Methodist. Avocations: golf, fishing, hunting, weight-lifting. Office: Horton Futures Adv PO Box 892 Amarillo TX 79105-0892 Home: 2204 Julian Blvd Amarillo TX 79102-1312

HORTON, THOMAS ROSCOE, business advisor; b. Fort Pierce, Fla, Nov. 17, 1926; s. Charles Montraville Horton and Ruby Mae (Swain) Warren; m. Marilou Deeming, Dec. 19, 1947; children— Susan, Jean, Marilyn BS, Stetson U., 1949, LHD (hon.), 1982; MS, U. Fla., 1950, PhD, 1954; LLD (hon.), Pace U., 1976; DLitt (hon.), U. Charleston, 1980. Instr., asst. headmaster Bolles Sch., Jacksonville, Fla., 1950-52; with IBM Corp., Armonk, NY, 1954-82; pres., CEO Am. Mgmt. Assn., NYC, 1982-89, chmn., CEO, 1989-91, chmn., 1991-92;

advisor Stetson U., DeLand, Fla., 1992-96; pres. emeritus Am. Mgmt. Assn., NYC, 2003. Chmn. The Comml. Bank, 2001-, Techna Health, LLC, 2001-; mem. adv. bd. Who's Who in Fin. and Industry, 1988—, Who's Who in Am., 1999—; panelist White House Conf. on Productivity, 1981; co-chair White House Conf. on Critical Infrastructure Assurance, 2000. Author: What Works for Me, 1986, Beyond the Trust Gap, 1990, The CEO Paradox, 1992, Information Security Governance: What Directors Need to Know, 2001, Information Security Oversight: Essential Board Practices, 2002; editor: Traffic Control--Theory and Implementation, 1965; columnist Mgmt. Rev., 1982-92, Dir. & Bd., 1998—; assoc. prodr. SHO Entertainment, Inc., 1997-2000. Life mem. Salvation Army, Am. Mgmt. Assn., 1990—; trustee Bethune-Cookman Coll., Daytona Beach, Fla., 1971-82, hon., 1982—; trustee Pace U., NYC, 1975-92, emeritus trustee, 1992—; dir. Assn. Governing Bds. Univ. and Coll., 1976-85, chmn., 1982-84, hon. dir., 1987-90; trustee Am. Grad. Sch. Internat. Mgmt., Glendale, Ariz., 1982-92, Stetson U. Bus. Sch. Found., 1992—; mem. econ. devel. com. City of DeLand (Fla.), 1992-98; trustee emeritus Stetson U., 1996—; bd. dir. Kids Voting USA, 1991-2000, chair, 1992-98; adv. bd. Am. C. of C. of Cuba in US, 1996—; bd. dir. Ctr. for Bd. Leadership. Washington, 1999—; bd. visitors The Bolles Sch., Jacksonville, Fla., 1998-2000. Fellow: Internat. Acad. Mgmt. (vice chancellor), Acad. Mgmt.; mem.: Svc. Corps Retired Execs., Mgmt. Exec. Soc., Assn. Internat. des Etudiants en Sci. Econ. et Comml. (hon. dir. 1990—), Am. Com. Edn. (bd. dirs. 1982—84), Internat. Exec. Svc. Corps, Nat. Coun. on Philanthropy (trustee, vice chmn. 1973—80), Korean Mgmt. Assn. (hon.), Conf. Bd. (sr.), Am. Mgmt. Assn. (life), ASME (hon.), Japan Mgmt. Assn. (hon.), Russian Econ. Soc. (hon.), Internat. Coun. for Innovation in Higher Edn., Corp. Women Dir. Internat. Colloquium (co-chair 2002—03), Inst. Internat Auditors (mem. internatl auditing stds. bd. 2001—), Nat. Assn. Corp. Dir. (mem. Blue Ribbon Commn. on Dir. Professionalism 1996, faculty mem., bd. dirs. 1996—, audit com. 1999, chair 1999—2001, bd. corp. strategy 2000, bd. effectiveness 2001, bd. risk oversight 2002), Pres. Assn. NYC (chmn. 1982—91), European Found. for Mgmt. Devel., Lake Beresford Yacht Club, DeLand Country Club, Sigma Phi Epsilon (co-founder Fla. Beta chpt. 1949—). Baptist. Office: Stetson U PO Box 8395 Deland FL 32720 E-mail: thorton@stetson.edu.

HORTON, THOMAS W. telecommunications executive; MBA, So. Meth. U., 1985; grad., Baylor U.; MBA, Southern Methodist U. V.p. Europe Am. Airlines, sr. v.p. fin., CFO; sr. v.p., CFO AT&T, 2002—. Office: AT&T 295 N Maple Ave Basking Ridge NJ 07920

HORTON, WILLIAM RUSSELL, retired utility company executive; b. Toronto, Ont., Can., Aug. 25, 1931; s. Russell Burton and Freda Catherine (Middleton) H.; m. Dorothy Viva Rye, Nov. 27, 1954; children: William Russell, Robert Freeman, Douglas Lloyd, Ronald Edward. BA Sci. in Mining Engring., U. Toronto, 1955. Engr. Imperial Oil Ltd., Calgary and Camrose, Alta., Can., 1955-56; engr., mgr. Black Sivalls & Bryson Ltd., Edmonton, 1956—65; v.p. Gamma Engring. Ltd., Edmonton, 1965-68; pres. Horton Engring. Ltd., Edmonton, 1968-2000, chmn., 2000—; mem. Alta Pub. Utilities Bd., Edmonton, 1973-76; chmn. Alta. Pub. Utilities Bd., Edmonton, 1976-83; exec. v.p. Can. Utilities Ltd., Edmonton, 1984-90. Bd. dirs. Can. Utilities Ltd., Atco Utilities Bus. Group; mem. Centre for Study Regulated Industries McGill U.; hon. mem. Can. Assn. Members Pub. Utility Tribunals. Mem. Assn. Profl. Engrs. Geologists and Geophysicists Alta. (life), Northwest Electric Light and Power Assn. (hon. life). Avocations: sports, music, reading. Home: 17490 Coral Beach Rd Winfield BC Canada V4V 1C1 Office: Can Utilities Ltd 1400-909 11th Ave SW Calgary AB Canada T2R 1N6 E-mail: wrhorton@cablelan.net.

HORTON-STEVENSON, RHONDA ANNA, writer, educator; b. Canyonville/Oregon, Iowa, Dec. 23, 1950; d. Jack Stevenson Harrison-Horton and Alyne Ruth (Stevenson) Horton. AS in Advanced Sci./ Fashion, Kirkwood C.C., Cedar Rapids, Iowa, 1971; MS in Marriage and Family Counseling (hon.), U. Nev., 1989; BS in Edn. Elem and Exceptional Children, Iowa State U., Ames, 1975; MS in Spl. Edn., Iowa State U., 1988; Edn. Specialist, U. Nev., 1990, PhD in Edn, Counseling, Marriage and Family, Psychology/Psychol. Analysis, 1996; MA, Prarie Grad. Coll., Calgary, Alberta, 2001. Cert. tchr. cons. ministry, Iowa, Ill., Nev., Mo., N.Y., Calif., Hawaii, Tex., Md., Minn., Jamaica, Alberta, Can., Eng. Colo. Essence Miss Universe Miss Universe Inc., Iowa, 1969—97, 1978, 1989, 1994—97; essence Miss Am. Miss Am., Inc., Iowa, 1989, 1994—96; tchr. righteousness Holy Essence Essene Ch., Iowa, Nev., Calif., N.Y., 1985, 1988; governess, cons. State of Iowa Chs., Cts., Schs. Miss Iowa, 1985; educator parents tng. practicum reading U. Nev., Las Vegas, 1988—89. Author, cons., proprietor Children's Mastries- Nat. Bus. Yr. 1992, Iowa, Colo., Nev., 1985—; tchr. spl. edn. Des Moines Pub. Schs., 1975—77; tchr., counsellor Polk County Juvenile Home, Des Moines, 1978—80; cons., supr. practicum students Iowa State U., Ames, Iowa, 1988—89; tchr. emotionally disturbed, Ames, 1995—. Author: (manual) Peace Be Forth You I & II, 1988—89 (Pulitzer prize, 1993), (children's book) Lovely,. The Porcupine and His Quils, 1988; author: (cons.) Food Creation-Preschool Early Elementary Respect, 1994—95 (Miss Iowa-Miss USA pub. project award, 1996), over 48 written works. Governess Miss Universe Inc.-Ct. Females, 1989—; coord. fitness desk Young Women's Christian Assn., Iowa, Greater Des Moines, 1998—2002; mem., counsellor Girls Scouts Am.-Women's Auxillary, 1957—; hostess sales Puppy Day Vets. Dr., 1959. Named Miss Universe, U.S. Internation Negotiation, 1969—95; recipient Nat. prize peace and beauty, U.S., Vietnam, multiple countries, 2000, Everlasting Life award, 1969, 1997. Mem. Holy Essence Essene Ch. Avocations: theater, reading, gardening, sewing, house designs.

HORTON-WRIGHT, ALMA IRENE, educator; b. Austin, Tex., July 05; d. Ollon and Willie; m. Henry S. Wright, June 25; children: Sheila, Stanley, Gregory, Gerry. AA in Liberal Arts, San Bernardino Valley Coll., Calif., 1976; AA, Western Okla. State U., Altus, 1984; BA, Calif. State U., San Bernardino, 1979, postgrad.; MA in edn., Prairie View A&M U., 1993. Cert. tchr., Calif., life credential, Tex. Tchr. speed reading, edn. office Altus (Okla.) AFB; tchr. adult edn. Altus Sch. Dist.; elem. tchr. Rialto (Calif.) Unified Sch. Dist., Austin Ind. Sch. Dist. Named Tchr.of Yr., 2001-02. Mem. NEA, Tex. State Tchrs. Assn., Calif. State U. Almuni Assn., Edn. Austin, Phi Delta Kappa. Austin Ret. Tchrs. Assn., Tex. Ret. Tchrs. Assn. Avocations: travel, reading, art activities.

HORTTOR, DONALD J. lawyer; b. May 3, 1932; s. Elmer J. and Cleda C. (Cox) Horttor; m. Jane Ann Ausherman, Mar. 22, 1959; children: Daun Ann, Bretton J. AB in Econs., U. Kans., 1953, JD, 1959; LLM in Taxation, NYU, 1961. Bar: Kans. 1959, U.S. Dist. Ct. Kans. 1959, U.S. Ct. Appeals (10th cir.) 1963, U.S. Supreme Ct. 1965, U.S. Tax Ct. 1965. Adj. prof. Washburn U. Law Sch., Topeka, 1965—76; assoc. Cosgrove, Webb and Oman, Topeka, 1959—63, ptnr., 1963—. Author: (pamphlet) Estate Planning, Why A Will, Kans. Estate Adminstrn. Fellow: Am. Coll. Trust and Estate Coun.; mem.: ABA, Kans. Bar Assn., Topeka Bar Assn., Topeka Country Club, Moose, Elks, Masons. Republican. Congregationalist. Office: 1100 Bank Am Tower Topeka KS 66603-3477

HORTY, JOHN FRANCIS, lawyer; b. Johnstown, Pa., Oct. 21, 1928; s. John Frank and Nancy Bolsinger (Dibert) H.; m. Christine Kennamer, June 1979; children: John Francis, Jon Michael, Kathryn Camille, Roger Lawrence, Jason Lawrence. BA cum laude, Amherst Coll., 1950; LLB, Harvard U., 1953. Bar: Pa. 1956, D.C., 1981. Prof. U. Pitts., 1956-68; pres. Aspen Systems Corp., Pitts., 1966-71; mng. ptnr. Horty, Springer & Mattern, P.C., Pitts., 1971—. Pres. Action Kit for Hosp. Law, Pitts., 1971—; chmn. bd. St. Francis Ctrl. Hosp., Pitts., 1973-99, St. Francis Med. Ctr., 1999-2000; vice chmn. St. Francis Health System, 1999-2000; chmn. Estes Park Inst., Denver, 1984—; chmn. Indigo Inst., Washington, 1988—; pres. Nat. Coun. Cmty. Hosps., Washington, 1974-2001; bd. dirs. Hosp. Coun. Western Pa., 1989-2000. Editor and pub. (manuals, newsletters, chpts.) Hospital Law Manual, 1956, Action Kit for Hospital Law, 1973, Action Kit for Hospital Trustees, 1977, Patient Care Law, 1981, Treatise on Hospital Law, 1977, Medical Staff Law, 1984. Named Hon. Fellow Am. Coll. Hosp. Execs., 1965; recipient award of honor Am. Hosp. Assn., 1970. Mem. ABA, Am. Hosp. Assn (life, hon.), Pa. Bar Assn., D.C. Bar Assn., Allegheny County Bar Assn., Ponte Vedra Country Club, Tournament Players Club. Republican. Avocation: golf. also: 637 Ponte Vedra Blvd Unit D Ponte Vedra Beach FL 32082-2974 Home and Office: Horty Springer & Mattern 4614 5th Ave Pittsburgh PA 15213-3663

HORUZSKO, ANATOLIJ, medical research scientist; b. Pinsk, Belarus, Oct. 10, 1953; s. Pavel Horuzsko and Anna Juskevich; m. Vera Portik-Dobos, Mar. 30, 1981; children: Julia Szonja, Daniel David. MD(hon.), Pediat. Med. Sch., Leningrad, Russia, 1976; PhD in immunology and allergy, Inst. of Exptl. Medicine, Russian Acad. of Sci., Leningrad, Russia, 1980; MD, Semmelweis U. of Medicine, Budapest, Hungary, 1986; PhD in clin. immunology and allergy, Hungarian Acad. of Sci., Budapest, Hungary, 1987. Lectr., sr. lectr. Pediatric Med. Sch., Leningrad, Russia, 1979—86; sr. lectr. Nat. Inst. of Hematology and Blood Transfusion, Budapest, Hungary, 1986—92; non-clin. scientist, grade 1 Nat. Inst. for Med. Rsch., London, 1992—95; sr. rsch. scientist Med. Coll. of Ga., Augusta, 1995—98, instr., 1998—2002, asst. prof., 2002—. Author: (over 40 studies) Dealing With Issues In Transplantation Medicine And Immunobiology. Recipient Prize of George Soros, George Soros Found., 1988, Internat. Rsch. award, Wellcome Trust, U.K., 1992—95, Internat. Human Frontier Sci. Program Orgn., Strasbourg, France, 1998, Internat. Union Against Cancer, Geneva, Switzerland, 1999, Roche Organ Transplantation Rsch. Found., Switzerland, 2001. Mem.: European Fedn. for Immunogenetics (assoc.), Hungarian Soc. for Immunology (assoc.), Brit. Soc. for Immunology (assoc.), AAAS (assoc.), Am. Assn. of Immunologists (assoc.). Office: Med Coll of Ga 1120 15th St Augusta GA 30912-2600 Home Fax: 706-721-8732; Office Fax: 706-721-8732. Personal E-mail: horuzsko@netzero.net. E-mail: horuzsko@immag.mcg.edu.

HORVATH, ANNETTE, home care health administrator; b. Bronx, N.Y., Mar. 12, 1963; d. Thomas and Roslyn DeGrazia; m. Leonard Horvath, Aug. 28, 1988; children: Jennifer, Rebecca. BSN, Lehman Coll., Bronx., 1996; MS in Adminstrv. Health Svc., Iona Coll., New Rochelle, N.Y., 1999. RN. Case mgr. Montifiore Hosp., Bronx, NY, 1993—98; project mgr. Jewish Home and Hosp., N.Y.C., 1998—99, dir. patient svcs. Bronx, 1999—2000; adminstr. Americare Inc., Bklyn., 2000—01, Village Care of N.Y., N.Y.C., 2001—. Mem.: NAFE, Women Health Mgmt., Health Care Providers, Women Arts Mus. Avocations: reading, cooking. Office: Village Care of NY 154 Christopher St New York NY 10014

HORVATH, ARPAD, engineering educator; b. Subotica, Yugoslavia, Jan. 28, 1969; came to U.S., 1993; s. Matyas and Katalin H.. Diploma in Engring., Tech. U. of Budapest, 1993; MS, Carnegie Mellon U., 1995, PhD, 1997. Postdoctoral rschr. Carnegie Mellon U., Pitts., 1997, rsch. faculty, 1998-99; asst. prof. U. Calif., Berkeley, 1999—. Program co-chair IEEE Internat. Symposium on Electronics and the Environment, Danvers, Mass., 1999; conf. co-chair, San Francisco, 2000, Denver, 2001; co-dir. NATO Advanced Rsch. Workshop, Budapest, 2000. Co-developer: model and software Economic Input-Output Analysis Life-Cycle Assessment (EIO-LCA), 1996—99; contbr. Fellow fellow, AT&T Found. Indsl. Ecology Faculty, 1999, 2001, 2002, NSF/Lucent Techs. Indsl. Ecology, 1998—2000. Mem.: ASCE (assoc.; assoc. editor Jour. Infrastructure Sys.). Office: Dept Civil Engring & Environ Engring U Calif 215 McLaughlin Hall Berkeley CA 94720-1712 E-mail: horvath@ce.berkeley.edu.

HORVATH, CSABA, chemical engineering educator, researcher; b. Szolnok, Hungary, Jan. 25, 1930; came to U.S., 1963; s. Gyula and Róza (Lányi) H.; children: Donatella, Katalin. Diploma in Chem. Engring., U. Tech. Scis., Budapest, Hungary, 1952, Dr. (hon.), 1986; PhD, J.W. Goethe U., Frankfurt-Main, Germany, 1963; MA (hon.), Yale U., 1979. Asst. in chem. tech. U. Tech. Scis., Budapest, 1952-56; chem. engr. Hoechst AG, Frankfurt am Main, 1956-61; research fellow Harvard U., Cambridge, Mass., 1963-64; research assoc. Yale U. Sch. Medicine, New Haven, 1964-69, assoc. prof., 1970-79, prof. chem. engring., 1979—, chmn. dept. chem. engring., 1987-93. Prof. chem. engring. Llewellyn West Jones Jr., 1993-98, Roberto C. Goizueta, 1998—; organizing chmn. Internat. Symposium on Column Liquid Chromatography, N.Y.C., 1984; organizing co-chmn. Internat. Symposium on Capillary Electrochromatography, San Francisco, 1997-2000; organizing co-chmn. 1st internat. symposium on capillary electrochromatography, San Francisco; chmn. Gordon conf. ion exchangers and reactive polymers. Co-author: Introduction to Separation Science, 1973; assoc. editor: Encyclopedia of Bioprocess Technology, 1999; editor: Series High Performance Liquid Chromatography, 1981—, Capillary Electrochromatography (spl. issue of Jour. of Chromatography), 2000; mem. editl. bd. 9 sci. periodicals; contbr. more than 300 rsch. papers and articles to sci. publs. Organizing chmn. 8th Internat. Symposium on Column Liquid Chromatography, N.Y.C., 1984; organizing co-chmn. Internat. Symposia on Capillary Electrochromatography, San Francisco, 1997-2000. Recipient S. Dal Nogare award Delaware Valley Chromatography Forum, 1978, Tswett medal 15th Internat. Symposium on Advances in Chromatography, 1979, Humboldt sr. U.S. scientist award Humboldt Found., Fed. Republic of Germany, 1982, EAS Chromatography award, 1986, Van Slyke award N.Y. Metro Sect. Am. Assn. Clin. Chemists, 1992, A.J.P. Martin award Chromatography Soc. U.K., 1994, Disting. Contbn. in Separation Sci. award Calif. Separation Sci. Soc., 1995, Nat. award N.E. Region Chromatography Discussion Group, 1997, Halász medal award Hungarian Soc. for Separation Sci., 1997, Golay award 21st Internat. Symposium on Capillary Chromatography and Electrophoresis, 1999, M. Widmer award The New Swiss Chem. Soc., 2000, medal Conn. Separation Sci. Coun., 2000, award Assn. Biomolecular Resource Facilities, 2001, Austrian Ehrenkreuz for Sci. and Art 1st class, 2002, Tobern Bergman medal Swedish Chem. Soc., 2003. Fellow AIChE, Am. Inst. Med. and Biomed. Engrs. (founding); mem. AAAS, Deutsche Gesellschaft fuer Chemisches Apparatewesen, Chemische Technik und Biotechnologie e.v., Am. Chem. Soc. (nat. chromatography award 1983, nat. separation sci. and tech. award 2001), Am. Ceramic Soc., Hungarian Chem. Soc. (hon.), Hungarian Acad. Scis. (external), Hungarian Soc. Separation Sci. (hon.), Conn. Acad. Sci. and Engring., Conn. Acad. Arts and Scis., Inst. Food Technologists, Sigma Xi. Home: PO Box 605 41 Temple Ct New Haven CT 06503-0605 Office: Yale U PO Box 208286 9 Hillhouse Ave New Haven CT 06511-6815 E-mail: csaba.horvath@yale.edu.

HORVATH, IMRE GABOR, television producer and director; b. Constanza, Romania, Oct. 13, 1940; came to U.S., 1947; s. Emory Zoltan and Gabriella H.; m. Jean Abounader; children: Adam Zoltan, Gillian Leslie. AB, Columbia U., 1961; MA, NYU, 1963. Supr. research Grolier Pub. Co., N.Y.C., 1962-64; editor, writer Crowell-Collier Pub. Co., N.Y.C., 1964-66; film editor CBS News, other cos., N.Y.C., 1966-68; asst. producer, film editor 60 Minutes CBS News, N.Y.C., 1968-75, producer, writer 60 Minutes, 1975-80; pres., exec. producer Rainbow Broadcasting Co. (Rainbow Media, Inc.), Los Angeles and N.Y.C., 1980—. Adj. assoc. prof. journalism Columbia U., N.Y.C., 1976-78. Producer, dir. numerous segments of 60 Minutes including Noah, 1979 (Emmy award 1979), (documentaries) Murder: No Apparent Motive, 1984, Acts of Violence, 1985 (Ace award nominations 1984, 85), Cops: Behind the Badge, 1986 (Gold plaque Chgo. Internat. Film Festival 1986); producer, writer Walk Through the 20th Century with Bill Moyers (Emmy award nomination 1985); exec. producer Crimes of Passion, ABC-TV, 1988-89 (Emmy award nomination 1989), Too Good To Be True, NBC-TV, 1994-95; dir. Unsolved Mysteries, Atlantis, A Century of Living (HBO), other programs, 1990—. Recipient Journalism award Robert F. Kennedy Found., 1982, Howard Blakeslee award for Med. Journalism Am. Heart Assn., 1976. Mem. Acad. TV Arts & Scis., Dirs. Guild Am., Writers Guild Am.

HORVITZ, HOWARD ROBERT, biology educator, researcher; b. Chgo., Ill., May 8, 1947; s. Oscar and Mary Horvitz; m. Martha Constantine-Paton, May 2, 1993; 1 child, Alexandra Constantine. BS in Math., BS in Econs., MIT, 1968; MA in Biology, Harvard U., 1972, PhD in Biology, 1974. Postdoctoral fellow Med. Rsch. Coun. Lab. Molecular Biology, Cambridge, Eng.; asst. to assoc. prof. biology MIT, Cambridge, 1978-86, prof., 1986—, career devel. assoc. prof. biology, Whitehead Inst., 1982-85, mem. sci. adv. bd. Howard Hughes program in neurosci., 1984-88, investigator Howard Hughes Med. Inst., 1988—, Whitehead prof. biology, 1999-2000, David H. Koch prof. biology, 2000—. Neurobiologist (neurology), geneticist (medicine) Mass. Gen. Hosp., Boston, 1989—; advisor dept. biochemistry and molecular biology Harvard U., 1984-90; mem. neurobiology adv. bd. Cold Spring Harbor Lab., 1984—; mem. sci. adv. bd. Hereditary Disease Found., 1987-93, collaborative rsch. group adv. com., 1988-93, cure HD initiative adv. com., 1996—; mem. sci. adv. bd., Jane Coffin Childs Meml. Fund for Med. Rsch., 1989-97; sci. adv. bd. Com. on Scholarly Comm. with People's Rep. of China, U.S. NAS, 1987-93, Ain-Shams Med. Genetics Ctr. Cairo, 1990-91; co-organizer Gordon Conf. on Devel. Biology, 1985; organizer biennial meeting Cold Spring Harbor Internat. Conf., 1985, coms., 1981, 87; mem. organizing com. biennial meeting Ea. Coast C. Elegans, Cambridge, 1988, 90; mem. sci. rev. com. Amyotrophic Lateral Sclerosis Assn., 1990-95, co-chair meetings 1991, 93; lectr. Harvey Soc., 1989; macrofil steering com. spl. programme for esch and tng. in tropical diseases, WHO, 1992-95; adv. bd. Umea (Sweden) Ctr. Molecular Pathogenesis, 1993-96; co-chair working group on preclin. models for cancer Nat. Cancer Inst., NIH, 1996—; mem. adv. coun. Nat. Ctr. for Human Genome Rsch., NIH, 1996—; mem. sci. adv. group Sanger Ctr., Cambridgeshire, Eng., 1994—; chair devel. biology review com. Swedish Found. for Strategic Rsch., 1996; mem. sci. adv. bd. Umea (Sweden) Ctr. Molecular Pathogenesis, 1993-96, Netherlands Cancer Inst. Site Vis. Com., 1998; mem. sci. adv. com. Warren Alpert Found. (prize), 1997—; external review bd. dept. molecular, cellular and devel. biology U. Colo., Boulder, 1996; mem. sci. adv. group U. Pa. Med. Ctr. Inst. Aging, 1995—; cons. sci. adv. bd. Idun Pharmaceuticals, Inc., 1993—, Axys Pharms. Inc., 1998—. Author: (with others) The Role of Intercelluar Signals: Navigation, Encounter, Outcome, 1979, Genetic Maps, Vol. 1, 1980, Nematodes as Biological Models, 1980, Development of the Nervous System, 1981, Repair and Regeneration of the Nervous System, 1982, The Nematode Caenorhabditis elegans, 1988; mem. editl. bds. Jour. Neurogenetics, 1982-88, Jour. Neurosci., 1984-89, Devel. Biology, 1985-95, Genes and Devel., 1986-98, Cell, 1987-99, Trends in Genetics, 1987—, Neuron, 1987-90, The New Biologist, 1989-92, Genetic Analysis: Techniques and Applications, 1990-95, Current Opinion in Neurobiology, 1990—, Current Biol., 1992-95, Annual Rev. Genetics, 1993-97, Cell Death & Differentiation, 1994—, Neurobiology of Disease, 1994—, Jour. Exptl. Therapeutics and Oncology, 1995—, Invertebrate Neurosci., 1994—, Devel., 1986-93, Cancer Rsch., 1995-2000, Procs. of the NAS, 1997—, Jour. Cell Biology, 1997-2000, Genome Biology, 1999—; patentee in field; contbr. numerous articles to profl. jours. Mem. adv. bd. World Health Orgn. Spl. Programme for Rsch. and Tng. in Tropical Diseases, Microfil steering com., 1992-95. Recipient Rsch. Career Devel. award NIH, 1981-86, Spencer award in Neurobiology, Columbia U., 1986, Warren Triennial prize Mass. Gen. Hosp., 1986, Molecular Biology award U.S. Steel Found., 1988, Method to Extend Rsch. in Time award NIH, 1991, V.D. Mattia award Roche Inst. Molecular Biology, 1993, Hans Sigrist award, 1994, Charles A. Dana award for pioneering achievements in health and edn. Inst. Medicine NAS, 1995, Ciba-Drew award for biomed. sci., 1996, Rosenstiel award Brandeis U., 1998, Passano award for the advancement med. sci., 1998, Alfred P. Sloan Jr. prize GM Cancer Rsch. Found., 1998, Gairdner Found. Internat. award, 1999, Paul Ehrlich and Ludwig Darmstaedter prize, Frankfurt, Germany, 2000, Segerfalk award, 2000, March of Dimes prize in devel. biology, 2000, Charles-Leopold Mayer prize French Acad. Scis., 2000, Louisa Gross Horwitz prize, 2000, Bristol-Myers Squibb Award for Disting. Achievement in Neuroscience, 2001, Genetics Society of America Medal, 2001, Nobel prize in physiology or medicine, 2002; Woodrow Wilson fellow, 1968, NSF predoctoral fellow, 1968-72, Muscular Dystrophy Assn. postdoctoral fellow, 1974-77. Fellow AAAS, Am. Acad. Arts and Scis., Am. Acad. Microbiology, Am. Acad. Microbilogy; mem. Am. Assn. Cancer Rsch., U.S. Nat. Acad. Scis., Genetics Soc. Am. (membership com. 1984-86, bd. dirs. 1990-92, 94-96, organizer ann. meeting 1989, v.p. 1994, pres. 1995), Soc. Devel. Biology (nominations com. 1989), Soc. Nematologists, Soc. Neurosci. (pub. info. com. 1993-95), Am. Soc. Cell Biology (organizing com. ann. meeting 1992, pub. policy com. 1993-96, joint steering com. pub. policy 1994-97, exec. com. 1995—), Am. Soc. Microbiology, Helminthological Soc. Washington. Office: MIT Dept Biology 68-425 77 Massachusetts Ave Cambridge MA 02139-4307

HORVITZ, JOHN C. management consultant; b. Boston, Sept. 30, 1935; m. Sandra Farber, Jan. 19, 1963. BA, Harvard Coll., 1957, MBA, 1959. Retail buyer R. H. Macy's Inc., N.Y.C., 1960—64; product mgr. Bristol Myers, N.Y.C., 1964—70; jr. v.p., mktg. Aramis divsn. Estee Lauder, N.Y.C., 1970—76, v.p., gen. mgr. Parfums Lauder Pret, 1976—78; pres. Warner Western Fragrances, a divsn of Warner Commn., N.Y.C., 1978—81, Horvitz & Assocs., Inc., N.Y.C., 1981—. Avocations: tennis, skiing, biking, music, gardening. Office: Horvitz & Assoc 77 Park Ave New York NY 10016

HORVITZ, MICHAEL JOHN, lawyer; b. Cleve., Feb. 15, 1950; s. Harry Richard and Lois Joy (Unger) H.; m. Jane Rosenthal, Aug. 25, 1979; children: Katherine R., Elizabeth R. BS in Econs., U. Pa., 1972; JD, U. Va., 1975; LLM in Taxation, NYU, 1980. Bar: Ohio 1975, Fla. 1976. Assoc. Hahn, Loeser, Freedheim, Dean & Wellman, Cleve., 1975-78; counsel Hollywood, Inc., Fla., 1978-79; assoc. Jones, Day, Reavis & Pogue, Cleve., 1980-85, ptnr., 1985-2000, of counsel, 2001—. Mem. adv. bd. Kirtland Capital Ptnrs., L.P., 1992—; chmn. Parkland Mgmt. Co., 1992—; vice chmn. Horvitz Newspapers, Inc., 1994—; pres. H.R.H. Family Found., 1992—; chmn. H.R.H. Family Trust, 1992—; bd. dirs. Zephyr Mgmt., Inc.; corp. advisor Internat. Mgmt. Group, 1999—. Trustee Jewish Cmty. Fedn. Cleve., 1993-99, 2002—, Case Western Res. U., Musical Arts Assn., 1992—, Cleve. Ctr. Econ. Edn., 1992-95, Am. Cancer Soc., Cuyahoga County unit, 1989-95, Hathaway Brown Sch., Mt. Sinai Med. Ctr., Cleve. chpt. Am. Jewish Com., 1984-95, Montefiore Home for the Elderly, 1982-90, Health Hill Hosp. for Children, 1982-95, bd. pres., 1987-89; bd. dirs. Cleve. Mus. Art, 1991—, pres. bd., 1996-2001, chmn. bd., 2001—; bd. dirs. U. Va. Law Sch. Found., 1999—, pres., 2002—. Office: Jones Day 901 Lakeside Ave E Cleveland OH 44114-1190 also: Parkland Mgmt Co 1001 Lakeside Ave E Ste 900 Cleveland OH 44114-1172

HORVITZ, PAUL MICHAEL, finance educator, educator; b. Providence, Aug. 6, 1935; s. Abraham and Rose (Gershkoff) H.; m. Carol Broomfield, Nov. 17, 1955; children: Marcia Ellen Cohen, Steven Jay. BA, U. Chgo., 1954; MBA, Boston U., 1956; PhD in Econs., MIT, 1958. Fin. economist Fed. Reserve Bank of Boston, 1957-60; asst. prof. Boston U., 1960-62; sr. economist, compt. of currency Washington, 1963-66; dir. rsch. FDIC, 1967-77; prof. banking and fin. U. Houston, 1977—2001, emeritus, 2001—. Author: Management of Bank Funds, 1981, Monetary Policy & the Financial System, 6th edit., 1987; co-editor Jour. Fin. Svcs. Rsch.; contbr. articles to profl. jours. Mem. Am. Econ. Assn., Am. Fin. Assn., Shadow Fin. Regulatory Com. Home: 150 Sugarberry Cir Houston TX 77024-7244 E-mail: paulhorvitz@aol.com.

HORWICH, ALLAN, lawyer; b. Des Moines, Apr. 8, 1944; s. Joseph Maurice and Bernice (Davidson) Horwich; m. Carolyn Ruth Allen, Feb. 28, 1975; children: Benjamin, Diana, Eleanor, Flannery. AB, Princeton U., 1966; JD, U. Chgo., 1969. Bar: Ill. 1969, U.S. Dist. Ct. (no. dist.) Ill. 1969, U.S. Ct. Appeals (7th cir.) 1971, U.S. Supreme Ct. 1976, U.S. Ct. Appeals (10th cir.) 1983, U.S. Dist. Ct. (ctrl. dist.) Ill. 1990, U.S. Dist. Ct. (ea. dist.) Wis. 1995, U.S. Dist. Ct. (ea. dist.) Mich. 1995, U.S. Ct. Appeals (6th cir.) 1996. Assoc. Schiff Hardin & Waite, Chgo., 1969-74; ptnr. Schiff Hardin and Waite, Chgo., 1975—, vice-chmn., 1989-95. Adj. prof. law Northwestern U. Sch. Law, 1999—2000, sr. lectr. law, 2000—; mem. adv. bd. Wall St. Lawyer. Contbr. articles to profl. jours. Home: 216 W Concord Ln Chicago IL 60614-5743 Office: Schiff Hardin & Waite 6600 Sears Tower Chicago IL 60606 E-mail: ahorwich@schiffhardin.com.

HORWICH, ARTHUR L. medical educator; AB, Brown U., 1972, MD, 1975. Prof. genetics and pediat. Yale U., New Haven, assoc. investigator Howard Hughes Med. Inst. Recipient Basil O'Connor Rsch. award; John A. Hartford Found. fellow. Mem.: NAS. Office: Dept Genetics Yale U Sch Medicine 333 Cedar St PO Box 208005 New Haven CT 06520-8005*

HORWICH, GEORGE, economist, educator; b. Detroit, July 23, 1924; s. Charles and Rose (Katzman) H.; m. Geraldine Lessans, Dec. 27, 1953; children: Ellen Beth, Karen Louise, Robert Lloyd, Susan Jean. Student, Wayne State U., 1942-43, 46, Ind. U., 1943-44; AM, U. Chgo., 1951, PhD, 1954. Lectr. econs. Extension Ctrs. Ind. U., Gar and Calumet, 1949-52, instr. econs. Bloomington, 1952-55; rsch. assoc. Nat. Bur. Econ. Rsch., N.Y.C., 1955-56; from asst. prof. to prof. econs. Purdue U., West Lafayette, Ind., 1956-99, chmn. econs. dept., 1974-78, Burton D. Morgan prof. for study pvt. enterprise, 1981-94, prof. emeritus, 1999—. Sr. rsch. assoc. Brookings Instn., Washington, 1958-62; sr. economist U.S. Dept. Energy, Washington, 1978-80; spl. asst. for contingency planning U.S. Dept. Energy, 1984; adj. scholar Am. Enterprise Inst., 1984—; collaborating scientist energy divsn. Oak Ridge Nat. Lab., 1988-94; mem. U.S. Treasury Cons. Group, Washington, 1969; cons. Fed. Res. Bank, Chgo., 1971; vis. prof. econs. U. Calif., San Diego, 1971-72, People's Univ. of China, Beijing, 1992, Kobe (Japan) U. Commerce, 1996-97; vis. scholar Victoria U., New Zealand, 1997; staff Ind. Coun. Econ. Edn., West Lafayette, 1974—. Ctr. Pub. Policy and Pub. Adminstrn., Purdue U., West Lafayette, 1977—; advisor Econ. Inst. Rsch. and Edn., Boulder, Colo., 1977—; cons. U.S. Dept. Energy,

1980-88, Fortune 500 cos., 1965—, U.S. Dept. State, Washington, 1982, 92, Hudson Inst., 1991; vis. prof. Yokohama (Japan) City U., 2000. Author: Money, Capital and Prices, 1964; (with others) Costs and Benfits of a Protective Tariff on Refined Petroleum Products After Crude Oil Decontrol, 1980, Energy: An Economic Analysis, 1983; (with D.L. Weimer) Oil Price Shocks, Market Response and Contingency Planning, 1984; Responding to International Oil Crises, 1988; editor: Monetary Process and Policy, 1967, (with P.A. Samuelson) Trade, Stability, and Macroeconomics, 1974; (with J.P. Quirk) Essays in Contemporary Fields of Economics, 1981; (with E.J. Mitchell) Policies for Coping with Oil-Supply Disruptions, 1982, Energy Use in Transportation Contingency Planning, 1983; (with G.J. Lynch) Food, Policy and Politics, 1989; contbr. articles to profl. jours. With U.S. Army, 1943-46, ETO. NSF grantee; Fulbright rschr., 1996-97. Mem. Internat. Assn. Energy Econs., Am. Econ. Assn., Midwest Econs. Assn., Mont. Pelerin Soc., Nat. Assn. Scholars, Phila. Soc., Assn. Pub. Policy Analysis and Mgmt. Home: 120 Seminole Dr West Lafayette IN 47906-2116 Office: Purdue U Dept Econs West Lafayette IN 47907-1310

HORWICH, HARVEY, printer, publisher; b. Chgo., Jan. 1, 1929; s. Hy and Lillian Horwich; m. June H. Brounson, Aug. 22, 1948; children: Bruce, amela, Jeffrey, Robert, Paul. BA, UCLA, 1951. Owner, mgr. Lenoir Printing, Long Beach, Calif., 1959—. Councilman City of Torrance, Calif., 1982—; mem. Torrance Planning Commn., Torrance Parks and Recreation Commn.; mem. mgmt. team Spl. Olympics. Named Outstanding Vol., Lions Club, Torrance, 1995, Citizen of Yr., Torrance C. of C., 1997. Mem. Printing Assn. L.A. (past pres.). Home: 5537 Michelle Dr Torrance CA 90503-1836

HORWIN, LEONARD, retired lawyer; b. Chgo., Jan. 2, 1913; s. Joseph and Jennie (Fuhrmann) H.; m. Ursula Helene Donig, Oct. 15, 1939; children: Noel Samuel, Leonora Marie. LLD cum laude, Yale U., 1936. Bar: Calif. 1936, U.S. Dist. Ct. (cen. dist.) Calif. 1937, U.S. Ct. Appeals (9th cir.) 1939, U.S. Supreme Ct. 1940. Assoc. Lawler, Felix & Hall, 1936-39; counsel Bd. Econ. Warfare, Washington, 1942-43; attache, legal advisor U.S. Embassy, Madrid, 1943-47; sole practice Beverly Hills, Calif., 1948—2002. Dir., lectr. Witkin-Horwin Rev. Course on Calif. Law, 1939-42; judge pro tempore Los Angeles Superior Ct., 1940-42; instr. labor law U. So. Calif., 1939-42. Author: Insight and Foresight, 1990, Plain Talk, 1931—; contbr. articles to profl. jours. U.S. rep. Allied Control Council for Ger., 1945-47; councilman City of Beverly Hills, 1962-66, mayor, 1964-65; chmn. transp. Los Angeles Goals Council, 1968; bd. dirs. So. Calif. Rapid Transit Dist., 1964-66; chmn. Rent Stabilization Com., Beverly Hills, 1980. Fellow Am. Acad. Matrimonial Lawyers; mem. ABA, State Bar Calif., Order of Coif, Balboa Bay Club, Aspen Inst., La Costa Country Club. Address: 434 El Camino Dr Beverly Hills CA 90212-4222 E-mail: lhorwin@linkline.com.

HORWITZ, ALLAN BARRY, publishing executive; b. Bklyn., July 10, 1947; s. Gerard and Rhoda Horwitz; m. Elizabeth Ruth Farkas, June 22, 1975; children: Aaron, Robert, Tara, Blake. BA, U. Hartford, 1969; postgrad., Coll. William and Mary, 1970, The New Sch. for Social Research, 1973. Account exec. Wall Street Jour., N.Y.C., 1970-72, sales strategy planner, 1972-74; acquisitions and new bus. ventures analyst Dow Jones & Co., Inc., N.Y.C., 1974-76; pub. TV News, N.Y.C., 1973—; chmn., chief exec. officer Modular Publs., Inc., N.Y.C., 1974—, also bd. dirs.; pres., chmn., bd. dirs. Community Publs. of Am., Inc., N.Y.C., 1979—. Mem. Blue Ribbon panel of judges Emmy Awards, 1987-95; judge Internat. Film and TV Festival, 1990-92, Nat. Sports Emmy Awards, 1990-95. Mem. Consumers Union. Democrat. Jewish. Avocations: water skiing, boating, reading, chess, computers. Office: Community Publs of Am Inc 80 8th Ave New York NY 10011-5126

HORWITZ, BARBARA ANN, physiologist, educator, consultant; b. Chgo., Sept. 26, 1940; d. Martin Horwitz and Lillian Bloom; m. John M. Horowitz, Aug. 17, 1970. BS, U. Fla., 1961, MS, 1962; PhD, Emory U., 1966. Asst. rsch. physiologist U. Calif., Davis, 1968-72, asst. prof. physiology, 1972-75, assoc. prof., 1975-78, prof., 1978—, chair animal physiology, 1991-93, chmn. neurobiology, physiology and behavior dept., 1993-98, vice provost acad. personnel, 2001—. Cons. Am. Inst. Behavioral Rsch., Palo Alto, Calif., 1980, Am. Inst. Rsch., Washington, 1993-99, NSF, Washington, 1981-84, NIH, Washington, 1995-99. Contbr. articles to profl. jours. Named Arthur C. Guyton Physiology Tchr. of the Yr., 1996, postdoctoral fellow, USPHS, 1966—68; recipient Disting. Tchg. award, 1982, U. Calif.-Davis prize for Tchg. and Scholarly Achievement, 1991, Pres.'s award for excellence in fostering undergrad. rsch., 1995. Fellow: AAAS; mem.: Phi Sigma (v.p. Davis chpt. 1983—, nat. v.p. 1989—), Phi Kappa Pi, Soc. Exptl. Biology and Medicine (exec. coun. 1990—94, pres.-elect 1999—2001, pres. 2001—03, past pres. 2003—), N.Am. Assn. for Study of Obesity (exec. coun. 1988—92), N.Y. Acad. Scis., Am. Physiology Soc. (edn. and program coms. coun. 1993—96, pres.-elect 2001—02, pres. 2002—03, past pres. 2003—), Sigma Xi (pres. Davis chpt. 1980—81), Phi Beta Kappa (pres. Davis chpt. 1991—92, 2000—02). Office: U Calif Dept Neurobiology Phys Davis CA 95616 E-mail: bahorwitz@ucdavis.edu.

HORWITZ, BERTRAND NATHAN, accounting and finance educator; b. Chgo., Mar. 12, 1927; s. Max Solomon and Esther (Green) H.; m. Hertha Ostre Horwitz, Oct. 25, 1952; children: Eve, Neal, Mara. AB, U. Chgo., 1949, MA, 1951; PhD, U. Minn., 1962. Assoc. Russian Rsch. Ctr., Cambridge, Mass., 1960—61; Sloan tchg. fellow MIT, 1962-63; asst. prof. U. Rochester, N.Y., 1964-67; assoc. to full prof. Syracuse (N.Y.) U., 1967-72; prof. Binghamton (N.Y.) U., 1972—. Vis prof. U. Chgo., 1978—79, Nat. Ctr. for Indsl. Sci. and Tech., Mgmt. Devel., China, 1981—82; cons. UN, 1984; vis prof. Nat. Ctr. for Indsl. Sci. and Tech., Mgmt. Devel., China, 1984; vis. prof. U. Internat. Bus. and Econs., Beijing, 1988; vis prof. Chinese U., Hong Kong, 1993—94, City U., Hong Kong, 1994—96, 1998—99, 2000. Co-author: (book) Financial Accounting and Corporate Decisions, 1982; author: (book) Soviet Industrial Accounting, 1969. With USN, 1945-46. Rsch. grantee NSF, 1979, 83; recipient Gov.'s award N.Y. State, 1992, Internat. Edn. and Bus. award U.S. Dept. Edn., 1988 91. Mem. Am. Acctg. Assn., Am. Econ. Assn., Fin. Execs. Inst. Jewish. Avocations: reading, running, fgn. langs. Home: 3317 Almar Dr Vestal NY 13850-2836 E-mail: horwitz@binghamton.edu.

HORWITZ, DAVID A. physician, scientist, educator; BA, U. Mich., 1958; MD, U. Chgo., 1962. Intern, resident Michael Reese Hosp., Chgo., 1966; rheumatology fellow Southwestern Med. Sch. U. Tex., 1969, instr. internal medicine Southwestern Med. Sch., 1968-69; from asst. prof. to assoc. prof. medicine Sch. Medicine U. Va., Charlottesville, 1969-79, prof. medicine, 1979-80; prof. medicine and microbiology, chief divsn. rheumatology and immunology sect. Sch. Medicine U. So. Calif., L.A., 1980—. Vis. prof. Clin. Rsch. Ctr., Harrow, Eng., 1976-77; vis. investigator Inperial Cancer Rsch. Fund, London, 1988-89; vis. scientist Nat. Inst. Arthritis, Musculoskeletal and Skin Diseases, NIH, Bethesda, Md., 2001-02. Contbr. more than 100 articles to profl. jours. Recipient James R. Klinnenberg award for rsch., Arthritis Found. Mem.: Am. Rheumatism Assn. (pres. 1985). Achievements include research in elucidation of lymphocytes, cytokines and immunologic circuits involved in the regulation of antibody production, characterization of pathologic abnormalities in immune regulation in subjects with Systemic Lupus Erythematosus; The generation of regulatory Tcell subsets ex-vivo, and their potential for the treatment of autoimmune diseases and to prevent graft rejection. Office: Divsn Rheumatology And Immunology 2011 Zonal Ave # 711 Los Angeles CA 90089-0110

HORWITZ, DAVID LARRY, pharmaceuticals company executive, researcher, educator; b. Chgo., July 13, 1942; s. Milton Woodrow and Dorothy (Glass) H.; m. Gloria Jean Madian, June 20, 1965; children: Karen, Laura. BA, Harvard U., 1963; MD, U. Chgo., 1967; PhD, 1968; MBA, Lake Forest Grad. Sch. Mgmt., 1991. Diplomate Am. Bd. Internal Medicine. Resident in internal medicine U. Chgo. Hosp., 1971-72; fellow in endocrinology U. Chgo., 1972-74; asst. prof., 1974-79; assoc. prof. U. Ill., Chgo., 1979-90; clin. prof. medicine, 1990-92; med. dir. Baxter Healthcare Corp., Deerfield, Ill., 1982-91; v.p. med. and profl. affairs, 1991-92; v.p. med. and regulatory affairs SciClone Pharms., San Mateo, Calif., 1992-95; exec. v.p., 1995-97; sr. v.p. Tech. Advanced Tissue Scis., La Jolla, Calif., 1998-2000; v.p. med. and regulatory affairs LifeScan (a Johnson and Johnson Co.), Milpitas, Calif., 2000—. Contbr. over 100 articles to profl. jours. Comdr. USNR, 1969-71. Recipient Outstanding Young Citizen of Chgo. award Chgo. Jr. C. of C., 1976, Outstanding Young Citizen Ill. award Jaycees, 1977. Fellow ACP; mem. Am. Diabetes Assn. (bd. dirs. No. Ill. affil. 1976-92, pres. 1987-89, R & D award 1974-76), Am. Assn. Clin. Nutrition, Endocrine Soc.

HORWITZ, DONALD PAUL, lawyer; b. Chgo., Feb. 5, 1936; s. Theodore J. and Lillian H. (Shlensky) H.; m. Judith Robin, Aug. 23, 1964; children: Terry Robin Kass, Linda Diane, Gail Elizabeth. BS, Northwestern U., 1957; JD, Yale U., 1960. Bar: Ill. 1961, D.C. 1961, U.S. Supreme Ct. 1966; CPA, Ill. With atty. gen.'s honors program Dept. Justice, 1961-63; atty. Gottlieb & Schwartz, Chgo., 1963-66; with Arthur Young & Co. CPAs, Chgo., 1966-72, ptnr., 1971-72; exec. v.p., sec., dir. McDonald's Corp., Oak Brook, Ill., 1972-90; ptnr. Sonnenschein, Nath & Rosenthal, Chgo., 1990—. Lectr. Northwestern U. Law Sch., Grad. Sch. Commerce, DePaul U., Chgo.; bd. dirs. Bernard Tech. Inc., 1997—, chmn. bd., 1998-2002; sec. System Capital Corp, 1996. Contbr. articles to profl. jours. Trustee Goodman Theatre/Chgo. Theatre Group, 1993—96, Evans Scholars Found., Western Golf Assn., 1984—87; pres., bd. dirs. Briarwood Country Club, 1972—73; caucus nominating com. Village of Glencoe, Ill., 1975—78, vice-chmn., 1988—89; bd. dirs. Northwestern Healthcare Network, 1990—94; vice-chmn., bd. dirs., chmn. bd. Highland Park Hosp., Lakeland Health Ventures and Northwestern Network, bd. govs., 1994—2000; chief legal officer adv. bd. Northwestern U. Kellogg Bus. Sch., 2000—; chmn. Midwest region Anti-Defamation League, 1994—95, mem. nat. commn., 1994—; exec. com. Yale Law Sch. Assn.; bd. dirs. Lakeland Health Ventures and Northwestern Network, 1986—94, McDonald's Family Charities, Inc., 2001, Scholl Sch. Podiatry, 2001—03, Chgo. Med. Sch./Finch U. Health Scis., 1993—2003, Found. for Podiatric Edn., 2002—03. Mem.: ABA, Am. Arbitration Assn. (arbitrator panel 1991—), Chgo. Bar Found. (trustee 1990—97), Chgo. Bar Assn., Ill. Bar Assn., Northmoor Country Club, Econs. Club, Standard Club.

HORWITZ, ELEANOR CATHERINE, information and education official; b. N.Y.C., Dec. 21, 1941; d. Fritz and Hedwig E.F. (Kramer) Jahoda; m. Paul Horwitz, Aug. 15, 1964; children: Gregory Douglas, Catherine Helen, Laura Elizabeth. BA, Swarthmore Coll., 1962; MA, NYU, 1967; MS, Cornell U., 1969; postgrad., Oreg. State U., 1969-70. Sci. tchr. New Lincoln Sch., N.Y.C., 1962-67; coordinator outdoor edn. Lane County Int. Edn. Dist., Eugene, Oreg., 1969-70; staff writer Billerica (Mass.) Banner, 1971-72; instr., writer Mass. Audubon Soc., Lincoln, 1972-75; pub. use specialist U.S. Fish and Wildlife Service, Concord, Mass., 1975; staff writer Soc. Am. Foresters, Washington, 1975-76; mem. Mass. Gov.'s Forestry Rev. Bd., Boston, 1976-77; chief info. and edn. Mass. Div. Fisheries and Wildlife, Westborough, 1977—. Mem. steering com. Sec.'s Adv. Group on Environ. Edn. Exec. Office of Environ. Affairs, Commonwealth of Mass., 1990-2000, co-chair, 1992-97, chair, 1997-98; bd. dirs. Mass. Wildlife Fedn., 1986—, v.p., 1989-95, 97—, pres., 1995-97. Author: Clearcutting, A View from the Top, 1974; author, editor: Ways of Wildlife, 1977 (ACI Book award 1978); editor: (mag.) Massachusetts Wildlife, 1977—; contbr. articles to popular mags. Active Concord Natural Resources Commn., 1976-82, chmn. 1979-80; trustee Concord Land Conservation Trust, 1988—, trustee Holbrook Island Trust, 1993-2000; MBA rep. West Concord Union Ch., 1998-2003; deacon W. Concord Union Ch., 2003—. Recipient R.E. Dimmick award Oreg. Wildlife Soc., 1970, citation Worcester County League Sportsmen's Clubs, 1987, citation Minutemen chpt. Ducks Unltd., 1987, Conservation award Mahar Fish & Game Assn., 1991, Woman of Yr. award N.E. County Quabbin Anglers Assn., 1991, Sportsman of Yr. New England Outdoor Writers, 1998, Spl. award for Wildlife edn., Mass. Sportsmen's Coun., 2003, Disting. Svc. award Ducks Unltd., 2003. Mem. Outdoor Writers of Am., New Eng. Outdoor Writers Assn. (membership sec. 1987-90, bd. dirs. 1987—, sec. 1990-93, 2001-2003, v.p. 1993-94, 99-2000, pres. 1994-95), Am. Forestry Assn. (life), New Eng. Conservation Info. and Edn. Assn. (chmn. 1986-87, 90-91), Mass. Wildlife Fedn., Wildlife Soc. (profl. cert., chmn. edn. com. 1974-76, 84-87, nominating com. 1990-91, Leopold award com. 1996-98, cert. of recognition 1978), Nashoba Sportsmen's Club, Concord Rod and Gun Club, Maynard Rod and Gun Club (hon.). Mem. United Ch. of Christ. Office: Mass Divsn Fisheries and Wildlife Westborough MA 01581

HORWITZ, ETHAN, lawyer; b. Binghamton, NY, May 9, 1952; s. Lester and Barbara (Goldstein) H.; m. Freddi Sue Finegood; children: Jessica Sara, Matthew Eli, Emily Crystal. BS, Poly. Inst., 1972; MS, NYU, 1974; JD, St. Johns U., 1976. Bar: N.Y. 1977. Assoc. Cooper, Dunham, Clark, Griffin & Moran, N.Y.C., 1976-77, Ladas & Parry, N.Y.C., 1977-80; from assoc. to ptnr. Darby & Darby, NYC, 1980—2002; ptnr. Goodwin Procter, LLP, NYC, 2002—. Author: (treatise) World Trademark Law and Practice, 1982; co-author: (treatise) Patent Litigation: Procedure and Tactics; co-editor: Intellectual Property Counseling and Litigation; mem. editl. bd. Trademark Reporter, 1980-82. Bd. dirs. Project Dorot, N.Y.C., 1977—, pres., 1984-89. Mem. N.Y. Patent Law Assn., U.S. Trademark Assn. (chmn. Western Europe com.), Inst. Trademark Agts. (overseas mem.), Internat. Assn. Protection Indsl. Property, Internat. Bar Assn. Fedn. Internat. de Conseils en Propriete Industrielle. Jewish. Office: Goodwin Procter LLP 599 Lexington Ave New York NY 10019

HORWITZ, IRWIN DANIEL, otolaryngologist, educator; b. Chgo., Mar. 31, 1920; s. Sol and Belle (Stern) H.; m. Isabel Morwitz, July 23, 1944; children— Steven, Judd, Clare. BS, U. Ill., 1941, MD, 1943. Intern Cook County Hosp., Chgo., 1944; resident Ill. Eye and Ear Infirmary, Chgo., 1946-48; practice otolaryngology Chgo., 1948—; clin. prof., head divsn. otolaryngology Chgo. Med. Sch., 1969; prof. Rush Med. Sch., 1976—; formerly chief divsn. otolaryngology Mt. Sinai Hosp., former pres. med. staff. Contbr. articles profl. jours. Served to capt., M.C. AUS, 1944-46. Fellow A.C.S.; mem. AMA, Chgo. Otol. and Laryngol. Assn., Am. Acad. Ophthalmology and Otolaryngology, Ill., Chgo. med. socs. Home: 1633 2nd St #106 Highland Park IL 60035-5719 Office: 9669 Kenton Ave Skokie IL 60076-1266

HORWITZ, JOY A. foundation administrator; b. Apr. 18, 1958; BA in European History and English, Cornell U.; JD, U. Pa. Assoc. Pepper, Hamilton and Scheetz, Phila.; assoc. Environ. program Pew Charitable Trusts, Phila., 1992—98, dir. legal affairs, 1998—. Chair Environ. Commn., Haddonfield, NJ. Office: Pew Charitable Trusts 2005 Market St Ste 1700 Philadelphia PA 19103-7077

HORWITZ, KENNETH MERRILL, lawyer, accountant; b. Atlanta, Oct. 11, 1943; s. Sidney A. and Lillian Ann (Rappaport) H.; m. Barbara Lynn Smith, June 23, 1968; children: Seth A., Lisa E. BS in Psychology, Ga. Inst. Tech., 1965; JD, Emory U., 1968; LLM, George Washington U., 1972. Bar: Ga. 1968, D.C. 1969, Tex. 1974. Sr. tax specialist IRS, Washington, 1969-74; assoc. McDonald, Sanders et al, Ft. Worth, 1974-76; ptnr. Laventhol & Horwath, Dallas, 1978-83, Coopers & Lybrand, Dallas, 1989, Washington, 1983-89; ptnr. gen. bus. & taxation Vial, Hamilton, Koch & Knox, Dallas, 1989—. Contbr. articles to profl. jours. Mem. ABA, AICPA, Tex. Bar Assn., Tex. Soc. CPAs (bd. dirs., bd. govs. CPE Found.), Dallas Bar Assn. (past chair internat. law sect.), Internat. Trade Assn. Dallas Ft. Worth (former treas.), Dallas Coun. World Affairs (bd. dirs.), Internat. Tax Assn. (chmn. Dallas chpt.). Office: Vial Hamilton Koch & Knox LLP 1717 Main St Ste 4400 Dallas TX 75201-7388

HORWITZ, MARCUS AARON, microbiologist, immunologist; b. Elmira, N.Y., May 3, 1946; s. Abraham and Rose (Hirsch) H.; m. Helene L. DesRuisseaux, Nov. 27, 1981; children: Joshua, Daniel. AB in Physics, Cornell U., 1968; MD, Columbia U., 1972. Diplomate Am. Bd. Internal Medicine, Am. Bd. Infectious Diseases. Resident in medicine Albert Einstein Coll. Medicine, Bronx, N.Y., 1972-74, fellow in infectious diseases, 1976-77; epidemic intelligence svc. officer Ctrs. for Disease Control and Prevention, Atlanta, 1974-76; NIH postdoctoral fellow The Rockefeller U., N.Y.C., 1977-80, asst. prof., 1980-84, assoc. physician, 1980-84; chief infectious diseases UCLA Sch. Medicine, L.A., 1985-92, prof. medicine and microbiology, immunology, genetics, 1985—. Chmn. scientific adv. bd. Am. Leprosy Found., Rockville, Md., 1990—; trustee Trudeau Inst., Saranac Lake, N.Y., 1994-97; mem. tuberculosis panel U.S. - Japan Coop. Med. Scis. Program, 1991-95. Mem. editl. bd., guest editor: Jour. of Clin. Investigation, 1989-96; editor: (book) Bacteria - Host Cell Interaction, 1988; patentee vaccine for Legionnaires' Disease, vaccine for tuberculosis, Exochelins. Cmdr. USPHS 1974-76. Recipient Alexander Langmuir award Ctrs. for Disease Control, Atlanta, 1976, Faculty Rsch. award Am. Cancer Soc., 1985. Fellow AAAS, Infectious Diseases Soc. Am. (Squibb award for Outstanding Rsch. 1991), Am. Soc. Clin. Investigation. Office: UCLA/Dept Medicine CHS 37-121 10833 Le Conte Ave Los Angeles CA 90095-1688 E-mail: MHorwitz@mednet.ucla.edu.

HORWITZ, MELVIN, lawyer, physician; b. N.Y.C., Nov. 20, 1926; m. Dorothy G. Horwitz. BA, Columbia U., 1945; MD, Harvard U., 1949; JD, Yale U., 1986. Bar: Conn. 1986. Resident in surgery Yale-New Haven Hosp., New Haven, 1959-52; resident Columbia-Presbyterian Med. Ctr., 1954-55; surgeon Manchester (Conn.) Meml. Hosp., 1956-86, chief of surgery, 1976-81, sr. surgeon emeritus, 1981—; rsch. cons., vis. lectr. dept. animal pathology and virology U. Conn., Storrs, 1962-73. Adj. prof. Western New Eng. Law Sch., Springfield, Mass., 1986-87; pres. Helapol Assocs., Manchester, 1987—; chmn. Nutmeg Inst. Rev. Bd., 1991-2001; cons. Inst. Medicine, Washington, 1985. Office: Helapol Assoc 223 Ludlow Rd Manchester CT 06040-4546

HORWITZ, PAUL, physicist; b. N.Y.C., Dec. 4, 1938; s. Louis David and Sylvia Helen (Laibman) H.; m. Eleanor Catherine Jahoda, Aug. 15, 1964; children: Gregory Douglas Lee, Catherine Helen, Laura Elizabeth. AB, Harvard U., 1960; MS, Columbia U., 1963; PhD, NYU, 1967. Rsch. assoc. Cornell U., Ithaca, N.Y., 1967-69, U. Oreg., Eugene, 1969-71; prin. rsch. scientist Avco Everett Rsch. Lab., Everett, Mass., 1971-79; sr. scientist Bolt, Beranek & Newman Inc., Cambridge, Mass., 1979-91; divsn. scientist Bolt, Branek & Newman Inc., Cambridge, Mass., 1991-94; prin. scientist, 1994-97; sr. scientist The Concord Consortium, 1997—. Contbr. articles to profl. jours. Recipient Founders Day award NYU, 1969, 2 EDUCOM Nat. awards for ednl. software, 1992; Am. Phys. Soc. Congl. fellow, 1975-76; GM Corp. scholar Harvard U., 1960. Mem. Am. Ednl. Rsch. Assn. Home: 32 Riverside Ave Concord MA 01742-3020 Office: 70 Fawcett St Cambridge MA 02138-1110

HORWITZ, RONALD M. business administration educator; b. Detroit, June 25, 1938; s. Harry and Annette (Levine) H.; m. Carol Bransky, Mar. 30, 1961; children: Steven, Michael, David, Robert. BS, Wayne State U., 1959, MBA, 1961; PhD, Mich. State U., 1964. CPA, Mich. Prof. fin. U. Detroit, 1963-73, 75-79; healthcare cons., dir. personnel devel. Arthur Young & Co., Detroit, 1974-75; prof. fin., dean Sch. Bus. Adminstrn. Oakland U., Rochester, Mich., 1979-90, acting v.p. for acad. affairs, 1992-93, prof. fin., 1991—2002, prof. emeritus of fin., 2002—. Contbr. articles to profl. jours. Bd. trustees Providence Hosp. and Med. Ctr., 1995—, The Roeper Sch., 1996—; pub. mem. Greater Detroit Health Coun., 1980—; mem. fin. com. Ascension Health, St. Louis, 1998-2001, audit com., 2001—; audit com. Daus. of Charity Nat. Health System, 1988-93; mem. adv. bd. Providence Hosp., Southfield, 1980-95. Stonier fellow Am. Bankers Assn., 1963. Mem. Healthcare Fin. Mgmt. Assn. (bd. dirs. 1976-80), Mich. Assn. CPA's (grantee 1960), Fin. Mgmt. Assn., Acctg. Aid Soc. Detroit (founder), Mich. Bridge Assn. (pres. 1974-76). Avocation: bridge (life master). E-mail: horwitz@oakland.edu.

HORWITZ, SARI, reporter; b. Tucson; BA in Polit. Sci., Bryn Mawr Coll.; M in Politics, Philosophy and Econs., Oxford U. Writer, editor Congl. Quar., Washington; reporter Washington Post. Recipient Pulitzer prize gold medal, 1999, Selden Ring award, 1999, Grand prize, Washington-Balt. Newspaper Guild, Morton Mintz award. Office: Washington Post 1150 15th St NW Washington DC 20071

HORWITZ, SETH, information technology executive; b. Phila., Apr. 12, 1957; s. Norman David and Beatrice Levy Horwitz; m. Marie Scearce, Jan. 2, 1981; children: Hannah Margaret Scearce, Nathan Aaron Scearce. BA, Pa. State U., University Park, Pa., 1979; MS, Drexel U., Phila., 1984. Dir. ops. Telebase, King of Prussia, Pa., 1985—2002; founder and dir. CommuniShare, Phila., 2002—. Office: CommuniShare 7224 Hazel Ave Upper Darby PA 19082 E-mail: seth@communishare.org.

HORWITZ, WILLIAM J. treasurer; b. St. Louis, Jan. 10, 1946; s. Harold S. and Henrietta B. Horwitz; children: Harris Saul, Pallas Hannah Eleanor. AB, Harvard U., 1967; MPhil, Yale U., 1969, PhD, 1971. Assoc. prof. classics dept. U. Okla., Norman, 1971-79; treas. Bride's House, St. Louis, 1979—. Contbr. articles to profl. jours. Recipient Woodrow Wilson fellowship, 1967, John Harvard Hon. scholarship, 1964, 66. Mem. Harvard Club of St. Louis (v.p. 1988-90, chmn. various coms. 1986-88), Yale Club of St. Louis. Office: Bride's House 1010 Locust St Saint Louis MO 63101-1306

HOSALKAR, HARISH SADANAND, pediatrician, orthopedist, surgeon, consultant; b. Calcutta, India, Sept. 19, 1972; s. Sadanand Ramchandra and Sujata Sadanand Hosalkar; m. Hetal Hosalkar, Mar. 19, 1998; 1 child, Hriday. MB, BChir, U. Mumbai, India, 1995; MS in Orthopedics, U. Mumbai, 1998; DO, Coll. Physicians and Surgeons, Mumbai, 1997. Bd. cert. orthopaedic surgeon specialized in pediat. orthopaedics. Intern K.E.M. Hosp., Mumbai, 1994—95, house officer, 1995, sr. house officer, 1996, registrar, 1996—97, sr. registrar, 1997—98; specialist registrar B.J. Wadia Hosp., Mumbai, 1998—99; lectr. K.B. Bhabha Hosp., Mumbai, 1999—2000; fellow Children's Hosp. Phila., 2000, Valley Children's Hosp., Fresno, Calif., 2000—01, Great Ormond St. Hosp., U. Coll. London, 2001, sr. fellow, 2002—. Dir. orthopaedics Kerkar's Gen. Hosp., Mumbai, 1999—2000; presenter in field. Contbr. articles to profl. jours. Faculty polio surgeon PNR Found., Bhaunagar, 1998—2000; coord. Plague Vaccination Team, Bombay, 1994; cmty. health worker Malavani Village, Mumbai, 1992—93. Named one of Best Citizens of India, 2003; recipient Ranbaxy award for awareness in Aids campaign, 1994, first prize and award, Leprosy Awareness and Mgmt., Ackworth Found., 1994, Dr. Premchand award for cmty. health work, Mumbai, 1995, Rashtriya Gaurav Pride of India award, 2002, Rashtriya Shiromani of India award, 2003. Fellow: Coll. Physicians and Surgeons; mem.: Am. Acad. Orthopaedic Surgeons, Limb Reconstruction Soc. N.Am., Pediat. Orthopaedic Soc. India (life), Maharashtra Orthopaedic Assn. (life), Indian Arthroscopic Assn. (life), Bombay Orthopaedic Soc. (life), Assn. Med. Cons. (life), Indian Med. Assn. (life), Pediat. Orthopedic Soc. N.Am. Avocations: bridge, singing, reading. Office: Childrens Hosp Philadelphia 2nd Fl Wood Bldg 34th St Civic Ctr Blvd Philadelphia PA 19104

HOSANG, ROBERT MICHAEL, research scientist; s. Bernard Otto Hosang and Patricia Hawco. Tchr. St. Joseph's Sch., 1953—62, Quincy H.S., 1965—68, Boston State Coll., 1970—73; ind. rschr., 1973—. Author: Gravity, 2001, The Frequency of Gravity, 2003, The Full Cycle, 2003. Mem.: Broadcast Music Inc. Personal E-mail: rmhosang@juno.com.

HOSEA, JULIA HILLER, communications executive, paralegal; b. Cin., Oct. 19, 1952; d. Clifford John and Nancy Carol (Elberg) Hiller; m. Jon Michael Ausman, Nov. 3, 1973 (div. 1978), m. Robert Arthur Hosea, Mar. 22, 1987 (dec. Dec. 12, 1998). BA, Allegheny Coll., 1975; cert., Inst. Paralegal Tng., Phila., 1975. Gen. paralegal Pettigrew & Bailey, Miami, Fla., 1975-76, Joseph J. Weisenfeld Law Offices, Miami, 1976-81; corp. paralegal Wood & Lamping, Cin., 1981-85; pension specialist Katz, Teller Brant & Hild, Cin., 1985-89; owner, mgr. Chrysalis Communications, Cin., 1989-90, The Hosea Group, Grand Junction, 1990-95; owner Ruby Canyon Textiles, Grand Junction, 1996—2992; mgr. Action Potential, LLC, 2002—03. Grant adminstr. for advance med. directives program in Colo., 2000—; adj. instr. Coll. Mt. St. Joseph, Cin., 1984-90. Contbr. articles to profl. publs. Mem. Cin. Paralegal Assn. (pres. 1984-85), Nat. Fedn. PAralegal Assn. (chmn. pension sect. 1986-87, editor Nat. Paralegal Reporter 1988-92). E-mail: jhosea@attbi.com.

HOSEK, JAMES ROBERT, economist; b. Evanston, Ill., Aug. 31, 1944; s. Walter Frank and Frances Miriam (Hoffman) H.; m. Susan DeWire, Sept. 10, 1966; children: Katherine, Adrienne, Peter. BA, Cornell U., 1966; MA, U. Chgo., 1970, PhD, 1975. Rsch. analyst Nat. Bur. Econ. Rsch., New Haven, 1970-73; assoc. economist RAND, Santa Monica, Calif., 1973-79, economist, 1979-83, sr. economist, 1983—, dir. def. manpower rsch. ctr., 1981-85, head dept. econs. and stats., 1985-90, corp. rsch. mgr., human capital, 1990-94, human capital and material resource policy, 1994-96. Mem. panel NAS, Washington, 1988; mem., chair econ. adv. coun. Calif. Inst. Fed. Policy Rsch., 1994—; founding mem. Advanced Transp. Industry Consortium, 1997—; prof. econs. RAND Grad. Sch., 1997—. Editor RAND Jour. of Econs., 1988—, Quadrennial Rev. Mil. Compensation, 2000-02; assoc. editor Abstracts of Working Papers in Econs., 1986-96; contbr. articles to profl. jours. Recipient

numerous rsch. grants; RAND Europe fellow, 2000. Fellow Interuniversity Sem. on Armed Forces and Soc.; mem. Am. Econ. Assn., Western Econ. Assn., Phi Eta Sigma. Avocations: bicycling, photography, hiking.

HOSEMANN, C. DELBERT, JR., lawyer; b. New Orleans, June 30, 1947; s. Charles D. and Patricia H.; m. Mary Lynn Lagen; children: Kristen Cullen, Charles Delbert III, Mark Mansfield. BBA, U. Notre Dame, 1969; JD, U. Miss., 1972; LLM in Taxation, NYU, 1973. Assoc. Dossett, Magruder & Montgomery, Jackson, Miss., 1973-78; ptnr. Magruder, Montgomery, Brocato & Hosemann, Jackson, 1978-88, Phelps Dunbar, L.L.P., Jackson, 1988—. Contbr. articles to profl. jours.; speaker in field. Mem. Miss. del. S.E. regional employee benefits liaison com. EP/EO Atlanta, 1986-88, chmn., 1992-93; mem. Leadership Jackson, 1991-92, bd. dirs., 1995-96; pres. Miss. Blood Svcs., Inc., 1994-95; Rep. nominee U.S. Congress 4th Congl. Dist., 1998; trustee Jackson State U. Devel. Found. Mem. ABA (employee benefits com., taxation sect., continuing legal edn. com. budget and fin. com.), Hinds County Bar Assn. (sec. 1980), Miss. State Bar Assn. (dir. young lawyers sect. 1976-78, taxation com.), Jackson Young Lawyers Assn. (pres. 1977-78). Office: Phelps Dunbar 200 S Lamar St Ste 500 Jackson MS 39201-4013

HOSEY, SHERYL LYNN MILLER, educator, editor, theater director; b. Phila., May 15, 1968; d. Roger Lee and Janice Catherine (Myers) M.; m. John William Hosey, July 8, 1994. AA, Bucks County C.C., Newtown, Pa., 1989; BFA summa cum laude, Va. Commonwealth U., 1992, MA, 1997; cert. in editing, Temple U., 1999. Cert. secondary sch. tchr., Pa. Instr. drama Va. Commonwealth U., Richmond, 1989-92; program support technician Va. Commonwealth U./Med. Coll. Va., Richmond, 1992-97; editl. svcs. adminstr. Meniscus Ltd., Bala Cynwyd, Pa., 1998-99; tchr., drama dir. Council Rock H.S. South, Holland, Pa., 1999—. Proofreader, editor. Fellow Nat. Writing Project Pa. chpt. West Chester U., 2000. Mem. Nat. Coun. Tchrs. English, Ednl. Theatre Assn., Phi Kappa Phi, Phi Delta Kappa. Avocations: acting, singing, reading, designing and making clothes, attending plays, symphony and ballet. Office: Council Rock High Sch South 2002 Rock Way Holland PA 18966 E-mail: mh@millerhosey.com.

HOSHAW, LLOYD, retired historian, educator; b. Benton, Ind., May 9, 1924; s. Walter and Gladys Ethel (Blue) H.; m. Evelyn F. Tyler, Dec. 24, 1954; children: Linda, John, James, Walter, David, Paul. BA, Goshen Coll., 1949; MA, Ind. U., 1951. Tchr. Winamac (Ind.) High Sch., 1952-55; instr. LaSalle(Ill.)-Peru-Oglesby Jr. Coll., 1955-65; history prof., dept. chair Rock Valley Coll., Rockford, Ill., 1965-88, history prof., 1988—2001; ret., 2001. Bd. dirs. Rock River Christian Coll. Author: A History of Eastern Civilizations, Vol I., 1994, Vol. II, 1995, 2d edit., 2001. With USN, 1944-45. Mem. VFW (life), Archeol. Inst. Am. (Rockford chpt.), Ill. State Hist. Soc., Rockford Hist. Soc. Baptist. Avocations: photography, travel. Home: 1860 Charlotte Dr Rockford IL 61108-6508

HOSHIELD, SUSAN LYNN, pediatric nurse practitioner; AA, North Cen. Mich. Coll., 1972, ADN, 1978; BSN, Lake Superior State U., 1990; MSN, U. Mich., 1993; student Internat. Health Program, Wayne State U., Detroit, 2000—. RN, PNP. Sales mgr. Petoskey Floral & Bridal, Petoskey, Mich., 1968-77; staff nurse NICU No. Mich. Hosp., Petoskey, 1978-88, primary nurse II/NICU, 1989-90, regional perinatal coord., 1990-95, infant apnea nurse coord., 1990-95; nursing faculty Lake Superior State U., Sault Ste. Marie, Mich., 1995-96; pediatric nurse practitioner Burns Clinic Med. Ctr., Petoskey, Mich., 1996-98; primary nurse NICU and pediatrics No. Mich. Hosp., Petoskey, Mich., 1999-2000, Wellness Inst. for Wholistic Living, Harbor Springs, Mich., 1999—2001; infant mental health specialist No. Mich. Cmty. Mental Health, Gaylord, 1999—2002; pediat. nurse practitioner Cmty. Free Clinic, Petoskey, 1999—; care mgr. No. Mich. Cmty. Mental Health, Gaylord, 2002—. Adv. bd. Mich. SIDS Alliance, Lansing, 1993-99, vice chair, 1996-97, chair, 1997-98; chairperson Children's Health Fair, Petoskey, 1991-95; adj. faculty Lake Superior State U., Sault Ste Marie, Mich., 1994. Author: (pamphlet) Infant Apnea Clinic, 1994. Adv. bd. sex edn. curriculum Harbor Springs, Mich., 1992-98; mem. Immunization Task Force, Charlevoix, Mich., 1994; adv. com. Mich. State U. Coop. Ext., Petoskey, 1992-95, Adolescent Health, Charlevoix, 1990-93; active Harbor Springs Cmty. Band, 1996—. Vol. Spotlight, Mich. SIDS Alliance, 1994; hon. chair March of Dimes WalkAmerica, 1994-95. Mem. AWHONN, Perinatal Assn. of Mich. (bd. dirs., sec. 1993-95), Mich. Assn. Apnea Profls., Nurses Assn. Pediat. Nurses and Practitioners, Mich. Nurses Assn. of Pediat. Nurses and Practitioners, Petoskey Area Bus. and Profl. Women (rec. sec. 1998-2000, 2d v.p. 2000-01, 1st v.p. 2001-02, pres., 2002-), No. Mich. Assn. Infant Mental Health (sec. 2000-02, pres., 2002-). Avocations: quilting, alternative health care practices, healing touch and therapeutic touch. Home: 421 Emmet St Petoskey MI 49770-2603 Office: 1165 Elkview Blvd Gaylord MI 49735 E-mail: shosh@youraccordion.com.

HOSHINO, YOSHIRO, industrial technology critic; b. Tokyo-Shi, Tokyo-Hu, Japan, Jan. 13, 1922; s. Teruoki and Matsue Hoshino; m. Kumiko Serizawa, July 7, 1954; children: Syuichiro, Kenjiro, Chieko, Tetsuro. B, Tokyo Inst. Tech., 1944, Dr., 1980. Asst. tech. staff Agy. of Tech., Tokyo, 1944-45, critic, 1945-62; prof. Ritsumeikan U., Kyoto, 1962-68, cirtic, 1968-81; prof. indsl. tech. Teikyo U., Tokyo, 1981-97, critic, 1997—. Hon. prof. N.E. U., Shenyang, China, 1985—. Author: Collected Works of Yoshiro Hoshino, 1977-79, Future of Civilization, 1980, Fundamental Problems on Latest Technology, 1986, Technology, Economy and Politics—Japan and China, 1945-1991, 1993. Avocation: driving. Home: 9-8-19 Chiyogaoka Asao-ku Kawasaki-shi Kanagawa-ken 215-0005 Japan

HOSICK, HOWARD LAWRENCE, cell biology educator, academic administrator; b. Champaign, Ill., Nov. 1, 1943; s. Arthur Howard and Eunice Irma (Miller) H.; m. Cynthia Ann Jacobson, June 15, 1968; children: Steven Cameron, Anna Elise, Rachel Victoria. BA, U. Colo., 1965; PhD, U. Calif., Berkeley, 1970. Postdoctoral fellow Karolinska Inst., Stockholm, 1970-72; asst. research biochemist U. Calif., Berkeley, 1972-73; asst. prof. Wash. State U., Pullman, 1973-78, assoc. prof., 1978-83, prof. cell biology, 1983—, chmn. dept. zoology, 1983-87, chmn. dept. genetics and cell biology, 1987-91. Vis. scientist U. Reading, Eng., 1978; disting. scientist Aichi Cancer Ctr., Nagoya, Japan, 1986; vis. scholar Cambridge U., 1994; rsch. com. Am. Heart Assn., 1989; grant rev. com. Nat. Cancer Inst., 1993—. Rev. editor In Vitro Cellular and Molecular Biology, 1986—; contbr. articles to profl. jours. Bd. govs. Internat. Assn. Breast Cancer Rsch., 1993—. Recipient H.S. Boyce award, 1981, Shell Faculty Devel. award, 1984, Cancer Rsch. award Eagles Club, 1989, G. and L. Pfeiffer Rsch. Found. award, 1992; fellow NIH, NSF, Am. Cancer Soc., Damon Runyan-Walter Winchell Cancer Fund, Fogarty Internat. Ctr., 1968—; grantee NIH, NSF, Am. Cancer Soc., Am. Inst. Cancer Rsch., Pfeiffer Found., 1973—, U.S. Army. Mem. Am. Soc. Cell Biology, Tissue Culture Assn., Am. Assn. Cancer Research, Internat. Assn. Breast Cancer Research. Lodges: Rotary. Democrat. Buddhist. Avocations: running, woodworking, model aviation. Home: 1185 NE Lake St Pullman WA 99163-3869 Office: Wash State U Sch Biol Scis Pullman WA 99164-4234 E-mail: hosick@wsu.edu.

HOSIE, STANLEY WILLIAM, foundation executive; b. Lismore, NSW, Australia, Apr. 28, 1922; came to U.S., 1945; s. Stanley James and Catherine Clare (Chisholm) H. BA, U. Queensland, Brisbane, Australia, 1945; Lic. in Theology, Cath. U., Washington, 1946, MA, 1948. Ordained priest Soc. of Mary, Roman Cath. Ch., 1946. Dean of studies Marist Coll., Lismore, 1949-57; founder, pres. Chanel Coll., Victoria, Australia, 1958-62; apptd. to hdqs. Soc. of Mary, Rome, 1963; biographer and peritus to Pacific Island nation Cath. Bishop Second Vatican Coun.; co-founder, CEO Found. for Peoples South Pacific (now Counterpart Internat.), Washington, 1966—2001; chmn. bd. Counterpart Internat. Theologian Conf. of Pacific Cath. Bishops, 2nd Vatican Coun.; dir. Am. Coun. Vol. Internat. Action, N.Y.C., 1976—89, treas., 1983—84; founder, CEO Santa Monica Entertainment Group Film Prodn. Co., 1994; apptd. Presdl. Adv. Com. on Vol. Fgn. Aid, 1988—93; spl. advisor MFM film of Morris West's "Shoes of the Fishermen". Author: The Swiss Conspiracy, 1976, The Boomerang Conspiracy, 1978, (biography) Anonymous Apostle, 1966, also numerous screenplays; spl. advisor to film Shoes of the Fisherman. Recipient Best Article Vatican II award Nat. Cath. Periodicals Assn., 1964. Mem. Writers Guild Am. East, Soc. des Oceanistes, Australian Coll. Edn. Democrat. Roman Catholic. Avocations: tennis, swimming. Office: Counterpart Internat 723 Palisacles Beach Rd #211 Santa Monica CA 90402

HOSKER, DONALD, materials research technician; b. Boston, June 21, 1961; s. Donald and Carlene Mary (Womack) H. BS in Math., Northeastern U., Boston, 1991, cert. mgmt. and bus. adminstrn., 1993. Lic. real estate sales assoc., Mass. Supr. New Eng. Duct Cleaning Co., Braintree, Mass., 1977-88; sales assoc. Ginino Realtors, Brockton, Mass., 1987-88; sr. materials rsch. technician rsch. and engring. group Morton Internat., Woburn, Mass., 1988-95; materials rsch. technician CVD rsch. dept. Thermo Trex Corp., Waltham, Mass., 1995-96, San Diego, Calif., 1996; CVD/diffusion equipment specialist Unitrode Corp., Merrimack, N.H., 1996-99, Tex. Instrument, Merrimack, N.H., 1999—. Sci.-by mail scientist Mus. of Sci., Boston, 1999—. Mem.: AAAS, N.Y. Acad. Scis., Mensa. Avocations: hiking, camping, scuba diving, dxing. Home: 45 Derry St Merrimack NH 03054-3134 Office: Tex Instrument Merrimack NH 03104 E-mail: dhosker@msn.com.

HOSKIE, LORRAINE, consumer products representative, poet; b. Nansemond County, Va., Aug. 26, 1953; m. Eddie Lewis Hoskie, July 7, 1972 (div. Oct. 1980); children: Jacqueline Marie, Quinton Lewis. BS, Va. Commonwealth U., 1977. Clk. Christian Children's Fund, Richmond, 1977—79, corr. rsch. clk., 1979—80; eligibility worker City of Richmond, 1982—83; substitute tchr. Sch. Bd., Richmond, 1983—86; telemarketer Energy Savs. Exterior, Richmond, 1995—96; CRT operator Snelling Pers. Svcs., Richmond, 1996; mail clk. Abacus, Richmond, 1997; office worker Kelly Svcs., Richmond, 1997; remittance processor Calipher, Inc., Richmond, 1997—2001; adminstrv. program specialist II VA Employment Commn., 2003—. Substitute tchr. Sch. Bd. of Franklin, Va., 1987; ch. sec. SDA-Ephesus, Richmond, 1981-82; vol. worker Bapt. Student Union Va. Commonwealth U., Richmond, 1971-72, math. tutor Spl. Svcs. Program, 1972. Sec. Ephesus Prison Ministry, 1996—; team sec. Ephesus Va. Dept. Correction, 1993-94. Named Golden Poet, World of Poetry, Sacramento, 1990, recipient award of merit cert., 1990; recipient Poet of Merit award Am. Poetry Assn., 1988, Appreciation award VA Dept. Corrections, 1994, Pres. award for literary excellence Nat. Authors Registry, 1994. Democrat. 7th Day Adventist. Avocations: crocheting, creative writing, music, poetry writing. Home: 3912 Chamberlayne Ave Apt D-17 Richmond VA 23227-4261 Office: VEC 703 E Main St Rm 123 Richmond VA 23218

HOSKING, NEVILLE JOHN, educational administrator; b. London, Jan. 10, 1948; s. David John and Violet Jean Hosking; m. Patricia Gail Hosking. BEd, U. Saskatchewan, Sask., Can., 1971, MEd, 1977, U. Victoria, B.C., Can., 1986; PhD, U. Oreg., 1990. Tchr., pring. Lloydminster (Alta., Can.) Pub. Schs., 1971-82; program cons. Prince Albert (Sask.) Schs., 1982-87, supr. curriculum, 1987-89; exec. dir. Saskatchewan Edn., Regina, Sask., 1990-93; grad. dir. Ea. Wash. U., Cheney, 1994-98, dean Coll. Edn., 1998-2000, vice provost acad. affairs, 2000—. Author: (textbook) Student-Centered Literacy Instruction in the Middle Years, 2000; contbr. articles to lit. jours. Grantee Title II Tchr. Enhancement, 1999-2002, Wash. State Sch. Improvement Commn. on Student Learning, 1998. Mem.: Can. Spl. Interest Group of Literacy (chair 1990—91), Am. Ednl. Rsch. Assn., Nat. Coun. for Accreditation of Tchrs. (bd. examiners), Nat. Staff Devel. Coun., Internat. Reading Assn. (chairperson Concern for Affect in Reading 2000—), Phi Delta Kappa (chpt. pres. 1995—97). Avocations: skiing, hiking, reading. Home: 628 W 24th Ave Spokane WA 99203 E-mail: nhosking@ewu.edu.

HOSKINS, ALEXANDER L. (PETE HOSKINS), zoological park administrator; b. Woodland, Calif., Sept. 1, 1947; s. Edgar and Betty (Stoner) H.; m. Sharon Paula Barr, May 19, 1990; children: Emily, David, Adam. BA in Polit. Sci., San Jose State U., 1969; MA in Pub. Adminstrn., U. Minn., 1971. Asst. to city mgr. City of Foster City, Calif., 1971-72; mgmt. analyst Mng. Dir.'s Office, City of Phila., 1972-80, exec. dir. Fairmount Park, 1980-88, commr. of streets, 1988-93; pres., CEO, Zool. Soc. Phila., 1993—. Contbr. articles to various publs. Exec. v.p. Chestnut Hill Cmty. Assn., 1974-76; trustee Cmty. Leadership Seminars, 1978-80, Unitarian Soc. Germantown, 1985-87; chmn. Delaware Valley Regional Horticulture Industry Coun., 1985-86, Phila. Independence Marathon, 1985-88 Recipient ann. award for meritorious mcpl. svc. Ctrl. Phila. Devel. Corp., 1986, honor award for restoration and revitalization Pa.-Del. chpt. Am. Soc. Landscape Architects, 1986, govt. svc. award Phila. sect. ASCE, 1990, govt. award for excellence in pub. adminstrn. Phila. regional chpt. ASAP, 1991, award for engring. excellence Cons. Engrs. Coun. N.J., 1991, William V. Donaldson award for civic price PhilaPride, 1992. Mem. Am. Pub. Works Assn. (Delaware Valley exec. com. 1992—). Office: Phila Zoo Garden 3400 W Girard Ave Philadelphia PA 19104-1196

HOSKINS, CARLTON L. legislative staff member; b. Owensboro, Ky., Mar. 8, 1971; s. Robert Martin and Marylou (Stine) H. BS in Polit. Sci., USAF Acad., 1994. Counterintelligence spl. agt. 902d Mil. Intelligence Group, Ft. Meade, Md., 1994-97; adjutant Allied Mil. Intel Btn., Sarajevo, Bosnia, 1997-98; chief of counterintelligence Def. Spl. Weapons Agy., Washington, 1998-99; social aide to U.S. Pres. The White Ho. Mil. Office, Washington, 1997-99; legis. asst. U.S. Sen. Arlen Specter, 1999—. Mem. Army-Navy Club (mem. polo team 1996—), Mil. Polo Team, Potomac Polo Club, City Tavern Club. Home: 1123 Independence Ave SE Washington DC 20003-1443

HOSKINS, CAROL NOLL, nursing educator, researcher; b. N.Y.C., Dec. 25, 1932; d. Victor Herbert and Rachel (Perkins) Noll; m. Donald William Hoskins, Dec. 19, 1955; children: Lauren Hoskins Lingley, David William, Bruce Noll. BSN, Cornell U., 1955; MA, NYU, 1973, PhD, 1978, U. Athens, Greece, 1998. RN. Pub. health nurse Vis. Nurse Svc. N.Y., N.Y.C., 1955—58; asst. prof. nursing NYU, N.Y.C., 1977—82, assoc. prof. nursing, 1982—87, prof. nursing, 1987—, dir. PhD program in nursing, 1990—, prin. investigator 3 phase program breast cancer rsch., 1990—. Author: Developing Research in Nursing and Health, 1998; co-author: Breast Cancer: Journey to Recovery, 2001; prin. author: (4-part video series) Journey to Recovery: For Women with Breast Cancer and Their Partners, 2002; contbr. articles to profl. jours. Case mgr. ARC Family Emergency Relief Svcs., 9/11. Grantee Nat. Inst. Nursing Rsch., Nat. Cancer Inst., 1999—; Sr. Fulbright scholar, Cornell U., 1955. Fellow: Am. Acad. Nursing (award); mem.: ANA, Fulbright Assn., Sigma Theta Tau. Avocations: swimming, skiing, quilting, gardening. Home: 3-24 Parsons Blvd Whitestone NY 11357 Office: NYU Steinhardt Sch Edn 246 Greene St New York NY 10003-6677 E-mail: cnh1@nyu.edu.

HOSKINS, DONALD W. medical association administrator; BS, Queens Coll., 1953; MD, Cornell U., 1957. Diplomate Am. Bd. Internal Medicine. Chief med. officer, med. dir., sr. v.p. med. affairs Continuum Health Ptnrs. (Beth Israel), 1997—; assoc. prof. clin. medicine Albert Einstein Coll. Medicine, Bronx, NY. Office: Beth Israel Med Ctr First Ave 16th St New York NY 10003

HOSKINS, IFFATH ABBASI, obstetrician-gynecologist; b. Karachi, Pakistan, June 18, 1951; came to U.S., 1977; d. Mohd Assan and Mehru Kazi Abbasi; m. William John Hoskins, Nov. 9, 1985; 1 child, Ahad Jamie;1 child, Maria Aisha. MD, Dow Med. Coll., Karachi, 1975. Diplomate Am. Bd. Ob-gyn. Intern St. Elizabeth Hosp., Washington, 1977—78, resident in psychology, 1978—79; resident in ob-gyn. Naval Hosp., Bethesda, Md., 1979—82; fellow high risk obstetrics Walter Reed Army Hosp., Washington, 1983-85, attending high risk obstetrics, 1985-87; dir. rsch. Bellevue Hosp., N.Y.C., 1987-90, chief obstetrics, 1990-97; assoc. prof. NYU Sch. Medicine, N.Y.C., 1994—; dir. residency program, chief dept. ob-gyn. NYU Downtown Hosp., N.Y.C., 1997—2002; dir. women's svcs. Meml. Health Univ. Med. Ctr., Savannah, Ga., 2002—. Attending NYU Downtown Hosp., N.Y.C. Contbr. over 75 articles to profl. jours. Bd. trustees March of Dimes, N.Y.C. Capt. USN, 1979—, with USMC, 2003, Iraq. Recipient Gold medal, Dow Med. Coll., Karachi, 1975. Fellow: ACS; mem.: ACOG (sec. N.Y. chpt. 1999—, Cmty. Svc. award 1999, Dist. Outstanding Svc. award 2001), Wash. Soc. Pathology. Republican. Moslem. Avocation: reading. E-mail: hoskiif@memorialhealth.com.

HOSKINS, JANET ALISON, anthropologist, film producer; b. Middletown, Conn., Apr. 24, 1954; d. Robert Wilson and Katharine Bail Hoskins; m. Valerio Valeri, Dec. 30, 1988 (dec. Apr. 25, 1998); children: Sylvana Sarasvati Valeri, Artemisia Katharine Valeri. BA in Anthropology, Pomona Coll., 1975; PhD in Anthropology, Harvard U., 1984. Prof. anthropology U. So. Calif., L.A., 1985—; resident scholar Inst. for Advanced Study, Princeton, NJ, 1990—91; vis. lectr. Social Anthropology Inst., Oslo, 1992—93; prof., chmn. of anthropology Monash U., Melbourne, Australia, 1994—96; rsch. fellow Rsch. Sch. for Pacific and Asian Studies, Canberra, Australia; Getty rsch. scholar Getty Rsch. Inst. for the History of Art and the Humanities, L.A., 2002—. Author: The Play of Time: Kodi Perspectives on Calendars, History and Exchange (Harry J. Benda prize in SE Asian Studies, 1996), Biographical Objects: How Things Tell the Stories of People's Lives; dir.: (film) Feast in Dream Village (Barbara Myerhoff Film Festival award, 1988); prodr.: Horses of Life and Death (Am. Anthrop. Assn. honors, 1990). Fellow Indonesian Rsch. fellow, Fulbright Commn., 1987, NEH, 1996, Indonesian Field Rsch., Wenner Gren Found. for Anthrop. Rsch., 2000; grantee, NSF, 1988. Mem.: Am. Anthrop. Assn., Am. Ethnol. Soc. Office: U So Calif University Park Campus Los Angeles CA 90089

HOSKINS, JOHN HOWARD, urologist, educator; b. Breckenridge, Minn., Mar. 18, 1934; s. James H. and Ruth (Johanson) H.; m. Nancy Weih, Aug. 3, 1957; children: William, James, Laura, Sara. BA in History, U. Iowa, 1956; BS in Medicine, U. S.D., 1959; MD, Temple U., 1961. Diplomate Am. Bd. Urology. Practice medicine specializing in urology, Sioux Falls, S.D., 1966-96; head sect. urology U. S.D. Sch. Medicine, Vermillon, 1977-93; ret., 1997. Maj. M.C. U.S. Army, 1967-69, Vietnam. Fellow ACS; mem. AMA, Am. Urol. Assn., Augustana Fellows, Masons, Shriners, Rotary. Republican. Methodist. E-mail: jnhoskins@msn.com.

HOSKINS, JOHN ROYCE, JR., organization program specialist; b. Pensacola, Fla., May 4, 1976; s. John Royce Hoskins Sr. and Carolyn H. Hoskins. BA in English, U. West Fla., 1999. Founder, pres. Books for Life Pub., Pensacola, Fla., 2000—01; program support specialist United Cerebral Palsy, Pensacola, Fla., 2001—. Student asst. to newsletter editor Escambia County Sch. Dist. Grants Mgmt., Pensacola, Fla., 1997—2000; chair essay contest African Am. Student Assn., Pensacola, Fla., 1999. Author: Love Ordained, vol. 1, 2001, The Revelation of John, and Other Poems, 2001, Ordered Steps, 2001; contbr. Avocations: basketball, drawing, website design, reading. Home: PO Box 179 Cantonment FL 32533 Office: Books of Life Pub PO Box 104 Cantonment FL 32533

HOSKINS, RICHARD JEROLD, lawyer; b. Ft. Smith, Ark., June 19, 1945; s. Walter Jerold and Emma Gladys Hoskins; children: Stephen Weston, Philip Richard. BA, U. Kans., 1967; JD, Northwestern U., 1970. Bar: N.Y. 1971, Ill. 1976, U.S. Supreme Ct. 1982. Assoc. Davis Polk & Wardwell, N.Y.C., 1970-73; asst. U.S. atty., So. Dist. N.Y., 1973-76; assoc. Schiff Hardin & Waite, Chgo., 1976-77, ptnr., 1978—. Adj. prof. U. Va. Law Sch., 1980-83, Northwestern U. Law Sch., 1992-98, sr. lectr., 1999—. Contbr. articles to profl. jours. Mem. vis. com. U. Chgo. Div. Sch.; Chancellor emeritus Episcopal Diocese of Chgo. Fellow Am. Coll. Trial Lawyers, Am. Bar Found.; mem. ABA, Ill. State Bar Assn., Chgo. Bar Assn., 7th Cir. Bar Assn., Assn. of Bar of City of N.Y., Chgo. Coun. Lawyers, Law Club Chgo., Met. Club (Chgo.), Univ. Club (Chgo.); bd. visitors and govs. St. John's Coll., Office: 6600 Sears Tower Chicago IL 60606

HOSKINS, WILLIAM JOHN, obstetrician, gynecologist, educator; b. Harlan, Ky., May 10, 1940; s. Lonnie S. and Joanne (Huff) H.; m. Betty Jean Gay, Sept. 10, 1960 (div. 1985); children: Tonya J., William John Jr.; m. Iffath Abbasi Ahson, Nov. 9, 1985; children: Ahad A., Mariya A. BA, U. Tenn., Knoxville, 1962; MD, U. Tenn., Memphis, 1965. Diplomate Am. Bd. Ob-Gyn., Am. Bd. Gynecol. Oncology. Commd. lt. USN, 1966, advanced through grades to capt.; intern Jacksonville (Fla.) Naval Hosp., 1966-67; med. officer Destroyer Squadron 8 USN, Mayport, Fla., 1967-68; resident in ob-gyn Oakland (Calif.) Naval Hosp., 1968-71; staff dept. ob -gyn Pensacola (Fla.) Naval Hosp., 1971—74; fellow in gynecol. oncology U. Miami, Fla., 1974-76; dir. gynecol. oncology Nat. Naval Med. Ctr., Bethesda, Md., 1976—86; assoc. prof. ob-gyn Uniformed Svcs. U., Bethesda, 1976-86; ret. USN, 1986; assoc. chief gynecology svc. Meml. Sloan-Kettering Cancer Ctr., N.Y.C., 1988-90, chief gynecology svc., 1990—, 1990—; assoc. prof. ob-gyn Cornell U. Med. Ctr., N.Y.C., 1986-90; prof. ob-gyn. Cornell U. Med. Coll., N.Y.C., 1990-94, vice chmn. protocol com. gynecol. oncology group, 1993-94, vice chmn. gynecologic oncology group, 1993—2002; Avon chair gynecologic oncology rsch. Meml. Sloan-Kettering Cancer Ctr., N.Y.C., 1995-96, dep. physician in chief disease mgmt. teams, 1996—; dir. Curtis & Elizabeth Anderson Cancer Ctr. at Memorial Health U. Med. Ctr., Savannah, Ga., 2001—; prof. ob-gyn. Mercer Med. Coll., Macon, Ga., 2001—. Chmn. ovarian com. Gynecol. Oncology Group, Phila., 1984-89. Editor: Principles and Practice of Gynecology and Oncology, 1992, 3d edit., 2000, Cancer of the Ovary, 1993, Cervical Cancer and Perinvasive Peoplasia, 1996, Cancer Management: A Multidisciplinary Approach, 1996, Handbook of Gynecologic Oncology, 2000, 2d edit., 2002, Atlas of Procedures in Gynecologic Oncology, 2003; contbr. over 224 articles to profl. jours., chpts. to books. Fellow Am. Coll. Obstetricians and Gynecologists (v.p. Navy sect. 1982-83), ACS; mem. Am. Gynecol. and Obstet. Soc., Soc. Gynecol. Oncologists (sec.-treas. elect 1992, sec.-treas. 1994—, coun. mem. 1988-91, pres. 1999), Soc. Gynecol. Surgeons, Internat. Gynecol. Cancer Soc., Am. Radium Soc., Am. Assn Cancer rsch., 1996—. Republican. Moslem. Office: Anderson Cancer Inst at Meml Health Univ Med Ctr 4700 Waters Ave Savannah GA 31404 Office Fax: 912-350-8199.

HOSKINS, WILLIAM KELLER, pharmaceutical executive, mediator/arbitrator, lawyer; b. Cin., Feb. 22, 1935; s. John Hobart and Gertrude Louise (Keller) H.; m. Elizabeth Ann Grimm, Aug. 5, 1961; children: Bruce, Andrew, John, Elizabeth, Allison. BA, Yale U., 1956; LLB, Harvard U., 1962. Bar: Ohio 1962, U.S. Dist. Ct. (so. dist.) Ohio 1963, U.S. Tax Ct. 1963, U.S. Ct. Appeals (6th cir.) 1964, N.Y. 1982, Mo. 1983. Assoc. Frost & Jacobs, Cin., 1962-68; gen. counsel Drackett Co., Cin., 1968-71, v.p., gen. counsel, 1971-81; assoc. gen. counsel Bristol Myers Co., N.Y.C., 1981, spl. counsel, 1982; v.p., gen. counsel, sec. Hoechst Marion Roussell (formerly Marion Labs. Inc.), Kansas City, Mo., 1982-97; gen. ptnr. Hoskins Group, Boston, 1998—; pres. Hoskins & Assocs., Boston, 1998—; mng. ptnr. Resolution Coun., LLP, Portland, Oreg., 2002—. Chmn. household div. Soap and Detergent Assn., N.Y.C., 1978-79, chmn. Chem. Spltys. Mfg. Assn., Washington, 1982; bd. dirs. Am. Arbitration Assn., N.Y.C., 1997—, Ferrrellgas, Inc., Kansas City, Mo., 2003—. Isotechnika, Inc., Edmonton, 2003--. Mem. Hamilton County Rep. Ctrl. Com., Ohio, 1970-81; sec.-treas. Marion Labs. Polit. Action Com., 1982-89; sec.-treas. polit. action com. Mid-Am. Com. Sound Govt., Lake Quivira, Kans., 1982-86; bd. dirs. Landmark Legal Found., Kansas City, 1995-2003, vice chmn., 2001-2003. Lt. (j.g.) USN, 1956-59. Mem. Mo. Bar Assn., Ohio Bar Assn., N.Y. Bar, Cin. Bar Assn., Harvard Law Sch. Alumni Assn. (bd. dirs. 1991-95). Roman Catholic. Home: 85 E India Row Apt 20B Boston MA 02110-3397 Office: Hoskins and Assocs Resolution Counsel LLP 85 E India Row Apt 20A Boston MA 02110-3397 Fax: 617-742-2368. E-mail: Bhoskins98@aol.com.

HOSKINSON, CAROL ROWE, middle school educator; b. Toledo, Mar. 10, 1947; d. Webster Russell and Alice Mae (Miller) Rowe; m. C. Richard Hoskinson, June 8, 1969; 1 child, Leah Nicole. BS in Edn., Ohio State U., 1968; MEd, Ga. State U., 1972. Tchr. Whitehall City Sch., Columbus, Ohio, 1968-69; tchr. DeKalb County Sch., Decatur, Ga., 1969-74, Mt. Olive Twp. Sch., NJ, 1974-75, DeKalb County Sch., Decatur, 1975-79, Fulton County Sch., Atlanta, 1991—. Substitute tchr. DeKalb County Schs., Decatur, 1980-91, Fulton County Sch., Atlanta, 1989-91. Pres. Esther Jackson PTA, Roswell, Ga., 1988-89; treas. Women of the Ch., Roswell, 1983-84; chairperson local sch. adv. Esther Jackson, Roswell, 1989-91; del. Women and Constn. Conv., Atlanta, 1988; mem. Supt.'s Adv. Com.; corr. sec. Chattahoochee HS PTSA, 1997-98; VIP dedicated hostess Olympic Games, Atlanta, 1996; treas. Chattahoochee Cotillion Club, 2000, 2001; mem. leadership team Holcomb Bridge Mid. Sch., 1999-2003. Named Vol. of Yr. Fulton County Schs., 1988-89. Mem. AAUW (v.p. Atlanta chpt. 1970-89, edn. scholarship honoree 1984, 86), Atlanta Lawn Tennis Assn., Roswell Hist. Soc., Roswell Hist. Preservation Com., Nat. Mid. Sch. Assn., Zoo Atlanta, High Mus. Art, Ga. PTA, Ohio State Alumni Assn., Ga. State Alumni Assn., Profl. Assn. Ga. Educators. Democrat. Presbyterian. Avocations: tennis, reading, education-related activities. Home: 1670 Branch Valley Dr Roswell GA 30076-3007

HOSLER, CHARLES LUTHER, JR., meteorologist, educator; b. Honey Brook, Pa., June 3, 1924; s. Charles Luther and Miriam Deichley (Stauffer) H.; m. Gladys Cheesbrough, 1947 (div.); children:Sharon Elizabeth, David Charles, Lynn Rebecca, Peter William; m. Anna R. Stahel, 1971. Student, Bucknell U., 1943-44, MIT, 1944-45; BS, Pa. State U., 1947, MS, 1948, PhD, 1951. Faculty Pa. State U., University Park, 1948—, prof. meteorology, 1960—, head dept. 1961-65, dean Coll. Earth and Mineral Scis., 1965-85, sr. v.p. rsch., dean Grad. Sch., 1985-92. Hydrographer Pa. Dept. Forests and Waters, 1949-59; meteorol cons., 1950—, vis. prof. colls., lectr. civic and profl. groups; condr. daily TV

weather program, 1957-67; spl. rsch. microphysics of clouds; chmn. bd. atmospheric scis. and climate Nat. Acad. Scis., 1984-86; mem. Nat. Sci. Bd., 1985-94; mem. nat. adv. com. on oceans and atmosphere; chmn. bd. trustees Univ. Corp. for Atmospheric Rsch., Boulder, Colo., 1981-85. Contbr. articles to profl. jours. Served to lt. (j.g.) USNR, 1943-46; lt. comdr. Res. Fellow Am. Meteorol. Soc. (councilor, pres. 1976); mem. Nat. Acad. Engring., Am. Geophys. Union Am. Chem. Soc. (regional lectr. 1971-72), AAAS, Sigma Xi (pres. Pa. State U. 1958, nat. lectr. 1972), Tau Beta Pi. Home: 1229 Smithfield Cir State College PA 16801-6426 Office: Pa State U 617 Walker Bldg University Park PA 16802-5014

HOSLER, ELIZABETH, management consultant; b. Barberton, Ohio, Mar. 1, 1964; d. Ernest Wade and Jean Heath Underwood; m. Michael J. Hosler, Sept. 4, 1950; children: Emilie, Mary Catherine. MBA, U. Dayton, 1993. CPA. Asst. mgr. Rax Restaurants, Columbus, Ohio, 1987-88; clk. The Ltd., Inc., Columbus, 1988-92. Mem. Nat. Mgmt. Assn. (treas. 1996-98). United Methodist. Avocation: playing pipe organ. Home: 430 E Moler St Columbus OH 43207-1241 Office: Solid Waste Authority Cen Ohio 6220 Young Rd Grove City OH 43123-9518

HOSLEY, MARGUERITE CYRIL, civic worker; b. Houston, July 29, 1946; d. Frederick Willard and Marguerite Estella (Arisman) Collister; m. Richard Allyn Hosley II, July 18, 1968; children: Richard A. III, Sean Frederick, Michelle Cyril. BS in Edn., U. Houston, 1968; postgrad., Tex. A&M U., 1970-71. Cert. tchr., Tex. Tchr. Sharpstown H.S., Houston, 1968-69, Bryan (Tex.) H.S., 1969-71; ins. asst. Farmers Ins., Stafford, Tex., 1981-83; adminstrv. asst., fin. asst. Christ United Meth. Ch., Sugarland, Tex., 1984-92; mem. planning and zoning commn. City of Sugarland, 1995-98; mem. Sugarland City Coun., 1998—; mayor pro tem City of Sugarland, 2000-2001. Pres. bd. dirs. Ft. Bend Boys Choir, 1984-85; docent Bayou Bend Collection and Gardens, Houston Mus. Fine Arts, 1994—, day chair, 1997-98, spl. event chmn. 1999-2000, group tour chmn., 2002-2003; mem. Ima Hogg Ceramic Cir., 1994—, social chmn., 1997-98; bd. dirs. Am. Cancer Soc., 1990-97; pres. Am. Cancer Soc. League, 1993-94; mem. Lone Star Stomp com. Ft. Bend Mus. Assn., 1991-97; parent vol. Ft. Bend Ind. Schs., 1980-94; raffle chmn. Ft. Bend Drug Alliance Gala, 1989; newsletter chmn. Am. Heart Assn. Guild, 1990-91, v.p., 1992-93; bd. dirs. Sugar Land Cultural Arts Found., 1999—, Battleship Tex. Found., 2001-2002. Named Ft. Bend Outstanding Woman, Ft. Bend County, 1992. Mem. Houston Ladies' Tennis Assn. (team capt.), Ft. Bend Mus., Sweetwater Country Club (bd. govs. 1990-93), Sweetwater Women's Assn. (treas. 1985-87, pres. 1987-88), Friends of Casa (charter mem.), Aggie Moms Club, Chi Omega Alumnae. Republican. Methodist. Avocations: tennis, dancing, reading, continuing education classes. Home: 427 W Alkire Lake Dr Sugar Land TX 77478-3527

HOSMAN, SHARON, elementary education educator; b. Springfield, Mo., May 20, 1939; d. Charles E. and Jewell A. (Allgood) Beckerdite; m. Ralph W. Hosman, Jan. 1, 1980; children: Kevin Cook, Melissa Cook, Shawn Cook. BS, SW Mo. State U., 1964, MS, 1980. Tchr. music Pleasant Hope (Mo.) Sch., 1964-66; elem. tchr. Willard (Mo.) Pub. Schs., 1966-93. Mem. Internat. Reading Assn., Am. Fedn. Tchrs. Methodist. Home: HC 80 Box 782 Camdenton MO 65020-8612

HOSMAN, SHARON LEE, music educator; b. Bisbee, Ariz., Nov. 2, 1943; d. Roy Lee and Virginia Baldwin (Bandel) H. BA, Loretto Heights Coll., 1965; MA, U. No. Colo., 1979. Tchr. Livermore (Calif.) Sch. Dist., 1965-66, Jefferson County Pub. Schs., Golden, Colo., 1966-97. Faculty rep. North Area Citizens Adv. Com., Arvada, Colo., 1979-81, S.I.P.C., Arvada, 1982-83, North Area Sch. Improvement Process Com., Arvada, 1984-91, North Area Accountability com., 1991-92. Piano accompanist for sch. groups, 1965-97. Mem. NEA, DAR, Jefferson County Edn. Assn., Colo. Edn. Assn., Music Tchrs. Nat. Assn., Colo. State Music Tchrs. Assn., Denver Area Music Tchrs. Assn., Musicians' Soc. Denver, Am. Guild Organists, Hereditary Order of First Families of Mass., Smithsonian, Denver Rescue Mission, Denver Dumb Friends League, St. Luke's Hosp. Aux. (life). Republican. Episcopalian. Avocations: art, music, drama, reading, gardening.

HOSMER, HILARY HOLDEN, computer systems educator; b. Worcester, Mass, Sept. 15, 1945; d. Humphrey Buttrick and Janet Wyatt Hosmer; m. Robert Burrell Holden, June 30, 1973; children: Katherine, Jonathan. BA, Bryn Mawr Coll., 1967; MEd, U. Mass., 1971, Vol. Peace Corps, Guiglo, 1967-69; race rels. cons. Fed. Desegregation Ctr. Dade County Pub. Sch., Miami, Fla., 1970-71; edn. rep. Honeywell Inc., Wellesley, Mass., 1972-74; programmer Mass. Hosp. Assn., Burlington, 1974-75; cons. Blue Cross/Blue Shield Inc., Boston, 1975-76; edn. specialist Digital Equipment Corp., Maynard, Mass., 1976-77; edn. coordinator, cons. tng. mgr. Interactive Data/Chase Econometrics, Waltham, Mass., 1980-81; instr. Bentley Coll., Waltham, 1981-86; mem. tech. staff MITRE Corp., Bedford, Mass., 1986-90; founder, pres. Data Security Inc., Bedford, 1990—; part-time dir. info. assurance Norman Data Def. Sys., 2000-01. Faculty cons., mem. steering com. Bay State Jr. Coll. Bus. Skills Tech. Writing Program, Waltham, 1983-85; founder, chair New Security Paradigms Workshop, 1992—; founder The Security Consortium, 1991; invited computer security amb. to China, 1994, 2000; keynote spkr. IFIP, Samos, Greece, 1996, ISAS, Caracas, Venezuela, 1997. Co-founder Students for Internat. Order and World Peace, 1966, Prospect Theater Workshop, 1970. Named citizen ambassador People to People, Europe, 1985, People's Republic China, 1986. Mem.: Computer Profls. for Social Responsibility, Am. Computer Mfrs., Bryn Mawr (Boston). Democrat. Unitarian Universalist. Avocations: theater, sailing, travel.

HOSOKAWA, DAVID, advertising executive; CEO TMP Worldwide, Inc., N.Y.C., vice chmn. Office: TMP Worldwide Inc 622 3rd Ave Fl 36 New York NY 10017-6707

HOSSAIN, M. IQBAL, pediatrician, researcher; b. Sirajganj, Rajshahi, Bangladesh, Jan. 1, 1961; s. Elius Uddin and Mosammot Hamida (Begum) Talukder; m. Rehana Yasmin, Oct. 9, 1986; children: M. Rezoan, Ibnat Aniqa. MB, BS, Rajshahi Med. Coll., Bangladesh, 1985; diploma in child health, Inst. Child Health, Bangladesh, 1990; postgrad., U. Calif., Davis, 2000. Intern Rajshahi Med. Coll. Hosp., Bangladesh, 1985-86; med. officer Sirajganj Children Hosp., Bangladesh, 1986-91, jr. cons., chief physician, 1991-93; med. officer Internat. Ctr. for Diarrhoeal-Diseases Rsch., Bangladesh, 1993-99, asst. scientist, 1999—. Contbr. articles to profl. jour. Joint sec. Chandpal Polli Chikitsa Kendro, Srirajganj, 1990—. Grantee Bangladesh Integrated Nutrition Project, 1998, USAID, 2000; travel scholar Internat. Congress on Coop. Rsch. with Devel. Countries, Basel, Switzerland, 1999; Fogarty fellow U. Calif., Davis, 2000; grantee US AID, 2000. Mem. Bangladesh Med. Assn., Bangladesh Pediat. Assn., Bangladesh Pvt. Med. Practitioner Assn. Moslem. Avocations: reading, indoor games, music. Home: 949/3/C East Shewrapana 1216 Dhaka Bangladesh Office: ICDDR B Mohakhali 1212 Dhaka Bangladesh E-mail: ihossain@dp.com., mhossain@ucdavis.edu.

HOSSAIN, MURSHED, physicist, researcher; b. Pathaliakandi, Homna, Comilla, Bangladesh, Nov. 21, 1950; came to U.S., 1979; s. Mohammad Abdul Alim and Mehar Nigar; m. Sufia Khatun, July 25, 1982; children: Chintan, Chetak. BSc with honors, Dacca U., Bangladesh, 1975, MSc, 1976; MS, Coll. William & Mary, 1981; PhD, Coll. William & Mary, Va., 1983. Cert. in therapeutic radiologic physics Am. Bd. Radiology. Jr. rsch. officer Forest Rsch. Inst., Chittagong, Bangladesh, 1977-78; sci. officer AEC, Dhaka, Bangladesh, 1978-79; staff scientist Inst. for Computer Applications in Sci. & Engring. NASA Langley Rsch. Ctr., Hampton, Va., 1983-85; assoc. rsch. scientist Courant Inst. Math. Scis., NYU, 1985-88; rsch. scientist Bartol Rsch. Inst., U. Del., Newark, 1988-91, sr. rsch. scientist, 1991-97; adj. faculty Rowan U., Glassboro, N.J., 1995-97, asst. prof. dept. chemistry and physics, 1998; clin. resident Thomas Jefferson U., Phila., 1998—99, instr., 1999—2001, asst. prof., 2001—. Mng. com. B.G. Press H.S., Tejgaon, Dhaka, Bangladesh, 1974-77; v.p. Dacca U. Physics Assn., 1975-76; joint sec. Sr. Forrest Rsch. Officers Assn., Forest Rsch. Inst., 1977-78. Contbr. articles to profl. jours. including Jour. Plasma Physics, Physics Fluids, Phys. Rev. Letters, Astrophys. Jour., Physics Letters, Computer Physics Comm., Phys. Rev., Med. Physics. Mem. Am. Assn. of Physicists in Medicine. Achievements include research in radiation therapy physics, on plasma transport, astrophysical convection, fluid and magnetofluid turbulence theory and simulation. Home: 1015 Sweet Cherry Ct Wilmington DE 19809 Office: Thomas Jefferson U Dept Radiation Oncology 111 S 11th St Philadelphia PA 19107-5084 E-mail: murshed.hossain@mail.tju.edu.

HOSSAIN, TARIQUE M. marketing science analyst, educator; arrived in U.S., 1989; s. Abdul Latif Miah and Halima Begum; m. Misty Khandokar, Apr. 18, 1998. MS, U. North Tex., 1991; PhD, Tex. A & M U., 1997. Sr. economist RRC, Inc., Bryan, 1997—99; mktg. sci. analyst Ipsos-Vantis, San Ramon, Calif., 1999—. Lectr. Calif. State U., Hayward, 2003—. Grantee, Norwegian State Ednl. Fund, 1988. Mem.: Inst. for Ops. Rsch. and the Mgmt. Sci., Omicron Delta Epsilon. Achievements include research in Econometric Test of Price Asymmetry in Retail Gasoline Market; modeler perceptual map using composite score. Office: IPSOS-Vantis 3130 Crow Canyon Pl San Ramon CA Office Fax: 703-738-1788.

HOSSLER, DAVID JOSEPH, lawyer, law educator; b. Mesa, Ariz., Oct. 18, 1940; s. Carl Joseph and Elizabeth Ruth (Bills) H.; m. Gretchen Anne, Mar. 2, 1945; 1 child, Devon Annagret. BA, U. Ariz., 1969, JD, 1972. Bar: Ariz. 1972, U.S. Dist. Ct. Ariz. 1972, U.S. Supreme Ct. 1977. Legal intern to chmn. FCC, summer 1971; law clk. to chief justice Ariz. Supreme Ct., 1972-73; chief dep. county atty. Yuma County (Ariz.), 1973-74; ptnr. Hunt, Kenworthy, Meerchaum and Hossler, Yuma, Ariz., 1974—. Instr. in law and banking, law and real estate Ariz. Western Coll.; instr. in bus. law, mktg., ethics Webster U.; instr. agrl. law U. Ariz.; co-chmn. fee arbitration com. Ariz. State Bar, 1990—; instr. employee/employer law U. Phoenix. Editor-in-chief Ariz. Adv., 1971-72. Mem. precinct com. Yuma County Rep. Ctrl. Com., 1974-2000, vice chmn., 1982; chmn. region II Acad. Decathalon competition, 1989; bd. dirs. Yuma County Ednl. Found. (Hall of Fame 2000), Yuma County Assn. Behavior Health Svcs., also pres., 1981; coach Yuma H.S. mock ct. team, 1987-94; bd. dirs. friends of U. Med. Ctr. With USN. Recipient Man and Boy award, Boys Clubs Am., 1979, Freedoms Found. award, Yuma chpt., 1988, Demolay Legion of Honor, 1991, Francis Woodward award, Ariz. Pub. Svc., 2000, named Vol. of Yr., Yuma County, 1981—82, Heart of Yuma award, 2000, voted Yuma's Best (atty.), 2001—02. Mem. ATLA, Am. Judicature Soc., Yuma County Bar Assn. (pres. 1975-76), Navy League, VFW, Am. Legion, U. Ariz. Alumni Assn. (nat. bd. dirs., past pres., hon. bobcat 1996, Disting. Citizen award 1997), Rotary (pres. Yuma club 1987-88, dist. gov. rep. 1989, dist. gov. 1992-93, findings com. 1996, dist. found. chair 1996-2000, co-chmn. internat. membership retention 2000-01, John Van Houton Look Beyond Yourself award 1995, Roy Slayton Share Rotary Share People award 1996, Al Face You Are the Key award 1997, Ted Day Let Svc. Light the Way award 1998, Rotary Found. citation for meritorious svc., Internat. Svc. Above Self award, Cliff Doctorman Real Happiness is Helping Others award, Disting. Svc. award). Episcopalian (vestry 1978-82). Home: 2802 S Fern Dr Yuma AZ 85364-2919 Office: Hunt Kenworthy Meerchaum and Hossler 330 W 24th St Yuma AZ 85364-6455 also: PO Box 2919 Yuma AZ 85366-2919 E-mail: dhossler@mindspring.com.

HOST, STIG, real estate company executive, oil company executive; b. Copenhagen, Sept. 26, 1926; came to U.S., 1941; s. Thorkil and Eli (Stallknecht) H.; m. Jeanne Grinnell, Feb. 24, 1951; children: N. George, Alexander (dec.), Christian T., T. Amory. AB in Econs., Harvard U., 1951; postgrad. in Bus., NYU, 1952-53. Bunker sales agt. Cory Mann George Corp., N.Y.C., 1950-53; cargo sales asst. Mobil Internat., N.Y.C., 1953-57; dir. cargo sales, Europe and North Africa Mobil Supply Co., Ltd., London, 1957-59; mng. dir. Mobil Sales (Internat.), Tokyo, 1959-61; v.p. crude and product sales Mobil Sales and Supply Corp., N.Y.C., 1961-65, exec. v.p. marine, indsl. and govt. sales, 1965-68; pres., gen. mgr. Mobil Oil Italiana, Rome, 1968-72; v.p., bd. dirs. Mobil Europe, Inc., London, 1972-73; vice-chmn., chief exec. officer Skaarup Shipping Corp., Greenwich, Conn., 1973-79; chmn., bd. dirs. Internat. Energy Corp., Stamford, Conn., 1979—. Chmn., bd. dirs. Internat. Marine Sales, Inc., Stamford, 1979—, Kriti Exploration, Inc., Houston, 1980—, Kriti Properties and Devel. Corp., Houston, 1985—; bd. dirs. Fla. Fuels, Inc., Miami, Fla.; mem. exec. and audit coms., bd. dirs. DeVegh Mut. Fund, N.Y.C., 1977-86; trustee, mem. exec. com. and audit coms. Alliance Internat. Fund, N.Y.C., 1980—02; trustee DLJ-Winthrop Focus Funds, N.Y.C., 1986-2001, Alliance Global Environ. Fund, 1990-2000, Alliance New Europe Fund, 1990—03, Alliance All Asia Investment Fund, 1994—03; chmn. Alexander Host Found., 1984—; exec. trustee Am. Scandinavian Found., 1987—; overseer Tufts U. Coll. Engring., 1990-93. Mem. Fulbright Commn., Rome, 1969-71; trustee Temple U., Rome, 1971-72, Overseas Sch. of Rome, 1966-71. Served as mcht. marine officer, 1943-46, ETO. Decorated Order of Grande Ufficiale, Govt. of Italy, 1970. Mem.: Am. Petroleum Inst. (25 yr. club), Harvard Univ. Alumni Assn. (nominations overseers and directors com. 1985—89, bd. dirs., chmn. comms. com., mem. continuing edn. com.,), Tokyo Club, Royal Automobile Club (London), Indian Harbor Yacht (Greenwich) (bd. dirs., audit com. 1973—78), N.Y. Yacht Club, Harvard Club (N.Y.C.) (chmn. long range planning 1978—82). Republican. Episcopalian. Home: 103 Oneida Dr Greenwich CT 06830-7127 Office: Kriti Mgmt Inc 345 E 37th St Rm 312 New York NY 10016-3256

HOSTER-BURANDT, NORMA J. musician, fundraiser; b. Phila., Sept. 29, 1956; d. Downey Delbert and Norma M. (Von Vital) H.; m. Timothy Lee Burandt; children: Jonathan Daniel Loudon, Jeremy Matthew Loudon. BMus Piano Performance summa cum laude, Temple U., 1978, MMus in Piano Pedagogy, 1980. Ordained deacon Presbyn. Ch. USA. Pvt. piano tchr., 1973—; devel. coord. Chesapeake (Va.) Gen. Hosp., 2001—. Piano tchr., accompanist Temple U. Music Prep., Phila., 1978-81; accompanist Choral Soc. Montgomery County, Blue Bell, Pa., 1991-93; founding accompanist Temple U. Children's Choir, Phila., 1992-99; organist Covenant Presbyn. Ch., Trenton, N.J., 1997-2001; accompanist Am. Choral Dirs. Assn. convs., 1996-98; accompanist in field; grants specialist Recording for the Blind & Dyslexic Nat. Headquarters, Princeton, N.J., 2000-01. Performances on local/nat. radio broadcasts, 1995, 97, 98; rec. artist Temple U. Children's Choir, 2001. Avocations: choral singing, needlecraft. Home: 202 North Hill Ln Chesapeake VA 23322-6604

HOSTERT, LEONA TERESSA, research librarian; b. Pitts., Oct. 13, 1933; d. Joseph C. and Mary T. (Chropka) Bajoras; m. Arthur H. Hostert, Aug. 9, 1958; children: Erik M., Wendy A. BS in Edn., Ind. State U., 1955; MLS, Duquesne U., 1965. Cert. secondary edn. educator, Pa. Spl. libr. Am. Electronic Labs., Colmar, Pa., 1982; libr. high sch. North Penn Schs., Lansdale, Pa., 1986—; pres. Lee's Rsch., Lansdale, Pa., 1985—. Access Pa. liaison North Penn Schs., Lansdale, 1986—. Bd. dirs. North Penn Symphony, Lansdale, 1986-88; planning commr. Upper Gwynedd Twp., Lansdale, 1987-89; area rep. Lansdale Rep. Party, Montgomery County, 1988-89. Mem. Pa. Sch. Libr. Assn., North Pa. Edn. Assn. (membership chair, rep. 1991—). Home: 423 N Brookside Dr Oxford PA 19363

HOSTETLER, ELSIE J. musician, music educator; b. Sugarcreek, Ohio, Apr. 8, 1942; d. Jonas B. and Lovina Hostetler. Student, Akron (Ohio) U., 1969-70. Cert. tchr. chord approach to piano, New Sch. Am. Music. Receptionist to office mgr. Milk, Inc., Akron, 1964-78; adminstr. Christian Tng. Ctr., St. Louis, 1987-88, music dir., 1989-91; music sec. Gospel Assembly Conv. Ctr., Louisville, 1992—; piano tchr. Red Bud, Ill., 1997—. Workshop leader EZ-Creative Piano, Red Bud, 1999—. Band dir., choir dir. Gospel Assembly Ch., Akron, 1959-78; asst. pianist, organist, instrumental tchr. Gospel Assembly Ch., St. Louis, 1981-91; music dir., pianist-organist Christian Assembly Ch., Millstadt, Ill., 1992—. Mem. Music Tchrs. Nat. Assn., Ill. State Music Tchrs. Assn. Home: 98 Jennys Way Smithton IL 62285-1656 E-mail: ezpiano98@aol.com.

HOSTETLER, KARL YODER, internist, endocrinologist, educator; b. Goshen, Ind., Nov. 17, 1939; s. Carl Milton and Etta LaVerne (Yoder) H.; m. Margaretha Steur, Dec. 17, 1971; children: Saskia Emma, Kirsten Cornelia, Carl Martijn. BS in Chemistry, DePauw U., 1961; MD, Western Res. U., 1965. Diplomate Am. Bd. Internal Medicine, Am. Bd. Endocrinology and Metabolism. Intern, resident in medicine Univ. Hosp. Cleve., 1965-69; fellow endocrinology Cleve. Clinic Found., 1969-70; postdoctoral fellow, lipid chemistry U. Utrecht, The Netherlands, 1970-73; asst. prof. medicine U. Calif., San Diego, 1973-79, assoc. prof. medicine, 1979-82, prof. medicine, 1982—; v.p. R&D Vical Inc., 1987—92. Assoc. editor: Jour. of Clin. Investigation, 1993-97; contbr. numerous articles to scholarly and profl. jours. Pres. San Diego County chpt. Am. Diabetes Assn., 1982-83. Recipient fellowship John Simon Guggenheim Found., 1980-81, Japan Soc. for Promotion of Sci., Tokyo, 1986. Mem. Am. Soc. Clin. Investigation, Am. Soc. Biochemistry and Molecular Biology, Western Soc. Clin. Investigation, Western Assn. Physicians, Am. Soc. Microbiology, Internat. Soc. Antiviral Rsch. Achievements include research in antiviral drugs design; phospholipid chemistry and biochemistry; drug induced lipid storage. Office: U Calif San Diego Dept Medicine 0676 La Jolla CA 92093 E-mail: khostetl@ucsd.edu.

HOSTETTER, AMOS BARR, JR., cable television executive; b. Jan. 12, 1937; s. Amos Barr and Leola (Conroy) Hostetter. BA cum laude, Amherst Coll., 1958; MBA, Harvard U., 1961. Asst. to v.p. fin. Am. & Fgn. Power Co., N.Y.C., 1958—59; investment analyst Cambridge (Mass.) Capital Corp., 1961—63; co-founder, exec. v.p. Continental Cablevision, Inc., Boston, 1963—80, pres., CEO, 1980—85, chmn., CEO, 1985—96; CEO MediaOne, Inc., Boston, 1996—2000; chmn. Pilot House Assoc., LLC; chmn., CEO Continental Cablevision, Inc. (name changed to Media One), 1985—; founder, bd. dirs. Cable Satellite Pub. Affairs Network, 1979—. Bd. dirs. Commodities Corp., Princeton, NJ; trustee various mut. funds Mass. Fin. Svcs., 1985—. Trustee Children's TV Workshop, N.Y.C., 1980—, New Eng. Med. Ctr. Hosp., Boston, 1982—; bd. overseers Mus. Fine Arts, Boston, 1987—; bd. dirs. Corp. Pub. Broadcasting, Washington, 1975—79, Walter Kaitz Found., 1981—. Named Man of Yr., Cablevision Mag., 1972. Mem.: Internat. Radio and TV Soc., Nat. Cable TV Assn. (nat. chmn. 1973—74, dir. 1968—75, 1982—, Larry Boggs award 1975), Amherst Coll. Soc. Alumni (pres. 1982—84, exec. com. 1982—, chmn. 1987—). Office: The Pilot House Lewis Wharf Boston MA 02110

HOSTETTER, ELIZABETH A. music educator; d. Charles Bernard and Esther Marie Jones; m. Wayne Kent Hostetter, Aug. 11, 1967; children: Karen Lee Kilpatrick, Lydia Ann. MusB with high honors, U. of Louisville, 1969, MusM, 1971; D Mus. Arts, Ariz. State U., 1990. Piano tchr. Opus 48 Sch. of Music, Inc., Anniston, Ala., —; organist Parker Meml. Bapt. Ch., Anniston, 1998—; asst. prof. of music Ala. State U., Montgomery. Dir. Opus 48 Sch. of Music, Inc, Anniston, 2001—02; adj. piano tchr. rand Canyon U., Phoenix. Trustee North Am. Mission Bd., Alpharetta, Ga., 1988—89. Recipient Regents Academic scholarship, Ariz. State U., 1986—88, Faculty Wives scholarship, 1986—87; grantee Grad. Students Assn. for Rsch., AZ State U., 1988. Mem.: Music Tchrs. Nat. Assn. (Amanda Penick Tchr. Enrichment grant 1999), Phi Kappa Lambda, Phi Kappa Phi. Republican. Baptist. Avocations: travel, reading, cooking.

HOSTETTER, JAMES WILLIAM, lawyer; b. Newark, Ohio, May 10, 1948; s. James O. and Joanne A. (Abel) H.; m. Lynn Susan Kudlack, June 19, 1971; children: Brad A., Eric A. BS, Wittenberg U., 1970; JD, Capital U., 1976. Bar: Ohio 1976, U.S. Dist. Ct. (so. dist.) Ohio 1977, U.S. Ct. Appeals (6th cir.) 2001, U.S. Supreme Ct. 1979; cert. mediator. Tchr. Berne Union Schs., Sugar Grove, Ohio, 1970-71, East Muskingum Schs., New Concord, Ohio, 1971-72; work-study coord. Licking County Schs., Newark, 1972-73; with legal divsn. Ohio Dept. Taxation, Columbus, 1973-76; ptnr. Schaller, Hostetter & Campbell, Newark, 1976-92; asst. pros. atty. Licking County Prosecutor's Office, Newark, 1976-79, 84-92; dir. of law City of Newark (Ohio), 1992—. Clk. Heath (Ohio) Civil Svc. Comn., 1981-83; real estate instr. Cen. Ohio Tech. Coll., Newark, 1978-83. Mem., pres. Lakewood Local Bd. Edn., Hebron, Ohio, 1980-84; mem. exec. com. Licking County Rep. party, Newark, 1982—; vol. Licking County United Way, Cancer Soc., Heart Fund, Newark. Mem. Ohio State Bar Assn., Ohio Mcpl. Attys. Assn., Licking County Bar Assn., Licking County C. of C., Newark Lions Club, Newark Maennerchor, Moose. Republican. Avocations: youth coaching, tennis, baseball. Office: Dir Law City of Newark 40 W Main St Newark OH 43055-5521 E-mail: jhostett@ci.newark.oh.us.

HOSTETTER, LAR-RIE DAWN, poet; b. Pascagoula, Miss., Jan. 24, 1972; Author numerous poems. Vol. Overton-Brooks VA Hosp., Shreveport, La., 2002, Am. Legion Post 388, Koran, La., 2001—02. Recipient Fire Muse award, Famous Poets Soc., 2001. Democrat. Baptist. Home: 139 Bluff Rd Ringgold LA 71068

HOSTETTLER, JOHN N. congressman; b. Evansville, Ind., July 19, 1961; s. Earl Eugene and Esther Aline (Hollingsworth) H.; m. Elizabeth Ann Hamman, Nov. 12, 1983; children: Matthew, Amanda, Jaclyn. BSME, Rose-Hulman Inst. Tech. Reg. profl. engr. Engr. So. Ind. Gas and Electric, Evansville, 1986-94; mem. U.S. Congress from 8th Ind. Dist., Washington, 1995—; mem. Agriculture and National Security coms.; mem. Judiciary Com. Vice chair House Armed Services Comm. Special Oversight Panel on Terrorism, 2001—. Deacon 12th Avenue Gen. Baptist, 1986-1995. Republican. Baptist. Office: US Ho of Reps 1214 Longworth HOB Washington DC 20515-0001*

HOSTETTLER, STEPHEN JOHN, naval officer; b. Evansville, Ind., Aug. 23, 1931; s. Ernest Hoffman and Frances Reitz (Bays) H.; m. Lucy Ann Ingalls, June 10, 1953; children: Katherine Ann, Stephen John Jr. BS, U.S. Naval Acad., 1953; MSE.E., U.S. Naval Postgrad. Sch., 1960; P.MD, Harvard Bus. Sch., 1969. Commd. ensign USN, advanced through grades to rear adm.; comdr. USS Halsey CG 23; program mgr. medium-range missile systems Naval Sea Systems Command, 1974-76; comdr. U.S. Naval Forces, Republic of Korea; sr. mem. Mil. Armistice Commn., UN Command, Republic of Korea, 1979-81; dir. surface combat systems divsn. Office Chief Naval Ops., Washington, 1981-82; dir. Joint Cruise Missile Office, Washington, 1982-86, ret., 1986; v.p., gen. mgr. Va. propulsion divsn. Atlantic Rsch. Corp., Alexandria, Va., 1986-92; ret., 1992—. Decorated Bronze Star medal., Def. Superior Svc. medal, Def. D.S.M., Legion of Merit

HOSTLER, CHARLES WARREN, former ambassador, international affairs consultant; b. Chgo., Dec. 12, 1919; s. Sidney Marvin and Catherine (Marshall) Hostler; 1 child, Charles Warren Jr. BA, U. Calif. at Los Angeles, L.A., 1942; MA, Am. U., Beirut, Lebanon, 1955, Georgetown U., 1950, PhD, 1956. Commd. 2d lt. U.S. Air Force, 1942, advanced through grades to col., 1955; ret., 1963; dir. internat. ops. McDonnell Douglas Corp., Middle East, 1965-67, mgr. internat. ops. Paris, 1963-65, mgr. internat. mktg., missiles and space, 1967-69; pres. Hostler Investment Co., Newport Beach, Calif., 1969-74; chmn. bd. Irvine (Calif.) Nat. Bank, 1972-74; dir. Wynn's Internat., Inc., Fullerton, Calif., 1971-74; dep. asst. sec. for internat. commerce, dir. Bur. Internat. Commerce, U.S. Dept. Commerce, Washington, 1974-76; regional v.p. Mid-East and Africa, E-Systems Inc., Cairo, Egypt, 1976-77; pres. Pacific SW Capital Corp., San Diego, 1977-89; ambassador U.S. Govt., Bahrain, 1989-93. Hon. consul gen. Kingdom of Bahrain, 1993—; adj. prof. polit. sci. San Diego State U., 1999—. Author: Turkism and the Soviets, 1957, The Turks of Central Asia, 1993, Soldier to Reality, 2003. Chmn. Calif. Contractors State Lic. Bd., 1973—79, San Diego County Local Agy. Formation Commn., 1979—89, Calif. State Park and Recreation Commn., 1983—89; pres. San Diego Consular Corps, 1996—98; chmn., bd. dirs. People-to-People Internat. Decorated Legion of Merit; recipient Eisenhower Disting. Svc. award, decorations from 9 nations, Fgn. Affairs award for Pub. Svc., U.S. State Dept. Mem.: VFW (life), Coun. Am. Ambs., Mid. East Inst. (bd. govs. 1962—80, 1993—), Vets. of Office of Strategic Svcs., Mil. Officers Assn. of Am. (life), Navy League (life). Office: 1101 First St # 302 Coronado CA 92118-1474

HOSTNIK, CHARLES RIVOIRE, lawyer; b. Glen Ridge, N.J., Apr. 8, 1954; s. William John and Susan (Rivoire) H. AB, Dartmouth Coll., 1976; JD, U. Puget Sound, 1979. Bar: Wash. 1980, U.S. Dist. Ct. (we. dist.) Wash. 1980, U.S. Dist. Ct. (ea. dist.) Wash. 1982, U.S. Ct. Appeals (9th cir.) 1983, Hoh Tribal Ct. 1984, Nisqually Tribal Ct. 1984, Puyallup Tribal Ct. 1984, Shoalwater Bay Tribal Ct. 1984, Skokomish Tribal Ct. 1984. Asst. atty. gen. Atty. Gen.'s Office State of Wash., Olympia, 1980-84; assoc. Kane, Vandeberg, Hartinger & Walker, Tacoma, 1984-87; ptnr. Anderson, Burns & Hostnik, Tacoma, 1988—. Trial and appellate judge N.W. Intertribal Ct. Sys., Edmonds, Wash., 1986—2000. Author: (chpt.) Washington Practice, 1989. Office: Anderson Burns & Hostnik 6915 Lakewood Dr W Ste A1 Tacoma WA 98467-3299

HOSTON, GERMAINE ANNETTE, political science educator; b. Trenton, NJ; d. Walter Lee and Veretta Louise H. AB in Politics summa cum laude, Princeton U., 1975; MA in Govt., Harvard U., 1978, PhD in Govt., 1981. Rsch. asst. Princeton U., NJ, 1973-75; tchg. asst. Harvard U., Cambridge, Mass., 1977-78; asst. prof. polit. sci. Johns Hopkins U., Balt., 1980-86, assoc. prof. polit. sci., 1986-92; prof. polit. sci. U. Calif., San Diego, 1992—, dir. Ctr. for

Democratization and Econ. Devel., 1993-99; founder, pres. Inst. Trans Pacific Studies in Values, Culture and Politics, 1999—. Vis. prof. L'Ecole des Hautes Etudes en Sci. Sociales, Paris, 1986, Osaka City U., Japan, 1990, U. Tokyo, 1991; faculty advisor Chinese lang. program Johns Hopkins U., 1981-92, undergrad. ethics bd., 1980-83, pub. interest investment adv. com., 1982-85, undergrad. admissions com., 1983-84, 86-89, pres.'s human climate task force, 1987, dir. undergrad. program, 1987, 88-89, mem. com. undergrad. studies, 1987-91, organizer comparative politics colloquium, 1987-89, dept. colloquium, 1987-89, 91-92; Japanese studies program com. U. Calif., San Diego, 1992—, Chinese studies program, 1994—, field coord. comparative politics, 1994—95, dir. grad. studies comparative politics, 1997-98; bd. dir. Inst. East-West Security Studies, NYC, 1990-97; Am. adv. com. Japan Found., 1992—; edn. abroad program com. U. Calif., 1996—; adv. com. Calif. Ctr. Asia Soc.; mem. com. tech. comms. Inst. East West Security Studies, 1997—; participant numerous workshops and seminars; lectr. in field. Author: Marxism and the Crisis of Development in Prewar Japan: The Debate on Japanese Capitalism, 1986, The State, Identity, and the National Question in China and Japan, 1994, (with others) The Biographical Dictionary of Neo-Marxism, 1985, The Biographical Dictionary of Marxism, 1986, Culture and Identity: Japanese Intellectuals During the Interwar Years, 1990, The Routledge Dictionary of Twentieth-Century Political Thinkers, 1992; mem. editl. bd. Jour. Politics, 1997—2001; contbr. articles to profl. jours. Active Md. Food Com., 1983-92, program concepts subcom. CROSS ROADS Com., Diocese of Md., 1987-88, outreach com. St. David's Episcopal Ch., Balt., standing commn. human affairs Gen. Conv. of the Episcopal Ch., 1991-97; chair peace and justice commn. Episcopal Diocese Md., 1984-87, co-chair companion diocese com., 1987-92, chair CROSS ROADS program bd., 1988-92; exec. bd. dir. Balt. Clergy and Laity Concerned, 1985-86; alternate, regular lay del. 69th Gen. Conv. of The Episcopal Ch., Detroit, 1988; trustee Va. Theol. Sem., 1988-2000; lay del. 70th Gen. Conv. of The Episcopal Ch., Phoenix, Ariz., 1991; dep. Nat. Conv. Episcopal Ch., 1988-93. Am. Legion Aux. scholar, 1972, Am. Logistical Assn. scholar, 1972-76; fellow Harvard U., 1975-77, NSF, 1975-77; Lehman fellow Harvard U., 1978-79, Fgn. Lang. and Area Studies fellow, 1978-79; fellow Am. Assn. Univ. Women Ednl. Found., 1979-80; Fgn. Rsch. scholar U. Tokyo, 1979, 82, 84, 85, 86, 91; Travel grantee Assn. Asian Studies, Japan-U.S. Friendship Commn., 1981; Internat. fellow Internat. Fedn. Univ. Women, 1982, 83; Postdoctoral grantee Social Sci. Rsch. Coun., 1983; fellow NEH, 1983; Kenan Endowment grantee Johns Hopkins U., 1984-85; fellow Rockefeller Found. Internat. Rels., 1985-88; Travel grantee Assn. Asian Studies, 1991; grantee Japan-US Friendship Commn., 1997; rsch. grantee Acad. Senate Com. on Rsch., 1996. Mem. Asia Soc. (trustee 1994—2000), Am. Polit. Sci. Assn. (mem. coun. 1991-93, mem. com. on internat. polit. sci. 1997—2003, v.p. 1998—), Assn. Asian Studies (mem. N.E. Asia coun. 1992-95, vice-chair N.E. Asia coun. 1993—94, nominated editor Jour. Asian Studies 1994, mem. coun. on fgn. rels. 1990—), Internat. Platform Assn., Pacific Coun. on Internat. Policy, Women's Fgn. Policy Group. Democrat. Episcopalian. Avocations: reading, cooking, sailing, tennis, working out. Office: 9921 Carmel Mountain Rd # 196 San Diego CA 92129 E-mail: ghoston@myesa.com.

HOTALING, ROBERT BACHMAN, community planner, educator; b. Syracuse, N.Y., July 19, 1918; s. Elliot Danforth and Florence (Bachman) Hotaling; m. M. Janet Kelley, Nov. 20, 1943 (dec.); children: Marilyn Kelley, Brock Elliot, William Austin, Richard Chapman; m. Jeanne Bryant, July 31, 1971 (dec.); m. Phyllis Hargrave, July 27, 2001. BS in Environ. Sci. and Forestry, Syracuse U., 1942; M of Urban and Regional Planning, Mich. State U., 1952. Staff dir. McFadzean, Everly Rose and Assocs., Chgo., 1946-49; dir. state and local planning R.I. Exec. Dept., Providence, 1952-55; tech. coord. for planning Interstate hwy. sytems through New England, R.I., Mass. and Conn., 1954-55; city planning dir., urban renewal planner Portland, Maine, 1955-57; acting dir., sec. Greater Portland Regional Planning Commn., 1956-57; prof. urban and regional planning Coll. Social Sci., Mich. State U., East Lansing, 1957-81; prof. lifelong edn. Inst. Community Devel., Mich. State U., East Lansing, 1957-81; prof. emeritus Mich. State U., 1981—; assoc. McKenna and Assocs., Farmington Hills, Mich., 1992—, Freeman, Smith & Assocs., Lansing, Mich., 1992—, Pub. Sector Cons., Lansing, 1992—. Pres. Urban Cons., Inc., 1962-66; pres., owner Robert B. Hotaling and Assoc., 1949—; expert witness to law firms, state and fed. agys., philanthropic orgns.; cons., lectr., seminarian Mich. Twp. Assn., 1963-81, Mich. Mcpl. League, 1978-94; mem. Mich. State Bd. of Registration for Profl. Community Planners, 1967-81, chmn., 1970-72, 76-79; cons. to state agys., polit. orgns. and corps. Author: Michigan Local Planning Commissioners Handbook (3 edits.), Michigan Township Planning and Zoning Handbook (2 edits.); chmn. editorial com. Mich. Laws Relating to Planning (3 edits.); contbr. articles to profl. jours. Mem. twp. planning commn. 1958-70, 87-94, 96-2001, chmn. 1969-70, 1998-2000, Meridan Twp., Ingham County, Mich.; mem. Meridian Twp. charter com., chmn., 1970-73; mem. Meridian Twp. Zoning Bd. of Appeals, 1969-70, 87, chmn. 1969-70; mem. strategic planning com. for planning future of Meridan Twp., Gov.'s State Legis. Zoning Revision Com., 1977-79; bd. dirs. Mich. Parks Assn., 1960-68; charter mem. Am. Inst. Cert. Profl. Cmty. Planners, 1954-81; mem. Mich. State Bd. Registration for Profl. Cmty. Planners State Exam. Com., 1969, 99, Am. Inst. Planners Nat. Exam. Com. for Profl. Planners, 1977-78; pres. Cadgewith Farms Homeowners assn., 2002—. Capt. C.E., U.S. Army, 1942-46. Recipient Meritorious Svc. award Mich. Mcpl. League, 1994. Mem. Mich. Soc. Consulting Planners (bd. dirs. 1979—). Episcopalian. Home and Office: PO Box 304 Haslett MI 48840-0304 Fax: 517-702-9615. E-mail: rbhjbh@aol.com.

HOTCHKISS, CHARLOTTE EVANS, veterinarian, researcher; b. Concord, Mass., Feb. 2, 1961; d. Gordon Goodwin and Doletha Watt Evans; m. Mark Talbot Hotchkiss, June 29, 1985; children: Laura, Arthur. AB, Bryn Mawr Coll., 1981; DVM, Cornell U., 1988; PhD, U. Fla., 1994. Instr. Yale U., New Haven, Conn., 1994-95; asst. prof. Wake Forest U. Sch. Medicine, Winston-Salem, N.C., 1995-2000; project dir. Nat. Ctr. for Toxicological Rsch., Jefferson, Ark., 2000—. Mem. AVMA, Am. Coll. Lab. Animal Medicine (planning com., 1999-2002), Am. Assn. for Lab. Animal Sci. Home: 10627 Pineview Dr Mabelvale AR 72103 Office: The Bionetics Corp 3900 NCTR Rd Jefferson AR 72079 Office Fax: 870-543-7065. E-mail: chotchkiss@nctr.fda.gov.

HOTCHKISS, EUGENE, III, retired academic administrator; b. Berwyn, Ill., Apr. 1, 1928; s. Eugene and Jeanette (Kennan) H.; m. Suzanne Ellen Troxell, Nov. 17, 1962; 1 dau., Ellen Sinclair. AB, Dartmouth Coll., 1950; PhD, Cornell U., 1960; LLD (hon.), Ill. Coll., 1976, Lake Forest Coll., 1993. Asst. to dean Dartmouth Coll., 1953-54, asst. dean, 1954-55, asso. dean, 1958-60; asst. dean Cornell U., Ithaca, N.Y., 1955-58; dean students, lectr. history Harvey Mudd Coll., Claremont, Calif., 1960-63, dean coll., 1962-68; exec. dean Chatham Coll., Pitts., 1968-70; pres. Lake Forest (Ill.) Coll., 1970-93, pres. emeritus, 1993—; interm pres. Eckerd Coll., 2000-01. Lt. (j.g.) USNR, 1950-53. Mem. Chgo. Coun. Fgn. Rels., Econ. Club, Chgo. Onnentsia Club, Caxton Club, Phi Beta Kappa, Phi Kappa Phi, Chi Phi. Office: Lake Forest Coll 555 N Sheridan Rd Lake Forest IL 60045-2338

HOTCHKISS, HARLEY N. professional hockey team owner; b. Tillsonburg, Ont., Can. BS in Geology, Mich. State U. CEO, gov. Calgary Flames, owner, gov. Bd. dirs. Conwest Exploration Co. Ltd., Nova Corp., Mich. State U. Found., Telus Corp.; chmn. NHL Bd. Govs., 1995—. Past chmn. Foothills Hosp. Bd.; vice chmn. Foothills Hosp. Found.; co-chmn. Pntrs. in Health Campaign. Office: Calgary Flames PO Box 1540 Sta M Calgary AB Canada T2P 3B9

HOTCHKISS, HEATHER A. social worker, consultant; d. John L. and Patrecia W. Hotchkiss. MSW, U. Denver, 1996. Mental health clinician Colo. Mental Health Inst. at Ft. Logan, Denver, 1990—95; cons. Colo. Dept. Edn., Denver, 1995—. Co-author: Making Standards Work: A Teachers Guide to Contextual Learning, 1999. Chair Colo. Sch. Social Work Com., Denver, 1998—2000. Named Colo. Sch. Psychologist Advocate of Yr., Colo. Soc. Sch. Psychologists, 2000—01; recipient Vision and Leadership award, Colo. Sch.-to-Career Partnership, 2001, All Means All School-to-Work award, 2000, Colo. Sch. Social Worker Distinction award, Colo. Sch. Social Work Com., 2002, Donn Brolin award, Coun. Exceptional Children, 2002. Mem.: NASW, Coun. for Exceptional Children. Office: Colo Dept of Edn 201 E Colfax Ave Rm 300 Denver CO 80203

HOTCHKISS, HENRY WASHINGTON, real estate broker and financial consultant; b. Meshed, Iran, Oct. 31, 1937; s. Henry and Mary Bell (Clark) H. BA, Bowdoin Coll., 1958. French tchr. Choate Sch., Wallingford, Conn., 1959-62; v.p. Chem. Bank, N.Y.C., 1962-80, v.p. Chem. Bank Internat. San Francisco, 1973-80; dir. corp. rels., mgr. Crédit Suisse, San Francisco, 1980-87, fin. cons., 1989—; with Dan Mello Real Estate, 1994—; bd. dirs. Calif. Coun. Internat. Trade, 1976-87; dir. Indonesia-U.S. Bus. Seminar, Los Angeles, 1979. Assoc. bd. regents L.I. Coll. Hosp., 1969-71, pres., 1971, bd. regents, 1971-73; bd. dirs. Gordonstown Am. Found., 1986—, pres., 1986-99; chmn. Captain Joshua Slocum Centennial Com. of Fairhaven, Mass., 1995-98; bd. dirs. Joshua Slocum Soc. Internat., Inc., 1998—. Capt. USAR, 1958-69. Mem. Mayflower Soc., SAR, Soc. of the Cin., Explorers Club N.Y. (treas. no. Calif. chpt. 1984-86), St. Francis Yacht Club (San Francisco). Home: 80 Fort St Fairhaven MA 02719-2812

HOTCHKISS, JOSEPH HENRY, toxicologist, educator; s. Magaret and Joseph Henry Hotchkiss; m. Kristie Marie Wallace, June 17, 1972; 1 child, Kelsey Lynne. PhD, Oreg. State U., Corvallis, 1979. Rsch. chemist Adolph Coors Brewing, Golden, Colo., 1970—74; pub. health fellow US Food & Drug Adminstrn., Washington, 1979—80; prof. and chair Cornell U. Dept. of Food Sci., Ithaca, NY, 1980—. Food chem. codex Nat. Acad. of Sci., Washington, 1989—98; joint expert com. on food additives (jecfa) FAO/WHO, Rome, 1998—2001; spl. govt. employee US Food & Drug Adminstrn., Washington, 2000—. Author: (text book author) Food Science. Fellow Fellow, Inst. of Food Technologists, 2002. Fellow: Inst. of Food Technologists (several 1980—2003, Fellow 2001). Achievements include research in Research related to food packaging and food safety/toxicology, governement regulation. Office: Cornell Univ Stocking Hall Ithaca NY 14850 Personal E-mail: jhh3@cornell.edu. E-mail: jhh3@cornell.edu.

HOTCHNER, AARON EDWARD, author; b. St. Louis, June 28, 1920; s. Samuel and Sally (Rossman) H.; children: Timothy, Holly, Tracy. AB, LLB, Washington U., St. Louis, 1941, LHD (hon.), 1992. Bar: Mo. 1941. Practiced law in, St. Louis, 1941-42; articles editor Cosmopolitan mag., 1948-50. V.p., treas. Newman's Own, Inc.; v.p. Hole in the Wall Gang Camp. Freelance writer short stories and articles in various mags. including Sat. Eve. Post, Esquire, Readers Digest, 1950—; TV playwright Playhouse 90, 1958-60; adapted major Hemingway works for TV including For Whom The Bell Tolls, 1958, The Killers, 1959; writer screenplay Adventures of a Young Man, 1961; author: The Dangerous American, 1958, Papa Hemingway: A Personal Memoir, 1966, revised, 1999, Treasure, 1970, King of the Hill, 1972, Looking for Miracles, 1974, Doris Day, 1976, Sophia, Living and Loving, 1979, The Man Who Lived at the Ritz, 1981, Choice People, 1984, Hemingway and His World, 1989, Blown Away, 1990, Louisiana Purchase, 1996, After the Storm, 2000, Dreams of Glory, 2001, The Day I Fired Alan Ladd, 2002; playwright: The Short Happy Life, 1961, The White House, 1964, The Hemingway Hero, 1967, Do You Take This Man?, 1970, Sweet Prince, 1980, Let 'Em Rot, 1987, Welcome to the Club, 1989, Courtroom Cantata, 1995, Exactly Like You, 1996, Papa Hemingway (rev.), 1999, Exactly Like You, 1999, After the Storm, 2000, The World of Nick Adams, 2001. Founding dir. Hole in the Wall Gang Fund. Served to maj. USAAF, 1942-46, NATOUS. Recipient Disting. Alumni award Law Sch., Washington U., 1992. Mem. Mo. Bar Assn., Writers Guild Am., Dramatists Guild, PEN, Authors Guild, Authors Guild Found. (bd. dirs.), Century Club. Address: 14 Hillandale Rd Westport CT 06880-5225

HOTCHNER, HOLLY, curator, museum director, conservator; BA in Art History and Studio Art, Trinity Coll., 1973; MA in Art History, diploma conservation, NYU, 1982. Exhbns. cataloguer, collections cataloguer Mus. Modern Art, N.Y.C., 1973-76; chief conservator N.Y. Hist. Soc., N.Y.C., 1984-88, dir. mus., 1984-95; dir. Am. Craft Mus., N.Y.C., 1996—. Bd. dirs. Alliance for Contemporary Glass, Friends of Fiber Art; chmn. bd. 235 E. 73rd Owners Corp., 1994-2000; mem. edn. com. Whitney Mus. Am. Art, 1994—; mem. bd. trustees N.Y. Landmarks Conservancy, 1996—; mem. adv. bd. Friends of Contemporary Ceramics; lectr., panelist, juror in field. Mem. Am. Assn. Mus., Art Table, Phi Beta Kappa. Office: Am Craft Mus 40 W 53rd St New York NY 10019-6106

HOTELLING, DAVID RAWSON, endocrinologist, educator; b. Riverside, Calif., Feb. 26, 1938; s. Kenneth Hotelling and Elizabeth (Gute) Rowland; m. Rebecca Riter, June 22, 1966; children: Kirstin, Kimberly. BA, Reed Coll., 1960; MD, U. Cin., 1964. Diplomate Am. Bd. Internal Medicine. Intern San Francisco Gen. Hosp., 1964-65; resident VA Hosp., U. Calif. San Francisco, 1966-67, Boston City Hosp., 1970-71; fellow in endocrinology Beth Israel Hosp., Boston, 1968-70; attending physician Maine Med. Ctr., Portland, 1971—, Mercy Hosp., Portland, 1971—; asst. clin. prof. medicine U. Vt., Burlington, 1990—. Lt. comdr. USNR, 1965-70. Fellow Am. Coll. Endocrinologists; mem. Am. Assn. Clin. Endocrinologists, Am. Assn. Internal Medicine, Am. Assn. Diabetes, Am. Endocrine Soc. Office: 190 Pine St Portland ME 04102-3513

HOTELLING, HAROLD, law and economics educator; b. N.Y.C., Dec. 26, 1945; s. Harold and Susanna Porter (Edmondson) H.; m. Barbara M. Anthony, May 4, 1974; children: Harold, George, James, Claire, Charles. AB, Columbia U., 1966; JD, U. N.C., 1972; MA, Duke U., 1975, PhD, 1982. Bar: N.C. 1973. Legal advisor U. N.C., Chapel Hill, 1972-73; instr. bus. law U. Ky., Lexington, 1977-79, asst. prof., 1980-84; asst. prof. dept. econs. Oakland U., Rochester, Mich., 1984-89; assoc. prof. econs. Lawrence Technol. U., Southfield, Mich., 1989—, chmn. dept. humanities social scis. and comm., 1994-99. Contbr. articles to profl. jours. Episcopalian. Home: 2112 Bretton Dr S Rochester Hills MI 48309-2952 Office: Lawrence Technol U Dept Humanities Southfield MI 48075 E-mail: hotelling@ltu.edu.

HOTELLING, KURT PAUL, music educator, writer; b. Durham, N.C., Oct. 3, 1958; s. William Edmondson and Virginia Keister Hotelling. MusB, N.C. Sch. of the Arts, 1980; student, Appalachian State U., 1987. Registered clergy ECKANKAR Religion Light and Sound of God, 2001; lic. tchr. State Bd. of Edn., N.C., 1987. Music tchr. Surry County Schs., Dobson, NC, 1987—88; programmer and trust asst. Wachovia Bank and Trust Co., N.A., Winston-Salem, NC, 1988—90; tchr. Forsyth Tech. Coll., Winston-Salem, 1990—92, Temp. Resources, Winston-Salem, 1992—94; tchr. - instrumental music Macon County Schs., Highlands, NC, 1994—95; tchr. / bandmaster Cherokee (N.C.) Ctrl. Schs., 1995—98; tchr. - instrumental music Duplin County Schs., Kenansville, NC, 1998—99; tchr. / bandmaster Cherokee (N.C.) Ctrl. Schs., 1999—; asst. dir. of student activities N.C. Sch. of the Arts, Winston-Salem, 1981—86. Author: (radio plays) The Hearken Theatre; actor: (radio plays) The Martian Archives; author: A Bridge of Doom, 1983; prodr.: (books for listening) A Bridge of Doom; composer: Invention in C minor, 1979, Swordsmen Arise Fanfare, 2000; author: Traversity: Demons and Demigods, 1995. Clergy Eckankar, Asheville, NC, 1994—2002. Recipient Outstanding Tchr. and Mentor, Brevard Coll., 1996. Mem.: Music Educators Nat. Conf. (assoc.). Democrat. Eckankar. Avocations: writing, sound production, cooking. Home: 991 Kirklands Creek Road Bryson City NC 28713 Office: Cherokee Central Schools 1501 Acquoni Road Cherokee NC 28719 Office Fax: 828-497-4472. Personal E-mail: abridgeofdoom@yahoo.com.

HOTES, ROBERT JOSEPH, architect; b. Lakewood, Ohio, Dec. 29, 1962; s. William Joseph and Catherine Mary (Hauptman) H. BS in Engring., Princeton U., 1985; MArch, U. Pa., 1991, cert. in hist. preservation, 1993. Jr. engr. Tippetts-Abbett-McCarthy-Stratton, Washington, 1981-82; jr. architect Metcalf and Assocs., Washington, 1983-84; architect Skidmore, Owings & Merrill, Washington, 1985-86, Bass, Gick & Mickley, Washington, 1986-88, Martin & Jones, Washington, 1989; archtl. conservator ICCROM, Rome, 1989; architect U. Pa., Phila., 1990; preservation intern Inst. Spetsproyectrestavratsiya, Moscow, 1990; architect Susan Maxman Architects, Phila., 1991-97; assoc. Susan Maxman & Ptnrs., Architects, Phila., 1998—2001; sr. assoc. DPK&A Architects, Phila., 2001—. Shareholder The Athenaeum of Phila.; adj. prof. Phila. U., 1997-99. Mem. Phila. Opera Guild; mem. alumni coun. com. cmty. svc. Princeton U., 1995—, chmn. class of 1985 reunion, 1995-2000, pres. class of 1985, 2000—, com. on reunions, 1999-2002, alumni rels. and comm. com., 2000—; mem. Arts and Bus. Coun. Greater Phila. Mem. AIA (assoc. dir. Phila. chpt. 1994, chmn. intern and assoc. affairs com. 1994, hist. preservation com. 1991—, chmn. 1995—, dir. 2003—, Young Arch. award 2000), Nat. Coun. Archtl. Registration Bds., Nat. Trust Hist. Preservation, Hist. Soc. Washington, Preservation Alliance Greater Phila. (advocacy com. 1998—), D.C. Preservation League, Assn. Preservation Tech., Soc. Archtl. Hists., Archs., Designers, Planners for Social Responsibility, Documentation and Conservation Bldg., Sites and Neighborhoods of Modern Movement, Friends Terra Cotta, Am. Inst. for Conservation of Historic and Artistic Works, Ptnrs. for Sacred Places, Cmty. Design Collaborative, Internat. Coun. on Monuments and Sites, Preservation Pa., Preservation Del., Preservation N.J., Hist. Soc. of Princeton, N.J., U. Pa. Preservation Alumni Assn., Grad. Sch. Fine Arts Alumni Assn.(bd. dirs. 2003-), Princeton Gay and Lesbian Alumni (bd. dirs. 1992—), Princeton Club (N.Y.), Princeton Club (Phila., bd. govs. 1995-2001), Center City Residents Assn., Washington Square West Civic Assn., Friends Louis I. Kahn Park, Friends Music at Princeton, Union League of Phila. Office: DPK&A Architects LLP 421 Chestnut St Philadelphia PA 19106-2415 Business E-Mail: rhotes@dpka.com. E-mail: rjhotes@alumni.princeton.edu.

HOTH, STEVEN SERGEY, lawyer, educator; b. Jan. 30, 1941; s. Donald Leroy and Ina Dorothy (Barr) H.; m. JoEllen Maly, July 29, 1967; children: Andrew Steven, Peter Lindsey. AB, Grinnell Coll., 1962; JD, U. Iowa, 1966; postgrad., U. Pa., 1968, Oxford (Eng.) U., 1973. Bar: US Ct. Appeals (8th cir.) 1966, US Tax Ct. 1967, US Ct. Claims 1967, US Dist. Ct. Iowa 1968, US Dist. Ct. ND 1968, US Dist. Ct. SD 1968, US Supreme Ct. 1973, US Ct. Appeals (7th cir.) 1982. Law clk. to chief justice (Lord of Foleshill) US Ct. Appeals (8th cir.), Fargo, ND, 1967-68; assoc. Hirsch, Adams, Hoth & Krekel, Burlington, Iowa, 1968-72, ptnr., 1972-91; pvt. practice Burlington, 1992—. Asst. atty. Des Moines County, Burlington, 1968-72, atty., 1972-83; alt. mcpl. judge, Burlington, 1968-69; lectr. criminal law Southeastern C.C., West Burlington, 1972-82; assoc. prof. polit. sci. Iowa Wesleyan Coll., Mt. Pleasant, 1981-82; Pres. of Amerail, Inc., Iowa Truck Rail, Amerial, Inc.; pres. Burlington Truck Rail, Burlington Short Line RR. Inc., Iowa Internat. Investments, Burlington Storage and Transfer; sec. Burlington Loading Co. Contbr. numerous articles to profl. jours. Chmn. Des Moines County Civil Svc. Commn.; trustee Charles H. Rand Lecture Trust; mem. Des Moines County Conf. Com., Des Moines County Conf. Bd.; dir. Burlington Med. Ctr. Staff Found.; moderator 1st Congl. Ch., Burlington; bd. dir. UN Assn.; clk. Burlington North Bottoms Levy and Drainage Dist.; bd. mem., pres. Burlington Cmty. Sch. Dist. Bd. Edn., chmn. commn. on ministry, mem. exec. com. Nat. Assn. Congl. Christian Chs., moderator; treas. 1st dist. Dem. Com.; bd. dir. Legal Aid Soc. Planned Parenthood Des Moines County. Recipient Chmn.'s award ARC, 1980; Reginald Heber Smith fellow in legal aid Cheyenne River Indian Reservation, Eagle Butte, SD, 1967-68. Mem. Missionary Soc.-Nat. Assn. Congl. Christian Chs., ABA (internat. sect., tax sect.), Iowa State Bar Assn. (liaison to Iowa Med. Soc.), Des Moines County Bar Assn., Am. Judicature Soc., Agrl. Law Com., Iowa Def. Coun., Iowa Archaeol. Soc., Soc. for German Am. Studies, Manorial Soc. Gt. Britain, Grinnell Coll. Alumni Assn. (bd. dir.), Malawi Soc., Burlington-West Burlington C. of C. (bd. dir.), Nat. Assn. Congrl. Christian Ch., Burlington Golf Club, New Crystal Lake Club (pres.), Elks, Eagles, Masons, Rotary. Office: PO Box 982 Hoth Bldg 200 Jefferson St Burlington IA 52601

HOTTEL, JERRY W. engineering executive, consultant; s. Clair L. and Betty L. Hottel; m. Karen M. Twist, Sept. 12, 1981; children: Brian J, Mark J, Leah M. BSME, Tri-State U., 1974. Registered profl. engr., Ohio, 1981. Project engr. BP Amoco, Toledo, 1975—79, sr. project engr. Cleve., 1979—90; project mgr. HWH Architects Engrs. Planners, Inc., 2000—. Engring. supt. BP Amoco, Cleve., 1982—89, staff engr., 1980—82, plant engr., 1975—78. Elder Lakewood Presbyn. Ch., Ohio, 1991. Mem.: ASME, Cleve. Soc. Profl. Engrs. (dir. 1996—2003). Christian. Avocations: camping, scouting. Office: Hwh Architects Engrs Planners Inc 1001 Lakeside Ave Suite 800 Cleveland OH 44114

HOTTENSEN, MARGARET M. lawyer; b. Norristown, Pa., Apr. 15, 1949; d. Joseph J. and Camelia (Sirianni) C.; m. George W. Hottensen, Jr. BA, U. Steubenville, 1971; JD, U. Notre Dame, 1974. Bar: Pa. 1974. Law clk. to judge Ct. Common Pleas, Montgomery County, Norristown, 1974-75; asst. dist. atty. Berks County, Reading, Pa., 1976-77; staff atty. Criminal Procedures Rules Com., Phila., 1978-79; assoc. regional counsel EPA, Phila., 1979—. Mem. ABA, Montgomery County Bar Assn., Notre Dame Club (Phila.), Wissahicken Skating Club (bd. dirs.), Delta Zeta. Republican. Roman Catholic. Home: 870 Flintlock Dr Lansdale PA 19446-5568 Office: EPA 1650 Arch Street Philadelphia PA 19103 also: 1650 Arch St Philadelphia PA 19103 E-mail: hottensen.margaret@epa.gov.

HOTTENSTEIN, ERIN, journalist; BA, Goucher Coll., 1996. News dir. KUGR/KYCS Radio, Green River, Wyo., 1996—97; anchor, prodr. KGWN TV, Cheyenne, Wyo., 1997—98; city/country reporter Wyo. Tribune-Eagle, Cheyenne, 1998—2000; reporter No. Colo. Bus. Report, Ft. Collins, 2001—. Named Newswoman of Yr., Wyo. AP Broadcasters Assn., 1997—98; recipient 1st and 2d Pl. Investigative Reporting award, Wyo. Press Assn., 1999, 2d Pl. Govt. Issue Reporting award, 2000, Vivian Castleberry award for news reporting, under 100,000 circulation, Assn. Women Journalists, 2000. Mem.: Investigative Reporters and Editors, Soc. Profl. Journalists.

HOTZ, HENRY PALMER, retired physicist; b. Fayetteville, Ark., Oct. 17, 1925; s. Henry Gustav and Stella (Palmer) H.; m. Marie Brase, Aug. 22, 1952; children: Henry Brase, Mary Palmer, Martha Marie. BS, U. Ark., 1948; PhD, Washington U., St. Louis, 1953. Asst. prof. physics Auburn U., Ala., 1953-58, Okla. State U., Stillwater, 1958-64; assoc. prof. Marietta Coll., Ohio. 1964-66; physicist, scientist-in-residence U.S. Naval Radiol. Def. Lab., San Francisco, 1966-67; assoc. prof. U. Mo., Rolla, 1967-71; physicist Qanta Metrix div. Finnigan Corp., Sunnyvale, Calif., 1971-74; sr. scientist Nuclear Equipment Corp., San Carlos, Calif., 1974-79, Envirotech Measurement Systems, Palo Alto, Calif., 1979-82, Dohrmann div. Xertex Corp., Santa Clara, Calif., 1982-86; sr. scientist Rosemount Analytical Div. Dohrmann, 1983-91; cons. Burlingame, Calif., 1991-2001; ret., 2001. Cons. USAF, 1958-62; mem. lectr. selection com. for Hartman Hotz Lectrs. in law, liberal arts U. Ark. Served with USNR, 1944-46. Mem. Am. Phys. Soc., Am. Assn. Physics Tchrs., AAAS, Phi Beta Kappa, Sigma Xi, Sigma Pi Sigma, Pi Mu Epsilon, Sigma Nu Lodges: Masons. Methodist. Home: 290 Stilt Ct Foster City CA 94404-1323

HOTZ, JEFFREY ALAN, anesthesiologist, educator; b. Hamilton, Ont., Can., July 15, 1960; BS, U. Toronto, 1982; MD, McMaster U., 1985. Diplomate Am. Bd. Anesthesiology. Intern Mt. Sinai Hosp., Toronto, Canada, 1985-86; resident anesthesiology U. Toronto, Toronto, Canada, 1987-91; fellow critical care medicine Hosp. Sick Children, Toronto, Canada, 1991-92; asst. prof. clin. anesthesiology U. Calif.-Davis Med. Ctr., Sacramento, 1992-98; assoc. prof. U. Calif., Calif., 1998—. Emergency physician Northwestern Hosp., Toronto, 1987-91; pediatric anes., Phoenxi Children;s Hosp., St. Joseph Hosp. Fellow: Royal Coll. Physicians; mem.: AMA, Can. Physicians and Surgeons Ont., Royal Coll. Physicians and Surgeons Can., Soc. Pediat. Anesthesiologists, Ont. Med. Assn., Can. Soc. Anesthesiologists, Ariz. Soc. Anesthesiologists, Am. Acad. Pediatrics, Am. Soc. Anesthesiologists. Address: 2901 N Ctrl Ave # 500 Phoenix AZ 85012

HOTZ, ROBERT LEE, science writer, editor; b. Hartford, Conn., Mar. 7, 1950; s. Robert B. and Joan (Willison) H.; m. Jennifer Hall Arlen, May 21, 1988; children: Michael Arlen, Robert Arlen. BA magna cum laude, MA, Tufts U., 1973. Tech. editor Intermetrics, Inc., Cambridge, Mass., 1973-76; reporter The News-Virginian, Waynesboro, 1976-79, The Pitts. Press, 1979-84; sci. writer The Atlanta Jour.-Constn., 1984-90, projects editor, 1991-93; sci. editor, 1993; sci. writer The L.A. (Calif.) Times, 1993—. Participant NSF Antarctica Expeditions, 1987, 95, 01. Author: Designs on Life: Exploring the New Frontiers of Human Fertility, 1991; contbr. articles to profl. pubs. Recipient Sci. Journalism award AAAS, 1977, 88, 97, Ga. Best Reporting award AP, 1986, Metro Staff Pulitzer Prize spot news, 1995, Walter Sullivan award Am. Geophys. Soc., 1995, Journalism award ASCE, 1995, Media award Nat. Mental Health Assn., 1996. Mem. Nat. Assn. Sci. Writers (bd. dirs.), Soc. Profl. Journalists (Ray Sprigle Meml. award 1982, 84, Nat. Mag. Writing award 2000), Sigma X (hon.), Nat. Press Club. Episcopalian. Office: The LA Times NY Bur 2 Park Ave 8th Fl New York NY 10016 Home: 120 West 15th St Apt 7E New York NY 10011 E-mail: leehotz@earthlink.net.

HOTZE, CHARLES WAYNE, publisher, printer; b. Moline, Ill., Feb. 19, 1919; s. Charles Edmund and Nellie (Gibbs) H.; m. Hazel Ann Tebbens, Dec. 20, 1956; children: Karen Ann, Carla Ann. BA, U. Ill., 1941. Pres., chmn. bd. Fowle Printing Co., Milw., 1953-55; pres. Pub. Clin. Med., Northfield, Ill.,

1954—, Med. Digest, Inc., 1955—, C. W. Hotze Bldg. Corp., 1956—, Pediatrics Digest, Inc., 1962—, Psychiatry Digest, 1962—, Dermatology Digest, 1963—, Ob/Gyn Digest, 1964—, Urology Digest, 1964—, Cardiology Digest, 1966, Med. Comm., Inc., 1968—; chmn. bd. Lake County Press, Inc., Waukegan, Ill., 1971-78; pres. K&C Land Devel. Corp., 1993—. O.R.L. Digest, 1971—, Ophthalmology Digest, 1971—, Orthopedics Digest, 1973—, Pharmacy Digest, 1978—, Veterinary Digest, 1978—, Radiology Digest, 1979, Anesthesiology Digest, 1981—. Served to 1st lt. Infantry, AUS, 1942-44. Mem. Soc. Acad. Achievement, Am. Med. Writers Assn., Pharm. Advt. Club, Midwest Pharm. Advt. Club, Ams. Armorial Ancestry, Mayflower Soc., SAR, Am. Legion, Benevolent and Protective Order of Elks, Psi Upsilon. Clubs: Sunset Ridge (Northfield, Ill.). Home: 1950 Sunset Ridge Rd Northfield IL 60093-1060 Office: PO Box 8021 Northfield IL 60093-8021

HOUBOLT, JOHN CORNELIUS, physicist; b. Altoona, Iowa, Apr. 10, 1919; s. John H. and Hendreika (Van Ingen) H.; m. Mary Morris, June 14, 1949; children: Mary Cornelia, Joanna, Julie. BS, U. Ill., 1940, MS, 1942; PhD, Swiss Fed. Inst. Tech., Zurich, 1958, hon. doctorate, 1975, Clarkson U., 1990. Bridge engr. I.C. R.R., 1940; city engr. Waukegan, Ill., 1941; aero. research scientist NASA, Hampton, Va., 1942-49; asso. chief dynamic loads div. NACA NASA, 1949-62; chief theoretical mechanics div. NASA, 1962-63; sr. v.p., dir. Aero Research Asso. Princeton Inc., N.J., 1963-76; chief scientist Langley Research Center, Hampton, Va., 1976-85. Cons. and adviser to govt. agys. and industry, 1985—; instr. grad. extension div. U. Va., 1944—, Va. Poly. Inst., 1958— ; exchange scientist Royal Aircraft Establishment, Eng., 1949; dir. Doweave, Inc., Walker-Gordon Labs.; Mem. Air Force Scientific Adv. Bd. Asso. editor: Jour. Spacecraft and Rockets. Recipient Rockefeller Pub. Svc. award, 1956, Exceptional Sci. Achievement award NASA, 1963, Structures, Structural Dynamics and Materials award AIAA, 1967, Disting. Civil Engring. Alumni award U. Ill., 1969, Illini Achievement award U. Ill., 1970, Dryden Rsch. lectr. award, 1972, Space Act award NASA, 1983, Pa. Engr. of Yr. award, 1989, U. Ill. Alumni award, 1997, Spirit of St. Louis medal, 2000. Fellow AIAA (hon. v.p. tech.); mem. Nat. Acad. Engrs., Tau Beta Pi, Chi Epsilon, Phi Kappa Chi, Sigma Xi. Achievements include rsch., numerous reports in aeros., aeroelasticity, structures, atmosphere turbulence, space flight and moon landing. Office: Langley Rsch Ctr NASA Hampton VA 23665

HOUCHARD, MICHAEL HARLOW, retired organization executive; b. Long Beach, Calif., Oct. 4, 1935; s. Harold Harlow and Michella (Mehle) H.; m. Merry Carol Filek, May 5, 1962; 1 child, Christina Carol. B. in Bus., U. Fla., 1962; M., U. Utah, 1975. Asst. mgr. W.T. Grant Co., St. Petersburg, Fla., 1962; with Fla. Indsl. Commn., Miami, 1962-65, U.S. Dept. Labor, Atlanta, 1965-91; fed. rep. Manpower Adminstrn., Atlanta, 1965-69, exec. asst., 1969-75; assoc. regional adminstr. Employment & Tng. Adminstrn., Atlanta, 1975-76, exec. asst., 1976-83, asst. regional adminstr., 1984-87, regional adminstr., 1987-91; ret., 1991; assoc. dir. Alliance for Employee Growth and Devel. Inc., Atlanta, 1991-98, ret., 1998. Mem. Am. Legion, Conyers, Ga., 1988-96; mem. citizen adv. com., Rockdale County Bd. Edn. With USN, 1954-58. Mem. Southeastern Employment & Tng. Assn., Internat. Assn. Personnel in Employment Security, Great Dane Club Mid-South (pres. 1968-70), Conyers Kennel Club (pres. 1984-85), Conyers/Rockdale C. of C. (chairperson edn. com.); mem. adv. com. Ga. Perimeter Coll.; mem. land use com. Rockdale County. Avocations: raising purebred dogs, gardening. Home: 3250 Gees Mill Rd NE Conyers GA 30013-1438 E-mail: lyceumfarm@aol.com.

HOUCHIN, JOHN FREDERICK, SR., human services administrator; b. Oak Park, Ill., Nov. 1, 1945; s. O. Boyd and Mary Ruth (Schroke) H.; m. Bette Louise Arnold, July 9, 1969; children: John Jr., David Locke. AA, Kemper Mil. Sch. & Coll., Boonville, Mo., 1966; BS, Ohio State U., 1968; EdD, U. Mass., 1987. Prog. dir. Cuyahoga County Assn. Retarded Citizens, Cleve., 1973-75; resdl. dir., asst. supt. Ohio Dept. Mental Health & Retardation, Broadview Devel. Ctr, Broadview Hts., Ohio, 1975-80; reg. mental retardation coord. Mass. Dept. Mental Health, Region IV A, Watertown, Mass., 1980-83; dir. devel. svcs. Mass. Dept. Mental Health, Belchertown State Sch., 1983-86; asst. reg. dir. Conn. Dept. Retardation, Region 6, Waterford, 1986-91; CEO G.B. Cooley Svcs. for Retarded Citizens, West Monroe, La., 1991-97; regional dir. Conn. Dept. of Mental Retardation, 1997-2000, dir. ops., 2000-01, dir. North Ctrl. region, 2001—. Mem. disability specialist program adv. bd. Manchester C.C., 2001—; lectr. in field. Contbr. book: Supported Employment Implementation, 1988. State adv. coun. Conn. Dept. Rehab. Svcs., Hartford, 1988-91; regional adv. coun. Region 8 Office Mental Retardation, 1992-94, chmn., 1993; mem. Monroe Beautification Bd., 1996-97; mem. Twin Cities Mayors Com. on Disabled, 1994-97; bd. dirs. Eastern Conn. Regional Transp. Consortium, 1997-2000. Capt. U.S. Army, 1969-72. Mem. Internat. Freelance Photographer Assn., Monroe C. of C., N.E. La. Camera Club (pres. 1993-94). Episcopalian. Avocation: photography. Office: North Ctrl Regional Dept Mental Retardation 270 Farmington Ave Farmington CT 06032-1953

HOUCK, JOHN DUDLEY, investment adviser, educator; b. Detroit, May 5, 1939; s. Horace Alonzo and Mae Edward (Snyder) H.; m. Carol Kay Houck, July 16, 1958; children: Sallie Mae Williams, Cheryl Ann Richard, Jonathan Matthew, Rebecca Cyrene Myers, James Timothy. AA, L.A. Valley Coll., 1964; BS in Bus. Econs., Pacific Western U., 1982; MS in Mgmt., Am. Coll. for Fin. Scis., 1994; MA in History, Gulf So. U., 1993; PhD in Edn., LaSalle U., 2002. Pres., CFO Western Pacific Fin. Svcs., Inc., L.A., 1976—. Adj. prof. U. Phoenix, Trinity Coll. Mem. Lds Ch. Avocations: golf, fishing, history. Office: Western Pacific Fin Svcs Inc c/o CEO 1036 E Avenue J # 212 Lancaster CA 93535-3840 E-mail: jdhouck@mail.uophx.edu.

HOUCK, PATRICIA ROSE, statistician, researcher; b. Pitts., Pa., Aug. 26, 1959; d. Bernard Sylvester and Josephine Zipfel; m. Robert William Houck, Aug. 22, 1981; children: William Joseph, Michael Robert. MSH in Biostats., U. of Pitts., 1988. Statis. svcs. adminstr. U. Pitts. Med. Ctr. Health Sys., Pitts., 1995—. Contbr. articles to profl. jours. Mem. Environ. Awareness Groups, Pitts. Recipient Reliability of Panic Disorder Severity Scale-Self Rating grantee, MHIRC-NIMH, 1999—2001. Mem.: Citizens Helping Our Cmty. (assoc.), Pitts. SAS Users Group (assoc.; sec. 1997—99). Democrat. Roman Catholic. Achievements include research in application of statistical methods in psychiatry and statistical consulting. Avocations: hiking, gardening. Office: UPMC Health Syst-WPIC 3811 O'Hara St Pittsburgh PA 15227 E-mail: houckpr@upmc.edu.

HOUE, POUL, education educator; b. Snedsted, Denmark, Feb. 4, 1946; s. Christen Houe and Mary Bangsgaard. Cand.mag., Aarhus U., Denmark, 1970. Pedagogy Certificate Danish Ministry of Edn., 1971. Instr. Marselisborg Tng. Coll., Aarhus, Denmark, 1969—70, Royal Danish Sch. of Edn., Aarhus, Denmark, 1971—73; rsch. assoc. Aarhus U., 1971—73; vis. assoc. prof. Uppsala U., Sweden, 1973—78; asst. prof. U. of Minn., Mpls., 1978—81, assoc. prof., 1981—84, prof., 1984—. Vis. prof. U. Amsterdam, Netherlands, 1988; adv. bd. mem. Wiener Studien zur Skandinavistik, Vienna, 1997—; cons. Ency. Brit., Chgo., 1999—2000; chair Internat. Isak Dinesen Conf., Internat. August Strindberg Conf. Author: (literary history) Fra Amerika til Danmark, Johannes V. Jensens lange rejse; editor (contributor): (cultural history) Documentarism in Scandinavian Literature, Images of America in Scandinavia; author: (literary history) Menneskelinien; editor (contributor): (intellectual history) Anthropology and Authority, (literary history) August Strindberg and the Other, (intellectual history) Soren Kierkegaard and the Word(s). Recipient Sabbatical Program award, Bush Found., 1986—87, Supplementary Sabbatical award, U. of Minn., 2001—02; grantee Rsch. grantee, Danish Rsch. Coun. for the Humanities, 1994—95; Am.-Scandinavian Found. granatee, 1986, 1993. Mem.: Johannes V. Jensen Ctr., Aarhus U., Soc. for the Advancement of Scandinavian Study, Internat. Assn. of Scandinavian Studies, Universitetsjubil[00e6]ets danske Samfund. Home: 1307 Boardwalk Ave Minneapolis MN 55411-3365 Office: University of Minnesota 9 Pleasant St SE Minneapolis MN 55455-0124 Office Fax: 612-624-8297. Personal E-mail: houex001@tc.umn.edu. E-mail: houex001@tc.umn.edu.

HOUGAARD, TODD LAMONT, photographer; b. Bountiful, Utah, May 10, 1967; s. Hugh Martin and LuCene Alta (Childs) H.; m. Joni Wilkin, Apr. 17, 1993; children: Dallin, Adam. BA, Brigham Young U., 1990. Chief photographer KBYU, Provo, Utah, 1990; news photographer KRNV, Reno, 1991-93; news photographer KUBC Las Vegas, 1993—94; sr. news photographer KSTU, Salt Lake City, 1994—. Prodr., photojournalist, editor: (documentary) The Great Salt Lake: Utah's Desert Sea, 1999 (Regional Emmy award 2000, Nat. Telly award 2000). Pres. elder's quorum 43rd ward LDS Ch., West Valley City, Utah, 1999-2002. Recipient Emmy award NATAS, 1998, 2000. Mem. Nat. Press Photographers Assn. (life, pres. Utah chpt. 2000-03, chair quarterly TV edit contest 2000—, assoc. dir. region IX 2001), Soc. Profl. Journalists (pres. Utah chpt. 2000-02, Utah Photographer of Yr. award 1998, 99, 2001, 2002, Utah Editor of Yr. award 1999, 2001—). Avocations: photographer, travel, family. Office: KSTU 5020 W Amelia Earhart Dr Salt Lake City UT 84116 Fax: (801) 536-1325. E-mail: thougaard@fox13.com., thougaard@msn.com.

HOUGE, TIMOTHY TODD, education educator; b. Jamestown, N.D., Sept. 5, 1961; s. Clifford Alvin and LuLaBelle Houge; m. Ethel Mae Houge, July 6, 1995; children: Amanda Michelle, Christina Marie. BS in Edn., Valley City State Coll., 1988; MEd, U. Nev., 1993, EdD, 2000. Elem. sch. tchr. Wichita (Kans.) Sch. Dist., 1988—90, Clark County Sch. Dist., Las Vegas, 1990—98, reading specialist, 1998—2000; asst. prof. elem. reading No. State U., Aberdeen, SD, 2000—. Sgt. U.S. Army, 1982—85. Office: Northern State Univ 1200 S Jay St Aberdeen SD 57401 Office Fax: 605-626-3102. E-mail: houget@northern.edu.

HOUGGARD, SANTA CAROL HALL, family nurse practitioner; b. Ermine, Ky., Nov. 9, 1940; d. Russell L. and Ila (Amburgey) Hall; m. Byron L. Houggard, Apr. 30, 1965; children: Teresa Bramlet, Sutherland, Ronald L. Diploma, Sch. Profl. Nursing, Harlan, Ky., 1961; BSN cum laude, U. San Diego, 1981, MS in Nursing, 1983. Cert. family nurse practitioner. Staff nurse Whitesburg (Ky.) Meml. Hosp., 1961-62; nurse USN, 1962-65; pvt. duty nurse, 1965-77; nurse practitioner North County Health Svcs., San Marcos, Calif.; clin. adminstr., nurse practitioner Mountain Health Project, Campo, Calif., 1977-79; instr. U. San Diego, 1983-85; ind. contractor family nurse practitioner, Santee, Calif., 1985-88; family nurse practitioner NAVCARE, San Diego, 1988-89, Mountain Health Ctr., Campo, 1989-91, So. Indian Health Coun., 1991-95; prof. nursing Ariz. Western Coll., Yuma, Ariz., 1998—. Lt. (j.g.) USN, 1962-65. Mem.: Ariz. Nurses Assn. (pres. Rio Colo.-Yuma Chpt.), ANA, Sigma Theta Tau. Home: 12124 S Sandra Ave Yuma AZ 85367-6026 E-mail: carol.hoggard@azwestern.edu.

HOUGH, JACK VAN DOREN, otologist; b. Lone Wolf, Okla., Sept. 12, 1920; s. Chapman Ernest and Hazel (Van Doren) H.; m. Joan Ingle, Dec. 29, 1943; children: Ted Chapman, Jack Van Doren Jr., Timothy Ingle, David Alliston. BS, Southeastern State U., 1939; MD, U. Okla., 1943. Diplomate Am. Bd. Otorhinolaryngology. Intern USN Hosp., Farragut, Idaho, 1944; resident, then fellow in otolaryngology U. Okla. Hosps., Oklahoma City, 1946-50; clin. instr. otorhinolaryngology U. Okla. Health Scis. Ctr., Oklahoma City, 1950 51, now clin. prof. otorhinolaryngology, head and neck surgery; pvt. practice Oklahoma City, 1951—. Bd. dirs. MAP Internat., Inc.; developer surg. techniques and instruments for hearing restoration and middle ear reconstrn., electromagnetic hearing devices, cochlear implants. Contbr. sci. articles and textbook chpts. to med. publs. Past ruling elder, Cen. Presbyn. Ch., Oklahoma City; founder, Covenant Community Ch. Oklahoma City, 1980, now session moderator. Decorated Bronze Star, recipient Presdl. Unit citation, Navy Dept. citation for heroism; recipient Harris P. Mosher award Triologic Soc., numerous awards from profl. orgns.; inducted into Okla. Hall of Fame, 1991. Mem. AMA, Am. Bd. Otolaryngology, Am. Acad. Otolaryngology-Head and Neck Surgery, Am. Otological Soc. (past pres., award of merit), Head and Neck Surgery of Am., Am. Triological Soc., Oklahoma County Med. Assn., Okla. Med. Assn., Okla. Acad. Medicine, Osler Soc., Am. Acad. Ophthalmologic and Otolaryngologic Allergy, Christian Med. Soc., Christian Soc. Otolaryngology-Head and Neck Surgeons (founder, past pres.), MAP Internat. (founder), Otosclerosis Study Group (past pres.), Audiology Soc., Von Bekesy Soc. (past pres.), Pan-Am. Assn. Otorhinolaryngology and Bronchoesophagology, Politzer Soc., Am. Sci. Affiliation, numerous other profl. orgns. Home: 9117 SW 22nd St Oklahoma City OK 73128-4918 Office: Hough Ear Inst 3400 NW 56th St Oklahoma City OK 73112-4404

HOUGH, MARK MASON, lawyer; b. Uniontown, Pa., Jan. 21, 1945; s. Carl H. and Ruth Ann (Mason) H.; children: Benjamin, Daniel; m. Sharon Fay Jesperson, Oct. 26, 1985. BA in Econs., U. Wash., 1966, JD, 1971. Bar: Wash. 1971, U.S. Dist. Ct. (we. dist.) Wash. 1973, U.S. Dist. Ct. (ea. dist.) Wash. 1976, U.S. Ct. Appeals (9th cir.) 1979. Staff atty. Bur. of Competition FTC, Washington, 1971-73; from assoc. to ptnr. Schweppe Krug & Tausend, P.S., Seattle, 1973-89; ptnr. Reed & McClure, Seattle, 1989-2000; prin. Riddell Williams, P.S., 2000—. Mem. ABA (sects. on bus., litigation and antitrust), Wash. State Bar Assn. (sect. on antitrust, litig., intellectual property and bus.). Office: Riddell Williams PS Ste 4500 1001 Fourth Ave Plaza Seattle WA 98154-1065 E-mail: mhough@riddellwilliams.com.

HOUGH, MICHAEL JAMES, sculptor, educator; b. Anaheim, Calif., Jan. 20, 1960; s. Richard Guy Hough and Barbara Jean (Dierberger) Moody; m. Ronelle Bingham, July 28, 1984; m. Tracy Lee Watts, Mar. 23, 1991; children: Timothy Michael Enke, Alden Richard Thomas, Lydia Drue. BA in Art, Calif. State U., Sacramento, 1983, MA in Art, 1989; MFA in Ceramic Sculpture, RISD, 1993. Graphic designer J.K. Bonum, Sacramento, 1980-86; mem. TV prodn. staff Sta. KVIE Channel 6, Sacramento, 1983-89; art tchr. El Sereno H.S., Fair Oaks, Calif., 1987-90; ceramics instr. RISD, Providence, 1991-93; art tchr. Snake River Correctional Facilities, Ontario, Oreg., 1993-96, Boise (Idaho) State U., 1994—97, Treasure Valley C.C., Ontario, 1994—97; ceramic artist Weiser (Idaho) Sculpture Works, 1983—97; prof. art Bridgewater (Va.) Coll., 1997—. Vis. artist Foresthill and Auburn Union Sch. Dists., Calif., 1984-91; mural painter Taylor Studios, Sacramento, South Lake Tahoe, and Carson City, Nev., 1988—; presenter Raku demonstrations Sacramento Open Studio Tours, 1989, 90; fin. dir., mem. 750 Gallery, Sacramento, 1987-89; dir. Witt Gallery, Calif. State U., Sacramento, 1985-86; kiln rm. mgr. RISD, 1991-93. One-man shows include 750 Gallery, Sacramento, 1987, ArtWorks Gallery, Fair Oaks, Calif., 1987, 89, Michael Himovitz Gallery, Sacramento, 1990, 93, 95, 96, Himovitz Pavillions, Sacramento, 1991, Habatat/Shaw Gallery, Farmington Hills, Mich., 1994, Gallery at Glendeven, Mendocino, Calif., 1994; group shows include Thesis Exhbn. RISD Roitman Gallery, Providence, Rhode Island, Grad. Exbhn., 1993, Habatat/Shaw Gallery, Mich., 1993, Farrell Collection, Washington, 1993, Holmes Fine Art Gallery, San Jose, Calif., 1993, Cafe au Clay Cup Invitational Lincoln Arts, Calif., 1994, Contemporary Crafts Gallery, Portland, 1994, The Potters Ctr., Boise, 1994, Michael Himovitz Gallery, 1994, Galos Fine Art, Idaho, 1995, San Bernardino Mus. Art, 1997, Coos Art Mus., Oreg., 1997, Miller Gallery, Bridgewater Coll., 1998, Sycamore House Gallery, Harrisonburg, Va., 1998, 99, Concord Coll., Athens, W.Va., 2001, Radford (Va.) U., 2001; Brevard (N.C.) Coll., 2002, Bridgewater Coll., 2002; exhibited in group shows Witt Gallery, Calif. State U., Sacramento, 1983, Rara Avis Gallery, Sacramento, 1985, 750 Gallery, Sacramento, 1987, 1988, Contemporary Crafts Gallery, Portland, Oreg., 1994, Corbin Art Ctr., Spokane, Wash., 1995, Michael Himovitz Gallery, Sacramento, 1997, Staunton (Va.) Augusta Arts, 1998, Staunton Augusta Art Ctr., 1999, Limn Gallery, San Francisco, 2000, Fredericksburg (Va.) Ctr. for Creative Arts, 2000, Art Mus. of Ams., Washington, 2001, Ridley Gallery, Rocklin, Calif., 2002; represented in permanent collections at Faviana Olivier, Boston, Pac-Tel Corp., Calif., Embassy Suites Hotel, South Lake Tahoe, Calif., Sacramento First Nat. Bank, Tower Corp., Sacramento, Hewlett Packard Co., Roseville, Calif.; represented in (books): Raku Pottery, 1991, Raku: A Practical Approach, 1991; contbr articles to profl. jours. Invitational-promotion fundraiser Sta. KXJZ, Sacramento, 1991. Avocations: collecting, gardening, cooking, traveling. Home: PO Box 97 New Hope VA 24469-0097 E-mail:.haugh@bridgewater.edu.

HOUGH, ROBERT ALAN, civil engineer; b. East Orange, N.J., Aug. 6, 1959; s. Robert Elmer and Margaret (Dean) H.; m. Marianthony Kiernan Hough. AB in Civil Engring., Lafayette Coll., 1981; MBA in Mgmt., Fairleigh Dickinson U., 1995. Registered profl. engr., N.J. Dept. head water/wastewater engring. dept. Van Note-Harvey Assocs., Princeton, NJ, 1981—2002, head dept., 1994—2002; twp. engr. Twp. of Woolwich, Gloucester County, NJ, 1993—2002; borough engr. Borough of Pennington, Mercer County, NJ, 2000—02; I/I project engr. Princeton Sewer Oper. Com., NJ, 2002—. Bd. engr. Bd. Pennington, Mercer County, N.J., 2000-2002. Class rep. Pingry Sch. Alumni Assn., 1977—, bd. dirs., 1981—; bd. dirs., pony league dir., mgr., coach Springfield Jr. Baseball League, Inc., 1985—, pres., 1989-90; mem. bd. Union County Regional H.S. Dist. No. 1, 1997, Springfield Twp. Planning Bd., 2000—. Mem. NSPE, ASCE, Am. Water Works Assn., N.J. Soc. Profl. Engrs., Water Environ. Fedn., N.J. Assn. Environ. Authorities, N.J. Soc. Mcpl. Engrs. Roman Catholic. Avocations: softball, golf. Home: 38 Tudor Ct Springfield NJ 07081-3023 Office: Princeton Sewer Opers Com c/o Burough of Princeton Monument Dr Princeton NJ 08542-0390

HOUGH, THOMAS HENRY MICHAEL, retired lawyer, educator; b. Midland, Pa., Aug. 4, 1933; s. Bert Patrick and Marguerite (Mullen) H.; m. Jocelyn Peltz, Aug. 20, 1956; children: Jocelyn, Thomas Henry Michael. AB, Dickinson Coll., 1955; JD, Dickinson Sch. Law, 1958. Bar: Pa. 1959, U.S. Ct. Appeals (3d cir.) 1975, U.S. Supreme Ct. 1970. Field atty. NLRB, Pitts., 1959-60; atty. United Steelworkers Am., 1960-68; ptnr. Lucchino, Gaitens & Hough, Pitts., 1968-79, Hough & Gleason, PC, Pitts., 1980-94, Barry Fasulo & Hough, PC, Pitts., 1994—2002, ret., 2002. Adj. assoc. prof. pub. sector arbitration and pub. sector collective bargaining Grad. Sch. Pub. and Internat. Affairs, U. Pitts., 1970-97.

HOUGHAM, NORMAN RUSSELL, financial services company executive; b. Correctionville, Iowa, Sept. 28, 1937; s. Russell Lowell and Geneva Marie (Lafferty) H.; m. Evelyn Joy Foley, Apr. 10, 1960; 1 child, Jill. Ed., Am. Inst. Banking, 1969; diploma, Sch. Bank Adminstrn., 1980. Clk. Earlham (Iowa) Savs. Bank, 1959-60; cashier Capital City State Bank, Des Moines, 1960-76; v.p. Brenton Nat. Bank, Des Moines, 1976-82; sr. v.p. Am. Fed. Savs. and Loan, Des Moines, 1982-90; mng. agt. Resolution Trust Corp., 1990-94; CFO Midwest Fin. Svcs. Ltd., 1995—. Bd. dirs. Earlham Swim Pool Devel. Corp., 1972; mem. bd. edn. Earlham Sch., 1986; bd. dirs., treas. Pioneer Pl. Retirement Homes, Earlham, 1998—; bd. dirs., chmn. fin. com. Earlham Ch. of Christ, 1999; trustee Earlham Pub. Libr., 1990. Recipient Bd. Dirs. award Des Moines chpt. Am. Inst. Banking, 1972, Instr. Appreciation award Inst. for Fin. Edn., 1983, award of merit Earlham Bd. Edn., 1986, Spl. Achievement award FDIC, 1992, Cert. of Appreciation RTC, 1992. Mem. Masons. Republican. Avocations: reading, teaching. Home: 235 NE 3d St PO Box 344 Earlham IA 50072-0344 Office: PO Box 277 Adel IA 50003-0277 E-mail: nhougham@aol.com., hougham@ncasi.com.

HOUGHTALING, PAMELA ANN, technology marketing professional, writer; b. Catskill, N.Y., July 8, 1949; d. Stanley Kenneth and Mildred Edythe (Fyfe) H. BA, Princeton U., 1971; M in Internat. Affairs, Russian Inst., Columbia U., 1974, cert., 1976. Internat. rels. analyst Libr. of Congress, Washington, 1974-75, U.S. GAO, Washington, 1976-77; pub. affairs specialist IBM Corp., Washington, 1977-81; sr. external programs analyst IBM World Trade Americas/Far East Corp., North Tarrytown, N.Y., 1981-82; mgr. labor affairs/bus. practices U.S. Coun. Internat. Bus., N.Y.C., 1982-84; comms. specialist-advt. IBM Corp., Boca Raton, Fla., 1984-86, staff comms. specialist White Plains, N.Y., 1986-88, comms. cons., 1988-90; sr. mktg. specialist Wang Labs., Bethesda, Md., 1990-93; pub. rels. dir. STG Mktg. Comm., 1993-94; mgr. mktg. comm. Cable & Wireless, Inc., Vienna, Va., 1994-95; contractor to Applied Physics Lab. Johns Hopkins U., Laurel, Md., 1998-99, tech. comms. cons., 1995—98; mktg. program mgr. Info. Tech. Lab. Nat. Inst. Stds. and Tech., Gaithersburg, Md., 2000—03; fellow U.S. Dept. Commerce Sci. and Tech., 2003—. Mem. Am. Mktg. Assn., Armed Forces Comms. and Electronics Assn., Nat. Assn. Sci. Writers.

HOUGHTELLING, AYRES, artist, architect, engineer; b. Defiance, Ohio, Feb. 12, 1912; s. Charles Wesley Houghtelling and Elizabeth Overbaugh; m. Lydia Amaddeo, Nov. 22, 1974. Student, San Mateo Coll., Stanford U. Allegorically depicted Shakespeare's works (two of which are permanently exhibited in Civici Mus., Venice, Italy), one man show includes The City of Paris, San Francisco; exhibited in group shows at San Francisco World's Fair, Fountainebleu Hotel, Omaha, Jocelyn Mus., Omaha, Plz. Hotel, Hollywood, Calif.; prin. archtl. works include 23 pavillions 1964 World's Fair, Air France, Am. Airlines, Am. Petroleum Inst., Beach-Nut Corp., Coca-Cola, Continental Iins., Christian Sci. Pavilion, Chrysler Corp., DeBeers Consolidated Mines, Ea. Airlines, Edison Electric Inst., Gen. Dynamics Corp., Iberian Airlines, L.I. Asn., Nat. Airlines, New England States Pavilion, N.Y. State Pavilion, Owens Corning Glass, Pharm. Mfrs., Proposed Space and Motion Theme, Travelers Ins., TWA Airlines, United Airlines; illustrator for several art books and Nasa publs.; inventor pull-top can opener. Home: 60 Sutton Pl S New York NY 10022

HOUGHTON, ALAN NOURSE, association executive, educator, consultant; b. Hartford, Conn., Jan. 17, 1924; m. Elizabeth T. Jones, Mar. 30, 1946; children: Alan Nourse, Elizabeth Boardman, John Barnard, Suzanne Tolles. AB cum laude, Harvard U., 1946, AM, 1951; postgrad., Columbia U., 1951, U. Conn., 1961, 62-63. Faculty Groton (Mass.) Sch., 1946-51; chmn. classics dept. Loomis Sch., Windsor, Conn., 1951-55; headmaster Pine Point Sch., Stonington, 1955-67, Renbrook Sch., West Hartford, 1967-73; exec. dir. Conn. Assn. Ind. Schs., 1974-89; ednl. cons. Madison, 1989-94. Mem. Sch. Bldg. Com., Lyme, Conn., 1959, Zoning Bd. Appeals, 1959-61, Zoning and Planning Commn., 1963-65, Bd. Fin., 1971-75, Lyme Dem. Town Com., 1957-63; trustee Blair Acad., Blairstown, N.J., Pine Point Sch., Stonington, Conn., Renbrook Sch., Country Sch., Madison, Conn.; corporator Hartford Hosp. 1st lt. USAAF, 1943-45. Decorated D.F.C., Air medal with three oak leaf clusters; Houghton Wing named for him at Pine Point Sch. Mem. Conn. Assn. Ind. Schs. (tchrs. edn. and profl. stds. rep. 1963-66, v.p., pres.), Classical Assn. New Eng., Mile Creek Beach Club (bd. govs. 1958-73), Harvard Club (N.Y.C.), Madison Winter Club, Phi Delta Kappa, Pi Eta. Home: 26 Sylvan Rd Madison CT 06443-3303

HOUGHTON, AMORY, JR., (AMO HOUGHTON), congressman; b. Corning, N.Y., Aug. 7, 1926; m. Priscilla Dewey Houghton; 4 children. BA, Harvard U., 1950, MA, 1952; PhD (hon.), Alfred U., 1963, Albion Coll., 1964, Cen. Coll., 1966, Clarkson Coll. Tech., 1968, Elmira Coll., 1982, Hartwick Coll., 1983, Houghton Coll., 1983. Exec. officer Corning Glass Works, 1951-86; mem. U.S. Congress from 29st N.Y. dist. (formerly 31st), Washington, 1987—; mem. internat. rels. com., ways and means com., chmn. oversight subcom., vice-chmn. subcom. on Africa. Mem. Grace Commn., Bus. Council N.Y. State, Bus. Adv. Commn. for Gov. N.Y., Labor-Industry Coalition for Internat. Trade. Trustee Brookings Instn. With USMC, 1945-46. Mem. Corning C. of C., Rotary. Republican. Office: US Ho of Reps 1111 Longworth Ho Office Bldg Washington DC 20515-3231*

HOUGHTON, ANTHONY, physics educator, research scientist; b. Heanor, Eng., Oct. 4, 1935; came to U.S., 1963; s. George and Florence G. (Frost) H.; m. Patricia Sanchez-Cerani, July 15, 1961. BSc, U. Birmingham, Eng., 1956, PhD, 1959. Rsch. physicist McMaster U., Hamilton, Ont., Can., 1960-63; asst. prof. physics Brown U., Providence, 1963-67, assoc. prof., 1967-71, prof., 1971—, chmn. dept. physics, 1992-98. Postdoctoral fellow Carnegie Inst. Tech., 1959-60, U. Calif., San Diego, 1959-60; vis. prof. Oxford (Eng.) U., 1970, 1998, U. Paris at Orsay, 1970, U.K. AEC, Harwell, Eng., 1971, U. So. Calif., 1975-76, Manchester (Eng.) U., 1976, U. Sussex, Eng., 1977, U. Heidelberg, Germany, 1977, 78, Dalhousie U. Halifax, N.S., Can., 1979, Imperial Coll., London, 1982-83, U. Calif., San Diego, 1989-90, U. Calif., Santa Barbara, 1998, numerous others; cons. Los Alamos Nat. Lab., 1988—. Contbr. numerous articles to profl. jours. Recipient rsch. grants. Fellow Am. Phys. Soc. Home: 173 Mathewson Rd Barrington RI 02806-4426 Office: Brown U Dept Physics Providence RI 02912-0001 E-mail: houghton@physics.brown.edu.

HOUGHTON, DAVID DREW, meteorologist, educator; b. Phila., Apr. 26, 1938; s. Willard Fairchild and Sara Nancy (Holmes) H.; m. Barbara Flora Coan, June 22, 1963; children: Eric Brian, Karen Jeanette, Steven Andrew. BS, Pa. State U., 1959; MS, U. Wash., 1961, PhD, 1963. Rsch. scientist Nat. Ctr. Atmospheric Rsch., Boulder, Colo., 1963-68; exch. scientist USSR Acad. Scis., Moscow, 1966; vis. scientist Courant Inst. Math. Scis., N.Y.C., 1966; asst. prof. dept. meteorology U. Wis., Madison, 1968-69, assoc. prof., 1969-72, prof., 1972-2001, chmn. dept., 1976-79, 91-94, prof. emeritus, 2001—. Scientist Internat. Sci. and Mgmt. Group for Global Atmospheric Rsch. Program, Bracknell, Eng., 1972-73; lectr. Nanjing U., People's Republic of China, 1980; vis. sr. scientist Nat. Meteorol. Ctr., Washington, 1988, Inst. Atmospheric Physics, Acad. Scis., Beijing, 2002; vis. scientist Inst. of Atmospheric Physics, Acad. of Scis., Beijing and Nanjing U., Nanjing, China, 1989; vis. cons. World Meteorol. Orgn., Geneva, 1997; vis. prof. Clark Atlanta U., 1998; trustee Univ. Corp. for Atmospheric Rsch., 1999-02. Contbr. articles to profl. jours.; editor-in-chief: Handbook of Applied Meteorology, 1985. Vice chmn. Planning Commn., Town of Dunn, Wis., 1977-81. NSF fellow, 1960-63. Fellow AAAS,

Am. Meteorol. Soc. (chmn. edn. and human resources commn. 1987-93, pres. 1995-96); mem. Phi Beta Kappa, Sigma Xi, Phi Kappa Phi. Mem. Rel. Soc. Of Friends. Office: U Wis Dept Atmos and Ocean Sci Madison WI 53706 E-mail: ddhought@facstaff.wisc.edu.

HOUGHTON, DIANE MURLEY, actor, vocalist; b. Boston, Feb. 6, 1935; d. John Taylor and Irene Hingley Murley; m. William R. Houghton, June 14, 1958; children: Rebecca Houghton Shrimpton, Adam Barrett. AB, Union Coll., Barbourville, KY, 1953—57. Cert. music tchr. grades 1-12 Ky., 1959. Actor: (with kentucky shakespeare festival) Lady Macbeth, Maria, Mistress Quickly, Nurse, Constance, Paulina, etc.; actor/singer (chicago area theater) Mrs. Hammerine in Steppenwolf Theater's Summer, Joanne in Company, Hattie Walker in Follies, Mrs. Hoffman in Working, Aunt Sally in Big River, 1st Female in Jacques Brell, Sadie in 70 Girls, 70, Aggie Powell in One Tough Cookie, (regional theater) Linda Loman in Death of a Salesman, Kate Keller in All My Sons, Sarah in Quilters, Dolly Levi in Hello, Dolly!, Vera Charles in Mame, Mrs. Lovett in Sweeney Todd, (off broadway) Jenny in Mamaleh!; actor: (nbc movie of the week) Elizabeth Mitchell in The Shadow of a Killer; singer: (chicago cabaret) Night Talk, a one woman cabaret show with Patrick Holland. Founder, dir. Fourth Revelation Teen Chorus, Louisville, 1971—75; landscape designer and gardener First Presbyn. Ch. & Bay Ridge Meth. Ch., Bklyn., 1999—2003. Mem.: Screen Actor's Guild, Actors Equity Assn.

HOUGHTON, JAMES RICHARDSON, glass manufacturing company executive; b. Corning, N.Y., Apr. 6, 1936; s. Amory and Laura (Richardson) H.; m. May Tuckerman Kinnicutt, June 30, 1962; children: James DeKay, Nina Bayard. AB, Harvard U., 1958, MBA, 1962. With Goldman, Sachs & Co., N.Y.C., 1959-61; with Corning Glass Works (name changed to Corning Inc. 1989), 1962-96; European area mgr. Corning Glass Works, Zurich, Switzerland, 1964-68, v.p., gen. mgr. consumer products divsn., 1968-71, vice chmn. bd., dir., chmn. exec. com., 1971-83, chmn. bd., CEO, 1983-96, 2002—, non-exec. chmn. bd., 2001—02. Bd. dirs. Met. Life Ins. Co., Exxon Mobile Corp.; mem. Harvard Corp. Trustee Corning Inc. Found., Corning Mus. Glass, Pierpont Morgan Libr., N.Y.C., Met. Mus. Art, Bus. Coun. With U.S. Army, 1959-60. Mem.: Corning Country; River, Harvard, Univ., Links (N.Y.C.); Brookline (Mass.) Country; Tarratine (Dark Harbor, Maine); Augusta (Ga.) Nat. Golf; Rolling Rock, Laurel Valley Golf (Ligonier, Pa.). Episcopalian. Office: Corning Inc MP HQ E2-6 One Riverfront Plz Corning NY 14831

HOUGHTON, KATHARINE, actress; b. Hartford, Conn., Mar. 10, 1945; d. Ellsworth Strong and Marion Houghton (Hepburn) Grant. BA, Sarah Lawrence Coll., Bronxville, N.Y., 1965. Founding mem. Pilgrim Repertory Co. (Shakespeare touring co. sponsored by Ky. Arts Commn.), 1971-72, SC Arts Commn., 1972, Miss. Arts Commn., 1973, Conn. Arts Commn., St. Joseph Coll., 1974; lectr. in field. Debut on Broadway stage in A Very Rich Woman, 1965; appeared in stage plays Charley's Aunt, New Orleans Repertory, 1966, The Front Page, Broadway, 1968, Ten O'Clock Scholar, Royal Poinciana Playhouse, Fla., 1969, The Private Ear/The Public Eye, Sullivan, Ill., 1969, Sabrina Fair, Ivoryton Playhouse, 1968, The Miracle Worker, Sullivan, Ill., A Scent of Flowers (Theatre World award), Off Broadway, 1969, Misalliance, Hartford Stage Co., 1970, The Taming of the Shrew, Actors Theatre, Louisville, 1970, Poor Richard, Tartuffe, 1970, Ring Around the Moon, Hartford Stage Co., 1970, Major Barbara, The Glass Menagerie, Actors Theatre of Louisville, 1971, Play It Again Sam, Actors Theatre of Louisville, 1971, Suddenly Last Summer, Ivanhoe, Chgo., 1973, The Prodigal Daughter, Kennedy Center, Washington, 1973, Bell, Book and Candle, Pensacola, Fla., 1974, The Rainmaker, Ind. Repertory Co., 1975, Spiders Web, Atlanta, 1977, Hedda Gabler, Nashville, 1978, Dear Liar, Dayton, Ohio, 1978, 13 Rue de L'Amour, Ind. Repertory Co., 1978, Antigone, Nashville, 1979, Uncle Vanya, Acad. Festival Theatre, Lake Forest, 1979, Forty Carats, Radford U. Theatre, Va., 1979, A Doll's House, St. Edward's U. Theatre, Tex., 1979, The Sea Gull, Pitts. Public Theatre, 1979, The Glass Menagerie, Pa. Stage Co., 1980, Taming of the Shrew, Pa. State Festival, 1980, Terra Nova, Actors Theatre of Louisville, 1980, The Merchant of Venice, South Coast Repertory, Costa Mesa, Calif., 1981, A Touch of the Poet, Yale Repertory Theatre, 1983, To Heaven in a Swing, Am. Place Theatre, N.Y.C., tour various theaters, 1983-85, Sally's Gone She's Left Her Name, Am. Festival Theatre, NH, 1984-86, Vivat, Vivat Regina, Mad Woman of Chaillot, The Time of Your Life, Children of the Sun, Mirror Repertory Co., N.Y.C., 1985, A Bill of Divorcement, Westport Country Playhouse, Conn., 1985, One Slight Hitch, Charlotte Repertory Co., 1986, To Heaven in a Swing, Amherst Coll., Bowdoin Coll., 1986, and Bronson Alcott Centennial Celebration, 1988, The Hooded Eye, West Bank Downstairs Theatre Bar, 1987, Ivoryton Playhouse, 1987, Murder in the Cathedral, West Point Cadet Chapel, 1987, The Leaves of Vallombrosa, 1988, Our Town, Broadway, 1988-89, Love Letters, Ivoryton Playhouse, 1989, To Kill A Mockingbird, Paper Mill Playhouse, NJ, 1991, Lettice & Lovage, Ivoryton Playhouse, 2002; motion pictures include Guess Who's Coming to Dinner, 1967, The Gardener, 1972, Eyes of the Amaryllis, 1981, Mr. North, 1987, Billy Bathgate, 1990, Ethan Frome, 1992, The Night We Never Met, 1992, Kalamazoo, 1993, Let It Be You, 1994, Best Kept Secret, Berkshire Theatre Festival, 2000, NJ Repertory Theatre, 2001, Sch. House Theatre, Croton Falls, NY, 20001 (motion picture) The Pursuit of Happiness, 2003; TV series The Adams Chronicles, 1975; TV mini-series I'll Take Manhattan, 1986; appeared on TV in Legacy of Fear, 1974, The Color of Friendship, 1981, (day-time serials) One Life to Live, 1989, All My Children, 1992; toured in Sabrina Fair, 1975, The Mousetrap, Arms and the Man, Dear Liar, 1976, The Streets of New York, Westport, Conn., Guildford, NH, Dennis, Mass., Denver, 1980; appeared in To True to Be Good, Acad. Festival Theatre, Lake Forest, Ill., 1977, Spingold Theatre, Waltham, Mass., 1977, Annenberg Center, Phila., 1977; author: (plays) To Heaven in a Swing, 1982, Merlin, 1984, Buddha, On The Shady Side, The Right Number, 1986, (book) The Marry Month of May, 1988; (stage prodns.) Phone Play, 1988, Good Grief, 1988, Mortal Friends, 1988 (stage prodn. premiere 1988), The Lick Penny Lover, 1988, Only Angels, 1997, (screenplays) The Heart of the Matter, 1989, Journey to Glasnost, 1990, Good Grief, 1991, Motherman, 1993, Acting in Concert, 1994, Spot, 1996, (play) Best Kept Secret, A Dangerous Liaison in the Cold War, 1998; co-author: Two Beastly Tales, 1975; editor: MHG: A Biography, 1989; written, performed in lectr. engagements: The Secret Life of Louisa May Alcott, Small Press Ctr., NYC, 1998, Women of AchievementSeries, The Mount, Lenox, Mass., 2002, My Grandmother's House Near the River, Conn. River Mus., 1999, The Wadsworth Atheneum, Conn., 1999, The Hope Club, Providence, 2000, The Cosmopolitan Club, NYC, 2002, Katharine Times Three, Conn. Hist. Soc., 1999, Wadsworth Atheneum, 2000, Denver Town Hall, 2001, Met. Mus. Art., NYC, 2001; appeared Larry King Live, 2003. Mem. Dramatists Guild.

HOUGHTON, MYRON JAMES, theology educator; b. Schenectady, N.Y., July 26, 1941; s. William James and Louise J. (Dlubac) Houghton. Diploma, Moody Bible Inst., 1962; BA, Pillsbury Coll., 1964; BDiv, Grand Rapids Bapt. Sem., 1967; M Liberal ARts, So. Meth. U., 1971; MA, St. Thomas Theol. Sem., 1977; ThD, Concordia Sem., St. Louis, 1986; PhD, Dallas Theol. Sem., 1993; cert. in orthodox theology, St. Stephen's Course of Studies, 1995. Ordained Bapt. Ch., 1966. Mem. faculty, chair theology dept. Denver Bapt. Bible Coll., 1971-83, Faith Bapt. Theol. Sem., Ankeny, Iowa, 1986—; mem. faculty theology dept. Faith Bapt. Bible Coll., Ankeny, 1983-86. Interim pastor Berean Bapt. Ch., Boulder, 1972-73, South Holly Bapt. Ch., Littleton, Colo., 1975-76, 80. Contbr. articles to profl. publs. Mem. Evang. Theol. Soc. Office: Faith Bapt Theol Sem 1900 NW 4th St Ankeny IA 50021-2152 E-mail: dr.m.houghton@netzero.net.

HOUGHTON, RAYMOND CARL, JR., education educator; b. Greenfield, Mass., May 26, 1947; s. Raymond Carl and Phyllis Irene (Richason) H.; m. Jan Marie Laws, Sept. 22, 1973; children: Raymond James, April Monica, Amy Rose. BS in Math., Norwich U., 1969; MS in Computer Sci., George Washington U., 1975; MSEE, Johns Hopkins U., 1980; PhD in Computer Sci., Duke U., 1991. Computer operator Norwich U., Northfield, Vt., 1967-69; specialist programmer power transformer dept. GE Co., Pittsfield, Mass., 1969-70, mathematician armament dept. Burlington, Vt., 1972-73; mem. tech. staff Computer Scis. Corp., Silver Spring, Md., 1974-75; data systems analyst computer security applications div. Nat. Security Agy., Ft. Meade, Md., 1975-78; computer scientist Inst. Computer Scis. and Tech./Nat. Bur. Standards, Gaithersburg, Md., 1978-83; instrnl. rsch. asst. dept. computer sci. Duke U., Durham, N.C., 1984-91; assoc. prof. dept. math. and computer sci. Augusta (Ga.) State U., 1987—93; lectr. Skidmore (N.Y.) Coll., 1993-95; pres. Cyber Haus Learning Ctrs., Delmar, NY, 1995—99. Bd. advisers, columnist Software Engring: Tools, Techniques, Practice, 1990-94, info. sys. delegate, Peoples Rep. China, 2000; adj. prof. SUNY Sch. Bus., Albany, 1997-2000; mission in understanding del. People to People Amb. Programs, Vietnam, 2002; spkr. in field. Contbr. articles to profl. jours. 1st lt. U.S. Army, 1971-72, Vietnam. Decorated Purple Heart; recipient Certs. of Recognition, U.S. Dept. Commerce, 1981, 83, Letter of Appreciation, Def. Comms. Agy., 1976. Mem.: IEEE, Assn. Computing Machinery, 101st Airborne Divsn. Assn., People to People Internat. Lutheran. Office: Cyber Haus 159 Delaware Ave #145 Delmar NY 12054-1369 E-mail: cyhous@msn.com.

HOUGHTON, RICHARD ARNOLD, research ecologist; b. Huntington, N.Y., Apr. 1, 1943; s. Richard A. and Phebe E. (Briggs) H.; m. Barbara T. Olsen (div.); children: Olsen, Graham; m. Susan M. Case, Aug. 27, 1977; children: Benjamin, Samuel. AB, Hamilton Coll., 1965; PhD, SUNY, Stony Brook, 1979; D (honoris causa), U. Munich, 1995. Rsch. asst. Brookhaven Nat. Lab., Upton, N.Y., 1966-74; rsch. assoc. Marine Biol. Lab., Woods Hole, Mass., 1975-84, asst. scientist, 1984-87; assoc. scientist Woods Hole Rsch. Ctr., 1987-89, sr. scientist, 1989—. Vis. sr. scientist NASA, Washington, 1993-94; mem. nat. tech. adv. com. Nat. Inst. Global Environ. Change, Davis, Calif., 1992-97. Contbr. articles to profl. jours. Mem., bd. dirs. Waldorf Assn. Cape Cod, Bourne, Mass., 1990-93. Grantee U.S. Dept. Energy, 1987, 90, 2001, 2002, NSF, 1987, EPA, 1991, 2000, 2001, 2002, 2003, NASA, 1995, 96, 97, 98, 2000, 2001, 2002, 2003. Mem. Am. Geophys. Union, Ecol. Soc. Am., Sigma Xi. Office: Woods Hole Rsch Ctr PO Box 296 Woods Hole MA 02543-0296 E-mail: rhoughton@whrc.org.

HOUGLAND, MARK ALLYN, writer; b. Schenectady, N.Y., Mar. 23, 1950; s. Russell Allyn and Bernice Virginia Hougland; m. Gail Ann Cronauer, Apr. 23, 1974; children: Adam Cronauer, Noah Cronauer. BA, Case Western U., 1972; MA, Ill. State U., 1975. Instr. St. Nobert Coll., West De Pere, Wis., 1975-79; tchr. Booker T. Washington H.S., Dallas, 1981-84; instr. Mountain View Jr. Coll., Dallas, 1993-97. Author: Chasing Tom, 1984, The Don Juan Killer, 1997, Quits, 1997, What Comes Around, 1999. Home and Office: 3815 Clover Ln Dallas TX 75220

HOUGLUM, BRUCE MONROE, music educator; b. Fargo, N.Dak., Feb. 19, 1946; s. Victor Monroe and Thelma Gudrun Houglum; m. Diane C. Berg, July 28, 1968; children: Kirsten, Karin. MusB, Concordia Coll., 1968; MusM, N.W. U., 1971. Dir. music Ulen (Minn.)-Hitterdal Pub. Schs., 1968—70, Round Lake (Ill.) Pub. Schs., 1971—72; dir. orch. Moorhead (Minn.) Pub. Schs., 1972—81, Fargo (N.Dak.) Pub. Schs., 1981—95; assoc. prof. music Concordia Coll., Moorhead, 1995—, dir. orch. Co-founder FM Youth Symphony, Moorhead; asst. condr. FM Symphony Orch., Moorhead, 1996—. Guest condr.: Music Festivals, 1995—. Named Tchr. of Yr., N.Dak. Music Educators Assn., 1991. Mem.: Nat. Sch. Orch. Assn. Home: 1121 49th Ave South Fargo ND 58104 Office: Concordia College 901 8th St South Moorhead MN 56562

HOUK, BENJAMIN NOAH, artistic director, choreographer; b. Seattle, Apr. 4, 1962; s. Robert Louis Houk and Marilyn Joan (Haugen) Sundin; m. Lauri-Michelle Rohde, July 11, 1991; children: Madeline, Katherine;children from previous marriage: Marissa, Skylar. Studied dance, Amherst Ballet Acad., 1978, Jan Collum Sch. Ballet, 1979, Jo Emery Sch., 1979-80, N.Y. studios, 1980-83, Robert Joffrey Workshop, 1981, Am. Ballet Ctr., 1980-83, Pacific NW Ballet, 1983—; student, U. Wash., 1988—. Prin. dancer Pacific Northwest Ballet, Seattle, 1983—; asst. dir. Bravo Ballet Arts in Edn. Program, Seattle, 1993-96; with Pacific Northwest Ballet, Seattle, 1987-89, soloist, 1987—, prin. dancer, 1989-96; M.C., coord. Joffrey, N.Y.C., 1983; artistic dir., choreographer Nashville Ballet, 1996-99; artistic dir. Fort Worth Dallas Ballet, 1998—2001; dir. Dance Acad., San Marcos, Calif., 2001—. Guest artist guest artist Orange County Ballet, Ithaca, NY, 1981, Koslovs and Friends, San Francisco, 1985, Ballet Oreg., Portland, 1988, Ballet Chgo., 1989, Nev. Dance Theatre, Las Vegas, 1990, Tacoma Perf. Dance Co., 1980, Nevada Festival Ballet, 1993—94, Maui Ballet Co., 1994; dance instr., lectr., 1984—. Dancer (ballets) Pacific Northwest Ballet include Romeo in The Tragedy of Romeo and Juliet, Sigfried in Swan Lake, Franz in Coppelia, The Prince in The Nutcracker, others include Albrecht in Giselle, Othello in The Moor's Pavane, choreographer Capriole Suite, 1988, By When, 1989, Shard, 1990, First Light, 1992, Schubert 2-4-5, 1994, Bete Noir, 1993, Across and Back, 1994, Nutcracker, 1995, Open Water, 1995, Aida, 1997, Passage, 1998, Swan Lake (after Petipa), 1998; TV appearance Disney Presents Bill Nye the Science Guy, 1994. Artistic dir. Benefit for the Homeless, Everett, Wash., 1990—91. Grantee Tacoma (Wash.) Arts Coun., 1986. Mem.: Am. Guild Mus. Artists. Avocations: reading, windsurfing, pottery, mountaineering, painting. Office: 1635 Rancho Santa Fe Ste 203 San Marcos CA 92069*

HOUK, KENDALL NEWCOMB, chemistry educator; b. Nashville, Tenn., Feb. 27, 1943; s. Charles H. and Janet Houk; 1 child, Kendall M.; m. Robin L. Garrell. AB, Harvard U., 1964, MS, 1966, PhD, 1968. Asst. prof. chemistry La. State U., Baton Rouge, 1968-72, assoc. prof., 1972-75, prof., 1975-80, U. Pitts., 1980-86, UCLA, 1986-91, chmn. dept. chemistry and biochemistry, 1991-94. Dir. chemistry divsn. NSF, 1988—90. Contbr. articles to profl. jours. Recipient Schrodinger medal World Assn. Theoretically Oriented Chemists, 1998. Fellow AAAS; mem. Internat. Acad. Quantum Molecular Sci., Am. Chem. Soc. (Cope Scholar award 1988, James Flack Norris award 1991, award for computers in chemistry and pharm. sci. 2003). Office: UCLA Dept Chemistry Biochemistry 405 Hilgard Ave Los Angeles CA 90095-9000

HOULE, ARTHUR JOSEPH, music educator; b. Lowell, Mass., Feb 5, 1955; s. Robert Joseph and Beatrice Dupré Houle; m. Azam Gousheguir, July 5, 1981; children: Bijan Andrew, Darius Brian. MusB in Piano Performance, U. Lowell, 1976; MusM in Piano Performance, New Eng. Conservatory, 1982; D of Musical Arts in Piano Performance and Pedagogy, U. Iowa, 1991. Piano faculty New Eng. Conservatory Ext. Divsn., Boston, 1978—80, Belmont (Mass.) Music Sch., 1978—83, Boston Conservatory Ext. Divsn., 1982—83, Dana Hall Sch. Music, Wellesley, Mass., 1983—86; grad. tchg. asst. U. Iowa, Iowa City, 1986—88; asst. prof. piano and head of the piano area U. ND, Grand Forks, 1988—90; asst. prof. piano and piano accompanying U. Tex., Austin, 1990—92; assoc. prof. piano, dir. keyboard studies Albertson Coll. Idaho, Caldwell, 1992—. Founder, artistic dir. ann. internat. festival for creative pianists (www.albertson.edu/music/pianofestival.htm) Albertson Coll. Idaho, Caldwell, 2000—, dir. ann. piano festival, 1995—2000; presenter in field. Composer: (music publ.) Cowboy Jazz; musician: (cd recording) Chopin Nocturnes (Critical acclaim), Music of Marjorie Burgess (Critical acclaim); contbr. articles to profl. jours. Recipient First prize Pi Kappa Lambda Scholarship Competition, New Eng. Conservatory, 1978, Second prize Original Instrumental Composition Competition, Music Umbrella Austin, 1991; grantee, Albertson Coll. Idaho, 1992—2002; NEH rsch. grantee, Albertson Coll. Idaho 1995, 96, 98, 02, 1995, 1996, 1998, 2002, Tchr. Scholarship grantee, Idaho Music Tchrs. Assn., 1998. Mem.: Idaho Music Tchrs. Assn., Music Tchrs. Nat. Assn., Coll. Music Soc. (chair profl. life initiative task force on assoc. profs. 2001). Achievements include research in classical improvisation, especially in music of Chopin. Significant influence on piano concerts, teaching, workshops, adjudicating, writing, and development of unique festival competition. Avocation: swimming. Home: 175 E Boise Ave Boise ID 83706 Office: Albertson Coll Idaho 2112 Cleveland Blvd Caldwell ID 83605 Office Fax: 208-459-5885. E-mail: ahoule@albertson.edu.

HOULE, JEFFREY ROBERT, lawyer; b. Biddeford, Maine, July 27, 1965; s. Marcel Paul and Lois Marie (Jackson) H.; children: Grace Morgan, Hunter Jackson. AB, Boston Coll., Chestnut Hill, Mass., 1987; JD, Western New Eng. Coll., Springfield, Mass., 1991; LLM in Taxation, Cert. in Employee Benefits Law, Georgetown U., Washington, 1992, LLM in Securities Regulation, 1995. Bar: D.C., N.Y., Conn., Mass., Maine. Pres. A.F.I. Investments, Springfield, Mass., 1988-91, Washington Capital Ventures, LP, Washington, 1995-98; law clk. Stones Solicitors, Exeter, Devon, Eng., 1989; jud. intern to the Hon. Joan Glazer Margolis U.S. Magistrate Judge, New Haven, Conn., 1990; legal intern Office of Atty. Gen. Robert Abrams, N.Y.C., 1990; analyst The Bur. of Nat. Affairs, Inc., Washington, 1992; assoc. Andros, Floyd & Miller PC, Hartford, Conn., 1992-94, Elias, Matz, Tiernan & Herrick LLP, Washington, 1994-98; founding ptnr. Greenberg Traurig LLP, McLean, Va., 1998—. Contbr. articles to profl. jours. With U.S. Army, 1984-86. Mem. ABA, The Army and Navy Club, The Federalist Soc.,The Tower Club, Phi Alpha Delta. Republican. Roman Catholic. Avocations: hiking, horseback riding, swimming, scuba diving, international travel.

HOULE, JOSEPH E. mathematics educator; b. Hartford, Conn., Oct. 11, 1930; s. Joseph E. and Rena (Cyr) H.; m. Constance Deschamps, June 19, 1954; children— Marie, Joseph, Celia, Elizabeth, Amy, Bernice. AB, Cath. U. Am., 1952, MA, 1954, PhD, 1959. From instr. to assoc. prof. math. Georgetown U., 1953-62; assoc. prof. Seton Hall U., 1962-63; prof. math. Pace U., N.Y.C., 1963-94, chmn. dept., 1963-70, dean Dyson Coll. Arts and Scis., 1971-90, vice provost, 1987-90. Dir. Ctr. for Applied Ethics, 1982-93, emeritus, 1994—; Internat. Exec. Svc. Corps. vol. exec. Ministry of Edn., Budapest, Hungary, 1991. Fellow N.Y. Acad. Scis. (chmn. sect. math. 1968-69), Phi Beta Kappa Soc.; mem. Math. Assn. Am., Sigma Xi. Roman Catholic. Home: A188 Harrogate 400 Locust St Lakewood NJ 08701-7411

HOULIHAN, DAVID PAUL, lawyer; b. Youngstown, Ohio, May 14, 1937; s. Paul V. and Delcie (Norman) H.; m. Marlene K. Betras, Aug. 13, 1960; children: Kevin, Rex, Laura, Brian. BS, Youngstown State U., 1959; postgrad., Purdue U., 1960; LLB, Georgetown U., 1964. Bar: D.C. 1965, U.S. Ct. Appeals (D.C. cir.) 1965, U.S. Supreme Ct. 1968, U.S. Ct. Internat. Trade 1976, U.S. Ct. Customs and Patent Appeals 1976, U.S. Ct. Appeals (Fed. cir.) 1982. Analyst U.S. Internat. Trade Commn., Washington, 1960-64; counsel U.S.-Japan trade council Stitt & Hemmendinger, Washington, 1964-68; ptnr. Daniels, Houlihan & Palmeter P.C., Washington, 1968-84, Mudge, Rose, Guthrie, Alexander & Ferdon, Washington, 1984-95, White & Case, Washington, 1995—. Lectr. Oxford U., Eng., 1972; chmn. Keidanren Seminar: Dumping, Customs and Tax Aspects of Transfer Pricing. Contbr. articles to profl. jours. Mem. ABA, D.C. Bar Assn., British-Am. C. of C. Democrat. Roman Catholic. Avocations: sailing, music. Address: White & Case 601 13th St NW Washington DC 20005-3807 Personal E-mail: dholihan@whitecase.com.

HOULIHAN, GERALD JOHN, lawyer; b. Cortland, N.Y., Aug. 26, 1943; s. Robert Emmett and Helen (Corsi) H.; m. Claudia C. Kitchens; children: Andrea, Gerald Jr., Maureen, Katherine, Colleen. BS, U. Notre Dame, 1965; JD, Syracuse U., 1968. Bar: N.Y. 1968, U.S. Dist. Ct. (we. dist.) N.Y. 1968, U.S. Ct. Appeals (2nd cir.) 1972, U.S. Supreme Ct. 1980, U.S. Ct. Appeals (5th cir.) 1981, U.S. Ct. Appeals (11th cir.) 1981, Fla. 1985, U.S. Dist. Ct. (so. dist.) Fla. 1985, U.S. Dist. Ct. (so. dist.) N.Y. 1986, U.S. Dist. Ct. (no. dist.) Fla. 1986, U.S. Ct. Appeals (4th and D.C. cirs.) 1987, U.S. Dist. Ct. (middle dist.) Fla., 1987. Assoc. Harris, Beach, Keating et al., Rochester, N.Y., 1968-72; asst. U.S. atty. U.S. Atty.'s Office, Rochester, 1972-81; sr. litigation counsel U.S. Dept. Justice, Rochester, 1981-82; chief asst. U.S. atty. U.S. Atty.'s Office, Miami, Fla., 1982-85; ptnr. Steel Hector & Davis, Miami, 1985-91; mem. Greenberg, Traurig, Hoffman, Lipoff, Rosen & Quentel, P.A., Miami, 1991-95; ptnr. Houlihan & Ptnrs., P.A., 1995—. Advocate Am. Bd. Trial Advocates. Belle L. Landry scholar Syracuse Soc. Mem. Fed. Bar Assn. (pres. 1993-94, bd. dirs. Miami chpt. 1988—), Order of Coif. Democrat. Home: 5191 SW 76th St Miami FL 33143-6015 Office: Houlihan & Ptnrs PA 2600 S Douglas Rd Ste 600 Miami FL 33134-6100 E-mail: gjhoulihan@aol.com.

HOULIHAN, PATRICK THOMAS, museum director; b. New Haven, June 22, 1942; s. John T. and Irene (Rourke) H.; m. Betsy Eliason, June 19, 1965; children: Mark T. and Michael D. (twins). BS, Georgetown U., 1964; MA, U. Minn., 1969; PhD, U. Wis., Milw., 1971. Asst. commr. N.Y. State Mus., Albany, 1980-81; dir. Heard Mus., Phoenix, 1972-80, S.W. Mus., L.A., 1981-87, Millicent Rogers Mus., 1988-93; writer, rschr. Ugo Prodns., L.A., 1993—2000; founding ptnr. Walkabout Books, LLC, 2000—.

HOUMES, BLAINE V. emergency physician, county medical examiner; b. Sept. 13, 1952; MD, U. N.D., 1988. Diplomate Am. Bd. Emergency Medicine. Intern Cook County Hosp., Chgo., 1988-89, resident, 1989-92; mem. staff Mercy Med. Ctr., Cedar Rapids, Iowa, 1992—; med. examiner Linn County, Cedar Rapids. Mem. Am. Coll. Emergency Physicians, Am. Acad. Emergency Medicine, Iowa Med. Soc., Am. Acad. Forensic Scis. Office: Linn County Emergency Med 701 10th St SE Cedar Rapids IA 52403-1251

HOUNSELL, JILLANN CUSICK, secondary education educator; b. Ridley Pk., Pa., Aug. 23, 1943; d. John Thomas and Ellen Lenore (Bauer) Cusick; m. Thomas Sidney Hounsell, Aug. 5, 1967; children: Dana Jeanne, Jillann Irene, Tamryn JoyEllen, Thomas Sidney Jr. BA, Westminster Coll., 1965; MEd, U. Del., 1969; EdD, Wilmington Coll., 2000. Sci. tchr. Newark Sch. Dist., 1965-67, planetarium dir., 1968-69, Alexis I. duPont Spl. Sch. Dist., Greenville, Del., 1969-79; sci. instr. Red Clay Consol. Sch. Dist., Wilmington, Del., 1980—. Assoc. dir. State Sci. Olympiad, Dover, Del., 1998-2003; adj. sci. instr. U. Del., Newark, 1999; field tester for properties of matter Smithsonian Nat. Sci. Resources Ctr.. Pres. PTA, Wilmington, 1982-84, Hockessin, Del., 1988-90; v.p. Del. State PTA, Dover, 1986-88; choir dir. Hockessin United Meth. Ch., 1992-96. Recipient Nat. Presdl. award for excellence in sci. and math. tchg., 1999, Environ. Educator or Yr. award, 2002. Mem. NEA, Del. State Edn. Assn., Del. Dept. Edn. (lead tchr., mem. state assessment com., state stds. com. 1998-00), Del. Tch rs. Sci., Del. Assn. Biology Tchrs. Republican. Avocations: stained glass, shell collection & identification, painting. Home: 735 Montgomery Woods Dr Hockessin DE 19707-9324 Office: H B duPont Mid Sch 735 Meeting House Rd Hockessin DE 19707-8508

HOUNSFIELD, GODFREY NEWBOLD, radiation scientist; b. Aug. 28, 1919; s. Thomas H. Ed., City and Guilds Coll., London; diploma, Faraday House Elec. Engring. Coll., London; MD (hon.), U. Basel, 1975; DSc (hon.), City U., 1976, U. London, 1976; DTech (hon.), U. Loughborough, 1976; D honoris causa, Cambridge U., 1992. Joined EMI Ltd., Hayes, Middlesex, Eng., 1951, head med. systems sect., cen. research labs., 1972-76, sr. staff scientist, 1977—. Professional fellow in imaging scis. Manchester U., 1978-86. Contbr. articles to sci. jours. Recipient Nobel prize in Physiology or Medicine, 1979; MacRobert award, 1972; Wilhelm-Exner medal Austrian Indsl. Assn., 1974; Ziedses des Plantes medal Physikalische Medizinische Gesellschaft, Würzburg, 1974; Prince Philip Medal award CGLI, 1975; ANS Radiation Industry award Ga. Inst. Tech., 1975; Lasker award Lasker Found., 1975; Duddell Bronze medal Inst. Physics, 1976; Golden Plate award Am. Acad. Achievement, 1976; Reginald Mitchell Gold medal Stoke-on-Trent Assn. Engrs., 1976; Churchill Gold medal, 1976; Gairdner Found. award, 1976; decorated comdr. Order Brit. Empire, 1976, knight, 1981. Fellow Royal Soc. Achievements include leading design team for 1st large all-transistor computer to be built in Gt. Britain; invented EMI-scanner computerized transverse axial tomography system for X-ray exam.; developed new X-ray technique (EMI-scanner system). Office: Ctrl Research Labs EMI Group Dawley Rd Hayes Middlesex UB3 1HH England

HOUPIS, CONSTANTINE HARRY, electrical engineering educator; b. Lowell, Mass., June 16, 1922; s. Harry John and Metaxia (Gourokous) H.; m. Mary Stephens, Aug. 28, 1960; children: Harry C., Angella S. Student, Wayne U., 1941-43; BS, U. Ill., 1947, MS, 1948; PhD, U. Wyo., 1971. Spl. rsch. asst. U. Ill., 1947-48; devel. elec. engr. Babcock & Wilcox Co., Alliance, Ohio, 1948-49; instr. elec. engring. Wayne State U., 1949-51; prin. elec. engr. Battelle Meml. Inst., Columbus, Ohio, 1951-52; prof. elec. engring. Air Force Inst. Tech., Wright-Patterson AFB, Ohio, 1952-96, prof. emeritus, 1997—. Guest lectr. Nat. Tech. U. Athens, 1958, 99, U. Patras, 1984, Weizmann Inst. Sci., 1984, U. Strathclyde, 1995, Binghampton U., 1996; sr. rsch. assoc. Air Force Rsch. Lab., 1981-97, sr. rsch. assoc. emeritus, 1997—. Author: (with J.J. D'Azzo) Feedback Control System Analysis and Synthesis, 1960, 2d edit., 1966; Principles of Electrical Engineering: Electric Circuits, Electronics, Energy Conversion, Control Systems Computers, 1968; Linear Control Systems Analysis and Design: Conventional and Modern, 1975, 4th edit., 1995, (with J.J. D'Azzo and Stuart N. Sheldon) Linear Control Systems and Analysis with MATLAB, 2003, 5d edit.; (with J. Lubelfeld) Outline of Pulse Circuits; (with G.B. Lamont) Digital Control Systems: Theory Software, Hardware, 1985, 2d edit., 1992; (with S. Rasmussen) Quantitative Feedback Theory: Fundamentals and Applications, 1999, (with J.F. D'Azzo and S.N. Sheldon) Linear Control System Analysis and Design with MATLAB, 2003, also articles on automatic controls in profl. jours. in U.S., U.K. and Europe. Served with AUS, 1942-46. Recipient Outstanding Engr. award Dayton Area Nat. Engrs. Week, 1962, Outstanding Civilian Career Svc. award, 1997, Outstanding Engring. Alumnus

award U. Wyo., 2002. Fellow IEEE; mem. Am. Soc. Engring. Edn., Am. Hellenic Edn. Progressive Assn., Tau Beta Pi, Eta Kappa Nu. Greek Orthodox. Home: 1125 Brittany Hills Dr Dayton OH 45459-1415 Office: Air Force Inst Tech Hobson Way WPAFB Dayton OH 45433-7765

HOUPIS, JAMES LOUIS JOSEPH, dean, biologist; b. Binghamton, N.Y., Oct. 11, 1956; s. Louis Harry and Annamarie Benenati Houpis; m. Valerie Wood, May 18, 1955; children: Ellas, Aaron, Joseph, Jacob. BA, U. Calif., Berkeley, 1978; MS, San Diego State U., 1984; Doctorate, U. Calif., Berkeley, 1989. Environ. scientist, project leader Lawrence Livermore Nat. Lab., Livermore, Calif., 1986—96; asst. dir. environ. scis. program So. Ill. U., Edwardsville, Ill., 1996—97, assoc. prof. dept. biol. scis., 1996—99, dir. environ. scis. program, 1998—2001, prof. dept. biol. scis., 1999—2001; dean Coll. Natural Scis. Calif. State U., Chico, Calif., 2001—, prof. dept. biol. scis., 2001—. Councilor-at-large Ill. State Acad. Sci., Springfield, 2000—01; session chair Air Pollution Workshop, Boone, NC, 1998—; co-chair sustainable forestry com. Dept. Energy, Office Indsl. Tech., Georgetown, 1995—96; vice-chair elevated CO2 session Air and Waste Mgmt. Ann. Meeting, Nashville, 1996. Assoc. editor: Jour. Environ. Quality, 2001—; contbr. Grantee, U.S. EPA, 1987—90, rsch. grantee, Calif. Air Resources Bd., 1991—92, Lawrence Livermore Nat. Lab., 1991—95, Nat. Inst. for Global Environ. Change, 1992—95, U.S. EPA, 2001—03. Mem.: Xi Sigma Pi, Sigma Xi (pres. So. Ill. U. 2000—01). Office: Calif State U Coll Natural Scis Chico CA 95929-0555 Office Fax: 530-898-4363. Business E-Mail: jhoupis@csuchico.edu.

HOUPT, JAMES EDWARD, lawyer; b. Calif., 1951; m. Leslie Ann Jones Houpt. BA with distinction, Calif. State U., Chico, 1976; JD cum laude, Harvard U., 1992. Bar: Va. 1992, D.C. 1992, U.S. Ct. Appeals (4th cir.) 1992, Md. 1993, Calif. 1997, U.S. Ct. Appeals (9th cir.) 1997. News dir. Sta. KNVR-FM, Paradise, Calif., 1978-80; anchor, reporter Sta. KHSL-AM-TV, Chico, 1980-85; sr. reporter Sta. KOLO-TV, Reno, 1985-89; assoc. Baker & Hostetler, Washington, 1992-97; assoc. of counsel, ptnr. Orrick, Herrington & Sutcliffe LLP, Sacramento, 1997—. Lectr. journalism Calif. State U., 1981, 85; adj. prof. law sch. U. Calif., Davis, vis. prof., 1999, 2000. Author: (booklet) Access to Electronic Records, 1990, The Libel Curtain: A Comparison of Canadian & American Libel Law, 1994, Going On-Line: Is the World Wide Web a Web for the Unwary?, 1996, Boarding a Moving Bus: Developing an Internet Risk Management Strategy, 1997, The Courts and the Internet. A Match Made in Hell?, 2000; contbr. articles to legal and gen. interest publs. With USN, 1970-74. Recipient Cert. of Merit, Calif.-Nev. AP TV-Radio Assn., 1983, 84, 86. Mem. ABA, Va. State Bar Assn., D.C. Bar, Calif. Bar Assn., VFW, Am. Legion. Avocations: photography, hiking, canoeing. Office: Orrick, Herrington & Sutcliffe LLP 400 Capitol Mall Ste 3000 Sacramento CA 95814-4497

HOUPT, JEFFREY LYLE, dean, psychiatrist, educator; b. Phila., Aug. 13, 1941; s. H. Lyle and Elizabeth (McAlpine) Houpt; m. Corinne A. Anderson, Dec. 28, 1964; children: Brian Jeffrey, Eric Robert. BS in Zoology, Wheaton Coll., 1963; MD, Baylor Coll. Medicine, 1967. Diplomate Am. Bd. Psychiatry and Neurology. Intern Boston City Hosp., 1967-68; resident in psychiatry Yale U., New Haven, 1968-71; staff med. officer Oak Knoll Naval Hosp., Oakland, Calif., 1971-73; adj. asst. prof. psychiatry Presbyn. Hosp., San Francisco, 1973-75; asst. prof. to prof. psychiatry Duke Med. Ctr., Durham, N.C., 1975-83; prof. psychiatry, chmn. dept. Emory U. Sch. Medicine, Atlanta, 1983-90; dean Sch. Medicine Emory U., Atlanta, 1988-96; dean Sch. Medicine, vice chancellor for med. affairs U. N.C., Chapel Hill, 1997—; CEO U. N.C. Health Sys., Chapel Hill, 1998—. Author: The Importance of Mental Health Services for General Health Care, 1979; contbr. articles to med. jours. Lt. comdr. USN, 1971-73 Fellow Am. Coll. Psychiatry (pres.), Am. Psychiat. Assn. Home: 51319 Eastchurch Chapel Hill NC 27517-8302 Office: U NC at Chapel Hill CB # 7000 Chapel Hill NC 27599-7000

HOURANI, LAUREL LOCKWOOD, epidemiologist; b. Carmel, Calif., Sept. 10, 1950; d. Eugene Franklin and Katherine Ruth (Miller) Betz; m. Ghazi Fayez Hourani, Feb. 28, 1984; children: Nathan, Danna, Lisa. BA, Chico State U., 1977; MPH, Am. Univ. Beirut, 1983; PhD, U. Pitts., 1990. Prog. evaluator Community Hosp. Monterey Peninsula, Carmel, Calif., 1978-81; instr./researcher Am. Univ. Beirut, 1981-85; predoctoral fellow U. Pitts., 1985-89; researcher, cons. V.A. Med. Ctr., Pitts., 1988-90; dir., tumor registry Med. Ctr. U. Calif. Irvine, Orange, 1990-92; epidemiologist Naval Health Rsch. Ctr., San Diego, 1993-95, head divsn. health scis., 1995-2001; sr. epidemiologist Rsch. Triangle Inst., Research Triangle Park, N.C., 2001—. Cons. Nat. Devel. Commn. South Lebanon, 1981-83. Author: No Water, No Peace, 1985; contbr. articles to profl. jours. Bd. dirs. Am. for Justice in Middle East, Beirut, 1982-85, Nat. Devel. Com., South Lebanon, 1983-85. Recipient grant V.A., Pitts., 1989, rsch. grant U. Rsch. Bd., Beirut, 1985. Mem. Am. Psychol. Assn., Am. Pub. Health Assn., Soc. for Epidemiologic Rsch.

HOURY, DEBRA, emergency physician, educator; MD, MPH, Tulane U., 1998. Resident in emergency medicine Denver Health Med. Ctr., 1998—2002, chief resident, 2001—02; assoc. dir. Ctr. for Injury Control, Atlanta, 2002—; asst. prof. Emory U., Atlanta, 2002—. Mem. editl. bd. Annals of Emergency Medicine; contbr. articles to profl. jours. Recipient Young Investigator award, Am. Coll. Emergency Physicians, 2000, Leadership award, Emergency Medicine Residents Assn., 2001, Academic Excellence award, EMRA, 2000, Leadership award, AMA Found., 2002; scholar, Emory U., 1994—98; Med. Student Rsch. grantee, So. Med. Assn., 1997—98, Resident Rsch. grantee, EMF, 2001—02, Riggs Career Devel. grantee, 2002—03. Mem.: AMA, APHA (Jay Drotman award 2002), Soc. Acad. Emergency Medicine, Am. Coll. Emergency Physicians, Kappa Kappa Gamma. Office: Emory Ctr for Injury Control 1518 Clifton Rd Ste 230 Atlanta GA 30322

HOUSE, CHARLETTA, librarian; b. Mobile, Ala., July 9, 1937; d. Charlie and Nevada (Travis) H. BS, Ala. State U., 1959; MLS, U.Md., 1973; MEd, Salisbury State U., 1993. Acquisitions asst. libr. Ala. A&M Libr., Normal, Ala., 1963-68; asst. libr. circulation dept. U. Md. Eastern Shore, Princess Anne, 1968-71, head circulation dept., 1972-83; circulation, reference libr. Salisbury (Md.) State U., 1984-86, reference, spl. collection libr., 1986—. Mem. Wicomico County Commn. of Women, Dem. Club of Wicomico County. Mem. AAUW, LWV, NAACP, Md. Libr. Assn., The Links, Inc., Kappa Delta Pi, Delta Sigma Theta Sorority, Inc. Methodist. Avocation: reading. Office: Salisbury Univ Blackwell Libr 1101 Camden Ave Salisbury MD 21801-6860

HOUSE, DONALD LEE, SR., software executive, private investor, management consultant; b. Covington, Ga., Aug. 7, 1941; s. Ben Luther and Almeda (Johnson) H.; m. Nickie Farguson, Oct. 19, 1962; children: Donald Lee Jr., Danielle Elizabeth. BS, Ga. Inst. Tech., 1963, MS, 1967. Process engr. E.I. Dupont, Chattanooga, 1966-68; asst. to pres. Jefferson (Ga.) Mills Inc., 1968; exec. v.p. Mgmt. Sci. Am. Inc., Atlanta, 1968-87; investor, bus. cons. Atlanta, 1987—2002; chmn. Clarus Corp., Atlanta, 1992-97, also bd. dirs.; chmn. Ockham Techs., 1999—. Bd. dir. Expeditor Sys., Transnexus, Nu Bridges, LLC, Afterbot, Inc.; Carreker, Inc.bd. dir.; mem. Ga. Tech. Presdl. adv. bd. 1st lt. U.S. Army, 1963—65. Named to Ga. Tech. Hall of Fame, 2000. Mem.: Tech. Assn. Ga. (bd. dir.). Republican. Avocations: reading, horse farm. Home: 2480 Spalding Dr Atlanta GA 30350-3600 E-mail: dhouse@att.net.

HOUSE, ERNEST ROBERT, education educator, educational evaluator; b. Alton, Ill., Aug. 7, 1937; s. Ernest House and Helen Lucille (Schumake) McDaniel) m. Donna Brown, Feb. 1, 1964; children: Kristin, Colby. AB, Washington U., St. Louis, 1959; MS, So. Ill. U., 1964; EdD, U. Ill., 1968. Cert. high sch. tchr., Ill. Tchr. English, Roxana (Ill.) High Sch., 1960-64; cons. Ill. demonstration project for gifted youth U. Ill., Urbana, 1964-65, dir. gifted program evaulation Coop. Ednl. Rsch. Lab., 1967-69, project dir., ednl. specialist, 1969-71, project dir., asst. prof. edn., 1971-75, assoc. prof., 1975-79, prof., 1979-85; vis. prof. U. Colo., Boulder, 1982, prof. edn., 1985—, dir. Lab. for Policy Studies, 1985—. Vis. scholar UCLA, 1976, Harvard U., Cambridge, Mass., 1980; mem. lab. rev. panel U.S. Dept. Edn., 1987—. Author: The Politics of Educational Innovation, 1974, (with Steve Lapan) Survival in the Classroom, 1978; Evaluating With Validity, 1980, Jesse Jackson and the Politics of Charisma, 1988, Professional Evaluation: Social Impact and Political Consequences, 1993, Values in Evaluation, 1999, Where the Truth Lies, 2002; mem. editorial bd. Ednl. Evaluation and Policy Analysis, 1971-81, 86—; editor-in-chief New Directions for Program Evaluation, 1982-85; columnist Evaluation Practice, 1984-88. Mem. rsch. staff Senator Adlai Stevenson of Ill., 1970, Ill. lt. gov. Paul Simon, 1972. Recipient Harold D. Lasswell prize Policy Scis. Policy Scis. Jour., 1989. Mem. Am. Ednl. Rsch. Assn. (program chmn. 1976, chmn. awards com. 1983), Am. Evaluation Assn. (Lazarfield award), Phi Beta Kappa. Democrat. Avocations: swimming, writing.

HOUSE, HAROLD VON, science educator, consultant; b. Brazil, Ind., Feb. 12, 1958; s. James Evan and Mary Lou (Shonk) House; m. Susan Cheryl Wythe, Aug. 18, 1976; children: Nancy Anne Cox, Kimberly Jane, Andrew Michael. BS, Ind. State U., Terre Haute, Indiana, 1976—80; EdS, Ind. State U., Terre Haute, 1990—2003; MS, U. Dayton, Ohio, 1983—86. Lic. Sch. Principal Ind., 1992, Sch. Dist. Supt. Ind., 2003, Spl. Edn. Dir. Ind., 2003. Mayor, mcpl. judge Village of Owensville, Ohio, 1983—87; vocat. coop. edn. dir. S. Vermillion Schs., Clinton, Ind., 1987—98; spl. edn. tchr. coord. Indpls. Pub. Schs., 1998—2001; adj. prof. Michiana Coll., South Bend, Ind., 2001—03; lead tchr. Ind. Dept. Corrections, South Bend, 2001—03. Bd. mem. Ohio Gov.'s State Adv. Group on Juvenile Justice and Delinquency Prevention, Columbus, 1983—87; profl. devel. site founder Butler U., Indpls. Pub. Schs.; leadersip devel. fellow Indpls. Pub. Schs., 1999—2000; bd. mem. Indpls. Police Dept. PAL Program, 2000—03. Vice chmn. Ind. Criminal Justice Inst., Indpls., 1990—2002; mem., Ind. chpt. Correctional Edn. Assn., Indpls., 2002—; at-large bd. mem. Ind. Correctional Assn., Indpls., 2003—. Named to Mktg. Edn. Hall of Fame, Am. Vocat. Assn., 1986, Am. Police Hall of Fame, Nat. Assn. of Chiefs of Police, 1988, All Am. Tchr. Team, USA Today, 1999; recipient Michael Jordan Fundamentals Award & Grant for Teachers, World Divsn. of Nike, 1999; Lilly Tchr. Creativity fellow, Lilly Endowment, 2000. Mem.: Nat. & Ind. Edn. Assn. (mem. 1976—2003), Ind. Chpt., Correctional Edn. Assn. (bd. mem. 2002—), Ind. Correctional Assn. (bd. mem. 2003—), Knute Rockne Meml. Kiwanis Club (mem. 2002—03). Democrat. Methodist. Avocation: campaign button collecting. Home: 3804 Palomino Cir Ste #3B South Bend IN 46628 Office: Ind Dept Correction 4650 Old Cleveland Rd South Bend IN 46628

HOUSE, JAMES STEPHEN, sociological social psychologist, educator; b. Phila., Jan. 27, 1944; s. James Jr. and Virginia Miller (Sturgis) H.; m. Wendy Fisher, May 13, 1967; children: Jeff, Erin. BA, Haverford Coll., 1965; PhD, U. Mich., 1972. From. instr. to assoc. prof. sociology Duke U., Durham, N.C., 1970-78; assoc. prof. sociology/assoc. rsch. scientist Survey Rsch. U. Mich., Ann Arbor, 1978-82, assoc. chair dept. sociology, 1981-84, prof. sociology, sr. rsch. scientist Survey Rsch. Ctr., 1982—, chair dept. sociology, 1986-90, dir. Survey Rsch. Ctr., Inst. Social Rsch., 1991-2001. Author: Work Stress and Social Support, 1981; co-editor: Sociological Perspectives on Social Psychology, 1995; assoc. editor Social Psychology Quar., 1988-91, Jour. Health & Social Behavior, 1997-2000, Internat. Ency. of the Social and Behavioral Scis., 2001; contbr. chpts. to books and articles to profl. jours. Guggenheim fellow, 1986-87. Fellow: AAAS, Soc. Behavioral Medicine, Am. Acad. Arts and Scis.; mem.: Soc. for Epidemiol. Rsch., Soc. for Psychol. Study of Social Issues, Acad. Behavioral Medicine Rsch., Am. Sociol. Assn., Inst. Medicine of NAS. Office: Univ Mich Inst Social Rsch PO Box 1248 Ann Arbor MI 48106-1248 E-mail: jimhouse@umich.edu.

HOUSE, JOHN WILLIAM, otologist; b. L.A., July 12, 1941; s. Howard and Helen House; m. Barbara Breithaupt, Mar. 28, 1993; children: Hans, Chris, Kurt, Steven, Kevin. BS, U. So. Calif., 1964, MD, 1967. Intern L.A. County-U. So. Calif. Med. Ctr., 1967-68; resident Glendale (Calif.) Adventist Hosp., 1971-72, L.A. County Med. Ctr., 1972-74; fellow Otologic Med. Group, L.A., 1974, pvt. practice, 1975—; pres. House Ear Inst., L.A., 1987—. Mem. editorial bd. Am. J. Otology, 1986—; contbr. articles to jours. in field. Admissions com. interviewer, U. So. Calif. Sch. Medicine, Los Angeles, 1976—; mem. Los Angeles County Sheriff's Res. Med. Co. Capt. U.S. Army, 1969-71. Recipient Hocks Meml. award Am. Tinnitus Assn., 1988; named Tchr. of Yr., U. So. Calif. Family Practice Dept., 1987. Fellow Am. Acad. Otolaryngology/Head and Neck Surgery; mem. AMA, Am. Neurotology Soc. (program chmn. 1976—, pres. 1998-99), Am. Otol. Soc. (past pres.), Triologic Soc., Am. Soc. Mil. Otolaryngologists, Pan-Am. Assn. Otorhinolaryngology Broncho Esophagology, Jonathan Club (Los Angeles). Avocations: skiing, computers, running, swimming. Office: House Ear Clinic Inc 2100 W 3rd St Fl 1 Los Angeles CA 90057-1922

HOUSE, KAREN ELLIOTT, company executive, former editor, reporter; b. Matador, Tex., Dec. 7, 1947; d. Ted and Bailey Elliott; m. Arthur House, Apr. 5, 1975 (div. Sept. 1983); m. Peter Kann, June 4, 1984; children: Hillary, Petra, Jason, Jade. BJ, U. Tex., 1970; postgrad. Inst. Politics, Harvard U. Edn. reporter Dallas Morning News, 1970-71, with Washington bur., 1971-74; regulatory corr. Wall Street Jour., Washington, 1974-75, energy and agr. corr., 1975-78, diplomatic corr., 1978-84, fgn. editor N.Y.C., 1984-89; v.p., Internat. Group Dow Jones & Co., 1989-95, pres. Internat. Group, 1995—; sr. v.p. Dow Jones Co pub. Wall St. Jour., 2002. Bd. dirs. Rand Corp.; mem. adv. bd. Ctr. Strategic Internat. Studies; dir. Coun. on Foriegn Rels. Trustee Boston U. Recipient Edward Weintal award for Diplomatic Reporting, Georgetown U., 1980-81, Edwin Hood award for Diplomatic Reporting Nat. Press Club, 1982, Disting. Achievement award U. So. Calif., 1984, Pulitzer prize for Internat. Reporting, 1984, Overseas Press Club Bob Considine award, 1984, 88; Harvard fellow, 1982. Fellow Nat. Acad. Arts and Scis. Home: 58 Cleveland Ln Princeton NJ 08540-3077 Office: Dow Jones & Co 200 Liberty St Fl 9 New York NY 10281-1003 E-mail: karen.house@dowjones.com.

HOUSE, STEPHEN EUGENE, information systems consultant; b. Pueblo, Colo., July 18, 1951; s. Floyd Eugene and Jewell (Brame) H.; m. Cheryl Virginia Ashby, Mar. 15, 1975; children: Deborah Lynne, Mark Stephen. BS in Bus. Info. Systems, West Coast U., 1992. Programmer Calif. Sch. Employees Assn., San Jose, 1976-79; programmer/analyst Marysville (Calif.) Joint Unified Sch. Dist., 1979-80; tech. lead Mervyns, Hayward, Calif., 1980-85, Lucky Stores, Inc., Dublin, Calif., 1985-87; project lead Northrop, Pica Rivera, Calif., 1987-92; tech. cons. Computer Profls. Inc., Charlotte, N.C., 1992-97; mem. profl. staff Compuware Corp., Charlotte, 1997—.

HOUSE, W(ILLIAM) MICHAEL, lawyer; b. Birmingham, Ala., Dec. 19, 1945; s. B. William and Kathryn Regina (Cantrell) H.; m. Kathryn House, Sept. 30, 1969; children: Tanner, Slade, Kate. BS, Auburn U., 1968; JD, U. Ala., 1971. Bar: Ala. 1971, D.C. 1992. Legal asst. to Congressman James M. Collins, Washington, 1971-72; atty. Ala. Supreme Ct., Montgomery, 1972-76; assoc. Odom, Argo, Enslen, Montgomery, 1976-79; chief of staff Sen. Howell Helfin, Washington, 1979-86; of counsel McNair Law Firm, Washington, 1986-88; ptnr. Shaw, Pittman et al, Washington, 1988-91, Hogan & Hartson, Washington, 1991—, chair legis group. Pres. Ala. Young Lawyers, 1976; chmn. Ala. Citizens Conf., Ala. State Courts, 1974-75; co-chmn. Potomac Group Dem. Nat. Com., 1987-93; mem. bus. adv. coun. Auburn Sch. Bus., 1990-93; mem. pres.'s cabinet U. Ala., 2000—. Capt. U.S. Army, 1971—80. Named Ala. Outstanding Young Man Ala. JC's, 1979. Mem. Ala. Bar Assn. (award of merit 1974), Am. Judicature Soc. (bd. dirs.), Soc. Internat. Bus. Fellows (bd. dirs.), Pi Kappa Alpha (bd. dirs. Meml. Found. 1980-86). Avocations: tennis, reading. Office: Hogan & Hartson 555 13th St NW Ste 800E Washington DC 20004-1161

HOUSEAL, BRIAN L. conservationist; b. Sept. 1950; m. Katherine Houseal; children: Ian, Patrick. Bachelor's, Colgate U.; Master's in Regional Planning, Syracuse U.; Master's in Landscape Arch., SUNY, Syracuse. Mem. U.S. Peace Corps, U.S. Agy. for Internat. Devel., World Bank, UNESCO; v.p. and regional dir. Mex. and Ctrl. Am. programs Nature Conservancy, dir. stewardship Latin Am.; exec. dir. Adirondack Coun., 2002—. Office: 103 Hand Ave Ste 3 PO Box D-2 Elizabethtown NY 12932*

HOUSE-HENDRICK, KAREN SUE, nursing consultant; b. San Francisco, July 16, 1958; d. Mathas Dean and Marilyn Frances (Weigand) House., Casa Loma Coll., 1985; AS in Nursing, SUNY at Albany, 1987. Psychiat. charge nurse Woodview Calabasas (Calif.) Hosp., 1985-87, Treatment Ctrs. Am., Van Nuys, Calif., 1987-88; cons., RN Valley Village Devel. Ctr., Reseda, Calif., 1988; plastic surg. nurse George Sanders, M.D., Encino, Calif., 1986—; nurse New Image Found., 1989—97, Mid Valley Youth Ctr., 1991—2000; dir. nursing Encino Surgicenter (Sanders), 1992—. Dir. nursing Devel. Tng. Svcs. for Devel. Disabled, 1988—95; nurse cons. New Horizons for Developmentally Disabled, 1993, Exceptional Children's Found., 2001—; nurse specialist, collagen and Botox trainer, 1998—. Instr., vol. ARC. Recipient Simi Valley Free Clinic Scholarship. Mem. Encino C. of C. Office: 16633 Ventura Blvd Ste 110 Encino CA 91436-1834 E-mail: khouse6783@aol.com., karen@drsanders.com.

HOUSEHOLDER, LARRY, state official, small business owner; m. Taundra Householder; children: Derek, Adam, Matthew, Nathan, Luke. Grad. in polit. sci., Ohio U., 1982. Commr. Perry County; Dist. 78 Ohio Ho. Rep., 2001—. Bd. chmn. Tri-County CAA; mem. L.F.C.P. Solid Waste Bd., Perry County Planning Commn. Coach Youth Baseball. Named Hon. State farmer, 1995. Mem.: NFIB, C.of C., Rules and Ref. Com. (chmn.), 33d Degree Scottish Rite, Aladdin Temple Shrine (amb.), Moose, Eagles, Lions, Grange, Farm Bur. Achievements include Speaker Householder running for state representative in 1996 where he has worked diligently to promote economic development, infrastructure, and improved education. Office: 77 South High St 14th Fl Columbus OH 43215-2500 Office Fax: 614-644-9494. Business E-Mail: rep78@ohr.state.oh.us.

HOUSEKNECHT, STEPHEN, artist, educator; b. Batavia, N.Y., Nov. 15, 1951; s. William K. and Marianne Houseknecht. A. A. Humanities, Genesee C.C., Batavia, NY, 1972; BA in Art, Buffalo State Coll., Buffalo, NY, 1975; MFA in Photography, SUNY at Buffalo, Buffalo, NY, 1980. Vis. rsch. curator and project developer of the houseknecht collection of photography NY State Mus., Albany, NY, 1991—92; instr. of photography and art history Genesee C.C., Batavia, NY, 1988—90; lectr., fine arts photography Buffalo State Coll., Buffalo, 1992—. Photographic history / exhibition, Genesee County History Dept/ Printing Glass Plate Negative Collection, phase 1 (NY State Coun. of the Arts Decentralization Program, 2002), photographic exhibition, Persistence Of Vision: Extended Family Album (NY State Coun. of the Arts Decentralization Program, 1993), rephotographic survey/ photo exhibition, Genesee: Then and Again, A Hundred Year Photographic Perspective (NY State Coun. of the Arts Decentralization Program, 1991), photographic exhibition, Persistence Of Vision: Extended Family Album (The NY State Legislature Local Initative Grant (Natural Heritage Trust), 1990), Persistence Of Vision: Extended Family Album A First Local Exhibition (NY State Coun. of the Arts Decentralization Program, 1989). Avocations: working with WWII aircraft, working with chow chows. Home: 10895 Warner Rd Darien Center NY 14040 Office: Upton Hall 114 Buffalo State College 1300 Elmwood Ave Buffalo NY 14222 E-mail: houseksj@buffalostate.edu.

HOUSEL, NATALIE RAE NORMAN, physical therapist; b. Syracuse, N.Y., July 25, 1959; d. Rudolf Anthony and Pauline Mary (Proia) Norman; m. Thomas Hugh Housel, June 25, 1988; children: Heather, Tommy and Tiffany (twins). BS in Phys. Therapy, Ithaca Coll., 1981; MA in Applied Psychology, Fairfield U., 1986; EdD in Curriculum and Instrn., U. Ctrl. Fla., 2002. Cert. geriatric clin. specialist Am. Bd. Phys. Therapy Specialties., diplomate wound care specialist Am. Acad. Wound Mgmt. Staff phys. therapist, N.Y., 1981-85; sr. phys. therapist Rome (N.Y.) Devel. Ctr., 1987-89; asst. dir. phys. therapy Tioga (N.Y.) Gen. Hosp. and Nursing Home, 1989-91, Corning (N.Y.) Hosp., 1991-92; asst. dir. rehab. svcs. Arnot Ogden Med. Ctr., Elmira, N.Y., 1992 93; sch. phys. therapist Collier County Pub. Schs., Naples, Fla., 1993-94; pvt. practice phys. therapist Ft. Myers, Fla., 1995-96; dir. phys. therapy Beverly Enterprises, Ft. Myers, Fla., 1995-96; therapy supr. Lee Meml. Health Sys. Health Park Care Ctr., Ft. Myers, Fla., 1996-97; rehab. mgr. occupl., speech and phys. therapy Lee Meml. Home Health, Fort Myers, Fla., 1997-98. Instr phys. therapy assts. Broome C.C., 1989, wound care nutrition for Hosp. Food Adminstrs., 1997; oral examiner for phys. therapy licensees N.Y. State, Albany, 1988-90; adj. faculty S.W. Fla. Coll., Ft. Myers, 2003—. Adult group leader Family Faith Formation, St. Columbkill Ch., Ft. Myers, Fla., 1996-97. Mem.: APA, Am. Acad. Wound Mgmt. Avocations: flute, piano, swimming. Home: 1626 N Hermitage Rd Fort Myers FL 33919-6409

HOUSEMAN, ALAN WILLIAM, lawyer; b. Colorado Springs, Colo., Apr. 23, 1943; s. Murl Clarence and Opal Juanita (Snyder) H.; m. Susan Hays Margolis, June 17, 1967; children: Alana Judith, Nora Suzanne. BA, Oberlin Coll., 1965; JD, NYU, 1968. Bar: Mich. 1968, U.S. Dist. Ct. (ea. dist.) Mich. 1969, U.S. Dist. Ct. (we. dist.) Mich. 1970, U.S. Ct. Appeals (6th cir.) 1973, U.S. Supreme Ct. 1976, D.C. 1979, U.S. Ct. Appeals (D.C. cir.) 1982, U.S. Ct. Appeals (3d cir.). Reginald Heber Smith fellow Wayne County Legal Services, Detroit, 1968-69; dir. Mich. Legal Services, Detroit, 1969-76; dir. research inst. Legal Services Corp., Washington, 1976-81; dir. Ctr. for Law and Social Policy, Washington, 1981—. Author: (with others) Legal Services History, 1984; contbr. articles to profl. jours. Chmn. Orgn. of Legal Svcs. Back-Up Ctrs., N.Y.C., 1973-75; vice chmn. Project Adv. Group, Washington, 1974-76. Recipient Recognition award Mich. Welfare Rights Orgn., 1975, Achievement award Project Adv. Group, 1979, 88, Nat. Equal Justice award, 1994. Mem. ABA, Nat. Legal Aid and Defender Assn. (chmn. civil com. 1975-77, recipient spl. award 1973, 88, 2000), Law and Soc. Assn., Soc. Am. Law Tchrs. Democrat. Mem. United Ch. Christ. Avocations: hiking, tennis, music. Home: 1715 Crestwood Dr NW Washington DC 20011-5333 Office: Ctr for Law and Social Policy 1015 15th St NW Ste 400 Washington DC 20005 E-mail: ahouse@clasp.org.

HOUSEMAN, ANN ELIZABETH LORD, educational administrator, state official; b. New Orleans, Mar. 21, 1936; d. Noah Louis and Florence Marguerite (Coyle) Lord; m. Evan Kenny Houseman, June 25, 1960; children: Adrienne Ann, Jeannette Louise, Yvonne Elizabeth. BA, Barnard Coll., 1957; MA, Columbia U., 1962; PhD, U. Del., 1969. State supr. reading Dept. Pub. Instrn., Del., 1977-79; prin. M.L. King Jr. Elem. Sch., Wilmington, Del., 1979-80; adminstr., exec. dir. Del. State Arts Coun., Wilmington, 1980-84; acting dir. Divsn. Hist. and Cultural Affairs State of Del., Wilmington, 1983-84; prin. P.S. du Pont Intermediate Sch., Wilmington, 1984-91; dir. Mid.-Atlantic States Arts Consortium, Balt., 1980-84. Mem. adv. bd. Rockwood Mus., Wilmington, 1981-94; bd. dirs. Opera Del., Inc., Wilmington, 1984-97, pres., 1991-93, dir. devel., 1994-95, coord. adv. bd., 1996; bd. dirs. Del. Theatre Co., Wilmington, 1984-90; bd. dirs. Aux. of Alfred I. duPont Hosp. for Children, 1997—, pres., 2000-01. Mem. Phi Delta Kappa. Republican. Presbyterian. E-mail: houseman@udel.edu.

HOUSEPIAN, EDGAR MINAS, neurosurgery educator; b. N.Y.C., Mar. 18, 1928; s. Moses Minas and Makrouhie (Ashjian) H; m. Marion Grace Lyon, Sept. 18, 1954; children: David Minas, Stephen Lyon, Jean Carleton Housepian. AB cum laude, Columbia U., 1949, MD, 1953; DSc (hon.), Nat. Acad. Scis. Armenia, 1997, Yerevan State Med. U., 1997. Intern in surgery U. Hosps. of Cleve., 1953-54, asst. resident in surgery, 1955-56, Neurol. Inst., N.Y.C., 1955-56, asst. resident in neurol. surgery, 1956, asst. resident in neurology, 1957-58, sr. resident in neurol. surgery, 1958-59; asst. resident in neuropathology Columbia Presbyn. Med. Ctr., N.Y.C., 1956; asst. prof. Columbia U., N.Y.C., 1967-76, prof., 1976-96, prof. emeritus neurol. surgery, 1997—, spl. adv. internat. affiliations to v.p. health scis., 1996—; asst. neurol. surgeon Columbia Presbyn. Med. Ctr., N.Y.C., 1959-61, asst. attending neurol. surgeon, 1961-64, assoc. attending surgeon, 1964-75, attending surgeon, 1975—. Asst. vis. neurol. surgeon Francis Delafield Hosp., N.Y., 1959-72; asst. attending neurol. surgeon N.Y. State Psychiat. Inst., 1962-80; attending neurol. surgeon VA Hosp., Bronx, 1962-69; cons. neurol. surgeon U.S. Naval Hosp., St. Albans, N.Y., 1963-74, Englewood (N.J.) Hosp., 1964—, Greenwich (Conn.) Hosp., 1965-91; mem. courtesy staff dept. surgery St. Luke's-Roosevelt Hosp. Ctr., N.Y., 1981—; guest lectr. Soviet Acad. of Sci., 1965; vis. prof. surg. neurology Edinburgh (Eng.) U., 1968; mem. search com. radiotherapy Columbia U., 1980-84, 88—, sec. staff com., 1962-68, mem. communicable disease and antibiotics com., 1966-75, mem. dean's ad hoc com. on nat. bds., 1974, mem. univ. senate exec. com., 1979-81, mem. fin. com. assn. of alumni of Physicians and Surgeons Coll., 1979—, mem. clin. rsch. adv. com. Cancer Rsch. Ctr., 1980—, mem. dean's adv. com. on continuing med. edn., 1987—, chmn. libr. and audiovisual com., 1972—, chmn. com. on human investigation, 1972—, mem. standing com. on edn., 1980—, chmn. credentials com., 1981—, active numerous other univ. coms.; mem. World Congress Ad Hoc TV Rev. Com., 1969; mem. claims rev. com. Med. Liability Mut. Ins. Co., 1978—; prin. investigator brain tumor chemotherapy sect., mem. comprehensive cancer sect. Nat. Cancer Inst., 1973-77; vis. prof. in surg. neurology Edinburgh U., 1968; vis. prof. Postgrad. Inst. Med. Edn. and Rsch., Chandigarh, India, 1981; guest lectr. Soviet Acad. Sci., 1965; active numerous other career related activities. Contbr. chpts. to books, articles to Jour. Neurosurgery, Jour. Neuropathology, Jour. Neuropathology and Exptl. Neurology, Jour. Nervous Mental Diseases, Perspectives in Neurol. Surgery, numerous others. Mem. med. adv. bd. Nat.

Neurofibromatosis Found., 1978-81; mem. adv. com. Armenian studies program Columbia U., 1972-80; trustee Gulbenkian Found., 1975—; dir. med. relief programs for diocese Armenian Ch. Lt. comdr. USNR, 1945-46, 61-91. Recipient Ellis Island medal of honor, 1994, Presdl. citation Republic of Armenia, 1994, Alumni Fedn. medal Columbia U., 1996; Donner Found. Rsch. fellow, 1956; Parkinson's Disease Found. Postdoctoral Rsch. fellow, 1959-61; Fulbright fellow, 1968; grantee Am. Cancer Soc., 1969-72, Nat. Cancer Inst., 1973-77. Fellow ACS; mem. AAAS, AMA, AAUP, Am. Acad. Neurol. Surgeons (Humanitarian award 2002), Am. Assn. Neurol. Surgeons, Am. Epilepsy Soc., Am. Trauma Soc., Am. Pain Soc., N.Y. Acad. Sci., N.Y. County Med. Soc., N.Y. State Med. Soc., Internat. Soc. Rsch. in Stereoencephalotomy (charter), Assn. for Rsch. in Nervous and Mental Diseases, N.Y. Soc. Neurosurgery (past pres.), Rsch. Soc. Neurol. Surgeons, N.Y. Neurol. Soc., Congress of Neurol. Soc., Soc. for Neurosci., N.Y. State Neurosurg. Soc. (past pres.), Internat. Assn. for the Study of Pain, Internat. Soc. on Disaster Medicine, Fulbright Alumni Assn., Internat. Brain Rsch. Orgn., World Fedn. Neuroscientists, Nat. Acad. Scis. Armenia, Phi Beta Kappa, Sigma Xi. Office: Columbia U Coll Physicians & Surgeons 710 W 168th St New York NY 10032-2603

HOUSER, DONALD RUSSELL, mechanical engineering educator, consultant; b. River Falls, Wis., Sept. 2, 1941; s. Elmont Ellsworth and Helen (Bunker) H.; m. Colleen Marie Collins, Dec. 30, 1967; children: Kelle, Kerri, Joshua. BS, U. Wis., 1964, MS, 1965, PhD, 1969. Registered profl. engr., Ohio. Instr. U. Wis., Madison, 1967-68; from asst. prof. to prof. Ohio State U., Columbus, 1968—2003, emeritus prof., 2003—, dir. Gear Dynamics and Gear Noise Rsch. Lab., 1979—, dir. Ctr. for Automotive Rsch., 1994-99. V.p. Gear Rsch. Inst., State Coll., Pa., 1990-99. Author: Gear Noise, 1991; contbg. editor Sound and Vibration mag., 1988-96; assoc. editor Jour. Mech. Design, 1993-94; mem. adv. bd. JSME Internat. Jour., 1996-2000; contbr. articles to profl. jours. Elder St. Andrews Presbyn. Ch., Columbus, 1972-75. Fellow ASME (legis. liaison Ohio coun. 1976-80, Century II medallion 1980); mem. Am. Gear Mfrs. Assn. (acad.), Soc. Automotive Engrs., Am. Helicopter Soc., Inst. Noise Control Engrs. Roman Catholic. Achievements include development of technology for measuring gear transmission error under load. Office: Ohio State U 206 W 18th Ave Columbus OH 43210-1189 E-mail: houser.4@osu.edu.

HOUSER, DOUGLAS GUY, lawyer; b. Oregon City, Oreg., July 11, 1935; s. Roy B. and Shirley (Knight) H.; m. Lucy Anne Latham, Sept. 1, 1961; children: Brooks Bonham, Bradley Knight, Anne Elizabeth. BA, Willamette U., 1957; JD, Stanford, 1960. Bar: Oreg. 1960. Practice in Portland, 1961—; ptnr. Bullivant, Houser PC, 1965—. Chmn. com. on continuing legal edn. Oreg. State Bar, 1969-70, chmn. com. jud. adminstrn., 1975, bd. bar examiners, 1970-72, mem. bd. bar govs., 1977-80, treas., 1979-80; judge protem Circuit Ct., 1973-77; gen. counsel NIKE, Inc., 1972-84, dir, 1972—; bd. overseers RAND Inst. for Civil Justice; gen. counsel Soc. Registered Profl. Adjusters; former gen. counsel Pacific N.W. Life Ins. Co.; lectr. Contbr. articles to profl. publs. Legal adviser Portland Sch. Dist. 1 Race and Edn. Com., 1963-64; mem. Eagle bd. Columbia-Pacific council Boy Scouts Am., 1962-70; past v.p., treas., bd. dirs. Waverley Children's Home; trustee Willamette U.; bd. visitors Stanford U. Sch. Law, 1978-80, 8991, 96-98, 98-2000, Willamette U. Law Sch., 1986; chmn. Oreg. State Jud. Fitness Commn., 1980—. Fellow Am. Bar Found. (life), Am. Coll. Trial Lawyers, Internat. Acad. Trial Lawyers; mem. ABA (past chmn. tort and ins. practice sect.), Multnomah County Bar Assn. (chmn. com. continuing legal edn. 1977), Oreg. Assn. Def. Counsel (dir. 1972-76, pres. 1976-77), Def. Research Inst. (bd. dirs. 1990-93, sec.-treas. 1993—), Fedn. Def. and Corp. Counsel (chmn. bd. dirs. 1991-92), Am. Judicature Soc. (bd. dirs. 1985-88), Internat. Assn. Def. Counsel, Stanford Law Soc. Oreg., Am. Law Inst., Nat. Jud. Coll. (adv. coun. 1990—), Willamette U. Alumni Assn. (pres. 1972-74, bd. trustees 1971—), Beta Theta Pi, Phi Delta Phi, Omicron Delta Kappa, Pi Gamma Mu. Republican. Episcopalian (trustee Diocese Oreg. 1972-75, sr. warden). Clubs: Waverly Country, Arlington, Multnommah Athletic. Home: 11621 SW Military Ln Portland OR 97219 Office: Bullivant Houser Bailey PC Portland OR 97204-2089

HOUSER, HAROLD BYRON, epidemiologist; b. North Liberty, Ind., Nov. 22, 1921; s. Edgar Allen and Gladys Chloe (Stillson) H.; m. Clara Jane Goin, Sept. 18, 1944; children: Cristene, Edgar, John, Susan, James. AB, Ind. U., 1942, MD, 1944. Intern U.S. Marine Hosp., New Orleans, 1944-45; resident Crile VA Hosp., Cleve., 1947-49; asst. prof. medicine SUNY, Syracuse, 1952-58; asst. prof. medicine and community health Case Western Res. U., 1958-64, assoc. prof., 1965-74, prof. epidemiology, 1974-92, prof. emeritus, 1992—, chmn. dept. biometry, 1975-85, chmn. dept. epidemiology and biostats., 1985-92; cons. in field. Contbr. numerous articles to profl. jours. Served with U.S. Army, 1945-47, 49-52. Recipient Group Lasker award Am. Pub. Health Assn., 1954, Disting. Civilian award Dept. Def., 1973 Fellow Infectious Diseases Soc.; mem. Am. Epidemiol. Soc. (pres. 1991). Home: #CS 9103 5950 N Fountains Ave Tucson AZ 85704 E-mail: halhous@aol.com.

HOUSER, JIM (JAMES COWING HOUSER JR., JIM HOUSER), painter, art educator; b. Dade City, Fla., Nov. 12, 1928; s. James C. and Martha (Futch) H.; m. Constance Woodward; children: James Jackson, Katrina J. BS, Ringling Sch. of Art, 1949; BFA, Fla. So. Coll., 1951; postgrad., Art Inst. Chgo., 1952; MFA, U. Fla., 1953. Exhibited at Grand Ctrl. Moderns Gallery, N.Y.C., 1966—; represented by Rudolph Galleries, Woodstock, N.Y., Coral Gables Fla., 1964-90, Gallery Camino Real, Boca Raton, Fla., 1972—, David Findlay Galleries, N.Y.C., 1974-84, Sherry French Gallery, N.Y.C., 1985. Sr. instr. art Ky. Wesleyan Coll., Owensboro, 1954-60, art chmn., 1964-70, dir. art gallery, 1974-91; art instr. Palm Beach C.C.; artist Notre Dame U., 1970; Cornell U., NYU, 1971: judge local and nat. art competitions; lectr. in field. Author: Color for the Artist, 1975, video texts; one man shows include Gallery Camino Real, 1972-89, 99, 2003, Brevard C.C., Cocoa, Fla., 1973, Valencia C.C., Orlando, Fla., 1974, David Findlay Galleries, N.Y.C., 1976, 78, 81, 83, Northwood Inst., 1986, Palm Beach C.C., 1988, numerous others in U.S. and Europe; exhibited in group shows at Dept. State Spl. Exhbn., Washington, 1967—, Major Fla. Artist Invitational Exhbn., Sarasota, Fla., 1981-92, North Miami Mus. and Art Ctr., North Miami, Fla., 1985, South Fla. Invitational Exhbn., 1991, Ft. Lauderdale Mus. Art, Men's Art Northwood U., West Palm Beach, Fla., 1994, Festival Internat. Peinture, Cagnes-sur-Mer, France, 2001; permanent collection at Boca Raton Mus. Art. Mem. selection com. Palm Beach Coun. Arts, 1987; mem. art rev. bd. scholarship awards Palm Beach Post-Times, 1982-87. Recipient Merit award Ft. Lauderdale Mus., 1974, Atwater Kent award 1977, 89, Akston Found. award 1977, Philip Hulitar award 1982, Four Arts award 1992, 93, Soc. Four Arts, West Palm Beach; established Connie and Jim Houser award for the Contempary Exhbn. Soc. of the Four Arts, 1996-2002. Mem. Soc. of the Four Arts (Cert. of Appreciation 1996, 10 other awards). Republican. Methodist. Avocations: music, photography, computer. Home and Office: 8338 SE Coconut St Hobe Sound FL 33455-2911

HOUSER, JIM See HOUSER, JIM

HOUSER, JOHN EDWARD, lawyer; b. Richmond, Va., Dec. 24, 1928; s. Aubrey Alphin and Winnifred (Savage) H.; m. Elizabeth Rives Pollard, Apr. 1, 1967; children— Allen Rives Cabell Lybrook, Andrew Murray Lybrook. B.S., U. Va., 1959, LL.B., 1959. Bar: Fla. 1959, U.S. dist. ct. (so. and mid. dists.) Fla. 1959, U.S. Ct. Appeals (5th cir.) 1963, U.S. Supreme Ct. 1970, U.S. Ct. Appeals (11th cir.) 1981. Assoc., Jennings, Watts, Clarke & Hamilton, Jacksonville, Fla., 1959-61, Howell, Kirby, Montgomery & Sands, Jacksonville, 1961-63; ptnr. Howell & Houser, Jacksonville, 1963-65; sole practice, Jacksonville, 1965—; lectr. on Long shore and Harbor works Comp. Act Loyola U., 1979, 88; dir. William P. Polythress & Co., Richmond, Neal F. Tyler & Sons, Jacksonville. Author: England's Legacy to America, 1996. Active Jacksonville U. Council, Jacksonville Symphony Assn., Fla. Hist. Soc., Jacksonville Hist. Soc., Cummer Gallery of Art, Jacksonville Art Mus.; mem. English-Speaking Union, dir., 1970-79, pres., 1974-78, nat. regional chmn., 1973-76, nat. dir., 1976-81; hon. sec. Live Oak Hounds; subscriber Exmoor Foxhounds; active Thomasville Landmarks, dir., 1991—, Thomasville Arts Guild, Thomasville Cultural Ctr., Thomas County Hist. Soc. Served with AUS, 1953-57. Mem. Internat. Assn. Indsl. Accident Bds. and Commns., Maritime Law Assn., Southeastern Admiralty Law Inst., Jacksonville Claimsmen Assn., Atlanta Claimsmen Assn., ABA, Jacksonville Bar Assn., Fla. Bar, Fla. Def. Scl. Assn., Am. Judicature Soc., Am. Arbitration Assn., Ga. Trust for His. Preservation, Nat. Trust Hist. Preservation, Fla. Inst. Pub. Affairs, Navy League, Jacksonville Assn. Def. Counsel, Def. Research Inst., Theta Delta Chi, Sigma Nu Phi. Clubs: Rotary Internat., River, Fla. Yacht, University (Jacksonville), Deerwood, Ponte Vedra River, Exchange, German, Ye Mystic Revellers, Univ., Princeton of N.Y., Glen Arven, Commonwealth (Richmond, Va.); 2300. Office: PO Box 873 Jacksonville FL 32201-0873

HOUSER, NATHAN, philosophy educator; b. Auburn, Ind., May 10, 1944; s. Frank F. and Viola M. (Hose) H.; m. Aleta Halme, Dec. 12, 1975; children: Jesse, Ezra. PhD, U. Waterloo, 1985. Asst. prof. philosophy Ind. U., Indpls., 1986-91, assoc. prof. philosophy, 1991-97, prof. philosophy, 1997—, prof. Am. studies, 1997—, founding faculty mem. Sch. of Informatics, 2000. Asst. editor Writings of Charles S. Peirce, Indpls., 1983-85, assoc. editor, 1985-93, gen. editor, 1993—; dir. Peirce Edition Project, 1993—; dir. Inst. Am. Thought, Charles S. Peirce Soc., 2003—. Adv. bd. Modern Logic Pub., 1993—; co-editor: Essential Peirce, 1992, vol. 2, 1998, Studies in the Logic of Charles Sanders Peirce, 1997. Fulbright-Hays fellowship, 1978; devel. grantee Prince Charitable Trusts, 1996, collaborative rsch. grantee Nat. Endowment for Humanities, 1997, 99, 01. Mem. Am. Philos. Assn., Soc. Advancement Am. Philosophy, Charles S. Peirce Soc., History of Sci. Soc., Semiotic Soc. Am., Assn. Documentary Editing. Office: CA545 IUPUI 425 University Blvd Indianapolis IN 46202-5148 E-mail: nhouser@iupui.edu.

HOUSER, RONALD EDWARD, lawyer, mediator; b. Fairbury, Nebr., Aug. 11, 1949; s. Edward Erle and Lois Charlotte (Dux) H.; m. Linda Marie Webber, June 13, 1971 (div. 1985); children: Angela Marie, Brian Edward, Darren James; m. Beatrice Virginia McMullen Bupp, July 24, 1993. DVM, U. Mo., 1974; MS, Ohio State U., 1979; JD, U. Ga., 1990. Bar: Ga. 1990, U.S. Dist. Ct. (mid., no. and so. dist.) Ga. 1990, U.S. Ct. Appeals (11th cir.) 1990, U.S. Ct. Mil. Appeals 1993, U.S. Supreme Ct. 1993. Asst. instr. Univ. Nebr., Lincoln, 1979-83; owner, mgr. Lincoln Animal Health Clinic, 1983-85; atty. Cook, Noell, Tolley, Bates & Michael, Athens, Ga., 1990—. Contbr. articles to profl. jours. Mem. Nebr. State Bd. Health, 1980-84. Mem. Nat. Lawyers Assn., Nebr. Vet. Med. Assn. (dist. pres. 1979-81), Christian Legal Soc., Res. Officers Assn., Am. Legion, Phi Alpha Delta, Sigma Xi. Avocations: sports, reading, gardening. Home: PO Box 502 Athens GA 30603-0502 Office: Cook Noell Tolley Bates & Michael LLP 304 E Washington St Athens GA 30601-2751

HOUSER, RUTH G. financial executive; b. Virginia Beach, Va., Feb. 25, 1953, BS in Acctg. cum laude, Wheeling Coll., 1975. CPA, Fla., Ga., W.Va. Sr. acct. Price Waterhouse, Pitts., 1975-79; mgr. Lockheed Space Opers. Co., Cape Canaveral, Fla., 1980-84; mgr. info. systems AT&T, Morristown, NJ, 1984—87, fin. dir. France and Italy Paris, 1987-89, mgr. acctg. policy Morristown, 1989-90, dir. billing svcs. Bridgewater, N.J., 1990-92, controller, Network Wireless Systems Morristown, N.J., 1992-93; fin. billing team dir. WorldPartners/WorldSource AT&T, Bridgewater, N.J., 1993-95; dist. mgr. Lucent Technologies Intellectual Property, Coral Gables, Fla., 1995-98; revenue assurance mgr. Data Networking Svcs., St. Petersburg, Fla., 1998-99; CFO, mergers and acquisitions mgr. Lucent Technologies, Tierra Verde, Fla., 1999—2001; contr. intellectual property Agere Sys., Orlando, Fla., 2001—. Vol. C. Dillon Libr., Bedminster, NJ, 1985, v.p. bd. trustees, 1988—92; sec., trustee Friends of C. Dillon Libr., 1992—95; committeewoman Bedminster Twp., 1995; trustee Ct. Against Spouse Abuse, St. Petersburg; treas. League to Aid Abused Children and Adults, St. Petersburg, 1999—2001, Cross of Lorraine Am. Lung Assn., 1999—2002, Disney 2002 Marathon, Orlando, Fla.; chmn. spring spectacular Ct. Against Spouse Abuse, St. Petersburg, 2001; mem. Heart of Fl. United Way Leadership Club, Fla., 2001; CFO Col. Potter Cairn Terrier Rescue, 2002—; committeewoman Somerset County Reps. Dist. 5, Bedminster, 1993—95. Recipient Cmty. Vol. award, Queen's Ct., Inc., 2001. Mem. AICPA, FICPA. Avocations: international travel, reading, sports. Home: 13524 Turtle Marsh Loop 611 Orlando FL 32837 Office: Agere Sys Rm 301C 1250 9333 John Young Pkwy Orlando FL 32819

HOUSE-SOREMEKUN, BESSIE, political science educator; b. Lanett, Ala. d. William Penn House Sr. and Jo Frances House; m. Maurice Soremekun, July 14, 2001; 1 child, Adrianna Midamba. BA Magna Cum Laude in English, Huntingdon Coll., 1978; MA in internat. studies, U. Denver, 1980, PhD in internat. studies, 1988. Asst. prof. to assoc. prof. Kent State U., Dept of Polit. Sci., Kent, Ohio, 1989—. Exec. dir., founder Ctr. for the Study and Develop. of Minority Bus., Kent, Ohio, 2003. Author: Confronting the Odds: African American Entrepreneurship in Cleveland, Ohio, 2002 (Henry Howe Book Award, 2003); co-editor: African Market Women and Economic Power: The Role of Women in African Economic Development, 1995; author: Class Development and Gender Inequality in Kenya, 1990. Grantee, Cleve. Found., 1999—2002, Ohio Bd. of Regents, 1997—99, Ohio Urban U. Program, 1995, 2000. Mem.: Assn. of Afro Life and Hist., African Studies Assn., Links, Inc., Kent Chpt., Phi Beta Delta, Alpha Beta, Sigma, Sigma, Sigma. Democrat. Methodist. Avocations: reading, writing books, writing poetry. Home: PO Box 22226 Beachwood OH 44122 Office: Kent State U Kent OH 44242 Office Fax: 330-672-5303. E-mail: bhouse@kent.edu.

HOUSE-WADE, SUSAN PATRICIA, writer, educator; b. Denver, Sept. 7, 1963; d. Albert Richard Jr. and June (McPherson) H. BA, U. Tex., 1984; MA, U. London, 2000. Bur. chief Southwest Newswire, Houston, 1984-90; acct. exec. Tichenor Media Sys., Houston, 1990-94; comm. cons. IES, Osaka, Japan, 1994-96; author, lectr. on Japan, 1996—; exhbn. co-organizer Japan Soc., Japan, 2001—. Vol. svcs. bd. dirs. Inst. Internat. Edn., Houston. Mem.: Clan MacPherson Assn., U. Tex. Ex-Students Assn. (London), Japan Soc. (London) (chmn. arts com. 2002—), Oriental Ceramic Soc. (London), Am. Women's Club (co-chmn. arts and antiques com. 2002—).

HOUSEWORTH, RICHARD COURT, state agency administrator; b. Harveyville, Kans., Jan. 18, 1928; s. Court Henry and Mabel (Lynch) H.; m. Laura Louise Jennings, Nov. 1, 1952; children: Louise, Lucile, Court. BS, U. Kans., 1950. Mgmt. trainee Lawrence Nat. Bank, Kans., 1951-52; pres. 1st Nat. Bank, Harveyville, 1952-55; exec. v.p. Ariz. Bank, Phoenix, 1955-87, cons., 1987-88; dir. Export-Import Bank of the US, Washington, 1988-91; alt. U.S. exec. dir. The Inter-American Devel. Bank, Washington, 1991-93; supt. of banks, Banking Dept. State of Ariz., 1993—. Past chmn. Conf. of State Bank Suprs., Washington. Past pres. Better Bus. Bur., Tucson; past chmn. bd. Pacific Coast Banking Sch. U. Wash.; past pres. Barrow Neurol. Inst. of St. Joseph's Hosp.; past chmn. Valley of the Sun Visitors and Conv. Bur. Served with U.S. Army, 1946-48. Recipient 1st Disting. Service award Scottsdale Jaycees, 1962 Mem. Ariz. C. of C. (1st pres., dir.), Tucson C. of C. (past pres.), Am. Inst. Banking (past pres. Maricopa chpt.), Ariz. Bankers Assn. (past pres.), Urban League of Phoenix (past chmn.), Paradise Valley Club, Met. Club, Phi Delta Theta. Republican. Episcopalian. Home: 5434 E Lincoln Dr # 83 Paradise Valley AZ 85253-4118 Office: Supt of Banks 2910 N 44th St Ste 310 Phoenix AZ 85018-7270 E-mail: houseworth@azbanking.com.

HOUSHIAR, BOBBIE KAY, language arts educator; b. Fort Smith, Ark., Nov. 28; d. Ernest and Virgil Straham. BA, Saginaw Valley State U., 1973; MA in Elem. Edn. Adminstrn., Cen. Mich. U., 1975, Cert. Gen. Edn. Adminstrn., 1978. Elem. tchr. Saginaw (Mich.) Pub. Schs., 1973-74, jr. high tchr., 1975-76, tchr. middle sch., 1983—; learning ctr. coord. Saginaw Valley State U., University Center, Mich., 1974-75, instr. reading, 1974-75; tchr. ESL Refugee Ctr. of Saginaw, 1982-83. Instr. ind. study Cen. Mich. U., Saginaw, 1988-90; tutor bilingual students Delta Coll., Saginaw, 1987-96; supr./student tchrs. Saginaw Pub. Schs., 1988—; oratorical/writing instr. Saginaw Pub. Schs., 1983—. Editor: Young Writers in Michigan, 1989. Vol. Saginaw County chpt. ARC, 1996-99; mem./vol. League of Cath. Women, Saginaw, 1976—. Recipient Recognition award Saginaw Infant Mortality Coalition award, Saginaw Cooperative Hosp., 1998, Educator of Yr. award, Saginaw Coop. Hosp., 1999, Excellence in Tchg. English Writing Skills award, Saginaw Bd. Edn., 2002, Accent on Achievement award, Saginaw Pub. Sch. Bd. of Edn., 2002, others. Mem. NEA, Saginaw Edn. Assn., Mich. Edn. Assn., Nat. Coun. Tchrs. of English, ASCD, Mich. Mid. Sch. Assn., Delta Sigma Theta. Democrat. Roman Catholic. Avocations: reading, student mentor, tennis, swimming, horses. Office: South Middle Sch 224 N Elm St Saginaw MI 48602-2651 Personal E-mail: Siamak67@cs.com. Business E-Mail: BHoushiar@spsd.net.

HOUSKE, SISTER VIRGINIA, music educator, organist; b. St. Hilaire, Minn., Mar. 22, 1932; d. Oscar John and Viola Louise (Wilson) H. AA, Corbett Coll., 1968; BS in Music Edn. magna cum laude, U. N.D., 1971; postgrad., S.W. Minn. State coll., 1973. Joined Sisters of St. Benedict, Roman Cath. Ch., 1953. Tchr. Little Oak Sch. Dist. 165, Thief River Falls, Minn., 1951-52; novice Order of St. Benedict, Crookston, Minn., 1953-54; elem. and music tchr. Sacred Heart Sch., East Grand Forks, Minn., 1955-57, 63-71, St. Joseph Sch., Moorhead, Minn., 1957-59, 72-73, Red Lake Falls, Minn., 1959-62, 73-75, Cathedral Sch., Crookston, Minn., 1962-63; music tchr. Assumption Sch., Barnesville, Minn., 1971-72, 75-80, Mt. St. Benedict Conservatory, Crookston, Minn., 1980—, organist, 1980—, Cathedral of the Immaculate Conception, Crookston, Minn., 1994—. Organist Villa St. Vincent Chapel, Crookston, 1981—; music libr. Mt. St. Benedict Monastery, Crookston, 1970—. Soprano and Latin cons. Crookston Cmty. Chorus, 1982—; accompanist, organist numerous local groups, Crookston, 1980—. Mem. Music Tchrs. Nat. Assn. (cert.), Am. Guild Organists (program com. 1997—), Minn. Music Tchrs. Assn. (cert., contest chair N.W. dist. 1998—), Suzuki Assn. Am., Suzuki Assn. Minn., Pi Lambda Theta. Roman Catholic. Avocations: calligraphy, cats. Home: Mount St Benedict Crookston MN 56716 Office: Mount St Benedict Conservatory 620 Summit Ave Crookston MN 56716-2799 E-mail: vhouske@msb.net.

HOUSLEY, PHIL F. professional hockey player; b. St. Paul, Mar. 9, 1964; Mem. USA hockey team World Cup Tournament, 1982; with Buffalo Sabers, 1982-90; defenseman Winnipeg Jets, St. Louis Blues, 1993, Calgary Flames, 1994—96, 1998—2000, Washington Capitals, 1996—98, Chgo. Blackhawks, 2001—. Mem. World Jr. Hockey Championship Team, 1982, World Nat. Chapionship Hockey Team, 1982, '86,'89, 2000, 01; mem. Hockey World Cup Champions, 1986; named to NHL All Star game 1984, 89-93, 2000, Silver medalist in 2002 Olympic Hockey Games Office: Chgo Blackhawks United Ctr 1901 W Madison St Chicago IL 60612

HOUSMAN, TAMARA SALAM, dermatologist; M.D., U. of Louisville, Louisville, KY, 1993—97. MD NC, 2000. Resident in dermatology Wake Forest Univ Sch. of Medicine, Winston Salem, NC, 2002—, rsch. fellow- dept. of dermatology, 2000—02. Mem.: Am. Acad. of Dermatology. Office: Dept of Dermatology WFUSM Medical Center Blvd Winston Salem NC 27103

HOUSNER, GEORGE WILLIAM, retired civil engineering educator, consultant; b. Saginaw, Mich., Dec. 9, 1910; s. Charles and Sophie Ida (Schust) Housner. BSCE, U. Mich., 1933; PhD, Calif. Inst. Tech., 1941. Registered Calif. Engr. U.S. Corps Engrs., L.A., 1941—42; ops. analyst 15th Air Force, Libya, 1943—45, 1945—45, prof. engring. Calif. Inst. Tech., Pasadena, 1945—, prof. emeritus earthquake engring.; earthquake engring. cons. Pasadena, 1945—. Mem. Gov.'s Earthquake Coun., 1971—76, L.A. County Earthquake Commn., 1971—72; chmn. com. on earthquake engring. NRC, 1983—92, com. on internat. decade natural hazard reduction, 1986—88; chmn. seismic adv. bd. CALTRANS, 1990—94. Author (3 textbooks) ; contbr. articles to profl. jours. Recipient Disting. Civilian Svc. award, U.S. War Dept., 1945, Bendix Rsch. award, Am. Soc. Engring. Edn., 1967, Nat. medal Sci., 1988, The Washington award, Western Soc. Engrs., 1995. Mem.: ASCE (von Karman medal 1972, Newmark medal 1981), NAS (adv. panel on earthquake hazard 1981—83), NAE (Founders award 1991), Japan Acad., Earthquake Engring. Rsch. Inst. (pres. 1954—65), Internat. Assn. Earthquake Engring (pres. 1969—73), Seismol. Soc. Am. (pres. 1977—78, medal 1981). Office: Calif Inst Tech Dept Engring & Applied Sci 1200 E California Blvd Pasadena CA 91125-0001*

HOUSTON, ALLAN WADE, professional basketball player; b. Louisville, Apr. 4, 1971; married. BA in African-Am. Studies, U. Tenn., 1993. Guard Detroit Pistons, 1993—96, New York Knicks, 1996—. Achievements include NBA Draft first round eleventh pick, 1993. Office: New York Knicks Madison Square Garden 2 Penn Plz New York NY 10121-0101

HOUSTON, CAROL OLSON, educator, accounting; b. Tacoma, Wash., Aug. 7, 1951; d. E. Goodwin and Dorothy (Brown) Olson; m. Arthur L. Houston, Jr., Sept. 8, 1984. BA in History and German, Pacific Luth. U., 1973, MBA in Acctg., 1979; PhD in Bus., U. Wash., 1986. CPA Wash. Corr. Creditanstalt Bankverein, Vienna, 1973-74; sr. clk. Internat. Inst. Applied Systems Analysis, Laxenburg, Austria, 1974-77; staff acct. Brink and Sadler CPA's, Tacoma, 1979-80; asst. prof. Pacific Luth. U., Tacoma, 1980-82, San Diego State U., 1986-92, assoc. prof., 1992—98, prof., 1999—. Presenter in field. Contbr. articles to profl. jours. Mem. Am. Acctg. Assn. (various offices 1989—), Calif. Soc. CPA's (San Diego chpt. bd. dirs. 1987-88), Acad. Internat. Bus., Golden Key Soc., Beta Gamma Sigma, Beta Alpha Psi. Office: San Diego State U Sch Acctg 5500 Campanile Dr San Diego CA 92182-0002

HOUSTON, C(LARENCE) STUART, radiologist, educator; b. Williston, N.D., Sept. 26, 1927; s. Clarence Joseph and Sigridur (Christianson) H.; m. Mary Isabel Belcher, Aug. 12, 1951; children: Stanley, Margaret, David, Donald. MD, U. Man., Winnipeg, Can., 1951; DLitt, U. Sask., Saskatoon, Can., 1987. Demonstrator in anatomy U. Sask., 1960-61, teaching fellow in radiology, 1963-64, lectr., 1964-65, asst. prof., 1965-67, assoc. prof., 1967-69, prof., 1969-95, emeritus prof., 1995—, head dept. med. imaging, 1982-87. Author: To the Arctic by Canoe, 1974, Pioneer of Vision, 1980, Arctic Ordeal, 1984, R.G. Ferguson, Crusader, 1991, Arctic Artist, 1994, Steps on the Road to Medicare, 2002, Eighteenth-Century Naturalists of Hudson Bay, 2003; editor jour. Can. Assn. Radiologists, 1976-81. Recipient Roland Michener Conservation award Can. Wildlife Fedn., 1986, Douglas H. Pimlott Conservation award Can. Nature Fedn., 1988, Ralph D. Bird award Man. Naturalists' Soc., 1989, Doris Huestis Speirs award Soc. Can. Ornithologists, 1989, Eugene Eisenmann medal Linnean Soc. N.Y., 1990, Sask. Order of Merit, 1992, Officer of Order of Can., 1993. Mem. Can. Soc. for History of Medicine (pres. 1987-89), Royal Coll. Physicians and Surgeons (mem. coun. 1984-90, chmn. specialty com. 1984-88), Am. Ornithologists' Union (mem. coun. 1978-80, chmn. memls. com. 1984—, v.p. 1990-91). Avocation: bird banding. Home: 863 University Dr Saskatoon SK Canada S7N 0J8 E-mail: houstons@duke.usask.ca.

HOUSTON, DAVID WINSTON, federal judge; b. 1944; BBA, U. Miss., 1966, JD, 1969. Spl. agt. FBI, 1969-72; ptnr. Houston, Chamberlin & Houston, 1972-83; asst. dist. atty. 1st Jud. Dist., 1975-76; atty. City of Aberdeen, Miss., 1976-83, former mcpl. judge; bankruptcy judge U.S. Bankruptcy Ct. (no. dist.) Miss., Aberdeen, 1983—. Mem. Nat. Conf. Bankruptcy Judges (bd. govs. 1984-87, 89-91, pres. 1993-94), Am. Coll. Bankruptcy, 1st Jud. Dist. Bar Assn., Miss. Bar Assn. (bd. bar commrs. 1982-85), Monroe County Bar Assn. Office: US Bankruptcy Ct (no dist) Fed bldg 301 W Commerce St Aberdeen MS 39730-2520 Fax: 601-369-2635. E-mail: david_houston@msnb.uscourts.gov.

HOUSTON, DOROTHY MIDDLETON, elementary education educator; b. LaGrange, Ga., Oct. 23, 1936; d. Robert Meriwether and Marie Elizabeth (Davis) Middleton; m. Richard Gray Houston Sr., June 3, 1956; children: Jean, Ann, Richard Jr., Thomas Sandy. BS in Edn., U. Ga., 1958, MEd, 1970. Tchr. Auburn (Ga.) Elem. Sch., 1958-59; tchr. phys. edn. DuPont Manual High Sch., Louisville, 1959-62; instr. women's dept. phys. edn. U. Ga., Athens, 1970-71; tchr. phys. edn. Woodstock (Ga.) Elem. Sch., 1971-72, Brumby Elem. Sch., Marietta, Ga., 1972-77, Murdock Elem. Sch., Marietta, Ga., 1977-81; tchr. Teasley Elem. Sch., Smyrna, Ga., 1981-95; ret., 1995. Childcare program adminstr. Internat. Student Conf., Toccoa, Ga., 1986; tchr. tng. Pub. Schs. Ga., 1969-92. Mem.: Cobb-Marietta Ret. Educators (pres. 2001—02), Phi Kappa Phi. Baptist. Avocations: fitness, recreational crafts, gardening. Home: 1849 Service Dr NE Marietta GA 30066-1917

HOUSTON, E. JAMES, JR., bank officer, consultant; b. Highland Park, Mich., Sept. 25, 1939; s. Ernest James and Frieda Mary (Milligan) H.; m. Ann Draper, Dec. 16, 1961; children: James Lee, Jay Douglas, m. M. Aleen Bateman, Sept. 1, 2001, 1 child, Chanda Brae. BS in Finance, Wayne State U., 1964, MBA, 1967. Asst. v.p. Bank of the Commonwealth, Detroit, 1957-69; v.p. Birmingham Bloomfield Bank, Mich., 1969-70, pres., 1970-71; exec. v.p. Fidelity Bank Mich., Birmingham, 1971; pres. Houston & Assocs., Inc., Birmingham, 1971-91; mgr. loan rev. Republic Bancorp Inc., Ann Arbor, Mich., 1991-93, mgr. loan control, 1993-94, loan control officer, 1994-95, v.p. loan control, 1995—2003; v.p. strategic asset mgmt. dept. Franklin Bank, N.A., Southfield, Mich., 2003—. Lectr. fin. Wayne State U. Sch. Bus. Adminstrn. Detroit, 1971—. Active Bloomfield Hills Hockey Assn.; pres. pro tem Village of Bingham Farms Village Council; chmn. Southfield Twp. Citizens' Com.; v.p. Hickory Hollow Homeowners Assn.; trustee Southeastern Oakland County Water Authority; mem. Community House Assn., Birmingham; bd. dirs. CATV Birmingham YMCA; mem. parents council Brookside Sch., Cranbrook, Mich.

pres. Brookside Sch. Dads Club; mem. Cranbrook Arena Com. Mem. Birmingham-Bloomfield C. of C., Greater Detroit C. of C. Clubs: Wayne State U. Alumni;. Lodges: Rotary. Republican. Presbyterian. Address: 1318 Jay St Waterford MI 48327

HOUSTON, ELIZABETH REECE MANASCO, correctional education consultant; b. Birmingham, Ala., June 19, 1935; d. Reuben Cleveland and Beulah Elizabeth (Reece) Manasco; m. Joseph Brantley Houston; 1 child, Joseph Brantley Houston III. BS, U. Tex., 1956; MEd, Boston Coll., 1969. Cert. elem. tchr., Calif., cert. spl. edn. tchr., Calif., cert. community coll. instr., Calif.; cert. adminstr., Calif. Tchr., elem. Ridgefield (Conn.) Schs., 1962-63; staff, spl. edn. Sudbury (Mass.) Schs., 1965-68; staff intern Wayland (Mass.) High Sch., 1972; tchr., home bound Northampton (Mass.) Schs., 1972-73; program dir. Jack Douglas Ctr., San Jose, Calif., 1974-76; tchr. specialist spl. edn., coord. classroom svcs., dir. alternative schs. Santa Clara County Office Edn., San Jose, Calif., 1976-94. Instr. San Jose State U., 1980—86, U. Calif., Santa Cruz, 1982—85, Santa Clara U., 1991—94; cons. Houston Rsch. Assocs., Saratoga, Calif., 1981—; mem. neighborhood accountability bd. County of Santa Clara Probation Dept., 2002—. Author: (manual) Behavior Management for School Bus Drivers, 1980, Classroom Management, 1984, Synergistic Learning, 1986, Learning Disabilities in Psychology for Correctional Education, 1992. Recipient President's award Soc. Photo-Optical Instrumentation Engrs., 1979, Classroom Mgmt. Program award Sch. Bds. Assn., 1984, Svc. to Youth award, Juvenile Ct. Sch. Adminstrs. of Calif., 1989-94; grantee Santa Clara County Office Edn. Tchr. Advisor Program U.S. Sec. Edn., 1983-84. Home: 12150 Country Squire Ln Saratoga CA 95070-3444

HOUSTON, FRANK MATT, dermatologist; b. New Orleans, Dec. 15, 1939; s. Matt Francis and Amanda Vallie (Welch) H.; m. Helen Butler, Apr. 24, 1965; children: F. Matt, Catherine E.C., Amanda J.B. BS, La. State U., 1960, MD, 1964. Diplomate Am. Bd. Dermatology. Intern Johns Hopkins U., Balt., resident; physician, dermatologist Greensboro (N.C.) Dermatology Assocs., 1970—. Cons. Moses H. Cone Hosp., Greensboro, N.C., Wesley Long Hosp. Greensboro, 1970—; adj. asst clin. prof. dermatology U. N.C. Sch. of Medicine, Chapel Hill, 1980—. Bd. dirs. Greensboro Hist. Mus., Greensboro Preservation Soc., Greensboro Symphony Soc., Greensboro Opera Co. Capt. U.S. Army, 1965-71. Fellow Am. Acad. Dermatology; mem. AMA. N.C. Soc. Medicine, Royal Coll. of Physicians, Am. Coll. Physicians, Am. Skin Assn. (scientific adv. com. to bd. dirs.), Greensboro City Club (bd. dirs.). Republican. Episcopalian. Avocations: travel, aerobics, music. Office: Greensboro Dermatology 2704 Saint Jude St Greensboro NC 27405-3670

HOUSTON, GERRY ANN, oncologist; b. Baldwyn, Miss., July 16, 1953; d. Jeff Davis and Frances Holland (Agnew) Goodson; m. Terry L. Houston, Dec. 18, 1976 (dec. May 1987); 1 child, Claire Holland; m. Abe John Malouf, July 23, 1988. BA, U. Miss., 1974, MD, 1978. Diplomate Am. Bd. Internal Medicine, Am. Bd. Medical Oncology, Am. Bd. Hospice and Palliative Care. Intern U. Med. Ctr., Jackson, Miss., 1978-79; resident U. Med. Ctr., Jackson, Miss., 1979-81, fellow oncology, 1981-83; ptnr. Jackson (Miss.) Oncology Assocs., 1987—. Staff physician Miss. Bapt. Med. Ctr., Jackson, 1983—, Ctr. Miss. Med. Ctr., Jackson, 1983—, St. Dominic Hosp., Jackson, 1983—, River Oaks Hosp., Jackson, 1983—, Univ. Med. Ctr., Jackson, 1983—; med. dir. Hospice Ministries, Jackson, 1989—; mem. exec. com. Bapt. Med. Ctr., 1994, chief of staff, 2003—; med. dir. Bapt. Comprehensive Breast Ctr., 1997—. Contbr. articles to profl. jours. Chmn. exec. com. Miss. divsn. Am. Cancer Soc., 1993-95, pres., bd. dirs., 1989-93. Clin. rsch. fellow Am. Cancer Soc. Fellow ACP; mem. AMA, Nat. Hospice Orgn., Acad. Hospice Physicians, So. Assn. Oncology, Am. Soc. Clin. Oncology, Alpha Omega Alpha. Episcopalian. Avocations: jogging, reading, snow skiing. Office: Jackson Oncology Assocs 1227 N State St Ste 101 Jackson MS 39202-2413 E-mail: ghouston@mbmc.org.

HOUSTON, GLORIA, author, educator, consultant; b. Marion, N.C., Nov. 24; d. James Myron and Ruth Houston; children: M. Diane Gainforth, Julie Ann Floen. BS, Appalachian State, 1963; MEd., U. S.Fla., 1983, PhD, 1989. Lit., writing cons. various orgns., 1979—; founding coord. Suncoast Young Authors Conf. Coll. Edn., U. So. Fla., Tampa, 1985-94, adjunct instr., 1982 87, vis. asst. prof., author-in-residence, 1989—; author-in-residence Western Carolina U., Cullowhee, NC, 1994—2002. Cons. IBM/Goodhousekeeping Tell Me a Story Project, 1989; lectr. in field; presenter workshops nationwide. Author: (juvenile and young adult) The Year of the Perfect Christmas Tree, 1988 (Pubs. Weekly best seller list, other commendations), Littlejim, 1990, My Great Aunt Arizona, 1991, Littlejim's Gift, 1994, Mountain Valor, 1995, Littlejim's Dreams, 1997, Bright Freedom's Song, 1998, How Writing Works, 2003, Miss Dorothy and Her Bookmobile, 2003; pub. numerous books; contbr. articles to various publs. and mags. Fla. Endowment for the Humanities scholar, 1988-89; recipient Disting. Alumnae award Appalachian State U., Excellence in Edn. award for Literacy from Partnerships in Edn., 1990. Mem. Authors Guild, Internat. Reading Assn. (Disting. Educator), Soc. Children's Book Writers. Avocations: travel, reading, folklore.

HOUSTON, GUY SPENCER, state legislator; b. Walnut Creek, Calif. m. Inge; 3 children. Pres. Residential Real Estate and Mortgage Fin. Co., 1991—; mayor Dublin, Calif.; mem., dist. 15 Calif. State Assembly, 2002—. Vice-chair Labor and Employment Com.; mem. Banking and Fin. Com.; chmn. Dublin Housing Authority; mem. Livermore-Amadore Valley Transit Authority. Mem. Alameda Ptnrs. in Edn., Dublin Youth Football. Republican. Mailing: PO Box 942849 Rm 4208 Sacramento CA 94249 Office: 734 3rd St Brentwood CA 94513*

HOUSTON, IVAN JAMES, insurance company executive; b. Los Angeles, June 15, 1925; s. Norman Oliver and Doris Talbot (Young) H.; m. Philippa Elizabeth Jones, July 15, 1946; children— Pamela, Kathleen, Ivan Abbott. BS, U. Calif., Berkeley, 1948; postgrad., U. Man., 1948-49; LLD, U. La Verne, 1993. With Golden State Mut. Life Ins. Co., L.A., 1948—, v.p., actuary, 1962-66, sr. v.p., actuary, 1966-70, pres., CEO, 1970-77, chmn., pres., 1977-80, chmn., CEO, 1980-90, chmn., 1990—. Bd. dirs. First Interstate Bank Calif., Pacific Telesis Corp., Family Savs. Mem. L.A. World Affairs Coun., 1970—; chmn. ctrl. region United Way, Inc., L.A., 1973-75, mem. corp. bd. dirs., 1973-80, v.p., 1973-75; bd. dirs. M & M Assn., L.A. Urban League, pres., 1977—; bd. fellows Claremont U. Ctr., 1972-80; bd. regents Loyola Marymount U., 1972-75, 79-82; bd. visitors Anderson Grad. Sch. Mgmt., UCLA, 1990-93; pres. City of L.A. Human Rels. Commn., 1993-95, 99-2000. With Inf. AUS, 1944-45. Decorated Purple Heart, Bronze Star; knight comdr. Order St. Gregory the Great. Fellow Life Office Mgmt. Inst.; mem. Am. Acad. Actuaries, Am. Soc. Pension Actuaries, Internat. Actuarial Assn., Los Angeles Actuarial Club, Conf. Cons. Actuaries (assoc.), Am. Coun. Life Ins. (dir.), Life Office Mgmt. Assn. (dir., mem. exec. com. 1972-75, chmn. 1979), Mil. Order of Purple Heart, Calif. C. of C. (dir.), Los Angeles Area C. of C. (dir.), Town Hall, Calif. Club, Cosmos Club, Kappa Alpha Psi, Sigma Pi Phi. Roman Catholic. Home: 5111 S Holt Ave Los Angeles CA 90056-1117 Office. 1999 W Adams Blvd Los Angeles CA 90018-3500 E-mail: ihouston@aol.com

HOUSTON, JAMES D. writer; b. San Francisco, Nov. 10, 1933; s. Albert Dudley and Alice Loretta (Wilson) H.; m. Jeanne Wakatsuki, Mar. 27, 1957; children: Corinne, Joshua, Gabrielle. BA in Drama, San Jose (Calif.) State U., 1956; MA in Lit., Stanford U., 1962. Lectr. in writing Stanford U., 1968-69, U. Calif., Santa Cruz, 1969-83, vis. prof., 1987-93; disting. vis. writer U. Hawaii, Honolulu, 1983-84; Allen T. Gilliland prof. telecom. San Jose State U., 1985-86; vis. writer U. Mich., Ann Arbor, fall 1985, U. Oreg., Eugene, 1994, George Mason U., Fairfax, Va., 1999. Mem. adv. bd. Squaw Valley Cmty. of Writers, Calif., 1990—, bd. dirs., 2001, Tandy Beal Dance Co., Santa Cruz, 1985-; adv. coun. Kiriyama Pacific Rim Book Prize, 2001; mem. PEN/Faulkner Found., Writers in Schs. Nat. Adv. Coun., 2002. Author: (novels) Between Battles, 1968, Gig, 1969 (Joseph Henry Jackson award 1967), A Native Son of the Golden West, 1971, Continental Drift, 1978, Love Life, 1985, The Last Paradise, 1998 (Am. Book award 1999), Snow Mountain Passage, 2001, others; (non-fiction) Californians: Searching for the Golden State, 1982 (Am. Book award 1983), The Men in My Life, 1987, In the Ring of Fire: A Pacific Basin Journey, 1997, others; co-author: (with Jeanne Wakatsuki Houston) Farewell to Manzanar, 1973, (with John R. Brodie) Open Field, 1975; films include Li'a, The Legacy of a Hawaiian Man, 1988, Listen to the Forest, 1991, The Hawaiian Way: The Art and Family Tradition of Slack Key, 1993, Words, Earth and Aloha: The Sources of Hawaiian Music, 1995 (Silver Maile award 1995), Luther Kahekili Makekau: A One Kine Hawaiian Man, 1997, The Sons of Hawaii: A Sound, A Band, A Legend, 2000; (with Jeanne Wakatsuki Houston and John Korty) Farewell to Manzanar, 1976 (NBC World Premiere movie 1976, Humanitas prize 1976); contbr. numerous articles to popular jours. Mem. Calif. Coun. for Humanities, San Francisco, 1983-87, cons., 1988—; mem. steering com. Pacific Rim Film Festival, Santa Cruz, 1988—. Wallace Stegner Writing fellow Stanford U., 1966-67, rsch. fellow East-West Ctr., Honolulu, 1984, Resident fellow Rockefeller Found., Bellagio, Italy, 1995; fiction grantee Nat. Endowment for the Arts, 1976. Mem. PEN West, Western Am. Lit. Assn. (Disting. Achievement award 1999), Calif. Studies Assn. (Carey McWilliams award 2000). Avocations: bluegrass music, ragtime piano, hatha yoga. Home and Office: 2-1130 E Cliff Dr Santa Cruz CA 95062 E-mail: jhouston@cruzio.com.

HOUSTON, JAMES GORMAN, JR., state supreme court justice; b. Eufaula, Ala., Mar. 11, 1933; s. James Gorman and Mildred (Vance) H.; m. Martha Martin, Dec. 3, 1955; children: Mildred Vance, J. Gorman III. BS, Auburn U., 1955; LLB, U. Ala., 1956, JD, 1969. Bar: Ala. 1956. Law clk. to chief justice Ala. Supreme Ct., Montgomery, 1956-57; ptnr. Houston & Martin, P.C., Eufaula, 1960-85; assoc. justice Ala. Supreme Ct., Montgomery, 1985—. County atty. Barbour County, Clayton, Ala., 1961-79. Contbr. numerous opinions to So. Reporter; contbr. articles to profl. jours. Mayor pro tem, alderman City of Eufaula, 1964-70; pres. Heritage Assn., Eufaula, Ala., 1979-82; mem. Ala. Commn. on Uniform State Laws. 1st lt. JAGC, USAF, 1957-60. Named Citizen of Yr., City of Eufaula, 1979; recipient Alumni Achievement in Humanities award Auburn Univ., 1993. Fellow Am. Bar Found.; mem. ABA, Ala. Bar Assn., Ala. State Bar (examiner 1979-82, disciplinary commn. 1984-85, state bar commr. 1982-85), Barbour County Bar Assn. (pres. 1975), Eufaula C. of C. (pres. 1974). Republican. Methodist. Office: Ala Supreme Ct 300 Dexter Ave Montgomery AL 36104-3741

HOUSTON, JOSEPH BRANTLEY, JR., optical instrument company executive; b. Birmingham, Ala., June 15, 1934; s. Joseph Brantley and Inez (Graben) H.; m. Elizabeth Reece Manasco; 1 child, J. Brantley III. AB in Astronomy, U. Tex., 1956; MS, Northeastern U., 1969. Commd. 2d lt. C.E., U.S. Army, 1956, advanced through grades to capt., 1968; optical engr. Perkin-Elmer, Wilton, Conn., 1961-64; mgr. massive optics, chief engr. underwater optical sys. Itek Corp., Lexington, Mass., 1964 71; asst. to pres. Kollmorgen E-O Divsn., Northampton, Mass., 1971-73; v.p. advanced devel. and spl. projects Itek Corp., Sunnyvale, Calif., 1973-81; founder Houston Rsch. Assocs., Saratoga, Calif., 1981—, Houston Tech. Internat., Inc., San Jose, Calif., 1991-97; founder, exec. dir. Forum for Mil. Applications of Directed Energy, Huntsville, Ala., 1989-96. Contbr. articles to profl. jours.; inventor. Recipient Outstanding Civilian Svc. medal U.S. Army, 1987. Fellow Internat. Soc. Optical Engring. (life; pres. 1977-78, advanced tech. advisor 1981—, Goddard award 1982); mem. Optical Soc. Am. (founder, chair Fabrication and Testing Tech. Group, editor Optical Workshop Notebook). Office: 12150 Country Squire Ln Saratoga CA 95070-3444

HOUSTON, STANLEY DUNSMORE, retired public relations executive; b. Toronto, July 17, 1930; s. Archibald Laing and Mary (Dunsmore) H.; m. Pauline Lennox, Oct. 20, 1955 (div. July 1975); children: Wayne Cameron, Scott Gregory, Kevin Edward; m. Suzanne Fogarty, Sept. 15, 1978 (div. Nov. 1990). Grad. secondary sch., Humberside Collegiate, Toronto, 1948. Journalist editor Toronto Telegram, 1948-59; exec. v.p. Pub. Rels. Svcs. Ltd., Toronto, 1959-72; pres., chief exec. officer The Houston Group Communications Ltd., Toronto, 1972-90; chmn., chief exec. officer Edelman Houston Group, Toronto, 1990-96. Dir. L'Agence des Relationnistes de Montreal, 1974, Toronto Waterfront Coun., 1988-92, Daniel J. Edelman, Inc., Chgo.; mem. editorial adv. bd. The Sponsorship Report, Toronto. Author feature articles Macleans, Mayfair, Saturday Night; organized World Curling Championship, 1959-69; founder Can. Ladies Curling Assn. and Championship, 1960; promoted 1st Can. World Cup Ski Race, 1965; inaugurated Can. Grand Prix auto race, 1967; created duMaurier Classic (LPGA major golf event), 1974. Mem. Can. Ladies Profl. Golf (pres. 1974), Ont. M.S. Soc. (dir. 1984-87), Can. Pub. Rels. Soc., Nat. Club, World Trade Ctr., Credit Valley Golf and Country Club, Variety Club of Ont., Tent 28.

HOUSTON, THOMAS PRICE, family physician, medical association official; b. Starkville, Miss., Aug. 27, 1951; s. P.D. Jr. and Jean Porter (Benison) H.; m. Cheryn Elizabeth Alten, July 1983; 1 child, Stephen. BA in Biology and Chemistry, U. Miss., Oxford, 1973; MD, U. Miss., Jackson, 1977. Diplomate Am. Bd. Family Practice. Resident in family practice U. Miss., Jackson, 1977-80, chief resident, 1979-80; asst. prof. family medicine Ohio State U., Columbus, 1981-83; assoc. dir. family practice residency program Floyd Med. Ctr., Rome, Ga., 1983-86; assoc. prof. family medicine, dir. family practice residency U. Kans. Sch. Med., Wichita, 1986-90; dir. dept. preventive medicine and pub. health AMA, Chgo., 1990-96, dir. sci. and pub. health adv. programs, 1996—. Dir. SmokeLess States Nat. Tobacco Prevention and Control Program, 1993—; co-chair 11th World Conf. on Tobacco or Health, 2000; cons. tobacco prevention and control for state, fed. and internat. govts. and agys. Author, editor AMA Guideline for Diagnosis and Treatment of Nicotine Dependence, 1994, assoc. editor Guides to the Evaluation of Permanent Impairment, 1994, editl. adv. bd. Tobacco Control: Internat. Jour., 1993—, editl. bd. Am. Jour. Preventive Medicine, 2001—; contbr. articles to med. jours. Bd. dirs. Ill. divsn. Am. Cancer Soc., Chgo., 1994—2002. Recipient The Surgeon Gen.'s medallion AMA, 1988, award for disting. svc. on behalf of Am.'s Youth, 1990; Carrier scholar U. Miss., 1969-73; grantee Robert Wood Johnson Found., 1993—. Fellow Am. Coll. Preventive Medicine (chmn. program planning com. ann. meeting 1997); mem. Am. Acad. Family Physicians (mem. health edn. com.). Methodist. Avocations: gardening, cooking, travel, music. Home: 817 Brighton Dr Wheaton IL 60187-8109 Office: Am Med Assn 515 N State St Chicago IL 60610-4325 Fax: 312-464-4111. E-mail: thomas_houston@ama-assn.orh.

HOUSTON, WHITNEY, vocalist, recording artist; b. East Orange, N.J., Aug. 9, 1963; d. John R. and Cissy Houston; m. Bobby Brown, July 18, 1992; 1 child, Bobbi Kristina Houston Brown. HHD (hon.), Grambling U. Trained under direction of mother, mem. New Hope Bapt. Jr. Choir, 1974, background vocalist Chaka Khan, Lou Rawls, Cissy Houston, 1978, appeared in Cissy Houston night club act, record debut (duet with Teddy Pendergrass) Hold Me, 1984, albums Whitney Houston, 1985, Whitney, 1986, I'm Your Baby Tonight, 1990, My Love Is Your Love, 1999, songs Greatest Love of All, Saving My Love For You, Didn't We Almost Have It All, You're Still My Man, I'm Your Baby Tonight, 1991, (duet with Mariah Carey from Prince of Egypt soundtrack) When You Believe, 1998, appeared in HBO TV spl. Welcome Home, Heroes, With Whitney Houston, 1991, fashion model Glamour Mag., Seventeen mag., 1981, actress (films) The Bodyguard, 1992, Waiting To Exhale, 1995, The Preacher's Wife, 1996 (Image award Outstanding Lead Actress in a motion picture, 1997), Scratch the Surface, 1997, Anything for You, 2000, (TV miniseries) Cinderella, 1997; prodr.: (films) The Princess Diaries, 2001. Founder The Whitney Houston Found. for Children, Inc. Nominee 4 times 1994, 87; recipient Grammy award for Best Female Pop Performance, 1985, Best Female R&B Vocal Performance, 2000, Winner Am. Music award, 1985 (2), 1986 (5), 1988 (2), 7 Am. Music awards, 4 #1 Single Record awardist of Yr. Billboard mag., 1986, BET Lifetime Achievement award, 2002. Office: care John Houston Nippi Inc 2160 N Central Rd Fort Lee NJ 07024-7547

HOUSTON, WILLIAM ORRIS, JR., oral and maxillofacial surgeon; b. Pueblo, Colo., Aug. 8, 1931; s. William O. and Vera Loretta (Hornback) H.; m. Betty Jean Freeman, Sept. 6, 1952; children: Kelly, Shelly. Student, St. Martin's Coll., Olympia, Wash., 1949-51; DDS, Creighton U., 1955; postgrad., U. Pa., 1958-59, Geisinger Med. Ctr., Danville, Pa., 1959-61. Diplomate Am. Bd. Oral and Maxillofacial Surgery. Pvt. practice, Boise, Idaho, 1961—2001; ret., 2001. Staff mem. St. Alphonsus Regional Med. Ctr., Boise, 1961—, bd. dirs., 1973-95; staff mem. St. Luke's Regional Med. Ctr., Boise, 1961—; cons. VA Med. Ctr., Boise, 1961— Bd. trustees Boise Ind. Sch. Dist., 1972-82. Recipient St. George medal Am. Cancer Soc., 1992. Fellow Am. Coll. Dentists, Internat. Coll. Dentists; mem. ADA, Idaho Dental Assn., Am. Assn. Oral and Maxillofacial Surgeons, Idaho Soc. Oral and Maxillofacial Surgeons, Rotary, KC. Republican. Roman Catholic. Avocations: skiing, fishing, camping. Home: 5521 Lubkin St Boise ID 83706-1027

HOUSTON, WILLIAM ROBERT MONTGOMERY, ophthalmic surgeon; b. Mansfield, Ohio, Nov. 13, 1922; s. William T. and Frances (Hursh) H.; B.A., Oberlin Coll., 1944; M.D., Western Res. U., 1948; m. Marguerite LaBau Browne, Apr. 25, 1968; children: William Erling Tenney, Marguerite Elisabeth LaBau, Selby Cabot Truitt Vanderbilt. Intern, Meth. Hosp. Bklyn., 1948-49, Ill. Eye and Ear Infirmary, Chgo., 1949-50; resident N.Y. Eye and Ear Infirmary, 1950-52; practice medicine specializing in ophthalmic surgery, Mansfield, 1952—; fellow retinal vascular disease NYU, 1968-69; mem. staffs Mansfield Gen. Hosp., Mansfield, N.Y. U. Bellevue Med. Center, N.Y.C.; assoc. prof. clin. ophthalmology N.Y. U. Sch. Medicine. Pres. Mansfield Symphony Soc., 1965-68, Mansfield Civic Music Assn., 1965; mem. Mansfield City Sch. Bd., 1962-65, v.p., 1965. Served to capt. M.C. USAF, 1952-55. Diplomate Am. Bd. Ophthalmology. Recipient Honor award Acad. Ophthalmology. Fellow Internat. Coll. Surgeons; mem. SR (color guard 1961-71), Nat. Geneal. Soc. (award of Merit), Ohio Hist. Soc. (life), Western Res. Hist. Soc. (life fellow), N.Y. Geneal. and Biog. Soc. (life), Ohio Geneal. Soc. (trustee 1955—). Editor, Ohio Records and Pioneers Families, 1970—. Address: 456 Park Ave W Mansfield OH 44906-3118

HOUT, MICHAEL, sociologist, educator; b. May 14, 1950; BA in Sociology and History, U. Pitts., 1972; MA in Sociology, Ind. U., 1973, PhD in Sociology, 1976. Asst. prof. U. Ariz., 1976—82, assoc. prof., 1982—85, U. Calif., Berkeley, 1985—88, prof., 1988—, chair dept. sociology, 1988—91, dir. Survey Rsch. Ctr., 1992—98. Vis. prof. U. Coll., Dublin, 1983—84, Dublin, 1991. Named Disting. Grad. Sch. Alumnus, Ind. U., 2000; fellow, John Simon Guggenheim Meml. Found., 1985—86; Tng. fellow, NIMH, 1972—76, Vis. fellow, Russell Sage Found., 1996—97. Mem.: AAAS, NAS, Sociol. Rsch. Assn., Am. Polit. Sci. Assn., Internat. Sociol. Assn., Population Assn. Am. (Clifford C. Clogg Meml. award 1996), Am. Sociol. Assn. Office: Survey Rsch Ctr 2538 Channing Way Berkeley CA 94720-5100 Office Fax: 510-643-6874. Business E-Mail: mikehout@uclink4.berkeley.edu.*

HOUTCHENS, BARNARD, retired lawyer; b. Johnstown, Colo., Aug. 5, 1911; s. Everet Harrison and Evelyn Mary (Barnard) H.; m. Margaret Belle Colvin, Dec. 28, 1940; children: John Barnard, Marilyn (dec.). BA, U. Nebr., 1933, LL.B., 1935; LL.D., U. No. Colo. at Greeley, 1963. Bar: Colo. 1935. Practiced in, Greeley, 1935-90; ret., 1990; city atty., 1941-47, 49-50. Mem. bar com. Colo. Bd. Law Examiners, 1947-81, chmn., 1968-81 Trustee State Colls., Colo., 1948-65, pres. bd., 1964-65; nat. sec.-treas. Assn. Gov. Bds. State Univs. and Allied Instns., 1960-62; bd. dirs. U. No. Colo. Found., 1975-79, pres., 1978-79. Fellow Am. Coll. Trial Lawyers; mem. ABA, Colo. Bar Assn., Weld County Bar Assn. (pres. 1946-47), Greeley Jr. C. of C., Greeley C. of C. (pres. 1951-52), Blue Key, Sigma Chi. Clubs: Rotary, Elks (past exalted ruler Greeley), Masons. Home: 1020 48th Ave Greeley CO 80634-2316

HOUTCHENS, ROBERT AUSTIN, JR., biochemist; b. Denver, Mar. 31, 1953; s. Robert A. and Lorna G. (Smyth) H.; m. Cynthia Susan Barth, July 24, 1976; children: Hilary, Graham. BS in Engring. Sci., Colo. State U., 1975, PhD, 1980. Grad. research asst. biochemistry dept. Colo. State U., Ft. Collins, 1976-80; sr. research chemist Dow Chem. Co., Midland, Mich., 1980-84, project leader, 1984-89, DowElanco, 1989-90; sr. rsch. scientist BIOPURE Corp., Boston, 1990-94, tech. mgr., 1994-96, sr. tech. mgr., 1996-97, assoc. dir. process devel., 1997—. Contbr. articles on biochemistry to profl. jours. Patentee in field. Fellow Boettcher Found. Mem. Am. Chem. Soc., AAAS, Sigma Xi, Tau Beta Pi Home: 22 Briar Dr Milford MA 01757-1069 Office: BIOPURE Corp 11 Hurley St Cambridge MA 02141-2110

HOUTSMA, PETER C. lawyer; b. Denver, 1951; BA in Polit. Sci. and Econs. magna cum laude, U. Colo., 1973; JD magna cum laude, Cornell U., 1976. Bar: Colo. 1976. Mem. Holland & Hart, Denver, 1976—. Mem. Am. Arbitration Assn. (panel arbitrators), Order of Coif, Phi Beta Kappa. Office: Holland & Hart PO Box 8749 Denver CO 80201-8749

HOUTZ, DUANE TALBOTT, hospital administrator; b. Kansas City, Mo., Apr. 28, 1933; s. Dudley and Helen (Talbott) H.; m. Margaret McNiel; children: Erik Siegfried, Jamie Houtz Harvey. BS, U. Kans., 1955; MHA, Washington U., St. Louis, 1960. Asst. dir. Shands Teaching Hosp. and Clinics, Gainesville, Fla., 1961-65; asst. prof. Ctr. for Health and Hosp. Adminstrn., U. Fla., Gainesville, 1964-65; adminstr., exec. v.p. Baptist Med. Ctr., Montclair-Birmingham, Ala., 1965-75; hosp. dir. Alton Ochsner Med. Found., New Orleans, 1975-77; pres. Morton F. Plant Hosp., Clearwater, Fla., 1977-92, pres. emeritus, 1992—; nat. advisor to the health care industry Pershing Yoakley & Assocs., P.C., 1995-99. Chmn. Southeastern Hosp. Conf., 1986-87; chmn., pres. SunHealth Care Plans Fla., 1986-87; bd. dirs. SunHealth Enterprises Inc., SunHealth Corp.; advisor Corrigo Health Care Solutions, LLC, 1998—. Contbr. articles to profl. jours. Bd. dirs. Cmty. Svc. Coun., Birmingham, 1972-75, United Way of Pinellas County, 1987-93, campaign chmn. med. divsn., 1992-94; bd. dirs. Fla. League for Nursing, 1989-98, Bay Area Hosp. Coun./Tampa Bay Hosp. Coun., 1990-95, Morton Plant Found., 1990-96; mem. Fla. Geriatric Rsch. Bd., 1993-98; adv. bd. Jr. League Pinellas County, 1993-94; mem. Vets. Affairs Mgmt. Assistance Coun., 1996—; vice-chmn. Sun Coast Health Coun., 1998-2003. Capt. USAF, 1955-58. Recipient Acad. award USAF Basic Flight Sch., 1956, award of merit Fla. Hosp. Rsch. and Edn. Found., 1993, Washington U. Hosp. Adminstrn. Program Alumni of Yr. award, 1996; fellow Birmingham Bapt. Hosp. Found., 1985. Fellow Am. Coll. Healthcare Execs. (Regents award 1992); mem. Nat. League Nursing (bd. dirs.), Am. Hosp. Assn. (vice-chmn. council nursing 1983, rsch. com.), Assn. Voluntary Hosps. Fla. (bd. dirs. 1979-83, pres. 1979-80), Fla. Hosp. Assn. (trustee, bd. dirs. 1979-82), Greater Clearwater C. of C. (Outstanding Citizen selection com. 1982, bd. govs. 1984-87, bd. govs. 1987-88), Pinellas Suncoast C. of C. (adv. coun. 1984-87), Kiwanis (pres. Birmingham chpt. 1970-71), Phi Delta Theta. E-mail: dhoutz1@tampabay.rr.com.

HOUTZAGER, MARIANNE JOHANNA (MARIAN DE BOYEN), writer, artist, photographer; b. The Hague, Aug. 31, 1953; d. Joseph Houtzager and Gisèle Van Boeyen. HAVO, NTI, Rotterdam, Holland, 1972. Author: (booklet) The Winterwren, 1994, The Orca, 1995, (book) Action Skoatter in the Lead, 2000; one-person shows include (gouaches) Town Hall Krimpen a/d Yssel, 1976, (photographs) Wolvega Racecourse, 1996; exhibited group shows (gouaches) Gallery Los, Krimpen a/d Yssel, 1977. Recipient Am. Medal of Honor. Mem.: Internat. Order of Merit. Avocations: drawing, photographing, private flying, co-owner trotting horse. Home: PO Box 143 2920 AC Krimpen a/d Yssel Netherlands E-mail: mdeboyen@wanadoo.nl.

HOUX, MARY ANNE, investments executive; b. Kansas City, Mo., Aug. 16, 1933; d. Rial Richardson Oglevie and Geraldine Marie (McHale) Oglevie; m. Phillip Clark Houx, May 12, 1962 (dec. Dec. 1974); 1 child, Clark Oglevie. BS in Edn., U. Kans., 1954. Tchr. Kirkwood (Mo.) Pub. Schs., 1954-55, Kansas City (Kans.) Pub. Schs., 1955-57; asst. to v.p. Woolf Bros., Kansas City, Mo., 1957-59; Midwest dir. C.A.R.E., Inc., Kansas City, 1959-62; legal sec. Phillip C. Houx, Chico, Calif., 1962-74; owner Mary Anne Houx Investments, Chico, 1974—. Trustee Chico Unified Sch. Dist. Bd., 1977-90; coun. person City of Chico, 1990-91; 3rd dist. supr. County of Butte, Calif., 1991—. Named Woman of Yr., Calif. Assembly, 2001. Mem. Calif. Sch. Bds. Assn. (pres. 1987-88), Greater Chico C. of C. (Athena award 1993). Republican. Roman Catholic. Office: PO Box 1087 Chico CA 95927-1087

HOUZE, HERBERT GEORGE, writer; b. Brockville, Ont., Can., Apr. 18, 1947; s. McLean and Grace Lynham (Sayce) H.; m. Carolyn Pierce Johnson, July 8, 1972 (div. May 1990); children: Jennifer E., Alexander J. M., Andrew W.; m. Christine Mary Reinhard, Sept. 13, 1996. BA, McMaster U., Hamilton, Ont., 1969; MA, Vanderbilt U., 1971. Curator of mil. history Chgo. Hist. Soc., 1973-76; curator Winchester Mus. Buffalo Bill Hist. Ctr., Cody, Wyo., 1983-91. Advisor Royal Mil. Coll. Can. Mus., Kingston, Ont., 1979—; dir. John McLaren & Sons Distillers Ltd., London and Perth, 1990—. Author: (books) Knightly Musings, 1988, The Sumptuous Flaske, 1989, To the Dreams of Youth, 1992, Winchester History, 1994, Colt Rifles & Muskets, 1996, Winchester Model 52, 1997, Winchester Bolt Action Rifles, 1998, Winchester Model 1876 Centennial Rifle, 2001, Arming the West, 2001, Colt Presentations, 2002. Mem. Arms and Armour Soc. London, Armor & Arms Club N.Y., Les Amis du Musee de Liege.

HOVAN, REBECCA S. music educator; b. Louisville, Ky., July 31, 1961; d. Kenneth G. and Jo Ann Stockdell; m. Michael L. Hovan; children: Samuel, Christopher. MusB, Mid. Tenn. State U., 1983; MusM, U. North Tex., 1985. Tchg. fellow in flute U. North Tex., Denton, 1984—85; instr. Mid. Tenn. State U., Murfreesboro, 1986—90; flute instr.-preparatory program U. Notre Dame, South Bend, Ind., 2000—01; flute instr. Grace Coll. and Theol. Sem., Winona Lake, Ind., 2000—03; assoc. lectr. Ind. U. South Bend, 1995—; flute instr. Goshen Coll., Goshen, Ind., 2000—. Prin. flute Elkhart County Symphony, Elkhart, Ind., 1993—, Mid. Tenn. Symphony, Murfreesboro, 1986—89; pers. mgr./music libr. Elkhart County Symphony, Elkhart, Ind., 1999—2001; presenter pedagogy workshops. Children's choir dir. Calvary Assembly of God, Elkhart, Ind., 1997—2000. Recipient state finalist collegiate artist competition, Music Tchrs. Nat. Assn., 1983. Mem.: Nat. Assn. Coll. Wind and Percussion Instructors (assoc.), Am. Fedn. Musicians (assoc.), Nat. Flute Assn. (assoc.; pedagogy com. 2002, winner masterclass competition 1985). Office: Music Dept Goshen Coll 1700 S Main St Goshen IN 46526-4724

HOVANESSIAN, SHAHEN ALEXANDER, electrical engineer, educator, consultant; b. Tehran, Iran, Sept. 6, 1931; came to U.S., 1949; s. Alexander and Jenik (Thadeus) H.; m. Mary Mashourian, Sept. 17, 1960; children: Linda Larsen and Christina Tchaparian (twins). BSEE, UCLA, 1954, MSME, 1955, PhDEE, 1958. Registered profl. engr., Calif. Research scientist Chevron Research Corp., La Habra, Calif., 1958-63; sr. scientist Hughes Aircraft Co., El Segundo, Calif., 1963-86; sr. tech. specialist Aerospace Corp., El Segundo, Calif., 1986-96; lectr. UCLA, 1962—; cons. engr. L.A., 1996—. Mem. adv. group for aerospace R & D NATO, 1985-87. Author: (with Louis A. Pipes) Matrix—Computer Methods in Engineering, 1969; Digital—Computer Methods in Engineering, 1969; Radar, Detection and Tracking Systems, 1973; Computational Mathematics in Engineering, 1976; Synthetic Array and Imaging Radars, 1980; Radar System Design and Analysis, 1984; Introduction to Sensor Systems, 1988; (with Khalil Seyrafi) Introduction to Electro-Optical Imaging and Tracking Systems, 1993; editor Computers and Elec. Engring., 1973-76. Inventor radar computer Fellow IEEE (U.S. del. Moscow 1973, disting. lectr.); mem. ASME, Sigma Xi, Tau Beta Pi. Democrat. Roman Catholic. Avocations: investments, real estate. Home: 3039 Greentree Ct Los Angeles CA 90077-2020 E-mail: shovaness@aol.com.

HOVANNISIAN, RICHARD G. Armenian and Near East history educator; b. Tulare, Calif., Nov. 9, 1932; s. Kaspar and Siroon (Nalbandian) H.; m. Vartiter Kotcholosian, Mar. 2, 1957; children: Raffi, Armen, Ani, Garo. BA in History, U. Calif., Berkeley, 1954, MA in History, 1958; cert. in Armenian, Coll. Arménien, Beirut, 1956; PhD in History, UCLA, 1966; hon. doctorate, Erevan State U., Armenia, 1994, Artsakh State U., 1997. cert. tchr., Calif. Tchr. Fresno (Calif.) City Schs., 1958-62; lectr. Armenian UCLA, 1962-69, prof. Armenian and Near Ea. history, 1969—; chair modern Armenian history Armenian Ednl. Found., 1987—; assoc. dir. G.E. von Grunebaum Ctr. Near Ea. Studies UCLA, 1979-95. Assoc. prof. history Mt. St. Mary's Coll., L.A., 1965-69; advisor Calif. Bd. Edn., Sacramento, 1984-85, 86-88; cons. on multicultural edn.; lectr. to univ. and cmty. groups and profl. confs. worldwide; mem. U.S.-USSR commns. Am. Coun. Learned Socs., 1985-91, U.S. project coord. for study contemporary ethnic processes in U.S. and USSR. Author: Armenia on the Road to Independence, 1967, 4th edit., 1984, The Republic of Armenia, vol. I, 1971, vol. II, 1982, vols. III-IV, 1996, The Armenian Holocaust, 1980, The Armenian Genocide in Perspective, 1986; The Armenian Genocide: History, Politics, Ethics, 1992, The Armenian People form Ancient to Modern Times, vol. I, The Dynastic Periods: From Antiquity to the Fourteenth Century, vol. II, Foreign Dominion to Statehood: The Fifteenth to Twentieth Century, 1997, Remembrance and Denial: The Case of the Armenian Genocide, 1998, Armenian Van Vaspurakan, 2000; author: (with others) Transcaucasia: Nationalism and Social Change, 1983, Le Crime de Silence: Le Génocide des Arméniens, 1984, A Crime of Silence, 1985, Toward the Understanding and Prevention of Genocide, 1984, Genocide: A Critical Bibliographic Review, 1988, Embracing the Other: Philosophical, Psychological, and Historical Perspectives on Altruism, 1992, Diasporas in World Politics, 1993, Genocide and Human Rights, 1993, Genocide: Conceptual and Historical Dimensions, 1994, The Legacy of History in Russia and the New States of Eurasia, 1994; editor: The Armenian Image in History and Literature, 1981, Islam's Understanding of Itself, 1983, Ethics in Islam, 1985, Poetry and Mysticism in Islam: The Heritage of Rumi, 1994, The Thousand and One Nights in Arabic Literature and Society, 1997, The Persian Presence in Islam, 1998, Religion and Culture in Medieval Islam, 1999, Enlightenment and Diaspora: The Armenian and Jewish Cases, 1999; chmn. editorial bd. Armenian Rev., Ararat, Haigazian Armenological Rev., Mitk, Human Rights Rev.: Jour. of Soc. for Armenian Studies; contbr. numerous articles to profl. jours. Calif. rep. Western Interstate Commn. for Higher Edn., 1978-94; bd. dirs. Facing History and Ourselves Found., Internat. Alert, Found. for Rsch. on Armenian Architecture, Internat. Inst. Holocaust and Genocide Studies, Armenian Nat. Inst., Ctr. for Comparative Genocide Studies, Sydney, Australia, Armenian Ctr. for Nat. and Internat. Studies, Armenia. Recipient Nat. Svc. award Armenian Nat. Com. of Am., 1978, Man of Yr. award Armenian Profl. soc., 1980, Citizen of Yr. award Armenian Am. Citizens League, 1981, Citizen of Yr. award United Armenian Cultural Assn. of Chgo., 1981, Recognition award Armenian Cultural Assn., Fresno, Calif., 1982, Man of Yr. award Rep. Assembly Armenian Ch. Am., 1983, Recognition award Armenian Ednl. Found., 1984, Mesrop Mashdots medal and citation Catholicos of Cilicia, Lebanon, 1984, Person of Yr. award Armenian Cultural Assns. Western U.S., 1985, Disting. Scholar award and medal Armenian Cultural Assns. U.S. and Can., 1986, Recognition Program award Armenian Assembly and Hamazkaine, Nor Seroont and Tekeyan Cultural Assns., 1987, Humanity award Facing History and Ourselves Found., 1988, Dadian award for advancement of Armenian culture Armenian Students Assn. Am., 1990, Disting. Svc. award Armenian Nat. Com. Western U.S., 1996, Disting. Achievement award Internat. Soc. for Traumatic Stress Studies, 1998, Movses Khorenatsi award and medal Republic Armenia, 1998, Pan-Kharpert Assn., 2000, also other citations and recognitions; grantee NEH, 1981-82, Calif. Coun. Humanities, 1985-86; Humanities Inst. fellow, 1972, Guggenheim fellow, 1974-75. Fellow Middle East Studies Assn. (mem. editorial bd.), Am. Assn. Advancement of Slavic Studies; mem. Armenian Acad. Sci. (academician), Am. Hist. Assn., Soc. for Armenian Studies (founder, pres. 1974-75, 90-92, book rev. editor jour., mem. editorial bd.), Oral History Assn., Nat. Assn. Armenian Studies (hon.), Armenian Ednl. Found. (hon.). Armenian Apostolic. Office: UCLA Dept History PO Box 951473 Los Angeles CA 90095-1473

HOVDA, THEODORE JAMES, lawyer; b. Forest City, Iowa, Oct. 15, 1951; s. Ernest J. and Doris (Goodnight) H.; m. Susan J. Miller, Feb. 24, 1973; children: Theodore James III, Lee Joseph, Margaux Ann. BS, Iowa State U., 1973; JD, U. Iowa, 1977. Asst. county atty. Hancock County, Garner, Iowa, 1977-78, county atty., 1979-98; mem. Riehm & Hovda, Garner, 1977-98, Hovda Law Office, 1998—. County chmn. Hancock County Rep. Ctrl. Com., 1979-98. Mem. Iowa Bar Assn., Hancock County Bar Assn., Dist. 2A Bar Assn., Rotary, Masons. Republican. Methodist. Home: 785 11th Street Pl Garner IA 50438-1848 Office: Hovda Law Office PO Box 9 395 State St Garner IA 50438-0009 Fax: 641-923-3108. E-mail: tshovda@kalnet.com.

HOVDE, F. BOYD, lawyer; b. Mpls., Aug. 7, 1934; s. Frederick L. and Priscilla L. (Boyd) H.; m. Alice Austell, Feb. 22, 1981; children by previous marriage: Frederick R., Debra L., Kristine L., Sarah L. AB, Princeton U., 1956; JD, U. Mich., 1959. Bar: Ind. 1959, U.S. Dist. Ct. (no. and so. dists.) Ind. 1959, U.S. Ct. Appeals (7th cir.) 1960, U.S. Supreme Ct. 1977. Assoc. Ice, Miller, Donadio & Ryan, Indpls., 1959-67, ptnr., 1967-69, Townsend, Hovde & Townsend, Indpls., 1969-77; mem. Townsend, Hovde, Townsend & Montross, P.C., 1977-84, Townsend, Hovde & Montross, P.C., 1984-97, F. Boyd Hovde, P.C., 1985—, Hovde Law Firm, 1997—. Mem. com. on character and fitness Ind. Supreme Ct., 1976-2000, rules of practice and procedure, 1980-92. Mem. Indpls. Bar Assn. (treas. 1969, v.p. 1974, pres. 1979), ABA (del. 1980-83), Ind. Trial Lawyers Assn. (bd. dirs. 1970—, pres. 1976-77), Assn. Trial Lawyers Am., Am. Coll. Trial Lawyers, Internat. Acad. Trial Lawyers, Ind. Coll. Trial Lawyers, Indpls. Jaycees (pres. 1963-64), Ind. Golf Assn. (pres. 1974-75), Western Golf Assn. (dir. 1969-81, v.p. 1972-81), Crooked Stick Golf Club (Carmel, Ind.), Pine Valley Golf Club (Celmenton, N.J.), Old Marsh Golf Club (Palm Beach Gardens, Fla.). Office: Hovde Law Firm Ste 205 10585 N Meridian St Indianapolis IN 46290-1068

HOVDESTAD, WAYNE ROY, petroleum engineer; b. Kyle, Can., Feb. 8, 1958; s. Roy Osmond and Joann Shirley (Hanscam) H.; m. Michelle Diane Trew, May 17, 1980 (div. Mar. 1996); 1 child, William Roy Patrick; m. Maria Anatolievna Sinkova, Aug. 17, 1997; children: Stephanie Maria, Katherine Anna. BE, U. Saskatchewan, Can., 1979; ME, U. Calgary, Can., 1989. Engr. Texaco Can., Calgary, 1979-82, supr. engr., 1983-89; bus. engr. Texaco Inc., Houston, 1982-83; bus. devel. ESSO Can., Calgary, 1990-91; sr. engr. Petronas, Kuala Lumpar, Malaysia, 1991-94; pvt. practice Calgary, 1994-95; sr. planner Qatar Gen. Petroleum Corp., Doha, 1996-2000; sr. mgmt. Eurogas Corp., Calgary, 2000—. Contbr. articles to profl. jours. Grantee Govt. Alberta, Can., 1986. Orthodox Christian. Avocations: Aikido, Karate, languages. Office: Eurogas Corp Ste 440 333-5th Ave SW Calgary AB Canada T2P 3B6 E-mail: wrhovdestad@shawlink.ca.

HOVEL, ESTHER HARRISON, art educator; b. San Antonio, Tex., Jan. 12, 1917; d. Randolph Williamson and Carrie Esther (Clements) Harrison; m. Elliott Logan Hovel, Sept. 30, 1935; children: Richard Elliott, Dorothy Auverne. BA, Incarnate Word Coll., 1935; postgrad., Oxford U., 1979, British Inst. Art, Florence, Italy, 1980. Civil svc. auditor U.S. Govt. Office of Price Adminstrn., San Antonio, 1942-44; interior decorator Parkway Interior Design Studio, El Paso, Tex., 1968-72; instr. stained glass and sculpture El Paso Mus. Art, 1972-78; tchr. sculpture Albuquerque Sr. Ctrs., 1983-85. Docent El Paso Mus. Art, 1972-82. Exhibited sculpture Museo De Artes, Juarez, Mexico, 1981 (1st place 1981). Bd. dirs. YMCA, Albuquerque, 1963-64 (plaque 1964); charter mem. and bd. dirs. Contact Lifeline Internat., Albuquerque, 1982-92 (2 plaques 1986, 90); mem. Com. on Bicentennial of U.S. Constitution, Washington and N.M., 1987-89. Recipient 2 medals Exxon Corp., 1986, 89, Medal of Merit Pres. Ronald Reagan, 1987; grantee Exxon Corp., 1986, 90. Mem. Jr. League Internat. (various offices 1948-97, emeritus mem.), Rotary "Anns" (various offices). Republican. Mem. Christian Ch. Avocations: sculpture, stained glass, oil painting, travel, volunteerism. Home: 7524 Bear Canyon Rd NE Albuquerque NM 87109-3847

HOVER, JOHN CALVIN, II, banker; b. Orange, N.J., May 13, 1943; s. John Curry and Edith Margaret (Hopkins) H.; m. Jacqueline Whitley, Sept. 4, 1997; 1 child, Margaret Riddle. BA in English Lit. U. Pa. 1965, MBA in Mktg., 1967; postgrad., Aspen Inst., 1988. With Chem. Bank, 1968-76; with corp. banking and personal banking U.S. Trust Co. of N.Y., N.Y.C., 1976-80, sr. v.p., div. mgr., pvt. banking, 1980-91, exec. v.p. asset mgmt., pvt. banking group, 1991-98; retired, 1999. Chmn. U.S. Trust Pvt. Equity Fund; bd. dirs. New Hope & Ivyland R.R., Pa., Penn Club N.Y., Tweedy Browne Fund Inc.; chmn. bd. overseers, U. Mus., Phila. Trustee U. Pa., Phila. Mem. St. Nicholas Soc., 1st Troop Phila. City Cav., Soc. Colonial Wars, St. Andrews Soc., Most Venerable Order of Hosp. of St. John of Jerusalem, Knickerbocker Club, Univ. Club, Psi Upsilon. Avocation: railroadiana. Home: PO Box 676 3039 Durham Rd Buckingham PA 18912 E-mail: jhover@erols.com.

HOVING, JOHN HANNES FORESTER, consulting firm executive; b. N.Y.C., July 18, 1923; s. Hannes and Mary Alma (Gilbert) H.; m. Anne Fisher Spiers, Feb. 1, 1958; children: Christopher, Karen Anne, Katherine Jean. BA in History, U. Chgo., 1947. Radio news editor, reporter Milw. Jour., Capital Times, Madison, Wis., 1947-51; asst. to chmn. Democratic Nat. Com., 1952-54; exec. positions Kefauver, Stevenson, Johnson, Humphrey, Sanford presdl. campaigns; asst. to presdl. asst. for trade policy 1962; v.p. exec. action Air Transp. Assn. Am., Washington, 1956-64; propr. cons. firm Washington, 1964-72; sr. v.p. Federated Dept. Stores, Inc., Cin., 1972-82; pres. The Hoving Group (cons. firm), Washington, 1982—. Chmn. Washington Theol. Consortium, 1993-96; mem. adv. bd. Fashion Inst. Design Merchandising; past dep. chmn. planning Dem. Nat. Com. With AUS, 1943-46. Decorated Purple Heart, Bronze Star Mem. Am. Assn. Polit. Cons., Met. Club, Nat. Press Club, Nat. Capital Dem., Queen City Club (Cin.), Lotos Club (N.Y.C.). Home: 415 Dogleg Dr Williamsburg VA 23188

HOVING, THOMAS, museum and cultural affairs consultant, author; b. N.Y.C., Jan. 15, 1931; s. Walter and Mary (Osgood Field) H.; m. Nancy Melissa Bell, Oct. 3, 1953; 1 dau., Petrea Bell. BA, Princeton U., 1953, MFA, 1958, PhD, 1959, HHD (hon.), 1968; LHD (hon.), Hofstra U., 1966; LLD (hon.), Pratt Inst., 1967; DFA (hon.), NYU, 1968; LittD (hon.), Middlebury Coll., 1968. Staff Medieval Met. Mus. Art and The Cloisters, 1959-65, curator, 1965-66; commr. parks N.Y.C., 1966-67; adminstr. Dept. Recreation and Cultural Affairs, 1967; dir. Met. Mus. Art, 1967-77; pres. Hoving Assocs., Inc., museum and cultural affairs cons. firm, 1977—; pres. spl. mus. exhibitions The Planning Corp., 1983-91; arts and entertainment corr. ABC-TV show 20/20, 1978-84; editor Connoisseur mag., 1981-91. Author: Guide to the Cloisters, 1964, The Chase, The Capture, 1975, Kuerners and Olsons; exhbn. catalogue, 1976, Two Worlds of Andrew Wyeth: A Conversation with Andrew Wyeth, 1978, Tutankhamun, The Untold Story, 1978, King of the Confessors, 1981, Masterpiece, 1986, Discovery, 1989, Making the Mummies Dance, 1993, Andrew Wyeth: Autobiography, 1995, False Impressions, The Search for Big Time Art Fakes, 1996, Greatest Works of Art of Western Civilization, 1997, Art for Dummies, 1999, The Art of Dan Namingha, 2000; contbr. articles on art, parks and recreation to profl. publs., mags. and newspapers. Past trustee Inst. Fine Arts NYU. Lt. USMC, 1953-55. Decorated knight Legion of Honor France; recipient Bronze medal Citizens Budget Com., 1966, Cue mag. award, 1966, Disting. Achievement award Advt. Club Am., 1966, Disting. Contbn. award Park Assn. N.Y.C., 1967, Elsie de Wolfe award Am. Inst. Interior Designers, 1967, Woodrow Wilson award Princeton U., 1977 Mem. AIA (hon.) Office: Hoving Assocs Inc 150 E 73rd St New York NY 10021-4362 E-mail: tomhoving@earthlink.net.

HOVIS, ROBERT HOUSTON, III, lawyer; b. Washington, Apr. 19, 1942; s. Robert Houston Jr. and Lera Frances (Robbins) H.; m. Mary Ann Jennings, Dec. 27, 1965. BS, U. Tenn., 1964, JD, 1966. Bar: Tenn. 1967, Va. 1967, U.S. Dist. Ct. (ea. dist.) Va. 1973. Asst. commonwealth atty. Fairfax County, Va., 1969-71, pvt. practice law, 1971—; prin. Robert H. Hovis III PC, Annandale, Va.; commr. in chancery Circuit Ct. Fairfax County, 1969—. Commr. in chancery Cir. Ct. Fairfax County, 1969—. Mem. adv. coun. Salvation Army, Annandale, 1984—; bd. dirs. Annandale C. of C., 1984. With U.S. Army, 1967-69, Germany. Mem. ATLA (cert. Nat. Coll. Advocacy 1981, cert. Med. Malprctice Advanced Coll. 1983), Va. Trial Lawyers Assn. (profl. negligence sect.), Va. State Bar, Fairfax County Bar Assn., Trial Lawyers for Pub. Justice (Va. state coord. 1993—), Fairfax County Cir. Ct. (ind. case evaluator), Ethridge Soc., Rotary (pres. 1983-84). Mem. ATLA (cert. Nat. Coll. Advocacy 1981, cert. Med. Malpractice Advanced Coll. 1983), Va. Trial Lawyers Assn. (profl. negligence sect.), Trial Lawyers Assn. Met. Washington, Fairfax County Bar Assn., Va. State Bar, Trial Lawyers for Pub. Justice (Va. state coord. 1993—), Fairfax County Cir. Ct. (ind. case evaluator), Ethridge Soc., Million Dollar Advocates Forum. Lodges: Rotary (pres. 1983-84). Democrat. Methodist. Home: 2700 Green Holly Springs Ct Oakton VA 22124-1457 Office: 4544 John Marr Dr Annandale VA 22003-3308

HOVLAND, KENNETH ROGER, ophthalmologist, educator; b. Kankakee, Ill., Jan. 15, 1936; s. Roger Williams and Esther Margaret (Grondahl) H.; m. Sue Pendleton Egbert, Dec. 18, 1960; children: Peter G., Katherine A., Douglas A., Sarah L. BS, U. Ill., 1958, MD, 1962. Diplomate Am. Bd. Ophthalmology. Intern Colo. Gen. Hosp., Denver, 1962-63; resident in ophthalmology U. Colo., Denver, 1963-66; fellow in retina Mass. Eye and Ear Infirmary, Boston, 1967-68; instr. U. Colo. Med. Ctr., Denver, 1968-71, asst. clin. prof. ophthalmology, 1971-78, assoc. clin. prof., 1978-87, clin. prof., 1987—; vice-chair dept. ophthalmology U. Colo. Health Scis. Ctr., Denver, 1995—. Internat. vol. CARE-MEDICO, Algeria, 1966, Project HOPE, Tunisia, 1970, Project ORBIS, Burma, China, others, 1984—. Fellow: Am. Acad. Ophthalmology (Honor award 1980, Sr. Achievement award 2002); mem.: Denver Med. ., Colo. Med. ., Colo. Ophthal. Soc., Schepens Internat. Soc., Assn. Rsch. Vision Ophthalmology, Retina Soc. Avocations: music, sailing, hiking. Office: 850 E Harvard Ave Ste 505 Denver CO 80210-5078

HOVSEPIAN, DAVID MINAS, radiologist; b. N.Y.C., July 6, 1955; s. Edgar Minas and Marion Lyon Housepian; m. Adrienne Welch, July 25, 1978. BA, Columbia U., 1982, MD, 1986. Intern Overlook Hosp., Summit, NY, 1986—87; resident Presbyn. Hosp., N.Y.C., 1987—91; fellow Thomas Jefferson U. Hosp., Phila., 1991—93; attending physician Barnes-Jewish Hosp., St. Louis, 1993—. Asst. prof. radiology Sch. Medicine Washington U., St. Louis, 1993—99, assoc. prof. radiology Sch. Medicine, 1999—; mem. adv. panel Guidant Corp., Menlo Park, Calif., 1997—99; examiner Am. Bd. Radiology, Tucson, 2000—. Mem. editl. bd.: Jour. of Vasc. Interventional Radiology, 1996—, Radiology, 1997—2001 (Spl. Distinction in Reviewing award, 94), cons. to editor:, 2001—, reviewer: Jour. Vasc. Interventional Radiology, 1987—. Scholar Macy scholar, 1981. Mem.: AMA, Am. Soc. Reproductive Medicine, Soc. Interventional Radiology, Radiol. Soc. N.Am., Am. Coll. Radiology. Avocations: reading, physical fitness, bicycling, golf, skiing. Office: Mallinckrodt Inst Radiology 510 S Kings Hwy Blvd Saint Louis MO 63110 Fax: 314-362-2276. E-mail: hovsepiand@mir.wustl.edu.

HOW, HOTON, electrical engineer; b. Taichung, Taiwan, Oct. 10, 1954; s. Pei-Yin How and Su-Yien Kao; m. Qian Zhan, Mar. 29, 1957; 1 child, Joan Chi. DSc, MIT, 1987. Adj. prof. Northeastern U., Boston, 1996—; pres. Hotech, Inc., Belmont, Mass., 2001—. Cons. ElectroMagnetic Applications, Inc., Boston, 1991—. Contbr. articles to profl. jours.; 8 patents in field, 8 patents pending. Grantee, NSF, 1994, 1996, 2002, 2003. Home: 262 Cliftion St Belmont MA 02478 Office: Hotech Inc 829 Concord St # C Cambridge MA 02138 Home Fax: 617-489-4565; Office Fax: 617-489-4565. Personal E-mail: hotonhow@hotech.com. E-mail: hotonhow@hotech.com.

HOWALD, JOHN WILLIAM, lawyer; b. St. Louis, Dec. 21, 1935; s. Herbert John and Irene Dorothy (Weber) H.; m. Nina M. Zierenderg, June 15, 1957 (div. 1970); children: Deborah A., Catherine A., Laura A., John William; m. Betty L. Curtis, Feb. 14, 1971 (div. 1999); 1 stepchild, Tracy L.; m. Nancy J. Owens, Mar. 1, 2003. BS, U. Mo., 1957; JD, St. Louis U., 1962. Bar: Mo. 1962, U.S. Dist. Ct. (ea. dist.) Mo. 1962, U.S. Ct. Appeals (8th cir.) 1965, U.S. Supreme Ct. 1985. V.p. sales Eureka Svc. and Equip. Co., Eureka, Mo., 1959-62; ptnr. Sheehan, Furtaw & Howald, Hillsboro, Mo., 1963-64, Thurman, Nixon, Smith & Howald, Hillsboro, 1964-70, Thurman, Nixon, Smith, Howald, Weber & Bowles, Hillsboro, 1970-80, Thurman, Smith, Howald, Weber & Bowles, Hillsboro, 1989-91, Thurman, Howald, Weber, Bowles & Senkel, Hillsboro, 1991-95, Thurman, Howald, Weber, Senkel & Norrick, L.L.C., Hillsboro, 1995—. Bd. dirs. LaBarque Ent. of Jefferson County, Hillsboro, 1965-2002, Rustic Hills Resort Ltd., Hillsboro, 1968—. Mem. Mo. Ethics Commn., 1994-98, vice-chmn., 1995-96, chmn., 1996-98. Lt. (j.g.) USN, 1957-59. Recipient Spl. award, Meramec Basin Assn., 1967, 69. Fellow Am. Bar Found., Am. Coll. Trust and Estate Counsel (Mo. chmn. 1987-92), mem. ABA, Estate Planning Coun. St. Louis (pres. 1990-91), Mo. Bar Assn. (bd. govs. 1975-87, Pres. Spl. award 1979), Jefferson County Bar Assn. (pres. 1963-64). Avocations: travel, golf. Home: 9662 W Vista Dr Hillsboro MO 63050-3112 Office: Thurman Howald Weber Senkel & Norrick LLC PO Box 800 One Thurman Ct Hillsboro MO 63050

HOWARD, ALAN CHARLES, retired English language educator; b. Manistee, Mich., Aug. 27, 1944; s. Edmund Witherell and Esther Marie (Watrous) Howard; m. Rosemary Tuller, Jan. 29, 1961 (div. June 1963); 1 child, Deborah; m. Lois Marie Zimmer, June 20, 1965 (div. May 1990); children: Jennifer, Rebecca; m. Judy Kay Miller, May 29, 1992. AB in English, Ctrl. Mich. U., 1967; MA in English, U. Mich., 1968. Lectr. English Southgate Tech. Coll., London, 1975-76; asst. prof. English Bay de Noc Community Coll., Escanaba, Mich., 1968-75, 76-95. Newspaper columnist, 1995—2001; author: (poetry) Longing for Latitude, 1998 (Midwest Indep. Pub. Assn. award, 1999), (novel) Come Back to Sorrento, 2001. Mem. Bay Area Campus Ministry, Escanaba, 1985-95; sec., v.p. PTO, Escanaba, 1983-85; chmn. Bay de Noc C.C. Global Awareness Com., 1989-95; mem. Escanaba City Recreation Bd., 1989-95; former mem. Escanaba Pub. Libr. Bd. Fulbright grantee, 1975-76, 91; named one of Outstanding Young Men of Am. U.S. Jaycees, 1977. Avocations: travel, photography, cooking, creative writing. Home and Office: 1322 N 16th St Escanaba MI 49829-1713

HOWARD, ALEX T., JR., federal judge; b. 1924; Student, U. Ala., 1942, student, 1946, Auburn U., 1942-44; JD, Vanderbilt U., 1950. U.S. probation officer, Mobile, Ala., 1950-51; ptnr. Johnstone, Adams, Howard, Bailey & Gordon, Mobile, 1951-86; U.S. commr. U.S. Dist. Ct. (so. dist.) Ala., 1956-70, judge, 1986—, chief judge, 1989-94, sr. judge, 1996—. Assoc. editor Am. Maritime Cases for Port of Mobile. Served to 2d lt. U.S. Army, 1943-46. Mem. ABA, Internat. Soc. Barristers, Internat. Assn. of Ins. Counsel, Maritime Law Assn. of U.S., Southeastern Admiralty Law Inst. (dir. 1978-80), Ala. Bar Assn., Ala. Def. Lawyers Assn. (dir. late 1950's), Mobile Bar Assn. (pres. 1973).

HOWARD, ALTON JOHNATHAN, publishing company executive; b. Monroe, La., Sept. 6, 1951; s. Alton Hardy and Mamie Jean H.; m. Chrysanne Howard, Dec. 27, 1971; children: Korie, Ryan, Ashley. BSBA, Harding U., 1973. V.p. Howard Bros. Discount Stores, Inc., Monroe, La., 1973-80; pres. Mid-South Devel., Inc., West Monroe, 1980—, Worldwide Found., West Monroe, 1980—, Howard Pub. Co., Inc., West Monroe, 1980—. Bd. dirs. Ouachita Christian Sch., 1979—; pres. coun. mem. Harding U., 1987—. Office: Howard Pub Co 3117 N 7th St West Monroe LA 71291-2227

HOWARD, ANDREW BAKER, lawyer; b. Watertown, N.Y., July 26, 1969; s. Courtland Rogers and Maryanne H.; m. Elizabeth Edge, June 8, 1996; children: Christopher Baker, Paul Andrew. BA cum laude, St. Lawrence U., 1991; JD cum laude, Union U., 1994. Bar: N.Y. 1995. Atty. Connor, Curran & Schram, Hudson, N.Y., 1994—; asst. dist. atty. Columbia County Dist. Atty., Hudson, 1995. Instr. Am. Inst. Banking, Albany, 1997—. Mem. N.Y. State Bar Assn., Columbia County Bar Assn., Justinian Soc., Columbia County C. of C. (bd. dirs.). Republican. Roman Catholic. Avocations: mountain biking, skiing, shooting. Home: 3075 Upper Main St Valatie NY 12184 Office: Connor Curran & Schram PC 441 E Allen St Hudson NY 12534-2422 E-mail: howard@ccslawfirm.com.

HOWARD, ARTHUR ELLSWORTH DICK, law educator; b. Richmond, Va., July 5, 1933; s. Thomas Landon and Marie Antoinette (Dick) H. BA, U. Richmond, 1954; LLB, U. Va., 1961; BA with honors, Oxford U., 1960, MA, 1965; LLD (hon.), James Madison U., 1983, U. Richmond, 1984, Campbell U., 1986, Coll. William and Mary, 1991, Wake Forest U., 2000. Bar: Va., D.C. 1961. Asso. Covington & Burling, Washington, 1961-62; law clk. to Supreme Ct. Justice Hugo L. Black, Washington, 1962-64; assoc. prof. law U. Va., Charlottesville, 1964-67, prof., 1967-76, White Burkett Miller prof. law and public affairs, 1976—, assoc. dean, 1967-69, dir. Ctr. for Pub. Svc., 1988-89, Roy L. and Rosamond Woodruff Morgan rsch. prof., 2001—. Bd. dirs. Am. Ditchley Found.; participant counsel sessions Gen. Assembly Va., 1969—70. Author: Commentaries on the Constitution of Virginia, 2 vols., 1974 (Phi Beta Kappa prize), The Road from Runnymede: Magna Carta and Constitutionalism in America, 1968, (with Baker and Derr) Church, State and Politics, 1982, Democracy's Dawn, 1991, Constitution-Making in Eastern Europe, 1993, Magna Carta: Text and Commentary, 1998; bd. editors The American Oxonian, 1968—, The Wilson Quar., 1977—. Chmn., exec. dir. Va. Commn. on Constl. Revision, 1968-69; chmn. Va. Commn. on Bicentennial of U.S. Constn., 1985-92; mem. Va. Ind. Bicentennial Commn., 1966-83; vice chmn. Magna Carta Commn. Va., 1965-66; Va. sec. Rhodes Scholarship Trust, 1970—; counselor to Gov. of Va., 1982-86; bd. dirs. James Madison Meml. Found., Jamestown-Yorktown Found., 2003—; hon. mem. High Table Christ Ch., Oxford, 2002. With U.S. Army, 1954-56. Recipient Disting. Prof. award U. Va., 1981, Randa medal Czech Republic, 1996; fellow Woodrow Wilson Internat. Center for Scholars, Smithsonian Instn., Washington, 1974-75, 76-77; fellow Ctr. Advanced Studies U. Va., 1970-71, 76-77, 82-83; Rhodes scholar Oxford U., 1958-60; Disting. Vis. scholar in residence Rhodes Ho., Oxford U., 2001 Mem. Va. Bar Assn. (v.p. 1970-71), Va. Acad. Laureates (chmn. 1981-92), Cosmos Club (Washington), Oxford and Cambridge Club (London). Episcopalian. Home: 627 Park St Charlottesville VA 22902-4654 Office: U Va Sch Law 580 Massie Rd Charlottesville VA 22903-1738

HOWARD, BARBARA SUE MESNER, artist; b. Princeton, N.J., Aug. 6, 1944; d. Maximilian Hutchinson and Ethel Gertrude (Vieten) Mesner; m. James Scott Howard, Dec. 26, 1967 (dec. Jan. 1998). Sculpture study, H.I. Gates, sculptor, Washington, 1965-66; BA, Hood Coll., Frederick, Md., 1966; postgrad., Rutgers U., 1967-69. Cert. tchr., N.J. Asst. buyer Jordan Marsh, Boston, 1966-67; sculpture instr. Princeton Art Assn., 1968-71, 77-78; art tchr. N.J. Pub. Schs., 1967-70; chmn. art dept. Stuart Country Day Sch., Princeton, 1970-76; artist Hightstown, N.J., 1977—. Exhibited in group shows Art Cons., Princeton, 1974, 75, 78, Gallery 100, Princeton, 1975, Betty Parson Gallery, N.Y.C., 1975, Hunterdon Art Ctr., Clinton, N.J., 1977, Squibb Gallery, Princeton, 1973, 82,

Art Masters Gallery, Princeton, 1984, Trenton City Mus., 1984, Grippi Gallery, N.Y.C., 1984, 85, 86, Gourgaud Gallery, 1986, N.J. Ctr. Visual Arts, Summit, 1987, Morris Mus., Morristown, N.J., 1987, A.D. Gallery, N.J. 1989-2003, Artworks Gallery, Art Ctr. Trenton, 1989, Williams Collection Gallery, Princeton, 1991, 92; Hood Coll. Centennial Alumnae Art Exhbn., 1993; Women's Studies Gallery Princeton U., 1995-96; represented in numerous pvt. collections. Fellow Mixed Media N.J. State Council on the Arts, 1985; recipient Purchase award Mercer County Artists Exhibition, 1983. Mem. Artworks, Artists Equity, fellow Mus.of Modern Art, patron Mahatten Theater Club, Smithsonian Assocs., Met. Mus. Art, Nat. Mus. Women in Arts (charter). Avocations: long distance swimming, biking, hiking. Studio: 451 S Main St Hightstown NJ 08520-3405 also: Eable Crag Lk Piercefield NY 12973 E-mail: nichet46@hotmail.com.

HOWARD, BARRY CHRISTOPHER, minister; b. Balt., Aug. 10, 1971; s. Dale Harley and Margaret Catherine Howard; m. Amie Joan Palumbo, Sept. 7, 1991; children: Noah Louis, Hillary Hope, Abraham Christian, Joshua Dale. BS in Bus. Adminstrn. summa cum laude, Regis U., 2000; student, Evangel Christian U. Am., 2000—. V.p. Youth With A Mission Denver, Arvada, Colo., 1990—. Min. Faith Bible Chapel, Arvada, 1996—. Cubmaster Pack 999, Arvada, 2002—03. Mem.: Colo. Soc. Colonial Wars (gov. 2002—), Colo. Soc. Sons and Daughters of the Pilgrims (dep. gov. 2002—), Nat. Soc. SAR (chaplain 1998—2000), Order of the Crown of Charlemagne in the USA, Presdl. Families Am. (chaplain 2001—03), Colo. Soc. Mayflower Descendants (chaplain 1998—2002), Phi Theta Kappa, Alpha Sigma Nu, One In A Thousand Soc., Cerebrals Soc. (v.p. 2002—), Colloquy, Intertel, Mensa. Republican. Achievements include development of World Advocates International NGO - Relief and Development Organization. Avocations: travel, classical guitar, chess. Home: 10939 West 59th Pl Arvada CO 80004 Office: Youth With A Mission Denver 12750 West 63rd Ave Arvada CO 80004 Home Fax: 303-424-2151; Office Fax: 303-424-2151. Personal E-mail: barrychoward@hotmail.com. E-mail: barryhoward@ywamdenver.org.

HOWARD, BERNARD EUFINGER, mathematics and computer science educator; b. Ludlow, Vt., Sept. 22, 1920; s. Charles Rawson and Ethel (Kearney) H.; m. Ruth Belknap, Mar. 29, 1942. Student Middlebury Coll., 1938-40; B.S., MIT, 1944; M.S., U. Ill., 1947, Ph.D., 1951. Staff mem. Radiation Lab. MIT, Cambridge, 1942-45; asst. math. U. Ill., Champaign-Urbana, 1945-49; sr. mathematician Inst. Air Weapons Rsch., U. Chgo., 1951, asst. to dir. Inst. for Systems Rsch., 1952-56, assoc. dir., 1956-60, assoc. dir. Labs. for Applied Sci., 1958-60; dir. Sci. Computing Ctr. U. Miami, Coral Gables, Fla., 1960-64, prof. math. and computer sci., 1960-91, prof. emeritus, 1991—, assoc. faculty Grad. Sch. of Internat. Studies, 1996—; chmn. bd. dirs. Sociocybernetics, Inc.; exec. sec. Air Force Adv. Bd. Simulation, 1951-54; cons. Systems Rsch. Labs, Inc., Dayton, Ohio, 1963-67, acting dir. math. scis. div., 1965; cons. Variety Children's Rsch. Found., Miami, 1964-66, Fla. Power & Light Co., Miami, 1968, Shaw & Assocs., 1964-75; vis. fellow Dartmouth Coll., Hanover, N.H., 1976; co-investigator Positron Emission Tomography Ctr., U. Miami Dept. Neurology/Mt. Sinai Med. Ctr., 1981-84. Creator Parabolic-Earth Radar Coverage Chart, 1944; co-creator: (with Henry W. Kunce) Sociocybernetics, 1971, Optimum Curvature, 1964, Optimum Torsion, 1974, (with J.F.B. Shaw) Principles in Highway Routing, (with James M. Syck) Twisted Splines, 1992. Chmn. bd. dirs. Blue Lake Assn., Inc., Miami, 1969-96, chmn. emeritus 1996—. Am. Soc. Engrng. Edn.-Office of Naval Research fellow Naval Underwater Systems Ctr., 1981, 82. Mem. Am. Math. Soc., Soc. Indsl. and Applied Math. (treas. S.E. sect. 1964), Am. Phys. Soc., Assn. Computing Machinery (chpt. chmn. 1969-70), IEEE, AAUP (chpt. sec. 1974-91), Sigma Xi, Phi Kappa Phi, Pi Mu Epsilon, Alpha Sigma Phi, Alpha Epsilon Lambda. Home: 7320 Miller Dr Miami FL 33155-5504 Office: U Miami Sci Computing Ctr Coral Gables FL 33124

HOWARD, BETTIE JEAN, surgical nurse; b. Balt., Sept. 26, 1926; d. Milton James and Elizabeth Maria (Morgan) Knight; m. Stanley Lewis Howard; children: Amanda J. Scott, Sarah L. Howard, Mary McK. Strobel, Elizabeth M. Shaner, Roderick S. Diploma, Church Home and Hosp., Balt., 1947. RN, Md.; cert. bd. gastroenterology nurse. Head nurse med.-surg. unit Church Home & Hosp., Balt., 1947-48; surg. pediat. staff nurse Johns Hopkins Hosp., Balt., 1948-51, surg. pediat. acting head nurse, 1951-52, otolaryngology endoscopy head nurse, 1952-56; pediat. emergency rm. triage nurse U. Md. Hosp., Balt., 1966-68; head nurse surg. endoscopy nurse U. Md. Med. Ctr., Balt., 1968—2002, endofiberscope team coord. perioperative/trauma, 2002—. Adv. bd. Astra Merck for Patient Self Mgmt. Programs; spkr. Soc. Internat. Gastroent. Nurses and Endoscopy Assocs. VIth Internat. Congress, Paris, 1996, VII Internat. Congress, Vienna, 1998. Contbr.: (book chpt. sect.) Policy and Politics for Nurses, 1993; contbr. articles to profl. jours. Chmn. Digestive Disease Nat. Coalition, Washington, 1993-95; coord. exec. panel Nat. Digestive Disease Info. Clearinghouse, NIH, Bethesda, Md., 1992-2002; adminstrv. bd. Grace United Meth. Ch., Balt., 1993-95. Mem. Soc. Gastroenterology Nurses and Assocs., Inc. (pres. 1988-89, Gabriele Schindler award 1991), Soc. Internat. Gastroenterol. Nurses and Endoscopy Assocs. (charter, spkr. 1998), Chesapeake Soc. Gastroenterology Nurses and Assocs. (charter, pres. 1981-83), Certifying Bd. Gastroenterology Nurses and Assocs. Inc. (pres. 1992-93). Republican. Avocations: reading, interior decorating, sewing, native-american collection. Home: 905 Saxon Hill Dr Cockeysville MD 21030-2905 Office: U Md Med Ctr 22 S Greene St Baltimore MD 21201-1544

HOWARD, BLAIR DUNCAN, lawyer; b. Alexandria, Va. s. T. Brooke and Elizabeth Duncan H.; m. Catherine Cremins; children: Thomas Brooke II, Caitlin Margaret. BA, U. Va., 1960; LLB, American U., 1963. Ptnr. Howard, Leino & Howard, Alexandria, Va., 1966—. Capt. USA, 1963-65. Named in Superstar Ohio Assn. Criminal Defense Lawyers, Columbus, 1994, One of Top Lawyers in Met. Washington, Washingtonian Mag. article, 1997. Fellow Am. Coll. Trial Lawyers; mem. ABA, ATLA, Alexandria Bar Assn., Va. State Bar Assn. (faculty professionalism course 1990-93). Office: Howard Morrison & Howard 1 Wall Street Warrenton VA 20186-3319

HOWARD, CARL, lawyer; b. Chgo., July 23, 1920; m. Kathleen Agnes Costello, May 10, 1953; 1 child, Carl. AB, DePauw U., 1942; JD, U. Calif., San Francisco, 1949. Bar: Calif. 1951. Supervising dep. corps. commr. State of Calif., San Francisco, 1951-69; supervisory asst., asst. house counsel Fed. Home Loan Bank of San Francisco, 1970-75; legal counsel Home Fed. Savs. and Loan Assn., San Diego, 1976-88, chmn. bd. dirs., 1985-86; assoc. Kerner, Colangelo & Imlay, 1976-86; sole practice, 1987-96. Lt. USNR, 1942-46, PTO. Mem. State Bar Calif., Am. Legion. Republican. Roman Catholic. Avocations: walking, golfing, bicycling. Home: 2450 Quintara St San Francisco CA 94116-1139

HOWARD, CAROL SPENCER, librarian, journalist; b. Great Bend, Kans., 1944; d. Thomas Glendon and Margaret Merle (Jackson) Spencer; m. William Neal Howard, Dec. 31, 1977 (div. July 1987); 1 child, Morgan William. BA in Journalism, English and Edn., Baylor U., 1967; MLS, U. Tex., 1974. Cert. libr. City desk reporter Waco (Tex.) News-Tribune, 1965-67; guest editor Mademoiselle mag., N.Y.C., 1966; womens' news reporter Houston Post, 1969; libr. Austin Ind. Sch. Dist., 1974—86, 1991—97, San Antonio Ind. Sch. Dist., 1989-90, Del Valle (Tex.) Ind. Sch. Dist., 1990-91; children's book reviewer Austin Am. Statesman, 1984-90. Freelance journalist, children's lit. cons. Contbr. articles to profl. jours. Fellow U. Tex., 1973-74. Home: PO Box 302019 Austin TX 78703-0034

HOWARD, CAROLE MARGARET MUNROE, retired public relations executive; b. Halifax, N.S., Can., Mar. 5, 1945; came to the U.S., 1965; d. Frederick Craig and Dorothy Margaret (Crimes) Munroe; m. Robert William Howard, May 15, 1965. BA, U. Calif., Berkeley, 1967; MS, Pace U., 1978. Reporter Vancouver (Can.) Sun, 1965; editl. assoc. Pacific N.W. Bell, Seattle, 1967-70, employee info. supr., 1970-72, advt. supr., 1972, project mgr. EEO, 1972-73, mktg. mgr., 1973, info. mgr., 1974-75; dist. mgr. media rels. AT&T, N.Y.C., 1975-77, dist. mgr. planning, 1977-78, dist. mgr. advt., 1978-80; media rels. mgr. Western Electric, N.Y.C., 1980-83; divsn. mgr. regional pub. rels. AT&T Info. Sys., Morristown, N.J., 1983-85; v.p., pub. rels. and comm. policy The Reader's Digest Assn., Inc., Pleasantville, N.Y., 1985-95; ret., 1995. Faculty profl. pub. course Stanford U., summer, 1993-95; bd. dirs. Andrew Corp. Author: On Deadline: Managing Media Relations, 1985, 2d edit., 1994, 3rd edit., 2000; contbg. author: Communicators' Guide to Marketing, 1987, Experts in Action: Inside Public Relations, 2d edit., 1988, Travel Industry Marketing, 1990, The Business Speakers Almanac, 1994, Majoring in the Rest of your Life, 2000, Marketing Communications, 2002; newsletter editor Wash. State Rep. Ctrl. Com., 1973-74; contbg. editor Pub. Rels. Quar.; pres. The Reader's Digest Found.; adv. bd. Pub. Rels. News, Pub. Rels. Rev., Jour. Employee Comm. Mgmt., Ragan Pub. Rels. Jour. Corp. adv. bd. Caramoor Ctr. for Music and the Arts; bd. dirs. The Hundred Club of Westchester, Inc., The Lila Acheson Wallace Fund for Met. Mus. of Art, Madison Square Boy's and Girl's Club of N.Y.C. Mem. Women in Comm. (bd. dirs. Wash. state 1973), Internat. Assn. Bus. Communicators, Pub. Rels. Soc. Am., Nat. Press Women, Wash. Press Women (bd. dirs. 1972), Issues Mgmt. Assn., Pub. Rels. Seminar, Am. Cancer Soc., Arthur Page Soc., Wisemen, The Aspen Club, La Paloma Country Club, Gray Wolf Ski Club, San Juan Outdoor Club, Pagosa Springs Arts Coun., Pi Beta Phi. Anglican. Home and Office: PO Box 5499 Pagosa Springs CO 81147-5499

HOWARD, CECIL BYRON, pediatrician; b. Wallins, Ky., Apr. 16, 1927; s. William Knott and Maggie (Cawood) H.; m. Rebekah Ann Buckley, Mar. 4, 1931; children: Mark Byron, Sally Ann Howard Truxal, Maggie Elizabeth Howard Ray. BA, Vanderbilt U., 1949, MD, 1953. Intern U. Va. Hosp., Charlottesville, 1953-54; resident U. Tex. Med. Br., Galveston, 1954-56; pediatrician pvt. practice, Maryville, Tenn., 1956—. Dir. Christian Ch. Found. Handicapped, 1983—; elder 1st Christian Ch., Maryville, 1961-2003; scoutmaster Boy Scouts Am., 1964-79, chmn. Tuckaleechee Dist. Great Smoky Mountain Coun., 1973-75; mem. Blount County D.H.S. Child Abuse Rev. Team, 1965-2002. With U.S. Army, 1945-47. Fellow Am. Acad. Pediatrics; mem. Blount County Med. Soc. (pres. 1973), Maryville Optimist Club (pres. 1973). Republican. Avocations: hiking, piano, reading. Office: 1103 E Lamar Alexander Pkwy Maryville TN 37804-5130

HOWARD, CHRISTOPHER PHILIP, business consultant; b. N.Y.C., Aug. 6, 1947; s. Murray and Hope (McGurn) H.; m. Danina Mary Hill, June 29, 1987; children: Sean, Stephen, Coby, Katherine, Sara. BA in Econs., Stanford U., 1968; MBA, Santa Clara U., 1970. Cert. mgmt. cons.; cert. profl. cons. to mgmt; cert. mgmt. acct.; cert. bus. counselor. Cons. Ernst & Ernst, CPAs, Phoenix, 1972-74; ops. mgr. Jensen Tools & Alloys Inc., Phoenix, 1974-77; CFO Pioneer Industries, Inc., Phoenix, 1977-80; sr. v.p. Health-Tech Mgmt., Inc., Phoenix, 1980-84; mng. prin. Howard and Assocs., Inc., Phoenix, 1984-87; consulting mgr. Grant Thornton, CPAs, Reno, 1987-89; mng. dir. Howard Consulting Group, Inc., Reno, 1989—2002; faculty mem. U. Nev., Reno, 1991—2001; CEO North Star Investors, Inc., 2002—. 1st lt. USAF, 1970-72. Mem. Inst. Cert. Mgmt. Accts., Nat. Bur. Cert. Cons., Inst. Cert. Mgmt. Cons., Inst. Bus. Appraisers, Inst. Mgmt. Cons., Inst. Cert. Bus. Counselors, Stanford U. Alumni Assn. Episcopalian. Office: Howard Consulting Group 695 Sierra Rose Dr Reno NV 89511 E-mail: chris@northstarinvestors.com.

HOWARD, CONSTANCE A. state representative; b. Chgo., Ill., Dec. 14, 1942; BS in Liberal Arts, MS in Corrections and Criminal Justice, Chgo. State U. Owner network mktg. bus.; mem. Ill. Ho. of Reps., 1994—. Alt. del. Dem. Nat. Conv., 1984, 1988; southside office coord. Braun for Senate, Chgo. Recipient LEAD award, Chgo. Tchrs. Union, Cert. of Appreciation, Ill. Coalition Against Domestic Violence, Twp. Officials Ill., Gapple Devel. Corp. Mem.: Nat. Polit. Congress Black Women, Ind. Voters Ill. (Best Freshman Voting Record Progressive Issues award), Cook County Dem. Women, Black Elected Officials Ill., Chgo. Urban League, Black Women's Network. Democrat. Office: 270-S Stratton Office Bldg Springfield IL 62706 Address: 8729 S State St Chicago IL 60619*

HOWARD, CYNTHIA, lawyer, county official; b. Northampton, Mass., July 14, 1951; d. Robert TenBroeck and Margaret Eleanor (McCleary) H.; m. Thomas A. Lubeck, Oct. 27, 1990; children: Alice, Jacob. BA, Oberlin Coll., 1973; JD, U. Minn., 1978. Bar: Minn. 1978, S.D. 1979, Washington 1991. Staff mng. atty. Dakota Plains Legal Svcs., Eagle Butte, S.D., 1978-81; pvt. practice Deadwood, S.D., 1981-86; dir. No. Hills Pub. Defender, Deadwood, 1986-89; asst. pub. defender Minnehaha County Public Defender, Sioux Falls, S.D., 1991-98; dir. Minnehaha County Office of Pub. Adv., Sioux Falls, 1999—. Bd. dirs. Black Hills Legal Svcs., Rapid City, S.D., 1981-87. Bd. dirs. YWCA, Sioux Falls, 1992-2001; mem. Sioux Falls Historic Preservatin Commn., 1992-96, Mem. S.D. State Bar Assn. (criminal pattern jury instrn. com. 1991-97, mem. ethics com. 1999—). Democrat. Presbyterian. Avocation: weaving. Office: Pub Adv 415 N Dakota Ave Sioux Falls SD 57104-2412

HOWARD, DAVID, ballet school administrator; b. London, June 14, 1937; came to U.S., 1966; s. Walter and Dorothy (Fell) Edwards. Grad., Arts Ednl. Sch., London, 1955; D (hon.), Oklahoma City U., 1998. Mem. faculty Sch. Ballet, Harkness House for Ballet Arts, N.Y.C., 1966—; prin. tchr. Harkness Ballet Co., N.Y.C., 1967—; dir. Sch. Ballet Harkness House for Ballet Arts, N.Y.C., 1969—; founder David Howard Sch. Ballet, N.Y.C., 1977; company teacher Am. Ballet Theater, 1990—2002. Am. judicator 1st Internat. Ballet Competition, Miss., 1979; co-dir., co-founder Northeastern Ballet Summer Sch., Bard Coll., 1979; assoc. artistic dir. Catskill Ballet Theatre, 1980; founder David Howard Dance Ctr., N.Y.C., 1986—; mem. founding bd. Swiss Profl. Sch., Zurich; guest tchr. Royal Ballet, 1986—87, 1993, 95, San Francisco Ballet, Juilliard Sch.; guest tchr., coach Am. Ballet Theatre, 1990—93, 1998—99, 2000—01, Bejart Ballet, 1992—94; guest tchr. Royal Ballet, 1998—2001; artistic advisor Nat. Dance Co. Mex., Mexico City, 1996—97; artistic assoc. Marin Dance Theatre, San Rafael, Calif., 1996—97; tng. David Howard Found., Seattle, Tulsa, Dallas, Erie, Pa., Boston, N.Y.C., 1990—96; tchr. steps Broadway Dance Ballet Acad., East N.Y.C., 1996—2001; tchr. N.Y. On The Rd., 1996—2001; tng. program Internat. Ballet Competition, Jackson, Miss., 1998; mem. faculty Joffrey/New Sch. U., N.Y.C., 1998—2002; tng. program Internat. Ballet Competition, 2002. Prin. dancer London Palladium, 1955—57, with Royal Ballet Eng., 1957—63, soloist, 1958—63, Nat. Ballet Can., 1963—64, appeared in (musical) Little Me, London, 1964—66; collaborator double album ballet music: ; with Royal Ballet, 1991—92, 1997—2001; with Royal Ballet, 2003—; with Finnish Nat. Ballet, 1999, Royal Swedish Ballet, 1977—, choreographer Rachmaninoff Suite, 1971—, Divertissement D'Adam, 1971—, Rossini Variations, 1973, Designs in Shades of Baroque, 1974, Fantasy, 1980; teaching record albums include David Howard in Class, rec. 25 video tapes, 125 CDs on ballet. Recipient Dance Master of Am. ann. award, 1983. Mem. Regional Dance Am. (dir. pres.), royal Acad. Dancing, London Actors Equity (Adeline Genee Silver medal for male dancers 1954). *I have followed with great enthusiasm the growth of dance in the United States and have dedicated myself to the development of ballet training in America and bring it to a higher level. I have devoted my time and effort to Regional Dance America, which reflects and contributes to the ever increasing size of ballet audiences across America. With this happening, no longer will the dancers who are developed each year have to seek employment within the long established European system of state-supported ballet houses.*

HOWARD, DAVID, educational administrator; b. Delaware, Ohio, Sept. 24, 1929; s. Dale David and Clarine (Morehouse) H. BA, Ohio Wesleyan U., 1953; student, Columbia U, 1961-62, 86, NYU, 1985-86. Lic. tchr., attendance coordinator, N.Y. News writer Australian Broadcasting Co., Sydney, 1955; editl. asst. N.Y. Times, N.Y.C., 1956-58; tchr. social studies N.Y.C. Bd. of Edn., 1958-82, hotel and shelter ednl. coord., 1982-89; asst. supr. N.Y.C. Truancy Patrol Teams, 1989—. Author: Night Lights Went Out, 1966, Casa Alhambra, 1968, Picker of the Kingdom, 1999, Springtime for Kelly, 2001. Reservist FEMA, N.Y.C., 1980—. Lt. col. USAFR, 1953-75. Mem. Mystery Writers of Am., English Speaking Union. Republican. Protestant. N.Y.C. Anchor & Saber. Home: 324 E 61st St Apt 20 New York NY 10021-8709

HOWARD, DAVID E. artist; b. N.Y.C., Jan. 25, 1952; s. John C. and Florence (Martino) H. Student, Ohio U., 1969-71; MFA, San Francisco Art Inst., 1974. Comml. photographer, Athens, Ohio, 1969-71; tchr. photography San Francisco Ctr. for Visual Studies, 1971-74, visual artist in photography, 1975—, dir., 1975—. Vis. instr. City Coll. San Francisco; grad. isntr. San Francisco Art Inst. Author: Photography for Visual Communicators, Objective Reality, 1972, monographs Realities, 1976, Perspectives, 1978, The Last Filipino Head Hunters, 2001, American Artist, 1990, Illusionistic Perceptions, Sacred Journey, 2003, Taschen, 2003; photography numerous periodicals including Village Voice, N.Y.C., San Francisco Chronicle, Artweek, N.Y. Art Revs., 1990, L.A. Reader, Tribal Arts mag., 1998, 2002, Filipinas, 1998, Patagonia Mag., 2002, TV Documentary series; one-man shows include G. Ray Hawkins Gallery, Images Gallery N.Y.C., U. Calif. Extension, John Bolles Gallery, San Francisco, Hirshhorn Mus., Smithsonian Instn., Washington, San Francisco Art Inst., Ohio U., Athens, Thomas J. Crowe Gallery, L.A., Madison (Wis.) Art Ctr., Lehigh U., Pa., Fourth Street Gallery, N.Y.C., Intersection Gallery, San Francisco, Third Eye Gallery, N.Y.C., Ctr. for Visual Studies, San Francisco, Hutchinson Community Coll., Kans., Hank Baum Gallery, San Francisco, Martin Webber Gallery, 1986, Marc Richards Gallery, L.A., 1987, E.Z.T.V., L.A., 1987, 88, G. Ray Hawkins Gallery, L.A., 1988, Fine Arts Mus. L.I., 1989, Phila. Mus. Art, 1990, San Jose, Calif., 2000; numerous group shows including Art Commn. Gallery, San Francisco, DeYoung Mus., San Francisco, Oakland (Calif.) Mus., Palace of Fine Arts, San Francisco, Camera Work, L.A., Erie (Pa.) Art Ctr., Vorpal Gallery, 1985, Cal. State U., 1988, San Francisco Pub. Libr., 1987, Video Refuses, 1986, Hadley Martin Gallery, San Francisco, 1987, Fine Art Mus. L.I., 1989, Chandler Gallery, Seattle, 1991; represented in collections Mus. Modern Art, N.Y.C., Oakland (Calif.) Mus., San Francisco Mus. Modern Art, City of San Francisco, De Saisset Art Gallery, Santa Clara, Calif., Whitney Mus. Am. Art, Hirshhorn Mus., Smithsonian Instn., Art Ctr., Waco, Tex., Memphis Brooks Mus., Memphis, Akron (Ohio) Art Mus., Am. Mus. Natural History, N.Y.C. Spl. Collections; pvt. collections; prodr. videotape New York's East Village Art Scene, 1985, California's Art Scene, 1986, others; prodr. exptl. films: Analysis of Realities, 1974, Levels of Consciousness, 1976, Levels of Reality; prodr., dir. Art Seen, TV comml. documentary series on contemporary art televised in N.Y.C., L.A., San Francisco, Miami, Fla., Portland, Oreg., New Orleans, San Francisco, aired PBS, 1994, T.V. show Keith Haring: Artist at Work, selected segments shown Whitney Mus., Hirschhorn-Smithsonian Instn.; internat. exhbns. 10th and 13th Internat. Exhbns. Contemporay Art, Royan, France, 34thand 41st Internat. Salons of Japan, Tokyo, and 5 cities, Mex. Exhbn., Ex Convento de Carman, Guadalajara, 31st Cork Film Festival, 1986, Chgo. Film Festival, 1986, 42nd San Francisco Internatl. Film Fest., 1999, Presidio Earth Days Fest., 1999; other mus., galleries, univs. in U.S. and Europe; produced and directed films New York's East Village Art Scene, 1985, California's Art Scene, Parts 1 & 2, Levels of consciousness, Levels of Reality; presenter weekly cable TV series; Blackstar syndicated photographer, N.Y.C. Recipient San Francisco Art Festival award. Home and Office: Visual Studies 49 Rivoli St San Francisco CA 94117-4306 E-mail: info@artexhibitionrentals.com.

HOWARD, DAVID L. music educator, conductor; b. Oklahoma City, Aug. 18, 1973; m. Andrea L. Weirick; children: Stuart, Abigail. MusB Edn., U. of Ctrl. Okla., 1997, MusM with honors, 1999. Cert. tchr. Okla. Choral dir. Monroney Jr. H.S., Midwest City, Okla., 1999—2001; min. of music Howard Meml. Bapt. Ch., Oklahoma City, 1999—; choral dir. Choctaw (Okla.) H.S., 2001—. Artistic dir./condr. Midwest Choral Soc., Midwest City, 2000—. Conductor (choral) Handel's Messiah, 2002; singer (recital): Robert Schumann's Dichterliebe, Op. 48, 1999, Songs of Travel by Ralph Vaughan Williams, and Let us Garlands Bring, Op. 18 by Gerald Finzi; singer: (opera) Mozart's Don Giovanni & Cosi Fan Tutte, and Verdi's La Forza del Destino, 1998, Die Fledermaus, 2003. Mem.: Internat. Fedn. for Choral Music, Internat. Arbeitgemeinschaft fur Hymnologie, Hymn Soc. of Gt. Britain & Ireland, East Ctrl. Okla. Choral Directors Assn. (v.p. 2002—), Music Educators Nat. Conf., Am. Choral Directors Assn., Pi Sigma Alpha. Home: 1725 Cherokee Tr Choctaw OK 73020 Personal E-mail: dlhoward@cleanweb.net.

HOWARD, DAVIS JONATHAN, lawyer, educator, writer; b. S.I., N.Y., Dec. 8, 1954; s. Royal Marwin and Muriel Lu (Russell) H. BA summa cum laude, Wagner Coll., 1976; JD, Yale U., 1982. Bar: N.Y. 1983, N.J. 1986, U.S. Dist. Ct. (so. and ea. dists.) N.Y. 1983, U.S. Dist. Ct. N.J. 1986, U.S. Ct. Appeals (3d cir.) 1987, U.S. Ct. Appeals (4th cir.) 1988, U.S. Ct. Appeals (2d cir.) 1994. Assoc. Robson & Miller, N.Y.C., 1983-85, Sills Cummis Zuckerman Radin Tischman Epstein & Gross, P.A., Newark, 1985-92; ptnr. Parry & Howard, P.A., Elizabeth, N.J., 1993-98; pvt. practice Staten Island, NY, 1998—2002. Lectr. law Rutgers U. Sch. Law, Newark, 1987-89; faculty legal seminars, symposiums; adjunct Coll. of Staten Island, CUNY, 1999. Contbr. articles to legal jours.; editor-in-chief, co-founder Shepard's N.J. Ins. Law and Regulation Reporter, 1991. Dir. alumni sch. com. Yale U., 1989-96. Mem.: ABA, ATLA, Am. Soc. Writers on Legal Subjects, Def. Rsch. Inst., N.Y. County Lawyers Assn., N.J. Bar Assn., N.Y. State Bar Assn., Scribes. Home and Office: 46 Longfellow Ave Staten Island NY 10301-4616 Fax: 718-816-4961. E-mail: dajho@aol.com.

HOWARD, DEAN DENTON, electrical engineer, researcher, consultant; BSE.E., Purdue U., 1949; MSE.E., U. Md., College Park, 1951. Elec. engr. Naval Research Lab., Washington, 1949-84; cons. in elec. engring. Kaman Corp., Alexandria, Va., 1984-94; cons. in field, 1994—. Instr. George Washington U., Washington, 1983-94. Author: (with others) Radar Handbook, 1990; co-author: Radar Handbook, 1970, Airborne Radar, 1961; contbr. articles to IEEE jour.; patentee (multiple) in monopulse radar and related fields. Served with USN, 1945-46 Recipient Radar Devel. award U.S. Navy, 1978, Meritorious Civilian Service award, 1980 Fellow IEEE; mem. Research Soc. Am. Avocation: ham radio W3PRH.

HOWARD, DESMOND KEVIN, professional football player; b. Cleveland, May 15, 1970; BA Comm. Studies, U. Mich. Wide receiver Washington Redskins, 1992-94; wide receiver, kick returner Jacksonville Jaguars, 1995, Green Bay Packers, 1996-97, Oakland Raiders, 1997-98; wide receiver Detroit Lions, 1999—. Named College Football Player of the Year, The Sporting News, 1991; recipient Heisman Trophy, 1991, Maxwell award, 1991, MVP Super Bowl XXXI, 1997. Office: Detroit Lions 1200 Featherstone Rd Pontiac MI 48342-1938 also: Detroit Lions Inc 222 Republican Dr Allen Park MI 48101

HOWARD, DONALD SEARCY, banker; b. Leadville, Colo., Aug. 13, 1928; s. Paul Parker and Amanda Jane (Searcy) H.; m. Phyllis Havey, Oct. 1, 1955; children: Steven, Julie, Rebecca, Martin BSBA, Northwestern U., 1950; MBA, Harvard U., 1955. Rsch. assoc. Bus. Sch., Harvard U., Boston, 1955-57; ofcl. asst. overseas div. Citibank, London, 1957; asst. cashier Citibank, N.A., N.Y.C., 1959-60, asst. v.p., 1960-63, v.p., 1963-69, dep. comptroller, 1969-72; sr. v.p.-fin. Citicorp-Citibank, 1972-79, exec. v.p., chief fin. officer, 1980-88; chief fin. officer Salomon Inc., N.Y.C., 1988-93. Mem. fin. acctg. stds. adv. com. Fin. Acctg. Found., Stamford, Conn., 1985-88; mem. Internat. Acctg. Stds. Adv. Commn., London, 1986-93; dir. Bank Leumi U.S.A., 1994—, Green Garden, Inc., Bedford, Pa., 1986-2002, Consolidated Purchasing Svcs., Bernardsville, N.J., 1987-99, dir., Howard Vending, Miami, 2001-, Green Garden Products LLC, Bedford, 2002—. Co-Author: Managing The Liability Side of the Balance Sheet, 1976, Evolving Concepts of Bank Capital Management, 1980 Chair emeritus trustees Cornerstone Sch., Jersey City, 1993-2002; trustee Vis. Nurse Assn. Ctrl. N.J., 1995-97. Lt. comdr. USNR, 1950-57, Korea. Mem. Am. Bankers Assn. (chief fin. officer's exec. com. 1984-87). Presbyterian. E-mail: Phyldonhow@aol.com.

HOWARD, EDWARD FRANCIS, lawyer; b. New Brighton, Pa., Oct. 4, 1942; s. Allen Michael and Mary Rosalie (Herbulock) H.; m. Eleanor Elizabeth Harding, Dec. 28, 1968. BA, Geneva Coll., 1966; JD, Harvard U., 1969. Bar: U.S. Dist. Ct. D.C. 1970, U.S. Supreme Ct. 1970. Legis. asst. U.S. Rep. Spark Matsunaga, Washington, 1970-75; gen. counsel U.S. Select Com. on Aging, Washington, 1975-79, Nat. Council on Aging, Washington, 1979-82; counsel for social security U.S. House. Select Com. on Aging, Washington, 1982-83; coord. pub. policy Villers Found., Washington, 1983-89; gen. counsel U.S. Bipartisan Commn. on Comprehensive Health Care, Washington, 1989-90; exec. v.p. Alliance for Health Reform, 1991—. Adj. faculty New Sch. for Social Rsch., 1980; ofcl. observer White House Confs. on Aging, 1981, facilitator, 1995. Contbr. articles to profl. jours. Chair pub. policy com. Am. Soc. on Aging, 1984-86, bd. dirs., 1986-88; mem. primary care journalism award selection com. Pew Health Professions Commn., 1995-99. With U.S. Army, 1961-63. Hunter Coll. fellow, 1987. Mem. ABA (commn. on legal problems of the elderly 1979-86), Nat. Acad. Social Ins., Covering Kids and Families Eligibility Policy Group, N. Am. Steering Com. on Global Med. Forum. Roman Catholic. Avocation: basketball.

HOWARD, ELIZABETH ANN BLANTON, courier service executive; b. Spindale, N.C., Mar. 14, 1934; d. John Lloyd and Monnie Clare (Geer) Blanton; m. Bill O. Howard, Aug. 13, 1950; children: Deborah Monnette Howard Gustafson, Michael Ray. Grad. H.S., Rutherfordton, N.C.; real estate student, U. S.C., 1965. Sales rep. Reserve Life Ins. Co., Rutherfordton, N.C., 1956-63; sec.,

salesperson Johnny Barker Real Estate, Columbia, S.C., 1963-65; sec. A.M. Pullen & Co., Columbia, 1963-65; owner, mgr. Ann's Sample Shop, Columbia, S.C., 1965-81; pres. Modubilt Corp., Columbia, 1965-75, First Comml. Assocs., Inc., Columbia, 1965-75, Ann's Rag Time Van, Columbia, 1979-88; sec., treas. Howard's Courier Svc., Inc., Rutherfordton, N.C., 1990-2000, v.p., 2000—. Bldg. project mgr. Gen. Svc. Adminstrn., 1960's. Contbg. editor: Creative Ways to Raise Funds and Activate Alumni, 1995; contbr. History Book for Spindale United Meth. Ch. Pres. Spindale Elem. PTA, 1956, Belvedere Elem. PTA, Columbia, S.C., 1963-66; bd. dirs. Rutherfordton, N.C. C. of C., 1991-92, 96-99; pres. Rutherford County Concert Assn.; bd. dirs. Habitat, 2001--. Named Sec. of Yr. WIOS Radio, Columbia S.C., 1967; recipient Charles Z. Flack award, Rutherfordton, N.C., 1992, award for svc. Am. Cancer Soc., 1996, Gov.'s award 2000. Mem. Sears Coun. of Career Women (charter), Rutherfordton Hist. Soc., Rutherfordton Ctrl. H.S. Alumni Assn. (pres. 1992—. All Class Reunion award 1992), Nat. Honor Soc.02099712 Democrat. Methodist. Avocations: travel, rehabilitation of older homes, reading. Home: 1198 Oak Springs Rd Rutherfordton NC 28139-8099 Office: PO Box 475 Spindale NC 28160-0475

HOWARD, GENE CLAUDE, retired lawyer, retired state senator; b. Perry, Okla., Sept. 26, 1926; s. Joe W. and Nell L. (Brown) Howard; m. Belva J. Prestidge, Dec. 28, 1979; children: Jean Ann, Joe Ted, Belinda Janice. JD, U. Okla., 1951. Bar: Okla. 1950, U.S. Ct. Mil. Appeals 1956, U.S. Supreme Ct. 1956. Ptnr. Howard & Widdows & Bufogle PC, and predecessors, Tulsa, 1952—; mem. Okla. Ho. of Reps., 1958-62, Okla. Senate, 1964-82, pres. pro tem, 1974-81. Mem. exec. com. Coun. State Govts., 1974—76; chmn. Okla. State and Edn. employees Group Ins. Bd., 1990—98; bd. dirs. Cubic Energy Corp., Local Okla. Bank; trustee Phila. Mortgage Trust, Okla. Coll. Savs. Plan. Mem. So. Growth Policy Bd., 1972—76; pres. Okla. Jr. Dems., 1954; del. Dem. Nat. Conv., 1964. With U.S. Army, 1944—46, PTO, lt. col. USAF, 1961—62. Mem.: Phi Delta Phi, Tulsa County Bar Assn. (Outstanding Young Atty. 1953), Okla. Bar Assn. Mem. Disciples Of Christ. Home: 2404 E 29th St Tulsa OK 74114-5619 Office: Howard Widdows & Bufogle PC 1500 Nations Bank Ctr 15W6 Tulsa OK 74119 E-mail: howardgc@swbell.net.

HOWARD, GEORGE HARMON, management consultant; b. St. John, Wash., Nov. 14, 1934; s. George Philip and Corrinne Cadwallader (Rippeteau) H.; m. Elizabeth Ann Ogden, Dec. 22, 1956 (dec. July 1991); children: Debra Ann Gollnick, Keith Philip, Corrie Lou Govostis, Stacia Elizabeth; m. Mary Katherine Collins, Nov. 4, 1999. BA, Wash. State U., 1957; MBA, Harvard U., 1967. Sales rep. Burroughs Corp., Spokane, Wash., 1957; various positions USAF, 1958-77; vice commdr. AF Contract Mgmt. Div., Kirtland AFB, N.Mex., 1978; mgr. corp. devel. Leisure Dynamics, Evergreen, Colo., 1978-80; pres. HBK Assocs., Inc., Evergreen, 1981-87; dir. ops. ILX Lightwave Corp., Bozeman, Mont., 1988-89; sr. cons. Matrix Mgmt. Group, Seattle, 1990-94; pres. HBK Assocs. Inc., Auburn, Wash., 1994—. Pres. Howard Farms, Inc., St. John, Wash., 1986—. Co-author: TFX Acquisition, 1966. Instr. Red Rocks Community Coll., Denver, 1986-87; del. Colo. Rep. Conv., Denver, 1984. Recipient Outstanding Sr. award Wash. State U., 1957, Legion of Merit award USAF, 1978, Bronze star USAF, 1968. Mem. Shrine, York Rite Bodies, Masonic Lodge, Order of Eastern Star, Wheatland Grange, Air Force Assn., Mil. Officers Assn. Am.. Republican. Episcopalian. Avocations: computers, boating, fishing. Home: 6358 S 298th Pl Auburn WA 98001-3040 Office: HBK Assocs 6358 S 298th Pl Auburn WA 98001-3040 E-mail: 76206.1417@compuserve-.com.

HOWARD, GERRY REA, music educator, singer, classical musician; b. Brady, Tex., Nov. 13, 1940; d. Willie Melvin and Mary Catherine (Brown) Howard; m. Leslie Wayne Templeton, July 28, 1961 (div. Feb. 1977); children: Todd Wayne Templeton, Gwen Marie Templeton; m. Harold James Roberts Jr., Sept. 24, 1977 (div. June 1998). Student, Sam Houston State U., 1959-60; MusB, U. Houston, 1962, postgrad., 1964-65; grad., North Tex. State U., 1966, Stephen F. Austin U., 1983; postgrad., East Tex. State U., 1984, Memphis State U., 1984-85, Las Vegas U., 1985. Cert. music tchr., 1-12, Tex., elem. tchr., 1-8, Tex., cert. music tchr., elem.-sec. (K-12), elem. edn. (K-8), Okla.; cert. Orff-Schulwerk levels I, II, III. Music tchr. Deer Park (Tex.) Ind. Sch. Dist., 1962-63, Dallas Ind. Sch. Dist., 1963, Richardson (Tex.) Ind. Sch. Dist., 1964-68; kindergarten tchr. Houston Ind. Sch. Dist., 1971, tchr. 1st grade, 1974-78; tchr. music Klein (Tex.) Ind. Sch. Dist., 1978-90; music tchr. grades 1-6 Choctaw (Okla.)-Nicoma Park Sch. Dist., Okla., 1993-98; choir/music tchr. grades 7-8 Aldine Middle Sch., Aldine Ind. Sch. Dist., 1998—99, Aldine Ind. Sch. Dist., Eckert Intermediate Sch., Houston, 1999—2002; ret., 2002. Pianist, mus. dir. 1960 Playhouse, 1979; pianist prodns. Klein Forest H.S., 1984-86, Klein H.S., 1987-90; singer Houston Symphony Chorale, 1960-62, Richardson Choral Club, 1963-64, Jeffrey Ross Chorale, Spring, Tex., 1988-89, Tomball (Tex.) Cmty. Ch., 1988-90, Oklahoma City Met. Chorus, 1994-96, Okla. Master Chorale, 1996-98. Organist St. Paul's Presbyn. Ch., Houston, 1975-77, Lakewood United Meth. Ch., Tex., 1978-80, Windwood Presbyn. Ch., Cypress, Tex., 1981-90, St. Timothy United Meth. Ch., Houston, 1998-99, Christ Redeemer Presbyn. Ch., 2002—; music dir. 1st Meth. Ch., Choctaw, Okla., 1990-93; handbell dir., organist St. Matthews United Meth. Ch., Okla., 1994-96. Recipient Tex. Pianist 2nd Pl. award Tex. Music Tchrs. Assn, 1959; Jesse Jones Foundation scholar, 1959, Houston 1st Pl. award-piano Houston Music Tchrs. Assn., 1959; Sam Houston State U. scholar, 1959, U. Houston scholar, 1960-62. Mem. NEA, Okla. Educators Assn., Music Educators Nat. Conf., Nat. Music Tchrs. Assn., Am. Guild Organists, Am. Guild of English Handbell Ringers, Inc., The Choristers Guild, Tex. Music Educators Assn., Tex. Tchrs. Assn., Klein Educators Assn., Okla. Music Tchrs. Assn., Okla. Kodály Educators, Kodály Educator Am., Am. choral Dirs.' Assn., Okla. Choral Dirs.' Assn., Okla. Orff-Schulwerk Assn., Am. Orff-Schulwerk Assn. (cert. levels I-III), Gulf Coast Orff-Schulwerk Assn., Sigma Alpha Iota (v.p. Houston alumni chpt. 1971-72, 99, Sword of Honor 1972). Republican. Avocations: oil painting, sewing, crafts, travel, watercolors. Home and Office: 6810 Clee Ln Spring TX 77379-4865 E-mail: ghoward9@ev1.net.

HOWARD, GLEN SCOTT, foundation executive, lawyer; b. Birmingham, Ala., May 28, 1950; s. Jack and Bernice (Koffman) H.; m. Lauren Oldak, Sept. 2, 1978; 1 chld, Gregory Alan. AB cum laude, Harvard Coll., 1971; JD, U. Chgo., 1974. Law clk. to chief judge U.S. Dist. Ct., Altanta, 1974-76; assoc. Sutherland, Asbill & Brennan, Washington, 1976-81, ptnr., 1981-96; gen. counsel, COO Fannie Mae Found., Washington, 1996-97, sr. advisor, 1997-99, sr. v.p., gen. counsel, 2000—. Performer radio show and record album: Classics Illustrated, 1984; contbr. articles to profl. jours. Bd. dirs. Davis Meml. Goodwill Industries, Washington, 1996--, vice-chair, 1999—; bd. dirs. Greater D.C. Cares, Washington, 1998—, chair, 2001—; pres. United Arts Orgn. Greater Washington, 2000—; bd. dirs. Leadership Washington, 2000—, Greater Washington Bd. Trade, 2002—; chair Greater Washington Bus. Philanthropy Summit, 1999-2002, September 11th Fund Distribution com., Greater Washington, 2001—; tchr. Temple Sinai Religious Sch., 1997—. Mem.: ABA, Choral Arts Soc. Democrat. Office: Fannie Mae Found 4000 Wisconsin Ave NW Washington DC 20016-2800 E-mail: ghoward@fanniemaefoundation.org.

HOWARD, GREGORY CHARLES, lawyer; b. Jan. 20, 1947; s. Robert L. and Nonamae (Lawlor) H.; m. Kathy Arlene Steinbacher, Oct. 1, 1983. Student, Clarkson Coll., 1965-67; BS, Boston U., 1969; JD, New Eng. Sch. Law, 1975. Bar: Mass. 1975, U.S. Dist. Ct. Mass. 1975, U.S. Supreme Ct. 1979. Assoc. Carmen L. Durso, Boston, 1975-77, Norris Kozodoy & Krasnoo, Boston, 1977-79; pvt. practice Boston, 1979-80; ptnr. Hoff Ernstoff & Howard, Boston, 1980-86; pres. Gregory C. Howard, PC, Boston, 1986—. Home: 5 Eliot Ave Chestnut Hill MA 02467-1455 Office: 28 State St Ste 1100 Boston MA 02109-1775 E-mail: greghoward@earthlink.net.

HOWARD, HAROLD CHARLES, provost, strategic planner, consultant; b. Loogootee, Ind., Mar. 28, 1926; s. Rodolophus Henry and Grace Mae (Carroll) H.; m. Gladys Marie Richardson, Dec. 17, 1949; children: Mark Allen, Carol Joy. BA, No. Baptist Coll., 1962; MA, Loyola U., Chgo., 1963, PhD, 1965. Ordained to ministry Bapt. Ch., 1952. Asst. supt. Jerry McAuley Mission, N.Y.C., 1945-46; parish min. Cypress Ave. Bapt. Ch., N.Y.C., 1946-52; staff evangelist Bapt. Gen. Conf., Chgo., 1952-60; grad. study fellow Loyola U., Chgo., 1962-65; prof. history, exec. v.p., dean Ea. Coll., St. Davids, Pa., 1966-78, v.p. strategic planning, dean non-traditional edn., 1988-93, provost, 1993—2003, acting pres., 1996, exec. v.p., 2003—; prin. Howard Assocs., Radnor, Pa., 1978-88. Dir. Am. Studies Inst., St. Davids, 1965-78; sr. cons. Main Event Mgmt. Corp., Sacramento, 1978-88; adv. bd. Franklin Fibre-Lamitex, Wilmington, Del., 1986-91; cons. Model-Netics, Arthur Andersen, St. Charles, Ill., 1986-87; mgmt. tng. cons. AXA Corp., France, 1988-90. Author: Tools for Strategic Planning and Tools for Mentoring Leaders. Active Temple Bapt. Ch., Univ. Planning Assoc., 1989—. Recipient Freedom Found. award, 1980; named Alumnus of Yr. Judson Coll. (formerly No. Bapt. Coll.), 1968. Mem. Phi Alpha Theta, Delta Mu Delta. Avocations: biking, hiking, reading, traveling abroad. Home: 51 Treaty Dr Wayne PA 19087-5510

HOWARD, HARRISON SABIN, literature educator; b. Phila., May 15, 1937; s. Morton Howard and Elizabeth Dinah Wasserman; m. Angela Falco Howard, June 5, 1962; children: Sabin Gilardi, Joshua Harrison. BA cum laude, Harvard U., Cambridge, MA, 1959; Bachelors Fgn. Trade, Am. Inst. Fgn. Trade, Phoenix, AZ, 1961; Masters History, NYU, New York, NY, 1968, PhD History, 1976. History & lit. tchr. Internat. Sch. of Milan, Milan, 1963—65; history & English tchr. Kew Forest Sch., Queens, NY, 1965—66; history tchr. Warwick Valley Pub. Sch., Warwick, NY, 1973—74, Profl. Children's Sch., New York, NY, 1975—80, Ethical Cultrure Fieldston Schools, New York, NY, 1980—. Author: (book) Romulo Gallegos y la Revolucion Burguera de Venezuela. Pvt. first class US Army, 1959—62, Nj / Ky. Fellow Fellowship for Caracas Venezuela, Orgn. Am. States, 1974-1975. Democrat. Episcopalian. Avocations: piano, mountain climbing, musical composition. Home: 142 West End Ave Apt 23N New York NY 10023-6128 Office: Fieldston School Fieldston Road Bronx NY 10471

HOWARD, HARRY CLAY, lawyer; b. Rockwood, Tenn., May 1, 1929; s. Harry Clay and Julia Roe (Cannon) H.; m. Mary Helen Harrison, June 12, 1951 (dec. Dec. 1997); children: Helen Howard Porter, Anne Howard Freihofer; m. Telside Matthews Strickland, Dec. 15, 1998. BA, Vanderbilt U., 1951; LLB, Emory U., 1955. Bar: Ga. 1955. Sr. ptnr. King & Spalding, Atlanta, 1956-92, ret. ptnr., 1993—. Bd. dirs. Avondale Mills Inc. Mem. coun. Emory Law Sch., 1975-85, chmn., 1976-77; bd. dirs. Cen. Atlanta Progress Inc., 1981-85, Wesley Woods Geriatric Hosps., 1987-93, chmn., 1988-92; trustee Wesley Homes Inc., 1961-93, chmn., 1981-86; past trustee Oglethorpe U., The Lovett Sch. 1st lt. USMC, 1951-53. Mem. Am. Law Inst., State Bar Ga., Atlanta Bar Assn., Lawyers Club Atlanta, Piedmont Driving Club, Peachtree Golf Club, Highlands Country Club, Phi Beta Kappa, Omicron Delta Kappa. Office: King & Spalding 191 Peachtree St NE Ste 4900 Atlanta GA 30303-1740

HOWARD, HERBERT HOOVER, broadcasting and communications educator; b. Johnson City, Tenn., Nov. 7, 1928; s. Bonnie Robert and Laura Elizabeth (Crumley) H.; m. Alpha Sells Day, Nov. 16, 1956; 1 child, Joseph David. BS, E. Tenn. State U., Johnson City, 1952, MS, 1955; cert., U. N.C., 1959; PhD in Mass Comm., Ohio U., 1973. Announcer, program dir. Sta. WJHL-AM-FM-TV, Johnson City, 1951-58; writer, announcer Sta. WCHL & WUNC-TV, Chapel Hill, N.C., 1958-59; from instr. to radio network mgr. U. Tenn., 1959-70, from asst. to assoc. prof. communications, 1970-80, prof. broadcasting, 1980-99, prof. emeritus, 1999—, asst. dean Coll. Communications, 1981-93, acting dean, 1990-91; assoc. dean, 1993-99. Mem. cmty. adv. bd. WSJK-WKOP Pub. TV, 1995—; pres. Tazewell TV Corp., 1996—. Author: Multiple Ownership in Television and Broadcasting, 1979, (textbook) Radio, TV, and Cable Programming, 1984, 94, Broadcast Advertising, 1979, 88, 91; contbr. articles to profl. jours. Mem. Soc. Profl. Journalists, Assn. Edn. in Journalism and Mass. Comms., Broadcast Edn. Assn. (Disting. Edn. Svc. award 2000), Optimists (So. Knoxville v.p 1972—, pres. 1974, lt. gov. Tenn. dist. internat. chpt. 1976). Republican. Presbyterian. Avocations: traveling, stamp collecting. Home: 1724 S Hills Dr Knoxville TN 37920-2937 Office: U Tenn 333 Communications Bldg Knoxville TN 37996-0001 E-mail: herbhoward1@att.net.

HOWARD, J. TIMOTHY, finance company executive; m. Debra Howard; children: Julia, Lauren. B in Econs. magna cum laude, M in Econs., UCLA. Fin. adv. Chase Econometric Assocs., 1975; v.p., sr. fin. economist Wells Fargo Bank, San Francisco; v.p., chief economist Fannie Mae, 1982, sr. v.p. econs. and planning, exec. v.p. econs., strategic planning and fin. analysis, 1987-88, exec. v.p. asset mgmt., 1988-90, exec. v.p., CFO, 1990—, vice chmn., 2003—. Bd. dirs. CarrAmerica Realty Corp. Trustee, mem. exec. com., officer The Washington Opera; trustee Holton-Arms Sch.; bd. dirs. Wharton Fin. Instns. Ctr. Office: Fannie Mae 3900 Wisconsin Ave NW Washington DC 20016-2892

HOWARD, J. WOODFORD, JR., political science educator; b. Ashland, Ky., July 5, 1931; s. J. Woodford and Florence Alberta (Stephens) H.; m. Valerie Hope Barclay, Apr. 10, 1960; 1 child, Elaine Howard Christ. BA summa cum laude, Duke U., 1952; M.P.A., Princeton U., 1954, MA, 1955, PhD, 1959. Instr. Lafayette Coll., Easton, Pa., 1958-59; postdoctoral fellow Harvard Law Sch., 1961-62; asst. prof. Lafayette Coll., 1959-62, Duke U., 1962-66, assoc. prof., 1966-67, Johns Hopkins U., 1967-69, prof. polit. sci., 1969-75, Thomas P. Stran prof., 1975-96, Thomas P. Stran prof. emeritus, 1996—, chmn. dept., 1973-75. Author: Mr. Justice Murphy: A Political Biography, 1968, Courts of Appeals in the Federal Judicial System, 1981 (cert. merit ABA 1982); mem. editl. bd. Law and Soc. Rev., 1975-76, 78-82, Am. Polit. Sci. Rev., 1977-81, Jour. Politics, 1979-93, Johns Hopkins U. Press, 1991-93; subject of essay in The Pioneers of Judicial Behavior, edited by Nancy Maveety, 2003; contbr. articles to profl. jours. Mem. history program adv. com. Fed. Jud. Ctr., 1989-95; trustee Balt. Mus. Art; mem. music com. Balt. Symphony Orch.; bd. dirs. Shriver Hall Concert Series; vestryman Ch. of Redeemer, Balt., 1988-90. Lt. USAF, 1955-57. Named to Hall of Fame, Floyd Co., Ky., 1957; recipient Outstanding Tchr. awards and citations, Lafayette Coll., 1960, Duke U., 1966, Johns Hopkins U., 1969, 1970, 1993, Pub. award, Harcourt Coll., 2001. Mem.: Law and Soc. Assn., Am. Judicature Soc., Nat. Capitol Area Polit. Sci. Assn. (coun. 1986—89), So. Polit. Sci. Assn., Am. Polit. Sci. Assn., Filson Hist. Soc., Supreme Ct. Hist. Soc., Princeton Club (N.Y.C.), 14 Hamilton St. Club (Balt.), Phi Beta Kappa, Omicron Delta Kappa. Office: Johns Hopkins U Dept Polit Sci Baltimore MD 21218-2685

HOWARD, JACK, labor relations consultant; b. Santa Ana, Calif., Aug. 26, 1924; s. Floyd Willie and Inez (Cooley) H.; m. Margaret Anne McKinnon, Aug. 25, 1950 (dec.); children: Marc, Anne. AB, U. Calif., Berkeley, 1948; MA, UCLA, 1952. Reporter Springfield (Ohio) Daily News, 1949-51; labor editor San Francisco Chronicle, 1952-60; chief investigator govt. information subcom. U.S. Ho. of Reps., 1960-63; spl. asst. to undersec. of Labor, 1963-64; adminstr. Neighborhood Youth Corps, 1964-66, Bur. of Work Programs, 1966-67; exec. asst. to Sec. Labor, 1968; v.p. Ednl. Scis. Programs, Inc., N.Y.C., 1969-71; sec.-treas., cons. William Benton Found., N.Y.C., 1971-80; asst. to pub. Ency. Brit., N.Y.C., 1971-73; asst. dir. Twentieth Century Fund, N.Y.C., 1974-76; asst. to pres. Am. Fedn. State, County and Mcpl. Employees AFL-CIO, 1976-97; ind. cons., 1997—. Internat. v.p. Am. Newspaper Guild-AFL-CIO, 1957-60 With AUS, 1943-46. Congl. fellow Am. Polit. Sci. Assn., 1957-58; Recipient Distinguished Svc. award Dept. Labor, 1965 Mem. ACLU. Home: 219 5th St NE Washington DC 20002-5919 E-mail: howardjack@hotmail.com.

HOWARD, JAMES FRANCIS, JR., medical educator, neurologist; b. Bellows Falls, Vt., May 3, 1948; s. James Francis Sr. and Elena Marie (Hippolitus) H.; m. Adrienne Lee Brown, May 25, 1974; children: Meghan Louise, Jeffrey Gates. BA, U. Vt., 1970, MD, 1974. Diplomate Am. Bd. Neurology and Psychiatry, Am. Bd. Electrodiagnostic Medicine; lic. physician, N.C., Va. Intern in medicine Albany (N.Y.) Med. Ctr. Hosp., 1974-75; resident in neurology U. Va. Sch. Medicine, Charlottesville, 1975-78, instr. neuromuscular disorders, 1978-79; asst. prof. neurology and medicine U. N.C. Sch. Medicine, Chapel Hill, 1979-85, assoc. prof., 1985-92, prof., 1992—. Assoc. editor: Jour. Clin. Neuromuscular Disease; contbr. numerous articles to profl. jours. Bd. dirs. Carolinas Myasthenia Gravis Found., Durham, NC, mem. med. adv. bd., 1981—. Recipient Tchr. Investigator Devel. award NIH, 1985, Outstanding Svc. award Myasthenia Gravis Found., 1994, 95, Physician of Yr. award, 1997. Fellow Am. Acad. Neurology, Am. Neurol. Assn., Am. Assn. Electrodiagnostic Medicine (chair coms., bd. dirs. 2002--); mem. Soc. Neurosci., N.Y. Acad. Scis., N.C. Neurological Soc. (pres. 1994). Avocations: sailing, snow skiing, philately, genealogy, model railroading. Office: U NC Dept Neurology 3114 Bioinformatics Bldg Chapel Hill NC 27599-7025 Business E-Mail: howardj@glial.med.unc.edu.

HOWARD, JAMES JOSEPH, III, utility company executive; b. Pitts., July 1, 1935; s. James Joseph Jr. and Flossie (Wenzel) H.; m. Donna J. Fowler; children: James J. IV, Catherine A., Christine A., William F. BBA, U. Pitts., 1957; MS, MIT, 1970. With Bell Telephone of Pa., Pitts., 1957-78, v.p., gen. mgr., 1976-78; v.p. ops. Wis. Telephone Co., Milw., 1978-79, exec. v.p., chief operating officer, 1979-81, pres., chief exec. officer, 1981-83, chmn., chief exec. officer, 1983; pres., chief operating officer Ameritech, Chgo., 1983-87, dir.; pres., chief exec. officer No. States Power Co., Mpls., 1987—, chmn., 1988—, Xcel Energy, 2000-2001. Bd. dirs. Walgreen Co., Deerfield, Ill., No. States Power Co., Mpls., Honeywell, Mpls., Fed. Res. Bank of Mpls., Ecolab, St. Paul, ReliaStar Fin., Mpls., Edison Electric Inst., Electric Power Rsch. Inst., chmn. Nuclear Energy Inst. Trustee U. St. Thomas, St. Paul. Sloan fellow MIT, 1969. Mem. Conf. Bd. N.Y.

HOWARD, JAMES KENTON, academic administrator, journalist; b. June 30, 1943; s. Arthur R. and Dora G. (Utt) H.; m. Lynn M. Marsh, Sept. 23, 1982; children: Lara L., James M. BA, U. Okla., 1965, MA, 1979; Inst. Ednl. Mgmt., Harvard U., 1991. Asst. dean students U. Okla., Norman, 1965-67, asst. to pres., 1967-68, asst. to v.p. for univ. rels. and devel., 1978; editor Northland Press, Flagstaff, Ariz., 1972-77; cons. Okla. Dept. Public Safety, Oklahoma City, 1977; asst. dean student affairs Northeastern State U., Tahlequah, Okla., 1978-79, dir. univ. svcs., 1979-82, asst. prof. journalism, 1979—, v.p. adminstrn., 1982-91, v.p. bus. and devel., 1991—, trustee NSU Found., 1981-90, 92—. Mem. Coun. Bus. Officers, Okla. State Regents for Higher Edn., 1982—; adv. dir. BancFirst, 1995—. Author: Ten Years With the Cowboy Artists of America, 1976. Bd. dirs. Friends of Mus. No. Ariz., 1974-77; chmn. No. Ariz. campaign March of Dimes, 1973-74; founding chmn. Cherokee County Cmty. Sentencing Coun., 1997—; No. Ariz. coord. Babbit for Atty. Gen. Campaign, 1974; trustee Flagstaff-Coconino County Pub. Libr., 1976-77, chmn. bd. trustees, 1976-77; pres. Indian Nations Soccer Coun., 1981-82; bd. dirs. Indian Nations coun. Boy Scouts Am., 1990-94, Okla. Found. for Excellence, 1996—; trustee Tahlequah Pub. Schs. Found., 1990-2000, founding chair, 1990-98; bd. dirs., exec. com. Leadership Okla., 1990-98, pres., 1994-95, mem. Class II, 1988-89; bd. dirs. Okla. Assn. of Coll. and Univ. Bus. Officers, 1993-98, pres., 1996-97; bd. dirs. Okla. Acad. for State Goals, 1993—, chair, 1999-2000; founding pres. Boys and Girls Club of Tahlequah, 1996-2000; pres., Coll. Assn. Liability Mgmt., 1996-98, 2002—; bd. dirs. Okla. Arts Inst., 1997—, Okla. Music Hall of Fame, 2000—, Communities Found. Okla., 2000-02. With USAF, 1968-72. Recipient Eason Book Collection award, 1965, Book Design award Rounce and Coffin Club of L.A., 1974-75, Citation of Profl. Merit Northeastern State U., 1991, Excellence in Okla. Leadership award, 1995, Disting. leadership award Nat. Assn. Cmty. Leadership, 1995-96. Mem. U. Okla. Assn. (life), Nat. Cowboy Hall of Fame and Western Heritage Ctr. (life), Tahlequah Area C. of C. (bd. dirs. 1985-88), Mensa, Rotary (past pres., Paul Harris fellow), Sigma Delta Chi, Kappa Tau Alpha, Lambda Chi Alpha. Office: Northeastern State U Adminstrn Bldg Ste 109 Tahlequah OK 74464

HOWARD, JAMES WEBB, investment banker, lawyer, engineer; b. Evansville, Ind., Sept. 17, 1925; s. Joseph R. and Velma (Cobb) H.; m. Phyllis Jean Brandt, Dec. 27, 1948; children: Sheila Rae, Sharon Kae. BS in Mech. Engring, Purdue U., 1949; postgrad., Akron (Ohio) Law Sch., 1950-51, Cleve. Marshall Law Sch., 1951-52; MBA, Case Western Res. U., 1962; JD, Western State Coll. Law, 1976. Registered profl. engr., Ind., Ohio. Jr. project engr. Firestone Tire & Rubber Co., Akron, 1949-50; gen. foreman Cadillac Motor Car div. GM, 1950-53; mgmt. cons. M.K. Sheppard & Co., Cleve., 1953-56; plant mgr. Lewis Welding & Engring. Corp., Ohio, 1956-58; underwriter The Ohio Co., Columbus, 1959; chmn. Growth Capital, Inc., Chgo., 1960-98; pvt. practice law San Diego, 1979-85. Pres. Meister Brau, Inc., Chgo., 1965-73, The Home Mart, San Diego, 1974-82; mng. agt., fin. instn. specialist FDIC/RTC, 1985-90; specialist in charge Office of FDIC-DOL, Portland, Oreg., 1986-87. Developer of "Lite" beer. Co-chmn. Chgo. com. Ill. Sesquicentennial Com., 1968. Served with AUS, 1943-46. Decorated Bronze Star, Parachutist badge, Combat Inf. badge. Mem. ASME, Nat. Assn. Small Bus. Investment Cos. (past pres.), State Bar Calif., Grad. Bus. Alumni Assn. Western Res. U. (past gov.), Masons, Tau Kappa Epsilon, Pi Tau Sigma, Beta Gamma Sigma. Methodist.

HOWARD, JEAN CATHERINE HART, photojournalist, educator; b. Oakland, Calif., May 14, 1948; d. Douglas Charles and Dorothy C. Stahle; m. John Terry Hart, May 5, 1973 (div. Apr. 1983); m. William Pratt Howard, Nov. 7, 1992; children: Samuel Douglas, William Maxwell. Student, Art Ctr. Coll. Design/UCLA, 1977; BA in Journalism, Broadcasting, Advtsg., U. Mo., 1971; Cert. in Photography and Applied Arts, Brooks Inst. Photography, Santa Barbara, Calif., 1989; MA in Photographic Comm., Ohio U., 1991. Dir. art, prodn., pub. rels. Success Mag. TRAID, Chgo., 1982-85; dir. corp. pub. rels. Working Woman mag. Hal Publs., N.Y.C., 1985-86; gen. illustrator Brooks Inst. Photography, Santa Barbara, Calif., 1986-88; photography intern Ventura (Calif.) Star-Free Press, 1988; photo editing intern The Courier-JOur., Louisville, Ky., 1990; photo editor, photographer The Palm Beach Post, West Palm Beach, Fla., 1990-2000; photo editor The Stuart (Fla.) News, 2000. Tchr. curricuium design, instr. pilot program basic elements of photography The Children's Creative Project, Santa Barbara, Calif., 1987; tchr. photography Sch Comm. U. Miami, Coral Gables, 1993, photojournalism II The Art Inst., Ft. Lauderdale, Fla., 1994, intro. to photography Palm Beach C.C., West Palm Beach, Fla., 1996; dir. Shows include Maine Photographic Workshop Gallery, Rockport, 1989, Siegfried Hall Ohio U., Athens, 1990, Spaulding U., Louisville, Ky., 1990, Palm Beach Internat. Airport, West Palm Beach, Fla., 1993, juried exhibn. Fla. artists, Coral Gables, 1994, Ft. Lauderdale (Fla.) Mus. Art 1994, Dutchess County Art Assn., Poughkeepsie, N.Y., 1994, Eissey Campus Theater Gallery Palm Beach C.C., 1996; creator corp. logos including L.A Heart Inst., UCLA Handicapped Found., FK Hubbard and Assocs.; creative dir Boyce Advtsg., Santa Monica, Calif., Personnel Jour., Santa Monica, Mother hood Maternity Shops, Santa Monica; actor: Actors Studio Workshop, L.A. Wisdom Bridge, Chgo., Northwestern U., Evanston, Ill. Vol. The Tennis Patrons, Washington, VISTA, Providence, R.I.; bd. dirs. Love Yourself Found. Santa Barbara, Calif., Juvenile Diabetes, West Palm Beach, Fla., Talent Bank St Vincent Heart Assn., L.A.; mem. Women's Cmty. Ctr., Santa Barbara; founding mem. Juvenile Justice for All project South Fla. chpt. Scholar, tchg. fellow Ohio U., 1990, South Fla. Visual and Media Arts fellow South Fla. Cultura Consortium-NEH, 1992; grantee Fla. Dance Coun., 1994, NEA, 1993; recipien Winner award print competition Photographic Soc. Am., 1987, Best Use o Pictures NPPA-U. Mo., 1992, 3d Pl. Pictorial 1994 So. Short Course Compe tition, Paul Myrhe award Penny-Mo. Journalism, 1995, 3d Pl. Sunshine award Fla. Soc. Profl. Journalism, Carville Pub. Svc. medal Fla. Soc. Newspape Editors, 1999, Nat. Assn. Op. Ed. Editors Best Theme Page, 2000; finalist Soro. Found. Media Group, N.Y. for Fla's. Youngest in Adult Persons, 2000, Best o Photojournalism award Nat. Press Photographers Assn., 2001, 1st pl. Featur award Palm Beach Post, 2001. Mem. Women in Comm., Advt. Women N.Y. Walter Williams Club, Delta Delta Delta. Avocations: reading, walking painting, swimming. Home and Office: 731 High St West Palm Beach Fl 33405-1454 E-mail: jeanhhoward@aol.com.

HOWARD, JEFF DAVID, volunteer, retired military officer; b. Dallas, Jun 14, 1961; s. M.J. and Mary E. Howard; children: Joshua Michael, Alliso Maggie. BS in Geog., U. Ctrl. Ark., 1983. Enlisted U.S. Army, 1979, advance through grades to maj., 1987, ret., 2003; claims examiner, mgr., clk. VA Regional Office, Little Rock, 1986-93. Artist numerous paintings. Vol. Multi cultural Ctr. Ft. Smith, Ark., 1998-2003, bd. dirs., 1998-2003; Red Kettl coord., procurement vol., vol. adminstrv. asst. The Salvation Army, Ft. Smith 1996-2003; missionary Fgn. Mission Bd., So. Bapt. Conv., Moscow, Yalta Ukraine, 1991; vol. Interfaith Disaster Recovery Ctr., Ft. Smith, 1996-97; vol bd. dirs. Alzheimer's Assn., Ft. Smith, 1997; vol. Ctrl. Christian Ch., Ft. Smith 1994—; dep. dir. gen. Internat. Biog. Ctr., Cambridge, Eng., 2003. Named Vol of Yr., Salvation Army, 1996, 97, 98, 99. Mem. Disabled Am. Vets. (Gol Leader award 1997), Am. Biography Soc. Avocations: painting, volunteering fine automobiles, collecting military and foreign country memorabilia, collecting coins and precious metals. Home: PO Box 2194 Fort Smith AR 72902-219

HOWARD, JEFFREY HJALMAR, lawyer; b. N.Y.C., Aug. 23, 1944; s Virgil Edward and Margaretta E. H.; m. Brenda H. Howard, June 19, 1966 children: Taggart Harrison, Brooke Kennedy. BA in Philosophy, Randolph Macon Coll., 1966; postgrad. (English Speaking Union scholar) U. Edinburg (Scotland), 1965; LLB, U. Va., 1969. Bar: D.C. 1970, U.S. Sup. Ct. 1978, Va 1987. Law clk. Circuit Ct., Montgomery County, Md., 1969-70; assoc Covington & Burling, Washington, 1970-74; assoc. gen. counsel for toxics pesticides and solid waste U.S. EPA, Washington, 1974-76; ptnr. Crowell & Moring, 1989—; lectr. antitrust and environ. law U. Va. 1976-89; lectr. enviror

law Peking U., Peoples Republic of China, 1986. Mem. ABA, D.C. Bar Assn., Va. Soc. Fellows, Order Coif, Alpha Psi Omega, Alpha Epsilon Pi, Delta Sigma Rho-Tau Kappa Alpha, Omicron Delta Kappa. Editorial bd. Va. Law Rev., 1967-69; contbr. chpts. to books and articles to profl. jours. Home: 1021 Duchess St Mc Lean VA 22102-2007 Office: 1001 Pennsylvania Ave NW Washington DC 20004-2505

HOWARD, JEFFREY R. judge; b. Claremont, N.H. BA, Plymouth St Coll-Univ N.H., 1978; JD, Law Ctr-Georgetown U, 1981. Assoc. atty. gen. Div. Legal Counsel; atty. Antitrust Div-Atty. Gen. Ofc., 1981; U.S. atty. Dist. of N.H., Concord, 1989—92; atty. gen. State of N.H., 1993—97; ptnr. Choate Hall & Stewart, 1997—2001; judge US Ct. Appeals 1st Cir., 2002—. Mem. atty. gen. adv. com. Attys. Gen. Thornburg & Barr. Office: 1 Warren Rudman US Courthouse 55 Pleasant St Concord NH 03301

HOWARD, JOAN ALICE, artist; b. N.Y.C., Apr. 28, 1929; d. John Volkman and Mary Alice Devlin; m. Robert Thornton Howard, June 26, 1949; children: Barbara Jo, Robert Thornton Jr., Gregory Lyon, Brian Devlin. Student, Hunter Coll., 1947-48, UCLA, 1967-68, Los Angeles Valley Coll., 1970-71. Dir., choreographer Acad. Dance, Floral Park and Forest Hills, N.Y., 1947-57; dir. dance. Cath. Parochial schs., N.Y.C., Bklyn., and Floral Park, N.Y., 1948-55; chair dept. dance Molloy Coll., 1958-67; artist sta. KNBC-TV, L.A., 1967-74, NBC, N.Y.C., 1974-78, sta. WNBC-TV, N.Y.C., 1978-79; artistic dir. Brookville (N.Y.) Sch., 1980-85; tchr. adult continuing edn. Lewisboro (N.Y.) Sch. Sys., 1995-98. Dir. dance N.Y.C. YMCA, 1948; founder, dir. Queens-Nassau Regional Dance Theatre, 1950-55; choreographer Molloy Coll. Dance Theatre, 1959-67; cons. pre-natal exercise, L.I., N.Y., 1980—; judge art show Westbury (N.Y.) Mural Project, 1979; art cons. Chase Manhattan Bank, 1994-96, curator Chase Manhattan Bank, Cross River, N.Y., 1993-94, art. cons. 1996-97; instr. continuing edn. Lewisboro Cross River, N.Y., 1996, 97, 98, Ridgefield, Conn., 1996, 97, 98; instr., speaker in field; instr. adult edn., Ridgefield and Lewisboro, N.Y., 1995-99; instr. all media Painted Fern Ct. Studio, 1998-2000, Brockgreen Gardens Murrells Inlet, S.C., 1999-2000; instr. painting Brookgreen Gardens and Art Works, Litchfield, S.C., 2001; instr. art Coastal Carolina U., Conway, S.C., 2002-03. One-woman shows include Dime Savs. Bank, Manhasset, N.Y., 1986-87, Ridgefield (Conn.) Guild Gallery, 1989-90, 91, 92, 93, Nardin Gallery Fine Arts, 1990, Chase Manhattan Bank, 1990-97, Manhasset Libr. Gallery, 1990-91, Hutchinson Gallery L.I. U., 1991, Rose Gallery, Kent, Conn., 1991, 92, 93, 94, Chelsea House, N.Y., 1991, Plandome Gallery, L.I., 1991, Sacco's, Ridgefield, 1991, Great Neck (N.Y.) Libr. Gallery, 1991, N.Y. Inst. Tech., Greenvale, N.Y., 1992, 93, Chase Manhattan Bank, Cross River, N.Y., 1992-93, 95-96, 96-97, Hicksville (N.Y.) Gallery, 1993, Chase Manhattan Bank, N.Y., 1995-97, Burroughs Chapin Mus., Myrtle Beach, S.C., 2003, Aldrich Mus., 1995, 96, Ridgefield Libr., 1997, Adam Broderick Image Group, mural project Logans, S.C., Januven Gallery, S.C., 2001-02; exhibited in group shows at Valley Ctr. Arts Gallery, L.A., 1968-72, Home Savs. & Loan Art Exhibits, L.A., 1969-70, Westwood Art Gallery, L.A., 1972, Onion Gallery, L.A., 1972, North Ridge Women's Ctr. Gallery, L.A., 1972, Great Neck (N.Y.) Ctr. Gallery, 1976, A&S Gallery, Manhasset, 1976, Gloria Vanderbilt Designers Showcase, 1978, Ridgefield (Conn.) Guild Artists, 1983, Manhasset Libr. Gallery, 1985-89, Great Neck House Gallery, 1986-87, Hutchins Gallery C.W. Post Coll., L.I., 1986-90 (awards 1986, 87, 88, 89, 90), Dime Savs. Bank, Manhasset, N.Y., European Am. Bank, 1988, Nardin Fine Arts, Cross River, N.Y., 1989, Plandome Gallery, N.Y.C., 1990, Aldrich Mus., 1992-93, Hicksville (N.Y.) Gallery, 1993, Ridgefield (Conn.) Guild of Artists Gallery, 1993, Rose Gallery, Hicksville Gallery, 1993, Chase Manhattan Bank, N.Y.C., 1993-94, Tchr. Cont. Edn. Lernsboro Sch. Dist., N.Y., 1995-96, Adam Broderick Image Group, Ridgefield, Conn., 1995-96, Navden Gallery, N.Y., 1996, Masters Art Show, Litchfield, S.C., 2001, Sea Mist Resort, Myrtle Beach. S.C., 2003, others; exhibited in juried shows Nassau County Mus. Fine Arts, Roslyn, N.Y., 1985, Plandome Gallery, 1987-88, Great Neck House Gallery, 1986-89 (hon. mention), East Meadow Libr. Gallery, 1988, Freeport Gallery, 1988, Shelter Rock Gallery, 1989, Ridgefield Gallery Portrait Show, 1989-90, Ridgefield Artists' Guild, 1989, 93, Nardin Gallery, 1989, Hutchins Gallery L.I. U., 1991, Rose Gallery, Kent, Conn., 1991, 92, 94, Chelsea House Mus. Cultural Commn., 1991, Manhasset Gallery, 1990-91, Sacco, Ridgefield, 1991, Great Neck Libr. Gallery, 1991, Chase Manhattan Bank, Cross River, N.Y., 1992-94, 95, Tchrs. Art Yorktown Artists Club, 1994, Aldrich Mus., 1993-94, Ridgefield (Conn.) Art Guild Gallery, 1993, 95, 96, 97, Hicksville (N.Y.) Art Gallery, 1993, Chase Manhattan Bank, N.Y., 1993, 94, 95, 96, 97, 98, HBO, N.Y.C., 1995, Ridgefield Libr. Gallery, 1997, instr. Brookgreen Gardens, Lichtfield, SC; murals, Logan's Roadhouse, SC, Adam Broderick Image grp., CT, Art Works Litchfield, S.C., 2000-02; choreographer contemporary ballet Crucifixion, 1960, Persephone, 1961, Cubes of Truth, 1962, Somewhere, 1965; appeared on radio show Coast to Coast on a Bus, 1939-47; Broadway prodn. Lady in the Dark, 1940-42; performed ballet in TV show Stars of Tomorrow, 1942, Sleeping Beauty, 1942; creator 7 murals Logam Road House, North Myrtle Beach, S.C., 4 paintings Eastport (N.Y.) Animal Hosp.; executor commd. work at color workshops All Media, 1998-2000, numerous others. Dem. committeewoman, Glen Cove, N.Y., 1954-58. Recipient Del Rey Perpetual Race championship trophy, 1974, Little Sabot Perpetual Race trophy, 1972-74, So. Calif. Women's Sailing Conf. sabot championship, 1972-74, 1st Woman trophy Olympic Regatta, 1973. Mem. Dance Educators Am., Manhasset Art Assn., Women's Sailing Com. of U.S. Yacht Racing Union (fund raiser 1980-81), Am. Women's C. of C. L.A., Tri-County Artists Ridgefield Art Guild, Waccemaw Art & Crafts Guild, Georgetown Watercolor Soc. Avocation: racing sail boats and rally cars. Home and Office: 4545 Painted Fern Ct Murrells Inlet SC 29576-6380

HOWARD, JOANNE FRANCES, marketing executive, funeral director, extended care coordinator; b. St. Louis, Feb. 5, 1953; d. Frank Henry and Evelyn Julia (Haeckel) Spellazza; m. Claude Lorrain Howard, May 20, 1978; children: Amy Julia, Laura Ann. BA, U. Mo., St. Louis, 1975; MS, Western Ill. U., 1976. Lic. funeral dir. Analyst Street Industries, Inc., St. Louis, 1977-78; rsch. analyst Gallup & Robinson Co., Princeton, N.J., 1978-80, Jack Eckerd Corp., Clearwater, Fla., 1980-82, sr. rsch. analyst, 1982-88; mktg. cons. Howard Assocs., 1986—; funeral dir. Pugh Funeral Home, Golden City, Mo., 1992—. Marketing executive, funeral director, extended care coordinator, research analyst; b. St. Louis, Feb. 5, 1953; d. Frank Henry and Evelyn Julia (Haeckel) Spellazza; m. Claude Lorrain Howard, May 20, 1978; children: Amy Julia, Laura Ann. BA, U. Mo.-St. Louis, 1975; MS, Western Ill. U., 1976. Lic. funeral director. Analyst, Streett Industries, Inc., St. Louis, 1977-78; research analyst Gallup & Robinson Co., Princeton, N.J., 1978-80, Jack Eckerd Corp., Clearwater, Fla., 1980-82, sr. research analyst, 1982-88; mktg. cons. Howard Assocs., 1986—; cons. Anson Lee Rector Inc., Tarpon Springs, Fla., 1982-83, Med-Op Clinics, Tarpon Springs, Fla., 1983-88; funeral dir., extended care coord. Pugh Funeral Home, Golden City, Mo., 1992—; analyst, cons. H.L. Pugh Assocs. Consulting, Golden City, 1992—. Editor monthly newsletter Florida West Coast chpt. Am. Mktg. Assn., 1982-83. Mem. Pinebrook Homeowners Assn., Largo, Fla., 1983-84. Mem. Am. Mktg. Assn. (past sec.-treas.), Mo. Funeral Dirs. Assn., Nat. Funeral Dirs. Assn., Mo. Inst. Funeral Profls. Democrat. Editor newsletter The Dead Beat—A Caregiver's Soapbox. Active Pinebrook Homeowners Assn., Largo, Fla., 1983-84 Mem. Am. Mktg. Assn. (past sec.-treas., newsletter editor Fla. West Coast chpt. 1982-83), Nat. Funeral Dirs. Assn., Mo. Funeral Dirs. Assn., Mo. Inst. Funeral Profls. Democrat. Home and Office: 708 SE 70th Ln Golden City MO 64748-8152 E-mail: editor@thedead-beat.com.

HOWARD, JOHN, federal agency administrator; MD, Loyola U., 1974; M of Occupational Health, Harvard Sch. Pub. Health, 1982; JD, UCLA, 1986; LLM, George Wash. U., 1987. Bd. Certified Occupational Physician. Internist UCLA Sch. Medicine Pulmonary Fellowship Program, Cedars-Sinai Med. Ctr., L.A.; med. dir. and chief clinician Philip Mandelker AIDS Prevention Clinic; asst. counselor to Under Sec. Health and Human Svcs.; asst. prof. environmental and occupational medicine U. Calif. at Irvine; chief Divsn. Occupational Safety and Health, State of Calif. Dept. Indsl. Rels., 1991—; dir. CDC, Nat. Inst. for Occupational Safety and Health (NIOSH), 2002—. Office: Hubert H Humphrey Bldg 200 Independence SW Rm 715H Washington DC 20201

HOWARD, JOHN ADDISON, former college president, institute executive; b. Evanston, Ill., Aug. 10, 1921; s. Hubert Elmer and Edith (Sackett) H.; m. Janette Marie Nobis, Aug. 11, 1951; children: Marie Starr, Steven Lamson, Martha Nobis, Katherine Louise. Student, Princeton U., 1939-42; BS, Northwestern U., 1947, MA, 1949, PhD, 1962; LL.D., Grove City Coll., 1972, Brigham Young U., 1976, Rockford Coll., 1980. Instr. French Palos Verdes Coll., Rolling Hills, Calif., 1947-49, dean students, 1949-51, v.p., 1950-51, pres., 1951-55; exec. vice chmn. Pres.'s Com. on Govt. Contracts, 1956-57; pres. Rockford (Ill.) Coll., 1960-77; dir. Rockford Coll. Inst., 1977-80; pres. The Rockford Inst., 1980-86, counselor, 1986-97; sr. fellow The Howard Ctr. Religion, Family & Soc., 1997—. Author: Detoxifying the Culture, 2001; contbg. author: Dilemmas Facing the Nation, 1979. Mem. U.S. Commn. on Marijuana and Drug Abuse, 1971-73, Pres.'s Task Force on Priorities in Higher Edn., 1969-70; pres. Ingersoll Found., 1983— . Served to 1st lt. AUS, 1942-45. Decorated Silver Star with oak leaf cluster, Purple Heart with oak leaf cluster.; Recipient Horatio Alger award, 1967; Educator of Yr. Religious Heritage Am., 1980 Mem. Am. Assn. Pres. Ind. Colls. and Univs. (pres. 1969-72), Phila. Soc. (pres. 1979-81), Rockford Country Club, Rotary, Phi Beta Kappa. Home: 1802 Birchwood Ln Rockford IL 61107-1878

HOWARD, JOHN KENNETH, accountant, consultant; b. Milw., May 2, 1946; s. John George and Marjorie Jean (Rastall) H.; children: Kenneth J., Rebecca L., Joseph B., Jessica M. BS in Acctg., Marquette U., 1969. CPA. Staff auditor Arthur Young & Co., Milw., 1969-74, audit mgr. Milw. & N.Y.C., 1974-78, prin., dir. audit Milw., 1978-81, ptnr., 1981-86; exec. v.p. Sharp Packaging Systems, Sussex, Wis., 1987-92; exec. v.p., COO, 1999—2001; acct. pvt. practice, Franklin, Wis., 1992—. Bd. dirs. Franklin Little League, 1983—; pres. Franklin Jaycees, 1981; dist. dir., regional dir. Wis. Jaycees, Milw., 1982-83. With U.S. Army Res., 1968-74. Recipient U.S. Jaycees M. Keith Upson Meml. award, Milw., 1983. Mem. AICPA, Wis. Inst. CPAs., Exec. Agenda. Roman Catholic. Avocations: fishing, gardening, coaching baseball. E-mail: jhowcpa@execpc.com.

HOWARD, JOHN KENNETH, secondary school educator; b. Greeley, Colo., Nov. 24, 1953; s. William Theodore Howard and Ruth Marie Metsker; m. Mary Catherine Howard, Aug. 4, 1984; children: Kenneth William, Thomas Richard. Bachelor's, U. No. Colo., 1976, U. Nebr., 1984, 99. Cert. tchr. Nebr., Colo. Tchr., coach Callaway (Nebr.) Pub. Schs., 1976-82, Grand Island (Nebr.) Ctrl. Cath. Sch., 1984—; libr. asst. Edith Abbott Meml. Libr., Grand Island, 1999—. Avocations: reading, walking, athletics, cooking. Home: 2215 W Koenig Grand Island NE 68803 Office: Grand Island Ctrl Cath 1200 N Ruby Grand Island NE 68803

HOWARD, JOHN LINDSAY, lawyer, forest industry company executive; b. Drumheller, Alta., Can., Nov. 18, 1931; s. Lindsay Lee and Nancy (Martin) H.; m. Jeannette Huguenin, Nov. 21, 1969. B.Comm., U. B.C., 1959, LL.B., 1961; LL.M., Harvard U., 1968; postgrad., McGill U., Montreal, Can., 1967. Bar: B.C. 1962, Que. 1967, Fed. Queen's Counsel 1977. Mem. Brahan, Dickerson & Howard, Vancouver, B.C., 1962-67, Tansey, de Grandpre, Montreal, 1968-71; asst. dep. minister Fed. Dept. Consumer and Corp. Affairs, Ottawa, Ont., 1971-79; sr. v.p. law and corp. affairs MacMillan Bloedel Ltd., Vancouver, 1979-96, cons., corp. dir., comml. law arbitrator, 1996—. Co-author: Proposals for a New Corporation Law for Canada, 1971, Proposals for a Securities Market Law for Canada, 1979. Home: PO Box 1132 Sooke BC Canada V0S 1N0 E-mail: johnhoward@shaw.ca.

HOWARD, JOHN LORING, retired trust banker; b. Auburn, N.Y., Apr. 12, 1935; s. Chauncey Frisbie and Ruth Dorothea (Burrows) H.; m. Catherine Edith Swaffin, July 1, 1961; children: John Loring, Jr., Sarah Catherine. BS, Cornell U., 1957; postgrad., NYU, 1961-62; grad. with distinction, Southwestern Grad. Sch. Banking, 1970. V.p. Chase Manhattan Bank, N.Y.C., 1961-77; sr. v.p., dir. mgr. RepublicBank Houston, 1978-82; sr. v.p., group mgr. RepublicBank Trust Co., Houston, 1983-87, NCNB Tex. Nat. Bank, Dallas, 1988-91, NationsBank of Tex., N.A., Dallas, 1992-95, v.p., 1996-99; ret., 1999. Elder Munn Avenue Presbyn. Ch., East Orange, N.J., 1963-64; chmn. troop com. Boy Scouts Am., New Providence, N.J., 1975-77, chmn. Polaris dist. Friends of Scouting, Houston, 1980-82, vice chmn. North Trail dist. com., Dallas, 1990-93, chmn., 1994-95, mem. Arrowhead dist. com., Austin, 1998—, chmn. Arrowhead dist. Friends of Scouting, 2001—; mem. fin. com. Spring Woods United Meth. Ch., Houston, 1981-84; treas Bethany Found., Inc., Austin, 2001—; vice chmn. bd. trustees Bethany United Meth. Ch., 2002, chmn., 2003—. 1st lt. USMC, 1957-60. Republican. Home: 10676 Bramblecrest Dr Austin TX 78726-1906

HOWARD, JOHN WAYNE, lawyer; b. Dec. 17, 1948; s. Joseph Leon and Irene Elizabeth (Silver) H.; m. Kathleen Amanda Busby, Oct. 7, 1978. BA, U. Calif., San Diego, 1971; JD, Calif. Western Sch. Law, 1976; postgrad., San Diego Inn of Ct., 1979, Hastings Coll. Advocacy, 1981; grad. Program of Instrns. for Lawyers, Harvard Law Sch., 1992. Bar: Calif. 1978, U.S. Dist. Ct. (so. dist.) Calif. 1978, U.S. Supreme Ct. 1989, Colo. 1989, U.S. Dist. Ct. (no. dist.) Calif., U.S. Dist. Ct. (ea. dist.) Calif., U.S. Ct. Appeals (9th cir.) 1995, U.S. Ct. Appeals (D.C. cir.) 1996, U.S. Ct. of Claims 1996. Assoc. Robert T. Dierdorff, San Diego, 1978-79; pvt. practice San Diego, 1979-82; ptnr. Howard & Neeb, San Diego, 1982-84; prin. John W. Howard and Assocs., San Diego, 1984-86; gen. counsel Ace Parking, Inc., 1986-89, CCCA Inc., 1989-93; pres. Individual Rights Found. Inc., 1993-95, Inst. for Constitutional Rights, Inc., 1995—, John W. Howard and Assoc., 1995—. Jud. arbitrator Superior Ct. Calif., 1983—. Chmn. San Diego County Indigent Def. Adv. Bd., 1981-84, mem. subcom. on def. monitoring and budget for Office Defender Svcs. of San Diego County; mem. select com. on small bus. Calif. State Assembly, 1983-90; chmn. San Diego Pub. Arts Adv. Bd.; mem. San Diego County Coun. of Com. Chairs; chmn. precinct orgn. Roger Hedgecock for Supt. Campaign Com., 1976, mem. steering com., 1976; chmn. steering com. Hedgecock for Mayor, 1982, Cleator for Mayor, 1986; chmn. Muscular Dystrophy Telethon, San Diego, 1983; vice chmn. San Diego Festival of Arts, 1983-84; pres. Bowery Theatre, San Diego, 1984-89; pres., bd. dirs. La Jolla Stage Co.; founder, bd. dirs. San Diego Theatre League; 1st v.p., bd. dirs. Muscular Dystrophy Assn.; bd. dirs. Patrick Henry Meml. Found., Brookneal, Va., The Poe Mus., Richmond, Va., San Diego Med. Oncology Rsch. Found., Ilan-Lael Found., Multiple Sclerosis Soc., Am. Ballet Found., Wellness Cmty., Teatro Macara Magica; bd. dirs., chmn. legal affairs subcom. Calif. Motion Picture Coun.; mem. adv. bd. dirs. San Diego Motion Picture Bur.; mem. pub. edn. com. Am. Cancer Soc.; founder, bd. dirs. San Diego Theatre Found., 1984—; mem. 44th Congl. Dist. Adv. Com.; mem. Com. to Re-Elect Congressman Bill Lowery; mem. San Diego County 4th Dist. Adv. Com. Mem. ABA, ATLA, Calif. State Bar Assn., Am. Corp. Counsel Assn., San Diego County Bar Assn. (chmn. superior ct. com. 2002—), Consumer Attys. Assn. L.A., U. Calif.-San Diego Alumni Assn. (past v.p., bd. dirs.), Calif. Western Sch. Law Alumni Assn., Friendly Sons of St. Patrick, Delta Kappa Epsilon, Phi Alpha Delta, Enright Inn of Ct., Am. Inns of Ct. Republican.

HOWARD, JOSEPH HARVEY, retired librarian; b. Olustee, Okla., Jan. 15, 1931; s. William Lester and Letitia Browder (Dickey) H.; m. Patricia Shaughnessy Schiebel, Apr. 10, 1980. B in Mus. Edn., U. Okla., 1952, MLS, 1957. Assoc. dir. pub. svcs. U. Colo. Libr., Boulder, 1960-63; vol. Peace Corps, Kuala Lumpur, Malaysia, 1963-65; head catalog dept. Washington U., St. Louis, 1956-67; asst. chief descriptive cataloging divsn. Libr. of Congress, Washington, 1967-68, chief descriptive cataloging divsn., 1968-72, chief serial record divsn., 1972-75, asst. dir. (cataloging) processing dept., 1975-76, asst. libr. for processing svcs., 1976-83; dir. Nat. Agrl. Libr., Beltsville, Md., 1983-94, ret., 1994. Author: Malay Manuscripts— A Bibliographical Guide, 1966. Served with AUS, 1952-54. Recipient Outstanding Svc. to Librarianship award U. Okla., 1979. Mem. ALA (Melvil Dewey medal 1995) Personal E-mail: jhhoward@comcast.net.

HOWARD, LEE MILTON, international health consultant; b. India, Nov. 9, 1922; s. John A. and Grace Mary (Lemen) H.; m. Maxwell C. Croft, June 22, 1946; children: Regan Ellis, Christine Baker, Kirk Anderson, Gene Reid. B.Sc., Baylor U., 1945; MD, Johns Hopkins U., 1947, M.P.H., 1958, Dr.P.H., 1959. Diplomate: Am. Bd. Preventive Medicine. Med. and surg. resident Church Home Hosp., Balt., 1947-50; mem. med. staff Clough Meml. Hosp., Ongole, Andhra, India, 1950-53; dir. Victoria Meml. Hosp., Warangal, Andhra, India, 1953-56; physician Med. Care Clinic, Johns Hopkins Hosp., 1957; U.S. adviser on malaria Philippines, 1960-62; U.S. regional malaria adviser Far East AID, 1962-64; chief malaria br. health div. AID, Washington, 1964-66; dep. dir. health svc. Office Tech. Coop. and Rsch., 1966-67, dir., 1967, Office Health, Devel. Support Bur., 1967-80; mem. expert co. on malaria WHO, 1966-79, chmn. com., 1970, adviser parasitic diseases, 1970; mem. U.S. del. World Health Assembly, 1969-79, WHO cons. on resource moblzn., 1979-81. AID devel. fellow, 1979-80; vis. asso. prof. parasitology Inst. Hygiene, U. Philippines, 1960—; vis. lectr. Johns Hopkins U. Sch. Pub. Health, Harvard Sch. Pub. Health, Yale U., Boston U., Tulane U.; vis. fellow Inst. Devel. Studies, U. Sussex, 1979; mem. U.S. del., PAHO directing coun.; chief office resource mblzn. PAHO, 1981-82, office of external affairs, 1982-87; cons. to AID, WHO, World Bank, 1987—; sec., mem. exec. com. Gorgas Meml. Inst., 1972; mem. U.S. Sr. Exec. Svc. Recipient Superior Honor award AID, 1974, Disting. Career Svc. award AID, 1987, Disting. Alumnus award Baylor U., 2001; rsch. fellow U.S. Armed Forces Epidemiol. Bd., 1958-59. Fellow Am. Pub. Health Assn., Royal Soc. Tropical Medicine and Hygiene; mem. Am. Soc. Tropical Medicine and Hygiene, Philippine Pub. Health Assn., Johns Hopkins U. Sch. Pub. Health Soc. Alumni (pres. 1984-85), Soc. Scholars (Johns Hopkins U.), Nat. Coun. Internat. Health (charter mem.), Diplomatic and Consular Officers Ret., Cosmos Club (Washington). Home: 647 Azalea Dr Apt 1 Rockville MD 20850-2012

HOWARD, LEWIS SPILMAN, lawyer; b. Knoxville, Tenn., Oct. 10, 1930; s. Frank Catlett and Lillian (Spilman) H.; m. Anne Robinson, Dec. 26, 1953 (div. 1976); children: Catherine C., Martha S., Lewis S. Jr., Laura A. (dec.). BSBA, JD, U. Tenn., 1953. Bar: Tenn. 1953, U.S. Ct. Mil. Appeals 1954, U.S. Dist. Ct. Ga. 1954, U.S. Dist. Ct. Tenn. 1956, U.S. Ct. Appeals (6th cir.) 1959. Ptnr. Kennerly, Montgomery, Howard & Finley, Knoxville, 1957-84, Howard & Ridge, Knoxville, 1984-99, Howard & Howard, Knoxville, 2000—. Gen. counsel Coal Creek Mining and Mfg. Co., Knoxville, 1969—, pres., 1971—. Vice chmn. Knoxville Bd. Edn., 1968-71. Capt. JAGC, USAR, 1953-56. Mem. ABA, Tenn. Bar Assn., Knoxville Bar Assn., Cherokee Country Club. Republican. Presbyterian. Avocation: boating. Home: 1604 Kenesaw Ave Knoxville TN 37919-7863 Office: Howard & Howard 4800 Old Kingston Pike Knoxville TN 37919-6478

HOWARD, LOU DEAN GRAHAM, elementary education educator; b. Conway, Ark., Aug. 11, 1935; d. Nathan Eldridge and Martha Regina (Sutherland) Graham; m. Robert Hunt Howard, June 4, 1961; 1 child, Kenneth Paul. BSE, U. Cen. Ark., 1957; MA, Vanderbilt U., 1960. Cert. sch. adminstr., prin./supr., curriculum specialist, mentor, grad. elem. Elem. tchr. Hughes (Ark.) Pub. Schs., 1957-59; supervisory tchr. Peabody Demonstration Sch., Nashville, 1959-61; elem. tchr. Orange County Pub. Schs., Orlando, Fla., 1965-68; elem. tchr., K-5 adminstr. Westchester Acad., High Point, N.C., 1968-77; tchr. alternative learning ctr.-mid. sch. Randolph County Pub. Schs., Archdale-Trinity, 1978; elem. tchr. Greensboro (N.C.) Pub. Schs., 1978-93, Guilford County Schs., High Point, N.C., 1993-97, ret., 1997. Contbr. articles to newspapers and AAUW Bull. Active Stephen Ministry, commnd. Stephen Leader, 2002; citizen ambassador program of People to People Internat. del. to U.S./China Joint Conf. on Women's Issues, Beijing, 1995; precinct chmn. county exec. com., state exec. com. of Dem. Party; mem. High Point (N.C.) Racial Justice Task Force. Mem.: AAUW (pres. N.C. state 1982—84, assn. nominating com. 1985—87, pres. High Point br. 1988—90, co-pres. 1998—2002, N.C. state parliamentarian 2002—, Gift honoree Ednl. Found.), NEA (sch. rep., mem. instrnl. and profl. devel. com.), ASCD, Clan Graham Soc. (sec. 1982—2002, Disting. Svc. award), N.C. Women's Orgns., Peabody Coll. Elem. Coun. (sec.), Ind. Schs. Assn., Assn. Childhood Edn. Internat. (past pres.), Order of The Golden Thistle (charter), Phi Delta Kappa, Delta Kappa Gamma (rsch. chair 1998—2000). Methodist. Home: 1228 Kensington Dr High Point NC 27262-7316

HOWARD, LOUNITA COOK, nonprofit executive director; b. Lebanon, Tenn., July 30, 1962; d. Gordon Lew and Sandra Marie (Davis) Cook; m. Bobby Le Howard, Feb. 19, 1983. BS, Middle Tenn. State U., 1985. Intern The Bus. Jour., Nashville, 1985; staff writer The Nashville Bus. Jour., 1985-86, The Lebanon Democrat, 1986-89, news editor, 1989-98; exec. dir. United Way of Wilson County, Lebanon, Tenn., 1998—; owner, pub. The Watertown Gazette, 2003—. Campaign coord. Wilson County United Way, 1990, mem. comms. com., 1991-92; mem. adv. bd. March of Dimes, Wilson County, 1991; grad. Leadership Wilson, 1995. Recipient Appreciation plaques Wilson County Edn. Assn., 1988, Enhanced 911 Wilson County, 1990; Sch. Bell award Tenn. Edn. Assn., 1988-89, Cert. of Recognition, 1990, Cert of Appreciation, March of Dimes, 1991, Mng. Editors awards Tenn. Assoc. Press. Mem. Tenn. Press Assn. (1st pl. award 1989-91, 95, 97-98), Soc. Profl. Journalists, Lebanon Bus. and Profl. Women's Club (2d v.p. 1993-94, 1st v.p. 1994-95, pres. 1995-96, Woman of Yr. 1994-95, Young Careerist 1990), Lebanon-Wilson County C. of C. (amb. 1997-2002), Lascassas-Milton Lions (treas. 1998-2001) Wilson Orgn. for Networking and Edn. (charter/founding mem., v.p. 2001-02, pres. 2002-03). Baptist. Avocations: home renovation, remodeling, gardening, reading. Office: United Way of Wilson County 102 E Main St PO Box 3541 Lebanon TN 37088-3541

HOWARD, LYN JENNIFER, medical educator; b. Buxton, U.K., Jan. 19, 1938; came to U.S., 1965; naturalized, 1971; d. Peter and Bess (Donnelly) Marsh; m. Burtis Howard, Mar. 13, 1965 (div. 1988); children: Peter Howard, Thia Howard; m. Jack Alexander, Sept. 10, 1995. BA, Oxford U., 1960, MA, BM, BCh, 1964. Diplomate Am. Bd. Internal Medicine, diplomate Am. Bd. Nutrition. Intern London Hosp., 1964-65, Kans. City Med. Ctr., 1965-66, resident, 1966-70; fellow in clin. nutrition and gastroenterology Vanderbilt Hosp., 1971-73; dir. clin. nutrition program Albany (N.Y.) Med. Coll., 1973-80, asst. prof. medicine, pediat., 1973-76, assoc. prof. medicine, pediat., 1977-84, prof. medicine, 1984—, head divsn. clin. nutrition, 1986—. Asst. dir. Clin. Studies Ctr., Albany Med. Ctr., 1973-78; attending physician Albany Med. Ctr. Hosp., 1973—; attending physician, cons. clin. nutrition Albany VA Hosp., 1973—; cons. pediat. gastroenterology St. Peter's Hosp., Albany, 1974—; med. dir. Albany Home Health Resources, 1991-92; mem. working group Nat. Commn. Digestive Diseases, 1977; mem. NIH Consensus Devel. Conf., 1978, nutrition rsch. directions, 1979, spl. study sect. clin. nutrition rsch. units, 1980, nutrition study sect., 1989-93; cons. AMA Drug Evaluations, 1982, Medicare, Blue Cross/Blue Shield S.C., 1987—; keynote spkr. Australian Soc. Parenteral and Enteral Nutrition, Perth, 1993, 1st Clin. Nutrition Symposium, Kuala Lumpor, Malaysia, 1994. Contbg. editor Nutrition Reviews, 1981-87, 89; mem. editl. bd. Jour. Drug-Nutrient Interactions, 1984, Contemporary Issues in Clin. Nutrition, 1985, Jour. Am. Soc. Parenteral and Enteral Nutrition, 1987-90; contbr. articles, abstracts to profl. jours., chpts. to books. Exec. dir. Oley Found. for Home Parenteral and Enteral Nutrition, 1983-87, pres., 1987-91, med. dir., 1991; pres. Camphill Found., Pa., 1994. Recipient Clifton C. Thorne Cmty. Svc. award, 1990, Physician of Yr. award Albany chpt. Crohn's Colitis Found. Am., 1991; elected 1st woman mem. Great Lakes Interurban Club, 1990; Major County scholar, 1956; grantee Nutrition Found., 1973-79, U.S. Dept. Agriculture, 1978-81, William F. Donner Found., 1983, Oley Found. for Home Parenteral and Enteral Nutrition Patients, 1983—, Home Health Care of Am., 1983-88, Hosp. for Incurables Found., 1987-88, 91, Schaeffer Found. for Faculty Devel., 1988. Fellow Royal Coll. Physicians, Am. Coll. Physicians, Am. Coll. Nutrition (dir. 1985-88); mem. Am. Bd. Nutrition (dir. 1980, pres. 1982-84), Brit. Med. Assn., Am. Soc. Parenteral and Enteral Nutrition (abstract selection com. 1980, nutrition support standards com. 1984, future directions com. 1991, OASIS working group 1991-92, award 1992), Am. Soc. Clin. Nutrition (rsch. com. 1978, edn. com. 1979, councilor 1982-85, chair post grad. clin. nutrition tng. com. 1983-88, clin. practice in health and disease 1991), Am. Inst. Nutrition, Am. Gastroent. Assn. (co-organizer post grad. tng. course 1987, tng. and edn. com. 1988-91, abstract selection com. 1989), N.Am. Soc. Pediat. Gastroenterology, Am. Fedn. Clin. Rsch. (abstract selection com. 1986), Alpha Omega Alpha. Office: Albany Med Coll Albany NY 12208

HOWARD, MARILYN HOEY, lawyer; b. Keene, N.H., Aug. 17, 1952; d. Thomas John and Arleen Carol (Grimmelman) Hoey; m. Charles Taylor Howard, Apr. 14, 1984; children: Joseph Dale, John Thomas. BA, Univ. Fla., 1975; JD, Duke Univ. Sch. Law, 1978. Bar: Fla. 1979, U.S. Cir. Ct. (5th and 11th cirs.) Fla. 1980. Sr. coun. Harris Corp., Melbourne, Fla., 1978-98. Mem. adv. bd. Indian River Nat. Bank, 1998—. Mem. Fla. Bar (chair corp. counsel com. Bus. Law Sect. 1996-98, chair quality of life, stress mgmt. com. 1995-97), Republican. Avocations: writing, poetry, italian. Home: 2552 King St NE Palm Bay FL 32905-4704 E-mail: marilena@juno.com.

HOWARD, MELVIN, financial executive; b. Boston, Jan. 5, 1935; s. John M. and Molly (Sagar) H.; m. Beverly Ruth Kahan, June 9, 1957; children: Brian David, Marjorie Lyn. BA, U. Mass., 1957; MS, Columbia U., 1959. Fin. exec. Ford Motor Co., Dearborn, Mich., 1959-67; v.p. adminstrn. Shoe Corps. of Am., Columbus, Ohio, 1967-70; contr., sr. v.p. fin., chief fin. officer Xerox Corp.,

1970-84, exec. v.p., chmn. fin. svcs., 1984-86, vice chmn. of bd., 1986-90, bd. dirs., 1982-90; pres., CEO Ehrlich Bober Fin. Corp., 1990-92; mng. dir. Taurus Adv. Group, 1993-94. Bd. dirs. Gould Pumps, Inc., Sector Mgmt., Inc. Trustee Nursing and Home Care, Commonwealth Coll. 1st lt. AUS, 1957. Mem. Birchwood Country Club, Frenchman's Creek Country Club, Beta Gamma Sigma. Home: 3139 Miro Dr S Palm Beach Gardens FL 33410-1285

HOWARD, MICHAEL ELIOT, historian, educator; b. London, Nov. 29, 1922; s. Geoffrey Eliot and Edith Julia Emma (Edinger) H. MA, U. Oxford, 1948, LittD, 1976, Leeds (Eng.) U.; DLitt, U. London, 1988. Asst. lectr. history Kings Coll. U. London, 1947-53, lectr. war studies, 1953-62; prof. war studies U. London, 1963-68; fellow higher defence studies All Souls Coll., Oxford, 1968-77; prof. history of war U. Oxford, 1977-80, regius prof. modern history, 1980-89; prof. history Yale U., New Haven, 1989-93. Pres. Internat. Inst. Strategic Studies, London. Author: The Franco Prussian War, 1961 (Duff Cooper Prize, 1962), Grand Strategy, vol. IV, 1971 (Wolfson award for history), War in European History, 1976, The Invention of Peace, 2002, The First World War, 2003, many others. Served to capt. Brit. Army, 1942-45. Decorated Mil. Cross His Majesty King George VI, comdr. Brit. Empire, companion of Honor; recipient Atlantic award, NATO, 1989; created Knight Bachelor, 1986. Fellow Brit. Acad., U.S. Acad. Arts and Scis., Athenaeum Club, Garrick Club (London). Anglican.

HOWARD, MICHAEL JOSEPH, communications executive, real estate developer; b. Detroit, Oct. 26, 1951; s. Thomas Angel and Margaret Jane (Uttenweiler) H.; divorced; children: Jennifer Paula, Daniel Joseph. Student, Schoolcraft Coll., 1971. Lic. real estate broker, Mich.; lic. residential builder, Mich. Mem. field svc. staff ITT, Southfield, Mich., 1971-81; pres. Howard Properties, Inc., Southfield, 1988—93, Allied Alarm Systems, Inc., Southfield, 1988—98, Allied Communications, Inc., Southfield, 1979—. Commr. Downtown Devel. Authority, Southfield, 1989—. Mem. Nat. Assn. Home Builders, Nat. Fedn. Ind. Bus., Mich. Assn. Home Builders, Mich. Pay Telephone Assn. (treas. 1986), Southfield C. of C., Optimist Club (charter). Republican. Roman Catholic. Avocations: numismatics, classic cars, boating. Office: Allied Communications Inc 17600 Northland Park Ct Southfield MI 48075-4321

HOWARD, MILDRED, sculptor; b. San Francisco, 1945; AA, cert. in fashion arts, Coll. Alameda, 1977; MFA in Fiberworks, John F. Kennedy U., 1985. One-woman shows include Mill Valley (Calif.) Old Post Office, 1984, Dade County Libr., Miami, Fla., 1985, Calif. State U., Hayward, 1987, Headlands Ctr. for the Arts, Sausalito, Calif., 1991, San Francisco Art Inst., 1991, Gallery Paule Anglim, San Francisco, 1991, 93, INTAR, N.Y.C., 1992, U. Art Gallery, Sonoma State U., Rohnert Park, Calif., 1992, San Jose (Calif.) Mus. Art, 1994, Hammonds House Galleries, Atlanta, 1994, Capp St. Project, San Francisco, 1994; group exhbns. include Security Pacific Gallery, San Francisco, 1992, Lew Allen Gallery, Santa Fe, 1992, Shea & Bornstein Gallery, Santa Monica, 1992, Creative Time, N.Y.C., 1992, Berkeley Art Ctr., 1992, Nina Nielsen Gallery, Boston, 1993, New Mus. Contemporary Art, N.Y.C., 1993, Calif. Crafts Mus., San Francisco, 1994, U. Calif. Berkeley Mus. Art, Sci. and Culture, 1994, Laney Coll., Oakland, Calif., 1994, The Mus. at Blackhawk, Danville, Calif., 1994, Hampton (Va.) U. Mus., 1994, Gallery Resche, Paris, 1994, Yerba Buena Ctr. for the Arts, San Francisco, 1994, Installation Gallery, San Diego, 1994, Jewett Hall Gallery, U. Maine, Augusta, 1994, CCAC, Oakland, 1994, Oakland Mus., 1994, Louis Stern Fine Arts, L.A., 1995, Gallery Concord, 1995, others; represented in permanent collections Oakland Mus., Wadsworth Atheneum, Hartford, Conn., Rene and Veronica di Rosa Found., Napa, Calif., pvt. collections. Recipient Bank of Am. award, San Francisco, 1975, Small Projects award Inter Arts Marin, San Rafael, Calif., 1984, Adaline Kent award San Francisco Art Inst., 1991; fellow in mixed media Calif. Arts Coun., 1990, Lila A. Wallace/Reader's Digest Internat. Traveling fellow, 1992-93. Office: c/o Porter Troupe Gallery 301 Spruce St San Diego CA 92103-5626

HOWARD, M(OSES) WILLIAM, JR., minister; b. Americus, Ga., Mar. 3, 1946; s. M. William and Laura (Turner) H.; m. Barbara Jean Wright, July 11, 1970; children: Matthew Weldon, Adam Turner, Maisha Wright BA, Morehouse Coll., 1968, L.H.D., 1984; M.Div., Princeton Theol. Sem., 1972; D.D., Miles Coll., 1979, Central Coll., 1980; LLD, Bloomfield Coll., 2001. Ordained to ministry Am. Baptist Ch., 1974; exec. dir. Black Council, Ref. Ch. in Am., N.Y.C., 1972-92; pres. N.Y. Theol. Sem., N.Y.C., 1992-00; pastor Bethany Baptist Ch., Newark, 2000—. Bd. dirs. Nat. Conf. Black Churchmen, 1975-80; moderator Commn. of World Council Chs. Program to Combat Racism, 1976-78; bd. dirs. Nat. Media Found.; pres. Nat. Council Chs., 1979-81; condr. Christmas services for hostages Am. embassy, Tehran, Iran, 1979; chmn. UN Seminar on Bank Loans to South Africa, Zurich, 1981; chmn. ecumenical delegation to Syria, 1984, instrumental (with Rev. Jesse Jackson) in obtaining release of Lt. Robert O. Goodman, USN; chair religious com. to welcome Nelson Mandela to U.S.A., 1990. Researcher: Born to Rebel - Autobiography of Benjamin Elijah Mays, 1967; editor: monthly newsletter Black Caucus RCA, 1973-92; pub., producer ann. lectureship, 1975-92. Active YMCA; trustee Trenton State Coll., 1981-82, Nat. Urban League; bd. dirs. Children's Def. Fund, The Independent Sector, founding mem. People for Am. Way; pres. Am. Com. on Africa, 1987-92; mem. Coun. Fgn. Rels., 1997—. Recipient Disting. Service award as chmn. Commn. on Justice, Liberation and Human Fulfillment, Disting. Alumnus award Princeton Theol. Sem., 1984; decorated comdr. Order Knights of Holy Sepulchre. Mem. NAACP, Assn. Theol. Schs. in U.S. and Can. (sec. 1998-2000), Sigma Pi Phi. Baptist. Office: Bethany Baptist Ch 275 W Market St Newark NJ 07103 E-mail: mwhoward@bethany-newark.org. *Perhaps the greatest challenge to humanity today is to see that our moral and ethical development catches up, and keeps pace with, our advances in technology.*

HOWARD, MURIEL A. academic administrator; Grad., CUNY; MA in Edn., SUNY, Buffalo, 1973, D in Edni. Orgn., Adminstrn., Policy, 1985. Asst. dir. Univ. Learning Ctr. SUNY, Buffalo, 1974-81, dir. University Learning Ctr., 1981-84, dir. Ednl. Opportunity Ctr., 1984-87, assoc. vice provost for spl. programs, 1987-90, asst. to pres., 1990-91, dep. to pres., 1991-92, v.p. pub. svc. and urban affairs, 1992-95; pres. Buffalo State Coll., N.Y., 1996—. Co-founder Buffalo Prep; co-chair adv. task force on gen. edn. SUNY Provost; bd. dirs. Merchants Mutual Ins. Co., Fleet Bank, Grace Manor Nursing Home, Greater Buffalo Devel. Found., Buffalo Mus. of Sci., Studio Arena Theatre. Bd. dirs. United Way Buffalo and Erie County (campaign chair 1999); mem. Erie County Exec.'s transition team (chair subcom. Youth Svcs. and Edn.). Recipient Governor's State Divsn. of Women award, Am. Jewish Com. Inst. of Human Rels. award, Disting. Alumni award U. Buffalo, Disting. Alumna award Staten Island Coll., Educator of Yr. award Black Educators Assn. of Western N.Y., 1991, award for Community Svc. Minority Bar Assn. W. N.Y., Disting. Alumnus award Catholic Campus Ministry, Award of Excellence Project WIN's, 1993; charter inductee W. N.Y. Women's Hall of Fame. Mem. Am. Assn. State Colls. and Universities (bd. mem.); mem. pres.'s bd. Nat. Collegiate Athletics Assn. Office: Buffalo State Coll GC 517 1300 Elmwood Ave Buffalo NY 14222-1004

HOWARD, NATHAN SOUTHARD, investment banker, lawyer; b. Marysville, Ohio, May 4, 1941; s. Cone Howard Jr. and Catherine (Southard) H.; divorced; children— Ercil Coleman, Lyndsay Christine BA, William and Mary Coll., 1962, JD, 1965. V.p. White Weld & Co., N.Y.C., 1972-75; v.p. Prudential-Bache Securities, Inc., N.Y.C., 1975-80, assoc. dir., 1980-82, mng. dir., 1985-89; dir. energy and utilities group Barclays de Zoete Wedd Corp. Fin., N.Y.C., 1990-93; v.p. energy divsn. Bank of New York, N.Y.C., 1993—. Bd. dirs. People Symphony Concerts, N.Y.C., 1982— Mem. ABA, N.Y. State Bar, N.Y. Soc. Securities Analysts, Bond Club N.Y., Univ. Club (N.Y.C.). Home: 19 East 80 St 3C New York NY 10021 Office: Bank of New York 1 Wall St 19th Fl New York NY 10286 E-mail: nhoward@bankofny.com.

HOWARD, PATRICK GENE, marine corps officer; b. Wheeling, Va., Nov. 28, 1945; s. Gene Edward and Margaret Anna (Fry) H.; m. Paula Lee Oberle, May 25, 1969; children: Brian, Michael, Marc. BS, U.S. Naval Acad., 1967; MPA, Shippensburg U., 1987. Commd. ensign USMC, 1967, advanced through grades to maj., 1995; comdg. officer 2d Bn., 10th Marines, 1981; head policy sect., exec. asst. Hqrs. Marine Corps; comdr. 11th Marines, 1990-92; sec. gen. staff Asst. Commandant Marine Corps Office, 1992-93; dir. pers. mgmt. divsn. Manpower and Res. Affairs Dept. Hdqs. Marine Corps, Washington, 1993-95; comdg. gen. Marine Corps Base, Camp Lejeune, N.C., 1995-97, dep. comdg. gen., 1997-99; dir. res. affairs divsn. USMC, Quantico, Va., 1999—. Decorated Legion of Merit with Combat V and gold star, Def. Meritorious Svc. Medal, Meritorious Svc. medal with gold star. Roman Catholic. Avocation: golf. Office: Marine Corps Base PSC Box 20004 Quantico VA 22134-9100

HOWARD, PIERRE, former state official; m. Nancy Elizabeth (Barnes); children: Christopher, Caroline. Grad., U. Ga., 1965, JD, 1968. Former mem. Ga. Senate, Atlanta, former asst. floor leader, former chmn. human resources com.; lt. gov. State of Ga., Atlanta, 1991-98; ptnr. Spl. Corp. Strategies, Atlanta, 1999—; co-founder Insider Advantage.com, Atlanta. Recipient Nathan Davis Award AMA, 1996. Mem. Phi Beta Kappa. Office: Insider Advantage.com 4401 Northside Pkwy. Ste 130 Atlanta GA 30327*

HOWARD, RICHARD RALSTON, II, medical health advisor, researcher, financier; b. Winnfield, Kans., May 26, 1948; s. Richard Ralston and Ione (Mayer) H. BBA, Loyola U., New Orleans, 1970; MPH, Tulane U., 1977, MS, 1984, DrPH, 1988. Researcher Loyola U., 1973; educator Dominican Coll., New Orleans, 1977; educator Sch. Pub. Health Tulane U., New Orleans, 1978-82, researcher Sch. Medicine, 1979-88; med. health advisor Howard Med. Clinic, Slidell, La., 1982-91; founder The Inst. Econ. Tech. Rsch., New Orleans, 1993—. NIH grantee, 1979; VA grantee, 1984. Mem. Internat. Platform Assn., Am. Assn. Individual Investors, Beta Beta Beta. Achievements include research on the impact of the health food industry on nutrition awareness, cocaine testing through quantitative tear analysis, vitamin C and ophthalmic wound healing. Home: 3531 Nashville Ave New Orleans LA 70125-4339

HOWARD, ROBERT ELLIOTT, former federal official, consultant, educator; b. Staten Island, N.Y., Feb. 19, 1933; s. David and Helen (Gresser) H.; m. Bulbul Batra, Mar. 24, 1957; children: Nina Howard Regan, Nicholas, Sarah. AB, Columbia U., 1952; DPhil, Oxford U., Eng., 1957. Rsch. fellow in physics Carnegie Inst. Tech., Carnegie-Mellon U., Pitts., 1958-60; rsch. physicist Nat. Bur. Standards, Washington, 1960-67; mem. profl. staff Office Mgmt. and Budget, Washington, 1968-87, dep. assoc. dir. for nat. security, 1987-90, assoc. dir. for nat. security and internat. affairs, 1990-93; vis. prof. Nat. Defense Univ., Washington, 1993-95; pres. Key Assocs., 1995—. Adj. prof. nat. security studies Georgetown U., Washington, 1993—2002; vis. rsch. physicist U.K. Atomic Energy Authority, Harwell, England, 1962. Contbr. numerous articles to profl. jours. Recipient Presdl. Meritorious Exec. award, 1987, Presdl. Disting. Exec. award, 1990; Fulbright fellow Indian Inst. Tech., New Delhi, 1966. Fellow Am. Phys. Soc. Republican. Avocations: walking, reading, arts, tennis. E-mail: rhoward9@erols.com.

HOWARD, ROBERT FRANKLIN, observatory administrator, astronomer; b. Delaware, Ohio, Dec. 30, 1932; s. David Dale and Clarine Edna (Morehouse) H.; m. Margaret Teresa Farnon, Oct. 4, 1958; children: Thomas Colin, Alan Robert, Moira Catharine BA, Ohio Wesleyan U., 1954; PhD, Princeton U., 1957. Carnegie fellow Mt. Wilson and Palomar Obs., Pasadena, Calif., 1957-59, staff mem., 1961-81; asst. prof. U. Mass., Amherst, 1959-61; asst. dir. for Mt. Wilson Mt. Wilson & Las Campanas Obs., Pasadena, 1981-84; dir. Nat. Solar Obs., Tucson, 1984-88, astronomer, 1988-98, astronomer emeritus, 1998—. Editor: Solar Magnetic Fields, 1971; editor: (jour.) Solar Physics, 1987-98; contbr. articles to profl. jours. Mem. Am. Astron. Soc. (Hale prize 2003), Internat. Astron. Union.

HOWARD, ROBERT STAPLES, newspaper publisher; b. Wheaton, Minn., Oct. 23, 1924; s. Earl Eaton and Helen Elizabeth (Staples) H.; m. Lillian Irene Crabtree, Sept. 2, 1945; children: Thomas, Andrea, William, David. Student, U. Minn., 1942, 45. Pub. various daily, weekly newspapers, 1946-55; pub. Chester, Pa. Times, 1955-61; Pres. Howard Publs. (18 daily newspapers), 1961—2002. With AUS, 1942-43; 2d lt. USAAF, 1944-45. Home: PO Box 1337 Rancho Santa Fe CA 92067-1337 Office: 2525 Pio Pico Dr Ste 202 Carlsbad CA 92008-0570

HOWARD, RON, director, actor; b. Duncan, Okla., Mar. 1, 1954; s. Rance and Jean Howard; m. Cheryl Alley, June 7, 1975; 4 children: Bryce, Jocelyn and Paige (twins), Reed. Student, U. So. Calif., Los Angeles Valley Coll. Co-chmn. Imagine Films Entertainment, L.A. Actor: (theatre) The Seven Year Itch, 1956, Hole in the Head, 1963; (films) The Journey, 1959, Five Minutes to Live, 1959, Music Man, 1962, The Courtship of Eddie's Father, 1963, Village of the Giants, 1965, Wild Country, 1971, Happy Mother's Day... Love George, 1973, American Graffiti, 1973, The Spikes Gang, 1974, The First Nudie Musical, 1976, Eat My Dust, 1976, The Shootist, 1976, Grand Theft Auto (also dir.), 1977, More American Graffiti, 1979, The Magical World of Chuck Jones, 1992; (TV, host/narrator) Frank Capra's American Dream, 1997; dir.: Night Shift, 1982, Splash, 1984, Cocoon, 1985, Gung Ho, (also exec. prodr.) 1986, No Man's Land, (also exec. prodr.) 1987, Willow, 1988, Parenthood (also co-author) 1989, Backdraft, 1991, Far and Away (also co-prodr., co-author) 1992, The Paper, 1994, Apollo 13, 1995 (Outstanding Directorial Achievement in Motion Picture award Dirs. Guild Am. 1996), Ransom, 1996, Edtv, 1999, dir. prodr. A Beautiful Mind, 2001 (Best Dir., Best Picture Oscar award 2002); actor, dir. prodr. Dr. Seuss-How the Grinch Stole Christmas, 2000; exec. prodr.: Clean and Sober, 1988, Vibes, 1988, Closet Land, 1991, Inventing the Abbotts, 1997, Hiller and Diller (TV, exec.), 1997, From the Earth to the Moon (mini series), 1998, Sports Night (TV series, exec.), 1998, Felicity (TV series, exec.), 1998, Student Affairs (TV), 1999, How to Eat Fried Worms, 1999, Detox, 1999, The PJs (TV series, exec.), Edtv, 1999, (TV Series) 24, 2001, The Beast, 2001, Arrested Development, 2003, co-prodr.: Stealing Harvard, 2002; regular TV series: The Andy Griffith Show, 1960-68, The Smith Family, 1971-72, Happy Days, 1974-80; other TV appearances include New Breed, Wonderful World of Disney, Gentle Ben, Laverne and Shirley, Twilight Zone, Danny Kaye Show, Fugitive, Dennis the Menace, Bonanza, Five Fingers, Gunsmoke, The F.B.I., 11th Hour, (TV movies) The Migrants, 1974, Locusts, 1974, Huckleberry Finn, 1975, Cotton Candy (co-writer, dir.) 1978, Act of Love, 1980, Bitter Harvest, 1981, Fire On the Mountain, 1981, Skyward (dir., co-exec. prodr.) 1981, Through the Magic Pyramid (dir., exec. prodr.) 1981, When Your Lover Leaves (co-exec./prodr.) 1983, Return to Mayberry, 1986, (voice) Osmosis Jones, 2001 (animation), Boarding School, 2002. Mem. AFTRA, SAG, Acad. Motion Picture Arts and Scis. Office: Richard Lovett CAA 9830 Wilshire Blvd Beverly Hills CA 90212

HOWARD, RUSSELL ALFRED, astrophysicist, researcher; b. Baltimore, Md., Aug. 17, 1941; s. Michael and Evelyn Howard; m. Rosalie Elizabeth Nasuta, Feb. 6, 1966; children: Geoffrey, Matthew. BS, Univ. Marlyand, College Park, MD, 1964; PhD, Univ. Md., College Park, MD, 1969. Resident assoc. Nat. Rsch. Coun., Wash., 1969—71; astrophysicist Naval Rsch. Lab, Wash., 1971—98, head, solar physics br., 1998—. Author: (book) Solar Physics; contbr. articles to profl. jours. Recipient Stellar Award, RNASA, Houston, TX, 2001, E.O. Hulburt Sci. Award, Naval Rsch. Lab, Wash., DC, 2002, Berman Publ. award, Naval Rsch. Lab, 2002, Tech. Transfer Award, Naval rsch. Lab., 1997. Mem.: Am. Astron. Soc., Solar Physics Div., Am. Geophys. Union. Home: 9936 Wood Grouse Court Burke VA 22015-2920 Office: Naval Research Lab Code 7660 Washington DC 20375

HOWARD, STEPHEN JAMES, clinical psychologist; b. Warsaw, Jan. 23, 1926; came to U.S., 1949; s. Maciej Halpern and Romana Kenig; m. Bozenna Emilia Howard, Aug. 6, 1960; 1 child, Jacqueline Ann. BA, U So. Calif., 1951; MA, L.A. State Coll., 1953; PhD, U. So. Calif., 1962. Bd. Cert. Diplomate Am. Bd. Profl. Psychology, 1967. Clin. psychologist L.A. County Juvenile Hall Clin., 1956-58; sr. clin. psychologist Calif. Youth Authoriy, Norwalk, Calif., 1958-62, Calif. Dept. Mental Hygiene, L.A., 1962-65; dir. program devel. San Fernando Valley Child Guidance Clin., Northridge, Calif., 1965-91; pvt. practice Studio City, Calif., 1962—. Assoc. clin. prof. U.C.L.A., 1996—, chmn/prof. advisory com. S.F.V. Child Guidance Clin., Northridge, Calif., 1997—, mem. mental health disaster team Am. Red Cross, L.A., 1992—, chmn. Countywide Interagency Com. Mental Health, 1977, 85. Contbr. to profl. jours. Chmn. Children & Youth Com., 1980-91; chairperson Citizen's Advisory Com., 1983. Recipient Certificate of Merit U.S. House of Reps., 1991, Commendation Resolution award Calif. Legis. Assembly, 1991, Appreciation & Recognition award County L.A., 1991, City of L.A., 1991. Fellow Soc. Personality Assesment; mem. APA, Calif. Psychological Assn. (pres., 1977), L.A. County Psychology Assn. (pres. 1974-75), Am. Soc. Abuse of Children. Democratic. Avocations: swimming, traveling, opera, ballet. Home: 13025 Woodbridge St Studio City CA 91604-1431 E-mail: DrSJHoward@aol.com.

HOWARD, STEPHEN L. chemical engineer; s. Marvin and Edith Howard; m. Diane Howard; children: Eric, Stephanie, James. BS in Chemistry, BS in Chem. Engring., U. Utah, 1984, PhD in Phys.-Analytical Chemistry, 1988. Chem. engr. U.S. Army Rsch. Lab., Aberdeen Proving Ground, Md., 1991—. Office: U S Army Rsch Lab Amsrl-Wm-Bd Aberdeen Proving Ground MD 21005

HOWARD, STEPHEN WRIGLEY, telecommunications executive; b. Buffalo, Sept. 7, 1940; '. Norman Wrigley and Vesta (Gow) H.; m. Eileen F. O'Neill (div. 1973); children: Elizabeth Anne, Amy Lindsay; m. Dimiti Ann Stegeman; 1 child, Sarah Winsome. BLS, Boston U., 1981. Underwriter Aetna Life & Casualty Co., Boston, 1963-66; mem. sales and mktg. staff New Eng. Telephone Co., Boston, 1966-82; mgr., cons. liaison AT&T, Morristown, N.J., 1983; ptnr. Howard Assocs., Lebanon, Maine, 1983—. Adj. faculty Boston U., 1982—, St. Joseph's Coll., Standish, Maine, 1995—; lectr., Software Inst., Andover, Mass., 1984-88; mem. tech. bd. Maine Tech. Inst., 2000—. Author software. Mem. Boston U. Alumnae Sch. Com., 1987—, Maine Sci. and Tech. Found., 1999—. Republican. Episcopalian. Avocations: tennis, forestry, trap and skeet. E-mail: showard@ha77.com.

HOWARD, TAMMY WILLIAMS, nurse practitioner; b. Tenn. d. Billy Clay and Joan Marie Williams; m. Steve Howard; children: Angelle Marie, Brett Davis, Clay Alan, LaShea Angelle. BSN, Tenn. Tech. U., Cookeville, 1986; MSN, U. Tenn., Knoxville, 1993. RN, Tenn.; cert. inpatient obstetric nurse, cert. womens health care nurse practitioner, cert. lactation cons. With Cumberland Med. Ctr., Crossville, Tenn., 1986-2001, patient edn. dept., 1998-2001; asst. prof. Tenn. Tech. U. Sch. Nursing, Cookeville, 2001—. Adj. faculty Tenn. Tech. U. Sch. Nursing, 1995-97; obstet. coord. DeKalb Gen. Hosp., Smithville, Tenn., 1991-93; location cons. Cookeville Regional Med. Ctr., 2002—. Mem.: Tenn. Nurses Assn., ANA, Tenn. Nurses Assn. ((pres. Dist. 9)), ANA.

HOWARD, TERRY THOMAS, obstetrician, gynecologist; b. Cleve., May 14, 1943; s. Henry and Paula H.; m. Phyllis C. Schaevitz, Aug. 21, 1965; children: Jennifer, Jason, Brian. AB magna cum laude, Columbia U., 1965; MD, Harvard Med. Sch., 1969. Diplomate Am. Bd. Ob-Gyn. Intern, resident gen. surgery Beth Israel Hosp., Boston, 1969-71; resident ob-gyn Boston Hosp. for Women (now named Brigham & Womens Hosp.), 1971-74; physician Chelmsford (Mass.) Med. Assocs., 1974-88, Harvard Cmty. Health Plan, Chelmsford, 1988-97, Harvard Vanguard Med. Assocs. (formerly Harvard Cmty. Health Plan), Chelmsford, 1998-2000; pvt. practice Chelmsford, 2000—. Trustee Lowell (Mass.) Gen. Hosp., 1987—. Bd. dirs. Friends of the Children Concert Band, Chelmsford, 1981—, Lowell Cmty. Health Ctr., 2002--; trustee Congregation Shalom, Chelmsford, 1993-96. Fellow Am. Coll. Obstetrics & Gynecology, Am. Coll. Surgeons; mem. Am. Soc. Reproductive Medicine.

HOWARD, THOMAS K. surgeon; b. Pitts., June 15, 1935; s. Charles Wooster and Edna Elizabeth (Greene) H.; m. Joan Clement, Dec. 19, 1959; children: Thomas, Jr., Kelley Clement, Christine Joan, Steven Charles. BS, U. Del., 1956; MD, Jefferson Med. Coll. of Phila., 1960. Diplomate Am. Bd. Orthop. Surgery. Active staff Carroll County Gen. Hosp., Westminster, Md., 1968-70, Gettysburg (Pa.) Hosp., 1968-75; chief of staff Elizabethtown (Pa.) State Crippled Children's Hosp., 1975-76; chief of surgery Hanover Gen. Hosp., 1982-84; pvt. practice, Hanover, Pa., 1968-96; cons. in orthopaedics. Chief staff Hanover Gen. Hosp., 1990-92. Bd. dirs. YMCA, Hanover, 1973, Hanover Hosp., 2001—; U.S. Cycling Fedn. ofcl. Lt. USN, 1961-64. Fellow Am. Acad. Ortho Surgeons (bd. councilors 1982-86); mem. Pa. Orthopaedic Soc. (pres. 1980-81), Pa. Med. Soc., Jefferson Orthopaedic Soc., Orthopedic Surgeons and Trauma Soc. (pres. 1995-97), Hanlon Soc. Republican. Methodist. Avocations: scuba diving, bicycle racing, fly fishing, travel, golf. Home and Office: 14 Holly Ct Hanover PA 17331-1348 E-mail: jthoward@blazenet.net.

HOWARD, VICTOR, management consultant; b. Montreal, Aug. 12, 1923; s. Thomas and Jean (Malkinson) H.; m. Dorothy Bode, Dec. 25, 1953. BA, Sir George Williams U., 1947, BSc, 1948; PhD, Mich. State U., 1954. Mech. design engr. Can. Vickers Ltd., Montreal, 1942-46; with Aluminum Co. Can., 1946-48, E.B. Badger Co., Boston, 1948-50; asst. prof. Mich. State U., 1952-56; social scientist Rand Corp., 1956-58; staff exec., pers. dir. System Devel. Corp., Santa Monica, Calif., 1958-66; staff cons. Rohrer, Hibler & Replogle, San Francisco, 1966-69; mng. dir. Rohrer, Hibler & Replogle Internat., London and Brussels, 1969-74, ptnr., 1974, mgr. San Francisco, 1974-88, dir., 1979-88; pres. V. Howard and Assocs., 1988—, The Inst. on Stress and Health in the Work Place, 1988—. Vice chair State Bd. Psychology, 1989-93. Trustee Masonic Homes, Calif. Fellow Brit. Inst. Dirs.; mem. APA, Western Psychol. Assn., Am. Coll. Forensic Examiners, U.S. Power Squadrons (comdr. Sequoia Squadron 1981, dist. comdr. 1987), Calif. State Mil. Res. (col. 1984), Reform Club, Hurlingham Club (London), Thames Motor Yacht Club (Molesey, Eng.), Order St. John of Jerusalem (chevalier), Sovereign Mil. Order of the Temple of Jerusalem (prior Priory of St. Francis, Grand Cross), Masons (33 deg.), Shriners, Sigma Xi. Home and Office: 5555 Montgomery Dr #20 Santa Rosa CA 95409-5597 E-mail: toralin@aol.com.

HOWARD, W. SCOTT, language educator; b. Englewood, N.J., Nov. 6, 1963; PhD, Univ. Wash., Seattle, Wash., 1998. Asst. prof. Dept. of English, Univ. Denver, Denver, 1998—. Office: Univ Denver 495 Sturm Hall Denver CO 80208

HOWARD, WALTER BURKE, chemical engineer; b. Corpus Christi, Tex., Jan. 22, 1916; s. Clement and Nell (Smith) H.; m. Virginia Kentucky Freeman, Feb. 14, 1942; children— Thomas Clement, Virginia Ann. BA, U. Tex., 1937, BS in Chem. Engring, 1938, MS, 1940, PhD, 1943. Registered profl. engr., Tex.; chartered engr., U.K. From sr. asst. to sr. chem. engr. Bur. Indsl. Chemistry, U. Tex., Austin, 1939-52; from sr. engr. to scientist Monsanto Chem. Co., Texas City, Tex., 1952-64; mgr. process safety, sci. fellow to disting. fellow Monsanto Co., St. Louis, 1965-81; process safety tech. cons., 1981—. Contbr. chapters to books, articles to profl. jours.; patentee in field. V.p. Texas City Sch. Bd., 1963-64; chmn. bd. dirs. Mainland Opportunity Sch., 1958-61; mem. area coun. Boy Scouts Am., 1958-60; active P.T.A.; trustee Austin Presbyn. Theol. Sem., 1961-64. Fellow Brit. Instn. Chem. Engrs., Am. Inst. Chem. Engrs. (dir., Walton/Miller award 1987, Ann. Inst. lectr. 1987), Am. Chem. Soc., Combustion Inst. Internat., Nat. Fire Protection Assn. (Disting. Svc. award 1984), Austin Engrs. Club (past dir.), Phi Beta Kappa, Sigma Xi, Phi Lambda Upsilon. Presbyterian (elder). Address: 2020 S 80th St Omaha NE 68124

HOWARD, WILLIAM GATES, JR., electronics company executive; b. Boston, Nov. 6, 1941; s. William Gates and Mary Louise (Creager) H.; m. Kathleen Louretta Shipp, June 4, 1983. B.E.E. with distinction, Cornell U., 1964, MS, 1965; PhD, U. Calif.-Berkeley, 1967. Asst. prof. dept. elec. engring. and computer scis. U. Calif.-Berkeley, 1967-69; group ops. mgr. Motorola Semicondr. Group, Mesa, Ariz., 1969-76; v.p., dir. tech. and planning Motorola Semicondr. Sector, Phoenix, 1976-83; v.p., dir. R&D Motorola Inc., Schaumburg, Ill., 1983-87; sr. fellow Nat. Acad. Engring., Washington, 1987-91; chmn. bd. dirs. Thunderbird Technologies, Inc. Dir. BEI Techs., Inc., Ramtron Internat Corp., Credence Sys. Corp., Xilinx, Inc., Sandia Corp.; chmn. semicondr. tech. adv. com. U.S. Dept. Commerce, 1978-83; chmn. adv. group on electron devices Dept. Def., 1982-99, mem. def. sci. bd., 1996—; mem. study com. on tech. and implications of VLSI, NAS, 1980; chmn. vis. com. on advanced tech. Nat. Inst. Stds. and Tech., 1988-92; chmn. Def. Sci. Bd. Task Force on Microelectronics Rsch. Facilities, 1991-92; mem. Sandia Pres. Adv. Coun.; chmn. bd. dirs. Credence Sys., Inc. Author: (with D.J. Hamilton) Basic Integrated Circuit Engineering, 1976, (with B. Guile) Profiting from Innovation, 1992; patentee (with J.B. Cecil) improved reference current source, ladder termination circuit, three terminal zener diode. Fellow AAAS, IEEE (vice chmn. circuits and systems soc. 1976-78); mem. Nat. Acad. of Engring., Sigma Xi, Phi Kappa Phi, Eta Kappa Nu, Tau Beta Pi. Office: 10642 E San Salvador Dr Scottsdale AZ 85258-6114

HOWARD, WILLIAM HERBERT, lawyer; b. June 27, 1953; s. Victor Jack and Dolores (Reiter) H.; m. Sara Conners Thomas, July 24, 1982; children: Claire Fontaine, Victoria Hill. BA, Case Western Res. U., 1975; JD, 1978. Bar: Ohio 1978, Pa. 1986, U.S. Dist. Ct. (so. dist.) Ohio 1978, U.S. Ct. Appeals (6th cir.) 1979, U.S. Dist. Ct. (ea. dist.) Pa. 1986, U.S. Ct. Appeals (3d cir.) 1987. Law clk. U.S. Dist. Ct. (so. dist.), Cin., 1978-80; assoc. Estabrook, Finn & McKee, Dayton, Ohio, 1980-83, Porter, Wright, Morris & Arthur, Dayton,

1983-85, Cozen O'Connor, Phila., 1985—87, ptnr., 1987—91, sr. ptnr., 1991—; Law clk. USD Ct. (m. dist.), Pa., 2003. Mem. ABA (sect. litigation ins. coverage litigation com., Natural Resources Environmental and Energy Law, Tort and Ins. Law), Ohio Bar Assn., Pa. Bar Assn. (civil litigation, environ., mineral and energy law sects., sports, ntertainment and art law com.), Phila. Bar Assn. (mem. environ. law com.). Republican. Roman Catholic. Avocations: running, fitness, home repairs/gardening, movies, music. Office: Cozen O'Connor 1900 Market St Philadelphia PA 19103-3527 Fax: 215-665-2013. E-mail: whoward@cozen.com.

HOWARD, WILLIAM MATTHEW, arbitrator, writer, lawyer; b. Oak Park, Ill., Dec. 16, 1934; s. William and Martha Geraldine (Herlock) H.; children: Matthew William, Stephanie Sue. BSBA, U. Mo., 1956, JD, 1958; postgrad., U. Nice, France, 1976, U. London, 1977; PhD, Ariz. State U., 1995. Bar: Mo. 1958, U.S. Supreme Ct. 1986; cert. mediator and arbitrator, Fla. Supreme Ct. Jr. ptnr. Bryan Cave, St. Louis, 1958-66; asst. to pres. Granite City (Ill.) Steel Co., 1966-69; pres. Thomson Internat. Co., Thibodaux, La., 1969-70; founder, pres., chmn. bd. The Catalyst Group, Phoenix, 1970-97; dean, ctr. adminstr. The Union Inst., San Diego, 1997-99; pres. Dispute Solutions, Inc., Scottsdale, Ariz., 1999—. Mem. adj. faculty U. Mo., Columbia, 1956-58, St. Louis U., 1958-61, Ariz. State U., 1994-96, Ottawa U., 1994-96, Nova Southeastern U., 1996-97; chmn. unauthorized practice law com. Mo. Bar, St. Louis, 1964-65; chmn. bd. N.V. Vulcaansoord, Terborg, The Netherlands, 1975-78, E. Chalmers Holdings, Ltd., Glasgow, Scotland, 1977-78; exec. com. Chem. Bank, Irvine, Calif., 1985-90; vis. lectr. UCLA, 1987; arbitrator Am. Arbitration Assn., N.Y.C., 1987—, N.Y. Stock Exch., 1987—, Nt. Assn. Securities Dealers, Chgo., 1987—, Nat. Futures Assn., Chgo., 1988—, Am. Stock Exch., N.Y.C., 1988; hearing officer Mo. Dept. Natural Resources, Jefferson City, 1987-89, Internat. Ct. Arbitration, 1993—, Inter-Am. Comml. Arbitration Commn., 1993—; mem. Fla. Automobile Arbitration Bd., 1997-98; bd. dirs. Xeric Corp., Denver, Phoenix. Editor newsletter Extras, 1970—; exec. producer: (motion picture) Twice a Woman, 1979; contbr. numerous articles and revs. to various jours. Bd. dirs. U. Mo. Alumni Assn., 1986, Breckenridge (Colo.) Film Festival, 1989, Actors Theatre Phoenix, 1990; mem. club adv. bd. Phoenix Art Mus., 1990; dir. Scottsdale Cultural Coun., 1991. Mem. Am. Arbitration Assn. (regional adv. com.), Soc. Profls. in Dispute Resolution, Fla. Acad. Mediators, Nat. Inst. Dispute Resolution, Mensa, Order of Coif. Avocations: literature, travel, theatre, visual arts, skiing. Office: PO Box 9249 Phoenix AZ 85068-9249 Fax: 602-674-3993. E-mail: howardbill@msn.com.

HOWARD, WILLIAM PERCY, physician; b. Canton, Miss., Dec. 29, 1947; s. John Wesley Griffin and Ann (Wallace) H.; m. Nancy Rose Moyers, May 25, 1980; children: John W.G. II, Ann Skidmore, Ashley Elizabeth. BS in Chem. Engring., Miss. State U., 1970; MD, U. Miss., 1979. Chem. engr. Miss. Chem. Corp., Yazoo City, 1970-75; resident Univ. Med. Ctr., Jackson, Miss., 1979-82; staff physician emergency physician MEA Med. Sys., Jackson, 1982-90, clin. staff physician, 1990—. Chmn. bd. dirs. 1st Intermed Corp., 1997—, Miss. Emergency Assn., 1997-99; mem. physicians adv. com. Blue Cross-Blue Shield, 1993—. Named Madison (Miss.) County Cattleman of Yr., 1991, Madison County Conservation Farmer of Yr., 2001, Miss. Angus Assn. Progressive Breeder of the Yr., 2003. Fellow Am. Acad. Family Practitioners; mem. AMA, Am. Angus Assn., Miss. State Med. Assn. Republican. Methodist. Avocations: antiques, history, architecture, cattle farming. Office: MEA Med Clinic 5606 Old Canton Rd Jackson MS 39211-4217

HOWARD-HILL, TREVOR HOWARD, English language educator; b. Wellington, New Zealand, Oct. 17, 1933; came to U.S. 1972; s. Roland Henry and Dulcie Helena (Howard) Hill; children: Miranda Caroline, Victoria, Penelope Anne Din, Christopher John, Dorothy Disterheft. BA, Victoria U., Wellington, N.Z., 1955; MA, Victoria U., 1957, PhD, 1960; DPhil, U. Oxford, Eng., 1971. Head cataloguing Alexander Turnbull Libr., Wellington, 1961-63; sr. rsch. fellow Oxford U. Computing Lab., 1965-70; lectr. English Univ. Coll., Swansea, Wales, 1970-72; assoc. prof. English U. S.C., Columbia, 1972-77, prof English, 1977-90, chmn. dept. English, 1990-91, C. Wallace Martin prof. English, 1990-99, Disting. prof. emeritus, 1999—, sr. rsch. fellow, Thomas Cooper Libr., 1999—. Coll. dir. S.C. Coun. Tchrs. English, 1982-85; bibliography/access panelist NEH, 1984, 86. Author: Ralph Crane, 1972, Literary Concordances, 1979, Middleton's Vulgar Pasquin: Essays on a Game of Chess, 1995, editor: Sir John van Olden Barnavelt, 1980, The Book of Sir Thomas More: Essays, 1989, A Game of Chess, 1990, Thomas Middleton's A Game of Chess, 1993, Middleton's Bridgewater Manuscript of A Game of Chess, 1995; mem. editl. bd. Lit. Rsch., 1986-94, Rev., 1992-2000, Shakespeare Notes, 1996—; compiler: Oxford Shakespeare Concordances, 1969-73, Index to British Literary Bibliography, 9 vols., 1969—, British Book Trade Dissertations to 1980, 1998, Shakespearian Bibliography and Textual Criticism, 2000; editor Papers of the Bibliog. Soc. Am., 1994—; co-editor Renaissance Papers, 1996-2000. Recipient Russell award for rsch. U. S.C., 1988; U. New Zealand fellow, 1958-59, NIRNS fellow Oxford U., 1966-67, fellow H.E. Huntington Libr., 1975, NEH, 1979, Guggenheim fellow, 1989, fellow Folger Shakespeare Libr., 1993, Brit. Libr. Ctr. for Book, 1994-95, Edinburgh U. Ctr. for Book, 1999. Mem. MLA, Modern Humanities Rsch. Assn., Soc. for Textual Scholarship, Shakespeare Assn. Am., New Zealand Libr. Assn., Bibliog. Soc. London, Bibliog. Soc. Oxford, Bibliog. Soc. Am. (coun. 1994-2000). Home: 823 Poinsettia St Columbia SC 29205-2039 Office: U SC Thomas Cooper Libr 107 Columbia SC 29208-0001 E-mail: ralphcrane@msn.com.

HOWARD-PEEBLES, PATRICIA N. clinical cytogeneticist; b. Lawton, Okla., Nov. 24, 1941; d. J. Marion and R. Leona (prestidge) Howard; m. Thomas M. Peebles, Aug. 16, 1975. BSEd, U. Ctrl. Okla., 1963; student, Randolph-Macon Coll. Women, 1964; PhD in Zoology (Genetics), U Tex. at Austin, 1969. Diplomate Am. Bd. Med. Genetics; cert. clin. cytogeneticist, med. geneticist. Sci. and history tchr. Piedmont (Okla.) Pub. Schs., 1963-64; biochem. technician biochemistry sect. biology divsn. Oak Ridge (Tenn.) Nat. Lab., 1964-66; instr. rsch. pediatrics dept. pediatrics, instr. cytotech. U. Okla. Health Scis. Ctr., Oklahoma City, 1971-72; asst. prof., dir. Cytogenetics Lab. U. So. Miss., Hattiesburg, 1973-77, assoc. prof., dir. Cytogenetics Lab., 1977-80; assoc. prof. dept. pub. health, staff Lab. Med. Genetics U. Ala., Birmingham, 1980-81; assoc. prof., dir. Cytogenetics Lab. dept. pathology U. Tex. Health Sci. Ctr., Dallas, 1981-85, prof., dir. Cytogenetics Lab., 1985-87; prof. dept. human genetics Med. Coll. Va., Richmond, 1987-2001; clin. cytogeneticist, dir. postnatal lab. Genetics & IVF Inst., Fairfax, Va., 1987-98, co-dir. cytogenetics lab., 1998-2000, genetic, cytogenetic cons., 2000—. Am. Cancer Soc. postdoctoral fellow dept. human genetics U. Mich. Med. Sch., Ann Arbor, 1969-70, dept. human genetics and devel. Coll. Physicians and Surgeons, Columbia U., N.Y.C., 1970-71; genetic cons. Ellisville (Miss.) State Sch., 1973-80; attending staff dept. pathology Parkland Meml. Hosp., Dallas County Hosp. Dist., 1981-87; mem. sci. adv. com. Fragile X Found., 1985-2002; mem. Internat. Standing Com. on Human Cytogenetic Nomenclature, 1991-96. Contbr. articles to profl. jours., chpts. to books; reviewer Am. Jour. Human Genetics, Am. Jour. Med. Genetics, Clin. Genetics, Human Genetics. Fellow Am. Coll. Med. Genetics (founding mem.); mem. AAAS, Am. Soc. Human Genetics, Assn. Genetic Technologists, Tex. Genetics Soc. (chmn. planning com. ann. meeting 1984), Delta Kappa Gamma, Sigma Xi. Baptist. E-mail: phpeebles@yahoo.com.

HOWARDS, STUART S. urologist, educator; b. Milw., Mar. 29, 1937; s. Harvey H. and Anne (Levin) H.; m. Carter N. Howards, Aug. 20, 1966; children: Penelope P., Hugh N. BA, Yale U., 1959; MD, Columbia U., 1963. Intern in surgery Peter Bent Brigham Hosp., Boston, 1963-64, resident in urology, 1968-71; resident in surgery Childrens Hosp., Boston, 1964-65; rsch. assoc. NIH, Bethesda, Md., 1965-68; asst. prof. urology and physiology U. Va., Charlotteville, 1971-74, assoc. prof., 1974-76, prof., 1976—, chief divsn. pediat. urology, 1986—; exec. sec. Am. Bd. Urology, Charlottesville, Va. Chmn. exam com. Am. Bd. Urology, 1985-91, trustee, 1986-92, pres., 1992-93, exec. sec., 1997—; sr. urologic advisor to dir. NIDDK/NIH. Editor: Infertility in the Male, 1991, 3d edit., 1997, Adult and Pediatric Urology, 1991, 3d edit., 1995; editor Jour. Urology, 1983-2000. Maj. USPHS, 1965-68. Recipient Career Investigation award NIH, 1973-78. Fellow Am. Acad. Pediats.; mem. Am. Urol. Assn. (Golden Cystoscope award 1981, Scott award 1990, Hugh Young award 1991, Disting. Svc. award 2001), Clin. Soc. Genitourinary Surgeons, Am. Soc. Reproductive Medicine (bd. dirs. 1994-96, treas. 1996—), Soc. Andrology, Genitourinary Surgeons, Am. Assn. Genito-Urinary Surgeons (sec.-treas. 1992-97), Am. Bd. Urology (trustee 1987-93, pres. 1993, exec. dir. 1997—), NIDDY, NIH (sr. urology advisor to the dir., 2002—), Nat. Bd. Med. Examiners. E-mail: ssh4e@virginia.edu.

HOWARTH, WILLIAM (LOUIS HOWARTH), education educator, writer; b. Mpls., Nov. 26, 1940; s. Nelson Oliver and Mary Watson (Prindiville) H. BA with highest distinction, U. Ill., 1962; MA, U. Va., 1963, PhD, 1967. Instr. Princeton (N.J.) U., 1966-68, asst. prof., 1968-73, assoc. prof., 1973-81, prof. English, 1981—. Mem. exec. com. Princeton Environ. Inst.; advisor Program in Environ. Studies, Program in Am. Studies Princeton (N.J.) U.; cons. Ctr. for Edits. of Am. Authors, 1974, Rockefeller Bros. Fund, 1976, Geraldine W. Dodge Found., 1981, Nat. Geog. Soc., 1984, Corp. for Pub. Broadcasting, 1986, NEH, 1987, Nat. Rural Studies Coun., 1988, Atlantic Ctr. for Arts, 1990, Santa Fe Environ. Coun., 1991, ALA, 1993, Assn. for the Study of Lit. and Environment, 1994, Kellogg Found., 1995, Arthur Vining Davis Found., 1998, AAAS, 2000. Author: Nature in American Life, 1972, The John McPhee Reader, 1976, The Book of Concord, 1982, Thoreau in the Mountains, 1982, Traveling the Trans-Canada, 1987, Mountaineering in the Sierra Nevada, 1989, Walking with Thoreau, 2001; author book chpts.; editor-in-chief: The Writings of Henry D. Thoreau, 1972-80; mem. numerous editl. bds.; editl. adviser numerous jours. and publs.; contbr. articles to profl. jours. Woodrow Wilson Found. fellow, 1966, Henry E. Huntington Libr. fellow, 1968, NEH fellow, 1977, John E. Annan BiCentennial Preceptor, Princeton, 1973, Pew and Templeton Founds. fellow, 2000. Mem. MLA, Am. Studies Assn., Thoreau Soc. Am. (pres. 1975-76), Am. Soc. Environ. History, Am. Lit. Assn., Nat. Geographic Soc. (contract writer 1978—), Nat. Rural Studies Coun. (assoc.), Assn. for the Study of Lit. and Environ. (adv. bd.), Am. Soc. Environ. History (adv. bd.), Ctr. for Am. Places (chmn. bd. dirs.), Phi Beta Kappa. Office: Princeton U 22 McCosh Hall Princeton NJ 08544-1607

HOWAT, JOHN KEITH, retired museum executive; b. Denver, Apr. 12, 1937; s. James Bowcott and Nancy Selden (Skinker) H.; m. Anne Hadley, June 21, 1958; children: Karen Louise, Laura Anne. Grad., Phillips Exeter Acad., 1955; BA, Harvard U., 1959, MA, 1962. Curator Hyde Collection, Glens Falls, N.Y., 1962-64; Ford fellow NYU Inst. Fine Arts, 1965—66; Chester Dale fellow Met. Mus. Art, N.Y.C., 1966 67, asst. curator dept. Am. paintings and sculpture, 1967-68, assoc. curator-in-charge, 1968-70, curator, 1970-82, chmn. depts. Am. art, 1982—2001. Mem. adv. com. archives Am. art Smithsonian Instn., 1969—; trustee Archives of Am. Art, 1988—, N.Y. Society Libr., 2002—. Author exhbn. catalogs John Frederick Kensett: An American Master, 1985, An American Paradise: The World of The Hudson River School, 1987, Art and the Empire City: New York, 1825-1861, 2000. Mem. Union Club, Grolier Club, Century Assn. Home: 1100 Park Ave New York NY 10128-1202

HOWATT, SISTER HELEN CLARE, former human services director, former college library director; b. San Francisco, Apr. 5, 1927; d. Edward Bell and Helen Margaret (Kenney) H. BA, Holy Names Coll., 1949; MS in Libr. Sci., U. So. Calif., 1972; cert. advanced studies, Our Lady of Lake U., 1966. Joined Order Sisters of the Holy Names, Roman Cath. Ch., 1945. Life tchg. credential, life spl. svcs. credential, prin. St. Monica Sch., Santa Monica, Calif., 1957-60, St. Mary Sch., L.A., 1960-63; tchr. jr. high sch. St. Augustine Sch., Oakland, Calif., 1964-69; tchr. jr. high math St. Monica Sch., San Francisco, 1969-71, St. Cecilia Sch., San Francisco, 1971-77; libr. dir. Holy Names Coll., Oakland, Calif., 1977-94; Spanish instr. Collins Ctr. Sr. Svcs., 1994-99; acct. St. Monica Sch., San Francisco, 1999—2002; libr. St. Martin de Porres Sch., Oakland, 2003—. Contbr. math. curriculum San Francisco Unified Sch. Dist., Cum Notis Variorum, publ. Music Libr., U. Calif., Berkeley. Contbr. articles to profl. jours. Recipient NSF grantee, 1966, NDEA grantee, 1966. Mem. Cath. Libr. Assn. (chmn. No. Calif. elem. schs. 1971-72). Home and Office: 4660 Harbord Dr Oakland CA 94618-2211

HOWDEN, FRANK NEWTON, Episcopal priest, humanities educator; b. Phila., Mar. 23, 1916; s. John George and Sarah Harvey (McFarlane) H.; m. Cornelia Jane Fenton, Oct. 7, 1943 (dec. Aug. 1981); children: Robert Newton, William John McFarlane, Susan Catherine Victoria Howden Blanchard, Sarah Jane Fenton; m. Mary Valerie Clark, Apr. 23, 1983. *Reverend Frank Newton Howden's father was born in Edinborough, Scotland, April 19, 1876. He was secretary and treasurer of Clyde Dock Company from 1902-1909. In 1910 he emigrated to Philadelphia, Pennsylvania, and worked for the Rapid Transport until 1918. Thereafter, his family lived in various parts of the Catskill Mountains in the state of New York. He died in 1954. The Reverend's mother, Sarah Harvey McFarlane, was born in Glasgow, Scotland, March 1, 1875, and died in September of 1964.* AB, U. of the South, 1940; STB, Gen. Theol. Sem., N.Y.C., 1943; MS, Ctrl. Conn. U., 1968; postgrad., McGill U., Montreal, Can., 1953-56. Ordained priest Episcopal Ch.; cert. tchr., Conn. Curate St. Peter's Ch., Auburn, N.Y., 1943-44, All Angels Ch., N.Y.C., 1944-45; priest in charge (vicar) St. John's Ch., Sewaren and Fords, N.J., 1945-48; rector St. Luke's Ch., St. Albans, Vt., 1951-56, Trinity Ch., Waterbury, Conn., 1956-66; history tchr. Woodbury (Conn.) H.S., 1966-69; prof. humanities Waterbury State Tech. Coll., 1970-82; rector Trinity Ch., Lime Rock, Conn., 1969-85, elected rector emeritus, 1985—. Pres. Priests' Fellowship, Conn., 1958-59; archdeacon New Haven County, Diocese of Conn., 1963-66, dean Litchfield Deanery, 1984-85. *Since retirement, the Reverend Frank Newton Howden has been busy writing his latest manuscript, Life of Christ.* Author: A Rule of Life, 1954, Life Here and Hereafter, 1992. 1st lt. Chaplain Corps, U.S. Army, 1948-51, chaplain Vt. Nat. Guard, 1952-56. Mem. St. Margaret's Soc. (assoc.), Over-Seas League (London), English-Speaking Union. Democrat. Avocations: photography, audio-visual presentations, preaching and taking services in Anglican churches. Home and Office: 9 Argyle Rd Southborough Tunbridge Wells TN4 0SU England

HOWDESHELL, DANIEL THOMAS, music educator; b. St. Petersburg, FL, July 30, 1954; s. Thomas Gibbons and Catherine Frances Howdeshell; m. Suzanne LoBaido, June 27, 1981; 1 child, Joseph. BAE, AZ State U, Tempe, AZ, 1976; MusM, U of AZ, Tucson, AZ, 1981. Cert. tchr. AZ. Tchr. Ash Fork Pub. Sch., Ash Fork, Ariz., 1976—77, Ft. Huachuca Acc. Sch., Ft. Huachuca, Ariz., 1978. Gen. mgr. Sierra Vista Symphony, Sierra Vista, Ariz., 1999—2000. Treas. Ft. Huachuca Ed. Assn., Ft. Huachuca, Ariz., 1993. Recipient Ed. of the Month, Phi Delta Kappa/ AZ, 2002, Mayor's Artist, City of Sierra Vista/ AZ, 2002. Mem.: Music Ed. Nat. Conf. Democrat. Roman Catholic. Achievements include co-founded Sierra Vista Symphony Orches. Avocations: astronomy, travel. Home: 3385 Plaza Candida Sierra Vista AZ 85650-7513 Office: Smith Middle Sch PO Box 12954 Fort Huachuca AZ 85670

HOWE, CANDACE JO-LYNN, writer; b. Berks County, Pa., June 23, 1966; d. Harry Daniel Mountz III and Donna Lee (Hewitt) Mountz. BA in psychology, Mass. Coll. of Liberal Arts, 1989. Cert. Psychiatric Therapist Psyciatric Inst. of Am., 1990. Residential counselor Ctr. for Humanistic Change, No. Adams, Mass., 1986—93; admissions clerk No. Adams Regional Hosp., 1986—89; psychiat. therapist Greylock Pavillion N.A.R.H., No. Adams, 1989—90; asst. dir. Ad Lib Inc., Pittsfield, Mass., 1994—99; ins. agent John Hancock Property Casualty, Pittsfield, 1992, census worker U.S. Dept of Treasury, Pittsfield, 2002. Adv. Com. of No. Berkshire County, No. Adams, 1994—95; voting mem. adv. bd. Dept. of Mental Health, Berkshires, Mass., 1994—96, human rights advocacy, Pittsfield, 1994; tchr. Mt. Greylock Christian Acad., No. Adams, 1999—2000. Contbr. articles; author: They Meant it for Evil, but God Meant it for Good. Telephone silicitor Mark of Dimes, No. Adams, 1991; pub. spkr. Consortium Conf. and Advocacy, Springfield, Mass., 1991; fundraiser Am. Stroke Assn., Springfield, 2002—. Recipient Letter of Commendation, Dept. Mental Retardation, 1992. Mem.: Am. Psychiat. Soc., Citizens Against Child Abuse, People for the Abusal Treatment of Animals. Democrat. Baptist. Avocations: writing, reading, history, bible study, computers, collecting old money, collecting old baseball, football and basketball cards. Home: 89 1/2 Liberty St North Adams MA 01247 Home Fax: 413-664-6637. E-mail: multyjody@aol.com.

HOWE, CARROLL VICTOR, construction equipment company executive; b. Kearny, N.J., Dec. 12, 1923; s. Wright and Ada (Hodge) H.; m. Nancy Osborne Stivers, Nov. 24, 1951 (div.); m. Priscilla Howland Greene, Mar. 1, 1957 (div.); children: Gregory Carroll, Christopher David; m. Eilene Crawley Pierson, Apr. 14, 1984 (div.). BA, Princeton U., 1947; MFA, Yale U., 1950. Writer, producer Pemeho Prodns., N.Y.C., 1950-51, free lance actor, writer, 1952-54; salesman Atlas Rigging Supply Corp., Newark, 1954-56, office mgr., 1956-57, sales mgr., 1957-58, v.p., 1958-62, pres., 1962-94, Arsco Industries, Inc., Newark, 1966-2000. Bd. dirs. Select Ins. Group of North Am., 1987-94. Author: Best One-Act Plays, 1949-1950, 1950, (play) The Long Fall, 1950, 1957, Best Short Plays, 1917-1957, 1957. Bd. dirs., pres. 15 Tenant Shareholders, Inc., N.Y.C., 1978-81, Alumni Coun. Yale U. Grad. Sch. Drama, 1988-94; mem. bd. govs. Newark Acad., Livingston, N.J., 1990-94; mng. ptnr. Crollar Assocs. Newark, 1983-94. Served from pvt. to 2d lt. USMCR, 1942-46, 1st lt. to capt., 1951-52. Recipient Applause award N.J. Theatre Group, 1989. Mem. Wildlife Conservation Soc., USA Track & Field, Boat/US, AAII, Am. Mensa Ltd., Quadrangle Club, Princeton Club Sarasota, Yale Club of Suncoast, Westhampton Yacht Squadron (treas. 1970-72, vice commodore 1972-74, commodore 1974-76, dir. 1976-80), Bradenton Yacht Club, Ivy League Club. Humanist. Home and Office: 2914 River Trace Circle Bradenton FL 34208 Fax: 941-744-1912.

HOWE, DANIEL WALKER, historian, educator; b. Ogden, Utah, Jan. 10, 1937; s. Maurice Langdon and Lucie (Walker) H.; m. Sandra Fay Shumway, Sept. 3, 1961; children: Rebecca, Christopher, Stephen. AB magna cum laude, Harvard U., 1959; MA, Oxford (Eng.) U., 1965; PhD, U. Calif., Berkeley, 1966. From instr. to assoc. prof. history Yale U., 1966-73; assoc. prof. history UCLA, 1973-77, prof., 1977-92, chmn. dept., 1983-87. Harmsworth vis. prof. Am. history, Oxford (Eng.) U., 1989-90, Rhodes prof. Am. history, 1992-2002; vis. prof. Yale U., 2001. Author: The Unitarian Conscience, 1970, The American Whigs: An Anthology, 1973, Victorian America, 1976, The Political Culture of the American Whigs, 1979, Making the American Self, 1997. Served to lt. U.S. Army, 1959-60. Kent fellow Danforth Found., 1964-66; Charles Warren Center for Studies in Am. History fellow, 1970-71; NEH fellow, 1975-76; Guggenheim fellow, 1984-85; Huntington Libr. fellow, 1992, 94, 2002-03. Fellow Royal Hist. Soc.; mem. Am. Hist. Assn., Orgn. Am. Historians, Soc. Historians Early Am. Rep. (pres. 2000-01), Soc. Am. Historians, Oxford and Cambridge Club (London). Episcopalian. Home: 3814 Cody Rd Sherman Oaks CA 91403-5019 E-mail: howe@history.ucla.edu.

HOWE, DEAN OTIS, JR., curator, consultant; b. Kansas City, Mo., Aug. 26, 1935; s. Dean Otis Howe and Eleanor Lewis Waddell. B, U. Cin., 1958. Curator, dir. Mimosa Ho. Mus., Covington, Kans., 1985—98, Linwood Lawn Ho. Mus., Lexington, Mo., 2000—. Cons. City of Northern, Ky., 1985—98. Mem.: Musical Box Soc. Internat., Automated Musical Instrument Collectors Assn. Avocations: furniture, piano restoration, research on authentic restoration on 19th Century. Home and Office: 110 S 15th St Saint Joseph MO 64501

HOWE, DRAYTON FORD, JR., lawyer; b. Seattle, Nov. 17, 1931; s. Drayton Ford and Virginia (Wester) H.; m. Joyce Arnold, June 21, 1952; 1 son, James Drayton. AB, U. Calif., Berkeley, 1953; LLB, U. Calif., San Francisco, 1957. Bar: Calif. 1958. CPA Calif. Atty. IRS, 1958-61; tax dept. supr. Ernst & Ernst, San Francisco, 1962-67; ptnr. Bishop, Barry, Howe, Haney & Ryder, San Francisco, 1968—. Lectr. on tax matters U. Calif. extension, 1966-76. Mem. Calif. Bar Assn., San Francisco Bar Assn. (chmn. client relations com. 1977), Calif. Soc. CPA's. Office: Bishop Barry Howe Haney & Ryder 2000 Powell St Ste 1425 Emeryville CA 94608-1861 E-mail: dhowe@bhhr.com.

HOWE, EDWIN A(LBERTS), JR., lawyer; b. Cleve., Jan. 21, 1939; s. Edwin Alberts and Helen Dorothy (Beck) H.; m. Margaret Joan Webber, Sept. 12, 1964; children: Christopher, Melissa, Katie. BA, Yale U., 1961; JD with honors, U. Mich., 1964. Bar: N.Y. 1965, U.S. Supreme Ct. 1976. Assoc. Debevoise and Plimpton, N.Y.C., 1964-70; ptnr. Howe & Addington LLP, N.Y.C., 1970-99, sr. counsel, 2000—. Founding dir. Interlakes Health Found., Inc., vice chmn. Trustee Garden City (N.Y.) Pub. Libr., 1982-86, chmn., 1986-88; trustee Village of Garden City, 1988-89; mem. Garden City Environ. Adv. Bd., 1994-98, Westport (Conn.) Land Acquisition Com., 1999-2001, Westport Archl. Rev. Bd., 2000-01; chmn. steering com. Project to Revitalize Downtown Ticonderoga, N.Y., 2002—, mem. steering com. Ticonderoga Comprehensive plan, 2003-, mem. Ticonderoga Econ. Devel. Com., 2003-; founding dir. and vice-chair, Inter-Lakes Health Found., 2003-. Fellow Inst. Dirs.; mem. ABA, Internat. Fiscal Assn., Counselors of Real Estate, Urban Land Inst., Nat. Real Estate Forum (chmn. 1996-2000, exec. dir. 2001—), Assn. of Bar of City of N.Y., N.Y. State Bar Assn., Internat. Bar Assn., Internat. Law Assn. (Am. Br.), Am. Soc. Internat. Law, Sky Club, Yale Club, No. Lake George Yacht Club, Lake George Assn., Rogers Rock Club. Republican. Episcopalian. Avocations: fishing, golf, reading, theatre, languages. Home: PO Box 350 Ticonderoga NY 12883-0350 Office: The Roseville Co LLC PO Box 598 Ticonderoga NY 12883-0598

HOWE, FISHER, management consultant, former government official; b. Winnetka, Ill., May 17, 1914; s. Lawrence and Hester (Davis) H.; m. Deborah Froelicher, June 4, 1945; children: Elizabeth, Shippen. AB, Harvard, 1935; student, Nat. War Coll., 1948. Salesman Coats & Clarks Thread Co., N.Y.C., 1935-40, Patons & Baldwins, Ltd., Yorkshire, Eng., 1936-37; mem. staff Office of Dir., OSS, Washington, London, Mediterranean, 1941-45; fgn. svc. officer Dept. State, 1945-68, spl. asst. under sec. of state, econ. affairs, 1945-46, dep. dir. Bur. Intelligence and Rsch., exec. sec., dir. exec. secretariat, 1956-58; dep. chief of mission and charge Am. Embassy, Oslo, Norway, 1958-62, The Hague, The Netherlands, 1962-65; mem. policy planning coun., 1965-68; exec. dir., asst. dean Johns Hopkins U. Sch. Advanced Internat. Studies, 1968-72; dep. exec. dir. Commn. on Orgn. of Govt. for Conduct of Fgn. Policy, Washington, 1973-75; sec., gen. adv. com. Energy R & D Adminstrn., 1975-77; dir. instl. rels. Resources for the Future, Inc., 1978-82; ptnr. Lavender/Howe & Assocs., Washington, 1982—. Author: Computer and Foreign Affairs, 1968, Fund Raising and the Nonprofit Board Member, 1988, Board Member's Guide to Fund Raising, 1991, Welcome to the Board, 1995, Board Member's Guide to Strategic Planning, 1997. Trustee Fountain Valley Sch., Colorado Springs, Colo., Pilgrim Soc., Plymouth, Mass., Support Ctr. Washington, Inst. Circadian Physiology, Boston. Served to lt. USNR, 1943-44, overseas svc. Mem. Metroplitan Club (Washington), Mill Reef. Address: Ingleside # 637 3050 Military Rd NW Washington DC 20015

HOWE, FLORENCE, English educator, writer, publisher; b. N.Y.C., Mar. 17, 1929; d. Samuel and Frances (Stilly) Rosenfeld AB, Hunter Coll., 1950; AM, Smith Coll., 1951; postgrad., U. Wis., 1951-54; DHL (hon.), New Eng. Coll., 1977, Skidmore Coll., 1979, DePauw U., 1987, SUNY Coll. Old Westbury, 1992, Pace U., 2000, Chatham Coll., 2000. Tchg. asst. U. Wis., Madison, 1951-54; instr. Hofstra Coll., 1954-57; lectr. English, Queens Coll., CUNY, 1956-57; asst. prof. English Goucher Coll., 1960-71; prof. humanities and Am. studies SUNY, Old Westbury, 1971-85; prof. English City. Coll. and Grad. Sch., CUNY, 1985-95, Grad. Sch./CUNY, 1995—2001; pres., dir. The Feminist Press at CUNY, 1970—2000. Vis. prof. U. Utah, 1973, 75, U. Wash., 1974, John F. Kennedy Inst. Am. Studies Free U. Berlin, 1978, Oberlin Coll., 1978, Denison U., 1979, MLA Summer Inst. U. Ala., 1979, Coll. of Wooster, 1980; found. edit. Women's Studies Quarterly, 1972-82. Author: The Conspiracy of the Young, 1970, Seven Years Later: Women's Studies Programs in 1976, 1977, Myths of Coeducation: Selected Essays, 1964-1984, 1984; editor: (with Ellen Bass) No More Masks! An Anthology of Poems by Women, 1973, Women and the Power to Change, 1975; (with Nancy Hoffman) Women Working: An Anthology of Stories and Poems, 1979; (with Suzanne Howard, Mary Jo Boehm Strauss) Everywoman's Guide to Colleges and Universities, 1982; (with Marsha Saxton) With Wings: An Anthology of Literature by and About Disabled Women, 1987; (with John Mack Faragher) Women and Higher Education in American History, 1988, Tradition and the Talents of Women, 1991, No More Masks, An Anthology of 20th Century American Women Poets, 1993, The Politics of Women's Studies: Testimony from 30 Founding Mothers, 2000, (with Jean Casella) Almost Touching the Skies: Women's Coming of Age Stories, 2000; mem. editl. bd. Women's Studies: An Interdisciplinary Jour., 1971—, SIGNS: Women in Culture and Society, 1974-80, Jour. Edn., 1976—, The Correspondence of Lydia Marie Child, 1977-81, Research in the Humanities, 1977—; contbr. articles to profl. jours. Named NEH fellow, 1971—73, Ford Found. fellow, 1974—75, Fulbright fellow, India, 1977, Mellon fellow, Wellesley Coll., 1979, Rockefeller Found. fellow, T. Bellagio, 1997; recipient Mina Shaughnessy award, Fund for Improvement of Post-Secondary Edn., 1982—83, U.S. Dept. State grant, 1983, 1993, Team awards, Rockefeller Found., Bellagio, 2001—03. Office: The Feminist Press at CUNY 365 Fifth Ave New York NY 10016-4309 E-mail: fhowe@gc.cuny.edu.

HOWE, GORDON, former professional hockey player, sports association executive; b. Saskatoon, Sask., Can., Mar. 31, 1928; arrived in U.S., 1944; s. Albert Clarence and Katherine (Schultz) Howe; m. Colleen Janet Joffa, Apr. 15,

1953; children: Marty Gordon, Mark Steven, Cathleen Jill, Murray Albert. Profl. hockey player with Detroit Red Wings Hockey Club (Nat. Hockey League), 1944—73, player, pres.; with Houston Aeros (World Hockey Assn.), 1971—73, New Eng. Whalers (World Hockey Assn.), Hartford, Conn., 1977—78, Hartford Whalers, NHL, 1980—82; spl. asst., mng. ptnr. Hartford Whalers, 1982—92. Named Canada's Athlete of Yr., 1963, 12-time mem., NHL 1st All-Star Team, 9-time mem., NHL 2d All-Star Team, Most Valuable Player and to 1st All-Star Team, World Hockey Assn., 1974; recipient Order of Can. medal, 1971, Hart Meml. Trophy, Art Ross Trophy, Lester Patrick Trophy. Mem.: Omaha Sports Hall of Fame, Mich. Sports Hall of Fame, Nat. League Hall of Fame. Congregationalist.

HOWE, JAMES EVERETT, investment company executive; b. N.Y.C., Mar. 30, 1930; s. Ernest Joseph and Gladys Montgomery (Sills) H.; m. Judith DePuy Keating, May 9, 1959; children: James E. Jr., David K. BA, Williams Coll., 1952; MBA, Columbia U., 1954. Chartered fin. analyst. Statistician J.P. Morgan & Co., N.Y.C., 1956-59; investment research officer Morgan Guaranty Trust Co., N.Y.C., 1959-65; sr. analyst Tri-Continental Corp., N.Y.C., 1965-80; asst. v.p., voting shareholder J&W Seligman & Co., N.Y.C., 1980-81; chmn. investment com. Charles Edison Fund, Newark, 1981—. Trustee Brook Found., N.Y.C., 1966-72, Charles Edison Fund, 1972—; bd. deacons Brick Presbyn. Ch., N.Y.C., 1963-66. 1st lt. USAF, 1954-56, ETO Recipient fin. award Wall Street Journal, 1954. Mem. N.Y. Soc. Security Analysts, Assn. for Investment Mgmt. and Rsch., Machinery Analysts N.Y. (charter, pres. 1967-68), Environ. Control Analysts N.Y. (charter, pres. 1975), Jamestowne Soc., Princeton Co. (charter, gov. 1993-94), Genesee Valley Club, Short Hills Club, Nassau Club, Alpha Kappa Psi. Republican. Presbyterian. Avocation: photography. Home: 33 Keats Rd Short Hills NJ 07078-2913

HOWE, JAMES TARSICIUS, retired insurance company executive; b. Calcutta, India, Nov. 20, 1924; came to U.S., 1975; s. Joseph Ne-Ching and Anna Su-Cheng (Huang) Hou; m. Juliana Wong, Feb. 8, 1948; children: Christopher, Celine, Catherine, Charles, Caroline. Diploma in Bus. Adminstrn., Chinese U., Hong Kong, 1969; postgrad. in Advanced Mgmt., Lingnam Inst. Bus. Adminstrn., Hong Kong. Trainee Bank of China, Calcutta, 1942-45, various managerial positions Calcutta and, Pakistan, 1945-51; mng. ptnr. import and export firm Karachi, Pakistan, 1951-54; various exec. positions Am. Internat. Underwriters (Pakistan) Ltd., 1954-65, Am. Internat. Underwriters (Far East) Inc., 1965-73; pres., mng. dir. Am. Internat. Underwriters, Hong Kong, 1973-75; asst. treas. Am. Internat. Group, Inc., N.Y.C., 1975—76, treas., 1976—81, v.p., 1981—92; ret., 1992. Bd. dirs., chmn. audit and conduct coms. A.I.G. Life Ins. Co. Ltd., Can.; bd. dirs., vice chmn. AICCO; ret. treas. C.V. Starr & Co., Inc., also numerous other subs.; advisor U.S. Congl. Adv. Bd.; staff AIG Assurance Co. of Can. Named hon. Ky. col., 1979; Knight Comdr. with star of Holy Sepulchre of Jerusalem, Roman Cath. Ch.Outstanding Spkr. of 20th Century, Internat. Biog. Ctr., London, 2000; admitted to The Millennium Hall of Fame, The Internat. Biog. Ctr., London, 1997. Mem.: Internat. Platform Assn., Internat. Real Estate Appraisers, Internat. Real Estate Inst., Nat. Assn. U.S. Corp. Treas., Am. Mgmt. Assn., Nat. Assn. Rev. Appraisers and Mortgage Underwriters (sr.), Serra Club (N.Y.C.), Royal Hong Kong Jockey Club, Am. Club Hong Kong (life absent mem.), Royal Hong Kong Golf Club (life absent mem.), Hong Kong Country Club, Chinese Cath. Club (life), KC (grand knight Short Hills coun.), Rotary. Home: Palace Pl Ste 3601 1 Palace Pier Ct Etobicoke ON Canada M8V 3W9

HOWE, JAY EDWIN, lawyer; b. Omaha, Apr. 13, 1940; m. Catherine B. Olesen; children: Joseph E., Olivia G. BA, U. Iowa, 1963, JD, 1966. Bar: Iowa 1966, U.S. Dist. Ct. (so. dist.) Iowa 1966. County atty. Adair County, Iowa, 1973-79; ptnr. Howe & Olesen, Greenfield, Iowa, 1979—. Served with U.S. Army, 1966-68. Mem.: Iowa Bar Assn., 1000 Friends of Iowa Club. Catholic Christian. Office: Howe & Olesen PO Box 86 Greenfield IA 50849-0086

HOWE, JOHN PRENTICE, III, health science center executive, physician; b. Jackson, Tenn., Mar. 7, 1943; s. John Prentice and Phyllis (MacDonald) H.; m. Tyrrell Flawn; children: Lindsey Warren, Brooke Olmsted, John Prentice IV. BA, Amherst Coll., 1965; MD, Boston U., 1969. Diplomate Am. Bd. Internal Medicine, internal medicine and cardiovascular disease. Research assoc. cellular physiology Amherst Coll., 1963-64; research assoc. cardiovascular physiology Boston U. Sch. of Medicine, 1966-67; lectr. medicine Boston U. Sch. Medicine, 1972-73; intern Boston City Hosp., 1969-70, asst. resident, 1970-71; rsch. fellow in medicine Harvard U., 1971-73, Peter Bent Brigham Hosp., 1971-73; survey physician Framingham Cardiovascular Disease Study, Nat. Heart and Lung Inst., 1971; asst. clin. prof. medicine U. Hawaii, 1973-75; from asst. prof. medicine to assoc. prof. U. Mass., 1975-85, assoc. prof., 1977-85, vice-chmn. dept. medicine, 1975-78, asst. dean continuing edn. for physicians, 1976-78, assoc. dean profl. affairs and continuing edn., 1978-80, acad. dean, 1980-85, vice chancellor, 1980-85, acting chmn. dept. anatomy, 1982-85; pres. U. Tex. Health Scis. Ctr., San Antonio, 1985-2000; pres., CEO Project Hope, Millwood, Va., 2001—. Prof. medicine, U. Tex. Health Sci. Ctr., San Antonio, 1985—; chief of staff, U. Mass. Hosp., 1978-80. Mem. editl. bd. Archives Internal Medicine, 1991—; contbr. articles to profl. jours., chpts. to books. Trustee S.W. Found. for Biomed. Rsch., San Antonio Med. Found., S.W. Rsch. Inst. Maj. M.C, U.S. Army, 1973-75. Alfred P. Sloan scholar Amherst Coll., 1962-65; recipient Ruth Hunter Johnson award Boston U. Sch. of Medicine, 1969 Fellow: Am. Coll. Chest Physicians, Am. Coll. Cardiology, ACP; mem.: Bexar County Med. Soc. (exec. com. 1985—2000, 1985—2000, pres. 1996), Tex. Soc. Biomed. Rsch. (past pres.), Tex. Med. Soc. (coun. med. edn. 1986—2001, ho. of dels. 1989—2001, pres.-elect 1997—98, pres. 1998—99), Am. Heart Assn. (fellow coun. clin. cardiology), AMA (coun. on sci. affairs 1993—2001, del. ho. dels. 1995—2001), Omicron Kappa Epsilon, Alpha Omega Alpha. Avocations: tennis, skiing. E-mail: jhowe@projecthope.org.

HOWE, JONATHAN THOMAS, lawyer; b. Evanston, Ill., Dec. 16, 1940; s. Frederick King and Rosalie Charlotte (Volz) H.; m. Lois Helene Braun, July 12, 1963; children: Heather C., Jonathan Thomas Jr., Sara E. BA with honors, Northwestern U., 1963; JD with distinction, Duke U., 1966. Bar: Ill. 1966, U.S. Dist. Ct. (no. dist.) Ill. 1966, U.S. Ct. Appeals (7th cir.) 1967, U.S. Tax Ct. 1968, U.S. Supreme Ct. 1970, U.S. Ct. Appeals (D.C. cir.) 1976, U.S. Ct. Appeals (9th cir.) 1980, U.S. Ct. Appeals (4th, 5th, 11th dirs.) 1983, U.S. Claims Ct. 1990. Ptnr. Jenner & Block, Chgo., 1966-85, sr. ptnr. in charge assn. and adminstrv. law dept., 1978-85; founding and sr. ptnr., pres. Howe & Hutton, Chgo., Washington & St. Louis, 1985—. Exec. and adv. coms. to Ill. Sec. of State to revise the Ill. Not for Profit Act, 1983-86; dir. Pacific Mut. Realty Investors, Inc., 1985-86; dir. cable TV options for public Chgo. Access Corp., 1995-97, Bostrom Corp., 2001—. Contbg. editor Ill. Inst. for Continuing Legal Edn., 1973—, Sporting Goods Bus., 1977-91, Meeting News, 1978-88, Meetings Mgr., 1988—, Meetings and Convs., 1991—; contbr. articles to profl. jours.; legal editor Meetings and Convs., 1990—. Mem. Dist. 27 Bd. Edn., Northbrook, Ill., 1969-89, sec., 1969-72, pres., 1973-84; chmn. bd. trustees Sch. Employee Benefit Trust, 1979-85; founding bd. dirs., pres. Sch. Mgmt. Found. Ill., 1976-84; mem. exec. com. Northfield Twp. Rep. Orgn., 1967-71; bd. deacons Village Presbyn. Ch. Northbrook, 1975-78, trustee, 1981-83; mem. Arts and Music Forum, 4th Presbyn. Ch., Chgo., 1990-93; spl. advisor Pres.'s Coun. Phys. Fitness and Sports, 1983-87, Duke Univ. Sch. of Law Bd. of Visitors (life mem.). Named Industry Leader of Yr., Meeting Industry, 1987, Sch. Bd. Mem. Yr. (twice), Ill. State Bd. Edn.; recipient Internat. Found. PaceSetters award Hospitality Sales Mktg. Assn., 1996. Fellow Internat. Forum of Travel and Tourism Advs., Am. Soc. Assn. Execs. (vice-chmn. legal com. 1983-86), Am. Bar Found.; mem. Internat. Assn. Conv. and Hosp. Indsl. Attys. (founder), ABA (antitrust sect. Nat. Inst. com., trade assn. law com. corp. banking and bus. law sect., sect. on litigation, adminstrv. law sect.; mem. internat. law com., continuing edn. com., tort and ins. practice, vice-chmn. com. sports law 1986—, standing com. meetings and travel 1988-93, spl. advisor 1993—), Task Force on Membership Benefits for Disabled Lawyers, Ill. Bar Assn. (antitrust sect., civil practice sect., sch. law sect., adminstrv. law sect.; co-editor Antitrust Newsletter 1968-70), Chgo. Bar Assn. (def. of prisoners com. 1966-83, antitrust law com. 1971—, continuing edn. com. 1977—, chmn. assn. and non-profit soc. law com. 1984-86), Am. Soc. Assn. Execs. (vice-chmn. legal com., founding mem. legal sect.), N.Y. Soc. Assn. Execs., Acad. Hospitality Industry Attys. (founder, bd. dirs. 1994—, pres. 2001—), Nat. Sch. Bds. Assn. (nat. bd. dirs. 1979-89, exec. com. 1981-89, sec.-treas. 1983-85, 2d v.p. 1985-86, pres. 1987-88, chmn. devel. com. 1982-87, pres. 1987-88), D.C. Bar Assn., Am. Judicature Soc., Ill. Assn. Sch. Bds. (pres. 1977-79, bd. dirs. 1971-88), Chi Bar Found. (life), Assn. Forum Chicagoland (assoc., formerly Chgo. Soc. Assn. Execs.), Nat. Sch. Bds. Found. (pres./trustee 1995-2002), U.S. C. of C. (legal coun. 1998—), Greater Washington Soc. Assn. Execs., Legal Club, Law Club, Mid-Am. Club, Tower Club, Univ. Club Chgo., Order of Coif, Psi Upsilon. Home: 126 W Delaware Pl Chicago IL 60610-3252 Office: 20 N Wacker Dr Ste 4200 Chicago IL 60606-9833 E-mail: jth@howehutton.com.

HOWE, LYMAN HAROLD, III, chemist, researcher; b. Wilkes-Barre, Pa., Nov. 5, 1938; s. Lyman Harold and Esther Madeline (Smith) H.; m. Mary Louise Reinhart, June 16, 1962; 1 child, Jennifer. BS, Duke U., 1960; MS, Emory U., 1961; PhD, U. Tenn., 1966. Rsch. assoc. Emory U., 1960-61; rsch. and teaching assoc. U. Tenn., 1962-66; rsch. chemist water mgmt. TVA, Chattanooga, 1966-97. Co-author publs. in field. Fellow ASTM (water com. results advisor 1976-97, Max Hecht award 1985, Award of Merit 1993); mem. Am. Chem. Soc., Am. Contact Bridge League (Ace of Clubs award, third place Chattanooga Club Master of Yr. award 1989, reviewer environ. sci. and tech. 1989), U.S. Chess Fedn. Clubs: Torch (1st v.p. chpt. 1981, pres. 1982-83, 2d v.p. 1984-88). Presbyterian. Home: 1241 Mountain Brook Cir Signal Mountain TN 37377-2127 E-mail: LymanHoweIII@msn.com.

HOWE, MARTHA MORGAN, microbiologist, educator; b. N.Y.C., Sept. 29, 1945; d. Charles Hermann and Miriam Hudson (Wagner) M.; m. Terrance Gary Cooper. AB, Bryn Mawr Coll., 1966; PhD, MIT, 1972. Postdoctoral fellow Cold Spring Harbor Lab, N.Y., 1972-74; asst. prof. bacteriology U. Wis., Madison, 1975-77, assoc. prof., 1977-81, prof., 1981-84, Vilas prof., 1984-86; Van Vleet prof. virology U. Tenn., Memphis, 1986—. Mem. genetic biology rev. panel NSF, 1980-82; mem. gen. rsch. support rev. com. NIH, Bethesda, 1982-86, mem. microbial physiology and genetics 2 study sec., 1997-2001; mem. sci. adv. com. instnl. rsch. grants Am. Cancer Soc., 1991-94. Assoc. editor Virology, 1983-92, Genetics, 1994; mem. editorial bd. Jour. Bacteriology, 1985-90; contbr. articles to profl. jours. and books. Recipient Rsch. Career Devel. award NIH, 1978; H.I. Romnes Faculty fellow U. Wis., 1981; Amoco Teaching award U. Wis., 1981. Fellow Am. Acad. Microbiology (bd. govs. 1991-99); mem. Am. Soc. Microbiology (chmn. divsn. H 1983, councillor divsn. H 1989-91, chmn. com. on awards 1990-96, pres.-elect 1999-2000, pres. 2000-2001, past pres. 2001-2002, Eli Lilly award 1985, ASM Founders Disting. Svc. award 1999), Am. Soc. Biochemistry and Molecular Biology, Genetics Soc. Am. (bd. dirs. 1989-91, program com. 1989-90). Office: U Tenn Dept Molecular Scis 858 Madison Ave Memphis TN 38163-0001 E-mail: mhowe@utmem.edu.

HOWE, PATRICIA MOORE, adult education educator; b. Woodside, N.Y., Oct. 10, 1938; d. James Preston and Florence (McGowen) Moore; m. Douglas C. Howe, Aug. 2, 1958; children: William, David, Timothy. BS in Lit., SUNY, Oneonta, 1972, MS in Edn., 1975. Cert. elem. and adult edn., Del. Tchr. Cecil County Bd. Edn., Elkton, Md., 1979-80; beginning reading instr. Chesapeake Job Corps Ctr., Port Deposit, Md., 1980-85; coord. adult programs U. Del., Newark, 1987-97, acad. coord., 1993-98, ret., 1998. Owner Edn. Works. Home: 23 Acorn Dr Elkton MD 21921-3209

HOWE, RICHARD CUDDY, state supreme court justice; b. South Cottonwood, Utah, Jan. 20, 1924; s. Edward E. and Mildred (Cuddy) H.; m. Juanita Lyon, Aug. 30, 1949; children: Christine Howe Schultz, Andrea Howe Reynolds, Bryant, Valerie Howe Winegar, Jeffrey, Craig. BS, U. Utah, 1945, JD, 1948. Bar: Utah. Law clk. to Justice James H. Wolfe, Utah Supreme Ct., 1949-50; judge city ct. Murray, Utah, 1951; individual practice law, 1952-80; justice Utah Supreme Ct., Salt Lake City, 1980—2002. Mem. Utah Constnl. Revision Commn., 1976-85. Chmn., original mem. Salt Lake County Merit Coun.; mem. Utah Ho. of Reps., 1951-58, 69-72, Utah Senate, 1973-78. Named Outstanding Legislator Citizens' Conf. State Legislatures, 1972 Mem. ABA, Utah Bar Assn., Sons of Utah Pioneers. Mem. Lds Ch.*

HOWE, RICHARD RIVES, lawyer; b. Portland, Oreg., Dec. 21, 1942; s. Hubert Shattuck Jr. and Anna Gertrude (Moody) H.; m. Elizabeth Anne Crowell, Aug. 29, 1964; 1 child, Richard Rives Jr. BA, Yale U., 1964; JD, Harvard U., 1967. Bar: N.Y. 1968, U.S. Ct. Appeals (2d cir.) 1973, U.S. Dist. Ct. (so. and ea. dists.) N.Y. 1973, U.S. Supreme Ct. 1973. Assoc. Sullivan & Cromwell, N.Y.C., 1967-74, ptnr., 1974—. Exec. com. Nat. Com. Am. Fgn. Policy, Inc., 2000—. Pres., bd. dirs. Peoples' Symphony Concerts, N.Y.C., 1983—, bd. dirs. Bar Assurance and Reinsurance Ltd., Bermuda, 1994—. Mem.: ABA (com. on corp. practice, fed. regulation securities com., legal options com.), Assn. Bar City N.Y., N.Y. State Bar Assn. (mem. exec. com. 1982—99, chmn. 1992—93, bus. law sect., chmn. securities regulation com. 1982—86), Pi Sigma Alpha, Phi Beta Kappa. Democrat. Home: 86 Woodfield Dr Short Hills NJ 07078-1654 Office: Sullivan & Cromwell Fl 32 125 Broad St Fl 32 New York NY 10004-2498 E-mail: hower@sullcrom.com.

HOWE, ROGER EVANS, mathematician, educator; b. Chgo., May 23, 1945; s. John Perry and Marilyn (Leilani) (Evans) H.; m. Carolyn (Rutter) Read Howe, Sept. 9, 1967; Nicholas Read, Katherine Joanna. BA, Harvard Coll., 1966; PhD in Math., U. Calif., Berkeley, 1969. Asst. prof. SUNY, Stony Brook, 1969-72, assoc. prof., 1972-74; prof. Yale U., New Haven, 1974—. Vis. mem. Inst. for Advanced Study, Princeton, NJ, 1971—72; guest prof. U. Bonn, Germany, 1973—74; vis. prof. Oxford (Eng.) U., 1978, Rutgers U., New Brunswick, NJ, 1989—90, U. Paris VII, 1996, Nat. U. Singapore, 1999, Hong Kong U. Sci. & Tech., 2002; fellow Inst. for Advanced Studies, Hebrew U. of Jerusalem, 1988; panel on math. learning NRC, 1999—2001; sci. adv. bd. Singapore Inst. Math. Scis., 2001—; math. portfolio rev. panel NSF, 2003—; steering com., undergrad. program coord. Park City Math. Inst., 2001—. Co-author: Non-abelian Harmonic Analysis, 1992; advisor Jour. die reine und angewandte Mathematik, 1985-97; editor Bull. Am. Math. Soc., 1988-90; mem. editl. bd. Math. Rsch. Letters, Hong Kong, 1993-96, Advances in Math., 1995-99, Transformation Groups, 1995-2001, Jour. Functional Analysis, 2000—; contbr. articles to profl. jours. Study panel RAND Math., 2000—03; steering com. CBMS Math. Edn. of Tchr. Report, 1998—2001. Guggenheim Found. fellow, 1983, Japan Soc. Promotion of Sci., Tokyo, 1993. Fellow Am. Acad. Arts and Scis., Conn. Acad. Sci. and Engring., Nat. Acad. Sci.; mem. Am. Math. Soc. (editor 1989-92, chair com. on edn. 2000—), Math. Assn. Am. (com. Lester R. Ford award), Nat. Coun. Tchrs. Math. Office: Yale U PO Box 208283 New Haven CT 06520-8283

HOWE, RONALD EVANS, lawyer, minister, small business owner; b. Charles City, Iowa, Feb. 17, 1945; s. Evans R. and Elizabeth (Atchison) H.; m. M. Kristin Petersmith, Aug. 16, 1970; children: Sarah Elizabeth O'Brien, Rachel Ellen Wolf, Michael Evans. Cert., Moody Bible Inst., 1966, AB, 1969, U. Iowa, 1968, JD, 1972; ThM, Dallas Theol. Sem., 1975. Lic. to ministry Ind. Mission Ch., 1966, ordained Evang. Free Ch. Am., 1990. Bar: Iowa 1972, Tex. 1973, U.S. Tax Ct. 1974. Atty. Law Offices of Gordon Macdowell, Dallas, 1972-75; sr. min. Elim Chapel, Winnipeg, Man., Can., 1975-85, Evang. Free Ch., Fresno, Calif., 1985—2001; broadcaster weekly radio program Free to Live, 1985—2001; owner, pres. Elimcare Cmty., 1992—, Elim Place, Inc., 1992—, Elim Gardens, LLC, 2000—; pres. Elimcare Ministries, 2001—; exec. dir. The Elimcare Found., 2001—. Adj. prof. Winnipeg Theol. Sem., 1975-85, Briercrest Grad. Sch., Caronport, Sask, Can., 1985-87; mem. adv. bd. Trinity Western U., Langley, B.C., Can., 1985-2002; bd. dirs. Haggai Inst., Winnipeg, 1977-85, Link Care Ctr., Fresno, 1985-2001; bd. govs. Winnipeg Bible Coll. and Sem., 1982-85; mem. exec. com. Fresno Christian Sch., 1985-2001; cons. Evang. Ministries Found., Fresno, 1999-2001; lectr. in field. Author: (booklet) Breakfast of Champions, 1984. Exec. dir. Cmty. Advocacy Found., 1999-2002. Recipient Mayor's Commendation for 10 Yrs. of Contbn. in Leadership to City of Fresno, 1995, Outstanding Bus. award for leadership in edn. Compact Fresno, 1998. Mem. North Fresno Rotary (bd. dirs. 2003—). Republican. Office: Elimcare 6276 N First St Ste 103B Fresno CA 93710 Business E-Mail: elimcare@sbcglobal.net. *The greatest challenge of my life is to be alert daily to the struggle of maintaining integrity between what I say and what I practice. This authenticity or lack thereof impacts my personal, family and professional life.*

HOWE, SANDRA JO, library director; b. St. Louis, Sept. 30, 1960; d. Raymond Lee and Elizabeth Ann Griffin; m. Steven Howe, June 24, 1977 (div. Nov. 1978); children: Beth Marie Howe, Ricky A. Rudd. Student, Culver-Stockton Coll., 1997-99. Pharmacy technician Grand Leader Pharmacy, Canton, Mo., 1981-87; mgr., cons. Mo. Pizza Co., Canton, 1993-96; asst. libr. Canton Pub. Libr., 1996-97, dir., 1997—. Mem. ALA, ACLU, Mo. Libr. Assn. Avocations: reading, promoting literacy, nature walks, gardening. Office: Canton Pub Libr 409 Lewis St Canton MO 63435-1529 E-mail: sjhowe@yahoo.com.

HOWE, THOMAS NOBLE, archaeologist, educator, architect; b. Sault Sainte Marie, Mich., Sept. 4, 1949; s. Donnell Conde Howe and Margaret Eleanor Frantz. BA German, Lawrence U., 1971; MA, Harvard U., 1975, PhD Fine Arts, 1985. Chair dept. art Southwestern U., Georgetown, Tex., 1990—97; assoc. dir. Palatine East Excavation, Rome, 1988—93; asst. director/architect Castle Copse Excavation, Great Bedwyn, England, 1983—86; instr. Harvard U., Cambridge, Mass., 1982—82; Brown disting. rsch. prof. Southwestern U., Georgetown, Tex., 2000—04; coordinatore generale (dir.) The Restoring Ancient Stabiae Found., Castellammare di Stabia, Italy, 2002—. Fellow Humanities Inst. U. Chgo., 1995—96. Author: (book) Vitruvius: Ten Books on Architecture (commentary and illustrations), 1999; author: (chief author/planner) (master plan (book) Restoring Ancient Stabia: Master Plan 2001, 2001; author: (author, co-editor) (book) The Romano-British Villa at Castle Copse, Great Bedwyn, 1997; author: The Invention of the Doric Order, 1985. Commr. Hist. Architecture and Rev. Commn., Georgetown, 2001—04. Mem.: Phi Beta Kappa. Home: 1205 Laurel Street Georgetown TX 78626 Home Fax: 512-883-4810; Office Fax: 512-863-1422. Business E-Mail: howet@southwestern.edu.

HOWE, VIRGINIA HOFFMAN, nurse administrator; b. Buffalo, Apr. 14, 1940; d. George C. Jr. and Mabel (Parrish) Hoffman; m. Lawrence T. Howe, Apr. 11, 1970; children: Daniel George, Timothy Kelly. AAS, Trocaire, 1977; BS in Community Health Nursing, SUNY, Buffalo, 1986. RN, N.Y. Assoc. coord. oper. rm. Buffalo Gen. Hosp., head nurse oper. rm. gen. surgery, oper. rm. staff nurse, nurse clinician otolaryngology and ear, nose, throat dept., nurse clinician divsn. plastic and reconstructive surgery, nursing instr., educator, discharge planning nurse, cmty. health nurse, nurse paralegal, infection control nurse, supr., cons.; nurse legal cons. Cons. in field. Mem.: Nurse Paralegal Cons., Legal Nurse Cons., Assn. Operating Rm. Nurses.

HOWE, WARREN BILLINGS, physician; b. Jackson Heights, N.Y., Oct. 25, 1940; s. John Hanna and Francelia (Rose) H.; m. Hedwig Neslanik, Aug. 7, 1971; children: Elizabeth Rose, Sarah Billings. BA, U. Rochester, 1962; MD, Washington U., St. Louis, 1965. Diplomate Am. Bd. Family Practice with CAQ in Sports Medicine, Nat. Bd. Med. Examiners. Intern Phila. Gen. Hosp., 1965-66; resident physician Highland Hosp./U. Rochester, 1969-71; family physician Family Medicine Clinic of Oak Harbor (Wash.), Inc., PS, 1971-92; student health physician, univ. team physician We. Wash. U., Bellingham, 1992—. Team physician Oak Harbor H.S., 1972-92; head tournament physician Wash. State H.S. Wrestling Championships, Tacoma, 1989—; attending physician Seattle Goodwill Games, 1990; clin. asst. prof. U. Wash. Sch. Medicine, 1975-82; bd. dirs. Nat. Operating Com. on Stds. for Athletic Equipment. Contbr. articles to profl. jours. and chpts. to books; editl. bd. The Physician and Sports Medicine Jour., 1984—. Bd. dirs. Oak Harbor Sch. Dist. #201, 1975-87; chmn. Oak Harbor Citizen's Com. for Sch. Support, 1988-90. Lt. comdr. USN, 1966-69, Vietnam. Recipient Disting. Svc. award City of Oak Harbor, 1984; Paul Harris fellowship Oak Harbor Rotary Club. Fellow Am. Coll. Sports Medicine (chair membership com. 1986-95), Am. Acad. Family Physicians; mem. Wash. State Med. Assn., Am. Med. Soc. for Sports Medicine (Humanitarian award 2002), Am. Coll. Health Assn. Presbyterian. Home: 4222 Northridge Way Bellingham WA 98226-7804 Office: WWU Student Health Ctr 2001 Bill McDonald Pkwy Bellingham WA 98225-9132

HOWE, WILLIAM HUGH, artist; b. Stockton, Calif., June 18, 1928; s. Edwin Walter and Eugenia (Mercante) H. AB, Ottawa (Kans.) U., 1951. Illustrator Western Auto Supply, Kansas City, Mo., 1952, Kansas City Mdse. Mart, 1953-56; comml. artist U.S. Army C.E., Kansas City, 1958-64, Howard Needles Tammen & Bergendoff Cons. Engrs., Kansas City, 1964-68, Urban & Regional Planning, 1968-70; freelance artist, 1970—. Exhibited paintings of butterflies Philbrook Art Ctr., Tulsa, Ft. Worth Children's Mus., Montserrat Gallery, N.Y.C., Witte Meml. Art Mus., San Antonio, Anthropology Mus., Chapultepec Park, Mexico City, Alice Sabatini Gallery, Topeka Pub. Libr., 2002, Powell Gardens, Kingsville, 2003; represented in permanent collections: Smithsonian Instn., Washington, Franklin Mint (Pa.), Cranbook Inst., Bloomfield Hills, Mich., U. Mich. Exhibits Mus., Ann Arbor, Oak Knoll Mus., Clayton, Mo., Am. Mus. Natural History, N.Y.C., Denver Mus. Natural History, Am. Baptist Assembly, Green Lake, Wis., Mowbray Union, Ottawa U., Kans., Cen. Mo. State Coll., Warrensburg, Mich. State U., East Lansing, U. Wyo. Art Mus., Laramie, San Diego Mus. Nat. History, Balboa Park, U. Ariz., Tuscon, Ill. State Mus. Art, Springfield, Mont. Hist. Soc., Helena, Wyo. State Art Mus., Cheyenne, Ariz. State U., Tempe, Milw. Pub. Mus., State Capitol Bldg., Denver, Denver Pub. Libr., Kansas City (Mo.) Mus. History Sci., Presdl. Palace, Tamazunchale, San Luis Potosi, Mexico, Ottawa (Kans.) Jr. H.S., others; Am. Heritage Wildlife cards Am. Butterflies, 1983, U. Kans., 1994, U. Calif. Berkeley, Allyn Mus. Entomology, Sarasota, U. Colo., Colo. State U., Calif. Acad. Scis., San Francisco, Oakland (Calif.) Mus., James Ford Bell Mus., U. Minn. (Mpls), Coutts Art Mus., 1997; Author-artist: Our Butterflies and Moths, 1964, The Butterflies of North America, 1975, Butterfly Chart of North America, 1979, Butterfly sect. Readers Digest North American Wildlife, 1980; co-author (with Carlos R. Beutelspacher Baights), U.N.A.M., Mexico City, 1984; one man shows Caroline Kingcade Gallery, North Kansas City, Mo., 1988, Coutts Mus. of Art, El Dorado, 1997, Dallas Mus. Natural History, Fair Park, 1999, George P. Spiva Art Ctr., Joplin, Mo., 1999, Alice Sabatini Art Gallery, Topeka, 2002, Shawnee County Libr., Topeka, 2002; TV show Hoy Mismo, 1986. Mem. Ottawa Community Arts Coun., Leavenworth Arts. Coun.; mem. Larry Hatteberg's "Kans. People" KAKE-TV, Wichita. Named Am. Artist Am. References, 1990. Mem. Jour. Lepidopterists Soc., Burroughs Nature Club, Audubon Soc. Mo., Central States Entomo. Soc., Los Angeles County Mus., Spiva Art Ctr., Dallas Mus. Natural History, Mus. Culture and Natural History, Harvard Botanical Mus.. Democrat. Episcopalian. Avocation: collecting butterflies in Mexico and Guatemala. Home: 822 E 11th St Ottawa KS 66067-3138

HOWELL, ALLY WINDSOR, lawyer, author, editor; b. Montgomery, Ala., Mar. 10, 1949; s. Elvin and Bennie Merle (Windsor) H.; m. Donna K. Graffander, Sept. 2, 1989; children: Christopher Darby, Joshua Darby, Jeremiah Graffander. BA, Huntington Coll., 1971; JD, Jones Sch. Law, 1974. Bar: Ala. 1974, U.S. Supreme Ct. 1977, U.S. Ct. Appeals (fed. cir.) 1983, U.S. Ct. Appeals (11th cir.) 1981, U.S. Tax Ct. 1979, U.S. Claims Ct. 1982, U.S. Dist. Ct. (mid. dist.) Ala. 1975, U. Dist. Ct. (so. dist.) Ala. 1978. Archivist Hist. Rsch. Ctr. Air U., Maxwell AFB, Ala., 1972-75; pvt. practice Montgomery, 1975-82, 83-01; atty.-editor West Group, Rochester, N.Y., 2001—. Adj. prof. Faulkner U., Montgomery, 1975—, adj. prof. Jones Law Sch., 1983—85; asst. atty. gen., chief legal sect. Ala. Medicaid Agy., Montgomery, 1982—83. Author: Alabama Civic Practice Forms, 1986, 3d edit., 1992, Alabama Torts Case Finder, 1988, Alabama Personal Injury and Torts, 1996, Trial Handbook for Alabama Lawyers, 2d edit., 1998. Co-founder, bd. dirs. Montgomery Inst., 2000—01; treas. bd. dirs. Gay Alliance of the Genesee Valley. Hon. lt. col., aide de camp Gov. Ala., 1974. Mem. ABA (contbr. editor profl. liability newsletter, litigation sect. 1990-92, co-editor trial techniques comm. newsletter), Assn. Trial Lawyers Am., Montgomery County Bar Assn. (newsletter editorial com. 1984-85), Nat. Bd. Trial Adv. (cert. civil litigation 1981, 86, 91, examiner ethics, evidence and civil procedure), Nat. Lesbian and Gay Law Assn. (bd. dirs. 1999-2001, vice co-chair 2000-2001, editor newsletter 2000—). Presbyterian.

HOWELL, ALVIN HAROLD, engineer, company executive, educator; b. Sedgwick, Kans., Feb. 5, 1908; s. George Alfred and Gertie (Johnson) H.; m. Helen Whitney, Sept. 7, 1934; children: Elizabeth, Alvin Harold, John Arthur, Gordon Howard. BS, U. Kans., 1929; student, Union Coll., Schenectady, 1929-30; MS, Mich. Coll. Mining and Tech., 1934; Sc.D., Mass. Inst. Tech., 1938. Registered profl. engr., Mass. Test engr. Gen. Electric Co., Schenectady, 1929-30; instr. Mich. Coll. Mining and Tech., 1931-34, research geophys. prospecting methods, summers 1931-34; research assoc. MIT, Cambridge, 1939-40; vis. prof., adminstrv. officer Radar Sch., 1942-43; asst. prof. elec. engring. Tufts U., Medford, Mass., 1940-41, assoc. prof., head dept. elec. engring., 1941-43, prof., head dept. elec. engring., dir. research, 1943-70, prof., dir. Balloon Astronomy Lab., 1970-78, emeritus prof., 1978—; devel. rocket and balloon type instrumentation; dir. Doble Engring. Co., 1960—, v.p., 1961-63, chmn. exec. com., 1969—, chmn. bd., 1979—. Mem. NRC; cons. on

tethered and free floating balloon systems Air Force Geophysics Lab. Author: (with others) Principles of Radar, 1944; Contbr. (with others) articles to profl. publs. Recipient Exceptional Service award USAF, 1955; Distinguished Service award Tufts U., 1973; Tufts Service citation Tufts U. Alumni Assn., 1974; lab. named in his honor Tufts U., 1984. Mem. IEEE, Am. Phys. Soc., AAAS, AAUP, Sci. Ballooning Assn. (v.p. 1975-78), Am. Soc. Engring. Edn., Sigma Xi, Eta Kappa Nu, Tau Beta Pi. Baptist. Achievements include development of balloon-borne telescope for tracking planets and stars and balloon-borne payload for precisely pointing at ground targets to permit radiometric and interferometric measurements at IR wave lengths. Home: 990 Massachusetts Ave Arlington MA 02476-4532 Office: Tufts U Dept Elec Engring Medford MA 02155

HOWELL, ARTHUR, lawyer; b. Atlanta, Aug. 24, 1918; s. Arthur and Katharine (Mitchell) H.; m. Caroline Sherman, June 14, 1941; children: Arthur, Caroline, Eleanor, Richard, Peter, James; m. Janet Kerr Franchot, Dec. 16, 1972. AB, Princeton U., 1939; JD, Harvard U., 1942; LLD (hon.), Oglethorpe U., 1972. Bar: Ga. 1942. Assoc. F.M. Bird, 1942-45; ptnr. Alston & Bird (and predecessor firms), 1945-89, of counsel, 1989—. Bd. dirs., gen. counsel Atlantic Steel Co., 1960-93; chmn., bd. dirs. Summit Industries, Inc.; bd. dirs. Enterprise Funds; chmn. emeritus bd. dirs. Crescent Banking Co.; past pres. Atlanta Legal Aid Soc.; emeritus mem. bd. dirs. Crescent Bank and Trust Co. Pres. Met. Atlanta Cmty. Svcs., 1956, dir., 1953—; pres. Cmty. Planning Coun., 1961—63; gen. chmn. United Appeal, 1955; spl. atty. gen. State Ga., 1948—55; spl. counsel, Univ. Sys. Ga. State Sch. Bldg. Authorities, 1951—70; adv. com. Ga. Corp. Code, 1967—; trustee, past chmn. Oglethorpe U.; trustee Princeton, 1964—68; emeritus trustee Atlanta Speech Sch., Westminster Schs., Atlanta, Episcopal H.S., Alexandria, Va., Morehouse Coll.; past trustee Inst. Internat. Edn., mem. exec. com., 1969—72; elder, trustee, chmn. bd. trustees Presbyn. Ch., 1985—89; past chmn. Atlanta Adv. Com. Pks. Named hon. alumnus Ga. Inst. Tech. Mem.: Am. Judicature Soc., Lawyers Club of Atlanta (past. pres.), Atlanta Bar Assn., Ga. Bar Assn., ABA, Am. Law Inst. (life), Soc. Colonial Wars, Princeton Club of N.Y., Nassau Club, Homosassa Fishing Club, Capital City Club, Phi Beta Kappa. Home: 200 Larkspur Ln Highlands NC 28741-8388 Office: Alston & Bird One Atlantic Ctr 1201 W Peachtree St Atlanta GA 30309-3424

HOWELL, BENJAMIN FRANKLIN, JR., geophysicist, educator; b. Princeton, N.J., June 12, 1917; s. Benjamin Franklin and Claire M. (Mead) H.; m. Constance M. Benson, June 30, 1943 (dec.); children: Barbara Carolyn, Catherine Ann (dec.), Bonnie Andrea, James Benjamin. AB, Princeton U., 1939; MS, Calif. Inst. Tech., 1942, Ph. D., 1949. Research engr. div. war research U. Calif. at San Diego, 1942-45; geophysicist United Geophys. Co., 1946-49; faculty Pa. State U., 1949—, prof. geophysics, 1953—, head dept. geophysics and geochemistry, 1949-63; asst. dean Grad. Sch. Pa. State U., 1968-70, assoc. dean, 1970-82, assoc. dean emeritus, 1982—. Chief cons. seismologist Vibratech Engring. Co., Hazleton, Pa., 1955-69 Author: Introduction to Geophysics, 1959, Earth and Universe, 1972, Introduction to Seismological Research: History and Development, 1990; Editor: Contributions in Geophysics in Honor of Beno Gutenberg, 1958. Fellow Am. Geophys. Union (sec. sect. tectonophysics 1956-59, sect. seismology 1959-63), Geol. Soc. Am.; mem. soc. Exploration Geophysics, Seismol. Soc. Am. (pres. 1963-64), Phi Beta Kappa, Sigma Xi. Baptist. Home: 1143 Smithfield Cir State College PA 16801-6424 Office: 406 Deike Bldg University Park PA 16802-2713 E-mail: howellbf@aol.com.

HOWELL, BRADLEY SUE, librarian; b. McKinney, Tex., July 15, 1933; d. Jessie Leonard and Carrie Pearl (Nickerson) LaFon; m. Richard Dunn Howell, May 18, 1957; children: Mark Richard, Celeste Ella, Jane Elizabeth. BS in Edn., So. Meth. U., 1955; MS in Libr. Sci., East Tex. State U., 1968. Tchr. J.B. Hood Jr. High Sch., Dallas, 1955-56, Mineral Wells (Tex.) Jr. High Sch., 1957-58; libr. Ascher Silberstein Sch., Dallas, 1963, San Jacinto Sch., Dallas, 1960-62, 65-81, Woodrow Wilson High Sch., Dallas, 1981—. Pres. Tex. United Meth. Hist. Soc., 1980—84, v.p., 2000—; sec. South Ctr. Jurisdiction Archives and history of United Meth. Ch., 1980—88; v.p. local ch. sect. The United Meth. Hist. Soc., 1989—95, chmn., 1995—99; pres. PTA Woodrow Wilson H.S., 1983—84; leader Camp Fire, Inc., 1970—; v.p. South Ctrl. Jurisdiction, Archives and History The United Meth. Ch., 2000—04. Recipient Wakan award Camp Fire, Inc., 1976, Hiltcni award, 19782, Sawnequas award, 1988, Gulick Vol. award, 1998, Terrific Tchr. award Tex. PTA, 1984, Jim Collins Outstanding award, 1986, Honor award Nat. Sch. Pub. Relation Assn., 1986, Dallas Positive Parents award, 1987, Golden Flame award, 1990; elected Woodrow Wilson H.S. Hall of Fame, 1999. Mem.: Am. Libr. Svcs. to Children (Newbery com. 1980), Tex. Libr. Assn. (chmn. archives and history roundtable 1990—92), Tex. Assn. Sch. Librs., Dallas Assn. Sch. Libns. (pres. 1975—76), Freedoms Found. and Valley Forge (pres. Dallas chpt. 1997—99, v.p. edn. 2003—), Pi Lambda Theta (Alpha Sigma chpt. pres. 1997—2002), Delta Psi Kappa, Phi Delta Kappa, Alpha Delta Pi, Delta Kappa Gamma (state achievement award 1988, Golden Gift Leadership Mgmt. award 1985). Democrat. Home: 722 Ridgeway St Dallas TX 75214-4453 Office: Woodrow Wilson High Sch 100 S Glasgow Dr Dallas TX 75214-4598

HOWELL, BRUCE INMAN, academic administrator; b. Roanoke Rapids, N.C., Mar. 12, 1942; s. Leroy Inman and Pauline (Massey) H.; m. Mable Lea Smith, Aug. 22, 1965; children: Bruce Inman Jr., Virginia Lea. BS in English and History, East Carolina U., 1964, MA in History and Sch. Adminstrn., 1965; postgrad., N.C. State U., 1971, 84, Mich. State U., 1971, Duke U., 1976, N.C. Bank Dirs. Coll., 1999. Cert. grad. tchr., prin., supr., N.C., investment banker, stock exchange and brokerage office procedures. Instr., grad. asst. East Carolina U., Greenville, N.C., 1964-65; stockbroker Interstate Securities Corp., Charlotte, N.C., 1968-70; dean continuing edn. Lenoir C.C., Kinston, N.C., 1970-75; pres. Sampson Tech. Coll., Clinton, N.C., 1975-80, Wake Tech. C.C., Raleigh, N.C., 1980—. Adj. prof. dept. adult and C.C. edn. N.C. State U., 1982—, gen. adv. com., 1982; mem. Wake County-Raleigh Pvt. Industry Coun., 1983-94, Raleigh Econ. Devel. Roundtable, 1984—, exec. com.; adv. N.C. govt. agys., Wake Co. Communities in Schs., 1990—; adv. Cen. Carolina Consortium, 1993-97, pres., 1996-97; mem. numerous ednl. commns. and task forces. Author: Debasement: A Problem of Imperial Rome, 1966, The Lenoir County Story, 1968; editorial bd. Community Coll. Review, N.C. State U., 1982-93; contbr. articles to profl. jours. Mem. Lenoir County Schs. Vocat. Adv. com., 1972-75, Econ. Devel. Com., Fuguay-Varina; bd. dirs. Lenoir County Heart Fund, 1972, Lenoir County Fair Assn., 1970, Branch Banking & Trust Co., Cary, N.C., 1980-98; chmn. bd. dirs. Crescent State Bank, 1998—; mem. Wake County Interagy. Coord. Coun., 1981; membership com. N.C. Lit. and Hist. Assn., 1978; mem. adminstrv. bd. Westminster United Meth. Ch., 1973-76; active First United Meth. Ch., Clinton, 1977-81, chmn. adminstrv. bd., 1978-80, White Plains, 1981—, trustee, 1997—. Grad. fellow East Carolina U., 1964-65; Kellogg Community Svcs. fellow, Lenoir Community Coll., 1971; named one of Outstanding Young Men Am., 1975, 77, 78, Jacyee of Yr., 1967, Outstanding Old Jaycee of Yr., 1971; recipient Chief Exec. Officer award So. Region Assn. Community Colls., 1989. Mem.: N.C. Assn. Colls. and Univs. (govtl. agys. liaison com. 1983—90, pres. 1993), Am. Numismatic Assn., Nat. Geneal. Soc., N.C. Employees Assn., N.C. Assn. Pub. C.C. Pres. (com. mem., pres. 1986—87), N.C. C.C. Adult Edn. Assn., So. Assn. Colls. and Schs. (evaluation com. 1982, 1990, 1992—94), Nat. Coun. Resource Devel., Am. Coun. on Edn, Am. Coun. on Edn., Rotary (Cary pres. 1999—2000), Execs. Club of Raleigh (pres. 1996—98), Cary C. of C. (econ. devel. com 1983—, edn. task force com. 1987—, bd. dirs. 2001—, chair edn. com. 2002—), Greater Raleigh C. of C. (adv. com. manpower resource devel. program 1980, leadership round table 1983—, higher edn. roundtable 1986—), Fuquay-Varina C. of C. (bd. dirs. 1987—90), Kappa Delta Pi, Phi Kappa Phi. Avocations: antiques, furniture refinishing, gardening, numismatics. Home: 1105 Queensferry Rd Cary NC 27511-6426 Office: Wake Tech Community Coll 9101 Fayetteville Rd Raleigh NC 27603-5655

HOWELL, CHARLES MAITLAND, dermatologist; b. Thomasville, N.C., Apr. 14, 1914; s. Cyrus Maitl and Lilly Mae (Ammons) H.; m. Betty Jane Myers, Feb. 12, 1949; children: Elizabeth Myers, Pamela Jane. BS, Wake Forest U., Winston-Salem, N.C., 1935; MD, U. Pa., 1937. Intern Charity Hosp., New Orleans, 1937-38; resident in medicine Burlington County Hosp., Mt. Holley, N.J., 1938-39; sch. physician Lawrenceville (N.J.) Sch., 1939-42; resident in pathology N.C. Baptist Hosp., Winston-Salem, 1947-48; resident in dermatology Columbia-Presbyn. Med. Ctr., N.Y.C., 1948-50; resident in allergy Roosevelt Hosp., N.Y.C., 1950-51; practice medicine specializing in dermatology Winston-Salem, 1951—. Mem. staff N.C. Bapt., Forsyth Meml. hosps.; mem. faculty Bowman Gray Sch. Medicine, Wake Forest U., 1951-86, head. sect., 1984-86, prof. dermatology, 1967-84, prof. emeritus, 1984, head sect., 1961-86, acting head sect., 1984-86. Served as officer M.C. AUS, 1942-46. Fellow Am. Acad. Dermatology, Am. Acad. Allergy; mem. N Am. Clin. Dermatol. Soc., N.Y. Acad. Scis. Clubs: Old Town (Winston-Salem); Bermuda Run Country (Clemmons, N.C.). Democrat. Baptist. Home: 1100 E Kent Rd Winston Salem NC 27104-1116 Office: 340 Pershing Ave Winston Salem NC 27103-2513

HOWELL, CONNIE RAE, critical care nurse; b. St. Charles, Ill., July 13, 1952; d. George and Genevieve B. (Zornow) H. Diploma, Evangelical Sch. Nursing, Oak Lawn, Ill., 1973. Cert. critical care nurse. Staff nurse U. Utah Hosp., Salt Lake City, 1977-79, U. Wash. Hosp., Seattle, 1979-83, Sherman Hosp., Elgin, Ill., 1983-87, Univ. Hosp. and Clinics, Madison, Wis., 1987-90, Sherman Hosp., Elgin, Ill., 1991—. Mem. AACN, Evangelical Sch. Nursing Alumnae Assn.

HOWELL, CONNIE SUE, state transportation dispatcher; b. Westerville, Ohio, Apr. 24, 1960; d. Fred Shimp and Martha Lee Jennings; 1 child from previous marriage, Jeremy James Deckling. Student, Columbus State C.C., Columbus, Ohio, 1999—. Cert. Comml. Ops. 1995. Mem.: Phi Theta Kappa. Office: 2855 W Dublin Granville Rd Columbus OH 43235-2712 Home: 107 Rupolo St Saint Paris OH 43222-9544

HOWELL, DONALD LEE, lawyer; b. Waco, Tex., Jan. 31, 1935; s. Hilton Emory and Louise Howell; m. Gwendolyn Avera, June 13, 1957; children: Daniel Liege, Alison Avera, Anne Turner. BA cum laude, Baylor U., 1956; JD with honors, U. Tex., 1963. Bar: Tex. 1963. Assoc. Vinson & Elkins, Houston, 1963-70, ptnr., 1970—, mem. mgmt. com., 1980-99. Capt. USAFR, 1956-59. Fellow Am. Bar Found., Tex. Bar Found., Houston Bar Found., Am. Law Inst.; mem. ABA, Am. Coll. Bond Counsel, Houston Bar Assn., Nat. Assn. Bond Lawyers (pres. 1981-82, bd. dirs. 1979-83), Attys. Liability Assurance Soc. (Bermuda bd. dirs. 1992—, chmn. 2000-02, U.S. bd. dirs. 1992—, chmn. 2000-02), Houston Club, Houston Ctr. Club, Order of Coif, Phi Delta Phi. Democrat. Episcopalian. E-mail: dhowell@velaw.com.

HOWELL, FRANCIS CLARK, paleo-anthropologist; b. Kansas City, Mo., Nov. 27, 1925; s. Edward Ray and Myrtle Marie (Clark) H.; m. Betty Ann Tomsen, June 17, 1955; children: Brian David, Jennifer Clare PhB, U. Chgo., 1949, MA, 1951, PhD, 1953. Instr. anatomy Washington U., St. Louis, 1953-55; asst. prof. to prof. anthropology U. Chgo., 1955-70; prof. anthropology U. Calif.-Berkeley, 1970-91, emeritus prof., 1991—. Contbr. numerous articles on human biol. and cultural evolution to profl. jours. Trustee L.S.B. Leakey Found., 1969—. Served with USN, 1944-46 Recipient Franklin L. Burr prize, Nat. Geographic Soc., 1993, Leakey prize L.S.B. Leakey Fedn., 1998, Charles Robert Darwin Lifetime Achievement award Am. Assn. Phys. Anthropologists, 1998. Fellow Am. Acad. Arts and Scis.; mem. Nat. Acad. Scis., Am. Philos. Soc., AAAS, Calif. Acad. Sci. (trustee 1975-1991, Fellows medal 1990), Acad. des Scis., Inst. de France. Home: 1994 San Antonio Ave Berkeley CA 94707-1620 Office: U Calif Mus Vertebrate Zoology Berkeley CA 94720-3160

HOWELL, GEORGE BEDELL, equity investing and managing executive; b. Schenectady, Sept. 19, 1919; s. Jesse M. and Grace (Gerhaeusser) H.; m. Mary Barbara Crohurst, July 10, 1944; children: Raymond Gary, Terry Barbara, Janice Patricia, Nancy Jo, George Bedell Jr. BS in Adminstrv. Engring., Cornell U., 1942. With GE, 1946-59; v.p. mfg. Leece Neville Co., Cleve., 1959-61, Royal Electric Co., Pawtucket, R.I., 1961-62; dir. ops. packaging equipment and product devel. Acme Steel Co. (merged with Interlake Steel Corp. 1965), 1962-64; v.p. adminstrv. svc. Interlake Steel Corp., Chgo., 1964-66, v.p. internat. divsn., v.p. Acme Products divsn., 1966-70; CEO Golconda Corp., Chgo., 1970-72; v.p. devel. Internat. Minerals & Chems. Corp., 1972-73, sr. v.p., pres. industry group, 1974-77, exec. v.p., 1977-81; pres., CEO Wurlitzer Co., 1982-86, chmn., pres., CEO, 1986-87, vice chmn., 1987-88; prin. Mid West Ptnrs., Chgo., 1988-89; gen. ptnr. Pfingsten Ptnrs., Chgo., 1989-94, ptnr., 1994—2003, mem. adv. bd., 2002—; chmn. Hallcrest Holding Corp., 1992-97, dir. exec. com., 1998—. Chmn. bd. trustees Village of Oak Brook, Ill., 1965-73, pres., 1973-79; trustee Christ Ch., Oak Brook, vice chmn., 1992-97, trustee emeritus, 1998; mem. univ. coun. Cornell U., 2001—. N.Y. State and Univ. scholar Cornell U., 1942. Mem. McGraw Wildlife Found., Chgo. Athletic Assn., Medinah Country Club, Ocean Reef Club (Fla.). Home: 5 Brighton Ln Oak Brook IL 60523-2323 Office: 520 Lake Cook Rd Ste 375 Deerfield IL 60015-5632 E-mail: ghowell@pfingsten.com., howellgb@aol.com. *Trust in God. Balance family, work, church and government service. Live every day of your life.*

HOWELL, GEORGE COOK, III, lawyer; b. New Orleans, June 27, 1956; s. George C. Jr. and Billie Grace (Webb) H.; children: Margaret Sloan, George C. IV. AB magna cum laude, Princeton U., 1978; JD, U.Va., 1981. Bar: Va. 1981, U.S. Dist. Ct. (ea. dist.) Va. 1982, U.S. Ct. Appeals (4th cir.) 1982. Law clk. U.S. Dist. Ct. (ea. dist.) Va., Alexandria, 1981-82; assoc. Hunton & Williams, Richmond, Va., 1982-89, ptnr., 1989—, team head tax & employee benefits, 1999—. Contbr. Va. Law Rev., 1980; editor-in-chief Va. Tax Rev., 1980-81; articles editor The Tax Lawyer, 1983-86, mng. editor, 1987-89. Mem. usher's guild 1st Presbyn. Ch., Richmond, 1986-90; participant Leadership Metro Richmond, 1987-88. Mem. ABA (taxation sect. chmn. remic task force 1987-88, chmn. mini-program on mortgage-backed securities 1988, chmn. subcom. on asset securitization 1988-90, corp. tax shelters tax force 2000-2001, vice chmn. com. on fin. trans. 1990-92, chmn. com. on fin. trans. 1992-94, sec. taxation 1995-97, sect. taxation coun., 1997-2000, vice chmn. comm. 2001-2003), Princeton Assn. Va. (treas. 1987-89, pres. 1989-91), Order of Coif, Phi Beta Kappa. Republican. Avocations: golf, tennis, basketball, running, the stock market. Office: Hunton & Williams 951 E Byrd St Ste 200 Richmond VA 23219-4074

HOWELL, GEORGE WASHINGTON, lawyer, consultant; b. Fairfield, Ala., Jan. 11, 1927; s. George Washington and Margaret Lorraine (Hamric) H.; m. Joan Cotty White, Sept. 4, 1954 (dec. Mar. 1993); children: Jeffrey Page, Jennifer Margaret; m. Patricia Van Metre Minkler, Oct. 24, 1993. Student, Emory U., 1944-45, U. S.C., 1945-46; BS in Math., U. Ala., 1948, JD, 1951. Bar: Ala. 1951, Miss. 1961. Atty. U.S. Steel Corp. TCI div., Fairfield, Ala., 1951-57; atty. Ingalls Shipbldg. Corp., Pascagoula, Miss., 1957-62, gen. counsel, 1962-66, v.p., gen. counsel, 1966-70, Litton Industries, Inc. Marine Group, Pascagoula, Miss., 1970-87, sr. counsel, 1988-92. Cons. on litgation State of Wash., Olympia, 1982-85; chmn. taxation comm. Shipbuilder's Council Am., Washington, 1966-70; dir. Miss. Econ. Council, Jackson, 1972-73; adj. prof. law U. Miss., Oxford, 1973-82 Originator Young Leaders Camps at Kanuga for At Risk Children, 1993; pres. South Miss. Festival of Arts, Pascagoula, 1962; mem. Miss. Com. for Humanities, Jackson, 1973-82; mem., pres. Pascagoula Sch. Bd., 1981-86; mem. Miss. Research and Devel. Council, Jackson, 1979-83; mem., vice chmn. Gov.'s Commn. on Efficiency and Economy in State Govt., 1970; mem. Gov.'s Adv. Com. on Edn. Conf., Jackson, 1972, Gov.'s Task Force on Pub. Edn. Reform, 1982, Govs's. Private Sector Council, Jackson, 1984-86; pres. Community Concert Assn., Pascagoula, 1981-83; Asheville Cmty. Hero Torch Bearer Olympic Games, 1996; dir. Kanuga Conf., Inc., 2000—. Served to comdr. USNR, 1944-87. Recipient Outstanding Contbn. award Miss. R & D Ctr., 1984, Merit award Pascagoula C. of C., 1966; mem. U. Ala. Baseball Team of Century award, 1993. Mem. ABA, Miss. Bar Assn., Birmingham Jr. C. of C. (pres. 1956), Pi Mu Epsilon, Omicron Delta Kappa, Pi Kappa Alpha Episcopalian. Avocations: gardening, tennis. Home and Office: 3 St Giles Pl Asheville NC 28803

HOWELL, HARLEY THOMAS, lawyer; b. Chgo., June 5, 1937; s. Harley W. and Geneva (Engelmann) H.; m. Aliceann A. McLaughlin, Apr. 23, 1983; children by previous marriage: Shelley A. Young, Rebecca L., Emily S. AB, Princeton U., 1959; JD, Yale U., 1962. Bar: Md. 1962, U.S. Supreme Ct. 1966, D.C. 1972. Law clk. to chief judge U.S. Ct. Appeals (4th cir.), 1962-63; assoc. Semmes, Bowen & Semmes, Balt., 1966-72, ptnr., 1972-92, Howell, Gately, Whitney & Carter LLP, Towson, Md., 1992-98, counsel, 1998-99; ptnr. Howell & Gately, Balt., 1999—2002, counsel, 2002—03. Mem. Gov.'s Commn. to Revise Annotated Code Md., 1975-85; mem. standing com. on rules of practice and procedure Ct. Appeals of Md., 1985-2000. Bd. dirs. Balt. Symphony Orch., 1975—, sec., 1986-2003, exec. com., 1986—; trustee Sheppard & Enoch Pratt Hosp., Towson, 1991—. Capt. JAG Corps, U.S. Army, 1963-66. Decorated Army Commendation medal. Fellow Am. Coll. Trial Lawyers, Am. Acad. Appellate Lawyers, Md. Bar Found.; mem. ABA, Md. State Bar Assn., Bar Assn. Balt. City, Balt. County Bar Assn., D.C. Bar Assn., Fed. Bar Assn., Wine and Food Soc., Wranglers Law Club (Balt.), Am. Coll. Barristers. Home: 1012 Chestnut Ridge Dr Lutherville Timonium MD 21093-1716 Office: Howell & Gately One Charles Ctr 19th Fl 100 N Charles St Baltimore MD 21201 E-mail: hthomas37@comcast.net.

HOWELL, JAMES BURT, III, retired agricultural products company sales consultant; b. Dec. 11, 1933; s. James Burt and Catharine Stanger (Sparks) H.; m. Lorraine Marie Chanatry, Feb. 18, 1995. BS with honors, Rutgers U., 1956; MBA, U. Del., 1980. Agrl. sales rep. Allied Chem. Corp., Phila., 1957-59; sales cons. Asgrow Seed Co. subs. Upjohn Co., Vineland, NJ, 1960—2002; ret., 2002. Bd. dirs. Advance Weight Systems, Inc., LaGrange, Ohio. Mem. ofcl. bd. (session) 1st Presbyn. Ch. of Cedarville, 1960—; admissions liaison officer U.S. Mil. Acad., West Point, N.Y., 1973—; chmn. Lawrence Twp. Zoning Bd. Adjustment. With U.S. Army, 1957, col. USAR. Recipient Burpee Hort. award Rutgers U., 1955. Mem.: Res. Officers Assn. U.S., Pesticide Assn. N.J., Vegetable Growers Assn. N.J., Nat. Defense Indsl. Assn., Alpha Zeta (Centennial Honor Roll 1997), Alpha Gamma Rho, Phi Beta Kappa. Home and Office: Asgrow Seed Co 23 Shadow Brooke Dr Bridgeton NJ 08302

HOWELL, JAMES EDWIN, economist, educator; b. Sterling, Colo., Mar. 6, 1928; s. James William, Jr. and Lois (Brown) H.; m. Linda Leinbach, 1965; children: Kenneth E., William J., Jan E., Caitlyn B. BA, Fresno State Coll., 1950; MA, U. Ill., 1951, Yale U., 1953, PhD, 1955. Instr. econs. and stats. Yale U., 1954-56; mem. staff Ford Found., 1956-58, 62, cons., 1958-72; Theodore J. Kreps prof. econs. Stanford U., 1958—, asso. dean Grad. Sch. Bus., 1965-70; vis. prof. econs. London Bus. Sch., 1992. Dir. gen. Internat. Inst. Mgmt. and Adminstrn., Berlin, 1970-72; dir. Stanford-Insead Advanced Mgmt. Program, European Inst. Bus. Adminstrn., France, 1979-81; sometime prof., lectr. U. Hawaii, U. Calif.-Berkeley, Stanford in Vienna, U. Pa., Nat. U. Singapore, London Bus. Sch.; vis. prof. Humboldt U., Berlin, 1995; cons. U.S. and Europe; bd. dirs. Edn. Devel. Corp. Author/co-author: Higher Education for Business, 1959, European Economics-East and West, 1967, Mathematical Analysis for Business Decisions, 1963, 2d edit., 1971, (with G. L. Bach) Economics, 11th edit., 1987. Served with AUS, 1946-47. Ford Found. faculty fellow Harvard U., 1959-60; NSF sr. postdoctoral fellow London Sch. Econs., 1963-64; recipient Davis award for lifetime achievement Stanford U., 1996. Mem.: University Club (N.Y.C.). Office: Stanford U Grad Sch Bus Stanford CA 94305

HOWELL, JEANETTE HELEN, retired cultural organization administrator; b. Portsmouth, Hampshire, Eng., June 2, 1925; arrived in U.S., 1976; d. Henry Augustus and Mary Scott (Randall) Butler-Frere; m. Reginald Robert Howell, Aug. 14, 1948; children: Josephine Thalia Howell, Robert Henry Adam Howell, Matthew Charles Howell. Student, High Wycombe Coll. Art, 1967-71, Sutton Sch. Art. Dir./owner Bourne End (pre-sch.), Bucks, Eng., 1965-69; adminstr. Historic Denver, Denver, 1980-83; mgr. II Bur. Conservation, State of Maine, Thomaston, 1987-90; dir. Lincoln County Hist. Assn., Wiscasset, Maine, 1990-93; ret., 1993. Founder Decorative and Fine Arts N.J., pres., 1977, co-founder Decorative and Fine Arts Soc. U.K., 1966, Decorative and Fine Arts Soc. N.J. ednl. lectrs. and seminars (pres. 1977); bazaar chmn. St. John's Cathedral, Denver, 1981; pres. Damariscotta (Maine) Arts Coun., 1984-86; sr. warden St. Andrew's Ch., Newcastle, Maine, 1992-96; co-founder Friends of Colonial Pemaquid (Maine), 1993; trustee Maine Archives and Mus., 1999—; bd. dirs. Lincoln Home Assisted Living. Nurse emergency med. hosp., Weymouth, Dorset, Eng., 1942-48. Recipient Americans-By-Choice Outstanding Svc. award Citizenship Day com., Denver, 1983, Appreciation award Maine Vols. in Parks, 1997. Mem.: Maine Archives and Mus. (v.p. 2000, pres. 2002—). Avocations: gardening, archaeology, history research, literature. Home: 534 Harrington Rd Pemaquid ME 04558-4214 E-mail: howell@lincoln.midcoast.com.

HOWELL, JOEL DUBOSE, internist, educator; b. Tex., May 11, 1953; s. Wilson and Nora (Levitas) Howell; m. Linda C. Samuelson, June 26, 1976; children: Jonathan Samuelson, Benjamin Samuelson. BS, Mich. State U., 1975; MD, U. Chgo., 1979; PhD in History and Sociology of Sci., U. Pa., 1987. Intern, resident in internal medicine U. Chgo., 1979-82; Robert Wood Johnson clin. scholar U. Pa., Phila., 1982-84; instr. U. Mich., Ann Arbor, 1984-86, asst. prof., 1986-90, assoc. prof., 1990-97, prof., 1997—, Victor Vaughan prof. history medicine, 2001—. Editor: (book) Technology and American Medicine Practice: 1880-1930, 1988, Medical Lives and Scientific Medicine at Michigan; author: Technology in the Hospital, 1995. Scholar Henry J. Kaiser Family Fedn. Faculty, 1989—92, Charles E. Culpeper Found. Med. Humanities, 1992—96. Fellow: ACP, Am. Osler Soc., Am. Assn. History Medicine. E-mail: jhowell@umich.edu.

HOWELL, JOEL WALTER, III, lawyer; b. Jackson, Miss., Dec. 25, 1949; s. Joel W. and Elizabeth (Harris) H.; m. Wilhelmina C. Pontus, June 25, 1983. BA, Millsaps Coll., 1971; JD, Columbia U., 1974. Bar: Tex. 1974, U.S. Ct. Appeals (5th cir.) 1974, Miss. 1975, U.S. Dist. Ct. (no. and so. dists.) Miss. 1975. Ptnr. Daniel, Coker, Horton, Bell & Dukes, Jackson, 1975-80; pvt. practice, Jackson, 1981—. Adj. faculty law sch. Miss. Coll., Jackson, 1988. Contbg. editor, case notes and comments editor Columbia Jour. Transnat. Law, 1973-74. Mem. ABA, ATLA, Tex. Bar Assn., Miss. Bar, Hinds County Bar Assn. (small firm practice com. 1993-94, chair 1995, computer columnist newsletter 1996—, webmaster 1997—), Miss. Trial Lawyers Assn., Miss. Def. Lawyers Assn., Def. Rsch. Inst., Miss. Bankruptcy Conf. Home: 50 St Andrews Dr Jackson MS 39211-2466 Office: PO Box 16772 5446 Executive Pl Jackson MS 39206-4103 E-mail: jwh3@mindspring.com.

HOWELL, JOHN FLOYD, insurance company executive; b. Mt. Juliet, Tenn., Dec. 24, 1932; s. Robert Lee and Rachel Mae (Draper) H.; m. Margaret Ann Herring, Dec. 27, 1955; children: John Floyd, Leigh Ann, Stephen Donelson. Student, Vanderbilt U., 1951-53; BA, U. Iowa, 1955, postgrad., 1955-56. Actuarial asst. Nat. Life & Accident Ins. Co., Nashville, 1963-64, asst. actuary, 1964-65, 2d v.p., 1965-71, v.p., 1971-81, sr. v.p., 1981-83, also dir.; v.p., chief actuary Ind. Life & Accident Ins. Co., 1984-88, sr. v.p., chief actuary, 1989-96, ret., 1996. Bd. dirs. Vol. Jacksonville, 1984-89, Mental Health Resource Ctr., Jacksonville, 1987-90, Fla. Meth. Bd. Pensions, 1988-96, Jacksonville Urban League, 1992-95; mem. adv. bd. Montgomery Bell Acad., 1995—. Fellow Soc. Actuaries; mem. Am. Acad. Actuaries, Richland Country Club (Nashville), Epping Forest Yacht Club (Jacksonville). Methodist. Home: 2200 Harding Pl #2 Nashville TN 37215-4145

HOWELL, JOHN MCDADE, retired university chancellor, political science educator; b. Five Points, Ala., Jan. 28, 1922; s. John William and Bettie Mae (Lee) H.; m. Gladys Evelyn David, Aug. 9, 1952; children: David Noble, Joseph Lee. AB, U. Ala., 1948, MA, 1949; PhD, Duke U., 1954. Instr. U. Idaho, 1950; instr. Randolph-Macon Woman's Coll., Lynchburg, Va., 1951-52, Duke U., 1952-53; asst. prof. Sweet Briar Coll., Lynchburg, 1953-54, Memphis State U., 1954-57; assoc. prof. East Carolina U., Greenville, N.C., 1957-61, prof., 1961-87, chmn. polit. sci. dept., 1963-66, dean Coll. Arts and Scis., 1966-69, dean Grad. Sch., 1969-73, vice chancellor for acad. affairs, 1973-79, chancellor, 1982-87. Author: (with others) Conflict of International Obligations and State Interests, 1972; Contbr.: (with others) chpts. to The International Law Standard and Commonwealth Developments, 1966, De Lege Pactorum, 1970; articles to profl. jours. Served with USAAF, 1942-45. Decorated Bronze Star medal. Mem. Phi Beta Kappa, Phi Kappa Phi, Pi Sigma Alpha. Home: 1953 Quail Ridge Rd Apt E Greenville NC 27858-5599

HOWELL, JOHN REID, mechanical engineering educator; b. Columbus, Ohio, June 13, 1936; s. Frederick Edward and Hilma Lavilla (Kief) H.; m. Arlene Elizabeth Pollitt, June 20, 1959 (div. 1974); m. Susan Gooch Conway, May 20, 1979; children: John Reid Jr., Keli Dianne, David Lee. BSChemE, Case Inst. Tech., 1958, MSChemE, 1960, PhD, 1962. Registered profl. engr. Aerospace engr. NASA Lewis Research Ctr., Cleve., 1961-68; assoc. prof. U. Houston, 1969-73, prof., 1973-78; dir. Energy Inst. U. Houston, 1975-78; vis. prof. mech. engring. U. Tex., Austin, 1978-79, prof., 1979-82, E.C.H. Bantel prof., 1982-90, Baker-Hughes Centennial prof. dept. mech. engring., 1990—, chmn. mech. engring. dept., 1986-90, dir. Ctr. for Energy Studies, 1988-91, assoc. dean for rsch. Coll. Engring., 1996-99. Dir. thermal transport and thermal

processing program NSF, 1994-95. Co-author: Thermal Radiation Heat Transfer, 1972, 4th edit., 2002, Design of Solar Thermal Systems, 1984, Fundamentals of Engineering Therdynamics, 1987, 2d edit., 1992; editor: Journal of Heat Transfer, 1995-2000; contbr. articles to profl. jours. Commr. Renewable Energy Resources Commn., Austin, 1980-81. Served to 1st lt. USAF, 1962-65. Recipient Spl. Svc. award NASA, 1965, Ralph Coats Roe award Am. Soc. Engring. Edn., 1987, Max Jakob award AIChE/ASME, 1998; named to Hon. Order Ky. Cols., 1980. Fellow ASME (Heat Transfer Meml. award 1991), AIAA (Thermophysics award 1990); mem. Russian Acad. Scis. (elected fgn. mem. 1999). Office: U Tex Dept Mech Engring 1 University Station C2200 Austin TX 78712 E-mail: jhowell@mail.utexas.edu.

HOWELL, JULIUS AMMONS, retired plastic surgeon; b. Thomasville, N.C., Apr. 14, 1914; s. Cyrus Maitland and Lillie Mae (Ammons) H.; m. Octavia Anne Southern, Oct. 20, 1951; children: Anne, Karen, Robin. LLB, Wake Forest U., 1935, BS, 1940; MD, U. Pa., Phila., 1943. Diplomate Am. Bd. Plastic & Reconstructive Surgery, Am. Bd. Otolaryngology. Chief plastic surgery sect. Bowman Gray Sch. Medicine, Winston Salem, N.C., 1959-84, prof. emeritus plastic surgery, 1984-2000; lectr. Sch. Law Wake Forest U., Winston Salem, N.C., 1978-94; pvt. practice Winston Salem, N.C., 1984-99; ret., 1999. Mem. medico-legal com. N.C. Med. Soc., Raleigh, 1960-93, S.E. Soc. Plastic Surgery; mem. adv. com. N.C. Indsl. com., Raleigh, 1976-86; trustee Blue Cross/Blue Shield, Chapel Hill, 1964-68. Co-author: Plastic Surgery, 1979. Julius Ammons Howell Endowed Chair Surgery named in his honor Bowman Gray Sch. Medicine, 1995. Mem. ACS; Am. Soc. Plastic & Reconstructive Surgery (medicolegal com.), Am. Assn. Plastic Surgeons. Baptist.

HOWELL, KAREN JANE, private school educator; b. Mpls., Apr. 24, 1946; d. John and Lorraine (Quale) Borgen; m. John Morris Howell; children: Laura, John. AS in Math. and Sci., Cottey Jr. Coll., Nevada, Mo., 1966; BS in Elem. Edn. Sci. and Math., U. No. Colo., Greeley, 1968; MS Science & Gifted Education, University Of Virginia, Alexandria, Va, 1980—83. Cert. 5/6th Grade Team Tchr. 1968, 6th Grade Gifted Tchr. 1971, K-6th Gifted Program Tchr. 1983. Team tchr. John Adams and Carver Elem. Schs., Colorado Springs, Colo., 1968—73; tchr. gifted 3-6th grade Math. and Sci. Washington Mill and Stratford Landing Elem. Schs., Alexandria, Va., 1973—83; tchr. gifted program Tokeneke Elem. Sch., Darien, Conn., 1983—85; 5-8th science, 1-8 art teacher Hillel Academy, Fairfield, Ct, 1985—. Art / science docent Smithsonian Instn. and Am. Mus. Nat. History, Washington, 1974—82; guide Discovery Mus., Bridgeport, Conn., 1985—. Author: (various workshops, teaching modules) Using Art Properties With Mus. Tours, 1980-1990, 1990, (teacher's guide) Motivational Techniques, Math Manipulatives, 1988,1992, 1994. Chairperson, bd. dirs. Fairfield (Conn.) Internat. Dance Co., 1990—2002; judge Conn. State Invention Conv., Hartford, 1983—87. Recipient Presdl. award for Excellence in Sci. Tchg., State of Conn., 1989, Presdl. award for Excellence in Math. Tchg., 1989, First Sci. Tchr. award, State Sci. Fair Conn., 1996, 1st Place, Middle Schs., Conn. State Sci. Fair, 1995, 1996, 1997, 1998, 1999. Mem.: NEA, Am. Chem. Soc., Nat. Math. Tchrs. Assn., Conn.. Earth Tchrs. Assn., Conn. Sci. Tchrs. Assn. (Conn. Sci. Tchr. of Yr. award 2002), Nat. Sci. Tchrs. Assn., Audubon Soc., Am. Mensa, Am. Ballet Theater (assoc.). Methodist. Avocations: ballet, jazz, dancing. Office: Hillel Academy 1571 Stratfield Rd Fairfield CT 06432 Personal E-mail: j.howell@comsoc.org.

HOWELL, NEIL, music educator; m. Jill Dacus, June 13, 1998. MusB in Edn., U. SC, 1988, MusM in Edn., 1991; degree in Sch. Adminstrn., Lincoln Meml. U., Harrogate, TN, 2003. Professional Teaching Certificate Ga., 1984. Dir. of bands Heritage H.S., Conyers, Ga., 1993—, Dreher H.S., Columbia, SC, 1993—94. Mem.: Phi Mu Alpha Sinfonia (life; pres., historian 1986—87, Outstanding Mem. 1987). Republican. Bapt. Avocations: markmanship, electrical engineering, travel. E-mail: nhowell@rockdale.k12.ga.us.

HOWELL, NELDA KAY, home economist, retired; b. Kinston, N.C., Apr. 30, 1938; d. John Franklin Sr. and Reba Ellen (Davis) H. BS in Home Econs., East Carolina U., 1960; MEd in Adult and C.C. Edn., N.C. State U., 1970. Home agt. agrl. ext. svc. N.C. State U., Hyde County, 1959-62; vocat. home econs. tchr. Richlands (N.C.) H.S. Onslow County Sch. Sys., 1962-65; home econs. ext. agt. N.C. State U., Craven County, 1965-71; assoc. dist. leader Piedmont Clemson (S.C.) U. Coop. Ext. Svc., 1971-84, dist. ext. chmn. Savannah Valley, 1984-87, dist. ext. dir. Savannah Valley, 1987-91; commr. Onslow County Hosp. Authority, 2001—; chair Onslow Ambulatory Svcs., 2003. Mem. land use and devel. com. Onslow County Comprehensive Plan, 2001—02; mem. policy com. Joint Land Use Study Onslow County, 2002—. Bd. dirs. Onslow Women's Ctr.; staff com. 1st Bapt. Ch. of Swansboro (sec. 2000-2001). Kellogg fellow Agrl. Policy Inst. N.C. State U., 1969; named Woman of Yr., Swansboro Area C. of C., 1999. Mem. AAUW (NC, state membership v.p. 1996-98, parliamentarian, 2001-02), N.C. Assn. Family and Consumer Scis. (Southeastern region treas. 1996-97), Swansboro Toastmasters (pres. 1997), Onslow County Coun. for Women (sec. 1994-95, co-chair 1999-2000), Women's Forum of N.C. (sec. 2001-02, treas. 2003-, bd. dirs. women united, 2003—), N.C. Women United (bd. dirs. 2003-04), East Carolina U. Alumni Assn. (sec. Onslow County chpt. 1998, treas. 2003—), Gamma Sigma Delta. Democrat. Baptist. Avocations: volunteering, reading, travel, public policy. Home: 109 Howell Rd Hubert NC 28539-3911 E-mail: nhowell@ec.rr.com.

HOWELL, RALPH RODNEY, pediatrician, educator, geneticist; b. Concord, N.C., June 10, 1931; s. Fred Lee and Grace Mary (Blackwelder) H.; m. Sarah Vosburg Esselstyn, Nov. 19, 1960 (dec.); children: Grace Meyer, Elizabeth Eriksson, John Esselstyn. BS, Davidson Coll., 1953; MD, Duke U., 1957. Intern Duke U., 1957-58, resident in pediatrics, 1958-59, research fellow in pediatrics and medicine, 1959-60; clin. assoc. and staff NIH, Bethesda, Md., 1960-64; assoc. prof. pediatrics Johns Hopkins U., Balt., 1964-72; pediatrician-in-chief Univ. Children's Hosp. at Hermann, Houston, 1972-87, chmn. med. bd., 1972-87; David Park prof. U. Tex. Med. Sch., Houston, 1972-89, chmn. dept. pediatrics, 1972-87; prof., chmn. dept. pediatrics U. Miami Sch. Medicine, 1989—2003, chmn. emeritus, prof., 2003—; sec. med. staff Jackson Meml. Hosp., Miami, 1992-93, v.p. med. staff, 1993-97, pres. med. staff, 1997-99; spl. asst. to dir. NICHD/NIH, Bethesda, Md., 2003—. Cons. pediat. M.D. Anderson Hosp. and Tumor Inst., 1972-89; mem. metabolism study sect. NIH, 1973-77, chmn. maternal and child health adv. com., 1983-86; mem. exec. com. Nat. Practitioner Data Bank, 1995-98; mem. nat. clin. adv. com. Nat. Found. March of Dimes, 1973-79; mem. nat. med. adv. bd., bd. dirs. Muscular Dystrophy Assn., chmn. sci. adv. bd.; vis. prof. Inst. Molecular Genetics, Baylor Coll. Medicine, Houston, 1988; chief pediat. Holtz Childrens Hosp., U. Miami-Jackson Meml. Med. Ctr., 1989-2003; mem. nat. adv. coun. Nat. Inst. Child Health and Human Devel., 1999—. Author: (with G.H. Thomas) Selected Screening Tests for Genetic Metabolic Diseases, 1973, (with F.H. Morriss, L.K. Pickering) Role of Human Milk in Infant Nutrition, 1986; contbr. articles to profl. jours. Trustee Jackson Lab. Bar Harbor, Maine, 1985-2003; dir. Rip van Winkle Found., Claverack, N.Y., 1987-92, pres., 1992—; bd. dirs. Congl. Ch. Found., Coconut Grove, Fla., Dr. John T. Macdonald Found., Coral Gables, Fla., 2003—. Served to sr. surgeon USPHS, 1960-64. Fellow AAAS, Am. Acad. Pediatrics (com. on genetics); mem. AMA (ho. of dels. 1998—), Am. Pediatric Soc., Soc. Pediatric Rsch., Houston Pediatric Soc. (pres. 1978-79), Tex. Med. Assn., Soc. Inborn Errors of Metabolism (pres. 1981), Miami Pediatric Soc., Fla. Med. Assn., Am. Coll. Med. Genetics (bd. dirs. 1991—, treas. 1995-96, pres.-elect 1997-98, pres. 1999—2000), Am. Coll. Med. Genetics (found. pres. 2003—), Nat. Human Genome Rsch. Inst. (chmn. ethical, social and legal issues rev. group 1996—), Pi Kappa Alpha, Cosmos Club (Washington). Home: L'Hermitage Villa 66 2000 S Bayshore Dr Miami FL 33133-3256 Office: U Miami Sch Medicine Dept Pediatrics D-820 PO Box 16820 Miami FL 33101-6820 E-mail: rhowell@jhu.edu.

HOWELL, ROBERT CHARLES, philosopher, educator; b. Indpls., Jan. 23, 1940; s. Robert Donald and Lorinda Catherine (Cottingham) Howell; m. Pamela Paige Fischer, Oct. 23, 1977; children: Robert Laurence, Katherine Kinney Elizabeth. BA, Kenyon Coll., 1961; MA, U. Mich., 1963, PhD, 1967. Asst. prof. U. Ill., Urbana, 1966—68, Stanford (Calif.) U., 1968—75; asst. prof. to prof. SUNY, Albany, 1975—. Vis. asst. Johns Hopkins U., Balt., 1974; vis. mem. Inst. Advanced Study, Princeton, NJ, 1982—83. Author: Kant's Transcendental Deduction, 1992. Fellow, ACLS, 1975—76; Fulbright-Hays fellow, Oxford U., 1965—66. Mem.: N.Am. Kant Soc., Am. Soc. Aesthetics, Am. Philos. Assn. Office: SUNY at Albany Dept Philosophy 1400 Washington Ave Albany NY 12222

HOWELL, R(OBERT) THOMAS, JR., lawyer, former food company executive; b. Racine, Wis., July 18, 1942; s. Robert T. and Margaret Paris (Billings) H.; m. Karen Wallace Corbett, May 11, 1968; children: Clarinda, Margaret, Robert. AB, Williams Coll., 1964; JD, U. Wis., 1967; postgrad., Harvard U., 1981. Bar: Wis. 1968, Ill. 1968, U.S. Dist. Ct. (no. dist.) Ill. 1968, U.S. Tax Ct. Assoc. Hopkins & Sutter, Chgo., 1967-71; atty. The Quaker Oats Co., Chgo., 1971-77, counsel, 1977-80, v.p., assoc. gen. corp. counsel, 1980-84, v.p., gen. corp. counsel, 1984-96, corp. sec., 1994-96; of counsel Seyfarth Shaw, Chgo., 1997—. Bd. dirs. Ill. Inst. of Continuing Legal Edn., Lawyers for Creative Arts. Editor (mags.) Barrister, 1975-77, Compleat Lawyer, 1983-87. Bd. dirs. Metro. Family Svcs.; bd. dirs. Chgo. Bar Found., 1987—, pres., 1991-93; trustee 4th Presbyn. Ch., Chgo., 1989-92, pres., 1994-96; bd. dirs. Chgo. Equity Fund, 1992-96. Capt. USAR, 1966-72. Mem. ABA, Ill. Bar Assn., Wis. Bar Assn., Chgo. Bar Assn. (bd. mgrs. 1977-79, chmn. young lawyers sect. 1974-75), LawClub Chgo., Econ. Club Chgo., Univ. Club Chgo. (bd. dirs. 1982-85, 87-88, v.p.). Presbyterian. Home: 853 W Chalmers Pl Chicago IL 60614-3233 Office: Seyfarth Shaw 55 E Monroe St Ste 4200 Chicago IL 60603-5863 E-mail: thowell@seyfarth.com.

HOWELL, ROGER EUGENE, music educator, musician; b. Marietta, Ga., Apr. 21, 1961; s. Roger S. Howell Jr. and Lois Musgrove Howell; m. Angela Joyetta Davy, Mar. 2, 1951; 1 child, Roger Eugene Howell Jr. MusB, Ga. State U., 1979—86; MusB in Edn., Kennesaw State U., 1998—2000. Cert. tchr. Ga. State Bd. Edn., 2000. Music specialist Lockheed Elem. Sch., Marietta, Ga., 2000—02, A. L. Burruss Elem. Sch., 2002—. Profl. pianist Swing Shift, Rio, Nightwind, Atlanta, 1985—. Music dir. Due West Meth. Ch., Marietta, 1981—90. Mem.: Profl. Assn. Ga. Educators, Ga. Music Educators Assn. Achievements include Orff-Schulwerk Level One Certification; Outstanding Senior in Music Education Award at Kennesaw State University; Yamaha Music in Education Training Certificate; Certificate in Excellence for completion of the Undergraduate Teacher Preparation Program at Kennesaw State University; Outstanding New Certified Teacher at Lockheed Elementary School. Home: 1082 Arden Dr Marietta GA 30008-3502 Office: A L Burruss 325 Manning Rd Marietta GA 30064

HOWELL, THOMAS, history educator; b. Houston, Jan. 20, 1944; s. John Thomas and Hazel (Hall) H.; m. Donna Jo Walker, Aug. 14, 1971; children: Catherine Jewel, Judith Hazel. BA, La. Coll., 1964; MA, La. State U., 1966, PhD, 1971. Instr. La. State U., 1967-68, La. Coll., Pineville, 1968-70, asst. prof., 1970-72, assoc. prof., 1972-77, prof., 1977, Crowell prof., 1984—, chmn. dept. history and polit. sci., 1975-95, chmn. divsn. social and behavioral scis., 1995-2000, chmn. divsn. history and polit. sci., 2000—. Lectr. La. Endowment for Humanities, 1983, 86, 87, 1990—96, 2001—, project dir., 1989, 2000, 03. Mem. La. Elections Integrity Commn., 1980—86, vice-chmn., 1981; coord. La. Civitan Youth Citizenship Seminar, 1975—76; commr. Gulf Coast Athletic Conf., 1981—; mem. NAIA Nat. Eligibility Commn., 1983—, chmn., 1994—; mem. hearing com. disciplinary bd. La. Bar Assn., 1995—2001. Mellon summer fellow, 1981; Fulbright lectr. U. Iceland, 1986-87; inductee Nat. Assn. Intercollegiate Athletics Hall of Fame, 1999. Mem. La. Hist. Assn., So. Hist. Assn., SW Assn. Pre-Law Advisers, Orgn. Am. Historians, Alpha Chi, Omicron Delta Kappa. Baptist. Home: 216 Myrtle St Pineville LA 71360-5164 Office: La Coll Dept History Pineville LA 71359-0001 E-mail: howell@lacollege.edu.

HOWELL, THOMAS LEE, composer, writer; b. Jacinto, Tex., Apr. 19, 1953; s. Robert and Bertha Howell; children: Tommy, Charity, Stormy. Artist; musician; comml. painter; artist and band leader Dark Star Prodn., 1977—97. Author: (novels) Hegira, 1999, Flyte, Fumar; author-composer: songs and lyrics incl. collection No Way Home; author: (autobiography) Ripples, 1999.

HOWELL, WELDON U., JR., lawyer; b. Dallas, July 16, 1947; s. Weldon U. and Betty (Temple) H.; m. Barbara Molina, July 14, 1973; children: Benjamin, Sarah. B.A., U. Ariz., 1969; postgrad. City London Poly. Sch., 1971; J.D., U. Tex., 1973. Bar: Tex. 1973, Calif. 1974, U.S. Dist. Ct. (cen., no., so. and ea. dists.) Calif., U.S. Ct. Appeals (9th cir.) 1984, U.S. Tax Ct. 1981, U.S. Ct. Claims 1981. Briefing atty to assoc. justice Supreme Ct. Tex., Austin, 1973-74; assoc. Schramm & Raddue, Santa Barbara, Calif., 1974-77, sr. ptnr., chmn. bus. and tax dept., 1977—; sr. ptnr. Howell Moore & Gough LLP, Santa Barbara. Bd. dirs., pres. Santa Barbara County Bd. Edn. Mem. Santa Barbara County Bar Assn. (chmn. tax sect. 1984, bd. dirs. 1986-88, pres. 1994), Barristers Club Santa Barbara (pres. 1977-78), Pi Kappa Alpha. Democrat. Clubs: Tennis of Santa Barbara (chmn., 1980). Home: 2525 Anacapa St Santa Barbara CA 93105-3511 Office: Howell Moore & Gough LLP 812 Presidio Ave Santa Barbara CA 93101-2210

HOWELL, WILLIAM ASHLEY, III, lawyer; b. Raleigh, N.C., Jan. 2, 1949; s. William Ashley II and Caroline Erskine Greenleaf; m. Esther Holland, Dec. 22, 1973. BS, Troy State U., 1972; postgrad., U. Ala., Birmingham, 1974-75; JD, Birmingham Sch. Law, 1977. Bar: Ala. 1977, U.S. Dist. Ct. (no. dist.) Ala. 1977, U.S. Ct. Appeals (5th cir.) 1977, U.S. Supreme Ct. 1982, U.S. Ct. Appeals (11th cir.) 1983, U.S. Dist. Ct. (mid. dist.) Ala. 1987. Atty. pub. defender divsn. Legal Aid Soc. of Birmingham, 1977—78, civil divsn. Legal Aid Soc. of Birmingham, 1978—81; dist. office atty. SBA, Birmingham, 1980—82, supervising atty. Ala. Dist., 1982—; spl. asst. U.S. Atty. (mid. dist.), Ala., 1988—, U.S. Atty. (so. dist.), Ala., 2002—. Part-time instr. legal and social environ. and human resources mgmt. Jefferson State C.C., Birmingham, 1993. Contbr. articles to profl. jours. Vol. reader Radio Reading Svc. Network for Blind, 1991—93; mem. Shelby County Econ. Devel. Coun., 1993—94, Hispanic Outreach Commn., 2000—01, Highland Crest Homeowners Assn., 2002—; del. state conv. Episc. Ch. of Ala., various yrs.; bd. dirs. Hoover Homeowners Assn., 1977—81, Southside Ministries, Inc., 1990—91, v.p. bd. dirs., 1990—91; bd. dirs. SafeHouse of Shelby County, Inc., 1990—93, vice chmn., 1991—93. Recipient Am. Jurisprudence Criminal Procedure Book award. Mem. ABA (sect. corporation, banking and bus. law), Nat. Parks and Conservation Soc. (life), Fed. Bar Assn. (sec. Birmingham chpt. 1980-81, del. nat. conv. 1993, 94, del. mid yr. meeting, 1994-95), Ala. Bar Assn. (com. on future of the profession 1978-81, 83-84, com. on quality of life 1992-93, sect. bankruptcy and corp. law, sect. bankruptcy and comml. law, sect. corp. counsel, sect. banking and bus. law), Nature Conservacy (life), Birmingham Bar Assn., Birmingham Venture Club, Sierra Club (life), Sigma Delta Kappa (v.p., Outstanding Sr. award 1977). Episcopalian. Office: US Small Bus Adminstrn 801 Tom Martin Dr Ste 201 Birmingham AL 35211-4436 Fax: 205-290-7443. E-mail: william.howell@sba.gov.

HOWELL, WILLIAM JAMES, state legislator; b. Washington, May 8, 1943; m. Cecelia Joy Stump; children: William F., Leland J. BSBA, U. Richmond; LLB, U. Va. Mem. Va. State Legis., 1988—, ho. spkr., mem. cts. of justice, mem. transp. com., mem. fin. com., mem. Chesapeake and its tributaries com. Republican. Baptist. Office: Gen Assembly Bldg PO Box 406 Richmond VA 23218-0406*

HOWELL, WILLIAM PAGE, real estate company executive; b. Carnegie, Okla., July 27, 1952; s. Herman Glen and Muriel Joyce (Raby) H.; 1 child, Blake Alexander Sewell-Howell. BS, Southwestern U., Weatherford, Okla., 1975; MS, U. Okla., 1976. Chief exec. officer, pres. Howell Assocs., Norman, Okla., 1976-84; dir. Saudi Arabian Investment Corp., Dallas, London, 1984-87; dir. acquisitions Mitsui Fudosan (N.Y.) Inc., N.Y.C., 1987-93; prin., ptnr. Peninsula Mgmt. Corp., N.Y.C., 1993—; pres. Howell Assocs. of N.Y., N.Y.C., 1993—; mng. ptnr. Cushman Peninsula Asset Mgmt. Group, N.Y.C., 1993—; chmn., pres. Boutique Hotels and Resorts, N.Y.C., 1998—; chmn., CEO, H.A.I. Investment Advisors, N.Y.C., 1999—. Dir. adv. bd. Comml. Property News, N.Y.C., 1990—. Demographics coord. Dem. Nat. Com., Atlanta, 1976-77. Mem. Urban Land Inst., Assn. Fgn. Investors in U.S. Real Estate, Fedn. Internat. Adminstrs. de Bein Conseils Immobiliers, Japan Soc., N.Y. Real Estate Club, Internat. Devel. Rsch. Coun. Avocations: flying, skiing, skydiving, fishing, golf. Home: 111 E 30th St Apt 10A New York NY 10016-7352

HOWELL, WILLIAM ROBERT, retail company executive; b. Claremore, Okla., Jan. 3, 1936; s. William Roosevelt and Opal Theo (Swan) H.; m. Judy Howell; children: Ann Elizabeth, Teresa Lynn. BBA, U. Okla., 1958. With J.C. Penney Co., Inc., 1958—, store mgr., 1968-69; dist. mgr., dir. Treasury Stores subs., Dallas, 1969-71, div. v.p., dir. domestic devel. N.Y.C., 1973-76, regional v.p., western regional mgr., 1976-79, sr. v.p., dir. merchandising, mktg. and catalog, 1979-81, exec. v.p., 1981-82, vice chmn. bd. dirs, 1982-83, chmn., chief exec. officer, 1983-97; chmn. emeritus J.C. Penney Co., Inc., Plano, Tex., 1997—. Bd. dirs. Exxon-Mobil Corp., Pfizer Corp., Bankers Trust Co., Halliburton Co., The Williams Cos., Am. Electric Power, Viseon. Mem. Bus. Coun., Dirs.' Table, Delta Sigma Pi, Beta Gamma Sigma.

HOWELLS, JOHN GWILYM, medical scientist; b. Anglesey, Wales, June 24, 1918; s. Richard David and Mary (Hughes) H.; m. Ola Margaret Harrison, Dec. 12, 1943; children: David, Richard, Cheryl, Roger. MBBS, London U., 1943, MD, 1950. House physician Charing Cross Hosp., London, 1943; trainee Gottingen (Germany) U., 1946; registrar Maudsley Hosp., London, 1947-49, Inst. Neurology, London, 1948; dir., rsch. dir. Inst. Family Psychiatry, U. Cambridge, Ipswich, England, 1949-83; tchr. U. Cambridge, Eng., 1974-83. Mem. East Anglian Regional Hosp. Bd., Cambridge, 1965-74; mem. faculty bd. clin. medicine U. Cambridge, 1974-77. Author: Family Psychiatry, 1963, Theory and Practice of Family Psychiatry, 1967, Nosology of Psychiatry, 1970, The Royal College of Psychiatry, Remember Maria, 1974, Principles of Family Psychiatry, 1975, Integral Clinical Investigation, 1982, Reference Companion to the History of Abnormal Psychology, 1983 (Acad. Book of Yr. 1985), Concept of Schizophrenia, 1990; editor: Modern Perspectives in Psychiary, 12 vols., 1965-85, World History of Psychiatry, 1974; co-author: Family Relations Indicator, 1967, Family and Schizophrenia, 1985, Family Diagnosis, 1985, Clematis, 1990, Guide to Clematis, 1990, Growing Clematis, 1994, The Rose and The Clematis, 1996, The Viticellas, 1998, Choosing Your Clematis, 2000. Capt. Royal Army Med. Corps, 1944-46. Disting. fellow Am. Psychiat. Assn., 1968; fellow WHO, 1961. Fellow Royal Coll. Psychiatrists (founder), Royal Soc. Medicine (life); mem. World Psychiat. Assn. (chmn. history of psychiatry), Brit. Med. Assn. (life). Achievements include promoting evolution of experiential psychopathology, vector psychiatry and family psychiatry. Fax: 01206-337-577.

HOWELLS, WILLIAM WHITE, anthropology educator; b. N.Y.C., Nov. 27, 1908; s. John Mead and Abby MacDougall (White) H.; m. Muriel Gurdon Seabury, June 15, 1929; children— Gurdon Howells Metz, William Dean SB, Harvard U., 1930, PhD, 1934; DSc (hon.), Beloit Coll., 1975, U. Witwatersrand, 1985. From asst. prof. to prof. anthropology U. Wis., 1939-54, prof. integrated liberal studies, 1948-54; prof. anthropology Harvard U., 1954-74, prof. emeritus, 1974—. Hon. fellow Sch. Am. Research, 1975 Author: Mankind So Far, 1944, The Heathens, 1948, Back of History, 1954, Mankind in the Making, 1959, rev. edit., 1967, The Pacific Islanders, 1973, Cranial Variation in Man, 1973, Evolution of the Genus Homo, 1973, Skull Shapes and The Map, 1989, Getting Here: The Story of Human Evolution, 1993, Who's Who in Skulls, 1995; editor: Early Man in the Far East, 1949, Ideas on Human Evolution, 1962, Paleoanthropology in the People's Republic of China, 1977, Am. Jour. Phys. Anthropology, 1949-54; assoc. editor Human Biology, 1955-74. Served as lt. USNR, 1943-46 Recipient Viking Fund medal in phys. anthropology, 1954 Fellow AAAS, Indian Anthrop. Assn. (fgn.), Am. Acad. Arts and Scis., Am. Anthrop. Assn. (pres. 1951, Disting. Service award 1978), Soc. Antiquaries London; mem. NAS, Austrian Acad. Scis., Mass. Hist. Soc., Am. Assn. of Physical Anthropologists (sec., treas. 1939-41, Charles R. Darwin Lifetime Achievement award 1992); corr. mem. Geog. Soc. Lisbon, Anthrop. Soc. Paris (Broca prix du Centenaire 1980), Anthrop. Soc. Vienna, Royal Soc. South Africa (fgn.), Soc. for Biol. Anthropology Spain (corr.), Tavern Club (Boston); Harvard Faculty Club. Home: 11 Lawrence Ln Kittery Point ME 03905-5104

HOWENSTINE, E. JAY, housing economist; b. Stanford, Ky., Aug. 12, 1914; s. E. Jay and Roberta (O'Bannon) H.; m. Elsie Craig Greenhalgh, Dec. 27, 1958; children: Robert Jay, Richard Allen, Judith Ann, Patricia Ann. BA, Miami U., Oxford, Ohio, 1936; MA, Ohio State U., 1938, PhD, 1942. Instr. in econs. No. Mich. U., Marquette, 1939-41; assoc. prof. Park Coll., Parkville, Mo., 1942-44; agrl. economist USDA, Washington, 1944-46; housing economist Nat. Housing Adminstrn., Washington, 1946-47; economist UN Relief and Rehab. Adminstrn., Washington, 1947-48; housing economist Internat. Labour Office, Geneva, 1948-67; internat. rsch. coord. HUD, Washington, 1967-86; cons. Internat. Cons. Svcs., Arlington, Va., 1986—. Bd. dirs. Arlington Housing Corp., 1984-92; co-covenor Coalition for Housing in Arlington, 1987—. Author: Compensatory Employment Programmes, 1968, Foreign Housing Subsidy Systems, 1974, Attacking Housing Costs, 1983, Housing Vouchers, 1986, The New Housing Shortage, 1993; bd. editors Cities, 1981—. Vice chair social responsibilties com. Unitarian Ch., Arlington. Ohio State U. fellow, 1938-39, scholar, 1936-38. Avocations: tennis, swimming, camping. Home: 2948 26th St N Arlington VA 22207-4959

HOWER, EDWARD, writer, journalist, educator; b. N.Y.C., NY, Jan. 10, 1941; s. Virgil Hower and Dorothy Condit; m. Alison Lurie; children: Daniel, Lana. BA, Cornell U., 1959—63; Diploma in Edn., Makerere U., Kampala, Uganda, 1963—64; MA, UCLA, 1968—71. Instr. Ithaca Coll., 1975—. Author: (novels) A Garden of Demons, Shadows and Elephants, The Pomegranate Princess, Queen of the Silver Dollar, Night Train Blues, Wolf Tickets, The New Life Hotel. Fellow Fulbright Lectureship, India, Fulbright/U.S. State Dept., 1990-91; grantee Nat. Endowment for the Arts Grant, Nat. Endowment for the Arts, 1976-77, N.Y. State Coun. on the Arts Grant, NY State Coun. on the Arts, 1982, Ingram Merrill Found. Grant, Ingram Merrill Found., 1985, Fulbright Sr. Rsch. Grant, India, Fulbright/U.S. State Dept., 1986-87. Mem.: PEN, Amnesty Internat. Home: 1409 Hanshaw Rd Ithaca NY 14850 Office: Ithaca Coll Ithaca NY 14850 Personal E-mail: edwardhower@hotmail.com.

HOWER, FRANK BEARD, JR., retired banker; b. Louisville, Ky., Nov. 26, 1928; s. Frank Beard and Katharine (Coffman) H.; m. Virginia W. Barker, Dec. 30, 1954; children: Frank Beard III, William. AB, Centre Coll., Danville, Ky., 1950. With Liberty Nat. Bank, Louisville, 1950-90, exec. v.p., 1967-71, pres., 1971-90, CEO, chmn. bd. dirs., 1973-90, ret., 1990. Bd. dirs. Falls City Industries, Inc., Louisville, Bank One, Ky., Norton Health Sys., Inc., Am. Life and Accident Ins. Co., Churchill Downs Inc., Anthem Inc.; chmn. Norton Kosair Childrens Hosp., Inc., 1983-84. Trustee J. Graham Brown Found., U. Louisville; chmn. regional adv. bd. Comptr. of Currency, 1976; mem. Ky. Registry of Election Finance, 1966-70, Ky. Econ. Progress Commn., 1964-70; vice chmn. Ky.-Tenn. Export Coun.; gen. chmn. United Appeal, 1969; chmn. Greater Louisville Fund for the Arts, 1976; v.p. Louisville Philharm. Orch., 1974-75; chmn. Regional Airport Authority of Louisville and Jefferson County, Louisville Devel. Com.; bd. dirs., chmn. U. Louisville; trustee, chmn. Ky. Ind. Coll. Found.; trustee Centre Coll.; mem. Actors Theatre Bd. Maj. USMCR, 1951-52, Korea. Mem. Am., Ky. bankers assns., Robert Morris Assos., Assn. Res. City Bankers, Louisville C. of C. (pres. 1973) Republican. Episcopalian.

HOWER, JEANNE LOUISE, landscape designer; b. Mpls., Apr. 24, 1948; d. Archie Edward and Joyce Loucille (Cleve.) Hower; divorced: 1 child, Angela Marie. Student in landscape design, Olympic Coll., 1983-85; student in interior design, Life Time Career, Grand Rapids, Minn., 1975-77. Receptionist Bradfords, Inc., Anoka, Minn., 1966-67; inspector quality Pioneer Plating Co., Mpls., 1967-68, Honeywell County, Mpls., 1968-72; owner Jeanne's Profl. Finishing, Brementon, Wash., 1976-79; interior designer Office Interiors of Seattle, 1979-82; landscape designer, owner Horizon's Landscape Design, Bremerton, Wash., 1986-97. Art dir. fairgrounds, Bremerton, 1978-81; crafts artist Artist Club, Bremerton, 1981-88; profl. gardener Gardener's Club, 1988-97. Floral, landscape and interior design projects. Affil. mem. Epilepsy Assn., Seattle, 1987-97, Nature Conservaory, 1990-97, Save the Whales, 1985-90. Mem. Am. Soc. Landscape Designer (affill.). Avocations: reading, gardening, collecting, crafts, saving the earth. Home and Office: 1733 Winfield Ave Bremerton WA 98310-4438

HOWER, PHILIP LELAND, semiconductor device engineer; b. Reading, Pa., Apr. 9, 1934; s. Frank B. and Gladys (Fox) H.; m. Suzanne Mulvey, Apr. 28, 1962; children: Benjamin L., Suzanne E. BSEE, Lehigh U., 1956; MSEE, U. So. Calif., 1958; PhDEE, Stanford U., 1967. Tech. staff Fairchild R&D, Palo Alto, Calif., 1966-71; adv. engr. Westinghouse R&D, Pitts., 1971-81; prin. scientist Unitrode Corp., Watertown, Mass., 1981-92; prin. engr. Unitrode Integrated Cirs., Merrimack, N.H., 1992-99; disting. mem. tech. staff Tex. Instruments, Manchester, NH, 1999—. Contbr. 40 articles to profl. jours. Fellow IEEE (life); mem. IEEE Power Electronics Soc. (William E. Newell award 1986, disting. lectr., 1999). Achievements include 7 patents in the field of semiconductor device design. Home: 315 Border Rd Concord MA 01742-4625 Office: Tex Instruments 50 Phillippe Cote St Manchester NH 03101 E-mail: phil_hower@ti.com.

HOWES, BRIAN THOMAS, lawyer; b. Sioux Falls, S.D., July 23, 1957; s. Thomas A. and Joyce L. (McFarland) H.; m. Robin Kay Schoonover, June 2, 1979; children: Phillip, Adam, Jason. BSBA in Acctg., BA in Polit. Sci., Kans. State U., 1979; JD, U. Kans., 1982. Bar: Mo. 1982, U.S. Dist. Ct. (we. dist.) Mo. 1982, U.S. Supreme Ct. 1989. Assoc. Shughart, Thomson & Kilroy, Kansas City, Mo., 1982-85; exec. v.p., COO, gen. counsel Tenenbaum & Assocs., Inc., Kansas City, 1985-95; ptnr., nat. dir. property tax svcs. Ernst & Young LLP, Kansas City, 1995-99; of counsel Shughart Thomson & Kilroy, P.C., Kansas City, 2000—. Pres. Nat. Coun. Property Taxation, 1999-2000. Contbr. articles to profl. jours; writer, speaker in field. Contbg. mem. Dem. Nat. Com.; bd. dirs. Kansas City Wheelchair Athletic Commn., 1987-89, Vol. Atty. Project, 1984—, Nat. Youth Sports Coaches Assn., 1994—. Mem. ABA, Kansas City Met. Bar Assn., Lawyers Assn. Kansas City, Am. Corp. Counsel Assn., Inst. for Profls. in Taxation, Internat. Assn. of Assessing Officers, Urban Land Inst. Episcopalian. Home: 4901 W 130th St Shawnee Mission KS 66209-1864 Office: Shughart Thomson & Kilroy PC Ste 1800 120 W 12th St Kansas City MO 64105-1929 E-mail: bhowes@kc.stklaw.com.

HOWES, JAMES GUERDON, communications company executive; b. Balt. s. James Harold and Edna Esther (Lowman) H. BS, U. Md., 1967, MBA, 1969. Staff asst. U.S. Senate, Washington, 1965-68; regional mktg. adminstrn. Hertz Corp., Balt., 1972-75; commr. aviation Dutchess County, Poughkeepsie, N.Y., 1975-80; airport dir. St. Petersburg-Clearwater (Fla.) Internat. Airport, 1980-2001; pres. Atlas Comm., Tampa, 2001—. Producer radio programs Choral Masterpieces, 1985-95, King of Instruments, 1983-95, Sacred Classics, 1995—. Committeeman Rep. Nat. Com. Campaign, Washington, 1974-84, Riverside Ch., N.Y.C., 1976-80; v.p. Boy Scouts Am., Largo, Fla., 1987-91, nat. coun. rep., 1992-96. Capt. USAF, 1969-72. Recipient So. divsn. Airport of Yr. Safety award, 1998. Mem. Am. Assn. Airport Execs., Southeastern Airport Mgrs. Assn. (pres. 1993-94), Belleair Country Club. Methodist. Avocations: flying, scuba diving, classical music, photography, white water rafting. Home: 41 Pine Wood Cir Safety Harbor FL 34695-5421 also: 6 Crow's Nest Hill Bailey's Bay CR 04 Bermuda Office: PO Box 5534 Baltimore MD 21285 E-mail: jghowes@compuserve.com.

HOWES, LORRAINE DE WET, fashion designer, educator; b. Port Elizabeth, South Africa, Dec. 24, 1933; came to U.S., 1957; d. Jacobus Egnatius and Johanna Elizabeth (Lowenburg) de W. Student, Sch. Fashion Design, Boston, 1957-58. Apprentice Jonathan Logan & Adam Leslie, Johannesburg, South Africa, 1953-55; apprentice, wookroom asst., model Norman Hartnell, designer to the Queen, London, 1955-57; model Peter Lumley Agy., London, 1955-57; designer, dept. mgr. Design Rsch. Inc., Cambridge, Mass., 1957-59; model Hart Agy., Boston, 1957-76; designer, mgr. Estabrook & Newell, Boston, 1959-62; designer, owner Lorraine de Wet, Boston, 1962-79; mem. adj. faculty dept. apparel design RISD, Providence, 1972-76, asst. prof., assoc. prof., 1976-82, acting head dept., 1976-79, head dept., 1979-99, prof., 1988-2000, prof. emeritus, 2000—, interim dean arch. and design, 2000-2001. Designer, cons. apparel industry and theatre, 1979—; dir. Hamilton Cornell Mass., 1986-2000; design and tech. edn. cons. apparel and textiles Hangzhou Econ. Commn., China, 1986-88; mem. individual grants panel Nat. Endowment for Arts, 1994. Named Faculty Mem. of Yr., RISD Alumni Assn., 1984-85; recipient John R. Frazier Excellence in Tchg. award RISD, 1993, Hon. Alumna award RISD, 1995, Helen Rowe Metcalf award 2003; named champion R.I. Pub. Links, 1983, 84. Mem.: Costume Soc. Am., Fashion Inst. Tech. Design Lab., Fashion Group. Avocation: golf. Office: RISD Dept Apparel Design 2 College St Providence RI 02903-2784

HOWES, SOPHIA DUBOSE, writer; b. Balt., Apr. 20, 1954; d. John Carleton and Marie Josephine (Meeth) Jones; m. Edward Phillip Howes, Jan. 26, 1996; 1 child, Michael Laurence. BFA with honors, NYU, 1982, MFA, 1994; JD, Fordham U., 2002. Legal asst. Skadden, Arps, Slate, Meagher & Flom, N.Y.C., 1984-93; script reader Haft Nassiter Co., N.Y.C., 1994; editl. assoc. Matthew Bender & Co. Inc., N.Y.C., 1994-97. Extern Fordham U. Sch. Law, Surrogate's Ct., N.Y.C., 1999; rsch. asst. Securities Arbitration Clinic, Fordham Law Sch., 2000, Writing Rsch., ECPAT, summer 2001. Author one act plays, including Better Dresses, Rosetta's Eyes, 1988, 1988, Adamov, 1992, two-act play The Poisoned Kiss, 1994; mem. staff Fordham Environ. Law Jour., 1999-2000, sr. notes and comments editor, 2000-01. Recipient Grad. award in playwriting, NYU-Tisch Sch. Arts, 1994, Seidman award for talent, 1982. Mem. Dramatists Guild. Avocation: mountain climbing. E-mail: edwardhowes@juno.com.

HOWES, THEODORE CLARK, claims examiner; b. Ridgefield, Conn., Dec. 25, 1929; s. Robert Clark and Phyllis Evelyn (Greene) H.; m. Anne Christine Tourgee, Sept. 28, 1968. BS, Springfield (Mass.) Coll., 1956. Cert. tchr., Mass. Claims examiner Geico, Chevy Chase, Md., 1967-78, U.S. Dept. Labor, Washington, 1978—. Innovator in use of laser for mil. application. Sgt. USAF, 1948-52. Mem. VFW, Soc. Mayflower Descendants, Alden Kindred Am., Am. Legion. Republican. Congregationalist. Avocations: hunting, fishing, gardening, horseback riding, antiques. Home: Fox Meadow Farm 17110 Bollinger School Rd Emmitsburg MD 21727-8721 Office: US Dept Labor 200 Constitution Ave NW Washington DC 20210-0001

HOWETT, JOHN CHARLES, JR., lawyer; b. Tampa, Fla., Feb. 11, 1946; s. John Charles and Martha Carlton (Durrance) H.; m. Mary K. Sheehan, Oct. 12, 1974; children: Timothy S., Julia K. BA, U. Pa., 1968; JD, Dickinson Sch. of Law, 1974. Bar: Pa. 1974, U.S. Supreme Ct. 1979. Law clk. Hon. Roy Wilkinson Commonwealth Ct. Pa., Harrisburg, 1974-75; sr. ptnr. Howett, Kissinger & Conley, P.C., Harrisburg, 1975—. Contbr. articles to profl. jours. 1st lt. U.S. Army, 1968-71, Vietnam. Mem. Pa. Bar Assn. (chmn. family law sect. 1995-96, bd. govs. 1978-81, 88-91, pres. young lawyers divsn. 1979-80), Am. Acad. Matrimonial Lawyers (pres. Pa. chpt. 1999-2000), Dauphin County Bar Assn. (pres. 1994-95, chmn. family law sect. 1990-91), Internat. Acad. Matrimonial Lawyers. Office: Howett Kissinger & Conley PC PO Box 810 130 Walnut St Harrisburg PA 17101-1612

HOWEY, JOHN RICHARD, architect, writer; b. New Haven, Jan. 13, 1933; s. Joseph Herman and Dorothy Pauline (Good) H.; m. Maria Andrea Hatges, Sept. 8, 1968; children: John Michael, Dorothy Anne. Student, Wooster Coll., 1951-52; BS, Ga. Inst. Tech., 1956, BArch, 1957. Registered architect Fla. With various archtl. firms, Fla. and Ga., 1958-63; pres. John Howey, Architect, AIA, Tampa, Fla., 1963-73, John Howey Assocs., Tampa, Fla., 1973—. Pres. Baypark, Inc., Tampa, 1988—. Prin. works include coll. bldgs. U. So. Fla., 1975, Louis Pappas Restaurant, Tarpon Springs, Fla., 1975 (honor design award AIA 1976), office bldg. 101 S. Franklin St., Tampa, 1980 (Fla. Preservation award 1984), Williers Residence, Tampa, 1980 (honor design award AIA 1981), modular urban transit shelters, 1977 (U.S. patent 1980, honor design award AIA 1985), Tehran, Iran Libr. Project, 1978, Baypark Pl. apt. bldgs., Tampa, 1989 (honor design award AIA 1989, Millenium Award of Honor, 2000), others; author: The Sarasota School of Architecture, 1995; co-author: Florida Architecture, A Celebration, 2000. With U.S. Army Corps of Engrs., 1957-58. Fellow AIA (Fla./Caribbean region Design Excellence Honor award 1985, Fla. ctrl chpt. Medal of Honor 1986); mem. Sertoma Club (bd. dirs. 1970-73), Exch. Club. Episcopalian. Achievements include featured in 1000 Architects, 2003; 100 of the World's Best Houses, 2003. Avocations: photography, painting. Home: 2538 W Palm Dr Tampa FL 33629-7314 Address: John Howey Assocs 121 W Whiting St Tampa FL 33602-5136 Office Fax: 813-229-1528. E-mail: jhoweyarch@tampabay.rr.com.

HOWIE, HENRY S., III, social worker, educator; b. Rock Hill, S.C., Mar. 3, 1963; s. Henry S. and Betty Jane Howie; m. Margaret Ann Sullivan, Oct. 21, 2000; 1 child, Henry Jedidiah. BA, Clemson U., 1985; MBA, Winthrop Coll., Rock Hill, S.C., 1988; MEd, Converse Coll., Spartanburg, S.C., 1999; MFA, Vt. Coll., 2002. Social worker Cherokee County Dept. of Social Svcs., Gaffney, SC, 1996—; adj. prof. of english Converse Coll., Spartanburg, SC, 2003—. Bd. dirs. Preservation Trust of Spartanburg. Contbr. short stories and essays to anthologies and collections; author: (book rev.) Two Novels by Mary Chesnutt, (novel chpts.) In Morgan's Shadow. Bd. dirs. Preservation Trust of Spartanburg, 2003. Mem.: Hub City Writers Project, Associated Writing Programs, Am. Mensa. Liberal. Unitarian Universalist. Avocations: writing, reading, music, walking, working puzzles and brain teasers. Home: 506 S Irwin Ave Spartanburg SC 29306 Office: PO Box 1369 Gaffney SC 29342 Personal E-mail: showie.1@juno.com.

HOWITT, ARNOLD MARTIN, university administrator, educator; b. N.Y.C., Jan. 6, 1947; s. Wilfred D. and Mildred (Wolch) H.; m. Maryalice Sloan; children: Matthew, Molly, Alexandra, Mark. BA, Columbia U., 1969; MA, Harvard U., 1971, PhD, 1976. Asst. prof. Brown U., Providence, 1974-76, Harvard U., Cambridge, Mass., 1976-80, assoc. prof., 1980-82, assoc. dir. Taubman Ctr. State and Local Govt., Kennedy Sch. Govt., 1983-93, exec. dir. Taubman Ctr. State and Local Govt., Kennedy Sch. Govt., 1993—. Exec. dir. Coop. Mobility Program, MIT, Cambridge, 1998-2001; cons. in field; part-time lectr. SUNY, Albany, 1984-92, U. Wash., Seattle, 1988—, dir. Exec. Session on Domestic Preparedness for Terrorism, Kennedy Sch. Govt., 1999-2003. Author: Managing Federalism, 1984; co-author, editor: Perspectives on Management Capacity Building, 1986, Countering Terrorism, 2003; contbr. articles to profl. jours. Office: Harvard U Kennedy Sch Govt 79 JF Kennedy St Cambridge MA 02138-5801

HOWITT, PAMELA TESLER, development and philanthropy association administrator; b. Providence, Apr. 10, 1955; d. Marvin Gerald and Marilyn (Schaffer) Tesler; m. Steven Samuel Howitt, Apr. 7, 1990. BFA, U. R.I., 1977; M in Profl. Studies magna cum laude, Pratt Inst., 1979. Dir. youth devel programs Pratt Inst., Bklyn., 1979-80, dir. alumni resources, 1980-85; maj. gifts devel. officer Columbia U., NYC, 1985-87; dir. devel. Columbia U./Columbia Presbyn. Med. Ctr., NYC, 1987-89; asst. dean for devel. and external rels. Grad. Sch. Design Harvard U., Cambridge, Mass., 1989-93; exec. dir. FirstFed Charitable Found., 1993-2001; pres. Devel. and Philanthropy, 1993—; exec. dir. Bay State Fed. Savs. Charitable Found., 1993—2001; donor svc. officer The RI. Found., 2001—. Cons., fundraiser in field. Author (documentary): Coping with Death and Dying with Adolescents Through Art Therapy. Mem.: Assn. Fundraising Profls., Advancement Network, Coun. on Founds., Planned Giving Group of New Eng., Planned Giving Group of R.I., Assn. Small Founds., Coun. for Advancement and Support of Edn., Univ. Club R.I.

HOWL, JOANNE HEALEY, veterinarian, writer; b. Mariemont, Ohio, Mar. 16, 1957; d. Joseph Daniel and Claire Helen (Baillargeon) H.; m. Arthur Wesley Howl, May 12, 1990; children: Bryan Arthur, Martha Grace Claire DVM, U. Tenn., 1987. Sr. lab. animal technician Lab. Animal Facility, Knoxville, 1983-84; gnotobiology technician U. Tenn., Knoxville, 1984-86; assoc. vet. Mynatt Vet. Clinic, Knoxville, 1987-89; veterinary med. officer USDA Animal and Plant Health Inspection Svcs., Raleigh, N.C., 1989-90; owner Creature Comfort Vet. Relief Svc., Laurel, Md., 1991-95; assoc. veterinarian Muddy Creek Animal Hosp., West River, Md., 1996-97; freelance writer, West River, Md., 1995—. Author: Your Cat's Life, 1999; editor VMAT-2 News, 1996—; contbr. articles to profl. jours. Dep. team leader Vet. Med. Assistance Team-2. Mem. AVMA, Am. Animal Hosp. Assn., Am. Assn. Feline Practitioners, Md. Vet. Med. Assn. (chmn. pub. rels. com. 1995-98, sec./treas. 1998-2002, pres. 1999-2000), Am. Acad. Vet. Disaster Medicine (sec./treas. 1998-2002). Episcopalian. Avocations: hiking, gardening, house remodeling. Home and Office: 4304 Tenthouse Ct West River MD 20778-9797

HOWLADER, M. MOSTOFA KAMAL, engineering educator; b. Jhalakati, Bangladesh, Mar. 1, 1967; s. Abdur Rob Howlader and Aleya Begum; m. Anjuman Ara Laiju. BSEE, Bangladesh U. Engring. and Tech., Dhaka, Bangladesh, 1991; MSEE, U. New Orleans, 1994; PhD in Elec. Engring., Va. Tech., 2000. Telecomm. engr. Bangladesh T&T Bd., Dhaka, 1991—92; grad. rschr. U. New Orleans, 1993—94; grad. rsch. fellow CREOL, U. Cen. Fla., Orlando, 1994—96; grad. rschr. Va. Tech., Blacksburg, 1996—2000; asst. prof. U. Tenn., Knoxville, Ala., 2000—. Contbr. Named Weston Fulton Prof., U. Tenn., 2001—03; recipient Basic Rsch. award in radio frequency engring., USAF Office of Rsch., 2001—03, Basic Rsch. award in signal processing, Oak Ridge Nat. Lab., 2001—02. Mem.: IEEE (mem. tech. program com. Computer Soc. 2000—), Photo-Optical Engring. Soc. Avocations: music, travel, swimming. Office: U Tenn 414 Ferris Hall 1508 Middle Way Dr Knoxville TN 37996 Office Fax: 865-974-5483. Business E-Mail: howlader@utk.edu.

HOWLAND, BETTE, writer; b. Chgo., Jan. 28, 1937; d. Sam and Jessie (Berger) Sotonoff; m. Howard C. Howland (div.); children— Frank, Jacob. BA, U. Chgo., 1955. Assoc. prof. com. social thought U. Chgo., 1993-97. Author: W-3, 1974, Blue in Chicago, 1978 (1st prize Friends of Am. Writers), Things to Come and Go, 1983, Trial, 1998, Calm Sea and Prosperous Voyage, 1999. Fellow Rockefeller Found., 1969, Marsden Found., 1971, Guggenheim Found., 1978, Nat. Endowment for the Arts, 1981, MacArthur Found., 1984. Jewish. Address: PO Box 405 Union Pier MI 49129-0405

HOWLAND, JACOB, philosopher, educator; b. Phila., Nov. 23, 1959; s. Howard Chase and Bette Sotonoff Howland; m. Jennifer Bryant Hayes, June 27, 1981; children: Abraham, Nathaniel. BA, Swarthmore Coll., 1981; PhD, Pa. State U., 1987. From asst. to assoc. prof. philosophy U. Tulsa, 1988—2002, prof. philosophy, 2002, McFarlin prof. philosophy, 2002—. Author: The Republic: The Odyssey of Philosophy, 1993, The Paradox of Political Philosophy, 1998; referee (numerous profl. jours.). Bd. dirs. Tulsa Jewish Retirement Ctr., 1998—; bd. trustees Okla. Found. Humanities, Oklahoma City, 1994—96; pres. bd. dirs. Heritage Acad., Tulsa, 1994—95. Richard M. Weaver fellow, Intercollegiate Studies Inst., 1986—87, grantee, Earhart Found., 1994. Jewish. Avocation: soccer. Office: Dept Philosophy and Religion U Tulsa 600 S College Ave Tulsa OK 74104-3189

HOWLAND, JAMES CHASE, retired engineer, consultant; b. Oregon City, Oreg., June 2, 1916; s. Arthur Cornell and Sade (Chase) H.; m. Ruth Louise Meisenhelder, June 14, 1941; children: Joyce, Eric, Mark, Peter. BS, Oreg. State U., 1938; MS, MIT, 1939. Registered profl. engr., Oreg. Engr. Standard Oil Co. Calif., El Segundo, 1939-41; cons. engr. CH2M Hill, Corvallis, Oreg., 1946—90. Bd. dirs. Madison Ave Task Force, Corvallis, 1974—, chmn. 1974-78; trustee Linfield Coll, McMinnville, Oreg., 1979—, Corvallis Riverfront Commn., 1994—; with Corvallis Planning Commn., 1957-70, Oreg. Water Resources Commn., Salem, 1987-93. Served with U.S. Army, 1941-46, PTO. Mem. ASCE (hon., engring. mgmt. award 1987), Profl. Engrs. Oreg., Oreg. Couns. Engrs. Council (pres., engr. yr. 1988), Tau Beta Pi. Republican. Presbyterian. Avocations: hiking, biking, making screen prints. Home: 2575 SW Whiteside Dr Corvallis OR 97333-1401 Office: CH2M Hill PO Box 428 Corvallis OR 97339-0428

HOWLAND, JOAN SIDNEY, law librarian, law educator; b. Eureka, Calif., Apr. 9, 1951; d. Robert Sidney and Ruth Mary Howland. BA, U. Calif., Davis, 1971; MA, U. Tex., 1973; MLS, Calif. State U., San Jose, 1975; JD, Santa Clara (Calif.) U., 1983; MBA, U. Minn., 1997. Assoc. librarian for pub. svcs. Stanford (Calif.) U. Law Library, 1975-83, Harvard U. Law Library, Cambridge, Mass., 1983-86; dep. dir. U. Calif. Law Library, Berkeley, 1986-92; dir. law libr., Roger F. Noreen prof. law U. Minn. Sch. of Law, 1992—, assoc. dean info. tech., 2001—. Questions and answers column editor Law Libr. Jour., 1986-91; memt. column editor Trends in Law Libr. Mgmt. & Tech., 1987-94. Mem. ALA, ABA (com. on accreditation 2001—), Am. Assn. Law Librs., Am. Assn. Law Schs., Am. Indian Libr. Assn. (treas. 1992—), Am. Law Inst. Office: U Minn Law Sch 229 19th Ave S Minneapolis MN 55455-0400

HOWLAND, KRISTINE NELSON, college administrator; b. Plymouth, Wis., May 11, 1947; d. Merland Walter and Harriet Mae (Radloff) Nelson; m. Robert Vaughan Howland, Dec. 30, 1977. AAS, SUNY, 1968; BS, Cornell U., 1978; MBA, Plymouth State Coll., 1989. Mgr., buyer John Lewton Apparel, Ithaca, N.Y., 1969-70; purchasing sec. Ithaca Coll., 1970-71, admstr. for spl. events, 1971-74; conf. coord. Cornell U., Ithaca, 1974-79; sales rep. trainee The Travelers Ins. Co., Inc., Syracuse, 1979-80; spl. projects coord. Groton (Conn.) Resources Organized Inc., 1980-81; dir. sales Sheraton Inn-Norwich, Conn., 1982-83, Norwich Inn & Spa, 1983-84; program coord. Keene State Coll., 1984-85, asst. to the pres., 1985-88, dir. of devel. and alumni affairs, 1988-94, dir. institutional advancement; v.p. for devel. Tiffin (Ohio) U., 1994-95; dir. major and planned gifts Goucher Coll., Balt., 1995—, acting v.p. for advancement, 2000—02; v.p. for univ. rels. and devel. Union Inst. and U., Cin., 2002—, Montpelier, Vt. V.p. N.H. Women in Higher Edn. State Planning Bd., 1991-93. Adult vol. and mem. Girl Scouts Am., 1954—; chair group travel devel. Southeastern Conn. Tourism Dist., Mystic, Conn., 1982-83, chair advt. com., 1983-84; mem. public rels. com. Greater Keene C. of C., 1984-94; mem. Corp. Child Care Group, Inc., Keene, 1985-89, v.p., 1987-89; mem. ednl. programs com. N.H. Coun. on Fund Raising, 1991-94; chair membership com. Chesapeake Planned Giving Coun., 1997-99, treas., 2000; founding mem., bd. dirs. Southeastern Conn. Tourism Dist., East Lyme, Conn., 1982-84. Recipient Judith A. Sturnick award N.H. Women in Higher Edn. Assn., 1993; named Founding Mem. of Major Gifts Exch. Md. chpt. Nat. Soc. of Fund Raising Execs., 1996-97. Mem. AAUW (pres. 1992-94), Chesapeake Planned Giving Coun., Cornell Club of Md., Cornell Club of N.Y., Coun. for Advancement and Support of Edn., Nat. Assn. of Women in Edn., Nat. Soc. for Fund Raising Execs., Md. Assn. of Women in Edn. Episcopalian. Avocations: reading, hiking, cooking. Office: Goucher Coll 1021 Dulaney Valley Rd Baltimore MD 21204-2753

HOWLAND, LLEWELLYN, III, publishing executive, writer; b. Boston, Aug. 21, 1937; s. Llewellyn and Sarah (Ives) Howland; m. Jessie Williams, June 3, 1967; children: Jessie Howland Cahill, Cornelius. BA, Harvard U., Cambridge, Mass., 1959. Sales rep. Harcourt Brace World, N.Y. C., 1961—62; literary agt. Sterling Lord Agy., N.Y. C., 1962—64; book editor Little, Brown & Co., Boston, 1965—77; Bookseller, writer freelance, Boston, 1977—. Cons., advisor Several Mus. Author (3 books, countless articles and revs.). Trustee Mystic Seaport Mus., Mystic, Conn., 1984—97, Old Dartmouth Hist. Soc., New Bedford, Mass., 2003—; mem. many maritime and art mus. Priv. U.S. Army, 1961—62. Mem.: Mass. Hist. Soc., Tavern Club, Boston. Avocations: book collecting, sailing, history. Home and Office: 100 Rockwood St Jamaica Plain MA 02130

HOWLAND, NINA DAVIS, historian; b. Wichita, Kans., June 2, 1939; d. Earle Rosco Davis and Kathrine Keene Laurie; m. Kenneth Eugene Howland, Sept. 27, 1959; children: Douglas Earle, Christopher Keene, Karen Laurie, Rebecca Kathrine. BA with high honors, U. Md., London Center, Eng., 1970; PhD, U. Md., College Park, 1983; MA with distinction, U. London, 1972. Instr. U. Coll., U. Md., College Park, 1978-79, 82, Hood Coll., Frederick, Md., 1981; archivist Nat. Archives, Washington, 1984-85; historian Office of Historian U.S. Dept. of State, Washington, 1985—. Editor: Foreign Relations of the United States, 1961-63, vol. XXI, Africa, 1995, Foreign Relations of the United States, 1964-68, vol. XVI, Africa, 1999, Foreign Relations of the United States, 1964-68, vol. XXII, Iran, 1999, vol. XXI Near East Region, Arabian Peninsula, 2000; divsn. chief Middle East, South Asia & African divsn., 2002—. Rsch. grantee William Randolph Hearst Found., 1980. Mem. Soc. for Historians of Am. Fgn. Rels., Soc. for History in Fed. Govt., Peace History Soc., Phi Kappa Phi. Home: 9808 E Bexhill Dr Kensington MD 20895-3223 Office: Office of Historian US Dept of State 2401 E St NW Dept of State Washington DC 20522-0001 Fax: 202-663-1289. E-mail: ninakenhowland@juno.com.

HOWLAND, RICHARD HUBBARD, architectural historian; b. Providence, Aug. 23, 1910; S. Carl Badger and Cora Augusta (Hubbard) H. AB, Brown U., 1931, also hon. doctor's degree; A.M., Harvard U., 1933; PhD, Johns Hopkins U., 1946. Fellow Agora excavations, Athens, Greece, 1936-38; instr. Wellesley Coll., 1939-42; chief pictorial records sect. OSS, 1943-44; founder dept. history art Johns Hopkins, 1947, chmn. dept., 1947-56; pres. Nat. Trust for Historic Preservation, 1956-60; chmn. dept. civil history Smithsonian Instn., Washington, 1960-67, spl. asst. to sec., 1968-85. Trustee Am. Sch. Classical Studies, Athens; founding mem. Am. Com. Internat. Commn. Historic Sites and Monuments. Author: (with Eleanor Spencer) Architecture of Baltimore, 1954, Greek Lamps and Their Survivals, 1958. Trustee Irish Georgian Soc., Evergreen Found. Decorated Order Brit. Empire, Order George I (Greece), U.S. Order St. John of Jerusalem. Fellow Royal Soc. of the Arts; mem. Soc. Archtl. Historians (founding mem.), English Speaking Union, Soc. Cincinnati (hon.), Md. Soc. Colonial Wars, Victorian Soc. in Am. (former pres.), Century Assn., Knickerbocker Club, 14 West Hamilton St. Club, Cosmos Club, Arts Club, Dacor-Bacon Club, City Tavern Club, Phi Gamma Delta. Home: 3900 Cathedral Ave NW Apt 712A Washington DC 20016-5299 Fax: 202-338-4384.

HOWLAND, RICHARD MOULTON, retired lawyer; b. Glen Cove, L.I., N.Y., Jan. 2, 1940; s. Richard Moulton and Natalie (Fuller) H.; m. Julie Rose Keschl, Sept. 28, 1974 (div.); children: Kimberly Merrill, Gillian Fuller. BA, Amherst Coll., 1961; JD, Columbia U., 1968. Bar: Mass. 1968. Assoc. firm Nutter, McLennen & Fish, Boston, 1968-69, DiMento & Sullivan, Boston, 1969-70; atty for students U. Mass., Amherst, 1970-74; practice law Amherst, 1974-2000; Legal Infirmary Amherst, 1997-98; ret., 2001. Adj. prof. U. Mass., 1972-76, Western New Eng. Coll. Sch. Law, 1993-94; vis. lectr. Amherst Coll., 1983, mock trial team coach, 1989-98; mock trial team coach Tufts Coll., 1998, Deerfield Acad., 1999-2000, Southwick H.S., 1999-2000; tchr. constnl. law, history, social studies Springfield H.S. Sci. and Tech., 2001—. Co-editor: Mass. Lawyers Weekly, 1979—94; emeritus:, 1994, statistician: New Eng. Blizzard, 1996—98, Conn. Pride, 1999—2000, Springfield Sirens Pro Soccer, 1999—2000. Asst. moderator Town of Leverett, 1988—93, moderator, 1993—96; mem. Leverett Sch. Bldg. Com., 1988—89; trustee Art Inst. Boston, 1990—92, Greenfield C. C. Found., 1991—97, Amherst Regional H.S. Coun., 1993—95, Amherst Hist. Soc., 1990—95; pres. Leverett PTO, 1981—85; mem. devel. com. Pioneer Valley H.S. of the Performing Arts, 1996—97; pres. Interfaith Housing Corp., Amherst, 1984—93; bd. dirs. Leverett Craftsmen and Artists, Inc., 1986—2001, treas., 1988—89, v.p., 1988—89, pres., 1989—2001; bd. dirs. Cmty. Multisvc. Inc., Northampton, Mass., 1987—93; trustee Wildwood Cemetery Assn., 1987—; bd. dirs., sec. Responsible Hospitality Inst., 1990—95; mem. host com. Russia-Amherst Exchange City of Petrozavadsk, 1988—; del. rep. Town of Amherst to Sister City, Kanegasaki, Japan, 1992—95; chair Amherst-Kanegasaki Sister Com., 1994—95; mem. bd. career com. Hampshire-Franklin Sch., 1995—98; cert. master ofcl. U.S. Assn. Track and Field, 1996—; Western Mass. track and field ofcl., 1995—; Western Mass. football ofcl., 1995—; referee FIFA Soccer, 1997—; active Connecticut Valley Soccer Ofcls. Assn., 1995—; collegiate water polo ofcl., 1997—2000; asst. coach varsity girls soccer Amherst Regional H.S., 1995—99; v.p. Western Mass. track and field, 2002—. Lt. j.g. USNR, 1961—65. Named Hon. Life Citizen, Town of Leverett, Mass., 2002. Mem. ABA (chmn. profl. liability com. Gen. Practice Sect. 1987-90, chmn. certification and specialization com. Gen. Practice Sect. 1992-95, chmn. family law com. 1995-96, chmn. certification, specialization and law sch. curriculum com. 1996-98, mem. coun. 1997-2001), Mass. Bar Assn. (chmn. com. on chem. dependency, Mass. Community Svc. award 1984), Franklin Bar Assn., Hampshire Bar Assn. (del. to Mass. Bar Assn., sec., v.p. 1986), Mass. Acad. Trial Lawyers, Amherst C. of C. (pres. 1985-93, Dakin medallion 1995), Nat. High Sch. Slavic Honor Soc. (hon.), Amherst Alumni Athletic Assn. (bd. dirs. 1995—), Skating Club (past v.p., treas. 1987-96, Amherst). Democrat. Home: 326 N Pleasant St Amherst MA 01002-1706 E-mail: rmh1240@hotmail.com.

HOWLAND, WILLARD J. radiologist, educator; b. Neosho, Mo., Aug. 28, 1927; s. Willard Jay and Grace Darlene (Murphy) H.; m. Kathleen V. Jones, July 28, 1945; children: Wyck, Candice, Charles, Thomas, Heather AB, U. Kans., 1948, MD, 1950; MA, U. Minn., 1958; DSc (hon.), Coll. Med. N.E. Ohio, 1990. Intern U.S. Naval Hosp., Newport, R.I., 1950-51; pvt. practice medicine Kans., 1951-55; resident Mayo Clinic, Rochester, Minn., 1955-58; radiologist Ohio Valley Gen. Hosp., Wheeling, W.Va., 1959-67, prof., dir. diagnostic radiology Med. Units U. Tenn., Memphis, 1967-68; dir., chmn. dept. radiology Aultman Hosp., Canton, Ohio, 1968-87, pres. med. staff, 1978; prof., chmn. radiology coun. Coll. Medicine N.E. Ohio U., Rootstown, 1976-87, program dir. integrated radiology residency, 1976-87. Author, co-author three books and rsch. papers in field. With U.S. Army, 1945-46, USN, 1950-51. Fellow Am. Coll. Radiology; mem. AMA, Radiol. Soc. N.Am., Am. Roentgen Ray Soc., Ohio State Radiol. Soc. (pres. 1980-81), Masons. Republican. Presbyterian. Office: 1405 Harbor Dr NW Canton OH 44708-3098

HOWLETT, CLIFFORD THEODORE, JR., (KIP HOWLETT), chemicals executive; b. Portland, Oreg., Oct. 19, 1945; s. Clifford T. and Lois (Ellis) H.; children: Beth, Ted, Michael; m. Marybeth Rossomando, Nov. 8, 1997. BA, Johns Hopkins U., 1967; JD, Willamette U., 1974. Bar: Oreg. 1974. Counsel, project dir. Western Environ. Trade Assn., Portland, 1973-75; v.p. environment and govt. affairs Ga.-Pacific Corp., Washington, 1988-94; vice-pres. for policy National Policy Forum, Wash., DC, 1994—. Chmn. Inter-Industry Wood Dust com., Washington, 1988—. Author: The Pitfalls and Possibilities of Planning, 1973, The Biomass Potential of Short Rotation Farms, 1977, Forest and Mill Residues as Potential Sources of Biomass, 1977. Mem. Alumni Schs. com. Johns Hopkins U., 1988—; bd. dirs. Boys and Girls Clubs of Greater Washington, 1999. With U.S. Army, 1968-70. Mem. ABA, Oreg. Bar Assn., Am. Paper Inst. (chmn. dioxin potency com. 1988—, chmn. joint occupational

health study com. with Nat. Forest Products Assn. 1988—), NAM (chmn. OSHA policy com. 1988—). Home: 6635 Byrns Pl Mc Lean VA 22101-4419 Office: Chlorine Chemistry Council 1300 Wilson Blvd Arlington VA 22209-2307

HOWLETT, D(ONALD) ROGER, art gallery executive, art historian; b. Syracuse, N.Y., Mar. 27, 1945; s. Donald Bliss and Dorothy Irene (Trautman) H. BA, Hamilton Coll., 1966; MA, SUNY, Cooperstown, 1967; postgrad., Yale U., 1968-69. Mem. curatorial dept. Garvan Coll., Yale U. Art Gallery, New Haven, 1967-68; mem. painting dept. Childs Gallery, Boston, 1970—, v.p., ptnr., 1972-83, pres., 1983—, N.Y.C., 1983-91. Councilor Emerson Gallery, Hamilton Coll., Clinton, NY, 1985—; trustee Lyme Acad. Fine Arts, Old Lyme, Conn., 1992—2002; founder New Eng. Print Fair, 1999; dir. New Eng. String Ensemble, 2003—. Author: Sculpture of Donald De Lue, 1990, William Partridge Burpee, 1991, The Lynn Beach Painters, 1998; collections arranged: George Luks (author catalog), 1973-74, Molly Luce: Eight Decades of the American Scene (author catalog), 1983; contbr. Am. Nat. Biography, 1999. Mem. Am. Assn. Mus., Soc. for Propagating the Gospel Among the Indians and Others in N.Am., Harvard Musical Assn., St. Botolph Club, Boston Athenaeum. Avocation: watercolorist. Home and Office: Childs Gallery 169 Newbury St Boston MA 02116-2834

HOWLETT, HOWARD THOMAS, JR., automotive sales consultant; b. Detroit, May 5, 1938; s. Howard Thomas and Lucille (Winter) H.; m. Dee Christy Howlett, Mar. 9, 1963; children: Howard III, Donald Christy. Student, Denison U.; degree in Printing Mgmt. and Advt., Ferris State U. Surg. technician Grace Hosp. Northwest Detroit, 1954-57; various positions including asst. to pres., prodn. mgr. Evans Winter Hebb Inc., Detroit, 1961-78; various mktg. and sales positions GM Corp., Chevrolet Motor divsn., Detroit-Buffalo, 1978-95; owner, prin. Howlett Cadillac Olds Pontiac, Inc., Jamestown, N.Y., 1995—. Bd. dirs. Grand Olds Gang Pitts.; pres. Good Olds Guys, Erie, Pa, Olds Connection, Buffalo, N.Y. Trustee W.C.A. Healthcare Sys.; corporator Hamot Hosp.; pres. Three Circles, Lakewood, N.Y.; chair Starflight, Inc.; sec. So. Tier Healthcare Sys.; bd. dirs. Chautauqua County Healthcare Network, vice chair. Mem. Hosp. Assn. of N.Y., Am. Hosp. Assn. (com. governance), Am. Coll. Healthcare Execs., Healthcare Trustees N.Y. State. Home and Office: 125 E Terrace Ave Lakewood NY 14750-1331

HOWLETT, MICHAEL JOSEPH, JR., lawyer; b. Chgo., July 10, 1948; s. Michael Joseph and Helen (Geary) H.; m. Kathleen Fitzgerald, Oct. 2, 1970; children— Elizabeth, Melissa, Catherine. B.A., St. John's U., Collegeville, Minn., 1970; J.D., U. Notre Dame, 1973. Bar: Ill. 1973, U.S. Dist. Ct. (no. dist.) Ill. 1975, U.S. Ct. Appeals (7th cir.) 1975, Ind. 1980, U.S. Supreme Ct. 1980. Law clk. U.S. Dist. Ct., U.S. Ct. Appeals, Chgo., 1973-75; asst. U.S. atty. no. dist. Ill., Chgo., 1975; ptnr. firm Moriarty, Hultquist & Howlett, Chgo. and South Bend, Ind., 1980-83; assoc. judge Cir. Ct. Cook County (Ill.), Chgo., 1983-86; counsel, Hayes & Power, 1986-87; ptnr. Pope & John, Ltd., Chgo., 1987—; spl. outside counsel ethics com. U.S. House of Rep., 1988, dep. spl. outside counsel com. on offl. conduct (ethics), 1988-89; pub. dir. Mid-Am. Commodity Exchange, Chgo., 1981-83; spl. dep. prosecutor St. Joseph County (Ind.), South Bend, 1981-83; pres. Lawyers Assistance Program, Chgo., 1989-90, dir., intervenor, 1984—; panel atty. Fed. Defender Program, Inc., U.S. Dist. Ct. (no. dist.) Ill., 1977-83; adj. prof. trial practice and civil procedure John Marshall Law Sch., Chgo., 1977-79, 83-84; mem. fed. criminal jury instrns. com. 7th Cir. Ct. Appeals, Chgo., 1981— ; lectr. profl. responsibility Loyola U. Law Sch., Chgo., 1984— ; lectr. trial practice U. Chgo. Law Sch., 1985—; vice chmn. Ill. Task Force on Gender Bias in the Cts., 1987—. Candidate Ill. lt. gov. Adlai Stevenson Solidarity Party, 1986; dir. Great Books Found., 1987— . Mem. Chgo. Bar Assn., Ill. Bar Assn., ABA, Ill. Judges Assn. (bd. dirs. 1984-86), Ill. Trial Lawyers Assn. Democrat. Roman Catholic. Office: Pope & John Ltd 444 N Michigan Ave Ste 2500 Chicago IL 60611-3997

HOWLEY, JAMES MCANDREW, lawyer; b. Dunmore, Pa., Oct. 3, 1928; s. Joseph Austin and Mary Helene (Ruddy) H.; m. Mary McDade; 1 child, Maura. BS, U. Scranton, 1952; LLB, U. Pa., 1955. Bar: Pa. 1956, U.S. Dist. Ct. (mid. dist.) Pa. 1956, U.S. Ct. Appeals (3d cir.) 1960. Pvt. practice, Scranton, Northeastern Pa., 1956—. Panel mem. and speaker at various legal symposiums; chmn. and commr. Pa. State Ethics Commn.; chmn. Gov.'s Spl. Trial Ct. nomination commn., Lackawanna County, Pa., 1987; disciplinary bd. Supreme Ct. Pa. hearing com., 1987; lawyer's adv. com. U.S. Ct. Appeals (3d cir.), 1983-86, U.S. Dist. Ct. (mid. dist.) Pa., 1981-86. Chmn. and trustee Marywood Coll., trustee St. Mary's Villa. Fellow Am. Coll. Trial Lawyers; mem. ABA, Pa. Bar Assn., Pa. Def. Inst., Am. Bd. Trial Advs. (cert.), Lackawanna County Bar Assn., Scranton C. of C. (bd. dirs.), Country Club of Scranton (pres. 1974-79), Friendly Sons of St. Patrick (pres. 1986). Roman Catholic. Avocation: golf. Home: 115 Maple Ave Clarks Summit PA 18411-2513 Office: 1000 Bank Towers 321 Spruce St Scranton PA 18503-1400 E-mail: jmhowley@aol.com.

HOWLEY, PETER ANTHONY, communications executive; b. Phila., Mar. 5, 1940; s. Frank Leo and Edith Jenkins (Cadwallader) H.; m. M. Mavin Renz, June 25, 1966; children: Tara Noel, Christina Maeve, Sean-Francis Cadwallader. B in Indsl. Engring., NYU, 1962, MBA in Mktg., 1970. Mem. mgmt. staff AT&T, White Plains, N.Y., 1965-73, MCI, Inc., N.Y.C., 1973-76; v.p., gen. mgr. Citizens Utilities Co., Kingman, Ariz., 1976-85; chmn., pres., CEO Centex Telemgmt., Inc., San Francisco, 1985-94; founder, chmn., pres., CEO, Air Power Comm., Inc., San Francisco, 1995-96; chmn. Western Ventures, San Francisco, 1994-98; co-founder, chmn., past pres., past CEO IPWireless, Inc., San Bruno, Calif., 1998—. Former bd. dirs. NetMoves, Inc.; bd. dirs. Woodbridge, N.J., Exodus Comm., Inc., Santa Clara, Calif., Worldport Comms., Inc., Houston; mem. adv. bd. NASDAQ Corp., 1992-94. Contbr. to numerous profl. publs. Dir. The Ind. Inst.; founder Am. Bus. Conf. Found. Capt. USAF, 1962-65, 68-69. Recipient Outstanding Achievement award USAF. Mem. Am. Bus. Conf. Roman Catholic. Avocations: skiing, tennis, running, sailing. Office: 135 Third St San Rafael CA 94901 E-mail: pahowley@aol.com.

HOWLEY, PETER MAXWELL, pathology educator; b. New Brunswick, N.J., Oct. 9, 1946; s. Bartholomew Maxwell and Grace (Size) Howley; m. Ann Margaret McElwee, Aug. 23, 1969; children: Cristin, Megan, Maura. AB, Princeton U., 1968; M Med. Sci., Rutgers U., 1970; MD, Harvard U., 1972. Diplomate Am. Bd. Pathology. Intern Mass. Gen. Hosp., Boston, 1972—73; commd. lt. USPHS, 1973, advanced through grades to capt., 1985; rsch. assoc. NIH, Bethesda, Md., 1973—75; resident in pathology Nat. Cancer Inst., Bethesda, 1975—77, prin. investigator, 1977—84, lab. chief, 1984—93; ret., 1993; George Fabyan prof. comparative pathology, chmn. dept. Harvard Med. Sch., Boston, 1993—. Mem. sci. adv. bd. ONYX Pharm. Co., Richmond, Calif., 1992—97, Baxter Internat., Deerfield, Ill., 1995—, Enanta Pharm. Co., Cambridge, Mass., 1999—; chair Nat. Cancer Policy Bd., 1997—2000. Editor: The Molecular Basis of Cancer, 1996, 2nd edit., 2001, Fields Virology, 4th edit., 2001; contbr. over 220 articles to med. jours. Recipient Wallace P. Rowe award, Nat. Inst. Allergy and Infectious Diseases, 1986, Meritorious Svc. award, USPHS, 1989, Paul Ehrlich-Ludwig Darmstaedter prize, Govt. of Germany, 1994. Fellow: AAAS, Am. Acad. Microbiology; mem.: NAS, Am. Acad. Arts and Scis., Inst. Medicine. Achievements include patent for Recombinant DNA Process Utilizing Papillomavirus DNA as a Vector. Office: Harvard Medical Sch Bldg D2-Rm 629 200 Longwood Ave Boston MA 02115-5701 E-mail: peter_howley@hms.harvard.edu.

HOWORTH, DAVID, producer, director; b. N.Y.C., Aug. 30, 1941; s. Marion Beckett and Dorothy Huldah (Cowing) H.; m. Bea Borges, May 6, 1967. AA, Santa Barbara (Calif.) C.C., 1970; student, UCLA, 1977, Am. Film Inst., L.A., 1982. V.p., co-owner Golden Coast Films, Santa Barbara, 1971-82, owner, prodr., dir., 1982—. Software developer, prodr. Internet Career Vision, Wildlife/Nature series, 1993; prodr., dir. Careers: Nursing, 1993; co-prodr., co-writer (ednl. picture) Just Beer, 1983. With USMCR, 1960-65. Recipient awards Columbus Internat. Film/Video Festival, 1993, Nat. Mental Health Assn., 1981, Excellence-Suitable for Family Viewing, No. Calif. Motion Picture and TV Coun., 1975. Mem. NATAS, AMA (acad. med. films), Internat. Interactive Comms. Soc., Greater Santa Barbara Advt. Club (pres. 1972). Avocations: historical films, records, swimming, boating. Office: Golden Coast Films H102 2020 Alameda Padre Serra # H102 Santa Barbara CA 93103-1756

HOWORTH, DAVID BISHOP, lawyer; b. Temple, Tex., Feb. 6, 1947; s. Marion Beckett and Mary Hartwell (Bishop) H.; m. Martha Ellen Peacock, Aug. 29, 1970; children: Katherine Somerville, Emily Hartwell. BA, Yale U., 1971; JD, U. Miss., 1975. ar: N.Y. 1976, Oreg. 1990, Wash. 1996, Miss. 2000, U.S. Dist. Ct. (so. and ea. dists.) N.Y. 1977, U.S. Ct. Appeals (2d cir.) 1984, U.S. Dist. Ct. Oreg. 1990, U.S. Ct. Appeals (9th cir.) 1991. Assoc. Dewey Ballantine, N.Y.C., 1975-77, 78-83, ptnr., 1984-90; asst. prof. law U. Miss., University, 1977-78, vis. assoc. prof. law, 2000—. Mem. ABA, N.Y. State Bar Assn., Assn. Bar City of N.Y. Home: 1420 S 10th St Oxford MS 38655 Office: Sch Law U Miss University MS 38677 E-mail: dhoworth@olemiss.edu.

HOWREY, EUGENE PHILIP, economics educator, consultant; b. Geneva, Ill., Dec. 1, 1937; s. Eugene Edgar and Ellen Pauline (Boord) H.; children: Patricia Marie, Richard Philip, Margaret Ellen, Mark McCall. AB, Drake U., 1959; PhD, U. N.C., 1964; MA (hon.), U. Pa., 1972. Asst. prof. econs. Princeton U., N.J., 1963-69; assoc. prof. econs. U. Pa., Phila., 1969-73; prof. econs. U. Mich., Ann Arbor, 1973—, prof. stats., 1978—. Cons. Mathematica, Inc., Princeton, 1965-75; guest lectr. Inst. Advanced Studies, Vienna, 1974, 76. Contbr. articles to profl. jours. Research grantee NSF, 1975, 79, 84 Mem. Ann Arbor Velo Club, Ann Arbor Bicycle Touring Club (pres. 1979-80), Phi Beta Kappa. Democrat. Roman Catholic. Avocation: bicycling. Home: 2152 Overlook Ct Ann Arbor MI 48103-2336 Office: U Mich Dept Econs Ann Arbor MI 48109 E-mail: eph@umich.edu.

HOWSE, CATHY L. writer, researcher, entrepreneur; b. Murfreesboro, Tenn., Dec. 16, 1955; d. John Edd Sr. and Elmira Howse; children; Gregory Simpson Jr., Brandon J. BS, Met. State Coll., Denver, 1987. Author: Ultra Black Hair, 1990, 2000, Ultra Black Hair Growth II, 1994. Achievements include development of a method for hair growth and lengthening for black women. Office: UBH Publs Inc PO Box 22678 Denver CO 80222 E-mail: mail@ubhpublications.com.

HOWSE, JENNIFER LOUISE, foundation administrator; b. Glendale, Calif., Jan. 31, 1945; d. Benjamin McCausland and Patricia Louise (Naylor) H. PhD in Linguistics, Fla. State U., 1973; LHD (hon.), SUNY, Bklyn., 1990. Rsch. asst., instr. Inst. Human Devel. Coll. Edn., Fla. State U., Tallahassee, 1967-69; dir. planning and evaluation Wakulla County (Fla.) Sch. System, 1969-72; dir. NARC/HEW Liaison Project Nat. Assn. for Retarded Citizens, Govtl. Affairs Office, Washington, 1972-73; dir. Developmental Disabilities Bur., dir. Bur. Tech. Assistance and Regulation Fla. Dept. Health and Rehab. Svcs., Tallahassee, 1973-75; exec. dir. Willowbrook Rev. Panel, N.Y.C., 1975-78; assoc. commr. N.Y. State Office Mental Retardation and Developmental Disabilities, N.Y.C., 1978-80; state commr. for mental retardation Dept. Pub. Welfare, Harrisburg, Pa., 1980-85; exec. dir. Greater N.Y. chpt. March of Dimes Birth Defects Found., N.Y.C., 1985-89, pres. White Plains, N.Y., 1990—. Advisor Ctr. for Family Life in Sunset Park, Bklyn., 1992—. Bd. dirs. Salk Inst., La Jolla, Calif., Nat. Health Coun., Washington, Barrier Island Trust, Tallahassee; mem. Kaiser Commn. on Future of Medicaid, Balt., 1992—. Office: March Dimes Birth Defects Found 1275 Mamaroneck Ave White Plains NY 10605-5298

HOWSE, ROBERT LLOYD, law educator, consultant; b. Toronto, Ontario, Canada, Aug. 21, 1958; s. Hebert Lloyd Howse and Susan Gladys Winsor; m. Denyse Marie Laure Goulet, June 23, 1984. BA with high distinction, U. Toronto, 1980; LLB (hon.), U. Toronto Faculty of Law, 1989; LLM, Harvard Law Sch., 1990. Mem., policy planning secretariat Dept. External Affairs, Govt. of Can., Ottawa, 1983—84; 3rd, 2nd sec., polit. and econ. Embassy of Can., Belgrade, Yugoslavia, 1984—86; asst. prof., assoc. prof. law U. Toronto, 1990—99; prof. law U. Mich., Ann Arbor. Reporter law of world trade orgn. Am. Law Inst., Phila., 2002—; mem. editl. adv. bd. European Jour. Internat. Law, Florence, Italy, 2001—, Legal Issues Econ. Integration, Amsterdam, Netherlands, 2001—; mem. group ind. experts European Commn., Global Governance Project, DG Trade, Brussels, 2001—02; assoc. dir. Ctr. Study State and Market, 1995—98; mem. faculty, m.i.l.e. program World Trade Inst., Berne, Switzerland, 2000—; vis. prof. law Harvard Law Sch., Cambridge, Mass., 1989—89. Co-author: The Regulation of International Trade, 2nd edition, Restorative Justice: A Conceptual Framework; co-editor: The Federal Vision; co-translator Alexandre Kojeve Outline of a Phenomenology of Right. Pro bono legal cons. Nat. Wildlife Fedn., Washington, 2000—02; co-founder Can. for All Canadians Referendum NO Com., Ottawa, 1992—92. Fellow, C.D. Howe Inst., 2001—. Avocations: creative writing, weightlifting, dogs. Home: 11980 Bemis Rd Manchester MI 48158 Office: U Mich Law Sch Hutchins Hall #337 Ann Arbor MI 48109-1215 E-mail: rhowse@umich.edu.

HOWSER, RICHARD GLEN, lawyer; b. Tulsa, Apr. 5, 1951; s. Richard Glen and Mary Ann Howser; m. Judith Anne Howser, Sept. 1, 1986; children: Crystal, Benton, Elizabeth, Richard. BA, U. Ill., 1973; JD, Loyola U., 1977. Assoc. Clausen Miller P.C., Chgo., 1977-83, ptnr., 1983—, dir., 1992—, corp. sec., 1996—. Treas. Wilmette (Ill.) Luth. Ch., 1991-95, pres., 1995-96; area chmn. New Trier Republican Orgn., Kenilworth, Ill., 1992—. Mem. ABA, Soc. Trial Lawyers, Ill. State Bar Assn., Chgo. Bar Assn. Avocations: soccer coach, sunday school teacher, gardener, history buff, politics. Office: Clausen Miller PC 10 S Lasalle St Ste 1600 Chicago IL 60603-1098

HOWSON, AGNES WAGNER, health educator; b. Lebanon, Pa., May 9, 1940; d. Lester Frederick and Mary Elizabeth (Engle) Wagner; m. Robert Douglas Howson, Mar. 25, 1961; children: R. Douglas, Geoffrey F., Eric M., Stephen M. AS, Becker Jr. Coll., 1960; AA in Edn., Brookdale C.C., 1971, AAS in Nursing, 1975; BS in Human Svcs., Thomas A. Edison State Coll., N.J., 1988; MA in Edn., Georgian Ct. Coll., 1995; PhD in Natural Health, Clayton Coll., Birmingham, Ala., 1998. RN, N.J.; cert. health edn. specialist. Substitute sch. nurse Middletown Twp. (N.J.), 1976-82; staff nurse Riverview Hosp., Red Bank, NJ, 1977-78, 80-81; clinic supr., counselor Planned Parenthood of Monmouth County, Shrewsbury, NJ, 1978, 87; staff cmty. health nurse MCOSS Nursing Svcs., Red Bank, NJ, 1983-89; nurse health educator Family Health Resource Ctr. Riverview Med. Ctr., Red Bank, NJ, 1989-92; health educator Blue Cross/Blue Shield Health Ctr., Eatontown, NJ, 1994-95; RN, diabetes educator Wellness Ctr. Jersey Shore Med. Ctr., Neptune, NJ, 1996-97; adj. prof. health studies Monmouth U., West Long Branch, NJ, 1998—2000; nurse clinician dept. clin. nursing edn. Riverview Med. Ctr., Red Bank, NJ, 1999—. Mem. Am. Holistic Nurses Assn., Am. Assn. Health Educators. Home: 128 Bruce Rd Red Bank NJ 07701-5605

HOWSON, CHRISTOPHER PAUL, medical association administrator, epidemiologist; married; 1 child. BA in Anthropology and Sociology, Swarthmore Coll., 1971; MS in Epidemiology and Biostatistics, U. Okla., 1976; PhD in Epidemiology, UCLA, 1983. Rschr. Mass. Gen. Hosp., Boston, 1971-74; sr. rschr. rural emphysema screening project U. Okla., 1974-76; dir. hypertension detection and follow-up program UCLA, 1987-93; sr. epidemiologist nutrition and metabolic studies Mahoney Inst. for Health Maintenance, Am. Health Found., N.Y.C., 1983-86; sr. program officer Inst. Medicine, NAS, Washington, 1986-91; assoc. dir. bd. internat. health Inst. of Medicine, NAS, Washington, 1991—98, dir. bd. internat. health, 1998—; v.p. for global programs March of Dimes, White Plains, NY, 1998. Office: March of Dimes 1275 Mamaroneck Ave White Plains NY 10605-5298

HOWZE, JOSEPH LAWSON EDWARD, retired bishop; b. Daphne, Ala., Aug. 30, 1923; s. Albert Otis and Helen Artamesa (Lawson) H.. BS, Ala. State U., 1948; postgrad., Phillips Coll., Gulfport, Miss., 1980; LLD (hon.), U. Portland, 1974, St. Bonaventure U., 1977, Manhattan Coll., N.Y.C., 1979; HHD (hon.), Sacred Heart Coll., Belmont, N.C., 1977, Lift Bible Crusade Coll., 1987, Belmont Abbey Coll., 1999, Christ the King Sem., 2002. Ordained priest Roman Cath. Ch. Pastor chs., Charlotte, Southern Pines, Durham, Sanford, Asheville, NC, 1959—72; aux. bishop Diocese of Natchez-Jackson, Miss., 1972—73, bishop, 1973—77, Diocese of Biloxi, Miss., 1977—2001. Mem. Miss. Health Care Commn.; mem. adminstrv. bd., vacation com. NOCB/USCC; mem. edn. com. USCC, mem. social devel. and world peace com.; liaison com. to Nat. Office of Black Catholics NCCB; trustee Xavier U., New Orleans; bd. dirs. Biloxi Regional Med. Ctr. Recipient Star of the Sea award, U.S. Conf. Cath. Bishops, 2002. Mem.: Knights of St. Peter Claver, KC. Democrat. Roman Catholic. Home: Po Box 1189 Biloxi MS 39532-1189*

HOXIE, FREDERICK EUGENE, history educator; b. Hoolehua, Hawaii, Apr. 22, 1947; s. John Wadman and Catherine (Agee) H.; m. Elizabeth Anne Schroder, July 11, 1970 (dec. Dec. 1983); children: Silas, Charles; m. Holly Frances Hanscom, Jan. 3, 1986; stepchildren: Stephen Hoskins, Philip Hoskins. BA, Amherst Coll., 1969, PhD in Humane Letters (hon.), 1994; MA, Brandeis U., 1976, PhD, 1977; PhD in Humane Letters (hon.), L.I. U., 2000. Tchr. Phila. Pub. Schs., 1969-70; high sch. tchr. Punahou Sch., Honolulu, 1970-72; asst. prof. Antioch Coll., Yellow Springs, Ohio, 1977-82, assoc. prof., 1982-83; dir. D'Arcy McNickle Ctr. for Am. Indian History, Newberry Libr., Chgo., 1983-94, v.p. rsch. and edn., 1994-98; Swanlund prof. history U. Ill., Urbana, 1998—. Cons. Cheyenne River Sioux Tribe, Eagle Butte, S.D., 1977-78, U.S. Senate Com. on Indian Affairs, Washington, 1989-90, Little Big Horn Coll., Crow Agency, Mt., 1990-98, Nat. Park Svc., Denver Support Ctr., 1997-98, Dept. of Justice, 2000-01. Author: A Final Promise, 1984, 2d edit., 2001, Parading Through History, 1995; editor: Indians in American History, 1988, 2d edit., 1997, Ency. of North American Indians, 1996, Talking Back to Civilization, 2001. Bd. dirs. Ill. Humanities Coun., Chgo., 1997-2003; trustee Nat. Mus. Am. Indian, Smithsonian, 1990-95, Amherst Coll., 2001—. Humanities fellow Rockefeller Found., 1984-85, fellow NEH, 1990-91. Mem. Am. Hist. Assn. (program chmn. 1992), Am. Soc. for Ethnohistory (pres. 1995-96), Orgn. Am. Historians (exec. bd. 1997-2000). Avocations: running, tennis. Office: U Ill Dept History 309 Gregory Hall 810 S Wright St Urbana IL 61801-3644 E-mail: hoxie@uicu.edu.

HOXIE, RALPH GORDON, educational administrator, author; b. Waterloo, Iowa, Mar. 18, 1919; s. Charles Ray and Ada May (Little) H.; m. Louise Lobitz, Dec. 23, 1953 (dec. 1992); m. Ada B. Edgerton, June 21, 1997. BA, U. No. Iowa, 1940; MA, U. Wis., 1941; PhD, Columbia, 1950; LLD (hon.), Chung-ang U., 1965; LittD (hon.), D'Youville Coll., 1966; grad., Air War Coll., 1971; LHD (hon.), Gannon U., 1988, Wesley Coll., 1989, U. No. Iowa, 1990, Shepherd Coll., 1992, Teikyo Post U., 1994, Long Island U., 1995, Fitchburg State Coll., 1997. Roberts fellow Columbia, 1946-47, Roberts travelling fellow, 1947-48, asst. to provost, 1948-49; asst. prof. history, gen. editor Social Sci. Found.; asst. to chancellor U. Denver, 1950-53; project asso. Columbia Bicentennial History, 1953-54; dean Coll. Liberal Arts and Scis., L.I. U., 1954-55; acting dean C. W. Post Coll., 1954-55, dean, 1955-60, provost, 1960-62, pres., 1962-68; chancellor L.I. U., 1964-68, cons., 1968-69; pres. Center for Study of Presidency, 1969-95; chmn. Ctr. for Study of Presidency, 1995-96, pres., chmn. emeritus, 1997—. Pub. mem. Fgn. Svc. officer selection bd. U.S. Dept. State; vis. lectr. U. Ala., U. Calif., Irvine, Columbia U., U. Colo., Colo. State U., U. Wyo., Chapman Coll., U. No. Colo., Colo. Coll., Gannon U., Gettysburg Coll., Heidelberg Coll., U. Kans., Kans. State U., Muskingum Coll., Post Coll., St. Francis Coll. N.Y., USAF Acad., Naval War Coll., Nat. Archives, Nat. War Coll., Oglethorpe U., U. Genoa, Italy, U. Pitts., U. Tex., El Paso, U Wis., Northwestern U., U. No. Iowa; bd. govs. Banque Continentale br. Franklin Nat. Bank. Author: John W. Burgess, American Scholar, 1950, Command Decision and the Presidency, 1977, (with others) A History of The Faculty of Political Science, Columbia University, 1955, Organizing and Staffing the Presidency, 1980; editor: Frontiers for Freedom, 1952, The White House: Organization and Operations, 1971, The Presidency of the 1970's, 1973, The Presidency and Information Policy, 1981, The Presidency and National Security Policy, 1984 ; editor Presdl. Studies Quar., 1970-95; contbg. author: (with others) Freedom and Authority in Our Time, 1953, The Coattailess Landslide, 1974, Power and the Presidency, 1976, Classics of the American Presidency, 1980, The Blessings of Liberty, 1987, Popular Images of American Presidents, 1988, Rating Game in American Politics, 1988, Science and Technology Advice to the President, Congress, and Judiciary, 1988, The American Presidency: Historical and Contemporary Perspectives, 1988, Points of View, 1988, The Presidency in Transition, 1989, Dictionary of American History, 1996, Points of View, 1998, Moral Authority of Government, 1999; contbr. articles to profl. jours. and encys. Bd. dirs. United Fund L.I., Bklyn. Inst. Arts and Scis., Tibetan Found., L.I. Coun. Alcoholism, Bklyn. chpt. ARC Greater N.Y.; chmn., pres. bd. dirs. Am. Friends Chung-ang U.; pres. Pub. Mems. Assn. Fgn. Svc.; trustee Air Force Hist. Found., U. No. Iowa Found., Nat. Inst. Social Scis., Kosciuszko Found. N.Y., Mackinac Coll., North Shore chpt. Am. Assn. UN, Downtown Bklyn. Assn., Coun. Higher Ednl. Instns. N.Y.C.; mem. adv. bd. L.I. Air res. Ctr.; co-founder, mem. adv. coun. Robert A. Taft Inst. Govt.; sec. Nassau County Commn. on Govt. Revision; co-chmn. Nassau-Suffolk Conf. Christians and Jews; dir., pres. Great-N.Y. Coun. Fgn. Students; bd. govs. Human Resources Ctr., N.Y. Korean Vets. Meml. Commn. Served to capt. USAAF, 1942-46; brig. gen. USAF ret. Decorated Meritorious Svc. medal, Legion of Merit, Korean Cultural medal, numerous other medals; recipient Disting. Svc. medal City N.Y., 1965, Alumni Achievement award U. No. Iowa, 1965, Alumni Achievement award Columbia U., 1997, Columbia award for Disting. Achievment, 1997; named Man of Yr. Paderewski Found., 1966, Man of Yr. Eloy Alfaro Found., 1966. Fellow Am. Studies Assn. Met. N.Y.; mem. Am. Hist. Assn., Internat. Assn. Univ. Pres., Am. Polit. Sci. Assn., Acad. of Polit. Sci., Navy League, Air Force Assn., Res. Officers Assn. (pres. Mitchel chpt.), V.F.W., Am. Legion, L.I. Assn. (dir.), Am. Polar Soc., Kappa Delta Pi, Pi Gamma Mu, Alpha Sigma Lambda, Delta Sigma Pi, Gamma Theta Upsilon. Clubs: Century Assn., Met., Columbia Univ. Faculty House (N.Y.C.); Met. (Washington); Bklyn., Montauk (Bklyn.); Old Westbury Golf and Country and Mill River (hon.). Episcopalian. Home: PO Box 248 Oyster Bay NY 11771-0248 Office: PO Box 248 Oyster Bay NY 11771-0248 E-mail: rghoxie@aol.com. *Each day I seek to ask how I can better serve others. Assuredly, in so serving, ours will be the richest of dividends and life takes on an ever-fuller meaning.*

HOXIE, ROBERT PRYNNE, retired entomologist; b. St. Louis, Mar. 14, 1936; s. Robert Lee Hoxie and Helen Louise Hughes. BS in Agr., U. Ariz., 1961; MS in Entomology, Mich. State U., 1974. Cryptographer U.S. Dept. Def., Ft. Ord, Calif., 1964-67; biol. rsch. technician USDA, East Lansing, Mich., 1967-75, support scientist in entomology Agrl. Rsch. Svc., 1975-86; entomologist USDA Agrl. Rsch. Svcs., West Lafayette, Ind., 1986-90, weed scientist, safety officer, 1990-98, ret., 1999. Contbr. articles to sci. and profl. jours. Mem. Coleopterist Soc., N.Y. Entomol. Soc., Sigma Xi. Home: 8134 W 400 N West Lafayette IN 47906 E-mail: rph6@mindspring.com.

HOXTER, ALLEGRA BRANSON, radio news and freelance writer; b. Detroit, Jan. 2, 1934; d. Henry Clay and Anita (Coniglio) B.; m. Curtis Joseph Hoxter, Jan. 2, 1981. MusB, U. Mich., 1954; student, New Eng. Conservatory, 1954-55; MALS, U. Mich., 1958; student, Vienna (Austria) Acad. Music and Dramatic Arts, 1959-60. Fgn. corr. UPI, Vienna, 1960-64; editor, translator Austrian Consulate Gen., N.Y.C., 1965-67; writer, translator Curtis J. Hoxter, Inc., N.Y.C., 1967-68; radio, TV newswriter NBC, N.Y.C., 1968; radio news writer, editor Sta. WCBS, N.Y.C., 1968-96. N.Y. Corr. Birmingham (Eng.) Evening Mail, 1974-81. Co-author: (hist. novel) Frontiers Aflame, 1987. Mem. Writers Guild Am. East (pres. 1979-81, chmn. nat. council 1981-83), TV and Radio Working Press Assn. (sec. 1988-99). Avocations: classical music, cooking, cats. Home: 34 Broadfield Rd New Rochelle NY 10804-2102

HOXTER, CURTIS JOSEPH, international economic adviser, public relations and public affairs counselor; b. July 20, 1922; s. Jacob and Hanna (Katzenstein) Hoxter; m. Grace Lewis, Feb. 4, 1945 (dec.); children: Ronald Alan, Victoria Ann, Audrey Theresa(dec.); m. Allegra Branson, Jan. 2, 1981. AB, NYU, 1948, MA, 1950. Staff contbr. AUFBAU-Reconstn., N.Y.C., 1939-40; feature writer, reporter L.I. (N.Y.) Daily Press, 1940-42; editor, writer, analyst Office War Info., N.Y.C., 1943-45; pub. info. officer Dept. State, 1945-47; dir. pub. rels. Internat. C. of C., 1948-53; info. cons. (Marshall Plan), Econ. Cooperation Adminstrn., Washington, 1950-55; exec. v.p. George Peabody and Assocs., Inc., 1953-56; pvt. practice, 1956—. Pub. rels. cons. various cos., fin. instns. and govt. agys.; columnist Scripps-Howard Newspapers; adviser U.S. Com. for UN Day; editl. advisor Internat. Economy mag.; advisor on internat. econ. and fin. problems to global agys., U.S. Del. Disarmament Conf., London; mem. internat. adv. bd. Bus. Week Chief Exec. Roundtable; exec. dir. adv. com. to Chancellor of Austria; mem. adv. com. Grad. Sch. Internat. Rels., U. Calif., San Diego; sr. advisor to pres. European Commn. Contbr. and commentator articles to nat. mags. and newspapers. With AUS, World War II. Decorated Order of Merit of the Republic of Austria, 1991. Mem. Met. (N.Y.C.), Econ. Club N.Y., Leewood Country Club, Coral Beach and Tennis (Bermuda), Univ. Club (Washington). Office: 380 Lexington Ave New York NY 10168-0002 E-mail: hoxterinc@aol.com.

HOY, GEORGE PHILIP, clergyman, county official; b. Indpls., Feb. 5, 1937; s. Clarence Augustus Hoy and Margaret Louise (Etter) Wooley; m. Barbara J. Turpen, Aug. 11, 1957 (dec. Feb. 1987); 1 foster child, Richard H. Johnson children: Rene Hoy Riegle, Sherri Hoy Haas, Matthew Philip; m. Sandra L. Knipe, July 30, 1999; stepchildren: Wendy Knipe Bredhold, Benjamin Knipe. BA, Ky. Wesleyan Coll., 1958; MDiv, So. Bapt. Theol. Sem., Louisville, 1962. Ordained to ministry United Ch. of Christ, 1962, Nat. Bapt. Conv. 1997. Pastor Union United Ch. of Christ, Evansville, Ind., 1962-72, Faith United Ch. of Christ, Ft. Wayne, Ind., 1975-80, St. Matthew's United Ch. of Christ, Evansville, 1981-87; dir. Youth Svc. Bur., Evansville, 1972—75; pastor St. Peter's United Ch. of Christ, Evansville, 1987—94; interim pastor Zion United Ch. of Christ, Henderson, Ky., 2003. Mem. faculty Brescia U., Owensboro, Ky., 1970-72; chaplain Evansville State Hosp., 1966-72, Fraternal Order Police, Evansville, 1982-92, chaplain, life mem.; dir. Tri-State Food Bank, Evansville, 1987-2000, ret. 2000; del. gen. synod Ind.-Ky. Conf., United Ch. of Christ, 1978-81; bd. dir. Vanderburgh County Cmty. Corrections. Religion columnist Evansville Press, 1983-93. Vol. Habitat for Humanity, Americus, Ga., 1980-81; active City-County Human Rels. Commn., Evansville, 1984-93; bd. dirs. Leadership Evansville, 1987-92, Outreach Ministries, Evansville, 1987-93; regional bd. adv. Ch. World Svc., 1987-2002; mem. Bread for the World, Amnesty Internat., Police Athletic League; active Vanderburgh County Coun., 1992—, pres., 1994-95, v.p., 1997; v.p. Vanderburgh County Coun., 1997; chmn. Vanderburgh County Soil and Water Conservation Dist.; chair fin. Pigeon Creek Greenway; chmn. hunger walk CROP; bd. dirs. Sustainable Evansville, Harvesting Inner City Ministries; pres. Evansville Area Cmty. Chs., chmn. Pastoral Rels.; Com. 1st Ebenezer Bapt.; city county data bd., preservation com., Old Liberty Bapt. Ch. Recipient Doing The Right Thing award, Evansville Psyc. Children's Ctr., 2002, ecumenical award Evansville Area Coun. of Chs., 1987, Native Am. award Coun. of Bear, Evansville, 1988, Individual Achievement award Leadership Evansville, 1998, Martin Luther King Jr. Cmty. Svc. award Black Leadership Conf., 2000, Starfish award Tri-State Food Bank, 2000, award for outstanding svc. to foster parents, Sagamore of the Wabash award, 2000, others; named to CROP Honor Roll, 1997, Hon. Order Ky. Cols., Hall of Fame, Ctrl. H.S., 2001. Mem. NAACP, ACLU, Internat. Brotherhood Magicians, Ind. Psychol. Assn., Tri-State Pastors Circle (pres. 1984-85), Northside Ministerial Assn., Interdenominational Ministers Alliance, Downtown Ministerial Assn., Evansville Tri-State Assn. (pres. 1972-75), Greenpeace, Silent Singers (hon.), Democrat. Avocations: music, art, drama, dance performing, model railroading. Home: 217 Cherry St Evansville IN 47713-1242 E-mail: revgph@aol.com.

HOY, HAROLD JOSEPH, marketing educator, retail executive, writer, military officer, editor, management consultant; b. Pine Grove, Pa., Jan. 10; s. Harold Jefferson and Naomi E. H.; m. Z. Jane Brown, July 2, 1960; children: Kathryn Burgess, Elisabeth Wermuth, Suzanne Hoy-Wong, Kristen Shugrue. BS, Pa. State U., 1955; MBA, U. Hartford, 1973, postgrad., U. Conn., 1981, Harvard U., 1986, Pa. State U., 1990, U. London, 2003. Gen. mgr. Montgomery Ward & Co., Chgo., 1963-67, D & L Stores, New Britain, Conn., 1967-81; prof. mktg. Ctrl. Conn. State U., New Britain, 1974-79; prof. U. Conn., Storrs, 1977-79; prof. mktg. and mgmt., faculty coun., grad. faculty Pa. State U., 1979-91; prof. Elizabethtown (Pa.) Coll., 1992—93; pres. H.J. Hoy Assocs. Mgmt. Cons., Pine Grove, Pa., 1979-99; mem. Woodrow Wilson Inst. Internat. Scholars, Washington, 1994-95. Founder, dir. Pa. State U. Small Bus. Devel. Ctr.; dir. U.S. Small Bus. Inst., Pa. State U., Harrisburg; dir. internat. rsch. scholars Harvard U., 1997; mem. Pa. State White House Conf. on Small Bus. and Fed. White House Conf. on Small Bus., Washington, 1987, CATO Inst., Washington, 2003. Author, editl. reviewer coll. book pubs. and acad. mgmt. and mktg. jours; contbr. articles to profl. jours, including Columbia U. Jour. of World Business. Eagle Scout, Boy Scouts Am.; Capt. 1st co. Gov.'s Foot Guard Ct. Army N.G., Hartford, Conn. 1st lt. Fin. Corps, U.S. Army; capt. Continental Army Command. Named Wisdom Hall of Fame fellow, 1997. Mem. Am. Mktg. Assn., Acad. Mktg. Sci., Acad. Internat. Bus., Internat. Coun. for Small Bus., Nature Conservancy, Masons (32 deg.), Nat. Sojourners, Royal Arch, Knights Templar, Sierra Club. Avocations: photography, international business research, philately.

HOY, MARJORIE ANN, entomology educator; b. Kansas City, Kans., May 19, 1941; d. Dayton J. and Marjorie Jean (Acker) Wolf; m. James B. Hoy; 1 child, Benjamin Lee AB, U. Kans., 1963; MS, U. Calif., Berkeley, 1966, PhD, 1972. Asst. entomologist Conn. Agrl. Expt. Sta., New Haven, 1973-75; rsch. entomologist U.S. Forest Svc., Hamden, Conn., 1975-76; asst. prof. entomology U. Calif., Berkeley, 1976-80, assoc. prof. entomology, 1980-82, prof. entomology, 1982-92, prof. emeritus, 1992—; Fischer, Davies and Eckes prof., dept. entomology and nematology U. Fla., Gainesville, 1992—; chmn. Calif. Gypsy Moth Sci. Adv. Panel, 1982—; mem. genetics resources adv. com. USDA, 1992—, mem. adv. com. agrl. biotech., 2000—02; mem. com. on biol. threats to agrl. plants and animals NRC and NAS, 2001—02; F.E. Guyton disting. lectr. Auburn (Ala.) U., 1997. Chmn. Calif. Gypsy Moth Sci. Adv. Panel, 1982—; mem. genetics resources adv. com. USDA, 1992—, mem. adv. com. agrl. biotech., 2000—01; F.E. Guyton disting. lectr. Auburn (Ala.) U., 1997; mem. com. on biol. threats to agrl. plants and animals NRC and NAS, 2001—02. Editor, co-editor: Genetics in Relation to Insect Managment, 1979, Recent Advances in Knowledge of the Phytoseiidae, 1982, Biological Control of Pests by Mites, 1983, Biological Control in Agricultural IPM Systems, 1985, Insect Molecular Genetics, 1994, 2d edit., 2003, The Phytoseiidae as Biological Control Agents of Pest Mites and Insects: A Bibliography, 1996, Managing the Citrus Leafminer, 1996; mem. editorial bd. Exptl. and Applied Acarology, Biol. Control, Biocontrol Sci. and Tech., Environ. Biosafety Rsch.; contbr. articles to profl. jours. Mem. Sec. Agrl.'s adv. com. agrl. biotechnology; cons. Pew Charitable Trust. Recipient citation for outstanding achievments in regulatory entomology Fla. Divsn. Plant Industry, 1995, USDA honor award Sec. of Agr., 1996, award for sci. Nat. Agri-Mktg. Assn., 1998, sr. faculty award U. Fla. chpt. Gamma Sigma Delta, 1998. Fellow AAAS, Royal Entomol. Soc. London, Entomol. Soc. Am. (mem. Pacific br. governing bd. 1985, Bussart award 1986, Founder's Meml. award 1992); mem. Nat. Acad. Scis. (com. on biol. threats to agr. plants and animals), NY Acad. Scis., Am. Genetic Assn., Internat. Orgn. Biol. Control (v.p. 1984-85), Am. Inst. Biol. Scis. (adv. coun. 1996-98, governing bd. 1999-2001), Acarological Soc. Am. (governing bd. 1980-84, pres. 1992), Soc. for Study of Evolution, Fla. Entomological Soc. (Team Rsch. award 1997, Outstanding Tchg. award 1999), Phi Beta Kappa, Sigma Xi (chpt. sec. 1979-81, Sr. Faculty Rsch. award 1996). Avocations: hiking, gardening, snorkeling. Home: 4320 SW 83rd Way Gainesville FL 32608-4131 Office: U Fla Dept Entomology and Nematology PO Box 110620 Gainesville FL 32611-0620 E-mail: mahoy@mail.ifas.ufl.edu.

HOYE, ROBERT EARL, systems science educator; b. Warwick, R.I., Jan. 12, 1931; s. S. Earl and Alice (Landry) H.; m. Patricia Buswell, Aug. 20, 1955 (dec. May 22, 2002); children: Robert Earl Jr., Joanne D., Peter M., Kathleen B. BA, Providence Coll., 1953; MS, St. John's U., N.Y.C., 1955; PhD, U. Wis., Madison, 1973. Instr. St. John's U., 1953-55; dir. guidance Middleboro (Mass.) Pub. Schs., 1955-56, Rutland (Vt.) Pub. Schs., 1956-57; dean Champlain (Vt.) Coll., 1957-58; supt. Frontier Regional Sch. Dist., Deerfield, Mass., 1958-60; New Eng. dir. Sci. Rsch. Assocs. subs. IBM, Chgo., 1960-65; nat. dir. Learning Systems div. Xerox Corp., N.Y.C., 1965-66; dir. Instrnl. Media Lab. U. Wis., Milw., 1966-73; asst. v.p. U. Louisville, 1974-81, prof. cmty. health Sch. Medicine, 1981-92, prof. urban policy, coord. grad. program in health systems, 1981-95, prof. edn., 1992-95, prof. emeritus, 1995—. Cons. to mgmt., Louisville, 1966—; mem. faculty health svcs. Walden U., 1988—, vis. prof. exec. leadership U. Sarasota, 1995-2001 Author: Index to Computer Based Learning, 1973; co-author: Home Health, 1996; editor Edn. Jour., 1968-73; also articles. Recipient cert. of merit San Diego State U., 1983, Grad. Teaching Excellence award U. Louisville, 1984, gold medal Project Innovation, 1984, Outstanding Faculty Mem. award Walden U., 2000. Fellow Am. Acad. Med. Adminstrs. (diplomate, chmn. editl. bd. 1986-94), Royal Soc. Health (Statesman in Healthcare Adminstrn. award 1992). Democrat. Roman Catholic. Home: 2238 Wynnewood Cir Louisville KY 40222-6342 E-mail: rhoye@waldenu.edu.

HOYER, LEON WILLIAM, physician, educator; b. Mpls., Mar. 6, 1936; s. Ludolf J. and Inez (Fuglesteen) H.; m. Diane Desmond Lawrence, Dec. 30, 1960 (dec. Aug. 2002); children: Helen Kristin, Sharon Anne, Erik William. AB, Harvard U., 1958; MD, U. Minn., 1962. Diplomate Am. Bd. Internal Medicine, Nat. Bd. Med. Examiners. Intern and asst. resident in medicine Presbyn. Hosp., N.Y.C., 1962-64; assoc. resident in medicine, fellow in hematology, asst. prof. medicine Strong Meml. Hosp.-U. Rochester Med. Ctr., 1966-70; prof. medicine, head hematology div. U. Conn. Sch. Medicine, Farmington, 1970-85; v.p. rsch. Holland Lab., ARC Biomed. Svcs., Rockville, Md., 1985-2000; adj. prof. genetics George Washington U., Washington, 1988-2000, prof. medicine, 1995-2000; mem. bd. supervisory dirs. Pharming NV, 2001. Chmn. med. and sci. adv. com. Nat. Hemophilia Found., N.Y.C., 1982-85; mem. hematology study sect. NIH, Bethesda, Md., 1976-80, 87-91. Editor: Factor VIII Inhibitors, 1984, Recombinant Technology in Hemostasis and Thrombosis, 1991, Inhibitors to Coagulation Factors, 1995; contbr. numerous articles and revs. to profl. publs., chpts. to books. J. Macy Found. faculty scholar, 1978-79, Murry Thelin Rsch. award Nat. Hemophilia Found., 1981, grantee Nat. Heart, Lung and Blood Inst., 1968-2000. Fellow ACP; mem. Am. Soc. Hematology (chair publs. com. 1990-96, councillor 1996-98), Am. Soc. Clin. Investigation, Internat. Soc. Thrombosis and Hemostasis (sci. and standardization com. 1985-90, v.p. XVIIth congress Washington 1999). Achievements include establishment and expansion of largest blood research institute in U.S.; research on the nature of hemophilia and Von Willebrand's disease. Home: 2014 Quay Village Ct Apt 202 Annapolis MD 21403-5228 E-mail: lhoyer@aol.com.

HOYER, MARY LOUISE, social worker, educator; b. Wausau, Wis., Dec. 4, 1925; d. Jacob and Julia (Anderson) Stuhlfauth; m. William Henriksen Hoyer, June 30, 1948; children: Mark Charles, Gail Maren. BS in Biochemistry, U. Minn., 1948; MSW, Cath. U., 1985, D of Clin. Social Work, 1994. Lic. cert. clin. social worker, Md.; bd. cert. diplomate in clin. social work. Rsch. biochemist NIH, Bethesda, Md., 1948-50; dir. Teller Tng. Ctr. Internat. Telephone and Telegraph, Washington, 1967-69; specialist employee devel. Civil Svc. Commn., Washington, 1969-75, supr. sys. sect., 1975-78; mgr. agy. assistance divsn. Office Pers. Mgmt., Washington, 1978-82; vol. counselor Comty. Crisis Ctr., Bethesda, 1980-82; classroom and field instr. Cath. U., Washington, 1986-91; clin. social worker St. Francis Ctr., Washington, 1985-88; pvt. practice as clin. social worker Bethesda, 1987—. Dep. exec. dir. task force on exec. devel. in sr. exec. svc.: Policy Initiatives for Reform of Civil Svc., Office of Pers. Mgmt., Washington, 1978-79. Contbr. rsch. articles to profl. jours. Precinct chairperson Dem. Action Group, Bethesda, 1962-66; fin. cons. Sch. Bd., Hamilton, Mont., 1950-54; cons. Internat. Visitors Info. Svc., Washington, 1962-66; vol. Md. Fair Housing, Bethesda, 1962-66. Legis. fellow U.S. Congress, Washington, 1980. Mem. NASW, Greater Washington Soc. Clin. Social Workers. Democrat. Lutheran. Home and Office: 5901 Lone Oak Dr Bethesda MD 20814-1845

HOYER, STENY HAMILTON, congressman; b. N.Y.C., June 14, 1939; s. Steen T. and Jean Baldwin (Slade) H.; m. Judith Elaine Pickett, June 17, 1961 (dec. Feb. 1997); children: Susan, Stefany, Anne. BS, U. Md., 1963; LLB, Georgetown U., 1966. Bar: Md. 1966. Exec. asst. to U.S. senator, 1962-66; mem. Haislip & Yewell, Marlow Heights, Md., 1966-69, Hoyer & Fannon, District Heights, Md., 1969-81; pvt. practice, 1981-89; mem. U.S. Congress from 5th Md. dist., 1981—; mem. appropriations com.; co-chmn. House Dem. steering com., 1989-94; ranking mem. Commn. on Security and Coop. in Europe; ranking mem. HAC. Mem. Md. Senate, 1966-78, pres., 1975-78, chmn. Prince George's County del., mem. fin., joint budget and audit coms., 1968, chmn. joint commn. on intergovtl. cooperation, 1971. Mem. Md. Bd. Higher Edn., 1978-81; mem. Balt. Council Fgn. Relations; bd. visitors U. Md. Sch. Pub. Affairs Mem. U. Md. Alumni Assn. (trustee), Phi Sigma Alpha, Omicron Delta Kappa, Delta Theta Phi, Sigma Chi. Democrat. Home: 40740 Parlett Morgan Rd Mechanicsville MD 20659-4708 Office: US House of Reps 1705 Longworth Hob Washington DC 20515-0001*

HOYERT, MARK SUDLOW, psychology educator; b. Coll. Pk., Md., July 14, 1959; s. John H. and E. Louise Hoyert; m. Cynthia Hoyert, June 10, 1991; children: Matthew, Shelby. BA in history, U. MD, 1982, BS in psychology, 1981; MA in psychology, Emory U., 1985, PhD in psychology, 1988. Prof. of psychology Ind. U. N.W., Gary, 1988—. Office: Ind U N W Psychology Dept Gary IN 46408

HOYLE, LAWRENCE TRUMAN, JR., lawyer; b. Greensboro, N.C., Oct. 6, 1938; s. Lawrence Truman and Martha Parks (Lane) H.; m. Molly Hoyle, Oct.1993; children: Eric L., Alison D. AB in History, Duke U., 1960; JD, U. Chgo., 1965. Bar: Pa. 1965, U.S. Dist. Ct. (ea. dist.) Pa. 1966, U.S. Ct. Appeals (3d cir.) 1966, U.S. Dist. Ct. (no. dist.) Miss. 1968, U.S. Supreme Ct. 1970, U.S. Ct. Appeals (4th, 5th and 11th cirs.) 1984, U.S. Ct. Appeals (D.C. cir.) 1988, U.S. Ct. Appeals (6th cir.) 2001. Assoc. Schnader, Harrison, Segal & Lewis, Phila., 1965-71; dep. atty. gen., chief civil litigation divsn. Pa. Dept. Justice, Harrisburg, Pa., 1971-72; exec. dir. Pa. Crime Commn., Harrisburg, Pa., 1972-74; ptnr. Schnader, Harrison, Segal & Lewis, Phila., 1974-85, Hoyle, Morris & Kerr LLP, Phila., 1985—2002, Hoyle, Fickler, Herschel, & Mathes LLP, 2003—. Lectr. Sch. Law, Temple U., 1969-71; mem. vis. com. Law Sch., U. Chgo., 1975-77, 88-90, 96-98, 2000-01; mem. nominating com. Pa. Appellate Ct., 1979-86; mem. Pa. Jud. Inquiry Rev. Bd., 1988-90. Bd. vis. Duke U. Trinity, 1992-99; bd. dirs. The Lighthouse, Phila., 1968-77, United Communities of S.E. Phila., 1983-86, Pub. Interest Law Ctr., Phila., 1976-2002, Fox Chase Cancer Ctr., 1992—; vol. atty. Lawyers' Com. for Civil Rights Under the Law, 1968; trustee Acad. Natural Scis., 1998—. Fellow Am. Bar Found., Am. Coll. Trial Lawyers (chair complex litigation com. 2000-03; mem. ABA, Pa. Bar Assn., Phila. Bar Assn., Racquet Club Phila., Blooming Grove Hunting and Fishing Club. Democrat. Home: 404 Spruce St Philadelphia PA 19106-4216 Office: Hoyle Fickler Herschel & Mathes 1 S Broad St Ste 1500 Philadelphia PA 19107 E-mail: lhoyle@hoylelawfirm.com.

HOYLE, WILLIAM VINTON, JR., lawyer; b. Newport News, Va., Apr. 8, 1949; s. William Vinton and Nancy Nelson (Granberry) H.; children: Tiffany Lynn, Suzanne Michelle. BA, Coll. of William and Mary, 1972; JD, U. Richmond, 1982; postgrad. in internat. law, Cambridge U., Eng., 1979. Bar: Va. 1982, U.S. Dist. Ct. (ea. and we. dists.) Va. 1982, U.S. Ct. Appeals (4th cir.) 1982, U.S. Supreme Ct. 1987. Journalist Newport News (Va.) Daily Press, Norfolk Virginian-Pilot, Richmond Times-Dispatch, 1970-79; ptnr. Hoyle, Corbett, Hubbard & Smith, Newport News, 1982-88, Hoyle & Allen, P.C., Newport News, 1989-91; pvt. practice Newport News, 1991—. Frequent planner, author, editor, lectr. Va. State Bar profl. seminars. Co-editor, contbg. author: Employment Law in Virginia, 1997—. Bd. dirs. Peninsula Legal Aid Ctr., Inc., 1990-2000. Mem. Assn. Trial Lawyers Am., Va. Trial Lawyers Assn., Va. Bar Assn., Va. State Bar, Newport News Bar Assn., Nat. Employment Lawyers Assn. Avocations: sailing, travel, writing.

HOYNES, LOUIS LENOIR, JR., lawyer; b. Indpls., Sept. 23, 1935; s. Louis L. and Catharine (Parker) H.; m. Judith E. Kass, Oct. 12, 1958 (div. 1979); children: Thomas M., William D., Ellen B.; m. Virginia Devin, Dec. 9, 1979. AB, Columbia U., 1957; JD cum laude, Harvard U., 1962. Bar: N.Y. 1963, U.S. Supreme Ct. 1967, U.S. Dist. Ct. (so. dist.) N.Y., U.S. Ct. Appeals (2d, 7th and 9th cirs.). Assoc. Willkie Farr & Gallagher, N.Y.C., 1962-68, ptnr., 1969-90; counsel Nat. League Profl. Baseball Clubs, 1970-90; sr. v.p., gen. counsel Wyeth (formerly) Am. Home Products Corp., 1990-2000; exec. v.p. gen. counsel Am. Home Products Corp. (now Wyeth), 2000—. Lectr. law Columbia U., N.Y.C., 1982-91; bd. dirs. Cytec Industries Inc.; trustee Food and Drug Law Inst., 1994-2002. Served to lt. USNR, 1957-59, PTO. Mem. ABA, N.Y. State Bar Assn., Assn. of City of Bar of N.Y., The Assn. Gen. Counsel. Home: 47 Cornwells Beach Rd Sands Point NY 11050-1305

HOYNG, PETER, humanities educator; b. Raesfeld, Westphalia, Germany, Mar. 5, 1960; s. Werner and Franziska Hoyng; m. Caroline Molina Y Vedia, June 14, 1988 (div. Aug. 1994). BA, U. Siegen, Germany, 1988; PhD, U. Wis., 1994. Mem. faculty U. Tenn., Knoxville, 1994—, chair German program, 1999—2002. Editor: On George Taboris Theater Works. Mem.: AAUP (pres. Knoxville 2001—02). Office: U Tenn 701 McClung Tower Knoxville TN 37996 Office Fax: 865-974-7096. E-mail: hoeyng@utk.edu.

HOYT, CHARLEE VAN CLEVE, gmanagement executive; b. Bluefield, W.Va., May 21, 1936; d. Charles Ives Van Cleve and Kathryn Margarete (Harden) Perrow; m. Ronald Reiner Hoyt, 1959 (div. 1983); children: Dean Christopher, Jason Allen. BA in Edn., U. Fla., 1959, MEd, 1962, postgrad., 1963-64. Cert. spl. edn. tchr. Tchr. Amherst County Schs., Elon, Va., 1958; tchr. spl. edn. Marion County Schs., Ocala, Fla., 1959-61; counselor Univ. Counseling Ctr., Gainesville, Fla., 1962-63, Sunland Tng. Ctr., Gainesville, 1963; mem. community faculty Minn. Met. State Coll., Mpls., 1972-83; mem. council City of Mpls., 1975-86; ptnr. Van Cleve Assocs., 1980-87, 91—; pres. Van Cleve, Doran & Bruno, Inc. 1987-91; corp. officer BAM Leasing Co., Inc., 1987-97; dir. human resources Pascua Yagu Tribe, 1988-95; adj. faculty U. Phoenix, Tucson, 1995—2002; vis. tchr. Tucson Unified Sch. Dist., 1995—2002; pres. Van Cleve Assocs., 1991—; bus. mgr. An Actor's Studio, 1996-98; mem. faculty Govt. Tng. Service, St. Paul, 1978-86, Ariz. Govt. Tng. Services; pres. Minn. Women in City Govt., St. Paul, 1978-79; mem. Met. Land Use Adv. Bd., St. Paul, 1978-83; bd. dirs. Transp. Adv. Bd., St. Paul, 1979-81; mem. conf. faculty League of Minn. Cities, St. Paul, 1979-82; bd. dirs. Met. Council Criminal Justice Adv. Bd., St. Paul, 1979-82; pres. Women in Mcpl. Govt., Nat. League of Cities, Washington, 1980-81, founder minority caucus coalition, 1982, dir., 1982-84; curriculum cons. Nat. Women's Edn. Fund, Washington, trainer, 1982-86; officer JTPA Grantee Orgn. Region IX, 1994—; commr. Pima County/Tuscon Women's Commn. Presenter numerous workshops; contbr. articles to profl. jours. Mem. Women Helping Women YWCA, 1987—; various offices with Republican Party, Minn., 1970-86 ; pres. Burroughs Elem. Sch. PTA, Mpls., 1973-74; panelist White House Conf., 1981; chmn. Senator Durenburger's Task Force on Women's Issues, Mpls., 1981-84; bd. dirs. Nat. Conf. Rep. Mayors and Council Mems., 1984-85; mem. Senator Durenburger's Intergovtl. Relations Adv. Com., Mpls., 1984-86; bd. dirs. Twin Cities Internat. Program, Mpls., 1983-86; participant Women's Dialogue US/USSR, Moscow, 1985; trustee Council Internat. Programs, Cleve., 1985-90; bd. dirs. At the Foot of the Mountain Theater, Mpls., 1985-86, Tucson Ctrs. for Women and Children, 1988-92; bd. dirs. GOP Feminists, Hamline U. Ctr. for Women in Govt.; mem. Nat. Women's Polit. Caucus, Hennepin County Women's Polit. Caucus; mem. Tucson Support for Success Team, 1986-92, Tuscon YWCA Women Helping Women; bd. dirs. Tucson Ctrs. Women and Children. Mem. Am. Soc. Training and Devel., Minn. Women Elected Ofcls. (pres. 1983-85), Izaak Walton League, Tucson C. of C. Methodist. Club: Remington Investment (pres. 1968-70) (Mpls.). Avocations: lapidary, music, handwork, camping, science fiction. Home: 6932 E 2nd St Tucson AZ 85710-1222

HOYT, CHARLES KING, architect, editor; b. Lakehurst, N.J., Apr. 23, 1938; s. Charles Freeland Hoyt and Maude Leslie King. BArch, U. Pa., 1961. Registered arch., N.Y., Conn. Arch. Harrison & Abromovitz, N.Y.C., 1963-66, Edward Larrabee Barnes, N.Y.C., 1966-69; archtl. dir. N.Y. State Urban Devel. Corp., N.Y.C., 1969-72; sr. editor Archtl. Record, 1972-97; pvt. practice house design and renovation Lyme, Conn., 1997—. Author: Buildings for Commerce and Industry, 1978, Public, Municipal and Community Buildings, 1980, Interior Spaces Designed by Architects, 1981, Cities, 1982, More Places for People, 1983; contbr. articles to profl. jours., encys. Fellow AIA (past chair Haskell awards com., N.Y.C. chpt. hist. bldgs. com.); mem. Soc. Archtl. Historians, Nat. Trust, Nature Conservancy. Republican. Home and Office: 484 Joshuatown Rd Lyme CT 06371-3034 E-mail: lymey1@usa.comm.

HOYT, CLARK FREELAND, journalist, newspaper editor; b. Providence, Nov. 20, 1942; s. Charles Freeland and Maude Leslie (King) H.; m. Jane Ann Hauser, Sept. 30, 1967 (div. Jan. 1978); m. Linda Kauss, Aug. 22, 1988. AB, Columbia Coll., 1964. Research asst. to U.S. Senator, Washington, 1964-66; reporter Lakeland (Fla.) Ledger, 1966-68; politics writer Detroit Free Press, 1968-70; Washington corr. Miami Herald, 1970-73; nat. corr. Knight Newspapers, Washington, 1973-75, news editor Washington bur., 1975-77; bus. editor Detroit Free Press, 1977-79, conv. editor, 1979-80, asst. to exec. editor, 1980-81; mng. editor Wichita Eagle-Beacon, Kans., 1981-85; news editor Washington Bur., Knight-Ridder Newspapers, 1985-87, bur. chief, 1987-93, v.p. news, 1993-99, Washington editor, 1999—. Recipient Pulitzer prize nat. reporting, 1973. Mem. Nat. Press Club (fin. sec., bd. govs, 1975), Gridiron Club. Home: 655 Mine Ridge Rd Great Falls VA 22066-2704 Office: 700 National Press Building Washington DC 20045-1701

HOYT, COLEMAN WILLIAMS, postal consultant; b. N.Y.C., Nov. 11, 1925; s. Colgate and Muriel (Williams) H.; m. Cecilia Lucia Guarana, Oct. 21, 1972; children: Coleman Williams, Andrew Erskine, Stephen Tecumseh. B of Naval Sci., Tufts U., 1945; BS, Yale U., 1948. With Reader's Digest Assn., Pleasantville, N.Y., 1948-87, mgr. book prodn., 1950-61, mgr. book subscription svc., 1961-63, mgr. subscription svc. RCA Victor Record Club, 1963-65, mgr. corp. distbn., 1965-76, v.p., dir. distbn., 1976-87; pvt. practice cons. Woodstock, Vt., 1987—. Mem. Postmaster Gen.'s Mailers Tech. Adv. Com., 1968—, chmn., 1971-73. Pub. mem. USIA inspection team, Lebanon, 1971; nat. trustee Outward Bound, Inc., 1972-88; trustee Vt. Land Trust, 1988-93, vice chmn., 1989-92; mem. dir. coun. Nat. Postal Mus., Smithsonian, Washington, 1995—. Ensign USNR, 1943-46. Recipient Disting. Svc. award U.S. Postal Svc., 1973, Donald Mumma award Graphics Comm. Assn., 1987, Miles Kimball award Mail Advt. Svc. Assn., 1987. Mem. Mag. Pubs. Assn. (chmn. postal com. 1974-80), Direct Mktg. Assn. (bd. dirs. 1973-79, chmn. govt. affairs com. 1983-86), Pub. Mems. Assn. of Fgn. Svc., Assn. Postal Commerce (bd. dirs. 1982—), Continuity Shippers Assn. (exec. dir. 1997—), Yale Club of N.Y., Squadron A Club, Lakota Club. Republican. Episcopalian. Home and Office: Saddlebow Farm 2351 N Bridgewater Rd Woodstock VT 05091-9670

HOYT, EARL EDWARD, JR., industrial designer; b. Binghamton, N.Y., July 16, 1936; s. Earl Edward and Lea (LaRue) H.; m. Bernice Phillips Maseritz, Aug. 20, 1960; children: Earl Edward III, Justin Phillips. B with honors in Indsl. Design, Pratt Inst., 1960. Designer Donald Deskey Assocs., N.Y.C., 1960-65; pres. The Hoyt Group Inc., Stone Ridge, N.Y., 1965—. Instr. Sch. Visual Arts, N.Y.C., Pratt Inst., Rutgers Sch. Package Engring.; lectr. in field. Awarded more than 85 patents in field. Served with U.S. Army, 1954-56. Recipient awards archtl. design concept Am. Inst. Architects, 1964, Package Yr. Package Design Mag., 1970, Grand/Excellence in Design and Quality Soc. Plastic Industy, 1972, design Am. Inst. Graphic Artists Competition, 1st prize splty. design innovation-1st prize household products-1st prize communication excellence N.J. chpt. Packaging Inst. USA, 1979, package yr. Food and Drug Packaging Mag., 1978, 80, Jupiter Engring. excellence in design Western Plastics Exposition, 1980, package design excellence Clio, 1978, 81, 87, outstanding packaging achievement N.J. Packaging Execs. Club, 1982, 83, 86 (best of show/package yr.). Mem. Indsl. Designers Soc. Am. Republican. Avocations: watercolor artist, skiing, fishing, outdoor activities, guitar. Home: 24 Woodland Rd Stone Ridge NY 12484-5514 Office: The Hoyt Group Inc PO Box 928 Woodstock NY 12498-0928 Fax: (845) 657-6024.

HOYT, HERBERT AUSTIN AIKIN, television producer; b. Buffalo, June 20, 1937; s. John Davidson Hill and Amie Dean (Aikins) Hoyt. BA, Yale Univ., 1959. Reporter Niagara Falls Gazette, NY, 1963-64; prodr., exec. prodr. WGBH Ednl. Found., Boston, 1965—2003; with Austin Hoyt Prodns., 2003—. Prodr. TV programs including The Advocates, 1969-74; Enterprise: The Wildcatter, 1981; Vietnam: A Television History, Tet 1968; L.B.J. Goes to War, 1964-65, (Emmy, Writers Guild of Am. awards); Reagan's New Federalism: Shift or Shaft?, 1983; The Nuclear Age, 1989; exec. prodr. Zoom, 1974-75; In Search of the Real America, 1975-78; Frontline Spl. Report: Crisis in Central America, 1985, Mexico, 1988; Korea: The Unknown War, 1990; Am. Experience: Eisenhower, 1993, The Windsors, 1994, 2002, The Churchills, 1996; American Experience: Carnegie, The Richest Man in the World, 1997, Reagan, 1998 (Peabody award), MacArthur, 1999 (Emmy award), PBS Millenium, 2000, American Experience: Chgo. City of the Century, 2003. Mem.: Somerset Club (Boston), Yale Club (N.Y.C.). Home and Office: 11 Wright St 3 Cambridge MA 02138

HOYT, JAMES LAWRENCE, journalism educator, athletic administrator; b. Wausau, Wis., July 18, 1943; s. Lawrence Beryl and Eleanor (Kischel) H.; m. Cheryl Johannes, July 23, 1966; children: Randall James, Rebecca Cheryl, Diane Caroline. BS, U. Wis., 1965, MS, 1967, PhD, 1970; postgrad., U. Pa., 1967-68. Reporter Sta. WTMJ-TV, Milw., 1965-67; prof. journalism Ind. U., Bloomington, 1970-73; writer, editor NBC News, Washington, 1972; prof. journalism U. Wis., Madison, 1973—; dir. U. Wis. Sch. Journalism, Madison, 1981-91. Chmn. athletic bd., faculty rep. NACC Big Ten Conf. Western Collegiate Hockey Assn., U. Wis., Madison, 1991-2001. Author: Mass Media in Perspective, 1984, Writing News for Broadcast, 1994; contbr. articles to profl. jours. Recipient Carol Brewer award Wis. Associated Press, 1996. Mem. Assn. for Edn. in Journalism and Mass Comm. (Disting. Broadcast Educator 2002), Radio-TV News Dirs. Assn., Broadcast Edn. Assn., Internat. Radio-TV Soc. (Frank Stanton fellow 2001). Methodist. Avocation: hockey. Home: 4709 Fond Du Lac Trl Madison WI 53705-4812 Office: U Wis Sch Journalism 821 University Ave Madison WI 53706-1412

HOYT, JOHN ARTHUR, humane society executive; b. Marietta, Ohio, Mar. 30, 1932; s. Claremont Earl and Margaret Adeline (Hawkins) H.; m. Gertrude Ellen Mohnkern, June 7, 1957; children: Margaret Rose, Karen Elizabeth, Anne Christine, Julie Kay. BA, Rio Grande Coll., 1954, DD, 1968; MDiv, Colgate Rochester Div. Sch., 1958; Dr honoris causa, U. Bucharest, Romania, 1995; LHD (hon.), St. Thomas U., Miami, Fla., 1998, U. St. Petersburg, Russia, 1997. Ordained to ministry Baptist Ch., 1957; pastor Allen Park (Mich.) Bapt. Ch., 1958-60, First Presbyn. Ch., Leroy, N.Y., 1960-64; sr. minister Drayton Ave. Presbyn. Ch., Ferndale, Mich., 1964-68, First Presbyn. Ch., Fort Wayne, Ind., 1968-70; pres. Humane Soc. U.S., Washington, 1970-91, chief exec., 1992-97; pres. emeritus, 1997—; pres. Humane Soc. Internat., Washington, 1991-94; pres., dir. Humane Soc. of Can., Toronto, 1994-98; vice chmn. bd. dirs. EarthKind Internat., Washington, London, 1991-98; pres. Earthkind, U.S., Washington, 1994-97. Author: Animals in Peril: How "Sustainable Use" is Wiping Out the World's Wildlife, 1994. Pres. Nat. Assn. for Humane and Environ. Edn., East Haddam, Conn., 1970-94, chmn. bd. dirs. 1973-95; trustee Rio Grande (Ohio) Coll., 1979-86, Lake Erie Coll., Painesville, Ohio, 1986-88; bd. dirs. The Am. Fondouk, Boston, 1986-97, Earth Day 1990, 1989-90, Global Tomorrow Coalition, 1989-94; pres. World Soc. for Protection of Animals, London, 1986-90, v.p., 1990-98; pres. dir. Ctr. for Respect Life and Environment, Washington, 1986-98; pres., dir. Internat. Ctr. Earth Concerns, Calif., 1994-98; dir. Grupo de los Cien, Mex., 1994-98, Counterpart Internat., Washington, 1997—; mem. Earth Charter Commn.; v.p. Internat. Devel. Conf., Washington, 1997-99; vice chmn., dir. East Restoration Corps., Washington, 1999—; dir. Sky Voyager, The Plains, Va., 2001—; pres., dir. Bear Castle Property Owners Assn., Bumpbass, Va., 2001—. Recipient Disting. Alumnus award Rio Grande Coll., Founders award for Humane Excellence ASPCA, 1991, George T. Angell Humanitarian award Mass. SPCA, 1992, Pres.'s Disting. Ministry award Sch. of Theology at Claremont, Calif., 1995, Reverence for Life Commendation Albert Schweitzer Inst. for the Humanities, 1998. Home: 320 Bear Castle Dr Bumpass VA 23024-4925 Office: Humane Soc US 2100 L St NW Ste 500 Washington DC 20037-1596

HOYT, KENNETH BOYD, educational psychology educator; b. Cherokee, Iowa, July 13, 1924; s. Paul Fuller and Mary Helen (Tinker) H.; m. Phyllis June Howland, May 25, 1946; children: Andrew Paul, Roger Alan, Elinore Jane. BS, U. Md., 1948; MA, George Washington U., 1950; PhD, U. Minn., 1954; Ed.D. (hon.), Crete Coll., 1981. Tchr., counselor Northeast (Md.) High Sch., 1948-49; dir. guidance Westminster (Md.) High Sch., 1949-50; tchg. asst. U. Minn., 1950-51, instr. ednl. psychology, 1951-54; asst. prof. U. Iowa, Iowa City, 1954-57, assoc. prof., 1957-60, prof. edn., 1961-69; dir. Splty. Oriented Student Research Program, prof. edn. U. Md., Silver Spring, 1969-74; dir. office career edn. U.S. Office Edn., 1974-82; disting. vis. scholar Embry Riddle Aero. U., 1982-84; Univ. Disting. prof. edn. Kans. State U., 1984—2003; dir. counseling high skills vo-tech career options program Kansas State U., 1993-98, prof. emeritus, 2003—. Cons. Ordnance Civilian Personnel Agy., 1954-60, Iowa Dept. Pub. Instrn., 1954-69, U.S. Dept. Labor, 1956-68, 65—, U.S. Office Edn., 1958—, Nat. Inst. Edn., 1973—. Author: (with L.A. Van Dyke) The Drop-Out Problem in Iowa High Schools, 1958, (with C.P. Froehlich) Guidance Testing, 1960, Selecting Employees for Developmental Opportunites and Guidance Services; Suggested Policies for Iowa Schools, 1963, Career Education: Contributions to an Evolving Concept, 1976, Career Education: Where It Is and Where It Is Going, 1981; co-author: Career Education: What It Is and How To Do It, 1972, Career Education and the Elementary School Teacher, 1973, Career Education in the Middle Junior High School, 1973, Career Education for Gifted and Talented Students, 1974, Career Education in the High School, 1977, Counseling for High Skills, 2001; Editor: Counselor Education and Supervision, 1961-65; Mem. editorial bd.: Personnel and Guidance Jour, 1960-63; Contbr. articles to profl. jours. Served with AUS, 1943-46. Fellow APA (divsn. 17); mem. Am. Counseling Assn. (pres. 1966-67, Arthur Hitchcock Outstanding Disting. Profl. Svc. award, 1994), Am. Vocat. Assn. (Outstanding Svc. award 1972), Assn. Counselor Edn. and Supervision (Disting. Svc. award 1965, Outstanding Career award 1990), Nat. Career Devel. Assn. (Eminent Career award 1981, pres. elect 1991-92, pres. 1992-93), Am. Sch. Counselors Assn., Am. Ednl. Rsch. Assn., Nat. Assn. for Industry Edn. Cooperation (vice-chmn. 1992—), Phi Delta Kappa. Home: 149 N Dartmouth Dr Manhattan KS 66503-3021 Office: Kans State U Coll of Edn 369 Bluemont Hall Manhattan KS 66506-5300 E-mail: khoyt@ksu.edu.

HOYT, KENNETH M. federal judge; b. 1948; AB, Tex. So. U., 1969, JD, 1972. Mem. firm Wickliff, King, Hoyt & Jones, 1972-75, Anderson, Hodge, Jones & Hoyt, 1975-79, Webster & Andrews, 1979-81; presiding judge 125th Civil Dist. Ct., 1981-82; pvt. practice law Kenneth M. Hoyt & Assocs., 1983-85; justice U.S. Ct. Appeals (1st cir.), 1985-88; judge U.S. Dist. Ct. (so. dist.)Tex., Houston, 1988—. Faculty trial advocacy program South Tex. Coll., 1981-82; adj. prof. Thurgood Marshall Sch. Law, 1983-84. Contbr. articles to profl. jours. Former bd. dirs. Bus. and Profl. Men's Club; judge trial advocacy program U. Houston, 1982-84, 87-88; former mem. Juvenile Justice & Delinquency Prevention Adv. Bd., Blue Ribbon Commn., Rev. Criminal Justice Corrections System, Referendum Force, Selection of Judges; former mem. adv. bd. Parents of Murdered Children and Coalition of Victims Rights; formerly active Salvation Army; former chmn. Capital Devel. Com., Wheeler Ave. Bapt. Ch.; past dir. Houston Lawyer's Referral Svc. With USNG, 1972-78. Decorated Am. Spirit medal; recipient Outstanding Community Svc. award Kendleton, Tex., Ethel Ranson Art & Literary Club award, Outstanding Acheivement award Thurgood Marshall Sch. Law Alumni Assn., 1986; named one of Most Outstanding Black Rep. South Tex. Mem. Nat. Bar Assn., State Bar Tex. (task force, minimum continuing legal edn.). Office: US District Courthouse Suite 11144 515 Rusk St Houston TX 77002-2605

HOYT, LUPÉ ANN GONZALEZ, social services administrator; b. San Pedro, Calif., Jan. 6, 1952; d. Pedro Meléndez and Nellie (Baldonado) González; m. Robert Alan Hoyt, Oct. 8, 1977; children: Karen Elena, David Elijah, Sylvia Carol. A in Bibl. Studies, Bethany Bible Coll.; BA in Psychology and Counseling, La. Bapt. U. Christian counselor Ashland Christian Counseling Svcs., Cin., 1999—2000; instr. Norwood (Ohio) Service League, Inc., 2001—02, Norwood (Ohio) Svc. League, 2002—. Instr. Temple Baptist Coll., Cin., 2000, Norwood Christian Acad., 2001-02. Vol. Fernside Ctr. for Grieving Children, Am. Cancer Soc. Mem. Am. Assn. Christian Counseling, Nat. Alliance Hispanic Health. Republican. Baptist. Avocations: botany, ancient history, loom weaving, navajo language and culture, herb gardens. Home: 4525 Floral Ave Cincinnati OH 45212-3251 Office: Norwood Service League Inc 5300 Montgomery Rd Cincinnati OH 45212

HOYT, MARY FINCH, author, editor, media consultant, former government official; b. Calif. 2 children. Free-lance mag. writer, speechwriter, formerly with Ladies' Home Jour. mag.; info. officer Peace Corps; pres. sec. to Mrs. Edmund Muskie, 1968; pres. sec. to Mrs. George McGovern, 1972; former ptnr. McClure, Schultz and Hoyt (pub. rels.).; press sec. to Mrs. Rosalynn Carter and East Wing coord. The White House, Washington, 1977-81; dir. communications Nat. Trust for Hist. Preservation, Washington, 1989-93; author, editor, media cons., 1993—. Author: American Women of the Space Age, 1966; author: (with Eleanor McGovern) Uphill: A Personal Story, 1974; author: East Wing: Politics, the Press and a First Lady, 2001. Mem. Presdl. Commn., 1977. Democrat.

HOYT, MICHAEL F. psychologist, writer; b. Chgo., Dec. 21, 1948; BS, UCLA, 1970; PhD, Yale U., 1976. Lic. psychologist Calif. Sr. staff psychologist Kaiser Permanente, San Rafael, Calif., 1979—; clin. faculty U. Calif., Sch. Medicine, San Francisco, 1981—; ind. cons., lectr., 1980—. Internat. workshop spkr. various countries, including U.S., Japan, Eng., Scotland, Ireland, Can., Mex., Finland, Hungary, Austria, others. Author: Brief Therapy and Managed Care, 1995, Some Stories are Better Than Others, 2000, Interviews with Brief Therapy Experts, 2001, The Present Is a Gift, 2003; editor: Constructive Therapies, vol. 1, 1994, Constructive Therapies, vol. 2, 1996, The Handbook of Constructive Therapies, 1998, The First Session in Brief Therapy, 1992. Recipient Disting. Presenter award, Internat. Assn. Marriage and Family Counselors, 1997. Mem.: APA (Continuing Edn. Disting. Spkr. 1995). Office: Kaiser Permanente Med Ctr Psychiatry Dept 820 Las Gallinas Ave San Rafael CA 94903 Business E-Mail: Michael.Hoyt@KP.org.

HOYT, MONT POWELL, lawyer; b. Oklahoma City, Apr. 3, 1940; s. Lester Dean and Paula (Powell) H.; m. Alice Nathalie Ryan, June 15, 1974; children: Mont Powell Jr., Kathleen, Michael, Caroline. BA, Northwestern U., 1962; JD, Okla. Law Sch., 1965; M in Comparative Law, U. Chgo., 1968. Bar: Okla. 1965, Tex. 1968. Law clk. U.S. Dist. Ct., Oklahoma City, 1965; stagiaire to French advocat Paris, 1967-68; assoc. Baker & Botts, Houston, 1968-75, ptnr., 1975-92; shareholder Verner, Liipfert, Bernhard, McPherson & Hand, Houston, 1993-94; ptnr. Hughes & Luce, Houston, 1994-2001, Shook, Hardy & Bacon, Houston, 2001—. Adj. prof. law U. Houston, 1970-76 Contbr. articles to profl. jours. Bd. dirs. French Am. Found., N.Y.C., 1979-85, Mexican Cultural Inst., 1991-95, Fgn. Policy Assn., 1991-93; mem. Latin Am. adv. bd. Americas Soc., 1992—. Mem. ABA (chmn. sect. internat. law and practice 1984-85), Internat. Bar Assn. (coun. sect. of energy and nat resources law 1983-86), Am. Law Inst., Am. Soc. Internat. Law, Am. Arbitration Assn., German Am. C. of C. (bd. dirs. 1978-94), InterAm. C. of C. (bd. dirs. 1991-99, chmn. 1996-98), U. Chgo. Law Sch. Alumni Assn. (v.p. 1990-91), Coun. on Fgn. Rels. (chmn. Houston 1991-92), Houston Country Club (Houston), Met. Club (Washington). Avocations: spanish language study, running, international affairs, ham radio. Office: PO Box 131026 Houston TX 77219-1026 E-mail: mhoyt@shb.com.

HOYT, ROGER FRANKLIN, physicist; b. Evergreen Park, Ill., Aug. 16, 1949; s. William Abe and Betty Jane H.; m. Jennifer Ann, June 24, 1978; children: Elizabeth, David. BS, U. Ill., Champaign/Urbana, 1971; MS, U. Calif., San Diego, 1975, PhD, 1978. Rsch. staff IBM, San Jose, 1982-94, mgr./program dir., 1994—. Rev. panel mem Nat. Rsch. Coun., Washington, 1992—98. Mem. editl. bd. Jour. Info. Storage and Processing, 1997—, IEEE Transactions on Magnetics, 2003—, contbg. author Magnetic Disk Drive, 1997—. Vestry mem. Episcopal Ch. Almaden, Calif., 1986-89; storage chmn., Nat. Electronics Initiative, 1996-. Corp. U.S. Army, 1971—78. Decorated Army Commendation medal. Fellow: IEEE (dir. San Francisco coun. 1996—97, editor-in-chief IEEE press 1997—98, 3d Millennium medal 2000); mem.: IBM Acad. of Tech., N.Y. Acad. Scis., Am. Phys. Soc. Republican. Episcopalian. Achievements include patents for inventions in field. Office: Hitachi Globl Storage Tech 5600 Cottle Rd San Jose CA 95193-0001 E-mail: roger.hoyt@sbcglobal.net.

HOYT, ROSEMARY ELLEN, trust advisor; b. Iowa City, Iowa, Apr. 12, 1949; d. Joseph Asa Hoyt and Mary Jane (Brobst) Vandermark; m. Louis O. Scott, Oct. 16, 1965 (div. Nov. 1968); children: Wayne L. Lawson, Jo Anna Jane Kollasch; m. David K. Duckworth, July 23, 1983 (div. Dec. 1994); 1 child, Mary Rose Duckworth. Cert. in applied banking/consumer credit, Am. Inst. Banking, 1988; BBA, So. Calif. U., 1992, MBA, 1997. Cert. in trust adminstrn; cert. trust ops. specialist; cert. in trust tax. Teller Community Bank of Fla., St. Petersburg, 1973-75; bookkeeper Chevron Svc. Sta., St. Petersburg, 1973-77, Landmark Bank, St. Petersburg, 1977-80; teller First Nat. Bank of Ely, Nev., 1981, Nev. Bank and Trust, Ely, 1982; asst. v.p. and trust officer First Nat. Bank Farmington, N.Mex., 1983-96; asst. v.p., trust officer Bank One, Dallas, 1997—. Pres., founder Day Camp Southside, St. Petersburg, 1976-77. Planning chmn. terr. 5 ann. meeting ARC, Farmington, 1990-91, babysitting instr., 1990-96, basic aid tng. instr., 1992, Project Read instr., 1994; coord. United Way, 1997. Recipient Appreciation award ARC, 1991. Mem. Fin. Women Internat. (by-laws com. 1990-91, treas. 1993-94), Nat. Assn. Trust Ops. Specialists (bd. dirs. 1992), Am. Bus. Women's Assn. (v.p. 1991, pres. 1992, Appreciation award 1989, Woman of Yr. 1995). Republican. Avocations: crocheting, cooking, gardening. Office: 1717 Main St 11th Fl Dallas TX 75243 E-mail: rehoyt@sbcglobal.net.

HOZA, STEVEN PAUL, museum curator, consultant, educator, conservator; b. Phoenix, May 30, 1962; s. John Stephen and Helen (Scheidel) H.; m. Marla Jean Imdieke, May 25, 1990. BA in History, Ariz. State U., 1986. Exhibit technician Ariz. State Capitol Mus., Phoenix, 1982-87; bookbinder, conservator Ariz. State Archives, Phoenix, 1987-90; registrar, curator Ariz. Hist. Soc., Tempe, 1990—; instr. Ctrl. Ariz. Coll., Casa Grande, 1997—. Author: PW: First Person Accounts of German POWs in Arizona, 1994, Best Place in the Country: First Person Accounts of Military Aviation in Arizona During WWII. Pres. Old Ch. Com., Tempe, 1989—; archivist Old Ch. Archives, Tempe, 1989—. Recipient Spkrs. Cert. Res. Officers Assn., 1997, 99. Mem. Falcon Field Assn. (hon.). Roman Catholic. Avocations: australian rules football, locating wwii aircraft crash sites, wwii american home front collecting. Office: Ariz Hist Soc 1300 N College Ave Tempe AZ 85281-1211 E-mail: steve.hoza@ahs.maricopa.gov.

HOZER, LESZEK, materials scientist, engineer; b. Blizyn, Kielce, Poland, Oct. 2, 1958; came to U.S., 1991; s. Tadeusz and Hanna Hozer; m. Joanna Kuciak, 1982; 1 child, Katarzyna. MS in Engring., Warsaw (Poland) Inst. Tech., 1982; PhD, Gdansk (Poland) Tech. U., 1987. Rsch. assoc., head nitride ceramics lab. Inst. Electronic Materials Tech., Warsaw, 1982-90; tech. asst. to pres. Electronic Materials Rsch. and Prodn. Ctr., Warsaw, 1990; postdoctoral assoc. MIT, Cambridge, 1991-94, rsch. assoc., 1994-97; mem. tech. staff Sarnoff Corp., Princeton, N.J., 1997-2000; advanced tech. project leader Cookson Electronics Assembly Materials Group, Jersey City, 2000—. Author: Ceramic Materials with Active Grain Boundaries, 1990, Semiconductor Ceramics: Grain Boundary Effects, 1994; contbr. articles to profl. jours.; patentee in field. Mem. Am. Ceramic Soc., Polish Ceramic Soc., Materials Rsch. Soc., Sigma Xi. Achievements include development of advanced silicon carbide materials including reaction-infiltrated composites for electronic and structural applications; development of low cost, ceramic on metal, plasma display back panel; development of lead free soldering materials. Office: Alpha Metals 600 Route 440 Jersey City NJ 07304 Fax: 201-434-2529. E-mail: lhozer@cooksonelectronics.com.

HOZESKI, BRUCE WILLIAM, English language and literature educator; b. Grand Rapids, Mich., Feb. 28, 1941; s. Gerard Thadeus and Dorothy Elizabeth (Platschore) H.; m. Kathleen Antoinette Tuma, Sept. 9, 1967; 1 child, Alison Michelle. AA, St. Peter's Coll., Balt., 1961; BA, Aquinas Coll., 1964; MA, Mich. State U., 1966, PhD, 1969. Instr. Lansing (Mich.) Community Coll., 1967-69; grad. asst. Mich. State U., East Lansing, 1964-69; from asst. prof. to prof. English Ball State U., Muncie, Ind., 1969—, dir. grad. programs in English, 1998—2001. Author: Hildegard of Bingen's Scivias, 1986, Hildegard of Bingen's Liber Vitae Meritorum, 1993, Hildegard of Bingen: The Book of the Rewards of Life, 1997, Hildegard von Bingen's Mystical Visions, 1998, Hildegard's Healing Plants: From Her Medieval Classic Physica, 2001; bibliographer: (with Lorrayne Y. Baird-Lange and Bege K. Bowers) An Annotated Chaucer Bibliography, 1989, 90, 91, 92, Studies in the Age of Chaucer; contbr. An Annotated Chaucer Bibliography, 1993, 94, 95, 96, 97, 98, 99, 2000, 01, 02, 03, Studies in the Age of Chaucer; mem. editl. bd. Classical and Modern Lit., A. Quar., 1988—; editor-in-chief, mng. editor Ball State U. Forum, 1984-90; contbr. chpts. to books, articles to profl. jours. Recipient Outstanding Faculty Svc. award Ball State U., Muncie, Ind., 1999-2000. Mem. Medieval Acad. Am., Early English Text Soc., New Chaucer Soc., The Medieval and Renaissance Drama Soc., Medieval Assn. Midwest (editor 1982-85, v.p. 2000-01, pres. 2001-02), Internat. Soc. Hildegard (exec. coun. 1989—, pres. 1984-89, treas. 2001—), Lambda Iota (exec. sec., treas. 1995—), Omicron Delta Kappa. Roman Catholic. Avocations: tennis, flower gardening. Home: 7404 W Augusta Blvd Yorktown IN 47396-9353 Office: Ball State U Dept English 2000 W University Ave Muncie IN 47306-0460 E-mail: bhozeski@bsu.edu.

HOZO, IZTOK, mathematician, educator; b. Ljubljana, Slovenia, May 28, 1963; s. Dzevad Hozo and Metka Kraigher-Hozo; m. Stela Pudar, Jan. 4, 1963; children: Mak, Irena. PhD, U. Mich., 1993. Prof. math. Ind. U. NW, Gary, 1994—. Contbr. articles to profl. jours. Mem.: AAUP, Math. Assn. Am. Office: Ind Univ NW 3400 Broadway Gary IN 46383 Office Fax: 219-981-4247.

HOZUMI, MOTOO, medical educator, researcher; b. Fukushima, Japan, Mar. 12, 1933; s. Akiine and Fumi Hozumi; m. Sakiko Wakabayashi, May 4, 1963; children: Yuko, Masamichi, Ayako. BSc, Tokyo U. Edn., 1956, MSc, 1958, Dsc, 1961. Rsch. mem. Nat. Cancer Ctr. Rsch. Inst., Tokyo, 1962-64, chief ctrl. lab., 1964-75; dir. dept. chemotherapy Saitama (Japan) Cancer Ctr. Rsch. Inst., 1975-93, dir., 1990-93; spl. rsch. Saitama (Japan) Cancer Ctr., 1993-96. Rsch. mem. Roswell Park Meml. Inst., Buffalo, N.Y., 1965-67; vis. prof. Showa U. Med. Sch., Tokyo, 1988-2001; cons. Japan Immunoresearch Inst., Takasaki, Japan, 1993-98. Author: Advances in Cancer Research, 1983, Ciba Foundation Symposium, 1990, Status of Differentiation Therapy, 1991, (rev. jour.) CRC Critical Rev. Oncol./Hematol., 1985, Internat. Jour. Hematology, 1998. Recipient Princess Takamatsu Cancer Rsch. Found. prize, 1974. Mem. AAAS, Japanese Cancer Assn. (councilor 1973-98, meritorious mem. 1999—), Japan Hematol. Soc. (councilor 1992-98, meritorious mem. 1999—), Am. Assn. for Cancer Rsch. Avocation: music. Home: 12-288 Fukasaku Minuma Saitama 337-0003 Japan

HRABOWSKI, FREEMAN ALPHONSA, III, university president; b. Birmingham, Ala., Aug. 13, 1950; s. Freeman A. II and Maggie (Geeter) H.; m. Jacqueline Coleman, Aug. 29, 1970; 1 child, Eric. BA, Hampton (Va.) Inst., 1970; MA, U. Ill., 1971, PhD, 1975. Asst. dean student svcs., vis. asst. prof. U. Ill., Champaign-Urbana, 1974-76; assoc. dean grad. studies Ala. A&M U., Normal, 1976-77; v.p. for acad. affairs, dean arts and scis. Coppin State Coll., Balt., 1977-87; exec. v.p. U. Md. Baltimore County, Balt., 1987-92, interim pres., 1992-93, dir. Meyerhoff scholarship program, 1989-93, pres., 1993—. Bd. dirs. Mercantile Safe Deposit & Trust Co., McCormick & Co. Co-author: Beating the Odds, 1998, Overcoming the Odds, 2002. Active Md. Gov.'s Commn. on State Taxes and Tax Structure, Annapolis, 1990, co-chair Md. Gov.'s Transition Policy Group on Edn., 1994-95, Gov's. Commn. on Devel. of Advanced Tech. Bus., 2003—; chair Md. Humanities Coun., Balt., 1991; bd. dirs. U. Md. Med. Sys., Balt. Mus. Art, Carnegie Instn. Washington, France/Merrick Found., Marguerite Casey Found., Md. Acad. Scis., Balt. Cmty. Found., Constellation Energy Group, Inc., Corvis Corp., Balt. Equitable Soc. Recipient 20 Yr. Outstanding Alumnus award Hampton U., 1990. Baptist. Home: 18 Aston Ct Owings Mills MD 21117-1439 Office: U Md Balt County Office of President 1000 Hilltop Cir Baltimore MD 21250-0001 E-mail: hrabowski@umbc.edu.

HRACHOVINA, FREDERICK VINCENT, osteopathic physician and surgeon; b. St. Paul, Minn., Sept. 2, 1926; s. Vincent Frank and Beatrice (Funda) H.; m. Joan Halverson, July 2, 1955 BA in Chemistry, Macalester Coll., St. Paul, 1948; DO, Kirksville Coll. Osteo. Med., Mo., 1956. Chemist Mpls.-St. Paul area, 1948-51; intern Clare Gen. Osteo. Hosp., Mich., 1956-57; pvt. practice Mpls. Minn., 1957-84; asst. prof. osteo. principles and practices Nova Southeastern U. Coll. Osteo. Medicine, Ft. Lauderdale, Fla., 1985-88; founder, pres. Physician Placement Svc., Fla. and Minn., 1973—; med. dir. Associated Bioscience, Inc., Mpls., 1992, Sera-Tec Biologicals Inc., Jacksonville, Fla., 1993-94; staff physician Allegheny Biologicals, Inc., Jacksonville, 1995-96; med. dir. Serologicals, Jacksonville, 1996; med. ins. examiner Hooper Holmes, Inc., St. Petersburg, Ft. Myers, Fla., 1997—; ins. med. examiner Examination Mgmt. Svcs., Inc., Tampa, Ft. Myers, Fla., 1998—. Bd. dirs. Internat. Acad. Osteopathic Medicine, lectr. Internat. Acad. Osteo. Medicine, Brussels, 1984; mem. Northlands Regional Med. Program, Inc., 1971—73, Health Svcs. Devel. Com., Regional Adv. Group; founder, faculty advisor Fla. Acad. Osteopathy Student Assn., Nova Southeastern U. Coll. Osteo. Medicine, Ft. Lauderdale, Fla., 1987; staff physician Centeon Bio-Svcs. Plasma Corp., St. Paul, 1998; v.p. med. rels., mem. adv. bd. Sinofresh Labs., Venice, Fla., 2002. Author: Microscopic Anatomy, 1952; Methods of Development of New Osteopathic Medical Colleges in the Next Millennium, 1977; contbr. articles to profl. jours.; patent pending in field. Mem. Crow Wing County (Minn.) Portage-Crooked Lake Preservation Soc., 1977—, Sr. Citizen Assn., Garrison, Minn., 1991—, Deerwood Civic and Commerce Assn., Deerwood, Minn., 1992—; chmn. street lights program Pinebrook South, Venice, Fla. Grantee Smith Kline & French Labs., 1973, 89, Hill Labs, Gusman Med. Equipment, 1987. Mem. Am. Coll. Osteo. Family Practice (life), Am. Osteo. Assn. (life, coun. fed. health programs, drug enforcement adminstrn. prescribers working com. 1974-75), Am. Acad. Osteopathy (life), Am. Assn. Sr. Physicians, Am. Osteo. Acad. Sports Medicine (life), Am. Blood Resources Assn., Am. Assn. Blood Banks, Gulf Coast Hibiscus Soc. (presdl. liason to Venice C. of C. 1996), Minn. Osteo. Assn. (life, pres. 1965-66, exec. dir. 1966-74, pub. rels. dir. 1974-75), Assn. Osteo. State Exec. Dirs. (pres. 1970-71, dir. 1971-74, founder nat. legis. sem. 1974), Fla. Soc. Coll. Osteopathic Family Practice (lectr. Mo. soc.), Fla. Acad. Osteopathy (bd. trustees, chmn. audit and membership com.), Fla. Osteo Found. (v.p.), Ga. Osteopathic Med. Assn. (chmn. Olympic com. 1995-96), Fla Osteo. Med. Assn. (Dade county chpt. chmn. osteo. lit. com., conv. chmn. dist. two 1994, dist. #7 Sarasota County, chmn. legis. com. dist. 11, v.p. dist. 7, long range planning com., mem. com., chmn. 175th ann. founder party), Fla. Osteopathic Med. Assn. (dist. 5, 7, 11), Internat. Acad. Osteo. Medicine (bd. trustees), Minn. Gymnastic Assn. (founder Floor Exercise 1962-72), Fla. Acad. Osteopathy Student Assn. at Southeastern Coll. Osteopathic Medicine (originator, advisor), Dade-Broward Osteopathic Med. County Soc., Duval County Osteopathic Soc., Sarasota County Osteo. Soc., Twin-City Model A Ford Club, Pierce Arrow Soc. (sec. Fla. region 1988, news reporter Arrow Driver Midwest region, Mpls., life, founder Midwest region, 1983, dir./treas., 1983-84, gen. chmn. Midwest region swapmeet, Golden Valley, MN, 1990, nat. dir. 1983-84, contbr. articles to Arrow Jour.), Venice C. of C. (mem. membership com., mem. amb. com.), Cadillac LaSalle Club (founder 1978, treas. North Star region 1978-83), Classic Car Club Am. (life, membership chmn. Minn. upper midwest region 1977, sec. 1978, Gold Coast region-Fla.), Antique Auto Club. Am. (life, news reporter St. Paul chpt., Minn. region, Ft. Lauderdale region, Jacksonville region, Venice chpt., Lemon Bay region, judge at nat. meet Venice, Fla. 1997), Breakfast club Mpls., Y.E.S. Club 1st Nat. Bank Deerwood (Minn.), Scottish Rite, Valley of St. Paul, Lions (Bay Lake, Minn. del. to internat. conv., Miami, Fla., 1989), Optimist Club (dir. Mpls. 1959-62, 69-72, pres. 1970-71, gen. chmn. fl. exercise Olympic gynmastic program 1959-65), Masons (life, Capitol City #217, St. Paul), Shriners (life mem. Zuhrah Shrine Temple, Mpls., fund raising com.), Phi Sigma Gamma (life, nat. pres. 1987-89, pres. grand coun. and found. 1987-89, grand coun. advisor and chmn. bd.), Arlington Shrine Club (Jacksonville), Cummer Gallery of Art and Gardens (Jacksonville), Arlington Preservation Soc. (Jacksonville), Venice Shrine Club (Fla.), Aadzuhma Shrine Club (Brainerd, Minn.), Manasota Fossil Club, Airstream Fla. Suncoast Club, Wally Byam Caravan Club, Internat. Airstream Inc. Home: 1238 Lucaya Ave Venice FL 34185-6407

HRANITZKY, RACHEL ROBYN, lawyer; b. Irving, Tex., Mar. 16, 1968; d. Dennis Rogers and Jeanne Beverly (Crooks) H. BA, Tex. Christian U., 1987, U. Tex., 1988; JD, So. Meth. U., 1995. Bar: Tex. 1995, U.S. Dist. Ct. (no. dist.) Tex. 1997, U.S. Dist. Ct. (ea. dist.) Tex. 1999, U.S. Dist. Ct. (so. and we. dists.) Tex. 2000. Tchr. Grapevine H.S., Tex., 1989—92; clk. to Hon. Candace Tyson, 44th Dist. Ct., Dallas, 1993; assoc. cons. Mesa, Inc., 1995; assoc. Hiersche, Hayward, Drakeley & Urbach, 1996—. Rsch. asst. William V. Dorsaneo, III, 1993-95; clinic atty. So. Meth. U. Legal Clinics, Dallas, 1995. Mem. ABA, ATLA, Dallas Bar Assn., Dallas Assn. Young Lawyers, Rotary Club, Jr. League Plano, Delta Theta Phi. Avocations: art, music, sports, cooking, dancing. Home: 11251 Newberry Dr Frisco TX 75035-8614 Office: 15303 Dallas Pkwy Ste 700 Addison TX 75001-4610 E-mail: rhranitzky@hhdulaw.com.

HRESAN, SALLY L. journalism educator; b. Beckley, W.Va., Jan. 15, 1946; BA, Sullins Coll., Bristol, Va., 1965; BS in Journalism, W.Va. U., 1967, MS in Journalism, 1977, EdD, 1990. Asst. copy supr. Dayton's Corp., Mpls., 1967-70; grad. asst. W.Va. U., Morgantown, 1970-73; pub. rels. dir. Powers Sch., Pitts., 1973-77; prof. journalism Shepherd Coll., Shepherdstown, W.Va., 1977—. Student publ. advisor Shepherd Coll., 1977-88, dir. journalism internship program, 1985—, curriculum designer communications dept., 1987—; media law cons. Sta. WXVA, Charles Town, W.Va., 1988-89; mem. faculty senate strategic planning com., profl. devel. com., campus jud. bd., hearing panel for cases of termination of employment, pres.'s blue ribbon com. on advisement and retention, subcom. on student/faculty advisement, student newspaper bd. advisors, 1990, coord. faculty devel. 1993—. Editor: (assoc.) Bootstrap mag., 1984-85. Coord., moderator Nat. park Svc. Employee Program, Harpers Ferry, W.Va., 1990; active Drive Against Diabetes Golf Tournament, South Mountain, Pa., 1989; publicity chmn. Old Opera House Theatre, Charles Town, 1981-84. Mem. Assn. Edn. for Journalism, Coll. Media Advisors, W.Va. Communications Assn. (sec.-treas. 1991), W.Va. Journalism Assn. (co-founder 1990), W.Va. Press Assn., W.Va. Univ. Study Group, Columbia Scholastic Press Assn., Nat. Press Photographers Assn. (women's com. 1991, rsch. coord. audio-visual program on access to news events 1991), SATNET (course coord. 1992—, chair com. on pedagogy and student learning 1993—, pres. faculty senate 1993—, facilitator, state and local coord. Great Tchr. Seminar 1994), Kappa Tau Alpha (dept. chmn. 1996-). Avocations: skiing, golf. Home: PO Box 1295 Shepherdstown WV 25443-1295 Office: Shepherd Coll 215 Knutti Hall College St Shepherdstown WV 25443

HRIBAR, JOHN ANTHONY, civil engineer, consultant; b. Pitts., Jan. 10, 1934; s. Rudolph and Mary (Porenta) Hribar; m. Kathleen Mary Tarker, July 9, 1967; children: Suzanne, John, Laura, Amy. BSCE, Carnegie Mellon U., 1956, MS, 1957, PhD, 1960. Asst. prof. civil engring. Carnegie Mellon U., Pitts., 1960—64, assoc. prof. civil engring., 1964—70; v.p., dir. Gen. Analytics, Inc., Monroeville, 1966—70, v.p., gen. mgr., 1970—74; treas., dir. GAI Cons., Inc., Monroeville, 1974—79, v.p., dir., 1979—2003. Dir., asst. sec. Terra Ins. Ltd., Hamilton, Bermuda, 1980—88; dir. Terra Ins. Co., Montpelier, Vt., 1988—2001. Contbr. articles to profl. jours. Mem.: ASCE, Am. Soc. Engring. Edn., Phi Kappa Phi, Sigma Xi. Roman Catholic. Avocation: reading. Home: 610 Driftwood Dr Pittsburgh PA 15238-2516 Office: GAI Cons Inc 570 Beatty Rd Monroeville PA 15146-1334

HRICAK, HEDVIG, physician, radiologist; came to U.S., 1972; MD, U. Zagreb, 1970; PhD, Karolinska Inst., 1992. Diplomate Am. Bd. Radiology 1978. Intern in radiology Hosp. M. Stojanovic, Zagreb, 1971-72, resident in radiology, 1972-73, St. Joseph Mercy Hosp., Pontiac, Mich., 1974-77; fellow in diagnostic radiology Henry ford Hosp., Detroit, sr. staff diagnostic radiology, 1978-81; asst. clin. prof. diagnostic radiology U. Mich., Ann Arbor, 1979-81; from asst. prof. to assoc. prof. U. Calif., San Francisco, 1982-86, prof. radiology, urology, radiation oncology, ob-gyn., 1986-99; chmn. dept. radiology Meml. Sloan-Kettering Cancer Ctr., NY, 1999—; prof. radiology Weill Med. Coll. Cornell U., NY, 2000—. Vis. prof. numerous univs., including Vanderbilt U., Nashville, 1997; vis. prof. Thomas Jefferson U. Hosp., Phila., 2000. Author books in field; assoc. editor, Jour. of Magnetic Resonance Imaging, 2001—, Radiology, 1998—, Jour. of Women's Imaging, 1996—, others; contbr. numerous articles to sci. and profl. jours. Recipient Marie Curie award, AAWR, 2002, Gold medal, ISMRM, 2003; grantee numerous grants in field, including NIH, Am. Cancer Soc., Nat. Cancer Inst.;, numerous hon. lectureships. Fellow Am. Coll. Radiology, Internat. Soc. Magnetic Resonance in Medicine, Soc. Uroradiology (corrs. mem., pres. 2001-03); mem. German Roentgen Soc., Acad. Radiology Rsch. (bd. dirs. 1997—), Radiol. Soc. N.Am. (chmn. pub. info. adv. bd. 1997-2002, bd. dirs. 2003—), Soc. for the Advancement of Women's Imaging (pres. 1997-99), Calif. Acad. Medicine (pres. 1999), Brit. Inst. Radiologists (hon.). E-mail: hricakh@mskcc.org.

HRICIK, LORRAINE E. bank executive; m. Nicholas DeGuercio; 2 children. B in Math. and Computer Sci., Ind. U., Pa., 1973; MBA, Columbia U., 1991. With Securities Industry Automation Corp.; exec. v.p. Chase Manhattan Bank (now J.P. Morgan); exec. v.p. and head J.P. Morgan Treasury Svcs. Mem. Chase Technology Governance Bd.; chair The Clearing House Interbank Payment Co. L.L.C. Adv. Bd.; mem Federal Reserve Bank of N.Y. Payments Risk Com., N.Y. Clearing House Steering Com.; bd. dirs. Internat. Ctr. N.Y. Inductee Academy of Women Achievers, YWCA, 1990. Office: Chase Manhattan Bank 270 Park Ave Fl 12 New York NY 10017-2089

HRINAK, DONNA JEAN, ambassador; b. Sewickley, Pa., Mar. 28, 1951; d. John and Mary (Pukach) H.; m. Gabino (Lou) Flores, July 15, 1977; 1 child, Wyatt A. Flores. BA, Mich. State U., 1972. State dept. officer Am. Embassy, Bogota, Colombia, 1979-81, former dep. prin. officer Warsaw, 1977-79, Mexico City, 1974-81, former min. counselor Teguciagalpa, Honduras, 1989-91; regional affairs officer for C.Am. Dept. State, Washington, 1982-84, dep. asst. sec. for inter-Am. affairs, 1991-93; dep. prin. officer U.S. Consultate Gen., Sao Paulo, Brazil, 1984-87; coord. Policy for Summit of Ams. 1994, 1993-94; amb. to Dominican Republic Santo Domingo, 1994-97; amb. to Bolivia-La Paz, 1197—2000; amb. to Venezuela, 2000—02; amb. to Brazil, 2002—. Named one of Ams. Ten Outstanding Young Working Women, Glamour mag., 1985. Mem. Am. Fgn. Svc. Assn., Exec. Women in Govt., Inter-Am. Dialogue Fgn. Policy Assn. Avocations: reading mysteries, playing tennis, watching baseball. Office: US Embassy SES Avenida das Nacaes 801 Lote 03 Quadra 70403-900 Brazil*

HRISTOVA, KRASSIMIRA RADOYKOVA, microbiologist, researcher; b. Sofia, Bulgaria, Feb. 17, 1964; d. Radoiko Gerov and Iordanka Asenova Hristov; m. Ivaylo Iliev Hristov, Mar. 1, 1987; 1 child, Radostina. MS with great distinction, Sofia U., 1987, PhD, 1993. Microbiologist Inst. Molecular Biology, Bulgarian Acad. Scis., Sofia, 1993-94; rsch. assoc. Nat. Bank for Indsl. Microorganisms and Cell Cultures, Sofia, 1994-98, mem. adv. bd.; postdoctoral rsch. assoc. U. Ill., Urbana-Champaign, 1998-2000, U. Calif., Davis, 2000—. Contbg. author: Bulgarian Antarctic Research, 1996; contbr. articles to sci. jours., including Environ. Microbiology, Applied and Environ. Microbiology, Biotech. and Biotech. Equipment. Postgrad. scholar Russian Fed. Govt., 1991, lab. scholar FEMS, Osnabruck, Germany, 1992; fellow UNESCO, Budapest, Hungary, 1995, Govt. of Que. fellow U. Sherbrooke, 1997. Mem. AAAS, Am. Soc. for Microbiology, Internat. Soc. for Microbial Ecology, Union Scientists in Bulgaria, Bulgarian Soc. for Microbiology. Office: U Calif LAWR Dept One Shields Ave Davis CA 95616 Fax: 530 752-1552. E-mail: krhristova@ucdavis.edu.

HRITZ, GEORGE F. lawyer; b. Hyde Park, N.Y., Aug. 28, 1948; s. George F. and Margaret M. (Callahan) H.; m. Mary Elizabeth Noonan; 1 child, Amelia C. Hritz. AB, Princeton U., 1969; JD, Columbia U., 1973. Bar: N.Y. 1974, D.C. 1978, U.S. Supreme Ct. 1979. Law clk. U.S. Dist. Ct. (ea. dist.) N.Y., N.Y.C., 1973; assoc. Cravath, Swaine & Moore, N.Y.C., 1974-77; counsel U.S. Senate Select Com. Ethics Korean Inquiry, Washington, 1977-78; ptnr. Moore & Foster, Washington, 1978-80, Davis, Weber & Edwards, N.Y.C., 1980-2000; assoc. ind. counsel Washington, 1986-89; ptnr. Hogan & Hartson, LLP, N.Y.C., 2000—. Mem. adv. com. U.S. Dist. Ct. (ea. dist.) N.Y., 1990—. Trustee Fed. Bar Found., 1998—; bd. dirs. gen. counsel exec. com. Internat. Rescue Com., 1982—; chmn. planning bd. Village of Sleepy Hollow, N.Y., 1993-97; bd. dirs. exec. com. Princeton in Africa, 2000—. Mem. Fed. Bar Coun., D.C. Bar Assn. Home: 29 Guinea Rd Greenwich CT 06830 Office: Hogan & Hartson LLP Ste 2500 875 Third Ave New York NY 10022 E-mail: gfhritz@hhlaw.com.

HRMA, PAVEL, materials scientist, educator; b. Prague, Czech Republic, Oct. 3, 1939; s. Jindrich and Marie Hrma. MS, Inst. Chem. Tech., Prague, 1961, PhD, 1969. Tech. mgr. Flat Glass Industry, Olovi, Czech Republic, 1961—63; rsch. scientist Czechoslovak Acad. Scis., Prague, 1969—81; sr. lectr. U. Sheffield, England, 1981—82; rsch. prof. Case We. Res. U., Cleve., 1982—89; staff scientist Pacific NW Nat. Lab., Richland, Wash., 1989—. Cons. Corning Industry, Corning, NY, 1986—89. Contbr. articles to profl. jours. Fellow: Am. Ceramic Soc.; mem.: Materials Rsch. Soc. Office: Pacific Northwest National Lab K6-24 PO Box 999 Richland WA 99352 Office Fax: 509-376-3108. E-mail: pavel.hrma@pnl.gov.

HRONES, STEPHEN BAYLIS, lawyer, educator; b. Boston, Jan. 20, 1942; s. John Anthony and Margaret (Baylis) H.; m. Anneliese Zion, Sept. 11, 1970; children: Christopher, Katja. BA cum laude, Harvard U., 1964; postgrad., U. Sorbonne, Paris, 1964-65; JD, U. Mich., 1968. Bar: Iowa 1969, Mass. 1972, U.S. Dist. Ct. Mass. 1973, U.S. Ct. Appeals (1st cir.) 1979, U.S. Tax Ct. 1985, U.S. Supreme Ct. 1991. Pvt. practice, Heidelberg, Germany, 1970-72; pvt. practice Boston, 1973-86; ptnr. Hrones and Harwood, Boston, 1986-90, Hrones and Garrity, Boston, 1990—. Clin. assoc. Suffolk U. Law Sch., Boston, 1979-82; faculty adv. Harvard Law Sch., 1988—; instr. Northeastern Law Sch., 1998, Mass. Continuing Legal Edn. Programs, 1988—. Author: How To Try a Criminal Case, 1982, Criminal Practice Handbook, 1995, 2d edit., 1999, Massachusetts Jury (Criminal) Instructions, 2d edit., 1999; contbr. articles to profl. jours. Trustee Orgn. for Assabet River, 1990-99; schs. and scholarship com. Harvard U.; fundraiser Harvard Coll. Fund, 1985—. Recipient Edward J. Duggan Pvt. Counsel award for zealous advocacy and outstanding legal svcs. to the poor Com. for Pub. Counsel Svcs., 2000; Fulbright scholar, 1968-69. Mem. ABA, ACLU, Nat. Assn. Criminal Def. Lawyers, Mass. Assn. Criminal Def. Lawyers, Mass. Bar Assn., Boston Bar Assn., Nat. Lawyers Guild, Fulbright Assn. Democrat. Avocations: squash, skiing, wind-surfing, vegetable gardening, reading. Home: 39 Winslow St Concord MA 01742-3817 Office: Hrones and Garrity Lewis Wharf Bay 232 Boston MA 02110 Fax: 617-227-3908. E-mail: sbhlaw@comcast.net.

HRUBAN, RALPH HARVEY, pathologist, educator; b. Chgo., July 28, 1959; s. Zdenek and Jarmila (Stanek) H.; m. Claire Elizabeth Desaulnier, May 26, 1985; children: Zoe Marie, Emily Anne, Carolyn Anna. BA, U. Chgo., 1981; MD, Johns Hopkins U., 1985. Lic. pathologist, Md. Intern in pathology Johns Hopkins Hosp., Balt., 1985-86, resident in pathology, 1986-88, chief resident in pathology, 1989-90, asst. prof. pathology, 1990-93, assoc. prof. pathology, 1993—99, prof. pathology, 1999—, asst. prof. otolaryngol head and neck surgery, 1993-95, assoc. prof. oncology, 1995—99, prof. oncology, 1999—, dir. divsn. cardiovascular-respiratory pathology, 1993—99, dir. divsn. gastrointestinal-liver pathology, 1998—. Pathologist Johns Hopkins Hosp., Blrt., 1990—. Meml. Sloan-Kettering fellow, 1988-89. Office: Johns Hopkins Hosp Dept Pathology Baltimore MD 21231

HRUSKA, ALAN J. lawyer; b. N.Y.C., July 9, 1933. BA, Yale U., 1955, LL.B., 1958. Bar: N.Y. 1959, U.S. Supreme Ct. 1970. Assoc. firm Cravath, Swaine & Moore, N.Y.C., 1958-67, ptnr., 1968—; chmn. planning and program com. 2d Circuit Jud. Conf., 1974-80; co-chmn. 2d Circuit Commn. Reduction of Burdens and Costs in Civil Litigation, 1977-80; commr. N.Y. State Exec. Adv. Commn. on Adminstrn. of Justice, 1981-83; chmn. bd. SoHo Press, Inc., 1986—; CEO The Talking Pictures Co., 2001—. Author: Borrowed Time, 1984. Bd. dirs. Legal Action Ctr., 2000—. Mem.: ABA, Fund for Modern Cts. (bd. dirs. 1994—), Inst. Jud. Adminstrn. (trustee 1978—92, pres. 1982—85, bd. dirs. 1992—2002), Fed. Bar Coun. (trustee 1976—, pres. 1984—86), Assn. Bar City of N.Y. (sec. 1965—66), N.Y. State Bar Assn., Am. Coll. Trial Lawyers, Ctr. for Pub. Resources (exec. com. 1984—2002). Office: Cravath Swaine & Moore 825 8th Ave Fl 38 New York NY 10019-7475

HRUTKAY, LIDELLA WILSON, lawyer, state legislator; b. Morgantown, W.Va., Nov. 24, 1960; d. Amos Clark and Bertha Marie (Eloi) W.; m. Mark Oliver Hrutkay, June 14, 1986; 1 child, Gregory James. BS in Bus., W.Va. U., 1983; JD, Ohio No. U., 1987. Bar: W.Va. 1989, D.C. 1990. Sec. Amos C. Wilson, L.C., Logan, W.Va., 1979-89, lawyer, 1989-93; lawyer, pres. Wilson and Hrutkay Law Offices, L.C., Logan, 1993—; mem. W.Va. Ho. of Dels., 2001—. Mem. W.Va. Ho. of Dels., Charleston. Rep. 7th senatorial dist. W.Va. Dem. Platform Com., Charleston, 2000. Mem. ABA, Nat. Orgn. Social Security Claiments Reps. (sustaining), W.Va. Bar Assn., Order Ea. Star. Avocations: bowling, cooking, fishing, camping, car races. Office: Wilson and Hrutkay Law Offices LC PO Box 1760 Logan WV 25601

HRUZ, PAUL W, pediatrician, endocrinologist, research scientist; m. Anne Brannan, June 15, 1991; children: Matthew, Margaret, Sean, Mary. PhD, Med. Coll. of Wis., Milw., WI, 1987—93; MD, Med. Coll. of Wis., Milw.. WI, 1987—94. Asst. prof. Wash. U., St. Louis, Mo., 2003—, instr., 2000—03, endocrinology fellow, 1997—2000; pediat. resident U. of Wash., Seattle, Wash., 1994—97. Recipient Most Outstanding Med. Student, NIH/NIDDK, 1993, Armond J Quick Award for Excellence in Biochemistry, Med. Coll. of Wis., 1994, Rsch. and Recognition Award, Nat. Inst. of Chemists, 1987. Mem.: AAAS, Am. Diabetes Assn., Endocrine Soc., AMA, Lawson Wilkins Pediatric Endocrine Soc. (assoc.), Am. Acad. of Pediat. (assoc.), Phi Lambda Upsilon, Alpha Omega Alpha, Phi Beta Kappa. Catholic. Achievements include research in Discovery of mechanisms by which HIV drugs cause diabetes. Avocation: zymurgy. Office: Washington University Box 8208 660 South Euclid Ave Saint Louis MO 63110 Office Fax: 314-286-2892. E-mail: hruz_p@kids.wustl.edu.

HRYCAK, MICHAEL PAUL, lawyer; b. Mpls., May 12, 1959; s. Peter and Rea Meta (Limberg) Hrycak; m. Rita Hrycak; children: Brandon Paul, Jared Michael. BA, Rutgers U., 1981, JD, 1989; MS, N.J. Inst. Tech., 1983. Bar: N.J. 1990, N.Y. 1990, Conn. 1990, D.C. 1992, U.S. Dist. Ct. N.J. 1990; U.S. Ct. Appeals (3d cir.) 1998, U.S. Ct. Appeals (4th cir.) 2000. Systems analyst RCA Astro-Electronics Divsn., Princeton, N.J., 1983-86; prin. atty. Law Office of Michael P. Hrycak, Westfield, N.J., 1990—. Lt. USNG, 1981-87, capt., 1987-96, maj., 1996-2003, lt. col., 2003—. Mem.: D.C. Bar Assn., Ukrainian Engrs. Soc. Am. (treas. 1984—2002), Ukrainian Am. Bar Assn., Conn. Bar Assn., N.Y. Bar Assn. Republican. Ukrainian Catholic. Avocations: skiing, backpacking, marksmanship, traveling, current events. Home: 129 Beech St Cranford NJ 07016 Office: 316 Lenox Ave Westfield NJ 07090-2138

HRYCAK, PETER, mechanical engineer, educator; b. Przemysl, Poland, July 8, 1923; came to U.S., 1949, naturalized, 1956; s. Eugene and Ludmyla (Dobrzanska) H.; m. Rea Meta Limberg, June 13, 1949; children: Maria (dec.), Michael Paul, Orest W.T., Alexandra Martha. Student, U. Tubingen, Germany, 1946-48; BS with honors, U. Minn., 1954, MS, 1955, PhD, 1960. Registered profl. engr., N.J. Adminstrv. asst. French Mil. Govt. in Germany, 1947-49; instr. mech. engring. U. Minn., Mpls., 1955-60; mem. tech. staff Bell Telephone Labs., Murray Hill, N.J., 1960-65; sr. project engr. Curtiss-Wright Corp., Woodridge, N.J., 1965; assoc. prof. mech. engring. N.J. Inst. Tech., 1965-68, prof., 1968-93, prof. emeritus, 1993—, dir. jet rsch. lab., 1966-93. Participant in Internat. and Nat. Conf. on Engring. and Applied Sci. Contbr. articles to profl. jours.; one of original Telstar designers. Bd. dirs. Ukrainian Congress Com. Am., Mpls., 1956-60, Plast Camp, East Chatham, N.Y., 1963-68; v.p. Ukrainian Music Found., 1977-97; pres. assn. Peremyschyna, 1993—. NASA grantee, 1967-68; NSF grantee, 1982-84. Mem. AIAA (sr.), ASME, Inst. Environ. Scis. (sr.), Ukrainian Engrs. Soc. Am. (pres. 1966-67), Am. Geophys. Union, Nat. Ukrainian Acad. Engring. Scis., Shevchenko Sci. Soc., Ukrainian Acad. Arts and Scis. in U.S.A., Sigma Xi, Pi Tau Sigma, Tau Beta Pi. Home: 19 Roselle Ave Cranford NJ 07016-2532 Office: NJ Inst Tech 323 Martin Luther King Jr Blvd Newark NJ 07102-1824

HRYCELAK, GEORGE J. surgeon; b. Salzburg, Austria, 1948; BS, U. Ill., 1969, MD, 1973. Diplomate Am. Bd. Surgery. Intern Cook County Hosp., Chgo., 1973-74, resident gen. surgery, 1974-78; attending surgeon Ill. Masonic Med. Ctr., Chgo., 1979—; clin. asst. prof. surgery U. Ill., 1981—; pvt. practice. Fellow ACS; mem. AMA, Ukrainian Med. Assn. N.Am. (exec. dir. 2001—). Office: 809 N Western Ave Chicago IL 60622-4637

HRYCIK, PAULINE EMILY, educator; b. Buffalo, Sept. 23, 1946; d. Roman and Isabelle Mary Waleszczak. BA in English, Edn., Niagara U., 1973; MS in Edn., Canisius Coll., 1976; postgrad., SUNY, Buffalo, 1983, 84. Cert. elem. tchr., secondary English, SAS administrv., drug educator. Itinerant tchr. Buffalo Pub. Schs., 1979; prin. K-8 Diocese of Buffalo, 1974-79; tchr. English, gifted-talented, adminstrv. asst, team leader Royalton-Hartland Sch. Dist., Middleport, N.Y., 1980-88; 8th grade English tchr. Medina (N.Y.) Cen. Sch. Dist., 1988—. Contbr. articles to profl. jours. Named Outstanding Tchr. of English N.Y. State Coun. Tchrs. English. Mem. Nat. Coun. Tchrs. English, N.Y. State Coun. Tchrs. English, AGATE, N.Y. State Mid. Sch., Medina Tchrs. Assn. (peer mediation trainer, conf. planning com., N.Y. state tchr. exam. grader 1993—). Home: 33 Garnet Rd Buffalo NY 14226-2505

HSI, DAVID CHING HENG, plant pathologist and geneticist, educator; b. Shanghai, May 17, 1928; came to US, 1948, naturalized, 1961; s. Yulin and Sue Jean (King) H.; m. Kathy S.W. Chiang, 1952; children: Andrew C., Steven D. BSA, St. John's U., Shanghai, 1948; MS, U. Ga., 1949; PhD, U. Minn., 1951. Grad. teaching asst. U. Minn., St. Paul, 1950; postdoctoral fellow US Cotton Field Sta., Sacaton, Ariz., 1951-52; mem. faculty N.Mex. State U., Las Cruces, 1952—, prof. plant pathology and genetics, 1968-92, prof. emeritus, 1992—. Cons. AID, Pakistan, 1970; coord. external evaluation panel Peanut Collaborative Rsch. Support Program, USA, West Africa, S.E. Asia, 1993-95; acad. exch. People's Republic China, 1978, 84, 85, Republic China, 1979, 81, 82, Brazil and Argentina, 1980, Australia, 1983, South Africa, 1981; judge sr. botany N.Mex. Sci. and Engring. Fair, 1979—; adj. prof. biology U. N.Mex., 1986—. Author rsch. papers in field; co-developer new crop cultivars. Past bd. dir., treas. Carver Pub. Libr., Clovis, N.Mex.; elder 1st Presbyn. Ch., Albuquerque, workship com. chmn., 1981-82, adult edn. com. chmn., 1988-91, pers. com., 1995-98; mem. nat. adv. coun. discipleship and worship Gen. Assembly United Presbyn. Ch. USA, 1978-81, mem. nat. theol. reflections working group, 1980-81, mem. ednl. and congl. nurture unit, 1991-93, N.Mex. Child Abuse Neglect Prevention Implementation Task Force, 1993-97; mem. bd. edn. Albuquerque Pub. Schs., 1982, sec. bd. edn., 1983, v.p., 1984; bd. dir. Mid. Rio Grande Coun. Govts., 1983, 84; chair Albuquerque Sisters Cities Bd., 1986-88; 1st v.p. Albuquerque Sister Cities Found., 1995-96, pres., 1996-98; chair Albuquerque Biopark Adv. Bd., 2003—; mem. com. higher edn. Gen. Assembly The Presbyn. Ch. (USA), 1991-93, preparation ministry com., Presbytery Santa Fe, 1993-98, chair, 1996-97; co-chair N.Mex. Advocates for Children and Families, 1993-95, vice chair, 1995-98; bd. dir. Greater Albuquerque Vol. Adminstr., 1992-95, 97-99, Project Change, 1994-98, v.p., 1996-98; v.p. Albuquerque Edn. Retirees, 1995-96, pres., 1996-98; v.p. Edn. Success Alliance, 1996-98; trustee All Faiths Receiving Home, 1997-2003; trustee, Sandia Prep Sch., 2001-03; bd. dir., v.p. Explora Sci. Ctr. and Children Mus. Albuquerque, 1998—, v.p., 2002--; v.p. The Friendship Force of N.Mex., 2001, pres., 2002. Recipient Disting. Rsch. award Coll. Agr. and Home Econs. N.Mex. State U., 1971, Disting. Svc. award, 1985, Albuquerque Human Rights awad, 1997; inducted into Sr. Citizen's Hall of Fame, 1993. Fellow AAAS (hon., coun. mem. 1998—, Southwestern and Rocky Mountain divsn., exec. com. 1993-95, pres.-elect 1995-96, pres. 96-97); mem. Internat. Soc. Plant Pathology, Am. Phytopath. Soc. (judge Internat. Sci. and Engring. Fair 1983), Nat. Sweet Potato Collaborators Group (chmn. sprout prodn. and root piece propagation com. 1982-84), Nat. Geog. Soc., Am. Peanut Rsch. and Edn. Soc. (chmn. site selection com. 1981, award com., pres.-elect 1981, pres. 1982), N.Mex. Acad. Sci. (chmn. com. 1980, pres. 1981, 82, treas. 1984-92, dist. scientist award 1984), Nat. Assn. Acad. Sci. (pres.-elect 1992-93, pres. 1993-94), N.Mex. Chinese Assn. (pres. 1983-84, 92-93, treas. 1985-86, past bd. dir.), Chinese Am. Citizens Alliance (v.p. Albuquerque lodge 1988-92, v.p. 2002—), Albuquerque Coun. for Internat. Visitors (v.p. 1988, pres. 1989-91), Sigma Xi (life, N.Mex. coord. centennial celebration, sr. editor commemorative pub. Frm Sundaggers to Space Exploration), Kiwanis Internat. (past pres. Clovis, past chmn. spl. program com., past bd. dir. Albuquerque). Home and Office: 2504 Griegos Pl NW Albuquerque NM 87107-2874 E-mail: Davidnkathyhsi@aol.com. *In grateful appreciation of my God-given talents and opportunities, my privileged academic trainings in China and U.S.A., and my professional experience and associations with world-wide scientists, I shall continue to contribute to the scientific advancement and practice, and to promote human understanding and international cooperation for the betterment of mankind and for the glorification of my Creator.*

HSI, DENISE CHUR-YEE TSO, investment consultant; b. San Francisco, Oct. 31, 1958; d. Thompson W.S. and Virginia C.H. (Leung) Tso; m. Edward Yang Hsi, Aug. 3, 1985; children: Edward Yang II, Clarissa Sian Li-hwa. AB in Journalism cum laude, U. So. Calif., 1981; postgrad., Loyola Marymount U., L.A., 1990—. Community rep. L.A. Unified Sch. Dist., 1978-80; exec. dir. student news svc. U. So. Calif., 1979-80; mktg. dir. Pacific Gold Designers, L.A., 1980-81; investment/property mgr. Colyear Devel. Corp., L.A., 1982-85; legal adminstr. O'Connor, Cohn, Dillon & Barr, San Francisco, 1985-86; exec. asst. Gibson, Dunn & Crutcher/WSGP Internat., Inc., L.A., 1986—. Bd. dirs. DEH Investments Ltd. Co-founder, editor newspaper Asian Pacific Lifeline, 1980. Mem. U. So. Calif. Pres.'s Circle, U. So. Calif. Jr. Aux., Alpha Gamma Delta (publicity coord. 1982, sec. 1982-83), Sigma Delta Chi, Alpha Mu Gamma. Republican. Avocations: tennis, squash, asian art, travel. Home: 819 S Ridgeside Dr Monterey Park CA 91754-3724 Office: Gibson Dunn & Crutcher Ste 4700 333 S Grand Ave Los Angeles CA 90071-3197

HSI, EDWARD YANG, lawyer, industrialist, medical venture capitalist, political advisor; b. Ann Arbor, Mich., May 30, 1957; s. Peter Hwei-Yang and Priscilla Lai-Fong (Lam) H.; m. Denise Chur-Yee Tso, Aug. 3, 1985; 2 children, Edward Yang II, Clarissa Sian Li-Hwa. BS, U. So. Calif., 1980; MBA, Duke U., 1983; JD, U. Calif., Davis, 1986. Bar: Calif. 1986, U.S. Dist. Ct. (cen. dist.) Calif. 1987, U.S. Ct. Appeals (9th cir.) 1987, U.S. Tax Ct. 1988, U.S. Supreme Court 1991. Tax intern Coca Cola Co., L.A., 1983, Lear Siegler Inc., Santa Monica, Calif., 1984; assoc. Lawler, Felix & Hall, L.A., 1986-87, Morrison & Foerster, L.A., 1987-89, Thelen, Marrin, Johnson & Bridges, L.A., 1989, Baker & McKenzie, Hong Kong, Singapore, 1989-92; of counsel Tilleke & Gibbins/Jones, Day, Reavis & Pogue, Bangkok, 1992—, Tilleke & Gibbins Cons., Ltd., Indochina, 1992—; group gen. counsel Humpuss Group Indonesia, Jakarta, Singapore, 1992-94; pres., CEO Humpuss Arun Aromatics Petrochemicals, Jakarta, Arun, Sumatra, 1994—96; exec. dir. Dharmala Group, Jakarta, 1997; vice chmn., CEO Asean Infrastructure Holdings Ltd., Jakarta, 1997—; chmn., CEO Asean Energy Group Ltd., Jakarta, 1998—. Spl. advisor to the shareholders Gunung Sewu Group and Duta Anggada Group, Jakarta, 1997; founder, prin. Grant Thornton Taira Hsi and Taira & Hsi, Internat. in cooperation with Kaye Scholer LLP, Jakarta, 1998—2000; advisor Govt. of Republic of Indonesia on a Policy Proposal for the Econ. Restoration of Province of Aceh, to chmn. of Indonesian Parliament DPR on a Nat. Econ. Revitalization Policy, 1998—99; mng. dir. Asia-Pacific region Mysmart Solutions, Inc., 2000—01; spl. advisor to chmn. Shingfa Group, Taipei, 2001—02; advisor Golkar Parliamentary Party of The Republic of Indonesia Del. to Taiwan to address Bilateral Internat. Cooperation in the Labor and Energy Sectors, 2002; bd. dirs. DEH Asia Ltd., VBP Ltd., AO Asia Ltd., Asia Beta Capital Ltd.; COO Pacific Republic Capital, a Med. Ventures Group, 2003—. Editor: Income Taxation of Foreign Related Transaction, 5 vols., 1987; contbr. articles on tax to profl. jours. Mem.: ABA, World Peace and Diplomacy Forum (mem. founding coun., Cambridge 2003—), L.A. County Bar Assn., State Bar Calif., U. Calif. Alumni Assn., Duke Alumni Assn., Hong Kong Stanley Residents' Assn., Tuen Ng Dragon Boat Races Festival (co-chmn., ATT and Baker & McKenzie entry), Indonesian Bus. Soc., Hong Kong Assn., Am. C. of C.-Hong Kong, Punahou Sch. Alumni Assn., Order of Coif, Phi Kappa Tau, Alpha Mu Alpha, Phi Delta Phi. Democrat. Avocations: southeast asian art, jazz drumming, classical music, anthropology, discipleship. Home: 819 S Ridgeside Dr Monterey Park CA 91754-3724 Office: Chase Plaza 21st Fl Jalan Jenderal Sudirman Kav 21 Jakarta 12910 Indonesia E-mail: eyhsi@yahoo.com.

HSI, ERIC D. hematopathologist; b. Kalamazoo, July 21, 1963; s. Richard. S.P. and Nancy N. Hsi. BA, Kalamazoo Coll., 1985; MD, U. Mich., 1990. Resident in pathology U. Mich., Ann Arbor, 1990-94, fellow in surg. pathology, 1994-95, fellow in hematopathology, 1995-96; asst. prof. pathology Loyola U. Med. Sch., Maywood, Ill., 1996-97; assoc. staff Cleveland Clin., Cleve., 1997-99, mem. staff, head sect. hematopathology, 1999—. Contbr. articles to profl. jours., including Nature, Human Pathology, others. Fellow Am. Soc. Clin. Pathologists; mem. Coll. Am. Pathologists, Am. Soc. Hematology, Soc. Hematopathology, Clin. Cytometry Soc., U.S. and Can. Acad. Pathology (Stowell Orbison award 1993). Office: Cleveland Clin Found L-11 9500 Euclid Ave Cleveland OH 44195-0001

HSIA, DAVID, health services researcher, administrator; b. NYC, Nov. 22, 1950; s. David Yi-Yung and Hsio Hsuan (Shih) H.; m. Susie Q. Lew, Nov. 12, 1991; children: Julie Lew Hsia, Katie Lew Hsia. BA, Haverford Coll., 1972; JD, Yale U., 1975; MD, U. Ill., 1984; MPH, Harvard U., Boston, 1982. Atty. Fed. Reserve Bd., Washington, 1975-79; intern VA Med. Ctr., Washington, 1984-85; resident Johns Hopkins, Balt., 1985-87; med. officer HHS Office of Inspector Gen., Washington, 1987-92, HHS Agy. for Healthcare Rsch. & Quality, Rockville, Md., 1992—. Detailee Nat. Performance Review, Washington, 1993-2000. Contbr. articles to profl. jours. including New Eng. Jour. Medicine, JAMA, Annals of Internal Medicine, Am. Jour. Pub. Health. Office: HHS-AHRQ 540 Gaither Rd Rockville MD 20850-6649

HSIA, FRANKLIN WEN-HAI, computer programmer, systems analyst, consultant; b. Taipei, Taiwan, Feb. 27, 1966; came to U.S., 1976; s. John and Daisy Chen-Chieh (Yu) H.; m. Deena S. Hsia. BA in Computer Sci., U. Buffalo, 1990. Program designer N.Y. State Sch. Bds. Assn., Albany, 1991-92; sr. computer programmer analyst N.Y. State Dept. Taxation and Fin., Albany, 1992-94, N.Y. State Dept. Health, Albany, 1994-95, assoc. computer programmer analyst, 1995-98, data comm. specialist, 1998—. Exec. cons. Get Connected!, Clifton Park, N.Y., 1996—. Cons. United Cerebral Palsy N.Y., Albany, 1995-96, mem. Sierra Club, Albany, 1996—. Recipient Best Practice award N.Y. State Forum Info. Resource Mgmt., 1996. Office: NY State Dept Health Empire State Plz C 148 Concourse Plz Albany NY 12237-0001 E-mail: get.connected@usa.net.

HSIA, SOPHIE S. language educator; b. Shanghai; came to U.S., 1973; d. Harvey J. and Helen (Tang) Hsia. MS, Georgetown U., 1976; EdD, Harvard U., 1989. Cert. in TESL. Lectr., rschr. Free U. Brussels, 1978-83; lectr., instr., tchg. fellow Tufts U., Lesley Coll., Northeastern U., Harvard U., 1986-90; assoc. prof. City U. Hong Kong, 1991-97; sr. fellow, assoc. prof. Nanyang Tech. U., Republic of Singapore, 2000—01; mem. online faculty U. Phoenix Sch. Advanced Studies, 2002—, area chair rsch. EdD program, 2003—. Mem. acad. program coun. U. Phoenix, Ariz., 2002—03. Sponsor Foster Parent Plan/Plan Internat., Warwick, RI, 1990—. Rsch. grantee Hong Kong Govt., others. Mem. APA, Am. Assn. Applied Linguistics. Home: 5555 N Sheridan Rd Apt 1816A Chicago IL 60640-1611 E-mail: shsia@email.uophx.edu.

HSIAO, KUANG-TING, mechanical engineer educator, researcher; s. Fong-Shen and Wong-Hsiu-Lang Hsiao; m. Juo-Wen Mao, Aug. 17, 2000. BS, Nat. Taiwan U., 1987—91; PhD, U. Del., 1994—2000. Postdoctoral fellow U. Del., Newark, Del., 1999—2000, rsch. assoc., 2000—03; asst. prof. mech. engring.

U. S. Ala., Mobile, 2003—. Mem.: SAMPE (assoc.), ASME (assoc.). Achievements include modeling transport phenomena in porous media in Liquid Composite Molding processes and developing intelligent, advanced materials processing technology; This technology utilizes computers to automatically design, monitor and control Liquid Composite Molding processes. Office: Mech Engring Dept EGCB 212 Univ Ala Mobile AL 36688 E-mail: kuangtinghsiao@yahoo.com.

HSIAO, MICHAEL S. electrical engineer, educator; b. Keelung, Taiwan; s. Ming-Yang Hsiao. PhD, U. Ill., 1997. Asst. prof. Rutgers U., Piscataway, N.J., 1997—; now with Va. Tech. NSF grantee, 2001. Mem. IEEE. Office: Rutgers U Dept Elec & Comp Engring 94 Brett Rd Piscataway NJ 08854-8058 E-mail: mhsiao@ece.rutgers.edu.

HSIEH, JIANG, research scientist; b. Beijing; s. Bai Zhang Xie and En Rong Gao; m. Lily Gong; children: Christopher, Matthew. PhD, Ill. Inst. of Tech., 1985—89. Sr. scientist Siemens Gammasonics, Inc., Hoffman Estate, Ill., 1984—86; principle rsch. scientist Siemens Gammasonics, Inc, 1986—89; sr. scientist GE Med. Systems, Milw., 1989—2000, chief scientist, 2000—. Contbr. over 90 papers, articles to profl. jours. Mem.: SPIE, IEEE. Achievements include over 85 US patents. Office: GE Medical Sys PO Box 414 W-1190 Milwaukee WI 53201 Office Fax: 262-312-7690. E-mail: jiang.hsieh@med.ge.com.

HSU, CHENG, decision sciences and engineering systems educator; b. Taipei, Taiwan, May 11, 1951; came to U.S., 1976; s. Chung-Yu and Te-Zeng (Yeh) H.; m. Susan Hsu; m. Susan; 1 child, Diana. BS in Indsl. Engring., Tunghai U., Taichung, Taiwan, 1973; MS, Ohio State U., 1978, PhD, 1983. Info. engr. China Tech. Cons., Inc., Taipei, 1975-76; grad. rsch. asst. Ohio State U., Columbus, 1977-80, grad. teaching assoc., 1980-82; asst. prof. decision scis. and engring. systems Rensselaer Poly. Inst., Troy, N.Y., 1982-88, assoc. prof., 1988-96, dir. undergrad. programs, 1989-91, dir. doctoral program, 1994—, prof., 1996—. Cons. Coopers & Lybrand, Albany, N.Y., 1988, Digital Equipment Corp., Nashua, N.H., 1991, Gen. Electric R&D, Schenectady, N.Y., 1995—; co-founder, bd. dirs. EnterNet, Inc., 2000—; patentee in field. Author: Enterprise Integration and Modeling: The Metadatabase Approach, 1996, Innovative Planning for Electronic Commerce and Enterprises: A Reference Model, 2000. Grantee GM, 1986—89, DEC, 1986—89, Johnson & Johnson, 1986—89 Aluminum Co. Am., 1992—95, Digital Equipment Corp., 1992—95, GE, 1986—95, GM, 1986—95, IBM, 1986—95, A T & T, 1987, NATO, 1988, State of N.Y., 1988, NSF, 1991—96, Samsung, 1995—98, U.S. Army, 1995—96, N.Y. State Dept. Transp., 1997—99, 2002—03. Mem. IEEE (sr.), ACM, Soc. Mfg. Engrs. (sr.), Prodn. and Ops. Mgmt. Soc., N. Am. Chinese Bus. Educators Assn. (bd. dirs. 1988-90). Republican. Home: 168 Maxwell Rd Newtonville NY 12110-4949 Office: Rensselaer Poly Inst 5219 CII Troy NY 12180-3590

HSU, CHUNG YI, neurologist; b. Taipei, Taiwan, China, Oct. 14, 1944; s. Huo and Jane (Wu) H.; m. Amy Yang, Sept. 27, 1974; children: Alice L., Virginia, Charles Y. MD, Nat. Taiwan U., Taipei, 1970; PhD, U. Va., 1975. Diplomate Am. Bd. Psychiatry and Neurology. NIH fellow Diabetes Rsch. Ctr., U. Va., Charlottesville, 1975-77; fellow dept. pharmacology Med. U. S.C., Charleston, 1977, intern dept. medicine, 1977-78, resident dept. neurology, 1978-80, chief resident dept. neurology, 1980-81, fellow clin. neuropharmacology, 1981, dir. neuropharmacology dept. neurology, 1981-89; dir. neuropharmacology div. restorative neurology Baylor Coll. Medicine, Houston, 1989-93; head cerebrovascular disease sect., dept. neurology Washington U. Sch. Medicine, St. Louis, 1993—2002; The Stein Family chair in neurology Barnes-Jewish Hosp., St. Louis, 2001—02; pres. Taipei Med. U., Taiwan, 2002—. Mem. adv. panel on drug info. U.S. Pharmacopeial Conv., Rockville, Md., 1985-90; mem. Nat. Inst. Neurol. Disease and Stroke, NIH, 1988-97, mem. nat. adv. bd. on med. rehab. rsch. Nat. Inst. Child Health and Human Devel., NIH, 1997-2001; mem. merit rev. com. neurobiology C, VA, 2000—. Mem. editl. bd. Stroke, Jour. Cerebral Blood Flow and Metabolism, Brain Rsch., Jour. Neurotrauma, Clin. Neuropharmacology, Jour. Med. Ethics and Humanities, Taiwan, Acta Neurologica Taiwanica; mem. guest editl. bd. Jour. Formosan Med. Assn.; editor 4 monographs; contbr. articles to profl. jours. Mem. rsch. and program evaluation com. Am. Heart Assn., 1998—; chair Bugher Found. award rev. com., 1999, 2000, 01. 2d lt. Taiwan Navy, 1970-71. Grad fellow U.Va. Sch. Medicine, Charlottesville, 1971-75; recipient Nat. Rsch. Svc. award USPHS, 1977, 81, NIH Tchr. Investigator Devel. award 1983-88, NIH Javits Neurosci. Investigator award, 1991-2001, Disting. Rschr. award Vivian L. Smith Found., 1993-94, Taiwanese Am. Found. award, 1997. Fellow Am. Acad. Neurology; mem. Am. Heart Assn. (fellow stroke coun., chair brain rev. com. 1996-97, rsch. program and devel. com. 1998—), Am. Neurol. Assn., Taiwan Stroke Soc., Taiwan Neurol. Soc., Internat. Soc. Cerebral Blood Flow and Metabolism, Neurotrauma Soc. (pres. 1992-93), N.Am. Taiwanese Prof. Assn. (pres. 1995-96), Taiwanese Assn. Charleston (pres. 1984-85), Dana Alliance for Brain Initiatives. Avocation: literature. Home: 538 Conway Village Dr Saint Louis MO 63141-5807 Office: Washington U Sch Medicine Dept Neurology Box 8111 660 S Euclid Ave Saint Louis MO 63110-1010

HSU, CORNELIA WANG MEI-CHIH, education educator; arrived in U.S.A., 1969; m. Justin Chin-Chung Hsu, Dec. 29, 1973; 2 children. BS, Providence Coll., Taiwan, 1967; MS, W.Va. Univ., Morgantown, W. Va., 1971. High sch. math tchr. Tainan Girls Middle Sch., Tainan, Taiwan, 1967—69; instr. St. Pauls Coll., Lawrenceville, Va., 1972—73, Morgan State Univ., Balt., 1973—. Cons. Urban Inst., Washington, 1973. Dep. sec. Global Alliance for Democracy and Peace, Washington, 2002. Mem.: Math. Assn. Am. Avocations: ballroom dancing, gardening, singing. Office: Dept Math Morgan State Univ Cold Spring Ln Hillen Rd Baltimore MD 21251

HSU, DONALD KUNG-HSING, educator, management consultant; b. Shanghai, People's Republic China, Apr. 17, 1947; came to U.S., 1970; s. Kuo Chung and Ching Hwa (Yang) H.; m. Salome Yu-Ching Hsiao, Mar. 18, 1972; 1 child, Douglas. BS, Nat. Cheng King U., Tainan, Taiwan, 1969; PhD, Fordham U., 1975. Rsch. assoc. Princeton U., 1975, Columbia U., 1976; instr. chemistry N.J. Inst. Tech., Newark, 1977-78; v.p. TCK Industries Inc., Bklyn., 1977-81; instr. data processing NYU, N.Y.C., 1980-82; asst. prof. physics and computer sci. St. Peter's Coll., Jersey City, 1978-83; coord. computer sci. program Felician Coll., Lodi, N.J., 1983-88; tech. instr. Dun and Bradstreet, Basking Ridge, N.J., 1988; assoc. prof. Dominican Coll., Orangeburg, N.Y., 1988—, dir. bus. adminstrn., 1990-96. Mktg. cons. Otsubo Internat., Ft. Lee, NJ, 1984—94, Yuasa Realty, Ft. Lee, 1995—; tech. project dir.computer grants Felician Coll., 1985—88; dir. mktg. TCT Fin., N.Y.C., 1995—2002, Fulton Group, NYC, 2002—; cons. in field. Contbr. articles to profl. jours. Sec., mem. exec. council Chinese Am. Acad. and Profl. Assn., N.Y.C., 1981-84. NASA fellow, 1975; NSF fellow, 1976, grantee, 1982-83. Mem. AAUP, IEEE (officer 1983-84), Assn. for Computing Machinery, Nat. Assn. Realtors, United Socs. of Engring. and Sci. of N.J. (pres. 1991-94), Cheng Kung U. Alumni Assn. Greater N.Y., Inc. (vice chmn.), Shanghai Tiffin Club (N.Y.C.; v.p. 1999—), World League Freedom and Democracy (pres. Greater N.Y. chpt. 1991—). Republican. Office: Dominican Coll Western Hwy Orangeburg NY 10962 E-mail: yanyou@hotmail.com.

HSU, GLORIA, piano teacher; b. Taipei, Taiwan, Mar. 26, 1959; d. Robert and Anna Chieu (Lu) Hsu. Student, Juilliard Sch., 1970-75; BA, Hayward (Calif.) U., 1992. Cert. profl. music tchr. Profl. piano tchr. MTNA, Calif., 1992—. Fundraiser for Vietnamese refugees S.I. Orphanage, 1980. Appeared on World Jour. fundraiser for Vietnamese Refugees. Great Neck Symphony Soc. winner Tchrs. of Piano, 1972. Mem. Music Tchrs. Nat. Assn. Democrat. Christian. Avocations: listening to medieval music, reading culture and history books. Home: 3371 Isherwood Way Fremont CA 94536-3566

HSU, IMMANUEL CHUNG YUEH, history educator; b. Shanghai, May 6, 1923; came to U.S., 1949, naturalized, 1962; s. Thomas K.S. and Mary (Loh) H.; m. Dolores Menstell, Apr. 14, 1962; 1 child, Vadim Menstell. BA, Yenching U., China, 1946; MA, U. Minn., 1950; PhD (Harvard-Yenching fellow), Harvard U., 1954. Postdoctoral research fellow Harvard U., 1955-58; vis. asso. prof. history, vis. prof. Harvard Summer Sch., 1961, 64, 68, 75; asst. prof. history U. Calif. at Santa Barbara, 1959-60, asso. prof., 1960-65, prof., 1965-91, chmn. history dept., 1970-72. Faculty rsch. lectr., 1971; mem. del. to Chinese Acad. Scis., Beijing, spring 1979, 80; vis. prof. Hamburg U., Germany, spring 1973, Stockholm U., 1990, Leningrad (St. Petersburg) U., 1991; Fulbright lectr., 1973; vis. Wei Lun prof. The Chinese U. Hong Kong, 1998. Author: Intellectual Trends in the Ch'ing Period, 1959, China's Entrance into the Family of Nations, 1960, The Ili Crisis: A Study of Sino-Russian Diplomacy, 1871-1881, 1965, The Rise of Modern China, 1970, 2d edit., 1975, internat. edit., 1975-76, 3d edit., 1983, 4th edit., 1990, 5th edit., 1995 (Commonwealth Lit. priz of Calif. 1971), 6th edit., 2000, Chinese trans., 2001-02; editor: Readings in Modern Chinese History, 1971, Late Ch'ing Foreign Relations, 1866-1905, in The Cambridge History of China, Vol. 11, 1980, China Without Mao, 1983, 2d edit., 1990. Guggenheim fellow, 1962-63; Nat. Acad. Scis. disting. scholar to China, spring 1983 Mem. Am., Pacific hist. assns., Assn. Asian Studies, Assn. Ch'ing Studies. Office: U Calif Dept History Santa Barbara CA 93106 E-mail: dhsu5@cox.net.

HSU, JOHN, anesthesiologist; b. Los Cruces, N.Mex., Sept. 16, 1962; s. Frank and Sumihsu Hsu; m. Sherie Hsieh, Sept. 24, 1988; children: Joffrey, Athena, Matthew. BS in Biochemistry, U. Calif., Riverside, 1984; MD, Loyola Med. Sch., Maywood, Ill., 1988. Staff anesthesiologist Lakewood (Calif.) Anesthesia Group, 1994; med. dir. Ctr. for Aesthetic Surgery, Brea, Calif., 1994, SBS Med. Mgmt., corona, Calif., 1995—. Cons. Yangsoft, Acton, Calif., 1994—. Mem. Am. Soc. Anesthesiology, Calif. Soc. Anesthesiologists, Am. Soc. Physician Execs. Office: SBS Med Mgmt 17532 Marengo Dr Rowland Heights CA 91748-4118

HSU, JOHN, physician scientist; MBA, Wharton Sch., Phila., 1995; MD, U. of Pa., 1995; MSCE, U. of Pa., Phila., 1999. Physician scientist Kaiser Found. Rsch. Inst., Oakland, Calif., 1999—2002. Office: Kaiser Found Rsch Inst 2000 Broadway 3rd Fl Oakland CA 94612

HSU, JOHN CHAO-CHUN, retired pediatrician; b. China, 1916; BS, U. Yenching, Peking, China, 1937; MD, U. Peiping Union Med. Coll., 1942; MPH, U. Mich., 1948; postgrad., Liverpool (Eng.) U., 1967. Diplomate Am. Bd. Pediatrics. Physician Nat. Inst. Health, Chungking, China, 1943-45; attending physician The 5th Mcpl. Hosp., Shanghai, China, 1946-47; postgrad. rsch. fellow Columbia U./Mt. Sinai Hosp., N.Y.C., 1948; rotating intern St. Elizabeth Hosp., Dayton, Ohio, 1950-51; resident in pediatrics Kaiser Found. Hosp., Oakland, Calif., 1953-54, Beth El Hosp., Bklyn., 1954-55; chief resident in pediatrics Royal Alexandra Hosp., Edmonton, Can., 1956-57; rsch. fellow Children's Hosp., L.A., 1958-59; pvt. practice specializing in pediatrics, L.A., 1959—. Fellow Royal Soc. Health (London), Royal Soc. Tropical Medicine and Hygiene (London), Am. Acad. Pediat., mem. AMA, APHA, Med. Coun. Can. (lic.). Home: PO Box 22683 San Francisco CA 94122-0683

HSU, KATHARINE HAN KUANG, pediatrics educator; b. Foochow, Fukien, China, Feb. 12, 1914; came to U.S., 1948; d. Wen Chen and Shu Fong (Huang) H.; m. T.L. Hsu, Apr. 26, 1941 (dec. Apr. 1990). BS, Yenching U., Beijing, 1935; MD, Peking Union Med. Coll., 1939. Intern Peking Union Med. Coll., 1938-39, resident, 1939-41; asst. prof. Baylor Coll. Medicine, Houston, 1953-60, assoc. prof., 1960-69, prof. pediatrics, 1970-79, prof. emeritus, 1979-94; ret., 1994. Recipient Disting. Achievement award Am. Thoracic Soc., 1994; named Internat. Woman Yr. Internat. Biog. Ctr., 1996-97. Avocation: photography. Home: 9427 Denbury Way Houston TX 77025-4036

HSU, KYLIE, language educator, researcher, linguist, educator; BA, U. Mich., 1980; MA, Calif. State U., Northridge, 1994; PhD, UCLA, 1996. Lang. and math. instr. U. Mich., Ann Arbor, 1976-80; asst. to pres. Am. GNC Corp., Chatsworth, Calif., 1980-86, exec. v.p., 1986-93; instr. in Chinese UCLA, 1994-95; dir. Lang. Inst. Pacific States U., L.A., 1996-97; asst. prof. Calif. State U., L.A., 1997—2002, assoc. prof., 2002—, assoc. chair dept. modern lang. and lit., 2003, assoc. dir. Chinese Studies Ctr., 1999—. Conf. chair Eng. Lang. Tchg. Conf., L.A., 1996; editor-in-chief Pacific States U. Newsletter, 1997; judge Chinese Poetry Recital Contest, L.A., 1997; manual evaluator Edwin Mellen Press, Lewiston, NY, 1998—; com. chair Major Tsai Scholarship in Chinese Studies, 1999. Author: (book) Discourse Analysis, 1998, Selected Issues in Mandarin Chinese Word Structure Analysis, 2002; mem. editl. bd. Multimedia Ednl. Resource Learning and Online Tchg., 2000—02; contbr. articles to profl. jours. Named one of 2000 Oustanding Scholars of 20th Century, 2000; recipient Hon. Sci. award, Bausch & Lomb, 1976; fellow, State of Calif., 1996—97; Olive M. Roosenraad Meml. scholar, 1976—80, Vieta Vogt Woodlock scholar, 1976—80, Lit., Sci. and Arts scholar, U. Mich., 1977—80, Alumnae Coun. scholar, 1976—80, Martin Luther King scholar, 1977—80, W. K. Kellog Found. scholar, 1977—78, James B. Angell scholar, 1979—80, Presdl. fellow/Rsch. grantee, U. Calif., Berkeley, 1996—97, Advanced Rsch. Lang. Acquisition grantee, U. Minn., Mpls., 2001, Regents-Alumni scholar, 1976—77. Mem.: IEEE (exhibits chair 1993), Assn. Linguistic Typology (scholar 1995), Am. Assn. Applied Linguistics (session chair 1995), Am. Coun. Tchg. Fgn. Langs. (panel chair 1997), Chinese Lang. Tchrs. Assn., Linguistic Assn. S.W. (organizer 31st ann. meeting), Phi Beta Kappa, Phi Kappa Phi. Office: Calif State U LA 5151 State University Dr Los Angeles CA 90032-8112 E-mail: kyliehsu@msn.com.

HSU, LIFANG, statistician, department chairman; b. Kaohsiung, Taiwan, Mar. 10, 1951; arrived in U.S., 1976; d. Yew Ting Hsu and Li Hwa Hwang; m. Pinyuen Chen, May 16, 1976; 1 child, Hannah Chen. BS in Math., Nat. ChengKung U., Tainan, Taiwan, 1973; MS in Math., U. Miami, 1978; MS in Applied Stats., U. Calif. Santa Barbara, Goleta, 1979, PHD in Math. Stats., 1983. Math. tchr. Nat. Panchiao H.S., Taipei, Taiwan, 1973—76; tchg. asst. Bucknell U., Lewisburg, Pa., 1976, U. Miami, Coral Gables, Fla., 1977—78, U. Calif. Santa Barbara, Goleta, 1978—83; asst. prof. SUNY, Oswego, 1983—89, Le Moyne Coll., Syracuse, NY, 1989—93, assoc. prof., 1993—2000, chair, prof., 2000—. Mem. exa.n com. Regent Coll., Albany, NY, 1994—96, on-line facilitator for stats., 2000—01. Contbr. articles to profl. jours. Summer Rsch. fellow, Air Force Office Sci. Rsch., Rome AFB, 1993, R&D grantee, LeMoyne Coll., Syracuse, 1990—91, 1992—93, 1995—96, 2001. Mem.: Math. Assn. Am., Am. Statis. Assn. (pres.-elect and program chair Syracuse chpt. 1997, pres. Syracuse chpt. 1998, mem. exec. com. Syracuse chpt. 1994—97, 1999—), Inst. Math. Stats. Avocations: drawing, swimming. Office: Le Moyne Coll 1419 Salt Springs Rd Syracuse NY 13214

HSU, MING-YU, engineering educator; b. Kweiyang, Kweichow, China, Dec. 4, 1925; s. Pei-Kung and Wan-Ju (Hsiao) H.; m. Chih-Ju Yao, Jan. 1, 1952; children: Chi-Hsing, Chi-Yun, Chi-En, Chi-Che, Chi-Cheng. BE, Nat. Kweichow U., 1948; Dipl.Engr., Delft Tech. U., The Netherlands, 1959. Registered profl. engr., Ill., Ga., Fla., S.C. Prof. Cheng-Kung U., Tainan, Taiwan, 1960-68; dir. Land Devel. Commn., Taipei, 1960-68; engring. cons. Ministry of Housing & Utilities, Sehba, Libya, 1968-71; sr. engr. Philipp Holzmann Ag., Hamburg, Fed. Republic of Germany, 1971-74, Weber, Griffith & Mellican, Galesburg, Ill., 1974-80; chief engr. Chatham Engring. Co., Savannah, Ga., 1980-82; sr. cons. Hussey, Gay, Bell & DeYoung, Inc., Savannah, 1982—; prof. Savannah Coll. of Art and Design, 1986—. Designed and constructed numerous indsl. office, apt. and comml. bldgs., marine structures including docks, loading platforms, marinas, shipyards and water and waste water treatment structures. Contbr. articles on structural engring. to profl. jours. Mem. Nat. Soc. Profl. Engrs., ASCE. Home: 1115 Wilmington Island Rd Savannah GA 31410-4508 Office: Hussey Gay Bell & DeYoung 329 Commercial Dr Savannah GA 31406-3630

HSU, PATRICK KUO-HENG, retired languages educator, librarian; b. Hefei, Anhui, China, July 3, 1936; came to U.S., 1965; s. Hsiang-Chang and Yi-Yun (Tan) H.; m. You-Wei Gina Wang, Feb. 1, 1962; children: David Shing, Jim Chi. BA, Nat. Cheng-Chi U., Mucha, Taipei, Taiwan, 1960; MSLS, Western Mich. U., 1968. Asst. libr. Ripon (Wis.) Coll., 1968-77, assoc. libr., 1977-85, libr., 1985; assoc. prof., libr. dir. Tex. Luth. U., Seguin, 1985-91, prof., univ. libr., dir. info. svc., 1991—2002. Dir. Univ. Students in Am. from Taiwan Consortium, Seguin, 1990-96. Translator, editor: A Selection of Modern One-Act-Plays, 1971; translator: Theory of Literature, 1976. Dir. Chinese Soc. San Antonio, 1989-95; mem. World Affairs Coun. San Antonio, 1993—, San Antonio Chinese Cult. Inst. (chmn. bd.), 1994-95; advisor Overseas Chinese Affairs Commn., Republic of China, 1994-96. Mem. ALA, MLA, Assn. Asian Studies, Chinese Lang. Tchrs. Assn., Tex. Libr. Assn., Seguin Lions. Avocations: travel, photography, chinese art collecting.

HSU, SHU-DEAN, hematologist, oncologist; b. Chiba, Japan, Feb. 21, 1943; came to U.S., 1972; s. Tetzu and Takako (Koo) Minoyama; m. San-San Hsu, Mar. 3, 1973; children: Deborah Te-Lan, Peter Jie-Te. MD, Taipei (Taiwan) Med. Coll., 1968. Diplomate Am. Bd. Internal Medicine, Am. Bd. Hematology, Am. Bd. Med. Oncology. Asst. in medicine Mt. Sinai Sch. Medicine, N.Y.C., 1975-77; asst. instr. medicine U. Tex., Galveston, 1977-78; lectr. in medicine Tex. A&M U., Temple, 1978-80; asst. prof. medicine U. Ark., Little Rock, 1980-83; practice medicine specializing in hematology-oncology Visalia (Calif.) Med. Clinic, 1983-00, Sequoia Regional Cancer Ctr., Visalia, 2000—. Chief hematology and oncology VA Med. Ctr., Temple, Tex., 1978-80. Contbr. articles to profl. jours. Fellow ACP; mem. N.Y. Acad. Scis., Am. Soc. Clin. Oncology, Am. Soc. Hematology, Calif. Med. Assn., Tulare County Med. Soc. Clubs: Visalia Racquet. Home: 3500 W Hyde Ave Visalia CA 93291-5620 Office: Sequoia Regional Cancer Ctr 602 W Willow Visalia CA 93291

HSU, STEPHEN MING, materials scientist, chemical engineer; b. Shanghai, Nov. 20, 1943; s. Chu-chen and Man-Yeo Hsu; m. Stella P. Lee, Sept. 8, 1968; children: Stephanie C., Vivian C. BSChemE, Va. Polytechnic Inst. State U., 1968; MSChemE, Pa. State U., 1972, PhD in Chem. Engring., 1976. Project engr. Dorr Oliver, 1968; rsch. engr. Amoco, 1974-78; group leader Nat. Inst. Stds. and Tech., Gaithersburg, 1978-85, chief ceramics divsn., 1985-92, group leader surface properties ceramics divsn., 1992—2002, leader nanomech. properties group, 2002—. Vis. prof. chem. engring. Pa. State U., 1991—92, adj. prof. chem. engring., 1983—97; adj. prof. materials scis. U. Md., 1994—98; Eshbach vis. fellow Ctr. Engring. Tribology Northwestern U., 1992; postdoctoral rsch. advisor NRC, 1980—; panelist nat. materials adv. bd. NAS, 1985, mem. com. on ceramic tribology, ant. materials adv. bd., 1986—87; chmn. Gordon Rsch. Conf. on Tribology, 1988, lectr., 80, 84, 86, 88, 92; mem. Nat. Steering Com. on Superconductivity Rsch. for Power Transmission, 1987—91; chair numerous confs.; nat. tech. coord. Internat. Energy Agy. Annex III on Advanced Materials, 2003—. Contbr. articles to profl. jours. Recipient Capt. Alfred E. Hunt meml. medal, 1980, Al Sonntag award 1991, Soc. of Tribologists and Lubricating Engrs.; Diamond Shamrock grad. fellow, 1971, Bronze medal for Superior Fed. Svc., Dept. Commerce, 1983, Silver medal for Meritorious Fed. Svc., 1990; fellow STLE, 2000. Mem.: ASTM (mem. petroluem products 1978—92, mem. recycled oil products 1979—87, mem. automotive products 1979—92, mem. analytical methods 1979—92, chmn. 1983—85, chmn. additive response of oils 1984—88, mem. oxidation methods 1987—92), TMS ASME (rsch. com. on tribology 1984—92), AICE, Am. Ceramics Soc. (mem. tribology working group 1985—86, dir. program on phase diagrams 1989—91), VAMAS (co-chmn. tech. working are on wear test methods 1995—, co-chmn. tech. working area on nanotech. 2001—), Orgn. Chinese Am. (founding pres. Chgo. chpt. 1976), Soc. Tribologists and Lubricating Engrs. (chmn. paper solicitation 1983, paper solicitation chmn. com. 1984, analytical com. 1985—86, chmn. ann. meeting program com. 1986, membership com. 1987—90, dir. 1987—94, steering com. mem. Wear Conf. 1995—97, sec., treas. Wear Materials Conf. 1997—99, v.p. 1999—, pres. 2001—, lubrication fundamentals com.), Soc. Automotive Engrs., Asian Pacific Am. Coun. (award 1987), Phi Lambda Upsilon, Phi Kappa Phi. Avocations: tennis, reading, bridge. Office: Nat Inst Stds and Tech Rm A265 Bldg 223 Mailcode 8520 I-270 & Quince Orch Gaithersburg MD 20899-0001 E-mail: stephen.hsu@nist.gov.

HSU, THOMAS TSENG-CHUANG, civil engineer, educator; b. Swatow, China, July 28, 1933; came to U.S., 1958; s. Benjamin D.H. and Lucy S.K. (Ma) Zi; m. Laura H.N. Ling, July 20, 1963; children: Lynne Ling, Mia Ming. BS, Harbin (China) Poly. U., 1957; MS, Cornell U., 1960, PhD, 1962. Engr. structural rsch. lab. Portland Cement Assn., Skokie, Ill., 1962-68; assoc. prof. structural engring. U. Miami, Coral Gables, Fla., 1968-73, prof., 1973-79, dept. chmn., 1974-78; vis. prof. dept. civil engring. Nat. Taiwan U., Taipei, 1979-80; prof. structural engring. U. Houston, 1980—, chmn., 1980-84, Moores univ. prof., 1998—. Eshbach disting. vis. prof. Tech. Inst., Northwestern U., 1991-92; prin. investigator NSF, Washington, 1970—; cons. Kaiser Transit Group, Dade County, Fla.; 1977-79. Author: Torsion of Reinforced Concrete, 1984, Unified Theory of Reinforced Concrete, 1993; contbr. articles to profl. jours. Recipient Rsch. medal Am. Soc. Engring. Edn., 1969, Award of Excellence, Halliburton Found., 1990; named Hon. Disting. Prof., Harbin Inst. Civil and Archtl. Engring., China, 1993. Fellow ASCE (Walter L. Huber Rsch. prize 1974), Am. Concrete Inst. (Leonard C. Wason medal 1965, Arthur R. Anderson award 1990). Home: 5034 Glenmeadow Dr Houston TX 77096-4212 Office: U Houston Dept Civil Environ Engring Houston TX 77204-0001

HSU, TSONG HAN, chemist, researcher; b. Linhai, Zheqiang, China, Oct. 10, 1922; arrived in U.S., 1962; s. pao sun Hsu and Fon wha Ho; m. Qi Wen Zhang Hsu, May 18, 1995; 1 adopted child, Wu Jun; m. Mayaung Tai Hsu, Nov. 6, 1950 (dec. Feb. 11, 1987). BS, Amoy (China) U., 1947; MS, Auburn U., Ala., 1964, PhD, 1968. Sr. scientist U.S. Plywood-Champion Papers, Brewster, NY, 1968—72; sr. rsch. and devel. chemist RSA Corp., Ardsley, NY, 1972—75; project dir. UN Internat. Devel. Orgn., Langoon, Myanmar, 1976—79; rsch. assoc. Jim Walter Rsch. Corp., St. Petersburg, Fla., 1980—82; sr. resin chemist Hillyard Chem. Co., St. Joseph, Mo., 1982—87. Fellow: Am. Inst. of Chemists. Achievements include patents in field of of adhesives. Home: 1548 81st Ave North Saint Petersburg FL 33704-4055

HSU, VINCENT P, epidemiologist; b. Bloomington, Ind., Aug. 30, 1968; s. King-Yi Eugene and Alice O Hsu; m. Grace Y Lai, Dec. 25, 2001. BS, Pacific Union Coll., 1986—91; MPH, UCLA, 1999—2000; MD, Loma Linda U., 1991—95. Diplomate Am. Bd. of Internal Medicine, 1998, Infectious Disease Am. Bd. of Internal Medicine, 2001. Asst. dir. Los Angeles County, Tb Control Program, 2000—01; epidemic intelligence svc. officer Centers for Disease Control and Prevention, Atlanta, 2001—. Lt. comdr. USPHS, 2001—03, Atlanta, GA. Decorated Crisis Response Svc. award USPHS. Mem.: ACP (assoc.). Avocations: triathlon, organ. Office: Centers for Disease Control and Preventi 1600 Clifton Rd MS A-34 Atlanta GA 30030 Office Fax: 404-639-3645.

HSU, YU KAO, aerospace scientist, mathematician, educator; b. Wukang, Hunan, China, Apr. 24, 1922; arrived in U.S., 1956, naturalized, 1972; s. Ming Yung and Zhu Ching (Liu) H.; m. Martha Tih Wang, Dec. 11, 1965; children: Timothy, Melinda Taylor. PhD, Rensselaer Poly. Inst., 1966. Rsch. asst. Rensselaer Poly. Inst., Troy, N.Y., 1962-66; asst. prof. aerospace engring. W.Va. U., Morgantown, 1966-71; assoc. prof. math. Univ. Coll., U. Maine, Orono, 1971-83, prof., 1983-93, prof. emeritus, 1993—. Inst. guest MIT, 1978; vis. fellow Princeton (N.J.) U., 1993; presented papers at NASA, 1993, NASA Lewis Rsch. Ctr., 1996. Author: Two-Phase Laminar Film Condensation, Applied Mathematics for Engineering Technology; contbr. articles to profl. jours. Summer faculty fellow Goddard Space Flight Ctr., 1987, 88, NASA Langley Rsch. Ctr., 1989. Mem. AIAA, Am. Math. Soc., Soc. Indsl. and Applied Math., Acad. Mechanics, Sigma Xi. Roman Catholic. Achievements include research and publications in pressure field caused by cone rotating in non-Newtonian liquid, also supercaritating hydrofoil, also non-steady molecular beam of strong shock structure problem, laminar film condensation. Home: 121 Juniper St Bangor ME 04401-4155

HSUEH, CHUN-TU, political scientist, historian, foundation executive; b. Canton, China, Dec. 12, 1922; came to U.S., 1949, naturalized, 1960; m. Cordelia Teh-hua Huang, Dec. 13, 1952. Cert., China Sch. Jornalism, Hong Kong, 1939; LLB, Chaoyang U., China, 1946, Raffles Coll., Singapore, 1946-49; MA, Columbia U., 1953, PhD, 1958; hon. doctorate, U. San Martin de Porres, Lima, Peru, 1984, Inst. Far Ea. Studies, Russian Acad. Scis., 1999. Research assoc. polit. sci. Stanford U., 1959-62; lectr. history U. Hong Kong, 1962-64; vis. assoc. prof. SUNY, Plattsburgh, 1964-65; assoc. prof. U. Md., College Park, 1965-68, prof. politics, 1968-92; pres. Huang Hsing Found., Md., 1990—. Prof. Columbia U., summer 1969, 89; sr. assoc. mem. St. Antony's Coll., Oxford U., 1969; vis. prof., acting dir. Free U. Berlin, 1970; prof. Harvard U., summer 1979, 84; vis. scholar Peking U., 1983, Hebrew U., Jerusalem, 1984; disting. vis. prof. Zhongshan U., Guangzhou, China, 1983—, Wuhan U., 1984—, Peking U., 1989—, Zhejiang U., 1992—, Hunan U., 1996—, Shandong U., 1999—; adv. prof. Fudan U., Shanghai, 1985—; vis. fellow Australian Nat. U., Canberra, 1985; rsch. assoc. Ctr. for Chinese Studies U. Calif., Berkeley, 1985-86; chmn. Washington and S.E. Regional Seminar on China, 1974-81; exec. dir. Asian Polit. Scientists Group in U.S.A., 1975-2000; mem. vis. com., dept. internat. rels. Lehigh U., 1979-85; pres., chmn., Huang Hsing Found., Md., 1990—; vis. prof. U. Hong Kong, Trinity term, 1985, hon. prof., 1991-96; hon. prof. People's U. China, 1993—. Fgn. Affairs Coll., Beijing, 1996—, Jianghan U., Wuhan, China, 1987—, Ningxia U., 1992—, Nanjing Normal U., 1996—, Grad. Sch., Chinese Acad. Social Scis., 1998—, The Confucius Acad.,

Shandong, 1998—; trustee Jinan U., Guangzhou, China, 1989—, Nanjing Normal U., 1997—, Nanjing U., 1998—; advisor Sun Yat-sen Found., Guangzhou, 1992—; bd. dirs. Atalntic Coun. U.S., Washington, 1994—; bd. dirs. Russian Rsch. Ctr. Chinese Acad. Social Scis., 1996—; hon. pres. Internat. Studies Assn., Shandong Province, 1998—; advisor Churchill Coll., U. Cambridge, 1998—, mem. exec. com.; bd. dirs. Atlantic Coun. Found., 1999—; hon. dir. Chaoyang Ctr. for Legal Studies, People's U. China, 2000—. Author: Huang Hsing and the Chinese Revolution, 1961, Chinese edit., 1980; editor, contbr. Revolutionary Leaders of Modern China, 1971, French edit., 1973, Dimensions of China's Foreign Relations, 1977, Asian Political Scientists in North America: Professional and Ethnic Problems, 1977, China's Foreign Relations: New Perspectives, 1982, Traditional Government in Imperial China: A Critical Analysis, 1982, The Chinese Revolution of 1911: New Perspectives, 1986, author/editor (books in Chinese with English title) People, Places and Politics, 1991, China and Her Neighbors: Prospects for the 21st Century, 1995, New Dimensions of China's Diplomacy, 1997, The New Russia: Politics, Economics and Diplomacy, 1997, Modernization of the Legal System and China's Economic Development, 1997, Confucianism and Modernization of Chinese Culture, 1998, Trade and Economic Relations Between China and Russia, 1999, China and Central Asia, 1999, Sun Tzu's Art of War and Its Value in Modern Times, 1999, Social Change in the Chinese Communities in Southeast Asia after World War II, 1999, Prospects for China's Relations with Europe in the 21st Century, 2000, Japan in Turbulence, 2001, A Strategic Study of Establishing a Maritime Shandong, 2000, Europe and China in the 21st Century, 2000, Social Life and Ideas Change in Modern China, 2001, The Cradle of Modern Chinese Jurisprudence: The History of Chaoyang University, 2001, Russian Siberia and the Far East, 2002, Central and Eastern Europe in Transition, 2002. Mem. Nat. Bicentennial Ethnic-Racial Coun., 1974-76, Nat. Com. on U.S.-China Rels., 1976—; mem. adv. com. Md. Bicentennial Commn., 1975-76; mem. nat. exec. com. Caucus for New Polit. Sci., 1973-75. Named hon. fellow Inst. Russian, East European & Ctrl. Asian Studies, Chinese Acad. Social Scis., 2000—, fgn. mem., Nat. Acad. Scis. of Ukraine, 2000. Mem.: Am. Polit. Sci. Assn., Western Returned Scholars Assn. (hon. chmn. Found. 1994—, Beijing, overseas hon. v.p.), Assn. for Asian Studies (chmn. com. on scholars of Asian descent 1981—84). Office: 14017 Wagon Way Silver Spring MD 20906-2065

HSUEH, EDDY C. surgeon, oncologist; b. Taichung, Taiwan, May 18, 1965; s. Yuan-tu Hsueh and Chai Hsu; m. Hui-ling Lee, Apr. 17, 1965; children: Joanne, Brandon. BA, U. Chgo., 1987, MD, 1991. Resident in gen. surgery SUNY, Bklyn., 1991—96; asst. dir. surg. oncology John Wayne Cancer Inst., Santa Monica, Calif., 1999—, dir. immunotherapy enhancement, 2000—. Recipient Young Oncologist Essay award, Am. Radium Soc., 1997, Mentored Clin. Scientist Devel. award, Nat. Cancer Inst., 2000—; grantee Tech. Transfer program, Calif. Dept. Health Svcs., 2000—02. Fellow: ACS (life); mem.: AMA (licentiate), Assn. for Academic Surgery (licentiate), Soc. Surg. Oncology (licentiate Best Clin. Rsch. award 1998), Am. Assn. for Cancer Rsch. (licentiate), Am. Soc. Clin. Oncology (licentiate Merit award 1997, 1998, 2000, Young Investigator award 1999, Career Devel. award 2001—). Achievements include research in elucidating the specific immunologic response in killing tumor cells; defining the predictive factors associated with cancer patient survival; development of novel strategy for immune mediated killing of cancer cells. Avocations: reading, travel, swimming. Office: John Wayne Cancer Inst 2200 Santa Monica Blvd Santa Monica CA 90404 Office Fax: 310-449-5261. E mail: echsueh@msn.com.

HSUEH, WEI, pathologist, educator; b. Inner Mongolia, China, Apr. 21, 1944; d. Hsing-ruh and Yu-ing H.; m. Frank Gonzalez-Crussi, 1978. MD, Nat. Taiwan U., Taipei, 1968; PhD, Ind. U., 1972. Diplomate Am. Bd. Pathology. Assoc. pathologist Children's Meml. Hosp., Chgo., 1978—; asst. prof. pathology Northwestern U. Med. Sch., Chgo., 1978-83, assoc. prof. pathology with tenure, 1983-90, prof. pathology, 1990—. Mem. GMA-2 study sect. NIH, 1992-96; mem. reversite site visit NIH/NICHD, 1992; spl. reveiwer NSF, March of Dimes, Chgo. Lung Assn., Scleroderma, NIH, 2000, 03, B.C. Health Rsch. Found., Can. Contbr. over 100 articles to profl. jours., 9 chpts. to books. Grantee Nat. Inst. Allergy and Infectious Diseases, 1979-84, NIH/Nat. Inst. Diabetes, Digestive and Kidney Diseases, 1984-2002, Nat. Inst. Child Health and Human Devel., 1994-99. Mem. Am. Assn. Investigative Pathologists, Am. Assn. Immunologists, Internat. Acad. Pathology. Office: Children's Meml Hosp 2300 N Childrens Plz Chicago IL 60614-3394

HTOO, MAUNG S. communications executive; b. Yonangyaung, Burma, Aug. 17, 1927; s. Li Than Pe and Daw Saw Yin; m. Loretta Anne Htoo, Jan. 19, 1953; children: Susan, Nancy, Rhonda, Naomi. BS, U. Maine, 1952, MS, 1954; PhD in Phys. Chemistry, Rensselaer Poly. Inst., Troy, N.Y., 1961. Rsch. chemist Internat. Paper Co., Gelns Falls, NY, 1954—61; mgr. tech. assurance labs. IBM Corp., Poughkeepsie, NY, 1961—92; prof. Rensselaer Poly. Inst., Troy, 1992—97; pres. Tech. Comm. Internat., Poughkeepsie, 1992—. Cons. IBM, 1982—92. Editor: Microelectronic Polymers, 1989; guest editor Polymer Engring. & Sci., 1972, 1975, 1978, 1981, 1984, 1987, 1990, 1993. Pres. Vassar Bros. Inst., Poughkeepsie, 1997—2003; chmn. Conservation Adv. Coun., La Alengo, NY, 2003—; dir. Dutchess County Sci. Fair, Poughkeepsie, 1989—. Fellow: Am. Inst. Chemists; mem.: IBM Acad. Tech., Soc. Plastics Engrs., Am. Chem. Soc. (sr.), N.Y. Acad. Scis., Rotary (pres. 1988—89), Sigma Xi. Achievements include patents for in field; design of chemical processes for semiconductor manufacturing plant; discovery of of several new organic semi-conductors. Avocations: reading, skiing, bicycling, walking. Home: 10 Rabbit Trail Rd Poughkeepsie NY 12603 Office: Technical Communications Internat 10 Rabbit Trail Rd Poughkeepsie NY 12603

HU, CHI YU, physicist, educator; b. Szchwan, China, Feb. 12, 1933; arrived in U.S., 1957, naturalized, 1974; s. T. C. and P. S. (Yang) Hu; children: Marica, Mark, Albert, Han Chin. BS, Nat. Taiwan U., 1955; PhD, MIT, 1962. Rsch. assoc. St. John's U., Jamaica, NY, 1962-63; asst. prof. physics Calif. State U., Long Beach, 1963-68, assoc. prof., 1968-72, prof., 1972—. NSF vis. prof. UCLA, 1988—90. Contbr. articles to prof. jours. Fellow NSF summer, 1965, 1976; grantee, NSF, 1969—70, 1986—88, 1988—90, 1990—, Calif. State U. Long Beach Found., 1965, 1966, 1970, 1972, Dept. Energy, 1986—88. Mem.: Am. Phys. Soc. Office: Calif State U Dept Physics Long Beach CA 90840-0001 Business E-Mail: chihu@csulb.edu.

HU, CHUANPU, pharmacologist; b. Harbin, China, 1961; arrived in U.S., 1986; s. Yuxian Hu; m. Wenyu Lu Hu. Undergrad., Cath. U. Louvain, Belgium, 1979—84, Licentiate, 1984; MS, U. Cin., 1988; PhD, Stanford U., 1993. Postdoctoral fellow Stanford (Calif.) U., 1994—96; math. statistician FDA, Rockville, Md., 1996—2000; sci. cons. Pharsight Corp., Cary, NC, 2000—01; pharmacometrician GlaxoSmithKline, Research Triangle Park, NC, 2002—. Contbr. chapters to books, articles to profl. jours. Mem.: Am. Statis. Assn. Office: GlaxoSmithKline PO Box 13398 Five Moore Dr Research Triangle Park NC 27709 Office Fax: 919-483-6380.

HU, DANIEL DAVID, lawyer; b. N.Y.C., 1960; BA, Rice U., 1982, MA, 1984; JD, U. Tex., 1986. Bar: Tex. 1986. Jud. clk. Hon. Norman W Black, Houston, 1986-88; assoc. Royston Rayzor, Houston, 1988-91; asst. U.S. atty. U.S. Attys. Office, Houston, 1992—. Mem.: Houston Asian Bar (commr., Tex. access to justice commn.), Lone Star Legal Aid (bd. mem.), State Bar Tex. Avocation: running. Office: US Attys Office PO Box 61129 Houston TX 77208-1129

HU, DAN-NING, ophthalmologist; b. Shanghai, Dec. 25, 1936; came to U.S., 1989; s. Bing-Kui and Hua-Li (Liu) H.; m. Yuk-Shan Chu, May 6, 1973; 1 child, Ying Wu. MD, Shanghai First Med. Coll., 1955; fellow, Johns Hopkins U., 1981. Chmn. dept. ophthalmology Chiuchang Hosp., Shanghai, 1970-79; dir. Zhabei Eye Inst. and Hosp., Shanghai, 1979-89; chmn., prof. dept. med. genetics and dept. ophthalmology Tiedao Med. Coll., Shanghai, 1984-89; vice-dir. Nat. Ctr. of Genetic Medicine, Shanghai, 1988-89; dir. Tissue Culture Ctr. N.Y. Eye and Ear Infirmary, N.Y.C., 1989—. Cons. Allergan, Inc., Irvine, Calif., 1993—; prof. dept. ophthalmology N.Y. Med. Coll., Valhalla, 1995—; cons. Pharmacia, Stockholm, 1993—, Kaoshing Med. U., Taiwan, 1999—; hon. prof. Shanghai First Hosp., China, 2000—; hon. prof. and dir. Myopia Inst., Wenzhou Med. Coll., 2000—; adv. prof. Fudan U.; hon. prof. Tong Ren Hosp. and Beijing Inst. Ophthalmology, 2001—. Author: Ophthalmic Genetics, 1988; assoc. editor: Pigment Cell Rsch., 1999—; mem. editl. com. Chinese Jour. Ophthalmology, 2002-; inventor in field. Recipient Chinese Med. Rsch. award Chinese Health Ministry, 1980; grantee NIH, Bethesda, Md., 1986, IPE Rsch. grant Glaucoma Found., N.Y.C., 1994. Mem.: Soc. Ocular Pigment Cell Rsch. (chmn. 1997—), Chinese Soc. Ophthalmology (com. 1979—90), Internat. Soc. Eye Rsch., Internat. Fedn. Pigment Cell Soc. (chmn. ocular/extracutaneous pigmentation expert group 1997—), Chinese Soc. Ophthalmic Genetics (chmn. 1979—89, award 1980), Chinese Soc. Med. Genetics (exec. com. 1986—89). Office: NY Eye & Ear Infirmary 310 E 14th St New York NY 10003-4201

HU, HAIJUN, atmospheric scientist, electrical engineer; b. Yanshi, Henan, China, Dec. 22, 1962; came to U.S., 1990; parents, Congjie Hu and Xiulian Wang. BS, Shandong U., 1983; MEng, Chinese Acad. Scis., 1987; PhD, Yale U., 1997. Asst. engr. Chinese Dept. Energy, Anyang, China, 1983-84; rsch. scientist Inst. Electronics Chinese Acad. Scis., Beijing, 1987-90; atmospheric scientist Airborne Rsch. Assocs., Inc., Waltham, Mass., 1996, Harvard U., Cambridge, Mass., 1997—. Contbr. numerous articles to profl. jours.; inventor, engr. in field. Co-recipient Advances in Sci. and Tech. award Chinese State Sci. and Tech. Commn., 1988. Mem. Am. Meteorol. Soc., Am. Geophys. Union. Avocations: reading, writing, travel. Home: 289B Summer St Arlington MA 02474-2819 Office: Harvard U Divsn Engring/Applied Scis 12 Oxford St Cambridge MA 02138-2902 Fax: (617) 495-4902. E-mail: hu@huarp.harvard.edu.

HU, JIAN, physicist, researcher; b. Chang Sha, Hunan, China, Dec. 23, 1956; s. Fang Yizhi and Daren Hu; m. Qiaoling Liang; 1 child, Yao. BS in Engring., Huazhong U. Sci. & Tech., China, 1982; PhD U. Edinburgh, Scotland, 1998. Chartered Physicist, UK. Rsch. asst. Nat. Inst. Power Sources, Tianjin, China, 1982—92, rsch. engr., 1987—92; rsch. assoc. Edinburgh U., 1998—99; rsch. fellow Napier U., Edinburgh, 1999—2001; scientist Nat. Renewable Energy Lab., Denver, 2001—. Contbr. articles to profl. jours. Assoc. mem. Scottish Internat. Resources Project, 1997—; headmaster Alba Cathay Chinese Sch., Edinburgh, Scotland, 1996—97. Recipient Outstanding Rsch. award, Chinese Govt., 1988. Mem.: IEEE (sr.), Inst. Physics (UK). Home: 1801 E Gerard Pl #123 Englewood CO 80110 Office: Nat Renewable Energy Lab 1617 Cafe Blvd Golden CO 80601 E-mail: hu2001j@hotmail.com.

HU, KE, medicinal chemist, pharmacologist; b. Dunhua, Jilin, China, Aug. 21, 1970; s. Zhi Cheng Hu and Rongrong Xu; m. Jin Chen. BS, Shenyang Pharm. U., Liaoning, China, 1993, PhD, 1998. Rsch. scientist Yale U., New Haven, 1999—2000, Roswell Park Cancer Inst., Buffalo, 2000—. Spkr. in field. Contbr. articles to profl. jours. Mem.: AAAS, Soc. Chinese Bioscientists in Am., Am. Assn. Pharm. Scientists, Am. Chemistry Soc., Am. Assn. Cancer Rsch. Achievements include 5 patents. Avocations: sports, travel, art, reading. Office: Roswell Pk Cancer Inst Dept Pharmacology Elm & Carlton Sts Buffalo NY 14263 E-mail: huke98@hotmail.com.

HU, KELLY, actress; b. Honolulu, Feb. 13; Grad., Kamehameha Sch. Actor: (films) Friday the 13th Park VIII, 1989, The Doors, 1991, Harley Davidson and the Marlboro Man, 1991, Surf Ninjas, 1993, No Way Back, 1995, Strange Days, Scorpion King, 2002, Fakin' Da Funk, 1997, Martial Law: The Movie, 1998; (TV films) The Bold and the Beautiful, 1987; (TV series) Star Command, 1996, Nash Bridges, 1996, Sunset Beach, 1997, Hollywood Squares, 1998, Martial Law, 1998; (TV films) American Eyes, 1991, numerous TV guest appearances, 1987—. Named Miss Teen USA, 1985, Miss Hawaii, 1993. Office: c/o Gage Group 9255 Sunset Blvd # 515 Los Angeles CA 90069

HU, LI, art educator; b. Shanghai, Sept. 16, 1950; s. Renzhi Hu and Keren He; m. Ping Li, Feb. 22, 1988; children: Yichen Hu, Elina Hu. BFA, Shanghai U., 1986; MFA, U. S.D., 1993. Art designer Xiechang Sewing Machine Co., Shanghai, 1977-83; asst. prof. Shanghai U., 1986-89; assoc. prof. U. Wis., Oshkosh, 1993—. Solo shows include North Central Coll., Naperville, Ill., 2002, Ripon (Wis.) Coll., 2001, Hopper House Art Ctr., Nyack, N.Y., 2001, So. Oreg. U., Ashland, 2001, Coll. of Siskiyous, Weed, Calif., 2000, 1078 Gallery, Chico, Calif., 2000, Lakeland Coll., Sheboygan, Wis., 2000, Morehead State U., Kent, 1999, U. Wis., Madison, 1999, Reno City Hall Gallery, 1999, Art Inst. and Gallery, Salisbury, Md., 1999, Art Ctr. in Orange, Va., 1999, Colo. State U., Ft. Collins, 1998, Coker Coll., Hartsville, S.C., 1998, Linfield State Coll., McMinnville, Oreg., 1998, McHenry County Coll., Crystal Lake, Ill., 1998, Chadron State Coll., Nebr., 1997, Kansas City Artists Coalition, Kansas City, Mo., 1997, Mont. State U., Billings, 1996, Corvallis Arts Ctr., Oreg., 1996, Minnetonka Ctr. for the Art, Wayzata, Minn., 1995, Bloominton Art Ctr., Minn., 1995, others; group shows include Ohio State U., Mansfield, 2002, Taipai Fine Art Mus., Taiwan, 2001, Leslie Powell Gallery, Lawton, Okla., 1997, 2000, Smithtown Twp. Arts Coun., St. James, N.Y., 1997, Korean Cultural Ctr., L.A.., 1996, Medici Art Ctr., Phila., 1996, San Francisco State U. Student Ctr. Art Gallery, Calif., 1995, Berkeley Art Ctr., Calif., 1995, Royal Garden Gallery, Copenhagen, 1987, Hunte Coll., N.Y., 1986, Kobe (Japan) Agr. Mus., 1986, Shanghai Art Mus., 1986, 87, 89, Coll. Visual Arts, St. Paul, 2001, Taipai Fine Art Mus., Taiwan, 2001 others; work collected at Sioux City Art Ctr., Iowa, U. S.D., Vermillion,, Ripon Coll., Wis., Coal and Oil Corp., Ji Lu, Japan, Art Corp. of Japan-China, Kobe, Japan. Recipient Hon. Mention Okla.: Centerfold, Seventh, Leslie Powell Gallery, Lawton and the U. of Sci. and Art, Chickacha, 1997, Faculty Devel. Rsch. grant U. Wis., Oshkosh, 1996, 1995, Juror's award Berkeley Art Ctr. Assn., Calif., 1995, others. Home: 4365 Bellhaven Ln Oshkosh WI 54904 E-mail: Hu@uwosh.edu.

HU, MICHAEL Z. chemical engineer, educator; b. Baoqing, Heilongjiang, China, Oct. 16, 1963; came to U.S., 1990; s. Tusheng and Zhangxian Hu; m. Lili Wang, July 5, 1989; children: Davis R., Angela M. BSChE, Nanjing U. Chem. Tech., MS in Chem. Engring., 1998; PhD in Chem. Engring., U. Idaho, 1993. Asst. prof. Nanjing U. Chem. Tech., 1988-90; postdoctoral rsch. assoc. Oak Ridge (Tenn.) Nat. Lab., 1993-95, devel. staff mem., prin. investigator, 1995—. Adj. prof. U. Tenn., Knoxville, 1997—; hon. prof. U. Md., College Park, 1999—, South China U. Tech., Guangzhou, 2002—; hon. guest prof. South China U. of Tech., Guangzhou, 2002—; chair for nanomaterials application conf. The Knowledge Found., Boston, 2000; chair nanosymposium ACERS Ann. Meeting, 2001, 2002. Assoc. editor Jour. Nanosci. and Nanotech., 2001—; contbr. numerous articles to profl. jours.; patentee in field. Recipient Tech. Achievement award U. Tenn./Battelle LLC, 2000, Significant Event award, 2000, Award of Merit for scholarly/profl. article Soc. for Tech. Comm., 2000; disting. grad. fellow U. Idaho, 1990; grantee DOE/BES/DMS, 1996, ORNL-LDRD, 1998, 99, 2000—, NSF, 1998-2000, DOE/TFA, 2000-02, others. Mem. Am. Ceramic Soc. (chair nanomaterial symposium 2001, 02, 1st place winner 2000, 1st prize poster award 1998), AIChE, Tau Beta Pi (life). Avocations: violin playing, tai chi, basketball, biking, music appreciation. Office: 1 Bethel Valley Rd Oak Ridge TN 37831-6181

HU, MING, pharmaceutical scientist; s. Hu and Chang; m. Yanping Hu; children: Vivian, William. PhD, U. Mich., Ann Arbor, 1988. Asst. prof. Wash. State U., Pullman, 1990—97, assoc. prof., 1997—. Founder Pullman Chinese Culture Ctr., Wash., 1997. Mem.: Am. Assn. of Pharm. Scientists, Am. Soc. of Pharmacology and Exptl. Therapeutics. Office: Dept Pharm Scis Wash State Univ Pullman WA 99164-6534 Office Fax: 509-335-5902.

HU, QIANG, research scientist, educator, engineer; arrived in U.S., 1995; s. Qi Hu and Liangzhen Liu; m. Yong Jiang; 1 child, Xinlei. MS, Zhejiang U., Hangzhou, China, 1981, PhD, 1990; MS, Wayne State U., 2002. Cert. AutoCAD, St. Clair Coll. Applied Arts and Tech., Ont., Can., 2001. Lectr. Jiangxi Poly. U., Nanchang, 1982—87; assoc. prof., lectr. Zhejiang U., Hangzhou, 1990—95; rsch. assoc. Wayne State U., Detroit, 1995—99, rsch. asst., instrnl. asst., 2001—02; product engr. AEROTEK Automotive Svcs., Dearborn, Mich., 1999—99; lectr. Oakland U., Rochester, Mich., 2002; project engr. Master Mfg., Inc., Mississauga, Canada, 2003—. Editor: (handbook) Concise Handbook of Machine Tools Design, 1994; contbr. articles to profl. jours. Grantee, Natural Nat. Sci. Found. China, 1994, Engring. Physics Inst. China, 1994. Achievements include patent for system and method for prediction sound radiation and scattering; research in prediction of sound radiation based on particle velocity measurements; modeling and simulation of pressure fluctuation inside automotive fuel injection system; modeling of dynamic cushioning performances of expanded plastics; optimal design of shockproof package. Home: 57 Weybridge Crescent Brampton ON L6V 3S3 Canada

HU, SHAOHUA, political scientist; b. Jinhu, China, Dec. 22, 1963; s. Jijian Hu and Boying Ge. PhD, Am. U., 1997. Rsch. asst. U.S. inst. Peace, Washington, 1994—98; vis. asst. prof. Colgate U., Hamilton, NY, 1999—2000, U. Aveiro, Portugal, 2000, Colby Coll., Waterville, Maine, 2000—; asst. prof. Wagner Coll., S.I., NY, 2001—. Author: Explaining Chinese Democratization, 2000; mem. editl. bd. Western Classics Internat. Rels., 1986—89. Pres. Chinese Students and Scholars Assn. Am. U., Washington, 1993—94. Fellow Rsch., Chinese Acad. Social Scis., Beijing, 1986—89. Mem.: Am. Polit. Sci. Assn. Home: 610 Victory Blvd # 3L Staten Island NY 10301 Office: Wagner Coll Dept Polisci 1 Campus Rd Staten Island NY 10301 Fax: 718 420 4158. E-mail: shu@wagner.edu.

HU, SHOUPING, education educator; m. Shaoqing Li, Oct. 30, 1998. PhD, Ind. U., 2000. Policy analyst Ind. U., Bloomington, 1999—2000; asst. prof. Seton Hall U., South Orange, NJ, 2000—. Recipient First prize for excellence in rsch. for young scholars, Peking U., 1995. Mem.: Assn. Study of Higher Edn., Am. Edni. Rsch. Assn. Office: Seton Hall University 400 South Orange Ave South Orange NJ 07079 Office Fax: 973-761-7642. Personal E-mail: hushoupi@shu.edu. E-mail: hushoupi@shu.edu.

HU, STEVE SENG-CHIU, scientific research company executive, academic administrator; b. Yangchou City, China, Mar. 16, 1922; s. Yubin and Shuchang (Lee) H.; m. Lily Li-Wan Liu, Oct. 2, 1977; children: April, Yendo, Victor. MS, Rensselaer Poly. Inst., 1940; PhD, MIT, 1942; postgrad., UCLA, 1964-66. Postdoctoral vis. rsch. fellow Calif. Inst. Tech., Pasadena, 1942-44; pres., mng. tech. dir. China Aircraft, China Motor Corp., Douglas Aircraft, various locations, 1943-48, Kelly Mining and Engring. Corp., Ariz., N.Mex. and N.Y., 1949-54; sys. engr., meteorol. sci. dir. RCA, Ariz., 1955-58; rsch. specialist Aerojet Gen., Calif., 1958-60; rsch. scientist Jet Propulsion Lab., Calif., 1960-61; mng. tech. dir. Huntsville divsn. Northrop Corp., Calif. and Ala., 1961-72; pres. Century Rsch., Inc. Scientific research company executive, academic administrator; b. Yangchou City, Kiangsu Province, Peoples Republic of China, Mar. 16, 1922; s. Yubin and Shuchang (Lee) H.; m. Lily Li-Wan Liu, Oct. 2, 1977; children: April, Yendo, Victor. MS, Rensselaer Poly. Inst., 1940; PhD, MIT, 1942; postgrad., UCLA, 1964-66. Postdoctoral vis. rsch. fellow Calif. Inst. Tech., Pasadena, 1942-44; pres., mng. tech. dir. China Aircraft Corp., China Motor Corp., Douglas Aircraft Corp's China Programs, Calif. and N.J. and N.Y., 1943-48, Kelly Mining and Engring. Corp., Ariz., N.Mex. and N.Y., 1949-54; systems engr., meteorol. sci. dir. R.C.A., Ariz., 1955-58; rsch. specialist Aerojet Gen., Calif., 1958-60; rsch. scientist Jet Propulsion Lab., Calif., 1960-61; mng. tech. dir. Huntsville div. Northrop Corp., Calif. and Ala., 1961-72; pres. Century Rsch., Inc.; bd. dirs. Am. Tech. Coll., pres., U. Am. United Rsch. Inst., Gardena, San Bernardino, Calif., 1973—; pres. U. Am. Found. and U. Am. Rsch. Found., Calif. and Taiwan, Republic of China, 1981—; bd. dirs., exec. v.p. Am. Astronautical Soc., Wash., 1963-70; cons. Hsin-Hwa Nuclear Reactor Program, Taiwan, 1954-58; prof. Auburn (Ala.) U., U. Ala., U. Ariz., U. So. Calif., L.A., 1957-73. Recipient Cert. of Merit and Cash award Commn. Aeronautical Affairs, Republic of China, 1945. Mem. Am. Astronautical Soc., AIAA, Nat. Assn. Tech. Schs., Shanghai Commerce/Industry Soc. (China, hon. chmn. 1991—). Recipient Cert. of Merit and Cash award Commn. Aeronautical Affairs, Republic of China, 1945. Mem. AIAA, Am. Atronautical Soc., Nat. Assn. Tech. Schs., Shanghai Commerce/Industry Soc. (china: hon. chmn. 1991—). Office: Office Sect Century Rsch Bldg 16935 S Vermont Ave Gardena CA 90247-5630

HU, TEH-WEI, economics educator; b. Shanghai, Oct. 10, 1937; came to U.S., 1961; married. PhD, U. Wis., 1967. Statis. analyst World Bank, Washington, 1962-63; asst. prof. Pa. State U., University Park, 1966-70, assoc. prof., 1970-72, prof., 1972-86, U. Calif., Berkeley, 1986—, chmn., 1990-93, assoc. dean, 2000—03. Cons. World Bank, 1985-93, Ford Found., 1983-88, Ministry of Health, People's Rep. of China, 1990—. Named Disting. in Social Svcs., Pa. State Alumni Assn., 1985, Disting. Alumni, Econs. Inst., U. Colo., 1992. Mem. Am. Econs. Assn., N.Am. Chinese Econs. Assn. (pres. 1987-89). Office: U Calif Sch Pub Health 412 Warren Hl Berkeley CA 94720-0001

HU, YIFAN, computational mathematician; b. Shanghai, Oct. 26, 1963; s. Wenxian Hu and Yinghua Ji; m. Yuan Wang, Oct. 24, 1963; children: Madeleine, Lucy. BSc with honors, Shanghai-Jiao-Tong, 1985, MSc with honors, 1988; PhD, Loughborough (Eng.) U., 1992. Chartered mathematician. Asst. lectr. Shanghai-Jiao-Tong U., 1988-89; sr. scientific officer CLRC Daresbury Lab., Warrington, Eng., 1992-97, 98-2001; sr. developer Wolfram Rsch. Inc., 2001—. Sr. devel. engr. Computational Dynamics, London, 1997-98 Fellow Inst. of Math. and its Applications. Achievements include research on new algorithms for parallel computing, new algorithms for optimization, new algorithms for sparse matrix ordering. Office: Wolfram Rsch Inc 100 Trade Center Dr Champaign IL 61820 Fax: 1-217-398-0747. E-mail: yifanhu@wolfram.com.

HU, YUN HANG, chemical engineer; PhD, Xiamen U., China, 1990. Sr. staff engr. Exxon Mobil Rsch. and Engring. Co., Annandale, NJ, 1998—2002; rsch. full prof. SUNY-Buffalo, Amherst, NY, 2002—, vis. scientist, 1995—98; assoc. prof. Xiamen U., 1992—95, asst. prof., 1990—92. Contbr. scientific papers to profl. jours. Mem.: AIChE, Am. Chem. Soc. Avocation: acting. Office: SUNY at Buffalo 303 Furnas Hall Amherst NY 14260 Office Fax: 716-645-3822. E-mail: yhu@buffalo.edu.

HU, ZHIYU, research scientist, educator; b. Kunming, Yunnan Province, China, June 30, 1965; s. Wenguo Hu and Ping Li; m. Hongzhi Li, June 2, 1965; children: Lydia, Liana. BS, Yunnan U., 1986; MA, Fisk U., 1995; PhD, U. Tenn., 2000. Asst. engr. Kunming Inst. Tech., Kunming, 1986—90; team leader and tchr. Yangbi Detachment of Vols. in Ednl. Svc., Yangbi, 1988—89; exchange vis. scholar U. Va., Charlottesville, 1990—93; gradute rsch. asst. Oak Ridge Nat. Lab., Oak Ridge, Tenn., 1995—2000; head Protiveris, Inc., Rockville, Md., 2000—02; staff scientist Oak Ridge Nat. Lab., Tenn., 2002—; rsch. asst. prof. U. Tenn., 2002—. Cons. Protiveris, Inc., Rockville, 2002—. Named Outstanding Vol. Tchr., Dept. of Edn. Yunnan Province, 1989; named to 11th Discover Mag. awards for technol. innovation, Discover Mag., 2000. Mem.: Microscopy Soc. Am., Materials Rsch. Soc., Electrochem. Soc., Am. Physics Soc., Sigma Pi Sigma. Office: Oak Ridge Nat Lab Bethel Valley Rd PO Box 2008 Oak Ridge TN 37831-6123 Office Fax: 865-574-6210. E-mail: huzn@ornl.gov.

HUA, SHIPING, political science educator; b. Hebei, China, Mar. 28, 1956; came to U.S., 1987; s. Jingwen and Suxia (He) H.; m. Jia Qin, Aug. 24, 1987; children: Xiaojia, James Hong. BA, Tianjin Fgn. Langs. Inst., China, 1982; MA, Chinese Acad. Social Sci., Beijing, 1986; PhD, U. Hawaii at Manoa, Honolulu, 1993. Degree assoc., vis. fellow East West Ctr., Honolulu, 1990-94; assoc. prof. polit. sci. Eckerd Coll., St. Petersburg, Fla., 1996—2003, Univ. Louisville, 2003—. Editor, translator: Reporting and Writing the News, 1987; author: Scientism and Humanism: Two Cultures in Post-Mao China, 1995, Chinese Political Culture, 2001. Mem. Am. Polit. Sci. Assn., Assn. Asian Studies. Office: 4200 54th Ave S Saint Petersburg FL 33711-4744 E-mail: huasp@eckerd.edu.

HUA, XIANXIN, cell and cancer biology educator; b. Tongshan, Hubei, China, Aug. 27, 1962; s. Chengda Hua and Donge Jia; m. Wei Gao, June 24, 1988; children: Connie, Michael. MD, Hubei Med. Coll., 1983; PhD, U. Tex. Southwestern Med. Ctr., Dallas, 1995. Postdoc. clin. scientist, Whitehead Inst., MIT, Cambridge, 1996-2000; asst. prof. cell biology, cancer biology, U. Pa., Phila., 2000—. Recipient Howard Temin award Nat. Cancer Inst., 1998, Career Devel. award Burroughs Welcome Fund, 1998, Rita Allen Scholar, 2002, Am. Cancer Soc. Rsch. Scholar, 2003. Em. AAAS. Office: Univ Pa 412 BRB 2/3 421 Curie Blvd Philadelphia PA 19104-6160

HUAMAN-MEJIA, ANTONIO, pathologist; b. Chota, Cajamarca, Peru, Nov. 8, 1929; s. Octavio and Genoveva (Mejia) H.; m. Rosa Ana Castillo, May 3, 1956; children: Rosa Ines, Ana Genoveva, Antonio Andres. MD, U. San Marcos, 1956; DrMed, U. Cayetano Heredia, 1973. Diplomate Am. Bd. Pathology, Am. Bd. Nuclear Medicine. Med. inspector Peruvian Social Security, Tacna, 1957-58; chief med. lab. So. Peru Copper Corp., Tacna, 1957-59; dir. lab. St. Francis Hosp., Topeka, 1963-79; cons. pathologist Damon Corp., Topeka, 1970-78; dist. coroner 4th Jud. Dist., Topeka, 1978-81; chief pathology Ministry Def. and Aviation, Tabuk, Saudi Arabia, 1981-84; med. dir. Kans.

Neurol. Inst., Topeka, 1985-86; chief pathology Security Forces Hosp., Riyadh, Saudi Arabia, 1986-89; chmn. Patol King Khaled Eye Hosp., Riyadh, 1989—97; asst. clin. prof. pathology King Saud U., Riyadh, 1992—97; asst. clin. prof. pathology and ophthalmology Kans. U., Kansas City, 1997—. Vis. prof. pathology, U. Health Scis., Antigua, W.I. Author: Expats and Scuds, 1997; contbr. articles to profl. jours. Fellow Coll. Am. Pathologists; mem. Am. Acad. Ophthalmologists, Internat. Acad. Pathology, Latin Am. Pathology Found. (pres. 1979-80), Colegio Medico Peruano, Internat. Soc. Geo. Ophthalmology. Democrat. Roman Catholic. Avocations: writing, graduate medical education. Home: 2637 SW Westport Dr Topeka KS 66614-2513

HUANG, BEN (HAIBIN HUANG), chemical engineer, researcher; b. Xian, Shanxi, China, Oct. 1, 1959; came to U.S., 1991; s. Yun Zhen and Wen Xian (Chen) Huang; m. Meng Qiu Zheng, Aug. 19, 1995; children: William Z., Catherine Y. BS, Xian Inst. Metallurgy, China, 1981; MS in Polymer Chemistry, U. Sci. & Tech. of China, Hefei, China, 1988; MS in Chem. Engring., U. S. Fla., 1994, PhD in Chem. Engring., 1997. Process engr. Shanxi Chem Design Co., Xian, China, 1982-85; asst. prof. S. China U. Tech., Guang Zhou, China, 1988-91; rsch. chemist Film Techs Internat., St. Petersburg, Fla., 1997-98, R&D mgr., 1998—. Contbg. co-author: Interfacial Aspects of Multicomponent Polymer Materials, 1997. Recipient Excellent Thesis award Anhui Acad. Soc., China, 1989. Mem. Am. Chem. Soc. Achievements include patents pending for; patents in field; invention of tech. to synthesize mono-distributed, polymer encapsulated particles with the emulsion polymerization method; development of three layered polymer matrix for fiber optical sensor. Avocations: hiking, travel, reading. Office: Film Techs Internat Inc 2544 Terminal Dr S Saint Petersburg FL 33712-1669

HUANG, C. P. engineering educator; b. Changhua, Taiwan, Taiwan, Oct. 4, 1941; s. Wan-ji and You Huang; m. Yu-chu Chang, June 9, 1946; children: Catherine Kailing, Calvin Kaiming. BS, Nat. Taiwan U., Taipei, 1965; MS, Harvard U., 1967, PhD, 1971. Registered profl. engr., Assn. of Profl. Engrs. Disting. prof. U. of Del., Newark, 1963—, chmn., 1966—2001. Recipient Gordon Maskew Fair award, Water Environment Fedn., 1998. Office: U Del 356 Du Pont Hall Newark DE 19716 Office Fax: 302-831-3640. E-mail: huang@ce.udel.edu.

HUANG, CHANG-SHAN, landscape architect, educator; b. Fushun, China, Feb. 28, 1959; came to U.S., 1985; s. Wei-Guo Huang and Shu-Mei Chen; m. Ying Shan, Feb. 10, 1985; 1 child, Kerry. B in Architecture, Tsinghua U., 1983; MLA, Pa. State U., 1992; MA, PhD, U. Pa., 1995. Registered landscape architect, Tex. Instr. Tsinghua U., Beijing, 1983-85; landscape arhcitect John Rahenkamp Cons., Inc., Phila., 1988-91; cmty. planner Michael Cabot Assn., Stroudsburg, Pa., 1992-95; assoc. prof. landscape architecture Tex. A&M U., College Station, 1995-2001, 2001—; prin. HHL Group, Inc., College Station, 2003—. Mem. Am. Inst. Cert. Planners, Am. Soc. Landscape Architects, Am. Planning Assn., Overseas Chinese Landscape Architects Assn. (pres. 2002-03), Phi Beta Delta. Avocations: landscape drawing, watercolor, photography, music, travel. Home: 803 Royal Adelade Dr College Station TX 77845-4441 Office: Tex A&M U Coll Architecture College Station TX 77843-0001 E-mail: cshuang@archone.tamu.edu.

HUANG, CHENG-TEH JAMES, linguistics educator; b. Hualien, Taiwan, China, June 4, 1948; s. Ching-Fa Huang and Hsui-O Chen; m. Hsiao-Y Emily Huang, Nov. 30, 1977; children: Yiching Deborah, David J. BA, Nat. Taiwan Normal U., Taipei, China, 1972; MA, Nat. Taiwan Normal U., Taipei, Taiwan, 1974; PhD, MIT, 1982. Asst. prof. U. Hawaii, Honolulu, 1982-83, Nat. Tsing Hua U., Hsinchu, Taiwan, 1983-85; from asst. prof. to assoc. prof. Cornell U., Ithaca, N.Y., 1985-90; prof. U. Calif., Irvine, 1989-2001, Harvard U., Cambridge, Mass., 2001—. Vis. prof. Linguistic Inst., 1986, 91, 97, U. Paris, 1991; dir. Summer Inst. Chinese Linguistics, Santa Cruz, 1991, Cornell, 1997. Co-editor: Squibs and discussions, 1987-89; mem. editl. bd. Lang. Rsch., 1984—, Jour. Japanese Linguistics, 1985—, Linguistic Inquiry, 1987—, Nat. Lang. and Linguistic Theory, 1987-91, Oxford Series Comparative Grammar, 1989—, Nat. Lang. Linguistics, 1991—, Syntax: Theoretical and Exptl. Approaches, 1997—, Jour. Generative Grammar, 1998—; editor-in-chief Contemporary Chinese Linguistics, 1994—, Studies in Contemporary Linguistic Theories, 1996—; contbr. articles to profl. jours. Fulbright fellow, 1978-82, Guggenheim fellow, 1988-89, Sr. Scholar fellow Chiang Ching-Kuo Found., 1996-97, fellow Ctr. Advanced Study Behavioral Scis., 1997-98. Mem. Linguistic Soc. Am. (mem. program com. 1992-95, mem. com. linguistic insts. and fellowships 1997), Internat. Assn. Chinese Linguistics (pres. 2000). Home: 43 Upland Rd Cambridge MA 02140 Office: Harvard U Dept Linguistics Cambridge MA 02138 E-mail: jhuang@ui.edu.

HUANG, DONGZHOU, civil engineer, researcher, engineering educator; b. Ruijin, China, Nov. 5, 1949; arrived in U.S., 1990; s. Ziquan and Youdi (Zhu) Huang; m. Yingying Shu, Feb. 10, 1979; 1 child, Yicheng. BS, Tongji U., 1974, MS, 1985, PhD, 1989. Asst. prof. Tongji U., Shanghai, 1980-88, assoc. prof., 1989—; rsch. assoc. prof. Fla. Internat. U., Miami, 1990-95, rsch. prof., 1995-97; engr. Fla. Dept. Transp., Miami, 1997-99; sr. rsch. scientist Structural Rsch. Ctr., Tallahassee, 1999—; prof. Fuzhou U., China, 1999—; hon. prof. Sch. Civil Engring. Shandong U., China, 2003—. Assoc. dir. Bridge Rsch. Ctr. Tongji U., Shanghai, 1986—90; hon. prof. sch. civil engring. Shandong U., China, 2003—, hon. prof. Sch. Civil and Hydraulic Engring., 2003—. Coauthor: (book) Stability and Vibration of Bridge Structures, 1991 (1st prize Best Publs. in China, 1993); contbr. chapters to books, over 50 articles to profl. jours. Mem.: ASCE, N.Y. Acad. Sci. Achievements include establishment of methods for analyzing dynamic responses/impact factors of multi-girder bridges, box girder bridges, curved girder bridges, arch bridges, cable-stayed bridges due to moving vehicles; found the basic relationship between static and dynamic responses as well as the relationship between impact factor and lateral load distribution factor; development of finite element methods for analyzing elastic and inelastic lateral buckling of truss and trussed-arched bridges, as well as for static and dynamic analysis of curved box girder bridges; a practical method for determining lateral load distribution factors of arch and beam bridges; a bridge load capacity rating method through test; design method of end zone reinforcement for precast-prestressed concrete beams. Office: Structural Rsch Ctr 2007 E Paul Dirac Dr Tallahassee FL 32310-3760 E-mail: dong.huang@juno.com.

HUANG, EUGENE YUCHING, civil engineer, educator; b. Changsha, China, Nov. 28, 1917; came to U.S., 1948, naturalized, 1962; s. Sam and Yi Yun (Chao) H.; m. Helen M. Woo, Aug. 20, 1955; children: Martha, Pearl, William, Mary, Priscilla, Stephen. *Eugene Huang's daughter, Martha, AB1978 Harvard, PhD 1999 Columbia, is a free-lance writer. His daughter, Pearl, SB 1980 MIT, PhD 1990 Princeton, is employed as director of oncology for Glaxo Smith Kline Co. Eugene's son, William, AB 1981 Harvard, JD 1986 Yale, PhD, 1998 University of California Berkeley, is an attorney in Washington DC. His daughter, Mary, AB 1984 Harvard, MD 1988 Duke, is an oncologist at Massachusetts General Hospital. His daughter, Priscilla, SB1986 MIT, MBA 1990 Pennsylvania, is employed as senior director of financial evaluation and analysis for Merck Co. His son, Stephen, BS 1990 Yale, MD 1995 Pennsylvania, is an endocrinologist at Boston Children's hospital.* MS, U. Utah, 1950; D.Sc., U. Mich., 1954. Registered profl. engr., Ill., Mich. Asst. engr. Chinese Nat. Hwy. Adminstrn., 1941-45, asso. engr., 1945-48; research asst. Engring. Research Inst., U. Mich., 1953-54; research asst. prof. civil engring. U. Ill., Urbana, 1954-58, asso. prof., 1958-63; prof. transp. engring. Mich. Tech. U., Houghton, 1963-84; acting head dept. civil engring., 1979-80; acting dean of grad. studies Mich. Tech. U., Houghton, 1981-83, prof. emeritus transp. engring., 1984—. Cons. transp. systems design, soil mechanics, 1954— Author: Overview of the American Transportation System, 1976; contbr. numerous articles on transp. design systems and research on materials for pavement to profl. jours. Recipient Faculty Research award Mich. Tech. U., 1967 Fellow ASCE; mem. AAAS, ASTM, NRC (transp. rsch. bd. 1954), Am. Soc. Engring. Edn., Assn. Asphalt Paving Technologists, Inst. for Opns. Rsch. and the Mgmt. Scis., Am. Ry. Engring. Assn., Sigma Xi, Chi Epsilon, Tau Beta Pi, Phi Tau Phi. Episcopalian. Home: 400 Garnet St Houghton MI 49931-1420

HUANG, GUIYOU, English studies educator, writer; b. Xinjiang, China, Dec. 24, 1961; came to U.S., 1989; s. Huang Honglai and Dong Xiuqin; m. Yufeng Qian; 1 child, George Ian. BA in English, Qufu Tchrs. U., 1983; MA in English, Peking U., 1989; PhD in English, Tex. A&M U., 1993. Instr. Qufu Tchrs. U., 1983-86; tchg. asst. Peking U., 1986-89; editl. asst. South Ctrl. Rev. Tex. A&M U., College Station, 1989-93, lectr., 1993-95; asst. prof. Kutztown U., Pa., 1995-2000, assoc. prof., 2000—03, prof., 2003—, dir. univ. honors program, 2000—, chair dept. English, 2002—. Author: Whitmanism, Imagism, and Modernism in China and America, 1997; editor: Asian American Autobiographers, 2001, Asian American Poets, 2002, Asian American Short Story Writers, 2003; contbr. articles to profl. jours. Recipient Profl. Devel. awards State Sys. Higher Edn. Pa., 1997-98, 2003. Mem. MLA, Am. Lit. Assn., Am. Studies Assn., South Cen. MLA, Frederick Douglass Inst. (founding mem.), Assn. for Asian Am. Studies. Avocations: swimming, travel, cooking, fishing, conversation. Home: 312 Susquehanna Trl Allentown PA 18104 E-mail: huang@kutztown.edu.

HUANG, HERTZ, market researcher, statistician; b. Yuandi, Maioli, Taiwan, Nov. 30, 1938; s. Hotz and Chaijo Wang Huang; m. Elizabeth T. Huang; 1 child, Henry W. M.S. in Stats., Iowa State U., 1970, PhD. in Stats., 1972. Sr. rsch. analyst Minn. State Dept. of Edn., St. Paul, 1974—77; Math. Stats. U.S. Dept. Health Edn. and Welfare, Washington D.C., 1977—78, U.S. Bur. of the Census, Washington D.C., 1978—79, supr. math. stats., 1979—94; pres. Taiwan Mktg. Rsch. Inc., Taipei, Taiwan, 1994—. Pres. and ctrl. com. mem. Formosan Assn. for Pub. Affairs, Washington D.C., 1991; pres. The Taiwanese Assn. of Am., 1990. Mem.: Am. Stats. Assn. (mem. 1970—). Home: 7005 Petunia St Springfield VA 22152 Office: Taiwan Marketing Research Inc 9F No51 Sung Chiang Rd Taipei Taiwan

HUANG, HSIEN-LU, electrical engineer; b. Hsiang-Hsiang, Hunan, China, Dec. 12, 1923; s. Shao-Ju and Ching (Yu) H.; m. Hui-Lien Peng Huang, Jan. 1, 1947; children: Su and Nan-Ching Chang, Kung and Janet Tu Huang, Chin and Samuel Lin, Hsin and Chris Lu, Sung-Ping and Emanuel Lin, Peter Sung-an and Nina Wang Huang. BSEE, Nat. Hunan U., 1944; MSEE, Va. Polytechnic Inst./State U., 1968, PhD in Elec. Engring., 1969. Cert. mgr. Rockwell Nat. Mgmt. Assn. Maj. Chinese Air Force, 1944-64, prodn. control chief, quality control officer, dep. squadron comdr., 1944-64; assoc. prof. in elec. engring. Taipei Inst. Technology, 1960-66; instr. in elec. engring. Va. Polytechnic Inst. and State U., Blacksburg, 1968-69; asst. prof. in elec. engring. W.Va. U., Morgantown, 1970-74; devel. design engr. Barber - Colman Co., Rockford, Ill., 1975-76 Bridgeport Machines Control Co., Horsham, Pa., 1977-79; sr. elec. engr. and reliability engr. specialist Ford Aerospace and Comms. Corp., Houston, 1979-85; lead reliability engr. Rockwell Space Opers. Co., Houston, 1986-96; mem. engring. staff United Space Alliance West, Houston, 1996—. Contbr. articles to profl. publs.; patentee candidate in field. Elder, advisor Phila. Chinese Bible Study Fellowship, Phila., 1977-79; elder, evangelist Clear Lake Chinese Ch., Houston, 1979—; founder, coord. Space Christians Fellowship & Bible Study, Clear Lake, Houston, Tex., 1980—. Recipient Nat. Fidelity/Diligence medal Pres. of Rep. of China, Taipei, 1955, Group Achievement award Lyndon B. Johnson Space Ctr., Houston, 1983. Fellow AIAA (assoc.); mem. IEEE (life), Nat. Mgmt. Assn. (cert. mgr.). Avocations: bible study, personal evangelism, christian fellowship, church visitation, family spiritual retreat. Home: 470 Buoy Rd Webster TX 77598-2505 Office: United Space Alliance-West 600 Gemini St Houston TX 77058-2754 E-mail: Hsien.L.Huang@usa-spaceops.com., hlhuang@email.com.

HUANG, HUEI-PING, research scientist; b. Taichung, Taiwan, Oct. 25, 1965; arrived in U.S., 1992; s. Kuochung and Ijih Huang. BSc, Nat. Ctrl. U., Chungli, Taiwan, 1987; MSc, Nat. Taiwan U., Taipei, 1989; PhD, U. Ill., 1997. Rsch. scientist Cooperative Inst. for Rsch. in Environ. Sci., U. Colo., Boulder, 1997—2002; postdoctoral rsch. fellow Lamont-Doherty Earth Obs., Columbia U., Palisades, NY, 2002—. Contbr. articles to profl. jours. Mem.: Am. Geophys. Union, Am. Meteorol. Soc. Achievements include among the first to find that the total angular momentum of the Earth's atmosphere increases under global warming. Office: Lamont-Doherty Earth Obs PO Box 1000 61 Route 9W Palisades NY 10964

HUANG, JACOB CHEN-YA, physician, city official; b. Chia-Yi, Taiwan, Dec. 25, 1937; came to U.S., 1966; naturalized, 1974; s. Chang-Chiang and Agenes Cheng-Jen H.; m. Vivian Lin, Oct. 3, 1970; children: Phyllis, Albert, Edward. Diplomate Am. Bd. Family Practice. Intern Taipei City Hosp., 1964-65, house officer in pediatrics, 1965-66; fellow in clin. pathology Albert Einstein Coll. Medicine-Lincoln Hosp., 1968-70; dir. pub. health N.Y.C. Health Dept., 1971—77; sr. pub. health officer N.Y. State Dept. Health, 1970—76; chief drug diagnostic sect. N.Y.C. chief med. examiner, 1968-79; resident in family medicine Lutheran Med. Ctr., N.Y.C., 1970-71; clin. assoc. prof. NYU, 1972-76; med. dir. Paterson City (N.J.) Health Dept., 1977—. Chmn. dept. family practice Dover (N.J.) Gen. Hosp. and Med. Center, 1980—; trustee N.J. Passaic PRO, 1987—; bd. dirs. ambulatory care adv. bd. Beth Israel Hosp., N.Y.C., 1972-76, cmty. adv. bd. ambulatory svcs. St. Vincent Med. Ctr., N.Y.C., 1972-76, COMED-IPA Inc., N.J., 1980—; bd. dirs. Mount Olive City (N.J.) Bd. of Health, 1993—; mem. Presdl. Bus. Commn., 2002. N.J. hon. chmn. physician adv. bd. Nat. Rep. Com., 2001; hon. chmn. bus. adv. coun., mem. Presdl. bus. commn. Rep. Party, 2002. Recipient Physician's Recognition award AMA. Fellow Am. Coll. Preventive Medicine, Am. Acad. Family Physicians; mem. Am. Public Health Assn., Am. Chinese Med. Assn. N.J. (pres., founder), N.J. Am. Acad. Family Physicians (trustee 1994—, bd. dirs. 1994—, exec. bd. dirs. 1995—), Chinese Am. Med. Soc. (bd. dirs.), Chinese Am. Physicians Network of N.J. (pres. 1997—), Columbia U. Sch. Pub. Health Alumni Assn. (exec. bd. 1992). Home: 3 Walnut Hill Dr Chester NJ 07930-3006 Office: Bartley Sq Rte 206 Flanders NJ 07836 E-mail: Huang5@aol.com.

HUANG, JAOU-CHEN, obstetrician-gynecologist, reproductive endocrinologist; b. Taipei, Taiwan, Aug. 15, 1955; MD, Nat. Taiwan U., 1980. Diplomate Am. Bd. Ob-Gyn., Am. Bd. Reproductive Endocrinology and Infertility. Intern Nat. Taiwan U. Hosp., Taipei, 1979-80, resident, 1982-85; intern Columbia Physicians & Surgeons-Harlem Hosp., NYC, 1987-88, resident, 1988-91; fellow Harvard Med. Sch.-Brigham & Women's Hosp., Boston, 1991-93; asst. prof. U. Tex., Houston, 1993—2000, assoc. prof., 2000—. Attending physician Hermann Hosp., Houston, 1993—. Fellow ACOG, Endocrine Soc.; mem. Am. Soc. Reproductive Medicine; Soc. for Gynecologic Investigation. Office: U Tex Women's Clinic 6410 Fannin St Ste 350 Houston TX 77030-3004 also: U Tex Health Scis Ctr 6431 Fannin St Ste 3-604 Houston TX 77030-1501

HUANG, JOSEPH CHEN-HUAN, civil engineer; came to U.S., 1962, naturalized, 1972; MS in Structural Engring., Va. Poly. Inst. and State U., 1964, PhD 1988; m. Elizabeth C. Huang, Sept. 3, 1966; children: Edith, Eleanor, Evelyn, Edna. Registered profl. engr. N.Y., N.J., Pa., Del., Md., Va., W.Va., N.C., Fla., D.C. Project engr. Green Assos., Inc., Balt., 1964-68; pres. Gen. Engring. Cons., Inc., Balt., 1968-76; chmn., CEO Highlights Engring. Corp., Towson, Md., 1976—; pres. HS Mgmt. and Svcs. Corp., 1992—. Mem. ASCE, Am. Concrete Inst., NSPE, Chinese Bus. Assn. Greater Washington (pres. 1993). Author; Prestressed Steel Structures, Strategies for Business; contbr. articles to profl. jours. Home: 3506 Templar Rd Randallstown MD 21133-2428 Office: 1248 E Joppa Rd Towson MD 21286-5805 also: 1045 Taylor Ave Baltimore MD 21286-8331 also: 825 N Hammonds Ferry Rd Ste B Linthicum Heights MD 21090-1355

HUANG, KERSON, physics educator; b. Nan Ning, Kwangsi, Peoples Republic of China, Mar. 15, 1928; came to U.S., 1947; s. Horton T. and Shi (Ng) H.; m. Julia M. Sheng, Sept. 9, 1956 (div. 1971); m. Rosemary E. Verducci, May 19, 1979; 1 child, Kathryn Camille. SB, MIT, 1950, PhD, 1953. Instr. MIT, Cambridge, 1953-55, asst. prof. physics, 1957-61, assoc. prof., 1961-66, prof., 1966—99, prof. emeritus, 1999—; fellow Inst. for Advanced Study, Princeton, N.J., 1955-57; hon. prof. Fudan U., Shanghai, Peoples Republic of China, 1980. Author: Quarks, Leptons and Guage Field, 1982, Statistical Mechanics, 1987, I Ching, 1987, Quantum Field Theory, 1998, Introduction to Statistical Physics, 2001; cons. editor: World Sci. Pub., Singapore, 1981—. Fellow Alfred P. Sloan Found., 1961-62, Guggenheim Found., Geneva, 1962, sr. fellow Fulbright Founf., Santiago, Chile, 1974. Fellow Am. Acad. Arts and Scis., Am. Phys. Soc. Office: MIT 77 Massachusetts Ave Rm 6309 Cambridge MA 02139-4307

HUANG, KUN LIEN, software engineer, scientist; b. Nantou, Taiwan, Jan. 20, 1953; came to U.S., 1984; S. Chai-Chang and Fei-Chei (Chi) H.; m. Sue Hui Lee, Mar. 24, 1981; 1 child, Wayne. BS, Nat. Taipei Inst. Tech., Taiwan, 1973, N.D. State U., 1986, MS, U. Mo., 1988. Mech. engr. Ta Tung Aluminum Co., Taipei, 1975-76, rsch. mgr. Tapei, 1976-77, prodn. tech. mgr., 1977-79, quality control mgr., 1979-84; computer programmer U. Mo., Columbia, 1988; systems analyst, programmer NCR Corp., San Diego, 1989-92; database cons. Gamma-Metrics, 1992-93; software engr. Sci. Applications Internat. Corp., 1993-95; Unix adminstr. Gen. Instrument Corp., 1995-98; sr. database mgr. Indusoft, Inc., 1998—. Cons. Computing Ctr., U. Mo., Columbia, 1987-88. Recipient Nat. scholarship Republic China Jaycees, Taipei, 1972. Mem. AAAS, San Diego Taiwanese Cultural Assn. Republican. Avocation: fishing. Home: 1232 Bernardo Ridge Pl Escondido CA 92029

HUANG, LIANG HSIUNG, microbiologist; b. I-Lan, Taiwan, July 16, 1939; came to the U.S., 1963; s. Kin Shi and A. Chaw (Huang) L.; m. Jane Huang, July 23, 1970; children: Grace, Amy. MS, U. Wis., 1965, PhD, 1971. Postdoctoral rsch. fellow Ohio State U., Columbus, 1972-73, U. Ga., Athens, 1973-75; rsch. scientist Pfizer Cen. Rsch., Groton, Conn., 1975-78, sr. rsch. scientist, 1978-83, sr. rsch. investigator, 1983-91, prin. rsch. investigator, 1991—. Mem. adv. com. Am. Type Culture Collection, Rockville, Md., 1989-92. Contbr. articles to Internat. J. Systemic Bacteriology, Applied Microbiology, Arch. Biochem. Biophys., Mycotaxon, Jour. Indsl. Microbiology, Mycologia, Can. Jour. Botany, Am. Jour. Botany, Jour. Antibiotics; mem. editorial bd. Antimicrobial Agts. and Chemotherapy, 1977-82, Jour. Antibiotics, 1990—; editor: U.S. Fedn. for Culture Collections Newsletter, 1987-88. Active Conservation Com., East Lyme, Conn. Mem. U.S. Fedn. for Culture Collections (v.p. 1988-90, pres. 1990-92, exec. bd. 1998-2000), Soc. for Indsl. Microbiology, Am. Soc. for Microbiology (selection com. J.R. Porter award 1989-91), Mycological Soc. Am., N.Y. Acad. Scis. Achievements include patents; action of gramicidin on mitochondria; discovery of new polycyclic ether antibiotics, of ansamycin antibiotics, of novel squalene synthase inhibitor, of novel quinolone compounds, of novel quinomycins, of novel macrolides, of novel efrotomycins, of novel rapamycins, of novel topoisomerase II inhibitor, and of new development type of ascocarp centrum; description of new genus of actinomycetes and new species of Nocardia, Actinomadura, Nocardiopsis, Catenuloplanes, Aspergillus, Penicillium, Eleutherascus, Gliocephalotrichum, Neurospora, Triangularia, and Zopfiella. Home: 23 Sunrise Trail East Lyme CT 06333-1129 Office: Pfizer Global R&D Groton Labs/Pfizer Inc Eastern Point Rd Groton CT 06340-4947 E-mail: liang_h_huang@groton.pfizer.com.

HUANG, LIMIN, chemist, researcher; b. Jiangyin, Jiangsu Province, China, Apr. 17, 1970; s. Mantang and Wenyu (Cai) Huang; m. Lingling Wei, Apr. 28, 1998. PhD in Chemistry, Fudan U., Shanghai, China, 1997. Rsch. asst. Fudan U., Shanghai, 1992—97, lectr., 1997—2000; postdoctoral rschr. U. of Calif., Calif., 2000—02; postdoctoral rsch. scientist Columbia U., N.Y.C., 2002—. Contbr. articles to profl. jours. Recipient TIAN Award, TIAN Fund, 1997, award, Guanghua Edn. Fund, 1994. Mem.: Am. Chem. Soc., Internat. Zeolite Assn., Material Rsch. Soc. Achievements include patents for Synthesis of composite mesomicroporous materials. Office: Columbia Univ 500 W 120th St New York NY 10027 Office Fax: 214-854-8257. Personal E-mail: lmhuang70@yahoo.com. Business E-Mail: lh2036@columbia.edu.

HUANG, LINDA CHEN, plastic surgeon; b. Ithaca, N.Y., July 24, 1952; MD, Stanford U., 1979. Chmn. plastic surgery St. Joseph Hosp., Denver. Office: 1578 Humboldt St Denver CO 80218-1638

HUANG, MEI QING, physics educator, researcher; b. Wuhan, Hubei, People's Republic China, Jan. 20, 1942; came to U.S., 1988; parents Gong Li and Hui Qin Xia Huang; m. Jin Song Chen, Jan. 6, 1938; children: Qun Chen, Li Chen. Grad. dept. physics, U. Sci. and Tech. China, Beijing, 1964. Asst. prof. dept. physics U. Sci. and Tech. China, 1964-70, 1970-78, instr., 1978-87, assoc. prof., 1987—, head div. magnetism, 1986-88; rsch. assoc. dept. MEMS Carnegie-Mellon U., Pitts., 1983-85, 88-91, rsch. scientist in advanced materials, 1991—. Participant Chinese-Am. coop program in atomic, molecular and condensed matter physics Chinese Acad. Sci. and Am. Physics Soc., 1988; presenter 5th, 6th, 30th, 34th-38th, 40th-47th Ann. Conf. on Magnetism and Magnetic Materials, Internat. Conf. on Rare Earth Applications and Devels., 11th, 12th, 17th Internat. Workshop on Rare Earth Magnets and Their Applications. Contbr. articles to Physica, Jour. Appleid Physics, Jour. Magnetism and Magnetic Materials, Jour. Less Common Metals. Recipient 3d prize of sci. and tech. Acad. Sci. China, 1988. Mem. Chinese Phys. Soc., Am. Phys. Soc. Achievements include patents pending for Cerium-free Mischmetal Fe-B-o Permanent Magnets; research in magnetic properties and structure of magnetic recording powder using magnetic measurements; electron microscopic investigation and Mossbauer spectrum analysis, magnetic properties and structure of rare earth intermetallic properties using X-ray diffraction and magnetic measurement; influence of hydrogen on the magnetic characteristics of$R_2Fe_{14}B$ system; magnetic and structural properties of $R_2Fe_{17}N_x$, $R_2(Fe, Co)_{17}N_x$, $(Sm, R)Fe_{17}N_x$ nitrides, $Fe_{16}N_2$, $RCo_{13-x}Si_x$, $RCo_{7-x}Zr_x$; sintering studies of permanent magent materials, metal bonded $Sm_2Fe_{17}N_x$ type magnets, synthesis and characterize structure and magnetic properties of Fe-Co alloy nanoparticles. Home: 2408 Hemlock Dr Dayton OH 45431-3407 Office: Air Force Rsch Lab Universal Energy Sys Inc 4401 Dayton-Xenia Rd Dayton OH 45432

HUANG, MICHAEL BAILOU, librarian; b. Shanghai, May 10, 1956; s. Yulin Huang and Shuru Tang; m. Helen Hui Shi, Sept. 29, 1984; 1 child, Jenny Junyan. BA in English Lit., Shanghai Tchrs. U., China, 1982; MLS, Clarion U., Pa., 1989; MEd, Elmira Coll., N.Y., 1997. Cert. libr. N.Y., 1990. Tchr. English Minhang H.S., Shanghai, 1982—88; ref. libr., head of interlibrary loan dept. Steele Meml. Libr., Elmira, 1990—97; sr. asst. libr. Oswego State U., 1997—99, SUNY Health Scis. Ctr. Libr., Stony Brook, NY, 1999—. Vis. scholar Capital Normal U. Libr., Beijing, 1998. Contbr. In the Turn of the Centuries: Retrospect and Prospect of Libraries, 1999, The 21st Century Libraries: Development and Transformation, 2000, Global Digital Library Development in the New Millennium, 2001; contbr. articles to profl. jours. Recipient Finest Paper award, China Soc. for Libr. Sci. Ann. Conf., 1999, 2002; grantee Prof. Devel. and Quality of Working Life grant, N.Y. State United Univ. Professions, 1998, Profl. Devel. grant, State U. Librs. Assn., 1998. Mem.: Med. Libr. Assn., State Univ. of N.Y. Librs. Assn., Chinese Aml. Librs. Assn., Med. Libr. Assn. (Outstanding Contbn. by a New Mem. award N.J.-N.Y. chpt. 2000). Home: 15 Lyndon Lne South Setauket NY 11720 Office: Suny Stony Brook Health Sciences Library 8034 Suny,Hsc Level 3 Rm 136 Stony Brook NY 11794-8034 Home Fax: 631-444-6649; Office Fax: 631-444-6649. Personal E-mail: michael.b.huang@sunysb.edu. Business E-Mail: michael.b.huang@sunysb.edu.

HUANG, PAN MING, soil science educator; b. Pu-tse, Taiwan, Sept. 2, 1934; arrived in Can., 1965; s. Rong Yi and Koh (Chiu) H.; m. Yun Yin Lin, Dec. 26, 1964; children: Daniel Chian Yuan, Crystal Ling Hui. BSA, Nat. Chung Hsing U., Taichung, Taiwan, 1957; MSc, U. Man., Winnipeg, Can., 1962; PhD, U. Wis., Madison, 1966. Cert. prof. agrologist. Asst. prof. soil sci. U. Sask., Saskatoon, Can., 1965-71, assoc. prof., 1971-78, prof., 1978—. Invited rsch. chair Nat. Taiwan U., 1996, 2003; nat. vis. prof., head dept. soil sci. Nat. Chung Hsing U., 1975-76; mem. agr. adv. bd. Lewis Pubs., 1991—; hon. prof. Huazhong Agr. U., 1992—, Guanxi Agrl U., 1993—, Henan Agrl. U., 1996—, Langzhou U., 1999—; acad. advisor Chinese Acad. Scis., 1996—. Author: Soil Chemistry, 1991, Environmental Soil Chemistry and Its Impact on Agriculture and the Ecosystem, 2000; mem. editl. bd.: Chemosphere, 1987—97, Pedosphere, 1990—, Trends in Agr. Sci., 1991—95, Advances in Environ. Sci., 1993, Geodema, 1994—, Soil Sci. Plant Nutrition, 1998—, Water, Air, and Soil Pollution, 1998—2001, Humic Substances in the Environment, 1998—; editor: 14 books; spl. editor, mem. editl. bd.: Water Pollution Rsch. Jour. Can., 1983—89, 1991—93, Agro's Ann. Rev. Crop Ecology, 1995—, mem. editl. adv. bd.: Trends in Soil Sci., 1995—; contbr. over 260 articles to profl. jours., over 28 referred rsch. papers in jours. and chpts. to books. Bd. dirs. Saskatoon Chinese Mandarin Sch., 1977-79, Saskatoon Soc. for Study Chinese Culture, 1983—. 2d lt. Taiwan Mil. Tng. Corps, 1957-59. Recipient Disting. Rschr. award, U. Sask., 1997; grantee UN Environment Programme, Nat. Scis. and Engring. Rsch. Coun. Can., numerous other agys., 1965—. Fellow: The World Innovation Found., Am. Soc. Agronomy, Soil Sci. Soc. Am. (rep. Clay Minerals Soc. 1979—83, chmn. divsn. S-9 1983—84, bd. dirs. 1983—84, editor spl. pub. 1986, Internat. Soil Sci. award com. 1986—87, assoc. editor 1987—92, Marion L. and Christie M. Jackson Soil Sci. award com. 1990—92, rep. to Internat. Union Pure and Applied Chemistry 1990—2000, fellow com. 1992—94, chmn.-elect divsn. S-2 1993—94, chmn. 1994—95, past chmn. 1995—96, spl. awards com. 1995—96, chair nominations com. divsn. S-2 1995—96, bd. dirs. 1995—96, editor spl. pub. 1998, Soil Sci. Rsch. award 2000), AAAS, Can. Soc. Soil Sci.; mem.: Can. Network Toxicology (team on metal speciation

1993—96), Internat. Union Pure and Applied Chemistry (assoc.; commn. environ. analytical chemistry 1993—95, titular mem. com. fundamental environ chemistry 1995—97, 1999—2001), Internat. Human Substances Soc. (leader Can. nat. chpt. 1992—), Internat. Assn. Study Clays (treas. 1993—2001), N.Y. Acad. Scis., Am.Chem. Soc., Internat. Union Soil Sci. (chmn. working group MO 1990—), Sigma Xi. Avocations: music, reading. Home: 130 Mount Allison Cres Saskatoon SK Canada S7H 4A5 Office: U Sask Dept Soil Sci Campus Dr 51 Saskatoon SK Canada S7N 5A8 E-mail: Huangp@sask.usask.ca.

HUANG, PENG, statistician; d. WeiYou Huang and JinLian Luo. MS, Rochester Inst. Tech., 1995; MA, U. Rochester, 1996, PhD, 2000. Mathematician Fuzhou Agr. Bur., Fuzhou, China, 1989—93; rsch. and tchg. asst. U. Rochester, NY, 1995—2000; asst. prof. Med. U. S.C., Charleston, 2000—. Author: (optimal design) minimum aberration two-level split plot design, 1995 (Shewell award Am. Soc. Quality Control, 1997). Recipient Excellence prize, Chinese Nat. Intelligent Open Competition Com., 1987, Robust Design award, Quality Engring. by Design Symposium, Rochester Inst. Tech., 1994; fellow Dean's fellow, U. Rochester, 1997—98; grantee, NIH & NINDS, 2002—; scholar Richard A. Freund scholar, Am. Soc. Quality Control, 1994. Mem.: The Internat. Biometric Soc., Am. Soc. for Quality Control, Am. Statis. Assn., Math Assn. Am., Inst. Math. Stats., Internat. Chinese Statis. Assn. Home: 1645 N Woodmere Dr Apt F-25 Charleston SC 29407 Office: Med Univ SC 135 Cannon St Ste 303 Box 250835 Charleston SC 29425 Office Fax: 1-843-876-1126. E-mail: huangp@musc.edu.

HUANG, PENG, science educator; b. Charleston, S.C., Mar. 8, 1971; s. William and Linda Huang. PhD, U. S.C., Columbia, 2001. Dir.: (exhibition) Incident of diabetic disease in South Carolina. Home: 1645 N Woodmere Dr Charleston SC 29407 Office: Med Univ South Carolina 130 Cannon St Ste 305 Charleston SC 29401 Home Fax: 843-224-3462. Personal E-mail: huangp@musc.edu.

HUANG, PINGSHENG, marketing professional, consultant; b. Guang Dong, China, Nov. 21, 1957; s. Zhiping Huang and Bingyan Li; m. Yi Jia Hong, Jan. 13, 1990; 1 child, Samson. BA, South China Normal U., 1982; MA, Seton Hall U., 1992; PhD, Walden U., 1995. Registered profl. devel. provider N.J. Lectr. Zhanjian (China) Norma Coll., 1982—87, Guangchou (China) U., 1987; prodn. supr. Tokai Internat., Tokyo, 1988; chief editor China Daily, Suriname, 1989; mktg. trainer Sun Moon Star, Inc., Piscataway, NJ, 1994—97; mktg. dir. Mini-Micro Supply, Inc., Piscataway, NJ, 1997—98; pres. Magi Compo Inc., Towaco, NJ, 1998—, with Social Security Adminstrn. Patentee in field. Mem.: China's Assn. Sci. and Tech., Assn. Math. Tchrs. N.J. (spkr. 2000). Avocations: badminton, tennis, bartending. Home: 20 Alpine Rd Towaco NJ 07082

HUANG, ROBERT, electronics manufacturing executive; BS, Kyushu U., Japan; MS, U. Rochester; MBA, MIT. Sales mgr. Advanced Micro Devices; founder Compac Microelectronics, 1980; founder, pres., CEO Synnex (formerly Compac Microelectronics), Fremont, Calif., 1992—. Office: Synnex Info Tech Inc 3797 Spinnaker Ct Fremont CA 94538

HUANG, ROGER DOMINIC, finance educator; b. Nov. 9, 1955; s. Peter Huang; m. Ying W. Huang, Nov. 19, 1982; children: Sean, Timothy, Evelyn. PhD, U. of Pa., 1980; BS in Indsl. Mgmt., Purdue U., 1975. Prof. of fin. Vanderbilt U., Nashville, 1998—2000; prof. fin. U. of Notre Dame, Ind., 2000—. Office: University of Notre Dame Mendoza College of Business Notre Dame IN 46556

HUANG, SHAWN SHAOPING, engineer; b. Changjian, Hainan, China, Aug. 15, 1963; came to U.S., 1987; married, 1989; children: Anthony Jianfeng, Elizabeth Joanna. B in Engring., Inst. Hydraulic & Elec. Engr., Wuchan, China, 1983; postgrad., Peking U., Beijing, 1983-84; MS, Inst. Atomic Energy, Beijing, 1983-86; PhD, U. Idaho, 1990. Grad. asst. Inst. Atomic Energy, Beijing, 1984-86, rsch. assoc., project leader, 1986-87; grad. asst. U. Idaho, Moscow, 1987-90; sr. rsch. engr. Exxon Prodn. Rsch. Co., Houston, 1990-2000; prin. prof. Halliburton Kellogg Brown & Root, Houston, 2000-01; chief engr. Phillips Petroleum Co., Houston, 2001—. Contbr. articles to profl. jours. including Am. Chem. Abstracts and Supercritical Fluid Sci. and Tech. Vol. fund distbn. agy. United Way Gulf Coast chpt., Houston, 1996-98; vol. Idaho Spl. Olympic Games, 1988. Mem. AIChE, Tau Beta Pi. Achievements include invention of a new process that increases the natural gas liquid recovery on a deepwater floating production system by 300 percent. Office: Phillips Petroleum Co 6330 West Loop South Houston TX 77401 E-mail: ShawnHuangV@cs.com.

HUANG, SHENG HE, medical educator; b. Lian Yuan, Hunan, China, Oct. 1, 1950; came to U.S., 1985; s. Yu-sheng Huang and Mei-Xiang Zen; m. Chun-Hua Wu, Sept. 8, 1978; children: Min, Wendy. Grad., 1st Mil. Med. U. China, 1973, Peking Union Med. Coll., 1981. Rsch. assoc. Peking Union Med. Coll., 1982-85; vis. asst. prof. Sch. Medicine U. Colo., Denver, 1985-86; postdoctoral fellow Childrens Hosp. L.A., 1986-89, rsch. assoc., 1989-97; asst. prof. rsch. Sch. Medicine U. So. Calif., L.A., 1997—. 1st author: (book) Clinical Use of Enzymes, 1984; inventor in field; mem. rev. bd. Jour. Molecular Biology and Biotech., 1999—. Recipient First award NIH, 1997, grant-in-aid Nat. Am. Heart Assn., 1999, grant-in-aid Am. Heart Assn., 1994. Mem. Am. Assn. Cancer Rsch., Am. Soc. Microbiology. Office: Childrens Hosp LA Divsn Infectious Disease 4650 W Sunset Blvd Los Angeles CA 90027-6062 E-mail: shhuang@hsc.usc.edu.

HUANG, SHOUHUA, electronics engineer; b. Hubei, China, Nov. 28, 1956; came to U.S., 1994; m. Dongmei; children: Davy, Andrew. BS, Nanjing U., 1980; ME, Wuhan Rsch. Inst. Posts and, Telecomm., Wuhan, 1986; PhD, Beijing U. Posts and Telecomm., 1992. Engr. Ministry of Aeronautics and Space of China, 1980-83, Wuhan Rsch. Inst. of Posts and Telecomms., Wuhan, 1986-88; postdoctoral fellow Tsinghua U., Beijing, 1992-94; rsch. assoc. U. So. Calif., L.A., 1994-95; rsch. engr. E-Tek Dynamics, Inc., San Jose, 1995-97; sr. engr. Osicom Technologies, Inc., San Diego, 1997-99, Jet Propulsion Lab., Pasadena, Calif., 1999—. Patentee in field; translator: (books) Guide to Programs 1992/National Natural Science Foundation of China, Guide to Programs 1993, National Natural Science Foundation of China; contbr. articles to profl. jours. Mem. IEEE (sr.), Optical Soc. Am., Internat. Soc. for Optical Engring. Achievements include rsch. on 6-channel OC-48 (6x2.4 gb/s) 9,000 km WDM optical comm. system, 6x2.4 Gbit/s circulating loop with 100 km DSF (Dispersion Shifted Fiber), LD characterization systems, numerous others. E-mail: shouhua.huang@jpl.nasa.gov.

HUANG, SUNG-CHENG, electrical engineering educator; b. Canton, China, Oct. 26, 1944; came to U.S., 1967; s. Hip-chung Wong and Chi-hung Chung; m. Caroline S. Soong, Sept. 4, 1971; children: Michael, Dennis. BSEE, Nat. Taiwan U., Taipei, 1966; DSc, Wash. U., 1973. Rsch. assoc. biomed. computer lab. Wash. U., St. Louis, 1973-74; project engr. Picker Corp., Cleve., 1974-77; asst. prof. UCLA Sch. Medicine, 1977-82, assoc. prof., 1982-86, prof., 1986—, Edward Farber lectr. U. Chgo., 1986. Mem. editl. bd. Jour. Nuc. Medicine, 1997—, Jour. Cerebral Blood Flow, 1989-92; dep. chief editor Jour. Cerebral Blood Flow and Metabolism, 1993—; contbr. over 200 articles to profl. jours. Recipient George Von Hevesy prize World Congress of Nuclear Medicine and Biology, 1982; grantee U.S. Dept. Energy, 1977—, NIH, 1977—. Mem. AAAS, IEEE, Soc. Nuclear Medicine, Soc. Cerebral Blood Flow. Achievements include patent for spread beam overlap method; development of various tracer techniques used for positron emission tomographic (PET) studies in nuclear medicine; research in computer tomographic image construction technique. Office: UCLA Sch Medicine Divsn Nuclear Medicine and Biophysics 10833 Le Conte Ave Los Angeles CA 90095-6948 E-mail: hhuang@mednet.ucla.edu.

HUANG, THOMAS SHI-TAO, electrical engineering educator, researcher; b. Shanghai, June 26, 1936; came to U.S., 1958; s. Chien Liang and Allen (Chien) H.; m. Margaret Y. Nee, Apr. 4, 1959; children: Caroline B., Marjorie A., Thomas T., Gregory T. BS, Nat. Taiwan U., Taipei, 1956; MS, MIT, 1960, ScD, 1963. Asst. prof. MIT, Cambridge, Mass., 1963-67, assoc. prof., 1967-73; prof. Purdue U., West Lafayette, Ind., 1973-80, U. Ill., Urbana, 1980—, William L. Everitt Disting. Prof., 1996—. Vis. prof. Swiss Inst. Tech., Zurich, U. Hannover, Federal Republic of Germany, U. Que., Can., others; cons. IBM, AT&T Bell Labs., MIT Lincoln Lab., Kodak, others. Author 2 books; editor 12 books; contbr. more than 400 articles to tech. jours. Recipient A. V. Humboldt U.S. Sr. Scientist award Alexander V. Humboldt Found., 1976-77; Honda Lifetime Achievement award, 2000; Guggenheim fellow, 1971-72; fellow Japan Assn. for Promotion of Sci., 1986. Fellow IEEE (Signal Processing Soc. Tech. Achievement award 1987, Soc. award 1991, Third Millennium medal 2000, Jack S. Kilby medal 2001), Optical Soc. Am., Internat. Assn. for Pattern Recognition (King-Sun Fu Prize, 2002), Internat. Optical Engring. Soc.; mem. NAE, Chinese Acad. Engring. (fgn.), Chinese Acad. Scis. (fgn.). Office: Univ Ill Beckman Inst 405 N Mathews Ave Urbana IL 61801-2325

HUANG, TING-CHIA, chemical engineering educator, researcher; b. Tainan, Taiwan, June 1, 1932; s. Tzuo and Nai (Yeh) H.; m. Juei-Chin Wan, Jan. 19, 1958; children: Ling-Yuang, Ling-Huei, Ping-Hsien, Chao-Cheng. BS, Nat. Cheng Kung U., Tainan, 1955; D Engring., U. Tokyo, 1979. Tchg. asst. dept. chem. engring. Nat. Cheng Kung U., 1956-60, instr., 1960-65, assoc. prof., 1965-68, prof., 1968—, chmn., dir. dept., 1981-87, v.p., 1995-97, acting pres., 1996-97; nat. chair prof. Ministry of Edn., 1997—2000. IAEA rsch. fellow Japan Atomic Energy Rsch. Inst., Tokai-mura, Ibaraki-Ken, 1962; rsch. assoc. U. Houston, 1969-70; tech. cons. ChiMeng Indsl. Co., Ltd., Hsin-Hua, Taiwan, 1979-99; cons. Ministry Edn., Taipei, Taiwan, 1988-94, Kang Hsiang Lan Pharmaceutice Co., Ltd., Yung-Kan Ind. Park, Tainan Syan, Taiwan, 1989—, Vedan Enterprise Corp., Shalu Taichung, Taiwan, 1999—. Author: Experimental Physical Chemistry, 1963, 20th edit., 1987, Chemical Engineering Thermodynamics, 1971, Physical Chemistry, 1978, 5th edit., 1990, Experiments in Physical Chemistry, 1983, 3d edit., 1988; regional editor Waste Mgmt. jour.; contbr. over 190 articles to profl. jours. Recipient Engring. Sci. award Hsu's Found., 1975, Engring. Acad. award Ministry Edn., 1979, Outstanding Rsch. award Ministry Edn., 1983, 84, Nat. Sci. Coun., 1986-94; named Outstanding Invited Rschr. Nat. Rsch. Coun., 1995-98. Mem. AIChE, Chinese Inst. Engrs. (best paper award 1975, 85, 96, 99, Outstanding Engring. Prof. award 1991), Chinese Inst. Chem. Engrs. (assoc. editor-in-chief jour. 1986-2000, Chin Kai-Ying award 1991, Best Paper award 1994, 95, 99, Chem. Engr. Inst. prize 1997), Chinese Chem. Soc., Soc. Chem. Engrs. Japan, Chinese Inst. Mining Engring. (Best Paper award 1989, 95), Phi Tau Phi. Avocations: reading, inventing, writing, music, table tennis. Address: 4th fl 23 Alley 17 Ln 133 Sec 2 Chong Hua E Rd Tainan 70104 Taiwan Office: Nat Cheng Kung U No 1 Ta'-Siue Rd Tainan 70101 Taiwan E-mail: tchuang@mail.ncku.edu.tw.

HUANG, VICTOR TSANGMIN, food scientist, researcher; b. Republic of China, Dec. 12, 1951; came to U.S., 1975; s. Shen Tan and Yeh Gee (Lai) H.; m. Jean Fong Chen, June 9, 1978; children: Hank Su, Andrea Su. BS, Hsing-Hua U., Hsin-Chu, Republic of China, 1973; MS, U. Chgo., 1977; PhD, Ohio State U., 1981. Teaching asst. U. Chgo., 1975-77; rsch. assoc. Ohio State U., Columbus, 1977-81; food scientist Pillsbury Co., Mpls., 1981—. Presenter dairy, baby and bakery product formulation field, 1977-94. Contbr. articles to profl. jours.; patentee frozen desserts and microwave food formulation fields in U.S. and Europe. Vice pres. Minn. Taiwanese Assn., Mpls., 1985. 2d lt. Taiwan Army, 1973-75. Mem. Am. Dairy Sci. Assn., Inst. Food Technologists, Am. Assn. Cereal Chemists, Am. Chem. Soc., Toastmasters (pres. Mpls. 1988). Office: Pillsbury Tech Ctr 330 University Ave SE Minneapolis MN 55414-1779

HUANG, VIVIAN WENHUEY CHEN, lawyer; b. Taipei, Taiwan, Aug. 10, 1942; came to U.S., 1968; d. Yi Song and Ling Yu (Lin) Chen; 1 child, Charlotte. BA in Law, Nat. Taiwan U., 1966; JD, Ind. U., 1971. Bar: Mass. 1975. Assoc. Mau Chun Chen's Law Office, Taipei, 1966-67; staff lawyer Urban and Econ. Devel. Com., Taipei, 1967-68; assoc. Ropes & Gray, Boston, 1973-89; of counsel Cuddy, Lynch & Bixby, 1990-92, Bloom & Witkin, 1992—; adv. coun. Gov. Mass., Boston, 1983—; founder, chmn. bd., pres., CEO, Asian Am. Bank & Trust Co., Boston, 1993-2001; chmn. bd., pres., CEO, August Fin. Holding Co., Inc., Boston, 2001—. Trustees Harry H. Dow Meml. Legal Assistance Fund, 1985—; advisory trustee Peabody & Essex Mus. of Salem, Mass., 1988-93, overseer, 1993-95. Mem. ABA, Mass. Bar Assn. (critical issue com. 1988—), Asian-Am. Lawyers Assn. Mass. (bd. dirs. 1983-88), Boston Bar Assn. (steering com. internat. law sect. 1983, chmn. Asian Pacific Rim com. 1988-90), Nat. Assn. Chinese Ams. (bd. dirs., sec. Boston chpt. 1983-94, v.p. 1990-92), Orgn. Chinese Ams. (bd. dirs. 1982-88). Democrat. Avocations: painting, skiing, tennis, hiking, music. Home: 30 Farrwood Dr Andover MA 01810-5233 Office: August Fin Holding Co Inc 150 Lincoln St Boston MA 02111 E-mail: vwchuang@august-financial.com.

HUANG, WENLIN, scientist, researcher; b. Wuhan, Hubei, China, Oct. 1, 1953; s. Zhudong Huang and Yuzheng Fong; m. Marilyn X. Zhou, Nov. 7, 1993; 1 child, Manli. BS, Three Gonges U., Yicheng, Hubei, China, 1975; PhD, Academia Sinica, Wuhan, China, 1986; postgrad., Princeton (N.J.) U., 1996. Rsch. asst. prof. Wuhan Inst. Vitology, 1986-88; dir., founder pharm. co. Wuhan, 1988-91; vis. fellow Princeton U., 1991-96, with rsch. staff, 1996-97; rsch. scientist Allegheny U., Phila., 1997-98; prof. Sen Yat-Sen Med. U., Guangzhou, China, 1998-2001; sr. rsch. scientist Advanced Vital Rsch. Inst., Yonkers, N.Y., 1998—. Guest prof. Fourth Mil. U., Xi An, China, 1998; v.p. US-China Econ. and Trading Promotion Coun., N.Y.C., 1999—; adv. bd. Microbiology Inst. Acad. Sci., Guangdong, China, 2000— Patentee in field. Recipient award NIH, 1995, 97, Nat. Sci. Found., 1998, Nat. Edn. Minister, China, 1999. Mem. AAAS, Soc. Chinese Am. Professors (bd. dirs. 1995—), Infectious Diseases Soc. Am., Soc. Microbiology Am., Am. Cancer Rsch. Assn., N.Y. Acad. Sci. Avocations: travel, reading. Home: 9629 Bustleton Ave Apt 213 Philadelphia PA 19115 E-mail: wl_huang@hotmail.com.

HUANG, YUNG-HUI, chemical engineer; b. Taipei, Taiwan, July 20, 1953; arrived in U.S., 1979; s. Lane-Chi and Yu-Bei (Tsai) Huang; m. I-Hung Huang, May 15, 1992; children: Caroline, Catherine. BS, Nat. Ctrl. U., Chung-Li, Taiwan, 1976; MS, U. S.C., 1982; PhD, U. Fla., 1986. Rsch. assoc. Auburn (Ala.) U., 1987-88, Mich. Molecular Inst., Midland, 1988-90; sys. engr. S3 Technologies, Columbia, Md., 1990-92; sr. process engr. Formosa Plastics Corp., Livingston, NJ, 1992-95; process mgr. J. M. Huber Corp., Havre de Grace, Md., 1995—. Vis. scholar Tech. U. Denmark, Lynby, 1985; organizer Polymer Symposium Sci., Engring. and Tech., Houston, 1995. Contbr. articles to profl. jours. 2d lt. Chinese Army, 1976—78. Mem.: AIChE, Soc. Advancement Materials and Process Engring., Soc. Plastics Engrs., Sigma Xi. Achievements include 3 patents in field. Avocations: basketball, tennis, music, literature, computer. Home: 1107 Jeanett Way Bel Air MD 21014-4685 Office: J M Huber Corp 907 Revolution St Havre De Grace MD 21078-3723 E-mail: HGSHH@Huber.com.

HUARD, DONALD V. psychologist, educator; b. Dearborn, Mich., May 9, 1932; s. George Raymond and Viola Margaret Huard; m. Marie Darlene Fournier, June 13, 1957 (dec. Nov. 2, 1981); children: Christopher Leon, Theresa Anne, David Donald, Gregory George; m. Margaret Eugenia Russell, July 2, 1982. AA, Phoenix C.C., Ariz., 1955; BS, Ariz State U., Tempe, 1957; MA, Ariz.State U., 1959, PhD, 1971. Lectr. in psychology Ariz. State U., 1960—62; prof. psychology and stats. Phoenix C.C., 1963—98, prof. emeritus. Emphasis editl. writer The Phoenix Gazette, 1980—81; assoc. editor The Maricopa County C.C. Jour., Phoenix, 1982—83. Author: (books) Behavioral Statistics, 1992, The Violence That Prevails, 1996, Teen Agers: What Will Drugs, Safe Sex Do to You?, 1997, Where Grandpa's Been: An Autobiography, 1999, Youth Deficit Disorder, 2001, You Need a Red Hat, 2002. Mem., contbr. Brady Campaign to Prevent Gun Violence, Wash. Cpl. U.S. Army, 1952—54, Alaska. Achievements include development of conditioning behavioral sci. lab at Phoenix Coll., 1965-80. Avocations: photography, travel, writing. Home: 1549 E Oriole Pl Prescott AZ 86303 E-mail: donderhead@juno.com.

HUARD, JAMES GERALD, mathematician, educator; b. Waterville, Maine, Mar. 1, 1948; s. Leslie John Huard and Ethelyn Lillian King. BA, U. Maine, 1969; MS, Yale U., 1972; PhD, Pa. State U., 1978. Vis. lectr. U. of Ga., Athens, Ga., 1976—77; vis. instr. So. Ill. U. Carbondale, 1977—79, vis. asst. prof., 1979—80; asst. prof. Niagara U., Lewiston, NY, 1980—84; from asst. prof. to assoc. prof. Canisius Coll., Buffalo, 1984—96, prof., 1996—. Editor: (book) The Collected Papers of Sarvadaman Chowla, Vol. I-III, 1999; contbr. articles to profl. jours. Summer Faculty fellow, Canisius Coll., 1988, 1994, 1998. Mem.: Math. Assn. of Am., Am. Math. Soc., Pi Mu Epsilon, Phi Kappa Phi, Phi Beta Kappa. Avocations: choral singing, house plants, nature walks. Office: Canisius Coll 2001 Main St Buffalo NY 14208-1098

HUASUN, QIN, diplomat; m. Jiang Hongmei; 2 children. Grad., Fgn. Affairs Inst. Info. dept., attache, 3d sec., 2d sec. to Sierra Leone Govt. People's Rep. China, 1961-80, dep. dir., counselor, dir. info. dept. Min. Fgn. Affairs, 1980-84, counselor, dep. permanent rep. Chinese mission to UN, 1984-87, amb., permanent rep. UN Vienna, 1987-90, dir.-gen. dept. internatl orgns. and confs. Min. Fgn. Affair, 1990-93, asst. min. fgn. affairs, 1993-95, permanent rep. People's Rep. China to UN N.Y.C., 1995-2000; mem. nat. com. Chinese People's Polit. Consultative Conf., 1998—2003, vice-chmn. fgn. affairs com., 2000—03; mem. China nat. com. Coun. Security Cooperation Asia Pacific, China. Mem. standing com., vice-chmn. fgn. affairs com. China Econ. and Social Coun., 2002—. Office: CSCAP China 3 Toutiao Taijichang, Beijing 100005 China

HUBAND, FRANK LOUIS, educational association executive; b. Washington, July 12, 1938; m. Carol Singer. BS, Cornell U., 1961, PhD, 1967; JD, Yale U., 1975. Bar: D.C. 1975, U.S. Patent Office, 1977; registered prof. engr., Tex. Asst. prof. elec. engring. and math. scis. Rice U., Houston, 1966-72; owner, pres. Engring. Systems, Houston, 1972-73; atty., advisor FEA, Washington, 1975-76; div. dir. NSF, Washington, 1976-90; exec. dir. Am. Soc. for Engring. Edn., Washington, 1990—; sec. gen. IACEE, 2002—. Cons. Tex. Instrument, 1968-75; lectr. George Mason U., Fairfax, Va., George Washington U. Author: Protection of Computer Systems and Software, 1986. Mem. IEEE, ABA, NSPE, Am. Chem. Soc., Am. Inst. Physics, Internat. Assn. for Continuing Engring. Edn. (sec. gen.). Office: Am Soc for Engring Edn 1818 N St NW Ste 600 Washington DC 20036-2476 E-mail: f.huband@asee.org.

HUBBARD, ARTHUR THORNTON, chemistry educator, electro-surface chemist; b. Alameda, Calif., Sept. 17, 1941; s. John White and Ruth Frances (Gapen) H.; children: David A., Lynne F. BA, Westmont Coll., 1963; PhD, Calif. Inst. Tech., 1967. Prof. chemistry U. Hawaii, Honolulu, 1967-76, U. Calif., Santa Barbara, 1976-86; Ohio eminent scholar and prof. chemistry U. Cin., 1986-99, dir. Surface Ctr., 1986-99; dir. Santa Barbara Sci. Project, 1999—. Chmn. Ohio Sci. and Engring. Roundtable, 1990-95. Co-editor Jour. Colloid and Interface Sci., 1993—; series editor Surfactant Science Series; editor: Encyclopedia of Surface and Colloid Science. Mem. Am. Chem. Soc. (assoc. editor jour. Langmuir 1984-90, vice chair surface and colloid div. 1999, chair-elect 2000, chair 2001, Kendall award 1989), Electrochem. Soc. (David C. Grahame award 1993), Am. Phys. Soc. Office: Santa Barbara Sci Project PO Box 42530 Santa Barbara CA 93140-2530

HUBBARD, DEAN LEON, university president; b. Nyssa, Oreg., June 17, 1939; s. Gaileon and Rhodene (Barton) H.; m. Aleta Ann Thornton, July 12, 1959; children: Melody Ann, Dean Paul John, Joy Marie BA, Andrews U., 1961, MA, 1962; diploma in Korean Lang., Yunsei U., Seoul, Korea, 1968; PhD, Stanford U., 1979. Dir. English Lang. Schs., Seoul, 1966-71; asst. to pres. Loma Linda U., Calif., 1974-76; acad. dean Union Coll., Lincoln, Nebr., 1976-80, pres., 1980-84, NW Mo. State U., Maryville, 1984—. Chair Acad. Quality Consortium, 1993-96; examiner Malcolm Baldridge Nat. Quality Award, 1993-96; judges panel Mo. Quality Award, 1994-96; adv. coun. edn. statistics U.S. Dept. Edn., 1997-99. Mem. ACE Leadership Devel. Coun., 1996—. Avocation: classical music. Office: NW Mo State U Office of President AD143 800 University Dr Maryville MO 64468-6001*

HUBBARD, DONALD, marine artist, writer; b. Bronx, N.Y., Jan. 15, 1926; s. Ernest Fortesque and Lilly Violet (Beck) H. (div.); children: Leslie Carol, Christopher Eric, Lauren Ivy, Cameron C. McNall; m. Kay Frances Boldt, Oct., 1998. Student, Brown U., 1944-45; AA, George Washington U., 1959, BA, 1958; student, Naval War Coll., 1965-66. Commd. ensign U.S. Navy, 1944, advanced through grades to comdr., 1965, served as naval aviator, 1944-67, ret., 1967; founder, operator Ocean Ventures Industries, Inc., Coronado, Calif., 1969-77, Sea Eagle Pubs., Coronado, 1988. Lectr. on marine art; SCUBA instr. Author: Ships-in-Bottles, 2d edit., 1988, A How To Guide to a Venerable Nautical Craft, 1971, Buddleschiffe: Wie Macht Man Sie, 1972, The Complete Book of Inflatable Boats, 1979, Where to Paddle in San Diego County and Nearby Mexico, 1992, Days of Yore: Rhymes and Other Writings, 1995, Neptune's Table: Cooking the Sea Food Exotics, 1997; editor The Bottle Shipwright, works featured in American Artist of the Bookplate, 1970-90; contbr. articles to various publs.; featured (TV series) House and Garden, What's My Hobby?, (mag.) Coastal Living, 2003. Decorated Air medal, U.S. Navy. Mem. Ships-in-Bottles Assn. (pres. N. Am. divsn. 1982—), Nature Printing Soc., Am. Soc. Bookplate Collectors and Designers, San Diego Watercolor Soc. (bd. dirs. 1981-82), San Diego Maritime Assn. Home and Office: 1022 Park Pl Coronado CA 92118-2822 E-mail: hubbarddon@aol.com.

HUBBARD, ELIZABETH, actress; b. N.Y.C. d. Benjamin Alldritt and Elizabeth (Wright) H.; divorced; 1 son, Jeremy Danby Bennett. AB cum laude, Radcliffe Coll.; postgrad., Royal Acad. Dramatic Art, London. Leading role: CBS daytime TV serial As the World Turns, 1984— (9 Emmy nominations for Best Leading Actress), NBC daytime TV serial The Doctors (Best Leading Actress Emmy), First Ladies' Diary (Best Leading Actress Emmy); appeared on Broadway in Present Laughter, Joe Egg, Time for Singing, Look Back in Anger, I Remember Mama (musical), others; appeared in off-Broadway prodn. Boys from Syracuse, Threepenny Opera (musicals); movie appearances include I Never Sang for My Father, The Bell Jar, Ordinary People, Center Stage; frequent guest TV talk shows. Former bd. dirs. Found. in Motion, Immigration and Refugee Svcs. of Am., U.S. Com. for Refugees. Recipient The Physicists Clarence Derwent award.

HUBBARD, ELIZABETH LOUISE, lawyer; b. Springfield, Ill., Mar. 10, 1949; d. Glenn Wellington and Elizabeth (Frederick) H.; m. A. Jeffrey Seidman, Oct. 27, 1974 (div. May 1982). BA, U. Ky., 1971; JD with honors, Ill. Inst. Tech.-Chgo. Kent Coll. Law, 1974. Bar: Ill. 1974, U.S. Dist. Ct. (no. dist.) Ill. 1974, U.S. Ct. Appeals (7th cir.) 1976, U.S. Supreme Ct. 1984. Atty. Wyatt Co., Chgo., 1974-75, Gertz & Giampietro, Chgo., 1975-81, Baum, Sigman, Gold, Chgo., 1981-98, Elizabeth Hubbard, Ltd., 1981-98, Hubbard & O'Connor, Ltd., Chgo., 1998—. Legal counsel NOW, Chgo., 1978-94, sec., 1977. Editor: Chgo. Kent Law Rev., 1970; supplement editor: Litigating Sexual Harassment and Sex Discrimination Cases, 1997—2003. Bd. dirs., mem. The Remains Theatre, 1985-94. Mem. Chgo. Bar Assn. (fed. civil procedure com.), Ill. State Bar Assn., Nat. Employment Lawyers Assn. (chair Ill. chpt. 1992-95, sec.-treas. 1997—). Home: 420 W Grand Ave Apt 4A Chicago IL 60610-4087 Office: Ste Six West 900 W Jackson Blvd Chicago IL 60607-3024 Fax: (312) 421-5310. E-mail: ehubbard@hubbardoconnor.com.

HUBBARD, FRED LEONHARDT, lawyer; b. Carlinville, Ill., Apr. 14, 1940; s. David Fred and Frances Pauline (Leonhardt) H.; m. Sharon L. Woodyard, Nov. 13, 1964; 1 child, Glenn Edward. BS in Commerce, U. Ill., 1961, JD, 1963. Bar: Ill. 1963. Ptnr. Lowenstein and Hubbard, Danville, Ill., 1965-73, Lowenstein, Hubbard & Smith, Danville, Ill., 1973-88, Hubbard, Smith & Kagawa, Danville, Ill., 1990 92, Gunn & Hickman, P.C., Danville, Ill., 1992-97, Fred L. Hubbard Law Office, Danville, Ill., 1997—. Chmn. Vermilion County Am. Cancer Soc., 1982-83; pres. Plankeshaw coun. Boy Scouts Am., 1984-85. Served to sgt., U.S. Army, 1963-69. Recipient Silver Beaver award Boy Scouts Am., 1980, also Dist. award of Merit. Mem. Vermilion County Bar Assn. (pres. 1991-92), Ill. State Bar Assn., Vermilion County Hist. Soc., Masons (33d degree). Republican. Methodist. Avocations: music, woodworking, photography, model railroading, antiques. Home: PO Box 434 Catlin IL 61817-0434 Office: 415 N Gilbert St PO Box 12 Danville IL 61834-0012

HUBBARD, GREGORY SCOTT, physicist; b. Lexington, Ky., Dec. 27, 1948; s. Robert Nicholas and Nancy Clay (Brown) Hubbard; m. Susan Artimissa Ruggeri, Aug. 1, 1982. BA, Vanderbilt U., 1970; postgrad., U. Calif., Berkeley, 1975-77. Lab. engr. physics dept. Vanderbilt U., Nashville, 1970-73; staff scientist Lawrence Berkeley Lab. Dept. Instrument Techs., Berkeley, 1974-80; dir. rsch. & devel. Canberra Industries, Inc., Detector Products Divsn., Novato, Calif., 1980-82; v.p., gen. mgr. Canberra Semiconductor, Novato, 1982-85; cons., owner Hubbard Cons. Svcs., 1978—. Cons. SRI Internat., Menlo Park, Calif., 1979—86, sr. rsch. physicist, 1986—87; divsn. staff scientist space exploration projects office Ames Rsch. Ctr., NASA, Moffett Field, Calif., 1987—90, chief space instrumentation and studies br., 1990—92, dep. chief space projects divsn., 1992—96, assoc. dir. space directorate, 1996—97, dep. dir. space directorate, 1997—99, assoc. ctr. dir., 1999—2001, dep. ctr. dir. rsch., 2001—02, ctr. dir., 2002—; mem. Fed. Sr. Exec. Svc.,

1997—; study mgr. Mars Pathfinder Mission, 1990—91, Ames project mgr., 1992—96; mission mgr. Lunar Prospector Mission, 1994—99; interim dir. NASA Astrobiology Inst., 1998—99; Mars program dir. NASA Hdqrs., 2000—01; mem. Columbia Accident Investigation Bd.; lectr in field. Recipient Exceptional Achievement medal, NASA, 1994, 2001, Outstanding Leadership medal, 1998, 1999, 2002, Laurels for Accomplishments in Space, Aviation Week, 1997, 1998; scholar Founders scholarship, Vanderbilt U., 1966. Fellow: AIAA; mem.: IEEE, Am. Phys. Soc., Internat. Acad. Astronautics, Nuc. Sci. Soc., Commonwealth Club Calif., Hon. Order Ky. Cols. Home: 103 Fey Dr Burlingame CA 94010

HUBBARD, HAROLD MEAD, environmental scientist, consultant; b. Beloit, Kans., Apr. 16, 1924; s. Clarence Richard and Elizabeth (Mead) H.; m. Doreen J. Wallace, Aug. 13, 1948 (div. 1975); children: Stuart W., David D.; m. Barbara Bell Czarnecki, May 9, 1976 (div. 1987), remarried Sept. 9, 1999. BS, U. Kans., 1948, PhD, 1951; DSc (hon.), Regis U., 1984. Instr. chemistry U. Kans., Lawrence, 1949-51; rsch. chemist, rsch. mgr., lab. mgr. E. I. DuPont de Nemours & Co., Inc., Wilmington, Del., 1951-69; dir. phys. sci. Midwest Rsch. Inst., Kansas City, Mo., 1970-75, v.p. rsch., 1976-78, sr. v.p. ops., 1979-82, exec. v.p., 1983-90; dir. Solar Energy Rsch. Inst., 1982-90; Spark M. Matsunaga disting. fellow in energy and environ. U. Hawaii at Manoa, 1991-96; pres., CEO Pacific Internat. Ctr. for High Tech. Rsch., Honolulu, 1992-95. Vis. sr. fellow Resources for the Future, 1990-91; bd. dirs. Guaranty State Bank; chmn. Nat. Rsch. Coun. bd. on energy and environ. sys., 1991-96. With U.S. Army, 1942-45. Mem. Mo. Acad. Sci. (councillor at large 1977-80), Tech. Transfer Soc. (v.p. 1978-79), Am. Chem. Soc., AAAS, N.Y. Acad. Scis., Am. Solar Energy Soc., Colo. Renewable Energy Soc. (pres. 1996-97), Sigma Xi, Delta Upsilon, Cosmos Club. Home: 3938 SW Linden Ct Lees Summit MO 64082-4643

HUBBARD, HARVEY HART, aeroacoustician, noise control engineer, consultant; b. Swanton, Vt., June 17, 1921; s. Horace Waite and Elbie (Hart) H.; m. Sadie Margaret Miller; children: Thomas W., Susan H., Pamela L., Walter R. BSEE, U. Vt., 1942. Engr. Westinghouse Mfg. Co., Pitts., 1942; br. chief NASA, Hampton, Va., 1945-59, asst. div. chief, 1959-80; sr. rsch. assoc. Coll. William and Mary, Williamsburg, Va., 1981-85; cons. Bionetics Inc., Hampton, 1985-87, Planning Rsch. Corp., Hampton, 1987—. Author over 130 book chpts. and tech. reports in aeroacoustics rsch. and noise control engring., 1949-99. Lt. col. USAF, 1942-45, PTO. Recipient Sonic Boom Rsch. award, 1968, Medal for Exceptional Sci. Achievement, 1969, NASA, medal for Disting. Pub. Svc., 1992. Fellow AIAA (assoc., Aeroacoustics medal 1979), Acoustical Soc. Am. (pres. 1989-90, Silver medal in noise 1978); mem. Inst. of Noise Control Engring. (pres. 1979). Presbyterian. Home: 325 Charleston Way Newport News VA 23606-1174

HUBBARD, HELEN MITCHELL, accountant, lawyer; b. Denver, Dec. 21, 1955; d. Albert Russell and Celia Marie (Phillips) Mitchell; m. Larry Dale Hubbard, June 16, 1974 (div. Aug. 1997); 1 child, Benjamin David. BBA, Tex. Tech U., 1975; JD magna cum laude, So. Meth. U., 1987. CPA, Tex.; Bar: Tex. 1987, D.C. 1995. Mem. sr. staff Price Waterhouse, Dallas, 1975-81; law clk. Judge Irving L. Goldberg U.S. Ct. Appeals (5th cir.), Dallas, 1987-88; assoc. Johnson & Gibbs, P.C., Dallas and Washington, 1988-94, Miller & Chevalier, Chartered, Washington, 1994-95; from assoc. to ptnr. Akin Gump Strauss Hauer & Feld, Washington, 1995-96; ptnr. Ernst & Young LLP, Washington, 1996—2002; tax legis. coun. U.S. Dept. of Treasury, 2002—. Adj. prof. Georgetwon U. Law Ctr., 1997—2001; v.p. 1661 Crescent Place, Inc., 1999-2000. Mem. ABA (chair tax acctg. com. 1996-98, vice chair govt. rels. com. 1999-2001, co-chair simplification task force 1999—2002, asst. sec. tax sect. 2001—02), AICPA, State Bar of Tex., D.C. Bar. Office: Dept of the Treasury 1500 Pennsylvania Ave Rm 3044 Washington DC 20220-2604 E-mail: helen.hubbard@do.treas.gov.

HUBBARD, HERBERT HENDRIX, lawyer; b. Balt., Sept. 20, 1922; s. Amberson Hardy and Louise Virginia (Hendrix) H.; m. Joanne Hileman Nottingham, June 5, 1948 (dec. Sept. 2002); children: Melissa Hubbard O'Donnell, Alison Hubbard. JD, U. Md., Balt., 1950. Bar: Md. 1950, U.S. Dist. Ct. Md. 1950, U.S. Ct. Appeals (4th cir.) 1953, U.S. Supreme Ct. 1963. Clk. to dist. judge U.S. Dist. Ct. Md., Balt., 1950-51; assoc. France, Rouzer & Harris, Balt., 1951-52, 54-59; asst. U.S. atty. Dist. Md., Balt., 1952-53, 1st asst. U.S. atty., 1953-54; atty., ptnr. Weinberg & Green, Balt., 1959—98; gen. counsel Forest Haven Nursing Home, Balt., 2001—; counsel Saul Ewing, Balt., 1998—2001, of counsel, 2001—. Founding dir. Devel. Credit Fund, Inc., Balt., 1984-96. Chmn., corp. devel. coun. Sheppard & Enoch Pratt Hosp., Balt., 1978-86. Mem. ABA, Md. Bar Assn. (founding, chmn. profl. liability ins. com. 1976-82), Bar Assn. Ins. Trust (trustee 1976-88), Legal Mut. Liability Ins. Soc. Md. (sr. v.p., gen. counsel, bd. dirs., exec. com. 1986—, founding dir.), Order of Coif, U. Md. Law Review. Episcopalian. Avocations: tennis, bridge. Home: Blakehurst 1055 W Joppa Rd Towson MD 21204 Office: 100 S Charles St Ste 1500 Baltimore MD 21201-2771 also: 701 Edmondson Ave Catonsville MD 21228

HUBBARD, JOHN RANDOLPH, retired academic administrator; b. Belton, Tex., Dec. 3, 1918; s. Louis Herman and Bertha (Altizer) H.; m. Lucille Luckett, Jan. 29, 1947 (div. Dec. 1983); children: Elisa, Melisse, Kristin. AB, U. Tex., 1938, A.M., 1939, PhD, 1950; L.H.D., Hebrew Union Coll., Los Angeles, 1971, Westminster Coll., Fulton, Mo., 1977; LL.D., Sch. of Ozarks, 1973, U. So. Calif., 1980. Pvt. sec. to ICC commr., 1939-41; teaching fellow U. Tex., 1946-48; vis. asst. prof. Brit. history La. State U., 1948; asst. prof. European history Tulane U., 1949-52, asso. prof., 1953-58, prof., 1958-65; dean Newcomb Coll., 1953-65; vis. asst. prof. European history Yale, 1952-53; chief edn. adviser U.S. AID, India, 1965-69; v.p. for acad. affairs, provost U. So. Calif., Los Angeles, 1969-70, pres., 1970-80, pres. emeritus, 1980—, John R. Hubbard Chair Brit. history, 1980—; U.S. amb. to India, 1988-89. Co-chmn. Indo-U.S. Subcommn. on Edn. and Culture, 1982—. Contbr.: articles and revs. to Jour. Modern History; other ednl. jours. Mem. bd. Tulane-Lyceum Assn., 1953-65, Isidore Newman Sch., 1953-65; mem. Region 12 selection com. Woodrow Wilson Fellowship Program, also chmn., 1955-65; mem. bd. U.S. Edn. Found., India; mem. Indian adv. bd. Women's Coll. Faculty Exchange program; pres. bd. Am. Internat. Sch., New Delhi; mem. So. Calif. adv. bd. Inst. Internat. Edn.; trustee Scholarships for Children of Am. Mil. Personnel; bd. dirs. Community TV So. Calif., Los Angeles. Served as an aviator in USN, 1941-46; flight instr. and patrol plane comdr. Atlantic and Pacific fleets; lt. comdr. Res. Decorated D.F.C., Air medals (4); chevalier des Palmes Académiques; Stella della Solidarietá Italiana Italy; Order of Taj 3d degree Iran; recipient Disting. Services to Higher Edn. in U.S. award Tulane U., New Orleans, 1976; Air U. award, 1976; Disting. Alumnus award U. Tex., Austin, 1978, Alben W. Barkley medal for disitng. svc., 1989. Mem. Am., Miss. Valley hist. assns., So. Hist. Soc. (exec. council 1954-56), Anglo-Am. Hist. Soc., Assn. Ind. Calif. Colls. and Univs. (trustee), Am. Council Edn. (commn. on fed. relations 1975-77), Assn. Am. Univs. (council on fed. relations 1975-79), Orgn. Am. Historians, Conf. Brit. Studies, Am. Council Learned Socs., Phi Beta Kappa, Phi Delta Kappa, Alpha Kappa Psi, Delta Kappa Epsilon, Omicron Delta Kappa. Clubs: Royal Aero (London), Athenaeum (London); Los Angeles Country; California (Los Angeles); University (N.Y.C.); Cosmos (Washington). Office: U So Calif Dept History Los Angeles CA 90089-0001 *The fear of false knowledge is the beginning of wisdom.*

HUBBARD, MICHAEL JAMES, lawyer; b. N.Y.C., Dec. 8, 1950; s. William Neil and Elizabeth (Terleski) H. AB, U. Mich., 1976; JD, Marquette U., 1979. Bar: Wis. 1980, Mich. 1980. Assoc. Kidston, Peterson P.C., Kalamazoo, 1980, Barbier, Goulet & Petersmarck, Mt. Clemens, Mich., 1981; pvt. practice Detroit, 1982-86, Belleville, Mich., 1990-98; assoc. Lawrence J. Stockler, P.C., Southfield, Mich., 1987; staff atty. Hyatt Legal Svcs., Southgate, Mich., 1988; assoc. Dunchock, Linden & Wells, Coruna, Mich., 1989. Mem. State Bar Mich. (criminal law, negligence, gen. practice sects.) Republican.

HUBBARD, PERRY, lawyer; b. Tarrant, Ala., Mar. 17, 1921; s. Lex Walter and Erline (Perry) H.; m. Carolyn Gates, Nov. 26, 1942; children: Perry, Carolyn L., Kathryn R., Edward H.; m. Margaret Cannon, Mar. 20, 1982. BS, U. Ala., 1943, LLB, 1945. Bar: Ala. 1945. Assoc. Spain, Davies, Gillion, Grooms & Young, Birmingham, Ala., 1945-48; asst. prof. law U. Ala., 1948-50; sole practice, Tuscaloosa, 1950-53; assoc. LeMaistre, Clement & Gewin, Tuscaloosa, 1953-61; ptnr. Hubbard & Waldrop, Tuscaloosa, 1961-84; of counsel Hubbard, Waldrop, Reynolds, Davis & McIl'wain, Tuscaloosa, 1984— ; adj. prof. U. Ala., 1950—. Mem. adv. com. on appellate rules to Ala. Supreme Ct. and U.S. Ct. Appeals 5th Cir. Mem. Tuscaloosa County Bar Assn. (pres. 1959), Ala. Bar Assn. (chmn. practice and procedure sect. 1965-68), Am. Coll. Trial Lawyers. Democrat. Methodist. Club: Indian Hills Country. Office: 808 Lurleen B Wallace Blvd N Tuscaloosa AL 35401-2116

HUBBARD, PETER LAWRENCE, lawyer; b. Syracuse, N.Y., Apr. 4, 1946; s. Bardwell B. and Barbara (Bowen) H.; m. Hannah R., June 21, 1967; 1 child, Brian C. BA, Syracuse U., 1968, JD, 1971; postgrad., Judge Advocate Gen.'s Sch., Charlottesville, Va., 1976. Bar: N.Y. 1972, U.S. Dist. Ct. (no. and we. dists.) N.Y. 1972, U.S. Ct. Appeals (2d cir.) 1983. Assoc. Smith & Sovik, Syracuse, N.Y., 1971-72; asst. dist. counsel U.S. SBA, Syracuse, 1972-80; mng. ptnr. Menter, Rudin & Trivelpiece, Syracuse, 1980—. Lectr. in field. Contbr. articles to profl. jours. Pres. Reachout Inc., County Drug Rehab. Agy., Syracuse, 1979; mem. bd. trustees Loretto Mgmt. Corp., Syracuse, 2001. Office: Menter Rudin & Trivelpiece 500 S Salina St Ste 500 Syracuse NY 13202-3300 E-mail: phubbard@menterlaw.com.

HUBBARD, ROBERT GLENN, former federal agency administrator; b. Apopka, Fla., Sept. 4, 1958; s. Charles Whistnant and Myrtle Jean (Dabbs) H. BA, BS, U. Cen. Fla., 1979; AM, Harvard U., 1981, PhD, 1983. Prof. econs. Northwestern U., Evanston, Ill., 1983-87; Russell L. Carson prof. econs. and fin. Columbia U., N.Y.C., 1988—; dep. asst. sec. U.S. Dept. Treasury, Washington, 1991-92; chmn. Coun. of Econ. Adv., Washington, 2001—03. John M. Olin fellow, Nat. Bur. Econ. Rsch., Cambridge, Mass., 1987-88; cons., U.S. Dept. State, Dept. Energy, Internat. Trade Commn., Social Security Adminstrn., Nat. Petroleum Coun., numerous pvt. corps.; chmn., U.S. Pres. Coun. Econ. Advs., 2001-2003. Editor: Asymmetric Information, Corporate Finance and Investment, 1989; contbr. numerous articles to profl. jours. Grantee, NSF, 1983—. Mem. Am. Econ. Assn., Econometric Soc., Royal Econ. Assn., Am. Fin. Assn. Republican. Presbyterian. Avocations: reading, theater, travel. E-mail: rgh1@columbia.edu.

HUBBARD, RUTH, biology educator; b. Vienna, Mar. 3, 1924; came to U.S., 1938; d. Richard and Helene (Ehrlich) Hoffmann; m. Frank Twombly Hubbard, Dec. 26, 1942 (div. 1951); m. George Wald, June 11, 1958; children: Elijah, Deborah Hannah. AB, Radcliffe Coll., 1944, PhD, 1950; DSc (hon.), Macalester Coll., 1991, U. Toronto, Ont., Can., 1991, So. Meth. U., 1997; LHD (hon.), So. Ill. U., Edwardsville, 1991. Lab. technician Tenn. Pub. Health Service, Chattanooga, 1945-46; fellow U. Coll. Hosp. Med. Sch., London, 1948-49; Guggenheim fellow Carlsberg Lab., Copenhagen, Denmark, 1952-53; research fellow Harvard U., Cambridge, Mass., 1950-52, 54-58, research assoc., lectr., 1958-74, prof., 1974-90, prof. emerita, 1990—. Vis. prof. M.I.T., Cambridge, 1972; cons. Boston Women's Healthbook Collective 1982—; Regents lectr. U. Calif, Berkeley, 2002. Author: (with Margaret Randall) The Shape of Red: Insider/Outsider Reflections, 1988; author: The Politics of Women's Biology, 1990, (with Elijah Wald) Exploding the Gene Myth, 1993, 97, 99, Profitable Promises: Essays on Women, Science and Health, 1995; editor: Women Look at Biology Looking at Women, 1979, Genes and Gender II, 1979, Biological Woman--The Convenient Myth, 1982, Woman's Nature: Rationalizations of Inequality, 1983, Reinventing Biology: Respect for Life and the Creation of Knowledge, 1995; contbr. more than 250 articles on sci. and women's issues to profl. and lay books and jours. Adv. coun. mem. Nat. Women's Health Network, Washington, 1980-85; bd. dirs. Coun. Responsible Genetics, Boston, 1982—, Boston Women's Health Book Collective, 1998-99; mem. adv. bd. Boston Women's Fund, 1983-85, 2000—; mem. adv. bd. Civil Liberties Union of Mass., 1990-91, 95—, bd. dirs., 1991-95. Recipient Paul Karrer medal Swiss Chem. Soc., 1967, Peace and Freedom award Women's Internat. League for Peace and Freedom, 1985, Feminist Marathoner award Boston chpt. NOW, 1991, Disting. Svc. award Am. Inst. Biol. Sci., 1992. Fellow AAAS; mem. Marine Biol. Lab. (trustee 1973-78, trustee emerita 1990—), Soc. Biol. Chemists, Nat. Women's Studies Assn., Phi Beta Kappa, Sigma Xi. Avocations: reading, music, yoga, swimming. Home: 21 Lake View Ave Cambridge MA 02138-3325

HUBBARD, STANLEY STUB, broadcast executive; b. St. Paul, May 28, 1933; s. Stanley Eugene and Didrikke A. (Stub) H.; m. Karen Elizabeth Holmen, June 13, 1959; children: Kathryn Elizabeth Hubbard Rominski, Stanley Eugene II, Virginia Anne Hubbard Morris, Robert Winston, Julia Didrikke Coyte. BA, U. Minn., 1955; hon. doctorate, Hamline U., 1995. With Hubbard Broadcasting, St. Paul, 1951—, pres., 1967—, chmn., CEO, 1983—; past chmn. US Satellite Broadcasting Co., Inc., 1981-99. Mem. broadcast adv. com. on comm. subcom. Ho. of Reps., 1977—79; mem. adv. com. on advanced TV, FCC, 1988—95; mem. US Nat. Inf. Infastructure Adv. Coun., 1994—96. Contbr. articles to profl. jours. Chmn. St. Croix Valley Youth Ctr., 1968—; trustee Hubbard Broadcasting Found.; bd. dirs. U. Minn. Found., Mpls., Am. Friends of Jamaica, Assn. Maximum Svc. TV, U. St. Thomas, Minn. Bus. Partnership; past advisor Gov.'s Crime Commn., Ramsey County Ice Arena Com.; past bd. dir. The Guthrie Theater, The Psychoanalytic Found. of Minn., Sci. Mus. of Minn.; past mem. Hazelden Adv. Com.; active Met. Airports Pub. Found. Adv. Bd. Recipient Mitchell Charnley award Northwest Broadcast News Assn., 1991, Internat. Humanitarian award Am. Friends of Jamaica, 1989, Arthur C. Clarke award Satellite Broadcasting and Comm. Assn., 1994, DreamMaker award Children's Cancer Rsch. Fund, 1994, Disting. Svc. award Nat. Assn. Broadcasters, 1995, Spurgeon award Boy Scouts Am., 1985, Avatar award Broadcast Cable and Fin. Mgmt., 1995, Human Rights award Am. Jewish Com., 1995, Cmty. Leadership award Mpls./St. Paul chpt. Alzheimer's Assn., 1995, Most Innovative Product award Minn. High Tech. Coun., 1995, Journalism Innovator award U. Nebr., 1996, Minn. Family Bus. award U. St. Thomas, 1996, Disting. Alumnus award Breck Sch., 1996, Minn. and Dakotas Entrepreneur of Yr. award, 1996, Heritage award US Hockey Hall of Fame, 1996, U. Minn. M Club Hall of Fame Lifetime Achievement award, 1996, Broadcasters' Found. Golden Mike award, 1997, Acad. of Achievement's Golden Plate award, 1997; named to Broadcasting and Cable Hall of Fame, 1991, Soc. Satellite Profl. Internat. Space Hall of Fame, 1992, Acad. Achievement's Golden Plate award, 1997, Broadcast Pioneer award Minn. Broadcasters Assn., 1998, John Hogan Disting. Svc. award Radio & TV News Dir. Assn., 2000, Promax TV Century award, 2003; inductee St. Croix Valley Athletics Hall of Fame, 2000, Pavek Mus. of Broadcasting Hall of Fame, 2001, ProMax TV Cent. Award, 2003; named one of First Fifty Giants of Broadcasting, Lib. Am. Broadcasting, 2003. Mem. Nat. Acad. TV Arts and Scis. (past chmn. bd. trustees, found. pres. 2003—, Minn. chpt. Silver Cir. award 2001), Broadcast Pioneers, Internat. Radio and TV Soc. Avocations: sailing and boating, reading, photography. Office: Hubbard Broadcasting Inc 3415 University Ave W Saint Paul MN 55114-2099

HUBBARD, STEVAN RALPH, biophysicist, educator; b. Sioux Falls, S.D., Dec. 19, 1957; s. Robert Earl and Joanne Marie (Lindgren) H.; m. Elizabeth Jane Albert, Dec. 27, 1986. BS, Cornell U., 1980; PhD, Stanford U., 1988. Postdoctoral rsch. scientist Columbia U., N.Y.C., 1988-93, assoc. rsch. scientist, 1993-95; asst. prof. pharmacology NYU, N.Y.C., 1995-2000, assoc. prof. pharmacology, 2000—. Achievements include determination of the three-dimensional structures of protein molecules by x-ray crystallography.

HUBBARD, SUSAN MARY, writer, English educator; b. Syracuse, N.Y., Sept. 6, 1951; d. Middleton John Schwartz and Dorothy Katharine Long; m. J. T. W. Hubbard, June 16, 1979 (div. Aug. 1994); children: Katherine Ada, Clare Adrienne; m. Robley Wilson, June 17, 1995. BA, Syracuse U., 1974, MFA, 1984. Reporter, columnist Evening Press, Binghamton, N.Y., 1974-76, Evening Sentinel, Ansonia, Conn., 1976-78; investigative reporter Jour.-Courier, New Haven, 1978; reporter Herald-Jour., Syracuse, 1979-80; tchg. asst. Syracuse U., 1981-84, instr., 1984-88; project editor ERIC Clearinghouse, 1986-87; sr. lectr. Cornell U., Ithaca, N.Y., 1988-95; writer in residence Pitzer Coll., Claremont, Calif., 1995; assoc. prof., assoc. chair dept. English U. Ctrl. Fla., Orlando, 1995—. Author: Walking on Ice, 1990 (Assoc. Writing Programs prize 1989), Blue Money, 1999; (Janet Heidinger Kafka prize 2000); co-editor: 100% Pure Florida Fiction, 2000; stories in Ploughshares, N.Am. Rev., TriQuar., Miss. Rev., Kalliope, S.E. Quar. Fellow, Aspen Writer's Conf., 1987; grantee Master Writer's grant, Nat. Writer's Voice, 1997. Mem.: Associated Writing Programs (mem. exec. bd. 1999—, pres. 2002—03). Office: U Ctrl Fla PO Box 161346 Orlando FL 32816-1346

HUBBARD, THOMAS C. ambassador; b. Ky., 1943; m. Joan Magnusson; 2 children. Grad., U. Ala., 1965. With U.S. Fgn. Svc., 1965—, polit./econ. officer, econ./comml. officer Fukuoka, Japan, mem. polit. section U.S. Embassy Tokyo, 1971-73, 78-81; econ. officer Japan Desk Dept. State, 1973-75; exec. sec. to delegation U.S. Mission to OECD, Paris, 1975, energy advisor; dir. tng. and liaison staff Bur. Pers. Dept. State, Washington, dep. dir. Philippine Desk, 1984-85, country dir. Philippines Desk, 1985-87; dep. chief of mission U.S. Embassy, Kuala Lumpur, Malaysia, 1987-89; minister-counselor Sr. Fgn. Svc., 1989-90; minister, dep. chief of mission U.S. Embassy, Manila, 1990-93; dep. asst. sec. for East Asian and Pacific Affairs Dept. State, Washington, 1993-96; amb. to Republic of the Philippines and Republic of Palau Manila, 1996—2001; amb. to Republic of Korea, 2001—. Legis. asst. Congressman Jim Leach, Iowa, 1981; prin. dep. asst. East Asian and Pacific Affairs Sec. of State, 2000—01. Mem. Phi Beta Kappa. Office: Chongo-gu Unit 15550 82 Sejong-ro Seoul Republic of Korea*

HUBBARD, WILLIAM BOGEL, planetary sciences educator; b. Liberty, Tex., Nov. 14, 1940; s. William Bogel and Marie Hubbard; m. Jean North Gilliland, June 8, 1963; children: Lynne Marie, Laurie North. BA, Rice U., Houston, 1962; PhD, U. Calif., Berkeley, 1967. Rsch. fellow Calif. Inst. Tech., Pasadena, 1967-68; asst. prof. astronomy U. Tex., Austin, 1968-72; assoc. prof. planetary scis. U. Ariz., Tucson, 1972-75, dir. Lunar and Planetary Lab., 1977-81, prof., 1975—. Cons. Lawrence Livermore (Calif.) Nat. Lab., 1972-86, NASA, 1994—; prin. investigator NASA, 1974—, NSF, 1970, 79, 83, 86-93; exch. scientist USSR Nat. Acad. Sci., 1973, mem. com. div. for planetary scis., 1985-88; mem. com. on planetary and lunar exploration NRC, 2003—. Contbr. articles to profl. jours.; assoc. editor: Icarus, 1980-2003. Fellow Japan Soc. for Promotion of Sci., Am. Geophys. Union; mem. AAAS, Am. Astron. Soc., Internat. Astron. Union, Am. Hereford Assn., Nat. Cattlemen's Beef Assn., Sigma Xi. Democrat. Episcopalian. Home: 2618 E Devon St Tucson AZ 85716-5506 Office: U Ariz Lunar & Planetary Lab Tucson AZ 85721-0092

HUBBARD, WILLIAM JAMES, library director; b. Grand Rapids, Mich., July 17, 1941; s. Willard Wright and Sara (Rast) H.; m. Barbara Ockun, Sept. 8, 1962; children: William, Thomas, James, Gregory. AB, Dartmouth Coll., 1963; MLS, SUNY, Geneseo, 1972. Engr., supr. Rochester (N.Y.) Telephone Corp., 1963-71; contract libr. Xerox Corp., Webster, N.Y., 1971-72; libr. circulation SUNY, Fredonia, 1973-75; libr. user svcs. Va. Poly. Inst. and State U., Blacksburg, 1975-80; dir. libr. svcs., dir.automation-networks, act. state libr. Va. State Libr., Richmond, 1980-88; univ. libr. Jacksonville (Ala.) State U., 1988—. Author: Stack Management, 1981; assoc. editor Ala. Librarian; contbr. articles to profl. jours. Mem. Ala. Libr. Assn., Nat. Assn. Scholars, Am. Soc. Info. Sci. and Tech., Assn. Knowledgework. Office: State U Univ Libr Jacksonville AL 36265 E-mail: williamj@hubbards.org., bhubbard@jsucc.jsu.edu.

HUBBARD, WILLIAM NEILL, JR., pharmaceutical company executive; b. Fairmont, N.C., Oct. 15, 1919; s. William Neill and Mary Emma (Fenegan) H.; m. Elizabeth Terleski, Dec. 28, 1945 (dec. Mar. 1984); children— William Neill III, Michael J., Mary E., Elizabeth A., Susan E.; m. Joyce Elaine Wixson, Apr. 3, 1987. AB, Columbia U., 1942; postgrad., U. N.C. Sch. Medicine; MD, NYU, 1944. Mem. house staff 3d med. div. Bellevue Hosp., N.Y.C., 1944-50; instr. medicine N.Y. U., 1950-53, asst. prof., 1953-59; asst. dean, then assoc. dean N.Y. U. Coll. Medicine, 1951-59; dean U. Mich. Med. Sch., 1959-70, assoc. prof. internal medicine, 1959-64, prof., 1964-70; dir. U. Mich. Med. Center, 1969-70; gen. mgr. pharm. div., v.p. Upjohn Co., 1970-72, exec. v.p., 1972-74, pres., 1974-84, dir., 1968-91. Dir. Johnson Controls, Inc., Consumers Power; bd. dirs. Pharm. Mfrs. Assn., 1978-80, 81-84, chmn. bd., 1980-81; chmn. coun. health care tech. Inst. Medicine of NAS, 1986-90; cons. USPHS; trustee N.Y. Acad. of Medicine, 1994-2002; bd. dirs. Pan-Am. Health and Edn. Found., 1996-2001. Mem. Nat. Adv. Commn. on Libraries, 1966-68; med. adv. com. W.K. Kellogg Found., 1959-67, trustee, 1979-92; mem. Gov.'s Adv. Com. on Edn. Health Care, 1965-69; trustee Bronson Meth. Hosp., 1970-84; chmn. Gov.'s Action Com. on Corrections, 1972-73; mem. panel ednl. consultants Commn. on Edn. for Health Adminstrn., 1973-75; mem. com. on med. edn. Brown U., 1974-77; mem. nat. sci. bd. NSF, 1974-80, cons. to bd., 1980-83; bd. dirs. Family Health Internat. (formerly Internat. Fertility Research Program), 1981-90; mem. bd. sci. and tech. for internat. devel. Nat. Acad. Scis., 1978-80, Council on Sci. and Tech. for Devel., 1978-83; bd. visitors in East Asian studies U. Mich., 1976-80; bd. overseers Morehouse Coll., 1976-81; bd. dirs. Nat. Med. Fellowships, Inc., 1973-75, Nat. Fund. Med. Edn., 1962-75; trustee Kalamazoo Coll., 1973-78, Columbia U., N.Y.C., 1981-89; mem. bd. regents Nat. Library of Medicine, 1963-67, 72-76, chmn., 1965-67, 74-76, cons., 1976-84; bd. dirs. Am. Near East Refugee Aid, 1977-82; dir. devel. council U. Mich., 1979-87; mem. population adv. panel Office of Technology Assessment, U.S. Congress, 1979-81; chmn. bd. visitors Med. Ctr. U. Mich., 1989-99; bd. visitors U. Mich. Sch. of Nursing, 1995-98, Columbia U. Sch. Nursing, 1990-99. Fellow ACP, Am. Acad. Arts and Scis., Royal Soc. Medicine; mem. AMA, Inst. Medicine of NAS, Harvey Soc., N.Y. Acad. Medicine, Soc. Alumni Bellevue Hosp., Mich. Med. Soc. (coun. 1960-62), Kalamazoo Acad. Medicine, Am. Soc. Clin. Pharmacology and Therapeutics, Assn. Am. Med. Colls. (pres. 1966-67), Jamestown Soc., Sigma Xi, Alpha Omega Alpha. Home: 3634 Woodcliff Dr Kalamazoo MI 49008-2513 Fax: 269-372-9305. E-mail: W.N.HUBBARD@worldnet.att.net.

HUBBE, HENRY ERNEST, financial forecaster, funds manager; b. Hamburg, Germany, Aug. 13, 1932; came to U.S., 1958; s. H.V. and Ingeborg M. (Schroeder) H.; m. Mary E. Wylie, 1961; children: John, Michael. BA, NYU, 1971, MBA, 1974. Area adminstr. Bank of Am. NT&SA, San Francisco, 1958-63; asst. v.p. Citibank N.Am., N.Y.C., 1963-74; sr. v.p. European Am. Bank, N.Y.C., 1974-84; pres. Internat. Treasury Cons., N.Y.C., 1984-94; mng. dir. Fintech (UK) Ltd., London, 1985-96, Fintech Asset Mgmt., London, 1985-96; pres. Fintech (USA) Ltd., N.Y.C., N.Y., 1996—. Mem. faculty Am. Inst. Banking, N.Y.C., 1974-83; guest speaker internat. confs., profl. orgns.; panel mem. Bus. Internat., London. Creator proprietary computer software; contbr. articles to profl. jours. Mem. Beta Gamma Sigma (v.p. 1971—). Avocation: golf.

HUBBEL, MICHAEL ROBERT, insurance company executive, educator; b. Grand Rapids, Mich., June 5, 1954; s. Robert Lewis and Irene Rose (Socha) H. AA, Lansing Community Coll., 1974; BA, Mich. State U., 1976; MBA, Coll. of Ins., 1994. CPCU. Rsch. analyst Farm Bur. Ins. Group, Lansing, Mich., 1971-81; sr. rsch. analyst Hastings (Mich.) Mut. Ins. Co., 1981-85; assoc. prof. ins., dir. ins. program Olivet (Mich.) Coll., 1985-89; v.p. informational resources Pioneer State Mut. Ins. Co., Flint, Mich., 1989-93; assoc. dir. Ctr. for Profl. Edn. Coll. of Ins., N.Y.C., 1993-95; assoc. prof. ins., dir. ins. Olivet (Mich.) Coll., 1995-2001, prof. risk mgmt. and ins., 2001—, chair dept. bus. and econs., 1996—2002, chair dept. ins. and risk mgmt., 2002—. Instr. risk mgmt. Lansing C.C., 1991, ins. Mich. State U. Coll. Bus., East Lansing, 1983-84, 88-89, continuing edn., 1985-92; mem. Mich. Ins. Bur. Agts. Edn. Adv. Coun., 1992-93, 95-2001; writer property-casualty test devel. panels Mich. Ins. Bur., 1989, 91; book reviewer Ins. Inst. Am., 1987, 90. Editor, creator monthly trade newsletter Third Thursday, 1981-82; adv. bd. Jour. of Internat. Ins.; contbr. articles to trade jours. and newsletters. Explorer advisor, mem. com. Chief Okemos coun. Boy Scouts Am., 1987-89; v.p. Grand Ledge Jaycees, 1982-83; mem. ins. adv. bd. Olivet Coll., 1990-92, Northwestern Mich. Coll., 1992; adminstr. Mich. Ins. Hall of Fame. Recipient Presdl. award Olivet Coll., 1988, 90, 98, 2002, 03, Award of Distinction Nat. Assn. Profl. Surplus Lines Offices. Mem. Soc. CPCUs (chpt. bd. dirs. 1989-90), Cen. Mich. Underwriters Assn. (pres. 1982-83), 1752 Club, Gamma Iota Sigma (assoc., advisor 1986-89, 95—, mem. nat. bd. trustees, v.p. 1990-92, pres. 1992-95). Lutheran. Avocations: sailing, skiing, golf, reading, writing. Office: Olivet Coll Mott 406 Olivet MI 49076

HUBBELL, BILLY JAMES, lawyer; b. Pine Bluff, Ark., May 21, 1949; s. Arley E. and Mary M. (Duke) H.; m. Judy C. Webb, Feb. 21, 1981; children: Jennifer Leigh, William Griffin. BE, U. Cen. Ark., 1971; JD, U. Ark, Little Rock, 1978. Bar: Ark. 1978, U.S. Dist. Ct. (ea. dist.) Ark. 1978, U.S. Ct. Appeals (8th cir.) 1987. Tchr. Grady (Ark.) High Sch., 1971-78; assoc. Smith and Smith, McGehee, Ark., 1978-79; ptnr. Smith, Hubbell and Drake, McGehee, 1979-86, Griffin, Rainwater & Draper, P.A., Crossett, Ark., 1987-90; dep. prosecuting atty. Ashley County, Ark., 1989-90; dist. judge Crossett, 1991—; pvt. practice, 1991—. Candidate Ark. Ho. of Reps., Lincoln County, 1984, 10th

Jud. Dist. Cir./Chancery Judge, 1998. Sgt. USAR, 1970-76. Mem. Ark. Bar Assn., S.E. Ark. Legal Inst. (chmn. 1984-85, Ashley County Bar Assn. (past pres.), Ark. Trial Lawyers Assn. Democrat. Seventh Day Adventist. Avocations: jogging, computers. Office: PO Box 574 Crossett AR 71635-0574 E-mail: bjhubbell@alltel.net.

HUBBELL, ERNEST, lawyer; b. Trenton, Mo., Aug. 28, 1914; s. Platt and Maud Irene (Ray) H.; m. Nevah Smith, Apr. 25, 1943; 1 child, Platt Thorpe. AA, North Cen. Mo. Coll. (formerly Trenton Jr. Coll.), 1934; JD, Georgetown U., 1938. Bar: D.C. 1937, Mo. 1938, U.S. Supreme Ct. 1946. Practiced in, Trenton, 1938-39, Jefferson City, Mo., 1939-42; pvt. practice, Kansas City, Mo., 1947-52; ptnr. Hubbell, Sawyer, Peak, O'Neal & Napier (formerly Hubbell, Lane & Sawyer), Kansas City, 1952—. Asst. atty. gen. Mo., 1939-43; first chmn. bench, bar com. 16th Jud. Cir. Ct., Kansas City, 1964-69, mem 16th Cir. Jud. Nominating Commn., 1970-75; mem. U.S. Cir. Judge Nominating Commn., 1977-80. Trustee Legal Aid and Defender Soc. Greater Kansas City, 1964-73; mem. Law Found. U. Mo. Kansas City, 1966-71; chmn. Nat. Council on Crime and Delinquency, 1966-76; pres. Hubbell Family Hist. Soc., 1981-85; mem. Soc. Fellows Nelson Art Gallery. With USAAF, 1943-44, capt. JAGC, 1944-46. Mem. ABA, Kansas City Met. Bar Assn. (pres. 1963-64, ann. Achievement award 1974, 1st ann. Litigator Emeritus award), Mo. Bar Assn., Assn. Trial Lawyers Am. (assoc. editor R.R. law sect. of jour. 1951—), Mo. Assn. Trial Attys. (pres. 1954, editor bull. 1955), Lawyers Assn. Kansas City, Lawyers Assn. St. Louis, Archeol. Inst. Am., Sierra Club (life). Episcopalian. Democrat. Club: Kansas City. Home: 1210 W 63d St Kansas City MO 64113-1513 Office: Hubbell Sawyer Peak O'Neal & Napier Power and Light Bldg 106 W 14th St Fl 12 Kansas City MO 64105-1914

HUBBELL, FLOYD ALLAN, physician, educator; b. Waco, Tex., Nov. 13, 1948; s. F.E. and Margaret (Fraser) H.; m. Nancy Cooper, May 23, 1975; 1 child, Andrew Allan. BA, Baylor U., 1971, MD, 1974; MS in Pub. Health, UCLA, 1983. Diplomate Am. Bd. Internal Medicine. Intern, then resident Long Beach med. program U. Calif., Irvine, 1975-78, asst. prof. medicine, 1981-89, assoc. prof. medicine and social ecology, 1989-97; prof. medicine and social ecology, 1997—; dir. primary care internal medicine residency U. Calif., Irvine, 1992-97, chief divsn. gen. internal medicine and primary care, 1992—2002, dir. Ctr. for Health Policy and Rsch., 1993—, chair dept. medicine, 2002—. Contbr. articles to profl. jours. Recipient Outstanding Tchr. award U. Calif., Irvine, 1985, 89. Fellow ACP; mem. APHA, Soc. Gen. Internal Medicine, Physicians for Social Responsibility. Democrat. Avocations: reading, skiing, water sports. Office: U Calif Health Policy Rsch 100 Theory # 110 Irvine CA 92697-5800 E-mail: fahubbel@uci.edu.

HUBBELL, JOHN HOWARD, radiation physicist; b. Ann Arbor, Mich., Apr. 9, 1925; s. Howard Adams Hubbell and Mildred Jeanetta (Lipe) Hubbell Dyson; m. Jean Garber Norford, June 11, 1955; children: Anne Virginia Hubbell Cooper, Shelton Eric, Wendy Jean Hubbell Carballo. BS in Engring. Physics, U. Mich., 1949, MS in Physics, 1950; doctor honoris causa, U. Cordoba, 1996. Rschr. x-ray crystal diffraction group Nat. Bur. Standards (name now Nat. Inst. Standards & Tech.), Washington, 1950-51; rschr. thermodynamics sect. Nat. Bur. Stds. (name now Nat. Inst. Stds. & Tech.), Washington, 1951, rschr. radiation theory group, 1951-62, dir. x-ray and ionizing radiation data ctr. Washington & Gaithersburg, Md., 1963-81, rschr. Ctr. for Radiation Rsch. Gaithersburg, 1982-88, rschr., cons. Photon and Charged Particle Data Ctr., 1988—. Mem. cross sect. evaluation working group Brookhaven (N.Y.) Nat. Lab., 1965—; cons. Lawrence Livermore (Calif.) Nat. Lab., 1966—, Lawrence Berkeley (Calif.) Nat. Lab., 1966—, Internat. Atomic Energy Agy., Vienna, 1987—, WHO, Geneva, 1989—; sec. task force on x-ray absorption coefficients Internat. Union Crystallography, 1979—; lectr. USSR Acad. Scis., 1979, People's Republic of China State Bur. Metrology, 1987, 93, India under Indo-U.S. Spl. Fgn. Currency Program, 1972, 74, 90; invited lectr. Japanese Soc. Radiol. Tech., Nagoya Ann. Conf., Kyoto, Osaka, 1995; vis. prof. U. Cordoba, Argentina, 1996. Author: Photon Cross Sections, Attenuation Coefficients and Energy Absorption Coefficients, 1969; editor: Jour. Applied Radiation and Isotopes, 1988—92; editor-in-chief: Radiation Physics and Chemistry, 1992—2001, cons. editor:, 2002—; contbr. articles to profl. jours. and encys., chapters to books. Scoutmaster, Boy Scouts Am., Washington, 1953-60; ch. sch. tchr. Foundry United Methodist Ch., Washington, 1963-78. With U.S. Army, 1943-45, ETO. Decorated Bronze Star; recipient Faculty medal Tech. U. Prague, 1982; named Outstanding Alumnus U. Mich. Nuc. Engring. Dept., 1995. Fellow Am. Nuc. Soc. (Radiation Industry award 1985, Profl. Excellence award 1990), Health Physics Soc. (chmn. gen. radiation protection sect., stds. com. 1984-90, Disting. Sci. Achievement award 2001), Am. Phys. Soc.; mem. Soc. Nuc. Medicine (Paul C. Aebersold award 1985), Internat. Radiation Physics Soc. (pres. 1994-97, sec. to adv. bd. 2000--), Radiation Rsch. Soc., Hubbell Family Hist. Soc., Internat. Higher Edn. Acad. Scis. Achievements include development of computationally tractable solutions for the (now called) Hubbell rectangular source integral and Epstein-Hubbell generalized elliptic-type integral. Avocations: eclipse chasing, playing harmonica. Home: 11830 Rocking Horse Rd Rockville MD 20852-2322 Office: Nat Inst Standards and Tech Mail Stop 8463 Rad Physics Bldg Rm C-314 Gaithersburg MD 20899-8463 E-mail: john.hubbell@nist.gov. *In this later stage of my life I view my global science connections more and more as an opportunistic tool toward realizing, incrementally at least, Teilhard de Chardin's envisioned "noosphere" (humanity as a caring communicating "thinking skin" of the earth), declaring the pragmatic and compelling authenticity of the option of a friendly cosmos as not only a place in which to live, but also to bravely wear as a suit of clothes, in contrast to the hostile and judgmental cosmos envisioned, dwelt in, and worn by many.*

HUBBELL, JOHN PLATT, pediatrician, educator; b. Palmerton, Pa., July 30, 1919; s. John Platt Hubbell and Dorothy Peters; m. Martha Gallison, June 3, 1944; children: Pamela Hubbell Robinson, John P. III, Deborah Hubbell-Hudak. AB, Williams Coll., 1940; MD, Harvard U., 1943. Cert. bd. cert. Am. Bd. Pediats. Intern, resident Children's Hosp., Boston, 1944—45, 1946—47; assoc. prof. pediats. Harvard Med. Sch., Boston, 1954—. Aattending pediatrician newborn nurseries Brigham and Women's Hosp., Boston, 1954—2003. Contbr. articles to profl. jours. Mem. vestry Ch. of the Redeemer, Ch. Hill, Mass., 1970. Lt. (j.g.) USNR, 1945—46, lt. (s.g.), lt. comdr. USNR, 1952—54. Mem.: Needham Ret. Men's Glee Club, The Country Club, Alpha Omega Alpha, Phi Beta Kappa. Democrat. Episcopalian. Avocations: golf, tennis, singing, bridge. Home: 65 Putnam St Needham Heights MA 02494

HUBBELL, KATHERINE JEAN, retired marketing professional; b. Norfolk, Va., Mar. 5, 1951; d. Lester Earle and Katherine Jean (Bush) Hubbell; m. Daryl Paul Domning, July 10, 1987; 1 child, Charlotte Roxanna Domning. BA in English, Clemson U., 1974, BS in Math., 1974; MBA in Mktg., Va. Polytech. Inst. & State U., 1991. Info. sys. engr. MITRE Corp., McLean, Va., 1975-79, mem. tech. staff Bedford, Mass., 1980-81; design engr. GE, Wilmington, Mass., 1979-80; budget assoc. nat. hdqrs. ARC, Washington, 1982-92; mktg. cons. Dominion Group, Vienna, Va., 1993-98; with Nat. Found. Women Bus. Owners, Washington, 1999—2001; ret. Prime Vol. Opportunities, 2002. Vol., recreation ARC Bethesda Naval Hosp., 1976—79; vol. Holy Cross Hospice, 1984—87; vol., allocations com. United Way Nat. Capitol Area, 1989—91; vol., database mgr. Nat. Christian Life Cmty. U.S., 1993—97, vol., strategic planning com. Christian Life Cmty. Mid-Atlantic Region, 1989—90, vol., co-chair, 1995—2001, vol., devel. officer, 2003—; vol., adv. com. The Arc of Montgomery County, 2000. Home: 9211 Wendell St Silver Spring MD 20901-3533

HUBBELL, WAYNE LESTER, ophthalmologist, educator, chemist, educator; b. Riverside, Calif., Mar. 24, 1943; s. Lester Glenn and Helyn Marie Hubbell; m. Cheryl Alice McAfee, Jan. 6, 1965; 1 child, Paul Wayne. BS in Chemistry, Oreg. State U., 1965; PhD in Chemistry, Stanford U., 1970; Doctorate (hon.), U. Pecs, Hungary, 1998. Prof. U. Calif., Berkeley, 1970—83, UCLA, 1983—. Contbr. articles to profl. jours. Finalist Sci. Talent Search, Westinghouse Corp., 1961; named Jules Stein prof., UCLA, 1983—, Jesse W. Beams Meml. Lectr. in Biophysics, U. Va., 1994, Zuffanti Lectr. in Chemistry, Northeastern U., 1996, Alexander M. Cruickshank Lectr., Gordon Rsch. Confs., 1997, Irving L. Schwartz Lectr., Mt. Sinai Sch. Medicine, 1998; recipient Teacher-Scholar award, Camille and Henry Dreyfus Found., Merit Rsch. award, Nat. Eye Inst., 1990—2000, Sr. Investigator award, Rsch. to Prevent Blindness, 1990, Rsch. award, Alcon Rsch. Inst., 1994, Sr. Investigator award, Rsch. to Prevent Blindness, 1999, Gold medal, Internat. Electron Paramagnetic Resonance Soc., 2000; fellow, Air Force Office Sci. Rsch.-NRC, 1969—70; Found. fellow, Alfred P. Sloan Found., 1973—75. Fellow: Biophysical Soc. (Elisabeth Roberts Cole award 1994), Am. Acad. Arts and Scis.; mem.: Am. Chem. Soc. Achievements include development of technique of site-directed spin labeling. Home: 1668 Michael Ln Pacific Palisades CA 90272 Office: Jules Stein Eye Inst UCLA Sch Medicine Los Angeles CA 90095 Office Fax: 310-794-2144. Personal E-mail: hubbellc@aol.com. E-mail: hubbellw@jsei.ucla.edu.

HUBBS, DONALD HARVEY, foundation executive; b. Kingman, Ariz., Jan. 3, 1918; s. Wayne and Grace Lillian (Hoose) H.; m. Flora Vincent, June 14, 1945; children: Donald Jr., Susan Tyner, Diane Schultz, Wayne, David, Adrienne Busk. BA in Edn., Ariz. State U., 1940; JD, Southwestern U., 1956. CPA; bar: Calif. 1956. Acct. Wright and Hubbs, LA, 1945-67; pvt. practice atty. LA, 1956-81; pres., dir. Conrad N. Hilton Found., LA, 1981-98, chmn. bd., CEO, 1998—. Bd. dirs. Vita Pakt Citrus Products Co.; regent Mt. St. Mary's Coll., 1983-98; bd. councilors U. So. Calif. Law Sch., 1992-99, Donald H. Hubbs Chair U of Houston Coll. of Hotel & Restaurant Mgmt. Hon. chief of the tribes of Kapatinga and Oku, Ghana, West Africa; spkr. So. Govs. Conf., 1986; chmn. Hilton Coll., Univ. Houston. 1st lt. (inf.) U.S. Army. Decorated Purple Heart; recipient Anne Sullivan medal Perkins Sch. for the Blind, 1992, Humanitarian award Nat. Coun. Juvenile and Family Ct. Judges, 1994, Humanitarian award Family Violence Prevention Fund, 2000, Spirit of Helen Keller award Helen Keller Internat., 1995. Mem. State Bar of Calif., So. Calif. Assn. for Philanthropy (pres. 1985-86), Riviera Country Club, LA Country Club. Avocations: cattle ranching, hunting, fishing, golfing. Home: 1658 San Onofre Dr Pacific Palisades CA 90272-2735 Office: Conrad N Hilton Found Ste 1000 10100 Santa Monica Blvd Los Angeles CA 90067-4100

HUBEL, DAVID HUNTER, physiologist, science educator; b. Windsor, Ont., Can., Feb. 27, 1926; s. Jesse Hervey and Elsie (Hunter) Hubel; m. Shirley Ruth Izzard, June 20, 1953; children: Carl Andrew, Eric David, Paul Matthew. BSc, McGill U., 1947, MD, 1951, DSc (hon.), 1978; AM (hon.), Harvard U., 1962; DSc (hon.), U. Man., 1983; DHL (hon.), Johns Hopkins U., 1990; DSci, U. Western Ont., 1993; DSc, Oxford U., 1994, Gustavus Adolphus Coll., 1994, Ohio State U., 1995; D (hon.), U. Madrid, 1997, Univ. Miguel, 1998; JD (hon.), Dalhousie U., 1998; D (hon.), U. Toronto, 2002. Intern Montreal Gen. Hosp., 1951—52; asst. resident neurology Montreal Neurol. Inst., 1952—53, fellow clin. neurophysiology, 1953—54; asst. resident neurology Johns Hopkins Hosp., 1954—55; rsch. fellow Walter Reed Army Inst. Rsch., Washington, 1955—58; sr. fellow neurol. scis. group Johns Hopkins U., 1958—59; faculty Harvard U. Med. Sch., 1959—, George Packer Berry prof. physiology, chmn. dept., 1967—68, George Packer Berry prof. neurobiology, 1968—82, John Franklin Enders U. prof., 1982—, rsch. prof. Neurobiology. Lectr. in field; George Eastman prof., Oxford, England, 1991—92; rschr. brain mechanisms in vision; spkr. in field. With AUS, 1955—58. Recipient Trustees award, Rsch. to Prevent Blindness, 1971, Lewis S. Rosentiel award for disting. work in basic med. rsch., 1972, Karl Lashley prize, Am. Philos. Soc., 1977, Louisa Gross Horwitz prize, Columbia U., 1978, Dickson prize in medicine, U. Pitts., 1979, Ledile prize, Harvard U., 1980, Nobel prize, 1981, Outstanding Sci. Leadership award, Nat. Assn. for Biomed. Rsch., 1990, City of Medicine award, 1990, Glen A. Fry medal, Coll. Optometry, Ohio State U., 1991, First Ann. George A. Miller lectr., Cognitive Neurosci. Soc., Gerald award, Soc. Neurosci., 1993, Helen Keller award, Helen Keller Eye Rsch. Found., 1995, Wilder Penfield Lecture, Montreal Neurological Inst., 1998, Frontiers in Neuroscience Lecture, Case Western Reserve U., 2000, Disting. Canadians Spkr. Series, Corpus Christi Coll., 2001. Fellow: AAAS, Am. Acad. Arts & Scis.; mem.: NAS, Academia Europaea (fgn. mem.), Royal Soc. London, Am. Philos. Soc. (Karl Spencer Lashley prize 1977), Johns Hopkins U. Soc. Scholars, Spanish Soc.Ophthalmology (hon.), Assn. Rsch. in Vision and Ophthalmology (Friedenwald award 1975), Soc. for Neurosci. (Bwditch lectr. 1966), Deutsche Acad. der Naturforscher Leopoldina (Grass lectr. 1976, Gerard award 1993), Am. Physiol. Soc., Sigma Xi. Home: 98 Collins Rd Waban MA 02468-2235 Office: Harvard U Med Sch Dept Neurobiology WAB213 220 Longwood Ave Boston MA 02115-5701*

HUBEN, BRIAN DAVID, lawyer; b. Inglewood, Calif., May 14, 1962; s. Michael Gerald and Dorothy (Withers) H.; m. Kathy Henson Johnson, Apr. 6, 1991; children: Kaitlin Johnson, Mariana Johnson. BA, Loyola Marymount U., 1984; JD, Loyola Law Sch., 1987. Bar: Calif. 1988, U.S. Dist. Ct. (no., ce., ea. and so. dists.) Calif. 1988, Ariz., 1994, U.S. Ct. Appeals (9th cir.) 1988, D.C. 1989, U.S. Supreme Ct. 1996. Assoc. Steinberg, Nutter & Brent, Santa Monica, Calif., 1988-89, Smith & Hilbig, Torrance, Calif., 1989-95, Robie & Matthai, L.A., 1995-99; spl. master State Bar of Calif., 1995-99; counsel Katten Muchin Zavis Rosenman, L.A., 1999—. Del. L.A. County Bar Assn. State Conv., 1990-99. Mem. instl. rev. bd. Torrance Meml. Med. Ctr., 1990-95. Mem. Calif. Bar Assn., D.C. Bar Assn., L.A. County Bar Assn., Loyola Marymount Univ. Alumni Assn. (dir., bd. dirs. 1995-01). Democrat. Roman Catholic. Avocations: travel, sports, current events. Office: Katten Muchin Zavis Rosenman 2029 Century Park E 26th Flr Los Angeles CA 90067-3012 E-mail: brian.huben@kmzr.com.

HUBER, SISTER ALBERTA, college president; b. Rock Island, Ill., Feb. 12, 1917; d. Albert and Lydia (Hofer) H. BA, Coll. St. Catherine, St. Paul, 1939; MA, U. Minn., 1945; PhD, U. Notre Dame, 1954. Mem. faculty Coll. St. Catherine, 1940—, prof. English, 1953-97; prof. emerita, 1997; chmn. dept. Coll. St. Catherine, 1960-63, acad. dean, 1962-64, pres., 1964-79. Trustee Avila Coll., Kansas City, Mo., 1986-97, St. Joseph's Hosp., St. Paul, 1971-80; pres. UN Assn. Minn., 1980-81; bd. dirs. St. Paul YMCA, 1986-92. Decorated Chevalier, Ordre des Palmes Acad.; recipient Outstanding Achievement award U. Minn. Alumni Assn., 1981. Mem. Phi Beta Kappa, Pi Gamma Mu. Office: 1724A Munster Ave Saint Paul MN 55116-3031

HUBER, ANN CERVIN, nurse; b. Balt., Dec. 1, 1941; d. John and Rose (Kortus) Cervin; m. Frank H. Huber, Sept. 26, 1964; children: Holly Ann, Joann Františka. Diploma, Union Meml. Hosp. Sch. Nursing, 1963; BSN, U. Md., 1994. RN, Md.; cert. community health nurse. Staff nurse Union Meml. Hosp., Balt., clin. nurse, 1963-74; pub. health nurse Balt. City Health Dept., 1975-79; community health nurse Harford County Health Dept., Bel Air, Md., 1979-94; coord. and AIDS case mgr. Harford County, 1994—2002. Active Czech and Slovak Heritage Assn. Md. Recipient Govs. Citation, 1990, 2002, Unsung Hero award Harford Coun. Cmty. Svcs., 1996, Heart to Heart award Harford County, 1997. Mem.: SOKOL (pres. 1986—88, bd. dirs. 1988—90, v.p. 1991—94, pres. 1994—96, v.p. 1996—97, pres. 2000—02, bd. dirs. 2002—, v.p. 2002—), ANA, Md. Classified Employees Assn. (treas. 1986—88), Md. Nurses Assn. (chmn. sunshine com., steering com.), Assn. Nurses AIDS Care, Sigma Theta Tau.

HUBER, COLLEEN ADLENE, artist; b. Concordia, Kans., Mar. 30, 1927; d. Claude Irve and Freda (Trow) Baker; m. Wallace Charles Huber, Oct. 18, 1945 (dec.); children: Wallace Charles II (dec.), Shawn Dale, Devron Kelly (dec.), Candace Lynette, Melody Ann. Student, UCLA, 1974-78; BA cum laude, Calif. Poly. U., 1983. Co-owner, artist The Rocket (community newspaper), Garden Grove, Calif., 1955-58; quick sketch artist Walt Disney Prodn. Co., Burbank, Calif., 1958-59; v.p., art dir. Gray Pub. Co., Fullerton, Calif., 1968-76; tchr. North Orange County Sch. Dist., La Palma, Calif., 1974-76; art dir. Shoppers Guide, Upland, Calif., 1979-81; pub., owner Community Woman/Huber Ad Agy., Anaheim, Calif., 1976-79; artist Bargain Bulletin Pub., Fallbrook, Calif., 1979-82; graphic artist, designer Van Zyen Pub., Fallbrook, 1982-83; cons. sales East San Diego Mag./Baker Graphics, Rancho San Diego, Calif., 1978-88; owner, artist Coco Bien Objet d'Art, Laguna Beach, Calif., 1986-92; instr. Camp Fire Inc., 1990-92, Coco Bien Objet d'Art, Temecula, Calif., 1992-93, Sun City, Calif., 1993—, Castle Rock, Wash., 1993—. Dir. edn. Art Acad., Orange County, 1992-94; instr. Lake Elsinore Community Ctr., 1992—, San Jacinto C.C., 1997-98; 2nd v.p., membership chair, Fine Art Inst., San Bernadina Mus., San Bernardino, Calif., 1998-99, rec. sec., 2000-02. Author: Gail, 1980 (1st Pl. award 1981, 2d Pl. award 1981); artist: Yearlings (2d Pl. award 1985), Penning (1st Pl. award 1987); exhibited at Temecula Art Coun. Wild Life Art Show, 1999, San Bernardino Mus., 2001 (1st pl. award); mfeatured artist San Bernardino Mus. Fine Arts Inst., 2001. Participant Art-A-Fair, Laguna Beach Festival Show. Recipient certs. North Orange County ROP, 1976-77, 2d pl. San Bernardino Art Show, 1995, Hon. Mention Nat. Orange Show, 1996, City of Lake Elsinore, 1997, 1st pl. award FAI San Bernardino Mus., 1999, 2001. Fellow Zonta (2d v.p. 1990-91), Laguna Beach C. of C. (docent gallery night 1988); mem. Exec. Women, Calif. Press Women Assn. (chmn. jr. journalism contest Orange County chpt. 1985-86, pres. 1986-87; yearly chair Taste of Valley art show 1997), Wildlife Art Assn. Republican. Roman Catholic. Avocations: baseball fan, golf, swimming, dancing, theatre. E-mail: cocobien@bigfoot.com.

HUBER, DON LAWRENCE, publisher; b. Milw., Aug. 17, 1928; s. Wallace Fred and Florence (Bleck) H.; m. Joan Mac Monnies, June 23, 1951. Student, Carthage (Ill.) Coll., 1946-48; BS in English, Northwestern U., 1950. Sales exec. sta. WOR (radio), N.Y.C., 1957-58; owner, gen. mgr. Sta. KALE-Radio, Pasco, Washington, 1958-60; mgr. advt. Standard Rate and Data Service, N.Y.C., 1961-70; v.p., pub. Computer and Communication Decisions, Hayden, N.J., 1970-87, VNU Bus. Press.; pvt. practice specializing in bldg. pvt. homes, 1990—. Painter oil landscape paintings, 1990—. Served with USN, 1946-48. Mem. Sales Execs. N.Y., Navy League, Am. Artists Profl. League, Salamagundi Club, Hudson Valley Art Assn. Clubs: Northwestern University (N.Y.C.). Home and Office: 24 Rolling Dr Glen Head NY 11545-2613 E-mail: donlhubr@aol.com.

HUBER, DONALD SIMON, physician; b. Clarendon, Pa., Apr. 18, 1929; s. Walter Casper and Mary Agnes (Earley) H.; m. Mary Hanks, Sept. 6, 1958; children: Donald Scott, Mark Walter, Mary Lisa. BA, Duke U., 1951, MD, 1954. Diplomate Am. Bd. Internal Medicine, Am. Bd. Allergy and Immunology. Intern Charity Hosp., New Orleans, 1954-55; resident internal medicine Tulane U. Hosp., New Orleans, 1955-56, 58-60; pvt. practice Huntsville, Ala., 1960-96 (ret. 1996); clin. assoc. prof. medicine Sch. Primary Med. Care, Huntsville, 1985—. Med. dir. Cmty. Free Clinic, 1998—. Lt. commdr. USN, 1956-58, USNR, 1958-60. Fellow Am. Coll. Allergists; mem. AMA, Am. Acad. Allergy and Immunology, Ala. Soc. Allergy and Immunology (pres. 1985), Huntsville Rotary Club (bd. dirs. 1978). Republican. Methodist. Avocation: traveling. Home: 507 Holmes Ave Huntsville AL 35801 E-mail: donhuber@knology.net.

HUBER, DOUGLAS CRAWFORD, pathologist; b. S. Charleston, W.Va., June 11, 1939; s. Abram Paul and Mary Ashley (Grow) H.; m. Deena Rae Freedman, Aug. 8, 1969; children: Adam Crawford, Laura Kristen; m. Angelika Madelon Pohl, June 3, 1961 (div. 1965); 1 child, Heidemarie Jutta. Student, Harvard U., 1958, 59; AB, Emory U., Atlanta, 1960; MD, Emory U. Sch. of Med., Atlanta, 1964. Cert. anatomic and clin. pathology, dermatopathology Med. Assn. Ga. Assoc. pathologist Baldwin County Hosp., Milledgeville, Ga., 1971-72, Leary Lab., Boston, 1972-73; lab. dir. Homer D. Cobb Mem. Hosp., Phenix City, Ala., 1973-79; gen. practitioner Leonard Morse Hosp., Natick, Mass., 1979-80; lab. dir. WellStar Douglas Hosp., Douglasville, Ga., 1980—; med. dir. Roche Biomedical Lab., Atlanta Div., Tucker, Ga., 1989-93; lab. dir. Wellstar Paulding Hosp., 1998—, Wellstar Cobb Hosp., 1999—. Deputy state commr. Coll. Am. Pathologists Lab. Inspection Program, Skokie, Ill., 1976-79; v.p. Ala. Assn. Pathologists, Birmingham, 1979; with WellStar Northwest Physicians Group, 1996—. Pres. Nam Vets of Ga., 1982-85; capt. with U.S Army, 1965-67. Fellow Coll. Am. Pathologists, Am. Soc. Clinical Pathologists.

HUBER, HENRY B. retired music educator; b. Cincinnati, Ohio, Jan. 24, 1942; m. Deanna K. Atkinson, July 10, 1965; 1 child, Scott. BA Music, Miami Univ., Oxford, OH, 1964; MA Ed., Univ. Cin., Cincinnati, OH, 1969. Cert. Counseling & Supervision Miami Univ., Oxford, OH, 1984. Music educator Hamilton City Schools, Hamilton, Ohio, 1964—66, NW Local Schools, Cincinnati, 1966—94; adj. faculty Xavier Univ., Cincinnati, 1999—. Mem.: Ohio Music Edn. Assn., Music Educators Nat. Conf., The Am. Guild of English Handbell Ringers (area v chair-elect 2001). Home: 3380 Rocker Drive Cincinnati OH 45239-4018 Home Fax: 513-741-8847.

HUBER, JEANNE LEONCE, development director, consultant; d. Marie Leonce Many; m. Mark Huber, Dec. 5, 1954. MBA, U. of New Orleans, 2001. V.p. mktg. United Way for the GNO Area, New Orleans, 1994—2001; devel. dir. La. SPCA, New Orleans, 2002—. Pres. Zonta Club of New Orleans, 2001—03, Am. Mktg. Assn., New Orleans, 1995—96. Recipient Role Model award, YWCA of New Orleans, 1998, Women of the Yr., Bus. & Profl. Women, 2002. Independent. Avocations: reading, volunteering, writing.

HUBER, JOAN ALTHAUS, sociology educator; b. Bluffton, Ohio, Oct. 17, 1925; d. Lawrence Lester and Hallie (Althaus) H.; ; m. William Form, Feb. 5, 1971; children: Nancy Rytina, Steven Rytina. BA, Pa. State U., 1945; MA, Western Mich. U., 1963; PhD, Mich. State U., 1967. Asst. prof. sociology U. Notre Dame, Ind., 1967-71; asst. prof. sociology U. Ill., Urbana-Champaign, 1971-73, assoc. prof., 1973-78, prof., 1978-83, head dept., 1979-83; dean Coll. Social and Behavioral Sci., Ohio State U., Columbus, 1984-92; coordinating dean Coll. Arts and Sciences, Ohio State University, Columbus, 1987-92, provost, 1992-93; sr. v.p., provost emeritus prof. Sociology emeritus, 1994. Author: (with William Form) Income and Ideology, 1973, (with Glenna Spitze) Sex Stratification, 1983. Editor: Changing Women in a Changing Society, 1973, (with Paul Chalfant) The Sociology of Poverty, 1974, Macro-Micro Linkages in Sociology, 1991. NSF research awardee, 1978-81 Mem. Am. Sociol. Assn. (v.p. 1981-83, pres. 1987-90), Midwest Sociol. Soc. (pres. 1979-80). Home: 2880 N Star Rd Columbus OH 43221-2959 Office: Ohio State U Dept Sociology 300 Bricker Hall 190 N Oval Mall Columbus OH 43210-1321 E-mail: huber.3@osu.edu.

HUBER, JOHN CHARLES, information technology executive, director; b. St. Louis, Feb. 13, 1940; s. George August Huber and Ethel Edith (Schall) Muehling; m. Sonia Ann Goldusky Huber, Aug. 25, 1962; children: Kris, Monica. BSEE, U. Mo.-Columbia, 1961, PhD, 1965; MBA, U. St. Thomas, St. Paul, Minn., 1982. Registered profl. engr., Minn. Sr. rsch. specialist 3M/Central Rsch. Labs, St. Paul, Minn., 1965-76; mktg. mgr. 3M/Commercial Chem. Divsn., St. Paul, Minn., 1976-81; nat. sales and mktg. mgr. 3M/Interactive Sys. Divsn., St. Paul, Minn., 1981-85; mgr. of new product devel. 3M Co./Telecom Sys. Divsn., Austin, Tex., 1985-95; exec. dir. Inst. for Invention and Innovation, Austin, Tex., 1995—. Edtl. adv. bd. mem. Fiber Optic Product News, Morris Plains, N.J., 1991-95. Author: Industrial Fiber Optic Networks, 1995, Managing Innovation, 2001; contbr. 44 articles to profl. jours. Mem. Vestry St. Paul's Epis. Ch., Hudson, Wis., 1973-80; bd. dirs. St. Croix Valley Arts Guild, Hudson, Wis., 1974-78, Zachary Scott Theatre Ctr., Austin, Tex., 1986-90. Recipient Leadership award Austin Bus. Cmty. for the Arts, 1988, Honor award for Disting. Svc. in Engring., U. Mo.-Columbia, 1999. Episcopalian. Achievements include research in inventive productivity. Avocations: history, antiques, photography, theater. Office: Inst for Invention and Innovation Ste 238X 500 E Anderson Ln Austin TX 78752-1207 E-mail: jchuber@InventionAndInnovation.org.

HUBER, LISA ANN MARI BRONES, public relations executive; b. Albert Lea, Minn., May 12, 1967; d. Max Beene and Marge Leene (Thrond) B. BA in Journalism, English, U. Iowa, 1989, JD, 1992. Bar: Calif. TV news anchor, reporter Sta. KIMT, Mason City, Iowa, 1992-94; TV news reporter Sta. WOI-TV, Des Moines, 1994-95; TV news anchor, reporter Sta. WHO-TV, Des Moines, 1995-99, Sta. WHAS-TV, Louisville, 1999—2002; dir. pub. rels. The Commonwealth Group, Louisville, 2002—. Mem. ABA, Internat. Assn. Bus. Comms., Calif. State Bar Assn., Soc. Profl. Journalists (1st Pl. award for minority affairs reporting TV, 2001), Pub. Rels. Soc. Am., Phi Delta Phi, Phi Beta Kappa. Lutheran. Avocations: travel, sports. Office: The Commonwealth Group 200 S 5th St Ste 400N Louisville KY 40202 E-mail: lbhuber@thecommonwealthgroup.com.

HUBER, MARIANNE JEANNE, art dealer, appraiser; b. Amboy, Ill., June 9, 1936; d. John Francis and Jeannette Marie (Wurth) Faivre; m. Robert L. Huber, Oct. 3, 1959; children: Michael Robert, Stephan Louis, Edward Francis. BA, Cardinal Stritch Coll., Milw., 1958. 6th grade tchr. St. Andrew's Sch., Rock Falls, Ill., 1958-59; jr. high tchr. Garside Sch., Mexico City, 1959-61; art dealer, cons. Huber Primitive Art, N.Y.C. and Dixon, Ill., 1963—; founder, pres. New World Art Svcs., N.Y.C. and Dixon, Ill., 1993—. Lectr., cons. Primitive Art Soc., Chgo., 1987, Freeport (Ill.) Art Mus., 1993, Indpls. Mus. Art, 1994, Nprstk Mus., Prague, Czech Republic, 1995; participant Maya Meetings, Austin, Tex., 1985—. Author: Echoes of a Distant Flute, 1984; co-prodr., author (documentary films) The Cuna, 1980, Nebaj, Cotzal and Chajul, 1987, 2003 Maya Calendar, 2004 Maya Calendar, collector, organizer traveling exhbns. The Cuna, 1980—. Election judge Ogle County, Ill., 1993—; committeewoman Dem. Precinct, 2002—. Mem.: LWV, AAUW, Ethnographic Art Soc., Am.

Appraisers Assn., Am. Soc. Appraisers, Am. Assn. Dealers in Ancient Oriental and Primitive Art, Phidian Soc., Ill. Dem. Women, Indpls. Met. Mus. Art, Internat. Platform Assn. (gov. 1993—), Delta Epsilon Sigma. Democrat. Avocations: hiking, wilderness camping, painting, piano, travel. Home and Office: 1012 Timber Trail Dr Dixon IL 61021-8934 E-mail: tellapple@aol.com., evalu8pc@aol.com.

HUBER, MARK, foundation administrator; b. Jacksonville, Fla., Dec. 5, 1954; s. John Joseph Jr. and Gloria R. Huber; m. Jeanne Leonce Huber, Mar. 28, 1987. BA in Liberal Arts, U. New Orleans, 1979, MA in Arts Adminstrn., 1987. Gen. mgr. Green Bay Symphony Orch., Wis., 1988—90; exec. dir. S.C. Philharmonic Orch., Columbia, 1990—93; ops. dir. La. Philharmonic Orch., New Orleans, 1993—94; sr. devel. officer Loyola U. New Orleans, 1994—97; chief devel. officer New Orleans Police Found., 1997—. Cons. Ctr. for Non Profit Resources, New Orleans, 1997—. Prodr.: (CD) New World Relampagos, 2000. Exec. bd. Wis. Citizens for the Arts, Milw., 1990; chmn. crime abatement com. New Orleans C. of C., 1998. Comdr. USNR, 1979—. Roman Catholic. Avocation: music performance and composition.

HUBER, MARY SUSAN, music educator; b. Buffalo, Feb. 14, 1946; d. Floyd M. Zaepfel and Thelma Zaeptel; m. David Conrad Huber, Dec. 27, 1971; children: David Conrad Jr., Kevin Michael. BS in Music, Daemen Coll., 1969; MEd in Music, State U. Buffalo, 1971; M in Ednl. Leadership, U. North Fla., 1991. Elem. music tchr. Maryvale Sch. Sys., Buffalo, 1969—74, Lakeland Prep, Orlando, Fla., 1980—81, North Shore Elem., Jacksonville, Fla., 1981—85, Loretto Elem., Jacksonville, 1985—89, Mandarin Oaks Elem., Jacksonville, 1989—90; mid. sch. choral dir. Mandarin Mid. Sch., Jacksonville, 1990—. Contbr. articles. Mem. citizens opinion rsch. forum County of Duval, Jacksonville, 1987; life mem. Duval County PTA, 1987—; mem. choir St. Joseph Cath. Ch., 1999—2002. Named Educator of Yr., Jaycee's, Jacksonville, 1987, Tchr. of Yr., Rotary, Mandarin, 1998. Mem.: Duval County Elem. Tchrs. Assn. (past elem. pres.). Republican. Roman Catholic. Home: 11068 Great Western Ln W Jacksonville FL 32257

HUBER, PAUL WILLIAM, biochemistry educator, researcher; b. Medford, Mass., July 23, 1951; s. William Francis and Catherine (Sheridan) H. BS, Boston Coll., 1973; PhD, Purdue U., 1978. NIH postdoctoral fellow U. Chgo., 1979-81, rsch. assoc., 1982-85; asst. prof. U. Notre Dame, Ind., 1985-92, assoc. prof., 1992—2003, assoc. chmn., 1993-97, prof., 2003—. Vis. fellow Yale U., 1997. Contbr. articles to profl. jours. Recipient John A. Kaneb award for undergrad. tchg., U. Notre Dame, 2001. Mem. AAAS, Am. Soc. Biochemistry and Molecular Biology. Home: 1215 E Irvington Ave South Bend IN 46614-1417 Office: U Notre Dame Dept Chemistry/Biochemistry Notre Dame IN 46556 Business E-Mail: huber.1@nd.edu.

HUBER, RICHARD GREGORY, lawyer, educator; b. Indpls., June 29, 1919; s. Hugh Joseph and Laura Marie (Becker) H.; m. Katherine Elizabeth McDonald, June 21, 1950 (dec.); children: Katherine, Richard, Mary, Elizabeth, Stephen, Mark. BS, U.S. Naval Acad, 1942; JD, U. Iowa, 1950; LLM, Harvard U., 1951; LLD (hon.), New England Sch. Law, 1985, Northeastern U., 1987, Roger Williams U., 1996. Instr. law U. Iowa, 1950; assoc. prof. law U. S.C., 1952-54; assoc. prof. Tulane U., 1954-57, Boston Coll., 1957-59, prof., 1959-90, dean, 1970-85; disting. prof. Roger Williams U., Bristol, R.I., 1993-95; prof. New England Sch. Law, Newton, Mass., 1995-99. Adj. faculty Boston Coll., 1999—. Contbr. articles and book revs. to profl. jours. Past chairperson pers. and fin. coms. Mass. chpt. Multiple Sclerosis Soc.; past pres. bd. trustees Beaver Country Day Sch. With USN, 1941-47, 51-52. Mem. ABA (del., mem. coun. legal edn. 1981-85, trustee law sch. admissions coun 1983-85), Soc. Am. Law Tchrs., Assn. Am. Law Schs. (pres. 1988-89), Coun. Legal Edn. Opportunity (pres. 1975-79), Am. Judicature Soc., Mass. Bar Assn., Mass. Bar Found. Democrat. Roman Catholic. Home: 406 Woodward St Waban MA 02468-1523 Office: 885 Centre St Newton MA 02459-1148 E-mail: richard.huber1@worldnet.att.net., huber@monet.bc.edu.

HUBER, RICHARD MILLER, American studies consultant; b. Ardmore, Pa., July 27, 1922; s. John Y. Jr. and Caroline (Miller) H.; divorced; children: Cintra Hutchinson Huber McGauley, Richard Miller Jr., Casilda Carter. BA, Princeton U., 1945; PhD, Yale U., 1953. Mem. faculty Princeton (N.J.) U., 1950-54; pres. Princeton Manor Constrn. Co., 1958-62; producer, moderator Sta. WHWH-AM-FM, Princeton, 1965-67; corr. Sta. WNET-TV, N.Y.C., 1967-68; dean Sch. Gen. Studies Hunter Coll., N.Y.C., 1971-77, exec. dir. div. continuing edn., 1977-82; asst. dir. TV and radio Nat. Endowment for the Humanities, Washington, 1983-84, spl. asst. to chmn., 1984-85; pres. Huber Assocs., Washington, 1985—. Pres. Prodn.-in-Progress, Inc., Washington, 1986-89; cons. Am. studies Dept. State and U.S. Info. Agy., 1989—. Author: Big All The Way Through: The Life of Van Sandvoord Merle-Smith, 1952, The American Idea of Success, 1971, rev. edn., 1987, How Professors Play the Cat Guarding the Cream: Why We're Paying More and Getting Less in Higher Education, 1992; editor: (with Wheaton J. Lane) New Jersey Historical Series, 31 vols., 1965. Mem. Coun. of Friends, Princeton U. Libr. 2nd lt. USAAF, 1942-45, Italy. Decorated Air medal; recipient N.J. Hist. Soc. award, 1965, award of merit Am. Assn. State and Local History, 1965, Author's award N.J. Assn. Tchrs. of English, 1965, award of recognition N.J. Hist. Commn., Trenton, 1983. Mem. Soc. Am. Historians, Am. Studies Assn. Republican. Episcopalian. Avocations: tennis, jogging, swimming. Office: Huber Assocs Ste 926 2950 Van Ness St NW Washington DC 20008-1120

HUBER, RITA NORMA, civic worker; b. Cin., July 16, 1931; d. Andrew Elwood and Mary Gertrude (Hille) Stewart; student Cin. Coll. Conservatory Music, 1949-50, Berlitz Sch., Cin., 1951-52; m. Justin G. Huber, July 17, 1954; children: Monica Ann, Sarah Marie, Rachel Miriam. Tchr. Russian lang. for officers' wives Ft. Sill, Okla., 1955-56; bd. dirs. United Community Svcs., Cedar Rapids, Iowa, 1969; founder, chairperson Linn County Consumers League, 1969-70; founder, pub. rels. dir. Cedar Rapids Rape Crisis Svcs., 1974—; owner/operator Huber Janitorial Svcs., 1982-84; chairperson Linn County Dem. Womens Club, 1966-67, Linn County Com., Eugene McCarthy for Pres., 1967-68; campaign mgr. Delores Cortez for Iowa Legislature, 1968, Jan V. Johnson for Iowa Legislature, 1970, Stanley Ginsberg for county supr. Linn County, 1974, E.L. Colton for Cedar Rapids pub. safety commr., 1977; chairperson Linn County Dem. Cen. Com., 1976-77, 88-90; state coord. Jerry Brown for Pres., 1976; chairperson Pat Kane for Linn County Recorder, 1982; chmn. Linn County Bd. Health, 1982-85; supr. Linn County, 1990-95; chairperson Linn County bd. Suprs., 1992; instr. parliamentary procedures Cedar Rapids Women's Community Leadership Inst., 1975-77; lectr. local colls. and svc. orgns.; tchr. conversational Russian, Pierce Elementary Sch., Cedar Rapids, 1976; instr. Russian, Community Edn. div. Kirkwood Community Coll.; mem. care rev. com. Pineview Care Ctr., Cedar Rapids, 1987-90. Named to Iowa Dem. Party DVP Hall of Fame, 1986, Linn County Dem. Party Hall of Fame, 2003; recipient Woman of Yr. award Women's Equality Day Cedar Rapids Iowa, 1993; Mem. Am. Inst. Parliamentarians. Roman Catholic (extraordinary minister of Eucharist). Composer: She is Risen, 1973. Home: 2050 Glass Rd NE Cedar Rapids IA 52402-3401

HUBER, ROBERT, biochemist, educator; b. Munich, Feb. 20, 1937; s. Sebastian and Helene (Kebinger) H.; m. Christa Huber, 1960; children: Ulrike, Martin, Robert, Julia Diploma, Tech. Universität Munich, 1960, PhD, 1963, Habilitation, 1968; D (hon.), Louvain, Belgium, 1987, U. Ljubljana, Slovenia, 1989; D for Medicine and Surgery (hon.), U. 'Tor Vergata', Rome, 1991; D (hon.), Univ. Nova de Lisboa, Portugal, 2000; Dr honoris causa, U. AutÓnoma de Barcelona, 2000. External prof. Tech. U. Munich, 1976; prof., dir. Max-Planck-Inst. for Biochemistry, Martinsried, Germany, 1972—. Editor Jour. Molecular Biology. Decorated grosse Verdienstkreuz mit Stern und Schulterband, Order for Merit for Sci. and Arts (Germany); recipient E.K. Frey medal Gesellschaft für Chirurgie, 1972, Otto Warburg medal Gesellschaft für Biologische Chemie, 1977, Emil van Behring medal U. Marburg, 1982, Keilin medal Biochem. Soc. London, Richard Kuhn medal Soc. German Chemists, 1987, E.K. Frey-E. Werle meml. medal, 1989, Kone award Assn. Clin. Biochemists, 1990, Sir Hans Krebs medal, 1992, Bayerischer Maximilianorden für Wissenschaft und Kunst, 1993, Linus Pauling medal, 1993, 94, Disting. Svc. award Miami Biotech. Winter Symposia, 1995, Max Tishler prize Harvard U., 1997, Max Bergmann medal U. Tübingen, 1997, co-recipient Nobel prize for chemistry, 1988. Fellow Royal Soc. London, Third World Acad. Scis., Am. Acad. Microbiology; mem. NAS (U.S.A.) (fgn. assoc.), European Molecular Biology Orgn. (coun. mem.), Japanese Biochem. Soc. (hon.), Deutsche Chemische Gesellschaft, Gesellschaft für Biologische Chemie, Am. Soc. Biol. Chemists (hon.), Swedish Soc. Biophysics (hon.), Bayerische Acad. der Wissenschaften, Deutsche Acad. der Naturforscher Leopoldina, Croatian Acad. Scis. and Art (corr.), Acad. Nazionale dei Lincei, European Molecular Biology Orgn. Office: Max Planck Inst Biochem Am Klopferspitz 18A Martinsried Munich 82152 Germany

HUBER, THOMAS P. lawyer; b. Watertown, Wis., Oct. 26, 1936; s. Frederick O. and Isabel Mary (Coogan) H.; m. Gloria A. Parrella, Dec. 30, 1961; children— Patrick, Christopher, Mary. B.S., Marquette U., 1959; LL.B., George Washington U., 1967. Bar: Hawaii 1968. Assoc. Cades Schutte Fleming & Wright, Honolulu, 1967-73, ptnr., 1973— . Pres. Protection and Advocacy Agy. of Hawaii, Honolulu, 1978-81, 83-84. Chmn. Task Force on Guardianship, Civil Commitment and Protective Services in Hawaii, Honolulu, 1980-83; bd. dirs. Cath. Charities, Honolulu, 1985—. Served to 1st lt. USMC, 1959-62. Mem. ABA, Hawaii Bar Assn. Roman Catholic. Club: Pacific (Honolulu). Home: 46-291 Auna St Kaneohe HI 96744-4110

HUBER, TONYA, teacher educator, writer; b. Lackawanna, NY, Feb. 28, 1958; d. H. Joseph and Elsie Garlick H. BS, Pa. State U., 1982, MEd, 1985, PhD, 1990. Assoc. prof. Wichita (Kans.) State U. Coll. of Edn., 1990—2002, prof., 2002—; internat. and overseas program faculty Coll. of N.J., Trenton, 1997—. Adv. Wichita State U.; cons., presenter in field. Author: Teaching in the Diverse Classroom: Learner-Centered Activities That Work, 1993, Quality Learning Experiences for ALL Students, 2002; founder, editor: Jour. Critical Inquiry Into Curriculum and Instrn., 1998—, assoc. editor: Multicultural Edn. Mag., —. Recipient Howard Soule Grad. fellow in Ednl. Leadership, Phi Delta Kappa, 1989. Mem.: Nat. Assn. for Multicultural Edn. (founder 1990, publs. com. 1993—2003, chair Nat. Leadership Inst. 1996, v.p. 2002—, Svc. award 1990—98). Avocations: free weights, western horseback riding, reading, theatre. Office: Wichita State U Dept Curriculum/Instrn 1845 Fairmount St Wichita KS 67260-0028 E-mail: tonya.huber@wichita.edu.

HUBER, VANDRA LEE, businesss educator, consultant; b. Salt Lake City, July 18, 1949; d. Fred L. and Twila Blanche (Jacobs) H.; m. Michael Krolewski, June, 1986. BS cum laude, U. Utah, 1971, MS in Econs., 1978; MBA, Ind. U., 1981, D Bus. Adminstrn. in Human Resources, 1982. Cert. bus. communicator. Reporter, editor Salt Lake City Tribune, 1971-77; dir. communications Utah Social Services, Salt Lake City, 1977-79; instr. Ind. U., Bloomington, 1979-82; asst. prof. Cornell U., Ithaca, N.Y., 1982-85; asst. prof. human resources and mgmt. U. Utah, Salt Lake City, 1985-87; asst. prof. human resources and organizational behavior U. Wash., Seattle, 1987-89, assoc. prof., 1989—. Cons. Boeing, AFL-CIO and other nonprofit orgns. Rochester, Salt Lake City, Seattle; mem. adv. bd. Cornell Inst. Social and Econ. Rsch., 1983-85. Author: Personnel and Human Resource Managment, 1993, Australian Personnel and Human Resource Management, 1992; contbr. over 65 articles to profl. jours. Treas. Community Crisis Ctr., Salt Lake City, 1978-79; awards chair, nat. auction coord. Scottish Terrier Club Am., 1993; lic. dog judge Am. Kennel Club. Social Sci. Research Council grantee, 1982; Richard Irwin Dissertation grantee, 1982. Mem. APA, Am. Inst. Decision Scis., Internat. Assn. Bus. Communicators (Intermountain Outstanding Communicator 1978), Acad. Mgmt. (Dorothy Harlow researcher 1986, ascendent scholar 1987, Fritz Roethlisberger 1988), Western Acad. Mgmt., Soc. Indsl. and Orgnl. Psychologists, Soc. Human Resource Mgrs., World at Work, Am. Comepnsation Assn. Democrat. Episcopalian. Avocations: handling, breeding and exhibiting scottish terriers. Home: 18831 NE 140th Pl Woodinville WA 98072-6301 Office: U Wash Sch Bus DJ-10 Seattle WA 98112

HUBER, VIDA SWARTZENTRUBER, nursing educator; b. West Liberty, Ohio, Mar. 27, 1937; d. L.L. and Nanna V. (Bender) Swartzentruber; m. Harold E. Huber, June 6, 1970; 1 child, Heidi Marie. Diploma, Milford Meml. Hosp., 1959; BSN, Eastern Mennonite Coll., 1961; MA in Nursing Edn., Columbia U., Tchrs. Coll., 1966, EdD, 1970. Staff nurse Milford Meml. Hosp., Del., 1959-60; nursing supr. County Rest Home, Greenwood, Del., 1959-60, 61-65; instr. nursing Milford Meml. Hosp., Del., 1961-64, ednl. dir., 1964; chmn., prof. Eastern Mennonite Coll., Dept. Nursing, Harrisonburg, Va., 1967-84; vis. prof. U. Va. Sch. Nursing, Charlottesville, Va., 1984-86; exec. dir. Va. Soc. Profl. Nurses, Harrisonburg, Va., 1987-88; prof., dept. head nursing James Madison U., Harrisonburg, Va., 1988-99, interim assoc. dean Coll. Integrated Sci. and Tech., 1999—2001, assoc. dean, 2001—, dir. Inst. for Innovation in Health and Human Svcs., 2001—. Speaker in field; bd. dirs. County Rest Home, Greenwood, Del., 1970-81, pres., 1980-81. Contbr. articles to profl. jours. Named Outstanding Young Women Am., 1973, Outstanding Educator AM. 1973, 75, one of Outstanding Nurses in Va., Va. Nurses Assn.; recipient Women's Caucus Award for Svc., 1992, James Madison Citizenship awrd, 2002.. Mem. ANA, Am. Assn. Colls. Nursing, Nat. League Nursing, Va. Assn. Colls. Nursing, Mennonite Nurses Assn. (project dir. 1988), Kappa Delta Pi, Pi Delta Kappa, Pi Lambda Theta, Sigma Theta Tou. E-mail: hubervs@jmu.edu.

HUBER, VIRGINIA ROLLO, photojournalist, educator, artist; d. Earl Eugene Rollo and Pauline Celeste Ritter; children: John, Laurie Huber Sheffler, James A. BS in Journalism-English, U. Ill., 1941; MAT in Art-Journalism, Whitworth Coll., Spokane, Wash., 1968. File clk. U.S. Army, Marion, Ill., 1941—42; reporter Decatur (Ill.) Rev., 1941—42; writer Scott Field Air Base, Belleville, Ill., 1942—43; asst. city editor Globe-Dem., St. Louis, 1943—45; co-owner, features, editls. York Daily News Times, York, 1947—55; contbr., art, writing Sacred Heart Hosp., Spokane, 1960—70; freelance feature writer Spokane Review-Chronicle, 1970—80; artist, instr. Rollo Fine Art, Port Orchard, Wash., 1999—; dir. art gallery U.S. Rte. 6 Tour Assn., Port Orchard, 2001—. Pianist, singer retirement cmtys., Silverdale, Port Orchard, Federal Way, Shelton, Wash., 1997—. Acrylic portrait, Innocence, BC Can. Regional Show, 1986 (Hon. Mention, 1994); rewrite (Almanac); author: stories on banking industry, real estate devel. on Puget Sound South Kitsap Bus. Jour., 2001. Writer Kitsap Ind., Port Orchard, Wash., 2000; reporter stories on banking industry, real estate devel. on Puget Sound South Kitsap Bus. Jour., Port Orchard, 2001. Mem.: South Kitsap Art Assn. (sec. 2002—), Peninsula Art League, Gig Harbor Cultural Arts, Pi Beta Phi, Theta Sigma Phi. Avocations: swimming, walking, photography, piano, singing. Home: Bldg 1 Apt 202 1790 Sidney Ave Port Orchard WA 98366 Office: Rollo Fine Art Bldg 1 Apt 202 1790 Sidney Ave Port Orchard WA 98366

HUBERMAN, ARIANA, language educator; b. Buenos Aires, Oct. 29, 1969;, U.S.1989; d. David Huberman and Juana Kivatinetz de Huberman. BA, Tufts U.; MA, PhD, N.Y. U., 2001. Tchg. asst. N.Y. U., N.Y.C., 1997—99, instr., 1999—2002; asst. prof. Alfred U., NY, 2002—. Archival asst. N.Y. U. Archives, N.Y.C., 1995—2000. Editor: (arts and lit.) Prisma Mag., 1990. Mac Cracken fellow, N.Y. U., 1994—99, Susan Eliakim Siman scholar, 1999, Penfield fellow, 2000—01. Office: Alfred Univ Saxon Dr Alfred NY 14802 E-mail: huberman@alfred.edu.

HUBERMAN, BENJAMIN, technology consultant; b. Havana, Cuba, Jan. 25, 1938; came to U.S., 1946; s. Henry and Marcella (Waisman) H.; m. Gisela Bialik, Oct. 13, 1963; children: Jonathan, Martin. AB, Columbia Coll., 1959; BS, Columbia U., 1960; diploma of Imperial Coll., U. London (Eng.), 1962. Sr. official Arms Control & Disarmament Agy., Washington, 1966-73, Nat. Security Coun., Washington, 1973-75; dir., policy evaluation Nuclear Regulatory Commn., Washington, 1975-77; sr. official Office Sci. and Tech. Policy, Washington, 1977-81; dep. sci. advisor to pres. White House, Washington, 1981; v.p. Cons. Internat. Group, Inc., Washington, 1982-88, pres., 1988-90, Huberman Cons. Group, Washington, 1990—; v.p. GBH Radio Inc., Fisher Island, Fla., 1997—. Bd. dirs. AETC Inc., San Diego; chmn. Chief Naval Ops. exec. panel Atlantic Coun., Washington. Lt. USN, 1960-66. Fulbright scholar, London, 1960-61. Mem. Coun. Fgn. Rels., Met. Club, Cosmos Club (Washington). Home: 5022 Fisher Island Dr Fisher Island FL 33109 Office: Huberman Cons Group 1090 Vermont Ave NW Ste 800 Washington DC 20005-4961

HUBERMAN, BERNARDO A, physicist; b. Buenos Aires, Nov. 7, 1943; arrived in U.S., 1966, naturalized, 1974; s. Leon and Sara Huberman; children: Lara M., Andrew D. PhD in Physics, U. Pa., 1971. Mem. rsch. staff Xerox Palo Rsch. Ctr., Calif., 1974-80, prin. scientist, 1983-84, rsch. fellow, 1985-2001; fellow HP Lab., Palo Alto, 2001—, dir. info. dynamics lab., 2001—. Vis. scientist Inst. Laue-Langevin, Grenoble, France, 1976; cons. prof. Stanford U., Calif., 1981—; vis. prof. U. Paris, 1981, U. Copenhagen, 1993, European Sch. Bus., 1999. Author: The Laws of the Web, 2001; contbr. articles to profl. jours. Trustee Aspen Ctr. Physics, Colo., 1980—. Fellow: Japan Soc. Promotion of Sci., Am. Phys. Soc.; mem.: AAAS. Office: HP Labs 1500 Page Hill Rd Palo Alto CA 94304

HUBERMAN, JEFFREY ALLEN, architect; b. Boston, Jan. 2, 1942; s. Sidney H. and Miriam (Walker) H.; m. Barbara Kemp, May 16, 1964 (div.); children: Amy Beth, Marc Walker. BArch, U. Fla., 1964. Designer Odell Assocs., Charlotte, N.C., 1964-67, Wolf-Johnson Assocs., Charlotte, 1967-69; designer, architect Wolf Assocs., Charlotte, 1970-71; ptnr. Gantt Huberman Architects, Charlotte, 1971—. Mem. N.C. Bd. Architecture, 1995—, sec., 1996-97, treas., 1997—, v.p., 1999—, pres., 2001-2003; bd. dirs. Green Hill Ctr. N.C. Art, 1998—. Chmn. annual fund drive Charlotte-Mecklenburg Arts and Sci. Coun., 1975-81, v.p., 1977-78, bd. dirs., 1977; bd. dirs. Charlotte Opera Assn., 1966-82, pres., 1979-81; pres. Children's Theatre, 1984-85, bd. dirs., 1981-87; bd. dirs. Temple Beth El, 1968-83, Charlotte-Mecklenburg Community Rels. Com., 1974-84, Planned Parenthood of Greater Charlotte, 1978-80, Charlotte Jr. Soccer Found., 1978-82, Tarradiddle Players, 1986-87; chmn. Charlotte Clean City Com., 1975-77; youth soccer coach, 1975-84; com. mem. Performing Arts Ctr. Adv. Ctr., 1983-85; adv. com. Charlotte/Douglas Internat. Airport, 1987-88, art adv. com., 1992—. Fellow AIA (chmn. honor awards com. 1972, treas. Charlotte, N.C. sect. 1976-77, chmn. audit com. 1987, bd. dirs. 1987-92, long range planning com. 1990, component resources com. 1992, pres. N.C. chpt. 1991, N.C. Archtl. Found. 1994, N.C. Gold medal 2002), Nat. Coun. Archtl. Registration Bd. (juror divsns. B and C archtl. registration exam. 1984-86, chmn. divsn. B graphic 1989, master jurors com. 1986, archtl. registration exam. com. 1996-97, intern devel. program com. 1998-2002, chair, 2000-2002, procedures and documents com. 2000—, chair reciprocity impediment task force 2002—, So. region sec. 2003—). Office: Gantt Huberman Architects 500 N Tryon St Charlotte NC 28202-2232

HUBERMAN, JONATHAN SERGE, venture capitalist; b. Washington, July 8, 1965; s. Benjamin and Gisela Bialik Huberman; m. Susan Lynn Lutzker, May 1, 1993; children: Mara, Adam. AB in Computer Sci., Princeton U., 1988; MBA, U. Pa., Wharton, 1992. Mktg. mgr. future archs. Cray Rsch., Inc., Mpls., 1988-90; case leader Boston Consulting Group, Chgo., 1992-95; gen. ptnr. Idanta Ptnrs., San Diego, 1995—. Bd. dirs. Iomega Corp., San Diego, Nano Nexus, Inc., Fremont, Calif., Teradiant, Inc., Santa Clara, Calif., Torrey Corp., Livermore, Calif. Avocations: ice hockey, skiing. Office: Idanta Ptnrs 9255 Towne Center Dr #925 San Diego CA 92121 Fax: 858-452-2013. E-mail: jonathan@idanta.com.

HUBERMAN, RICHARD LEE, lawyer; b. Lynn, Mass., Dec. 6, 1953; s. Irving Morris and Selma Edythe (Wolk) H. AB, Harvard U., 1975, JD, 1978. Bar: Mass. 1979, D.C. 1979. Atty. Office of Rail Pub. Counsel, Washington, 1978-80; counsel subcom. on commerce, consumer protection and competitiveness (formerly commerce, transp. and tourism) U.S. Ho. of Reps., Washington, 1980-95, mem. prof. staff Com. on Edn. and Workforce, 1995—97; pvt. practice Washington, 1997-98; counsel to commr. and chmn. Occupl. Safety and Health Rev. Commn., Washington, 1998—. Mem. ABA, Mass. Bar Assn., Harvard Law Sch. Assn. Clubs: Harvard (Washington). Democrat. Home: 2141 P St NW Apt 302 Washington DC 20037-1031 Office: Occupl Safety and Health Rev Commn 1120 20th St NW Washington DC 20036 E-mail: rhuberman@oshrc.gov.

HUBERT, BARBARA BOEKLEN, pharmaceutical company executive; b. Fort Belvoir, Va., Aug. 26, 1952; d. Francis Albert Boeklen and Dorothy Froehlich; 1 child, Jason Shane Gress. BS in Chemistry, Va. Commonwealth U., 1976; MBA in Sci. Tech. and Innovation, George Washington U., 1985. Rsch. technician Phillip Morris Rsch., Richmond, Va., 1972-75; chemist A.H. Robins Co., Richmond, 1975-80; asst. dir. stds. devel. U.S. Phrmacopeia, Rockville, Md., 1980-99, dir. exec. sec. office, 1999-2001, dir. pharmacopeial edn., 2001—02, dir. sales and mktg. reference stds. and edn., 2002—. Mem. Assn. for Internat. Practical Tng. (bd. dirs. 1996-98), Am. Assn. of Pharm. Scientists (chair analytical pharm. quality sect. 1995, 96, exec. coun. 1994-96chair elect 1994-95, sec., treas. 1993-94), Am. Chem. Soc. Avocation: horsewoman. Office: US Pharmacopeia 12601 Twinbrook Pkwy Rockville MD 20852-1790

HUBERT, FRANK WILLIAM RENE, retired university system chancellor; b. Milam County, Tex., June 2, 1915; s. Jonce Sherod and Lura Gertrude (White) H.; m. Mary Julia Glidden, June 15, 1940; children: Frank William Rene, Mary Katherine. BA, U. Tex., 1938, MA, 1946, PhD, 1950; LL.D., Baylor U., 1979; LLD, Tex. Coll., 1992. Dir. Lutcher Stark Boys, Inc., Orange, Tex., 1938-44; prin., dir. secondary edn. Stark Sr. High Sch., Orange, 1946-48; research fellow, curriculum and instrn. U. Tex., 1948-49; adminstrv. asst. Found. Sch. Program Act div. Tex. Auditor's Office, Austin, 1949-50, dir. div., 1949-50; dir. div. profl. standards, also div. tchr. edn. Tex. Edn. Agy., Austin, 1950-55; supt. schs. Orange Ind. Sch. Dist., 1955-59; dean Sch. Arts and Scis., Tex. A&M U., College Station, 1959-65, dean Coll. Liberal Arts, 1965-69, dean Coll. Edn., 1969-79, dir. basic div., 1959-60, chancellor, 1979-82, chancellor emeritus, 1983—. Exec. sec. Tex. Bd. Exam. Tchr. Edn., 1952-55; mem. com. 75 U. Tex.; pres. Tex. Conf. Tchr. Edn., 1959; mem. Nat. Council Accreditation Tchr. Edn., 1953-55; v.p. S.W. Ednl. Devel Corp., 1966-67, pres., 1967-68; mem. Nat. Adv. Commn. on Mexican-Am. Edn., U.S. Office Edn., 1967-69; adv. council U.S. Command and Gen. Staff Coll., 1972-75; pres. Corp. Research and Engring. in Edn., 1969-2000; mem. bd. cons. Center for Research and Edn. Free Enterprise, 1977-80; mem. Tex. Adv. Com. Tech.-Vocat. Edn., 1978-80, Gov.'s Com. Pub. Edn., 1966-69 Mem. Charter Change Commn., Orange, 1958; trustee Tex. Coll., 1987-94. Served with AUS, 1944-46. Mem. NEA, Orange Edn. Assn. (pres. 1943-44), Assn. Tex. Colls. and Univs. (pres. 1965-66), Am. Tex. Assns. Sch. Adminstrs., Am. Acad. Polit. and Social Sci., Philos. Soc. Tex., Tex. Tchrs. Assn. (chmn. com. tchr. edn. and profl. standards 1955-60), Sons Republic Tex., Coushatta Camellia Soc. (pres. 1991-92), Am. Camellia Soc. (edn. com. 1991-93). Home: Apt A101 2410 Memorial Dr Bryan TX 77802-2841

HUBERT, HELEN BETTY, epidemiologist; b. N.Y.C., Jan. 22, 1950; d. Leo and Ruth (Rosenbaum) H.; m. Carlos Barbaro Arostegui, Sept. 11, 1976 (div. May 1987); 1 child, Joshua Daniel Hubert. BA magna cum laude, Barnard Coll., 1970; MPH, Yale U., 1973, MPhil, 1976, PhD, 1978. Rsch. assoc. Yale U., New Haven, 1977-78; rsch. epidemiologist Nat. Heart, Lung and Blood Inst., Bethesda, Md., 1978-84; rsch. dir. Gen. Health, Inc., Washington, 1984-87; sr. rsch. scientist Stanford (Calif.) U., 1988—. Peer rev. Am. Jour. Epidemiology, Am. Jour. Pub. Health, Chest, Jour. AMA (JAMA), Archives Internal Medicine; contbr. articles to profl. jours., chpts. to books. NIH grantee, 1997—. Mem. Am. Coll. Epidemiology, Soc. Epidemiol. Rsch., Assn. Rheumatology Health Profls., Phi Beta Kappa, Sigma Xi (grant-in-aid for rsch. 1978). Office: Stanford Univ Med Ctr 701 Welch Rd Ste 3305 Palo Alto CA 94304-1701

HUBERT, JEAN-LUC, chemicals executive; b. Metz, Moselle, France, Mar. 13, 1960; s. Andre and Franziska (Schmidt) H. Diplome Ingenieur, Diplome Detudes Approfondies, Ecole Centrale Paris, 1982; MS in Mech. and Nuclear Engring., Northwestern U., 1985; M in Project Mgmt. with distinction, Keller Grad. Sch., 1996. Simulation engr. Didier Werke, Wiesbaden, Germany, 1981; engr. Iron and Steel Rsch. Inst., Metz, France, 1983; cryogenic applications engr. L'Air Liquide, Paris, 1985—86; R&D mgr. cryogenic refrigeration processes Liquid Air Corp., Countryside, Ill., 1986—89, project mgr. new processes devel. group, 1989—93; concurrent multi project mgr., primary metals and combustion, mktg. and applications group Air Liquide America Corp, Countryside, Ill., 1993—95; applied tech. engring. dept. mgr. Air Liquide Am. Corp., Countryside, Ill., 1995—99, mgr. ctrl. engring. dept., bus. devel. group, 1999—2001; mgr. customer equipment and installation design Air Liquide Am. LP, Houston, 2001—. New process devel. cons. Liquid Air Corp./Energy Systems, Lake Charles, La., 1987-90, BIG3/INS, Houston, 1990-91, exceptional ops. mgr., coord. subcontractors, regional svc. and sales coord. applications unit, 1992-93; air liquide group expert, tech. ops. Bulk Sytems, 2003—. Patentee cryogenic food freezing, cryogenic embrittlement processes, pipeline rehab. processes, multi-step combined mech./thermal stripping processes, supercritical chemical extraction processes, ozone based food sanitizing processes. 2d lt. French Navy, 1982-83. Tuition fellow Georges Lurcy Found., 1984, Henri Blanchenay fellow French Inst., 1984, Bieneck/Didier fellow, Fed. Rep. Ger., 1984, Northwestern U. Rsch. assistantship, 1984. Mem.

ASME, Inst. Food Technologists (profl.), Internat. Inst. Refrigeration, Iron and Steel Soc. Achievements include 7 US, Canadian and 2 European patents for High Efficiency Linear Freezer, for Method and Apparatus for Enhancing Production Capacity and Flexibility of a Multi-tier Refrigeration Tunnel, for Process and Apparatus for Embrittling and Subsequently Removing an Outer Protective Coating of a Pipe or Pipeline, and for Efficiency Process and Apparatus for same and for a fast efficient, low-cost stripping process of non-metallic layers from steel substrates, for supercritical CO2 pressure swing absorption based cleaning methods and systems and for process and equipment for sanitizing food using ozone. Home: 16402 Willingham Way Houston TX 77095 Office: Air Liquide America LP 12800 W Little York Houston TX 77041 Business E-Mail: jean-luc.hubert@airliquide.com. E-mail: Dillingen@att.net.

HUBLER, JULIUS, artist; b. Granite City, Ill., Dec. 11, 1919; s. Voyle and Marie (Lewedag) H.; m. Loretta Lanter, Apr. 26, 1943; children: Stuart Alden, Ann Marlowe McClure. BS, S.E. Mo. U., 1943; MA, Ed.D., Columbia U., 1951. Sci. tchr. Wibaux High Sch., Mont., 1942-43, Ashton High Sch., Idaho, 1943-45; art instr. CCNY, 1946-48; prof. art SUNY-Buffalo, 1948-82; freelance artist Buffalo, 1982—; painter, graphic designer, sculptor, photographer. One-man exhbn. Albright-Knox Mus., Buffalo, 1991, Rodman Hall Nat. Exhbn. Ctr., St. Catharines, Ont., Can., 1991; exhibited in group shows Taipei Mus. Fine Arts, 1983-88, 94, Internat. Miniature Print Biennial, 1989, Salon de Peiture et d'Estambe Montreal, Que., Can., Silvermine, New Canaan, Conn., 1994; named in books: Endgrain-Contemporary Wood Engraving in North America, 1994, An Engravers Globe, London, 2001; contbr. articles to profl. publs. Mem. Western N.Y. Peace Ctr. Deans scholar; State U. Iowa grad. scholar, 1944; Arthur W. Dow scholar Columbia U., 1947; disting. service awardee U. Buffalo, 1958; recipient Silvermine award, 1999. Mem. AAUP (bd. dirs., pres. N.Y. state chpt. 1956-60), Soc. Am. Graphic Artists (Warren Mack Meml. purchase award 1962), NAD (assoc., Samuel F.B. Morse medal 1977, Anonymous prize 1980, Leo Meissner prize 1989), Amnesty Internat., Brit.-N.Am. Philatelic Assn., Buffalo Stamp Club, Helvetia Am. Club. Clubs: Buffalo Stamp, Helvetia Am. *One is in debt to an endless number of people living and dead. Many have paid a horrible price. Change and, hopefully progress, are rarely welcome. Products of imagination testify to the necessary sacrifice, dedication, strength and vision. It is not a matter of formal education but vigilant attention to life, beliefs and purposes.* Died Jan. 11, 2003.

HUBLEY, REGINALD ALLEN, publishing executive; b. New Rochelle, N.Y., Aug. 21, 1928; s. Reginald McDonald and Eleanor Francis (Stock) H.; m. Karleen J. Smith, Apr. 7, 1979; children: Brandon, Caroline, Matthew. BS in Commerce and Fin., Bucknell U., 1952. With McGraw Hill Pub. Co., N.Y.C., N.J., 1952-54; dist. mgr. Elec. Constrn. and Maintenance, and Elec. Wholesaling publs., Cleve., 1954-59, sales mgr. N.Y.C., 1959-63, pub., 1963-69, Nucleonics Week, Nucleonics & Sci. Research, N.Y.C., 1966-69, Aviation Week and Space Tech., N.Y.C., 1969—, Am. Machinist, N.Y.C., 1976—; v.p. European ops. McGraw-Hill Pub. Co., London, 1979-87, v.p. internat., 1987-88, ret., 1988. Cons. British Aerospace, The Economist London, Nikkei Bus. Pub. Tokyo, 1988-90. Served with USN, 1946-48, PTO. Fellow Inst. of Dirs., London; mem. Internat. Fedn. Periodical Pubs. (exec. com.), Aviation Hall of Fame (bd. nominations 1971—) Republican.

HUBNER, ROBERT WILMORE, retired business machines company executive; b. Seattle, Mar. 21, 1918; s. Robert G. and Thurza (Wilmore) H.; m. Katherine L. Huick, Apr. 4, 1942 (dec. June 1996); children: Melissa, Robert Wilmore; m. Patricia Craig, Jan. 24, 1997. Grad., U. Wash., 1941. With IBM, 1941-43, 43-78, dir. recruitment, 1956, exec. asst. to exec. v.p., 1957, sales mgr. data processing div., 1957-59, exec. asst. to chmn. bd., 1959-61, dir. mktg., 1961-65, v.p. mktg., 1965-68, v.p., group exec., 1968-71, sr. v.p., mem. mgmt. com., 1972-78, ret., 1978. Mem. emeritus adv. bd. Grad. Sch. Bus., U. Wash.; trustee emeritus South Street Seaport, N.Y.C., Nat. Trust for Historic Preservation; past trustee Maritime Ctr. at Norwalk, Conn.; past trustee Edgartown (Mass.) Reading Rm. Mem. N.Y. Yacht Club (N.Y.C., past trustee), Wee Burn Club (Darien, Conn.), Edgartown Yacht Club (Mass., past commodore), Edgartown Golf Club, Riomar Country Club (Vero Beach, Fla.), Cruising Club Am. (past trustee), Pilgrims Club. Home: 911 Greenway Ln Vero Beach FL 32963-2109

HUBSCHMAN, HENRY A. lawyer; b. Newark, N.J., Aug. 12, 1947; s. Morris and Esther (Weissman) H.; m. Joanne L. Goode; children: Lilly, Josie, Ellis, Nathan. BA summa cum laude, Rutgers U., 1969; JD magna cum laude, M Pub. Policy, Harvard U., 1973. Bar: Mass. 1973, N.J. 1974, D.C. 1974, Ohio 1994. Law clk. U.S. Dist. Ct. Mass., Boston, 1973-74; assoc. Fried, Frank, Harris, Shriver & Jacobson, Washington, 1974-77, 79-80, ptnr., 1980-92; v.p., gen. counsel, bus. devel. GE Aircraft Engines, Cin., 1992-97; pres., CEO GE Capital Aviation Svcs., Stamford, Conn., 1997—. Exec. asst. to Sec. HUD, Washington, 1977-79; bd. dir. Fed. Nat. Mortgage Assn., 1979-81. Jewish. Home: 37 Hillside Rd Greenwich CT 06830-4834 Office: GE Capital Aviation Svcs 201 High Ridge Rd Stamford CT 06905-3417

HUCHRA, JOHN PETER, astronomer, educator; b. Jersey City, N.J., Dec. 23, 1948; s. Mieczyslaw Piotr and Helen Ann Huchra; m. Rebecca M. Henderson; 1 child, Harry Matthew. BS, MIT, 1970; PhD, Calif. Inst. Tech., 1976. Ctr. fellow Ctr. for Astrophysics, Cambridge, Mass., 1976-78; astronomer Smithsonian Astrophys. Obs., Cambridge, Mass., 1978-89, sr. astronomer, 1989—; lectr. dept. astronomy Harvard U., Cambridge, Mass., 1979-84, prof. dept. astronomy, 1984—2002, Robert O. and Holly Thomis Doyle prof. cosmology, 2002—; assoc. dir. Ctr. for Astrophysics, Cambridge, Mass., 1989—98; dir. F.L. Whipple Observatory, 1994-98. Mem. coun. Space Telescope Sci. Inst., Balt., 1987-95; chmn. working group on galaxy radial velocities Internat. Astron. Union, Paris, 1988—; chmn. large astron. data base working group NASA/IPAC, Washington, 1988-92; mem. astronomy and astrophysics survey Optical Panel, NAS, NRC, 1989-90; adv. bd. and vis. com. Arecibo Obs., Ithaca, N.Y., 1989-92; users com. Cerro Tololo Inter-Am. Obs., La Serena, Chile, 1989-91; vis. com. ESO, 1993-97; mem. NRC Com. on Astronomy and Astrophysics, 1994-2001, co-chmn. 1997-2001; mem. AURA, bd. dirs., 1995-, chair, 2001—; mem. NRC bd. on physics and astronomy, 1997-2003, chair, 2000-03; chair NOAO Future Directions Com., 1998-99. Contbr. chapters to books to profl. jours. Rsch. grantee, NASA, 1979—, Smithsonian Inst., 1980, NSF, 1984-89, 99—. Fellow AAAS (Newcomb Cleve. award 1990), Am. Phys. Soc. AIP (pub. policy com. 1988-95); mem. NAS, Am. Acad. Arts and Scis., Am. Astron. Soc. (pub. bd. chmn., 1986-88, councilor 1998-2001, sci. editor Astrophys. Jour. 1998-2003), Royal Astron. Soc., Astron. Soc. of the Pacific, Am. Phys. Soc. Astrophysics Divsn. (exec. com. 1996-97), Nat. Environ. Leadership Coun., Wilderness Soc., Nat. Audubon Soc., Mass. Audubon Soc., Union of Concerned Scientists, Nature Conservancy, Trustees of Reservations, Appalachian Trail Conf., Am. Contract Bridge League, Greenpeace, Green Mtn. Club, Appalachian Mtn. Club, Sierra Club, Sigma Xi, Gamma Nu. Achievements include discovery of Comet Huchra, of nearest gravitational lens; revision of cosmic distance scale; completion of first and second Center for Astrophysics Redshift Survey; measurement of infall of our Milky Way Galaxy into the Virgo Cluster; discovery of Great Wall of galaxies, 2 Micron All Sky Survey. Office: Harvard-Smithsonian Ctr Astrophysics 60 Garden St Cambridge MA 02138-1516 E-mail: huchra@cfa.harvard.edu.

HUCHTON, PAUL JOSEPH, JR., pediatrician; b. El Paso, Tex., Mar. 15, 1934; s. Paul Joseph Sr. and Eugenia Cregor (Kimbrough) H.; m. Sheila Ann Borsian, June 1, 1963; children: Hadley Ann Bernhard, David Morgan, Amy H. Anderson, Karen H. Hammer. BA, U. Tex., 1954; MD, Vanderbilt U., 1958. Diplomate Am. Bd. Pediat. Intern Vanderbilt U. Hosp., Nashville, 1958-59; resident U. Chgo., 1959-60; from resident to chief resident U. Colo., Denver, 1960-61; pvt. practice specializing in pediat., El Paso, 1963—. Mem. staff Providence and Sierra Med. Ctr., El Paso. Mem. Tex. Med. Assn. (del., counsellor 1970-93), El Paso County Med. Soc. (pres. 1985), Rotary Club El Paso (pres. 1980, Paul Harris award 1983). Republican. Mem. Vestry St. Francis On The Hill. Avocations: long distance cycling, computers. Office: 1515 N Oregon St El Paso TX 79902-4042 E-mail: phuchton@elp.rr.com.

HUCK, DANIEL N. lawyer, educator; b. Parkersburg, W.Va. m. Deborah McDaniel, Dec. 21, 1991; 1 child, Joseph Frumenti. BA, Bucknell U., 1984; JD, Northeastern U., 1987; MA, Marietta Coll., 2001; D in Edn., W.Va. U., 2001. Dep. atty. gen., atty. gen. City of Charleston, 1987-90; gen. counsel to gov. State of W.Va., Charleston, 1990-94; atty. Huck & Gillooly, Charleston, 1994-95; city atty. City of Charleston, W.Va., 1995-96; dist. mgr. Am. Gen. Fin. Svcs., Charleston, 1995-97; atty. Allen Guthrie & McHugh, Charleston, 1997-99; instr. Marshall U., Huntington, W.Va., 1999-2001; asst. prof. Marietta (Ohio) Coll., 2001—. Chmn. W.Va. Gov.'s Juvenile Justice Com., Charleston, 1995-98, W.Va. Regional Jail Correctional Authority, Charleston, 1996-2001. Contbr. articles to profl. jours. Mem. Charleston Mcpl. Planning Commn., 1995-98. Mem. ABA, ARC, W.Va. Bar Assn., Omicron Delta Kappa, Phi Delta Kappa. Avocations: numismatics, chess, guitar, traveling. Home: 8 Sylvan Way Marietta OH 45750-9626

HUCK, ELIZABETH LOUISE, radiologist; b. St. Louis, July 15, 1966; d. William Frank and Katharine Ann Hrach; m. Rodney Irwin Huck, Dec. 19, 1997. BA in Biology, St. Louis U., 1988; DO, Kirksville Coll., 1992. Intern Deaconess Med. Ctr., St. Louis, 1992-93, resident, 1993-97; radiologist Ctrl. Radiology Group, St. Louis, 1997-98, Berland Radiology, St. Louis, 1998—. Grantee Mo. Assn. of Osteo. Physicians and Surgeons, 1990; scholarship Found. of St. Louis, 1984, Westlake Found., 1984. Mem. AMA, Am. Osteo. Coll. of Radiology, Am. Osteo. Assn., Am. Roentgen Ray Soc., Radiol. Soc. of N.Am. Avocations: reading, crafts, travel. Home: 16910 Westridge Oaks Dr Wildwood MO 63040 Office: Berland Radiology 774 N New Ballas Rd Saint Louis MO 63141-6716

HUCK, JOHN LLOYD, pharmaceutical company executive; b. Bklyn., July 17, 1922; s. John Lloyd and Adrienne (Warner) H.; m. Dorothy Bertha Foehr, Nov. 20, 1943; children: Lloyd E., Jeanne Huck Leslie-Hughes, Virginia Huck Stalcup. BS in Chemistry, Pa. State U., 1946. Research chemist Hoffmann-LaRoche, Nutley, N.J., 1946, sales rep., 1948, dir. sales tng., 1951, asst. gen. sales mgr., 1955, dir. product devel., 1958; dir. mktg. Merck Sharp & Dohme Div., West Point, Pa., 1958; v.p. mktg. planning MSD div., 1966, v.p. sales and mktg., 1968, exec. v.p., 1969, exec. v.p., gen. mgr., 1972, pres., 1973; sr. v.p. Merck & Co., Rahway, N.J., 1975, exec. v.p., 1977, dir., 1977-86, pres., chief operating officer, 1978-85, chmn. bd., 1985-86; chmn. bd., chief exec. officer Nova Pharm. Corp., Morristown, N.J., 1986-88, chmn. bd., 1988-91. Patentee in field. Trustee Pa. State U., 1977-92, v.p., 1985-88, pres. bd., 1988-91; trustee Morristown Meml. Health Found., Inc., N.J., 1979-96, chmn. bd., 1986-88; trustee Geraldine R. Dodge Found. 1st lt. USAAF, 1942-46. Alumni fellow Coll. Medicine Pa. State U., 1980, Coll. of Sci., 1983; named to Nutley Hall of Fame, 2003. Mem. Morris County Golf Club, Piper's Landing Golf Club. Republican. Presbyterian. Home: 1 Carriage Hill Dr Morristown NJ 07960-6994

HUCK, L. FRANCIS, lawyer; b. Pittsfield, Mass., May 5, 1947; s. Lewis Francis Joseph and Rosemary (Ahearn) H.; m. Natalie Anne Murphy, June 10, 1978; children: Amelia Emerson, Rosemary Alice, Charles Randolph. AB, Harvard U., 1969; JD, Stanford U., 1972. Assoc. Simpson, Thacher & Bartlett, NYC, 1972-79, ptnr. N.Y.C., 1980—. Mem. Harvard Club N.Y.C., Wee Burn Club. Democrat. Home: 90 Inwood Rd Darien CT 06820-2427 Office: Simpson Thacher & Bartlett 425 Lexington Ave Fl 15 New York NY 10017-3954

HUCK, LARRY RALPH, manufacturing executive, sales consultant; b. Yakima, Wash., Aug. 10, 1942; s. Frank Joseph and Helen Barbara (Swalley) H.; m. Peggy L. Huck; 1 child, Larry Ralph II. Student, Wash. Tech. Inst., 1965-66, Edmonds Coll., 1966-67, U. Wash., 1967-69, Seattle C.C., 1969-70. Salesman Kirby Co., Seattle, 1964-68, sales mgr., 1968-69; salesman Sanico Chem. Co., Seattle, 1968-69, Synkoloid Co., Seattle, 1970-71; tech. sales rep. Vis. Queen divsn. Ethyl Corp., Seattle, 1971-75; western sales mgr. B & K Films, Inc., Belmont, Calif., 1975-77; pres. N.W. Mfrs. Assocs., Inc., Bellevue, Wash., 1977-86, pres. combined sales group, 1984, 86-96; nat. sales mgr. Gazelle Inc., Tomah, Wis., 1979-81; dir. sales J.M.J. Mktg. E.Z. Frame divsn., 1984-85; nat. accounts mgr. Upnorth Plastics, St. Paul, 1984-87; gen. mgr. Otool Co., 1996-98; N.W. sales mgr. Roberts Consol. divsn. Q.E.P. Inc., 1998-2000; dist. sales mgr. State Indsl. Products, Cleve., 2000—. V.p. Bellevue Nat. Little League; basketball cord. Cath. Youth Orgn., Sacred Heart Ch.; head baseball coach Pierce Coll., Tacoma. With USMC, 1959-66. Mem. Nat. Coun. Salesmen's Orgns., Mfrs. Agts. Nat. Assn., Am. Hardware Mfrs. Assn., N.W. Mfrs. Assn. (pres.), Hardware Affiliated Reps., Inc., Door and Hardware Inst., Internat. Conf. Bldg. Ofcls., Am. Baseball Coaches Assn., Marine Corps. Assn., 1st Marine Divsn. Assn., 3d Marine Divsn. Assn. (life, v.p.). Roman Catholic. Office: 521 Elma Ave NE Renton WA 98059-4844

HUCKABEE, HARLOW MAXWELL, lawyer, writer; b. Wichita Falls, Tex., Jan. 22, 1918; s. Edwin Cleveland and Gladys Idella (Bonney) H.; m. Gloria Charlotte Comstock, Jan. 10, 1942; children: Bonney M., David C., Stephen M. BA, Harvard U., 1948; JD, Georgetown U., 1951. Bar: U.S. Dist. Ct. D.C. 1952, U.S. Ct. Appeals (D.C. cir.) 1952. Cashier br. office Columbian Nat. Life Ins. Co., Boston, 1935-40; lawyer Fed. Housing Adminstrn., Washington, 1955-56; trial lawyer, criminal sect., tax divsn. U.S. Justice Dept., Washington, 1956-63; lawyer IRS, Washington, 1963-67; trial lawyer organized crime and racketeering sect. U.S. Justice Dept., Washington, 1967-68, trial lawyer criminal sect., tax divsn., 1968-80. Author: Lawyers, Psychiatrists and Criminal Law, 1980, Mental Disability Issues in the Criminal Justice System: What They Are, Who Evaluates Them, How and When, 2000; contbr. articles to profl. jours. and legal publs. including Diminished Capacity Dilemma in the Federal System, 1991. Maj. U.S. Army, 1940-45, 48-55, ETO, Korea; lt. col. USAR, 1961. Methodist. Home: 5100 Fillmore Ave Apt 913 Alexandria VA 22311-5048

HUCKABEE, MICHAEL DALE, governor; b. Hope, Ark., Aug. 24, 1955; m. Janet McCain, May 25, 1974; children: John Mark, David, Sarah. BA in Religion magna cum laude, Ouachita Bapt. U., Arkadelphia, Ark., 1976; postgrad., Southwestern Bapt. Theol. Sem., Ft. Worth, 1976-77. Ordained to ministry So. Bapt. Conv., 1974. Pastor Walnut Street Bapt. Ch., Arkadelphia, 1974-75, Immanuel Bapt. Ch., Pine Bluff, Ark., 1980-85, Beech Street 1st Bapt. Ch., Texarkana, Ark., 1986—; lt. gov. State of Ark., 1993-96, gov., 1996—. Founder, past pres. Am. Christian TV Sys., Pine Bluff; pres. Ark. Bapt. Conv., 1989-91. Chmn. So. Govs. Assn., So. Technology Coun., So. Internat. Trade Coun. Republican. Home: 1800 Center St Little Rock AR 72206-1418 Office: Office of the Gov State Capitol Rm 250 Little Rock AR 72201-1088*

HUCKABY, GARY CARLTON, lawyer; b. Lanett, Ala., July 12, 1938; s. Carl Walker and Mary Evelyn (Meriwether) H.; m. Jeanne Davey Huckaby, Feb. 23, 1963; children: Gary Jr., John Stephen, Michael Stewart. BA, U. Ala., 1960, JD, 1962. Bar: U.S. Supreme Ct. 1963, U.S. Ct. of Mil. Appeals 1963, U.S. Ct. Appeals (5th and 11th cirs.) 1963, U.S. Dist. Ct. (no., middle and so. dists) Ala. 1963. Law clk. to chief justice Ala. Supreme Ct., Montgomery, 1962-63; asst. U.S. Sen. Lister Hill, Washington, 1963; ptnr. Smith, Huckaby & Graves, Huntsville, Ala., 1966-85, Bradley, Arant, Rose & White, Huntsville, 1985—; dir. Ala. Ctr. for Law & Civic Edn., 1992—. Dir. coun. Internat. Visitors of Huntsville-Madison County, 1983-89, Tenn. Valley Boy Scouts Am., 1975-79, Mental Health Assn. Madison County, 1970-78, Ala. Law Sch. Found., 1981—; pres. Huntsville-Madison County Mental Health Bd., 1977-80, Madison County Heart Assn., 1968; active Citizens Com. on Higher Edn. of Ala. Legis., 1976, judicial sect. of Huntsville-Madison County Local Govt. Study Com., 1969. Capt. USAF, 1963-66. Fellow Am. Bar Found., Am. Coll. Trial Lawyers; mem. ABA (bd. govs. 1990-91, house of delegates, chmn. standing com. on lawyer referral and info. services 1982-85, chmn. spl. com. on delivery of legal services 1976-79, standing com. on lawyers pub. service responsibility 1987-90, consortium on legal services and the pub. 1976-79, task force on pub. edn. 1978, standing com. on lawyers in the armed forces 1971-73), Ala. State Bar (pres., bd. commrs. 1981-87, exec. com. 1982-83, 84-85, 87-88, chmn. governance com. 1986-87, action group on professionalism, disciplinary bd. 1981-87; recipient award of merit 1986), Huntsville-Madison County Bar Assn. (pres. 1977-78, chmn. grievance com. 1976, bench and bar relations 1981, convention host com. 1971, law day com. 1968), Am. Judicature Soc. (former bd. dirs.), Rotary. Democrat. Episcopalian. Home: 701 Greene St SE Huntsville AL 35801-4232 Office: Bradley Arant Rose & White 200 Clinton Ave W Ste 900 Huntsville AL 35801-4900

HUCKABY, MARK ANSON, paramedic, educator, emergency medical services specialist; b. Columbia, Tenn., Aug. 25, 1965; s. Paul and Mildred Louise (Tomlin) H. Cert. paramed. tech., Vol. State Community Coll., Gallatin, Tenn., 1986. Lic. paramedic, Tenn; cert. EMT/paramedic, Tex, Ohio, adv. EMS instr., Tex., ACLS/BLS instr., ACLS regional faculty, advanced BTLS instr., others. Firefighter/paramedic Maury Co., Tenn., 1981; pub. safety operator/dispatcher Williamson County, Tenn., 1990; supr. paramedics The General Jackson, Opryland USA, Inc., Opryland Hotel, The Grand Ole Opry, Nashville, 1986; sr. emergency med. technician, paramedic Nashville Fire Dept., 1987. EMS del. to USSR/Europe Citizen Amb. Program; paramed. tech. preceptor Vol. State C.C., Gallatin, Tenn., 1989; supr. health and emergency med. svcs. Fiesta Tex. Theme Park, San Antonio, 1991; EMS educator MEDIC Inc., San Antonio, 1994; educator in allied health San Antonio Coll.; tech. resource specialist Tex. Dept. Health, Bur. Emergency Mgmt., 1996, assoc. dir. EMS, 97, EMS specialist, 98; corp. mgr. health svcs. Six Flags Theme Parks, 1998; critical care instr./coord. Grant Med. Ctr., Columbus, Ohio, 2001; ind. health and safety cons., 01. Staff writer EMS Messenger, mem. conf. staff and faculty, mem. leadership acad. faculty; text reviewer Appleton and Lange Pub., Jones and Bartlett Pub.; mem. editl. rev. bd., advanced CISD team mem. Tex. EMS mag. Mem. med. com. Tex. Spl. Olympics. Mem. ARC, ASTM (f-30 EMS com., f-24 EMS com.),, Am. Heart Assn., Nat. Assn. EMTs, Nat. Paramedic Soc., Nat. Assn. EMS Educators, Nat. Assn. EMS Quality Profls., Nat. Assn. EMS Physicians, Tenn. Paramedic Soc., Tex. Assn. EMTs, United Paramedics (Nashville chpt.), Internat. Assn. Fire Fighters, Internat. Assn. Fire Chiefs (EMS sect., Indsl. sect.).

HUCKEBA, EMILY CAUSEY, retired elementary school educator; b. Carrollton, Ga., Aug. 26, 1941; d. Edward Clark and Audie Farmer Causey; m. Dale Malloy Huckeba, Aug. 27, 1961; 1 child, Catherine Nan. BS Elem. Edn., West Ga. Coll., 1962, M Edn., 1977. 2nd grade tchr. Whitesburg (Ga.) Elem. Sch., 1962—63; 1st grade tchr. Ctrl. Elem. Sch., Carrollton, Ga., 1963—68, Roopville (Ga.) Elem. Sch., 1968—96, music tchr., 1996—98, substitute tchr., 1998—2001. Mem. alumni coun. West Ga. Coll., Carrollton, 1991—93; pilot tchr. Whole Lang. Program Roopville (Ga.) Elem. Sch., 1993—95. Charter mem. Roopville Hist. Soc., 1984—; organist, pianist Roopville Bapt. Ch., 1960—. Mem.: NEA, Ga. Music Educators Assn., Carroll Heard Ret. Tchrs., Ga. Assn. Educators, Alpha Delta Kappa. Baptist. Home: 1135 S Hwy 27 Roopville GA 30170-2516

HUCKEBY, ED D. academic administrator, composer, conductor; b. Ada, Okla., July 9, 1948; s. Cecil S. and Lula F. Huckeby; m. Latricia A. Wilson, June 5, 1970; children: Angela Dawn Corr, Amanda Deanne Davis. BA in Edn., East Ctrl. State Coll., 1970; M in Music Edn., U. Okla., 1974; EdD, Okla. State U., 1989. Cert. tchr., adminstr. State Dept. Edn., Okla. Dir. bands Allen (Okla.) Pub. Schs., 1968—70; dir. instrumental music Poteau (Okla.) Pub. Schs., 1970—76; dept. head, dean grad. sch. Northwestern Okla. State U., Alva, 1976—98; exec. dir. Tulsa (Okla.) Ballet Theatre, Inc., 1998—99; chief academic and oper. officer/assoc. v.p. for academic affairs Northeastern State U., Broken Arrow, Okla., 1999—. Mem. Educators Leadership Acad., Edmond, Okla., 1999—2000, Mayor's Arts Task Force, Tulsa, 2002—03; pres. Higher Edn. Cultural Roundtable, Tulsa, 2002—03; edn. chair Broken Arrow Leadership Acad. Composer: over 120 published works. Co-chair Tulsa Area United Way Campaign, Broken Arrow, 2002—03. Named to Hall of Fame, Okla. Bandmasters Assn., 1996; recipient Serious Music award, ASCAP, 2002. Mem.: Broken Arrow C. of C., Rotary Internat. Avocations: music, golf, travel. Home: 4832 W Dallas St Broken Arrow OK 74012 Office: Northeastern State University 3100 E New Orleans Broken Arrow OK 74014 Office Fax: 918-449-6019. Personal E-mail: huckeby@nsuok.edu. E-mail: huckeby@nsuok.edu.

HUCKINS, HAROLD AARON, chemical engineer; b. Cambridge, Mass., Nov. 28, 1924; s. Harold Aaron and Julia E. (Nugent) H.; m. Elizabeth L. Kearns, Nov. 15, 1952; children: Richard W., Robert M., Christopher N., Patricia A., Leslie K. BSChemE, Northeastern U., 1945; ASME, Lowell Inst., 1946; postgrad., Boston U., 1947-49, U. Pitts., 1950-52. Chem. process engr., asst. project mgr. Monsanto Chem. Co., Boston-Everett, Mass., 1945-49; sr. process engr., group leader Koppers Co. Chem. Div., Pitts., 1949-53; mgr. pilot plants, project mgr. Sci. Design Co., Inc., N.Y.C., 1953-66; v.p. tech. ops. Oxirane Chem. Co., Princeton, N.J., 1966-73; v.p. tech. assessment Halcon SD Group, N.Y.C., 1973-85; pres. Princeton Advanced Tech., Inc., 1985—. Dir. Assn. Cons. Chemists and Chem. Engrs. div., N.Y.C., 1990-93, program chair, 1992-93; dir. Materials Tech. Inst., St. Louis, 1976-85; spkr. local groups/TV global energy trends; presenter in field. Co-author: The Chemical Plant, 1966; contbr. articles to profl. jours. Fellow AIChE (chair ctrl. Jersey sect. 1976-77, dir mgmt. divsn. 1981-82, dir. materials engring. and sci. divsn. 1992-93, chmn. chem. tech. materials com. 1983-84, chmn. John Fritz medal commn. 1989, chmn. entrepreneurial forum 1994—, Chem. Engring. Practice award 1994); mem. Am. Soc. Materials, Am. Chem. Soc., Am. Ceramic Soc. Nat. Assn. Corrosion Engrs. (conf. chmn. 1984), Comml. Devel. Assn., Mensa Internat., Country Club of Hilton Head Island, Port Royal Racquet Club, Hilton Head Ski Club (bd. dirs.). Achievements include patents for chemical process technology. Home and Office: Princeton Advanced Tech Inc 4 Bertram Pl Hilton Head Island SC 29928-3936 Fax: 843-689-9212. E-mail: hhuckins@hargray.com.

HUCKMAN, MICHAEL SAUL, neuroradiologist, educator; b. Newark, Aug. 20, 1936; s. Louis Fillmore and Mollie (Lehman) H.; m. Beverly Joy Blachman, Aug. 2, 1964; children: Andrew Garfield, Robert Steven. AB, Princeton U., 1958; MD, St. Louis U., 1962. Rotating intern, then resident in radiology Phila. Gen. Hosp., 1962-63, 65-68; fellow in neuroradiology Edward Mallinckrodt Inst. Radiology, Washington U., St. Louis, also univ. instr. radiology, 1968-70; mem. faculty Rush Med. Coll., Chgo., 1970—, prof. radiology, 1978—; dir. sect. neuroradiology Rush-Presbyn.-St. Luke's Med. Center, 1970—; mem. faculty Cook County Grad. Sch. Medicine, 1972-91. Cons. Nat. Ctr. for Health Care Tech., 1980-81; sec.-gen. XVI Symposium Neuroradiologicum, 1994-98. Mem. editorial bd. Jour. Computer Assisted Tomography, 1976-94, Radiographics, 1983-87, Applied Radiology, 1987-89; cons. editor Am. Jour. Roentgenology, 1990-91; contbr. articles to med. jours. Served with USNR, 1963-65. Spl. fellow Nat. Inst. Neurol. Diseases and Blindness, 1968-70 Fellow Am. Coll. Radiology; mem. AMA, Am. Soc. Neuroradiology (sec. 1980-83, pres. elect 1986-87, pres. 1987-88, editor-in-chief Am. Jour. Neuroradiology 1989-97, editor emeritus 1998—, archivist 1998—, Gold medal 1999), Radiol. Soc. N.Am. (Gold medal 2002), Am. Soc. Head and Neck Radiology, Am. Roentgen Ray Soc., Assn. Univ. Radiologists, European Soc. Neuroradiology, World Fedn. Neuroradiol. Socs. (historian 1993-97, v.p. 1997—, pres.-elect 1998, pres. 2002—), Ill. Med. Soc., Ill. Radiol. Soc., Chgo. Med. Soc., Blockley Radiol. Soc., Soc. for Scholarly Publ., Japanese Soc. Neuroradiology (hon.), Coun. Biology Editors, Soc. Fifth Line, Indian Soc. Neuroradiology (hon. life), Sigma Xi, Phi Delta Epsilon. Clubs: Princeton Alumni of Chgo. (trustee 1982-84), Caxton. Jewish. Home: 175 E Delaware Pl Apt 7401 Chicago IL 60611-1731 Office: 1753 W Congress Pky Chicago IL 60612-3809 E-mail: m.huckman@comcast.net.

HUCKSHOLD, WAYNE WILLIAM, elementary education educator; b. St. Louis, Mar. 5, 1952; s. Albert Clarence and Jane Martha (Stewart) Huckshold; m. Paula Louise Ransin, June 14, 1977 (div. Apr. 1987); 1 child, Kristen Louise. BS in Edn., U. Mo., 1976, MEd, 1977. Cert. elem. edn. K-8, phys. edn. K-9, health edn. K-12, sci. 7-9, Mo.; Nat. Coun. Accreditation of Tchr. Edn.; cert. personal trainer Am. Coun. Exercise. Tchr. grade 3 Camdenton (Mo.) R-III, 1977-81, coach football, track and cross country, 1978-81; fitness instr., athletic trainer Columbia (Mo.) Sports Medicine, 1981-84; student athletic trainer U. Mo., Columbia, 1983-84, grad. tchg. asst., 1984-85; elem. tchr. Francis Howell Sch. Dist., St. Charles, Mo., 1985-91, elem. tchr. phys. edn., 1991—, mem. supt.'s comm. coun., 1992-93. Master's swim coach West County YMCA, Chesterfield, Mo., 1991—, personal trainer, 1992— ; level 2 swim coach Am. Swimming Coaches Assn., 1997—; head women's varsity swim coach Francis Howell H.S., 1998—99; asst. head coach U.S.S. Swim Team, St. Peter's Rec-Plex, 1997—2000; new tchr. mentor Francis Howell Sch. Dist., 1996—. Olympic Torch relay runner Winter Olympic Games, Columbia, Mo., 2002. Named YMCA Endurance Athlete of Yr., YMCA, St. Louis, 1990; grantee Union Electric Co., St. Louis, 1989; fellow Tchrs. Acad. Class 1994, Network for Ednl. Devel., Danforth Found., 1993-94. Mem. NEA, AAHPERD, Mo. Edn. Assn., Francis Howell Edn. Assn., Mo. Alliance for Health, Phys. Edn., Recreation and Dance, U.S. Phys. Edn. Assn., Nat. Assn. for Sport and Phys. Edn., Assn. for Advancement Health Edn. Avocations: running, swimming, biking, triathlons, spending time with family and friends. Home: 1549 Milbridge Dr Chesterfield MO 63017-4611 Office: Francis Howell Sch Dist Warren Elem Sch 141 Weiss Rd Saint Peters MO 63376 E-mail: whuckshold@yahoo.com.

HUCKSTEAD, CHARLOTTE VAN HORN, retired home economist, artist; b. Garwin, Iowa, Jan. 13, 1920; d. George Loren and Esther Olive (Carver) Van Horn; m. Lowell Raine Huckstead (dec.); children: Karen C., Roger H., Martha E., Paul R., Sarah S. BS, U. Wisc., 1942; BFA, Boise (Idaho) State U., 1989. Merchandising Montgomery Ward, Chgo. and Santa Monica, Calif., 1941-42; "Rosie the Riveter" WWII, Chgo. and Beloit, Wis., 1942-46; woman's editor Dairyland News, Milw., 1950-54; interior designer, cons., tchr. South Bend, Marshfield, Wis., Merced, Calif., 1952-69; extenion home economist U. Minn., Rochester, 1973-78; dir. food svcs. Milton (Wisc.) Sch. Dist., 1978-85; artist, 1952—. Painting and sculpture. Vol. Idaho Genealogy Libr., 1994—99, Dakoto County Hist. Soc., 2000—03; treas. Wis. Food Svcs. Assn., 1980—85; leader/mem. Girl Scouts Am., 1934—78; bd. dirs. Rock County Hist. Soc., Janesville, Wis., 1979—84, Milton Hist. Soc., 1979—85. Mem. AAUW, Nature Conservancy, Idaho Hist. Soc. (vol. 1985-99), Idaho Centennial Art Group (sec. 1991, show chmn. 1992, historian 1993-95), Idaho Water Color Soc., Morrison Ctr. Aux. (vol. 1986-99, bd. dirs. 1992-93, 97-99, Auxilian of Yr. 1995), Boise State Alumni Assn., Audubon Soc., Ch. Women United (editor 1985-86), Sierra Club, Boise Art Mus., Wis. Alumni Assn., Friends of Hist. Mus. Boise. Protestant. Avocations: reading, history, archaeology, theatre, travel.

HUDACHEK, SUSAN MARIE, contracts specialist; consultant; b. Steubenville, Ohio, Apr. 20, 1957; d. Joseph Michael and Edna Rita (Garish) H. AS in Liberal Arts, W.Va. No. C.C., Weirton, 1977; BA in Psychology, Wheeling Jesuit U., 1979; MPH, U. Pitts., 1982. Coordination asst. Rehab. Inst. Pitts., 1982-87; admissions coord. Wightman Ctr. for Nursing and Rehab., Pitts., 1987-88; program dir. HealthSouth Harmarville Rehab. Ctr., Pitts., 1989-93; program assoc. United Way, Pitts., 1994-95; support svcs. coord. UPMC Shadyside Hosp., Pitts., 1995-96, reimbursement specialist, 1996-98; provider contracts specialist Highmark Blue Cross Blue Shield, Pitts., 1998—. Cons. in field, 1993-98. Mem.: APHA, Western Pa. Myasthenia Gravis Assn. Democrat. Roman Catholic. Avocations: travel, information technology, reading, dogs and cats. Home: 5647 Callowhill St Pittsburgh PA 15206

HUDACSKO, DENNIS WAYNE, b. New Brunswick, NJ, Dec. 13, 1945; s. Dennis and Mary Valerie (Haydu) Hudacsko; m. Mary Joan Tatu, July 29, 1977 (div. Aug. 1993); children: Elyse Coelle, Marc Denes; m. Karen Annette Sagan, Jan. 23, 1995. BA cum laude, Rutgers U., 1972, M in City and Regional Planning, 1975. Planning asst. Planning & Design Assocs., Somerset, N.J., 1972-73; planner Union County Planning Bd., Elizabeth, N.J., 1973-75; sr. planner Union County Mgr., Elizabeth, N.J., 1975-76; dir. planning City of Elizabeth, 1976-86, Piscataway (N.J.), 1986-87, Candeub, Fleissig & Assocs., Springfield, N.J., 1987-89; with T&M Assocs., Middletown, NJ, 1989—97; propr. Dennis W. Hudacsko- Zoning & Planning Consulting, Bedminster, NJ, 1997—. Instr. Rutgers U. Extension, New Brunswick, N.J., 1976-77, Union Coll., Cranford, N.J., 1987—; mem. Union County Econ. Devel. Program Com., 1973-86; bd. advs. Middlesex County Air Quality Program, New Brunswick, 1974-76. Editor: (newsletter) Advanced Planning, 1976-86. Bd. dirs. Citizen's League of Elizabeth, 1986—; commr. Riverside (NJ) Planning Bd., 1971—72; mem. NJAPA Legislative Com., 1992—, Bedminster Township Planning Bd., 1998—; mem. Bedminster Township Environ. Commn., 1999—; mem. Bedminster Township Landscape Adv. Com., 2000—, Raritan Watershed Mgmt. Plan Tech. Adv. Com., 2001, Habitat for Humanity, site selection com., 1997—. Served to sgt. USAF, 1966—70. Grantee EPA, HUD, Food and Drug Adminstrn., Dept. Transp., 1978. Mem. Am. Planning Assn., Urban Land Inst., Am. Inst. Cert Planners, N.J. Profl. Planners, Mensa. Mem. Reformed Ch. of Am. Club: Central Jersey Bike (Metuchen). Avocation: bicycle touring. Office: Zoning & Planning Consulting 135-2 Cowperthwaite Rd Bedminster NJ 07921

HUDAK, CHRISTINE ANGELA, nursing informatics educator, specialist nursing informatics; b. Cleve., Dec. 13, 1950; d. Ernest J. and Helen M. (Orovets) H. BSN, Case Western Res. U., 1974; MEd in Post-Secondary Edn., Cleve. State U., 1980, PhD, 1998. Pub. health nurse Vis. Nurse Assn. of Cleve., 1974-75; clin. preceptor physician's asst. program Cuyahoga Community Coll., Cleve., 1975-77; staff nurse MetroHealth Ctr. for Skilled Nursing Care, Cleve., 1977-78; staff devel. instr. The MetroHealth System, Cleve., 1978-82, instr. in continuing edn., 1982-85, health care analyst, info. specialist, 1985-87; coord. clin. info. systems tng. Metro Health System, Cleve., 1987-90, mgr. specialized instnl. progs., 1990-94; mgr. user support svcs. Metro Health Sys., Cleve., 1994-95; lectr., lead instr. nursing informatics Case Western Res. U., Cleve., 1995-98, asst. prof. nursing informatics and mgmt., 1998—. Coord. MS in nursing informatics program Case-Western Res. U., 2002—; instr. in health care info. systems adult degree program Capital U., Cleve.; instr. div. continuing edn. Cleve. State U.; clin. instr. nursing info. systems Case Western Res. U., 1990, part-time instr. nursing info. systems, 1990-95. Mem. Am. Assn. Artificial Intelligence, Ctr. Profl. Ethics (charter), Ednl. Computer Consortium Ohio, Midwest Alliance for Nursing Informatics, Am. Assn. Nursing Informatics, Hosp. Info. and Mgmt. Systems Soc., Nat. League for Nursing, Phi Delta Kappa, Pi Lambda Theta, Sigma Theta Tau. Office: Case Western Res U Frances Payne Bolton Sch Nursing 10900 Euclid Ave Cleveland OH 44106-4904 E-mail: cah16@po.cwru.edu.

HUDAK, JOSEPH DAVID, forensic engineer, educator, police investigator; b. Pottstown, Pa., Feb. 11, 1956; s. Joseph Andrew and Eleanore Barbara (Pierzchala) H.; children: Meredith Rebecca, Jonathan Michael, Wesley Robert; m. Joann Marie Kempf. BS in Civil Engring. with honors, Drexel U., 1979. Accredited accident reconstructionist Accreditation Commn. for Traffic Accident Reconstruction. Civil engr. IU Conversion Systems, Horsham, Pa., 1980-82, VFL Tech., Malvern, Pa., 1982-84; state trooper Pa. State Police, Harrisburg, 1984-2000; assoc. Robson-Lapina Inc. Forensic Engrs., Lancaster, Pa., 2000—. Adj. faculty Tex. A&M U., 1995—; pres., forensic engring. cons. iE Forensic Cons., Inc., Newfoundland, Pa., 1997—; alternate rep. ACTAR bd. dirs., 1995-2000. Contbr. articles to profl. publs.; presenter in field of traffic homicide investigations. Mem. ASCE (assoc.), Soc. Automotive Engrs. (assoc.), Nat. Assn. Traffic Accident Reconstructionists and Investigators, Md. Assn. Traffic Accident Invesigators, Fraternal Order Police, Rotary, Tau Beta Pi, Chi Epsilon. Avocations: reading, sports, martial arts, stone masonry, weight training. Home: RR 1 Box 167C Newfoundland PA 18445-9772 Office: Robson-Lapina Inc Forensic Engrs 350 New Holland Ave Lancaster PA 17602-2301

HUDAK, MICHAEL JOHN, environmentalist, writer, photographer; b. Johnson City, N.Y., Dec. 4, 1952; s. Michael Hudak and Alice Emily Rosner. BA, SUNY, Binghamton, 1975, PhD, 1985; MS, Northwestern U., 1977. Cons. Digital Equipment Corp., Maynard, Mass., 1985—85; rsch. scientist Siemens Corp. Rsch., Princeton, NJ, 1986—91; dir. Pub. Lands Without Livestock, Binghamton, 1999—. Resource person grazing task force Sierra Club, San Francisco, 1999—2000, chair end comml. grazing subcom., 2000—00; editl. cons. VivaVegie Soc., N.Y.C., 2001—02. Author: The Last Children of Charles Richard Trayhorn, 1992; photos included in Welfare Ranching, 2002. Office: Pub Lands Without Livestock 38 Oliver St Binghamton NY 13904-1516

HUDAK, THOMAS F(RANCIS), finance company executive; b. Donora, Pa., Jan. 29, 1942; s. Thomas Joseph and Ann Marie (Petrus) H.; m. Dorothy Ann Palko, July 27, 1963; children: Diana Lynn, Debra Ann, Thomas David. BS, St. Vincent Coll., 1963; MBA, Ohio State U., 1968. Bar: C.P.A., Ohio. Accountant Coopers & Lybrand, Columbus, Ohio, 1963-65; dept. mgr., data processing Western Electric Corp., Columbus, 1965-66; fin. controls mgr. Indsl. Nucleonics Co., Columbus, 1966-69; sr. v.p. fin., chief fin. officer G.C. Murphy Co., McKeesport, Pa., 1969-85, chmn. bd., 1981-85; pres. Hudak & Assocs. Treas. Mack Realty Co., McKeesport, Murphy Devel. Corp., Court House Village Co., Spotsylvania Realty Co.; bd. dirs., pres. Terry Farris Stores, Inc.; mem. adv. bd. Liberty Mut. Ins. Co.; corp. comptr. PPG Industries, Inc., Pitts., 1986-89; chmn. bd. dirs., pres. Continental Plastics, Inc., 1989-95; bd. dirs. RXI Corp. Bd. dirs., pres. G.C. Murphy Co. Found. Mem. AICPA, U.S. C. of C., Fin. Execs. Inst. (dir. Pitts. chpt. 1982-85), Risk and Ins. Mgmt. Soc., Nat. Retail Mchts. Assn. (dir. fin. div. 1982-85), Nat. Assn. Corp. Dirs., Machinery and Allied Products Inst. (fin. coun.), Assn. Spice Traders, Assn. Dressings and Sauces, Peanut Butter and Nut Processors Assn.

HUDDLE, DONALD LEROY, economist, educator; b. L.A., Calif., Jan. 1, 1933; s. Roy Lee and Elaine Maude (Armstrong) Huddle; m. Germaine Buchard, Aug. 20, 1958 (div. 1977); children: Clarissa, Gerard, Richard, Roy; m. Bernardine Huddle, Oct. 29, 1988. BS, UCLA, 1959, MA, 1960; PhD, Vanderbilt U., 1964. Instr. Vanderbilt U., Nashville, 1963-64; asst. prof. Rice U., Houston, 1964-67, assoc. prof., 1967-69, prof., 1970-92, prof. emeritis, 1992—. Vis. prof. Yale U., New Haven, 1966—67; cons. U.S. Dept. of Def., Houston, 1967—68, Shell Oil Corp., Houston, 1974—78, U.S. C. of C. Future Studies Com., Houston, 1983—85, various legal orgns., 1971—; guest radio and TV, 1964—. Contbr. articles to profl. jours.; mem. editl. bd. So. Econ. Jour., 1970—74. Referee Woodrow Wilson Found., Washington, 1992—95; appointee task force on immigration State of Tex., 1982—86, NAFTA, 1991—92; pres. First Unitarian Ch., Houston, 1970. Grantee, U.S. Dept. of Def., 1964—65, NSF, 1971—75, Agy. Internat. Devel., 1975—77, Carrying Capacity Network, 1992—98; scholar, Yale U., 1966—67; Nat. Def. fellow, Vanderbilt U., 1960—63. Mem.: ACLU, NEH (proposal evaluation com., Stephen minister 1998—2003), Western Econ. Assn., Am. Acad. Polit. and Social Sci. (referee), Econ. Devel. and Cultural Change (referee), Am. Econ. Assn. Avocations: tennis, backpacking, travel, meditation. Office: Rice U PO Box 1892 Houston TX 77251-1892

HUDDLE, FRANKLIN PIERCE, JR., diplomat; b. Providence, May 9, 1943; s. Franklin Pierce and Clare (Scott) H.; m. Chanya Sawangrot, May 13, 1988; 1 child, Pavarage. BA, Brown U., 1965; postgrad., Columbia U., 1965-66; MA, Harvard U., 1970, PhD, 1978. Coord. Arabic affairs Peace Corps, Bisbee, 1968-69; instr. Harvard U., Cambridge, Mass., 1970-74; with Dept. of State, Washington and abroad, 1974—, charge d'affaires Rangoon, Burma, 1990-94; dir. Pacific Island Affairs, 1994-96; consul gen. Bombay, 1996-99, Toronto, 1999—2001; amb. to Tajikistan, 2001—. Author: Libyan Arabic, 1966; author, editor: Let's Go Europe, 1971; co-author: Nationalities of the USSR, 1975; photography shows in Thailand, Nepal and Washington, 1980, 81, 84; patentee rocket coatings, 1960. Recipient Rivkin award; Ford Found. grantee; Wayland scholar. Mem. Phi Beta Kappa. Avocations: piano, chess, ice skating. Office: 7090 Dushanbe Place Dulles VA 20189-7090

HUDDLESON, EDWIN EMMETT, III, lawyer; b. Oct. 20, 1945; s. Edwin Emmet and Mary (Taeusch) H.; m. Andra Nan Oakes, July 8, 1978; children: Michael, Jonathan. BS, Stanford U., 1967; JD, U. Chgo., 1970. Bar: Calif. 1970, D.C. 1977, Md. 2001. Law clk. to Judge Charles M. Merrill U.S. Ct. Appeals (9th cir.), 1970—71; civil divsn. U.S. Dept. Justice, Washington, 1971—77. Chmn. Ct. Rules Com. DC Bar, 2001—; com. on procedures U.S. Ct. Appeals (DC cir.), 2002—. Author: Waiver of Miranda Rights, 1969, Confidentiality for Editorial Process, 1978, Treatise on Equipment Leasing, 1989, Appellate Advocacy, 1991, Environmental Law Protections for Lenders, 1994, Leasing Is Distinctive!, 2003; mem. U. Chgo. Law Rev., 1968-70, comment editor, 1969-70; originator Harold Leventhal Talks; contbr. articles to profl. jours. Fellow Am. Bar Found.; mem. ABA (chmn. com. on leasing 2002—), Am. Law Inst. Home: 1962 Upshur St NW Washington DC 20011-5354 Office: The Woodward Building 733 15th St NW Ste 719 Washington DC 20005 E-mail: huddlesone@aol.com.

HUDDLESTON, CHARLES B. surgeon, educator; b. Sedalia, Mo., Nov. 18, 1952; s. Charles M. and Dorothy G. Huddleston; children: Laura, Rachel, Alexander. BA, U. Mo., 1974; MD, Vanderbilt U., 1978. Diplomate Am. Bd. Surgery, Am. Bd. Thoracic Surgery. Intern in internal medicine Vanderbilt Med. Ctr., 1978-79, resident in gen. surgery, 1979-86, resident in CT surgery, 1986-88; fellowship in pediat. CT surgery Hosp. for Sick Children, London, 1988-89; assoc. prof. surgery SUNY Health Sci. Ctr., Syracuse, 1989-90, Washington U. Sch. Medicine, St. Louis, 1990—, prof. surgery. Dir. heart transplant program, dir. lung transplant program, chief pediat. cardiothoracic surgery St. Louis Children's Hosp., 1994—. Capt. USNR, 1994—. Mem. Phi Beta Kappa. Methodist. Home: 428 Edgewood Clayton MO 63105

HUDDLESTON, JEFFREY LAWRENCE, music educator; b. Greenville, Miss., Oct. 5, 1962; s. Roy P. and Emma Dukes Huddleston; m. Delphimé Rice, Aug. 3, 1985; children: Madeline, Jeffrey II. BME, Miss. Valley State U.; MusM, U. of Miss., 1985. Cert. tchr. Tenn. Orff music tchr. Crump Elem. Sch., Memphis, 2000—01; dir. of jazz studies Overton H.S., Memphis, 2001—. Bd. dirs. New Hope Cmty. Devel. Assoc., Memphis, 2000—02. Mem.: Music Educators Nat. Conf. Democrat. Baptist. Avocations: travel, swimming, reading. Office: Overton HS 1770 Lanier Lane Memphis TN 38125 Home: 610 Bonnie Dr Oakland TN 38060 Personal E-mail: jhuddlesto@aol.com. E-mail: jhuddlesto@aol.com.

HUDDLESTON, JOSEPH RUSSELL, judge; b. Glasgow, Ky., Feb. 5, 1937; s. Paul Russell and Laura Frances (Martin) H.; m. Heidi Wood, Sept. 12, 1959; children: Johanna, Lisa, Kristina. AB, Princeton U., 1959; JD, U. Va., 1962, LLM, 1997. Bar: Ky. 1962, U.S. Ct. Appeals (6th cir.) 1963, U.S. Supreme Ct. 1970. Ptnr. Huddleston Bros., Bowling Green, Ky., 1962-87; judge Warren Cir. Ct. Divsn. I, Bowling Green, Ky., 1987-91, Ky. Ct. appeals, Bowling Green, 1991—2003, sr. judge, 2003—. Mem. Adv. Com. for Criminal Law Revision, 1969-71; exec. com. Ky. Crime Commn., 1972-77. Named Ky. Outstanding Trial Judge, 1990. Fellow Am. Bar Found.; mem. ABA, Ky. Bar Assn. (ho. of dels. 1971-80), Assn. Trial Lawyers Am. (state del. 1981-82), Ky. Acad. Trial Attys. (bd. govs. 1975-87, pres. 1978), Bowling Green Bar Assn. (pres. 1972), So. Ky. Estate Planning Coun. (pres. 1983), Rotary Internat. (Paul Harris fellow), Bowling Green-Warren County C. of C. (bd. dirs. 1987-91), Port Oliver Yacht Club (commodore), Commonwealth Yacht Club. Democrat. Episcopalian. Home: 644 Minnie Way Bowling Green KY 42101-9210

HUDDY, MARGARET, artist, writer, educator; b. Phila., July 4, 1939; m. Norman Walter Huddy, June 6, 1959; children: Kathleen, Teresa, John, Bernadette. Student, Moore Coll. Art, 1957-59, Monterey Peninsula Coll., 1964-66. Art tchr. Marymount Jr. Sch., Arlington, Va., 1969-76, Coastal Carolina C.C., Jacksonville, N.C., 1978-80, Farifax County Adult Edn., Springfield, Va., 1980-86, Art League Sch., Alexandria, Va., 1991—2003, Corcoran Coll. Art and Design, Washington, 1999—2003. Contbr. articles. Recipient 2d prize for watercolor, 1998, 1st prize So. Watercolor Soc., 1999. Mem. Am. Watercolor Soc. (signature mem., CFS medal 1994), Nat. Watercolor Soc. (award 1997, 2003), Va. Watercolor Soc. Roman Catholic. Office: Torpedo Factory Art Ctr 105 N Union St # 203 Alexandria VA 22314-3217 E-mail: Mhuddy@huddy.com.

HUDEL, CHESTELLA ALVIS, athletics educator; b. Temple, Okla., Jan. 13, 1931; d. James Chester and Jewel (McCain) Alvis; m. William August Hudel, June 14, 1952 (dec. June 1962); children: Mary Hudel Rinne, Nancy Hudel Parten, Joan Hudel Patrick. BS in Child Devel., Tex. Women's U., 1950. Tchr. Port Arthur (Tex.) Ind. Sch., 1950-53, Ridgewood Park Pre-Sch., Dallas, 1962-86; trainer Red Cross, Dallas, 1975—; adapted aquatics dir. YWCA, Dallas, 1975—. Trainer water safety instrs. Red Cross, Dallas, 1975-96; coach Spl. Olympics, 1993-98; educator Down's Syndrome Guild/Dallas Ind. Sch. Dist., 1994-96; counselor for breast cancer survivors Encore YWCA/Komen Found., Dallas, 1995-98. Elder Northridge Presbyn. Ch., Dallas, 1979-98; com. on adminstrn. YWCA, Dallas, 1980-86; mem. Northridge Learning Ctr. Bd., Northridge Presbyn. Ch., Dallas, 1987-97; swim program leader Light House for the Blind, 1986-90, Tom Landry Ctr. Baylor Hosp., 2003—; resource person Parent to Parent, 1993. Recipient Golden Rule award J.C. Penny, Dallas, 1983, Extra Step award Red Cross, Dallas, 1989, Spirit of Red Cross award, 1990, GM Vol. Spirit award GM, Dallas, 1992, George Washington medal of honor Freedom Found. Valley Forge, Dallas, 1997; named Vol. of the Yr., Helping Agys. Serving Richardson, Tex., 1990. Mem. Assn. for Retarded Citizens. Avocations: journal and scrapbook making, piano, bridge, bible study. Home: 6015 Sandhurst Ln Apt A Dallas TX 75206-4726

HUDES, NANA BRENDA, marketing professional; b. N.Y.C., Nov. 25; d. Harry and Anita Lorraine (Seiken) Richter; m. Barton Hudes, Sept. 2, 1958 (div. Sept. 1972); children: Layne A., Michael F., Meredith A. Student, Skidmore Coll.; BA magna cum laude, Pace U., 1974; MS with honors, Coll. of New Rochelle, 1976. Dir. mail mktg. mgr. Pergamon Press, Elmsford, N.Y., 1979-80, spl. sales mgr., 1980-81; mktg. mgr. Knowledge Industry Publs., White Plains, N.Y., 1981-82, Grolier Electronic Pub., Danbury, Conn., 1982-84, dir. mktg., 1984-86; mktg. mgr. R.R. Bowker, New Providence, N.J., 1986-88, mktg. dir., 1988-91, sr. dir. mktg., 1991-99. Tchr. social studies Rye Neck (N.Y.) Mid. Sch., 1978-79; pres. NH Assocs., Mktg. Cons., 2000-01; dir. libr. mktg. Columbia U. Press, 2001—. Dist. leader, county committeeperson Dem. Party, Matawan Twp., N.J., 1964. Home: 233 E 69th St New York NY 10021-5414 E-mail: nhudes@mindspring.com.

HUDGENS, ANN YOUNG, librarian, counselor; b. Louisville, Ky., Feb. 11, 1931; d. Paul L. and Leona (Pardue) Young; m. Raymond D. Hudgens, July 8, 1949; children: Eric E., Teresa Herndon. BA, Union U., 1964; MA, Peabody Coll., 1970, MLS, 1974; EdD, Tenn. State U., 1989. Cert. sr. psychol. examiner, sch. counselor K-12, tchr. K-8, Tenn. Tchr. Anderson Sch., Brownsville, Tenn., 1964-66, Boyd-Buchanan, Chattanooga, 1966-68; libr., tchr. David Lipscomb U., Nashville, 1968—98. Book reviewer Christian Chronicle, 1992. Driver, tchr. Inner City Ministry, Nashville, 1988—. Mem. Nashville Psychol. Assn., Tenn. Assn. Psychol. Examiners. Republican. Mem. Church of Christ. Avocations: sign language, camp work, grandmothering. Office: David Lipscomb Univ 3901 Granny White Pike Nashville TN 37204-3903

HUDGINS, CATHERINE HARDING, business executive; b. June 25, 1913; d. William Thomas and Mary Alice (Timberlake) Harding; m. Robert Scott Hudgins IV, Aug. 20, 1938; children: Catherine Harding Adams, Deborah Ghiselin, Robert Scott V. BS, N.C. State U., 1933; postgrad., N.C. Sch. for Deaf, 1933-34. Tchr. N.C. Sch. for Deaf, Morganton, 1934-36, N.J. Sch. for Deaf, Trenton, 1937-39; sec. Dr. A.S. Oliver, Raleigh, 1937, Robert S. Hudgins Co., Charlotte, N.C., 1949—, v.p., treas., 1960—; also bd.dirs.; ret. Mem. Jr. Svc. League, Easton, Pa., 1939; project chmn. ladies aux. Profl. Engrs. N.C., 1954-55, pres., 1956-57; pres. Christian H.S. PTA, 1963; program chmn. Charlotte Opera Assn., 1959-61, sec., 1961-63; sec. bd. Hezekiah Alexander House Aux., 1949-52, treas., 1983-84, v.p., 1984-85, pres., 1985-89; sec. Hezekiah Alexander Found., 1986—; past chmn. home missions, annuities and relief Women of Presbyn. Ch., past pres. Sunday Sch. class. Named Woman of Yr. Am. Biog. Soc., 1993. Mem. N.C. Hist. Assn., English Speaking Union, Internat. Platform Assn., Mint Mus. Drama Guild (pres. 1967-69), Internat. Biog. Ctr. Eng. (dep. dir. gen.), Heritage Found. (pres. 1994), Empower Am. (leadership coun. 1995), Daus. Am. Colonists (state chmn. nat. def. 1973-74, corr. sec. Virginia Dare chpt. 1978-79, 84-85, state insignia chmn. 1979-80), DAR (nat. chmn.'s assn., rec. sec. nat. officers club 1990—, chpt. regent 1957-59, chpt. chaplain 1955-57, N.C. program chmn. 1961-63, state chmn. nat. def. 1973-76, state rec. sec. 1977-79, hon. state regent for life, chmn. N.C. Geneal. Register 1982, nat. vice chmn. S.E. region Am. Indians 1989—, rec. sec. Nat. Officers Club 1990-92, v.p. N.C. State Officer's Club 1991-92, pres. 1992-94), Children Am. Revolution (N.C. sr. pres. 1963-66, sr. nat. corr. sec. 1966-68, sr. nat. 1st v.p. 1968-70, sr. nat. pres. 1970-72, hon. sr. nat. pres. life 1972—, 2d v.p. Nat. Officers Club, 1st v.p. 1977-79, pres. 1979-81), Huguenot Soc. N.C., Carmel Country Club (Charlotte), Viewpoint 24 Club (v.p. 1986, pres. 1987). Home: 1514 S Wendover Rd Charlotte NC 28211-1726

HUDIAK, DAVID MICHAEL, academic administrator, lawyer; b. Darby, Pa., June 27, 1953; s. Michael Paul and Sophie Marie (Glowaski) H.; m. Veronica Ann Barbone, Aug. 28, 1982; children: David Michael, Christopher Andrew, Jonathan Joseph. BA, Haverford Coll., 1975; JD, U. Pa., 1978. Bar: Pa. 1979, U.S. Dist. Ct. (ea. dist.) Pa. 1979, NJ 1981, U.S. Dist. Ct. NJ 1981. Assoc. Jerome H. Ellis, Phila., 1978-79, Berson, Fineman & Bernstein, Phila., 1979-80; pvt. practice Aldan, Pa., 1980-81; dir. tng. paralegal program PJA Sch., Upper Darby, Pa., 1982—, acting dir., 1983-89, dir., 1989—; v.p. The PJA Sch., Inc., 1989—, bd. dirs.; v.p., sec.-treas., bd. dirs. 7900 West Chester Pike Corp., 1994—. Mem. staff Nat. Ctr. Ednl. Testing, Phila., 1982-87; instr. Villanova (Pa.) U., 1985. Mem. Havertown Choristers; active U. Pa. Light Opera Co., 1977—84; mem. 10th Synod Archdiocese of Phila., 2002; active mem., parish coun., lector, cantor St. Eugene Parish. Mem. ABA, Pa. Bar Assn., Founders Club Haverford Coll. Office: PJA Sch 7900 W Chester Pike Upper Darby PA 19082-1917

HUDICK, ANDREW MICHAEL, II, finance executive; b. Holly Springs, Miss., May 11, 1958; s. Joseph Frank and Marie Carmella (Peters) Hudick; m. Anne-Marie Gwynn, Oct. 3, 1998. BSCE, U. Va., 1980; Cert. fin. planner, Coll. for Fin. Planning, 1982, MS in Retirement Planning, 1991. Cert. fin. planner, Coll. for Fin. Planning, 1982. Engr. Norfolk & Western Rwy., Roanoke, Va., 1980-81; prin., founder, head Fee-Only Fin. Planning, L.C., Roanoke, 1981—. Adj. faculty Va. Polytech. and State U., 1994—96. Contbr. Bd. dirs. Assn. retarded Citizens, Roanoke, 1985, Mental Health Assn., Roanoke, 1984—86, treas., 1986; chmn. spkrs. bur. United Way Roanoke Valley, 1985—86. Named Outstanding Vol., Va. Skyline Girl Scout Coun., 1986, One of Top 60 Fin. Advisors, Worth Mag., 1994, One of Top 200 Fin. Advisors, 1996, One of Top 250 Fin. Advisors, 1997, One of Top 300 Fin. Planners, 1998, One of Top 120 Fin. Advisors for Physicians, Med. Econs. Mag., 1998, One of Top 150 Fin. Advisors, 2000, One of Top 100 Fin. Advisors, Mut. Fund Mag., 2001; recipient Disting. Svc. award, Mental Health Assn., 1984, 1986, Outstanding Svc. award, United Way Roanoke Valley, 1986, One of Top 100 Fin. Advisors, Mut. Fund Mag., 2002. Mem.: Internat. Bd. Stds. and Practices for Cert. Fin. Planners (bd. examiners 1989—93), Internat. Assn. Fin. Planning (pres. 1987—88), Nat. Assn. Personal Fin. Advisors (v.p. 1993, treas. 1994, pres. 1995—96, bd. dirs.), Inst. Cert. Fin. Planners (cert.), Toastmasters (treas. Roanoke 1984—85, pres. 1985, gov. dist. 66 1986, advanced spkg. cert.). Avocation: handball, croquet, bridge. Office: Fee-Only Financial Planning LC 355 Campbell Ave SW Roanoke VA 24016-3624

HUDIK, MARTIN FRANCIS, hospital administrator, educator, consultant, writer; b. Chgo., Mar. 27, 1949; s. Joseph and Rose (Ricker) H.; m. Eileen Hudik; 1 child, Theresa Margaret. BS in Mech. and Aerospace Engring., Ill. Inst. Tech., 1971; BPA, Jackson State U., 1974; MBA, Loyola U., 1975; postgrad., U. Sarasota, 1975-76; AAS in Engring., Morton Coll., 1969. Cert. health care safety mgr., hazard control mgr., hazardous materials mgr., OSHA hazardous materials response instr., hazardous materials incident comdr., disaster coord., police instr., Ill., security cert. instr., Ill. With Ill. Masonic Med. Ctr., Chgo., 1969-94, dir. risk mgmt., 1974-79, asst. adminstr., 1979-94; facilities engring. mgr. Bethany/Adv. Hosp., 1997-98; health care cons., 2000—; bus. mgr. St. Bernadine Parish, 2001—. Capt. tng. divsn. Cicero (Ill.) Police Dept., tng. and internal affairs divsn., aux. divsn., 1971-99, U.S. Dept. Commerce, 2000, ind. cons., 2000; instr. Nat. Safety Coun. Safety Tng. Inst., Chgo., 1977-85; cons. mem. Coun. Tech. users Consumer Products, Underwriters Labs., Chgo., 1977-96; instr., lt. U.S. Def. Civil Preparedness Agy. Staff Coll., Battle Creek, Mich., 1977-85; liaison officer to Cook County Emergency Svcs.; asst. dir. Emergency Svcs. and disaster Agy. Town of Cicero, 1988-97; pres. Cook County Emergency Mgmt. Coun., 1991-92; exec. bd., pres. U.S. Postal Svc. Postal Customer Adv. Coun., Cicero, 1996-99; mem. exec. bd. Chicagoland Postal Adv. Coun., 1994—; exec. bd. advisor Cicero PCAC, 1998—. Pres. sch. bd. Mary Queen of Heaven Sch., Cicero, 1977-79, 84-86, Mary Queen of Heaven Ch. Coun., 1979-81, 83-86, St. Leonard Parish Coun., 1998-2001, I.M.M.C. Employee Club, 1983-86; co-chmn. Archdiocese of Chicago Deanery IV-C, 1999—; mem. Cath. Edn. Com., 2000—, Archdiocese of Chgo. Pastoral Coun., 2000—. Recipient Presdl. Sports award, Amateur Athletic Union, 1978, 1980, 1981, 2000, Meritorious Svc. award, Town of Cicero, 1990, Spl. Svc. award Underwriters Lab., 1992, medal of Merit, 1996, Emergency Svcs. Achievement award, 1997, Police Achievement award, 1998, Spl. Svc. award, Cook County Sheriffs Dept., 1993, Excellence in Svc. award, U.S. Postal Svc., 1997, Outstanding Effort award, 1998, Outstanding Svcs. award, Cicero Postal Coun., 1998, Svc. Recognition award, 1999, Outstanding Performance award, 2001, Volunteerism award, U.S. Postal Svc., 2002, Svc. Recognition award, Archdiocese of Chgo., 2003; scholar state scholar, Ill., 1969—71. Mem. Am. Coll. Healthcare Execs., Am. Soc. Hosp. Risk Mgmt., Nat. Fire Protection Assn., Am. Soc. SafetyEngrs. (profl.), Am. Soc. Law and Medicine, Ill. Hosp. Security and Safety Assn. (co-founder 1976, founding pres. 1976-77, hon. dir. 1977-82), Cath. Alumni Club Chgo. (bd. dirs. 1983-84, 86), Mensa, Masons (Berwyn, Ill. chpt.), KC (mem. 4th degree cardinal coun., Svc. award 2002), Pi Tau Sigma, Tau Beta Pi, Alpha Sigma Nu. Republican. Roman Catholic. Home: 2116 S 51st Ct Cicero IL 60804-2345 Office: 6845 Riverside Dr Berwyn IL 60402-2231

HUDKINS, JAMES ALLEN, accountant; b. Oakland, Calif., June 3, 1953; s. Robert Getty and Violet Mildred (Williamson) H. AA in Bus., Coll. of Alameda, 1973, AA in Computers, 1999; BA in Acctg., San Francisco State U., 1975. CPA, Calif. Tax auditor State of Calif., Monterey, 1975-76; audit sr. Fox & Co., CPA's, Oakland, 1976-78; sr. acct., auditor Wallace, Meyer & Co., CPA's, Oakland, 1978-80; mgr., broker, appraiser Pacific Bus. Sales, Oakland, 1980-85; mgr., appraiser Valuation Counselors, Inc., San Francisco, 1985-87; mortgage broker Fin. Transaction Corp., Alameda, Calif., 1987-89; pvt. practice

Alameda, 1989—. Mem. Nat. Eagle Scout Soc., Northwestern Pacific R.R. Hist. Soc. Libertarian. Lutheran. Avocations: hiking, history, geography, movies, reading, railroads. Home and Office: 3319 Central Ave Alameda CA 94501-3110 E-mail: JAHudkins@prodigy.net.

HUDKINS, JOHN W. lawyer; b. Inglewood, Calif., Jan. 12, 1946; s. Ralph Emerson and Genevieve Delores H.; m. Diana Byler, Feb. 16, 1969. BA, Calif. State U., Hayward, 1968; MBA, U. Nev., Las Vegas, 1971; JD, U. of Pacific, 1976; LLM, George Washington U., 1983. Bar: Iowa 1976, Calif. 1977, U.S. Ct. Mil. Appeals 1976, Fla. 1995. Commd. 2d lt. USAF, 1968, advanced through grades to lt. col., 1983, ret., 1988; sr. counsel Aerojet-Gen. Corp., Sacramento, 1988-94; dir. bus. mgmt. Olin Ordnance, Downey, Calif., 1994-95, sr. counsel St. Petersburg, Fla., 1995-96, v.p., chief counsel, 1996-97; v.p., dep. gen. counsel Primex Tech., Inc., St. Petersburg, Fla., 1997-2001; dep. gen. counsel Gen. Dynamics Ordnance and Tactical Sys., 2001—. Bd. dirs. Vandenberg Fed. Credit Union, Lompoc, Calif., 1983-85, Prince William (Va.) County Soccer Assn., 1985-88. Mem. ABA (pub. contract law sect.), Nat. Security Indsl. Assn. (chair legal com.). Home: 1339 Forestedge Blvd Oldsmar FL 34677-5119 Office: Gen Dynamics Ordnance and Tactical Sys 10101 9th St N Saint Petersburg FL 33716 E-mail: jwhudkins@stp.gd-ots.com.

HUDNALL, JARRETT, JR., management and marketing educator; b. Rhome, Tex., Oct. 6, 1931; s. Jarrett and Katherine (Wilson) H.; m. Sarah Ruth Warren, Nov. 24, 1955; children: Jarrett Joseph, William Warren, Katherine Lee, Thomas Wilson. Student, Arlington (Tex.) State Coll., 1948-50; BBA, U. Tex., Austin, 1953, MBA, 1956; PhD, U. Ala., 1966. Lectr. U. Tex., 1955-56; asst. prof. Arlington State Coll., 1956-58; instr. U. Ala., 1958-61; asst. prof. La. Tech. U., 1961-62, assoc. prof. mktg., 1962-67, prof., head dept. bus., 1967-77; exec. Superior Supply Co., Inc., 1978-83, P&A div. Ciba-Geigy, 1983-84; v.p. Rohcar, Inc., 1984-90; prof. mgmt. and mktg. Stephen F. Austin State U., Nacogdoches, Tex., 1985-92; dean coll. bus. and commerce U. West Ala., Livingston, 1992-94; prof. mktg. Miss. U. for Women, Columbus, 1994—2002; emeritus; emeritus designee Assn. Collegiate Bus. Schs. & Programs, 2002—. Vice pres. Ctrl. Asian Cons., LLC; bd. dirs. SBI; cons. firms in chem. fertilizer, petroleum, farm equipment mfg., bus.; cons. agrl. and econ. devel. products W. Republic of Uzbekistan, 1995; vis. prof. mktg. Huron U., London, 2000, 02. Author: (with A.L. Secyle) Compensation of Retail Department Store and Specialty Store Salesman in Major Texas Cities, 1957, Attitudes of Gulf Service Station Dealers Toward Minor Tuneup and Repair Work, 1963, An Economic Analysis of Income and Employment in a Four-State Deep South Region, 1950-60, 1966. Lt. AUS, 1953-55. Gulf Oil Corp. fellow, 1963. Mem. Am. Mktg. Assn., So. Mktg. Assn., S.W. Fedn. Allied Disciplines, Am. Collegiate Retailing Assn., So. and Southwestern Bus. Dean's Assn., Small Bus. Inst. Dirs.' Assn., Allied Academies, Sigma Iota Epsilon, Beta Gamma Sigma, Alpha Kappa Psi, Kappa Delta Pi. Democrat. Baptist. Home: 1003 Lakeview Dr Ruston LA 71270-5233 E-mail: jhud@cox-internet.com.

HUDNALL, STANLEY DAVID, pathology and laboratory medicine educator; b. Auburn, Ala., May 28, 1951; BS, U. of S.C., 1973; MD, Med. U. of S.C., 1978. Lic. anatomical and clin. pathology Am. Bd. of Pathology, hematology Am. Bd. of Pathology. Resident in pathology Yale U. Sch. of Medicine, New Haven, 1978—82; rsch. fellow in pathology Harvard Med. Sch., Boston, 1982—84; asst. prof. of pathology UCLA Sch. of Medicine, L.A., 1984—92, Baylor Coll. of Medicine, Houston, 1992—94; prof. of pathology U. of Tex. Med. Br., Galveston, 1994—. Chief divsn. of hematopathology U. Tex. Med. Br., Galveston, 1994—. Contbr. rsch. articles and book chpts. Recipient Carolina scholarship, U. of S.C., 1969—73. Fellow: Coll. of Am. Pathology; mem.: Am. Soc. for Investigative Pathology, U.S. - Can. Acad. of Pathology, Am. Soc. for Microbiology, Am. Soc. of Hematology, Phi Beta Kappa. Achievements include patents pending for techniques for rapid identification of human herpesviruses. Office: U Tex Med Br 301 University Blvd Galveston TX 77555-0741 E-mail: shudnall@utmb.edu.

HUDNER, PHILIP, lawyer, rancher; b. San Jose, Calif., Feb. 24, 1931; s. Paul Joseph and Mary E. (Dooling) H.; m. Carla Raven, Aug. 6, 1966; children: Paul Theodor, Mary Carla. BA with great distinction, Stanford U., 1952, LL.B., 1955. Bar: Calif. 1955. Lawyer Pillsbury, Madison & Sutro, San Francisco, 1958—, ptnr., 1970-99, Botto Law Group, San Francisco, 1999—; rancher San Benito County, Calif., 1970—. Asst. editor: Stanford Law Rev., 1954-55; author articles on estate and trust law. Pres. Soc. Calif. Pioneers, 1976-78, Louise M. Davies Found., 2002—, Drum Found., 1985—. Served with U.S. Army, 1956-58. Fellow Am. Bar Found.; mem. Internat. Acad. Estate and Trust Law (steering com. 1974-75, exec. coun. 1980-85), San Benito County Saddle Horse Assn., Order of Malta, Phi Beta Kappa, Pacific Union Club, Lagunitas Country Club, Frontier Boys, Bohemian Club, Rancheros Visitadores. Democrat. Roman Catholic. Office: Botto Law Group 180 Montgomery St Fl 16 San Francisco CA 94104-3104 Fax: 415-364-0075. E-mail: phudner@bottolaw.com.

HUDNUT, DAVID BEECHER, retired leasing company executive, lawyer; b. Cin., Feb. 21, 1935; s. William Herbert and Elizabeth Allen (Kilborne) H.; m. Robin Fraser, Apr. 12, 1958; children: David Beecher, Marjorie Elizabeth, Joshua Fraser, John Marshall, Benjamin Parker. AB, Princeton U., 1957; JD, Cornell U., 1962. Bar: N.Y. 1962, U.S. Supreme Ct. 1967. Assoc. Hughes, Hubbard & Reed, N.Y.C., 1962-67; with Ind. and chem. products div. Ford Motor Co., 1967-69; v.p. U.S. Leasing Internat., Inc., San Francisco, 1969-76, sr. v.p., 1976-90. Bd. dirs. Gary. D. Nelson Assocs., Inc., 1995—, Bread and Roses, 1995-2001, chmn., 1999-2001, Cameron House Found., 1979-98, pres., 1980-92; bd. dirs. Svcs. for Srs., 1970-96, pres. 1990-92, No. Calif. Presbyn. Homes, 1971-77, chmn., 1973-76, 79-86; bd. dirs. Edgewood Children's Ctr., 1979-86, Ind. Colls. No. Calif., 1981-84; mem. adv. bd. Alumnae resources, 1982-94; mem. Calif. Hist. Soc., 1986-92, pres. 1989-91; mem. Calif. Hist. Found., 1997—, chmn., 1999—. Home: 9 Via Capistrano Belvedere Tiburon CA 94920-2030

HUDNUT, ROBERT KILBORNE, clergyman, author; b. Cin., Jan. 7, 1934; s. William Herbert and Elizabeth (Kilborne) H.; m. Mary Lou Lundell; children by previous marriage: Heidi, Robert Kilborne, Heather, Matthew. BA with highest honors, Princeton, 1956; M.Div., Union Theol. Sem., N.Y.C., 1959. Ordained to ministry Presbyn. Ch., 1959; asst. minister Westminster Presbyn. Ch., Albany, N.Y., 1959-62; minister St. Luke Presbyn. Ch., Wayzata, Minn., 1962-73, Winnetka (Ill.) Presbyn. Ch., 1975-94. Exec. dir. Minn. Pub. Interest Research Group, 1973-75; Co-chmn. Minn. Joint Religious Legis. Coalition, 1970-75 Author: Surprised by God, 1967, A Sensitive Man and the Christ, 1971, A Thinking Man and the Christ, 1971, The Sleeping Giant: Arousing Church Power in America, 1971, An Active Man and the Christ, 1972, Arousing the Sleeping Giant: How to Organize Your Church for Action, 1973, Church Growth Is Not the Point, 1975, The Bootstrap Fallacy: What The Self-Help Books Don't Tell You, 1978, This People-This Parish, 1986, Meeting God in the Darkness, 1989, Emerson's Aesthetic, 1996, Call Waiting, 1999. Pres. Greater Met. Fedn. Twin Cities, 1970—72; chmn. Citizens Adv. Com. on Interstate 394444, 1971—75; mem. planning commn. City of Cottage Grove, Minn., 2001—; chmn. Dem. Party 33d Senatorial Dist. Minn., 1970—72, Minnetonka Dem. Party, 1970—72; fusion candidate for mayor City of Albany, 1961; nat. chmn. Presbyns. for Ch. Renewal, 1971; bd. dirs. Minn. Coun. Chs., 1964—70; trustee Princeton U., 1972—76, Asheville (N.C.) Sch., 1979—2003. Rockefeller fellow, 1956; named Outstanding Young Man Minnetonka, 1967; recipient Distinguished Service award Minnetonka Tchrs. Assn., 1969 Mem. Phi Beta Kappa. Home and Office: 7145 65th St S Cottage Grove MN 55016-1130 E-mail: rkhudnut@aol.com.

HUDNUT, WILLIAM HERBERT, III, senior resident fellow, political scientist; b. Cin., Oct. 17, 1932; s. William Herbert Jr. and Elizabeth (Kilborne) H.; m. Beverly Guidara; children: Michael Conger, Laura Anne, Timothy Norton, William Herbert IV, Theodore Beecher, Christopher Shew. BA magna cum laude, Princeton, 1954; MDiv summa cum laude, Union Theol. Sem., N.Y.C., 1957; DD (hon.), Hanover Coll., 1967, Wabash Coll., 1969; LLD (hon.), Butler U., 1980, Anderson Coll., 1982, Franklin Coll., 1983, Millikin U., 1987, Ind. U., 1994, Elmhurst Coll., 1996; LLD (hon.), Youngstown State U., 2002; LittD (hon.), U. Indpls., 1981; DPS (hon.), Blackburn Coll., 1987. Ordained to ministry Presbyn. Ch., 1957; asst. minister Westminster Ch., Buffalo, 1957-60; pastor 1st Presbyn. Ch., Annapolis, Md., 1960-63; dir. Westminster Found., Annapolis, 1960-63; sr. minister 2d Presbyn. Ch., Indpls., 1963-72; mem. 93d Congress from Ind., 1973-74; dir. dept. community affairs Ind. Central U., Indpls., 1975; mayor City of Indpls., 1976-91; fellow Inst. Politics Harvard U., 1992; sr. fellow Hudson Inst., Indpls., 1992-94; pres. Civic Fedn., Chgo., 1994-96; sr. resident fellow The Urban Land Inst., Washington, 1996—. Mem. Presdl. Adv. Com. on Federalism, 1981-84. Author: Minister/Mayor, 1987, The Hudnut Years in Indianapolis, 1976-1991, 1995, Cities on the Rebound, 1998, Halfway to Everywhere, 2003; editor: Union Sem. Quar. Rev., 1956-57; contbr. sermons, articles to profl. publs. Mem. Bd. Pub. Safety, Indpls., 1970-71, Rep. Nat. Com., 1987; pres. Anne Arundel County Mental Health Assn., 1961-63; pres., bd. dirs. Marion County Mental Health Assn., 1966-68, Westminster Found., Purdue U., 1969-73; bd. dirs. Cmty. Svc. Coun. Met. Indpls., 1964-68, Family Svc. Assn., 1966-72, Flanner House, 1968-72; pres. trustees Darrow Sch., New Lebanon, N.Y., 1968-75; Task Force on Fed. Deficit, 1981; mem. Adv. Commn. on Intergovtl. Rels., 1984-90; bd. dirs. Indpls. Ctr. for Adv. Rsch., 1976-91, Humane Soc., 1983-91; trustee Roosevelt Ctr. Am. Policy Studies, Washington, 1984-87; Pleasant Run Children's Home Found. bd., 1992-94, Children's Home & Aid Soc. Ill., 1994-96; co-vice chmn. Alliance for Redesigning Govt., 1992-2000; mem. Police Found. Bd., 1997—; mem. Nat. Assn. Securities Dealers Regulation Bd., 1996-98, Nat. Adjudicatory Coun., 1998; mem. accreditatio bd. Am. Planning Assn., 1998—2001; mem. Town Coun., Chevy Chase, Md., 2000—; active Millenial Housing Com., 2000—2001. Recipient William Booth award Salvation Army, 1984, Russell G. Lloyd disting. svc. award Ind. Assn. Cities and Towns, 1985, Rosa Parks award Am. Assn. for Affirmative Action, 1992, Woodrow Wilson award Princeton U., 1986, disting. urban mayor award Nat. Urban Coalition, 1987; named All-Pro City Mgmt. Team, City and State mag., 1986, 89, 92; fellow Nat. Acad. Pub. Adminstrn., 1994—. Mem. Columbia Club Indpls. (bd. dir. 1994-96), Kiwanis, Masons (33 deg.), Phi Beta Kappa. Office: The Urban Land Inst 1025 Thomas Jefferson St NW Washington DC 20007-5201 E-mail: bhudnut@uli.org. *Life is relationships, and whatever we can do to enlighten and strengthen each other, in the family circle, among our friends, in business, in society at large, will help. This requires ardor and self-surrender, faith, hope and humor.*

HUDSON, ALAN C.H. music educator, tropical fruit farmer; s. George Clyde and Lydia Helena Hudson; m. Cathy Lee Horne, Jan. 6, 1973; children: Emma Jean, Amanda Lynn. B in Music Edn., Boston U., 1973. String tchr. Milford (Mass.) Schs., 1973—74; gen. music tchr. Airbase Elem. Sch., Miami, 1974—75, orch. tchr., Redland Mid. Sch., Miami, 1975—98, Coral Reef Sr. H.S., Miami, 1998—. Recipient Fla. Orchestral Tchr. of Yr. award, Am. String Tchrs. Assn., 2002. Mem.: Fla. Orchestral Assn. (v.p. 1998—98). Avocations: lychee farming, violin repair.

HUDSON, ALAN PAUL, microbiologist, educator, research scientist; b. Batavia, N.Y., Dec. 7, 1948; s. Eldon North and Helen Louise Hudson; m. Judith Ann Whittum, Dec. 24, 1983. PhD, CUNY, 1978. Asst. prof. microbiology MCP-Hahnemann Sch. Medicine, Phila., 1986—92, assoc. prof. microbiology, 1992—97; assoc. prof. microbiology Sch. Medicine Wayne State U., Detroit, 1997—2000, prof. microbiology Sch. Medicine, 2000—. Grantee, NIH, various pvt. founds., VA Med. Rsch. Svc. Mem.: Am. Soc. Microbiology. Achievements include discovery of defined host-pathogen interaction for Chlamydia during reactive arthritis. Office: Wayne State U Sch Medicine 540 East Canfield Ave Detroit MI 48201 E-mail: ahudson@med.wayne.edu.

HUDSON, ANTHONY WEBSTER, retired federal agency administrator, minister; b. Durham, NC, Mar. 23, 1937; s. Emanuel and Adele (Nixon) H.; m. Glenda Buchanan, Jan. 18, 1964 (div. Dec. 1996; children— April Lynn, Verna Lea; m. Maude Harrison, Aug. 23, 1997. Student, Rutgers U., 1954-59, Columbia, 1960-62, George Washington U., 1967-69, Wesley Theol. Sem., 1991-95. Ordained chaplain United Ch. of Christ, 1995. Pers. mgmt. specialist U.S. Civil Service Commn., N.Y.C., 1962-65; tng. officer personnel div. Washington, 1966; tng. officer Bur. Tng., 1967; coordinator Project 250 Bur. Tng., 1968-70; dir. personnel, 1970-74; dir. fed. EEO, 1974-77; staff dir. personnel Def. Logistics Agy., 1977-92; assoc. minister People's Congregational Ch., 1995-2001; chaplain Springvale Terrace, from 1995; interim min. Lincoln Congl. Temple, from 1999. Chmn. personnel adminstrn. faculty USDA Grad. Sch. Contbr. to Ency. of Edn, 1971, Homily Service, 2001. Trustee Govt. Svcs., Inc., Washington; chmn. merit pers. bd. Md.-D.C. Park and Planning Commn., Silver Spring, 1974-86; mem. Fed. Pers. Mgmt. Career Bd.; pres. bd. dirs. Worldwide Assurance for Employees of Pub. Agys.; chmn. Montgomery County Merit Sys. Protection Bd., 1989-95. 1st lt. arty. U.S. Army, 1959-60. Recipient Spl. citation U.S. Civil Service Commn., 1969, William A. Jump Meml. award, 1970. Meritorious Svc. award Def. Logistics Agy., 1980, Exceptional Svc. award, 1986; inducted into Def. Logistics Agy. Hall of Fame, 1998. Mem. ASTD (exec. bd., chmn. cmty. svcs. 1966-68), D.C. Sociol. Soc., Am. Personnel and Guidance Assn., Soc. Personnel Adminstrn. (exec. com. 1971-74), Internat. Personnel Mgmt. Assn. (exec. coun. 1977). Am. Sociol. Assn. (employment com. 1971-74), Am. Fgn. Svc. Assn., NAACP, Am. Soc. on Aging, Coll. of Chaplains, Phi Sigma Delta. Home: Chevy Chase, Md. Died Aug. 9, 2003.

HUDSON, BARBARA, religious writer, actor; b. St. James, Minn., Feb. 2, 1921; d. Lloyd Edwin and Lois (Hardin) H.; m. Jesse Wilbert Powers, Oct. 27, 1946 (div. Apr. 1970); children: Jean Lois, Cathy Colleen; m. Lawrence Kneeland Dudley, Dec. 5, 1971 (div. Apr. 1979). BA, U. Iowa, 1942; MA, U. So. Calif., 1952. Tchr. drama, speech Southgate (Calif.) H.S., 1944-45; youth dir. Hollywood (Calif.) Presbyn. Ch., 1945-47; tech. writer secret publications Litton Industries, Canoga Park, Calif., 1959—61; assoc. prof. Calif. Luth. U., Thousand Oaks, 1961-75; missionary Calvary Cmty. Ch., Westlake Village, Calif., 1980—. Author: The Henrietta Mears Story, 1958, Where Is God, 1970, God's Power in Your Life, 1971, Bridge of Nothing Less, 1975, (videos) Women of the Bible, 1990; writer, prodr., dir. (pageant) Here I Stand, 1967, Bridge of Nothing Less, 1975, Forward in Faith, 1975, God of the Mountain, 1952-57; contbr. articles to profl. jours.; internat. touring in one woman show Women of Glory, 1982—. 2d lt. in 1st officer's class USMCWR, 1943—45, U.S. Mem. Gamma Phi Beta, Zeta Phi Eta, Pi Kappa Delta (Diamond award 1939). Republican. Home: Box 3722 Thousand Oaks CA 91359 Office: PO Box 3722 Thousand Oaks CA 91359

HUDSON, BRADFORD TAYLOR, management educator; b. Ithaca, NY, Dec. 17, 1962; s. John Boswell and Sandra Lee (Chermak) H. BA, U. Pa., 1984; M in Profl. Studies, Cornell U., 1993. Sr. cons. TQM Group, Boston, 1993-94; pres. Hudson Cons., 1994—2001; asst. prof. Boston U., 1995-96, 2002—; CEO Bay Tower, Inc., Boston, 1998-2000. CEO Brandpoint.com, Cambridge, 1996-98, chmn., 1998-2001; guest lectr. Harvard U., Cambridge, 1998-99. Contbr. articles to profl. publ. Page to spkr. US Ho. Reps., Washington, 1980; aide Presdl. Inaugural Com., Washington, 1981. Lt. (O-3) USN, 1984-89. Decorated Navy Achievement medal and Battle "E" commendation USN, 1989; named among Top 100 Ind. Restaurant Co. in USA, Restaurants and Instns. Mag., 1999-2000. Episcopalian. Office: Boston Univ Ste 200 808 Commonwealth Ave Boston MA 02215 E-mail: bhudson@bu.edu.

HUDSON, CELESTE NUTTING, education educator, reading clinic administrator, consultant; b. Nashville, Sept. 18, 1927; d. John Winthrop Chandler and Hilda Bass (Alexander) Nutting; m. Frank Alden Hudson III, Dec. 30, 1948 (dec.); m. Robert Daniel Quartell, June 3, 1989; children: Frank Alden Hudson IV (dec.), Jo Ann Hudson Algermissen, Celeste Jane Hudson Norman, Jack Winthrop N. Hudson. BS, Oreg. Coll. Edn., 1952; MS, So. Ill. U., 1963, PhD, 1973. Cert. tchr., Tenn., Oreg., Mo., Iowa. Tchr. pub. schs., Crossville, Tenn., 1949-51, Salem, Oreg., 1952-53, West Walnut Manor, Mo., 1953-54, Normandy Sch. Dist., St. Louis County, Mo., 1954-66; reading coord. Sikeston (Mo.) Pub. Schs., 1966-69, Charleston, Mo., 1969-72; traveling cons. Ednl. Devel. Labs., Huntington, N.Y., 1970-71; mem. clin. staff So. Ill. U. Reading Ctr., 1972; asst. prof. edn. St. Ambrose Coll., 1972-75, U. Tenn., Chattanooga, 1975-76; project dir. Learning Skills Ctr. St. Ambrose U. (formerly St. Ambrose Coll.), 1976-80, asst. prof. edn., 1976-78, assoc. prof., 1979-86, prof., 1986-94, prof. emeritus, 1995—. Dir. elem. edn. St. Ambrose U., 1972-94, chmn. dept. edn., 1980-84, divsn. chmn., 1984-87, faculty vice-chair, 1989-90, faculty chair, 1990-91; cons. in field. Author: Handbook for Remedial Reading, 1967, Cognitive Listening and the Reading of Second Grade Children, 1973, The Effect of Visual Fatigue on Reading, 1990, Longitudinal Study of Children in Clinical Reading, 1994. Mem. Kimberly Village Bd., Davenport, Iowa, 1979-83; chmn. worship com., Asbury Meth. Ch., 1985-90, choir, 1978-98, mem. bell choir, 1995-97; co-chmn. Sarah Cir., 1996-99; mem. Trinity Hosp. Aux., 2001—. Mem.: AARP, DAR (Hist. Soc., real granddaughter), AAUW (Lit. club), AAUP, Normandy Ret. Tchrs. Assn., Orgn. Tchr. Educators Reading, Davenport Area Ret. Tchrs. Assn., Assn. Tchrs. Educators, Internat. Reading Assn. (Scott County coun.), Iowa Assn. Colls. Tchr. Edn. (exec. bd. 1989—92), United Daus. of Confederacy, United Daus. of the Confederacy (3rd v.p. 1966—70), New Eng. Women (pres.-elect 1994—95, pres. 1996—2003), Renaissance Dance Club, Real Granddaughter Club, Quad City Women's Investment Club (treas. 2001—), Original Music Students Club (corr. sec. 1995—96), Bettendorf Lionels (treas. 1998—2002), Phi Delta Kappa, Kappa Delta Pi (sponsor 1974—96), Alpha Delta Kappa (past pres.). Address: St Ambrose U Box E 140 518 W Locust St Davenport IA 52803-2829

HUDSON, CHARLES DAUGHERTY, insurance executive; b. La Grange, Ga., Mar. 17, 1927; s. J.D. and Janie (Hill) H.; m. Ida Cason Callaway, May 1, 1955; children: Jane Alice Hudson Craig, Ellen Pinson Hudson Harris, Charles Daugherty, Ida Hudson Russell. Student, Auburn U., 1945-48, LHD (hon.), 1992; LLD, La Grange Coll.; LHD (hon.), Mercer U., 1987. Ptnr. Hudson Hardware Co., La Grange, 1950-57, Hammond-Hudson Ins. Agy., La Grange, 1957-58, owner, 1958-78; pres. Hammond, Hudson & Holder INc., 1978-94, chmn. bd., 1994—. Bd. dirs., mem. exec. com. Citizens & So. Nat. Bank, La Grange, 1964-90; bd. dirs. Citizens & So. Ga. Corp., Citizens & So. Nat. Bank, Atlanta, C&S Investment Advisors, Inc., Atlanta, C&S Ga. Corp.; acting pres. La Grange Coll., 1979-80; v.p., bd. dirs. la Grange Industries, 1956—, Hudson Maddox Enterprises, 1965-95; ptnr. PCH Properties, 1981—; chmn. bd. dirs. First Annuity Corp., La Grange; bd. dirs., chmn. trust com. NationsBank of Ga. Recipient Pres.'s award Colonial Life Ins. Co., 1966, 69-70, 75-80, Disting. Alumni award Ga. Mil. Acad.-Woodward Acad., 1971, Disting. Svc. award Ga. Hosp. Assn., 1980, Respect Law award Optimists Assn., 1977, Van Landingham Commitment to Edn. award, 1996, Pub. Svc. award Ga. Assn. AIA, 1977, Leading Producer award Aetna Life and Casualty, 1979; Paul Harris fellow, 1984. Mem. Am. Legion, Ga. Assn. Ind. Ins. Agts., Ga. Sch. Bd. Assn. (area dir.), SAR, Amicale de Group LaFayette (hon.). Chattahoochee Valley Art Assn., La Grange C. of C. (bd. dirs.), Newcomen Soc. N.Am., Ga. Hosp. Assn. (trustee 1980—), U. Ga. Gridiron Secret Soc., Highland Country Club (chmn. bd. 1999—), Lafayette Club, Commerce Club Atlanta, Aetna Life and Casualty Presidents, Masons, Shriners, Elks, Rotary (pres. 1964-65), Sigma Alpha Epsilon, Beta Gamma Sigma. Home: 407 Country Club Rd Lagrange GA 30240-2031 Office: Hammond Hudson & Holder Inc 206 W Haralson St Lagrange GA 30240-2722

HUDSON, CHRISTOPHER GILES, social worker, educator; b. Casper, Wyo., June 24, 1949; s. Benjamin and Jean (Barlow) H.; m. Barbara Berger, Dec. 10, 1983; children: Daniel, Elisabeth. BA, U. Chgo., 1971, MA, 1974; PhD, U. Ill., Chgo., 1983. Cert. by Acad. Cert. Social Workers. Psychiatric social worker Northeast Hosps., Chgo., 1974-75; sch. social worker Bd. Edn., Chgo., 1975-76; caseworker Jewish Family Svc., Chgo., 1977-80; asst. prof. social work George Williams Coll., Downers Grove, Ill., 1983-86, East Carolina U., Greenville, N.C., 1987; assoc. prof. Salem (Mass.) State Coll., 1987-92, prof., 1992—, exec. dir. Ctr. for Applied R&D, 1997—2001. Bd. dirs. Family Network, Salem, 1989—; pres. Northshore Mental Health Bd. Dept. Mental Health, Mass., 1998-2002. Editor Dimensions of State Mental Health Policy, 1991; author: An Interdependency Model of Homelessness, 1999; contbr. articles to profl. jours. Recipient Rschr. of Yr. award Alliance for the Mentally Ill., Mass., 1999; fellow NIMH, 1981, 82; Fulbright sr. fellow, Hong Kong, 2002-03. Mem. NASW (Mass. chpt., bd. dirs. 1990-94, 98-2000), Coun. on Social Work Edn., Acad. Cert. Social Workers. Office: Salem State Coll 352 Lafayette St Salem MA 01970-5348

HUDSON, CHRISTOPHER JOHN, publisher; b. Watford, Eng., June 8, 1948; s. Joseph Edward and Gladys Jenny Patricia (Madgwick) Hudson; m. Lois Jeanne Lyons, June 16, 1979; children: Thomas, Ellen, Ronald, Timothy, Jonas. BA with honors, Cambridge U., Eng., 1969, MA with honors, 1972. Promotion mgr. Prentice-Hall Internat., Eng., 1969-70, area mgr., 1970-71, mktg. mgr., 1971-74, dir. mktg., 1974-76, asst. v.p., 1976; group internat. dir. I.T.T. Pub., N.Y.C., 1976-77; pres. Focal Press, Inc., N.Y.C., 1977-82; v.p., pub. Aperture Found. Inc., N.Y.C., 1983-86; head publs. J. Paul Getty Trust, L.A., 1986—. Author: Guide to International Book Fairs, 1976; pub. Aperture, 1983-86, J. Paul Getty Mus. Jour., 1986—. Mem. adv. coun. Nat. Heritage Village, Kioni, Greece; mem. trade with eastern Europe com. Assn. Am. Pubs., N.Y., 1976-79, internat. fairs com., 1986-88. Mem.: Internat. Assn. Scholarly Pubs. (sec.-gen. 1994—97, chmn. internat. contracts com.), Internat. Pubs. Assn., U.S. Mus. Publ. Group (chmn. 1989—), Internat. Assn. Mus. Publs. (Frankfurt, Fed. Republic Germany chmn. 1992—95), Hellenic Soc. (London), Travelers' Century Club (bd.dirs.), Oxford & Cambridge Club (London). Avocations: rural preservation projects in england, greece and california. Office: J Paul Getty Mus 1200 Getty Ctr Dr Ste 1000 Los Angeles CA 90049-1687

HUDSON, DARRIL, political scientist, educator; b. Trousdale, Okla., Dec. 18, 1931; s. Frank Wilks Hudson and Emma Lee (Jackson) Van Meter. BA, U. Calif., Berkeley, 1954; MSc in Internat. Rels., London Sch. Econs & Polit. Sci, 1960, PhD, 1965. Lectr. U. Md. Overseas Program, 1959-67; assoc. prof. Md. State Coll., Princess Anne, Md., 1967-68; prof. Calif. State U., Hayward, 1968-93, prof. emeritus, 1993—; vis. prof. Am. U., Paris, 1992-93. Resident dir. German program Calif. State U., Heidelberg, Fed. Republic Germany, 1990-91; Fulbright prof. U. Heidelberg, 1981-82. Author: A Visitor's Guide to American Home Cooking, 1989, The World Council of Churches in International Affairs, 1978, The Ecumenical Movement in World Affairs, 1968. 1st lt. Intelligence Svc., U.S. Army, 1955-58. Rsch. fellow Alexander von Humboldt Found., Bonn, Heidelberg, Fed. Republic Germany, 1966-67, 75, 89; recipient H.C. Richards prize Gray's Inn, London, 1965. Mem. Am. Friends of Paris Opera, Conservatory of Music San Francisco, San Francisco Opera Assn. Democrat. Avocations: cooking, writing, travelling. Home: 443 Fair Oaks St San Francisco CA 94110-3618 E-mail: darrilh@yahoo.com.

HUDSON, DENNIS LEE, lawyer, retired government official, arbitrator, educator; b. St. Louis, Jan. 5, 1936; s. Lewis Jefferson and Helen Mabel (Buchanan) H.; children: Karen Marie, Karla Sue, Mary Ashley. BA, U. Ill., 1958; JD, John Marshall Law Sch., 1972. Bar: Ill. 1972, U.S. Dist. Ct. (so. and no. dists.) Ill. 1972. Ins. IRS, Chgo., 1962-72; spl. agt. GSA, Chgo., 1972-78, spl. agt.-in-charge, 1978-83, regional insp. gen., 1983-87; supervisory spl. agt. Dept. Justice-GSA Task Force, Washington, 1978; arbitrator Circuit Ct. Cook County, Ill., 1987-93; prof. criminal justice Coll. of DuPage, Glen Ellyn, Ill., 1996—. Mem. adv. bd. Suburban Law Enforcement Acad., Glen Ellyn, Ill., 1999—; mem. adv. bd. campus police Coll. DuPage, Glen Ellyn, 1999—; deacon Grace Luth. Ch., La Grange, Ill., 1977—81; lay eucharistic min. All Sts. Episcopal Ch., Western Springs, Ill., 1999—; bd. govs. Theatre Western Springs, Ill., 1978—81, 1991—92; bd. dirs. Pendulum Theatre Co., Chgo., 2001—. With U.S. Army, 1959—61. John N. Jewett scholar, 1972, Am. Jurisprudence shcolar, 1972. Mem. ABA, Ill. Bar Assn. Office: Coll Dupage Bus & Svcs Div 22D St Lambert Rd Glen Ellyn IL 60137 E-mail: hudsond@cdnet.cod.edu.

HUDSON, DONALD J. retired stock exchange executive; b. Vancouver, B.C., Can., Sept. 26, 1930; BA in Econs. and Math., U. B.C., 1952; LLD (hon.), Simon Fraser U., 1993. With Shell Oil Co. of Can. Ltd., 1952-53; dir. sales devel. Can. Pacific Airlines, Vancouver, 1953-64; sr. v.p. Pacific div. T. Eaton Co., Ltd., Vancouver, 1964-81; pres. Vancouver Stock Exch., 1982-95. Bd. dirs. Internat. Fin. Ctr., Vancouver; trustee Endowment Fund YMCA Greater Vancouver; past chmn. bd. govs., Simon Fraser U., 1988-90; past chmn., bd. trustees, St. Paul's Hosp., 1983-85. Mem.: Vancouver Club, Vancouver Lawn Tennis Club.

HUDSON, EDWARD RANDALL, JR., gas, oil industry executive; b. Ft. Worth, Tex., July 24, 1934; s. Edward Randall and Josphine Terrell (Smith) H.; m. Ann Frasher, Sept. 19, 1959; children: Edward Randall III, Frasher Hudson Pergande. BA, U. Tex., 1955; JD, Harvard U., 1958. Owner, oil prodr. Hudson Oil, Ft. Worth. Vice-chmn. cultural property com. U.S. Info. Agy.; bd. dirs. Kimbell Art Found., Aspen Ctr. Physics; sec. bd. dirs. Burnett Found.; chmn. bd. dirs. Modern Art Mus. Ft. Worth; nat. com., founding co-chmn. bd. dirs. Aspen Art Mus. Mem. Ft. Worth Club, River Crest Country Club, Argyle, Knickerbocker, Steeplechase, Order of the Alamo, Phi Beta Kappa. Avocations:

art collector contemporary U.S. and folk art. Home: 55 Westover Ter Fort Worth TX 76107-3106 also: 750 Castle Creek Dr Aspen CO 81611-1138 Office: Hudson Oil 616 Texas St Fort Worth TX 76102-4696 E-mail: eh34@compuserve.com.

HUDSON, EDWARD VOYLE, linen supply company executive; b. Seymour, Mo., Apr. 3, 1915; s. Marion A. and Alma (Von Gonten) H.; m. Margaret Carolyn Greely, Dec. 24, 1939; children: Edward G., Carolyn K. Student, Bellingham Normal Coll., 1933-36, U. Wash., 1938. Asst. to mgr. Natural Hard Metal Co., Bellingham, 1935—37; ptnr. Met. Laundry Co., Tacoma, 1938—39; propr., mgr. Peerless Laundry & Linen Supply Co., Tacoma, 1939—. Propr. Ind. Laundry & Everett Linen Supply Co., 1946-74, 99 Cleaners and Launderers Co., Tacoma, 1957-59; chmn. Tacoma Pub. Utilities, 1959-60; trustee United Mut. Savs. Bank; bd. dirs. Tacoma Better Bus. Bur., 1977—; mem. regional bd., SBA, 1965. Pres. Wash. Conf. on Unemployment Compensation, 1975-76; pres. Tacoma Boys' Club, 1970; v.p. Puget Sound USO, 1972-91; elder Emmanuel Presbyn. Ch., 1974—; past campaign mgr., pres. Tacoma-Pierce County United Good Neighbors. Recipient Disting. Citizen's cert. USAF Mil. Airlift Com., 1977; U.S. Dept. Def. medal for outstanding pub. svc., 1978. Mem. Tacoma Sales and Mktg. Execs. (pres. 1957-58), Pacific NW Laundry, Dry Clearning and Linen Supply Assn. (pres. 1959, treas. 1965-75), Internat. Fabricare Inst. (dir. dist. 7, treas. 1979, pres. 1982), Am. Security Coun. Bd., Tacoma C. of C. (pres. 1965), Air Force Assn. (pres. Tacoma chpt. 1976-77, v.p. Wash. state 1983-84, pres. 1985-86), Navy League, Puget Sound Indsl. Devel. Coun. (chmn. 1967), Tacoma-Ft. Lewis Olympia Army Assn. (past pres.), Elks Club (vice chmn. bd. trustees 1984, chmn. 1985-86), Shriners (potentate 1979), Masons, Scottish Rite, Tacoma Club, Tacoma Country and Golf Club, Jesters Club, Rotary (pres. Tacoma chpt. 1967-68), Tacoma Knife and Fork Club (pres. 1964). Republican. Home: 3901 N 37th St Tacoma WA 98407-5636 Office: Peerless Laundry & Linen Supply Co 2902 S 12th St Tacoma WA 98405-2598

HUDSON, FRANKLIN, real estate developer, lawyer; b. N.Y.C., Nov. 1948; s. Alec N. Hudson. BBA., Sam Houston State U., 1971; JD, St. Mary's U., 1974. Bar: Tex. 1975, U.S. Dist. Ct. (so. dist.) Tex. 1979, U.S. Supreme Ct., U.S. Ct. of Appeals, Atlanta, New Orleans and San Francisco, Mem. Nat. Assn. Home Builders, Nat. Multi Family Council, State Bar Assn. Tex. Office: c/o PO Box 460029 Houston TX 77056-8029

HUDSON, FRANKLIN DONALD, diversified company executive, consultant; b. Asheville, N.C., July 21, 1933; s. Halbert Austin and Lillian Naomi (Cook) H.; m. Rosemary Wheatley, Dec. 1, 1956; children: Lawrence Jamison, Lauren Jean. B.E.E., Yale U., 1955; MBA, NYU, 1962; postgrad., Pace U., 1972-75. Sales rep. RCA, N.Y.C., 1959-62; Latin Am. gen. mgr. Fed. Pacific Electric Co., P.R., 1962-68; dir. mktg. GTE Sylvania, 1968-71; dir. Home Equipment div. Singer Co., N.Y.C., 1971-75; v.p. internat. Corometrics Med. Systems, Inc., Wallingford, Conn., 1975-78; v.p. planning and devel. Norlin Corp., White Plains, N.Y., 1978-81; founder, exec. v.p. Integrated Genetics, Inc., 1981-85; founder, bd. dirs. Organogenesis Inc., 1985-89; founder, pres. TSI Corp., 1987-90, Protarga, Inc., 1990-93; biotech. cons., 1995—; pres., dir. VIMRX Pharms., Inc., Stamford, Conn., 1994-95. Chmn. Bio-Brite, Inc., 1990—; adj. prof. NYU, Boston U. Mem. Conn. Rep. Fin. Com., 1968-74; asst. dir. Campaign for Yale, 1978; trustee Quinsigamond Coll., 1989-92; mem. bd. overseers Boston Symphony Orch., 1993-2002. Capt. USAF, 1956-58. Mem. Russell Trust Assn., Assn. Yale U. Alumni (bd. dirs.), Longwood Cricket Club, Sippican Tennis Club, Kittansett Club, Mory's Club, Hawk's Nest Golf Club, Tau Beta Pi. Episcopalian.

HUDSON, FREDERICK BERNARD, management consultant; b. Chgo., Oct. 29, 1947; s. Joseph Thomas and Nellie (Parham) H.; m. Yvonne Marjorie Hudson, July 9, 1994. BA, Wayne State U., 1969; postgrad., Yale U., 1969—70; MA, New Sch. Social Rsch., 1975. Registered city planner, Am. Inst. City Planners, 1979. Adminstr. cmty. rels. for N.J. Odyssey Ho., N.Y.C., 1971-73; spl. program asst. Nat. Urban League, N.Y.C., 1973-75; rsch. assoc. Afram Assocs., N.Y.C., 1975; program cons. City Univ. Rsch. Found., N.Y.C., 1975-76; project dir. Elon Michels and Assocs., Detroit, 1977—78; staff analyst Detroit City Coun., 1978-79; vis. asst. prof., coord. So. Ill. U., Edwardsville, 1979-80; dir. pub. rels. Frederick Douglass Creative Arts Ctr., N.Y.C., 1981-82; ednl. officer Am. Bus. Inst., N.Y.C., 1986-89; pres. Centaur Consultants, N.Y.C., 1983—. Mem. faculty Coll. New Rochelle, So. Ill. U., Ednl. Found. Dist. Coun. 37 (local of Am. Fedn. State, County and Mcpl. Employees); Am. Bus. Inst. Mgmt. and Comm. cons. to Coro Found., Asia Pacific Found., NuArtist Prodns., Milw. Ednl. Found., New Future Found., MicroBanking Network, AT & T, Reality Ho., Nat. Drug Prevention Week, Fed. Emergency Mgmt. Adminstrn., Yale Coun. Cmty. Affairs, N.J. Dept. Correction, and various candidates for state and nat. polit. offices; presenter in field. Prodr. (TV program) Take It to the Hill, 1995-99; guest and commentator numerous TV and radio programs, including HBO and ABC News; contbr. opinion columns to mags., poems to lit. jours. and anthology; co-author (jazz oratorio) Let Us Now Praise Righteous Men, 1969; author: What's In a Number? An Evaluation of a Title I Program, 1965, A Business Plan for a Multi-National Entertainment E-Commerce Business, 2000; screenwriter (TV drama) Things We Take, 1992; prodr. (TV series) The Undercover Man, 1993-95. Organizer Nat. Action Network, 1995—, Oct. 22 Movement, 2000—, Internat. Action Ctr., 2000—; hon. chmn. small bus. adv. coun. Nat. Rep. Congl. Com. Recipient Mayor's commendation, City of Newark, 1974, Emerging New Writer award, PEN, 1984, Outstanding Achievement in Poetry Silver award cup Internat. Soc. Poets, 2002, 03; name inscribed on Wall of Tolerance, Montgomery, Ala., 2002. Mem. Am. Mgmt. Assn., Film Video Arts Assn., Mensa. Office: Centaur Consultants 1510 E 172 St Ste 4 Bronx NY 10472 E-mail: fhdson@aol.com.

HUDSON, HAROLD JORDON, JR., retired insurance executive; b. Kansas City, Mo., Mar. 10, 1924; s. Harold Jordan and Fannie (Jenkins) H.; m. Patricia Louise Orr, Oct. 1, 1949. BS, U. Mo., 1945, LL.B., 1948; grad., Advanced Mgmt. Program, Harvard U., 1968. Bar: Mo. 1948. Practiced in, Kansas City, until 1952; atty. Comml. Union Co., Kansas City, 1952-53, Cleve., 1953-56; with Gen. Reins. Corp., N.Y.C., 1956-83, asst. sec., 1958-61, sec., 1961-62, v.p., 1963-68, sr. v.p., 1968-70, pres., 1970-71, 1971-72, chief exec. officer, 1971-83, chmn., 1973-83, also dir. Chmn. Reins. Assn. Am., 1975-76. Mem. Mo. Bar, Phi Delta Phi, Kappa Alpha. Clubs: Brook (N.Y.C.); Indian Harbor Yacht, Greenwich Country (Greenwich, Conn.); Cat Cay Yacht (Bahamas); Card Sound Golf. Office: PO Box 10350 Stamford CT 06904-2350

HUDSON, JEFFREY REID, lawyer; b. Santa Monica, Calif., Mar. 15, 1952; s. Caswell Hadden and Donna Rita (Mazzulla) H.; children: Joan Louise, Reid Adams. BA, Claremont McKenna Coll., 1974; JD, Harvard U., 1978. Bar: Calif. 1978. Assoc. Gibson, Dunn & Crutcher, L.A., 1978-85, ptnr., 1986—. Office: Gibson Dunn & Crutcher 333 S Grand Ave Ste 4400 Los Angeles CA 90071-3197

HUDSON, JOHN BOSWELL, sociologist, educator; b. Decatur, Ill., Dec. 1, 1930; s. George Taylor and Margaret Shirley (Boswell) H.; m. Sandra Lee Cermak, Mar. 16, 1957; children: Scott Martin, Bradford Taylor. Student, Reed Coll., 1948-51; BA, U. Oreg., 1952; MA, U. Wash., 1956; postgrad., Cornell U., 1957-60, PhD, 1963. Asst. prof. sociology Humboldt State U., Arcata, Calif., 1960-61, Cornell U., Ithaca, N.Y., 1961-64, Lehigh U., Bethlehem, Pa., 1964-65, Syracuse (N.Y.) U., 1965-66; rsch. assoc. Harvard U., 1966-67; rsch. sociologist Mass. Dept. Mental Health, Boston, 1967-68; sr. sociologist Abt Assocs., Inc., Cambridge, Mass., 1968-69; prof. sociology Trent U., Peterborough, Ont., Can., 1969-73; asst. adminstr. Brockton (Mass.) Multi-Svc. Ctr., 1973-74; lectr. bus. adminstrn. Northeastern U., Boston, 1974-76; cons. Cambridge, 1976-78; pres., treas. Cambridge Condominium Collaborative, Inc., 1978-86, chmn., treas., 1986-93; dir. edn. and tng. DeWolfe New Eng., 1994, v.p. for organizational devel., 1995-97. Vis. scientist dept. behavioral scis. Harvard Sch. Pub. Health, summers 1971, 72, winter-spring, 1973; lectr. real estate Boston U., 1988-90. Author: Creativity and Innovation, 1966, Functional Analysis as a Strategy for Studying Social Change and Stability, 1967, Policy-Oriented Basic Research, 1969, Social Policy and Theoretical Sociology, 1970, An Empirical Validation of Hypothesis-Generating Strategies, 1970, Social Structure and Culture: A Conceptual Analysis, 1971, Perspectives on Offender Rehabilitation, 1971, The Structure of Innovation, 1971, A Proposal for a Center of Innovation, 1971, Nursing Education in Transition, 1972, Residential Care for the Mentally Retarded, 1972, The Interface Between Theory and Practice, 1979, Theory, Practice, and Paradigm Shifts, 1992. Mem. mgmt. com. Sch. Nursing, Peterborough Civic Hosp., 1970-72; bd. dirs. Brockton Area Assn. for Retarded Citizens, 1974-75; mem. City Mgr.'s Cable TV Adv. Com., Cambridge, 1979-85; chmn. Cambridge Condominium Network, 1979-86; docent U. Iowa Mus. Art, 1998—; bd. dirs. Coun. Internat. Visitors to Iowa Cities, 1999-2000, Iowa Arts Coun., 2002--; elected del. Imagine Iowa 2010, 2001. Social Sci. Rsch. Coun. fellow Stanford U., summer 1964; Recipient award of merit Peterborough Assn. for Mentally Retarded, 1972; named Cambridge Realtor of Yr., Greater Boston Real Estate Bd., 1993. Mem. Nat. Assn. Realtors (cert. real estate brokerage mgr. 1989, cert. internat. property specialist 1994, cert. residential specialist 1994, chair internat. adv. group 1997, mem. internat. ops. com. 1997-98), Cmty. Assns. Inst. (named Colleague of Yr. New Eng. chpt. 1985), New Eng. Sociol. Assn. (treas. 1979-82, v.p. 1987-90, pres.-elect 1990-91, pres. 1991-92, Pioneer award 1991). Home: 782 Westside Dr Iowa City IA 52246-4341 E-mail: John.B.Hudson@att.net.

HUDSON, JOHN IRVIN, retired career officer; b. Louisville, Oct. 12, 1932; s. Irvin Hudson and Elizabeth (Reid) Hudson Hornbeck; m. Zetta Ann Yates, June 27, 1954; children: Reid Irvin, Lori Ann, John Yates, Clark Ray BS in Bus. Mgmt., Murray State U., 1971. Commd. 2nd lt. USMC, 1954, advanced through grades to lt. gen., 1987; comdg. officer Marine Fighter Attack Squadron 115, Vietnam, 1968, Marine Corps Air Sta., Yuma, Ariz., 1977-80; asst. wing comdr. 2nd Marine Air Wing, Cherry Point, N.C., 1980-81; comdg. gen. Landing Force Tng. Command/At.,4th Marine Amphibious Brigade, Norfolk, Va., 1981-83, 3rd Marine Aircraft Wing, El Toro, Calif., 1985-87, First Marine Amphibious Force, Campen, Calif., 1986-87; dep. chief staff for manpower Hdqrs. USMC, Washington, 1987-89; dir. U.S. Marine Corps Edn. Ctr., Quantico, Va., 1983-85; ret. active duty Hdqrs. USMC, Washington, 1989. Apptd. to Ariz. State Transp. Bd., 1994-2000, chmn. 1999; apptd. commr. Ariz. Power Authority, 2000—; apptd. bd. dirs. Greater Yuma Port Authority, chmn., 2000-02; operating bd. dirs. Yuma Regional Med. Ctr., 2001—. Decorated DFC, DSM, Bronze Star, Air medals, Silver Hawk; flew 308 combat missions in Vietnam in F-4 Phantom; inductee Early and Pioneer Naval Aviators' Assn., 1998. Mem. VFW, Golden Eagles, Marine Corps Aviation Assn. (life), Marine Corps Assn., Marine Corps Hist. Soc., Order of Daedalians (life). Avocations: sports, sailing, hunting, fishing. Home: 12439 E Del Rico Yuma AZ 85367-7366

HUDSON, JOHN LESTER, chemical engineering educator; b. Chgo., 1937; s. John Jones and Linda Madeline (Panozzo) H.; m. Janette Glenore Caton, June 29, 1963; children: Ann, Barbara, Sarah. BS, U. Ill., 1959; MS in Engring., Princeton U., 1960; PhD, Northwestern U., 1962. Registered profl. engr., Ill. Asst. prof. chm. engring. U. Ill.-Urbana, 1963-69, assoc. prof., 1969-75; prof., chmn. dept. chem. engring. U. Va., Charlottesville, 1975-85, mem. Ctr Advanced Studies, 1985-86, prof., 1986-88, Wills Johnson prof., 1988—. Mgr. Ill. Div. Air Pollution Control, Springfield, 1974-75; cons. to various industires and govt. agys., 1966— Contbr. articles to profl. jours. Recipient sr. Humboldt prize, 1989; NSF fellow, 1962, Fulbright fellow, 1961-63, 82-83. Mem. AIChE (Wilhelm award 1991), Am. Chem. Soc. Home: 1920 Thomson Rd Charlottesville VA 22903-2419 Office: U Va Dept Chem Engring 102 Engineers Wy Box 400741 Charlottesville VA 22904-4741 E-mail: hudson@virginia.edu.

HUDSON, JUDITH ANNE, developmental psychologist, researcher; PhD in Developmental Psychology, CUNY, 1984. Asst. prof., psychology SUNY, Albany, NY, 1984—87; assoc. prof. psychology Rutgers U., New Brunswick, 1987—. Rsch. dir. Douglass-Psychology Child Study Ctr., New Brunswick, NJ, 1988—. Editor: Knowing and Remembering in Young Children. Fellow: APA (divsn. 7); mem.: Valentine Chatenay Soc., Cognitive Develoment Soc., Soc. for Rsch. in Child Devel., Am. Psychol. Soc. Office: Dept Psychology Rutgers U 53 Ave E Piscataway NJ 08854-8040

HUDSON, KAREN ANN SAMPSON, music educator; b. Greenville, Mich., Nov. 1, 1946; d. Elton J. Sampson and Freda Sampson Grunwald; m. James Gary Hudson, May 23, 1970; children: Alexander E., Annemarie M., Elaine K., Veronica L. BA, U. Mich., 1968. Piano tchr. Karen Hudson's Piano Studio, Reno, 1994—. Lay Carmelite Little Flower Lay Carmelites, Reno, 1997—. Mem.: Nat. Music Tchrs. Assn., Autism Soc. Am. Democrat. Home: 2055 Severn Dr Reno NV 89503

HUDSON, KATE, actress; b. L.A., Calif., Apr. 19, 1979; m. Chris Robinson, Dec. 31, 2000. Actor: (films) Desert Blue, 1998, Ricochet River, 1998, 200 Cigarettes, 1999, About Adam, 2000, Gossip, 2000, Almost Famous, 2000 (Golden Globe award for Best Supporting Actress, 2001), Dr. T and the Women, 2000, The Cutting Room, 2001, The Four Feathers, 2002, How to Lose a Guy in 10 Days, 2003, Alex and Emma, 2003, Le Divorce, 2003; (TV series) Party of Five, 1996, EZ Streets, 1997.*

HUDSON, KATHERINE MARY, manufacturing company executive; b. Rochester, N.Y., Jan. 19, 1947; d. Edward Klock and Helen Mary (Rubacha) Nellis; m. Robert Orneal Hudson, Sept. 13, 1980; 1 child, Robert Klock. Student, Oberlin coll., 1964-66; BS in Mgmt., Ind. U., 1968; postgrad., Cornell U., 1968-69. Various postitions in fin., investor rels., communications, gen. mgr. instant photography Eastman Kodak Co., Rochester, 1970-87, chief info. officer, 1988-91, v.p., gen. mgr. printing and pub. imaging, 1991-93; pres., CEO W.H. Brady, Milw., 1994—, Brady Corp., Milw., 1999—. Bd. dirs. CNH Global N.V. Mem. adv. coun. Ind. U. Sch. Bus., 1994—; trustee Alverno Coll., 1994—; bd. dirs. Med. Coll. Wis., 1995—. Recipient Chief of the Yr. award Info. Week Mag., 1990, Athena award Rochester C. of C., 1992, WESG Breaking Glass Ceiling award, 1993, Sacajewea award, 1995; Lehman fellow N.Y. State, 1968; named Wis. Bus. Leader of Yr., 1995. Republican. Avocations: golf, fishing, creative writing. Office: Brady Corp 6555 W Good Hope Rd PO Box 571 Milwaukee WI 53201-0571 E-mail: kathy_hudson@bradycorp.com.

HUDSON, MANLEY O., JR., lawyer; b. Boston, June 25, 1932; s. Manley O. and Janet (Aldrich) H.; m. Olivia d'Ormesson, July 1, 1971 (dec. May 2000); children: Nicholas Aldrich, Antonia Maria Conchita. AB, Harvard U., 1953, LL.B., 1956. Bar: N.Y. 1964. Law clk. Justice Stanley Reed, U.S. Supreme Ct., Washington, 1956-57; assoc. Cleary, Gottlieb, Steen & Hamilton, 1958-68, ptnr., 1968—2001. Contbr. articles to profl. jours. Mem. Coun. Fgn. Rels., Century Assn. Office: Cleary Gottlieb Steen & Hamilton City Place House 55 Basinghall St London EC2V 5EH England Business E-Mail: mhudson@cgsh.com.

HUDSON, MARGUERITE W. secondary school educator; b. Pitkin, La., June 10, 1929; BS, Northwestern State U., 1949; MA in Edn., No. Colo. U., 1951; MA in English Arts, Northwestern State U., 1969. Tchr. scis. Ouachita Parish H.S., Monroe, La., 1949—50, Haynesville (La.) High Sch., 1951—61, Bossier High Sch., Bossier City, La., 1961—69; instr. English Bossier Parish C.C., Bossier City, 1970—79, Centenary Coll., Shreveport, La., 1982—83; tchr., supr. Ga. Mil. Acad., Barksdale AFB, 1980—90; sch. bd. mem., pres. Bossier Sch. Bd., Benton, La., 1991—98; ret., 1991. Named one of 100 Outstanding Women of Century. Mem.: NEA, La. Educators Assn. Democrat. Baptist. Avocation: water skiing, dancing, creative writing class, travel, Bridge. Home: 4497 Palmetto Rd Benton LA 71006

HUDSON, MARK WOODBRIDGE, lawyer; b. Pasadena, Calif., May 14, 1940; s. Victor Stuart and Mary Charlotte (Woodbridge) H.; m. Marsha Fae Alderson, Dec. 20, 1969; children: Peter, Ashley, Holly. BA, U. Calif., Berkeley, 1961; JD, U. Calif., Hastings, 1967. Bar: Calif., 1968, U.S. Dist. Ct. 1968, U.S. Ct. Appeals (9th cir.) 1968. Atty. Dunn, Hart & McDonald, San Francisco, 1968-73; assoc. Sedgwick, Detert, Moran & Arnold, San Francisco, 1973-78, ptnr., 1979—98; atty. Fortune, Drevlow, O'Sullivan, Ciotoli & Hudson, San Francisco, 1998—. 1st lt. U.S. Army, 1961-63. Mem. Calif. Bar Assn., Assn. Def. Counsel, San Francisco Bar Assn. Democrat. Home: 15 Robertson Ter Mill Valley CA 94941-3358 Office: Drevlow O'Sullivan Ciotoli & Hudson 560 Mission St San Francisco CA 94105

HUDSON, MARY KAY, executive; b. Memphis, May 27, 1948; d. Charles Page Parrish and Mary Geneva Parks; m. Henry Alexander Hudson Jr., Nov. 8, 1969. BS in Edn., Memphis State U., 1970. Officer Turkey Pine Plantation, Inc. Author: Register of Qualified Soldiers/Patriots of the American Revolution Buried in Tennessee, 2000; contbr. articles to mags. Dir. Millington (Tenn.) Resource Ctr., Mid South Hosp., Memphis, 1990-91; exec. sec. Millington C. of C., 1991-92; pres. Med.-Dental Officer Wives Club, Naval Air Sta., Millington, 1986-87, Officer Wives Club, Millington, 1994-95. Mem.: Descs. of Early Settlers of Shelby County Tenn. and Adjoining Counties, Early Settlers of Marshall County Miss., Nat. Soc. Sons and Daus. Antebellum Planters 1607-1861, Nat. Soc. So. Dames Am., U.S. Daus. 1812 (organizer Piomingo chpt., pres. 1991—94), Nat. Soc. Colonial Dames XVII Century (vol. genealogist 1997—), Nat. Soc. DAR (organizer River City chpt. 1990, vol. genealogist 1998—, chpt. regent for life 2000—), Sons and Daus. Pilgrims (Tenn. branch gov. 1999—2001, hon. life Tenn. br. gov.), Dames of Ct. Honor (Tenn. state pres. 1999—2001, hon. life Tenn. state pres.), Colonial Dames of Am., United Daus. of Confederacy (pres. Gayoso chpt. 1998—2000, Jefferson Davis medal 2000, Winnie Davis medal 2000), Colonial Order of Crown (life), Jamestowne Soc. (life; organizing gov. First Miss. Co. 2000—), Nat. Soc. Daus. Founders and Patriots Am. (life), Nat. Soc. Magna Charta Dames and Barons (life), Presdl. Families of Am. (life), Order Ams. Armorial Ancestry (life), The Phantagenet Soc. (life), The Soc. Descendants of Knights of Most Noble Order of Garter (life). Avocations: genealogy, travel, tennis, growing irises, collecting early postcards. Home: PO Box 653 Sumrall MS 39482-0653

HUDSON, MCKINLEY, army officer, retired zoo deputy director; b. Cin., May 13, 1941; BS, Ctrl. State U., Wilberforce, Ohio, 1963; MS, So. Ill. U., 1974; MA, Naval War Coll., Newport, R.I., 1986. Commd. 2d lt. U.S. Army, 1963, advanced through grades to col., 1985, retired, 1993, commdr. 548th composite support battalion, 1983-85, commdr. 80th area support group, 1986-88, chief of staff mil. traffic mgmt. command Oakland, Calif., 1988-93; dep. dir. Nat. Zoological Park Smithsonian Instn., Washington, 1994—2002. Decorated Legion of Merit, Bronze Star with Oak Leaf cluster. Mem. Assn. U.S. Army, Assn. Am. Zoos and Aquariums, U.S. Army Transp. Corps. Regiment (Disting. Mem. Regiment 1993), Nat. Defense Transp. Assn. (Nat. award for disting. svc. 1992), Kappa Alpha Psi. Home: 13 Cabin Creek Ct Burtonsville MD 20866

HUDSON, MICHAEL CRAIG, political science educator; b. New Haven, Conn., June 2, 1938; s. Robert Bowman and Joan (Loram) H.; m. Vera George Wahbe, June 16, 1963; children: Leila Olga, Aida Joan. BA with honors, Swarthmore Coll., 1959; MA, Yale U., 1960, PhD, 1964; Cert. in Arabic, Princeton U., 1961. History tchr. Am. Community Sch., Beirut, 1962-63; instr. Swarthmore (Pa.) Coll., 1963-64; asst. prof. Bklyn. Coll., CUNY, N.Y.C., 1964-70; assoc. prof. Johns Hopkins U., Sch. Advanced Internat. Studies, Washington, 1970-75; assoc. to prof. Georgetown U., Washington, 1975—; dir. Georgetown U. Ctr. for Contemporary Arab Studies, Washington, 1976—89, 1999—2000, 2003—; Seif Ghobash prof. of Arab studies Sch. Fgn. Svc. Georgetown U., Washington, 1980—. Bd. dirs. Nat. Council on U.S./Arab Rels., Washington; cons., lectr. U.S. State Dept.; commentator on Middle Ea. affairs to U.S. and internat. news media; lectr. at univs. in Mid. East, Europe, Japan, China, Australia. Mem. editorial bd. Internat. Jour. of Middle East Studies, 1980-86, Cambridge U. Press Mid. East Studies, 1989-98; author: The Precarious Republic (Lebanon), 1968, Arab Politics: The Search for Legitimacy, 1977; co-author: World Handbook of Political and Social Indicators, 1972; editor: The Palestinians: New Directions, 1990, Middle East Dilemma: The Politics and Economics of Arab Integration, 1999; contbr. numerous articles to jours. in field. Bd. dirs Ctr. for Middle East Studies, Macquarie U., Sydney, Australia. Robert R. McCormick fellow Yale U., 1959-63, fellow Ford Found., 1970-71, Guggenheim fellow, 1975-76, Fulbright fellow, 1994; grantee Am. Philos. Soc., 1965, 68. Fellow Middle East Studies Assn. of N.Am. (pres. 1987); mem. The Middle East Inst., Am. Polit. Sci. Assn., Internat. Studies Assn., Coun. on Fgn. Rels., Am. Inst. Yemeni Studies. Avocations: drawing, painting, book collecting, swimming, running. Office: Georgetown U Ctr for Contemporary Arab Studies Sch Fgn Svc 251 Intercultural Ctr Washington DC 20057-1020 E-mail: hvdsonm@georgetown.edu.

HUDSON, MICHAEL DARREN, agricultural economics educator; m. Lisa J. Maul, Dec. 6, 1991; children: Nathaniel Thomas, Haley Elisabeth. BS, West Tex. A&M U., 1992; MS, Tex. Tech U., 1994, PhD, 1997. Assoc. prof. Miss. State U., Mississippi State, 1998—. Editor: (book) Proceedings: FTAA, the WTO, and Domestic Farm Policy; contbr. book, articles to profl. jours. Den leader Boy Scouts Am., Starkville, Miss., 2001—02. Nat. Rsch. Initiative grantee, USDA, 1999—2001. Mem.: Miss. Agrl. Econs. Assn. (pres. 2001—02), Western Agrl. Econs. Assn., So. Agrl. Econs. Assn., Food Distbn. Rsch. Soc. (editl. bd. mem. 1999—2002), Am. Agrl. Econs. Assn. (v.p. agribusiness sect. 2002—), Am. Econ. Assn.

HUDSON, MICHEL COLETTE, consultant; b. Houston; d. Arthur James and Dorothy Ann (Newton) Rutrough; m. Scott V. Hudson; 1 child, David. BA, U. St. Thomas, Houston, 1982. Cert. fund raising exec. CFRE Profl. Certification Bd., 2001. Dir. devel. info. systems U. St. Thomas, Houston, 1983—85; coord. alumni/devel. rsch. and records U. Mo., Columbia, 1987—90, mgr. alumni/devel. rsch. and records, 1990—95; dir. devel. svcs. Seton Healthcare Network, Austin, Tex., 1995—97, v.p. devel. svcs., 1997—2001; campaign mgr. centennial campaigns The Seton Fund, Austin, Tex., 2001—01; owner Gnu Gap Consulting, Round Rock, Tex., 2001—. Online instr. FUNDCLASS, 1998, 2003; instr. fund raising mgmt. cert. program U. Tex., Austin, 2000—; instr. Austin C.C. Ctr. for Cmty.-Based and Nonprofit Orgns., 2003; presenter in field. Contbr. articles to profl. jours. Membership svcs. coord., hospitality chair Columbia Art League, 1993—95; v.p. Columbia Choral Ensemble, 1994—95. Mem.: Writers League Tex. (fundraising com. 1998—99), Am. Prospect Rsch. Assn.-Mo. Chpt. (pres., v.p., newsletter editor/pub. 1992—95), Internat. Assn. Theater and Stage Employees (trustee 1994—95), Assn. Profl. Rschrs. for Advancement (pres., conf. chair, membership svcs. dir. 1994—2001, Disting. Svc. award 2003), Cir. of Friends (sec./publ. design 1997—2003). Office: Gnu Gap Consulting 1805 Gnu Gap Round Rock TX 78664 E-mail: gnugap@yahoo.com.

HUDSON, MILES, retired special education educator; b. Brewer, Maine, Aug. 22, 1940; s. Fredrick and Elsie (Bailey) H. BS, U. Maine, Farmington, 1963. Cert. spl. edn. tchr., Maine, Mass. Founder, program coord. spl. edn. program, Millinocket, Maine, 1963-68; founder spl. edn. class MDI H.S., Bar Harbor, Maine, 1968-70; unit leader spl. edn. Methuen (Mass.) Pub. Schs., 1970-74; vocat. spl. edn. tchr. Minuteman Vocational Tech. H.S., Lexington, Mass., 1974-80; spl. edn. tchr. Dr. Franklin Perkins Schs., Lancaster, Mass., 1980-83; head tchr. for autistic and psychotic children Devereaux Found., Rutland, Mass., 1985-86; vocat. instr. Bangor (Maine) Mental Health Inst., 1986-87; program dir. Capacito Learning Ctr., Ellsworth, Maine., 1986-87; spl. edn. tchr., founder summer program Town of Jonesport (Maine) Schs., 1987-90; ret., 1992. Mem. Countywide Regional Tchr. Support Com. Author: Survey of Special Education Classes in Maine, 1963. Home: 307 S Lubec Rd Lubec ME 04652-9627

HUDSON, MILLER NEWTON, public agency manager, consultant; b. St. Louis, Sept. 29, 1945; s. Miller Newton Hudson and Mary Alene Howard; m. Caren Lee Harnest, Nov. 10, 1966 (div. Oct. 1983); children: Byron Richard, Lara Camille; m. Catherine Marie Moyer, Sept. 21, 1985, (div. Dec. 2002). BS in Psychology, U. Md., 1967. Test ctr. mgr. AT&T, Washington, 1967-71; installation mgr. Mountain Bell, Denver, 1972-83; audit mgr. U.S. West, Denver, 1984-86; pvt. practice pub. policy cons. Denver, 1987—98; exec. dir. Colo. Intermountain Fixed Guideway Authority, Denver, 1998—. Dir. excise and licenses City and County Denver, 1987-88. Author (play) Campaigning, 1992 (Best New Play award 1992); contbr articles to profl. jours. State rep. Colo. Legislature, Denver, 1979-83; Dem. party chmn. Denver County, 1983-85; bd. chmn. Kids Voting Colo., Denver, 1994-98. Lt. USN, 1968-70. Named Outstanding Young Leader, Lions Club, Denver, 1980, Outstanding Vol., Assn. Retarded Citizens, Denver, 1988. Avocations: skiing, trail building, hiking, camping, writing. Home: 4906 W 32nd Ave Denver CO 80212 Office: Colo Intermountain Fixed Guideway Authority PO Box 377 Dumont CO 80436 E-mail: mnhwriter@aol.com.

HUDSON, NOEL, artist; b. San Francisco, Dec. 27, 1943; d. Robert Denfeld and Isobel Franklin (Shaw) H.; m. Thomas Donald Reidy, Feb. 20, 1977. BA in Art, Scripps Coll., 1965; MA in Art, Claremont Grad. U., 1972. Instr. in art, ceramics Calif. H.S., Whittier, 1967-70; instr. in art Tachikawa Mid. Sch., Tachikawa AFB, Japan, 1970-73; instr. in painting and drawing Riverside (Calif.) City Coll., 1974; instr. in ceramics, off-loom fiber Redondo Beach (Calif.) H.S., 1974-80; instr. in painting, drawing, design N.Mex. Highlands U., Taos, 1981-83; instr. in drawing No. N.Mex. C.C., Taos, 1991-92; instr. in painting and color theory U. N.Mex., Albuquerque, 1992-93; instr. in painting,

drawing, design, color theory and art history Santa Fe C.C., N.Mex., 1993—. Mem. various coll. coms. Santa Fe C.C.; coord. art tour Taos Art Assn., 1983—84; art cons. Taos Elem. Schs., 1983; bd. dirs. Capitol Art Found., Santa Fe, 2002—. One-woman shows include Wichita Art Mus., 1986, Montoya y Montoya Gallery, Denver, 1989, Southwest Passage Gallery, San Juan Capistrano, Calif., 1991, Greg Flores Gallery, Taos, 1994, The Albuquerque Mus., 1995—2003, Expressions in Fine Art Gallery, Santa Fe, 1997, Sumner & Dene Creations in Art, San Diego, 1998, Represented in permanent collections The Harwood Mus. Art, Taos, Santa Fe C.C., The Capitol Art Collection., N.Mex. State Capitol, Santa Fe. Democrat. Avocations: spiritual investigation, travel, hiking, reading. Home: 59 Balsa Rd Santa Fe NM 87508-8259 Office: Santa Fe CC 6401 Richards Ave Santa Fe NM 87508-4887

HUDSON, PATRICIA ANN SIEGEL, association management specialist; b. Louisville, Mar. 29, 1955; d. Roy John and Theresa (Preate) Siegel. BS in human svc., Pa. State Univ., Scranton, 1977; M psychosocial sci., cert. cmty. psychologist, Pa. State U., Scranton, 1982. Field rep. Am. Cancer Soc., Bethlehem, Pa., 1978-80; teen dir. YWCA, Harrisburg, Pa., 1980-82, mgr. membership devel. AAUW, Washington, 1982-85; mgr. membership Boat Owners Assn., U.S. (BOAT/US), Alexandria, Va., 1985-88; asst. v.p. leadership and membership devel. Nat. Assn. Home Builders, Washington, 1988-95; prin. Siegel and Assoc. Internat., San Francisco, 1995—; founder and pres. Ctr. for Excellence in Assn. Leadership. Cons. to membership based assn., San Francisco, 1995—. Contbg. author: The National Chpt. Partnership, 1993; co-author: Thriving on Change: Discovering the Power of Your Assn. to Affect Soc. Change, 1999; Beyond Membership Mktg.: Developing on Innovative Plan that Guarantees Results, 1999; Get Them Active! Using Icebreakers, Energizers and Summerizers to Enhance Group Productivity, 1999. Recipient Award for Disting. Svc. in Cmty. Psychology, Pa. State U. Harrisburg Campus, 2000. Mem. Am. Soc. Assn. Exec.; cert. trainer, presenter conf. and meetings 1990-95; bd. dir. 1993-95; edn. com. 1995; charter chmn. chpt. rels. sect. 1993-95; award of membership excellence, 1992; cert. assn. exec. 1990. Avocations: reading, travel, walking. Office: 236 W Portal Ave # 782 San Francisco CA 94127-1423

HUDSON, RALPH P. physicist; b. Wellingborough, Eng., Oct. 14, 1924; came to U.S., 1949, naturalized, 1960. s. Harold and Ada (Jenkinson) H.; m. Nancy Brisby, July 9, 1947, children: Geoffrey R., Wendy E. BA, Merton Coll., Oxford U., 1944, MA, PhD, Oxford U., 1949; DSc (hon.), Purdue U., 2001. Sci. officer U.K. Ministry Supply, Birmingham, Eng., Montreal, Que. and Chalk River, Ont., Can., 1944-46; vis. lectr. Purdue U., 1949-50, asst. prof., 1950-51; with Nat. Bur. Standards, Washington, 1951-80, chief cryogenic physics sect., 1954-61, chief heat div., 1961-78; dep. dir. Center for Absolute Phys. Quantities, 1978-80; dir. publs. Internat. Bur. Weights and Measures, Sèvres, France, 1980-89; program dir. low temperature physics NSF, Washington, 1989-92. Cons. in field, 1993—; guest worker fundamental constants data ctr. Nat. Inst. Stds. & Tech., 1998—. Editor: Metrologia, 1980-89, editl. cons., 1995—. Mem. U.K. Home Guard, 1941-43, U.K. Atomic Energy Program, 1944-46. Recipient Silver and Gold medals Dept. Commerce, 1957; Samuel Wesley Stratton award Nat. Bur. Standards, 1964; Edward U. Condon award, 1976; Guggenheim fellow, 1960-61 Fellow Am. Phys. Soc., Franklin Inst. (John Price Wetherill medal 1962); mem. Cosmos Club (Washington). Achievements include spl. rsch. on behavior of matter near absolute zero temperature; first demonstrated the non-conservation of parity in the weak interactions. Home: 5500 Uppingham St Chevy Chase MD 20815-5508 E-mail: ralph.hudson@nist.gov.

HUDSON, RAYMOND ANTHONY, physician; b. Buffalo, Aug. 18, 1921; MD, SUNY, 1944. Intern Erie County Med. Ctr., Buffalo, 1944-45, resident, 1945-46, 48-49; cardiology fellow SUNY, Buffalo, 1949-51; attending Sisters Charity Hosp., Buffalo. Assoc. clin. prof. medicine SUNY, Buffalo. Fellow Am. Coll. Cardiology, Med. Soc. State N.Y. Office: 529 Kings Hwy Buffalo NY 14226-4542

HUDSON, RICHARD L. retired educator, clergyman; b. Watertown, N.Y., Dec. 1, 1920; s. Milo Alfred and Marion (Davidson) H.; m. Beatrice Evalin Olson, Apr. 23, 1955; children: Margery Elise, Pamela Kristine. AB, Syracuse U., 1944, PhD, 1970; BD, Yale U., 1947, STM, 1950. Ordained to ministry United Meth. Ch., 1947. Asst. minister Rome (N.Y.) Meth. Ch., 1946-48, Meth. Ch., Parish, N.Y., 1950-54; commentator Religion Makes News, Sta. WSYR, Syracuse, N.Y.; dir. pub. rels. Syracuse Area United Meth. Ch., 1954-56; minister Meth. Ch., Carthage, N.Y., 1956-58; Cokesbury fellow, grad. asst. Syracuse U., 1958-61; mem. faculty Wyoming Sem., Kingston, Pa., 1961-64, New Eng. Coll., Henniker, N.H., 1964-83, prof., 1971-83, prof. emeritus, 1983—, dean humanities, 1970-71. Adj. prof. history Post Coll., Waterbury, Conn., 1985-91, Quinnipiac Coll., Hamden, Conn., 1987-97. Author: A Burden for Souls, 1950, A Student's Guide to the New Testament, 1963, The Challenge of Dissent, 1970; editor: The Only Henniker on Earth, 1980. Chmn. Henniker Hist. Soc., 1976-83; docent Canterbury Shaker Village, 1975-83, New Haven Colony Hist. Soc., 1984-93, bd. dirs. 1988-90. Mem. Mayflower Soc., Theta Chi Beta, Tau Theta Upsilon, Tabard. Home and Office: 44 Cloudland Rd North Haven CT 06473-4006

HUDSON, RICHARD MCLAIN, JR., journalist, researcher; b. L.A., June 18, 1925; s. Richard McLain Hudson and Helen Theodora Grant; m. Helen Aurora Lundstrom, Dec. 6, 1958; children: Lucinda, Anne. BS, U. Minn., 1946. Teaching asst. econs. U. So. Calif., L.A., 1946-47; editor Monrovia (Calif.) Daily News-Post, 1948-50, Pasadena (Calif.) Star-News, 1950-52, Stars & Stripes, Darmstadt, Germany, 1953-54, Picture News, N.Y.C., 1955-57; mng. editor Caracas (Venezuela) Daily Jour., 1958-60; founding editor War/Peace Report, N.Y.C., 1960-77, Global Report, N.Y.C., 1977—. Exec. dir. Ctr. for War/Peace Studies, N.Y.C., 1960—; host weekly TV series Global Forum, Peace Through the UN, 1986-87; prin. arch. Binding Triad Sys. Global Decision-Making. Author: (with Ben Shahn) Kuboyama and the Saga of the Lucky Dragon, 1965. Mem. Dem. County Com., N.Y., 1980-92. Ensign, USN, 1944-46. Mem. UN Corrs. Assn., World Federalist Assn. (bd. dirs. 1980—). Avocations: fishing, photography, tennis, biking. Home: 150 W 80th St New York NY 10024-6310 Office: Ctr for War/Peace Studies 180 W 80th St # 211 New York NY 10024-6301 E-mail: hudson@cwps.org.

HUDSON, ROBERT FRANKLIN, JR., lawyer; b. Miami, Fla., Sept. 20, 1946; s. Robert Franklin and Jane Ann (Reed) H.; m. Edith Mueller, June 19, 1971; children: Daniel Warren, Patrick Alexander. BSBA in Econs., U. Fla., 1968, JD, 1971; summer cert., U. London, 1970; LLM in Taxation, NYU, 1972. Bar: Fla. 1971, N.Y. 1975. Law clk. to judge Don N. Laramore U.S. Ct. Claims, Washington, 1972-73; assoc. Wender, Murase & White, N.Y.C., 1973-77; ptnr. Arky, Freed, Stearns et al, Miami, 1977-86, Baker & McKenzie, Miami, 1986—, mem. policy com., 1990-93, mem. client credit com., 1992-99, mng. ptnr. Miami office, 1996-98; N. Am. Tax Practice Group Mgmt. com., 2000—. Mem. adv. bd. Tax Mgmt., Inc., Washington, 1986—, Fgn. Investment N.Am., London, 1990-96; legal counsel to her majesty's Britanic Counsel, Miami. Author: Federal Taxation of Foreign Investment in U.S. Real Estate, 1986; contbr. articles to legal publs. Bd. dirs. Fla. Philharmonic, 1996-97, Performing Arts Ctr. Found., 1994—, vice chmn. 2000—; bd. dirs. Concert Assn. Fla., 1992—, exec. com., 1993 98, vice chmn., 1994-98; bd. dirs. Camillus House, 2003—. Mem. ABA, Fla. Bar Assn. (chmn. tax sect. 1989-90, Outstanding Spkr. 1995), Internat. Fiscal Assn. (v.p. S.E. region U.S. br. 1985-92, exec. coun. 1987—), Inter-Am. Bar Assn., Internat. Bar Assn., Internat. Tax Planning Assn., Coll. Tax Lawyers, World Trade Ctr. (bd. dirs. 1992-94), S.E./U.S. Japan Assn., Japan Soc. South Fla. (chmn. pub. affairs com. 1991-93, bd. dirs. 1993-2000, treas. 1995-96, pres. 1996-99 Democrat. Methodist. Avocations: sking, boating, photography, travel, hiking. Office: Baker & McKenzie 1111 Brickell Ave Ste 1700 Miami FL 33131-3257 E-mail: bob.hudson@bakernet.com.

HUDSON, ROBERT PAUL, medical educator; b. Kansas City, Kans., Feb. 23, 1926; s. Chester Lloyd and Jean (Emerson) H.; m. Olive Jean Grimes, Aug. 1, 1948 (div. 1963); children: Robert E., Donald K., Timothy M.; m. Martha Isabelle Holter, July 10, 1965; children: Stephen, Laurel. BA, U. Kans., 1949, MD, 1952; MA, Johns Hopkins U., 1966. Instr. U. Kans., Kansas City, 1958-59, assoc. in medicine, 1959-63, asst. prof., 1964-69, assoc. prof., 1969—, prof., chmn. history of medicine, 1969-95, ret. Author: Disease and Its Control, 1983; mem. editl. bd. Bull. History of Meidcine, Balt., 1981-94; contbr. articles to profl. jours. 1st lt. U.S. Army, 1953-55. Master ACP; mem. Am. Assn. for History of Medicine (pres. 1984-86), Am. Osler Soc. (bd. govs., pres. 1987-88). Home: 12925 S Frontier Rd Olathe KS 66061-8647 Office: Kans U Med Ctr 39th And Rainbow Blvd Kansas City KS 66160-0001 E-mail: rhudsonku@aol.com.

HUDSON, RONALD MORGAN, aviation planner; b. Anniston, Ala., May 7, 1954; s. James Alphus and Mildred Christine (Morgan) H.; m. Marsha Carol Smith, Dec. 27, 1974 (div. Oct. 1989); children: Jereme Brandon, Sara Elizabeth; m. Connie M. Luckey, Nov. 13, 1993. BS in Aviation Mgmt., Auburn U., 1976. Aviation planner Wainwright Engring. Co., Montgomery, Ala., 1978-81, Ralph Burke Assocs., Park Ridge, Ill., 1981-85; sr. assoc. mgr. aviation Knight Architects, Engrs., Planners, Inc., Chgo., 1985-96; assoc. ptnr. Hanson Profl. Svcs. Inc., Oak Brook, Ill., 1996—. Mem. Am. Planning Assn., Am. Inst. Cert. Planners, Am. Assn. Airport Execs., Ill. Pub. Airports Assn. Avocations: biking, travel. Home: 1710 E Oakton St Arlington Heights IL 60004-5000 E-mail: ronaldhudson@comcast.net.

HUDSON, ROY DAVAGE, retired pharmaceutical company executive; b. Chattanooga, June 30, 1930; s. Roy and Everence (Wilkerson) H.; m. Constance Joan Taylor, Aug. 31, 1956; children: Hollye Lynne, David Kendall. BS, Livingstone Coll., 1955; MS, U. Mich., 1957, PhD, 1962; MA, Brown U., 1968; LL.D., Lehigh U., 1974, Princeton, 1975. Asst. prof. pharmacology U. Mich. Sch. Medicine, 1961-66; assoc. prof. med. sci. Brown U. Sch. Medicine, 1966-70, assoc. dean grad. sch., 1966-69; pres. Hampton U., 1970-76; dir. rsch. planning and coordination Parke, Davis Pharm. Co., Ann Arbor, Mich., 1976; v.p. rsch. planning Warner Lambert/Parke-Davis Pharm. Rsch. Divsn., Ann Arbor, 1977-79; mgr. sci. liaison Upjohn Co., Kalamazoo, 1979-81, mgr. CNS diseases rsch., 1981—85, dir. CNS diseases rsch., 1985-87; v.p. pharm. rsch. divsn. Europe Upjohn Co., Brussels, 1987-90; corp. v.p. pub. rels. Upjohn Co., Kalamazoo, 1990-92, ret., 1992. Adj. prof. Black Americana studies Western Mich. U., Kalamazoo, 1993; interim exec. dir., CEO Guidance Clinic, Kalamazoo, 1993; interim pres. Livingstone Coll., Salisbury, N.C., 1995-96; dir. Parke-Davis & Co., United Va. Bank-Citizens and Marine, United Va. Bankshares, Comerica Bank-Mich., Chesapeake and Potomac Telephone Co. of Va. Contbr. articles to profl. jours., chpts. to books. Mem. screening com. Danforth Grad. Fellowships, 1962-78; mem. adv. council Danforth Grad. Fellows program Danforth Found., 1972-79; chmn. Va. Com. on Selection Rhodes Scholars, 1973; mem. Commn. on Fed. Relations, Am. Council on Edn., 1972-76, bd. dirs., 1973-76; mem. adv. council to dir. NIH, 1974—; Mem. R.I. Commn. Econ. Devel., 1967-69, R.I. Urban League scholarship com., 1966-70; mem. inst. policy commn. So. Regional Edn. Bd.; bd. dirs. Afro-Am. Soc. Conn. Coll., Kalamazoo Area Math and Sci. Ctr., Kalamazoo Area Academic Achievement Program, ARC; bd. dirs., v.p. Nat. Assn. Equal Opportunity in Higher Edn.; trustee Brown U., Livingstone Coll., Peninsula United Community Services, Spelman Coll. Served with USAF, 1948-52. Recipient Disting. Alumni award Livingstone Coll.; Outstanding Civilian Service award U.S. Army.; Danforth Grad. fellow, 1955-61 Mem. Am. Soc. Pharmacology and Exptl. Therapeutics, Peninsula C. of C., NAACP (life, 1st v.p., Golden Heritage), AAAS, N.Y. Acad. Scis., Sigma Xi, Phi Kappa Phi, Phi Sigma, Beta Kappa Chi, Kappa Delta Pi, Omega Psi Phi, Gamma Alpha, Alpha Kappa Mu. Home: 7057 Oak Highlands Dr Kalamazoo MI 49009-7508 E-mail: r.d.hudson@worldnet.att.net.

HUDSON, SAMUEL CAMPBELL, JR., art educator, artist, sculptor, portraitist; b. Richmond, Va., Aug. 25; s. Samuel Campbell Sr. and Kizzie Morse (Barker) H.; m. Susan Holley Hudson (dec. 1966); children: Samuel Campbell III, Kimberly Ann; m. Sara Caroline Magers, Aug. 16, 1973. AA, Coll. William & Mary, 1963; BFA, Va. Commonwealth U., 1973; MFA, U. N.C., 1975. Art instr. U. N.C., Greensboro, 1973-74, Guilford Tech. C.C., Jamestown, N.C., 1974-76; asst. prof. art Nazareth Coll. Rochester, NY, 1978—83; prof. art, dean student affairs Studio Sch. Visual Rsch., Rochester, 1983-87; asst. prof. art, dir. O'Connor Gallery Rosary Coll., River Forest, Ill., 1988-98. Vis. artist Davidson C.C., Lexington, N.C., summer 1976; vis. prof. design U. Miss., University, 1976-77; dir. A.W. Mitchell & Co., Inc., Fredericksburg, Va., 1990-99; editl. adviser Collegiate Press, Alta Loma, Calif., 1991-93; cons. Greensboro Artists' League, 1985-87; art dir., founding ptnr. Capital Ideas, Inc., Richmond, Va., 1963-66; judge 14th Annual Keuka Lake Art Show, Hammondsport, N.Y., 1980, 1st Annual Poster Competition N.Y. Assn. Retarded Children, Rochester, 1980, Oak Park (Ill.) Art League Fall Festival '89 Exhibit; juror Annual Nazareth Coll. Art Student Competition and Exhbn., Rochester, N.Y., 1979-83; judge, juror Greensboro Artists' League's 13th Annual Nat. Painting, Drawing, and Sculpture Competition, 1982, Annual Rosary Coll. Fine Arts Club Competition and Exhbn., River Forest, Ill., 1991-93; cons. visual studies Cons. Assocs., Chgo., 1997—. One man shows include Ctrl. YWCA Art Gallery, Richmond, 1961, Richmond Profl. Inst., 1963, Weatherspoon Mus., Greensboro, N.C., 1975, Greensboro Coll., 1978, Little Gallery, Rochester, 1982, Studio Gallery Ctr. Creative Arts, Greenboro, 1986, O'Connor Gallery, River Forest, Ill., 1989, others; group exhbns. include Mariners Mus., Newport News, Va., 1967 (award), 68 (award), Va. Mus. Fine Arts, Richmond, 1967 (award), also travel exhbn., 1967-69, The 21st Nat. Art on Paper, 1984 (award 1985), The Marietta 11th Nat., 1977 (award 1978), Nat. On-Paper Show '82, 1982 (award 1982), Salmagundi Annual Summer Show, N.Y.C., 1982, 83, 84, 85,U. N.C.-Greensboro, 1986, Wehterholt Galleries, Washington, 1991, 92, 93, River Forest (Ill.) Pub. Lib. Gallery, 1993, others. Gallery asst. Civic Arts Coun. Kid Art, Oak Park, Ill., 1993; curator, judge Fra Angelico Art Found., River Forest, 1992; judge, juror Midwest Assn. Religious Talent, Milw., 1992. Grantee W.T.D. Pumphery Found., 1983-85. Mem. AAUP, Coll. Art Assn. Am., Nat. Trust for Hist. Preservation, Kappa Pi. Democrat. Avocations: in-line skating, weight-training, furniture design. Home: 149 W Park Dr Lombard IL 60148-3320

HUDSON, SHEILA DONNETTE, waste management administrator; b. Dayton, Ohio, Feb. 9, 1961; d. James R. Hudson and Shirley Lawson Spangler. BS in Agr., U. Tenn., 1984, MPH in Occupl./Environ. Health & Safety, 1995. Cert. hazardous materials mgr. Rsch. technician Oak Ridge Nat. Lab., 1988-91; environ. technician Lockheed Martin Energy Sys., Oak Ridge, 1991-93, waste disposal coord., 1993-96; waste specialist Pacific We. Techs., Oak Ridge, 1996-97; mgr. transp./waste mgmt. Molten Metal Tech., Oak Ridge, 1997-98; mgr. transp./waste ops. Brit. Nuc. Fuel, Inc., Oak Ridge, 1998—. Democrat. Avocations: horseback riding, hiking, softball, canoeing, travel. Home: 760 Old Emory Rd Clinton TN 37716-6058 Office: BNFL Inc ETTP Hwy 58 Portal 8 Oak Ridge TN 37831 Fax: 423-241-5041. E-mail: shudson878@cs.com.

HUDSON, STANTON HAROLD, JR., public relations executive, educator, academic administrator; b. Syracuse, NY, Jan. 28, 1951; s. Stanton Harold Sr. and Lucille (Shea) Hudson. Cert. in lang. and history, L'Univ. de Caen, France, 1970; BA in History/Polit. Sci., Canisius Coll., 1972; postgrad., SUNY, Buffalo, 1974-76, Syracuse U., 1995-98. Legis. asst., asst. pub. rels. dir. Erie County Rep. Com., Buffalo, 1971-73; dir. pub. rels. and fin. Greater Niagara Frontier Coun. Boy Scouts Am., Buffalo, 1977-79; dir. pub. rels. Ellis Singer & Webb Advt., Buffalo, 1979-80; asst. v.p., mgr. mktg. communications M&T Bank, Buffalo, 1980-85; exec. dir. Shea's Ctr. Performing Arts, Buffalo, 1986; pres. Hudson Mktg. Comm., Buffalo, 1987-88; sr. dir. advt. and pub. rels. Blue Cross Western N.Y., Inc., Buffalo, 1988-91; prin. Fredrickson & Hudson Assocs., Buffalo, 1991-92, Hudson & Assocs. Pub. Rels., Inc., Buffalo, 1992—. Asst. prof. Canisius Coll., 1993—, dir. grad. program orgnl. comm. & devel., 1995—. Editor: (newsletter) M&T Bank Observer, 1981—82 (Project PICA Grand award United Way Buffalo and Erie County); mng. editor: newsletter Blue Cross Ink, 1991. Mem. nat. coun. Am. Lung Assn., 1999—, mem. nat. bd. dirs., 2000—, mem. audit oversight com., 1999—, mem. nat. action panel on tobacco, 2001—03, mem. mktg. and comms. com., 2000—, vice chmn., 1999—2000, mem. tobacco control steering com., task force on mktg., 1996—99, revenue generation com., 1998—99; chmn. pub. rels. and mktg. coms. Greater Buffalo chpt. ARC, 1989—92, bd. dirs. Greater Buffalo chpt., 1991—92; bd. dirs. ARC Blood Svcs., N.Y.-Pa. Region, 1993—2003; bd. dirs., exec. com. Greater Buffalo Opera Co., 1991—93; trustee, mktg. com. Theodore Roosevelt Inaugural Nat. Hist. Site Found., 1994—, co-chair 2001 Pan Am. Expo. centennial celebration com.; bd. dirs. Buffalo Coun. on World Affairs, 1994—2002, co-chair mktg. com., 1994—98; Success By 6 awareness com. Buffalo and Erie County United Way, 1997—, leadership coun., 1998—; bd. dirs. East Hill Found., 2000—; exec. com. Erie County Cultural Resources Adv. Bd., 2000—, 2003—; chmn. Erie Niagara Tobacco-Free Coalition, 1999—2000, 2003—; mem. nat. customer svc. team Am. Lung Assn., 1998—99. Recipient Gold Star award, Nat. Adv. Agy. Network, 1979, Gold Quill award, Internat. Assn. of Bus. Communicators, 1984, Francis V. Hanavan Meml. award, Am. Lung Assn. We. N.Y., 1997, CEO's award, 2002, Brotherhood/Sisterhood award, Nat. Conf. for Cmty. and Justice, 1999, Pres. award, Theodore Roosevelt Inaugural Nat. Hist. Site Found., 2002. Mem.: Western NY Grantmakers Assn. (v.p. 2003—), Coordinated Care Mgmt. Corp. (mktg. com. 1994—98), Western N.Y. Comms. Steering Com. (chair 1991—92), Am. Mktg. Assn. (v.p. comms. Buffalo/Niagara chpt. 1991—92), Pub. Rels. Soc. Am. (treas. Buffalo/Niagara chpt. 1986—89, pres.-elect 1989—90, pres. 1990—91, treas. N.E. dist. 1992, nat. continuing edn. bd. 1993—95, chmn. 1994, chair N.E. dist. 1994, treas. 1994—96, nat. nominating com. 1995, nat. assembly del. 1997—2000, nat. commn. pub. rels. edn. 1997—, universal accreditation bd. 1998—2000, mem. profl. devel. task force 2001—, nat. assembly del. 2003—, mem. ednl. affairs com. 2003—, mem. ednl. affairs task force 2003, counselors acad. educators sect., mem. Coll. Fellows, Practitioner of the Yr. Buffalo/Niagara chpt. 1993, Excalibur award 1993, 1994, 1995, 1997, Nat. Paul M. Lund Pub. Svc. award 1997), Pub. Rels. Student Soc. Am. (nat. profl. advisor 1996—2000, nat. faculty advisor 2003—), Rotary (past dir.). Avocations: theater, jazz, reading, travel. E-mail: shud012851@aol.com.

HUDSON, SUNCERRAY ANN, analyst, research grants manager; b. San Francisco, Jan. 20, 1960; d. Charles Hudson and Nan Katherine (Coleman) Wagoner. BA, U. San Francisco, 1982; student, S.E. C.C., San Francisco, 1988; student in Orgl. Mgmt., U. Phoenix, San Francisco, Calif., 2003—. Stock transfer clk. Bank Calif., San Francisco, 1983-85; prin. clk. U. Calif., San Francisco, 1985-87, adminstrv. asst. II, 1987-88, adminstrv. asst. III, 1988-95, adminstrv. analyst, 1995—; ind. dealer Nat. Safety Assocs., Inc., San Francisco, 1990-92. Art cons. Artistic Impressions, Inc., 1994—96; mem. Notary Pub. Commn., 1997—; shape rite distbr., 1997—99. Mem.: Nat. Coun. Negro Women, Acad. Bus. Officers' Group, Am. Soc. Notaries, Sharing the Wealth Social Club, Gamma Phi Delta. Avocations: donating to various orgns. and the homeless, rollerskating, reading. Office: U Calif Campus Box 0440 521 Parnassus Ave San Francisco CA 94122-2722

HUDSON, TAJQUAH JAYE, managed health care executive; b. Paris, Tex., Oct. 16, 1959; d. Bob and Ramona (Pollan) Dennison. BS, E. Cen. Okla. State U., 1981; MS in Health, Wichita State U., 1987; cert. managed care exec. program, U. Mo., 1997. Diplomate Am. Coll. Health Care Execs. Program coord. Valley View Hosp., Ada, Okla., 1982-85; mgr. regional mktg., communications EQUICOR-Equitable HCA Corp., Wichita, Kans., 1986-89; regional adminstr. Aetna Health Plans, Overland Park, Kans., 1989 92; chief bus. and strategic devel. officer U. Kans. Med. Ctr., Kansas City, 1992—98, sr. v.p. bus. and strategic devel., 1999—. Speaker in field. Home: 15216 Johnson Dr Shawnee KS 66217

HUDSON, TIMOTHY LEON, nursing educator; b. Macon, Ga., Sept. 30, 1971; s. Leon Radford Hudson and Janice Lynette Bassett; m. Rebecca Lynn McAfee, June 24, 1995; children: Blakely, Jacob. AS in Nursing, Ga. Southwestern U., 1993, BS in Nursing, 1995; MS in Adminstrn., Ctrl. Mich. U., 1999; MEd, Okla. U., 2001; PhD candidate in Bus. Adminstrn., Touro U. Internat., 2001—. Diplomate Am. Coll. Healthcare Execs., cert. healthcare exec. Am. Coll. Healthcare Execs.; CCRN, AACN, nursing adminstr., AACN. Charge nurse gen. surg. unit Sumter Regional Hosp., Americus, Ga., 1993 95; charge nurse surg. intensive care unit Walter Reed Army Med. Ctr., Washington, 1996-99; asst. head nurse emergency med. treatment 212th Mobile Army Surg. Hosp., Miesau, Germany, 1999-2001, chief staff devel. Landstuhl (Germany) Regional Med. Ctr., 1999-2001; nurse presdl. svc. White House Med. Unit, Washington, 2001—. Nuc., biol. and chem. med. officer 212th MASH and Landstuhl Regional Med. Ctr., 1999—2001; chem., biol. and radiological officer White House Med. Unit, 2001—; chief decontamination team Landstuhl Regional Med. Ctr., 1999—2001, mock code coord., 1999—2001, Walter Reed Army Med. Ctr., 1997—99; mem. adj. faculty European divsn. U. Md. Author: Modular Instruction Manual, 1998; med. topics editor: Soldier, Airman, Sailor and Marine Internet Newsletter, 1999—2001; editor (critical care newsletter): Walter Reed Army Med. Ctr., 1997—99; editor: (med. nursing newsletter), 1996—97. Foster parent Kaiserslautern (Germany) Mil. Cmty. Foster Care Program, 1999—2001; cmty. vol. Army Cmty. Svc., Kaiserslautern, Germany, 1999—2001. Capt. U.S. Army, 1995—. Recipient Parachutist badge, U.S. Army, 1993, Air Assault badge, 1997, Army Achievement medal, 1997, 98, Meritorious Svc. medal, 1999, 2001, Army Commendation medal, 2000, Kosovo Campaign medal, 2000, Mil. Outstanding Vol. Svc. award, 2001, award NATO, 2000; named Outstanding Young Man of Am., 1998. Mem. ANA, Am. Assn. Critical Care Nurses, Ga. Nurses Assn. Home: 6153 Green Hollow Ct Springfield VA 22152 Office: White House Med Unit 1600 Pennsylvania Ave Washington DC 20500 Office Fax: 202-757-2529. E-mail: tlhudson@hotmail.com.

HUDSON, WALTER TIREE, artist; b. Lynchburg, Va., Apr. 10, 1943; s. Randolph Ward Hudson and Frances Anderson Tyree. Grad. h.s., Campbell County, Va.; student, Ctrl. Va. C.C., 1997, Stratford Career Inst., 2001. Owner Linchberg Folk Arts, Lynchburg, Doggywood Lit. Prodns. Exhibitions include The Framery, 1985—2000, Seven Hills Art Club, 1985—88, Amelia Pride, 1988, Lynchburg Pub. Libr., 1987—, Lynchburg Recreation Dept., 1988—2001, Daily Bread, 1989—, Adult Daycare Ctr.-Va. Bapt. Hosp., 1989—94, Va. Episcopal Sch., 1993—97, Lynchburg Art Festival, 1991, Elks Nat. Home, 1992, Ehrich's Optitions, 1992—2002, G.H. Vander Elst Collection, 1993, U. Tex., Houston, 1993, Lynchburg Fine Arts Ctr., Lynchburg PO, 1994, Lynchburg Voter Registration Office, 1995, Free Clinic of Va., 1995, Irby L. Hudson Collection, 1995, Lynchburg Social Svcs., 1987—99, Lynchburg Pub. Housing Authority, 1986—2000, Va. Episcopal Sch., 1988—2002, Robert Hicks Collection, 1992, 101 Quinlan St., 1996, Doggiewood Collection, 1996, Linchbird and Linchberg "1997", De Z Night Jump, 1997, 707 Mansfield Street, 1998, Ah Holloween Spring, 1998, Spring Fling, 1998—99, Blue Berg, 1998, Community Market, 1999, Linchbird, Red, White and Blue, 1999, West End Story, 1999, Crossus "99", WSET TV News, 1999, Haley's, 2000, Cornucopia, 2000, Mental Blocks, 2000, Calif. Poly of San Luis Obispo, 2000, KSU Found. Gift of Manhattan Kans., 2000, The Mormon Auction, 1999, Linchberg Berginia, 2000, E.C. Glass HS, 2000, Lynchburg Jour., 2001, Social Svcs., 2001, Facetous Art, 2002, Art Diploma, 2003. Active Ct. St. United Meth. Ch. With U.S. Army, Airborne, 1960-63. Mem. Lynchburg Stamp Club, Blue Ridge All Airborne Club. Republican. Mem. Lds Ch., Mormon, Baptist. Avocations: stamp collecting, reading, walking. Home: 3475 Fort Ave Apt 326 Lynchburg VA 24501-3834

HUDSON, WENDY JOY, software manager; b. New Brunswick, N.J., May 27, 1955; d. Herbert Roy Hudson and Dorothy Louise (Kaepernik) Hansen; m. William Howard Hudson, June 12, 1982. BA in Computer Sci., Rutgers U., 1977, MS in Computer Sci., 1979. Computer cons. Bell Labs., Holmdel, N.J., 1977-79; sr. mem. tech. staff Concurrent Computer, Tinton Falls, N.J., 1979-81, mgr., 1981-83, sr. mgr., 1983-89, prin. mgr., 1989-91; mgr. Transarc, Pitts., 1991-92; group mgr. Ilex Sys., Shrewsbury, N.J., 1992-95; mgr. IBM, Dayton, N.J., 1995 97, Lucent Techs., Bell Labs., Holmdel, N.J., 1997—. Contbr. articles to profl. jours. Mem. Assn. Computing Machinery. Republican. Episcopalian. Avocations: genealogy, skiing, bicycling, traveling. Home: 619 High Bridge Rd Colts Neck NJ 07722-1320 Office: Lucent Techs Bell Labs Crawfords Corner Rd Holmdel NJ 07733-2611

HUDSON, WILLIAM JEFFREY, JR., manufacturing company executive; b. Ill., May 20, 1934; s. William J. Sr. and Olga Georgevna (de Tarnowsky) H.; m. Margaret Royal, June 11, 1957; children: William J. III, Scott D., Robert C. BS in Elec. Engring., M. Cert. Elec. Engring., Cornell U., 1957; postgrad., Drexel U., 1959-61. With AMP Inc., Harrisburg, Pa., 1961—, market rschr., 1961-65, mgr. product planning Syscom, 1965, product mgr. Selective Signal, 1965-67, new product mgr. Capitron, 1967-73, new product mgr. Electron Devices Divsn., 1973-76, mgr. Devel. Engring. Circuit Components Divsn., 1976-77, mgr. Signal Components Divsn., 1977-81, group dir. connector and electronic products group, 1981-82, divisional v.p. connector and electronic products group, 1982-83, divisional v.p. Far East ops. Tokyo, 1983-89, corp. v.p. Asia/Pacific, 1989-91, exec. v.p. internat. Harrisburg, 1991-92, pres., CEO, 1993-98, vice chmn., 1998—99, also bd. dirs. Bd. dirs. Goodyear Tire and Rubber Co., Keithley Instruments, Inc., Carpenter Tech. Corp., Applied Systems Intelligence, Inc., Cornell U. Coun. Engring. Adv. Coun.; mem. investment com. High Street Capital, 1999—. Contbr. articles to profl. jours.; 12 patents in field. Bd. dirs. Pinnacle Health Found., 1994—, Elderport, Inc.,

2001—, Applied Systems Intelligence, Inc., 2002—; mem. bd. advisors Hershey Med. Ctr., 1994-2000; chmn. Pa. Export Trade Com., 1995-96; bd. dirs., exec. com. Team Pa., 1995—, work force investment bd. mem., chmn. employment stats. com., 1999—; mem. Pa. Human Resource Investment Coun., 1996—, chmn., 1996-99 Lt. (j.g.) USN, 1957-61. Mem. Nat. Elec. Mfrs. Assn. (exec. com., bd. govs. 1994-99), Nat. Assn. Mfrs. (exec. com., bd. dirs. 1993-98, vice chmn. 1997-98), Elec. Mfrs. Club (bd. dirs. 1993-98), Bus. Roundtable, U.S. Coun. Internat. Bus. (exec. com., chmn. Pa. Export Trade Coun., 1995-96, Team Pa. Human Resource Investment Coun., 1996-99, others).

HUDSON, WILLIAM L. conductor; Studies with Anthony Gigliotti, Max Rudolph, Erich Leindorf; grad., Phila. Mus. Acad., U. Pa., Yale U.; conducting student, Tanglewood Music Festival, Curtis Inst. Music, Phila. Conservatory. Condr., music dir. Fairfax Symphony Orch., Annandale, Va. Prof. music, condr. opera prodns. and symphony orch. U. Md.; faculty mem. Conducting Inst. Am. Symphony Orch. League; music dir. Shenandoah Valley Music Festival, 1979—. Bd. dirs. No. Va. Youth Symphony, Fairfax (Va.) Chorale Soc.; mem. adv. panel Fairfax County Coun. Arts; hon. chmn. Fairfax Spotlight on Arts, 1990. Recipient Outstanding Music Dir./Condr. award Washington Area Music Assn., 1985. Office: Fairfax Symphony Orch PO Box 1300 Annandale VA 22003-9300

HUDSON, WILLIAM MARK, insurance company executive, owner; b. Parkersburg, W.Va., Oct. 30, 1932; s. Morton Arden and Dorthy (Medealf) H.; m. Margie Webb, Oct. 3, 1953; children: William Mark II, Jay Lynn, Janet. Student, Fla. U., 1964-65, Fla. LaSalle U., 1971. Mgr. W.T. Grant Co., several cities, 1954-65; owner, agent Bill Hudson Ins. and State Farm Ins. Co., Orange Park, Fla., 1965-2001; ret., 2001. Pres. BILMARJA, Inc., Orange Pk., 1987—; owner Atlantic Travel, 1998-99. Chmn. Clay County (Fla.) Transp. Authority, 1988-90, 95-96; owner Get a Way Travel, Orange Park, 1994-98, Atlantic Travel Deltona, 1998-99; elder, chmn. fin. com. St. Giles Presbyn. Ch., Orange Prk, 1990—; treas. Clay County C. of C., 1987-88; mem. stewardship com. St. Augustine Presbyn. Ch., chmn. planned giving com., 1996-2000; bd. dirs., pres. Clay County Gator Club, 1998—, pres. 2002—; pres. Gator Caravan, U. Fla., 1997—. Sgt. USMC, 1951-54. Mem. Rotary (bd. dirs. 2002—, Paul Harris fellow 1983, Morocco Patrol (capt. 1989-90), Shriners (pres. Motor Corp. 1974-75, pres. Patrol Assn. 1989-90, sec. southeastern Motor Corps 1972-74), Masons (vice chmn. 1996-97, pilgramage com. 1993-94, chmn. membership com. 1990-93), Order of Demolay, Knights Comdr. of Ct. of Honour, Legion of Honor (dean 1996-97). Republican. Presbyterian. Avocations: helping burned and crippled children, boating, motor home travel.

HUDSON, YEAGER, philosophy educator, minister; b. Meridian, Miss., Aug. 14, 1931; s. William Ernest and Effie (Yeager) H.; m. Margaret Louise Hight, Dec. 20, 1953; children: Paul Brinton, Gareth Yeager. AB, Millsaps Coll., 1954; STB, Boston U., 1958, PhD, 1965; MA (hon.), Colby Coll., 1977. Ordained to ministry United Methodist Ch., 1963. Instr. philosophy Colby Coll., Waterville, Maine, 1959-65, asst. prof., 1965-70, assoc. prof., 1970-77, prof., chmn. dept., 1977-89, Charles A. Dana prof. philosophy, 1994-99, Charles A. Dana prof. emeritus, 1999—. Fulbright lectr. Ahnednager Coll., (India), 1967-68 Author: Emerson and Tagore: The Poet as Philosopher, 1988, Philosophy of Religion, 1990; editor: Profile of a College, 1972, Philosophy of Religion: Selected Readings, 1991, Rending and Renewing the Social Order, 1996, Technology, Morality and Social Policy, 1998, Globalism and the Obsolescence of the State, 1999, Cultural Integrity and World Community, 2000, Responsible Religious Belief: The Limits of Entitlement, 2002; co-editor: Revolution, Violence and Equality, 1990, Philosophical Essays on the Ideas of a Good Society, 1988, Terrorism, Justice and Social Values, 1991, Communitarianism, Liberalism and Social Responsibility, 1991, The Bill of Rights: Bicentennial Reflections, 1993, Freedom, Dharma and Rights, 1993, The Social Power of Ideas, 1995. Mem. Am. Philos. Assn., N.Am. Soc. for Social Philosophy (bd. officers), Am. Inst. Indian Studies (trustee 1980—), Assn. Asian Studies. E-mail: ylhudson@gwi.net. *There is widespread agreement among the thinkers and seers of nearly every society concerning the highest ideals according to which humans should live. The tragedy is that we still lack the moral will to put our ideals into effect in practical international affairs.*

HUDSON-YOUNG, JANE SMITHER, investor; b. Altavista, Va., July 5, 1937; d. Victor Nelson and Eloise (Reynolds) Smither; m. J. Lee Hudson, May 15, 1954; 1 child, Michael Edward; m. Gordon M. Young, July 9, 1989. AAS in Mgmt. summa cum laude, Ctrl. Va. C.C., 1978. Adminstrv. asst. Altavista H.S., 1954-55; with Lane Co. Inc., Altavista, 1956-89, exec. sec. to chmn. bd., 1976-81, exec. sec. to chmn. exec. com., 1981-84, spl. asst. for pub. rels. comms., 1984-86, account exec. nat. accounts, 1986, asst. sales mgr. contract divsn., 1986-87, mktg. adminstr., 1988-89; realtor R.B. Carr & Co., Altavista, 1980-87, assoc. broker, 1985-87; mem. adv. bd. Am. Fed. Savs. and Loan, 1985-89. Corr. Lynchburg (Va.) News, 1966-72. Mem. town coun. Town of Altavista, 1980-86; sec. Altavista Cmty. Improvement Coun., 1981-82; mem. bd. deacons First Bapt. Ch., Altavista, 1980-83. Home and Office: 1100 Heritage Plantation Dr Pawleys Island SC 29585-6749

HUDSON-ZONN, ELIZA, nurse, psychologist; b. Monrovia, Liberia, Dec. 12, 1956; arrived in U.S., 1978; d. Hartzell Gleh and Joan Eliza (Roberts) Killen; m. Henry Clay Hudson, July 28, 1979 (div. Apr. 1985); 1 child, Kimberly Clayde; m. Mawuli Sonny Zonn, July 31, 1988; 1 child, Jewel Lorraine. BA in Psychology, BSC in Nursing, U. So. Miss., 1984. RN, N.J., Tex. Pvt. duty nurse Maxim Healthcare, Inc., South Orange, NJ, 1990—; critical care nurse Midpoint Profl. Agy., East Orange, 1988; supervising nurse Interim Healthcare, Inc., Morristown, NJ, 1990—; staff nurse Montclair (N.J.) Gen. Hosp., 1989—91; pvt. nurse Beth-Israel Med. Ctr., Newark, 1988—92; staff nurse United Children's Hosp., Newark, 1989—92; critical care nurse Nat. Staffing Assocs. Inc., East Orange, 1989—; DON New Cmty. Extended Care, Newark, 2003—. Charge nurse Cmty. Psychiat. Ctr., Houston, 1993; dir. nursing med. day care New Cmty. Extended Care Ctr., Newark, 2003—. Rural health vol. Red Cross Liberia, Monrovia, 1973—74; women's refugees health adv. Union Sierra Leone for Liberia, 1990—95; human rights adv. Movement for Justice in Africa, 1975—; mem. Women Refugees Health Advocate Union Sierra Leone for Liberia, 1990—95; coord., health svcs. dir. Liberian Cmty. Assn. N.J., 2001; membership recruiter Student Unification Party, Monrovia, 1975—76; counselor Providence Bapt. Ch., 1975, St. Elmo Bapt. Ch., 1982. Recipient Pub. Svc. award East Miss. Bapt. Women Conv., 1972; So. Bapt. Conv. scholar, 1978-84, Nat. Bapt. Conv. scholar, 1972-84. Mem.: Suehn Acad. Alumni Assn. (recruiter 1995, founding mem. 1995). Democrat. Avocations: reading, writing, athletics, decoration, antiques collecting. Home: 64 Hillyer St Orange NJ 07050 Office: New Cmty Extended Care Med Day Care II Newark NJ 07107

HUDSPETH, ALBERT JAMES, biomedical researcher, educator; b. Houston, Nov. 9, 1945; s. Chalmers Mac and Demaris H. (DeLange) Hudspeth; m. Ann Maurine Packard, Feb. 12, 1977; children: James Chalmers, Ann Maurine Demaris. BA, Harvard U., 1967, MA, 1968; PhD, 1973, MD, 1974. Mem. biology faculty Calif. Inst. Tech., Pasadena, 1975—83; prof. physiology U. Calif., San Francisco, 1983—89; former prof. cell biology and neurosci. U. Tex. Southwestern Med. Ctr., Dallas, 1989—95; now F.M. Kriby prof. Rockefeller U., NYC, 1995—; investigator Howard Hughes Med. Inst., 1993—. Mem. bd. dirs. Drafaess Rsch. Found.; adv. com. mem. Burroughs Welcome Fund; mem. NIDCO. Recipient W. Alden Spencer award, N.Y. Acad. Sciss., 1985, Javits Neurosci. Investigator award, NIH, 1985—91, Cole award, Biophys. Soc., 1991, Claude Pepper award, NIH, 1991—93, Dana award, Charles A. Dana Found., 1994, L.S. Rosenstiel award, Brandeis U., 1997, Hitchcock Lectureship, U. Calif. Berkely, 1999, others. Mem.: NAS, Phi Beta Kappa, Alpha Omega Alpha. Office: Rockefeller Univ Campus Box 314 1230 York Ave New York NY 10021-6399 E-mail: hudspaj@rockvox.rockefeller.edu.

HUDSPETH, CHALMERS MAC, lawyer, educator; b. Denton, Tex., Oct. 18, 1919; s. Junia Evans and Ethel (Burns) H.; m. Demaris Eleanor De Lange, Jan. 30, 1945; children: Albert James, Thomas Richard, Helen Demaris. BA, Rice U., Houston, 1940; JD, U. Tex., 1946. Bar: Tex. 1946. Pvt. practice, Houston, 1947—; of counsel De Lange Hudspeth McConnell and Tibbets LLP, 1988—; asst. prof. law U. Tex. at Austin, 1946-47; lectr. govt. Rice U., 1947—, bd. govs., 1980-89, trustee, 1982-89, trustee emeritus, 1989—. Bd. dirs. Stewart Title Guaranty Co. Contbr. articles to profl. jours. Mem. bi-racial com. Houston Ind. Sch. Dist., 1955-56; trustee, v.p. Brown Found., 1983-89. Served to lt. USNR, 1942-45. Fellow Am. Bar Found., Tex. Bar Found.; mem. ABA, Tex. Bar Assn., State Bar Tex. (dir. 1966-68, v.p. 1968-69), Houston Philos. Soc. (pres. 1964-65), Petroleum Club of Houston, Chancellors, Order of Coif, Phi Delta Phi. Office: De Lange Hudspeth McConnell & Tibbets LLP Eight Greenway Plz Ste 1300 Houston TX 77046

HUDSPETH, GREGG WILLIAM, landscape architect; b. Canyon, Tex., Nov. 14, 1959; s. Elmer and Winnie H. B of Landscape Arch., Tex. Tech. U., 1982. Registered landscape architect, Tex., Ala., Fla., Ga., S.C., Tenn., N.C., Pa., La. Landscape architect Richardson Verdoorn, Inc., Austin, Tex., 1983—87, Niles Bolton Assocs., Atlanta, 1987—. 1st lt. USAF, 1982-83. Mem. Am. Soc. Landscape Architects (pres. Ga. chpt. 1992-93), Am. Planning Assn., Congress for the New Urbanism. Avocation: golf. Office: Niles Bolton Assocs 3060 Peachtree Rd NW Ste 600 Atlanta GA 30305-2236

HUDSPETH, HARRY LEE, federal judge; b. Dallas, Dec. 28, 1935; s. Harry Ellis and Hattilee (Dudney) H.; m. Vicki Kathryn Round, Nov. 27, 1971; children: Melinda, Mary Kathryn. BA, U. Tex., Austin, 1955, JD, 1958. Bar: Tex. 1958. Trial atty. Dept. Justice, Washington, 1959-62; asst. U.S. atty. Western Dist. Tex., El Paso, 1962-69; assoc. Peticolas, Luscombe & Stephens, El Paso, 1969-77; U.S. magistrate El Paso, 1977-79; judge U.S. Dist. Ct. (we. dist.) Tex., El Paso, 1979—; chief judge U.S. Dist. Ct. (we. dist) Tex., El Paso, 1992-1999. Bd. dirs. Sun Carnival Assn., 1976, Met. YMCA El Paso, 1980-88. Mem. Travis Cnty Bar Assn., U. Tex. Ex-students Assn. (exec. coun. 1980-86), Chancellors, Order of Coif, Phi Beta Kappa. Democrat. Mem. Christian Ch. (Disciples Of Christ). Office: US Dist Ct We Dist Tex 903 San Jacinto Ste 440 Austin TX 78701

HUDSPETH, HARVEY GRESHAM, history educator; b. Clarksdale, Miss., Oct. 17, 1955; s. Joseph MacDonald Hudspeth and Martha Lou Shelton; m. Mary Ruth Chambley, May 25, 1999. BA in History and Polit. Sci., U. Miss., 1978, JD, 1981, PhD in History, 1994. Bar: Miss. 1981, U.S. Dist. Ct. (no. dist.) Miss. 1981, U.S. Dist. Ct. (so. dist.) Miss. 1984, U.S. Ct. Appeals (5th cir.) 1985, Ill. 1989. Staff atty. Miss. Sec. of State, Jackson, 1981-83; pvt. practice Gulfport, Miss., 1983-85; land analyst Shell Oil Co., Houston, 1985-87; title examiner 1st Am. Title, Chgo., 1987-89; credit adminstr. Citicorp, Chgo., 1989-90, tchg. asst. U. Miss. University, 1991-94; history program coord., asst. prof. history Mississippi Valley State U., Itta Bena, Miss., 1994-2000, assoc. prof., 2000—. Presenter in field. Contbr. to books: Tennessee Encyclopedia of History, 1998, Booker T. Washington: Essays, 1998, Encyclopedia of the Supreme Court, 2001, Encyclopedia of the Gilded Age, 2003, Franklin D. Roosevelt and the Transformation of the Supreme Court, 2002; contbr. articles to profl. jours. Chmn. Com. to Elect Joe Hudspeth Pub. Svc. Commr., Miss., 1983. Recipient Miss. Humanities Coun. Tchr. of Yr. award, 2001. Mem. Am. Hist. Assn., Orgn. Am. Historians, Miss. Hist. Assn., Gulf South Hist. Assn., So. Conf. on Afro-Am. Studies, Inc., Econ. and Bus. Hist. Soc. (trustee 2000-2001, pres.-elect 2001-2002, pres. 2002-), Miss. Bar Assn., Ill. Bar Assn. Republican. Presbyterian. Avocations: travel, politics, reading. Home: 14000 Hwy 82 West PO Box 5045 Itta Bena MS 38941 Office: Mississippi Valley State U 14000 Highway 82 W Itta Bena MS 38941-1401

HUDSPETH, STEPHEN MASON, lawyer; b. Pitts., Jan. 22, 1947; s. Harold Mason and Edna Mary (Lawrenson) H.; m. Rebecca Anne Ellis, Apr. 3, 1971; children: David, Catherine. BA, MA magna cum laude, Yale U., 1968, JD, 1971. Bar: N.Y. 1973, Pa. 1973, U.S. Dist. Ct. (so. and ea. dists.) N.Y. 1973, U.S. Ct. Appeals (2d cir. 1973), Mass. 1974, U.S. Dist. Ct. (ea. dist.) Pa. 1975, U.S. Ct. Appeals (1st cir.) 1976, U.S. Ct. Appeals (3d cir.) 1977, U.S. Supreme Ct. 1980, Maine 1987. Assoc. Lord, Day & Lord, N.Y.C., until 1979, ptnr., 1979-86, Coudert Bros., N.Y.C., 1986—, mem. exec. com., 1990-93, also head litigation dept., 1994—. Adj. asst. prof. bus. law Wagner Coll., 1973-83. Co-author: Transfer Pricing under U.S. Law, 1995; contbr. articles to profl. jours., chpts. to books. Vestryman St. Alban's Episcopal Ch., S.I., N.Y., 1979-85, warden, 1985-87; chmn. Stewardship Commn., Diocese of N.Y., 1987-95; vestryman St. Matthew's Episcopal Ch., Wilton, Conn., 1989-92, warden, 1992-95; bd. dirs. Union Theol. Sem., 2000—. Capt. C.E., USAR, 1968-73. Mem. ABA, N.Y. State Bar Assn., Assn. Bar City N.Y., Phi Beta Kappa. Office: Coudert Bros 1114 Ave of Americas 4th Fl New York NY 10036-7710

HUDZINSKI, LEONARD GERARD, social sciences educator, researcher; b. Aug. 14, 1946; BA in Psychology and Sociology, Findlay (Ohio) Coll., 1968; MSW, U. Mich., 1971; PhD, U. Pitts., 1975. Diplomate Clin. Social Work Examiners. Tchg. asst. dept. sociology Findlay Coll., 1966-68; psychology specialist Lyster Army Hosp., Ft. Rucker, Ala., 1969-70; psychiat. social worker Toledo (Ohio) Mental Health Ctr., 1972; instr. in applied social rsch. and social work Med. Coll. Ohio, 1974-77; head divsn. clin. social work Ochsner Med. Instns., New Orleans, 1977—2001; ret., 2001. Dir. Ochsner Ctr. for Elimination of Smoking; asst. clin. prof. psychiatry La. State U. Med. Ctr.; asst. clin. prof. Tulane Med. Ctr.; instr., social scis. dept., Tahoe Coll. South Lake Tahoe, Calif.; psychology and sociology faculty Lake Tahoe C.C., 2002-; program dir., adminstr. State of Ohio Epilepsy Deinstitutionalization Assistance Program, 1976-77. Contbr. articles to profl. jours.; mem. editorial bd. Headache Quar., 1989—. Bd. dirs. Biofeedback Certification Inst. Am., Wheat Ridge, Colo., 1995. With U.S. Army, 1968-70. Fellow Am. Assn. for Study of Headache; mem. Assn. for Advancement of Behavior Therapy, Assn. Applied Psychophysiology and Biofeedback, La. Assn. Applied Psychophysiology and Biofeedback (past pres.), Am. Assn. for Study of Headache, NASW, La. Assn. for Clin. Social Work Vendorship (bd. dirs., treas., pres.), ACSW, Am. Fedn. for Clin. Rsch. Home: P O Box 1182 Zephyr Cove NV 89448

HUEBNER, EMILY ZUG, judicial administrator; b. Bryn Mawr, Pa., Apr. 17, 1942; d. Harry Coover and Anne (Mayer) Zug; m. John Stephen Huebner, June 16, 1962; children: Christopher, Jeffrey. BA, Goucher Coll., 1964, MEd, 1965. Alumni specialist Am. U., Washington, 1978-80, conf. coord., 1980-83, program specialist, 1983-87, assoc. dir. contract programs, 1987-90; tng. adminstr. Fed. Jud. Ctr., Washington, 1990-91, asst. dir. ct. edn., 1991-95, dir. ct. edn., 1995—. Cons. adult learning Coll. Bd., N.Y.C., 1985-88; cons. Coun. for Adult and Experienced Learning, Chgo., 1988-90. Contbr. articles to profl. jours. Mem. exec. bd. United Way/United Black Fund, Washington, 1988-91. Recipient Vol. Svc. award United Way/United Black Fund, 1990. Mem. Higher Edn. Group (pres. 1993-94), Am. Soc. Tng. and Devel. (Continuous Svc. award 1990), Assn. for Continuing Higher Edn. (chair human resources 1988-89), Women Adminstrs. in Higher Edn. Home: 6102 Cromwell Dr Bethesda MD 20816-3410 Office: Fed Jud Ctr 1 Columbus Cir NE Washington DC 20002-8000

HUEBNER, JOHN STEPHEN, geologist; b. Bryn Mawr, Pa., Sept. 9, 1940; s. John Mudie and Elizabeth (Converse) H.; m. Emily Mayer Zug, June 16, 1962; children: Christopher Converse, Jeffrey Worrell. AB magna cum laude, Princeton U., 1962; PhD, Johns Hopkins U., 1967. Rsch. geologist U.S. Geol. Survey, 1967-97. Cons. NASA, 1976-78; lectr. George Washington U., 1971; sec.-treas. Am. Geol. Inst., 1974-75. Assoc. editor Jour. Geophys. Rsch., 1977-79; Contbr. articles profl. jours. Pres. Wood Acres Citizens Assn., 1977—78; sec. Cosmos Club Found., 1998—99, treas., 1999—2003. Recipient Meritorious Svc. award U.S. Dept. Interior, 1995. Fellow Mineral. Soc. Am. (bd. dirs. 1985-88, recipient MSA award 1978); mem. AAAS, Geochem. Soc. (treas. 1972-75), Am. Geophys. Union, Geol. Soc. Washington (sec. 1972, v.p. 1991, pres. 1992, bd. dirs. 2000-2001), Cosmos Club Washington (treas. 2003), Sigma Xi. Home: 6102 Cromwell Dr Bethesda MD 20816-3410 E-mail: shuebner@radix.net.

HUEBNER, SISTER ROSEMARITA, nun, art educator; b. Neenah, Wis., Jan. 21, 1932; d. Carl William and Frances Clare (Wagner) H. Student, Oshkosh State U., 1950-51; BA, Mt. Mary Coll., Milw., 1961; MS in Art, U. Wis., 1965, MFA, 1967. Prof. Mt. Mary Coll., Milw., 1970—, chmn. art dept., 1970—87, 1994—2002; adminstr., v.p. Sch. Sisters Notre Dame, Milw., 1987-92. Mem. adv. bd. Lakefront Festival Art, Art Mus. Milw., 1978-2001. Recipient Spl. Pres.'s award Wis. Art Edn., 1981, Art Educators award City of Milw., 1988; Lifetime Achievement award Wis. Designer Crafts Coun., 2003. Mem. Am. Crafts Coun., Enamelist Soc., Wis. Designer Crafts Coun. (sec. 1998-2001, award 1982), Milw. Area Tchrs. Art (award 1998), Great Lakes Enamel Guild (co- founder, execd. com.). Democrat. Roman Catholic. Home: 7988 N 94th St Milwaukee WI 53224 Office: Mt Mary Coll 2900 Menomonee River Pky Milwaukee WI 53222 E-mail: huebner@mtmary.edu.

HUEBSCHER, HERBERT, electrical engineer, educator; b. Vienna, Feb. 6, 1926; arrived in U.S., 1938; s. Jacob and Toni Huebscher; m. Lucille Blanche Pion, Dec. 9, 1951; children: Robert K., Eric M., Toni R. BEE CCNY, 1947; MS, Adelphi U., Garden City, N.Y., 1961; MBA, Adelphi U., 1981. Engr. RCA, N.Y.C., Camden, NJ, 1947—49, Garod Majestic TV, Bklyn., 1949—51, Fairchild Camera Instrument Co., Queens, NY, 1951—52; project mgr. Kollsman Instrument Corp., Elmhurst, NY, 1952—56; v.p. strategic planning Hazeltine Corp., Greenlawn, NY, 1956—88; asst. prof. C.W Post Campus, Long Island U., Coll Mgmt., Brookville, NY, 1988—96; retired, 1996. Bd. dirs. Denton Green Housing, Garden City Park, NY, 2001—. Lt. j.g. USN, 1944—47, PTO. Achievements include patents for hand-held identification system; automatic car locating system. Avocations: genealogy, photography. Home: 37 Leslie Ln New Hyde Park NY 11040 E-mail: huebsch@optonline.net.

HUEFNER, DIXIE SNOW, special education educator; b. Washington, Dec. 7, 1936; m. Robert Paul Huefner, July 30, 1960; children: Steven Frederick, Eric William; m. Robert Paul Huefner. BA in Polit. Sci., Wellesley Coll., 1958; MS in Spl. Edn., U. Utah, 1977, JD, 1986. Clin. instr. dept. spl. edn. U. Utah, 1978-86; jud. clk. to hon. Stephen H. Anderson U.S. Ct. Appeals (10th cir.), 1986-90; clin. asst. prof. dept. spl. edn. U. Utah, Salt Lake City, 1986-89, vis. asst. prof. dept. spl. edn., 1989-90, asst. prof. dept. spl. edn., 1990—94, assoc. prof., 1994—99, prof., 1999—. Presenter in field. Contbr. articles prof. jours.; author: (book) Getting Comfortable with Spl. Edn.Law /Christopher-Gordon Pub., 2000; co-author: Edn. Law and the Pub. Sch./ Christopher-Gordon Pub., 1998. Apptd. to Utah State Bd. Edn. Adv. Com. on the Handicapped. Mem. ABA, Coun. for Exceptional Children, Learning Disability Assn., Learning Disability Assn. Utah, Nat. Assn. for Retarded Citizens, Women Lawyers Utah, bd. mem. Utah parent ctr., Edn. Law Assoc.. Office: U Utah Dept Spl Edn 1705 E Campus Ctr Dr Rm 221 Salt Lake City UT 84112-9253

HUEFNER, ROBERT P. political science educator; b. Logan, Utah, Apr. 18, 1936; s. Paul and Wynona (Musser) H.; m. Dixie Snow, July 30, 1960; children: Steven F., Eric W. BS in Civil Engring., U. Utah, 1958; M of City Planning, MIT, 1960; DBA, Harvard U., 1972. Assoc. planner Salt Lake County, Salt Lake City, 1960-63; state planning coor. State of Utah, Salt Lake City, 1963-67; White House fellow U.S. Treasury, Washington, 1967-68; from asst. prof. to prof. U. Utah, Salt Lake City, 1972—, dir. Ctr. for Pub. Adminstrn., 1972-85, Matheson prof. polit. sci., 1988—2002, dir. Matheson Ctr. Health Studies, 1988—2002. Mem. Commn. on Operation of U.S. Senate, Washington, 1975-76; gubernatorial transition coord. State of Utah, Salt Lake City, 1984; cons. U.S. Dept. HEW, Washington, 1973-74. Editor, author: Changing to National Health Care, 1992; contbr. chpts. to books, articles to profl. jours. Bd. dirs. and exec. com. Coalition for Utah's Future, Salt Lake City, 1990—; vice chair, chair Utah Tax Rev. Commn., Salt Lake City, 1984-94; chair Utah State Health Coun., Salt Lake City, 1981-85; vice chair Gov.'s Com. on Exec. Reorgn., Salt Lake City, 1977-79; mem. steering com. Envision Utah, Salt Lake City, 1998—. Recipient Cmty. Svc. award LWV, 1996, Faculty Cmty. Svc. award U. Utah Alumni Assn., 1996, Disting. Svc. award Utah Pub. Health Assn., 1993, Disting. Svc. award U. Utah, Disting. Svc. to State Govt. award Nat. Govs. Assn., 1984. Fellow Am. Inst. Cert. Planners; mem. Am. Planners Assn., Am. Polit. Sci. Assn., Am. Soc. for Pub. Adminstrn., Am. Soc. Bioethics and Humanities, Utah Soc. for Pub. Adminstrn. (Spl. award 1985), Internat. Assn. Bioethics. Home: 24 U St Salt Lake City UT 84103-4301 Office: U Utah Dept Polit Sci Rm 25polit 260 S Central Campus Dr Salt Lake City UT 84112-9199

HUELS, STEVEN MARK, physicist, mathematician, astronomer; b. Dunkirk, N.Y., Oct. 12, 1960; s. Robert Paul and Agnes Eve (Grzeskowiak) H. BS in Physics and Math. with honors, SUNY, Fredonia, 1982; MS in Astronomy, Pa. State U., 1984. Rsch. asst. Lord Corp., Erie, Pa., 1980-81, SUNY Rsch. Found., Fredonia, 1981-82; grad. asst. N.Mex. State U., Las Cruces, 1982-83, Pa. State U., University Park, 1983-84; quality control lab. mgr. Chem. Process and Supply Corp., Dunkirk, N.Y., 1985-89; sci. writer Am. Coll. Testing Program, Iowa City, 1990-92; sr. lab. analyst Dunkirk Environ. Lab., 1992—. Recipient scholarship N.Y. State Bd. Regents, 1978, Anne Walker Meml. scholarship, 1978, Bausch and Lomb Hon. Sci. medal, 1978, Ruth Tice Callahan award for Acad. Excellence, 1979, Fredonia Alumni Assn. Freshman award, 1979. Mem.: Friends of Lowell Observatory, Internat. Dark-Sky Assn., Marshall Martz Meml. Astron. Assn., Nat. Weather Svc. Coop. Observer, The Planetary Soc., Soc. Photo-Optical Instrumentation Engrs., N.Y. Acad. Scis., Pa. State U. Alumni Assn. (life), Am. Phys. Soc. (astrophysics and chem. physics divsns.) (life), Theta Psi Omicron, Pi Mu Epsilon (mem. N.Y. Pi chpt.), Phi Eta Sigma. Republican. Roman Catholic. Home: 843 Central Ave Dunkirk NY 14048-3346 Office: Wright Park Dr Dunkirk NY 14048 E-mail: shuels@members.nyas.org.

HUELSMANN, THOMAS J. retired music educator; b. Stillwater, Minn., Mar. 20, 1945; m. Mary C. Collison, Aug. 10, 1968; children: Jennifer, Melanie, Frederick. BA in music, Coll. of St. Thomas, 1962—66, MA in tchg., 1966—67. Tchr., instrumental music South Wash. County Schools, Cottage Grove, Minn., 1967—2001; adj. lectr., music U. of St. Thomas, St. Paul, 1992—2000. Pres. St. Croix Friends of the Arts, Stillwater, Minn.; bass trombonist Mpls. Civic Orch., Minneapolis, Minn., 1977—85; substitute tchr., music Stillwater Area Schools, Stillwater, Minn., 2001—. Arranger/transcriber (band and choir composition) Oh, How Beautiful the Sky, 1978. Camp coord. Woodbury Youth Orch., Minn., 2001. Recipient Honor Faculty, Pk. H.S., Cottage Grove, Minn., 1979, 2001. Mem.: Music Educators Nat. Conf., Internat. Assn. of Jazz Educators, Nat. Band Assn. Avocations: music arranging, camping, canoeing, hunting, fishing. Home: 401 S Greeley St Stillwater MN 55082 Personal E-mail: tjhuels@attbi.com.

HUEMER, MICHAEL, philosophy educator; b. Hollywood, Calif., Dec. 27, 1969; PhD, Rutgers U., 1998. Asst. prof. U. of Colo., Boulder, 1998—. Author: (book) Skepticism and the Veil of Perception; editor: Epistemology: Contemporary Readings. Mem.: Am. Philos. Assn. Office: U Colo Philosophy Dept Boulder CO 80309-0232

HUENEFELD, THOMAS ERNST, financial consultant, retired banker; b. Cin., July 7, 1937; s. Carl Ernst and Catherine Louise (Messer) H.; m. Catherine Ann Cogburn, Feb. 5, 1960; children: Richard Ernst, Amy Cogburn. BS in Bus. Adminstrn., U. Fla., 1961; grad. Nat. Comml. Lending Grad. Sch., U. Okla., 1975. Cert. comml. lender Am. Bankers Assn.; cert. lender-bus. banking Inst. Cert. Bankers. Mgmt. trainee Huenefeld Co., Cin., 1961—62, asst. sec., buyer, 1963—65; credit analyst First Nat. Bank Cin. (now U.S. Bank, N.A.), 1966—68, asst. cashier, 1968—69, asst. v.p., 1969—75, v.p., 1975—83, sr. v.p., 1983—96; ret., 1996. Cons. Star Banc Corp. (now U.S. Bancorp), Cin., 1997-98; dir. Wolf Machine Co., S. Eastern Materials Corp., Archiable Electric Co., Eastern Machinery Co., Ninth St. Garage, Inc., Logan & Kanawha Coal Co., Inc., Safegard Corp. Author: Pittsburgh's Historic East End: In and Around Point Breeze 1914, 2001. Bd. mgrs. Emanuel Cmty. Ctr., Cin., 1965-70, pres., 1968-70; trustee Huenefeld Meml., Inc., Cin., 1965-72, treas., 1965-69; trustee Funds for Self Enterprise, Cin., 1972-76, pres., 1973-76; trustee Cin. Musical Festival Assn., 1976-82, mem. exec. com., 1977-79; trustee Betts House Rsch. Ctr., 1999-2002, Cmty. Ltd. Care Dialysis Ctr., Cin., 1978-85; trustee Mercantile Libr., 1979-2001, v.p., chmn. fin. com., 1983-88, life mem., 2001-; trustee MagnaCare Health Plan, 1988-91, v.p., chmn. fin. com., 1990-91; trustee Spring Grove Heritage Found., 2001-, Ohio Hist. Soc. Found., 2002—; adv. bd. Riemenschneider Bach Inst. Baldwin-Wallace Coll., 1988—; mem. history adv. bd. Cin. Mus. Ctr., 1997—; mem. adv. bd. Scarlet Oaks Retirement Comm., 1998—, Emery Ctr. Corp., 1999-2002. Mem. Am. Fin. Assn. (life), Fin. Mgmt. Assn. (life), Risk Mgmt. Assn. (life), Cin. Assn. Credit and Fin. Mgmt. (dir. 1972-76), Am. Inst. Banking, Newcomen Soc. N.Am., Ohio Hist. Soc. (life, trustee 2001-), Ohioana Libr. Assn. (life), Cin. Hist. Soc. (life, trustee 1979-87, mem. exec. com. 1983-85, v.p. 1985-89), Cin. Preservation Assn. (trustee 1989-95, adv. bd. 1995—), Cincinnatus Assn. (exec. com. 1983-84), Cin. Country Club, Queen City Club, Bankers Club, The Assemblies (chmn. 1972-73), Univ. Club (bd. govs. 1982-89), Univ. Club Cin. Found. (trustee 1989-96), Fanfare (pres. 1979-80), Friends William Howard Taft Birthplace (trustee 1997-03), Sigma Chi. Republican. Methodist. Home and Office: 3440 Principio Ave Cincinnati OH 45208-4240

HUENEMANN, RODNEY KARL, state administrator, executive; b. Mason City, Iowa, Dec. 8, 1954; s. Karl Gerhardt and Cecilia Elfrieda (Mettler) H.; m. Karen Lynn Fisher, Sept. 22, 1979; 1 child, Brandon. BA in Sociology and Social Work, U. No. Iowa, 1977. Devel. dept. dir. Upper Des Moines Opportunity, Emmetsburg, Iowa, 1977-84; program planner Iowa Office for Planning and Programming, Des Moines, 1984-85, program adminstr., 1985-86; chief Iowa Bur. Cmty. Svcs., Iowa Dept. Human Rights, Des Moines, 1986-98; adminstr., cmty. svcs. adminstrn. Ariz. Dept. Econ. Security, Phoenix, 1998-2000, planner div. policy and program devel., 2000—. Part-time county corr. Des Moines Register, 1982-84; part-time property mgr. Edward Wordrip, Westport, Conn., 1985-88; spkr. in field. Mem. Palo Alto County Rep. Party Ctrl. Com., Emmetsburg, 1979-83; initiator, co-chair Iowa State Homeless Assistance Coordinating Com., Des Moines, 1990-94; mem. staff/parish rels. com. 1st United Meth. Ch., Des Moines, 1995-97. Recipient Pub. Policy award Mid Iowa Cmty. Action, Marshalltown, 1995. Mem. Nat. Assn. Cmty. Action Agys. (cert. cmty. action profl., mem. edn. com. 1990-94, mem. cert. adv. group 1990-94), nat. Assn. for State Cmty. Svcx. Programs (bd. dirs. 1987-93, mem. mgmt. info. syss. 1989-92, ways and means com. 1995—). E-mail: rhuenemann@mail.de.state.az.us.

HUENING, WALTER CARL, JR., retired consulting application engineer; b. Boston, Feb. 10, 1923; s. Walter Carl and Gladys (Whittemore) H.; m. Margaret Laurence McGeary, Aug. 5, 1944 (dec. 1986); children: Peter Carl, Susan Laurence Huening Locke; m. Elizabeth Ann Young Wright, Apr. 9, 1988. BSEE magna cum laude, Tufts U., 1944. Registered profl. engr., N.Y., Ohio. Instr. elec. engring. Tufts U., Medford, Mass., 1946-48; distbn. engr. plant engring. dept. GE, Lynn, Mass., 1948-50, application engr. indsl. power engring. Schenectady, N.Y., 1952-56, product planner protective devices dept. Plainville, Conn., 1956-58, design engr. vacuum cleaner dept. Cleve., 1958-59, application engr. comml. and mcpl. dept. Schenectady, 1960-62, application engr. steel mill, 1962-68, cons. application engr. indsl. power engring., 1968-89. Mem. U.S. nat. com. Internat. Electrotech. Commn., tech. advisor on Tech. Com. 73 matters, 1972-89. Contbr. tech. papers to jours. and chpts. to books; patentee vacuum cleaner latch. Lt. comdr. USNR, 1944-46, 50-52, ret. Fellow IEEE (life, R. H. Kaufmann award 1988, Indsl. and Comml. Power Systems Dept. Achievement award 1989, prizes for papers 1970, 82); mem. Tau Beta Pi. Independent. Avocations: photography, collecting recorded traditional jazz music. Address: 1229 Godfrey Ln Niskayuna NY 12309-1241 E-mail: whueningjr@aol.com.

HUERTA, SERGIO, physician, researcher; b. Mexico City, Dec. 21, 1966; s. David Huerta and Edelmira Yepez; m. Hsiao Ching Li, June 19, 1999. MD, UCLA Sch. of Medicine, Los Angeles, Calif., 1994—98; BS, U. of Calif., LA, Los Angeles, Calif., 1990—92; AA, West LA Coll., Culver City, Calif., 1988—90. Doctor of Medicine Med. Bd. of Calif., Calif., 2001. Surg. resident U. of Calif., Irvine, Orange, Calif., 1998—; fellow in nutritional oncology UCLA Ctr. for Human Nutrition, Los Angeles, Calif., 2000—02. Inaugural chmn. of the western student med. forum residents' sect. Western Student Med. Forum and the Am. Fedn. for Med. Rsch., Carmel, Calif., 2001—02, chmn. of the western student med. forum residents' sect., 2002—03; founder and provider of a clinic mng. obesity in an indigent population Venice Family Clinic, Venice, Calif., 2001—02. Author: (book) The Pocket Rev. of Surgery, (manuscript) Manuscript in Cancer Rsch.; co-author (manuscript) Manuscript in Annals of Surgery; author: (manuscript) Manuscript in Surgery, Manuscript in Am. Surgeon, Manuscript in Surg. Rounds, Manuscript in Am. Surgeon, Manuscript in Surgery, Manuscript in Digestive Diseases and Sciences; co-author (manuscript) Manuscript in Jour. of Surg. Rsch.; author: (manuscript) Manuscript in Cancer Rsch. (Minority in Cancer Rsch., 2001), Manuscript in Jour. of Gastrointestinal Surgery, Manuscript in Am. Jour. of Clin. Nutrition. Recipient Emil Bogen Rsch. Prize, UCLA Sch. of Medicine, June 1998, Minority Scholar-in-Tng. Award, Am. Assn. for Cancer Rsch., April 2002, Minority in Cancer Rsch. Award, February 2002, Travel Award, Am. Fedn. for Med. Rsch., February 2002, Minority in Cancer Rsch. Award, Am. Assn. for Cancer Rsch., October 2001, Minority Scholar-in-Tng. Award, February 2002; fellow Fellowship in Nutritional Oncology, Nat. Institute of Health, 2000-2002, Outstanding Rsch. Fellow Award, UCLA Ctr. for Human Nutrition, June 2002; grantee Pilot Feasability Study ($ 15, 000), 2001; scholar Travel Award, Am. Inst. for Cancer Rsch., July 2000. Mem.: AMA, North Am. Assn. for the Study of Obesity, Am. Assn. for Cancer Rsch., Am. Gastroent. Assn. Office: UCLA Ctr for Human Nutrition 12-217 Warren Hall 900 Veteran Ave Los Angeles CA 90095 Office Fax: 310-206-5264. Personal E-mail: shuerta@pol.net. E-mail: shuerta@pol.net.

HUESCA DORANTES, PATRICIA, researcher; d. Elia Dorantes Falconi and Jose Luis Huesca Rodriguez; m. Brian Keith Martin, Feb. 18, 1996; 1 child, Itxel Brianna Martin-Huesca. B.A. Internat. Rels., ITESM, NL. Mexico, 1990—94; Master of Pub. Affairs, The U. of Tex. at Dallas, Richardson, Texas, 1997—99; P.D. Degree in Polit. Economy, The U. of Tex. at Dallas, Richardson, TX, 1997—2001. Geographic and Information Systems UTD, Tex., 1999. Instl. rsch. assoc. The U. of Tex. at Dallas, Richardson, TX, Tex., 1999—. Author: The Emergence of Multiparty Competition in Mexican Politics; co-author: Bldg. a GIS Database for Space and Facilities Mgmt. Fellow Intro. to Mandarin Chinese, Chinese Govt., 1995. Mem.: Am. Econ. Assn., [00b7] The Acad. of Polit. Sci. (assoc.). Achievements include patents pending for Space Inventory Database. Office: The University of Texas at Dallas PO Box 830688 AD 29 Richardson TX 75083-0688 Office Fax: 972-883-2451. E-mail: phuesca@utdallas.edu.

HUESTIS, CHARLES BENJAMIN, former academic administrator; b. Seattle, Jan. 27, 1920; s. Claude Erwin and Eloise Marie (Pettit) H.; m. Kathryn Alice Porter, Mar. 1, 1942; children: Stephen Porter, Jeffrey Charles, Robin Rebecca. Student, Griffin Murphy Coll., Seattle, 1938-39, U. Calif. Berkeley, 1946. With Seattle First Nat. Bank, 1941; acct. Rheem Mfg. Co., Richmond, Calif., 1946-51, chief acct. aircraft div. Downey, Calif., 1951-54, corp. comptroller, 1954-56; v.p., treas. Hall-Scott Inc., Berkeley, Calif., 1956, exec. v.p., dir., treas., 1956-57; adminstrv. cons. Overseas Nat. Airways, Oakland, Calif., 1957-58; controller El Segundo div. Hughes Aircraft Co., 1958-59, controller Tucson div., 1959, treas., chmn. finance com., 1960-66, v.p., 1962-66; v.p., treas., dir. Am. Mt. Everest Expdn., 1963; v.p. bus. and finance Duke U., Durham, N.C., 1966-83, sr. v.p., 1983-85, sr. v.p. emeritus, 1985—; dir. Technomics, Inc., Falls Church, Va., 1966-76; chmn. bd. Sta. WDBS, 1970-76. Bd. dirs. Santa Barbara (Calif.) Research Ctr., 1959-66; bd. dirs., mem. exec. com. Research Triangle Found., Research Triangle Park, N.C., 1969-85; trustee Research Triangle Inst., Research Triangle Park, 1967-79, Sierra Club Found., 1969-79; commr. N.C. Marine Fisheries, 1985-87; trustee N.C. Nature Conservancy., 1977-86, 87-96, chmn., 1979-83; bd. dirs. N.C. Ednl. Facilities Fin. Agy., 1987-91—; climbing leader Duke-Gettysburg Expdn. to Kurdistan, 1982. Served with U.S Army Signal Corps, 1942-45. Mem. Explorers Club (v.p. research and edn. 1987-88), Am. Alpine Club. Home: 1803 Woodburn Rd Durham NC 27705-5724 Office: Duke U Durham NC 27706

HUESTIS, DOUGLAS WILLIAM, physician, pathologist; b. London, Ontario, Can., Mar. 21, 1925; s. Richard Douglas and Marie Marguerite (Hinde) H.; m. Rosemary Lucille Colford, June 11, 1955; children: Lucy Mary, Marilyn Joan, Andrew Charles, Karen Ann, Peter Douglas. MD, McGill U., Montreal, Que., 1948. Cert. anatomic pathology, clin pathology Pathologist, asst. dir. labs. Western Pa. Hosp., Pitts., 1955-60; instr. pathology Univ. Pitts., 1955-60; dir. Chas. Hymen Blood Ctr. Mount Sinai Hosp. Med. Ctr., Chgo., 1960-69; assoc. prof., pathology Chgo. Med. Sch., 1960-66, prof. clin. pathology, 1966-69; prof. pathology, chief transfusion medicine Univ. Ariz., 1969-93, prof. emeritus, 1993—; med. dir., blood program Southern Ariz. Red Cross, 1970-77. Mem. nat. blood. resource program Nat. Heart & Lung Inst., Bethesda, Md., 1970-74; coun. on immunohematology Am. Soc. Clin. Pathologists, Chgo., 1965-70; bd. dirs. Am. Assn. of Blood Banks, Chgo., 1964-70; chmn. med. adv. com. Southern Arizona Red Cross Blood Program, 1987-96. Author: Practical Blood Transfusion, 1969, 76, 81, 88; contbr. articles to sci. jours.; chpts. to books. Exch. scientist Soviet-Am. Health Exch. Nat. Insts. of Health, Moscow, 1976; coun. North Am. Internat. Soc. Blood Transfusion, Paris, 1976-82; expert mem. bd. dirs. Vox Sanguinis Found., Basel, Switzerland, 1987—. With Canadian Army, 1944-45. Mem. Am. Assn. Blood Banks (John Elliott award, 1975), Am. Soc. clin. Pathologists, Internat. Soc. Blood Transfusion, British Blood Transfusion Soc. Avocations: writing, gardening, music, art. Home: 3525 N Tin Star Pl Tucson AZ 85745-4130

HUETTNER, RICHARD ALFRED, lawyer; b. N.Y.C., Mar. 25, 1927; s. Alfred F. and Mary (Reilly) Huettner; m. Eunice Bizzell Dowd, Aug. 22, 1971; children: Jennifer Mary, Barbara H. Stead. Marine Engrs. License, N.Y. State Maritime Acad., 1947; BS, Yale U. Sch. Engring., 1949; JD, U. Pa., 1952. Bar: D.C. 1952, N.Y. 1954, U.S. Ct. Mil. Appeals 1953, U.S. Ct. Claims 1961, U.S. Supreme Ct. 1969, U.S. Ct. Appeals (fed. cir.) 1982, also other fed. cts, registered to practice U.S. Patent and Trademark Office 1957, Canadian Patent Office 1968. Engr. Jones & Laughlin Steel Corp., 1954-55; assoc. atty. firm Kenyon & Kenyon, N.Y.C, 1955-61, mem. firm, 1961-96, of counsel, 1996-98; specialist patent, trademark and copyright law. Trustee N.J. Shakespeare Festival, 1972-79, sec., 1977-79; trustee Overlook Hosp., Summit, N.J., 1978-84, 86-89, vice chmn. bd. trustees, 1980-82, chmn. bd. trustees, 1982-84; trustee Overlook Found., 1981-89, chmn. bd. trustees, 1986-89, emeritus trustee, 1991; trustee Colonial Symphony Orch., Madison, N.J., 1972-82, v.p. bd. trustees 1974-76. pres. 1976-79; chmn. bd. overseers N.J. Consortium for Performing Arts, 1972-74; mem. Yale U. Council, 1978-81; bd. dirs. Yale Communications Bd., 1978-80; chmn. bd. trustees Center for Addictive Illnesses, Morristown, N.J., 1979-82; rep. Assn. Yale Alumni, 1975-80, chmn. com. undergrad. admissions, 1976-78, bd. govs., 1976-80, chmn. bd. govs., 1978-80; chmn. Yale Alumni Schs. Com. N.Y., 1972-78; assoc. fellow Silliman Coll., Yale U., 1976—; bd. dirs., exec. com. Yale U. Alumni Fund, 1978-81; mem. Yale Class of 1949 Council, 1980—; bd. dirs. Overlook Health Systems, 1984—. Served from midshipman to lt. USNR, 1945-47, 1952-54; cert. JAGC 1953; Res. ret. Recipient Yale medal, 1983, Disting. Svc. to Yale Class of 1949 award, 1989, Yale Sci. and Engring. Meritorious Svc. award, 1992. Fellow: AAAS, N.Y. Bar Found.; mem.: ABA (life), Fed. Bar Coun., Yale Sci. and Engring. Assn. (v.p. 1973—75, pres. 1975—78, exec. bd. 1972—79), Am. Judicature Soc., Internat. Patent and Trademark Assn., Ret. Officers Assn. (life), N.Y. Intellectual Property Law Assn. (life; chmn. com. mtgs. 1961—64, chmn. com. econ. matters 1966—69, 1972—74), Am. Intellectual Property Law Assn. (life), N.Y. County Lawyers Assn., N.Y. Acad. Scis., Assn. Bar City N.Y., N.Y. State Bar Assn., Yale (N.Y.C.); Yale of Central N.J. (Summit) (trustee 1973-88, pres. 1975-77), Morris County Golf (Convent, N.J.); The Graduates (New Haven). Home: 20 Chadwell Place Morristown NJ 07960-6945 Fax: 973-455-7165. E-mail: huettnerrichard@aol.com.

HUEY, F. B., JR., minister, theology educator; b. Denton, Tex., Jan. 12, 1925; s. F.B. and Alma Gwendolyn (Chambers) H.; m. Nonna Lee Turner, Dec. 22, 1950; children: Mary Anne Huey Lisbona, Linda Kaye Huey Miller, William David. BBA, U. Tex., 1945; MDiv, Southwestern Bapt. Theol. Sem., 1958, PhD, 1961. Ordained to ministry So. Bapt. Conv., 1956. Pastor Bolivar Bapt. Ch., Sanger, Tex., 1956-59, Univ. Bapt. Ch., Denton, 1959-61; prof. Old Testament So. Brazil Bapt. Theol. Sem., Rio de Janeiro, 1961-65, Southwestern Bapt. Theol. Sem., Ft. Worth, 1965-95, chmn. D in Ministry program, 1978-79, assoc. dean for PhD program, 1984-90; ret., 1995. Pastor Rush Creek Bapt. Ch., Arlington, 1989-93; guest prof. Bapt. Theol. Sem., Ruschlikon, Switzerland, 1971-72; guest prof. Canadian So. Bapt. Sem., Cochrane, Can., 1996. Author: Exodus: Bible Study Commentary, 1977, Chinese edit., 1983, Yesterday's Prophets for Today's World, 1980, Chinese edit., 1991, Jeremiah: Bible Study Commentary, 1981, Chinese edit., 1982, Numbers: Bible Study Commentary, 1981, Chinese edit., 1988, Ezekiel-Daniel, 1983, (with others) Student's Dictionary for Biblical and Theological Studies, 1983, Helps for Beginning Hebrew Students, 1981, Jeremiah-Lamentations: New American Commentary, 1993; translator: (with others) New American Standard Bible, 1971, New International Version Bible, 1978, International Children's Version Bible, 1983; editor Southwestern Jour. Theology, 1975-78; contbr. articles to profl. jours. Named Disting. Alumnus Southwestern Bapt. Theol. Sem., 2001. Mem. Soc. Bibl. Lit., Nat. Assn. Profs. Hebrew, Nat. Assn. Bapt. Profs. Religion, Delta Sigma Pi, Beta Gamma Sigma, Theta Xi. Home: 6128 Whitman Ave Fort Worth TX 76133-3547 E-mail: fbhuey@aol.com.

HUEY, GEORGE IRVING, JR., software consultant; b. Chula Vista, Calif., June 8, 1957; s. George I. Sr. and Grace C. (Beck) H. BSEE, Ctrl. Mo. State U., 1980. Computer programmer Bendix Corp., Kansas City, Mo., 1978-82; software cons. Info. Industries Inc., Kansas City, 1982-83; systems mgr. Aramco Svcs. Co., Houston, 1983-84; sr. system tech. specialist Saudi Aramco, Saudi Arabia, 1985-87, supr. comm. ops. data systems support unit, 1987-90; sr. sys. cons. Intergraph, Huntsville, Ala., 1991-95; prin. cons. Microsoft Corp., Redmond, Wash., 1995—. Internat. cons. Intergraph, Huntsville, 1991-95. Author software applications. Mem. Nat. Athlete Strength Assn. (powerlifter, submaster 1991—, 3d pl. 1992 nat. regionals, 2d pl. 1993 nat. regionals), PADI Dive Club (dive master). Avocations: computer, scuba diving, powerlifting, reading science fiction. Home: 3824 Horizon Court Naperville IL 60564 E-mail: ghuey@microsoft.com.

HUEY, JOHN WESLEY, JR., editor; b. Atlanta, Apr. 18, 1948; s. John Wesley and Helen (Cahill) Huey; m. Kathryn White (div. 1981); 1 child, John Wesley IV; m. Sue Yeargan (dec. 1986); m. Kate Ellis, 1993; 1 child, Cole. BA in English, U. Ga., 1970. Reporter DeKalb New Era, Decatur, Ga., 1972-74, Atlanta Constn., 1974-75, Wall St. Jour., Dallas, 1975-79, bur. chief Atlanta, 1979-82, mng. editor Brussels, 1982-83, editor, 1983-84, sr. spl. corr. Atlanta, 1984-86; Atlanta bur. chief, 1986—88; contbg. editor Fortune mag., 1988; editor Southpoint mag., Atlanta, 1989—90; sr. editor Fortune mag., 1990—95; mng. editor Fortune, 1995—2001; editorial dir. Time Inc., 2001—. Mem. adv. bd. Grady Coll., U. Ga. Served to lt. (j.g.) USN, 1970-72. Mem.: ASME, Coun. on Fgn. Rels. Methodist. Office: Time Inc 1271 Avenue Of The Americas New York NY 10020-1300 E-mail: Laura_Whitaker@timeinc.com.

HUEY, J(OSEPH) WISTAR, III, import/export executive; b. Balt., Dec. 8, 1938; s. J. Wistar, Jr. and Louisa Thompson (Macgill) H.; m. Rebecca MacRae Wilson, Feb. 2, 1963 (div. 1975); children: Cameron MacRae, Elizabeth Stewart, Rebecca Macgill, Joseph Wistar IV; m. Lucia Coy Humes, Dec. 6, 1975 (div. 1980); m. Mary Joyce Noell, Sept. 8, 1998. BA, Johns Hopkins U., 1962. Underwriter emeritus Firemans Fund Ins. Co., Balt., 1962-70; v.p. comml. ins. Stump, Harvey & Cook, Inc., Balt., 1970-77; sr. account exec. Tongue Brooks & Co., Inc., Balt., 1977-85; v.p. comml. ins. Wye Ins., Inc., Balt., 1985-89; v.p. mktg. Ins., Inc., Balt., 1989-91; founder, CEO Chesapeake Antique & Classic Motorcars, Ltd., Balt., 1991—2000, mktg. dir., cons.; founder Scottish Highlands and Islands Tour Consultancies, Ltd., 2000—. Cons., dir. Mortons Gourmet and Wine Importers Internat., Ltd., Balt.; bd. dirs. Gaumer Enterprises, Balt., C.J. Dugan Real Estate, Balt., Talbott and Talbott Lingual Rsch. Labs., Inc., Balt.; chmn. bd. dirs. H.E.D. Telecons., Inc.; mktg. dir., cons. Gross Coate 1658, Easton, Md. Mem. Internat. Platform Assn., Md. Hist. Soc., Bentley Driver's Club. Avocations: highland bagpipes, banjo, guitar, chess, bridge. Home: Greystone Ste 303 3700 College Ave Ellicott City MD 21043-4663

HUEY, WARD L(IGON), JR., retired media executive; b. Dallas, Apr. 26, 1938; s. Ward Ligon and Irene Helen (Freeman) H.; m. Marian Kennedy Powell, Oct. 28, 1961; children: Ward L. III, David Powell. BA, So. Meth. U., 1960. Successively with dept. prodn., sales svc. mgr. local sales, regional sales mgr., gen. sales mgr. Sta. WFAA-TV, Dallas, 1960-67, sta. mgr., 1972-75; v.p., gen. mgr. Belo Broadcasting Corp., Dallas, from 1975; vice chmn. bd. dirs., pres. broadcast div. A. H. Belo Corp., Dallas, 1987—2001. Chmn. affiliate bd. govs. ABC-TV, 1981-82, chmn. bd. TV Operators Caucus, 1989. Mem. exec. com. So. Meth. U. Meadows Sch. Arts, 1986—, Goodwill Industries Dallas, 1978-79, State Fair Tex., 1992—; bd. dirs. Children's Med. Found. Tex., Dallas, 1985-94, Dallas Found., 1993—; trustee So. Meth. U., 1996—. Named Disting. Alumni, Highland Park H.S., 1998, Pioneer of Yr., Tex. Broadcasters, 2000; named to, Broadcasting and Calbe Hall of Fame, 1999; recipient Disting. Alumni award, So. Meth. U., 2000. Mem. Maximum Svc. TV Assn. (vice chmn. 1988-94), TV Bur. Advt. (past bd. dirs., exec. com. 1984-88), Assn. Broadcast Execs. Tex. (bd. dirs. 1977-78), Dallas Advt. League (bd. dirs. 1975-76), Salesmanship Club Dallas (pres. 1992-93), Dallas Country Club. Methodist. Avocations: skiing, boating, swimming, golf, music.

HUFBAUER, GARY CLYDE, lawyer; b. San Diego, Apr. 3, 1939; s. Clarence Clyde and Arabelle Maxwell (McKee) H.; children: Randall Clyde Revelle (dec.), Ellen Arabelle Scripps, Romain Clyde; m. Valerie Parra, 1996. AB, Harvard U., 1960; PhD, King's Coll., Cambridge U., Eng., 1963; JD, Georgetown U., 1980. Bar: D.C. 1980, Md. 1980. Mem. faculty dept. econs. U. N.Mex., Albuquerque, 1963-74, prof., 1970-74; dir. internat. tax staff U.S. Dept. Treasury, Washington, 1974-77; dep. asst. Sec. Treasury, Internat. Trade and Investment Policy, 1977-80; mem. firm Rose, Schmidt, Chapman, Duff & Hasley, Washington, 1980-85; dep. dir. Internat. Law Inst., Georgetown Law Ctr., Washington, 1980-82; Wallenberg prof. fin. Georgetown U., Washington, 1985-92; dir. studies Coun. on Fgn. Rels., N.Y.C., 1997-98; sr. fellow Inst. Internat. Econs., Washington, 1982-85, 92-97, 98—. Mem. Harvard Devel. Adv. Svc., Pakistan, 1967-69; vis. prof. Stockholm Sch. Econs., 1974, Cambridge U., 1973, Georgetown U., 1975. Author: Economic Sanctions Reconsidered, 1990, World Capital Markets, 2001. Ford Found. fellow, 1966-67; Fulbright rsch. scholar, 1973 Mem. Am. Econ. Assn., Nat. Economists Club. Episcopalian. Office: Inst for Internat Econs 1750 Massachusetts Ave NW Washington DC 20036-1903

HUFF, C(LARENCE) RONALD, public policy and criminology educator; b. Covington, Ky., Nov. 10, 1945; s. Nathaniel Warren G. and Irene Opal (Mills) H.; m. Patricia Ann Plankenhorn, June 15, 1968; children: Tamara Lynn, Tiffany Dawn. BA, Capital U., 1968; MSW, U. Mich., 1970; PhD, Ohio State U., 1974. Social worker Franklin County Children's Svcs., Columbus, Ohio, 1968; social work intern Pontiac (Mich.) State Hosp. and Family Svc. Met. Detroit, 1969-70; dir. psychiat. social work Lima (Ohio) State Hosp., 1970-71; chief psychiat. social worker N.W. Cmty. Mental Health Ctr., Lima, 1971-72; grad. tchg. assoc. sociology Ohio State U., 1972-74; asst. prof. social ecology U. Calif., Irvine, 1974-76; asst. prof. sociology Purdue U., 1976-79; assoc. prof. pub. policy/mgmt. Ohio State U., Columbus, 1979-87, dir. Criminal Justice Rsch. Ctr., 1979-99, prof., 1987-99, prof. emeritus, 1999—, dir. Sch. Pub. Policy and Mgmt., 1994-99; dean Sch. Social Ecology U. Calif., Irvine, 1999—, prof. criminology, law and society, 1999—. Vis. prof. U. Hawaii, 1995; cons. Bur. Justice Stats., Nat. Inst. Justice, Nat. Inst. Corrections, Nat. Inst. Juvenile Justice and Delinquency Prevention, U.S. Senate Jud. Com., NSF, FBI, others; expert witness fed. and state cts. Author: Youth Violence: Prevention, Intervention, and Social Policy, 1999, Convicted But Innocent: Wrongful Conviction and Public Policy, 1996, (Outstanding Acad. Book award Choice Mag., 1996), The Gang Intervention Handbook, 1993, Gangs in America, 1990, 2d edit., 1996, 3rd edit., 2002, House Arrest and Correctional Policy: Doing Time at Home, 1988, The Mad, The Bad, and The Different: Essays in Honor of Simon Dinitz, 1981, Attorneys as Activists: Evaluating the American Bar Association's BASICS Program, 1979, Contemporary Corrections: Social Control and Conflict, 1977, Planning Correctional Reform, 1975, and others; mem. editl. bd. various jours.; contbr. articles to profl. jours., chpts. to books. Recipient Nat. Security award Mershon Found., 1980, prize New Eng. Sch. Law, 1981, Outstanding Tchg. award, 1985, Donald R. Cressey award Nat. Coun. on Crime and Delinquency, 1992, Paul Tappan award Western Soc. Criminology, 1993, Herbert Bloch award Am. Soc. Criminology, 1994; grantee ABA, 1974-77, Purdue U., 1978, Dept. Justice, 1978-79, 85-88, 91-95, Ohio Dept. Mental Health, 1982-83, 84-85, 85-87, Gov.'s Office Criminal Justice, 1985-88, 92-95, 98, Ohio Dept. Youth Svcs., 1989-90, Ohio State U./Ohio Bd. Regents, 1990-92. Fellow Western Soc. Criminology, Am. Soc. Criminology (exec. bd., pres.-elect 1999-2000, pres. 2000-01, Herbert Bloch award 1994); mem. Acad. Criminal Justice Scis., Nat. Coun. on Crime and Delinquency, Phi Kappa Phi, Phi Beta Delta. Office: U Calif Irvine Sch Social Ecology 300 Social Ecology I Irvine CA 92697-7050 E-mail: rhuff@uci.edu.

HUFF, DANNY W. paper products executive; Asst. to group contrs. budgets and planning to dir. corp. reporting and asst. to corp. contr. Georgia Pacific Corp., 1979—82, dir. project analysis, 1982—84, dir. corp. finance, 1984—92, assistant treasurer, 1992—93, treasurer, 1993—96, v.p., treas., 1996—99, exec. v.p. fin., CFO, 1999—. Office: Georgia-Pacific Corp 133 Peach Tree St NE Atlanta GA 30303

HUFF, DAVID L. geography educator; BS, U. Oreg., 1955; MBA, U. Wash., 1957, PhD, 1960. Now Century Club prof. depts. geography and mktg. adminstrn. U. Tex., Austin. Office: Univ Tex Dept Of Geography Austin TX 78712

HUFF, GAYLE COMPTON, advertising and marketing executive; b. Washington, Nov. 28, 1956; d. Walter Dale and Jeanne (Parker) C.; m. Lanny Ross Huff, May 22, 1982 (div. 2002). B in Gen. Studies, U. Mich., 1978. Mgr. br. merchandising CBS Records, Chgo., 1978, local promotion, mktg. mgr. Indpls., Boston, N.Y.C., 1978-81; spl. projects supr. Pickwick Internat. Musicland Group, Mpls., 1981-82; account exec. Campbell-Mithun Advt., Mpls., 1982-85; mktg. mgr., communications Universal Foods Corp., Milw., 1985-86; nat. advt. mgr. Thorobred Advt. Agy. (Jockey Internat., Inc.), Wis., 1986-88, dir. consumer and trade advt., 1988-89, v.p. advt., 1990-92; dir. mktg./advt. Allen-Edmonds Shoe Co., Port Washington, Wis., 1993-95; v.p., dir. Fin. Mktg. Plus Direct Mktg. Group, Libertyville, Ill., 1995-97; dir. mktg. & merchandising AR Accessories Group Inc., Milw., 1997-98; v.p. creative svcs. Tucker-Knapp Integrated Mktg. Comms., Schaumburg, Ill., 1998-2000; sr. mgr. creative svcs. Discover Fin. Svcs. (Morgan Stanley Dean Witter), Riverwoods, Ill., 2000—. V.p., sec. Java Masters, Inc., 1992—. Recipient Discover Leadership award, Discover Fin. Svcs. Inc., 2000, 2001. Mem. Traffic Audit Bur. for Media Measurement (bd. dirs. 1988-93), Assn. Nat. Advertisers (print adv. com., out of home advt. com. 1989-92). Avocations: dancing, gymnastics, conga drumming. Office: Discover Fin Svcs 2500 Lake Cook Rd # 2W Deerfield IL 60015-3851 E-mail: gaylehuff@discoverfinancial.com.

HUFF, JANE VAN DYKE, secondary education educator; b. Marshall, Mo., Aug. 7, 1948; d. Leonard Scott and Bertha Mae (Carmean) Van Dyke; m. George Sweat Huff, June 27, 1970; children: Ethan Van Dyke, Katherine Van Dyke. BA cum laude, So. Meth. U., 1970. Cert. tchr. K-8, Mo. Tchr. 2d grade Marshall Pub. Schs., 1970-73, substitute tchr. K-12, 1985-93, tchr. 6th grade social studies, 1993—. Organist Marshall 1st United Meth. Ch., 1971—; bd. dirs. Marshall Pub. Edn. Found., 1993—, Marhsall Pub. Schs. Citizens' Adv. Bd., 1988-94, Marshall Philharm. Orch., 1980—, pres., 1990—; bd. dirs. Marshall Mcpl. Bd., 1985—, Marshall Cmty. Chorus, 1989-2001. Named Outstanding Educator, Marsaline Br. NAACP, 2002; recipient Mo. Scholars Acad. Excellence in Tchg. award, 2001. Mem. Mo. State Tchrs. Assn., Marshall City Tchrs. Assn. (Outstanding Tchr. award 2002), Phi Beta Kappa, Alpha Kappa Delta. Avocations: music, musical accompaniment. Home: 331 E North St Marshall MO 65340-2225

HUFF, JANET HOUSE, special education educator; b. Kansas City, Mo., Sept. 5, 1947; d. Arthur and Juanita House; m. William E. Huff, Dec. 20, 1975; children: Ryan, Anesi. BS in Edn., Emporia State U., 1970; MA in Edn., U. Phoenix, 1998, adminstr. license, 2001. Cert. Type A psychology, educationally handicapped and spl. tchr. I, Colo., Type D Elem./Middle. Tchr. spl. edn. Kansas City (Kans.) Unified Sch. Dist., 1970-73, S.W. Bd. Coop. Svcs., Cortez, Colo., 1973-74, Mesa County Valley Sch. Dist. 51, Grand Junction, Colo., 1974-86, Bakersfield (Calif.) City Schs., 1986-89, Fresno (Calif.) Unified Sch. Dist., 1989-90, Cherry Creek Sch. Dist. 5, Englewood, Colo., 1990-92, Jefferson County Sch. REI, 1992—. Lutheran. E-mail: jhuff@jeffco.k12.co.us.

HUFF, JAY, music educator; b. Lubbock, Tex., Jan. 16, 1926; s. Joseph Alexander and Zelta Myrtle Huff; m. Mary Ellen Peck, Sept. 19, 1950; m. Mollie Marie O'Meara, Mar. 23, 1979; children: Cheryl Jean Krause, Ronald Paul. MusB, Colo. U., 1948, MusM, 1951; PhD, Northwestern U., Evanston, Ill., 1965. Asst. prof. No. State Coll., Aberdeen, SD, 1952—54, S.F. Austin State U., Nacogdoches, Tex., 1954—59; violinist San Antonio Symphony, 1959—60, Mpls. Symphony, 1960—61; asst. prof. Milliken U., Decatur, Ill., 1963—65; assoc. prof. Ohio State U., Columbus, 1965—88, assoc. prof. emeritus, 1988—. Editor (translator): A Treatise on the Practice of Mensural Music in the Italian Manner, 1972, An English Translation of Part VI of Walter Odington's De Speculatione Musice, 1973, For Making Organum; composer: (musical core) Centennial, 1970, The Night Thoreau Spent in Jail, 1970. With U.S. Army, 1944. Avocation: classical literature. Home: 180 Arlene Ct SE Rio Rancho NM 87124-2713

HUFF, JOHN DAVID, church administrator; b. Muskegon, Mich., Nov. 20, 1952; s. Lucius Barthol and Marian (Brainard) H.; m. Diane Lynn Church, May 17, 1975; children: Joshua, Jason, Jessica. B in Religious Edn., Reformed Bible Coll., 1977; MA in Sch. Adminstrn., Calvin Coll., 1983; postgrad., Western Mich. U., 1984-93. Cert. ch. educator. Dir. edn. 1st Christian Reformed Ch., Visalia, Calif., 1977—79, Bethany Reformed Ch., Grand Rapids, Mich., 1979—83, Haven Reformed Ch., Kalamazoo, 1983—90, exec. dir. ops., 1990—93; exec. dir. Manitoqua Ministries, Frankfort, Ill., 1993—2002; pastor

preaching and adminstrn. First Reformed Ch., DeMotte, Ind., 2002—. Cons. David C. Cook Pubs., 1988-90, Office Evangelism Reformed Ch. in Am., 1987-91; tchr. trainer, mem. renewal forum Synod of Mich. Reformed Ch. in Am., 1987-90; regional evangelism trainer Synod of Mid-Am., 1995-2002; bd. dirs. Chgo. Christian Counseling Ctr., 1995-2000, bd. officer, 1996-2000; v.p. Illiana Classis Reformed Ch. in Am., 1999, pres., 2000; Denominational "Refocus Leaders" facilitator Classis Illiana, 1998-2000, Classis Chgo., 1999-2001; mem. adj. faculty Trinity Christian Coll., 1996; adj. prof. Reformed Bible Coll., 2000. Author: Effective Decision Making for Church Leaders, 1988, Leader's Guide for Out of the Saltshaker and into the World, 1988. Vice-chmn. Youth Com. Bill Glass Crusade, Visalia, 1978, chmn. Cen. Valley Ch. Workers Conf., Visalia, 1978; mem. Youth Com. City-Wide Easter Svcs., Visalia, 1979; trustee Reformed Bible Coll., Grand Rapids, 1984-91, exec. com., 1985-91, asst. sec. bd. dirs., 1986-87, sec. bd. dirs., 1987-90; chmn. S.W. Mich. Christian Discipleship Com., 1984-85. Recipient DeVos award Reformed Bible Coll., 1977; Mich. State scholar, 1970. Mem. Bibl. Archeol. Soc., Christian Educators-Reformed ch. Am., Inst. for Am. Ch. Growth (cons. 1986-93), Christian Mgmt. Assn. Cen. Valley Youth Ministers (sec. 1978-79), Alban Inst., Am. Camping Assn. (bd. dirs. Ill. chpt. 1995-98), Christian Camping Internat., Delta Epsilon Chi. Republican. Avocations: reading, racquetball, golf, civil war information. Home and Office: 9991 W 1200 N Demotte IN 46310 E-mail: JohnHuff@netnitco.net. *Half of being smart is knowing what you're dumb at!.*

HUFF, JOHN GARDNER, child welfare specialist, state official; b. Chgo., Nov. 24, 1951; s. Norman M. Huff and Florence Lightfoot; m. Judith Helen Wood, Aug. 30, 1980; 1 child, Walter Norman. AA, Lincoln (Ill.) Coll., 1973; BS, Ill. State U., 1975; MA, Govs. State U., University Park, Ill., 1978. Cert. 6-12 tchr., Ill. Substitute tchr. Chgo. Bd. Edn., 1975-78, 92-93; indsl. safety cons. Ill. Dept. Commerce and Cmty. Affairs, Chgo., 1978-81; revenue collector Ill. Dept. Revenue, 1981-91; employment specialist Ill. Dept. Employment Security, 1993-94; child welfare specialist Ill. Dept. Children and Family Svcs., 1995—. Pub. mem. collection agy. licensing and disciplinary bd. Ill. Dept. Profl. Regulation, Springfield, 1989—2002. Author: Information Sources for Parents of African-American Children, 1998, 99—; editor: DCFS Purchase of Service Resource Info. Guide, 1998—, Precinct committeeman McLean County Rep. Com., 1974-75, Du Page County, 2000—; alt. del. Rep. Nat. Com., Kansas City, Mo., 1976; libr. trustee Village of Lyons, Ill., 1985-94; regional sch. trustee Cook County, Chgo., 1985-94. Named Ky. Col., Commonwealth of Ky., 1988, Ala. Col., State of Ala., 1988, Tex. Adm., State of Tex., 1999. Mem. Masons (master 1979). Avocation: collecting political campaign items. Home: 4911 Bryan Pl Downers Grove IL 60515-3621 Office: Ill Dept Child and Family Svcs 1026 S Damen Ave Chicago IL 60612 E-mail: jhuff@idcfs.state.il.us.

HUFF, ROBERT WHITLEY, obstetrician, gynecologist, educator; b. San Antonio, 1937; MD, Baylor U., 1966. Diplomate Am. Bd. Med. Genetics, Am. Bd. Ob-Gyn., Am. Bd. Maternal and Fetal Medicine. Intern Ben Taub Gen. Hosp., Houston, 1966-67; resident in ob-gyn. Bexar County Hosp., San Antonio, 1969-72; prof. U. Tex., San Antonio, 1972—. Mem. staff Med. Ctr. Hosp., San Antonio. Office: U Tex Health Sci Ctr ObGyn Mail Stop 7836 7703 Floyd Curl Dr San Antonio TX 78284-6200

HUFF, RONALD GARLAND, mechanical engineer; b. Toledo, Ohio, Dec. 29, 1930; s. Blenn Chalmer and Helen Ester (Schling) H.; m. Nancy Carroll Warns, June 29, 1957; children: Dennis Lee, Deborah Lynn. BSME, U. Toledo, 1953. Aero. engr. Nat. Adv. Com. for Aeronautics, Cleve., 1955-58; aerospace tech. NASA, Cleve., 1958-87; cons./proprietor Ronald G. Huff & Assocs., Cleve., 1986—. Contbr. articles to profl. jours. Photographer North Olmsted Band Boosters, Ohio, 1974-80; active PTA, North Olmsted, 1969-72. 1st lt. U.S. Army, 1953-55. Mem. ASME (chmn. winter ann.meeting 1986), AIAA. Congregationalist. Achievements include patents on supersonic jet noise suppressor; method for measuring internal hot gas side wall temperatures in thin wall generatively cooled rocket engines, multi-fold side branch muffler. Home and Office: Huff & Assocs 3741 Cinnamon Way Westlake OH 44145-5717

HUFF, ROSEMARY BOWERS, music and voice educator; b. Krebs, Okla., Dec. 14, 1924; d. Harvey Henry and Hilda Magdalene (Kiple) Bowers; m. Howard Farmer Huff, June 10, 1951 (dec. Sept. 16, 2001); children: Carol Celeste Huff Hicks, Angela Kay, Gloria Ann Huff Graham, Craig Kenton. AB in Music Edn., Park Coll., 1947; M Sacred Music, Union Theol. Sch. Sacred Music, N.Y.C., 1951. Ordained to ministry Christian Ch. (Disciples of Christ), 1951. Tchr. music Harper-Maize (Kans.) Pub. Sch., 1947-49; music educator divsn. overseas ministries Christian Ch. (Disciples of Christ), Tokyo, 1951-62; min. music Willow Rd. Christian Ch., Enid, Okla., 1963-69, Ctrl. Christian Ch., Enid, 1970-80; organist, choir dir. Phillips Theol. Sem., Enid, 1968-80; min. music Bethany Christian Ch., Tulsa, 1980-89; pvt. tchr. piano and voice, Enid, 1965-80, Tulsa, 1980—. Judge Tri-State Music Festival, Enid, 1970-99. Recipient Honored Min.'s award Christian Ch. (Disciples of Christ), 1992. Mem. Assn. Disciple Musicians (planning coun. 1986-89), Hymn Soc. Am., Nat. Music Tchrs. Assn., Okla. Music Tchrs. Assn. (cert. piano and voice tchr.), Tulsa Accredited Music Tchrs. Assn. (dir. accreditation 1986-89), Hyechka Music Club. Democrat. Avocations: music, art. Home: 3715 E 81st Pl Tulsa OK 74137-1602

HUFF, RUSSELL JOSEPH, public relations and publishing executive; b. Chgo., Feb. 24, 1936; s. Russell Winfield and Virgilist Marie (McMahon) H.; m. Beverly Diane Staschke, 1968; 1 child, Michelle Lynn. BA in Philosophy cum laude, U. Notre Dame, 1958; BS in Theology, Cath. U. Santiago (Chile), 1960; MA in Comm. Arts, U. Notre Dame, 1968. Ordained priest Roman Cath. Ch., 1962. Exec. editor Cath. Boy and Miss., Notre Dame, Ind., 1963-68; mng. editor Nation's Schs., McGraw Hill, Chgo., 1968-70; v.p. pub. affairs Homart Devel. Co., Chgo., 1971-76; dir. pub. rels. Sears, Roebuck Co. Internat. Ops., Chgo., 1976-82; dir. pub. affairs Sears Roebuck Found. Internat. Projects, Chgo., 1981-82; sr. v.p., sales and mktg. dir. Mineca Internat., Inc., Chgo., 1982-84; v.p., pub. rels. Lofino Poppa Devel. Corp., Sarasota, Fla., 1984-85; pres., co-owner R.J. Huff & Assocs., Inc., Sarasota, 1985—2001; real estate broker Sarasota, 1985-2001. Author: Come Build My Church, 1966, On Wings of Adventure, 1967, Wings of WWII, 1985 (award 1986), Companion to Wings of World War II, 1987, Winging It, Vols. I and II, 1992; editor, pub. (quar. jour.) Wings and Things of the World, 1987-93, Wings and Things of the World for Sale, 1993-95; cons., editl. contbr. Aviation Treasures, 1995—; sr. editor The Nobody's Fool Fin. Market Analyst Pub., 1996-98. Care min. leader Ch. Incarnation Parish Coun., 1998-2002; future planning and rev. com., stewardship comm. chmn., Internat. Peace and Justice chmn., Recipient Outstanding Mag. award Cath. Press Assn., 1965, 67; named for Best Cover, Nation's Schs., 1968; cert. Gemol. Inst. Am.; cert. jr. coll. tchr., Calif. Mem. Pub. Rels. Soc. Am. (accredited 1976—), Chicagoland Mil. Collectors Soc. (dir. quar. expositions 1981-82), Am. Soc. Mil. Insignia Collectors, Orders and Medals Soc. Am., Nat. Fgn. Trade Coun., Pub. Affairs Coun., Conf. Bd., Internat. Bus. Coun., Internat. Vis. Ctr. Chgo., Ptnrs. of the Ams. (cert. for advancement L.Am. rels. 1980), São Paulo Ptnrs. (cert. for advancement Brazil-U.S. rels. 1979, dir. Ill.), Chgo. Assn. of Commerce and Industry, U.S.-Spanish C. of C. of Middle West (dir.), War Memorabilia Collectors Soc. (exec. dir.). Roman Catholic. Office: 4062 Kingston Ter Sarasota FL 34238-2632 E-mail: russhuff@comcast.net.

HUFF, SARA DAVIS, nursing manager; b. Moundville, Ala., May 16, 1935; d. George W. and Maggie A. (Callahan) Davis; m. Eugene H. Huff, May 21, 1956 (div. June 1992); children: John Davis Huff, Timothy Eugene Huff. RN, Druid City Hosp. Sch. Nursing, Tuscaloosa, Ala., 1956; BS, Oglethorpe U., 1980. CNOR. RN, oper. rm. Druid City Hosp., Tuscaloosa, 1956-58; asst. head nurse, thoracic cardiovascular St. Joseph's Hosp., Atlanta, 1958-60; charge nurse/open heart thoracic Emory U. Hosp., Atlanta, 1960-64, edn. coord. oper. room, 1974-75; oper. rm. supr. H. Egleston Hosp. for Children, Atlanta, 1964-73; nurse cons. Cons. Surg. Svcs., Atlanta, 1986-92; dir. surg. svcs. Northside Hosp., Atlanta, 1975-86; staff nurse oper. rm. Northlake Hosp., Atlanta, 1990-92; dir. surg. svcs. Atlanta Hosp., 1989-90, Newton Gen. Hosp., Covington, Ga., 1992—98; clin. resource mgr. Emory Dunwoody Med. Ctr., Atlanta, 2002—. Spkr. in field. Mem. AORN (nat. bd. dirs. 1980-84, gen. AORN nat. congress 1980, other coms.), ANA, Assn. of Oper. Rm. Nurses of Atlanta (Nurse of Yr. 1975), Atlanta Area Oper. Rm. Suprs. (chmn. 1973-75). Home: 2534 Warwick Cir NE Atlanta GA 30345-1632 E-mail: graceD8669@aol.com.

HUFF, SHEILA LINDSEY, secondary education educator, coach; b. Rockport, Ind., Oct. 29, 1951; d. William Nathaniel and Thelma Cordelia (Crawley) Lindsey; m. Aug. 7, 1976 (div. 1984); children: Aaron Drake, Andrew Christopher. BS, Ind. State U., 1973, MS, 1975. Cert. health and phys. edn. tchr., Ind., lic. secondary administrn. and supervision. Asst. dir. residence hall Ind. State U., Terre Haute, 1973-74, dir. residence hall, 1974-76; coach boys tennis Evansville (Ind.) Vanderburgh Sch. Corp., 1976-78, girls track coach, 1976—, girls volleyball coach, 1985-89, tchr. phys. edn. and recreation, summer 1985-90; asst. prin. Glenwood Middle Sch.; assoc. prof. U. So. Ind.; prin. Glenwood Mid. Sch., 2000; prof. U. So. Ind., 2001. Instr. in CPR, ARC, Evansville, 1980-90; advisor Health Profls. Adv. Bd., Evansville, 1989-90; interim prof. U. So. Ind., Evansville, 1989—, assoc. prof., 1990—; asst. athletic dir. Bosse H.S., 1995—. Community instr. ARC, Evansville, 1986-90; bd. dirs. YWCA, 2000-2003; pres. exec. bd. Washington Ave. Ctr., 2003 Mem. AAHPERD, NEA, Nat. Assn. Secondary Sch. Prins., Ind. Assn. Secondary Sch. Prins., Ind. Tchrs. Assn., Ind. Health, Phys. Edn. and Recreation Assn. Evansville Tchrs. and Coaches Assn. Baptist. Avocations: reading, crafts, sports, cooking. Home: 1706 N Thomas Ave Evansville IN 47711-4452

HUFF, WILLIAM BRAID, retired publishing company executive; b. Lynn, Mass., Apr. 18, 1950; s. Harold Butler and Mary Stewart (Braid) Huff; m. Karen Murphy, May 4, 1985; children: Thomas Murphy, Kathryn Braid. BS, Bowdoin Coll., 1972; MBA, Darthmouth Coll., 1974. CPA Mass. Staff acct. Arthur Andersen, Boston, 1974—76; contr. Affiliated Broadcasting, Boston, 1976—82, treas., 1982—86, sr. v.p., 1984—86; contr. Affiliated Publs., Boston, 1982—86, v.p., 1986—89, CFO, 1989—91, exec. v.p., CFO, 1991—97; sr. v.p., CFO Boston Globe Newspaper Co., 1992—97, pres., CFO, 1997—2001. Chmn. Morgan Meml. Goodwill; v.p. Wayland Pub. Sch. Found. Mem.: AICPAs, Mass. Soc. CPAs, Weston Golf. Republican. Episcopalian. Avocations: skiing, soccer, golf. Home: 5 Sherman Bridge Rd Wayland MA 01778-1213

HUFFAKER, E. WAYNE, artist; b. Flin Flon, Man., Can., June 14, 1933; s. Marvin F. and Janice (Barton) H.; m. Shirley K. Huffaker, Apr. 3, 1951 (dec. 1968); children: Tony, Gary, Laura, Renee; m. Linda S. Huffaker, May 21, 1984; 1 child, Brandon. AA, Ventura (Calif.) Coll., 1968. Info. svcs. supr. Conoco, Inc., Houston, 1956-95. Automobilia artist done for commn., mag., books and box-lid art, as well as speculation pieces to offer as originals or ltd. edit. prints. With USNR, 1950-62. Mem. Am. Soc. Aviation Artists, Inc., Colored Pencil Soc. Avocations: sports, custom and classic cars. Home: 19606 Spring Sage Ct Houston TX 77094-2627 Office: PMB 168 925 S Mason Rd Katy TX 77450-3874

HUFFER, MELISSA WYNNE CLEM, accountant; b. Staunton, Va., Oct. 16, 1966; d. Samuel Helms and Patsy Ann (Doome) Clem; m. Robert Louis Huffer, Dec. 30, 1994; children: Charles Reese, Alexandria Quinn. BS in BA, BS in econs., Bridgewater (Va.) Coll., 1989. CPA, Va.; cert. aerobic and fitness instr., body pump instr. Acct. R.L. Persinger & Co., Staunton, 1989-91, Elmore, Hupp & Co., Staunton, 1991-95; treas., CEO Huffer & Co., Inc., Staunton, 1995—; owner, mgr. Melissa C. Huffer, CPA, Staunton, 1998—. Biometics distbr., 2000—. Fin. sec. 1st Presbyn. Ch., Staunton, 1997-2000; rec. sec. Izaak Walton League of Am., Staunton, 1994, 99-2001. Mem. DAR (treas. 1997-2001), AICPA, Va. Soc. CPAs, Aerobics and Fitness Assn. Am. Republican. Presbyterian. Avocations: dance, weight training, photography, gardening, biking. Home and Office: 2002 3d St Staunton VA 24401-3026 E-mail: cpa1@ntelos.net.

HUFFINE, COY LEE, retired chemical engineer, consultant; b. Knoxville, Tenn., Apr. 2, 1924; s. Coy Mann and Inez Belle (Story) H.; m. Virginia Elizabeth Browne, Mar. 31, 1951; children: Jeremy Bennett, Lucinda Jane. BS, U. Tenn., 1945, MS, 1947; PhD, Columbia U., 1953. Prin. engr. aircraft nuclear propulsion program Gen. Electric Co., Oak Ridge and Cin., 1951-59; research ceramist Gen. Electric Research Lab., Schenectady, 1959-60; project mgr. devel. and mfg. Apollo spacecraft Heat Shield, space sys. div. Avco Corp., Lowell, Mass., 1960-67; with IBM, Rochester, Minn., 1968-87, mgr. component tech., info. systems div., 1980-87. Cons. and lectr. in field; lay-lectr. on history and philosophy of sci. Unitarian-Universalist Ch. Served with USN, 1945-46. Mem. Am. Inst. Chem. Engrs., AIME, Nat. Inst. Ceramic Engrs., Am. Ceramic Soc., N.Y. Acad. Scis., Sigma Xi Home: 2247 5th Ave NE Rochester MN 55906-4017

HUFFINGTON, ANITA, sculptor; b. Balt., Dec. 25, 1934; d. Norris Jackson and Agnes (Hook) H.; m. Manuel Rubin Duque, Sept. 17, 1957 (div. Nov. 1964); 1 child, Lisa Huffington Duque; m. Henry Sutter, Dec. 4, 1964. BA, CCNY, 1973, MFA, 1975. Resident La Napoule (France) Art Found., 1996. One-woman exhbns. include U. Ark., Fayetteville, 1982, Valley House Gallery, Dallas, 1986, Benton Gallery, Southampton, NY, 1989, Ark. Art Ctr., Little Rock, 1990, O'Hara Gallery, NYC, 1994, 96, 99, 2001, U. Ctrl. Ark., Conway, 1997, Triangle Gallery, San Francisco, 1998, Lisa Kurts Gallery, Memphis, 1999, 2003, Morris Mus., Augusta, Ga., 2004, Walton Art Ctr., Fayetteville, Ar., 2004; 2-person show Lisa Kurts Gallery, 1995; 3-person shows Louis Stern Gallery, West Hollywood, Calif., 1996, Triangle Gallery, San Francisco, 1996; group exhbn. include Internat. Women's Art Festival, NYC, 1976, U. Ark., Fayetteville, 1978, 92, Ark. Arts Ctr., Little Rock, 1979-81, Territorial Restoration Gallery, Little Rock, 1981, Harris Gallery, Houston, Tex., 1981-93, Sculptural Arts Mus., Altanta, 1982, Benton Gallery, Southampton, NY, 1988, Kornbluth Gallery, Fair Lawn, NJ, 1989, The Art Show, 7th Regiment Armory, NYC, 1989-2003, Ft. Smith (Ark.) Art Ctr., 1990, Salon de Mars, Paris, 1992, U. Pa., Phila. US Artists Art Fair, Pa. Acad., 1992-2002, ARTexas, Dallas, 1993-94, Art Fair Seattle, 1995-97, Art Miami (Fla.), 1996, 98, Triangle Gallery, San Francisco, 1996, 99, 2000, Am. Acad. Arts and Letters, NYC, 1997, Columbus (Ga.) Mus. and Miss. Mus. Art, Jackson, 1997, Am. Acad. Arts and Letters, 1997, Two Sculptors, Inc., NYC, 1998, Valley House Gallery, Dallas, 1998, Art Palm Beach, 1998, 99, 2000, 01, Dallas Internat. Art and Antiques Fair, 2000-02, Hist. Ark. Mus., Little Rock, 2001, Met. Mus. Art, NYC, 2002, others; works in permanent collection of Met. Mus. of Art, NYC, 2003; featured in various profl. publ., mag., newspapers, and videos. Recipient Jimmy Ernst award Am. Acad. Arts and Letters, 1997, others; Visual arts fellow Ark. Arts Coun.

HUFFINGTON, ROY MICHAEL, business executive, former ambassador; b. Tomball, Tex., Oct. 4, 1917; s. Roy Mackey and Bertha (Michel) H.; m. Phyllis Gough, Oct. 26, 1945; children: R. Michael, Terry Huffington Dittman. BS, So. Meth. U., 1938; MA, Harvard U., 1941, PhD, 1942, grad. advanced mgmt. program, 1976; LHD, So. Meth. U., 1990. Tchg. fellow Harvard U., Cambridge, Mass., 1939-42, instr. geology, 1942; sr. geologist, divn. exploration geologist Humble Oil and Refining Co., Houston, 1946-56; pres. Roy M. Huffington, Inc., Houston, 1956-83, chmn. bd., 1956-90, chmn., pres., 1993—; U.S. amb. to Austria, Vienna, 1990-93. Bd. dirs. Huffco Group, Inc., Houston; bd. dirs. Am. Petroleum Inst., Washington, 1983-90, 93—; bd. dirs. Brookings Inst., Washington, 1984-88, mem. exec. com., 1993-2002, hon. life trustee, 1988-90, 93—; chmn. Salzburg Seminar, 1994—, bd. dirs., 1992-94. Contbr. articles to profl. jours. Bd. dirs. Tex. Med. Ctr., 1989-90, 93—, Houston Mus. Natural Sci., 1981-86, Kid Care, Inc., Houston, 1993-2003; trustee Huffington Found., 1987—, Baylor Coll. Medicine, 1986-90, 93-99, trustee emeritus, 1999—, chmn. devel. bd. Huffington Ctr. on Aging, 1999—; trustee Webster U., Vienna, 1992-2002, George Bush Libr. Found., Tex. A&M U., 1993—; bd. visitors M.D. Anderson Cancer Ctr., 1980-90, 93-99, sr. mem., 1999—; bd. visitors Sheltering Arms Found. for Elderly, 1994-97, Claremont Sch. Politics and Econs., Claremont Grad. U., 1995-2002; bd. govs. Mid. East Inst., 1982-88; devel. bd. U. Tex. Health Sci. Ctr., 1981-90, 93—, life mem., 1997—; dir. The Rothko Chapel, 1996-2002; mem. leadership com. James A. Baker III Inst. for Pub. Policy, Rice U., 1993—. Lt. comdr. USNR, 1942-45, USNR, 1942-54. Decorated Bronze Star with combat V, Grosse Goldene Ehrenzeichen (Austria), 1997; recipient Alumni Achievement award Harvard U. Bus. Sch., 1982, Oil Drop award petroleum divsn. ASME, 1985, Gold Medallion Oil Pioneer award Indonesian Govt., 1985, John Rogers award Southwestern Legal Found., 1987, Disting. Alumni award So. Meth. U., 1988, Internat. Businessman of Yr. award Houston World Trade Assn., 1988, Amb. of Yr. award Diplomatic Club, Vienna, 1992, Disting. Svc. award Permian Basin sect. Soc. Econ. Paleontologists and Mineralogists, 1996, Woodrow Wilson award for corp. citizenship Woodrow Wilson Internat. Ctr. for Scholars, 2001, Henry Lawrence Gantt medal ASME, 2001, Founding Father award, Pertamina, Jakarta, Indonesia, 2002; named to Tex. Bus. Hall of Fame, 1992. Fellow AAAS (life), Geol. Soc. Am. (trustee 1988-90, hon. found. trustee 1991—); mem. Am. Assn. Petroleum Geologists (Michel T. Halbouty Human Needs award 1991, trustee assoc. found. 1980-90, 93—), Ind. Petroleum Assn. Am. (dir. 1979-80), U.S. Oil and Gas Assn., Tex. Ind. Prodrs. and Royalty Owners Assn., Tex. Oil and Gas Assn. (dir. 1972-84, Disting. Svc. award 1988), Houston Geol. Soc., Am. Inst. Profl. Geologists, 25-Yr. Club of the Petroleum Industry, Internat. Assn. for Energy Econs. Washington (pres.'s adv. coun. 1997—), All-Am. Wildcatters (chmn. 1986-87), Asia Soc. N.Y. (chmn. 1982-89, trustee 1978-82, hon. life trustee 1989-90, 93—), Am. Austrian Found. N.Y. (trustee 1993—), The U.S. Indonesia Soc. (Washington, dir. 1994—), Coun. on Fgn. Rels., World Econ. Forum, Coun. Am. Ambs., Interferon Found. (vice chmn., co-founder, 1979-90), U.S. Navy League, Nat. Petroleum Coun., SAR, Coronado Club (Houston), The Houston Club (bd. dirs. 1967-70, v.p. 1969-70), The Houston Country Club (mem. ho. com. 1979-81), Met. Club N.Y.C. (mem. govs. adv. bd. 1974-77), Met. Club of Washington, Petroleum Club of Houston (mem. food com. 1966-67, mem. fin. com. 1969-70, bd. dirs. 1978-80, 1st v.p. 1980-81), Alpha Tau Omega (bd. govs. Found. 1993—, Disting. Alumni award 1987). Republican. Presbyterian. Office: PO Box 4337 Houston TX 77210-4337

HUFFMAN, CAROL KOSTER, retired elementary school educator; b. L.I., N.Y., Nov. 4, 1933; d. Harry C., Jr. and Mary M. (Wilchin) Koster; m. William Leslie Huffman. BS, Hofstra U., 1954, MS, 1967. Cert. elem., art, nursery and spl. edn. tchr. N.Y., advanced Irlen screener I and area coord. Dir. Child's World Sch., New Orleans; in-svc. instr. Half Hollow Hills Schs., Dix Hills, NY, resource, self-contained program, art and learning strategies tchr.; instr. in spl. edn. Hofstra U., Hempstead, NY; cons. curriculum, spl. edn. and reading; ret. Rschr. identification and ednl. accomodations students with visual disabilities affecting schoolwork. Editor: The Communicator, The Phoenix, Williamsburg Directory Sect. Former del. N.Y. State Retirement Sys.; former bd. dirs. Win-Gate Village Club, Orlando, Fla.; chair Neighborhood Beautification Grant Com., 2002—03. Recipient award, Orange County, Fla., 2001—02, 2002—03. Mem.: AFT, Half Hollow Hills Tchr. Assn., N.Y. State United Tchrs., Kappa Delta Pi, Kappa Pi.

HUFFMAN, DAVID GEORGE, electrical engineer; b. Fresno, Calif., Apr. 13, 1965; s. Fred Norman and Sharon (Richardson) H.; m. Johnnie Ann Valtierra, Sept. 21, 1991; children: Matthew Christopher Kenerly, Makenna Francisca-Elise. BSEE, Fresno State U., 1988. From field engr. to pres. Power Systems Testing Co., Fresno, Calif., 1988—2002, pres., 2002—. Mem. Internat. Electronic and Electrical Engrs. Assn., Eta Kappa Nu. Avocations: golf, model building, reading, traveling, skydiving. Office: Power Systems Testing Co 4688 W Jennifer Ave Ste 108 Fresno CA 93722-6418

HUFFMAN, DELTON CLEON, JR., pharmacy association executive; b. St. Louis, Feb. 18, 1943; s. Delton Cleon and Kathryn (Saegesser) H.; m. Judy Hill, Aug. 11, 1962; children— Kimberly Lea, Jeffrey Keith. BS in Pharmacy (Archer Drug Co. scholar), U. Ark., 1966; PhD, U. Miss., 1971. Pharmacist Crank Drug Co., Inc., Little Rock, 1966—67; asst. prof., dir. div. pharmacy adminstrn. U. Tenn. Coll. Pharmacy, Memphis, 1970—73, asso. prof., chmn. dept. pharmaceutics, 1973; exec. v.p. Am. Coll. Apothecaries, 1971—, also prof., chmn. dept. pharmacy, 1974—89, vice chancellor adminstrn., 1984—89; exec. dir. Nat. Cmty. Pharmacists Assn. Mgmt. Inst., Alexandria, Va., 1989—99, sr. v.p. practice and mgmt., 1992—99. Contbr. articles to profl. lit. Recipient Lederle Faculty award, 1971; NDEA fellow, 1967-70; Am. Found. for Pharm. Edn. fellow, 1967-70 Fellow Am. Coll. Apothecaries; mem. AAAS, Am. Assn. Colls. Pharmacy, Am. Pharm. Assn., Nat. Cmty. Pharmacists Assn., Tenn. Pharm. Assn., Okla. Pharm. Assn. (hon.), Ark. Pharm. Assn. (hon. life), Am. Soc. Assn. Execs., Kappa Psi, Rho Chi. Home: 6020 Willoughby Oak Ln Bartlett TN 38135-1464 Office: 2830 Summer Oaks Dr Bartlett TN 38134-3811

HUFFMAN, DURWARD ROY, college system official, electrical engineer; b. Little Mountain, S.C., Jan. 22, 1939; s. Roy Otho and Mabel Amanda (Huffstettler) H.; m. Lillian Hope Farrell, Apr. 18, 1959; children: Donald Durward, Heatherlyn. BSEE, Heald Engring. Coll., 1963; MSEE, U. Colo., 1966; EdD in Higher Edn., U. Sarasota, 1980. Registered profl. engr., Pa. Asst. design engr. Westinghouse Elec. Corp., Sunnyvale, Calif., 1963-64; instr. elec. engring. U. Colo., Boulder, 1965-67; elec. engr. Corning (N.Y.) Glass Works, 1967-68; sr. process control engr. Corning Glass Works, Wellsboro, Pa., 1968; assoc. prof. elec.-electronic engring. tech. Luzerne County C.C., Wilkes-Barre, Pa., 1968-73, chmn. dept., 1971-73; faculty Midlands Tech. Coll., Columbia, S.C., 1973-75; assoc. dean Nashville State Tech. Inst., 1976-87, acting dean instrn., 1985-86; pres. No. Maine Tech. Coll., Presque Isle, 1987-2001; acad. officer Maine C.C. Sys., Augusta, 1994-2001, chief acad. officer, 2001—. Presenter in field; chair tech. accreditation commn. Accreditation Bd. Engring. and Tech., 1989-90. Editor-in-chief, Jour. Engring. Tech., 1990-92, pub. editor, 1987-89. Mem. steering com. Ctrl. Aroostook County (Maine) Job Opportunity Zone, 1988-91; bd. dirs. Leaders Encouraging Aroostook Devel., 1988-2001, sec., 1988-93; bd. dirs. Maine Rsch. and Productivity Coun., 1988-92; mem. pub. policy com. Maine Alzheimer's Assn., 2001—. Fellow Accreditation Bd. Engring. and Tech.; mem. IEEE (sr.), Am. Soc. Engring. Edn. (divsn. engring. tech. exec. bd. 1981-82, sec. 1982-84), Am. Tech. Edn. Assn., Am. Assn. C.C. (commn. on cmty. and workforce devel. 1995-97, com. on academic, student, cmty. devel. 1998-2001), Engring. Tech. Leadership Inst. (mem. exec. com. 1978-79, 86-87), New Eng. Assn. Schs. and Colls. (chairperson accreditation team 1990, 95, 97, 98, team mem. 1994-96), Rotary (chairperson com. on vocat. svc. 1988-89, dist. 7810 scholarships subcom. 1996-2000), Presque Isle Club, Eta Kappa Nu. Republican. Avocation: vol. work accreditation postsecondary ednl. instns. and programs. Office: Maine CC Sys 323 State St Augusta ME 04330-7131

HUFFMAN, EDGAR JOSEPH, oil company executive; b. Hartford City, Ind., Aug. 24, 1939; s. Floyd Edgar and Elizabeth Jean Huffman; m. Margaret Mary Brenet, May 3, 1980; children: Donovan L. Walker, Maryanne Ramiriz. BBA, Ind. Cen. U., 1961; MA, NYU, 1968. V.p. corp. profitability Valley Nat. Bank, Phoenix, 1978—82, v.p. corp. planning, 1982—85; v.p., chief exec. officer Visa Industries Ariz., Phoenix, 1985—95. Chmn. bd. dirs. Montessori Day Schs., Inc., Phoenix, 1981; bd. dirs. Basic Earth Scis., Calpcco III, Denver. Home: 1710 E Cinnabar Ave Phoenix AZ 85020-1915 E-mail: ehuffman@mdpsc.org.

HUFFMAN, GREGORY SCOTT COMBEST, lawyer; b. Austin, Tex., Dec. 19, 1946; s. Calvin Combest and Olive Agnes (Weaver) H.; m. Mary L. Murphy, Feb. 1, 1986. Student, Stanford U., France, 1966—67; BA in History with great distinction, Stanford U., 1969; postgrad., London Sch. of Econs., 1971—72; JD, Harvard U., 1973. Bar: Tex. 1973, U.S. Dist. Cts. Tex. 1974, U.S. Ct. Appeals (5th cir.) 1975, U.S. Supreme Ct. 1976. From assoc. to sr. ptnr. Thompson & Knight, Dallas, 1973—, also dir. Chief editor (monographs) Texas Free Enterprise and Antitrust Act, 1984-90, Texas Antitrust and Related Statutes, 1991—. Pres. Northern Hills Neighborhood Assn., 1980; bd. dirs. Common Cause of Tex., 1979-81, Love Field Citizens Action Commn., 1980-83, Appleseed Found., 1996-2001; adminstrv. chmn., bd. dirs. Tex. Appleseed, 1996-2001; active Tex. Supreme Ct. Adv. Com. on Professionalism. Fellow Tex. Bar Found., Dallas Bar Found.; mem. ABA (antitrust and litigation sect.), Tex. Bar Assn. (antitrust and litigation sect., chmn. unlawful practice law com. 1981-83, chmn. lawyer referral svc. com. 1982-83, bd. legal specialization 1974-77, chmn. antitrust and bus. litigation sect. 1991-92, bd. dirs. 1983—, task force on unauthorized practice of law, author of reports, presdl. citation 2000, cert. of merit 2001), Dallas Bar Assn. (antitrust sect., sec.-treas. 1981, chmn. unauthorized practice law com. 1979, chmn. lawyer referral svc. com. 1980-81, chmn. profl. svcs. com. 1986-87, chmn. spkrs. com. 1999-2000, chmn. CLE com. 2001, bd. dirs. antitrust sect. 1981, 89-2002, bd. dirs. litigation sect. 1988), Harvard Law Sch. Assn. Tex. (pres. 1987-88), Tower Club Dallas, Phi Beta Kappa, Sigma Alpha Epsilon. Methodist. Home: 8234 Garland Rd Dallas TX 75218-4417 Office: Thompson & Knight 1700 Pacific Ave Ste 3300 Dallas TX 75201-4693

HUFFMAN, JAMES THOMAS WILLIAM, oil exploration company executive; b. Norman, Okla., Mar. 27, 1947; s. Thomas William and Dorlese M. (Hicks) H.; children: Laura Anne, Christopher James. BBA, Baylor U., 1970. CPA. Mgr. Arthur Andersen & Co., Houston, 1970-76; sr. mgr. Price, Waterhouse & Co., Denver, 1976-79; v.p. Credo Petroleum Corp., 1978-80, pres., 1980-81, chmn., chief exec. officer, 1981—, also dir. Dir. Huffman Heat

Exchangers Inc.; dir. XF&R, Inc.; pres., dir. SECO Energy Corp.; pres., dir. United Oil Corp. Mem. AICPA, Tex., Colo. socs. CPAs, Petroleum Landman, Ind. Petroleum Assn. Am., Ind. Petroleum Assn. Mountain State, Petroleum Accts. Soc.

HUFFMAN, JAMES LLOYD, law educator; b. Ft. Benton, Mont., Mar. 25, 1945; s. Roy E. and Menga (Herzog) H.; m. Leslie M. Spencer, Sept. 11, 1956; children: Kurt Andrew, Erica Leigh, James Spencer, Claire Menga, Margaret Murray. Student, Stanford U., 1963-64; BS, Mont. State U., 1967; MALD, Fletcher Sch. Law and Diplomacy, 1967-68; JD, U. Chgo., 1972. Bar: Mont., U.S. Ct. Appeals (Fed. cir.), U.S. Supreme Ct. Asst. prof., then assoc. prof. Lewis and Clark Law Sch., Portland, Oreg., 1973-78, prof. law, 1978—, assoc. dean, 1978-80, dir. natural resources law inst., dean, 1993—, Erskine Wood Sr. prof. law, 2001—. Vis. prof. Auckland U. (N.Z.), 1980-81, U. Oreg. Law Sch., 1988, U. Athens, 1988-89; mem. com. socioecon. effects of earthquake prediction Nat. Acad. Scis., 1977-80. Author: The Allocation of Water to Instream Flows: A Comparative Study of Policy Making and Technical Information in the States of Colorado, Idaho, Montana and Washington, 1980, Government Liability and Disaster Mitigation: A Comparative Study, 1986; contbr. articles to profl. jours. Bd. mem. Bishop Street Funds. NSF grantee, 1976-77, 81-84; Office of Water Rsch. Dept. Interior grantee, 1978-80; Raymond fellow, 1973. Mem. Am. Soc. Legal History, Rocky Mountain Mineral Law Found. Home: 5340 SW Hewett Blvd Portland OR 97221-2254 Office: Lewis & Clark Sch Law Portland OR 97219 Business E-Mail: huffman@lclark.edu.

HUFFMAN, JOAN BREWER, history educator; b. Springfield, Ohio, Aug. 18, 1937; d. James Clarence and Berniece (Notter) Brewer; m. James Russell Huffman, Aug. 21, 1959; children: Jill Elizabeth, Jean Elaine. AB, Ohio U., 1959; MA, Ga. State U., 1968, PhD, 1980. Adj. prof. Wesleyan Coll., Macon, Ga., 1981-82; instr. history Macon State Coll., 1968-72, asst. prof., 1972-81, assoc. prof., 1981-86, prof., 1986-2000, prof. emerita, 2000—; owner The Printed Page, Macon, Ga., 1993-97, Picture Perfect, 1995—. Chmn. History adv. com. U. Sys. Ga., 1986—87. Contbr. articles to profl. jours. Mem., bd. dirs. Oklahatchee Pk., Perry, Ga., 1966-68, Macon State Coll. Found., 1985-90, Ga. Humanities Coun., Atlanta, 1983-87. Katharine C. Bleckley scholar English-Speaking Union, 1977; recipient Gov.'s award in the humanities, 1998. Mem. N.Am. Conf. on Brit. Studies, Am. Hist. Assn., Southern Hist. Assn. (membership com. 1988-89), Ga. Assn. Historians (pres. 1982-83), Phi Beta Kappa, Phi Alpha Theta (award 1978). Home: 135 Covington Pl Macon GA 31210-4445 E-mail: huffmanj@bellsouth.net.

HUFFMAN, JOHN CURTIS, chemist; b. Kokomo, Ind., Dec. 9, 1941; s. Millard William and Lorene Gladys (Patmore) H.; m. Carolyn Jean Nash, Sept. 4, 1964; children: John Nash, Charles Curtis. BS in Chemistry, Ind. U., 1964, MS in Chemistry, 1968, PhD in Chemistry, 1974. Crystallographer Ind. U., Bloomington, 1968-74, dir. Molecular Structure Ctr., 1974—, sr. scientist in chemistry, 1984—, dir. Informatics Rsch. Inst., 2002—, adj. prof. informatics, 2003—. Pres. Xtelletx Software, Bloomington; cons. various drug and chem. cos. Contbr. over 800 articles to profl. jours. Vol. Boy Scouts Am. Recipient Polyhedron Best Paper award Pergamon Press, 1987. Mem. AAAS, Am. Crystallographic Assn., Am. Chem. Soc., Am. Inst. Physics, Sigma Xi. Avocation: computer programming. Office: Ind U Chemistry Dept Bloomington IN 47405

HUFFMAN, LOUISE TOLLE, middle school educator; b. Tallahassee, Fla., July 24, 1951; d. Donald James and Mary Alice (McNeill) Tolle; m. Terry Lee Huffman, July 17, 1976; children: Cody McNeill, Hunter Tolle. BSED in Spl. Edn./Elem. Edn., So. Ill. U., 1973; MSEd, No. Ill. U., 1979. Cert. elem. tchr., spl. edn. tchr. Ill. Title I reading tchr., Tonica, Ill., 1973-74; learning disabilities tchr. St. Charles, Ill., 1974-78; spl. edn. tchr. McWayne Elem. Sch., Batavia, Ill., 1978-80; tchr. grades 1, 3, 4, and 5 Steeple Run Elem. Sch., Naperville, Ill., 1980-98; tchr. Kennedy Jr. H.S., Naperville, 1998—. Com. to develop dual maj. in elem. edn. and sci. Benedictine U., Lisle, Ill., 1999—2000; curriculum developer Brookfield (Ill.) Zoo, 2001—02; facilitator of tchr. workshops Jurica Sci. Mus./ Benedictine U., Lisle, 1992—; facilitator sci. workshops Mus. Sci. and Industry, Chgo., 1991—96; Hamline U., St. Paul, 1990—93; Saturday Morning TV Sci. tchr. Dist. 203, Naperville, 1994; author Earth Rhythms Saturday Sch. program Benedictine U., 1996; tchr. summer sci. workshop Golden Apple Found., 1999—; mem. steering com. World Sch. Adventure Learning St. Thomas U., St. Paul, 1992—94; steering com. World Sch. Adventure Learning Hamline U., 1995, 2002. Co-author: Antarctica: A Living Classroom, 1991; contbg. author: Project Circles: The World School for Adventure Learning, 2002; contbr. articles to Cobblestone Mag., Good Apple Newspaper, Children's Digest; author of poetry. Bd. dirs. Cmty. United Meth. Ch. Sojourners Sunday Sch., Naperville, 1995-2000; confirmation class tchr. Cmty. United Meth. Ch., 1999-2001. Recipient award of Excellence, Ill. Sci. Tchrs. Assn., 1992, 1996, Golden Apple award, 2002, tchr. rsch. assistantship in Antarctica, NSF, 2001—03; grantee, Naperville Edn. Found., 1994, 2002, Jeanine Nicarico Lit. grant, 1999. Methodist. Office: Kennedy Junior High Sch 2929 Green Trails Dr Lisle IL 60532-6262 E-mail: lhuffman@ncusd203.org.

HUFFMAN, PATRICIA JOAN, retired accounting coordinator; b. Elmira, N.Y., Mar. 29, 1941; d. F. John and Alice E. (Patterson) Garbay; m. Edward L. Huffman, May 28, 1960; children: Debra L. Palmer, Thomas E., Matthew M. AA in Bus. Adminstrn., AA in Data Processing, Corning C.C., 1984; BS in Acctg., Elmira Coll., 1991. Clk. typist Hardinge's Bros., Elmira, N.Y., 1959-62, Gen. Precision Labs., Pleasantville, N.Y., 1965-66; data entry clk. Reader's Digest, Pleasantville, 1966-68, Elmira Data Processing, 1968-69; acctg. clk. Am. LaFrance, Elmira, 1969-73, GE, Elmira, 1973-75, Elmira Star-Gazette, 1975-77; various temporary positions Manpower, Elmira, Corning, N.Y., 1980, 84-85; pers. clk. Atlantic & Pacific Tea Co., Horseheads, N.Y., 1980-82; from sales tax clk. to acctg. coord. Corning, Inc., 1985-96, ret., 1996—, 1996. Author: (poem) Those Black Nights/Where Dreams Begin, 1993 (Editor's Choice award 1993), In Sorrow/Outstanding Poets of 1994 (Editor's Choice award 1994), Remember the Good Times My Love/Dance on the Horizon, 1994 (Editor's Choice award 1994), Lissa/Best Poems of 1995 (Editor's Choice award 1995), Prairie Rattler/Best Poems of 1996, (Editor's Choice award 1996), The Night My Cat Died/Best Poems of the '90s (Editor's Choice award 1996), Pray the Rosary/Best Poems of 1998 (Editor's Choice award 1998). V.p. Ladies of Charity, 1992—96, pres., 1996—98, sec., 1984—86; bd. dirs. N.E. reg. v.p. Ladies of Charity U.S.A., 1999—2002, sec., 2001; lector St. Mary Our Mother Ch., Horseheads, NY, 1986—90, Eucharistic min., 1996—. Mem. Internat. Soc. Poets (mem. adv. panel mem. 1993—, Internat. Poet of Merit award 1993-95). Avocations: poetry writing, charity work. Home: 110 Hillcrest Rd Elmira NY 14903-7981 E-mail: pathuffman@hotmail.com.

HUFFMAN, PATRICIA NELL, entrepreneur; b. Springfield, Mo., Sept. 25, 1947; d. Rex Eugene and Helen Marie (Appleby) Riggs; m. Frank Dale Huffman, June 18, 1966 (div. Apr. 2003); children: Chad, Heather, Tyler. Student, Joplin Jr. Coll., 1966. Saleswoman Sta. KTVJ-TV, Joplin, Mo., 1972—77; designer, mktg. ADI-Comml. Interiors, Tulsa, 1983—84; pres., designer Bittersweet, Inc., Joplin, 1984—89; founder, pres. By Invitation Only, 1986—89. Co-owner, bd. dirs., sec. J Town Billiards, Sports Bar and Grill, 1999—; cons. in field. Designer country gift items, 1978—. Vol. Mental Health Ctr., Joplin, 1965, Am. Heart Assn., Joplin, 1980, Family Self Help Ctr., Joplin, 1981—, United Way, Joplin, 1982; pres. Women's Support Group, Joplin, 1983-85, Family Violence Coun., 1996-97, bd. dirs., pres. bd.; bd. dirs. Children's Ctr., 1997-2001; co-founder S.A.F.E. Coalition, 1989-97. Recipient Women Helping Women award, 1998, House Resolution No. 785 for volunteerism with children and women State of Mo., 1994. Mem. Exch. Club (Book of Golden Deeds award for outstanding volunteerism with women and children 1996). Avocations: bridge, creative writing, billiards, painting, illustrating and writing children's books. Office: PO Box 2159 2502 S Main St Joplin MO 64803-2159 E-mail: Jtownbilliards@aol.com., paintinglibra@sbcglobal.net.

HUFFMAN, ROBERT ALLEN, JR., lawyer; b. Tucson, Dec. 30, 1950; s. Robert Allen and Ruth Jane (Hicks) H.; m. Marjorie Kavanagh Rooney, Dec. 30, 1976; children: Katharine Kavanagh, Elizabeth Rooney, Robert Allen III, Simeon Ross. BBA, U. Okla., 1973, JD, 1976. Bar: Okla. 1977, U.S. Dist. Ct. (no. dist.) Okla. 1977, U.S. Ct. Appeals (10th cir.) 1978, U.S. Supreme Ct. 1982. Assoc. Huffman, Arrington, Kihle, Gaberino & Dunn, Tulsa, 1977-81, ptnr. 1981-97, ptnr. Edwards & Huffman LLP, 1997—. Mem. ABA, Tulsa County Bar Assn., Fed. Energy Bar Assn. Republican. Roman Catholic. Clubs: Southern Hills Country (Tulsa). Home: 5937 S Columbia Ave Tulsa OK 74105-7319 Office: Edwards & Huffman LLP 6626 E 101st Ste 100 Tulsa OK 74137 E-mail: rhuffman@edwardshuffman.com.

HUFFMAN, WALTER B. army officer; b. Keesler AFB, Miss., Oct. 8, 1944; m. Anne Robison; children: Burl, Becky, Ross. BS, Tex. Tech U., 1967, MEd, 1968, JD with highest honors, 1977. Commd. 2d lt. U.S. Army, 1968, advanced through grades to maj. gen.; judge adv. in various assignments including Desert Shield/Desert Storm, 1977-97; judge advocate gen. U.S. Army, 1997—. Editor-in-chief Tex. Tech Law Rev. Decorated Legion of Merit with one oak leaf cluster, Bronze Star medal with 2 oak leaf clusters. Office: US Army Army Pentagon Rm 1e739 Washington DC 20310-0001

HUFFMAN-HINE, RUTH CARSON, adult education administrator, educator; b. Spencer, Ind., Sept. 13, 1925; d. Joseph Charles Carson and Bess Ann Taylor; m. Joe Buren Hine; children: Paulette Walker, Larry K., Annette M. AA in Fine Arts, Ind. Cen. Coll., 1967; BS in Edn., Butler U., 1971; MS in Adult Edn., Ind. U., 1976; PhD in Ednl. Adminstrn., Greenwich U., 1995. Cert. elem. edn. Subs. tchr. Met. Sch. Dist. Wayne Twnshp., Indpls., 1956-60; tchr. of homebound Met. Sch. Dist. Decatur Twnshp., Indpls., 1964-66; adult edn. tchr. Met. Sch. Dist. Wayne Twnshp., Indpls., 1971-75, adminstr. adult edn., 1975—. Cons. Ind. Adoption System, Indpls., 1985—; regional rep. Ind. Assn. Adult Adminstrs., 1984—; program rep. Ind. Literacy Coordinators, Indpls., 1985—; speaker, mem. literacy research and evaluation com. Ind. Adult Literacy Coalition, Indpls., 1980-86. Author: Driving Regulations and Courtesies, It Happened at the Pond, 1997, We Build Walls, 1999; co-author Learning for Everyday Living, 1978, Table Approach to Education, 1984, Developing Educational Competencies for Individuals Determined to Excel, 6 vols., 1980 (ERIC System award 1980), (ERIC System award 1985), Collection, Evaluation, Dissemination of Special Research Projects, 1984, Automobile Driving Rules and Regulations, 1988. Vice com. person Rep. Orgn., Indpls., 1968-72; charter mem., sec. Project READ, LITERACY, 1988. Recipient Extra Mile award Met. Sch. Dist. Wayne Twp., 1990. Mem. Internat. Reading Assn. (Celebrate Literacy award 1984), Ind. Assn. for Adult & Continuing Edn. (treas. 1984—, pres. 1990-93, Outstanding Adult Educator 1979), Beta Phi Delta (pres. 1986—), Beta Phi, Delta Kappa Gamma (v.p. 1985-86, fellowship chmn. 1982-84), Phi Delta Kappa. Republican. Mem. Christian Ch. Avocations: reading, music, bicycling. Home: 138 Abner Creek Pkwy Danville IN 46123-9602 Office: Adult Basic Edn Ctr 5248 W Raymond St Indianapolis IN 46241-4700

HUFFMAN-KLINKOWITZ, JULIE ANN, genealogist, researcher; b. Mason City, Iowa, May 28, 1956; d. Garth Wayne Huffman and Shirley Jean Bond; m. Jerome Francis Klinkowitz, May 27, 1978. BA, U. No. Iowa, 1977, MA, 1982. Co-author: Kurt Vonnegut: A Comprehensive Bibliography, 1987, The Descendants of John Bond (1661) of Beverly, Massachusetts, 1992, David Elliott, Loyalist, and His Descendants, 1995; author: Some of the Descendants of William Shaw of Surry County, N.C., 1996, Some of the Ancestors and Descendants of William Brocklin Smith of Bledsoe County, Tennessee, 1998, The Descendants of Wawrzyniec (Lawrence) John Chmielewski and Florentyna (Florentine) Jakubczak in America, 2003.

HUFFSTETLER, PALMER EUGENE, lawyer; b. Shelby, N.C., Dec. 21, 1937; s. Daniel S. and Ethel (Turner) H.; m. Mary Ann Beam, Aug. 9, 1958; children: Palmer Eugene, Ben Beam, Brian Tad. BA, Wake Forest U., 1959, JD, 1961. Bar: N.C. 1961. Practiced in Kings Mountain, N.C., 1961-62, Raleigh, N.C., 1962-64; with State Farm Ins. Co., Orlando, Fla., 1962; gen. legal counsel Carolina Freight Corp., Cherryville, N.C., 1964-93, sec., 1969-90, sr. v.p., 1969-89, exec. v.p., 1985-93, pres., 1993-95; ret., 1995; pres., CEO Blue Chip Inc., 1997-99. Author, composer: Senior Man on Carolina Line, Fifty Years Ago. Chmn. Cherryville Zoning Bd. Adjustment, 1967-70; active N.C. Gasoline and Oil Insp. Bd., 1974-76; class chmn. Wake Forest Coll. Fund, 1971-79, decade chmn., 1981-82; governing body, chmn. adminstrv. com. So. Piedmont Health Systems Agy., 1975-77; mem. Cherryville Econ. Devel. Commn., 1982-87, Cherryville Econ. Devel. Com., 1995-97; pres. Cherryville Devel. Corp., 1986—; bd. dirs. C. Grier Beam Truck Mus., 1982-2002, pres. 1982-96; bd. dirs. Schiele Mus., Gastonia, N.C., 1985-88, Gaston Meml. Hosp., 1990-93, vice-chmn. bd.; active N.C. Gov.'s Hwy. Safety Commn., 1985-88, Gov.'s Bus. Com., N.C., 1993-95; v.p. Ctrl. and So. Rate Bur., 1984-89; trustee Brevard Coll., 1987-93. Mem. N.C. State Bar, N.C. Bar Assn. (mem. adminstrv. bd. 1965-69, 71-72, chmn. adminstrv. bd., trustee 1970-73, fin. com. 1994-2002). Methodist. Home: 2141 Fairways Dr Cherryville NC 28021-2115

HUFNAGEL, GLENDA ANN LEWIN, human relations educator and administrator; b. Ronake, Ala., Apr. 13, 1948; d. Clifford Herbert and Gladys (Halsey) Lewin; children: Lisa, Jessica. BS, U. Okla., 1976, MA, 1979, M in Human Rels., 1990, PhD, 1999. Asst. prof. Ctrl. State U., Edmond, Okla., 1984-85, Oklahoma City C.C., 1976-84, Rose State Coll., Midwest City, Okla., 1984-90, U. Okla., Norman, 1991—, asst. dir. human rels. advanced program, 1997—. V.p. People Energy, Oklahoma City, 1984-85; pres. Comm. Cons., Norman, Okla., 1982—; adj. asst. prof. Russel Sage Coll., Albany, N.Y., 1989—; mem. bd. dirs. Bethesda Alternatives, Norman. Contbr. articles to profl. jours. Bd. dirs. Women's Resource Ctr., Norman, Okla., 1980-85, advisor, 1985—; advisor Norman's Battered Women's Shelter, 1985—. Mem. Nat. Women's Studies Assn., NOW, South Ctrl. Women's Studies Assn. (pres. 1995—), Phi Kappa Phi (charter). Democrat. Avocations: camping, reading, travel, sewing, photography. Home: 1704 Homeland Ave Norman OK 73072-5743 Office: U Okla Dept Human Rels 1704 Homeland Norman OK 73072 E-mail: gahafnagel@ou.edu.

HUFSCHMIDT, MAYNARD MICHAEL, resources planning educator; b. Catawba, Wis., Sept. 28, 1912; s. John Jacob and Emma Lena (Von Arx) H.; m. Elizabeth Louise Leake, July 5, 1941; children: Emily Ann, Mark Andrew. BS, U. Ill., 1939; MPA, Harvard U., 1955, DPA, 1964. Planner Ill. State Planning Commn., Chgo., 1939-41; engr. U.S. Nat. Resources Planning Bd., Washington, 1941-43; budget examiner U.S. Bur. Budget, Washington, 1943-49; program staff mem. Office of Sec., Dept. Interior, Washington, 1949-55; research asso. Grad. Sch. Public Adminstrn., Harvard U., 1955-65; prof. depts. city and regional planning, environ. scis. and engring. U. N.C., Chapel Hill, 1965—; fellow Environ. and Policy Inst., East-West Center, Honolulu, 1979-85, acting dir., 1985-86, sr. cons., 1986-89, sr. fellow, 1990-94. Cons. U.S. Bur. Budget, 1961, Council Econ. Advisers, 1965-67, Nat. Acad. Scis., 1967, 69-70, Pan-Am. Health Orgn., 1967, 70, WHO, 1970, 71, 76, 77, Resources for Future, 1955, 56, 72-74 Author: (with Arthur Maass and others) Design of Water-Resource Systems, 1962, (with Myron B. Fiering) Simulation Techniques for Design of Water-Resource Systems, 1966; Editor: Regional Planning— Challenge and Prospects, 1969; editor: (with Eric L. Hyman) Economic Approaches to Natural Resource and Environmental Quality Analysis, 1982, (with David E. James and others) Environment, Natural Systems and Development: An Economic Valuation Guide, 1983, (with John A. Dixon) Economic Valuation Techniques for the Environment, 1986, (with K. William Easter and John A. Dixon) Watershed Resources Management, 1986, (with Janusz Kindler) Approaches to Integrated Water Resources Management in Humid Tropical and Arid and Semiarid Zones in Developing Countries, 1991, (with Michael Bonell and John S. Gladwell) Hydrology and Water Management in the Humid Tropics, 1993. Recipient Clemens Herschel award Boston Soc. Civil Engrs., 1958, Pub. Svc. award U.S. Dept. Interior, 1994; named Friend of Univs. Coun. on Water Resources, 1990; sr. postdoctoral rsch. fellow NSF, 1971. E-mail: eastwestplanner@aol.com.

HUFSTEDLER, SETH MARTIN, lawyer; b. Dewar, Okla., Sept. 20, 1922; s. Seth Martin and Myrtle (Younts) H.; m. Shirley Ann Mount, Aug. 16, 1949; 1 child, Steven. BA magna cum laude, U. So. Calif., 1944; LL.B., Stanford U., 1949. Bar: Calif. 1950. Pvt. practice, L.A.; assoc. Lillick, Geary & McHose, 1950-51; with Charles E. Beardsley, 1951-53; ptnr. Beardsley, Hufstedler & Kemble, 1953-81, Hufstedler, Miller, Carlson & Beardsley, 1981-88, Hufstedler, Kaus & Ettinger, L.A., 1988-94; Hufstedler & Kaus, 1994-95; sr. of counsel Morrison & Foerster LLP, 1995—. Mem. Calif. Jud. Coun., 1977—78. Legis. editor Stanford U. Law Rev., 1948-49. Sec. regional planning coun. United Way, 1971-75; co-chmn. Pub. Commn. County Govt., L.A., 1975-76, 89-92; trustee AEFC Pension Fund, 1978-82; mem. Calif Citizens Commn. on Tort Reform, 1976-77; bd. visitors Stanford Law Sch., chmn., 1972-73. Lt. (j.g.) USNR, 1943-46. Mem. ABA (chmn. action commn. to reduce ct costs and delay 1979-81, mem. coun. sr. bar div. 1986-89, chmn. 1987-88), Los Angeles County Bar Assn. (trustee 1963-65, 66-70, pres. 1969-70, Shattuck Price award 1976), State Bar Calif. (bd. govs. 1971-74, pres. 1973-74, Bernard Witlan medal 2002), Am. Judicature Soc., Am. Law Inst., Am. Coll. Trial Lawyers, Am. Bar Found. (bd. govs. 1975-86, pres. 1982-84), Chancery Club (pres. 1974-75), Order of Coif, Phi Beta Kappa, Phi Kappa Phi, Delta Tau Delta. Democrat. Office: Morrison & Foerster 555 W 5th St Ste 3500 Los Angeles CA 90013-1024

HUFSTEDLER, SHIRLEY MOUNT (MRS. SETH M. HUFSTEDLER), lawyer, former federal judge; b. Denver, Aug. 24, 1925; d. Earl Stanley and Eva (Von Behren) Mount; m. Seth Martin Hufstedler, Aug. 16, 1949; 1 son, Steven Mark. BBA, U. N.Mex., 1945, LLD (hon.), 1972; LLB, Stanford U., 1949; LLD (hon.), U. Wyo., 1970, Gonzaga U., 1970, Occidental Coll., 1971, Tufts U., 1974, U. So. Calif., 1976, Georgetown U., 1976, U. Pa., 1976, Columbia U., 1977, U. Mich., 1979, Yale U., 1981, Rutgers U., 1981, Claremont U. Ctr., 1981, Smith Coll., 1982, Syracuse U., 1983, Mt. Holyoke Coll., 1985; PHH (hon.), Hood Coll., 1981, Hebrew Union Coll., 1986, Tulane U., 1988. Bar: Calif. 1950. Mem. firm Beardsley, Hufstedler & Kemble, L.A., 1951-61; practiced in L.A., 1961; judge Superior Ct., County L.A., 1961-66; justice Ct. Appeals 2d dist., 1966-68; circuit judge U.S. Ct. Appeals 9th cir., 1968-79; sec. U.S. Dept. Edn., 1979-81; ptnr. Hufstedler & Kaus, L.A., 1981-95; sr. of counsel Morrison & Foerster LLP, L.A., 1995—. Emeritus dir. Hewlett Packard Co., US West, Inc.; bd. dirs. Harman Internat. Industries. Mem. staff Stanford Law Rev, 1947-49; articles and book rev. editor, 1948-49. Trustee Calif. Inst. Tech., Occidental Coll., 1972-89, Aspen Inst., Colonial Williamsburg Found., 1976-93, Constl. Rights Found., 1978-80, Nat. Resources Def. Coun., 1983-85, Carnegie Endowment for Internat. Peace, 1983-94; bd. dirs. John T. and Catherine MacArthur Found., 1983—2002; chair U.S. Commn. on Immigration Reform, 1996-97. Named Woman of Yr. Ladies Home Jour., 1976; recipient UCLA medal, 1981. Fellow Am. Acad. Arts and Scis.; mem. ABA (medal 1995), L.A. Bar Assn., Town Hall, Am. Law Inst. (coun. 1974-84), Am. Bar Found., Women Lawyers Assn. (pres. 1957-58), Am. Judicature Soc., Assn. of the Bar of City of N.Y., Coun. on Fgn. Rels. (emeritus), Order of Coif. Office: Morrison & Foerster LLP 555 W 5th St Ste 3500 Los Angeles CA 90013-1024

HUG, CARL CASIMIR, JR., anesthesiology and pharmacology, educator; b. Canton, Ohio, Dec. 20, 1936; s. Carl Casimir and Aimee Cecelia (McArdle) H.; m. Marilyn Ann France, May 12, 1956; children: Patricia Ann DeStephano, Michael Stephen, Joan Marie Daniel, Mary Lynn Higgins, Lori Renee Mauldin. BS in Pharmacy summa cum laude, Duquesne U., 1958; PhD in Pharmacology, U. Mich., 1963, MD with distinction, 1967. Diplomate Am. Bd. Anesthesiology (bd. dirs. 1984-96, v.p. 1990-92, pres. 1992-93). From instr. to assoc. prof. pharmacology U. Mich., Ann Arbor, 1963-71; from assoc. prof. anesthesiology and pharmacology to emeritus prof. Emory U. Sch. Medicine, Atlanta, 1972—, dep. chmn. for rsch., 1987-95, dep. chmn. for acad. affairs, 1995—2001; faculty assoc. Emory U. Ctr. for Ethics, 2001—. Vis. rsch. prof. U. Leiden, The Netherlands, 1982. Author: Alfentanil: Pharmacology and Uses in Anesthesia, 1984; editor Pharmacokinetics of Anaesthesia, 1984; editor Anesthesiology, 1979-88. Chmn. St. Francis Sch. Bd., Ann Arbor, Mich., 1967—71; coach Little League, Ann Arbor, 1967—71; active Corpus Christi Cath. Ch., Stone Mountain, Ga., 1972—96, St. John Neumann Cath. Ch., Liburn, Ga., 1997—; bd. dirs. Found. for Anesthesiology Edn. and Rsch., 1993—2003, v.p., 1995—98, pres., 1998—2001. Named Tchr. of Yr. Emory U. Anesthesiology, 1989, hon. lectr. at multiple Univs. Fellow Royal Coll. Anaesthetists (Eng.) (hon.), Australian and New Zealand Coll. Anaesthetists (hon.); mem. Belgian Soc. Anesthesia and Reanimation (hon.), Am. Soc. Anesthesiologists (mem., chmn. various coms. 1976—, Rovenstine lectr. 1999). Office: Emory Univ Hosp Dept Anesthesiology 1364 Clifton Rd NE Atlanta GA 30322-1104 E-mail: carl_hug@emoryhealthcare.org.

HUG, JAMES EDWIN, religious organization executive; b. Omaha, May 10, 1941; s. Edwin Joseph and Dorothy Ann (Spellecy) H. AB in Philosophy, Spring Hill Coll., 1965, MA in Philosophy, 1966; MA in Christian Spirituality, St. Louis U., 1973; PhD in Christian Ethics, U. Chgo., 1981. Ordained Jesuit priest, 1972. Instr. in philosophy Creighton U., Omaha, 1966-69; mem. editorial staff Theology Digest, 1969-73; lectr. in Christian spirituality St. Louis U., 1972-73; instr. in Christian ethics Jesuit Sch. Theology, Chgo., 1978-80; sr. fellow Woodstock Theol. Ctr., Washington, 1981-85; rsch. dir. Ctr. of Concern, Washington, 1986-88, exec. dir., 1989—. Bd. dirs. Internat. Devel. Conf., Washington; cons. The Cath. Healthcare Assn. Author: Scripture Sharing on Bishops' Pastoral, 1987; co-author: Social Revelation: Profound Challenge for Christian Spirituality, 1987; editor, contbr.: Dimensions of the Healing Ministry, 1989; editor: Tracing the Spirit: Communities, Social Action..., 1983. Bd. dirs. Cen. Am. Refugee Ctr., Washington, 1983-85, Religious Task Force on Cen. Am., Washington, 1988-98, U.S. Cath. Mission Assn., Washington, 1988-94; adv. bd. Ctr. for Mission Rsch. and Study Maryknoll, Maryknoll Mission Assn. of the Faithful, 1996-2001. Mem. Soc. Christian Ethics, Cath. Theol. Soc. Am. Office: Ctr of Concern 1225 Otis St NE Washington DC 20017-2516 E-mail: jhug@coc.org.

HUG, PROCTER RALPH, JR., federal judge; b. Reno, Mar. 11, 1931; s. Procter Ralph and Margaret (Beverly) H.; m. Barbara Van Meter, Apr. 4, 1954; children: Cheryl Ann English, Procter J., Elyse Marie Pasha. BS, U. Nev., 1953; LLB, JD, Stanford U., 1958. Bar: Nev. 1958. Mem. Springer, McKissick & Hug, 1958—63, Woodburn, Wedge, Blakey, Folsom & Hug, Reno, 1963—77; U.S. judge 9th Circuit Ct. Appeals, Reno, 1977—2002, U.S. chief judge, 1996—2000; sr. judge, 2002—. Dep. atty. gen. State of Nev., 1971—76; v.p. dir. Nev. Tel. & Tel. Co., 1958—77. Mem. bd. regents U. Nev., 1962—71, chmn., 1969—71; bd. visitors Stanford Law Sch.; mem. Nev. Humanities Commn., 1988—94; vol. civilian aid sect. U.S. Army, 1977. Lt. (j.g.) USNR, 1953—55. Named Alumnus of Yr., U. Nev., 1988; recipient Outstanding Alumnus award, 1967, Disting. Nevadan citation, 1982. Mem.: ABA (bd. govs. 1976—78), Stanford Law Soc. Nev. (past pres.), U. Nev. Alumni Assn. (past pres.), Nat. Assn. Coll. and Univ. Attys. (past mem. exec. bd.), Nat. Judicial Coll. (bd. dirs. 1977—78, 2001—), Am. Judicare Soc. (bd. dirs. 1975—77). Office: US Ct Appeals 9th Cir US Courthouse Fed Bldg 400 S Virginia St Ste 708 Reno NV 89501-2181

HUG, RICHARD ERNEST, environmental company executive; b. Paterson, N.J., Jan. 11, 1935; s. Gustave T. and Nelly (Rutishauser) H.; m. Lois-Ann Schack, Sept. 1, 1956; children: Donald R., Cynthia A. BS, Duke U., 1956, M in Forestry, 1957; DHL, U. Balt., 1991. Engr. forest products divsn. Koppers Co., Inc., Pitts., 1957-62, tech. rep., 1962-66, tech. sales rep., 1966-68, area sales mgr., 1968-70, mgr. product devel., 1970-72, gen. mgr. laminated products, 1972-73, v.p., gen. mgr. environ. systems divsn., 1973-74, corp. v.p., 1973-83; pres., CEO, owner Environ. Elements Corp., Balt., 1983-88, chmn., CEO, 1988-90, chmn., 1990-95, chmn. emeritus, 1995—; owner, chmn. Deco-Sign Products, Inc., 1991—; owner, CEO, chmn. Hug Enterprises, Inc., 1991—; owner, chmn. The Great Am. Car Wash, etc., Inc., 1992—. Mem. Md. Health Resources Planning Commn., 1984-88; bd. dirs. Nat. Aquarium, Balt., 1981-94, chmn., 1988-91; bd. dirs. Nat. Aquarium Found., 1995—. Bd. dirs. Blue Cross-Blue Shield Md., 1973-94, Boy Scouts Am., Balt., 1974-85, Greater Balt. Com., 1978, 84-88, Loyola Coll. Md., 1982—, U. Md. Med. System, 1984-95, U. Md. Med. System Found., 2000—, Jr. Achievement Ctrl. Md., 1985-95, Duke U. Sch. Environ., 1986—, chair, 1988-95, Am. Auto Assn., Md., 1988—, Mid Atlantic Am. Auto Assn., 1990—, Md. Internat. Ctr., 1984-95, Downtown Balt. Ctr., 1991-94, Walters Art Mus., 1992-97, Environ. Forum, 1993-95, Hospice Chesapeake, 1993-98, Diehl Graphsoft, 1996-2000, Marco Group, 1985—, Annapolis Ctr., 2001—; campaign chmn. United Way Ctrl. Md., 1979, 80, chmn., 1987-89; chmn. finance Ellen Sauerbrey for Gov., 1994-98, Md. Rep. Party, 1999-2000, Bob Ehrlich for Gov., 2001—, Md. Bush for Pres. Campaign, 1999-2000; bd. dirs. Kennedy Krieger Inst., 1981—, chair, 1984-86; bd. dirs. Ind. Coll. Fund. Md., 1978-88; bd. dirs. Balt. Symphony Orch., 1989—, CEO coun., 1988-90; mem. chancellor's adv. coun. U. Md., 1990-2002; bd. regents Univ. Sys. Md., 2003-; chair Md. Leadership, 1995-96; chmn. Md. U.S. Olympics Commn., 1987-88; mem. Young Pres.'s Orgn., 1974-85, chmn., 1980. Eagle scout, 1950; Pres. medal Loyola Coll., 1992. Mem. Chesapeake Pres. Orgn. (chmn. 1994-95, CEO 1986-2002), Water and Wastewater Equipment Mfrs. Assn. (bd. dirs. 1983-88), Inst. Clear Air Cos. (bd. dirs. 1980-94, pres. 1990-94), Nat. Assn. Mfrs. (bd. dirs. 1983-94), Md. Ctr. Bus. Mgmt. (bd. dirs. 1984-95, chmn. 1987-92), Md. Bus. Responsibility Govt. (bd. dirs. 1995—), Md. C. of C. (bd. dirs. 1981-95, v.p. 1981-84, chmn. 1985-87), Ctr. Club (bd. govs. 1993—, membership chmn. 1994-2000, v.p.

1997—, Silver Beaver award 1985, Nat. Outstanding Fund Raiser 1992). Home: 992 Stonington Dr Arnold MD 21012-1654 Office: Environ Elements Corp 3700 Koppers St Baltimore MD 21227-1020

HUGE, HARRY, lawyer; b. Deshler, Nebr., Sept. 16, 1937; s. Arthur and Dorothy (Vor de Strasse) H.; m. Reba Kinne, July 2, 1960; 1 child, Theodore. AB, Nebr. Wesleyan U., 1959; JD, Georgetown U., 1963. Bar: Ill. 1963, D.C. 1965, S.C. 1985. Assoc. Chapman & Cutler, Chgo., 1963-65; from assoc. to ptnr. Arnold & Porter, Washington, 1965-76; sr. ptnr. Donovan, Leisure, Rogovin, Huge & Schiller, Washington, 1976-92, Shea and Gould Internat., Washington, 1992-94; ptnr. Powell Goldstein Frazer & Murphy, Washington, 1995—2002, Harry Huge Law Firm LLP, 2002—. Chmn. Oncostasis, Inc., Charleston, S.C.; chmn., trustee United Mine Workers Health and Retirement Funds, 1973-78; chmn. bd. dirs. Hollings Cancer Ctr. Med. U. S.C., Charleston; trustee Shook and Fletcher Asbestos Settlement Trust, Washington, 2002—. Contbr. articles to legal jours. Pres. Voter Edn. Project, Atlanta, 1974-78; mem. Pres.'s Gen. Adv. Com. Arms Control, 1977-81; trustee Nebr. Wesleyan U., 1978—; mem. task force local govt. Greater Washington Rsch. Ctr., 1981-82; spl. master Friends for All Children, Inc., U.S. Dist. Ct. D.C.; mem. Nat. Tobacco Settlement Arbitration Panel, Durham, N.C. With U.S. Army, 1960; officer USNG, 1960-65. Mem.: ABA (co-chmn. legis. com. litigation sect. 1981), Inst. Human Virology (bd. dirs. U. Md. Balt. 1996—2001), D.C. Bar Assn. (bd. profl. responsibility 1976—81). Home: 25 E Battery St Charleston SC 29401-2740 Office: Harry Huge Law Firm LLP 901 Ninth St NW Washington DC 20004-2505 Office Fax: 202-318-1261.

HUGENBERG, PATRICIA ELLEN PETRIE, product designer; b. N.Y.C., Oct. 17, 1934; d. Milton John Petrie and Miriam Lois Lampke-Rubenstein-Petrie; m. George John Hugenberg, Jan. 18, 1958; 1 child, Kurt John James. Student, Briarcliff Jr. Coll., 1954, U. Calif., Berkeley, 1966. Guidette NBC, N.Y.C., 1956; designer, resch. developer Designs for Prodn., Sausalito, Calif.; inventor games, toys, med. items, Sigi Design, San Francisco; pres. PPH Designs. Mem. pending bd. Milton & Carroll Petrie Found. for New Millenium, N.Y.C. Photographer: (book cover jacket) Baltimore; prin. works include plexiglass knitting needles, plexiglass embedded light space age stardust galaxy hammocks, space age crutch, new saddle design for mobile riding easels, kitchen veg-garnisher punch; patents pending in field. Mem. NRA. Avocations: music, oil painting, horseback riding, traveling, gardens. Home and Office: 10 Leeward Rd Belvedere CA 94920-2321

HUGG, GERALDINE BERTHA NOVOTNY, retired gerontology specialist, journalist; b. N.Y.C., Oct. 15, 1913; d. Jerry Joseph and Bertha Ann (Strnad) Novotny; m. Alan Eddy Hugg, Mar. 10, 1982 (dec. Feb. 1997). BA in Journalism, U. Wis., 1949; MS in Pub. Rels., Boston U., 1953. lic. profl. gerontology U. Mich., Drake U. Departmental sec. U. Conn., Storrs, 1933-41, departmental asst., 1941-43, asst. editor, publs. editor divsn. comm., 1950-60; specialist Inst. Gerontology, U. Conn., 1960-67; dir. Windham Area Sr. Ctr., Willimantic, Conn., 1967; cons. and field rep. Conn. State Dept. Aging, Hartford, 1967-76; ret., 1976. Advisor Conn. Coun. Sr. Citizens, 1960—; attended 9th Internat. Gerontol. Congress, Kiev, Russia, 1972. Contbg. editor Seniorage, 1976-2001; contbr. columns various newspapers. Vol. social action and edn. Conn. Soc. Gerontology, 1961-99, pres., 1981-83; participant Am. Exch. Corps, Caucuses, Russia, 1980, USSR People to People Program, China, 1994, South Africa, 1995, Russia and Estonia, 1996; active the Capitol Region Conf. Chs., 1996—; advcate for justice and peace Capitol Region Conf. of Chs., Hartford, Conn., 1997—; mem. Conn. Campaign to Abolish Nuclear Weapons, 1997; co-chmn. Conn. Coalition on Aging, Inc., Hartford, 1976-80; mem. United Srs. in Action, 1997—; mem. advocacy justice and peace Capitol Region Conf. Chs., Hartford, Conn., 1996— . Sgt. USMCR, 1943-45. Recipient David C. King award, Conn. Soc. Gerontology, Hartford, 1985—98, award 100 Years of Women, U. Conn., Storrs, 1993, ofcl. citation, Conn. State Gen. Assembly, 2000, Walter P. Reuther Disting. Svc. award, 2000. Mem. Nat. Coun. on Aging (life), Nat. Coun. Sr. Citizens (life, mem. com. to establish 1st set of stds. for sr. ctrs.), Conn. Coun. Sr. Citizens, (v.p.), Czechoslovak Am. Club (pres. 1939-60), Zonta Internat. Club of West Hartford (bd. dirs. 1970—), Womens Internat. League Peace and Freedom, Ch. Women United (Conn. chpt. adv. bd. 1984), Czechoslovak Culture Group, United Srs. in Action (vol. activist), UN Assn. (Greater Hartford, Conn.). Democrat. Unitarian Universalist. Avocations: swimming, oil painting, hiking. Home: 275 Steele Rd Apt 422 West Hartford CT 06117-2716

HUGGARD, JOHN PARKER, lawyer; b. Midland, Tex., Dec. 7, 1945; s. Peter John and Dorothy (Sampson) H. BA, U. N.C., 1971, JD, 1975; MA, Duke U., 1989. Bar: N.C. 1975, U.S. Dist. Ct. (ea. dist.) N.C. 1975, U.S. Ct. Appeals (4th cir.) 1975, U.S. Tax Ct. 1976, U.S. Ct. Claims 1976, U.S. Ct. Customs 1977, U.S. Ct. Mil. Appeals 1977, U.S. Dist. Ct. D.C. 1979, U.S. Supreme Ct. 1979, U.S. Ct. Internat. Trade 1981, U.S. Ct. Customs and Patent Appeals 1982; cert. fin. planner; chreterd fin. cons. Sr. ptnr. Hensley & Overby, Raleigh, N.C., 1975-88, Huggard, Obiol & Blake, PLLC, Raleigh, 1988—; alumni disting. prof. Law and Econs. N.C. State U., Raleigh, 1975—. Author: The Adminstration of Decedents' Estates in North Carolina, 1985, North Carolina Estate Settlement Guidebook, 1995, Living Trust/Living Hell-Why You Should Avoid Living Trusts, 1998, Investing with Variable Annuities, 2002; contbr. articles to profl. publs. With USMC, 1964-68, capt. USNR. Mem. ABA, Am. Bus. Law Assn., Assn. Trial Lawyers Am., N.C. Bar Assn., N.C. Acad. Trial Lawyers, N.C. Coll. Advocacy, Acad. Outstanding Tchrs., Wake County Bar Assn., Phi Beta Kappa. Democrat. Roman Catholic. Avocation: flying. Home: 8621 Kings Arms Way Raleigh NC 27615-2029 Office: Huggard Obiol & Blake PLLC 124 Saint Marys St Raleigh NC 27605-1809

HUGGETT, MONICA, performing company executive; Artistic dir. Portland Baroque Orch., Oreg. Office: Portland Baroque Orch 1425 SW 20th Ave Ste 102 Portland OR 97201-2485

HUGGINS, AMY BRANUM, music educator; b. Memphis, Dec. 20, 1954; d. Leon and Scharlene Oney Branum; m. R. David Huggins, May 8, 1976; children: Alexander, Stephanie. MusM in Edn. with Kodaly emphasis, Holy Names Coll., Oakland, Calif., 1985; MusB in Edn., Peabody Conservatory of Music, 1976. Pvt. piano instr., Balt., 1973—; early music tng. faculty prep. divsn. Peabody Conservatory of Music, Balt., 1976—83, music theory faculty prep. divsn., 1976—83, curriculum designer prep. divsn., 1976; condr., founder The Pine Grove Madrigals, Balt., 1976—; vocal music specialist Pine Grove Elem. Sch., Balt., 1976—; master tchr., supr. of student tchrs. Peabody Conservatory of Music, Shenandoah Conservatory of Music, Towson State U., U. of Md., Loyola Coll., Balt., 1978—; organizer, dir. choral festivals Balt. County Pub. Schs., Balt., 1980—90; instr. Children's Chorus of Md., Balt., 1983—86; curriculum designer Balt. County Pub. Schs., 1991; pvt. voice instr. Balt., 1997—; cons. Children's Chorus of Md., Balt., 1998—99; dir., co-founder The Am. Kodaly Inst., Balt., 2000—; instr. grad. studies program Loyola Coll. in Md., Balt., 2001—. Kodaly clinician, cons. Orgn. of Am. Kodaly Educators, Moorhead, Minn., 1978—, Md. United Specialists in Kodaly, Balt., 1978—. Author: (book) Elements: A Sight Singing and Rhythm Reading Book for Beginners, 1982, Kodaly, American Style, 2001, Folk Guitar for the Music Educator, 2002, 5-String Banjo for the Music Educator, 2003; contbr. articles to profl. jours. Bd. dirs., sec. Children's Chorus of Md., 1981—83. Scholar, Mu Phi Epsilon Alumni Assn., 1975. Mem.: OAKE (overseer 1997—98, chair nat. conf. planning com. 1997—98, 1983—85, overseer tchr. tng. com. 1983—85, 1997—98), MENC, The VoiceCare Network, Soc. for Rsch. in Music Edn., Soc. for Music Tchr. Edn., Md. Music Educators Assn., Am. Choral Dirs. Assn., Orgn. of Am. Kodaly Educators (v.p. 1983—85, 1997—98), Md. United Specialists in Kodaly (pres. 1996—98, 1982—84, 1998—99, mem. at large 1995—96, sec. 1980—82), Mu Phi Epsilon. Home: 307 Southway Baltimore MD 21218 Office: Am Kodaly Inst Ste 202 100 E Pennsylvania Ave Baltimore MD 21286 Office Fax: 410-494-4673. Personal E-mail: amybhuggins@yahoo.com. E-mail: amybhuggins@hotmail.com.

HUGGINS, BOB, college basketball coach; b. Morgantown, W.Va., Sept. 21, 1953; s. Charles Huggins; m. June Ann Fillman; children: Jenna Leigh, Jacqueline. BS magna cum laude, U. W.Va., 1977, MA in Health Adminstrn., 1978. Grad. asst. basketball coach U. W.Va., Morgantown, 1977-78; asst. basketball coach Ohio State U., Columbus, 1978-90; head coach Walsh Coll., Canton, Ohio, 1980-83; asst. basketball coach U. Ctrl. Fla., Orlando, 1983-84; head basketball coach U. Akron, Ohio, 1984-89, U. Cin., 1989—. Mem. basketball coaching staff U.S. World Univ. Games team, 1993. Founder Bob Huggins Found., 1997-98. Named Coach of the Yr. dist. 22 NAIA, 1981-82, 1982-83, area 6, 1982-83, Mid-Ohio Conf., 1981-82, 1982-83, Ohio Valley, 1984-85, Metro Conf., 1989-90, Dapper Dan Man of Yr., 1986-87, dist. 4 USBWA, 1991-92, Conf. USA, 1996-98, 98-99, 99-2000, Mideast Coach of Yr. Basketball Times, 1991-92, 95-96, Co-Nat. Coach of Yr., 1991-92 Hoop Scoop mag., finalist for AP Coach of Yr., 1991-92, Ohio Coll. Coach of Yr. Columbus Dispatch, 1991-92, 1995-96, Nat. Coll. Coach of Yr., Playboy Mag., 1992-93, Midseason Coach of Yr. USA Today, 1991-92 season, Mideast Coach of Yr. Basketball Times, 1995-96 season, Nat. Coach. of Yr. Basketball Times, 1997-98 season, The Sporting News, 1999-2000 season, ESPN.com, 2001-02 season; recipient Ray Meyer award Gt. Midwest conf., 1991-92, 92-93. Achievements include his 500-172 record (.744) amassed during his 21 seasons as a head coach ranks him second in winning percentage and 19th in victories among active Division 1 mentors; his string of 11 consecutive NCAA tournament appearances is the third-longest active streak; his teams have won over 20 games in all but three of his 21 campaigns and he has averaged 23.8 victories a season, 27.4 wins per campaign over the past seven years; he has compiled a 332-100 record (.769) in his 13 years at Cincinatti, making him the most winning coach in terms of victories and percentage in the school's rich basketball history. Office: Univ Cincinnati Men's Basketball 340 Shoemaker Ctr Cincinnati OH 45221-0001

HUGGINS, CHARLES EDWARD, obstetrician, gynecologist, educator; b. Hartsville, S.C., Nov. 16, 1944; s. Charles Witherspoon Huggins and Frances Sue (Fountain) Evans; m. Mary Ellen Esto, May 29, 1966; children: Chadwick Edward, Laura Ruth, Mary Elizabeth. BS, Wofford Coll., 1965; MD, Med. U. S.C., 1969. Diplomate Am. Bd. Ob-Gyn. Intern Strong Meml. Hosp., Rochester, 1969-70; resident in ob-gyn. Med. U. S.C. Hosp., Charleston, 1970-74; chief of ob-gyn. Roper Hosp., Charleston; chmn. ob-gyn. dept. Bon Secours St. Francis Hosp., Charleston, 1999—. Clin. assoc. prof. Med. U. S.C.; mem. exec. bd. Roper Hosp., Charleston,1992-95, perinatal adv. bd., Charleston, 1992-95. Leader Boy Scouts of Am., Mt. Pleasant, S.C., 1978-88; coach Hungry Neck Internat. Soccer, Mt. Pleasant, 1978-88. Lt. Cmdr. USN, 1974-76. Fellow ACOG, South Atlantic Assn. Ob-Gyn. (chair state com. 1995-98); mem. AMA, Am. Fertility Soc., NYAS, S.C. Med. Assn., Charleston County Med. Soc., Pi Kappa Phi (archon 1962—), Phi Rho Sigma. Presbyterian. Fax: (843) 577-4193.

HUGGINS, CHARLOTTE SUSAN HARRISON, secondary school educator, author, travel specialist; b. Rockford, Ill., May 13, 1933; d. Lyle Lux and Alta May (Bowers) Harrison; m. Rollin Charles Huggins Jr., Apr. 26, 1952; children: Cynthia Charlotte Peters, Shirley Ann Cooper, John Charles. Student, Knox Coll., 1951-52; AB magna cum laude, Harvard U., 1958; MA, Northwestern U., 1960, postgrad., 1971-73; cert. in conversation French, Berlitz Lang. Sch. Asst. editor Hollister Publs., Inc., Wilmette, Ill., 1959—65; tchr. advanced placement English New Trier H.S., Winnetka, Ill., 1965—, master tchr., 1979, leader tchr., 1988. With Task Force Commn. on Grading, 1973—74; Sabbatical project 1 yr. world travel History-Lit. Prospectus; cons. Asian Studies New Trier, 1987—88; mem. New Trier Supts. Commn. on Censorship, 1991; critic tchr. Northwestern U.; cons. McDougall-Littel's Young Writer's Manual, 1985—88; asst. sponsor Echoes, 1981—, Trevia, 1982, 83; sponsor New Trier News, 1988—; pres. Harrison Farms, Inc., Lovington, Ill., 1976—; spkr. North Suburban Geneal. Soc., 1990; presenter Asian lit. Ill. Humanities Coun., 1992, Nat. Scholastic Press Assn., No. Ill. Sch. Press Assn., 1992, 93, 94; instr., travel expert New Trier Adult Edn. Keys to the World's Last Mysteries, 1986—. Author: A Sequential Course in Composition Grades 9-12, 1979, A History of New Trier High School, 1982, Passage to Anaheim: An Historical Biography of Pioneer Families, 1984, Cambodia: A Place in Time, 1987; author: (video tapes) The Glory That was Greece, 1987; author: The World of Charles Dickens, 1987; editor: The Cornog Years, 2002. Women's bd. St. Leonard's House, Chgo., 1965—75; active Ctrl. Sch. PTA Bd., Wilmette, Ill., 1960—64; assocs. bd. Northwestern U. Settlement, Chgo., 1965—, pres., 1999—, fund-raising com., 1997—, ctrl. bd. com., 2003—. Recipient Citizenship award, DAR, 1953, award, Phi Beta Kappa, 1957, Am. Legion, 1959, Cert. of Merit Graphic Arts Competition, Printing Industries of Am., 1983, 1st pl. award, Am. Scholastic Press Assn., 1990, Cert. of Merit, Am. Newspaper Pubs. Assn., 1990. Mem.: DAR (historian 1999—2000, regent 2000—02, parliamentarian 2002—), ASCD, MLA, NEA, IRTA, Ill. Journalism Edn. Assn. (sec. 1997—97, awards chmn., bd. dirs., Life Achievement award 2001), New Trier Edn. Assn. (sec. 1992, pres.-elect 1994, pres. 1995—96, parliamentarian 2003—), Ill. Assn. Tchrs. English, Ill. Edn. Assn., Nat. Scholastic Press Assn. (conv. del. 1991, spring conf. rep. 1991—92, 1992—93, 1993—94, presenter fall and spring conv. 1993—94, spring conf. rep. 1994—95, presenter fall and spring conv. 1994—95, 1994—95, spring conf. rep. 1995—96, presenter fall and spring conv. 1995—96, 1996—, newspaper judge, All-Am. Newspaper award 1990—91, Life Achievement award 2001), Nat. Coun. Tchrs. English, Harvard U. Alumni Assn. (admissions candidate interviewer), Radcliffe Coll. Alunmae Assn., Knox Coll. Alumni Assn., Terra Mus. Chgo. (charter), Chgo. Farmers, Mary Crane League, Women Comm., Inc., Nat. Huguenot Soc., Quill and Scroll (bd. dirs. 1992—93, George Gallup award 1990), Ill. Huguenot Soc., Columbia Scholastic Press Assn. (del. 1990, newspaper judge), Jr. Aux. U. Chgo. Cancer Rsch. Bd., Northwestern U. Alumni Assn., Art Inst. Chgo. (life), New Trier Ret. Tchrs. Assn. (newsletter editor), Lyric Opera (assoc.), Univ. Club Chgo., Mich. Shores Club, Women's Club Willmette, Pi Beta Phi (North Shore Chgo. alumnae bd., publicity chair). Home: 700 Greenwood Ave Wilmette IL 60091-1748 Office: 385 Winnetka Ave Winnetka IL 60093-4238

HUGGINS, ELAINE JACQUELINE, nurse, retired army officer; b. San Jose, Calif., Mar. 26, 1954; d. William Burt and Edith Gwendolyn (Schindler) Moreland; m. Bruce Carlton Allanach, Oct. 8, 1976 (div. Oct. 1989); stepchildren: Dawn Louise, Christopher Bruce, Jeffrey Scott, Sean Michael; m. Michael Henry Huggins, Dec. 8, 1991; children: Phoebe Marie, Chloe Anne, Michael Henry Jr.; stepchildren: Abbey Rose, Jamin Michael. BSN, U. Md., 1976; MSN, Med. Coll. Ga., 1988; postgrad., Calif. Inst. Integral Studies. RN, Ga., Md., Calif. Commd. 1st lt. Nurse Corps U.S. Army, 1972, advanced through grades to maj., 1986; staff nurse gen. medicine-oncology Walter Reed Army Med. Ctr., Washington, 1976-78, team leader gen. medicine-oncology, 1978-79, head nurse med. splty. ward, 1979-80; asst. head nurse gynecol. oncology unit Tripler Army Med. Ctr., Honolulu, 1980-81, head nurse med. splty. clinic, 1981-83; staff nurse orthopedics Eisenhower Army Med. Ctr., Ft. Gordon, Ga., 1983-84, patient edn. coord., 1984-85, head nurse recovery rm., 1985-86; head nurse oncology/neurology unit Letterman Army Med. Ctr., Presidio of San Francisco, 1988-89, clin. nurse psychiat. unit, 1989-90, chief nursing adminstrn. E/N, 1990-92, ret., 1992; case mgr. Vis. Nurses Pomona, Claremont, Calif., 1993-94; nursing supr. Vis. Nurses Assn./Hospice of Pomona, San Bernadino, Calif., 1994-95, quality risk resource mgr., 1995-96; performance improvement mgr. Santa Barbara Vis. Nurses Assn., 2000—01; dir. edn. performance improvement and credentialising 30th Med. Group, Vandenburg AFB, Calif., 2001—. Sabbatical to Australian outback with rsch. interests in cross-cultural health care and spirituality in health care, 1996—99; freelance writer, cons., 1999—2000; mem. adj. faculty Sch. Nursing U. Phoenix-So. Calif. Campus, 1995—96; owner Hugg 'Ems Telephone Peer Counseling, 2002—03; lectr. in field. Contbr. articles to nursing, mil., and med. publs. Mem. pub. edn. com. Am. Cancer Soc., Honolulu, 1982. Recipient Humanitarian Svc. medal, 1990. Mem. Am. Diabetes Assn., Am. Assn. Diabetic Educators, Grad. Student Nurses Assn. (sec. 1986-87), ANA, Mensa, Sigma Theta Tau. Avocations: reading, walking, beach combing. Home: 164 Auriga Ave Lompoc CA 93436-1216 Office: 30th Med Group 338 South Dakota Ave Vandenberg AFB CA 93437 E-mail: elaine.huggins@vandenberg.af.mil.

HUGGINS, JAMES BERNARD, corporate executive; b. Parkersburg, W.Va., June 5, 1950; s. Bernard Alonzo and Evelyn Belle (Wiblin) H.; divorced; 1 Stepchild, Jeremy Hawk; children: Jennifer Ashton, James B.A. III. AA, W.Va. U., Parkersburg, 1970; BA, W.Va. U., Morgantown, 1972; PhD in Internat. Bus., U. Wexford, Switzerland, 2001. Asst. Office of Senate Majority Whip, Washington, 1973-76; office mgr. U.S. Sen. Robert C. Byrd, Washington, 1976-93, state dir., 1985-91; prof. staff mem. U.S. Senate Appropriations Com., Washington, 1991-93; sr. mng. assoc. Linton Mields Reisler & Cottone, Washington, 1992-94; pres. The Cottone & Huggins Group, Washington, 1994—; chmn. Ctr. for Sino-Am. Trade. Co-chmn. Nat. Legis. Liaison Com.; dir. Fed. Liaison. Col. USAF/CAP; maj.- gen. U.S. Svc. Commd. Decorated Disting. Svc. medal with 5 oak leaf clusters, others. Mem. Nat. Conf. State Socs. (treas. 1980), W.Va. Soc. Washington (pres. 1980-82), W.Va. U. Alumni Assn. (nat. capital chpt.). Democrat. Epsicopalian. Avocations: sailing, flying, scuba diving. Office: The Cottone and Huggins Group 601 Pennsylvania Ave NW Ste 900 S Washington DC 20004

HUGGINS, ROBERT BRIAN, nonprofit organization official; b. Schenectady, N.Y., Apr. 11, 1953; s. Lawrence P. and Mary A. (Flynn) H. BS, Villanova U., 1975; MBA, Temple U., 1980; grad. mgmt. skills program, Nat. Acad. for Voluntarism, Alexandria, Va., 1994. Mktg. analyst Phila. Saving Fund Soc., 1976-77, advt. mgr., 1978-80, dir. advt., 1981-84, dir. spl. projects, 1985-86; account exec. United Way Southeastern Pa., Phila., 1987-89, sr. account exec., 1990-95, asst. v.p., 1996—. E-mail: rbhuggins@juno.com.

HUGHART, THOMAS ARTHUR, minister; b. Morgantown, W.Va., Feb. 21, 1932; s. Joseph Marvin and Helen Hood (Williams) H.; m. Gloria Joyce Wiley, Feb. 1, 1958; children: Andrew William, Heidi Ellen, Bradford David. BA, Coll. of Wooster, 1953; MDiv, Union Theol. Sem., N.Y.C., 1956; STD, San Francisco Theol. Sem., San Anselmo, Calif., 1982. Ordained to ministry Presbyn. Ch. (U.S.A.), 1956. Assoc. min. Watchung Presbyn. Ch., Bloomfield, N.J., 1956-59; pastor Bedford (N.Y.) Presbyn. Ch., 1959-89, co-pastor, 1989-95; interim sr. pastor First Presbyn. Ch., Greenwich, Conn., 1995-97, Ctrl. Presbyn. Ch., N.Y.C., 1997-99; pres. Ethics Mgmt. Consultants, Inc., Bedford, N.Y., 1999—; interim pastor All Souls Parish, Port Chester, NY, 2000—01. Mem. Presbyn. Conf. Assn., N.Y.C., 1985-2000; moderator Presbytery of Hudson River, 1975. Democrat. Home: 459 Old Post Rd PO Box 447 Bedford NY 10506-0447 Office: Ethics Mgmt Consultants Inc Box 447 459 Old Post Rd Bedford NY 10506-1029 E-mail: Ethicscon@aol.com.

HUGHES, ALFRED CLIFTON, archbishop; b. Boston, Dec. 2, 1932; s. Alfred Clifton and Ellen Cecelia (Hennessey) H.. AB, St. John's Sem. Coll., 1954; STL, Gregorian U., Rome, 1958, STD, 1961. Ordained priest Roman Cath. Ch., 1957, ordained bishop Roman Cath. Ch., 1981. Asst. pastor St. Stephen's Parish, Framingham, Mass., 1958—59, Our Lady Help of Christians, Newton, Mass., 1961—62; lectr. St. John's Sem., Brighton, 1962—65, spiritual dir., 1965—81, rector, 1981—86; aux. bishop Archdiocese of Boston, 1981—93; regional bishop of Merrimack Region, 1986—90; vicar for adminstrn. Archdiocese of Boston, 1990—93; bishop of Baton Rouge, 1993—2001; coadjutor archbishop of New Orleans Archdiocese of New Orleans, 2001—02, archbishop of New Orleans, 2002— . Chmn. com. on doctrine U.S. Cath. Conf. Bishops, 1991—94, com. on use of catechism, 1995—. Author: Preparing for Church Ministry, 1979, Spiritual Masters, 1999; chmn. editl. bd.: Nat. Dir. for Catechesis; contbr. articles to profl. jours. Recipient Mellon and Davis Founds. grant, 1976. Mem.: Catholic Theol. Soc. Am. Roman Catholic. Office: Archdiocese of New Orleans 7887 Walmsley Avenue New Orleans LA 70125-3496*

HUGHES, ALLEN, music critic; b. Brownsburg, Ind., Dec. 28, 1921; s. Maurice McKinley and Bess (Collyer) H.; m. Marian Nina Berklich, Mar. 28, 1964. Student, George Washington U., 1940-42; BA, U. Mich., 1946, B.Mus., 1947; postgrad., N.Y. U., 1948-50. Lectr. music Toledo Mus. Art, 1946-47; asst. editor, critic Mus. Am., 1950-53; free-lance writer Paris, France, 1953-55; music critic N.Y. Herald Tribune, 1955-60; mem. music faculty Bklyn. Coll., 1958-60; music critic N.Y. Times, 1960-61, asst. dance critic, 1961-62, dance critic, 1962-65, music critic, 1965-86. Served to lt. (j.g.) USNR, 1943-46. Office: 1255 N Gulfstream Ave Sarasota FL 34236

HUGHES, ANN HIGHTOWER, retired economist, international trade consultant; b. Birmingham, Ala., Nov. 24, 1938; d. Brady Alexander and Juanita (Pope) H. BA, George Washington U., 1963, MA, 1969. Asst. U.S. trade rep. Exec. Office of Pres., Washington, 1978-81; dep. asst. sec. trade agreements Dept. Commerce, Washington, 1981-82, dep. asst. sec. Western Hemisphere, 1982-95; dir. C & M Internat., Washington, 1995-97; ret. Recipient meritorious exec. award Pres. of U.S., 1982, 88, disting. exec. award, 1993.

HUGHES, ANN NOLEN, psychotherapist; b. Ft. Meade, Md. d. George M. and Georgie T. Nolen; m. Edwin L. Hughes, Oct. 21, 1961; 1 child, Andrew G. BS in Psychology, Rollins Coll., 1985, MA in Counseling, 1986; student in pub. speaking and human rels., Dale Carnegie Inst., 1981; student, Duke U., 1950-52. Lic. mental health counselor; nat. cert. counselor; nat. cert. gerontl. counselor. Supr. top secret control, audio/visual small parts supply U.S. Army, Continental U.S. and Tokyo; adminstrv. sec. Sys. Devel. Corp., Rand Corp., Santa Monica, Calif.; adminstrv. asst., editor, exec. sec., adminstrv. sec. Aerospace Corp., El Segundo, Calif.; staff therapist Circles of Care, Melbourne, Fla. Developer program for leading divorce support groups for Brevard Women's Ctr. Various leadership positions PTA, Pittsford, NY, Brookfield, Wis., 1968—81; mem. Brevard Cmty. Chorus, 1991—, adv. bd., 1997; docent Space Coast Sci. Ctr., 1991—92; vol. ref. desk Suntree-Viera Libr., 1997—98; mem. Citizen's Emergency Response Team (CERT), 1999—2001. Mem. DAR, Fla. Coun. on Aging, Mental Health Counselors Assn. of the Space Coast, Space Coast PC Users Group, Nat. Geneal. Soc., Geneal. Soc. South Brevard, Suntree Country Club, Suntree Master Homeowners Assn. (Twin Lakes rep. 1997—), Brevard County Alumnae Assn. of Kappa Kappa Gamma, Kappa Kappa Gamma. Presbyterian. Avocations: photoimaging, fitness, genealogy, voice, choral singing. Office: PO Box 410162 Melbourne FL 32941-0162

HUGHES, AUSTIN LELAND, biological sciences educator; b. Washington, Sept. 10, 1949; s. Edward Riley and Josephine (Nicholls) H.; m. Mary Ann Hughes, Apr. 23, 1980; children: Austin Leland, Helen W. AB, Georgetown U., 1969; MS, W.Va. U., 1980; PhD, Ind. U., 1984. Asst. prof. Pa. State U., University Park, 1990-96, assoc. prof., 1996-97; prof. biol. scis. U. S.C., Columbia, 2000—, dir. Biotech. Inst., 2002—. Author: Evolution and Human Kinship, 1988, Adaptive Evolunion of General Genomes, 1999; mem. editl. bd. Immunogenetics, 1991—; contbr. more than 150 articles to sci. jours. Recipient Ryan Philosophy medal Georgetown U., 1969; NIH Rsch. Career Devel. awardee, 1992-97. Mem. Soc. for Study of Evolution, Soc. for Molecular Biology and Evolution. Roman Catholic. Office: Y SC 700 Sumter St Columbia SC 29208-0001

HUGHES, B. WAYNE, retail executive; 2 children. BS, UCLA. Dir. Pub. Storage Inc., Glendale, Calif., 1980—, pres., co-CEO, 1980—91, chmn. bd. dirs., CEO, 1991—, Pub. Storage Properties XI, Inc. and affilated cos., 1990—98. Office: Pub Storage Inc 701 Western Ave Ste 200 Glendale CA 91201

HUGHES, BARNARD, actor; b. Bedford Hills, N.Y., July 16, 1915; s. Owen and Madge (Kiernan) H.; m. Helen Stenborg, Apr. 19, 1950; 2 children. Student, Manhattan Coll., DHL (hon.), 1989. Stage debut with Shakespeare Fellowship Co. in The Taming of the Shrew, N.Y.C., 1934; actor (plays) including Please, Mrs. Garibaldi, 1939, Herself, Mrs. Patrick Crowley, 1939, The Ivy Green, 1949, Dinosaur Wharf, 1951, The Teahouse of the August Moon, 1956, A Bell for Adano, 1957, Home of the Brave, 1957, The Will and The Way, 1957, Enrico IV, 1958, A Majority of One, 1959, Advise and Consent, 1960, Rosmersholm, 1962, A Doll's House, 1963, The Advocate, 1963, Nobody Loves and Albatross, 1963, Hamlet, 1964, I Was Dancing, 1964, Generation, 1965, Hogan's Goat, 1965, How Now Dow Jones, 1967, The Wrong-Way Light Bulb, 1969, Sheep on the Runway, 1970, Line, 1971, Abelard and Heloise, 1971, Older People, 1972, Hamlet, 1972, Much Ado About Nothing, 1972 (Tony nomination 1973), Uncle Vanya, 1973, The Good Doctor, 1973, The Merry Wives of Windsor, 1974, Pericles, Prince of Tyre, 1974, All Over Town, 1974, The Three Sisters, 1977, The Devil's Disciple, 1977, 78, Da, 1978 (Tony award Best Actor 1978, Outer Critics Circle award 1978), Homeward Bound, 1980, Iceman Cometh, 1981, 85, Translations, 1981, Tartuffe, 1982, Angels Fall, 1982, 83, End of the World, 1984, The Sky is No Limit, 1984, You Can't Take It With You (Abbey Theatre, Dublin, Ireland), 1989, Prelude to A Kiss, 1990, Da, 1999, (Olympia Theatre, Dublin, Ireland) 1993, Waiting in the Wings, 1999, (films) including The Young Doctors, 1961, Hamlet, 1964, Midnight Cowboy, 1969, Where's Poppa?, 1970, Deadhead Miles, 1970, The Pursuit of Happiness, 1971, The Hospital, 1971, Cold Turkey, 1971, Rage, 1972, Sisters, 1973, Oh God!, 1977, First Monday in October, 1981, Tron, 1982, Best Friends, 1982, Maxie, 1985, Where are the Children?, 1986, The Lost Boys, 1987, Da (Olymoia Theatre, Dublin, Ireland), 1988, Doc Hollywood, 1991, Sister Act II: Back in the Habit, 1993, Odd Couple II, 1997, The Cradle Will Rock, 1998, (TV movies) including Guilty or Innocent: The Sam Sheppard Murder Case, 1975, 1975, Tell Me My

Name, 1977, See How She Runs, 1978, Homeward Bound, 1980, The Sky's No Limit, 1984, Agatha Cristie's A Carribean Mystery, 1983, Night of Courage, 1986, A Hobo's Christmas, 1987, Day One, 1989, Home Fires Burning, 1989, Guts and Glory: The Rise and Fall of Oliver North, 1989, The Incident, 1990, Miracle Child, 1993; star: (TV series) Doc, 1975-76, Mr. Merlin, 1981-82, The Cavanaughs, 1986-87, Blossom, 1991-93. With U.S. Army, 1943-45, No. Africa, Italy. Recipient St. Clair Bayfield award, 1973; elected to Theatre Hall of Fame, 1991. Office: Howard Aronson Withum Smith Brown 328 Newman Springs Rd Red Bank NJ 07701-5654

HUGHES, BLAKE, retired architectural institute administrator, publisher; b. N.Y.C., June 24, 1914; s. Ferdinand Holme and Ines (de Cordova) H.; m. Betty Jean Wolf, Aug. 26, 1951; children: Diane Elizabeth, Brian Blake. Degre de civilisation, Sorbonne U., Paris, 1935; AB summa cum laude, Dartmouth Coll., 1936; postgrad., Columbia U., 1936-37. Salesman Edward B. Smith & Co., Smith, Barney & Co., investment bankers, N.Y.C., 1936-38, N.Y. Life Ins. Co., 1939-40; promotion mgr. Engring. News Record, Constrn. Methods, McGraw-Hill Inc., N.Y.C., 1947-50; promotion mgr., dir. mktg. Archtl. Record F.W. Dodge Corp., N.Y.C., 1951-61; assoc. pub. Archtl. Record McGraw-Hill Inc., N.Y.C., 1961-68, pub. Archtl. Record, 1968-80, pub. House & Home, 1976-77; pres. Internat. Inst. for Architecture, Washington, 1978-81. Author: A Lifetime's Too Short, 2002, Good Job, 2002, (novels) A Lifetimes Too Short, (short stories) Good Job. Trustee Unity (Maine) Coll., 1965-75; pres. Internat. Archtl. Found., 1973-78; bd. dirs. Nat. Home Improvement Coun., 1976-77. Lt. USNR, 1940-45. Decorated Order of Fatherland War (Russia). Mem. Union Internat. Architects (archtl. critics com. 1978-80), Appalachian Housing Inst. (bd. dirs.), Charleston Artist Guild (pres. 1990-91), English Speaking Union (pres. Charleston chpt. 1995-96), Carolina Yacht Club, Phi Beta Kappa, Delta Sigma Rho. Home: 109 E Bay St Apt 2C Charleston SC 29401-2549

HUGHES, BRADLEY RICHARD, business executive; b. Detroit, Oct. 8, 1954; s. John Arthur and Nancy Irene (Middleton) H.; m. Linda McCants, Feb. 14, 1977; children: Bradley Richard Jr., Brian Jeffrey. AA, Oakland Coll., 1974; BS in Journalism, BJ, U. Colo., 1979, MBA in Fin. and Mktg., 1981, MS in Telecommunications, 1990. Cert. office automation profl., cert. systems profl. Buyer Joslins Co., Denver, 1979; mktg. adminstr. Mountain Bell, Denver, 1980 82; ch. cons. AT&T Info. Systems, mktg. exec. AT&T, Denver, 1983-86, acct. exec., 1986-87; mktg. mgr. U.S. West, Denver, 1987-95; dir. U. Colo. Coll. Engring., Denver, 1995—. Exec.-on-loan U. Colo. Coll. Engring. Contbr. articles to bus. publs. Bd. dirs. Brandychase Assn.; state del., committeeman Republican Party Colo.; dir. Inst. for Govt. Innovation; bd. dirs. Olmsted Pavilion, dir. Colo. Chess Acad. Mem. IEEE, Assn. MBA Execs., U.S. Chess Fedn., Internat. Platform Assn., Mensa, Intertel, Assn. Telecommunications Profls., Am. Mgmt. Assn., Am. Mktg. Assn., Info. Industry Assn., Office Automation Soc. Internat., World Future Soc., Triple Nine Soc., Internat. Soc. Philos. Inquiry, Assn. Computing Machinery. Republican. American Baptist. Home: 5759 S Jericho Way Aurora CO 80015-3653 Office: U Colo Coll Engring PO Box 104 Denver CO 80201-0104

HUGHES, BRIAN LEE, music educator; b. Lansing, Mich., May 10, 1957; s. Harry and Thala Mildred Hughes; m. Coleen Ruth Schaefer, July 9, 1988; 1 child, Caitlyn Rose. B Music Edn., Olivet Coll., 1982; MusM in Edn., U. No. Iowa, 1992, MusM in Conducting, 1993. Dir. music Don Bosco H.S., Gilbertville, Iowa, 1983—87, First Bapt. Ch., Moline, Ill., 1988—91; dir. bands Alleman H.S., Rock Island, Ill., 1987—91; condr. Dubuque (Iowa) Youth Symphony, 1994—2002; asst. condr. Dubuque Symphony Orch., 1996 2002; dir. instrumental music, chmn. dept. Loras Coll., Dubuque, 1993—, arts and lecture chmn., 1997—; founder, condr. Tri-State Wind Symphony, Dubuque, 1995—. Cons. Dubuque Symphony Orch., 1995—2001; bd. dirs. Dubuque Arts Coun., 1999. Author: (program notes) Dubuque Symphony Orch., 1995—2001, Cedar Falls Symphony, 2000—. Candidate Grand Ledge (Mich.) Sch. Bd., 1975, 1976. Recipient Condr. prize, Hradee Kralove (Czech Republic) Philharm., 1999, Western Bohemia Philharm., Marianske Lazne, Czech Republic, 2000. Mem.: Condrs. Guild, Iowa Band Masters Assn., Music Educators Nat. Conf. Avocations: reading, camping, travel, golf. Home: 1297 Langworthy St Dubuque IA 52001-6422 Office: Loras Coll 1450 Alta Vista St Dubuque IA 52004-0178

HUGHES, BYRON WILLIAM, lawyer, oil exploration company executive; b. Clarksdale, Miss., Nov. 8, 1945; s. Byron B. and Francis C. (Turner) H.; m. Sarah Eileen Goodwin, June 23, 1973 (div.); children: Jennifer Eileen, Stephanie Ann. BA, U. Miss., 1968; JD, Jackson Sch. Law (now Miss. Coll. Law), 1971. Bar: Miss. 1971, U.S. Supreme Ct. 1975; cert. real estate appraiser. Atty., abstractor Miss. Hwy. Dept., 1971-76; atty., ind. landman Byron Hughes Oil Exploration Co., Jackson, Miss., 1976-92; prosecutor, child support enforcement atty. Miss. Dept. Human Svcs., 1992—. Tchr. high sch.; real estate broker. Mem. ABA, Miss. Bar Assn., Hinds County Bar Assn., Bolivar County Bar Assn., Am. Judicature Soc., Nat. Assn. Real Estate Appraisers, Miss. Child Support Assn., Miss. Assn. Petroleum Landmen, Ala. Landmen Assn., Black Warrior Basin Petroleum Landmen Assn., Am. Assn. Petroleum Landmen (cert. profl. landman 1991), Ole Miss. Alumni Assn., Miss. Coll. Alumni Assn., Miss. Art Assn., Cleve. Exch. Club, Sigma Delta Kappa. Methodist. Home and Office: PO Box 1485 Jackson MS 39215-1485

HUGHES, CHRISTOPHER ADAM, conductor, educator; s. Ronald Dee and Kathleen Ann Hughes. BA magna cum laude, Western State Coll., 1994; MMus, VanderCook Coll. of Music, Chgo., 1997; postgrad., U. of Colo., Boulder, 2002—. Lic. profl. educator Colo. Dept. of Edn. Dir. of instrumental music Grand Junction Ctrl. H.S., Grand Junction, Colo., 1994—2000; instrumental music condr. Smoky Hill H.S., Aurora, Colo., 2000—02; grad. asst./educator U. of Colo., Boulder, 2002—. First vice-president Colo. Band Directors Assn., Denver, 1997—2001; honor ensemble condr., Denver, Craig, Delta, Greeley, Westminster, Colo., 1999—2002; cmty. band condr. Performer Colo. Brass Band, 1991—, Rocky Mountain Brass Works, 2000—. Scholar Grad. Tchg./Rsch. Assistantship, U. of Colo. Mem.: Coll. Band Dirs. Nat. Assn., Colo. Music Educators Assn., Am. Sch. Band Dirs. Assn., Internat. Trumpet Guild, Kappa Delta Pi. Avocations: restoration of 1957 Chevrolets, domestic and international travel, mountain climbing, sight seeing. Home: 3940 S Hannibal Street Aurora CO 80013

HUGHES, CLAUDE L. endocrinologist; s. Claude L. and Elizabeth B. Hughes; m. Linda A. Sakiewicz; children: Maureen C., Patrick R., Gavin C. BS magna cum laude, East Carolina U., 1973; MD, Duke U., 1980, PhD, 1981. Diplomate Am. Bd. Ob-gyn, Am. Bd. Reproductive Endocrinology. Asst., assoc. and rsch. prof. dept. ob-gyn Duke U., Durham, NC, 1985—2000, cons. prof. dept. ob-gyn, 2000—; assoc. prof. depts. comparative medicine and ob-gyn Wake Forest U., Winston-Salem, NC, 1994—97; prof. dept. ob-gyn UCLA, 1998—2000; dir. med. and sci. svcs. Quintiles, Inc., Research Triangle Park, NC, 2001—. Women's guild endowed chair and dir. Ctr. Women's Health, CSMC, L.A., 1998—2000. Bd. dirs. then chmn. bd. dirs. Am. Livestock Breeds Conservancy, Pittsboro, NC, 1994—2003; vol. head coach men's rugby football club U. N.C., Chapel Hill, 2001—03. Named Outstanding Alumnus, East Carolina U., 1998; recipient NAMS/DuPont Protein Technologies Soy Rsch. award, N.Am. Menopause Soc., 2002; Grad. fellow U. Glasgow, Scotland, The Rotary Found., 1974—75. Mem.: Soc. Reproductive Endocrinology and Infertility, Bayard F. Carter Soc., Am. Soc. Reproductive Medicine, Drug Info. Assn., Soc. for the Study of Reproduction, Am. Coll. Women's Health Physicians, Am. Acad. Pharm. Physicians, Soc. Toxicology, Endocrine Soc., Am. Assn. Small Ruminant Practitioners (assoc.). Achievements include patents for phytoestrogens and hormone combinations in human health; research in the effects of natural and environmental hormone-like chemicals on reproduction, development and health. Avocations: rugby, breed conservation. Office: Med and Sci Svcs Quintiles PO Box 13979 Research Triangle Park NC 27709-3979 E-mail: claude.hughes@quintiles.com.

HUGHES, CLYDE MATTHEW, religious denomination executive; b. Huntington, W.Va., Dec. 7, 1948; s. Donald Lee and Audrey Arlene (Stevers) H.; m. Linda May Daniels, June 10, 1972; children: Crystal, Dustin, Tina, Wesley, Timothy, Penny, Heidi, Robin. Diploma, Amb. Bible Inst., London, Ohio, 1972; BA, Cedarville (Ohio) Coll., 1974; MA, Meth. Theol. Sch. in Ohio, 1980; DD, Heritage Bible Coll., Dunn, N.C., 1994. Ordained to ministry Internat. Pentecostal Ch. of Christ, 1974. Pastor Internat. Pentecostal Ch. of Christ, Hillsboro, Ohio, 1981-82, nat. dir. Sunday sch. London, 1976-82, dir. ch. ministries, 1982-84, asst. gen. overseer, 1984-90, gen. overseer, chmn. gen. bd., 1990—. Mem. nat. com. Mission Am., 1997—; bd. dirs. Beulah Heights Bible Coll., Atlanta, 1982—, chmn. bd. 1990-96. Editor-in-chief The Pentecostal Leader; contbr. articles to religious publs. Chmn. bd. dirs. Locust Grove Rest Home, 1990-98. Mem. Nat. Assn. Evangs. (bd. dirs. 1990—2001), Madison County Evang. Assn. (bd. dirs. 1990-2001), London Ministerial Assn., Chs. United with Israel (bd. gov. 2002-), Mission Am. (nat. com. 1997-), Pentecostal/Charismatic Chs. N.Am. (bd. dirs. 1994—, exec. com. 2001), Internat. Pentecostal Press Assn., N. Am. chpt. exec. com., 2001—. Mem. Internat. Pentecostal Ch. Of Christ. Home: 7040 Danville Rd London OH 43140-9766

HUGHES, DAVID HENRY, manufacturing company executive; b. Orlando, Fla., Dec. 20, 1942; s. Harry C. and Pauline B. Hughes; m. Rebecca Wilkins; 1 child, Kristin E.; m. Linda Cooper, Apr. 26, 1986; children: Patrick, Shelby. BS, U. Fla., 1965, JD, 1967. Mgmt. trainee Hughes Supply Inc., Orlando, 1968-72, pres., chief operating officer, 1972 74, pres., chief exec. officer, 1974-86, chmn., chief exec. officer, 1986—, also dir. Bd. dirs. Sun Banks Inc., Orlando, SunTrust Banks Inc., Atlanta. Active Orlando Regional Healthcare Sys. Mem. Fla. Bar Assn., Fla. Coun. of 100. Republican. Avocations: golf, fishing.*

HUGHES, DAVID MICHAEL, oil service company executive, rancher; b. Knoxville, Tenn., Mar. 20, 1939; s. Cleo L. and Lucille (Farmer) H.; m. Louise Love, Mar. 17, 1960 (div. 1971); children: David Michael Jr., Sheryl Lynn; m. Elizabeth Grove, Mar. 16, 1974; children: Christopher Grove, Andrew Carter. BCE, U. Tenn., 1962. Founder, owner World Wide Divers, Inc., Morgan City, La., 1962-69; founder, past chmn. bd. Oceaneering Internat., Inc., Houston, 1969-90; founder, owner Broken Arrow Ranch, Ingram, Tex., 1975—; founder, pres. Tex. Wild Game Coop., Ingram, 1981—, Game Ranching, Inc., Ingram, 1986—. Bd. dirs. Oceaneering Internat., Inc., 1969—. Author: Broken Arrow Ranch Cookbook, 1984; patentee underwater corrosion meter, underwater camera and a device for identifying a characteristic of an object or the contents of a container. Chmn. Hist. Preservation Com., Ingram, 1986—; mem. Adv. Coun. Tex. Marine Sci. Inst., 1980-91; hon. chmn. Hunters for the Hungry, 1991—, nat. chmn. Named "Who's Who in Tex. Food and Wine", Dallas Morning News Poll, 1992; named industry pioneer Offshore Energy Hall of Fame, 1999. Mem. Assn. Diving Contractors (pres. 1967-71, Galletti award 1981), Exotic Wildlife Assn. (pres. 1987-89), Chi Epsilon (nat. conv. del. 1961). Republican. Avocations: woodworking, cooking. Home: Broken Arrow Ranch Inc PO Box 530 Ingram TX 78025-0530

HUGHES, DAVID ROBERT, gaming company executive; b. Holyoke, Mass., Dec. 28, 1962; s. Charles Russell and Kathleen McAnulty; m. Patricia McKeon, June 24, 1995. BS in Acctg., Richard Stockton Coll. N.J., 1986. CPA, N.J. Sr. auditor Pratt Corp., Atlantic City, 1987; fin. acctg. and reporting mgr. Trump Org., Atlantic City, 1988-95; fin. and casino contr. Hemmeter Enterprises, Denver, 1995; v.p., dir. of fin. Mohegan Sun Casino, Uncasville, Conn., 1996; v.p. fin. Sun Internat., Uncasville, 1997; CFO, sr. v.p. Resorts Casino Hotel, Atlantic City, 1997-2000; CEO Sun Cruz Casinos LLC, Dania Beach, Fla., 2000—. Adj. prof. Atlantic C.C., Mays Landing, N.J., 1993 94; table mem. N.J. Casino Control Commn., Atlantic City, 1999. Named One of Top 40 Execs. under 40 N.J. Business mag., 1998. Mem. AICPA, N.J. Soc. CPAs. Republican. Roman Catholic. Avocations: golf, billiards, classical guitar, wine conniseur. Home: 611 Open Meadow Rd Frederick MD 21703 E-mail: david.hughes@att.net.

HUGHES, DEAN THOMAS, English language educator, writer; b. Ogden, Utah, Aug. 24, 1943; s. Emery T. and Lorraine Pierce Hughes; m. Kathleen Hurst, Nov. 23, 1966; children: Thomas, Amy, Robert. BA, Weber State U., 1967; MA, U. Wash., 1968, PhD, 1972; postdoctoral seminar, Stanford U., 1975, Yale U., 1978. Prof. English Cen. Mo. State U., Warrensburg, Mo., 1972-80; writer Provo, Utah, 1980-97; prof. English Brigham Young U., Provo, 1997—2002. Author: (nonfiction) The Mormon Church: A Basic History, 1986, Lullaby and Goodnight, 1992, Baseball Tips, 1993, Great Stories from Mormon History, 1994, (with Tom Hughes) We'll Bring the World His Truth: Missionary Adventures from Around the World, 1995, (children's and young adult fiction) Under the Same Stars, 1979, Switching Tracks, 1982, Nutty and the Case of the Mastermind Thief, 1985, Theo Zephyr, 1987, Family Pose, 1989, Lucky Breaks Loose, 1990, Rookie Star, Vol. 5, Angel Park All-Stars, 1990, Lucky Fights Back, 1991, Up to Bat, Vol. 12, Angel Park All-Stars, 1991, Total Soccer, Vol. 6, Angel All-Stars, 1992, Lucky the Detective, 1992, Nutty's Ghost, 1993, Find the Power, 1994, Backup Soccer Star, 1995, Team Picture, 1996, Brad and Butter: Play Ball!, 1998, Now We're Talking, Vol. 5, Scrappers, 1999, Home Run Hero, Vol. 3, Scrappers, 1999, Soldier Boys, 2001 (NY Pub. Lit. Best Book for Teenage 2001, nominee Heartland award 2002), others, (novels) Rumors of War, Vol. I, Children of the Promise, 1997, Since You Went Away, Vol. 2, Children of the Promise, 1997, Far From Home, Vol. 3, Children of the Promise, 1998, When We Meet Again, Vol. 4, Children of the Promise, 1999, As Long As I Have You, Vol. 5, Children of the Promise, 2000, (Hearts of the Children series) The Writing on the Wall, Vol. 1, 2001, Troubled Waters, Vol. 2, 2002. Mem. lit. bd. trustees Provo City, 1988-94, 96-2000; bd. dirs. Brigham Young Acad., Provo, 1997-2000, Provo Theatre Co., 1999-2000, Domestic Violence Coalition, Provo, 1997-2000. Named Disting. Utahn, State of Utah, 1996, 100 Most Prominent Utah Authors, Utah State U., 1991, Mo. Authors, Key to Mo. Authors, Mo. Libr. Assn., 1987; recipient Editor's choice award, 1990, Best Books for the Teen Age, N.Y. Pub. Libr., 1993, Best Book in Children's and Young Adult Lit., Assn. Mormon Letters, 1993, 1997-98 Best Fiction award Ind. LDS Booksellers Assn., 1998, Best Novel 1998, Assn. for Mormon Letters, 1999, 1998 Excellence in Writing award, 1999, 1998-99 Book of Yr. award Ind. LDS Booksellers Assn., 1999, Frankie and John K. Orton LDS Lit. award, 1999. Mem. Soc. Children's Bookwriters, Author's Guild, Assn. for Mormon Writers. Democrat. Mem. Lds Ch. Avocations: skiing, golf, travel. Home: PO Box 307 Midway UT 84049

HUGHES, EDWARD JOHN, artist; b. North Vancouver, B.C., Feb. 17, 1913; s. Edward Samuel Daniell and Katherine Mary (McLean) H.; m. Fern Rosabell Irvine Smith, Feb. 10, 1940 (dec. 1974). Grad., Vancouver Sch. Art, 1933; D Fine Art (hon.), U. Victoria, 1995; DLL (hon.), Emily Carr Inst. Art & Design, Vancouver, B.C., 1997, Malaspina Univ.-Coll., Nanaimo, B.C., 2000. Exhbns. include retrospective, Vancouver Art Gallery, 1967, Surrey Art Gallery, Art Gallery of Greater Victoria, Edmonton Art Gallery, Calgary Glenbow Gallery, 1983-85, Nat. Gallery Can., Beaverbrook Gallery, Fredericton, 1983-85; represented in permanent collections, Nat. Gallery Can., Ottawa, Art Gallery Ont., Toronto, Vancouver Art Gallery, Montreal Mus. Fine Art, Greater Victoria Art Gallery; ofcl. Army war artist, 1942-46. Served with Can. Army, 1939-46. Recipient Can. Council grants, 1958, 63, 67, 70 Mem. Royal Can. Acad. Arts, Order of Can. Presbyterian. Address: 2449 Heather St Duncan BC Canada V9L 2Z6

HUGHES, EDWARD T. retired bishop; b. Lansdowne, Pa., Nov. 13, 1920; Student, St. Charles Sem., U. Pa. Ordained priest Roman Cath. Ch., 1947. Ordained titular bishop Segia and aux. bishop Phila., 1976—86; 2d bishop Diocese of Metuchen, NJ, 1986—97, ret., 1997.

HUGHES, EDWARD THOMAS, retired English educator, consultant; b. Elmira, N.Y., June 4, 1942; s. Henry Michael and Irene (Husar) H.; m. Judy Ann Lawrence, Sept. 20, 1969; children: Susan Jill, Anne-Marie. BA, SUNY, Albany, 1964, MA, 1968, MS, 1974. Cert. tchr. English, sch. adminstrn. and supervision, sch. dist. adminstrn. Tchr. English Horseheads (N.Y.) Ctrl. Schs., 1964-67, Shenendehowa Ctrl. Schs., Clifton Park, N.Y., 1967-99, chairperson English, 1973-99. Adj. prof. tchr. edn. SUNY, Albany, 1988-91; supr. student tchrs. Coll. St. Rose, 2000-; chairperson Profl. Performance Rev. Com. Shenendehowa Ctrl. Sch., Clifton Park, 1991-93, 96-99; participant field tests Nat. Bd. Profl. Teaching Stds., U. Pitts., Conn., 1993; cons. Project Lead The Way. Contbr. articles to Schenectady Sunday Gazette. Eucharistic minister St. Edward's Cath. Ch., Clifton Park, N.Y., 1990—, faith formation com., 1989-92; host chairperson Am. Field Svc. Shenendehowa Pub. Libr., Clifton Park, 1980-85, bd. trustees, v.p., 1994-95. Named Outstanding Educator Cornell U., 1990, Educator of Excellence award N.Y. State English Coun., 1997. Mem. ASCD, Shenendehowa PTA (Life), English Educators Assn. (treas. capital dist.). Roman Catholic. Avocations: classical music, collecting figurines, reading.

HUGHES, EDWIN LAWSON, retired information technology executive; b. Pittsburg, Kans., Aug. 11, 1924; s. Edwin Byron and Vera (Lawson) H.; m. Ann Turner Nolen, Oct. 21, 1961; 1 child, Andrew George; children from previous marriage: John Lawson, James Prescott. BSEE, Mo. Sch. Mines, 1949; MSEE, U. Ill., 1950. Registered profl. engr., Fla. Rsch. assoc. digital computer lab. U. Ill., 1949-53; rsch. assoc. Internat. Telemeter Corp., L.A., 1953-54; with Lockheed Missile Sys. Divsn., L.A., 1954-56; group leader Systems Devel. Corp., Santa Monica, Calif., 1957-60; tech. dir. Gen. Motors, Oak Creek, Wis., 1960-71; v.p. engring. Xerox Corp., Webster, N.Y., 1971-81, Santec Corp., Amherst, N.H., 1981-82; chmn., pres., chief exec. officer Fla. Data Corp., Melbourne, 1982-83; pvt. practice cons. Melbourne, 1984-88; ret. Contbr. articles and papers to profl jours.; inventor computers, copiers; patentee in field. Com. mem. Boy Scouts Am., Pittsford, N.Y., 1974-76; mem. Brevard Cmty. Chorus. With U.S. Army, 1943-46, ETO. Mem. IEEE (sr., life), Space Coast PC Users Group (pres. 1991-95, 97-99, sec. 1988-91, treas. 1995-97), Suntree Country Club. Republican. Avocations: skiing, choral singing, tennis, home computers. Home and Office: 447 Pauma Valley Way Melbourne FL 32940-1918 E-mail: elhughes@cfl.rr.com.

HUGHES, ERIC SCOTT, music educator; b. Troy, NY, Apr. 6, 1974; s. John Robert and Ernestine Julia Hughes. MusB, SUNY, Potsdam, 1992—96; MA, George Mason U., 1996—97. Tchr. instrumental music East Ramapo Ctrl. Sch. Dist., Spring Valley, NY, 1997—2000; tchr. instrumental music . Niskayuna (NY) Ctrl. Sch. Dist., 2000—. Mem.: Music Educators Nat. Conf., NY State Sch. Music Assn., Kappa Delta Pi. Avocation: tennis. Home: 14 James Street Cohoes NY 12047 Office: Niskayuna Central School District 1626 Balltown Road Niskayuna NY 12309 Personal E-mail: ericscotthughes@aol.com.

HUGHES, FRANCIS P. medical organization executive; Exec. v.p. Am. Bd. Anesthesiology, Raleigh, NC. Office: Am Bd Anesthesiology 4101 Lake Boone Trl Ste 510 Raleigh NC 27607-7506

HUGHES, GEORGE MAXWELL KNIGHT, pharmaceutical company executive, retired; b. Wallasey, Eng., July 10, 1928; came to U.S., 1954; s. Arthur Trevor and Gwendolyn Mary (Jones) H.; m. Christine Anne Rofe, Sept. 21, 1954 (div. 1996); children: Jane K., Mark K. BA, Cambridge (Eng.) U., 1950, PhD, 1954. Rsch. chemist, asst. to v.p. rsch., then dir. rsch. adminstrn. Pfizer-Rsch., Groton, Conn., 1959-69; dir. sys. and planning Pfizer Pharms., N.Y.C., 1969-72, v.p. adminstrn., 1972-75, v.p. diagnostics products Columbia, Md., 1980-81, v.p. sys. and comm. N.Y.C., 1981-89; v.p., gen. mgr. Pfizer Med. Sys., Columbia, 1975-80, ret., 1992; vis. prof. Coll. Info. Sci. and Tech., Drexel U., Phila., 1990-92, rsch. prof., 1992—2000, adj. prof., 2001—. Mem. panel on healthcare tech. assessment Inst. Medicine, Washington, 1986-90. Patentee in chemistry; contrb. papers to numerous publs. Capt. U.K. Army, 1946-48. Avocations: golf, bridge, computing. Home and Office: 4882 N Newport Island Dr Vero Beach FL 32967

HUGHES, GORDON F. research scientist, electrical engineer; b. L.A., Sept. 9, 1937; s. Thomas Whitsett and Elizabeth Hughes; m. Shirley Gordon, Nov. 4, 1982; children: Laura Marie, Eric Thomas. BS in Physics, Calif. Inst. Tech., 1959, MSEE, 1961, PhDEE, 1963. Aerospace scientist Autonetics, Anaheim, Calif., 1963-69; prin. scientist Xerox Palo Alto Rsch. Ctr., L.A., 1969-82; sr. dir. engring. Seagate Tech., Scotts Valley, Calif., 1982-97; sr. project scientist U. Calif., San Diego, 1997—; assoc. dir. Ctr. Magnetic Recording Rsch., 1997—. Cons. Hughes Magnetics, San Diego, 1970—. Contbr. over 48 articles to profl. publs.; patentee in field. Fellow IEEE. Avocation: flying. Office: U Calif San Diego Ctr Magnetic Recording Rsch 9500 Gilman Dr La Jolla CA 92093-0401 E-mail: gfhughes@ucsd.edu.

HUGHES, GRACE-FLORES, business exeucitve; b. Taft, Tex., June 11, 1946; d. Adan Flores and Catalina San Miguel; m. Harley Arnold Hughes, May 25, 1980. BA, U. D.C., 1977; MPA, Harvard U., 1980. Sec. Dept. Air Force Kelly AFB, San Antonio, 1967-70, Pentagon-Office Sec. of Def., Washington, 1970-72; program asst., social sci. analyst HEW, Washington, 1972-78; social sci. analyst, acting dir. Office Hispanic Ams. HHS, Washington, 1978-81; vis. prof. Nebr. Wesleyan U., Lincoln, 1982-83, U. Nebr., Omaha, 1984; spl. asst. SBA, Washington, 1985-88, assoc. adminstr. for minority small bus., 1988; dir. community rels. Dept. Justice, Washington, 1988-92; pres. Grace, Inc., Alexandria, Va.; v.p. for intergovtl. affairs USTAK, LLCcs., Inc. Spl. asst. Reagan/Bush '84 Campaign, Nebr. and Washington, 1984, 50th Presdl. Inaugural, Washington, 1984-85, Office Pub. Liaison, The White House, 1985. Author: The Bureaucrat, Categorized Workforce, 1992; co-author: New Book of Knowledge, 1980; chair adv. bd. Harvard Jour. Hispanic Policy, 1989—; The Use and Abuse of Diversity Mag., 1994, Hispanic Mag., 1996. Adv. mem. U.S. Senate Rep. Task Force, Washington, 1988-91; alumni exec. bd. J.F. Kennedy Sch. Govt., Harvard U., Cambridge, Mass., 1989-93; mem. Rep. Hispanic Assembly, 1984—; apptd. by Gov. Allen of Va. to Bd. for Profl. and Occpl. Regulations, 1994—, Bd. for Agr. and Consumer Svcs., 1997—; bd. dirs. Hispanic Found. for Arts; apptd. by Pres. Bush Fed. Svc. Impasses Panel, 2000. Recipient Excellence award Nev. Econ. Devel. Corp., 1988, Leadership award Am. GI Forum, Omaha, 1989; named one of 100 Most Influential Hispanics in U.S. Hispanic Bus. Mag., 1988. Mem. Assn. Pub. Adminstrs. (Outstanding Pub. Svc. award 1990), Hispanic Bus. Roundtable, Coun. in Excellence in Govt. (prin.), Fedn. Rep. Women, Mex.-Am. Women's Nat. Assn., Univ. Club (Washington). Episcopalian. Avocations: tennis, jogging, aerobics, equestrian. Home and Office: 5208 Bedlington Ter Alexandria VA 22304-3551

HUGHES, JAMES BAKER, JR., retail executive, consultant; b. Englewood, Calif., Nov. 15, 1938; s. James Baker Hughes Sr. and Mary Alma (Nettleton) Gaston; m. Jeanette Ann Martin, July 20, 1968; children: Heather, Hollis Ann. BS, U. Houston, 1961. CPA, Tex. V.p. Deep River Armory, Inc., Houston, 1958—65, pres., 1965—88, European Arms Assocs., 1961—88, Consol. Munitions Corp., 1968—88; sales mgr. Tex-Products Machinery & Supply, 1989—92, acct., 1992—97; mng. dir. Transportes Pesados Ams. S.A., Guatemala City, Guatemala, 1997—98; dir. internat. projects INTECCSA, 1997—98; dir. fgn. projects Sarco, Inc., Sterling, NJ, 1998—; dir. Interactive Sys., Inc., Houston, 1999—2001; mgr. Stone Canyon Ranch, Travis County, 1995—; sr. tax acct. Gray & Assocs., PC, Lago Vista, 2002—. Instr. continuing edn. U. Houston, 1976-77; assoc. prodr. Chisos Film Prodns., Houston, 1969-70; cons. State of Mex. Police Dept., 1976-78, Smithsonian Instn., 1988; CFO, treas. Bald Eagle Mining Co., 1995-98; dir. internat. projects Blue Wave Studios, Houston, 1999-2000; bd. dirs. West View Internat. Corp., Houston. Author: Confederate Gunmakers, 1961, Mexican Military Arms, 1968, The New Model Russian Revolver, A Brief History, 1999, The Gatling Gun Notebook, 2000; contbr. more than 50 articles to profl. jours.; inventor range gun finding sight. Rep. campaign worker Harris County, Tex.; active St. Martin's Episcopal Ch., Houston, 1954-95, Trinity Episcopal Ch., Marble Falls, Tex., 2001—; bd. dirs. Young Reps. Harris County, 1968, Lago Vista Acad., 2002--; dir. fin. Inst. for Rsch. on Small Arms in Internat. Security, Alexandria, Va., 1993—; treas. Sean Ashley House, Houston, 1993-97, adv. dir., 1997—; historian MexicoHistory-Net, 2000—. Recipient Bronze Benefactor Medal Royal Life Saving Soc., 1978. Mem. Nat. Rifle Assn. (life), Houston Gun Collectors Assn. (life, pres. 1960-61), Inst. Internac. De Historia Mil. in Mexico City (hon.), Horseshoe Bay Club (Marble Falls, Tex.), Meml. Drive Coutnry (pres. 1978-79), Racquet (Houston). Republican. Avocations: hunting, fishing, white-water rafting. Office: PO Box 4838 Lago Vista TX 78645-0055 E-mail: jimhughes@ev1.net.

HUGHES, JAMES MITCHELL, epidemiologist; b. Pitts., Aug. 11, 1945; s. James Paul and Adelaide (Mitchell) H.; m. Pamela Mary Parsons, June 12, 1971; children: Andrew Saban, Mitchell Parsons. BA, Stanford U., 1966, MD, 1971. Diplomate Am. Bd. Preventive Medicine, Am. Bd. Internal Medicine, Am. Bd. Infectious Diseases. Intern U. Wash., Seattle, 1971-72; epidemic intelligence svc. officer Ctr. for Disease Control, Atlanta, 1973-75; resident internal medicine U. Wash., Seattle, 1972-73, 75-76; fellow infectious diseases U. Va., Charlottesville, 1976-78; chief water-related diseases activity, asst. chief enteric diseases br. Bur. Epidemiology, Ctr. for Disease Control, Atlanta, 1978-81; chief surveillance and prevention br., asst. dir. med. sci., hosp. infections program Ctr. for Infectious Diseases, Ctrs. for Disease Control, Atlanta, 1981-83, dir. hosp. infections program, 1983-88; dep. dir. Nat. Ctr. for Infectious Diseases, Ctr. for Disease Control, Atlanta, 1988-92; dir. Nat. Ctr. for Infectious Diseases, Ctrs. for Disease Control and Prevention, 1992—; clin. assoc. prof. Emory U., Atlanta, 1993-2001; clin. prof. dept. medicine Emory U. Sch. Medicine, 2001—. Clin. assoc. prof. divsn. geographic medicine, dept.

medicine, U. Va., Charlottesville, 1979-82; clin. asst. prof. divsn. infectious diseases, dept. medicine Emory U., Atlanta, 1981-93; staff physician Atlanta VA Hosp., 1989—; adj. prof. dept. epidemiology Rollins Sch. Pub. Health, Emory U., 1994—. Contbr. articles to profl. jours., chpts. in books. Baseball coach North Decatur (Ga.) Youth Assn., 1981-90; pres. Westchester Sch. PTA, Decatur, 1986-87. Asst. surgeon gen. USPHS, 1973-75, 76—. Recipient Meritorious Svc. medal USPHS, Atlanta, 1986, Outstanding Svc. medal, 1989, Disting. Svc. medal, 1997. Fellow ACP, AAAS, Infectious Diseases Soc. Am.; mem. APHA, Inst. of Medicine, Am. Soc. Microbiology, Am. Soc. Tropical Medicine and Hygiene, Am. Epidemiol. Soc., Royal Soc. Tropical Medicine and Hygiene, Soc. Epidemiol. Rsch., U. So. Calif. Alumni Assn. (bd. govs. 1995-97), Stanford U. Alumni Club Ga. (pres. 1980-82). Avocations: sports, travel. Office: NCID Mail Stop C12 CDC 1600 Clifton Rd NE Atlanta GA 30329-4018 E-mail: jmh2@cdc.gov.

HUGHES, JAMES PAUL, physician; b. Wilkinsburg, Pa., Apr. 9, 1920; s. Paul S. and Sara C. (Coleman) Hughes; m. Adelaide C. Mitchell, June 21, 1944; 1 child, James Mitchell. BS, U. Pitts., 1944, MD, 1945; D in Indsl. Medicine, U. Cin., 1952. Diplomate Am. Bd. Preventive Medicine. Intern St. Francis Hosp., Pitts., 1945—46; resident in pathology Univ. Hosps., Cleve., 1948—49; fellow in indsl. medicine Kettering Lab. U. Cin., 1949—51; physician The Tex. Co., 1951—52, The Ethyl Corp., Cin., 1952—57; chief Bur. Indsl. Health Dept. Health City of Cin., 1952—55; med. dir. Kaiser Aluminum & Chem. Corp., Oakland, Calif., 1957—82; sr. ptnr. Hughes-Lewis Assocs., Oakland, Calif., 1982—88; asst. prof. indsl. medicine U. Cin., 1952—55; assoc. prof. preventive medicine Ohio State U., 1955—57; exec. v.p., dir. Kaiser Found. Internat., 1967—76; project dir. U.S. Peace Corps Health projects, 1966—68, USAID med. relief project, Port Harcourt, Nigeria, 1970—72, Health Svcs. on Bandama River project, Kossou, Côte d'Ivoire, 1970—72; v.p. health svcs. Kaiser Industries Corp., 1972—74; clin. assoc. prof. occupl. medicine U. Calif., San Francisco, 1979—96; med. dir. occupl. health svcs. Merritt Peralta Med. Ctr., Oakland, Calif., 1982—86. Mem. hearing bd. Bay Area Air Quality Mgmt. Dist., Calif., 1989—98; mem. U. Calif. Pres.'s Coun. on Nat. Labs., Lawrence Berkeley, Lawrence Livermore, Los Alamos; mem. panel on environment, safety and health, 1993—98. Author (with N.H. Proctor): Chemical Hazards of the Workplace, 1978, 1996; editor-in-chief Health Hazards of the Workplace Report, 1989—91. Chmn. com. for Industry Coun. Tropical Health, Harvard U. Sch. Pub. Health, 1969—76. Served to capt. U.S. Army, 1946—48. Decorated Officier de l'Ordre Nat. Ivoirien Abidjan. Fellow: ACP, Am. Coll. Occupl. and Environ. Medicine (past pres., Health Achievement award 1972, Kehoe award 1982, Knudsen award 1996); mem.: Inst. Medicine NAS. Home: 124 Guilford Rd Piedmont CA 94611-3805

HUGHES, JEROME MICHAEL, education foundation executive; b. St. Paul, Oct. 1, 1929; s. Michael Joseph and Mary (Molloy) H.; m. Audrey M. Lackner, Aug. 11, 1951; children— Bernadine, Timothy, Kathleen, Rosemarie, Margaret, John BA, Coll. of St. Thomas, St. Paul, 1951; MA, U. Minn., 1958; EdD, Wayne State U., 1970; postdoctoral fellow, U. Minn., 1985. Tchr. Shakopee Sch. Dist., Minn., 1951-53, St. Paul Sch. Dist., 1953-61, counselor, 1963-66, rsch. asst., 1966-67, edn. cons., 1968-87; mem. Minn. Senate, St. Paul, 1966-93, chmn. edn. com., 1973-83, chmn. elections and ethics com., 1983-93, pres., 1983-93; mem. faculty U. Minn., 1986-95; pres. Minn. Edn. Found., Roseville, 1992—; mem. nat. legis. coun. AARR, 2002—. Mem. Edn. Commn. of States, Denver, 1973-93; mem. Nat. Cmty. Edn. Adv. Coun., Washington, 1980-83; mem. Nat. Conf. State Legislature State/Fed. Assembly, 1983-93; adj. faculty U. Minn., 1986-95. Chair Goodwill/Easter Seals, 1993-95; bd. dirs. Nat. Parenting Assn. Minn., 1994-97, State Legis. Leaders Found., 1985-93; nat. legis. coun. AARP, 2002—. Mott fellow, 1967-68, Ford Found. fellow George Washington U., 1974-75, Bush Summer fellow, U. Calif., 1975; Disting. Policy fellow George Washington U., 1977-78; postdoctoral fellow U. Minn., 1980-81; recipient Pennell award Minn. Fedn. Tchrs., 1974; Disting. Svc. award Minn. Elem. Sch. Prins. Assn., 1982; named Community Educator of Yr. Minn. Community Edn. Assn., recipient other awards Mem. Phi Delta Kappa. Democrat. Avocations: travel, reading, discussion, exercise. Office: Minn Edn Found PO Box 13643 Roseville MN 55113-0643

HUGHES, JOHN, chemical company executive; b. St. David's, Wales, Apr. 10, 1943; came to U.S., 1964; s. Essex James and Mary Ann Hughes; m. Linda Kay Petersen; children: Stacey Ann, Bradford James. BS in Chemistry, U. Wales, 1964; MBA, U. Chgo., 1968. With AMCOL Internat., Arlington Heights, Ill., 1965—, now chmn. Office: AMCOL Internat 1500 W Shure Dr Arlington Heights IL 60004-1443

HUGHES, JOHN J. federal judge, educator; b. 1946; BS, Villanova U., 1968, JD, 1971. Bar: N.J. 1971. Law clk. N.J. Dept. Law and Pub. Safety, Trenton, 1971; assoc. Sterns & Greenberg, Trenton, 1972; asst. N.J. pub. defender for Essex and Hunterdon regions Office Pub. Defender, Trenton, 1972-75; asst.-in-charge Trenton-Camden offices Office Fed. Pub. Defender for N.J. Dist., 1976-91; magistrate judge for N.J., U.S. Dist. Ct., Trenton, 1991—. Lectr. Widener U. Sch. Law; mem. Jud. Conf. Com. on Defender Svcs. Bd. dirs. Mobile Meals Trenton; trustee Georgian Court Coll., Newgrange Sch. Outreach Ctr. Fellow Am. Bar Found.; mem. ABA, Fed. Magistrate Judges Assn., N.J. Bar Assn., Assn. Criminal Def. Lawyers N.J. (Chief Judge Lawrence A. Whipple Meml. award), Brehon Law Soc., Seton Hall Law Sch. Inn Ct. (master), Mercer County Am. Inn of Ct. (master, pres.). Office: 6000 US Courthouse 402 E State St Trenton NJ 08608-1507

HUGHES, JOHN RUSSELL, physician, educator; b. DuBois, Pa., Dec. 19, 1928; s. John Henry and Alice (Cooper) H.; m. Mary Ann Dick, June 14, 1958; children: John Russell Jr. (dec.), Christopher Alan, Thomas Gregory, Cheryl Ann. AB summa cum laude, Franklin and Marshall Coll., 1950; BA with honors, Oxford (Eng.) U., 1952, MA with honors, 1955, DM (hon.), 1976; PhD, Harvard U., 1954; MD, Northwestern U., 1975. Neurophysiologist NIH, 1954-56; dir. electroencephalography dept. Meyer Hosp., SUNY, 1956-63; dir. div. lab. scis., including electroencephalography Northwestern U. Med. Center, 1963-77, prof. neurology, 1968—; dir. EEG and Epilepsy Clinic, U. Ill. Med. Center, 1977—; staff U. Ill. Hosp., Community Hosp., Geneva, Delnor Hosp., St. Charles; dir.neurophysiology Humana-Michael-Reese Med. Ctr., 1992—. Cons. Chgo. VA Westside Hosp., Mercyville and Copley Meml. Hosp., Aurora, Ill., others; participant debate on brain death BBC-TV; bd. dirs. Am. Bd. EEG and Neurophysiology; participant Am. Med. EEG Assn.; rep. Internat. Fedn. EEG and Clin. Neurophysiology lectr. tour of Africa, 1989; keynote speaker Internat. Course of Neurophysiology, Oxford U., 1993, invited speaker, 1996, 99, 02; invited spkr. Damascus Med. Sch., Syria, 1998, Royal Soc. of Medicine, London, 2003; lectr. in field. Author: Functional Organization of the Diencephalon, 1957, Atlas on Cerebral Death and Coma, 1976, Chinese Translation, 1997, Japanese Translation, 1998, EEG in Clinical Practice, 1982, 2d edit., 1994, EEG Evoked Potentials in Psychiatry and Behavioral Neurology, 1983; contbr. articles to profl. jours. Command Surgeon, USAR, 1986-90, with Army Med. R & D Command, 1990—, mobilization replacement for maj. gen., comdr. Recipient Alumni award Franklin and Marshall Coll., 1978, Lifetime Achievement award Am. EEG and Clin. Neurophysiol. Soc., 2000. Mem. Am. Electroencephalography Soc. (treas. 1965-68), Eastern Electroencephalography Soc. (sec.-treas. 1961-64), Ctrl. Electroencephalography Soc., Am. Med. EEG Assn. (bd. dirs.), Am. Bd. EEG and Neurophysiology (bd. dirs.), Internat. EEG and Clin. Neurophysiology (bd. dirs.), Am. Acad. EEG (bd. dirs.), Brit. Soc. of neurophysiology (hon.), Chgo. Acad. Medicine, Am. Epilepsy Soc., Am. Physiol. Soc., Soc. Neuroscis., Am. Acad. Neurology, Phi Beta Kappa, Sigma Xi (lectr. 1960—) Achievements include research on coding in central nervous system, new theory on neural mechanisms in olfaction, electro-clin. correlations in different types of epilepsy, organic aspects in juvenile delinquency. Home: 720 Roslyn Ter Evanston IL 60201-1722 Office: U Ill Consultation Clinic Epilepsy 912 S Wood St Chicago IL 60612-7325 E-mail: JHughes@uic.edu. *Always be ahead of your colleagues in every endeavor by having done it before they do. Do what you must do now to leave time for innovation later.*

HUGHES, JOHN W. film producer, screenwriter, film director; b. Lansing, Mich., Feb. 18, 1950; m. Nancy Ludwig; children: John III, James. With Needham Harper & Steers, Chgo.; copywriter, creative dir. Leo Burnett Co.; editor National Lampoon; founder, pres. Hughes Entertainment, 1985—. Screenwriter: National Lampoon's Class Reunion, 1982, National Lampoon's Vacation, 1983, Mr. Mom, 1983, Nate and Hayes, 1983, National Lampoon's European Vacation, 1985, (as Edmond Dantes), 101 Dalmations, 1996, Maid in Manhattan, 2002, Just Visiting, 2001; screenwriter, prodr.: Pretty in Pink, 1986, Some Kind of Wonderful, 1987, The Great Outdoors, 1988, National Lampoon's Christmas Vacation, 1989, Home Alone, 1990, Career Opportunities, 1990, Dutch, 1991, Home Alone 2: Lost in New York, 1992, Dennis the Menace, 1993, Baby's Day Out, 1994, Miracle on 34th Street, 1994, 101 Dalmations, 1996, Flubber, 1997, Home Alone 3, 1997, Reach the Rock, 1998; screenwriter, dir.: Sixteen Candles, 1984, Weird Science, 1985; screenwriter, dir., prodr.: The Breakfast Club, 1985, Ferris Bueller's Day Off, 1986, Planes, Trains and Automobiles, 1987, She's Having a Baby, 1988, Uncle Buck, 1989, Curly Sue, 1991; prodr.: Only the Lonely, 1991, NewPort South, 2001; TV writer: Home Alone 2, 2002, National Lampoon's American Adventure, 2000. Recipient Commitment to Chgo. award, 1990; named NATO/ShoWest Prodr. of Yr., 1990. also: c/o Michael Wimer Creative Artists Agy 9830 Wilshire Blvd Beverly Hills CA 90212-1804

HUGHES, J(OHNSON) DONALD, history educator, editor; b. Santa Monica, Calif., June 5, 1932; s. Johnson and Vannelia Anna (Blanchfield) H.; m. Pamela Louise Peters, June 8, 1964; children: Peter, Melissa, Joy. AB, UCLA, 1954; S.T.B., Boston U., 1957, PhD, 1960; postgrad., Am. Sch. Classical Studies, Greece, 1966-67. Asst. prof. history U. Denver, 1967-72, assoc. prof. history, 1972-77, prof. history, 1977—, Evans prof., 1994—, chair dept. history, 2000—01. Author: Ecology in Ancient Civilizations, 1975; In The House of Stone And Light, 1978 (Nat. Pk. Service award 1977-78); North American Indian Ecology, 1983, Pan's Travail: Environmental Problems of the Ancient Greeks and Romans, 1994, An Environmental History of the World: Humankind's Changing Role in the Community of Life, 2001; editor: Ecological Consciousness, 1981, The Face of the Earth: Environment and World History, 2000; editor Environ. Rev., 1983-85, mem. editl. bd., 1986-95; mem. editl. bd. Environ. Ethics, 1981-89, Environ. History, 1995—. Boston U. fellow, 1957; Danforth Found. assoc., 1965—; Lindbergh grantee, 1987. Mem. Am. Inst. Archaeology, Am. Soc. Environ. History (exec. bd. 1983-85, Disting. Svc. award 2000), Forest History Soc., Am. Hist. Assn., Phi Beta Kappa. Home: 2580 S University Blvd Apt 1001 Denver CO 80210-6159 Office: U Denver Dept History Denver CO 80208-0001

HUGHES, KAYLENE, historian, educator; b. Modesto, Calif., Aug. 4, 1952; BA, Miami-Dade (Fla.) Jr. Coll., 1972, Fla. Internat. U., 1976; MA, Fla. State U., 1977, PhD, 1985. Intern Fla. State Dept. Archives Records Mgmt., Tallahassee, 1977; Claims Control Supr. Sys. Devel. Corp., Tallahassee, 1978-81; editl. asst. Fla. Hotel and Motel Jour., Tallahassee, 1983-85; dir. edn., rsch. mgr. Fla. Hotel and Motel Assn., Tallahassee, 1985-87; historian U.S. Army Aviation & Missile Command, Redstone Arsenal, Ala., 1987—. Grad. asst. Fla. State U., Tallahassee, 1976-77, tchg. asst., 1981-83; adj. instr. history John C. Calhoun C.C., Huntsville, Ala., 1990—. Author: Florida's Lodging Industry: The First 75 Years, 1987, The Missile's Red Glare, 1992, Redstone Army Airfield: A Tradition of Aviation Support, 1992, Redstone Arsenal's Role in Operation Desert Shield/Desert Storm, 1992; contbr. articles to jours. and newspapers. Grantee Fla. State U., 1983. Mem. Phi Alpha Theta (sec. 1982-85), Phi Theta Kappa. Home: 342 Pawnee Trl SE Huntsville AL 35803-2280 E-mail: kaylene.hughes@redstone.army.mil.

HUGHES, KEITH WILLIAM, banking and finance company executive; b. Cleve., July 1, 1946; s. Delmar Vern and Margaret Virginia Hughes; m. Cheryl Foster, Aug. 30, 1969; 1 child, Amy. BS, Miami U., Oxford, Ohio, 1968, MBA, 1969. Mktg. mgr. Continental Bank, Chgo., 1970-73; exec. v.p. broker/dealer subs. Assos. Corp., 1973-74; v.p. mktg. Northwestern Nat. Bank, 1974-76; sr. v.p. Crocker Bank, San Francisco, 1976-81; exec. v.p., dir. Assocs. Corp., Dallas, 1981-85, sr. exec. v.p., 1985-88, vice-chmn., 1988-91, pres., chmn, CEO, 1995-96; chmn., CEO Assocs. First Capital Corp. (merged with Citigroup 1999), 1996—99; vice chmn., dir. Citigroup, 1999—2000; corp. bd. dirs. Carreker, 2003—. Active United Way (chmn. Dallas campaign), Cancer Found., Dallas Mus. of Art. Mem. Am. Bankers Assn., Bank Mktg. Assn., Consumers Bankers Assn., Nat. Consumer Fin. Assn., Olympic Club (San Francisco), Los Colinas Country Club (Tex.), Crescent Club (Dallas), Ocean Reef Club (Key Largo).

HUGHES, KENNETH MARTIN, planner; b. Dubuque, Iowa, Oct. 12, 1952; s. Vernon Owen and Rose Adelaide Hughes; m. Ellen Rhoda Kemper, May 27, 1990; children: Melissa, Christopher. Degree in sociology and urban studies, U. Notre Dame, 1974; MA in Urban Affairs, Va. Tech., 1976. Senate aide to Sen. Edward Kennedy, Washington, 1977-80; lobbyist nat. coalition, 1981-83; congl. aide to Rep. Dave Obey, 1983-85; exec. dir. Inst. Transp. and Devel. Policy, Washington, 1984-88; lobbyist Sierra Club, Santa Fe and Washington, N.Mex., 1986-88, 91-93; program analyst N.Mex. State Land Office, Santa Fe, 1993-94; regional planning bur. chief Local Govt. divsn. State of N.Mex., Santa Fe, 1994—. Bd. dirs., co-founder Inst. for Transp. and Devel. Policy, Washington; adj. prof. U. N.Mex., 1997-2003. Dir. League Am. Bicyclists, Balt.; co-chair Citizens Environ. Task Force, Santa Fe, 1990-94; chair State Bicycle, Equestrian and Pedestrian Com., N.Mex., 1995-97; vice-chair City's Bicycle Com., Santa Fe, 1992; mem. adv. bd. 1000 Friends of N.Mex., 1997—. Named Profl. Planner of Yr., N.Mex. chpt. Am. Planning Assn., 1997; Knight Found. fellow in cmty. bldg., 2001. Mem. Am. Inst. Cert. Planners, Rio Grande chpt. Sierra Club (energy and transp. chair 1991—). Democrat. Roman Catholic. Avocations: bicycling, cross-country skiing.

HUGHES, KENT HIGGON, economist; b. Portland, Oreg., Feb. 23, 1941; s. John Kenneth and Gwladys (Higgon) H.; m. Virginia Carrington Sammon; children: John Kenneth, Jeff, Krista. BA, Yale U., 1962; LLB, Harvard U., 1965; PhD, Washington U., 1976. Bar: D.C. 1971. Fellow Internat. Legal Ctr., Sao Paulo, Brazil, 1967-69; atty. Urban Law Inst., Washington, 1970-71; legis. counsel Office of Sen. Vance Hartke, Washington, 1971-72; analyst Congl. Rsch. Svc., Washington, 1973-76; sr. economist Joint Econ. Com., Washington, 1977-82; legis. dir. Office Sen. Gary Hart, Washington, 1983-84; staff dir. trade subcom. Ho. Reps. Fgn. Affairs Com., Washington, 1985-87; chief economist Dem. policy com. U.S. Senate, Washington, 1987-90; pres. Coun. on Competitiveness, 1990-93; assoc. dep. sec. of commerce U.S. Dept. of Commerce, Washington, 1993-99; pub. policy scholar Woodrow Wilson Internat. Ctr., Washington, 1999-2001; dir. project on Am. and the global economy Woodrow Wilson Ctr., 2001—. Author: Trade, Taxes, Transnationals, 1979; contbr. articles to profl. jours. Mem. ABA, Am. Econ. Assn., D.C. Bar Assn. Avocations: languages, rugby, collecting political memorabilia. Home: 4961 Allan Rd Bethesda MD 20816-2721 Office: Woodrow Wilson Internat Ctr One Woodrow Wilson Plaza 1300 Pennsylvania Ave NW Washington DC 20004-3027 E-mail: Hugheske@wwic.si.edu.

HUGHES, KEVIN JOHN, lawyer; b. St. Cloud, Minn., July 27, 1936; s. Fred James and Valeria Mary (Spaniol) H.; m. Joanne Margaret Robertson, July 27, 1936; children: Anne, Thomas, Jennifer, James, Emily. BA in Philosophy and Polit. Sci., St. John's U., Collegeville, Minn., 1958; JD, U. Minn., 1962. Bar: Minn. 1962, U.S. Dist. Ct. Minn. 1963, U.S. Ct. Appeals (8th cir.) 1973, U.S. Supreme Ct. 1973. Law clerk Minn. Supreme Ct., 1962-63; assoc. Fred J. Hughes Atty., St. Cloud, 1963; ptnr. Hughes Thoreen & Sullivan, Hughes Thoreen Mathews & Knapp, St. Cloud, 1964-94, Hughes Mathews PA, St. Cloud, 1994—. Bd. dirs. Ctrl. Minn. Cmty. Found., United Way, YMCA. 1st lt. U.S. Army, 1959. Mem.: Nat. Health Lawyers Assn., Minn. State Bar, St. Cloud C. of C. Home: 295 Waite Ave S Saint Cloud MN 56301-7335 Office: Hughes Mathews PO Box 548 Saint Cloud MN 56302-0548 E-mail: khughes@hughesmathews.com.

HUGHES, KEVIN PETER, lawyer; b. N.Y.C., Sept. 8, 1943; s. George and Mae (Kilduff) H.; m. Margaret Ellen Comiskey, Nov. 18, 1967; children: Erin, Cara, Deirdre. BA, Manhattan Coll., 1965; JD, St. John's U., 1968. Bar: N.Y. 1968, U.S. Dist. Ct. (so. dist., ea. dist.) N.Y. 1971, U.S. Ct. Appeals (2d cir.) 1975, U.S. Supreme Ct. 1980. Law clerk to justice N.Y. Ct. Appeals, Albany, 1968-70; assoc. Weil, Gotshal & Manges, N.Y.C., 1970-77, ptnr., 1977—. Arbitrator Am. Arbitration Assn., N.Y.C., 1984—. Mem. ABA (litigation sect.), N.Y. State Bar Assn., Plandome Country Club (Manhasset, N.Y.), Eagle Creek Golf and Country Club (Naples, Fla.) Republican. Roman Catholic. Avocations: skiing, golf. Home: 27 Chapel Rd Manhasset NY 11030-3601 Office: Weil Gotshal & Manges 767 5th Ave Fl Concl New York NY 10153-0119 E-mail: kevin.hughes@weil.com.

HUGHES, LIBBY, writer; b. Pitts, Aug. 11, 1932; d. Lloyd Alfred and Vera Abby (Walker) Pockman; m. R. John Hughes, Aug. 20, 1955 (div. 1988); children: Wendy E., Mark E. BA, U. Ala., 1954; MFA, Boston U., 1955. Profl. actress, Kenya, S. Africa, 1955-59; drama critic and feature writer Cape Cod Newspapers, 1977-86, assoc. pubr., 1977-81, pubr., 1981-85. Pres. Desert Starfield Prodn., 1994; theatre critic www.capecodtoday.com. Author: Bali, 1969, Margaret Thatcher, 1989, Benazir Bhutto, 1990, Nelson Mandela, 1992, Good Manners for Children, 1992, H. Norman Schwarzkopf, 1992, West Point, 1992, Valley Forge, 1992, Colin Powell, 1996, School Manners Workbook, 1998, Christopher Reeve, 1997, Tiger Woods, 2000, Yitzhak Rabin, 2001, George W. Bush, 2003; editor: Ginger Rogers Autobiography, 1989, 91; playwright: Sin in the Attic (Chatham Drama Guild award 1999-2000), Pasta and Curry (New Opera and Musical Theatre Initiative award 2000), 26 others; theater reviewer www.capecodtoday.com Bd. dir. Wisdom Inst., 1984-86, Cape Cod Mus., 1984-86. Recipient Songwriting award, Eventide Arts Festival of Cape Cod, 2001. Mem. ASCAP, Dramatists Guild, Authors Guild, Ala. Wildlife Rescue Svc. (pres. 1988-89), Nat. Soc. Arts and Letters (chpt. pres. 1984-86, protocol officer 1984-86), Nat. League Am. Pen Women. Avocations: theatre, news, wildlife, breeding rhodesian ridgebacks. Home: June to August 23 Grove Lane Brewster MA 02631 also: September to May 988 Memorial Dr #81 Cambridge MA 02138 E-mail: libhughes@aol.com.

HUGHES, LINDA J. newspaper publisher; b. Princeton, B.C., Can., Sept. 27, 1950; d. Edward Rees and Madge Preston (Bryan) H.; m. George Fredrick Ward, Dec. 16, 1978; children: Sean Ward, Kate Ward. BA, U. Victoria (B.C.), 1972; LittD (hon.), Athabasca U., 1997; hon. diploma in journalism, Grant MacEwan C.C., Edmonton, Alta., Can., 1999. With Edmonton Jour., Alta., Can., 1976—, from reporter to asst. mng. editor, 1984-87, editor, 1987-92, pub., 1992—. Southam fellow U. Toronto, Ont., Can., 1977-78; recipient Disting. Citizen award Grant MacEwan C.C., 1999. Office: Edmonton Journal 10006 101st St PO Box 2421 Edmonton AB Canada T5J 2S6

HUGHES, LORRAINE WILLIAMS, credit counselor, housing specialist; b. Roanoke Rapids, N.C., June 28, 1948; d. Reginald Alton and Marie Carpenter Williams; m. Wilson Almond Hughes; children: Kevin Lee, Karen Ann. Credit counselor, housing profl. Choanoke Area Devel. Assn., Inc., Rich Square, NC, 1994—. Author: Second Chance For Cora, 2001, The Path to Dignity, 2003. Mem.: N.C. Housing Counselors.

HUGHES, LYNN NETTLETON, federal judge; b. Houston, Sept. 9, 1941; m. Olive (Allen). BA, U. Ala., 1963; JD, U. Tex., 1968; LLM, U. Va., 1992. Bar: Tex., 1966. Pvt. practice, Houston, 1966-79; judge Dist. Ct. Tex., Houston, 1979-85; U.S. dist. judge So. Dist. Tex., Houston, 1985—. Adj. prof. South Tex. Coll. Law, 1973—, U. Tex., 1990-91, 2000-01; Tex. del. Nat. Conf. State Trial Judges, 1983-85; cons. Tex. Jud. Budget Bd., 1984; lectr. Tex. Coll. Judiciary, 1983; mem. task force on revision rules of civil procedure Supreme Ct. Tex., 1993-94; cons. on constn. Moldova, 1993, European Community, 1989, Ukraine, 1995, Romania, 1996, Albania, 1997; mem. jud. adv. bd. Law and Econs. Ctr., George Mason U., 1999—. Mem. adv. bd. Houston Jour. Internat. Law, 1981—, chmn., 1989-99. Trustee Rift Valley Rsch. Mission, 1978—; mem. St. Martin's Episcopal Ch.; dir. Houston World Affairs Coun., 1997—, co-chair 1999-00. Mem.: FBA (bd. dirs. Houston chpt. 1986—89), ABA, Am. Inns of Ct. XV (pres. 1986—92), Houston Philos. Soc. (exec. com. 2000—03), Am. Anthrop. Assn., Am. Soc. Legal History, Am. Judicature Soc., Tex. State Bar (nominations com. jud. sect. 1983, ct. cost, delay and efficiency com. 1981—90, vice chmn. 1984—86, selection, compensation and tenure state judges com. 1981—85, vice chmn. 1982—83, liaison with law schs. com. 1987—92, plain lang. com. 1989—96), Houston Bar Assn., Maritime Law Assn., Am. Law Inst., Coun. on Fgn. Rels., Houston Com. Fgn. Rels. (chmn. 2003—). Office: US Ct Hse 11122 515 Rusk St Houston TX 77002-2605 Home: PO Box 61565 Houston TX 77208

HUGHES, MARCIA MARIE, lawyer, consultant, motivational speaker; b. Montrose, Colo., Oct. 12, 1949; d. John Atkinson and Catherine Marie (Buskirk) H.; m. James Terrell, Dec. 26, 1990; 1 child, Julia. BA, U. Colo., 1972; JD with honors, George Washington U., 1976; MA in Psychology, U. Colo. Bar: Colo. 1976, U.S. Dist. Ct. Colo. 1976, U.S. Ct. Appeals (10th cir.) 1976. Adminstrv. aide Bur. Accounts Treasury Dept., Washington, 1972-73; legis. aide to Congresswoman Patricia Schroeder Washington, 1973-74; legal intern Consumer Product Info. Ctr., Washington, 1974-75, Media Access Project, Washington, 1975-76; law clk. to Hon. William E. Doyle U.S. Ct. Appeals (10th cir.), Denver, 1976-77; asst. atty. gen. Colo. Atty. Gen.'s Office, Denver, 1977-79; spl. asst. to dir. Colo. Dept. Health, Denver, 1979-81; assoc. Rothgerber, Appel, Powers & Johnson, Denver, 1982-85; ptnr. Cockrel, Quinn & Creighton, Denver, 1985-87; pres. Hughes, Duncan & Dingess, Denver, 1987-90, Marcia M. Hughes, P.C., Denver, 1990-99, Collaborative Growth, L.L.C., 1993—; exec. dir. Pntrs. Mentoring Assn., 1998-2000. Pub. spkr. on emotional intelligence, the 2% solution, orgnl. growth, interpersonal dynamics, negotiation strategies, spirit in the workplace. Bd. dir. Visiting Nurse Assn., Jefferson County chpt. ARC, 1999-2000, Influence Denver X, Capitol Hill United Neighborhoods, 1977-86; v.p. Nat. Assn. Neighborhoods, 1980-81; bd. dir. Ecumenical Housing Corp., 1982-85; participant Leadership Denver, 1984-85; active Big Sisters Colo., Denver, 1987-93; vice chmn. Kempe Children's Found., bd. dir., 1991-95, chair pub. affairs com.; bd. dir. Colo. Found. Children and Families, 1993-96, pres., 1995-96; apptd. mem. family issues task force Colo. Legislature. Named one of Outstanding Young Women in Colo., 1980, Big Sister of Yr., 1991. Mem. Colo. Profl. Soc. on Abuse of Children (bd. dirs.), Colo. Bar Assn. (chmn. environ. sect., officer 1982-86), Colo. Hazardous Waste Com. (chmn. 1982-85). Avocations: writing, hiking, gardening, reading. Home: PO Box 10758 Golden CO 80401-0610

HUGHES, MARGARET EILEEN, law educator, former dean; b. Saskatoon, Sask., Can., Jan. 22, 1943; d. E. Duncan and Eileen (Shaver) Farmer; m. James Roscoe Hughes, May 21, 1966; children: Shannon Margaret, Krista Lynn. BA, U. Sask., 1965, LLB, 1966; LLM, MSW, U. Mich., 1968. Asst. prof. law U. Windsor, Ont., Can., 1968-71, assoc. prof. law, 1971-75; exec. interchange Dept. Justice, Ottawa, 1975-77, counsel, 1977-78; prof. law U. Sask., 1978-84; dean law U. Calgary, Canada, 1984-89, prof., 1989—, assoc. v.p. human resources, 2001—. Faculty sr. univ. adminstrs.'s course Centre Higher Edn., R & D, Banff, Can., 1990—; bd. dirs. Indsl. Rels. Rsch. Group; co-chair Annual Labour Arbitration Conf., 1990-2000. Contbr. articles to profl. jours. and chpts. to books. William Cooke fellow U. Mich. Faculty Law, 1966-68. Mem. Law Soc. Alta., Law Soc. Sask., Legal Edn. Soc. Alta. (bd. dirs. 1984-89), Law Soc. Alta. (legal edn. com. 1984-89), Can. Assn. Law Tchrs., Council Can. Law Deans (sec. 1986-87, chmn. 1987-88), Can. Inst. Resources Law (exec. com. 1984-89, bd. dirs. 1984-89), Can. Research Inst. for Law and Family (exec. com. 1986-88, bd. dirs. 1986-89, 97-2001). Avocations: swimming, skiing. Office: U Calgary Human Resources 2500 University Dr NW Calgary AB Canada T2N 1N4

HUGHES, MARIJA MATICH, law librarian; b. Belgrade, Yugoslavia; came to U.S., 1960, naturalized, 1971; d. Zarija and Antonija (Hudowsky) Matich. BA in Music, Mokranjac, Belgrade; BA in English, U. Belgrade and Calif. State U.; MLS, U. Md.; student, McGeorge Sch. Law; MHA in Health Care Adminstrn., George Washington U., 1985, M. in Adminstrv. Scis., 1989. Counselor, gen. mgr. Career Counseling Service, Sacramento, Calif., 1962-64; sec. to mgr. Sacramento State Coll., 1965-66; student librarian High John program U. Md., Fairmont Heights, 1967; reference librarian Calif. State Law Library, Sacramento, 1968; head reference library-faculty liasion librarian Hastings Coll. Law U. Calif., San Francisco, 1969-72; head law librarian AT&T, Washington, 1972-73; chief law librarian Nat. Clearinghouse Library, U.S. Commn. on Civil Rights, Washington, 1973-86; tech. info. specialist U.S. Dept. Labor, OSHA, Tech. Date Ctr., 1988—; owner, pub. Hughes Press. Author (compiler): The Sexual Barrier, Legal and Econ. Aspects of Employment, vols. 1 and 2, 1970—73, The Sexual Barriers: Legal, Medical, Economic and Social Aspects of Sex Discrimination, 1977, Computer Health Hazards, 1990, 1993, Computer Health Hazards, Eng. translation, 1996, Sick From Computers, 1994, Computers, Antennas, Cellular Telephones and Power Lines Health Hazards, 1996, Shadow at the Ball, 2001; contbr. articles. Mem. Cellular Phone Task Force. Mem. Am. Assn. Law Librs., Bioelectromagnetics Soc., Consumer Utilities Bd. Home: 2400 Virginia Ave NW Apt C501 Washington DC 20037-2644

HUGHES, MARY ELIZABETH, interior designer; b. Charleston, W.Va., Sept. 7, 1940; d. Denver Lewis and Ida Frances (Fink) Morgan; children: George Charles IV, Justin Morgan, Mary Frederick. Student, Randolph-Macon Woman's Coll., 1958-60; BS, W.Va. U., 1963; AAS, Art Inst. Pitts., 1981. Cert. secondary edn., interior design. French tchr. Kanawha County Schs., Charleston, W.Va., 1963-64, Marshall County Schs., Moundsville, W.Va., 1964-70; sr. designer Boury, Inc. Contract Design, Wheeling, W.Va., 1985-87; head designer Stone and Thomas Design Studio, Wheeling, 1987-88; dir. archtl. design Boury, Inc. Contract Design, Wheeling, 1980-92; owner Hughes Design Gallery, Glen Dale, W.Va., 1981-92; pres., CEO Hughes Design Gallery, Inc., Wheeling, 1993—. Guest lectr. history of furniture Art Inst. Pitts., 1990. Mem. Hist. Landmarks Commn., Marshall County, W.Va., 1986—90; mem. adv. com. W.Va. Dept. Culture and History, 1992; mem. interior furnishings com. W.Va. Gov.'s Mansion, Charleston, 1986—, chmn., 1998—; pres. Jr. League Wheeling, 1976—78; mem. stewardship commn. Episcopal Diocese of W.Va., Charleston, 1988—90; mem. Episcopal Endowment Fund. Com., W.Va., 1990—92; vacancy cons. Episcopal Diocese W.Va., 1993—98; bd. dirs. W.Va. Mansion Preservation Found., Charleston, 1989—; bd. dirs., past pres. No. Panhandle Behavioral Health Ctr., W.Va., 1981—91, Northwood Found., 1994—2000; mem. found. bd. dirs. W.Va. No. C.C., 1991—, v.p., 1993—2000, pres., 2000—; bd. dirs. Wheeling Symphony, 1995—, pres. elect, 2001—03. Named Interior Design Alumni of Yr. Art Inst. Pitts., 1990. Mem. Am. Soc. Interior Designers (profl., pres. Pa. West chpt. 1998-99), Internat. Interior Design Assn., Sandcrest Found. (bd. dirs.), Rotary, Chi Omega, Kappa Delta Pi, Alpha Delta Kappa. Democrat. Avocations: bicycling, walking, swimming, gardening, reading. Home: 509 Wheeling Ave Glen Dale WV 26038-1639 Office: Hughes Design Gallery 600 National Rd Wheeling WV 26003-6598

HUGHES, MARY KATHERINE, lawyer; b. July 16, 1949; d. John Chamberlain and Marjorie (Anstey) H.; m. Andrew H. Eker, July 7, 1982. BBA cum laude, U. Alaska, 1971; JD, Willamette U., 1974; postgrad., Heriot-Watt U., Edinburgh, Scotland, 1971. Bar: Alaska 1975. Ptnr. Hughes, Thorsness, Gantz, Powell & Brundin, Anchorage, 1974-95; mcpl. atty. Municipality of Anchorage, 1995-2000; of counsel Hughes, Thorsness, Powell, Huddleston & Bauman, 2001—. Trustee Willamette U., 1997—; bd. visitors WUCL, 1978—2001; bd. dirs. Alaska Repertory Theatre, 1986—88, pres., 1987—88; commr. Alaska Code Revision Commn., 1987—94; active U. Alaska Found., 1985—, trustee, 1990—; bd. visitors U. Alaska, Fairbanks, 1994—2002, bd. regents, 2002—; bd. dirs. Anchorage Econ. Devel. Corp., 1989—, chmn., 1994; active Providence Anchorage Adv. Coun., 1993—, Providence Alaska Found., 1998—, chair, 2002—; lawyer rep. 9th Cir. Jud. Conf., 1995—2000; pres., trustee Alaska Bar Found., 1984—98, trustee, 2001—. Fellow: Am. Bar Found.; mem.: Internat. Mcpl. Lawyers Assn. (state chair 1995—96, regional v.p. 1997—2000), Anchorage Assn. Women Lawyers (pres. 1976—77), Alaska Bar Assn. (bd. govs. 1981—84, pres. 1983—84), Soroptimists (pres. 1986—87), Delta Theta Phi. Republican. Roman Catholic. Home: 1592 Coffey Ln Anchorage AK 99501-4977 E-mail: mkhughes@acsalaska.net.

HUGHES, MARY SORROWS, artist; b. Washington, Oct. 28, 1945; d. Howard Earl and Martha Jane (Summerville) Sorrows; m. Frank Broox Hughes, May 22, 1967; 1 child, Broox Bradley. BA in Art, Centenary Coll., 1967, BA in Edn., 1978. Draftsman for civil engring. dept. Texaco, New Orleans, 1967-70; owner, freelance artist Shreveport, La., 1979—. Illustrator Total Tales, 1984; included in The Best of Watercolor, 1995, Best of Watercolor: Painting Color, 1997, Floral Inspirations, 1998, Splash 7: The Qualities of LIght, 2002; represented in permanent collections Southwestern Electric Power Co., Shreveport, Burgess Corp. Collection, Calif.; featured artist Watercolor Mag., 2003, Phila. House Auction and Fund Raiser for AIDS, 2003. Bd. dirs. Child Care Svcs., Inc. of N.W. La., Shreveport, 1987-91, pres., 1991; Artport Airport Exhibit and Fundraiser for AIDS, Shreveport, 1991-2002; worker Habitat for Humanity, Shreveport, 1992, 94; trustee St. Luke's Meth. Ch., Shreveport, 1993-95, chair bldg. com., 1986; bd. dirs. Shreveport Art Guild, Friends of the Meadows Mus., 2000-03. Recipient Gary, Field, Landry & Bradford award La. Women Artists, Baton Rouge, 1994. Mem.: Hoover Watercolor Soc. (pres. 1986, treas., publicity chair, others, Jurors Choice award 2001, Transparent Watercolor award 2003), La. Artists (pres. 1994, 1998), Watercolor West (Yarka St. Petersberg Mdse. award 1995, Signature Mem. award 1996, W. Burgess Purchase prize 1998), Southwestern Watercolor Soc. (Signature Mem. award 1991, Edgar A. Whitney award 1992, Ansel Merchandise award 1999, Canson-Talons Inc. award 2000, chosen as one of 10 artists for Hwy. Haiku 2002), Med. Aux. Wives Club. Democrat. Avocations: exercise, gardening, travel, reading, playing the flute. Home: 530 Atkins Ave Shreveport LA 71104-4448 Studio: 1700 Creswell Ave Shreveport LA 71101-4726 E-mail: maryhughes@marysorrowshughes.com.

HUGHES, MICHAEL PATRICK, artist; b. Chgo., Dec. 25, 1950; s. William George and Patricia Ann (Guilfoil) H.; m. Dorothea Sofia Savage, May 11, 1977 (div. June 1987); 1 stepchild, Stefani Savage; m. Deborah Kay Horewitz, Aug. 5, 1991 (div. June 1997). AA in Fine Arts, L.A. Valley Coll., 1975; BFA in Painting, Otis Art Inst., 1977; MFA in Art & Design, Calif. Inst. Arts, 1980. Tchr. Ragan Art Acad., 1997—2000, dir., 2001—. One-man shows include Calif. Inst. Arts, 1979, 80, West Colo. Gallery, Pasadena, Calif., 1980, The Art Dock, L.A., 1985, Orlando Gallery, Sherman Oaks, Calif., 1986, 87, Jose Drudis-Biada Art Gallery, L.A., 1990; group shows include Calif. Inst. Arts, 1980, 81, Lehigh U. Art Gallery, Bethlehem, Pa., 1983, Calif. State U. Art Gallery, San Bernardino, 1982, Future Perfect Gallery, L.A., 1984, Tortue Gallery, Santa Monica, Calif., 1987, Downey Mus. Art, 1988, The Tanzmann Assocs., L.A., 1989, Boritzer/Gray Gallery, Santa Monica, 1991, 98, Touchstone Ctr. Arts, Pitts., 1992, Brand Libr. Art Galleries, Glendale, Calif., 1992, Mt. San Antonio Coll. Art Gallery, Walnut, Calif., 1993, Downtown Arts Devel. Assn., L.A., 1994, 93, others; represented in permanent collections at Lee & Paulette Arnone, Capitan, N.Mex., Steve Sharpe, Somis, Calif., Joseph A. Hardy Sr., Farmington, Pa., Ellie Blankfort, L.A., Chaim Ben Basat, Sepulveda, Calif., Mr. & Mrs. Murray Horewitz, Connellsville, Pa., Downey Mus. Art, Rudy & Chris Andl, Thousand Oaks, Calif., Miki Warner, Malibu, Calif., Carl Schlossberg, Encino, Calif., Jack Sullivan, San Gabriel, Calif., Mr. & Mrs. Robert Taylor, L.A., Ben Tunnel, L.A., William Bingham, Encino, Calif., Richard Godfrey, L.A., others; large scale sculptural commns. Bank of Am., L.A., 1993, also pvt. collection. Avocations: cooking, golf.

HUGHES, MICHAEL RANDOLPH, evangelist; b. Newport News, Va. s. Luke Jr. and Patsy Ruth (Jewell) H.; m. Carolyn Delight Williamson, Mar. 20, 1981; children: Amanda, Patsy. Diploma, Memphis Sch. Preaching, 1976; cert. in theology, Ala. Christian Sch. Religion, 1982, BA, 1984; MS, Troy State U., 1987; MA, So. Christian U., 2001. Min. Newport News Ch. of Christ, 1977-80, 81-83, Ch. of Christ of Clyattville, Ga., 1980-81, 83-85, City Boulevard Ch. of Christ, Waycross, Ga., 1985-87, Hampton (Va.) Ch. of Christ, 1988-92; instr. Bible Ga. Christian Sch., Dasher, 1985-87; min. Green's Lake Road Ch. of Christ, East Ridge, Tenn., 1992-97; min., elder Marion (Ark.) Ch. of Christ, 1997—; prof. So. Christian U., Montgomery, Ala., 1999—. Dir., instr. Bible, Idlewild Christian Camp, Surry, Va., 1977-80; youth worker Ga. Christian Children's Home, Dasher, 1985-87; missionary Mil. Outreach, Germany, 1988-90, Chs. of Christ, India, Malaysia, Taiwan, 1992—; program analyst HB Software, 1996—; co-founder, co-owner HB Software, 1997—. Author: Tax Record System, 1980; contbr. articles to relgious publs. Cmty. organizer North End Huntington Heights Preservation Assn., Newport News, 1977—80; tax preparer VITA, Valdosta, Ga., 1986—87; mem. Ark. Gov.'s Steering Com. on Abstinence Edn., 2000—01; elected ofcl., chmn. Crittenden County Ark. Rep. Ctrl. Com., 2000—02; chmn. 1st Cong. Dist. Ark./Ea. Region, 2002—; chmn. ea. region 1st Congl. Dist. Rep. Party of Ark., 2002—. Recipient award of merit Memphis Sch. Preaching, 1977. Mem. Givens Orgn., Memphis Sch. Preaching Alumni Assn. (bd. dirs. 1991-95, 98—). Avocations: coin collecting, tennis, bowling. Home: 72 Military Rd PO Box 209 Marion AR 72364-0209 Office: Marion Ch Christ PO Box 209 Marion AR 72364-0209

HUGHES, MICHAELA KELLY, actress, dancer; b. Morristown, N.J., Mar. 31; d. Joseph Francis and Mary Elizabeth (Coughlin) H. Scholarship student, Houston Ballet Acad., 1970-73; part-time scholarship student, Sch. Am. Ballet, 1971. Founder, owner Classic Stocking Co., 1992—. Child actress with Alley Theatre, Houston, 1969, 71, mem. Houston Ballet, 1974, Eliot Feld Ballet, N.Y.C., 1975—, prin. dancer, 1974-79, mem. Am. Ballet Theatre, 1979-81; Broadway appearances include On Your Toes, 1982, as Gloria Upson in Mame, 1983, Raggedy Ann, 1986, as Cassie in A Chorus Line, 1987, Anything Goes, 1988, (films) Hellfighters, A Chorus Line, Alice, The Human Quality; appeared as Fiona in Another World (serial), Loving, Saturday Night Live, Veronica's Closet (sitcom), numerous television commls. Mem. AFTRA, SAG, AEA, Am. Guild Mus. Artists.

HUGHES, OWEN WILLARD, artist; b. Fremont, Ohio, Mar. 31, 1919; s. George Alfred and Maude Alice (Wilson) H.; m. L. Virginia Peddicord, Apr. 5, 1942; 1 child, Sue Ellen. Grad., Famous Artists Sch., Westport, Conn., 1964; degree, Rochester Inst. Tech., 1970; grad., Sch. Modern Photography, 1984. Artist, sign painter Consolidated Outdoor Display Co., Fremont, 1938-40; cartoonist, artist Ohio Power Co., Tiffin, 1940-41; artist, sign. painter, airplane nose artist 8th and 9th air forces USAF, 1941-45; supr. art and sign work 9th Troop Carrier Command Display at USAF Exhibit, Eiffel Tower, Paris, 1945; artist, sign painter Consolite Outdoor Display Co., Fremont, 1945-48, Hughes-Park Art & Signs, Fostoria, Ohio, 1948-52, Rogers Indsl. Display Co., Cleve., 1952-53; artist, silk screener Murray-Ohio Bicycle Co., Cleve., 1953-54; artist, carton designer Victor Wagner & Son Folding Cartons, Cleve., Buffalo, 1954-59, Bloomer Bros., Riegel, Rexham, Fibreboard, Foldpak, Newark, 1959-81; owner Hughes Art & Signs, Newark, 1981—2003. Artist Nat. War Plane Mus., Elmira, N.Y., 1986—, U.S. Aviation Mus., Willowick, Ohio, 2001—. Nose art Doc of the 7 Dwarfs on last B-29 Superfortress, Wichita, Kans., 2002; compiler: hist. book, including artwork for 441st troop carrier group. Staff sgt. USAAF, 1942-45, ETO. Mem. The Eighth Air Force Hist. Soc., 10th Air Depot Group Assn., Nat. Warplane Mus., U.S. Aviation Mus., Toastmasters Internat., Lions. Republican. Methodist. Avocations: coin collecting, stamp collecting, model railroading, photography, camping. Home and Office: 320 E Miller St Newark NY 14513-1518

HUGHES, PATRICIA NEWMAN, academic administrator; b. Vicksburg, Miss., Apr. 16, 1964; d. Horace Wilbur Sr. and Florence (Hearn) Newman; m. Tommy Wade Hughes, Dec. 29, 1990; children: Newman Price, Dylan Wade; stepchildren: Amber Brooke, Kala Marie. BA, Miss. State U., 1986. Coord. prospect rsch. Office of Devel. Miss. State U., 1989-93, coord. prospect mgmt. Office of Devel., 1993-96, coord. prospect and donor rels. Office of Devel., 1997-98, asst. dir. devel., 1998—2002; dir. spl. giving programs Miss. State U. Found., 2002—. Mem.: Assn. Fundraising Profls., Coun. Advancement and Support of Edn., Assn. Profl. Rschrs. for Advancement. Baptist. Avocations: reading, boating, camping. Office: Miss State U PO Drawer 6149 200 Walker Rd Mississippi State MS 39762 E-mail: thughes@foundation.msstate.edu.

HUGHES, PAUL ANTHONY, minister, musician, songwriter, author, publisher; b. Tulsa, Sept. 14, 1957; s. James Barrie and Naomi Ruth (Kinard) H. BS in Indsl. Distbn., Tex. A&M U., College Station, 1980; MDiv in Christian Edn., Assemblies of God Theol. Sem., Springfield, Mo., 1986; postgrad., Baylor U., 1987. Ordained to ministry Assemblies of God, 1989. Pastoral asst., adult tchr., asst. supt. Magnolia Hill Assembly of God, Livingston, Tex., 1988-90; tchr. Bible, musician, religious writer, songwriter, 1990—; asst. pastor First Assembly of God, Liberty, Tex., 1992-94. Adult Bible tchr. Evangel Assembly of God, Houston, 1994-96; instr. Tex. Sch. Bus., Houston, 1999—. Editor, pub.: Spiritual Insight newsletter, 1995—; contbr. articles, book revs.; owner, pub. Pneumatikos website, Biblical Spirituality website, Divine Parody website. Singles dir., prayer emphasis dir. Grace Assembly of God, Houston, 1996 98; founding pastor West Loop Ch., Houston, 1999-2002. Home: 1111 Woods Dr Liberty TX 77575-3609 E-mail: westloop@yahoo.com. *"Truth is just truth; you can't have opinions about truth." - Peter Schickele.*

HUGHES, RICHARD GARY, engineering educator; b. Grand Forks, N.D., Apr. 26, 1960; s. Robert George and Clarice Irene Hughes; m. Amy Jo Miller, Aug. 14, 1982; children: Randall George, Michael Richard. BS, N.Mex. Inst. Mining and Tech., Socorro, 1982; MS, Stanford U., 1995, PhD, 1999. Registered profl. engr., Colo. Prodn. engr. Tenneco Oil Co., Englewood, Colo., 1983—86; mgr. Stewart Title, Englewood, 1986—87; petroleum engr., project mgr. Softsearch/Dwights Energy Data, Denver, 1987—90; tchg. affiliate Stanford (Calif.) U., 1998, rsch. asst., 1993—99; asst. prof. U. Okla., Norman, 1999—. Cons., Norman, 1999—. Mem.: Am. Soc. for Engring. Educators, Am. Geophys. Union, Soc. Petroleum Engrs. Office: U of Okla T 301 100 E Boyd Norman OK 73019

HUGHES, ROBERT DAVIS, III, theology studies educator; b. Boston, Feb. 16, 1943; s. Robert Davis and Nancy (Wolfe) Hughes; m. Barbara Brunn, June 12, 1965; children: Robert David, Thomas Dunstan. BA, Yale U., 1966; MDiv, Episcopal Divinity Sch., 1969; MA, U. Toronto, Ont., Can., 1973, PhD, 1980. Ordained deacon Episcopal Ch., 1969, ordained priest Episcopal Ch., 1970. Assoc. rector Good Shepherd Ch., Athens, Ohio, 1969-72; vicar Epiphany Ch., Nelsonville, Ohio, 1969-72; asst. curate St. Anne's Ch., Toronto, 1972-75; instr. Sch. Theology U. of the South, Sewanee, Tenn., 1977-80, asst. prof. systemic theology, 1980-84, assoc. prof. systemic theology, 1984-92, prof. systematic theology, 1992—, faculty trustee, 2000—, Norma and Olan Mills prof. div., 2001—. Bd. dirs. Anglican Ctr. Christian Family Life, Sewanee, 1981—; mem. dept. edn. ecumenical commn., alcohol and drug commn. Diocese Tenn., 1981—88, mem. gen. bd. exam. chaplains, 2001—. Contbr. articles to various publs. Soloist Toronto Chamber Soc., 1975—77; pres., soloist Sewanee Chorale, 1979—84; vol. Cmty. Chest Boy Scouts Am., Sewanee, 1979—84; pres. Sewanee Chem. Dependency Assn., 1982; trustee St. Andrew's Sewanee Sch., 1997—. Fellow, Forum, 1998—; Episcopal Ch. Found. fellow, 1972—, Kent fellow, Danforth Found., 1975—77, Sabbatical grantee, Mercer and Conant Funds, 1984, 1991, 1998, Vis. scholar, Div. Sch. U. Cambridge, 1998. Mem.: AAUP (v.p. chpt. 1982—83, pres. 1985—87, v.p. state conf. 1990—94, pres. 1994—96, nat. coun. 1997—2000, v.p. chpt. 2001—), Soc. Christian Spirituality, Am. Acad. Religion, Soc. Anglican and Luth. Theologians (sec.-treas. 1986—95, v.p. 1995—96, pres. 1996—97), Crystal Lake Yacht Club (Frankfort, Mich.), E.Q.B. Club (bd. dirs. 1981—83). Office: Sch of Theology 335 Tennessee Ave Sewanee TN 37383-0001 E-mail: rhughes@sewanee.edu.

HUGHES, ROBERT HARRISON, former agricultural products executive; b. Puunene, Hawaii, Mar. 23, 1917; s. Robert Edwin and Alice Thayer (Walker) H.; m. Nadine Jeannette Hegler, Aug. 24, 1940 (div. 1983); children: Robert Lawrence, Linton Alice, Carole Nadine.; m. Judith R. Gething, Jan. 28, 1983. B.Sc. in Sugar Tech, U. Hawaii, 1938. With Hawaiian Comml. & Sugar Co., 1939—62, sugar mill supt., 1962—65; prodn. mgr., v.p. tech. services C. Brewer & Co., Ltd., Honolulu, 1965-69, sr. v.p. Hawaiian ops., 1969-77, exec. v.p., 1977-80, dir. subs., 1966-80; pres. Hawaiian Sugar Planters Assn., Aiea, 1981-85; dir. Mauna Loa Resources Inc., 1986-95. Mem. bd. regents U. Hawaii, 1961-66; trustee Hawaii Conf. Found., 1966-85, Hawaii Loa Coll., 1980-89, Moloka'i Mus. and Cultural Ctr., 1984-91, Hawaiian Hist. Soc., 1990-94, U. Hawaii Found., 1963-65, 73-78, pres., 1967-68; bd. dirs. Hawaii Multi-Cultural Ctr., 1979-81, Samaritan Counseling Ctr. Hawaii, 1985-91; chmn. adv. bd. Cancer Rsch. Ctr., Hawaii, 1979-81; pres. Hawaii conf. United Ch. of Christ, 1962-63. Mem. Hawaiian Sugar Planters Assn. (dir. 1972-80), Hawaiian Hist. Soc. Home: 1080 S Beretania #902 Honolulu HI 96814-1445

HUGHES, ROBERT MERRILL, control system engineer; b. Glendale, Calif., Sept. 11, 1936; s. Fred P. and Gertrude G. H.; 1 child, Tammie Lynn Cobble. AA, Pasadena City Coll., 1957. Registered profl. engr., Calif., Nev.; lic. gen. bldg. contractor. Engr. Aerojet Gen. Corp., Azusa, Calif., 1957-64, 66-74; pres. Automatic Electronics Corp., Sacramento, 1964-66; specialist Perkin Elmer Corp., Pomona, Calif., 1974-75; gen. mgr. Hughes Mining Inc., Covina, Calif., 1975-76; project mgr. L&A Water Treatment, City of Industry, Calif., 1976-79; dir. Hughes Industries Inc., Alta Loma, Calif., 1979—. Pres. Hughes Devel. Corp., Carson City, Nev.; chmn. bd. Hughes Mining Inc., Hughes Video Corp. Patentee in field. Mem. AIME, Nat. Soc. Profl. Engrs., Instrument Soc. Am., Am. Inst. Plant Engrs. Republican. Office: PO Box 915 Carson City NV 89702-0915

HUGHES, SARAH, figure skater; b. Great Neck, N.Y., May 2, 1985; Student, Yale U. Mem. U.S. Olympic Team, Sydney, 2000. Competitive history includes: 3d place North Atlantic Novice, 1996, 1st place North Atlantic Novice, 1997, 1st place North Atlantic Novice, 1998, 2d place Mexico Cup, 1998, 1st place Eastern Jr., 1998, 1st place U.S. Championships Jr., 1998, 2d place Hungarian Trophy, 1998, 4th place U.S. Championships, 1999, 7th place World Championships, 1999, 1st place World Jr. Team Selection Competition, 2d place World Jr. Championships, 1999, 2d place ISU Jr. Grand Prix, 2d place Hershey's Kisses (Team USA), 1999, 1st place Vienna Cup, 1999, 4th place Skate America, 1st place Keri Lotion vs. The World (Team USA-1st place), 1999, 5th place World Championships, 2000, 3d place Trophee Lalique, 1999, 3d place U.S. Championships, 2000, 2d place Internat. Figure Skating Challenge (Team USA-2d place), 2000, 2d place U.S. Championships, 2001, 2d place, Skate America, 2001, 1st place, Olympic Winter Games, 2002. recipient Sullivan award, 2002, ESPY award for best olympian; names USOC Sports Woman of the Yr., 2002, March of Dimes Sports Woman of the Yr., 2002 Avocations: reading, tennis, violin. Office: USFSA 20 1st St Colorado Springs CO 80906-3624

HUGHES, SHARON MARY, trade association executive; b. Chgo., July 28, 1952; d. George Ingersoll and Rose Myrtle (Reed) H. BA in Polit. Sci. and Comm. cum laude, Am. U., 1980, MS in Bus., Govt. Rels., 1985. Freelance photographer, N.Y.C., 1972-76; advt. account exec. R.L. Newport and Co., N.Y.C., 1976-78; direct mail advt. mgr. John Wanamaker's, Phila., 1981-83; legis. intern U.S. Congressman James Florio, Washington, 1985; asst. dir. legis. affairs Nat. Food Processors Assn., Washington, 1985-87; mgr. govt. affairs Synthetic Organic Chem. Mfrs. Assn., Washington, 1987-89; exec. v.p. Nat. Coun. Agrl. Employers, Washington, 1989—. U.S. employer rep. Internat. Labour Orgn. High-Level Meeting on Achieving Equality in Employment for Migrant Workers, 2000; U.S. employer advisor 88th and 89th Session, Internat. Labor Conf, 2000, 01. Mem., sodalist Holy Rosary Ch. Sodality, Washington, 1989— (sec. 1997-99). Mem. Women in Govt. Rels. (bd. dirs. 1996-98, co-chmn. environ. task force 1988-89, mem. agrl. task force 1989-90, co-chmn. congl. rels. com. 1992-93), Am. League Lobbyists (bd. dirs. 2002—, sec. 2003—), Am. Soc. Assn. Execs. (cert. assn. exec.), Greater Wash. Soc. Assn. Execs., Boys and Girls Clubs of Greater Washington (bd. dir., 2001—), Phi Kappa Phi. Roman Catholic. Avocations: photography, skiing, golf, history, travel. Office: Nat Coun Agrl Employers 1112 16th St NW Ste 920 Washington DC 20036-4825 Fax: 202-728-0303. E-mail: hughes@NCAEonline.org.

HUGHES, SPENCER EDWARD, JR., retired financial executive, consultant; b. Bklyn., Sept. 6, 1933; s. Spencer Edward and Marie (Carey) H.; m. Diane E. Woods, June 15, 1963; children: Spencer Edward III, David Charles, Charles Woods. BA, Columbia Coll., 1955; postgrad., NYU, 1959-60; MBA in Fin., Hofstra U., 1961. Mem. staff L.I. Lighting Co., Hicksville, N.Y., 1958-64, mgr. investor relations, 1964-83, asst. treas., 1984-93; pvt. practice corp. fin. and investor rels. cons., 1993-95; ret., 1995. 1st lt. USAF, 1955-57. Mem. Corp. Transfer Agts. Assn. (bd. dirs. 1968-75). Avocations: sailboat racing, tennis, golf. Home: 3357 Trinidad Ct Punta Gorda FL 33950-6375 E-mail: shughesjr@comcast.net.

HUGHES, STANLEY JOHN, mycologist; b. Llanelli, S. Wales, Sept. 17, 1918; emigrated to Can., 1952, naturalized, 1967; s. John Thomas and Gertrude (Roberts) H.; m. Lyndell Anne Rutherford, Oct. 11, 1958; children— Robert Conway, Glenys Anne, David Stanley. B.Sc. with honors, U. Wales, Aberystwyth, 1941, M.Sc., 1943, D.Sc., 1954. Asst. to adv. mycologist Nat. Agrl. Advisory Ser. U. Wales, 1941-45; asst. mycologist Commonwealth Mycological Inst., Kew, Eng., 1945-52; mycologist Research br. Agr. Can. Central Exptl. Farm, Ottawa, Ont., 1952-58, sr. mycologist, 1958-62; prin. mycologist Rsch. br. Agr. Can. Central Exptl. Farm (Ctr. for Land and Biol. Resources Rsch., 1962-83; hon. rsch. assoc., 1983—. Sr. research fellow New Zealand Dept. Sci. and Indsl. Research, 1963; Exchange scientist Nat. Research Councils of Can. and Brazil, 1974 Contbr. articles in field to profl. jours. Recipient Jakob Eriksson Gold medal, 1969; George Lawson medal, 1981 Fellow Royal Soc. Can., Linnean Soc. London (fgn. mem.); mem. Mycological Soc. Am. (pres. 1975; Disting. mycologist award 1985); British Mycological Soc. (fgn. v.p. and honorary mem. 1987), Internat. Mycological Assn. (v.p. 1977-83, hon. v.p. XVI internat. botanical congress 1999). Mem. United Ch. of Can. Home: 360 Hamilton Ave Ottawa ON Canada K1Y 1C5 Office: Ea Cereal/Oilseed Rsch Ctr Agrl and Agri-Food Can Ctrl Exptl Farm Ottawa ON Canada K1A 0C6 E-mail: sjhughes@sympatico.ca.

HUGHES, STELLA PLATT, sociology educator; b. Rapid City, S.D., Aug. 25, 1929; d. George Lee Platt and Josephine Ann Paulson; m. William Lewis Hughes, June 9, 1950; children: Elizabeth Holderman, James, Judith Cockrell, Michael. BS in Psychology, Okla. State U., 1973, MS in Corrections, 1976, PhD in Sociology, 1981. Undergraduate acad. counselor Okla. State U., Stillwater, 1981, lectr. dept. sociology, 1982, adj. asst. prof., 1982-88; assoc. prof. dept. liberal arts S.D. Sch. Mines and Tech., Rapid City, 1989-93, prof. dept. social scis., 1993-96, prof. emeritus, 1996—. Cons. Okla. Hwy. Safety Office, 1985-88, HHS, 1992, 93, USDA, 1994; faculty assoc. Office Juvenile Sys. Oversight Okla. Commn. Children and Youth, 1986, U.S. Dept. Justice, 1986-87; project dir. Okla. Commn. Children and Youth/Dept. Mental Health, 1986; program evaluator S.D. Sch. Mines and Tech., 1992-93. Contbr. articles to profl. jours. Asst. leader, leader Girl Scouts Am., Stillwater, Okla., 1964-66; rep. to state bd. Okla. Assn. Children Learning Disabilities, Stillwater, 1971-72; bd. dirs. Cmty. Action Found., Stillwater, 1971-76, chmn. bd. dirs., 1974-76; bd. dirs. Sheltered Workshop Payne County, Stillwater, 1972-73; vol. counselor Payne County Vol. Program Misdeameanants, Inc., Stillwater, 1974-75; mem. steering com. Payne-Noble Family Planning, Stillwater, 1975-80; judge High Plains Sci. and Engring. Fair, 1990—, mem. sci. rev. com., 1991-94; mem. U.S. Senator Tom Dashle's Health Adv. Group, Rapid City, 1991—; bd. dirs. Black Hills Symphony Orch., Rapid City, 1996-99, v.p., 1997-99. Mem. AAAS, Norwegian-Am. Hist. Soc., Sons Norway, Nat. Geneal. Soc., Am. Sociol. Assn., Soc. Study Social Problems, Rsch. Soc. Alcoholism, Great Plains Sociol. Assn., Midwest Sociol. Soc., Southwestern Social Sci. Assn., New Eng. Hist. and Geneal. Soc., Alpha Kappa Delta. Avocations: genealogy, travel. Home: 6118 Greenleaf Ct Rapid City SD 57702-8845

HUGHES, SUE MARGARET, retired librarian; b. Cleburne, Tex. d. Chastain Wesley and Sue Willis (Payne) H. BBA, U. Tex., Austin, 1949; MLS, Tex. Woman's U., 1960, PhD, 1987. Sec.-treas. pvt. corps., Waco, Tex., 1949-59; asst. in public services Baylor U. Library, Waco, 1960-64, acquisitions librarian, 1964-79, acting univ. librarian, summer 1979, dir. Moody Library, 1980-89; interim univ. libr. Baylor U., Waco, 1989-91, spl. materials cons., 1991-92; ret., 1992. Mem. AAUP, ALA, Southwestern Library Assn., Tex. Library Assn., AAUW, Brazor Forum, Hist. Waco Found., Delta Kappa Gamma, Beta Phi Mu, Beta Gamma Sigma. Clubs: Altrusa. Methodist.

HUGHES, TERESA LEE, lawyer, educator; b. Little Rock, Mar. 6, 1953; d. William Lindsay and Lillian Phyllis Cloud; m. Thomas Morgan Hughes III, Aug. 10, 1974; 1 child, Gwyneth Leigh. BA in Humanities, Hendrix Coll., 1975; JD, U. Ark., Little Rock, 1978. Bar: Ark. 1978, U.S. Dist. Ct. Ark. 1978. Ptnr. Hughes & Hughes PA, Searcy, Ark., 1978—. Former adj. prof. Ark. State U., Beebe. Pres. White County Dem. Women, 1993; chmn. com. White County Dems., 1994-2000; chmn. White County Election Com., 1994-2000; trustee White County Libr. Sys., 1987-97, chmn. bd. trustee, 1995-97; sec. Gov.'s Commn. Librs., 1997; trustee White County CASA, 1999-2002. Mem. Ark. Trial Laywers Assn., Ctrl. Ark. Debtor-Creditor Bar Assn., Bus. & Profl. Women Beebe (sec. 1998-99, pres. 1995, Woman of the Yr. 1989), White County Bar Assn. (pres. 1993), Ark. Assn. Women Lawyers. Office: Hughes & Hughes 407 W Arch Ave Searcy AR 72143-5202 E-mail: hughesfirm@aol.com

HUGHES, THOMAS LOWE, foundation executive; b. Mankato, Minn., Dec. 11, 1925; s. Evan Raymond and Alice (Lowe) H.; m. Jean Hurlburt Reiman, May 7, 1955 (dec. Dec. 1993); children: Thomas Evan, Allan Cameron; m. Jane Dudley Casey Kuczynski, Nov. 25, 1995. BA summa cum laude, Carleton Coll., 1947, LHD (hon.), 1974; BPhil and MA in Politics (Rhodes scholar), Balliol Coll., Oxford (Eng.) U., 1949; LLB, JD, Yale U., 1952; LLD (hon.), Washington Coll., 1973, Denison U., 1980, Fla. Internat. U., 1986; HHD (hon.), Washington and Jefferson Coll., 1979. Bar: Minn. 1952, U.S. Supreme Ct. 1960, U.S. Dist. Ct. D.C. 1968. Profl. staff mem. U.S. Senate Subcom. on Labor and Labor-Mgmt. Relations, Com. on Labor and Pub. Welfare, 1951-52; assoc. prof. polit. sci. and internat. rels. U. So. Calif., 1953; asso. prof. polit. sci. and internat. relations Trinity Coll., Tex., 1954, George Washington U., 1957-58; exec. sec. to gov. of Conn., 1954-55; legis. counsel Sen. Hubert Humphrey, 1955-58; adminstrv. asst. U.S. Rep. Chester Bowles, 1959-60; spl. asst. to under sec. state Dept. State, 1961, dep. dir. intelligence and research, 1961-63, dir. intelligence and research with rank of asst. sec. state, 1963-69; minister, dep. chief mission Am. embassy, London, 1969-70; planning and coordination staff Dept. State, 1970-71; pres., trustee Carnegie Endowment for Internat. Peace, 1971-91, pres. emeritus, hon. trustee, 1991—. Former chmn. nuclear proliferation and safe-

guards adv. panel Office Tech. Assessment, Congress U.S.; co-chmn. Coun. P.R.-U.S. Affairs; internat. adv. bd. Battelle, Pacific Northwest Nat. Lab.; vis. sr. rsch. fellow German Hist. Inst., Washington. Author: The Hohenzollerns; editor: Indian Chiefs of Southern Minnesota; mem. editorial bd. Fgn. Policy Mag., 1971—, chmn., 1971-91; contbr. articles to nat. periodicals. Vol. Kibbutz Ein Hashofet, Israel, 1950; trustee, sec. German Marshall Fund U.S., 1972-82; mem. Trilateral Commn., 1973-83; trustee Am. Inst. Contemporary German Studies, Am. Acad., Berlin, Social Sci. Found., U. Denver; former bd. govs. Ditchley Found., Eng.; vis. com. Ctr. for Internat. Studies, Harvard U., 1971-76; bd. visitors Ctr. for German and European Studies, Georgetown U.; bd. dirs. Arms Control Assn.; mem. adv. coun. Woodrow Wilson Sch., Princeton U.; mem. adv. bd. Fundacion Luis Munoz Marin, San Juan, P.R.; chmn. U.S.-U.K. Bicentennial Fellowships Com. on Arts, 1975-78; mem. adv. com. Hubert H. Humphrey Inst. Pub. Affairs U. Minn.; staff dir. platform com. Dem. Nat. Conv., 1960. Served to maj. JAGC, USAF, 1952-54. Recipient Arthur S. Fleming Outstanding Pub. Svc. award, 1964. Mem. Institut Internat. de Geopolitique Paris, N.Y. Coun. Fgn. Rels., Inst. Current World Affairs (trustee), Internat. Inst. Strategic Studies London (trustee Am. com.), Am. Acad. Diplomacy, Am. Assn. Rhodes Scholars, Washington Inst. Fgn. Affairs (pres., mem. exec. com.), Atlantic Coun. U.S. (bd. dirs.), Oxford-Cambridge Assn. Washington (former chmn.), Women's Fgn. Policy Group, New England Hist. Geneal. Soc., Scottish Genealogy Soc., Soc. Mayflower Descs., Mid-Atlantic Club (chmn.), Cosmos Club, Century Assn. (N.Y.C.), Oxford (Eng.) Union, Knight of St. John (Johanniterorden, Balley Brandenburg), Phi Beta Kappa, Phi Delta Phi. Episcopalian. Office: German Hist Inst 1607 New Hampshire Ave NW Washington DC 20009-2562 E-mail: thoshughes@aol.com.

HUGHES, THOMAS MORGAN, III, lawyer; b. Racine, Wis., June 14, 1949; s. Thomas Morgan and Rosemary (Navratil) H.; m. Teresa Lee Cloud, Aug. 10, 1974; 1 child, Gwyneth Leigh. B.B.A., U. Wis.-Madison, 1971; J.D., St. Louis U., 1974. Bar: Ark. 1974, U.S. Dist. Ct. (ea. dist.) Ark. 1974. Sole practice, Beebe, Ark., 1974-78; ptnr., Hughes & Hughes, Searcy, Ark., 1978— ; instr. Ark. State U., Beebe, 1975. City atty. City of Beebe, 1975-76; treas. Beebe Indsl. Devel. Corp., Beebe, 1983— ; judge City Ct., Beebe, 1985-87, Beebe Mcpl. Ct., 1987—. Mem. White County Bar Assn. Prs. 1996), Beebe C. of C. (pres. 1984—), Kiwanis (pres. 1981-82, bd. dirs. 1979—). Democrat. Home: 807 W Louisiana St Beebe AR 72012-2623 Office: Hughes & Hughes PO Box 91 Searcy AR 72145-0091

HUGHES, THOMAS PARKE, history educator; b. Richmond, Va., Sept. 13, 1923; s. Hunter Russell and Mary Bronaugh (Quisenberry) H.; m. Agatha Chipley, Aug. 7, 1948; children: Thomas P. (dec.), Agatha H., Lucian P. BME, U. Va., 1947, PhD, 1953; D (hon.), Royal Inst. Tech., Stockholm, 2000, Northwestern U., 2001. Instr. U. Va., Charlottesville, 1951-54; asst. prof. history Sweet Briar (Va.) Coll., 1954-56; assoc. prof. history Washington and Lee U., Lexington, Va., 1956-63, M.I.T., Cambridge, 1963-66; prof. history Inst. Tech., So. Meth. U., Dallas, 1969-73; mem. faculty U. Pa., Phila., 1973-94, prof. history and sociology of sci., 1973-94, Andrew W. Mellon prof., 1987-94, prof. emeritus, 1994—. Vis. assoc. prof. history Johns Hopkins U., Balt., 1966-69; Torsten Althin prof. Royal Inst. Tech., Stockholm, 1985-90; founding rsch. prof. Tech. Univ., Darmstadt, Fed. Republic Germany, 1986-87; vis. rsch. prof. Wissenschaftszentrum Berlin, 1988-94; vis. prof. MIT, 1991, 93, 94—, E.T.H. Zürich, 1997, Stanford U., 1999—. Author: Elmer Sperry: Inventor and Engineer, 1971 (Dexter prize), Networks of Power: Electrification in Western Society 1980-1930, 1983 (Dexter prize), American Genesis: A Century of Invention and Technological Enthusiasm 1870-1970, 1989 (Pulitzer Prize finalist); editor: (with Agatha C. Hughes) Lewis Mumford: Public Intellectual, 1990, Rescuing Prometheus, 1998, Systems, Experts, and Computers, 2000. Chmn. Nat. Rsch. Coun. com., 1996—99; mem. adv. coun. Smithsonian Inst., 1984—90. Served to lt. (j.g.) USN, 1943—46. Fulbright postdoctoral fellow, Germany, 1958—59, NSF fellow, 1975, Inst. Advanced Study fellow, Berlin, 1983, Guggenheim fellow, 1986. Mem. Nat. Acad. Engring., Soc. History of Tech. (pres. 1978-80, Leonardo da Vinci medal 1984), Soc. Social Studies Sci. (Bernal prize 1990), History of Sci. Soc. (coun. 1976-79), Am. Acad. Arts and Scis., Johns Hopkins U. Soc. of Scholars, Swedish Royal Acad. of Engring. Scis., Am. Philos. Soc., Phi Beta Kappa. E-mail: thughes@sas.upenn.edu.

HUGHES, TIMOTHY F. mechanical engineer, consultant; b. Olean, N.Y., Sept. 8, 1961; s. Robert and Patricia Hughes. BS in Mech. Engring., Grove City Coll., 1983; MBA, Canisius Coll., 1999. Lic. profl. engr., Pa., 1989, cert. energy mgr., Assn. Energy Engrs., 2002, Leadership in Energy and Environmental Design, US Green Bldg. Coun., 2002. Engr. KLH Engrs., Pitts., 1983—84; mech. engr. Robson & Woese Consulting Engrs., Rochester, NY, 1984—89; divsn. engr. Niagara Mohawk Power Corp., Buffalo, 1989—2000; sr. project engr./bus. devel. C&S Engrs., Buffalo, 2000—. Pres. East Aurora (N.Y.) Cmty. Nursery, 1999—2001. Mem.: Am. Soc. Heating, Refrigeration and Air Conditioning Engrs., Am. Soc. Energy Engrs., Mu Kappa Tau, Beta Gamma Sigma. Office: C&S Engrs 90 Broadway Buffalo NY 14203 Office Fax: 716-847-1454. Personal E-mail: tim.hughes@verizon.net. E-mail: thughes@cscos.com.

HUGHES, VESTER THOMAS, JR., lawyer; b. San Angelo, Tex., May 24, 1928; s. Vester Thomas and Mary Ellen (Tisdale) H. Student, Baylor U., 1945-46; BA with distinction, Rice U., 1949; LLB cum laude, Harvard U., 1952. Bar: Tex. 1952. Law clk. U.S. Supreme Ct., 1952; assoc. Robertson, Jackson, Payne, Lancaster & Walker, Dallas, 1955-58; ptnr. Jackson, Walker, Winstead, Cantwell & Miller, Dallas, 1958-76, Hughes, Luce, Hennessy, Smith & Castle, Dallas, 1976—, Hughes & Hill, Dallas, 1979-85, Hughes & Luce, Dallas, 1985—. Bd. dirs. Exell Cattle Co., Amarillo, Tex., LX Cattle Co., Amarillo, Austin Industries, Dallas, Sammons Enterprises, Inc.; adv. dir. First Nat. Bank Mertzon; sr. tax counsel Cmtys. Found. of Tex., Inc.; mem. adv. com. Tex. Supreme Ct., 1985-93. Contbr. articles on fed. taxation to profl. jours. Bd. dirs. Juvenile Diabetes Found. Inc., Dallas, 1982—; trustee Dallas Bapt. U., 1967-77; v.p., trustee, exec. com. Tex. Scottish Rite Hosp. for Children, 1967—; bd. overseers vis. com. Harvard Law Sch., 1969-75. 1st lt. JAGC U.S. Army, 1952-55. Mem. ABA (coun. sect. taxation 1969-73), Tex. Bar Assn., Dallas Bar Assn., Am. Law Inst. (coun. 1958—), Am. Coll. Tax Counsel, Ctr. for Am. and Internat. Law, Am. Coll. Trust and Estate Counsel, Met. Club (Washington), Harvard Club (N.Y.C.), Masons, Order Ea. Star, Phi Beta Kappa, Sigma Xi. Democrat. Baptist. Avocations: traveling, community and church activities, reading. Office: Hughes & Luce 1717 Main St Ste 2800 Dallas TX 75201-4685

HUGHES, W. JAMES, optometrist; b. Shawnee, Okla., Oct. 15, 1944; s. Willis J. and Elizabeth Alice (Nimohoyah) Hughes. BA in Anthropology, U. Okla., 1966, MA in Anthropology, 1972; OD, U. Houston, 1976; MPH, U. Tex., 1977. Lic. optometrist Okla., Tex., W.Va. Commd. med. officer USPHS, 1966, advanced through grades to capt./optometrist, 1993; physician's asst. Houston, Dallas, 1969-70; teaching asst. in clin optics U. Houston, 1973-74; contact lens rsch. asst., 1974; Wesley Jessen Contact Lens Rep., 1974-76; extern eye clinic Tuba City Indian Hosp., 1975; Indian Health Svc. optometrist Eagle Butte, S.D., 1976; optometrist vision care project Crockett Ind. Sch. Dist., 1977; vision care program dir. Bemidj Area Indian Health Svc., 1977-78; optometrist Navajo Area Indian Health Svc., Chinle Health Ctr., 1978-79, Shiprock USPHS Indian Hosp., 1979—; chief vision care program No. Navajo Med. Ctr., 1994—; dir. eye clinic USPHS No. Navajo Med. Ctr., Shiprock, N.Mex. Adj. prof. So. Calif. Coll. Optometry, L.A., U. Houston Coll. Optometry, 1978—, So. Coll. Optometry, Memphis, 1980—; Navajo area Indian Health Svc. rep. to optometry career devel. com. USPHS. Contbr. articles to profl. jours. Sgt. U.S. Army, 1966-69, Capt, USPHS, 1993—. Decorated Bronze Star, Purple Heart; recipient House of Vision award, 1974, Cmty. Health Optometry award, 1976; Better Vision scholar, 1973-76. Mem. Am. Pub. Health Assn., Am. Optometric Assn., Tex. Optometric Assn. Commd. Officers Soc., Assn. Am. Indian Physicians, Beta Sigma Kappa. Democrat. Roman Catholic.

HUGHES, WALTER THOMPSON, physician, pediatrics educator; b. Cleve., May 16, 1930; s. Walter Thompson and Millie Hasentine (Collette) H.; m. Frances J. Skinner, Nov. 24, 1957; children: Carla, Gregory, Christopher. MD, U. Tenn., 1954. Diplomate Am. Bd. Pediatrics. Resident in pediatrics U. Tenn. Coll. Medicine, Memphis, 1955-57, prof. pediatrics and microbiology, 1969-77, prof. pediatrics, 1981—; mem. St. Jude Children's Rsch. Hosp., Memphis, 1969-77, mem., chair dept. infectious diseases, 1981-95; mem. staff Walter Reed Army Med. Ctr., Ft. Detrick, Md., 1957-59; pvt. practice pediatrics Cleve., 1959-61; instr. to prof. U. Louisville Sch. Medicine, 1961-69; Eudowood prof. pediatrics, dir. div. infectious diseases Johns Hopkins U. Sch. Medicine, Balt., 1977-81; Arthur Ashe chair in pediat. AIDS rsch. St. Jude Children's Rsch. Hosp., Memphis, 1993-98, emeritus mem., 1998—. Capt. U.S. Army, 1957-59. Fellow Am. Acad. Pediatrics; mem. Am. Pediatric Soc., Infectious Diseases Soc. Am., Soc. Pediatric Rsch., Pediatric Infectious Diseases Soc. (pres. 1983-85). Republican. Methodist. Home: 854 River Park Dr Memphis TN 38103-0804 Office: St Jude Children's Rsch Hosp 332 N Lauderdale St Memphis TN 38105-2729 E-mail: walter.hughes@stjude.org., FHU577483@aol.com.

HUGHES, WAUNELL MCDONALD (MRS. DELBERT E. HUGHES), retired psychiatrist; b. Tyler, Tex., Feb. 6, 1928; d. Conrad Claiborne and Bernice Oletha (Smith) McDonald; m. Delbert Eugene Hughes, Aug. 14, 1948; children: Lark, Mark, Lynn, Michael. BA, U. Tex., Austin, 1946; MD, Baylor U., 1951. Intern VA Hosp., Houston, 1951-52; resident Parkland Hosp., Dallas, 1964-67; pvt. practice gen. medicine Tyler, 1952-64; acting chief psychiatry svc. VA Hosp., Dallas, 1967-68, asst. chief, 1968-73, chief Mental Hygiene Clinic and Day Treatment Ctr., 1973-82, unit chief acute inpatient psychiatry Med. Ctr., 1982-88; clin. instr. psychiatry Southwestern Med. Sch., U. Tex. Health Sci. Ctr., Dallas, 1968-88; psychiat. cons. Dallas Family Guidance Clinics, 1990. Chmn. pre-sch. vision and hearing program Pilot Club, Tyler, 1960-64. Mem. Am. Med. Women's Assn. (pres. Dallas 1980-81, archivist 1997—), Am. Psychiat. Assn., Am. Group Psychotherapy Assn. (pres. Dallas chpt. 1984-86), North Tex. Soc. Psychiat. Physicians (co-chair mental health/mental retardation pro bono clinic com. Dallas chpt. 1989-91, mem. patient advocacy com. 1992—), Dallas Area Women Psychiatrists (archivist 1985—, pres. 1997-99), Alpha Epsilon Iota (pres. 1950-51). Home: 3428 University Blvd Dallas TX 75205-1834 E-mail: dhu6763151@aol.com.

HUGHES, WILLIAM ANTHONY, retired bishop; b. Youngstown, Ohio, Sept. 23, 1921; s. James Francis and Anna Marie (Philbin) H.. Degree, St. Charles Sem., Balt., St. Mary's Sem., Cleve.; MA in Edn., Notre Dame U., 1956. Ordained priest Roman Cath. Ch., 1946. Pastor chs., Boardman and Massillon, Ohio, 1946—55; prin. Cardinal Mooney H. S., Youngstown, Ohio, 1956—65; supt. schs. Diocese of Youngstown, 1965—72, Episcopal vicar of edn.., 1972—73, vicar gen., 1973—74; aux. bishop, 1974—79; bishop of Covington, 1979—; ret., 1995. Office: Cathedral of Assemption 1140 Madison Ave Covington KY 41011-3116

HUGHES, WILLIAM EARLE, lawyer; b. June 14, 1944; s. Robert Earle and June Alice (Eldridge) Hughes; m. Cheryl Christine Dempsey, Oct. 4, 1963; children: Christine, Robert, Alexander. BA, The Citadel, 1965; JD, Harvard U., 1968. Bar: Mass. 69, Okla. 78. Assoc. Herrick and Smith, Boston, 1970—73; asst. U.S. atty. U.S. Dept. Justice, Boston, 1973—78; assoc. Doerner, Stuart, S.D. and A., Tulsa, 1972—89, ptnr., 1982—89. Fulbright scholar and vis. prof. U. Tunis, Tunisia, 2000—01. Capt. U.S. Army, 1968—70, Vietnam. Decorated Bronze Star. Mem.: Okla. Bar Assn. Republican. Roman Catholic. Home: 1020 E 18th St Tulsa OK 74120-7407 E-mail: bluegilltwo@earthlink.net.

HUGHES, WILLIAM FOSTER, career officer, surgeon, obstetrician, gynecologist; b. Lexington, Va., July 1, 1944; s. John Anderson Jr. and Mary Elizabeth (Shaner) H.; m. Susan Lee Aplegate, July 12, 1969; children: Carolyn Michelle, John Robert, Jennifer Marie. BS, U.S. Mil. Acad., 1966; MD, Med. Coll. Va., 1978; postgrad., U.S. Army War Coll., 1989. Diplomate Nat. Bd. Med. Examiners, Am. Bd. Ob-Gyn. Commd. 2nd lt. U.S. Army, 1966, advanced through the grades to col., 1990; combat infantryman-platoon leader, co. comdr. U.S. Army, Vietnam, 1967-68, attack helicopter pilot, 1970-71; airfield comdr. Tipton Army Airfield, Ft. Meade, Md., 1971-74; intern in ob-gyn. Tripler Army Med. Ctr., Honolulu, Hawaii, 1978-79, resident in ob-gyn., 1979-82; staff physician Martin Army Cmty. Hosp., Ft. Benning, Ga., 1982-86; divsn. surgeon 101st Airborne Divsn., Ft. Campbell, Ky., 1986-88; command surgeon U.S. Special Ops. Command, MacDill Air Force Base, Fla., 1989-93; hosp. comdr. Darnall Army Cmty. Hosp., Ft. Hood, Tex., 1993-95; v.p. prodn. Info. Co., 1997—; cons. Med Nat., Inc., 1999—. Asst. prof. dept. ob-gyn. Tex. A&M U., College Station, 1994—; cons. Army Surgeon Gen., 1995-96. Decorated Silver Star, DFC, Purple Heart. Fellow ACOG, ACS; mem. Am. Coll. Physician Execs. Avocations: golf, fishing, running. Home: 712 Coyote Cir Harker Heights TX 76548 E-mail: bhughes578@aol.com.

HUGHES, WILLIAM JEFFREY, lawyer; b. San Gabriel, Calif., Dec. 6, 1951; s. William Drennan and Rosetta Jane (Duff) H. B.A., Stanford U., 1973; J.D., Hastings Coll., 1977; M.L., London Sch. Econ., 1979. Bar: Calif., 1977, U.S. Dist. Ct. (no. dist.) Calif. 1977, U.S. Ct. Appeals (9th cir.) 1980, U.S. Supreme Ct. 1982. Assoc. Alexander Anolik, P.C., San Francisco, 1978-80; mem. Brooks & Hughes, San Leandro, Calif., 1980-83; inheritance tax referee State of Calif., Alameda County, 1981-83; gen. counsel Bicara, Ltd., Carson, Calif., 1983—; dir. Food Wholesalers Am., Carson, 1984— . Contbr. articles to profl. jours. Mem. Thomas Scotto Scholarship Fund Com., San Francisco, 1981-82. Mem. Los Angeles County Bar Assn. Democrat. Office: Bicara Ltd PO Box 58834 Los Angeles CA 90058-0834 Home: 2633 Manoa Rd Honolulu HI 96822-1767

HUGHES, WILLIAM JOHN, former congressman, diplomat; b. Salem, N.J., Oct. 17, 1932; s. William W. and Pauline H.; m. Nancy L. Gibson; children: Nancy Lynne, Barbara Ann, Tama Beth, William John. AB, Rutgers U., 1955, JD, 1958, LLD (hon.), 1995; LHD (hon.), Mt. Vernon Coll., 1984; LLD (hon.), Richard Stockton State Coll., 1994, Glassboro State Coll., 1992; AA (hon.), Cumberland County Coll., 1994. Bar: N.J. 1959. Ptnr. Loveland, Hughes & Garrett, Ocean City, N.J., 1968-78; 1st asst. pros. atty. Cape May County, N.J., 1960-70; mem. 94th-103rd Congresses from 2d N.J. dist., Washington, D.C., 1974-95; amb. to Panama U.S. Dept. State, 1995-98; Clifford P. Case prof. pub. affairs Rutgers U., 1997; disting. scholar ethics and pub. policy Richard Stockton Coll. N.J., Pomona, 1999—; prof. Rutgers U., 1999—; of counsel Riker, Danzig, Scherer, Hyland & Perretti, LLP, 2000—. Bd. govs. Shore Meml. Hosp., Sommers Point, N.J., 1972-76. Recipient Ann. Planning award Am. Planning Assn., 1979, Disting. Citizen award Atlantic Area coun. Boy Scouts Am., 1982, Legislator of Yr. award VFW, 1982, Pres.'s award Nat. Dist. Attys. Assn., 1982, Legis. Leadership award Nat. Assn. Chain Drug Stores, 1984, Humanitarian citiation Food Mktg. Chain Drug Stores and N.J. Food Council, 1984, Legis. award Nat. Assn. Police Orgns., 1984, Legis. Achievement award Fed. Law Enforcement Officers Assn., 1984, Man of Yr. award Girl Scouts Am., 1986, Legis. award N.J. Foster Parents Assn., 1986, Leo Fraser Super Achiever award Juvenile Diabetes Found., 1987, Arthur E. Armitage Sr. Disting. Alumni award Rutgers U., 1987, Disting. Info. Processing Pub. Service award Data Processing Mgmt. Assn., 1987, Rutgers U. medal, 1992, Distinction in Pub. Svc. award Am. Rivers, 1993, Congressional Advocacy award, 1994, Spirit of South Jersey award South Jersey Devel. Coun., 1994, Career Achievement award in pub. svc. N.J. Edn. Assn., 1995; named Congressman of Yr., Nat. Assn. Police Orgns., 1986, Hall of Disting. Alumni award Rutgers U., 1997, Jefferson medal award N.J. Intellectual Property Law Assn., 1995, Judge John F. Gerry award for adminstrv. justice, 2000, South Jerseyan of Yr. award Rand Inst.,2003 Pub. Affairs, Rutgers U. Fellow Am. Bar Found.; mem. ABA, N.J. Bar Assn., Ocean City Hist. Soc. (bd. dir. 1972-76), Ocean City C. of C. (bd. dir. 1960—), Exch. of Ocean City Club (pres. 1965-66, Nat. Big E. award 1965), Masons (master lodge, Worshipful Master 1969). Democrat. Episcopalian. Home: 1019 Wesley Rd Ocean City NJ 08226-4754 E-mail: ambjack1@aol.com.

HUGHES, WILLIAM LEWIS, former university official, electrical engineer; b. Rapid City, S.D., Dec. 2, 1926; s. Clarence William and Newell (Chase) H.; m. Stella Marie Platt, June 9, 1950; children: Elizabeth Helen, James Edward, Judith Lee, Michael George. BS in Elec. Engring, S.D. Sch. Mines and Tech., 1949; MS, Iowa State U., 1950, PhD, 1952; DSc (hon.), S.D. Sch. Mines and Tech., 2000. Broadcast and TV engr., 1946-49; mem. faculty Iowa State U., 1949-60; prof. elec. engring., 1959-60; prof. elec. engring., head Sch. Elec. Engring., Okla. State U., Stillwater, 1960-76, Clark A. Dunn prof. engring., 1976-86, dir. Engring. Energy Lab., 1976-86; pres. InEn Corp, 1972-88; v.p. S.D. Sch. Mines and Tech., Rapid City, 1988-93; pres. Dakota Alpha Inc., 1994—. Chmn. ad hoc com. NAS, 1976, 79, mem. bd. sci. and tech. in devel., 1983; chmn. NAS/Philippine Govt. del. to Philippines, 1978, Indonesia, 1979, India, 1979, 85, 89, Thailand, 1990, 93; cons. industry and govt.; mem. indsl. com. TV frequency allocation studies FCC, 1957-59. Author: Nonlinear electrical Networks, 1960; also articles; co-author: Lines, Waves and Antennas, 1961, 2d edit., 1973; contbr. sects. to 6 engring. handbooks. Served with USNR, World War II. Named S.D. Profl. Engr. of Yr., S.D. Engring. Soc., 1995. Fellow IEEE; mem. NSPE (life, Disting. Svc. award 1997), Sigma Xi, Sigma Tau, Tau Beta pi, Eta Kappa Nu, Pi Mu Epsilon. Achievements include patentee nonlinear systems, color TV systems, direct energy conversions systems. Home: 6118 Greenleaf Ct Rapid City SD 57702-8845 E-mail: bhughesrc@aol.com.

HUGHES, WOODROW MILTON, real estate broker; b. Birmingham, Ala., June 22, 1950; s. Woodrow W. and Helen Hughes; m. Gloria Adams Hughes, June 3, 1995. BA, U. Ala., 1973. Broker assoc. RE/MAX Greater Atlanta, 1988-2000; broker-owner Atlanta Relocation, Stockbridge, Ga., 2000—; broker assoc. Metro Brokers GMAC, 2001. Spkr. in field. Capt. U.S. Army, 1973-81. Mem. Atlanta Bd. Realtors (tech. com. 1998-99). Avocations: gardening, alabama football, astronomy, atlanta braves baseball. Home: 211 Whitesand Bay Dr Stockbridge GA 30281-6202

HUGHEY, DAVID VAUGHN, business administration educator, educational consultant; b. Henderson, Nev., Jan. 19, 1944; s. Vaughn V. and Janet R. (Taborsky) H. BA, Kent State U., 1967; postgrad., So. Ill. U., 1967-68; PhD, U. Pitts., 1977; BS, Internat. Coll., Newlands, Cayman Islands, 1987, M of Acctg., 1994, MS, 1995. Cert. instr. anthropology and biology Calif. C.C. Instr. bus. Stautzenberger Coll., Findlay, Ohio, 1988; acct., bookkeeper JEF Transport Co., Findlay, 1988-91; sr. lectr. biology U. Findlay, 1991; asst. prof. applied behavioral scis. Nat.-Louis U., Atlanta, 1991-92; prof. human resources, dean Internat. Coll., Newlands, 1992-95, prof. bus. adminstrn., dean, 1995-2000, prof. bus. adminstrn., 2000—01, ednl. cons., 2002—; acct. Alumco/Aluminite, 2003. Tax preparer Jackson Hewitt, 2003—; acct. Alumco, 2003—. Contbr. articles and revs. to profl. jours. and books. Contbr. Cayman Islands Nat. Mus., Georgetown, 1996-2001. With U.S. Army, 1969-71. Predoctoral fellow Andrew Mellon Found., 1974-76. Fellow Am. Anthropol. Assn.; mem. Caribbean Studies Assn. (life), Am. Acctg. Assn., N.Y. Acad. Scis., Inst. Mgmt. Accts., Pi Gamma Mu (hon.). Episcopalian. Avocations: poetry, photography, chess. Office: 137 Sears Rd Chehalis Cayman Islands E-mail: profdave@hotsheet.com., dvhughey@lycos.com., profdave@inbox.net., drdavehughey@netzero.net.

HUGHEY, RICHARD KOHLMAN, author, lawyer; b. Chgo., July 6, 1934; BA cum laude, Santa Clara U., 1958, JD cum laude, 1963. Bar: Calif. 1964, U.S. Ct. Appeals (9th cir.) 1964, U.S. Supreme Ct. 1972. Atty. Pacific Gas & Elec. Co., San Francisco, 1963-69, Berry, Davis & McInerny, Oakland, Calif., 1969-71; ptnr. Caputo, Liccardo, Rossi & Kohlman, San Jose, 1971-75; lectr. law, dir. CLE Santa Clara (Calif.) U., 1975-80; mng. editor Bancroft-Whitney Co., San Francisco, 1980-91, Lawyers Coop. Pub. Co., Rochester, N.Y., 1992-94; history and lit. biography writer, 1995—; columnist Mountain Democrat, Placerville, Calif., 1997—. Author: Jeffers Country Revisited: Beauty Without Price, 1996, Computer Technology in Civil Litigation, 1990, Trial Lawyers Manual, 1978, Jeffers in Antrim, 2003, El Dorado: California's Empire County, 2003; co-author: Petroglyphs: Poetry and Fiction, 1994, Hey Lew: Homage to Lew Welch, 1997; editor: Am. Jury Trials, 1980—90, Proof of Facts, 1982—90; bd. editors Calif. State Bar Jour., 1972—75, editor-in-chief Santa Clara Law Rev., 1961—63. Mem. citizen's adv. commn. U.S. Postal Svc., San Francisco, 1989—92; mem. adv. bd. Commn. on Future of the Cts., Jud. Coun. of Calif., 1992. Avocation: photography.

HUGHS, MARY GERALDINE, accountant, social service specialist; b. Marshalltown, Iowa, Nov. 28, 1929; d. Don Harold Sr. and Alice Dorothy (Keister) Shaw; m. Charles G. Hughs, Jan. 31, 1949; children: Mark George, Deborah Kay, Juli Ann, Grant Wesley. AA, Highline C.C., 1970; BA, U. Wash., 1972. Asst. contr. Moduline Internat., Inc., Chehalis, Wash., 1972-73; contr. Data Recall Corp., El Segundo, Calif., 1973-74; fin. adminstr., acct. Saturn Mfg. Corp., Torrance, Calif., 1974-77; sr. acct., adminstrv. asst. Van Camp Ins., San Pedro, Calif., 1977-78; asst. adminstr. Harbor Regional Ctr., Torrance, Calif., 1979-87; active bookkeeping svc., 1978—. Instr. math. and acctg. South Bay Bus. Coll., 1976-77; treas., bd. dirs., Harbor Fed. Credit Union. Author: Iowa Auto Dealers Assn. Title System, 1955, Harbor Regional Center Affirmative Action Plan, 1980, Harbor Regional Ctr. Financial Format, 1978, Provider Audit System, 1978, Handling Client Funds, 1983. Sec. Pacific N.W. Mycol. Soc., 1966-67. Recipient award Am. Mgmt. Assn., 1979. Mem. Beta Alpha Psi. Republican. Mem. Ch. of Christ. Home and Office: 32724 Coastsite Dr Unit 107 Rancho Palos Verdes CA 90275 E-mail: mghughs@earthlink.net.

HUGHSTON, THOMAS LESLIE, JR., lawyer; b. Spartanburg, SC, July 25, 1943; s. Thomas Leslie and Eunice (Poole) Hughston; m. Mary Anne McLean, May 30, 1943; children: Karen, Greer, Mary. BA, The Citadel, 1965; JD, U. S.C., 1968. Bar: S.C. 1968, U.S. Dist. Ct. S.C. 1968. Assoc Nicholson & Nicholson, Greenwood, SC, 1968—72; ptnr. Bishop & Hughston, Greenwood, 1972, Bishop, Hughston & Daniel, Greenwood, 1983—85; resident cir. judge U.S. Ct. Appeals 8th Jud. Dist.; ret. judge, 1998—. Mcpl. judge City of Greenwood, 1973—75; pub. defender Greenwood and Abbeville Counties, SC, 1973—75. Recipient Disting. Svc. award, S.C. Mcpl. Assn., 1981. Mem.: S.C. Bar Asssn., Greenwood County Bar Assn. (pres. 1980), Kiwanis. Baptist. Office: 100 Broad St Rm 368 Charleston SC 29401-1564 Home: 9 Wentworth St Charleston SC 29401

HUGLER, EDWARD CHARLES, lawyer, federal and state government; b. Phila., Feb. 7, 1950; s. Edward Tarman and Lavina Rita (Kelchner) H.; m. Anna Louise Wolgast, June 13, 1987; children: Samuel Rives, Sarah Elizabeth. BA, U. Md., 1973; JD, Sch. of Law, Pepperdine U., 1976. Bar: D.C., Calif. Atty. advisor to adminstrv. law judge, Office of Hearing and Appeals U.S. Dept. of the Interior, 1977-78; atty., advisor, Office of the Solicitor U.S. Dept. of Labor, 1978-81, counsel for Standards and Legal Advice, Office of the Solicitor, 1981-88, dep. assoc. solicitor, Office of the Solicitor, 1988-89, dep. adminstr. for Coal Mine Safety and Health, Mine Safety and Health Adminstrn., 1989-91, dep. asst. sec. for Mine Safety and Health, 1991-98, acting asst. sec. for Mine Safety and Health, 1993-94; adminstr. for metal and nonmetal safety and health U.S. Dept. of Labor/Mine Safety and Health Adminstrn., 1998-99; dep. asst.,sec. for info. tech. U.S. Dept. Labor, 1999-2000; dep. asst. sec. for adminstrn. and mgmt. ops. Office of Asst. Sec. Adminstrn. & Mgmt., U.S. Dept. of Labor, Washington, 2000—. Office: Office of Asst Sec Adminstrn & Mgmt 200 Constitution Ave NW Washington DC 20210-0001 E-mail: hugler-edward@dol.gov.

HUGO, NORMAN ELIOT, plastic surgeon, medical educator; b. Beverly, Mass., Sept. 23, 1933; s. Victor Joseph and Helen Bernadette (Box) Hugo; m. Geraldine P Tonry, Oct. 10, 1959; children: Helen, William, Geraldine, Norman, Catherine. BA, Williams Coll., 1955, DSc (hon.), 1989; MD, Cornell U. Med. Coll., 1959. Diplomate (dir 1982-88, vice chmn 1987-88, residency rev comt, accreditation coun, grad med educ, 1994-98) Am Bd Plastic Surg. Intern, resident Cornell U. Surg. Svc., Bellevue Hosp., N.Y.C., 1959-63; resident N.Y. Hosp.-Cornell Med. Ctr., 1963-65, univ. instr. surgery, 1966-65; asst. prof. Ind. U.; asst. chief plastic surgeon Walter Reed Army Med. Ctr., 1967-69; assoc. prof. U. Chgo., 1969-71; chief plastic and reconstructive surgery Michael Reese Hosp., Chgo., 1969-71, Passavant Hosp., Chgo., 1971-79; assoc. prof. Northwestern U., Chgo., 1971-82; dir. plastic surgery Lakeside VA Hosp., 1971-77; chief plastic and reconstructive surgery Columbia U.-Presbyn. Med. Ctr., N.Y.C., 1982-95; prof. Columbia U. Coll. Physicians & Surgeons, 1982-98, prof. emeritus, 1998—. Maj MC AUS, 1967—69. Mem.: AMA (del 1983—88), ACS, Am Burn Soc, NY Acad Sci, Soc Head and Neck Surgeons, Asn Acad Surg, Am Clefts Palate Soc, Plastic Surg Research Coun, Chicago Soc Plastic Surg (secy 1979—81, vpres 1981—82), Am Soc Aesthetic Plastic Surg (secy 1979—82), Am Asn Plastic and Reconstructive Surg (trustee 1982—84), Am Soc Plastic and Reconstructive Surgeons (trustee 1981—84, historian 1982—84, vpres 1985—86, pres-elect 1986—87, pres 1987—88, bd dirs educ found), Touchdown Club Am (dir. 2002—), Union Club (New York City) (gov. 2002—), Williams Club. Home: 37 Carriage Ln New Canaan CT 06840-4401 Office: Columbia U Coll Physicians and Surgeons 161 Fort Washington Ave New York NY 10032-3713

HUGUENIN, NANCY HOFFMAN, behavioral psychologist; b. Franklin, Pa., May 12, 1947; d. Kelse Monjar and Eleanor (Jelken) Hoffman; m. Robert Louis Huguenin, June 21, 1969. BS in Psychology, U. Pitts., 1969; MA in Psychology, Boston U., 1971, PhD, 1978. Grad. tchg. fellow in psychology Boston U., 1969-74, psychology instr., 1972; rsch. assoc. Ednl. Rsch. unit Eunice Kennedy Shriver Ctr. for Mental Retardation, Inc., Waltham, Mass., 1977-80; postdoc-

toral fellow in applied behavior analysis R.I. Hosp., Providence, 1978-80; dir. Programmed Instrn. Lab., Grad. Sch. U. Mass., Amherst, 1980-85, staff assoc. Computing Ctr., 1980-81, staff assoc. Grad. Sch., 1981-85; behavioral psychologist Mental Retardation unit Coastal Cmty. Counseling Ctr., Hingham, Mass., 1985-87; behavioral psychologist Mental Retardation Clin. Team, South Shore Assn. for Retarded Citizens, Inc., Hingham, 1987-89; clin. supr. in psychology Walter E. Fernald State Sch., Waltham, Mass., 1989-93; pres. Behavior Analysis & Tech., Inc., Groton, Mass., 1993—. Adj. asst. prof. psychology U. Mass., 1980-87; referee Jour. Behavior Therapy and Exptl. Psychiatry, 1974-78, Rsch. in Developmental Disabilities, 1993; mem. Fernald Ctr. Human Rights Com., Fernald Ctr., Belmont, 1995—; behavioral cons. Monson Devel. Ctr., Palmer, Mass., 1981-85, Milton (Mass.) Pub. Schs., 1985, Greater Plymouth Assn. for Retarded Citizens, Kingston, 1989, South Shore Collaborative, Hingham, 1986-97, Bi County Collaborative, North Attleboro, Mass., 1993-98, Greater Waltham Assn. for Retarded Citizens, Waltham, 1995-97, Walpole Pub. Schs., 1995, South Norfolk County Assn. for Retarded Citizens, Westwood, Mass., 1995, Horace Mann Ednl. Assocs., Littleton, Mass., 1996, Hingham Pub. Schs., 1996-97, 2001, Hudson (Mass.) Pub. Schs., 1996, Assabet Valley Collaborative, Marlboro, 1996-2000, Boylston Pub. Schs., 1996-97, 99, Lighthouse Sch., Inc., Chelmsford, 1997-98, Charmss Collaborative, Randolph, Mass., 1999-2000, Inst. for Profl. Practice, Lunenberg, Mass., 1999-2000; behavior in-svc. trainer Work, Inc., North Quincy, Mass., 1997, 99-2000, South Shore Collaborative, Hingham, 1999, Kelleher Ctr., Arlington, Mass., 1999, Dr. Franklin Perkins Schj., Lancaster, Mass., 2002; ednl. cons. Judge Rotenberg Ednl. Ctr., Canton, Mass., 2000; workshop presenter Parents of Tots, Wakefield, Mass., 2001. Mem. editl. bd. Transitions in Mental Retardation, 1984-87; contbr. articles to profl. jours. including Jour. Exptl. Child Psychology, Jour. Exptl. Analysis of Behavior, Rsch. in Devel. Disabilities. Mem. APA, AAAS, Am. Assn. on Mental Retardation (psychology divsn. chairperson N.E. Region X 1983-86), Assn. for Behavior Analysis, Assn. for Advancement of Behavior Therapy, Am. Acad. on Mental Retardation, Eastern Psychol. Assn., Phi Beta Kappa, Psi Chi. Democrat. Avocations: singing, reading, walking, observing nature, traveling. Office: Behavior Analysis and Tech Inc PO Box 327 61 Long Hill Rd Groton MA 01450-1239

HUHEEY, MARILYN JANE, ophthalmologist, educator; b. Cin., Aug. 31, 1935; d. George Mercer and Mary Jane (Weaver) H. BS in Math., Ohio U., Athens, 1958; MS in Physiology, U. Okla., 1966; MD, U. Ky., 1970. Diplomate Am. Bd. Ophthalmology. Tchr. math. James Ford Rhodes H.S., Cleve., 1956-58; biostatistician Nat. Jewish Hosp., Denver, 1958-60; life sci. engr. Stanley Aviation Corp., Denver, 1960-63, N.Am. Aviation Co., L.A., 1963-67; intern U. Ky. Hosp., 1970-71; emergency room physician Jewish Hosp., Mercy Hosp., Bethesda Hosp., Cin., 1971-72; ship's doctor, 1972, resident in ophthalmology Ohio State U. Hosp., Columbus, 1972-75; practice medicine specializing in ophthalmology Columbus, 1975—. Mem. staff Univ. Hosp., Grant Hosp., St. Anthony Hosp., 1975-79; clin. asst. prof. Ohio State U. Med. Sch., 1976—, dir. course ophthalmologic receptionist/aides, 1976; mem. Peer Rev. Sys. Bd., 1986-92, exec. com., 1988-92; mem. Ohio Optical Dispensers Bd., 1986-91; bd. dirs. Ctrl. Ohio Radio Reading Svc., 1997—; mem. Ohio Bd. Cosmetology, 1999—. Dem. candidate for Ohio Senate, 1982; mem. Wicked Investment Club, 1998—, pres. 1999—. Fellow Am. Acad. Ophthalmology, mem. AAUP, Am. Assn. Ophthalmologists, Ohio Ophthalmol. Soc. (bd. govs. 1984-89, del. to Ohio State Med. Assn. 1984-88), Franklin County Acad. Medicine (profl. rels. com. 1979-82, legis. com. 1981-89, edn. and program com. 1981-88, chmn. 1982-85, chmn. cmty. rels. com. 1987-90, chmn. resolution com. 1987-92, mem. fin. com. 1988-92), Ohio Soc. Prevent Blindness (chmn. med. adv. bd. 1978-80), Ohio State Med. Assn. (dr.-nurse liaison com. 1983-87), Columbus EENT Soc., Am. Coun. of the Blind (bd. dirs. 1995-96), Life Care Alliance (pres. sustaining bd. 1987-88), United Way (planning com. 1992-93), LWV, Columbus Coun. World Affairs, Columbus Bus. and Profl. Women's Club, Columbus C. of C., Grandview Area Bus. Assn., Federated Dem. Women Ohio, Columbus Area Women's Polit. Caucus, Columbus Met. Club (forum com. 1982-85, fundraising com. 1983-84, chmn. 10th anniversary com. 1986), Mercedes Benz Club (dir. 1981-83), Zonta (program com. 1984-86, chmn. internat. com. 1983), Herb Soc., Phi Mu. Home: 2396 Northwest Blvd Columbus OH 43221-3829 Office: 1335 Dublin Rd Ste 25A Columbus OH 43215-1000

HUHN, RICHARD DALE, physician; b. Washington, Sept. 3, 1953; s. Richard Howard and Ruthmae (Brundage) H.; m. Margaret Zinkand, Mar. 21, 1980; children: Jessica Anne, Richard Andrew, Robert Christopher. BS in Chemistry magna cum laude, BS in Biology, Am. Univ., 1976; MD, U. Md., Balt., 1980. Diplomate Nat. Bd. Med. Examiners, Am. Bd. Internal Medicine, hematology subspeciality, Am. Bd. Clin. Pharmacology. Resident medicine Med. Sch. Brown U., Providence, 1980-83, fellow clin. pharm. med., 1985-88; staff physician Cleve. Dept. Health Welfare, 1983-85; asst. mem. St. Jude Children's Rsch. Hosp., Memphis, 1988-90; asst. med. dir. Sandoz Pharm. Co., East Hanover, N.J., 1990-92; asst. prof. medicine & clin. pharmacology U. Medicine & Dentistry N.J.-Robert Wood Johnson Med. Sch., New Brunswick, 1992-96, acting. dir. Clin. Rsch. Ctr., 1995-96; staff fellow hematology br. Nat. Heart Lung Blood Inst./NIH, 1996-98; med. dir. G.D. Searle & Co., 1998-99; assoc. prof. Coriell Inst. Med. Rsch., 1999—. Mem. sci. rev. bd. Cancer Inst. N.J., New Brunswick, 1994-96; presenter in field. Contbr. numerous articles to profl. jours. Recipient Clin. Investigator award NIH/NCI, 1990, Faculty Devel. award PhRMA, 1993. Mem. ACS, Am. Soc. Hematology, Nat. Assn. Scholars, Am. Fedn. Clin. Rsch., Am. Soc. Clin. Pharmacology & Therapeutics, Internat. Soc. Exptl. Hematology, Internat. Soc. Hematotherapy & Graft Engring., Am. Assn. Blood Banks, Phila. Coll. Physicians. Avocations: woodworking, carpentry, gourmet cooking. Home: 42 Mile Dr Chester NJ 07930-2803 Office: Coriell Inst for Med Rsch 403 Haddon Ave Camden NJ 08103 E-mail: huhnr@att.net.

HUHNKE, JR. BILLY GENE, music educator; b. Worland, Wyo., Sept. 23, 1955; s. Billy Gene Huhnke, Sr. and Sharon Lee Fech; children: Spencer David Huhnke, Stephen Carl Huhnke, Jessika Mari Huhnke, Nikolas Thomas Huhnke. MusB in Edn., U. of Wyo., 1974—78; MusM in Conducting, U. of Utah, 1990—91. Cert. tchr. Utah State Bd. Edn., 2002. Dir. of bands Lyman Pub. Schools, Wyo., 1978—83, Pk. City Sch. Dist., Park City, Utah, 1983—. Pres., bldg. rep. Pk. City Edn. Assn., Utah, 1987—95; v.p. Utah Assn. of Jazz Educators, 1997—98; v.p. of jazz Utah Music Edn. Assn., 1995—96; chapperne, asst. dir., performer Utah Ambassadors of Music Europe, 2001—01. Founding bd. mem. Pk. City Teen Ctr.; mem. Salt Lake Symphonic Winds, 1993—2000, Dem. State Legislature Campaign, Utah, Pk. City Performing Arts Found., 1995—2002, Jazz Arts of the Mountain West, Utah, 1996—2002, Pk. City Internat. Jazz Festival. Na NA. Recipient Utah Rural Schools Music Tchr. of the Yr., Utah Rural Schools Assn., 1989. Mem.: Nat. Band Assn., Utah Band Assn., Intenational Assn. of Jazz Educators, Utah Asociation of Jazz Educators, Music Educators Nat. Conf. (MENC), Utah Music Educators Assn. (UMEA) (v.p. jazz 1996—97), NEA, Utah Edn. Assn., Pk. City Edn. Assn. (pres., bldg. reprentative 1987—96). Independent. Avocations: traveling, reading, fly fishing, skiing, rollerblading, music. Home: PO Box 67 Park City UT 84060 Office: Park City School District 2700 Kearns Blvd Park City UT 84060 Personal E-mail: bhuhnke@darnfastnet.com. E-mail: bhuhnke@parkcity.k12.ut.us.

HUHS, JOHN I. international lawyer; b. Galveston, Tex., Sept. 18, 1944; s. Roy E. and Martha Mae (Hansen) H.; m. Vivian C. Swindley, 1970 (div. 1978). BA, U. Wash., 1966; MBA, JD, Stanford U., 1970. Bar: N.Y. 1971, D.C. 1981. Internat. cons. Satra Cons. Corp., N.Y.C., 1970-73; sr. staff White House Office Mgmt. & Budget Nat. Security, Internat. Affairs, Washington, 1974-75; ptnr. Pisar & Huhs, N.Y.C., 1976-84; sr. v.p., gen. counsel Tendler, Beretz Assocs., Ltd., N.Y.C., 1985-87; pvt. practice N.Y.C., 1987-88; ptnr., chmn. internat. dept. LeBoeuf, Lamb, Greene & MacRae, N.Y.C., 1989—. Prin. Ctr. for Excellence in Govt., 1984—99. Contbr. articles on internat. law, bus. and fin. to profl. jours.; comment editor Stanford Law Rev., 1967-69. Mem. bd. visitors Stanford Law Sch., 1996-98. Mem.: ABA (chmn. com. on Soviet and Ea. European law 1982—85, chmn. com. internat. comml. trans. 1985—90, coun. sect. internat. law and practice 1988—92, rep. to Union Internat. Avocats 1991—94), D.C. Bar Assn., N.Y. State Bar Assn. (chmn. internat. investment devel. com. 1987—91), Assn. of Bar of City of N.Y. (internat. trade com. 1987—89, com. Newly Ind. States of former Soviet Union 1989—2000), 175 E. 74th Corp. (pres.), Univ. Club N.Y.C., Order of Coif. Home: 175 E 74th St New York NY 10021-3218 Office: LeBoeuf Lamb Greene MacRae 125 W 55th St New York NY 10019-5369 E-mail: jhuhs@llgm.com.

HUI, DAFENG, ecologist, statistician; b. Fengxian, Jiangsu, China, Dec. 26, 1964; m. Yin Liu, Oct. 26, 1968; 1 child, Lucy Ya. PhD, U. of Okla., 2002. Lectr. Yangzhou U., 1984—2001; postdoctoral rsch. assoc. U. of Okla., Norman, 2002—. Author: (book) Practical Statistical Analysis System (SAS) Usage; contbr. scientific papers to profl. jours. Recipient 2d Class Achievements award of science and tech. improvement, Ministry of Edn. of China, 1999, 2d Class award of course constrn. in biometry and quantitative genetics, Jiangsu Province Edn. Com., China, 1997. Mem.: Am. Geog. Union, Ecol. Soc. of Am. Office: U Okla 770 Van Vleet Oval Norman OK 73019

HUI, ERIC KA-WAI, virologist, researcher; b. Hong Kong, Nov. 27, 1968; s. Chung Hung Hui and Li Hing Cheng; m. Ya-Ju Lo, Nov. 13, 1972. PhD, Nat. Yang Ming U., Taiwan, ROC, 1999; MSc, Fu Jen Cath. U., 1992, BSc, 1990. Postdoctoral rschr. Dept. microbiology, immunology and molecular genetics, UCLA Sch. of Medicine, Calif., 1999—. Rsch. asst. Dept. Pharmacology, Chang Gung U., Tao Yuan, Taiwan, Taiwan, 1992—93. Author (freelance writer): (popular scientific mag.) Movies magnifier (Life Sciences in Movies). Recipient Outstanding Rsch. Article award, Liver Disease Prevention & Treatment Rsch. Found., 1999, Outstanding Poster Presentation Award, Yang Ming Acad. Symposium, 1999. Mem.: Soc. of Chinese Bioscientists in Am., The Am. Soc. for Microbiology (wash. dc, usa 1994), The Am. Soc. for Cell Biology (wash. dc, usa 1994), The Am. Soc. for Virology (assoc.). Achievements include research in Virus particle formation and virus maturation. Home: Rm 3105 Sui Ming House Chai Wan Hong Kong Hong Kong Office: UCLA Sch of Medicine 10833 Le Conte Ave Los Angeles CA 90095-1747 Office Fax: 310-206-3865. Personal E-mail: ekwhui@yahoo.com.hk. E-mail: ekwhui@ucla.edu.

HUI, HO-WAH, pharmaceutical scientist; b. Hong Kong, June 20, 1957; came to U.S., 1976; s. Ching-Choi and Choy-Hing (Yong) H.; m. Julia Ying Chow, July 24, 1982; children: Jessica, Joanna. BS in Pharmacy with distinction, U. Wis., 1980, MS in Pharmaceutics, 1983, PhD in pharmaceutics, 1985. Registered pharmacist. Intern in pharmacy Madison (Wis.) Gen. Hosp., 1980-81; teaching asst. pharmacy U. Wis., Madison, 1981-83, research asst. pharmacy, 1983-85; rsch. pharmacist Abbott Labs., North Chicago, Ill., 1985-87; also bd. seminar com. Abbott Labs, North Chicago, Ill.; sr. rsch. scientist Abbott Labs., North Chicago, Ill., 1987-91, rsch. investigator, 1991-94, assoc. rsch. fellow vol. soc., 1994—. Chmn. Exploratory Projects Discussion, Abbott Labs., 1988. Author: Oral Drug Products, 1987; contbr. articles to profl. jours. Counsellor, dir. Awana Youth Club, Vernon Hills/Highland Park, Ill., 1987—; pres. Madison Chinese Christian Fellowship, 1984, bd. dirs. exec. com., 1982-83; steering com. Chinese Christian Union. Ch., Chgo., 1986—, trustee, 1992—. Recipient Merck Sharp and Dohme scholarship U. Wis., 1984. Mem. Am. Pharm. Assn., Am. Assn. Pharm. Scientists (chmn. pharmaceutics and drug delivery publicity 1995, 96, chmn. drug delivery program 1990-91), Chicagoland Pharm. Discussion Group (chmn. membership com. 1993-96, program com. 1996-2002, chmn. 2003-), Lake County Chinese Am. Assn. (pres. 1994-95, bd. dirs. 1995-98), Far East Broadcasting Co.-Chgo. (chmn. bd. dirs. 1997-2001). Avocations: swimming, table tennis, playing violin, singing.

HUIBERTS, PIETER J. development chemist; b. Woerden, Utrecht, The Netherlands, Nov. 20, 1971; arrived in U.S., 1998; s. Dirk Huiberts and Marianne Huiberts-Klok. BSc in Biochemistry, Hogeschool, West-Brabant, Etten-Leur, The Netherlands, 1998. Cert. safe microbiologic techniques. Intern FMC BioProducts, Rockland, Maine, 1997-98; analytical chemist Biowhittaker Molecular Applications, Rockland, 1999, devel. chemist Walkersville, Md., 2000—02, rsch. chemist, database specialist, 2002, Cambrex Biosci. Walkersville Inc., 2002—. Home: #402 160C Willowdale Dr Frederick MD 21702 Office: Cambrex Biosci Walkersville Inc 8830 Biggs Ford Rd Walkersville MD 21793 Office Fax: 301-845-4868. E-mail: phuiberts@yahoo.com., piet.huiberts@cambrex.com.

HUIE, CAROL P. information systems educator; b. Kingston, Jamaica; AAS, Hostos Community Coll., N.Y.C., 1986; BSc, Lehman Coll., N.Y.C., 1988; MS, CCNY, 1994; postgrad., CUNY, 1994—99, Nova Southeastern U., 2001—. Patient acct.coord. New Rochelle Med. Ctr., New Rochelle, NY, 1988-91; coll. lab tech. Hostos Community Coll., Bronx, NY, 1991-98, instr., 1994—2000, asst. professor, 2000—. Dean's list, Hostos Community Coll., 1986. Mem.: IEEE, Assn. Computing Machinery, Schomburg Ctr. Rsch. Black Culture, Consortium for Computing in Small Colls., Delta Pi Epsilon. E-mail: tennishuie@aol.com.

HUIE, GEORGETTE LYNN, social services administrator; b. San Francisco, Apr. 22, 1951; d. George and Isabel (Chin) H. BS in Math., Calif. State U., Hayward, 1973, MS in Math., 1976; postgrad., McCormick Theol. Sem., Chgo., 1998—2002. K-adult tchg. credential, Calif. Lectr. math. U. San Francisco, 1977-78, San Francisco State U., 1978-79; sys. engr. IBM, San Francisco, 1979-92, sales specialist, 1993-97; urban ministry resident Center City Chs., Hartford, Conn., 2002—. Moderator Presbytery of San Francisco, Berkeley, Calif., 1990; mem. exec. com., bd. dirs. Nat. Coun. Chs., N.Y.C., 1992-95; sec., bd. dirs. San Francisco Food Bank, 1994-99; vice chmn., chmn. bd. dirs. Presbyn. Ch. (U.S.A.) Found., Jeffersonville, Ind., 1997; bd. dirs. New Covenant Trust Co. Recipient cert. of recognition Calif. Senate, 1991. Democrat. Avocations: golf, music. Office: Center City Chs Inc 40 Pratt St Ste 210 Hartford CT 06103-1601

HUIE, ROBERT ELLIOTT, research chemist; b. Atlanta, Jan. 24, 1945; s. Robert Elliott Huie and Margaret (Haddon) Wigley; m. Yee Yin Au, Aug. 3, 1973 (div. Sept. 1988); children: Robert Elliott, Amanda May, Jessica Lai; m. Gilda Borbe, June 18, 1996. BA, Macalester Coll., 1966; PhD, U. Md., 1972. Rsch. chemist Nat. Inst. Stds. and Tech., Gaithersburg, Md., 1967-96, group leader, 1996—. Vis. scientist phys. chemistry dept. Cambridge (Eng.) U., 1975-76; conf. chair Internat. Conf. Chem. Kinetics, 1993, 97, 2001; commn. mem. Internat. Union of Pure and Applied Chemistry, 2000-01; com. mem. NASA Panel Data Evaluation. Contbr. over 165 articles to profl. jour.; assoc. editor Internat. Jour. Chem. Kinetics, 1997—. Mem. Am. Chem. Soc., Am. Geophys. Union, Sigma Xi. E-mail: robert.huie@nist.gov.

HUIE, ROLAND EUGENE, JR., director, music educator; b. Mobile, Ala., Feb. 26, 1956; s. Roland Eugene Huie Sr. and Martha Kathryn Atchison; m. Melody Ann Collins, June 9, 1979; children: Roland Eugene III, Patrick Lloyd. MusB in Edn., U. So. Miss., 1978, MusM in Edn., 1979. Cert. tchr. La., 1979. Band dir. St. Bernard Parish Schs., La., 1979—82, dir. bands, 1982—90, St. Tammany Parish Schs., Slidell, 1990—94, Mandeville, 1994—. Site chmn. St. Tammany Parish Honor Band, Mandeville, 1990—90, 1998—98, 2001—02, 2002—; co-chmn. La. Music Educators Dist. Honor Band, Hammond, 1994—; mentor tchr. St. Tammany Parish Schs., 1996—. Performer Musical Arts Assn., Slidell, 1990—93, Mandeville Cmty. Band, 1995—99, Northshore Big Band, Slidell, 1994—98, St. Timothy United Meth. Orch., Mandeville, 1994—2002, St. Timothy Brass Choir, 2001—02, 1st Bapt. Ch. of Mandeville Orch., 1996—2002. Mem.: La. Bandmasters Assn. (assoc.), Assn. of Dirs. (assoc.), La. Music Educators Assn. (assoc.), Music Educators Nat. Conf. (assoc.), Sigma Phi Epsilon (life), Kappa Kappa Psi (life). R-Consevative. Home: 305 Concord Dr Mandeville LA 70471 Office: Fontainebleau High Sch 100 Bulldog Dr Mandeville LA 70471 Personal E-mail: huies@bellsouth.net. E-mail: rehfhs@stpsb.k12.la.us.

HUITT, JIMMIE L. rancher, oil, gas, real estate investor; b. Gurdon, Ark., Aug. 21, 1923; s. John Wesley and Almedia (Hatten) H.; m. Janis C. Mann, Oct. 30, 1945; children— Jimmie L., Jr., Allan Jerome BS in Chem. Engring., La. Tech. U., 1944; MS in Chem. Engring., U. Okla., 1948, PhD, 1951. Research engr. Mobil Oil Corp., Dallas, 1951-56, Gulf Research Co., Pitts., 1956-67; ops. coordinator Kuwait Oil Co., London, 1967-71; gen. mgr. Gulf Oil-Zaire, Kinshasa, 1971-74; mng. dir. Gulf Oil-Nigeria, Lagos, 1974-76; sr. v.p., exec. v.p. Gulf Oil Exploration and Prodn. Co., Houston, 1976-81, pres., 1981-85; rancher Four Jays Ranch, Industry, Tex., 1986—. Contbr. articles to profl. jours.; patentee in field Served to 1st lt. U.S. Army, 1944-47 Mem. Soc. Petroleum Engrs. (chmn. various coms. 1956—), Masons, Shriners. Republican. Office: Four Jays Ranch PO Box 236 Industry TX 78944-0236

HUIZENGA, GEORGIANA R. public library director, storyteller; b. Painesville, Ohio, Aug. 11, 1945; d. George Blair and Mildred Louise (Cone) Sheers; m. Keith Garrett Huizenga Jr., Aug. 12, 1967; children: Jennifer Lynn, Andrew Blair. BA, Bowling Green State U., 1967. Libr. assoc. Bowling Green (Ohio) State U., 1967-68; ref. libr. Wood County Pub. Libr., Northwood, Ohio, 1970-80, br. libr., 1980-93; libr. dir. Harris-Elmore (Ohio) Pub. Libr., 1993—. Columnist: (book rev.) Suburban Press newspaper, 1981-84; author numerous poems. Sec., charter mem. Woodmore Acad. Boosters, Elmore, 1994-97, v.p., 1999-2000, pres., 2000-01; pres. Ch. Coun., Elmore, 1985, 98; mem. Prin. Comm. Team, Elmore, 1993-98, Cmty. Woodmore H.S., Elmore, 1994, 95, mem. supts. adv. com., 2001; mem. governance bd. SEO. Mem. ALA, Ohio Libr. Coun. (membership com. 1995-98, small librs. divsn.), Ohio Pub. Libr. Info. Network (libr. issues task force 1994-96), Elmore Study Club (pres. 1997-98), Pride n' Joy Mother's Club (pres. 1979-80, 94-95), Elmore Kiwanis (treas. 2000-01, pres. 2002—). Democrat. United Ch. of Christ. Avocations: reading, storytelling, public speaking, writing, volunteering. Home: 16020 W Portage River South Rd Elmore OH 43416-9710 Office: Harris-Elmore Pub Libr PO Box 45 328 Toledo St Elmore OH 43416 E-mail: Huizenge@oplin.lib.oh.us.

HUIZENGA, H. WAYNE, entrepreneur, professional sports team executive; b. Evergreen Park, Ill., Dec. 29, 1939; s. G. Harry and Jean (Riddering) Huizenga; m. Martha Jean Pike, Apr. 17, 1972; children: H. Wayne Jr., H. Scott, Ray, Pamela Ann. Student, Calvin Coll., 1957-58. Vice chmn., pres., chief operating officer Waste Mgmt. Inc., Oak Brook, Ill., 1968-84; chmn. Huizenga Holdings, Inc., Ft. Lauderdale, Fla., 1984—; chmn., chief exec. officer Blockbuster Entertainment Corp., Ft. Lauderdale, 1987-94; owner Florida Marlins, Miami, 1992-99, Fla. Panthers, Sunrise, Fla., 1993—; chmn. Boca Resorts, Inc., Boca Raton, Fla., 1996—, AutoNation Inc., Ft. Lauderdale, 1999—. Owner Miami Dolphins and Pro Player; chmn. AutoNation, 1994—, Boca Resorts, Inc., Republic Svcs., Extended Stay Am. Mem. Fla. Victory Com., 1988-89, Team Repub. Nat. Com., Washington, 1988-90; organizer Broward Victory 90 PAC, Ft. Lauderdale, 1989-90. Recipient Entrepreneur of Yr. award Wharton Sch. U. Pa., 1989, Excalibur Award Bus. Leader of Yr. News/Sun Sentinel, 1990, Silver Medallion Brotherhood award Broward Region Nat. Conf. Christians and Jews, 1990, Laureates award Jr. Achievement Broward and Palm Beach Counties, 1990, Jim Murphy Humanitarian Award The Emerald Soc., 1990, Entrepreneur of Yr. award Disting. Panel Judges Fla., 1990, Man of Yr. Billboard/Time Mag., 1990, Man of Yr. Juvenile Diabetes Found., 1990, Fla. Free Enterpriser of Yr. award Fla. Coun. on Econ. Edn., 1990, commendation for youth restricted video State of Fla. Office of Gov., 1989, Hon. Mem. Appreciation award Bond Club Ft. Lauderdale, 1989; honored with endowed teaching chair Broward Community Coll., 1990. Mem. Lauderdale Yacht Club, Tournament Players Club, Fisher Island Club, Ocean Reef Club, Cat Cay Yacht Club, Coral ridge Country Club, Linville Ridge Country Club. Avocations: golf, collecting antique cars. Office: Huizenga Holdings 450 E Las Olas Blvd Ste 1500 Fort Lauderdale FL 33301-4212

HUIZENGA, JOHN ROBERT, nuclear chemist, educator; b. Fulton, Ill., Apr. 21, 1921; s. Harry M. and Josie B. (Brands) H.; m. Dorothy J. Koeze, Feb. 1, 1946; children: Linda J., Jann H., Robert J., Joel T. AB, Calvin Coll., 1944; PhD, U. Ill., 1949. Lab. supr. Manhattan Wartime Project, Oak Ridge, 1944-46; instr. Calvin Coll., Grand Rapids, Mich., 1946-47; assoc. scientist Argonne Nat. Lab., Chgo., 1949-57, sr. scientist, 1958-67; professorial lectr. chemistry U. Chgo., 1963-67; prof. chemistry and physics U. Rochester, 1967-78, Tracy H. Harris prof. chemistry and physics, 1978-91, Tracy H. Harris prof. emeritus chemistry and physics, 1991—, chmn. dept. chemistry, 1983-88. Vis. prof. Joliot-Curie Lab., U. Paris, 1964-65, Japan Soc. for Promotion of Sci., 1968; chmn. Nat. Acad. Sci.-NRC Com. on Nuclear Sci., 1974-77; mem. energy rsch. adv. bd. Dept. Energy, 1984-90; numerous adv., vis. coms. to univs., govt. and nat. labs. Author: (with R. Vandenbosch) Nuclear Fission, 1973; (with W.U. Schröder) Damped Nuclear Reactions, 1984; Cold Fusion: The Scientific Fiasco of the Century, 1992; contbr. articles to profl. jours. Fulbright fellow Netherlands, 1954-55; Guggenheim fellow Paris, 1964-65; Guggenheim fellow Berkeley, Calif., 1973; Guggenheim fellow Munich, W.Ger., 1974; Guggenheim fellow Copenhagen, 1974; recipient E.O. Lawrence award AEC, 1966, Leroy Rundle Grumman medal, 1991; named Disting. Alumnus Calvin Coll., 1975 Fellow AAAS, Am. Phys. Soc., Am. Acad. Arts and Scis.; mem. NAS (chmn. NAS-NRC com. on nuclear and radiochemistry 1988-91), Am. Chem. Soc. (award for nuclear applications in chemistry 1975), Phi Beta Kappa, Sigma Xi, Phi Kappa Phi. Home: 43 McMichael Dr Pinehurst NC 28374-6702

HUJSAK, RUTH JOY, musician, educator; b. Buffalo, May 13, 1924; d. Frederic Cecil and Elfrieda (Fell) Detenbeck; m. Edward Josef Hujsak, June 27, 1953; children: Michael Kim, Jonathan Todd. MusB, U. Rochester, 1945. Cert. piano tchr. Instr. piano, organ, theory Marion (Va.) Coll., 1945-46; pianist Miss. State U. for Women, Columbus, 1946-47; pvt. music studio, concert work Kenmore, N.Y., 1947-53; lectr. harp U. Calif. San Diego, La Jolla, 1968-95; instr. harp San Diego State U., 1970-84; lectr. harp Point Loma Nazarene U., San Diego, 1977-95; instr. harp U. San Diego, 1980-84. Fellow Ctr. Mus. Experiment, U. Calif., San Diego, 1974; bd. dirs. Friends of Music, 1990—; propr. Mina-Helwig Co., 1976—; CEO Perigee West Co., 1989-95. Composer harp music, 1975—; contbr. articles to mags. Mem. music com. La Jolla Presbyn. Ch., 1980-92, also elder; past v.p. Cmty Music Sch. Buffalo. Recipient scholarship Schmitz Sch. Piano, 1948. Mem. Musicians Assn. San Diego, Chromatic Club Buffalo (life, pres. 1950), Mus. Merit Soc. San Diego (bd. dirs.), Am. Harp Soc. (chmn. religious music com., pres. San Diego chpt.), World Harp Congress. Sigma Alpha Iota (life). Republican. Avocations: reading, cooking, health foods. Home: 8732 Nottingham Pl La Jolla CA 92037-2128

HUKEL, DENNIS RANDALL, industrial designer, translator; b. Fullerton, Calif., Sept. 21, 1952; s. Ramon E. and Wanda Laverne Hukel; m. Susan Ellen Dietrich; children: Rebecca Michelle, David Michael. Diploma, Criss Bus. Coll., Anaheim, Calif., 1972. Piping designer Fluor Corp., Irvine, 1973—82; drafter, designer Irvine Ranch Water Dist., 1984—2000; trans., proofreader Lockman Found., La Habra, Calif., 1997—; design technician Berryman & Henigar, Santa Ana, Calif., 2000—. Vol. cons. Concordant Publ. Concern, Santa Clarita, Calif. Author: Perpetual Calendar, 1972; author, editor Morphological Dictionary of G.N.T. Nouns, 1992. Mem.: Internat. Orgn. Septuagint and Cognate Studies, Am. Philol. Assn., Soc. Biblical Lit. Avocations: Indo-European linguistics, history, sociology. Home: 400 S Flower St # 89 Orange CA 92868 Office: Berryman & Henigar 2001 E 1st St Santa Ana CA 92705 E-mail: hukel@bhiinc.com.

HUKINS-RODRIGUE, DANA ANN, community health nurse; b. Raceland, La., Nov. 1, 1964; d. Herman Cecil and Diana Ann (Chiasson) H. BSN, Nicholls State U., Thibodaux, La., 1986. RN LA. Nurse II, staff pediatrics nurse South La. Med. Ctr., Houma, 1986-88; nurse, pub. health nurse III Lafourche Parish Health Unit, Thibodaux, 1988—. Mem. Nicholls State U. Nursing Honor Soc., Sigma Theta Tau (Xi Zeta chpt.).

HULA, KEVIN WILLIAM, political scientist, educator; b. Topeka, Apr. 1, 1965; s. Harold Lloyd and Anna Marie Hula; m. Susan Joyce Hula, July 30, 1994; children: Megan Joyce, Brennan William, Keanan Robert. BA, U. Kans., 1987; AM, Harvard U., 1991, PhD, 1995. Asst. prof. polit. sci. Loyola Coll., Balt., 1994-2000, assoc. prof. polit. sci., 2000—. Author: Lobbying Together: Interest Group Coalitions in Legislative Politics, 1999; abridger (textbook) Challenge of Democracy, 2000, 5th edit., 2003; contbr. (book) Interest Group Politics, 4th edit., 1995, Interest Group Connection, 2d edit., 2003. Advisor InterVarsity Christian Fellowship, Balt., 1995—. Jacob K. Javits fellow U.S. Dept. of Edn., 1987-91, Rsch. fellow The Brookings Inst., Washington, 1992-93; Newman scholar Loyola Coll., Balt., 2000—. Mem. Am. Polit. Sci. Assn. (Emerging Scholar for Yr. 2000), Internat. Studies Assn. (web editor Intelligence Studies sect. 2000—), Midwest Polit. Sci. Assn., So. Polit. Sci. Assn. Presbyterian. Office: Loyola Coll Md 4501 N Charles St Baltimore MD 21210

HULBERT, LINDA ANN, academic librarian; b. Racine, Wis., Nov. 10, 1947; d. David and Ruth (Alk) H.; m. A. Kent Rissman, Dec. 1, 1991; m. Shelley B. Plattner, Aug. 24, 1969 (div. 1976). BA, Washington U., St. Louis, 1969; MLS, U. Iowa, Iowa City, 1973; MA in Pub. Adminstrn., St. Louis U., 1993. Sch. librarian Parkway Sch. Dist., St. Louis, 1969-70, Mehlville Sch. Dist., St. Louis,

1970-71; adj. lectr. in libr. science Syracuse U., 1985; med. ref. libr. U. Iowa Health Scis. Ctr., Iowa City, 1973-77; collection devel. librarian SUNY, Health Scis. Ctr., Syracuse, 1977-87; asst. dir. tech. svcs. St. Louis U., 1988-98; dir. tech. and access svcs. So. Ill. U., Edwardsville, 1998—2002; assoc. dir. tech. svc. U. St. Thomas, St. Paul, 2002—. Cons. in field. Mem. ALA, N.Am. Serials Interest Group, Med. Libr. Assn. (membership com. 1980-83), St. Louis Med. Libraries (chair 1984-86). Avocations: downhill skiing, biking, walking, reading. Office: O'Shaugnessy Frey Libr U St Thomas 2115 Summit Ave St Paul MN 55105 Home: 6801 Telemark Trail Edina MN 55436

HULBERT, PAUL WILLIAM, JR., paper, lumber company executive; b. Washington, June 21, 1944; s. Paul William and Charlotte Mary (Johnson) Hulbert; m. Katherine Bren, Aug. 10, 1985; children: Paul William III, Jennifer Linda, Brian. BA in History, Denison U., 1966; MBA, U. Mich., 1971. Contr. Wickes Land Devel., Saginaw, Mich., 1969—71; mng. dir. Wickes Europe, The Hague, Netherlands, 1971—75; v.p. corp. devel. Wickes Corp., San Diego, 1975—77; sr. v.p., gen. mgr. Wickes Lumber, Saginaw, 1978—80; sr. v.p., group officer Wickes Cos., Inc., San Diego, 1980—82, Sequoia Supply, Irvine, Calif., 1982—85; pres. Sequoia Supply Divsn. Wickes Corp., Irvine, Calif., 1985—86; pres. Sequoia Supply, Inc., Irvine, 1987—89, Prime Source, Inc., Dallas, 1990—. Avocations: sports, coaching youth sports, golf. Office: Prime Source Inc PH#: 972-417-3701 1800 John Connally Dr Ph 4173701 Carrollton TX 75006-5403

HULBERT, RICHARD WOODWARD, lawyer; b. Cambridge, Mass., Sept. 24, 1929; s. Woodward Dennis and Clifford (Halliday) H.; m. Dorothy Marie Hanni, Apr. 21,1954; children: Jonathan, Ann, Laura, Mary. AB, Harvard U., 1951, LLB, 1955. Bar: N.Y. 1956. Assoc. Cleary, Gottlieb, Steen & Hamilton, N.Y.C., 1955-65, ptnr., 1966-83, 89-96, Paris, 1983-89, mng. ptnr. N.Y.C., 1979-84, of counsel, 1997—. Lectr. in law U. Calif., Berkeley, 1988; adj. prof. NYU Law Sch., 1990—; vice chmn. internat. ct. arbitration Internat. C. of C., 1994-99. Trustee Bklyn. Mus., 1992—, Bklyn. Bot. Garden, 1982-98, 99—; mem. Internat. C. of C. Commn. Internat. Arbitration, 2001—. Sheldon fellow in history Harvard U., 1951-52 Mem. ABA, N.Y. Bar Assn., Assn. of Bar of City of N.Y., Bklyn. Bar Assn., N.Y. County Lawyers Assn., Am. Law Inst., Century Assn., India House, Heights Casino. Democrat. Home: 141 Henry St Brooklyn NY 11201-2501 Office: Cleary Gottlieb et al 1 Liberty Plz New York NY 10006-1470 E-mail: rhulbert@cgsh.com.

HULBERT, SAMUEL FOSTER, college president; b. Adams Center, N.Y., Apr. 12, 1936; s. Foster David and Wilma May (Speakman) H.; m. Joy Elinor Husband, Sept. 3, 1960; children: Gregory, Samantha, Jeffrey. BS in Ceramic Engring., Alfred U., 1958, PhD, 1964. Registered profl. engr., La, S.C. Asst. varsity and freshman football coach Alfred U. (N.Y.), 1959—61; lab. instr. N.Y. State Coll. Ceramics, Alfred, 1958—59; instr. math and physics Alfred U., 1960—64; asst. prof. ceramic and metall. engring. Clemson U. (S.C.), 1964—68, head divsn. interdisciplinary studies, assoc. prof. materials and bioengring., 1968—71; assoc. dean engring research and interdisciplinary studies, prof. materials engring. and bioengring., dir. materials engring. and bioengring., 1970—73; prof. bioengring., dean Sch. Engring. Tulane U., New Orleans, 1973—76; pres.-designate spl. asst. to pres. Rose-Hulman Inst. Tech., Terre Haute, Ind., 1976, pres., 1976—. Bd. dirs. Ind. Bus. Modernization & Tech. Corp., Thomas & Skinner, Inc., Old Nat. Bank, Interactive Intelligence, Inc., Centerfield Capital Ptnrs. Mem. editorial bd. Jour. Biomed. Materials Rsch., 1970—, Interactive Intelligence, 2001-; contbr. articles in field of biomaterials and artificial organ design to profl. jours. Recipient medal Italian Soc. Orthopaedics, 1973, Delitala medal Instituto Ortopedico Rizzoli, 1973, Clemson award for outstanding contbns. to biomaterials, 1973, George Winters award European Soc. Biomaterials, 1982, Founder's award Soc. Biomaterials, 2001, Lifetime Achievement award Ind. Health Industry Forum, 1996, Ernst & Young Supporter of Indiana Entrepreneurship award, 1998, Chapman S. Root award Hospice of the Wabash Valley, 2000. Fellow Am. Inst. for Med. and Biol. Engring., Am. Biomaterials Scis. and Engring., Internat. Acad. Ceramics; mem. Am. Soc. Artificial Internal Organs, Biomed. Engring. Soc., Soc. Biomaterials (dir. 1974—, pres. 1975-76, founder's award 2001, William C. Hall award 2001), Am. Ceramic Soc., Nat. Inst. Ceramics Engrs., Am. Soc. Engring. Edn., Ind. Colls. and Univ. Assn., Ind. Colls. of Ind., Ind. Conf. Higher Edn., Assn. Ind. Tech. Univs. (sec., treas. 1977-78, pres. 1987-90), Presidents of Ind. Colls. and Univs., Vigo County Hist. Soc. (dir. 1979—, pres. 1995—), Keramos, Blue Key, Ind. Acad., Internat. Acad. Ceramics, Rotary, Sigma Xi. Republican. Office: Rose Hulman Inst Tech Office of Pres 5500 Wabash Ave Terre Haute IN 47803-3999

HULBERT, STEPHEN THOMPSON, academic administrator; BS in Edn., Worcester (Mass.) State Coll., 1966; MEd, U. Mass., Amherst, 1968; DEd, SUNY, Albany, 1972. Dir. student activities and residence life Western New England Coll., Springfield, Mass., 1968-70; cons. Univ. Assocs. Inc., Washington, 1971-72; exec. asst. to the pres. Mansfield (Pa.) U., 1972-77; v.p. for fin. and adminstrn. Slippery Rock (Pa.) U., 1977-88; v.p. adminstrv. svcs., treas. bd. trustees U. Northern Colo., Greeley, 1988-91, interim pres., 1991, sr. v.p., 1992-94, provost, v.p. for acad. affairs, 1994-96; commr. higher edn., CEO R.I. Bd. of Govs. for Higher Edn., Providence, 1996-99; chancellor U. Mont.-Western, Dillon, 1999—2003; pres. Nichols (La.) State U., 2003—. Govs. cabinet State of R.I. and Providence Plantations; mem. R.I. Juvenile Justice Oversight Commn. Mcpl. coun. Grove City, Pa., 1986-88; adv. bd. Franklin Regional Hosp., Franklin, Pa., 1985-88; mem. exec. bd. Longs Peak coun. Boy Scouts Am., 1991-96, disting. citizen com. chair, 1992, others; mayor's adv. task force City of Greeley, 1992-96, U. No. Colo. Found., Inc., 1991-96, R.I. Children's Crusade for Higher Edn., 1996-99, U. of No. Colo. Rsch. Corp., Inc., 1988-96, chair 1994-96, vice chair 1992-94, corp. treas. 1988-92; steering com. Edn. Comms., 1988—99; bd. govs. Colo. Alliance for Sci., 1995-96. Mem. Am. Assn. for Higher Edn., Nat. Assn. Intercollegiate Athletics (coun. pres.), Frontier Athletic Conf. (chair coun. pres. 2000-03), Phi Delta Kappa. Home: 906 E 1st St Thibodaux LA 70301 Office: Nicholls State U PO Box 2001 Thibodaux LA 70310 Fax: 985-448-4003. E-mail: pres-sth@nicholls.edu.

HULBURT, LUCILLE HALL, artist, educator; b. Portland, Oreg., Oct. 31, 1924; d. Allen Bergen and Agnes Edna (Davis) Hall; m. Frank Theodore Hulburt, Nov. 28, 1943; children: Robert, Carol Davalos, Clarke. Grad. h.s., Whitefish, Mont. Asst. milliner, illustrator Hat Co., N.Y.C., 1944; cafe owner, operator San Diego, 1950—52; profl. artist Vancouver, Wash., 1978—; resident artist Artist's Gallery 21, Vancouver, 1988—. Tchr. children and adult art clases, schs. and home studio, Vancouver, 1978—; artist in residence Wash. State Arts Commn., 1987-88; co-founder, coop. Artists Gallery 21, Vancouver, 1988—; cons. nat. Western Art Show and Auction, Trails West, Vancouver; organizer, com. mem. ann. Summer Art at the Ctr., Vancouver, 1986; judge/jurist art exhibits at county fairs, western art shows various locations in Wash. and Oreg., 1980—. Founder, pres. Boundary Assn. Retarded Children, Bonners Ferry, Idaho, 1964-65; com. mem. 1st Bldg. Com., Columbia Arts Ctr., Vancouver, 1980-81; bd. mem. Local Arts Promotion, Vancouver, 1992, 93. Recipient Best of Show award Western Art Show and Auction, Chinook, Mont., 1983, 84, Community Svc. award Arts Coun., Clark County, Wash., 1988, Windsor-Newton award Watercolor 91, 1991. Mem. S.W. Wash. Watercolor Soc. (co-founder, pres. 1979, 80, 84), Soc. Washington Artists (Grumbacher Silver medal 1990), Am. Artists Profl. League, Order Ea. Star (life), N.W. Watercolor Soc. Avocations: gardening, sewing, swimming. Office: Hulburt Studio 5515 NE 58th St Vancouver WA 98661-2146

HULDEEN, GERALD ALVIN, retired music educator; b. Ida Grove, Iowa, Apr. 23, 1935; s. Alvin Reuben and Florence A. Huldeen; m. Mabel Helen Huldeen, Aug. 5, 1956; children: Kirk, Kala, Jay. B Mus. Edn., Morningside Coll., Sioux City, Iowa, 1956; MMus, State U. S.D., 1963. Cert. tchr., Iowa. Band dir. Panora (Iowa) Cmty. Schs., 1956-59, Sioux Valley Cmty. Schs., Peterson, Iowa, 1959-64, Manning (Iowa) Cmty. Schs., 1964-75; ins. rep. Horace Mann Educators, Springfield, Ill., 1975-77; music tchr., band dir. Sioux City (Iowa) Cmty. Schs., 1977-95; ednl. rep. Mid-Bell Music Co., Sioux City, 1995-99. Adjudicator Iowa H.S. Music Assn., Boone, 1974—, Nebr. Music Edn., Elkhorn, Nebr., 1979—; instrumental music curriculum chair Sioux City Cmty. Sch., 1993-94. County del. Dem. party, Carroll, Iowa, 1976; v.p. Iowa QRP Radio Assn., Des Moines, 1998—; bd. dirs. Sooland Amateur Radio Assn., Sioux City, Iowa, 1997, 99—; vis. chmn. Mended Hearts, chpt. 41, Sioux City, 1998-02, pres. Mended Hearts, 2002—. Named Tchr. of Yr., Manning Jaycees, 1974. Mem. Iowa Band Masters Assn., N.W. Iowa Bandmasters (Ret. Band Master award 1998). Democrat. Lutheran. Avocations: amateur radio, bicycling. Home: 2909 S Olive St Sioux City IA 51106-4229 E-mail: WB0T@arrl.net.

HULING, TIMOTHY OLIVER, composer, educator; b. Santa Barbara, Calif., Aug. 27, 1976; s. Patricia Ruth and Rodney Craig Huling. MusB, Berklee Coll. Of Music, 1995—98. Orchestrator Hummie Mann's Visaje Music, Inc, Mercer Island, Wash., 1999—; prof. Bellevue C.C., Wash., 2000—. Composer AUDISEE Sound and Music, Seattle, 1999—2001; core faculty mem. Pacific N.W. Film Scoring Program, Seattle, 2000—; tchr. Music Works N.W., Bellevue. Orchestrator (imax film) Cyberworld, 3D, (film) PT Barnum; composer: (films) Behind Barbed Wire, Shag Carpet Sunset. Mem.: Seattle Composers Alliance. Home: 600 N 85th St #306 Seattle WA 98103 Office: Visaje Music Inc 8403 SE 53rd Pl Mercer Island WA 98040 Personal E-mail: thuling27@attbi.com.

HULKA, BARBARA SORENSON, epidemiologist, educator; b. Mpls., Mar. 1, 1931; d. Herbert Fritchof and Mable (Alquist) Sorenson; m. Jaroslav Fabian Hulka, Nov. 13, 1954; children: Carol Ann, Gregory Fabian, Bryan Herbert. BS, Radcliffe Coll., 1952; MS, Juilliard Sch. Music, 1954; MD, Columbia U., 1959, MPH, 1961. Diplomate Am. Bd. Preventive Medicine, lic. physician Pa., N.C. Research asst. prof. U. Pitts., 1966—67; asst. prof. U. N.C., Chapel Hill, 1967—71, assoc. prof., 1972—76, prof., 1977—, chmn. dept. epidemiology, 1983—93, Kenan prof., 1987—. Adj. prof. medicine Duke U. Med. Ctr., Durham, NC, 1982—; chair epidemiology and disease study sect., 1981—83, NIH, 1979—80; mem. Endpoint Rev. Safety Monitoring and Adv. Com. Breast Cancer Prevention Trial, Nat. Surg. Adjuvant Breast and Bowel Project, 1992—98; bd. sci. counselors Nat. Cancer Inst., 1980—94; mem. Inst. of Medicine com. toxic shock syndrome, NAS, 1981—82; mem. Sci. Rev. and Evaluation Bd. subcom. VA, 1983—85; mem. subcom. on long-term effects of short-term exposure to chem. agts. NAS, 1985; mem. preventive medicine and pub. health test com. Nat. Bd. Med. Examiners, 1985—88; mem. consensus conf. on smokeless tobacco Nat. Cancer Inst. Panel, 1986; mem. WHO Task Force on Safety and Efficacy of Fertility Regulating Methods, 1989—96; counsellor Internat. Soc. for Environ. Epidemiology, 1990—91; mem. Pres.' Cancer Panel Spl. Commn. on Breast Cancer, Nat. Cancer Inst., 1992—93; mem. bd. scientific counselors divsn. cancer etiology Nat. Cancer Inst., NIH, 1992—94; chair WHO steering com. of task force Epidemiologic rsch. in reproductive health, WHO, 1989—96; mem. steering com. for collaborative group on hormonal factors in breast cancer Oxford (Eng.) U., 1997—; mem. WHO Sci. and Tech. ADv. Group Human Reprodn. Program, Geneva, 1997—; mem. nat. sci. panel to the fed. jud. on silicone breast implants, 1996—99; mem. Nat. Adv. Environ. Health Scis. Coun. for Nat. Inst. Environ. Health Scis., 1998—2001. Mem. editl. bd.: Postgrad. Medicine, 1985—87, assoc. editor: Cancer Epidemiology, Biomarkers and Prevention, 1995—97; contbr. chapters to books, articles to profl. jours. Bd. dirs. Am. Cancer Soc., 1993—96. Recipient Disting. Achievement award, Am. Soc. Prevention Oncology, 1991; fellow travel study fellow, WHO, 1978; grantee, Health Resources Adminstrn., 1975—77, tng. grantee in cancer epidemiology, Nat. Cancer Inst., 1980—, prostate cancer grantee, 1983—85. Fellow: Royal Soc. Medicine; mem.: NAS (Inst. Medicine 1988, mem. com. crossroads nuc. test 1994—96, mem. commn. antiprogestins 1992—93, mem. com. passive smoking 1985—86, mem. Bd. on Environ. Studies and Toxicology/BEST 1997—, mem. commn. on life scis. nat. rsch. coun. 1998—2001), APHA (governing coun. 1976—78, chmn. epidemiol. sect. 1976—77), Am. Coll. Preventive Medicine (bd. regents 1986), N.C. Pub. Health Assn. (stats. and epidemiology sect. 1975, award for excellence), Am. Epidemiol. Soc., Soc. Epidemiol. Rsch. (pres. 1975—76, exec. com. 1973—77), Am. Coll. Epidemiology (Abraham Lilienfield award 1994), Delta Omega. Home: 2317 Honeysuckle Dr Chapel Hill NC 27514 Office: U NC Sch Pub Health Dept Epidemiol CB 7400 2104 E Mcgavran Chapel Hill NC 27599-0001

HULKA, JAROSLAV FABIAN, obstetrician, gynecologist; b. N.Y.C., Sept. 29, 1930; s. Jaroslav Hugo and Milada (Touskova) H.; m. Barbara E. Sorenson, Nov. 13, 1954; children— Carol Ann, Gregory Fabian, Bryan Herbert. BA, Harvard U., 1952; MD, Columbia U., 1956. Diplomate: Am. Bd. Ob-Gyn. Intern Roosevelt Hosp., N.Y.C., 1956-57; resident Sloane Hosp. for Women, Columbia-Presbyn. Med. Center, N.Y.C., 1957-60; Josiah Macy, Jr. fellow Columbia-Presbyn. Med. Center, 1960-61; practice medicine specializing in Ob-Gyn, 1961—; asst. prof. Ob-Gyn U. Pitts. Sch. Medicine, 1961-66, asso. mem. grad. faculty, 1962-66, acting chmn. dept. Ob-Gyn, 1963-64; asso. prof. dept. Ob-Gyn Sch. Medicine, U. N.C., Chapel Hill, 1967-76, prof. dept. Ob-Gyn and dept. maternal and child health, 1976-96. Author: Textbook of Laparoscopy, 1985, 3d edit., 1997; patentee in field. Assoc. dir. Carolina Population Center, 1967-74. Recipient Excel award Soc. of Laparoendoscopic Surgeons, 1994. Fellow ACOG; mem. Soc. for Gynecol. Investigation, Am. Assn. Gynecol. Laparoscopists (pres. 1980), Am. Fertility Soc., Soc. Reproductive Surgeons (founding), N.C. State Bar (bd. legal specialization 1990-96), Planned Parenthood Fed. Am. (chair nat. med. com. 1991-94), Soc. Physicians for Reproductive Choice and Health (founding). Achievements include development of and teaching of worldwide use of clips for female sterilization by laparoscopy; demonstration of local anesthesia for safer procedures. Home: 2317 Honeysuckle Rd Chapel Hill NC 27514-1716 Office: Population Ctr 123 W Franklin St Chapel Hill NC 27516-2524 E-mail: jhulka@unc.edu.

HULL, BRETT A. hockey player; b. Belleville, Ont., Can., Aug. 9, 1964; s. Bobby Hull. Student, U. Minn., Duluth, 1984-86. Profl. hockey player Calgary Flames, 1986—88; with St. Louis Blues, 1988—96; forward Dallas Stars, 1999—2001, Detroit Red Wings, 2001—. Player NHL All-Star Team, 1989—94, AHL All-Star 1st Team, 1986—87, NHL All-Star 1st Team, 1989—90, 1991—92. Named NHL Player of Yr., The Sporting News, 1989—90, 1991—92, All-Star Game MVP, 1992; recipient Lady Byng Meml. Trophy, 1989, 1990, Hart Meml. Trophy, 1990—91, Freshman of Yr. award, WCHA, 1984—85, Dudley Garrett Meml. Trophy, 1986—87, Dodge Ram Tough award, 1989—90, 1990—91, Lester B. Pearson award, 1990—91, Pro Set NHL Player of Yr. award, 1990—91. Achievements include Leader in Goals Scores, NHL, 1989-92; Stanley Cup Champions, Dallas Stars, 1999, Detroit Red Wings, 2002. Office: Detroit Red Wings Joe Louis Arena 600 Civic Center Detroit MI 48226

HULL, CATHY, artist, illustrator; b. N.Y.C., Nov. 4, 1946; d. Max H. and Magda M. (Stern) H.; m. Neil S. Janovic; 1 child, Julie. BA, Conn. Coll., 1968; cert., Sch. Visual Arts, N.Y.C., 1970. Instr. illustration and portfolio Sch. Visual Arts, N.Y.C., 1983-94, Parsons Sch. Design, N.Y.C., 1994—. Juror The 6th World Cartoon Gallery, Skopje, 1974, Soc. Pub. Designers, N.Y.C., 1982, Soc. Illustrators, N.Y.C., 1983, The Biennale of Humor, Fredrikstad, Norway, 1987, The 6th Internat. Simavi Cartoon Competition, Istanbul, Turkey, 1988; mem. exec. bd. Friends of H.S. of Art and Design. Contbr. to anthologies, books, mags. and newspapers including Time, Penthouse, Newsweek, Esquire, Playboy, MSNBC, Fortune, Wall Street Jour., Washington Post, Forbes, Chgo. Tribune, Ency. Brit., Disney, Sports Illustrated, N.Y. Times, Bus. Week, Travel and Leisure, Money, others; group shows include The 17th Nat. Print Exhbn., Bklyn., 1970, AIGA Show, N.Y.C., 1970-71, 74, Printing Industries Am., 1971, Soc. Illustrators, 1973, 80, 85, 94, 2001, World Cartoon Gallery, Skopje, 1972-75, Art Dir.'s Club, 1974, 82, Internat. Cartoon Exhbn., Istanbul, Turkey, 1974, Switzerland, 1974, 78, 80, 82, 90, Athens, Greece, 1975, Soc. Publ. Designers, 1974, 82, Musée de Beaubourg, Paris, 1977, Pacific Design Ctr., L.A., 1980, The Md. Inst., 1981, Scottsdale (Ariz.) Ctr. for Arts, 1981, Soc. Newspaper Design, 1984-85, Butler Inst. Am. Art, Youngstown, Ohio, 1983, Am. Peace Poster Exhibit, 1985, Quebec City Exhbn., Society of Illustrators, 2002; represented in permanent collections including Mus. Caricatures and Cartoons, Basel, Switzerland, Soc. Illustrators Advt. Ann. show, Smithtown Twp. Arts Coun.; designer playing cards sold at Cooper Hewitt Mus., N.Y., N.Y. Pub. Libr., L.A. County Mus. Art, St. Louis Art Mus., Chgo. Mus. Art, Nat. Mus. Scotland, Seibu, Japan, Contemporary Mus. of Honolulu, Contemporary Mus. San Diego, High Mus. Atlanta, Meml. Exhbn., Mus. Am. Illustration, 2002, Herbert F. Johnson Mus. of Art, 2002, Cornell U., Karikatur and Cartoon Mus., Basel, Switzerland, 2003. Exec. bd. Friends of the H.S. Art and Design, 2002—. Office: 180 E 79th St New York NY 10021-0437 E-mail: cmhull@aol.com.

HULL, CHARLES WILLIAM, retired special education educator; b. East St. Louis, Ill., Feb. 23, 1936; s. William Semple Hull and Jessie Marie (Brennan) Poole; m. Beverly Kay Julian, Aug. 19, 1967; 1 child, William Kenneth. BA in Econs., Cen. Meth. Coll., 1964; MEd, Olivet Nazarene Coll., 1974; AA (hon.), Joliet Jr. Coll., 1987. Tchr. elem. grades Taft Sch., Lockport, Ill., 1965-67; tchr. spl. edn. S.W. Cook County Coop. Assn. for Spl. Edn., Oak Forest, Ill., 1967-99; ret., 1999. Permanent exhibits include Tchr's Ret. Office Bldg., Springfield, Ill. Past bd. dirs., v.p., chmn. fund raising Easter Seals Will and Grundy Counties; dist. leader Am. Cancer Soc., 1984, residential campaign chmn., 1985; vol., mem. adv. bd. Big Bros.-Big Sisters Will County; Cub Scouts com. chmn. Boy Scouts Am., 1980-81, commr. Rainbow coun., bd. dirs. troop 61; choir, past trustee Faith United Meth. Ch.; Will County walkathon chmn. March of Dimes, 1979; chmn. Canal Days events Will County Hist. Soc., 1987; mem. Nat. Trust for Hist. Preservation, Lockport Area Geneal. Hist. Soc.; bd. dirs. Joliet Project Pride, Will County Project Pride, 2000-03; life mem. Friends of Ill. and Mich. Canal. Cpl. USMC, 1955-58. Recipient Congl. Medal of Merit, 1985, Frederick Bartleson Meml. award Will County Hist. Soc., 1985, Citizen of Week award Sta. WBBM, Chgo., 1985, Leadership award Am. Cancer Soc., 1985, Outstanding Svc. award Big Bros.-Big Sisters Will County, letter of commendation Pres. of U.S., 1986, 89, Disting. Svc. award Joliet Jr. Coll., 1987, Citizen of Month award Southtown Economist, plaque KC; inducted into Joliet/Will County Hall of Pride, 2002. Mem. 1st Marine Divsn. Assn., Coalition for Citizens with Disabilities in Ill. (life), Will County Old-Timers Baseball Assn., Am. Legion, Masons (32 degree), Shriners (pres. Joliet club 1983, Shriner of Yr. 1989), KC, Medina Temple, Cumberland Scottish Rite Club, Lions (pres. Manhattan club 1984, chmn. youth and fgn. exch. dist. 1986-87, bd. dirs. Lockport chpt.), Will County Hist. Soc. (pres. 1989), Joliet Area Ret. Tchrs. Assn., Ill. Ret. Tchrs. Assn., Pleasant Hill Hist. Soc., Royal Order Scotland. Republican. Methodist. Home: PO Box 429 Pleasant Hill TN 38578

HULL, CORDELL WILLIAM, business executive; b. Dayton, Ohio, Sept. 12, 1933; s. Murel George and Julia (Barto) H.; m. Susan G. Ruder, May 10, 1958; children: Bradford W., Pamela H., Andrew R. B.E., U. Dayton, 1956; MS, MIT, 1957; JD, Harvard U., 1962. Bar: Ohio 1962; Registered profl. engr., Mass. Atty. Taft, Stettinius & Hollister, Cin., 1962-64, C & I Girdler, Cin., 1964-66; gen. counsel, treas., pres. C&I Girdler, Internat., Brussels, 1966-70; v.p. Bechtel Overseas Corp., San Francisco, 1970-73; pres., dir. Am. Express Mcht. Bank, London, 1973-75; v.p., treas. Bechtel Corp. and Bechtel Power, San Francisco, 1975-80; pres. Bechtel Fin. Services, San Francisco, 1975-82; v.p., chief fin. officer Bechtel Group Inc., 1980-85; pres. Bechtel Power Corp., 1987-89, dir.; chmn. Bechtel Enterprises, 1990-95. Bd. dirs. Fremont Group, Inc., Darby Overseas Ltd., Gilead Scis.; chmn. Audit Comm.; bd. dirs. Gilead Scis.; dir. Fed. Res. Bank San Francisco, 1988—90. Mem. Knickerbocker Club, Pacific Union Club, Menlo Country Club. also: 400 Oyster Point Blvd Ste 410 South San Francisco CA 94080

HULL, DAVID GEORGE, aerospace engineering educator, researcher; b. Oak Park, Ill., Mar. 27, 1937; s. John Lawrence Hull and Elizabeth Christine (Carstensen) Meyer; m. Meredith Lynn Kiesel, June 2, 1962 (div. July 1980); children: David, Andrew, Matthew; m. Vicki Jan Poole, June 30, 1983; children: Katherine, Emily. BS, Purdue U., 1959; MS, U. Wash., 1962; PhD, Rice U., 1967. Staff assoc. Boeing Sci. Research Labs., Seattle, 1959-64; research assoc. Rice U., Houston, 1964-66; asst. prof. U. Tex., Austin, 1966-71, assoc. prof., 1971-77, prof., 1977-85, M.J. Thompson Regents prof., 1985—. Cons. several aerospace cos. Assoc. editor 2 jours.; reviewer several engring. jours.; contbr. more than 55 articles to profl. jours. Recipient/co-recipient more than 50 grants and contracts; recipient award Best paper, AAS/AIAA Space Flt. Mechanics Conf., Albuquerque, 1995. Mem. AIAA (assoc. fellow, atmospheric flight mechanics tech. com. 1974-77, guidance and control tech. com. 1984-87), AAS (sr. mem.), Delta Tau Delta (treas. Purdue U. 1958-59). Office: U Tex ASE/EM C0600 Austin TX 78712-0235

HULL, DENNIS JACQUES, counselor; b. Orange, N.J., June 8, 1945; s. Jacques Lionel and Ora May (Holdman) H.; m. Elizabeth Ann Martin, Sept. 7, 1969; 1 child, Jonathan. BA in Psychology, Calif. State Univ., Hayward, 1968, MS in Counseling, 1975. Cert. counselor Nat. Bd. Cert. Counselors, Inc. Counselor L.A. Harbor Coll., Wilmington, Calif., 1979-84, Western Nev. C.C., Carson City, 1984-86, coord. counseling svcs., 1987-94, dir. counseling svcs., 1994—. With USAF, 1968-72. Mem. Am. Counseling Assn., Calif. Assn. Counseling Devel., Calif. C.C. Counselors Assn. (bd. dirs., so. conf. chair 1983-84). Office: Western Nev Cmty Coll 2201 W College Pkwy Carson City NV 89703-7316

HULL, DWIGHT SIGWORTH, II, engineer; b. Des Moines, Dec. 18, 1943; s. Dwight Sigworth Sr. and Betty (Carlson) H.; m. Judith Ann Miller, Dec. 23, 1966; children: Andrew, Emily. BS in Fire Protection and Safety Engring, Ill. Inst. Tech., 1966; MBA, Wayne State U., 1972. Registered profl. engr. Tenn. Asst. mgr. Mich. Insp. Bur., Detroit, 1966-72; chief engr. Frank B. Hall & Co., Detroit, 1972-76; coord. fire protection and security Tenn. Valley Authority div. Power Prodn., Chattanooga, 1976—. Mem. Mayor's Engring. Adv. Coun., chattanooga, 1982—; advisor Chattanooga State Tech. U., 1985—. 1st lt. C.E., U.S. Army, 1966-69, Vietnam. Mem. Am. Soc. Safety Engrs. (profl.), Nat. Fire Protection Assn., Soc. Fire Protection Engrs. (chpt. pres., v.p.). Methodist. Avocations: golf, antique restoration. Home and Office: 10528 Aspen Ridge Ln Knoxville TN 37932-1555 E-mail: w-dshfpe2@bellsouth.net.

HULL, EDMUND J. ambassador; b. Keokuk, Iowa, Dec. 1949; married; 2 children. Diploma with honors, Princeton U.; postgrad. in strategic issues with Sir Michael Howard, Oxford U., 1986—87. Numerous positions including dir. No. Gulf Affairs during the Gulf War; dep. chief of mission and charge d'Affaires U.S. Embassy, Cairo, 1993—96; former dir. Office of Peacekeeing; former acting coord. for counterterroism U.S. Dept. of State; U.S. amb. to Yemen, 2001—. Vol. Peace Corps, Tunisia, 1971—73. Recipient Meritorious Honor award, Superior Honor awards, U.S. Dept. of State, Baker-Wilkins award, 1995. Office: DOS Amb 6330 Sanaa Pl Washington DC 20521*

HULL, ELAINE MANGELSDORF, psychology educator; b. Houston, Aug. 15, 1940; d. Paul August and Mary Eleanor (Stephens) Mangelsdorf; m. Richard Thompson Hull, May 30, 1962; 1 child, Geoffrey Alaric (dec.). BA, Austin Coll., Sherman, Tex., 1963; PhD, Ind. U., 1967. Asst. prof. psychology SUNY, Buffalo, 1967-73, assoc. prof., 1973-86, prof., 1986—, dir. biopsychology grad. program, 1986—. Author: Study Guide to Accompany Kalat's Biological Psychology, 1981, 2000; contbr. Recipient Chancellor's award for excellence in teaching SUNY, Buffalo, 1975, award for teaching SUNY Students Assn., 1986, N.Y. State Union of Univ. Profls. Excellence award 1990. Mem. APA, AAAS, Soc. for Neurosci., Internat. Soc. for Psychoneuroendocrinology, N.Y. Acad. Scis. Democrat. Avocations: jogging, classical music. E-mail: emhull@buffalo.edu.

HULL, ELIZABETH ANNE, retired English language educator; b. Upper Darby, Pa., Jan. 10, 1937; d. Frederick Bossart and Elizabeth (Schmik) H.; m. Dean Carlyle Beery, Feb. 5, 1955 (div. 1962); children: Catherine Doria Beery Pizarro, Barbara Phyllis Beery Wintczak; m. Frederik Pohl, July 1984. Student, Ill. State U., 1954-55; AA, Wilbur Wright Jr. Coll., Chgo., 1965; B in Philosophy, Northwestern U., 1968; MA, Loyola U., Chgo., 1970, PhD, 1975. Teaching asst. Loyola U., Chgo., 1968-71; prof. English, coord. honors program William Rainey Harper Coll., Palatine, Ill., 1971-2001; ret., 2001. Judge nat. writing competition Nat. Coun. Tchrs. of English, 1975—, John W. Campbell award, 1986—. Co-editor: (with F. Pohl) Tales from the Planet Earth; contbr. articles to profl. jours. Pres. Lexington Green Condominium Assn., Schaumburg, Ill., 1982-84; bd. dirs. Hunting Ridge Homeowner's Assn., Palatine, 1984-86; Dem. candidate for U.S. Ho. of Reps. for 8th Congl. Dist. Ill., 1996; bd. dirs. N.W. Cmty. Hosp. Aux., 2001—; steering com. Constituency on Vols. Ill. Hosp. Assn., 2001—. Recipient Northwestern U. Alumni award for Merit, 1995, Thomas Clareson award Sci. Fictin Rsch. Assn., 1998, Excellence award Nat. Inst. for Staff and Orgnl. Devel., 1998. Mem. MLA, Midwest MLA, Popular Culture Assn., Sci. Fiction Rsch. Assn. (editor 1981-84, sec. 1987-88, pres. 1989-90), Ill. Coll. English Assn. (pres. 1975-77), World Sci. Fiction Assn. (N.Am. sec. 1978—, pres. Honors coun. Ill. region 1992-93), Palatine Area LWV (bd. dirs. 1991—, v.p. 1995-96, pres. 1998-2000), Am. Assn. for Women in C.C. (v.p. comm., bd. dirs. Harper Coll. chpt. 1993-96). Home: 855 Harvard Dr Palatine IL 60067-7026

HULL, FRANK MAYS, federal judge; b. Augusta, Ga., Dec. 9, 1948; d. James M. Hull Jr. and Frank (Mays) Pride; m. Antonin Aeck, Apr. 16, 1977; children: Richard Hull Aeck, Molly Hull Aeck. AB, Randolph-Macon Women's Coll., 1970; JD cum laude, Emory U., 1973. Bar: Ga. 1973, U.S. Ct. Appeals (5th cir.) 1973, U.S. Dist. Ct. (no. dist.) Ga. 1974, U.S. Ct. Appeals (11th cir.) 1982. Law clk. to Hon. Elbert P. Tuttle U.S. Ct. Appeals (5th cir.), Atlanta, 1973—74; assoc. Powell, Goldstein, Frazer & Murphy, Atlanta, 1974—80, ptnr., 1980—84; judge State Ct. Fulton County, Atlanta, 1984—90, Superior Ct. Fulton County, Atlanta, 1990—94, U.S. Dist. Ct. (no. dist.) Ga., 1994—97, U.S. Ct. Appeals (11th cir.), 1997—. Mem. commn. on family violence State of Ga., 1992—94, commn. on gender bias in jud. sys., 1988—90. Mem. Leadership Atlanta, 1986—, program co-chair criminal justice com., 1988—89; Sunday sch. tchr. Cathedral St. Philip, Atlanta, 1983—88, children's com., 1981—82, outreach com., 1989—91; bd. dirs. Met. Atlanta Mediation Ctr., Inc., 1976—79, Atlanta Vol. Lawyers Assn., 1988—91. Fellow, AAUW, 1973—. Mem.: ABA (fin. sec. long range planning com. tort and ins. practice sect. 1979—82, chmn. contract documents divsn., forum com. on constrn. industry 1983—85, edtl. staff jour. 1981—85, vice chmn. fidelity and surety law com. 1978—85), Nat. Assn. Women Judges, Ga. Assn. Women Lawyers, Atlanta Bar Assn., Am. Judicature Soc. (bd. dirs. 1990—96), Ga. Bar Assn., Order of Coif. Office: US Ct of Appeals 56 Forsyth St NWRm 300 Atlanta GA 30303-2289

HULL, FREDERICK ALBERT, artist; b. Norfolk, Va., July 27, 1931; s. William Barr and Velma Beatrice Hull; m. Joan Arnold, Aug. 4, 1956; children: Frederick William, Christopher John. BA in Art, Calif. State U., Sacramento, 1971, MPA, 1977. Chief of design dept. Reed & Reese Corp., Pasadena, Calif., 1961—63; asst. br. chief graphic br. 323 Flying Tng. Wing, Mather AFB, Calif., 1963—72; art and prodn. editor The Navigator mag. Dept Air Force, Mather AFB, Calif., 1972—87; syndicated cartoonist Adventure Features Syndicate newspapers, Glendale, Calif., 1976—90; instr. journalism Calif. State U., Sacramento, 1981; dir., writer, artist Hull Features Syndicate, Am. Internat. Features, Calif. and Mo., 1991—95; sr. signature artist, master painter No. Calif. Artists Inc., Carmichael, 1995—; also bd. dirs. No. Calif. Artists Inc. NCA, Carmichael. Designer, publ. asst. dir. Calif. State Mil. Mus., Sacramento, 1982-92; mem. art show and promotion bds. Sacramento Fine Art Ctr., Carmichael, 1997—. Maj. U.S. Army, 1954-56, with Calif. State Mil. Reserve, 1982-96. Recipient numerous nat. and internat. juried show awards for oil painting. Mem.: Sigma Delta Chi, Phi Kappa Tau. Avocations: sailing, bike riding, jogging, weightlifting, woodworking. Home: 2512 G St Sacramento CA 95816

HULL, GRAFTON HAZARD, JR., social work educator; b. Great Bend, Kans., Nov. 24, 1943; s. Grafton H. and Mary Kathryn (Hagerty) H.; m. Jannah Mather; children: Michael, Patrick, Robert Hurn, Jacob Hurn. BS, U. Wis., Madison, 1967; MSW, Fla. State U., 1969; EdD, U. S.D., 1979. Social worker Cen. State Hosp., Milledgeville, Ga., 1969; chief social work sect. Mental Hygiene Cons. Svc., Ft. Knox, Ky., 1969-71; social worker, then social work supr. Manitowoc County Dept. Social Svc., Manitowoc, Ky., 1971-74; asst. prof., chair dept. sociology Morningside Coll., Sioux City, Iowa, 1974-79; assoc. prof., chair dept. social welfare U. Wis., Whitewater, 1979-82, prof., chair dept., 1982-88, prof., chair dept. social work Eau Claire, 1988-93; dir. Sch. Social Work S.W. Mo. State U., Springfield, 1993-96; dir. divsn social work Ind. Univ. NW, Gary, 1996-2000; dir. BSW program U. Utah, Salt Lake City, 2000—. Site visitor Coun. Social Work Edn., Washington, 1981—, cons. in field. Co-author: The Generalist Model of Human Services Practice, Understanding Generalist Practice, Building the Undergraduate Social Work Library, Case Studies in Generalist Practice, Generalist Practice with Organizations and Communities, The Macro Skills Workbook; cons. editor Jour. Social Work Edn., 1989-95, Aretê, 1993—, Advances in Social Work, 2000—, Jour. Baccalaureate Social Work, 2002-; contbr. articles to profl. jours. Bd. dirs. Gary Neighborhood Svcs.; mem. Hoosier Boys Town Pub. Policy com.; chmn. Landmarks Commn., Whitewater, 1982-88; city councilman, mem. Planning and Architecture Rev. Commn., City of Whitewater, 1987-88. Capt. U.S. Army, 1969-71. Recipient Wis. Social Work Educator of Yr., 1991, City of Whitewater Hist. Preservation award, 1988, Outstanding Svc. award U. Wis.-Eau Claire, 1993, Outstanding Social Worker award Ind. House of Reps., 1999. Mem. NASW (chair west ctrl. Wis. br. 1989-91), Baccalaureate Program Dirs. Assn. (pres. 1991-93), Coun. Social Work Edn. (commn. on accreditation 1987-93, bd. dirs. 1993-96), Wis. Coun. Social Work Edn. (pres. 1984-91), Inst. Advancement Social Work Rsch. (sec.-treas. 1993-95), Mo. Consortium of Social Work Edn. Programs (pres. 1995-96), Ind. Assn. for Social Work Edn. (exec. com. 1999-2000). Democrat. Avocations: travel, writing. Home: 2781 E Amberwick Ln Sandy UT 84093 Office: U Utah Sch Social Work Salt Lake City UT 84112 E-mail: GHull@socwk.utah.edu.

HULL, GRETCHEN GAEBELEIN, lay worker, writer, lecturer; b. Bklyn., Feb. 5, 1930; d. Frank Ely and Dorothy Laura (Medd) Gaebelein; m. Philip Glasgow Hull, Oct. 24, 1952; children: Jeffrey R., Sanford D., Meredyth Hull Smith. BA magna cum laude, Bryn Mawr Coll., 1950; postgrad., Columbia U., 1950-52; DLitt (hon.), Houghton Coll., 1995. Major presenter Internat. Coun. on Bibl. Inerrancy, Chgo., 1986; guest lectr. London Inst. on Contemporary Christianity, 1988; lectr. at large Christians for Bibl. Equality, St. Paul, 1988-2000; major presenter Presbyn. Ch. (U.S.A.) Nat. Abortion Dialogue, Kansas City, Mo., 1989; disting. scholar lectr. Thomas F. Staley Found., Stony Brook, N.Y., 1991. Elder Presbyn. Ch. (U.S.A.); mem. Madison Ave. Presbyn. Ch., N.Y.C.; vis. prof. Regent Coll., Vancouver, B.C., 1992. Author: Equal to Serve, 1987; (with others) Women, Authority and the Bible, 1986, Applying the Scriptures, 1987, Study Bible for Women (New Testament), 1996, The Global God, 1998, The Gospel with Extra Salt, 2000, The IVP Women's Bible Commentary, 2002; editor Priscilla Papers, 1989-99; contbg. editor Perspectives, 1992—; mem. edtl. bd. Prism, 1994—; contbr. articles to religious mags. Trustee Cold Spring Harbor Village Improvement Soc., 1966-69, Soc. of St. Johnland, Kings Park, N.Y., 1972-75. Mem. Woman's Union Missionary Soc. Am. (bd. dirs. 1954-71), Presbyns. United for Bibl. Concerns (bd. dirs. 1973-75), L.I. Presbytery (gen. coun. 1981-83), Christians for Bibl. Equality (bd. dirs. 1987-94), Latin Am. Mission (trustee 1989-95), Evangelicals for Social Action (bd. dirs. 1991-99, 2001—), Network Presbyn. Women in Leadership (steering com. 1994-98), Presbyns. for Renewal (bd. dirs. 1994-2000). Home and Office: 63 Meadow Lakes Hightstown NJ 08520

HULL, HERBERT MITCHELL, plant physiologist, researcher; b. La Jolla, Calif., Aug. 19, 1919; s. Daniel Ray and Emma (Kammeyer) H.; m. Mary Randall Mattison, Mar. 4, 1950; children: Laurinda Lee, Daniel James. AA, Pasadena City Coll., 1939; BS, U. Calif., Berkeley, 1946; PhD, Calif. Inst. Tech., 1951. Research fellow Calif. Inst. Tech., 1949-52; plant physiologist U.S. Dept. Agr., Tucson, 1952-78; prof. renewable natural resources U. Ariz., 1966-85, prof. emeritus, 1985—. Served as meteorologist and pilot USAAF, 1941-46. Fellow AAAS, Ariz.-Nev. Acad. Sci.; mem. Am. Soc. Plant Biologists, Bot. Soc. Am., Sigma Xi, Alpha Zeta. Presbyterian. Home: 4040 W Sweetwater Dr Tucson AZ 85745-9757

HULL, J(AMES) RICHARD, retired lawyer, business executive; b. Keokuk, Iowa, Dec. 5, 1933; s. James Robert and Alberta Margaret (Bouseman) H.; m. Patricia M. Kiesner, June 14, 1958; children— Elizabeth Ann Hull Whims, James Robert, David Glen. BA, Ill. Wesleyan U., 1955; JD, Northwestern U., 1958. Bar: Ill. 1958, Fla. 1978. V.p., sec., gen. counsel Honeggers & Co., Inc., Fairbury, Ill., 1959-65, also bd. dirs.; staff atty. Am. Hosp. Supply Corp., Evanston, Ill., 1965-68, chief atty., asst. sec., 1968-70, corp. sec., 1970-71, corp. sec., corp. gen. counsel, 1971-79, gen. counsel, 1979-84; sr. v.p., sec., gen. counsel Household Internat. Inc., Northbrook, Ill., 1984-93, sr. v.p., of counsel, 1993-94; ret. Mem. planning com. Northwestern U. Corp. Counsel Inst., 1992-93, chmn. Northwestern Corp. Counsel Ctr., 1993. Bd. trustees, bd. visitors Ill. Wesleyan U.; pres. Prestancia Cmty. Assn. Fellow Am. Bar Found., Am. Law Inst.; mem. ABA, Ill. Bar Assn., Fla. Bar Assn., Chgo. Bar Assn. (chmn. corp. law dept.), North Shore Gen. Counsels, Northwestern U. Sch. Law Alumni Assn. (pres.), Sigma Chi, Legal Club (Chgo.), Law Club (Chgo.), Skokie Country Club (Glencoe, Ill.), Gator Creek Golf Club (Sarasota, Fla.), T.P.C. Club (Prestancia, Fla.), Prestancia Cmty. Assn. (pres. 1995-96), Champion Hills Golf Club (Hendersonville, N.C.), Hendersonville Country Club. Home (Winter): 4634 Mirada Way #24 Sarasota FL 34238 Home (Summer): 21 LaCoste Dr Hendersonville NC 28739 *Success will come to those who plan and rehearse. Set your goals, define your strategies and implement your tactics. Your goals must always determine and never justify the means toward achievement.*

HULL, JANE DEE, former governor, former state legislator; b. Kansas City, Mo., Aug. 8, 1935; d. Justin D. and Mildred (Swenson) Bowersock; m. Terrance Ward Hull, Feb. 12, 1954; children: Jeannette Shipley, Robin Hillebrand, Jeff, Mike. BS, U. Kans., 1957; postgrad., U. Ariz., 1972-78. Spkr. pro tem Ariz. Ho. of Reps., Phoenix, 1993, chmn. ethics com., chmn. econ. devel., 1993, mem. legis. coun., 1993, mem. gov.'s internat. trade and tourism adv. bd., 1993, mem. gov.'s strategic partnership for econ. devel., 1993, mem. gov.'s office of employement implementation task force, 1993, spkr. of house, 1989-93, house majority whip, 1987-88; sec. of state State of Arizona, Phoenix, 1993—97; gov. State of Ariz., Phoenix, 1997—2003. Bd. dirs. Morrison Inst. for Pub. Policy, Beatitudes D.O.A.R., 1992, Ariz. Town Hall, Ariz. Econs. Coun.; mem. dean's coun. Ariz. State U., 1989-92; assoc. mem. Heard Mus. Guild, Cactus Wren Rep. Women, ; mem. Maricopa Med. Aux., Ariz. State Med. Aux., Freedom Found., Valley Citizens League, Charter 100, North Phoenix Rep. Women, 1970, Trunk 'N Tusk Legis. Liaison Ariz. Rep. Party, 1993; Rep. candidate sec. of state, 1994. Recipient Econ. Devel. award Ariz. Innovation Network, 1993. Mem. Nat. Orgn. of Women Legislators, Am. Legis. Exch. Coun., Nat. Rep. Legislators Assn. (Nat. Legislator of Yr. award 1989), Soroptimists (hon.). Republican. Roman Catholic.*

HULL, JANE LAUREL LEEK, retired nurse, administrator; b. Ontario, Calif., July 4, 1923; d. William Abram and Susan Bianca (Pethick) Leek; m. James B. Hull, Oct. 10, 1944 (dec.); children: James W., William P., Kenneth D. RN, Columbia Presbyn. Sch. Nursing, 1944; BA, Redlands U., 1977. RN Calif., N.Y., Pa. Spr. obstetrics Mid-Valley Hosp., Peckville, Pa., 1945-46; sch. and surg. nurse acute nursing Scranton (Pa.) State Hosp., 1947-52; nurse San Antonio Cmty. Hosp., Upland, Calif., 1953-55; office nurse H.L Archibald, Upland, 1965; vis. nurse Pomona West End, Inc., Pomona, Calif., 1968-73, exec. dir. Claremont, Calif., 1973-92, pres., 1991-92, Pomona (Calif.) West End Inc., Claremont, Calif., 1991. Tchr. ARC nursing course to high sch. students; cons. Livingston Meml. Vis. Nurse Assn. Ventura, Calif., organizer homemaker dept. in Vis. Nurse Assn., 1972. Co-developer plugs for in-dwelling Foley catheters, 1963. Treas. PTA, Pomona, Calif.; vol. exec. dir. Inland Hospice Assn., 1979-80, mem. accreditation commn., 1988-89; vol. Nat. Found. for Hospice/Home Care, 1988. Recipient Woman Achiever award, Pomona Valley, 1983, Excellence in Edn. award Nat. Assn. Home Care, 1988. Mem. Am. Assn. Ret. Persons (local coord.), Calif. Nurses Assn. (pres. dist. 53, 1958), Calif. Assn. for Health Svcs. at Home (dir.), Calif. League Nursing, Nat. Homecaring Coun. (dir.), Home Care Aide Assn. Am. (chmn.), Nat. Assn. Home Care (bd. dirs.), Zonta (pres. 1976). Home: 543 W F St Ontario CA 91762-3117

HULL, JOHN DANIEL, IV, lawyer; b. Washington, Feb. 27, 1953; s. John Daniel III and Arlene (Reemer) Hull. BA cum laude, Duke U., 1975; JD, U. Cin., 1978. Bar: DC 1980, U.S. Dist. Ct. DC 1983, U.S. Ct. Appeals (DC cir.) 1984, U.S. Ct. Appeals (10th cir.) 1986, Md. 1989, Pa. 1989, U.S. Dist. Ct. (we. dist.) Pa. 1989, U.S. Ct. Appeals (3d cir.) 1989, U.S. Supreme Ct. 1989, Calif. 2002, U.S. Dist. Ct. (so. dist.) Calif. 2002. Legis. asst. 93d & 96th U.S. Congresses, Washington, 1974, 78-81; assoc. Rose, Schmidt & Dixon, Washington, 1981-87, ptnr., 1988-92, Hull McGuire PC, Pitts., Washington, and San Diego, 1992—. Mem.: U. Cin. Law Rev., 1976—77, editor student articles:, 1977—78. Fellow Congress of Ctr. for Internat. Legal Studies, Salzburg, Austria. Mem.: ABA, Calif. Bar Assn., Internat. Bar Assn., Pa. Bar Assn., Md. Bar Assn., Bar Assn. DC, Internat. Bus. Law Consortium, Tara Club, Duke Club. Office: Hull McGuire PC 32d Fl US Steel Tower 600 Grant St Pittsburgh PA 15219-2702 also: Hull McGuire PC 888 17th St NW Ste 1000 Washington DC 20006 also: Hull McGuire PC 701 B St Fl 10 San Diego CA 92101 E-mail: jdhull@hullmcguire.com.

HULL, KATHLEEN ANN, humanities educator; b. Louisville, Jan. 12, 1956; d. Richard Ostrander and Eileen (Powers) Hull; m. Ernest G. Jacob, Apr. 23, 1983; 1 child, Allison Jacob. BA in History and Philosophy of Sci., McGill U., 1978; MA in Philosophy, Johns Hopkins U., 1981; PhD in Theol. and Religious Studies (hon.), Drew U., 1996. Rsch. assoc. Ctr. for Health Policy Studies, Columbia, Md., 1981—83; asst. to the headmistress The Barnard Sch., N.Y.C., 1983—85; adj. asst. prof. Fairleigh Dickinson U., Madison, NJ, 1992—96; adj. assoc. prof. NYU, N.Y.C., 1996—. Lectr. in field. Contbr. Vol. union organizing com. NYU ACT-UAW, N.Y.C., 2000—02. Recipient Art of Tchg. prize, NEA, 2001, Faculty award for tchg. excellence, NYU, 2002, Helen LaPage and William Hale Chamberlain prize, Drew U., 1996; Johns Hopkins U. fellow. Mem.: AAUP (chpt. v.p. 2000—02, chpt. co-pres. 2002—), Soc. for Women in Philosophy, Soc. for Advancement of Am. Philosophy, Assn. for Core Texts and Courses, Am. Philos. Assn. Home: 547 Saint Mark's Ave Westfield NJ 07090

HULL, LEWIS WOODRUFF, manufacturing company executive; b. Scranton, Pa., Oct. 16, 1916; s. Robert Alonzo and Clara Lucelia (Woodruff) H.; m. Margaret (Burns) Carson, June 7, 1947; children: Arthur, Martha, Stephen, Rebecca. BS in Chem. Engring., MIT, 1938. Divsn. mgr. F. J. Stokes Co., Phila., 1938—52; bd. dir. Hull Corp., Warminster, Pa., 1952—2002; pres. Hull Vac Pump Corp., Warminster, 2002—, Hull Freeze-dry Corp., Warminster, 2002—. Bd. dir. Hull Internat. Ltd., Girvan, Scotland, Hull-Japan Ltd., Tokyo, Penn Engring. and Mfg. Inc., Danboro, Pa., Advanced System Design, Evergreen, Colo., Willow Grove Bancorp, Maple Glen, Pa., Pa. Free Enterprise Found., Erie, Pa. (v.p.), Hull-Finmac Inc., Warminster, Pa.; dir. Mid-Atlantic Employers Assn., Trooper, pa. Contbr. articles to profl. jours.; patentee in field. Bd. dir. Heritage Conservancy, Doylestown, Pa. Mem. Plastics Pioneers Assn. (past pres.), Am. Vacuum Soc. (past pres.), Rotary. Republican. Avocations: sailplaning, tennis. Home: 277 W Bristol Rd Southampton PA 18966-1070 Office: HullVac Pump Corp 73 Steamwhistle Dr Warminster PA 18974-4875

HULL, LOUISE KNOX, retired elementary educator, administrator; b. May 24, 1912; d. William E. and Ruby Joe (Bradshaw) Knox; m. Berrien J. Hull, Jan. 1, 1953. BS in Edn., S.W. Mo. State U., 1933; postgrad., U. Colo., 1939, Northwestern U., 1945; MA in Edn., NYU, 1951. Cert. elem. and secondary tchr., Mo. Elem. tchr. R12 Sch. Dist., Springfield, 1936-70, supr. tchr., 1956-70, mem. adv. com. to supt., 1955-57; ret., 1970. Chmn. Christian edn. com. Westminster Presbyn. Ch., 1953-66, trustee, 1983-86, chmn. bd. trustees, 1986, circle chmn., 1986-89, mem. women's adv. bd., 1987-89, rep. witness and fin. com., 1990, pres. Women of Ch., 1970-73, 90-92, pres. bd. trustees, 1983-86; life mem. Wilson Creek Found., Springfield, 1954-67; sec. greene County Hist. Soc., Springfield, 1960-96, also life mem.; mem. Springfield Little Theater Guild, 1970—, Hist. Preservation Soc., Springfield, 1980—; docent Mus. of Ozarks, Springfield, 1976-85; chmn. dist. III, John Calvin Presbytery, 1974-76, sec., 1977-80; vol. St. John's Regional Med. Ctr., 1970-78. Mem. Springfield Ret. Tchr. Assn. (life), Mo. Ret. Tchr. Assn. (life), Ozarks Genealogy Soc. (sec. 1985-87, pub. info. rep. 1987-89), DAR, Mo. Fedn. Women's Clubs (chmn. home life com. 1986-89), Springfield City Fedn. Women's Club (pres. 1990-92), Brige Dept. of Sorosis, 1995-2003; Audubon Dept. of Sorosis; Sorosis Club (pres. Springfield 1980-82, chmn. hobby dept. 1986-88, 94-96, chmn. fine arts dept. 1988-90, mem. perpetual endowment com. 1992-96, chmn. 1994, parliamentarian 1998-2000, chmn. Audubon dept. 2000-02, sec. bridge dept. 1995—), Ch. Women United, Alpha Delta Pi (treas. house corp. 1932-60), Alpha Delta Kappa (sec. 1965-67, corr. sec. Psi chpt. 1990-92).

HULL, MARGARET RUTH, artist, educator, consultant; b. Dallas, Mar. 27, 1921; d. William Haynes and Ora Carroll (Adams) Leatherwood; m. LeRos Ennis Hull, Mar. 29, 1941; children: LeRos Ennis, Jr., James Daniel. BA, So. Meth. U., Dallas, 1952; postgrad., So. Meth. U., 1960-61; MA, North Tex. State U., 1957; postgrad., R.I. Sch. Design, 1982. Art instr. W.W. Bushman Sch., Dallas Ind. Sch. Dist., 1952-57, Benjamin Franklin Jr. High Sch., Dallas, 1957-58, Hillcrest H.S., Dallas, 1958-61, dean, pupil personnel counselor, 1961-70; designer, coord. curriculum writing visual art cluster Skyline H.S., Dallas, 1970-76; developer curriculum writing/writing art cluster Booker T. Washington Arts Magnet H.S., Dallas, 1976-82, coord. visual arts careers cluster, 1976-82, artist, ednl. cons., 1982-96. Tchr. children's painting Dallas Mus. Fine Art, 1956-70; mus. reprodns. asst. Dallas Mus. Art, 1984-93. Group shows include Dallas Mus. Fine Arts, 1958, Arts Magnet Faculty Shows, 1978-82, Arts Magnet H.S., Dallas Art Edn. Assn. Show, 1981, D'Art Membership Show, Dallas, 1982-83; represented in pvt. collections. Trustee Dallas Mus. Art, 1978—84; vol. League Dallas Mus. Art, 1982—2002. Mem. Tex. Designer/Craftsmen, Craft Guild Dallas, Fiber Artists Dallas, Dallas Art Edn. Assn., Tex. Art Edn. Assn., Nat. Art Edn. Assn., Dallas Counselors Assn. (pres. 1968), Delta Delta Delta.

HULL, MCALLISTER HOBART, JR., retired university administrator; b. Birmingham, Ala., Sept. 1, 1923; s. McAllister Hobart and Grace (Johnson) H.; m. Mary Muska, Mar. 23, 1946; children: John McAllister, Wendy Ann. BS with highest honors, Yale, 1948, PhD in Physics, 1951. Tech. asst. Los Alamos Lab., 1944-46; From instr. to asso. prof. physics Yale U., 1951-66; prof. physics, chmn. dept. Oreg. State U., 1966-69, State U. N.Y. at Buffalo, 1969-72, dean Grad. Sch., 1972-74, dean. grad. and profl. edn., 1974-77; provost U. N.Mex., 1977-85, counselor to pres., 1985-88, prof. emeritus physics, 1988—. Adviser to supt. schs., Hamden, Conn., 1958-65 Author papers, books, chpts. in books, articles in encys. Bd. dirs. Western N.Y. Reactor Facility, 1970-72; trustee N.E. Radio Obs. Corp., 1971-77; pres. Western Regional Sci. Labs., 1977; chmn. tech. adv. com. N.Mex. Energy Research Inst., 1981-83, mem., 1983-88; co-chmn. Nat. Task Force on Ednl. Tech., 1984-86. Served with AUS, 1943-46. Faculty fellow Yale U., 1964-65 Fellow Am. Phys. Soc.; mem. Am. Assn. Physics Tchrs. (chmn. Oreg. sect. 1967-68) E-mail: machull@unm.edu. *Experience says that everyone is sometimes wise, no one is always wise. One mustdevelop the willingness to listen for wisdom from whatever source, the judgment to identify it, the skill to use it: only in this way can one's talents, however modest or extensive, be optimally enhanced and the number of wasted efforts minimized.*

HULL, PATRICIA ANN, nursing administrator; b. Johnstown, Pa., May 26, 1942; d. Willard Earl and Florence Merritt; m. Bruce Edward Dunn, July 31, 1965 (div. Aug. 1975); children: Rachel Dunn Allen, Kelly Dunn Thomas, Heather Dunn Wyant; m. Harry Edwin Hull, May 21, 1988 (dec. 1996). Diploma in nursing, Conemaugh Hosp. Sch. Nursing, Johnstown, 1963. Cert. gerontol. nurse. Staff nurse Conemaugh Hosp., 1963-64; head nurse, supr. 1710 USAF Hosp., Savannah, Ga., 1964-66; part-time staff nurse Rochester (N.Y.) Gen. Hosp., 1966; part-time supr., clinic emergency rm. U. Miami (Fla.), 1967-68; staff supr. Arbutus Park Manor, Johnstown, 1979-92, dir. nursing, 1992—. Dist. rep., sec. Western Pa. Conf. United Meth. Bd. Health and Welfare, 1987-92; mem. Christ United Meth. Ch., Johnstown, health and welfare chmn., 1986-91, Stephens min., 1994—, trustee, adminstrv. bd., 1980-92; vol. ARC, Johnstown flood, 1977, blood drives; former Brownie, Girl Scout leader, Talus Rock Girl Scout Coun. 1st lt. USAF Nurse Corps, 1964-66; bd. dirs. Cambria County Br., Alzheimer's Assn. Recipient State of Pa. Gerontol. Nursing Study grant Indiana U. Pa., 1992. Mem. Pa. Assn. Dirs. Nursing Adminstrn/Long Term Care, Am. Soc. Long Term Care Nurses, Health Ministries Assn. (P.A.L.M. chpt.). Avocations: profl. artist, ecology. Home: 1128 Boyd Ave Johnstown PA 15905-4413 Office: Arbutus Park Manor 207 Ottawa St Johnstown PA 15904-2337

HULL, PHILIP GLASGOW, lawyer; b. St. Albans, Vt., Feb. 17, 1925; s. Charles Herman and Gladys Gertrude (Glasgow) H.; m. Gretchen Elizabeth Gaebelein, Oct. 24, 1952; children: Jeffrey R., Sanford D., Meredyth Hull Smith. AB, Middlebury Coll., 1949; LLB, Columbia U., 1952. Bar: N.Y. 1952, Fla. 1977. Staff mem. subcom. on adminstrn. internal revenue laws, com. on ways and means U.S. Ho. of Reps., Washington, 1951; assoc. Winthrop, Stimson, Putnam & Roberts, N.Y.C., 1952-63, ptnr., 1964-97, sr. counsel, 1998-2000, Pillsbury Winthrop, N.Y.C., 2001—. Mem. Sch. Revenue Com., Cold Spring Harbor, N.Y., 1963-65; bd. dirs. Eagle Dock Found., Cold Spring Harbor, 1971-74, People's Symphony Concerts, N.Y.C., 1977—, L.I. Philharm., 1979-81; trustee L.Am. Mission, Miami, Fla., 1969-79; elder Ctrl. Presbyn. Ch., Huntington, N.Y., 1956-78; mem. nat. mssions bd. United Presbyn. Ch., U.S.A., 1967-73; trustee Madison Avenue Presbyn. Ch., N.Y.C., 1989-94, pres., 1993-94; mem. Lloyd Harbor Conservation Adv. Coun., 1973-77. With U.S. Army, 1943-46. Ellis fellow, Kent scholar, Stone scholar Columbia U. Mem. Am. Coll. Trust and Estate Counsel, 1979-2002, N.Y. State Bar Assn., Fla. Bar Assn., Christian Legal Soc. (bd. dirs. 1984-97), Fellowship Christians in Univs. and Schs. (trustee 1983-90), Univ. Club N.Y.C. (bd. dirs. 1986-90), Cold Spring Harbor Beach Club, Blue Key, Phi Beta Kappa. Office: Pillsbury Winthrop One Battery Park Plz New York NY 10004-1490

HULL, RAYMOND WHITFORD, public relations executive; b. Cohoes, N.Y., Oct. 13, 1946; s. Raymond W. and J. Ruth (Barber) H. BS, Syracuse U., 1971. Spl. asst. to Gov. Nelson A. Rockefeller, Albany, N.Y., 1971; conf. asst. to commr. N.Y. State Dept. Environ. Conservation, Albany, 1971-74; exec. dir. Spl. Joint Legis. Commn. on Petroleum Distbn., Albany, 1974-75; asst. headmaster Hoosac Sch., Hoosick, N.Y., 1975-77; area coordinator N.Y. State Assembly, Albany, 1977-79; staff dir. N.Y. State Senate Com. on Energy, Albany, 1979-85; dir. pub. affairs Niagara Mohawk Power Corp., Albany, 1985-89; pub. affairs cons. Albany, 1990-96; assoc. commr. N.Y. State Dept. Motor Vehicles, Albany, 1996—. V.p. Rensselaer City Sch. Bd., N.Y., 1981-86; treas. bd. trustees Hoosac Sch., 1974-81, Rennsselaer City Hist. Soc., 1980—, pres., 1994; trustee Rennselaer county hist. Soc., 1986-94. Mem.: Ft. Orange (Albany); SAR (N.Y.C.). Republican. Episcopalian. Avocations: historical architecture, art. Home: The Patroon Agts House 15 Forbes Ave Rensselaer NY 12144-1622 E-mail: RayHull@aol.com.

HULL, RICHARD FRANKLIN, insurance brokerage executive; b. N.Y.C., Nov. 8, 1931; s. Washington and Emily G. (Stevenson) H.; children: Richard Franklin, David Townsend, Christopher Cornelius. Student, U. Va., 1953. Underwriter Crum & Forster Group, N.Y.C., 1953-56; pres. Hull & Co., Washington, 1956-62, Ft. Lauderdale, Fla., 1962—. Served with USMC, 1950-53. Mem. Am. Assn. Mng. Gen. Agts., Nat. Assn. Profl. Surplus Lines Assn., Ill. Surplus Lines Assn., Nat. Assn. Ins. Agts., Fla. Assn. Ins. Agts., Profl. Ins. Agts. Assn., Ind. Agts. Assn., Balboa Bay Club, Lauderdale Yacht Club, Lago Mar Country Club, Lloyd's Yacht Club, Rod and Reel Club, Ocean Reef Club, Lyford Cay Club, Cat Cay Club, Jockey Club, Royal Nassau Sailing Club, City of London Club. Home: 2401 Del Lago Dr Fort Lauderdale FL 33316-2301 Office: 2150 S Andrews Ave Fort Lauderdale FL 33316-3432 E-mail: rhull@hullco.com.

HULL, RITA PRIZLER, retired accounting educator; b. Lone Tree, Iowa, Mar. 29, 1936; d. Ernest Ralph and Mildred Lennis (Huskins) Prizler; m. J.W. Hull, May 29, 1954 (div. 1963); children: Mark, Marshall; m. John O. Everett, Sept. 1, 1976. BA in Acctg., Augustana Coll., Rock Island, Ill., 1967; MA in Acctg., Western Ill. U., 1973; PhD in Bus. Adminstrn., Okla. State U., 1978. CPA, Ill.; cert. internal auditor, Ill. Auditor Price Waterhouse & Co., Chgo., 1967-70; asst. prof. acctg. Bowling Green (Ohio) State U., 1976-78; assoc. prof. No. Ill. U., DeKalb, 1978-82; prof. Va. Commonwealth U., Richmond, 1982-2001. Contbr. articles, papers to profl. publs. Recipient Outstanding Women award Greater Richmond area, YWCA, 1995. Mem. AICPA, NOW (treas. Richmond chpt. 1987-88), Am. Soc. Women Accts. (treas. Richmond chpt. 1986-87, sec. 1987-88, pres. 1988-90, nat. bd. dirs. 1990-93, nat. sec. 1991-92, nat. v.p. 1992-93, Nat. Woman of Achievement award, 1994), Am. Acctg. Assn. (Trueblood seminars com. 1987-88, acctg. educator awards com. 1988-90, awards evaluation com. 1990-91, chmn.-elect gender issues in acctg. sect. 1991-92, chmn. 1992-93, coun. 1992-93), Inst. Internat. Auditors, Acad. Acctg. Historians. Democrat. Unitarian-Universalist. Avocations: travel, reading, gardening. Home: 810 Keats Rd Richmond VA 23229-6520 Office: Va Commonwealth U 1015 Floyd Ave Richmond VA 23284-9000 E-mail: ritahullcpa@verizon.net.

HULL, ROBERT GLENN, retired financial administrator; b. Ottumwa, Iowa, Sept. 14, 1929; s. C. Glenn and DeElda L. (Davidson) H.; m. Donna Marie Hastriter, Jan. 26, 1951; children: Cynthia Ann Hull Williams, Steven Kent. BA, Friends U., 1956; MS, Emporia Kans. State U., 1966. With Nat. Coop. Refinery Assn., McPherson, Kans., 1957-91, treas., comptroller, 1968-76, v.p. finance, 1976-91. Dir. Jayhawk Pipeline Corp., Clear Creek Cos. Bd. dirs. Central Coll., McPherson. Served with USAF, 1951-55. Mem. Fin. Execs. Inst., Nat. Assn. Accountants for Coops., Am. Petroleum Inst., Delta Pi Epsilon. Clubs: Petroleum, McPherson Country. Republican. Methodist. Home: 417 S Grand St Mcpherson KS 67460-4912 E-mail: rhull7@cox.net.

HULL, ROGER HAROLD, academic administrator; b. NYC, June 18, 1942; s. Max Harold and Magda Mary (Stern) H.; children: Roberto Franklin, Lincoln Macgregor. AB cum laude, Dartmouth Coll., 1964; LL.B., Yale U., 1967;

LL.M., U. Va., 1972, S.JD, 1974; LHD, Rockford Coll., 1988; LLD, Beloit Coll., 1992. Bar: N.Y. 1968. Assoc. firm White & Case, N.Y.C., 1967—71; spl. counsel to gov., Va., 1971—74; spl. asst. to chmn., dep. staff dir. Interagy. Task Force Law of Sea, NSC, 1974—76; v.p. devel. Syracuse U., 1976—79, v.p. devel. and planning, 1979—81; pres. Beloit (Wis.) Coll., 1981—90, Union Coll., Schenectady, 1990—; chancellor Union U., 1990—. Mem. U.S. del. Law of Sea Conf., 1974-76; adj. prof. Syracuse Univ. Law Sch., 1976-81; bd. visitors Coll. William and Mary, Williamsburg, Va., 1970-74; mem. pub. instns. task force Assn. Gov. Bds., 1975. Author: The Irish Triangle, 1976; co-author: Law and Vietnam, 1968. Co-founder, vice chair Schenectady 2000. Named Schenectady County Person of Yr., 1998, Patroon, 1999, Schnectady C. of C. Exec. of Yr., 2002 ; recipient Cmty. Leadership award, 1999. Mem. Am. Soc. Internat. Law, Univ. Club, Millbrook Golf and Tennis Club. Office: Union Coll Pres Office Schenectady NY 12308

HULL, RONALD R. human resources specialist; s. Ralph Earl Hull; 1 child, Timothy Ronald. MS in Pub. Adminstrn., Calif. State U., LA, 1983. Dir. human resource svcs. Calif. State U., Long Beach, Calif., 1988—99; mgr. compensation svcs. U. Calif., LA, 2003. Mem.: Coll. Univ. Profl. Assn. Human Resources (treas. 1998—2002, Hugh Avery award 2002). Personal E-mail: ronhull@sbcglobal.net.

HULL, SUZANNE WHITE, writer, retired administrator; b. Orange, NJ, Aug. 24, 1921; d. Gordon Stowe and Lillian (Siegling) White; m. George I. Hull, Feb. 20, 1943 (dec. Mar. 1990); children: George Gordon, James Rutledge, Anne Elizabeth Hull Sheldon. BA with honors, Swarthmore Coll., 1943; MSLS, U. So. Calif., 1967. Mem. staff Huntington Libr., Art Gallery and Bot. Gardens, San Marino, Calif., 1969-86, dir. adminstrn. and pub. svcs., 1972-86, also prin. officer. Cons. Women Writers Project, Brown U., 1989-2001. Author: Chaste, Silent and Obedient, English Books for Women, 1475-1640, 1982, 88, Women According to Men: The World of Tudor-Stuart Women, 1996, Japanese edit., 2003; editor: State of the Art in Women's Studies, 1986. Charter pres. Portola Jr. HS PTA, LA, 1960-62; pres. Children's Svc. League, 1963-64, YWCA, LA, 1967-69; alumni coun. Swarthmore Coll., 1959-62, 83-86, mem.-at-large, 1986-89; adv. bd. Hagley Mus. and Libr., Wilmington, Del., 1983-86, Betty Friedan Think Tank, U. So. Calif., 1985-93, Early Modern Englishwoman: A Facsimile Libr. Essential Works, 1995-2001; hon. life mem. Calif. Congress Parents and Tchrs.; bd. dirs. Pasadena Planned Parenthood Assn., 1978-83, adv. com., 1983—; founder-chmn. Swarthmore-LA Connection, 1984-85, bd. dirs., 1985-92; founder Huntington Women's Studies Seminar, 1984, steering com., 1984-91, adv. bd., 1991-96; organizing com. Soc. for Study of Early Modern Women, 1993-94; mem. women's com. art collections and botanical gardens. Mem. Monumental Brass Soc. (U.K.), Renaissance Soc., Brit. Studies Conf., Western Assn. Women Historians, Soc. Study of Early Modern Women, Authors Guild, Beta Phi Mu (chpt. dir. 1981-84). Home: Apt 203 211 S Wilson Ave Pasadena CA 91106 Office: 1151 Oxford Rd San Marino CA 91108-1218

HULL, THOMAS CLINTON, mathmatics educator; b. Warwick, RI, Nov. 5, 1969; s. Richard James and Catherine Ray Hull; life ptnr. Sarah-Marie Belcastro. PhD in Math., U. of RI, 1997. Math. prof. Merrimack Coll., North Andover, RI, 1997—. Vis. prof. U. of Cin., 2002—. Author: (book) Origami, Plain and Simple, Russian Origami; editor: (procs. book) Origami3: Proceedings of the Third International Meeting of Origami Science, Mathematics, and Education; art exhbn., Five Intersecting Tetrahedra and other works. Project NExT Fellow, The Math. Assn. of Am., 1998. Mem.: Math. Assn. of Am., Am. Math. Soc., Origami U.S.A. (bd. mem. 1995—2003). Achievements include research in Numerous results on geometry of origami crease patterns. Avocation: ultimate frisbee. Office: Dept of Math Merrimack Coll North Andover MA 01845 E-mail: thull@merrimack.edu.

HULL, WILLIAM EDWARD, theology educator; b. Birmingham, Ala., May 28, 1930; s. William Edward and Margaret (King) H.; m. Julia Wylodine Hester, July 26, 1952; children: David William, Susan Virginia. BA, Samford U., 1951; MDiv, So. Bapt. Theol. Sem., Louisville, 1954, PhD, 1960; postgrad., U. Gottingen, Germany, 1962-63, Harvard U., 1971. Ordained to ministry Bapt. Ch., 1950. Pastor Beulah Bapt. Ch., Wetumpka, Ala., 1950-51, Cedar Hill Bapt. Ch., Owenton, Ky., 1952-53, 1st Bapt. Ch., New Castle, Ky., 1953-58; from instr. to assoc. prof. So. Bapt. Theol. Sem., Louisville, 1954-67, prof., 1967-75, dean theology and provost, 1969-75; pastor 1st Bapt. Ch., Shreveport, La., 1975-87; provost Samford U., Birmingham, Ala., 1987-96, Univ. prof., 1987-2000, rsch. prof., 2000—. Author: Gospel of John, 1964, Broadman Bible Commentary, 1970, Beyond the Barriers, 1981, Love in Four Dimensions, 1982, The Christian Experience of Salvation, 1987, Southern Baptist Higher Education: Retrospect and Prospect, 2001, (with others): Professor in the Pulpit, 1963, The Truth That Makes Men Free, 1966, Salvation in Our Time, 1978, Set Apart for Service, 1980, Celebrating Christ's Presence Through the Spirit, 1981, The Twentieth Century Pulpit, Vol. II, 1981, Minister's Manual, 1983-87, 2000, 02, Biblical Preaching: An Expositor's Treasury, 1983, Preaching in Today's World, 1984, Heralds to a New Age, 1985, Getting Ready for Sunday: A Practical Guide for Worship Planning, 1989, Best Sermons 2, 1989, The University Through the Eyes of Faith, 1998, Southern Baptist Higher Education: Retrospect and Prospect, 2001; contbr. articles to profl. publs. Mem. Futureshape Shreveport (La.) Commn., 1985-87. Recipient Denominational Svc. award Samford U., 1974, Liberty Bell award Shreveport Bar Assn., 1984, Brotherhood and Humanitarian award NCCJ, 1987, Charles D. Johnson Outstanding Educator award Assn. So. Bapt. Colls. and Schs., 1999. Mem. Nat. Assn. Bapt. Profs. Religion (pres. 1967-68), Am. Acad. Religion, Soc. Biblical Lit., The Club (Birmingham), Vestavia Country Club (Birmingham), Rotary, Phi Kappa Phi, Phi Eta Sigma, Omicron Delta Kappa. Baptist. Home: 435 Vesclub Way Birmingham AL 35216-1357

HULME, MARY ANN PRIM KUMM, women's health nurse, administrator; b. Galion, Ohio, July 25, 1952; d. Walter Herman and Mary Elizabeth (Prim) Kumm; m. Roy Allan Hulme, Jan. 8, 1977; children: Eric A., Ann E. BSN, Capital U., 1974; MSN, Case Western Res. U., 1993. RN, Ohio; cert. in ob-gyn., inpatient ob-gyn., neonatal nursing ANCC. Staff and charge nurse, labor and delivery St. Ann's Hosp., Columbus, Ohio, 1974-76, head nurse, dir. ob-gyn. outpatient clinic, 1976-77; clin. nurse, sr. clin. nurse, head nurse mgr. labor/delivery Univ. Hosps., Cleve., 1977-94; head nurse mgr. labor/delivery antepartum U. Hosps. Cleve., Cleve., 1994-98, head nurse mgr. labor and delivery, 1998—2003, adminstr. risk prevention, quality and accreditation Dept. Ob-gyn., 2003—. Clin. instr. maternity and gynecology nursing Case Western Res. U., Cleve., 1986—, Kent State U., 1995—; cons. case/care mgmt., 1999. Contbr. articles to profl. jours. With United Way Svcs., 1998. Recipient Pre Gold medal U.S. Figure Skating Assn. Mem. Ohio Orgn. Nurse Execs. (program chair, bd. dirs.), Assn. Womens Health, Obstet. and Neonatal Nursing, Assn. Oper. Room Nurses, Cleve. Skating Club (past bd. dirs., co-chmn. skating com.), Sigma Theta Tau. Lutheran. Avocations: ice dancing, curling, running. Home: 16070 S Park Blvd Cleveland OH 44120-1673

HULNICK, DONALD H. radiologist; b. N.Y.C., May 28, 1951; s. George Herman and Elsie Post Hulnick; children: Blake, Molly. BA, Brown U., 1973; MD, NYU, 1977. Diplomate Am. Bd. Radiology. Resident then fellow in radiology NYU Med. Ctr., 1978-82; attending physician Bellevue Hosp., N.Y.C., 1982-88, NYU Hosp., 1982-88, co-dir. divsn. gastrointestinal radiology and body computed tomography, 1985-88; attending physician Danbury (Conn.) Hosp., 1988—, vice chmn. dept. radiology, 1996—2000. Pres. Danbury Radiol. Assocs., P.C., 1996-98. Contbr. articles to profl. jours. Named Gold Medal Exhibitor, Am. Roentgen Ray Soc., Boston, 1985; recipient Editor's Recognition awards Jour. Radiology, 1986, 87. Office: Dept Radiology Danbury Hosp 24 Hospital Ave Danbury CT 06810-6099 E-mail: Hulnickdh@aol.com.

HULSBOS, CORNIE LEONARD, civil engineering educator; b. Given, Iowa, Aug. 23, 1920; s. Neal and Elizabeth (Van Klaveren) H.; m. Elsie Marthe Hallas, June 21, 1945; children: Susan, Betty, David. BS, Iowa State U., 1941, MS, 1949, PhD, 1953. Registered profl. engr., Iowa. With Am. Bridge Co., 1941-46; mem. faculty Iowa State U., 1946-60, prof. civil engring., 1957-60; research prof. civil engring., chmn. structural concrete div. Fritz Engring. Lab., Lehigh U., 1960-65; prof. civil engring., chmn. dept. U. N.Mex., Albuquerque, 1965-85, prof. emeritus, 1985—; mem. com. concrete bridges Transp. Research Bd., 1962-84, chmn., 1971-77, mem. com. field testing bridges, 1965-80. Fellow ASCE (sec. treas. Iowa sect. 1957-60, 1st v.p. Lehigh Valley sect. 1964-65, chmn. Albuquerque br. 1968-69), Am. Concrete Inst.; mem. Am. Soc. Engring. Edn., Sigma Xi, Tau Beta Pi, Phi Kappa Phi, Chi Epsilon, Pi Mu Epsilon. Home: 7608 Palo Duro Ave NE Albuquerque NM 87110-2315 E-mail: chulsbos@aol.com.

HULSE, DEXTER CURTIS, manufacturing executive; b. Woodland, Calif., Oct. 6, 1952; s. Dexter Curtis Hulse and Geraldine Ezabell (Ratliff) Curtis; children: Sandra Marie, Jennifer Lynn; m. Sherry Matson, Dec. 17, 2002. B.Indsl. Engring., Shawnee State U., Portsmouth, Ohio, 1973; Deg. in Computer Aided Design, Shawnee State U., 1992, BS in Mfg. Edn., 2000. Numerical control operator Lodge & Shippley, Cin., 1973—76; journeyman machinist Nat. Mine Svc. Co., Ashland, Ky., 1976—86; regional mgr. A.L. Williams Mktg., Minford, Ohio, 1982—87; pres. D & D Emergency, Wheelersburg, 1987—88; gen. gmr. Dexter Mfg., 1988—93; instr. Shawnee State U., 1988—2002; sr. insp. Piketon Uranium Enrichment Facility Lockheed Martin Utility Svc., 1995—98; instr. computer aided design U. Cin., Clermont, 2002—. Mem. computer-aided design adv. bd. Shawnee State U., 1990-94; CAD/CAM instr. Buckeye Hills Career Ctr., Rio Grande, Ohio, 1998-2002; cons. Scioto Bus. Cons., Wheelersburg, 1986-95. Vol. fireman Porter Twp. Fire Dept., Wheelersburg, 1984-87. Mem. Ch. Nazarene. Avocations: canoeing, atv's, computers. E-mail: dexterhulse@hotmail.com.

HULSE, ROBERT DOUGLAS, high technology executive; b. Niagara Falls, N.Y., Aug. 16, 1943; s. Robert Edwin and Helen Louise (Kenny) H.; m. Nancy Louise Musser, Aug. 20, 1966 (div. 1986); children: Anne Warren, Robert Alexander; m. Karen Alice Karlberg, Dec. 31, 1987. AB, Princeton U., 1965; SMChemE, MIT, 1966, SM in Mgmt., 1968. Mgr. bus. analysis Halcon Internat. Inc., N.Y.C., 1968-73, dir. bus. planning, 1973-76; v.p., gen. mgr. Halcon Catalyst Industries, Little Ferry, N.J., 1976-82; v.p. planning & devel. Engelhard Industries, Iselin, N.J., 1982-84; pres., chief exec. officer i-STAT Corp., Princeton, N.J., 1984-86, Sunstone Inc., Dayton, N.J., 1986-87; vice chmn. Princeton Entrepreneurial Resources, 1988-90; pres., chief exec. officer SDTX Technologies, Inc., Princeton, 1989—; v.p. bus. devel. Enzon, Inc., Piscataway, N.J., 1991-94; exec. dir. The Sage Group, Bridgewater, N.J., 1995—, also bd. dirs.; COO, Hemispherx Biopharma, Inc., Phila., 1996-97; gen. ptnr. SAE Ventures, New Canaan, Conn., 1997-2001. Cons. in field; dir. SDTX Technologies, Inc., Princeton, 1989—; pres., dir. Captiva Technologies, Princeton, 1989—; dir. Carnegie Venture Resources, Inc., Princeton, The Sage Group, Bridgewater. Dir. Gotham Light Opera Soc., N.Y.C., 1969-73; treas. Bloomingdale House of Music, N.Y.C., 1979-84. Named Univ. scholar Princeton U., 1961. Mem. The Licensing Execs. Soc., Soc. Competitive Intelligence Professionals, The Union League Club, Doubles, Sigma Xi, Phi Beta Kappa. Republican. Episcopalian. Avocations: chess, tennis. Home: 706 Sayre Dr Princeton NJ 08540-5835 Office: The Sage Group Inc 245 Rte 22 W Ste 304 Bridgewater NJ 08807-2560 E-mail: Doughulse@aol.com.

HULSE, RUSSELL ALAN, physicist; b. N.Y.C., Nov. 28, 1950; s. Alan Earle and Betty Joan (Wedemeyer) Hulse. BS, Cooper Union, 1970; MS, U. Mass., 1972, PhD, 1975. Rsch. assoc. Nat. Radio Astronomy Observatory, Charlottesville, Va., 1975—77; mem. tech. staff Princeton (N.J.) U. Plasma Physics Lab., 1977—80, staff rsch. physicist, 1980—84, rsch. physicist, 1984—92, prin. rsch. physicist, 1992—. Contbr. articles to profl. jours. Recipient Nobel prize in physics, 1993. Fellow: Inst. of Physics, Am. Phys. Soc.; mem.: Soc. for Industrial & Applied Math, Am. Astron. Soc. Avocations: clay target shooting, bird watching, cross-country skiing, canoeing, hiking. Office: Plasma Physics Lab MS32 C-Site B 145 A PPL Princeton NJ 08543-0451

HULSEBOSCH, DANIEL JOSEPH, historian, educator; b. Scarsdale, N.Y., Nov. 6, 1965; s. Edward J. and Jane Mangan Hulsebosch. AB, Colgate U., 1987; JD, Columbia U., 1991; AM, Harvard U., 1991, PhD, 1999. Asst. prof. Sch. of Law St. Louis (Mo.) U., 1999—. Cons. in field. Contbr. articles to profl. jours. Fellow Samuel I. Golieb fellowship, N.Y. U. Sch. of Law, 1998—99; grantee Whiting fellowship in the Humanities, Harvard U., 1996—97. Mem.: Soc. for Historians of the Early Republic, Am. Soc. for Legal History, Omohundro Inst. for Early Am. History and Culture (assoc.), Phi Beta Kappa. Office: Saint Louis University School of Law 3700 Lindell Boulevard Saint Louis MO 63108 Office Fax: 314-977-3332.

HULSEY, RACHEL MARTINEZ, secondary school educator, columnist; b. Laredo, Tex., Jan. 30, 1950; d. Manuel Conrado and Julia (Solis) Martinez; children: John Travis, Marisa Andrea, Joseph Robert. BA, Our Lady of the Lake U., 1971; MA, U. Tex., 1977. Tchr. Harlandale Mid. Sch., San Antonio, 1971-77; reading supervisor Harlandale I.S.D., San Antonio, 1977-83; English tchr. Judson Ind. Sch. Tchr., San Antonio, 1983—; columnist SA Herald, 2002—. Writing trainer N.J. Writing Project in Tex., San Antonio, 1992—, reading trainer, 1995—, 6-Traits Trainer, 2001—, curriculum writer, 2001—; cons. in field. Mem. NEA, Tex. State Edn. Assn., San Antonio Romance Authors, Alamo Writers Assn. Roman Catholic. Avocations: writing, reading, collecting books, dancing, exercising.

HULSHOF, KENNY, congressman; b. Sikeston, Mo., May 22, 1958; m. Renee Lynn Howell. BS, U. Mo., 1980; JD, U. Miss., 1983. Mem. U.S. Congress from Mo. 9th Dist., 1997—, Ways & Means Com., Stds. of Ofcl. Conduct Com., Ho. Budget Com., Ho. Ethics Com. Rep. candidate for Boone County Prosecutor, 1992, U.S. House, 1994, 96. Republican. Roman Catholic. Office: Ho of Representatives 412 Cannon Washington DC 20515-2509*

HULSTAERT, FRANK, pharmaceutical company executive; b. Ghent, Belgium, July 4, 1960; s. Armand and Cecile (Poppe) H.; m. Martine Snoeck, Jan. 18, 1990; children: Eva, Lars. MD, State U. Ghent, 1985; MSc in Informatics, Free U. Brussels, 1992; postgrad., Limburgs U. Ctr., Diepenbeek, Belgium, 1993-94. Lic. physician, Belgium. Resident in internal medicine Univ. Hosp. Ghent, 1986-87; cons. in software Applied Artificial Intelligence N.V., Brussels, 1987-88; assoc. physician Becton Dickinson Immunocytometry Sys. Europe, Erembogem, Belgium, 1988-92; clin. rsch. physician Sandoz (Novartis), Brussels, 1992-97; head clin. R&D dept. Innogenetics, Ghent, 1997—. Contbr. articles to profl. jours.; inventor in field. Res. officer Med. Dept. NATO, 1985-86. Fellow Royal Coll. Physicians (U.K.), Faculty of Pharm. Medicine. Avocation: tennis. Office: Innogenetics NV Technologiepark 6 B-9052 B-9052 Ghent Belgium E-mail: frankhul@innogenetics.com.

HULSTON, JOHN KENTON, lawyer, director; b. Dade County, Mo., Mar. 29, 1915; s. John Fred and Myrtle Rosa (King) H.; m. Ruth Amis Luster, Dec. 18, 1944; 1 son, John Luster. AB, Drury Coll., Springfield, Mo., 1936; JD, Mo. U., Columbia, 1941, D (hon.), 1997. Bar: Mo. 1941, U.S. Supreme Ct. 1949. Tchr., coach Ash Grove (Mo.) High Sch., 1936-38; pvt. practice law Springfield, 1946—; co-founder, dir., v.p., sec. Reed Oil Co., Big Spring, Tex., 1951-68, Pioneer Oil Co., Ft. Worth, 1954-79; operator, chmn. Copperhead Hill farms (beef production), 1955-98; chmn. Bank of Ash Grove, 1959—, Citizens Home Bank, Greenfield, Mo., 1966—; pres. Bank of Springfield, 1968-69, Bank of Billings, 1987—; vice chmn., dir., mem. exec. com. Centerre Bank of Springfield (now Bank of Am.), 1969-89; sec., dir., v.p., mem. exec. com. Ozark Air Lines Inc. (now Am. Air Lines), St. Louis, 1971-86, sec., dir., v.p., 1984-88. Instr. real estate law Drury Coll., 1948-64; vis. lectr. corp. law E.R. Breech Sch. Bus., 1953. Author: West Point and Wilson's Creek 1861, 1955, An Ozarks Boy's Story, 1971, An Ozarks Lawyer's Story, 1976, History of Bank of Ash Grove, 1883-1983, 1983, A Look at Dade County, Missouri, 1905-85, 1985, Panhandle Profiles, 1889-1989, 1989, Lester E. Cox, 1895-1968, 1992, Moments in Time, 2001; (with Paul W. Barrett) Harry S. Truman v. J. William Chilton, 1991; contbr. articles to profl. jours. Chmn. Wilson's Creek Nat. Battlefield Commn., 1969-79; vice chmn. Springfield Home Rule Charter Commn., 1953; chmn. Springfield City Charter Commn., 1977; pres. Greene County Estate Planning Coun., 1952; trustee Springfield Pub. Libr., 1957-63, Drury Coll., 1966-96, life trustee, 1996—; trustee State Hist. Soc. Mo., 1974—, CoxHealth, 1959—, pres., 1966, chmn., 2001-03; chmn. Greene County Dems., 1947-48; introduced Pres. Harry S. Truman at 1st Whistle Stop Speech, Springfield, July 5, 1948; presdl. elector, 1948; mem. Mo. Civil War Centennial Commn., 1961-65; trustee U. Mo. Jefferson, 1976-82, Mo. U. Law Sch. Found., Columbia, pres., 1985-87; co-founder Civil War Round Table of the Ozarks, 1948, Wilson's Creek Battlefield Found., 1952, Greene County Hist. Soc., 1962, The Hist. Mus. Springfield-Greene County, 1974; mem. devel. fund bd. Mo. U., Columbia, 1986-90. Maj. U.S. Army, WWII, 1941-46. Recipient Springfield Young Man of Year award, 1950, Disting. Alumni award Drury Coll., 1974, Springfieldian of Year award, 1978, The Missourian award, 1998, Spl. commendation U.S. Dept. Interior, Nat. Park Service, 1981, Faculty-Alumni Gold medal award Mo. U., Columbia, 1988, Citation of Merit Mo. U. Law Sch., Disting. Svc. award Mo. U. Alumni Assn., 1993; inductee into Mo. Writers Hall of Fame, 1995. Fellow Am. Bar Found. (life); mem. ABA (real property, probate/trust reporter Mo. 1974-96), Am. Judicature Soc., Am. Acad. Hosp. Attys., Am. Soc. Law, Ethics and Medicine, Mo. Bar Assn. (1st chmn. legal aid 1952), Springfield Met. Bar Assn. (pres. 1973, Disting. Atty. award 2002), Springfield C. of C. (pres. 1950, 51, 54), Supreme Ct. of Mo. Hist. Soc. (co-founder, trustee 1984-90), SAR, Order of Coif, Masons (32 deg.), Shriners (potentate 1963), Jester, Hickory Hills Country Club (Springfield), Phi Delta Phi, Kappa Alpha Order. Democrat. Presbyterian. Home: 1300 E Catalpa St Springfield MO 65804-0134 Office: 2060 E Sunshine St Springfield MO 65804-1815 *Awareness of one's limitations sometimes is the spur to sustained effort creating worthwhile achievements.*

HULTBERG, JOHN, artist; b. Berkeley, Calif., Feb. 8, 1922; s. John Waldemar and Mabel Olive (Hammer) H.; m. Hilary Editha Blesh, June 9, 1948 (div. 1956); children: Carl Rudolph, Stephanie Maria; m. Lynne Drexler, Sept. 1985. AB, Fresno State Coll., 1943; student, Calif. Sch. Fine Arts, 1947-49, Art Students League, N.Y.C., 1949-51. Exhibited San Francisco Mus. Art, 1947-49, Los Angeles Mus., 1949, New Talent show, Mus. Modern Art, 1952, one man shows Korman Gallery, N.Y.C., 1953, Martha Jackson Gallery, N.Y.C., 1955, Corcoran Gallery, Washington, 1955, Butler Art Inst., Ohio, 1955, UN Exhibit, San Francisco, 1955, Galerie Rive Droit, Paris, 1954-55, Galerie Nina Dausset, Paris, 1954, Galeria Spazio, Rome, 1955, Mus. Modern Art, Rome, 1955, Guild Hall, East Hampton, N.Y., 1955, I.C.A., London, 1956, others; rep. in collections Met. Mus. Art, Whitney Mus., Roy R. Neuburger, Edward Root, Michel Tapie.; author 5 books. Served as lt. (j.g.) USNR, 1943-46. Recipient prize San Francisco Mus. watercolor ann., 1948; prize San Francisco oil ann., 1941; hon. mention Los Angeles Centennial painting exhibit, 1949; 1st prize Corcoran Biennial Exhibit, Washington, 1955; prize Congress for Cultural Freedom Exhbn. for painters under 35, Europe, 1955; hon. mention Carnegie Internat. Ex-hon., 1955; Norman Harris medal at 65th ann. exhbn. Art Inst. Chgo.; Altman prize NAD, 1972, 85, Shatlov award, 1983, also another award; Albert Bender fellow San Francisco, 1949; Guggenheim fellow, 1956; Nat. Endowment Arts grantee, 1981 Mem. NAD Home: 141 W 73rd St New York NY 10023-2916

HULTGREN, DENNIS EUGENE, farmer, management consultant; b. Union County, S.D., Mar. 19, 1929; s. John Alfred and Esther Marie (Johnson) H.; m. Nelda Ethelyn Olson, Aug. 3, 1957; children: Nancy Hultgren Forsythe, Jean Hultgren Doty, Jahn Dennis, Ruth Dorothy Hultgren Henneman. Grad. high sch. Farmer, Union County, 1953—. Commr., chmn. Union County Planning and Zoning Bd., 1972-83; mem. bd. bylaw revision Union County Electric Co., 1983-85. Pres. bd. Union Creek Cemetry, 1958—; pres. bd. mgrs. Union-Sayles Watershed Dist., 1965-70; exec. bd. S.D. Farm Bur., Union County, 1996—, pres., 1998—; treas. Sioux Valley Twp., Union County, 1980—; treas., bd. dirs. W. Union Sch., 1957-67; chmn. Union County Sch. Bd., 1961-68; pres. Alcester (S.D.) Sch. Bd., 1970-77; chmn. Alcester PTA, 1967-68; mem. tech. bd. rev. Southeastern Coun. Govts., Sioux Falls, 1976-77; bd. dirs. Siouxland Interstate Met. Planning Coun., Sioux City, 1977-83, sec. coun. ofcls., 1978-83; bd. dirs. Old Opera House Cmty. Theater, Akron, Iowa, Akron Area Action Assn., 1983-85, Akron Devel. Corp., 1985-90; Rep. precinct committeeman, 1970, Union County Rep. Ctrl. Com., 1970—; chmn. S.D. State Bd. Equalization, 1987-95, S.D. State Resolutions Com.; mem. synod stewardship bd. Western Iowa Synod Luth. Ch., 1987-90, elected synod assembly bus. and coun. com., 1991-93, synod bus. and coun. com., 1997-99, synod coun. Western Iowa Synod, 1997-2000; S.D. del. Rep. nat. Conv., New Orleans, 1988. Served with AUS, 1951-53, Korea. Decorated Combat Infantry Badge, 3 Bronze Battle Stars; recipient Outstanding Dedication and Svc. award Old Opera House Cmty. Theatre, 1984, Sioux City Siouxland Disting. Citizen award Siouxland Interstate Met. Planning Coun., 1983, Jefferson award Sta. KELO-TV, 1985, Outstanding Cmty. Svc. award Lions Internat., 1985. Mem. NRA, Farm Bur., Farmers Union (exec. bd. Union County 1987-90), S.D. Livestock Feeders Assn., Nat. Cattlemen's Assn., Associated Sch. Bds. S.D. (Merit award 1976), Am. Legion (exec. bd. Akron 1978-92, comdr. Akron 1980-81, 85-86, historian 1981-96, trustee 1983-90, 96—, vice comdr. 9th dist. 1989, chmn. athletics and contest com. Dept. of Iowa Am. Legion, 1991-92, 97-99, 2002-03, judge adv. 9th dist. Iowa 1993—), VFW (Alcester, S.D., vice-comdr. 1995-97, comdr. 2000-02). Lutheran (mem. bd. 1967-70, 82-84, 90-93, 2001—, lay chmn. 1970, 82-93, chmn. centennial com. 1974, chmn. 125th anniversary com. 1999, chmn. ch. bd. 2001-03). Address: Hulteboda Farm 47953 309th St Akron IA 51001-7575

HULTGREN, GLENN M. chiropractor; b. Westby, Mont., Dec. 27, 1932; s. Luther E. and Mae Agnes (Englar) H.; m. M. Marylou Johnston, Feb. 26, 1955; children: Bonnie, Robert, Barry, Bethel. Student, Jamestown Coll., 1950-52; DC, Palmer Coll. Chiropractic, Davenport, Iowa, 1955. Cert. Internat. Chiropractors Coun. Imaging. Pvt. practice, Bismarck, ND, 1955—58, Fort Collins, Colo., 1958—. Mem. Bd. Chiropractic Examiners, Colo., 1982-88; mem. Ctr. for Bioethics and Human Dignity, Chgo., 1997—; pres. Christian Bioethics Awareness, Inc. Mem. Am. Back Soc., AAAS, Christian Chiropractors Assn. (exec. sec. 1958—), Colo. Chiropractic Assn. (pres. 1974), Congress Chiropractic State Assns. (pres. 1977-80), Gideons. Home: 1913 Sequoia Fort Collins CO 80525 Office: 4745 Boardwalk Bldg C-1 Fort Collins CO 80525 E-mail: gmhultgren@bigplanet.com.

HULTIN, JERRY MACARTHUR, dean, lawyer; b. Lansing, Mich., May 17, 1942; s. Arthur Frederick and Donna (Prevey) H.; m. Jill Foreman, June 27, 1965; children: Jeremy Foreman, Jedd Foreman. BA, Ohio State U., Columbus, Ohio, 1960—64; JD, Yale Law Sch., New Haven, CT, 1969—72. Bar: Ohio 1972, U.S. Dist. Ct. (so. dist.) Ohio 1973, U.S. Ct. Appeals (6th cir.) 1975, U.S. Supreme Ct. 1979. Ptnr. Taylor and Hultin, Columbus, Ohio, 1972—74, Moots, Hultin, Weinberger & Cope, Columbus, Ohio, 1975—80; coo Hydron and HydroHorse, Columbus, Ohio, 1980—82; ceo Novatech, Columbus, Ohio, 1982—83; chmn. Hultin & Associates, Inc., Columbus, Ohio, 1984—94; ptnr. Jefferson Partners, Washington, 1994—97; under sec. of the navy Dept. of Def., Washington, 1997—2000; dean Stevens Inst. of Tech., Hoboken, NJ, 2000—. Chief coun. Joint Select Com. on Workers Compensation, Columbus, 1975-76; exec. com. CETA Strike Force, Columbus, 1983-84; trustee, chmn. Savs. & Loan Assurance Corp., Columbus, 1985-88; bd. dirs. Fed. Home Loan Mortgage Corp., McLean, Va.; mem. Chief of Naval Ops. Exec. Panel, 1994—. Sponsor (book and study) The Global Century: Globalization and National Security. Chmn. Columbus Cable Commn., 1977-78; pres. ACTV-Access Cable, Columbus, 1984-86; treas., chmn. Participation 2000, Inc., 1988—. Lt. USN, 1964-69. Lt. USN, 1964—60, Vietnam, Western Pacific and California. Decorated Navy Unit Commendation and various Vietnam-era medals Dept. of Def., Disting. Pub. Svc. Medal Dept. of Navy, Dept. of Def. Mem.: Nat. Economist Club. Achievements include development of Revolution in Business Affairs in Department of the Navy; Navy Marine Corps Intranet; Thirty Something for young naval officers. Avocations: running, squash, tennis, golf, music. Home: 2 Ninth Street Hoboken NJ 07030 Office: Howe School of Technology Management Stevens Institute Castle Point on Hudson Hoboken NJ 07030 Office Fax: 201-216-5385. Personal E-mail: jhultin@stevens.edu. E-mail: jhultin@stevens.edu.

HULTMAN, CHARLES WILLIAM, economics educator; b. Oelwein, Iowa, Apr. 6, 1930; s. John William and Alma (Loeb) H.; m. Irene Oliver, June 7, 1957; children: Susan, Gregory. BA, Upper Iowa U., 1952; MA, Drake U., 1957; PhD, U. Iowa, 1960. Asst. prof. U. Ky., Lexington, 1960-64, prof. econs., 1967-98, chmn. dept., 1969-71, CSX prof. bus. and pub. policy, 1988-98, assoc. dir. Ctr. for Devel. Change, 1971-73, assoc. dean for rsch., 1976-85, prof. emeritus, 1998—; tchr. English, Luth. Ch., Pingxiang, China, summer 1999. Vis. assoc. prof. U. Calif., 1964-65, prof. of banking and fin. Univ. Coll., Dublin, Ireland, 1990; fall semester Ford Found. prof. Fudan U., Shanghai, China, 1989. Author: International Finance, 1963, American Business and the Common Market, 1964, Problems of Economic Development, 1967, Ireland in the World Economy, 1969, (with M. Wasserman, R. Ware) International Economics, 1969, Comparison of Projected Unemployment Insurance Costs, 1973, The Environment of International Ban King, 1990; book rev. editor Internat. Devel. Rev.; mem. editorial adv. bd. Sage Papers in Internat. Studies, assoc. editor internat. econs. Wall Street Rev. Books; acting editor: Jour. Growth

and Change, 1979-86. Chmn. Ky. Coun.Econ. Advisors, 1976-85; mem. So. Growth Policies Bd., 1976-90. With U.S. Army, 1952-55. Fulbright lectr. Ireland, 1967-68 Mem. Eastern Econ. Assn. (exec. bd. 1980-84) Lutheran. Home: 3341 Crown Crest Rd Lexington KY 40517-2809

HULTQUIST, STEVEN JOHN, lawyer; b. Sioux City, Iowa, Jan. 29, 1949; s. Robert Edward and Betty (Van Dyck) H.; m. Judith Ann Raymond, July 10, 1972 (div. May 1981); m. Donna Marie DeMichele, Nov. 18, 1981 (div. Feb. 1995); 1 child, Liana Rose; m. Debra R. Ashe, July 29, 1998. BSChemE, Wash. U., 1970, MSChemE, 1972; JD, Fordham U., 1979. Bar: U.S. Patent and Trademark Office 1976, N.Y. 1980, Calif. 1981, U.S. Dist. Ct. (cen. dist.) Calif. 1982, U.S. Ct. Appeals (9th cir.) 1982, Conn. 1984, U.S. Ct. Appeals (fed. cir.) 1985, N.C. 1987. Lab. researcher Carboline Co., St. Louis, 1969-72; patent engr. Union Carbide Co., Tonawanda, N.Y., 1972-74, patent trainee N.Y.C., 1974-76, patent agt., 1976-80, patent atty., 1980-81, Tosco Corp., L.A., 1981-82; patent counsel Am. Cyanamid Corp., Stamford, Conn., 1982-85; pvt. practice Weston, Conn., 1985-86; assoc. Olive & Olive P.A., Durham, N.C., 1986-87, ptnr., 1988-89; of counsel Harlow, Derr & Stark, Research Triangle Park, N.C., 1990; ptnr. Harlow, Stark, Hultquist, Evans & London, Research Triangle Park, 1990-92; prin. Intellectual Property/Tech. Law, Research Triangle Park, 1992. Adj. prof. engring. N.C. State U., 1994-97; chmn. Incutech Com., 1987, Tech. Exch. Com., 1989; pres. Tri-Letix Corp., 1995-97; v.p. CaroTech LLC, 1995-96, pres., 1996-99; bd. dirs. Coun. Entrepreneurial Devel. Author: North Carolina General Practice Deskbook, 1995—; editor Tech. Exch. Newsletter; patentee in semiconductor mfg., material scis. fields; contbr. articles to profl. jours. Fundraiser YMCA of Wake County, Raleigh, N.C., 1988. Mem. ABA (Intellectual Property Law Chpt. Deskbook award 1998), N.C. Bar Assn. (intellectual property sect., counsel mem. 1992-95), Copyright Law Assn., Durham C. of C., Coun. for Entrepreneurial Devel., N.C. Acad. Trial Lawyers, Licensing Exec. Soc., Sigma Xi (sec. Research Triangle Park chpt. 2000-2002). Republican. Presbyterian. Avocations: civic affairs, bus. devel. and networking, pro bono law, psychology of learning. Home: 100 Steeple Chase Ln Chapel Hill NC 27517-7436 Office: 1414 Raleigh Rd Ste 201 Chapel Hill NC 27517- E-mail: hultquist@iptl.com.

HULTSTRAND, CHARLES JOHN, architect; b. Mt. Vernon, Ohio, Dec. 26, 1951; s. Donald M. and Marjorie R. (Richter) H.; m. Kathi, Brooke, Andrew, Caroline, Clay, Kristi, Scott. BSE, Princeton U., 1974; MArch, Rice U., 1977. Registered architect, S.C. Assoc., project designer Golemon & Rolfe Architects, Houston, 1977-83; prin., exec. v.p., dir. of design The Boudreaux Group, Inc., Columbia, S.C., 1983—. Guest lectr. Clemson (S.C.) U. Coll. Architecture, 1993-97; mem. steering com. Onions & Orchids Award Program, Columbia, 1988, jury mem., 1989; mem. steering com. Columbia R/UDAT Commn., 1987; v.p. Terrace Lake, Inc.; bd. dirs. Columbia Devel. Corp. Pres. parent tchr. fellowship Ben Lippen Sch., Columbia, 1991-94, mem. bd. mgrs., 1991—, v.p. bd., 1995-2000; mem. fundraising com., 1993-2002; deacon Cornerstone Presbyn. Ch., Columbia, 1988-91, First Presbyn. Ch., Columbia, 1997-99, 2000-03, vice chmn., 2001-02, chmn., 2003; pres. Yokemen Svc. Orgn., 1982-83; vol. ARC Hurricane Hugo Relief, 1990, SCETV Fundraising, Columbia, 1991. Mem. AIA (pres. S.C. chpt. 1996, v.p./pres.-elect S.C. chpt. 1995, sec.-treas. S.C. chpt. 1993-94, chmn. spkrs. bur. 1988-90, dir. Columbia sect. 1988-90, chmn. govt. affairs commn. S.C. chpt. 1990-93, bd. dirs., advisor intern devel. program 1990-94, state engr.'s com. 2002), S.C. Archtl. Soc. (bd. dirs./sec. 1997-99), Columbia Design League (bd. dirs. 1997-98), Columbia Coun. Archs. (pres. 1986-87, bd. dirs. 1984-87), Princeton Alumni Assn. S.C. (treas. 1990-94), Greater Columbia C. of C. Avocations: reading, walking, tennis, golf. Office: The Boudreaux Group PO Box 5695 Columbia SC 29250-5695 E-mail: chultstrand@boudreauxgroup.com.

HULTSTRAND, DONALD MAYNARD, bishop; b. Apr. 16, 1927; s. Aaron Emmanuel (H.) and Selma Avendla (Liljegren) Hultstrand; m. Marjorie Richter, June 11, 1948; children: Katherine Ann, Charles John. BA summa cum laude, Macalester Coll., 1950; BD summa cum laude, Colgate-Rochester Theol. Sem., 1974; DD honoris causa, Nashotah Divinity Sch., 1986. Ordained priest Episcopal Ch., 1953, consecrated bishop Episcopal Ch., 82. Vicar St. John's Episcopal Ch., Worthington, Minn., 1953—57; rector Grace Meml. Ch., Wabasha, Minn., 1957—62, St. Mark's Episcopal Ch., Canton, Ohio, 1962—68, St. Paul's Episcopal Ch., Duluth, Minn., 1969—75; assoc. rector St. Andrew's Episcopal Ch., Kansas City, Mo., 1968—69; exec. dir. Anglican Fellowship of Prayer, 1975—79; rector Trinity Episcopal Ch., Greeley, Colo., 1979—82; bishop Episcopal Diocese of Springfield, Ill., 1982—91; exec. bd. Episcopal Radio (TV Found.), Atlanta, 1982—87, Anglican Fellowship of Prayer, 1968—93; adv. bd. Episcopal Boys' Homes, Salinas, Kans., 1983—91; com. of execs. Ill. Conf. Chs., 1982—91; mem. House of Bishops, 1982—, mem. Minn. Standing Com., 1970—73. Chmn. Minn. Examining Chaplains, 1954—61; chaplain Pewsaction Fellowships U.S.A., 1983—92; pres. Living Ch. Found., 1992—2002; advisor Diocesan Youth of Minn., 1956—60. Author: The Praying Church, 1978, And God Shall Wipe Away All Tears, 1968, Intercessory Prayer, 1972, Upper Room Dialogues, 1980, Revelations of Effective Prayer, 1995; co-author: The Parish as a Center of Prayer, 1996. Bd. dirs. Sr. Citizens Housing, Duluth, Minn., 1972—75, St. Luke's Hosp., Duluth, 1969—75; pres. Low-Rent Housing Project, Greeley, 1979—82. Served with USNR, 1945—46. Named hon. canon, Diocese of Ohio, Cleve., 1967; recipient Disting. Svc. award, Young Life Minn., 1974. Mem.: Pi Phi Epsilon. Episcopalian. Address: 1701 S Le Homme Dieu Dr NE Alexandria MN 56308-8504

HUM, VANCE YORK, technology consulting executive; b. San Francisco, Apr. 19, 1948; s. Bing Wai and Jean Bik-Tsun (Pong) H.; m. Carolyn Hwa Cheung, July 2, 1972; children: Matthew Ta, Christina Lee, Jonathan Derek-Lee. Bsee, u. mD., 1971; postgrad., George Washington U., 1977-83, U. Md., 1983—. Engr. Singer-Link Divsn., Silver Spring, Md., 1970; engr., field engr. Bendix Field Engring., Columbia, Md., 1971-72; primary examiner U.S. Patent & Trademark Bd., Arlington, Va., 1972-83; v.p. ops. Cheung Labs., Inc., Lanham-Seabrook, Md., 1983-86; v.p. fin. Cheung Labs. Inc., Lanham-Seabrook, Md., 1985-86; v.p. ops. Century Techs., Inc., Silver Spring, 1988-89; CEO, bd. dirs. Marc's Distbg., Inc., Jessup, Md., 1987-88; CEO, pres. I.M. Systems Group, Inc., Kensington, Md., 1986-87, 89—. Chmn. bd. dirs. I.M. Systems Group, Inc., Md., 1989—; chmn. audit/supervisory com. Lee Fed. Credit Union, Washington, 1977-83; mem. adv. bd. Pacific Savs. and Loan Assn., McLean, Va., 1979-80; chmn. strategic planning com. Nat. Assn. Corp. Dirs., Balt.-Washington, 1989; mem. No. Va. Technology Coun., 2001. Troop treas. Boy Scouts Am., Bethesda/Chevy Chase, Md., 1993—. Mem. Herndon (Va.) C. of C., Monte Jade Sci. and Tech. Assn. Greater Washington D.C. Area (bd. dirs. 1999), No. Va. Tech. Coun. (hon. co-chair bus. adv. coun. 2003). Avocations: tennis, golf, Karate, skiing, gardening, jiu-jitsu. Office: IM Sys Group Inc 3401 Bexhill Pl Kensington MD 20895-3105

HUMANN, L. PHILLIP, bank executive; Chmn., pres. & CEO SunTrust Banks, Inc., Atlanta, 2000—. Office: Suntrust Banks Inc 303 Peachtree St NE Atlanta GA 30308-3201

HUMANN, RICHARD, artist; s. Richard Charles Human and Estella Marie Chonko; m. Susan Darmiento, Nov. 6, 1993. AAS, Harriman Coll., 1981. Represented by Lance Fung Gallery, NYC, 1997—. Installation, Psycho Killer, Evidence of My Being, A Childish Fear, exhibitions include Palazzo Zorzi, Venice Biennale, Venice, 2003, Kemi (Finland) Art Mus., Archivio Emily Harvey, Venice, Italy, 2003, Body Lang., Karolyn Sherwood Gallery, Des Moines, 2003, Possessions for Judgment Day, Project Row Houses, Houston, TX, exhibited in group shows at NY Art, S*MOVA (Sonoma Mus. of Visual Arts, Sonoma, CA, 2002, Mapping the Vicinity, Voorkamer Gallery, Lier, Belgium, 2002, Ssamzie Site Specific, Ssamzie Space, Seoul, Korea, 2001, The Last Waltz, Gallery St. Gertrud, Malm, Sweden, 2000, The Planet Art Gallery, Cape Town, South Africa, 1998, 5 from Williamsburg, Leo Kamen Gallery, Toronto, Can., 1998.

HUMAR, ABHINAV, transplant surgeon, clinical researcher; b. Udaipur, Rajasthan, India, Mar. 25, 1965; s. Jagmohan and Yash Humar; m. Priya Davada, Dec. 29, 1991; children: Rishab, Pooja. MD, U. Ottawa, Can., 1988. Frcs Royal Coll. of Physicians and Surgeons, 1995, Transplant Surgeon U. of Minn./ MN, 1997. Assoc. prof. U. Minn., Mpls., 1998—. Dir. living donor transplant program U. Minn., Mpls., 2001—. Mem.: Am. Soc. Transplant Surgeons. Achievements include research in development of cadaver split liver transplants for adult recipients. Avocations: tennis, skating. Office: University of Minnesota 420 Delaware St SE Minneapolis MN 55455 Office Fax: 612-624-7168. E-mail: humar001@umn.edu.

HUMBACH, MIRIAM JANE, marketing and financial professional; b. N.Y.C., May 18, 1965; d. William Walter and Mildred (Wender) H. BA in Bus.-Econs./Psychology, SUNY, Oneonta, 1986; MBA, Adelphi U., 1996; MS in Acctg., Pace U., 2002. Fin./acctg. staff The N.Y. Times Co., N.Y.C., 1987-92, media svcs. rsch. asst., 1992-93; circulation/staff asst. N.Y. Times Co., N.Y.C., 1993-95, mktg. cns., rsch. analyst, 1995—. Editor: Rethinking Equity Trading at Nasdaq, 1998, The Electronic Call Auction: Market Mechanism and Trading Building a Better Stock Market, 2001. Mem.: NAFE, Beta Alpha Psi (dir. cmty. svc.). E-mail: mjhumbach@yahoo.com.

HUMBLE, MONTY GARFIELD, lawyer; b. Cameron, Tex., Dec. 20, 1951; s. Don Garfield Humble and Betty Sue (Maedgen) French; m. Donell Lou Moss, Mar. 12, 1976 (div. June 1981); m. Macy A. Melton, Oct. 23, 1993; children: Megan Elizabeth, John Marshall, Nicole Marie, Crawford Melton. BA, U. Tex., 1974, JD, 1976. Assoc. Clark, Thomas, Winters and Shapiro, Austin, Tex., 1972-82, Vinson & Elkins, Houston, 1982-86, ptnr. Dallas, 1986—. Bd. dirs. Ft. Worth Ballet, 1990-94, Dallas Opera, 1987-92, Tex. Gen. Counsel Forum, 2001—, Tex. Nanotech. Initiative, 2002—; mem. external rsch. adv. coun. U. Tex., Dallas; gen. counsel Superconducting Super Collider Devel. Authority, 1987-94; mem. Leadership Dallas, 1988; mem. legal advisors Dallas City Charter Revision Com., 1990; mem. Greater Dallas Planning Coun.; mem. adv. coun. U. Tex. Dallas External Rsch., 2002. Fellow Dallas Bar Found.; mem. ABA, State Bar Tex., Nat. Assn. Bond Lawyers (steering com. 1985-87, 94-96, bd. dirs. 2001—, treas. 2002—), Health Care Fin. Mgrs. Assn. (bd. dirs. 1990-92), Crescent Club, Bent Tree Country Club, Phi Beta Kappa. Republican. Office: Vinson & Elkins LLP 2001 Ross Ave Ste 3700 Dallas TX 75201-2975 E-mail: mhumble@velaw.com.

HUME, BRIT (ALEXANDER BRITTON HUME), journalist; b. Washington, June 22, 1943; s. George and Virginia Powell (Minnigerode) H.; m. Clare Stoner, Feb. 10, 1965 (div. 1992); children: Louis, Virginia, Alexander Jr. (dec.); m. Kim Schiller, June 1, 1993. BA, U. Va., 1965. Reporter Hartford (Conn.) Times, 1965-67, UPI, Hartford, Conn., 1967, Balt. Evening Sun, 1968; fellow Washington Journalism Ctr., 1969; reporter Jack Anderson Column, Washington, 1970-72; freelance journalist Washington, 1973; cons. ABC News, Washington, 1973-76, corr., 1976-97; columnist Washington Post Writers Group, 1987-99; chief Washington corr., mng. editor Fox News, Washington, 1997—. Author: Death and the Mines, 1971, Inside Story, 1974. Recipient Emmy award, 1992; named Best in Bus. by Am. Journalism Rev., 1992, 94. Mem. Met. Club, Chevy Chase Club, St. Andrews Soc. Episcopal. Office: FOX News 400 N Capitol St NW Ste 550 Washington DC 20001-1502

HUME, CAMERON R. ambassador; married; 4 children. Grad., Princeton U.; LLB, Am. U. With U.S. Fgn. Svc., 1970—, vice consul, advisor on human rights U.S. Mission to UN, mem. Sec. of State's planning staff, desk officer South Africa, polit. counselor, Beirut, dir. field sch. Tunis, advisor on Middle East, U.S. Mission to UN, 1986-90, sr. advisor, 1990, dep. chief of mission U.S. Embassy to Holy See, 1991-94, minister-counselor for polit. affairs U.S. Mission to UN, 1994-97, amb. Democratic and Popular Republic of Algeria, 1997—2000, amb. Republic South Africa, 2001—. Author: The United Nations, Iran and Iraq, 1994, Ending Mozambique's War, 1994; contbr. articles to profl. jours. Coun. on Fgn. Rels. fellow, 1975-76, Harvard U. Ctr. for Internat. Affairs fellow, 1989-90; U.S. Inst. of Peace guest scholar, 1994. Mailing: United States Embassy PO Box 9536 Pretoria 0001 South Africa Office: United States Embassy 877 Pretoria St Pretoria 0001 South Africa*

HUME, ELLEN HUNSBERGER, media analyst, journalist; b. Chevy Chase, Md., Apr. 24, 1947; d. Warren Seabury and Ruth (Pedersen) H.; m. John Shattuck, Feb. 14, 1991; 1 child, Susannah; stepchildren: Jessica, Rebecca, Peter. BA, Harvard U., 1968; PhD (hon.), Daniel Webster Coll., 1990, Kenyon Coll., 2001. Reporter Somerville (Mass.) Jour., 1968-69; feature writer Santa Barbara (Calif.) News Press, 1969-70; pub. service dir., copy writer KTMS Radio, Santa Barbara, 1970-72; edn. reporter Ypsilanti (Mich.) Press, 1972-73; bus. reporter Detroit Free Press, 1973-75; met. reporter L.A. Times, 1975-77, congl. reporter, 1977-83; White House corr., polit. writer Wall St. Jour., Washington, 1983-88; exec. dir. Shorenstein Ctr. on Press and Politics Harvard U., Cambridge, Mass., 1988-93; moderator The Editors TV program, Montreal, Que., 1990-93; adj. lectr. Kennedy Sch. Govt., 1991-93, Medill Sch. Journalism, 1993-94. Commentator Washington Week in Rev. PBS-TV, 1973—88, CNN, 1993—97; exec. dir. The Democracy Project PBS, 1996—98; cons. US-AID, 2002, Knight Found.; bd. dirs. Internews. Kennedy Inst. Politics fellow, Harvard U., 1981, Annenberg Washington Program fellow, 1993—95, sr. rsch. fellow, U. Mass., Boston, 2003. Mem.: Nat. Press Club, Coun. of Fgn. Rels. Methodist. Address: 121 Hunnewell Ave Newton MA 02458 E-mail: ellen.hume@umb.edu.

HUME, JAMES BORDEN, corporate professional, foundation executive; b. Halifax, N.S., Can., Nov. 6, 1950; s. Thomas White and Elizabeth Mae (Spears) Hume; m. Penelope Ann Morris, June 3, 1972; children: Kathryn Ann, David Stuart. BA, U. Calgary, Alta., Can., 1972. Chartered Acct. V.p. TIW Industries Ltd., Ottawa, Ont., Can., 1978-80; pres. Hume Mgmt. Cons. Ltd., Calgary, 1980-85, Kanesco Holdings Ltd., Calgary, 1985—. Pres. The Kahanoff Found., Calgary, 1984—; bd. dirs. Can. West Found., Ecotrust Can., Southwestern Resources Group, The Kahanoff Found., Calgary, Hudson Bay Co. Fellow, Inst. Chartered Accts., 2002. Mem.: Can. Inst. Chartered Accts. Office: Kahanoff Found 400 Third Ave SW Ste 4206 Calgary AB Canada T2P 4H2

HUME, PATSY DISEKER, politician; b. Dec. 31, 1929; BA, Baylor U., 1950; postgrad., Emory U., 1966-67. Tchr. Randolph AFB Elem. Sch., Tex., 1949-51, Eubank Elem. Sch., Albuquerque, N.Mex., 1956-57; elem. sch. libr. DeKalb County, Ga., 1967-74; middle sch. libr. Alief, Tex., 1974-77. Precinct chmn. Lincoln County Reps., N.Mex., 1990—2002, chmn., 1983—88, co-chair yearbook com., 1993—94, mem. fundraising com., 1993—94, mem. candidate recruitment, 1993, dep. registration officer, 1983—94, rep. to exec. bd., 1994—95, 1st vice chmn., 1995—96, chmn., 1996—97, parliamentarian, 1999—; mem. state ctrl. com. N.Mex. Reps., 1983—97; treas. Federated Rep. Women, 1980—84, 1987—90, county ctrl. com., 1983—, by-laws chmn., 1999—, state ctrl. com., 1999—, parliamentarian, 2000—; chmn. by-laws, standing rules com., parliamentarian Federated Rep. Women of Lincoln County, 2003—. Home: HC 67 Box 56 Nogal NM 88341

HUME, SUSAN RACHEL, finance and economics educator; b. Englewood, N.J., Aug. 25, 1952; d. Philip and Anna Ann (Petrowski) Nachtigal; m. John Elliott Hume, Dec. 27, 1975; children: Philip John, Scot Elliott. BA, Douglass Coll., 1974; MBA, Rutgers U. Grad. Sch. Mgmt., 1976; PhD, CUNY, 2003. Bank analyst N.Y. Fed. Res. Bank, 1976-77, sr. credit analyst, 1977-79; sr. comml. loan officer 1st Pa. Bank, Phila., 1979-81; asst. v.p. Mfrs. Hanover Trust Co., N.Y.C., 1982-83, v.p., 1983-84, dept. head, hedge funding and asset liability mgmt., 1984-88; adj. assoc. prof. fin. and econs. Rider Coll., 1988-90; asst. adj. prof. Fairleigh Dickinson, Madison, N.J., 1991-93; adj. prof. dept. fin. and econs. Baruch Coll., N.Y.C., 1993—. Mem. Douglass Alumnae Endowment Fund Fin. Com., 1985—; pres. Douglass Coll. Class of 1974, 1990-; mem. internat. seminar interest rate risk mgmt. N.Y. Inst. Fin., N.Y.C., 1990-92. Mem. choir, Sunday Sch. tchr. Presbyn. Ch., Glendale; mem. investment com. Glendale Presbyn. Ch.; active Boy Scouts Am., PTO Cedar Hill and Ridge H.S.; former chairperson McGinn Elem. Sch. PTA Reading Program. Recipient Heller alumni award Rutgers U., 1976. Mem.: Beta Gamma Sigma.

HUMENIK, FRANK, science educator, consultant; b. Brooklyn, Ny, May 26, 1937; s. Frank Joseph and Pauline Humenik; m. Sue Anne Humenik; children: Kerry Knoll, David. PhD, Ohio State U., Columbus, Ohio, 1969, MS, 1966, BSCE, 1963. Coord. animal waste mgmt. program NC State U., Raleigh, 1997—, educator and assoc. dept. head biology and agrl. engring., extension leader Raliegh, 1973—87, educator and dept. head biology and agrl. and civil engring. Raleigh, 1969—73; educator. Cons. DeKalb Swine Breeders, DeKalb, Ill., 1975—80; project/fellowship reviews EPA, Washington, 1972—2002; expert witness U.S. Dept. Justice, 2000—01. Contbr. articles to profl. jours.; co-author (book) Livestock Waste Management, 1992, Managing Livestock Waste to Preserve Environmental Quality, 2000. Fellow: Am. Soc. of Agrl. Engineers; mem.: Am. Soc. of Agrl. Engineers (chmn. 1975), USDA Grant, Nat. Ctr. for Manure and Animal Waste Mgmt. (dir. 2002), Nat. USDA Rsch. Ext. Initiative on Animal Waste (co-chair 2002), Sigma Xi. Office: North Carolina State University 909 Capability Drive Raleigh NC 27695 Office Fax: 919-513-1023. E-mail: frank_humenik@ncsu.edu.

HUMES, CHARLES WARREN, counselor, educator; b. Cambridge, Mass. s. Charles W. and Alice E. H.; m. Marilyn A. Harper, Aug. 7, 1965; children: Rebecca Ellyn Gelber, Malinda Maye Sneary. MA, NYU, 1952; EdM, Springfield Coll., 1956; EdD, U. Mass., 1968. Lic. profl. counselor, Va.; cert. profl. counselor, Ariz. Sch. psychologist Westfield (Mass.) Pub. Schs., 1955-62, dir. guidance, 1962-70; assoc. prof. Springfield (Mass.) Coll., 1968-70; dir. pupil svc. and spl. edn. Greenwich (Conn.) Pub. Schs., 1970-80; assoc. prof. No. Va. Grad. Ctr. Va. Tech. U., Falls Church, 1980-88; prof., 1988-93; prof. emeritus, 1993—; pvt. practice, 1985—95; co-owner Clipper Press, 1996—. Author: Pupil Services: Develpment, Coordination, Administration, 1984, Contemporary Counseling: Services, Applications, Issues, 1987, Descendants of Nicholas Humes of Massachussetts, Vols. 1 and 2, 1996-99; book rev. editor: Sch. Counselor, 1984-93; contbr. over 60 articles on counseling to profl. jours. V.p. Westfield Area Child Guidance Clinic, 1963-65, pres., 1965-66; mem. Greenwich Hosp. Nursing Coun., 1970-75. Mem.: SAR (registrar/genealogist Palo Verde, Ariz. chpt. 1997—2000, 2002), ACA (cons.), APA, Ariz. Counselors Assn., Conn. Assn. Counselor Edn. and Supervision (pres. 1979—80), Nat. Geneal. Soc., Phi Kappa Phi, Phi Delta Kappa (v.p. Va. Tech. 1982—83), Ariz. Soc. Mayflower Descendents (state membership chmn. 2002—). Home and Office: 15038 E Palomino Blvd Fountain Hills AZ 85268

HUMES, GRAHAM, investment banker; b. Williamsport, Pa., Oct. 8, 1932; s. Samuel and Elenor (Graham) H.; m. Elizabeth Schwartz Hershey, June 17, 1978; children: Margaret, Kathryn, Malcolm, Elizabeth, John Hershey, Lisa Hershey. BA, Williams Coll., 1954; MBA, Harvard U., 1958. Mng. ptnr. Butcher & Singer, Inc., Phila., 1958-74; sr. v.p. Girard Bank-Mellon Bank, Phila., 1974-87; mng. dir. Legg Mason Wood Walker, Inc., Phila., 1987-93; founder, gen. dir. CARESBAC, St. Petersburg, Russia, 1993-95. Chmn. Cherry Valley (NY) Spring Water Co.; bd. dir. Brunschwig & Fils, Inc., N. White Plains, NY, presiding dir., Technitrol Inc., Trevose, Pa., Baltic Cranberry Corp., St. Petersburg, Russia, George M. Leader Family Corp., Hershey, Pa.; trustee Fgn. Policy Rsch. Inst., Phila., Presbyn. Childrens Village, Rosemont, Pa. Mem. Merion Cricket Club, Phila. Club, Harvard Bus. Sch. Club. Republican. also: PO Box 368 Cherry Valley NY 13320-0368

HUMES, H(ARVEY) DAVID, nephrologist, educator; b. Honolulu, Nov. 20, 1947; s. William and Nancy Humes; m. Dolores Humes; 1 child, Michael David. BA, U. Calif., Berkeley, 1969; MD, U. Calif., San Francisco, 1973. Diplomate Am. Bd. Internal Medicine. Intern Moffit Hosp. and U. Calif. Hosps., San Francisco, 1973-74; resident U. Calif. Hosps., San Francisco, 1974-75; clin. fellow nephrology U. Pa. Hosp., Phila., 1975-76; rsch. fellow lab. kidney & electrolyte physiology Peter Bent Brigham Hosp., Boston, 1976-77; from instr. to asst. prof. medicine Peter Bent Brigham Hosp./Harvard Med. Sch., Boston, 1977-79; from asst. prof. to assoc. prof. internal medicine U. Mich., Ann Arbor, 1979-86, prof. internal medicine, 1986—, John G. Searle prof., chmn. internal medicine, 1996-2000; founder, gen. ptnr., mgr. EpiGenesis, LLC; founder, dir., chief sci. officer Nephros Therapeutics, Inc.; founder, pres. Innovative Biotherapies, Inc. Founder, pres. Innovative Biotherapies, Inc.; mem. sci. adv. bd. NephRx; cons. Sandoz Pharm., Bristol-Meyers-Squibb, Sterling-Winthrop, AmGen., Dow Chem.; dir., chief Nephrology Rsch. Labs., U. Mich., Ann Arbor, 1980-81; chief med. svc. VA Med. Ctr., Ann Arbor, 1983-96, chmn. internal medicine, 1996-2000. Editor: Current Opinion in Internal Medicine, 2001—; editor-in-chief: Kelley's Textbook of Internal Medicine, 1997—2001; mem. editl. bd. Am. Jour. Medicine, 1997—; mem. editl. bd.: Seminars in Nephrology, 1993—, Internat. Yearbook of Nephrology, 1989—; contbr. articles to profl. jours. Grantee Nat. Kidney Found., 1981-85, 87-88, PHS, 1987—, VA, 1982—, Am. Heart Assn., 1982-87, 94-95. Fellow: AAAS, ACP; mem.: Am. Soc. Artificial Internal Organs (trustee), Ctrl. Soc. Clin. Rsch. (past pres.), Nat. Kidney Found. Mich., Nat. Kidney Found. (Pres. award), Internat. Soc. Nephrology, Am. Fedn. Clin. Rsch., Am. Soc. Nephrology, Am. Heart Assn., Am. Soc. Clin. Investigation, Assn. Prof. Medicine, Am. Physiol. Soc., Phi Beta Kappa, Alpha Omega Alpha. Achievements include development of bioartificial kidney; research in cellular basis of acute renal failure, biochemical basis of aminoglycoside-induced acute renal failure, cyclosporine nephrotoxicity, lipid alterations in ischemic acute renal failure, free-radical-induced mitochondrial injury, molecular basis of renal repair in acute renal failure, molecular basis of kidney tubulogenesis. Office: U Mich Med Sch Box 0644 7220 MSRB III 1150 W Medical Ctr Ann Arbor MI 48109

HUMES, JAMES CALHOUN, lawyer, communications consultant, writer, educator; b. Williamsport, Pa., Oct. 31, 1934; s. Samuel Hamilton and Elenor Kathryn (Graham) H.; m. Dianne Stuart, July 25, 1957; children: Mary Stuart Quillen, Rachel Bailey. Student, Hill Sch., Stowe Sch., Eng., Williams Coll., 1953-55; AB, George Washington U., 1959, JD, 1962. Bar: Pa. 1963. Mem. Pa. Ho. of Reps., Harrisburg, 1962-65; exec. dir. Phila. Bar Assn., 1967-69; presdl. asst. policy planning sect. White House, Washington, 1969-70; dir. Office Policy and Plans, U.S. Dept. State, Washington, 1970-72; presdl. asst. White House Staff, Washington; White House cons. to Pres. Ford, Washington, 1976-77; Woodrow Wilson fellow Smithsonian Instn., Washington, 1982-83; adj. prof. Williams Coll., 1986-87; Ryals Chair Leadership and Lang. U. So. Colo., Pueblo, 1997—. Mem. U.S. Commn. for UNESCO; adj. prof. U. Pa., 1985-99; editl. advisor Pres. Ford's memoirs A Time To Heal. Author: Sweet Dream, 1966, Instant Eloquence, 1973, Podium Humor, 1975, Roles Speakers Play, 1976, How to Get Invited to the White House, 1977, Winston Churchill: Speaker of the Century, 1980, Talk Your Way to the Top, 1980, Standing Ovation, 1988, Sir Winston Method, 1991, The Benjamin Franklin Factor, 1992, My Fellow Americans, 1992, Citizen Shakespeare, 1993, Wit and Wisdom of Churchill, 1994, Wit and Wisdom of Benjamin Franklin, 1995, Wit and Wisdom of Abraham Lincoln, 1996, Confessions of a White House Ghost Writer, 1997, Nixon's Ten Commandments of Statecraft, 1998, Eisenhower and Churchill: The Partnership that Saved the World, 2001, Speak Like Churchill Stand Like Lincoln, 2002, Which President Killed a Man, 2002, Winston Churchill, 2003. Decorated Order of Brit. Empire. Fellow Royal Soc. of Art; mem. SAR, St. Nicholas Soc. NY, Soc. Pilgrims, Soc. Cin., Order of Magna Charta, Union League Club, Phila. Cricket Club, Brook Club (NY). Republican. Presbyn. Home: 4404 Turnberry Cres Pueblo CO 81001-1162

HUMICK, THOMAS CHARLES CAMPBELL, lawyer; b. N.Y.C., Aug. 7, 1947; s. Anthony and Elizabeth Campbell (Meredith) H.; m. Nancy June Young, June 7, 1969; 1 child, Nicole Elizabeth Campbell. BA, Rutgers U., 1969; JD, Suffolk U., 1972; postgrad., London Sch. Econs.-Polit. Sci., 1977-78. Bar: N.J. 1972, U.S. Ct. Appeals (3d cir.) 1976, U.S. Supreme Ct. 1977, N.Y. 1981. Law clk. Superior Ct. N.J., 1972-73; assoc. Riker, Danzig, Scherer & Debevoise, Newark and Morristown, N.J., 1973-77; ptnr. Francis & Berry, Morristown, 1978-84, Dillon, Bitar & Luther, Morristown, 1985-92, Schenck, Price, Smith & King, Morristown, 1992—. Arbitrator U.S. Dist. Ct. N.J., 1985—; del. to Jud. Conf. for 3d Jud. Cir. U.S., 1975-79; mem. dist. X ethics com. N.J. Supreme Ct., 1983-87; mem. jud. selection com. Morris County, 1995-99. Contbg. author: Valuation for Eminent Domain, 1973; mem. editl. bd. Suffolk U. Law Rev., 1970-71, N.J. Lawyer, 1993-94. Trustee Peck Sch., 1993-98; trustee Richmond Fellowship N.J., 1982-89, pres., 1984. Mem. ABA, FBA, N.J. Bar Assn., Morris County Bar Assn. (trustee 1995-2000), Bay Head Yacht Club. Republican. Presbyterian. Home: PO Box 191 Oldwick NJ 08858-0191 Office: Schenck Price Smith & King 10 Washington St Morristown NJ 07963-0905 E-mail: tcch@spsk.com.

HUML, DONALD SCOTT, manufacturing company executive; b. Lake Geneva, Wis., May 8, 1946; s. Robert Francis and Shirley (Roberts) H.; m. Joyce Cora Featherstone, Oct. 2, 1965; children: Tiffany Lynn, Alison Michelle, Andrew Scott. BBA, Marquette U., 1969; MBA, Temple U., 1980. Mgr. treasury ops. Allis-Chalmers Corp., West Allis, Wis., 1970-73; dir. fin. services CertainTeed Corp., Valley Forge, Pa., 1973-75, asst. treas., 1975-78, v.p., treas., 1978-81, v.p., comptroller, 1981-83, v.p., div. pres., 1983-86, v.p., group pres., 1986-89, v.p., chief fin. officer, 1989-90; v.p., CFO Saint-Gobain Corp., Valley Forge, Pa., 1990-94; sr. v.p., CFO Snap-on Inc., Kenosha, Wis., 1994—2002;

CFO Greif, Inc., Delaware, Ohio, 2002—. Mem. adv. bd. Marquette U. Sch. Bus. Adminstrn. Mem. Am. Mgmt. Assn., Fin. Execs. Inst., Conf. Bd. CFO Coun., Leading CFOs, Beta Gamma Sigma. Republican. Roman Catholic. Avocations: tennis, running, reading. Home: 1808 Wingate Dr Delaware OH 43015 Office: Greif Inc 425 Winter Rd Delaware OH 43015 E-mail: don.huml@greif.com.

HUMLICEK, EVELYN CLARICE, volunteer, retired nursing educator; b. Tamora, Nebr., Apr. 10, 1923; d. George Edward and Anna Marie (Polacek) H. BS in Nursing, Creighton U., Omaha, 1947; MS in Edn., U. Omaha, 1953; M Nursing Adminstrn., U. Minn., 1958. RN. Staff nurse St. Joseph's Hosp., Omaha, 1945-47; instr. St. Joseph's Hosp. Sch. of Nursing, Omaha, 1947-50; assoc. chief nursing edn. VA Med. Ctr., Omaha, 1950-85. Mem. Nebr. Medicare Beneficiary Adv. Com., 1989—. Counselor Vol. Intervening for Equity, Omaha, 1985—, Am. Assn. Ret. Persons., Omaha, 1986—, tax counselor for elderly; mem. life long learning adv. com. Met. C.C., Omaha, 1993—. Recipient Outstanding Career award chief med. dir. VA, Washington, 1985. Mem. Nebr. Nurses' Assn. (Profl. Achievement award dist. II 1976). Avocations: geneology, travel, bridge. Home: 4220 Spring St Omaha NE 68105-3351

HUMMEL, DANA D. MALLETT, librarian; BA in Art History, Smith Coll., 1957; MA in Libr. and Info. Sci., Denver U., 1968; postgrad., Def. Lang. Inst., 1961, Instituto Mexicano-Norteameric, 1962, John F. Kennedy Ctr. for Spl., 1974, Nat. War Coll., 1976, No. Va. Bus. Sch., 1978, Cath. U. Am., 1981; diploma, U. Italiana per Stranieri, Perugia, Italy, 1997. Head libr., adminstrn. Howard AFB, Libr., C.Z., 1969-70; asst. libr. Holmes Intermediate Sch., 1970-71; tchr. Spanish and substitute tchr. J.E.B. Stuart H.S., 1972-77; sec. Office of exec. dir.-Africa The World Bank, 1978-79; personal sec. to rector Falls Ch. (Va.), 1979-81; mgr. Info. Svcs. Ctr. BDM Internat., subs. Ford Aerospace Co. (now Northrop Grumman), McLean, Va., 1981-88. Mem. vestry Falls Ch. Epis. Ch., 1982; del. Rep. State Conv., 1981, 86; pres. Ravenwood Civic Assn., 1979-80, 80-81, 81-82; rep. Mason Dist., Fedn. Civic Assns.; mem. ann. plan rev. task force Mason Dist., 1981-82; gov. trustee Fairfax County Pub. Libr. Bd., 1982-00, chmn. bd. trustees Fairfax County; lead fund raiser Smith Coll., 1998-2002; active St. Boniface Epis. Ch. Named Outstanding Woman of Yr., Fairfax County Bd. Suprs. and Com. of Women, 1982. Mem. AAUP, ALA, Am. Soc. for Info. Sci., Spl. Libr. Assn., Va. Libr. Assn., D.C. Libr. Assn., Women in Def., Villa D'Este Assn. (bd. dirs. 1995-98, pres. 1997-98), Jr. League Sarasota, Fla., Tournament Players Club Prestancia, Fla., The Field Club, Marie Selby Botanical Gardens, The Smith Club of Sarasota. Home: 7355 Villa D Este Dr Sarasota FL 34238-5649

HUMMEL, GENE MAYWOOD, retired bishop; b. Lancaster, Ohio, Nov. 12, 1926; s. Ivan Maywood and Anna Mildred (Black) H.; m. R. Jeannine Lane, June 17, 1950; children: Gregory L., G. Michael. Student, Miami U., Oxford, Ohio, 1944, Dartmouth Coll., 1944-45; BS in Agr, Ohio State U., 1949, BS in Agrl. Engring, 1950. Supr. North Am. Aviation Inc., Columbus, Ohio, 1951-57; prodn. control chief Martin Co., Orlando, Fla., 1957-61; ordained to ministry Reorganized Ch. of Jesus Christ of Latter Day Saints, 1961; ministerial asst. to Center Stake bishop, Independence, Mo., 1961-63; bishop San Francisco Bay Stake, 1964-70, 1968-70, Center Stake, 1970-72; bishop, mem. Presiding Bishopric Internat. Ch., 1972-88, presiding bishop, 1988-92; ret., 1992. Dir. Health Care Systems, Inc., 1983-92, Ctr. Place Improvement Inc., Independence, Cen. Profl. Bldg., Inc., Independence, E.A. Smith Retirement Ctr., Inc., Cen. Devel. Assn., Inc., Boatmans Bank of Kansas City, Mo.; dir., v.p. Systems Communication, Inc., Independence, 1975-92. Mem. corp. body Independence Sanitarium and Hosp., 1972-92; bd. dirs. Mid-Am. Health Network, Kansas City, 1983-92. With USNR, 1944-45. Reorganized Ch. Of Jesus Christ Of Latter-Day Saints.

HUMMEL, GREGORY WILLIAM, lawyer; b. Sterling, Ill., Feb. 25, 1949; s. Osborne William and Vivian LaVera (Guess) H.; m. Teresa Lynn Beveroth, June 20, 1970; children: Andrea Lynn, Brandon Gregory. BA, MacMurray Coll., 1971; JD, Northwestern U., 1974. Bar: Ill. 1974, U.S. Dist. Ct. (no. dist.) Ill. 1974. Assoc. Rusnak, Deutsch & Gilbert, Chgo., 1974-78; ptnr. Rudnick & Wolfe, Chgo., 1978-97; mem. Bell, Boyd & Lloyd LLC, Chgo., 1997—. Editor Jour. Criminal Law & Criminology Northwestern U., 1973-74; co-author: Illinois Real Estate Forms, 1989; contbr. articles to law jours. Mem. gov. coun. Luth. Gen. Hosp. Advocate Health Care Sys.; trustee Mac Murray Coll., Jacksonville, Ill., 1986-2001; trustee, sec.-treas. Homes for Children Found; bd. advisors Chgo. area coun. Boy Scouts Am., ChildServ; trustee Nat. Inst. Constrn. Law and Practice. Mem. Internat. Bar Assn. (past co-chmn. com. internat. constrn. projects), Am. Coll. Constrn. Lawyers (past pres.), Urban Land Inst. (trustee), Urban Land Inst. Found. (gov.), Chgo. Dist. Coun. (past chmn.), Lambda Alpha Internat. (Ely chpt. past pres.). Office: Bell Boyd & Lloyd LLC 3 1st Nat Plaza 70 W Madison St Ste 3300 Chicago IL 60602-4207 E-mail: ghummel@bellboyd.com.

HUMMEL, KAY JEAN, physical therapist; b. Cleve., Apr. 24, 1943; d. Lloyd Elmer and Olive Agnes (Latou) Hetherington; m. Charles William Hummel (div. Feb. 1984); children: Patrick H., Robin E. BA, Miami U., Oxford, Ohio, 1965; cert. in phys. therapy, Columbia U., N.Y., 1966. Lic. phys. therapist, La.; cert. ofcl. Games Uniting Mind and Body. Staff phys. therapist St. Joseph's Hosp., Chgo., 1966-68, Wrightwood Extended Care Facility, Chgo., 1967-68, Suburban Hosp., Bethesda, Md., 1969, Holy Cross Hosp., Silver Spring, Md., 1969-70; asst. chief phys. therapist Community Gen. Hosp., Syracuse, N.Y., 1970-76; itinerant phys. therapist Caddo Parish Schs., Shreveport, La., 1976—; pvt. practice Shreveport, 1985—. Games Uniting Mind & Body, Inc. classifer and cert. ofcl. Mem. U.S. Cerebral Palsy Athletic Assn. (regional classifier), Presbyn. Women: Presbytery of the Pines Coord. Team, North La. Scottish Soc., elder, Presbyn. Ch., Kappa Delta Alumni Assn. Office: 3004 Knight St Shreveport LA 71105-2506

HUMMEL, MARIAN, retired art teacher, photographer; b. Bethlehem, Pa., May 12, 1943; d. Donald Clare and Helen Florence (Harman) Conner; m. Gerard G. Hummel, June 29, 1998. BA in Fine Arts, Fairleigh Dickinson U., 1966; MA in Visual Arts, William Paterson Coll., Wayne, N.J., 1971, postgrad., 1991. Cert. art tchr., supr., prin., N.J. Tchr. art Hopatcong Sch. Sys., Lake Hopatcong, N.J., 1966-67; art instr. Am. Acad. for Girls, Istanbul, Turkey, 1967-68; art. instr. Boonton Twp. (N.J.) Sch. Sys., 1968-99, gifted/talented coord., 1989-99. Photographer for greeting cards; exhibited photographs in shows at Kemerer Mus., Bethlehem, Pa., 1974, Jockey Hollow Gallery, Morristown, N.J., 1979, Bergen Cmty. Mus., 1981; photos in permanent collection Lehigh U., Bethlehem. VOL. FOR ANIMAL SHELTERS. Recipient awards for tchg. and for photography. Mem ASCD, Art Educators N.J., Boonton Twp. Edn. Asn. (v.p. 1989-99, negotiations chair 1989-99). Republican. Presbyterian. Avocations: landscape and travel photography, reading, walking.

HUMMEL, MARILYN MAE, elementary education educator; b. Cleve., June 20, 1931; d. John Winfield and Meta E. (Timm) H. BS, Ohio U., 1953. Cert. elem. educator. Elem. tchr. Lakewood (Ohio) Bd. of Edn., 1953-83. Mem. Centennial Planning Com., Lakewood, Ohio 1989; vol. United Way, Lakewood Hosp. Jennings scholar, 1969-70; named Tchr. of the Yr., Franklin Sch., 1983. Mem.: Lakewood Hist. Soc., Kiwanis Club, Coll. Club West, Delta Kappa Gamma. Republican. Presbyterian.

HUMPHREVILLE, JAMES EDWIN, conductor; b. Lorain, Ohio, Sept. 25, 1930; s. George Dewey and Elizabeth (Caple) H.; m. Ada May Schleig, Aug. 31, 1952; children: Kim Elizabeth, Scott Douglas. BMus, Ohio Wesleyan U., 1952; MA, Columbia U., 1961; profl. diploma, U. Conn., 1969. Cert. music tchr., Conn. Tchr. Danbury (Conn.) High Sch., 1957-61, dir. choirs, 1961-75; supr. music Danbury Pub. Schs., 1975-90; mem. affiliate faculty music Western Conn. State U., Danbury, 1960-70; condr. Danbury Concert Chorus, 1967-85; music dir.- condr. Danbury Symphony Orch., 1977-2000, music dir. and condr. emeritus, 2000—; condr. Conn. Opera Alliance, Redding, 1994-97. Bd. dirs. Danbury Concert Assn., 1967-80; mem. music edn. adv. com. Conn. State Bd. Edn., Hartford, 1973-76. With U.S. Army, 1952-55. Mem. Am. Fedn. Musicians, Conn. Music Educator Assn. (pres. 1971-73), Danbury Musicians Assn. (v.p. 1991-97), Music Educator Nat. Conf. (east divsn. bd. 1971-73), Masons, Lions Club. Avocations: scuba diving, travel. Home: 9 Cedar Crest Dr Danbury CT 06811-4227 Office: Danbury Music Ctr 256 Main St Danbury CT 06810-6635

HUMPHREY, CHESTER BOWDEN, cardio-thoracic surgeon; b. Marblehead, Mass., July 29, 1939; s. Leonard Graves and Mary Louise (Bowden) H.; m. Joyce Claire Jazwinski, Mar. 20, 1971; 1 child, Andrew Bowden. BS, Dickinson Coll., 1961; MD, Temple U., 1965. Diplomate Am. Bd. Thoracic Surgery, Am. Bd. Surgery. Intern Hartford Hosp., 1965-66, resident in gen. surgery, 1966-71; resident in thoracic and cardiovascular surgery Naval Regional Med. Ctr., San Diego, 1973-75; cardio-thoracic surgeon Cardiothoracic and Vascular Surgeons, P.C., 1976—. Adv. com. Town of West Hartford (Conn.) Paramedics, 1989—. Comdr. USN, 1970-76. Fellow Am. Coll. Surgeons, Am. Coll. Cardiology, Am. Coll. Chest Physicians; mem. Soc. for Thoracic Surgeons, Denton Cooley Surg. Soc., New England Soc. for Vascular Surgery. Office: Cardiothoracic & Vascular Surgeons PC 85 Seymour St Ste 325 Hartford CT 06106-5522

HUMPHREY, CRAIG REED, social studies educator; b. Grand Rapids, Mich., Oct. 14, 1942; s. Roger and Ruth Reed Humphrey; m. Catherine Elaine Clark, Aug. 6, 1966; children: Michelle Ruth, Gwen Allison. BA, Bowling Green State U., Ohio, 1964; MA, Brown U., Providence, 1967; PhD, Brown U., 1971. Asst. prof. Coll. of William and Mary, Williamsburg, Va., 1969—71, Pa. State U., University Park, 1971—77, assoc. prof., 1977—2001, assoc. prof. emeritus of sociology and demography, 2001—. Vis. assoc. prof. Yale U., New Haven, 1996—97. Co-author: (book) Environment, Energy and Society, 2002, (anthology) Environment, Energy and Society: Exemplary Works, 2003. Pres. Cmty. Land Trust, State College, Pa., 2002—. Mem.: Rural Sociol. Soc. (assoc. editor 2002—), Am. Sociol. Assn. (sect. pres. 1986—88, chair sect. on environment and tech. 1986—88). Democrat. Episcopalian. Avocations: sailing, gardening, writing, physical fitness. Home: 227 W Prospect Ave State College PA 16801 Office: Pa State Univ Dept Sociology 215 Oswald Tower University Park PA 16802

HUMPHREY, DIANA YOUNG, fund raiser; b. Balt., Feb. 7, 1938; d. Edwin Parson and Elizabeth Miller (Hoskins) Young; m. David Henry Carls, July 27, 1963 (div. Dec. 17, 1997); children: Peter Van Patten Carls, Elizabeth Roy Carls, Susan Montanye Carls; m. George Lee Humphrey, May 22, 1999. AB, Smith Coll., Northampton, Mass., 1960. Lic. real estate broker, Mass., 1978. Fgn. rights sales Little, Brown & Co., Inc., Boston, 1960-63, speech writer DNA Rsch., N.Y.C., 1963-64; vol. fund raiser John V. Lindsay, N.Y.C., 1964-65, Smith Coll., Northampton, Mass., 1970-75, 90-95, Smith Coll. Club, Concord, Mass., 1976-89, Jr. League of Boston, 1967—; bd. mem. devel. Ctr. House, Inc., Boston, 1981-94; fund raiser events Boston Symphony Orch., 1975—; dir. edn. Hawthorne Ptnrs. Inc. Fund raising, events Mass. Soc. for Prevention of Cruelty to Children, Boston, 1997—. Editor: Huntington Hartford Gallery Modern Art, N.Y.C., 1963. Speechwriter, Nelson A. Rockefeller Presdl. campaign, N.Y.C., 1963-64; active John V. Lindsay for Mayor, N.Y.C., 1964-65; mem., chmn. Wayland (Mass.) Planning Bd., 1976-81, Wayland Housing Partnership, 1987—; mem. Patriots' Trail coun. Girl Scouts U.S. Mem. Jr. League of Boston, Weston Golf Club. Episcopalian. Avocations: golf, travel, gardening, singing, politics. Home: 42 Cutting Cross Way Wayland MA 01778-3845

HUMPHREY, DORIS DAVENPORT, publishing company executive, consultant, educator; b. Woodbury, Tenn., June 3, 1943; d. Luther and Gladys (Alexander) Davenport; m. John Sparkman Humphrey, Sept. 15, 1941 (dec.); children: Heather, Holly. BS, Middle Tenn. State U., 1965; MBE, Ga. State U., 1972, EdS, 1977, PhD, 1983; postgrad., Bryn Mawr Coll., 1989. Sec., coord. creative svcs., asst. to pres. Noble-Dury & Assocs., Nashville, 1965-69; asst. account exec. McCann-Erickson & Assocs., Atlanta, 1969-70; adj. and full-time instr. DeKalb C.C., 1970-79; coord. internship program Raymond Walters Coll., U. Cin., 1980-83, chmn. dept. office adminstrn., 1981-86; asst. dean bus. and office mgmt. Delaware County C.C., Media, Pa., 1987-90; pres. Career Solutions Tng. Group, Paoli, Pa., 1990. Lectr. in field; curriculum cons. Author: The Medical Office: A Reference Manual, 1997, Pediatric Associates, P.C., 2004, School to Work Series, 1994, 2001, Quick Skills Series, 2002; pub. Career Launcher, 1998, Reality, 1999, It's for Real, 2001, Hands on Academics, 2002. Former trustee Harcum Coll., 1996—2002; elder Presbyn. Ch., 1999—2002; bd. dirs. Main Line C. of C. Mem. Nat. Bus. Edn. Assn., Am. Vocat. Assn., Friend Bus. Edn. State Pa., Delta Pi Epsilon. Presbyterian.

HUMPHREY, EDWARD WILLIAM, surgeon, medical educator; b. Fargo, N.D., Dec. 6, 1926; s. Edward W. and Minnie (Ramstad) H.; m. Noreen Sander, Sept. 23, 1950; children: Katherine Lisa, Joan Karen. BA, U. Minn., 1948, MD, 1951, PhD in Physiology, 1959. Mem. faculty U. Minn. Med. Sch., Mpls., 1958-94, prof. surgery, 1965-94; prof. emeritus, 1994—; interim chair U. Minn. Med. Sch., Mpls., 1993-94; mem. staff VA Hosp., Mpls., 1958-94, chief surg. svc., 1962-93. Author: Manual of Pulmonary Surgery, 1982, (with D. McQuarrie) Reoperative General Surgery, 1992, 2d edit., 1996; contbr. articles to profl. jours. Mem. A.C.S., Minn. Surg. Soc., Am., Central surg. assns., Soc. Univ. Surgeons, Am. Physiol. Soc., Am. Soc. Cell Biology, Am. Assn. Thoracic Surgery, Soc. Internat. De Chirurgie, Soc. Exptl. Biology and Medicine, Sigma Xi, Alpha Omega Alpha. Achievements include research in fields of cancer, pulmonary physiology, biological transport, thoracic surgery. Home: 95 Harbour Passage Hilton Head Island SC 29926-1264

HUMPHREY, GEORGE MAGOFFIN, II, plastic molding company executive; b. Cleve., Mar. 19, 1942; s. Gilbert Watts and Louise (Ireland) H.; m. Marguerite Burton, June 19, 1964 (div. 1989); children: Mary O., Sandra; m. Patience Ryan, June 22, 1991. BA, Yale U., 1964; JD, U. Mich., 1967. Bar: Ohio 1967. Sales rep. Hanna Mining Co., Cleve., 1970-72, European rep., 1972-77, sales rep., 1977-78, mgr. sales, 1978, v.p. sales, 1978-80, sr. v.p. fin., 1980-81, sr. v.p. sales, dir., 1981-84; mng. dir. Russell Reynolds Assocs., Cleve., 1984-87; gen. ptnr. Philips Industries, Ltd., Cleve., 1987-94; pres. Extrudex, Cleve., 1990—. Trustee Cleve. Mus. Art, Cleve. Mus. Natural History, Cleve. Scholarship Programs, Inc., Univ. Hosps. Cleve. Served to capt. USMC, 1967-70. Mem. Union Club (Cleve.). Republican. Episcopalian. Home: 18 W Mather Ln Bratenahl OH 44108-1158 Office: Extrudex 310 Figgie Dr Painesville OH 44077-3028

HUMPHREY, JOHN JULIUS, university program director, historian, writer; b. Booneville, Miss., Jan. 22, 1926; s. George Duke and Josephine (Robertson) H.; m. Mary Margaret Ryan, Jan. 19, 1949 (dec. June 1996); children: George Duke II, Laurie Ann. BS, Miss. State U., 1945; BA, U. Wyo., 1946, MA, 1964, postgrad., 1964-68, U. Ariz., 1969-71. Pres. J.J. Humphrey Co. Inc., Laramie, Wyo., 1947-68; lectr. History U. Ariz., Tucson, 1969-71, asst. dir. placement, 1969-70, dir. scholarships, awards, 1970-72, dir. office of scholarships and fin. aid, 1972-84, dir. scholarship devel., 1970-91; asst. to pres. western area Cumberland Coll., Williamsburg, Ky., 1991; v.p. bus. affairs Tucson Coll. Arts and Scis., 1992. Sec. Baird Found., Tucson, 1970—; bd. dirs. Bendalin Fund, Phoenix, 1976—, Cacioppo Found., Tucson, 1986—; cons. DeMund Found., St. Louis, 1970—; mem. Pres. Club U. Ariz. Found.; mem. Ariz. Assn. Fin. Aid Officers, 1970-91, pres., 1973-74; pres. Ariz. Coll. & Univ. Faculty Assn., 1972-73. Ivinson Meml. Hosp. Bd., Laramie, 1964-68. Recipient Spl. award U. Ariz. Black Student Govt., 1983, Black Alumni, 1990; study grantee U. Ariz., 1993—. Mem. Am. Indian Alumni Assn. (Spl. Appreciation for Svc. in Scholarships Native Ams. award 1982), Mormon History Assn., Masons (32 degree, Knight York Cross of Honor), Shriners. Methodist. Home: 5602 E Holmes Tucson AZ 85710

HUMPHREY, LOIS ELLEN, librarian; b. Coos Bay, Oreg., Aug. 21, 1932; d. James Follett Houston and Lillette Anna (Carlson) Laneway; m. Thomas Harold Humphrey, Aug. 29, 1952; children: Denise, Ellen, Megan, Jane. BS, U. Oreg., 1959, MLS, 1969. Librarian Marshfield H.S., Coos Bay, 1959—60, Coquille (Oreg.) H.S., 1976—. Adv. bd. Coos County Edn. Svc., Coos Bay, 1977—. Mem.: Coquille Edn. Assn. (bldg. rep. 1982, 1984, v.p. 1989—90, pres. 1990—91), Coos Bay Libr. Assn. (life; officer 1976—), Northwest Quilters, Friends of Wilsonville Libr. (life), Coos Sand and Sea Quilters (charter), South Coast Wave Walkers (v.p. 1991), Cmty. Concert Assn. Coos Bay (bd. dirs. 1965—), Coos Hist. Soc. (life), Coos Bay Jr. Women's Club (pres. 1962—63), South Coast Running Club (treas. 1988—), Sons and Daus. Oreg. Pioneers (life), Delta Kappa Gamma (scholarship com.), P.E.O. Sisterhood (state area edn. chmn., chpt. pres. 2000—02). Episcopalian. Home: 6576 SW Stratford Ct Wilsonville OR 97070-6787

HUMPHREY, LOUISE IRELAND, civic worker, equestrienne; b. Morehead City, N.C., Nov. 1, 1918; d. R. Livingston and Margaret (Allen) Ireland; m. Gilbert W. Humphrey, Dec. 27, 1939; children: Margaret (Mrs. K. Bindhart), George M. II, Gilbert Watts. Educated pvt. schs. Nurse's aide ARC, 1944-64. Past. dir. Nat. City Bank, Cleve., Nat. City Corp., Cleve. 1981-86. Trustee Mus. Arts Assn.; hon. trustee, past pres. Vis. Nurse Assn.; hon. trustee Lake Erie Coll.; life trustee United Way Cleve.; trustee Archbold Med. Ctr. and Hosp., Thomasville, Ga.; hon. trustee Case Western Res. U., Bus. Coun. Internat. Understanding Inc.; bd. dirs. Monticello (Fla.) Opera Ho.; mem., former trustee, 2d v.p. Jr. League Cleve.; past pres., hon. chmn. bd. dirs. Met. Opera Assn., NY; bd. dirs. Lincoln Ctr., NY, Thomas County Entertainment Found.; past pres. No. Ohio Opera Assn.; mem. adv. bd. Coll. Vet. Medicine U. Fla., Gainesville; mem. Ohio Arts Coun., 1975—85; treas., trustee Wildlife Conservation Fund Am.; former master Foxhounds Chagrin Valley Hunt, Gates Mills, Ohio; past dir., zone v.p. U.S. Equestrian Team Inc., now hon. life dir.; mem. Garden Club Cleve.; bd. dirs., past pres. Nat. Homecaring Coun.; treas., bd. dirs. Wildlife Legis. Fund Am. Conservation Fund; past pres. bd. dirs. Thomasville Cultural Ctr.; bd. dirs. Cmty. Found. North Fla.; commr. Fla. Game & Fresh Water Fish, 1984—99. Home: Box 91102 Woodfield Springs Plantation Tallahassee FL 32309

HUMPHREY, MATTHEW J. manufacturing specialist; b. Bandon, Oreg., Oct. 2, 1963; s. Kenneth Price and Shirley Ann (McAllister) H.; m. Cindy Lynne Humphrey, May 6, 1989; children: Emily Rose, Marina Lynne, Jonathon Caleb, Noelle Violet, Seth Martin(dec.). BA in French, Portland State U., Oreg., 2000. Author: Treasure in Heaven, 2000, Cape Blanco, 2001; singer: (CD) Christmas Lullabies, 2001. Specialist 1st class U.S. Army, 1986—90. Mem.: Toastmasters Internat. Republican. Evangelical. Avocations: writing, singing.

HUMPHREY, NEIL DARWIN, retired university president; b. Idaho Falls, Idaho, May 20, 1928; s. Clair Pierce and Freda (Hatfield) H.; m. Mary Pat Smith, Aug. 21, 1950; children: Ann Humphrey Melcher, Therese Humphrey Hymer. BA in Polit. Sci., Idaho State U., 1950; MS in Govt. Mgmt., U. Denver, 1951; EdD, Brigham Young U., 1974; LHD (hon.), U. of Akron, 1991; LLD (hon.), U. Nev., 1995. Exec. sec. Nev. Taxpayers Assn., 1955-59; budget dir. State of Nev., Nev., 1959-61; bus. mgr. U. Nev., 1961-64, v.p. fin., 1964-67, acting pres., 1967-68; chancellor U. Nev. System, 1968-77; pres. U. Alaska, 1977-78; v.p. for fin. affairs Youngstown (Ohio) State U., 1978-79, exec. v.p., 1979-84, pres., 1984-92. Bd. dirs. First Fed. Savs. and Loan of Youngstown, 1984-1992, bd. dirs. Comml. Intertech Corp., 1985-200 Home: 1404 Copper Point Cir Reno NV 89509-6262

HUMPHREY, OWEN EVERETT, retired education administrator; b. Wautoma, Wis., Oct. 25, 1920; s. Marion A. and Flora A. (Helms) H.; m. Billye A. Cox, Apr. 6, 1946 (dec. Dec. 1974); children: Reba, Ivye. BS, U. Wis., Whitewater, 1947; MS, U. Ark., 1949; advanced cert., U. Ill., 1954. Life gen. supervisory cert. grades K-14. Elem. classroom tchr. Four Corners Sch., Plainfield, Wis., 1941-42; jr. high art and sci. tchr. Jefferson Sch., Sheboygan, Wis., 1947-48; elem. classroom tchr. and prin. Holcomb, Mo., 1949-50, Lincoln Sch., Mattoon, Ill., 1950-55; supervising prin. various elem. schs., Peotone, Ill., 1955-57; elem. tchr. Nameoki Sch., Granite City, Ill., 1957-59; elem. prin. Maryville Sch., Granite City, 1959-67; curriculum coord. Sch. Dist. #9, Granite City, 1967-79; adminstrv. asst. Regional Supt. of Schs., Madison County, Ill., 1979-81, 85-87; ret., 1987. Leader parent study groups Ea. Ill. U., Mattoon, 1950-54; PTA field unit organizer Ill. Congress of Parents and Tchrs., Mattoon, 1952-54; coord. local dist. planning Sch. Dist. #9, Granite City, 1973-79; rep. Ill. State Curriculum Coun., Springfield, 1980-81. Co-author: The Greening of Gateway East, 1984; contbr. poetry to Nat. Libr. of Poetry anthologies; contbr. articles to profl. jours. Dir. chorus Area Coun. PTA, Mattoon, 1950-54, Granite City Area Coun. PTA, 1957-59; dir. Granite City Steel Mixed Chorus, 1958-60; actor Creative Arts Theatrical Soc., 1992--. Sgt. U.S. Army Infantry, 1942-45, ETO. Recipient Area Coun. PTA award Granite City, Ill., 1979. Mem. NEA (life), ASCD (life), Ill. ASCD (life, bd. dirs.), Internat. Poets Soc. (life), Creative Arts Theatrical Soc. (bd. govs.), Miners Inst. Found. (bd. dirs. 2002-03), Phi Delta Kappa (Gateway East chpt. sec., historian, v.p., pres., Svc. Key award 1984, George H. Reavis Assoc. award 1991). Avocation: composing music and lyrics. Home: 18 Wilson Park Dr Granite City IL 62040-3550

HUMPHREY, PATRICIA BUSLEE, statistician, researcher; d. Roger Martin and Shirley Remquist Buslee; m. Thomas Joseph Humphrey, July 19, 1981; children: Emma Margaret, Ceba Lynn. BA, Ft. Lewis Coll., 1976; MA, U. of N.Mex, 1978; PhD, U. of Alaska, 1995. Staff mem. Los Alamos (N.Mex.) Nat. Lab., 1980—82, sect. leader, 1982; computer analyst Planning Rsch. Corp., Albuquerque, 1982—84; sys. analyst EG&G, Albuquerque, 1984; programmer/analyst Fairbanks (Alaska) North Star Borough, 1984—89; vis. asst. prof. of stats. U. of Alaska, 1996—97; asst. prof. of stats. Ga. So. U., Statesboro, 1997—. Contbr. articles to profl. jours. Math. team coach Statesboro (Ga.) H.S., 1999—2003. Mem.: Math. Assn. of Am. (newsletter editor SIGMAA on Stats. Edn. 1998—). Avocation: reading. Office: Ga So U PO Box 8093 Statesboro GA 30460

HUMPHREY, PHYLLIS A. writer; b. Oak Park, Ill., July 22, 1929; d. Richard William and Antoinette (Chalupa) Ashworth; m. Herbert A. Pihl, Sept. 13, 1946 (div. 1957); children: Christine Pihl Gibson, Gary Fraizer Pihl; m. Curtis H. Humphrey, June 21, 1965; 1 child, Marc. AA, Coll. San Mateo, Calif., 1972; postgrad., Northwestern U., 1945-47. Ptnr. Criterion House, Oceanside, Calif., 1972—. Author: Wall Street on $20 a Month, 1986, Golden Fire, 1986, Sweet Folly, 1990, Flying High, 1995, Once More With Feeling, 1998, Tropical Nights, 2000, Choices, 2001, North by Northeast, 2001, Charade, 2002; author radio scripts Am. Radio Theatre, 1983-84; contbr. short stories and articles to popular mags. Mem. Mensa. Republican. Christian Sci. Ch. Avocations: reading, travel. Office: Criterion House PO Box 586295 Oceanside CA 92058-6295

HUMPHREY, ROGER GAVIN, music educator; b. Alma, Mich., Apr. 1, 1948; s. Wallace Otto and Margaret Louise Humphrey; m. Barbara Elaine Mead, Oct. 20, 1979; children: Alexis Sylvon Gorlock, Joshua Jacob Strieff- ;children: Shawn Aileen Acosta-Arellano, Eric Jay Lovejoy. Guitar instr. Marshalls Sch. of Music, Lansing, Mich., 1981—, Olivet Coll., Mich., 1988—, Alma Coll., Mich., 1992—. Owner/pres. First Music, St. Louis, 1995. Author: (book) Learning the Guitar Vol. I & Vol. II, My 1st Guitar Book, My 2nd Guitar Book, etc. Elder Peace Luth. Ch., Alma, Mich., 1994—98. E-4 USAF, 1967—71, Mich. and Japan. Grant, U. S. Govt., 1976—78. Mem.: Phi Mu Alpha. Independent. Lutheran. Avocation: bicycling. Office: Olivet College Arts/Communications Dept 320 S Main St Olivet MI 49076-9406 Personal E-mail: humphreyroger@netscape.net. E-mail: rhumphrey@olivetcollege.edu.

HUMPHREY, SAMUEL STOCKWELL, town official, physicist; b. Canton Center, Conn., Apr. 25, 1923; s. Harold William and A. Genevieve (Stockwell) H.; m. Mary Elizabeth Mills, Feb. 4, 1945; children: Warren Mills, Kenneth Stockwell, Marianne Ruth. BS, U. Conn., 1948; MA, Wesleyan U., Middletown, Conn., 1950; postgrad., U. Utah, 1961-63. Enlisted USAF, 1942, advanced through grades to lt. col., 1966, ret., 1971; physicist Wesleyan U., 1948-51; cons. physicist Canton, Conn., 1971-74; tchr. physics Canton (Conn.) High Schs., 1973-74, real estate broker, 1975-93; first selectman Town of Canton, 1983-87, selectman, 1989-91, mem. bd. fin., 1997—; mgr. Cherry Brook Farm LLC. Dir. Conn. Conf. Municipalities, Conn. Interlocal Risk Mgmt. Agys. (CIRMA), 1987; bd. dirs. Sundown Ski Patrol, Inc.; mem. policy bd. and exec. com. Capitol Region Coun. of Govts., 1983-87; cons. physicist RCA, Burlington, Mass., 1971-74, Martin Marietta, Orlando, Fla., 1971-72; co-founder Simsbury (Conn.) Bank & Trust Co.; researcher in field. Author, editor numerous studies and reports. Trustee, treas. 1st Congl. Ch., Canton Ctr., 1972-85; chmn. Hist. Dist. Commn., Canton, 1972-80, Mcpl. Bd. Fin., Canton, 1975-83, 97—; justice of peace State of Conn., 1974—. Recipient numerous awards and decorations USAF and Philippines; Wesleyan U. fellow, 1948-50. Mem. Optical Soc. Am. (emeritus), Air Force Assn., Conn. Christmas Tree Growers Assn. (bd. dirs. 1984-90, v.p. 1990, pres. 1992-95), New Eng. Christmas Tree Assn. (dir. 1990—), Hanscom Flying Club (Bedford, Mass., pres. 1955-59), Skiesta Club (pres. 1964-68), Sigma Xi (assoc.), Sigma Pi Sigma. Republican. Mem. United Ch. of Christ. Avocation: ski patrol. Home: Box 150 96 Barbourtown Rd Canton Center CT 06020-0150 E-mail: sshumphrey@aol.com.

HUMPHREY, SANDRA MCLEOD, psychologist; b. Salt Lake City, Aug. 6, 1936; d. Murdoch John McLeod and Virginia Carol (Matthews) Sveeggen; m. Brian Neil McLeod Humphrey, Sept. 16, 1961; children: Jade, Brandon, Tricia. BA, U. Minn., 1958, MA, 1961. Lic. cons. psychologist Minn. Clin. psychologist Anoka-Metro (Minn.) Regional Treatment Ctr., 1961-92. Cons. in field. Author: A Dog Named Sleet, 1984, If You Had to Choose, What Would You Do?, 1995, It's Up to You. . .What Do You Do, 1999, Keepin' it Real, A Young Teen Talks with God, 2003, If You Had to Choose, What Would You Do?, 2003; contbr. articles to profl. jours., stories to children's mags. Vol. Death Row Prison Ministry, 1985—, Damascus Way Prison Ministry, Mpls., 1987—, Foster Care Rev. Bd., 1986, Our Saviour's Shelter, Mpls., 1988; confirmation mentor Oak Knoll Ch., 1992—, vol. Youth Ministry Team, 1992—, tchr. Sun. sch., 1992—. Mem.: Soc. Children's Book Writers and Illustrators. Avocations: tennis, swimming, writing, reading, pets. Home: 19 Westwood Rd Minnetonka MN 55305-1587 E-mail: Sandra305@aol.com.

HUMPHREY, STEPHEN M. paperboard company executive; b. Oct. 10, 1944; BS, Siena Coll., 1967. With GE Co., 1967—81; pres. on-hwy. products bus. Rockwell Internat. Corp., 1981—94; chmn., pres., CEO Nat. Gypsum Co., Charlotte, NC, 1994—96; pres. CEO Riverwood Internat. Corp. Atlanta, 1997—2003, also bd. dirs. Riverwood Internat. Corp., Atlanta, pres., CEO Graphic Packaging Corp. (formerly Riverwood Internat. Corp.), Atlanta, 2003—. Office: Graphic Packaging Corp Ste 1400 3350 Riverwood Pkwy SE Atlanta GA 30339-6401*

HUMPHREY, SUSANNE MARGUERITE, information scientist; b. Shanghai, Jan. 1, 1945; arrived in U.S., 1950; d. Richard and Amalie (Schlamowicz) Kriss; m. Andrew Clifton Humphrey, Mar. 16, 1970; 1 child, Andrew Clifton Jr. BA, U. Md., 1965, MLS, 1969. Indexer Nat. Libr. Medicine, Bethesda, Md., 1965-66, searcher, 1967-68, database mgr., 1969-70, thesaurus specialist, 1971-81, researcher, 1982-84, rsch. project leader, 1985—. Reviewer NSF grant proposals; cons. AAAS, Washington, 1987—88; referee Jour. Am. Soc. Info. Sci. Tech., Proceedings of ASIST Ann. Meeting, Genome Biology. Author: Databases: A Primer for Retrieving Information by Computer, 1986 ; contbr. chpt. in book Expert Systems in Libraries, 1990; editor: (newsletter) SIG/CR News, 1990-91; contbr. chpts. to books and articles to profl. jours. Fellow AAAS; mem. IEEE, Am. Soc. Info. Sci. Tech. (chmn. Spl. Interest Group 1990), Med. Libr. Assn., Am. Chem. Soc., Assn. Computing Machinery, Acad. Health Infro. Profls. (Sr.). Achievements include creation and development of MedIndEx (Medical Indexing Expert) System, an interactive knowledge-based (i.e. artificial intelligence) prototype for indexing medical journal articles; journal descriptor and semantic type indexing system for automatic indexing of medical text. Office: Nat Libr Medicine 8600 Rockville Pike Bethesda MD 20894-0002

HUMPHREY, WATTS SHERMAN, technical executive, author; b. Battle Creek, Mich., July 4, 1927; s. Watts Sherman Humphrey and Katharine (Strong) Osborne; m. Barbara Fallon, May 22, 1954; children: Katharine Pickman, Lisa Fish, Sarah DeCamello, Watts Jr., Peter, Erica Jarrett, Christopher. BS in Physics, U. Chgo., 1949, MBA, 1951; MS in Physics, Ill. Inst. Tech., 1950; PhD in Software Engring. (hon.), Embry Riddle Aero. U., 1998. Electronics engr. Fermi Inst. U. Chgo., 1949-51, dir. sci. pers. Chgo. Midway Lab., 1951-53; mgr. computing devel. Sylvania Electric Products, Natick, Mass., 1953-59; instr. computer design Northeastern U., Boston, 1956-59; with IBM, White Plains, N.Y., 1959-86, mgr. teleprocessing systems devel., 1959-64, dir. systems application engring., Armonk, N.Y., 1964-65, dir. time sharing systems, White Plains, 1965-66, dir. programming, 1966-68, v.p. tech. devel., Armonk, 1968-70, dir. Endicott (N.Y.) Labs., 1970-72, dir. policy devel., Armonk, 1972-79, dir. tech. assessment, White Plains, 1979-83, dir. programming quality and process, Poughkeepsie, N.Y., 1983-86; dir. software process program Software Engring. Inst. Carnegie Mellon U., Pitts., 1986-91, fellow, 1991—. Chmn. adv. bd. IBM Systems Rsch. Inst., N.Y.C., 1973-82. Author: Switching Circuits with Computer Applications, 1958, Managing for Innovation, Leading Technical People, 1987, Managing the Software Process, 1989, A Discipline for Software Engineering, 1995, Managing Technical People, Innovation, Teamwork and the Software Process, 1997, Introduction to the Personal Software Process, 1997, Introduction to the Team Software Process, 1999, Winning with Software: an Executive Strategy, 2002; contbr. numerous articles to profl. jours. ; (mem. editl. bd.) Jour. Sys. and Software, 1988-96, Software Process, Improvement and Practice, 1996-, Empirical Software Engring., 1996-. Bd. examiners Malcolm Baldridge Nat. Quality Award, 1991; sci. adv. com. Std. System Ctr. USAF, 1989-92. With USN, 1944-46. Recipient Aerospace Software Engineering award Am. Inst. of Aeronautics and Astronautics, 1993, Boeing award for leadership and innovation in software process improvement, 2000; Watts Humphrey Software Quality Inst. in Chennai, India, named in his honor, 2000. Fellow IEEE (editorial bds. Spectrum 1982-83, The Institute 1982-83, reviewer Software 1984, Computer 1984, IBM System Jour. 1989); mem. Assn. for Computing Machinery, Inst. for Radio Engrs. (chmn. computer sect. 1959). Republican. Achievements include patents in field. Avocations: running, skiing, duplicating bridge. Office: Carnegie Mellon U Software Engring Inst 4500 5th Ave Pittsburgh PA 15213-2612

HUMPHREYS, BETSY L. librarian; BA, Smith Coll.; MLS, U. Md. Assoc. dir. libr. ops., asst. dir. health svcs. rsch. info. Nat. Libr. Medicine NIH. Contbr. articles to profl. jours. Fellow Am. Coll. Med. Informatics; mem. Inst. Medicine Nat. Acad. Sciences, Acad. Health Info. Profls. (disting. mem.), Am. Med. Informatics Assn., Med. Libr. Assn., Assn. Health Svcs. Rsch. Office: Nat Libr Medicine NIH 8600 Rockville Pike Bldg 38 Bethesda MD 20894-0001

HUMPHREYS, DAVID HARDING, plastic surgeon; b. N.Y.C., May 9, 1947; s. John Sanford and Leonie Kinsley (Harding) H.; m. Joan Ellen Heller, Dec. 1, 1971; children: Justin H., Samuel B., Nathaniel H., Nicholas M. BA, St. John's Coll., Annapolis, Md., 1970; MD, U. Cin., 1979. Diplomate Am. Bd. Otolaryngology, Am. Bd. Plastic Surgery; lic. physician, Tex., N.C. Intern gen. surgery Baylor Affiliated Hosps., Houston, 1979-80, gen. surgery resident, 1980-81, resident in otolaryngology, 1981-84; resident in plastic surgery Cronin-Brauer-Biggs Clinic/St. Joseph's Hosp., Houston, 1984-86; pvt. practice Asheville, N.C., 1986—; active staff Meml. Mission Hosp., Asheville, 1987—, St. Joseph's Hosp., Asheville, 1987—, chief plastic surgery sect., 1988-89; staff physician Thom's rehab. Hosp., Asheville. Lectr. in field. Contbr. articles to profl. jours. Fellow ACS, Am. Acad. Otolaryngology-Head and Neck Surgery; mem. Am. Soc. Plastic and Reconstructive Surgeons, Southeastern Soc. Plastic and Reconstructive Surgeons, N.C. Soc. Plastic, Maxillofacial and Reconstructive Surgeons, Am. Cleft Palate Assn., Lipoplasty Soc. N.Am., Buncombe County Med. Soc., N.C. Med. Soc., Pan Am. Assn. Oto-Rhino-Laryngology. Office: Plastic Surgery Center 5 Livingston St Asheville NC 28801-4407

HUMPHREYS, DONALD D. oil company executive; BS, Okla. State U.; MBA, U. Penn. Various positions Exxon Corp., 1976—97, v.p., contr., 1997—99; v.p.. contr. Exxon Mobil Corp., 1999—. Office: Exxon Mobil Corp 5959 Las Colinas Blvd Irving TX 75039

HUMPHREYS, JEAN SURRATT, social sciences educator; b. Midland, Tex., Dec. 20, 1957; d. Marshall England and Margaret Nash Surratt; m. John R Humphreys, May 29, 1982; children: Lauren Ann, Jordan Nash, Joshua Neal. MA - Sociology, Baylor U., Waco, Texas, 1978—81. Teacher's Certification - Mathematics/Sociology Tex., 1979. Math tchr. Kimball HS, Dallas, 1980—82; math. tchr. LaVega HS, Bellmead, Tex., 1982—83; asst. prof. / dept. coord. Dallas Bapt. U., Dallas, 1992—. Site based decision team Young Jr. High/Ditto Elem., Arlington, Tex., 1996—2000; publications/spirit Martin Football Booster Club, Arlington, Tex., 2002—03; tournaments Martin Basketball Booster, Arlington, Tex., 2002—03; officer Parent Tchr. Assn./ Martin High/Young Jr./Ditto Elem., Arlington, Tex., 1990—2003. Recipient Alpha Chi, East Tex. Bapt. U., 1976-1978; fellow Sociology, Baylor U., 1978-1979. Mem.: Assn. for the Sci. Study of Religion (treas. 1998—2001), Southwestern Sociol. Assn., Soc. for Applied Sociology. Office: Dallas Baptist U 3000 Mountain Creek Parkway Dallas TX 75211 E-mail: jean@dbu.edu.

HUMPHREYS, JOSEPHINE, novelist; b. Charleston, S.C., Feb. 2, 1945; d. William Wirt and Martha (Lynch) Humphreys. AB, Duke U., 1967; MA, Yale U., 1968. Author: Dreams of Sleep, 1984 (Ernest Hemingway Found. award 1985), Rich in Love, 1987, The Fireman's Fair, 1991, Nowhere Else on Earth, 2000 (So. Book award 2001). Recipient Lyndhurst Found. prize, 1985, Hillsdale prize, 1993; Guggenheim fellow, 1984; Woodrow Wilson Found. fellow, 1967, Danforth Found. fellow, 1967. Fellow So. Writers. Home and Office: care Harriet Wasserman Agy 137 E 36th St Ste 190 New York NY 10016-3528

HUMPHREYS, KENDRA SUE, adult education educator; b. Christopher, Ill., Oct. 23, 1958; d. Ray Edmond Williams, Ellen Jane Williams; m. Paul Robert Humphreys; children: Amber Lipe, Ryan, Jason. AA, John A. Logan Coll.; BS in Edn., So. Ill. U., 1992, MS in Edn., 1993, PhD in Edn., 2001. Instr. Rend Lake Coll., Ina, Ill., 1992—93, John A. Logan Coll., Carterville, Ill., 1993—99; program mgr. adult edn. So. Ill. U., Carbondale, 1999—. Trainer John A. Logan Bus. and Industry Ctr., Carterville, 1994—99; devel. skills tng. specialist So. Ill. U., Carbondale, Ill., 1995—96; instr. Trico H.S., Campbell Hill, Ill., 1996—99; presenter Egyptian Ednl. Svc. Ctr., Southern, 1996—96, Kaskaskia Coll., Centralia, 1998—98. Co-author: The Big Picture, 1995; author: (manual) Computer-Assisted Instruction Manual for English Instructors at JALC, 1996. Mem.: Area Planning Coun. (vice chair 2000—). Home: 449 Humphreys Rd Elkville IL 63932 Office: So Ill Univ 500 C Lewis Ln Carbondale IL 62901-6704 Office Fax: 618-453-5305. Personal E-mail: hmphreys@siu.edu. Business E-Mail: hmphreys@siu.edu.

HUMPHREYS, KENNETH KING, engineer, educator, association executive; b. Pitts., Jan. 19, 1938; s. Meredith Harold and Olga (Adamitis) H.; m. Harriet Elizabeth Moss, May 6, 1961; children: Kenneth King, Keith Alan, Kevin James, Karen Elizabeth. BS, Carnegie Inst. Tech., 1959, postgrad., 1961-62, U. Pitts., 1965; MS, W. Va. U., 1967; PhD, Kennedy Western U., 1990. Registered profl. engr., Pa., N.C., W.Va.; cert. cost engr. U.S., Mex., Internat. Tech. asst. Applied Research Lab.-U.S. Steel Corp., 1959-60, tech. assoc., 1960-62, asst. technologist Universal, Pa., 1962-63, assoc. research engr., 1963-65; cost engr. W. Va. U. Coal Research Bur., Morgantown, 1965-67, sr. staff and cost engr., 1967-71, asst. dir., 1971-81; asst. prof. Coll. Mineral and Energy Resources-W. Va., Morgantown, 1970-73; assoc. prof. Coll. Mineral and Energy Resources-W. Va. U., Morgantown, 1973-76, prof., 1976-82, adj. prof., 1982-92, asst. to dean, 1971-77, chmn. minerals program, 1978-81, asst. dean acad. affairs, 1979-82; exec. dir. Am. Assn. Cost Engrs., 1971-92. Engring. cons. metallurgy and fuel tech., 1963-82; engring. cons. cost engring. and project mgmt., 1993—. Author: Basic Cost Engineering, 1981, 2d edit., 1986, 3d edit., 1996, What Every Engineer Should Know About Ethics, 1999; editor: Control and Management of Capital Projects, 2d edit., 1992, reprint edit., 1998; co-author, co-editor: Basic Mathematics and Computer Applications for Coal Preparation and Mining, 1983; co-author, assoc. editor: Coal Preparation, 4th edit., 1979; co-author, editor: Project and Cost Engineers' Handbook, 2d edit., 1984, 3d edit., 1993; co-author, co-editor: Mechanical Estimating Guidebook, 5th edit., 1987, 6th edit., 1995; co-author, editor: Jelen's Cost and Optimization Engineering, 3d edit., 1991; editor: Effective Project Management Through Applied Cost and Schedule Control, 1996; contbr. articles to prof. jours.; patentee in field. Leader Allegheny Trails, Piedmont and Mountaineer area couns. Boy Scouts Am., 1961—, dist. commr. Mountaineer area coun., 1969-72, dist. tng. chmn., 1972-74, 90, chmn. coun. tng., 1975-77, exec. bd., 1987-89, leadership devel. com., area 6 East Cen. region, 1977-79, dist. commr. Piedmont coun., 1996-97, rechartering com., 1997-99, asst. dist. commr., 1999—, internat. rep., 2001-; deacon 1st Presbyn. Ch., Morgantown, W.Va., 1968-70, ruling elder, 1972-75, 90-92, pres. congregation, 1975-77; deacon Waldensian Presbyn. Ch., Valdese, N.C., 1995-97, treas., 1995-96. Recipient Silver Beaver award Mountaineer Area Coun. Boy Scouts Am., 1973, Disting. Silver Beaver award Boy Scouts Am., 1990; recipient dist. award of merit Mountaineer Area Coun. Boy Scouts Am., 1969, Woodbadge award Mountaineer Area Coun. Boy Scouts Am., 1971, 50-Year Vets. award Boy Scouts Am., 1998, Het Schaap mit vijf Poten award Royal Netherlands Industries Fair, 1977; named Hon. West Virginian Gov. West Virginia, 1974. Fellow Assn. Cost Engrs. (U.K.), Assn. Advancement Cost Engring. Internat., Assn. Advancement Cost Engring. (nat. chmn. 1969-71, 98—, Mem. of Moment, nat. bd. dirs. 1971, exec. dir. 1971-92, award of merit 1993, award recognition 1979, pub. Cost Engring. mag. 1981-92, co-editor trans. 1982-92, pres. No. W.Va. sect. 1989-91, pres. Catawba Valley, Charlotte, N.C. sect. 1994-96), Assn. Italiana di Ingegneria Economica; mem. NSPE, Soc. Mexicana de Ingenieria Economica Financiera y de Costos (Mex.), Cost Engring. Assn. So. Africa, Internat. Cost Engring. Coun. (sec.-treas. 1976—, disting. internat. fellow), Profl. Engrs., N.C. (ethics steering com. 1995—, chmn. ethics com. 1999-2001, Engr. of Yr. award 1999), W.Va. Soc. Profl. Engrs. (bd. dirs. 1971-76, 83-92, v.p. 1980-81, pres. 1982-83, W.Va. Engr. of Yr. 1986), Morgantown Soc. Profl. Engrs. (pres. 1969-70, bd. dirs. 1970-76), Am. Assn. Engring. Socs. (bd. govs. 1979-83), Coun. Engring. Splty. Bds. (pres.-elect 1990-92, pres. 1992-93), Sigma Xi, Beta Theta Pi (asst. gen. sec. 1987-91), Alpha Phi Omega. Democrat. Home and Office: 1168 Hidden Lake Dr Granite Falls NC 28630-8592 E-mail: icec@icoste.org.

HUMPHREYS, KIRK, mayor; b. Okla. City, 1950; m. Danna Humphreys; 3 children. BA, U. Okla., 1972. Pres. Gibraltar Ivestments, Inc., Oklahoma City, 1989—; mayor Oklahoma City, 1998—; mem. adv. bd. U.S. Conf. of Mayors. Office: Office of the Mayor City Hall 200 N Walker Ave Ste 302 Oklahoma City OK 73102-2232*

HUMPHREYS, LLOYD GIRTON, research psychologist, educator; b. Lorane, Oreg., Dec. 12, 1913; s. John Pryor H. and Gertrude (Stephenson) H.; m. Dorothy Jane Windes, Dec. 27, 1937 (dec. July 12, 1995); children: John Daniel, Michael Stephenson, Margaret Anne, Susan Jeanne. BS, U. Oreg., 1935; MA, Ind. U., 1936; PhD, Stanford U., 1938. Instr. Northwestern U., 1939-42, asst. prof., 1945-46; assoc. prof. U. Wash., 1946-48, Stanford U., Calif., 1948-51; rsch. psychologist U.S. Air Force, San Antonio, 1951-57, mem., Sci. Adv. Bd. Office of Chief of Staff, 1959—62; prof. psychology U. Ill., Champaign-Urbana, 1957—, chmn. dept. psychology, 1959-69, acting dean Coll. Liberal Arts and Scis., 1979-80. Asst. dir. sci. edn. NSF, 1970-71; mem. bd. human resource data and analyses NRC, 1974-77, Commn. on Human Resources, 1978-82; mem. Ill. Gov.'s Blue Ribbon Commn. on Occupational Licensing, 1977-78; bd. dirs. Am. Insts. for Rsch., 1978-94; mem. expert com. on pediatric neurobehavioral evaluations EPA, 1983, cons. clean air sci. adv. com., mem. sci. adv. bd., 1983. Editor Psychol. Bull., 1964-68, Am. Jour. Psychology, 1968-80. Mem. com. on techniques for the enhancement of human performance NRC, 1985-88; mem. sci. adv. group for Project A and Bldg. the Career Force of Army Rsch. Inst., 1982-93; cons. RGI, Inc. Served from 2d lt. to capt. USAAF, 1942-45. Recipient Rsch. award Am. Ednl. Rsch. Assn., 1995, Ednl. Testing Svc. in Psychometrics award, 1995, Career Rsch. award APA Divsn. 5, 1997, Career Rsch. award Soc. Exptl. Multivariate Rsch., 2000. Mem. AAAS (chmn. sect. I 1962-63, v.p. 1963, council 1974-77, chmn. sect. J 1979-80), Psychometric Soc. (pres. 1959-60), Psychonomic Soc. (chmn. governing bd. 1962-63), Soc. Exptl. Psychologists, Am. Psychol. Soc., Chmns. Grad. Tng. Depts. Psychology (chmn. 1962-66), Phi Beta Kappa, Sigma Xi, Beta Gamma Sigma, Phi Delta Kappa, Delta Upsilon Home: 20710 E County Rd 1800 N Oakland IL 61943 Office: U Ill Dept Psychology 603 E Daniel St Champaign IL 61820-6232

HUMPHREYS, LOIS H. realtor; b. Abingdon, Va., Sept. 25, 1931; d. Howard Barnett Hagy and Deltia Sylvia Caudill; m. Paul Everett Humphreys, Apr. 15, 1951; children: Richard Everett, Jill Hagy Humphreys Dalton. Student, Am. Floral Arts, 1969. Cert. floral designer. Dental asst. Drs. Loving and Buchanan, Bristol, Abingdon, Va., 1949-51; sales staff Maxine's, Abingdon, 1955-65; sec. Gentrys Furniture, Abingdon, 1966-68; audio visual coord. Washington County Schs., Abingdon, 1968-70; retail merchant Humphreys Flowers and Gifts, Abingdon, 1969-87; realtor Va. Realtors Assn., Abingdon, 1976-93. Mem. Archtl. Rev. Bd., 1988—; chairperson Mount Rogers Planning Commn. Disabilities Bd., Marion, Va., 1988-98. Coun. mem. Town of Abingdon, 1988—, mayor, 1998—. Named Women of Yr., Abingdon Bus. and Profl. women, 1991-92. Mem.: DAR, C. of C., Abingdon United Meth. Women (pres. 1998—2002), Johnston Meml. Ladies Aux., Va. PTA (life). Avocations: doll collecting, traveling, family activities. Home: 790 Birdie Dr Abingdon VA 24211-3602 also: PO Box 789 Abingdon VA 24212-0789

HUMPHREYS, PAUL WILLIAM, philosophy educator, consultant; b. London, Jan. 17, 1950; came to U.S., 1971; s. William Edward and Florence C. (Didcock) H.; m. Diane Gail Snustad, July 14, 1984; children: Emily Victoria, Alexandra Elizabeth. BSc, U. Sussex, U.K., 1971; MA, MS, Stanford U., 1974, PhD, 1976. From asst. to assoc. prof. philosophy U. Va., Charlottesville, 1978-91, prof., 1991—, chmn., 1996-97, 99—; v.p. Assn. for Founds. Sci., 1995-99. Seminar dir. NEH, Va., 1991, 95; cons. EPA, CDC, BCG. Author: Chances of Explanation, 1989, Extending Ourselves, 2004; editor: Synthese, 1991—98, Foundations of Science, 1993—98, Oxford Studies in the Philosophy of Science, 1999—. Recipient Travel award Fulbright, 1971, Scholars award NSF, 1984. Mem. Am. Philos. Assn., Philosophy Sci. Assn. (mem. gov. bd. 1997-2000), Keswick Soc. (chmn. 2000—). Home: 323 Kent Rd Charlottesville VA 22903-2409 Office: U Va Dept Philosophy PO Box 400780 Charlottesville VA 22903-4780

HUMPHREYS, ROBERT LEE, advertising executive; b. Burbank, Calif., Dec. 30, 1924; s. Robert E. and Nancy Lucille (Gum) H.; m. Marie Dorthea Wilkinson, May 10, 1951; children: Dina Lizette, Gia Monique Thompson. BS in Mktg., UCLA, 1947. Merchandising rep. Life mag., L.A., 1947-48; promotion mgr. Fortune mag., N.Y.C., 1948-49; copywriter BBDO, L.A., 1950-51; account exec. KNBC-TV, L.A., 1951-52; v.p., account group mgr. Foote, Cone & Belding, L.A., 1952-62; CEO, chmn. emeritus Western divsn. Grey Advt., Inc., L.A., 1962-2000, dir., 1963-92; pres. Humphreys Seminars, L.A., 2000—. Dir. William O'Neil Fund, Beverly Hills, Calif. Featured guest on Corp. Viewpoint, PBS, 1978. Founding pres. UCLA Chancellor's Assocs., 1967—; founding chmn. Motorcycle Safety Coun., 1966; founding vice chmn. UCLA Found., 1967—; mem. president's circle Los Angeles County Mus. Art, 1983—; bd. dirs. Advt. Industry Emergency Fund, Banning Park Mus., 1991-96. Mem. Am. Advt. Fedn. (bd. dirs. 1982-92), World Affairs Coun., Hollywood Radio and TV Soc. (bd. dirs. 1976-82), L.A. Advt. Club (bd. dirs. 1974-76), Sierra Club (life), Bel Air Bay Club, Phi Gamma Delta. Home and Office: 12830 Parkyns St Los Angeles CA 90049-2630

HUMPHREYS, ROBERT RUSSELL, lawyer, consultant, arbitrator; b. Eugene, Oreg., May 7, 1938; s. Russell Wallace and Roberta Lois (Bennett) H.; m. Natalia Dimitrievna Lucenko; children: Tatyana Roberta, Grigori Robert. BA, U. Wash., 1959; LLB, George Washington U., 1965. Bar: Va. 1965, D.C. 1966, U.S. Dist. Ct. (D.C.) 1966, U.S. Ct. Appeals (D.C. cir.) 1985, U.S. Ct. Appeals (4th cir.) 2000, Ct. Fed. Claims 2001. Law clk. Barco, Cook & Patton, Washington, 1963-64, Keller & Heckman, Washington, 1964; mgr. pub. affairs services Air Transport Assn. Am., Washington, 1965-66; asst. to v.p. fed. affairs, 1966-71; spl. counsel com. on labor and human resources U.S. Senate, Washington, 1971-77; commr. Rehab. Services Adminstrn., HEW, Washington, 1977-80; ptnr. Hoffheimer & Johnson, Washington, 1980-83, Humphreys & Mitchell, Washington, 1983-88; cons. MARC Assocs., Inc., Washington, 1988-94; pvt. practice law, Washington, 1988—; pres. The Humphreys Group, Washington, 1991-95; pres., ceo Jennings Randolph Inst., Washington, 1998—; hearing officer State of N.C., 2002. Spkr. nat., internat. confs. Author: Compliance Manual on Americans with Disabilities Act; contbr. articles to profl. jours. Incorporator, bd. dirs., treas., counsel Nat. Ctr. for Barrier-Free Environ., 1975-77, 81-84; bd. dirs. Va. Spl. Olympics, 1982-84. Mem. D.C. Bar Assn., George Washington U. Law Alumni Assn., Va. State Bar, Phi Delta Phi. Achievements include being the prin. Senate draftsman for Black Lung Benefits Act, 1972, Rehab. Act, 1973, Randolph-Sheppard Act Amendments, 1974, Black Lung Benefits Reform Act, 1977.

HUMPHREYS TROY, PATRICIA, communications executive; b. Birmingham, June 3, 1946; m. Stephen Richard Troy; 1 child, David. BS in Edn., Auburn U., 1968, MEd, 1969; cert. advanced study in edn., Loyola Coll., 1989; cert., Inst. Orgn. Mgmt., U.S. Chamber at U. Del., 1999. Grad. tchg. asst. Auburn U., 1968—69; asst. libr. McKendree Coll., 1969—71; adj. instr. Chapman Coll., 1972—75; libr. Wroxeter-on-Severn, 1978—80; adminstrv. dir., media dir. Chesapeake Acad.1, 1980—89; pres., CEO Bay Media Inc., 1989—, Next Wave Group LLC, 2001 . Vice chair bd. trustees, chair strategic planning com. Anne Arundel Health Sys. and Anne Arundel Med. Ctr.; exec. dir. Assn. for Women in Comms. Unit pres. Am. Cancer Soc., 1986—92; pres. Panhellenic of Annapolis, 1976—; Pres. Cultural Arts Found. Anne Arundel County, 1995—99; pres. Greater Severna Park Coun., 1990—93; chair Small Area Plan for Severna Park, Anne Arundel County, 1997—2002, Anne Arundel County Cancer Control Task Force, 1994—96; bd. trustees, founding vice chair Chesapeake Acad., 1980—. Named One of Md.'s Top 100 Women, Daily Record, 1997, 1999, Bus. Leader of Yr., Anne Arundel Trade Coun., 1996, Women in Bus. Advocate, Md. Small Bus. Assn., Independence Day Parade Grand Marshal, Greater Severna Park Chamber, 1993; recipient Exec. citation for cmty. svc., Anne Arundel County, 1999, Disting. Alumni award, Leadership Anne Arundel, 1997, TWIN award, Anne Arundel County YWCA, 1996. Mem.: Am. Soc. Assn. Exec. (cert.), Anne Arundel Trade Coun./Annapolis and Anne Arundel County Chamber (edn. chmn. 1990—), Am. Bus. Women's Assn. (pres. Severn River/Md. Capital chpt. 1980—, Woman of Yr. Severn River 1991, Bus. Assoc. of Yr., Severn River 1992, named among Top 10 Women in Bus. 2003), Women in Comms. (pres. Md. profl. chpt. 1991—). Office: Ste S-28 780 Ritchie Hwy Severna Park MD 21146

HUMPHRIES, ASA ALAN, JR., biologist, educator, dean; b. Anniston, Ala., Sept. 6, 1924; s. Asa Allen and Myree (Adamson) Humphries; m. LaNelle Wright, Sept. 10, 1949 (dec. 1969); children: Susan Myree, David Alan, Ann Wesley; m. Laurie Cecilia Lee, July 22, 1972; 1 child, Laura Catherine. AB, Emory U., 1948, MS, 1949; AM, Princeton U., 1952, PhD, 1953. Instr. biology Emory U., Atlanta, 1949-50, from asst. prof. to assoc prof. dept. biology, 1954-67, prof. biology, 1967-81, chmn. dept. biology, 1974-81; anatomy instr. U. Va. Sch. Medicine, Charlottesville, 1953-54; prof. Transylvania U., Lexington, Ky., 1981-94, prof. emeritus, 1994—, v.p., dean, 1981-83, exec. v.p., dean, 1983-91, dean spl. programs, 1991-94, dean emeritus, 1994—. Mem. editl. bd.: U. Press Ky., 1981—94; contbr. articles to profl. jours. Trustee Lexington Clin. Found., 1986—; bd. dirs. Ky. Inst. Internat. Studies, 1990—94, Operation Read, Lexington, 1993—99, 2001—02. With U.S. Army, 1943—46. Recipient Ann. Rsch. award, Assn. S.E. Biologists, 1956, Transylvania medal, 2001; fellow, NATO, NSF, Procter, Princeton U., 1952—53; grantee Rsch., NSF, NIH, Rockefeller Found., 1959—. Mem.: AAAS, Soc. Devel. Biology, Optimist Club Internat., Alpha Tau Omega, Omicron Delta Kappa (leadership hon.), Sigma Xi. Democrat. Home and Office: 2009 Des Cognets Ln Lexington KY 40502-3040 E-mail: asa.humphries@gte.net.

HUMPHRIES, EDNA BEVAN, music educator, choir director; b. Cheyenne, Wyo., Sept. 21, 1922; d. Christopher Henry Droegemueller and Charlotte Adelheit Mueller; m. Elmer Wayne Bevan, Nov. 4, 1944 (div. Dec. 1988); children: David Wayne, Ronn Merrill, Paul Bevan (dec.), Philip Neal; m. John B. Humphries, Feb. 18, 1989. BS, U. Minn., 1943. Nat. and state cert. piano tchr. Freelance writer, Seattle, 1955—; piano tchr., 1955—; organist Luth. Ch., Seattle, 1950—80, choir dir., 1965—80; dir. bell choir John Knox Presbyn. Ch., Seattle, 1989—2002, Glendale Luth. Ch., Seattle, 1989—, Southminster Presbyn. Ch., Seattle, 2002—. Author: Christian Finger Plays and Games, 1955. Mem.: Wash. State Music Tchrs. Assn. (past treas., past pres. South King County chpt.). Avocation: square and folk dancing. Home: 830 SW Shoremont Ave Seattle WA 98166-3646

HUMPHRIES, EDWARD FRANCIS, lawyer; b. S.I., N.Y., May 25, 1957; s. Robert Edward and Joan D. (Mauter) H.; m. Colleen Kennedy, July 21, 1990; 1 child, Stephen Edward. BBA, Bernard M. Baruch Coll., 1981; JD, Fordham U., 1984. Bar: N.J. 1984, U.S. Dist. Ct. N.J. 1984, N.Y. 1985, U.S. Dist. Ct. (ea. and so. dists.) N.Y. 1985, U.S. Dist. Ct. (we. dist.) N.Y. 1987, Pa. 1990, Hawaii 1990, U.S. Supreme Ct. 1990, U.S. Dist. Ct. Hawaii 1991. Assoc. Amabile & Erman, Bklyn., 1984-86, 87-92, ptnr., 1993—; assoc. Pegalis & Wachsman, Great Neck, N.Y., 1986-87. Trustee Soc. Hill East Condominium Assn., East Brunswick, N.J., 1987-90, pres., 1988-90; co-chmn. Homeowners Assn. Coun. East Brunswick, 1988-90; vice-chmn. East Brunswick Planning Bd., 1989-90; pres. East Brunswick Rep. Club, 1989-91; mem. strategic planning com. Staten Island Acad., 2003. Recipient Morton Wollman medal in Mgmt. Bernard Baruch Coll., 1981. Mem. N.Y. State Bar Assn., Hawaii Bar Assn., Princess Bay Boatman's Assn. (vice commodore 2002—, bd. dirs. 2002—), Beta Gamma Sigma, Sigma Iota Epsilon. Republican. Roman Catholic. Home: 451 Manor Rd Staten Island NY 10314-2963 Office: Amabile & Erman 1000 South Ave Staten Island NY 10314-3430

HUMPHRIES, J. BOB, lawyer; b. Birmingham, Ala., Nov. 18, 1946; BS, Fla. State U., 1968, MBA, 1972, JD cum laude, 1971. Bar: Fla. 1972, Ga. 1974. Atty. Fowler, White, Gillen, Boggs, Villareal and Banker P.A., Tampa, Fla. Bus. editor Fla. State U. Law Rev., 1971. Chmn. bd. Tampa-Hillsborough County Pub. Libr., 1986-87; trustee Cmty. Found. Tampa Bay; bd. dirs., exec. mem. Tampa Bay Performing Arts Ctr.; bd. dirs. Tampa Bay Downtown Partnership;

sec. Performing Arts Ctr. Found. Mem. ABA, State Bar Ga., Fla. Bar (chmn. tax sect., mem. environ. and land use law sect., corp., banking and bus. law sect., and real property, probate and trust law sect.), Phi Delta Phi. Office: Fowler White Gillen Boggs Villareal and Banker 501 E Kennedy Blvd Ste 1700 Tampa FL 33602-5239 E-mail: bhtaxlaw@fowlerwhite.com.

HUMPHRIES, JOAN ROPES, psychologist, educator; b. Bklyn., Oct. 17, 1928; d. Lawrence Gardner and Adele Lydia (Zimmermann) Ropes; m. Charles C. Humphries, Apr. 4, 1957; children: Peggy Ann, Charlene Adele. BA, U. Miami, 1950; MS, Fla. State U., 1955; PhD, La. State U., 1963; cert., W2RN Cable. Registered lobbyist State of Fla. Part-time instr. psychology dept. U. Miami, Coral Gables, Fla., 1964—66; prof. behavioral studies dept. Miami-Dade Coll., 1966—. Presenter, lectr. in field cruise ship Costa Romantica. Editl. staff, maj. author The Application of Scientific Behaviorism to Humanistic Phenomena, 1975, Rev. Edit., 1979, prodr. & host, Sigma Series video, cert.for TV Strategies in Global Modern Academia: Issues and Answers in Higher Education, 1993—94, Strategies in Global Modern Academia: Issues and Answers in Higher Education II, 1995; prodr.: (video series) Strategies in Global Modern Academia: Issues and Answers in Higher Education, III, 1996—97, Strategies in Global Modern Academia: Issues and Answers in Higher Education, IV, 2001—02, W2RN (cert.). Mem. Biofeedback Delegation, China, 1995; mem. Citizen Amb. Program Psychic Arts Delegation to Russia, 1997, Am. Mus. Natural History; life mem. Pastorius Home Assn., Inc., 2001; mem. Citizen Amb. Program Vizcayans Mus., Aldren Kindred of Am., Inc., Nat. Trust Hist. Preservation, The Charles F. Menninger Soc., People to People; mem. ladies aux. Fla. Soc. SAR; mem. Nat. Mus. Women in Arts; mem. women's history month com. Jr. Honor Women Recognition, women's leadership seminar. Recipient award in hon. of women recognition, Women's Hist. Month com. and Women's Leadership Seminar, 2003. Mem.: AAUP (Miami-Dade Coll. chpt., past v.p. Fl. conf. 1986—88, pres. 1986—, mem. exec. bd. Fl. conf. 1989—90, former v.p., sec.), AAAS, AAUW (life; former v.p. Tamiami br. 1983—88, Appreciation award 1977), APA (life), Dade-Monroe Psychol. Assn., Fla. Psychol. Assn., Biofeedback Soc. Fla. (pres. 1990—), Noetic Scis., N.Y. Acad. Scis. (life), Assn. Applied Psychophysiology and Biofeedback, Inst. Evaluation, Diagnosis and Treatment (past v.p. 1975—87, pres. 1987—, former bd. dirs.), Internat. Soc. for Study Subtle Energies and Energy Medicine (charter), Physicians for Social Responsibility, Am. Psychol. Soc. (charter), Biofeedback Soc. Am. (pres. 1989—), Am. Inst. Parliamentarians, Pilgrim John Howland Soc., Hist. Homeowners Coral Gables, Heredity Order Descs. of Colonial Govs., Regines in Miami, North Campus Spkrs. Bur. (Cmty. Lecture Series award), Internat. Platform Assn. (bd. govs. 1979—, Silver Bowl award 1993), Mexico Beach C. of C. (bus. 1991—95), Colonial Dames 17th Century, Soc. Mayflower Descs. (elder William Brewster colony), Cellar Club, Coral Gables Country Club (life), Jockey Club (life), Phi Lambda Pi, Phi Lambda (Founder's Plaque 1976, Appreciation award 1987). Democrat. Achievements include research in biofeedback and human consciousness. Home: 1311 Alhambra Cir Coral Gables FL 33134-3521 Office: Miami Dade Coll North Campus 11380 NW 27th Ave Miami FL 33167-3418

HUMPHRIES, JOHN O'NEAL, physician, educator, university dean; b. Columbia, S.C., Oct. 22, 1931; s. Arthur Lee and Helen Elliott (O'Neal) H.; m. Mary Ellen Cregan, Mar. 13, 1954; children: Arthur Thomas, Ellen Cregan, John Elliott. BS, Duke U., 1952; MD, Johns Hopkins U., 1956. Diplomate Am. Bd. Internal Medicine (mem. bd. subsplty. cardiovascular disease 1974-79). Intern Johns Hopkins Hosp., 1957; asst. resident Osler Med. Service, Osler Med. Svc., 1958-60, resident physician pvt. med. svc., 1962-64, staff physician, 1962-79; rsch. fellow in cardiology U. London, St. George's Hosp., 1960-61, Johns Hopkins U. Med. Sch., 1956-57, 61-62, mem. faculty, 1964-79, Robert L. Levy prof. cardiology, 1975-79, prof. medicine, 1976-79; O.B. Mayer Sr. and Jr. prof. medicine U. S.C., Columbia, 1979-86, prof. medicine, 1979-96; disting. prof. medicine, dean emeritus, 1997—; chmn. dept. medicine U. S.C., Columbia, 1979-87, dean Sch. Medicine, 1983-94. Contbr. articles to med. publs.; mem. editl. bd. various jours. Bd. dirs. Md. Ballet, Balt., 1975-78. Master ACP (bd. govs. for S.C. chpt. 1986-90), Am. Coll. Cardiology (bd. govs. for Md. chpt. 1973-76); mem. Am. Fedn. Clin. Rsch., Am. Heart Assn. (fellow coun . clin. cardiology, chmn. postgrad. edn. com., exec. com. 1972-75), Cen. Md. Heart Assn. (pres. 1972-73), Md. Heart Assn. (pres. 1976-77), Assn. Univ. Cardiologists, Am. Clin. and Climatol. Assn., Alpha Omega Alpha. Office: U SC Sch Medicine Columbia SC 29208-0001

HUMPHRY, DEREK, association executive, writer, speaker; b. Bath, Somerset, Eng., Apr. 29, 1930; came to U.S., 1978; m. Royston Martin and Bettine (Duggan) H.; m. Jean Edna Crane, May 5, 1953 (dec. Mar. 1975); children: Edgar, Clive Stephen; m. Ann Wickett Kooman, Feb. 16, 1976 (div. 1990); m. Gretchen Crocker, 1991. Student pub. schs. Reporter Evening News, Manchester, Eng., 1951-55, Daily Mail, London, 1955-63; editor Havering Recorder, Essex, Eng., 1963-67; sr. reporter Sunday Times, London, 1967-78; spl. writer L.A. Times, 1978-79; founder, exec. dir. Hemlock Soc. N.Am., L.A., 1980-92, pres., 1988-90. Author: Because They're Black, 1971 (M.L. King award 1972), Police Power and Black People, 1972, Jean's Way, 1978, Let Me Die Before I Wake, 1982, The Right To Die, 1986, Final Exit, 1991, 3d edit., 2003, Dying with Dignity, 1992, Lawful Exit, 1993, Freedom To Die, 1998. With Brit. Army, 1948-50. Recipient Socrates award for right-to-die activism, 1997, George Saba medal for svcs. to world euthanasia movement, 2000. Mem. World Fedn. Right-To-Die Socs. (newsletter editor 1979-84, 92-94, sec.-treas. 1983-84, pres. 1988-90), Ams. Death with Dignity (v.p. 1993), Hemlock Soc. No. Calif. (v.p. 1994), Euthanasia Rsch. and Guidance Orgn. (pres. 1993—). Home and Office: 24829 Norris Ln Junction City OR 97448-9559 Fax: 541-998-1873. E-mail: dhumphry@efn.org.

HUMPHRY, JAMES, III, librarian, publishing executive; b. Springfield, Mass., July 21, 1916; s. James and Elizabeth Lucy (Ames) H.; m. Priscilla Eaton, Dec. 26, 1942; children: Susan H. Fitch, Elizabeth Ames Schnabel. AB, Harvard U., 1939; MS, Columbia U., 1941. Reference asst. N.Y. Pub. Library, 1939-41, 46, chief map divsn., 1946; librarian, prof. bibliography Colby Coll.; bus. mgr. Colby Coll. Press, 1947-57; chief librarian Met. Mus. Art, 1957-68; v.p. H.W. Wilson Co., Bronx, 1968-82, pres., dir. found., 1995-2000, also bd. dirs., 1968—; prof. Pratt Inst., Bklyn., 1982-98. Lectr. Columbia Sch. Libr. Svc., 1967-68; vis. assoc. prof. Grad. Sch. Libr. Studies, U. Hawaii, 1983; libr. cons. Am. Heritage, 1965-68, John Wiley & Sons, 1966-69, Coun. Advancement Small Colls., 1956, Gossage Regan Assocs., N.Y.C., 1988-96; coord. Maine Libr. Assn. for ALA sponsored Library Services bill, 1948-49, 55-57; nat. bd. Libr. Presdl. Papers, 1967-69; adminstr. grants-in-aid program N.Y. State Council Arts, 1967-68 Compiler, Library of Edwin Arlington Robinson, 1950; Editor: (with Carl J. Weber) Fitzgerald's Rubaiyat, 1959; Contbr. articles to mags. and jours. Trustee, chmn. adv. com. Archives Am. Art, 1967-88; mem. fine arts vis. com. Harvard U., 1967-73; mem. adv. council St. John's U. Congress for Librarians, 1963-67; bd. dirs. Huguenot YMCA; trustee N.Y. Met. Reference and Research Library Agy., 1967-77, Westchester Library System, 1974-83, New Rochelle Pub. Libr., 1977-87, Thomas Paine Nat. Hist. Assn., 1980-96; pres. Westchester Libr. System. 1980-82, New Rochelle Pub. Library 1979-80, 82, New Rochelle Pub. Libr. Found., 1994-96. With AUS, 1942-46, maj. U.S. Army, 1951-54; lt. col. USAR. Mem. ALA (councilor 1959-63, 67-69, chmn. com. on Wilson index reference services div. 1959-65, mem. subscription books com. 1963-66), Met. Mus. Art Employees Assn. (pres. 1961-63, gov. 1958-66), Maine Library Assn. (pres. 1955-56), Am. Assn. Museums (chmn. library group), Archons of Colophon (convener 1963-65), N.Y. Library Assn. (cons.), Spl. Libraries Assn. (chpt. vice chmn., chmn. mus. group 1962-64, N.Y. conf. chmn. 1967), Assn. Coll. and Research Libraries (pres., dir. 1966-69), Internat. Council Museums (corr.) Clubs: Grolier, N.Y. Library (council 1959-67, pres. 1965-66), Harvard (N.Y.C.). Office: 950 University Ave Bronx NY 10452-4224 Home: 31 Kirkland Village Cir Bethlehem PA 18017-4753 Fax: 610-691-4939.

HUMPREYS, NATALIA ALEXANDRA, mathematician; b. Leningrad, USSR, Russia, July 26, 1972; d. Alexandr Sergeevich Bondarev and Vera Leopoldovna Bondareva; m. John Morris Humphreys, June 21, 1997. PhD in Math., Ohio State U., 1999; MS Math., St. Petersburg State U., 1993; BS. Math., St Petersburg State U., 1992. Actuarial analyst Watson Wyalt & Co., Dallas, 2002—; lectr. Purdue U., 1999—2002, Ohio State U., 1999, grad. student, 1993—99. Author: (research) Jour. of Math Analysis and Application, 2000, Jour. of Approximation Jalory, 1999, Izvestiya Getv Collection of Sci. works, 1998. Grantee AWM workshop grant, Assn. for Women in Math., 1999. Mem.: Math. Assn. of Am., Am. Math. Soc. Avocations: swimming, bicycling. Home: 5738 Caruth howen Ln Apt 236 Dallas TX 75206 Office: Watson Wyatt & Co Suite 4200 2001 Ross Avenue Dallas TX 75201

HUMWAY, RONALD JIMMIE, accountant, former state agency administrator; b. Little Rock, Aug. 1, 1945; s. James Joseph and Rosalie (Ferguson) H.; m. Deborah Ann Northcutt, June 26, 1970; children: James Russell, Zachary Paul. AA, Southwestern Coll., Oklahoma City, 1967; BS in Econs., Oklahoma City U., 1969; BS in Acctg., U. Ark., Little Rock, 1978. CPA, Ark.; cert. fraud examiner. Field auditor Holiday Inns, Inc., Memphis, 1969-70; field auditor, supr. Ark. Div. Legis. Audit, Little Rock, 1970—2000, regional mgr. Jonesboro, 1985-99; chief fiscal officer Mid-South Health Sys., Inc., Jonesboro, Ark., 2000—01; pvt. practice as acct. and tax profl. Paragould, Ark., 2001—. Served with USAR, 1963-71. Mem. AICPA, Assn. Govt. Accts. (sec.-treas. Ctrl. ARk. chpt. 1976-77), SCV, Assn. Cert. Fraud Examiners. Baptist. Avocations: coin collecting, photography, golf. Home: 2709 White Cir Jonesboro AR 72404-6961 Office: 1801 W Kingshighway Ste 10 Paragould AR 72450-

HUNCHAREK, MICHAEL STEPHEN, oncologist; b. N.Y.C., July 25, 1961; s. Peter Huncharek, Irene Huncharek; life ptnr. LaMar Wheeler; children: Cyrus, Mia. BA, Vassar Coll, 1983; MPH, Yale U., 1986; MD, Boston U., 1991. Tech. specialist SUNY Stony Brook Sch. Medicine, 1983—84; cons. Bracewell and Patterson, Washington, 1985—86; intern Cambridge Hosp., Harvard Med. Sch., Mass., 1991—92; resident Mass. Gen. Hosp., Harvard Med. Sch., Boston, 1992—96; fellow Harvard Sch. Pub. Health, Boston, 1994—95; asst. med. dir. MetaWorks, Inc., Boston, 1996—97; contractor U.S. Pub. Health Svc./U.S. Secret Svc, Atlanta, 1997—98; dir. Meta-Analysis Rsch. Group, Stevens Point, Wis., 1997—; asst. prof. U. S.C. Sch. Medicine, Columbia, 1998—99; attending radiation oncologist Marshfield Clinic Cancer Ctr., Marshfield, Wis., 1999—. Cons. Blatt and Fales, Charleston, SC, 1985—87, Schering-Plough, Kenilworth, NJ, 1996—98, Bernard Lerner Inc., Chgo., 1996—97, Warner Lambert Corp., Kenilworth, NJ, 1999—2000; adv. com. Cornell U. Med. Coll./SPORE Grant, N.Y.C., 1999—; mem. rsch. com. Marshfield Med. Rsch. Found., Marshfield, 2000—. Author over 100 articles to profl. jours. Grantee, Schering-Plough Rsch. Inst., 1998, 1998, Bayer, Inc., 1998, Lyons, Lavey Nickel and Swift, 1998, Schering Plough Rsch. Inst., 1999, Warner-Lambert, 2001. Fellow: Am. Coll. Angiology; mem.: Am. Soc. Therapeutic Radiology and Oncology, Am. Assn. Cancer Rsch., Am. Coll. Epidemiology, Sigma Xi. Avocations: photography, flying, travel. Office: Marshfield Clinic Cancer Ctr c/o St Michael's Hosp 900 Il Ave Stevens Point WI 54481 Office Fax: 715-340-3080. Business E-Mail: Metaresearch@hotmail.com.

HUND, EDWARD JOSEPH, lawyer; b. May 3, 1945; s. Edward J. and Josephine A. (Hoover) Hund; m. Marty M. Anderson, June 29, 1970; children: Corie Elizabeth, Cyrus Anthony, Hanna Christine. Student, Creighton U., 1963—64; AB in Polit. Sci., Hays Coll., 1967; JD, Washburn U., 1970. Asst. county atty. Sedgwick County, Wichita, Kans., 1971—72; assoc. Smith, Shay, Farmer, Wetta, Wichita, Kans., 1972—75, ptnr., 1975—84, Focht, Hughey & Hund, Wichita, 1984—. Pres. Legacy of Justice Found., 2002—. 1st lt. NG USAR, 1968—74. Mem.: Wichita Bar Assn. (pres. young lawyers 1978), Kans. Bar Assn. (sec.-treas. 1981), Kans. Trial Lawyers Assn. (pres. 1991), Am. Bd. Trial Advocates (pres. Kans. chpt. 1995), Am. Trial Lawyers Assn. (bd. govs. 1994—95), ABA, Lions (v.p. 1979), East Y Mens Club (Wichita chpt.) (pres. 1980). Democrat. Congregationalist. Home: 325 Brookfield St Wichita KS 67206-1901 Office: Bradshaw Johnson & Hund 200 W Douglas Ave Ste 100 Wichita KS 67202-3001

HUNDELT, CRAIG THOMAS, realtor, engineering executive; b. St. Louis, Oct. 23, 1947; s. Lester William and Lydia Pearl Hundelt; m. Norma E. Colon-Munoz, Feb. 14, 1976 (div. Dec. 1995); children: Miguel, Elizabeth. BSBA, U. Denver, 1975; postgrad., U. Houston. Cert. energy mgr. Agrl. commodity sales rep. James McLain, St. Louis, 1975-76; v.p. mech. divsn. Consol. Mech. and Elec. Inc., St. Louis, 1976-82; mgr. of plant ops. Normandy Osteo. Hosps., St. Louis, 1982-86; facility mgr. VA Med. Ctr., St. Louis, 1987-95, engring. tech., 1995-99, voluntary svc. specialist, 1999—; comml. residential realtor Prudential Select Properties, St. Louis, 2002—. Owner real estate properties. Combat medic, psychiatric technician U.S. Army, 1969—70, Vietnam. Recipient Competent Toastmaster award, Toastmasters Internat. Mem. Sheet Metal A/C Contractors Nat. Assn., Hosp. Engrs. and Maintenance Assn. of St. Louis (pres. 1986-87), Am. Soc. of Hosp. Engring., Assn. Energy Engrs. Avocations: music, history. Office: Prudential Select Properties 13275 Manchester Rd Saint Louis MO 63131 E-mail: craighundelt@cs.com.

HUNDER, GENE GERALD, physician, educator; b. Lake City, Minn., Feb. 7, 1932; s. Tilman James and Melita Henrietta (Bremer) H.; m. Ingeborg Anne Hanson, May 6, 1990; children: Heidi, Jennifer, Gregory,Grant, Naomi, Stephanie. Student, St. Olaf Coll., 1950-52; BA, U. Minn. (Mpls.), 1954, MD, 1958, MS, 1963. Diplomate Am. Bd. Internal Medicine. Intern. Strong Meml. Hosp., Rochester, N.Y., 1958-59, resident, 1959-61, Mayo Clinic, Rochester, Minn., 1961-64; instr. internal medicine Mayo Grad. Sch., Rochester, Minn., 1966-67, asst. prof. internal medicine, 1968-73, assoc. prof., 1973-78, prof., 1978—, full mem. internal medicine, 1981—, cons. internal medicine and rheumatology; prof. internal medicine Mayo Clinic Mayo found., Rochester, Minn., 1978—; head sect. rheumatology Mayo Clinic, 1976-81. Chmn. rheumatology rsch. com., 1976-81, 87, clin. investigator tng. program Mayo Grad. Sch., 1981-84, chmn. div. rheumatology 1987-96; Philip Showalter Hench lect. Ariz. Med . Soc., Phoenix, 1965; Charles W. Thomas lectr. Med. Coll. Va., Charlottesville, 1979; Carl Pearson lectr. Los Angeles County Med. Assn., 1983; Henry J. Lehrhoff lectr. Clarkson Hosp., Omaha, 1989, Nana Swartz lectr. Swedish Med. Soc., 1994, Gilbert Galens Meml. lectr. William Beaumont Hosp., Detroit, 1995. Co-author: Physical Examination of the Joints, 1978; editor: Rheumatology, 1978, Atlas of Rheumatology, 1998, 2002, Mayo Clinic on Arthritis, 1999, 2002; assoc. editor: Jour. Lab and Clin. Medicine, 1979-81; editor Jour. Current Opinion in Rheumatology, 1992-2000, Jour. Arthritis Care and Rsch., 2000—; mem. editl. bd. Jour. Rheumatology, 1982—, Jours. Musculoskeletal Medicine, 1983-2001, Annals Internal Medicine, 1998-2001, ISI List of Frequently Cited Clin. Investigators. Mem. ho. dels. Arthritis Found., Atlanta, 1980-83, trustee, 1985; mem. exec. com. Minn. Arthritis Found., Mpls., 1984-90. Fellow ACP; Nu Sigma Nu scholar, 1995; Minn. Med. Found. acad. scholar, 1995. Mem. AMA, Am. Bd. Internal Medicine, AAAS. Ctrl. Soc. Clin. Research (mem. program com.), Am. Soc. Clin. Rheumatology (pres.), Am. Coll. Rheumatology (mem. exec. com. 1976-77, v.p. cen. region 1987, pres. cen. region, 1989, bd. dirs. 1988-92, Master award 1997), Phi Beta Kappa, Alpha Omega Alpha. Republican. Lutheran. Home: RR 1 Box 132B Zumbro Falls MN 55991-9725 Office: Mayo Clinic 200 1st St SW Rochester MN 55905-0002

HUNDERSMARCK, LAWRENCE F. theology studies educator; b. Passaic, NJ, June 3, 1951; s. Frederick and Katherine Hundersmarck; m. Kathleen Flaherty, June 19, 1976; children: Christopher, Maria, Kathleen. BS, U. Scranton, 1973; MA, Providence Coll., 1974, U. Dayton, 1976; PhD, Fordham U., 1982. Prof. dept. philosophy and religious studies, dir. Ctr. for Religious Studies Pace U., Pleasantville, NY, 1981—, founding chmn. dept. philosophy and religious studies, 1985—97. Vis. prof. Fordham U., N.Y.C., 1979—, St. John Neumann, N.Y.C., 1986—99; cons. honors program and critical thinking program Dover Union Sch. Dist., Dover Plains, NY, 1996—; lectr. in field. Contbr. articles to ref. books. Mem.: Medieval Acad. Am., Am. Cusanus Soc. (exec. bd. 1997—). Avocations: skiing, in-line skating, golf, hiking, camping. Office: Pace U 861 Bedford Rd Pleasantville NY 10570-2799 Home: 21 North Farm Dr Dover Plains NY 12522 Office Fax: 914-773-3785 . E-mail: lhundersmarck@pace.edu.

HUNDERT, EDWARD M. academic administrator; b. Woodbridge, N.J. m. Mary Hundert; 3 children. BS in Math. and History of Sci. and Medicine, summa cum laude, Yale U., 1978; MA in Philosophy, Politics and Econs., first class honors, Oxford U., 1980; MD, Harvard U., 1984. Diplomate Am. Bd. Neurology and Psychiatry. Med. intern Mount Auburn Hosp., Cambridge, Mass., 1984—85; resident in adult psychiatry, rsch. fellow, Labs. for Psychiatric Rsch. McLean Hosp., Belmont, Mass., 1985—88, chief resident, 1987—88; clin. fellow in psychiatry Harvard Med. Sch., Boston, 1984—88, instr. psychiatry, 1988—90, asst. prof. psychiatry, 1990—93, asst. prof. med. ethics, 1990—97, assoc. dean for student affairs, 1990—97, assoc. master, William B. Castle Soc., 1992—97, assoc. prof. psychiatry, 1994—97, faculty fellow, Harvard U. Mind/Brain/Behavior Initiative, 1996—99; prof. psychiatry U. Rochester Sch. Medicine and Dentistry, 1997—2002; prof. med. humanities U. Rochester (N.Y.) Sch. Medicine and Dentistry, 1997—2002, sr. assoc. dean for med. edn., 1997—2000, dean, 2000—02; pres. Case Western Res. U., Cleve., 2002—, prof. biomed. ethics, 2002—. Asst. psychiatrist McLean Hosp., Belmont, 1988—94, hosp. ethicist, 1988—97, assoc. psychiatrist, 1995—97; psychiatrist Strong Meml. Hosp., Rochester, NY, 1997—2002. Author: Philosophy, Psychiatry and Neuroscience: Three Approaches to the Mind, 1989, Lessons from an Optical Illusion: On Nature and Nurture, Knowledge and Values, 1995. Mem.: Phi Beta Kappa. Office: Case Western Res U Adelbert Hall 216 10900 Euclid Ave Cleveland OH 44106-7001*

HUNDLEY, CAROL MARIE BECKQUIST, music educator; b. L.A., Oct. 19, 1936; d. Paul Albert and Virginia Mary (Noll) Beckquist; m. Norris Cecil Hundley, Jr., June 8, 1957; children: Wendy Michelle Hundley Harris, Jacqueline Marie Hundley Reid. Student, Mt. St. Mary's Coll., 1954-55; AA, Mt. San Antonio Coll., 1956; postgrad., Calif. State U., L.A., 1981-82, 85-86. Tchr. pvt. piano studio, Arcadia, Calif., 1955-58, Pacific Palisades, Calif., 1965-95; vocal coach Corpus Christi Sch., Pacific Palisades, Calif., 1980-95, dir. instrumental music, 1980-95. Vocal and instrumental accompanist Theater Palisades, Pacific Palisades, 1986-87, music arranger, 1970-95; accompanist in field. Author: (play) Bach to Broadway, 1986, The Spirit of America, 1987; arranger and choreographer in field. Piano recitals Tuesday Musicale Jrs., Pasadena, Calif., 1950-54; accompanist Arcadia (Calif.) Women's Club, 1953-54; choral music provider Optimist Club, Pacific Palisades, 1989-92. Recipient scholarship Tuesday Musical Srs., 1954, Mt. St. Mary's Coll., 1954. Mem.: Santa Barbara Symphony League. Democrat. Roman Catholic. Avocations: reading, walking, composition and improvisation, dancing, interior decorating. E-mail: hundley@history.ucla.edu.

HUNDLEY, FREDERICK EUGENE, JR., music educator, consultant; b. Norfolk, Va., Nov. 1, 1968; s. Frederick E. Hundley, Sr. and Delorse I Hundley; m. Mary Evelyn Sasser, Dec. 19, 1963; children: Andrew Murphy, Lauren Murphy. MusB, Ga. So. U., 1991, MusM in Edn., 1993; EdS in Computer Tech., Nova Southeastern U., 2002; PhD in Computer Tech., Nova Southwestern U., 2003. Cert. Music Tchr. Ga. Prof. Std. Commn., 1993. Educator Savannah Christian Prep. Sch., Savannah, Ga., 1992—96, Emanual County Bd. of Edn., Swainsboro, Ga., 1996—. Computer cons. Ed-Comm, Inc., Swainsboro, Ga., 1998—; Musician Statesboro Cmty. Band, Statesboro, Ga., 1996—98, Savannah Cmty. Orch., Savannah, Ga., 1994—95; pianist First Bapt. Ch., Swainsboro, Ga., 1999—2000, ch. orch. mem., 1996—2002. Scholar William J. Deal scholarship for Musical Achievement, Music Dept. Ga. So. U., 1990. Mem.: PA of Ga. Educators, Assn. for Computing Machinery, Music Educators Nat. Conf., Tau Beta Sigma, Phi Mu Alpha Sinfonia (sec. 1990—91). Baptist. Avocations: reading, tennis, swimming, racquetball. Home: 108 Pate Street Swainsboro GA 30401 Office: Emanuel County Board of Education 201 North Main Street Swainsboro GA 30401 Personal E-mail: fhundley@bellsouth.net. E-mail: ghundley@emanuel.k12.ga.us.

HUNDLEY, LARRY WILLIS, aerospace company executive; b. Lewisburg, Ohio, Feb. 24, 1942; s. Frank Willis and Hilda Florence (Houdeshell) H.; m. Gerri Ann Yen, Sept. 12, 1964; children: Gregory, Tracy. BS, Edison State Coll., 1980; MBA, Am. Grad. U., 1984. Cert. contract mgr. Prodn. scheduler The Goodyear Tire & Rubber Co., Akron, Ohio, 1962-67, sr. contract mgr., 1967-84, mgr. contract adminstrn., 1985-86; mgr. contract mgmt. Goodyear Aerospace Corp., Akron, 1985-86; mgr. corp. contract mgmt. Loral Systems Croup, Akron, 1986-88; mgr. govt. compliance Aircraft Braking Systems Corp., 1988-90, dir. contract mgmt., 1990-93, dir. procurement and contracts, 1993—. Adv. bd. Nat. Contract Mgmt. Assn., Vienna. Editor: (newsletter) NCMA Northcoast News, 1985-90 (Graalman award 1985). Chief marshall NEC World Series of Golf, Akron, 1984-95; coach Cath. Youth Orgn., Cuyahoga Falls, Ohio, 1983; area chmn. YMCA, Akron, 1989. Ssgt. U.S. Army, 1966-72. Recipient Civic Achievement award, Jr. C. of C., Akron, 1990. Fellow Nat. Conctact Mgmt. Assn. (chap. pres. and nat. dir. 1984-90); mem. Am. Defense Preparedness Assn., Tau Kappa Epsion, Fraternal Order Eagles. Republican. Roman Catholic. Avocations: golf, clubmaking, sailing, antique restoration. Home: 462 W Willowview Dr Akron OH 44319-2951 E-mail: lwhundley@yahoo.com.

HUNDLEY, NORRIS CECIL, JR., history educator; b. Houston, Oct. 26, 1935; s. Norris Cecil and Helen Marie (Mundine) H.; m. Carol Marie Beckquist, June 8, 1957; children: Wendy Michelle Hundley Harris, Jacqueline Marie Hundley Reid. AA, Mt. San Antonio Coll., 1956; AB, Whittier Coll., 1958; PhD (Univ. fellow), UCLA, 1963. Instr. U. Houston, 1963-64; asst. prof. Am. history UCLA, 1964-69, assoc. prof., 1969-73, prof., 1973-94, prof. emeritus, 1994—, chmn. exec. com. Inst. Am. Cultures, 1976-93, chmn. univ. program on Mex., 1981-94, acting dir. Latin Am. Ctr., 1989-90, dir. Latin Am. Ctr., 1990-94. Exec. com. U. Calif. Consortium on Mex. and the U.S., 1981-86; adv. com. Calif. water atlas project Calif. Office Planning and Research, 1977-79 Author: Dividing the Waters: A Century of Controversy Between the United States and Mexico, 1966, Water and the West: The Colorado River Compact and the Politics of Water in the American West, 1975, The Great Thirst: Californians and Water 1770s-1990s, 1992, Las aquas divididas: Un siglo de controversia entre México y Estados Unidos, 2000, The Great Thirst: Californians and Water-A History, 2001; co-author: The Calif. Water Atlas, 1979, California: History of a Remarkable State, 1982; editor: The American Indian, 1974, The Chicano, 1975, The Asian American, 1976; co-editor: The American West: Frontier and Region, 1969, Golden State Series, 1978-2002; mng. editor Pacific Hist. Rev., 1968-97; mem. editl. bd. Jour. San Diego History, 1970-79, Calif. Hist. Soc., 1980-89; contbr. articles to profl. jours. Bd. dirs. John and LaRee Caughey Found., 1983-2000, Henry J. Bruman Ednl. Found., 1983-2003, Forest History Soc., 1987-93. Recipient award of merit Calif. Hist. Soc., 1979; Am. Philos. Soc. grantee, 1964, 71, Ford Found. grantee, 1968-69, U. Calif. Water Resources Ctr. grantee, 1969-72, 91, 2000, Sourisseau Acad. grantee, 1972, NEH grantee, 1983-89, Hewlett Found. grantee, 1986-89, U. Calif. Regents faculty fellow in humanities, 1975, Guggenheim fellow, 1978-79, Hist. Soc. So. Calif. fellow, 1996—; Whitsett lectr., 2000. Mem. Am. Hist. Assn. (exec. coun. Pacific Coast br. 1968-97, v.p. 1993-94, pres. 1994-95), Western History Assn. (coun. 1985-88, 93-97, pres. 1994-95, Winther award 1973, 79), Orgn. Am. Historians. Office: UCLA Dept History Los Angeles CA 90095-1473 E-mail: hundley@history.ucla.edu.

HUNDLEY, RONNIE, academic administrator; b. Columbus, Ga., July 18, 1950; s. Jack and Gwendolyn B. (Sasser) Hawthorne; m. Kathy A. Marcure, Apr. 28, 1972; children: Noel, Rhonda, Maria. BSME in Engring., U. Wash., 1974; MSME, Navy Postgrad., 1982, Degree of Engr., 1984. Registered profl. engr., Wash. Dir. engring. tech. Henry Cogswell Coll., Everett, Wash., 1989-91, acad. dean, 1991-93, pres., 1993—. Comdr. USN, 1968-89. Mem. ASME, Am. Assn. Higher Edn. Avocations: hiking, watercolor. Office: Henry Cogswell Coll 3002 Colby Ave Everett WA 98201-4012 E-mail: r.hundley@henrycogswell.edu.

HUNDT, PAUL ANTHONY, financial planner; b. La Crosse, Wis., June 9, 1942; s. Bernard and Catherine (Schams) H.; m. Patricia Arnold, Oct. 26, 1974; children: Peter A., Mary Elizabeth. BS in Am. History, St. Mary's U. Minn., 1964; postgrad., U. San Francisco, 1967-68. CFP, 1978. Lawn equipment sales mgr. Internat. Harvestor Co., Madison, Wis., 1968-69; account exec. Merrill Lynch Pierce Fenner & Smith, Milw., 1969-73; fin. planner Hundt Fin. Svcs., Inc., Milw., 1973—; real estate developer Hundt Properties Co., La Crosse County, Wis., 1976—. Bd. dirs. Fin. Planning Assn., Milw. chpt., 1994—. Author: The Economic and Political History of the Township of Washington, LaCrosse County Wisconsin, 1853-1900, 1964, Investing-Why You Should Seek A Business Owner's Double Digit Rate of Return, Why You Should Consider the Paul Hundt Personal Investment Strategy, 1998; contbr. articles to periodicals. Mem., del. Rep. Party Wis., Waukesha County, 1975—; founder, CEO, bd. chmn. Aquinas Academy, Menomonee Falls, Wis., 1989—; mem. Regnum Christi. Lt. USNR, 1965-68; co-founder, bd. dirs. Ridge History Park, Inc., La Crosse County, Wis. Mem. Bd. Adv. ITS Asset Mgmt, L.P., Rotary Club Brookfield, Wis. (sec. 1986-87, Paul Harris fellow 1982). Roman Catholic. Avocations: model railroading, gardening, golf, skiing, tennis. Office: Hundt Fin Svcs Inc 165 Bishops Way Ste 128 Brookfield WI 53005-6215

HUNDT, REED ERIC, information industry advisor, lawyer; b. Ann Arbor, Mich., Mar. 3, 1948; s. Neal H. and Viola (Pullan) H.; m. Elizabeth Ann Katz, Oct. 26, 1980; children: Adam Elias, Nathaniel Pullan, Sara. BA, Yale U., 1969, JD, 1974. Bar: U.S. Dist. Ct. Md. 1974, U.S. Ct. Appeals (4th cir.) 1975, U.S. Dist. Ct. (cen. and no. dists.) Calif. 1976, U.S. Ct. Appeals (9th cir.) 1976, U.S. Supreme Ct. 1977, U.S. Tax. Ct. 1978, U.S. Ct. Appeals (3d cir.) 1979, U.S. Dist. Ct. D.C. 1980, U.S. Ct. Appeals (D.C. cir.) 1980. Law clk. to presiding justice U.S. Ct. Appeals (4th cir.), Balt., 1974-75; assoc. Latham & Watkins, Washington, 1975-81, ptnr., 1982-94; chmn. FCC, Washington, 1994-97; prin. Charles Ross Ptnrs., LLC, Washington, Md., 1997—; sr. adv. McKinsey & Co. Mem. adv. com. and tchr. Yale Law Sch. and Yale Sch. of Mgmt.; bd. dirs. Allegiance Telecom, Inc., Northpoint Commn. Inc., Novell Inc., 1998—, Phone.com, Inc., Global Connect Partners, Core Express, Inc., Sigma Networks; spl. adv. Madison Dearborn Partners; venture ptnr. Benchmark Capital. Book rev. editor Yale U. Law Rev., 1974-75; author: (chpt. 9) Antitrust Adviser '85; contbr. articles to profl. jours. Mem. Environ. Task Force of Dem. Policy Com., Washington, 1986. Recipient Voice for Children Leadership award, Disting. Svc. award, Nat. Assn. of Elem. Sch. Principals, Nat. Assn. of Sec. Sch. Principals, Helen Keller Outstanding Pub. Svc. award, Am. Found. for the Blind. Mem. ABA.

HUNEKE, JOHN GEORGE, minister; b. Bklyn., Aug. 6, 1931; s. John Jacob and Adelaide (Peper) H. BA, Columbia U., 1953; MDiv, Luth. Theol. Sem., Phila., 1956; ThM, Harvard U., 1958. Ordained to ministry United Luth. Ch. Am., 1958. Asst. pastor Holy Trinity Luth. Ch., Bklyn., 1957-59; asst. to the pastor Trinity Luth. Ch., Middle Village, Queens, N.Y., 1959-60; pastor St. John's Luth. Ch., Greenpoint, Bklyn., 1960-73, Luth. Ch. of the Reformation, Bklyn., 1973—. Instr. religion Wagner Coll., S.I., 1957-58; stewardship com. Met. N.Y. Synod, Evang. Luth. Ch. Am., 1966-73. Author: Our Church 1867-1967, 100 Years, 1967, St. John's Lutheran Church, Our Church, February 13, 1898-1998, 100 Years, 1967, Lutheran Church Reformation, 1998. Bd. govs. Greenpoint Br. YMCA, Bklyn., 1963-73. Mem. Ordained Clergy Evang. Luth. Ch. Am. (Timotheans). Avocation: fishing. Home: Ridgewood 6016 Palmetto St Flushing NY 11385-3241 Office: Luth Ch Reformation 105 Barbey St Brooklyn NY 11207-2201 *As a Pastor for forty-five years, I have found satisfaction in my endeavor to be compassionate, to be present (to be there) where people hurt, and to have vision of the mission and message of justification by God's grace through faith. As the years go by, life becomes more meaningful to see other people realize that God loves all of us.*

HUNEYCUTT, ALICE RUTH, lawyer; b. New Haven, Jan. 10, 1951; d. C. Jerome and Alberta (Piner) H.; m. Howard Mark Bernstein, Nov. 28, 1981; children: Ashley Laughton, Laura Whitney. BA in History, Duke U., 1972; JD, U. Miami (Fla.), 1979. Bar: Fla. 1980, U.S. Dist. Ct. (so. dist.) Fla. 1980, U.S. Ct. Appeals (5th cir.) 1980, U.S. Dist. Ct. (mid. dist.) Fla. 1982, U.S. Ct. Appeals (11th cir.) 1982. Corp. counsel Burger King Corp., Miami, 1980-82; assoc. Stearns Weaver Miller Weissler Alhadeff & Sitterson, P.A., Tampa, Fla., 1982-84, ptnr., 1984—. Bd. dirs. Am. Heart Assn., Tampa, 1986-91, chmn. elect, 1988-89, chmn. 1990-91. Mem. ABA (corp., banking and bus law sect.), Fla. Bar Assn. (pres.'s Pro Bono Svc. award 1987), Fla. Assn. Women Lawyers. Democrat. Methodist. Home: 1400 72nd Ave NE Saint Petersburg FL 33702-4610 Office: 401 E Jackson St Ste 2200 Tampa FL 33602-5251 E-mail: ahyneycutt@swmwas.com.

HUNG, FRANK CHIEN-HSIN, chemist, researcher; b. Taiwan, Nov. 27, 1961; s. Po-Yang and Yu-Erh Hung; m. Chia-Hun Lin, June 3, 2000; 1 child, Fiona E. BA, CUNY, 1991; MS, Rutgers U., 1996. Sr. scientist Hoffmann La-Roche Inc., Nutley, NJ, 1990—. Office: Hoffmann L-Roche Inc 340 Kingsland St Nutley NJ 07110

HUNG, JAMES CHEN, engineer, educator, consultant; b. Foochow, Republic of China, Dec. 18, 1929; s. David Shen and Pearl C. (Chao) H.; m. Sufenne Huang, Apr. 3, 1958; children: John Y., Samuel M., Stephen T. BEE, Nat. Taiwan U., 1953; MEE, NYU, 1956, DEng, 1961. Registered profl. engr., Tenn. Instr. NYU, 1956-61; asst. prof. U. Tenn., Knoxville, 1961-62, assoc. prof., 1962-65, prof., 1965-84, disting. service prof., 1984-99, prof. emeritus, 1999—. V.p. Poly-Analytics, Inc., Knoxville; hon. prof. Nanjing U. Aerospace & Astrophysics, 1989, South China U. Tech., 1994, Hunan U., Peoples Republic of China, 1996; cons. prof. Northwestern Poly. U., Chongqing U., S.W. China Tchrs. U., 1984—. Contbr. articles to profl. jours. Recipient Technology award NASA, 1969, Cert. NASA, 1970, Brooks Disting. Engring. Prof. award, U. Tenn., 1973. Fellow: IEEE (editor IEEE Trans. on Indsl. Electronics 1991—95, gen. chmn. internat. symposium on indsl. electronics, Xian, China 1992, gen. chmn. internat. conf. indsl. tech. 1994, 1996, tech. activity bd. 1998—99, gen. chmn. internat. symposium on indsl. electronics, L'Aquila, Italy 2002, tech. track chair internat. conf. indsl. electronics 2003, Anthony J. Hornfeck Svc. award 1995, Eugene Mittelmann Achievement award 2000, Millennium medal 2000), Indsl. Electronics Soc. (v.p. 1996, pres.-elect 1997, pres. 1998—99); mem.: Phi Kappa Phi, Eta Kappa Nu, Tau Beta Pi, Sigma Xi. Methodist. Office: U Tenn Knoxville TN 37996-0001

HUNG, LI-SHAN, music educator; b. Taipei, Taiwan, July 27, 1968; d. Kang-Hui Hung and Chu-chih Tsai; m. Min-Chian Liu, July 18, 1998. BA, Nat. Taiwan Normal U., 1991; MusM, Johns Hopkins U., 1993, D of Musical Arts, 1999. Lectr. U. Pacific, Stockton, Calif., 2001—. Performer: numerous piano recitals. Recipient Rose Marie Milholland Award in piano performance, 1996, Annie Wentz Meml. Prize in Chamber Music and Piano Accompanying, 1994. Mem.: Steinway Soc. of Bay Area (bd. dirs.), Chinese Music Tchrs. Assn. No. Calif., Music Tchrs. Assn. Calif. (v.p. Los Altos br. 2001—02), Pi Kappa Lambda. Avocations: hiking, travel. Home: 1583 Nilda Ave Mountain View CA 94040 Office: Univ of Pacific 3601 Pacific Ave Stockton CA 95211-0110*

HUNG, MEI-JONG CHOW, social worker; b. Taipei, Taiwan, Republic China, Oct. 7, 1937; s. Wen-tung Yeh Chow; m. Chao-huang Hung, Mar. 24, 1964; children: Jennifer Ching-yi, John Ching-tsung. BS, Nat. Taiwan U., 1960; MSW, Simmons Coll. Sch. Social Work, 1963. Cert. social worker, hypnotherapist. Mental health counselor Taipei Pub. Health Teaching Demonstration, 1963-66; asst. prof. Taiwan U., 1964-66; social work supr. Johns Hopkins Hosp., Balt., 1969-71; pvt. practice social work Columbia, Md., 1972—. Vol. cmty. recreational social work, 1988—; prodr. Opera Internat., Washington, 1999—, prodr., 2002—. WHO fellow. Mem. NASW, Acad. Cert. Social Workers. Home and Office: 7255 Meadow Wood Way Clarksville MD 21029-1714 Address: PO Box 140 Fulton MD 20759-0140

HUNG, PAUL PORWEN, biotechnologist, educator, consultant; b. Taipei, Taiwan, Sept. 30, 1933; s. Yao-Hsun and Shiu-Chin (Wu) H.; m. Nancy Kay Clark, May 4, 1956; children: Pauline E., Eileen K., Clark D. BS in Arts and Sci., Millikin U., 1956; PhD in Biochemistry, Purdue U., 1960; DSc (hon.), Millikin U., 1997. Head molecular virology and biology Abbott Labs., North Chicago, 1960-81; gen. mgr. Bethesda Rsch. Lab., Gaithersburg, Md., 1981-82; asst. v.p. Wyeth Ayerst Labs., Radnor, Pa., 1982-95, disting. rsch. fellow, 1993-95; adj. prof. Northwestern U. Med. Sch., Chgo., 1975-86; chmn. bd. RDNA Corp., Bryn Mawr, Pa., 1995—, Global Briotech Inc., Taiwan, 1998—. Mem. Nat. Vaccine Adv. Com., Washington, 1990-95; cons. Am. Inst. Biol. Sci., Washington, 1992, UN Indsl. Devel. Orgn., Vienna, Austria, 1981; vis. prof. Stanford U., 1969-1970. Author: (chpt.) Recombinant DNA, 1991, Hepatitis Vaccine, 1991; contbr. over 270 articles to profl. jours. Named Disting. Alumni of Yr., Purdue U., 1994, Alumnus of Yr., Millikin U., 2001; recipient Taiwanese Am. Found. Sci. and Tech. award, 2001. Mem. Am. Soc. Biochemistry and Molecular Biology, Am. Assn. Cancer Rsch., Internat. Assn. Biol. Standardization, Am. Inst. Chemists, Am. Soc. Microbiology, Am. Chem. Soc., AAAS, N.Y. Acad. Sci., Medalion Soc./Millikin U. Achievements include patents in field. Home: 506 Ramblewood Dr Bryn Mawr PA 19010-2041 Fax: 525-3595; Home Fax: 610-525-3595. E-mail: pphung@prodigy.net.

HUNG, WILLIAM MO-WEI, chemist; b. Chekiang, China, Sept. 17, 1940; came to U.S., 1966; s. Jordon T. and I-Hsing (Chang) H.; m. Julia Tsui, July 20, 1968; children: Berwyn, Calvin. BS, Nat. Chung-Hsing U., 1963; PhD, U. Mass., 1970. Rsch. and teaching asst. U. Mass., Amherst, 1967-70; rsch. assoc. The Ohio State U., Columbus, 1970-74; sr. rsch. chemist Hilton-Davis Chem. Co., Cin., 1974-80, dir. chem. rsch., 1980-84, sr. rsch. fellow, 1984-87; staff rsch. scientist CIBA Vision Corp., Atlanta, 1987-92, rsch. fellow, 1992-94; head organic chemistry Tech. Resource Internat. Corp., Alpharetta, Ga., 1995—. Contbr. articles to profl. jours. 2d lt. Air Force of Republic of China, 1963-64, Taiwan. Fellow The Am. Inst. Chemists, Am. Chem. Soc. Achievements include patents for ultraviolet radiation absorbing agent for bonding to an ocular lens, tinted contact lenses with reactive dyes, novel color formers for transfer imaging dye and imaging systems. Home: 4062 Dover Ave Alpharetta GA 30004-1282 Office: Tech Resource Internat Corp 1525 Bluegrass Lakes Pkwy Alpharetta GA 30004-7713 E-mail: wmh@tricorporation.com.

HUNGATE, JOSEPH IRVIN, III, information technology executive; b. San Antonio, Nov. 17, 1956; s. Joseph Irvin Jr. and Betty Lou (Hatzenbuehler) H.; m. Santa Michelle Haines, May 15, 1993; children: Brittany Nicole, Annabel Sue, Charlotte Elizabeth. BS in Computer Sci., U. S.C., 1979, MS in Computer Sci., 1981; postgrad., U. Va., 1982-83. Tchg. asst. U. S.C., Columbia, 1979-81; sr. systems analyst GE, Charlottesville, Va., 1981-85; mgr. software devel. TRW, Fairfax, Va., 1985-88, prin. investigator, 1996 97, mgr. field engring. London, 1988-93; supervisory computer scientist Nat. Inst. Stds. and Tech. U.S. Dept. Commerce, Gaithersburg, Md., 1993 96; supervisory computer scientist Office of Insp. Gen., U.S. Dept. Commerce, 1997-99; assoc. dir. info. resource mgmt. office Ctrs. for Disease Control, Atlanta, 1999-2000; asst. inspector gen. info. technology, chief info. officer Treas. Insp. Gen. Tax Adminstrn., Washington, 2000—, chairperson exec. resource bd., 2001—. Mem. EIA Working Group RS-511, Detroit, 1983-85; recruitment coord. Affirmative Action, Fairfax, 1986-88; spl. liaison European Workshop on Open Sys., Brussels, 1993-96; chmn. Open Sys. Implementator's Workshop, Gaithersburg, 1993-97. Mem. Va. Student Aid Found., Charlottesville, 1985—; vol. coord. blood svcs. ARC, Fairfax, 1985-88; vol. Arlington County (Va.) Dem. Com., 1985-88; bd. dirs. Hungate Family Hist. Soc., Inc., Chevy Chase, Md., 1989—. Recipient commendation USN, London, 1990; scholar S.C. Ednl. Found., 1975. Mem. Computer Soc. of IEEE, Assn. for Computing Machinery, Am. Mgmt. Assn., Sigma Phi Epsilon. Methodist. Avocations: collecting wine, golf, sailing, skeet, travel. Home: 5818 N 27th St Arlington VA 22207 Office: 1125 15th St Ste 700A Washington DC 20005 E-mail: joseph.hungate@tigta.treas.gov.

HUNGER, J(OHN) DAVID, business educator; b. May 17, 1941; s. Jackson Steele and Elizabeth (Carey) H.; m. Betty Johnson, Aug. 2, 1969; children: Karen, Susan, Laura, Merry. BA, Bowling Green (Ohio) State U., 1963; MBA, Ohio State U., 1966, PhD, 1973. Selling supr. Lazarus Dept. Store, Columbus, Ohio, 1965-66; brand asst. Procter and Gamble Co., Cin., 1968-69; asst. dir. grad. bus. programs Ohio State U., Columbus, 1970-72; instr. Baldwin-Wallace Coll., Berea, Ohio, 1972-73; prof. U. Va., Charlottesville, 1973-82; strategic mgmt. prof. Iowa State U. Coll. Bus., Ames, 1982—. Prof. bus. George Mason U., Fairfax, Va., 1986-87; past pres. bd. dirs. Iowa State U. Press; cons. to bus., fed. and state agys. Author (with T.L. Wheelen): Strategic Management and Business Policy, 1983, 8th rev. edit., 2002, An Assessment of Undergraduate Business Education in the U.S., 1980, Cases in Strategic Management, 1987, Essentials of Strategic Management, 1997, 3d edit., 2003; author: Concepts in Strategic Management and Business Policy, 2000, 2d edit., 2002; contbr. articles to profl. jours. Capt. Mil. Intelligence, U.S. Army, 1966-68. Decorated Bronze Star. Mem. Acad. Mgmt., N.Am. Case Rsch. Assn. (pres.), Soc. for Case Rsch. (past pres.), Strategic Mgmt. Soc., US Assn. for Small Bus. and Enterpreneurship (past v.p.). Office: Iowa State U Coll Bus 300 Carver Hall Ames IA 50011 E-mail: jdhunger@iastate.edu.

HUNGERFORD, DAVID SAMUEL, orthopedic surgeon, educator; b. Rochester, NY, May 4, 1938; s. Francis Samuel and Marjorie Ellen (Wilson) H.; m. Uta-Heide Jung, July 20, 1962; children: Marc Wilson, Kyle Sasha, Lars Daniel. BA, Colgate U., 1960; MD, U. Rochester, 1964. Diplomate Am. Bd. Orthopaedic Surgery. Asst. prof. orthopaedic surgery Johns Hopkins U., Balt., 1972-78; chief orthopaedic surgery VA Hosp., Balt., 1975-80, Good Samaritan Hosp., Balt., 1972—, chief div. arthritis surgery, 1979—2001; assoc. prof. orthopaedic surgery Johns Hopkins U. Sch. Medicine, Balt., 1978-86, prof. orthopaedic surgery, 1987—. Cons. Balt. City Hosp., 1972-85, Children's Hosp., 1972-80, East Balt. Med. Ctr., 1972-78; co-dir. Johns Hopkins U. Ctr. for Osteonecrosis Rsch. and Edn., 1995—; bd. dirs. Nat. Osteonecrosis Found. Author: Progress in Orthopaedics, 1977, Ischemia and Necroses of Bone, 1980, Total Knee Arthroplasty: A Comprehensive Approach, 1984, Total Hip Arthroplasty: A New Approach, 1984, Bone Circulation, 1984, Disorders of the Patello Femoral Joint, 1990, Videobook of Total Knee Arthroplasty, 1994; founding editor Jour. Arthroplasty, 1985-93. Elder Cen. Presbyn. Ch., Balt., 1974-83; dir. Crippled Children's United Rehab. Effort, 1997—, Christian Orthopaedic Ptrs., 1997—; chmn. bd. Med. Assistance Program Internat., 1998—. Maj. U.S. Army, 1969. Recipient George Hoyt Whipple award, 1965; named Disting. So. Orthopedist, So. Orthopedic Assn., 2002; Colgate U. scholar, 1956-59, GM scholar, 1956-59, U. Rochester scholar, 1959-61, Girdlestone Meml. scholar Oxford U., Eng., 1969-70; fellow USPHS, Paris, 1961-62, Carl Berg traveling fellow, 1973. Mem. Johns Hopkins Med. and Surg. Soc., Md. Orthopaedic Soc., Arthritis Found., Md. Soc. Rheumatic Diseases, Am. Rheumatism Assn., Orthopaedic Rsch. Soc., Hip Soc., Am. Assn. Orthopaedic Surgeons, Am. Assn. Hip Knee Surgeons, Soc. Internat. de Chirurgie Orthopedique et de Traumatologie, Knee Soc. (pres. 1994). Republican. Home: 10715 Pot Spring Rd Cockeysville Hunt Valley MD 21030-3019 Office: Good Samaritan Hosp Profl Office Bldg G-1 5601 Loch Raven Blvd Baltimore MD 21239-2991 also: Johns Hopkins U Sch Medicine Dept Orthopaedic Surgery Baltimore MD 21205 Business E-Mail: dhunger@jhmi.edu.

HUNGERFORD, GARY A. insurance executive, columnist, author, editor; b. Bklyn., Apr. 20, 1948; s. Jean and Ann H.; m. Eleanor Haragsim, Oct. 4, 1969. BBA cum laude, The Coll. of Ins.: N.Y.C., 1974; MBA, The Coll. of Ins., 1978; grad., U.S. Army Svc. Rifle Small Arms Firing Sch., 1992. CPCU, 1976, ASLI, 2001. With Guardian Life Ins. Co., 1965-67, Providence Washington Ins. Co., 1967-68, The Atlantic Cos., 1968-74, Midland Ins. Co., 1974-76, Drake Ins. Co. of N.Y., 1976-78, Mead Reinsurance Corp., 1978-80, Yorktown Indemnity Co., 1980-82, Tri-County Facilities, Ltd./Tri-County Facilities N.J., Inc., 1982-85; pres., CEO Spl. Risk Facilities, Ltd., Lindenhurst, N.Y., 1985—; chmn., CEO CompuPub. Svcs., Ltd., Lindenhurst, 1987—; chmn. Hungerford Arms Co., Ltd., Lindenhurst, 1988—; v.p., dir. Protective Ins. Agy., Ridgewood, N.Y., 1983—. Past editor, pub. Lindenhurst's Chamber News, 1990-95; former columnist The South Bays' News, Lindenhurst's Chamber News, the Suffolk Alliance of Sportsmen's Newsletter, The Bullet. Author: NYSRPA's Education and Training Directory, 1992, History of New York State Rifle and Pistol Association, 1997, Atlantic Mutual's No-Fault Automobile Insurance Manual ; contbr. numerous ins.-related articles to profl. jours. Sponsor U.S. Olympic Shooting Team; life mem. The N.Y. State Conservation Coun.; mem. Glock Sport Shooting Found.; mem. N.Y. Senate Small Bus. Adv. Com. With U.S. Army, 1968-70. Mem. Soc. CPCU, Soc. for Ins. Rsch., Ind. Ins. Agts. Assn., Casualty and Surety Soc. N.Y., Profl. Ins. Agts. N.Y., Profl. Ins. Wholesalers Assn., Coll. Ins. Alumni Assn., Ind. Ins. Agts. N.Y., Coll. Ins. MBA Soc., Lindenhurst C. of C. (past chmn.), Nat. Assn. Desktop Publishers, M-1 Carbine Collectors Assn., Inc., Garand Collectors' Assn., L.I. Computer Assn., NRA (life, mem. field support team, polit. preference com. 1992, Inst. for Legis. Action, Polit. Victory Fund, cert. firearms instr., Golden Eagles), Citizens' Com. for Right To Keep and Bear Arms (life), N.Y. State Rifle and Pistol Assn. (life, past bd. dirs., past chmn. fin. com., past chmn. range com., past printing com., past hist. com., past omnibus com.), Northeastern Arms Collectors Assn., Internat. Game Fish Assn., N.Am. Fishing Club (charter), N.Am. Hunting Club (life), Nassau County Fish and Game Assn., Bass Anglers' Sportsman's Soc., Suffolk Alliance of Sportmen (del., firearms chmn., past v.p., dir.), Whitetails Unltd., Lindenhurst Lions Club, Old Bethpage Rifle and Pistol Club (trustee), Nat. Assn. Federally Lic. Firearms Dealers, Second Amendment Found. (life), United Gamefish Anglers, Inc. (life), Law Enforcement Alliance of Am. (life), L.I. Beach Buggy Assn., Shooters' Com. on Polit. Edn. (life), Wildlife Forever, Izaak Walton League, N.Y. Sportfishing Fedn. (life, del.), Varmint Hunters Assn. (life), Gun Owners Am. (life), Theodore Roosevelt Conservation Assn., L.I. Dahlia Soc. Republican. Avocations: chess, fishing, hunting, shooting sports, computers, photography. Office: Spl Risk Facilities Ltd 101 N Wellwood Ave Lindenhurst NY 11757-4001

HUNING, DEVON GRAY, actress, dancer, audiologist, veterinary technician, photographer, video producer and editor; b. Evanston, Ill., Aug. 23, 1950; d. Hans Karl Otto and Angenette Dudley (Willard) H.; divorced; 1 child, Bree Alyeska. BS with honors, No. Ill. U., 1981, MA, 1983; AAS in Vet. Tech. with honors, Colo. Mountain Coll., 2000. Actress, soloist, dancer, dir. various univ. and community theater depts., Bklyn., Chgo. and Cranbrook, B.C., Can., 1967—; audiologist, ednl. programming cons. East Kootenay Ministry of Health, Cranbrook, 1985-89; contractor, cons., trainer ednl., clin. and indsl. audiology BC, Wash., Oreg., 1989—97; ind. video prodn./photographer, 1979—; owner Maxaroma Espresso and Incredible Edibles, 1993-95, vet. technician specializing in exotics and avianix, writing and edn. rsch., 2000—; vol. NDMS/VMAT, 2001—. Master of ceremonies East Kootenay Talent Showcase, EXPO '86, Vancouver B.C., Can., 1986; creator, workshop leader: A Hearing Impaired Child in the Classroom, 1986. Producer, writer, dir., editor (video) Down With Decibels, 1992; author: Living Well With Hearing Loss: A Guide for the Hearing-Impaired and Their Families, 1992. Sec., treas. Women for Wildlife, Cranbrook, 1985-86; assoc. mem. adv. bd. Grand County Community Coll., Winter Park, Colo., 1975-77; assoc. mem. bd. dirs. Boys and Girls Club of Can., Cranbrook, 1985. Mem. Phi Theta Kappa. Avocations: snow and water skiing, scuba diving, dancing, marine animals, studying animal behavior. E-mail: d_huning@hotmail.com.

HUNKELE, LESTER MARTIN, III, retired federal agency administrator; b. Bklyn., Aug. 16, 1947; s. Lester Martin Jr. and Agnes Veronica (Tarpey) H.; m. Diane Kathryn Sotiridy, Mar. 30, 1974. BS, U.S. Mil. Acad., 1969; MS in Constrn. Engring., Purdue U., 1975; diploma, Indsl. Coll. Armed Forces, 1988. Registered profl. engr., Va.; cert. plant engr.; cert. constrn. mgr. Commd. 2d lt. U.S. Army, 1969, advanced through grades to capt., 1979; lt. col. USAR, 1990; ret., 1995; logistics officer 809 Engring. Bn., 1970-71, engr. officer, 1970-71; engr. officer army engring. sch. U.S. Army, Ft. Belvoir, Va., 1971-74, asst. area engr. Balt. dist. C.E., 1975-79, resigned, 1979; civil engr. office chief engrs. Dept. Army, Washington, 1979-81, asst. chief constrn. mgmt. office chief army res., 1981-83; asst. head facilities HQs USMC, Washington, 1983-85; dir. facilities office asst. sec. def. res. affairs Dept. Def., Washington, 1985-88, prin. dir. materiel and facilities, 1988-89; dep. asst. sec. for facilities Dept. Vets. Affairs, Washington, 1989-92, dep. asst. sec. facilities oversight, 1992-93; exec. dir. Pa. Ave. Devel. Corp., Washington, 1993-96; exec. project mgr. Gen. Svcs. Adminstrn., Washington, 1996; project exec. Clark Constrn. Group, 1996-99; assoc. v.p. DMJMH&N, Arlington, Va., 1999-2001, v.p., 2001—02, sr. v.p., 2002—. Mem. ASCE, NSPE (mem. govt. adv. group), CMAA, Am. Inst. Plant Engrs., Soc. Am. Mil. Engrs. (dir. Washington chpt. 1984-88), Fed. Exec. Inst. Alumni Assn. (membership chmn. 1987), West Point Soc. (co-founder Annapolis chpt. 1986—), Urban Land Inst., Lambda Alpha. Avocations: sailing, skiing, scuba diving. Home: 3259 Chrisland Dr Annapolis MD 21403-4352 Office: DMJMH&N 1525 Wilson Blvd Arlington VA 22209 E-mail: les.hunkele@dmjmhn.com.

HUNKER, FRED DOMINIC, internist, medical educator; b. Montgomery, Ala., Nov. 13, 1947; s. Joseph Frederick and Frances Cecelia (Armbruster) H.; m. Edith Margaret McCulloch, Sept. 25, 1976; children: Marie Elizabeth, Emily Kathleen, Jacob Dominic. BA in English, Creighton U., 1969; MD, U. Nebr., 1974. Diplomate Nat. Bd. Med. Examiners; diplomate in internal medicine, pulmonary medicine and sleep medicine Am. Bd. Internal Medicine. Intern U. Ala. Sch. Medicine, Birmingham, 1974-75, resident, chief resident and instr. medicine, 1975-77, 78-79, fellow in pulmonary medicine, 1977-78, clin. asst. prof., 1979-93, clin. assoc. prof., 1993—. Founder Montgomery Pulmonary Cons., P.A., 1979; pres. med. staff St. Margaret's Hosp., 1986-88; pres. med. staff Bapt. Med. Ctr., 2001-03. Contbr. articles to profl. jours. Bd. dirs. Am. Lung Assn. Ala., Ala. pres., 1997-99; physician vol. Project Hope, Maceio, Brazil, 1973; bd. dirs. Queen of Mercy Elem. Sch., 1986-91, Combined Montgomery Cath. Schs., 1992-2002; chmn. Physician's divsn. United Way Campaign, 1987-88, co-chair profl. divsn., 1999-2000; mem. Leadership Montgomery Class X, 1993-94. Knight Comdr. with star Equestrian Order of the Holy Sepulchre, 1990—. Fellow Am. Coll. Chest Physicians; mem. AMA, Am. Thoracic Soc. (coun. of chpt. reps., state rep. 1988-94, tng. and continuing med. edn. com. 1992-94), Ala. Thoracic Soc. (pres. 1986-87), Nat. Assn. Med. Dirs. of Respiratory Care, Med. Assn. State of Ala., Med. Soc. Montgomery County (pres. 1988-89, bd. censors 1989-96, M.D. of Yr. 2003), Montgomery C. of C., KC (3d degree), Capitol City Club. Roman Catholic. Avocations: fishing, wing shooting. Home: 1595 Gilmer Ave Montgomery AL 36104-5619 Office: Montgomery Pulmonary Cons 1440 Narrow Lane Pky Montgomery AL 36111-2654 E-mail: fhunker@knology.net.

HUNKINS, RAYMOND BREEDLOVE, lawyer, rancher; b. Culver City, Calif., Mar. 19, 1939; s. Charles F. and Louise (Breedlove) H.; m. Mary Deborah McBride, Dec. 12, 1967; children: Amanda, Blake, Ashley. BA, U. Wyo., 1966, JD, 1968. Ptnr. Jones, Jones, Vines & Hunkins, Wheatland, Wyo., 1968—. Local rules com. U.S. Dist. Ct., 1990—; spl. counsel U. Wyo., Laramie, State of Wyo., Cheyenne; mem. faculty Western Trial Adv. Inst., 1993-95, Wyo. Supreme Ct. Commn. Jud. Salary and Benefits, 1996-98; ; owner Thunderhead Ranches, Albany and Platte Counties, Wyo.; gen. ptnr. Split Rock Land & Cattle Co.; spl. asst. atty. gen., Wyo.; bd. dirs. Found. for Laramie, Laramie Peak Mus. Chmn. Platte County Reps., Wheatland, 1972-74, chmn. adv. coun. Coll. Commerce and Industry, U. Wyo., 1978-79; bd. dirs. U. Wyo. Found., 1996-2002, Found. Laramie, 2002—, Laramie Peak Mus., 1989—; bd. advisors Am. Heritage Ctr., 1995-99; active Gov.'s Crime Commn., 1970-78; pres. Wyo. U. Alumni Assn., 1973-74, commr. Wyo. Aeronautics Commn., 1987-98; moderator United Ch. Christ, 1997-98; Rep. candidate for Gov. Wyo., 2002. With USMCR, 1956-60. Recipient Big Horn Mountain Roundup Pax Irvine award, 1989, Outstanding Advisor award Phi Delta Theta, 1968. Fellow Am. Coll. Trial Lawyers (Wyo. state chmn. 1998-2000, nat. ethics com. 2000—), Internat. Soc. Barristers, Am. Bd. Trial Advs.; mem. ABA (aviation com. 1980-86, forum com. on constrn. industry litigation sect.), Wyo. Bar Assn. (chmn. grievance com. 1980-86, mem. com. on civil pattern jury instrns. 1999-2002, state bar-law sch. com., bench-bar rels. com.), Wyo. Trial Lawyers Assn. (past pres.), Lions, Elks. Office: Jones Jones Vines & Hunkins PO Drawer 189 9th and Maple Wheatland WY 82201

HUNN, MAX W. freelance/self-employed photojournalist; b. Rock Island, Ill., Dec. 10, 1914; s. Wilbur Bennett and Wilhelmina Mary Hunn; m. Beatrice Desjardin Hunn, Aug. 17, 1984; 1 child, Sandra Fo Piano;children: Linda Bair, Sandra Peters. BA in Journalism History, Grinnell Coll., 1937. Reporter Daily Dispatch, Moline, Ill., 1937—40, chief photographer, 1940—42; photo editor Pan Am. World Air, Miami, Fla., 1946—55; freelance photojournalist Fla., 1955—. Lt. USN, 1942—46. Mem.: WWII USN Armed Guard. Presbyterian. Avocations: travel, fishing.

HUNNICUTT, CHARLES ALVIN, lawyer; b. LaGrange, Ga., Dec. 7, 1950; s. William Oliver and Mary Olivia (Leggett) Hunnicut. BS, Am. U., 1972; JD, U. Ga., 1975; LLM, U. Brussels, Belgium, 1976. Bar: Ga. 1975, D.C. 1978, U.S. Dist. Ct. D.C. 1978, U.S. Ct. Appeals (D.C. cir.) 1978, U.S. Ct. Internat. Trade 1980, U.S. Ct. Appeals (fed. cir.) 1981, U.S. Supreme Ct. 1981. Dep. dir. State of Ga. Office, Brussels, 1975-76; ops. mgr. Presdl. Pers. The White House, Washington, 1976-77; exec. asst. to under sec. internat. trade U.S. Dept. Commerce, Washington, 1977-80; legal advisor to chmn. Internat. Trade Commn., Washington, 1980-87; ptnr. Robins, Kaplan, Miller & Ciresi, Washington, 1987-96, mng. ptnr., 1989-91; advisor to Govt. of Ukraine on accession to Gen. Agreement on Tariffs and Trade World Trade Orgn., Kiev, 1994-95; asst. sec. for aviation and internat. affairs U.S. Dept. Transp., Washington, 1996-99; ptnr. Robins, Kaplan, Miller & Ciresi, Washington, 1999—2003, mem. exec. bd., 2003—, exec. bd., 2003—. Adj. prof. Am. U. Coll. Law, Washington, 1988—91. Bd. visitors U. Ga. Sch. Law., 2000—. Mem.: Internat. Bar Assn., Am. Soc. Internat. Law (exec. coun. 1999—2002, chair budget com. 2000—), Washington Fgn. Law Soc. (pres. 1987—88), Ga. State Bar, Bar Assn. D.C., FBA, ABA (internat. trade steering com., air and space law forum). Democrat. Presbyterian. Office: Robins Kaplan Miller & Ciresi 1801 K St NW Ste 1200 Washington DC 20006-1307 E-mail: cahunnicutt@rkmc.com.

HUNNICUTT, RICHARD PEARCE, metallurgical engineer; b. June 15, 1926; s. James Ballard and Ida (Black) H.; m. Susan Haight, Apr. 9, 1954; children: Barbara, Beverly, Geoffrey, Anne. BS in Metall. Engring., Stanford U., 1951, MS, 1952. Metallurgist Gen. Motors Rsch. Labs, 1952-55; sr. metallurgist and processes Firestone Engring. Lab., 1957-58; head phys. scis. group Dalmo Victor Co., Monterey, 1958-61, head materials lab., 1961-62; v.p. Anamet Labs., Inc., Monterey, 1962-82, exec. v.p., 1982—. Partner Pyrco Co. Author: Pershing, A History of the American Medium Tank T20 Series, 1971, Sherman, A History of the American Medium Tank, 1978, Patton, A History of the American Main Battle Tank, vol. 1, 1984, Firepower, A History of the American Heavy Tank, 1988, Abrams, A History of the American Main Battle Tank, vol

2, 1990, Stuart, A History of the American Light Tank, vol. 1, 1992, Sheridan, A History of the American Light Tank vol. 2, 1995, Bradley: A History of American Fighting and Support Vehicle, 1999, Halftrack, A History of American Semi-tracked Vehicles, 2000, Armored Car: A History of American Wheeled Combat Vehicles, 2002. Served with AUS, 1943-46. Mem. AIME, ASTM, Electrochem. Soc., Am. Soc. Metals, Am. Welding Soc., Am. Soc. Lubrication Engrs. Research on frictional behavior of materials, development of armored fighting vehicles. Home: 9432 Swan Lake Dr Granite Bay CA 95746-7205

HUNNICUTT, VICTORIA ANNE WILSON, educator; b. Tyler, Tex., July 23, 1944; d. Leroy G. and N. Joseline (Bobo) Wilson; m. John Walter Hubble, July 29, 1967 (div. Oct. 1972); m. Buford D. Hunnicutt, Aug. 1, 1982. BA, Emory and Henry Coll., 1966; MEd, Mercer U., 1970; Ed Specialist, U. Ga., 1993; EdD, Ga. So. U., 1998. Tchr. Spanish/English Marion (Va.) Sr. H.S., 1966-67; tchr. Spanish Ballard Hudson Middle Sch., Macon, 1967-68; reading specialist Robins AFB Sch. System, Warner Robins, Ga., 1973-74, Spanish tchr., 1968-70, classroom tchr., 1970-86, computer/sci. specialist, 1986-90, prin. Robins Elem. Sch., 1991, curriculum coord., 1990-99; asst. prof. Early Childhood Ga. Coll. and State U., Macon, 1999—. Adj. prof. Tift Coll., Forsyth, Ga., 1985-88, Ft. Valley State Coll., 1993-99. Treas. Bibb County Dem. Women, Macon, Ga., 1986-88, membership chair 1989-93. Mem.: Nat. Coun. Tchrs. Math., NSTA, ASCD, Nat. Coun. Tchrs. English, Aerospace Edn. Found. (nat. bd. trustees 1998—, nat. sec. 2000—03, Tchr. of Yr. 1995, Jane Shirley McGee award 1990, Medal of Merit 1990, Exceptional Svc. award 1997, George C. Hardy award for excellence in aerospace edn. 1999, Pres.'s citation 2001), Air Force Assn. (treas. chpt. 296 1989—91, v.p. 1991—92, v.p. for aerospace edn. chpt. 296 1991—, v.p. for aerospace edn. Ga. State AFA 1992—97, v.p. chpt. 296 1993—94, regional v.p. for aerospace edn. 1997—, v.p. 1998—, v.p. for aerospace edn. Ga. State AFA 1998—), Ga. Assn. Tchr. Educators, Ga. Coun. Tchrs. of Math., Ocmulgee Audubon Soc. (edn. chair 1986—93), Nat. Audubon Soc., HOPE Coun. (pres. 1994—95), Internat. Reading Assn., Ga. Coun. of Internat. Reading Assn., Nat. Coun. Tchrs. of English, Bus. and Profl. Womens Club (Woman of Achievement local, regional, and state levels 1999), Phi Delta Kappa (chpt. sec. 2002—). Democrat. Methodist. Avocations: reading, gardening. Office: Ga Coll and State Univ 100 College Station Dr Macon GA 31206-5100 E-mail: vhunnicu@mail.gcsu.edu.

HUNSAKER, ANDETTA ROTILLA, physician, medical educator; d. Hollibert Eastwald and Carmella Phillips; m. Robert Pearson Hunsaker, July 10, 1994. MD, Loma Linda U., 1983. Cert. Nat. Bd. Med. Examiners, 1983. Attending physician Brigham and Women's Hosp., Boston, 1994—; asst. prof. Harvard Mediacl Sch., Boston, 2001—. Contbr. articles to profl. jours. Mem.: Soc. Thoracic Radiology, Am. Coll. Radiology, Am. Roentgen Ray Soc., Radiol. Soc. N.Am. Republican. Seventh Day Adventist. Avocations: church activities, decorating, gardening, cooking, violin. Office: Brigham and Womens Hosp 75 Francis St Boston MA 02115 Office Fax: 617-264-6802. Personal E-mail: ahunsaker@partners.org. E-mail: ahunsaker@partners.org.

HUNSAKER, JILL ANN, public health administrator; b. Wheatridge, Colo., Oct. 28, 1968; d. William J. and Janet Lavon (Jeanneret) H. BA in Psychology & Sociology, U. Colo., 1991; MPH, U. No. Colo., 1998. Residentialtreatment counselor Alternative Homes for Youth, Lakewood, Colo., 1991-94, asst. dir. emacipation program, 1994-95; teen outreach specialist Jefferson County Dept. Pub. Health, Lakewood, Colo., 1995-97; adminstrv. program specialist Colo. Dept. Pub. Health & Environment, Denver, 1997-99, health planner, 1999—. Head gymnastic coach Jefferson County Pub. Schs., Golden, Colo., 1992—96. Mem. Nat. Fedn. Interscholastic Ocfls. Assn., Colo. Pub. Health Assn. (com. mem. 1997). Democrat. Avocations: jogging, piano, biking, waterskiing. Home: 1204 S Pennsylvania St Denver CO 80210-1533 Office: Colo Dept Pub Health & Environment 4300 Cherry Creek Dr S Denver CO 80246

HUNSAKER, RICHARD KENDALL, lawyer; b. L.A., June 2, 1960; s. Richard Allan and Patricia Kendall (Cook) H.; m. Laura Constance Haile, Oct. 8, 1988; children, Charles Nicholas, Laura Caroline. BA, U. Ill., 1982, MA, 1983; JD, Washington U., St. Louis, 1986. Bar: Ill. 1986, U.S. Dist. Ct. (cen. and no. dists.) Ill. 1987, U.S. Ct. Appeals (7th cir.) 1990, Wis. 1992. Speech coach Champaign (Ill.) Central High Sch., 1979-81; instr. speech communications, asst. debate coach U. Ill., Urbana, 1982-83; assoc. Heyl, Royster, Voelker & Allen, Springfield, Ill., 1986-87, Rockford, Ill., 1987-93, ptnr., 1994—2002, Edwardsville, Ill., 2002—. Author: Advanced Real Estate Law in Illinois - Environmental Liabilities, 1992, (with others) Advanced Real Estate Law in Illinois: Environmental Liability, 1992. Mem. ABA (tort and ins. practice, litigation and natural resources, energy and environ. law sects.), Ill. Bar Assn. (assoc., ins. law sect. 1990-92, civil practice and procedure, workers compensation, tort law and environ. control law sects.), Ill. Assn. Def. Trial Counsel (co-chair fall seminar), St. Clair County Bar ASsn., Madison County Bar Assn., Seventh Cir. Bar Assn., Def. Rsch. Inst. Methodist. Avocations: golf, biking, backpacking. Home: 14 Saffrin Hill Glen Carbon IL 62034 Office: Heyl Royster Voelker & Allen Mark Twain Plaza II 103 W Vandalia St PO Box 467 Edwardsville IL 62025-0467 E-mail: rhunsaker@hrva.com.

HUNSAKER, RODERICK CASON, Mem. ABA. Club: University of Boston (v.p. 1983-84, gov. 1984—). Office: John Hancock Mut Life Ins Co PO Box 111 Boston MA 02117-0111

HUNSAKER, SCOTT LESLIE, gifted and talented education educator; b. Provo, Utah, Oct. 22, 1953; s. Melvin J and Ruth Lofthouse (Pulsipher) H.; m. Rebecca Naser, June 2, 1982; children: Adam Scott, Jacob Christian, Rachel Noelle. BA cum laude, Brigham Young U., 1977, MEd, 1982; PhD, U. Va., 1991. Classroom tchr. Alpine Sch. Dist., Orem, Utah, 1977-85, gifted coord. American Fork, Utah, 1986-87; rsch. asst. U. Va., Charlottesville, 1987-91; asst. prof. U. Ga., Athens, 1991-95, Utah State U., Logan, 1995-2000, assoc. prof., 2000—, chmn. ednl. policies curriculum subcom., 2002—. Presenter workshops and papers to internat., nat., state, and local confs. Co-author: Suggestions for Program Development in Gifted Education; contbr. articles to profl. jours. Mem. Mormon Tabernacle Choir. Named Coll. of Edn. Tchr. of Yr., Utah State U., 2002; Governor's fellow U. Va., 1989. Mem. Am. Edn. Rsch. Assn., Nat. Assn. Gifted Children (bd. dirs. 1992-98, edn. commn. 1999-2002, creativity div. chair 1989-90, John C. Gowan Grad. Student award 1989, Early Leader award 1991), Coun. Exceptional Children/The Assn. for Gifted, Utah Assn. for Gifted Children (3rd v.p. of publs. 1999-2001, pres. 2001-2003, past pres., 2003—). Mem. Lds Ch. Avocation: presidential trivia. Office: Dept Elem Edn Utah State Univ Logan UT 84322-2805 E-mail: scotthunsaker@usu.edu.

HUNSBERGER, ROGER MOORE, web site design company executive, writer, lumber company executive, musician; b. Washington, May 4, 1951; s. Emerson Franklin and Anne Chandler (Moore) H.; m. Linda Elizabeth Fleming, Aug. 16, 1969; children: Michelle Lynn Schahn, Eric John. Degree broadcast comms., RCA Insts., Inc., N.Y.C., 1972; student, Minn. Supreme Ct. Cont. Edn., St. Paul, 1986-89. Owner The Woodsmith, Mankato, Minn., 1975—79; terr. rep. Wadena (Minn.) Saw Mills, 1979—83; systems mgr. Indsl. Lumber & Plywood, Inc., Mpls., 1983—89; nat. sales mgr. Can. Forest Products, Ltd., Boise, Idaho, 1989—91; freelance writer St. Paul and Mpls., 1989—; owner A Writer on the Web, LLC, 1997—2001; creator, designer Xtravar.com, 2000—. Bassist The Basscats, 2002—; cons., writer Orgn. Random Lengths Publs., Eugene, Oreg., 1992—; creator, presenter mgmt. seminars U. Minn., 1992. Author: Mark of the Coyote, 1990, Sojourn, 1994; contbr. articles to profl. jours. Mem. election com. Minn. House-Mark Piepho campaign, Mankato, 1977-82; chair fin. com. Holy Rosary Parish, Mankato, 1978-80. Mem.: NRA, The Hunsberger Assn., The One Percent Club. Avocations: photography, hiking, woodworking, target shooting. Office: 3328 47th Ave S Minneapolis MN 55406-2345 E-mail: r.hunsberger@att.net.

HUNSINGER, DOYLE J. electronics executive; b. Hazelton, Pa., Nov. 12, 1947; s. Doyle J. and Doris Adele (Price) H.; m. Diane Barbara Trivigno, Oct. 12, 1968; children: Doyle III, Dana. BS in Mktg., Fairleigh Dickinson U., 1974. Various positions Sears, Roebuck & Co., Watchung, N.J., 1966-79; mdse. asst. Sears New York Group, Wayne, N.J., 1979-81; v.p., treas. CMF Key Services, Kenilworth, N.J., 1983-85; pres. CMF Bus. Supplies, South Plainfield, N.J., 1985—, DSI Delivery Sys., Inc., South Plainfield, N.J., 1987—, CMF Design Sys. Inc., South Plainfield, 1987-96; CFO, bd. dirs. McCook Tech., Huntington Beach, Calif., 1997-98; pres., CEO Media Techs., Tijuana, Mex. Mem. distbr. council Memorex Corp., Santa Clara, Calif., 1983-86, also 3M; chmn. Media Recycling, South Plainfield, N.J. Open space adv. com. Somerset County, 2002—; cons. Union County (N.J.) Dist. 1 Adv. Bd., 1985—92; capt. Watchung Fire Dept., 1980—83, trustee, 1988—92; mem. Somerset County Open Space, 2002—; committeeman Somerset County Rep. Orgn., Watchung, 1974—, mcpl. chmn., 1990—, fin. chmn., 1996—, exec. com., 1996—; treas. Watchung Candidates Com., 1983—92; vice chmn. Somerset County Rep. Orgn., 2000—, vice chmn., treas.; commr. Somerset City Park Commn., 2003—; fin. chmn. Wilson Meml. Ch., 1984—, bd. dirs., 1977—79, 1983—; v.p., coach Watchung Little League Baseball, 1982—83; scoring chmn. N.J. Synchronized Swimming, 1982—84. With USNG, 1967—74. Mem.: Nat. Office Products Assn., N.J. Exempt Fireman's Assn., Ctrl. Jersey C. of C. (3M distbr. coun. 1993—94), Union County C. of C., Watchung Fire (pres. 1979), Optimists (sec. Watchung club 1975—76). Avocation: fishing. Home: 701 Valley Rd Plainfield NJ 07069-6148 Office: CMF Bus Supplies Inc PO Box 339 South Plainfield NJ 07080-0339

HUNSINGER, PETER, publishing executive; Sales re., advt. mgr. Gourmet, 1985, advt. dir., 1986—93, pub., 1993—97, Arch. Digest, 1997—99; publisher Vanity Fair Magazine, N.Y.C., 1999—2003; pub. GQ Mag., 2003—. Office: GQ The Conde Nast Publications 4 Times Sq New York NY 10036-6522

HUNSPERGER, ELIZABETH JANE, art and design consultant, educator; b. Phila., Aug. 30, 1938; d. Francis Charles and Elizabeth Julia Thorpe; m. Robert George Hunsperger, Sept. 13, 1958; 1 child, Lisa Marie. AA in Design, Santa Monica Coll., 1974; student, UCLA, 1975-76; BA in Art History, U. Del., 1978; postgrad., Rutgers U., 1978-81; MA in Edn., Del. State Coll., 1993; postgrad. in ednl. technology, U. Del. Designer Huntingdon Mills, Phila., 1960-63, Rothschild's, Ithaca, N.Y., 1963-65, Cornell U., Ithaca, 1965-67; freelance designer Malibu, Calif., 1967-76; art and design cons., lectr. Art & Sci. Assocs., Newark, Del., 1980—, Galena, Md., 2001—. Art tchr. Cath. Diocese of Wilmington, 1988-95, Kent County High Sch., Md., 2002-; art and spl. edn. tchr. Red Clay Consolidated Sch. Dist. A.I. duPont H.S., Greenville, Del., 1995-97, Shorehaven Sch., Chesapeake City, Md., 1997-99, A.I. duPont Inst., Wilmington, Del., 1999—; with Leech Sch., 1994; cons. Arts and Sci. Assocs., Ednl. and Design Svcs., Newark, Del., 1995—; coord. Delmarva Edn. Action Learning Project; educator Kent County (Md.) Pub. Schs., 2002. Exhbns. include Malibu Art Assn. Show, 1973-74, Newark Art Show, 1987-88. Founding mem. bd. dirs., v.p. Newark Housing Ministry, Inc., 1983-94, pres., 1989-91; mem. social concerns com. and drug and alcohol task force Del.; active Coun. Exceptional Children. Recipient Outstanding Svc. award YWCA, Santa Monica, Calif., 1972, award of recognition Missionhurst, 1982, Gov.'s Vol. of the Yr. award State of Del., 1990. Mem. Nat. Art Edn. Assn., Am. Craft Coun., Art Educators of Del. (bd. dirs., pres.), Debutante Assemlby Club (N.Y.C.). Episcopal. Home: 14040 S Mill Rd Galena MD 21635 E-mail: elizabeth_hunsperger@usa.net.

HUNSTEIN, CAROL, state supreme court justice; b. Miami, Fla., Aug. 16, 1944; AA, Miami-Dade Jr. Coll., 1970; BS, Fla. Atlantic U., 1972; JD, Stetson U., 1976, LLD (hon.), 1993. Bar: Ga. 1976; U.S. Dist. Ct. 1978; U.S. Ct. Appeals 1978; U.S. Supreme Ct. 1989. Legal practice, Atlanta, 1976-84; judge Superior Ct. of Ga. (Stone Mt. cir.), 1984-92; justice Supreme Ct. of Ga., Atlanta, 1992—. Chair Ga. Commn. on Gender Bias in the Judicial System 1989—; pres. Coun. of Superior Ct. Judges of Ga., 1990-91; adj. prof. Sch. Law Emory U., 1991—. Bd. dirs. Ga. Campaign Adolescent Pregnancy Prevention, 1992—; chair Ga. Child Support Commn., 1993, 98, Supreme Ct. Equality Commn. Recipient Clint Green Trial Advocacy award 1976, Women Who Made A Difference award Dekalb Women's Network 1986, Outstanding Svc. commendation Ga. Legislature, 1993, Cmty. Svc. award Emory U. Legal Assn. for Women Students., 1993, Gender Justice award Ga. Commn. Family Violence, 1999, Margaret Burns award ABA, 1999; inducted to Fla. Atlantic U. Hall of Fame, 1993. Mem. Ga. Assn. of Women Lawyers, Nat. Assn. of Women Judges (dir. 1988-90), Bleckley Inn of Ct., State Bar Ga. Office: Supreme Ct Ga 244 Washington Street Atlanta GA 30334-9007 E-mail: hunsteic@supreme.courts.state.ga.us.*

HUNSUCKER, ROBERT DUDLEY, physicist, electrical engineer, educator, researcher; b. Portland, Oreg., Mar. 15, 1930; s. Robert Deets and Johnnie Morris (Kuykendal) H.; m. Judith Mary Cotter, Apr. 28, 1956 (dec. Nov. 1980); children: Edith Louise, Jeanne Marie, Cynthia Lee; m. Phyllis Marie Hoover, July 25, 1981. BS in Physics, Oreg. State U., 1954, MS in Physics, 1958; PhDEE, U. Colo., 1969. Asst. prof. Geophysics Inst. U. Alaska, Fairbanks, 1958-64, assoc. prof. Geophysics Inst., 1971-78, prof. Geophysics Inst., 1978-87; physicist Nat. Bur. Standards, Boulder, Colo., 1964-67; sr. project leader ITS Office of Telecommunications Sci., Boulder, 1967-71; prof. emeritus physics and elec. engring., sr. cons. U. Alaska, Fairbanks, 1988—. Radio propagation cons.; adj. prof. Pa. State U., Oreg. Inst. Technology. Author 2 Tech. Books; editor (in chief): Radio Sci., 1995—2002; assoc. editor: URSI Radioscience Bull., 1998—; contbr. articles to profl. jours. Served to lt. USNR, 1954-67. Fellow AAAS, IEEE (Alaska Engr. of Yr. Alaska sect. 1988, recipient outstanding achievement award IEEE region 6, 1988); mem. Am. Geophys. Union, U.S. Commission Internat. Union of Radio Sci., Sigma Xi, Sigma Pi Sigma, Eta Kappa Nu. Republican. Avocations: private pilot, fishing, amateur radio operation, writing. E-mail: rdhrpc1@aol.com.

HUNT, ALBERT R. newspaper executive; b. Charlottesville, Va., Dec. 4, 1942; s. Albert R. and Ann G. (Lillard) H.; m. Judy C. Woodruff, Apr. 5, 1980; children: Jeffrey Woodruff, Benjamin Woodruff, Lauren Ann Lee. BA in Polit. Sci., Wake Forest U., 1965. Reporter Wall St. Jour., N.Y.C., 1965-67, Boston, 1967-69, Washington, 1969-71, polit. reporter, 1972-83, bur. chief, 1983-93, exec. editor, 1993—. Author: (with others) American Elections of 1980, American Elections of 1982, American Elections of 1984, Elections American Style, 1987; participant in TV program CNN Capital Gang. Bd. visitors Wake Forest U., Winston-Salem, N.C., 1979-85, trustee, 1987; bd. dirs. Ottaway Newspapers, Inc.; sr. adv. bd. Shorenstein Barone Ctr. for Press, Politics and Pub. Policy, Harvard U., Cambridge, Mass.; pres. Dow Jones Newspaper Fund, 1993. Mem. Am. Polit. Sci. Assn. (congl. fellowship adv. com. 1981—). Office: Wall St Jour 1025 Connecticut Ave NW Ste 800 Washington DC 20036-5419

HUNT, BARNABAS JOHN, priest, religious organization administrator; b. Sayre, Pa., Jan. 6, 1937; s. Clarence Elmer and Margarite Frances (Bennett) H. BS in Edn., Pa. State U., 1958; postgrad., Elmira Coll., 1960-61, Portland (Oreg.) State U., 1969-70, Clackamas C.C., 1970-71, Mt. Hood Community Coll., 1973-74. Joined Soc. St. Paul, 1961, ordained priest Episcopal Ch. 1984, installed and seated as hon. canon of St. Paul's Cathedral, San Diego, 2000; cert. h.s. tchr. H.s. tchr. Pub. Schs., Candor, N.Y., 1958-61; headmaster St. Luke's Sch., Soc. St. Paul, Gresham, Oreg., 1961-64; lic. adminstr. St. Jude's Nursing Home, Inc., Portland and Sandy, Oreg., 1964-73; assoc. rector Soc. St. Paul, Palm Desert, Calif., 1975-89, rector, 1989—; brother in charge St. Paul's Press, Sandy, Oreg., 1969-76. Treas. Desert Samaritans for Elderly, 1997-98. Mem. Tri-County Bd., Oreg. Agy. on Aging, 1971-76; pres. Sandy C. of C., 1972; mem. Sandy City Coun., 1975-76, candidate for City Coun., City of Palm Desert, 1986; pres. St. Jude's Home, Inc., Oreg., 1989—; pres. adv. bd. The Carlotta, 1985-92, vice chmn. resource devel. fund bd., 1993-97; bd. dirs. St. Paul's Episcopal Home, Inc., San Diego, 2000—; chpt. mem. St. Paul's Episocal Cathedral, San Diego, 2000—. Fellow Am. Coll. Health Care Adminstrs. (pres. Coll. Found. 1984-87); mem. Nat. Guild Churchmen (pres. 1982—), Conf. on Religious Life in Anglican Communion (v.p. 1992-97, archivist 1982—). Episcopalian. Home and Office: Soc of St Paul Inc PO Box 34548 San Diego CA 92163-4548 Fax: 619-542-8585.

HUNT, CHARLOTTE DUMARESQ (DEMI), artist, writer; b. Cambridge, Mass., Sept. 2, 1942; d. William Morris Rosamond Pier Hunt; m. Tsi-Si Huang; 1 child, John. BA, Immaculate Heart Coll., 1962; MA, China Inst., 1976. Author: The Book of Moving Pictures, 1979, Under the Shade of the Mulberry Tree, 1979, Where Is It?, 1980, Liang and the Magic Paintbrush, 1980, The Leaky Umbrella, 1980, The Adventurea of Marco Polo, 1981, Three Little Elephants, 1981, Follow the Line, 1981, Where is Willie Worm?, 1981, Cinderella on Wheels, 1982, Peek-A-Boo, 1982, Watch Harry Growl, 1984, Demi's Find the Animals A B C: An Alphabet-Game Book, 1985, Demi's County the Animals 1 2 3, 1986, Dragon Kites & Dragonflies: A Collection of Chinese Nursery Rhymes, 1986, So Soft Kitty, 1986, Fuzzy Wuzzy Puppy, 1986, Chen Ping and His Magic Axe, 1987, Cuddly Chick, 1987, Fluffy Bunny, 1987, Demi's Opposites, 1987, Downy Duckling, 1987, Fleecy Lamb, 1987, The Hallowed Horse: A Folktale from India, 1987, A Chinese Zoo: Fables and Proverbs, 1988, Demi's Reflective Fables, 1988, Find Demi's Dinosaurs: An Animal Game Book, 1989, Jolly Koala Bear, 1989, Roly Poly Panda, 1989, Demi's Basket of Books, 1989, Demi's Christmas Surprise, 1990, The Empty Pot, 1990, Find Demi's Baby Animals, 1990, The Magic Boat, 1990, Demi's Sea Creatures: An Animal Game Book, 1991, The Artist and the Architect, 1991, Chingis Khan, 1991, Little Bitty Bunny, 1992, Little Chick Chick, 1992, In the Eyes of the Cat: Japanese Poetry for All Seasons, 1992, Little Baby Lamb, 1992, Demi's Dozen Farm Friends, 1992, Little Lucky Ducky, 1993, Demi's Secret Garden, 1993, Demi's Dragons and Fantastic Creatures, 1993, Demi's Dozen Good Eggs, 1993, Demi's Dozen Dinosaurs, 1994, Santa's Furry Friends, 1994, The Magic Tapestry; A Chinese Folktale, 1994, The Firebird, 1994, The Stonecutter, 1995, Buddha, 1995, The Dragon's Tale and Other Animal Fables of the Chinese Zodiac, 1996, Su Tong Po, 1996, Buddha Stories, 1997, One Grain of Rice, 1997, The Greatest Treasure, 1998, Dalai Lama, 1998, Kung-Hsi Fa-Ts' Ai!: Happy New Year Kung-Hsi, 1998, Gandhi, 2001, The Emperor's New Clothes, 2000, The Legend of Saint Nicholas, 2003; illustrator: The Classic of Tea, 1974, Bamboo Hats and a Rice Cake, 1993, The Magic Gold Fish: A Russian Folktale, 1995, Grass Sandals: The Travels of Basho, 1997, King Midas, The Golden Touch, 2002, Muhammad, 2002, The Legend of St. Nicholas, 2003. Fulbright scholar, Gujarat, India, 1963-64.

HUNT, CHERYL RUTH, librarian; b. Providence, Aug. 3, 1946; d. Frederick Briggs and Ruth Armstrong (Robbins) Grant; m. Joseph Martin Hunt, Apr. 23, 1983; 1 child, Heather Ruth. BSBA in Acctg., Bryant Coll., 1975; MLS, U. R.I., 1978. Cert. U.S. patent and trademark rsch. specialist. U.S. patent and trademark rsch. rep. Providence Pub. Libr., 1972—89, bus. reference libr., 1978—89, sr. children's libr./Knight Meml. Libr. Br., 1989—. Contbr. articles to profl. jours. Leader 4-H Millennium Libr. Club. Mem. Patent Dipository Libr. Assn. (asst. chmn. fin. com. 1987-89), Patent Documentation Soc., R.I. Invention Conv. for Kids (judge), Bringing Kids and Inventions Closer Together. Avocations: horses, exercising, arts and crafts. Home: PO Box 21 Harmony RI 02829-0021 Office: Providence Pub Libr 225 Washington St Providence RI 02903-3283

HUNT, DAVID EVANS, lawyer; b. Wilkes-Barre, Pa., May 10, 1953; s. James Dixon and Twyla (Burkert) H.; m. Denise M. Barbera, Aug. 21, 1976 (div. 1984); 1 child Christopher Evans; m. Elizabeth S. Pearce, Sept. 5, 1987; children: Alexandra Stacy, Thomas Dixon. AB, Dartmouth Coll., 1975; JD, U. Chgo., 1978. Bar: N.Y. 1979, U.S. Dist. Ct. (so. and ea. dists.) N.Y. 1979, Maine 1982, U.S. Dist. Ct. Maine 1982, U.S. Tax Ct. 1982, Fla. 1999. Assoc. Debevoise & Plimpton, N.Y.C., 1978-81; ptnr. Pierce, Atwood, Scribner, Allen, Smith & Lancaster, Portland, Maine, 1981-92, McCandless & Hunt, Portland, Maine, 1992-97; sole practitioner Portland, 1997—. Adj. prof. U. Maine Law Sch., Portland, 1991—92, Portland, 2000—02. Co-author: Maine Will and Trust Forms Annotated, 1994, Maine Estate Administration, 1996. Officer, dir. Maine Estate Planning Coun., Portland, 1986-94. Fellow: Am. Coll. Trust and Estate Counsel (state chair 1997—2001, regent 2001—03); mem.: ABA, Cumberland County Bar Assn., N.Y. State Bar Assn., Maine State Bar Assn., Fla. Bar, Woodlands Club. Episcopalian. Avocations: classical Latin, skiing. Home: 6 Highland St Portland ME 04103-3005 Office: 511 Congress St Portland ME 04101-3411 E-mail: dhunt@mainewills.com.

HUNT, DAVID FORD, lawyer; b. Ft. Worth, Apr. 7, 1931; s. John Greffrey and Bernice (Ford) H. BS, North Tex. State U., 1954; JD, Vanderbilt U., 1960. Bar: Tex. 1961, U.S. Dist. Ct. (no. dist.) Tex., U.S. Dist. Ct. (we. dist.) Tex., U.S. Dist. Ct. (ea. dist.) Tex.U.S. Ct. Appeals (5th and 11th cir.), U.S. Supreme Ct. Law clk. to U.S. dist. judge No. Dist. Tex., 1960-62; pvt. practice, Dallas, 1962-94; ptnr. Jenkens & Gilchrist, P.C., Dallas, 1980-92, of counsel, 1993-94; atty. pvt. practice, Denton County, Tex., 1995—. Chmn. com. on admissions Dist. 6 Tex. State Bd. Law Examiners, 1978-87 Contbr. articles to legal jours. Co-chmn. pollwatchers com. Dallas County Republican Com., 1964; Sec. Bootstrap Ranch, 1972-74; pres. So. Methodist U. Lambda Chi Edn. Found., 1972-76, dir. Internat. Lambda Chi Edn. Found., 1966-68. Served with AUS, 1954-56. Mem. Tex. Bar Assn., Tex. Bar Found., Vanderbilt U. Law Sch. Alumni Assn. (pres. Dallas chpt. 1972-75), Lambda Chi (chancellor 1966-68). Home and Office: 1849 Bridle Bit Rd Flower Mound TX 75022-6571

HUNT, DAVID G. state representative, coalition executive; b. Port Angeles, Wash., Nov. 10, 1967; s. Harley D. and Karin V. Hunt; m. Tonia M. Moore, Dec. 14, 1970; children: Andrew, Emily. Student, Columbia U., 1990. Cmty. rep. to US Congresswoman Louise Slaughter, Rochester, NY, 1990-96; field dir., outreach cons. Oregonians for Quality Healthcare, Portland, 1996-97; dist. dir. US Congresswoman Darlene Hooley, Salem, Oreg., 1997-99, US Congressman Brian Baird, Vancouver, Wash., 1999-2001; exec. dir. Columbia River Channel Coalition, Portland, Oreg., 2001—. Mem. Oreg. City Sch. Bd., 1999—2003; nat. pres. Am. Bapt. Ch., 2002—03. Mem. Rotary. Democrat. Home: 18411 SE Wilmot St Portland OR 97267 Office: Columbia River Channel Coalition 6208 N Ensign St Portland OR 97217 E-mail: hunt@inetarena.com.

HUNT, DAVID WALLINGFORD, lawyer; b. Washington, Sept. 27, 1952; s. Donald Harvey and Dorothy Walter (Johnson) H.; m. Sylvia Fortney, Aug. 10, 1974; 1 child, David Wallingford Jr. BA with high distinction, U. Va., 1974, JD, 1977. Bar: Ga. 1977, D.C. 1982, U.S. Ct. Appeals (5th cir.) 1981, U.S. Ct. Appeals (11th cir.) 1982. Law asst. Ga. Supreme Ct., Atlanta, 1977-78; atty. Troutman, Sanders, Lockerman & Ashmore, Atlanta, 1978-80; counsel Turner Broadcasting System, Inc., Atlanta, 1980-81; atty. O'Neill & Haase, P.C., Washington, 1981-84, ptnr., 1985-86; prin. Taubman, Hunt, Hodin & Costelloe, P.C., Washington, 1986-87; mem. Swidler & Berlin chartered, Washington, 1987—; gen. counsel Congl. Award Bd., Washington, 1986—. Mem. editorial bd. Va. Law Review, 1975-77. Pres. Windgate of Arlington, Va., 1982-84. Dillard fellow U. Va., Charlottesville, 1976-77. Mem. ABA, Ga. Bar Assn., D.C. Bar Assn., Order of the Coif, Phi Beta Kappa. Episcopalian. Home: 5850 Aspen Wood Ct Mc Lean VA 22101-2501 Office: Swidler & Berlin 3000 K St NW Fl 3 Washington DC 20007-5109

HUNT, DONNELL RAY, retired agricultural engineering educator; b. Danville, Ind., Aug. 11, 1926; s. Ray Hadley and Sarah Leona (Booty) H.; m. Dorothea Marie May, Sept. 2, 1951; children: David Carter, DeAnne Elizabeth. BS, Purdue U., 1951; MS, Iowa State U., 1954; PhD, Iowa State, 1958. Registered profl. engr., Ill. Instr. to assoc. prof. agrl. engring. Iowa State U., Ames, 1951-60; assoc. prof. U. Ill., Urbana, 1960-68, prof., 1968-96, asst. dean, dir. coop. edn. program Coll. Engring., 1986-96. Cons. in field. Author: Farm Power and Machinery Management,10th edit., 2001, Farm Machinery Mechanisms, 1972, Engineering Models for Agricultural Production, 1986. Served with U.S. Army, 1945-46. Fulbright awardee Ireland, 1968-69 Fellow Am. Soc. Agrl. Engrs.; mem. Am. Soc. Engring. Edn. Republican. Presbyterian.

HUNT, EARL STEPHEN, federal agency administrator; b. Chattanooga, Nov. 28, 1948; s. Earl Gladstone Jr. and Mary Anne (Kyker) Hunt; m. Edeltraut Gilgan, Sept. 6, 1986. BA with honors, Emory and Henry Coll., 1971; MA, Am. U., 1973; PhD, U. Va., 1979; MLS, CAS, Syracuse U., 2000. Instr. Fla. So. Coll., Lakeland, 1980-81; edn. cons. Nashville, N.Y.C., 1980-82; editor, cons. Washington, 1982-86; sr. rsch. analyst U.S. Dept. Edn., Washington, 1986—94, sr. internat. rels. specialist internat. affairs staff Office Undersecretary Edn., 2002—; planning dir. Nat. Libr. Edn., 1995—2002; mgr. U.S. Network Edn. Info., 1997—. Mem. drug prevention task force U.S. Dept. Edn., Washington, 1986—89; cons. U.S. Dept. Labor, Washington, 1990—, NSF, Washington, 1990—, U.S. Trade Rep., Washington, 1999—, U.S. Dept. Homeland Security, Washington, 2001—. Co-editor: (book) The Apocalyptic Premise: Nuclear Arms Debated, 1982; author: Drug Prevention Curricula, 1993, Mapping the World of Education: The Comparative Database System, 1994, Professional Workers as Learners, 1992, A Guide to the International Interpretation of U.S. Education Program Data, 1993; co-author: Classification of Instructional Programs, 1990, 2d edit., 2000; contbr. articles to profl. jours. Mem. Sangamore-Brooks Ln. Citizens' Assn., Bethesda, 1990—. Grantee, USIA, 1982. Mem.: Acad. Polit. Sci., Am. Assn. Higher Edn., Nat. Contract Mgmt. Assn., Phi Delta Kappa, Blue Key, Phi Gamma Mu, Alpha Phi Omega (life). Methodist. Avocations: reading, travel, gardening, cooking. Home: 5209 Sangamore Rd Bethesda MD 20816-2324 Office: US Dept Edn Internat Affairs Staff OUS Rm 6W242 FB6 400 Maryland Ave SW Washington DC 20202 Fax: 202-401-2508. Business E-Mail: stephen.hunt@ed.gov.

HUNT, EFFIE NEVA, former college dean, former English language educator; b. Waverly, Ill., June 19, 1922; d. Abraham Luther and Fannie Ethel (Ritter) H. AB, MacMurray Coll. for Women, 1944; MA, U. Ill., 1945, PhD, 1950; postgrad., Columbia U., 1953, Univ. Coll., U. London, 1949-50. Key-punch operator U.S. Treasury, 1945; spl. librarian Harvard U., 1947, U. Pa., 1948; Instr. English U. Ill., 1950-51; librarian Library of Congress, Washington, 1951-52; asst. prof. English Mankato State Coll., 1952-59; prof. Radford Coll., 1959-63, chmn. dept. English, 1961-63; prof. Ind. State U., 1963-86; dean Ind. State U. (Coll. Arts and Scis.), 1974-86, dean and prof. emerita, 1987—. Author articles in field. Fulbright grantee, 1949 50 Mem. AAUP, MLA, Nat. Council Tchrs. English, Am. Assn. Higher Edn., Audubon Soc. Home: 3365 Wabash Ave Apt 4 Terre Haute IN 47803-1655 Office: Ind State U Root Hall Eng Dept Terre Haute IN 47809-0001

HUNT, FRANCIS HOWARD, retired navy laboratory official; b. Emporia, Kans., Apr. 12, 1919; s. Frederick Raymond and Mabel (Holmes) Hunt; m. Kathleen McLean, June 4, 1945 (dec. Sept. 1992); children: Deborah Mary, Laurie Jane, Peter Raymond; m. Mary Alice Fish, July 16, 1993. BA, Wesleyan U., 1941. Supr. records Columbia U. divsn. War Research, New London, Conn., 1941—43, tech. editor, writer, 1943—44; with U.S. Navy Underwater Sound Lab., Fort Trumbull, New London, Conn., 1945—70, successively asst. to asst. tech. dir., 1945—47, staff asst. to tech. dir., head tech. info. divsn., 1947—60, assoc. tech. dir. for administrn., 1960—70; assoc. dir. center operations Naval Underwater Systems Ctr., Newport, RI, 1970—76. Mem. East Lyme Zoning Bd. of Appeals, 1956—, sec., 1960—78, chmn., 1978—97; charter mem. East Lyme Flood and Erosion Control Bd.; past mem. Niantic (Conn.) Boy Scout Com., East Lyme Jr. High Sch. Planning Com.; mem. Conn. Fedn. Planning and Zoning Agencies. Bd. dirs. E. Lyme Pub. Libr., 1962—83, Child Guidance Clin. So.Eastern Conn., 1959—62; justice of peace, 1985—; bd. dirs. East Lyme Nursing Assn., 1964—66. Served with AUS, 1944—45. Decorated Purple Heart, Bronze Star Medal WWII, Battle of the Bulge; named Melvin Jones Fellow for Dedicated Humanitarian Services, Lions Clubs Internat. Found., 1997; recipient Outstanding mem. Town Comm., East Lyme C. of C., 1972, 1981. Mem.: IEEE (life), Nat. Assn. Ret. Fed. Employees, Gov. William Bradford Compact, Nat. Huguenot Soc. (chaplain gen. 1993—95), Conn. Soc. SAR (mem. bd. mgrs. 1980—87, registrar 1984—87, Patriot medal 1987, Silver good citizenship medal 1992), Conn. Huguenot Soc. (pres. 1990—96), Conn., Lebanon, Columbia hist. socs., Soc. Colonial Wars in Conn., Soc. of Cin. in Conn., Soc. Mayflower Descendents in Conn., New Eng. Historic Geneal. Soc., Conn. Soc. Genealogists, R.I. Geneal. Soc., Lions (past pres. Niantic club). Baptist. Home: 2 Strawberry Ln Niantic CT 06357-1936

HUNT, FREDERICK TALLEY DRUM, JR., association executive; b. Martinique, French West Indies, Sept. 19, 1947; s. Frederick Talley Drum and Eleanor Conly H.; m. Acacia Lynn Graham, Dec. 4, 1976. Ba, Vanderbilt U., 1970. Dir. program devel. manufactured Housing Inst., Washington, 1973-74; pres. Hunt Assocs., Washington, 1974-75; asst. dir. field svcs. Nat. Assn. Life Underwriters, 1975-77; dir. comm., govt. liaison Am. Acad. Actuaries, Washington, 1977-80; pres. Soc. Profl. Benefit Adminstrs., 1980—. Pres., owner Hunt Mgmt. Sys., 1982—; advisor White House, Congress, others; spkr. in field. Contbr. articles to profl. jours. Mem.: Soc. Cin., Miles River Yacht Club, Met. Club, Aztec Club of 1847. Home: Westmoreland Hills 5308 Blackistone Rd Bethesda MD 20816-1803 also: 228 Riverside Rd Edgewater MD 21037-1505 Office: Hunt Mgmt Systems 2 Wisconsin Cir Ste 670 Chevy Chase MD 20815-7043

HUNT, GEORGE WILLIAM, priest, magazine editor; b. N.Y.C., Jan. 22, 1937; s. George Aloysius and Grace Winifred (Jordan) H. AB, Fordham U., 1961, MA, 1963; PhL, Woodstock Coll., 1961, STL, 1967; STM, Yale U., 1968; PhD, Syracuse U., 1974; DHL (hon.), Spring Hill Coll., 1991, Loyola Coll., Balt., 1993, Fairfield U., 1996. Joined S.J., 1954; ordained priest Roman Cath. Ch., 1967. Asst. prof. St. Peter's Coll., Jersey City, 1968-70; assoc. prof. Le Moyne Coll., Syracuse, N.Y., 1973-81; vis. prof. Georgetown U., Washington, 1983-84; pres., editor in chief Am. mag., N.Y.C., 1984-98; dir. Arch. Hughes Inst. of Religion and Culture Fordham U., Bronx, N.Y., 1999—. Author: (literary criticism) John Updike and the Three Great Secret Things, 1980 (Christianity lit. award 1981), John Cheever: The Hobgoblin Company of Love, 1983.Y Trustee Boston Coll., 1985—, Carnegie Coun. on Ethics and Internat. Affairs, 1986—, Holy Cross Coll., Worcester, Mass., 1990—, Loyola Coll., Balt., 1994—, Le Moyne Coll., Syracuse, 1995—; trustee emeritus U. Detroit, 1984—. Roman Catholic. Home and Office: Fordham U Arch Hughes Inst Religion and Culture 441 E Fordham Rd Bronx NY 10458-5149

HUNT, GERALD G., JR., architect, real estate broker; b. Cedar Rapids, Iowa, Aug. 16, 1942; s. Gerald George and Rae Louise Hunt; m. Mary Susan Vida, Dec. 28, 1974 (div.); children: Jordan, Tyler, Justin. BArch, U. Colo., 1971. Lic. arch., Colo.; real estate broker Colo. Arch. Everett/Zeigel Archs., Boulder, Colo., 1969—72; arch., ptnr. dbh Partnership-Archs., Boulder, 1972—76; arch., owner Bud Hunt Assocs., Boulder, 1976—78; arch., ptnr. Hunt/Zmistowski Archs., Boulder, 1978—80; arch., owner Archtl. Consultants, Centennial, Colo., 1980—. Pres. Archs. and Planners of Boulder, 1975—77; subcom. chair long range planning Boulder Valley Sch. Dist., 1986. Fundraising chair Am. Field Svc. Student Exch.-State of Colo., 1992. With U.S. Army, 1967—69, Vietnam. Mem.: Am. Legion. Avocations: woodworking, travel. Home: 6237 S Lafayette Pl Centennial CO 80121 Office: Archtl Cons & Auld Lang Syne RE 6237 S Lafayette Pl Centennial CO 80121

HUNT, GERALD WALLACE, lawyer; b. Portland, Oreg., Oct. 31, 1939; BSBA in Econs., U. Denver, 1961, JD, 1964; LLM in Taxation, Washington U., 1981. Bar: Colo. 1964, Ariz. 1968, Tex. 1996, Alaska 1999, cert.: Ariz. Bd. Legal Specialization (tax specialist). Asst. trust officer The Ariz. Bank, Phoenix, 1967-69; atty. Westover, Keddie, et al, Yuma, Ariz., 1969-73; pvt. practice law Yuma, 1973-74; atty. Hunt & Clark, Yuma, 1974-75, Hunt, Stanley & Hossler, Yuma, 1975-96, Hunt, Tallan & Hossler, Yuma, 1996-97, Hunt, Kenworthy and Hossler, Yuma, 1998—2002, Hunt, Kenworthy, Meerchaum & Hossler, Yuma, 2002—. Treas. Excel Group, Yuma, 1998—99, chair, 2000—02; bd. dirs. Greater Yuma Port Authority, 2000. Fellow: Am. Coll. Trust and Estate Counsel; mem.: ABA, Tex. Bar, Alaska Bar, Colo. State Bar, Ariz. State Bar, Internat. Mcpl. Lawyers Assn. Office: Hunt Kenworthy Meerchaum & Hossler 330 W 24th St Yuma AZ 85364-6455

HUNT, GORDON, lawyer; b. L.A., Oct. 26, 1934; s. Howard Wilson and Esther Nita (Dempsey) H. BA in Polit. Sci, UCLA, 1956; JD, U. So. Calif., 1959. Bar: Calif. 1960. Law clk. Appellate Dept., Superior Ct. L.A. County, 1959-60; mem. firm Behymer & Hoffman, Los Angeles, 1960-65; partner firm Behymer, Hoffman & Hunt, Los Angeles, 1965-68; ptnr. firm Munns, Kofford, Hoffman, Hunt & Throckmorton, Pasadena, 1969-90, Hunt, Ortman, Blasco, Palffy & Rossell, Pasadena, 1990-95; mem. Hunt, Ortman, Blasco, Palffy & Rossell Inc., 1995—. Lectr. UCLA, various yrs.; chmn. legal adv. com. Assoc. Gen. Contractors Calif., 1985; arbitrator L.A. Superior Ct., State of Calif. Author: Construction Surety and Bonding Handbook; co-author: California Construction Law, 16th edit.; contbr. numerous articles to legal jours. Mem. ABA, Calif. Bar Assn. (del. Conv. 1964-69), L.A. County Bar Assn. (real property com. 1965-66, exec. com. 1970-72, sec. 1972-73, vice chmn. 1972-75, chmn. real property sect. 1975-76, co-chmn. continuing edn. bar com. 1969-71), Am. Arbitration Assn. (arbitrator, mediator). Office: 301 N Lake Ave Fl 7 Pasadena CA 91101-4108 E mail: goff@hobpr.com.

HUNT, H(AROLD) KEITH, business management educator, marketing consultant; b. Apr. 16, 1938; married; 8 children. BS in Mktg. and Mgmt., U. Utah, 1961, MBA, 1962; PhD in Mktg., Northwestern U., 1972. Instr. Imperial Valley Coll., El Centro, Calif., 1962-64; teaching asst. Northwestern U., 1964-66, instr., 1966-67; asst. prof. bus. adminstrn. and journalism U. Iowa, 1967-73; cons., staff mem. Office Policy Planning and Evaluation, FTC, Washington, 1973-74; assoc. prof. bus. adminstrn. U. Wyo., Laramie, 1974-75; assoc. prof. bus. mgmt. Brigham Young U., Provo, Utah, 1975-78, prof., 1978—. Participant, chmn. various workshops, seminars, meetings; research expert, cons., expert witness on consumer research FTC, 1974-81; cons., expert witness div. drug advt. FDA, 1975-82; cons., adv. on consumer research Consumer and Corp. Affairs Can., 1978-82. Editor: Advances in Consumer Research, vol. 5, 1977; co-editor conf. proc. (with Frances Magrabi) Interdisciplinary Consumer Research, 1980, (with Ralph Day) Consumer Satisfaction/Dissatisfaction and Complaining Behavior, 8 vols., 1975-85, Jour. 1988—. Elected to Orem City Coun., Utah, 1986-93. Recipient Maeser Research award Brigham Young U., 1981; scholar-in-residence adv. dept. U. Ill., 1979; vis. research scholar Coll. Home Econs., U. Ala., 1980; vis. research scholar dept. mktg. and transp. U. Tenn., 1981; NSF grantee, 1975-77 Mem. Assn. Consumer Research (pres. 1979, exec. sec. 1983-2000, 1st Disting. Svc. award 1989), Am. Acad. Advt. (pres. 1982-83, exec. sec. 1983-86, elected fellow 1987), Am. Mktg. Assn., Soc. Consumer Psychology, Am. Council on Consumer Interests, Beta Gamma Sigma, Kappa Tau Alpha, Omicron Delta Epsilon, Phi Kappa Phi Home: 835 E High Country Dr Orem UT 84097-2370 Office: Brigham Young U Grad Sch Mgmt 632 TNRB Provo UT 84602-1133 E-mail: hkhunt@byu.edu.

HUNT, HEATHER M. lawyer; b. Madison, Wis., June 21, 1971; d. Charles Leonard Wnukowski and Nancy M. Marek; m. Rick J. Hunt, July 11, 1992. BS cum laude, U. Wis., Eau Claire, 1993; JD, U. Wis., Madison, 1997. Bar: Wis. 1997, U.S. Dist. Ct. (we. dist.) Wis. 1997. Intern Legal Assistance to Institutionalized Persons Program, Madison, 1995-96, LaCrosse County Dist. Atty.'s Office, LaCrosse, 1996, Wis. Supreme Ct., Madison, 1996; shareholder Wiley Colbert Norseng Cray Herrell & Flory, S.C., Chippewa Falls, Wis., 1997—. Note and comment editor U. Wis. Law Rev., 1995-97. Bd. dirs. Chippewa Valley Cultural Assn., Inc., 1997—, Leave A Legacy--Chippen Valley. Mem. Chippewa County Bar Assn., State Bar of Wis. Home: 921 W Willow St Chippewa Falls WI 54729-2149 Office: Wiley Colbert et al 119 1/2 N Bridge St Chippewa Falls WI 54729-2404 E-mail: hhunt@wileylaw.com.

HUNT, HELEN, actress; b. L.A., June 15, 1963; d. Gordon and Jane Hunt. TV appearances include Amy Prentiss, The Swiss Family Robinson, The Fitzpatricks, It Takes Two, Having Babies, Land of Little Rain, Weekend, Mary Tyler Moore Show, Family, St. Elsewhere; TV movies include Pioneer Woman, All Together Now, Death Scream, The Spell, Transplant, Angel Dusted, Child Bride of Short Creek, The Miracle of Cathy Miller, Desperate Lives, Quarterback Princess, Bill: On His Own, Choices of the Heart, Sweet Revenge, Why Are You Here?, Murder In New Hampshire: The Pamela Smart Story, 1991, In the Comfort of Darkness, 1992; TV series Mad About You, 1992-99 (Emmy nomination, Lead Actress - Comedy, 1993, 94, Golden Globe award for Best Actress, musical or comedy, 1994, 95, Emmy award for Best Leading Actress in a Comedy series, 1996); films include Rollercoaster, 1977, Girls Just Want To Have Fun, 1985, Trancers, 1985, Empire, 1985, Peggy Sue Got Married, 1986, Project X, 1987, Miles From Home, 1988, Next Of Kin, 1989, The Waterdance, 1992, Only You, 1992, Bob Roberts, 1992, Mr. Saturday Night, 1992, Kiss of Death, 1995, Twister, 1996, As Good As It Gets, 1997 (Acad. award Best Actress in a Leading Role 1997), Twister: Ride It Out, 1998, Twelfth Night, 1998, Dr. T and the Women, 2000, Pay It Forward, 2000, Cast Away, 2000, What Women Want, 2000, Curse of the Jade Scorpion, 2001; plays include: Life (X)3, 2003 Address: Connie Tavel Mgmt 9171 Wilshire Blvd Beverly Hills CA 90210-5530*

HUNT, HERBERT GAGE, III, accounting and tax educator; b. Barre, Vt., Dec. 24, 1952; s. Herbert Gage Jr. and Violet Ann (Rivers) H.; m. Pamela Lee Collier, June 30, 1974; 1 child, Jonathan. BA in Psychology, U. Vt., 1974, MBA in Acctg., 1978; PhD in Acctg., U. Colo., 1982. CPA, Colo. Instr. acctg. U. Vt., Burlington, summer 1978, asst. prof., 1987-90, assoc. prof., 1990-95, prof. acctg. and tax edn., 1995—2001; instr. acctg. U. Colo., Boulder and Denver, 1978-81, lectr. acctg. Denver, 1981-82; asst. prof. Pa. State U., University Park, 1982-87; prof. acctg. Calif. State U., Long Beach, 2002—. Contbr. articles to profl. jours.; editl. rev. bd. Acctg. Rev., 1989-93. Recipient Zimel Resnick MBA award U. Vt., 1978. Mem. Am. Acctg. Assn. (doctoral consortium fellow 1980), Am. Taxation Assn., Beta Gamma Sigma. Avocations: running, bicycling. Home: 3745 Roxanne Ave Long Beach CA 90808-2342 Office: Calif State U Long Beach Coll Bus Adminstrn Accountancy Dept 1250 Bellflower Blvd Long Beach CA 90840-8504 E-mail: hhunt@csulb.edu.

HUNT, J. B. transportation executive; Chmn. J.B. Hunt Group, Lowell, Ark., sr. chmn. Office: JB Hunt Transport Services Inc 615 JB Hunt Corporate Dr Lowell AR 72745

HUNT, JAMES BAXTER, JR., lawyer, retired governor; b. Guilford County, N.C., May 16, 1937; s. James Baxter and Elsie (Brame) Hunt; m. Carolyn Joyce Leonard, Aug. 20, 1958; children: Rebecca Hunt Hawley, James Baxter Hunt III, Rachel Nilender, Elizabeth Amigh. BS in Agrl. Edn., N.C. State U., 1959, MS in Agrl. Cons., 1962; JD, U. N.C., 1964. Bar: N.C. 1964. Econ. advisor H.M. Govt. of Nepal for Ford Found., 1964—66; ptnr. Kirby, Webb and Hunt, 1966—72; lt. gov. State of N.C., 1973—77, gov., 1977—85, gov., 1993—2001; ptnr. Poyner and Spruill, Raleigh, NC, 1985—93; mem. Womble Carlyle Sandridge & Rice, Raleigh, 2001—. Originator, bd. dirs. Triangle East; chmn. N.C. State U. Emerging Issues Forum; bd. visitors Wake Forst U.; founding chmn. Nat. Bd. for Profl. Tchg. Stds., 1987, Nat. Ctr. for Pub. Policy and Higher Edn., 1998. Author: Rally Around the Precinct, 1968. Trustee Atlantic Christian Coll.; mem. Carnegie Forum on Edn. and Econ. Task Force on Tchg. as a Profl., 1986; chmn. Nat. Commn. on Tchg. and Am.'s Future, 1994; state pres. Young Dems., 1968; del. Dem. Nat. Conv., 1968. Named Outstanding Young Man of Yr., Wilson Jr. C. of C., 1969, Outstanding Govt. Ofcl. in Cmty. Edn., Nat. Assn. Cmty. Edn., 1977; recipient 1st Harry S. Truman award, Nat. Young Dems., 1975, James Bryant Conant award, Edn. Commn. States, 1984, Nat. 4-H Outstanding Alumnus award, 1984, Soil Conservation Honors award, 1986, Child Health Adv. award, Am. Acad. Pediat., 1994, Friend of Edn. award, Horace Mann League, 1999. Mem.: Nat. Govs. Assn. (chmn. task force on technol. innovation mem. exec. com., chmn. edn. com. states and nat. task force on edn. for econ. growth 1982—83, leadership team on controlling crime and violence 1994, chmn. nat. edn. goals panel 1997—). Presbyterian. Office: Womble Carlyle Sandridge & Rice 150 Fayetteville St Mall Ste 2100 PO Box 831 Raleigh NC 27602

HUNT, JAMES CALVIN, academic administrator, physician; b. Lexington, N.C., Sept. 11, 1925; s. James Lee and Sarah Della (Frank) H.; m. Irene Kivett, Sept. 17, 1949; children— James Calvin, Michael S., Cynthia Irene. AB, Catawba Coll., 1949; MD, Bowman Gray Sch. Medicine, 1953; MS, U. Minn., 1958; ScD, Wake Forest U., 1992. Intern N.C. Bapt. Hosp., Winston-Salem, 1953-54; resident, fellow Mayo Grad Sch. Medicine, Rochester, Minn., 1954-58; practice medicine, specializing in internal medicine (cardiovascular-renal diseases) Rochester, 1958-78; cons., instr. to asst. prof. dept. medicine Mayo Clinic and Mayo Med. Sch., 1958-63, assoc. prof., chmn. div. nephrology, 1963-72, prof., chmn. dept. medicine, 1973-78; prof., assoc. dean clin. ednl. programs Mayo Med. Sch., 1972-74; prof. medicine U. Tenn., Memphis, 1978—, dean Coll. Medicine, 1978-81, v.p. health affairs, chancellor Univ. Health Scis. Ctr., 1981-93, univ. disting. prof., dir. clin. scholars program, 1993—2001, v/p/ health affairs, chancellor emeritus, 2001—. Mem. adv. coun. Nat. Heart, Lung and Blood Inst., NIH, 1976-81. Contbr. articles to med. jours. Pres. Nat. Kidney Found., 1973-76; trustee Le Bonheur Children's Med. Ctr., 1981-93, Christian Bros. Coll., 1983-95; mem. cmty. adv. bd. Bapt. Meml. Hosp., 1986—; mem. Congl. Tech. Adv. Coun., 1987-96, chair, 1995-96; mem. bd. dirs. Memphis Downtown Neighbors Assn., 1995-99, pres., 1997-98; mem. adv. bd. Goals for Memphis, 1987-95; bd. dirs. Memphis YMCA, Bapt. Meml. Coll. of Health Scis., 1995—, chair acad. affairs com., 1998—; mem. adv. bd. Rhodes Coll.; bd. dirs. Memphis Riverfront Devel. Corp., 1999—, sec. 2000-02. With USAAF, 1943-46, ETO. Recipient Disting. Svc. award Bowman Gray Sch. Medicine, Wake Forest U., 1975, Disting. Alumnus award Catawba Coll., 1974, Educator of Yr. award Memphis State U., 1986, Outstanding Alumnus award Mayo Found., 1991, Gift of Life award Nat. Kidney Found., 1991. Fellow A.C.P., Am. Coll. Cardiology, Am. Heart Assn. (council on circulation); mem. Internat., Am. socs. nephrology, Internat. Soc. Hypertension, Soc. Nuclear Medicine, Council for High Blood Pressure Research, Am. Soc. Internal Medicine, AMA, Am. Soc. Clin. Pharmacology and Therapeutics, Sigma Xi, Alpha Omega Alpha, Phi Rho Sigma. Home and Office: 3381 Moss Rose Dr Memphis TN 38115-4263

HUNT, JEFFREY BRIAN, lawyer; b. Huntington, W.Va., Sept. 23, 1958; s. Bernard Ray and Nadine Dora (Meadows) H.; m. Krista Moorman, May 14, 1983. BA magna cum laude, Marshall U., 1980; JD summa cum laude, U. Ky., 1983. Bar: Mo. 1983, Ill. 1984, U.S. Ct. Appeals (8th cir.) 1984. Assoc. Lewis & Rice, 1983-93; ptnr. Lewis, Rice & Fingersh, L.C., St. Louis, 1993—2002, Gallop, Johnson & Neuman, L.C., St. Louis, 2002—. Adj. instr. Washington U., St. Louis, 1983-89, 96—. Mem. ABA (vice chair TTIPS sect. civil procedure and evidence 1996—), Bar Assn. Met. St. Louis, Order of Coif, Omicron Delta Kappa. Democrat. Methodist. Avocations: tennis, softball, baseball, basketball, golf. Home: 2220 Stonegate Manor Ct Chesterfield MO 63017-7126 Office: Gallop Johnson & Neuman LC 101 S Hanley Ste 1600 Saint Louis MO 63105 E-mail: jbhunt@gjn.com.

HUNT, JERRY MACON, SR., retail executive; b. Memphis, May 7, 1932; s. Macon Henry and Frances Wilkins H.; m. June Brand, Oct. 24, 1948; children: June H. Pitney, Jerry M. Jr., Virginia H. Corley. Grad. high sch., Hogansville, Ga. Laborer Macon Hunt Lumber Co., Hogansville, Ga., 1948-49; owner Wholesale Lumber Producer, Hogansville, Ga., 1949-54; yard foreman Lockridge-Rodgers Lumber Co., East Point, Ga., 1954-56; sales cons. Flowers Lumber Co., East Point, Ga., 1956-59; v.p. Brand Elec. Co., Avondale Estates, Ga., 1959-61; owner, pres. All Elec. Dist., Inc., Decatur, Ga., 1961-97; retired, 1997—. Independent. Baptist (Primitive Bapt. minister).

HUNT, JOHN DAVID, retired banker; b. Worcester, Mass., May 2, 1925; s. John J. and Honorea B. (Tully) H.; m. Claire A. Sullivan, June 25, 1949; children: Barbara A., Kathryn R. AB, Brown U., 1949; postgrad. Advanced Mgmt. Program, Harvard U., 1973; DBA (hon.), Anna Maria Coll., 1982. Accountant Harry W. Wallis & Co., Worcester, 1949-50; with Worcester County Nat. Bank (now Fleet Bank), 1952—; asst. v.p. Worcester County Nat. Bank (now Shawmut Worcester County Bank N.A.), 1959-61, v.p., 1961-69, sr. v.p., 1969-73, exec. v.p., 1973-77, pres., 1977-87, chmn. bd., 1983, chmn. exec. com., 1987-90, ret., 1990. Bd. dirs. Worcester Bus. Devel. Corp., pres., 1981-82, chmn., 1987-99; trustee Allmerica Investment Trust, 1977-95, Allmerica Securities Inc., 1977-95, Mass. Biotech Rsch. Inst., 1985-98; instr. Am. Inst. Banking, 1957-60. Chmn. fund drive Greater Worcester United Appeal, 1972; Bd. dirs. United Cerebral Palsy Assn. Worcester County, 1957-67, bd. dirs. U. Mass. Medical Ctr. Found.; Worcester Better Bus. Bur., 1964-69, Catholic Charities Worcester, 1971-75, United Way Worcester, NCCJ, 1979-86; trustee Hahnemann Hosp., 1966-78, Assumption Coll., 1975-80; corporator St. Vincent Hosp.; mem. Worcester Redevel. Authority, 1983-85; adv. bd. dept. mgmt. Worcester Poly. Inst.; chmn. Civic Ctr. Commn., 1985 90; trustee Fund Edn. in Econs., 1980-85, chmn., 1984-85; bd. dirs. Worcester Mcpl. Research Bur., Inc., 1985-89. Served to lt. USNR, 1943-47, 50-52. Recipient Outstanding Young Man award Worcester County, 1961, Isaiah Thomas award Advt. Club Worcester, 1987, Peace medal State of Israel, 1987. Mem. Am. Inst. Banking, Robert Morris Assocs. (bd. govs. 1966-71, pres. New Eng. chpt. 1969-70), Am. Bankers Assn. (governing council), Mass. Bankers Assn., bd. govs. (1974-79, chmn. 1977), Worcester Area C. of C. (chmn. 1984, bd. dirs. 1980-99), Alpha Delta Phi. Clubs: Worcester County Brown, Worcester, Worcester Country, Oyster Harbors. Republican. Roman Catholic. Home: 770 Salisbury St Worcester MA 01609-1155

HUNT, JOHN EDWIN, insurance company executive, consultant; b. Ozark, Ala., Jan. 13, 1918; s. Tim Atticus and Ada (Arnold) H.; m. Winnifred Prichard; children: Jacqueline, John Edwin Jr., Geoffery, Scott, Richard; md. 2d Leona Snowden. Student, Columbus U., Washington, 1938-40, Pace U., 1940-41; diploma in banking, Am. Inst. Banking, 1942; diploma in ins., Travelers Ins. Co., 1944. Aide to regional adminstr., chief auditor Fed. Housing Adminstrn., Washington, 1938 40; with trust dept. Riggs Nat. Bank, Washington, 1940-42; asst. trust officer Fla. Nat. Bank, Jacksonville, 1942-44; asst. mgr. Travelers Ins. Co., Jacksonville, 1944-45, gen. agt. regional br., 1945-58; pres. John E. Hunt & Assocs., Tallahassee, 1972-84; chmn. bd. dirs. Hunt Ins. Group-Spl. Law Enforcement Agy. and Self-Ins. Fund Adminstrn., Tallahassee, 1984-97; pres. John Hunt & Assocs., Miami, Fla., 1958-72; chmn. emeritus Hunt Ins. Group, Tallahassee, 1997—. Pres. Ins. Cons. and Analysts, Tallahassee, 1972-95. Past chmn. pvt. industry coun. Pres. Reagan's Job Tng. Partnership Act; past mem. Gov's Adv. Coun. for Ins.; founder Fla. Police Chiefs Edn. & Rsch. Found., Inc.; trustee, mem. pres.'s coun. Fla. So. Coll., Lakeland, 1986-97. trustee emeritus, 1997—. Mem. Fla. Assn. Surplus Lines, Fla. Assn. Ins. Agts., Com. of 99 (past pres., bd. dirs., law enforcement com. 1984-85), Greater Miami Mortgage Brokers Assn. (pres. 1964-65), Fla. Jr. C. of C. (nat. dir., state v.p. 1950-52), Fla. Police Chiefs Assn. (hon., life), Fla. Sheriffs Assn. (hon., life), Killearn Golf and Country Club, Fla. Econ. Club, Tiger Bay Club, Govs. Club, Masons, Shriners, Elks (life). Republican. Avocation: yachting. Home: PO Box 14015 Tallahassee FL 32317-4015 Office: Hunt Ins Group Inc 3606 Maclay Blvd S Tallahassee FL 32312

HUNT, JOHN MORTIMER, JR., classical studies educator; b. Bryn Mawr, Pa., Sept. 21, 1943; s. John Mortimer and Ruth Pierson (Ott) H. AB, Lafayette Coll., 1965; MA, Bryn Mawr Coll., 1968, PhD, 1970. From asst. prof. to assoc. prof. classical studies Villanova (Pa.) U., 1970-91, prof., 1991—, chmn. dept. classical studies, 1993-99, dir. classical studies, 1999—. Instr. Latin Lafayette Coll., Easton, Pa., 1970; vis. assoc. prof. U. Calif., Santa Barbara, 1978—80. Mem. editl. bd. Classical Philology, 1976—2001; contbr. articles to profl. publs. Cornell U. fellow, 1965—66. Mem.: Delano Kindred, Roger Williams Family Assn., Colonial Soc. Pa., Soc. Colonial Wars in Pa., Soc. Mayflower Descs. Pa. (state historian 1999—2000, editor The Pa. Mayflower), Pa. Soc. S.R., Franklin Inn Club, Ancient and Honorable Artillery Co. Mass. Episcopalian. Avocations: genealogy, early American history, opera. Office: Villanova U Dept Classical and Modern Langs & Lits Villanova PA 19085-1699

HUNT, J(ULIAN) COURTENAY, artist; b. Jacksonville, Fla., Sept. 17, 1917; s. Julian Schley and Ruth Rosalind (Loftin) Hunt. Student, Ringling Sch. Art, Farnsworth Sch. Art. Tchr. pvt. classes painting. One-man shows include Cummer Gallery, Jacksonville, exhibited in group shows at Palm Beach Art Gallery, Soc. Four Arts, Palm Beach, Audubon Artists Am., N.Y.C., Allied Artists Am., Atlanta High Mus., St. Augustine (Fla.) Art Assn., Sarasota (Fla.) Art Assn., Nortno Art Gallery Palm Beaches, Represented in permanent collections U. Fla., Gainesville, Jacksonville U., City Hall of Jacksonville, Duval County Cir. Ct., Jacksonville Ind. Life Ins Co., P.A.S.T.A. Gallery, St. Augustine, Fla. With USAF, ETO. Home and Office: 2248 Carnes St Orange Park FL 32073

HUNT, LAMAR, professional football team executive; b. Aug. 2, 1932; s. H.L. and Lyda (Bunker) H.; m. Norma Hunt; children: Lamar, Sharron, Clark, Daniel. BS, So. Meth. U., 1956. Founder, owner Kansas City Chiefs, NFL, 1959—, pres., 1959-76, chmn., 1977-78; founder, pres. AFL, 1959; (became Am. Football Conf.-NFL 1970); pres. Am. Football Conf., 1970—. Bd. dirs. Profl. Football Hall of Fame, Canton, Ohio. Named Salesman of Yr., Kansas City Advt. and Sales Execs. Club, 1963, Southwesterner of Yr., Tex. Sportswriters Assn., 1959. Office: Kans City Chiefs 1 Arrowhead Dr Kansas City MO 64129-1651

HUNT, LAWRENCE HALLEY, JR., lawyer; b. July 15, 1943; s. Lawrence Halley Sr. and Mary Hamilton (Johnson) H.; m. Katherine Collins; children: Caroline Smith, Laura Hamilton, Darwin Halley. AB, Dartmouth Coll., 1965; cert., Inst. d'Etudes Politiques, Paris, 1966; JD, U. Chgo., 1969. Bar: N.Y. 1970, Ill. 1971, U.S. Ct. Appeals (9th cir.) 1980, U.S. Ct. Appeals (2d cir.) 1981, U.S. Supreme Ct. 1981. Assoc. Davis Polk & Wardwell, N.Y.C., 1969-70, Sidley & Austin, Chgo., 1970-75; ptnr. Sidley Austin Brown & Wood, Chgo., 1975—, mem. exec. com., 1985—2002. Mem. securities adv. com. Ill. Sec. of State, Springfield, Ill., 1977—87; prof. grad. program fin. svcs. law Ill. Inst. Tech.-Chgo.-Kent Coll. Law, 1987—99. Mng. editor U. Chgo. Law Review, 1968-69. James B. Reynolds scholar Dartmouth Coll., 1965-66. Mem.: ABA (com. on commodity regulation, past chmn. subcom. on futures commn. merchants, past mem. exec. coun.), Internat. Bar Assn. (past chmn. bus. law com. sub-com. futures and options), Indian Hill Club, Chgo. Club, Mid-Day Club. Office: Sidley Austin Brown & Wood Bank One Plz 10 South Dearborn St Chicago IL 60603 E-mail: lhunt@sidley.com.

HUNT, LORRAINE T. lieutenant governor; m. Charles Hunt; 3 children. Former pres., CEO Perri Inc.; founder, also bd. dirs. Continental Nat. Bank; lt. gov. State of Nev., 1998—, pres. Senate, 1999—. Bd. dirs. First Security Bank Nev.; chmn. bd. trustees Las Vegas Convention and Visitors Authority; former commr. and vice chair Nev. Commn. on Tourism; dir. Nev. Hotel/Motel Assn.; vice chmn. Nev. Motion Picture Found., Nev. Motion Picture Commn. Commr. Clark county Commn., 1995-99. Republican. Office: 101 N Carson St Ste 2 Carson City NV 89701-4786 also: 555 E Washington Ave Ste 5500 Las Vegas NV 89101-1081*

HUNT, MARK ALAN, museum director; b. Topeka, May 21, 1949; s. Ira B. and Marjorie May (McConnell) H.; m. Cynthia E. Rush, Feb. 21, 1976; children: Alexander Rush, Alice Claire. BA magna cum laude, Washburn U., 1971; MA, Cooperstown Grad. Programs, N.Y. State U. Coll., Oneonta, 1982; grad., Mus. Mgmt. Inst. U. Calif., Berkeley, 1983. Dir. Plymouth (Mich.) Hist. Mus., 1976; curator exhibits Kans. Hist. Soc., Topeka, 1976, asst. dir. mus., 1976-79, dir. mus., 1979-88, dir. mus. and hist. sites, 1988-90; dir. Nat. Scouting Mus., Murray (Ky.) State U., 1990-96, Ronald Reagan Presdl. Libr. and Mus., Simi Valley, Calif., 1996-2000; dep. dir./curator Franklin D. Roosevelt Libr., Hyde Park, N.Y., 2000—. Cons. Menninger Found., 1980, Nat. Endowment Humanities, 1974, 75, 77, 1978, Mus. Assessment Program; instr. mus. adminstrn., U. Kans., 1987-89; mem. adv. coun. Ea. Ill. U. Hist. Adminstrn. Program, 1992-96. Contbr. articles to profl. jours. Bd. dirs. Mulvane Art Ctr., Washburn U., 1988-89, Land Between the Lakes Assn., 1994-96; mem. master planning com. Ward-Meade Hist. Park, 1986-89; mem. Bus. Coun. for Arts, 1990-96; grad. Leadership Murray, 1994, Murray Tourism Commn., 1995-96; mem. Ventura County (Calif.) Cultural Tourism Collaborative, 1998-2000, Moorpark (Calif.) Coll. Found. Bd., 1999. Recipient award for excellence Kans. Mus. Assn., 1991; Wiseman scholar, 1967-68, Washburn scholar, 1968-71; Clark fellow, 1973-74, Alumni fellow Washburn U., 1998. Mem. Am. Assn. State and Local History (chmn. state membership com. 1976-85, cons., mem. program com. ann. meeting 1988, 92, mem. edn. com. 1981-84, mem. local arrangements com. ann. meeting 1985, mem. membership task force 1993-97, mem. nat. governing coun. 1991-95, mem. profl. std. and ethics com. 2001—), Mountain Plains Mus. Assn. (mem. bd. 1977, Kans. rep.), Calif. Assn. Mus. (dist. rep. on CAM bd. 1998-99), Kans. Mus. Assn. (pres. 1978-80, Excellence award 1991), Ky. Assn. Mus. (bd. dirs. 1994-96), Am. Assn. Mus. (mem. accreditation vis. com., mem. mus. studies task force 1988-89), Southea. Mus. Assn. (bd. dirs. 1995-96), Murray-Calloway County C. of C., Kappa Sigma, Phi Kappa Phi. Methodist. Home: 16 Yates Blvd Poughkeepsie NY 12601-5006 Office: Franklin D Roosevelt Libr 4079 Albany Post Rd Hyde Park NY 12538-1917 E-mail: mark.hunt@nara.gov.

HUNT, MARTHA, sales executive, researcher; b. N.Y.C., May 17, 1924; d. Paul Andrew and Monika (Dobberstein) Pankau; children: Philip Brian Hunt, Susan Monica Hunt. Student, Syracuse U., 1943-47. Asst. controller Commonwealth Fund, N.Y.C., 1947-50; sales tech. Caldwell & Bloor, Mansfield, Ohio, 1958-64; sales promotion mgr. Vita Craft Corp., Shawnee, Kans., 1964-91, cons., 1964—. Mem. Meeting Planners Internat., Kans. City, 1982—. Author and editor: cookbooks, 1965-91. Pres. LWV, Akron, Ohio, 1951-53; gov. Soroptimists, 1978-80, bd. dirs., Phila., 1978-80, coord. 1980-84, pres., Kansas City, 1973-74; bd. dirs. Kansas City chpt. Shepherd's Ctr., 1972—; nat. bd. dirs. Shepher's Ctrs. Am., 1990—; bd. dirs. Rose Brooks Ctr., 1979-86, v.p., 1984-85; bd. dirs., founder Safehome, Inc., 1979—, hon. chmn. as founder for Celebration of Safehome 1980-2000, 2000; pres. Metro Citizens Crusade Against Crime, Kansas City., 1983. Recipient Meritorious Svc. award, Kans. City Police Dept., 1975, Disting. Govs. award, Soroptimist Internat. Am., Phila., 1978-79, 79-80, Woman of Distinction award Santa Fe Trail Girl Scouts, 1993, Soroptimist Internat. Am., 1995, Milan Hulbert Humanitarian award Sales Profls. Internat., 1996, Mother of Our Movement award Kans. Coalition Against Sexual and Domestic Violence, 1999, Kansas City Chiefs/NFL Cmty. Quarterback award, 2002. Mem. Kappa Kappa Gamma (pres. 1948-49), Alumnae Assn. (N.Y.C.). Republican. Presbyterian. Avocations: traveling, volunteering. E-mail: mhunt5607@aol.com.

HUNT, MARTIN KYLE, corporate strategist; m. Jacqueline E. Hunt, 1995. BA, Swarthmore Coll., 1990; MBA, Harvard Bus. Sch., 1994. Internal cons. The Prudential, Newark, N.J., 1990-93; rsch. assoc. Harvard Bus. Sch., Boston, 1993-94; mgmt. cons. AMS, Inc., Fairfax, Va., 1994-97; sr. corp. strategist Unicom Corp., Chgo., 1997—; v.p. corp. initatives group MBNA Am. Bank, 1999—. Author: History of Black Business: The Coming of America's Largest African-American-owned Business, 1999. Avocations: tennis, business history.

HUNT, MARY ALICE, library science educator; b. Lima, Ohio, Apr. 14, 1928; d. Blair T. and Grace (Henry) H. BA, Fla. State U., Tallahassee, 1950, MA, 1953; PhD, Ind. U., Bloomington, 1973. Instr., librarian Fla. State U., Tallahassee, 1955-61, asst. prof., 1961-74, assoc. prof., 1974-82, prof., 1982-95, assoc. dean, 1986-95, prof. emerita, 1995—. Author: Transitions: An Informal History of a School Celebrating its 50th Anniversary, 1997; co-author: (book) Multimedia Indexes, Lists, etc., 1975; editor: (book) Multimedia Approach To Children's Literature, 1983, (periodical) FSU/SLIS Alumni Newsletter, 1966-95, Florida Libraries, 1961-67; assoc. editor: (book) Folders of Ideas for Library Excellence, 1991. Mem. ALA (councilor at large 1986-94, 96-2000), Southeastern Library Assn., Fla. Assn. Media in Edn., Delta Kappa Gamma, Pi Lambda Theta (life), Pi Kappa Phi, Beta Phi Mu. Avocations: gardening, reading, photography, pastel drawing and watercolor painting. Home: 1603 Kolopakin Nene Tallahassee FL 32301-4733

HUNT, MARY ELIZABETH, religious studies educator; b. June 1, 1951; BA magna cum laude, Marquette U., Milw., 1972; M of Theol. Studies, Harvard Div. Sch., 1974; MDiv, Jesuit Sch. Theology, Berkeley, Calif., 1979; PhD, Grad. Theol. Union, Berkeley, Calif., 1980. Vis. prof. theology ISEDET, Frontier Internship in Mission, Buenos Aires, 1980-82; co-dir., co-founder Women's Alliance for Theology, Ethics and Ritual, Silver Spring, Md., 1983—; vis. asst. prof. religion Colgate U., Hamilton, N.Y., 1986-87; rsch. fellow Ctr. for Study of Values in Pub. Life, Harvard Div. Sch., 2000-01. Lectr., condr. workshops in field; adj. assoc. prof. women's studies program Georgetown U., 1995-99; women's adv. com. Concilium. Author: Fierce Tenderness: A Feminist Theology of Friendship, 1990; mem. editl. bd. Jour. Feminist Studies in Religion, Jour. Religion and Abuse, Theology and Sexuality Jour.; editor: Good Sex: Feminist Perspectives from the World's Religions; contbr. articles to profl. jours. Recipient Isaac Hecker award Paulist Ctr., Boston, Prophetic Figure award Women's Ordination Conf., prize Crossroad Women's Studies, 1990. Mem. Am. Acad. Religion, Alpha Sigma Nu. Office: Women's Alliance Theology 8035 13th St Ste 5 Silver Spring MD 20910-4870 Fax: 301-589-3150. E-mail: mhunt@hers.com.

HUNT, MARY MELINDA, artist; b. Calgary, Alta., Can., May 16, 1958; d. Charles Warren and Patricia Gayford Hunt; children: Emily Hunt Olfson, Rachel Hunt Olfson. BA, Reed Coll., 1981; BFA, Mus. Art Sch., Portland, Oreg., 1981; MFA, Yale U., 1985. Author: (book) Hart Island; pub. art work, Circle of Hope, 1994, Letters to a Forest, 1995. Recipient Conn. Commn. on Arts award, 1987, Project award, N.Y. State Coun., 1995, Media award, 2000. Democrat. E-mail: huntolfson@earthlink.net.

HUNT, MAURICE ARTHUR, English educator, researcher; b. Lansing, Mich., Oct. 30, 1942; s. Elmore Clare and Irene Elizabeth H.; m. Pamela Helene Coyle, June 24, 1978; children: Alison, Jeffrey, Andrew, Thomas. BA, U. Mich., 1964; MA, U. Calif., Berkeley, 1966, PhD, 1970. Instr. English Coll. Marin, Kentfield, Calif., 1970-73; lectr. English Dominican Coll., San Rafael, Calif., 1974-75; vis. asst. prof. English Ariz. State U., Tempe, 1980-81; from asst. to assoc. prof. English Baylor U., Waco, Tex., 1981-93, prof. English, 1993—, chair dept. English, 1996—. Mem. adv. bd. writing ctr. Tex. A&M U., College Station, Tex., 1985—; dir. Baylor Advanced Placement Inst., Waco, 1994-95, Baylor Freshman Composition Program, Waco, 1982-98; mem. exec. com. S. Ctrl. Renaissance Conf., College Station, 1988-90. Author: Shakespeare's Romance of the Word, 1990, Shakespeare's Labored Art, 1995; editor: Approaches to Teaching "The Tempest" and Other Late Romances, 1992, "The Winter's Tale": Critical Essays, 1995, Approaches to Teaching Shakespeare's "Romeo and Juliet", 2000; assoc. editor Papers on Lang. and Lit., 1996—, The Upstart Crow: A Shakespeare Jour., 1990—; mem. editl. bd. Shakespeare and the Classroom, 1993—; contbr. articles to profl. jours. Fundraiser United Way Bay Area, San Francisco, 1976-80; bd. dirs. Alameda County Tng. and Employment Bd., Oakland, Calif., 1977-78. Rsch. grantee Baylor U., 1986—. Mem. MLA, Fulbright Grants (mem. so. region, mem. nat. screening com.), Shakespeare Assn. Am., Greater Lansing Area Sports Hall of Fame, S. Ctrl. Renaissance Conf. (mem. exec. com. 1984—), Internat. Assn. Univ. Profls. English, Phi Beta Kappa. Democrat. Episcopalian. Avocations: jogging, sports. Home: 321 Oakwood Ln Hewitt TX 76643-3027 Office: 500 Speight Ave Waco TX 76798-7404 E-mail: mauricehunt@Baylor.edu.

HUNT, MICHAEL ALLEN, psychologist, educator; b. Austin, Tex., Apr. 6, 1947; s. Darryl Allen Hunt and Opal Margarite Hunt. MA, U. Houston, 1981. Food stamp caseworker Dept. Pub. Welfare, San Antonio, 1969—71, AFDC eligibility caseworker San Antonio and Houston, 1970—73; emergency caseworker Harris County Child Protective Svcs., Houston, 1972—74; prin. investigator Dolphin Rsch. Team U. Houston-Clear Lake, 1985—. Adj. human scis. and humanities U. Houston-Clear Lake; adj. prof. social scis. Coll. of Mainland. Mem. Seabrook (Tex.) Wetlands Adv. Bd. Mem.: APA, Am. Psychol. Soc., Tex. Marine Mammal Stranding Network (bd. dirs. 1988—). Avocations: kayaking, camping, hiking, art, writing. Office: U Houston-Clear Lake 2700 Bay Area Blvd Houston TX 77058-1098 Office Fax: 281-283-3397. Personal E-mail: huntm@cl.uh.edu. Business E-Mail: huntm@cl.uh.edu.

HUNT, MICHAEL O'LEARY, wood science and engineering educator; b. Louisville, Dec. 9, 1935; s. George Henry and Tressie (Truax) H.; children: Elizabeth H. Schwartz, Lynne T. Lattimer, Michael O. Jr. BS, U. Ky., 1957; M.Forestry, Duke U., 1958; PhD, N.C. State U., 1970. Product engr. Wood Products div. Singer Co., Pickens, S.C., 1959-60; asst. prof. wood sci. Purdue U., West Lafayette, Ind., 1960-70, assoc. prof., 1970-79, prof., 1979—, dir. Wood Rsch. Lab., 1979—2002. Contbr. articles over 80 articles to profl. jours. Chmn. campus preservation com. Wabash Valley Trust for Historic Preservation, Lafayette. Recipient Servaas Meml. award Hist. Landmarks Found. of Ind., 1994, H. Fannon award Lafayette Neighborhood Housing Svcs., 1998, Downie Meml. award Wabash Valley Trust, 2002. Mem. Forest Products Soc. (pres. 1990-91, Fred Gottschalk Meml. award 1984), Soc. of Wood Sci. and Tech., Rotary. Achievements include patent for lightweight, high-performance structural particleboard. Office: Purdue Univ Wood Rsch Lab West Lafayette IN 47907-2033

HUNT, PETER JAMES, management consultant, statistics educator; b. Trenton, N.J., Nov. 23, 1940; s. Cyril James and Mary (Fassetti) H. BS, Pa. State U., 1965; MS, U. Detroit, 1968; PhD, U. Akron, 1974. Dir. rsch. Human R&D, St. Petersburg, Fla., 1974-75; pres. Productivity Mgmt. Cons., Clearwater, Fla., 1976—. Author: Program Evaluation, 1976, Statistics for Managers, 1978, Statistical Process Control, 1985, Total Quality Management, 1991, A Manual for Guage/Measurement Process Assessment, 1992, Design of Experiments for Batch Manufacturing, 1998. Cpl. USMC, 1965-71. Mem.: Am. Soc. Quality. Episcopalian. Avocations: sailing, mountain climbing, scuba diving, flying. Office: Productivity Mgmt Consultants 849 Harbor Island Clearwater FL 33767-1807

HUNT, PHILIP CHARLES, engineer, consultant; b. Concord, Mass., Nov. 3, 1958; s. Philip Walter and Evelyn Elise (Roessler) Hunt; m. Xing Wang, Mar. 1, 1998. BA, U. Denver, 1980; AS, Wentworth Inst., 1984; MS summa cum laude in Engring., So. Calif. U. Profl. Studies, 2002. Product field mgr. Moore Business Forms, Wellesley Hills, Mass., 1984—86; sr. cons. Gerald T. Reilly & Co., Milton, Mass., 1986-88; product mgr. Info. Systems Assocs., Mobile, Ala., 1988—92; product mgmt. liaison engr. Microsystems Software, Framingham, Mass., 1992—97; engring. support analyst BMC Software, 1998-99; pre-sales engr. Harte-Hanks, 1999-2000; sr. sales cons. Informatica Corp., 2000—01; client support mgr. US Power Solutions, 2001. Mem.: IEEE, Computer Soc. of IEEE, Mensa, Tau Alpha Pi. Home: 9 Arcadia Cir Marlborough MA 01752-6452 E-mail: philip-hunt@comcast.net.

HUNT, RAY L. petroleum company executive; b. 1943; s. H. L. and Ruth (Ray) Hunt; m. Nancy Ann Hunt; 5 children. BBA, So. Meth. U., 1965. With Hunt Oil Co., Dallas, 1958—; chmn., pres., CEO Hunt Consolidated Inc., Dallas, 1994—. Exec. com., bd. trustees So. Mich. U.; bd. trustees Ctr. for Strategic & Internat. Studies, Washington. Named to Tex. Bus. Hall of Fame, 1992. Mem.: Am. Petroleum Inst. (exec., pub. policy com., chmn. 1991—94). Office: Hunt Consolidated Inc 1445 Ross At Field Dallas TX 75202

HUNT, ROBERT G. construction company executive; b. Feb. 15, 1948; BS in bus., Ball State U.; MS in Engring., Purdue U. Joined Huber, Hunt & Nichols Inc., Indpls., 1974, from field engr. to divsn. mgr., pres. Phoenix and Tampa, CEO Indpls., 1999—; pres. The Hunt Corp., Indpls. Office: Hunt Construction Group 2450 S Tibbs Ave Indianapolis IN 46241*

HUNT, ROBERT GARY, medical consultant, oral and maxillofacial surgeon; b. San Diego, July 10, 1945; s. Harvey E. and Pauline A. (Nazarovic) H.; m. Diane G. Hunt, Apr. 26, 1975; 1 child, Christine G. AA, Mesa Coll., San Diego, 1971; BS in Medicine, MD, U. nebr., 1979; DDS, U. So. Calif., 1976. Diplomate Am. Bd. Oral and Maxillofacial Surgery, Nat. Bd. Med. Examiners; lic. physician, Calif., Nebr.; lic. dentist, Calif., Nebr. Oral and maxillofacial surgeon in pvt. practice, San Diego, 1981—. With USAF, 1965-70. Fellow Am. Assn. Oral and Maxillofacial Surgeons, Am. Coll. Oral and Maxillofacial Surgeons, Internat. Coll. Surgeons, Internat. Soc. Plastic, Aesthetic and Reconstructive Surgery, Am. Coll. Oral Implantology; mem. AMA, ADA, So. Calif. Acad. Oral Pathology, Mensa, Omicron Kappa Upsilon, Phi Kappa Phi, Alpha Tau Epsilon, Delta Sigma Delta, others. Home: 2240 Sunset Blvd San Diego CA 92103-1120

HUNT, ROBERT GAYLE, former government official; b. Greeley, Colo., Aug. 2, 1933; s. Ray and Myrtle Marie (Dunham) Hunt; m. Harriet Gertrude McNeel, June 10, 1955 (div. 1978); children: Leslie Lynn Hunt Cowen, Linda Jean, Julia Gail Hunt Walsh, Gregg Bryan, Robert John. BA, U. No. Colo., 1955; MPA, Syracuse U., 1957; student, Fed. Exec. Inst., Charlottesville, Va., 1973, Western Exec. Sem. Ctr., (fed. govt.), 1991. Various positions housing and cmty. devel. programs HUD, Washington, 1957-79; spl. asst. to dep. asst. sec. FHA, 1979-89; dir. mgmt. svcs. divsn., 1989-97; ret., 1997. Pres. Kings Park Civic Assn., Springfield, Va., 1966-67; elder Providence Presbyterian Ch., Fairfax, Va., 1968-71, 79-82, 1986-89; pres. Fairfax County Fedn. Citizens Assn., 1970-71; chmn. Citizens for Sch. Bonds, 1973; mem. Fairfax County Sch. Bd., 1973-77; pres. Social Ctr. for Psychiat. Rehab., Inc., 1983-85; pres. Fairfax Com. of 100, 1986-88; bd. dirs. No. Va. Mental Health Assn., 1988-94, v.p., 1992-93, vice-chmn.; Fairfax County Adv. Task Force on Cultural Facility, 1988-89; spokesperson Clean Water Coalition, 1970; supt. Fairfax County Pub. Sch., cmty. adv. com., 1971-1972, 1997-99; mem. pres.'s cir. Psychiat. Rehab. Svcs., Inc., 1994—, mem. planned giving com., 1996-97; chmn. Cmty. Ministry No. Va., 1984-86, 96-2000. Named Outstanding Citizen, Kings Park Civic Assn., 1975; recipient citations Fairfax County Sch. Bd., 1973, Disting. Svc. award, 1977, Citizen of Yr. award Fairfax County, Va., 1999, Washington Post trophy, 1999. Mem. Chesapeake Harbour Yacht Club (Annapolis, Md.). Avocation: sailing. Home: 8910 Cromwell Dr Springfield VA 22151-1120 E-mail: robhuu@aol.com.

HUNT, ROBERT WILLIAM, theatrical producer, arts management consultant; b. Seattle, June 8, 1947; s. William Roland and Margaret Anderson (Crowe) Hunt; m. Marcie Loomis, Aug. 24, 1968 (div. Dec. 1975); 1 child, Megan; m. Susan Moyer, June 17, 1989 (div. Oct. 1997); children: Donovan, Jillian. BA, U. Wash., 1969. CPA Wash. Data processing cons. Arthur Andersen & Co., Seattle, 1968-78; owner, cons. Robert W. Hunt & Assocs., Seattle, 1978—; exec. prodr. Village Theatre, Issaquah, Wash., 1979—. Developer Francis J. Gaudette Theatre, Issaquah, Wash., 1994; cons. San Francisco Mus. Modern Art, 1981—90, Mus. of Flight, Seattle, 1983—90, Met. Mus. N.Y.C., 1984—85; contracted for acquired mgmt. Everett (Wash.) Performing Arts Ctr., 1998—. Prodr.: Eleanor, 1987, Heidi, 1989, Charlie and the Chocolate Factory, 1989, Book of James, 1990, Funny Pages, 1991, Jungle Queen Debutante, 1991, Glimmerglass, 1995, City Kid, 1995, Bootlegger, 1996, 4:00 AM Boogie Blues, 1998, Crossing Over, 1999, Making Tracks, 2000, Play It By Heart, 2000, Cupid and Psyche, 2001, The Ark, 2001, Searching 4Y, 2001, Six Wives, 2002, Oue Red Flower: Letters from 'Nam, 2002. Chmn. com. Seattle Arts Commn., 1975—78; treas. Arts Resource Svcs., Seattle, 1976—78; gen. mgr. Musicomedy Northwest, Seattle, 1977—79; bd. dirs. Theatre Puget Sound; past treas., bd. dirs. Bellevue Fed. Little League. Grantee, Seattle Arts Commn., 1978—79, Wash. State Arts Commn., 1980—, King County Arts Commn., 1980—, Nat. Endowment for Arts, 1992—. Mem.: Nat. Alliance for Musical Theatre (past treas., bd. dirs.), Seattle Rotary. Office: Village Theatre 303 Front St N Issaquah WA 98027-2917 E-mail: RHunt@villagetheatre.org.

HUNT, ROGER, former state legislator; m. Sharon Hunt; 3 children. BA, Augustana Coll.; JD, U. S.D.; MA, George Washington U. Mem. S.D. Ho. of Reps., 1991—2001, mem. judiciary and edn. coms., spkr. of ho., 1999—2001; atty., tchr. S.D. State Legislature. Mem. Judge Advocate Gen. Corps USN, 1962—84. Address: 48190 265th St Brandon SD 57005-7205

HUNT, ROGER SCHERMERHORN, healthcare administrator; b. White Plains, NY, Mar. 7, 1943; s. Charles Howland and Mildred Russell (Schermerhorn) H.; m. Mary Adams Libby, June 19, 1965; children: Christina Markle, David. BA, DePauw U., 1965; MBA, George Washington U., 1968. Adminstrv. resident Lankenau Hosp., Phila., 1966-68; asst. adminstr. Hahnemann Med. Coll. and Hosp., Phila., 1968-71, hosp. dir., 1971-74, assoc. v.p., hosp. adminstr., 1974-77; dir. Ind. U. Hosp., Indpls., 1977-84; pres. Luth. Gen. Hosp., Pk. Ridge, Ill., 1984-90; pres., CEO Fontbonne Health Sys., Toronto, Canada, 1990-92; sr. v.p. Northwestern Healthcare Network, Chgo., 1993-96; pres., CEO ViaHealth, Rochester, NY, 1996-99; prin. Hunt Healthcare, Deerfield, Ill., 1999—2002; CEO, BroMenn Healthcare Sys., Bloomington, Ill., 2002—. Chmn. Alliance of Indpls. Hosp., 1981; pres. United Hosp. Services, 1979-81; assoc. prof. hosp. adminstrn. Ind. U. Sch. Medicine, 1977-84; vice chmn. Pa. Emergency Health Services Council, 1975-77; pres. Chester County Emergency Med. Service Council, 1971-77. Pres. Wayne Area Jr. C. of C., 1970-71, state dir., 1971-72; bd. dir. Rochester Philharm. Orch., 1998-99, Cmty. Cancer Ctr., 2002—. Fellow Am. Coll. Healthcare Exec. (regent for Ind. 1984, Ill. 1988-90, Postgrad. tng. award 1968); mem. Am. Hosp. Assn., Hosp. Assn. of NY State (bd. dir. 1998-99), Ind. Hosp. Assn. (bd. dir. 1982-84), Met. Chgo. Healthcare Coun. (bd. dirs. 1986-95), DePauw U. Alumni Assn. (bd. dir. 1988-94), Greater Rochester Metro C. of C. (bd. dir. 1998-99), Comm. Cance Ctr. (bd. dir., 2002-) Office: BroMenn Healthcare PO Box 2850 Bloomington IL 61702-2850 E-mail: Rogerhunt@earthlink.net.

HUNT, RONALD FORREST, lawyer, director; b. Shelby, N.C., Apr. 18, 1943; s. Forrest Elmer and Bruna Magnolia (Brackett) H.; m. Judy Elaine Shultz, May 19, 1965; 1 child, Mary AB, U. N.C., 1966, JD, 1968. Bar: N.C. 1968, D.C. 1973. Mem. staff SEC, Washington, 1968-69, legal asst. to chmn., 1970-71, sec. of commn., 1972-73; dep. gen. counsel, sec. Student Loan Mktg. Assn., Washington, 1973-78, sr. v.p., gen. counsel, sec., 1979-83, exec. v.p., gen. counsel, 1983-90; pvt. practice New Bern, NC, 1991—99. Vice chmn. First Capital Corp., Southern Pines, N.C., 1984-90; bd. dirs. Student Loan Mktg. Assn., Washington., SLM Corp., Reston, Va., e-Numerate Solutions, Inc., McLean, Va.; chmn. bd. dirs. Nat. Student Loan Clearinghouse, Reston, 1993-95, 97—. Trustee Warren Wilson Coll., Asheville, NC; mem. Montgomery County (Md.) Commn. Landlord and Tenant Affairs, 1976—81, chmn., 1979—81; bd. dirs. D.C. chpt. ARC, 1976—83; trustee Arena Stage, Washington, 1984—89, Washington Theatre Awards Soc., 1988—90. Republican. Presbyterian. Avocations: sailing; gardening.

HUNT, RONALD J. academic administrator; Assoc. prof., dental ecology UNC, Sch. Dentistry, 1986—88, prof., dental ecology, 1990—92, asst. dean, 1992—98, assoc. dean, 1998—99; dean, Med. Coll., Va. Sch. Dentistry Va. Commonwealth U. Richmond, 1999—. Office: PO Box 980566 Richmond VA 23298

HUNT, SEAN EMMET, anesthesiologist; b. Salem, Mass., Apr. 10, 1952; s. Robert Francis and Elizabeth Mary (Kelley) H.; m. Catherine Louise O'Donnell, Apr. 30, 1983; children: Christopher, Matthew. BS, Boston Coll., 1974, MS, 1976; MD, Tufts U., 1980. Diplomate Am. Bd. Anesthesiology. Intern New Eng. Med. Ctr., Boston, 1980-81, resident in anesthesia, 1982-84; resident in surgery St. Elizabeth's Hosp. Boston, 1981-82; sr. staff physician Lahey Clinic, Burlington, Mass., 1984-91; physician Exeter (N.H.) Hosp., 1992-99, Addison Gilbert Hosp., Gloucester, Mass., 1995-99; med. dir. anesthesia svcs. Hunt Ctr., Danvers, Mass., 1994—99; physician Beverly (Mass.) Hosp., 1991-99; med. dir. Ambulatory Surgery Ctr. Dartmouth-Hitchcock, Manchester, N.H., 1999—. Asst. prof. anesthesiology Dartmouth Med. Sch. Mem. Am. Coll. Physician Execs., Am. Soc. Anesthesiologist (author ASA Self Education and Evaluation Program 1987-91), Mass. Soc. Anesthesiologists (dist. rep. 1995-99), Soc. Cardiovascular Anesthesiologists, N.H. Med. Soc., N.H. Soc. Anesthesiologists (sec., treas. 2002--). Roman Catholic. Avocations: alpine skiing, mountain biking, hiking, golf, cross country skiing. Office: Dartmouth Hitchcock 100 Hitchcock Way Manchester NH 03104-4125 E-mail: sean.e.hunt@hitchcock.org.

HUNT, SWANEE G. public policy educator, former ambassador; b. Dallas, May 1, 1950; m. Charles Alexander Ansbacher; 3 children. BA, Tex. Christian U., 1972; MA, Ball State U., 1976; MA in Religion, Iliff Sch. of Theology, 1977, PhD, 1986; PhD (hon.), Webster U., 1994. Founder, chmn. Hunt Alternatives Fund, 1981—; co-founder, co-dir. Karis Community, 1980-83; min. pastoral care Capital Heights Presbyn. Ch., 1983; commr., vice chair Denver Community Mental Health Commn., 1983-87; with Gov. Policy Acad. on Families and Children at Risk, 1989-90; chair Colo. Coord. Coun. Housing and the Homeless, 1989-92; U.S. amb. to Austria, 1993-97; dir. women and pub. policy program Kennedy Sch. Govt. Commr. Rufugees United Nations High. Composer The Witness Cantata, 1985. Bd. dirs. Ctr. Reproductive Law and Policy, Charter Fund, Am. Mental Health Fund Nat. Adv. Bd., Colo. Children's Campaign, Denver Civic Ventures, Inc., The Missing Half, Pub. Edn. Coalition, U. Colo. Ctr. Health Ethics and Policy Rev. Bd., 1987-89, Women and Founds./Corp. Philanthropy; co-founder, trustee Women's Found. Colo.; trustee U. Denver; chair Mayor's Human Capital Agenda Coun., 1992-93; co-chair Denver Initiative Children and Families. Recipient Martin Luther King Humanitarian award U. Colo., 1992, NCCJ, 1992, Denver Urban Ministries, 1991, United Meth. Ch., 1989, Internat. Women's Forum, 1989, Sta. KUSA-TV, 1989, Caring Connection, 1989, Nat. Mental Health Assn., 1985, Mental Health Assn. Colo., 1984, 94, Mile High award United Way, 1993, Am. Heritage award Anti-Defamation League, 1995, Cordon Bleu du Saint Esprit Peace award, 1996, Humanitarian Lifetime Svc. award Denver Holocaust Awareness, 1997, Together for Peace award, 1997, 3 decorations Austrian Govt., 1997, Amb. award The Conflict Ctr., 1997, Inst. for Internat. Edn. award, 1998. Office: 168 Brattle St Cambridge MA 02138-3309 also: Kennedy Sch Govt 79 Jfk St Rm T110A Cambridge MA 02138-5801

HUNT, T(HOMAS) W(EBB), retired religion educator; b. Mammoth Spring, Ark., Sept. 28, 1929; s. Thomas Hubert and Ethel Clara (Webb) H.; m. M. Laverne Hill, July 22, 1951; children: Melana Claire Hunt Monroe. MusB, Ouachita Bapt. U., 1950; MusM, N. Tex. State U., 1957, PhD, 1967. Faculty Southwestern Bapt. Theol. Sem., Ft. Worth, 1963-87; life cons. for prayer Bapt. Sunday Sch. Bd., Nashville, 1987-94, ret., 1994. Lectr. in field; confs. on the five continents; mem. adv. coun. Life Action Ministries; mem. bd. ref. Union U., adv. coun. Life Action Ministries, bd. reference Union U. Author: The Doctrine of Prayer, 1985, Music in Missions, 1986, The Disciple's Prayer Life, 1988, Church Ministry Prayer Manual, 1994, The Mind of Christ, 1995, In God's Presence, 1995, From Heaven's View, 2002, The Life-Changing Power of Prayer, 2002; founder, author: course in music in missions. Bd. dirs. Life Action Ministries; Union Univ. Home: 3915 Cypress Hill Dr Spring TX 77388-5798 *In a rapidly changing world, we rely on a God who does not change.*

HUNT, VALERIE VIRGINIA, electrophysiologist, educator; b. Larwill, Ind., July 22, 1916; d. Homer Henry Hunt and Iva Velzora Ames. BS in Biology, Fla. State Coll., 1936; MA in Physiol. Psychology, Columbia U., 1941, EdD in Sci. Edn., 1946; DD, Phoenix Inst., San Diego, 1984. Sci. tchr. Anniston (Ala.) H.S., 1936-38; asst. anatomy nursing dept. Columbia U., N.Y.C., 1939-40; chmn. health edn. Boston YWCA, 1942-43; instr. Columbia U. Tchrs. Coll. and Coll. Physicians and Surgeons, N.Y.C., 1943-46; asst. prof. U. Iowa, Iowa City, 1946-47; assoc. prof., dir. divsn. phys. therapy UCLA, 1947-64, prof. physiology, dir. electromyographic lab., 1964-80, prof. emeritus, 1980—; dir. BioEnergy Fields Lab. BioEnergy Fields Found., Malibu, Calif., 1980—; CEO Malibu Pub. Co., 1995—. Cons. Nat. Bd. YWCA, 1943-46, Nat. Early Childhood Edn., 1948-50, UCLA Sch. Engring. Prosthetics Inst., 1949-51, Calif. Dept. Edn., 1950-60, Chrysler Motor Co. Space Divsn. Rsch., 1952, NASA Space Biology, 1958; field reader U.S. Dept. HEW, 1958-65; reviewer sci. textbooks McMillan Pub., Prentice-Hall, McGraw-Hill, W.B. Saunders & Co., 1959-67; cons. Fetzer Found. Energy Field Rsch., 1989, Heart Math Found., 1992. Author: Recreation for the Handicapped, 1955, Corrective Physical Education, 1967, Movement Education for Preschool, 1972, Guidelines for Movement Behavior: Curricula for Early Childhood Education, 1974, Infinite Mind: Science of the Human

Vibrations of Consciousness, 1993, Mind Mastery Meditations, 1997, Naibhu, 1998; contbr. articles to profl. jours. Pres. United Cerebral Palsy, L.A., 1947-51; mem. adv. com. Harlan Shoemaker Clinic for Neurol. Disabilities, 1948-53; bd. dirs. Found. for Jr. Blind, 1949-52, Crippled Children Soc., 1953-58, YWCA, L.A., 1955-65; adv. com., Internat. Congress for Exceptional Children, 1964-72, Rory Found., L.A., 1998—; vestry bd. mem. St. Matthew Episcopal Ch., L.A., 1965-69. Rsch. grantee USPHS, 1957-61, Adelphi Found., 1960-63, Rolf Found., 1965-71; recipient Heritage award Calif. Dance Educator Assn., 1987, N.B. Rudman award Found. Exceptional Leadership, 1995; Dame Order of St. John of the Ams., 1996. Mem. NSF, N.Y. Acad. Scis., Pi Lambda Theta, Kappa Delta Pi. Avocations: travel, gardening, music, art, lecturing. Office: BioEnergy Fields Found PO Box 6653 Malibu CA 90264-6653 E-mail: vhunt@bioenergyfields.org.

HUNT, WAYNE ROBERT, SR., state government official; b. Mt. Holly, NJ, Feb. 23, 1948; s. Edward Middleton Sr. (deceased) and Sarah Isabel (Pope) H.(deceased); m. Elizabeth Evans Caputi, Oct. 23, 1982; children: Brandi Leigh, Wayne Robert Jr., Joshua David, Jacob Cody. BSBA, William Jewell Coll., 1970; MPA, Rutgers U., 1993; student, Command and Gen. Staff Coll., 1995. Cert. pub. mgr., facilitator. Mgr. Edward M. Hunt & Son Inc., Mt. Holly, NJ, 1970—79; spl. staff officer mech. sect., engrng. divsn. N.J. Dept. Def., Trenton, NJ, 1979—82, asst. bur. chief facilities mgmt. bur., 1982—88; contracting officer/bur. chief installations divsn. ops. bur NJ Dept. Mil. and Vets. Affairs, Lawrenceville, 1986—94; dir. installations div. NJ Dept. Mil and Vets Affairs, Lawrenceville, 1994—99, chief info. officer, 1999—2003; chief Fin. & Info. Office, 2003—. Field assoc. orgnl. leadership development sc. Nat. Guard Bur., 1986-92. Deacon New Life Christian Ch.; past pres. Union Fire Co. #2. Lt. col. NJ Army Nat. Guard, 1970—; Battalion Cmmdr; anti-terrorism-force protection section chief; Sch. Bd. Dir., Morrisville Sch. Bd. Recipient Proclamation for Svc. to State, Gov. James J. Florio, 1993, Cert. of Recognition, Drumthwacket Found., 1992, Letter of Appreciation, N.J. Statue of Liberty Svc., N.J. Dept. Mil. and Vets. Affairs Group award, 1995, NGANJ Pres. award, 1997, Rancocas Valley Regional HS VIP Hall of Fame, 1997; N.J. State Teamwork Award, Meritorious Svc. medal, (5) Army Commendation medals. Mem. ASPA (Cert. Achievement 2002), Internat. Facilities Mgmt. Assn., Am. Mgmt. Assn., Constrn. Specifications Inst., Pub. Sector Mgr. Assn., N.J. Soc. Cert. Pub. Mgr., Am. Acad. Cert. Pub. Mgr., past pres. N.G. Exec. Dir. Assn. (2d v.p., chmn. nominations com., by-laws com.), N.G. Assn. of US (Dist. Svc. medal 2003, Am. Medal Honor 2003), N.G. Assn. of NJ (sec. 1987—, Pres.'s award 1997), 114th Regimental Assn., Trenton Arty. Officers Assn., Enlisted Assn. NJ, Trinity Ctr. Conflict Mgmt., Masons (32 deg.), Elks, Pi Alpha Alpha. Avocations: golf, camping, jogging, weight training. Home: 247 N Pennsylvania Ave Morrisville PA 19067-1103 Office: NJ Dept Mil and Vet Affairs 101 Eggerts Crossing Rd Lawrenceville NJ 08648-2805

HUNT, WILLIAM B. cardiopulmonary physician; b. Lexington, N.C., Sept. 27, 1927; s. William B. and Maxine (Cox) H.; married; children: William B., III, Anne, Alex, Sarah. BS, Wake Forest U., 1948; MD, Bowman Gray Sch. Medicine, Winston Salem, N.C., 1953. Diplomate Am. Bd. Internal Medicine, Am. Bd. Allergy and Immunology. Intern, resident U. Va., Charlottesville, 1953-55, resident, fellow, 1957-59, assoc. prof., 1960-75, asst. dean Sch. Medicine, 1972-75; fellow gastroenterology Bowman Gray Sch. Medicine, Winston Salem, 1959-60; instr. internal medicine N.Y. Med. Coll., N.Y.C., 1959-60; from clin. assoc. prof. medicine to clin. prof. medicine East Carolina Sch. Medicine, Greenville, N.C., 1975 —; staff physician Craven Regional Med. Ctr., New Bern, N.C., 1975—, med. dir. cardiopulmonary svcs., 1975-95. Cons. N.C. Health Dept., TB Control Br., 1997-2000; TB control physician Craven County Health Dept., 1999—; mem. N.C. TB Peer Rev. Com., 1996—. Pres. Ea. Area Health Edn. Ctr., 1990-95. Recipient Douglas Southhall Freeman award Va. Lung Assn., 1975, Disting. Alumnus award Bowman Gray Sch. Medicine, 1973, Robert Bageant award Va. Soc. Respiratory Care, 1987. Fellow Am. Coll. Chest Physicians, Am. Thoracic Soc., Am. Coll. Physicians; mem. N.C. Med. Soc. (councillor 1978, exec. com. 1981), Va. Thoracic Soc. (pres. 1974), N.C. Thoracic Soc. (pres. 1984), N.C. Lung Assn. (pres. 1986), Craven Pamlico Jones Med. Soc. (pres. 1984). Democrat. Episcopalian. Avocations: skiing, golf, flying, sailing, tennis. Home: 1617 King Mountain Rd Charlottesville VA 22901

HUNT, WILLIAM E., SR., retired state supreme court justice; b. 1923; BA, LLB, U. Mont., JD, 1955. Bar: 1955. Judge State Workers' Compensation Ct., 1975-81; justice Mont. Supreme Ct., Helena, 1984—2001.

HUNT-CLERICI, CAROL ELIZABETH, retired academic administrator, counselor; b. N.Y.C., Mar. 14, 1938; d. William Laubach and Mary Alice (Grace) Hunt; m. Francis Anthony Clerici, May 17, 1958; children: Francis Anthony Clerici Jr., David William Clerici, Paul Camilio Clerici. AB, Boston Coll., 1987, MA, 1990. Faculty pers. asst. academic v.p. office Boston Coll., Chestnut Hill, Mass., 1984-99; psychol. counselor Summerhill Ho., Norwood, Mass., 1989—2003; ret., 2003. Rep. staff adv. senate Boston Coll., Chestnut Hill, 1981—98, vice-chair, 1985—86, chair, 1986—88, Chestnut Hill, 1990—91; sec. Martin Luther King Jr. Com., 1989—98. Rep. Walpole (Mass.) Town Hall Meeting, 1977—82; vol. Friends of Wrentham; treas. CAMY 5K Run, DAVID 5K Walk Race. Mem.: APA (assoc.). Avocations: theater, reading, music, travel.

HUNTE, BERYL ELEANOR, mathematics educator, consultant; b. N.Y.C. BA, CUNY-Hunter Coll., 1947; MA, Columbia U., 1948; PhD, NYU, 1965. Instr. math. So. U., Baton Rouge, 1948-51; tchr. math. Bloomfield (N.J.) H.S., 1951-57; tchr. maths. Friends Sem., N.Y.C., 1957-62; asst. prof. maths. Rockland C.C., Suffern, N.Y., 1962-63; instr. maths., supr. tchr. trainees NYU, N.Y.C., 1964; chmn. dept. math. Borough of Manhattan C.C., N.Y.C., 1964-67, 70-73, prof. maths., 1970-95, prof. maths. emerita, 1996, acting dean students, 1985-87, acting dean acad. affairs, 1987-88; dean for spl. projects CUNY, 1988-89. Assoc. U. Seminar on Higher Edn., Columbia U., N.Y.C., 1989-95. Author: (with others) (textbook) Mathematics Through Statistics, 1973. NSF fellow, summer 1960, 1963-64, Chancellor's Faculty fellow CUNY, 1980. Mem. N.Y. Acad. Scis., Am. Math. Soc., CUNY Acad. for Humanities and Scis. (bd. dirs. 1991—, first v.p. 1994—), UN Assn. N.Y.C. (bd. dirs., sec. 1980-86). Avocations: opera, concerts, ballet, bridge.

HUNTEN, DONALD MOUNT, planetary scientist, educator; b. Montreal, Mar. 1, 1925; came to U.S., 1963, naturalized, 1979; s. Kenneth William and Winnifred Binnmore (Mount) H.; m. Isobel Ann Rubenstein, Dec. 28, 1949 (div. Apr. 1995); children: Keith Atherton, Mark Ross; m. Ann Louise Sprague, May 21, 1995. B.Sc., U. Western Ont., 1946; PhD, McGill U., 1950. From research asso. to prof. physics U. Sask. (Can.), Saskatoon, 1950-63; physicist Kitt Peak Nat. Obs., Tucson, 1963-77; sci. adv. to asso. adminstr. for space sci. NASA, Washington, 1976-77; prof. planetary scis. U. Ariz., Tucson, 1977-88, Regents prof., 1988—. Cons. NASA, 1964—. Author: Introduction to Electronics, 1964; (with J.W. Chamberlain) Theory of Planetary Atmospheres, 1987; contbr. articles to profl. jours. Recipient Pub. Svc. medal NASA, 1977, 85,96, medal for exceptional sci. achievement, 1980, Space Sci. award Com. on Space Rsch., 2000. Mem.: AAAS, Can. Assn. Physicists (editor 1961—63), Royal Soc. Can., Nat. Acad. Scis., Internat. Assn. Geomagnetism and Aeronomy, Internat. Union Geodesy and Geophysics, Internat. Astron. Union, Am. Astron. Soc. (chmn. divsn. planetary scis. 1977), Am. Geophys. Union (John Adam Fleming medal 1998), Am. Phys. Soc., Cosmos Club (Washington), Explorers Club. Home: 3445 W Foxes Den Dr Tucson AZ 85745-5102 Office: U Ariz Dept Planetary Scis Tucson AZ 85721-0001

HUNTER, ALBERT DALE, sociology educator, poet; b. Jamestown, N.Y., Mar. 4, 1942; s. Leland Roy and Emma Delight (Blanchard) Hunter; m. Ann Elizabeth Grice, Dec. 21, 1961 (div.); children: Allyson Lee, Andrew David; m. Renee Denise Weber, Mar. 17, 1990; children: Christian Devin, Adam McKeagan. BA, Cornell U., 1964; MA, U. Chgo., 1967, PhD, 1970. Lectr. U. Chgo., 1967—68; asst. prof. sociology Wesleyan U., Middletown, Conn., 1968—71; assoc. prof. sociology U. Rochester, NY, 1971—76; prof. sociology Northwestern U., Evanston, Ill., 1976—. Cons. City of Atlanta, 1973, Inst. Man and Sci., Renseelerville, NY, 1974, EPA/CDC, Love Canal, NY, 1980; vis. fellow Yale U., 1980, London Sch. Econ., 1990, U. Edinburgh, 1998. Author: Symbolic Communities, 1974, The Rhetoric of Social Research, 1990; co-author: Multi-method Research, 1989. Commr. City Plan Commn., Evanston, 2001—. Mem.: Am. Sociol. Assn. (chair cmty. sect. 1978—80). Home: 1040 Elmwood Ave Evanston IL 60202 Office: Northwestern U 1810 Chicago Ave Evanston IL 60202

HUNTER, ALLISON MARIE, web site designer; b. Summit, NJ, Dec. 15, 1967; d. William Arthur and Katherine Hall Hunter; m. Cary Eugene Wolfe, June 1, 2002. MFA, Rensselaer Poly. Inst., Troy, NY, 1995—97; MFA diploma (equiv. to MFA), Ecole Cantonale d'Art de Lausanne, Lausanne, Switzerland, 1987—90. French Eurocentre, 1987. Web designer (self-employed) Allison Hunter Web Design, LLC, Albany, NY, 2002—; curatorial asst. Tang Tchg. Mus. and Art Gallery, Saratoga Springs, 2001—02; lectr. Dept. of Art, Rensselaer Poly. Inst., Troy, NY, 2000—01; new media specialist Dept. of Mktg. and Media Rels., Rensselaer Poly. Inst., Troy, NY, 1999—2000. Artist com. mem. Arts Ctr. of the Capital Region, Troy, NY, 1998—2003. Author: (article) Sculpture Mag., article for how design magazine, wrote 2 articles for www.ebr.com. Recipient Artist in Residence, Banff Ctr. for the Arts, Banff, Alta., Can., 1997, Ctr. for Metamedia, Plasy, Czech Republic, 1998, Europos Parkas, Vilnius, Lithuania, 1999, Open-Air Art Mus., Pedvale, Latvia, 2001-02, Purchase Prize, U. at Albany Art Mus., Albany, NY, 2002, Artist in Residence, Pirkkala Sculpture Symposium 03, Pirkkala, Finland, 2003; fellow Grad. Fellowship, U. at Albany, 1998; grantee SOS, NYFA, 1999-2003. Mem.: Albany-Colonie Chamber of Commerce, Coll. Art Assn., Graphic Artists Guild.

HUNTER, BARBARA WAY, public relations consultant; b. Westport, N.Y., July 14, 1927; d. Walter Denslow and Hilda (Greenawalt) Way; m. Austin F. Hunter, Jan. 24, 1953; children: Kimberley, Victoria. BA, Cornell U., 1949. Assoc. editor Topics Pub. Co., N.Y.C., 1949-51; publicist Nat. Dairy Product Corp., N.Y.C., 1951-53; account exec. Sally Dickson Assn., 1953-56; assoc. D-A-Y Pub. Relations (div. Ogilvy & Mather Co.), N.Y.C., 1964-70, exec. v.p., 1970-84, pres., 1984-89, Hunter & Assocs., Inc., 1989-97, chmn., 1997-2000. Bd. dirs. Mr. Steak Inc., Denver, Great River Arts Inst. Trustee Cornell U., Ithaca, N.Y., 1980-85; life mem. Cornell U. Coun.; bd. dirs. Point O'Woods Assn., Fire Island, N.Y., 1980-87, 2002—, pres., 2003—. Recipient Sparkplug award Internat. Foodservice Mfrs. Assn., 1970, Matrix award N.Y. Women in Communications Inc., 1980, Entrepreneurial Woman award Women Bus. Owners, 1981, Nat. Headliner award Women in Communications Inc., 1984. Fellow Pub. Rels. Soc. Am. (pres. 1984, pres.-elect 1983, treas. 1982, pres. N.Y. chpt. 1980, Nat. Gold Anvil award 1993); mem. Found. Pub. Rels. Rsch. and Edn. (trustee 1982, 84), Walpole Hist. Soc. (bd. dirs. 2002-), Cornell Club of N.Y., The Club at Point O'Woods. also: 31 Wentworth Rd Walpole NH 03608

HUNTER, BEATRICE TRUM, editor; b. N.Y.C., Dec. 16, 1918; d. Gabriel and Martha (Engle) T.; widowed. BA, Bklyn. Coll., 1940; MA, Columbia U., 1942. Tchr. N.J. Pub. Schs., Bellevue, Newark, 1940-45, N.Y.C. Pub. Schs., 1945-55; food editor Consumers' Rsch. Mag., 1975—. Author: The Natural Foods Cookbook, 1961, Gardening Without Poisons, 1964, Consumer Beware!, 1971, Food Additives and Your Health, 1972, The Natural Foods Primer, 1972, The Baking Sampler, 1972, Yogurt, Kefir and Other Milk Cultures, 1973, Fermented Foods and Beverages, 1973, Beatrice Trum Hunter's Favorite Natural Foods, 1974, Golden Harvest Kitchens, 1974, Food and Your Health, 1974, The Mirage of Safety, 1975, The Great Nutrition Robbery, 1978, The Sugar Primer, 1979, How Safe is the Food in Your Kitchen, 1981, The Sugar Trap and How to Avoid It, 1982, Wheat, Miller and Other Grains, 1982, Brewer's Yeast, Wheat Germ and Other High Power Foods, 1982, Gluten Intolerance, 1987, Grain Power, 1994, others; co-author: (chpts.) The Healthy School Handbook, 1995, Cambridge History of Food, 2000; author: (book) Food and Your Health, 2003, Water and Your Health, 2003. Recipient Jonathan Forman award, Soc. Clin. Ecology, 1980, Lifetime Achievement award, Nat. Nutrition Foods Assn., 2001. Mem.: Human Ecology Action League (bd. dirs. 1972—), Weston A. Price Found. (hon.), Internat. Coll. Applied Nutrition (hon.), Environ. Health Care Orgn. (hon.), Price Pottenger Nutrition Found. (hon.), Am. Acad. Environ. Medicine (hon.). Avocations: ice crystal photography, traveling. Home and Office: 243 Falls Rd Deering NH 03244-6302

HUNTER, BEVERLY CLAIRE, research scientist, educator; b. Pitts., Apr. 19, 1941; d. Eldon Clare and Ethel Mae (Kamer) Roberts m. Harold G. Hunter, Jan. 7, 1966; children: Cynthia Claire, Gregory Shawn. BA cum laude (Nat. Merit scholar), U. Pitts., 1963. Computer programmer U.S. Navy, 1964-65; systems engr. IBM Corp., 1965-66; dir. instructional programming Human Resources Rsch. Orgn., Alexandria, Va., 1966-68, sr. staff scientist, 1970-87; staff scientist Matrix Rsch., Alexandria, 1969; lead scientist BBN Corp., 1993-98; scientist Boston Coll., 1998-99; pres. Piedmont Rsch. Inst., Amissville, Va., 1999—. Cons. U.S. Congress, U.S. Office Edn., Bell Labs., Telenet Comms.: pres. Targeted Learning Corp., 1983-89; adj. prof. U. San Francisco, 1985-86; v.p. Piedmont Rsch. Ctr., 1979-80; peer reviewer, NSF, program mgr. rsch. on tchg. and learning, 1989-93. Co-author: Learning Alternatives in U.S. Education: Where Student and Computer Meet, 1975, Computer Literacy, 1982; Author: My Students Use Computers, 1984 Guide to Learning Resources for Users of IBM Personal Computers, Scholastic U.S. History Data Bases, 1985, Scholastic U.S. Government Data Bases, 1985, Scholastic Life Science Data Bases, 1985, Scholastic Physical Sciences Data Bases, 1985, Scholastic World Geography Data Bases, 1986, Scholastic Poetry and Mythology Data Bases, 1986, Scholastic Literature Data Bases, 1986, Scholastic Constitution Then and Now Data Files, 1987, Scholastic Weather and Climate Data Files, 1987, Working with the U.S. Congress, 1988, Online Searching in the Curriculum, 1989; Scientists at Work hypermedia data base; editor Edn. and Computing Internat. Jour.; contbr. articles to publs. Grantee, N.S.F., 1979—2002. Mem.: Rappanhannock League Environ. Protection (bd. dirs.), Nature Conservancy, Assn. Computing Machinery. Home: 130 Mossie Ln Amissville VA 20106-4152 Office: Piedmont Rsch Inst 130 Mossie Ln Amissville VA 20106-4152

HUNTER, BILLIE MARIE, social worker, educator; b. Dallas, Aug. 10, 1936; d. Alvis W. and Margie B. (Hall) Lindsey; m. E. Royce Hunter, Aug. 30, 1955 (dec. Apr. 1999); children: Gina Marie, Lindsey Royce(dec.), Hollianne. BA, U. Sci. and Arts in Okla., Chickasha, 1980; MSW, U. Okla, 1983. Lic. clin. social worker, Okla. Realtor, OK, 1969-80; social worker Dept. Human Svcs., Ct. Related and Community Svcs., Anadarko, Norman, OK, 1980-85; therapist Cen. Okla. Community Mental Health Ctr., Norman, 1985-86; program dir. Esteem Counseling Ctr. Tulsa Psychiatric Ctr., 1986-88; program mgr. eating disorders unit Hillcrest Hosp., Tulsa, 1988-89; social worker/therapist Sigonella Naval Air Sta., Italy, 1989-92; familty advocacy rep. Family Svc. Ctr. Naval Surface Warfare Ctr., Dahlgren, Va., 1992-93; dist. coord. Children's Initiative Network Century Healthcare, Inc., Tulsa, 1993-96; mgr. family advocacy treatment Altus Air Force Base, Okla., 1996-97; dir. Kennedy Girls Home, Hobart, Okla., 1997-99; retired, 1999; part-time in home/cmty. based therapist NorthCare, Inc., Norman, 2001—. Tchr. Tulsa Jr. Coll., 1986-87; adj. asst. prof. in social work U. Okla., 1994-95. Vol. Tulsa chpt. ARC, 1987-88; mem. Norman Cmty. Choral Soc. Mem.: Norman Newcomers Club (pres. 2002—03). Avocations: travel, reading mysteries/cryptograms, word puzzles, cooking, interior decorating.

HUNTER, BRINCA JO, education specialist; b. Athens, Ga., Feb. 24, 1940; d. Mattie Maude Patton; m. Levis Eugene Hunter, May 6, 1961 (dec. 1994); children: Daphne M. Inman, Jason L. BS in Spl. Edn., U. Akron, 1977, MS in Ednl. Supervision, 1992; PhD in Ministry, Shalom Sem., 1999. Instr. Medina (Ohio) County Bd. Mental Retardation and Devel. Disabilities, 1969-88, edn. specialist, 1988-99, ret., 1999; registrar Springs of Life Bible Coll. and Shalom Sem., 1999—. Mem. Medina City Citizens Adv. Com., 1978-84; bd. dirs. YWCA, Medina, 1978-84, Springs of Life Min., fin. sec. 2d Bapt. Ch., Medina, 1978-82. Mem. ASCD, AAUW, Am. Assn. Mental Retardation, Profl. Assn. Retardation (gen. bd. dirs. 1996—, adult svcs. bd. 1995—, scholar 1982). Democrat. Avocations: crafts, reading. Home: 226 N Harmony St Medina OH 44256-1938

HUNTER, BROTHER EAGAN (DONALD J. HUNTER), retired education educator; b. Cedar Rapids, Iowa, June 9, 1922; s. John William and Nellie (Connors) H. BA, U. Iowa, 1944; MEd, U. Tex., 1971. Tchr. Churchill Jr. H.S., Galesburg, Ill., 1944-45, Ctrl. Cath. H.S., South Bend, Ind., 1946-47, Msgr. Coyle H.S., Taunton, Mass., 1947-50; tchr., vice prin., dir. studies Notre Dame H.S., Sherman Oaks, Calif., 1950-61, prin., 1978-80; tchr., vice prin., dir. studies St. Francis H.S., Mountain View, Calif., 1961-64, prin., 1964-70, Notre Dame H.S., Biloxi, Miss., 1971-77; mem. staff St. Edward's U., Austin, 1977-78, prof. edn., 1980-2000. Pres. Archdiocese of L.A. English Com., 1951-53, Guidance Coun., 1955-60; cons. So. Assn. Colls. and Schs., 1974-77, State of Miss., Dept. Edn., 1974-77; reg. advisor Nat. Cath. Edn. Assn., Secondary Sch. Dept., 1974-77, reg. cons., 1977-80; del. Gov.'s Conf. on Edn., Miss., 1975; bd. trustees St. Edward's U., Austin, 1978-80; mem. liturgical commn. Diocese of Austin, 1980-88, coun. of religious, 1983, adminstrv. coun. mem., 1986-88; liaison rep. Intercollegiate Studies Inst., Inc., 1983-98, Tex. Elem. Prins. and Suprs. Assn., 1984-93; mem. sch. bd. St. Michael's Cath. Acad., Austin, 1984-85; mem. state selection com. U.S. Senate Youth Program, 1986; del. Study Mission to People's Rep. of China, 1987; liaison rep. Tex. Acad. Skills Project, 1988-89; del. Nat. Cath. Edn. Assn.'s Reg. Congress for Tex., Ark., Okla., N.Mex. from Diocese of Austin, 1991; mem. adv. com. Diocese of Austin, Tex., 2002—, com. cons. Contbr. numerous articles to profl. jours. Dir. Assocs. of Holy Cross in Prayer, 2000—. Recipient Disting. Profl. Svc. award Nat. Assn. Sec. Sch. Prins., 1978, Ednl. Leadership-Austin award St. Michael's Acad., 1992, Selective Service citations Pres. U.S., 1975. Home and Office: Saint Edward's Univ 3001 S Congress Ave Austin TX 78704-6425 E-mail: eagenh@admin.stedwards.edu.

HUNTER, BUDDY D. holding company executive; b. Wilsontown, Mo., Feb. 28, 1930; s. Harold H. and Marie (Miller) H.; (div.); children— Bruce, Beverly, Brenda, Brett BS, Northeast Mo. State U., 1950. Pres. S.P. Wright & Co., Springfield, Ill., 1956-69; chmn. bd., pres., chief exec. officer AMEDCO Inc., St. Louis, 1969-86; chmn. Huntco Inc., Chesterfield, Mo., 1986—. Bd. dirs. Mark Twain BancShares, St. Louis, Svc. Corp. Internat., Houston, Cash Am. Investments, Ft. Worth, numerous other cos. Bd. dirs. Meml. Med. Ctr.; exec. adv. council Breech Sch. Bus., Drury Coll., Springfield, Mo. Capt. USAF, 1951-56 Mem. Masons, Shriners. Avocations: tennis; skiing; jogging. Office: Huntco Inc 14323 S Outer 40 Dr #600N Chesterfield MO 63017-5747

HUNTER, BYNUM MERRITT, lawyer; b. Greensboro, N.C., June 13, 1925; s. Hill McIver and Annie (Merritt) H.; m. Ann Fulenwider, June 22, 1957 (div. 1968); children: Ann Shirley, Mary Parker; m. Mary Lane Yancey, Aug. 7, 1969 (div. 1978); m. Mary Bonneau McElveen, June 13, 1980; 1 son, Bynum Jr. AB, U. N.C., 1945, JD, 1949. Bar: N.C. 1949. Ptnr. Smith & Moore LLP. Served with USNR, 1943-46, 51-53. Fellow Am. Coll. Trial Lawyers, Am. Bar Found. (life mem.); mem. ABA, Internat. Assn. Def. Counsel, Am. Judicature Soc., Greensboro Bar Assn. (pres. 1965-66) 4th Cir. Jud. Conf., N.C. Bar Assn., Zeta Psi, Phi Delta Phi. Clubs: Rotary. Home: 710 Country Club Dr Greensboro NC 27408-5714 Office: Smith & Moore LLP Ste 1400 PO Box 21927 300 N Green St Greensboro NC 27420-1927 E-mail: bynum.hunter@smithmoorelaw.com.

HUNTER, CARL GLENN, retired commissioner; b. Little Rock, Aug. 30, 1923; s. Robert Weir and Jewel Monette Hunter; m. Mary Anid Scott, Jan. 20, 1945; children: Carl Scott, David Albert. BS in Agr., U. Ark., 1945. Cert. hon. master gardener U. Ark. Ext. Svc., biologist The Wildlife Soc., instr. Ark. Law Enforcement Acad., Prescott Coll., ARiz., U. Ark. Little Rock. Asst. chief game mgmt. Ark. Game and Fish Commn., Little Rock, 1942—57, asst. dir., 1977—87; gen. mgr. Wingmead Plantation, Stuttgart, Ark., 1957—77. Agt., author Ozark Soc. Found., Little Rock, 1984—2001; horticulturist Wildflowers of Ark., Little Rock, 1987—2001; rep. Ark. Conservation Coalition, Little Rock, 1990—2001. Author: Wildflowers of Arkansas, 1984, Trees, Shrubs & Vines of Arkansas, 1989, This Cup, 1991, Autumn Leaves & Winter Berries in Arkansas, 1995, The Piano Player, 1997, Poems & Pieces, 2003; contbr. articles to profl. jours. Named Outstanding Alum, U. Ark., 1998. Mem.: Ozark Soc., Ark. Native Plant Soc. Avocations: photography, botany, gardening, landscaping, music. Home: 18 Pointer Dr Alexander AR 72002 Office: Wildflowers of Ark 18 Pointer Dr Alexander AR 72002

HUNTER, DANIEL CLYDE, JR., retired surgeon, educator; b. Ephraim, Utah, 1922; s. Daniel C. Sr. and Mary Gwyneth (Evans) H.; m. Mary Margaret Webb, June 4, 1945; children: Daniel III, Mary Kathryn, David, Karen, Christopher, Susan, Rebecca, Scott, Curtis, Joseph. BA, U. Utah, 1943, MD, 1946; pathologist, U. Mich., 1951, surgeon, 1953. Diplomate Am. Bd. Surgery. Intern, resident U. Mich. Hosp., Ann Arbor, 1946-48, 50-51, fellow, 1951-53, asst. prof. surgery, 1953-60; surgeon McKay Dee Hosp., Ogden, Utah, 1960-99; ret., 1999—. Clin. asst. prof. surgery U. Utah, 1960-70. Fellow ACS; mem. Am. Coll. Occupl. and Environ. Medicine, Soc. for Surgery of Alimentary Tract, Western Surg. Assn., Utah State Med. Soc., Ogden Surg. Soc., Soc. Bariatric Surgeons.

HUNTER, DAVID GEORGE, physician, researcher; b. Boston, Oct. 28, 1957; s. Donald George and Marie Ann Hunter; m. Michele Trucksis, Oct. 7, 1990; children: Adam J., Luke T. BSEE, Rice U., 1979; PhD in Cell Biology, Baylor Coll. Medicine, 1984, MD, 1987. Diplomate Am. Bd. Ophthalmology. Intern Framingham (Mass.) Union Hosp., 1987; resident in ophthalmology Mass. Eye & Ear Infirmary, Harvard Med. Sch., Boston, 1988-91; assoc. prof. ophthalmology and biomed. engring. Johns Hopkins U., Balt., 1991—2002, mentor biomed. engring. grad. students; chair ophthalmology Children's Hosp., Boston, 2002—. Author: Last Minute Optics, 1996; inventor, patentee in field; contbr. articles to profl. jours. Recipient Richard S. Ross Clinican Scientist award Johns Hopkins U., Young Investigator award Whitaker Found., Lew R. Wasserman Merit award Rsch. to Prevent Blindness. Fellow Am. Acad. Ophthalmology; mem. IEEE, Am. Assn. for Pediat. Ophthalmology and Strabismus, Assn. for Rsch. in Vision and Ophthalmology. Democrat. Home: 84 Draper Rd Wayland MA 01778- Office: Children's Hosp Boston Ophthalmology-Fegan 4 300 Longwood Ave Boston MA 02115 E-mail: hunterdgh1@hotmail.com.

HUNTER, DONALD FORREST, lawyer; b. Mpls., Jan. 30, 1934; s. Earl Harvey and Ruby Cecilia (Lagerson) H.; m. Marlys Ann Zilge; Jeffrey, Cheri, Kathryn. BA, U. Minn., 1961, JD, 1963. Bar: Minn. 1963, U.S. Dist. Ct. Minn. 1965, U.S. Ct. Appeals (8th cir.) 1965, Ill. 1977, U.S. Dist. Ct. (no. dist.) Ill. 1991, U.S. Supreme Ct. 1986. Assoc., then ptnr. Gislason, Dosland, Hunter & Malecki, New Ulm, Minn., 1963-76; exec. v.p., sec., gen. counsel Wirtz Prodn. Ltd. Ice Follies/Holiday on Ice, Chgo., 1976-79; ptnr. Gislason, Dosland, Hunter & Malecki, Mpls., 1979-99; of counsel Gislason & Hunter, 1999—. Chmn. bd. dirs. Chgo. Milw. Corp., 1977-81; pres. Chgo. Milw. R.R., 1977-81; bd. dirs. First Security Bank, Chgo.; bd. dirs., officer First Security Bancorp, Inc., Chgo., 1993—; bd. dirs., sec. Wirtz Corp., Chgo. Blackhawk Hockey Team and related cos. Fellow Am. Coll. Trial Lawyers; mem. ABA, Am. Judicature Soc., Minn. Bar Assn. (bd. of govs. 1973-76), 5th Dist. Bar Assn. (pres. 1971-72), Hennepin County Bar Assn., Minn. Def. Lawyers Assn. (bd. dirs. 1976), Internat. Assn. Ins. Counsel, U.S. Supreme Ct. Hist. Assn. Office: Gislason & Hunter PO Box 5297 9900 Bren Rd E Ste 215E Hopkins MN 55343-9666

HUNTER, DOUGLAS LEE, ministry executive, former elevator executive; b. Greeley, Colo., May 3, 1948; s. Delmer Eural and Helen Converse (Haines) H.; m. Janet Lee Snook, May 26, 1970; children: Darin Douglas, Joel Christopher, Eric Andrew, Jennifer Lee. BA, U. Sioux Falls, 1979; postgrad., N.Am. Bapt. Sem., Sioux Falls, S.D., 1977-79. Elevator constructor Carter Elevator Co., Inc., Sioux Falls, 1971-72, rep., 1972-74, contr., 1974-78, sec.-treas., 1978-82, v.p., 1982-87, pres., 1987-93; ptnr. Lifters Ltd., Sioux Falls, 1984-90, CEO, 1987-96; v.p. Fellowship or Cos. Christ, Internat., 1994-97; pres. Media Asia, 1997-99; Atlanta regional dir. Christian Leadership Concepts, 1999-2000; exec. Ravi Zacharias Internat. Min., 2000—. Bd. dirs. Home Fed. Savs. Bank, HF Fin. Corp.; U.S. del. Forum Bus. in Vietnam, Ho Chi Minh City, 1993; guest lectr. Nat. Econs. U., Hanoi, Vietnam, 1995. Mem. gen. bd. Christian Ch., Indpls., 1984-88; mem. regional bd. Christian Ch. in the Upper Midwest, Des Moines, 1985-87; bd. dirs. Glory House, Sioux Falls, 1983-86; leader Bible Study Fellowship, Sioux Falls, 1981-92; vice chmn. Greater Sioux Empire Billy Graham Crusade, 1986-87; mem. internat. bd. dirs. Fellowship of Cos. for Christ Internat., 1993-95; bd. dirs. Am. Mongolia Found., 1992-99; active S.D. Trade Del. to Mongolia, 1993-99; trustee N.Am. Bapt. Sem., 1989-2001; bd. dirs. Providence Christian Acad., 1998—2002, chmn., 1999—2002. Named Outstanding Young Religious Leader Sioux Falls Jaycees, 1974. Mem. S.D. Family Bus. Coun., Sen. Larry Pressler's Small Bus. Adv. Com., Nat. Assn. Elevator Contrs., Nat. Assn. Elevator Safety Authorities, Constrn. Specifications Inst., Christian Businessmen's Com. U.S., Sioux Falls C. of C. Republican. Avocations: golf, tennis, reading, music. Home: 695 Wyndham Place Cir Lawrenceville GA 30044-3629 Office: RZIM Ste 250 4275 Peachtree Corners Cir Norcross GA 30092 E-mail: doug.hunter@rzim.org.

HUNTER, DUNCAN LEE, congressman; b. Riverside, Calif., May 31, 1948; m. Lynne Layh, 1973; children: Robert Samuel, Duncan Duane. JD, Western State U., 1976. Bar: Calif. 1976. Pvt. practice, San Diego; mem. U.S. Congress from 52nd Calif. dist., 1981—; mem. armed svcs. com. With U.S. Army, 1969-71, Vietnam. Decorated Air medal, bronze star. Mem. Navy League. Republican. Baptist.*

HUNTER, DURANT ADAMS, executive search company executive; b. North Adams, Mass., Nov. 25, 1948; s. Richard Andrew and Lucy (Adams) H.; m. Sara Hoagland, June 10, 1978; children: John, Abigail. AB, U. N.C., 1971; MPA, George Washington U., 1973. Staff asst. to Congressman Silvio O. Conte U.S. Ho. of Reps., Washington, 1971-72; program dir. Internat. Mgmt. and Devel. Inst., Washington, 1973-74; asst. v.p. J.P. Morgan Co., N.Y.C., 1974-81; v.p., COO James Hunter Machine Co., North Adams, 1981-83; exec. v.p. HM Internat., Wellesley, Mass., 1983-85; mng. dir. Boyden Internat., Boston, 1985-89; ptnr. Gardiner Stone Hunter Internat., Boston, 1989-92; pres., CEO Pendleton James Assocs. Inc., Boston, 1992-2000; CEO Whitehead Mann Inc., 2000—. Mem. Wellesley Planning Bd., 1983-86; bd. dirs. Boys and Girls Clubs, Boston, 1988—, Wide Horizons Children's Svcs., Waltham, Mass., 1989—, Mass. Cultural Coun.; trustee The Wang Ctr. for the Performing Arts, Boston, 1995—, The Fessenden Sch., Newton, Mass., 2000-2003; bd. dirs. Mass. Cultural Coun. Mem.: Hole-in-the-Wall Golf Club (Naples, Fla.), Ekwanok Country Club (Manchester, Vt.), Royal Automobile Club (London), The Country Club (Brookline, Mass.), Univ. Club (N.Y.C.), Bus. Assoc. Club (pres. 1989). Home: 153 Ridgeway Rd Weston MA 02493-2724 Office: 1 International Pl Boston MA 02110-2602

HUNTER, EARLE LESLIE, III, retired professional association executive; b. Juneau, Alaska, Nov. 23, 1929; s. Earle and Mary Uinta (Kirk) H.; m. Helen Doreen Dawson, Jan. 19, 1954; children: Barbara, James, Robert. BS, Ill. Coll. Optometry, Chgo., 1956, OD, 1957, DOS, 1988, New Eng. Coll. Optometry, 1995. Practice optometry, Juneau, 1957-59, McMinnville, Oreg., 1959-71; dir. clinics Pacific U., Forest Grove, Oreg., 1971-74; dir. primary care Am. Optometric Assn., St. Louis, 1974-78, asst. exec. dir., 1978-84, interim exec. dir., 1984-85, dep. exec. dir., 1985-87, exec. dir., 1987-95; ret., 1995—99, spl. asst. to the dean U. Mo. Sch. Optometry, 1999-2001. Sec. Z.80 com. Am. Nat. Stds. Inst., 1974-95. Contbr. articles to profl. jours. County chmn. various gubernatorial campaigns; vice chmn. Oreg. Health Commn., 1971-74. Named Optometrist of Yr., Oreg. Optometric Assn., 1971, Jr. Citizen of Yr., Jaycees, McMinnville, 1961. Fellow APHA, Am. Acad. Optometry; mem. Optical Soc. Am., Am. Soc. Assn. Execs. (com. 1981-93), St. Louis Soc. Assn. Execs. (pres. 1983-84), U.S. C. of C. (assn. com.), Tomb and Key, Univ. Club (St. Louis), Masons, Elks, Beta Sigma Kappa. Republican. Episcopalian. Avocations: sailing, golf. Home: 213 Orchard Ave Saint Louis MO 63119-2523

HUNTER, ELMO BOLTON, federal judge; b. St. Louis, Oct. 23, 1915; s. David Riley and Della (Bolton) H.; m. Shirley Arnold, Apr. 5, 1952; 1 child, Nancy Ann (Mrs. Ray Lee Hunt). AB, U. Mo., 1936, LLB, 1938; Cook Grad. fellow, U. Mich., 1941; PhD (hon.), Coll. of Ozarks, 1988. Bar: Mo. 1938. Pvt. practice, Kansas City, 1938-45; sr. asst. city counselor, 1939-40; ptnr. Sebree, Shook, Hardy and Hunter, 1945-51; state circuit judge Mo., 1951-57; Mo. appellate judge, 1957-65; judge U.S. Dist. Ct., Kansas City, Mo., 1965—97, now sr. judge. Instr. law U. Mo., 1952-62; mem. jud. selection Elmo B. Hunter Citizens Ctr., Am. Judicature Soc. Contbr. articles to profl. jours. Mem. Bd. Police Commrs., 1949-51; Trustee Kansas City U., Coll. of Ozarks; fellow William Rockhill Nelson Gallery Art. 1st lt. M.I., AUS, 1943-46. Recipient 1st Ann. Law Day award U. Mo., 1964, Charles E. Whittaker award, 1994, SAR Law Enforcement Commendation medal, 1994, citation of Merit Mo. Law Sch., 1996. Fellow ABA; mem. Fed., Mo. bar assns., Jud. Conf. U.S. (mem. long range planning com., chmn. ct. adminstrn. com.), Am. Judicature Soc. (bd. govs., mem. exec. com., pres., chmn. bd., Devitt Disting. Svc. to Justice award 1987), Acad. Mo. Squires, Order of Coif, Phi Beta Kappa, Phi Delta Phi. Presbyterian (elder).

HUNTER, EVAN (ED MC BAIN), author; b. N.Y.C., Oct. 15, 1926; s. Charles F. and Marie (Coppola) Lombino; m. Anita Melnick, Oct. 17, 1949 (div.); children: Ted, Mark, Richard; m. Mary Vann Finley, June 1973 (div.); 1 stepdau., Amanda Eve Finley; m. Dragica Dimitrijevic, 1997. Student, Cooper Union, 1943-44; BA, Hunter Coll., 1950. Author: The Blackboard Jungle, 1954, Second Ending, 1956, Strangers When We Meet, 1958, A Matter of Conviction, 1959, The Remarkable Harry, 1960, The Wonderful Button, 1961, Mothers and Daughters, 1961, Happy New Year, Herbie, 1963, Buddwing, 1964, The Paper Dragon, 1966, A Horse's Head, 1967, Last Summer, 1968, Sons, 1969, Nobody Knew They Were There, 1971, Every Little Crook and Nanny, The Easter Man, 1972, Come Winter, 1973, Streets of Gold, 1974, The Chisholms, 1976, Me and Mr. Stenner, 1977, Walk Proud, 1979, Love, Dad, 1981, Far from the Sea, 1983, Lizzie, 1984, Criminal Conversation, 1994, Privileged Conversation, 1996, Candyland, 2001, The Moment She Was Gone, 2002; also mystery novels under pseudonym Ed McBain: The Pusher, Cop Hater, The Mugger, 1956; The Con Man, 1957, Killer's Choice, 1957, Killer's Payoff, Lady Killer, 1958, Killer's Wedge, 'Til Death, King's Ransom, 1959, Give the Boys a Great Big Hand, The Heckler, See Them Die, 1960, Lady, Lady, I Did It, 1961, The Empty Hours, Like Love, 1962, Ten Plus One, 1963, Ax, 1964, The Sentries, 1965, He Who Hesitates, Doll, 1965, Eighty Million Eyes, 1966, Fuzz, 1968, Shotgun, 1969, Jigsaw, 1970, Hail, Hail, the Gang's All Here, 1971, Sadie When She Died, Let's Hear It for the Deaf Man, 1972, Hail to the Chief, 1973, Bread, 1974, Where There's Smoke, 1975, Blood Relatives, 1975, So Long As You Both Shall Live, 1976, Guns, 1976, Long Time No See, 1977, Goldilocks, 1978, Calypso, 1979, Ghosts, 1980, Rumpelstiltskin, 1981, Heat, 1981, Beauty and the Beast, Ice, 1983, Jack and the Beanstalk, 1984, Lightning, 1984, Snow White and Rose Red, 1985, Eight Black Horses, 1985, Cinderella, 1986, Another Part of the City, 1986, Poison, 1987, Puss in Boots, 1987, Tricks, 1987, McBain's Ladies, 1988, The House That Jack Built, 1988, Lullaby, 1989, McBain's Ladies, Too, 1989, Downtown, 1989, Vespers, 1990, Three Blind Mice, 1990, Widows, 1991, Kiss, 1992, Mary, Mary, 1993, Mischief, 1993, There Was a Little Girl, 1994, And All Through the House, 1994, Romance, 1995, Nocturne, 1997, The Big Bad City, 1999, The Last Dance, 2000, Money, Money, Money, 2001, Candyland, 2001, Fat Ollie's Book, 2003; writer screenplays: Strangers When We Meet, 1960, The Birds, 1962, Fuzz, 1972, Walk Proud, 1979, Dream West, 1986; stage plays: The Easter Man, 1964, The Conjuror, 1969. Served with USNR, 1944-46. Named Lit. Father of Year, 1961; recipient Profl. Achievement award Hunter Coll., 1981, Grand Master award Mystery Writers of Am., 1986, Diamond Dagger award, Brit. Crime Writers Assn., Frankfurt Original e-book award, best fiction, 2002. Mem. Phi Beta Kappa.

HUNTER, FLOYD DORE, lawyer; b. Alliance, Ohio, Apr. 18, 1934; s. William and Celeste (Dore) H.; m. Vanetta Elizabeth McFeely, June 15, 1957; children— Kevin, Vanetta E., Kent. B.S., U.S. Coast Guard Acad., 1956; J.D., George Washington U., 1964. Bar: U.S. Ct. Appeals (D.C. Cir.) 1964, U.S. Ct. Mil. Appeals 1967, U.S. Supreme Ct. 1968, Mass. 1973, U.S. Ct. Appeals (1st cir.) 1976. Commd. ensign U.S. Coast Guard, 1956, advanced through grades to comdr., 1969; ret., 1976. assoc. Hoch & Flanagan, P.C., 1976-79, prin., 1979-85; prin. Flanagan & Hunter, P.C., 1985—. Mem. Acton and Acton-Boxborough Regional Dist. Sch. Coms., 1978-84; selectman, Acton, 1984— . Mem. ABA (chmn. standing com. legal assistance for mil. personnel 1978-84, standing com. lawyer referral and info. service 1984—), Mass. Bar Assn., Boston Bar Assn., Maritime Law Assn. Home: 3 Foster St Acton MA 01720-5406 Office: 211 Congress St Boston MA 02110-2410

HUNTER, FORREST WALKER, lawyer; b. Arlington, Va., Jan. 25, 1950; s. Dallas Walker and Ann Arsell (Wheat) H.; m. Susan Gladys Zsamer, June 8, 1974; children: Andrew Chastain, Alison Christian. BA, U. Va., 1972; JD, Emory U., 1975. Bar: Ga. 1975, U.S. Dist. Ct. (no. dist.) Ga. 1978, U.S. Ct. Appeals (5th cir.) 1978, U.S. Ct. Appeals (11th cir.) 1981, U.S. Dist. Ct. (mid. dist.) Ga. 1982, U.S. Dist. Ct. (so. dist.) Ga. 1983, U.S. Ct. Appeals (6th cir.) 1988, U.S. Dist. Ct. (we. dist.) Mich. 1994, U.S. Ct. Appeals (7th cir.) 1996, U.S. Dist. Ct. (ea. dist.) Tex. 1999, U.S. Dist. Ct. (no. dist.) Ind. 2002. Atty. Office Chief Counsel IRS, Dept. Treasurey, Washington, 1975-77, sr. atty. Office. Regional Counsel Atlanta, 1977-81; assoc. Jones, Bird & Howell and Alston & Bird, Atlanta, 1981-85; ptnr. Alston & Bird, Atlanta, 1985—. Bd. dirs. Boys and Girls Clubs of Metro Atlanta, 1984. Mem. Am. Health Lawyers Assn., Ga. Acad. Hosp. Attys., Lawyers Club Atlanta, Atlanta Bar Assn., U. Va. Alumni Assn., Emory U. Alumni Assn. Office: Alston & Bird 1 Atlantic Ctr Atlanta GA 30309-3424

HUNTER, GARRETT BELL, investment banker; b. N.Y.C., Apr. 11, 1937; s. John W. and Helene (Bond Lipe) H.; m. Lynn M. Cowell, Oct. 6, 1962; children: Lee, Andrew, Sarah. AB in Philosphy, Brown U., 1960; MBA in Fin., NYU, 1965; postgrad., Stonier Grad. Sch. Banking, 1973. V.p. Midlantic Nat. Bank, Newark, 1960-73, Nat. State Bank, Elizabeth, N.J., 1973-77; sr. v.p. R.I. Hosp. Trust Nat. Bank, Providence, 1977-89; pres. Bus. Devel. Co. of R.I., 1989—. Bd. dirs. Lab-Volt, Farmingdale, N.J., Bus. Devel. Co. of R.I., Providence, R.I., Atlantek, Inc., Wakefield, R.I.; adv. bd. Andera Inc., Providence. Home: 150 Tamarack Dr East Greenwich RI 02818-2204 E-mail: ghunter@bdcri.com.

HUNTER, GEORGE GILL, III, religious studies educator; b. Louisville, June 25, 1938; s. George Gill Jr. and Barbara Deborah (Craig) H.; m. Charlotte Sooter Swor, June 12, 1967 (div. Jan. 1973); 1 child, Gill; m. Ella Fay Hunter, Jan. 6, 1975; children: Monica, Donald. BA, Fla. So. Coll., Lakeland, 1960; BD, Emory U., Atlanta, 1963; ThM, Princeton Theol. Sem., 1964; PhD, Northwestern U., Evanston, Ill., 1972. Ordained to ministry, Meth. Ch., 1965. Pastor First Meth. Ch., Dade City, Fla., 1964-65; staff Meth. Bd. Evangelism, Nashville, 1965-72; asst. prof. Perkins Sch. Theology, So. Meth. U., Dallas, 1972-77; asst. gen. sec. for evangelism United Meth. Bd. of Discipleship, Nashville, 1977-83; dean Sch. of World Mission and Evangelism Asbury Theol. Sem., Wilmore, Ky., 1983—2001, Disting. prof., 2001—. Founder Acad. for Evangelism, 1975—, pres., 1995-97. Author: The Contagious Congregation, 1979, Church Growth: Strategies that Work, 1980. To Spread the Power, 1987, How to Reach Secular People, 1992, Church for the Unchurched, 1996, The Celtic Way of Evangelism, 2000, Leading and Managing a Growing Church, 2000, Getting Serious About Outreach: Recovering Apostolic Ministry and Evangelism, 2003. Recipient The Philip award United Meth. Assn. of Evangelists, 1980. Mem. Am. Soc. for Church Growth (co-founder, pres. 1989, McGavran award 1996), Acad. for Evangelism (Finney award 2002), Mission Soc. for United Methodists, Internat. Sports Sci. Assn. Democrat. Avocation: weightlifting. Home: 94 Summertree Dr Nicholasville KY 40356 Office: Asbury Theological Sem Sch of World Mission/Evang Wilmore KY 40390 E-mail: george_hunter@asburyseminary.edu.

HUNTER, HARLEN CHARLES, orthopedic surgeon; b. Estherville, Iowa, Sept. 23, 1940; s. Roy Harold and Helen Iola (King) H.; m. JoAnn Wilson, June 30, 1962; children: Harlen Todd, Juliann Kristin. BA, Drake U., 1962; DO, Coll. Osteo. Med. and Surgery, Des Moines, 1967. Diplomate Am. Osteo. Bd. Orthop. Surgery, Am. Osteo. Acad. Sports Medicine. Intern Normandy Osteo. Hosp., St. Louis, 1967-68, resident in orthops., 1968-72, chmn. dept. orthops., 1976-77; founder Orthopedics and Sports Medicine, PC, Bedford, Ind. Founder, orthop. surgeon Mid-States Orthop. Sports Medicine Clinics of Am., Ltd. SPORTS Med. Ctrs., Chesterfield, Mo., Fairview Heights, Ill., Jerseyville, Ill., Herman, Mo., 1977-99, Hunter Trauma Team, 1988-92; founder, pres. Life Style Health Systems, 1992; assoc. prof. orthop. Kansas City Coll. Osteopathy, 1993; adj. prof. Lake Erie Coll. Osteo. Medicine, 1995—; mem. staff Normandy Osteopathic, 1972-90, Outpatient Surgery Ctr., St. Louis, 1990-99, Luth. Med. Ctr., 1989-99, St. Joe's of Kirkwood, 1990-99, Bedford Med. Ctr., Dunn Meml.; clin. instr. Kirksville Coll. Osteo. Medicine; orthop. cons., team physician to high schs.; pres. Health Specialists, Inc.; program dir. sports medicine Family Physicians, 1993, 94; sponsor, lectr. sports and occupl. emergency medicine, 1997—; host weekly TV program Raceology Weekly Spl. on Motorsports; mem. med. adv. bd. Mo. Athletic Activities Assn.; cons. sports medicine Sports St. Louis newspaper; founder Ann. Sports Medicine Clinic for Trainers and Coaches, 1 yr. fellowship in sports medicine; nat. lectr. various social, profl. orgns.; adj. clin. assoc. prof. Coll. Osteo. Surgery, Des Moines; orthop. surgeon Iowa State Boys Basketball Tournament, 1966-85; founder Mobile Sports Medicine Semi Truck, 1988, Hunter Sports Medicine Clinic, Belleville, Ill.; sponsor U.S. Biathalon Assn., 1989; staff photographer Ind. Motor Speedway, 1973—, Daytona Internat. Speedway, 1979-96; adv. bd. Motorsport Rsch. Group Human Performance Internat., Daytona Beach, Fla., 1990—; mem. Sports Medicine Commn. Ind. State Med. Assn. Co-author: Motorsports Medicine, 1992; host daily radio program Making a Difference, For Your Health; contbr. articles to profl. jours. Mem. adv. bd. Bedford Salvation Army. Recipient Clinic Spkr. award Iowa H.S. Baseball Coaches Assn., 1982, 83, Hall of Fame award Mo. Athletic Trainers Assn., 1987, Sibley Medallion award for outstanding svc. Lindenwood U., Ann. Outstanding Soccer Player of Yr. award Mo. Athletic Club, Hunter 100 Stock Car Race, Peveley, Mo., Bob Scott Photography award Indpls. Motor Speedway, 2002; named Businessman of Yr., Nat. Rep. Congl. Com., 2003; Harlen C. Hunter Sports Complex named in his honor Lindenwood U., St. Charles, Mo., 1988. Fellow Am. Coll. Osteo. Surgeons, Am. Osteo Acad. Orthops. (past chmn. com. on athletic injuries), Am. Osteo. Acad. Sports Medicine; mem. Am. Osteo. Assn., Mo. Assn. Osteo. Physicians and Surgeons (medallion award 1990), Am. Coll. Sports Medicine, Am. Orthop. Soc. Sports Medicine (del. sports medicine exch. program to China 1985), AMA, Am. Coll. Occupational Medicine, Ind. Med. Assn. (sports medicine com. 1999—), Ind. Osteo. Assn. (trustee 2003—), St. Louis Met. Med. Assn., Sports Car Club Am. (med. dir. pro racing 1989-91), World Congress Motorsport Scis., St. Louis Auto Racing Club (Amb. award 1989, 91), 500 Old Timers Club, The Butler Soc., Elks, Lions, Masons, Shriners. Republican. Methodist. Home: 604 Heltonville Rd E Bedford IN 47421-9250 Office: Ortho & Sports Medicine 2900 16th St Bedford IN 47421-3510

HUNTER, HERBERT ERWIN, aerospace engineer; b. Washington, June 11, 1934; s. Herbert C. and A. Paula (Dieterich) H.; m. Helen Louise Shelhorse, June 11, 1956 (div. 1978); children: Erwin, David, Shirley Black, Patricia Copeland, Linda Markiewicz; m. Jeanne Theresa Parent, Nov. 25, 1978; stepchildren: Richard Kinsella, William Kinsella, Katey McMahon, Philip Kinsella. BS in Aerospace Engring., U. Md., 1956; MS in Aerospace Engring., Calif. Inst. Tech., Pasadena, 1957, PhD in Aerospace Engring., 1960. Dept. mgr. AVCO Corp., Wilmington, Mass., 1963-73; pres., founder, chmn. bd. dirs. Adapt Svc. Corp., Reading, Mass., 1973-83; assoc. fellow Nichols Rsch. Corp., Huntsville, Ala., 1983-94; co-founder Applied Data Trends, Inc., Huntsville, 1994, pres., 1994-2000, pres. emeritus, 2000—, dir., 1994—. Dir. QPC, Inc., 2000—. Contbr. articles to Jour. Aerospace Scis., Jour. Math Physics, Jour. Climate Applied Meteorology, Jour. Atmospheric Ocean Tech. With USAF, 1960-63. Mem. AAAS, AIAA, Am. Meteorol. Soc., Soc. of Photo-Optical Instrumentation Engrs. Baptist. Home: 8912 Hogan Dr SE Huntsville AL 35802-3436 Office: Applied Data Trends Inc PO Box 4445 Huntsville AL 35815-4445 E-mail: herbhunter@aol.com.

HUNTER, HERBERT M. science educator; b. Harrisburg, Pa., Mar. 19, 1943; s. Maggie A. Hunter; m. Lovyenne D. Hunter, Jan. 2, 1972 (div. June 30, 2002); 1 child, Brian M.; m. Sharon W. Hunter; stepchildren: Luke Wolf, Benjamin Wolf. AS in arts & sci., Cmty. Coll. Phila., 1968; BS in social sci., Pa. State U., Univ. Park, 1970; MA in African Am. studies, Boston U., 1971, PhD in sociology, 1981. Sr. tchg. fellow Boston U., 1972—74; asst. prof. Roxbury Cmty. Coll., Mass., 1974—76, Pa. State U., Middletown, 1978—85; assoc. prof. Ind. U. Pa., 1985—96, prof., 1996—. Author: Race, Class, and World Systems, 1987, The Sociology of O.C. Cox, 2000; contbr. chapters to books. Sgt. USMC, 1961—66. W.E.B. DuBois fellow, Harvard U., 1976—77. Mem.: Am. Sociol. Assn., Phi Kappa Phi. Independent. Home: 11735 N 131st Way Scottsdale AZ 85259 Office: Ind Univ Pa McElhaney Hall Indiana PA 15701 Business E-Mail: hmhunter@iup.edu.

HUNTER, HOWARD OWEN, academic administrator, law educator; b. Brunswick, Ga., Oct. 14, 1946; m. Susan Frankel, Nov. 27, 1971; 1 child, Emily Atwood Plotkin. BA in Russian Studies, Yale U., 1968, JD, 1971. Bar: Ga. 1971. Assoc. atty. Hogan & Hartson, Washington, 1971-72, Hansell, Post, Brandon & Dorsey, Atlanta, 1972-76; asst. prof. Emory U. Sch. Law, Atlanta, 1976-79, assoc. prof., 1979-82, assoc. dean, 1979-80, prof., 1982—, prof. law, dean, 1989-2001, provost, exec. v.p. for acad. affairs, 2001—. Dir. Ga. Vol. Lawyers for the Arts, Inc., 1975-89, sec., 1975-77, treas., 1978-80, v.p., 1980-82, pres., 1984-87; vis. prof. law U. Va. Sch. Law, Charlottesville, 1982-83; hon. prof. law U. Hong Kong, 1986; vis. Mills E. Godwin prof. law Coll. William & Mary, Williamsburg, Va., 1989; mem. Chief Justice Commn. on Professionalism, 1990—, Supreme Ct. Commn. on Indigent Def., 2000—; bd. trustees Fed. Def. Program, 1991-97; lectr. in field. Author: Freedom of Information Handbook: Georgia, 1979, Modern Law of Contracts: Breach and Remedies, 1986, supplements, 1987, 88, 89, 90, 91, 92, 93, Modern Law of Contracts: Formation, Performance, Relationships, 1987, supplements, 1988, 89, 90, 91, 92, 93, Modern Law of Contracts, revised edit., 1993, supplements, 1994, 95, 96, 97, 98, 2d rev. edit., 1999, supplements, 2000, 01, (with Mogens Pedersen) Recent Reforms in Swedish Higher Education, 1980; contbr. articles to profl. jours.; mem. editl. bd. Jour. of Contract Law, 1988—. Fulbright Sr. scholar U. Sydney, 1988. Mem. ABA, Assn. Am. Law Schs., Am. Law Inst. (mem. consultative com. on revisions to article 2 of UCC), State Bar Ga. (mem. editl. bd. Ga. State Bar Jour. 1977-82), Decatur-DeKalb Bar Assn., Atlanta Bar Assn. (vol. lawyer project on illegal Cuban immigrants 1985-87, vol. lawyer in representation of Cuban inmates at fed. prison in Talladega, Ala. 1988, bd. dirs. internat. transaction sect. 1995—), Inst. Continuing Legal Edn. (vice-chmn. bd. trustees 1993-97), Inst. Continuing Judicial Edn. (bd. trustees 1989-2001). Avocations: cycling, jogging, fishing, travel. Office: 404 Adminstrn Bldg Emory Univ Atlanta GA 30322 E-mail: hunter@emory.edu.

HUNTER, JACK DUVAL, retired lawyer; b. Elkhart, Ind., Jan. 14, 1937; s. William Stanley and Marjorie Irene (Upson) H.; m. Marsha Ann Goodsell, Nov. 14, 1958 (dec.); children: Jack, Jon, Justin. BBA, U. Mich., 1959, LLB, 1961. Bar: Mich. 1961, Ind. 1962. Atty. Lincoln Nat. Life Ins. Co., Ft. Wayne, Ind., 1961-64, asst. counsel, 1964-68, v.p., gen. counsel, 1975-79, sr. v.p., gen. counsel, 1979-86, exec. v.p., gen. counsel, 1986-99. Asst. gen. counsel, asst. sec. Lincoln Nat. Corp., Ft. Wayne and Phila., 1968-71, gen. counsel, 1971-2002, v.p., 1972-79, sr. v.p., 1979-86, exec. v.p., 1986-2002. Life trustee Ind. Nature Conservancy, chmn. bd. trustees, 1993-95. Recipient Oak Leaf award Nature Conservancy, 1997. Mem. ABA, Ind. State Bar Assn., Allen County Bar Assn., Assn. Life Ins. Counsel (pres. 1995-96), Am. Coun. Life Ins. (chmn. legal sect. 1991). E-mail: jack.hunter2@verizon.net.

HUNTER, JAMES AUSTEN, JR., lawyer; b. Phoenix, June 19, 1941; s. James Austen and Elizabeth Aileen (Holt) H.; m. Donna Gabriele, Aug. 24, 1973; 1 child, James A. AB, Cath. U. Am., 1963, LL.B., 1966. Bar: N.Y. 1967, Pa. 1975, U.S. Supreme Ct. 1974. Assoc. firm Sullivan & Cromwell, N.Y.C., 1967-74; assoc. firm Morgan, Lewis & Bockius, LLP, Phila., 1974-77, ptnr., 1977—. Staff: The Yale Law Jour. Home: 1001 Red Rose Ln Villanova PA 19085-2118 Office: Morgan Lewis & Bockius LLP 1701 Market St Philadelphia PA 19103-2903 E-mail: jhunter@morganlewis.com.

HUNTER, JAMES GALBRAITH, JR., lawyer; b. Phila., Jan. 6, 1942; s. James Galbraith and Emma Margaret (Jehl) H.; m. Pamela Ann Trott, July 18, 1969 (div.); children: James Nicholas, Catherine Selene; m. Nancy Grace Scheurwater, June 21, 1992. B.S. in Engring. Sci., Case Inst. Tech., 1965; J.D., U. Chgo., 1967. Bar: Ill. 1967, U.S. Dist. Ct. (no. dist.) Ill. 1967, U.S. Ct. Appeals (7th cir.) 1967, U.S. Ct. Claims, 1976, U.S. Ct. Appeals (4th and 9th cirs.) 1978, U.S. Supreme Ct. 1979, U.S. Dist. Ct. (cen. dist.) Ill. 1980, Calif. 1980, U.S. Dist. Ct. (cen. and so. dists.) Calif. 1980, U.S. Ct. Appeals (5th cir.) 1982, U.S. Ct. Appeals (fed. cir.) 1982. Assoc. Kirkland & Ellis, Chgo., 1967-68, 70-73, ptnr., 1973-76; ptnr. Hedlund, Hunter & Lynch, Chgo., 1976-82, Los Angeles, 1979-82; ptnr. Latham & Watkins, Hedlund, Hunter & Lynch, Chgo. and Los Angeles, 1982— . Served to lt. JAGC, USN, 1968-70. Mem. ABA, State Bar Calif., Los Angeles County Bar Assn., Chgo. Bar Assn. Clubs: Metropolitan (Chgo.), Chgo. Athletic Assn., Los Angeles Athletic. Exec. editor U. Chgo. Law Rev., 1966-67. Office: Latham & Watkins Sears Tower Ste 5800 Chicago IL 60606-6306 also: 633 W 5th St Los Angeles CA 90071-2005

HUNTER, J(AMES) PAUL, English language educator, literary critic, historian; b. Jamestown, N.Y., June 29, 1934; s. Paul W. and Florence I. (Walmer) H.; children: Debra, Lisa, Paul III, Anne, Ellen Harris. AB, Ind. Central Coll., 1955; MA, Miami U., Oxford, Ohio, 1957; PhD, Rice U., 1963. Instr., U. Fla., Gainesville, 1957-59, Williams Coll., Williamstown, Mass., 1962-64; asst. prof. U. Calif., Riverside, 1964-66; assoc. prof. English Emory U., Atlanta, 1966-68, prof., 1968-80, chmn. dept., 1973-79; prof. English, dean Coll. Arts and Sci., U. Rochester, N.Y., 1981-86; prof. English U. Chgo., 1987—, Chester D. Tripp prof. humanities, 1990-96, Barbara E. and Richard J. Franke prof. humanities, 1996—2001; dir. Franke Inst. for the Humanities, 1996—2001, Franke prof. emeritus, 2001—; prof. of English U. of Va., 2001—. Gen. editor Bedford Cultural Edits., 1994—. Author: The Reluctant Pilgrim, 1966, Occasional Form, 1975, Norton Introduction to Poetry, 8th edit., 2002, Norton Introduction to Literature, 8th edit., 2001, New Worlds of Literature, 2d edit., 1994, Before Novels, 1990; co-editor: Rhetorics of Order/Ordering Rhetorics, 1989; editor: Norton Critical Edition of Mary Shelley's Frankenstein, 1996. Sr. advisor Andrew W. Mellon Found., 1999—. Guggenheim fellow, 1976-77, NEH fellow, 1985-86, Nat. Humanities Ctr. fellow, 1986, 95-96. Mem. MLA, Am. Soc. 18th Century Studies (Louis Gottschalk prize 1991, 2d v.p. 1994-95, 1st v.p. 1995-96, pres. 1996-97), Southeastern Am. Soc. 18th Century Studies (pres. 1977-78), So. Atlantic MLA (pres. 1992-93), N.E. Am. Soc. 18th Century Studies (pres. 1982-83). E-mail: jph7f@virginia.edu.

HUNTER, JODY JEAN, association executive, naturalist; b. Glen Cove, N.Y. d. William T. and Lois Hunter; m. Joseph A. Herbert, Jr., Nov. 30, 1998; stepchildren: Mary Herbert, Nancy Herbert. BS in Park Mgmt. and Conservation magna cum laude, U. N.H., 1980. Cert. in food svc. sanitation; CPR; advanced life saving. Park mgr. Fairfax County Park Authority, Fairfax, Va., 1980-86; adminstrv. asst. The Wilderness Soc., Washington, 1988-89, Internat. Chiropractors Assn., Washington, 1986-88, membership coord. Arlington, Va., 1989-93, dir. membership svcs., 1993—. Spl. events coord. Arlington Uncommon Market Food Coop., 1990—, bd. dirs., 1987—91, sec., 1989; vol. No. Va. Regional Park Authority, Fairfax Station, 1999, Arlingtonians for a Clean Environment, 2000—; vol. membership coord. No. Va. Land Trust, 2000—, Signature, Gunston and Shakespeare Landsberg theaters, 1996—. Mem.: The Nature Conservancy, Nat. Honor Soc., Am. Soc. Assn. Execs., Sr. Key U. Honor Soc., Phi Kappa Phi. Avocations: wildflower appreciation, nature walking, edible foods identification, worldwide adventure travel. Home: 5652 8th St N Arlington VA 22205-1020

HUNTER, JOHN GRAHAM, investment management company executive; b. Edinburgh, Mar. 28, 1943; s. David and Catherine Valentina (Quillete) H.; m. Eileen Shannon, Nov. 1, 1969 (div. Mar. 1991); children: John, Sharryn. Assoc., Chartered Inst. of Mktg. Trainee Britannic Assurance, 1963-66, mgr., 1966-80; mktg. dir. Tyndall Holdings Plc, 1981-88, Refuge Overseas, Guernsey, 1988-92; chmn., CEO Apollo Investment Ltd., Guernsey, 1993—. Chmn. Action Rsch. for Multiple Sclerosis, Guernsey, 1986. Mem. United Club, Guernsey Sporting Club, Royal Channel Island Yacht Club. Avocations: literature, travel, golf. Home: Oakstone House Rue de la Lande Vale Guernsey GY3 5BQ Channel Islands

HUNTER, JOHN LESLIE, lawyer; b. Miss., Aug. 15, 1946; m. Judy G. Hunter; children: John Leslie II, Lee Joseph, Kristy Lynn. BS, Miss. State U., 1969; JD, U. Miss., 1972. Bar: U.S. Dist. Ct. (no. dist.) Miss. 1972, U.S. Dist. Ct. (so. dist.) Miss. 1973, U.S. Ct. Appeals (5th cir.) 1974, U.S. Supreme Ct. 1978, U.S. Dist. Ct. (so. dist.) Ala. 1980, U.S. Ct. Appeals (11th cir.) 1981. Ptnr. Cumbest Cumbest Hunter & McCormick, Pascagoula, Miss., 1973—. Atty. Jackson county Port Authority. Mem. ABA, Assn. Trial Lawyers of Am. (sustaining mem.), Am. Bd. Trial Advocates, Miss. Bar Assn. (past exec. com. bd. commrs.), Miss. Trial Lawyers Assn. (sustaining), Jackson County Bar Assn. Presbyterian. Office: Cumbest Cumbest Hunter McCormick 729 Watts Ave PO Box 1287 Pascagoula MS 39568-1287 E-mail: jlh@cchmlawyers.com, jlh@cableone.net.

HUNTER, J(OHN) ROBERT, insurance consumer advocate; b. New Orleans, Nov. 20, 1936; s. J. Robert and Alberta M. (Cox) H.; m. Carole A. Means, Mar. 6, 1976; children: Laura Jeanne, James Douglas, John Robert, III. BS, Clarkson U., 1958; grad. Program for Sr. Mgrs., Harvard U., 1976. Dir. of ins. Atlantic Mut. Ins. Co., 1960-61; supervisory actuary Ins. Svcs. Office, N.Y.C., 1961-67; asst. actuary Mut. Ins. Rating Bur., N.Y.C., 1967-71; chief actuary Fed. Ins. Adminstrn., HUD, Washington, 1971-74, acting adminstr., 1974-76, adminstr., 1976-77, dep. fed. ins. adminstr., 1977-80; founder, pres. Nat. Ins. Consumer Orgn., 1980-93; ins. commr. State of Tex., 1993-94; dir. ins. Consumer Fedn. Am., Arlington, Va., 1994—. Author: Taking the Bite Out of Insurance, 1980, Profitability and Investment Income in Property Casualty Insurance, 1983, Insurance in California, 1986, Pay at the Pump Private No Fault Auto Insurance,

1992, Proposition 103 Revisited: A Consumer Triumph, 1993, Auto Insurance, Progress but More to Be Done, 1995, America's Distrous Disaster Insurance System, 1998, Premium Deceit, 1999, Texas Tort Reform's Incredible Shrinking Savings, 1999, Changes in State Insurance Department Resources, 2000, California Auto REgulation The Best in Nation, 2001, Medical Malpractice Insurance: Stable Losses/Unstable Rates, 2002, Home Insurance Rates Rise Sharply, 2003, Insurers Undermine Terrorism Insurance Law, 2003. Pres. Freeport (N.Y.) Cmty. Chorale, 1970-71; pres., founder Rockville (Md.) Musical Theatre, 1974-75; vestryman Christ Ch., Alexandria, 1982-84, 91-93. Recipient award for excellence Sec. HUD, 1977, Ester Peterson award for consumer lifetime achievement. Fellow Casualty Actuarial Soc.; mem. Am. Acad. Actuaries, Internat. Actuarial Assn. Home: 2202 24th St N Arlington VA 22207-4904 E-mail: loonlakeme@aol.com.

HUNTER, KENNETH M. business information systems educator; b. Muskgeon, Mich., Jan. 11, 1943; s. Merlin Arthur and Dorothy Elaine Hunter. PhD, U. Wis., 1968. Asst. prof. math. La. State U., Baton Rouge, 1968—71; prof. William James Coll., Allendale, Mich., 1971—78; assoc. prof. Sangamon State U., Springfield, Ill., 1978—79; sys. analyst Baxter Travenol Labs., Chgo., 1979—80; assoc. prof. U. Pacific, Stockton, Calif., 1980—83; asst. prof. San Francisco State U., 1983—84, prof. bus. info. sys., 1988—; assoc. prof. Aquinas Coll., Grand Rapids, Mich., 1984—85; sys. analyst W.W. Engring. and Sci., Grand Rapids, Mich., 1985—88. Democrat. Achievements include patents for search engines, fuzzy finite state non-deterministic automata.

HUNTER, LARRY DEAN, lawyer; b. Leon, Iowa, Apr. 10, 1950; s. Doyle J. and Dorothy B. (Grey) H.; m. Rita K. Barker, Jan. 24, 1971; children: Nathan (dec.), Allison. BS with high distinction, U. Iowa, 1971; AM, JD magna cum laude, U. Mich., 1974, CPhil in Econs., 1975. Bar: Va. 1975, Mich. 1978, Calif. 1992. Assoc. McGuire Woods & Battle, Richmond, Va., 1975-77; asst. counsel, internat. counsel Clark Equipment Co., Buchanan, Mich., 1977-80; ptnr. Honigman, Miller, Schwartz and Cohn, Detroit, 1980-93; asst. gen. counsel Hughes Electronics Corp., L.A., 1993-98, corp. v.p., 1998—; sr. v.p., gen. counsel DIRECTV, Inc., El Segundo, Calif., 1996-98; chmn. pres. DIRECTV Japan Mgmt., Inc., Tokyo, 1998-2000. Mem. faculty Wayne State U. Law Sch., Detroit, 1987-89. Mem. Order of Coif. Home: 1101-B S Catalina Ave Redondo Beach CA 90277 Office: Hughes Electronics Corp 2250 E Imperial Hwy El Segundo CA 90245 E-mail: larry.hunter@hughes.com.

HUNTER, LARRY LEE, retired electrical engineer; b. Versailles, Mo., Mar. 5, 1938; s. Donnan Kleber and Molly Opal (Roe) H.; m. Marcella Ann Avey, Feb. 1, 1959; children: Cynthia Lynn Hunter Morency, Stuart Roe. BSEE, U. Mo., 1963; MBA, Fla. Inst. Tech., 1984. System test engr. McDonnell Aircraft Corp., St. Louis, 1963-65; design engr. Magnavox Co., Urbana, Ill., 1965-66, R&D engr., 1966-67; project engr. LTV Electrosystems, Garland, Tex., 1967-68, systems engr., 1968-70; program mgr. Dorsett Electronics, Tulsa, 1970-73, Harris Corp., Melbourne, Fla., 1973-75, bus. area mgr., 1975—85; v.p. mktg., engring., program mgmt. Teledyne Lewisburg, Tenn., 1985-88; pres. L.H. Assocs., Columbia, Tenn., 1988-90; founder, gen. mgr. Precision Cable div. AMP Inc., Harrisburg, Pa. and Greensboro, NC, 1990-96, dir. global cable sys. bus. group, 1996-97; pres. L. Hunter Assocs., Inc., Tampa, Fla., 1997—2001. Contbr. articles to profl. jours. Mem.: IEEE, Eta Kappa Nu. Republican. Methodist. Achievements include inventor of medical thermometer. Home: 16309 E Course Dr Tampa FL 33624-1127

HUNTER, LELAND CLAIR, JR., management consultant; b. Phila., Feb. 22, 1925; s. Leland Clair and Lillian Mae (Failor) H.; m. Elva Joy Charlton, July 5, 1946; children: Charlton Lee, Steven Kent, Brian Scott, Donna Joy. BS, Villanova U., 1948; postgrad., Columbia U., 1944-45; MBA, Fla. Research Inst., 1971; grad., Advanced Mgmt. Program, Harvard U., 1973. Test engr. Gen. Electric Co., Phila., 1949-50; with Fla. Power & Light Co., 1950-88, v.p. indsl. relations, 1966-72, v.p. transmission and distbn., 1972-73, group v.p., 1973-78, sr. v.p., 1978-88; pres. Leland Hunter Mgmt. Cons., Miami, 1988—; chmn. Hunter, Voehl and Lewis, 1995—; conf. co-chair Nat. Youth Crime Prevention Conf.; editor Charlton Pub. Co., 1998, pres., 2001. Mem. spl. labor com. Sec. of Labor U.S., 1975-76; mem. Labor and Mgmt. Polit. Action Com. for Utility Industry, 1977, Gov.'s Adv. Coun. Productivity, 1981—; pres. Leland Hunter Mgmt. Cons. Vice chmn. adv. com. Dade County (Fla.) Sch. Bd., 1966; bd. govs. Gold Coast AAU, 1967-68; bd. dirs. Crime Commn. of Greater Miami, 1974— ; chmn. bd. Victoria Hosp., 1984-88; dir. Pro-Fish of Fla.; Fla. Lawyers Prepaid Legal Services Inc. Crime Commn. of Greater Miami, 1980— ; bd. advisors Stetson U.; mem. bus. adv. com. Brookings Instn., Washington; exec. v.p. Atlantic Gamefish Found.; mem. Blue Ribbon Com. to Save Miami's Fin. Future, 1996; mem. County Mgrs. Com. to Stop Corruption in Dade County Politics, 1999. Served with USN, 1943-46. Recipient Key to City Toledo and Coral Gables Fla.). Mem. Am. Soc. Tng. Dirs. (pres. local chpt. 1955-56), Fla. Athletic Club (pres. 1962), Coral Gables Country Club, Univ. Miami Club. Home and Office: 7881 SW 180th St Miami FL 33157-6216

HUNTER, LORIE ANN, women's health nurse; b. Royal Oak, Mich., Aug. 8, 1969; d. Ronald and Rose Katherine (Thurman) Ladziak. BSN, Mercy Coll. Detroit, 1991. RN. Nurse extern Detroit Med. Ctr.- Sinai Hosp., 1989-91, nurse, 1991—. Mem. NAACOG, NLN, Mich. Coll. Nursing. Home: 3367 Kilmer Dr Troy MI 48083-5082 E-mail: loriehunter@msn.com.

HUNTER, LYNN, sales executive, writer, elementary school educator; b. Bronx, N.Y., Apr. 25, 1949; d. Harvey and Pearl (Weinstock) Handelsman; m. Casey Scott Hunter, Oct. 1, 1988. BA, Bklyn. Coll., 1970, MS, 1973; EdD, Nova Southeastern U., Ft. Lauderdale, Fla., 1995. Tchr. Bd. Edn. N.Y.C., Bklyn., 1970-80; prodr., writer WNYE-TV Bd. Edn., Bklyn., 1979-82; assoc. prodr. Broadway Prodns., N.Y.C., 1979-83; mktg. mgr. Account-A-Call, N.Y.C., 1980-85; spl. cons. Open Ct. Pub., Peru, Ill., 1985-89, ednl. rep., 1990-94, Ky. Ednl. TV, Lexington, 1988-92; regional mgr. Creative Publs., Mountainview, Calif., 1994—; distance learning coord. NYC Dept. Edn., 2001—. Judge Emmy awards children's TV, NATAS, N.Y.C., 1990—; mem. adv. bd. reading Open Ct. Pub., Peru, 1992—94; sales cons., pres. Edn. Media Enterprises, Jackson, NJ, 1992—; learning coord. N.Y.C. Bd. Edn.; ind. sales rep. variety textbook cos., N.Y. and N.J.; pub. rels. officer Brick Twp. Sch. Dist., 1998—2001. Author (children's book): Meet the Dooples, 1998, The Dooples and the Shapes, 2002; author, creator characters Dooples, prodr., writer pub. svc. announcements, WNYE-TV, 1989. Mem. ASCD, NATAS, NAFE, Nat. Coun. Tchrs. Maths., Am. Ednl. Rsch. Assn., Internat. Reading Assn., Assn. Math. Tchrs. N.J., N.J. Math. Coalition (adv. bd. 1992-94), N.Y. Assn. fo Edn. of Young Children. Home and Office: 51 Whitesville Rd Jackson NJ 08527-5116 also: 770 Anderson Ave Cliffside Park NJ 07010

HUNTER, MARK JOHN, lawyer, photographer; b. Alpena, Mich., Dec. 22, 1956; s. Francis Raymond and Evelyn Joan (Hoodlet) Hunter. BA in U.S. History, Mich. State U., 1979, BA in Graphic Design, 1981; A in Concrete Tech., Alpena CC, 1987; JD, Ohio No. U., 1995. Bar: Mich. 1996. Freelance photographer, Alpena, 1974—; mfg. mgr. Concrete Product Industry, Mass., 1987—89; attendant Hunter Funeral Home, Alpena, 1995—; pvt. practice Alpena, 1996—. Ex-officio mem. Alpena County Planning Commn., 1999—2002; vice chmn. Alpena County Rep. Com., 2001—02; mem. Alpena County Rep. Exec. Bd., 2003—, mem. exec. com., 2003—04; bd. dirs. Sunrise Mission Shelter, Alpena, 2000. Mem.: World Wildlife Fund, Mich. Land Use Inst., Eagles Club of Ossineke, Moose Lodge. Avocations: political theory, prisoners of conscience, world development, reading biographies. Office: 310 W Chisholm St Alpena MI 49707 E-mail: ehunter@i2k.com.

HUNTER, MATTIE, human services executive; b. Chgo., June 1, 1954; d. Lucious and Flabe (Davis) H. BA, Monmouth (Ill.) Coll., 1976; MA, Jackson (Miss.) State U., 1982. Summer counselor Chgo. Housing Authority, 1972-76; asst. mgr. Whitney's Fashions, Chgo., 1976; tng. specialist City Colls. of Chgo., 1977-81; youth service worker Dept. Human Services City of Chgo., 1977-81; program dir. Human Services Devel. Inst. Chgo., 1982-85, exec. asst. to pres., 1985—. Conf. planner, community liaison, and mktg. Bakeman & Assocs., Chgo., 1986—. Author: (newsletter) Nat. Elk Alcoholism Commn., 1982. Mem. Community Devel. Adv. Council City of Chgo., 1986; mem. steering com. Cook County Democratic Women, Chgo., 1985—; staff asst. Polit. Action Conf. of Ill., Chgo., 1984—; vol. Warren county Rep. Orgn., Monmouth, 1975; fundraiser Nat. Polit. Congress of Black Women, Chgo., 1985—; vol. coordinator Hands Across Am., Chgo., 1986, March of Dimes Telethon, Chgo., 1979-81, Muscular Distrophy, Chgo., 1980, 81, 85, local adv. council Chgo. Housing Authority, 1968-76; precinct coordinator congl. dist. race, Chgo., 1980, 1976, 3rd Ward Regular Democratic Orgn., Chgo., 1970-72; asst. ward coordinator Washington for Mayor City of Chgo., 1983; surveyor Joint Ctr. for Polit. Studies, Washington, 1973; ambassador of mercy United Way, Chgo.; vice chmn. adv. council Chgo. Intervention Network Dept. of Human Services, 1985—, convocations com. Monmouth Coll., 1973-74, cultural affairs com., 1975-76; bd. dirs. Black Leadership Roundtable of Ill., Chgo., 1986—. Named one of Outstanding Young Women Am., 1985; recipient award of Appreciation, Dept. Human Services City of Chgo., 1981, award of Gratitude, Human Resources Devel. Inst. Chgo., 1984. Mem. Notaries Assn. of Ill., Inc., Nat. Black Alcoholism Council (chmn. Orgn. Devel. Com., award of Appreciation), Nat. Forum Black Pub. Adminstrs., Nat. Assn. for Female Execs. Democrat. Baptist. Avocations: volleyball, softball, bowling. Home: 5604 S Prairie Ave Apt 3 Chicago IL 60637-5306*

HUNTER, MICHAEL, publishing executive; b. Atlanta, Dec. 11, 1941; s. Joel H. and Eleanor Johnson; m. Katherine Garlick, Aug. 2, 1975. BA cum laude, Harvard U., 1964; postgrad., Columbia U., 1965-67. Dir. Spectrum Books, Prentice-Hall Inc., Englewood Cliffs., N.J., 1974-80; pres. Gen. Pub. div. Prentice-Hall Inc., Englewood Cliffs., N.J., 1980-85; pres. Hunter Pub. Co., N.Y., 1985—. Mem. Am. Assn. Pubs. (exec. council Gen. Pub. div.) Clubs: University (N.Y.C.). Home: 239 S Beach Rd Hobe Sound FL 33455-2511 Office: Hunter Pub Co 130 Campus Plz Edison NJ 08837-3936 E-mail: hunterp@bellsouth.net.

HUNTER, MICHAEL JAMES, state government official, lawyer, educator; b. Enid, Okla., July 2, 1956; s. James Chester Hunter and Phyllis Merle Brinker; m. Cheryl Lynn Plaxico, Dec. 26, 1981; children: Barret Michael, Hayden Brock. BA in History, Okla. State U., 1978; JD, U. Okla., 1982. Bar: Okla. Ptnr. Crabtree & Miller, Okla. City, 1981-85, George, Moore, Hammons & Hunter, Okla. City, 1985-87; of counsel Musser & Bunch, Okla. City, 1987-93; gen. counsel Okla. Corp. Commn., 1993-94; chief of staff Congressman J.C. Watts, Jr., 1995-99; sec. of state State of Okla., 1999—2002; COO Am. Coun. Life Insurers, 2002—. Del. Rep. Nat. Conv., Detroit, 1980, New Orleans, 1988; chmn. Rep. Caucus, 1988-90; state rep. Okla. Ho. of Reps., Okla. City, 1984-90, mem. Constitution Revision Study Commn. Named One of Okla.'s Best Legislators, The Daily Oklahoman, Okla. City, 1987; recipient Legis. Appreciation award, Okla. Dist. Atty.'s Assn., Okla. City, 1988. Mem. Okla. Bar Assn., Okla. County Bar Assn. Republican. Presbyterian. Avocations: baseball, books, movies. Office: ACLI 101 Constitution Ave NW Washington DC 20001 Fax: 202-572-4702.

HUNTER, MILTON, army officer; b. Houston, May 1, 1943; married; 2 children. BS in Archtl. Engring., Wash. State U., 1967; M in Engring., U. Wash., 1978; grad. Exec. Devel. Program, U. Va., 1988; postgrad., Tex. A&M U., 1990, Harvard U., 1994; DSc (hon.), N.J. Inst. Tech., 1997. Registered profl. engr., D.C. Commd. 2d lt. U.S. Army, 1967, advanced through grades to maj. gen.; instr. Tactical Bridging br., dept. applied engring. U.S. Army Engr. Sch., Ft. Belvoir, Va.; with U.S. Army Corps of Engrs., comdr. and dist. engr. Seattle Dist., comdg. gen., divsn. engr. South Pacific, San Francisco, chief of staff, comdg. gen., divsn. engr. North Atlantic divsn. N.Y., to 1997, condg. gen., divsn. engr. North Atlantic divsn., 1997-2000, dep. chief of engrs., dep. comdr., 2000—. Decorated Legion of Merit (2), Bronze Star medal, DSM, others; recipient Disting. Alumni award Wash. State U., 1991; named to Outstanding Young of Am., 1979. Fellow Soc. Am. Mil. Engrs.; mem. Army Engr. Regtl. Assn., Assn. U.S. Army, Tau Beta Pi. Office: US Army Corps of Engrs 441 G St NW Washington DC 20314

HUNTER, M(ILTON) REED, JR., lawyer; b. Salt Lake City, Oct. 5, 1932; s. Milton Reed and Ferne (Gardner) H.; m. Mary Anne Shumway, Dec. 19, 1968; children: Edward Lund, Anne Leslie, Maria Lynne, Jefferson Reed. BA with honors, Brigham Young U., 1953; JD, U. Utah, 1961. Bar: Utah 1961, Calif. 1969, U.S. Ct. Appeals (10th cir.) 1961, U.S. Ct. Appeals (9th cir.) 1969, U.S. Supreme Ct. 1978. Asst. atty. gen. Utah State Atty. Gen.'s Office, Salt Lake City, 1961-68; staff atty. Continuing Edn. of the Bar, U. Calif., Berkeley, 1968-71; assoc., ptnr. Goldstein, Barceloux & Goldstein, San Francisco, 1971-84; v.p., atty. Fadem, Berger & Norton, Santa Monica, Calif., 1984-89; sole practitioner Encino, Calif., 1989-90; ptnr. Crosby, Heafey, Roach & May, L.A., 1990-2000; sole practitioner, 2000—. Contbr. articles to profl. jours. Sgt. U.S. Army, 1953-55, Germany. Mem. Calif. State Bar, Calif. Acad. Appellate Lawyers (pres. 1979-80; chair state bar com. on appellate cts. 1985), Los Angeles County Bar Assn. (condemnation com.), Mensa, Phi Kappa Phi, Phi Alpha Theta. Republican. Mem. Lds Ch. Avocations: music, film, tennis, travel. Home and Office: 1359 Amesbury Cir Salt Lake City UT 84121 E-mail: reed@mariahunter.com.

HUNTER, PATRICIA PHELPS, physician assistant; b. Nyack, N.Y., Oct. 11, 1952; d. Everett Edward and Evelyn Phelps; m. George Patton Hunter, June 26, 1982; children: Eric I., Kurt A. BA in Psychology & Spanish magna cum, Oneonta State U., 1974; BS in Physician Asst., Hahnemann Med. U., 1981; MS in Pub. Health, West Chester U., 1984. Rsch. asst. Oneonta (N.Y.) State U., 1973-74, Dartmouth Med. Sch., Hanover, N.H., 1974-76; paramedic San Francisco Ambulance, 1977-79; physician asst. Montgomery Hosp., Norristown, Pa., 1981—. Fellow Am. Acad. Physician Assts. (cert.); mem. Assn. for Retarded Citizens, Nat. Orgn. Rare Disorders, Nat. Orgn. Apraxia and Dyspraxia, Variety Club Camp and Devel. Ctr Parents' Group (treas. 1999—). Avocations: skiing, scuba diving. Home: 331 Collegeville Rd Collegeville PA 19426-3030 Office: Montgomery Fornance Family Practice 1330 Powell St Ste 409 Norristown PA 19401

HUNTER, PATRICIA RAE (TRICIA HUNTER), state official; b. Appleton, Minn., June 15, 1952; d. Harlan Ottowa and Clara Elizabeth (Tryhus) H.; m. Clark Waldon Crabbe, May 28, 1978 (div. July 1994); 1 child, Samantha Marcantonio. AS in Nursing, Good Samaritan Hosp., Phoenix, 1974; BS in Nursing, U. San Diego, San Diego, 1981; M Nursing, UCLA, 1985. RN; cert. oper. rm. nurse. Surg. svcs. educator Stanford Hosp., 1983-85; oper. rm. supr. Alexian Bros., San Jose, Calif., 1985-86; dir. surg. svcs. Cmty. Hosp. Chula Vista, Calif., 1986-89; mem. Calif. State Assembly, San Diego, 1989-92; spl. asst. Gov. Wilson Office Statewide Health Planning and Devel., Sacramento, 1993-94; commr. Calif. Med. Assistance Commn., Sacramento, 1994-98, sr. v.p., mng. dir., 1998—, The Flannery Group, San Diego, 1997—2002; pvt. practice Hon. Tricia Hunter Legis. Advocated Cons., 2002—. Bd. mem. Premier Home & Health, Phoenix, 1994-95; cons. Summit Schs., Ontario, Calif., 1992-93, hosp., Monterey, Calif., 1984—; mem. adv. bd. Alheimers Assn., San Diego, 1990-92, Arthritis Found., 1990-92. Pres. Calif. Rep. League, 1995-97. Named Rockie Legislator of Yr., Calif. Psychol. Assn., 1990, Legislator of Yr. Calif. Nurse Practitioners Assn., 1992; recipient Alice Pauly award Nat. Women Polit. Caucus, San Diego, 1991. Mem. ANA (v.p. 1982-85), Assn. Oper. Rm. Nurses, NWPC, Bus. and Profl. Orgn., Rotary (bd. mem. 1993-94), San Diego Red Cross (bd. mem.), Sigma Theta Tau (leadership award 1991). Republican. Lutheran. Home: 3260 E Fox Run Way San Diego CA 92111-7723 Office: Hon Tricia Hunter 1121 Lane St Ste 409 Sacramento CA 95814 E-mail: thunter930@aol.com.

HUNTER, RICHARD EDWARD, retired physician; b. Worcester, Mass., May 30, 1919; s. William and Catherine (Powers) H.; m. M. Minta Shaw, Jan. 30, 1993; children: Todd Wayne, Elayne Cheryl, Jill Elizabeth, Amy Louise. AB, Clark U., 1941; MD, Boston U., 1944. Diplomate Am. Bd. Ob-Gyn. Intern Worcester City Hosp., 1944-45; resident in gen. surgery Framingham (Mass.) Union Hosp., 1947; resident in ob-gyn Mercy Hosp., Balt., 1947-49; practice medicine specializing in ob-gyn Worcester, 1949—; prof. dept. ob-gyn U. Mass., Worcester, 1976—, chmn. dept. ob-gyn, 1976-89, emeritus prof., 1989—; ret., 1999. Contbr. articles to med. jours. Served with U.S. Army, 1945-47. Mem. ACS, ACOG, New Eng. Assn. Gynecologic Oncologists, Soc. Gynecologic Oncology, Boston Obstetric Soc., New Eng. Cancer Soc., Am. Soc. Clin. Oncology, Soc. Gynecologic Surgeons, Royal Soc. Medicine. Republican. Office: 55 Lake Ave N Worcester MA 01655-0002 Home: 340 May St Worcester MA 01602

HUNTER, RICHARD SAMFORD, JR., lawyer; b. Montgomery, Ala., May 8, 1954; s. Richard Samford and Anne (Arendell) H.; m. Jane Messer, June 28, 1981; children: Richard Samford III, Benjamin Arendell. Student, Berklee Coll. of Music, 1974—75; BA, U. N.C., 1977; JD, Cumberland Sch Law of Samford U., 1980. Bar: N.C. 1980, U.S. Dist. Ct. (ea. and ctrl. dists.) N.C. 1981; cert. Am. Bd. Trial Advs. Assoc. Green & Mann, Raleigh, N.C., 1980-82, Smith, Debnam, Hibbert & Pahl, Raleigh, 1982-85; ptnr. Futrell, Hunter & Bingham, Raleigh, 1985-97. Pres., North Carolina Acad. of Trial Lawyers, 1993-94; pres. elect, 1992-93; exec. comm., 1987-94; bd., 1984-87; chair, Auto Torts Sect., 1998—, program chmn. media law U. N.C., Chapel Hill, 1983 84; mem. faculty NCATL Nat. Inst. Trial Advocacy, 1987; lectr. in field. Author: How to Try a Civil Case, 1986, Traumatic Medicine, 1988, Insurance Law for the General Practitioner, 1992, North Carolina Bar Assn. Desk Book, 1992, Traumatic Medicine, 1988, Inadequate Offer? Try that P.I. Case, 1995; composer, performer (TV musical) The Tomorrow Show, 1975; contbr. articles to profl. jours. and mags. including Trial Briefs Mag., Fourth Quarter. Corp. fund raiser United Way, Wake County, N.C., 1984-85; mem. clergy's sermon evaluation com. Christ Episc. Ch., Raleigh; bd. dirs. Raleigh Chamber Music Guild, 1986-88; bd. dirs. Food Bank of N.C., 1990—. Fellow Roscoe Pound Found. Fellow So. Trial Lawyers Assn., Roscoe Pound Found.; mem. ABA (litig. sect.), ATLA, Am. Bd. Trial Advocates (cert.), N.C. Bar Assn. (litig. sect.), Wake County Bar Assn. (bd. dirs. 1987, 88, chmn. 1988), Assn. Trial Lawyers Am. (Stalwart fellow Roscoe Pound Found.), N.C. State Bar, N.C. Acad. Trial Lawyers (speaker various seminars, chmn. speakers bur. 1984-85, bd. govs. 1986—, v.p. pub. svc. and info. com. 1988-90, v.p. membership 1990-91, v.p. legis. 1991—, pres. 1993-94, exec. com. 1987-94, chmn. auto torts sect. 1998—, mem. edn. com. 1985-88, pres.-elect 1992-93, bd. dirs. 1984-87, co-chair auto torts sect. 1998-99, U. N.C. journalism press law seminar, 1983, 84), Kiwanis, Sphinx, Phi Alpha Delta. Democrat. Avocations: sports, music, hunting, fishing. Home: 813 Graham St Raleigh NC 27605-1124 Office: 133 Fayetteville Street Mall Ste 300 Raleigh NC 27601-2908 Fax: 919-831-8734. E-mail: hunteratty@aol.com.

HUNTER, ROBERT FREDERICK, lawyer; b. Ft. Worth, June 7, 1937; s. Homer Alexander and Pauline (Steely) H.; m. Elisabeth Loader, July 1, 1961 (div. Sept. 1982); children: Homer Alexander II, Robert Frederick Jr.; m. Barbara Bailey, June 7, 1984. BBA, BS in Civil Engring., Tex. A&M U., 1960; MS, M.I.T., 1964; JD, So. Meth. U., 1974. Bar: Tex. 1975. Mo. 1976. Pres., chief exec. officer Hydro-Air Engring., St. Louis, 1974-84; sole practice Dallas, 1985-86; ptnr. Ashley and Welch, Dallas, 1987-90; pvt. practice Dallas, 1990—. Mem. ABA, ASCE, Tex. Bar Assn., Mo. Bar Assn., Phi Delta Phi. Lodges: Rotary (pres. 1970). Republican. Avocations: cameras, woodworking. Home: 3517 Villanova St Dallas TX 75225-5008

HUNTER, ROBERT GRAMS, retired English language educator; b. Milbank, S.D., Nov. 12, 1927; s. Donald Raymond and Esther (Grams) H.; m. Anne Ziesmer, Aug. 25, 1956; children: Timothy, Catherine. BA, Harvard, 1949; MA, Columbia, 1957, PhD, 1962. Instr. Robert Coll., Istanbul, Turkey, 1949-52; successively instr., asst. prof., asso. prof. Dartmouth, 1959-70; Kenan prof. English Vanderbilt U., Nashville, 1970-82; Frensley prof. English So. Meth. U., Dallas, 1982-97; ret., 1997. Author: Shakespeare and the Comedy of Forgiveness, 1965, Shakespeare and the Mystery of God's Judgments, 1976. Served with AUS, 1952-54. Home: 5923 Hillcrest Ave Dallas TX 75205-2262

HUNTER, SALLY IRENE, interior designer; b. East Liverpool, Ohio, Oct. 8, 1936; Charles E. and Thelma E. (Rice) H. BA, Kalamazoo Coll., 1958. Certified Am. Soc. Interior Designers. Interior designer The Higbee Co., Cleve., 1958-70; interior designer, v.p., dir. of design Harrisons Fine Furniture and Interiors, Lakewood, Ohio, 1970—. Mem. Nat. Trust Hist. Preservation. Mem. Am. Soc. Interior Designers (profl.), Cleve. Mus. Art, Cleve. Zool. Soc. Home: 22535 Detroit Rd Rocky River OH 44116-2056 Office: Harrisons Fine Furniture & Interiors 14518 Detroit Ave Lakewood OH 44107-4317 Fax: 216-521-9163.

HUNTER, STEPHEN, film critic, writer; b. Kansas City, Mo., 1946; 2 children. Grad., Northwestern U., 1968. Film critic, writer Washington Post, 1997—; copy reader, book rev. editor, feature writer Balt. Sun, 1971, critic, 1981; film critic Washington Post, 1997. Author: (book) Master Sniper, 1980, Second Saladin, 1982, Spanish Gambit: A Novel, 1985, Day Before Midnight, 1989, Point of Impact, 1993, Dirty White Boys: A Novel, 1994, Violent Screen: A Critic's 13 Years on the Front Lines of Movie Mayhem, 1995, Black Light, 1996, Time to Hunt: A Novel, 1998, Hot Springs: A Novel, 2000, Pale Horse Coming: A Novel, 2001. With U.S. Army. Finalist Pulitzer prize (2); recipient Am. Soc. Newspaper editors award for disting. writing in criticism, 1998, Pulitzer prize for criticism, 2003. Office: The Washington Post 1150 15th St NW Washington DC 20071

HUNTER, SUE PERSONS, former state official; b. Hico, Tex., Aug. 21, 1921; d. David Henry and Beulah (Boatwright) Persons; m. Charles Force Hunter: children: Shelley Hunter Richardson, Kathy Hunter McCullough, Margaret Hunter Brown. BA, U. Tex., 1942. Air traffic controller CAA (now FAA), San Antonio, Houston, 1942-52; writer Bissonet Plaza News, 1969-72; coord. Goals for La., 1971-74; adminstrv. dir. Jeff Publs. Inc., 1974; press sec. Jefferson Parish Dist. Atty., 1972-75; comm. cons., 1975-78; adminstr. Child Support Enforcement Divsn., 1979-85. Contbg. editor: The Jeffersonian, 1975—76. Pres. United Ch. Women East Jefferson, La., 1958-59; mem. LWV Jefferson Parish, La., 1961—, pres., 1961-63, bd. dirs., 1993-96; bd. dirs. LWV of La., 1962-67, pres., 1967-71; mem. probation svcs. com. Cmty. Svc. Coun., Jefferson, 1966-73, v.p., 1970-72; mem. Goals Found. Coun. Met. New Orleans, 1969-75, sec. 1970, 72; mem. Goals La. Task Force State and Local Govt., 1969-70; pres. MMM Investment Club, 1969-72; bd. dirs. New Orleans Area Health Planning Coun., 1969-75, Friends of Westminster Tower, 1986, Coun. for Internat. Visitors, 1990—, pres., 1991-93, programmer, 1994—; bd. dirs. Jefferson Twenty Five, 1991—, v.p., 1995-96, pres., 1997-98; mem. adv. coun. La. State Health Planning, 1971-76, title I adv. coun. La. State Dept. Edn., 1970-72; vice chmn. Jefferson Women's Polit. Caucus, 1977-78, chmn., 1979, treas., 1980; Nat. Women's Polit. Caucus, 1997—; bd. dirs. New Orleans Area/Bayou-River Health Sys. Agy., 1978-82, pres., 1980, 81; mem. Task Force for La. Talent Bank of Women, 1980; exec. bd. La. Child Support Enforcement Assn., 1980-86, pres., 1982-84; bd. dirs. legis. chmn. Nat. Child Support Enforcement Assn., 1983-86; mem. Gov.'s Commn. on Child Support Enforcement, 1984-88, mem. La. Statewide Health Coordinating Coun., 1980-83, mgmt. com. edn. fund LWV La., 1988-89; clk. of session Parkway Presbyn. Ch., 1998-2002. Recipient Outstanding Citizens award Rotary Club, Metairie, La., 1962, River Ridge award, 1976, Great Lady award East Jefferson Gen. Hosp. Aux., 2000. Mem. Am. Assn. Individual Investors (pres. New Orleans chpt. 1986-88), New Orleans Panhellenic (pres. 1956-57), Fgn. Rels. Assn. (bd. dirs. New Orleans chpt. 1992-2001, sec. 1996-99, 1st v.p. 1999-2001), Les Pelicaneers (pres. 1988-90), Earn and Learn Investment Club (pres. 1992-94), Dir.'s Cir., The Oxford Club, Alpha Xi Delta (pres. New Orleans City Panhellenic 1957-58). Home: 210 Stewart Ave New Orleans LA 70123-1457

HUNTER, TIM BRADSHAW, radiologist, educator; b. Balt., Aug. 15, 1943; s. Leo Lauren and Naomi (Bradshaw) H. BA, DePauw U., 1966; MD, Northwestern U., Chgo., 1968; BS, U. Ariz., 1980. Diplomate Am. Bd. Radiology. Fellow, Dept. Radiology, Coll. Medicine U. Ariz., Tucson, 1975, from asst. prof. to assoc. prof. radiology, 1975-87, prof., 1987—, dir. Tucson Breast Ctr., 1986-90; dir. Divsn. of Abdominal Imaging, Tucson, 1987-90; chief of staff Univ. Med. Ctr., Tucson, Ariz., 1993-94. Chmn. Soc. for Computer Applications in Radiology, Harrisburg, Pa., 1989; pres. Ariz. Radiological Soc., 1982; memb. bd. Ariz. Allopathic Med. Examiners, 1997—. Editor: The Computer in Radiology, 1986; sr. editor: Radiologic Guide to Medicial Devices and Foreign Bodies, 1994. Pres. Internat. Dark-Sky Assn., Tucson, 1988-97, Tucson Amateur Astronomy Assn., 1 989-91. Lt. USN, 1961-71, Vietnam. Am. Coll. Radiology fellow, 1991. Mem. Phi Beta Kappa, Alpha Omega Alpha. Republican. Achievements include patent for CCD mammography. Office: Univ Ariz Dept Radiology AHSC 1501 N Campbell Ave Tucson AZ 85724-0001

HUNTER, TODD LEE, secondary school music educator; b. Phoenixville, Pa., July 7, 1954; s. Edward Gilmore and Mary Louise (Miller) H.; m. Deborah Ann Johnson, Oct. 9, 1976 (dec. Mar. 1996); 1 child, Lauren Elizabeth; m. Michele Suzanne DeLaunay, July 19, 1997; 1 child, Paul, Vanessa Victoria. B Music Edn., Mansfield U. of Pa., 1976; MusM in Edn., West Chester U. of Pa., 1983. Cert. music tchr., Pa. Instrumental and gen. music tchr. Minersville (Pa.) Area H.S., 1977-80; instrumental music tchr. Berwick (Pa.) Area Sr. H.S., 1980-87; music and instrumental music tchr. Ctrl. Bucks West H.S., Doylestown, Pa., 1987-88; music, instrumental music tchr., head dept. Dallas

(Pa.) Sr. H.S., 1988—. Prin. trombone Bloomsburg (Pa.) U. and Cmty. Orch., 1976—, Schuylkill Symphony Orch., Pottsville, Pa., 1991-93; mem. trombone sect. Susquehanna Valley Chorale Orch., Selinsgrove, Pa., 1985-91; trombonist, vocalist, mem. aux. percussion sect. Daddy-O and the Sax Maniax, Scranton and Wilkes Barre, Pa., 1992—. Musician Gene Dempsey Orch., Scranton, 1980—, Penn Ctrl. Wind Band, Lewisburg, Pa., 1996—. Mem. NEA, Pa. Music Educators Assn., Music Educators Nat. Conf., Pa. State Edn. Assn., Phi Mu Alpha Sinfonia, Kappa Kappa Psi. Avocations: performing, arranging music, hunting, fishing, travel. Home: 382 Fowlersville Rd Bloomsburg PA 17815-6964 Office: Dallas Sr HS PO Box 2000 Dallas PA 18612-0720 E-mail: toddbone@ptdprolog.net.

HUNTER, TONY (ANTHONY REX HUNTER), molecular biologist, educator; b. Ashford, Kent, Eng., Aug. 23, 1943; came to U.S., 1971; s. Ranulph Rex and Nellie Ruby Elsie (Hitchcock) H.; m. Philippa Charlotte Marrack, July 19, 1969 (div. 1974); m. Jennifer Ann Maureen Price, June 8, 1992; children: Sean Alexander Brocas, James Samuel Alan. BA, U. Cambridge, Eng., 1965, MA, 1966, PhD, 1969. Rsch. fellow Christ's Coll., U. Cambridge, 1968-71, 73-75; rsch. assoc. Salk Inst., San Diego, 1971-73, asst. prof., 1975-78, assoc. prof., 1978-82, prof., 1982—, Am. Cancer Soc. Rsch. Prof., 1992—. Adj. prof. biology U. Calif. San Diego, La Jolla, 1982—. Contbr. articles to sci. jours. Recipient award, Am. Bus. Found. for Cancer Rsch., 1988, Katharine Berkan Judd award, Meml. Sloan-Kettering Cancer Ctr., 1992, Internat. award, Gairdner Found., 1994, Hopkins Meml. award, 1994, Mott prize, GM Cancer Rsch. Found., 1994, Feodor Lynen medal, 1999, J. Allyn Taylor Internat. prize in medicine, John P. Robarts Rsch. Inst. and C.H. Stiller Meml. Found., 2000, Keio Med. Sci. prize, Keio U. Med. Sci. Fund, Tokyo, 2001, Sergio Lombroso award in cancer rsch., Weizmann Inst. Sci., 2003, City of Medicine award, Durham Health Ptnrs., 2003. Fellow Am. Acad. Arts and Scis., Royal Soc. London, Royal Soc. for Arts, Mfrs. and Commerce; mem. NAS (fgn. assoc.), European Molecular Biology Orgn. (assoc.). Avocations: white water rafting, desert camping. Home: 4578 Vista de la Patria Del Mar CA 92014-4150 Office: Salk Inst Biol Studies Molecular-Cell Biology Lab 10010 N Torrey Pines Rd La Jolla CA 92037-1099 E-mail: hunter@salk.edu.

HUNTER, VICTOR LEE, marketing executive, consultant; b. Garrett, Ind., Mar. 1, 1947; s. John Joseph and Martha May (Brown) H.; m. Linda Ann Loudermilk, Dec. 19, 1969; children: Jed, Andrew, Matthew, Holly. BS, Purdue U., 1969; MBA, Harvard U., 1971. Dir. mktg. Kreuger, Inc., Green Bay, Wis., 1971-75; pres. B&I Furniture, Milw., 1975-81, Hunter Bus. Group, LLC, Milw., 1981—. Bd. dirs. Wm. K. Walthers Co., Milw. Author: Business-to-Business Marketing: Creating a Community of Customers, 1997. Lay leader United Meth. Ch., Whitefish Bay, Wis., 1985; mem. exec. com. Greater Milw. Conv. and Visitors Bur. Mem. Direct Mktg. Assn., Wis. Pres.' Orgn., Bus. to Bus. Direct Mktg. Coun., Strategic Accounts Mgmt. Assn. (bd. dirs.). Office: Hunter Business Group PO Box 12970 Milwaukee WI 53212-0970

HUNTER, WILLIAM DENNIS, lawyer; b. Boise, Idaho, June 26, 1943; s. William Gregory and Lorene (Persilla) H.; m. Jane Emily Porter, Apr. 30, 1966; children: Keith Alan, Elise Aubrey. BA, Stanford U., 1965; JD, U. Calif., San Francisco, 1973. Bar: Calif. 1973, U.S. Dist. Ct. (no. dist.) Calif. 1974, U.S. Ct. Appeals (9th cir.) 1974, U.S. Supreme Ct. 1996. Assoc. Pettit & Martin, San Francisco, 1973-79, ptnr., 1980-92, counsel, 1993-95, Collette & Erickson LLP, San Francisco, 1995-2000; regional counsel The Nature Conservancy, San Francisco, 2000—. Bd. dirs. City Celebration, Inc., San Francisco, 1984-91, pres., 1989-91. Recipient Service award Calif. Nature Conservancy, 1987. Mem. ABA, Calif. State Bar Assn., San Francisco Bar Assn., Nat. Assn. Installation Devel. (regional dir. 1993-2000), Order of coif. Democrat. Office: The Nature Conservancy 201 Mission St 4th Fl San Francisco CA 94105

HUNTER, WILLIAM SCHMIDT, engineering executive, environmental engineer; b. Bellwood, Pa., Mar. 24, 1931; s. William Franklin and Mary Mildred (Schmidt) H.; m. Barbara Ruth Crosland (dec. Mar. 1959); m. Sandra Lee Showalter, Aug. 26, 1961 (dec. Sept. 1991); m. Mary Elizabeth Tyson, Sept. 6, 1997; children: Felicia Fawn, Clarissa Cay, Patricia Schmidt. BSME, Lehigh U., 1953. Registered profl. engr., Pa. Project engr. W.Va. Pulp & Paper Co., Tyrone, Pa., 1953-56, plant engr. Williamsburg, Pa., 1956-61; project engr. St. Regis Paper Co., DeFeriet, N.Y., 1961-62; plant engr. Ga. Pacific Corp., Lyons Falls, N.Y., 1962-67; sr. project engr. Allied Paper Co., Kalamazoo, Mich., 1967-69, Hammermill Paper Co., Erie, Pa., 1969-80; chief engr. Stora Newton Falls, N.Y., 1980-81, v.p. engring., 1981-90, dir. environ. affairs, 1990-95, Appleton Papers Inc., Newton Falls Mill, Newton Falls, N.Y., 1995-97; coord. econ. renewal program Clifton-Fine Econ. Devel. Corp., Wanakena, N.Y., 1999-2001, treas., 2001—. Councilman Williamsburg Borough Coun., 1961; mem. legis. adv. com. to state assemblywoman, 1994—98; pres., trustee Edinboro (Pa.) Presbyn. Ch., 1978—79; bd. dirs. Am. Cancer Soc., Lewis County, NY, 1995—97; vice chmn. Solid Waste Disposal Authority, St. Lawrence County, NY, 1992, 1993, chmn., 1994, 1995, 1996, 1997; com. chmn. Explorer Scouts Boy Scouts Am., Williamsburg, Pa., 1959; mem. com. Devel. Authority North Country Solid Waste Mgmt., Lewis, Jefferson and St. Lawrence Counties, NY, 1994, 1995, 1996; mem. Residents Com. to Protect the Adirondacks, 1996—; mem. The Adirondack Coun., 1997—; bd. dirs. Clifton-Fine Hosp. Bd. Mgrs., 2001—. Mem. ASME, TAPPI, Altoona Engring. Soc. (bd. dirs. 1955-58), Adirondack Nature Conservancy, Sierra Club, Nature Conservancy. Avocation: amateur radio. Home: 23 Colby Rd Star Lake NY 13690-3137 Office: Clifton-Fine Econ Devel Corp PO Box 115 Wanakena NY 13695 E-mail: whunter@northnet.org.

HUNTER BLAIR, PAULINE CLARKE, author; b. Kirkby-in-Ashfield, Eng., May 19, 1921; d. Charles Leopold and Dorothy Kathleen (Milum) Clarke; m. Peter Hunter Blair, Feb., 1969. BA with honors, Somerville Coll., Oxford U., Eng., 1943. Free-lance writer, 1948—. Lectr. Author (writing as Pauline Clarke): (novels) The Pekinese Princess, 1948, The Great Can, 1952, The White Elephant, 1952, Smith's Hoard, 1955, The Boy with the Erpingham Hood, 1956, Sandy the Sailor, 1956, James, The Policeman, 1957, James and the Robbers, 1959, Torolv The Fatherless, 1959, 2d edit., 1973, The Lord of the Castle, 1960, The Robin Hooders, 1960, James and the Smugglers, 1961, Keep the Pot Boiling, 1961, The Twelve and the Genii, 1962 (Libr. Assn. Carnegie medal, 1962, Lewis Carrol Shelf award, 1963, Deutsche Jugend Buchpreis, 1968), Silver Bells and Cockle Shells, 1962, James and the Black Van, 1963, Crowds of Creatures, 1964, The Bonfire Party, 1966, The Two Faces of Silenus, 1972; author: (under pseudonym Helen Clare) Five Dolls in a House, 1953, Merlin's Magic, 1953, Bel The Giant and Other Stories, 1956, Five Dolls and the Monkey, 1956, Five Dolls in the Snow, 1957, Five Dolls and Their Friends, 1959, Seven White Pebbles, 1960, Five Dolls and the Duke, 1963; author: (under pseudonym of Helen Clare) The Cat and the Fiddle and Other Stories from Bel, the Giant, 1968; author: (writing as Pauline Hunter Blair) The Nelson Boy, 1999, A Thorough Seaman, 2000, Warscape, 2001, Jacob's Ladder, 2003; book reviewer, contbr.: Times Lit. Supplement. Mem.: Brit. Soc. Authors. Home: Church Farm House Bottisham Cambridge CB5 9BA England Office: care Curtis Brown Ltd Haymarket House 28/29 Haymarket London SW1Y 4SP England also: care John Cushman Assocs Inc 24 E 38th St New York NY 10016-2502

HUNTER-BONE, MAUREEN CLAIRE, magazine editor; d. Eugene Francis and Audrey Dolores (Connellan) Hunter; m. Stanley Bone, Nov. 2, 1974; children: John Hunter Bone, Caroline Vandervoort Bone. BA in English lit., St. Mary's Coll., Notre Dame, Ind., 1968. Writer Scholastic Mags., N.Y.C., 1968-69, from asst. editor to editor, 1969-79; freelance writer N.Y.C., 1979-87; sr. editor 3-2-1 Contact Mag., N.Y.C., 1987; editor Kid City Mag., N.Y.C., 1988-90, editor-in-chief, 1990-91; editor-in-chief Kid City and Ghostwriter mags. Ghostwriter Books, Ghostwriter Newspaper Feature, N.Y.C., 1991-94; v.p., editor-in-chief juvenile periodicals Children's TV Workshop, N.Y.C., 1994—. Author: First Follow Nature, 1970, Adventures with a 3-Spined Stickleback, 1972. Mem. nat. ednl. adv. com. U.S. Bicentennial Com., Washington, 1988-91; bd. advisors Epiphany Community Nursery Sch., N.Y.C., 1987-92. Mem. Am. Soc. Mag. Editors (screening judge for nat. mag. awards 1993-96), Ednl. Press Assn. (bd. dirs. 1991-93, Disting. Achievement award 1988-95). Avocations: painting, music. Office: Childrens TV Workshop One Lincoln Plz New York NY 10023

HUNTER-STIEBEL, PENELOPE, art historian; b. Washington; d. Burton Leath and Beulah (Wooten) H.; m. Gerald G. Stiebel; 1 child, Hunter. BA, Barnard Coll., 1968; MA, NYU, 1971. With Met. Mus. of Art, N.Y.C., 1969-83, asst. curator, 1975-79, assoc. curator, 1979-83; curatorial cons. N.Y.C., 1983-86; prin. Rosenberg & Stiebel, Inc., N.Y.C., 1986-2000; consulting curator of European art Portland (Oreg.) Art Mus. Exhbn. curator Met. Mus. Art, Rochester (N.Y.) Meml. Art Gallery, Detroit Inst. Art, Philbrook Mus., Portland (Oreg.) Mus. Art. Editor: Stroganoff: The Palace and Collections of a Russian Noble Family, 2000, Stuff of Dreams from the Paris Musee des Arts Decoratifs, 2002, Triumph of French Painting: 17th Century Masterpieces, 2003. Office: 252 E 68th St New York NY 10021

HUNTINGTON, EARL LLOYD, lawyer, retired natural resources company executive; b. Orangeville, Utah, Sept. 2, 1929; s. Lloyd S. and Hannah Annette (Cox) H.; m. Phyllis Ann Reed; children: Jane, Ann, Stephen. BS, U. Utah, 1951, JD, 1956; LL.M., Georgetown U., 1959. Bar: Utah 1956, D.C. 1959, N.Y. 1966, Conn. 1988. Trial atty. Dept. Justice, Washington, 1956-63; counsel Texasgulf Inc., NYC, 1963-74, v.p., gen. counsel, 1974-81, sr. v.p., gen. counsel, 1981-90, also bd. dir., 1981-94; sr. v.p., gen. counsel, dir. Elf Aquitaine Inc., 1982-90, ret., 1990. Case note editor U. Utah Law Rev., 55-56. Served with U.S. Army, 1951-53. Mem. Monarch Country Club, Country Club Darien, Order of Coif, Phi Delta Phi, Beta Gamma Sigma.

HUNTINGTON, HILLARD GRISWOLD, economist; b. Boston, Apr. 10, 1944; s. Hillard Bell and Ruth Smedley (Wheeler) H.; m. Honor Mary Griffin, Sept. 30, 1972; children: Honora Redmond, Emma Anne Hillard. BS, Cornell U., 1967; MA, SUNY, Binghamton, 1972, PhD, 1974. Staff economist Fed. Energy Adminstrn., Washington, 1974-77; dir., sr. economist Data Resources, Inc., Washington, 1977-80; exec. dir. Energy Modeling Forum Stanford (Calif.) U., 1980—. Vol. U.S. Peace Corps., Pub. Utilities Authority, Monrovia, Liberia, 1967-69; vis. rsch. assoc. Inst. Devel. Studies, U. Nairobi, Kenya, 1972-73; mem. joint U.S.-U.S.S.R. Nat. Acad. Sci. Panel on Energy Conservation, 1986-90; peer rev. panel Nat. Acid Precipitation Assessment Program Task Force, Ctrs. for Excellence Govt. Can., Nat. Petroleum Coun., Commn. for Environ. Coop. N.Am.; cons. Argonne Nat. Lab., Electric Power Rsch. Inst., others. Editor Macroeconomic Impacts of Energy Shocks, 1987, N. Am. Natural Gas Markets: selected tech. studies, 1989, Designing Competitive Electricity Markets, 1998. Life fellow Clare Hall, Cambridge (Eng.) U. Fellow U.S. Assn. for Energy Econs. (sr., pres. 1997), Internat. Assn. Energy Econs. (sr., v.p. publs. 1990-92, program chmn. N.Am. conf., program chmn. internat. conf.), Am. Statis. Assn. (com. on energy stats. 1992-94), Am. Econ. Assn. Home: 305 Hermosa Way Menlo Park CA 94025-5821 Office: Stanford U 450 Terman Ctr Stanford CA 94305-4026 E-mail: hillh@stanford.edu.

HUNTINGTON, JAMES CANTINE, JR., equipment manufacturing company executive; b. Detroit, Mar. 21, 1928; s. James Cantine and Joanna (Donlon) H.; m. Bettyanne Hopkins, Sept. 21, 1973; children: James, Ann, Patricia, Carol, Judith, Amy. B.E.E., Cornell U., 1950. Mktg. exec. Harnischfeger Corp., Milw., 1953-62; cons. Milw., 1962-64; mgr. Colt Industries, Beloit, Wis., 1964-67; v.p., dir. Clark Equipment Co., Buchanan, Mich., 1967-76; sr. v.p. Am. Standard, Inc., 1976-88; ret., 1988. Served with AUS, 1945-47, 50-53. Mem. Constrn. Industry Mfrs. Assn., Delta Kappa Epsilon, Tau Beta Pi, Eta Kappa Nu. Home: 613 Twin Pine Rd Pittsburgh PA 15215-1568

HUNTINGTON, LAWRENCE SMITH, investment banker; b. NYC, June 13, 1935; s. Prescott B. and Sarah H. (Powell) H.; m. Olivia Hallowell (div.); children: Christopher Bowditch, Charles Stewart Butler, Matthew Hallowell; m. Caroline Ballard BA, Harvard U., 1957; LL.B., New York Law Sch., 1964, LLD (hon.), 1998. With Fiduciary Trust Co. Internat., N.Y.C., 1961-2000, pres., CEO, 1973-99, chmn. bd., CEO, 1983-2000. Dir. Bus. Execs. for Nat. Security, 1993-2000, Woods Hole Rsch. Ctr., 1994—, chmn., 1997—. Bd. dirs. St. Luke's-Roosevelt Hosp., N.Y.C., 1974, chmn., 1975-81, 96-2001; bd. dirs. World Wildlife Fund, Washington, 1977-96, chmn., 1984-86, mem. nat. coun., 1996-2002; bd. dirs. Trinity Ch., N.Y.C.; bd. dirs. Citizens Budget Com., N.Y.C., 1970—, trustee, 1970—, chmn. 1978-84, The Commonwealth Fund, 1989—, N.Y. Law Sch., 1984—, chmn., 1992-97, Opsail, 1992—; mem. adv. bd. N.Y. State Common Retirement Fund Investment Com., 1981-87; dir. Josiah Macy, Jr. Found., 1981—; trustee Santa Fe Inst., 1988-98; trustee South Street Seaport, 1988—, chmn., 1999—; mem. adv. bd. NASD Internat. Mkts., 1994-99. Lt. USCG, 1959-61 Mem.: Explorers Club, N.Y. Yacht Club (trustee, commodore 2002—), Am. Alpine Club, Century Assn.

HUNTINGTON, ROBERT GRAHAM, environmental business consultant; b. Mt. Holly, N.J., Mar. 12, 1934; s. Harold Graham and Mary Helen (Curtis) H.; m. Patricia Ann Pearsall, Jan. 28, 1956; children: Gracia Curtis, Anne Wolcott Huntington Fielden. BSME, Union Coll., 1956; MS in Engring., Harvard U., 1959, postgrad., 1968. Prin. devel. engr. Carrier R&D Corp., Syracuse, N.Y., 1959-60; corp. v.p. Am. Air Filter Corp., Louisville, 1960-85; v.p. Allis Chalmers Corp., Milw., 1979-85; sr. v.p. Rsch. Cottrell Corp., Branchburg, N.J., 1985-86; sr. v.p., subs. dir. Environtl. Elements Corp., Balt., 1986-96; owner, prin. Huntington Cons., Cooperstown, N.Y., 1994—. Pres. Indsl. Gas Cleaning Inst., Alexandria, 1982-84, dir., 1965-85; chmn. Environtl. Industry Coun., Washington, 1985-94; adv. bd. Power Industry Coun., Detroit, 1989-94 Patentee in field. Trustee bd. advisors Union Coll., Schenectady, 1989—2001, past chmn., mem. dean's engring. coun., 1989; past pres. Glimmer Glass Opera Guild; past bd. dirs. Pro Musica Rara, Balt., Glimmer Glass Opera Co., Cooperstown, NY. With U.S. Army, 1956—59. Mem.: Internat. Execs. Svc. Corps, Assn. Iron and Steel Engrs., Samuel Huntington Hist. Preservation Trust, Hon. Order Ky. Cols., Susquehanna Soc. for Prevention Cruelty to Animals (bd. dirs. 1995—2002), Mohican Club (Cooperstown), Ctr. Club (Balt.), Cooperstown Country Club. Presbyterian. Avocations: performing arts, educational leadership, historic preservation, technology, civic contribution. Home: 13 Main St Cooperstown NY 13326-1329 E-mail: byngh@capital.net.

HUNTINGTON, ROBERT HOWARD, business management executive; b. Mpls., Mar. 25, 1955; s. Robert Howard and Cecelia (Benchak) H.; m. Susan Mary McCafferty; children: Ashley, Aidan. BA, Middlebury Coll., 1978, MA, 1983; MBA, Dartmouth Coll., 1985; EdD, Harvard U., 1997. Asst. mgr. Gen. Foods Corp., White Plains, 1985-87, Allied Domecq Quick Svc. Restaurants, Dunkin' Donuts/ Baskin-Robbins /Togo's Eateries, Randolph, Mass.; dir. Allied Domecq Retailing USA, Dunkin' Donuts/Baskin-Robbins, Randolph, Mass., 1991-96, v.p., 1996—. Tchg. fellow grad. sch. edn. Harvard U., Cambridge, Mass., 1991-92, instr. summer sch., 1991; tchg. asst. Harvard Ext. Sch., 1988-90; bd. trustees Lasell Coll., Newton, Mass., 1998—. Bd. dir. First Parish Unitarian-Universalist, Medfield. Fellow: Phi Beta Kappa; mem.: Sierra Club. Home: 70 Adams St Medfield MA 02052-1614 Office: Allied Domecq Quick Svc Restaurants 14 Pacella Park Dr Randolph MA 02368-1773

HUNTINGTON, THOMAS ROBERT, surgeon; b. St. Paul, Minn., 1953; MD, U. Ariz., 1975. Diplomate Am. Bd. Surgery, Am. Bd. Surg. Intern Vanderbilt U. Hosp., Nashville, Tenn., 1975-76; resident in surgery U. Ariz. Hosp., Tucson, 1976-77, 78-81; pvt. practice Boise, Idaho, 1982—. Hosp. appts.: St. Alphonsus Hosp., Boise, St. Luke's Hosp., Boise. Fellow ACS, Internat. Coll. Surgeons. Office: 222 N 2nd St Ste 107 Boise ID 83702-6129

HUNTLEY, DIANE E. dental hygiene educator; b. Concord, N.H., Oct. 1, 1946; d. George Williams and Esther A. (Gadwah) H. AS, Fones Sch. Dental Hygiene, Bridgeport, Conn., 1966; BA, U. Bridgeport, Conn., 1968; MA, SUNY, Buffalo, 1971; PhD, Kans. State U., 1985. Registered dental hygienist. Dental hygienist various gen. practice dentists, Conn., Colo., 1966-76; clin. instr. Fones Sch. Dental Hygiene, 1971-74; asst. prof. U. Colo. Dental Sch., Denver, 1974-76; asst. prof. dental hygiene Wichita (Kans.) State U., 1976-82, assoc. prof., 1982—. Vol. hygienist Good Samaritan Clinic, Wichita, 1989-90, 92—. Contbr. articles to profl. jours. Mem. dental adv. bd. United Meth. Urban Ministries, Wichita, 1990-92; mem. P.A.N.D.A. Coalition of Kans. Exec. Com., 1995—. Mem.: AAUP (Wichita State U. chpt. sec.treas. 1988—91), Am. Dental Hygienists Assn. (editl. dir. 1983—85, historian 1993—2001), Kans. Dental Hygienists assn. (del. 1989—93, treas. 1998—2000, parliamentarian 1998—2001, trustee 2000—03), Wichita Dental Hygienists Assn. (pres. 1982—83, treas. 1988—90, trustee 1990—91), Am. Dental Edn. Assn., Apha Eta, Phi Kappa Phi. Office: Wichita State U 1845 Fairmount St Wichita KS 67260-0144

HUNTLEY, JAMES ROBERT, government official, international affairs scholar and consultant; b. Tacoma, Wash., July 27, 1923; s. Wells and Laura H.; m. Colleen Grounds Smith, May 27, 1967; children by previous marriage: Mark, David, Virginia, Jean. BA magna cum laude in Econs., Sociology, U. Wash., 1948, postgrad. sociology and internat. relations (Carnegie fellow), 1951; MA in Internat. Relations, Harvard U., 1956. Cons. Wash. Parks Recreation Commn., Olympia, 1949-51; exchange of persons officer U.S. Fgn. Service, Frankfurt, Nuremberg, Germany, 1952-54; dir. cultural center USIA, Hof/Saale, Germany, 1954-55; USIA postgrad. scholar Harvard U., 1955-56; asst. to Pres.'s coordinator for Hungarian relief Washington, 1956; European regional affairs officer USIA, Washington, 1956-58; dep. pub. affairs officer U.S. Mission to European Communities, Brussels, 1958-60; mem. U.S. Delegation to Atlantic Congress, London, 1959; sec. organizing com. Atlantic Inst., Brussels and Milan, 1960, exec. officer and co-founder Paris, 1960-63; dir. Atlantic Inst. (N.Am. Office), Washington, 1963-65; founder, sec. Com. Atlantic Studies, 1963-65; sec. edn. com. NATO Parliamentarians Conf., Brussels, 1960-64; program asso., internat. affairs div. Ford Found., N.Y.C., 1965-67; sec. gen. Council Atlantic Colls., London, 1967-68; ind. writer, cons., lectr., internat. affairs Guildford, Eng., 1968-74; founder, sec. Assn. Mid-Atlantic Clubs, 1970-74; founder, sec. gen. Standing Conf. Atlantic Orgns., 1972-74; rsch. fellow, sr. advisor to pres. on internat. affairs Battelle Meml. Inst., Seattle, 1974-83; pres., chief exec. officer Atlantic Council of U.S., Washington, 1983-85; ind. cons., author internat. affairs, 1985—. European corr., environ. affairs Saturday Rev./World, 1972-74; Corrs. World Wide, London, 1970-74; European corr. Non-Profit Report, 1970-74 Author: The NATO Story, 1965, (with W.R. Burgess) Europe and America - The Next Ten Years, 1970, Man's Environment and the Atlantic Alliance, 1972, Uniting the Democracies, 1980, Pax Democratica—A Strategy for the 21st Century, 1998, 2d edit., 2001; contbr. articles to profl. jours. Bd. dirs. Internat. Standing Conf. Phlanthropy, 1969-74, Assn. to Unite Democracies, 1976-94, Seattle Com. Fgn. Rels., 1975-78, World Affairs Coun. Seattle, 1975-83, adv. bd. 1986—, Bainbridge Island Land Trust, 1994-97; founding chmn. Coms. for a Cmty. of Democracies, 1979-92; co-founder 21st Century Found., 1987-91; mem. adv. bd. 21st Century Trust, London, 1988—; co-founder Next Century Initiative, 1992-95, New Century Initiative, 1996-99, pres. 1996-98; co-founder, v.p. Coun. for Cmty. of Democracies, 1999—. Recipient Disting. Eagle Scout award 1995; named Kappa Sigma Man of Yr., 1999. Mem. Rainier Club (Seattle), DACOR (Washington). Home and Office: 1213 Towne Rd Sequim WA 98382-8049 E-mail: huntleypax@aol.com. *For a full life, embrace a worthy cause. Mine is the unity of the democracies. America's most precious asset is its free political system. It can be successfully defended only if we merge our force, our hearts and our fortune with like-minded peoples. Like-mindedness is not simply a gift of history; it must be cultivated. My life's aim has been to forge consensus among the democracies as a prelude to the creation of a free, just, and durable world order.*

HUNTLEY, ROBERT ROSS, physician, educator; b. Wadesboro, N.C., Sept. 6, 1926; s. George W. and Louise (Ross) H.; m. Joan Cornoni, Apr. 10, 1976; children: Katherine, Robert, Julia, Elizabeth, Jeffress. BS in Chemistry, Davidson Coll., 1947; MD, Bowman-Gray Sch. Medicine, 1951. Diplomate: Am. Bd. Preventive Medicine (trustee 1974-78), Am. Bd. Family Practice. Intern U. Mich. Hosp., Ann Arbor, 1951-53; resident, fellow N.C. Meml. Hosp., Chapel Hill, 1959-62; pvt. practice medicine Warrenton, N.C., 1953-58; from instr. to assoc. prof. medicine and preventive medicine U. N.C., Chapel Hill, 1959-68; asso. dir. Nat. Center for Health Services Research, HEW, 1968-70; prof., chmn. dept. community and family medicine Georgetown U., 1970-89, prof. emeritus, from 1989; pres. Georgetown U. Community Health Plan, Inc., 1972-80. Chmn. health care tech. study sect. HEW, 1978—82; adj. prof. dept. family medicine U. N.C. Sch. Medicine, 1994—99. Editor various profl. books; contbr. articles to profl. jours. Served with USN, 1945—46. Mem.: Acad. Medicine Washington (emeritus), N.C. Med. Soc., D.C. Med. Soc., Assn. Tchrs. Preventive Medicine (pres. 1974—75). Democrat. Methodist. Died Dec. 8, 2002.

HUNTLEY, ROBERT STEPHEN, newspaper editor; b. Winston-Salem, N.C., Mar. 6, 1943; m. Linda Fabry; children: Kristine Elizabeth, Katherine Vallie. BA in Journalism, U. N.C., 1965. Reporter UPI, various locations, 1965-69, writer, editor broadcast and gen. news depts. Chgo., 1969-77, exec. editor nat. broadcast dept., 1977-78; bur. chief Commodity News Svc., Chgo., 1978-79, U.S. News & World Report, Chgo., 1979-82, assoc. editor Washington, 1982-85, sr. editor, 1985-86; reporter, rewrite specialist Chgo. Sun Times, 1986-90, met. editor, 1990-91, asst. mng. editor/metro, 1991-97; editl. page editor, 1997—. Bd. dirs. City News Bur., Chgo, 1993-97, pres., 1996; media fellow Hoover Instit. Stanford U., 2001 V.p. Ill. Freedom of Info. Coun., 1994. Recipient Stick-O-Type award for feature writing Chgo. Newspaper Guild, 1987, Appreciation cert. for outstanding contbns. to freedom of info. Nat. Ctr. Freedom of Info. Studies at Loyola U.-Chgo., 1993; Media fellow Hoover Instn., Stanford U., 2001. Mem. Ill. Freedom of Info. Coun. (v.p. 1994). Office: Chgo Sun-Times 401 N Wabash Ave Chicago IL 60611-5642

HUNTLEY, WILLIAM BARNEY, educator; b. Feb. 19, 1933; AB, Duke U; BD, Yale U; PhD, Duke U. Chaplain Ch. of St. Mary Westminster (Mo.) Coll., Mo., 1964-74, chmn. divsn. humanities, 1969-72, dean of students, 1972-74; assoc. dean Waseda U., Tokyo, 1986-87; chair dept. religious studies U. Redlands (Calif.), 1977-82, 84-86, 1997—, dir. Asian studies program, 1991—2002, Crawford prof. of religious studies, 2000—. Author: Experiencing Japan; contbr. articles to profl. jours. Scholar-in-residence Reitaku U., Kashiwa, Japan, 1988-89. Address: 1474 Pacific St Redlands CA 92373-6936 E-mail: bill_huntley@redlands.edu.

HUNTLEY, WILLIAM THOMAS, III, investor, consultant; b. Greensboro, North Carolina, Mar. 13, 1935; s. William Thomas II and Lillian H.; m. Gladys Louise (Bowden), Aug. 11, 1953; children: David C., William Thomas IV, Charlton A., Kimberly Patrick. BA in Econ., Davidson Coll., N.C., 1958. CPCU. Field rep. Aetna Casualty and Surety Co., Atlanta, 1958—62; marine dept. mgr. Chubb and Son, Inc., Atlanta, Dallas, 1962—67; sr. v.p. Pritchard and Jerden, Inc., Atlanta, 1967—96; mng. gen. ptnr. Huntley and Bradley, Ltd., Partnership, Roswell, Ga., 1995—. Com. chmn. Peach Bowl, 1969-75. Mem. Coun. of Ins. Agt. and Brokers (pres. 1990-91), Atlanta Assn. Ind. Ins. Agt. (pres. 1979-80), Ind. Ins. Agt. Ga. (bd. dirs. 1979-81), Atlanta C. of C. (chair sports com. 1969), Atlanta Athletic Club, Golf Club Amelia Island. Republican. Presbyterian. Avocations: golf, numismatics, investing. Home: 1807 Atlantic Pl Amelia Island FL 32034-5818 Office: Huntley and Bradley LP 2030 Riverside Rd Roswell GA 30076-4026

HUNTON, RICHARD EDWIN, family practice physician; b. Boonville, Ind., Dec. 23, 1924; s. Edwin Chandler and Nellie Celicia (Wright) H.; m. Agnes Katherine Setser, Aug. 22, 1953; children: Jennifer Leigh, Richard Edwin Jr. AA, George Washington U., 1947, AB, 1949, MD, 1952. Diplomate Am. Bd. Family Practice, Nat. Bd. Med. Examiners. Intern Gallinger Mcpl. Hosp., Washington, 1952-53; resident Spartanburg (S.C.) Gen. Hosp., 1953-54; staff physician Scurry Clinic, Greenwood, S.C., 1954-89; locum tenens Carolina Health Ctrs., Greenwood, 1990—. Mem. med. staff Self Regional Healthcare, Greenwood, 1954—, chief of staff, 1976, dir. med. edn., 1981-89, clin. asst. prof. family medicine, 1980-93, institutional rev. bd., 1980—. Author: Formula For Fitness, 1966; film prodr. Constrictive Pericarditis, 1956. Trustee Faith Home Rehab. Ctr., Greenwood, 1979-80. With U.S. Army, 1943-45. Decorated Purple Heart, Bronze star. Fellow Am. Acad. of Family Practice (state bd. dirs. 1972-76); mem. AMA, Am. Acad. of Family Physicians, Disabled Am. Vets., Gideons Internat., Phi Eta Sigma, Phi Beta Kappa. Baptist. Avocations: organ, piano, woodworking, photography, shooting sports. Home: 112 Wendover Rd Greenwood SC 29649-8923 E-mail: drhunton@greenwood.net.

HUNTOON, ANN KRISTEN, performing arts association administrator, music educator; b. Syracuse, N.Y., June 26, 1959; d. Richard Benson and Jean Robb Huntoon; m. Ronald C. Knuth; children: Daniel Charles Knuth, David Lambert Knuth. Diploma, RN, Mount Carmel Sch. Nursing, Columbus, Ohio, 1980; MusB, U. Wis., Stevens Point, 2001. RN Wis. RN oper. rm./recovery rm. W.Va. U. Hosp., Morgantown, 1982—84; RN surg. cardiac ICU Cleve. Clinic, 1984—85; RN surg. ICU St. Joseph's Hosp., Marshfield, Wis., 1985—86, RN cardiac rehab. nurse clinician, 1991—92; pvt. music instr. Marshfield, 1996—; arts adminstr. Boxwood Music Ltd., Balt., 2002—; substitute tchr. Marshfield Pub. Schs., 2003—. 2nd flute Ctrl. Wis. Symphony Orch., Stevens Point,

1999—; pres. bd. dirs. Boxwood Festival, Ltd., Balt., 1999—. Mem. worship and music com. First Presbyn. Ch., Marshfield, 1990—, elder, 2001—02. Mem.: PEO, Marshfield Arts Adv. Coun., Upper Midwest Flute Assn. (bd. mem. 1999—2002), Nat. Flute Assn., Omicron Delta Kappa, Pi Kappa Lambda, Phi Kappa Phi. Avocations: reading, music. Home: 713 S Oak Ave Marshfield WI 54449 Office: Boxwood Music Ltd 714 Wyndhurst Ave Baltimore MD 21210

HUNTOON, PETER WESLEY, geoscience consultant; b. West Orange, N.J., Aug. 27, 1942; s. Perry Speer Huntoon and Mary Elizabeth Klemann; m. Susan Beatrice Burma (dec. Nov. 1970); m. Victoria Anne Gillespie, Jan. 8, 1971 (div. 1989); 1 child, Trey Huntoon; life ptnr., Kathleen Vera Kimball. Student, Ariz. State Coll., 1961-63; BS, U. Ariz., 1966, MS in Hydrology, 1968, PhD in Hydrology, 1970. Cert. profl. geologist, Wyo. Gd. Profl. Geologists, 1992; cert. profl. hydrogeologist, Am. Inst. Hydrology, 1984; cert. Ground Water Profl., Assn. Ground Water Sci. and Engring., 1987. Asst. prof. geology U. Nebr., Lincoln, 1971-74; prof. geology and geophysics U. Wyo., Laramie, 1974-98; chair and prof. environ. studies U. Nev., Las Vegas, 1998-99; cons. Boulder City, Nev., 1999—. Interim dir. Water and Energy Rsch. Inst., U. Guam, Mangilao, 1985; vis. scientist, Inst. Karst Geology, Chinese Acad. Geol. Scis., Guilin, China, 1990. Author: Territorials, A Guide to U.S. Territorial National Bank Notes, 1980, United States Large Size National Bank Notes, 1995; author (map) Geologic Map of the Eastern Grand Canyon National Park and Vicinity, 1980 (Excellence in Publ. award Nat. Park Cooperating Assns. 1980), (map) Geologic Map of Canyonlands National Park and Vicinity, Utah, 1982; ; contbr. articles to profl. jours. Mem. Albany County Planning Commn., Laramie, 1989. Recipient Best Spkr. awards, Wyo. Geol. Assn., 1988, 90, 93, 94. Fellow Geol. Soc. Am. Democrat. Avocations: hiking, rafting, spelunking, numismatics. Home and Office: 1403 Garnet Boulder City NV 89005 E-mail: peter.huntoon@att.net.

HUNTOON, ROBERT BRIAN, chemist, food industry consultant; b. Braintree, Mass., Mar. 1, 1927; s. Benjamin Harrison and Helen Edna (Worden) H.; m. Joan Fairman Graham, Mar. 1, 1952; children: Brian Graham, Benjamin Robert, Elisabeth Ellen, Janet Lynne, Joelle. BS in Chemistry, Northeastern U., 1949, MS, 1961. Analytical chemist Mass. Dept. Public Health, microbiologist Met. Dist. Commn., 1950-53; rsch. and devel. chemist Heveatex Corp., Melrose, Mass., 1953-56; with Gen. Foods Corp., 1956-70, acting quality control mgr., 1965-67, head group rsch. and devel. Tarrytown, N.Y., 1967-70; dir. quality control U.S. Flavor div. Internat. Flavors & Fragrances, Teterboro, N.J., 1970-83, mgr. tech. svcs., 1983-87, mgr. product devel., 1987-89, cons., 1989-92; ind. cons. product devel., 1989—. Contbr. articles on flavor and food quality control to profl. and co. publs.; patentee gelatin compositions and mfg. processes. Served with USCG, 1945-46. Mem. Essential Oils Assn. (com. mem.), Flavor and Extracts Mfg. Assn. (com. mem.), Am. Chem. Soc., Inst. Food Technologists, Internat. Platform Assn., Indsl. Mgmt. Club (v.p. 1967) (Woburn), Croton Yacht Club, Saugus River Yacht Club (treas. 1967-68). Republican. Presbyterian. Office: 7 Scotland Hill Park Chestnut Ridge NY 10977-5908

HUNTRESS, BETTY ANN, retired small business owner, retired elementary school educator; b. Apr. 29, 1932; d. Emmett Slater and Catherine V. (Kihlmire) Brundage; m. Arnold Ray Huntress, June 26, 1954; children: Catherine, Michael, Carol, Alan. BA, Cornell U., 1954. Tchr. h.s., Bordentown, N.J., 1954-55; tchr. Midland (Mich.) Pub. Schs., 1968—98; ret., 1998. Asst. to prof. Delta Coll., Northwood Inst., Midland; tchr. Midland Pub. Schs., 1998—2000; owner, mgr. The Music Stand, Midland, 1979—82. Bd. dirs. Midland Ctr. for Arts, 1978-86, v.p., 1980-84, Friends of the Ctr., 1985—; charter bd. mgrs. Matrix Midland Ann. Arts and Sci. Festival, 1977-80; cons. Girl Scouts U.S., 1964-76; bd. dirs. Literacy Coun. Midland County, 1986-94, sec., 1987-91; active Mich. Internat. Coun., 1975-76, Midland Hist. Soc., 1990—, Dow Chem. Centennial Com., 1996-98; mem. Presbyn. ch. choir, 1963—. Named Midland Musician of Yr., 1977. Mem. AAUW (dir. 1962-73, pres. 1971-73, mem. Mich. state divsn. 1983-85, bd. dirs. 1993-95, Outstanding Woman as Agt. of Change award 1977, fellowship grant named in her honor 1976), LWV (bd. dirs. 1986-90, com. charter schs. 1995-99), Music Soc. Midland Ctr. for arts (dir. 1971-86, chmn. 1976-79), Midland Symphony League Soc. (2d v.p. 1995-99), Cmty. Concert Soc., Women's Study Club of Midland (pres. 1995-96), Friends of Libr., Kappa Delta Epsilon, Pi Lambda Theta, Alpha Xi Delta. Presbyterian. Home: 5316 Sunset Dr Midland MI 48640-2536 Personal E-mail: arnhunt@concentric.net.

HUNTRESS, WESLEY THEODORE, JR., scientist; b. Washington, Apr. 11, 1942; s. Wesley Theodore and Elizabeth Agnes (Moran) H.; m. Roseann Albano, June 22, 1973; 1 child, Garret. BS, Brown U., 1964; PhD, Stanford U., 1968. Scientist Jet Propulsion Lab., Pasadena, Calif., 1968-88; dep. dir earth sci. NASA, Washington, 1988-90, dir. solar system exploration, 1990-93, assoc. adminstr. space sci., 1993-98; dir. geophys. lab. Carnegie Instn. Washington, 1998—. Office: Geophys Lab Carnegie Instn Washington 5251 Broad Branch Rd NW Washington DC 20015-1305

HUNTSINGER, JAMI L. English educator; b. El Paso, Tex., Jan. 11, 1960; d. James D and Marilyn J Huntsinger. BS, U. of SD, Vermillion, SD, 1982, MA, 1989; PhD, U. of N.Mex, Albuquerque, NM, 1997. Tchg. asst. U. of N.Mex at, Albuquerque, 1986—97, Univerisity of SD, SD, 1986—97; prof. U. of Mex. at Valencia Campus, Los Lunas, N.Mex., 2001—. Mem.: MLA, ASLE, NCTE. Avocations: gardening, hiking, camping.

HUNTSINGER, JERALD E. advertising executive; Founder Huntsinger & Jeffer, Richmond. Office: Huntsinger & Jeffer 809 Brook Hill Cir Richmond VA 23227

HUNTSMAN, JON MEADE, chemical company executive; b. 1937; BS, U. Pa., 1959; MBA, U. So. Calif., 1970. With Olson Bros, Inc., North Hollywood, Calif., from 1961; assoc. adminstr. HEW, spl. asst. to the pres., 1971-72; with Huntsman Container Corp., Salt Lake City, 1972-83, Huntsman Chem. Corp. Salt Lake City, 1982—; CEO Huntsman Corp., Salt Lake City, 1996-2000, chmn., 2000—. Pres. mission LDS Ch., Washington, 1980-83. Office: Huntsman Corp 500 Huntsman Way Salt Lake City UT 84108-1235*

HUNTSMAN, JON MEADE, JR., federal agency administrator; b. Palo Alto, Calif., Mar. 26, 1960; s. Jon Meade and Karen (Haight) H.; m. Mary Katherine Cooper, Nov. 18, 1983; children: Mary Anne, Abigail, Elizabeth, Jon III. AB, U. Pa., 1987. Spl. asst. to chmn. Rep. Nat. Com., Washington, 1982; staff asst. White House, Washington, 1983; state dir. Utah Reagan-Bush campaign, Salt Lake City, 1984; v.p., dir. Huntsman Pacific Chem. Corp., Taipei, Taiwan, 1987-88; dep. asst. sec. Internat. Trade Adminstrn., Washington, 1989-90; dep. asst. sec. commerce for E. Asia and the Pacific U.S. Dept. Commerce, Washington, 1990-91; Dep. USTR Off. U.S. Trade Rep., Washington, 2001—. Chmn. U.S.-China Comml. Commn. Groups, Washington, 1990-91, U.S.-Mongolia Trade Facilitation Group, 1990-91; exec. sec. U.S.-Thailand Joint Comml. Commn., 1990-91, U.S. Pacific Islands Joint Comml. Commn., 1990-91. State dir. Utah Reagan-Bush campaign, Salt Lake City, 1984; chmn. Utah Reagan-Bush Inaugural Com., Salt Lake City, 1985; nat. del. Rep. Conv., 1984, 86. Mem. Internat. Club Washington, Asia Soc. Republican. Mem. Lds Ch. Office: Exec Off of the Pres US Trade Repr 600 17th Street NW Washington DC 20508-4801

HUNTSMAN, LEE, university provost, academic administrator; BSc in elec. engring., Stanford U., 1963; PhD in biomedical engring., U. Pa., 1968. Dir. ctr. for bioengineering U. Wash., 1980—96, assoc. dean for sci. affairs, sch. of medicine, 1993—96, provost, v.p. acad. affairs, 1997—, interim pres., 2002—. Mem. Whitaker Found. Governing Com., 1994—98; chmn. Working Gorup on Rev. of Bioengineering and Tech. Instrumentation Develop. Rsch. for the Ctro for Sci. Rev of the NIH, 1998. Fellow: Am. Ins. of Med. and Biol. Engring., Am. Assn. for the Advancement of Sci. Office: Office of the Pres U of Wash 301 Gerberding Hall Box 351230 Seattle WA 98195

HUNTSMAN, PETER R. chemicals executive; Started as truck driver Huntsman Corp., Salt Lake City, 1993—, various mgmt. positions in several of co.'s gobal divsns., v.p. Polymers, sr. v.p. purchasing and logistics, pres. Huntsman Petrochemical Corp., pres., COO, CEO, 2000—. Office: Huntsman Corp 500 Huntsman Way Salt Lake City UT 84108*

HUNTTING, CYNTHIA COX, artist; b. San Francisco, Sept. 2, 1936; d. E. Morris and Margaret (Storke) Cox; m. Edward Tyler Huntting Jr., Mar. 8, 1969 (div. 1974). BA, Smith Coll., 1958; San Francisco Art Inst., 1959. Artist Emporium White House, San Francisco, 1958-61; artist, staff Pace Program Stanford U., 1962-64; artist World Affairs Council No. Calif., San Francisco, 1964-67; artist pvt. practice San Francisco, 1968—. Mem. Modern Art Council Bd. San Francisco Mus. Modern Art, 1970-78. Active Jr. League San Francisco, Inc. Mem. Birnam Wood Golf Club (Montecito, Calif.), Town and Country, Calif. Tennis. Republican. Episcopalian. Avocations: tennis, fly fishing. Home and Office: 2720 Lyon St San Francisco CA 94123-3815

HUNTWORK, JAMES RODEN, lawyer; b. Milw., May 6, 1948; s. Daniel Lawrence and Gladys (Roden) H.; m. Patience Tipton Huntwork, July 7, 1972; children: Andrew Stuart, Sarah Noel. BA with distinction, Shimer Coll., 1968; JD, Yale U., 1972, MA Econs., 1973. Bar: Mass. 1972, Ariz. 1977. Atty. Sullivan & Worcester, Boston, 1972-77, Jennings, Strouss & Salmon, Phoenix, 1977-91, Fennemore Craig, Phoenix, 1992-98, Salmon, Lewis & Weldon, Phoenix, Ariz., 1998—. Dir. exec. com. Phoenix Econ. Growth Corp., 1987-91; state ballot security chmn. Ariz. Rep. Party, Phoenix, 1992—; originator The Comml. Law Project for Ukraine, 1991—; mem. Ariz. Ind. Redistricting Commn., 2001—. Co-recipient Judge Learned Hand Human Rels. award Am. Jewish Com., 1992. Mem. ABA, Ariz. Bar Assn., Maricopa County Bar Assn., Phoenix C. of C. (N.Am. Free Trade Task Force 1991-95). Republican. Office: Ste 200 2850 E Camelback Rd Phoenix AZ 85016-4316 E-mail: jrh@huntwork.net., jrh@slwplc.com.

HUNZICKER, WARREN JOHN, research consultant, physician, cardiologist; b. Lawrence, Kans., Sept. 26, 1920; s. Carl John and Edith (Glenn) H.; m. Marjorie Jean Owen, Apr. 16, 1946; children— Karen Hunzicker Putnam, Kathleen Ann AB, U. Kans., 1942, MD, 1944; postgrad. in medicine, Harvard U. Hosps., Peter Bent Brigham and Boston City Hosps., 1946-48. Intern St. Luke's Hosp., 1944-45; practice medicine specializing in cardiology Spokane, Wash., 1948-51, 54-58; med. dir. Nat. Life & Accident Co., Nashville, 1958-60; v.p., med. dir. Kansas City Life, Mo., 1960-80; sr. v.p. med. N.Am. Reassurance, N.Y.C., 1980-86. Assoc. clin. prof. medicine U. Mo., Kansas City, 1961-82; dir. M.I.B. Inc., Boston; med. cons. Life Ins. Med. Research Fund, Washington, 1983-97; bd. dirs. Kansa City Life Ins. Co. Contbr. articles to profl. jours. Served to lt. M.C., USNR, 1941-46, 52-53, Korea Levine fellow in cardiology Harvard U. (Peter Bent Brigham Hosp.), 1951-52 Fellow Am. Coll. Cardiology; mem. AMA, Council Life Ins. (chmn. med. sect. 1971-72), Assn. Ins. Med. Dirs. (exec. council 1971-73), Mo. Med. Assn., Union League of N.Y.C. Republican. Methodist. Avocation: fishing. Home: 1248 Stratford Rd Kansas City MO 64113-1326

HUO, BONNIE KWAN, artist; b. China, Nov. 23, 1949; d. Hok Pui and Tai Wah (Wong) Kwan; m. Rex W.C. Huo, Feb. 10, 1972; 1 child, Alina. BA, U. Calif., Berkeley, 1971; postgrad. diploma in edn., U. Hong Kong, 1972. Sole proprietor Anything Aesthetic, Hong Kong, 1987—. One-woman exhibits include Kowloon Shangrila Hotel, Hong Kong, 1989, Shenzhen Art Mus., China, 1993, Letty's Gallery, Vancouver, 1994, Pristine Harmony Art Ctr., Taipei, 1995, Modest Art Gallery, Toronto, Traditional Chinese Cultural Soc., Montreal, 1996, Melbourne Chinese Mus. & Sydney Chinese Culture Ctr., 1998, World Jour. Gallery, San Francisco, 2000, World Jour. Gallery, L.A., U. Indpls., Shenzhen Art Mus., 2003; represented in permanent collections Singapore Nat. Mus., Shenzhen Art Mus., Australia Chinese Mus., U. Indpls., Sotheby's Fine Modern Chinese Painting Auction. Recipient Cert. of Honor Suprs. of City and County of San Francisco and numberous art awards. Mem. Hong Kong Lingnan Art Assn. (vice chair), Fedn. Can. Artists, Fedn. Chinese Can. Artists in Vancouver, Hong Kong Artists Assn., Hong Kong Lan Ting Soc. (com. mem.), Internat. Calligraphy Alliance (Hong Kong chpt.), Asia Soc. Arts Am. Avocations: traveling, attending cultural events, reading, poetry. Fax: (852) 2838-9362. E-mail: ufomail@netfront.net.

HUO, SHOUQUAN, research scientist, educator; m. Yumin Li, July 3, 1967; 1 child, Lily. BS, Zhengzhou U., China, 1988, MS, 1991; PhD, Nanjing U., China, 1994. Vis. scientist Inst. for Molecular Sci., Okazaki, Japan, 1995—96; Coe rsch. fellow Hokkaido U., Sapporo, Japan, 1996—97; vis. assoc. prof. Qufu Normal U., China, 1997—98; postdoctoral rsch. assoc. Purdue U., West Lafayette, Ind., 1998—2002; sr. rsch. chemist DSM Pharms., Inc., Greenville, NC, 2002—. Author: (book) Handbook of Organopalladium Chemistry for Organic Synthesis, Titanium and Zirconium in Organic Synthesis, (invited review) Studies on the cyclometallation of ferrocenylimines (Fist-class Rsch. Achievement Award, 1996); contbr. articles to profl. jours. Mem.: Japan Chem. Soc., Am. Chem. Soc., Sigma Xi. Office: DSM Pharms Inc 5900 NW Greenville Bvld Greenville NC 27834-1887

HUO, XIAOMING, mathematician, educator; PhD, Stanford U., 1993—99. Prof. Ga. Inst. of Tech., 1999—. Contbr. articles to profl. jours. Recipient First Prize In Internat. Math. Olympiad, IMO orgn. com., 1989. Mem.: Inst. of Math. Stats. Achievements include development of var. toolboxes for signal processing. Office: School of ISyE 765 Ferst Dr Atlanta GA 30332

HUOT, RACHEL IRENE, biomedical educator, research scientist, physician; b. Manchester, N.H., Oct. 16, 1950; d. Omer Joseph and Irene Alice (Girard) Huot. BA in Biology cum laude, Rivier Coll., 1972; MS in Biology, Cath. U. Am., 1976, PhD in Biology, 1980; MD, La. State U. Health Sci. Ctr., Shreveport, 2000. Sr. technician Microbiol. Assocs., Bethesda, Md., 1974-77; chemist Uniformed Svcs. Univ. of Health Scis., Bethesda, 1977-79; biologist Nat. Cancer Inst., Bethesda, 1979-82; postdoctoral fellow S.W. Found. for Biomed. Rsch., San Antonio, 1982-85, asst. scientist, 1985-87, staff scientist, 1987-88; instr. U. Tex. Health Sci. Ctr., San Antonio, 1988-89; asst. prof., dir. basic urologic rsch. La. State U., New Orleans, 1990-96; resident in family practice Aultman Hosp., Canton, Ohio, 2001—02, U. Minn./Mayo Clinic, Waseca, 2002—. Judge sr. divsn. Alamo Regional Sci. Fair, San Antonio, 1989—90. Contbr. Vol. ARC, Christus Schumpert Hosp., Shreveport; patient educator vol. Martin Luther King Clinic, Shreveport, 1996—2000. Recipient Rsch. Svc. award, NIH, 1983—86, Searle Young Investigator award, 1994; grantee, NSF, 1972—74. Mem.: AMA, AAUW, LWV, AAAS, Minn. Acad. Family Practice, Am. Acad. Family Practice, Am. Soc. Experiment Biology, St. Vincent De Paul Soc., N.Y. Acad. Scis., Soc. In Vitro Biology, Fedn. Am. Scientists, Am. Soc. Cell Biology, Am. Assn. Cancer Rsch., Am. Soc. Microbiology, Sierra Club, Sigma Xi, Delta Epsilon Sigma, Iota Sigma Pi. Democrat. Roman Catholic. Avocation: Avocations: drawing, painting, road-racing, reading, Volksmarching. Home: 405 N 5th St Apt 416 Mankato MN 56001

HUPP, JAMES R. academic administrator; MD, U. Conn.; DMD, Harvard Sch. Dental Medicine; JD, Rutgers U.; MBA, Loyola U. Cert. Oral and Maxillofacial Surgery. Resident in internal medicine UCLA Med. Ctr.; resident in oral and maxillofacial surgery U. Conn.; chair U. Medicine and Dentistry N.J., 1989—94; prof. and chair, dept. dentistry U. Md., Baltimore, 1994—2002; dean, Sch. Dentistry U. Miss. Med. Ctr., 2002—. Office: 2500 N State St Jackson MS 39216

HUPPAUF, BERND RUDIGER, educator; b. Waldenburg, Germany, Oct. 19, 1942; came to U.S., 1994; s. Walter and Hertha H.; m. Barbara Arnscheid; children: Anna, Fabian, Markus. DPhil, Tubingen U., Germany, 1970. Asst. prof. Tubingen U., Germany, 1970-73, Regensburg U., Germany, 1973-76; prof. U. New South Wales, Australia, 1976-93, NYU, N.Y.C., 1994—. Author: Von Sozialer Utopie, 1971; co-author: Methodendiskission, 1972, 95; editor: Ansichten vom Krieg, 1984, War, Violence and Modernity, 1997. Home: 1 Washington Square Village New York NY 10012 Office: 19 University Pl New York NY 10003-4556

HUPPE, ALEX, public relations executive; b. Princeton, N.J., June 18, 1947; s. Bernard F. and Mary Lois (McMaster) Huppe; m. Lindsay Dearborn, Dec. 26, 1970 (div. 1990); m. Barbara C. Mulligan, Oct. 12, 1991. BA with honors, Harpur Coll., 1969; MA, U. Va., 1971. Prof. English Western Piedmont C.C., Morganton, NC, 1971-79, asst. to pres., 1979-80; asst. dean Boston U., 1980-85; dir. news Dartmouth Coll., Hanover, N.H., 1985-95; dir. pub. affairs Harvard U., Cambridge, Mass., 1995—99, v.p., cons., 1999—. Rschr. Smith/Huppe Rsch., Boston, 1980—85; adj. prof. English Maine Maritime Acad., 2002—; adv. bd. Harpur Coll., 1998—. Co-author: (book) Alaska National Communication Program, 1982. Pres. River City Arts, 1993—95; mem. SUNY Binghamton Alumni Bd., 2003—; chmn. bd. dirs. Celo Health and Edn. Corp., Burnsville, NC, 1973—78; bd. dirs. Assocs. Boston Pub. Libr., 1997—2002, Castine Hist. Soc., 2001—. Mem.: NATAS (New Eng. chpt. gov. 1983—87, dir., Disting. Svc. award 1987), Ivy League News Dirs. (sec. 1988—91), Pub. Rels. Soc. Am. (exec. bd. counselors higher edn. 1998). Avocations: sailing, skiing, auto restoration.

HUPPER, JOHN ROSCOE, lawyer; b. N.Y.C., June 16, 1925; s. Roscoe Henderson and Dorothy Wallace (Healy) Hupper; m. Joyce Shirley McCoy, July 14, 1952; children: John R. Jr., Gail J., Craig W. AB, Bowdoin Coll., 1949; LLB, Harvard U., 1952. Bar: N.Y. 1954, U.S. Supreme Ct. 1960. Assoc. Cravath, Swaine & Moore LLP, N.Y.C., 1952-60, ptnr., 1961-95. Trustee Allen-Stevenson Sch., 1968—96; bd. dirs. Travelers Aid Soc., NY, 1962—79, Legal Aid Soc., N.Y.C., 1971—76; overseer Bowdoin Coll., 1970—82, trustee, 1982—95. With U.S. Army, 1943—46. Fellow: Am. Coll. Trial Lawyers; mem.: ABA, N.Y. Supreme Ct. (mem. com. character and fitness appellate divsn. 1st dept. 1992—, spl. master 1982—), Assn. Bar City of N.Y., N.Y. County Lawyers Assn., N.Y. State Bar Assn., Down Town Assn., Union Club, Univ. Club, Apawamis Club. Republican. Home: 105 E 67th St New York NY 10021-5901 Office: Cravath Swaine and Moore LLP 825 8th Ave New York NY 10019-7475

HUR, ROBERT KYOUNG, law clerk; b. N.Y.C. s. Young and Haesook Hur. AB magna cum laude with highest honors, Harvard U., 1995; JD, Stanford U., 2001. Assoc. Boston Cons. Group, 1996—98; summer assoc, Kirkland & Ellis, Washington, 2000; law clk. to the Hon. Alex Kozinski U.S. Ct. Appeals (9th cir.), Pasadena, Calif., 2001—02, law clk to the Hon. William H. Rehnquist U.S. Supreme Ct., Washington, 2002—. Exec. editor: Stanford Law Rev., 2000—01; contbr. articles to legal jours. Head alumni giving Stanford U. Law Class of 2001, 2001—. Recipient Briggs fellowship, Harvard U., 1995. Mem.: Order of Coif.

HUR, STEPHEN PONYI, civil engineer, management consultant, educator; b. Beijing, Hopei, China, Jan. 27, 1947; came to U.S., 1982; s. Mingan and Wenshien (Lu) H.; m. Lian Lihua Chiang, Mar. 8, 1975; children: Harry Yenhung, Cathy Chiayi. BS, Chungyuan U., 1968; MSCE, W. Va. U., 1973; Mgmt. Devel. Program cert., Taiwan U., 1982. Civil engr. Asia Cement Corp., Hsinchu, Taiwan, 1969-71; plant engr. Oriental Chem. Fiber Corp., Hsinchu, 1973-76; assoc. prof., chmn. civil engring. dept. Minghsin Coll. Engring., Hsinchu, 1976-78; gen. mgr. Join Engring. Cons., Taipei, 1978-83; sec., treas. Postech Construction Co., Belmont, Calif., 1983-86; pres. Standard Products, Foster City, Calif., 1984—. Tech. adviser Pacific Camus Corp., Taipei, 1979-82; v.p. Long Bon Development Co., Taiwan, 1992—; mng. dir. Long Jee Holding Co., Malaysia, 1999—; chmn. Ko Hun Construction Co., Taiwan, 2000—; lectr. civil engring. dept. Tankang U., Taipei, 1980-90. Author: Construction Management, 1977, Modern Masonry, 1980, Small R.C. Building Design, 1981, Industrialized Housing, 1981, Small Business in USA, 1988, The English-Speaking Chinese, 1990, The Story of English Language, 1991. Mem. Am. Concrete Inst., Soc. Theoretical and Applied Mechanics, Chinese Inst. Engrs., The Smithsonian Assn., People to People Internat., Internat. Platform Assn. Avocation: chinese classical music and opera. Office: Standard Products 999C Edgewater Blvd # 171 San Mateo CA 94404-3777 also: Long Jee Holding Co 22-01A 165 Jalan Ampang Kuala Lumpur 50450 Malaysia E-mail: pyhur@mstc.kohun.com.tw.

HUR, SU-RYONG, physician, anesthesiologist; b. Korea, Feb. 8, 1942; s. Hyung Keun and JaeKyung (Kim) H.; m. Myung Ja; children: Jennifer, Steven, Michelle. MD, Seoul Nat. U., 1966. Diplomate Am. Bd. Anesthesiology. Intern Union Hosp., Fall River, Mass., 1966-67; resident St. Vincent's Hosp, Worcester, Mass., 1967-68, Mass. Gen. Hosp., Boston, 1968-71; staff anesthesiologist St. Michael's Hosp., 1975—; asst. prof. anesthesiology Med. Coll. Wis., 1971-75, mem. clin. faculty anesthesiology, 1976—. Contbr. articles to profl. jours. Fellow Am. Coll. Anesthesiologists; mem. AMA, Internat. Anesthesia Rsch. Soc., Am. Soc. Anesthesiologists, Korean Am. Med. Assn., Wis. Soc. Anesthesiologists, State Med. Soc. of Wis., Med. Soc. of Milw. County, Milw. Soc. of Anesthesiologists. Office: St Michael Hosp Dept Anesthesiology 2400 W Villard Ave Milwaukee WI 53209-4999 Home Fax: 262-241-3415; Office Fax: 414-527-5145.

HURABIELL, JOHN PHILIP, SR., lawyer; b. San Francisco, June 2, 1947; s. Emile John and Anna Beatrice (Blumenauer) H.; m. Judith Marie Hurabiell, June 7, 1969; children; Marie Louise, Michele, Heather, John Philip Jr. JD, San Francisco U., 1976. Bar: Calif. 1977. Atty. pvt. practice, San Francisco, 1977-86; ptnr. Huppert & Hurabiell, San Francisco, 1985—. Pres. San Francisco S.A.F.E., Inc., 1983-88, pres. emeritus, 1988—. Editor, primary author: C.A.L.U. Business Practices Guidelines, rev. edit., 1980. Treas. Rep. election coms.; 1st v.p. Bling Babies Found., 1989-91, bd. dirs., sec., 1995-97, 98-2000; bd. dirs. Calif. State Mining and Mineral Mus., 1990-93. With USN, Vietnam. Decorated Navy Commendation medal. Mem. ATLA, Calif. Bar Assn., San Francisco Trial Lawyers Assn., Lawyers Club San Francisco, St. Thomas More Soc., St. Francis Hook & Ladder Soc. (trustee), The Family Club, Ferrari Club Am. (pres., chmn. Pacific region 1997-98, regional dir. 1998—2001, nat. legal chmn. 2000—), Golden Gate Breakfast Club, KC, Alhambra Lodge (organizing regional dir. 1983-85). Roman Catholic. Avocations: racing vintage automobiles, fly fishing. Office: Huppert & Hurabiell 3101 Clement St San Francisco CA 94121-1615

HURAS, WILLIAM DAVID, retired bishop; b. Kitchener, Ont., Can., Sept. 22, 1932; s. William Adam and Frieda Dorothea (Rose) H.; m. Barbara Elizabeth Lotz, Oct. 5, 1957; children— David, Matthew, Andrea BA, Waterloo Coll., Ont., 1954; BD, Waterloo Sem., Ont., 1963; MTh, Knox Coll., Toronto, Ont., 1968; MDiv, Waterloo Luth. U., 1973; DD (hon.), Wilfred Laurier U., Waterloo, 1980, Huron Coll., London, Ont., 1989. Ordained to ministry Luth. Ch. in Am., 1957. Pastor St. James Luth. Ch., Refrew, Ont., 1957-62, Advent Luth. Ch., North York, 1962-78; bishop Eastern Can. Synod Luth. Ch. in Am., Kitchener, 1978-85, Eastern Synod Evangel. Luth. Ch. in Can., 1986-98. Mem. exec. com. Can. sect. of Luth. Ch. in Am., 1969-79; mem. exec. com. Luth. Merger Commn., Can., 1978-85; pres. Luth. Council Can., 1985-88; chmn. Group Svcs. Inc., Evangelical Luth. Ch. in Can., 1993—2001; mem. Anglican-Luth. Jt. Working Group, 1995—2001. Bd. govs. Waterloo Luth. U., 1966-75, Waterloo Luth. Sem., 1973-75, 78—. Mem. Order of St. Lazarus of Jerusalem (Ecclesiastical Grand cross 1985). Lutheran. E-mail: huras@golden.net. *We are called by God and God covets an affirmative response. To say "yes" to God is to say "yes" to all of life and to all of God's people.*

HURCOMB, LAURA GRACE, visual artist; b. Glendale, Calif., Aug. 13, 1963; d. Doris Irene (Gleason) H.; m. Richard Halvorsen, Feb. 26, 1984; children: Jordan, Logan Hurcombhalvorsen. Student, Johnson County Cmty. Coll., 1993-95; BFA, Kansas City (Mo.) Art Inst., 1998; postgrad., U. Mo., Kans. City, 2001—. Art tchr. Midland Acad., Shawnee, Kans., 1993-95; visual artist H Studios, Overland Park, Kans., 1996—98, HUR Studio, Kans. City, Kans., 1998—, digital imager DeCloud Studio, Overland Pk., 1998—2000. Photographer Studio Fine Arts Dept. U. Mo., Kans. City, 2003, tchg. asst. Studio Fine Arts Dept., 03. Prin. works include sculpture Toy and Miniature Mus., Kans. City, Mo.; executed Murals Pleasentill, Mo., 1997; exhibited in group shows at City of Hanstholm Denmark, 1997, Unitarian Ch., 1997, Loomin Eleven Opie Gallery, 1999, PVI, Overland Park, 2000. Art tchr. Boys & Girls Club Kans. City, 1995-96; muralist Bartel Hall Storytellers, Kans. City, 1997; exhibition Famous Foot Wear, A Benefit to Stamp Out AIDS Kans. City Art Inst., 1997. Merit scholar Kans. City Art Inst., 1995. Mem. Nat. Assn. Photoshop Profl., Sons of Norway. Adventist. Avocations: surfing the www, music, animals, gardening. E-mail: hurgrace@hotmail.com.

HURD, BYRON THOMAS, retired publishing executive; b. Roseville, Mich., 1933; s. Clark Frank and Evelyn (Sybelden) H.; m. Barbara Jean Ekeroth; children: Thomas E., Roger A., J. Douglas, James B. BSBA in Advt. and Mktg., Wayne State U., 1954. Sales mgr. Detroit Free Press, 1954-55, Milne & Jones, Royal Oak, Mich., 1955-56, Detroit Times, 1956-59; account mgr. Milne Circulation Sales, Inc., Bloomfield Hills, Mich., 1959-65; agt. Bankers Life Co., Des Moines, Iowa, 1965-66; promotion mgr. Chgo. Today, Chgo. Tribune, 1966-74; owner, cons. Circulation Specialists, Homewood, Ill., 1974-77; exec.

dir. circulation The Star Newspapers, Chicago Heights, Ill., 1977-95; ret., 1995. Panelist, discussion leader, session master, com. mem. No. Ill. Newspapers Assn., DeKalb. Contbr. Publishers handbook, 1988. Elder, pres. governing bd. Flossmoor (Ill.) Community Ch., 1988. Mem. Cen. States Circulation Mgrs. Assn., Suburban Newspapers Am. (conf., sem. com. mem.), Audit Bur. Circulation (voting rep.), Circulation Mgmt. Ill., Rotary (dir. community svc. 1978-79, dir. internat. svc. 1979-80, sec. 1981-82, v.p. 1982-83, pres. 1983-84, dist. dir. pub. rels. 1984-86, dist. govs. aide 1986-87, dist. dir. vocat. svc. 1987-88, host Soviet Emerging Leaders 1988, Finnish 1989, dist. dir. group study exchange with India 1990, dist. conf. com. master ceremonies 1987-88, dist. conf. com. chmn. 1989-90), Flossmoor Country Club (sports and pastimes com. mem. 1988), Bentwater Golf Club, Internat. Golfing Fellowship of Rotary (lifetime), U.S. Golfing Fellowship of Rotary (lifetime). Avocations: golf, skiing, racquetball, drawing, painting.

HURD, DAVID NORMAN, federal judge; b. 1937; BS, Cornell U., 1959; JD with honors, Syracuse U., 1963. Bar: N.Y. 1963, U.S. Supreme Ct. 1970. Pvt. practice, 1963-70; ptnr. O'Shea, Griffin, McDonald, Hurd and Stevens, Rome, N.Y., 1970-91; U.S. Magistrate judge Utica, 1991-99; judge U.S. Dist. Ct. (no. dist.) N.Y., Utica, 1999—. Mem. Am. Coll. Trial Lawyers, N.Y. State Bar Assn., Oneida County Bar Assn., Rome Bar Assn., Albany County Bar Assn., Order of the Coif. Office: US Courthouse Rm 300 10 Broad St Utica NY 13501-1233

HURD, ERIC RAY, rheumatologist, internist, educator; b. Columbus, Kans., July 5, 1936; s. Myron Alexander and Isobel (Moore) H.; m. Beverly Jean Button, June 14, 1962; children: Sherryl Lynn, Susan Rae, Brent Eric. BS, U. Tulsa, 1958; MD, U. Okla., 1962. Intern St. John's Hosp., Tulsa, 1962-63, resident in internal medicine, 1963-65; research fellow U. Tex., Dallas, 1965-67, instr. internal medicine, 1967-68, asst. prof., 1968-73, assoc. prof., 1973-80, prof., 1980—. Cons. rheumatologist, attending physician Parkland, VA Hosps.; dir. John Peter Smith Hosp. Arthritis Clinic, Ft. Worth; chief rheumatology VA Hosp., 1982—, mem. immunology research merit rev. bd.; assoc. Baylor Arthritis Ctr., 1981—; mem. med. and sci. com. North Tex. Arthritis Found., bd. med. dirs., 1988—, chmn. profl. edn. com.; traveling guest lectr. Tex. Med. Assn., Belgium and Fed. Republic Germany, 1990. Contbr. articles to profl. jours. Served to maj. U.S. Army, 1963-74. Recipient Clin. Scholar award Arthritis Found., 1975-77; named Outstanding Cons. Faculty Mem. John Peter Smith Hosp., 1983-84, Outstanding Part-time Clin. Prof. John Peter Smith Hosp., 1989-90. Mem. ACP, Am. Assn. Immunologists, Am. Fedn. Clin. Research, Am. Rheumatism Assn. (cooperating clinics com. 1968-74, Founding Fellow 1986), Tex. Rheumatism Assn. (sec.-treas. 1976-79, 2d v.p. 1979-80), Tex. Med. Soc., Dallas County Med. Soc., Phi Eta Sigma. Democrat. Methodist. Office: Arthritis Ctrs of Tex 712 N Washington Ave Ste 200 Dallas TX 75246-1632

HURD, GALE ANNE, film producer; b. L.A., Oct. 25, 1955; d. Frank E. and Lolita (Espiau) H. Degree in econs. and communications, Stanford U., 1977. Dir. mktg. and publicity, co-producer New World Pictures, L.A., 1977-82; pres., producer Pacific Western Prodns., L.A., 1982—. Producer: (films) The Terminator, 1984 (Grand Prix Avoiriaz Film Festival award), Aliens 1986 (nominated for 7 Acad. awards, recipient Best Sound Effects Editing award, Best Visual Effects award Acad. Picture Arts & Scis.), Alien Nation (Saturn award for best sci. fiction film), The Abyss, 1989 (nominated for 4 Acad. awards, Best Visual Effects award), The Waterdance, 1991 (2 TFP Spirit awards, 2 Sundance Film Festival awards), Cast a Deadly Spell, 1991 (Emmy award), Raising Cain, 1992, No Escape, 1994, Safe Passage (Beatrice Wood award for Creative Achievement), 1994, The Ghost and the Darkness,(Acad. award) 1996, The Relic, 1996, Going West in America, 1996, Dante's Peak, 1997, Virus, 1997, Dead Man on Campus, 1997, Armageddon, 1998, Dick, 1999, Clockstoppers 2002 The Hulk, 2003 (TV series) Adventure, Inc., 2002; exec. producer: (films) Switchback, 1997, Tremors, 1990, Downtown, 1990, Terminator 2, 1991 (winner 3 Acad. awards), Witch Hunt, 1994, Sugartime, 1995; creative cons. (TV program) Alien Nation, 1989-90. Juror Focus Student Film Awards, 1989, 90; chmn. Nicholl Fellowship Acad. Motion Picture Arts & Scis., 1989—; mem. Show Coalition, 1988—; mem. Hollywood (Calif.) Women's Polit. Com., 1987—; mem. U.S. Film Festival Juror; bd. dirs. IFP/West, Artists Rights Found.; trustee Am. Film Inst.; bd. dirs. L.A. Internat. Film Festival, Coral Reef Rsch. Found., Ams. for a Safe Future; mentor Peter Stark Motion Picture Producing Program, Sch. of Cinema-TV, U. of So. Calif., Women in Film Mentor Program. Recipient Spl. Merit award Nat. Assn. Theater Owners, 1986, Stanford-La Entrepreneur of Yr. award Bus. Sch. Alumni L.A., 1990, Fla. Film Festival award, 1994, Women in Film Crystal award, 1998, Ind. Vision award Temucala Film Festival, 2001; named Prodr. of Yr., Stunt Awards, 2003. Mem. AMPAS (prodr.'s br. exec. com. 1990—, festival grants com.), Am. Film Inst. (trustee 1989—), Americans for a Safe Future (bd. dirs. 1993—), Prodr.'s Guild Am. (bd. dirs.), Women in Film (bd. dirs. 1989-90,2000—), Inst. for Rsch. on Women and Gender (nat. adv. panel 1997—), Feminist Majority, The Ocean Consrvancy, Heal the Bay, Reef Check Internat. Seakeepers Soc., Mulholland Tomorrow, The Trusteeship, Phi Beta Kappa. Avocations: scuba diving, paso fino horses. Office: Valhalla Motion Pictures 8530 Wilshire Blvd Ste 400 Beverly Hills CA 90211

HURD, J. NICHOLAS, executive recruiting consultant, former banker; b. Boston, Dec. 10, 1942; m. Joan Hinton; children: Jennifer H. Auber, Marshall H., P. MacKenzie. BA in Econs., Hobart Coll., 1965; postgrad., Stanford U. Bus. Sch., Grad. Sch. Credit and Fin. Mgmt., summers 1971-73; grad. Advanced Mgmt. Program, Harvard U., 1979. Dist. mgr. Mfrs. Hanover Trust, N.Y.C., 1965, 74-77; sr. v.p. Hartford (Conn.) Nat. Bank, 1977-82; exec. v.p. Old Stone Bank, Old Stone Corp., Providence, 1982-84; mng. dir. Russell Reynolds Assocs., Inc., Boston, 1985—; dir. Emersons Investment Mgmt., Boston. Corporate overseer Ptnrs. Healthcare Sys., Boston, 1990-99. Bd. overseers The Huntington Theatre Co., Boston. Mem. R.I. Country Club (Barrington), Southport Yacht Club (West Southport, Maine), Moorings Club (Vero Bch., Fla.), Harvard Club (Boston). Office: Russell Reynolds Assocs Inc Old City Hall 45 School St Ste 3D Boston MA 02108-3296

HURD, JERRIE, writer; b. Idaho Falls, Idaho, Apr. 3, 1949; d. Jared Wirkus and Colleen Nielsen; m. Jon Hurd, June 30, 1967; children: Devin Jared, Ethan Jon. BA, U. Colo., 1969; MFA, U. Oreg., 1981. Author: Miss Ellie'sPurple Sage Saloon, 1995, Kate Burke Shoots the Old West, 1997, The Lady Pinkerton Gets Her Man, 1997. Bd. trustees Autry Mus. of Western Heritage, 2002—. Mem. Women Writing the West (pres., founder 1996-98), Weste Writers Am. (bd. dirs. 1998-2000), Women of West Mus. (bd. dirs., treas. 1996-2002). Democrat. Office: PO Box 12 Boulder CO 80306-0012

HURD, JOHN R. lawyer; b. San Francisco, May 4, 1942; BA, Harvard U., 1964; student, U. Ctrl. del Ecuador; LLB, U. Tex., 1967. Bar: Tex. 1967. Mem. Vinson & Elkins L.L.P., Houston. Office: Vinson & Elkins 2500 First City Tower 1001 Fannin St Ste 3300 Houston TX 77002-6706 Address: 10 Blenheim San Antonio TX 78209

HURD, MARK V. manufacturing executive; B in Bus. Adminstrn., Baylor U., 1979. COO Teradata (divsn. NCR Corp.), 2000—03; pres. NCR Corp., 2001—, COO, 2002—03, CEO, 2003—. Bd. visitors sch. bus. Duke U. Office: 1700 S Patterson Blvd Dayton OH 45479*

HURD, MARY K. civil engineer, writer; BSCE, Iowa State U., Ames; postgrad, U. Chgo., U. Mich., U. Ill. Assoc. editor spl. tech. publs. Am. Concrete Inst., 1966-67, staff engr., 1967-76; engr.-writer, cons., 1976-80, 90—; engring. editor Concrete Constrn. Mag., Addison, Ill., 1983-90, editor, 1981-83; pres. engr. publs. Farmington Hills, Mich. Past chmn. bd. dirs. Concrete Improvement Bd. Author: (book) Formwork for Concrete, 1963, 6th edit. 1995; contbr. numerous articles in field to profl. jours. including Constrn. Specifier, Concrete Internat., Jour. Am. Concrete Inst., Internat. Jour. of Ferrocement, Revista IMCYC Mexico, Pub. Works, Concrete Constrn., Concrete Prodr., PCI Jour.; presenter and organizer in field. Recipient Profl. Achievement in Engring. Citation award Iowa State U., 1982, Outstanding Achievement award Concrete Improvement Bd. Detroit, 1990. Mem. ASCE (life), Am. Concrete Inst. (hon. mem., past mem. bd. dirs., organizing chmn. com. 124 concrete aesthetics, com. 347 formwork for concrete, past pres. Mich. chpt., Constrn. Practice award 1982, 88, Delmar L. Bloem Disting. Svc. award 1990, Arthur Y. Moy award Mich. chpt. 1994, Henry C. Turner medal 1995); mem. Am. Soc. Concrete Contractors, Precast/Prestressed Concrete Inst. (profl.), The Concrete Soc. (U.K.), Constrn. Writers Assn., Tau Beta Pi, Phi Kappa Phi. Address: 33742 Lyncroft Rd Farmington Hills MI 48331-3647

HURD, PAUL GEMMILL, lawyer; b. Salt Lake City, Nov. 23, 1946; s. Melvin and Marjorie Hurd. BS, Portland State U., 1968; JD, Lewis and Clark Coll., 1976. Bar: Oreg. 1976, Wash. 1984, U.S. Dist. Ct. Oreg. 1980, U.S. Ct. Appeals (9th cir.) 1981, U.S. Supreme Ct. 1988. Sr. dep. dist. atty. Multnomah County Dist. Atty., Portland, Oreg., 1976-80; trial counsel Burlington No. R.R., Portland, 1980-84; asst. gen. counsel Freightliner LLC, Portland, 1984-89, assoc. gen. counsel, 1989—2002, gen. counsel, sec., 2002—. Trustee Leukemia Assn. of Oreg., Portland, 1984-90. Mem. Oreg. Bar Assn., Wash. Bar Assn., Multnomah Bar Assn., Am. Corp. Counsel Assn. (bd. dirs. N.W. chpt.), Nat. Inst. for Trial Adv. (diplomate 1982), Associated Oreg. Industries (bd. dirs. 2002—). Republican. Presbyterian. Avocations: cross country skiing, reading history, bicycling. Office: Freightliner LLC Legal Dept PO Box 3920 Portland OR 97208-3920

HURD, PHILIP JUSTIN, executive search consultant; b. Cleve., June 20, 1961; s. Justin G. and Claudia L. Hurd; m. Janet Kelley; children: Audrey, Grace, Anne. BSEE, Rensselaer Poly. Inst., Troy, N.Y., 1983; MSEE, Northeastern U., Boston, 1987. Cert. personnel cons. Sr. engr. Digital Equipment Corp., Marlboro, Mass., 1983-87; sr. cons. Winter, Wyman & Co., Waltham, Mass., 1987-91; pres. Lynx, Inc., Lexington, Mass., 1991—. Office: Lynx Inc 35 Bedford St Ste 3 Lexington MA 02420-1506

HURD, RICHARD NELSON, pharmaceutical company executive; b. Evanston, Ill., Feb. 25, 1926; s. Charles DeWitt and Mary Ormsby (Nelson) H.; m. Jocelyn Fillmore Martin, Dec. 22, 1950; children: Melanie Gray, Suzanne Dewitt. BS, U. Mich., 1946; PhD U. Minn., 1956. Chemist Gen. Electric Co., Schenectady, N.Y., 1948-49; R&D group leader Koppers Co., Pitts., 1956-57; rsch. chemist Mallinckrodt Chem. Works, St. Louis, 1957-63, group leader, 1963-66, Comml. Solvents Corp., Terre Haute, Ind., 1966-68, sect. head, 1968-71; mgr. sci. affairs G. D. Searle Internat. Co., Skokie, Ill., 1972-73, dir. mfg. and tech. affairs, 1973-77; rep. to internat. tech com. Pharm. Mfrs. Assn., Skokie, Ill., 1973-77; v.p. tech. affairs Elder Pharms., Bryan, Ohio, 1977-81; v.p. rsch. & devel. U.S. Proprietary Drugs & Toiletries div. Schering-Plough Corp., Memphis, 1981-83; v.p. sci affairs Moleculon, Inc., Cambridge, Mass., 1984-88; v.p. regulatory affairs Pharmaco-LSR, Inc., Austin, Tex., 1989-94; prin. Hurd & Assocs., Inc., Evanston, ILL., 1994—. Contbr. articles to profl. jours.; patentee in field. Mem. Ferguson-Florissant (Mo.) Sch. Bd., 1964-66; bd. dirs. United Fund of Wabash Valley (Ind.), 1969-71. With USN, 1943-46, 53-55. E.I. DuPont de Nemours & Co., Inc. fellow, 1956. Fellow AAAS; mem. Am. Acad. Dermatology (life), Am. Soc. Photobiology, Am. Chem. Soc., N.Y. Acad. Sci., Am. Pharm. Assn., Am. Assn. Pharm. Scientists, Food and Drug Law Inst., Drug Info. Assn., Sigma XI, Mich. Shores Club (Wilmette, Ill.). Presbyterian. Achievements include codevelopment of Ralgro and Oxsoralen; research in thioamides as a class of organic compounds; development of macrocyclic synthetic routes for natural products; development of psoralens for photochemotherapy of dermatologic disorders. E-mail: hurdreg@earthlink.net.

HURD, RUTH, publishing executive; Publisher The Thomas Register of Am. Mfrs., N.Y.C., 1985—. Office: The Thomas Register 5 Penn Plz Fl 9 New York NY 10001-1810*

HURD, SUZANNE SHELDON, retired federal agency health science director; b. Elmira, N.Y., Dec. 17, 1939; d. Victor Sheldon H. BS, Bates Coll., 1961; MS, U. Wash., 1963, PhD, 1967. Post-doctoral fellow U. Calif., Berkeley, 1967-69; grants assoc. NIH, Bethesda, Md., 1969-70; health sci. adminstr. Nat. Heart, Lung and Blood Inst., Bethesda, 1970-78, dep. dir. div. lung diseases, 1979-84, dir. divsn. lung diseases, 1984-99; acting dir. Nat. Inst. Nursing Rsch., Bethesda, 1994-95; acting dir. Women's Health Initiative Nat. Heart, Lung and Blood Inst., Bethesda, 1997-99; sci. dir. global initiative for asthma Med. Comm. Resources, Inc., Gig Harbor, Wash., 2000, sci. dir. global initiative chronic obstructive lung disease, 2000—. Mem. Am. Thoracic Soc. E-mail: shurd@prodigy.net.

HURDLE, CLINT, professional athletics manager; b. Big Rapids, Mich., July 30, 1957; m. Karla Hurdle; 1 child, Ashley. Mgr. Colo. Rockies, 2002—, hitting instr., 1994—96. Office: Co Rockies 2001 Blake St Denver CO 80205

HURDLE, THOMAS GRAY, retired urologist; b. Roanoke, Va., Nov. 15, 1919; s. Grover Cleveland and Bronna (Garrison) H.; m. Eloise Spence, Mar. 14, 1945; children: Patricia Ann, Marilyn Sue, Edward Thomas. BS, Roanoke Coll., 1942; MD, Med. Coll. Va., 1945. Diplomate Am. B. Urology. Intern Doctor's Hosp., Washington, 1945-46; preceptorship urology Dr. A.A. Creecy, Newport News, Va., 1948-52; resident urology VA Med. Teaching Group Hosp., Memphis, 1952-53, chief resident urology, 1953-54; urologist VA Hosp., Fayetteville, N.C., 1954-55; attending physician, cons. urology Highsmith-Rainey Meml. Hosp., Fayetteville, 1954-2001. Cons. Sampson County Meml. Hosp., Clinton, N.C., 1954—, Betsy Johnson Meml. Hosp., Dunn, N.C., 1956-65; attending physician, cons. Cape Fear Valley Hosp., Fayetteville, 1956—; sec. Cumberland County Med. Soc., Fayetteville, 1956-63. Contbr. article to Va. Med. Jour., 1950, Jour. Urology, 1955. Mem. Lions, Hampton, Va., 1950-52. With Med. Corp., U.S. Army, 1943-45, 46-48. Award named in his honor Cumberland County Med. Soc., 1992. Fellow ACS; mem. AMA, Am. Urol. Assn., Carolina Urol. Assn. (sec. 1985-87, pres.-elect 1987-88, pres. 1988-89), Cumberland County Med. Soc. (pres. 1965, chmn. awards com. 1964—), Am. Assn. Clin. Urologists, N.C. State Med. Soc. (life, 50 Yr. Club), So. Med. Assn. Republican. Methodist. Avocations: gardening, woodworking. Home: 234 Courtyard Ln Fayetteville NC 28303-4605 Office: Fayetteville Urology Assocs 1786 Metromedical Dr Fayetteville NC 28304-3861

HURET, BARRY S. marketing professional, consultant; b. N.Y.C., 1938; s. Benjamin and Anna (Berko) H.; m. Marilynn Moskowitz, Feb. 1961; children: Abbey, Eric. BA with honors, Cornell U., 1961; MBA with distinction, NYU, 1970. Asst. sales engr. Westinghouse Corp., Pitts., 1962-64; sales engr. MultiAmp Corp., Cranford, N.J., 1964-65; sales engr., regional mgr., nat. sales mgr. Gould, Inc., St. Paul, 1965-77; successively mktg mgr., v.p. mktg., v.p. new bus. ventures Exide Corp., Horsham, Pa., 1977-82; nat. sales mgr. battery sales div. Panasonic Indsl. Co., Secaucus, N.J., 1982-86, asst. gen. mgr. battery sales group, divsn. head, 1986-97; pres., CEO Huret Assocs., Inc., 1997—. Past dir., bd. dirs. Lithium Tech. Corp., Matsushita Storage Battyer Corp. Am.; sr. assoc. Kline Group; former sr. counselor Mastushita Storage Battery Co. Am.; past chmn. battery sect. accessory divsn. Electronic Industries Assn.; exec. rev. bd. Power 94, Power 95, Power 96; cons. Battery Rsch. Lab. Rutgers U., GIGA ExperNet; chmn. Battery Sessions, Battery Track Portable by Design, 1998—; cons. ibattery.com, 1998—; expert witness battery litigation, 1999—. Author: A User Friendly Guide to Selecting Rechargeable Batteries. 1st lt. U.S. Army, 1961—62. Recipient Hector Lazo Meml. Mktg. award NYU, 1970, Alumni Key, 1970. Mem. Cornell U. Alumni (former v.p. class of 1959), Phi Beta Kappa. Home: 484 Kings Rd Yardley PA 19067-4652 E-mail: bhuret@comcast.net.

HURLBERT, ROGER WILLIAM, information service industry executive; b. San Francisco, Feb. 18, 1941; s. William G. and Mary (Greene) H.; m. Karen C. Haslag, Nov. 6, 1982; children: Sage, Mica, Chula, Monk, Morris, Cassie. BS in Community Devel., So. Ill. U., 1965. Newspaper editor and reporter various, San Francisco Bay Area, 1958-62; pvt. practice investigation Ill., 1963-65; advisor San Francisco Planning Urban Rsch. Assn., 1969-87; pres. Sage Info. Svcs., Glen Ellen, Calif., 1988—. Compiler U.S. Land Data Base, 1972—. Pres. Haight-Ashbury Neighborhood Coun., San Francisco, 1959-61. With U.S. Army, 1966-68, Vietnam. Recipient Cert. of Merit, San Francisco Coun. Dist. Mchts. Assn., 1972. Mem. Real Estate Info. Profls. Assn. (sec. 1998-03), Direct Mktg. Assn., Mail Advt. Svc. Assn. Internat., League of Men Voters (v.p. 1959—), Internat. Assn. of Assessing Officials. Democrat. Office: Sage Info Svcs 13606 Arnold Dr PO Box 1832 Glen Ellen CA 95442-1832

HURLBURT, HARLEY ERNEST, ocean modeling and prediction scientist; b. Bennington, Vt., Apr. 12, 1943; s. Paul Rhodes and Evelyn Arlene (Lockhart) H.; m. Cheryl Elaine Finch, Jan. 10, 1998. BS in Physics (scholar), Union Coll., Schenectady, 1965; MS, Fla. State U., 1971, PhD in Meteorology, 1974. NASA trainee Fla. State U., 1970-72; postdoctoral fellow advanced studies program Nat. Ctr. Atmospheric Rsch., Boulder, Colo., 1974-75; staff scientist JAYCOR, Alexandria, Va., 1975-77; oceanographer Naval Rsch. Lab. and related orgns., Stennis Space Ctr., Miss., 1977—, br. head, 1983-85. Adj. faculty marine sci. U. So. Miss., Stennis Space Ctr., 1993—; adj. faculty meteorology Fla. State U., Tallahassee, 1995—; mem. nat. adv. panels NASA satellite surface stress working group, 1981-84, minerals mgmt. svc. interagy. adv. group, 1982-89, world ocean circulation experiment working group on numerical modeling, 1984-96, USN space oceanography working group, 1986-89; co-chmn. working group on global prediction sys., ocean prediction workshop, 1986; internat. working group on acoustic monitoring of world ocean Sci. com. Oceanic Rsch., 1991-98; internat. working group on modelling subarctic North Pacific circulation North Pacific Marine Sci. Orgn., 1994-95; mem. sci. steering team Internat. Global Ocean Data Assimilation Experiment, 1998—; mem. NASA High Resolution Ocean Topography Sci. Working Group, 2001, NASA Wide Swath Ocean Altimeter Sci. Working Group, 2002-03; project leader to develop the world's first eddy-resolving global ocean prediction model for USN, 1987-2001. Contbr. numerous articles to profl. jours. V.p. Burgundy Citizens Assn., 1976-77. Weather officer USAF, 1965-69. Recipient Disting. Scientist medal 13th Internat. Colloquium, Liege, Belgium, 1981, Publ. award for best basic rsch. paper Naval Ocean R&D Activity, 1980, 90; grantee Office Naval Rsch., 1975-77, 84—, Dept. Energy, 1975-78, Tex. A&M U., 1976, Office of Naval Tech., 1987-93, Space Warfare Sys., 1989-94, Advanced Rsch. Projects Agy., 1993-95, Strategic Environ. Rsch. and Devel. Program, 1994-95, Def. Dept. High Performance Computing Challenge, 1997—, Nat. Ocean Partnership Program, 1997—; case study on Eddy-resolving Global Ocean Modeling and Prediction included in 2000 Computerworld Smithsonian Collection archived in Smithsonian's Nat. Mus. Am. History's permanent rsch. collection. Mem. Am. Meteorol. Soc., Am. Geophys. Union, Oceanography Soc., Phi Sigma Kappa, Sigma Xi (Kaminski Publ. award 1991), Sigma Tau, Chi Epsilon Pi. Methodist. Achievements include research on the oceanic onset of El Nino and the dynamics of loop current eddy shedding in the Gulf of Mexico; discovery of the impact of upper ocean-topographic coupling via flow instabilities on upper ocean current pathways, including the Gulf Stream in the Atlantic and the Kuroshio in the Pacific; transition of the world's first eddy-resolving global ocean prediction system to the Naval Oceanographic Office for operational use. Home: 507 Hermitage Ct Pearl River LA 70452-3903 Office: Naval Rsch Lab Code 7304 Bay Saint Louis MS 39529 E-mail: hurlburt@nrlssc.navy.mil.

HURLBUT, ROBERT HAROLD, health care services executive; b. Rochester, N.Y., Mar. 9, 1935; s. Harold Leroy and Martha Irene (Fincher) H.; m. Barbara Cox, June 14, 1958; children: Robert W., Christine A. Hurlbut Bean. Student, Coll. Hotel Adminstrn., Cornell U., 1953-56. Adminstr., dir. Pillars Nursing Home, Rochester, 1956—, Elmcrest Nursing Home, Churchville, N.Y., 1960—, Elm Manor Nursing Home, Canandaigua, N.Y., 1960—, Penfield Nursing Home, Rochester, 1963—, Avon (N.Y.) Nursing Home, 1964—, Newark (N.Y.) Nursing Home, 1965—, Lakeshore Nursing Home, Rochester, 1972—. Bd. dirs. HSBC, Strong Meml. Hosp.; organizer, adminstrv. dir. hdqrs. Rohm Svcs. Corp., Rochester, 1964—; organizer, pres. hdqrs. Vari-Care Inc., Rochester, 1969—93; commr. N.Y. State Ins. Fund; mem. Cornell U. Hotel Sch. Adv. Coun. Trustee U. Rochester; St. John Fisher Coll., 1983—98; trustee emeritus; mem. adv. bd. U. Rochester; trustee Eastman Dental Ctr. Found.; pres. Hurlbut Trust, 1994; mem. bd. govs. Strong Meml. Hosp., 1992—97, chmn.-elect bd. dir. Fellow Am. Coll. Health Care Adminstrs.; mem. Greater Met. C. of C. (past chmn. bd. dirs.), Genesee Valley Club, Oak Hill Club, Cornell Soc. Hotelmen, Lambda Chi Alpha. Home: 200 Sheldon Rd Honeoye Falls NY 14472-9316 Office: Hurlbut Trust 740 East Ave Rochester NY 14607-2107

HURLBUT, TERRY ALLISON, pathologist; b. Richmond, Va., Nov. 24, 1957; s. Terry A. and Evelyn I. (Randlette) H.; m. Sharon L. Clouston, Oct. 24, 1998. BS, Yale Coll., 1980; MD, Baylor Coll. Medicine, 1985. Pathology residency Vanderbilt U., Nashville, 1986-89; fellowship pathology Dartmouth Med. Sch., Hanover, N.H., 1989-91; pathology residency Monmouth Med. Ctr., Long Branch, N.J., 1991-93; clin. pathologist Kimball Med. Ctr, Lakewood, N.J., 1993-95; dir. informatics Lakewood Pathology Assn., 1993-99; clin. pathologist Meml. Hosp. Burlington County, Mt. Holly, N.J., 1996-99. Co-author: The Laboratory Consultant, 1992; contbr. article to profl. jours. Fellow Coll. Am. Pathologists. Baptist. Home: 5 Grosvenor Rd Short Hills NJ 07078 E-mail: hurlbutta@comcast.net.

HURLEY, ALFRED FRANCIS, historian, academic administrator emeritus, retired air force officer; b. Bklyn., Oct. 16, 1928; s. Patrick Francis and Margaret Teresa (Coakley) H.; m. Joanna Helen Leahy, Jan. 24, 1953; children: Alfred F., Thomas J., Mark P., Claire T., John K. BA summa cum laude, St. John's U., 1950; MA, Princeton U., 1958, PhD, 1961. Enlisted USAF, 1950, commd. lt., 1952, tng. officer, instr. navigator, 1952—56; from instr. to asst. prof. history USAF Acad., 1958—63, prof., head dept. history, 1966—80; navigator, exec. officer USAF Hdqrs., Germany, War Plans Staff, Joint Chiefs of Staff, 1963—66; bd. mem. Acad. Bd., 1977-80; advanced through grades to brig. gen. USAF, ret., 1980; v.p. adminstrv. affairs U. North Tex. (formerly North Tex. State U.), Denton, 1980-82, pres., 1982-2000, prof. history, 1981—; chancellor U. North Tex. Sys., 2000—02. Mem. adv. com. USAF hist. program sect. USAF, Washington, 1982-86, chmn., 1984-86; mem. bd. visitors Air U., 1993-97. Author: Billy Mitchell, Crusader for Air Power, 1964, (rev. edit.), 1975; contbg. author: Winged Shield, Winged Sword, History of the USAF, 1997; co-editor: Air Power and Warfare, 1979. Decorated Legion of Merit (2); Guggenheim fellow, 1971-72, Eisenhower Inst., Smithsonian fellow, 1976-77; recipient Pres.'s medal St. John's U., 1990. Mem.: Tex. Philos. Soc. (2d v.p. 2002—), Dallas Citizens Coun. (bd. dirs. 2000—02), North Tex. Commn. (bd. dirs. 1986—2000, chmn. 1995—97), Alliance for Higher Edn. of North Tex. (trustee 1983—89, chmn. coun. of pres. 1989—90), Tex. Coun. Pub. Univ. Pres. and Chancellors (chmn. 1987—89), Coalition Urban and Met. Univs. (co-chair 1993—2002, mem. exec. com. 2002—), Am. Hist. Assn. (chmn. NASA fellowship com. 1993—94), Am. Coun. Edn. (commn. leadership 1993—96), Am. Assn. State Colls. and Univs. (coun. state reps. 1989—92), Air Force Hist. Found. (trustee 1980—), Soc. for Mil. History (trustee 1973—78, 1981—85). Roman Catholic. Home: 828 Skylark Dr Denton TX 76205-8012 Office: U North Tex Dept History Denton TX 76203-0650

HURLEY, ALLYSON KINGSLEY, dentist; b. Buffalo, June 15, 1949; d. Norman and Marion (Legler) Kingsley; m. Lawrence Joseph Hurley, May 28, 1977; children: Michael William, Kathryn Elizabeth. Student, Barat Coll., 1967-68; degree in dental hygiene, Marquette U., 1970, BS, 1971; DDS, Howard U., 1977. Pvt. practice dental hygiene, Washington, 1971-77; resident VA Hosp., Lyons, N.J., 1977-78; gen. practice dentistry Chatham, N.J., 1978—. Attending dentist Overlook Hosp., Summit, N.J., 1979—, dir. resident adminstrn., 1980-85, mem. edn. com., 1981-86; clin. instr. dental hygiene Union County Tech. Inst., Scotch Plains, N.J., 1979-81, mem. selection com. for dental dept., 1987; coord. kindergarten-4th grades dental health program Chatham Boro Sch. System, 1978-92; active oral cancer screening program Chatham Boro Jr. Women's Club, 1980-82. Editor, contbg. author newsletter Word of Mouth, 1981—; author (booklet) Your Child's Teeth, 1984; contbg. author Love Is the Best Medicine, 2001; one-person shows of nature photographs. Alumni recruiter Marquette U., Morris County, N.J., 1977-83; bd. dirs. Am. Cancer Soc., Morris County, 1981-83; chair Scholarship Found. of the Chathams, Inc., 1985-95. Recipient 3 awards for nature photography. Master Acad. Gen. Dentistry; mem. ADA, Am. Acad. Cosmetic Dentistry (accredited mem.), N.Am. Nature Photography Assn., N.J. Acad. Cosmetic Dentistry (pres. 2000—), Tri-County Dental Soc. (bd. dirs. 1982-83), Internat. Dental Lectr. Internat. Platform Assn., N.Y. Acad. Scis., Columbia U. Dental Study Club, No. N.J. Women's Study Club (pres. 1980-82, 86—, sec. 1983-86), Newcomer's Club Chatham Township, Acad. of Esthetic and Restorative Dentistry Study Club. Republican. Roman Catholic. Office: Allyson Kingsley Hurley DDS 58 Main St Chatham NJ 07928-2104

HURLEY, AMY ELIZABETH, human resources educator; b. New Britain, Conn., Aug. 4, 1961; d. Roberta (Burnes) Hurley; m. Amory Evan Hanson. BS in Bus. Adminstrn., U. Fla., 1983; MBA, N.Y. Inst. Tech., 1987; PhD in Mgmt. NYU, 1994. Asst. prof. Cath. U. Am., Washington, 1994-97; assoc. prof., chair human resources and career counseling Chapman U., Orange, Calif., 1997—. Faculty adv. Omicron Delta Kappa; rsch. fellow Ctr. Leadership and Career Studies Emory U., 1992-97. Contbr. articles to profl. jours. Torchbearer selected

by United Way and U.S. Olympic Com., 1996; bd. dirs. HIV Arts Found., founding mem.; vol. Starlight Found., 1992. Recipient Meritorious award Starlight Found., 1987-95. Mem. APA, Soc. Indsl./Orgnl. Psychology, Acad. Mgmt. (nat. exec. bd.). Office: Chapman U One University Dr Orange CA 92866-4804

HURLEY, BRUCE PALMER, artist; b. Tacoma, May 9, 1944; s. Gerald Baynton and Donna Ray (Whealey) H.; m. Ivy Jane Partridge; 1 child, Paul George. BS in Edn., Oreg. Coll. Edn., 1968. Cert. secondary edn. tchr. One-man shows include Goldberg's, 1966, Hillsboro Pub. Libr., 1969, 1971, Valley Art Assn., Forest Grove, 1971, 1974, exhibited in group shows at Portland Art Mus., 1970, Northwest Artist Workshop, 1979, Sun Bird Gallery, 1986, Sunriver Juried Show, 1986, 1992, Beaverton Arts Showcase, 1990, 1991, 1992, 1993, 1994, 1996, 1997, 1998 (1st place watercolor), 2003, Represented in permanent collections Oreg. Coll., Oriental Medicine, David Wheeler, Washington, Libr. of Am. Psychiat. Assn., Schools Med. Plz., Tigard, Oreg., Atty. Mark Olson, N.Y.C., Nicholas S. Law, Cambridge, Eng., Washington County Pub. Svc. Bldg., Hillsboro, Oreg., Portland Habilitation Ctr., others; author: Planet Ploob Vacation, 1992, Divine Soliloquy, 1994; inventor numerous paintings, drawings and sculptures. Mem. Portland Art Mus. Recipient Cmty. Svc. award Beaverton Arts Commn., 1993, Royal Patronage award Hutt River, Australia, 1995. Mem. Theosophical Soc. Avocations: musicology, camping, raw foods, naturopathy, mysticism. Home: 251 NW Bailey St Hillsboro OR 97124-2903

HURLEY, CHERYL JOYCE, book publishing executive; b. Pitts., Oct. 30, 1947; d. John and Violet der Norsek; m. Kevin Hurley, July 27, 1974. Lang. and lit. cert., Université de Lyon, France, 1968; AB, Ohio U., 1969; MA, U. Mich., 1971. Research assoc. MLA, N.Y.C., 1972-74, dir. spl. programs, 1974-79; pub. The Library of America, N.Y.C., 1979—, pres., 1988—. Cons. in field. Contbr. articles to profl. jours. Trustee French Inst./Alliance Francaise, 1992—, v.p., exec. com., 1994—, chmn. libr. com., 1996—, adv. com. N.Y. 100 Centennial, 1997-98; mem. humanities adv. coun. N.Y. Pub. Libr., 1996—; trustee Samuel H. Kress Found., 1999—; mem. dean's adv. bd. Rackham Grad. Sch. U. Mich., 2000-. Rackham fellow, 1969—70. Mem.: Assn. Internationale de Bibliophilie, Am. Antiquarian Soc. (councillor 1999—), Bridgehampton Club, Colony Club, Grolier Club, Century Assn., Phi Beta Kappa. Home: 1172 Park Ave New York NY 10128-1213 Office: Libr of Am 14 E 60th St New York NY 10022-1006

HURLEY, DAVID HOWARD, physicist; b. Alexandria, Va., Jan. 16, 1965; s. Mary Alphin and Homer Howard Hurley; m. Miho Sakuraoka. PhD, Johns Hopkins U., 1993—97. Postdoctoral fellow NSF, Sapporo, Japan, 1997—99; staff scientist INEEL, Idaho Falls, Idaho, 1999—. Postdoctoral fellowship, NSF and NRC, 2002. Achievements include research in acoustic confinement, picosecond acoustics. Home: 3493 Summit Run Trail Idaho Falls ID 83404 Office: Ineel PO Box 1625 Idaho Falls ID 83415-2209 E-mail: hurldh@inel.gov.

HURLEY, DEAN C. bank executive, lawyer; b. South Weymouth, Mass., Oct. 16, 1954; s. Dean C. and Neva (Richards) H.; m. Laura Ann Beck, Apr. 5, 1997; children: Mackenzie Katherine, Caroline Jeanette, Margaret Neva. BS, Fairleigh Dickinson U., 1976, MBA, 1978; JD, N.Y. Law Sch., 1985. Bar: N.J. 1985, D.C. 1986. Asst. ops. mgr. Fieldcrest Mills, Inc., N.Y.C., 1976-77; spl. projects mgr. Citicorp Credit Svcs. Inc., N.Y.C., 1978-86; v.p., dir. fin. planning First Jersey Nat. Corp., Jersey City, 1986-88; v.p. asset strategies A/L. Mgmt. Dae Ichi Kangyo Bank div. The CIT Group, 1988-95; v.p. portfolio sales group Keenan, McDevitt & Co., Inc., 1996-98; v.p. debt, currencies, commodities and derivatives comml. mortgage acquisitions group Société Générale, N.Y.C., 1998—2003, dir. debt, currencies, commodities and derivatives comml. mortgage backed securitization group, 2003—. Active Christian Ctr.; trustee, recording sec. Livingston Symphony Orch., 1993-97. Mem.: Nat. Assn. Securities Dealers, Omicron Delta Epsilon, Phi Delta Phi. Republican. Avocations: piloting pvt. aircraft, power boating. Home: 23 Cider Mill Ln Port Murray NJ 07865-3202 Office: Société Générale 1221 Avenue Of The Americas New York NY 10020-1001

HURLEY, ELIZABETH, actress, model, producer; b. Hampshire, Eng., June 10, 1965; m. Hugh Grant. Student, London Studio Ctr. Head devel. Simian Films, London and L.A., 1994—; model, cosmetic rep. Estee Lauder. Actress appearing in TV programs and movies including (films) Die Tote Stadt, 1987, Rowing with the Wind, 1988, Bloody Atlantic, 1991, The Orchid House, 1991, Passenger 57, 1992, El Largo Invierno, 1992, Beyond Bedlam, 1993, Goldeneye, 1995, Mad Dogs and Englishmen, Austin Powers: International Man of Mystery, 1997, (TV movies) The Shamrock Conspiracy, 1995, Samson and Delilah, 1996, Permanent Midnight, 1998, Edtv, 1999, My Favorite Martian, 1999, Austin Powers: The Spy Who Shagged Me, 1999, The Weight of Water, 2000, Bedazzled, 2000, Servicing Sarah, 2002, (TV series) Cristabel, 1989, Rumpole and the Barrow boy, 1989, Sharpe II, 1995; host (TV spl.) The World of James Bond, 1995; prodr. Mickey Blue Eyes, 1999. Office: Creative Artists Agy 9830 Wilshire Blvd Beverly Hills CA 90212-1804

HURLEY, FRANCIS T. retired archbishop; b. San Francisco, Jan. 12, 1927; Grad., St. Patrick Sem., Menlo Park, Calif., Cath. U. Am. Ordained priest Roman Cath. Ch., 1951, consecrated bishop 1970. With Nat. Cath. Welfare Conf., Washington, asst. sec., 1958—68; assoc. sec. Nat. Cath. Welfare Conf. (now U.S. Cath. Conf.), 1968—70; titular bishop Daimlaig, aux. bishop Diocese of Juneau, Alaska, 1970—71; bishop of Juneau Alaska, 1971—76; archbishop of Anchorage, 1976—2001. Roman Catholic.*

HURLEY, FRANK THOMAS, JR., realtor; b. Washington, Oct. 18, 1924; s. Frank Thomas and Lucille (Trent) H.; m. Betty Guisinger, Aug. 9, 1997. AA, St. Petersburg Jr. Coll., 1948; BA, U. Fla., 1950. Reporter St. Petersburg (Fla.) Evening Independent, 1948-53; editor Arcadia (Calif.) Tribune, 1956-57; reporter Los Angeles Herald Express, 1957; v.p. Frank T. Hurley Assocs., Inc. Realtors, 1958-64, pres., 1964—. Sec., dir. Beau Monde, Inc., 1977-79. Author: Surf, Sand and Post Card Sunsets, 1977, Pass-a-Grille Vignettes, 1999. Elected St. Petersburg Beach Bd. Commrs., 1965—69; chmn. Pinellas Coutn Traffic Safety Coun., 1968—69; apptd. mem. Pinellas County Hist. Commn., 1993—, chmn., 2003; pres. Pass-A-Grille Cmty. Assn., 1963; mem. St. Petersburg Mus. Fine Arts, St. Pete Beach Aesthetic and Hist. Rev. Bd., chmn., 1994—96; apptd. mem. Pinellas County Sesquicentennial Coord. Com., 1995; pres. Gulf Beach Bd. Realtors, 1969; bd. govs. Palms of Pasadena Hosp., 1979—86. With USAAF, 1943—46. Mem. Fla. Assn. Realtors (dir., dist. v.p. 1971), St. Petersburg Suncoast Assn. Realtors (life, Ambassadors award 1994), St. Petersburg Beach C. of C. (dir., pres. 1975-76, Citizen of Yr. award 1983), Fla. Hist. Soc., Ky. Col., Am. Legion, Pass-A-Grille Yacht Club, Sigma Delta Chi, Sigma Tau Delta. Home: 2808 Sunset Way Saint Petersburg Beach FL 33706-4133 Office: 2506 Pass A Grille Way Saint Petersburg Beach FL 33706-4160

HURLEY, HARRY JAMES, JR., dermatologist, educator; b. Phila., Oct. 10, 1926; s. Harry James and Margaret (McHenry) Hurley; m. Jeanne Florence Geiger, July 15, 1950; children: Susan, Harry James III, Jeffrey, Marilyn, Nancy. Student, St. Joseph's Coll., Phila., 1943—45; MD, Jefferson Med. Coll., Phila., 1949; DSc in Medicine, U. Pa., 1958. Cert. Am. Bd. Dermatology. Rotating intern Fitzgerald-Mercy Hosp., Darby, Pa., 1949—50, resident in ob-gyn., 1950—51; resident in dermatology and syphilogy U. Pa. Hosp., 1951—53; rsch. fellow USPHS, 1955—56; mem. faculty U. Pa. Sch. Medicine, 1956—59, assoc. prof. dept. dermatology, 1962—68, prof. clin. dermatology, 1978—; prof. dermatology, chief sect., chief dermatol. sect. coll. hosp. Hahnemann Med. Coll., Phila., 1959—62; chief dermatology Phila. Gen. Hosp., 1962—73; asst. exec. dir. Am. Bd. Dermatology, 1985—92, exec. dir., 1993—. Attending dermatologist Fitzgerald-Mercy Hosp., 1956—80, Bryn Mawr Hosp., 1956—75, Am. Oncologic Hosp., Phila., 1960—62, U. Pa. Hosp., 1962—80; chmn. adv. bd. Nat. Program Dermatology, 1974—75; pres. Dermatology Found., 1975—76; cons., advisor in field. Editor: Jour. Geriatric Dermatology, 1993—; contbr. Capt. M.C. USAR, 1953—55. Recipient Rsch. Recognition award, Phila. chpt. Nat. Cystic Fibrosis Found., 1959, Clarence E. Shaffrey medal and award, St. Joseph's U., 1980, Finnerud award, Dermatol. Found., 1991. Fellow: ACP (chmn. self-assessment program sect. dermatology 1976); mem.: Phila. Dermatol. Soc. (editor proc. 1968—69, pres. 1970—71), Coll. Physicians Phila., Delaware County Med. Soc., Pa. Med. Soc., Pa. Acad. Dermatology (pres. 1969—70, Disting. Svc. commendation 1973), Soc. Investigative Dermatology, Am. Dermatol. Assn. (bd. dirs. 1977—82, pres. 1983—84), AMA (chmn. residency rev. com. 1979—82), Am. Acad. Dermatology (bd. dirs. 1972—75, chmn. coun. govtl. liaison 1974—75, mem. nominating com. 1977—80, chmn. nominating com. 1987, chmn. audit com. 1988—89, hon. mem., Everett Fox lectr. and award 1994), Am. Bd. Dermatology (examiner 1974—83, exec. com. 1978—79, chmn. edn. com. 1979—84, v.p. 1982—83, pres. 1983—84, bd. dirs., exec. dir. 1993, exec. cons. 2001—, Disting. Svc. award 1984), Overbrook Golf Golf Club (bd. dirs. 1988—, v.p. 1993), Alpha Epsilon Delta. Address: Amer Bd Dermatology Henry Ford Hosp One Ford Pl Detroit MI 48202-3450

HURLEY, JANET LEE, university health service administrator; b. Schenectady, N.Y., Sept. 8, 1948; m. Harry Spencer Turner; children: Scott Ashley, Jeffrey Douglas. BS, Miami U., Oxford, Ohio, 1970; MS, Kansas State U., 1980; PhD, U. Ky., 1993. Tchr. Lafayette Elem. Sch., Norfolk, Va., 1970-72, Roberts Pk. Elem. Sch., Norfolk, 1972-74, Westford (Vt.) Village Sch., 1974-76; coord. Univ. of Mid-Am. Kansas State U., Manhattan, 1978-80, coord. spl. projects, 1980-81, specialist continuing edn., 1981-85; assoc. dean continuing edn. U. Ky., Lexington, 1985-93, adminstr. univ. health svc., 1993—. Editor: History and Practice of College Health, 2002. Bd. dirs. YWCA, Lexington, 1995-98, Coll. of the Finger Lakes, Corning, N.Y., 1991-97, Tates Creek Band Boosters, Lexington, 1994, 95, 96. Fellow Am. Coll. Health Assn.; mem. Nat. Univ. Continuing Edn. Assn. (Program of Excellence award 1987, 92, Robertson Leadership award 1988, Advancing the Profession award 1992). Office: U Ky Univ Health Svc B-163 Ky Clinic Lexington KY 40536-0001 E-mail: jhurley@uky.edu.

HURLEY, JOHN ARTHUR, national security advisor; b. NYC, Aug. 22, 1935; s. John Herbert and Alice Carolyn (Lubeck) H.; m. Margaret Allen Boocock, Nov. 25, 1961 (div. 1980); children: John A. (Jack) III, Sarah Brett Hurley Dewing; m. Eileen Bridget Hayes, Feb. 14, 1987. BA in Econs., Rutgers U., 1957; MA in Internat. Rels., Am. U., 1966; MS in Mgmt., Nat.-Louis U., 1995. Rsch. analyst Dept. State, Washington, 1962-65; budget examiner Bur. Budget, Washington, 1965-70; asst. divsn. chief Office Mgmt. and Budget, Washington, 1970-73; asst. commr. US Customs Svc., Washington, 1973-78, regional commr. Balt., 1978-82, dep. asst. commr. Washington, 1984-86; customs attaché US Customs Svc., Am. Embassy, London, 1986-92, area dir., 1992-96, dep. exec. dir., 1996—2001; ret., 2001; nat. security advisor. Adj. prof. mgmt. subjects, 1995—. 1st lt. USAF, 1959-62, brig. gen. (ret.) USAFR. Decorated Legion of Merit. Mem. Internat. Assn. Chiefs of Police (internat. policy com.), Fed. Law Enforcement Officers, Sr. Exec. Assn., Phi Beta Kappa; mem., Cold War Mus. Bd. of Dir. (2003-), CSC - Dyn Corp. Co. Avocations: reading, tennis, horseback riding, railroads, teaching. Home: 9001 Cherrytree Dr Alexandria VA 22309-2902 Office: CSC Dyn Corp Co Nat Security Programs Divsn 6101 Stevenson Ave Alexandria VA 22304 E-mail: hurleyja@aol.com.

HURLEY, JOHN KENNETH, real estate and merchant banking executive; b. Washington, Nov. 28, 1931; s. Frank T. and Lucille (Trent) H.; m. June Carol Morgan, June 19, 1954 (div. 1976); children: Sean Kenneth, Kathleen Patricia; m. Joyce Carol Winemiller, Mar. 30, 1980 (div. 1990). AA, St. Petersburg Jr. Coll., 1952; BS, Fla. State U., 1954. Chmn. of bd. Frank T. Hurley Assocs., Inc., St. Petersburg Beach, Fla., 1954—; pres. Hurley Marine Corp., St. Petersburg Beach, 1980—, Pass-a-Grille Trading Co., St. Petersburg Beach, 1982—, J. Kenneth Hurley Co., St. Petersburg Beach, 1984—. Ptnr. Joyce Hurley Natural Food Products, St. Petersburg Beach, 1982-94; mng. dir. Baytree Investors, St. Petersburg Beach, 1993-97; guest lectr. more than 40 colls. and univs. Pub. Palma Ceia - MacDill News, Tampa, Fla., 1972-76; pub. poet in numerous periodicals and anthologies. Bd. dirs. Orthomolecular Research Ctr., St. Petersburg Beach, 1955-85; chmn. Zoning and Planning Bd., St. Petersburg Beach, 1968-71; pres. Friends St. Petersburg Beach Library, 1976-78. Mem. Gulf Beach Seminole Bd. Realtors, Slocum Soc., Ky. Cols. Republican. Mem. United Ch. of Christ. Club: Pass-a-Grille (Fla.) Yacht (sec. 1978-80). Avocations: yachting, tennis; cert. master for passenger vessels. Home: 2122 W Vina Del Mar Blvd Saint Petersburg FL 33706-2842 Office: 2506 Pass A Grille Way Saint Petersburg FL 33706-4160

HURLEY, KEVIN, publishing executive; Past v.p., pub. Home Mechanix, N.Y.C.; past exec. v.p., pub. Springhouse (Pa.) Corp., now pres. Office: Springhouse Corp PO Box 908 Spring House PA 19477-0908

HURLEY, LAWRENCE JOSEPH, lawyer; b. Plainfield, N.J., Nov. 17, 1946; s. Luke Michael and Gertrude Marie (Bremer) H.; m. Allyson J. Kingsley, May 28, 1977; children: Michael William, Kathryn Elizabeth. BS, U. Dayton, 1969; JD, Cath. U. Am., 1974. Bar: N.J. 1974, U.S. Dist. Ct. N.J., 1974, D.C. 1976, N.Y. 1980, U.S. Ct. Appeals (3rd cir.) 1980, U.S. Dist. Ct. (ea. and so. dists.) N.Y. 1981, U.S. Ct. Appeals (2nd cir.) 1981, U.S. Ct. Appeals (D.C. cir.) 1982. Law clk. Superior Ct. N.J., New Brunswick, 1974-75; assoc. Lynch, Mannion, Lutz & Lewandowski, New Brunswick, 1975-76, Stryker, Tams & Dill, Newark, 1976-79; atty. AT&T, Basking Ridge, NJ, 1979-85; chief asst. prosecutor econ. crimes and ofcl. corruption Morris County Prosecutor's Office, Morristown, NJ, 1985—89; ptnr. Voorhees & Acciavatti, Morristown, 1989-91; sr. atty. AT&T, 1991—96; labor and employment counsel Lucent Techs., Murray Hill, NJ, 1996—99, mng. labor and employment corp. counsel, 1999—2001, mng. litigation, labor and employment counsel, 2001—. With U.S. Army, 1969-71. Decorated Bronze Star and Army Commendation medal U.S. Army. Mem. ABA (litig. sect. 1976-86, labor law sect. 1981-86, criminal law sect. 1985-91, labor law sect. 1991—), N.J. State Bar Assn. (labor law sect. 1981—). Office: Lucent Techs Rm 3A518 600 Mountain Ave New Providence NJ 07974

HURLEY, LINDA KAY, psychologist; b. Kansas City, Mo., June 4, 1951; d. James O. and Phyllis L. (Steil) Hurley; m. Thomas O'Connell. BS, U. Mo., 1973; BA, Am. U., 1978, MA, 1983, PhD, 1986. Lic. psychologist, Tex. Assoc. psychologist Tarrant County Mental Health/Mental Retardation, Ft. Worth, 1983-84; intern in med. psychology Oreg. Health Scis. U., Portland, 1984-85; instr. in pediatrics and psychology U. Tex. Southwestern Med. Ctr., Dallas, 1985-88, asst. prof., 1988-96; psychologist, dir. tng. Child Study Ctr., Ft. Worth, 1990-91; pediatric & clin. child psychologist Ft. Worth Pediatrics, 1991—2002; pvt. practice Hurst, Tex., 2003—. Trustee Ronald McDonald House (Friends of Children, Inc.), 1986-89. Co-author: (with Michael C. Roberts) Managing Managed Care, 1997. With USAF, 1974-77. Mem. APA (clin. psychology divsn., clin. child psychology sect.), Ft. Worth Area Psychol. Assn. (treas. 1994, pres.-elect 1996, pres. 1997, past-pres. 1998), Soc. Pediat. Psychology (bd. dirs.), Assn. Advancement of Behavior Therapy, Soc. Rsch. in Child Devel., Tex. Psychol. Assn., Ft. Worth Camera Club (bd. dirs. 1997-99), Phi Kapppa Phi. Avocations: cooking, music, photography. Office: 1500 Norwood Drive Ste 306 Hurst TX 76054 Mailing: PO Box 820261 North Richland Hills TX 76182-0261

HURLEY, MIKE (JOHN MATHIAS GERETSCHLAEGER), English language educator; b. St. Paul, Aug. 21, 1939; BS, N.D. State U., 1962; MA, Ind. U., 1972; MA in Tchg., Bridgewater State Coll., 1982. Enlisted USN, 1962, commd. ensign, 1964, advanced through grades to lt. comdr., 1971; resigned, 1986; seaman, journalist USS Independence, 1963-64; press escort officer UN Command, Seoul, 1964-65; asst. public affairs officer Sixth Naval Dist., Charleston, 1965-67; asst. head orientation Chief of Navy Info., The Pentagon, 1968; instr. Def. Info. Sch., Fort Harrison, Ind., 1969-71; force public affairs officer U.S. Naval Forces, Vietnam, 1971-72; resigned USN, 1972; exec. dir. Cmty. Svc. Officers, Fall River, Mass., 1973-75; assoc. dir. Citizens for Citizens, Fall River, 1975-83; assoc. prof. Bridgewater (Mass.) State Coll., 1984—. Pub. Segregansett Press, Bridgewater, 1990—; elec. bookseller Mudhopper Books, 2000—. Contbr. short fiction to profl. publs. under personal and pen names. With USNR, 1983-86. Avocation: philatelist. Office: Segregansett Press PO Box 545 Bridgewater MA 02324-0545 E-mail: tewagar@aol.com., mike@mudhopperbooks.com.

HURLEY, WILLIAM JOSEPH, retired information systems executive; b. N.Y.C., June 14, 1939; s. William and Anna Rita (Hubschman) H.; m. Dorothy Ann Mellett, Sept. 23, 1961 (dec.); children: William, Terrianne, Barbara, Daniel; m. Marianne F. Jordan, Mar. 17, 1990. BBA, Pace U., 1968, MBA, 1973. Dir. info. system Gen. Foods Corp., White Plains, N.Y., 1973-79; dir. systems devel. Securities Industry Automation Corp., N.Y.C., 1979; dir. mgmt. info. systems Schering Plough Corp., Kenilworth, N.J., 1979-81, sr. dir. mgmt. info. systems, 1981-83, v.p. mgmt. info. service, 1983-88; v.p. world wide info. systems Technicon Corp., Tarrytown, N.Y., 1988-90; dir. info. systems Miles Inc., Tarrytown, 1990-95. Pres. New City (N.Y.) vol. Fire Engine Co. 1, 1979-81; commr. New City Fire Dist., 1983-94. Served with USMC, 1956-59. Mem. Soc. Info. Mgmt., Assn. Systems Mgmt. (v.p. 1981), Am. Legion. Republican. Roman Catholic. Avocation: financial planning. Home: Unit 504 3150 N A1A Fort Pierce FL 34949-8868 E-mail: bhurley317@aol.com.

HURLEY, WILLIAM JOSEPH, business executive; b. Phila., July 26, 1940; s. Thomas Patrick and Louise Catherine (Culhane) H.; m. Rosemary Anne Gorman, Aug. 17, 1963; children: William J. Jr., Sharon A., Sean T., Megan M. BS in Chemistry, Villanova U., 1962; PhD in Chemistry, Princeton U., 1967. Rsch. chemist DuPont Co., Wilmington, Del., 1967-71, Parlin, N.J., 1971-73, rsch. supr., 1973-74, Rochester, N.Y., 1974-80, tech. mgr. Wilmington, 1983-86, venture mgr., 1986-88, tech. mgr., 1988-89, lab. dir. Circleville, Ohio, 1989-93, mgr. tech. pers. Wilmington, 1993-94, mgr. corp. bus. devel., 1994-99; devel. mgr. P.O. Magnetics, B.V., Eindhoven, The Netherlands, 1981-83; pres. Innovatech LLC. Adj. prof. Villanova U., 1998—, Pa. State U., 1999. NSF fellow, 1966. Mem. Am. Chem. Soc. (Outstanding Student award 1962). Avocations: boating, hiking, tennis.

HURLIN, DAN, actor, theater director; Artistic dir. Andy's Summer Playhouse, Wilton, NH, 1987—93; instr. Bowdoin Coll., Bennington Coll., Barnard Coll., Princeton U., Sarah Lawrence Coll.; dir. Pupet Lab at Arts St. Ann's, Bklyn. Dir.: No(thing so powerful as) Truth, 1995, Constance and Ferdinand, 1991, The Jazz Section, 1989, A Cool Million, 1990, Quintland, 1992, The Day the Ketchup Turned Blue, 1997, The Shoulder, 1998, Everyday Uses for Sight, 2000. Recipient Village Voice OBIE award, 1990, New York Dance and performance Award, A.K.A. Bessie, 2000; grantee Guggenheim Fellowship, 2002. Office: 72-74 E 3rd St #5B New York NY 10003

HURLOCK, JAMES BICKFORD, retired lawyer; b. Chgo., Aug. 7, 1933; s. James Bickford and Elizabeth (Charls) Hurlock; m. Margaret Lyn Holding, July 1, 1961; children: James Bickford III, Burton Charls, Matthew Hunter. AB, Princeton U., 1955; BA, Oxford U., 1957, MA, 1960; JD, Harvard U., 1959. Bar: N.Y. 1960, U.S. Supreme Ct. 1967. Assoc. White & Case, N.Y.C., 1959—66, ptnr., 1967—2000; ret., 2000. Bd. dirs. Orient Express Hotels, Ltd., Stolt Offshore S.A. Trustee N.Y. Presbyn. Hosp., Parker Sch. Fgn. and Comparative Law, Woods Hole Oceanog. Inst.; chmn. Internat. Devel. Law Org., U.S. Assn. for UNHCR. Recipient Rhodes scholarship, 1955. Mem.: ABA, Am. Assn. Internat. Law, Am. Law Inst., N.Y. State Bar Assn., N.Y. Yacht Club, River Club. Republican. Episcopalian. Home: 46 Byram Dr Greenwich CT 06830-7008 Office: White & Case 1155 Avenue Of The Americas New York NY 10036-2787 E-mail: jhurlock46byram@aol.com.

HURN, RAYMOND WALTER, minister, religious order administrator; b. Ontario, Oreg., June 27, 1921; s. Walter H. and Bertha Sultana (Gray) H.; m. Madelyn Lenore Kirkpatrick, Dec. 30, 1941; children: Constance Isbell, Jacqueline Oliver. BA, So. Nazarene U., 1943; DD (hon.), So. Nazarene U, 1967; postgrad., U. Tulsa, 1946-47, Fuller Sem., Pasadena, Calif., 1978-81. Ordained to ministry Ch. of Nazarene, 1943. Pastor Ch. of Nazarene chs., Kans., 1943-59; dist. supt. Ch. of Nazarene, West Tex. dist., Tex., 1959-68; dir. home missions and ch. extension Internat. Hdqrs. Ch. of Nazarene, Kansas City, Mo., 1968-85, gen. supt., 1985-93. Author: Mission Possible, 1973, Black Evangelism, Which Way from Here, 1973, Spiritual Gifts Workshop, 1977, Finding Your Ministry, 1980, Mission Action Sourcebook, 1980, Unleashing the Lay Potential in the Sunday School, 1986, The Rising Tide: New Churches for the New Millenium, 1997. Recipient Exec. award Am. Inst. Ch. Growth, 1980, B award Bethany So. Nazarene Univ., 1982, Heritage award So. Nazarene U., 1993, Lifetime Achievement award Assn. of Nazarene Bldg. Prof., 1993, Multicultural Fellowship award, 1993; named Gen. Supt. Emeritus, 23rd Gen. Assembly of the Ch. of the Nazarene, 1993. Address: 17500 W 119th St #1101 Olathe KS 66061

HURNYAK, CHRISTINA KAISER, lawyer; b. Noblesville, Ind., Dec. 22, 1949; d. Albert Michael and Lois Angie (Gatton) Kaiser; m. Cyril Hurnyak, June 24, 1972. BA cum laude, Wittenberg U., 1972; JD, SUNY-Buffalo, 1979. Bar: N.Y. 1980, Pa. 1996, U.S. Dist. Ct. (we. dist.) Pa. 1998. Mem. support staff McKinsey & Co., Inc., mgmt. cons., Chgo., 1972-75; law clk. Justice Norman J. Wolf, N.Y. Supreme Ct., Buffalo, 1980-81; assoc. Dempsey & Dempsey, Buffalo, 1979-80, 81-90, Grossman, Levine & Civiletto, Niagara Falls, N.Y., 1990-95, Tarasi, Tarasi & Fishman, P.C. (formerly Tarasi Law Firm), Pitts., 1998—. Mem. ABA, ATLA, Pa. State Bar Assn., Pa. Trial Lawyers Assn.. Allegheny County Bar Assn. Democrat. Lutheran. Office: Tarasi Tarasi & Fishman PC 510 3rd Ave Pittsburgh PA 15219-2107

HURON, ROBERT LAWRENCE, photojournalist; b. New Rochelle, N.Y., Dec. 4, 1944; s. Lawrence Hall and Renee (Kelly) H. Sales rep. various photographic retail stores, N.Y. Met. Area, 1965-70; photography lab. technician varous labs., N.Y. Met. Area, 1965-75; freelance photographer/journalist pvt. practice N.Y. Met. Area, N.Y. Met. Area, 1975—. Contbr. to books Spectacular Railroad Photography, 1988, Diesel Locomotive Rosters, 2d edit., 1986; contbr. photos, articles to transp. mags. Bd. dirs. Long Island Commuters Assn., Locust Valley, N.Y., 1978—. Mem. Internat. Freelance Photographers Orgn. (master photographer), Photo Press Internat., Ctrl. Elec. R.R. Assn., Rwy. and Locomotive Hist. Soc., Elec. Railroaders Assn., Carson Long Inst. Alumni Assn. Avocations: R.R. and transportation historian, writer. Home: 111 Valley Ave Locust Valley NY 11560-2040

HURON, RODERICK EUGENE, minister, writer; b. Chesapeake, Ohio, Dec. 5, 1934; s. Raymond Clarence and Minnie Opal (Williams) Huron; m. Autumn June Hostetter, July 24, 1956; children: Lila Kay Huron Albinger, Eric Scott, Sara Lynn Huron Myers. BA, Ky. Christian Coll., 1956; MEd, U. Pitts., 1967; postgrad., U. Akron, 1968—70. Ordained to ministry Christian Chs. and Chs. of Christ, 1958; cert. meeting profl. Min. Highlawn Ch. of Christ, Huntington, W.Va., 1956—57; youth min. 1st Christian Ch., Canton, Ohio, 1957—62; min. LaBelle View Ch. of Christ, Steubenville, Ohio, 1962—67, West Akron Ch. of Christ, Ohio, 1968—71; missionary Toronto Christian Mission, 1971—75; sr. min. North Industry Christian Ch., Canton, 1976—84; dir.-elect N.Am. Christian Conv., Cin., 1984—86, conv. dir., 1986—97; pres. Meeting Excellence, 1997—2001; min. of membership devel. Lakeside Christian Ch., Ft. Mitchell, Ky., 1997—, min. involvement Lakeside Park, 1997—; dir. svc. learning Cin. Bible Coll. and Sem., 2003—. Quest on various TV and radio programs. Author: Do You Know Who You Are, 1976, Checkpoint, 1979 (Sherwood E. Wirt award Billy Graham Evangelist Assn.), Christian Minister's Manual, 1984 (Gold Medallion award Evang. Christian Pub. Assn.), Say Hello to Life, 1984, Bible Stories for Children, 1995; contbr. articles to religious jours. Republican. Mem. Christian Ch.

HURST, CHARLES WILSON, lawyer; b. Salt Lake City, July 4, 1957; s. John Vann and Myra (Kasik) Piscane; m. Karen Buck, Jan. 5, 1985, children: Jeanette Q., Daniel C., Brian K., Matthew C., Robert W. Student, U. Chgo., 1975-77; BA cum laude, Wesleyan U., Conn., 1979; JD, Duke U., 1983. Bar: Pa. 1983, U.S. Dist. Ct. (ea. dist.) Pa. 1985, Calif. 1986, U.S. Dist. Ct. (cen. dist.) Calif. 1990. Assoc. Saul, Ewing, Remick & Saul, Phila., 1983-85, Wyman Bautzer Kuchel & Silbert, Orange County, Calif., 1985-89, ptnr., 1990, Snell & Wilmer LLP, Orange County, 1990—. Dir. Pacific Art Found., 1994-2000; trustee Pegasus Sch., 1996—, vice chair, 2003. Mem. ABA (comml. leasing com. of real property, probate and trust law sect.), Orange County Bar Assn. Office: Snell & Wilmer 1920 Main St Ste 1200 Irvine CA 92614-7230 E-mail: churst@swlaw.com.

HURST, DEBORAH, pediatric hematologist; b. Washington, May 9, 1946; d. Willard and Frances (Wilson) H.; m. Stephen Mershon Senter, June 14, 1970; children: Carlin, Daniel. BA, Harvard U., 1968; MD, Med. Coll. Pa., 1974. Diplomate Nat. Bd. Med. Examiners, Am. Bd. Pediatrics, Am. Bd. Pediatric Hematology-Oncology. Intern Bellevue Hosp., NYU Hosp., N.Y.C., 1974-75, resident in pediatrics, 1975-76; ambulatory pediatric fellow Bellevue Hosp., N.Y.C., 1976-77; hematology, oncology fellow Bellevue Hosp., Columbia U., N.Y.C., 1977-80; assoc. hematologist Childrens Hosp. Oakland, Calif., 1980-92; asst. clin. prof. U. Calif. San Francisco Med. Ctr., 1992—; med. dir. Bayer

Corp., Berkeley, Calif., 1992-98; sr. dir. clin. devel. Chiron Corp., Emeryville, Calif., 1998—. Hematology cons. Assn. Asian/Pacific Community Health Orgns., Oakland; dir. Satellite Hematology Clinic/Valley Childrens Hosp., Fresno, Calif., 1984-92; cons. state dept. epidemiology Calif. State Dept. Health, Berkeley, 1992; chelation cons. lead poisoning program Childrens Hosp., Oakland, 1986-92. Contbr. articles to profl. jours. Vol. cons. lead poisoning State Dept. Epidemiology and Toxicology, Berkeley, 1986-92. Fellow Am. Acad. Pediatrics; mem. Am. Soc. Hematology, Am. Soc. Gene Therapy, Am. Soc. Clin. Oncology, Am. Soc. Pediat. Hematology/Oncology, Nat. Hemophilia Found., Internat. Soc. Thrombosis and Hemostasis. Office: Chiron Corp 4560 Horton St MS120 Emeryville CA 94608-2900

HURST, GREGORY SQUIRE, director, producer, investment executive; b. Oak Park, Ill., Dec. 1, 1947; s. Claude Squire Hurst and Marcia (Tooker) Allen; m. Joyce Barbara Baum, Apr. 4, 1981; children: Alexander Squire, Adam Spencer. BS, Miami U., Oxford, Ohio, 1969; MA, U. Wis., 1973; MFA, U. N.C., 1975; postgrad., U. Pa., 2003. Dir. theater Wayland Acad., Beaver Dam, Wis., 1969-73; instr. acting U. N.C., Chapel Hill, 1973-75; chmn. theater dept. Tarkio (Mo.) Coll., 1975-77; producing artistic dir. Pa. Stage Co., Allentown, 1979-88, George St. Playhouse, New Brunswick, N.J., 1988-97; v.p. investments, fin. advisor UBS Paine Webber Inc., N.Y.C., 1999—, ins. coord. br. office, 2001—. Artistic dir. Mule Barn Theatre, Tarkio, 1975-77; mem. theater panel Mo. Arts Coun., St. Louis, 1975-77, Pa. Coun. Arts, Harrisburg, 1982-85; cons. Found. Devel. Am. Profl. theatre, N.Y.C., 1983; on-site evaluator Nat. Endowment Arts, Washington, 1984-97; mem. mus. theater task force Rockefeller Found., Phila., 1985; founding mem. Playmakers Reperatory Theatre, 1975; vis. prof. Rutgers U., 1989; sr. lectr. Duke U., 1995-96. Librettist (mus. play) Song of Myself, 1981; stage dir. (world premieres) Feathertop, Great Expectations, (with Hinton Battle) Shim Sham, (with John Spencer) Walk out of Water, (with Estelle Parsons) Forgiving Typhoid Mary (named One of Best 5 Plays in Am., Time mag. 1991), Greetings, Copperhead, (with Cady Huffman and John Cullum) Jekyll and Hyde, (with Joel Higgins, Christine Andreas) Fields of Ambrosia, West End London Aldwych Theatre, 1996, (with Michael Rupert) Relativity, Sing a Christmas Song, (with Laura Innes and Gabrielle Carteris) Les Liaisons Dangereuse; nat. tour The Acting Co. The Glass Menagerie; prodr. (with Calista Flockhardt) Zara Spook and Other Lures, (with Bebe Neuwirth) Just So, (with Alison Janey) Idioglossia, (With Eli Wallach and Anne Jackson) Spunky & the Fitz; dir. TV shows General Hospital, One Life to Live, Another World, The Guiding Light. Area leader Allentown and Cen. Jersey United Way, 1981-92; exec. v.p., bd. dirs. Stage Dirs. and Choreographers Found., 1989-92, pres., 1992-98, East Coast Dirs. Coun. Recipient Downtown Improvement award City of Allentown, 1987, Outstanding Contbn. award Theatre Assn. Pa., 1988, Vision, dedication, leadership award SDC Found., 1998; Tony nomination for best musical Swinging On A Star; named Best Dir. in N.J. Belmont Avenue Social Club, 1994, Les Liaisons Dangereuse, 1989. Mem. Soc. Stage Dirs., Dramatist Guild, Dirs. Guild Am. (coun. mem. 1997-99), Actors Equity Assn., U. N.C. N.J. Alumni Club (pres. 1999—), Knights of the Vine, Phi Kappa Tau. Democrat. Avocations: golf, antiques, travel, swimming, gourmet cooking, wine collecting. Home: 3 Fernwood Ct East Brunswick NJ 08816-3333 E-mail: gsquireh@aol.com., gsquireh@home.com., gregory.hurst@ubspainewebber.com.

HURST, JEFFREY PAUL, agricultural products executive; b. South Dayton, NY, June 5, 1952; s. Kenneth Arthur and Marian Delight Hurst; m. Cheryl Greben Hurst, June 12, 1976 (div. Oct. 2002); children: Helen Ann, Lisa Marie. BS, U. Ky., 1974; MS, U. Wis., 1976. Animal nutritionist Culpeper (Va.) Farmers' Co-op., 1976—88; gen. mgr. I.D.O. Feed and Supply Corp., Fall River, Wis., 1988—. Pres. Va. State Feed Assn., 1983. Mem.: Am. Animal Sci. Assn., Am. Dairy Sci. Assn. Avocations: golf, guitar, running, investing, martial arts. Office: IDO Feed and Supply Corp PO Box 127 Fall River WI 53932 E-mail: hurst@powercom.net.

HURST, KENNETH THURSTON, publisher; b. London, Apr. 3, 1923; came to U.S., 1947, naturalized, 1953; s. Ralph Thurston and Karen (Tottrup) H.; m. Joan Gee Dec. 10, 1994; children: Lincoln, Brian, Maria Therese. Student pvt. schs. Account exec. Hutzler Advt. Agy., Dayton, Ohio, 1948-53; advt. and promotion mgr. McGraw-Hill Book Co., N.Y.C., 1953-58; advt, and publicity mgr. Hawthorn Books, Inc., N.Y.C., 1958-61; gen. mgr. Prentice-Hall of India Pvt. Ltd., New Delhi, 1961-63; v.p., gen. mgr. Prentice-Hall Internat., Inc., Englewood Cliffs, N.J., 1963-70, exec. v.p., 1970, now pres. Dir. Internat. Book Distbr., Ltd., Prentice-Hall S.E. Asia Ltd., Prentice-Hall India Ltd.; State Dept. adviser to Brazil and Burma; adviser AID Mission to Turkey, 1964, Morocco, 1965; cons. U.S. Info. Agy., U. N.C., U. Scranton, SUNY, MIT, Faculty Folio mag.; lectr. State Dept. Program Bur., NYU, Rockland Community Coll., U. Scranton, Drew U., Wagner Coll., Lake Forest (Ill.) Coll., Olivet (Mich.) Coll., Rosemont Coll., Pa., Oberlin Coll., Ohio, Corning Coll., N.Y., U. Cen. Fla., U. So. Fla., Edison C.C., Pepperdine Coll., Calif., Chestnut Hill (Pa.) Coll., Spearfish Coll., S.D., Rockpoint Colony, Cornell U., Stanford U., Russell Sage Coll., Fla. State U.; faculty ann. pubs. seminar; co-chmn. Internat. Sports Awards, 1982, Pub. Hall of Fame, 1984; mem. policy bd. Ctr. for the Book; chmn. Books Across the Sea. Co-author: Books for National Growth, 1965, Indian Publishing Since Independence, 1980, American Books Abroad, 1986, Spiritual Insights for Daily Living, 1986; author: Live Life First Class, 1985, Paul Brunton: A Personal View, 1988, Living the Good Life, 1989; contbr. articles to profl. jours. Mem. Spiritual Adv. Coun., Elizabeth Kubler-Ross Ctr.; mem. com. to balance budget Ctr. Applied Rsch. in Edn., Internat. Inst. Integral Scis.; trustee Valley Cottage Free Libr.; chmn., mem. nat. exec. coun. Spiritual Frontiers Fellowship; chmn. N.Y. Easter Seal dr., 1983, Paul Brunton Philosophic Found.; bd. dirs. Ctr. for Positive Living; pres., bd. dirs. Collier County Friends of Libr. Assn.; mem. Lee County Libr. Adv. Bd.; v.p. Las Vistas Assn. With Fleet Air Arm Royal Navy, 1942-47. Recipient Presdl. E award and E Star, Pub. Hall of Fame. Mem. Asia Soc., St. John's Old Boys' Assn., Assn. Am. Pubs. (chmn. internat. div., chmn. del. to India 1979, 84, to Thailand 1981), Am. Mgmt. Assn., Inst. Bus. Planning, Mensa, Acad. Religion (trustee), Inst. Near-Death Studies (bd. dirs.), Circumnavigators Club, Forum Club (bd. dirs.), Eng. Speaking Union (bd. dirs.), Internat. Club Fla., Overseas Press Club, Fla. Coun. Humanities, Neapolitan Club, Boston Athletic Club, Publishers Club, Englewood Club (gov.), Rotary (bd. dirs.). Republican. Episcopalian. E-mail: joanhurst@webtv.net.

HURST, LAURENDA LEE, library director, music educator; b. Muncie, Ind., Aug. 31, 1948; d. Martin Lewis Hurst, Retta Mae Hurst; m. Schuyler Townsend (div. Mar. 4, 1991); children: Schuyler Muench Townsend, Rebecca Lee Townsend McDole. BSc, Ball State U., 1992; MLS, Ind. U., 1996. Cert. tchr. Ind., 1992. Clk. Greentown Pub. Libr., Greentown, Ind., 1979—87, asst. dir., 1987—99, Tipton County Pub. Libr., Tipton, Ind., 1999—; pvt. music instr. Hurst Music Studio, Greentown, Ind., 1973—. Author: (plays) Greentown Once Upon a Time, 1998. Sec. Greentown Area Residents Assn., Greentown, 1999—2002; mem. Greentown Area Bus. Assn., Greentown, 1999—2002; pres. Ea. Parent Tchr. Orgn., Greentown, 1979—84; bd. dir. Ea.Howard Performing Arts Assn., Greentown, 2000—03. Grantee, Tipton Cmty. Found., 2000, 2002, Build Ind. grant, State of Ind., 2000, Am. Libr. Assn., 2001. Mem.: Ind. Libr.Fedn. (district II sec., treas. 1995—2003), Kokomo Morning Musicale (pres. 1985—87), Greentown Lion's Club, Tipton Rotary Club (cmty. resource chmn. 2001—02). Avocations: musical theater, live concerts, reading. Home: 802 East Hall Street Greentown IN 46936 Office: Tipton County Public Library 127 East Madison Street Tipton IN 46072 Office Fax: 765-675-4475. Business E-Mail: rhurst@tiptonpl.lib.in.us.

HURST, LELAND LYLE, natural gas company executive; b. Mooreland, Okla., Oct. 16, 1930; s. Lewis Walter and Ellen Sarah (Riggs) H.; m. Karen Lee Lamkin, Jan. 24, 1969; children: Courtney Anne, Caroline Leigh. BS in Indsl. Engring., Okla. State U., 1952; MS in Petroleum Engring., U. Tulsa, 1958. Registered profl. engr., Okla. With Amoco Prodn. Co., 1958-80; engr. Amoco Prodn. Co. (various locations), 1958-68; staff engr. Amoco Prodn. Co., Calgary, Alta., Can., 1968-70, div. engr. supr. Denver, 1970-73, area supt. Liberal, Kans., 1973-74, asst. div. engr. Denver, 1974-75, gas sales mgr., 1975-80; v.p. Amoco Gas Co., Houston, 1980-81, pres., dir., 1981-86; v.p. mktg. KN Energy Inc., Gasco Inc., 1986-87; v.p. interstate ops., exec. v.p. Gasco Inc., 1987-88, sr. v.p. ops., 1988-95, also bd. dirs., 1992-95; exec. v.p., dir. Indsl. Mechanics Inc., 1987-95, Sunflower Pipeline Co., 1988-95, Rocky Mountain Gas Co., 1992-95, 1992-95, No. Gas Co. Wyo., 1992-95, 1992-95. Bd. dirs., v.p. KN Front Range Oper. Co., KN Wattenberg Co., KN Wattenberg Ltd. Liability Co.; bd. dirs. RMNG Gathering Co., TCP Gathering Co.; v.p. Panola/Rusk Gatherers, Am. Energy Holdings, Inc., Am. Gas Storage, L.P., Am. Gathering, L.P., Am. Processing, L.P., Am. Oil and Gas Corp., Am. Pipeline Co., Am. Webb, Inc., AOG Holdings, Inc., AOG Mgmt., Inc., Caprock Pipeline Co., Red River Gas Pipeline Corp., Red River Pipeline, L.P., RRP Fin. Corp., Webb/Duval Gatherers, Westar Transmission Co., 1995. With Chem. Corps U.S. Army, 1953-55. Served with Chem. Corps U.S. Army, 1953-55. Mem. Rocky Mountain Gas Men's Assn. (bd. dirs. 1977), Soc. Petroleum Engrs. (editl. com. 1953-55), Rocky Mountain Oil and Gas Assn. Colo. (pres. 1995-97, indsl. mechanic chmn. 1995—), Natural Gas Men of Houston-New Orleans (v.p.), Houston Club, Denver Petroleum Club. Republican.

HURST, MARY JANE, English language educator; b. Hamilton, Ohio, Sept. 21, 1952; d. Nimrod and Leckie Gaines; m. Daniel L. Hurst, June 5, 1974; 1 child, Katherine Jane. BA summa cum laude, Miami U., 1974; MA, U. Md., 1980, PhD, 1986. Tchr. Groveport (Ohio) H.S., 1974-77; tchg. asst. U. Md., College Park, 1978-79, master tchr., 1979-82; asst. prof. English, Tex. Tech U., Lubbock, 1986-92, assoc. prof., 1992-99, prof., 1999—, assoc. dean Coll. Arts and Scis., 2000—. Vis. scholar Stanford U., summer 1987; steering com. Nat. Cowboy Symposium, Lubbock, 1988-89. Author: The Voice of the Child in American Literature, 1990; tech. editor: HTLV-I and the Nervous System, 1989; book rev. editor S.W. Jour. Linguistics, 1995-98; contbr. articles to profl. jours. Active Lubbock Cultural Affairs Coun., 1986-92, Lubbock Symphony Guild, 1992—; vol. Meals on Wheel, Lubbock, 1986-97, Habitat for Humanity, Lubbock, 1986-97, Interfaith Hospitality Network, 1998—. Mem.: MLA, AAUP (regional v.p. 1990—94), AAUW (alt. fellowships panel in linguistics 1988—90), South Ctrl. MLA, Coll. Tchrs. English Tex., Linguistic Assn. S.W. (pres. 1996—97, exec. dir. 1998—2001), Linguistic Soc. Am., Phi Beta Kappa, Alpha Lambda Delta, Sigma Tau Delta, Phi Kappa Phi. Avocations: geneaology, travel, west highland white terriers. Office: Tex Tech U Dept English Lubbock TX 79409

HURST, MATTHEW THOMAS, music educator; b. Norwood, Mass., July 21, 1968; s. Thomas Frazier and Rosemary Hurst; m. Karen Elaine Matz, July 9, 2000; stepchildren: Meridythe Lynn Donnan, Seth Anthony Donnan. BA, Montclair State Coll., 1991; MA, SUNY Stony Brook, 1997. Cert. EMT-Defibrillation N.Y. State Dept. Health Bur. Emergency Med. Svcs., 1998; Pub. Sch. Music Tchr. N.Y., 1997, Pub. Sch. Elem. Tchr. N.Y., 1997, Essentials of Firefighting-FireFighter I N.Y., 1996, Tchr. Music N.J. Dept. Edn., 1991. Instrumental music tchr. Sat. Music and Arts Program Montclair Pub. Schs., Montclair, NJ, 1987—92; saxophone instr. Music Prep. divsn. Montclair State Coll., Upper Montclair, NJ; music intern Ctr. for Performing Arts USDAN, Wheatly Heights, NY, 1989; music educator Bayport-Blue Point Sch. Dist., Bayport, NY, 1993—. Vol. firefighter and EMT-defibrillation North Babylon Fire Co., North Babylon, NY, 1996—98; prin. saxophonist Garden State Concert Band, NJ, 1991—92, Bloomfield Civic Band, Bloomfield, NJ, 1991—92; saxophonist Garden State Big Band, NJ, 1991—92; guest condr. Bloomfield Youth Band, Bloomfield, NJ, 1989, 1991. Recipient Semper Fidelis Award, U.S. Marines Youth Found. and Marine Corps League, 1986, Charles Lutton Award, Phi Mu Alpha Sinfonia and Montclair State Coll. Dept. of Music, 1987, Outstanding Young Men of Am., 1990, Outstanding Student Tchr. Award, Montclair State Coll., Sch. of the Fine and Performing Arts, 1991; scholar Musical Merit Award, USDAN Ctr. for the Creative and Performing Arts, 1984; Edna McEachern Scholarship Award, Montclair State Coll. Dept. of Music, 1988. Mem.: Suffolk County Music Educator's Assn., Music Educator's Nat. Conf., Soc. for Encouraging the Arts in Bayport-Blue Point Schools, Phi Mu Alpha Sinfonia (life; Lambda Mu chpt. pres. & v.p. 1988—90). Roman Catholic. Avocations: fine & performing arts, culinary arts, bicycling. Home: 21 School St Hampton Bays NY 11946 Office: Bayport-Blue Point Schl Dist 189 Academy St Bayport NY 11705

HURST, ROBERT JAY, securities company executive; b. N.Y.C., Nov. 5, 1945; s. Kurt and Jeanette (Sachs) H.; children: Alexander, Amanda. BA, Clark U., 1966; M in Govt. Adminstrn., U. Pa., 1968, Pub. Fin. fellow, 1969. With investment banking divsn. Merrill Lynch, Pierce, Fenner & Smith, Inc., N.Y.C., 1969-74, v.p., 1974, Goldman, Sachs & Co., N.Y.C., 1974-80, gen. ptnr., 1980—. Mem. mgmt. com. Goldman Sachs & Co., 1990, co-head investment banking divsn., 1996, head investment banking divsn., 1996-99, mem. exec. com., 1995, vice chmn., 1997; bd. dirs. IDB Holding Corp., VF Corp., Goldman Sachs Group, Inc., AirClic, Inc., Constellation Energy Group. Mem. bd. overseers Wharton Sch. U. Pa., mem. coun. fgn. rels.; trustee Com. Econ. Devel.; vice chmn. bd. trustees Whitney Mus. Am. Art, Nat. Gallery Art; chmn. Jewish Mus., 1991; bd. dirs. Nat. Found. Tchg. Entrepreneurship; trustees coun. Nat. Gallery Art. Mem. Univ. Club., Atlantic Golf Club (Bridgehampton), Sunningdale (N.Y.), Maroon Creek Club (Aspen). Office: Goldman Sachs & Co 85 Broad St Ground Fl New York NY 10004-2456

HURT, JENNINGS LAVERNE, III, lawyer; b. Sanford, Fla., Oct. 25, 1952; s. Jennings Laverne Jr. and Virginia (Ludwig) H.; m. Maribeth O'Connor, June 24, 1978; children: Jennings Laverne IV, Matthew Alexander, Natalie Elizabeth, Joseph Connor. AA, Seminole Jr. Coll., 1972; BSBA, U. Fla., 1974; JD with honors, Cumberland Sch. Law, 1977. Bar: Fla. 1977, U.S. Dist. Ct. (mid. dist.) 1978, U.S. Dist. Ct. (no. and so. dists.) Fla. 1982, U.S. Ct. Appeals (11th cir.) 1988; cert. trial lawyer Nat. Bd. Trial Advocacy. Assoc. D'Aiuto, Walker & Buckmaster, P.A., Orlando, Fla., 1977-79; ptnr. Anderson & Hurt, P.A., Orlando, 1979-87; mng. ptnr. Rissman, Weisberg, Barrett & Hurt, P.A., Orlando, 1987—. Contbr. articles to profl. jours. Recipient Am. Jurisprudence award, 1974. Mem. ABA, Orange County Bar Assn., Fla. Bar Assn. (bd. cert. trial lawyer), Fla. Def. Lawyers Assn., Def. Rsch. Inst., Cen. Fla. Med. Malpractice Claims Assn. (treas. 1992-95). Republican. Roman Catholic. Avocations: golf, tennis. Home: 1655 Barcelona Way Winter Park FL 32789-5614 Office: Rissman Weisberg Barrett & Hurt PA 201 E Pine St 15th Fl Orlando FL 32801-2738 E-mail: bucky.hurt@rissman.com.

HURT, MICHAEL CARTER, lawyer; b. Kokomo, Ind., Sept. 7, 1943; s. Eldon Carter and Jane Ann (McCool) H.; m. Susan Clay Lines, Jan. 18, 1964; children— Michael Carter II, Justin Patrick. J.D., U. Pacific, 1973. Bar: Wis. 1973, U.S. Dist. Ct. (ea. dist.) Wis. 1973, U.S. Ct. Appeals (7th cir.). Legal intern Sacramento County Pub. Defender, Sacramento, 1971-73; assoc. Laubenheimer, Patrick & Maegli, Menomonee Falls, Wis., 1973-74; ptnr. Patrick & Hurt, Menomonee Falls, 1974-86; pvt. practice, 1986—; chmn. SE Wis. Corrections Adv. Com., Waukesha, 1978— ; cir. ct. commr. Waukesha County Cir. Ct., 1983— ; acting family ct. commr. Waukesha County Family Ct., 1983— . Bd. mgrs. Tri-County YMCA, Menomonee Falls, 1975-87; panel mem. United Way of Waukesha County, 1981— ; vol. XIII Winter Olympic Games, Lake Placid, N.Y., 1980. Served to sgt. USAF, 1966-70. Mem. Wis. State Bar, Waukesha County Bar, Menomonee Falls C. of C. (bd. dirs. 1976-82), Phi Alpha Delta (chpt. justice 1971-73, outstanding mem. 1973). Republican. Methodist. Lodge: Kiwanis. Home: N87w15611 Kenwood Blvd Menomonee Falls WI 53051-2911 Office: N84w15959 Appleton Ave Menomonee Falls WI 53051-3044

HURT, WILLIAM, actor; b. Washington, Mar. 20, 1950; m. Mary Beth Hurt (div. 1982); m. Heidi Henderson, Mar. 5, 1989; children: Alexander, Sam. Grad., Tufts U., 1972; student, Juilliard Sch. Appeared with Oreg. Shakespeare Festival prodn. A Long Days Journey into Night, 1975, N.Y.C.; actor: (stage) debut in Henry V, 1977, also My Life, 1977, Ulysses in Traction, Lulu, 1978, Fifth of July, 1978, Hamlet, 1979, Mary Stuart, 1979, Childe Byron, 1981, The Diviners, 1981, The Great Grandson of Jedediah kohler, 1982, Richard II, 1982, A Midsummer Night's Dream, 1982, Hurlyburly, 1984, Joan of Arc at the Stake, 1985, Love Letters, 1989, Beside Herself, 1989, Ivanov, 1991, (films) including Altered States, 1980, Eyewitness, 1981, Body Heat, 1981, The Big Chill, 1983, Gorky Park, 1983, Kiss of the Spider Woman 1984 (Best Actor award Cannes Film Festival 1985, Acad. award for best actor 1985), Children of a Lesser God (nominated Acad. award for best actor 1986), 1986, Broadcast News, 1987 (nominated Acad. award for best actor), A Time of Destiny, 1988, The Accidental Tourist, 1988, I Love You To Death, 1990, Alice, 1990, The Doctor, 1991, Until the End of the World, 1991, Mr. Wonderful, 1993, The Plague, 1993, Trial by Jury, 1994, Second Best, 1994, Smoke, 1995, Michael, 1996, Jane Eyre, 1996, Un divan à New York, 1996, Shakespeare's Sister, 1997, Loved, 1997, Dark City, 1997, Lost in Space, 1998, One True Thing, 1998, Sunshine, 1999, Do Not Disturb, 1999, The 4th Floor, 1999, Artificial Intelligence: AI, 2001, Changing Lanes, 2002, Tuck Everlasting, 2002, The Blue Butterfly, 2002, The Tulse Luper Suitcases: The Moab Story, 2003, (T.V. appearances) including The Best of Families, 1977, Verna: USO Girl, 1980, All The Way Home, 1981, Dune, 2000, The Flamingo Rising, 2001, Masterspy: The Robert Hanssen Story, 2002; mem. Circle Repertory Co., N.Y.C; appeared in Chekhov's Ivanov at Yale Repertory Theatre, New Haven, Conn., 1990. Recipient 1st Spencer Tracy Award, 1988, for outstanding screen performances and profl. achievement, Theatre World award Work with Circle Repatory Theatre, 1978. Office: c/o Hilda Quille/William Morris 151 S El Camino Dr Beverly Hills CA 90212-2704*

HURT, WILLIAM HOLMAN, investment management company executive; b. L.A., Mar. 29, 1927; s. Holman G. and Mary E. (Ortloff) H.; m. Sheridan Ann Stephens, Aug. 10, 1950 (div. May. 1970); children: Kelley Anne Hurt Purnell, Kathleen Constance, Courtney Diana Hurt MacMillan; m. Sarah Sherman, May 28, 1970. BS magna cum laude, U. So. Calif., 1949; MBA, Harvard U., 1951. With Dean Witter & Co., Los Angeles, 1951-71, ptnr., 1959, sr. v.p., 1968-70, exec. v.p., dir., mem. exec. com., dir. mktg. and rsch., 1969-71; vice chmn. bd., chmn. exec. com. Capital Rsch. Co., 1972-77; chief exec. office Capital Group, Inc., L.A., 1978-82; chmn. Capital Strategy Rsch., Inc., 1982—. Adv. com. Coldwell Banker Funds, 1978-99. Mem. bd. councilors Grad. Sch. Bus., U. So. Calif., L.A., 1978-88, vis. com., 1990-96; bd. dirs. L.A. Children's Hosp., 1985— . Served with USNR, 1945-46. Mem. Calif. Club, L.A. Athletic Club, N.Y. Athletic Club, Phi Kappa Phi, Beta Gamma Sigma, Kappa Alpha. Republican. Office: 333 S Hope St Los Angeles CA 90071-1406

HURTEAU, GILLES DAVID, retired obstetrician, gynecologist, educator, dean; b. Cornwall, Ont., Can., Nov. 28, 1928; s. Joseph A. and Antoinette (St-Laurent) H.; m. Janine Anita Carriere, June 16, 1956; children: Michele, Jean, Louise, Pierre, Gilles Andre. BA, U. Ottawa, 1951; MD, CM, McGill U., 1955. Licentiate, Med. Council Can., 1956; cert. in ob-gyn, 1961. Instr. and clin. asst. Yale U. Med. Sch., New Haven, 1961-62; asst. prof. U. Ottawa Med. Sch., Ont., 1963-66, assoc. prof., 1966, prof. and chmn. dept. ob-gyn, 1967-76, dean Sch. Medicine, 1976-89, dean faculty health scis., 1978-89; exec. dir./registrar Royal Coll. Physicians and Surgeons Can., Ottawa, 1990-95. Bd. govs. U. Ottawa, 1995, chmn. exec. com., vice-chmn. bd. 2003—; bd. dirs. Assoc. Med. Svcs. Inc., Ont. Mem. editorial bd. European Jour. Ob-Gyn and Reproductive Biology, 1970-78; contbr. articles to profl. jours., chpts to books. Mem. council Ottawa-Carleton Dist. Health Council, 1978-84; jt. rsch. rev. task force Ont. Council Health, 1977-81, bd. dirs. Ont. Cancer Treatment and Rsch. Found. 1983-92, Physicians Svcs. Inc. Found. Ont., 1984-86, 95-2001. Fellow Royal Coll. Physicians and Surgeons Can. (coun. 1970-78, v.p. 1976-78), Royal Coll. Physicians Ireland (1994—); mem. Coun. Ont. Faculty of Medicine (1976-89), Assn. Can. Med. Colls. (pres. 1981-82). Home: 31 Durham (Priv)-Unit 203 Ottawa ON Canada K1M 2J1 E-mail: gilles.hurteau@sympatico.ca. *Ce que nous connaissons est peu de chose; ce que nous ignorons est immense.*

HURTER, ARTHUR PATRICK, economist, educator; b. Chgo., Jan. 29; s. Arthur P. and Lillian T. (Thums) H.; m. Florence Evalyn Kays; children— Patricia Lyn, Arthur Earl BSChemE, MSChemE, MA in Econs., PhD in Econs. Northwestern U. Chem. engr. Zonlite Rsch. Lab., Evanston, Ill., 1957-58; assoc. dir. Rsch. Transp. Ctr., Northwestern U., Evanston, 1963-65; asst. prof. dept. Indsl. Engring. and Mgmt. Scis. Tech. Inst., Northwestern U., 1962-66, prof. 1970—; prof. of transp., 1992—; chmn. dept. Northwestern U., 1969-89, assoc. prof. fin. Grad. Sch. Mgmt., 1969-70, prof., 1970—. Faculty mem. Newspaper Mgmt. Ctr., Transp. Ctr., 1989—; cons. U. Chgo., ESCOR, Sears Roebuck & Co., Standard Oil of Ind., Ill.; bd. dirs. Ill. Environ. Health Rsch. Ctr., 1972-77; mem. com. Sci. Tech. Adv., Ill. Inst. Natural Resources, 1980-84. Author: The Economics of Private Truck Transportation, 1965, Facility Location and the Theory of Production, 1989; contbr. articles to profl. jours. Pres. Coun. St. Scholastical H.S., 1972-80; elder Granville Ave. Presbyn. Ch., 1976-89; deacon 1st Presbyn. Ch., Evanston, trustee, 2003—. Grantee Resources for the Future 1964, Office of Naval Research, 1965, NSF, Social Sci. Research Council dissertation fellow Mem. Am. Econ. Assn., Regional Sci. Assn., Ops. Research Soc. Am., Inst. Mgmt. Scis., Inst. Indsl. Engrs., Sigma Xi, Phi Lambda Upsilon, Tau Beta Pi, Alpha Pi Mu (Disting. Engr. award). Home: 1505 W Norwood St Chicago IL 60660-2414 Office: Dept Indsl Engring Mgmt Sci Technological Inst Northwestern U Evanston IL 60208-0001

HURTT, FRANCES SCOTT, author; d. Fred Lee and Leona Lee Scott; m. Larry E. Hurtt, June 21, 1974; children: Jason Scott, Jeremy Brandon, Justin Matthew. BA in English and Sec. Edn., Ark. Coll., Batesville, 1974. Cert. sec. tchr., Ark., Mo.; cert. childbirth educator, lactation cons. Tchr. English Salem (Ark.) Sch., 1975-79, Marvel (Ark.) Pub. Sch., 1979-81, Seymour (Mo.) Sch., 1981-83; substitute tchr. Springfield (Mo.) R-12 Schs., 1983-85; mgr. pub. Metropolitan Pub. Co., Springfield, 1985-86; cert. childbirth educator Nat. Assn. Childbirth Educators, 1986-90; med. asst., dir. employee edn. Levi Harrison, Ark., 1991-95. Cons. in field. Author: EHBE - the First 50 Years 2000; contbr. articles to profl. jours. Baptist. Avocations: crafts, singing, church.

HURVICH, LEO MAURICE, experimental psychologist, educator, vision researcher; b. Malden, Mass., Sept. 11, 1910; s. Julius Solomon and Celia (Chikinsky) Hurvich; m. Dorothea Jameson, Oct. 23, 1948 (dec. 1998). BA, Harvard U., 1932, MA, 1934, PhD, 1936; MA (hon.), U. Pa., 1972; DSc (hon.), SUNY, 1989. Asst. dept. psychology Harvard U., Cambridge, Mass., 1936-37, instr. psychology, 1937-40; researcher Grad. Sch. Bus. Adminstrn., Harvard U., Boston, 1940-47; research psychologist Eastman-Kodak Co., Rochester, N.Y., 1947-57; prof. psychology, chmn. Washington Square Coll., NYU, 1957-62, prof. U. Pa., Phila., 1962-79, prof. emeritus, 1979—, mem. Inst. Neurol. Scis. 1962—, mem. Inst. for Rsch. in Cognitive Sci., 1990—2000. Vis. prof. Ctr. Visual Sci. U. Rochester, NY, 1974; adv. mem. vision com. NRC-NAS, Washington; mem. rsch. adv. com. Lighthouse Internat.; fellow Ctr. Advanced Study in Behavioral Scis., Stanford, Calif., 1981—82; mem. vis. com. MIT, 1977—83. Author: Color Vision, 1981, (with D. Jameson) The Perception of Brightness and Darkness, 1966; editor: (with D. Jameson) Visual Psychophysics-Handbook of Sensory Physiology, 1972; assoc. editor: Jour. Optical Soc. Am., 1980-84; topical editor color vision Color Rsch. and Application, 1992-94; contbr. articles to profl. jours. Mem. NRC-NAS com. on U.S. currency study, 1984-86. Recipient Howard Crosby Warren award Soc. Exptl. Psychologists, 1971, Deane B. Judd-AIC award Association Internationale de la Couleur, 1985, fellow John Simon Guggenheim Found., 1964-65, Hermann von Helmholtz award Cognitive Neurosci. Inst.,1987. Fellow: Am. Acad. Arts & Scis., Am. Psychol. Soc. (William James Fellow), Am. Psychol. Assn. (del. inter soc. color coun. 1955—82, Disting. Sci. Contbr. award 1972), NY Acad. Scis., Optical Soc. Am. (Edgar D. Tillyer medal 1982); mem.: Vision Sci. Soc., Rsch. Group in Color Vision Deficiencies, Inter-Soc. Color Coun. (I.H. Godlove award 1973), Internat. Brain Rsch. Orgn. (contbr. to Ency. of Neurosci. on Color Vision Deficiencies), Soc. Neurosci., Psychonomic Soc., Nat. Acad. Scis., Ea. Psychol. Assn., Sigma Xi, Phi Beta Kappa. Home: One Fifth Ave New York NY 10003 Office: Univ Pa 3815 Walnut St Philadelphia PA 19104-3604

HURWICH, ROBERT ALLAN, lawyer, multimedia, manufacturing and services company executive; b. South Bend, Ind., Nov. 1, 1941; s. Abe and Carolyne C. (Neisner) H.; m. Judith A. Jones, May 31, 1969; children: Katherine A., David A. AB, Harvard U., 1963, LLB, 1966. Bar: N.Y. 1967; U.S. Dist. Ct. (ea. dist.) N.Y. 1968, U.S. Dist. Ct. (so. dist.) N.Y. 1968, Conn. 1990. Law clk. U.S. Dist. Ct. (ea. dist.) N.Y., 1966-68; assoc. Cravath, Swaine & Moore, N.Y.C., 1968-75; gen. counsel, sec. Moore McCormack Resources, Inc. Stamford, Conn., 1975-89, v.p., 1979-89; pvt. practice, 1990-93; v.p. adminstrn., gen. counsel, sec. Lynch Corp., Greenwich, Conn., 1994—. Office: Lynch Corp 8 Sound Shore Dr Ste 290 Greenwich CT 06830-7272

HURWICZ, LEONID, economist, educator; b. Moscow, 1917; arrived in U.S. 1940; LLM, U. Warsaw, Poland, 1938; DSc (hon.), Northwestern U., 1980; honoris causa, U. Autónoma de Barcelona, Spain, 1989; D of Econs. honoris causa, Keio U., Tokyo, 1993; LLD (hon.), U. Chgo., 1993; D honoris causa Warsaw Sch. Econs., Poland, 1994. Rsch. assoc. Cowles Commn. U. Chgo. 1944—46; from assoc. prof. to prof. Iowa State U., Ames, 1946—49; prof. econ., math. and stats. U. Ill., 1949—51, U. Minn., Mpls., 1951—99, Regents prof., 1969—88, Regent's prof. emeritus, 1988—, Carlson prof. econs. 1989—92, prof. econs., 1992—. Vis. prof. econs. Stanford U., Calif., 1955—5 1958—59, Harvard U., Cambridge, Mass., 1969—71, U. Calif., Berkeley 1976—77, Northwestern U., Evanston, Ill., 1988—89, U. Calif., Santa Barbara

1998, Calif. Inst. Tech., 1999; Fisher lectr. U. Copenhaben, 1963; hon. prof. Ctrl. China U. Sci. and Tech., Wyhan, 1984; vis. lectr. People's U., Beijing, 1986, Tokyo U., 1982, Australian Econometric Mtgs., Melbourne, 1997; vis. Fulbright lectr. Bangalore U., India, 1965—66; vis. disting. prof. econs. U. Ill., 2001; invited lectr. Chuo U., Keio U., UN U., Inst. Adv. Studies (symposium participation), Tokyo, 1999, Symposium Devel. Western China, Chongqing, 2000, Pub. Econ. Theory Conf. Warwick U., England, 2000; cons. Econ. Design, Istanbul, 2000, Ctr. china U. Sci. and Tech., Wuhan, 2000, Peking U., 2000. Co-author (co-editor (with K.J. Arrow): Studies in Resource Allocation Processes, 1977; co-author: (co-editor (with K.J. Arrow and J. Uzawa) Studies in Linear and Non-Linear Programming, 1958; co-author: (co-editor (with J.S. Chipman) Prefences, Utility and Demand, 1971; co-author: (co-editor (D. Schmeidler and H. sonnenschein) Social Goals and Social Organization, 1985; editor: Econ. Design, 1993, Review of Econ. Design, 1997, Jour. of pub. Econ. Theory, 1999, Advances in Mathematical Economics, 1999, Econs. Bull., 2001; mem. adv. bd.: Jour. of Math. Econs.; contbr. articles to profl. jours. Recipient Nat. medal Sci., 1990; fellow, Ctr. Advances Studies in Behavioral Scis., 1955—56; scholar Sherman Fairchild Disting. scholar, Calif. Inst. Tech., 1984—85. Fellow: Am. Econ. Assn. (disting., lectr. 1972), Econometric Soc. (pres. 1969); mem.: NAS, Am. Acad. Arts and Scis. Office: Univ Minn Dept Econs 271 19th Ave S Minneapolis MN 55455-0430 E-mail: hurwicz@tc.umn.edu.

HURWITZ, ARTHUR ANDREW, immunologist, educator; b. Waltham, Mass., Apr. 21, 1965; s. Israel Samuel and Eleanor Moran Hurwitz; m. Julie Zawel, Aug. 4, 1990; children: A. J., Sammy. BS in Biology and French, Tufts U.; PhD, Albert Einstein Coll. Medicine, 1994. Postdoctoral fellow U. Calif., Berkeley, 1994-99; asst. prof. SUNY Upstate Med. U., Syracuse, 1999—. Reviewer Jour. Immunology, Bethesda, Md., 1998—. Postdoctoral fellow Dept. Def. Breast Cancer Rsch. Program, 1997-99; recipient Young Investigator award CaPCURE Found., 1999—, Dept. Def., 2001—. Mem. Am. Assn. Immunologists. Office: SUNY Upstate Med U 2204 Weiskotten Hall 766 Irving Ave Syracuse NY 13210 Fax: (315) 464-5849. E-mail: hurwitza@mail.upstate.edu.

HURWITZ, BARRIE JAMES, neurologist; b. Wolverhampton, England, Feb. 12, 1943; s. Israel and Margaret Wilson H.; m. Jean Gertrude, Mar. 2, 1969; children: Lynne, Karen, Steven. MBBCh, Witwatersrand U. Med. Sch., 1968. Diplomate Am. Bd. Psychiatry & Neurology. Intern Johannesburg Gen. Hosp., 1968-69, sr. house officer, 1970, resident in internal medicine, 1971-73, med. officer, sr. staff cardiology, 1974; fellow in neurology Cornell U. Med. Coll., N.Y.C., N.Y., 1974-76; asst. neurologist N.Y. Hosp., N.Y.C., 1974-76; neurologist N.Y. Hosp, N.Y.C., 1976-77; clin. asst. prof. neurology Temple U., Phila., 1977-78; from asst. to assoc. prof. neurology Duke U. Med. Ctr., Durham, N.C., 1978—. Grantee NIH, 1991—. Fellow Coll. Phys. South Africa; mem. Royal Coll. Physicians London, Edinburgh and Glasgow, Royal Soc. of Med. Office: Duke U Med Coll Dept Neurology PO Box 3184 Durham NC 27710-0001

HURWITZ, JOEL MICHAEL, lawyer; b. Lancaster, Pa., May 25, 1951; s. Leon Arnold and Helen (Lubit) H.; m. Jill Rosenheim, July 10, 1983; children: Jacqueline, Michael. BA, U. Pitts., 1973; MBA in Corp. Fin., U. Chgo., 1975, JD, 1976. Bar: Ill., 1976. Lawyer law divsn. The First Nat. Bank of Chgo., 1976-77; shareholder Lurie, Sklar & Simon, Ltd., Chgo., 1977-87; ptnr. Neal, Gerber & Eisenberg, Chgo., 1987—2002, Arnstein & Lehr, Chgo., 2002—. Instr. real estate law Chgo.-Kent Law Sch., 1980-81; dir. Capitol Analysts Network, Inc., Bethesda, Md., 1997—. Dir. Jewish Vocat. Svcs., Chgo., 1987-94; bd. dirs. Lawyers Com. for Better Housing, Chgo., 1978-81, Anti-Defamation League, 1992—, civil rights com., 1995—; bd. dirs. Chgo./Wis. region Assoc. Nat. Commrs., 1998—; co-chair Midwest civil rights com., 1995—; head coach Am. Youth Soccer Orgn., Highland Park, Ill., 1995-97; mem. sch. bd. High Sch. Dist. 113, 2001-. Mem. U. Pitts.-Pitt. Club of Chgo. (exec. com., chmn. Midwest scholarship 1994-98), Std. Club. Avocations: golf, investments. Office: Arnstein & Lehr 120 S Riverside Plz Chicago IL 60606 E-mail: jmhurwitz@arnstein.com.

HURWITZ, JOHANNA (JOHANNA FRANK), writer, librarian; b. N.Y.C., Oct. 9, 1937; d. Nelson and Tillie (Miller) Frank; m. Uri Hurwitz, Feb. 19, 1962; children: Nomi, Beni. BA, Queens Coll., 1958; MLS, Columbia U., 1959. Libr. children's sect. N.Y. Pub. Libr., 1959-64; lectr. in children's lit. Queen's Coll., N.Y.C., 1965-69; libr. Calhoun Sch., N.Y.C., 1968-75, New Hyde Park (N.Y.) Sch. Dist., 1975-77; libr. children's sect. Great Neck (N.Y.) Pub. Libr., 1978-92. Author: Busybody Nora, 1976, Nora and Mrs. Mind-Your-Own-Business, 1977, The Law of Gravity, 1978, Much Ado About Aldo, 1978, Aldo Applesauce, 1979, New Neighbours for Nora, 1979, Once I Was a Plum Tree, 1980, Superduper Teddy, 1980, Aldo Ice Cream, 1981, Baseball Fever, 1981, The Rabbi's Girls, 1982, Tough-Luck Karen, 1982, Rip-Roaring Russell, 1983, DeDe Takes Charge!, 1984, The Hot and Cold Summer, 1984, The Adventures of Ali Baba Bernstein, 1985, Russell Rides Again, 1985, Hurricane Elaine, 1986, Yellow Blue Jay, 1986, Class Clown, 1987, Russell Sprouts, 1987, The Cold and Hot Winter, 1988, Teacher's Pet, 1988, Anne Frank: Life in Hiding, 1988, Hurray for Ali Baba Bernstein, 1989, Russell and Elisa, 1989, Astrid Lindgren: Storyteller to the World, 1989, Class President, 1990, Aldo Peanut Butter, 1990, School's Out, 1991, E Is for Elisa, 1991, Roz and Ozzie, 1992, Ali Baba Bernstein, Lost and Found, 1992, The Up and Down Spring, 1993, Make Room for Elisa, 1993, Leonard Bernstein: A Passion for Music, 1993, New Shoes for Silvia, 1993, A Word to the Wise, 1994, School Spirit, 1994, A Llama in the Family, 1994, Ozzie on His Own, 1995, Birthday Surprises, 1995, Elisa in the Middle, 1995. Even Stephen, Down and Up Fall, 1996—, Spring Break, 1997, Ever-Clever Elisa, 1997, Helen Keller: Courage in the Dark, 1997, Faraway Summer, 1998, Starting School, 1998, A Dream Come True, 1998, Llama in the Library, 1999, Just Desserts Club, 1999, Summer with Elisa, 2000, Peewee's Tale, 2000, One Small Dog, 2000, Lexi's Tale, 2001, Russell's Secret, 2001, Oh No, Noah!, 2002, PeeWee & Plush, 2002, Dear Emma, 2002, Ethan, Out & About, 2002, Ethan at Home, 2003, Elisa Michaels, Bigger and Better, 2003. Recipient Bluebonnet award Tex. Libr. Assn., 1987, Wyoming Indian Paintbrush award 1987, W.Va. Children's Book award 1989, Sunshine State award Fla. Libr. Assn., 1990, Miss. Children's Book award Miss. Libr. Assn., 1990, S.C. Children's Book award, 1990, Garden State award N.J. Sch. Libr. Assn., 1991, 94, Weekly Reader Book Club award, 1993. Mem. PEN, Author's Guild, Soc. Children's Book Writers, Amnesty Internat. Address: 10 Spruce Pl Great Neck NY 11021-1904

HURWITZ, MARK HENRY, sales executive; b. Newark, Dec. 2, 1951; s. Murry L. and Elaine (Goldsmith) Hurwitz; m. Patricia B. Zeitler, Oct. 21, 1984; 1 child, Sarah Elizabeth. BA in Fine Arts Edn. cum laude, Kean Coll. N.J., 1974, MA in Fine Arts Edn. magna cum laude, 1982. Cert. tchr. N.J. Art tchr. Montgomery HS, Skillman, NJ, 1974-82; sales coord. Burger's Motorcycles, Three Bridges, NJ, 1982-85; acct. exec. Roger Wade Prodns., N.Y.C., 1985-88; v.p. sales Slide Sys., Inc., N.Y.C., 1988-2001, Big Color Sys., Inc., Mahwah, NJ, 2001—. Editor: (newsletter) Brigade Courier, 1987, Express, 1988; freelance photographer N.Y. Times Mag., 1979; cons. : (documentaries) Liberty! The American Revolution, 1997. Mem.: 3d N.J. Regiment (pres., comdr. 1990—92, paymaster 1977—78), Nat. Eagle Scout Assn., Brigade Am. Revolution (dir. pub. rels. 1976—87, nat. bd. mem.-at-large 1979—82, 1987—90, pres., comdr. 1993—97, past pres., comdr. 1997—99). Democrat. Jewish. Avocations: revolutionary war living history, motorcycling, photography. Home: 396 Meisel Ave Springfield NJ 07081-2316 Office: Big Color Systems Inc 24 Industrial Ave Upper Saddle River NJ 07458-2302 E-mail: jerseyblue3@comcast.net., markh@bigcolorsystems.com.

HURWITZ, MARK S. political scientist, educator, lawyer; b. N.Y.C., Nov. 3, 1960; s. Marvin S. and Patricia A. Hurwitz; m. Sheralee Shera Hurwitz, Sept. 12, 1992; children: Rachel M., Jacob B., Matthew C. BA, SUNY, Buffalo, 1983; JD, Bklyn. Law Sch., 1987; MA, Mich. State U., 1996, PhD, 1998. Bar: N.Y. 1988, Maine 1990. Assoc. lawyer Hoffinger, Friedland, Dobrish, Bernfeld & Stern, N.Y.C., 1987—94; instr. Mich. State U., East Lansing, 1994—98; asst. prof. polit. sci. U. Utah, Salt Lake City, 1998—99, SUNY, Buffalo, 1999—. Adv. com., dept. polit. sci. SUNY, Buffalo, 2000—; faculty cons., advanced placement program Ednl. Testing Svc., U. Nebr., Lincoln, 2001, Lincoln, 02. Contbr. articles to profl. jours. Legis. intern Gov. Conn., Washington Office, 1982; vol. Temple Beth Am Thanksgiving Food Drive, Amherst, NY, 1999—. Grantee Rsch., Baldy Ctr. Law and Social Policy, U. Buffalo, 2001—03. Mem.: Midwest Polit. Sci. Assn., Am. Polit. Sci. Assn. Office: U Buffalo Dept Polit Sci 520 Park Hall Buffalo NY 14260

HURWITZ, SOL, writer, consultant; b. Washington, Aug. 31, 1932; s. Morris Aaron and Rose (Honig) H.; m. Nina Deutch, May 3, 1959; children: Linda, Mark Aaron, Laura. BA, Harvard U., 1953, postgrad., 1955-56, advanced mgmt. program, 1977. Various communication and broadcasting positions, Washington, 1956-60, N.Y.C., 1960-66; assoc. dir. info. Com. for Econ. Devel., N.Y.C., 1966-67, dir. info., 1967-72, v.p., 1972-80, sr. v.p., 1980-90, pres., 1990-97, trustee, 1990—. Bd. dirs. Albert Shanker Inst., Washington, Families and Work Inst., N.Y.C. Contbr. articles to N.Y. Times, Washington Post, Christian Sci. Monitor, Barron's, Harvard Mag., others. Trustee Rye (N.Y.) Bd. Edn., 1970-76; overseer Colby Coll., Waterville, Maine, 1980-2001. With USN, 1953-55. Mem. Coun. on Fgn. Rels., Harvard Club N.Y.C., Manursing Island Club (Rye). Avocations: single sculling, hiking, tennis, music, theater. Home and Office: 800 Forest Ave Rye NY 10580-3202

HURWITZ, TED H. sports conference administrator; b. Bronx, N.Y., Aug. 5, 1938; s. Solomon David and Betty (Fine) H.; m. Norma Figueroa, May 31, 1970; children: David, Lina, Amy. BS in Math., CCNY, 1961; MS in Phys. Edn., Lehman Coll., 1971. Sr. programmer System Devel. Corp., Paramus, N.J., 1961-64; sr. systems analyst Am. Airlines, Briarcliff Manor, N.Y., 1964-67; freshman basketball coach CCNY, 1968-69; athletic dir., basketball coach, tennis coach Lehman Coll., Bronx, 1969-91; exec. dir. CUNY Athletic Conf., 1991—. Player, coach Maccabi Tel Aviv, 1968; cons. summer camps Town of Greenburgh, N.Y., 1989-99. Named to CCNY Athletic Hall of Fame, 1996, Inaugural class Lehman Coll. Athletic Hall of Fame, 1999. Avocations: basketball, tennis, dancing, reading. Home: 101 Old Mamaroneck Rd Apt 3a2 White Plains NY 10605-2433 Office: CUNY Athletic Conf Lehman Coll Bronx NY 10468 E-mail: thurwitzlc@aol.com.

HURYN, CHRISTOPHER MICHAEL, lawyer; b. Akron, Ohio, June 1, 1967; s. Michael Alexander and Eileen Ruth (McFadden) H.; m. Leslie Marie Vitale, Oct. 9, 1993; children: Samuel, Jacob, Natalie. BS in Bus. cum laude, Miami U., Oxford, Ohio, 1989; JD, U. Akron, 1993. Bar: Ohio 1993, U.S. Dist. Ct. (no. dist.) Ohio 1994, U.S. Ct. Appeals (6th cir.) 1994. Jud. law clk. to Hon. Frank J. Bayer, Summit County Ct. Common Pleans, Akron, 1990-93; ptnr. Tzangas, Plakas, Mannos & Recupero, Canton, Ohio, 1993—. Dean's Club scholar, Sch. Law scholar and Judge and Mrs. Charles Sacks scholar U. Akron Sch. Law, 1992-93. Mem. Ohio Bar Assn., Ohio Acad. Trial Lawyers, Stark County Acad. Trial Lawyers (trustee 1997). Office: Tzangas Plakas Mannos Et Al 454 Citizens Bldg Canton OH 44702

HUSA, KAREL, composer, conductor, educator; b. Prague, Czechoslovakia, Aug. 7, 1921; came to U.S., 1954, naturalized, 1959; s. Karel and Bozena (Dongresova) H.; m. Simone Perault, Feb. 2, 1952; children: Catherine, Anne-Marie, Elizabeth, Caroline. M summa cum laude, Conservatory and Acad. Music, Prague, 1945, 47; grad., Conservatoire de Paris, France, 1948; license for conducting, Ecole Normale de Paris, 1947; MusD (hon.), Coe Coll., 1976, Cleve. Inst., 1985, Ithaca Coll., 1986, Baldwin-Wallace Conservatory, 1991, Hartwick Coll., 1997, New Eng. Conservatory, 1998; DHL (hon.), Coll. St. Vincent, 1996; ArtsD (hon.), Masaryk U., Czech Republic, 2000, Acad. Musical Arts, 2000. Guest condr. Czechoslovak Radio, Prague, 1945-46; guest condr. orchs. in Hamburg, Brussels, Paris, Zurich, Suisse Romande, London, Manchester, Prague, Stockholm, Hong Kong, Singapore, Buffalo, N.Y.C., Boston, Rochester, N.Y., Balt., San Diego, Syracuse, N.Y.; faculty Cornell U., Ithaca, N.Y., 1954—, prof. music, 1954—, dir. univ. symphony and chamber orchs., 1972-92, Kappa Alpha prof. music emeritus. Composer: Symphony, 1953, Fantasies for Orchestra, 1957, Divertimento for Brass, 1959, Poem for Viola and Orchestra, 1959, Elegy and Rondeau for Saxophone and Orchestra, 1961, Divertimento for String Orchestra, 1948, String Quartet No. 2, 1952, Portrait for String Orch., 1953, Mosaiques for Orchestra, 1961, Fresque for Orchestra, rev. 1964, Sonatina for Piano, 1943, Sonatina Violin and Piano, 1945, Sonata for Piano, 1949, Evocations of Slovakia for Clarinet, Viola and Cello, 1951, Eight Duets for Piano, 1955, Twelve Moravian Songs, 1956, Poem for Viola and Orchestra, 1962, Serenade for Woodwind Quintet and Orchestra, 1963, Concerto for Brass Quintet and Orch., 1965, Two Preludes; flute, clarinet, bassoon, 1966, Music for Percussion, 1966, Concerto for alto saxophone, concert band, 1967, String Quartet No. 3, 1968 (Pulitzer prize 1969), Music for Prague; for Band, 1968, for Orch., 1969, Apotheosis of this Earth for Winds, 1970, Concerto for Percussion and Winds, 1971, Two Sonnets from Michelangelo for Orch, 1971, Concerto for Trumpet and Wind Orch., 1973, Apotheosis of this Earth for Chorus and Orch, 1973, Sonata for Violin and Piano, 1972-73, The Steadfast Tin Soldier; for narrator and orch., 1974, Sonata for Piano, No. 2, 1975, Monodrama, ballet for orch, 1975, An American Te Deum; for mixed chorus, baritone solo, band and organ, 1976, for orch., 1978, Landscapes for Brass Quintet, 1977, Fanfare for Brass Ensemble, 1980, Pastoral for Strings, 1980, Three Moravian Songs, 1981, The Trojan Women, ballet for orch., 1981, Sonata a Tre, 1982, Concerto for Wind Ensemble, 1982 (Sudler award 1983), Cantata, 1983, Smetana Fanfare for Wind Ensemble, 1984, Variations for Violin, Viola, Cello and Piano, 1984 (Friedheim award 1986), Symphonic Suite for Orch., 1984, Intrada for Brass Quintet, 1984, Concerto for Orchestra, 1986, Concerto for Organ and Orch., 1987, Frammenti for Organ solo, 1987, Concerto for Trumpet and Orch., 1987, Concerto for Violoncello and Orch., 1988 (Grawemeyer award 1993), String Quartet No. 4, 1990, Youth Overture, 1991, Cayuga Lake (Memories), 1992, Concerto for Violin and Orch., 1993, Five Poems for Wood-Wind Quintet, 1994, Les Couleurs Fauves, 1995, Midwest Celebration Fanfare, 1996, Celebration for Orchestra, 1997, Postcard from Home, 1997, Song, for Mixed Chorus, 2000, others; commns. from, UNESCO, Koussevitsky Found., Nat. Endowment for Arts, Friends of Music at Cornell, Fine Arts Found. Chgo., Ithaca Coll., U. Ga., Chgo. Symphony Orchestra, Butler U., Washington Music Soc., Coe Coll., N.Y. Philharmonic, U. So. Calif., Kerze Found., also others.; editor: French Baroque Music: Reconstructions of Old French Baroque works by Lully and Delalande, 1961-68. Recipient prize Prague Acad. Arts, 1948, French Govt. award, 1946-47, L. Boulanger award, 1952, Pulitzer prize in music, 1969, Acad. Inst. Arts and Letters award, 1989, Grawemeyer award U. Louisville, 1993, Serge Koussevitzky Music Found. award, 1993, Czech Republic's medal of merit of 1st degree Pres. V. Havel, 1995, medal of Honor, City of Prague, 1998; Guggenheim fellow, 1964-65. Mem. Internat. Inst. Arts and Letters (life), Am. Acad. Arts and Letters, Belgian Royal Acad. Arts and Scis., Am. Music Ctr., Am. Acad. Arts and Letters, Internat. Soc. Contemporary Music, French Soc. Composers, Am. Fedn. Musicians, Kappa Gamma Psi (hon.), Kappa Kappa Psi (hon.), Delta Omicron (hon.), Phi Mu Alpha (hon.). Avocations: painting, sports. Home: 4535 S Atlantic Ave Apt 2106 Port Orange FL 32127-7047 Office: Cornell U Dept Music Ithaca NY 14853 *As long as there will be museums, concerts, orchestras, libraries, our works will be measured against the masterpieces of the past. For this reason, the search for technical perfection must continue even today, in addition to new ideas and contents. One cannot exist without the other.*

HUSAIN, ALIYA NOOR, pathologist; b. Karachi, Sindh, Pakistan, Sept. 27, 1956; came to U.S., 1981; d. Zahid and Khadija (Minhaj) Omar; m. Syed Shaghil Husain, Mar. 31, 1983; children: Ameena, Ayesha, S. Omar. MBBS, King Edward Med. Coll., Pakistan, 1980. Diplomate Am. Bd. Pathology, Am. Bd. Pediatric Pathology. Asst. prof. Loyola U. of Chgo., Maywood, Ill., 1987-94, assoc. prof., 1994-2000, prof., 2000—01; assoc. prof. U. Chgo., 2002—. Contbr. articles to profl. jours. Mem. U.S. and Can. Acad. Pathology, Soc. Pediatric Pathologists. Avocations: bridge, golf, tennis. Office: U Chgo Pathology MC 6101 5841 S Maryland ave Chicago IL 60637

HUSAIN, SHUJAAT, music educator; b. Calcutta, Bengal, India, May 19, 1960; s. Vilayat Khan Husain and Monisha Khan; m. Parveen Khan, Mar. 29, 1984; 1 child, Fiza Khan. Prof. Music U. Wash., Seattle, 1997—. Home: 5238 Whitaker Ave Encino CA 91436*

HUSAIN, TAQDIR, mathematics educator; b. Matiamau, India, July 16, 1929; emigrated to Can., 1961, naturalized, 1966; s. Abdul Razzaq and Mashooqa (Beg) Ali; m. Martha Tempelhof, Mar. 30, 1959; children: Asra, Ahmad, Masud. BA, Muslim U., Aligarh, India, 1950, MA, 1952; PhD, Syracuse U., 1960. Lectr. Muslim U., 1952-53, Forman Christian Coll., Lahore, Pakistan, 1955-57; instr. Syracuse (N.Y.) U., 1957-61; asst. prof. Ottawa (Ont., Can.) U., 1961-64; assoc. prof. McMaster U., Hamilton, Ont., 1964-67, prof., 1967-94, prof. emeritus, 1995—. Chmn. dept. math. scis. McMaster U., 1967-73, 79-82. Author: Open Mapping and Closed Graph Theorems in Topological Vector Spaces, 1965, Introduction to Topological Groups, 1966, Topology and Maps, 1977, Barrelledness in Topological and Ordered Vector Spaces, 1978, Multiplicative Functionals on Topological Algebras, 1983, Orthogonal Schauder Bases, 1991; assoc. editor: Can. Jour. Math, 1979-86; contbr. articles to profl. jours. Recipient Internat. prize Friedric Vieweg und Sohn Pub. House, Braunschweig, West Germany, 1963; Tata research fellow Tata Inst., Bombay, India, 1953-55 Mem. Am. Math. Assn., Am. Math. Soc., Canadian Math. Soc. (council 1969-75).

HUSAR, WALTER GENE, neurologist, neuroscientist, educator; b. Jersey City, Sept. 24, 1956; s. Walter and Ksenia H. (Dawybida) H. BS in Biology summa cum laude, St. Peter's Coll., Jersey City, 1978; MS in Microbiology, Rutgers U., 1982; MD, UMDNJ-N.J. Med. Sch., 1988. Diplomate Nat. Bd. Med. Examiners; lic. physician, N.J., N.Y. Adj. instr., then adj. lectr. microbiology St. Peter's Coll., 1979-84; intern in neurology and internal medicine U. Medicine and Dentistry N.J., Newark, 1988-89, resident, then adminstrv. chief resident in neurology, 1989-92, instr. dept. neuroscis. to asst. prof. neuroscis., 1992-99, 99—, attending physician dept. neuroscis. U. Hosp., 1992—; staff attending physician VA Med. Ctr., East Orange, N.J., 1992—; cons. physician dept. medicine divsn. neurology Holy Name Hosp., Teaneck, N.J., 1992—, 1992—; attending physician St. Clare's Hosp. (formerly N.W. Covenant Med. Ctr.), Denville, N.J., 1997—; pvt. practice Denville, 1997—; regional staff Newton (N.J.) Meml. Hosp., 2001—. Mem. bd. health Twp. of East Hanover, N.J., 1993—, v.p., 1996-97, pres., 1998—; mem. stroke coun. Am. Heart Assn., 1992-96. Fellow Acad. Medicine N.J.; mem. AMA, Med. Soc. N.J., Morris County Med. Soc., Am. Acad. Neurology (assoc.), Am. Assn. Electrodiagnostic Medicine (assoc.). Home: 10 Christine Dr East Hanover NJ 07936-3039 Office: Ctrl Morris Neurology 145 Diamond Spring Rd Denville NJ 07834-2744

HUSARIK, ERNEST ALFRED, educational administrator; b. Gary, Ind., July 2, 1941; m. Elizabeth Ann Bonnette; children: Jennifer, Amy. BA in History, Olivet Nazarene U., 1963; MS in Ednl. Adminstrn., No. Ill. U., 1966; PhD in Ednl. Adminstrn. and Curriculum Devel., Ohio State U., 1973. Supt. Ontario (Ohio) Pub. Schs., 1973—75, Euclid (Ohio) Pub. Schs., 1975—86, Westerville (Ohio) Pub. Schs., 1986—2000, Carmel Clay Sch. Corp., 2000—01; ednl. specialist MS Cons. Inc. Past pres. Sch. Study Coun. Ohio, gd. govs. Westerville Fund; mem. adv. and distbn. com. Martha Holden Jennings Found.; pres. Westerville chpt. Am. Heart Assn.; past chmn. Franklin County Ednl. Coun.; past mem. alumni adv. coun. Ohio State U.; bd. dirs. Carmel Symphony. Named Ohio Supr. of Yr., 1994; named one of top 100 Edn. Adminstrs. N.Am., Exec. Educator, 1993. Mem.: ASCD, Hamilton-Boone County Ednl. Svc. Ctr. (chmn.), Franklin County Area Supt.'s Assn. (exec. com.), Ind. Assn. Pub. Sch. Supts., Ohio Assn. Supervision and Curriculum Devel., Ohio State U. Edliners (pres.), Sci. and Math. Achievement Required for Tomorrow, Ohio Math. and Sci. Coalition (exec. bd.), Buckeye Assn. Sch. Adminstrs. (bd. dirs., pres., Disting. Svc. award 2001), Am. Assn. Sch. Adminstrs., Olivet Nazarene U. Alumni Assn. (past mem. alumni bd. dirs.), Carmel C. of C., Westerville Area C. of C. (bd. dirs.), Rotary (pres. Westerville, Rotarian of Yr.), Sigma Tau Delta, Phi Delta Kappa (past chpt. pres.). Home: 1029 Wood Glen Rd Westerville OH 43081-3240 Office: 1029 Wood Glen Rd Westerville OH 43081-3240 E-mail: edwardH568@aol.com.

HUSARIK, STEPHEN, music educator; b. Chgo., May 23, 1944; s. Stephen Husarik Sr. and Inez Medley. MusB with honors, U. Ill., 1970, MusM, 1972, postgrad., 1972-77; PhD, U. Iowa, 1983. Tchg. asst. U. Ill., Urbana, 1972-74; lectr. Sampson C.C., Clinton, N.C., 1976; tchg. asst. U. Iowa, Iowa City, 1977, 79; instr. Lewis U., Lockport, Ill., 1978, Trinity Coll., Palos Hills, Ill., 1980; instr. music and humanities Moraine Valley Coll., Palos Hills, Ill., 1984-89; head carillonneur Westark Coll., Ft. Smith, Ark., 1995—, instr. music and humanities, 1992—2001; full prof. U. Ark., Ft. Smith, 2002—. Sr. editor Am. Keyboard Artists, 1987-92; co-author: A History of Westark Coll., 1999, (online question database) Reality Through the Arts, 2000; editor Who's Who in the Humanities, 1990-92; contbr. numerous articles to Piano Quar., Am. Music, Clavier mag., Nat. Assn. Humanities Edn. Jour., Classical Mag.; rec. artist: (piano solos) Pictures at an Exhbn. by Mussorgsky, Scott Joplin and the Ragtime Classics. Field reader Council for Post-Secondary Edn., Washington, 1987. Recipient Nat. Edpress Assn. award, 1987, Master Tchr. award Whirlpool, 2000, Tchr. of Yr. award Ark. Distance Learning Assn., 2002, Excellence in Online Tchg. award Ark. Distance Learning Assn., 2003; grantee NEH, 1984, 89, 94, Ark. Humanities Coun., 1997. Mem. Am. Musicol. Soc., Am. Liszt Soc., Guild of Carillonneurs of N. Am., Coll. Music Soc., Nat. Assn. Humanities Edn. (newsletter editor 1993-94), Westark Coll. Faculty Senate (chair 1998), Westark Coll. Assn. (chair 1999). Home: 9817 Jenny Lind Rd Finana Hills Fort Smith AR 72908 Office: Univ Ark Ft Smith Humanities Divsn Box 3649 Fort Smith AR 72913-3649 E-mail: shusarik@uafortsmith.edu.

HUSBAND, JOHN MICHAEL, lawyer; b. Elyria, Ohio, Apr. 7, 1952; s. Clint F. and Emma H.; m. Jan Lee Umbenhour, Sept. 15, 1975; children: Heather, John. BS, Ohio State U., 1974; JD, U. Toledo, 1977. Law clk. U.S. Ct. Appeals (10th cir.), Denver, 1977-78; ptnr. Holland & Hart, Denver, 1978—, chair labor and employment law dept., 1991-96; counsel Western Gov.'s Office, Denver, 1984. Editor, The Colorado Lawyer, Employment and Labor Rev., 1984—; co-editor Colo. Employment Law Letter. Bd. dirs. Colo. Safety Assn., 1984—, Denver Four Mile House, Town of Bow Mar, 1987-90; mem. Denver Leadership Assn.; sec., treas. Colo. Safety Assn., 1988—; bd. govs. U. Toledo Coll. Law. Inductee Elyria Sports Hall of Fame, 1997; fellow Coll. Labor and Employment Lawyers. Mem. ABA (labor law sect., individual rights and responsibilities com., co-chair pub. subcom. individual rights and responsibilities com. 1998-2003, co-chair complex and class litigation subcom.), Assn. Trial Lawyers Am., Nat. Inst. Trial Advocate, Ohio Bar Assn., Colo. Bar Assn. (labor sect.), Denver Bar Assn. Home: 5280 Ridge Trl Littleton CO 80123-1410 Office: Holland & Hart LLP PO Box 8749 555 17th St Ste 2900 Denver CO 80202-3979

HUSBY, DONALD EVANS, engineering company executive; b. Mpls., Nov. 30, 1927; s. Olaf and Elsie Louise (Hagen) H.; m. Beverly June Tilbury, Sept. 24, 1949. BS, S.D. State U., 1952. Student engr., jr. asst., sr. engr., mgr. new products Westinghouse Electric Corp., Cleve., 1952-72; engrng. mgr., v.p. engrng. lighting div. Harvey Hubbell, Inc., Christiansburg, Va., 1972-76; pres. Elliptipar Inc., West Haven, Conn., 1976-78; fellow engr., mgr. engrng. sect. Westinghouse Electric Corp., Vicksburg, Miss., 1978-82; engrng. mgr. new products devel. Cooper Industries Crouse-Hinds LTG Products div., 1982-84; utility sales mgr. central region Cooper Lighting, Mpls., 1985-89; chief exec. officer Husby & Husby Inc., Madison, Minn., 1990—. Mem. indsl. adv. counsel Underwriters Labs.; provider ednl. seminars in lighting, tech. expert for NVLAP, NIST, U.S. Dept. Commerce. Contbr. articles to profl. jours.; patentee in field. With USN, 1945—47. Fellow Illuminating Engrs. Soc. (chmn., sec., dir., Disting. Service award 1989); mem. Internat. Municipal Signal Assn., Soc. Plastics Engrs., Nat. Elec. Mfrs. Assn., Am. Nat. Standards Inst., Am. Soc. Quality Control, Am. Soc. Engrng. Physicists, Miss. Engrng. Soc., D.C. Soc. Profl. Engrs., Designers Lighting Forum., Mensa Internat., Toastmasters Internat. Mem. Christian Ch. Home and Office: 705 5th Ave PO Box 66 Madison MN 56256-0066

HUSE, EUGENE FRANKLIN, newspaper publisher; b. Norfolk, Nebr., Jan. 17, 1927; s. Eugene Franklin and Lucy (Neubold) H.; m. Karla Amelia Schnurr, Dec. 30, 1957; children: Mary Elizabeth Huse Olsen, William Harris. BA, U. Minn., 1950. Asst. pub. Norfolk Daily News, 1950-56, pub., 1956—, pres., 1961—. Pres. Bellevue (Nebr.) Leader Co., 1984-98, WJAG, Inc., 1961—. Pres. Greater Norfolk Corp. With USNR, 1945-46. Mem. Nebr. Press Assn. (bd. dirs. 1984-93, pres. 1991-92). Republican. Episcopalian. Office: Norfolk Daily News PO Box 977 Norfolk NE 68702-0977 E-mail: jhuse@norfolkdailynews.com.

HUSE, JAMES G. federal agency administrator; b. Medford, Mass. Grad., Boston Coll., 1965. From spl. agt. to asst. dir. U.S. Secret Svc.; asst. inspector gen. for investigations Office Inspector Gen., Social Security Adminstrn., dep. inspector gen., acting inspector gen., inspector gen., 1999—. Officer U.S. Army, Vietnam. Office: Social Security Adminstrn Office Inspector Gen 6401 Security Blvd Ste 300 Baltimore MD 21235-0001

HUSEBOE, ARTHUR ROBERT, American literature educator; b. Sioux Falls, S.D., Oct. 6, 1931; s. Carl and Lillian Ruth (Auby) H.; m. Doris Louise Eggers, May 27, 1953. BA, Augustana Coll., 1953; MA, U. S.D., 1956; PhD, Ind. U., 1963; LHD (hon.), Dana Coll., 1984. Teaching assoc. Ind. U., Bloomington, 1959-60; instr. U. S.D., Vermillion, 1960-61; prof. Augustana Coll., Sioux Falls, S.D., 1961—. Pres. S.D. Humanities Found., Sioux Falls, 1994-96, Fedn. of State Humanities Couns., Washington, 1988-91; exec. dir. Nordland Heritage Found., Sioux Falls, 1980—, Ctr. Western Studies, Augustana, 1989—; NEH regional heritage chair, 1989—. Author: An Illustrated History of the Arts in South Dakota, 1989, Sir George Etherege, 1987, Herbert Krause, 1985, Sir John Vanbrugh, 1976. Bd. dirs. S.D. Symphony, Sioux Falls, 1966—; mem. Nordland Fest Assn., Sioux Falls, 1975—. With U.S. Army, 1953-55. Recipient Gov.'s award in the Arts State of S.D., 1989; NEH grantee, 1975-77, 79-83, 92-94; named to S.D. Hall of Fame, 2001. Mem. MLA, We. Lit. Assn. (pres. 1976-77), Norwegian-Am. Hist. Assn., S.D. Hist. Soc. Lutheran. Avocations: travel, theater, classical music. Home: 813 E 38th St Sioux Falls SD 57105-5939 Office: Ctr for Western Studies Augustana Coll Box Sioux Falls SD 57197-0001 E-mail: arthur_huseboe@augie.edu.

HUSELID, BOYD LYNN, secondary school educator; b. Clinton, Minn., May 8, 1941; s. Bernard Otto Huselid and Laura Rose Huslid; m. Kathryn Kay Huselid; children: Heidi LaRee, Mark Nathan. BA, Concordia Coll., 1963; MS, Mankato State U, 1980. Physics tchr. Glenwood (Minn.) H.S., 1963—70, Lindbergh H.S., Minnetouk, 1970—82, Litchfield (Minn.) H.S., 1983—. Office: Litchfield Public Schools 901 N Gilman Litchfield MN 55355 Home: 30133 Briorwood Rd Paynesville MN 56362-9613

HUSHEN, JOHN WALLACE, manufacturing company executive; b. Detroit, July 28, 1935; s. J. Wallace and Hilda Carol (Jean) H.; m. Margaret Corinne Aho, Apr. 25, 1959 (div. May 1978); children: Susan Lisa, Jane Louise, Peter Matthew; m. Lane Gay Johnston, Feb. 8, 1985; 1 child, John Case. BA, Wayne State U., 1958. Reporter The Detroit News, 1959-66; campaign press sec. Griffin for Senate, Mich., 1966; press sec. U.S. Senator Robert P. Griffin, Washington, 1967-70; dir. pub. info. U.S. Dept. Justice, Washington, 1970-74; dep. press sec. Pres. Gerald R. Ford, Washington, 1974-76; dir. govt. relations Eaton Corp., Washington, 1976-79, dir. pub. affairs Cleve., 1979-81, v.p. govt. rels. Washington, 1981-91, v.p. corp. affairs Cleve., 1991-99. Trustee Citizens League Rsch. Inst., Cleve., press, 1998-2000; trustee YMCA, Cleve. Mem. Former Senate Aides, Senate Press Secs. Assn. (pres. 1969-70), Capitol Hill Club. Avocations: skiing, golf.

HUSHING, WILLIAM COLLINS, retired corporate executive; b. St. Louis, Jan. 22, 1918; s. Sumner Kinney and Anne (Sandner) H.; m. Mary Hardy, Jan. 10, 1946 (dec. 1986); children: Druscilla (dec.), Rebecca Ann. BS in Elec. Engring, U.S. Naval Acad., 1939; MS in Naval Constrn. and Engring, MIT, 1944; student, Harvard Bus. Sch., 1962; DSc (hon.), U. N.H., 1968. Commd. ensign U.S. Navy, 1939, advanced through grades to rear adm., 1967; aide, spl. asst. to chief (Bur. Ships), 1955-57; indsl. engr., comptroller U.S. Naval Shipyard, Mare Island, Calif., 1957-60; supr. shipbldg. U.S. Navy, Electric Boat div. Gen. Dynamics Corp., Groton, Conn., 1960-64; comdr. Naval Shipyard, Portsmouth, N.H., 1964-69; retired, 1969; exec. v.p. Bath Iron Works, 1969-70; pres. Forster Mfg. Co., Inc., 1970-71; mgmt. cons. Kensington Mgmt. Cons., Inc., Stamford, Conn., 1972-78; pres. Maine Multi-Power, Inc., Bath, 1979-91. Decorated Navy Commendation medal, Legion of Merit with Star. Mem. Am. Soc. Naval Engrs. Lutheran. Home: 1640 Twelve Oaks Way Apt 103 North Palm Beach FL 33408-3265

HUSKETH, ALMA ORMOND, language educator; b. Doves, N.C., Aug. 17, 1918; d. William Henry and Ella Carrie (White) Ormond; m. Edward Thomas Husketh Jr., June 11, 1943 (dec. May 1986); children: Edward Thomas III, William Ormond, Craig Moss. BA in English, U. N.C., Greensboro, 1939; MS in Libr. Sci., U.N.C., Chapel Hill, 1966. Tchr. Eng. Granville County Bd. Edn., Oxford, NC, 1934—44, 1946—61, libr., 1961—80; tchr. Eng. Lenoir Bd. Edn., Kinston, NC, 1944—46; instr. Eng. Vance-Granville C.C., Hernderson, NC, 1980—94, Columnist Butler-Creedmoor News, NC, 1988—2003. Author: (poem) Values, 1999. Tchr., Sunday sch. supt. Banks United Meth. Ch., Franklinton, NC, 1939—2003. Mem.: N.C. Ret. Sch. Personnel, Saturday Book Club, Alpha Delta Kappa. Democrat. Methodist. Avocations: walking, reading. Home: 3577 Brassfield Rd Creedmoor NC 27522

HUSKEY, DOW THOBERN, lawyer; b. Sept. 23, 1946; s. Dow Thobern Huskey and Helen (Weathersbee) Morris; m. Julie Beth Coursin, May 17, 1975; children: Dow, III, Whitney. BS, Samford U., 1970; JD, Cumberland Sch. Law, 1976. Bar: Ala. 1977, U.S. Dist. Ct. (mid. dist.) Ala. 1977, U.S. Ct. Appeals (5th cir.) 1977, U.S. Ct. Appeals (11th cir.) 1981, U.S. Supreme Ct. 1981. Ptnr. Huskey & Etheredge, Dothan, 1977—82, Johnson Huskey Hornsby & Etheredge, Dothan, 1982—87; pvt. practice Dothan, 1987—. Author: (non-fiction) Landlord and Tenant, The Law in Alabama, 1980, Damages, The Law in Alabama, 1985. Pres. Houston County chpt. Am. Cancer Soc., Dothan, Ala., 1979—81, Houston County chpt. Ala. Soc. Crippled Children and Adults, Dothan, 1982—83. Mem.: Soc. Ala. Def. Lawyers Assn., Am. Judicature Soc., Assn. Trial Lawyers Am., Nat. Assn. Coll. and Univ. Attys., Ala. Trial Lawyers Assn. (bd. govs. 1980—85), Rotary (pres. 1990—91). Republican. Episcopalian. Home: 27 Hampton Way Dothan AL 36305-6319 Office: 112 W Adams St Dothan AL 36303-4528

HUSKEY, HARRY DOUGLAS, information and computer science educator; b. Whittier, N.C., Jan. 19, 1916; s. Cornelius and Myrtle (Cunningham) H.; m. Velma Elizabeth Roeth, Jan. 2, 1939 (dec. Jan. 1991); children: Carolyn, Roxanne, Harry Douglas, Linda; m. Nancy Grindstaff, Sept. 10, 1994. BS, U. Idaho, 1937; student, Ohio U., 1937-38; MA, Ohio State U., 1940, PhD, 1943. Temp. prin. sci. officer Nat. Phys. Labs., Eng., 1947; head machine devel. lab. Nat. Bur. Standards, 1948; asst. dir. Inst. Numerical Analysis, 1948-54; asso. dir. computation lab. Wayne U., Detroit, 1952-53; asso. prof. U. Calif., Berkeley, 1954-58, prof., 1958-68, vice chmn. elec. engring., 1965-66, prof. info. and computer sci. Santa Cruz, 1968-85, prof. emeritus, 1985—; dir. Computer Center, 1968-77, chmn. bd. info. sci., 1976-79, 82-83. Vis. prof. Indian Inst. Tech., Kanpur; (Indo-Am. program), 1963-64, 71, Delhi U., 1971; cons. computer div. Bendix, 1954-63; vis. prof. M.I.T., 1966; mem. computer sci. panel NSF, Naval Research Adv. Com.; cons. on computers for developing countries UN, 1969-71; chmn. com. to advise Brazil on computer sci. edn. NAS, 1970-72; project coord. UNESCO/Burma contract, 1973-79; mem. adv. com. on use microcomputers in developing countries NRC, 1983-85. Co-editor: Computer Handbook, 1962. Recipient Disting. Alumni award Idaho State U., 1978, Pioneer award Nat. Computer Conf., 1978, IEEE Computer Soc., 1982; U.S. sr.scientist awardee Fulbright-Alexander von Humboldt Found., Mathematisches Institut der Tech. U. Munich, 1974-75, 25th Ann. medal ENIAC; inducted into U. Idaho Alumni Hall of Fame, 1989. Fellow AAAS, ACM, IEEE (edit. bd., editor-in-chief computer group 1965-71, Centennial award 1984), Brit. Computer Soc.; mem. Am. Math. Soc., Math. Assn. Am., Assn. Computing Machinery (pres. 1960-62), Am. Fedn. Info. Processing Socs. (governing bd. 1961-63), Sigma Xi. Achievements include designing SWAC computer, Bendix G-15 and G-20 computers. Home: 10 Devant Ln Bluffton SC 29909-4534 Office: U Calif Computer & Info Sci Santa Cruz CA 95064 E-mail: hhuskey@davtv.com.

HUSMAN, CATHERINE BIGOT, retired insurance company executive, actuary; b. Des Moines, Feb. 10, 1943; d. Edward George and Ruth Margaret (Cumming) Bigot; m. Charles Erwin Husman, Aug. 5, 1967; 1 child, Matthew Edward. BA with highest distinction, U. Iowa, 1965; MA, Ball State U., 1970. Actuarial asst. Am. United Life Ins. Co., Indpls., 1965—68, assoc. actuary, 1971—74, group actuary, 1974—84, v.p., corp. actuary, 1984—97, v.p., chief actuary, 1997—2002; cons., 2002—. Mem. group tech. com. Mut. Life Ins. Co., 1986-98; mem. profitability studies com. Life Office Mgmt. Assn. Inc., 1991-99. Mem. women's adv. com. United Way Cen. Ind., 1991-93; bd. dirs., mem. fin. com., St. Elizabeth's Home, 1991-99, sec., 1994, mem. exec. com., treas., 1995; bd. dirs., mem. adminstrv. svcs., mem. exec. com. Heritage Place, 1993-99, treas., 1995-99; mem. Exec. Svc. Corps, 2002—; docent Pres. Benjamin Harrison Home, 2002—. Fellow Soc. Actuaries; mem. Am. Acad. Actuaries, Actuaries Club Ind., Ky. and Ohio, Actuarial Club Indpls. (pres. 1979-80), Kiwanis (bd. dirs.), Phi Beta Kappa. Republican. Roman Catholic. Avocations: reading, tennis. Home: 1411 N Claridge Way Carmel IN 46032-8333 E-mail: cbhusman@earthlink.net.

HUSNEY, ELLIOTT RONALD, lawyer, financier; b. Mpls., July 24, 1940; s. Edward and Betty (Malca) H.; m. Gloria Lynne Rudd, Dec. 15, 1962; children: Ronald Edward, Kenneth Logan, Evan James. AA, U. Minn., 1960; BSBA, U. Denver, 1962, JD, 1965. Bar: Colo. 1966. Staff examiner Nat. Assn. Security Dealers Inc., 1965-66; trial atty. U.S. SEC, 1966-68; house counsel Denver Corp., 1968-69, Colo. Corp., 1969-70; v.p. Petro Search Inc., Denver, 1970-71; pres. Denver Venture Capital, Inc., 1972-75; ptnr. Husney & Pansing, Denver, 1975-77; of counsel Pansing & Pansing; chmn. Elliott Enterprise Group, Denver, 1977-86; pres. Walden Banking Ptnrs. Ltd., 1987—. Pres. Am. Heliothermal Corp., 1977-79; chmn, U.S. Israel Investments, 1977-83; chmn. Vital Sci. Corp. divsn. Vital Sci., Ltd., 1985-88, also dir.; dir. Pro Care Industries; pres. Elliott R. Husney PC, 1990—; ptnr. Dean McClure, Eggleston & Husney, 1990-94; of counsel McClure & Eggleston, 1995-96; spl. ltd. ptnr. Wolf Ventures, 1996-98, ptnr., 1998-2000, pres. Am. Jewish Com., 2001-. Bd. dirs. Am. Jewish Com., 1982—85, 1995—, Am.-Israel Friendship League, 1983—84. Recipient Young Leadership award Allied Jewish Fedn. of Denver; named Man of Yr. Denver Jaycees, 1978. Mem.: Denver Bar Assn.

HUSS, ALLAN MICHAEL, lawyer; b. Chgo., Sept. 29, 1949; s. Henry A. and Emily (Rosenheim) H.; m. Sandra Joyce Cohn, Aug. 16, 1970 (dec. Mar. 1992); children: Leah E., Samantha J.; m. Susan Irene Stanley Stallard, July 17, 1993; stepchildren: Michelle E. Stallard, Adam J. Stallard. BS, Mich. State U., 1970; JD, U. Cin., 1973. Bar: Ohio 1973, Mich. 1982. Staff atty. U. S. FTC, Cleve., 1973-81; sr. staff counsel Daimler Chrysler Corp. (formerly Chrysler Corp.), Detroit, 1982—. Mem. fed. adv. com. FTC, 1985-87; chmn. joint com. on admission to bar, Cuyahoga County, Ohio, 1980-81. Mem. ABA, State Bar Mich. (chmn. antitrust sect. 1995-96), Greater Cleve. Bar Assn. Avocation: computers. Home: 4934 Peggy St West Bloomfield MI 48322-4420 Office: DaimlerChrysler Corp 485-13-65 1000 Chrysler Dr Auburn Hills MI 48326-2766

HUSS, DONALD EDWIN, JR., musician; b. Portsmouth, Va., Dec. 21, 1956; s. Donald Edwin and Sue Lineburger Huss; m. Marcie Lewis, Dec. 28, 1985; 1 child, Wesley Harrison. MusB, Greensboro Coll., 1979; MusM, Fla. State U., 1982. Ordained deacon United Meth. Ch., 97. Instr. music South Ga. Coll., Douglas, 1982—84; dir. music First United Meth. Ch., Douglas, Ga., 1984—89, min. music Trinity United Meth. Ch., Sumter, SC, 1989—96; min. worship and arts Wesley Meml. United Meth. Ch., High Point, NC, 1996—. Mem. Robert Shaw Festival Singers, Carnegie Hall, N.Y.C., 1995—96, N.Y.C., 2000—01; guest condr. Piccolo Spoleto Festival, Charleston, SC, 1992, Charleston, 2001, Charleston, 03. Performer, recitalist: Sumter County Fine Arts Series, 1994, Cin. Music Club, 1994, Piedmont Artists Series, 1998. Bd. dirs. Sumter County Fine Arts Assn., 1992—94, High Point Cmty. Concerts Assn., 1998—2000, High Point U. Chapel, 1998—. United Meth. scholar, Greensboro Coll., 1975, Theodore Presser Nat. Music scholar, 1979. Mem.: NC Music Tchrs. Assn., Am. Guild Organists (dean 1998—99), Western NC Fellowship (pres. 2000—03), Pi Kappa Lambda. Avocations: reading, piano, singing. Home: 707 Florham Dr High Point NC 27262 Office: Wesley Meml United Meth Ch 1225 Chestnut Dr High Point NC 27262 Fax: 336-884-4313. E-mail: ehuss@wesleymemorial.org.

HUSS, WILLIAM LEE, computer analyst; b. Freedom, Wis., May 18, 1956; s. Donald John and Elaine Mary (Vandenberg) H.; m. Beth Ellen Braun, Oct. 4, 1980 (div. Sept. 1984); m. Carol Ann Lindemann, Dec. 26, 1987. BBA, U. Wis., Oshkosh, 1978. CPA, Wis. Staff acct. Clifton, Gunderson & Co., Neenah, Wis., 1979-80; contr., sec.-treas. Chief Equipment, Inc., Oshkosh, 1980-83; tax and systems mgr. Exptl. Aircraft Assn., Oshkosh, 1983-89; acctg. prof. Marian Coll., Fond du Lac, Wis., 1986-89; v.p. fin., sec., treas. Weaver's Bus. Interiors, Inc., Milw., 1989-92; acctg. mgr. The Tribute Cos., Inc., Delafield, Wis., 1993-96; contr. Saelens Corp., Johnson Creek, Wis., 1996-97; info. systems cons. Omni Resources, Inc., Brookfield, Wis., 1998; tech. architect SBC, Milw., 1998—. Acctg. instr. Fox Valley Tech. Inst., Oshkosh, 1980-92. Adv. editor book revs. McGraw Hill Book Co., 1983. Vol. Big Brother, 1976-89; pres., bd. dirs. Big Bros. of Oshkosh, 1985-88. Fellow Wis. Inst. CPA's; mem. Am. Inst. CPA's. Roman Catholic. Avocations: astronomy, reading, bicycling, racquetball, coin and book collecting. Home: N68 W27126 Oakdale Ln Sussex WI 53089-2340 Office: SBC 722 N Broadway Milwaukee WI 53202-4396 E-mail: wh8451@sbc.com.

HUSSAIN, ANEELA NAUREEN, physician; d. M A and K Jawed; children: Sahar Iqbal, Samra Iqbal, Adel Iqbal. Diplomate American Board of Family Practice ABFP, 2000. Asst. prof. SUNY-Downstate Med. Ctr., Bklyn., 1999—. Attending physician SUNY-Downstate Med. Ctr., Bklyn. Sch. physician. Fellow Fellow, Nassau Acad. of Medicine, Bd. of Directors. Mem.: AAFP (licentiate; sec., nassau acad. of family physicians 2000—02). Achievements include first to Fellow, Nassau Academy of Medicine.

HUSSAIN, BASIT, computer engineer, writer; b. Rawalpindi, Pakistan, Oct. 30, 1962; arrived in U.S., 1986; MSEE, U. Miami, Fla., 1988; PhD, U. Miami, 1991. Sr. rsch. assoc. Ctr. for Med. Imaging, Miami, 1995-97; security arch. Perot Systems, Tampa, Fla., 1997-2000; chief tech. officer eTrango Inc., Fremont, Calif., 2000, Fourth House Security Inc., Tampa, Fla., 2000—. Contbr. articles to profl. jours.; patentee in field. Recipient Joyce Jury award, Neural Networks Rsch., 1989. Mem.: IEEE. Avocation: Avocations: chess, bridge, inventions, writing. Office: 12000 28th St N 2d Fl Saint Petersburg FL 33176 E-mail: basit@4hsinc.com.

HUSSAIN, HAMID, physician; b. Karachi, Pakistan, July 20, 1962; s. Mohammed and Zalbunnisa (Sattar) H.; m. Shakeela Haroon, July 1, 1991; children: Hamza, Haaris, Hanzala. Cert., BMB Sch., Karachi, Pakistan, 1978; MD, Sind Med. Coll., Karachi, Pakistan, 1988. Diplomate Am. Bd. Internal Medicine, Am. Bd. Gastroenterology. Intern in internal medicine Maimonides Med. Ctr., Bklyn., 1993-94, resident in internal medicine, 1994-96, fellow in gastroenterology, 1996-99; fellow in hepatology/liver transplant Temple U. Hosp., Phila., 1999-2000; attending physician Commonwealth Health Ctr., Saipan, 2001, St. Tammany Regional Med. Ctr., LSU, Wash., 2001—. Mem. AMA, ACP, Am. Coll. of Gastroenterology, Am. Gastroenterology Assn., N.Y. Soc. of Gastroenterology. Avocations: reading, travel. Home: 200 St Ann Dr #914 Mandeville LA 70471 Office: La State U Washington-St Tammany Regional Med Ctr 400 Memphis St PO Box 40 Bogalusa LA 70429 E-mail: hh0762@aol.com.

HUSSAIN, MOINUDDIN SYED, geologist, reservoir engineer, consultant; b. Hyderabad, India, Dec. 28, 1931; s. Karimuddin Syed and Hafeeza Begum (Khan) H.; m. Aziza Moin Quadri, Aug. 20, 1942; children: Qutub, Ayesha, Arju. BS, Osmania U., Hyderabad, 1954; DIC, Imperial Coll., London, 1963; MS, London U., 1964. Registered profl. geologist, Calif. Asst. groundwater geologist Groundwater Devel. Orgn., Lahore, Pakistan, 1955-56; test geologist Std. Vacuum Oil Co. (ESSO), Karachi, Pakistan, 1956-62; superintending geologist Oil and Gas Devel. Corp., Karachi, Pakistan, 1962-69; mgr. exploration/projects Dawood Petroleum Ltd., Karachi, Pakistan, 1969-73; project geologist Hallenbeck McCoy and Assoc., Berkeley, Calif., 1973-75; sr. geologist Dow Chem. Co., USA, Houston, 1975-81; sr. internat. geologist Union Tex. Petroleum Corp., Houston, 1981-85; cons. Hycarbex, Inc., Houston, 1985-93; cons. in petroleum, energy, groundwater Katy, Tex., 1993—. Mem. adv. bd. Petroland Exploration Inc., Houston, 1985—; advisor Dawood Group of Industries, Karachi, 1969-73; del. to Pakistan, U.S. Dept. of Energy; mem. (with Dept. of Energy) Presdl. Mission to Pakistan, 1994-95. Founding mem. Internat. Explorationist Group, Houston, 1984. Mem. Am. Assn. Petroleum Geologists (cert. geologist, alt. del. 1984, Cert. of Recognition award 1987), Bangladesh Geol. Soc. (life), Pak-Am. Petroleum Soc. (founder 1983), Houston Geol. Soc. (Svc. award 1985). Republican. Muslim. Achievements include research on petroleum potential of Pakistan and Bangladesh resulting in several oil and gas discoveries; introduction of API stds. in these countries to replace Soviet technology; establishment of oil producing trend in San Marcos Arch area, Tex. thru Austic Chalk Formation; preparation of feasability studies for establishment of refineries, power plants, fertilizer plants, pig iron plants, LPG projects; design of oil and gas pipelines groundwater resource evaluation and development, basin evaluation, project development and implementation; petroleum exploration and development in the Middle East and Far East; petroleum crude and products market development. Office: Petroland Exploration Inc PO Box 218341 Houston TX 77218-8341 E-mail: energyexpln@ev1.com.

HUSSAIN, NAYYER, economics educator; b. Karachi, Sind, Pakistan, Apr. 8, 1951; arrived in U.S., 1981; s. Mazhar and Hussaina (Begum) H.; m. Nafisa Vali, July 28, 1984; children: Mustafa, Ali. BA, U. Karachi, 1976, MBA, 1979; MA, Calif. State U., 1983; PhD, U. Pitts., 1988. Sales officer Hussain Sons, Karachi, 1974-76; asst. mktg. mgr. Ummal Quwain Asbestos Ind., United Arab Emirates, 1979-81; tchg. asst. U. Pitts., 1983-84, tchg. fellow, 1984-88; asst. prof. Tougaloo (Miss.) Coll., 1988-91, assoc. prof., 1992—98, chmn. econs. dept., 1989-91, chmn. social sci. divsn., 1991-94, asst. v.p. for acad. affairs, 1994-95, acting v.p. for acad. affairs, 1995—96, v.p. fiscal affairs, 1996—98; fin. advisor Legg Mason Wood Walker, 1999—2001; dir. bus. affairs MedCentral Coll. Nursing, Mansfield, Ohio, 2001—. Named Outstanding Tchr., Madison County C. of C., 1991, Higher Edn. Appreciation Day Working for Acad. Excellence award Miss. State Legislature, 1994. Mem. Am. Econ. Assn. (editl. asst. Pitts. 1983-88), Rotary, Omicron Delta Epsilon. Avocations: reading, movies, model building. Office: MedCtrl Coll Nursing 335 Glessner Ave Mansfield OH 44903 Home: 1978 Park Ave West Mansfield OH 44906 E-mail: teeseeker@yahoo.com.

HUSSAIN, SYED TASEER, biomedical educator, researcher; b. Lahore, Pakistan, Sept. 18, 1943; came to U.S., 1970; s. S. Fayyaz and Riaz (Fatima) H. BS, Punjab U., Pakistan, 1963, BS with honors, 1964, MS, 1965; PhD, U. Utrecht, The Netherlands, 1969. Instr. Howard U. Coll. Medicine, Washington, 1972-73, asst. prof., 1973-76, assoc. prof., 1977-85, prof. anatomy, 1985—. Dir. gen. Pakistan Mus. of Natural History, Pakistan Sci. Found., Islamabad, 1985-87; grants reveiwer NSF, 1980—, NATO, 1987—, Nat. Geog. Soc., 1985—; frequent invited spkr. on evolutionary processes, biological changes, climate change and human health. Author, co-author over 50 publs. and several book chpts., contbr. articles to profl. jours. Grantee Smithsonian Instn., 1974-94, NSF, 1977—, Nat. Inst. Environ. Health Scis., 1994. Fellow Pakistan Acad. Geol. Scis.; mem. AAAS, Am. Assn. Anatomy, Soc. Vertebrate Paleontology. Achievements include research in evolution in locomotion and hearing mechanism in mammals; human health and forced climate change; influence of increased temperatures on diseases. Office: Howard Univ Coll Medicine 520 W St NW Washington DC 20001-2337

HUSSEIN, ZIAD A. electromagnetics scientist, researcher; b. Beirut; came to U.S., 1982, naturalized, 1998; s. Ali and Nawal Hussein; 1 child, Jennifer. BS, U. Mass., 1986; MS, Calif. State U., Northridge, 1991; postgrad., UCLA, 1994. Grad. rsch. asst. Calif. State U., 1987-89; mem. tech. staff Jet. Propulsion Lab., Calif. Inst. Tech., Pasadena, 1991—. Prin. investigator cryospheric advanced sensor NASA Instrument Incubator Program, 2002—. Contbr. articles to sci. jours., including IEEE Geosci. and Remote Sension, IEEE Antennas Digest, IEEE Geosci. and Remote Sensing Digest, Progress in Electromagnetic Rsch. Recipient cert. of recognition NASA, 1997, 99, 01. Mem. IEEE Geosci. and Remote Sensing Soc., IEEE Antennas and Propagation Soc. (session chmn., mem. tech. program com. 1995), IEEE Microwave Theory and Techniques Soc., Antennas Measurements Technique Assn. (orgn. com. 1994). Avocations: hiking, skiing. Home: 1401 N Los Robles Ave Apt 10 Pasadena CA 91104-5540 Office: Caltech/Jet Propulsion Lab 4800 Oak Grove Dr Pasadena CA 91109-8001 E-mail: ziad.a.hussein@jpl.nasa.gov.

HUSSEINZADEH, NADER, gynecologist, oncologist; b. Rasht, Iran, Aug. 5, 1944; MD, Nat. U., Iran, 1971. Diplomate Am. Bd. Ob-Gyn. Intern Greater Balt. Med. Ctr., 1974, resident in ob-gyn., 1975, 1977—79, Johns Hopkins U., Balt., 1976—77; fellow in gynecol. oncology Georgetown U., Hershey, Pa., 1979—80, Pa. State U., Hershey, 1983; mem. faculty U. Cin. Med. Ctr., prof., dir. gynecology/oncology; pvt. practice Univ. Ob-Gyn. Assocs., Cin. Prof., dir. gynecol. oncology U. Cin. Mem. ACOG, ACP, Assn. Am. Soc. Colposcopy and Cervical Pathology, Gynecol. Oncology Group, Soc. Gynecol. Oncologists, Am. Soc. Clin. Oncology Office: Greater Cincinnati Ob-Gyn Assocs 222 Piedmont Ave Ste 5100 Cincinnati OH 45219-4221 also: U Cin Sch Medicine Dept Ob-Gyn 231 Albert Sabin Way Cincinnati OH 45267-0526

HUSSEY, WARD MACLEAN, lawyer, former government official; b. Providence, Mar. 13, 1920; s. Charles Ward and Agnes (Shaw) H.; children—Thomas Ward, Carolyn Anne Hussey Bourdow, Wendy Ellen Hussey Addison. AB, Harvard U., 1940, LLB, 1946; MA, Columbia U., 1944. Bar: D.C. 1946. With Office of Legis. Counsel, U.S. Ho. of Reps., 79th to 100th Congresses, Washington, 1946-89, dep. legis. counsel, 1970-72, legis. counsel, 1972-89; adviser to fgn. govts. on tax reform, 1989—. Co-author: Basic World Tax Code, 1992, rev. edit., 1996. With USNR, 1942-46. Fellow Harvard Internat. Tax Program (sr.). Home: 312 Princeton Blvd Alexandria VA 22314-4719

HUSSEY, WILLIAM BERTRAND, retired foreign service officer; b. Bellingham, Wash., Oct. 23, 1915; s. Bertrand Brokaw and Ruth (Axtell) H.; m. Fredricka Boone, Dec. 31, 1940 (div. 1957); children: Christina, Pamela, Eva, William Bertrand, Peter; m. Piyachart Bunnag, May 20, 1959. BS, Boston U., 1938; postgrad., UCLA, 1939-40, Naval War Coll., 1953-54. Asst. housing mgmt. supr. U.S. Housing Authority, 1941-42; chmn. London (Eng.) Liaison Group, also State Dept. rep., 1948-52; spl. State Dept. rep., Rome, 1949, Paris, 1950. Chmn. regional conf., Dhahran, Saudi Arabia, 1949, chief civil-mil. relations sect., Munich, Germany, 1952-53, adminstrv. officer, Frankfurt, Germany, 1953-55, attache, Rangoon, Burma, 1955-56, consul, Chiengmai, Thailand, 1957-59; acting dep. chief plans and devel. staff Bur. Ednl. and Cultural Affairs, Dept. State, 1959-60, dep. chief cultural presentations div., 1960-61; mem. del. regional confs. in, Beirut, Lebanon and Kampala, Uganda, 1960; group leader Nat. Strategy Seminar, Asilomar, Calif., 1960; counselor of embassy, Lome, Republic of Togo, 1961-65, Blantyre, Malawi, 1965-66; charge d'affaires Am. embassys, Maseru, Lesotho, and Tananarive, Madgascar, 1966-67, Port Louis, Mauritius, 1967-68; UN rep., Western Pacific, Apia, Western Samoa, 1969-74, fgn. affairs cons., 1974—; del. UN Law of Sea Conf., 1975-80; assoc. v.p. Los Angeles Olympic Organizing Com., 1982-84; dir. govt. relations Statue of Liberty Centennial, Liberty Weekend, 1986. Served with U.S. Mcht. Marine, 1930-33; served to lt. comdr. USN, 1942-48, ETO; PTO capt. Res. Recipient Superior Service award Sec. of State, 1986. Address: 5563B Via Portora Laguna Woods CA 92653-6960 *We must learn from mistakes. The measure is less the occasional stumble than how quickly and sharply the common cadence of our heritage is restored.*

HUSSMAN, WALTER E., JR., publishing executive; Degree, U. N.C., 1968. Pub., owner Ark. Dem., Little Rock, 1974—91; pres., CEO Ark. Dem. Gazette Little Rock, 1991—. Pres. WEHCO Media, CEO; prin., owner Camden (Ark.) News, El Dorado (Ark.) News-Times, Hot Springs (Ariz.) Sentinel-Record, Magnolia (Ark.) Banner-News, Texarkana (Tex.) Gazette, KWEH FM radio Camden, KCMC AM radio, Texarkana, KTAL FM and TV, Texarkana, Shreveport, La. Bd. visitors U. N.C., Chapell Hill, NC. Office: Ark Dem Gazette 121 E Capitol Ave Little Rock AR 72201*

HUST, BRUCE KEVIN, lawyer; b. Cin., Aug. 16, 1957; s. George Julius and Shirley Mae (Glaser) H. BA, U. Cin., 1979; JD, No. Ky. U., 1985. Bar: Ohio 1986, U.S. Dist. Ct. (so. dist.) Ohio 1987, U.S. Ct. Appeals (6th cir.) 2000. Pvt. practice, Cin., 1986—; trial counsel Hamilton County Pub. Defender's Office, Cin., 1988—2000. Vol. Lawyers Project, Cin., 1986-87, 90—; precinct exec. mem. Hamilton County Rep. Ctrl. Com., 1988—. With Ohio Naval Militia 1988-94; journalist USNR, 1994—. Mem. Ohio State Bar Assn., Cin. Bar Assn. Ohio Assn. Criminal Def. Lawyers, Masons, Odd Fellows. Mem. United Ch. of Christ. Avocations: reading, current events, politics, writing and performing comedy. Home: 4247 Delridge Dr Cincinnati OH 45205-2025 Office: 30 E Central Pkwy Ste 100 Cincinnati OH 45202-1120 Office Fax: 513-421-7794.

HUSTAD, THOMAS PEGG, marketing educator; b. Mpls., June 15, 1945; s. Thomas Earl Pegg and John Charles and Dorothy Helen (Anderson) H.; m. Sherry Ann Thomas, Jan. 30, 1971; children: Kathleen, John. BS in Elec. Engring., Purdue U., 1967, MS in Mgmt., 1969, PhD in Mktg., 1973. Vis. asst. prof. Purdue U., West Lafayette, Ind., 1971-72; asst. prof. Faculty of Adminstrv. Studies York U., Toronto, Ont., Can., 1972-74, assoc. prof. 1974-76, assoc. prof., mktg. area coord., 1976-77; assoc. prof. mktg. Kelley Sch. Bus. Ind. U., Bloomington-Indpls., 1977-82, prof., 1982—. Chmn. MBA program Ind. U. Ann. Bus. Conf., 1983—85, chmn. program, 1983, 84 co-founder Exec. Forum; adj. prof. philanthropic studies, 1992—96; vis. prof. City U. Hong Kong, 1997, Ljubljana U., Slovenia, 1998, 2000, Steinbeis U. Berlin, 1998—2000, CEU Bus. Sch., Budapest, Hungary, 2003; exec. dir. Ind. U. Internat. Bus. Forum, 1981—85; cons. N.Am. corps. Govt. of Can.; cond.

seminars for U.S., Singapore, Can., European, Asian and Venezuelan industry; mem. selection com. Outstanding Corp. Innovator award, 1978—. Author: Approaches to the Teaching of Product Development and Management, 1977, (with others) PDMA Handbook of New Product Development, 1996; editor-in-chief: International Competition: The American Challenge, 1986, Managing the Product Development Process, 1989, Product Development: Prospering in a Rapidly Changing World, 1990; founder, editor-in-chief Jour. Product Innovation Mgmt., 1986-2000; contbr. articles to books and profl. jours. Fulbright fellow, 1987, fellow Ind. U. Ctr. for Entrepreneurship and Innovation, John Kosin Faculty fellow, 1993-2003; Crawford fellow of Product Innovation, 1993; recipient Eli Lilly MBA Tchg. Excellence award, 1990, Editorship award Elsevier Sci. Pub. Co., 1993, Kelley award for innovative tchg., 1999, Kelley Svc. award 2000, Anbar Emerald Golden prize for practical applications and originality, 2000; named Best Bet Tchr., Bus. Week Mag.; Thomas P. Hustad Best Paper award named in his honor, 1998. Mem.: European Inst. Advanced Studies in Mgmt. (chair ann. conf. 2003), Product Devel. and Mgmt. Assn. (v.p. confs. 1979, pres.-elect 1980, pres. 1981, dir. 1982—83, chmn. publ. com. 1982—84, sec./treas. 1984—96, mgr. assn. office 1984—96, bd. dirs. 1984—2000, program. chmn.3rd ann. conf., Presdl. award 1987), Am. Mktg. Assn. (award 1973), Brown U. Alumni Assn. (Assoc. Alumni award 1963), Internat. Assn. Jazz Record Collectors, Ancient and Hon. Arty. Co., Beta Gamma Sigma, Tau Beta Pi, Phi Eta Sigma. Home: 3101 Daniel St Bloomington IN 47401-2421 Office: Ind U Kelley Sch Bus 1309 E 10th St Bloomington IN 47405-1701 E-mail: hustad@indiana.edu.

HUSTED, RALPH WALDO, former utility executive; b. Martinsville, Ill., Apr. 2, 1911; s. Seth and Mary (Church) H.; m. Margaret Walden, Mar. 18, 1937; children: Catherine (Mrs. William R. Burleigh), David W. LL.B., Benjamin Harrison Law Sch., 1936. Bar: Ind. 1935. With Indpls. Power & Light Co., 1929—, sec., counsel, 1957-64, v.p. legal, sec., 1964-73, exec. v.p. adminstrn., 1973-74, pres., chief exec. officer, 1974-75, chmn. bd., chief exec. officer, 1975-76. Hon. trustee Intercollegiate Studies Inst., Inc., Wilmington, Dela.; bd. dirs. Liberty Fund, Indpls. Mem. Ind., Indpls., Am. bar assns. Home: Union, Ky. Died Aug. 7, 2000.

HUSTED, RUSSELL FOREST, research scientist; b. Lafayette, Ind., Apr. 4, 1950; s. Robert Forest and Miriam Ruth (Jackson) H.; m. Nancy Lee Driscoll, Oct. 25, 1969 (div. Feb. 1986); children: Jacqueline Marie, Randall Forest; m. Ruth Elaine Hurlburt, Nov. 12, 1988. BS in Chemistry with highest distinction, Colo. State U., 1972; PhD in Pharmacology, U. Utah, 1976. Post-doctoral fellow dept. medicine U. Iowa, Iowa City, 1976-79, rsch. scientist dept. medicine, 1979-81, 1982—; asst. prof. U. Conn. Sch. Medicine, Farmington, 1981-82. Contbr. articles to profl. jours. Mallinckrodt scholar Colo. State U., 1968. Mem. AAAS, Am. Soc. Nephrology, Am. Physiol. Soc., Soc. Gen. Physiology, N.Y. Acad. Sci., Sigma Xi. Democrat. Methodist. Office: Univ Iowa 3180 Medical Labs Iowa City IA 52242 E-mail: russell-husted@uiowa.edu.

HUSTED, STEWART WINTHROP, dean, marketing educator, consultant; b. Roanoke, Va., Oct. 22, 1946; s. John Edwin and Kathryn Faye (Stewart) H.; m. Kathleen Lixey, June 22, 1974; children: Ryan Winthrop, Evan William. BS, Va. Poly. Inst. & State U., 1968; MEd, U. Ga., 1972; PhD, Mich. State U., 1977. Mgmt. trainee Macy's Dept. Stores, Atlanta, 1967; trainee Heironimus Dept. Stores, Roanoke, Va., 1967; mktg. edn. coord. and tchr. Towers HS, Decatur, Ga., 1972-75; vocat. counselor Lansing Comm. Coll., Mich., 1975-76; from asst. prof. to prof. bus. Ind. State U., Terre Haute, 1977-89; Donaldson Brown disting. prof. bus. Lynchburg Coll., Va., 1989—2003, dean Sch. Bus., 1994—2002; Frederik Wachmeister prof., vis. chair Va. Mil. Inst., Va., 2002—03, John W. and Jane M. Roberts chair in free enterprise bus., 2003—. Reviewer McGraw-Hill, NYC, 1983-87, Southwestern Pub. Co., 1987, Dryden Press, 1993; liaison officer US Mil. Acad., 1987-95. Author: (with Sam Certo, Max Douglas) Business, 1st edit., 1984, 2d edit., 1987, 3rd edit., 1990, (with Ralph Mason, Pat Rath) Marketing Practices and Principles, 4th edit., 1986, 5th edit., 1995, (with others) Cooperative Occupational Education, 6th edit., 2003, (with Dale Varble and James Lowry) Principles of Modern Marketing, 1989, Marketing Fundamentals, 1993; contbr. articles to profl. jours., chpts. and cases to books. Rep. to curriculum consortium MarkEd, Ind. Dept. Pub. Instrn., 1978-85, also trustee; bd. dirs., treas. Big Bros./Big Sisters, 1977-80; bd. dirs., mem. exec. com. Lynchburg Bus. Devel. Ctr., 1999-2002. Served to lt. col. USAR, 1968-96, ret. 1996. Col. Va. Militia, 2002—. Named to Mktg. Edn. Hall of Fame, 1974; U.S. Office Edn. EPDA Nat. fellow, 1975-76. Mem. Am. Mktg. Assn. (pres. Blue Ridge chpt. 1991-92), Am. Soc. Tng. and Devel. (exec. com. sales and mktg. div. 1991), Mil. Order of World Wars, Delta Pi Epsilon, Beta Gamma Sigma, Epsilon Delta Epsilon (Research award 1978), Mu Alpha Mu, Phi Kappa Phi, Phi Eta Sigma. Methodist. Home: 2224 Surrey Pl Lynchburg VA 24503-3042

HUSTED, WILLIAM ARMSTRONG, sales executive; b. London, Feb. 25, 1937; s. John Grinnell Wetmore and Helen Armstrong Husted. BS, Hobart Coll., 1959. Jr. analyst group actuarial divsn. Met. Life Ins. Co., N.Y.C., 1959-60, sr. analyst group actuarial divsn. dividend sect., 1961-63, sr. retention analyst group customer rels. and adminstrn. staff, 1964-70; distbr. Amway, Bedford, N.Y., 1976-98; ind. bus. owner Quixtar, Bedford, NY, 1999—. Mem. Rep. Presdl. Legion of Merit, Washington, 1980—; mem. nat. adv. bd. Black America's Polit. Action Com., Hagerstown, Md., 1996—; rep. Congrl. Order Liberty, 1993, Congl. Order Freedom, 1995; founding prodr. GOP-TV, 1994—; nat. mem. Libr. of Congress, Washington, 1990— (mem. chmn. adv. bd., 1995); hon. educator St. Joseph's Indian Sch., 1997—; life mem. Rep. Nat. Com., 2002—. Royal Patronage bestowed Principality of Hutt River Province, 1994-95. Mem.: Consumer Reports (life), Kappa Alpha Soc. (mem. exec. coun. 1962—65). Episcopalian. Avocations: collecting stamps, signed first edition books and fine antiques. Home and Office: 46 Greenwich Rd Bedford NY 10506-1509

HUSTOLES, MARY JO, elementary education educator; b. Detroit, May 5, 1952; d. Robert Nelson Henderson and Mary Josephine (Henderson) Thornton; m. Paul John Hustoles; children: Elizabeth Anne, Brian Edward. BS in Spl. Edn., Wayne State U., 1973; MS in Learning Disabilities, NW Mo. State U., 1980; EdS in Elem. Edn., Mankato (Minn.) State U., 1991. Tchr. learning disabilities Claremont (Mo.) Elem. Sch., 1977-78, Shenandoah (Iowa) Elem. Sch., 1978-83, Smylie Wilson Jr. High Sch., Lubbock, Tex., 1983-84, Lafayette High Sch., Oxford, Miss., 1984-85; tchr. Jefferson Elem. Sch., Mankato, 1985-86, Hoover Elem. Sch., North Mankato, 1986-2001; ednl. cons., curriculum specialist Everyday Math. SRA/McGraw-Hill Pub. Co., Chgo., 2001—. Grade level leader tchr. Dist. 77, Mankato, 1991-93; presenter nat. and internat. workshop reading, writing, "Everyday Math." Mem.: ASCD, Nat. Coun. Tchrs. of Math. Avocations: walking, reading, jogging. Home: 120 Center St Mankato MN 56001-3862

HUSTON, CHRISTOPHER WORTH, rehabilitation medicine physician; b. U.S. Army Camp Zama, Japan, July 9, 1958; s. Robert Maxe and Nobuko (Iefuji) H.; m. Lisa Jean Warner, Apr. 1, 1992. BS in Food Sci. and Tech., Oreg. State U., 1981; MD, Oreg. Health Scis. U., 1985; M Rehab. Medicine, U. Wash., 1989. Diplomate Am. Bd. Phys. Medicine and Rehab., Am. Bd. Electrodiagnostic Medicine, Nat. Bd. Med. Examiners. Commd. 2d lt. U.S. Army, advanced through grades to maj.; resident in phys. medicine and rehab. U. Wash., 1985-89; asst. chief phys. medicine and rehab. William Beaumont Army Med. Ctr., El Paso, Tex., 1989-91; chmn. continuing med. edn. com. Walter Reed Army Med. Ctr., Washington, 1991-92, assoc. program dir. phys. medicine and rehab., 1991-93, staff physiatrist phys. medicine and rehab. svc., 1991-93, asst. chief phys. medicine and rehab. svc., 1992-93; asst. prof. clin. neurology Uniformed Svcs. U. Health Scis., Bethesda, Md., 1992-93; resigned U.S. Army, 1993; physiatrist Mountain Vista Med. Group, Scottsdale, Ariz., 1993-95; fellow in spine medicine, dept. rehab. medicine U. Pa., Phila., 1995-96; mem. staff hosp. of U. Pa., Phila., 1995-96, The Orthopedic Clinic, Phoenix, 1996—. Physician advisor, bd. dirs. med. retention bd. U.S. Army Mil. Dist. Washington, 1992-93; mem. staff Scottsdale Meml. Hosp.-North; lectr., presenter in field; clin. assoc. dept. rehab. medicine U. Pa., 1995-96; cons. Phoenix Suns, NBA, Phoenix Mercury, WNBA, Phoenix Rattlers, Arena Football League. Contbr. articles, abstracts to profl. publs. Fellow Am. Acad. Phys. Medicine and Rehab., Am. Assn. Electrodiagnostic Medicine; mem. AMA, Assn. Acad. Physiatrists (diplomate), Physiatric Assn. of Spine, Sports and Occupl. Rehab., Phi Kappa Phi, Alpha Lambda, Phi Eta Sigma. Avocations: running, golf. Office: The Orthopedic Clinic 9377 E Bell Rd # 231 Scottsdale AZ 85260

HUSTON, DANIEL CLIFF, geophysicist; b. Anchorage, June 29, 1955; s. Arthur Cliff and Allie Mae (Ogdon) H.; m. Holly Hunter, Oct. 10, 1992; children: Lana Marie, Hayley Allison. BS in Geology and Geophysics, marine option program cert., U. Hawaii, 1980; MA in Geological Scis., U. Tex., 1987. Surveyor Trans Alaska Pipeline, 1975-78; geologist R&M Cons., Anchorage, 1980; geophysicst U.S. Minerals Mgmt. Svc., Anchorage, 1981-83; rsch. asst. Miss. Canyon Project, Austin, 1983-84; project SEER U. Tex. Inst. Geophysics, Austin, 1983-87; geophys. intern Sohio Petroleum Co., San Francisco, summer 1984; geophysicist leader advanced seismic methods group Unocal Sci. and Tech. Divsn., Brea, Calif., 1987-90; sr. geophysicist Unocal Oil and Gas Divsn., Houston, 1991-96; founder, v.p. Hunter 3-D Inc. (geophys. consulting firm), 1996—, Creekside Exploration, Inc. (oil and gas exploration firm), 1999—. Pres. Creekside Exploration, Inc., 1999—; presenter in field. Contbr. articles to profl. jours. Fellow U. Tex. Indsl. Assocs., 1983. Mem. Am. assn. Petroleum Geologists, Soc. Exploration Geophysicists (presenter workshop 1984, ann. conv. 1986, regional conv. 1989). Methodist. Avocations: travel, scuba diving, skiing, weightlifting, reading history. Home: 1635 Creekside Dr Sugar Land TX 77478-4203

HUSTON, HARRIETTE IRENE OTWELL (REE HUSTON), retired county official; b. Kans. d. Harry C. Otwell and Fannie (Mitchell) Otwell Geffert; m. Dan E. Huston, Jan. 21, 1951; children: Terry Dane, Dale Curtis, Ronald William, Randal Philip. BS, Kans. State Coll., 1951. Cert. life and health ins. agt. Wash.; wastewater operator in tng. Wash. Tchr., Kans., 1955-68, 1955—68; assoc. home economist McCall's Patterns Co., N.Y.C., 1959-62; counselor, co-owner Dunhill Seattle Pers., 1968-75; enrollment officer, trainer, adminstrv. sec. Teller Tng. Insts., Seattle, 1975-76; life and health ins. agt. Lincoln Nat. Sales, Seattle, 1976-77; office mgr., adminstrv. sec. ARA Transp. Group, Seattle, 1977-78; asst. to the pres. Pryde Corp., Bellevue, Wash., 1978-80; sr. sec. Municipality of Met. Seattle, 1980-92, project asst., 1992-93; adminstrv. specialist II King County Dept. Met. Svcs. (formerly Municipality of Met. Seattle), 1993-95; ret., 1995. Substitute tchr. Sequim (Wash.) Pub. Schs., 1996—. Co-author: (book) Homemaking Textbook, 1956; contbr. articles to profl. jours. Sec. exec., mem. gen. bd. Bellevue Christian Ch., Disciples of Christ, 1976—77, chmn. flowers com., 1978—83, elder, 1978, deacon, 1987; mem. choir Sequim Presbyn. Ch., 1994—98, elder, 1996—99, chair congl. life com., 1996—99, co-chair rummage and antique extravaganza, 1996, 1998, mem. Presbyn. Women, 1994—, program chmn., 2000—; vol. Steven's Min., 2000—; bd. dirs., sec. Surrey Downs Cmty. Club, Bellevue, 1983—85; vol. leader, coord. Linking Home and Sch. Through Workplace, 1992—93; vol. Sequim-Dungeness Hosp. Guild Thrift Shop, 1999—; vol. group health coop. Sr. Caucs of Callam County, 1997—99; vol. Puget Sound Blood Ctr., Sequim, 1999—; mem. Nat. Women's History Mus., Washington, 2002—. Recipient certs. of Merit, Metro Hdqrs., Seattle, 1981—83, 1986, 1989. Mem.: AAUW. Avocations: flower arranging, bridge, interior decorating, home remodeling, lavender crafts. Home: 1783 E Sequim Bay Rd Sequim WA 98382-7657

HUSTON, JOHN CHARLES, law educator; b. Chgo., Mar. 21, 1927; s. Albert Allison and Lillian Helen (Sullivan) H.; m. Joan Frances Mooney, Aug. 1, 1954; children: Mark Allison, Philip John, Paul Francis James; m. Inger Margareta Westerman, May 4, 1979. AB, U. Wash., Seattle, 1950; JD, U. Wash., 1952; LLM, NYU, 1955. Bar: Wash. 1952, N.Y. 1964, U.S. Dist. Ct. (we. dist.) Wash. 1953, U.S. Ct. Appeals (9th cir.) 1953, U.S. Tax Ct. 1977, U.S. Supreme Ct. 1993. Assoc. Kahin, Carmody & Horswill, Seattle, 1952—53; teaching fellow NYU Law Sch., 1953—54; asst. prof. NYU, 1953—57; asst. co-dir. U. Ankara Legal Rsch. Inst., Turkey, 1954—55; asst. prof. Syracuse U., NY, 1957—60, assoc. prof., 1960—65, prof., 1965—67; prof., assoc. dean U. Wash., Seattle, 1967—73, prof. law, 1973—96, prof. emeritus, 1996—. Of counsel Carney, Badley, Smith & Spellman, Seattle, 1987—2002, Smith McKenzie Rothwell & Barlow, P.S., Seattle, 2002—; vis. prof. U. Stockholm, 1986, U. Bergen, 1989, Bond U., Australia, 1991. Author: (with Redden) The Mining Law of Turkey, 1956, The Petroleum Law of Turkey, 1956, (with Mucklestone and Cross) Community Property: General Considerations, 1971, (with Price and Treacy) 4th edit., 1994, (with Sullivan and others) Administration of Criminal Justice, 16, 2d edit., 1969, (with Miyatake and Way) Japanese International Taxation, 1983, supplements through 1997, (with Cross and Shields) Community Property Desk Book, 1977, 2d edit., 1989, supplement, 1997, (with Williams) Permanent Establishment, 1993. With USNR, 1945-46; capt. USAFR. Mem.: ABA, Internat. Fiscal Assn. (past regional v.p., past mem. coun.), Japanese Am. Soc. Legal Studies, King County Bar Assn., Wash. State Bar Assn. (chmn. tax sect. 1984—85), Am. Coll. Trust and Estate Coun. Office: 700 Logan Bldg 500 Union St Seattle WA 98101 Fax: 206-525-1758. E-mail: huston@att.net.

HUSTON, JOHN DENNIS, English educator; b. NYC, Sept. 21, 1939; s. A. Arthur H. and Jacquelin (Buchenau) Hawkins; m. Priscilla Jane, June 13, 1964 (div. July 1985); children: Katherine, Penn; m. Lisa B. Bryan, Aug. 8, 1988; stepchildren: Rudy Bryan, Kirby Bryan. BA, Wesleyan U., 1961; MA, Yale U., 1964, PhD, 1966. Instr., English Yale U., New Haven, 1966-67, asst. prof., 1967-69; assoc. prof. Rice U., Houston, 1969-80, prof., English, 1980—, Minnie Stevens Piper prof., 2002. Dir. freshman humanities Rice U., 1988-94, 1999-2003; master Hanszen Coll., 1978-82, 92-98. Author: Shakespeare's Comedies of Play, 1981; co-editor: Classics of the Renaissance Theater, 1969. Named CASE Prof. of Yr., 1989-90, Disting. Alumnus Wesleyan U., 1991; recipient Wilbur Cross medal Yale Grad. Sch., 1992; Minnie Stevens Piper Prof., 2002. Mem. Coll. English Assn. (bd. dir. 1989-92), Phi Beta Kappa. Democrat. Avocations: running, racquetball, squash, skiing, fishing. Home: 4115 Mcduffie St Houston TX 77098-3419 Office: Rice U Dept English PO Box 1892 Houston TX 77251-1892 E-mail: jdhuston@rice.edu.

HUSTON, JOHN WILSON, air force officer, historian; b. Pitts., Mar. 6, 1925; s. James Leslie and Kathryn Rachel (Ray) H.; m. Dorothy Winters Bampton, Aug. 27, 1960; children: Ann, John. BA, Monmouth Coll., 1948; MA, U. Pitts., 1950, PhD, 1957. Served as 1st lt. USAAF, 1943-45; advanced through grades to maj. gen. USAF Res., 1976; recalled to active duty as chief Office of Air Force History, Dept. Air Force, Washington, 1976—; lectr. history U. Pitts., 1949-56; prof. U.S. Naval Acad., Annapolis, 1956-76, chmn. dept. history, 1971-76. Vis. prof. U. Rochester, 1964, Ball State U., 1965, 67, U. Md., 1969; Disting. vis. prof. USAF Acad., 1994-95. Author: American Air Power Comes of Age: General Henry H. "Hap" Arnold's World War II Diaries, 2001. Decorated D.S.M., D.F.C. with oak leaf cluster, Air medal with 3 oak leaf clusters, Joint Service Commendation medal, Air Force Commendation medal. Home: 115 E Lake Dr Annapolis MD 21403-4444 Office: Hdqrs USAF AF/CVAH Bolling Afb Washington DC 20332-0001

HUSTON, KATHLEEN MARIE, library administrator; b. Sparta, Wis., Jan. 7, 1944; BA, Edgewood Coll., 1966; MLS, U. Wis., Madison, 1969. Libr. Milw. Pub. Libr., 1969-90; city libr. Milw. Pub. Libr. System, 1991—. Office: Milwaukee Pub Libr 814 W Wisconsin Ave Milwaukee WI 53233-2309

HUSTON, KENT ALLEN, rheumatologist; b. Wichita, Kans., May 14, 1944; s. George W. and Elizabeth H.; m. Janet Kay Heims, June 12, 1968 (div. 1985); children: Kent K., Heather J., Elizabeth K.; m. Susan Jolene Held, Dec. 2, 1990; 1 child, Boris H. BA, U. Kans, lawrence, 1966; MD, U. Kans, Kansas City, 1970. Diplomate Am. Bd. Internal Medicine and Rheumatology. Intern Wesley Med. Ctr., Wichita, 1970-71; resident in internal medicine Mayo Clinic, Rochester, Minn., 1971-75, fellow in rheumatology, 1975-77; pres. Mid-Am. Med. Cons., Kansas City, Mo., 1977-91, Ctr. Rheumatic Disease, Kansas City, 1991—. Preceptor U. Kans. Sch. Medicine, 1978—; clin. assoc. prof. U. Mo.-Kansas City Med. Sch., 1982—; mem. organizing com. Mid-Am. Rehab. Hosp.; dir. Mo. State Regional Arthritis Ctr., 1988—. Contbr. to profl. publs. Bd. dirs. Western Mo. chpt. Arthritis Found., 1980-90, chmn. med. and sci. com., 1984-87; mem. Mo. Arthritis Adv. Bd., Jefferson City, 1984—. Capt. USAF, 1971-73. Fellow ACP; mem. AMA, Am. Soc. Internal Medicine, Am. Coll. Rheumatology, Southwest Clin. Soc., Kansas City Met. Med. Soc., Kansas City Rheumatism Soc. (pres. 1991—). Avocations: backpacking, tennis, golf, photography, woodworking. Office: Ctr Rheumatic Disease 4330 Wornall Rd Kansas City MO 64111-3217

HUSTON, MARGO, journalist; b. Waukesha, Wis., Feb. 12, 1943; d. James and Cecile (Timlin) Bremner; m. James Huston, Dec. 9, 1967 (div.); 1 son, Sean Patrick. AB in Journalism, Marquette U., 1965. Editl. asst. Marquette U., Milw., 1965-66; feature editor, reporter Waukesha Freeman, 1966-67; feature reporter Milw. Jour., 1967-70, reporter Spectrum, women's and food sects., 1972-79, editl. writer, 1979-84, polit. reporter, 1984—, asst. picture editor, 1985-91, copy editor, 1992-95; reporter Milw. Jour Sentinel (merger Milw. Jour. and The Sentinel), 1995-99; mem. working bd. Cath. Herald, 2000—01; freelance journalist Milw., 2001—. Instr. mass comm. U. Wis., Milw. Mem. European Project Interreligious Learning, 2002—. Recipient Penney-Mo. award for consumer abortion series, 1977, Pulitzer Prize for investigation into plight of elderly, 1977, Clarion award, 1977, Knight of Golden Quill award, Milw. Press club, 1977, Wis. AP writing award, 1977, Spl. award Milw. Soc. Profl. Journalists, 1977, Penney-Mo. Paul Myhre award for excellence, 1978, By-Line award Marquette U. Coll. Journalism, 1980, Wis. UPI Best Editl. award, 1982, Wis. Women's Network award for journalist achievement for women's issues, 1983, Dick Goldensohn Fund award, 1991, 1st place award for investigative reporting Inland Press Assn., 1997, 98, 2d award Enterprise interpretive reporting Wis. Newspaper Assn., 1998; Wis. Arts Bd. Literary Arts grantee, 1992. Mem. European Project for Interreligious Learning, Milw. Press Club (Hall of Fame 2000).

HUSTON, NANCY LOUISE, writer, educator; b. Calgary, Alta., Can., Sept. 16, 1953; arrived in France, 1973; d. James Palmer Huston and Mary-Louise (Kester) Engels; m. Tzvetan Todorov, May 18, 1981; children: Léa, Alexandre. BA, Sarah Lawrence Coll., 1975; diploma in semiology, Ecole de Hautes Etudes, Paris, 1977; PhD (hon.), U. Montréal, 2000, Guelph U., 2003. Writer-in-residence Am. U. Paris, 1989; instr. women's studies Columbia U., Paris, 1982-88; vis. prof. French Lit. U. Mass., Amherst, 1990; vis. prof. French Lit. Harvard U., Cambridge, 1994. Author: Les Variations Goldberg, 1981 (prix Contrepoint), Plainsong, 1993, Cantique des Plaines, 1993 (prix du Gouverneur-Gènèral, prix Lucioles, prix Suisse-Can.), La Virevolte (prix L de Limoges, prix Louis-Hèmon de l'Acadèmie Languedoc), Tombeau de Romain Gary, 1995, Désirs et réalités, 1995, The Goldberg Variations, 1996, Slow Emergencies, 1996, Instruments des ténèbres, 1996 (Prix Goncourt des Lycéens, Prix Elle-Quebec, Prix du Livre Inter), Instruments of Darkness, 1997, L'Empreinte de l'ange, 1998 (prix des Libr. Quebec, Grand prix des Lectrices de Elle), Prodige, 1999 (Prix Aliénor d'Aquitaine), The Mark of the Angel, 1999 (Can. Jewish Book award for fiction, 2000, Talking Book of Yr. award, 2000), Prodigy, 2000, Dolce Agonia, 2001 (Prix Odyssée du Livre), Une Adoration, 2003, An Adoration, 2003, (nonfiction) Dire et Interdire, 1980 (prix Dinct-Sangle de l'Academie Français), Nord perdu, 1999 (Prix Marianne), Losing North, 2002. Decorated Chevalier de l'Ordre des Arts et des Lettres; recipient several exploration grants, Can. Coun., several writing grands, Centre Nat. des Lettres, Halif prize, Royal Acad. French Lang. and Lit., Belgium, 1998. Avocations: harpsichord, piano, yoga.

HUSTON, SALLY ANN, pharmacist; d. John Stephen and Mildred Juanita Pederi; m. Douglas R. Huston. MS, U. N.C., 1999. Registered pharmacist Ohio Bd. of Pharmacy, Mich. Bd. of Pharmacy. Contbr. articles and abstracts to profl. publs. Recipient Regents' fellowship, U. of Mich., Bd. of Regents, 1999—2002, student rsch. grant, Ctr. for the Edn. of Women, 2002, rsch. grant, Wyeth-Ayerst Pharms., 1998—99; fellow, Am. Found. for Pharm. Edn., 2000—03. Mem.: Am. Assn. of Colls. of Pharmacy, Am. Pharmacists' Assn., Phi Kappa Phi, Rho Chi (treas. 1977—78). Office: U Mich Coll Pharm 428 Church St Ann Arbor MI 48109-1065 Office Fax: 734-615-8171. E-mail: hustons@umich.edu.

HUSTON, SAMUEL RICHARD, health facility executive; b. Newton, Iowa, Apr. 21, 1940; s. Marshall Dwight and Miriam Evelyn (Peake) H.; m. Ann M. Huston; children: Carmen Colleen, Christopher Dwight. BA, U. No. Iowa, 1962; MA, State U. Iowa, 1964. Asst. adminstr. med. ctr. Hosp. of Vt., Burlington, 1964-66; assoc. dir. No. New Eng. Regional Med. Program, Burlington, 1966-68; asst. adminstr. Univ. Hosp. Cleve., 1968-70, from assoc. adminstr. to exec. v.p., COO, 1974—86; assoc. dir. Duke Hosp., Durham, N.C., 1970-72; pres., CEO Lehigh Valley Hosp. Ctr., Allentown, Pa., 1986—87, Allentown Hosp.-Lehigh Valley Hosp. Ctr., Pa., 1987—90; CEO Lehigh Valley Health Network, Lehigh Valley Hosp., Allentown, Pa., 1990—93; pres., CEO St. Luke's Med. Ctr., Cleve., 1994-97, St. Luke's Found. of Cleve., 1997-99; prin. Jay Alix and Assocs., 1999-2000; pres., CEO ViaHealth Sys., Rochester, NY, 2000—. Avocations: reading, music, hunting, golf. Home: 5 Roxbury Ln Pittsford NY 14534 Office: ViaHealth System c/o Rochester Gen Hosp Portland Ave Rochester NY 14621 E-mail: sam.huston@viahealth.org.

HUSTON, STEVEN CRAIG, lawyer; b. Morris, Ill., June 3, 1954; s. Raymond P. and Evelyn M. (Bass) Huston; m. Nina Huston. BA, Ill. Coll., 1977; JD, John Marshall Law Sch., 1980; MBA, Northwestern U., 1989. Bar: Ill. 1980, U.S. Dist. Ct. (no. dist.) Ill. 1980, U.S. Ct. Appeals (7th cir.) 1980. Assoc. Siegel, Denberg et al, Chgo., 1980-83; staff atty. William Wrigley Jr. Co., Chgo., 1983-84, asst. sec. legal, 1984-94, asst. v.p. legal, 1994-96, counsel North Am., 1996—2001; v.p., gen. counsel Symons Corp., 2002—03; v.p., gen. counsel, sec. Dayton Superior Corp., 2003—. Bd. dirs. SOS Am. Mem.: ABA, Am. Corp. Counsel Assn., Chgo. Bar Assn.

HUSZAGH, FREDRICK WICKETT, lawyer, educator, information management company executive; b. Evanston, Ill., July 20, 1937; s. Rudolph LeRoy and Dorothea (Wickett) H.; m. Sandra McRae, Apr. 4, 1959; children: Floyd McRae, Fredrick Wickett II, Theodore Wickett II. BA, Northwestern U., 1958; JD, U. Chgo., 1962, LLM, 1963, JSD, 1964. Bar: Ill. 1962, U.S. Dist. Ct. D.C. 1965, U.S. Supreme Ct. 1966. Market rschr. Leo Burnett Co., Chgo., 1958-59; internat. atty. COMSAT, Washington, 1964-67; assoc. Debevoise & Liberman, Washington, 1967-68; asst. prof. law Am. U., Washington, 1968-71; program dir. NSF, Washington, 1971-73; assoc. prof. U. Mont., Missoula, 1973-76, U. Wis., Madison, 1976-77; exec. dir. Dean Rusk Ctr., U. Ga., Athens, 1977-82; prof. U. Ga., 1982—. Chmn. TWH Corp., Athens, 1982—; chmn. Profession Mgmt. Techs., Inc., Athens, 1993-96; cons. TWH Scv. Corp.; cons. Pres. Johnson's Telecommunications Task Force, Washington, 1967-68; co-chmn. Nat. Gov.'s Internat. Trade Staff Commn., Washington, 1979- 81. Author: International Decision-Making Process, 1964, Comparative Facts on Canada, Mexico and U.S., 1979; editor Rusk Ctr. Briefings, 1981-82; contbr. articles to publs. Mem. Econ. Policy Coun., N.Y.C., 1981-89. NSF grantee, 1974-78. Republican. Presbyterian. Home: 151 E Clayton St Athens GA 30601-2702 Office: U Ga Law Sch Athens GA 30602 E-mail: huszagh@twhcorp.com.

HUSZAR, ARLENE CELIA, lawyer, mediator; b. N.Y.C., May 1, 1952; d. Charles and Dora (Toffoli) H.; m. Victor M. Yellen, May 6, 1978; 1 child. Mariette Huszar Yellen. BA, Fla. Atlantic U., 1973; JD, U. Fla., 1976. Bar: Fla. 1977, U.S. Dist. Ct. (mid. and no. dists.) Fla. 1978, U.S. Ct. Appeals (5th and 11th cirs.) 1978, D.C. 1979, U.S. Supreme Ct. 1982; cert. fed. and cir. ct. mediator, arbitrator. Pvt. practice, Gainesville, Fla., 1977-80; exec. dir. Fla. Instl. Legal Svcs., Gainesville, 1980—2001; deputy ct. adminstrv. 8th Judicial Circuit, Fla., 2001—. Author: (with others) Adoption, 1992, Termination of Parental Rights, 1997. Mem. City of Gainesville Citizens Adv. Com. for Cmty. Devel., 1976-79, Fla. Bar Com. on the Legal Needs of Children, 1984-85; mem. steering com. juvenile law sect. Nat. Legal Aid and Defender Assn., 1986-87; vice chmn. Alachua County Citizens Adv. Com., Dept. Criminal Justice Svcs., 1986-95; precinct committeewoman Alachua County Dem. Exec. Com., 1986-96; Queen of Peach parish coun. (sec. 1995-97, pres. 1998). Named one of Outstanding Young Women of Am., 1975. Mem. ATLA, Fla. Acad. Profl. Mediators, North Ctrl. Fla. Mediation Coun. (sec. 1999-2000, pres. 2000-02). Roman Catholic. Office: 201 E University Ave Gainesville FL 32601-4969

HUT, PIET, astrophysics educator; b. Utrecht, Holland, Sept. 26, 1952; came to U.S., 1981. s. Jan Lambertus Hut and Jenneke Johanna Hut-Broekroelofs; m. Eiko Ikegami, July 26, 1991. MS, U. Utrecht, 1977; PhD, U. Amsterdam, Holland, 1981. Asst. prof. astronomy dept. U. Calif., Berkeley, 1984-85; mem. Inst. for Advanced Study, Princeton, N.J., 1981-84, prof., 1985—. Contbr. articles to prof. jours. Mem. Am. Astron. Soc., Dutch Astron. Club, Astron. Soc. Japan. Office: Inst for Advanced Study Olden Ln Princeton NJ 08540

HUTCHENS, DENNIS WADE, anesthesiologist; b. Ashland, Ala., Aug. 25, 1963; s. Eugene Garlington and Betty Francis Hutchens; m. Laurie Sean Thornton, June 17, 1989; children: Courtney Rebekah, Abigail Frances, Dennis Wade III. BS, U. Ala., 1985; MD, U. South Ala., 1989. Bd. cert. Am. Bd.

Anesthesiology. Intern Marshall U. Hosp., Huntington, W.Va., 1989—90; resident U. Miss. Med. Sch., Jackson, 1990—93; pvt. practice anesthesiology, 1994—2001; staff anesthesiologist U. South Ala. Med. Ctr., Mobile, 2001—. Mem.: AMA, Am. Soc. Anesthesiologists, Phi Kappa Phi. Baptist. Avocations: travel, French horn. Home: 501 Hurtleigh Way Mobile AL 36608

HUTCHENS, EUGENE GARLINGTON, college administrator; b. Birmingham, Ala., Nov. 26, 1929; s. Wallace Luther and Reydonia (Corry) H.; m. Betty Frances Goode, Aug. 26, 1951; children: Dale Eugene, Wayne Goode, Dennis Wade. BA, Samford U., 1952; ThM, New Orleans Bapt. Theol. Sem., 1970; MS in Econs., U. Mo.-Columbia, 1972; D Arts in Theology, Emmanuel Sem., 1999. Ordained to ministry, 1952. Min. North Brewton (Ala.) Bapt. Ch., 1952-56, 1st Bapt. Ch., Ashland, Ala., 1956-63, Highlands Bapt. Ch., Huntsville, Ala., 1963-67; tchr. pub. schs. Huntsville, 1967-71; instr. econs. N.W. Ala. State Jr. Coll., 1972-77, acting pres., 1981, dir. Tuscumbia campus, 1977-89; adminstrv. asst. Shoals C.C., 1989-93, asst. to dean, 1993-95; pastor emeritus Weeden Heights Bapt. Ch., Florence, 1995; prof. Emmanuel Sem., 1995—. Owner radio stas., WKNI AM, Lexington, Ala., WFIX, Rogersville, Ala., 1991-96, mem. Ala. Bapt. State Exec. Bd., 1961-63; v.p. Ala. Bapt. State Pastors Conf., 1966, Ala. Bapt. Hist. Commn., 1992-2000. NSF grantee, 1971-72. Mem. NEA, Ala. Edn. Assn., Ala. Jr. and C.C. Assn. (exec. com. 1981-84), Phi Theta Kappa. Home: 801 E 2nd St Tuscumbia AL 35674-2206

HUTCHENS, GAIL R. chemist; b. Bentonville, Ark., Aug. 22, 1938; d. Sidney Baxter and Mary Dena Maurine (Harral) Rakes; m. Charles Verlin Hutchens, Mar. 4, 1967 (dec. 2002); children: David Charles, Kimberly Gail. Student, Ark. State Tchrs. Coll., 1955—58; grad., U. Tenn., 1961. Exec. v.p. Galbraith Labs., Inc., Knoxville, Tenn., 1959—93; analytical svcs. supr. Materials Engring. & Testing, Oak Ridge, Tenn., 1993—96, Techmer PM, LLC, Clinton, Tenn., 1996—. Emergency first responder instr. Video editor Democrates, Knoxville, TN, 1998. Mem. ASTM, Assn. Offcl. Analytical Chemists, Soc. Plastic Engrs. (local sect. sec. 2002-03), Am. Chem. Soc., Crestwood Hills Garden Club (pres. 1968-69), Small Chem. Bus. (sec. 1974-75), Beta Club Honor Soc., Alpha Chi. Avocation: diving instruction. Office: Techmer PM LLC 1 Quality Cir Clinton TN 37716-4017 E-mail: ghutchens@Techmerpm.com.

HUTCHENS, MICHAEL D. lawyer; b. Chgo., Jan. 13, 1960; s. Duane Eugene and Deborah Ann (Hoffman) H.; m. Christie Lynn Simons, July 2, 1983; children: Camille Gwendolyn Maxwell. BA, Coll. St. Thomas, St. Paul, 1982; JD, Hamline Law Sch., 1985. Bar: Minn. 1985, U.S. Dist. Ct. (4th cir.) 1986. Ptnr. Meagher & Geer, Mpls., 1986—. Arbitrator Am. Arbitration Assn., Mpls., 1990—. Mem. Minn. Def. Lawyers Assn. Office: Meagher & Geer 33 S 6th St Ste 4200 Minneapolis MN 55402-3788

HUTCHENS, NICKI JEAN, software developer; b. Saratoga Springs, N.Y., Feb. 13, 1959; d. Charles Edward Hutchens and Margaret Tallman; m. Robert Wack, Sept. 1, 1978 (div. May 1980); children: Jedidiah Robert, Jessie Margaret. BS in Mgmt. Info. Sys., Empire State Coll., 1995. Data libr. GE, Syracuse, N.Y., 1988-90, data mgr., 1990-93; programmer, analyst Gaylord Inf. Systems, Syracuse, 1994-96; systems engr. Electronic Data Systems, Charleston, S.C., 1996-97; lead programmer analyst Systems and Computer Tech., Columbia, SC, 1997—2000; software devel. CSI, Charleston, SC, 2000—02; sr. sys. programmer FedEx Corp., Collierville, Tenn., 2002—. Mem. AWANA Internat. (guards leader 1996—). Republican. Baptist. Avocations: running, reading, teaching.

HUTCHENS, TYRA THORNTON, physician, educator; b. Newberg, Oreg., Nov. 29, 1921; s. Fred George and Bessie (Adams) H.; m. Betty Lou Gardner, June 7, 1942; children: Tyra Richard, Robert Jay, Rebecca (Mrs. Mark Pearsall). BS, U. Oreg., 1943, MD, 1945. Diplomate: Am. Bd. Pathology, Am. Bd. Nuclear Medicine. Intern Minn. Gen. Hosp., Mpls., 1945—46; AEC postdoctoral research fellow Reed Coll., Med. Sch. U. Oreg., 1948—50; NIH postdoctoral research fellow Med. Sch. U. Oreg., 1951—53; mem. faculty Oreg. Health Scis. U., 1953—, prof., chmn. dept. clin. pathology, 1962—87, prof. emeritus, 1987—, prof. radiotherapy, 1963—71, allied health edn. coord., 1969—77. Vis. lectr. radiobiology Reed Coll., 1955, 56 Mem. adv. bd. Oreg. Regional Med. Program, 1968-75; mem. statuatory radiation adv. com. Oreg. Bd. Health, 1957-69, chmn., 1967-69; founding trustee Am. Bd. Nuc. Medicine, 1971-77, 82-84, sec., 1973-75, 84-85 ; voting rep. Am. Bd. Med. Specialties, 1973-78, chmn. com. long range planning, 1976-78; mem. sci. adv. bd. Armed Forces Inst. Pathology, 1978-83; chmn. Portland Com. on Fgn. Affairs, 1990-91. Lt. (j.g.) M.C., USNR, 1946-48. Charter mem. Acad. Clin. Lab. Physicians and Scientists, Soc. Nuc. Medicine (de Hevesey Nuc. Medicine Pioneer award 1995), Am. Coll. Nuc. Physicians; mem. AMA, Oreg. Pathologists Assn. (pres. 1968), Pacific N.W. Soc. Nuc. Medicine (pres. 1958), Coll. Am. Pathologists (bd. govs. 1967-74, pres. 1977-79, chmn. commn. on internat. affairs 1979-83, chmn. planning com. 1987 World Congress Pathology), Am. Soc. Clin. Pathologists (bd. registry med. technologists 1967-71), World Assn. of Socs. of Pathology (bur. of pathology 1981-87, 89-93, v.p. 1985-87, pres. 1989-91, chmn. commn. on world stds. 1981-86, Gold Headed Cane award 1995), World Pathology Found. (pres. 1987-89, trustee 1989-91), Assn. Clin. Pathologists (hon.), Italian Soc. Lab. Medicine (hon.), Phi Beta Kappa, Sigma Xi, Alpha Omega Alpha. Achievements include research and publications on radioactive carbon tracer studies of lipid metabolism, clinical radioisotope techniques. Home: 17480 Holy Names Dr #420 Lake Oswego OR 97034 Office: Oreg Health and Sci U 3181 SW Sam Jackson Park Rd Portland OR 97201-3011 E-mail: tyhutch@comcast.net.

HUTCHENS, WAYNE GOODE, anesthesiologist; b. Ashland, Ala., Apr. 21, 1959; s. Eugene Garlington and Betty Frances Hutchens; m. Kathy Windham Hutchens, June 26, 1982. BS cum laude, Sanford U., 1981; MD, U. Ala., 1985. Bd. cert. Am. Bd. Anesthesiology. Intern Carraway Meth. Med. Ctr., Birmingham, Ala., 1986—89; resident U. Ala. Sch. Medicine, Birmingham, Ala., 1989; anesthesiologist New London Anesthesiology Pain and Consultants, Atlanta, 1989—. Clarinetist Briarlake Orch. Mem.: AMA, Med. Assn. Ga., Am. Soc. Anesthesiologists, Phi Kappa Phi, Lambda Chi Alpha. Avocation: licensed air plane pilot. Home: 3522 Greystone Cir Atlanta GA 30341

HUTCHEON, LINDA ANN, English language educator; b. Toronto, Aug. 24, 1947; d. Vincent Roy and Elisa (Rossi) Bulfon Bortolotti; m. Michael Alexander Hutcheon, May 30, 1970. BA, U. Toronto, 1969, PhD, 1975; MA, Cornell U., 1971. Prof. McMaster U., Hamilton, Ont., Can., 1976-88, U. Toronto, 1988—. Vis. prof. U. Toronto, 1980-81, 81-82, 84-85, U. Wis., Madison, 1995, U. Ga., 1998, U. Queensland, Australia, 2001, U. Mich. Inst. for the Humanities, 2003. Author: Narcisstic Narrative, 1980 (choice award, 1980), Formalism and the Freudian Aesthetic, 1984, A Theory of Parody, 1985, 2000, A Poetics of Postmodernism, 1988, The Canadian Postmodern, 1988, The Politics of Postmodernism, 1989, 2002, Splitting Images, 1991, Irony's Edge, 1995; author: (with M. Hutcheon) Opera: Desire, Disease, Death, 1996; author: Bodily Charm: Living Opera, 2000; assoc. editor: RS/SI, 1982—84, U. Toronto Quar., 1993—; mem. (editl. bd.) Texte, Toronto, 1983—, English Studies in Can., 1984—94, Italian Canadiana, 1984—, Textual Practice, 1987—2003, Can. Rev. Comparative Lit., 1987—, Can. Poetry, 1987—93, PMLA, 1990—92, Essays on Can. Writing, 1992—, Contemporary Lit., 1992—, Modern Fiction Studies, 1993—, CLIO, 1994—, Parallax (U.K.), 1994—. Woodrow Wilson Found. fellow, 1969, Social Scis. and Humanities Rsch. Coun. Can. fellow, 1983, 93-95, 96-99, 2000-2003, co-fellow maj. collaborative rsch. initiatives, 1996-2000; Can. Coun. fellow, 1972-75, Killam Found. fellow, 1978-80, 86-88, Connaught fellow, 1991-92, Guggenheim fellow, 1992-93. Mem. MLA (del. assembly 1985-88, exec. coun. 1992-96, 2d v.p. 1998, 1st v.p. 1999, pres. 2000), AAAS (elected), Assn. Can. Coll. and Univ. Tchrs. English (exec. mem. 1978-81), Can. Comparative Lit. Assn. (sec.-treas. 1981-83), Internat. Comparative Lit. Assn. (coord. com. lit. history 1992-97).

HUTCHEON, PETER DAVID, lawyer; b. S.I., N.Y., Sept. 11, 1943; s. Peter and Helen Christine (Buckley) H.; m. Elizabeth Ann Demy, June 8, 1969 (div. Jan. 1986); children: Rececca Leigh, Douglas Ian; m. Barbara Mary Silver, Feb. 14, 1986; 1 child, Peter Silver. BA, Williams Coll., 1965; postgrad., Ludwig-Maximilian Universität, Munich, 1965-66; JD, Harvard U., 1969. Bar: N.Y. 1970, N.J. 1975. Assoc. White & Case, N.Y., 1968-75, Norris, McLaughlin & Marcus, P.A., Somerville, N.J., 1975-76, mem., 1976—. Chmn. N.J. Corp. and Bus. Law Study Commn., 1989—; mem., sec. adv. com. N.J. Bur. Securities, 1993-2001, chmn., 1994-2001. Contbr. articles to profl. jours. Chmn. bd. mgrs. St. Andrews Soc. of N.Y., 1986—87; deacon United Reformed Ch., Somerville, 1977—80; elder Bound Brook Presbyn. Ch., 1996—99. Dankstipendium scholar govt. of the Fed. Republic of Gemany, 1965. Mem. ABA (chmn. sect. of sci. and tech. 1986-87), N.J. State Bar Assn. (chmn. banking law sect. 1982-83, chmn. corp. and bus. sect. 1990-92), N.Y. State Bar Assn., German-Am. Lawyers Assn., Nat. Conf. of Lawyers and Scientists (del. 1988-91), Princeton Area Alumni Assn. of Williams Coll. (pres. 1981-89), Clan Donald (N.Y.). Avocations: wine tasting, singing. Office: Norris McLaughlin & Marcus PA PO Box 1018 721 Rt 202/206 Somerville NJ 08876

HUTCHEON, WALLACE SCHOONMAKER, history educator; b. N.Y.C., June 27, 1933; s. Wallace Schoonmaker and Dorothy Mae (Tate) H.; m. Margaret Marie Crossen, Sept. 29, 1963; children: Dorothy Lee, Hillary Ann. BS in Agrl. Econs., Pa. State U., 1954; MA in History, George Washington U., 1969, MPhil in History, 1971, PhD in History, 1975. Commd. ensign U.S. Naval Res., 1955, advanced through grades to comdr., 1970; comm. officer Fawtulant Naval Air Sta., Key West, Fla., 1955-59; edn. officer USS Kitty Hawk, 1962-64; air intelligence officer CVW-2, 1964-66, intelligence analyst DIA, 1966-70; released to inactive duty, 1970; ret., 1976; lectr. George Mason U., Fairfax, Va., 1970; instr. St. Marys Coll., Md., 1971; asst. prof. history No. Va. C.C., Annandale, 1971-75, assoc. prof., 1975-80, prof., 1980—, head dept., 1974—. Asst. chmn. divsn. social scis. and pub. svcs., 1979-; mgmt. tng. cons. Health Resources Adminstrn., HEW, Hyattsville, Md., 1978; cons. mil. evaluations program Am. Coun. Edn., Washington, 1980; cons. coll. hist. textbooks Houghton-Mifflin Co., Boston, Mass., 1992-; mem. adv. bd. Annual Editions, Dushkin Pub. Co.; pub. spkr. Mariners Mus., D.C. Historian Luncheon, others; cons. coll. history textbooks McGraw-Hill Co., 2003. Author: Robert Fulton: Pioneer of Undersea Warfare, 1981; contbr. to manuscripts collection U.S. Navy History Divsn. Mem. History of the City of Fairfax Roundtable, 1995-98; history day judge George Mason U., 1990-2002. Recipient Outstanding Contbns. to Edn. award, Alumni Fedn. No. Va. CC, 1993, 1995, 2003, Golden Apple award, Student Govt., 1999—2000. Mem. U.S. Naval Inst., Orgn. Am. Historian, No. Va. Assn. History (bd. dirs. 1994, v.p. 1994), U.S. Capitol Hist. Soc., Delta Chi. Democrat. Episcopalian. Avocations: swimming, reading, music, theatre. Home: 4425 Village Dr Fairfax VA 22030-5642 Office: No Va CC 0333 Little River Tpke Annandale VA 22003-3743 E-mail: whutcheon@nvcc.us.

HUTCHERSON, CHRISTOPHER ALFRED, marketing, recruiting and educational fundraising executive; b. Memphis, June 13, 1950; s. Alfred Wayne Hutcherson and Loretta (Morris) Kindsfather; m. Glenda Ann Champ, May 22, 1971 (dec. 1995). BS, U. Houston, 1972, MA in Adminstrn., 1977, postgrad., 1977-79. Cert. tchr. and adminstr., Tex. Pvt. music instr. Spring Br. and Pasadena Ind. Sch. Dists., Tex., 1968-75; jr. high and high sch. band dir. Deer Park (Tex.) Ind. Schs., 1972-80; recruiter M. David Lowe Personnel, Houston, 1981; sales dir. Instl. Financing Svcs., Benicia, Calif., 1982-85, sales mgr., 1985-87; nat. tng. dir. Champion Products and Svcs., San Diego, 1987-88, west coast and midwest sales mgr., 1988-89; pres. Camelot, Inc., Auburn, Calif., 1989-91; pres., CEO Camelot Telephone Assistance Program, Inc., Folsom, Calif., 1991-92; nat. dir. sales and mktg. edn. and devel. Nat. Scrip Ctr., Inc., Santa Rosa, Calif., 1992-95; exec. v.p. Scrip Plus Inc., Fresno, Calif., 1995-96; chmn., pres., CEO Children's Heroes, Inc., Grass Valley, Calif., 1996—2001; pres. Hutcherson Cons., 1989—; pres. bus. devel. Heroes, Inc., 2002—; exec. v.p. NBO Sys., Inc., Salt Lake City, 2002—. Fund raising cons. non-profit orgns., 1982—; spkr. in field; creator kitchen table mktg. sys., 1992. Pres. Sunshine Valley Homeowners Assn., 2000—01; choir dir. St. Hyacinth Ch., Dear Park, 1979—81; vice chmn. ch. coun., 1980; bd. dirs. Students in Free Enterprise, 2003; judge Tex. jr. high and high sch. bands, 1974—81; regional band chair, 1973—77; founder Tex. Region XIX Jr. High Band Competition, 1973; 1st chair clarinet Tex. All-State Band, 1968; pres. Glenda Hutcherson Heroes Found., 1996—; founder, pres. Children's Heroes Fund.; creator Heroes Reward Card Program, 1996—2001, Children's Heroes Brand, 1997. Mem. Kappa Kappa Psi (v.p. Outstanding Mem. award 1970). Republican. Mem. Lds Ch. Avocations: golf, reading, movies. Home: 201 E South Salt Lake City UT 84111-

HUTCHESON, J. STERLING, allergist, immunologist, physician; b. Richmond, Va., Apr. 17, 1936; s. James P. and Daisy-Clarke (Lorentz) H.; m. Nancy Montgomery Sanders, May 20, 1961; children: Anne Farrar McCausland, Betsy Dulaney. Student, Roanoke Coll., Va., 1953-55; BA, U. Va., 1955-57; MD, The Johns Hopkins U., 1957-61. Diplomate Am. Bd. Allergy and Clin. Immunology. Intern in medicine U. Va., Charlottesville, Va., 1961-62; resident in medicine Med. Coll. Va., Richmond, Va., 1962-64; fellow in allergy and immunology U. Va., Charlottesville, Va., 1964-65; asst. prof. medicine Med. Coll. Va., 1967-68; staff Nalle Clinic, Charlotte, 1968-89; pvt. practice Carolina Asthma and Allergy Ctr., 1990—. Founder Allergy Clinic USAF Acad. Hosp., Colo., 1965-67; cons. Blue Cross/Blue Shield of N.C., 1985-2002; adj. assoc. prof. pediats. U. N.C. Sch. Medicine, Carolinas Med. Ctr., Charlotte, 1997-2000. Bd. trustees Charlotte County Day Sch., 1974-85; bd. dirs. Friends of Music Queens Coll., 1994-96. Capt. USAF M.C. Fellow Am. Acad. Allergy, Asthma and Immunology, Am. Coll. Allergy, Asthma and Immunology; mem. Southeastern Allergy Assn., N.C. Soc. Allergy and Clin. Immunology (former pres.). Episcopalian. Avocations: gardening, hiking, classical music, reading. Home: 4200 Arbor Way Charlotte NC 28211-3812 Office: Carolina Asthma & Allergy Bldg 400 2711 Randolph Rd Charlotte NC 28207-2027

HUTCHESON, JACK ROBERT, hematologist, medical oncologist; b. Rock Hill, S.C., Dec. 26, 1946; s. Jack Robert and Lillian Massey (Dunlap) H.; m. Charlene Marie Dixon, Sept. 14, 1974; children: Gregory Allen, Julia Lynn. BS in Biology, Wake Forest U., 1969; MD, Med. U. S.C., 1973. Diplomate in internal medicine, hematology, oncology Am. Bd. Internal Medicine. Straight med. intern U. Md. Hosp., Balt., 1973-74, resident in medicine, 1974-76; fellow in hematology Med. U. S.C., Charleston, 1976-78; fellow in oncology Emory U., Atlanta, 1978-79; oncologist, hematologist Oncology and Hematology Assocs. of S.W. Va. Inc., Roanoke, 1979—; med. dir. Carilion Health Sys. Oncology Svc. Line, Roanoke, 1996—. Instr., assoc. investigator in hematology Med. U. S.C./VA Hosp., Charleston, 1977-78; assoc. prof. medicine U. Va., Roanoke. Contbr. articles to med. jours. Pres. Scottish Soc. Va. Highlands, Roanoke, 1996, 2000, 01; chair com. on smoking cessation Va. br. Am. Cancer Soc., Roanoke, 1980; mem. Vets. Corps. of Artillary, N.Y. Decorated Most Venerable Order of Hosp. of St. John of Jerusalem, knight grand cross Order of St. Catherine of Sinai, Caballero Grand Cruz Order Don Carlos I (Portugal), Knight Grand Cross Mil. Hospitalier Order of St. Lazarus, knight grand cross Order Crown of Thorns; recipient Berson Yalow award, Soc. Nuclear Medicine, 1977; grantee for hematology, VA Career Devel., 1977—78. Fellow ACP; mem. Am. Soc. Clin. Oncology, Am. Soc. Hematology, St. Andrews Soc. Presbyterian. Avocations: Jaguar auto restoration, genealogy, Scottish/Celtic activities, bagpipes. Home: 2860 S Jefferson St Roanoke VA 24014-3320 Office: Oncol and Hematol Assocs 2013 S Jefferson St Roanoke VA 24014-2419 E-mail: jack.hutchesonjr@usoncology.com.

HUTCHESON, JERRY DEE, manufacturing company executive; b. Oct. 31, 1932; s. Radford Andrew and Ethel Mae (Boulware) H.; m. Lynda Lou Weber, Mar. 6, 1953; children: Gerald Dan, Lisa Marie, Vicki Lynn. BS in Physics, Ea. N.Mex. U., 1965; postgrad., Temple U., 1962, U. N.Mex., 1965. Registered profl. engr., Calif. Rsch. engr. RCA, 1959—62; sect. head Motorola, 1962—63; rsch. physicist Dikewood Corp., 1963—66; sr. mem. tech. staff Signetics Corp., 1966—69; engring. mgr. Litton Sys., Sunnyvale, Calif., 1969—70, Fairchild Semiconductor, Mountain View, Calif., 1971; equipment engr., group mgr. Teledyne Semiconductor, Mountain View, 1971—74; dir. engring. DCA Reliability Labs., Sunnyvale, 1974—75; founder, prin. Tech. Ventures, San Jose, Calif., 1975—; CEO VLSI Rsch., Inc., 1981—. Contbr. Dem. precinct committeeman, Albuquerque, 1964—66. With USAF, 1951—55. Mem.: NSPE, Am. Soc. Test Engrs., Soc. Photo-Optical Instrumentation Engrs., Semiconductor Equipment and Materials Inst., Calif. Soc. Profl. Engrs., Profl. Engrs. Pvt. Practice, Masons. Presbyterian. Office: VSLI Rsch 1754 Technology Dr Ste 117 San Jose CA 95110-1320

HUTCHESON, JOHN AMBROSE, JR., history educator; b. Winston-Salem, NC, July 18, 1944; s. John Ambrose and Virginia Lee (Tillotson) H.; m. Marilyn Louise Beaver, July 15, 1967; children: Virginia Louise, Catherine Leigh. AB, U. N.C., 1966, MA, 1968, PhD, 1973. Asst. prof. history Dalton (Ga.) State Coll., 1974-90, assoc. prof. history, 1990-97, prof. history, 1997—, chair divsn. bus. adminstrn. and social sci., 1997-99, chmn. divsn. soc. sci., 1999—. Author: Leopold Maxse and the National Review, 1989; contbr. articles to profl. jours. Bd. dirs. Creative Arts Guild, Dalton, sec., 1994-99, pres., 1999-2001. Mem. Am. Hist. Assn., So. Hist. Assn., So. Conf. Brit. Studies (exec. coun. 1995-98, pres. 1999-2001), Carolinas Symposium on Brit. Studies (pres. 1995), Ga. Assn. Historians, World History Assn., Phi Alpha Theta. Democrat. Episcopalian. Home: 2204 Mathis Ln Dalton GA 30720-2942 Office: Dalton State Coll 213 College Dr Dalton GA 30720-3745 E-mail: jhutcheson@em.daltonstate.edu.

HUTCHESON, MARK ANDREW, lawyer; b. Phila., Mar. 29, 1942; s. John R. and Mary Helen (Willis) H.; m. Julie A. Olander, June 13, 1964; children: Kirsten Elizabeth, Mark Andrew II, Megan Ann. BA, U. Puget Sound, 1964; LLB, U. Wash., 1967. Bar: Wash. 1967, U.S. Dist. Ct. (we. and ea. dists.) Wash., U.S. Ct. Appeals (9th cir.), U.S. Supreme Ct. Staff counsel Com. on Commerce U.S. Senate, Washington, 1967-68; assoc. Davis Wright Tremaine, Seattle, 1968-72; ptnr. Davis, Wright Tremaine, Seattle, 1973—; mng. ptnr., chief exec. officer Davis Wright Tremaine, Seattle, 1989-94; chmn. Davis, Wright Tremaine, Seattle, 1994—. Mem., co-founder labor law com. Nat. Banking Industry, 1984—. Co-author: Employer's Guide to Strike Planning and Prevention, 1986; contbr. articles to profl. jours. Chmn., trustee Virginia Mason Hosp., Seattle, 1980—, Overlake Sch., Redmond, Wash., 1984-89, Epiphany Sch., Seattle, 1982-84, Legal Aid for Wash. Fund, 1991—; bd. dirs. Vis. Nurse Svcs., Seattle-King County, 1985-88; trustee Pacific N.W. Ballet, 1991-99, Pacific N.W. Assn. Ind. Schs., 1996-98. Nelson T. Hartson scholar U. Wash., 1966; Deerfield fellow Heritage Found., Deerfield, Mass., 1963. Mem. ABA (health care forum, employment law sect.), Seattle-King County Bar Assn. (employment law sect.), Am. Acad. Hosp. Attys., Am. Hosp. Assn. (labor rels. adv. com. 1978—), Coll. Labor and Employment Lawyers, Greater Seattle C. of C. (bd. dirs. 1991-94), Rainier Club, Seattle Tennis Club, Univ. Club, Order of Coif. Episcopalian. Avocations: sailing, tennis, skiing, reading, travel. Office: Davis Wright Tremaine 2600 Century Sq 1501 4th Ave Seattle WA 98101-1688 E-mail: markhutcheson@dwt.com.

HUTCHESON, RICHARD ERVIN, philosophy educator, academic administrator; b. Washington, Jan. 20, 1928; s. Samuel Joseph and Ruth (Nunnery) H.; m. Elizabeth Martz, June 4, 1953 (dec. Jan. 1999); children: Sara Ann, Amy Tabatha. AB, Coll. of William and Mary, 1952; MA, Harvard U., 1954, PhD, 1962; cert., Harvard Inst. Ednl. Mgmt., 1974. Asst. prof. Wofford Coll., Spartanburg, S.C., 1957-59; assoc. asst. prof. Allegheny Coll., Meadville, Pa., 1959-67; assoc. prof. philosophy, spl. asst. to pres. Kans. State U., Manhattan, 1967-69; prof., chmn. dept. philosophy St. Mary's Coll., Notre Dame, Ind., 1969-72; dean of arts and scis., prof. philosophy SUNY, Potsdam, 1972-84, v.p., 1984-85, prof. emeritus, 1990—. Fellow Rockefeller Found., 1952. Mem. Am. Philos. Assn., Metaphys. Soc. Am. Democrat. Avocations: reading, writing, listening to music, travel. Home: 387 Savage Farm Dr Ithaca NY 14850-6505

HUTCHESON, THOMAS WORTHINGTON, trade association official; b. Lake Forest, Ill., July 1, 1958; s. Harold Randolph and Minna Margaret (Adams) H. BA, U. Mass., 1980, MEd, 1987, EdD, 1993. Music tchr., 1975—; instr. edn. U. Mass., Amherst, 1987-89, v.p. Grad. Student Senate, 1988-89, rsch. asst. dept. econs., 1989-91; rsch. cons. Nat. Priorities Project, Northampton, Mass., 1991-92; estate cons. Sandwich, Mass., 1996-99; music critic The Recorder, Greenfield, Mass., 1996-99; project coord. Bonnyvale Environ. Edn. Ctr., Brattleboro, Vt., 1996-99, cons., 1992; policy asst. Organic Trade Assn., Greenfield, Mass., 1999-2000, policy coord., 2000—02, assoc. policy dir., 2002—. Contbr. articles to profl. jours.; musician, 1974—; arranger choral works: Welcome, Yule!, 1994—; dir. Shapeshifters vocal quartet, 1997-2001. Chmn. Pub. Transp. Com., Amherst, 1989-90; chmn. Franklin Regional Planning Bd., Greenfield, Mass., 2002—, local emergency planning com., 2002—; mem. Overall Econ. Devel. Program Policy Com., Greenfield, 1996-99, Greater Franklin Regional Comprehensive Econ. Devel. Strategy Com., 1999—; chmn. Com. on Elec. Industry Deregulation, Greenfield, 1996-99. Mem.: Am. Soc. Assn. Execs., Internat. Soc. for Ecol. Econs., Am. Planning Assn. Democrat. Mem. Soc. Of Friends. Avocations: Morris dance, family archives, traditional music. Home: 21 Madison Cir Greenfield MA 01301-2723 Office: Organic Trade Assn 60 Wells St Greenfield MA 01301-9654 E-mail: thutcheson@ota.com.

HUTCHIN, NANCY LEE, process engineering and change management consultant; b. Ft. Belvoir, Va., June 16, 1949; d. Walter James and Iyllis Elizabeth (Lee) H.; m. Stephen Lawrence Guiland Nov. 27, 1970 (div. 1983); children: Kai-Long Stephen Guiland, Petra Lee Guiland; m. John Edward Money, Jun. 7, 1986 (div. 1994). BA summa cum laude, U. Md., 1973, MA, 1976. Prin. sci. B-K Dynamics, Rockville, Md., 1978-86; sr. cons. James Martin Assoc., Reston, Va., 1986-88; cons. San Diego, 1989-95; cons. employee SAIC, San Diego, 1993-95; staff cons. Intergraph, Reston, 1995-99; practice mgr., bid and proposal mgr., program mgr. Keane Fed. Sys., Inc., Rockville, Md., 1999—2002; capture mgr. Gen. Dynamics Network Sys., Rockville, 2003—. Contbr. editor Enterprise Reengineering, 1994-96; assoc. pub. Black Riders, 1994-96; program com. Tools & Methods for Bus. Engring. Conf., 1995; mem. program com. Nat. Bus. Process Reengring. Conf., 1996, 98, SDPS Integrated Design and Process Tech. Conf., 1996, 98; bd. dirs. Strategic Info. Mgmt. & Tech. Solutions, Inc., Ogden, Utah; track chair changing human behavior Europe 98 Process and Knowledge Mgmt. Conf., London, 1998; program com. Women Execs. in State Govt. Leadership Conf. 2001, Lake Tahoe, Calif.; presenter in field. Contbr. articles to profl. jours. Bd. dirs. Exec. Women's Round Table. Mem. Women in Tech. DC chap., Soc. of Info. Mgmt., Soc. Design and Process Sci. Avocations: walking, travel, blues music.

HUTCHINGS, GEORGE HENRY, food company executive; b. Fort Worth, June 23, 1922; s. George H. and Emma (Harder) H.; m. Edith Van Gils, Mar. 23, 1946 (dec.); children: Mark Dennis Lisa Ellen; m. Elizabeth T. Storey, Apr. 10, 1968 (dec.). Student, Tex. A&M, 1940-42. Analyst mktg. research Frito Food Mfg., Dallas, 1946, mgr. mktg. research Los Angeles, 1946-57, div. sales mgr. San Mateo, Calif., 1958-60, div. gen. mgr., 1961, v.p., 1961-62; v.p. for ops. Western zone, 1962—; pres. Nalley's, Inc., Tacoma, 1964, Nalley's div. W.R. Grace & Co., 1966—, ret., 1972-81; pres. Wash. Beverages, Inc., Tacoma, 1972-81. Dir., mem. exec. com. Puget Sound Nat. Bank, Tacoma; cons. 1964-83; dir. mem. examining com. Key Bank of Wash., Tacoma, 1993-94, ret., 1994. Served to capt. USAAF, 1942-46. Decorated D.F.C., Air medal with 7 clusters. Mem. Tacoma Country and Golf Club, Masons. Lutheran. Home: 7419 North St SW Tacoma WA 98498-5213 *A man must know what he stands for before he can logically take a stand against anything.*

HUTCHINGS, JOHN BARRIE, astronomer, researcher; b. Johannesburg, Republic of South Africa, July 18, 1941; arrived in Can., 1967; BSc, Witwatersrand U., Johannesburg, 1962; MSc, Witwatersrand U., 1964; PhD, U. Cambridge, Eng., 1967. Rsch. scientist Dominion Astrophys. Obs., Nat. Rsch. Coun. Can., Victoria, B.C., 1967—. Author numerous rsch. papers and revs., 1964—. Recipient Gold medal Sci. Coun. B.C., 1983, Royal Jubilee medal, 2002. Fellow Royal Soc. Can.; mem. Internat. Astron. Union, Am. Astron. Soc., Can. Astron. Soc. (Beals award 1982). Office: Dominion Astrophys Obs 5071 W Saanich Rd Victoria BC Canada V9E 2E7 E-mail: john.hutchings@nrc-cnrc.gc.ca.

HUTCHINGS, PETER LOUNSBERY, retird insurance company executive, director; b. N.Y.C., Nov. 1, 1943; s. Robert Spaulding and Kathryn Eleanor (Lounsbery) H.; m. Marsha Kayser, May 27, 1966 (div. 1980); children: Michael, Daniel; m. Martha Deborah Wolfgang, Jan. 16, 1983 BA, Yale U., 1964. CLU, ChFC, FSA. Mem. actuarial program MONY, N.Y.C., 1964-68, dir. group systems, 1969, asst. v.p., 1970-73; v.p., actuary Blue Cross and Blue Shield of Greater N.Y., N.Y.C., 1973-77, sr. v.p., 1977-83; ptnr. Kwasha Lipton, Fort Lee, N.J., 1983-87; exec. v.p., CFO Guardian Life Ins. Co. Am., N.Y.C., 1987—2001. Pres. bd dirs. 300 CPW Corp., 1995-98; pres., bd. dirs. Park Ave. Life (Guardian sub.), 1998-2001, Vis. Nurse Svc. of N.Y., 1999—; bd. dirs. Well Choice. Active 14th St. Bus. Improvement Dist., N.Y.C., 1992-99, pres., 1995-99; bd. dirs. 14th St.-Union Sq. Local Devel. Corp., 1993-99, Children's Orch. Soc., 1999—, Downtown Alliance, 2000-02, Rubin Mus. Art, 2002—; mem. N.Y. Organ Donor Network, 2002—, Friends of Wertheim Nat. Wildlife Refuge, 1999—. Fellow Soc. Actuaries; mem. Am. Acad. Actuaries, Actuarial Soc. Greater N.Y. (pres. 1992-93). Avocations: photography, music, travel. Home: 300 Central Park W Apt 14B New York NY 10024-1513 E-mail: mdwplh@mac.com.

HUTCHINS, CARLEEN MALEY, acoustical engineer, consultant; b. Springfield, Mass., May 24, 1911; d. Thomas W. and Grace (Fletcher) Maley; m. Morton A. Hutchins, June 6, 1943; children: William Aldrich, Caroline. AB, Cornell U., 1933; MA, NYU, 1942; DEng (hon.), Stevens Inst. Tech., 1977; DFA (hon.), Hamilton Coll., 1984; DSc (hon.), St. Andrews Presbyn. Coll., 1988; LLD (hon.), Concordia U., Montreal, Que., Can., 1992. Tchr. sci. Woodward Sch., Bklyn., 1934-38, Brearley Sch., N.Y.C., 1938-49; asst. dir., asst. prin. All Day Neighborhood Schs., N.Y.C., 1943-45. Sci. cons. Coward McCann, Inc., 1956-65, Girl Scouts Am., 1967-65, Nat. REcreation Assn., 1957-65; permanent sec. Catgut Acoustical Soc., Montclair, N.J., 1962-2000; exec. dir. New Violin Family Assn. Inc., 2000—; hon. cons. Catgut Acoustical Soc., Inc., 2000—; maker violins. Author: Life's Key, DNA, 1961, Moon Moth, 1965, Who Will Drown the Sound, 1972; author (with others): Science Through Recreation, 1964; contbr. violin acoustics sect. Grove's Dictionary of Music and Musicians, 1964, 96; editor: (2 vols.) Musical Acoustics, Part I, Violin Family Components, 1975, Musical Acoustics, Part II, Violin Family Functions, 1976, The Physics of Music, 1978, Research Papers in Violin Acoustics, 1973-94, 96; contbr. articles to profl. jours. in Sci. Am. Jour. of the Acoustical Soc. Am., Jour. Audio Engring. Soc., Physics Today, Am. Viola Soc., Catgut Acoustical Soc. Martha Baird Rockefeller Fund for Music grantee, 1966, 68, 74; Guggenheim fellow, 1959, 61; recipient several spl. citations in music, Carleen Maley Hutchins medal (1st recipient) Catgut Acoustical Soc., Hon. Fellowship award Acoustical Soc. Am., 1998; NSF grantee, 1971, 74. Fellow AAAS (electorate nominating com. 1974-76, Outstanding Performance in the Scis. award 1994), Audio Engring. Soc. (life), Acoustical Soc. Am. (emeritus, membership com. 1980-86, exec. coun. 1984-87, medal and awards com. 1987-89, nominating com. 1987-88, Silver Acoustics Medal 1981, tech. com. music acoustics 1964—, chmn. pres.'s ad hoc com. 1987-88, archives com. 1988—, mem. com. on women 1989-97); mem. So. Calif. Violin Makers Assn. (hon.), Viola da Gambda Soc. Am. (hon.), Scandinavian Violin Makers Assn. (hon.), N.Y. Viola Soc., Guild Am. Luthiers, Am. Viola Soc., Violoncello Soc., Amateur Chamber Music Players Assn., Am. Philos. Soc. (award violin acoustics 1968, 81), Mich. Violin Makers Assn., Materials Rsch. Soc., Three O'Clock Club, Dot and Cirle, others, Sigma Xi, Pi Lambda Theta, Alpha Xi Delta. Home and Office: 42 Taylor Dr Wolfeboro NH 03894 E-mail: nvfa@att.net.

HUTCHINS, DIANE ELIZABETH RIDER, librarian; b. Kearny, N.J., June 25, 1951; d. Thomas Lindsay and Dorothy Jane (Sommer) Rider; m. Clifford James Hutchins, Feb. 14, 2002. MusB magna cum laude, Westminster Choir Coll., 1973; MLS, Fla. State U., 1993. Intern preservation dept. U. Fla., Gainesville, 1993, intern free-net libr. Tallahassee (Fla.) Free-Net, 1993; reference libr. Broward County Main Libr., Ft. Lauderdale, Fla., 1994-95; libr., instr. Art Inst. Ft. Lauderdale, 1995-96, dir. Learning Resource Ctr., 1996-98; dean Nevin C. Meinhardt Meml. Libr., 1998-99; collection devel. coord. Washington State Libr., 1999—2002, program mgr. collection mgmt., 2002—. Vice chair, assoc. mem. com. S.E. Fla. Libr. Info. Network, 1996-97, chair assoc. mem. com., 1997-98, ex officio mem. bd. dirs. S.E. Fla. Libr. Info. Network, 1996-99; spl. librs. rep. Fla. Libr. Network Coun., 1998-99. Soloist St. Paul's Chapel, Columbia U., N.Y.C., 1973, Ch. of St. Mary the Virgin, N.Y.C., 1974. Recipient Outstanding Leadership award Wash. State Libr., 2000; Fla. State U. fellow, 1993-94, Coll. Tchg. fellow, 1992-93; Louis Shores scholar, 1992-93. Mem. Spl. Librs. Assn. (dir. Fla. and Caribbean chpt. 1997-99; Fla. rep., steering com. South Atlantic Regional conf. 1997-99), Geneal. Soc. Southwestern Pa., Sierra Club, Phi Kappa Phi, Beta Phi Mu. Avocations: vegetarian cooking, genealogy, the internet, reading. Office: The Wash State Libr PO Box 42460 Olympia WA 98504-2460 E-mail: dhutchins@secstate.wa.gov.

HUTCHINS, EDITH ELIZABETH, accountant; b. Prince Frederick, Md., July 14, 1966; d. Aaron Ray and Alma Marie (Phillips) H.; 1 child, Jonathan Alexander Sawyer. BS in Acctg. summa cum laude, Hampton (Va.) U., 1988; MS in Taxation, Am. U., 2001. CPA Md. Staff acct. Deloitte & Touche, Morristown, N.J., 1988-89; account exec. KEZB Radio, El Paso, Tex., 1990; cost acct. Helen of Troy, El Paso, 1990; payroll adminstr. Calvert County Pub. Schs., Prince Frederick, Md., 1992—. Fin. cons., Prince Frederick, 1993—; tax preparer, Lexington Park, 1993—; writer, prodr. radio commls., 1990. Vol. Calvert County NAACP, 1996. Mem. AICPA, Md. Assn. CPAs, Alpha Kappa Alpha. Democrat. Avocations: missionary work, acting, golfing, tennis, travel. Home: 650 Gunsmoke Cir Lusby MD 20657-5156 E-mail: eeh_cpa@yahoo.com.

HUTCHINS, FRANK MCALLISTER, advertising agency executive; b. Rochester, N.Y., July 7, 1922; s. Francis Irving and Barbara Woodward (Arnold) H.; m. Jeanne Mathilda Bahn, Aug. 24, 1945; children: Katharine Arnold, Virginia Ann, Patricia Arms, Constance Anne. AB, Dartmouth Coll., 1947, MBA, 1948. Editor-in-chief Dartmouth Yearbook, 1943; bus. mgr. Dartmouth Daily Newspaper, 1947-48; account exec. Hutchins Advt. Co., Inc., Rochester, 1948-50, v.p., gen. mgr., 1950, pres., treas., from 1951, chmn. bd., CEO, until 1971; chmn. exec. com. Hutchins/Darcy, Inc., 1971-75, chmn. bd., CEO, 1976-77; chmn., CEO, Hutchins/Young & Rubicam Inc., Rochester, 1978-82, chmn., 1983-89, Hutchins/DAC Group, Rochester, 1998—. Trustee Vista Family of Funds, N.Y.C., 1982-94. Bd. dirs. United Way, Rochester, pres., 1974-75; bd. dirs. YMCA, Rochester, pres., 1969-71; trustee, mem. exec. com. Rochester Inst. Tech., 1968—, chmn. bd., 1981-84, hon. vice chnm., 2002—; trustee, mem. exec. com. Internat. Mus. Photography, 1975—; trustee, mem. exec. com., chmn. devel. com. Paul Smith's Coll. Arts & Scis., 1989—, vice chmn. of bd., 1995—; trustee Adirondack Pk. Inst., 1989—, pres., 1989-93, v.p. devel., 1993—; mem. alumni coun. Dartmouth Coll., 1969-72. With OSS, AUS, 1943-45; as 2d lt. inf., 1945-46. Mem. Rochester C. of C. (trustee 1970—, pres. 1978), Rochester Advt. Coun. (chmn. bd. 1957, bd. dirs.), Greater Rochester Visitors Assn. (chmn. bd. 1989-91, exec. com., bd. dirs. 1965—), Rochester Jr. C. of C. (pres. 1952-53), Am. Assn. Advt. Agys. (sec.-treas. 1972-73), Dartmouth Club (pres. Rochester chpt. 1951-52), Country Club of Rochester (pres. 1960-61, bd. stewards 1973-76), Genesee Valley Club, Theta Delta Chi. Episcopalian (vestryman, sr. warden St. Paul's Episcopal Ch., Rochester). Home: 75 Indian Spring Ln Rochester NY 14618-2527 Office: Hutchins/DAC 400 Midtown Tower Rochester NY 14604-2069

HUTCHINS, GROVER MACGREGOR, pathologist, educator, consultant; b. Balt., Aug. 17, 1932; s. Grover and Elmore (Lawrence) H.; m. Loretta Helen Bajkowska, July 29, 1956; children: Diana, David, Sally. BA, Johns Hopkins U., 1957, MD, 1961. Intern, then resident Johns Hopkins Hosp., Balt., 1961-65, pathologist, 1967—, dir. autopsy pathology, 1976—98; rsch. fellow Scripps Clinic and Rsch. Found., La Jolla, Calif., 1965-66; instr. in pathology Sch. Medicine, Johns Hopkins U., Balt., 1966-67, asst. prof., 1967-73, assoc. prof., 1973-83, prof. pathology, 1983—. Editor: Autopsy Performance & Reporting, 1990, An Introduction to Autopsy Technique, 1994; contbr. articles to profl. publs., chpts. to books. Cpl. U.S. Army, 1952-54. Mem. Coll. Am. Pathologists (autopsy com. 1986-2002, advisor forensic pathology com. 1988-95, chmn. autopsy com. 1991-95, mem. commn. on anatomic pathology 1991-95), Phi Beta Kappa, Alpha Epsilon Delta, Alpha Omega Alpha. Democrat. Episcopalian. Home: 1 Stratford Rd Baltimore MD 21218-1145 Office: Johns Hopkins Hosp Dept Pathology 600 N Wolfe St Baltimore MD 21287-0005

HUTCHINS, JOAN MORTHLAND, manufacturing executive, farmer; b. Pasadena, Calif., Aug. 8, 1940; d. Andrew and Constance Amelia (Gordon-Grant) Morthland; children: Andrew E. Bush, Georgia R. Bush, Alan S., Paul M. AB, Radcliffe Coll., 1961; hon. degree, Royal Coll. Music, London, 1979; AAS, SUNY, Farmingdale, 1985. Jr. mathematician Shell Devel. Co. (Shell Oil), Emeryville, Calif., 1961-63; mathematician Corp. for Econ. and Indsl. Rsch., London, England, 1964-65; mgmt. cons. McKinsey & Co., N.Y.C., 1965-67; v.p. devel. Compotite Corp., L.A., 1985-87, pres., 1987-89, pres., CEO, 1989—, MBH Farms, Inc., Elizaville, NY, 1986-2001, chmn., 2001—. Editor McKinsey & Co. Mgmt. Scis. News Bull., 1965-67; contbr. articles to profl. jours. Mem. bd. overseers Harvard U., Cambridge, Mass., 1994-2000, pres., 1999-2000, mem. overseers vis. com. Harvard athletic dept., 1986-91, mem. overseers vis. com. Arnold Arboretum, 1995—, chmn., 1997—, mem. overseers vis. com. Harvard Grad. Sch. Edn., 1995—, vice chmn., 2003—, Harvard music dept.; bd. dirs., v.p. Royal Music Found., N.Y.C., 1978-90; trustee Bowdoin Coll. Summer Music Festival, Brunswick, Maine, 1978-88, L.I. Biol. Assn., Cold Spring Harbor, N.Y., 1986-88; mem. adv. bd. Harvard U. Com. on Environment, 2001—. Mem. Am. Nat. Stds. Inst. (nat. waterproofing stds. com. 1988—), Harvard Alumni Assn. (bd. dirs. 1990-93, nominating com. overseers and dirs., 2000-03), Harvard-Radcliffe Club L.I. (pres. 1988-90). Avocations: skiing, music, sports, ice hockey, travel. Home: 8 Seawanhaka Pl Oyster Bay NY 11771-1629 Office: Compotite Corp 355 Glendale Blvd Los Angeles CA 90026-5032

HUTCHINS, KAREN LESLIE, psychotherapist; b. Denver, Sept. 9, 1943; d. Kimball Frederick and Bonnie Illa (Small) H.; divorced; 1 child, Alec Klinghoffer. BA, U. Denver, 1965; MA, George Washington U., 1972. Lic. profl. counselor, chem. depencency counselor, registered sex offender treatment provider, Reiki master Shamanic healing, cert. Nat. Bd. Clin. Hypnotherapists. Tchr. Washington Schs., 1966-70; asst. housing adminstr. George Washington U., Washington, 1970-72; counselor/instr. No. Va. C.C., Annandale, 1972-77, Austin (Tex.) C.C., 1977-80; co-owner Hearts Day Care, Austin, 1980-81; supr./therapist MaryLee Resdl. Treatment, Austin, 1981-82; child protective svc. worker Dept. Human Resources, Austin, 1982-84; probation officer Adult Probation Travis County, Austin, 1984-90; lead therapist Cottonwood Treatment Ctrs., Bastrop, Tex., 1990-91; psychotherapist Austin, 1991—. Presenter at confs. Vol. trainer Hotline, Austin, 1993—. Mem.: ACA, Tex. Counselors Assn., Tex. Assn. Addiction Profls., Found. for Shamanic Studies, Internat. Soc. for Study of Dissociation, Internat. Soc. Trauma and Stress Studies. Democrat. Jewish. Avocations: sewing, bird watching, animal tending, making custom jewelry. Office: Cicada Recovery Svcs 3004 S 1st St Austin TX 78704-6388

HUTCHINS, PETER EDWARD, lawyer; b. Nashua, N.H., Jan. 20, 1958; s. Edward Peter and Joyce Martha Hutchins; m. Kathy Hutchins; 1 child, Jamie. BA cum laude, Dartmouth Coll., 1980; JD magna cum laude, Boston Coll., 1983. Bar: N.H. 1983, U.S. Dist. Ct. N.H. 1983. Ptnr. Wiggin & Nourie, P.A., Manchester, N.H., 1983-98, Hall & Hess, PA, Manchester, 1998—. Basketball referee, cert. Internat. Assn. Approved Basketball Officials, N.H., 1992—; girls softball umpire, cert. N.H. Softball Umpires Assn., 1994—. Mem. N.H. Bar Assn. (v.p., pres. 2001-02). Avocation: officiating high school sports. Office: Hall Stewart Murphy Brown & Hutchins 80 Merrimack St Manchester NH 03101

HUTCHINS, ROBERT AYER, architectural consultant; b. N.Y.C., Oct. 19, 1940; s. Robert Senger and Evelyn Reed (Brooks) Hutchins; m. Saran Niel Morgan, Jan. 4, 1964; children: Amey, Elisabeth, Margaret. BA, Harvard U., 1962, MArch, 1965; MDiv, McCormick Theol. Sem., 1992. Cert. Nat. Coun. Archtl. Registration Bds., 1976; registered architect, Ill. Architect Skidmore, Owings & Merrill, Chgo., 1966—89, ptnr., 1980—89. Pres. Chgo. Architecture Found., 1983—86, v.p., 1986—89. Mem. Protestants for the Common Good, 2000—02; v.p., bd. dirs. Lincoln Park Zool. Soc., Chgo., 1976—91; bd. govs. Met. Planning Coun., Chgo., 1977—; bd. trustees McCormick Theol. Sem., 1990—91. Mem.: AIA (corp.), Chgo. Presbytery Svc. Corps., Chgo. Cultural Affairs Adv. Bd. (vice chmn. 1984—90).

HUTCHINS, STEVEN EDWARD, plastics company executive, writer; b. Hillsdale, Mich., July 24, 1969; s. Loren E. and Janice C. Hutchins; m. Stephenie Beth Phelps; 1 child, Brianna Bricker. Student, Jackson C.C., 1993—96. Area coord. Teleflex Automotive, Hillsdale, Mich., 1988—97; prodn. supr. Collins & Aikman, St. Joseph, Mich., 1997—2000, Kalfact Plastics Co., Rockford, Mich., 2000—. Coord. Collins & Aikman, St. Joseph, Mich., 1997—2000. Author: (book) The Fish of a Thousand Casts: Tales of Mischief and Mayhem in the Great Outdoors, 2002; columnist: Woods N Water News, Midwest Outdoors. Vol. river watch Mich. Dept. of Natural Resources, Cadillac, 2001—. Avocation: fishing. Personal E-mail: thousandcasts@ameritech.net.

HUTCHINS, TRAVER, publishing executive; Former mgr., corp. sales Lang Commn.; CEO and founder MediZine, Inc., 1997—. Office: Medizine 298 Fifth Ave 2nd Fl New York NY 10001

HUTCHINS, WILLIAM BRUCE, III, utility company executive; b. Tuscaloosa, Ala., Jan. 28, 1943; s. William B. Jr. and Mildred Louise (Lemley) H.; m. Priscilla Nichols, Oct. 30, 1965; children: Frances, Christopher. BS in Acctg., U. Ala., 1966, MBA, 1978; postgrad., Harvard U., 1987. Cert. mgmt. acct. Jr. acct. Ala. Power Co., Birmingham, 1966-67, So. Co. Services, Inc., Atlanta, 1971-72; sr. acct. Ala. Power Co., Birmingham, 1972-74, asst. to comptroller, 1974-75, asst. to exec. v.p., 1975-76, mgr. fin. and rev. planning, 1976-80, gen. mgr. fin. planning, 1980-81, asst. treas., 1981-83, v.p., treas., 1983-91, sr. v.p., chief fin. officer, 1991-94, exec. v.p., CFO, 1994—. Served to capt. USAF, 1967-71. Mem. Beta Gamma Sigma, Beta Alpha Psi, Omicron Delta Epsilon. Office: Ala Power Co PO Box 2641 Birmingham AL 35291-0001

HUTCHINSON, ANN, management consultant; b. East Stroudsburg, Pa., May 15, 1950; d. David Ellis and Susie (Ingalls) Hutchinson; m. Paul Harrison McAllister, Jan. 2, 1986. BS in Vocat. Edn., Fla. Internat. U., 1985; MBA, Pepperdine U., 1990. Cert. advanced vocat. tchr. Fla., cmty. coll. educator Ariz., pub. mgr. Motorcycle technician, Ft. Lauderdale, Fla., 1973-78; machinist, 1978-79; instr., motorcycle tech. Sheridan Vocat. Tech. Sch., Hollywood, Fla., 1979-85; adminstr., tng. program Am. Honda Motorcycle Divsn., Torrance, Calif., 1985-86, curriculum developer motorcycles svc. tech., 1986-90, coll. program coord., 1990-94; ednl. devel. dir. Clinton Tech. Inst., Phoenix, 1994-96; dep. mgr. tng. unit Ariz. State Dept. Econ. Security, Phoenix, 1996-99, mgmt. cons. office of total quality, 1999-2001; instrnl. sys. specialist Bur. Land Mgmt. Nat. Tng. Ctr., 2001—. Adj. faculty Ariz. State U., 2001—; chmn. high tech. acad. steering com. Pasadena (Calif.) United Sch. Dist., 1991—94; ednl. cons. Ctr. for Occupation R & D Sch.-to-Work Awards, 1994—97; mem. cert. pub. mgr. program adv. bd. Ariz. State U., 1998—2001. Examiner Gov.'s Award for Excellence, 1997—99; mem. Ams. With Disabilities Act com. Ariz. Dept. Econ. Security, 1995—2001; mem. Desert Hill Improvement Assn., 1996—, bd. dirs., editor, 1998—99, v.p., 1999—2001, pres., 2001—; examiner Ariz. State Quality Awards, 1997—2002, mem. tech. integrity coun., 2003—. Recipient State of Ky. Col. award, 1990, Quality award examiner, Az. State, 1997—2002, Quality award tech. integrity coun., 2002—. Mem.: ASTD, Am. Vocat. Assn., Vocat. Indsl. Clubs Am. (co-chmn. motorcycle tech. com. 1988—90, 1994—95, automotive nat. tech. com. 1990—94, adv. Hollywood, Fla. 1979—85), Cert. Pub. Mgr. Assn., Am. Motorcycle Assn., Toastmasters Internat. (Zenger Miller cert. 1996—). Avocation: Avocations: hiking, camping, st. motorcycle riding. Office: Bur Land Mgmt Nat Tng Ctr Office Total Quality 9828 N 31 Ave Phoenix AZ 85051 E-mail: behomes@attglobal.net.

HUTCHINSON, ASA, federal agency administrator; b. Benton County, Ark., Dec. 3, 1950; m. Susan Burrell; children: Asa III, Sarah, John, Seth. BS in Acctg., Bob Jones U.; JD, U. Ark. Atty. U.S. Dist. Ct. (we. dist.) Ark., 1982-85; ptnr. Karr & Hutchinson, Ft. Smith, Ark., 1986-96; rep. Ark. 3rd dist. U.S. House of Reps., 1996—2001; adminr. drug enforcement admin. U.S. Dept. Justice, Washington, 2001—03; under sec. for border and transp. security dept. Homeland Security, Washington, 2003—. Judiciary com. U.S. Congress, subcom. crime, subcom. constitution, transp. and infrastructure com., subcom. Water Resources and Environment, subcom. aviation, intelligence com., ethics com., intellectual property subcom.; co-chair Freshmen Bipartisan Campaign Finance Reform Task Force; apptd. to Speakers Task Force for Drug-Free Am.; co-chmn., chmn. Rep. Ctrl. Com. of Ark., 1990-95; past mem. Ark. Jud. Ethics Commn., Ark. Election Commn., Ark. Election Law Revision Commn.; condr. democracy workshops in Russia, 1994; del. White House Conf. on Aging, 1995; past bd. mem. Western Ark. chpt. Alzheimer's Assn. Named one of Ten Outstanding Young Leaders in Ark., Ark. Jaycees, 1986. Republican. Office: Dept Homeland Security 3801 Nebraska Ave NW Washington DC 20016*

HUTCHINSON, BARBARA WINTER, elementary school educator; b. Pitts., Dec. 20, 1952; d. Raymond Francis and Dorothy (Kunkel) Winter; m. Matthew Hutchinson, June 8, 1973; children: Matthew Martin, Jennifer Elizabeth. BA, Westminster Coll., 1974. Cert. tchr., Pa. Tchr. Shaler Area Sch. Dist., Glenshaw, Pa., 1975-84, North Allegheny Sch. Dist., Pitts., 1984—, staff devel. leader, 1991—. Mem. dist. adv. coun., profl. issues com. North Allegheny Sch. Dist., Pitts., 1993—, mem. instrnl. responsibility com., 1996-98, total quality in edn. process com., 1996-98, quality improvement team, 1996-97, strategic planning com., 1999—, total quality steering com., 1999-2000, negotiating team, 1999-2000, mem. profl. edn. com., 1998—; mem. mid. sch. day com., 2001—; presenter coop. learning workshops. Author: Primary Assistance, 1979, History of the Avonworth School District, 1990; co-author curriculum materials. Mem. Cmty. Presbyn. Ch. Ben Avon, Pa., 1976—; pres., program dir. Ben Avon Area Hist. Assn., 1988-2003; bd. dirs., sec., program chair Avon Club Found., 1990-93; mem. Ben Avon Centennial Com., 1990-93; co-leader local troop Girl Scouts U.S., 1991-92; bd. dirs. Sacred Heart Sch., Pitts., 1991-92. Recipient Found. Excellence award, 1996, Citation for Tchg. Excellence, Pa. Ho. of Reps., Outstanding Secondary Social Studies Program of Yr. award Pa. Coun. Social Studies Tchrs., 2002. Mem. Am. Fedn. Tchrs., North Allegheny Fedn. Tchrs. (mem. exec. coun. 1992-96, treas. 1996-98, secondary v.p. 1998-99, 1st v.p. 1999-2000, pres. 2000—), Pa. Fedn. Tchrs., Phi Delta Kappa. Avocations: sewing, wood refinishing, reading, writing, home decorating. Home: 205 Hillvue Dr Seven Fields PA 16046 Office: Marshall Middle Sch 5145 Wexford Run Rd Wexford PA 15090-7458 E-mail: bhutchinson@northallegheny.org.

HUTCHINSON, CHARLES EDGAR, engineering educator; b. Parkersburg, W.Va., Dec. 18, 1935; s. Charles Edgar and Elizabeth Hana (Eggleton) H.; m. Elva Anneta Butland, Aug. 20, 1960; children: Charles Edgar IV, John Mathew. BEE, Ill. Inst. Tech., 1957; MEE, Stanford U., 1961, PhD, 1963. Instr. USN ROTC, 1959-60; tchg. asst. Stanford (Calif.) U., 1960-63; lectr. UCLA, 1963-65; assoc. prof. U. Mass., Amherst, 1965-69, prof., 1969-84, acting assoc. dean acad. affairs, 1977, acting assoc. dean research affairs, 1977-78, head dept. electrical and computer engring., 1978-82; prof., dean Thayer Sch. Engring. Dartmouth Coll., Hanover, NH, 1984-94, 97-98, John H. Krehbiel Sr. prof. for emerging technologies, 1994—2003, emeritus, 2003—. Lectr. Sch. Medicine, Boston U., 1971-72; cons. The Analytic Scis. Corp., Reading, Mass., 1967-98, Molex, Inc., 1988—, Baxter Health, 1992-2003, Tally Sys., Inc., 1997—; bd. dirs. Markem Corp., Keene, N.H., Hypertherm, Inc., Hanover, N.H., Med. Media Sys., Inc., Lebanon, N.H., Dilion Tech., Inc., Newport News, Va., Microchips, Cambridge, Mass. Lt. USN, 1957-60. Mem. IEEE (chmn. edn. com. 1983-86, bd. govs. profl. group on aerospace and electronic sys. 1983-86, profl. groups on automatic control and on computers), Am. Soc. Engring. Edn. (chmn. computers in edn. divsn. 1975-77, New Eng. sect. 1965—), Assn. for Media-Based Edn. for Engrs. (vice chmn. 1983, bd. dirs. 1980-84), Sigma Xi, Eta Kappa Nu (nat. bd. dirs. 1966-69, chmn. nat. publicity com. 1968-73, faculty advisor 1966-68, 74-76), Tau Beta Pi (profl. 1967). Republican. Avocations: horse showing, horse breeding. Home: 89 Apple Blossom Ln Canaan NH 03741 Office: Dartmouth Coll Thayer Sch Engring Hanover NH 03755

HUTCHINSON, CHARLES SMITH, JR., book publisher; b. Topeka, Oct. 17, 1930; s. Charles S. and Cecil Marguerite (Weidenhamer) H.; m. Elizabeth Dunbar Hall, June 16, 1956; children: Amy Elizabeth, Todd Charles. BA, Principia Coll., 1952. Editor-in-chief, sec., dir. Burgess Pub. Co., Mpls., 1955-65; editor-in-chief coll. and profl. books, dir. Reinhold Book Corp., N.Y.C., 1965-68; editor-in-chief profl. and reference books Van Nostrand Reinhold Co., N.Y.C., 1968-70; pres., chmn. bd. dirs. Dowden, Hutchinson and Ross, Inc., Stroudsburg, Pa., 1970-78, v.p., sec., 1978-80; v.p. Hutchinson Ross Pub. Co., Stroudsburg, 1980-83; sci. pub. Van Nostrand Reinhold Co., N.Y.C., 1984-86; mng. dir. Hutchinson Assocs., Prescott, Ariz., 1987-91; pres. Geosci. Press, Inc., Tucson, 1989—, Harbinger House, Inc., Tucson, 1992-94; mng. ptnr. Picacho Peak Press, L.L.C., Tucson, 1994-2001. Bd. dirs. Hist. Farms Assn., Stroudsburg, 1980-86, pres., 1985-86; treas. Stroudsburg chpt. Kiwanis, 1977-78, v.p., 1978-80, pres., 1980-81. Recipient NuJay award Mpls. Jaycees, 1957, Disting. Pres. award Kiwanis, 1981. Fellow Geol. Soc. Am.; mem. Pub. Assn. of the West, Soc. Southwestern Authors (bd. dirs. 2000-01). Home: 5520 N Camino Arenosa Tucson AZ 85718-5416

HUTCHINSON, CRAIG LEWIS, internist; b. Cin. BS, U. Wis., 1976; MD, Med. Coll. Wis., 1980. Diplomate internal medicine and infectious disease Am. Bd. Internal Medicine. Resident in internal medicine Mich. State U., East Lansing, 1980-83; regional med. dir. Mich. Dept. Corrections, Lansing, 1983-97; fellow in infectious disease U. South Fla., Tampa, 1997-99; Mich. med. dir. Correctional Med. Svcs., Lansing, 1999—. Fellow Am. Coll. Physicians. Office: Correctional Med Svcs 2378 Woodlake Dr Ste 280 Okemos MI 48864-6016 E-mail: chutchinson@cmsstl.com.

HUTCHINSON, DAVID MICHAEL, economist; b. Washington, Feb. 11, 1944; s. Edmond Carlton Hutchinson; m. Helen Kwok-Wai Ho, Jan. 30, 1988; children: Michael Breton, Elena Michelle. BA in Econ., Southwestern U., 1964; postgrad, Fgn Svc. Sch. Econ., 1974-75; MA in Econ., George Washington U., 1979. Sys. analyst Brown Engring. Co., Huntsville, Ala., 1964-65; internat. economist Office East West Trade U.S. Dept. State, Washington, 1967-69, program officer Office Export Adminstrn., 1970-77; dep. dir. Market Expansion Divsn. Office Textiles & Apparel U.S. Dept. Commerce, Washington, 1980-88, spl. asst. to dep. asst. sec. textile Apparel Consumer Goods, 1988-95, acting dep. asst. sec. Textiles Apparel Consumer Goods, 1995, 2000—02, dir. Office Textiles Apparel, 1995—, mem. Sr. Exec. Svc., 2002—. With USAR, 1966-72. Avocations: computers, piano, guitar, squash, reading. Home: 9100 Town Gate Ln Bethesda MD 20817-4113

HUTCHINSON, DENNIS JAMES, law educator; b. Boulder, Colo., Dec. 28, 1946; s. Dudley Isom and Jane Wilcox (Sampson) H.; children: Kathryn Wood, David, Jane. Office: U Chgo Law Sch 1111 E 60th St Chicago IL 60637-2776 E-mail: dhutch@law.uchicago.edu.

HUTCHINSON, ELAINE FRANCES, secondary education educator; b. Nanticoke, Pa., Jan. 9, 1938; d. William Henry and Frances Elizabeth (Redwood) H. BS, East Stroudsburg U., 1959; MEd, West Chester U., 1971. Sci., history and humanities classroom tchr. Phoenixville (Pa.) Area Sch. Dist., 1959-97; ret., 1997. Author ednl. activities, curriculum in field. Sec. Booster Club, Phoenixville, 1992—95; active Home and Sch. Assn., Phoenixville, 1992—97; bd. dirs. Stepping Stones Pre-Sch.; vol., interpretive guide Nat. Pk. Svc., 1997—; coord. Phoenixville CROP Walk, 1997—. Named Outstanding Leader in Secondary Edn., 1976, Outstanding Sci. Tchr., Jaycettes, 1984; recipient Mayor's Spl. award, 2000. Mem.: NEA (ret.), Phoenixville Area Edn. Assn. (past pres.), Pa. State Edn. Assn. (ret.), Nat. Sci. Tchrs. Assn., Delta Kappa Gamma (rec. sec. 1994—98, past pres., Alpha Alpha State Album of Distinction 2002), Bus. and Profl. Women's Club (membership chmn. 1991—94, past pres.), Kiwanis. Baptist. Avocations: travel, photography, reading, flower arranging, ecology.

HUTCHINSON, JANET LOIS, historical society administrator; b. Washington, May 2, 1917; d. Lewis Orrin and Gertrude Elizabeth Hutchinson; divorced; 1 child, Jefferson Troy Siebert. Grad., So. Sem. and Jr. Coll., Buena Vista, Va., 1936; student, N.Y. Sch. Expression, 1923-30, Christine Dobbins Sch. Dance; studied with, Maude Adams, Clare Tree Major, 1934-35. Owner Broadlawn Inn Art Gallery, Camden, Maine, 1955-64; dir. Old Merchants House Mus., N.Y.C., 1962-63, Hist. Soc. Martin County, Stuart, Fla., 1965-91, Elliott Mus., Stuart, 1965-91, House of Refuge Mus., Stuart, 1965-91, dir. emeritus, 1991—; pres., editl. cons. Hutchinson/Paige, Stuart, 1991—. Editl. cons. History of East Stuart, Fla. Author: Tiny Timid's Christmas Wish, 1953, The History of Martin County, 1975; editor: History of East Stuart Florida, 1999; host: (TV interview show) Chronicle. Active Nat. Hist. Preservation Soc., Nat. History Soc., Fla. History Soc.; bd. dirs. Pioneer Occupationa Ctr. for Handicapped, St. Michael's Pvt. Sch.; adv. bd. St. Joseph's Coll. and Fla. Inst. of Tech. Named Woman of Yr., AAUW, 1975. Fellow: Nat. Arts Club; mem.: DAR (Halpatiokee chpt.), Nat. Soc. Lit. and Arts, Nat. Pen Women (hon.), Smithsonian Instn., Antique Car Assn., Salmagundi Club. Home: 1023 NW Spruce Ridge Dr Stuart FL 34994-9513

HUTCHINSON, JANIS FAYE, humanities educator, researcher; d. James and Alice Rose Hutchinson. BA, U. Ala., Tuscaloosa, 1975; M in Anthropology, U. Ala., 1980; PhD, U. Kans., 1984; MPH, U. Tex., Houston, 1997. Asst. prof. Wichita (Kans.) State U., 1983—84; prof. U. Houston, 1984—. Dir. African Am. studies U. Houston, 2001—02. Author: Cultural Portrayals of African Americans; contbr. articles to profl. jours. Chair HIV Outreach and Prevention Edn., Houston, 2000—02. Recipient Visionaries of Excellence award, Nat. Women Achievers, Houston, 1996. Mem.: Assn. Black Anthropologists (pres. 1997—99), Am. Anthrop. Assn. (adv. bd. 2001—02). Avocations: travel, museums, music. Office: U Houston 4800 Calhoun St Houston TX 77204-5020 Fax: 713-743-4287. E-mail: jhutchinson@uh.edu.

HUTCHINSON, JOHN WOODSIDE, mechanical engineer, educator; b. Hartford, Conn., Apr. 10, 1939; s. John Woodside and Evelyn (Eastburn) Hutchinson; m. Lizzi Spanggaard; children: Leif, David, Robert. BS, Lehigh U., 1960; MS, Harvard U., 1961, PhD, 1963; DSc (hon.), Royal Inst. Tech., Stockholm, 1985, Tech. U. Denmark, Lyngby, 1992, Northwestern U., Evanston, 2002. Asst. prof. Harvard U., Cambridge, Mass., 1964-69, Gordon McKay prof. applied mechanics, 1969—. Contbr. articles to profl. jours. Fellow, Guggenheim Found., 1974. Fellow: ASME (Araprd L. Nadai award 1991, Timoshenko medal 2002); mem.: NAS, NAE, ASTM (Irwin medal 1982), AAAS. E-mail: hutchinson@husm.harvard.edu.

HUTCHINSON, LESLIE JULIAN, preventive medicine physician; b. Cin., June 22, 1957; s. Joseph Edward and Evelyn (Moss) H.; m. Stephanie Ellyn Leffingwell, Dec. 22, 1989. BS, Xavier U., 1978; MD, U. Cin. Coll. of Medicine, 1984; MPH, The Johns Hopkins U., 1990. Diplomate Am. Bd. Preventive Medicine Specialist in Occupl. Medicine; MD, Calif., Ga.; registered hazardous substances profl. Chemist EPA, Cin., 1982; Ctrs. for Disease Control vis. program staff fellowship Nat. Inst. for Occupl. Safety and Health, Cin., 1984; resident in internal medicine Wright State U., Dayton, Ohio, 1984-85; med. officer Agy. for Toxic Substances and Disease Registry, Atlanta, 1986-92; occupl. medicine resident Emory U., Atlanta, 1992-93; adj. assoc. prof. environ. and occupl. health Emory U. Sch. Pub. Health, Atlanta, 1990—; pres. HLM Consultants, Atlanta, 1993—. On-site peer reviewer Tex. Air Control Bd., Galveston, 1987-88; mem. Emory U. Acad. Adv. Coun. on Occupl. and Environ. Health, Atlanta, 1989—; v.p., chief med. officer Internat. Inst. Environ. Risk Mgmt., U. S.W. Tex., San Marcos, 1997—. Contbr. articles to profl. jours. Instr. med. coll. admission text preparation program for minority students Atlanta U., 1987-90. Recipient Performance Mgmt. and Recognition System award Dept. Health and Human Svcs., 1989, Spl. Act or Svc. award Dept. of Health and Human Svcs., 1992, Xavier U. Achievement and Nat. Merit scholarships, Xavier Biology prize. Fellow Am. Coll. Occupl. and Environ. Medicine; mem. Nat. Environ. Health Assn., Delta Omega, Alpha Omega Alpha, Sigma Pi Sigma. Avocations: photography, oriental philosophy. Office: HLM Consultants 214 Wynfield Way Auburn GA 30011-2849 E-mail: hlm@mindspring.com.

HUTCHINSON, LYNDA RONETTE (BILLIE HOLIDAY JR., PRINCESS OF JAZZ, MUNCHIE), vocalist, musician, comedian; b. Queens, NY, Dec. 28, 1965; d. Roy Radcliff and Rachel Isabella (Outten) Hutchinson; children: Myisha Daunique Odom, Zaire chase Arzelle. At, LI U., Bklyn., 1991—96. Founder, CEO Diva Soul Records, 2003—. Singer: (performer) Empire Tech. Sch., 1989, LI U., 1991, Two Steps Down Jazz Club, 1992—94, Titus Walker's Ujjaama Black Theatre, 1991, Apollo Theatre, 2000, 2001, Lenox Lounge Jazz Club, 2002—, Cotton Club, 2002—, St. Nick's Pub, 2000—, (contestant) Showtime at the Apollo, 1994, Sylvia's 30 Anniversary, 1993, performer radio; author: (book of poetry) Lend Me Your Ear, 1992. Participant Nat. Action Network Freedom March, 1993. Finalist N.Y.C. Housing Authority Talent Search, 1998; recipient Cert. Achievement, Internat. Mannequins, Inc., 1995, Certification award, Project Enterprise, 2002, Mel Edwards award, 2003. Mem.: Harlem Arts Alliance, New Amsterdam Musical Assn. Home: Apt 16-G 2370 First Ave New York NY 10035

HUTCHINSON, MARK ROBERT, orthopaedic surgeon; s. Jack E. and Alice Marie Hutchinson; m. Susan Gusich, Apr. 8, 1989; children: Michael, Allison. BS, U. of Ill., 1979, MD, 1987. Cert. Am. Bd. of Orthopaedic Surgeons N.C., 1993. Dir. sports medicine U. of Ill., 1993, assoc. prof. orthop. and sports medicine, 1993. Founder Chgo. Sports Medicine Soc., 1994; fellow Am. Coll. of Sports Medicine, 1995, bd. trustees, 2002—; fellow Ky. Sports Medicine, Lexington, Ky., 1992—93, Am. Acad. of Orthop. Surgeons, Rosemont, Ill., 1995; head team physician USA Gymnastics, Indpls., 1995—2000; master instr. Arthroscopy Assn. of North Am., Rosemont, Ill., 1998; treas. Ill. Assn. of Orthop. Surgeons, Chgo., 2002—. Author chpts. and profl. pubs. Mem. Am. Coll. of Sports Medicine, Indpls., 2002—; pres. Chgo. Sports Medicine Soc., 1994. Pan Pacific Traveling Fellowship, Am. Orthop. Soc. for Sports Medicine, 2002. Fellow: Am. Acad. of Orthop. Surgeons, Am. Coll. of Sports Medicine; mem.: U.S.A. Gymnastics, Ill. Assn. of Orthop. Surgeons (treas.), Chgo. Sports Medicine Soc. (pres., v.p., treas.), Am. Orthop. Soc. for Sports Medicine, Arthroscopy Assn. of North Am. Office: 209 Med Scis South 839 South Wolcott Chicago IL 60612 Home Fax: 312-996-9025; Office Fax: 312-996-9025. Personal E-mail: mhutch@uic.edu. E-mail: mhutch@uic.edu.

HUTCHINSON, MICHAEL CLARK, lawyer; b. Quincy, Mass., Feb. 25, 1953; s. William Thomas and Marguerite J. (Gunning) H. BA cum laude, Bowdoin Coll., 1975; JD cum laude, Suffolk U., 1979. Bar: Minn. 1980, U.s. Dist. Ct. Minn. 1980. Law clk. 7th Jud. Dist. Ct., Moorhead, Minn., 1979-81; asst. county atty. Clay County Atty.'s Office, Moorhead, Minn., 1981-83; assoc. Clinton & O'Gorman P.A., Cottage Grove, Minn., 1983-90; asst. county atty. Washington County Atty.'s Office, Stillwater, Minn., 1990—. Mem. Minn. State Bar Assn., Washington County Bar Assn., Lions Club (pres. local club 1989-90). Roman Catholic. Office: Washington County Atty Office PO Box 6 Stillwater MN 55082-0006 E-mail: Mike.Hutchinson@co.washington.mn.us .

HUTCHINSON, PARK WILLIAM, JR., theatre educator; b. Lancaster, Pa., Apr. 14, 1935; s. Park William and Thelma Mae (Beam) H.; m. Patsy Ann Flory, Aug. 15, 1955 (div. May 1981); 1 child, Suzanne Flory Hutchinson; m. Jeri Ann McElroy, Sept. 18, 1982. BA, Franklin Marshall Coll., 1957; BD, Princeton Theol. Sem., 1960; MA, Columbia U., 1962; PhD, Northwestern U., 1968. Instr. Tougaloo (Miss.) Coll., 1962-64, asst. prof., 1964-65, dir. speech & theater, 1962-65; asst. prof. theatre R.I. Coll., Providence, 1968-71, assoc. prof., 1971-74, prof., 1974—, coord. grad. theatre programs, 1982—, chair dept. theater and dance, 1996-98, chair dept. music theater and dance, 1998-2001. Dir. dance & drama Mathewson St. United Meth. Ch., Providence, 1969-75; dir. R.I. Gov.'s Sch. for Youth in the Arts, Providence, 1970-72; art. dir. NewGate Theatre, Providence, 1991-92. Dir. over 100 plays and readings, 1957—. Mem. exec. bd. R.I. Festival Theatre, Providence, 1971, Coll. of Fellows, New Eng. Theatre Conf., Boston, 1987—; theatre coord. R.I. Arts in Edn. Project, Providence, 1970-72. Danforth Found. fellow, 1965-66, 67-68; grantee R.I. Com. for Humanities, 1975—, R.I. Coun. Arts, 1978—; recipient Trinity Rep Pell award for disting. svc. to the arts, 2003. Mem. Assn. Theatre in Higher Edn., Phi Beta Kappa. Avocations: hist. portrayals: Jefferson, Thoreau, Wilde, Poe, Darrow, etc. Home: 7 Wadsworth Ave Smithfield RI 02917-4109 Office: RI Coll 600 Mount Pleasant Ave Providence RI 02908-1924

HUTCHINSON, PETER ARTHUR, artist; b. London, Mar. 4, 1930; s. Arthur William Woodhams and Linda Mary Woodhams (West) Hutchinson. BFA, U. Ill., 1960. Author art books; contbr. articles, short stories to profl. publs.; one-man shows include John Gibson Gallery, N.Y.C., 1990, James Mayor Gallery, London, 1996, Galerie Damasquine, Brussels, 1997, Galerie Bugdahn und Kaimer, Düsseldorf, Germany, 1998, Galerie Helga De Alvear, Madrid, 1998, Kunstverein, Ulm, Germany, 1998, Holly Solomon Gallery, 1998, Biennale De France, Lyon, 1998, Galerie Lucien-Durand, Paris, 1999, Galerie Blancpain/Stepczynski, Geneva, 2001, Lance Fung Gallery, N.Y.C., 2002; exhibited in group shows including Mus. Modern Art, N.Y.C., 1969, Acad. Art, Berlin, 1988, Herter Gallery, U. Mass. Traveling Exhbn., 1989, Torch Gallery, Amsterdam, 1998. Mem. visual arts com. Fine Arts Work Ctr., Provincetown, Mass., 1979-85, 88-89. Fellow Aspen Ctr. for Arts, 1970-71, NEA, 1974, D.A.A.D., Berlin, 1988; grantee Adolph and Esther Gottlieb Found., 1987, Krasner-Pollack Found., 1989. Mem. Am. Rock Garden Club. Avocations: botany, history, biology, horticulture. Home: 10 Holway Ave Provincetown MA 02657-1327 E-mail: hutchinson2@capecod.net.

HUTCHINSON, ROBERT JOSEPH, writer; b. Tacoma, Wash., Nov. 12, 1957; s. A'lan Stanton and Mary Jane Hutchinson; m. Glenn Ellen Duncan, Jan. 6, 1990; children: Robert John, James Timothy, William Kelly, Mary Helen, Jane Anne. BA in Philosophy, Seattle U., 1981. Hawaii bur. chief The Hollywood (Calif.) Reporter, 1986-88; mng. editor Hawaii Mag., Irvine, Calif., 1988-90. Author: The Absolute Beginner's Guide to Gambling, 1996, When in Rome: A Journal of Life in Vatican City, 1998; editor: The Book of Vices, 1995. Roman Catholic. Avocations: Aikido, skiing, squash.

HUTCHINSON, THOMAS CUTHBERT, ecology and environmental educator; b. Sunderland, Eng., Feb. 18, 1939; emigrated to Can., 1967; s. Walter and Margaret Amelia (Bell) H.; s. Vivien Coyne, Sept. 8, 1961 (div. 1981); 1 dau., Sally Louise; m. Magda Havas, 1982. BS with honors in Botany, Manchester (Eng.) U., 1960; PhD in Ecology, Sheffield (Eng.) U., 1966. Sir James Knott fellow Newcastle (Eng.) U., 1964-67; asst. prof. dept. botany Toronto U., 1967-71, assoc. prof., 1971-74, prof., 1974-90, chmn. dept., 1976-82; assoc. dir. Inst. Environ. Scis., U. Toronto, 1974-76; prof. faculty of forestry U. Toronto, 1978-90; prof., chair environ. and resource study Trent U., Petersborough, Ont., 1991-94, prof. environ. resource studies program Petersburg, 1994—. Chmn. com. environ. quality criteria NRC Can.; dir. Oliver Ecol. Ctr., Trent U., 1999—. Co-author: Environmental Consequences of Nuclear War, 1986; editor: Heavy Metals in Environment, 1977, Acid Rain Effects on Forests, Crops and Wetlands, 1987; co-editor: Acid Rain Effects on Vegetation, 1980; editor: Environ. Revs., 1990—; assoc. editor : Jour. Applied Ecology, —, Ecotoxicology, —, Environ. Pollution, —, Environ. Health, —; contbr. articles. Mem. Royal Agrl. Winter Fair Ont. Com., 1992—. Recipient Faculty Alumni award U. Toronto, 1984, Civic medal City of Toronto, 1991. Fellow Royal Soc. Can. (Miroslaw Romanowski medal 1998), Explorers Club; mem. Am. Agronomy Soc., Coun. of Nat. Scis. and Engring. Rsch. (pres. 1994—), Can. Bot. Assn. (George Lawson medal 1982, Trent faculty rsch. award 1998), Am. Ecol. Soc., Brit. Ecol. Soc., Arctic Inst. N.Am., Rare Breeds Can. (bd. dirs. 1992—), Can. Cotswold Longwool Assn. (sec.-treas. 1993—). Home: RR # 2 Indian River ON Canada K0L 7B8 Office: Trent U Environ Resource 1600 W Bank Dr Peterborough ON Canada K9J 7B8 E-mail: THutchinson@trentu.ca.

HUTCHINSON, TIM, former senator; b. Bentonville, Ark., 1949; children: Jeremy, Tim, Joshua. MA in Polit. Sci., U. Ark. Co-owner, mgr. Sta. KBCV-FM, 1982-89; mem. 94th-98th Congresses from Ark., 1984-88, 106th Congress from 3rd Ark. dist., 1993; senator from Ark. U.S. Senate, 1997—2003; sr. advisor Dickstein, Shapiro, Morin, & Oshinsky, Washington, 2003—. Instr. history John Brown U., Siloam Springs, Ark.; mem. U.S. Senate armed svcs. com., health, edn., labor and pensions, com., vets.' affairs com., spl. subcom. on aging. Active Northwest Ark. C.C. Found. Named rep. of Yr. Ark. Fraternal Order Police, 1988, 90, Ark. Assn. of Chiefs of Police, 1990, 91. Mem. Bentonville Bella Vista C. of C., Bentonville Kiwanis Club. Republican. Baptist. Office: 2101 C St NW Washington DE 20037*

HUTCHISON, ANDREW SANDFORD, archbishop; LTh, Trinity Coll., 1969, DD (hon.), 1994, Monteal Diocesan Theol. Coll., 1993; DCL (hon.), Bishops U., 2003, DCL (hon.). Ordained deacon, priest, bishop. Asst. curate Christ Ch., Toronto, 1969; rector Parish of Minden, Haliburton Highlands, Ont., Can., 1970-74, St. Francis Ch., Toronto, 1974-81, St. Luke Ch. East York, Toronto, 1981-84; rector, dean Christ Ch. Cathedral, Montreal, 1984-90; bishop Diocese of Montreal, 1990—; bishop ordinary Can. Forces, Ottawa, 1997—; archbishop Montreal and Met. Ecclesiastical Province Can., 2002—. Pres. Montreal Diocesan Theol. Coll.; vis. Bishop's U., Lennoxville; bd. govs. Lakefield Coll., Ontario, 1994-97. Mem. Christian Ch. Office: Montreal Diocese 1444 Union Ave Montreal QC Canada H3A 2B8

HUTCHISON, BARBARA BAILEY, singer, songwriter; Recipient Grammy award for Best Musical Album for Children "Sleepy Time Lullabyes", 1996. Home: 7261 Kingston Rd Fairview TN 37062-8251 E-mail: barbara@bbhsings.com.

HUTCHISON, CHARLOTTE PANCOAST (SHERRY HUTCHISON), civic worker; b. Phila., Jan. 13, 1919; d. Charles Snowden and Minnie Loretta (Percell) P.; m. Lawrence O. Hutchison, May 18, 1945 (dec. Mar. 1988); children: Perry, Lawrence. AB, Bryn Mawr Coll., 1940. Mem. pers. com. Friends Com. on Nat. Legislation, 1994-2000. Contbr. poetry to Saturday Evening Post, 1943-45. Newsletter editor Women's Internat. League for Peace and Freedom, Des Moines, 1981—89; Iowa com. Am. Friends Svc. Com., 1977—93; joint oversight com. Iowa Peace Network, Des Moines, 1976—2002; newsletter editor Des Moines Valley Friends Meeting, 1971—; discipline rev. com. Iowa Yearly Meeting of Friends, 1989—96, 2002—; platform com. Polk County Dist. and State Dem. Party, 1972—88, 1998, 2000, 2002. Recipient Woman of Achievement award Greater Des Moines YWCA, 1990, Dorothy Towne award Iowa Coun. for Internat. Understanding, 1999. Mem. Amnesty Internat. (case coord. 1986-94), LWV, Nat. Soc. Colonial Dames (v.p. Des Moines Borough 1991-92). Mem. Soc. Of Friends. Avocations: photography, writing for newsletters. Home: 1328 Birch Ln Des Moines IA 50315-3020

HUTCHISON, CLAUDE B., JR., federal agency administrator; Grad., U. Calif., Berkeley; MBA, Harvard U. Chmn. Smith and Crowley Inc.; mng. dir. strategic mktg. group LEGC, Inc.; dir. Office Asset Enterprise Mgmt. Dept. Vets. Affairs, Washington, 2001—. Served with USNR. Office: US Dept Vets Affairs Mgmt 810 Vermont Ave NW Washington DC 20420

HUTCHISON, DEBORAH L. critical care nurse; b. Manhattan, Kans., Jan. 8, 1953; d. Patrick J. Sr. and Charlene S. (Baughman) Donnellan; m. James C. Hutchison III, Aug. 7, 1981; children: Todd, Jason, Tommy, Cynthia, Susan, Melissa. Diploma, St. John's Sch. Nursing, 1989; BS in Psychology cum laude, S.W. Mo. State U., 1983, MS in Biology, 1986. RN; cert. critical care. Grad. teaching asst. S.W. Mo. State U., Springfield; burn technician St. John's Hosp., Springfield, 1989-90, nurse, surg. intensive care unit, 1990—. Mem. ACLS, Am. Assn. Critical Care Nurses.

HUTCHISON, DORRIS JEANNETTE, retired microbiologist, educator; b. Carrsville, Ky., Oct. 31, 1918; d. John W. and Maud (Short) H. BS, Western Ky. State Coll., 1940; MS, U. Ky., 1943; PhD, Rutgers U., 1949. Instr. Russell Sage Coll., 1942-44, Vassar Coll., 1944-46; research asst. Rutgers U., 1946-48, research assoc., 1948-49; instr. Wellesley Coll., 1949-51; asst. Sloan-Kettering Inst., N.Y.C., 1951-56, assoc., 1956-60, assoc. mem., 1960-69, mem., 1969-90, mem. emeritus, 1990—, sect. head, 1956-90, acting chief div. exptl. chemotherapy, 1965-66, div. chief drug resistance, 1967-72, co-head lab. exptl. tumor therapy, 1973-74, lab. head drug resistance and cyto-regulation, 1973-84, coordinator field edn., 1975-81. Instr. Sloan-Kettering div. Cornell U. Grad. Sch. Med. Sci., N.Y.C., 1952-53, rsch. assoc., 1953-54, asst. prof., 1954-58, assoc. prof., 1958-70, prof. microbiology, 1970-90, prof. emeritus, 1990—, chmn. biology unit, 1968-74, assoc. dir., 1974-87; assoc. dean Cornell U. Grad. Sch. Med. Sci., 1978-87, asst. dean Cornell U., Ithaca, 1978-87; mem. Meml. Sloan-Kettering Cancer Ctr., 1984-90, mem. emeritus, 1990—; del. dir. Am. Cancer Soc., Inc., 1986-90. Bd. dirs. Westchester div. Am. Cancer Soc., 1976-90, exec. com., 1976-91; project chmn. Target 5, 1977-80, v.p., 1979-81, pres., 1981-83, sec., 1983-87, charter mem. So. Westchester Unit, 1984, pres., 1984-86. Named to Order of Ky. Cols., 1988; recipient Disting. Alumna, Western Ky. U., 2003; faculty fellow, Vassar Coll., 1946, USPHS fellow, 1951—53, Phillippe Found. fellow, Paris, 1959, Doris J. Hutchison fellowship established in her honor, 1999. Fellow N.Y. Acad. Sci., Am. Acad. Microbiology (charter), N.Y. Acad. Medicine (assoc.); mem. AAAS, Am. Assn. for Cancer Edn., Am. Assn. Cancer Research (emeritus), Harvey Soc., Genetics Soc. Am., Am. Inst. Nutrition, Am. Soc. for Microbiology (hon., councilor N.Y.C. br. 1954-58, pres. N.Y.C. br. 1958-60, nat. councilor 1961-63, chmn. nat. meeting 1967, mem. pres.'s fellowship com. 1973-76, chmn. 1975-76), Soc. for Cryobiology (hon. mem.), Am. Genetic Assn., Internat. Soc. Biochem. Pharmacology, N.Y. Soc. Ky. Women (pres. 1988—), N.Y. Found. Ky. Women (pres. 1990-2000), Bronxville Field Club, Elizabeth Hamilton Cullem Svc. Club, 2000—. Achievements include numerous publs. antibiotics and chems. effective in treatment of Tb and leukemia, reports on mechanisms explaining how leukemic cells become resistant to treatment; searches for more effective antileukemia drugs. Home: Southgate Bronxville NY 10708 *Achieving goals and providing support and guidance to others, who also wished to become contributors to the well-being of mankind, have been prime concerns to me. The slings and arrows during this time have been totally offset by the personal satisfaction felt as a result of our intangible and tangible achievements.*

HUTCHISON, ELIZABETH DORAN, social worker, educator; b. White County, Tenn., Feb. 24, 1945; d. James Marion and Beulah Mae (Manus) Doran; m. David Paul Hutchison, Aug. 31, 1968; children: Bradford, Abigail. BA in Sociology, Maryville Coll., 1967; MSW, Washington U., St. Louis, 1969; PhD in Social Welfare, SUNY, Albany, 1988. Social worker Barnes Hosp., St. Louis, 1969-72; screening social worker Jewish Hosp., St. Louis, 1972-73; cons. Holyoke (Mass.) Nursing Home, 1975-77, Mpcl. Nursing Home, Holyoke, 1976-77; social worker Belchertown (Mass.) State Sch., 1977; cons., educator Franklin/Hampshire CMHC, Northampton, Mass., 1977-80; asst. prof. Elms Coll., Chicopee, Mass., 1980-87, Va. Commonwealth U., Richmond, 1987—. Author: Dimensions of Human Behavior, 2d edit., 2003; contbr. articles to profl. jours. Vol. Parents Anonymous, Richmond, 1990. Mem. NASW, Coun. Social Work Edn. Democrat. Avocation: walking. Office: Va Commonwealth Univ Sch Social Work 6295 Edsall Rd Alexandria VA 22312

HUTCHISON, JANE CAMPBELL, art history educator, researcher; b. Washington, July 20, 1932; d. James Paul and Leone Bailey (Warrick) H. BA fine arts, Western Maryland Coll., 1954; MA art history, Oberlin Coll., 1958; PhD art history, U. Wis., 1964. Tech. illustrator/ Dept. Model Basin U.S. Navy, Washington, 1954-56; rsch libr. Toledo Mus. of Art, 1957-59; teaching asst. U. Wis., Madison, 1959-60,61-63; vis. asst. prof. Temple U., Phila., summer 1968; from instr. to assoc. prof. U. Wis., Madison, 1964—, prof., 1975—, dept. chmn., 1977-80, 92-93. Expert witness U.S. Dist. Ct. (so. dist.) N.Y., 2000; cons. in field. Author: Master of the Housebook, 1972, Early German Artists, vol. 8, 1980, vol. 9, 1981, vol. 9 part 2, 1991, vol. 8 part 6, 1996, Albrecht Dürer: A Biography, 1990 (German edit., 1994), Albrecht Durer: A Guide to Research, 2000; mem. editl. bd. Studies in Iconography, 1997—, Source, 2003, Sixteenth Century Jour., 2003. Pres. Madison chpt. AAUP, 1979-81, Midwest Art History Soc., 1983-85, treas., 2001—; sec.-treas. Historians of Netherlandish Art, 1995-99; pres. St. Andrew's Soc. Madison, 1995—; mem. spl. com. on arts funding Wis. State Legis. Coun., 2000-01. Grad. fellow Oberlin Coll., 1955-57, fellow U. Wis., 1959-60, 61-63, Fulbright fellow Rijksuniversiteit Utrecht, Netherlands, 1960-61, rsch. grantee NEH, Germany, 1982, German Acad. Exch. Svc., Germany, summer 1989; Grant in aid Am. Coun. Learned Soc., Amsterdam, 1984; recipient Alumni award Western Md. Coll. Trustees, 1987. Mem. AAUP (pres. Madison chpt. 1979-81), Internat. Coun. Mus., Am. Assn. Mus., Medieval Acad. Am., Coll. Art Assn., Univ. Club U. Wis. (bd. dirs. 1976-80, pres. 1980), Wis. Assn. Scholars (v.p. Madison chpt. 1990-95), Midwest Art History Soc. (pres. 1983-85, treas. 2001--), Historians of Netherlandish Art (treas. 1995-99), Print Coun. Am., Wis. Acad. Scis., Arts and Letters, Minerva Soc. Home: 2261 Regent St Madison WI 53705-5321 Office: U Wis Dept Art History 800 University Ave Madison WI 53706-1414 E-mail: jchutchi@facstaff.wisc.edu.

HUTCHISON, KAY BAILEY, senator; b. Galveston, TX, July 22, 1943; d. Allan and Kathryn Bailey; m. Ray Hutchison. BA, U. Tex., 1992, LLB, 1967. Bar: Tex. 1967. TV news reporter, Houston, 1969-71; pvt. practice law, 1969-74; press sec. to Anne Armstrong Rep. Nat. Com., 1971; vice-chair Nat. Transp. Safety Bd., 1976-78; asst. prof. U. Tex., Dallas, 1978-79; sr. v.p., gen. counsel Republic Bank Corp., Dallas, 1979-81; pntr. Boyd-Levinson, Ltd., Houston and Dallas, 1981-91; mem. Tex. Ho. of Reps., 1972-76; elected treas. State of Tex., 1990; U.S. senator from Tex. Washington, 1993—; mem. appropriations com., commerce, sci. and transp. com., environment and pub. works com., rules and adminstrn. com. Mem., chmn. Military Constrn. Subcom., commerce, sci. and transp. com. (chmn. Aviation subcom.), enciron-ment and pub. works com., rules and adminstrn. com.; chmn., bd. visitors, US Military Acad. at West Point, US Delegate to Commn. on Security and Cooperation in Europe (The Helsinki Commn.); owner McCraw Candies; co-founder Fidelity Nat. Bank. Recipient Eagle award valued commitment to our nation's Hispanic Cmty., 1993; named Rep. Woman of Yr. Nat. Fedn. Rep. Women, 1995, Outstanding U. Tex. Alumnus, 1995, Texan of Yr. Tex. Legis. Conf., 1997; named to Tex. Women's Hall of Fame, 1997. Fellow, U. Tex. Law Alumni Assn. (pres. 1985-86). Republican.*

HUTCHISON, STANLEY PHILIP, retired lawyer; b. Joliet, Ill., Nov. 22, 1923; s. Stuart Philip and Verna (Kinzer) H.; m. Helen Jane Rush, July 25, 1945; children: Norman, Elizabeth. BS, Northwestern U., 1947; LLB, Ill. Inst. Tech., 1951. Bar: Ill. 1951. Legal asst. Washington Nat. Ins. Co., Evanston, 1947-51, asst. counsel, 1951-55, asst. gen. counsel, 1955-58, assoc. gen. counsel, 1958-60, gen. counsel, 1960-63, v.p., gen. counsel, dir., 1963-66, exec. v.p., gen. counsel, dir., 1966-67, exec. v.p., gen. counsel, sec., dir., 1967-70, chmn. exec. com., 1970-73, vice-chmn. bd., 1974-75, chmn. bd., CEO, 1976-88; pres. Wash. Nat. Corp., 1970-83, CEO, 1978-88, chmn. bd., 1983-88; ret., 1988-98. Bd. dirs. Washington Nat. Corp. Pres.'s coun. Nat. Coll. Edn., 1977-88, adv. coun. Kellogg Grad. Sch. Mgmt. Northwestern U., 1981-88; bd. dirs. Evanston Hosp. Corp., 1983-88. Lt. (j.g.) USNR, 1942-46. Mem. Assn. Life Ins. Counsel, Am. Coun. Life Ins. (bd. dir. 1977-81, 84-88), Ill. Life Ins. Coun. (bd. dir. 1978-86, pres. 1983-85), Inc. Econs. Soc. Am. (bd. dir. 1977-85, chmn. 1981-82), Health Ins. Assn. Am. (bd. dirs. 1982-88, chmn. 1987-88). Home: 7501 E Thompson Peak Pky #501 Scottsdale AZ 85255 E-mail: carefreesh@aol.com.

HUTCHISON, VICTOR HOBBS, biologist, educator; b. Blakely, Ga., June 15, 1931; s. Joseph Victor and Veva (Hobbs) H.; m. Theresa Dokos, Dec. 14, 1952; children: Victoria Ann, John Christopher, David Michael, Kenneth Hobbs. BS, N. Ga. Coll., 1952; MA, Duke, 1956, PhD, 1959. Instr. Duke, 1957-58, faculty fellow, So. Fellowship Fund fellow, 1958-59; mem. faculty U. R.I., 1959-70, prof. biology, 1968-70; dir. Inst. Environ. Biology; 1966-70; prof., chmn. dept. zoology U. Okla., Norman, 1970-80, George Lynn Cross research prof. zoology, 1979-2001, rsch. prof. emeritus, 2001—. Research prof. Universidad de Los Andes, Bogotá, Colombia, 1965-66; prin. investigator Nat. Geog. Soc.-U. R.I. herpetological expdn. to Colombia, 1964-65, Nat. Geog. Soc.-U. Okla. expdns. to Lake Titicaca, 1975, to Cameroon, 1981 Editor Animal Natural History series, 1991—; rsch. and articles on heat tolerances of lower vertebrates, effects of day-length on metabolism and temperature tolerance of lower vertebrates, physiology of lower vertebrates, physiol. ecology of amphibians and reptiles, respiration in amphibians, behavioral thermoregulation. Guggenheim fellow, 1965-66 Fellow AAAS; mem. Am. Inst. Biol. Sci., Am. Soc. Ichthyologists and Herpetologists (pres. 1988), Am. Physiol. Soc., Ecol. Soc. Am., Herpetologists League (exe. com. 1968-71), Soc. Study Amphibians and Reptiles (bd. govs. 1986-88, pres. 1998-99), Explorers Club, Sigma Xi, Phi Sigma, Phi Kappa Phi. Achievements include demonstration of facultative endothermy in brooding pythons; research on role of skin in amphibian respiration; development of standardized method for determination of critical thermal maximum in animals. Home: 2010 Crestmont Ave Norman OK 73069-6414 Office: U Okla Dept Zoology Norman OK 73019-0001

HUTCHISON, WILLIAM EDWARD, JR., military officer, aerospace engineer; b. Plattsburgh, N.Y., June 20, 1960; s. William Edward and Mary Gallagher Hutchison. BS with hons. in Psychology, Duke U., 1982; BS cum laude in Aerospace Engring., The U. of Tex., Austin, Tex., 1996; MS in Engring and Mgmt., MIT, 2000, PhD in Earth, Atmospheric, and Planetary Sci., 2003. Commd. lt. USAF, 1982, advanced through grades to maj., 1999, comm software team chief, 1983—86, f-15 fighter pilot Kadena AB, Japan, 1986—90, t-38 instr. pilot Sheppard AFB, Tex., 1990—94, resigned from active duty 1994; t-38 instr. pilot USAF Res., Randolph AFB, Tex., 2000—; rsch. scientist MIT, Cambridge, Mass., 2003—. Contbr. articles to profl. jours. Buddy walk organizer Nat. Down Syndrome Soc., Lexington, Mass., 2002—03. Decorated 5th Air Force Tip of the Spear Safety award Hq 5th Air Force Command Commendation medal USAF, Combat Readiness Medal, Commendation medal recipient Captain's award, Duke U. Lacrosse Team, 1982; fellow, NASA, 1997 Tex. Space Grant Consortium, 1997; scholar AFROTC scholarship, Duke U. 1979—82, MIT, 1998—2003. Mem.: Duke Club of Boston (assoc.), MIT Club of Boston (assoc.), Phi Kappa Phi, Kappa Alpha (assoc.). Avocations: running bicycling, weightlifting, hiking, camping. Home: 2 Old Colony Lane Apt 1 Arlington MA 02476 Office: Massachusetts Institute of Technology Building 54 520 77 Massachusetts Avenue Cambridge MA 02139 Personal E-mail hutch@mit.edu.

HUTCHISON, WILLIAM ROBERT, history educator; b. San Francisco May 21, 1930; s. Ralph Cooper and Harriet (Thompson) H.; m. Virginia Quay Aug. 16, 1952; children: Joseph Cooper, Catherine Eaton, Margaret Sidney Elizabeth Quay. BA, Hamilton Coll., 1951, DHL (hon.), 1991; BA (Fulbright scholar), Oxford U., 1953, MA, 1957; PhD, Yale U., 1956; MA (hon.), Harvard U., 1968. Instr. history Hunter Coll., 1956-58; assoc. prof. Am. studies Am. U. 1958-64, prof. history and Am. studies, 1964-68; Charles Warren prof. history of religion in Am. Harvard U., 1968—2000; master Winthrop House, 1974-79 USIA lectr. E. Asia & Pacific, August, 1983; Charles Warren rsch. prof. Harvard U., 2000—. Vis. assoc. prof. history U. Wis., 1963-64 Author: The Transcendentalist Ministers: Church Reform in the New England Renaissance, 1959, The Modernist Impulse in American Protestantism, 1976, Errand to the World: American Protestant Thought and Foreign Missions, 1987; Religious Pluralism in America: The Contentious History of a Founding Ideal, 2003; editor

American Protestant Thought, the Liberal Era, 1968; co-editor and joint author: Missionary Ideologies in the Imperialist Era, 1982; editor and joint author: Between the Times: The Travail of the Protestant Establishment in America, 1900-1960, 1989; co-editor and joint author: Many are Chosen: Divine Election and Western Nationalism, 1994; contbr. articles to profl. jours. Recipient Brewer prize Am. Soc. Ch. History, 1957; Am. Religious Book award, 1976; Guggenheim fellow, 1960-61; fellow Charles Warren Ctr. for Studies in Am. History, Harvard, 1966-67; Fulbright Sr. Research scholar Free U., Berlin, 1976; Fulbright Disting. lectr. in Am. history India, summer 1981; Fulbright Western European Regional Research grantee, 1987; Fulbright Disting. lectr. in Am. hist. and rel., Indonesia, 1993; Olaus Petri lectr., Uppsala U. (Sw.), 1996. Mem. Am. Hist. Assn., Orgn. Am. Historians, Am. Studies Assn., Am. Soc. Ch. History (pres. 1981), Unitarian Universalist Hist. Soc., Mass. Hist. Soc., Phi Beta Kappa. Democrat. Mem. Soc. Of Friends. Home: 4 Ellery Square Cambridge MA 02138 Office: Widener N, Harvard Univ Cambridge MA 02138

HUTH, BRIAN JUSTIN, ESL educator, poet; b. Apple Valley, Calif. BA in Asian Studies, U. Cin., 1997. ESL tchr. Berlitz Internat. Inc., San Diego, 1998—. Com. mem. Performance and Time Arts, Cin., 1999—2000. Author: Midnight Boxcar Magic, 1999. Individual Artist grantee, City Cin., 1998.

HUTH, EDWARD JANAVEL, physician, editor; b. Phila., May 15, 1923; s. Edward Gaston and Suzanne Madeleine (Janavel) H.; m. Carol Elizabeth Monnik, Apr. 6, 1957; children: John Edward, James Janavel. BA, Wesleyan U., Middletown, Conn., 1945; MD, U. Pa., 1947. Diplomate Am. Bd. Internal Medicine, Nat. Bd. Med. Examiners. Intern Hosp. of U. Pa., 1947-48, resident medicine, 1949-51, ward physician, 1951-61; mem. Diagnostic Clinic, 1959-61; postdoctoral fellow Life Ins. Med. Research Fund, 1952-53; spl. research fellow USPHS, Univ. Coll. Hosp., London, Eng., 1957-58. Asst. instr. pharmacology U. Pa. Sch. Medicine, Phila., 1948-49, assoc. in medicine, 1951-58, asst. prof. medicine, 1958-61; assoc. prof. comparative medicine Sch. Vet. Medicine, 1963-68; adj. asst. prof. medicine U. Pa. Sch. Medicine, 1966-71, assoc. prof. clin. medicine, 1971-74, adj. clin. prof. medicine, 1974-78, adj. prof. medicine dept. medicine Assoc. Faculty, 1978-91; asst. prof. medicine Woman's Med. Coll., Phila., 1961-62, assoc. prof., 1962-65; chmn. com. on 4th edit. CBE Style Manual Coun. Biology Editors, 1971-78, chmn. com. on 6th edit., 1990-95; biomed. comms. study sect. NIH, 1972-76; chmn. subcom. 10 of Com. Z39 Am. Nat. Stds. Inst., 1974-77; mem. UNISIST Working Group on Primary Sources of Info., UNESCO, Paris, 1973-74; bd. regents Nat. Libr. Medicine, 1979-83; office med. applications of rsch. NIH, 2001—; expert com. on info. devel. and dissemination US Pharmacopeia, 2002—. Author: Medical Style and Format, 1987, How to Write and Publish Papers in the Medical Sciences, 1990, Writing and Publishing in Medicine, 1998, SI Units for Clinical Medicine, 1998, Medicine in Quotations, 2000; asst. editor Annals of Internal Medicine, 1960-63, assoc. editor, 1963-71, editor, 1971-90, editor emeritus, 1990-93, 95—, book rev. editor, 1990-93, 95-96, interim editor, 1994-95; editor Online Jour. Current Clin. Trials, 1991-94, also articles; mem. editl. bd. Nat. Med. Jour. India, 1991—, Transactions and Studies of the Coll. Physicians Phila., 2002—; adv. bd. Croatian Med. Jour., 1998—; rev. editor Pa. Geneal. Mag., 2003. Served with AUS, 1943-46, PTO. Fellow ACP, AAAS (coun. 1968, editor Online Jour. Current Clin. Trials 1991-94), Royal Coll. Physicians (London), Am. Med. Writers Assn. (pres. 1967-68); mem. Coun. Biology Editors (dir. 1970-75, chmn. 1973-74), European Assn. Sci. Editors, Coll. Physicians Phila., Soc. for Scholarly Pub. (dir. 1988-92), Phi Beta Kappa, Sigma Xi, Alpha Omega Alpha, Zeta Phi. Home and Office: 1124 Morris Ave Bryn Mawr PA 19010-1712

HUTH, LESTER CHARLES, lawyer; b. Tiffin, Ohio, Nov. 21, 1924. JD, U. Notre Dame, 1951. Bar: Ohio 1951. Pvt. practice, Fostoria, Ohio, 1954-97. Tiffin, Ohio, 1997—; acting mcpl. judge, Fostoria, 1970, city solicitor, 1954-56, 60-64, police prosecutor, 1964-68; magistrate Common Pleas Ct., Seneca County, Ohio, 1995—; legal counsel to St. Wendelin Parish, Fostoria, 1972-96, Cmty. Hospice, 1992—; atty. Selective Svc. Bd. Appeals, 1956-75. Clk. city council, Fostoria, 1957-58; sec.-treas. Karrick Sch. Handicapped Children, 1956-77; adviser to Fostoria Family and Child Svc., 1977-83. Recipient Certs. of Appreciation Pres. Lyndon Johnson, 1966, SSS, 1975. Mem. Mem. Ohio Bar Assn., Senece County Bar Assn., C. of C. (dir. 1970-71), Fostoria Jaycees (founding pres. 1954), Fostoria A.M. Exchange Club. Home and Office: 80 Northwood Dr Tiffin OH 44883-1997

HUTH, THOMAS JOSEPH, retired surgeon; b. Cin., Mar. 15, 1921; s. Edwin C. Huth and Clara Beal; m. Margie Marie Heringer, Aug. 5, 1950; children: Margaret, Regina, Timothy, Daniel. MD, U. Cin., 1948. Diplomate Am. Bd. Surgery. Intern Cin. Gen. Hosp., 1948-49; resident in gen. practice St. Elizabeth Hosp., Covington, Ky., 1949-50; resident in pathology Good Samaritan/U. Hosp., Cin., 1954, U. Hosp., Cin., 1954—55; fellow surgery Louisville VA Hosp., 1955-59; surgeon St. Elizabeth Hosp., Covington; ret. Mem. ACS (emeritus), Am. Coll. Chest Physicians, Am. Thoracic Soc.

HUTH, WILLIAM EDWARD, lawyer; b. South Bend, Ind., July 26, 1931; s. Edward Andrew and Margaret Mary (Emonds) H.; m. Mary Pamela Hall, Aug. 11, 1962; children: Katharine Louise, Stephen Edward (dec.), Alan Edward. BS, U. Dayton, 1952; JD, Yale, 1957. Bar: N.Y. 1958, U.S. Dist. Ct. (so. dist.) N.Y. 1959, Mich. 1962, U.S. Dist. Ct. (ea. dist.) Mich. 1962, U.S. Supreme Ct. 1969, Pa. 1975, Conn. 1978. Assoc. Kelley, Drye, Newhall & Maginnes, N.Y.C., 1958-61; group counsel Chrysler Corp., Detroit, 1962-72; ptnr. Ziegler, Dykhouse, Wise & Huth, Detroit, 1973-74; assoc. gen. counsel Westinghouse Electric Corp., Pitts., 1974-76; asst. sec., asst. gen. counsel Combustion Engring., Inc., Stamford, Conn., 1976-90; ptnr. Huth, Grinnell & Flaherty, Stamford, 1991-2000. Adj. prof. law Wayne State U., Detroit, 1969-74, adj. prof. law Pace U. Sch. of Law, 1999-2001. Contbr. articles to profl. publs. 1st lt. AUS, 1952-54. Mem. ABA (antitrust sect., internat. law sect., bus. law sect.), Am. Soc. Internat. Law, Am. Arbitration Assn. (Blue Ribbon Panel Arbitrators, internat. panel, mem. corp. coun. com.), ICC Arbitration Com., U.S. Coun. for Internat. Bus. (ICC arbitration com.), Chartered Inst. Arbitrators (London), Inter-Pacific Bar Assn., Internat. Bar Assn., Conn. Bar Assn. (chmn. corp. coun. sec. 1991-94), Assn. of Bar of City of N.Y., Westchester-Fairfield Corp. Counsel Assn. (pres. 1987, bd. dirs. 1984-88), U.S. C. of C. (mem. antitrust adv. coun.), Yale Club N.Y.C., The Army and Navy Club (Washington), Indian Harbor Yacht Club (Greenwich), Order of Coif. Roman Catholic. Home: 39 Balmaha Ct Fairfield CT 06825-1173 Office: PO Box 320298 Fairfield CT 06825 E-mail: huthwe@ix.netcom.com.

HUTSON, BETTY SWITZER, art educator, artist; b. Brunswick, Mo., Aug. 14, 1930; d. Henry William and Pearl Evelyn (Sayler) Switzer; m. Don L. Hutson, Sept. 7, 1952; children: Eric, Sheila Hutson, Robin Hutson-Montoya, Heather Hutson Daye. BFA, Ctrl. Meth. Coll., 1952; postgrad., U. Mo., 1953-54, Kansas City Art Inst., 1958-60, Avila Coll., 1981; MA in Art Edn., U. Mo., Kansas City, 1986. Cert. tchr. grades K-12, Mo. Elem. art cons. Md. Pub. Schs., Rockville, 1954-58; art instr. Ruskin High Sch., Hickman Mills, Mo., 1958-60, East High Sch., Kansas City, Mo., 1961-62, N.E. Sr. High Sch., Kansas City, 1964-65; dir. edn. All Souls Unitarian Ch., Kansas City, 1975-77; art instr. Westport Jr. High Sch., Kansas City, 1977-87; art instr., cons. De LaSalle Edn. Ctr., Kansas City, 1987-88; art instr. Nelson Mus. Art, Kansas City, 1987-88; visual arts resource tchr. Kansas City Middle Sch. Arts, 1988—99; ret., 1999. Art instr. U. Md., College Park, summer, 1956; resource cons. U. Mo., Kansas City, 1984-86; arts ptnrs. devel. Kansas City Sch. Dist. Learning Exch., 1985-86; curriculum author, task force mem. Kansas City Middle Sch. the Arts, 1988-90, Paseo Acad. Fine & Performing Arts, Kansas City, 1988-90; supervising tchr. student and practicum tchrs. Rockhurst Coll., Kansas City, 1976-92, Avila Coll., Kansas City, 1976-92, U. Mo., Kansas City, 1976-92, 94, Truman U., 1996-97, Park U., 1997-98. Author: Sampling the Basics, 1985; one-woman shows include Unitarian Gallery, 1987, 2001, Lebanon Gallery, 1988, Tchrs. Credit Union Gallery, 1989-90, Le Fou Frog, 2002-03; exhibited in group shows at Unitarian Gallery, Kansas City, 1985, 87, 89, 91, 93, 95, 97, 99, 2001, Nelson Mus. Art, Kansas City, 1989, Fed. Res. Bank, Kansas City, 1990, Kaw Valley Gallery, Kansas City, 1990, Blue Springs (Mo.) Art Exhbn., 1990, 91, Heartland Art Festival, St. Joseph, Mo., 1990-93, Allied Arts Coun., St. Joseph, 1990-93, Bruce Watkins Cultural Ctr., Kansas City, 1993, 94, 95, Muse Gallery, Kansas City, 1995, Kansas City Artists Coalition, 2000, Ashby-Hodge Art Gallery, 2001, Cultures w/o Borders Exhbn., 2001, Open Studios, 2001, 02, others; illus. Children's History of AME Church, 1997. Den mother, art leader Boy Scouts of Am., Raytown, Mo., 1967-69, Girl Scouts of Am., Raytown, 1969-75; vol. AIDSWalk 1998, 99, 2000, 01, 02, 03, Habitat for Humanity, 1992, 93, 94, 96, 2002, soup kitchen Ward Chapel AME, World Federalists, Kansas City, 1989—, Scholastic Arts Regional Com.; vol., fundraiser Peaceworks, Kansas City, 1986—; vol., leader, officer PTA, Kansas City, 1965-76; Jr. Great Books, Picture Lady, Headstart, Planned Parenthood, Friends of the Zoo; trustee All Souls Unitarian-Universalist, 1976-79, 96-99; vol. usher various orgns.; bd. dirs. Unitarian Gallery, 1989—, curator Elizabeth Layton exhibit, 1992. Recipient Disting. Svc. award All Souls Unitarian Ch., Kansas City, 1977, Outstanding Tchr. award Westport Jr. High Sch., Kansas City, 1987, Excellence in Tchtg. Art award, 1995. Mem. AAUW (v.p. 2002-, art study chmn.), Nat. Art Edn. Assn., Art Edn. Connection (Svc. award 1991-92), Mo. Art Edn. Assn. (Outstanding Art Tchr. 1992), Friends of Art-Nelson Mus. Art, Demeters (pres. 1978-80, 90-91, v.p. 1965-68, 79, 89, co-pres. 2001-03, Svc. award 1987), Kansas City Artists Coalition, Mo. Mid. Sch. Assn. Democrat. Unitarian Universalist. Avocations: travel, swimming, gardening, drawing, painting. Home: 7625 Baltimore Ave Kansas City MO 64114-1813

HUTSON, JEFFREY WOODWARD, lawyer; b. New London, Conn., July 19, 1941; s. John Jenkins and Kathryn Barbara (Himberg) Hutson; m. Susan Office, Nov. 25, 1967; children: Elizabeth Kathryn, Anne Louise. AB, U. Mich., 1963, LLB, 1966. Bar: Ohio 1966, Hawaii 1971. Assoc. Lane, Alton & Horst, Columbus, Ohio, 1966-74, ptnr., 1974—. Arbitrator commercial construction panel Am Arbitration Asn, 1976—. Trustee, vice-chair 6 Pence Sch, 1983—88; mem comt creeds and professionalism Ohio Supreme Ct, 1989—90; chair, bd dirs NW Counseling Servs, 1990—92; regional vpres Def Research Inst, 1991—93. Lt comdr USNR, 1967—71. Fellow: Columbus Bar Found, Ohio State Bar Found, Am Bar Found, Am Col Trials Lawyers, Am Arbit Asn; mem.: Faculty Def Coun Trail Acad, Int Asn Def Counsel, Columbus Bar Asn, Ohio Asn Civil Trial Attys, Ohio Bar Asn, Athletic Club, Scioto Country Club. Avocations: cycling, reading, music. Office: Lane Alton & Horst 175 S 3rd St Ste 700 Columbus OH 43215-5100

HUTSON, MELVIN ROBERT, lawyer; b. Decatur, Ala., Dec. 7, 1947; s. John Robert and Katie Louise (Waddell) H.; m. Margaret Ann Shaddix; children: Melvin, Rachael, Katie, Jamie. BS, U. Ala., 1968, JD, 1971. Bar: Ala. 1971, Ga. 1972, S.C. 1975, D.C. 1978. Atty. NLRB, Atlanta, 1971-73; ptnr. Thompson Mann & Hutson, Greenville, S.C., 1974-98, Melvin Hutson, PA, Greenville, 1998—. Bd. dirs. Primesco, Inc., Mutual Savings Life Ins. Co., Inc. Chmn. bd. dirs. World Cancer Rsch. Fund, London, 1994—; chmn. AGC Labor Lawyers Coun., 1989-90, Am. Inst. Cancer Rsch., 1982—. Mem. ABA (mem. com. on devel. of law under nat. labor relations act 1977—, chmn. subcom. on labor mgmt. litigation). Home: 1307 N Main St Greenville SC 29609-4716 Office: PO Box 88 Greenville SC 29602-0088 E-mail: mel.hutson@scbar.org.

HUTT, EVELYN ANN, geriatrician, researcher; b. Tawngii, Burma, July 17, 1952; d. Martin Perry and Thelma Pearl Hutt; m. Norm Aaronson, June 14, 1998; children from previous marriage: Eliana Rosa Mastrangelo, Levi Noah Mastrangelo. BA, U. Chgo., 1974; MD, U. Colo., 1985. Diplomate Am. Bd. Internal Medicine, cert. of added qualification in geriatrics Am. Bd. Internal Medicine. Resident in internal medicine U. Minn., Mpls., 1985—88; fellow in geriatrics Stanford U., Palo Alto, Calif., 1988—90; dir. Sr. Plus, Denver Health Med. Ctr., 1990—95; physician Kaiser Permanente, Denver, 1995—98; asst. prof. U. Colo. Health Scis. Ctr., Denver, 1998—; dir. program for rsch. in long term care for veterans VAMC, Denver, 2000—. Mem. collaborative decision making com. Bromwell Elem. Sch., Denver, 1997—98; bd. dirs. Cmty. Talmud Torah, Denver, 1999—2000. Mem.: Physicians For Human Rights, Am. Geriat. Soc. (New Investigator award 2000). Liberal. Jewish. Avocation: triathlons.

HUTT, LAURENCE JEFFREY, lawyer; b. N.Y.C., Dec. 15, 1950; s. George Joseph and Miriam Martha (Cohen) H.; children: Marcie Arin, Ethan Lance, Amanda Rachel, Denver Allison. BA in History, U. Pa., 1972; JD, Stanford U., 1975. Bar: Calif. 1975, Colo., 1995. Assoc. Kadison, Pfaelzer, Woodard, Quinn & Rossi, L.A., 1976-82, ptnr., 1982-87; shareholder Quinn, Kully and Morrow, L.A., 1987-96; ptnr. Arnold & Porter, L.A., 1996—. Judge pro tem L.A. Mcpl. Ctr.; judge pro tem settlement officer L.A. Superior Ct. Bd. dirs. Western Ctr. on Law and Poverty, 1999—2002. Mem. State Bar Calif. (mem. exec. com. conf. del. 1992-95, legis. chair and vice chair 1994-95), L.A. County Bar (del. to Calif. State Bar Conv. 1980-92, 97-98, 2002—, mem. del. exec. com. 1989-92, 2002—, del. chair 1991-92, state cts. com. 1989-93, vice chair 1989-90, chair superior cts. subcom. 1988-89, Calif. jud. sys. com. 1988-90, liaison bench and bar com. 1988-90, mem. jud. elections evaluation com. 1999—), Constnl. Rights Found. (bd. dirs. 2003-, high sch. moot ct. scoring att., coach 1985-90), Order of Coif, Phi Beta Kappa. Avocations: wine tasting, theater, film. Office: Arnold & Porter 777 S Figueroa St Fl 44 Los Angeles CA 90017-5800

HUTT, PETER BARTON, lawyer; b. Buffalo, Nov. 16, 1934; s. Lester Ralph and Louise Rich (Fraser) H.; children: Katherine Zurn, Peter Barton, Sarah Henderson, Everett Fraser. BA magma cum laude, Yale U., 1956; LLB, Harvard U., 1959; LLM, NYU, 1960. Bar: N.Y. 1959, D.C. 1961, U.S. Supreme Ct. 1967. Assoc. Covington & Burling, Washington, 1960-68, ptnr., 1968-71, 75—; chief counsel FDA, Washington, 1971-75. Bd. dirs. Cognetix, Inc., Salt Lake City, CV Therapeutics Inc., Palo Alto, Calif., PhaseForward, Inc., Waltham, Mass., Microban Internat. Ltd., N.Y.C., Momenta, Inc., Cambridge, Mass.; mem. adv. com. to dir. NIH, 1976—81; mem. com. on rsch. tng. NAS, 1976—80; bd. dirs. Calif. HealthCare Inst., San Diego; counsel to Alcoholic Beverage Med. Rsch. Found., 1984—85, chmn. bd. dirs., 1986—92; mem. Nat. Com. to Rev. Current Proc. for Approval of New Drugs for Cancer and AIDS, Nat. Cancer Inst., 1988—90; mem. nat. bd. Scripps Clinic and Rsch. Found., La Jolla, 1977—85, La Jolla, 1990—95; mem. internat. bd. Scripps Instns. of Medicine and Sci., 1995—, Ctr. for Study Drug Devel., Tufts U. Ctr., 1976—99, Ctr. for Advanced Studies, U.Va., 1982—, Inst. for Health Policy Analysis, 1982—, Am. Pharm. Inst., Washington, 1988—92; mem. Com. on Food Laws and Regulations, Inst. Food Tech.; mem. adv. com. Progress and Freedom Found., 1994—97; mem. adv. bd. Frazier Healthcare Investments, Seattle, 1993—, Sprout Group, N.Y. and Menlo Park, 1993—, Polaris Venture Ptnrs., Waltham, 1995—, Vanguard Medica Ltd., Guildford, England, 1993—99, Sherbrook Capital Health & Wellness Fund, Lexington, Mass., 1999—, Burrill Neutraceuticals Adv. Bd., San Francisco, 2000—; mem. various panels U.S. Congl. Office Tech. Assessment; lectr. on food and drug law Harvard U., 1994—, Stanford U., 1998; mem. adv. bd. Columbia U. Sch. Pub. Health, 1997—. Author: (with Patricia Wald) Dealing with Drug Abuse, 1972, (with Richard Merrill) Food and Drug Law, 1991, (with Bruce Kuhlik) Understanding Export Law, 1998; editor-in-chief U.S. Food Labeling Law, 1991—; contbg. editor: Legal Times of Washington, 1978-86; mem. editorial bd. various jours.; editor: Food and Drug Law: An Electronic Book of Harvard Law School Student Papers. Bd. dirs. Sidwell Friends Sch., Washington, 1976-84; bd. dirs. Legal Action Ctr., N.Y.C., 1976-2003, vice-chmn., 1984-98; bd. dirs. Found. for Biomed. Rsch., 1976-2003, vice chmn., 1989— ; trustee Washington Lawyers Com. for Civil Rights & Urban Affairs, 1976—, Food and Drug Law Inst., 2001—; bd. dirs. Soc. Risk Analysis, 1985-88, 89-92, counsel, 1992—; mem. vis. com. Harvard Sch. Pub. Health, 1980-86. Recipient award of merit FDA, 1972, 75, Disting. Svc. award HEW, 1974, Underwood-Prescott award MIT, 1977. Fellow: Soc. Risk Analysis; mem.: Inst. Medicine of NAS (Devel. of Drugs and Vaccines Against AIDS roundtable 1988—94, bd. on health care svcs. 1998—2002), Met. Club (Washington). Episcopalian. Home: 402 Prince St Alexandria VA 22314-3114 Office: Covington & Burling 1201 Pennsylvania Ave NW Washington DC 20004-2401

HUTTAR, CHARLES ADOLPH, retired language educator; b. Austin, Tex., July 8, 1932; s. Adolph Herbert and Leora White Huttar; m. Joy Anne Culbertson; children: Lydia Anne Brown, Sarah Elizabeth Anderson, Rachel Marie Vos, Charles Nathan, Julia Ruth Huttar Bailey, Elizabeth Joy Naka, Thomas Wyatt. AB, Wheaton Coll., 1952; MA, Northwestern U., 1953, PhD, 1956. Asst. prof. to assoc. prof. of English, dept. chair Gordon Coll., Wenham, Mass., 1955—66; prof. English Hope Coll., Holland, Mich., 1966—96, chmn. dept. English, 1971—76, prof. of English emeritus, 1996—. Rsch. fellow The Johns Hopkins U., Balt., 1980, Cornell U., Ithaca, NY, 1983; hon. rsch. fellow U. of Glasgow, Glasgow, Scotland, Great Britain and Northern Ireland, 1995; adv. bd. Mythlore (jour.), L.A., 1987—. Co-author: (book) Island Grove Campground: A Centennial History, 1999; editor: Imagination and the Spirit, 1971; co-editor: Word and Story in C. S. Lewis, 1991 (Mythopoeic Soc. Scholarship Award, 1992), The Rhetoric of Vision: Essays on Charles Williams, 1996 (Mythopoeic Soc. Scholarship Award, 1997), Scandalous Truths: Essays by and about Susan Howatch. Recipient Grant-in-Aid, Folger Shakespeare Libr., 1961, Disting. Svc. Award, Rotary Club, 1999; grantee, Am. Philos. Soc., 1967—78. Mem.: Milton Soc. of Am., MLA of Am. (life), Guild of Scholars of the Episcopal Ch., Conf. on Christianity and Lit. (sec. 1958—60, pres. 1966—68, bd. dirs. 1974—78, 1994—2003), Charles Williams Soc., Rotary Club (sec. 1996—2001). Home: 188 W 11th St Holland MI 49423 Office: Hope College POBox 9000 Holland MI 49422-9000 Business E-Mail: huttar@hope.edu.

HUTTEN, ANGELA CLARE, special education educator; b. Rockford, Ill., Dec. 1, 1938; d. Elmer Edward and Alice Caroline (Bassetti) Englund; m. Francis Joseph Hutten, June 23, 1962; children: Caroline, Edward, Rosemary. BA in English, No. Ill. U., 1961, MS in English Edn., 1967. Cert. tchr. grades K-12 regular edn., learning disabilities, socially and emotionally disorders, lang. arts, Ill. English tchr. Ela-Vernon H.S., Lake Zurich, Ill., 1961-62, Waukegan (Ill.) Twp. H.S., 1962-65; spl. edn. tchr. Waukegan (Ill.) Unit Dist. 60, 1972—. Mem. curriculum coun. Waukegan (Ill.) Pub. Schs., 1980-84, site-based adv. com., 1991—. Bd. dirs., v.p. AAUW Nursery Sch., Waukegan, 1970-74; mem. Friends of the Waukegan (Ill.) Pub. Libr., 1975—, treas., 1984, v.p., 1990-92, pres., 1998-2002. Mem. AAUW (Waukegan br. treas. 1976-77, v.p. 2002--), Am. Fedn. Tchrs. (nat. trainer), Ill. Fedn. Tchrs., Lake County Fedn. Tchrs. (Waukegan coun. sec. 1982-2001, local site coord. Ednl. Rsch. and Dissemination Program 1989—, coord. profl. devel.), Delta Kappa Gamma (Beta Upsilon chpt. sec. 1985-86), Phi Delta Kappa (chpt. 1123 v.p. 1990-91, conv. del. 1994-95). Avocations: reading, education research, furniture refinishing, needle point. Home: 2912 Carriage Ln Waukegan IL 60085-3116 Office: Lake County Fedn Tchrs 248 Ambrogio Dr Gurnee IL 60031-3373

HUTTENBACH, DIRK ERIK, psychiatrist; b. Amsterdam, The Netherlands, Feb. 6, 1938; came to U.S., 1953; naturalized, 1959; s. Gunter William and Berte Marie H.; m. Muriel Lee Patterson, June 6, 1964; children: William P., Eric, Marisa, Laura Lee. BSChemE, Case Western Res. U., 1959; MD, SUNY, Syracuse, 1965. Diplomate in gen., child and adolscent psychiatry Am. Bd. Psychiatry and Neurology, cert. addiction medicine Am. Soc. Addiction Medicine. Intern Kaiser Found. Hosp., San Francisco, 1965-66; resident in psychiatry Langley Porter Neuropsychiat. Inst., U. Calif. Med. Ctr., San Francisco, 1966-69, child psychiatry fellow, 1968-70; pvt. practice gen. psychiatry San Francisco, 1969-70; pvt. practice Smyrna, Ga., 1996—; pvt. practice child, adolescent and adult psychiatry Cobb County, Ga., 1972—; mem. staff Scottish Rite Children's Hosp., 1999—, Well Star Kennestone Hosp, 1973—, Ridgeview Psych. Inst., 1977 . Emergency psychiatrist Community Mental Health Svcs., San Francisco Gen. Hosp., 1969-70. TV guest appearances include The Today Show, NBC, 1989, The Sonya Freeman Show, CNN (Cable News Network), 1989; contbr. articles to profl. publs. Mem. spl. edn. profl. adv. com. Cobb County Pub. Schs., 1975-76, mem. drug-free schs. adv. bd., mem. youth suicide pub. awareness com., 1987-89; bd. dirs., mem. policy and procedures com. Cobb County Children's Shelter, 1981-89, mem. adv. com., 1989—; mem. adv. bd. Coun. for Children, Inc.; bd. dirs. Cobb County Emergency Aid Assn., 1973-81. Maj. Med. Svc. Corps, U.S. Army, 1970-72. Fellow Am. Psychiat. Assn., Am. Acad. of Children and Adolescent Psychiatry; mem. AMA (Continuing Med. Edn. awards), Med. Assn. Ga. (del. from Cobb County Med. Soc. 1985—), Ga. Psychiat. Physicians Assn. (chmn. task force on adolescent urine drug screening 1986—, chmn. awards com. 1999—), Ga. Assn. for Children with Learning Disabilities (Cobb County chpt.), Cobb County Med. Soc. (chmn. subcom. on adolescent drug abuse 1983—, pub. rels. chmn. 1990-92), Atlanta Holland Club. Avocations: reading, travel, current events. Office: 4015 S Cobb Dr SE Ste 210 Smyrna GA 30080-6316

HUTTENBACK, ROBERT ARTHUR, academic administrator, educator; b. Frankfurt, Germany, Mar. 8, 1928; s. Otto Henry and Dorothy (Marcuse) H.; m. Freda Braginsky, July 12, 1954; 1 dau., Madeleine Alexandra. BA, U. Calif. at Los Angeles, 1951, PhD, 1959; postgrad., Sch. Oriental and African Studies, U. London, Eng., 1956-57. Mem. faculty Calif. Inst. Tech., Pasadena, 1958-78, asst. prof., 1960-63, assoc. prof., 1963-66, prof. history, 1966-78, master student houses, 1958-69, dean students, 1969-72, chmn. div. humanities and social scis., 1971-77; chancellor U. Calif., Santa Barbara, 1977-86. Cons. Jet Propulsion Lab., Pasadena, 1966-68 Author: British Relations with Sind, 1799-1843, An Anatomy of Imperialism, 1962, (with Leo Rose and Margaret Fisher) Himalayan Battleground-Sino-Indian Rivalry in Ladakh, 1963, The British Imperial Experience, 1966, Gandhi in South Africa, 1971, Racism and Empire, 1976, (with Lance Davis) Mammon and the Pursuit of Empire, 1986, Kashmir and the British Raj - the 101 Years Lifespan of an Indian Princely State, 2003.. Served to 1st lt. U.S. Army, 1951-53.

HUTTER, ADOLPH MATTHEW, JR., cardiologist, educator; b. Fond du Lac, Wis., Feb. 22, 1937; s. Adolph Matthew and Janet (Kay) H.; m. Sylvia H. Murray, June 18, 1960; children: Janice Marie, Adolph Joseph, Elizabeth Kay, Matthew Murray, Jonathan James. BS summa cum laude, Georgetown U., 1959; MD, U. Wis., 1963. Diplomate Am. Bd. Internal Medicine, Am. Bd. Cardiovascular Diseases; lic. physician, Mass. Med. intern Strong Meml. Hosp., Rochester, N.Y., 1963-64; clin. assoc. Nat. Cancer Inst., Bethesda, Md., 1964-66; asst. resident Strong Meml. Hosp., 1966-67, assoc. resident, 1967-68; fellow in medicine (oncology) Georgetown U. Sch. Medicine, Washington, 1965-66; clin. and rsch. fellow in cardiology Mass. Gen. Hosp., Boston, 1968-70; instr. medicine Harvard U. Med. Sch., Boston, 1970-72, asst. prof., 1972-76, assoc. prof., 1976-99, prof., 1999—. Vis. prof. 100 univs. and med. ctrs., 1979-96; asst. in medicine Mass. Gen. Hosp., 1970-72, asst. physician, 1972-76, assoc. physician, 1976-84, physician, 1984—, assoc. dir. CCU, 1970-81, dir., 1981-86, chmn. med. intensive care coord. com., 1986-94; cardiologist Boston Bruins hockey team, 1972—, New Eng. Patriots football team, 1982—. Contbr. over 100 articles to med. jours. Trustee The Roxbury Latin Sch., 1988-90, mem. soc. of fellows, 1995—. Recipient Howard H. Blakeslee award, Am. Heart Assn., 1974; fellow, Roxbury Latin Sch. Fellow: AAAS, ACP, European Soc. Cardiology, Am. Coll. Cardiology (chmn. 1987—90, v.p. 1990—91, pres. 1992—93, past pres. 1993—94, mem. program com. on sci. sessions 1975—76, mem. credentials com. 1976—83, chmn. 1981—83, asst. sec. 1981—82, sec. 1984—85, mem. long-range planning com. 1981—83, mem. ACCEL com. 1982—90, mem. ACCEL edn. bd. 1987—90, 1993—, mem. strategic planning com. 1988—92, mem. exec. com. 1990—94, trustee 1981—85, 1987—95, chmn. govt. rels. com. 1993—, chmn. chpt. rels. com. 1993—, mem. chmn. award com. 1993—95, mem. tech. and practice exec. com. 1994—), Coun. on Clin. Cardiology of Am. Heart Assn. (mem. com. on postgrad. edn. 1972—75, mem. com. on sci. sessions program 1973—75, mem. sci. sessions com. 1979—81, vice chmn. com. on cardiovasc. disease of elderly 1987—90); mem.: Mass. Med. Soc., Am. Clin. and Climatol. Assn., U. Wis. Med. Alumni Assn., Alpha Omega Alpha. Roman Catholic. Avocations: tennis, golf. Office: Mass Gen Hosp Ambulatory Care Ctr 15 Parkman St Ste 467 Boston MA 02114-3117 E-mail: ahutter@partners.org.

HUTTER, ROBERT GRANT, lawyer, educator; b. Cleve., May 7, 1948; s. Russell G. and Tresa V. (Ireland) H. B.S.Ch.E., Va. Poly. Inst., 1969; J.D., U. Md., 1973; M.B.A., St. Bonaventure U., 1978. Bar: N.Y. 1980, U.S. Dist. Ct. N.Y. Chem. engr. Westinghouse, Balt., 1969-73; prof. law Alfred U., N.Y., 1974— ; ptnr. Sootheran & Hutter, Andover, N.Y., 1981— . Contbr. numerous articles and book revs. to profl. publs. Mem. N.Y. State Bar Assn., Allegany County Bar Assn. (chmn. real estate law com. 1983—). Home: RR 1 Box 81H Wellsville NY 14895-9801 Office: 15 Main St Andover NY 14806

HUTTNER, LOUISE ANN, mathematician, educator; b. Trenton, N.J., June 22, 1946; d. Walter Anthony and Helen Lasek; m. Bruce Alan Huttner, Dec. 4, 1976; children: Walter, Janet. BA in Math., Trenton State Coll., 1968, MA in Math., 1973. Cert. secondary sch. tchr. math., supr. N.J. Math. tchr. Hightstown (N.J.) H.S., 1968—69, Princeton (N.J.) H.S., 1969—72, Haddonfield (N.J.) H.S., 1972—75, Delran (N.J.) H.S., 1975—80; adj. instr. math. Burlington County Coll., Pemberton, NJ, 1980—88, coll. prof. math., 1988—. Author: (workbooks for Calculus I) Mathcad Project I, II, III, IV, 1995, (workbooks for Calculus II) Mathcad Project I, II, 1996; author: (internet course) Calculus I, 2002, Calculus II, 2000. Mem. ch. coun. St. Paul's Luth. Ch., Mt. Holly, NJ, 1998—2000, Sunday sch. tchr., 1980—94. Mem.: NEA, N.J. Edn. Assn., Phi Theta Kappa (advisor Pemberton, N.J. chpt. 2000—). Office: Burlington County Coll 3331 State Rte 38 Mount Laurel NJ 08054

HUTTNER, SIDNEY FREDERICK, librarian; b. Portal, N.D., Feb. 18, 1941; s. Frederick W. and Fern May (Nolting) H.; m. Elizabeth Ann Stege, Oct. 24, 1981; 1 child, Erica Marie. BA in Tutorial Studies, U. Chgo., 1963, MA in Philosophy, 1969. Asst. head spl. collections U. Chgo. Libr., 1970-80; head George Arents Rsch. Libr. Syracuse (N.Y.) Libr., 1980-84; curator spl. collections U. Tulsa Libr., 1984-98; head spl. collections U. Iowa Librs., 1999—. Author: A Register of Artists, Engravers, Booksellers, Bookbinders, Printers and Publishers in New York City, 1821-1842, 1993. Fellow Woodrow Wilson Found., 1963-64. Avocation: bookbinding. Home: 5 Glendale Cir Iowa City IA 52245-3208 Office: Spl Collections U Iowa Librs Iowa City IA 52240-1420 E-mail: sid-huttner@uiowa.edu.

HUTTO, EARL, retired congressman; b. Midland City, Ala., May 12, 1926; s. Lemmie and Ellie Hutto; m. Nancy Myers, July 8, 1967; children: Lori, Amelia Ann. BS, Troy State U., 1949; postgrad., Northwestern U., 1951; LLD, Troy State U., 1983. Tchr. Cottonwood (Ala.) High Sch., 1949-51; sports and program dir. Sta. WDIG, Dothan, Ala., 1951-54; sports dir. Sta. WEAR-TV, Pensacola, Fla., 1954-60; pres. Sta. WPEX-FM, Pensacola, 1960-65; sports dir. Sta. WSFA-TV, Montgomery, Ala., 1961-63; sports dir., state news editor Sta. WJHG-TV, Panama City, Fla., 1963-74; mem. Fla. Ho. of Reps., 1972-78, 96th-103rd Congresses from 1st Fla. dist., 1978-94. Mem. Armed Svcs. com., Merchant Marine Fisheries com.; chmn. subcom. Coast Guard Navigation, 1987-88, readiness subcom, 1989-94; chmn. tech. transfer panel, 1983, spl. ops. panel, 1984-89. Chmn. state govt. divsn. United Way, 1976-77; exec. bd. Gulf Coast coun. Boy Scouts Am.; deacon 1st Bapt. Ch., Pensacola, Fla.; bd. dirs. Bapt. Hosp., Hospice of N.W. Fla., Pensacola Hist. Soc.; pres. Earl Hutto Found.; trustee Nat. Naval Aviation Mus., 1979-2002. With USN, 1944-46. Recipient State Leadership award Sunshine State Assn. for the Blind, 1973; Legislator of Yr. award Fla. Assn. Retarded Children, 1974; Woodmen of the World Conservation award, 1974; Conservationist of Yr. award Bay County Audubon Soc., 1975; Legis. award Fla. Assn. Community Colls., 1978; Watchdog of Treasury award Nat. Associated Businessmen, 1979-80, 86, 88, 90; Alumnus of Yr. award Troy State U., 1980; Christian Statesman award, 1981; Leadership award Am. Security Council, 1982-87; Guardian of Small Bus. award Nat. Fedn. Ind. Businesses, 1986, 88, 90, Disting. Svc. award U.S. Navy League, 1988, Leg. award Nat. Assn. Renting Law Adminstrs., 1988, Am. Sec. Co. Eagle of Freedom award, 1990-91, Legislator of Yr. award Am. Sec. Co., 1992, Peace In Strength award, 1991, Disting. Svc. award Am. Logistics Assn., 1994, Lynn Rylander award Am. Def. Preparedness Assn., 1994, Charles Dick medal of merit U.S. Nat. Guard Assn., 1994. Mem. Troy State U. Alumni Assn., Earl Hutto Found. (pres.), Civitan Club (dep. gov. Ala.-West Fla. dist. 1967-71). Democrat. Home: 3459 River Gardens Cir Pensacola FL 32514-8162

HUTTO, RICHARD JAY, lawyer; b. Fitzgerald, Ga., Oct. 7, 1952; s. O.J. and Reba Ivalow (Gossett) H.; m. Katherine Anne Johnston, Aug. 3, 1991; children: Katherine Tod, Bradley Martin. BA, U. Ga., 1974; JD, Mercer U., 1984. Bar: Ga., 1984, D.C., 1985. Polit. coord. Jimmy Carter Presdl. Campaign, Atlanta, 1975-76; Carter family appointments sec. The White Ho., Washington, 1977-78; asst. to Lt. Gov. Zell Miller Lt. Gov. Zell Miller, Atlanta, 1978; program coord. White Ho. Conf. on Small Bus., Washington, 1979-80; dir. spl. projects White Ho. Conf. for Children and Youth, Washington, 1980-81; atty. Barrett, Montgomery and Murphy, Washington, 1984-87; v.p. Challenger Ctr. Space Sci. Edn., Alexandria, Va., 1987-89; pvt. practice Alexandria, Va., 1989-93; asst. v.p. devel. Mercer Univ., Macon, Ga., 1995-96. Commr. for Arts, City of Alexandria, 1989-93; mng. dir. The Grand Opera House, Macon, Ga.; Gov.'s appointee Ga. Coun. for Arts, 1995—, chmn., 1997-99; bd. dirs. So. Arts Fedn., 1997-99; pres. Macon-Bibb County Conv. and Visitors Bur.; exec. dir. Jekyll Island Found., 2000—; dir. planned giving Wesleyan Coll., 2001-02; dir. devel. Ga. Music Hall of Fame, 2002—. Decorated knight of merit Sacred Mil. Constantinian Order St. George. Mem. Nat. Assembly State Arts Agys. (bd. dirs.), Royal Overseas Club (London), Macon C. of C. (bd. dirs.). Roman Catholic. Avocations: book collecting, travel. Home: 1269 Jackson Springs Rd Macon GA 31211-1731

HUTTON, CAROLE LEIGH, newspaper editor; b. Framingham, Mass., Aug. 23, 1956; d. James and Norma Inez (Vitali) Hamilton; m. Tom Huff. B Journalism, Mich. State U., 1978. Editor Natick (Mass.) Sun, 1978—79; reporter, city editor, mng. editor Hammond (Ind.) Times, 1979—87; dir. publs. CNA Ins. Cos., Chgo., 1987—88; day city editor, accent editor Detroit News, 1988—90; city editor Detroit Free Press, 1992—95, dep. mng. editor for news, 1995—96, mng. editor, 1996—2002, exec. editor, 2002—. Tutor Detroit Pub. HS, 1994—94. Named one of 100 Most Influential Women in S.W. Mich., Crain's Detroit (Mich.) Bus.; recipient Local News Coverage award, Hoosier State Press Assn., 1982. Mem.: Assoc. Press Mng. Editors, Mich. AP Editors Assn. (pres., bd. dirs. 2000—), Am. Soc. Newspaper Editors, IAP Mng. Editors. Office: Detroit Free Press 600 W Fort St Detroit MI 48226-2706*

HUTTON, EDWARD LUKE, diversified public corporation executive; b. Bedford, Ind., May 5, 1919; s. Fred and Margaret (Drehobl) H.; m. Kathryn Jane Alexander; children— Edward Alexander, Thomas Charles, Jane Clarke BS with distinction, Ind. U., 1940, MS with distinction, 1941; LLD (hon.), Ind. U., Cumberland Coll., 1992. Dep. dir. Joint Export Import Agy. (USUK), Berlin, 1946-48; v.p. World Commerce Corp., 1948-51; asst. v.p. W.R. Grace & Co., 1951-53, cons., 1960-65, exec. v.p., gen. mgr. Dubois Chems. div., 1965-66, group exec. Specialty Products Group and v.p., 1966-68, exec. v.p., 1968-71; cons. internat. trade and fin., 1953-58; fin. v.p., exec. v.p. Ward Industries, 1958-59; pres., CEO Chemed Corp., Cin., 1971-2001, chmn., dir., 1993—, Omnicare, Inc., Cin., 1993—2003, Roto-Rooter, Inc., 2003—. Chmn. bd. dirs. Nat. San. Supply Co., 1983-97. Co-chmn. Pres.'s Pvt. Sector Survey on Cost Control, exec. com., subcom.; former trustee Millikin U., 1973-84. 1st lt., U.S. Army, 1945-47. Recipient Disting. Alumni Svc. award Ind. U., 1987. Mem. AAUP (governing bd. dirs. 1958—), Econ. Club, Princeton Club, Univ. Club, Queen City Club, Bankers Club. Home: 6680 Miralake Ln Cincinnati OH 45243-2722 Office: Chemed Corp 255 E 5th St Ste 2600 Cincinnati OH 45202-4700 E-mail: ehutton@chemed.com.

HUTTON, ERNEST WATSON, JR., urban designer, city planner; b. Ft. Myers, Fla., Oct. 25, 1944; s. Ernest Watson and Vera (Bowling) H.; m. Gretchen Bachrach, June 20, 1970 (div.); children: Elizabeth, Elinor; m. Anne Moore, Apr. 20, 1996; stepchildren: Philip, Alexander, Marya Mezzatesta. BA, Princeton U., 1966; BArch., U. Pa., 1968, MArch., M in City Planning, 1970. Sr. urban designer Jonathan Devel. Corp., Mpls., 1970-73, New Community Enterprises, Mpls., 1972-73, Arlen Realty & Devel. Corp., N.Y.C., 1973-74; sr. assoc. Llewelyn-Davies Internat., N.Y.C./Toronto/London, 1974-80; ptnr. Buckhurst Fish Hutton Katz Inc., N.Y.C., 1980-92; prin. Hutton Assocs., Inc., N.Y.C., 1993—. Mem. Union Square Alliance, 1995—; bd. dirs. Ky.-W.Va. Coal & Mining Co., 1996—. Author: (with others) Cultural Facilities in Mixed Use Development, 1986; editor Principles for Rebuilding Lower Manhattan, 2001; prin. works include Pitts. Cultural Dist./CNG Tower/Benedum Ctr., 1980-87 (HUD Nat. Merit award), Roanoke Vision Plans/Neighborhood Partnership, 1980-81, 86-87, 93,2000-01 (Am. Planning Assn. Nat award 1987), Hartford Riverfront Recapture Plan, 1981-85, 96-97 (Nat. Waterfront award 1997), Knoxville Downtown/Riverfront Plan, 1987-92, Rutland (Vt.) Downtown Plan, 1988-89, 95, Charlotte Arts Dist., 1986-91, Akron Downtown Plan, 1993-94, Conn. Scenic Byway Plan, 1994-98 (USDOT Design in Transp. nat. award 2000), Buffalo InnerHarbor Plan, 1997-98, Jamestown N.Y. Downtown Plans, 1988-2001, Jamaica Devel. Plan, 1999-2001, Southampton N.Y. Town Planning, 1998-2003, The Preserve Cmty. Plan, 2002-03, New York New Visions Lower Manhattan Devel., 2001-03 (AIA Nat. award, 2003). Fellow Inst. Urban Design; mem. Mayors Inst. City Design, (charter) Am. Inst. Cert. Planners, (charter mem.) Am. Planning Assn., (assoc.) AIA (co-chair, NYC planning urban design com., 2002—, N.Y. Citation for excellence in outreach 2003), New York New Visions (exec. com. 2001—), Congress for New Urbanism, Urban Land Inst., Am. Vaudeville Inc. (pres., bd. dirs. 1989-92), Lucille Ball Comedy Festival (mng. prodr. 1991), Cap and Gown Club (Princeton, N.J.). Home: 172 Pacific St Brooklyn NY 11201-6214 Office: Hutton Assocs Inc 9th Fl 22 W 19 St New York NY 10011-7910 E-mail: ehutton@huttonassociates.com.

HUTTON, JOHN EVANS, JR., surgery educator, retired military officer; b. N.Y.C., Sept. 9, 1931; s. John Evans and Antoinette (Abbott) H.; m. Barbara Seward Joyce, Apr. 15, 1961; children: John III, Wendy, James, Elizabeth. BA, Wesleyan U., 1953; MD, George Washington U., 1963. Diplomate: Am. Bd. Surgery, Am. Bd. Med. Examiners. Commd. 2d lt. USMC, 1953, advanced through grades to capt., 1962; discharged USMCR; commd. capt. U.S. Army, 1963, advanced through grades to brig. gen., 1989, intern, resident in gen. surgery Walter Reed Army Med. Ctr., 1963-68, fellow vascular surgery, 1969-70, asst. chief vascular surgery, 1970-71, mem. staff gen. surgery svcs., 1969-71, chief dept. surgery, 1981-84, White House physician, 1984-86, physician to the Pres., 1987-88, chief surgeon 91st Evacuation Hosp., Republic of Vietnam, 1968—69, chief vascular surgery, asst. chief gen. surgery Letterman Army Med. Ctr., 1971-74, chief gen. and vascular surgery, program dir., gen. surgery residency Letterman Army Med. Ctr., 1975-81; comdr. 47th Field Hosp., Honduras, 1984; commanding gen. Madigan Army Med. Ctr. U.S. Army, Tacoma, 1989-92; ret., 1992; prof. surgery, chief div. gen. surgery, dept. surg. Uniformed Svcs. U. Sch. Medicine, Bethesda, Md., 1992—, mem. faculty senate, 1996—99, mem. students promotion com., 1993-96, 2002—, mem. instl. rev. bd., 1993-96, mem. com. appointments, promotion and tenure, 1998-99, pres. elect faculty senate, 1997; pres. faculty senate Uniformed Svcs. U. Health Scis., Bethesda, 1998. Assoc. clin. prof. surgery U. Calif., San Francisco, 1978-81, mem. dean's adv. group, 1998-99; assoc. prof. surgery, vice chmn. dept. surgery Uniformed Svcs. U. Health Scis., Bethesda, 1981-84, prof. surgery, 1985—; clin. prof. surgery Tulane U. Sch. Medicine, 1988—, George Washington Sch. Medicine, Washington, 1985—. Contbr. articles, photographs to profl. publs., chpts. to books. Mem. men and boys choir Grace Cathedral, San Francisco, 1971-75. Decorated D.S.M., Bronze Star, Meritorious Svcs. medal with oak leaf cluster, Army Commendation Medal, Navy Commendation Medal, Joint Svc. Commendation Medal, Vietnam Svc. medal with four bronze svc. stars, Nat. DSM with two bronze svc. stars, Naval Occupation medal, WWII, Vietnam Honor medal 1st class, Vietnam Cross of Gallantry; recipient Barron Dominique Larrey award for excellence in surgery, Disting. Svc. medal, Uniformed Svcs. U. Sch. Medicine, 2000. Fellow: ACS; mem.: Soc. for Mil. Cons. to Armed Forces (councilor 1988—89, v.p. 2000, pres. 2001), Acad. Medicine Washington D.C., Chesapeake Vascular Soc., Soc. Mil. Vascular Surgery, Am. Assn. for Surgery of Trauma, Soc. Clin. Vascular Surgery, Am. Assn. for Vascular Surgery, Bay Surg. Soc. (hon.), U.S. Naval Acad. Sailing Squadron, St. Francis Yacht Club (membership com. 1978—81). Republican. Episcopalian. Avocations: music, photography, competitive sailing, coaching. Home: 1707 Priscilla Dr Silver Spring MD 20904-1610 Office: Uniformed Svcs U Health Scis Dept Surgery 4301 Jones Bridge Rd Bethesda MD 20814-4712

HUTTON, MARY J. guidance counselor; b. Kansas City, Mo., Nov. 21, 1951; d. Bill H. and Vera M. (Needels) Harmon; m. Douglas L. Hutton, June 1, 1974; children: Dylan M., Marissa S. Cert. in Elem. Edn., Northwest Mo. State U., 1973; M in Counseling, U. Iowa, 1985. Tchr. Mid-Buchanan Community Sch., St. Joseph, Mo., 1973-74; co-dir. Adolescent Ctr. FAMCO, Cedar Rapids, Iowa, 1974-76; employment specialist State of Iowa, Iowa City, 1976-80; employment mgr. Mercy Hosp., Iowa City, 1980-85; guidance counselor Linn Mar Community Sch., Cedar Rapids, 1985—. Mem. St. Paul's United Meth. Ch. Mem. NEA, Linn Mar Edn. Assn., Iowa Assn. for Counselors. Avocations: needle work, reading, children, tae kwon do (black belt). Home: 2366 Towne House Dr NE Cedar Rapids IA 52402-2228 Office: Bowman Woods 151 Boyson Rd NE Cedar Rapids IA 52402-1415

HUTTON, PAUL ANDREW, history educator, writer; b. Frankfurt, Germany, Oct. 23, 1949;, naturalized; s. Paul Andrew and Louise Katherine (Johnson) Hutton; m. Vicki Lynne Bauer, 1972 (div. 1985); 1 child, Laura; m. Lynn Terri Brittner, Dec. 31, 1988 (div. 1996); children: Lorena, Paul; m. Tracy Lee Cogdill, Aug. 7, 2001. BA, Ind. U., 1972, MA, 1974, PhD, 1981. Editorial asst. Jour. Am. History, Bloomington, Ind., 1973-77; instr. history Utah State U., Logan, 1977-80, asst. prof., 1980-84, U. N.Mex., Albuquerque, 1984-86, assoc. prof., 1986-96; prof. U. N. Mex., Albuquerque, 1996—. Author: Phil Sheridan and His Army, 1985; editor: Ten Days on the Plains, 1985, Soldiers West, 1987, The Custer Reader, 1992, (series) Eyewitness to the Civil War, 1991-93, Frontier and Region, 1997; assoc. editor Western Hist. Quar., 1977-84; editor N.Mex. Hist. Rev., 1985-91. Active Little Bighorn Battlefield Indian Meml. Adv. Com., Nat. Park Svc., 1994-2002. Recipient Evans Biography award Brigham Young U., 1986, Paladin award Mont. Hist. Soc., 1991, Western Heritage award Nat. Cowboy Hall of Fame, 1996, 99, 2003; named Mead Disting. Rsch. fellow Huntington Libr., 1988. Mem. Orgn. Am. Historians (Ray A. Billington award 1986), Western Hist. Assn. (exec. dir. 1990—), Soc. for Mil. History, Western Writers Am. (exec. bd. 1997-99, pres. 2002—, Spur award 1985, 2002, Pres. award 1998, Stirrup award, 2000), Writers Guild Am. West. Office: U NMex Dept History Albuquerque NM 87131-0001 E-mail: wha@unm.edu.

HUTTON, WILLIAM MICHAEL, manufacturing executive; b. Herrin, Ill., June 15, 1948; s. William T. and Violet (Childress) Hutton; m. Lois A. Piontkowski, Sept. 7, 1968; children: Cynthia L., Pamela. BS in Mgmt. Scis., So. Ill. U., 1972; MA in Ops. Mgmt., Norwich U., 1991; PhD in Bus. Adminstrn., Kennedy-Western U., 2003. Cert. foodservice profl., SME mfg. engr. Mgr. machining ops. Ingersoll-Rand, Phillipsburg, NJ, 1973-83; mgr. of mfr. Bendix Aerospace Corp., Eatontown, NJ, 1983-84; v.p. ops. Follett Corp., Easton, Pa., 1984-87, pres., COO, 1988-95; CEO Wilkra Co., Inc., Portland, Pa., 1995, also bd. dirs.; ptnr. Filtration Mfg. Co.; founder, pres. Omega Tools, Inc. Cons. to small mfg. co.; exec. in residence So. Ill. U., 1991—, guest lectr. Coll. Bus.; guest lectr. Moravian Coll.; bd. dirs. Bustin Industries. Author: (book) Competitive Strategy, A Heuristic Model for Linking Manufacturing and Marketing, 1992, Organizational Adaptation Through Strategic Reorientation, A Study of the Gas Distribution Industry. Chmn. adv. bd. Coll. Bus. and Adminstrn. So. Ill. U., 1989—, Ben Franklin Inst., 1991—; bd. dirs. Forum Lehigh Valley. Named to Hall of Fame Coll. Bus., So. Ill. U., 1994; recipient Alumni Achievement award, 1992, Ben Franklin Innovation award, 2002. Mem.: Soc. Mfg. Engrs., Ducks Unlimited, Grouse Soc., Young Pres.'s Orgn., So. Ill. U. Alumni Assn. Republican. Roman Catholic. Avocations: computer-aided design, springer spaniel training, fly fishing, upland hunting. Home: 4640 Hillview Dr Nazareth PA 18064-8525 Office: Omega Tools Co Inc PO Box 217 Portland PA 18351 E-mail: hutton@ptd.net.

HUTTON, WINFIELD TRAVIS, management consultant, educator; b. LA, Aug. 17, 1935; s. Travis Calhoun and Frances (Gardemann) H. BS in Mgmt. summa cum laude, Ohio State U., 1956, MBA, 1957, PhD, 1959. Consumer economist Fed. Res. Bank Atlanta, 1959-62; prof. econs. Hunter Coll., CUNY, 1962-68; prof. European divsn. U. Md., 1968-79, 93-99; prof. Troy State U.-Europe, Germany, 1979-93. Cons. on mgmt., mktg. and econs. in Europe, 1968—. Author: (mgmt. computer simulations) City Finance, 1994, Simanage, 1998; author computer programs for rsch. stats.; contbr. articles to profl. jours. Lay reader St. Alban's Episcopal Ch., Kaiserslauten, Germany, 1981-88. Mem. AAUP, Am. Mktg. Assn. (manuscript reviewer 1983-94), Am. Econ. Assn., Beta Gamma Sigma. Avocations: opera, folk dancing, walking, cycling, travel. Address: 15138 Stone Ln N Apt B106 Shoreline WA 98133-6259 also: Goethestr 66 19053 Schwerin Germany

HUTZ, REINHOLD JOSEF, physiologist, educator; b. Salzburg, Austria, Mar. 18, 1956; came to the U.S., 1959; s. Josef and Eva (Strauch) H.; m. Irene Maria O'Shaughnessy, May 21, 1983; children: Erika, Michael, Peter. BS, Loyola U., 1978, MS, 1980; PhD, Mich. State U., 1983. Rsch. assoc. Wis. Regional Primate Rsch. Ctr., Madison, 1983-86, affiliate scientist, 1987—; asst. prof. biol. scis. U. Wis., Milw., 1986-92, assoc. prof., 1992-98, prof., 1998—, assoc. dean rsch. grad. sch., 2003—. Assoc. adj. prof. Med. Coll. Wis., Milw., 1991—; standing mem. NIH ALTX-4 study sect., 2001—05. Cons. editor Am. Jour. Primatology, 1990—, Primates; referee Endocrinology, Biology of Reproduction, 1983—; contbr. articles to Jour. Med. Primatology, Endocrinology, Biology of Reprodn., Chem. Biolog. Interactions, Molecular Cell Endocrinology. Mem. exec. com. Milw. Donauschwaben German Soc., Milw., 1991—, music dir., 1991—. Grantee NIH, 1992, 95—. Mem. Internat. Soc. Primatologists (treas. 1992-96), Endocrine Soc., Soc. Study Reproduction, AAAS, Am. Soc. Primatologists (program chair 1990-92). Democrat. Roman Catholic. Achievements include research in effects of natural and xenobiotic estrogens, growth factors and environmental molecules (such as dioxins) on ovarian function. Home: 4830 N Bartlett Ave Milwaukee WI 53217-6016 Office: U Wis 3209 N Maryland Ave Milwaukee WI 53211-0413

HUTZELMAN, MARTHA LOUISE, lawyer; b. Hamilton, Ohio, Jan. 2, 1958; d. Donald Evert and Jeanne Louise (Thompson) H.; 1 child, Isolda Marie Meade. BA, Ohio No. U., 1979; JD, U. Ariz., 1982. Bar: Okla. 1983, Va. 1995, U.S. Tax Ct. 1991. Tax staff acct. Arthur Andersen & Co., Oklahoma City, 1982-83; benefits tax counsel Kerr-McGee Corp., Oklahoma City, 1983-91; sr. trial atty. IRS, Washington, 1991-95; shareholder Bosley Hutzelman, Alexandria, Va., 1995—. Mem. ABA (mem. employee benefits com. tax sect. 1996—, chair employee benefits com. tort and ins. practice sect. 2001, mem. joint com. employee benefits). Home: 9025 Andromeda Dr Burke VA 22015-3504 Office: Bosley Hutzelman 675N Washington St Ste 202 Alexandria VA 22314-1934 E-mail: mhutzelman@upensionlaw.com.

HUTZLER, LISA ANN, mental health nurse, adult clinical psychologist; b. Marietta, Ohio, Oct. 8, 1955; d. Donald Hayes and Winifred Maxine (Clark) Hutzler; m. Ernest Edwin Miller Jr., May 24, 1980; children: Nathan Andrew Miller, Daniel Seth Miller. BA in Psychology, Marietta Coll., 1977; AAS, Parkersburg Community Coll., W.Va., 1980; MA in Psychology, W. Va. Grad. Coll., 1995. RN, W.Va. Nurse adult psychiat. unit Cuyahoga Falls (Ohio) Gen. Hosp., 1982-83; staff nurse adult mental health St. Joseph's Hosp., Parkersburg, 1980-82, 85-91; personal care nurse Braley and Thompson, Vienna, W.Va., 1992-93; staff nurse Health South Western Hills Regional Rehab. Hosp., Vienna, 2002—. Vol. Boy Scouts Am./standard first aid instr., ARC. Mem. ANA, W.Va. Nurses Assn.

HUURMAN, WALTER WILLIAM, pediatric orthopaedic surgeon, educator; b. Rochester, N.Y., Mar. 16, 1936; s. Walter U. and Anna Mae (Lennon) H.; m. Lindsay Ann McGuiness, Dec. 16, 1967; children: Sean Patrick, Anne Lindsay. BS, U. Notre Dame, 1958; MD, Northwestern U., 1962. Diplomate Am. Bd. Orthopaedic Surgery. Intern Cook County Hosp., Chgo., 1962-63; flight surgeon USS Hornet, San Diego, 1964-66, NAS Miramar, San Diego, 1966-68; resident in orthopedic surgery Naval Regional Med. Ctr., Oakland, Calif., 1968-71; dir. pediatric orthopaedics USN, Oakland, Calif., 1973-77; prof. pediatrics and orthopaedics U. Nebr., Omaha, 1977—; dir. pediatric orthopedics U. Nebr./Children's Meml. Hosp., Omaha, 1977. Bd. dirs. Nat. Alumni, Northwestern U. Mem. editl. bd. Jour. Pediat. Orthopaedics, 1981-83, Jour. Bone and Joint Surgery, 1983-87, Pediatrics in Rev., 1995—; reviewer Clin. Orthopaedics and Related Rsch., 1985—, Jour. Am. Acad. Orthopaedic Surgeons, 1998—; contbr. articles to sci. and profl. jours. Pres., chmn. bd. dirs. Nebr. Arthritis Found., 1984. Capt. USN, 1963-77; res., 1980-95, ret. Fellow Am. Acad. Orthopaedic Surgery, Am. Acad. Pediatrics (chmn. orthopaedic sect. 1986-89), ACS; mem. AMA, Am. Orthopaedic Assn., Omaha Midwest Clin. Soc. (pres. 1994), Nebr. Orthopaedic Soc. (pres. 2000—), Pediat. Orthopaedic Soc. N.Am.(bd. dirs. 1994-2000), Acad. Orthopaedic Soc., Northwestern U. Feinberg Sch. Medicine Alumni Assn. (pres.-elect 2003—). Roman Catholic. Achievements include a pending patent for a club foot treatment device. Office: U Nebr Med Ctr 600 S 42nd St Omaha NE 68198-1002

HUVANE, KEVIN, talent agent; Talent agt. Creative Artists Agy., Beverly Hills, Calif. Office: Creative Artists Agy 9830 Wilshire Blvd Beverly Hills CA 90212-1825

HUVOS, ANDREW, internist, cardiologist, educator; b. Budapest, Hungary, Apr. 23, 1930; came to U.S., 1950; s. Julian Gyula and Magdolna (Matyas) H.; m. Monique Chatriot, June 8, 1959; children: Christine, Anne, Philip. Student, Free U. Brussels, 1948-50, Harvard U., 1951; MD, Boston U., 1955. Diplomate Am. Bd. Internal Medicine, Am. Bd. Cardiovascular Disease. Resident in medicine Yale-New Haven Med. Ctr., 1955-59; fellow in cardiology Mass. Gen. Hosp., Boston, 1961-63; physician-in-charge cardiac catheterization lab. Univ. Hosp., Boston, 1963-70; chief cardiology Faulkner Hosp., Boston, 1970-74, chief medicine, 1974-95; lectr. medicine Harvard Med. Sch., Boston, 1974-86; lectr. medicine and physiology Boston U. Sch. Medicine, 1976—95; prof. medicine Tufts U. Sch. Medicine, Boston, 1985-97, prof. emeritus, 1997—. Dir. Tufts Assoc. Health Plan, 1979-81. Contbr. articles to med. jours., chpts. to books. Chmn. bd. trustees Ecole Bilingue, Inc., Arlington, Mass., 1970-74; trustee Boston Med. Libr., 1981-85. Capt. M.C., U.S. Army, 1959-61. Recipient Excellence in Teaching award Boston U. Sch. Medicine, 1974; USPHS grantee, 1977-83. Fellow: ACP, Mass. Med. Soc. (del., mem. com. on med. edn. 1981—95), Am. Heart Assn., Am. Coll. Chest Physicians (pres. New Eng. States chpt. 1981—83), Am. Coll. Cardiology; mem.: Roxbury Clin. Record Club, Dorchester Med. Club, Alpha Omega Alpha. Presbyterian. Avocations: opera, classical music. Office: Faulkner Hosp Boston MA 02130

HUXFORD, J. DAVID, retired sales representative; b. Syracuse, N.Y., Jan. 2, 1925; s. James H. and Marion Louise (McNally) H.; m. Theodora Annette Weeks, Oct. 31, 1946; four children. BA in Econs., Notre Dame U., 1951. Supply & cost mgr. L.A.B. Corp., Skaneateles, N.Y., 1953-58; contract sales Pitts. Plate Glass Co., Syracuse, 1958-62; archl. rep. PPG Industries, Inc., Skaneateles, 1962-75; contract sales B.R. Johnson & Son, Inc., Syracuse, 1975-77; mfr.'s rep. Roberts-Gordon Inc., Buffalo, Syracuse, 1978-92. Pres. Prodrs. Coun., Syracuse chpt., 1968-69; first industry mem. pres. Constrn. Specifications Inst., Syracuse chpt., 1974-75; trustee Village Bd., Skaneateles, 1963-64, N.Y. State Hunter Instr., 1953-86, chmn. planning bd., 1990—, Nat. Rifle Assn. (life Mem.). Ret. Capt. USMC Reserve, 1942-63. Home: 52 Fennell St Skaneateles NY 13152-1122 Office: Skaneateles Library Association 49 East Genesee Street Skaneateles NY 13152

HUXLEY, SIR ANDREW (SIR ANDREW FIELDING HUXLEY), physiologist, educator; b. London, Nov. 22, 1917; s. Leonard and Rosalind (Bruce) H.; m. Jocelyn Richenda Gammell Pease, July 5, 1947 (dec. Mar. 2003); children: Janet Rachel, Stewart Leonard, Camilla Rosalind, Eleanor Bruce, Henrietta Catherine, Clare Marjory Pease. BA, Cambridge (Eng.) U., 1938, MA, 1941, ScD (hon.), 1978; MD (hon.), U. Saar, 1964, Marseille U., 1979, Humboldt U., Berlin, 1985, Ulm U., 1993, Charles U., Prague, 1998; DSc (hon.), U. Sheffield, Eng., 1964, U. Leicester, 1967, London U., 1973, U. St. Andrews, Scotland, 1974, U. Aston, Birmingham, Eng., 1977, U. Western Australia, 1982, Oxford U., 1983, U. Pa., 1984, Harvard U., 1984, U. Keele, 1985, East Anglia U., 1985, U. Md., 1987, Brunel U., 1988, U. Hyderabad, 1991, Glasgow U., 1993, Witwatersrand U., 1998; LLD (hon.), U. Birmingham, 1979, Dundee U., 1984; Dr (hon.), York U., 1981, Toyama Med. and Pharm. U., 1995; DHL (hon.), NYU, 1982. Mem. rsch. staff Anti-Aircraft Command, 1940-42, Admiralty, 1942-45; fellow Trinity Coll., Cambridge, 1941-60, 90—, hon. fellow, 1967-90, master, 1984-90, dir. studies, 1952-60. Demonstrator dept. physiology Cambridge U., 1946—50, asst. dir. rsch. dept. physiology, 1951—59, reader exptl. biophysics, 1959—60; Jodrell prof. U. Coll. London, 1960—69, Royal Soc. rsch. prof., 1969—83; emeritus prof. London U., 1983—, hon. fellow, 1980—; fellow Royal Soc. London, 1955—, Croonian lectr., 1967, mem. coun., 1960—62, 1977—79, pres., 1980—85; Herter lectr. Johns Hopkins U., 1959; Jesup lectr. Columbia U., 1964; Forbes lectr., 66; Florey lectr., 82; Blackett Meml. lectr., 84; Fullerian prof. Royal Inst., London, 1967—73; Hans Hecht lectr., Chgo., 1975; Sherrington lectr Liverpool U., 1976—77; Centenary Colloquium lectr. Berlin Inst. Physiology, 1977; Cecil H. and Ida Green vis. prof. U. B.C., 1980; 6th ann. Darwin Lecture, 82; Romanes Lecture Oxford U., 1983; Tarner lectr. Trinity Coll., Cambridge, 1988; Maulana Abul Kalam Azad Meml. Lecture, New Delhi, 91; C.G. Bernhard lecture Stockholm, 1993; Davson lecture Am. Physiol. Soc., 1998; Wartenweiler lecture Internat. Soc. of Biomechanics, Calgary, 1999. Author: Reflections on Muscle, 1980; editor Jour. Physiology, 1950-57, chmn. bd. Publs. on analysis of nerve conduction (with Hodgkin), physiology of striated muscle, devel. of interference microscope and ultramicrotome. Trustee Brit. Mus. (Natural History), 1981-90, Sci. Mus., 1984-88; mem. Agrl. Rsch. Coun., 1977-80, Nature Conservancy Coun., 1985-88, Animal Procedures Com., 1987-95. Decorated knight bachelor, Order of Merit, Grand Cordon of Sacred Treasure Japan; recipient (with A.L. Hodgkin and J.C. Eccles), Nobel Prize for physiology or medicine, 1963, Swammerdam medal, Soc. for Advancement of Natural Scis., Medicine and Surgery, Amsterdam, 1997, Copley medal, Royal Soc., 1973; fellow, Imperial Coll. Sci., Tech. and Medicine, 1980, Queen Mary and Westfield Coll., 1987, Royal Holloway and Bedford New Coll., 1994. Fellow Royal Acad. Engring. (hon.), Inst. Biology (hon.), Royal Soc. Can. (hon.), Royal Soc. Edinburgh (hon.), Royal Coll. Physicians (hon.), Acad. Med. Sci. (hon.), Indian Nat. Sci. Acad. (fgn.); mem. Physiol. Soc. (hon., rev. lectr. on muscular contraction 1973), Internat. Union Physiol. Scis. (pres. 1986-93), Brit. Biophys. Soc., Found. for Sci. and Tech., Royal Acad. Scis., Letters and Fine Arts Belgium (assoc.), Muscular Dystrophy Campaign (chmn. med. research com. 1974-81; v.p., 1981—), Royal Instn. Gt. Britain (hon.), Anat. Soc. Gt. Britain and Ireland (hon.), Am. Acad. Arts and Scis. (hon.), Am. Philos. Soc. (Penrose lectr. 1986), Brit. Assn. Advancement Sci. (pres. 1976-77), Leopoldina

Acad. (hon.), NAS (U.S.) (fgn. assoc.), Royal Acad. Medicine Belgium (assoc.), Dutch Soc. Scis. (fgn.), Royal Danish Acad. Sci. (hon.), Am. Soc. Zoologists (hon.), Royal Irish Acad. (hon.), Japan Acad. (hon.). Home and Office: Manor Field 1 Vicarage Dr Grantchester Cambridge CB3 9NG England

HUXLEY, HUGH ESMOR, molecular biologist, educator; b. Birkenhead, Eng., Feb. 25, 1924; s. Thomas Hugh and Olwen (Roberst) H.; m. Frances Fripp; 1 child, 3 stepchildren. BA, Cambridge (Eng.) U., 1948, MA, 1950, PhD, 1952, ScD, 1964; DSc (hon.), Harvard U., 1969, U. Chgo., 1974, U. Pa., 1975, U. Leicester, 1989. Rsch. student molecular biology unit Med. Rsch. Coun., Cavendish Lab., Cambridge, 1948-52, sci. staff, 1954-55; external staff dept. biophysics Med. Rsch. Coun., U. Coll., London, 1956-61, Med. Rsch. Coun. Lab. Molecular Biology, London, 1962-87, joint head structural studies divsn., 1974-84, dep. dir., 1977-87; prof. biology rosenteil Basic Med. Scis. Rsch. Ctr., Brandeis U., Waltham, Mass., 1987-97, dir., 1988-94, prof. emeritus, 1997—. Editor: Progress in Biophysics and Molecular Biology, 1960-66; mem. editl. bd. Jour. Cell Biology, 1959-63, Jour. Molecular Biology, 1962-70, 79-86, 90-93, Jour. Cell Sci., 1966-70; contbr. articles to profl. jours. Officer RAF, 1943-47. Decorated Mem. Order Brit. Empire; recipient Feldberg prize, 1963, Hardy prize, 1965, Louisa Gross Hurwitz prize, 1971, Internat. Feltrinelli prize, 1974, Gairdner award, 1975, Baly medal Royal Coll. Physicians, 1975, E.B. Wilson medal Am. Soc. Cell Biology, 1983, Albert Einstein award World Cultural Coun., 1987, Franklin medal, 1990, Disting. Scientist award Electron Microscopy Soc. Am., 1991; Commonwealth Fund fellow Mass. Inst. Tech., 1952-54, Christ's Coll. fellow Cambridge U., 1954-56, hon. fellow, 1981, King's Coll. fellow, 1961-67, Churchill Coll. fellow, 1967-87. Fellow Royal Soc. (Royal medal 1977, Copley medal 1997), Am. Biophysical Soc.; mem. NAS (hon. fgn. assoc.), Physiol. Soc., Brit. Biophys. Soc., European Molecular Biology Orgn., Am. Acad. Arts and Scis. (hon. fgn.), Danish Acad. Scis., Leopoldina Acad. Home: 349 Nashawtuc Rd Concord MA 01742-1616 Business E-Mail: huxley@brandeis.edu.

HUXLEY, MARY ATSUKO, artist; b. Stockton, Calif., Mar. 5, 1930; d. Henry K. and Kiku H. (Kisanuki) Taniguchi; m. Harold Daniels Huxley, 1957. Student, Armstrong Coll., Berkeley, Calif., 1950, San Francisco Art Inst., 1968; pvt. studies with, Thomas C. Leighton, 1970-75. Art show judge regional art clubs, corps., pvt. orgns., and county fairs, 1972-03. Solo shows include Artists' Coop., San Francisco, 1973, 75, 76, The Univ. Club Invitational, San Francisco, 1976, I. Magnin, San Mateo, 1976, Palo Alto Med. Found., 1992, Galerie Genese, San Mateo, 1993; exhibited in juried group shows at Catharine Lorillard Wolf Art Club, N.Y.C., 1979, Knickerbocker Artists of Am., N.Y.C., 1979, Salmagundi Club Ann., N.Y.C., 1981, Butler Inst. Am. Art, Youngstown, Ohio, 1982, Am. Artists Profl. League, N.Y.C., 1982, 83, 86, 87, 88, Oil Painters of Am. Ann. Nat. Juried Shows, Gallery at Long Grove, Ill., 1993, 94, Taos, N.Mex., 1997, Oil Painters of Am. Ann. Pacific Coast Regional Juried Show, Jones & Terwilliger Gallery, Carmel, Calif., 1997, San Francisco Ann. Art Festival, 1970-74, Renaissance Gallery, Santa Rosa, Calif., 1973, Paramount Theater, Oakland, Calif., 1974, Met. Club Invitational, San Francisco, Marin Soc. Artists Ann., Ross, Calif., 1976, 79, Soc. Western Artists Ann., San Francisco, 1976, 78, 80, Peninsula Art Assn. Ann., Belmont, Calif., 1980, Fresno (Calif.) Fashion Fair Ann., 1981, 84, De Saisset Gallery, U. Santa Clara, Calif., 1979, Lodi (Calif.) Ann. Grape and Art Festival, 1970, 71, 72, 73, 74, 75, 76, 77, 78, 79, 81, San Mateo County Ann. Floral Fiesta, 1975, 76, 77, 78, 79, 81, Charles & Emma Frye Mus. Gallery, Seattle, 1975, Redwood City Women's Club Ann. Flower Show, 1978, Fremont Art Assn. Anns., 1987, 88, 89, John Muir Med. Ctr. invitational, 1999-2000, 3 Com-Synopsis Invitational Traveling Exhibit, 2000-01; numerous others; represented in numerous pvt. and corp. collections in U.S., Europe and Asia. Recipient Marjorie Walter Spl. award San Mateo County Exhbn., 1975, Gold medallion and 1st award San Mateo County Fair Fine Arts Exhbn., 1976, Best of Show award Cultural Arts of Palo Alto and Palo Alto Art Club, 1979, Best of Show and 1st award U. Art Ctr. and Palo Alto Art Club Ann., 1981, Spl. Merit award Oakland Art Assn., John Muir Med. Ctr. Ann., 1989, 1st award Burlingame Art Soc. Anns., 1976, 77, 1st award Redwood City Women's Club Ann. Flower Show, 1978, 1st award Soc. Western Artists Palo Alto Med. Ctr. Ann., 1983, 1st award Soc. Western Artists John Muir Med. Ctr. Ann., 1986, 1st award Fremont Art Assn. Ann., 1989, numerous others. Fellow Am. Artists Profl. League; mem. Soc. Western Artists (signature, trustee 1986-97, bd. dirs. 1972-75, 98, chmn. juried exhbns. 1972-81), Am. Soc. Classical Realism, Oil Painters Am. (signature), Allied Artists Am., Marin Soc. Artists (signature). Studio: PO Box 5467 San Mateo CA 94402-0467

HUXTABLE, ADA LOUISE, architecture critic; b. N.Y.C. d. Michael Louis and Leah (Rosenthal) Landman; m. L. Garth Huxtable. AB magna cum laude, Hunter Coll.; postgrad., Inst. Fine Arts, NYU; hon. degrees, Harvard U., Yale U., NYU, Washington U., U. Mass., Oberlin Coll., Miami U., R.I. Sch. Design, U. Pa., Radcliffe Coll., Oberlin Coll., Smith Coll., Skidmore Coll., Md. Inst., Mt. Holyoke Coll., Trinity Coll., LaSalle U., Pace Coll., Pratt Inst., Colgate U., Hamilton U., Williams Coll., Rutgers U., Finch Coll., Emerson Coll., C.W. Post Coll. at L.I. U., Cleve. State U., Bard Coll., Fordham U., Parsons Sch. Design, Mass. Coll. Art, Nottingham U., England. Asst. curator architecture and design The Museum of Modern Art, N.Y.C., 1946-50; Fulbright fellow for advanced study in architecture and design Italy, 1950, 52; free-lance writer, contbg. editor to Progressive Architecture and Art in America, 1950-63; architecture critic N.Y. Times, N.Y.C., 1963-82, mem. editorial bd., 1973-82; Cook lectr. in Am. instns. U. Mich., 1977; Hitchcock lect. U. Calif.-Berkeley, 1982. Corp. vis. com. Harvard U. Grad. Sch. Design, Sch. Visual and Environ. Arts; mem. adv. bd. Am. Trust Brit. Libr.; archtl. cons. Nat. Gallery, London, J. Paul Getty Trust, L.A., San Francisco Pub. Libr., Mus. Contemporary Art, Chgo., Kansas City Art Mus.; archtl. critic The Wall Street Jour., 1996—. Author: Pier Luigi Nervi, 1960, Classic New York, 1964, Will They Ever Finish Bruckner Boulevard?, 1970, Kicked a Building Lately?, 1976, The Tall Building Artistically Reconsidered: The Search for a Skyscraper Style, 1985, Goodbye History, Hello Hamburger 1986, Architecture Anyone? 1986, The Unreal America: Architecture and Illusion, 1997. Recipient 1st Pulitzer prize for disting. criticism, 1970, Spl. award Nat. Trust for Historic Preservation, 1971, Archtl. Criticism medal AIA, 1969, medal for lit. Nat. Arts Club, 1971, Diamond Jubilee medallion City N.Y., 1973, Mayor's Cultural award, 1984, Woman of Yr. award AAUW, 1974, Sec.'s award for conservation U.S. Dept. Interior, 1976, Thomas Jefferson medal U. Va., 1977, Archtl. Criticism medal Acad. d' Architecture Française, 1988; Guggenheim fellow for studies in Am. architecture, 1958, MacArthur fellow, 1981-86, fellow Ctr. for Scholars and Writers, N.Y. Pub. Libr., 1999-00; Henry Allen Moe prize Humanities Am. Philosophical Soc., 1992. Fellow Am. Acad. Arts and Scis., Royal Inst. Brit. Architects (hon.), AAAL; mem. AIA (hon.), Am. Acad. Arts and Letters, Soc. Archtl. Historians. Home: 969 Park Ave New York NY 10028-0322

HUYBRECHTS, STEVEN MARC, space system technologist; b. Dover, N.H., Dec. 29, 1969; s. Marc Huybrechts and Brigitte Duces, John Strawhorn (Stepfather) and Ellida Yngente(Stepmother); m. Wendy Marie Cubbison, Oct. 11, 2002; children: Rachel Johnson, Caden, Taryn. BSc in Physics and Computer Sci., McGill U., Montreal, Can., 1991; MS in Aero. and Astron. Engring., Stanford U., 1992, PhD in Aero. and Astron. Engring., 1995. Rschr. Ctr. for Spacecraft Component Tech., Kirtland AFB, N.Mex., 1992—99, chief, 1999—2002. Recipient Arthur S. Flemming award, Flemming Found. and Georgetown U., 2000, Stellar award, Rotary Nat. Award for Space Achievement, 2000, Sci. and Tech. Achievement award, Air Force Materiel Command, 1997. Fellow: AIAA (sub-com. chair, conf. chair 1999—2002). Achievements include development of many enabling technologies for future space systems. Office: Air Force Rsch Lab 3550 Aberdeen Ave Kirtland Afb NM 87117-5776 Personal E-mail: smhuybrechts@stanfordalumni.org.

HUYCK, MARGARET HELLIE, psychology educator; b. Waterloo, Iowa, Apr. 14, 1939; d. Ole Ingeman and Mary Elizabeth (larsen) Hellie; m. William Thomas Huyck, June 24, 1961; children: Elizabeth, Karin. BA, Vassar Coll., 1961; MA, U. Chgo., 1963, PhD, 1970. Lic. psychologist, Ill. Asst. prof. Ill. Inst. Tech., Chgo., 1969-75, assoc. prof., 1975-89, prof. dept. psychology, 1990—. Vis. lectr. U. Oslo, 1977-78; lectr. Provident Hosp. Sch. Nursing, Chgo., 1964-66, Am. Soc. Aging, 1989-91; cons. Northwestern U., Evanston, Ill., 1973-79, Elgin (Ill.) Mental Health Ctr., 1975-77, No. Trust Bank, Chgo., 1981-85, Evanston Hosp., 1992-93, Metro. Family Svcs., 1998—. Author: Growing Older, 1974; co-author: Adult Development, 1982. Bd. mem. S.E. Chgo. Commn. Recipient Rsch. award NIMH, 1982-86. Fellow Gerontol. Assn. Am., Gerontol. Soc. Am. (sec. 1991-94); mem. APA (sci. policy fellow Office Behavioral and Social Sci. Rsch./NIH 1997-98), Older Women's League Ill. (pres. 1994-97, 2000—). Unitarian-Universalist. Office: Ill Inst Tech Inst Psychology Chicago IL 60616-3732 E-mail: mhhuyck@sbcglobal.net.

HUYETT, DEBRA KATHLEEN, elementary education educator; b. Massillon, Ohio, Oct. 10, 1955; d. William Wilbur and Vivian Delores (Anderson) H. BA, Stetson U., 1978. Cert. elem. and early childhood edn. tchr., Fla. Dir. assistance and long distance operator Gen. Telephone, Myrtle Beach, S.C., summer 1974-76; desk clk. Bon Villa Motel, Myrtle Beach, summer 1976-79; tchr. Lake Orienta Elem. Sch., Altamonte Springs, Fla., 1978-88, Bear Lake Elem. Sch., Apopka, Fla., 1988-2000; outreach specialist Seminole County Sch. Bd., 2000-01; reading specialist Goldsboro Math., Sci. and Tech. Magnet Elem. Sch., 2001—. Curriculum rep. Lake Orienta Elem. Sch., 1980-88, v.p. PTA, 1984-85; mem. Sch. Adv. Bd., 1995-97. Campaign vol. City Coun. Rep., Massillon, 1973; counselor Orange County Jail Ministry, Orlando, Fla., 1988-91; cmty. counselor EurAuPair, 1996-98. Named to Most Admired Men and Women of the Yr., 1995. Mem. Fla. Reading Conv. (chairperson Orlando chpt. 1983-84, chairperson for transp. and tours 1985-86), Seminole Edn. Assn. (faculty rep. Sanford, Fla. chpt. 1980-81), Seminole County Reading Coun. (rep. for Goldsboro 2001—), Delta Kappa Gamma. Republican. Baptist. Avocations: travel, reading, beach. Home: 893 Little Bend Rd Altamonte Springs FL 32714-7514 E-mail: DKH551010@aol.com.

HUYGENS, REMMERT WILLIAM, architect; b. Haarlem, The Netherlands, Apr. 19, 1932; came to U.S., 1956, naturalized, 1963; s. Willem and Antoinette (Bruynzeel) H. Diploma dept. architecture, Amsterdam HTS, 1955. With Marcel Breuer, N.Y.C., 1956; pvt. practice architecture Boston, 1960—. Prin. works include: Campus Rivers Country Day Sch., Weston, Mass., 1960, Longy Concert Hall, Cambridge, Mass., 1966, Interfaith Religious Ctr. Columbia, Md., 1967, campus N.H. Coll., Manchester, 1969-81, The Village of Loon Mountain, Lincoln, N.H., 1973—, Cath. Med. Ctr. Manchester, 1974, Milford (Conn.) Pub. Libr., 1976, Village Green at Stowe, Vt., 1980—, rsch. bldgs. for Biogen Inc., Cambridge, Mass. and Geneva, 1980, Indian Head Nat. Bank, Nashua, N.H., 1981, Pub. Lib., Framingham, Mass., 1982, Teradyne Circuits Inc., Nashua, 1983, Riverview office tower, Cambridge, 1985, Cochituate Place office bldg., Framingham, 1986 One Memorial Drive office tower, Cambridge, 1986, Constitution Office Complex, Boston, 1987, Water's Edge Resort, Westbrook, Conn., 1987, Franklin Park Zoo, Boston, 1989, Ipswich (Mass.) Country Club, 1989; office parks, residential communities and pvt. residences in U.S., Holland, France, Switzerland, Malaysia, corp. headquarters and rsch. facilities for Genzyme Corp., Enzytech Inc., BioSurface Technology Inc., ImmunoGen Inc., Digital Equipment Corp., urban planning Guangzhou, China, 100 story office tower, Guangzhou, China, 1990, work exhibited at N.Y. Archtl. League, N.Y. Mus. Modern Art, N.Y., Brockton Art Ctr., Boston Arch. Ctr.; works pub. in numerous books and jours., U.S., Eng., Holland, Italy, Japan, France, Belgium, Germany, China, others, including: Arch. Record, Archtl. Forum, AIA Jour., Am. Home, House and Garden, Progressive Arch., House Beautiful, N.Y. Times, Boston Globe. Recipient Abu-Dhabi Conf. Ctr. award, 1st award Internat. Masonry Inst., Modern Architecture award, Conseil d'Architecture, d'Urbanisme et de l'Environment (CAUE), France, others. Fellow AIA (Progressive Architecture Design awards, Honor awards New England regional coun., award of merit R.I. chpt., Conn. Soc. Architects./AIA Design award). Office: R W Huygens Arch Inc 125 Old Connecticut Path Wayland MA 01778-3201

HUYGHE, PATRICK ANTOINE, writer, editor; b. Newport News, Va., Aug. 28, 1952; s. Alain Emile and Gladys Huyghe; m. Carolyn Ann Schoemer, Oct. 23, 1988; 1 child, Alexandra. BA in Psychology, U. Va., 1974; MS in Pub. Comm., Syracuse U., 1976. Staff editor US Mag. N.Y. Times, N.Y.C., 1977-78; staff writer Newsweek Focus, Newsweek, Inc., N.Y.C., 1980; contbg. editor Sci. Digest, Hearst Mags., N.Y.C., 1981-84; sci. writer-in-residence Va. Poly. and State U., Blacksburg, 1986; ind. prodr. Innovation Sta. WNET, N.Y.C., 1987-90; freelance writer N.Y., 1979-2000; contbg. editor Omni, Gen. Media Internat., 1995-98; editor-in-chief Paraview Pub., N.Y.C., 2000—. Cons. Liberty Sci. Ctr., Jersey City, 1992, The Anomalist Website, 1995—, Petrosains Discovery Ctr., Malaysia, 1996—97, Small Comets Website, U. Iowa, 1997—. Author: (book) Glowing Birds, 1985, Columbus Was Last, 1992, The Field Guide to Extraterrestrials, 1996, Swamp Gas Times, 2001; co-author: The Big Splash, 1990, The Field Guide to Bigfoot, Yeti, and Other Mystery Primates Worldwide, 1999, The Field Guide to UFOs, The Field Guide to Ghosts and Other Apparitions, 2000. Fellow, Josiah Macy Found., 1985, Hopkins Found., 1996. Mem.: Soc. Sci. Exploration, Nat. Assn. Sci. Writers, Authors Guild. Address: PO Box 577 Jefferson Valley NY 10535-0577

HUYLER, JEAN WILEY, communications executive, consultant; b. Seattle, Mar. 30, 1935; d. Othello Phillip and Agnes Olivia (Snarr) Dickert; m. Richard Wiley, Apr. 1955 (div. 1963); children: Richard Kenneth Jr., Cynthia Jean; m. Garey Heath Huyler, Mar. 2, 1968 (div. 1972). BA, Marylhurst Coll., 1978; MA in Social Scis., Pacific Luth. U., Parkland, Wash., 1979; DLitt, Fairfax U., New Orleans, 1989; Degree in Hypnotherapy, Tacoma Coll., 1990. Ordained to ministry ReCreationists Assembly, 1991. Bur. mgr., reporter Lynnwood (Wash.) Enterprise, 1961-63; city editor, reporter/photographer Everett (Wash.) Daily Herald, 1963-71; spl. sects. editor Seattle Post-Intelligencer, 1971; sr. econ. editor Rainier Bancorp., Seattle, 1971-72; assoc. editor, women's editor Valley Newspapers, Kent, Wash., 1973-75; CEO Jean Wiley Huyler Comm., Gig Harbor, Wash., 1975—, EdCom-UpCom-One Step Beyond-TravCom, Gig Harbor, Wash., 1981—97. Environ. editor-writer Bonneville Power Adminstrn.-U.S. Dept. Interior, Portland, Oreg., 1976-77; comm. svc. dir. Wash. State Sch. Dirs. Assn., Olympia, 1977-81. Author: Communications is a People Process, 2d edit., 1981, Crisis Communications, 2d edit., 1981, De-mystifying the Media, 2d edit., 1981; editor, designer: For the Record: Tacoma Schools, 1984 (Nat. Sch. Pub. Rels. Assn. award 1985), Lifespan Learning on Centerstage of the Future, 1988, Learning to Learn: New Techniques for Corporate Education, 1989. Min. ReCreationists Assemlby, 1990—; minister and spiritual healer various orgns. Recipient Superior Performance award Wash. Press Assn., 1964, Communicator of Achievement, 1987, Pres.'s award, 1994, Nat. Excellence in Edn. Comms. award Nat. Assn. State Edn. Dept. Info. Officers, 1979, numerous other nat. and regional cmty. svc. and comm. awards. Mem. Nat. Fedn. Press Women (exec. bd. 1971-91, v.p. 1973-75, pres. 1975-77, Communicator of Achievement award 1988), Wash. Press Assn. (pres. 1971-73), Nat. Guild Hypnotists. Avocations: travel writing and photojournalism, adventuring.

HUYNH, QUANG KHAI, biochemist; b. Tuyhoa, Phu Yen, Vietnam, Jan. 10, 1952; s. Dieu H. and Chon Luong; m. Michiko S. Huynh, Aug. 1, 1979; children: Linda, Vicky, Amy. BS, Chiba U., Japan, 1975; MS, U. Osaka Pref., Japan, 1977; PhD, Osaka U., Japan, 1981. Rsch. scientist Monsanto, St. Louis, 1987-90, sr. rsch. specialist, 1990-94, assoc. fellow, 1996-2000; sr. rsch. scientist Monsanto Co./Searle, St. Louis, 1994-96; sci. fellow Pharmacia Corp., St. Louis, 2000—. Sr. rsch. biochemist Monsanto Co., St. Louis, 1985; post doctoral rsch. assoc. U. Tex., Austin, 1981. Contbr. over 40 articles to profl. jours. Grantee NIH, 1981-85; recipient Spl. award Robert A. Welch Found., 1985. Mem. AAAS, Protein Soc., Inflammation Rsch. Soc., Am. Soc. Biochemistry and Molecular Biology. Home: 1905 Powderhorn Pass Ct Wildwood MO 63011 Office: Pharmacia Corp/Monsanto Co 800 W Lindbergh Blvd Saint Louis MO 63167 E-mail: quang.k.huynh@pharmacia.com.

HUYPENS, JOZEF MARIA ALFONS, communication consultant; b. Geel, Antwerp, Belgium, Mar. 7, 1948; s. Robert Huypens and Maria Vangeel; m. Bertje Sterckx, July 28, 1969 (dec. Apr. 1999); children: Sven, Inge. Lic. Social Scis., Cath. U. Leuven, 1971, Doctor Comml. Scis., 1980. Journalist Gazet Van Antwerpen, Belgium, 1971-85, dep. editor-in-chief, 1985-91, editor-in-chief, 1991-96; prof. U. Antwerp, Belgium, 1992—, U. Leuven, Belgium, 1998—; gen. mgr. Communicado Int., Belgium, 1996—. Author: De Plaatselyke Nieuwsfabriek, 1980; co-author: Public Relations Non-Profit Organization, 1983; editor: Media en Politiek, 1999; contbr. articles to profl. publs. Senator Jaycees Internat., 1982—; pres. Vrienden Van Ter Wende, 1988—. Mem. Orde Van den Prince. Avocations: squash, music. Home: 's Hertogenlaan 58 3000 Leuven Belgium Office: Communicado Int 'S Hertogenlaan 58 3000 Leuven Belgium E-mail: jhuypens@communicado.be.

HUYSMAN, ARLENE WEISS, psychologist, educator, writer; b. Phila., 1929; d. Max and Anna (Pearlene) Weiss; m. Pedro Camacho; children: Pamela Claire, James David. BA, Shaw U., 1973; MA, Goddard Coll., 1974; PhD, Union Inst. Grad., 1980. Diplomate Am. Bd. Psychol. Specialties, Med. Psychology, 1997. Actress, dir. Dramatic Workshop, N.Y.C., 1956—68; music and drama critic and columnist Orlando (Fla.) Sentinel Star, 1966—68; psychodramatist Volusia County Guidance Ctr., Daytona Beach, Fla., 1966—68; free-lance journalist, 1968—70; psychodramatist Psychiat. Inst. Jackson Meml. Hosp., Miami, 1972—77; dir. Adult Day Treatment Ctr., 1974—77, Lithium Clinic, 1976—77; psychodramatist South Fla. State Hosp., Hollywood, 1971—72; psychotherapy supr., Neurosci. program coord. Miami Heart Inst., 1984—; clin. dir. Family Workshop, 1985—, Adult Day Treatment Ctrs., 1987—; founder, dir. Geriatric Adult Day Treatment Ctrs. Adj. asst. prof. Med. Sch. U. Miami, 1976—; adj. prof. Union Inst., 1992—, Antioch U., 1995—; specialist in Bi Polar Disorders, U. Wis., 1980—. Author: A Mother's Tears, 1998, 2002, The Postpartum Effect: Deadly Depression in Mothers, 2003. Mem. adv. panel Fine Arts Coun. Fla., 1976—77. Recipient Best Dirs. award and Best Actress award, Fla. Theatre Festival, 1967. Mem.: APA, Fla. Assn. Practicing Psychologists (bd. dirs., pres.), World Fedn. Mental Health, Am. Assn. Group Psychotherapy and Psychodrama, Am. Soc. Aging, Internat. Assn. Group Psychotherapy, Mental Health Assn. Dade County, Dade County Psychol. Assn. (bd. dirs.), Fla. Psychol. Assn., Am. Coll. Forensic Examiners, Fedn. Partial Hospitalization Study Groups, Moreno Acad., Union Inst. Grad. Alumni Assn. (bd. dirs., southeastern rep., pres.-elect). Office: Ctr Psychol Growth 3050 Biscayne Blvd Miami FL 33137-4143 E-mail: drhuysman@yahoo.com .

HUZURBAZAR, APARNA V. statistician; arrived in U.S., 1979; BA in Math., Claremont McKenna Coll., 1986; BS in Aerospace Engring., U. Colo., 1988; PhD in Stats., Colo. State U., 1994. Assoc. prof. of stats. U. N.Mex, Albuquerque, 1996—; statistician RAND Corp., Santa Monica, Calif., 2002—. Sec., treas. Com. of Pres. of Stats. Socs., Alexandria, Va., 2001—; Biometrics Soc. rep. to AAAS Internat. Biometrics Soc., Washington, 2002—. Author: (book) Flowgraph Models for Multistate Time to Event Data, (book chpt.) Advances onMethodological and Applied Aspects of Probability and Statistics; contbr. articles to profl. jours. Grantee, NSF, 1996—99. Mem.: AAAS, Assn. for Women in Sci., Internat. Biometric Soc., Inst. of Math. Stats., Am. Statis. Assn. (pres. 2000, v.p. Albuquerque chpt. 1999). Office: U NMex Dept Stats Albuquerque NM 87131-1141 E-mail: aparna@stat.unm.edu.

HVASS, SHERYL RAMSTAD, lawyer; BA, U. Minn., 1972; JD with honors, U. N.D., 1975. Bar: Minn. 1975, N.D. 1975, U.S. Dist. Ct. Minn. 1975, U.S. Dist. Ct. N.D. 1975, D.C. 1978, U.S. Ct. Appeals (8th cir.), U.S. Supreme Ct. 1978. Asst. Hennepin County Pub. Defender, 1975-78; asst. U.S. atty. U.S. Dist. Ct. Minn., 1978-81; assoc. Henson & Efron, PA, 1981-82; adj. prof. law sch. law Hamline U., 1983-86; judge Hennepin County Ct., Mpls., 1982-86; ptnr. Rider, Bennett, Egan & Arundel, Mpls., 1986-99; commr. Dept. of Corrections, St. Paul, 1999—. Co-chair Fed. Practice Com. for Dist. Minn., 1980-82; mem. faculty Nat. Inst. for Trail Advocacy, 1983—; chmn. Minn. Sentencing Guidelines Commns. Active Greater Mpls. Girl Scouts Am. Coun., 1992—, nominations com. 1993; bd. dirs. Mpls. Children's Med. Ctr., 1992, ethics com., 1993; mem. adv. coun. Women's Intercollegiate Athletics, U. Minn., 1987—, vice chair, 1988-89, chair, 1989-91; bd. dirs. YMCA Met. Mpls., 1986—, co-chair program svcs. com. 1987-88, chair pub. rels./pub. affairs com. 1988-92, vice-chmn. 1992—; bd. mgmt. Downtown YMCA, 1984-87; bd. dirs. Search Inst., 1984-88; active Minn. Women's Econ. Roundtable, 1985—; bd. visitors U. N.D. Law Sch., 1982—, U. Minn. Law Sch., 1997—. Recipient Women to Watch award, 1983, Karen Gibbs Women of Achievement award Twin West C. of C., 1985, Civil Justice award Am. Bd. Trial Advocates, 1992. Fellow ABA (life, mem. exec. coun. nat. conf. bar pres. 1992-93, standing com. on assn. comm. 1992-95); mem. Fed. Bar Assn. (sec. Minn. chpt. 1981-83), Nat. Assn. Women Judges (chair site selection com. 1984-85, co-chair judicial selection com. 1985-86), Internat. Soc. Barristers, Minn. State Bar Assn. (chair young lawyers sect. 1981-81, chair legal edn. and admissions com. 1982-84, task force on minority hiring 1986-87, exec. com. 1990—, pres. 1997), Minn. Judges Assn. (chair jury instrn. com. 1984-86, exec. com. 1984-86), Minn. Women Lawyers (exec. com. 1978-83, chair speakers bur. 1978-79, pres. 1981-82), Hennepin County Bar Assn. (vice chair young lawyers com. 1977, sec. 1988-89, treas. 1989-90, pres. 1991-92), Assn. State Correctional Adminstrs. (chair rsch. adv. com.). E-mail: sramstadhvass@co.doc.state.mn.us.

HWANG, CORDELIA JONG, chemist; b. N.Y.C., July 14, 1942; d. Goddard and Lilly (Fung) Jong; m. Warren C. Hwang, Mar. 29, 1969; 1 child, Kevin. BA, Barnard Coll., 1964; MS, SUNY, Stony Brook, 1969. Rsch. asst. Columbia U., N.Y.C., 1964-66; analytical chemist Veritron West, Inc., Chatsworth, Calif., 1969-70; asst. lab. dir., chief chemist Pomeroy, Johnston & Bailey Environ. Engrs., Pasadena, Calif., 1970-76; chemist Met. Water Dist. So. Calif., L.A., 1976-79, rsch. chemist, 1980-91, sr. chemist, 1992—2000, sr. rsch. chemist, 2001—. Mem. Joint Task Group on Instrumental Identification of Taste and Odor Compounds, 1983-85, instr. Citrus Coll., 1974-76; chair Joint Task Group on Disinfection by-products: chlorine, 1990. Mem. Am. Chem. Soc., Am. Water Works Assn. (cert. water quality analyst level 3, Calif.-Nev.), Am. Soc. Mass Spectrometry. Office: Met Water Dist So Calif 700 Moreno Ave La Verne CA 91750-3303 E-mail: chwang@mwd.dst.ca.us.

HWANG, DAVID HENRY, playwright, screenwriter; b. L.A., Aug. 11, 1957; s. Henry Yuan and Dorothy Yu (Huang) H.; m. Kathryn A. Layng, Dec. 17, 1993; 1 child, Noah. BA in English, Stanford U., 1979; postgrad., Yale Drama Sch., 1980-81. Playwright: FOB, 1980 (Obie award 1981), The Dance and the Railroad, 1981 (CINE Golden Eagle award 1982), Family Devotions, 1981, Sound and Beauty, 1983, The Sound of a Voice, 1984, As the Crow Flies, 1986, Rich Relations, 1986, M. Butterfly, 1988 (Tony award for best play 1988, Outer Critics Circle award for best Broadway play 1988, Pulitzer prize for drama nomination 1988), (musicals) 1000 Airplanes on the Roof, 1988, Bondage, 1992, Face Value, 1993, Trying to Find Chinatown, 1996, Golden Child, 1996-98 (Obie award 1997, Tony nomination Best Play 1998), The Silver River, 1997, (adaptation) Peer Gynt, 1998; librettist: The Voyage, 1992; screenwriter: (films) M. Butterfly, 1993, Golden Gate, 1994, (television) Forbidden Nights, 1990. Mem. Pres.'s Com. Arts and Humanities, 1994—. Fellow Rockefeller Found., 1983, Guggenheim Found., 1984, Nat. Endowment Arts, 1987; recipient Drama-Logue award 1980, 86, 98, John Gassner award, 1988. Mem. Dramatists Guild (bd. dirs. 1988—). Democrat. Office: Writers & Artists Agy care William Craver 19 W 44th St Ste 1000 New York NY 10036-6095 also: Creative Artists Agy 9830 Wilshire Blvd Beverly Hills CA 90212-1804

HWANG, HUE-HWA, geochemist; b. Taipei, Taiwan, July 28, 1961; arrived in U.S., 1987; d. Yun-Chin Hwang and Fang-Tsi Lo; m. Alexandros Trellakis, July 18, 1995 (div. Dec. 1998); 1 child, Alice Trellakis. BS, Nat. Taiwan U., 1984, MS, 1987; PhD, U. Ill., 1996. Tchg. asst. Nat. Taiwan U., Taipei, 1984—87; asst. staff geochemist Ill. State Geol. Survey, Champaign, 1989—96, assoc. geochemist, 1996—. Mem.: Am. Geophys. Union, Geol. Soc. Am., Sigma Xi. Office: Ill State Geol Survey 615 E Peabody Dr Champaign IL 61820

HWANG, JOHN DZEN, information systems educator; b. Shanghai, Sept. 8, 1941; came to U.S., 1956; s. John Ding and Sylvia H.; m. Gloria Hoi-Hoon Lum, June 17, 1967; children: John Dar, Andrew Cherng, Audrey Ming. BSEE, U. Calif., Berkeley, 1964; MA, Oreg. State U., 1966, PhD, 1968. Ops. rschr. Army Weapons Command, Rock Island, Ill., 1970-71; program mgr. Army Air Mobility R&D Lab., Moffett Field, Calif., 1971-75; divsn. chief Def. Comm. Agy., Arlington, Va., 1975-82; assoc. dir. Fed. Emergency Mgmt. Agy., Washington, 1982-96; gen. mgr. Info. Tech. Agy. City of L.A., 1996-99; prof. dept. info. sys. Calif. State U., Long Beach, 1999—. Editor: Analytical Concepts of Command and Control, 1976. Capt. U.S. Army, 1968-70. Univ. fellow Dept. Def., Harvard Bus. Sch., Boston, 1981. Home: 2157 Moreno Dr Los Angeles CA 90039-3061 E-mail: jdhwang@csulb.edu.

HWANG, MICHAEL TIAN-CHUNG, university president; b. Nan Cheng, Jiangxi, China, Mar. 5, 1941; came to U.S., 1964; s. Lu Xian and Hui Quing Wang Hwang; m. Grace Lee Piang, Apr. 4, 1968; children: Joseph, Jean. BA, Tamkang U., Taipei, Taiwan, 1964; MEd, Mercer U., 1967; EdD, Drake U., 1988; DSc, Shenandoah U., 1997. V.p. acad. rsch. programs Oklahoma City U., 1984-88; vis. scholar Harvard U. Grad. Sch. Edn., Cambridge, Mass., 1989; prof., dean internat. studies Tamkang U., 1990-96; pres. Armstrong U., Oakland, Calif., 1997—. Office: Armstrong U 1608 Webster St Oakland CA 94612 E-mail: info@armstrong-u.edu.

HWANG, PAUL MINGYOU, cardiologist; b. Seoul, Korea, June 23, 1963; came to U.S., 1976; s. Robert W. and Catherine B. (Johe) H. MD, PhD, Johns Hopkins U., 1993. Resident U. Calif., San Francisco, 1993-96; cardiology fellow Johns Hopkins Hosp., Balt., 1996-2001; investigator NHLBI NIH, Bethesda, 2001—; asst. prof. medicine Johns Hopkins U., Balt., 2001—. Fellow Howard Hughes fellow; grantee, NIH; scholar Fulbright scholarship. Mem. Am. Coll. Cardiology (assoc.), Phi Beta Kappa. Office: NHLBI NIH MSC 1650 Rm 7B15 10 Center Dr Bldg 10 Bethesda MD 20892

HWANG, ROLAND, lawyer; BSME, U. Mich., 1971, MBA, 1976; JD, Wayne State U., 1980, LLM, 1984. Bar: Mich. 1981, U.S. Dist. Ct. (we. dist.) Mich. 1981. Asst. atty. gen. State of Mich., Lansing, 1988—. Mem. adv. com. Madonna Coll. Legal Assistance Tng. Program, Livonia, 1982-88. Contbr. articles, reports to profl. jours. Chmn. Gov.'s Adv. Commn. on Asian Am. Affairs, Lansing, Mich., 1986-90; mem. state adv. bd. U.S. Commn. on Civil Rights, 1988—, chair 1997-2002. Fellow State Bar Mich. Found.; mem. State Bar Mich., Am. Citizens for Justice (treas. 1983, sec. 1985-86, pres. 1992-94), Soc. Automotive Engrs., Assn. Chinese Ams. Detroit (pres. 1982), Asian Am. Bar Assn. Mich. (co-founder 1986, pres. 1986-87), Internat. Inst. of Metro Detroit Inc. (bd. dirs. 1990-97, 2000—, pres. 1995-96, 2000-2001), Econ. Club (Detroit), Phi Alpha Delta. Avocation: reading. E-mail: hwangr@michigan.gov .

HWANG, TE-LONG, neurologist, educator; b. Hualien, Taiwan, Republic of China, Nov. 4, 1943; came to U.S., 1976; s. Tien-Fu and Tien (Liu) Hwang; m. Ai-Yu Chau; children: Tang-Hau Jimmy, Tang-Chieh George. MD, Nat. Def. Med. Ctr., Taipei, Taiwan, 1970. Intern New Brunswick (N.J.) Affiliated Hosps., 1976-77; pathology resident North Shore Univ. Hosp., Manhasset, N.Y., 1977-79; neurology resident U. Tex. Med. Sch., Houston, 1979-82; neuro-oncology fellow U. Tex. M.D. Anderson Cancer Ctr., Houston, 1983-85; attending neurologist VA Hosp., Topeka, Kans., 1986-88, Columbia, S.C., 1988—. Assoc. prof. U. S.C. Sch. Medicine, Columbia, 1988-94, prof., 1994—, chief neurology, 2002-. Mem. Am. Acad. Neurology, Am. Stroke Assn., Nat. Stroke Assn., World Fedn. Neurology (neurosonology rsch. group), S.C. Neurol. Assn. Home: 7 Birchbark Ct Columbia SC 29229-9002 Office: 3555 Harden Street Ext Columbia SC 29203-6894 E-mail: tlh@gw.mp.sc.edu.

HWANG, WENKE, health services researcher; b. Taipei, Taiwan, June 1960; s. Tsing-tsu and Dan-hai Hwang; m. Ching-chuan Yang; children: Sandra, Grace, Alan. BA, Nat. Chung-hsing U., Taipei, Taiwan, 1982, MA, 1984; PhD, U. of Md., 1996. Asst. scientist ctr. for hosp. fin. & mgmt. Johns Hopkins Med. Inst., Balt., 1999—. Cons. in field. Contbr. columns in newspapers, articles to profl. jours. Fellow, Ctr. for Medicare and Medicaid Svc., 1996; grantee, NIH. Mem.: Am. Pub. Health Assn., Acad. Health Svc. & Rsch. Office: Ctr for Hospital Finance and Management 624 N Broadway Room 307 Baltimore MD 21205 Office Fax: (410)9552301. Business E-Mail: whwang@comcast.net.

HWU, WEN-JEN, physician, oncologist, educator; b. Taiwan, Republic of China, Nov. 19, 1949; divorced; 2 children: Ai-Jen Poo, Ting Poo. BS in chemistry, Nat. Tsinghua U., Taiwan, 1971; MS in Chemistry, Duquesne U., 1975; PhD in Chemistry, Carnegie-Mellon U., 1976; MD, U. Calif., Irvine, 1982. Diplomate Am. Bd. Internal Medicine, Am. Bd. Med. Oncology; MD, Calif., Conn., N.Y. Rsch. fellow in endocrine biochemistry Purdue U., West Lafayette, Ind., 1976; rsch. fellow in neurophysiology, dept. physiology U. Calif., Irvine, 1976-78; intern and resident in internal medicine U. Calif. Irvine Coll. of Medicine and Med. Ctr., Orange, 1982-85; rsch. fellow in immunology Howard Hughes Med. Inst., Yale U. Sch. Medicine, New Haven, Conn., 1985-86; fellow in med. oncology Yale U. Sch. Medicine, New Haven, 1986-89, fellow in molecular biology, 1987-89, lectr. dept. molecular biophysics and biochemistry, 1987-89, instr. dept. internal medicine, 1989-91, co-dir. GU cancer unit, 1989-92, asst. prof. medicine, 1991-97, assoc. prof., 1997-98, Cornell U., Ithaca, NY, 2001—. Assoc. attending physician melanoma sect. Clin. Immunology Svcs., Meml. Sloan-Kettering Cancer Ctr., N.Y.c., 1999—; lab. instr. gen. chemistry, Duquesne U., Pitts., 1971-73; instr. organic and phys. chemistry labs., Carnegie-Mellon U., Pitts., 1973-75; postdoctoral rsch. fellow dept. physiology, U. Calif., Irvine, 9176-78; acting chief sect. hematology/oncology, VA Med. Ctr., West Haven, Conn., 1994-95, acting dir. cancer ctr., 1994-95; dir. melanoma unit comprehensive cancer ctr., Yale U. Sch. Medicine, New Haven, 1992-98; mem. adv. bd. Am. Cancer Soc., Conn. and South Cen. Middlexex-Meriden-Wallingford Units, 1989-98; chmn. Melanoma Tumor Bd., Yale Cancer, Ctr., 1994-98, Genitourinary Tumor Bd., 1994-98, mem. protocol rev. com., 1995-98. Contbr. numerous articles to sci. and profl. jours. Recipient Clin. Oncology award Am. Cancer Soc., 1986. Mem. ACP, Conn. Oncology Assn., Am. soc. clin. Oncology, Am. Fedn. Med. Rsch., Am. Assn. Cancer Rsch. Office: Meml Sloan-Kettering Cancer Ctr 1275 York Ave New York NY 10021

HWYNN, JULIE HUYNH, internal medicine physician; b. Saigon, Vietnam; came to U.S., 1979; d. Mark and Jackie; m. Phu Nguyen, Jan. 18, 1996; 1 child, Jett. BS, U. Calif., Irvine, 1990; MD, Chgo. Med. Sch., 1995. Resident in medicine Cook County Hosp., Chgo., 1995-98; staff physician Louis M. Weiss Meml. Hosp., Chgo., 2000; pvt. practice Garden Grove (Calif.) Primary Care Medicine, 2001—. Vol. clin. exposure program Chgo. Med. Sch., 1996, vol. Chgo. Med. Sch. Cares/HIV edn., 1993. Vol. Midwood Cmty. Hosp., Stanton, Calif., 1988-90, Cypress (Calif.) Coll., 1986. Recipient Humanitarian awards Cook County Hosp., Chgo., 1997, 98; Buena Pk. (Calif.) Women's Coll. scholar, 1985-86. Mem. ACP, AMA (life), Am. Acad. Ambulatory Care, Am. Soc. Internal Medicine, mem. Vietnamese Med. Assn. USA, Am. Acad. Med. Acupuncture, Am. Acad. Cosmetic Surgery, Calif. Med. Assn., Orange County Med. Assn., Golden Key, Alpha Epsilon Delta, Alpha Gamma Sigma. Avocations: acupuncture, tennis, swimming, music, laser cosmetic surgery.

HYAMS, HAROLD, lawyer; b. Bklyn., May 19, 1943; s. Frank Charles and Celia (Silverstein) H.; m. Simone Elkeharrat, Nov. 18, 1973; children: Gabriel, Galite, Emilie, Jonathan. BA, U. Vt., 1965; MA in Latin Am. Studies, Georgetown U., 1966; JD, Syracuse U., 1970. Bar: N.Y. 1971, Ariz. 1974, U.S. Dist. Ct. Ariz. 1974, U.S. Ct. Appeals (9th cir.) 1974, U.S. Supreme Ct. 1995. Asst. to the gen. counsel Am. Express Co., N.Y.C., 1970-72; atty. Legal Aid Soc., Bklyn., 1973; ptnr. Harold Hyams and Assocs., Tucson, 1974—. Mem. panel of arbitrators Am. Arbitration Assn., N.Y.C., 1971-73. Mem. Commn. on Ariz. Environ., 1988. Mem. Am. Bd. Trial Advs., Ariz. Trial Lawyers Assn., Pima County Bar Assn., Assn. Trial Lawyers Am. (adv. bd. trial advocates 1990, cert. specialist in personal injury and wrongful death 1991). Avocation: travel. Home: 3175 N Elena Maria Tucson AZ 85750-2915 Office: 680 S Craycroft Rd Tucson AZ 85711-7197

HYATT, KENNETH E(RNEST), diversified manufacturing executive; b. Canton, Ga., Aug. 14, 1940; s. Spurgeon Ernest Hyatt and Grace Marian Lorentzson; m. Anne King Rogers, Nov. 19, 1966; children: Ava Rogers, Grace Marian, Kenneth Ernest Jr. BSCE, Ga. Inst. Tech., 1962, MS in Indsl. Mgmt., 1966. Gen. supr. engring. Ga. Marble Co., Sylacauga/Tate, Ala., 1966-68, div. mgr. Sylacauga, Ala., 1968-71, v.p. Atlanta, 1971-74, exec. v.p., 1974-76, pres., 1976-84; v.p. and group exec. Jim Walter Corp., Tampa, Fla., 1984-86, exec. v.p., COO, 1986-88, pres., CEO, 1988-90; chmn., pres., CEO, Celotex Corp., 1990-95, Walter Industries, 1995-2000; pres. Hyatt & Assocs., Tampa, Fla., 2000—. Bd. dirs. Barnett Bank of Tampa. Lt. USN, 1962-65. Episcopalian. Avocations: hunting, fishing, building furniture. Office: Hyatt & Assocs 2202 N Westshore Blvd Ste 200 Tampa FL 33607-5749

HYATT-SMITH, ANN ROSE, non-profit organization executive, consultant; b. Portchester, N.Y., Sept. 25, 1953; d. David M. and Lenore Hyatt; m. Geoffrey D. Smith, June 24, 1984. BA in Lit., State U. Coll., Oneonta, N.Y., 1975; M in Profl. Studies, New Sch. for Social Rsch., 1986. Asst. to sec.-gen. Israel Interfaith Com., Jerusalem, 1977-79; field rep. United Jewish Appeal/Fedn. Jewish Philanthropies, N.Y.C., 1979-81; asst. v.p. United Way of N.Y.C., 1981-83; dir. devel. Hebrew Arts Sch., Merkin Concert Hall, N.Y.C., 1983-84; asst. dir. devel. St. Vincent's Hosp. and Med. Ctr. N.Y., N.Y.C., 1984-86; program mgr. Bernd Brecher and Assocs., Inc., N.Y.C., 1986-88; pres. Hyatt Smith Assocs., White Plains, N.Y., 1988-91; dir. devel. The Shield Inst., N.Y.C., 1991-95; dir. devel. and alumni rels. Sch. Law, Pace U., White Plains, N.Y., 1995-99; dir. devel. Mercy Coll., Dobbs Ferry, N.Y., 2000-01; dir. devel. and external rels. Blythedale Children's Hosp., Valhalla, NY, 2001—. Adj. faculty New Sch. for Social Rsch. and Learning Alliance. Fundraising chmn. White Plains H.S. Athletic Fund, Inc., 1999—2002; v.p., treas. Village Ind. Dems., N.Y.C., 1985—86. Mem.: Planned Giving Group of Greater N.Y., Women in Fin. Devel., Assn. Healthcare Profls., Assn. Devel. Officers, Assn. Fundraising Profls. (advanced cert. fund raising exec., ethics com. 1998—2000, pub. adv. com. 1998—2000). Jewish.

HYBL, WILLIAM JOSEPH, lawyer, foundation executive; b. Des Moines, July 16, 1942; s. Joseph A. and Geraldine (Evans) H.; m. Kathleen Horrigan, June 6, 1967; children: William J. Jr., Kyle Horrigan. BA, Colo. Coll., 1964; JD, U. Colo., 1967. Bar: Colo. 1967. Asst. dist. atty. 4th Jud. Dist. El Paso and Teller Counties, 1970-72; pres., dir. Garden City Co., 1973—; dir. Broadmoor Hotel, Inc., 1973—, also vice-chmn., 1987—; chmn., CEO, trustee El Pomar Found., Colorado Springs, Colo., 1973—; pres. U.S. Olympic Com., 1991-92,96-2000. Dir. USAA, San Antonio, Kinder Morgan Inc., Houston, FirstBank Holding Co. of Colo., Lakewood; mem. Colo. Ho. Reps., 1972-73; spl. counsel The White House, Washington, 1981; U.S. rep. to 56th Gen. Assembly of U.N., 2001-02. Pres. Air Force Acad. Found.; sec.; vice chmn. bd. U.S. Adv. Commn. on Pub. Diplomacy, 1990-97; civilian aide to sec. of army, 1986—. Capt. U.S. Army, 1967-69. Republican.

HYDE, ALAN LITCHFIELD, retired lawyer; b. Akron, Ohio, Nov. 4, 1928; s. Howard Linton Hyde and Katharine (Pennington) Litchfield; m. Charlotte Griffin Ross, July 10, 1954; children: Elizabeth Hyde Moore, Pamela. AB magna cum laude, Amherst Coll., 1950; JD, Harvard U., 1953. Bar: Ohio 1953, U.S. Dist. Ct. (no. dist.) Ohio 1955. Assoc. Thompson, Hine and Flory, Cleve., 1953-64, ptnr., 1964-93; ret., 1993. Hon. consul, Mexico, 1969—74. Contbr. articles to profl. jours. Trustee Planned Parenthood Greater Cleve., Inc., 1960-79, 80-81, pres. bd. trustees, 1977-79; sec., gen. counsel Greater Cleve. Growth Assn., 1972-74, 86-88, bd. dirs., 1974-80, 82-86, 88-93; trustee Cleve. World Trade Assn., 1978-81; trustee Cleve. Coun. World Affairs, 1980-93, mem. exec. com., 1980-83. Mem. ABA, Inter-Am. Bar Assn. (coun., com. on Latin Am. Devel.), Greater Cleve. Internat. Lawyers Group, Tavern Club (Cleve.), Chagrin Valley Hunt Club (Gates Mills, Ohio). Republican. Episcopalian.

HYDE, CLARENCE BRODIE, II, oil company executive; b. Ft. Worth, Oct. 22, 1937; s. Clarence Edgar and Frances McCain (Williams) H.; m. Sylvia Flower, June 5, 1960; children: C. Brodie III, Brooke Allison, Brett Kinlock, Blair Elizabeth. BS, Tex. Wesleyan Coll., 1961, LLD (hon.), 1996; MBA, U. Tex., 1963; grad., So. Meth. U., 1973. V.p., asst. mgt. lending group, chmn. loan com. Ft. Worth Nat. Bank, 1964-76; ind. oil prodr. Ft. Worth, 1976-78; pres., chmn. bd. Hyde Oil & Gas Corp., Ft. Worth, 1978—; pres. Hyde Resources Corp., 1997—, Hyde Energy Corp., 1993—. Mem. exec. com., dir. River Plz. Nat. Bank, Ft. Worth, 1983-86; trustee, v.p., treas. The Hyde Found., Ft. Worth, 1981—. Bd. dirs. Tarrant County chpt. Salvation Army, 1969-79, chmn. bd., 1972-74; trustee Trinity Valley Sch., Ft. Worth, 1970; mgmt. com. Camp Amon Cartr, Ft. Worth, 1970-76, adv. mem., 1976—; trustee Tex. Wesleyan Coll., 1971-96, chmn. bd., chmn. exec. com., 1990-94; bd. dirs. Big Bros. Tarrant County, 1971; trustee W.A. Moncrief Radiation Ctr., Ft. Worth, 1971-99, v.p., 1986-99; bd. dirs., mem. exec. Harris Hosp., Ft. Worth, 1971-88, Harris Meth. Health Systems, 1983-87; bd. dirs., treas. Tarrant County chpt. ARC, 1971-73, bd. dirs., 1989-91; bd. dirs., exec. com. Ft. Worth Opera Assn., 1971-99, v.p., treas., 1972-74; bd. dirs., exec. com. Hurst-Euless (Tex.)-Bedford Hosp., 1973-80; bd. dirs. Ft. Worth Arts Coun., 1972-95, pres., 1973-75; chmn. Cmty. Pride Campaign, 1972; bd. dirs. Ann Waggoner Scholarship Fund, 1984—; fin. com. Ft. Worth Country Day Sch., 1985-89; pres. MRC-Trans Co. (subs. Moncried Radiation Ctr.), 1987-94; bd. dirs. Cancer Care Svcs., 1994-95, adv. bd. dirs., 1995—; dir. Ft. Worth Pub. Libr. Found., 1996-2002. Named Alumnus of Yr., Tex. Wesleyan Coll., 1985. Mem. Ind. Petroleum Assn. Am., Tex. Ind. Prodrs. & Royalty Owners Assn., Tex. & Southwestern Cattle Raisers Assn., Tex. Hosp. Assn., Rivercrest Country Club, Shady Oaks Country Club (Ft. Worth), Steelechase Club (Ridotto), Ft. Worth Petroleum Club, Crescent Club (Dallas). Republican. Methodist. Avocations: hunting, fishing, travel. Home: 8 Westover Rd Fort Worth TX 76107-3103 Office: Hyde Oil & Gas Corp 6300 Ridglea Pl Ste 1018 Fort Worth TX 76116-5778

HYDE, DAVID ROWLEY, lawyer; b. Norwalk, Conn., Aug. 21, 1929; s. Thomas Arthur and Mary Julia (Sass) H.; m. Valerie Rosemary Worrall, Dec. 30, 1961; children: Meredith Ellen, Timothy Worrall. AB, Yale U., 1951, LL.B., 1954. Bar: Conn. 1954, N.Y. 1956, U.S. Supreme Ct. 1969. Assoc. Cahill Gordon & Reindel, N.Y.C., 1954-59, 64-65, ptnr., 1966-90, sr. counsel, 1991—; chief civil div. U.S. Atty.'s Office, 1961-63. Home: 35 W 12th St New York NY 10011-8501 Office: Cahill Gordon & Reindel 80 Pine St Fl 17 New York NY 10005-1790

HYDE, GERALDINE VEOLA, retired secondary school educator; b. Berkeley, Calif., Nov. 26, 1926; d. William Benjamin and Veola (Walker) H.; m. Paul Hyde Graves, Jr., Nov. 12, 1949 (div. Dec. 1960); children: Christine M. Graves Klykken, Catherine A. Graves Hackney, Geraldine J. Graves Hansen. BA in English, U. Wash., 1948; BA in Edn., Ea. Wash. U., 1960, MA in Edn., 1962. Cert. tchr. K-16, Wash.; life cert. specialist in secondary edn., Calif. English educator Sprague (Wash.) Consol. Schs., 1960-62, Bremerton (Wash.) Sch. Dist., 1962-63, Federal Way (Wash.) Sch. Dist., 1963-66; English, journalism and Polynesian humanities educator Hayward (Calif.) Unified Sch. Dist., 1966-86; ret., 1986. Charter mem. Hist. Hawaii Found., Honolulu, 1977-; founding mem. The Cousteau Soc., Inc., Norfolk, Va., 1973-; life mem. Hawaiian Hist. Soc., Honolulu, 1978-; mem. Molokai Mus. and Cultural Ctr., Kaunakakai, 1986-, Bishop Mus. Assn., Honolulu, 1973-, Mission House Mus., Honolulu, 1994, Bklyn. Hist. Assn., N.Y., 1994, Berkshire Family History Assn., Pittsfield, Mass., 1994-, Richville (N.Y.) Hist. Assn., 1994-, Swanton (Vt.) Hist. Soc., 1998-, N.Y. Geneal. and Biog. Soc., 1999-, New Eng. Hist. Genealogic Soc., 1998-, Gouverneur Hist. Assn., NY, 1998-, New Wing Luke Asian Mus., Seattle, 1994, Upham Family Soc., Inc., Melrose, Mass., 2001-, Calif. Ret. Tchrs Assoc. 2003. Mem. Libr. Congress Assocs. (charter), Nature Conservancy of Hawai'i, Smithsonian Inst. (contbg.), Nat. Geog. Soc., Nat. Trust Historic Preservation, Calif. Ret. Tchrs. Assn., Jr. League Spokane, U. Wash. Alumni Assn. (life), Ea. Wash. U. Alumni Assn. (life). Episcopalian. Avocations: historic and ecologic preservation, genealogy, shell collecting, needlework, crafts. Home: 5051 El Don Dr Apt 1301 Rocklin CA 95677-4470

HYDE, HARRY, JR., technical writer, editor, consultant; b. Phila., Apr. 12, 1925; s. Harry Edwin and Edna Augusta (Hubbard) H. BS, Temple U., 1950, EDM, 1961, MA, 1975. Pub., mng. editor The Delco Vet., Drexel Hill, Pa., 1946—58, Bryn Mawr, Pa., 1958-76; stats. clk. Bur. Census, Phila., 1950-51; claims examiner Social Security Adminstrn., Phila., 1951-52; adminstrv. asst. Harris Sales co., Lansdowne, Pa., 1952; rsch. asst. Rheem Mfg. Co., Phila., 1952-54, tech. pubs. cons., comms. specialist Drexel Hill, Pa., 1954—55, 1956—57, 1963—64, Bryn Mawr, 1967-68, 69-70, 71-77, 94-96, Swarthmore, Pa., 1996—; engring. asst. Chrysler Corp., Newark, Del., 1955-56; tchr. Brown Prep. Sch., Phila., 1956; tech. writer Burroughs Corp., Phila., 1957-58, Radnor, Pa., 1958-59; tech. writer, editor RCA Svc. Co., Cherry Hill, Princeton, Riverton, N.J., 1959-63; instr. Rutgers U., Camden, NJ, 1961—63; tech. editor, Applied Physics Lab. Johns Hopkins U., Silver Spring, Md., 1964-65; sr. tech. publs. engr. Martin Marietta Corp., Orlando, Fla., 1965-67; mng. editor Valley Voice, Bryn Mawr, Pa., 1966-96, Swarthmore, Pa., 1996—; tech. publications mgr. Dynasciences Corp., Blue Bell, Pa., 1968-69; reports coordinator Penn. Rsch. Assoc. Inc., Phila., 1970; mng. editor Continuing Education, Phila., 1970-71; publisher, mng. editor Areas Concern, Bryn Mawr, Pa., 1971-96; exec. dir. Concerned Citizens of the Delaware Valley, Bryn Mawr, Pa., 1974-96, Swarthmore, Pa., 1996—; tech. writer/editor RCA Corp., Gen. Electric Co., Martin Marietta Corp., Camden/ Moorestown, NJ, 1977-94. Contbr. articles; editor: South Jersey Guide ot Events and Places, 1977; columnist: New Am., 1974; columnist Delaware Valley Industry, 1974—75. Co-founder, chair Del. Valley Assn. Rail Passengers, Bryn Mawr, Pa., 1972—78, Del. Valley Citizens Com. Better Transp., 1972—93; co-founder Concerned Citizens Del. Valley, Bryn Mawr, 1974—96, 1996—, Concerned Citizens Swarthmore, 1996—; co-founder, coord. Shore-Train Riders Club, Camden, NJ, 1976—89; v.p. Raoul Wallenbert Com. Grtr. Phila., 1982—92; bd. dirs. Main Line Reform Temple Beth Elohim, Wynnewood, Pa., 1969—72; bd. dirs. Drexel Hill br. Jewish Cmty. Ctr. Long Beach Island, Beach Haven, NJ, 1959—71; mem. Jewish Labor Com., N.Y.C., 1983—; nat. bd. dirs. Am. Vets. Com., 1950—51, 1963—64, 1965—71, sec. Chester chpt., 1946, sec. Haverton chpt., 1946—47, chmn., 1947—48, exec. sec. Del. County chpt., 1948—49, chmn., 1949—53, chmn. Delaware Valley chpt., 1953—65, 1968—74; bd. dirs. Drexel Hill br. ARC, 1954—58; bd. dirs. S.E. Pa. chpt. Ams. for Dem. Action, Phila., 1990—; mem. regional citizens com. Del. Valley Regional Planning Commn., Phila., 1994—; steering com. Alliance for a Sustainable Future, Ambler, Pa., 1995—; bd. dirs. Sustainable Soc. Action Project, Upper Darby, Pa., 1991—; mem. Info. Resources Com., Swarthmore, Pa., 1998—. With U.S. Army, 1943—46, PTO. Named to Pa. Voter Hall of Fame Commonwealth of Pa., 1997. Mem.: AFL-CIO, Internat. Fedn. Profl. and tech. Engrs., Nat. Assn. Railroad Passengers (bd. dirs. 1978—80). Democrat. Jewish. Avocations: reading, research, development of new ideas. Home and Office: PO Box 561 Swarthmore PA 19081

HYDE, HENRY JOHN, congressman; b. Chgo., Apr. 18, 1924; s. Henry Clay and Monica (Kelly) H.; m. Jeanne Simpson, Nov. 8, 1947; children: Henry J., Robert, Laura, Anthony. Student, Duke U., 1943-44; BS, Georgetown U., 1946; JD, Loyola U., Chgo., 1949. Bar: Ill. 1950. Mem. Ill. Gen. Assembly, 1967-74, U.S. Congress from 6th Ill. dist., 1975—; mem. internat. rels. com., chmn. jud. com. With USN, 1944-46. Mem. Chgo. Bar Assn. Republican. Roman Catholic. Office: US Ho of Reps 2110 Rayburn Washington DC 20515-0001*

HYDE, HERBERT LEE, lawyer; b. Bryson City, N.C., Dec. 12, 1925; s. Ervin M. and Alice (Medlin) H.; m. Kathryn Long, Dec. 25, 1949; children: Deborah, Lynn, Karen, Benjamin, Jane, William. AB, W. Carolina U., 1951; JD, NYU, 1954. Bar: N.C. 1954, U.S. Dist. Ct. (we. dist.) N.C. 1954, U.S. Ct. Appeals (4th cir.) 1957, U.S. Supreme Ct. 1962, U.S. Dist. Ct. (mid. dist.) N.C. 1975, U.S. Dist. Ct. (ea. dist.) N.C. 1980. Ptnr. Van Winkle, Buck, Wall, Starnes & Hyde, Asheville, N.C., 1954-79; sole practice Asheville, 1979—. Sec. N.C. Dept. Crime Control and Pub. Safety, Raleigh, 1979. Author: Genuine Hyde, 1976, My Home is in the Smoky Mountains, 1998, Of Truth and Freedom, 2001, Living and Learning, Just Natural, 2001, Mountain Speaking, 2002; writer (song) The Cold Icy Waters of Swain. Senator N.C. Senate, Raleigh, 1964-66, 1990-94; mem. N.C. Ho. of Reps., Raleigh, 1972-76; chmn. Dem. Exec. Com. of Buncombe County, Asheville, 1988—; chmn. Dem. Congl. Dist. 11, 1988-90, N.C. State Dems., 1990—, chmn., 1993. Named N.C. Bar Assn. Gen. Practice Hall of Fame, 1999. Mem.: Am. Coll. Trial Lawyers. Democrat. Home: 93 Eastview Cir Asheville NC 28806-1130 Office: PO Box 7266 Asheville NC 28802-7266

HYDE, HOWARD LAURENCE, lawyer; b. Boston, Sept. 4, 1957; s. Morris Morton and Evelyn Lee (Weinstein) H.; m. Nancy J. Paulu, May 18, 1985; children: Emma Catherine, Benjamin Tuttle. AB, Dartmouth Coll., 1979; JD, Harvard U., 1982. Bar: Mass. 1983, D.C. 1987, U.S. Dist. Ct. Mass. 1984, U.S. Ct. Appeals (1st. cir.) 1984. Jud. clk. Minn. Supreme Ct., St. Paul, 1982-83; assoc. Gaston Snow & Ely Bartlett, Boston, 1983-86, Arnold & Porter, Washington, 1986-91, spl. counsel, 1992—. Mem. ABA (Bus. law sect.). Avocations: fly fishing, canoeing. Office: Arnold & Porter 555 12th St NW Washington DC 20004-1206 E-mail: Howard_Hyde@aporter.com.

HYDE, JANET SHIBLEY, psychologist, educator; b. Akron, Ohio, Aug. 17, 1948; d. Grant O. and Dorothy Mae Shilbey; m. John DeLamater; children: Margaret, Luke. BA, Oberlin Coll., 1969; PhD, U. Calif., Berkeley, 1972. Asst. prof. psychology Bowling Green State U., Ohio, 1972—76, assoc. prof., 1976—79, Denison U., Granville, Ohio, 1979—83, prof., 1983—86, acting provost, 1985—86; prof. psychology and women's studies U. Wis., Madison, 1986—. Author: (book) Half the Human Experience: The Psychology of Women, 1976, Understanding Human Sexuality, 1979; contbr. articles to profl. jours. Fellow: APA, Soc. Rsch. Child Devel., Soc. Sci. Study Sex. Democrat. Episcopalian. Home: 2015 Chadbourne Ave Madison WI 53726-4046 Office: U Wis Dept Psychology Madison WI 53706

HYDE, LAWRENCE HENRY, JR., industrial company executive; b. Cambridge, Mass., July 10, 1924; s. Lawrence Henry and Catherine I. (McMahon) H.; m. Lois A. Crehan, May 31, 1947; children— Abigail Ellen, Stephen Lawrence, Lawrence Henry III. AB, Harvard U., 1946, MBA, 1947. With Ford Motor Co., 1947-65, dir. internat. purchasing office, 1960-62; v.p. Philco, 1962-64; with Harris Corp., Cleve., 1965-73; from dir. internat. ops. to group v.p. internat. Am. Motors Corp., Detroit, 1974-83, v.p. internat., 1974-77; group v.p., pres. AM Gen. Corp., 1977-81, exec. v.p., 1982-83; with LTV Corp., 1983-85; divsn. pres. AM Gen., 1983-85; with Harris Graphics Corp., 1985-86, also chmn. bd. dirs.; with Sonex Rsch., Inc., 1986—, also chmn. bd. dirs., 1986-93, pres., 1997—. Bd. dirs., chmn. Karnak Investments, Ltd., Bermuda; chmn. U. Investment Fund Cairo. Trustee Am. U., Cairo. Office: Sonex Rsch Inc 23 Hudson St Annapolis MD 21401-3100

HYDE, MICHAEL ARTHUR, chemical company executive; b. Kingston, Ont., Apr. 17, 1942; s. Arthur Edwin and Isabell Mary (Moran) H.; m. Monica Jill Hill, Sept. 9, 1964 (div. 1972); children: David Michael, Andrew Tyler; m. Yoko Igaya, May 19, 1981; children: Keri Kazumi, Amanda Izumi. BS in Engring., Queen's U., Kingston, Ont., 1965. Registered profl. engr., Ont. Tech. mgr. constrn. divsn. rsch. Dow Chem. Can., Sarnia, Ont., 1971-76; dist. sales mgr. constrn. divsn. Toronto, 1980-83; nat. sales mgr. constrn. divsn., 1984-85; mgr. new ventures and diversification, 1986-88; dir. environ. affairs plastics dept., 1989—; dir. Ont. govt. affairs, 1994—. Dir. rsch. Dow Chem. Japan, Gotemba, Japan, 1976-80; v.p., sec. Mod-Lok Wall Sys. Ltd., Vancouver, B.C., Can., 1986-88; mem. Fire Test Bd., Ottawa, Ont., 1974-76; opportunity and innovation's industry cons. com. Min. Enterprise. Patentee in field. Chair Can. Chem. Prodrs./Sarnia Constrn. Assn. Retail Sales Tax Working Group. Mem. Ont. Indsl. Roofing Assn. (bd. dirs. 1981-84), Assn. Profl. Engrs., Constrn. Specs. Can. Conservative (dir., sec. treas., policy com., mem. exec. com.), Recycling coun. Ont. (chmn. pub. affairs com., mem product stewardship com., mgmt. com.), Environ. and Plastics Inst. Coun. (recycling and degradability sub-coms., Canplast award 1991), Corps. Supporting Recycling (corp. mem.) Collecte Selectif Quebec (corp. mem.), Can. Polystyrene Recycling Assn. (chmn. 1989-91), Can. Plastics Industry Assn. (nat. environ. health and safety com.), Vinyl Coun. Can. (mem. oper. com. and crisis response coms.), Plastic Film Mfrs. (recycling com.), Bus. Rsch. Netwwork, Can. Chems. Prodrs. Assn. (Ont. regional exec. com.), Ont. Region Bus. Econ. and Govt. Com. (chmn., Merit award 2001), Thursday Group and The Industry Network for City of Toronto, Global Climate Change Liaison Group. Avocations: swimming, boating, water skiing, cross-country skking. Home: 61 Greengrove Crescent Don Mills ON Canada M3A 1H8 Office: Dow Chem Can Inc PO Box 363 Don Mills ON Canada M3C 2S7 E-mail: mhyde@dow.com.

HYDE, REBECCA MEDWIN, financial consultant; b. Frederick, Md., Aug 30, 1947; d. William Herbert and Clella Evelyn Hyde. BA, Cath. U. Am., 1969 tchr. edn. cert., Towson State Coll., 1971; M Liberal Arts, Johns Hopkins U. 1973. Cert. fin. planner. Sr. jumbo underwriter, asst. v.p. Chase Home Mortgage Corp., Woodland Hills, Calif., 1988—95; fin. advisor Am. Express Fin Advisors, Columbia, Md., 1995—. Guest lectr. U. Balt. Sch. Law, 2000—01 Mem.: Fin. Planning Assn. Home: 5764 Stevens Forest Rd # 421 Columbia MD 21045 Office: Am Express Fin Advisors Ste 501 5950 Symphony Woods Rd Columbia MD 02104 Fax: 410-772-0494. E-mail: rebeccamhyde@yahoo.com

HYDE, THOMAS D. lawyer; Sr. v.p., sec., gen. counsel Raytheon Co. Lexington, Mass., 1994—2001; exec. v.p. for legal and corp. affairs Wal-Mart Stores, Inc., 2001—. Office: Wal-Mart Stores, Inc 702 SW Eighth St Bentonville AR 72716

HYDER, ANTHONY K. academic administrator, science educator; BS in Physics, U. Notre Dame, 1964; MS in Space Physics, Air Force Inst. Tech. 1964, PhD in Nuclear Physics, 1971. With Air Force Office of Sci. Rsch.; sci advisor Office of Under Sec. of Def. Rsch. and Advanced Tech., 1989—90; dir Space Power Inst., assoc. v.p. rsch. Auburn U., 1982—91, rsch. fellow Space Power Inst., 1991—95; assoc. v.p. grad. studies and rsch., prof. physics and aerospace engring. U. Notre Dame, Ind., 1993—. Mem. Air Force Sci. Adv. Bd. 1990—96; sci. adv. bd. Def. Intelligence Agy., 1990—95. Co-author (with D Flood): Spacecraft Power Systems, 1998; co-author: Defense Conversion Strategies, 1996, The Behavior of Systems in the Space Environment; contbr. Recipient R&D award, USAF; fellow Doctoral fellow, Air Force Inst. Tech. Mem.: AIAA, IEEE, Omicron Delta Kappa, Sigma Pi Sigma, Tau Beta Pi

Achievements include research in in the interaction of spacecraft with the space environment. Office: Univ of Notre Dame 501a Main Bldg 225 Nieuwland Science Bldg Notre Dame IN 46556-5670

HYE, A. electrical engineering educator; BSc, Punjab U., Lahore, Pakistan, 1967; BS, Engring. U., Lahore, 1978; MS, U. Bridgeport, Conn., 1987; PhD, Pacific Western U., L.A., 1990. Registered profl. engr., Conn. Sys. engr. Pitney Bowes, Stratford, Conn., 1990-91; mem. faculty dept. elec. engring. Fairfield (Conn.) U., 1991—. Mem. IEEE, NSPE, Conn. Soc. Profl. Engrs. Office: Fairfield U Dept Electrical Engring Fairfield CT 06430

HYLAND, GEOFFREY FYFE, energy service company executive; b. Montreal; B in Engring., McGill U., Montreal, 1966; MBA, York U., Toronto, Ont., Can., 1972. Pres., COO Shaw Industries Ltd, Toronto, Ont., 1987, pres., CEO, 1994—. Bd. dir. ShawCor Ltd., Enerflex Sys., Ltd., Exco Techs. Ltd., Fortis Inc. Office: ShawCor Ltd 25 Bethridge Rd Toronto ON Canada M9W 1M7 E-mail: ghyland@shawcor.com.

HYLAND, PATRICIA ANN (PAT HYLAND), writer; b. Buffalo, N.Y., Jan. 3, 1938; d. William Edward and Genevieve Martha (Warner) Pfister; m. William Lloyd Hyland, Aug. 30, 1958; children: Jennifer, Jeffrey, Todd, Timothy, Brian. BS in Bus. Adminstrn., St. Joseph's Coll., N. Windham, Maine, 1984; BSN, Mercy Coll. Nursing, San Diego, 1958. Author: Presidential Libraries and Museums: An Illustrated Guide, 1995; conbtr. articles to profl. publs. Spkr. presdl. libraries, nat. archives and hist. groups. Mem. Washington Ind. Writers. Home: 6505 Kalmia St Springfield VA 22150-1138

HYLAND, WILLIAM FRANCIS, lawyer; b. Burlington, N.J., July 30, 1923; s. Theodore J. and Margaret M. (Gallagher) H.; m. Joan E. Sharp, Apr. 20, 1946; children: William Francis, Nancy E. Hyland Wiley, Stephen J., Emma L. Hyland McCormack, Margaret M. Hyland Frank, Thomas M. BS in Econs, U. Pa., 1944, LL.B., 1949; D.H.L., Hahnemann Med. Sch. and Hosp., 1976. Bar: N.J. 1949, U.S. Supreme Ct. 1960. Of counsel Riker, Danzig, Scherer, Hyland & Perretti, Morristown, N.J.; atty. gen. N.J., 1974-78. Mem. N.J. Gen. Assembly from Camden County, 1954-61; speaker of house, 1958, acting gov., N.J., 1958; chmn. N.J. Sports and Expn. Authority, 1978-82, commr., 1974-84; pres. N.J. Bd. Pub. Utility Commrs., also mem. cabinet govs. Meyner, Hughes, Byrne, N.J., 1961-68, 74-78; chmn. N.J. Atomic Energy Council, 1968-69, N.J. Commn. Investigation, 1969-71; co-chmn. Reapportionment Commn.; chmn. Brazilian Mission Com., 1962-65; permanent del. Fed. Jud. Conf. 3d Circuit.; del.-at-large Dem. Nat. Conv., 1964, del., 1968; assoc. trustee U. Pa., 1960-74. Served as officer USNR, 1943-46, ETO, PTO. Decorated knight Order of St. Gregory (Pope Paul VI), 1964; recipient Distinguished Service award Camden County Jaycees, 1954, Outstanding Young Man in Govt. N.J. award N.J. Jaycees, 1958, Myrtle Wreath award Camden County So. N.J. region Hadassah, 1977, Pub. Service award Anti-Defamation League of B'nai B'rith, 1982; named Outstanding Citizen of N.J. Advt. Club. N.J., 1979 Mem. ABA (fellow N.J. chpt.), Camden County Bar Assn. (pres. 1959), Nat. Assn. R.R. and Utilities Commrs. (exec. com. 1965-68), Nat. Assn. Attys. Gen. (exec. com. 1975-78, v.p. 1976, pres. elect 1977-78), Phi Kappa Psi. Home: 1 Polo Club Rd Far Hills NJ 07931-2474 Office: Riker Danzig Scherer Hyland & Perretti Headquarters Plz 1 Speedwell Ave Ste 2 Morristown NJ 07960-6823

HYLANDER, WALTER RAYMOND, JR., retired civil engineer; b. July 22, 1924; s. Walter Raymond and Mary Howard (Douglass) H.; m. Marjorie Jean Gunter, Mar. 8, 1951; children: Walter Raymond, Joyce Elizabeth. BS, U.S. Mil. Acad., 1945; MS in Civil Engring., MIT, 1950. Registered profl. engr., N.Y., Miss. Commd. 2d lt. U.S. Army, 1945, advanced through grades to col., 1969, ret., 1973; tng. dir. Bechtel Power Corp., Grand Gulf, Miss., 1974-76; tng. and adm. mgr. Saudi-Arabian Bechtel Co., Jubail, 1976-77; tng. dir. St. Regis Paper Co., Montecello, Miss., 1978-79; chief civil engr. Bechtel Power Corp., Grand Gulf, 1979-86. Chmn. Panel of Experts on Mine Warfare, NATO, London, 1962-65; sr. advisor on engr. tng., Vietnam, 1967-68; mem. U.S. Army Com. on Mil. History, West Point, N.Y., 1972-73; mem. U.S. ACDA, Washington, 1968-69. Contbr. articles to profl. jours. Fellow: ASCE. Methodist. Home: Rosswood Plantation 2513 Red Lick Rd Lorman MS 39096 E-mail: whylander@aol.com.

HYLBERT, PAUL, construction executive; Various field and corp. pos., including mngr. dir. Wickes Europe, and sr. v.p. and gen. mgr. Wickes Lumber, 1966—90; pres. PrimeSource, 1990—2001; pres., CEO Lanoga Corp., Redmond, Wash., 2001—. Mem.: Nat. Bldg. Materials Distbrs. Assn. (pres. 1993). Office: Lanoga Corp 17946 NE 65th St Redmond WV 98052*

HYLTON, JOHN BAKER, music educator, university administrator; b. Connersville, Ind., Mar. 9, 1950; s. Joe Lewis and Betty (Baker) H.; m. Doris Ella Berkemeyer, Mar. 12, 1982; children: Mark, Jerry, Susan. BS in Music Edn., Gettysburg Coll., 1972; MEd, Pa. State U., 1976, EdD, 1980. Choral dir., tchr. music York (Pa.) City Sch. Dist., 1972-77; tchg. asst. Pa. State U., Univ. Park, 1977-80; asst. prof. music U. Mo., St. Louis, 1980-86, assoc. prof., 1986-95, prof., 1995—, chmn. dept. music, dir. fine arts outreach program, 1995-2000, assoc. vice chancellor acad. affairs, 2000—02, founding dean Coll. Fine Arts and Comm., 2002—. Author: Comprehensive Choral Music Education, 1995; mem. editl. bd. Mo. Jour. Rsch. in Music Edn.; editor: Mo. Jour. Rsch. in Music Edn., 1994—96; mem. editl. bd. Update: Applications of Music Edn. Rsch., 1990—96; contbr. Named Mo. Choral Conductor of Yr., 1993; recipient Alumni Achievement award, Pa. State U., 1999, Chancellors award for excellence in svc., U. Mo. at St. Louis, 2001, Merit award, St. Louis Suburban Music Educators, 1998. Mem.: Soc. for Music Tchr. Edn., Soc. for Rsch. in Music Edn., Music Educators Nat. Conf., Am. Choral Dirs. Assn. (life, newsletter editor 1988—96), Phi Kappa Phi, Phi Delta Kappa, Phi Mu Alpha Sinfonia. Avocations: battlefield guide Gettysburg Nat. Mil. Park, church musician, Hiking, civil war history. Office: U Mo at St Louis Coll Fine Arts & Comm 8001 Natural Bridge Rd Saint Louis MO 63121-4401 E-mail: johnhylton@umsl.edu.

HYLTON, MYLES TALBERT, lawyer; b. Pearisburg, Va., Apr. 22, 1954; s. Joseph Gordon and Ruby Viola (Clarkson) H.; 1 child, Jessica Kathleen. BSME, U. Mich., 1977, MSME, 1978; JD, U. Va., 1983. Bar: Va. 1983, U.S. Ct. Appeals (4th cir.) 1983, U.S. Patent Office 1985. Mech. engr. White Motor Co., New River, Va., 1979-80; assoc. Gentry, Locke, Rakes & Moore, Roanoke, Va., 1983-86, Stone & Hamrick, Radford, Va., 1986-89; ptnr. Pavin, Wilson, Barnett & Hopper, Roanoke, 1990-95; pvt. practice, Roanoke, 1995—. Mem. Va. Trial Lawyers, Assn. Trial Lawyers Am., Nat. Assn. Criminal Def. Lawyers, Soc. Automotive Engrs. Republican. Avocations: baseball, racquetball, weight lifting, boxing, scuba diving. Home: 1812 Sheffield Rd SW Roanoke VA 24015-3022 Office: 23 Franklin Rd SW Roanoke VA 24011-2403

HYLTON, THOMAS JAMES, author; b. Reading, Pa., Dec. 20, 1948; s. William Harold and Mary Harriet (Kitzmiller) H.; m. Frances Wismer, Aug. 31, 1970. BA, Kutztown U. of Pa., 1970. Reporter The Mercury, Pottstown, Pa., 1970-86, editl. writer, 1986-94. Author: Save Our Land, Save our Towns: A Plan for Pennsylvania, 1995; prodr., host (PBS) Save Our Land, Save Our Towns, 2000. Co-founder Trees Inc., Pottstown, 1983; co-founder Preservation Pottstown, 1984, 10,000 Friends of Pa., 1998. Recipient Am. Planning Assn. award, 1988, 90, 94, Honor award Nat. Trust for Hist. Preservation, 1997, Pulitzer prize for editl. writing, 1990; Pulliam fellow, 1993. Republican. Presbyterian. Home: 222 Chestnut St Pottstown PA 19464-5508 E-mail: hylton@ptdprolog.net.

HYMAN, ABRAHAM, electrical engineer; b. Bklyn., Mar. 8, 1934; s. Rubin and Regina (Holzman) H.; m. Marianne Daniel, June 19, 1955; children: Debra Hyman Rathauser, Lori Hyman Rones, Karen Hyman Cantor. BEE, Poly. Inst. Bklyn., 1945; MS, Newark Coll. Engring., 1954. Registered profl. engr., N.Y. Chief elec. engr. Med. Equipment R&D Lab., Fort Totten, N.Y., 1955-64; head lab. Office Naval Rsch., Port Washington, N.Y., 1964-66; tech. adminstr. AEC, Upton, N.Y., 1966-71; supr. indsl. hygienist Dept. Labor, Westbury, N.Y., 1971-80, regional indsl. hygienist N.Y.C., 1980-84; mgr. health and safety Unisys Corp., Great Neck, N.Y., 1984-95; safety and health cons. New Hyde Park, N.Y., 1995—; cons. Winthrop U. Hosp., Mineola, NY. Adj. prof. York Coll., Queens, NY, 1974—78; cons. Poison Control Ctr., Mineola, NY, 1981—; adj. assoc. prof. Staten Island Coll., NY, 1983—95; lectr. Queensboro C.C., Queens, NY, 1994—96. Patentee in field. Bd. dirs. Am. Lung Assn., East Meadow, 1974-99. Mem. IEEE, Am. Acad. Environ. Engrs. (diplomate), NSPE, Am. Conf. Indsl. Hygienists, Sci. Rsch. Soc. Am., Sigma Xi. Avocations: photography, swimming, bicycling. Home and Office: 142 Claudy Ln New Hyde Park NY 11040-1635 E-mail: marab6@aol.com.

HYMAN, ALBERT LEWIS, cardiologist, educator; b. New Orleans, Nov. 10, 1923; s. David and Mary (Newstadt) H.; m. Neil Steiner, Mar. 27, 1964; 1 son, Albert Arthur. BS, La. State U., 1943; MD, 1945; postgrad., U. Cin., U. Paris, U. London, Eng. Diplomate: Am. Bd. Internal Medicine. Intern Charity Hosp., 1945-46, resident, 1947-49, sr. vis. physician, 1959-63; resident Cin. Gen. Hosp., 1946-47; instr. medicine La. State U., 1950-56, asst. prof. medicine, 1956-57; asst. prof. Tulane U., 1957-59, assoc. prof., 1959-63, assoc. prof. surgery, 1963-70, prof. rsch. surgery in cardiology, 1970—, prof. clin. medicine Med. Sch., 1983—, adj. prof. pharmacology Med. Sch., 1974—, dir. Cardiac Catheterization Lab., 1957—, Mayerson meml. lectr. in physiology, 2000. Sr. vis. physician Touro Hosp., Touro Infirmary, Hotel Dieu; chief cardiology Sara Mayo Hosp.; cons. in cardiology USPHS, New Orleans Crippled Children's Hosp., St. Tammany Parish Hosp., Covington La. area VA, Hotel Dieu Hosp., Mercy Hosp., East Jefferson Gen. Hosp., St. Charles Gen. Hosp.; electrocardiographer Metairie Hosp., 1959-64, Sara Mayo Hosp., Touro Infirmary, St. Tammany Hosp.; cons. cardiovascular disease New Orleans VA Hosp.; cons. cardiology Baton Rouge Gen. Hosp., U.S. Dept. Justice, Fed. Social Security Agy.; Barlow lectr. in medicine U. So. Calif., 1977; mem. internat. sci. com. IV Internat. Symposium on Pulmonary Circulation, Charles U., Prague; Mayerson meml. lectr. dept. physiology Tulane Med. Sch., 1999; Plenary lectr. gene therapy Internat. Congress Pulmonary Circulation, Prague, 1999; vis. prof. medicine SUNY, Stony Brook, 2001; vis. prof. pharmacology U. South Ala. Med. Sch., 2001; invited lectr. in field. Mem. editorial bd. Jour. Applied Physiology; contbr. over 250 articles to profl. jours. Recipient award for rsch. of the Hadassah, 1980, Vis. Scientist award Wellcome Found., Univ. Coll., London, 1991, Disting. Achievement award Am. Heart Assn., 1992, 93, Dickinson-Richards lectr., 1990, Albert Hyman award for excellence in cardiology Tulane U. Med. Sch., 1997, Disting. Achievement award in sci. and rsch. Orleand Parish Med. Soc., 2001; Tulane Med. Sch. Sect. on Cardiology fellow, 1997. Fellow ACP, Am. Coll. Chest Physicians, Am. Coll. Cardiology, Am. Fedn. Clin. Rsch.; mem. AAUP, Am. Heart Assn. (fellow coun. on circulation, fellow coun. on clin. cardiology, mem. coun. on cardiopulmonary medicine, regional rep. coun. clin. cardiology, chmn. sci. com. cardiopulmonary coun. 1981, chmn. cardiopulmonary coun., rsch. com. bd. dirs., editl. bd. mem. Circulation Rsch., edit. bd. mem. Am. Jour. Physiology, Heart Disease and Stroke, Jour. Applied Physiology, Dickinson Richards Meml. Lectr. 1986, 92, Disting. Sci. Achievement award 1990, 93), La. Heart Assn. (v.p. 1974, Albert L. Hyman Ann. Rsch. award, Wellcome Rsch. Found. Vis. Scientist award Univ. Coll. London 1992, Disting. Achievement award outstanding sci. contbns. to cardiopulmonary medicine), Am. Soc. Pharmacology and Exptl. Therapeutics, So. Soc. Clin. Investigation (chmn. membership com.), So. Med. Soc. (Seale-Harris award 1988), Am. Physiol. Soc., N.Am. Soc. Pacing and Electrophysiology, Orleans Surg. Soc. (hon.), New Orleans Surg. Soc. (hon.), N.Y. Acad. Scis., Nat. Am. Heart Assn. (vice-chmn. rsch. com.), Alpha Omega Alpha. Achievements include research in cardiopulmonary circulation. Home: 5467 Marcia Ave New Orleans LA 70124-1052 Office: 3601 Prytania St New Orleans LA 70115-3610

HYMAN, ANDREW THEODORE, patent lawyer, physicist; b. Boston, Mar. 3, 1962; s. Lester Samuel Hyman and Helen Reeder Sidman. BS, U. Mass., 1987; JD, Lewis and Clark Coll., 1994. Bar: Conn. 1996, DC 1998, Mass. 2002, U.S. Patent Office 2000, U.S. Supreme Ct. 2000. Sci. data editor MIT Lincoln Lab., Lexington, Mass., 1989-90; mgr. Hostelling Internat., Knoxville, Md., 1995-2000; telecom. advisor Appalachian Trail Conf., Harpers Ferry, W.Va., 1997-2000; atty. Ware, Fressola, Vander Der Sluys & Adolphson, Monroe, Conn., 2000—. Contbr. articles to Findlaw's Writ, Am. Math. Monthly, Am. Jour. Physics, European Jour. Physics, Nuovo Cimento, Denver Jour. Internat. Law; referee Am. Jour. Physics, 1999. Bd. mem. Yankee Coun. Hostelling Internat., 2001—. Decorated Army Achievement medal U.S. Army, Wiesbaden, Germany, 1984. Achievements include discovery of parameter-independent formulation of classical electrodynamics; proposal of a new Whitehead-type theory of relativistic gravitation. Avocations: hiking, swimming. Office: 755 Main St PO Box 224 Monroe CT 06468-0224 E-mail: ahyman@aol.com.

HYMAN, BRUCE MALCOLM, ophthalmologist; b. N.Y.C., May 22, 1943; s. Malcolm A. and Sylvia S. H.; AB, Columbia U., 1964; MD, NYU, 1968. Intern in surgery Albert Einstein Coll. Medicine/Bronx Mcpl. Hosp., 1968-69; resident in ophthalmology Manhattan Eye, Ear and Throat Hosp., N.Y.C., 1971-74; pvt. practice medicine specializing in ophthalmology, N.Y.C., 1974—; tchr. attending surgeon Manhattan Eye, Ear and Throat Hosp., 1974—; med. cons. U.S. Seaplane Pilots Assn., 1975—, Health Ins. Plan Greater N.Y., 1977—; ophthalmologist to Hotel Trades Coun., Hotel Assn. N.Y.C., 1974—; attending ophthalmologist Roosevelt Hosp., N.Y.C., 1979—, dir. adult outpatient ophthalmology, 1980—; police surgeon N.Y.C., 1977—, dep. chief police surgeon, 1978—; attending ophthalmologist Doctors Hosp., 1979—, Le Roy Hosp., 1979—, St. Luke's Hosp., 1980—; outpatient ophthalmologist N.Y. Hosp., 1975-77; clin. ophthalmologist Columbia Coll. Physicians and Surgeons, 1981—. Served with USPHS, 1969-71. Diplomate Am. Bd. Ophthalmology. Fellow ACS; mem. N.Y. State, N.Y. County med. socs., Am. Acad. Ophthalmology and Otolaryngology. Contbr. articles to profl. jours. Office: 133 E 64th St New York NY 10021-7045

HYMAN, EDWARD JAY, forensic psychologist, cognitive and information scientist, consultant, educator, television news commentator; b. Roslyn, NY, Oct. 25, 1947; s. Herbert H. and Edith (Tannenbaum) H.; m. Deborah Anne McDonald, May 1, 1986; children: Cameron Scott, Devon Edward. AB, Columbia U., 1969; postgrad., Harvard U., 1969-70; PhD, U. Calif., Berkeley, 1975. Diplomate Am. Bd. Forensic Medicine, Am. Bd. Forensic Examiners, Am. Bd. Psychol. Specialties, lic. psychologist Calif. Editl. asst. Huntley-Brinkley Report NBC News, NYC, 1969; coord. Ctr. for Ednl. Change U. Calif., Berkeley, 1970-72, sr. fellow Ctr. for Social Rsch., 1972-74; intern Calif. Health Dept., Santa Cruz, Calif., 1974; lectr. U. Calif., Berkeley, 1975-76, asst. dean, 1976-77; chmn. bd. Assn. for Advanced Tng., LA, 1977-79; asst. prof. U. San Francisco, Calif., 1979-81; sci. dir. Ctr. for Social Rsch., Berkeley, Calif., 1981—; assoc. prof. psychiatry, psychology and law Ctr. Social Rsch., Berkeley, Calif., 1981-85; news commentator KRON-TV, 1981—88; prof. Ctr. Social Rsch., Berkeley, Calif., 1985-96, R. Nevitt Sanford prof. psychiatry, psychology & law, 1996—; news commentator NBC Network News, 1975—88, CBS Network News, 1988—, ABC Network News, 1990—. Cons. Union Am. Hebrew Congregations, 1967, Std. Oil Co., San Francisco, 1976—77, Exxon USA, 1976—77, Edison Electric Inst., Washington, 1977—80, NBC-TV, 1977—, Natural Resources Def. Coun., 1977—, Pacific Gas and Electric, 1986, PBS, 1997—, Frontline, 1997—, Weekend Today, 1997—; clin. dir. Inst. Labor & Mental Health, 1982—83. Co-author: Life Stress, 1983, Herbert Marcuse Festschrift, 1988; contbr. sci. papers and articles to profl. jour. Chair pub. rels. Tamalpais High Found., 2001—. Regents scholar U. Calif., 1974-75. Fellow: Calif. Inst. Forensic Scis.; mem.: APA, AAAS, AAUP, Am. Psychology-Law Soc., Am. Coll. Forensic Examiners, Soc. Psychol. Study Social Issues, Assn. Family and Conciliation Cts., Soc. Personality Assessment (conv. forensic issues chair), Am. Child Abuse Prevention Soc. (bd. dirs. 1975—, clin. dir. 1979—81, intern 1975—77), Internat. Congress Psychology (conv. com. 1980), Internat. Soc. Applied Psychology, Am. Coll. Forensic Psychology, Internat. Soc. Polit. Psychology (conv. com. 1987), Calif. Psychol. Assn., Am. Inst. Decision Scis., Alumni Club Columbia U. (No. Calif. bd. mem. 1995—, recruiting chair 1985—). Office: Ctr for Social Rsch 2029 Durant Ave Ste 301 Berkeley CA 94704 Office Fax: 415-388-5009.

HYMAN, HAROLD M. history educator, consultant; b. Bklyn., July 24, 1924; s. Abraham and Rebecca (Hermann) H.; m. Ferne Beverly Handelsman, Mar. 11, 1946; children: Lee Rosenthal, Ann Root, William Hyman. BA with honors, U. Calif. L.A., 1948; MA, Columbia U., 1950, PhD, 1952; LHD (hon.), Lincoln Coll., 1984. summer instr. Columbia U., 1953, U. Wash., 1960, Bklyn. Coll., 1962, U. Chgo., 1965; vis. asst. prof. UCLA, 1955-56; sr. Fulbright lectr. in Am. History and Law, grad. faculty polit. sci. U. Tokyo, 1973; faculty of law Keio U., 1973; adj. prof. legal history Bates Coll. Law U. Houston, 1977, of Am. legal history U. Tex. Law Sch., 1986; Meyer vis. disting. prof. legal history NYU Sch. Law, 1982-83; cons. and spkr. in field. Asst. prof. Earlham Coll., 1952-55; assoc. prof. Ariz. State U., 1956-57; prof. UCLA, 1957-63, U. Ill., 1963-68; William P. Hobby Prof. History Rice U., 1968-96, William P. Hobby prof. history emeritus, 1997—. Speaker in field. Author: Era of the Oath: Northern Loyalty Tests During the Civil War and Reconstruction (Albert J. Beveridge award Am. Hist. Assn. 1981), 1954, To Try Men's Souls: Loyalty Tests in American History (Sidney Hillman Found. prize 1960), 1981, Stanton: The Life and Times of Lincoln's Secretary of War, 1962, Soldiers and Spruce: Origins of the Loyal Legion of Loggers and Lumbermen: The Army's Labor Union of World War I, 1963, A More Perfect Union: The Impact of the Civil War and Reconstruction on the Constitution, 1973, Union and Confidence: The 1860s, 1976, (with William Wiecek) Equal Justice Under Law: Constitutional History, 1833-1880, 1982, paperback, 1983, Quiet Past and Stormy Present? War Powers in American History, 1986, American Singularity: The 1787 Northwest Ordinance, the 1862 Homestead-Morrill Acts, and the 1944 GI Bill, 1986, Oleander Odyssey: The Kempners of Galveston, 1870-1980, (Coral H. Tullis Meml. prize Tex. A&M U. Press 1990, T. R. Fehrenbach Book award Tex. Hist. Comsn. 1990, Ottis Lock Endowment award E. Tex. Hist. Assn. 1991), 1990, The Reconstruction Justice of Salmon P. Chase: In re Turner and Texas v. White, 1997, Character and Craftsmanship: A History of Houston's Vinson & Elkins Law Firm, 1917-1990s, 1998; editor (with Ferne B. Hyman) The Circuit Court Opinions of Salmon Portland Chase, 1972; contbr. numerous articles to profl. jours. Elected lay mem. Houston Bar Assn. Grievance Com., 1985-88; mem. numerous U. coms. The Constitution, Law, and Am. Life in the Nineteenth Century: A conf. named in his honor, Rice U. and NYU Sch. Law, 1989; named U.S. Presdl. appointee to permanent com. Oliver Wendell Holmes Trust, 1993-2001. Mem. Am. Hist. Assn. (numerous coms. and offices), Am. Soc. Legal History (pres . 1993-95), Orgn. Am. Historians (various coms. and offices), So. Hist. Assn. Avocation: fishing. Office: Rice University Dept History-MS 42 PO Box 1892 Houston TX 77251-1892

HYMAN, JEROME ELLIOT, lawyer; b. Rosedale, Miss., Dec. 26, 1923; s. Mose and Mary Ann (Sprecher) H.; m. Isabelle Miller, July 1, 1960. AB, Coll. William and Mary, 1944; LL.B. magna cum laude (Fay diploma), Harvard U., 1947. Bar: N.Y. 1949, D.C. 1960. Mem. fgn. funds control staff Dept. Treasury, U.S. Mil. Govt., Frankfurt and Berlin, Germany, 1945-46; law clk. to judge U.S. Ct. Appeals, Boston, 1947-48; assoc. firm Cleary, Gottlieb, Steen & Hamilton, N.Y.C., 1948-58, ptnr., 1959-93, sr. counsel, 1994—; trustee, mem. exec. com. Practising Law Inst., N.Y.C., 1972-97, v.p., 1979-86, pres., 1986-96, chmn. bd. trustees, 1996-97, chmn. emeritus, 1997—; sr. v.p., gen. counsel Pan Am World Airways, Inc., 1982-84. Bd. editors: Harvard Law Rev., 1945-47. Pres. Lexington Dem. Club, N.Y.C., 1956-58; counsel N.Y. Com. for Stevenson, 1956; del. various Dem. state and jud. convs.; alumni mem. Harvard Law Sch. Placement Com., 1976-79; nat. chmn. maj. gifts com. Harvard Law Sch. Fund, 1978-80; mem. overseers com. to visit Harvard Law Sch., 1986-92; trustee Lawyers' Com. for Civil Rights Under Law, 1981—; trustee Citizens Budget Commn., N.Y.C., 1991-94, trustee emeritus, 1994—; trustee Endowment Assn. of the Coll. of William and Mary, 1997—; mem. dean's adv. bd. Harvard Law Sch., 2000—, exec. com., 2003—. Fellow Am. Bar Found., Phi Beta Kappa Soc.; mem. ABA, Assn. Bar City N.Y. (chmn. com. corp. law 1984-87), Am. Law Inst., Am. Judicature Soc., N.Y. County Lawyers Assn., Tribar Opinion Commn., Harvard Law Sch. Assn. N.Y.C. (trustee 1980-83, v.p. 1984-85, pres. 1985-86), Nat. Harvard Law Sch. Assn. (mem. coun. 1990-93, mem. exec. com. 1991-93), Sky Club. Home: 1125 Park Ave Apt 10B New York NY 10128-1243 Office: Cleary Gottlieb Steen & Hamilton One Liberty Plaza New York NY 10006-1470 E-mail: jehyman23@hotmail.com., jhyman@cgsh.com.

HYMAN, LAWRENCE ROBERT, psychiatrist; b. Amsterdam, N.Y., Dec. 7, 1940; s. Morris Arthur and Bertha (Berkman) H.; m. Lois Armstrong Wilson, June 27, 1978; children: Elyse Michelle, Michael Louis, Joshua William. BA, Ohio Wesleyan U., 1963; MD, Chgo. Med. Sch., 1968. Intern then resident U. Wis., Madison, 1968-72; guest worker NIH, Bethesda, Md., 1973-76; asst. prof. Johns Hopkins Sch. Medicine, Balt., 1976-78; resident George Washington U., Washington, 1978-80; asst. clin. prof. U. Md., Balt., 1981-84; pvt. practice Columbia, Md., 1981—; active staff dept. psychiatry Howard County Gen. Hosp., Columbia, Md., 1981—; chief exec. officer Orchard Hill Treatment Ctr. for Chem. Dependency, Columbia, 1987-93; dir. Howard Behavioral Rsch. Group, 1999—, Lawrence R. Hyman MD and Assocs., 1993—. Cons. Family Therapy Inst., Rockville, Md., others; bd. dirs. Closecall Am., Inc. Contbg. editor Gould Med. Dictionary, 1979; contbr. articles to profl. jours. Adv. bd. Nat. Kidney Found., Balt., 1971. Maj. M.C., AUS, 1972-76. Recipient USPHS Rsch. Career Devel. award, 1977; NIH fellow, 1972; NIH grantee. Mem. Am. Psychiat. Assn., Md. Psychiat. Soc., Med. and Chirurgical Faculty State of Md., Howard County Med. Soc., Am. Orthopsychiat. Assn. Avocations: sailing, marathons. Home: 3681 Folly Quarter Rd Ellicott City MD 21042-1452 Office: # 201 11055 Little Patuxent Pky Columbia MD 21044

HYMAN, LEONARD STEPHEN, financial consultant, economist, writer; b. N.Y.C., June 5, 1940; s. Milton and Elsie (Reiter) H.; m. Judith N. Siegel, July 4, 1965; children: Andrew S., Robert C. BA, N.Y. U., 1961; MA, Cornell U., 1965. Fin. analyst Chase Manhattan Bank, N.Y.C., 1965-72; ptnr. H.C. Wainwright & Co., N.Y.C., 1972-77; v.p. Wainwright Securities, N.Y.C., 1977-78; v.p., head utility rsch. group Merrill Lynch Capital Markets, N.Y.C., 1978-94, first v.p., 1987-94; pres. Pvt. Sector Advisors, Inc., Sleepy Hollow, N.Y., 1994—. Mng. dir. Fulcrum Internat., Ltd., 1995-96; sr. industry advisor Salomon Smith Barney, Inc. 1997—2002; sr. assoc., cons. R.J. Rudden Assocs., 2002—; mem. bd. advisors Electric Power Rsch. Inst., 1993-99, Enertech Capital, 1999—, Excelergy, 2000—, Internat Found. Rsch. in Exptl. Econ., 2000—; mem. lunar energy enterprise case study task force NASA, 1988-89. Author: America's Electric Utilities, 1983; co-author: The New Telecommunications Industry, 1987, The Water Business, 1998, A Blueprint for Transmission, 1999; contbr. Electric Power Strategic Issues, 1983, The Future of Electrical Energy, 1986, Deregulation and Diversification of Utilities, 1988, The Electric Industry in Transition, 1994, The Virtual Utility, 1997, Power Systems Restructuring, 1998, Pricing in Competitive Electricity Markets, 2000; editor: The Privatization of Public Utilities, 1995; contbr. article to profl. jours.; mem. editl. bd. Forum for Applied Research and Public Policy, 1993—2002, Cogeneration and Competitive Power Jour., 1999—. Mem. Pa. Task Force on Electric Utility Efficiency, Harrisburg, 1982-83; mem. adv. com. U.S. Congress-Office Tech. Assessment, Washington, 1983, 86-87, 87-88, 92-93; mem. North Am. Elec. Reliability Coun. Elec. Reliability Panel, 1997. Mem. AAAS, Soc. Utility Regulatory Fin. Analysts (bd. dirs.), N.Y. Soc. Security Analysts, Fin. Analysts Fedn., Inst. Chartered Fin. Analysts, U.S. Energy Assn., Phi Beta Kappa. Democrat. Jewish. Avocations: travel, music, canoeing. Home and Office: Private Sector Advisors Inc 34 Fremont Rd Tarrytown NY 10591-1118 E-mail: lhyman@rjrudden.com.

HYMAN, LESTER SAMUEL, lawyer; b. Providence, July 14, 1931; s. Carl and Alice (Adelman) H.; m. Helen Reeder Sidman, Sept. 19, 1959 (div. 1982); children: David, Andrew, Elizabeth. AB, Brown U., 1952; LLB, Columbia U., 1955. Bar: D.C. 1955, Mass. 1955, U.S. Supreme Ct. 1957. Atty. SEC, Washington, 1955-57; chief asst. to Gov. State of Mass., Boston, 1962-64, sec. commerce, 1964-65; sr. cons. HUD, Washington, 1966-67, ptnr. Leva, Hawes & Symington, Washington, 1969-82; founding ptnr. Swidler & Berlin, Washington, 1982—, sr. of counsel. Lectr. John F. Kennedy Sch. Govt. Harvard U., 1968-69; bd. dirs. CDS Internat., 1988-94. mem. Internat. Oberver Team for nat. election in Haiti, 1990. Author: U.S. Policy Towards Liberia, 1822-2003: Unintended Consequences?, 2003. Bd. dirs. Ctr. Nat. Policy, Washington, 1980—; bd. advisors Close-Up Found.; bd. govs. Am. Jewish Commn., 1980-84; Dem. chmn., Mass., 1967-69, del. Dem. Nat. Conv., 1968, mem. Dem. Charter Reform Commn., 1970, D.C. Cmty. Humanities, 1988-90; bd. dirs. Cmty. Coll. of Brit. V.I., 1989—, Young Artists, 1989-94; mem. adv. bd. Internat. legal Studies Program, Washington Coll. Law, Am. U., 1990—; apptd. by Pres. Clinton to Franklin Delano Roosevelt Meml. Commn., 1994; trustee Norton Simon Mus. of Art, Pasadena, Calif., 1995-97; mem. U.S. Presdl. Del. to Guatamalan Peace Accord Singing, 1996; bd. dirs. Brit VI Natl. Park Trust, 1999, U. of Dist. of Columbia Fdn., 2002. Named Outstanding Young Man of Yr., Greater Boston Jr. C. of C., 1964. Mem. Performing Artists Soc. Am. (mng. dir. 1997), Internat. Intellectual Property Inst. (dir. 1998—). Home: 3826 Van Ness St NW Washington DC 20016-2228 Office: Swidler Berlin Shereff Friedman 3000 K St NW Ste 300 Washington DC 20007-5116 E-mail: lshyman@aol.com., lshyman@swidlaw.com.

HYMAN, LEWIS NEIL, investment company executive, investment advisor; b. Johnstown, Pa., Aug. 5, 1949; s. Albert and Helene (Rose) H.; 1 child, Hannah Rose. BA magna cum laude, U. Pitts., 1971, JD, 1974. Bar: Pa. 1974, U.S. Dist. Ct. 1974, U.S. Supreme Ct. 1974; registered investment advisor. Asst. dist. atty. Allegheny County Dist. Atty.'s Office, Pitts., 1974-79; pvt. practice lawyer Pitts., 1979-82, 89-91; investment banker Smith Barney, N.Y.C., Phila., 1982-86; v.p. investment banking and market devel. FGIC, Inc., N.Y.C., 1987-89; pres. The Hartwood Group, Pitts., 1991—, Hartwood Advisors, Inc., Pitts., 1991—; officer Strategic Benefits Group, Inc., Pitts., 1991-95. Lectr. U. Pitts., 1989-91, Allegheny C.C., Pitts., 1989-91, Pa. State U., Pitts., 19890-91, Joseph M. Katz Grad. Sch. Bus./U. Pitts., 1995. Bd. trustees Jewish Chronicle, Ctrl. Scholarship & Loan Referral Svc., Temple Sinai. Univ. scholar U. Pitts., 1971. Mem.: Pa. Bar Assn., Phi Beta Kappa. Avocations: tennis, golf, swimming, photography, sculpture, skiing. Office: The Hartwood Group 5401 Walnut St Pittsburgh PA 15232-2276 E-mail: hartwoodgroup@worldnet.att.net.

HYMAN, MARY BLOOM, science education programs coordinator; m. Sigmund M. Hyman, 1947 (dec.); children: Carol Hyman Piccinini, Nancy Louise. BA, Goucher Coll., 1971; MS, Johns Hopkins U., 1977. Asst. dir. Edn. Md. Sci. Ctr., Balt., 1976-81, dir. edn., 1981-90; coord. sci. edn. programs Loyola Coll., Balt., 1990—, coord. Inst. for Child Care Edn., 1992—. Trustee Goucher Coll., Franklin & Marshall Coll., Lancaster, Pa., 2003--; active Baltimore County Pub. Schs. Com. for Sch.-Based and Sch.-Linked Child Care; bd. dirs. Balt. Sch.-Age Child Care Alliance, Johns Hopkins U. Ctr. Talented Youth; mem. Gov.'s Task Force on Compensation of Child Care Providers, 1995-96. Recipient Disting. Women award Gov.'s Office, Annapolis, Md., 1981; Meritorious Svc. award Johns Hopkins U., 1983; Outstanding Svc. to Sci. Edn. award. Assn. Sci. Dept. Chairmen Balt. County Pub. Schs., 1989. Mem. Md. Assn. Sci. Tchrs. (bd. dirs.), Phi Beta Kappa, Phi Delta Kappa. Home: 10815 Longacre Ln Stevenson MD 21153-0665 E-mail: mhyman@loyola.edu.

HYMAN, MELVIN, speech-language pathologist, consultant; b. Bklyn., June 20, 1927; s. Isadore and Lillian (Pincus) H.; m. Joy Anne Kirk, June 10, 1973; 1 child, Ilana M. Hyman-Levin. BA, Bklyn. Coll., 1949; MA, Ohio State U., 1950, PhD, 1955. Cert. Am. Speech Lang. Pathology and Audiology, Ohio Bd. Speech-Lang. Pathology and Audiology. Prof., chair comm. disorders Bowling Green (Ohio) State U., 1952-90; owner, speech-lang. pathologist Hyman Hearing and Speech Ctr., Toledo, Ohio, 1985—. Cons. St. Vics Med. Ctr. and Hosp., Toledo, 1970—, Wood County Hosp., Bowling Green, 1979—, St. Lukes Hosp., Toledo, 1985—, Fulton County Health Ctr., Wauseon, Ohio, 1987—. Author: Rehabilitation After Trauma, 1962, Alaryngeal Speech, 1971, Index to Speech Language Hearing, 1979; contbr. chpts. to books. Bd. mem. Easter Seal Soc., Bowling Green, 1956-64, Northwest Ohio Family Svcs., Toledo, 1981-88, Lucas County Am. Cancer Soc., Toledo, 1994—, Toledo Ballet Assn, pres., 1988; past chmn. bd. dirs. N.W. Heart Assn., 1964, Ohio divsn. Am. Cancer Soc., 1978; bd. dirs. Toledo Legal Aid Soc., 1996— (past chmn. emeritus). Fellow Am. Speech-Lang. Pathology and Audiology (Pioneer award 1992, past pres.) Ohio Speech and Hearing Assn. (award 1996, hon. 1974); mem. Internat. Torch CLub (past pres. Toledo chpt.). Jewish. Avocations: opera, theatre, story telling. Home: 5123 Cambrian Rd Toledo OH 43623-2623 Office: Hyman Hearing & Speech Ctr 5950 Airport Hwy Toledo OH 43615-7382 E-mail: jmhyman@aol.com.

HYMAN, MICHAEL BRUCE, lawyer; b. Elgin, Ill., July 26, 1952; s. Robert I. and Ruth (Cohen) H.; m. Leslie Bland, Aug. 14, 1977; children: Rachel Joy, David Adam. BSJ with honors, Northwestern U., 1974, JD, 1977. Bar: Ill. 1977, U.S. Supreme Ct. 1989. Asst. atty. gen. Antitrust div. State of Ill., Chgo., 1977-79; trial atty. Much Shelist Freed Denenberg Ament & Rubenstein, Chgo., 1979-85, ptnr., 1985—. Chmn. panelist various continuing legal edn. seminars. Columnist Editor's Briefcase, CBA Record, 1988-90, 93—, The Red Pencil, 1986-89; contbr. chpt. to book, articles to profl. jours.; host (cable TV program) You and the Law, 1995—. Trustee North Shore Congregation Israel, Glencoe, 1980-89, 95-2001, v.p., 1987-89. Mem.: ABA (assoc. editor 1985—89, sect. litig., chmn. antitrust litig. com. 1987—90, mng. editor 1989—90, editor-in-chief Litig. News 1990—92, task force on civil justice reform 1991—93, chmn. monographs and unpub. papers com. 1992—95, editor-in-chief Litig. Docket 1995—2001, jud. divsn. lawyers conf., membership com. chair 1999—2003, Tips From the Trenches 2001—02, chmn. consumer and personal rights litig. com. 2002—, divsn. mem. chair 2002—, exec. com. 2002—), Chgo. Bar Found. (bd. dirs. 2003—), Decalogue Soc. Lawyers (trustee 2001—, co-chair CLE programs 2001—, fin. sec. 2002—03, sec. 2003—, rec. sec. 2003—), Am. Soc. Writers on Legal Subjects (chair book award com. 1997—), Ill. Bar Assn. (antitrust coun. 1981—87, vice chair, sec., co-editor newsletter 1982—85, chmn. coun. 1985—86, rep. on assembly 1986—92, chmn. bench and bar sect. coun. 1990—91, professionalism com. 1992—95, chair 1993—94, rep. on assembly 1994—99, vice chair ARDC com. 1995—96, cable TV com. 1995—, chair ARDC com. 1996—97, chair 1997—99, bench and bar sect. coun. 1998—2003, rep. on assembly 2001—), Chgo. Bar Assn. (editor-in-chief CBA Record 1988—90, bd. mgrs. 1992—94, editor-in-chief CBA Record 1993—, CBA News 1994—98, vice chair class action com. 1999—2000, chair 2000—01, 2d v.p. 2003—). Jewish. Avocations: writing, abraham lincoln. Office: Much Shelist Freed Denenberg Ament & Rubenstein 191 N Wacker Dr Ste 1800 Chicago IL 60606-1615 E-mail: mbhyman@muchshelist.com.

HYMAN, MILTON BERNARD, lawyer; b. L.A., Nov. 19, 1941; s. Herbert and Lillian (Rakowitz) Hyman; m. Sheila Goldman, July 4, 1965; children: Lauren Davida, Micah Howard. BA in Econs. with highest honors, UCLA, 1963; JD magna cum laude, Harvard U., 1966. Bar: Calif. 1967. Assoc. Irell & Manella LLP, L.A., 1970-73, ptnr., 1973—. Co-author: Partnerships and Associations: A Policy Critique of the Morrisey Regulations, 1976, Consolidated Returns: Summary of Tax Considerations in Acquisition of Common Parent of Subsidiary Member of Affiliated Group, 1980, Tax Aspects of Corporate Debt Exchanges, Recapitalization and Discharges, 1982, Tax Strategies for Leveraged Buyouts and Other Corporate Acquisitions, 1986, Preservation and Use of Net Operating Losses and Other Tax Attributes in a Consolidated Return Context, rev. edit., 1992, Collier on Bankruptcy Taxation, 1992, Real Estate Workouts and Bankruptcies, 1993, Current Corporate Bankruptcy Tax Issues, 1993, Tax Strategies for Corporate Acquisitions, Dispositions, Financing, Joint Ventures, Reorganizations, and Restructurings, 1995; author: A Transactional Encounter with the Partnership Rules of Subchapter K: The Effects of the Tax Reform Act of 1984, 1984, Net Operating Losses and Other Tax Attributed of Corporate Clients, 1987. Past pres., bd. dirs. Sinai Temple, West Los Angeles, Calif. Capt. JAGC, U.S. Army, 1967-70. Sheldon traveling fellow Harvard U., 1966-67. Mem. ABA (chmn. com. affiliated and related corps. 1981-83, chmn. corp. tax com. 1999-2000), Calif. State Bar Assn., Am. Law Inst. (fed. income tax project tax adv. group 1976—), Masons, Phi Beta Kappa. Jewish. Office: Irell & Manella LLP Ste 900 1800 Avenue Of The Stars Los Angeles CA 90067-4276

HYMAN, MISTY DAWN, Olympic athlete; b. Mesa, Ariz., Mar. 23, 1979; d. Steve and Margaret Hyman. Student, Stanford U. Recipient Gold medal 200-meter butterfly Sydney Olympics, 2000, Bronze medal 200-meter butterfly, Gold medal 4 x 400-meter medley relay (team) World Championships, 1998; winner 3 individual NCAA titles, 1998, mem. 2 championship relay teams NCAA, 1998; named NCAA Swimmer of Yr., 1998. Office: USA Swimming 1 Olympic Plz Colorado Springs CO 80909-5746

HYMAN, MONTAGUE ALLAN, lawyer, educator; b. N.Y.C., Apr. 19, 1941; s. Allan Richard and Lilyan P. (Pollock) H.; m. susann Podell, Jan. 25, 1965; children: Jeffrie-Anne, Erik. BA, Syracuse U., 1962; JD, St. Johns U., 1965. Bar: N.Y. 1965, U.S. Dist. Ct. (so. and ea. dists.) N.Y. 1967, U.S. Ct. Appeals (2d cir.) 1982, U.S. Supreme Ct. 1973. Assoc. Warburton, Hyman, Deeley & Connolly, Mineola, NY, 1965-67; ptnr. Hyman & Deeley, 1967-69, Koeppel, Hyman, Sommer, Lesnick & Ross, 1969-72, Hyman & Hyman, P.C., Garden City, 1972-80, Costigan, Hyman, Hyman & Herman, P.C., Mineola, 1980-87, Certilman, Haft, Balin, Buckley, Adler & Hyman, 1988—, Certilman Balin Adler & Hyman, 1988—. Lectr. Hofstra U., Adelphi U., Columbia Appraisal Soc., Practicing Law Inst.; chmn. bd. Edn. and Assistance Corp. Contbr. articles to profl. jours. Bd. trustees North Shore L.I. Jewish Health System. Mem. Nassau County Bar Assn., N.Y. State Bar Assn., Inst. Property Taxation. Office: Certilman Balin Adler & Hyman LLP 90 Merrick Ave East Meadow NY 11554-1571 E-mail: ahyman@certilmanbalin.com.

HYMAN, MORTON PETER, shipping company executive; b. N.Y.C., Jan. 9, 1936; s. Irving S. and Dora (Pfeffer) H.; m. Chris Oliphant Stern, Mar. 18, 1979; children: Sarah Anne, David Jacob. BA, Cornell U., 1956, LLD with distinction, 1959; DHL (hon.), N.Y. Med. Coll. Bar: N.Y. 1960. Assoc. Proskauer Rose Goetz & Mendelsohn, N.Y.C., 1959-63; officer, dir. Overseas Discount Corp., N.Y.C., 1963—, pres., 1983—; officer, dir. Overseas Shipholding Group, Inc., N.Y.C., 1969—, pres., 1971—, CEO, 1999—; also chmn., bd. dirs. Vice chmn. bd. Discount Bank and Trust Co., 1999-2002. Bd. editors Cornell Law Rev. Vice-chmn. N.Y. State Health Planning Commn., 1977-78; mem. Pub. Health Coun. N.Y., 1971-95, vice chmn., 1975-85, chmn., 1985-95; co-chmn. N.Y. State Health Issues Forum; chmn. N.Y. State Health Care Capital Policy Adv. Com., 1982-94; chmn. bd. trustees Beth Israel Med. Ctr., Continuum Health Ptnrs, Inc.; chmn. bd. trustees St. Luke's-Roosevelt Hosp. Ctr.; vice chmn. N.Y. Eye and Ear Infirmary; vice-chmn. bd. regents Long Island Coll Hosp.; chmn. N.Y. State Joint Exec. and Legis. Task Force on Delivery of Health Care, 1977-80; chmn. N.Y. State Joint Exec. and Legis. Com. on Residential Health Care Facilities, 1977-80; trustee The Brearley Sch., 1993-97; mem. pres. coun. United Hosp. Fund; bd. dirs. United Jewish Appeal Fedn., 1986-91; mem. bd. overseers Albert Einstein Coll. Medicine of Yeshiva U. 2d lt. AUS, 1956-57. Fellow N.Y. Acad. Medicine; mem. N.Y. Bar Assn., Harmonie Club, Order of Coif, Phi Kappa Phi Republican. Home: 998 5th Ave New York NY 10028-0102 Office: Overseas Shipholding Group Inc 511 Fifth Ave New York NY 10017-4903

HYMAN, NEIL HYMAN, surgeon, educator; b. N.Y.C., Mar. 21, 1958; s. Abe M. and Serene J. Hyman; m. Jennifer S. Shapiro, Sept. 6, 1986; children: Eric, Seth. BA, U. Pa., 1980; MD, U. Vt., 1984. Diplomate Am. Bd. Gen. Surgery, Am. Bd. Colorectal Surgery. Intern Mt. Sinai Med. Ctr., N.Y.C., 1984-85, surg. resident, 1984-89; fellow in colon and rectal surgery Cleve. Clinic, 1989-90; from asst. to assoc. prof. surgery U. Vt. Coll. Medicine, Burlington, 1990—2003, prof. surgery, 2003—; surgeon Fletcher Allen Health Care, Burlington, 1990—, chief divsn. gen. surgery, 2000—. Office: Fletcher Allen Health Care 3 Timber Ln South Burlington VT 05403-7205 E-mail: neil.hyman@vtmednet.org.

HYMAN, ROGER DAVID, lawyer; b. Oak Ridge, Tenn., Apr. 23, 1957; s. Marshall Leonard and Vera Lorraine (McKinney) H.; m. Elsa Laurencio, children: Cristina Alicia, James Marshall. BA, Vanderbilt U., 1979; JD, U. Tenn., 1984. Clk. Oak Ridge Nat. Lab., 1977-78, 81; air personality, news reporter Stas. WKDA, WKDF, Nashville, 1979; program dir. Sta. WBIR-FM, Knoxville, Tenn., 1979-80; assoc. atty. Hindman & Holt, Attys., Knoxville, Tenn., 1984-85; asst. atty. gen. State of Tenn., Knoxville, 1986-95; with Law Offices of Roger D. Hyman Powell, Tenn., 1995-97; ptnr. Hyman & Carter, PLLC, Powell, Tenn., 1997—. Bd. dirs. Knoxville Christian Sch., 1991-93. Democrat. Mem. Ch. of Christ. Home: 2713 Windemere Ln Powell TN 37849-3782 Office: Hyman & Carter PLLC PO Box 1304 Powell TN 37849-1304 E-mail: RDHymanLAW@aol.com.

HYMAN, SEYMOUR, capital and product development company executive; b. N.Y.C., June 19, 1927; s. Morris and Fannie (Baumwall) H.; m. Sandra Kammerman, Feb. 25, 1973. BS, N.Y. State Maritime Coll., 1948; student, Bklyn. Poly. Inst., 1944-45, Columbia, 1949-51; MS, N.Y. U., 1949. Chief mfg. engring. U.S. Naval Clothing Factory, Bklyn., 1950-51; chief indsl. engr. Peter Pan Mfg. Co., E. Newark, N.J., 1951-53; chief prodn. engr. Seampruf Inc., N.Y.C., 1953-54; founder, pres., chmn. bd. Herculite Protective Fabrics, Inc., N.Y.C., 1954-76; vice chmn. bd. Eckmar Corp., N.Y.C., 1969-75; co-founder pres., chmn. bd. Health-Chem. Corp., N.Y.C., 1971-76; pres. Delta Ventures Corp., N.Y.C., 1977—. Served with USNR, 1945-48. Mem. Soc. Plastic Engrs. Clubs: Mason (Shriner). Home: 425 E 58th St New York NY 10022-2300

HYMAN, STEVEN EDWARD, federal agency administrator, psychiatrist, educator; BA summa cum laude, Yale U., 1974; BA with honors, MA in History and Philosophy of Sci., U. Cambridge, Eng., 1976; MD cum laude, Harvard U., 1980. Diplomate Am. Bd. Psychiatry and Neurology. Intern in medicine Mass. Gen. Hosp., Boston, 1980-81, clin. and rsch. fellow in endocrinology and neurology, 1983-84, rsch. fellow in molecular biology, 1984-88, dir. rsch. dept. psychiatry, 1990-96, dir. divsn. addictions, 1992-95, supr. psychiatric residents, 1984—, dir. neurosci. and biolo. psychiatry curriculum for residents, lectr., 1986—; clin. fellow in medicine Harvard U., Boston, 1980-81, clin. fellow in psychiatry, 1981-84, rsch. fellow in genetics, 1984-87, from instr. in psychiatry to asst. prof. psychiatry Harvard Med. Sch., Boston, 1987-92, assoc. prof. psychiatry, 1993-98, prof. psychiatry, 1998—; dir. NIMH, Rockville, Md., 1996—2001; provost Harvard U., Cambridge, Mass., 2001—. Mem. sci. coun. NARSAD, 1996—; mem. adv. com. Howard Hughes Med. Inst., 1998—, Riken Brain Scis. Inst., Tokyo. Author: (with G.W. Arana) Handbook of Psychiatric Drug Therapy, 1987, 2d edit., 1991, 3d edit. (with G.W. Arana, J.R. Rosenbaum), 1995, (with E. Nestler) The Molecular Foundations of Psychiatry, 1993; editor numerous textbooks; mem. editl. bd. Jour. Geriat. Psychiatry and Neurology, 1987-96, Psychosomatics, 1988-96, Harvard Rev. Psychiatry, 1992—, Am. Jour. Med. Genetics, 1992—, Jour. Neurochemistry, 1994—, Archives Gen. Psychiatry, 1996—, Molecular Psychiatry, 1996—, Neurobiology of Disease, 1996—. Mellon fellow, 1974-76, Dupont-Warren fellow, 1983-84, Langhlin fellow Am. Coll. Psychiatry, 1983; recipient Laughlin award Nat. Psychiatric Endowment Fund, 1984, Physician Scientist award NIDDK, 1985-90, Philip Isenberg award for best tchr. selected by graduating residents McLean Hosp., 1985, Rsch. Scientist Devel. award level 2, 1995-96. Mem. APA, Am. Coll. Neuropsychopharmacology, Soc. Neurosci., Soc. Biolo. Psychiatry. Office: Harvard U Massachusetts Hall Cambridge MA 02138

HYMAN, WILLIAM JAY, internist, oncologist; b. L.A., Mar. 30, 1959; MD, Baylor U., 1985. Diplomate Am. Bd. Internal Medicine, Am. Bd. Oncology; cert. Am. Bd. Hospice and Palliative Medicine. Resident in internal medicine U. Cin., 1985-88; fellow in med. oncology Baylor U. Coll. Medicine, Houston, 1988-90; pvt. practice Tyler, Tex. Mem. staff Med. Ctr. Hosp., Tyler; attending internist Mother Francis Hosp. Mem. Am. Soc. Clin. Oncology, Tex. Med. Assn. Office: Tex Oncology Tyler Cancer Ctr 910 E Houston St Ste 100 Tyler TX 75702-8363

HYMEL, L(EZIN) J(OSEPH), lawyer, former prosecutor; b. Baton Rouge, July 2, 1944; s. Lezin Joseph Sr. and Alma K. Hymel; m. Linda N. Hymel, Oct. 6, 1973; children: Traci Lyn, Shea Roach Bonaventure, Kimberly Kaye. BS in Geology, La. State U., 1966, JD, 1969. Bar: La., U.S. Dist. Ct. (ea. dist.) La., U.S. Dist. Ct. (mid. dist.) La., U.S. Dist. Ct. (we. dist.) La., U.S. Ct. Appeals (5th cir.). Pvt. practice, Baton Rouge, 1969—70; staff atty. Office State Atty. Gen., Baton Rouge, 1970—71, asst. atty. gen., 1972—78, dir. criminal divsn., 1992—93; asst. dist. atty. Office 19 Jud. Dist. Atty., Baton Rouge, 1978—79; city judge Baton Rouge City Ct., 1980—83; state dist. ct. judge criminal divsn. 19th Jud. Dist. Ct, Baton Rouge, 1983—90, state dist. ct. judge civil divsn., 1991—92; U.S. atty. Office U.S. Atty., Dept. Justice, Baton Rouge, 1994—2001; ptnr. Sharp Henry Cerniglia Calvin Weaver & Hymel, Baton Rouge, 2001—. Office: Sharp Henry Cerniglia et al Ste C 15171 So Harrells Ferry Rd Baton Rouge LA 70816 Fax: (225) 755-1065. E-mail: ljhymel@sharphenry.com.

HYMER, TABITHA KIM, music educator, writer, photographer; b. Pitts., Kans., Sept. 7, 1960; d. Robert Fredrick and Joyce Elaine Hartmann; m. Dale Ray Hymer, July 29, 1978 (div. July 22, 1999); children: Joshua Bohannon, Clover Shea Baker, (Hymer). MusB Edn.(hon.), U. of Ctrl. Ark., 2003. Cert. Tchr. of Music in Piano Music Tchr's. Nat. Assn., 2002. Ind. piano tchr. Self-employed, Clinton, Ark., 1993—; piano tchr. U. of Ctrl. Ark., Conway, 2001—. Freelance photographer and writer Ark. Dem. Gazette, Little Rock, 2000—. Scholar Valerie-Klipsch Music Scholarship, U. of Ctrl. Ark., 2001. Mem.: Alpha Chi (hon.). Mem. Church Of Christ. Avocations: music, rollerblading, travel, art, gardening.

HYMES, DELL HATHAWAY, anthropologist, educator; b. Portland, Oreg., June 7, 1927; s. Howard Hathaway and Dorothy (Bowman) H.; m. Virginia Margaret Dosch, Apr. 10, 1954; 1 adopted child, Robert Paul; children: Alison Bowman, Kenneth Dell; 1 stepchild, Vicki (Mrs. David Unruh). BA, Reed Coll., 1950; MA, Ind. U., 1953, PhD, 1955; postgrad., UCLA, 1954-55; degree (hon.), U. Turino, Italy, 2002. From instr. to asst. prof. Harvard U., 1955-60; from assoc. prof. to prof. U. Calif., Berkeley, 1960—65; prof. anthropology U. Pa., 1965-72, prof. folklore and linguistics, 1972-88, prof. sociology, 1974-88, prof. edn., 1975-88, dean Grad. Sch. Edn., 1975-87; prof. anthropology and English U. Va., 1987-90, Commonwealth prof. anthropology, 1990-98, Commonwealth prof. English, 1990-98, emeritus, 1998—. Bd. dirs. Social Sci. Rsch. Coun., 1965-67, 69-70, 71-72. Author: Language in Culture and Society, 1964, The Use of Computers in Anthropology, 1965, Studies in Southwestern Ethnolinguistics, 1967, Pidginization and Creolization of Languages, 1971, Reinventing Anthropology, 1972, Foundations in Sociolinguistics, 1974, Soziolinguistik, 1980, Language in Education, 1980, In Vain I Tried to Tell You, 1981, (with John Fought) American Structuralism, 1981, Essays in the History of Linguistic Anthropology, 1983, Vers la Competence de Communication, 1984, Ethnography, Linguistics, Narrative Inequality, 1996; assoc. editor: Jour. History Behavioral Scis., 1966-93, Am. Jour. Sociology, 1977-80, Jour. Pragmatics, 1977—; contbg. editor: Alcheringa, 1973-80, Theory and Society, 1976-96; editor: Language in Society, 1972-92. Trustee Ctr. for Applied Linguistics, 1973-78. With AUS, 1945-47. Fellow Ctr. Advanced Study Behavioral Scis., 1957-58, Fellow Clare Hall, Cambridge, Eng., Guggenheim fellow, 1969-70, Nat. Endowment for Humanities sr. fellow, 1972-73. Fellow Am. Acad. Arts and Scis., Am. Folklore Soc. (pres. 1973-74), Brit. Acad.; mem. Am. Anthrop. Assn. (exec. bd. 1968-70, pres. 1983), Am. Assn. Applied Linguistics (pres. 1986), Linguistic Soc. Am. (exec. bd. 1967-69, pres. 1982), Coun. on Anthropology and Edn. (pres. 1978), Consortium Social Sci. Assns. (pres. 1984-85), Folklore Fellows Finland. Home: 205 Montvue Dr Charlottesville VA 22901-2022

HYMOWITZ, THEODORE, plant geneticist, educator; b. N.Y.C., Feb. 16, 1934; s. Bernard and Ethel (Rose) H.; m. Ann Einhorn, Dec. 25, 1960 (div. 1985); children: Madeleine, Sara, Jessica; m. Barbara E. Bohen, June 11, 1989 (div. 1998). BS, Cornell U., 1955; MS, U. Ariz., 1957; PhD, Okla. State U., 1963. Agronomist IRI Rsch. Inst., Campinas, Brazil, 1964-66; from asst. to assoc. prof. U. Ill., Urbana, 1967-75, prof., 1975—. With U.S. Army, 1957-59. Recipient Rsch. award Land of Lincoln Soybean Assn., 1990, Funk award, 1991; scholar Loeb Found., Stillwater, Okla., 1961-62, Fulbright scholar, 1962-63. Fellow AAAS, Linnean Soc. London, Am. Soc. Agronomy, Crop Sci. Soc. Am. (Frank N. Meyer medal 1988). Achievements include research in the establishment of chromosomal map of the soybean, inheritance of the absence of seed lectin in soybeans, elucidation of genomic relationships among species in the genus Glycine, development of soybean cultivar lacking the Kunitz trypsin inhibitor, history of the introduction of the soybean to N.Am. Office: U Ill Dept Crop Sci 1102 S Goodwin Ave Urbana IL 61801-4730

HYNEK, FREDERICK JAMES, architect; b. Minot, N.D., May 24, 1944; s. Frederick Frank and Esther Irene (Hermanson) H.; m. Jane Rebecca Lowitz, June 9, 1966; children: Tyler James, Scott Anthony. BArch, N.D. State U., 1967. Intern archtl. firms, Bismarck, N.D., 1967-72; architect Gerald W. Deines, Casper, Cody, Wyo., 1972-73; v.p. Gerald Deines and Assocs., 1973-77; propr. Fred J. Hynek AIA/Architect, Cody, Wyo., 1977-80; pres. Design Group, P.C., Architects/Planners, Cody, Wyo., 1980-86, CHD Architects, Cody, Wyo., 1986-94; CEO Cathexes, Inc., Reno, Nev., 1994-95; project mgr. Merrick and Co., Denver, 1995-97. Coordinating architect Jefferson County Sch. Dist., Lakewood, 1998-2000; prin. Reseutek Design Group, Denver; adj. faculty archtl. tech. dept., Arapahoe C.C., Littleton, Colo.; mem. cert. of need rev. bd. State of Wyo., 1984-87, selection com. for archtl. students for Western Interstate Commn. for Higher Edn. Profl. Student Exch. Program, U. Wyo., 1979-94. Mem. editl. adv. bd. Symposia Magazine, 1981-82. Bd. dirs. Cody Stampede Inc., 1977-82, Cody Nordic Ski Found., Park County Libr. Found.; chmn. archtl. adv. comms. City of Cody, Cody Econ. Devel. Coun., 1982-84; coach Absaroka Ski Assn., Bill Koch Youth Ski League, 1990-94; mem. Planning Commn., Town of Parker, 1997-98, Cody County Am. (Amb. of Yr. 1990). Served with USAR, 1967-68. Mem. AIA (dir. Wyo. chpt. 1976-83, pres. 1980, 81, sec./treas., 1990-91), Coll. Fellows of Am. Inst. of Architects; conf. chmn. Western Mountain region 1977 (mem. awards jury 1981, 92, treas. 1982-86) chmn. design awards N.D. 1981, 97, 2 awards for Excellence in Archtl. Design Wyo. chpt.), U.S. Ski Assn., U.S. Ski Coaches Assn., Profl. Ski Instrs. of Am. Cody County C. of C. (dir., pres. 1982). Republican. Presbyterian. Office: Ste 620 1512 Larimer Denver CO 80202-1621 Home: 16910 E Carlson Dr # 225 Parker CO 80134-6805 E-mail: fhynek@reseutek.com.

HYNES, AEDHMAR, public relations executive; married; 3 children. Econs degree, Univ. Coll., Galway, Ireland; postgrad. diploma in mktg. With London office Text 100, regional dir. N.Am. ops., 1997—. Office: Text 100 Corp San Francisco 2d Fl 30 Hotaling Pl Fl 2D San Francisco CA 94111-2201 Fax: (415) 836-5991. E-mail: ryand@text100.com.

HYNES, GARRY, theatre director; b. Ballaghadereen, Ireland; Grad., U. Coll. Galway; DLL (hon.), Nat. U. Ireland, 1997. Founder Druid Theatre Co. Galway, 1975—, artistic dir., 1975-91, 95—, The Abbey Theatre, 1991-94. Prodns. include: The Playboy of the Western World, Bailegangaire, Conversations on a Homecoming, Wood of the Whispering, 'Tis a Pity She's a Whore, Lovers' Meeting, The Loves of Cass McGuire, The Beauty Queen of Leenane (Tony award for dir. of a play 1998), The Leenane Trilogy, A Whistle in the Dark, King of the Castle, The Plough and the Stars, The Power of Darkness, Famine, Portia Coughlan, The Man of Mode, The Love of the Nightingale, The Colleen Bawn, The Lonesome West, A Skull in Connemara, Mr. Peter's Connections, Sive, 2002, On Raftery's Hill, 2000. DLL (hon.) Nat. Coun. of Ednl. Awards, 1988. Home: 42 Raymond St Dublin 8 Ireland Office: The Druid Theatre Co Chapel Ln Galway Ireland also: RTE Donnybrook Dublin 4 Ireland E-mail: garryhynes@aol.com.

HYNES, HUGH BERNARD NOEL, biologist, educator; b. Devizes, Eng., Dec. 20, 1917; s. Harry George Claude and Anna Minnie Lucy (Meyer) H.; m. Mary Elizabeth Hinks, Oct. 24, 1942 (dec. Jan. 1999); children: Richard Olding, Elisabeth Anne, Andrew John, Julian David. BSc, U. London, 1938, PhD, 1941, DSc, 1958, U. Waterloo, 1983, U. New Brunswick, 2003. With Brit. Ministry Agr., 1941, Brit. Colonial Agrl. Ser., 1942-46; faculty U. Liverpool, Eng., 1947-64; prof. biology U. Waterloo, Ont., Can., 1964-83, Disting. prof. emeritus, 1983—. Cons. in field. Author: The Ecology of Running Water; contbr. numerous articles to profl. jours. Decorated Can. Centennial medal; recipient Naumann/Thienemann medal, Internat. Limnological Assn. Fellow Royal Soc. Can.; mem. Freshwater Biol. Assn., Internat. Assn. Theoretical and Applied Limnology, N.Am. Benthol. Soc. Home: 127 Iroquois Pl Waterloo ON Canada N2L 2S6 E-mail: nhynes@sciborg.uwaterloo.ca.

HYNES, JAMES, writer; b. Okemos, Mich., Aug. 23, 1955; s. Glendon and Mary Hynes. BA, U. of Mich., 1973—77; MFA, U. of Iowa, 1987—89. Author (novels) The Wild Colonial Boy, The Lecturer's Tale, Kings of Infinite Space, (novellas) Publish and Perish. James Michener fellow, Iowa Writers' Workshop, 1989-1990.

HYNES, PATRICIA MARY, lawyer; b. N.Y.C., Jan. 26, 1942; BA, CUNY, 1963; LLB, Fordham U., 1966. Bar: N.Y. 1966, U.S. Dist. Ct. (so. and ea. dists.) N.Y. 1969, U.S. Ct. Appeals (2d cir.) 1982. Law clk. Hon. Joseph C. Zavatt U.S. Dist. Ct. (ea. dist.) N.Y., 1966-67; asst. U.S. atty. U.S. Dist. Ct. (so. dist.) N.Y., 1967-82, exec. asst. U.S. atty., 1980-82, chief ofcl. corruption and spl. pros. unit, 1978-80, chief consumer fraud unit, 1971-78, mem. civil divsn., 1967-71; ptnr. Milberg Weiss Bershad Hynes & Lerach LLP, N.Y.C., 1983-99, of counsel, 2000—. Adj. prof. law Fordham U., 1978—83; lectr. trial advocacy Harvard U. Law Sch., 1983; lectr. Practising Law Inst.; mem. criminal justice act peer rev. panel U.S. Dist. Ct. (so. dist.) N.Y., 1982—83, mem. discovery com. 1982—84, mem. civil litig. com., 1983—84, chmn. merit selection panel for N.Y. magistrate judges, 2002—. Mem. Fordham Law Rev., 1964-66; mem. editl. bd. N.Y. Law Jour., 1994—. Mem. NYC Charter Revision Commn., 2002. Gov.'s Exec. Adv. Com. on Adminstrn. Criminal Justice, 1981—82, N.Y. Gov.'s Commn. on Govt. Integrity, 1987—90, Mayor's Adv. Com. on Jud. 1994—2001; chairperson N.Y. Regional Consumer Protection Coun. 1971—72. Named one of 50 Top Women Lawyers, Nat. Law Jour., 1998, 2001. Fellow: Am. Coll. Trial Lawyers; mem.: ABA (chair govt. litig. com. litig. sect. 1984—87, chair securities litig. com. 1987—89, coun. litig. sect. 1989—92, chair pre-trial practice and discovery com. 1992—94, standing com. on fed. jud. 1995—2000, chair 2000—01, criminal justice sect.), Legal Aid Soc. (bd. dirs. 1998—), N.Y. Coun. Def. Lawyers, Fed. Bar Coun. (trustee 1983—91, treas. 1987—90, v.p. 1990, 1996—), N.Y. State Bar Assn. (consumer affairs com. 1974—78, criminal law com. 1980—84, police law and policy com. 1981—83, sec. 1982—84, ho. dels. 1983—84, exec. com. 1984—88, second century com. 1988—92, del. to ABA, ho. dels. 1990—94, chair fed. cts. com. 1992—95

del.), Assn. of the Bar of the City of N.Y., Am. Law Inst (spl. adviser 1995—2001), Fordham Law Alumni Assn. Office: Milberg Weiss Bershad Hynes & Lerach LLP One Penn Plz New York NY 10119

HYNES, RICHARD OLDING, biology researcher, educator; b. Nairobi, Kenya, Africa, Nov. 29, 1944; s. Hugh Bernard Noel and Mary Elizabeth (Hinks) H.; m. Fleur Marshall, July 29, 1966; children: Hugh Jonathan, Colin Anthony. BA with honors, U. Cambridge, Eng., 1966, MA, 1970; PhD, MIT, 1971. Asst. prof. biology MIT, Cambridge, 1975-78, assoc. prof., 1978-83, prof. dept. biology, 1983—, assoc. head dept. biology, 1985-89, head, 1989-91, dir. Ctr. for Cancer Rsch., 1991-2001, Daniel K. Ludwig prof. cancer rsch., 1999—; investigator Howard Hughes Med. Inst., Chevy Chase, Md., 1988—. Author: Fibronectins, 1990; editor Tumor Cell Surfaces and Malignancy, 1979, Surfaces of Normal and Malignant Cells, 1979; contbr. articles to profl. jours. Guggenheim Found. fellow, 1982; recipient internat. award Gairdner Found., 1997. Fellow AAAS, Am. Acad. Arts and Scis., Royal Soc. London; mem. Inst. Medicine NAS,, Nat. Acad. Scis. Office: MIT Ctr Cancer Rsch EI7-227 77 Massachusetts Ave Cambridge MA 02139-4307 E-mail: rohynes@mit.edu.

HYNES, SAMUEL, English language educator, author; b. Chgo., Aug. 29, 1924; s. Samuel Lynn and Margaret (Turner) H.; m. Elizabeth Igleheart, July 28, 1944; children: Miranda, Joanna. BA, U. Minn., 1947; MA, Columbia U., 1948, PhD, 1956. Mem. faculty Swarthmore Coll., 1949-68, prof. English lit., 1965-68; prof. English Northwestern U., Evanston, Ill., 1968-76, Princeton U., 1976-90, Woodrow Wilson prof. lit., 1978-90, Woodrow Wilson prof. lit. emeritus, 1990—. Author: The Pattern of Hardy's Poetry, 1961 (Explicator award, 1962), William Golding, 1964, The Edwardian Turn of Mind, 1968, Edwardian Occasions, 1972, The Auden Generation, 1976, Flights of Passage, 1988, A War Imagined, 1990, The Soldiers' Tale, 1997 (Robert F. Kennedy Book award, 1998), The Growing Seasons, 2003; editor: Further Speculations by T.E. Hulme, 1955, The Author's Craft and Other Critical WRitings of Arnold Bennett, 1968, Romance and Realism, 1970, Complete Poetical Works Thomas Hardy, Vol. I, 1982, Vol. II, 1984, Vol. III, 1985, Vols. IV and V, 1995, Thomas Hardy, 1984, Complete Short Fiction of Joseph Conrad, vols. I-III, 1992, vol. IV, 1993. Served to maj. USMCR, 1943-46, 52-53. Decorated Air medal, DFC; Fulbright fellow, 1953-54, Guggenheim fellow, 1959-60, 81-82, Bollingen fellow, 1964-65, Am. Coun. Learned Socs. fellow, 1969, 85-86; NEH sr. fellow, 1973-74, 77-78, 89-91. Fellow Royal Soc. Lit.; mem. Phi Beta Kappa. Home: 130 Moore St Princeton NJ 08540-3359

HYNES, THOMAS N. (TOBY HYNES), automotive company executive; BBA, Hillsdale Coll.; MBA, Stanford U. Various key positions in sales and ops. Ford Motor Co., 1969, regional mgr. Ford and Lincoln-Mercury divsns., pres., COO Primus Fin. divsn., 1995-99; pres., gen. mgr. Gulf States Toyota Inc., Houston, 1999 . Office: Gulf States Toyota 7701 Wilshire Pl Dr Houston TX 77040*

HYODO, HARUO, radiologist, educator; b. Honai-chyo, Nishiuwa-gun, Ehime, Japan, Mar. 3, 1928; B of Medicine, Tokushuma U., 1959, MD, 1966. Chief clinic of radiology Nat. Kochi Hosp., 1963-65; chief divsn. of radiology Ehime Prefectural Ctrl. Hosp., 1970-77; prof. dept. radiology Dokkyo U. Sch. Medicine, Mibu, Tochigi, Japan, 1977-90; dir. emeritus Ikeda Meml. Hosp., Sukagawa, Fukushima, Japan, 1990—; asst. dir. Fukuda Meml. Hosp., Mooka, Tochigi, 1993—. Guest prof. Dokkyo U. Sch. Medicine, 1994—, Tenjin (China) 2d Med. Coll., 1986—. Patentee in field. With Japanese Navy, 1944-45. Mem. German Radiol. Soc., Japanese Radiol. Soc. (cert. radiologist), Japanese Soc. Med. Imaging Tech. (pres. ann. gen. mtg. 1989-90), Japan Biliary Assn. (hon.; pres. ann. congress 1987-88), Japanese Med. Imaging Tech. Assn. (councilor 1980-95), Japanese Soc. Angiography and Interventional Radiology (hon.). Avocations: photography, motoring, bowling, fishing. Home: 1-9-3 Saiwai-chou Mib-machi Shimotsuga-gun Tochigi 321-0203 Japan Office: Fukuda Meml Hosp 3-10 Namiki-chou Mooka Tochigi 321-43 Japan

HYSER, RAYMOND M. humanities educator; b. Akron, Ohio, Jan. 31, 1955; s. Raymond and Geraldine K. Hyser; m. Pamela A. Hyser, May 26, 1990; children: Kelsey, Marshall, Christopher. BS in Edn., Ga. So. U., 1977, MA, 1979; PhD, Fla. State U., 1983. Instr. Ga. So. U., Statesboro, 1979—80; asst. prof. James Madison U., Harrisonburg, Va., 1983—89, assoc. prof., 1989—98, prof., 1998—. Adj. faculty Fla. State U., Tallahasee, 1983. Co-editor: Voices of the American Past, 2001; co-author: No Crooked Death, 1991 (Outstanding Book, Myers Ctr. for the Study Human Rights, 1992). Recipient Philip Klein prize, Pa. Hist. Assn., 1988. Mem.: So. Hist. Assn., Orgn. Am. Historians, Soc. for Historians of the Gilded Age & Progressive Era. Avocations: golf, camping, hiking. Home: 98 Laurel St Harrisonburg VA 22801 Office: James Madison Univ Faculty Dept Harrisonburg VA 22807

HYSLOP, GARY LEE, retired librarian; b. Oakland City, Ind., June 8, 1944; s. H. Boyd and Berniece (McKinney) H. BA, Oakland City U., 1966; MS, Ind. State U., 1974; MLS, Ind. U., 1987. Tchr. Ind. and Ohio Pub. Schs., 1967—77; mgr., officer F & M Fed. Savs. & Loan, Bloomington, Ind., 1977-81; broker, realtor Properties Unltd., Bloomington, 1981-82; tchr. Howe (Ind.) Mil. Sch., 1982-84, Madison (Ind.) Schs., 1984-86; asst. libr. Calif. State U., Bakersfield, 1988-91; dir. admissions and placement Sch. Libr. and Info. Sci. Ind. U., Bloomington, 1991-93; dir. Curriculum Materials Ctr. U. Cen. Fla., 1993-2000. Vol. Kern County Beethoven Festival, Bakersfield, 1988; bd. dirs. Bakersfield Community Theatre, 1989-91, nominating com., 1990-91; bd. regents/united faculty of Fla. task force on libr. issues Fla. State U. System, 1997-98. Recipient Meritorious Performance and Profl. Promise award Calif. State U., 1989, Excellence in Librarianship award U. Ctrl. Fla., 1999. Mem. ALA, SELA, Fla. Faculty Assn., UCF Librs. (personnel adv. com.), Fla. Assn. Coll. Rsch. Librs. (bd. dirs. 1994-97), 15th Ann. Task Force of the Libr. Instrn. Round Table, United Faculty of Fla. (senator 1997-99, chpt. sec.). Avocations: keyboard instruments, volunteerism, travel, writing fiction. Office: U Cen Fla Curriculum Materials Ctr Oviedo FL 32765-7025 E-mail: ghyslop@mail.ucf.edu., garyhyslop@hotmail.com.

HYSLOP, RICHARD STEWART, law educator; b. Kitchener, Ont., Can., May 23, 1944; s. Stewart Lees and Joyce Elaine (Slater) H. B.A., Calif. State U., Fullerton, 1966; M.A., U. Calif. Irvine, 1967; J.D., UCLA,1970. Bar: Calif. 1971, U.S. Dist. Ct. (cen. dist.) Calif. 1971, U.S. Supreme Ct. 1982, U.S. Ct. Appeals (9th cir.) 1982, U.S. Tax Ct. 1982. Mem. faculty Calif. State Poly. U. Pomona, 1970—, assoc. prof. govt. and Am. studies, 1975-79, prof., 1979—, assoc. v.p. acad. affairs, 1978-79, coordinator Am. Studies, 1975— ; assoc. Friedemann & Menke Orange, Calif., 1973-78, 81-84; cons. Nat. Multilingual Multicultural Materials Devel. Ctr., Pomona, 1977-80, law sch. admissions test Am. Testing Service, Princeton, 1981-83. arbitrator Am. Arbitration Assn., Los Angeles, 1976— . Author: (with Crane Miller) California: Geography of Diversity, 1983: (with others). Essays in American History and Culture, 1983. Recipient Disting. Tchr. award Calif. State Poly. U., 1974. Mem. Am. Culture Assn., Western Social Scis. Assn., Can. Studies in U.S., Western Can. Studies Group, Pi Gamma Mu. Home: 1147 Picaacho Dr La Habra CA 90631-8031 : is 3801 W Temple Ave Pomona CA 91768

HYSON, CHARLES DAVID, economist, consultant; b. Hampstead, Md., Dec. 29, 1915; s. Harry Perry and Rose (Miller) H.; m. Winifred Chandler Prince, Sept. 7, 1946; children— David Prince, Pamela Chandler Hyson Martin, Christopher Perry. AB, St. John's Coll., Annapolis, 1937; MS, U. Md., 1939; MA, Harvard, 1942, PhD, 1943. Agrl. economist FCA, 1939—40; staff Surplus Mktg. Adminstrn., Washington, 1940—41; resident tutor, then sr. tutor Harvard U., 1942—49, rsch. assoc., 1943—44, resident cons. Grad. Sch. Pub. Adminstrn., 1943—49, instr. econs., 1946—48, assoc. dir. mktg. rsch. program, 1948—49; regional economist, then chief prices and cost of living br. U.S. Bur. Labor Stats., 1944—46; indsl. economist Fed. Res. Bank Boston, 1946—48; asst. econ. commr. ECA Mission to Norway, Oslo, 1949—50; trade specialist, staff spl. rep. in Europe Paris, 1950; spl. asst. to chief of mission ECA, Mut. Security Agy., Lisbon, Portugal, 1950—52; dep. dir. U.S. Ops. Mission to Portugal, Mut. Security Agy., FOA, ICA, 1952—55; spl. rep. to Portugal ICA, 1955—57, chief Western Europe div., 1957—59, chief European Div., 1959—60; assigned to Nat. War Coll., 1960—61; counsellor of embassy for econ. affairs Am. embassy, Lisbon, 1955—57; dep. dir. for exec. staffing AID, Washington, 1961—62; adviser for econ. affairs Office Material Resources, AID, 1962—63; spl. asst. for econ. and trade affairs AID, 1963—74; cons. economist, 1975—. Dep. nat. coordinator, dep. exec. dir. Cabinet Com. Export Expansion, 1964; mem. White House Conf. on Internat. Coop., 1965; mem. Internat. Secretariat; econ. advisor on human skills in decade of devel., San Juan, PR, 1962. Contbr. numerous articles to econ. jours., books, also monographs. Decorated comdr. Order of Merit, Portugal Fellow Royal Econ. Soc.; mem. Am. Fgn. Service Assn., Am. Acad. Polit. and Social Sci., Am. Econ. Assn., Am. Agrl. Econ. Assn., N.Y. Acad. Scis., AAAS Clubs: Harvard (Washington); Keene Valley (N.Y.) Country; Ausable (St. Huberts, N.Y.); Adirondack Mountain. Address: 7407 Honeywell Ln Bethesda MD 20814-1019 *We live unrelentingly in an age defined by economics; therefore it is vital that the earth's resources be used wisely.*

HYTIER, ADRIENNE DORIS, French language educator; d. Jean and Katharine (Hytier) Matson. BA summa cum laude, Barnard Coll., 1952; MA, Columbia U., 1953, PhD, 1958. Instr. French Vassar Coll., 1959-61, asst. prof., 1961-66, assoc. prof., 1966-70, prof. French, 1970-96, Lichtenstein Dale prof. French, 1974-96. Vis. assoc. prof. Columbia U., 1966, U. Calif., 1968—69. Editor for French lit.: The 18th Century: A Current Bibliography Since 1970, 25 vols., Two Years of French Foreign Policy: Vichy 1940-42, 1958, 2d edit., 1974, Les Dépêches diplomatiques du Comte de Gobineau en Perse, 1959, La Guerre, 1975, 4th edit., 1991; contbr. articles to profl. jours. Decorated chevalier des Palmes Académiques; fellow Guggenheim Found., 1967-68. Mem. MLA, Am. Soc. 18th Century Studies, NE Soc. for 18th Century Studies, Internat. Soc. 18th Century Studies, Phi Beta Kappa. Home: 71 Raymond Ave Poughkeepsie NY 12603-0372 Office: Vassar Coll Box 372 Poughkeepsie NY 12604-0001

HYUN, MYUNG-KWAN, investment company executive; b. Sept. 2, 1941; married; 2 sons. BA in Law, Seoul Nat. U., 1963; MA in Econs., Keio U., 1974. CEO Samsung Corp., Seoul, Korea; vice chmn., CEO Samsung. Office: Samsung Corp 310 Taepyung-ro 2-ga Chung-gu CPO Box 1144 Seoul 100-102 Republic of Korea

IACOBUCCI, FRANK, lawyer, educator, jurist; b. Vancouver, B.C., Can., June 29, 1937; s. Gabriel and Rosina (Pirillo) I.; m. Nancy Elizabeth Eastham, Oct. 31, 1964; children— Andrew Eastham, Edward Michael, Catherine Elizabeth. B of Commerce, U. B.C., Vancouver, 1959, LLB, 1962; LLM, Cambridge U., Eng., 1964, Diploma in Internat. Law, 1966; LLD (hon.), U. B.C., 1989, U. Toronto, 1989, U. Ottawa, 1995, U. Victoria, 1996, Law Soc. Upper Can., 2000, McGill U., 2003, U. Waterloo, 2003. Bar: Ont. 1970, Queen's Counsel, 1986. Assoc. Dewey Ballantine et al, N.Y.C., 1964-67; assoc. prof. law U. Toronto, 1967-71, prof. law, 1971-85, assoc. dean faculty of law, 1973-75, v.p. internal affairs, 1975-78, dean faculty of law, 1979-83, v.p., provost, 1983-85; vis. fellow Wolfson Coll., Cambridge, Eng., 1978; dep. min. of justice and dep. atty. gen. Govt. of Can., Ottawa, Ont., 1985-88; chief justice Fed. Ct. of Can., Ottawa, 1988-90; justice Supreme Ct. Can., Ottawa, 1991 . Mem. Permanent Ct. of Arbitration, 1997—; former cons. Ont., Alta., Can govts.; mem. Ont. Securities Commn., Toronto, 1982-85; dir. Cambridge Can. Trust, 1984-91; mem. Can. Jud. Coun., 1988-91, exec. com., edn. com.; gov. Can. Jud. Centre, 1989-91; gov. Nat. Jud. Inst., 1992—; mem. adv. coun. Internat. Centre Criminal Law Reform and Criminal Justice Policy, 1991-93, dir. 1993—. Co-author: Canadian Business Corporations, 1977, Cases and Materials on Partnerships and Canadian Business Corporations, 1983; co-editor: Materials on Canadian Income Tax, 6th edit., 1985; contbr. chpts. to books, articles to profl. jours. Mem. Islington Residents and Ratepayers Assn., 1971-85; dir. Multicultural History Soc., Ont., 1976-88; v.p. Nat. Congress Italian Cans., 1980-83, dir. Toronto dist., 1979-83; v.p. Can. Inst. Advanced legal Studies, 1981-85, bd. govs., 1981-85, 91-98; mem. adv. com. Faculty of Law, McGill U., 1996—; mem. adv. bd. Inst. Can. Studies, U. Ottawa, 1998—. Named hon. citizen Cepagatti (Pescara), Italy, 2001, hon. citizen, Mangone, Italy, 1996; recipient Law Soc. medal, Law Soc. Upper Can., 1987, Ordine al merito, Nat. Congress Italian Canadians, Toronto Dist., 1989, 125th Anniversary of Confedn. Can. medal, 1992, Lion d'Or award, Ordre des Fils d'Italie au Can., Montreal, 1995, Cosentino dell'Anno award, Fedn. of Clubs Cosentini of Ont., 1995, Man of the Yr. award, Can. Italian Bus. and Profl. Assn. Toronto, 1985, Italo-Can. of the Yr. award, Confratellanza Italo-Canadese, Vancouver, 1985, Commendatore dell'Ordine Al Merito della Repubblica Italiana, 1993, Man of Yr. award, Brotherhood Interfaith Soc., Vancouver, Can., 1999, Medaglia d'Argento del Pres. della Repubblica Italiana, 2000, Can.-Italian Nat. award, 2000, Premio Italia nel mondo, Italy in the World award, 2001, Valigia d'Oro award, 2002; Newton Rowell fellow, Can. Inst. Internat. Affairs, 1962, McKenzie-King traveling fellow, U. B.C., 1963, hon. fellow, St. John's Coll., Cambridge U. Fellow Am. Coll. Trial Lawyers (hon.); mem. Can. Bar Assn., Le Club de Golf Rivermead (Aylmer, Quebec), Sigma Tau Chi, Phi Gamma Delta (Disting. Fiji award 1987). Avocations: tennis, golf, other sports. Office: Supreme Ct Can Wellington St Ottawa ON Canada K1A 0J1

IACOBUCCI, GUILLERMO ARTURO, chemist; b. Buenos Aires, May 11, 1927; came to U.S., 1962, naturalized 1972. s. Guillermo Cesar and Blanca Nieves (Brana) I.; m. Constanina Maria Gullich, Mar. 28, 1952; children: Eduardo Ernesto, William George. MSc, U. Buenos Aires, 1949, PhD in Organic Chemistry, 1952. Rsch. chemist E.R. Squibb Rsch. Labs., Buenos Aires, 1952-57; rsch. fellow in chemistry Harvard U., Cambridge, Mass., 1958-59; prof. phytochemistry U. Buenos Aires, 1960-61; sr. rsch. chemist Squibb Inst. Med. Rsch., New Brunswick, N.J., 1962-66; head bio-organic chemistry labs. Coca-Cola Co., Atlanta, 1967-74, asst. dir. corp. R&D, 1974-87, mgr. biochemistry and basic organic chemistry group, 1988-93, ret., 1993. Adj. prof. chemistry Emory U., 1975—. Contbr. articles on organic chemistry to sci. jours.; patentee in field. John Simon Guggenheim Meml. Found. fellow, 1958. Fellow Am. Inst. Chemists; mem. AAAS, Assn. Harvard Chemists, Am. Chem. Soc., N.Y. Acad. Scis., Am. Soc. Pharmacognosy, Phytochem. Soc. N.Am., Smithsonian Instn., Planetary Soc., Sigma Xi. Achievements include structure/activity correlations and molecular design of sweeteners; use of enzymes in asymmetric organic synthesis; natural products chemistry. Home: 2660 Peachtree Rd NW Apt 28E Atlanta GA 30305-3680 Office: Emory U Dept of Chemistry 1515 Pierce Dr NE Atlanta GA 30322-1003

IACONO, JAMES MICHAEL, research center administrator, nutrition educator; b. Chgo., Dec. 11, 1925; s. Joseph and Angelina (Cutaia) I.; children: Lynn, Joseph, Michael, Rosemary. BS, Loyola U., Chgo., 1950; MS, U. Ill., 1952, PhD, 1954. Chief Lipid Nutrition Lab. Nutrition Inst. Agrl. Rsch. Svc. USDA, Beltsville, Md., 1970-75, dep. asst. adminstrv. nat. program staff Washington, 1975-77, assoc. adminstr. office human nutrition, 1978-82, dir. Western Human Nutrition Rsch. Ctr. San Francisco, 1982-94. Adj. prof. nutrition Sch. Pub. Health UCLA, 1987—. Author over 100 rsch./tech. publs. and chpts. in books relating to nutrition and biochemistry and lipids. With U.S. Army, 1944-46. Recipient Rsch. Career Devel. award NIH, 1964-70. Fellow Am Heart Assn. (coun. on arteriosclerosis and thrombosis), Am. Inst. Chemists; mem. Am. Inst. Nutrition, Am. Soc. Clin. Nutrition, Am. Oil Chemists Soc. E-mail: JIacono25@aol.com.

IAFALLO, DEBORAH LYNN, geriatrics nurse; b. Silvercreek, N.Y., June 26, 1960; d. William Harold and Isabelle Carmen (Delgado) Paterson; m. Joseph Rocco Iafallo, Jr., Feb. 14, 1985; children: Aaron Joseph, Ryan Rocco. AAS, Trocaire Coll., 1994; BSN, Daemen Coll., 2000. RN, N.Y.; bd. cert. gerontol. nursing. Resident care coord. Father Baker Manor, Orchard Park, N.Y., 1994-97, nursing supr., 1997-99, insvc./infection control coord., 1999—2002; asst. dir. nursing Weinburg Campus, 2002— . Mem. Trocaire Coll. Alumni, Sigma Theta Tau. Lutheran. Avocations: painting, camping, biking. Home: 4553 Winding Woods Ln Hamburg NY 14075-5453

IAMELE, RICHARD THOMAS, law librarian; b. Newark, Jan. 29, 1942; BA, Loyola U., L.A., 1963; MSLS, U. So. Calif., 1967; JD, Southwestern U., L.A., 1976. Bar: Calif. 1977. Cataloger U. So. Calif., L.A., 1967-71; asst. cataloger L.A. County Law Libr., 1971-77, asst. ref. libr., 1977-78, asst. libr., 1978-80, libr. dir., 1980—. Mem. ABA, Am. Assn. Law Librs., Calif. Libr. Assn., So. Calif. Assn. Law Librs., Coun. Calif. County Law Librs. (pres. 1981-82, 88-90). Office: LA County Law Libr 301 W 1st St Los Angeles CA 90012-3140

IAMMARTINO, NICHOLAS R. corporate communications executive; B in Chem. Engring., Cooper Union; M in Chem. Engring., NYU; MBA in Fin., Adelphi U. Process engr. Esso Rsch. and Engring. Co., 1969-71; bus. and tech. news writer Chem. Engring. mag. McGraw-Hill, 1971-76; chem. industry securities analyst Merrill Lynch, 1976-78; from sr. writer to bus. pubs. mgr. dept. corp. comm. Celanese Corp., 1979-85; corp. mgr. fin. comm. and adminstrn. Philip Morris, Inc., 1985; dir. fin. comm. Borden, Inc., N.Y., 1986-89, dir. external comm., 1989, dir. pub. affairs, 1994-95, v.p. pub. affairs, 1995—. Bd. dirs. Borden Found., Inc.; mem. assn. bd. Columbus Zool. Pk. Assn. Office: Borden Inc 180 E Broad St Columbus OH 43215-3799

IANNACCONE, CYNTHIA JEAN, painter, illustrator; b. Rochester, N.Y., June 5, 1949; d. Joseph John and Alma Jean (Harris) I. BFA, Noval Scotia Coll. Arts/Design, 1973; MA, Marywood U., 1996. Cert. art edn. tchr., N.Y. Art tchr., mus. educator U. Rochester's Meml. Art Gallery, 1993—2001. Mem. Genessee Valley Calligraphers Guild, Soc. Children's Book Writers and Illustrators.

IANNACONE, RANDOLPH FRANK, lawyer; b. Paterson, N.J., Nov. 19, 1953; s. Anthony and Dorothy Mae (Russo) I. BSc in Pharmacy, St. John's U., N.Y.C., 1979; JD, N.Y. Law Sch., 1990. Bar: N.Y. 1990, U.S. Dist. Ct. (no., so. and ea. dists.) N.Y. 1990, U.S. Ct. Appeals (2d cir.) 1990, N.J. 1991, U.S. Dist. Ct. N.J. 1991, U.S. Ct. Appeals (11th cir.) 1993, U.S. Fed. Ct. of Claims, 1995, U.S. Tax Ct. 1995, U.S. Dist. Ct. (we. dist.) N.Y. 1999, U.S. Supreme Ct. 2000. Community pharmacist Dan Drug Co., Englewood, N.J., 1979-85; v.p., tech. dir. Reliance Packaging Corp., Paterson, 1985-87; assoc. Bower & Gardner, N.Y.C., 1990-91; with Med. Malpractice Ins. Assn., N.Y.C., 1991-93, pres. Middle Village Law Assocs. PC, NY, 1993—2002; v.p., sec., treas. Middle Village Law Assocs., P.C., NY, 2002—. Mem. faculty Marino CLE Inst., 2003—. Mem. West Paterson (N.J.) Jaycees, 1979-81; mem. Allendale (N.J.) Rep. Party, 1985—. Mem. ABA, N.Y. State Bar Assn., N.Y. County Lawyers (med. malpractice com. 1990—), N.J. Bar Assn., Assn. Trial Lawyers Am., Am. Pharm. Assn. (coord. continuing edn. com. Trenton com. 1979-82), Bklyn. Bar Assn. (mem. mediation panel 2002—), Queens County Bar Assn., Columbia Lawyers Assn., Bar Assn. of Criminal and Civil Cts. of N.Y.C. (bd. dirs. 2002—), Lions (bd. dirs. Middle Village club), Flushing Lawyers Club, Blackstones Lawyers Club, Order of The Barrister, Rho Chi, Phi Alpha Delta Avocations: computers, golf, photography, music. E-mail: riannacone@law-center.com.

IANNI, FRANCIS ALPHONSE, state official, former army officer; b. New Castle, Del., Aug. 2, 1931; s. Francisco and Mary (Marcozzi) I.; m. Ann Louise Wiggin, Apr. 16, 1955 (div.); children: Steven, Christina, Marisa, Jeanne, Marjorie; m. Carmela Jane Marsilii Carroll, Aug. 8, 1994. BS, U.S. Mil. Acad., 1954; M.MA & S., U.S. Command and Gen. Staff Coll., 1963; MA, U. Va., 1966. Served with Del. N.G., 1945-50; commd. 2d lt., inf. U.S. Army, 1954, advanced through grades to maj. gen., 1977; ret., 1977; adj. gen., 1977-81; dir. Hwy. Safety, 1981-88. Adj. prof. Goldey-Beacom Coll., Wilmington, 1988—. Author: World War One Remembered, 1993. Decorated Silver Star, Def. Superior Service medal, Legion of Merit with oak leaf cluster, Bronze Star, D.F.C., Air medal. Mem. Assn. U.S. Army, N.G. Assn., VFW, Am. Legion. Roman Catholic. Home: 807 Seville Ave Wilmington DE 19809-2130 Office: 4701 Limestone Rd Wilmington DE 19808-1927

IANNICELLI, JOSEPH, chemical company executive, consultant; b. N.Y.C., Aug. 5, 1929; s. Peter and Catherine (Gugliotti) I.; m. Betty Peterson, June 28, 1978; children: Mark, Rex, Gina. SB, MIT, 1951, PhD, 1955. Rsch. chemist Textile Fibers, E.I. DuPont, Wilmington, Del., 1955-60; tech. dir. Clay Div. J.M. Huber, Macon, Ga., 1960-70; founder, chief exec. officer Aquafine Corp., Brunswick, Ga., 1970—, Aero-Instant Corp., Brunswick, Ga., 1988—; co-founder IMPEX Corp., Brunswick, Ga., 1988—. Cons. Consol. Goldfields Australia, Sydney, 1976-78, Rio Tinto, Madrid, 1980-82, Hoganes, Malmo, Sweden, 1984. Author: Evaluation and Comparison of Crossfield and Solenoid Field Magnetic Filters, 1981, co-author: A Survey-Benneficiation of Industrial Minerals, 1980; contbr. over 30 articles to profl. jours. Pres. Ga. Tidewater Conservation Assn., Brunswick, 1991—92; govt. appointment as mem. Jekyll Island (Ga.) Citizens Resource Coun., 1995—97; foreman Glynn County Grand Jury, Brunswick, 1989; chmn. Glynn County Bd. Edn., 2002; bd. dirs. Jekyll Island (Ga.) Citizens Assn., 1992—96, pres., 1993—95. Recipient Rsch. grant NSF, 1980, 84, Elec. Power Rsch. Inst., 1980, Resolution of Commendation, Ga. Ho. of Reps., 1995. Fellow Am. Inst. Chemists; mem. Tech. Assn. of Pulp and Paper Industry (chmn. pigments com. 1971-72). Achievements include over 100 patents including paramagnetic separator and process, silane modified organo clays, mercaptan scrubber; performed first high temperature superconducting magnetic separation of minerals as part of a team consisting of Aquafine, DuPont and Sumitomo, 1996. Home: 28 Saint Andrews Dr Jekyll Island GA 31527-0901 Office: Aquafine Corp 3963 Darien Hwy Brunswick GA 31525-2423 E-mail: iannicelli@aquafinecorp.com.

IANNONE, ABEL PABLO, philosophy educator; b. Buenos Aires, Sept. 18, 1940; arrived in U.S., 1967; s. Nicolás Emilio and Marcelina (Diaz) Iannone; m. Mary Kathryn Garrow; children: Alejandra Emilia, Catalina Patricia. Student, U. Nacional Buenos Aires, 1958-62, 64-66; BA in Philosophy, UCLA, 1969; MA in Philosophy, U. Wis., Madison, 1972, PhD in Philosophy, 1975. Lectr. in philosophy U. Wis., Madison, 1974-75; asst. prof. philosophy U. Tex., Dallas, 1975-78, Iowa State U., Ames, 1982, Cen. Conn. State U., New Britain, 1983-86, assoc. prof., 1986-93, prof., 1993—. Vis. asst. prof. dept. philosophy Inst. for Environ. Studies U. Wis., Madison, 1977, 78, hon. fellow, 79, 80, 82; postdoctoral fellow U. Fla., Gainesville, 1982—83; vis. prof. dept. philosophy Henson Coll. Pub. Affairs and Continuing Edn. Dalhousie U., Halifax, NS, Canada, 1987. Author: Astérida, 1973, Philosophy as Diplomacy, 1994, Philosophical Ecologies, 1999, Dictionary of World Philosophy, 2001, Technology and Global Society, 2002, Business and Global Society, 2003; editor: Contemporary Moral Controversies in Technology, 1987, Contemporary Moral Controversies in Business, 1989, Through Time and Culture, 1994; contbr. articles to various publs. Mem.: AAAS, Argentine-N.Am. Assn. Advancement of Sci., Tech. and Culture, Am. Philos. Assn., Phi Beta Kappa. Office: Ctrl Conn State U 1615 Stanley St New Britain CT 06053-2439 E-mail: iannoneapablo@netscape.net.

IANNONE, DOROTHY, visual artist, writer; b. Boston, Aug. 9, 1933; arrived in Germany, 1967; d. William Iannone and Sarah (Nicoletti) Pucci; m. James Phineas Upham, Dec. 17, 1958 (div. Aug. 1967). BA, Boston U., 1957; postgrad., Brandeis U., 1957-58. Trans. agent U.S. Army Base, Boston, 1951—53; co-dir. Stryke Gallery, N.Y.C., 1963—67. Instr. open workshop, Coll. Art, West Berlin, 1977 and 1979; guest artist Rijks Academie, Amsterdam, 1982, 84, Jan Van Eyck Academie, Maastricht, Holland, 1982, 83, Enschede Academie, 1983. Author: Story of Bern, 1970, The Berlin Beauties, 1978, The Whip, 1980, Censorship and the Irrepressible Drive Toward Love and Divinity, 1983, 3d edit., 2002, Courting Ajaxander, 1993; (with Dieter Roth) Dieter and Dorothy: Their Correspondence in Words and Works 1967-1998, 2001; one woman-shows include Stryke Gallery, N.Y.C., 1964-67, Galerie Hansjörg Mayer, Stuttgart, 1967, Galerie Handschin, Basel, 1969, Galerie Wilbrand, Cologne, 1971, Eat Art Galerie, Düsseldorf, 1971, Galerie Jule Hammer, West Berlin, 1971, Galerie Steinmetz, Bonn, 1973, Galerie Edith Wahlandt, Schwäbisch-Gmund, West Germany, 1973, Galerie Sum, Reykjavik, 1974, Galerie Ben Vautier, Nice, France, 1975, Galerie 38, Copenhagen, 1975, Galerie Bama, Paris, 1976, Studio Galerie, Mike Steiner, Berlin, 1977, M. Würthle and O. Wiener Galerie, Berlin, 1977, Haus am Lutzow Platz, Berlin, 1978, Basel Art Fair, Galerie Mike Steiner, Switzerland, 1979, Neue Galerie Stadt Aachen, Ludwig Collection, Germany, 1980, Galerie Wallner, Malmö, Sweden, 1981, Nikolaj, Copenhagen, 1982, Galerie Ars Viva, Berlin, 1982, Galerie Rosenberg, Zürich, 1984, Boekie Woekie, Amsterdam, 1986, Petersen Galerie, Berlin, 1989, Galerie Bernhard Steinmetz, Bonn, Germany, 1990, Kunstfonds, Kunstraum, Bonn, 1990, Kunst-Werke, Berlin, 1992, Galerie Armin Hundertmark, Cologne, Germany, 1994, Galerie Roche, Bremen, Germany, 1995, Basel Art Fair, Galerie Stähli, Zürich, Switzerland, 1995, Galerie Holtmann, Cologne, 1996, New Soc. Fine Arts, Berlin, 1997, Mus. Modern Art, Arnhem, Holland, 1998, Boekie Woekie, Amsterdam, 1998, Galerie Andy Jllien, Zürich, 2001, Galerie Barbara Wien, Berlin, 2001-02, Laura Mars Group, Berlin, 2002; selected group exhbns. include Galerie Zwirner, Cologne, 1967, Kunsthalle, Bern, Switzerland, 1969, Kunsthalle, Düsseldorf, Germany, 1969, Edinburgh (Scotland) Festival of Arts, 1970, San Antonio Show, Galerie Bama, Paris, 1975, Mus. Modern Art, Paris. 1976, 80, Fondation Maeght, St. Paul-de-Vence, France, 1976, Studio du Passage 44, Brussels, 1976, Neue Galerie Stadt Aachen, Germany, 1976, Maison de la Culture, Rennes, France, 1977, Galerie Camomille, Brussels, 1984, Centre Georges Pompidou, Paris, 1985. Kunst-und Museumsverein, Wuppertal Germany, 1987, The Concealed Mus., Akademie der Kunste, Berlin, 1987-88, Galerie Petersen, Berlin, 1988, Galerie Marlene

Frei, Zürich, 1988, Fondation Danae, Pouilly, Valdampierre, France, 1988, Fondazione Mudima, Milan, 1990, Mus. Modern and Contemporary Art, Nice, 1991, Kunsthalle, Düsseldorf, 1992, Mus. Modern Art, Saint-Etienne, France, 1993, Haus am Lutzow Platz, Berlin, 1993, The Books of Artists, Inst. for Fgn. Rels., Berlin, 1995, Goethe Inst., Tel Aviv, 1995, Mus. Contemporary Art, Marseille, France, 1997, Kunsthalle, Steyr, Austria, 1998-99, Hommage à Dieter Roth, Galerie Heinz Holtmann, Cologne, 1998, NORD/LB Galerie, Braunschweig, Germany, 1999, Dieter Roth Acad., Basel, Switzerland, 2000, Pécs, Hungary, 2001, Reykjavik, Iceland, 2002, Springhornhof Kunstverein, Neuenkirchen, Germany, 2001, Coninx Mus., Zürich, 2002-03, Soc. Friends of Young Art, Baden-Baden, 2003; permanent collections include Mus. Drawings and Prints, Berlin, Nat. Mus. Women in the Arts, Washington, Ludwig Collection, Neue Galerie Stadt Aachen, Germany, Mus. Modern Art, St. Etienne, France, Bibliotheque Nationale, Paris, Kunst Mus., Basel, Berlinische Galerie, Berlin. Grantee Berlin Artists' Program, 1976, Art Found. Bonn, 1988, Women Artists' Program, Berlin Senate, 1994. Mem. Phi Beta Kappa. Home: Leonhardtstrasse 2 14057 Berlin Germany

IANNONE, PATRICK PAUL, optics scientist, researcher; b. Bklyn., July 11, 1962; s. Pasquale and Amelia Iannone; m. Carla Ruth Powers; children: Olivia Miranda, Gwen Marie, Ruby Elizabeth. BS in Applied Physics, Columbia U., 1984; PhD in Elec. Engring., Princeton U., 1994. Mem. tech. staff AT&T Bell Labs., Holmdel, NJ, 1985—96, AT&T Labs - Rsch., Middletown, NJ, 1996—. Contbr. articles to profl. jours. Mem.: Optical Fiber Conf. (networking subcom. 2000—02, chair networking subcom. 2002), IEEE Laser and Electro-Optics Soc. (meetings chair 2001—03, elected mem. bd. govs. 2002—). Achievements include patents in field. Office: AT&T Labs - Rsch 200 S Laurel Ave Middletown NJ 07748

IANNUZZI, JOHN NICHOLAS, lawyer, author, educator; b. N.Y.C., May 31, 1935; s. Nicholas Peter and Grace Margaret (Russo) I.; m. Carmen Marina Barrios, Aug. 1979; children: Dana Alejandra, Christina Maria, Nicholas Peter II, Alessandro Luca; children from previous marriage: Andrea Marguerite, Maria Teresa. BS, Fordham U., 1956; JD, N.Y. Law Sch., 1962. Bar: N.Y., U.S. Dist. Ct. (so. and ea. dists.) N.Y. 1964, U.S. Dist. Ct. (no. and we. dists.) N.Y. 1965, U.S. Ct. Appeals (2d cir.) 1965, U.S. Supreme Ct. 1971, U.S. Dist. Ct. Conn. 1978, U.S. Tax Ct. 1978, U.S. Ct. Appeals (5th and 11th cirs.) 1982, U.S. Ct. Appeals (4th cir.) 1988, Wyo. 1994. Assoc. Law Offices of H.H. Lipsig, N.Y.C., 1962, Law Offices of Aaron J. Broder, N.Y.C., 1963; ptnr. Iannuzzi & Iannuzzi, N.Y.C., 1963—. Adj. prof. trial advocacy Fordham U. Law Sch. Author: (fiction) What's Happening, 1963, Part 35, 1970, Sicilian Defense, 1974, Courthouse, 1977, J.T., 1984, (non-fiction) Cross-Examination: The Mosaic Art, 1984, Trial Strategy and Psychology, 1992, Handbook of Cross-Examination, 1999, Handbook of Trial Strategy, 2000. Mem. ABA, N.Y. County Bar Assn., N.Y. Criminal Bar Assn., Columbian Lawyers Assn., Lipizzan Internat. Fedn. (v.p.). Roman Catholic. Home: 118 Via Settembre 9 Rome Italy Office: Iannuzzi & Iannuzzi 74 Trinity Place New York NY 10006 also: 775 Park Ave Huntington NY 11743-3976 also: 345 Franklin St San Francisco CA 94102-4427 also: 1592 Pine Ave W Montreal QC Canada also: 120 Adelaide St W Toronto ON Canada H3B 3G3 E-mail: jni@iannuzzi.net.

IANZITI, ADELBERT JOHN, industrial designer; b. Napa, Calif., Oct. 10, 1927; s. John and Mary Lucy (Lecair) I.; m. Doris Moore, Aug. 31, 1952; children: Barbara Ann Ream, Susan Therese Shifflett, Joanne Lynn Lely, Jonathan peter, Janet Carolyn Kroyer. Student, Napa Jr. Coll., 1947, 48-49; AA, Fullerton Jr. Coll., 1950; student, UCLA, 1950, Santa Monica C.C., 1950-51. Design draftsman Basalt Rock Co., Inc. (div. Dillingham Heavy Constrn.), Napa, 1951-66, chief draftsman plant engring., 1966-68, process designer, 1968-82, pres. employees assn., 1967; now self-employed indsl. design cons. Vice-pres. Justin-Siena Parent-Tchr. Group, 1967. Recipient Editor's Choice award for Outstanding Achievement in Poetry, Nat. Libr. of Poetry, 1994. Mem. Aggregates and Concrete Assn. no. Calif. (vice-chmn. environ. subcom. 1976-77), Constrn. Specifications Inst., Native Sons of the Golden West, Nat. Italian Am. Found., World Affairs Coun. No. Calif., Internat. Platform Assn., Commonwealth of Calif. Club. Home and Office: 2650 Dorset St Napa CA 94558-6110

IAQUINTA, LEONARD PHILLIP, university official; b. Kenosha, Wis., Aug. 1, 1944; s. Anthony Sam and Mary Natalie (Gallo) I. *The Gallo and Iaquinta ancestors migrated to the USA from Calabria, the beautiful mountainous southernmost province of mainland Italy. Mr. Iaquinta's maternal grandparents are from the Torcaso and DiCello, and Perri families. They lived near the western coast of Calabria in Platania. His paternal grandparents lived near the eastern coast. Grandmother Arabia from Santa Severina lived in view of the ancient hilltop castle, now stunningly renewed as a learning center and museum. Grandfather Iaquinta lived nearby in smaller Roccabernarda.* BJ, Northwestern U., 1966; M in Journalism, Columbia U., 1967. Dir., cons. World Studies Data Bank Acad. for Ednl. Devel., N.Y.C., 1969-76; dir. field svcs. for alumni rels. Northwestern U., Evanston, Ill., 1977-81; dir. nat. alumni program Columbia U., N.Y.C., 1981-82; devel. officer, alumni dir. Bklyn. Coll. (CUNY), 1982-86; dir. devel. and alumni affairs Ind.-Purdue Univs., Ft. Wayne, 1986-95, Northeastern Ill. U., Chgo., 1995-2001; asst. dean, dir. devel. and alumni rels. Coll. Engring. and Applied Scis. U. Wis., Milw., 2001—03, devel. officer, 2003—. Spkr. various profl. confs. *Mr. Iaquinta specializes in institution building and program development. At Northeastern Illinois University, he led reinvention of the offices of development and alumni affairs. Additionally, he led the 1998-99 marketing and communications planning team which conducted extensive market research and wrote a marketing and communications plan which included specific goals and action steps. At U. Wis., he creted the first profl. devel. and alumni program for engring. and computer sci., increasing philanthropic funds and performance. Mr. Iaquinta's most recently published article, "Selection Savvy, Seven Steps to Hiring A Campaign Consultant," was in CASE Currents, May 1999.* Assoc. editor: Notes on Negotiating, 1974; contbr. articles to profl. jours.; author various devel. manuals. Exec. dir. Kenosha United Way, 1976-77. Recipient 4 nat. alumni programming and fundraising awards Council for Advancement and Support of Edn., 1981, 84, 88, 98; 15 Who Care awards, Vol. Connection of Switchboard of Ft. Wayne, 1990. Mem. Assn. Fundraising Profls., Coun. for Advancement and Support of Edn., East Wis. Planned Giving Coun., Rotary, Sigma Delta Chi. Mem. Congregational Ch. Avocations: gardening, reading, travel. Home: 9507 74th St Kenosha WI 53142-8194 Office: Univ Devel Office Hefter Conf Ctr 3271 N Lake Dr Milwaukee WI 53211-3125 E-mail: LPIaquinta@cs.com.

IAQUINTO, JOSEPH FRANCIS, electrical engineer; b. Phila., Nov. 9, 1946; s. Francis Edward Iaquinto and Maria Carmina (Mancini) Feldman; m. Jo-Carol Maniscalco, Nov. 21, 1977; children: Joseph Michael, Jonathan Franklin. BSEE, Drexel U., 1969; MSEE, Stanford U., 1971. Registered professional engineer, Pa., Va. Teaching asst. Stanford (Calif.) U., 1969-71; sr. project engr. GM Corp., 1971-75; regional system engring. mgr. Memorex Corp., King of Prussia, Pa., 1975-77; sr. prin. engr. Computer Sci. Corp., Falls Church, Va., 1977-80; dir. devel. Tesdata Systems Corp., Tyson's Corner, Va., 1980-82; staff engr. HRB-Singer Co., Lantham, Md., 1982-84; sr. staff engr. Lockheed Electronics Co., Vienna, Va., 1984-86; mem. tech. staff MRJ div. Perkin Elmer, Oakton, Va., 1986-89; system engr. Ford Motor Co., Dearborn, Mich., 1989-93; engring. mgr. A.C. Nielsen, Dunedin, Fla., 1993-94; mgr. sys. engring. E'On Corp., Reston, Va., 1994-95; mem. tech. staff TASC, Reston, Va., 1995—. Author: Memorex 1380 Internal and Lesson Plan, 1977, Simulation of Microwave Propagation in the Atmosphere, 1987; co-author: (with H. Brandt) Control Engineering Application to Automobiles, 1973; author: (with others) Secure Internetwork Data Communications, 1979, Mission Planning System Specification, 1985; contbr. articles to tech. publs. Instr. ARC, Mich. and Pa., 1971-77; treas. Macomb County Young Reps., Sterling Heights, Mich., 1975; councilman Longacre PTA, Farmington, Mich., 1990-92. Recipient acad. scholarship Phila. Sch. System. Mem. IEEE, Nat. Soc.Profl. Engrs., Inst. Soc. Am. Roman Catholic. Achievements include development of first microprocessor based direct digital engine fuel control algorithm at GM, of first microcomputer based direct digital wheel lock control algorithm at GM; co-invention of a classified secure network inter network communications protocol; co-conversion of classical signal processing algorithms to massively parallel computer algorithms; modification of system engineering technology to suit automotive electronics applications; invented methodology to use FMEAs and reliability engineering processes to create robust Network Management & Control system for wireless/wireline data communications network.

IAROCCI, KENT ALEXANDER, newswriter, home improvement contractor; b. Mamaroneck, N.Y., Jan. 12, 1958; s. Joseph Thomas and Norma Louise (MacDonald) I.; m. Karen Anne Morehead, Oct. 13, 1989 (div. 1990). Grad. H.S., Rye, N.Y., 1976. With C.B.S. Publs., Inc., Greenwich, Conn., bldg. supt., 1978-81; HVAC helper C.A.P.C.O. Svc., Pleasantville, N.Y., 1981-82; stores clerk Margaret Chapman Sch., Hawthrone, N.Y., 1982-83; auto and truck salesman Crabtree Mitsubishi, New Rochelle, N.Y., 1983-84, Fleet Chevrolet Corp., Mt. Vernon, N.Y., 1986-87; home improvement contractor Handyman Plus, New Rochelle, 1988-94, Rye, 1995—; newspaper reporter Martinelli Publs., Yonkers, N.Y., 1993; bus monitor, clk. Upper County Pky. Limousine Svc., New Rochelle, 1994-96; publ. Circa 1993 Publ., 1993, Grandview Press, 1994. Caddy Bonnie Briar Country Club, Larchmont, N.Y., 1996-97. Author: So You Thought So, 1993, Grandview Press, 1994, 3d edit., 2001. Platinum mem. Republican Nat. Com., 2000. Mem. Internat. Platform Assn., N.Y. Caledonian Club. Episcopalian. Avocations: singing, writing, reading, walking. Home and Office: 5 Charlotte St Rye NY 10580-2703

IARUSSI, DAVID MAURICE, firefighter, farmer; b. Natick, Mass., Sept. 19, 1962; s. Oswald V. and Mary Ann Iarussi; m. Sandra L. Iarussi, June 20, 1987; children: Hayley, Tyler, Anthony. Grad. high sch., Ashland, Mass., 1981. Part-time firefighter Ashland Fire Dept., 1980-84, full-time firefighter, 1984-94, pub. info. officer, 1998—, lt., 1999—; mechanic Indian Spring Shell, Ashland, 1981-84; plumber Thomas Shahood Plumbing, Framingham, Mass., 1984-94; farmer Iarussi Family Farm, Medway, Mass., 1998—. V.p. Ashland Cable Access Bd., 1993-94. Mem. Ashland Fire Dept. Assn. (v.p. 1996-97, Firefighter of Yr. award 1999, 1st ann. Lt. William C. Fuller Pride and Professinalism award 2001), Profl. Firefighters Union (v.p. Local 1893 1998-99), Mass. Farm Bur. Roman Catholic. Avocations: stamp collecting, collecting fire memorabilia, collecting indian memorabilia, environmental protection, outer space. Office: 70 Cedar St Ashland MA 01721-1923 E-mail: afd50dmi@aol.com.

IASIELLO, DOROTHY BARBARA, clinical social worker, former brokerage company executive; b. Bklyn., Oct. 6, 1949; d. Albert William (dec.) and Josephine (Accardo) Rehorn; m. John Joseph Iasiello Jr., May 5, 1974. AAS in Mktg., N.Y.C. C.C., 1969; BS in Econs., Coll. Staten Island, 1978; MS in Social Work, Columbia U., 2000. With J.P. Morgan Securities, N.Y.C., 1978-81, asst. treas. sales, 1981-84, asst. v.p. sales, 1984-88, v.p. sales adminstrn. mgmt., 1988-91, v.p. sales, 1991-95; bus. cons., 1996—98; clin. social work practitioner, 2000—. Roman Catholic. Avocations: reading, foreign and domestic travel.

IATESTA, JOHN MICHAEL, lawyer; b. Orange, N.J., Dec. 29, 1944; s. Thomas Anthony and Marie Monica I.; m. Paulina Clare Pascuzzi, July 11, 1971. BS magna cum laude, Seton Hall U., 1967, JD cum laude, 1976; MS, Fordham U., 1968; LLM in Corp. Law, NYU, 1986. Bar: N.J. 1976, U.S. Dist. Ct. N.J. 1976, U.S. Ct. Appeals (3d cir.) 1981, N.Y. 1982, U.S. Supreme Ct. 1985. Law sec. to presiding judge appellate div. Superior Ct. N.J., Trenton, 1976-77; assoc. Wilentz, Goldman & Spitzer, Woodbridge, N.J., 1977-81, D'Alessandro, Sussman & Jacovino, Florham Park, N.J., 1981-83; corp. counsel, 1983—, Rhodia Inc., Cranbury, N.J. Recipient Book prize Tchrs. Coll. Columbia U., 1967. Mem. ABA, N.J. Bar Assn., Am. Corp. Counsel Assn., Order of the Cross & Crescent, Delta Epsilon Sigma, Kappa Delta Pi. Office: Rhodia Inc 259 Prospect Plains Rd Cranbury NJ 08512 E-mail: john.iatesta@us.rhodia.com.

IAVICOLI, MARIO ANTHONY, lawyer; b. Camden, N.J., Aug. 11, 1939; s. Vito Anthony and Angelina Jessie (Marchionese) I.; m. Arlene V. LeDonne, July 6, 1963; children— Michelle, Denise, Laura. BME, Drexel U., 1962; JD, U. Pa., 1965. Bar: N.J. 1965. Assoc. Samuel P. Orlando, Camden, 1965-66, Ballen & Batoff, Camden, 1966-68; ptnr. Maressa, Console & Iavicoli, Berlin, N.J., 1968-72; first asst. prosecutor Camden County, 1972-74; pvt. practice Pennsauken, N.J., 1974-79, Haddenfield, 1980—; counsel to spkr. N.J. Gen. Assembly, 1970-72, N.J. Automobile Ins. Study Commn., 1970-74, Camden County Charter Study Commn., 1974, Camden County Republican party, 1974-76, N.J. Rep. party, 1976—; solicitor Haddenfield Borough, 1980—. Author: No Fault and Comparative Negligence in New Jersey, 1973; Drafter: N.J.'s No Fault Law and other companion legislation, 1970-73. Chmn. Camden County Rep. Com., 1978— ; Rep. state committeeman, 1976— ; mem. Electoral Coll. from, N.J., 1976; solicitor Pennsauken Twp., 1975— ; Vice pres. Haddonfield Home Sch. Assn., 1972-73; Bd. dirs. Drexel U. Class Endowment Fund; trustee Haddonfield Civic Assn. Named One of N.J.'s 5 Outstanding Young Men, 1974; recipient Ocean County Bar Assn. award, 1975 Mem. Camden County Jr. C. of C. (counsel 1967-68), ABA, N.J. Bar Assn., Camden County Bar Assn (trustee 1996-98, sec. 1998-99, treas. 1999-2000, 2d v.p. 2000-01, 1st v.p. 2001-02, pres.-elect 2002-03, pres. 2003—), Sons of Italy, Drexel U. Alumni Assn. (v.p. 1991—), Rotary. Roman Catholic. Home: 340 Marquis Rd Haddonfield NJ 08033-4011 Office: 43 Kings Hwy W Haddonfield NJ 08033-2128 E-mail: mario.iavicoli@verizon.net.

IBACH, ROBERT DANIEL, JR., library director; b. Lynch, Nebr., Dec. 31, 1940; s. Robert Daniel Sr. and Mabel Bertine (Selstad) I.; m. Paula Joanne Hubbling, June 11, 1977. B.R.E., Detroit Bible Coll., 1963; BD, Grace Theol. Sem., Winona Lake, Ind., 1966, ThM, 1969; MLS, Ind. U., 1975. Ordained minister, 1989. Libr. Grace Coll. and Sem., Winona Lake, 1969-86; library dir. Dallas Theol. Sem., 1986—. Archaeologist Heshbon (Jordan) Expedition, 1971-76; library cons. Inst. of Holy Land Studies, Jerusalem, 1989. Author: Archaeological Survey of the Hesban Region, 1987; contbg. author: Hesban After 25 Years, 1994, Dictionary of Biblical Imagery, 1998; periodical revs. editor: Bibliotheca Sacra, 1988—; contbr. articles to profl. jours., 1972—. Mem. Soc. Bibl. Lit., Am. Theol. Libr. Assn., Am. Libr. Assn., Tex. Libr. Assn. Home: 3229 Colby Cir Mesquite TX 75149-1875 Office: Dallas Theol Sem 3909 Swiss Ave Dallas TX 75204-6496

IBAÑEZ, ALVARO, patent design company executive, artist; b. Bucaramanga, Santander, Colombia, Jan. 18, 1951; came to U.S., 1981; s. Epimenio and Maria Delia (Muñoz) I.; m. Marta Cecilia Arias, Dec. 30, 1971 (div. Dec. 1991); children: Carlos Humberto, Alvaro Antonio, Diana Saray, Sandra; m. Denise DeVries, Sept. 6, 1997; children: Elena, Austin, Paul, Delia Denise. Fine arts, David Manzur Acad., Bogotá, Colombia, 1972; structural draftman, ACA-DITEC, Bogotá, Colombia, 1974. Elem. tchr. German Pena Sch., Bogotá, Colombia, 1971; with sales dept. Grolier Internat., Bogotá, Colombia, 1973-74; civil engring. draftsman Adminstrv. Dept. Cmty. Action, Bogotá, Colombia, 1974-76; gen. ins. mgr. Gilabert & CIA, Santa Marta, Colombia, 1976-77; farmer El Roble Ranch, Santa Marta, Colombia, 1976-77; sales mgr. Onix Ltda., Bucaramanga, Colombia, 1977-78; owner, mgr. Distrisiba Ltda., Bucaramanga, Colombia, 1977-80; sales mgr. Coramex Andina Ltda., Bogotá, Colombia, 1980-81; with Radian, Inc., Alexandria, Va., 1984—, Birch, Stewart, Kolasch & Birch, Falls Church, Va., 1985—, Diversified Technologies, Alexandria, Va., 1986—; pres., founder A-Ibañez Art Design, Inc., Falls Church, Va., 1985—; founder Sunrise Studio Gallery, Kilmarnock, Va., 1996—, Pennie & Edmonds, L.L.P., Washington, 1998—. Freelance Pub. Health Ctr., Bogotá, Colombia, 1971-74, Guillermo Victorino SA, Bogotá, 1973-74, Felix A. Clavijo Co., Bogotá, 1973-75, Metron Publicity, Bucaramanga, Colombia, 1977-80, Tulio Ramirez, 1980-81, Fabio Hernandez Salazar, Bogotá, 1980-81; with Lascaris Design Group Internat., Washington, 1984. One-man shows include Georgetown Streets, Washington, 1981, Sovran Bank CC, Springfield, Va., 1985; exhibited in group shows at David Manzur Acad., Bogotá, Colombia, 1974, Dicas Fine Arts Ctr., Bogotá, Colombia, 1979, Santander Indsl. U., Bucaramanga, Colombia, 1979, Arlington Ctr., Va., 1982, Falls Church Recreation Park, Va., 1982, Latin Am. Art League, Alexandria, Va., 1991, Desfile de las Americas, Washington, 1993, Martin Luther King Meml. Libr., Washington, 1994, 96, Art Mus. Ams.-Orgn. Am. States, Washington, 1994, Strathmore Hall Arts Ctr., North Bethesda, Md., 1994, AT&T, Oakton, Va., 1994, Washington, 1994, Cultural Mexican Inst., Washington, 1994, Montgomery County Exec. Office Bldg., Rockville, Md., 1994, Bell Atlantic, Arlington, Va., 1994, Silver Spring, Md., 1994, Torpedo Factory Art League, Alexandria, Va., 1994, Moscoso Gallery, Washington, 1995, Fla. Mus. Hispanic and Latin Am. Art, Miami, 1995, Montgomery County Exec. Office Bldg., Rockville, Md., 1995, NASA Hdqs., Washington, 1995, Pan Am. Health Orgn., Washington, 1995, SED Ctr., Washington, 1996, (retrospective) Falls Church (Va.) Recreation Ctr., 1997, Bell Atlantic Hdqrs., Arlington, Va., 1997, D.C. Arts in the Alley/Georgetown U., Washington, 1998, Moca Gallery, Washington, 1998, Del Ray Artisans, Alexandria, 1998, Barnes & Noble Seven Corners, Falls Church, 1998. Sponsor World Vision, Tacoma, Wash., 1987—, Child Devel. Ctr., Falls Church, Va., 1989—, Crystal Cathedral, Glandale, Calif., 1992—, Beverley Hills United Meth. Ch., Alexandria, Va., 1997, Arts in the Alley Georgetown, D.C., 1998. Recipient 1st prize drawing Prismacolor Contest, 1958. Mem. Worldwide Fine Art Promotions, Hispanic Museo Art, Art League, Torpedo Factory. Republican. Avocations: paint, gardening, music, travel. Home: A Ibañez Art Design Inc PO Box 1060 197 Whittaker Line Kilmarnock VA 22482-3123 E-mail: aibanez@rivnet.net.

IBANEZ, JANE BOURQUARD, management training consultant, lecturer; b. New Orleans, Oct. 11, 1947; d. Albert John and Josephine (Vachetta) Bourquard; m. Manuel Luis Ibanez, Oct. 16, 1970; children: Juana, Vincent, William, Marc. BS, U. New Orleans, 1970. Lab. researcher in organic chemistry U. New Orleans, 1967-68, genetics lab. instr., 1968-69, fitness instr., 1972-90, yoga meditative instr., 1972—, stress mgmt. instr., 1980—; profl. lectr., stress mgmt. cons., 1972—. Bd. examiners Tex. Supreme Ct., 1993—; guest lectr. U. New Orleans, Tex. A&M, Kingsville, ABWA Conv., South Tex. Banker's Assn., others; chmn. Spohn Kleberg Hosp., Kingsville, 1997-99; adv. com. KEDT TV Pub. Broadcasting. Author producer: (audiotapes) Childhood Stress, 1985, Yoga Workout, 1985, Jane's Way Mini Workout, 1986. Chmn. Tex. A&M U.-Kingsville Fund for Instnl. Advancement, Kingsville, 1989—98, also presdl. asst.; pres. Am. Cancer Soc., Kingsville, 1992—94; mem. South Tex. Celebrity Weekend Com., 1992—, Cmty. Cancer Adv. Com., 1995—; chmn. First Friday, 2000; mem. Christus Spohn Cmty. Diabetes Adv. Bd., 2002—; chair art gala com. South Tex. Inst. Art, 2003; trustee S. Tex. Inst. of Art, 2003—, Spohn Kleberg Hosp, 1991—99; mem. devel. bd. Spohn Kleberg Hosp., Kingsville, 1990—98, trustee, 1991—, chmn., 1998—99; chmn. devel. bd. Am. Heart Assn., Kingsville, 1990—95; bd. dirs. Corpus Christi Women's Shelter, 1991—95; trustee South Tex. Ranching and Heritage Festival, Tex., 1992—98; mem. casting adv. bd. KEDT -PBS. Mem. AAUW, U. New Orleans Fitness Club (pres. 1975-89). Roman Catholic. Avocations: meditation, walking, cooking, writing, reading. also: 2319 Prentiss Ave New Orleans LA 70122-5309 E-mail: mannyandjane@aol.com.

IBARGUEN, ALBERTO, newspaper executive; b. Rio Piedras, P.R., Feb. 29, 1944; s. Albert E. and Angelica (Bigas) I.; m. Susana E. Lopez, Jan. 8, 1969; 1 child, Diego. BA in History, Wesleyan U., Middletown, Ct., 1966; JD, U. Pa., 1974. Bar: Conn. 1974. Atty. Legal Aid Soc., Hartford, Conn., 1974-76; dir., counsel Conn. Election Commn., Hartford, 1976-77; ptnr. Cloud & Ibarguen, Hartford, 1977-78; atty. Updike, Kelly & Spellacy, Hartford, 1978-79; dep. gen. coun., v.p. public affairs, v.p. pvt banking Conn. Nat. Bank, Hartford, 1979-84; sr. v.p. Hartford Courant, 1984-86, exec. v.p. ops. Newsday/N.Y. Newsday, N.Y.C., 1986-95; pub. El Nuevo Herald, Miami, Fla., 1995-98; v.p. The Miami Herald, 1995-98, pub., 1998—; chmn. Miami Publishing Co., 1998—. Bd. dirs. Lincoln Ctr. for Performing Arts, N.Y.C., 1990-96, Dade County Found., Com. to Protect Journalists, Fla. Philharm., Pub. Broadcasting Sys., 1997—; trustee Wesleyan U., 1992-95, Smith Coll., 1995-97; mem. bus. commn. Met. Mus. Art, 1990-95. Mem. N.Y. Athletic Club. Office: The Miami Herald One Herald Plaza Miami FL 33132-1693*

IBAZEBO, EHIREME ANTHONY, physician; came to U.S., 1996; MD, U. Jos. Tng. Austin State Hosp. an affiliate of U. Tex. Health Sci. Ctr., San Antonio, 1996-2000; med. dir. Svcs. Texoma, Denison, Tex., 2000—. Recipient Resident Teaching award, 1999, 2000, award Exemplary Performance, 2000. Mem. AMA, Am. Psychiat. Assn., Tex. Med. Assn., Tex. Soc. Psychiat. Physicians. Avocations: music, biking, movies, novels, tennis, squash. Office: 101 E Jones St Sherman TX 75090

IBBOTSON, PATRICIA ANN, nurse, author; b. Detroit, Nov. 17, 1940; d. Russell and Sophia (Nigbor) I. Diploma in nursing, Mercy Sch. Nursing, Detroit, 1961. RN, Mich. From staff nurse to clin. nursing supervisor Wayne County Gen. Hosp., Westland, Mich., 1961-84; corp. screening nurse Fairlane Health Sys., Birmingham, Mich., 1986-91; occupl. health nurse Ford Motor Co., Dearborn, Mich., 1990—99. Author: Eloise Poorhouse, Farm, Asylum and Hospital 1839-1984; 2002. Avocations: genealogy, travel. Home: 22036 Nowlin St Dearborn MI 48124-2733

IBBOTSON, ROGER G. financial educator; b. Chgo., May 27, 1943; s. Arthur E. and Margaret B. (Weuthrich) I.; m. Jody L. Sindelar, 1983. BS, Purdue U., 1965; MBA, Ind. U., 1967; PhD, U. Chgo., 1974. Economist Bank of Japan, 1969; bond portfolio mgr., treas.'s office U. Chgo., 1971-75, asst. prof. fin. Grad. Sch. Bus., 1975-79, sr. lectr. fin. and exec. dir. Ctr. for Research in Security Prices, 1979-84; prof. Yale U. Sch. Mgmt, 1984—; chmn. Ibbotson Assocs., Inc., Chgo., 1979—; ptnr. Zebra Capital Mgmt., 2001—. Recipient Graham and Dodd award, 1980, 82, 84, 2001, James Vertin award AIMR, 2002. Mem. Am. Fin. Assn., Am. Econ. Assn., Fin. Mgmt. Assn. Author: (with Rex Sinquefield) Stocks, Bonds, Bills, and Inflation, 3d edit., 1982, (with Gary Brinson) Global Investments, 1993, (with J.C. Francis) Investments, 2002. Home: 75 Old Hartford Tpke Hamden CT 06517-3524 Office: 8 S Michigan Ave Ste 707 Chicago IL 60603-3357

IBBOTT, GEOFFREY STEPHEN, physicist; b. London, Mar. 23, 1949; s. Frank Alfred and Gladys Josephine (Gilbert) I.; m. Suzan Helen Doro, Feb. 14, 1969 (div. 1971); 1 child, Brian Richard; m. Diane Lorraine McCollum, Dec. 2, 1989. BA, U. Colo., 1979; MS, U. Colo. Health Sci., 1981; PhD, Colo. State U., 1993. Cert. radiol. physics Am. Bd. Radiology. Sr. instr., med. physicist U. Colo. Health Scis. Ctr., Denver, 1974-90; lectr., med. physicist Yale-New Haven Hosp., 1990-94; assoc. prof., dir. physics U. Ky. Med. Ctr., Lexington, 1994—2000; assoc. prof., chief outreach physics, dir. radiol. physics ctr. UT M.D. Anderson Cancer Ctr., Houston, 2001—. Mem. exam. panel Am. Bd. Radiol., 1993—. Assoc. editor Jour. of Med. Physics, 1982-99; contbg. author: The Selection and Performance of Radiologic Equipment, 1985: author: (booklet) Performance Evaluation of Hyperthermia Equipment, 1989; co-author: Radiation Therapy Physics, 1995; contbr. articles to profl. jours. Recipient Meml. award for profl. achievement Rocky Mountain chpt., Health Physics Soc., 1973, Farrington Daniels award, Med. Physics Jour., 1996. Fellow Am. Assn. Physicists in Medicine (pres. 1999), Am. Coll. Radiology; mem. Am. Soc. Therapeutic Radiology and Oncology (pres. coun. on ionizing radiation measurements and stds., 2002-03). Achievements include research on radiation response of mouse taste organ, development of polymer-gel dosimeter. Office: Dept Radiation Physics UT MD Anderson Cancer Ctr 1515 Holcombe Blvd Houston TX 77030

IBDAH, JAMAL A. medical educator; b. Jenin, Jordan, Nov. 18, 1956; s. Ahmad Ibrahim and Arifa Abdul-Rahman Ibdah; m. Mary R. Cantwell, Sept. 23, 1958; children: Khalid Jamal, Malik, Zain. MD, Jordan U. Sch Med, Amman, Jordan, 1975—82; PhD, Med. Coll. of Pa., 1984—87. Cert. Am. Bd. of Internal Medicine, 1994, Am. Bd. of Gastroenterology, 1998. Postdoctoral fellow in biochemistry Med. Coll. of Pa., 1987—88; asst. prof. in biochemistry U. of Jordan, 1988—91; resident, Internal Medicine Wake Forest U. Sch. of Medicine, 1991—94; fellow, Gastroent. Washington U. Sch. of Medicine, 1994—97; asst. prof., Internal Medicine, Gastroent. Wake Forest U. Sch. of Medicine, 1997—2001, assoc. prof., Internal Medicine, Gastroent., 2001—. Contbr. articles to var. profl. jours. Recipient North Am. Conf. for Gastroent. Fellows Award for an Outstanding Program Presentation, Am. Coll. of Gastroenterology, 1997; grantee Career Devel. Award (KO8), NIH, 1997-2002, Innovative Seed Grant in Clin. Rsch. in Liver Diseases, Am. Digestive Health Found., 1998-1999, Rsch. Grant in SIDS, Mar. of Dimes, 1999-2002, Investigator Award (RO1), NIH, 2001-2006. Mem.: Am. Soc. of Biochemistry and Molecular Biology, Am. Soc. of Human Genetics, Am. Assn. for the Study of Liver Diseases, Am. Gastroent. Assn. Achievements include development of an animal mouse model for an inherited disease in children that cause inability to breakdown fat. This model provided for the first time a genetic link to sudden infant death syndrome; published studies that, for the first time, provided an explanation for a serious liver disease in pregnant women and its assn. with an inherited disease in the fetus; published evidence that screening certain infants for a genetic mutation can be life saving. Home: 5224 Huntscroft Ct Winston Salem NC 27106 Office: Wake Forest U Sch Medicine Medical Center Blvd Winston Salem NC 27157 Office Fax: 336-716-6376. E-mail: jibdah@wfubmc.edu.

IBEN, ICKO, JR., astrophysicist, educator; b. Champaign, Ill., June 27, 1931; s. Icko and Kathryn (Tomlin) I.; m. Miriam Genevieve Fett, Jan. 28, 1956; children: Christine, Timothy, Benjamin, Thomas. BA, Harvard U., 1953; MS,

U. Ill., 1954, PhD, 1958. Asst. prof. physics Williams Coll., 1958-61; sr. rsch. fellow in physics Calif. Inst. Tech., Pasadena, 1961—64; assoc. prof. physics MIT, Cambridge, 1964-68, prof., 1968-72; prof. astronomy and physics, head dept. astronomy U. Ill., Champaign-Urbana, 1972-84, prof. astronomy and physics, 1972-89, disting. prof. astronomy and physics Urbana, 1989—99, disting. prof. emeritus, 2000; holder of Eberly family chair in astronomy Pa. State U., 1989-90. Vis. prof. astronomy Harvard U., 1966, 68, 70; vis. fellow Joint Inst. for Lab. Astrophysics U. Colo., 1971—72; vis. prof. astronomy and astrophysics U. Calif., Santa Cruz, 1972; vis. prof. physics and astronomy Inst. for Astronomy U. Hawaii, 1977; adv. panel astronomy sect. NSF, 1972—75; vis. com. Aura Observatories, 1979—82; vis. scientist astronomical coun. Union Soviet Socialist Rep. Acad. Sci., 1985; sr. vis. fellow Australian Nat. U., 1986; vis. prof. U. Bologna, Italy, 1986, Hokkaido U. Grad. Sch. Sci., 2001; sr. rsch. fellow U. Sussex, England, 1986; George Darwin lectr. Royal Astronomical Soc., London, 1984; McMillin lectr. Ohio State U., 1987; vis. eminent scholar U. Ctr. Ga., 1988; guest prof. Christian Albrechts U. Kiel, 1990; sr. fellow Nicolaus Copernicus Astron. Ctr., Warsaw, 2002. Contbr. articles to profl. jours. John Simon Guggenheim Meml. fellow, 1985-86; recipient Eddington medal Royal Astron. Soc., 1990. Fellow Japan Soc. for Promotion of Sci.; mem. Am. Astron. Soc. (councilor 1974-77, Henry Norris Russell lectr. 1989), U.S. Nat. Acad. of Scis., Internat. Astronom. Union. Home: 3910 Clubhouse Dr Champaign IL 61822-9280 Office: U Ill Dept of Astronomy 1002 W Green St Urbana IL 61801-3074

IBERALL, ALTHEA RUTH, computer scientist, playwright; b. Washington, May 3, 1949; d. Arthur Saul and Helene Rubenstein Iberall; m. Ron Aaronson, Sept. 4, 1974 (div. Sept. 1975). BA, NYU, 1975; MS, Boston U., 1978; PhD, U. Mass., 1987; Masters Professional Writing, U. So. Calif., L.A., 2001. Computer operator Norton Lilly, N.Y.C., 1971-73; computer programmer Citicorp, N.Y.C., 1973-76; sys. programmer Wang Labs., Lowell, Mass., 1977-79; mgr. product devel. Coleco Industries, Hartford, Conn., 1979-80; assoc. prof. Rensselar Poly. Inst., Hartford, 1980-87; vis. assoc. prof. U. Waterloo, Ontario, 1987; rsch. scientist U. So. Calif., L.A., 1988-94; mng. dir. Entertainment Tech. Ctr. U. So. Calif., L.A., 1994-2000; chief scientist United Internet Techs., L.A., 2000-2001. Trainer Contracted Computer Tng., L.A., 1993-94; bd. dirs. Little Blue Prodns., L.A. Co-author: Computer Architecture, 1985, The Grasping Hand, 1994; co-editor: Dextrous Robot Hands, 1990; prodr. plays at The Out Theatre, 2002, 03; author of poetry. Mem. Assn. for Computing Machinery, Soc. for Neurosci. Avocation: poetry slamming. E-mail: thea.iberall@verizon.net.

IBERGS, HARRY, musician, educator, music company executive; b. Winston-Salem, N.C., 1958; s. Herbert and Mirdza Ibergs. MusB, U. of N.C., 1981; MusM, U. of Tennessee, Knoxville, 1983; D of Mus. Arts in Vocal Performance/Vocal Sci. and Pedagogy, U. of Colo., 1988. Exec. dir. Rocky Mountain Opera Ednl. Touring Co., Denver, 1988—; v.p. Capital Connectors, Denver, 2002—. Adj. faculty Front Range C.C., Fort Collins, Colo.; asst. head tennis profl. Vienna (Va.) Golf and Country Club, 1977; asst. tennis dir. Young Folk Tennis Devel. Program, Winston-Salem, NC, 1974—76; adj. faculty Colo. State U., Fort Collins, 2000—02; adj. instr. U. of Colo., Boulder, 1983—88, U. of Tenn., Knoxville, 1981—83; part-time instr. U. of N.C., Chapel Hill; tennis dir. North Jeffco Pk. and Recreation Dist., Arvada, Colo., 1990—93; head tennis profl. Miami Golf and Country Club, Dayton, Ohio, 1980, Fonderlac Golf and Country Club, Poland, Ohio, 1979; asst. head tennis profl. Springfield (Va.) Golf and Country Club, Springfield, 1978; founder, dir. ednl. touring co.; dir. exec. coaching The Corp. Voice. Singer: (featured soloist) Opera, Art Song, and Oratorio (Nat. Assn. Tchrs. of Singing award, 1981). Vol. instr. for disabled skiers Nat. Sports Ctr. for the Disabled, Winter Park, Colo., 1994—2000. Mem.: Nat. Assn. of Tchrs. of Singing (assoc.). Achievements include development of vocal technique in the corporate world; design of structured vocal development and practice technique for singers; development of adaptive tennis for the disabled; instruction of adaptive skiing for spinal cord injuries. Avocations: skiing, tennis, fitness, bicycling, scuba diving.

IBERS, JAMES ARTHUR, chemist, educator; b. Los Angeles, June 9, 1930; s. Max Charles and Esther (Imerman) I.; m. Joyce Audrey Henderson, June 10, 1951; children: Jill Tina, Arthur Alan. BS, Calif. Inst. Tech., 1951, PhD, 1954. NSF post-doctoral fellow, Melbourne, Australia, 1954-55; chemist Shell Devel. Co., 1955-61, Brookhaven Nat. Lab., 1961-64; mem. faculty Northwestern U., 1964—, prof. chemistry, 1964-85, Charles E. and Emma H. Morrison prof. chemistry, 1986—. Recipient Disting. alumni award Calif. Inst. Tech., 1997. Mem. NAS, Am. Acad. Arts and Sci., Am. Chem. Soc. (inorganic chemistry award 1979, Disting. Svc. in the Advancement of Inorganic Chemistry award 1992, Linus Pauling award 1994), Am. Crystallographic Assn. (Buerger award 2002). Home: 2657 Orrington Ave Evanston IL 60201-1760 Office: Northwestern U Dept Chemistry Evanston IL 60208-3113 E-mail: ibers@chem.northwestern.edu.

IBERTI, ELISSA TATIGIKIS, painter, costume designer, educator, independent curator; d. Thomas H. and Mary E. Tatigikis; m. Joseph E. Iberti, Aug. 19, 1978; 1 child, Piero S. BFA, State Univ. Coll., Buffalo, 1977; MFA, Pratt Inst., 1979. Adj. asst. prof. visual arts Dowling Coll., Oakdale, NY, 1993—98, asst. prof. visual arts, 1998—. Freelance costume designer, NYC, 1999—2003. Costume design, Revenge of the Space Pandas, Charlotte's Web. Costume design and wardrobe mentor Packer Collegiate Inst., Bklyn., 2000—03. Fellow Ford Found. fellow, Pratt Inst., 1977—79. Mem.: Foundations in Art Theory and Education (FATE), Coll. Art Assn. Office: Dowling College Visual Arts Dept Idle Hour Blvd Oakdale NY 11769 Personal E-mail: ibertie@dowling.edu. E-mail: ibertie@dowling.edu.

IBISON, MICHAEL, physicist, researcher; b. Wallasey, Cheshire, United Kingdom, July 23, 1959; s. John Craig and Patricia Mary Ibison; life ptnr. Laurie Brooke Douglas; children: Jessica Gamble, Devin John Gamble. BSc in Electronics, U. of Southampton, Eng., 1980; PhD in Laser Physics, U. of Southampton, 1984. Rsch. fellow IBM, Winchester, England, 1989—90; cons. automatic image analysis Agfa-Gevaert, Antwerp, Belgium, 1991—94; vis. rsch. scholar Princeton U., NJ, 1994—97; sr. rsch. physicist Inst. for Advanced Studies at Austin, Tex., 1997—. Dir. Designflex Ltd., Bournemouth, Hampshire, United Kingdom, 1991—; cons. Davy-McKee Engring., Poole, Dorset, United Kingdom, 1990—91. Contbr. Grantee Acad. of Consciousness Studies grantee, Fetzer Found. / Princeton U., 1994; Rank Prize Fund scholar, 1986. Mem.: Planetary Soc., Soc. for Sci. Exploration, Am. Phys. Soc., AAAS. Advaita Vedanta. Achievements include patents for Algorithm for automatic analysis of X-ray irradiation images. Avocation: squash. Office: Institute for Advanced Studies at Austin 4030 West Braker Ln Ste 300 Austin TX 78759 Office Fax: 512-346-3017. E-mail: ibison@earthtech.org.

IBLER, GEROLD, finance company executive, consultant; b. Graz, Austria, Nov. 11, 1968; s. Gerold and Elisabeth Ibler; m. Theresa Ibler; children: Mia Cecile Scarbrough, Whitney Michelle Scarbrough, Nicolette Brooke. M. jur, Karl-Franzens-U.Graz, Austria, 1992, Dr iur, 1996; MBA, U. Miami, 1993. Mgr. PricewaterhouseCoopers, Miami, Fla., 1995—2000; European counsel Ferrell Schultz, Miami, Fla., 2000—; mng. dir. Boardroom Acctg. & Cons. Svcs., Miami, Fla., 2000—. Mem.: ABA, Miami City Club. Office: Ferrell Schultz 201 S Biscayne Blvd 34th Floor Miami FL 33131 Office Fax: 305-371-5732. E-mail: gibler@ferrellschultz.com.

IBRAHIM, GEORGE W. physician, health facility administrator; b. Lebanon, Nov. 17, 1936; m. Jean; 1 child, Alastair. Diplomate Am. Bd. Family Practice. Pres. Highland Med. & Diagnostic Clinic, Sebring, Fla., 1980—. Pres., bd. dirs. Health Ctr. Office: Highlands Med & Diagnostic Clinic 6721 US 27 S Sebring FL 33876

IBRAHIM, IBRAHIM AWAD, adult education educator; s. Awad Ibrahim and Thoraya Khater; m. Zahra Zakinasser, Nov. 27, 1987; children: Salma, Mohammad-Yasser, Maha, Dalia. MB, BChir, Cairo U., 1979; MPH, Tulane U., 1984; PhD, Va. Commonwealth U., 1997. Dir. quality mgmt. King Fahd Gen. Hosp., Jeddah, Saudi Arabia, 1993—96; prof. Pa State U., State College, 1997—; assoc. prof. epidemiology and biostatistics U. So. Miss. Ctr. for Cmty. Health, Hattiesburg, 2003—. Cons. preventive medicine King Abdul Aziz Naval Base Hosp., Jubail, Saudi Arabia, 1987—90. Mem.: APHA (health adminstrn. sect. coun. 2002—). Office: Pa State Univ 116 Henderson Bldg University Park PA 16802 also: U So Miss Ctr for Cmty Health PO Box 5122 Hattiesburg MS 39406 Office Fax: 814-863-2905. E-mail: iai2@psu.edu.

IBRAHIM, IBRAHIM N. bishop; b. Telkaif, Mosul, Iraq, Oct. 1, 1937; came to U.S., 1978; s. Namo Ibrahim and Rammo Yono. Grad., Mosul Sem., Iraq, 1951, St. Sulpice Sem., Paris, 1962; STD, Rome, 1975. Dir. sem., Baghdad, Iraq, 1964-68; assoc. pastor St. Joseph Ch., Baghdad, 1975-78; pastor Chaldean Ch., Los Angeles, 1979-82; bishop Chaldean Church of U.S.A., Southfield, Mich., 1982—; first Bishop Eparch Eparchy of St. Thomas the Apostle/Chaldean Cath. Diocese Am., Detroit, 1985—. Chaldean Catholic. Home: Chaldean Diocese USA 25603 Berg Rd Southfield MI 48034-2556

IBRAHIM, MOUNIR LABIB, physician, psychiatrist; b. Cairo, July 26, 1948; s. Labib and Olga (Bassili) I. Diploma, Cairo U., 1967, Diploma Sch. of Medicine, 1972. Diplomate Am. Bd. Psychiatry and Neurology, also with added qualifications in geriatric psychiatry. Psychiat. resident Behman Psychiat. Hosp., Cairo, 1974-76; intern, resident Rass-El-Tin Hosp., Alexandria, Egypt, 1972-74; postdoctoral tng. St. Barnabas Med. Ctr., N.J., 1979; house officer, resident in psychiatry/behavioral medicine Bowman Gray Sch. Medicine, Winston-Salem, N.C., 1980-84, asst. prof. dept. psychiatry, 1985-87; med. dir. psychiatry and dir. psychiat. edn. Forsyth Meml. Hosp., Winston-Salem, 1987-95; pvt. practice in gen. psychiatry Winston-Salem, 1987—; clin. assoc. prof. Bowman Gray Sch. of Medicine, Winston-Salem, 1992—; med. dir., partial psychiat. hospitalization program No. Hosp. of Surry County, Mt. Airy, N.C., 1996, Caldwell meml. Hosp., Lenoir, N.C., 1996-98, Alexander Cmty. Hosp., Taylorsville, N.C., 1997-98. Presenter in field. Contbr. articles to profl. jours. Recipient 6th Ann. Nancy C.A. Roeske M.D. Cert. of Recognition for Excellence in Med. Student Edn., 1996. Mem. Christian Med./Dental Soc. Avocations: travel, reading, music, spiritual growth. Office: 1400 Millgate Dr Ste A Winston Salem NC 27103-1338

ICAHN, CARL C. arbitrator, options specialist, corporation executive; b. Queens, N.Y., 1936; m. Liba Icahn; 2 children BA, Princeton U., 1957; postgrad., NYU Sch. Medicine. Apprentice broker Dreyfus Corp., N.Y.C., 1960-63; options mgr. Tessel, Patrick & Co., N.Y.C., 1963-64, Gruntal & Co., 1964-68; chmn., pres. Icahn & Co., N.Y.C., 1968—, chmn., chief exec. officer ACF Industries Inc., Earth City, Mo., 1984—, also bd. dirs.; chmn., bd. dirs., pres., chief exec. officer Trans World Airlines Inc., N.Y.C., 1986—. Chmn., bd. dirs. Bayswater Realty & Capital Corp. Office: Icahn & Co Inc 100 S Bedford Rd Mount Kisco NY 10549-3425 Address: ACF Industries 620 N 2nd St Saint Charles MO 63301-2081*

ICE, DIANA CAROLYN, librarian, writer; BA, U. Calif., Berkeley, 1968; MALS, U. Mich., 1969. Cert. pub. libr. Writer, Burlingham, NY, 1989—; assoc. editor Am. Life Pub. Co., Hurley, NY, 1989—96; libr. SUNY Coll., Oneonta, NY, 1975—88, Orange County CC, Middletown, NY, 1972—75, Creighton U. Alumni Meml. Libr., Omaha, 1969—72. Author: A Bird in Hand and Other Stories, Easy Herb Cooking for Busy People. Mem.: Nat. Writers Assn. (v.p. Hudson Valley chpt. 1989—96), Sci. Fiction and Fantasy Workshop (chmn. welcome com. 1990—2002). Episcopalian. Avocations: reading, needlework, gardening.

ICE, SUSAN M. psychiatrist; b. Reading, Pa., Aug. 1, 1946; d. John Tyndall and Mildred Rothermel Ice; m. Steven E. Samuel, Oct. 8, 1977 (div. 1985); m. Yiannis A. Koukoulis, Oct. 11, 1990; 1 child, Jessica Lindsay Samuel. BA, Johns Hopkins U., 1969, MD, 1972. Bd. cert. Am. Bd. Psychiatry and Neurology. Psychiatrist Lahey Clinic, Boston, 1977-80, McLean Hosp., Belmont, Mass., 1980-82; dir. eating disorders program Belmont Ctr., Phila., 1982-99; med. dir. The Renfrew Ctr., Phila., 1999—. Mem. Am. Psychiat. Assn., Pa. Psychiat. Assn., Phila. Psychiat. Soc. Presbyterian. Avocations: jogging, tennis, traveling, reading. Office: Renfrew Ctr of Phila 475 Spring Ln Philadelphia PA 19128-3918

ICENHOWER, DELLA MAUDE, retired school librarian; b. Dalby Springs, Tex., July 18, 1929; d. Clarence Winston and Sarah Della (Young) Dalby; m. James Robert Icenhower, June 3, 1951; 1 child, John Dalby. BS, U. North Tex., 1950; MEd, Tex. A&M U., Commerce, 1955. Tchr. Pewitt Ind. Sch. Dist., Naples, Tex., 1950, Lufkin (Tex.) Ind. Sch. Dist., 1951, Falls County Schs., Rosebud, Tex., 1952-56, Borger (Tex.) Ind. Sch. Dist., 1956-64, Fritch (Tex.) Ind. Sch. Dist., 1964-68; sch. libr. Childress (Tex.) Ind. Sch. Dist., 1967-70, Mansfield (Tex.) Ind. Sch. Dist., 1970-90. Steering com. Mansfield Ind. Sch. Dist., 1994—, technology com., 1997—, supt. search com., 1980-81, election ofcl., 1991—, vol., 1990—; mem. adv. bd. Mansfield Pub. Libr., 1976—. Mem. Delta Kappa Gamma, Phi Delta Kappa, Alpha Delta Kappa, Model A Ford Club. Democrat. Baptist. Home: 1 Circle Park Ct Mansfield TX 76063-3210 E-mail: jimdelicen@aol.com.

ICENOGLE, RONALD DEAN, software engineer, writer, physical chemist; b. Bismarck, N.D., May 5, 1951; s. Grover Donald and Mary Adeline (Parks) I.; m. Maria Cecilia Co., Apr. 26, 1987; children: Paul Steven, James Andrew. BS, Mich. State U., 1974; MS, Cornell U., 1977, PhD, 1981; BA in Edn., Ea. Washington U., 1996. Lab. technician N.D. State U., Fargo, 1974-75; tchg. asst. Cornell U., Ithaca, N.Y., 1975-77, grad. rsch. asst., 1977-80; rsch. chemist Shell Devel. Co., Houston, 1980-85; writer on philosophy and sci. Spokane, Wash., 1985-87; sr. devel. engr. Teknor Apex Co., Pawtucket, R.I., 1987-89; writer Spokane, Wash., 1990-96; agt. N.Y. Life Ins. Co., Spokane, 1991; ind. ins. mktg. agt. Spokane, 1991-92; registrar Ind. Order Foresters, Spokane, Wash., 1992; tchr. Olympia (Wash.) Sch. Dist., 1996-98, Pub. Schs. Personnel Coop., Olympia, Wash., 1998-99; info. tech. applications specialist Dept. Labor and Industries, Tumwater, Wash., 1999—. NIH predoctoral trainee, Cornell U., 1977-80. Author: Science and Moral Choice, 1996; co-inventor, 5 U.S. patents low-smoke polypropylene insulation compounds, also fgn. patents; contbr. articles to profl. jours. Counselor Nat. Music Camp, Interlochen, Mich., summers 1972-75; kayak guide Whitewater Challengers, White Haven, Pa., 1978-80. Mem.: PEN, Authors Guild, N.Y. Acad. Scis., Am. Chem. Soc., Phi Kappa Phi, Kappa Delta Pi, Phi Beta Kappa. Republican. Roman Catholic. Avocations: running, whitewater kayaking, yoga. Home: 3630 Joshua Way SE Olympia WA 98501-0917 E-mail: ricenogle@aol.com.

ICERMAN, LARRY, advanced technology business consultant, research and development administrator; b. Muncie, Ind., Sept. 22, 1945; s. Charles and Janelyn (Mock) I. BS in Aeronautics and Astronautics, MIT, 1967; MS in Applied Mechanics, U. Calif., San Diego, 1968, PhD in Engring. Sci., 1976; MBA in Fin., San Diego State U., 1976. Asst. prof. Washington U., St. Louis, 1976-79, assoc. prof., 1979-80; dir. N.Mex. Energy Inst., Las Cruces, N.Mex., 1980-81, N.Mex. State U. Energy Inst., Las Cruces, 1982-83, N.Mex. Energy R&D Inst., Santa Fe, 1984-86, N.Mex. R&D Inst., Santa Fe, 1986-89; pres. Icerman & Assocs., Santa Fe, 1989—. Bd. dirs. Coronado Ventures Forum, Santa Fe, Stolar Horizon, Inc., Raton, N.Mex. Co-author: Energy: Demands, Resources, Impact, Technology, and Policy, 1974, 76,2d edit., 78, 3d edit., 81, revised edit., Energy: Non-Nuclear Energy Technologies, 1975, 77, 2d revised edit., 84, revised and enlarged edit., Renewable Resource Utilization for Development, 1981; mem. editorial bd. Energy: The Internat. Jour., 1979 90. Bd. dirs. Tri-Area Assn. for Econ. Devel., Pojoaque, N.Mex., 1990—; mem. ednl. coun. MIT, Cambridge, Mass., 1981—; trustee, Valles Caldera Trust, Los Alamos, N.Mex. Spl. Recognition for Energy Innovation award U.S. Dept. Energy, 1985, Energy Innovation awards, 1986, 88. Mem. AAAS, AIAA, Am. Chem. Soc., N.Mex. Entrepreneurs Assn. (bd. dirs. 1990-93). Home and Office: 2999 Calle Cerrada Santa Fe NM 87505-5393

ICHAPORIA, PALLAN R. pharmaceutical marketing executive; b. Bombay, Aug. 15, 1952; came to U.S., 1976; s. Rustomji E. and Navajbai Rustomji (Umrigar) I.; m. Hutoxi Ichaporia, May 27, 1952; children: Burjor, Rashna, Farida. MBA, Phillips U., 1981; DBA, Okla. U., 1988. Mktg. & sales profl. Lamb Svcs., Okla., 1976-86, Bristol Myers Squibb, Evansville, Ind., 1986—. Author: The Gathas of Asho Zarathushtra, 1993; co-author: (with Helmut Humbach) The Heritage of Zarathushtra: A New Translation of His Gathas, 1994, Translation of Zamyad Yasht with Commentary and Glossary, 1997; contbr. articles to profl. jours.

ICHIISHI, TATSURO, economics and mathematics educator; b. Seoul, Dec. 16, 1943; came to U.S., 1970; s. Jitsuro and Tomiko Ichiishi; m. Barbara Ann Franklin, Sept. 7, 1973 BA in Econs., Keio U., Tokyo, 1966, MA in Econs., 1968; MA in Math., U. Calif., Berkeley, 1973, PhD in Econs., 1974. Rsch. assoc. Keio U., Tokyo, 1968-73; vis. rsch. fellow Cath. U. Louvain, Heverlee, Belgium, 1974-75; lectr., rsch. assoc. Northwestern U., Evanston, Ill., 1975-76; asst. prof. Carnegie-Mellon U., Pitts., 1976-80; assoc. prof. U. Iowa, Iowa City, 1980-83, prof., 1983-86, Ohio State U., Columbus, 1987—, Hitotsubashi U., Tokyo, 2001—02. Vis. prof. Bilkent U., Ankara, Turkey, 1997; guest prof. Keio U., Tokyo, 1999. Author: Game Theory for Economic Analysis, 1983, The Cooperative Nature of the Firm, 1993, Microeconomic Theory, 1997; editor (with Abraham Neyman and Yair Tauman): Game Theory and Applications, 1990; editor: (with Thomas Marschak) Markets, Games and Organizations: Essays in Honor of Roy Radner, 2002; series editor Math. Econs. and Game Theory, 2000—, assoc. editor Rev. Econ. Design, 1997—, mem. editl. bd. Internat. Jour. Game Theory, 1997—, Advances in Mathematical Economics, 1998—, Games and Economic Behavior, 1998—; contbr. articles. Recipient Nikkei-Tosho Bunka Sho award Nihon Keizai Shinbun and Japan Ctr. for Econ. Rsch., 1994; CORE fellow, 1974-75; NSF grantee, 1978-82, 82-85, 92-96. Mem.: Game Theory Soc. Office: Ohio State U Dept Econs 1945 N High St Columbus OH 43210-1172

ICHIKAWA, AKIKO, artist, editor; b. Sagamihara, Japan, June 21, 1973; arrived in U.S., 1976; d. Iekuni and Takako Ichikawa. BA in Visual Art with honors, Brown U., 1994; MFA, Hunter Coll., 1999. Editl. asst. Monthly Rev. Press, N.Y.C., 1994—96, book editor, 1996—97; editl. rschr. Mademoiselle, N.Y.C., 1997—99, Vogue, N.Y.C., 1999—. Co-curator show Summer Storage, N.Y.C., 2000; residency Djerassi, Calif., 2002, Longwood Arts Project, Bronx, NY, 2002—03. Two person show, EiE, Bklyn., 1999, P.S. 122 Gallery, N.Y.C., 2000, Momenta Art, Bklyn., 2000, exhibited in group shows at Providence Art Club, 1994, Henry St. Settlement, N.Y.C., 1998, 49 1/2 First Ave., 1999, Elizabeth Found. for Arts, 2000, Midway Contemporary Art, St. Paul, 2002, Andrew Kreps, N.Y.C., 2003; contbr. articles to profl. jours. Finalist, Pub. Art Fund, N.Y.C., 2001; recipient Roberta Joslin award, Brown U., 1994; grantee, Change, Inc., 2002; Project grant, Artists Space, N.Y.C., 2000. Office: PO Box 1045 Cooper Sta New York NY 10276 E-mail: ichikawaah@hotmail.com.

ICHINO, YOKO, ballet dancer; b. Los Angeles, Cali. Studied with Mia Slavenska, L.A. Mem. Joffrey II, N.Y.C., Joffrey Ballet, N.Y.C., Stuttgart Ballet, Fed. Republic Germany; tchr. ballet, 1976; soloist Am. Ballet Theatre, 1977-81; guest appearances, 1981-82; prin. Nat. Ballet Can., Toronto, Ont., 1982-90. Various guest appearances including World Ballet Festival, Tokyo, 1979, 85, Tokyo Ballet, 1980, with Alexander Godunov and Stars, summer, 1982, Sydney Ballet, Australia, N.Z. Ballet, summer 1984, Ballet de Marseille, 1985-87, Deutsche Opera Ballet Berlin, 1985-90, Munich Opera Ballet, 1987-90, Australian Ballet, 1987, 89, Staatsoper Berlin, 1989, 90, Komische Opera, Berlin, 1991-93, David Nixon's Dance Theater, Berlin, 1990, 91, Birmingham Royal Ballet, 1990-93, Deutsche Opera Ballet, Berlin, 1994-95; tchr. Australian Ballet, 1989, Birmingham Royal Ballet, 1991, 93, Nat. Ballet of Can., 1993, Cullberg Ballet, Sweden, 1994, Nat. Ballet Sch., 1994, 95, Ballet de Monte-Carlo, 1994, Geneva Ballet, 1995-98, Nederlands Dance Theater, 1995, Rambert Dance, 1995, Royal Winnipeg Ballet, 1999; tchr. numerous ballet workshops; dir. profl. program Ballet Met, 1995-2003; guest master tchr., coach No. Ballet Theatre, 2002. First Am. women recipient medal Third Internat. Ballet Competition, Moscow, 1977.

ICHINOSE, SUSAN M. lawyer; b. Honolulu, Mar. 5, 1944; d. Eugene T. and Harriet C. (Toi) I.; m. Martin D. Plotnick, Aug. 3, 1983; 1 child, Andrei I. AB, George Washington U., 1968; JD, Richardson Sch. of Law, Honolulu, 1977. Bar: Hawaii 1977, U.S. Dist. Ct. Hawaii 1977, U.S. Ct. Appeals (9th cir.) 1978, U.S. Supreme Ct. 1985. Assoc. Mukai Ichiki Raffetto & MacMillan, Honolulu, 1977-80, ptnr., 1981-84; mng. ptnr. Miller & Ichinose, Honolulu, 1985-91; ptnr. Foley Maehara Judge Nip & Chang, 1991-95; dir. Simons & Ichinose, 1995-99; pres. Hawaii Women Lawyers, 1997-98; pvt. practice Honolulu, 1999—. Mem. nat. panel of arbitrators Am. Arbitration Assn., 1990—; adj. prof. Richardson Sch. of Law, 1985, 87, 91, 93; lawyer rep. U.S. Dist. Ct. Hawaii 9th cir. jud. conf., 1999-02, lawyer rep. 9th cir. conf. exec. com., 2002—; dir. Hawaii Women Lawyers, 1998-99, legis. co-chair, 2001-02. Commr. Gov.'s Adv. Commn. on Librs., Honolulu, 1982-84; trustee Friends of Libr. of Hawaii, Honolulu, 1984-87. Mem. ABA, Hawaii Bar Assn. (dir. 2000-01), Am. Inns of Ct. (bencher). Office: 701 Bishop St Honolulu HI 96813-4814 E-mail: smilaw@lawyer.com.

ICHIYAMA, DENNIS YOSHIHIDE, design educator, consultant, administrator; b. Aiea, Hawaii, May 28, 1944; s. Edwin Kiyotada and Florence Fusae (Inoshita) I. BFA, U. Hawaii, 1966; MFA, Yale U., 1968; postgrad., Allgemeine Gewerbeschule, Basel, Switzerland, 1975-77. Instr. U. Bridgeport, Conn., 1968-70; sr. graphic designer Graphic Communications Ltd., Hong Kong, 1970-71; instr. Carnegie-Mellon U., Pitts., 1971-74; asst. prof. Cornell U., Ithaca, N.Y., 1974-75; assoc. prof. Ind. U., Bloomington, 1977-78; asst. prof. U. Ill., Chgo., 1978-79; assoc. prof. Wichita (Kans.) State U., 1979-81; prof., chmn. divsn. art and design Purdue U., West Lafayette, Ind., 1985-92, head dept. visual and performing arts, 1993—. Design cons. U.S. Postal Svc., Washington, 1986, Purdue U. Press, West Lafayette, 1989—, Interior Design Educators Coun., Ithaca, 1985-87; vis. scholar U. Iowa Ctr. for the Book, 1990; fellow to Ctr. for Artistic endeavor Purdue U. Sch. Liberal Arts, 1992; artist-in-residence Hamilton Wood Type & Printing Mus., Wis., 1999-2000; bd. dir. Coll. Art Assn., 2002—. Design work exhbns. in Can., U.S., Germany, Finland, France, Czechoslovakia; exhibited in shows at Centre Georges Pompidou, 1985, Poster Biennale, Warsaw, 1982, Biennale of Graphic Design, Brno, Czechoslovakia, 1982, 92, Columbia U. Rare Book and Manuscript Libr.; represented in collection of the Plakatsammlung of the Kunstgewerbemuseum, Zurich, Rochester Inst. of Tech. Libr., N.Y., Lahti Art Mus., Finland, Stern Book Arts and Spl. Collections Ctr., San Francisco Pub. Libr., Purdue U. Librs., The Ruth and Marvin Sackner Archive of Concrete and Visual Poetry; author essays in Contemporary Designers, 1985, T Y P O G R A M S, Pure Type Forms, 2000, The Hamilton Type Specimen Sheets Portfolio, 2001, book revs.; book reviewer Choice (ALA, Assn. Coll./Rsch. Librs.). Grantee Nat. Endowment for Humanities, 1984; IAC master fellow Ind. Arts Commn., 1985, 2001, Nat. Endowment for Arts, 1989, Individual Artist program grantee, 2001-03; Ctr. for Creative Endeavors fellow Purdue U., 1992, 2003—. Mem. Am. Ctr. for Design, Am. Inst. Graphic Arts, Graphic Design Educators Assn., Alliance Typographique Internat., Nat. Coun. Art Adminstrs. (nat. bd. dirs. 1998—), Internat. Coun. Fine Arts Deans, Coll. Art Assn. Am. (nat. bd. dirs. 2002—), Arts Ind. (state coun. 1993-99), Hui na opio o Hawaii (advisor 1986-93), Greater Lafayette Music Art. Buddhist. Avocations: swiss posters, artists books, chinese and japanese seals, printing history, hand bookbinding and letterpress printing. Office: Purdue U Dept Visual/Performing Arts Bldg 552 W Wood St West Lafayette IN 47907 E-mail: diad@purdue.edu.

IDASZAK, JEROME JOSEPH, economic journalist; b. Chgo., Dec. 28, 1945; s. Joseph Edward and Estelle Charlotte (Grelecki) I.; m. Geraldine Rae Fehst, Sept. 4, 1976; children: Alexander Jerome, Joshua Adam. BJournalism, Northwestern U., Evanston, Ill., 1967, MJournalism, 1968. Reporter Rockford Morning Star, Ill., 1968-70; reporter Chgo. Tribune, Deerfield, Ill., 1974-76; fin. reporter Chgo. Sun Times, 1976-82, fin. columnist, 1982-90, Washington corr., 1985-90; freelance writer and editor, 1991; assoc. editor Kiplinger Washington Editors, 1992—. Fin. commentator Sta. WBBM-AM, Chgo., 1984-85; contbr. Sta. WBEZ-FM, Chgo., 1987-93; grad. journalism instr. Northwestern U., 1984; instr. Inst. for Exptl. Learning, 2002-03. Author: (newspaper series) Farm problems, 1983 (Peter Lisagor award 1984); Asian economy & growth, 1979 (Peter Lisagor award 1980). Vol., U.S. Peace Corps, 1970-72. Brookings Instn. fellow, 1979. Mem. Soc. Profl. Journalists, Nat. Returned Peace Corps. Vols., Chgo. Headline Club (bd. dirs. 1980-85, pres. 1984-85).

IDDINGS, KATHLEEN, poet, editor, publisher, consultant; b. Ohio, June 25, 1945; d. Ralph Myers and Ruth Amelia Wolfe. BS in Edn., Miami U., Oxford, Ohio, 1968. Tchr. various Ohio schs., 1962-74; freelance photojournalist La Jolla, Calif., 1976-80; freelance pub. rels. mgr. San Diego, 1980-81; cons., 1981—; editor, pub. La Jolla Poet's Press, 1981—. Poetry cons. San Diego City Schs., 1990; resident Djerassi Artists' Colony, 1990. Author: (poetry) Sticks, Friction & Fire, 2001, 5 other books of poetry. Fellow, NEA, 1989; grantee, PEN, 1988, 1990, Calif. Arts Coun., 1994, Carnegie Authors; scholar, Napa

Poetry Conf. Mem.: PEN, San Diego Ind. Scholars, Associated Writers Program, Acad. Am. Poets, Univ. Club, Calif. San Diego Faculty Club (Chancellor's Assoc. 1999—2002). Democrat. Unitarian Universalist. Avocations: poetry readings, photography, college lectures, poetry contest judge. Office: La Jolla Poets Press PO Box 8638 La Jolla CA 92038-8638

IDDINS, BRENDA WALKER, nurse; b. Birmingham, Ala., Aug. 26, 1958; d. Eddie Clyde and Sybil Lucille (Lusk) Walker. Assoc. in Nursing, Jefferson State Jr. Coll., 1979; BSN, U. Ala., Birmingham, 1985, MSN, 1987, postgrad. cert. FNP, 1995. Cert. family nurse practitioner. Staff RN Univ. Ala. Birmingham Hosp., 1979-80, charge nurse, 1980-85, part-time staff RN, 1985-86, part-time transport RN, 1983-84, part-time rsch. nurse, 1985, clin. nurse specialist, 1987-92, lung transplant coord., 1992-93, rsch. coord., 1993-95; nurse practitioner, dir. student health svcs. Samford U., 1995-97; family nurse practitioner Bapt. Health Ctr., Lincoln, Ala. Item writer Nat. Coun. Licensure Examination for Registered Nursing, 1992; mem. test devel. com. ANCC, 1992-96. Mem. ANA, Am. Acad. Nurse Practitioners, Sigma Theta Tau.

IDE, ROY WILLIAM, III, lawyer; b. Geneva, Ill., Apr. 23, 1940; s. Roy William and Jenny (Coleman) Ide; m. Gayle Marie Oliver, Jan. 21, 1967; children: Logan, Jennifer, Lucienne. BA cum laude, Washington and Lee U., 1962; LLD, U. Va., 1965; MBA, Ga. State U., 1972. Bar: Ga. 1967, D.C. 1994, U.S. Ct. Appeals (5th and 11th cirs.) 1967, U.S. Supreme Ct. 1969. Law clk. Judge Griffin Bell U.S. Ct. Appeals (5th cir.), 1965—66; assoc. King & Spalding, Atlanta, 1966—71; ptnr. Huie, Sterne & Ide, Atlanta, 1971—77, Kutak Rock (and predecessor firm), Atlanta, 1978—92, mng. ptnr., Atlanta office, vice-chair, chmn. fin. dept., chmn. healthcare dept.; ptnr. Long, Aldridge & Norman; sr. v.p., spl. counsel E.F. Hutton and Co., Inc., 1985—87; spl. counsel, mng. dir. Prescott, Ball & Turben, 1988—. Former bd. dirs., mem. exec. com. Atlanta Com. for Olympic Games. Named one of Atlanta's Five Outstanding Men of Yr., 1976; recipient Arthur Van Briesen award, Nat. Legal Aid and Defender Assn., 1977. Mem.: ABA (ho. of dels., chair young lawyer's divsn. 1976, chair genl practice sect. 1983—84, chair spl. com. on drug crisis 1991—92, 1992—93, pres.-elect 1992—93, pres. 1993—94, immediate past pres. 1994—), Ga. Bar Assn. (bd. govs.). Office: McKenna Long & Aldridge LLP 303 Peachtree St NE Ste 5300 Atlanta GA 30308 Office Fax: 404-527-8566. E-mail: bide@mckennalong.com.

IDEKER, TREY, computational biologist, molecular biologist; b. Memphis, June 24, 1972; s. Raymond Edwin Ideker, Mary Lou Ideker; m. Kristyn Gray. BS in Elec. Engring. and Computer Sci., MIT, 1994, MS in Elec. Engring. and Computer Sci., 1995; PhD in Molecular Biotechnology, U. Wash., 2001. Rsch. scientist Loral Infrared and Imaging Sys., Lexington, Mass., 1991—95; database cons. Klinikum Rechts der Isar, Munich, 1995—96; rsch. fellow Whitehead Inst., Cambridge, 2001—03; asst. prof. dept. bioengring. U. Calif., San Diego, 2003—. Cons. Genstruct, Cambridge, 2001—, Pfizer, Cambridge, 2001—. Fellow, Achievement Rewards for Coll. Scientists, 1996—98. Mem.: Internat. Soc. for Computational Biology. Achievements include pioneering research in the nascent field of systems biology; invention of methods for modeling cellular systems and circuitry. Avocations: running, piano, guitar, scuba diving, travel. Office: U Calif San Diego Bioengring 9500 Gilman Dr La Jolla CA 92093-0412 E-mail: trey@bioeng.ucsd.edu.

IDING, ALLAN EARL, lawyer; b. Milw., Apr. 29, 1939; s. Earl Herman and Erna Adeline (Albrecht) I.; m. Anne Louise Chaconas, July 9, 1961; children: Kent Earl, Krista Anne Templeman, Bradford A., Andrea Beth Brozynski. BS, Marquette U., 1961, LLB, 1963; DHL (hon.), Nashotah (Wis.) House, 1990. Bar: Wis. 1963, U.S. Dist. Ct. (ea. dist.) Wis. 1963, U.S. Ct. Appeals (7th cir.) 1963. Law clk. U.S. Ct. Appeals (7th cir.), Chgo., 1963-64; assoc. Whyte Hirschboeck Dudek, S.C., Milw., 1964-71, mem., 1971—. Trustee Nashotah House, 1976—; pres., bd. dirs. Wis. DeMolay Found., Milw., 1985—, Wis. Health and Ednl. Facilities Authority, 1978-85, Wis. Masonic Home, Inc.; bd. dirs. Wis. Masonic Home, Inc.; pres., bd. dirs. Todd Wehr Found., Inc.; mem. Wauwatosa (Wis.) Police and Fire Commn., 1978-83. Mem. Blue Mound Golf and Country Club (sec., bd. dirs.), Masons (grand master Wis. 1981-82). Republican. Episcopalian. Avocation: golf. Home: 9212 Wilson Blvd Milwaukee WI 53226-1729 Office: Whyte & Hirschboeck Dudek SC Ste 2100 111 W Wisconsin Ave Milwaukee WI 53203-2501 E-mail: aiding@whdlaw.com.

IDINI, ANTONIO GIONVANNI, education educator; b. Sassari, Sardinia, Aug. 8, 1958; arrived in U.S., 1988; s. Pietro Gavino Idini and Maria Francesca Palitta; m. Bridgett R. Longust, Dec. 20, 1991 (div. Feb. 15, 2000). Laurea, Univ. Degli Studi Di Sassari, Italy, 1986; MA Am. Indian studies, Univ. Ariz., Tuscon, 1992, PhD, 1998. Lectr. of Italian Univ. So. Calif., L.A., 2000—. Fullbright Scholarship, 1988—89. Buddhist. Avocations: movies, poetry. Office: Univ So Calif Dept of French and Italian THH 135 Los Angeles CA 90089-3059

IDIYATULLIN, DJAUDAT SHAVKATOVICH, research associate; b. Kazan, Tatarstan, Russia, Sept. 16, 1957; s. Shavkat Galievich Idiyatullin, Farida Sungatovna Idiyatullina; m. Farida Raisovna Dautova; children: Airat, Aigul Idiyatullina. Ph.D, Kazan State University, Russia, 1993—96. Rsch. assoc. U. Minn., Mpls. Author: (patent) Bulletin of Russian patents, 1996, 1990, 1986; contbr. articles to profl. jours. including; Jour. Magnetic Resonance, Applied Magnetic Resonance, Biochemistry, Protein Science, Solid State Nuclear Magnetic Resonance, Magnetic Resonance Imaging. Mem.: New York Academy of Science. Home: 2816 Silver LN NE #105 Minneapolis MN 55421 Office: U Minn 6-155 Jackson Hall 321 Church Street SE Minneapolis MN 55455 Personal E-mail: idiat001&tc.umn.edu. Business E-Mail: idiat001&tc.umn.edu.

IDLER, ELLEN LOUISE, education educator; b. Pittsburgh, Pa., July 27, 1952; d. Charles Christian William and Kathryn Douglass Idler; m. Philip Ayers; children: Emmeline Idler Ayers, Alexander Douglass Ayers. BA, Coll. of Wooster, 1970—74; MA, Rutgers U., 1975—76; PhD, Yale U., 1979—85. Prof. Rutgers U., 1985—. Author: (book) Cohesiveness and Coherence: Religion and the Health of the Elderly, (article) Jour. of Gerontology (John Templeton Exemplary Paper Prize in Religion and Social Sci., 1998), Am. Jour. of Sociology, (article) Social Forces, Jour. of Health and Social Behavior, Am. Jour. of Epidemiology, Am. Jour. of Pub. Health. Elder Hillsborough Ref. Ch., Hillsborough, 1990—2002. Recipient Phi Beta Kappa, Coll. of Wooster, 1974, FIRST Award, Nat. Inst. on Aging, 1987-1992; fellow Rockefeller Bros. Fund Sem. Fellowship, Rockefeller Found., 1974, Charlotte W. Newcombe Fellowship, Woodrow Wilson Found., 1983, Vis. Tchg. and Rsch. Faculty, Danish Med. Rsch. Coun., 1999. Fellow: Gerontol. Soc. of Am. (Fellow 2001). Office: Rutgers University 30 College Ave New Brunswick NJ 08901 Personal E-mail: idler@rci.rutgers.edu. E-mail: idler@rci.rutgers.edu.

IDOL, JAMES DANIEL, JR., chemist, educator, inventor, consultant; b. Harrisonville, Mo., Aug. 7, 1928; s. James Daniel and Gladys Rosita (Lile) I.; m. Marilyn Thorn Randall, 1977. AB, William Jewell Coll., 1949; MS, Purdue U., 1952, PhD, 1955, D.Sc. (hon.), 1980. With Standard Oil Co., Ohio, 1955-77, rsch. supr., 1965-68, rsch. mgr., 1968-77; mgr. venture rsch. Ashland Chem. Co., Columbus, Ohio, 1977-79, v.p., dir. corp. R & D, 1979—88; disting. prof. materials sci. and ceramics sch. engring. Rutgers U., New Brunswick, NJ, 1988—2002, dir. polymer sci. ctr. for advanced materials via immiscible polymer processing, 2002—. Adv. bd. NSF Presdl. Young Investigators Awards, Nat. Inst. Sci. and Tech., 1997—; cons. in field; lectr. chem. engring. dept. Northwestern U., 1978, Stanford U., 1982-83, U. Calif., Berkeley, 1986, Yale U., 1988 U. Chgo., 1998; lectr. Lawrence Berkeley Lab., 1985-86; v.p., program coord. 1st N.Am. Chem. Congress, 1975; program coord. 1st Pacific Rim Chem. Cong., 1979; indsl. rep. U.S. Coun. for Chem. Rsch., 1983—, governing bd., 1985—; panel on frontiers in fossil fuel energy rsch. NRC, 1986, com. on tracking toxic wastes, 1989-93, panel on polymers in the environ. Internat. Union of Pure and Applied Chemistry, 1996, com. on energy conservation in processing of indsl. materials; adv. bd. U. Tex., Tex. A&M, Ohio State U., Purdue U., Okla. State U., Ariz. State U., U. Mass., Case Western Reserve U., 1965-75; com. polymers recycling Internat. Union Pure and Applied Chem., 1993—; mem. U.S. Coun. Chem. Rsch., 1981-89, gov. bd. 1985-88. Chmn. editl. adv. bd.: Indsl. & Engring. Chemistry Jour., 1976—84, mem. editl. adv. bd.: Chem. and Engring. News, 1977—81, Am. Chem. Soc. Symposium Series, 1978—84, Advances in Chemistry Series, 1979—84, Chem. Week Mag., 1980—82, Sci., 1986—91, Jour. Applied Polymer Sci., 1988—; contbr. chapters to books, articles to profl. jours., handbooks and encys. Active Cleve. Welfare Fedn. Recipient Modern Pioneer award NAM, 1965, Disting. Alumnus citation William Jewell Coll., 1971 Fellow AAAS, Am. Inst. Chemists (life; bd. dirs. 1981—, vice-chmn. 1986, chmn. 1987, Chem. Pioneer award 1968, Mems. and Fellows lectr. 1980); mem. Nat. Acad. Engring., Soc. Plastics Industry, Soc. Mfg. Engrs.-Composite Group, Am. Chem. Soc. (indsl. and engring. chemistry divsn., chmn. 1971, chem. innovator designation Chem. and Engring. News mag. 1971, adv. bd. Petroleum Rsch. Fund, 1974-76, Joseph P. Stewart Disting. Svc. award 1975, Creative Invention award 1975), Am. Mgmt. Assn. (R&D coun. 1985-88, Coun. award for Disting. Svc. pkg. coun. 1989-97, mfg. and tech. coun. 1997—), Dirs. of Indsl. Rsch., Am. Inst. Chem. Engrs., Licensing Execs. Soc., Soc. Plastics engrs., Indsl. Rsch. Inst. (rep., chmn. bd. editors 1983-86), Plastics Pioneers Assn., Soc. Chem. Industry (Perkin medal 1979), Ind. Acad. Sci., Catalysis Soc. (Ciapetti award/lectureship 1988), Cleve. Athletic Club, Cosmos Club (Washington), Worthington Hills Country Club, Masons, Shriners, Sigma Xi, Alpha Chi Sigma, Theta Chi Delta, Kappa Mu Epsilon, Alpha Phi Omega, Phi Gamma Delta. Mem. Christian Ch. (Disciples Of Christ). Achievements include invention of process for manufacture acrylonitrile (over 80 plants in 30 countries-this ammoxidation process was designated as Nat. Hist. Chem. Landmark 1996 by Am. Chem. Soc; patents in field. Office: Dept Ceramic & Materials Eng 607 Taylor Rd Rutgers Univ Piscataway NJ 08854-8065

IDOS, ROSALINA VEJERANO, secondary school educator; b. Ligao, Philippines, Mar. 18, 1944; arrived in U.S., 1987; m. Salvador Salcedo Idos, Dec. 21, 1969; children: Nathaniel, Rey, Lady Lou. BSc in Edn., U. of the East, Philippines, 1965; MSc in Edn., Nat. U., 2000. Cert. single subject tchg. in English, social studies, Filipino Calif., 1989. Tchr. Mayon H.S., Ligao City, Philippines, 1965—67; master tchr. in charge of student tchrs. U. of the East, Manila, Philippines, 1967—69, prof., 1969—87; tchr. San Diego Unified Sch. Dist. Morse H.S., San Diego, 1988—. Workshop presenter in field; curriculum writer Project Inclusion San Diego City Schs., San Diego, 1993—95. Recipient Outstanding Tchr. award, U. Calif., 1995—96, Educator of the Decade award, Filipino-Am. Educators Assn. San Diego, 1999, Svc. award, Fgn. Lang. Coun. San Diego, 1999, Recognition award, Filipino-Am. Educators of Calif., 2000. Fellow: Calif. Fgn. Lang. Project; mem.: San Diego Internat. Lang. Network (leadership team), Filipino-Am. Parents Assn. (adv. 1993—), Kaisahan Club (adv. 1990—). Roman Catholic. Avocations: reading, writing. Home: 6333 Viewpoint Ct San Diego CA 92139 Office: Morse High School 6905 Skyline Drive San Diego CA 92114

IDOURAINE, AHMED, nutritionist, food chemist, tissue culture engineer; b. Souk El-Had, Algiers, Algeria, Jan. 22, 1948; came to U.S., 1983; s. Mohamed Idouraine and Fatma Kennoud; m. Ghania Benkherouf, Nov. 4, 1997; children: Melissa-Sara, Nassim Charif, Ameen Redha. BS in Food Tech., Nat. Inst. Agronomy, Algiers, 1977; MS in Food Scis., U. Ariz., 1987, PhD in Nutritional Scis., 1993. Rsch. team leader agr. chemistry Sonatrach, Algiers, 1977-81; instr. food sci. dept. Nat. Inst. Light Industries, Boumerdes, Algeria, 1981-83; rsch./tchg. asst. dept. nutrition & food sci. U. Ariz., Tucson, 1985-93; rsch. assoc. Harrington Arthritis Rsch. Ctr., Phoenix, 1994-96; dir. rsch. & devel. Verigen Inc., Scottsdale, Ariz., 96-98, Verigen Transplant Svc. Internat., Phoenix, 1998—2001; rschr. Sun Health Rsch. Inst., Phoenix, 2002—. Contbr. numerous articles to profl. jours., numerous abstracts and presentations; patentee in field. McClelland scholar U. Ariz., 1991, Food Sci. scholar, 1992, Sonatrach scholar, 1983-87. Mem. Inst. Food Technologists, Am. Assn. Cereal Chemists, Ariz. Soc. Food Technologists, N.Y. Acad. Scis., Sigma Xi, Gamma Sigma Delta. Achievements include patents in field. Avocations: jogging, swimming. E-mail: vtsi@earthlink.net.

IDRIS, AHAMED H. emergency medicine physician; b. N.Y.C., 1947; MD, Rush Med. Coll., 1979. Diplomate Am. Bd. Internal Medicine, Am. Bd. Emergency Medicine. Resident in internal medicine Cook County Hosp., Chgo., 1979-83; dir. emergency medicine rsch. Shands Tchg. Hosp., Gainesville, Fla. Chair nat. basic life support sub-com. Am. Heart Assn.; med. liaison, dir human space flight rescue team NASA; cons. NIH. With M.C. U.S. Army, 1967—71. Decorated Bronze Star medal. Office: U Fla Coll Medicine Dept Emergency Medicine PO Box 100186 Gainesville FL 32610-0186

IDZIK, DANIEL RONALD, retired lawyer; b. Depew, N.Y., Jan. 20, 1935; s. Daniel Henry and Ann Mary (Kolakowski) I.; m. Kathleen Osborne, Oct. 6 1989; children by previous marriage: Christopher, Rebecca, Laura, Susan. BS, SUNY, Buffalo, 1956; LLB, Harvard U., 1963. Bar: N.Y. 1964. Exec. v.p. U.S. Nat. Student Assn., Phila., 1956-57; assoc. sec. World Univ. Svc., Geneva, 1957-60; chief counsel N.Y. State Senate Commn. on Labor and Industry, Albany, 1965; from assoc. counsel to gen. counsel Booz, Allen & Hamilton, Inc., N.Y.C., 1967-98; ret., 1998. Chmn. Philharmonia Virtuosi, Westchester County, N.Y., 1988-90, pres. 1987-88, bd. dirs. 1985-91; pres. Coun. for Arts in Westchester, 1983-85, bd. dirs., 1980-85; chmn., Friends of Neuberger Mus., Purchase, N.Y., 1991-93, pres., 1990, bd. dirs., 1987-97; bd. dirs. Buffalo State Coll. Found., 1985—, Jacob's Pillow, 1996—, LongBoat Key Ctr. Arts, 2000—, pres., 2002-. Recipient Disting. Alumni award SUNY Buffalo, 1986, Arts award Coun,. for the Arts in Westchester, 1990. Mem. Harvard Club of N.Y. (mem. bd. mgrs. 1997-2000). E-mail: daniel_idzik@post.harvard.edu.

IDZIK, MARTIN FRANCIS, lawyer; b. Depew, N.Y., Apr. 2, 1942; s. Daniel Henry and Ann Mary (Kolakowski) I.; m. Patricia Ann O'Brien, Aug. 7, 1965; children: Andrew, Amy. BS, Canisius Coll., 1963; JD, U. Notre Dame, 1966. Bar: N.Y. 1966. Assoc. Phillips, Lytle et al., Buffalo, 1971-76, ptnr., 1977-78, Jamestown, N.Y., 1979—. Bd. trustees Randolph Children's Home, 1993—99. Acting village justice, East Aurora, N.Y.,1972-79; bd. dirs. Chautauqua County Humane Soc., 1989-93, Downtown Jamestown Devel. Task Force, 1988-92, Jamestown YMCA, 1985-87, N.Y. State affiliate of Am. Heart Assn., 1983-85, Southwestern chpt. Am. Heart Assn., 1981-85, Jamestown Cmty. Learning Coun., 1995—, Roger Tory Peterson Inst., 2000—; chmn. fund for the Arts in Chautauqua County, 1984-88; pres. Arts Coun. Chautauqua County, 1982-84, United Way South Chautauqua County, 2000-01; mem. Jamestown Civic Ctr. Task Force, 1982-86, N.Y. State Mgmt. Atty.'s Conf., 1978—. Capt. JACG, U.S. Army, 1967-71. Mem. ABA, N.Y. State Bar Assn., Erie County Bar Assn., Jamestown Bar Assn. (pres. 1991-92), No. Chautauqua County Bar Assn., Sportsmen's Club (Stow, N.Y.). Office: Phillips Lytle Hitchcock 8 E 3rd St PO Box 1279 Jamestown NY 14702-1279 E-mail: midzik@phillipslytle.com.

IENNER, DON, music company executive; Co-founder,exec. v.p. Millennium Records, 1977—83; v.p. promotion, later exec. v.p., gen. mgr. Arista Records, 1983—89; chmn. Columbia Records Group, N.Y.C., 1994—; pres. Columbia Records, N.Y.C., 1989. Office: Columbia Records 550 Madison Ave New York NY 10022-3211

IERARDI, ANNE MARIE, pastoral counselor, artist; b. Boston, Mar. 4, 1953; d. John Lee Ierardi and Theresa Christine Verrochi. BA in Art, Emmanuel Coll., 1974; MDiv, Episcopal Div. Sch., 1985; DMin, Boston U., 1990. Dir., counselor Healthsigns Ctr. Inc., Boston, 1982-89, Yarmouthport, Mass., 1991—; field site supr. Lesley Coll., Cambridge, Mass., 1984-86; assoc. pastor, adj. prof. United Parish of Carver, Mass., 1988-90; counselor Interfaith Counseling Ctr., New Bedford, Mass., 1990-92; asst. pastor Federated Ch. of Orleans, Mass., 1993-95; chaplain Hospice of Cape Cod, Sandwich, Mass., 1995-97. Graphic and prodn. artist, Boston, 1976-84; adj. prof. Lesley Coll., 1984-86; mem. com. ch. and ministry United Ch. of Christ, Cape Cod, Mass., 1999. Vol. Vista, Horton, Kans., 1975-76; bd. dirs. Cape Cod Coun. Chs., Hyannis, Mass., 1993-96; mem. Cmty. Leadership Inst., Hyannis, 1993—; pres. New Eng. Women Mins., 1999-2000. Fellow Episcopal Div. Sch., 1987-88. Fellow Am. Assn. Pastoral Counselors (cert.); mem. Mass. Mental Health Counselors Assn. Democrat. Avocation: guitar. Home: 408 Main St Yarmouth Port MA 02675-1823 Office: Healthsigns Ctr Inc 408 Main St Yarmouth Port MA 02675-1823 E-mail: starfish@massmed.org.

IERARDI, ERIC JOSEPH, school system administrator; b. Bklyn., May 11, 1950; s. Joseph and Angelina (Vitale) I. BA, St. Francis Coll., 1973; MEd, Fordham U., 1987. Asst. dir. James A. Kelly Local Hist. Studies Inst., 1973; St. Francis Coll. tchr. St. Bartholomew's Sch., 1974-78; tchr. Our Lady of Grace Sch., Bklyn., 1978-86, St. Mary Star of Sea Sch., 1986-87, asst. on edn. to Bklyn. borough pres., 1979; dist. rep., mgr. Congressman Stephen J. Solarz, 1981-82; prin. St. Francis Xavier Sch., Vicksburg, Miss., 1987-89, St. Francis Paola Sch., Bklyn., 1989-91, St. Pius V, Jamaica, Queens, N.Y., 1991-96; adminstr. David A. Boody Intermediate Sch. 228, Bklyn. Instr. prof. Hinds C.C., Miss.; U.S. delegate Gruppo Savoia, 2000. Author: Gravesend: The Home of Coney Island, 1975, Gravesend: Brooklyn, Coney Island & Sheepshead Bay, 1996, Brooklyn in the 1920s, 1998; contbg. editor Bklyn. Mag., 1978-79. Past mem. Cmty. Planning Bd. 11, Bklyn.; past pres. Gravesend Dem. Club; commr. deeds City N.Y.; apptd. U.S. del. GRUPPO SAVOIA. Named Hon. Mayor, Gravesend, Eng., 1977, Knight Officier, Order of Merit of Savoy, 2002, Honored Guard, Royal Tombs at the Pantheon in Rome, 2003; recipient Calabrian of Yr. award Brutium Cultural Club, 1979; knighted, named to Order of Merit of Savoy, His Royal Highness Prince Victor Emmanuel IV of Savoy, 1999. Mem. Assn. Tchrs. Social Studies, Columbia Tchrs. Assn., Gravesend Hist. Soc. (pres.), Circolo Culturale Club, Univ. S. Fla. Club, Order Sons of Italy. Democrat. Roman Catholic. Home: PO Box 5 Upper Black Eddy PA 18972-0005 Office: IS 228 228 Avenue S Brooklyn NY 11223-2746

IEYOUB, RICHARD PHILLIP, state attorney general; b. Lake Charles, La., Aug. 11, 1944; s. Phillip Assad and Virginia Khoury Ieyoub; m. Caprice Brown, Feb. 3, 1995; children: Amy Claire, Nicole Anne, Brennan Jude, Richard Phillip Jr., Khoury Myhand, Christian Brown. BA in history, McNeese State U., 1968; JD, La. State U., 1972. Bar: La. 1972, U.S. Supreme Ct. Spl. prosecutor to atty. gen. State of La., Baton Rouge, 1972—74; assoc. Camp, Carmouche, Lake Charles, 1974—76; mem. Stockwell, Sievert, Lake Charles, 1976—78, Baggett, McCall, Singleton, Ranier, Ieyoub, Lake Charles, 1978—; pvt. practice Lake Charles; dist. atty. Calcasieu Parish, 1985—92; atty. gen. State of La., 1992—. Instr. criminal law McNeese State U.; chmn. La. Drug Policy Bd. Active La. Commn. on Law Enforcement; apptd. by gov. to adv. bd. D.A.R.E., La.; chmn. New Orleans Met. Crime Task Force, Gov's. Military Adv. Commn.; active President's Commn. on Model State Drug Laws, 1992—; parish coun. Immaculate Conception Cathedral Parish, Lake Charles; bd. dirs. S.W. La. Health Counseling Svcs., Crime Stoppers of Lake Charles, St. Jude Children's Rsch. Hosp., 1998—99; vice-chmn. La. coord. Coun. on the Prevention of Drug Abuse and Treatment of Drug Use; bd. dirs. La. State U. Alumni Assn. Named Outstanding Pub. Ofcl. for Diocese Lake Charles, 1990; recipient Disting. Alumnus award, McNeese State U., 1994, Legis. Leadership award, Nat. Coun. Against Drinking and Driving, 1996, Ochsner Humanitarian award, 1998. Mem.: ABA (vice-chmn. prosecution function com.), So. Attys. Gen. Assn. (elected chmn.), S.W. La. Bar Assn. (exec. com. 1979), Nat. Coll. Dist. Attys. (bd. regents 1991), La. Dist. Attys. Assn. (pres., bd. dirs. 1989—90), Nat. Assn. Attys. Gen. (exec. working group on prosecutorial rels.), Nat. Dist. Attys. Assn. (pres., bd. dirs. 1990—91), La. Bar Assn. (lectr. criminal law), Nat. Assn. Criminal Def. Lawyers, Assn. Trial Lawyers Am., Sierra Club. Democrat. Roman Catholic. Office: Justice Dept PO Box 94095 Baton Rouge LA 70804-4095*

IEZZA, ANITA KAY, physician assistant; b. Austin, Tex., Oct. 11, 1956; d. Bobby Ray and Elizabeth Frances (McDowell) Hazen; m. Joseph Thomas Iezza, Jan. 5, 1982 (div. Sept. 1993); children: Joseph Thomas, Jr. (dec.), Anita Elizabeth. BS, Physician Assoc., Trevecca Nazarene Coll., Nashville, 1979; MS, L.I. U., 1998. Physician asst. Montefiore Med. Ctr., Bronx, N.Y., 1979—, sr. physician asst., 1992—, HIV primary care trainer, 1991-92. Programs and edn. region v.p. Chpt. 21 Parents Without Ptnrs., Westchester County, N.Y., 1995-96. V.p. Parents Club, St. Catharine Acad., 2001-2002, pres., 2002-03. Mem.: NY State Physician Asst. Assn., Am. Acad. Physician Assts. Roman Catholic. Avocations: art, music, jazz, sports, reading books. Office: Montefiore Med Ctr 111 E 210th St Bronx NY 10467-2401

IFFT, LEWIS GEORGE, III, company administrator; b. Uniontown, Pa., July 21, 1951; s. Lewis George Jr. and Miriam Katherine Wilson; m. Kathleen Marie Andersen, Mar. 26, 1983; children: Christopher Andrew Ifft, Jonathan Lewis Ifft. BS in Bus. Adminstrn., Bowling Green (Ohio) State U., 1973; MBA, Rensselaer Polytechnic Inst., Troy, N.Y., 1979. Ops. mgr. Battery Products Divsn. Union Carbide Corp., 1973-80; asst. reg. mgr. Eastern Region TransAmerica Corp., Elizabeth, NJ, 1980-82, reg. mgr. Eastern Region, 1982, regional mgr. Central Region Chgo., 1982-89; v.p. The Fred Barbara Co., Chgo., 1989-90; v.p., gen. mgr. Global Intermodal Systems, 1990—. Mem. bd. dirs. Global Intermodal Systems, Inc., San Ramon, Calif. Presbyterian. Office: Global Intermodal Systems 11700 Wallisville Rd Houston TX 77013-3421 E-mail: lifft@gmodal.com.

IFFY, LESLIE, medical educator; b. Budapest, Hungary, May 17, 1925; came to U.S., 1969; s. Zoltan and Rozsa (Lantos) I.; m. Maureen B. Deeney. MD, U. Budapest, Hungary, 1949; MD (hon.), Semmelweis U., Budapest, 1993. Diplomate Am. Bd. Ob-Gyn. Resident, fellow Országos Testnevelési és Sportegészségügyi Intézet Hosp. Ministry of Health, Budapest, 1951-56; fellow U. Wash., Seattle, 1964; asst. prof. Temple U., Phila., 1969-70; assoc. prof. U. Ill., Chgo., 1971-72, Jefferson Med. Coll., Phila., 1972-73; prof. U. Medicine and Dentistry of N.J., Newark, 1974—; dir. obstetrics U. Hosp., Newark, 1974—. Contbr. over 190 articles to profl. jours. and chpts. to books; editor: Perinatology Case Studies, 1978, 85, Obstetrics and Perinatology, 1981 (in English and Spanish), Operative Perinatology, 1984 (in English, Spanish and Japanese), Operative Obstetrics, 2d edit., 1992. Recipient Dr. Robert Jardine Rsch. prize U. Glasgow, 1963, Ford Found. rsch. fellowship, Seattle, 1964, hon. fellowship Hungarian Obstet. Soc., 1986. Fellow Royal Coll. Surgeons (Can.); mem. Cen. Assn. Ob-Gyn. (life), Chgo. Gynecol. Soc., Am. Coll. Legal Medicine (bd. dirs. 1989-95), Royal Coll. Physicians (Edinburgh, Scotland, licentiate), Royal Faculty Physicians and Surgeons (Glasgow, Scotland, licentiate), Romanian Soc. Obstetricians and Gynecologists (hon.). Avocations: music, chess, literature. Home: PO Box 550 5 Robin Hood Rd Summit NJ 07901 Office: NJ Med Sch UMDNJ 150 Bergen St Newark NJ 07103 E-mail: iffylnj@aol.com.

IFTEKHARUDDIN, KHAN M. engineering educator, researcher; b. Rajshahi, Bangladesh, Dec. 25, 1966; s. Muhammad Azharuddin and Khaleda Khanom; m. Khondker T. Saeeda, Aug. 9, 1994. BS, Bangladesh Inst. Tech., Rajshahi, 1989; MS, U. Dayton, 1990—91, PhD, 1995. Sr. sys. engr. BDM Internat., Dayton, 1994—97; prin. rsch. engr. Timken Rsch., Canton, Ohio, 1997—98; asst. prof. N. D. State U., Fargo, 1998—2000, U. Memphis, 2000—. Summer rsch. faculty Air Force Rsch. Lab., Dayton, 2000, Dayton, 01. Editor: (jour.) Optical Engring., 1999, 2001, Optics and Laser Tech., 2000; author: (book chpt.) Optical Interconnection, 1997; contbr. papers to tech. jours. and confs. Recipient Best Paper award, 1998; grantee, Army Rsch. Office, 2000—02, Air Force Rsch. Lab., 2001, St. Jude Children's Hosp., 2001—02, ND EPSCoR, 1999—2000, NSF, 2001—03, Whitaker Found., 2000—03. Mem.: Am. Soc. of Engring. Edn., Internat. Soc. for Photo Instrument Engr. (mem. publ. com. 2002, conf. organizer 1998—), IEEE (sr.), Optical Soc. of Am. Office: U Memphis 206 Engring Sci Bldg Memphis TN 38152

IGALI, DANIEL (DANIEL IGALI BARALADEI), Olympic athlete; b. Eniwari, Nigeria, Feb. 3, 1975; arrived in Can., 1994; s. Maureen Matheny. Student in Mass Comm., Nigeria; student, Simon Fraser U. Named Nat. Wrestling Champion, Nigeria, 1990, African Wrestling Champion, Cairo, 1993, World Champion Wrestler, Ankara, Turkey, 1998, Athlete of Yr., Can., 1999, 2000; recipient Wrestling Gold medal, Olympics, 2000. Avocations: Kabaddi, watching wrestling movies, soccer, surfing the Internet. Office: 8876-140 St PO Box 16531 Surrey BC Canada V3W 2P5*

IGE, DAVID Y. state legislator; b. Jan. 15, 1957; m. Dawn Ige; children: Lauren, Amy, Matthew. BSEE, U. Hawaii, 1979, MBA in Decision Scis., 1985. Sr. adminstr. Hawaiian Telephone Co.; electronics engr., analyst Pacific Analyst Corp.; mem. Hawaii Ho. of Reps., Honolulu, 1986-93, Hawaii Senate, Dist. 17, Honolulu, 1994—; chair edn. and tech. com., mem. ways and means com. Hawaii Senate, Honolulu, mem. transp. and intergovtl. affairs com. Mem. Pearl City Cmty. Assn., Newtown Estates Cmty. Assn. Mem. IEEE. Democrat. Office: State Capitol 415 S Beretania St Honolulu HI 96813-2407*

IGER, ROBERT A. broadcast executive; b. N.Y.C., 1951; m. Willow Bay, Oct. 1995; children: Kate, Amanda, Max. Grad. magna cum laude, Ithaca Coll. Studio supr. ABC-TV, 1974—76; various pos. ABC-TV Sports, 1976—85; former v.p. program planning, development ABC Sports, 1985—87, v.p. program planning and acquisition, 1987—88; exec. v.p. ABC TV Network Group, 1988—89, pres., 1992—94, ABC Entertainment, 1989—92; exec. v.p.

Capital Cities/ABC Inc., N.Y.C., 1993—94, pres., COO, 1994—96; pres. ABC, Inc., N.Y.C., 1996—99; chmn. ABC Group, 1999—; pres. The Walt Disney Co., 2001. Trustee Ithaca Coll. Office: The Walt Disney Co 5005 Buena Vista St Burbank CA 91521-0001

IGGERS, GEORG GERSON, history educator; b. Hamburg, Germany, Dec. 7, 1926; came to U.S., 1938, naturalized, 1949; s. Alfred G. and Lizzie (Minden) I.; m. Wilma Abeles, Dec. 23, 1948; children: Jeremy, Daniel, Karl Jonathan. BA, U. Richmond, 1944, DHL, 2001; AM, U. Chgo., 1945, PhD, 1951; postgrad., New Sch. Social Rsch., 1945-46; doctorate (hon.), Philander Smith Coll., 2002. Instr. U. Akron, Ohio, 1948-50; assoc. prof. Philander Smith Coll., Little Rock, 1950-57; from assoc. prof. to prof. Dillard U., New Orleans, 1957-63; assoc. prof. Roosevelt U., Chgo., 1963-65; prof. history SUNY, Buffalo, 1965—, disting. prof., 1978-97, chmn., 1981-84, disting. prof. emeritus, 1997—. Mem. Conf. Group Ctrl. European History, vice chmn., 1989-90, chmn., 1990-91; vis. prof. U. Ark., Fayetteville, 1956-57, 64, U. Rochester, 1970-71, U. Leipzig, Germany, 1992; vis. assoc. prof. Tulane U., New Orleans, 1958-60, 63; vis. scholar Technische Hochschule Darmstadt, Germany, 1991, Forschungsschwerpunkt zeithistorische Studien, Potsdam, Germany, 1993; fellow Woodrow Wilson Ctr. Internat. Scholars, Washington, 1993 94; vis. prof. Aarhus (Denmark) U., 1998, Zentrum für Zeithistorische Forschung, Potsdam, Germany, 1998, U. New Eng. (Australia), 1999, Internat. Forschungszentrum Kulturwissenschaften, Vienna, 2000, U. Vienna, 2002. Author: The Cult of Authority, 1958, The German Conception of History, 1968, New Directions in European Historiography, 1975, Geschichtswissenschaft im 20 Jahrhundert, 1993, Historiography in the Twentieth Century, 1997; co-author (with Wilma Iggers) Zwei Seifen der Geschichte, 2002; editor: (with Harold T. Parker) International Handbook of Historical Studies, 1979, The Social History of Politics, 1986, (with James Powell) Leopold von Ranke and the Shaping of the Historical Discipline, 1990, Ein anderer historischer Blick Beispiele ostdeutscher Sozialgeschichte, 1991, Marxist Historiography in Transformation, 1991; co-editor Storia della Storiografia jour., Geschichtswissenschaft der DDR als Forschungsproblem, Historische Zeitschrift, Sonderband 27, 1998; mem. editl. bd. Zeitschrift für Geschichtswissenschaft, History and Theory. Bd. dirs., counselor Draft and Mil. Counseling Ctr., Buffalo, 1967-89; bd. dirs.Citizens Coun. Human Rels., Buffalo, 1965—; chmn. edn., exec. coms. NAACP, Little Rock, 1951-56, chmn. edn. com., New Orleans, 1957-63, bd. dirs, Buffalo, 1965—, chmn. edn. com., 1965-75, co-chmn. health com., 1979-85. Fellow Guggenheim Found., 1960-61, Rockefeller Found., 1961-62, NEH, 1971-72, 78-79, 85-86, Ctr. Interdisciplinary Rsch., Bielefeld, Fed. Republic Germany, 1986-87; hon. fellow Fulbright Commn. 1978-79, 85-86, 87; recipient Kittler award Technische Hochschule Darmstadt, 1988, Alexander von Humboldt Rsch. prize 1993. Mem. Internat. Commn. Historiography (v.p. 1980-95, pres. 1995-2000, exec. com. 2000—), Am. Hist. Assn., German Studies Assn., Acad. Scis. of German Dem. Republic (fgn. mem. 1990-92). Office: Dept History Park Hall SUNY Buffalo NY 14260-4130 E-mail: iggers@acsu.buffalo.edu.

IGLAUER, EDITH, writer, reporter; b. Cleve., Mar. 10, 1917; arrived in Can., 1976; d. Jay and Bertha G. (Good) I.; m. Philip Hamburger, Dec. 24, 1942 (div. 1966); children: Jay Philip Hamburger, Richard Shaw Hamburger; m. John Heywood Daly, Mar. 1, 1976 (dec. Feb. 1978). BA, Wellesley Coll., 1938; MS, Columbia U., 1939. Freelance writer, 1939—. Author: The New People, The Eskimo's Journey Into Our Time, 1966 (Outdoor Sci. Club award), Denison's Ice Road, 1975, 3d edit., 1992, Inuit Journey, 1979, revised edit., 2000, Seven Stones: A Portrait of Arthur Erickson, Architect, 1981, Fishing with John, 1988, 3d edit., 2000 (Shortlisted Gov. Gens. award), The Strangers Next Door, 1991; contbr. articles to newspapers and popular mags. Active Harbour Commn., Pender Harbour, B.C., 1993-95; bd. dirs. Grips, Sechelt Peninsula, 1996-98, Francis Point Marine Park Soc., 1998—, Haig-Brown Inst., 2003—. Geneva scholar Sch. Internat. Studies, 1937; recipient Woodrow Wilson Prize in modern politics Wellesley Coll., 1938, Cleve. Creative Achievement in Lit.award Womens City Club, 1983, Short-Listed, Gov. Gen's award for Non-Fiction, Can., 1988. Mem. Authors Guild, Writers Union Can., Cosmopolitan Club, N.Y., Cleve. Play House Club. Democrat. Avocations: swimming, travel, cooking, grandchildren. Home: PO Box 116 VON 1S0 Garden Bay BC Canada Office: The New Yorker Mag 4 Times Sq New York NY 10036-6561 Fax: 604-883-9322. E-mail: edaly@dccnet.com.

IGLEHART, DONALD LEE, engineering educator; b. Balt., May 11, 1933; s. Marion and Ruth (Billen) Iglehart; m. Sheralee Florence Hill, July 15, 1961; children: Kent Steven, Mark Stuart. BE in Physics, Cornell U., 1956; MS, Stanford U., 1959, PhD, 1961. Asst. prof., assoc. prof. Cornell U., Ithaca, NY, 1962—67; prof. Stanford U., Stanford, Calif., 1967—. Contbr. Lt. USN, 1956—58. Mem.: Inst. Ops. Rsch. and Mgmt. Scis. (John von Neumann Theory prize 2002), Nat. Acad. Engring. Avocations: tennis, piano. Home: 922 Talman Dr Stanford CA 94305 Office: Stanford Univ Stanford CA 94305

IGLEWICZ, BORIS, statistician, educator; b. Omsk, USSR, Oct. 11, 1939; came to U.S., 1952, naturalized, 1959; s. Solomon and Faiga (Brucker) I.; m. Raja Brody, May 24, 1973; children— David, Alana. BS, Wayne State U., 1962; MA, 1963; PhD, Va. Poly. Inst., 1967. Instr. math. Mich. Tech. U., 1963-64; asst. prof. stats. Case Western Res. U., 1967-69; assoc. prof. stats. Temple U., 1969-74, prof., 1974—, dir. Ph.D. program in stats., 1970-76, chmn. dept., 1978-82, dir. biostats. group, 1992-93, dir. biostats. rsch. ctr., 1993—. V.p., dir. Meco Metals Corp., 1974; vis. prof. Harvard U., 1984-85 Author: (with J. Stoyle) An Introduction to Mathematical Reasoning, 1973, (with D.C. Hoaglin) How to Detect and Handle Outliers, 1993; contbr. articles to profl. jours., chpts. to books. NIH fellow, 1964-67; advanced rsch. fellow Harvard U., 1978; recipient Musser Leadership award, 2001, Don Owen award 2003. Fellow: Am. Statis Assn. (pres. Phila. chpt. 1981—83, W.J. Youden award 2001), Royal Statis. Soc.; mem.: Internat. Stats. Inst., Am. Soc. Quality (sr.), Inst. Math. Stats., Biometric Soc., Beta Gamma Sigma, Pi Mu Epsilon, Sigma Xi. Home: 1912 Rolling Ln Cherry Hill NJ 08003-3328 Office: Temple U 1810 N 13th St Dept Stats Philadelphia PA 19122

IGNACIO, REINERE JOHN DY, research scientist; b. Manila, May 26, 1972; s. Reynaldo Mendoza and Lorna Dy I. BS, U. Ill., 1998. Instr. Naval Med. Ctr., Oakland, Calif., 1994-95; sr. rsch. assoc. Pierce Milw., 1998—. Mem. Nat. Sci. Adv. Coun. Alverno Coll., Milw., 2000—. Vol. tchr. Cath. East Elem. Sch., Milw., 2000. With USN, 1991-95. Mem. AAAS, Protein Soc., Soc. Biomolecular Screening. Home: 1533 E Royall Pl 10 Milwaukee WI 53202 Office: Pierce Milw 2202 N Bartlett Ave Milwaukee WI 53202 Fax: 414-227-3759. E-mail: ray.ignacio@perbio.com.

IGNAGNI, JOSEPH ANTHONY, humanities educator, associate dean; b. Royal Oak, Mich., May 13, 1959; s. Antonio and Vanna Ignagni; m. Darlene Ignagni, Aug. 21, 1982; 1 child, Chelsea. BS, Mich. State U., 1981; MS, Purdue U., 1984; MA, Mich. State U., 1986, PhD, 1990. Prof. U. Tex., Arlington, 1989—, assoc. dean Coll. Liberal Arts, 1998—2001. Contbr. articles to profl. jours. including Rev. Politics, Am. Politics Quar., Am. Jour. Polit. Sci., Polit. Rsch. Quar., among others. Mem. Am. Polit. Sci. Assn., Am. Jud. Soc., Midwest Polit. Sci. Assn., Western Polit. Sci. Assn., Southwestern Polit. Sci. Assn., Acad. Disting. Tchrs., Phi Alpha Delta, Phi Kappa Phi. Office: U Tex Arlington Dept Polit Sci Box 19539 Arlington TX 76019

IGNARRO, LOUIS J. pharmacology educator; b. Bklyn., May 31, 1941; BA in Pharmacy, Columbia U., 1962; PhD in Pharmacology, U. Minn., 1966. Prof. dept. molecular and med. pharmacology UCLA Sch. Medicine, 1985—; prof. of pharmacology Tulane Univ. School of Med., 1979—85; hon. Ph.D. Univ. of Madrid, Lund, Gent, and North Carolina. Contbr. articles to profl. jours. Recipient Rsch. Career Devel. award, USPHS, 1975—80, Nobel prize in Medicine, 1998, Merck Research Award, 1974; fellow postdoctoral, NIH, 1966—68. Mem.: NAS, Alpha Omega Alpha (hon.). Achievements include research in biochemical, physiological, and pathophysioilogical roles of nitric oxide and cyclic GMP in mammalian cell function; the transcriptional, translational and catalytic regulation of constitutive and inducible nitric oxide synthases; the role of other biochemical pathways in the regulation of biosynthesis and metabolism of nitric oxide; the biochemical and chemical mechanisms by which nitric oxide elicits cytotoxic effects on invading target cells and microorganisms; the role of nitric oxide as a neurotransmitter in non-adrenergic non-cholinergic neurons innervating various issues. Office: UCLA Sch Medicine Dept Molecular & Med Pharmacology 23-315 Chs 10833 Leconte Ave Los Angeles CA 90095-1735*

IGNATIEV, ALEX, physics researcher; b. Wehingen, Germany, Feb. 14, 1945; U.S. citizen; married; two children. BS, U. Wis., 1966; PhD in Material Sci., Cornell U., 1972. Postdoctoral fellow material sci. SUNY, Stony Brook, 1971-73; from asst. prof. to assoc. prof. physics and chemistry U. Houston, 1974-83, prof. physics and chemistry, 1983—; assoc. dir. Magnetic Info Rsch. Lab., 1984-89. Mem. energy lab. U. Houston, 1975—; lectr. physics Aarhus U., Denmark, 1977-78; Fulbright sr. scholar, 1983; assoc. dir. Space Vacuum Epitaxy Ctr., 1986-88, dir. 1988—; task leader Tex. Ctr. for Superconductivity, 1987—; dir. Tex. Ctr. superconductivity and advanced materials, 2002-. Assoc. editor Vacuum, Space Forum, Research Trends; contbr. numerous articles to profl. jours. Mem. AIAA, AAAS, ASME, IEEE, SPIE, Internat. Acad. Astronautics, Am. Phys. Soc., Am. Vacuum Soc., Am. Chem. Soc., Internat. Solar Energy Soc, The Materials Rsch. Soc., Sigma Xi. E-mail: ignatiev@uh.edu.

IGNATONIS, SANDRA CAROLE AUTRY, special education educator; b. Dixon Mills, Ala., June 6, 1942; d. Charles Franklin Autry; m. Algis Jerome Ignatonis, June 15, 1968; children: Audra Carole, David Jerome. BA, Samford U., 1964; cert. in Gifted Edn., Kennesaw State U., 1989. Cert. tchr., Ga. Tchr. Jefferson County Bd. Edn., Birmingham, Ala., 1964, Huntsville (Ala.) Bd. Edn., 1964-71, Epiphany Cath. Sch., Miami, Fla., 1981, Cobb County Bd. Edn., Marietta, Ga., 1982, Bartow County Bd. Edn., Cartersville, Ga., 1990-92, Sequoria Group, Inc., Roswell, Ga., 1996; with Atlanta real estate divsn. Regions Bank, Atlanta, 1997—. Mem. Sch. Self-Governance Com., Emerson, Ga., 1990-91, Soccer Adv. Bd., Marietta, 1985-89; judge, mem. Social Sci. Fair Competitions, Huntsville, 1964-71. Team mom Metro N. Youth Soccer Assn., Marietta, 1991-92; block parent Somerset Subdivision, Marietta, 1982-86, block capt., 1998-99; polit. chmn. Student Nat. Edn. Assn., Samford U., Birmingham, Ala., 1963-64; bd. dirs. Somerset Homeowners Assn., 1998-99. Recipient grant Samford U. Faculty, 1963. Mem. Ga. Supporters of Gifted, Profl. Assn. Ga. Educators. Republican. Roman Catholic. Avocations: tennis, bowling, gardening, needle work, reading. Office: Regions Bank 400 Embassy Row 6600 Peachtree Dunwoody Rd NE Atlanta GA 30328-1649

IGNAZITO, MADELINE DOROTHY, music educator, composer; b. Long Branch, N.J., Mar. 12; d. Henry George Jr. and Katherine (Manuel) Pigage; m. Martin Donald Ignazito, Feb. 15, 1969; children: Karen Ignazito-Cripps, Susan Ignazito-Wilhelm. BMus, Westminster Coll., 1962; MMus, U. Hartford, 1966. Nat. cert. tchr. music in piano, compostion and theory. Tutor Hartt Coll., West Hartford, Conn., 1964-66; music tchr. Hazlet (N.J.) Twp., 1966-69, Champaign, Ill., 1970-81, Charleston, Ill., 1981—; keyboard, aural theory instr. Lakeland Coll., Mattoon, Ill., 1985 88, music tchr., 1992-95. Composer Variations and Fugue, 1979 (Mu Phi Epsilon nat. 1st place), duet for violins and flute, 1987, Alchemies, 1999. Recipient Achievement award Mu Phi Epsilon, 1962, Composer's award Hartt Coll. Alumnae, 1965. Mem. Ill. State Music Tchrs. Assn. (state theory syllabus chair 1988-94), Coles County Art Coun. (pres., music dir. 1986-89), Charles Area Music Tchrs. Assn. (pres., co-founder 1986-99), Champaign Urbana Music Tchrs. Assn. (pres., co-chair 1998-2000), Zonta (fin. v.p. 1996-97, pres.-elect 1999-2000 pres 2001-2003, treas. 2003—, One award 1999), Tues. Morning Club (pres. 1997-98), Mu Phi Epsilon. Avocations: math puzzles, gardening, emboidery, swimming, walking. Home: 13961 E County Road 620N Charleston IL 61920-7831

IGNERI, DAVID SEBASTIAN, elementary education educator, lifeguard; b. Bklyn., July 4, 1944; s. Marco and Margaret (Marzullo) I.; m. Nancy Reilly Goldberg, Feb. 9, 1969 (div. Nov. 1974); 1 child, Lisa Anne; m. Elisabeth Kenyatta Strachan, Aug. 4, 1990; 1 child, Giovanni. BS in Edn., Brockport State U., 1966; MS in Edn., Long Island U., 1969, MA in History, 1972; profl. cert. in African studies, St. John's U., 1976; PhD in History, Union Inst., 1992; MALS in Am. Studies, Stony Brook U., 1997. Cert. elem. tchr. K-6, social studies tchr. 7-12, N.Y. Elem. tchr. Centereach (N.Y.) Pub. Schs., 1967-68, Brentwood (N.Y.) Pub. Schs., 1968-70, Patchogue Medford (N.Y.) Pub. Schs., 1970-98. Lectr. on historic topics, N.Y., 1988—; adj. prof. history Dowling Coll., Oakdale, N.Y., 1999-2001, L.I. Univ., 2002-2003. From lifeguard to chief lifeguard The Town of Brookhaven, N.Y., 1961-94. Recipient Commendation letters Town of Brookhaven, 1988, 93, longevity awards Brookhaven Recreation Dept., 1985, 90. Roman Catholic. Avocations: college prof. and profl. historian, physical conditioning. Home: 23 E 6th St Patchogue NY 11772-2315 E-mail. docig1@aol.com.

IGNOFFO, CARLO MICHAEL, insect pathologist-virologist; b. Chicago Heights, Ill., Aug. 24, 1928; s. Joseph and Lucy (Sardo) I.; m. Florence F. Mielcarek, Sept. 3, 1949. BS, No. Ill. U., 1950; MS, U. Minn., 1954, PhD, 1957. Asst. prof. Iowa Wesleyan Coll., Mt. Pleasant, 1957-59; insect pathologist U.S. Dept. Agr., Brownsville, Tex., 1959-65; dir. entomology Internat. Minerals & Chems. Corp., Wasco, Calif. and Libertyville, Ill., 1965-71; lab. dir. U.S. Dept. Agr., Columbia, Mo., 1971-91; prof. dept. entomology U. Mo., 1974—. Served with Chem. Corps U.S. Army, 1954-56. Mem. AAAS, Internat. Orgn. Biol. Control (pres. 1974), Am. Inst. Biol. Scis., Soc. Invertebrate Pathology (editorial bd. 1965-68, assoc. editor 1992—, treas. 1968-70), Entomol. Soc. Am. Achievements include isolating, commercializing 1st viral pesticide; patentee in field. Office: Research Park 1503 S Providence Rd Columbia MO 65203-3535 E-mail: ignoffoc@missouri.edu.

IGO, DONALD JAMES, economist; b. Plymouth, Mass., June 28, 1926; s. James Edward and Mary Lucy (Cavicchioli) I.; m. Doris Therese Grandmont, Oct. 6, 1951; children: Susan Draper, James, Joseph, Karen Kenton. AB in Econs. cum laude, Harvard U., 1950; MA in Econs., Am. U., 1958. Economist, cost engr. RAND Corp., Bethesda, Md., 1961-62; mem. tech. stafff Rsch. Analysis Corp., McLean, Va., 1962-68; economist Fed. R.R. Adminstrn., Washington, 1968-70; various positions U.S. Dept. Transp., Washington, 1970-82, asst. for energy policy, 1982—98; ret., 1998. Contbr. chpts. to profl. publs. With USN, 1946-48. Mem. Am. Econ. Assn., Learning in Retirement Inst. at George Mason U., Nat. Economists Club. Home: 6209 Cloud Dr Springfield VA 22150-1019 E-mail: don628@aol.com.

IGO, GEORGE JEROME, physics educator; b. Greeley, Colo., Sept. 2, 1925; s. Henry J. and Ida J. (Danielsen) I.; m. Nancy Tebow, May 12, 1953; children: Saffron, Peter Alexander. AB, Harvard Coll., 1949; MS, U. Calif., Berkeley, 1951, Phd, 1953. Postdoctoral Yale Univ., 1954, Brook Haven Nat. Lab., Upton, N.Y., 1955-57; instr. Stanford Univ., Palo Alto, Calif., 1957-59; guest prof. Univ. Heidelberg, Germany, 1960; staff mem. Lawrence Berkeley (Calif.) Lab., 1961-66, Los Alamos (N.Mex.) Nat. Lab., 1966-68; prof. UCLA, 1969—. With U.S. Army, 1944-46. Recipient Fulbright Travel award, 1960, Saclay, France, 1970, Sr. Scientist award Alexander von Humboldt Found., 1991, 95. Fellow Am. Phys. Soc. Office: UCLA Dept Physics 405 Hilgard Ave Los Angeles CA 90095-9000

IGOU, RAYMOND ALVIN, JR., orthopedic surgeon; b. Esterville, Iowa, Dec. 2, 1933; s. Raymond Alvin Sr. and Pearl Mildred (Christiansen) I.; m. Barbara Igou, Jan. 17, 1958 (div. June 10, 1980); children: Raymond Alvin III, Yvette Sharon; m. Jane Ann Leboda, Jan. 4, 1991 (wid. Apr. 2003). BS, N.Mex. State U., 1955; MD, Boston U., 1965. Diplomate Am. Bd. Orthopedic Surgery; lic. mortgage broker, Fla. Surg. internship Univ. Hosp., Boston, 1965-66; orthopedic resident Boston U. Sch. of Medicine, 1971-75; owner, operator Grant Buie Med. Ctr., Hillsboro, Tex., 1966-71; assoc. dir. dept. orthop. surgery, chief scoliosis clinic Boston City Hosp., 1975—, dir. rehab. svcs. City of Boston dept. health and hosps., 1975-80; asst. prof. ortho surg. Boston U. Sch. Medicine, 1979; med. dir. dept. rehab. svcs. New Eng. Meml. Hosp., Stoneham, Mass., 1979-95, chief orthopedic surgery, trustee, 1987—, chief of staff, 1989-90; orthopedic surgeon in pvt. practice, Stoneham, 1975—; chmn. dept. surgery Boston Regional Med. Ctr. (formerly New Eng. Meml. Hosp.), Stoneham, 1995. Sr. staff mem. Boston City Hosp., Univ. Hosp.; gen. ptnr. New Eng. MRI, L.P., 1989—; pres. Med Ptnrs. Ltd., 1988—; mem. Coun.-Boston Regional Med. Ctr., 1987, Gov.'s Adv. Coun. Indsl. Accidents, 1995; mng. gen. ptnr. WCPR Hartford Data Dispatch Ptnrs. Host talk show WALE, Providence, 1995-96; contbr. articles to profl. jours. Mem. Zoning and Planning Commn., Hillsboro, Tex., 1969-71; city councilman, Hillsboro, 1967-71; mem. Indsl. Found., Hillsboro, 1969-71. Capt. U.S. Army, 1955-60. Fellow Am. Acad. Orthopedic Surgeons; mem. Mass. Med. Soc., Boston Orthopedic Club, Freemasons, York Rites, Scottish Rites, Shriners. Republican. Avocations: flying, coin collecting. Home: 611 Revere Beach Blvd Revere MA 02151-4709 Office: Ortho Surgery and Sports Medicine Inc Ste 209 3 Woodland Rd Stoneham MA 02180-1713

IGUSA, JUN-ICHI, mathematician, educator; b. Japan, Jan. 30, 1924; came to U.S., 1953; s. Shiro and Rui (Fukushima) I.; m. Yoshie Yamamoto, Oct. 7, 1948; children— Kiyoshi, Takeru, Mitsuru. MA, Tokyo Imperial U., 1945; PhD, Kyoto (Japan) U., 1953. Assoc. prof. Kyoto (Japan) U., 1949-53; research assoc. Harvard U., 1953-55; mem. faculty Johns Hopkins, 1955—, prof. math., 1961-93, prof. emeritus, 1993—, J.J. Sylvester chair, 1986-93. Chmn. bd. dirs. Japan-U.S. Math. Inst. Johns Hopkins U., 1987-93. Author: Theta Functions, 1972, Forms of Higher Degree, 1978, Local Zeta Functions, 2000; editor-in-chief: Am. Jour. Math., 1978-93. Mem. Math. Soc. Japan, Am. Math. Soc., Phi Beta Kappa. Home: 14209 Greencroft Ln Hunt Valley MD 21030-1111

IGWE, GODWIN JOSEPH, chemical engineer; b. Omoku, Nigeria, Jan. 1, 1952; came to U.S., 1988, naturalized citizen, 1998; s. Christianah (Ellah) I.; m. Rose C. Okoroego, Jan. 7, 1971; children: Maureen, Chukwudi, Chukwuemeka. BSChemE, U. Kiel, 1977; MPhil, U. Leeds, U.K., 1981; PhD, U. Bradford, Eng., 1983. Registered profl. engr., Tex. Dir. Flopetrol (Schlumberger) Nigeria Ltd., Lagos, Nigeria, 1985-87; dir./mem. governing coun. Rivers State Govt. Sch. of Basic Studies, Port Harcourt, Nigeria, 1987-88; prof. chem. engring. Prairie View (Tex.) A & M U., Prairie View, 1989-91; sr. staff engr. Conoco Inc., Ponca City, Okla., 1992-93; sr. rsch. engr. DuPont Ctrl. R&D, Wilmington, Del., 1993—2002. Cons. Core Labs. Integrated Environ. Svcs., Western Atlas Corp., Houston, 1991; prof. chem. engring. U. Benin, Nigeria, 1990; vis. prof. chem. engring. Tex. A&M Dept. Chem. Engring., College Station, Tex., 1988-89; sr. lectr. Dept. of Chem. and Petrochem. Engring., Rivers State U. of Sci. and Tech., Port Harcourt, 1984-88; chem. engr. Schleicher & Schull, GmbH Filter Mfrs., Dassel, Germany, 1976; world bank cons., 1989—. Author: Needle Felts in Gas and Dust Filtration, Surface Structure of Needle-felted Gas Filters: Microscopical Examination Techniques, Powder Technology and Multiphase Systems; contbr. articles to profl. jours. including Jour. of Magyar Textiltechnika, Jour. of Indsl. Engring. Chemistry Rsch., Jour. of Chem. Engring. and Tech., Jour. of the Textile Inst., Indian Jour. of Tech., others. Robert S. McNamara fellowship World Bank, 1988, Alexander von Humboldt fellowship, 1992. Mem. AIChE (bd. dirs. environ. divsn. 1997-2000, dir. fuel and petrochem. divsn. 2002-2005), Soc. of Petroleum Engrs., Water Environ. Fedn., The Metal Soc., Am. Filt. and Sep. Soc. (editl. bd.), Internat. Soc. African Scientists (v.p.). Achievements include patents on organic destruction of contaminants in soil and polyamide, polyurethane micro blend and process; research on surface area measurement and gas permeametry at sub-atmospheric pressures, influence of some production parameters on the characteristics of needle felts for air filtration. Home: 16 Anderson Ln Newark DE 19711-3064 Office Fax: 302-234-4548. E-mail: goddyigwe@aol.com.

IHARA, LES, JR., state legislator; b. Honolulu, Apr. 19, 1951; BA in Liberal Studies, U. Hawaii. Comms. dir. cmty. devel. orgn.; mem. Hawaii Ho. of Reps., 1986-94, Hawaii Senate, Dist. 9, 1994—; mem. judiciary com., econ. devel. com. Hawaii Senate; mem. labor com. Hawaii State Senate. Chmn. Oahu Dem. Party, 1982-84, 90-94; del. Hawaii State Constl. Conv., 1978; mem. Ala Wai Watershed Assn., Waikiki Residents Assn. Mem. Kaimuki Bus. and Profl. Assn., Kapahulu Bus. Assn., Kaimuki Lions Club. Democrat. Office: Hawaii State Capitol 415 S Beretania St Rm 217 Honolulu HI 96813-2407

IHARA, MICHIO, sculptor; b. Paris, Nov. 17, 1928; naturalized, U.S., 2001; s. Usaburo and Shigeko (Shinkai) I.; m. Doreen Joyce Kaplan, July 7, 1966; 1 child, Akeo. BFA, Tokyo U. Fine Arts, 1953. Fulbright fellow MIT, 1961-62, rsch. assoc., 1962-64; instr. Musashino U. Fine Arts, Tokyo, 1966-69. One-man shows Kanegis Gallery, Boston, 1964, Tokyo Gallery, 1970, Staempfli Gallery, N.Y.C., 1977, 80, 84; numerous group shows in Japan and U.S., 1957-74; important works include marble mural Chuo-koron Pub. Co, Tokyo, 1957; copper relief 275 Wyman St. Office Bldg, Waltham, Mass., 1963; altar canopy Josenji Temple, Tokyo, 1965; metal screen Imperial Theatre, Tokyo, 1966; relief Internat. Christian U, Tokyo, 1967, Fuji Film Co. Bldg, Tokyo, 1969; sculpture Internat. Sculptors Symposium, Osaka, 1970, Wellesley (Mass.) Office Park, 1973, Fitchburg (Mass.) Pub. Library; civic sculpture, Auckland, N.Z., 1977, Constellation Place, Balt., 1978; metal screen Rockefeller Center, N.Y.C., 1978, Neiman-Marcus, Beverly Hills, Calif., New World Hotel, Hong Kong, Pavilion Hotel, Singapore; wall sculpture S.E. Bank, Miami, 1983; suspended sculptures Marriott Marquis Hotel, N.Y.C., 1985, wall sculpture Harvard U., 1985, 89, wind sculpture, Tallahassee City Hall, 1989, tower sculpture Tokyo City Hall, 1991, suspended sculptures AT&T Plaza, Chgo., 1991, Colorado Springs Airport, 1994, Wall Sculpture Ikenoue Ch., Tokyo, 1995, suspended sculpture Lorillard Headquarters, N.C., 1997, interactive sculpture Cyclelight, Boston 1st Night, 1993, suspended sculpture New Eng. Med. Ctr. Hosp., Boston, 2000, sculptures Yokohama Crematorium, Japan, 2002, suspended sculpture Crowne Plz. Hotel, N.Y., 2002, Suspended Sculpture 101 Constitution Ave. Bldg., Washington, D.C., 2003. Trustee The Artists Found. Mass. JDR 3d Fund grantee, 1970-71; recipient award Mass. Council Arts and Humanities, 1974, Nat. Inst. Arts and Letters/Am. Acad. Arts and Letters award in art, 1973, award Fgn. Min. of Japanese Govt., 1999; Graham Found. fellow, 1963-64; MIT Center for Advanced Visual Studies fellow, 1970-73 Mem. Japan Artists Assn. Address: 63 Wood St Concord MA 01742-2225 E-mail: michio.ihara@sprintmail.com.

IHDE, DON, philosophy educator, university administrator; b. Hope, Kans., Jan. 14, 1934; s. Melvin Millard and Nell Pearl (Reikeman) I.; m. Carolyn W. Ihde (div.); children: Leslie Ann, Lisa Ihde-Costa, Eric Martin; m. Linda Einhorn, Apr. 4, 1985; 1 child, Mark Hillel. BA, U. Kans., 1956; MDiv, Andover Newton Theol. Sem., 1959; PhD, Boston U., 1964; prof. honoraria, El Rosario U., Bogota, Columbia, 1982. Asst. prof. So. Ill. U., Carbondale, 1964-67, assoc. prof., 1968-69, SUNY, Stony Brook, 1969-70, prof., 1971-86, dean humanities and fine arts, 1985-90, leading prof., 1986—, disting. prof., 1997—. Author: Hermeneutic Phenomenology, 1971, Sense and Significance, 1973, Listening and Voice, 1976, Experimental Phenomenology, 1977, Technics and Praxis: A Philosophy of Technology, 1979, Existential Technics, 1983, Conequences of Phenomenology, 1986, Technology and the Life World, 1990, Instrumental Realism, 1991, Philosophy of Technology, 1993, Postphenomenology, 1993, Expanding Hermeneutics, 1998, Bodies in Technology, 2001; editor: The Conflict of Interpretations (Paul Ricouer); (with Richard M. Zaner) Phenomenology and Existentialism, 1973, Selected Studies in Phenomenology and Existential Philosophy, vol. IV, 1974, Interdisciplinary Phenomenology, vol. VI, 1977; (with Hugh J. Silverman) Selected Studies in Phenomenology and Existential Philosophy, vols. IX, XI, 1985, (with Evan Selinger) Chasing Technoscience, 2003; mem. editorial bd. Ind. U. Press, Northwestern U. Press. Recipient Jr. award So. Soc. for Philosophy and Psychology, 1966; summer rsch. fellow So. Ill. U., 1966, 67, 68, 69; Fulbright rsch. fellow U. Paris, 1967-68, sr. fellow NEH, 1972, vis. rsch. fellow Australian Nat. U., 1985, vis. scholar U. Sydney, 1991; grantee SUNY, Stony Brook, 1970, NSF, 1981. Mem. AAAS, Am. Philos. Assn. (mem. program com. 1976, 88, nominating com. 1981-83), Am. Psychol. Assn. (mem. sect. D), Heidegger Conf., Husserl Circle, Merleau-Ponty Circle, Nat. Assn. Sci., Tech. and Soc., Soc. Phenomenology and Existential Philosophy (exec. co-dir. 1972-75, 81-84), Soc. Philosophy and Tech. (bd. dirs. 1983-86, editor Ind. series), Phi Beta Kappa. Office: SUNY Dept Philosophy Stony Brook NY 11794-0001

IHDE, MARY KATHERINE, retired mathematics educator; b. St. Louis, Jan. 19, 1942; d. Harold Orville and Katharine Marie Nanninga; m. Daniel Carlyle Ihde, Dec. 22, 1968; children: Steven Carlyle, Douglas Harold. BA in Math., Northwestern U., 1964; MS in Math. Edn., Stanford U., 1968. Cert. tchr., N.Y., Calif., Md. Tchr. math. Shawnee Mission (Kans.) H.S. Dist., 1964-67; math. specialist Columbia Grammar and Prep. Sch., N.Y.C., 1969-72; tchr. math. Georgetown Visitation Prep. Sch., Washington, 1981-84; lectr. math. Mt. Vernon Coll., Washington, 1984-85; tchr. math. Nat. Cathedral Sch. for Girls, Washington, 1985-93, chmn. dept., 1989-92; inst. math. Maryville U., St. Louis, 1994-95, Webster U., St. Louis, 1994-95; tchr. math., curriculum coord. Whitfield Sch., St. Louis, 1995-96; math. curriculum cons., 1996—2002; ret., 2002. Recipient 2nd place state level competition award Mathcounts, 1992, 4th place, 1993; fellow Shell Oil Corp., 1967-68. Mem. Nat. Coun. Tchrs. Math., Pi Lambda Theta. Address: 10805 Chicobush Dr NW Albuquerque NM 87114-5550

IHEANACHO, VITALIS A, education educator, researcher; b. Lagos, Nigeria, Jan. 4, 1961; s. Innocent E and Innocnet A Iheanacho; m. Adaku Agwawuma Ahaotu, Jan. 13, 2003. PhD, U. of North Tex., 1985—93. Asst. prof. Voorhees Coll., Denmark, SC, 1996—2001; assoc. prof. Alcorn State U., Miss., 2001—.

Asst. prof. S.C. State U., Orangeburg, 2000—01. Prelaw adviser Alcorn State U., 2001—03. Mem.: Am. Polit. Sci. Assn. Roman Catholic. Avocations: reading, travel, jogging. Office: Alcorn State U 1000 Alcorn Dr Alcorn State MS 39182 E-mail: victory102@hotmail.com.

IHLANFELDT, WILLIAM, investment company executive, consultant; b. Belleville, Ill., Dec. 12, 1936; s. Raymond William and Olivia Anna (Boycourt) I.; m. D. Jeannine Huguelet, May 7, 1978; children: Troy, Kimberly, Holly. BS, Ill. Wesleyan U., 1959, LLD, 1980; MA, Northwestern U., 1963, PhD, 1970. Adminstr. Monticello Coll., Godfrey, Ill., 1959-60; tchr., coach Rich Twp. H.S., Park Forest, Olympia Fields, Ill., 1960-64; dir. fin. aid Northwestern U., Evanston, Ill., 1964-67, dean admission and fin. aid, 1973-78, v.p. instnl. rels., 1978-96; mng. dir. Hartline Investment Corp., Chgo., 1997—. Chmn. pub. policy Consortium Financing Higher Edn., Cambridge, Mass., 1979-83; chmn. Fedn. Ill. Ind. Colls. and Univs., Springfield, 1981-83; chmn. Fedn. Com. on State Funding, 1993-95; Student Loan Mktg. Assn., Washington, 1975-95, CyberMark, 1995-96, Constrn. Loan Assn., 1995-98; cons. in field. Author: Achieving Optimal Enrollments and Tuition Revenues, 1980; contbr. chpts. to books, articles to profl. publs. Founder, Northwestern U. Chgo. Action Project, Evanston, 1966; pres., CEO Northwestern U./Evanston Rsch. Park, 1986-96; co-founder Ill. Ind. Higher Edn. Loan Authority, Northbrook, 1981; founder Ill. Rsch. Park Authority, 1986. Wieboldt Found. grantee, 1966, 67, 68. Mem. Indian Hill Club (Winnetka, Ill.), Gainey Ranch Golf Club, Phi Delta Kappa. Avocations: tennis, golf, skiing. E-mail: wihlanfeldt@cox.net.

IHNAT, MICHAEL ANTHONY, administrative assistant; b. Balt., Md., Dec. 23, 1960; s. Gerard Joseph and Mary Elizabeth Ihnat; m. Milagros deLeon, Oct. 7, 1989; children: Robert Joseph, Michelle Sue. Asst. casting dir. Phillmar Casting, Winter Park, Fla., 1996—97; temp. adminstrv. asst. Staffing Solutions, Orlando, Fla., 1997—2000; adminstrv. asst. Freeman Decorating Co., Orlando, Fla., 2000—. Actor Clarissa Explains it All, Nickelodeon; nat. spokesperson s Omaha Steaks, Home Shopping Network; former radio disc jockey; musician. Co-author (with M. Ihnat): The Performers International Guidebook, 2000. Staff sgt. USAF, 1980—87. Decorated Good Conduct Medal with one bronze oak leaf cluster USAF, Meritorious Svc. award. Mem.: Actors Aritst Committed to Succeed (exec. v.p. 2001—02). Avocations: acting, writing, archery, camping, martial arts. Office: The Performers International Guidebook PO Box 771271 Orlando FL 32877-1271 Home Fax: 407-313-5894; Office Fax: 407-313-5894. Personal E-mail: mmihnat@msn.com. E-mail: mmihnat@msn.com.

IHRIE, ROBERT, oil, gas and real estate company executive; b. Phila., Jan. 4, 1925; s. Theodore Richard and Ella Martha (Anderson) I.; m. Dorothy Myrtle Waltz, July 8, 1944 (div. 1983); children: Robert Jr., Richard William, David Wayne, Nancy Ellen; m. Nancy Jean Joseph, June 8, 1984 BS, valedictorian, Ursinus Coll., 1943; MBA with high distinction, Harvard U., 1947. From process engr., econ. analyst, foreman, head tng. dept. to head bus. analysis dept. Esso Standard Oil Co., Baton Rouge, 1947-59; head demand and supply coord. and planning dept. Exxon Corp., N.Y.C., 1959-62; asst. dep. adminstr. AID, asst. sec. of state Dept. State, Washington, 1962-64; v.p. Lippincott and Margulies, Inc., N.Y.C., 1965-68; sr. v.p. Am. Trading and Prodn. Corp., Balt., 1968—, also bd. dirs. Bd. dirs. Am. Trading Real Estate Properties, Balt. With U.S. Army, 1943-46. Baker scholar Harvard Grad. Sch. Bus., 1947; recipient Presdl. Citation. Mem. Am. Contract Bridge League (life master 1977). Presbyterian. Avocations: roller dance skating, coaching softball, theater, travel. Home: 212 E Ridgely Rd Lutherville Timonium MD 21093-5239 Office: Am Trading & Prodn Corp PO Box 238 Baltimore MD 21203-0238

IHRIG, JUDSON LA MOURE, chemist; b. Santa Maria, Calif., Nov. 5, 1925; s. Harry Karl and Luella (LaMoure) I.; m. Gwendolyn Adele Montz, July 22, 1950; children— Kristin, Neil Marshall. BS, Haverford Coll., 1949; MA, Princeton U., 1951, PhD, 1952. Asst. prof. chemistry U. Hawaii, 1952-58, assoc. prof., 1958-72, prof., 1972-94, dir. honors program, 1958-64, 87-95, dir. liberal studies program, 1973-79, chmn. chemistry dept., 1981-86; prof. emeritus, 1994—. Cons. chemistry local firms. Author publs. in field. Served with AUS, 1945-46. Mem. Am. Chem. Soc., Phi Beta Kappa, Sigma Xi. Home: 386 Wailupe Cir Honolulu HI 96821-1525 Office: U Hawaii 2545 The Mall Honolulu HI 96822-2233

IIDA, SHUICHI, physicist, educator; b. Kobe, Hyogo-Ken, Japan, Jan. 30, 1926; s. Shunzoh and Sono (Ueda) Iida; m. Kyoko Matsuoka, Apr. 29, 1955; children: Mariko Takahara, Junko Kose. BS in Physics, U. Tokyo, 1947, PhD in Physics, 1958. Asst. prof. U. Tokyo, 1952-58, assoc. prof., 1958-68, prof., 1968-86, prof. emeritus, 1986; prof. Teikyo U., Sagamiko, Kanagawa, Japan, 1988-89, Utsunomiya, Japan, 1989-96. Vis. prof. AT&T Bell Labs., Murray Hill, NJ, 1961—63. Contbr. articles to profl. jours. Mem.: Japan Inst. Metals, Magnetics Soc. Japan, N.Y. Acad. Scis., Japan Soc. Powder and Powder Metallurgy, Physics Soc. Japan, Magnetics Soc. of IEEE, Am. Physics Soc. Achievements include research in ferrites; grand unifying frame for physics; electromagnetism; joint-use of MKSP and SI unit systems; correct representation for electromagnetic momenta; solution of Poincaré paradox; transient energy principle; proof for perfect diamagnetism of perfect conductors; essential q-number theory in biophysics; frontier notion principle; wave particle dualism; EPR problem; cold fusion; livelex f3 structure or filamentary current loops for c-number structure of lepton and hadron particles; electromagnetic origin of particle masses; trefoiled knot structure for proton; electromagnetic origin of weak and strong interactions; parasiton state pion in nuclei; contraparticles for neutrinos and pions; Iida diagram for parity violation problems; chipped photon mechanism for redshifts and denial of big-bang cosmology; finding of Iida metric with denial of black hole having surpassed Schwarzschild metric with Einstein equation; Iida structure for electronic order of magnetite; symmetric location of proton for hydrogen bond of ice; proposal for ECTJ mechanism for flagellar motor and strict proof for unified unrestricted Larmor diamagnetism and cyclotron motion; discovery of third fire and explosive proton-electron annihilation in type II supernovae. Home and Office: 4-23-11 Funabashi Setagaya-ku Tokyo 156-0055 Japan

IIJIMA, CHRIS K. law educator; b. NYC, Dec. 19, 1948; s. Takeru and Kazuko (Ikeda) I.; m. Karen Asakawa (div. Aug. 1991); m. Jane Ann Dickson, Feb. 17, 1993; children: Alan Kando, Christopher Takeru. BA, Columbia U., 1969; JD, N.Y. Law Sch., 1988. Bar: N.Y. 1989, U.S. Dist. Ct. (so. and ea. dists.) N.Y. 1989. Jud. clk. U.S. Dist. Ct. (so. dist.) N.Y., N.Y.C., 1988-90; litigation assoc. Friedman & Kaplan, N.Y.C., 1990-93; lawyering instr. NYU Sch. Law, N.Y.C., 1993-95; asst. prof., dir. lawyering process program Western New Eng. Coll. Sch. Law, Springfield, Mass., 1995-98; assoc. prof., dir. pre-admission program William S. Richardson Sch. Law, Honolulu, 1998—. Bd. dirs. Na Loio Pub. Interest Legal Ctr., Honolulu; mem. Manoa Network for Minority Students, Honolulu, 1998—. Bd. advisors Rosenberg Fund for Children, Springfield, Mass., 1997—; bd. dirs. Homeless Solutions, Inc., 2001—. Mem.: Soc. Am. Law Tchrs. (bd. dirs. 2002—). Office: William S Richardson Sch Law 2515 Dole St Honolulu HI 96822-2328 E-mail: iijimac@hawaii.edu.

IINUMA, HIROICHI, international economics and trade educator, researcher; b. Nakano, Tokyo, Japan, July 8, 1931; s. Yoshimitsu and Haru (Honda) I.; m. Chizuko Yoneda, Apr. 4, 1975. BA, Meiji U., Tokyo, 1954, MA, 1958, postgrad., 1961—64, Dr. in Comml. Sci., 2000. Tchr. Waseda Bus. High Sch., Tokyo, 1958-66; lectr. Wako U., Tokyo, 1966-69, assoc. prof., 1969-74, prof., 1974—2000, head dir. guidance counseling for students, 1977—80, 1991—94, dean faculty of econs., 1980—82, dir., trustee, 1980—82, prof. emeritus, 2000—. Lectr. Tokyo Fuji U., 1965—, Meiji U., Tokyo, 1971—2002, Josai U., 2002—, Takasaki City U. Econs., Gunma, 1973—98; chmn. JETRO Internat. Trade Advisers steering com., 1995—2001; vice chmn. Asian Market Econs. Rsch. Assn., 1997—. Author: Foreign Trade Principles and Practices, 1973, The Change and Future Perspective in International Trade, 1999, The Change and Future Perspective in International Economics and Trade, 2002; co-author: Business Administration, 1977. Mem.: Sci. Coun. Japan (liaison commr. field of internat. econs. study), Japan Soc. Internat. Econs., Japan Soc. for Study Bus. Adminstrn., Union Nat. Econ. Assns. in Japan (trustee 1990—), Japan Acad. Fgn. Trade and Bus. (chief sec. 1967—70, bd. dirs. 1970—, pres. 1995—99, spl. adviser 1999—, dir. 2001—), Soc. Mktg. and Distbn., All Kanto Rsch. Group Assn. for Fgn. Trade (chmn. 1980—83, 1985—89, 1992—98, sr. adviser 1998—). Home and Office: 1-58-10 Hirao Inagi Tokyo 206-0823 Japan

IJIRI, YUJI, accounting and economics educator; b. Kobe, Japan, Feb. 24, 1935; came to U.S., 1959; s. Takejiro and Hiroko (Hanno) I.; m. Tomoko Nishimura, June 17, 1962; children: Lisa, Yumi. LLB, Ritsumeikan U., Kyoto, Japan, 1956; MS, U. Minn., 1960; PhD, Carnegie Mellon U., 1963; LLD (hon.), DePaul U., 1990; DSc in Bus. Adminstrn. (hon.), Bryant Coll., 1991. CPA, Japan. Staff mem. Price Waterhouse & Co., Tokyo, 1957-59; asst. prof. grad. sch. bus. Stanford (Calif.) U., 1963-65, assoc. prof. grad. sch. bus., 1965-67; prof. grad. sch. indsl. adminstrn. Carnegie Mellon U., Pitts., 1967-75, Robert M. Trueblood prof. acctg. and econs., 1975-87, Robert M. Trueblood univ. prof. acctg. and econs., 1987—. Cons. Gulf Oil Corp., Pitts., 1968-85. Co-author: Skew Distributions and the Sizes of Business Firms, 1977, Kohlers Dictionary for Accountants, 6th edit., 1983, New Directions in Creative and Innovative Management, 1988; author: Momentum Accounting and Triple-Entry Bookkeeping, 1989; editor: Creative and Innovative Approaches to the Science of Management, 1993. Named inductee Acctg. Hall of Fame, Ohio State U., 1989. Fellow Acctg. Researchers Internat. Assn. (pres. 1979-81); mem. Am. Acctg. Assn. (pres. 1982-83, Outstanding Educator 1987), Fin. Execs. Inst. (chpt. bd. dirs. 1977-81), Beta Alpha Psi. Home: 5 Bayard Rd Apt 118 Pittsburgh PA 15213-1904 Office: Grad Sch Indsl Adminstrn Carnegie Mellon U Pittsburgh PA 15213

IKARD, FRANK NEVILLE, JR., lawyer; b. Wichita Falls, Tex., June 26, 1942; s. Frank Neville and Jean (Hunter) I.; children: Frank III, Jean, Charles; m. Kathleen P. Ikard, Feb. 14, 1998. BA, U. Tex., 1965, JD, 1968. Bar: Tex. 1968; cert. Tex. Estate Planning and Probate Law Bd. of Legal Specialization. Assoc. then ptnr. Clark, Thomas, Winters, & Shapiro, Austin, Tex., 1968-84; mng. ptnr. Jenkens & Gilchrist, Austin, 1985-88; ptnr. Johnson & Gibbs, Austin, 1988-92, Ikard & Golden, Austin, 1992—. Bd. dirs. Paramount Theatre, Austin, 1988-89, pres. bd. dirs., 1991-92; mem. Greater Austin Crime Commn. Fellow Am. Coll. Probate Counsel, Tex. Bar Found.; mem. Am. Coll. Trust and Estate Coun. (fiduciary litigation com. 1991-2001), Tex. Acad. Real Estate (pres. probate and trust law coun. 1988-89), State Bar Tex. (chmn., sec.-treas. legis. com. real estate, probate trust law sect. 1983-84, coun. chmn.), Travis County Bar Assn., Tarry House, Headliners, U. Tex. Club. Avocations: fly fishing, photography. Home: 1107 Gaston Ave Austin TX 78703-2507 Office: Ikard & Golden 106 E 6th St Ste 500 Austin TX 78701-3666 E-mail: fni@ikardgolden.com.

IKAWA-SMITH, FUMIKO, anthropologist, educator; b. Kobe, Japan, Sept. 10, 1930; arrived in Canada, 1960; d. Jokei and Sachi (Nakano) Ikawa; m. Takao Sofue, Jan. 1955 (div. 1958); m. Philip Edward Lake Smith, Nov. 1959; 1 child, Douglas Philip Edward. BA, Tsuda Coll., Tokyo, 1953; student Tokyo Met. U., 1954-55; AM in Anthropology, Radcliffe Coll., 1959; PhD in Anthropology, Harvard U., 1974. Asst. prof. McGill U., Montreal, Can., 1968-74, assoc. prof., 1974-79, chmn. dept. anthropology, 1975-80, prof., 1979—, dir. Ctr. East Asian Studies, 1983-88, chmn. dept. East Asian langs. and lits., 1983-88, assoc. acad. vice prin., 1991-96. Vis. prof. Canadian studies Kwansei Gakuin U., Japan, 1996-97. Editor: Early Paleolithic in South and East Asia, 1978, Proceedings of the First Meeting of The Social Sciences Association of Canada, 1989; mem. editl. bd. Anthrop. Sci., 1998—. Fellow Am. Anthrop. Assn. (exec. mem.-at-large archeology divsn. 1988-90), Current Anthropology (assoc.); mem. Pacific Sci. Assn. (life), Soc. Am. Archeology, Japan Studies Assn. Can. (acting pres. 1988-90, pres. elect 1998-99, pres. 1999-2000), Indo-Pacific Prehistory Assn. (exec. com. 1990-98), Can. Asian Studies Assn. (chair Japan com. 1991-94), Quebec-Japan Bus. Forum (bd. mem. 1998-2000). Avocations: horticulture, piano. Home: 3955 Ramezay Ave Montreal QC Canada H3Y 3K3 Office: McGill U Dept Anthropology 855 Sherbrooke St W Montreal QC Canada H3A 2T7 E-mail: fumiko.ikawa-smith@mcgill.ca.

IKEDA, CLYDE JUNICHI, plastic and reconstructive surgeon; b. Kobe, Japan, 1951; s. Paul Tamotsu and Kazu Ikeda. BA, SUNY, Binghamton, 1973; MD, N.Y. Med. Coll., Valhalla, 1979. Resident St. Vincent Hosp., N.Y.C., 1979-83, Francis Meml. Hosp., San Francisco, 1983-86; med. dir. Burn Ctr. St. Francis Meml. Hosp., San Francisco, 1992—2001, med. examiner, 1993—, med. dir. Wound Healing Ctr., 1994—2001; dir. Hosp. de la Familie, 2000—. Asst. clin. prof. plastic surgery U. Calif., San Francisco, 1998—. Fellow Am. Coll. Surgeons. Office: 1199 Bush St Ste 640 San Francisco CA 94109-5977

IKEDA, KAZUYOSI, physicist, poet; b. Fukuoka, Japan, July 15, 1928; s. Yosikatu and Misao (Misumi) I.; m. Mieko Akiyama, Nov. 20, 1956; children: Hiroko Ikeda Yamaguti, Yosihumi. *Father, Yosikatu Ikeda (deceased), as director of a gas company in Fukuoka, Japan, devoted his life to the development of the gas industry and the popularization of gas utilization in the city. Mother, Misao Ikeda, aged 95, has helped her husband for many years, taking care of all household matters. Wife, Mieko Ikeda, studied English literature at Fukuoka Women's University and, as a young girl, was trained to play the piano, which continues to be her hobby. Wife's father, Rokurobee Akiyama (deceased), was a university professor of German literature and published many literary books. Daughter, Hiroko Yamaguti, married, has a Master of Arts degree and is teaching linguistics in a university. Son, Yosihumi Ikeda, studied in the Faculty of Literature of Kyushu University and is highly interested in translating English.* 1st degree Rigakusi, Kyushu U., Fukuoka, Japan, 1951, DSc, 1957; D Environ. Sci. (hon.), Internat. Earth Environment U., 1993; DLitt (hon.), London Inst. Applied Rsch., 1995; diploma of honor, Inst. Affaires Internat., 1995, European Acad. Arts, 1999, Internat. Assn. Educators World Peace, 1999, Internat. Rels., 1999, Inst. Intercultural Studies Ala., 1999; DSc (hon.), World Acad., 1995; DHum honoris causa, Intl Acad. Culture/Polit. Sci., 1999. Asst. dept. physics Kyushu U. Faculty Sci., Fukuoka, 1956-60, assoc. prof. dept. physics, 1960-65; assoc. prof. dept. applied physics Osaka (Japan) U. Faculty Engring., 1965-68, prof. theoretical physics dept. applied physics, 1968-89, prof. theoretical and math. physics dept. math. scis., 1989-92, prof. emeritus, 1992—. Pres. Internat. Earth Environment U., Japan, 1995—, prof. theoretical physics, 1992—; bd. adv. coun. Ansted U., 1999—; prof. Internat. Assn. Educators for World Peace, 1999—. *Kazuyosi Ikeda, Doctor of Science, Honorary Doctor of Literature, is a scientist and poet. He has made outstanding contributions to science as a professor of theoretical physics and mathematical physics at Osaka University, publishing more than 100 papers and numerous books. His sphere of achievement is wide, ranging from statistical mechanics of an assembly of molecules to mechanical theory of a comet. In particular, his unique, rigorous mathematical theory of phase transitions and singularities has been widely noticed and very highly evaluated in the international academic world. He is also an eminent poet who has published numerous poems, in beautiful seven and five syllable meter, in Japanese and English. His unique poems on myriad subjects, based on his sincere love of creation, have gained many enthusiastic, admiring readers throughout the world.* Author: Haar's Thermostatistics, 1960, Modern Developments in Thermodynamics, 1974, Statistical Thermodynamics, 1975, Mechanics Without Use of Mathematical Formulae--From a Moving Stone to Halley's Comet, 1980, Invitation to Mechanics--From the Fundamentals of Calculus to the Motion of a Comet, with Appendix on a comet in ancient times, 1985, (collection of poems) Bansyoo Hyakusi, 1986, Basic Mechanics, 1987, Basic Thermodynamics--From Entropy to Osmotic Pressure, 1991, The World of God, Creation and Poetry, 1991, Poems on the Hearts of Creation, 1993, Mountains, 1995, North South East and West, 1996, Graphical Theory of Relativity, 1998, Hearts of Myriad Things in the Universe, 1998, Kazuyosi's Poetry on the Animate and the Inanimate, 1998, Poems on Love and Peace, 1998, Songs of the Soul, 1999, Hearts of Innumerous Things in Heaven and Earth, 2000, Kazuyosi's Poems on Myriad Things-For Global Brotherhood and World Peace, 2001, The World of Hearts, 2002, Peace Offerings, 2003, Men and Nature, 2003; editor Modern Poetry, 1996—; contbr. more than 100 articles to profl. jours.; author serialized poems, essays on poetry. Hon. founder, Japan rep. Olympoetry Movement, 1992—. Recipient Yukawa Commemorative Scholarship award Yukawa Found., 1954, World Biographical Hall of Fame award Hist. Preservations Am., 1990, prize Catania e il suo Vulcano, Accademia Ferdinandea Sci. Lettere Arti, 1994, Order of Good Neighbors, Olympoetry Movement Fund, 1996, Albert Einstein Acad. Cert. award for outstanding achievement Albert Einstein Internat. Acad. Found., 1998, Internat. Artistic-Literary prize of Primavera Catanase, Accademia Ferdinandea, Sci. Lettere Arte, 1997, Pandit prize Indian Coun. Natural Medicine Rsch., 1999, Diplome de Reconnaisance Edn. Ecologique, Assn. Internat. des Educateus pour la Paix Mondiole, 1999, Diplome ad Honores, Acad. Europeene des Arts, 1999, Diploma of Honor, Internat. Assn. Educators for World Peace, 1999, Diploma in Internat. Rels. Inst. for Internat. Rels. and Intercultural Studies of Ala. U., 1999, Prize Oscar 2000, Accademia Ferdinandea Sci. Lettere Arte, 2000, Gran Premio d'Autore, Edizioni U., 2000, New Millennium Michael Madhusuden award for best poetry Michael Madhusuden Acad., 2000, Oscar prize, 2000, Accademia Ferdinandea Sci. Lettere Arte, 2000, New Millenium Michael Madhusudan award Best Poetry Michael Madhusudan Acad., 2000, Netaj Subbash Chandra Bose Nat. award for Excellence in field of poetry and environ. sci. Jagruthi Kiran Found., 2001, Internat. Lit. prize Libro d'Oro Edizioni U., 2001; named Knight of Yr., Internat. Writers and Artists Assn., 1995, Knight Templar Order, Lofsensic Ursinius Order, Holy Grail Order, Universal Knights Order, San Ciriaco Order, 1995, Order of Pegasus Highest Degree, Olympoetry Movement Fund, 1996, Pandit prize, Indian Coun. of Natural Medicine and Rsch., 1999, Cultural Doctorate in Poetical Lit., World U. Roundtable, 1999, Best World Poet of Yr. award Poets Internat., 1999, Poet of Millennium award Internat. Poets Acad., 2000, Grand prize author Edizioni Universum, 2000, Netaji Subbash Chandra Bose Nat. award excellence in poetry and environ. sci. Jigruthi Kiran Found., 2001, Premio Letterario Internat., Global Peace and Friendship award India-European Union Friendship Soc., 2001, Ivory Eagle award Home of Letters, 2001, Sphatika (India) Internat. Poet award Supreme Governing Body of Sphatika Prakashana, 2001, Internat. Peace prize United Cultural Conv. USA, 2002, Mandakini Lit. award Internat. Poetry Soc. Bareilly, 2002, Excellence in World Poetry award Internat. Poets Acad., 2002, Voice of Kolkata award Kolkata Lit. Soc., 2003; decorated Knight comdr. Sovereign Order of Ambrosini's, 2001. Libro d'Oro Edizioni Universum, 2001. Fellow United Writers' Assn. (life), World Lit. Acad. (life), Internat. Poets Acad. (life, Internat. Eminent Poet award 1993); mem. N.Y. Acad. Scis., Am. Biog. Inst. Rsch. Assn. (dep. gov. 1989—, continental gov. 1998—), World Inst. Achievement (life), Lifetime Achievement Acad. (life, Golden Acad. award 1991), Phys. Soc. Japan (com. mem. 1970—, exec. com. centenary 1976-77, chmn. Osaka br. 1976-77, 83-84, editor jour. 1976-78), Internat. Biog. Assn. (life patron 1990—), Internat. Biog. Ctr. (dep. dir. gen. 1989—, vice consul 2002—), World Acad. Arts and Culture (life), World Congress of Poets (life), Confedn. Chivalry (mem. grand coun. 1991—, Chevalier Grand Cross 1991), Accademia Ferdinandea Scienze Lettere Arti (academician of honor 1994—), Order Internat. Fellowship (charter 1994—), World Parnassians Guild Internat. (hon. dir. 1995—), Acad. M.I.D.I. (senator 1995—), Coun. of States for Protection of Life (senator 1995—, minister plenipotentiary for Asian States 1999—), Academia Argentina (academician 1995—), Internat. Parliament for Safety and Peace (Medalla al Merito 1995, senator 1999—, minister plenipotentiary for Japan 1999—), Modern Poets Soc. (bd. dir. 1996—), Accademia Internazionale Trinacria Lettere-Arte-Scienze (academician of merit 1997—), Leading Intellectuals of the World (founding charter mem. 1998—), Internat. Govs. Club, London Diplomatic Acad. (founder 2000—), Planet Soc., Profs.-Students Coalition Unification North East West South (chmn. Osaka U. br. 1987—), Profs. World Peace Acad. (dir. Osaka br. 1988—), Nat. Coalition Unification North East West South (chmn. Osaka br. 1988—), World Peace Acad. (academician 1999—), Academie Scientifique Internat. Vie Univers (sci. academician environ. scis. 1999—), Academia Ecologia (hon. 1999—), Internat. Poetry for Peace Assn. (regional coord. Japan and Asia Pacific 2000—), Jagruthi Kiran Found. (hon. life 2000—), Am. Order of Excellence (founding mem. 2000—), Michael Madhusdan Acad. (chief exec. 2001—), Karuna India Soc. (patron 2001—), Chetana Lit. Group (patron-in-chief 2001—), Katha Kshetre (patron 2001—), Inst. der Affaires Internationales (corr. mem., rep. Japan 2002—), Internat. Honour Soc. (founding mem. 2002—). Home: Nisi-7-7-11 Aomadani Minoo-si Osaka 562-0023 Japan Office: Osaka U Fac Engring Dept Math Scis 2-1 Yamadaoka Suita-si Osaka 565-0871 Japan

IKELS, CHARLOTTE F. anthropology educator, researcher; b. Cambridge, Mass., Sept. 26, 1943; d. Carl Alfred and Gertrude Marie Ikels; m. Ezra F. Vogel, Nov. 3, 1979. BA in Anthropology, Harvard U., Cambridge, Mass., 1964; MAT in Social Studies, Harvard Grad. Sch. Edn., Cambridge, Mass., 1965; PhD in Anthropology, U. Hawaii, Honolulu, 1978. Educator Bedford H.S., Bedford, Mass., 1965—68, Va. Union U., Richmond, Va., 1968—72; rschr. Harvard Grad. Edn., Cambridge, Mass., 1978—85; asst. prof. Case Western Res. U., Cleveland, Ohio, 1985—92, assoc. prof., 1992—98, prof., 1998—. Co-editor Jour. of Cross-Cultural Gerontology, 1985—95. Co-author: (book) The Aging Experience, 1994 (Kalish, 1995); author: The Return of The God of Wealth (Leeds, 1996), Aging And Adaptation. Grantee Conf. Grant, Nat. Inst. on Aging, 1992, Rsch. Grants, Com. for Scholarly Communication with China, 1991,1998; Armington Professorship, Case Western Res. U., 1997-1999. Mem.: Am. Soc. of Law, Medicine, and Ethics, Gerontol. Soc. of Am., Am. Anthrop. Assn., Assoc. for Asian Studies. Birding. Avocation: biking. Office: Dept of Anthropology Case Western Res U 10900 Euclid Avenue Cleveland OH 44106 Office Fax: 216-368-5334. E-mail: cxi@po.cwru.edu.

IKENBERRY, HENRY CEPHAS, JR., lawyer; b. Cloverdale, Va., Mar. 23, 1920; s. Henry Cephas and Bessie (Peters) I.; m. Margaret Sangster Henry, July 3, 1943; children: Anna Catherine Ikenberry Fawell, Mary Margaret Ikenberry Rauck. BA, Bridgewater Coll., 1947; JD, U. Va., 1947. Bar: Va. 1947, W.Va. 1948, D.C. 1948, U.S. Supreme Ct. 1954, U.S. Ct. Claims 1972, U.S. Ct. Appeals (fed. cir.) 1982. Asso. firm Steptoe & Johnson, Washington, 1947-49, 50-53, partner, former chmn. exec. com., 1953-85, of counsel, 1986-92; asst. counsel Gen. Aniline & Film Co., N.Y.C., 1949-50. Mem. com. on unauthorized practice D.C. Ct. Appeals, 1972-76. Ruling elder Chevy Chase Presbyn. Ch., Washington, 1970-72; trustee Mary Baldwin Coll., Staunton, Va., 1979-92, mem. exec. com., 1987-92; life mem., dean's counsel Univ. Va. Sch. Law. Lt. comdr. USNR, 1941-46, ETO, PTO, Okinawa, The Philippines. Recipient Alumni citation Bridgewater Coll., 1960; named Ky. col., 1973 Mem. Bar Assn. D.C. (chmn. com. on corp. law 1960-61, com. comml. bus. law 1969-72), Raven Soc., Am. Legion, Metropolitan Club, Chesapeake Bay Yacht Club, Chevy Chase Club, Talbot Country Club (Easton, Md.), Order of Coif, Phi Delta Phi, Tau Kappa Alpha. Home: Pine Lodge 26783 Miles River Rd Easton MD 21601-5013 also: PO Box 1518 Easton MD 21601-8929 also: Box N-308 8101 Connecticut Ave Chevy Chase MD 20815

IKENBERRY, JUDITH LIFE, social and charitable organization volunteer, writer; b. Indpls., Jan. 7, 1936; d. Homer Lawrence and Mary (Banks) Life; m. Stanley O. Ikenberry, Aug. 24, 1958; children: David L., Steven O., John P. BS, Purdue U., 1953-57; MS, Mich. State U., 1957-59. Instr. Mich. State U., Lansing, 1959-60; home mgmt. specialist Pa. State U., State College, 1970-79. Author: Family Food Management Nutrition, 1976; contbg. author The President's Spouse, 1984. Chmn. Lincoln Acad. Convocation and Ball, Champaign, Ill., 1981-82; mem. Ill. Art Coun., 1987-95, Gov.'s Office of Vol. Action, 1985, Women's Bd. of Field Mus., Chgo., 1985-95. Named Disting. Citizen of Yr. Arrowhead Council of the Boy Scouts Am., 1988. Mem. Spouses Council of the Nat. Assn. of State U. and Land Grant Colls. (chmn. 1986-88). Presbyterian. Avocations: travel, botanical art-watercolor, cooking, sailing. Home: 104 Meadow Dr Urbana IL 61801

IKENBERRY, STANLEY OLIVER, education educator, former university president; b. Lamar, Colo., Mar. 3, 1935; s. Oliver Samuel and Margaret (Moulton) Ikenberry; m. Judith Ellen Life, Aug. 24, 1958; children: David Lawrence, Steven Oliver, John Paul. BA, Shepherd Coll., 1956; MA, Mich. State U., 1957, PhD, 1960, LHD (hon.); LLD (hon.), Millikin U.; LHD (hon.), Millkin U., Ill. Coll., Rush U., W.Va. U., Towson State U., U. Nebr., Bridgewater (Va.) Coll., Bradley U., Shepherd Coll., Roosevelt U., Juniatta Coll., Pa., 2003, Northeastern U. Instr. office evaluation svc. Mich. State U., 1958—60, instr. instl. rsch. office, 1960—62; asst. to provost for instl. rsch., asst. prof. edn. W.Va. U., 1962—65, dean coll. human resources and edn., assoc. prof. edn., 1965—69; prof., assoc. dir. ctr. study higher edn. Pa. State U., 1969—71, sr. v.p., 1971—79; pres. U. Ill., Urbana, 1979—95, pres. emeritus, Regent prof., 1995—; pres. Am. Coun. on Edn., Washington, 1996—2001. Bd. dirs. Pfizer, Inc., N.Y.C., Aquila Inc., Kans. City; pres. bd. overseers Tchrs. Ins. and Annutiy Assn./Coll. Retirement Equities Fund. Named hon. alumnus, Pa. State U. Fellow: Am. Acad. Arts and Scis.; mem.: Assn. Am. Univs. (past chmn.), Tavern Club (Chgo.), Cosmos Club (Washington), Mid-Am. Club, Comml. Club Chgo. Office: U Ill 347 Education 1310 S 6th St Champaign IL 61820

IKERD, SHIRLEY TEMPLE, financial planner; b. Meadville, Miss., Mar. 19, 1942; d. Morris Lee and Grace Cotten Temple; m. William L. Ikerd, June 19, 1960; children: Stephanie Ikerd Holland, Trina Ikerd Welch. Elem., Miss. Coll., Clinton, MS. Cert. Cosmetologist McComb Cosmetology Sch. Sec., clk. Franklin Tax Assessor Office, Meadville, Miss., 1963—65; kindegarten tchr.

Meadville Meth. Ch., Meadville, Miss., 1970—71; hairdresser Shirley's Beauty Shop, Meadville, Miss., 1976—86; billing coord., purchaser Profl. Health Care Services, Meadville, Miss., 1997—2002. Adv. bd. Bank of Franklin, Meadville, Miss., 1992—95; mem. Libr. Bd., Meadville, Miss., 1970—72. Author: (poem) Lasting Mirage (Editor's Choice, 1997), Poetry's Elite (Editor's Choice, 2000), Days Gone By (Editor's Choice, 1997). Recipient First pl., Fashion & Styles State Show, Jackson, MS, 1977, 2d pl., Model of the Yr., Natchez, MS, 1980—81, Cert. of Recognition, Family Support Leader, Desert Storm, US Army, 1991. Avocations: reading, writing, sewing, exercise, art. Home: PO Box 703 Meadville MS 39653

IKLE, DORIS MARGRET, energy executive; b. Frankfurt, Germany, May 28, 1928; came to U.S., 1937; d. Richard and Sonia (Pappenheimer) Eisemann; m. Fred Charles Ikle, Dec. 23, 1959; children: Judith, Miriam. BA, NYU, 1949, MA, 1953; postgrad., Columbia U., 1957. Economist Nat. Bur. Econ. Rsch., N.Y.C., 1949-54, Am. Bankers Assn., 1954-56, Rand Corp., Santa Monica, Calif., 1957-60, Inst. Energy Analysis, Washington, 1976-77; founder, pres. CMC Energy Svcs., Bethesda, Md., 1977—. Cons. U.S. Dept. Commerce, Washington, 1975-76; adv. council Am. for Energy Independence, 1985—. Author: The Complete Energy Audit Book, 1980; (software) Energy Audit Systems, 1984; contbr. articles to profl. jours. Office: CMC Energy Svcs 7300 Pearl St Bethesda MD 20814-3321

IKLÉ, FRED CHARLES, former federal agency administrator, policy advisor, defense expert; b. Fex, Switzerland, Aug. 21, 1924; s. Fritz A. and Hedwig M. (Huber) I.; m. Doris Eisemann, Dec. 23, 1959; children: Judith, Miriam. MA in Social Sci, U. Chgo., 1948, PhD in Sociology, 1950. Research assoc. Columbia Bur. Applied Social Research, 1950-54; mem. social sci. dept. Rand Corp., Santa Monica, Calif., 1955—61, head social sci. dept., 1968—73; research assoc. Ctr. for Internat. Affairs Harvard U., 1962-63; prof. polit. sci. Mass. Inst. Tech., 1964-67; dir. U.S. ACDA, Washington, 1973-77; chmn. Conservation Mgmt. Corp., 1978-81, 88—; under-sec. for policy Dept. Def., Washington, 1981-88; Disting. scholar Ctr. for Internat. and Strategic Studies, 1988—. Mem. Dept. Def. Policy Bd.; bd. dirs. Telos Corp.; mem. adv. bd. RAND Drug Policy Ctr.; mem. Nat. Com. on Terrorism, 1999-00, Gov. Smith Richardson Found., 1996—; chmn. U.S. Com. for Human Rights in North Korea. Author: The Social Impact of Bomb Destruction, 1958, How Nations Negotiate, 1964, Every War Must End, 1971. Mem. Internat. Inst. Strategic Studies, Coun. Fgn. Rels., Met. Club. Republican. Home: 7010 Glenbrook Rd Bethesda MD 20814-1223 Office: Ctr Strategic & Internat Studies 1800 K St NW Washington DC 20006-2202

IKLÉ, RICHARD ADOLPH, lawyer; b. Mineola, N.Y., Mar. 25, 1930; s. Adolph M. and Ruth Clark; children: Roger Scott, Lisa Kristina, Richard Keith. BA, Amherst Coll., 1953; JD, Columbia U., 1960. Bar: N.Y. 1961, Fla. 1975. Ptnr. Thacher, Proffitt & Wood, NYC., 1960—90; supervisory counsel FDIC, NYC, NJ, Washington, 1990—. Deacon Cmty. Ref. Ch., Manhasset, NY, 1975—80, elder, 1980—82. Lt. USNR, 1953—56. Mem.: ABA, Fla. Bar Assn., N.Y. State Bar Assn., Manhasset Bay Yacht Club (Port Washington, N.Y.). Avocations: sailing, mountain climbing.

IKRANAGARA, KAY, educational association administrator, educator; b. Council Bluffs, Iowa, Sept. 19, 1943; d. J. Bruce Glassburner and Eleanor Schlott; married; children: Innosanto, R. Biko. BA, U. Calif., Berkeley, Calif., 1966, MA, 1969; PhD, U. Hawaii, 1975. Instr. Ohio State U., Columbus, Ohio, 1989—91; asst. World Bank XVII Project Midwest Univs. Consortium, Jakarta, Indonesia, 1991—92; cons. comm. tng. program Indonesian Nat. Secretariat, Jakarta, 1992—94; exec. dir. Internat. Edn. Found., Jakarta, 1994—99; assoc. dir. Ctr. for Internat. Edn. and Devel. Assistance Ind. U., Bloomington, Ind., 1999—. Author: Tatabahasa Melayu Betawi, 1988. Office: Indiana Univ 201 N Indiana Ave Bloomington IN 47408

ILACQUA, ROSARIO SALVATORE, securities analyst; b. Albany, N.Y., Aug. 12, 1927; s. Anthony and Carmela (Gerasia) I. BS, Siena Coll., 1950; MS, Columbia U., 1955. Chartered fin. analyst. With L.F. Rothschild, N.Y.C., 1957-87, ptnr., 1972-87; with Nikko Securities, 1987-90, Rothschild Inc., 1990-99, Monness, Crespi, Hardt & Co., 2000—. With USNR, 1945-46. Mem. Nat. Assn. Petroleum Investment Analysts (pres. 1977), N.Y. Soc. Security Analysts, Oil Analysts Group N.Y. (pres. 1972), Assn. for Investment Mgmt. and Rsch. (chmn. corp. info. com.), N.Y. Athletic Club. Home: 2 Horatio St Apt 15J New York NY 10014-1645 Office: 767 Third Ave New York NY 10017

ILCHMAN, ALICE STONE, foundation administrator, former college president, former government official; b. Cin., Apr. 18, 1935; d. Donald Crawford and Alice Kathryn (Biermann) Stone; m. Warren Frederick Ilchman, June 11, 1960; children: Frederick Andrew Crawford, Alice Sarah. BA, Mt. Holyoke Coll., 1957; MPA, Maxwell Sch. Citizenship, Syracuse U., 1958; PhD, London Sch. Econs., 1965; LHD, Mt. Holyoke Coll., 1982, Franklin and Marshall Coll., 1983. Asst. to pres., mem. faculty Berkshire C.C., 1961-64; lectr. Ctr. for South and S.E. Asia Studies U. Calif., Berkeley, 1965-73; prof. econs. and edn., dean Wellesley (Mass.) Coll., 1973-78; asst. sec. ednl. and cultural affairs Dept. State, 1978; assoc. dir. ednl. and cultural affairs Internat. Comm. Agy., 1978—81; advisor to sec. Smithsonian Instn., 1981; pres. Sarah Lawrence Coll., Bronxville, N.Y., 1981-98; chmn. bd. Rockefeller Found., N.Y.C., 1995—2000. Dir. Jeannette K. Watson Fellowships, 1999—; intern, asst. to Sen. John F. Kennedy, 1957; dir. Peace Corps Tng. Program for India, 1965-66; chmn. com. on women's employment NAS; sr. advisor Thomas Watson Found., 1999—; bd. dirs. NYNEX, Seligman Group of Investment Cos. Author: The New Men of Knowledge and the New States, 1968, (with W.F. Ilchman) Education and Employment in India, The Policy Nexus, 1976. Trustee Mt. Holyoke Coll., 1970-80, Mass. Found. for Humanities and Pub. Policy, 1974-77, East-West Ctr., Honolulu, 1978-81, Expt. in Internat. Living, The Markle Found., The Rockefeller Found., chmn. bd. dirs., acting pres., 1998; trustee The U. of Cape Town, South Africa, Corp. Adv. Bd., Hotchkiss Sch.; mem. Smithsonian Coun., Yonkers Emergency Fin. Control Bd., 1982-88, Am. Ditchley Found. Program Com., Internat. Rsch. and Exch. Bd., Com. for Econ. Devel., The Masters Sch., Save The Children, Chamber Music Soc. Lincoln Ctr.; bd. dirs. Pub. Broadcasting Corp., 2000—. Hon. fellow Wadham Coll., Oxford U. Mem. NOW Legal Def. Edn. Fund, Coun. Fgn. Rels., Century Assn. (N.Y.C.), Bronxville Field Club. Home: 18 Highland Cir Bronxville NY 10708-5908 Office: Jeannette K Watson Fellowships 31st Fl 810 Seventh Ave New York NY 10019 E-mail: ailchman@jkwatson.org.

ILCHMAN, WARREN FREDERICK, university administrator, foundation director, educator; b. Denver, Sept. 6, 1933; s. Frederick Warren and Imogene (Trovinger) I.; m. Alice Crawford Stone, June 11, 1960; children: Frederick Andrew Crawford, Alice Sarah Crawford. BA, Brown U., 1955; PhD, Cambridge (Eng.) U., Eng., 1959. Asst. prof. Ctr. Devel. Econs. Williams Coll., Williamstown, Mass., 1960-64; from asst. prof. to prof. polit. sci. U. Calif., Berkeley, 1965-73, dir. Ctr. South and Southeast Asian Studies, 1970-73; vis. prof., research assoc. Ctr. Population Studies, Harvard U., Cambridge, Mass., 1973-74; prof. polit. sci. and econs., dean arts and scis. Grad. Sch., Boston U., 1974-76; program adviser internat. div. Ford Found., N.Y.C., 1976-80; v.p. for research and grad. studies SUNY, Albany, 1980-83, provost Nelson A. Rockefeller Coll. Pub. Affairs and Policy, 1983-87, dir. Rockefeller Inst. Govt., 1983-87, exec. v.p., 1987-90; pres. Pratt Inst., Bklyn., 1990-93; exec. dir. ctr. Philanthropy Ind. Univ., Indpls., 1993-97; dir. Paul and Daisy Soros Found., N.Y.C., 1998—. Author: Professional Diplomacy in the U.S, 1961, New Men of Knowledge and the Developing Nations, 1966, Professionals as Agents of Change, 1968, The Political Economy of Change, 1969, rev. edit., 1998 (translated into French, Spanish, Japanese, Hindi and Arabic), Political Economy of Development, 1972, Comparative Public Administration and The Conventional Wisdom, 1973, Policy Sciences and Population, 1975, Education and Employment: The Policy Nexus, 1976, New York in the Year 2000, 1986, Caring and Coping, 1986, Capacity to Change, 1997, Philanthropy and the World's Tradition, 1998, Westchester Cmty. Found. Bd. dirs. The Masters Sch., The Gen. Theol. Sem.; mem. Am. Friends of the Anglican Ctr. in Rome. Marshall scholar U.K.; recipient Harbison prize Danforth Found., 1969 Mem. Am. Soc. Pub. Adminstrn. (Burchfield award 1965), Asia Soc., Am. Polit. Sci. Assn., N.Y. Acad. Pub. Adminstrn. (Al Smith award), Assn. Asian Studies, Nat. Acad. Pub. Adminstrn., Univ. Club, Bronxville Field Club, Phi Beta Kappa. Episcopalian. Home: 18 Highland Cir Bronxville NY 10708-5908 Office: Paul and Daisy Soros Fellowship Program 400 W 59th St New York NY 10019-1105 E-mail: wilchman@sorosny.org.

ILES, EILEEN MARIE, bank executive; b. Highland Park, Ill., Sept. 29, 1965; d. Dennis Jay and Ida Sigrid (Calderelli) Connolly; m. Kenneth Robert Iles, Dec. 14, 1985; children: Kevin Andrew, Eric Robert. Student, U. Ill., Chgo., 1983-85; BBA in Acctg. and Mktg. Mgmt., U. N.Mex., 1988, M in Acctg., 1992. Acct. Charter Bank for Savs., Albuquerque, 1989-90, bank acctg. supr., 1990-91, asst. contr., 1991-2000, asst. v.p., 1992-2000; engagement mgr. Crowe Chizek & Co., LLP, 2000, sr. engagement mgr., 2000—. Instr. acctg. U. N.Mex., Albuquerque, 1994-99, Albuquerque Tech. Vocat. Inst., 2000; cons. in field. Mem.: Assn. Cert. Fraud Examiners, Inst. Internal Auditors, Inst. Mgmt. Accts. Office: One MidAm Plz PO Box 3697 Oak Brook IL 60522-3697 E-mail: eiles@crowechizek.com.

ILES, ROGER DEAN, business educator; b. Detroit, June 11, 1950; s. Virgil Llewellyn and Mary Elizabeth (Lynn) I.; m. Gail Ann Swatzell, Jan. 10, 1971; 1 child, Gwendolyn Christine. AA, Regents Coll., 1990; BS magna cum laude, Crichton Coll., 1992; MBA, U. Memphis, 1997. Enlisted USN, 1969, advanced through grades to chief electronics technician, 1969-89; ret., 1989; switchman Mich. Bell Telephone Co., Dearborn, 1968-69; controller, alumni advisor Crichton Coll., Memphis, 1989-99. Mem. adj. faculty, mem. capital campaign steering com. Crichton Coll., Memphis, 1998—; mem. adj. faculty U. Memphis, 1998—; mem. online faculty U. Phoenix, 2003—; chmn., mgr. Shade Tree Engring., Inc., Munford, Tenn., 1992—. Mem. Gideons Internat. (area dir., pres. Tipton County South Camp). Republican. Baptist. Avocations: auto racing, target shooting. Home: 59 Jennifer Cv Brighton TN 38011-6056 Office: 2359 Beaver Rd Ste A Brighton TN 38011-6215 Fax: 901-837-0499. E-mail: etcsw@email.uophk.edu.

ILETT, FRANK, JR., trucking company executive, educator; b. Ontario, Oreg., June 21, 1940; s. Frank Kent and Lela Alice (Siver) I.; m. Donna L. Andlovec, Apr. 3, 1971; children: James Frank, Jordan Lee. BA, U. Wash., 1962; MBA, U. Chgo., 1969. CPA, Idaho, Ill., Wash. Acct. Ernst & Young, Boise, Cleve., Spokane, 1962-69, mgr. Boise, 1970-72, regional mgr. San Francisco, 1972-73; treas. Interstate Mack, Inc., Boise, 1973-81, pres., CEO, 1981-82; pres. Interstate NationLease, Inc., Boise, 1975-81, Contract Carriers, Inc., Boise, 1983-89, Ilett Transp. Co., Boise, 1985-90; chmn. Carriers/West, Inc., Salem, Oreg., 1986-89; CFO, White GMC Trucks, 1988-92; v.p., CFO, May Trucking Co., Payette, Idaho, 1992-94; acct., mng. ptnr. Frank Ilett, Jr., CPA, Boise, 1994—. Spl. lectr. Boise State U., 1964-67, 94—, St. Mary's Grad. Sch., Moraga, Calif., 1989-92 ; v.p. I.D.E.A.L., Inc., Nampa, Idaho, 1997-2002; cons. Calif. Hosp. Commn., 1973, Idaho Hosp. Assn., 1974; chmn. Mack Truck Western Region Distbr. Coun., 1979-82; nat. distbr. adv. com. Mack Trucks, Inc., 1980-82; dir. stds. enforcement Idaho State Bd. Accountancy, 1983-84; contr. Idaho Stampede, 2002—. Contbr. articles to profl. jours. Recipient Outstanding Prof. award KPMG, 2003; named Arthur Andersen Outstanding Acctg. Prof., 1996, 2001. Mem.: ACIPA, SAR, Gen. Soc. Mayflower Descs., Crane Creek Country Club, Shriners, Masons, Alpha Kappa Psi (Outstanding Bus. Prof. award 1997, named Disting. Faculty Mem., Coll. Bus. 2002). Episcopalian. Home: 1701 Harrison Blvd Boise ID 83702-1015 Office: 1910 University Dr Boise ID 83725 E-mail: frankilett@msn.com.

ILEY, MARTHA STRAWN, music educator; b. Marhsville, NC, June 1, 1925; d. Stephen Hasty and Lila Faircloth Strawn; m. Bryce Baxter Iley, Aug. 7, 1948; children: Deborah Iley Hodde, Sheila Iley McLean, Cheryl Iley Lindstrom, Stephanie Iley Salb. BA, East Carolina Tchrs. Coll., 1946; MA, Western Ky. State Coll., 1947; MusM, Winthrop Coll., 1973; EdM, U. NC, Charlotte, 1974; EdD, Nova U., 1979; M Theol. Studies, Gordon-Conwell Theol. Sem., 1998. Cert. Music Tchrs. Nat. Assn. Music tchr. Lincolnton City Sch., 1947—48, Alexander Graham Jr. HS, Charlotte, NC, 1948—52, Charlotte Country Day Sch., 1955—59; min. music Providence Bapt. Ch., Charlotte, 1954—57, Carmel Bapt. Ch., Charlotte, 1968—70, 1975—76; project dir. music edn. Ctrl. Piedmont C.C., Charlotte, 1974—83; founder, chmn. bd. dirs. Met. Music Ministries, Charlotte, 1984—. Editor: (newsletter) ARTY-FACTS, 1983. Bd. dirs., sec. Charlotte Cmty. Concert Assn., 1980—93; dir. recital series Shepherd Ctr., Charlotte, 1980—83; adjudicator piano and voice various orgns., NC, 1980—. Recipient Disting. Music Alumni award, East Carolina U., 2002. Mem.: Charlotte Piano Tchrs. Forum (bd. dirs., pres. 1979—81), Charlotte Clergy Assn., NC Music Tchrs. Assn. (cert. chmn., v.p. 1981—83), Charlotte Music Club (bd. dirs.). Republican. Baptist. Avocations: writing, painting. Home: 10151 Robinson Church Rd Harrisburg NC 28075-6607 Office: Met Music Ministries Inc 1311 Paddock Cir Charlotte NC 28209-2443 Office Fax: 704-529-0256.

ILFELD, BRIAN MICHAEL, anesthesiologist; b. San Francisco, Nov. 5, 1966; s. Frederic William Ilfeld and Lydia Goldman Ingham; m. Jenny Kline Kline, June 3, 2001. BA, Pomona Coll., 1988; MD, U. Calif., San Francisco, 1995. Diplomate Am. Bd. Anesthesiologists. Resident anesthesiology U. Calif., San Francisco, 1997—2000; fellow regional anesthesiology Coll. Medicine U. Fla., Gainesville, 2001—02, asst. prof. Coll. Medicine, 2002—. Contbr. articles to profl. jours. Mem.: Internat. Anesthesia Rsch. Soc., Calif. Soc. Anesthesiologists, Fla. Soc. Anesthesiologists, Am. Soc. Regional Anesthesiologists, Am. Soc. Anesthesiologists, Phi Beta Kappa. Avocations: backpacking, skiing, travel, reading.

ILG, CHRISTOPHER PAUL, secondary school educator, music educator; b. Rocky River, Ohio, Jan. 12, 1966; s. Noel Stephen and Frances Marie Ilg; m. Kate Elizabeth Bruening, Dec. 30, 2000; 1 child, Emma Elizabeth. MusB in Edn., Cleve. (Ohio) State U., 1990. Cert. tchr. Ohio, 1990. Prin. organist St. Joseph Ch., Avon Lake, Ohio, 1978—87; HS and mid. sch. choral dir. Highland Local Schs., Medina, Ohio, 1991—. Music dir. St. Paul Luth. Ch., Sharon Ctr., Ohio, 1992—. Composer: (plays) Must The Show Go On?!. Organist St. Paul Luth. Ch., 1992—2002. Mem.: Am. Choral Dirs. Assn. (life). Liberal. Lutheran. Avocations: running, swimming, weightlifting, bicycling. Home: 5952 Emerald Lakes Drive Medina OH 44256 Office: Highland Local Schools 3880 Ridge Road Medina OH 44256

ILGEN, DANIEL RICHARD, psychology educator; b. Freeport, Ill., Mar. 16, 1943; s. Paul Maurice and Marjorie V. (Glasser) I.; m. Barbara Geiser, Dec. 26, 1965; children: Elizabeth Ann, Mark Andrew. BS in Psychology, Iowa State U., 1965; MA, U. Ill., 1968, PhD in Indsl.-Orgnl. Psychology, 1969. Asst. prof. dept. psychology U. Ill., Urbana, 1969-70; instr. Dutchess County C.C., Poughkeepsie, NY, 1971-72; from asst. prof. to prof. dept. psychol. scis. Purdue U., West Lafayette, Ind., 1972-83, area head indsl.-orgnl. psychology, 1978-83; Hannah prof. organizational behavior depts. mgmt. and psychology Mich. State U., East Lansing, 1983—. Vis. assoc. prof. dept. mgmt. and orgn. U. Wash., Seattle, 1978-79; vis. prof. dept. mgmt. U. Western Australia, 1991, 2000. Co-author (with J.C. Naylor and R.D. Pritchard): A Theory of Behavior in Organizations, 1980; co-author: (with E.J. McCormick) Industrial Psychology, 1985; co-editor (with E. Pulakos): The Changing Nature of Performance, 1999; co-editor: (with C. Hulin) Computational Modeling of Behavior in Organizations, 2000; co-editor: (with W. Borman and R. Klimoski) Industrial and Organizational Psychology, The Comprehensive Handbook of Psychology, vol. 12, 2002; contbr. ; editor: Organizational Behavior and Human Decision Processes, 1998—2001. Capt. M.I., U.S. Army, 1970-72. Grantee Purdue U. Found., 81-82, U.S. Army Rsch. Inst., 1974-82, Office Naval Rsch., 1982-86, 90—. Fellow Am. Psychol. Assn. (edn. tng. com., coun. reps. 1985-87), Soc. Indsl. and Organizational Psychology of Am. Psychol. Assn. (pres. 1987-88, Disting. Sci. Contbn. award 2001), Am. Psychol. Soc., Acad. Mgmt. (Herbert Heneman Jr. Disting. Lifetime Contbn. award 2002); mem. Soc. Orgnl. Behavior, Sigma Xi. Office: Mich State U Depts Mgmt And Psychol East Lansing MI 48824-1117 E-mail: Ilgen@msu.edu.

ILITCH, MARIAN, professional hockey team executive, food service executive; m. Michael Ilitch; children: Denise Ilitch Lites, Ron, Mike Jr., Lisa Ilitch Murray, Atanas, Christopher, Carole. Owner, sec.-treas. Detroit Red Wings, Detroit Tigers Baseball Team, 1993—, also bd. dirs.; sec.-treas., vice chair Little Caesar Internat.; sec.-treas. Olympia Arenas, Inc., Fox Theatre. Office: Little Ceasars Enterprises 2211 Woodward Ave Detroit MI 48201-3400 also: Detroit Tigers Tiger Stadium 2121 Trumbull St Detroit MI 48216-1343 Office: Detroit Red Wings Joe Louis Arena 600 Civic Center Detroit MI 48226

ILITCH, MICHAEL, professional hockey team executive; m. Marian Ilitch; children: Denise Ilitch Lites, Ron, Mike Jr., Lisa, Atanas, Christopher, Carole. Founder, owner Little Caesars Restaurant, 1959—; owner, pres. Detroit Red Wings Hockey Team, 1982—; founder Blue Line Distbg., Am.'s Pizza Cafe; owner Olympia Arenas, Inc. (formerly Olympia Stadium Corp.), 1983—, Adirondack Red Wings Hockey Team, Detroit Dr. of Arena Football League; owner, chmn., former pres. Detroit Tigers Baseball Team. Little Caesars Love Kitchen program, 1985—. With USMC, 4 yrs. Recipient Lester Patrick trophy, 1991, Bus. Statesman award, Harvard Bus. Sch. Club Detroit, 1990, Joe Louis award, Sports Illustrated Mag. and Detroit Inst. Arts, Humanitarian of Yr. award, March of Dimes. Office: Detroit Red Wings 600 Civic Center Dr Detroit MI 48226-4419 also: Detroit Tigers Tiger Stadium 2100 Woodward Ave Detroit MI 48201-3470 also: Little Caesars Enterprizes 2211 Woodward Ave Detroit MI 48201-3467

ILK, OZLEM, statistics educator, researcher; b. Ankara, Turkey, Apr. 14, 1976; d. Sebehattin and Hatice Ilk. BS, Mid. East Tech. U., Turkey, 1997; MS, Iowa State U., 2000. Rsch. asst. Mid. East Tech. U., Ankara, Turkey, 1997—; exch. visitor Iowa State U., Ames, 1998—, phd candidate, 2002—. Statis. programmer Iowa State U., Ames, 2002—. Scholarship For Grad. Studies, Mid. East Tech. U., 1998—. Avocations: basketball, jogging, travel. Personal E-mail: oilk@iastate.edu.

ILKIN, BAKI, diplomat; Turkish amb. to Copenhagen; spl. advisor to fgn. min. Govt. of Turkey; Turkish amb. to The Hague; Turkish amb. to USA, 1998—. Office: Embassy of the Republic of Turkey 2525 Massachusetts Ave NW Washington DC 20008-2826 Fax: 202-659-0744.

ILLANGASEKARE, TISSA HARISCHANDRA, engineering educator, researcher; b. Kandy, Central Province, Sri Lanka, Feb. 19, 1949; s. James and Anula Illangasekare; m. Malkanthi Paulis D.V.N.M. Paulis; children: Samantha, Tushani. PhD, Colo. State U., 1974—78; M in Engring., Asian Inst. Tech., Bangkok, Thailand, 1972—74; BSc with honors, U. Ceylon, Peradeniya, Sri Lanka, 1967—71. Cert. profl. engr., 1981, profl. hydrologist. Instr. U. Ceylon, Peradeniya, Sri Lanka, 1971—72; rsch. asst., prof. civil engring. Colo. State U., Fort Collins, Colo., 1978—83; asst. prof. civil engring. La. State U., Baton Rouge, 1983—86; assoc. prof. civil and environ. engring. U. Colo., Boulder, 1986—89, prof. civil and environ. engring., 1990—98; AMAX disting. chair environ. sci. and engngring., prof. civil engring. Colo. Sch. Mines, Golden, Colo., 1998—date. Dir. Ctr. Exptl. Study Subsurface Environ. Processes (CESEP), Golden, 2001—date; NRC rev. panel Nat. Acad. Sci. and Engring., 2000. Author about 150 tech. publs. ; assoc. editor Jour. of Hydrology, 1990—, Water Resources Research, American Geophysical Union, 1995—2001, Jour. Contaminanat Hydrology, 1997—, mng. editor Hydrology, Earth Sci. Rev., 2000—. Sr. senator Faculty Senate at Colo. Sch. Mines, Golden, 2000—. Named Distinguished Chair, Colo. Sch. Mines, 1998; grantee numerous Rsch. grants. Mem.: ASCE, Am. Inst. Hydrology, Nat. Groundwater Assn., Soc. Indusl. and Applied Math., Geol. Soc.of Am., Am. Geophysical Union (Unsaturated Zone com. 1995—). Home: 5222 Pinehurst Dr Boulder CO 80301-3791 Office: Colo Sch Mines 1600 Illinois St Golden CO 80401-1887 Office Fax: 303 273 3311. Business E-Mail: tissa@mines.edu.

ILLE, BERNARD GLENN, insurance company executive, director; b. Ponca City, Okla., Feb. 8, 1927; s. Frank Louis and Marie (Cornwell) I.; m. Mary Lou Allen, Aug. 23, 1952; children— Meredith, Les, Frank BBA in Fin., U. Okla., 1950. CLU. Agt. Phoenix Mutual Life, Hartford, Conn., 1950-54; gen. agt. Farmers and Bankers Life, Wichita, Kans., 1954-56; asst. v.p. agy. United Founders Life, Oklahoma City, 1956-58, agt. v.p., 1958-60, exec. v.p., dir. agy., 1960-66, pres., 1966-88, pres., CEO, 1988-94, First Life Assurance Co., Oklahoma City, 1994—; pres. BML Cons., Oklahoma City, 1994—; apptd. receiver Mid-Continent Life Ins. Co., Oklahoma City, 1999-2000. Bd. dirs., chmn. audit com., LSB Industries, (NYSE); bd. dirs. Oklahoma City, Quail Creek Bank, Oklahoma City, Landmark Nat., Upper Marlboro, Md.. Organizer Big Brothers, Oklahoma City, 1960; past pres., organizer Nat. Football Found., Oklahoma City, 1969. Recipient Young Pres. Orgn. award, 1966, U. Okla. Kappa Alpha Man of Half Century award. Mem. Okla. Life. Ins. Guaranty Assn. (chmn. 1984-94), Okla. Assn. Life Ins. Cos. (past pres. 2 terms), Exec. Svc. Corps. Okla. (chmn.), Quail Creek Golf and Country Club (organizer), Oak Tree Golf and Country Club, Petroleum Club, PGA West Country Club (Palm Springs, Calif.), La Quinta Golf and Country Club (Palm Springs), Carmel (Calif.) Valley Golf and Country Club, Palm Beach Golf and Polo Club (West Palm Beach), Kiawah Country Club (Kiawah Island, S.C.), Order Knights of Holy Sepulchre. Democrat. Roman Catholic. Home: 11004 Magnolia Park Oklahoma City OK 73120-5210 Office: BML Cons PO Box 21080 Oklahoma City OK 73156-1080 Fax: 405-755-8289.

ILLES, JUDY, medical researcher, radiologist; d. Herman and Ibolya Illes; m. Hendrik F. Machiel Van der Loos, Dec. 14, 1984; children: Hendrik Z. Adriaan Van der Loos, Kiah Ileana Van der Loos. BA, Brandeis U., 1981; MA, McGill U., 1983; PhD, Stanford (Calif.) U., 1987. Dir. strategic rsch. devel. Dept. of Radiology Stanford (Calif.) U., 1991—2001, sr. rsch. scholar Stanford (Calif.) Ctr. for Biomedical Ethics and Dept. of Radiology, 2001—. Pres. Illes & Assocs., Cons. in Rsch. Design and Devel., Woodside, Calif., 1995—; co-founder Stanford (Calif.) Brain Rsch. Ctr. Stanford (Calif.) U., Stanford, exec. dir. Stanford (Calif.) Brain Rsch. Ctr. Editor: Ethical Challenges in Advanced Neuroimaging, Emerging Ethical Issues in MRI; author: The Strategic Grant-Seeker: Conceptualizing Fundable Research in the Brain and Behavioral Sciences. Mem.: AAAS, Women in Neuroscience (pres.-elect 2003—), Acad. of Aphasia, Cognitive Neuroscience Soc., Soc. for Neuroscience, Internat. Neuropsychological Assn., Assn. of U. Radiologists, Am. Soc. for Bioethics and Humanities. Office: Stanford Center for Biomedical Ethics 701 Welch Rd Palo Alto CA 94304-5748 Office Fax: 650-724-6131.

ILLGEN, JOEL R. music educator; b. Ill., May 29, 1968; s. Gerald and Sharon Illgen; m. Susan J. Illgen, Aug. 4, 1989; children: Joel, Taylor, Janey, Tyndale. MusB, Oral Roberts U., 1990. Band dir. Acad. Ctrl. Pub. Sch., Tulsa, Okla., 1991, Kellyville (Okla.) Pub. Sch., 1991—94, Grove (Okla.) Pub. Sch., 1994—. Chmn. jr. HS clinic N.E. Okla. Band Dirs. Assn., Tulsa, 1995, chmn. HS clinic, 97. Baseball coach Grove (Okla.) Little League, 2001—02; bi-vocational youth min. Grove (Okla.) First Bapt. Ch., 1995—2001; bi-vocational music min. Elk River Bapt. Ch., Grove, 2002—. Named Young Bandmaster of Yr., Phi Beta Mu, 1996. Mem.: Okla. Music Adjudicators Assn., Nat. Assn. Music Educators, Internat. Assn. Jazz Edn., Okla. Music Educators Assn. (chmn. jazz divsn. 1999—2000). Avocations: playing music, camping, composing music, fishing. Office: Grove High School PO Box 450789 Grove OK 74345 Fax: 918-786-6454.

ILLIANO, ANTONIO, language educator, researcher; b. Monte di Procida, Naples, Italy, Apr. 21, 1934; arrived in U.S., 1960; s. Fausto Illiano and Luigina Scotto; m. Elfriede R. Illiano, June 4, 1962; 1 child, Vincent A. DLitt, Univ. Naples, Naples, Italy, 1958; PhD, Univ. Calif., Berkeley, Calif., 1966. Instr. Univ Calif., Santa Barbara, Calif., 1963—66; asst. prof. Univ. Oregon, Eugene, Oreg., 1967—68, Univ. N.C., Chapel Hill, NC, 1969—73, assoc. prof., 1973—81, prof., 1982—. Assoc. editor Forum Italicum, SUNY at Stonibrook; series editor Dictionary of Literary Biography, Detroit. Author: Introduzione alla critica pirandelliana, 1976, Metapsichica e letteratura in Pirandello, 1982, Per l'esegesi del Corbaccio, 1991, Morfologia della narrazione mazoniana, 1993, Sulle sponde del Prepurgatorio, 1997, Da Boccaccio a Pirandello, 1997, Dalla Vita Nuova a Palomar, 1999, Invito al romanzo d'autrice, 2001; co-editor (translator): The Italian Madrigal, 1971, On humor, 1974; co-translator Poeti e filsofi medievali, 1975, (filmscript) Forum Italicum, 1982; co-editor: 20th Century Italian Poets, 1992, Italian Culture, 1993. Mem.: Montesi d'America, Am. Assn. of Tchrs. of Italian. Home: 400 Ridgecrest Dr Chapel Hill NC 27514 Office: Univ NC Chapel Hill NC 27599

ILLNER-CANIZARO, HANA, physician, oral surgeon, researcher; b. Prague, Czechoslovakia, Nov. 2, 1939; came to U.S., 1968; d. Evzen Pospisil and Emilie (Chrastna) Pospisilova; m. Pavel Illner, June 14, 1963 (div. 1981);

children: Martin Illner, Anna Illner; m. Peter Corte Canizaro, Nov. 1, 1982. MD, Charles U., Prague, 1961. Diplomate Am. Bd. Oral Surgery. Resident in oral surgery Inst. of Health, Pribram, Czechoslovakia, 1961-63; attending physician Oral Surgery Clinic, Prague, 1963-68; rsch. assoc. dept. surgery U. Tex. Southwestern Med. Sch., Dallas, 1969-72, instr. surgery, 1972-74, U. Wash. Sch. Medicine, Seattle, 1974-77; asst. prof. surgery Cornell U. Med. Coll., N.Y.C., 1977-81, assoc. prof. surgery, 1981-83, Tex. Tech U. Health Scis. Ctr., Lubbock, 1984-88, prof. surgery, 1988—. Site visitor NIGMS Postdoctoral Tng. Grant, Bethesda, Md., 1987. Mem. editorial bd. Circulatory Shock, N.Y.C., 1981—; manuscript reviewer Surgery, Gynecology and Obstetrics, Chgo., 1985—; contbr. chpts. to books, articles to profl. jours. Grantee NIH, 1979-83, 87-92, Tex. Tech U. Health Scis. Ctr., 1985-86, U.S. dept. Army, 1988-90; Fogarty Sr. Internat. fellow, 1991-92. Mem. Shock Soc. Avocations: remodeling of historical homes, gardening, skiing, pottery. Home: 4622 8th St Lubbock TX 79416-4722 Office: Tex Tech U Health Scis Ctr 3601 4th St Lubbock TX 79430-0001

ILOGIENBOH, CAROLINE O. protective services official, publishing executive; b. Ubiaja, Edo, Nigeria, July 31, 1957; arrived in U.S., 1987; d. Augustine Asa and Esther Oniha Omoifo; m. Ephraim Eghehi Ilogienboh, Feb. 26, 1988; children: Ebinehita, Ofure, Nemedia. BA, U. Alta., Edmonton, Alta., Can., 1982. Cert. criminal justice counselor Addiction Profls. Cert. Bd NJ. Adminstrv. officer Nigerian Telecom., Lagos, 1983—87; social worker Cmty. Svc. N.J., East Orange, 1988—89; probation officer Superior Ct. N.J., East Orange, 1989—; pub. Sun Rose Pubs., East Orange, 2001—. Mem. adv. bd. Minority Concerns Com., Newark, 1999—, Essex County Coalition-Teen Pregnancy, East Orange, NJ, 2000—, Sch. Based Com., Orange, NJ, 2003. Author: Jayda's Story-Lost at Crossroads, 2001, The Return of Tyreek, 2002, poetry. Recipient Appreciation award, Probation Assn. N.J., Atlantic City, 2001. Mem.: Watchung Heights Neighborhood Assn. (program chair 1999—). Avocations: reading, travel, swimming, writing, sewing. Address: PO Box 2314 East Orange NJ 07019 Office: Essex Vicinage Probation Svcs 7th Fl 60 Evergreen Pl East Orange NJ 07018

ILOGU, NOEL OBIAJULU, physician; b. Ibadan, Oyo, Nigeria, Dec. 15, 1961; came to U.S., 1994; s. Edmund Christopher and Elizabeth Chineze (Obiago) I.; m. Sandra Nneka Ike, July 15, 1995; children: Chudi, Chisom, Tobenna. MD, U. Benin, Nigeria, 1985. Diplomate Am. Bd. Internal Medicine. Sr. house officer NHS Hosps., U.K., 1988-92; career registrar Burnley (Eng.) Gen. Hosp., 1992-94; resident St. Peter's U. Hosp., New Brunswick, NJ, 1994—97; pvt. practice, Somerset, N.J., 1997—. Cons. on tobacco issues in Africa, Lagos, Nigeria, 1997—. Contbr. articles to profl. jours. Mem. ACP, Am. Soc. Internal Medicine, Am. Soc. Addiction Medicine, Med. Soc. N.J., Royal Coll. Physicians (Edinburgh), NAACP. Office: 81 Veronica Ave Ste 204 Somerset NJ 08873

ILSON, BERNARD, public relations executive; b. N.Y.C. s. Abraham and Goldie Itzkowitz; m. Carol Ruth Geller; children: David, James. BA, Bklyn. Coll.; MA, Columbia U.; PhD, NYU, 1998. Writer NBC TV, N.Y.C., 1955-57; acct. exec. David Alber Assocs., N.Y.C., 1957-58; v.p. Rogers, Cowan and Brenner, N.Y.C., 1958-63; pres. Bernie Ilson, Inc., N.Y.C., 1963—. Founder Hall of Fame of Am. Humor; past/present clients include The Ed Sullivan Show, The Beatles at Shea Stadium, All in the Family, The Monkees, The Patridge Family, Grammy Awards, Entertainer of Yr. Awards, Motown Records, Tony Bennett, Liberty Mut. Ins. Co., Control Data Corp., Am. Soc. for Hypertension, Missoula Children's Theater, Silver Dollar City, Branson, Mo., Mack Ave. Records, Stax Records, Bell Records, Grand Ole Opry, Hee Haw, The Negotiation Inst., Liberty Mut. Legends of Golf, NBC TV Network, Simon and Schuster, The City of Mobile Tricentennial, Games Workshop, Marketplace series on pub. radio, Soupy Sales, Ken Burns Statue of Liberty TV spl. Watercolor artist: Bklyn. Mus. Biennial Watercolor Show, 1954; one-man shows: Keulik Gallery, N.Y.C., Nemisis Galley, N.Y.C.; pub., founder Ilson's Inside Information, 1991—; guest appearances (Beatles expert) CBS-TV, ABC Radio Network, Westwood One Radio Network, CNN TV Network. Mem. Writers Guild Am., Acad. TV Arts and Scis., Country Music Assn., Mobile C. of C., Kappa Delta Pi. Clubs: Explorers. Avocations: painting, fishing. Office: 65 W 55th St New York NY 10019-4913

ILSTAD, GEIR ARE, venture capitalist; b. Norway, Mar. 19, 1955; s. Johan Julius and Rønnaug Synnøve (Kristensen) I.; children; Bergen Burnett, Alexandra Burnett. Degree in Econs., U. Fribourg, Switzerland, 1980; BS, MBA, Menlo Sch. Bus., Atherton, Calif., 1982. Prin. Ilstad Group, Menlo Park, 1981; mgr. Bergen Bank A/S, Oslo, 1982-85; ptnr. SØR Invest A/S, 1984; project mgr. corp. fin. A.S. Factoring Finans, Oslo, 1985-86; pres., chmn. Prudent Mgmt., Inc., Menlo Park, 1986—. Mem. Nesodden Speed Skating Club, 1969-75, Unge Høyre, Nesodden, Norway, 1971. Served with paratroopers Norwegian Army, 1975-76. Mem. Norwegian Bus. Forum (bd. dirs.). Avocations: jogging, tennis, gardening, carpentry, cooking. Home and Office: Prudent Mgmt Inc PO Box 275 Los Altos CA 94023-0275

ILTIS, HUGH HELLMUT, plant taxonomist-evolutionist, educator; b. Brno, Czechoslovakia, Apr. 7, 1925; came to U.S., 1939, naturalized, 1944; s. Hugo and Anne (Liebscher) I.; m. Grace Schaffel, Dec. 20, 1951 (div. Mar. 1958); children: Frank S., Michael George; m. Carolyn Merchant, Aug. 4, 1961 (div. June 1970); children: David Hugh, John Paul. BA, U. Tenn., 1948; MA, Washington U., St. Louis and Mo. Bot. Garden, 1950, PhD, 1952. Rsch. asst. Mo. Bot. Garden, 1948-52; asst. prof. botany U. Ark., 1952-55; asst. prof. U. Wis.-Madison, 1955-60, assoc. prof., 1960-67, prof., 1967-93, prof. emeritus, 1993—, curator herbarium, 1955-67, dir. univ. herbarium, 1967-93, dir. emeritus, 1993—. Vis. prof. U. Va., Biol. Sta., 1959; world-wide lectr. in field; expdns. to Costa Rica, 1949, 89, Peru, 1962-63, Mex., 1960, 71, 72, 77, 78, 79, 81, 82, 84, 87, 88, 90, 93, 94, 95, 96, Guatemala, 1976, Ecuador, 1977, St. Eustatius, P.R., 1989, USSR, 1975, 79, Nicaragua-Honduras, 1991, Venezuela, 1991, Hawaii, 1967; mem. adv. bd. Flora N.Am., 1970-73, Gov. Wis. Commn. State Forests, 1972-73; rsch. assoc. Mo. Bot. Gardens, Bot. Rsch. Inst. Tex.; co-instigator Reserva Biosfera Sierrra de Manantlán, Jalisco, Mex. Author: articles flora of Wis. and Mex., Capparaceae, biogeography, evolution of maize, human ecology, especially innate responses to, and needs for, nature, beauty, diversity and wild nature.; co-author: Flora de Manantlan, 1995, Atlas of the Wisconsin Prairie and Savana Flora, 2000, Checklist of the Vascular Plants of Wis., 2001; editor: Extinction or Preservation: What Biological Future for the South American Tropics?, 1978. With U.S. Army, 1944—46, ETO. Recipient Biologia award, U. Tenn., 1948, Feinstone Environ. award, SUNY, Syracuse, N.Y., 1990, Conservation award, Conservation Coun. Hawaii, 1990, Nat. Wildlife Fedn. Spl. Achievement award, 1992, Puga medal, U. de Guadalajara, Mex., 1994, Disting. Alumnus award, Missouri Bot. Gardens, 1999. Fellow AAAS, Linnean Soc. (London); mem. Am. Inst. Biol. Scis., Bot. Soc. Am. (Merit award 1996), Soc. Econ. Botany (Econ. Botanist of Yr. award 1998), Am. Soc. Plant Taxonomists (Asa Gray award 1994), Internat. Assn. Plant Taxonomy, Soc. Bot. Mex., Soc. Study Evolution, Ecol. Soc. Am., Wis. Acad. Arts, Sci. and Letters, Forum for Corr.-Internat. Ctr. Integrative Studies, Nature Conservancy (co-founder and trustee emeritus Wis. chpt., Nat. Oakleaf award 1963), Wilderness Soc., Sierra Club, Nat. Parks Assn., Citizens Natural Resources Assn. Wis., Natural Resource Def. Coun., Environ. Def. Fund, Friends of Earth, Zero Population Growth, Negative Population Growth, Soc. Conservation Biology (Disting. Achievement award 1994), Natural Areas Assn., Sigma Xi, Phi Kappa Phi. Achievements include co-discoverer Zea diploperennis, Z. nicaraguensi and lycopersicom chmielewskii (high sugar-content wild tomatoes). Home: 2784 Marshall Pky Madison WI 53713-1023 Office: U Wis Dept Botany 430 Lincoln Dr Madison WI 53706-1313 Fax: 608-262-7509. E-mail: tscochra@facstaff.wisc.edu. *If we are to remain healthy and sane, we must concern ourselves with the concept of an Optimum Human Environment, one which must include large portions of the wild and natural environment that shaped our bodies and minds through natural selection over the past millions of years. Hence, only in the preservation of nature, of the world's wild ecosystems and their species, and in a clear comprehension of evolution and the consequent urgent need to reduce both the world's human population and its unsustainable trashing of the environment, can we find the foundations for a meaningful new ethic that will insure a livable world for our children. For their sake, we have to become good ancestors and learn to live within limits.*

IM, JAEMO, research scientist; b. Seoul, Republic of Korea, Dec. 1, 1965; s. Jong Tae Lim and Gae Ja Chun; m. Su Young Cho, Jan. 19, 1973; 1 child, Joanna Juwon. MS, Stanford U., 1991; PhD, Northwestern U., 1998. Process engr. Applied Materials, Santa Clara, Calif., 1991—93; rsch. assoc. Argonne Nat. Lab., Ill., 1998—2000; device scientist Agere Systems, Alhambra, Calif., 2000—. Author: (book) Ferroelectric Thin Films, 1997, In Situ Real-Time Characterization of Thin Films, 2000; contbr. articles to profl. jours. Mem. Light of Love Mission Ch., Pasadena, Calif., 2001—03. Fellow, Seiwha Found., 1988; scholar, Northwestern U., 1994. Mem.: Materials Rsch. Soc. (Grad. Student award 1998), Sigma Xi (assoc.). Achievements include patents pending for elimination of destructive processes in capacitors for non-volatile ferroelectric random access memories; design of 10 Gb/s Avalnche Photo Detector; 40 Gb/s PIN Photo Detector; research in designed and constructed a novel in-situ real time surface characterization system (ToF-ISARS); microwave frequency electric-field tunable devices. Home: 2852 Ashley Dr Pasadena CA 91107 Office: Agere Systems 2015 West Chestnut St Alhambra CA 91803 Personal E-mail: jaemue@hotmail.com. E-mail: imjaemue@yahoo.com.

IM, KUN SHIN, information scientist, educator; s. Chang Seok Im and Won Hee Kim. PhD, Yonsei U., Seoul, Korea, 1995, U. S.C., 2000. Vis. asst. prof. U. of Calif., Riverside, 1999—2000; asst. prof. U. of Colo., Denver, 2000—. Contbr. articles to profl. jours. 2d lt. U.S. Army. Mem.: Beta Gamma Sigma (life). Avocations: golf, basketball, travel, movies. Office: University of Colorado at Denver PO Box 173364 Campus Box 165 Denver CO 80217-3364 E-mail: kim@carbon.cudenver.edu.

IMADE, LUCKY OSAGIE, political scientist, educator; b. Kano, Nigeria, Dec. 18, 1957; arrived in U.S., 1983; s. Gabriel Agho and Jant Agho Imade; m. Ayowie H. Imade, Dec. 31, 1991; children: Olivia, Lucky Imade, Jr. BA, Shaw U., 1987; MA, Clark U., Atlanta, 1993, PhD, 1995. Instr. polit. sci. Ga. Perimeter Coll., Atlanta, 1995—97; coord. internat. programs Shaw U., Raleigh, NC, 1997—. Fulbright scholar, 1999—2000. Mem.: Edo Soc. Rsch. (pres. 1999—). Avocations: soccer, reading, tennis, travel, basketball. Office: Shaw U 118 E South St Raleigh NC 27601 E-mail: limade@shawu.edu.

IMAM, M. ASHRAF, materials scientist, educator; b. Patna, Bihar, India, Sept. 7, 1945; came to U.S. 1970; s. Naimuddin Ahmad and Zakia (Begum) Ahmad; m. Shamim Akhtar, June 22, 1979; children: Nabil S., Rahil U., Mariam S. BS, Ranchi U., India, 1966; MS, Carnegie-Mellon U., 1972; DSc, George Washington U., 1976. Rsch. assoc. George Washington U., Washington, 1976-78, rsch. scientist, 1978-81, adj. prof., 1981—; guest scientist Nat. Inst. Standard, Gaithersburg, Md., 1974—; sr. rsch. scientist Geo-Centers Inc., Newton, Mass., 1981-84; metallurgist Naval Rsch. Lab., Washington, 1984—. Contbr. articles to profl. jours.; editor: Structure and Deformation of Boundaries, 1986, Advances in Low-Carbon High Strength Ferrous Alloys, 1993, Advanced Materials and Processing, 1998. MRL fellow Carnegie Mellon U., 1971-72, CSIR fellow, 1966-68; recipient George Kimbell Burgess award, 2003. Fellow Am. Soc. of Metals Internat.; mem. ASM, The Minerals, Metals, Materials Soc. (titanium com. 1980—, phys. metallurgy com. 19805, mech. metallurgy com. 1980—), Sigma Xi. Achievements include 8 patents. Home: 1159 Mill Garden Ct Great Falls VA 22066-1845 Office: Naval Rsch Lab Code 6320 4555 Overlook Ave SW Washington DC 20375-0001 E-mail: imam@anvil.nrl.navy.mil.

IMANA, JORGE GARRON, artist; b. Sept. 20, 1930; came to U.S., 1964, naturalized, 1974. s. Juan S. and Lola (Garron) I.; m. Cristina Imana; children: George, Ivan. Grad. fine arts acad., U. San Francisco Xavier, 1950. cert. Nat. Sch. for Tchrs., Bolivia, 1952. Prof. art. Nat. Sch. Tchrs., Sucre, 1954-56; prof. biology Padilla Coll., Sucre, 1956-60; head dept. art Inst. Normal Simon Bolivar, La Paz, Bolivia, 1961-62; propr., mgr. The Artists Showroom, San Diego, 1973—. Over 100 one-man shows of paintings in U.S., S. Am., and Europe, 1952—, including: Gallery Banet, La Paz, 1965, Artists Showroom, San Diego, 1964, 66, 68, 74, 76, 77, San Diego Art Inst., 1966, 68, 72, 73, Constrast Gallery, Chula Vista, Calif., 1966, Univ. de Zulia, Maracaibo, Venezuela, 1969, Spanish Village Art Ctr., San Diego, 1974, 75, 76, La Jolla Art Assn. Gallery, 1969, 72-93, Internat. Gallery, Washington, 1976, Galeria de Arte L'Atelier, La Paz, 1977, Mus. Nat., La Paz, 1987, 88, Casa del Arte, La Jolla, Calif., 1987, Simon Patino Found., Bolivia, 1994; numerous group shows including: Fine Arts Gallery, San Diego, 1964, Mus. Modern Art, Paris, 1973; exhibits in galleries of Budapest, Hungary, 1975, Moscow, 1975, Warsaw, Poland, 1976; represented in permanent collections: Mus. Nat., La Paz, Mus. de la Univ. de Potosi, Bolivia, Mus. Nat. de Bogota, Colombia, S. Am. Ministerio de Edn., Managua, Nicaragua, Bolivian Embassy, Moscow and Washington, also pbt. collections in U.S., Europe and Latin Am.; executed many murals including; Colegio Padilla, Sucre, Bolivia, 1958, Colegio Junin, Sucre, Bolivia, 1959, Sindicato de Construccion Civil, Lima, Peru, 1960. Hon. consul of Bolivia, So. Calif., 1969-73. Served to lt. Bolivian Army, 1953. Recipient Mcpl. award Sucre, Bolivia, 1958. Mem. San Diego Art Inst., San Diego Watercolor Soc., Internat. Fine Arts Guild, La Jolla Art Assn. Home: Apt 212 2510 Torrey Pines Rd La Jolla CA 92037-3424

IMBARUS, AURA, language educator, consultant; b. Sibiu, Romania, July 2, 1971; arrived in US, 1997; d. Stefan Ioan and Aurelia Imbarus; m. Mihai Chiorean, Sept. 2, 1996. BA, Lucian Blaga U., Sibiu, 1995, MA, 1996, PhD, 2002. Cert. tchr. Calif. Asst. prof. English State U. Lucian Blaga, Sibiu, 1995—97; English tchr. Le Conte Humanities Magnet, LA, 1998—2000; English instr. LA City Coll., 1999—2000; English tchr. West H.S., Torrance, Calif., 2000—. English instr. Sylvan Learning Ctr., LA, 1998—99, LA Harbor Coll., Wilmington, Calif., 2000—, Long Beach (Calif.) City Coll., 2002—; ESL instr. El Camino Coll., Torrance, 2001—; interview operator Gallup Pool, Sibiu, 1993—97; head news dept. Radio Contact, Sibiu, 1993—97; mem. editl. bd. Jour. Hosp. Librarianship. Author: Research of Language & Literature, 2000; contbr. articles to profl. jours. Named Outstanding H.S. Tchr., U. Calif., 2001—02. Mem.: AAUW, MLA, Nat. Coun. Tchrs. English, Calif. Tchrs. Assn. Avocations: reading, swimming, ice skating, painting. Home: # 463 384 S Miraleste Dr San Pedro CA 90732-6068 Office: West HS 20401 Victor St Torrance CA 90503 Personal E-mail: auraimbarus@hotmail.com.

IMBAULT, JAMES JOSEPH, manufacturing executive; b. Muskegon, Mich., Oct. 31, 1944; s. Joseph Lionel and Ruth Pauline (Schutter) I.; m. Vallery Ann Rumisek, Dec. 29, 1967; children— Michelle, Allan. A.S., Muskegon Community Coll., 1965; B.S. Mech. Engrng. with honors, Mich. Tech. U., 1967; postgrad. UCLA, 1972-73. Sr. mem. tech. staff RCA, E.A.S.D., Van Nuys, Calif., 1968-74; mech. engrng. mgr. Litton Italia SPA, Rome, Italy, 1974-78; electromech. engrng. mgr. Incosym, Inc., Westlake Village, Calif., 1978-82, v.p., 1982-88, also dir.; dir. ops. Precision Products Plant Northrop, Norwood, Mass., 1988-97; v.p., gen. mgr. Electroswitch, Weymouth, Mass., 1997—. Patentee in field. Recipient Meritorious Performance award Muskegon Community Coll., 1965; Mich. Tech. U. scholar, 1965-67. Mem. Nat. Soc. Profl. Engrs., ASME, AIAA, Mich. Tech. U. Alumni Assn., Pi Tau Sigma, Tau Beta Pi, Phi Kappa Phi. Republican. Home: 12 Hayden Dr Foxboro MA 02035-1127

IMBEAU, STEPHEN ALAN, allergist; b. Portland, Oreg., Nov. 25, 1947; s. David A. and Marjory Anne (Jacobsen) I.; m. Shirley Ruth Burke, Aug. 18, 1979; children: Stephanie Frances, Andrew Paul, Charles Burke. BA, U. Calif., Berkeley, 1969; MD, U. Calif., San Francisco, 1973. Diplomate Am. Bd. Internal Medicine, Am. Bd. Allergy. Intern U. Wis., Madison, S.C., 1973-74, resident in internal medicine, 1974-75, resident in allergy, 1976-78, resident in infectious diseases, 1978-79; pvt. practice Florence, S.C., 1980—. Budget and control bd. S.C. Data Oversight Com., 1993—98; founder Coastal Growth Ptnrs. (a Venture Capital Co.), 1997; bd. dirs. Joint Coun. Allergy and Immunology; gen. ptnr. Venture Fund, 2001—, Coastal Growth Ptnrs., 1997—, Trelys Investments, Venture Capital Co., 1997—; co-owner profl. hockey team Columbia Infernos; mem. practicing physicans adv. coun. U.S. HHS Health Care Financing Adminstrn., 2000—03; commr. S.C. Dept. Health, 2003—. Contbr. articles to profl. jours. Chmn. Florence Symphony Orch., 1985-91; bd. dirs. Big Bros., 1989-92, Am. Lung Assn., 1982-86, Florence County Progress, chmn. 1993-95. Fellow ACP; mem. AMA (S.C. alt. del. 1992-98), Am. Acad. Allergists, S.C. Med. Soc. (trustee 1988-90, sec. bd. 1990-94, treas. 1995-97, S.C. Ambassador of the Yr. 1995, pres.-elect 1997, pres. 1998-99), Am. Acad. Allergy, Asthma and Immunology (alt. del. to AMA 1999—), Joint Coun. Allergy Immunology (bd. mem., sec. 2002—), Florence County Med. Soc. (pres. 1984-85), Lions (pres. 1987-88). Avocations: reading, hunting, stamp collecting. Home: 950 Park Ave Florence SC 29501-5734 Office: 8W E Cheves St Ste 420 Florence SC 29506-2769

IMBER, RICHARD JOSEPH, physician, dermatologist; b. Darby, Pa., Apr. 9, 1944; s. Joseph and Geraldine (Frances) I.; m. Helen Lee Stick, Nov. 18, 1971. BS, U. Dayton, 1966; MD, Temple U., 1970. Diplomate Am. Bd. Dermatology. Intern Denver Presbyn. Med. Ctr., 1970-71; resident dept. dermatology U. Colo. Health Sci. Ctr., 1971-74; chief of dermatology USAF Acad., Colorado Springs, 1974-76; sr. staff dermatologist Colo. Permanente Med. Group, Denver, 1976-83; dermatologist Denver Skin Clinic, 1983—. Asst. clin. prof. dermatology U. Colo. Med. Sch., Denver, 1974—. Contbr. articles to profl. jours. Maj. USAF, 1974-76. Fellow Am. Acad. Dermatology; mem. Pacific Dermatologic Assn., Colo. Med. Soc., Denver Med. Soc., Colo. Dermatologic Soc. (sec.-treas. 1980, v.p. 1981, pres. 1982). Avocation: scuba diving. Home: 4020 S Bellaire St Englewood CO 80110-5028 Office: Denver Skin Clinic 2200 E 18th Ave Denver CO 80206-1205

IMBERT, RICHARD CONRAD, insurance company executive, real estate developer; b. N.Y.C., Jan. 30, 1941; s. Henry A. and Patricia (Boyer) I.; married; children: Peter, Cynthia, Elise; m. Susan Fusaro. Grad. h.s., Amityville, N.Y. Underwriter Ins. Co. N.Am., Hempstead, NY, 1961—64; sales exec. Ashby Lee Biedler, Inc., N.Y.C., 1964—67, pres., 1967—74, Fisher-Biedler, Inc., Amityville, 1974—85, Am. Profl. Agy., Inc., Amityville, 1974—, R.C.I. Industries Inc., Amityville, 1980—, IMP Properties, Inc., Amityville, 1975—; pres., CEO Windmill Manor Farms, Inc., 2000—. V.p. L.I. Polymers, Hauppauge, N.Y., 1988; bd. dirs., chmn. bd. Polymerix, Inc., N.J., 1985-91; ptnr. Sheraton Hotel, Hauppauge. Chmn. bishop's appeal com. St. Martin of Tours Roman Cath. Ch., Amityville, 1985, trustee, 1987-90, bishop's coun of stewarts, 1990; mem. Rep. Senatorial Inner Circle, Pres. Adv. Com.; trustee L.I. Aquarium, Bay Shore, N.Y., 1997; dep. commr. of police Amityville Police Dept., 2000—. Named Man of the Yr., L.I. Aquarium, 2000. Mem. N.Y. State Thorobred Owners Assn., Southward Ho Country Club (West Islip, N.Y.), Unqua Corinthian Yacht Club (commodore 1981-82). Republican. Avocations: yachting, scuba. Office: RCI Industries Inc 95 Broadway Amityville NY 11701-2728

IMBRIE, ANDREW WELSH, composer, educator; b. N.Y.C., Apr. 6, 1921; s. Andrew C. and Dorothy (Welsh) I.; m. Barbara Cushing, Jan. 31, 1953; children: Andrew, John (dec.). AB, Princeton U., 1942; MA, U. Calif.-Berkeley, 1947. Instr. music U. Calif., Berkeley, 1947, 49-51, asst. prof., 1951, assoc. prof., 1957-60, prof., 1960-91, Jerry and Evelyn Hemmings Chambers chair dept. music, 1989-92. Composer-in-residence Tanglewood Music Ctr., Lenox, Mass., summer 1991; guest prof. Brandeis U., 1982, U. Ala., 1992, U. Chgo., 1994, 96-97, Northwestern U., 1994, NYU, 1995, Fromm prof., Harvard U., fall, 1997. Compositions include 3 symphonies, 5 string quartets, trios, sonatas, songs, orchestral and choral works, works for various chamber ensembles, Angle of Repose (opera), 3 piano concerti, concerti for violin, cello and flute, Dance-cantata Prometheus Bound, Requiem in memoriam John Imbrie (Grammy award nomination 2000), Adam (cantata). Bd. dirs. Koussevitzky Found.; bd. govs. San Francisco Symphony, 1982-91. Recipient Circle award N.Y. Music Critics, 1943-44; Alice M. Ditson fellow Columbia U., 1946-47; fellow Am. Acad. in Rome, 1947-49; grantee Nat. Inst. Arts and Letters, 1950; Guggenheim fellow, 1953-54, 60-61; merit award Boston Symphony Orch., 1955; creative arts award Brandeis U., 1958; Naumburg award, 1960; grantee Nat. Found. on Arts and Humanities; composer in residence Am. Acad. Rome, 1967-68; recipient Walter Hinrichsen award Columbia U., 1971 Mem. Am. Acad. Arts and Letters, Am. Acad. Arts and Scis., Phi Beta Kappa. Clubs: Bohemian (San Francisco). Home: 2625 Rose St Berkeley CA 94708-1920

IMBROGNO, CYNTHIA, magistrate judge; b. 1948; BA, Indiana U. Pa., 1970; JD cum laude, Gonzaga U., 1979. Law clk. to Hon. Justin L. Quackenbush U.S. Dist. Ct. (Wash. ea. dist.), 9th circuit, 1980-83; law clk. Wash. State Ct. of Appeals, 1984; civil rights staff atty. Ea. Dist. of Wash., 1984-85, complex litigation staff atty., 1986-88; with Preston, Thorgrimson, Shidler, Gates & Ellis, 1988-90, Perkins Coie, 1990-91; magistrate judge U.S. Dist. Ct. (Wash. ea. dist.), 9th circuit, Spokane, 1991—. Office: 740 US Courthouse 920 W Riverside Ave Spokane WA 99201-1010

IMBUS, SHARON HAUGHEY, neuroscience nurse; b. Norfolk, Va., Jan. 7, 1947; d., Everett Wayne and Bettie Louise Haughey; m. Charles Eugene Imbus, June 14, 1969; children: Edward Allen, Andrew Haughey. BSN, Ohio State U., 1969, MSN, 1971. RN, NP, Calif.; BLS instr. Charge nurse Children's Hosp., Columbus, Ohio, 1969-71; staff nurse L.A. County-U. So. Calif. Burn Ctr., 1971-72; biostatistician U. So. Calif., L.A., 1973-78; dir., spl. studies L.A. County-U. So. Calif. Burn Ctr., 1978-86; clin. specialist/nurse practitioner Imbus Fortanasce Neurology Ctr., Arcadia, Calif., 1989-2001; dir. neurol. rsch., clin. specialist/nurse practitioner Charles E. Imbus, MD, Inc., 1997—. Legal nursing cons., 1992; cert. ACE aerobis cinstr./rehab. staff Meth. Hosp., Arcadia, 1990; mem. ethics com. Meth. Hosp. of So. Calif., Arcadia, 1986—; speaker Internat. Ethics Conf., San Francisco, 1979. Contbr. articles to profl. jours. Mem.: Am. Assn. Neurosci. Nurses, Am. Burn Assn., Calif. Nurses Assn. Roman Catholic. Avocations: aerobic dancing, fitness, reading. Office: Charles E Imbus MD Inc 665 W Naomi Ave Ste 202 Arcadia CA 91007-7563

IMEL, JOHN MICHAEL, lawyer; b. Cushing, Okla., Aug. 4, 1932; s. Arthur Blaine and Hazel Monnet (Kelly) I.; m. Patricia Ann Carney, July 31, 1954; children: Blythe Michele, Kathryn Ann, Dixie Lynn, Sally Louise. BS, U. Okla., 1954, JD, 1959. Bar: Okla. 1959, U.S. Dist. Ct. (no. dist.) Okla. 1961, U.S. Ct. Appeals (10th cir.) 1961, U.S. Supreme Ct. 1962, U.S. Dist. Ct. (we. dist.) Okla. 1967, U.S. Dist. Ct. (ea. dist.) Okla. 1971. Asst. atty. County of Tulsa, 1959—60; mcpl. judge City of Tulsa, 1960—61; U.S. atty. U.S. Dept. Justice, Tulsa, 1961—67; ptnr. Moyers, Martin, Santee Imel & Tetrick, Tulsa, 1967—. Regent U. Okla., Norman, 1981-88, chmn., 1987-88; trustee Children's Med. Ctr., Tulsa, 1979-84. Capt. USNR, 1954-56. Fellow Am. Bar Found., Am. Coll. Trial Lawyers (state chmn. 1987-88); mem. Am. Inns of Ct. (program chmn. 1989-90, Exemplary Leadership award 1996), So. Hills Country Club (bd. govs. 1993-99), Tulsa Club (pres. 1990), Rotary (pres. 1968-69). Democrat. Methodist. Avocations: golf, swimming, tennis, reading. Home: 3920 E 58th Pl Tulsa OK 74135-7823 Office: Moyers Martin Santee Imel & Tetrick 401 S Boston Ste 1100 Tulsa OK 74103 E-mail: imel@moyersmartin.com.

IMERSHEIN, WILLIAM LEONARD, trimmings company executive, retired; b. N.Y.C., Aug. 21, 1922; s. Louis Emil and Rosetta Charlotte (Kaufman) I.; m. Norma Berman, June 20, 1948; children: Ruth Elizabeth, Judith Anne, Sara Louise. BS in Textile Engring., Ga. Tech., Atlanta, 1947. Sec.-treas., CEO Novelty Cord & Tassel Co., Inc., Bklyn., 1947-2000, ret., 2000. Hon. trustee Temple Sinai L.I., Lawrence, N.Y., Greater N.Y. Fedn. Reform Synagogues, 1994; troop leader, merit badge dean, committeeman Boy Scouts Nassau County, 1934—. With US Army, 1942-46, ETO. Jewish.

IMES, DANIEL ALAN, music educator; s. Armond Russell Imes Jr. and Bonnie Imes; m. Jill Veronica Isaac, July 12, 1986; 1 child, Emma Grace. MusB, Morehead State U., 1982—86; MA in edn., Western Ky. U., 1989—92. Cert. tchg. Ky., 1986. Band dir. Green H.S., Franklin Furnace, Ohio, 1986—88, Campbellsville H.S., Ky., 1988—. Mem.: Hon. Order of Ky. Colonels, Kappa Delta Pi, Phi Beta Mu Internat. Bandmasters' Frat., Phi Mu Alpha Sinfonia. R Conservative. Baptist. Home: 202 Wildflower Drive Campbellsville KY 42718 Office: Campbellsville HS 230 W Main St Campbellsville KY 42718

IMESCH, JOSEPH LEOPOLD, bishop; b. Grosse Pointe Farms, Mich., June 21, 1931; s. Dionys and Margaret (Margelisch) I.. BS, Sacred Heart Sem., 1953; student, N.Am. Coll., Rome, 1953-57; STL, Gregorian U., Rome, 1957. Ordained priest Roman Cath. Ch., 1956. Sec. to Cardinal Dearden, 1959—71; pastor Our Lady of Sorrows Ch., Farmington, Mich., 1971—77; titular bishop of Pomaria, aux. bishop of Detroit, 1973—79; asst. bishop N.W. region, 1977—79; bishop of Joliet, 1979—. Office: Chancery Office 425 Summit St Joliet IL 60435-7155*

IMHOF, SUSAN ANNE, poet; b. Alexandria, Va, May 22, 1967; d. William Anthony and Nancy Louise (Davis) I.; m. Chad Wollerton; children: Evan Davis Wollerton, Spencer Champe Wollerton. BA in English, U. Va., 1989; MFA in

Poetry, Warren Wilson Coll., 1994. Editor Blue Penny Quar., Charlottesville, Va., 1997-98; freelance poet, writer, editor, tchr., 1994—; editor The Workcare Group, Charlottesville, Va., 1999—2001. Author: (periodicals) Va. Quarterly Rev., Seneca Rev., New Va. Rev., Iris, Willow Rev., S.E. Rev., others. Reader Va. Festival of the Book, Charlottesville, 1996—2002; mem. poetry troupe For Crying Out Loud, 1990—; participant People's Poetry Gathering, 2001; Bd. dirs. Westminister Child Care Ctr., Charlottesville, 1998—99. Recipient Wagenheim Prize for Fiction, 1989. E-mail: imhof@cstone.net E-mail: wollertn@cstone.net.

IMHOFF, RICHARD JAMES, trust company executive, financial planner; b. Boonville, June 4, 1958; s. James Alvin and Clara Mae (Hurt) I.; m. Angela Marie Hutchinson, Dec. 28, 1979; children: Anna Michelle, Danielle Dominique. Student, Columbia (Mo.) Coll., 1976-78, Coll. for Fin. Planning, 1987, Nicholls State U., 1988; BS in Bus. Adminstrn., Drury Coll., 1996. CFP®, Accredited Asset Mgmt. Specialist. Rep., fin. planner NIS Fin. Svcs. Inc., Kansas City, Mo., 1979-84, Waddell and Reed Fin. Svcs./United Investors Life Ins. Co., Kansas City, Mo., 1984-85, IDS Fin. Svcs., Houma, La., 1985; asst. v.p., trust officer Premier Bank South La., Houma, 1985-89; trust officer Ctrl. Trust Bank, Jefferson City, Mo., 1989—2003; v.p., trust officer Empire Bank, Springfield, Mo., 1989—2003; trust officer Ozark Mountain Bank, Branson, Mo., 2003; sr. v.p. Sterling Trust Co., Springfield, 2003—. Instr. Ozark Empire chpt. Ctr. for Fin. Tng. Bd. dirs Springfield Pub. Schs. Found.; pres. parish coun., mem. fin. com. mem. planned giving com. St. Agnes Cathedral; mem. planned giving com. Springfield Cath. Schs. Mem. Fin. Planning Assn., Greene County Estate Planning Coun. (pres.), K.C. Republican. Avocations: tennis, basketball. Office: Sterling Trust Co Inc 2870 S Ingram Mills Rd Ste D Springfield MO 65804 Business E-Mail: rimhoff@sterlingtrust.biz.com.

IMHOFF, WALTER FRANCIS, investment banker; b. Denver, Aug. 7, 1931; s. Walter Peter and Frances Marie (Barkhausen) I.; m. Georgia Ruth Stewart, June 16, 1973; children: Stacy, Randy, Theresa, Michael, Robert. BSBA, Regis U., Denver, 1955; D Pub. Svc. (hon.), Regis U., 1991. Asst. v.p. Coughlin & Co., Denver, 1955-60; pres., chief exec. officer Hanifen, Imhoff Inc., Denver, 1960-2000; mng. dir. Stifel, Nicolaus & Co., 2000—; dir. Republic Fin. Corp., 2001—. Guest lectr. U. Colo., 1976 Trustee Regis Coll., 1975—95, treas., 1976—79, vice chmn., 1981, chmn., 1982—89, life trustee, 1998—; bd. dirs. NCCJ, 1980—89, chmn., 1986—89, life trustee, 1998—; bd. dirs. Arapahoe Libr. Found., 1990—94, Channel 6 Edni. TV, treas., 1996—97, vice chmn., 1997—98, chmn., 1998—99; bd. dirs. Highland Hills Found., 1993—, Denver Area coun. Boy Scouts Am., 1986—, v.p., 1989—; bd. dirs. St. Joseph's Hosp., mem. exec. com., 1991, vice chmn., 1994, chmn., 1995—98; bd. dirs. Kempe Children's Found., 1992, chmn., 1994—97; bd. dirs. 9 Who Cares, 1998—, Caring for Colo., 2001—; chmn. Colo. Concern, 1988—, St. Joseph Hosp. Found., 2000—; chmn. exec. com. 2% Club, 2000—; trustee Irish Cmty. Ctr., 2001. Named Outstanding Alumnus Regis Coll., 1970 Mem. Bond Club Denver (pres. 1965), Colo. Mcpl. Bond Dealers Assn. (pres. 1973), Mid-Continent Securities Industry Assn. (dir. 1972-75), Securities Industry Assn. (chmn. S.W. region 1991-95, dir. 1993-96), Nat. Assn. Security Dealers, Pub. Securities Assn. (dir. 1972-75), Denver C. of C. (bd. dirs. 1986 91, treas. 1989-91), Rose Hosp. Found., Centennial C. of C. (vice chmn.), NCCJ, Alpha Kappa Psi, Alpha Sigma Nu. Clubs: Denver (pres. 1981-82). Republican. Roman Catholic. Home: 10432 E Ida Pl Greenwood Village CO 80111-3753 Office: 1125 17th St Ste 1600 Denver CO 80202-2024

IMIG, JOHN DAVID, medical educator; b. Bloomington, Ill., Nov. 20, 1962; m. Melinda L. Peel, June 9, 1984; children: Allyson E., Emily R. BA in Biology magna cum laude, Blackburn Coll., Carlinville, Ill., 1985; PhD in Physiology, U. Louisville, 1990. Postdoctoral fellow Med. Coll. Wis., Milw., 1990-93; instr. rsch. physiology Tulane U. Sch. Medicine, New Orleans, 1993-95, rsch. asst. prof. physiology, 1995-98, asst. prof. physiology, 1998—2001; assoc. prof. physiology Med. Coll. Ga., Augusta, 2001—. Various editorial positions with profl. jours.; contbr. articles to profl. jours. LeRoy Edn. Assn. scholar, 1981, faculty Blackburn Coll. scholar, 1982, 84; Merck Sharp & Dohme fellow, 1992, NIH fellow, 1992-95; Young Investigator awardee Am. Soc. Hypertension. Fellow Am. Heart Assn. (coun. kidney in cardiovascular disease, high blood pressure rsch.); mem. Am. Physiol. Soc., Micorcirculatory Soc., Golden Key. Home: 1195 Rivershyre Dr Evans GA 30809-8209 Office: Med Coll Ga Vascular Biology Ctr 1120 15th St Augusta GA 30912-2500

IMIG, WILLIAM GRAFF, lawyer, lobbyist; b. Omaha, Aug. 13, 1941; s. Jacob H. and Gretchen (Kirk) I.; m. Joyce Stevens, Dec. 18, 1976; children: Scott, Kari, Steven. BA, Cornell U., 1963, LLB, 1965. Bar: Colo. 1965, U.S. Ct. Appeals (10th cir.) 1965, U.S. Supreme Ct. 1969. Assoc. Sherman & Howard, Denver, 1965-66; v.p., shareholder Ireland, Stapleton, Pryor & Pascoe, Denver, 1970-92; pvt. practice, Denver, 1992—. Colo. counsel Nat. Assn. Ind. Insurers, Des Plaines, Ill., 1971—; Colo. legis. counsel Allstate Ins. Cos., 1982—. Bd. editors Cornell Law rev., 1964-65. Chmn. Colo. Gov.'s Auto Insurance Task Force, 2002; trustee Colo. chpt. Nat. Multiple Sclerosis Soc., 1995-2000; mem. Auto Ins. Roundtable. Capt. JAGC, U.S. Army, 1966-70. Mem. Colo. Bar Assn. (bd. govs. 1974-77, pro bono award 1985), Colo. Assn. Commerce and Industry (chmn. tort reform coun., chmn. auto ins. roundtable), City Club of Denver, Denver Law Club, Phi Kappa Phi. Republican. Episcopalian. Home and Office: 1795 Monaco Pky Denver CO 80220-1644

IMLAH, MARYPAT, sales, advertising and marketing executive; b. Bklyn., Oct. 25, 1957; d. Kenneth William Joseph and Ann Marie (Beckley) Olivarius; m. Craig Alexander Imlah, Sept. 18, 1982; children: Christopher Edward, Jamison Robert, Meghan Patricia. BS in Mktg. and Comm., Ramapo State Coll., N.J., 1979; MBA in Mktg. and Mgmt., Fairleigh Dickinson U., 1985. Rschr., pub. rels. MacNeil/Lehrer Report Sta. WNET-TV, N.Y.C., 1977; salesperson Terrace Realty, Montvale, N.J., 1977-79; direct mail advt. copywriter Prentice-Hall, Inc., Englewood Cliffs, N.J., 1979-81; editor, promotional designer Beauty & Barber Supply Inst., Englewood, N.J., 1981-83; nat. dir. advt. and pub. rels. Emerson Radio Corp., North Bergen, N.J., 1983—, Oakton, Va., 1983—. Founder, pres. Imagery Print & Advt., Print Brokerage Design Agy., Promotional Items. E-mail: imagerypnt@aol.com.

IMMEL, BARBARA K. management consultant; b. Bakersfield, Calif., July 31, 1956; m. Joseph Herbert Immel, Jr., Aug. 31, 1979; children: Joseph Herbert Immel, III, Elizabeth Logan. BA in English, U. Calif., Santa Barbara, 1978, single subject tchg. credential, 1979; grad., Stanford Profl. Pub. Course, 1981, Stanford U. Exec. Pub. Course, 1982, grad., 2002, Buckley Sch. Pub. Speaking, 2000, grad., 2001. Asst. to pres. Vet. Practice Pub. Co., Santa Barbara, 1980—81; tech. editor I-III Syva Co., Palo Alto, Calif., 1982—86; adminstr. Syntex Corp., Palo Alto, Calif., 1986—92; compliance mgr. Chiron Corp., Emeryville, Calif., 1993—95; cons. pres. Immel Resources, LLC, Petaluma, Calif., 1995—. Vol. libr. Career Action Ctr., Palo Alto, Calif., 1982—86; instr. U. Calif. Berkeley Ext., 1995—2000, co-dir. drug devel. course, 1998—2000; guest lectr. undergrad. pharmacology course U. Calif., Berkeley, 1999—; cons. in field. Columnist: Biopharm mag., 1996—2001; contbr. articles to profl. jours. Scholar Pres. scholar, U. Calif. Santa Barbara, 1974—78. Mem.: Drug Info. Assn., Am. Soc. for Quality, Regulatory Affairs Profl. Soc., Pharm. Rschrs. and Mfrs. Am. (tng. com. 1988—92), Parenteral Drug Assn. Avocations: reading, travel, beading, ribbon embroidery, quilting. Office: Immel Resources LLC Ste B 616 Petaluma Blvd North Petaluma CA 94952 E-mail: immel@immel.com.

IMMELT, JEFFREY R. diversified technology and services company executive; b. Cincinnati, Ohio, Feb. 19, 1956; s. Joseph and Donna Immelt; m. Andrea Immelt; 1 child. BA in Applied Math., Dartmouth Coll., 1978; MBA, Harvard U., 1982. With GE Corp. Mktg., 1982; various positions GE Plastics, 1982-89; v.p. consumer svc. GE Appliances, 1989-91, v.p. worldwide mktg. and product mgmt.; v.p., gen. mgr. GE Plastics Am., 1992-96; pres., CEO GE Med. Sys., 1997—2000; pres., chmn. elect GE Co., 2000—01, chmn., CEO, 2001—. Office: GE 3135 Easton Tpke Fairfield CT 06431-0002

IMMERMAN, NEIL, academic administrator, computer scientist; BS, MS, Yale U., 1974; PhD, Cornell U., 1980. Grad. program dir., prof. computer sci. U. Mass., Amherst. Author: (book) Descriptive Complexity, 1999. Co-recipient Gödel prize in theoretical computer sci., 1995; recipient Guggenheim fellowship, 2003—04. Fellow: Assn. for Computing Machinery. Office: U Mass Dept Computer Sci Rm 374 140 Governor's Dr Amherst MA 01003-9264*

IMMERMAN, WILLIAM JOSEPH, film company executive; b. NYC, Dec. 29, 1937; s. Nathan and Sadye (Naumoff) I.; children: Scott, Eric, Lara. BS, U. Wis., 1959; JD, Stanford U., 1963. Bar: Calif., 1964. Dep. dist. atty. LA County, LA, 1963-65; v.p. bus. affairs Am. Internat. Pictures, LA, 1965-72; sr. v.p. 20th Century Fox Film Corp., LA, 1972-77; prod. Warner Bros. Pictures, LA, 1977-79; pres. Scoric Prod., Inc., LA, 1977—, Salem Prod., Inc., LA, 1978—, Distbn. Expense Co., LA, 1986-95; of counsel Barash and Hill, LA, 1983-93, Kenoff and Machinger, LA, 1993-2000; pres. Immkirk Fin. Corp., 1987-2000; pvt. practice Santa Monica, Calif., 2000—01; sr. exec. v.p., COO Crusader Entertainment, LLC, 2000—. Chmn. Cinema Group, Inc., LA, 1979-82; vice-chmn. Cannon Pictures, Inc., LA, 1989-90; cons. to pres. Pathe Comm. Corp., LA, 1988-89; dir. Heritage Entertainment Corp., LA, 1987-91. Dir. The Thalians, LA, 1978-99. Capt. USAR, 1959-68. Mem. Assn. Motion Picture and TV Producers (bd. dir. 1972-77), Ind. Film and Distbr. Assn. (bd. dir. 1966-70), Acad. Motion Picture Arts and Sci., State Bar Calif, Los Angeles County Bar Assn. Avocations: tennis, theater, sporting events, travel. Office: Crusader Entertainment LLC 132 B S Lasky Dr Beverly Hills CA 90212 E-mail: bimmerman@earthlink.net.

IMMKE, KEITH HENRY, lawyer; b. Peoria, Ill., Jan. 18, 1953; s. Francis William and Pearl Lenora (Kime) I. BA, U. Ill., 1975; JD, So. Ill. U., 1978. Bar: Ill. 1978, U.S. Dist. Ct. (so. and ea. dist.) Ill. 1979. Assoc. Lawrence E. Johnson & Assocs., P.C., Champaign, Ill., 1979-87; staff atty. Dept. Ins. State Ill., Springfield, 1987-88; legal counsel Underground Storage Tank program (now Divsn. Petroleum and Chem. Safety), 1988-98; asst. legal counsel Office Fire Marshal State Ill., 1988—. Legal counsel Underground Storage Tank Program (now Div. Petroleum and Chem. Safety 1988-98), asst. legal counsel; Office Fire Marshal State Ill., 1998—. Mem. ABA, Ill. State Bar Assn., U. Ill. Alumni Assn., Phi Kappa Phi, Pi Sigma Alpha, Phi Alpha Delta. Office: State Ill Office Fire Marshal Div Petroleum and Chem Safety 1035 Stevenson Dr Springfield IL 62703-4259

IMMONEN, GERALD MATTHEW, artist; b. Detroit, Apr. 16, 1936; Cert., Cooper Union, N.Y.C., 1958; BFA, Yale U., 1960, MFA, 1962. Prof. art R.I. Sch. Design, Providence, 1963—. Exhibited in group shows at Smithsonian Inst., Washington, 1965-67, Yale U., New Haven, 1967, Smith Coll. Mus. of Art, Northampton, Mass., 1975, Mus. of Art, RISD, 1981, Charles Cowles Gallery, N.Y.C., 1984, 86, Forum/Zurich Art Fair, Switzerland, 1984, Art Embassy Program, 1989—, Virginia Lynch Gallery, Tiverton, R.I., 1993, Cornell U., Ithaca, N.Y., 1994; solo exhbn. at Finnish Am. Contemporary Artist Series at Finnish Am. Heritage Ctr., Suomi Coll., Hancock, Mich.; exhbn. series From the Beginning. Contemporary Finnish-American Artists Series Retrospective, 2003-04; represented in permanent collections at Met. Mus. Art, N.Y.C., Memphis Brooks Mus. Art, Chase Manhattan Bank, N.Y., Herbert P. Johnson Mus. Art, Cornell U., Ithaca, N.Y., Bucknell U., Bethlehem, Pa.; one-man shows include Finnish-Am. Suomi Coll., Hancock, Mich., Taichung Mcp. Cultural Ctr., Taiwan, 1998. Recipient Alice Kimball traveling fellow, 1960; R.I. State Coun. on Arts grantee, 1984; recipient John Frazier award for Excellence in Tchg., R.I. Sch. Design, 1990 Home: 19 Creighton St Providence RI 02906-1518 Office: RI Sch Design 2 College St Providence RI 02903-2784

IMPARATO, ANTHONY MICHAEL, vascular surgeon, medical educator, researcher; b. N.Y.C., July 29, 1922; s. Silverio and Olga (Santilli) I.; m. Agatha Maria Petriccione, Dec. 19, 1943. children: Maria April Imparato, Karen Elsa Imparato Cotton. AB, Columbia U., 1943; MD, NYU, 1946. Diplomate Am. Bd. Surgery; cert. spl. qualifications in gen. vascular surgery. Intern U.S. Naval Hosp., Bklyn., 1946-47; fellow in anatomy NYU Med. Sch., 1949-50; successively intern, asst. resident in surgery, resident, chief resident in surgery NYU Med. Center Bellevue Hosp., 1950-56; mem. faculty NYU Med. Center, 1956—, dir. div. vascular surgery, 1975-92, prof. surgery, 1975—2000, prof. emeritus surgery, 2000—. Leader People-to-People delegation in vascular surgery: western Europe 1982, Soviet Union, 1985; ops. com. "Cooperative VA Study on Asymptomatic Carotid Stenosis", 1983-87 and Nascet, 1987-92; hon. pres. Societa Italiana Prevenzione Ictus Cerebrale, 1997, 98; lectr. in field. Contbr. over 175 articles in field, over 35 chpts. to textbooks. Served as officer M.C. USNR, 46-49, 50. Grantee NIH, 1976-81. Fellow ACS, Am. Coll. Cardiology; mem. Am. Heart Assn. (fellow Stroke Coun.), Am. Surg. Assn., Soc. for Vascular Surgery (pres. 1984-85), Internat. Cardiovascular Soc., Soc. Clin. Vascular Surgery, Soc. Angiologia Uruguay, Royal Australasian Coll. Surgeons (hon.), Soc. Internat. Chirurgie, N.Y. Regional Vascular Soc. (cofounder, pres. 1982-84), N.Am. Soc. Pacing and Electrophysiology (founding mem.), James IV Assn. Surgeons (dir., treas.), Lithuanian Vascular Soc. (hon.), Alpha Omega Alpha. Office: NYU Faculty Practice Area 530 1st Ave Ste 6-f New York NY 10016-6402

IMPELLIZZERI, ANNE ELMENDORF, insurance company executive, non-profit executive; b. Chgo., Jan. 26, 1933; d. Armin and Laura (Gundlach) Elmendorf; m. Julius Simon Impellizzeri, Oct. 12, 1961 (dec.); children: Laura, Theodore (dec.). BA, Smith Coll., 1955; MA, Yale U., 1957. CLU; ChFC. With Met. Life Ins. Co., N.Y.C., 1959-88, asst. v.p., corp. social responsibility, 1978-80, v.p., 1980-85, v.p. group ins., 1985-88; v.p. N.Y.C. Partnership, 1988-90; pres., CEO Blanton-Peale Inst., N.Y.C., 1990-98; exec. dir. Russel Wright's Manitoga, Garrison, NY, 1998—2001. Bd. dirs. Women's City Club of N.Y., 2002—, Bard Music Festival, 1990—, Nuveen Funds, 1994—, Support Ctr. for Nonprofit Mgmt., 1995—2000, Scenic Hudson, 1997—, treas., 1999—2002; trustee Smith Coll., 1991—96; mem. Bus. Urban Issues coun. The Conf. Bd., 1981—85, chair, 1983—85. Trustee Lakeland Bd. Edn., Westchester County, N.Y., 1967-71, pres., 1970-71; bd. dirs. Nat. Safety Coun., 1974-80; pres. Am. Assn. Gifted Children, 1975-85, chair, 1985-90. Named to Acad. of Women Achievers, YWCA N.Y., 1978; Fulbright grantee, 1955-56. Mem. Assn. Yale Alumni (bd. govs. 1985-88), Phi Beta Kappa.

IMPERATO, JOSEPH EDWARD, otolaryngologist; b. N.Y.C., Aug. 13, 1936; s. Salvatore James and Rose Ausilia (Leggio) I.; children: Rose, Joseph. BS, St. Peter's Coll., 1969; MD, U. Parma, Italy, 1971. Bd. eligible Am. Bd. Otolaryngology, Am. Bd. Disability Evaluating Physicians; lic. N.Y., N.J., Maine; cert. Ednl. Coun. Fgn. Med. Grads. Intern N.Y. Med. Coll., Flower 5th Ave Hosp., Met. Hosp. Ctr., N.Y.C., 1972-73, resident gen. surgery, 1973-74; resident ear nose throat N.Y. Eye and Ear Infirmary, N.Y.C.; fellow Montefiore Hosp ear nose throat, N.Y.C., 1977-78, Lenox Hill Hosp. ear nose throat, N.Y.C., 1978-79; pvt. practice ear, nose and throat N.Y.C., 1980-91; examining physician I N.Y. State Worker's Compensation Bd., N.Y.C., 1992-96; disability physician pvt. practice, 1996—. Cons. ear, nose and throat, Internat. Ctr. for the Disabled, N.Y.C., 1981-84; sr. ear, nose, throat specialist Nassau Queens Med. Group, (part time), 1984-89. Vol. physician Cath. Med. Mission to Honduras, 1984. Mem. AMA, AAAS, N.Y. State Med. Soc., N.Y. County Med. Soc., Surgical Soc. N.Y. Med. Coll., N.Y. Acad. Scis., 99+. Roman Catholic. Home: Ste 2AF 28 Greenwich Ave New York NY 10011-8362

IMPERATO, JOSEPH JOHN, lawyer, composer; b. Jersey City, N.J., Mar. 14, 1956; s. Joseph Francis Imperato and Edith Roslyn (Dubin) Schwimmer. Student, Oberlin Coll., 1974 76; BA, Fla. State U., 1978, JD, 1981. Bar: Fla. 1983; court-cert. forensic audio expert, 2003. Trial atty., tng. instr. Office of Pub. Defender, Miami, Fla., 1982—. Lectr., mock trial coach Dade County sec. schs. and univs., Miami, 1993—; owner ImperaTunes Music, 1997—. Composer musical scores Fox TV Network, 1992-94; composer comml. jingles, 1975— (Addy award 1976), original songs, 1974— (Billboard Mag. Songwriting award 1995); composer, producer original childrens' musicals, 1997—. Mem. ASCAP, Audio Engring. Soc. Office: Office of Pub Defender 1320 NW 14th St Miami FL 33125-1609 E-mail: imperato@sprynet.com.

IMPERATO, JOSEPH PHILIP, radiation oncologist, educator; b. Bronx, N.Y., July 15, 1955; s. Gioacchino Maggiorino and Josephine (Cioffi) I.; m. Jean Ann Dienhoffer, Sept. 25, 1982; children: Diane Marie, Joseph Daniel. BA magna cum laude, Holy Cross Coll., Worcester, Mass., 1976; MD, SUNY, Syracuse, 1980. Diplomate Am. Bd. Radiology, Am. Bd. Therapeutic Radiology. Asst. prof. radiology SUNY Upstate Med. Ctr., Syracuse, 1984-85, Northwestern U. Med. Sch., Chgo., 1986—; attending physician Lake Forest (Ill.) Hosp., 1986—, med. dir. radiation oncology, 1991—. Radiation oncology cons. Aramco Med. Facility, Dhahran, Saudi Arabia, 1991. Contbr. articles to profl. jours. Bd. dirs. Ill. divsn. Am. Cancer Soc., Chgo., 1993—, 2d v.p., 1994-96, 1st. v.p., 1996-98, pres., 1998-2000; bd. dirs. Y-ME, Chgo., 1994-97. Fellow Am. Coll. Radiology; mem. Am. Soc. Clin. Oncology, Am. Soc. Therapeutic Radiology and Oncology, Am. Coll. Radiology, Radiologic Soc. N.Am., Phi Beta Kappa, Alpha Omega Alpha. Republican. Roman Catholic. Avocations: computers, chess, working out. Office: Lake Forest Hosp 660 N Westmoreland Rd Lake Forest IL 60045-1696

IMPERATO, PASCAL JAMES, physician, healthcare administrator, writer, historian; b. NYC; s. James Anthony and Madalynne Marguerite (Insante) Imperato; m. Eleanor Anne Maiella; children: Alison Madalynne, Gavin Humbert, Austin Clement. BS, St. John's U., 1958, DSc (hon.), 1977; MD, SUNY, Downstate Med. Ctr., 1962; M in Pub. Health and Tropical Medicine, Tulane U., 1966, DSc (hon.), 1996. Diplomate Am. Bd. Preventive Medicine, Nat. Bd. Med. Examiners. Fgn. fellow Assn. Am. Med. Colls., Kenya, Tanzania, Uganda, 1961; intern in internal medicine L.I. Coll. Hosp., 1962-63, resident in medicine, 1963-65; fgn. rsch. fellow Tulane Univ.-U. del Valle, Cali, Colombia, 1965; N.Y. Acad. Medicine/Glorney Raisebeck fellow Tulane U., New Orleans, 1965-66; med. epidemiologist smallpox eradication-measles control program Ctrs. Disease Control/USPHS, Mali, 1966-72; dir. Bur. Infectious Disease Control, N.Y.C. Dept. Health, 1972-74, prin. epidemiologist, dir. immunization program, 1972-74, 1st dep. commr., 1974-77, dir. pub. health residency tng. program, 1974-77; chmn. N.Y.C. Swine Influenza Immunization Task Force, 1976-77; commr. health N.Y.C., 1977-78; chmn. N.Y.C. Bd. Health, 1977-78; chmn. bd. N.Y.C. Health and Hosps. Corp., 1977-78; chmn. exec. com. N.Y.C. Health Systems Agy., 1977-78; acting health services adminstr. N.Y.C., 1977-78; clin. instr. dept. medicine Cornell U. Med. Coll., N.Y.C., 1972-74, asst. clin. prof., 1974-78, asst. clin. prof. dept. pub. health, 1974-77, assoc. clin. prof., 1977-78, adj. prof., 1979-2000; clin. assoc. prof. dept. preventive medicine and cmty. health SUNY Health Sci. Ctr., Bklyn., 1974-77, lectr., 1977-78, prof., chmn., 1978-94, disting. svc. prof. and chmn., 1994-2001, disting. svc. prof., chmn., dir. master pub. health program, 2001—. Mem. staff N.Y. Hosp. 1972-78, L.I. Coll. Hosp., 1973—, State U. Hosp., 1978—, Kings County Hosp., 1978—; lectr. dept. cmty. medicine Mt. Sinai Sch. Medicine, CUNY, 1974-90; lectr. dept. health adminstrn. Sch. Pub. Health, Columbia U., 1982-89; cons. N.Y. State Dept. Edn., 1982-87, NAS, 1985; med. cons. Africa bur. US AID, 1974; med. dir. R&D and Epidemiology Island Peer Rev. Orgn., 1991—. Author: Doctor in The Land of the Lion, 1964, (with Osa Johnson) Last Adventure, 1966, Bwana Doctor, 1967, The Treatment and Control of Infectious Diseases in Man, 1974, The Cultural Heritage of Africa, 1974, A Wind in Africa: A Story of Modern Medicine in Mali, 1975, What To Do About the Flu, 1976, African Folk Medicine, 1977, Historical Dictionary of Mali, 1977, 3rd edit., 1996, Dogon Cliff Dwellers: The Art of Mali's Mountain People, 1978, Medical Detective, 1979, (with Eleanor Imperato) Mali: A Handbook of Historical Statistics, 1982, The Administration of a Public Health Agency: A Case Study of the New York City Department of Health, 1983, Buffoons, Queens and Wooden Horsemen, 1983, (with Greg Mitchell) Acceptable Risks, 1985, (with Robert I. Goler) Early American Medicine, 1987, Arthur Donaldson Smith and the Exploration of Lake Rudolf, 1987, Mali: A Search for Direction, 1989, (with Eleanor Imperato) They Married Adventure: The Wandering Lives of Martin and Osa Johnson, 1992, Quest for the Jade Sea: Colonial Competition Around an East African Lake, 1998, Legends, Sorcerers, and Enchanted Lizards: Door Locks of the Bamana of Mali, 2001, editor: Acquired Immunodeficiency Syndrome: Current Issues and Scientific Studies, 1989; Historical and Contemporary Aspects of Communicable Disease Control, 1996, (with Ronald E. Coons and J. Winthrop Aldrich) Over Land and Sea: Memoir of an Austrian Rear Admiral's Life in Europe and Africa, 1857-1909 (Ludwig Ritter von Höhnel), 2000; contbr. articles to profl. jours.; cons. editor N.Y. State Jour. Medicine, 1983, dep. editor, 1983-86, editor, 1986-93; editor Jour. Cmty. Health, 1985—; mem. editl. bd. Explorers Jour., 1979-88, Am. Jour. Chinese Medicine, 1985-2001, The Pharos, 1995—; mem. med. adv. bd. Med. Herald, 1992—; chairperson publs. com. Annals of Epidemiology, 1996-99. Bd. trustees Milton Helpern Libr. Legal Medicine, 1977—89; hon. trustee Martin & Osa Johnson Safari Mus., 1964—; mem. adv. bd. Physicians for Social Responsibility, 1983—; mem. NY State Bd. Medicine, 1985—95, vice chmn., 1990—93, chmn., 1993—95; mem. bd. zoning & appeals Village of Plandome Heights, NY, 1986—90, trustee, 1990—92; mem. sci. adv. bd. Explorers Club, 1988—93; chmn. NYC Met. Area Task Force on Syphilis, 1990—91; mem. bd. regents LI Coll. Hosp., 1992—2000; mem. NY State Coun. on Grad. Med. Edn., 1994—98; co-chmn. adv. commn. on pub. health NYC Coun., 1994—2001; mem. NY State Bd. Profl. Med. Conduct, 1994—; mem. Fulbright Selection Com. for Africa, 1999—2002, NYC Mayor Eliot Giuliani's Health Care Adv. Group, 1993; bd. dir. numerous orgs., 1977—78. Lt. comdr. USPHS, 1966—69. Recipient Meritorious Honor award Dept. State, 1971, US AID Meritorious Honor award, 1970, Outstanding Alumnus award Tulane U., 1978, Delta Omega Nat. Merit award, 1978, Frank Babbot award SUNY, 1980, Disting. Alumni Achievement award SUNY, 1987, Spl. Svc. award USPHS, 1987, Pub. Health Achievement award NYC Dept. Health, 1999, Nat. Acads. Practice Interdisciplinary Creativity award, 2000, Clark-Curran award SUNY, 2002; Fulbright scholar, North Yemen, 1985. Master: ACP (James D. Bruce Meml. award 2003); fellow: Am. Coll. Preventive Medicine, Am. Coll. Epidemiology, Royal Soc. Tropical Medicine & Hygiene; mem.: African Studies Assn., NY Soc. Tropical Medicine (v.p. 1976—77, pres. 1989—90), Am. Soc. Tropical Medicine & Hygiene, Author's Guild, Explorers Club, Alpha Omega Alpha, Delta Omega. Roman Catholic. Office: Box 43 450 Clarkson Ave Brooklyn NY 11203-2056

IMPERATO-MCGINLEY, JULIANNE LEONORE, endocrinologist, educator; b. N.Y.C., Sept. 22; d. Thomas and Marian (Crispinelli) Imperato; m. Patrick W. McGinley, Aug. 27, 1966; children: Alexandra Claire, Ian Patrick McGinley. BS in Chemistry cum laude, Coll. Mt. St. Vincent, 1961; MD with hons. in Pub. Health, SUNY, 1965. Intern in internal medicine St. Vincent's Hosp. and Med. Ctr., N.Y.C., 1965-66, resident in internal medicine, 1966-68; fellow in reproductive endocrinology NYU and Lenox Hill Hosps., N.Y.C., 1968-69; NIH fellow in endocrinology Cornell U. Med. Coll., N.Y.C., 1969-72; asst. physician The N.Y. Hosp., N.Y.C., 1969-72, physician to out-patient dept., 1972-75, asst. attending, 1975-81; from instr. in medicine to asst. prof. medicine Cornell U. Med. Ctr., N.Y.C., 1972-81; assoc. attending physician The N.Y. Hosp., N.Y.C., 1982—; assoc. prof. medicine Cornell U. Med. Coll., N.Y.C., 1982-93, assoc. dir. Gen. Clin. Rsch. Ctr., 1991-93, chief sect. androgen physiology divsn. endocrinology, 1992—, dir. Gen. Clin. Rsch. Ctr., 1993—, chief divsn. endocrinology, 1993—, prof. medicine, 1993-98, Rochelle Belfer prof. medicine, 1998—2001; disting. prof. endocrinology in med. Abby Rockefeller Mauzé, 2001—. Cons. prof. Nat. U. Pedro Henriquez Urena, Santo Domingo, Dominican Republic, 1987, St. Vincent's Hosp. and Med. Ctr., N.Y.C., 1978—; mem. internat. adv. bd. 3rd Internat. Conf. on Geriat. Nephrology and Urology, 1991-92; expert ad hoc grant reviewer behavioral medicine study sect. NIH, 1984, ad hoc mem. biopsychology study sect., 1982, ad hoc mem. site visit team biophysiology study sect., 1981; organizing com. Serono Symposium on Sexual Differentiation, 1982; plenary lectr. Merck Med. Adv. Coun. Meeting, St. Andrews, Scotland, 1991, European Soc. for Pediat. Endocrinology, Vienna, Austria, 1990; mem. Gordon Rsch. Conf., Plymouth, N.H., 1986; Macomber lectr. in human sexuality Harvard Med. Sch., Dept. Ob-Gyn., Boston, 1980. Assoc. editor Jour. Clin. Endocrinology and Metabolism, 1993—; reviewer: Acta Endocrinologica, Archives of Internal Medicine, Clin. Endcrinology, Endocrine Revs., Endocrinology, Jour. Clin. Endocrinology and Metabolism, Jour. Urology, New England Jour. Medicine; contbr. over 100 articles to profl. jours. NIH fund rschr.; active fundraising and drug donations The Robert Reid Cabral Children's Hosp., Santo Domingo, 1988—. Recipient award for outstanding clin. rsch. Dominican Pediat. Endocrine Soc., 1988, Rsch. award 1st prize Am. Acad. Pediats., sect. urology, 1984, Nicholas Pichardo award and lectr. for outstanding rsch. contbns. to advancement of medicine in Dominican Republic, Santo Domingo, 1980, also numerous rsch. grants. Mem. AAAS, Am. Fedn. for Clin. Rsch., Endocrine Soc. (chair, lectr. symposium on steroid 5a-reductase ann. meeting San Antonio 1992, membership com. 1989-91, chair membership com. 1991-92, chair meetings 1984-88), N.Y. Acad. Scis., Soc. for Study of Reprodn., Harvey Soc., Women in Endocrinology, Kappa Gamma Pi. Roman Catholic. Achievements include Defined the condition of 5a-reductase deficiency in man. Office: NY Hosp-Cornell U/Weill Med Coll Divsn Endocrin/Gen Clin Rsc 525 E 68th St New York NY 10021-4870

IMPERIAL, HENRY L. internist; b. Irosin, Philippines, Apr. 24, 1963; s. Joaquin Sr. and Avelina (Li) I. BS in Med. Tech., Far Ea. U., 1984, MD, 1988. Diplomate Am. Bd. Internal Medicine. Med. resident in primary care internal medicine U. Medicine and Dentistry N.J. Robert Wood Johnson Med. Sch., New Brunswick, 1991-94; primary care/internal medicine physician Browns-

ville (Tex.) Cmty. Health Ctr., 1994—, asst. med. dir., 1996, med. dir., 1996—. Cmty. faculty East Tex. Area Health Edn. Ctr., 1995—; continuous quality improvement program chmn. Brownsville Cmty Health Ctr., 1996—; clin. asst. prof. cmty. faculty U. Tex. Med. Br., Galveston, 1997—; clin. asst. prof. U. Tex. Health Sci. Ctr., San Antonio, 2000—. Pres. student coun. Far Ea. U. Sch. of Med. Tech., 1983-84. Mem. AMA (Physicians Recognition award 1997-2000, 2000—), ACP, Tex. Med. Assn./Cameron Willacy Med. Soc., Migrant Clinicians Network. Roman Catholic. Avocations: travel, wine/cuisine, tennis/chess. Office: Brownsville Cmty Health Ctr 2137 E 22nd St Brownsville TX 78521-2908 Office Fax: (956) 546-2056. E-mail: hlimperial@hotmail.com.

IMPREVEDUTO, ANTHONY NEIL, state legislator; b. Jersey City, Apr. 11, 1948; s. Rocco and Ann (Ferrone) I.; m. Susan Jane Zaluski, 1971; children: Loren Ann, Jamie Lee. BS, Rider Coll., 1971; MA, Seton Hall U., 1975. Assemblyman dist. 32 N.J. State Assembly, 1988—. Committeman Secaucus Municipality, N.J., 1979-80, coun., 1981—; pres. RVG Corp., Secaucus, 1973-80; ptnr. Impreveduto Family Partnership, 1983—, Secaucus 83 Assn., Newark, 1983—; pres. Secaucus 84 Orgn., 1984-89. Bus. dept. supervisor Secaucus Bd. Edn., 1971—; founder New Dem. Orgn.; past pres Holy Name Soc. Immaculate Conception Ch. Mem. Nat. Assn. Secondary Sch. Prins. & Supervisors, Am. Legis. Exch. Coun., N.J. Prins. & Supervisors Assn., Rotary. Address: 400 Plaza Dr Secaucus NJ 07094-3605*

IMRAY, THOMAS JOHN, radiologist, educator; b. Milw., Nov. 11, 1939; s. George William and Genevieve (Bresnehan) I.; m. Carla Marie Rake, Aug. 17, 1963; children: John Scott, Jean Ann, Jeff William. BA, Marquette U., 1961, MD, 1965. Diplomate Nat. Bd. Med. Examiners, Am. Bd. Radiology (guest examiner 1975-76, 79, 85-2002). Intern St. Mary's Hosp., San Francisco, 1965-66; resident in radiology U. Minn., Mpls., 1966-70, instr., 1969-70; asst. prof. Med. Coll. of Wis., Milw., 1973-77, assoc. prof., 1977-80, U. Calif., Irvine, 1980-82; prof. and chmn. dept. radiology U. Nebr. Med. Ctr., Omaha, 1982-96, prof. dept. radiology, 1996—. Vis. prof. Vanderbilt U., Nashville, 1976, 82, U. Wis., Madison, 1978, SUNY Downstate Med. Ctr., Bklyn., 1978, Harvard Med. Sch., Boston, 1980, Loyola U. Sch. Medicine, Maywood, Ill., 1980, UCLA-Wadsworth VA Hosp., 1981, UCLA, 1982 Northwestern U. Sch. Medicine, Chgo., 1984, Meth. Hosp., Indpls., 1984, U. Mo., Kans. City, 1985, U. Iowa, Iowa City, 1986, U. Ark., Little Rock, 1987, Keio U. Sch. Medicine, Tokyo, 1989, Mich. State U., 1993. Contbr. articles to profl. jours. Mem. Tech. Task Force on Diagnostic Radiology Nebr. Dept. Health, 1983-84; Major U.S. Army M.C., 1970-73. Co-recipient Magna Cum Laude in Sci. Exhibits award Am. Soc. Neuroradiology, 1987; GE grantee, 1985-87. Fellow Am. Coll. Radiology; mem. AMA (rep. to radiology residency rev. com., 1987), Radiol. Soc. N. Am. (award 1981, 82), Am. Coll. Radiology (com. on satellite communications 1981-83), Am. Roentgen Ray Soc. (award 1986), Assn. Univ. Radiologists, Soc. Chmn. Acad. Radiology Depts., Am. Soc. Uroradiology, Nebr. State Radiol. Soc., Nebr. State Med. Assn., Omaha Metro Med. Soc., Omaha Mid-West Clin. Soc. (hosp. and svc. exhibits com. 1984, award 1986), Omaha C. of C. (task force on edn. 1983-85, edn. coun. steering com. 1984, edn. coun. 1985), Rotary Internat. (program com. 1986), Marquette U. Club (bd. dirs. Omaha chpt., 1987), Alpha Omega Alpha (alumni and faculty mems. com., 1986). Roman Catholic. Avocation: swimming. Office: Nebr Health Sys Dept Radiology 981045 Nebr Med Ctr Omaha NE 68198-1045

IMRE, CHRISTINA JOANNE, lawyer; b. Gary, Ind., Oct. 25, 1950; d. Joseph and Ruth Leone I.; m. Richard Long, Dec. 31, 1991. BA, Mt. St. Mary's Coll., L.A., 1972; MA, U. Notre Dame, 1974; JD, Loyola Law Sch., L.A., 1980. Bar: Calif. 1980, U.S. Ct. Appeals (ninth cir.) 1982, U.S. Dist. Ct. (ctrl. dist.) Calif. 1983, U.S. Dist. Ct. (no. dist.) Calif. 1988,U.S. Dist. Ct. (so. dist.) Calif. 1995, U.S. Supreme Ct., 2000. Assoc. Lascher & Lascher, Ventura, Calif., 1980-83, Law Office of Errol Berk, Ventura, Calif., 1983-84, Pachter, Gold & Schaffer, L.A., 1984-87; sr. atty. Kornblum & McBride, L.A., 1987-89; ptnr. Horvitz & Levy LLP, Encino, Calif., 1989—2000, Crosby, Heafey, Roach & May, Los Angeles, 2000—02, Sedgwick, Detert, Moran & Arnold, LLP, Los Angeles, 2002—. Bd. govs. Calif. Continuing Edn. of Bar, Berkeley, Calif., 1996-2000; chair Calif. Continuing Edn. of Bar Joint Adv. Com., Berkeley, 1995; editorial bd. L.A. Lawyer Mag., L.A., 1996-99; cons. Handling Civil Appeals, Berkeley, 1996, Calif. Trial Practice, Berkeley, 1995; lectr. in field. Editor-in-chief: Loyola of Los Angeles International & Comparative Law Journal, 1979-80; monthly columnist CEB Civil Litigation Reporter; contbr. articles to profl. jours. and chpts. to books. Named one of 50 Most Powerful Women in L.A. Law, L.A. Business Journal, 1998; Loyola Law Sch. fellow, 1979-80, U. Notre Dame fellow, 1972-74. Mem. L.A. County Bar Assn., Defense Rsch. Inst., So. Calif. Defense Counsel Assn. Avocations: music, shakespeare, history, philosophy. Office: Sedgwick Detert Moran & Arnold LLP 801 S Figueroa St 18th Fl Los Angeles CA 90017 E-mail: christina.imre@sdma.com.

IMRHAN, SHEIK NAZIR, industrial engineer, educator; b. Bagotsville, Demarara, Guyana, Jan. 4, 1950; came to U.S., 1979; s. Imran and Husna B. Imrhan; m. Victorine Lall, May 10, 1975; children: Sabine M., Savina N. BSc, U. Guyana, Turkeyen, 1973, diploma in edn., 1975; MS in Stats., MS in Indsl Engring., U. Ala., Tuscaloosa, 1981; PhD, Tex. Tech U, 1983. Registered profl. engr., Tex. Master high schs., Georgetown, Guyana, 1968-75; shift mgr., chemist Guyana Sugar Corp., Wales, 1975-76; master Grand Turk Island High Sch., Turks and Caicos Islands, 1976-79; teaching asst. U. Ala., 1979-81, vis. asst. prof., 1984; rsch. asst. Tex. Tech U., Lubbock, 1981-83; asst. prof. La. Tech U., Ruston, 1984-87; assoc. prof. indsl. engring. U. Tex., Arlington, 1987—. Conf. presenter; indsl. cons. in musculoskeletal injuries. Author: Help! My Computer is Killing Me: Preventing Aches and Pains in the Computer Workplace, 1996, Preventing Aches and Pains from Computer Work, 2000; editor Internat. Jour. Indsl. Ergonomics, Internat. Jour. Indsl. Engrs.; contbr. articles on ergonomics and human factors to profl. jours. and conf. procs. Mem. Inst. Indsl. Engrs., Human Factors Soc. Am., Ergonomics Soc., North Tex. Human Factors Soc. (bd. dirs.-elect 1989-90). Avocations: reading, oil painting. Home: 5110 Trail Head Dr Arlington TX 76013-5321 Office: U Tex PO Box 19017 Arlington TX 76019-0001 E-mail: imrhan@imse.uta.edu.

IMSANDE, JOHN DAVID, geneticist, researcher, educator; b. Grass Range, Mont., June 14, 1931; s. Louis H. and Freda M. (Dengel) I.; m. Elizabeth Blanchard, June 2, 1956 (div.); children: Carol Imsande Batastini, Louis D.; m. Marica F. Doerschug, Aug. 13, 1976. BA in Edn (Math.), U. Mont., 1953; MS in Chemistry, Mont. State U., 1956; PhD in Biochemistry, Duke U., 1960. Postdoctoral fellow U. Calif. Berkeley, 1960-61; lectr., postdoctoral fellow Princeton (N.J.) U., 1961-62; asst. prof. Case Western Res. U., Cleve., 1962-64, assoc. prof. dept. biology, 1964-69; assoc. prof. genetics and biochemistry Iowa State U., Ames, 1969-73, prof. genetics, 1973—90, prof. agronomy and genetics, 1990-2000, prof. emeritus, 2001—. Vis. scientist U. Edinburgh, Scotland, 1968-69; vis. prof. U. Calif., San Diego, 1976-77; vis. prof. dept. agriculture U. Queensland, Brisbane, Australia, 1986-87, 90-91. Author: (chpt.) The ENZYMES-Pyrophosphorylases, Methods in Enzymology, 1961, Biology of the Rhizobiaceae, 1981; contbr. over 60 articles to profl. jours. Cpl. U.S. Army, 1953-55. NIH fellow USPHS, 1957-60, 60-62; grantee NIH, USDA. Democrat. Home: 5422 Arrasmith Trl Ames IA 50010-9231 Office: Iowa State U Dept Of Agronomy Ames IA 50011-0001 E-mail: jimsande@iastate.edu.

IMUS, DON, radio host; b. July 23, 1940; m. Deirdre Imus. Radio host WNBC, 1971-88, WFAN, 1988—; TV host MS/NBC, 1996—. Author: God's Other Son; co-author: (with Fred Imus) Two Guy's Four Corners, 1997; appeared on Prime Time Live, Larry King, David Lettermen, 60 Minutes, The Today Show. Host radiothon CJ Found. for Sids and the Tomorrow's Children's Fund, 1990—. Recipient three Marconi awards; named Major Market Personality of the Year, Syndicated Personality of the Year; Named Emerson Radio Hall Fame, Nat. Assn. Broadcasters Broadcasting Hall of Fame, Time Mags. Most Influential Ams., 1997. Office: Westwood One Entertainment 1675 Broadway New York NY 10019-5820 also: care WFAN-AM 34-12 36th St Astoria NY 11106

IMWINKELRIED, EDWARD JOHN, law educator; b. San Francisco, Sept. 19, 1946; s. John Joseph and Enes Rose (Gianelli) I.; m. Cynthia Marie Clark, Dec. 30, 1978; children— Marie Elise, Kenneth West BA, U. San Francisco, 1967, JD, 1969. Bar: Calif. 1970, Mo. 1984, U.S. Supreme Ct. 1974. Prof. law U. San Diego, 1974-79; prof. law Washington U., St. Louis, 1979-85, U. Calif.-Davis, 1985—. Disting. faculty mem. Nat. Coll. Dist. Attys., Houston, 1978— Author: Evidentiary Foundations, 1980, 5th rev. edit., 2002, Uncharged Misconduct Evidence, 1984, rev. edit., 1999, The New Wigmore: Evidentiary Privileges, 2002; co-author: McCormick, Evidence, 5th edit., 1999, Materials for Study of Evidence, 1983, 5th edit., 2002, Scientific Evidence, 1986, 3d edit., 1999, Pretrial Discovery: Strategy and Tactics, 1986, rev. edit., 1999, Courtroom Criminal Evidence, 1987, 3d edit., 1998, California Evidentiary Foundations, 1988, 3d edit., 2000, Dynamics of Trial Practice, 1989, 3d edit., 2002, Exculpatory Evidence, 1990, 2d edit., 1996, Florida Evidentiary Foundations, 1991, 2d edit., 1997, Illinois Evidentiary Foundations, 1991, 2d edit., 1997, Texas Evidentiary Foundations, 1992, 2d edit., 1998, New York Evidentiary Foundations, 1993, 2d edit., 1997, Evidentiary Distinctions, 1993, Colorado Evidentiary Foundations, 1997; contbg. editor Champion pub. Assn. Criminal Def. Lawyers, 1983, Courtroom Law Bull. Mem. Am. Acad. Forensic Sci., ABA (continuing edn. com. 1983-84), Am. Assn. Law Schs. (chmn. evidence sect. 1983) Democrat. Roman Catholic. Avocation: jogging. Home: 2204 Shenandoah Pl Davis CA 95616-6603 Office: U Calif Law Sch Davis CA 95616

INABINET, GEORGE WALKER, JR., retired state agency administrator; b. Cameron, S.C., Sept. 24, 1927; s. George Walker and Elizabeth (Wolfe) I.; m. Helen Ruth Davis, Sept. 27, 1947; children: Pamela Ruth, Jeffrey Walker. Cert. EE, S.C. Area Trade Sch., Columbia, 1949; Bus. Mgmt. degree, U. S.C., 1951; electronics engr. cert., Nat. Radio Inst., Washington, 1967. Asst. dir. S.C. Dept. Hwys., Columbia, 1951-53; adminstr. transp. S.C. Dept. Edn., Columbia, 1953-90. Chmn. Boy Scouts Am., Sandy Run, S.C., 1965-70; pres. Sandy Run Cmty. Club, 1966-70, S.C. Football Ofcls. Assn., Columbia, 1971-72; mem. White House Coun. on Youth, Washington, 1972-76; chmn. Calhoun County Tri-Centennial Commn., 1970; chmn. adminstrn. bd. Mt. Zion United Meth. Ch., Sandy Run, 1952-75; mem. Gov.'s Com. on Comm.; vice chmn. Calhoun County Planning Commn., 1996—, Calhoun County Facilities Com.; pres. ch. coun. Sandy Run Luth. Ch. Named to S.C. Football Ofcls. Hall of Fame, 2000. Mem. Assn. Pub. Safety Communications Officers (pres. 1979-81), Assn. Pub. Communications Officers (v.p. 1979-80, pres. 1980-81), S.C. Assn. Pupil Transp. (v.p. 1981-82, pres. 1982-83), Am. Legion (chmn. state oratorical com. 1989-97, mem. nat. commn. on Americanism), Masons, Shriners. Avocations: golf, fishing, swimming, all spectator sports. Home: Windy Hill 2496 Old State Rd Swansea SC 29160-9350

INABINET, LAWRENCE ELLIOTT, retired pharmacist; b. Orangeburg, S.C., June 15, 1933; s. Boysie Benjamin and Alrona Minerva (Robinson) I.; m. Velma Vincent Ferguson (div.); children: Rhett Elliott, Bonny Susan Murphy. BS in Pharmacy, U. S.C., 1963. Registered pharmacist, S.C. Retail pharmacist chain and ind. drug stores, 1963-69; staff hosp. pharmacist S.C. State Hosp., Columbia, S.C., 1969-71; staff pharmacist Hawthorne Pharmacy, Columbia, S.C., 1971-72, Hemingway (S.C.) Pharmacy, 1990-93, Revco Drug Stores, Marion, S.C., 1993-95; pharmacy supr. S.C. Dept. Corrections, Columbia, 1972-79; retail pharmacist Ind. Drug Stores, 1979-84; hosp. pharmacist Baker Hosp., North Charleston, S.C., 1984-86; asst. dir. pharmacy Marion (S.C.) Meml. Hosp., 1986-90. Author: (text) Civilian-Military Time Converter; patentee medicating device for animals, timepiece for converting mil. to civilian time and vice versa, 1997; contbr. poems to pubs. Deacon Bapt. ch. With USN, 1954-58. Mem. Am. Legion, Masons (past master, masonic knight templar), Kappa Psi. Avocations: guitar, song writing, sports cards, music. Home: 1704-A Greenwood Park Marion SC 29571-9406

INABNET, WILLIAM BARLOW, III, surgeon; b. Greensboro, N.C., Aug. 4, 1965; s. William Barlow Inabnet, Jr. and Pamela Inabnet; m. Kathleen Thornton, Feb. 10, 2000. BS in Biology, U. N.C., 1987, MD, 1991. Asst. prof. surgery Mt. Sinai Sch. oedicine, N.Y.C., 1998—. Fellow: ACS. Episcopalian. Achievements include development of surgical techniques. Office: Mount Sinai Med Ctr 5 East 98th St Box 1259 New York NY 10029 Office Fax: 212-410-0111.

INCANDELA, GERALD JEAN-MARIE, artist; b. Tunis, Tunisia, Feb. 19, 1952; came to U.S., 1977; s. Laurent and Gilda (Solina) I. BA, Janson De Sailly, Paris, 1970; postgrad., U. of Nanterre, Paris, 1971-73. One man shows include Felicity Samuel Gallery, London, 1978, Gallery Jean Chauvelin, Paris, 1978, Charles Cowles Gallery, N.Y., 1981, Robert Fraser Gallery, London, 1984, Mus. Modern Art, Oxford, Eng., 1986, Paul Kasmin, N.Y., 1988, SEBU, Japan, 1990; exhbns. in group shows at Hal Bromm Gallery, 1975, Grey Art Gallery, 1977, Corcoran Gallery, 1978, Jacksonville (Fla.) Mus., 1981, The Drawing Ctr., N.Y.C., 1982, Met. Mus. of N.Y.C., 1982, Mus. of Modern Art, 1983, Walker Art Ctr., 1986, J. Paul Getty Mus., Santa Monica, 1998, Galerie Beyeler, Basel, 2002. Home and Office: 88 Lexington Ave New York NY 10016-8943

INCAPRERA, FRANK PHILIP, internist; b. New Orleans, Aug. 24, 1928; s. Charles and Mamie (Bellipanni) I.; m. Ruth Mary Duhon, Sept. 13, 1952; children: Charles, Cynthia, James, Christopher, Catherine. BS, Loyola U. of South, 1946; MD, La. State U. Med. Sch., 1950. Diplomate Am. Bd. Internal Medicine. Intern Charity Hosp., New Orleans, 1950-51, resident, 1951-52, VA Hosp., New Orleans, 1952-54; practice medicine specializing in internal medicine New Orleans, 1957-97; med. dir. Internal Medicine Group, 1973-97, chief med. officer, 1997-99. Med. dir. Owens-Ill. Glass Co., New Orleans, 1961-85, Kaiser Aluminum Co., Chalmette, La., 1975-84, Tenneco Oil Co., Chalmette, 1978-84, Luth. Nursing Home, 1990-99; assoc. med. dir. Cigna Health Plan of La., 1991-99; co-founder Med. Ctr. E. New Orleans, 1975; clin. assoc. prof. medicine Tulane U. Sch. Medicine, 1971-87, clin. prof. medicine, 1987-99, clin. prof. medicine La. State U., 1994-; adv. bd. Healthcare New Orleans, 1991-96; mem. New Orleans Bd. Health, 1966-70. Bd. dirs. Meth. Hosp., 1971-97, sec. 1992-96, Chateau de Notre Dame, 1977-92, New Orleans Opera Assn., 1975—; mem. New Orleans Human Rels. Com., 1968-70; bd. dirs. Emergency Med. Svcs. Coun., 1977-86, pres. La. southeastern region, 1979-81; bd. dirs. New Orleans East Bus. Assn., 1980-99, v.p. 1981-83; bd. dirs. Luth. Towers, 1988-89, Peace Lake Towers, 1988-89, La. State U. Med. Ctr. Found. Bd., 1989-91, Cristo Sana, 1997—; mem. pastoral care adv. com. So. Bapt. Hosp., 1982-83; mem. pres.'s adv. bd. coun. Loyola U. of South, 1989-96. Capt. USAF, 1955-57. Named Man of Yr., St. Gabriel Holy Name Soc., 1964; recipient Lifetime award Outstanding Svc., Cefalutana Soc., La., 1998, Pres.'s award, New Orleans East Bus. Assn., 2000, Andrew Jackson Higgins award, Mayor's Mil. Adv. Com., 2002, Founders award, Italian-Am. Fedn. of the S.E., 2003. Master: ACP (gov. 1995—99, Laureate award 1993); mem.: AMA, La. Soc. Internal Medicine (exec. com. 1975—98, pres. 1983—85), La. State Med. Soc. (v.p. 1975—76, Continuing Med. Edn. award for Outstanding Contributions to advancement of continuing med. edn. in La. 2001), La. Occupl. Medicine Assn. (pres. 1971—72), New Orleans Acad. Internal Medicine (pres. 1969), Orleans Parish Med. Soc. (sec. 1972—74, Outstanding Physician award 2000), La. Med. Soc. (v.p. 1975—76), Am. Coll. Physicians Execs., Am. Geriatrics Soc., La. State U. Med. Sch. Alumni Assn. (pres. 1989—90, Alumnus of Yr. 1996), New Orleans East C. of C. (dir. 1979—85), Optimists Club (bd. dirs. New Orleans 1964—69), Blue Key, Order of St. Louis, Alpha Omega Alpha (Beta chpt., Vol. Clin. Faculty award 2003), Delta Epsilon Sigma. Home: 2218 Lake Oaks Pky New Orleans LA 70122-4345 E-mail: fincaprera@aol.com.

INCAUDO, JOSEPH AUGUST, engineering company executive; b. 1940; MA, UCLA, 1961; MBA, Harvard U., 1964. CPA, Calif. Cons., auditor Touche Ross & Co., L.A., 1964-68; contr. Bullocks, L.A., 1969-76; v.p. ops. May Co., L.A., 1976-78; v.p. fin. Tobias Kotzin Corp., L.A., 1978-80; v.p., CFO Vinnell Corp., Alhambra, Calif., 1980-83; exec. v.p., CFO Aecom Tech. Corp., L.A., 1983—. Bd. dirs. Resource Scis. of Arabia Ltd., Inst. of Social and Econ. Policy in the Middle East, John F. Kennedy Sch. Govt., Harvard U. Office: Aecom Tech Corp 555 S Flower Ste Ste 3700 Los Angeles CA 90071-2300

INCE, LAUREL T. music educator; b. Gonzales, Tex. m. Joe C. Ince; children: Joe C. Ince, Jr.(dec.), Mark A., Susan I. Burns, William C. BMus, Trinity U., 1950. Piano tchr. Ince Piano Studio, Gonzales, 1950—. Performer various internat. workshops, Austria, Can., Switzerland, Scotland, France; south ctrl. coord. music Link Found., 1990—. Contbr. articles to profl. jours. Advisor City Coun., Gonzales; accompanist First Bapt. Ch., Gonzales; pres. Sesame Club, Gonzales. Recipient Tchr. of Yr. award, Austin Music Tchrs. Assn., 1995, Pillar of the Point award, Inspiration Point Fine Arts Colony. Mem.: Nat. Guild Piano Tchrs., Tex. Music Tchrs. Assn. (state pres., Tchr. of Yr. award 1995), Nat. Fedn. Music Clubs (life; chmn. FAMA 1991, recording sec., lectr., performer), Tex. Fedn. Music Clubs (state pres., founder jr. state festival 1975), Sigma Alpha Iota (life). Avocations: entertaining, travel. Home: 723 St Francis Str Gonzales TX 78629 Home Fax: 830-672-5808. Personal E-mail: ljince@gvec.net.

INCROPERA, FRANK PAUL, mechanical engineering educator; b. Lawrence, Mass., May 12, 1939; s. James Frank and Ann Laura (Leone) I.; m. Andrea Jeanne Eastman, Sept. 2, 1960; children: Terri Ann, Donna Renee, Shaunna Jeanne. BSME, MIT, 1961; MS, Stanford U., 1962, PhD, 1966. Jr. engr. Barry Controls Corp., Watertown, Mass., 1959; thermodynamics engr. Aerojet Gen. Corp., Azusa, Calif., 1961; heat transfer specialist Lockheed Missiles and Space Co., Sunnyvale, Calif., 1962-64; mem. faculty Purdue U., 1966-98, prof. mech. engring., 1973-98, head dept., 1989-98; dean of engring. U. Notre Dame, Ind., 1998—. Cons. in field. Author: Introduction to Molecular Structure and Thermodynamics, 1974, Fundamentals of Heat Transfer, 1985, 90, 96, 2001; Fundamentals of Heat and Mass Transfer, 1981, 85, 90, 96, 2001, Liquid Cooling of Electronic Devices by Single-Phase Convection, 1999; also articles. Recipient Solberg Teaching award Purdue U., 1973, 77, 86, Potter Teaching award, 1973, Von Humboldt sr. scientist award Fed. Republic Germany, 1988; named One of the 100 most frequently cited engrs. in the world Inst. for Sci. Info., 2000. Fellow ASME (Melville medal 1988, Heat Transfer Meml. award 1988, Worcester Reed Warner award 1995); mem. Am. Soc. Engring. Edn. (Ralph C. Roe award 1982, George Westinghouse award 1983), Nat. Acad. Engring. Achievements include invention of bloodless surg. scalpel. Office: U Notre Dame Coll Engring 257 Fitzpatrick Hall Notre Dame IN 46556 E-mail: fpi@nd.edu.

INCULET, ION I. electrical engineering educator, research director, consultant; b. Iasi, Moldova, Romania, Feb. 11, 1921; arrived in Can., 1948; s. Ion C. and Ruxanda (Basota) I.; m. Marion Elsie Smith, Aug. 25, 1951; children: Richard, Catherine, Diana. Diploma in engring., Politechnica, Bucuresti, Romania, 1944; M in Engring. Sci., Laval U., Que., 1962; DTechSc (hon.), Bucuresti U., Romania, 1993; DSc (hon.), We. Ont. Can. U., 1996. Advance devel. engr. Can. GE, Peterborough, Ont., 1948-56, mgr. engring., Que., 1956-64; prof. elec. engring. U. Western Ont., London, 1964—, dir. environ. engring., 1966-68, dir. Applied Electrostatics Rsch. Ctr., 1986—. Pres. Elstat, Ltd., London, 1972—; cons. in field. Author: 1 book; contbr. over 110 articles to profl. jours., book chpts., holder 27 patents. Recipient T.C. Keefer medal Can. Soc. Civil Engring., 1994-95. Fellow IEEE (Centennial medal 1984), Can. Acad. Engring., Inst. Electrostatics of Japan; mem. NSPE (engring. medal 1984), Industry Applications Soc. IEEE (Outstanding Achievement award 1983), Romanian Acad. (hon.). Avocation: skiing. Home: 81 Lloyd Manor Crescent London ON Canada N6H 3Z4 Office: U Western Ont Engring Bldg Electrostatics Rsch Ctr London ON Canada N6A 5B9 E-mail: iinculet@julian.uwo.ca.

INDENBAUM, DOROTHY, musician, researcher; b. N.Y.C., Nov. 24; d. Abraham and Celia (Pine) Shapiro; m. Eli Indenbaum; children: Arthur, Esther. BA, Bklyn. Coll., 1942; MS, Queens Coll., 1962; PhD, NYU, 1993. Prof. Dalcroze Sch. Music, N.Y.C., 1957-93, chmn., 1995—; prof. Hunter Coll., N.Y.C., 1970-77. Assoc. dir. Aviva Players, N.Y.C., 1977—. Performed piano with chamber music ensembles. Chmn. Am. Jewish Congress, 1958-60, YIVO, 1980—, Bohemian Club, 1980—, 92nd St YMHA, 1985—. Mem. Am. Women Composers (bd. dirs. 1988-93), Internat. Alliance for Women in Music (bd. dirs. 1993—), Sonneck Soc., League for Yiddish, Musicians Club (bd. dirs. 1983—), Sigma Alpha Iota (program chmn.).

INDICK, JANET, sculptor, educational administrator; b. Bklyn., Mar. 3, 1932; d. Charles and Sarah (Goldsmith) Suslak; m. Benjamin Philip Indick, Aug. 23, 1953; children: Michael Korie, Karen Leigh Indick Maizel. BS in Art, Hunter Coll., 1953, postgrad., 1954, New Sch., 1961-62. Tchr. kindergarten pub. schs., Elizabeth, N.J., 1953-54; dir. nursery sch. Teaneck Jewish Ctr., N.J., 1964-92. Mem. Teaneck Arts Adv. Bd., 1982—88. (prin. works) Netzach Yisrael, Teaneck Jewish Ctr., 1974, Etz Chaim, 1981, Sanctuary Wall Menorah, 1983, Temple Beth Rishon, Wyckoff, N.J., 1981, 1983, Menorah, Franklin Lakes Pub. Sch., 1983, North Shore Synagogue, Syosset, N.Y., 1993, Temple Sharey Telfilo Israel, South Orange, N.J., 1993, (one-woman shows) Discovery Art Gallery, Clifton, N.Y., 1976, Mari Art Gallery, Westchester, N.Y., 1983, Hebrew Tabernacle, N.Y.C., 1984, Chubb Corp., Basking Ridge, N.J., 1985, Edward Williams Gallery Fairleigh Dickinson U., Hackensack, N.J., 1986, Vineyard Gallery, N.Y.C., 1986, Maurice M. Pine Gallery Fairlawn (N.J.) Pub. Libr., 1990, Quietude Garden Gallery, East Brunswick, N.J., 1991—92, Vineyard Gallery, N.Y., N.Y., 1986, Bergen Mus. Art & Sci., Paramus, N.J., 1994, N.Y.C. Boathouse Cafe, 1998, Kerygma Gallery, Ridgewood, N.J., 1999, Interchurch Ctr., N.Y., 1999, Solo Outdoor Sculpture Exhibition Broadfoot Gallery, Boonton, N.J., 2000—01, Atrium Gallery J.C.C., Washington Twp., N.J., 2002, Johnson & Johnson Co., Skillman, N.J., 2003, (exhibitions) Morris Mus., N.J., 1979, 1984, Newark Mus., 1982, Jersey City Mus., 1983, Hebrew Tabernacle, N.Y.C., 1984, Parsons Gallery, 1984, Lillian Heidenberg Gallery, 1984—96, Schering-Plough Corp., Madison, N.J., 1987, Kerygma Gallery, Ridgewood, N.J., 1988—2000, Marabella Gallery, N.Y.C., 1989, So. Vt. Art Ctr., Manchester, 1990, Nat. Assn. Women Artists Traveling Exhbns., 1989—90, 1996, Traveling Exhbns., 1998—99, Fgn. Traveling Exhbns., India, 1989—90, Columbus (Ohio) Mus. Fine Art, 1989—90, Balt. Mus. Art, 1989—90, Marunouchi Gallery, N.Y.C., 1994, Waterside Gallery, West Stockbridge, Mass., 1995, L'Atelier Gallery, Piermont, N.Y., 1994—96, Polo Gallery, Edgewater, N.J., 1994—2000, Goethe Mus., Weimar, Germany, 2000—01, Staaliche Mus., Berlin, 2000—01, Grounds for Sculpture, Hamilton, N.J., 2001, Musedu Monnai, Paris, 2002, Mus. Wroclaw, Poland, 2002, Can. War Mus., Ottawa, 2002, Am. Numis. Mus., Colorado Springs, Colo., 2002, N.Y. Ind. Art Fair, N.Y.C., 2002, (permanent collections) Jane Voorhees Zimmerli Art Mus. Rutgers U., New Brunswick, N.J., Corp. Towers Perrin, N.Y.C., AMP Corp., Harrisburg, Pa., Myron Mfg. Corp., Maywood, N.J., Chiropractic Health Care, Bergenfield, N.J., Bergen Mus., Paramus, Weingroup Equities Corp., N.Y.C., Hubbards Cupboard Corp., Edison, N.J., Rosenthal Art Equities, N.Y.C., Franklin Lakes Pub. Schs., Temple Beth Rishon, Wykoff, North Shore Synagogue, Syosset, Temple Sharey Tefilo, South Orange, Teaneck Jewish Ctr., Broadfoot Collection, Boonton, Internat. Sculpture Ctr. Collection III; Represented in permanent collections The Millenium Collection NAWA, New York, The Nat. Mus. of Women in the Arts, Washington, D.C., one-woman shows include Johnson & Johnson Co., N.J., 2003. Recipient Charlotte Dunwiddie Meml. award, Medallic Art Pen & Brush, 2001, Medal of Honor, Nat. Arts Club, 2001, C.A. Brown award, Medallic Art Pen and Brush, 2000, Internat. award, Manhattan Arts, 1999, Merit award, IFFRA/AIA Forum on Religious Art/Architecture, 1984, Sculpture award, Nat. Assn. Painters and Sculptors, 1980, Nat. Assn. Painters, 1978, Art in the Park, Paterson, NJ, 1977; grantee Fellowship grant in Sculpture, N.J. State Council on the Arts, 1981. Mem.: Fedn. Internationale de la Medaille, Medallic Art Soc. of Can., Am. Medallic Sculpture assn., Sculpture Assn. of N.J., Am. Numis. Soc., Artists Equity, Catherine Lorillard Wolfe Art Club (bd. dirs. 1994—96, 2000—02, sculpture chair 2001—03, 1st Sculpture award 1999, Medal of Honor in Sculpture 2001, H.W. Frismuth Bronze Sculpture award 2000, Presidents award 1996, Corp. award Sculpture 1995, H.W. Frismuth Bronze Sculpture award 1992), N.Y. Soc. Women Artists (sculpture chair 1999—2000), Nat. Assn. Women Artists (pres. 1997—99, advisor 2000—, Aluminum Sculpture Merit award 2000, Gretchen Richardson Meml. sculpture award 2001, Merit award in Sculpture 2000, Jeffrey Childs Willis Meml. award 1997, Clara Shainess Meml. award Sculpture 1994, Pauline Law award 1974). Democrat. Jewish. Home: 428 Sagamore Ave Teaneck NJ 07666-2626 E-mail: janetindick@aol.com.

INDIVIGLIA, SALVATORE JOSEPH, artist, retired naval officer; b. N.Y.C., Nov. 16, 1919; s. Joseph and Alfonsina Barbara (Gaeta) I.; widower Jan. 1986; children: Barbara Ann (dec.), Joseph, Lawrence, Dianne. BA, Pratt Inst., 1948; AS, U.S. Naval Acad., 1976. Mural painter asst. Crimi Studio, N.Y.C., 1939-42; art dir. Advt. Printin Co., N.Y.C., 1946-63; art tchr. Mechanics Inst., N.Y.C., 1962-66; v.p. Vogue Wright Studios, N.Y.C., 1963-80; dir. art Electrographic Corp., N.Y.C., Chgo., 1968-70; artist, account exec. Chelsea Photo/Graphics, Inc., N.Y.C., 1981-84. Ofcl. USN combat artist, Washington, 1960-89. Exhibited in group shows at Smithsonian Inst. Operations Palette, 1965, Joe and Emily Lowe Found., 1955, 1963 (Liquitex award, 1997); painter Am. Artist Mag., 1971, painter watercolors USN Combat Art Collection, N.Y. State Naval Militia, 1962, 1991, 1994, 1996—2003, featured USN combat artist, Channel 12 TV, N.Y., 2001. Comdr. USNR, 1962-79. Decorated Croce Al Merito Di

Guerra (Italy), Vietnamese Cross of Gallantry with palm. recipient U.S. Naval Acad. Supertintendent's award, 1983. Roman Catholic. Avocations: playing guitar, singing country & western music. Home: 974 Lorraine Dr Franklin Square NY 11010-1813

INDRITZ, MARY ELOISE STOIKES, pharmacy researcher; b. Madison, Wis., May 23, 1960; d. Gerald Leonard and Dorothy Jane (Dunn) S.; m. Austin N. Indritz, Aug. 24, 1996; children: Jack Philip Ernest, Paige Dorothy Mildred. BS in Pharmacy, Drake U., 1983; MS in Pharmacy Practice, N.D. State U., 1985; postgrad., U. Minn., 1994—. Resident VA Med. Ctr., Fargo, N.D., 1983-85; staff pharmacist Strong Meml. Hosp., Rochester, N.Y., 1985-86, Park Ridge Hosp., Rochester, 1986-88, clin. coord., 1988-89; supr. clin. svcs. Sisters of Charity Hosp., Buffalo, 1989-91; dir. pharmacy St. Francis Med. Ctr., Buffalo, 1989-91; clin. pharmacist A.O. Fox Meml. Hosp., Oneonta, N.Y., 1991-92; pharmacy supr. St. Joseph's Hosp., St. Paul, 1992-94. Contbr. articles to profl. jours. E.R. Squibb & Sons scholar, 1985; recipient Albert P. Prescott/Glaxo Leadership award, 1993, Albert B. Prescott Leadership award; N.Y. State Rsch. and Edn. Found., 1990. Fellow Am. Soc. Health-Sys. Pharmacists; mem. AAUW, APHA, Am. Sociol. Assn., Am. Pharm. Assn., N.Y. State Coun. Hosp. Pharmacists (pres. 1990-92), Rochester Area Soc. Hosp. Pharmacists (pres. 1987-89), Minn. Soc. Hosp. Pharmacists, Am. Soc. Hosp. Pharmacists (com. 1991—), N.D. Soc. Hosp. Pharmacists, Minn-Dakota Soc. Hosp. Pharmacists (sec. 1984-85), Gamma Phi Beta, Lambda Kappa Sigma, Rho Chi. Avocations: reading, skiing, biking, traveling, cooking. Home: 921 Bayless Ave Apt E Saint Paul MN 55114-1151 E-mail: stoi0005@ctc.umn.edu.

INDURSKY, ARTHUR, lawyer; b. Bklyn., Jan. 1, 1943; s. David and Anne (Levine) I.; m. Deanne Fiedler, Mar. 26, 1967; 1 child, Blake. BBA, CCNY, 1964; JD, Bklyn. Law Sch., 1967. Bar: N.Y., 1968. Entertainment counsel Columbia Pictures, N.Y.C., 1969-72; mng. ptnr. Grubman Indursky & Schindler P.C., N.Y.C., 1973—. Bd. dirs. Alliance Artists and Rec. Cos.; guest spkr. Can. Rec. Industry Seminar, 1986, Entertainment Law Soc., Bklyn. Law Sch., 1987, 92, Copyright Soc., 1988, Disting. Alumni Lecture Series Bklyn. Law Sch., 1989, Hofstra Law Sch., 1995. Bd. dirs. T.J. Martell Found. for Leukemia, Cancer and AIDS Rsch., 1993—. Recipient 1st Ann. Alumni Achievement award Bklyn. Law Sch., 1992, Outstanding Leadership award Meml. Sloan Kettering Cancer Ctr., 1994, City of Hope award, 1995, Jule Styne Humanitarian award Childrens Hearing Inst., 1998. Office: Grubman Indursky & Schindler PC 152 W 57th St New York NY 10019-3310

INDYK, MARTIN S. diplomat; b. London, July 1, 1951; BE, Sydney U.; PhD in Internat. Rel., Australian Natl. U. Spec. asst. to the pres. & sr. dir. for Near East & So. Asian affairs Natl. Sec. Council, 1993—95; deputy dir. current intelligence for the Mid-East Australia, 1978; exec. dir Washington Inst. for Near East Policy, 1985—93; U.S. amb. to Israel U.S. Dept. of State, 1995—97, 2000—01; asst. sec. Near Ea. affairs, 1997-2000; sr. mem. Sec. Christopher's Mid-East peace team; White House Rep. U.S.-Israel Sci. & Tech. Commission; adj. prof. Johns Hopkins Sch. Adv. Internat. Studies; dir. Saban Ctr. for Middle East Policy. Fellow sr. fellow, Brookings Inst. Office: The Brookings Inst 1775 Mass Ave NW Washington DC 20036 Fax: 202-797-6003.

INEZ, DONNA LEE, hospital administrator; b. Flushing, N.Y. d. Walter and Ruth (Pringle) Jackowski; m. Virgil Inez, May 30, 1968. BS, So. Conn. State U., New Haven; EdM, Rutgers U., New Brunswick, N.J. RN, Conn.; cert. BLS instr. Asst. supr. med.-surg. Morristown (N.J.) Meml. Hosp., 1969-72; LPN instr. Morristown Sch. Practical Nursing, 1972-78, nursing edn. instr., 1973-90; nursing edn. instr., clin. info. system coord. Morristown Meml. Hosp., 1984-90; asst. dir., clinical coord. patient care sys. Gen. Hosp. Ctr. Passaic, N.J., 1990-99; ret., 1999. Mem. ANA, Am. Med. Informatics Assn., N.J. State Nurses Assn. (com.), Sigma Theta Tau. Home: 63 Grove Ave Morris Plains NJ 07950-2025

INFANTE-OGBAC, DAISY INOCENTES, sales executive, marketing executive, real estate broker; b. Marbel, The Philippines, Aug. 3, 1946; came to U.S., 1968; d. Jesus and Josefina (Inocentes) I.; children: Desiree Josephine, Dante Fernancio, Darrell Enerico; m. Rosben Reyes Ogbac, Jan. 30, 1987. AA with highest honors, Notre Dame of Marbel, Philippines, 1963; AB in English magna cum laude, U. Santo Tomas, Manila, 1965, BS in Psychology, 1966; MA in Comms., Fairfield U., 1971. Real estate broker, Fla. Columnist, writer Pinoy News mag., Chgo., 1975-76, Philippine News, Chgo., 1977-80; cons. EDP Cemco Systems, Inc., Oak Brook, Ill., 1980-81; pres. Daisener, Inc., Downers Grove, Ill., 1980-82; cons. EDP Robert J. Irmen Assocs., Hinsdale, Ill., 1981-82; pres. Data Info. Systems Corp., Downers Grove, Ill., 1982-84; broker, co. mgr. Gen. Devel. Corp., Chgo., 1984-86; columnist, writer Via Times, Chgo., 1984-86; owner, pres. Marbel Realty, Chgo., 1984-88; exec. v.p. Dior Enterprises, Inc., Chgo., 1986-88; real estate sales mgr. M.J. Cumber Co., Grand Cayman, Cayman Islands, 1988-89, Vet. Real Estate, Orlando, Fla., 1989-90; sales mgr. All Star Real Estate, Inc., Orlando, 1990-92; ruby network mktg. exec. Melaleuca, Inc., 1991—; pres. Dior Enterprises, Inc., Orlando, 1992—; prin., owner All Travel, Inc., 2002—. Bd. dirs. Network Mktg. Alliance, 1996—; team leader, sr. team leader The Winners Circle, 1998-99; mem. Orlando Distbn. Ctr. for Healthpower Internat. Inc., 2000—. Author: Songs of Love, Prayer, and Worship to the Lord, 1998, Poems of My Youth, 1982; (lyrics and music) My First Twenty Songs, 1981, The Lord is My Rock; featured contbr. poems; American Poetry Anthology, vol. VIII, no. 4, Best New Poets of 1987, Journey of the Mind, 1995; composer lyrics and melody The Lord in My Rock, 2001; inventor fryer-steamer. Sec. Movement for a Free Philippines, 1984; active DO Pindy Orgn., 2003. Mem. NAFE, Am. Soc. Profl. Exec. Women, Philippine C. of C. (sec. Chgo. chpt. 1985), Bayanihan Internat. Ladies Assn., Lions (twister Fil-Am. club 1978-79). Roman Catholic. Avocations: bowling, swimming, racquetball, tennis. E-mail: iysiad@yahoo.com., diorentintl@yahoo.com.

INFINGER, GLORIA ALTMAN, retired nursing administrator; b. Charleston, S.C., Feb. 16; d. Norman B. and Gladys V. Risher; m. Norman M. Infinger, May 21, 1961; children: Robert M., Michael S. Diploma, Med. U.S.C., 1962. RN, S.C.; register cen. svc. technician. Nurse Med. U. S.C. Med. Ctr., Charleston, 1962-68, nursing supr., asst. dir. evening shift, 1974-86, mgr. sterile processing, 1986-94, sterile processing cons., 1994; office nurse John Aycock, M.D., Mt. Pleasant, S.C., 1968-69; asst. head nurse Charleston Meml. Hosp., 1969-73. Part-time RN Med. U. S.C., 1995-98; part-time salesperson Margiotta's Inc., 1998—. Mem. S.C. Assn. for Hosp. Ctrl. Svc. Pers. (founder 1992), Internat. Assn. Hosp. Ctrl. Svc. Material Mgmt., S.C. State Employees Assn., S.C. State Quilters Guild, Cobbleston Quilters Guild Charleston. Office: Margiotta's Sewing Machine Ctr 874 Orleans Rd Unit 5 Charleston SC 29407-4857

INFOSINO, IARA CIURRIA, management consultant; b. Campinas, Sao Paulo, Brazil, Aug. 24, 1952; came to the U.S., 1982; d. Humberto and Mafalda (Pavan) C.; m. Konstantinos Stavropoulos, Feb. 2, 1980 (div.); m. Charles J. Infosino, Feb. 24, 1995; 1 child, Melissa Rose. BS in Math., São Paulo State U., São José do Rio Preto, Brazil, 1974; MS in Applied Math., UNICAMP, Campinas, Brazil, 1982; PhD in Ops. Rsch., Stanford U., 1989. H.S. tchr. Colegio Santo Andre, São Jose'do Rio Preto, Brazil, 1973-74; tchg. asst. UNESP, São Jose'do Rio Preto, Brazil, 1974; asst. prof. Bus. Sch., São Jose'do Rio Preto, Brazil, 1973-75, UNICAMP, Campinas, Brasil, 1978-82; sr. cons. SynQuest, Inc. (formerly Bender Mgmt. Cons.), Arlington, Va., 1989—2001. Mem. INFORMS Inst. Avocations: dancing, good books, plays, fitness exercises, movies.

INFUSINO, ACHILLE FRANCIS, financial and administrative support executive; b. Kenosha, Wis, Feb. 8, 1953; s. Frank and Irene (Rende) I.; m. Joyce Marie, Nov. 22, 1975; children: Daniel, Nicholas, Jaclyn, Timothy. BA, Carthage Coll., 1982; MBA, Marquette U., 1987. Pres. Infusino Bros. Constrn. Co., Inc., Kenosha, 1987—, Cellular City Comm., Kenosha, 1987—; founder, sr. project mgr. Project Mgmt. Cons., Kenosha, 1994-2000; v.p. procurement and operational asset mgmt. ATC Leasing Co., Kenosha, 2000—02, sr. UP & gen. mgr., 2002—. Instr. Carthage Coll., 1990; adj. prof. advanced fin. mgmt. U. Wis., Parkside, 2000—; bd. dirs. Bank of Kenosha. Bd. dirs. Kenosha Area Devel. Corp., 1981-87, Salvation Army Adv. Bd., Kenosha, 1983-85; pres. St. Joseph's Interparish Jr. High Sch., Kenosha, 1986-91; chmn. Bd. Building Appeals, City of Kenosha, 1986-88. Mem. Italian Am. Soc., MBA Execs., Assn. Constrn. Insps., Environ. Assessment Assn. Avocations: youth athletic programs, little league baseball. Office: Bd of Trustees St Josephs HS 3614 16th Pl Kenosha WI 53144-3376 also: ATC Leasing 4316 39th Ave Kenosha WI 53144-1962

ING, CLARENCE SINN FOOK, preventive medicine physician, ophthalmic surgeon; b. Stockton, Calif., Oct. 1, 1938; s. Clarence S. and Isabel L. (Low) I.; m. May Chan, July 9, 1961; children: Michael, Stephen, Jeffrey, Daniel, Michelle. BA, La Sierra U., 1959; MD, Loma Linda U., 1963, MPH, 1990. Diplomate Am. Bd. Ophthalmology, Am. Bd. Preventive Medicine. Intern San Joaquin Gen. Hosp., Stockton, Calif., 1963-64; dir. emergency med. svc. St. Francis Hosp., Lynwood, Calif., 1966, Cmty. Hosp. San Gabriel, Calif., 1967; resident ophthalmology Hollywood Presbyn. Hosp., L.A., 1967-70; med. missionary Bella Vista Hosp., Mayaguez, P.R., 1970-78; staff physician Wildwood (Ga.) Sanitarium & Hosp., 1978-81; med. missionary, chief staff Armer Ishoda Meml. Hosp., Majuro, Marshall Islands, 1981-82; med. missionary Youngberg Adventist Hosp., Singapore, 1982-89, resident preventive medicine Loma Linda U. Med. Ctr., 1990-91; med. missionary, dir. Wellness Ctr. Youngberg Adventist Hosp., Singapore, 1992-97; med. dir. Weimar Inst., 1997-2000; pres. Newstart Med. Clinic, 1997—. Capt. U.S. Army, 1964-66. Fellow Am. Acad. Ophthalmology, Am. Coll. Preventive Medicine. Avocations: alpine skiing, scuba diving, golf, jogging, tennis. Office: Weimar Inst PO Box 486 20601 W Paoli Ln Weimar CA 95736-0486 Fax: 530-637-4443. E-mail: csfing@juno.com.

INGAGLIO, DIEGO AUGUSTUS, dentist; b. Phila., Dec. 4, 1922; s. Salvatore and Maria Concetta (Giordano) I.; m. Geraldine Jean Capizzi, July 11, 1948; children: Marie, Francene. DDS, U. Pa., 1947. With Phila. Mouth Hygiene Dept., 1947-50; asst. clin. dir. Emerson R. Sausser Med. Dental Clinic, Jefferson Hosp., Phila., 1950-51; pvt. practice dentistry Drexel Hill, Pa., 1953—. Staff Suburban Gen. Hosp., Norristown; mem. Congressional Adv Bd. Editor-in-chief U. Pa. Dental Jour., 1945-47. Intergenerational com., Upper Twp. Elem. Sch.; past pres. mature adults, Reesurrection Ch., Marmora, N.J., lector for mass readings, mem. Friends for Life com.; mem. Resurrection Ch. Liturgy Group; mem. vocations com. Diocese of Camden. With AUS, 1943-45, 51-53. Fellow Acad. Gen. Dentistry, Acad. Dentistry Internat., Royal Soc. Health; mem. ADA, AAAS, Pa. Dental Assn., Chester-Delaware County Dental Assn., Am. Internat., Philadelphia County Soc. Clin. Hypnosis, Nat. Space Inst., Phila. Physhodontontic Soc. (past pres.), Royal Soc. Hygiene, Nat. Ass.n Fed. Lic. Firearms Dealers, NRA, Cape May County Serra Group (pres. 2002—, trustee, v.p. in charge of membership), Heritage Found., Omicron Kappa Upsilon, Psi Omega. Address: 670 Breckley Rd Marmora NJ 08223-1158 E-mail: daimarmora@aol.com.

INGALLS, EVERETT PALMER, III, lawyer; b. Portland, Maine, Nov. 21, 1947; s. Everett Palmer and Joyce (Iveney) I.; m. Susan Wilson, Feb. 15, 1992; 1 child, Abigail Valentine. AB, Brown U., 1969; JD, Harvard U., 1972. Bar: Maine 1972, U.S. Dist. Ct. Maine 1972. Assoc. Pierce Atwood, Portland, 1972-77, mem., 1977—. Area chmn. Harvard Law Sch. Fund, Cambridge, Mass., 1978-82; pres. Portland Widows' Wood Soc., 1982-86; bd. dirs. Portland Stage Co., 1979-82; pres. Portland Performing Arts, 1992-94; pres. planned giving com. Maine Med. Ctr., 2002—. Fellow Am. Coll. Trust & Estate Counsel; mem. ABA (real property, probate & trust law and taxation), Harvard Law Sch. Assn. in Maine (pres. 1982-85), Phi Beta Kappa. Home: 125 Neal St Portland ME 04102-3209 Office: Pierce Atwood One Monument Sq Portland ME 04101 E-mail: eingalls@pierceatwood.com.

INGALLS, MARIE CECELIE, former state legislator, retail executive; b. Faith, S.D., Mar. 31, 1936; d. Jens P. and Ida B. (Hegre) Jensen; m. Dale D. Ingalls, June 20, 1955; children: Duane (dec.), Delane. BS, Black Hills State Coll., 1973, MS, 1978. Elem. tchr. Meade County Schs., Sturgis, S.D., 1957-72, Faith Sch. Dist. 46-2, 1973-76; elem. prin. Meade Sch. Dist. 46-1, Sturgis, 1976-81; owner, operator Ingalls, Sturgis, 1978-99; mem., asst. majority whip S.D. House Reps., Pierre, 1986-92; lobbyist S.D. Legislature. Former sec. S.D. Rep. Orgn; Rep. nominee S.D. Commr. Sch. and Pub. Lands, 1998. Recipient Woman of Achievement award City of Sturgis, 1986, Retail Bus. of Yr. 1998. Mem. S.D. Cattlewomen, S.D. Stockgrowers (edn. chair), S.D. Farm Bur. (bd. dirs. dist. V 1993-2001), Meade County Farm Bur., Faith C. of C. (pres. 1989), Sturgis C. of C. (past bd. dirs.), Key City Investment Club. Republican. Lutheran. Avocations: knitting, crocheting, piano, reading. Home: 17054 Opal Rd Mud Butte SD 57758

INGALLS, PAMELA LYNN, artist, educator; b. Spokane, Wash., June 10, 1957; d. Richard David and Marjorie Denise (Barry) Ingalls. Student, Accademia Delle Belle Arte, Florence, Italy, 1977-78; BA in Art, Gonzaga U., 1979. Resident artist, chore supr. Jesuit Vol. Corps, Seattle, 1980-81; graphic artist Tourmap Co., Spokane, 1982-86; painter Vashon Island, Wash., 1986—; apprentice Ron Lukas' Painting Studio, Seattle, 1992-95; art instr. Blue Heron Ctr. for Arts, Vashon Island, 1994—; artist-in-residence Belfast, Ireland, 1999—. Juror art exhbn. Western Wash. State Fair, Puyallup, 1997, Canterbury Faire, Kent, Wash., 1998; exhbn. advisor Blue Heron Ctr. for Arts, Vashon Island, 1997, Mercer Island Juried Art Exhibit, 2002, Eastside Assn. Fine Arts, 2003. Exhibited in over 125 including group shows Tacoma (Wash.) Art Mus., 1997 (Hon. Mention 1997), North Valley Art League Ann., Redding, Calif., 1998 (Best of Show 1998), Am. Women Artists Ann., 1998 (3d pl. 1998), Okla. Art Workshops, 1997 (Pres.'s award 1997), Desert Caballeros Mus., Wickedburg, Ariz., 2002, others. Creator after sch. art classes Blue Heron Ctr. for Arts, Vashon Island, 1992-98, bd. dirs.; art tchr. inner-city kids Readiness to Learn Grant, Seattle, 1994-98; participant Bethlehem Peace Pilgrimage, 1982-83. Recipient over 60 awards including Merit award Batavia Soc. Artists, 1997, Merit award Nat. Oil and Acrylic Painters Soc., 1995, 97, 1st prize Juan de Fuca Internat. Juried Show, 1997. Mem. Nat. Oil and Acrylic Painters Soc., Am. Artists Profl. League, Allied Artists of am., Oil Painters of Am., Women Painters of Wash. (exhbn. coord. 1992-98, 3d pl. award 1997, 1st pl. award 1998, 1st pl. award 2001). Home: PO Box 263 Vashon WA 98070-0263

INGALLS, ROBERT LYNN, physicist, educator; b. Spokane, Wash., June 15, 1934; s. Keith Irving and Ruth Louise (Strauss) I.; m. Liisa Vasama, Jan. 28, 1961 (div. Apr. 1993); children: Karen Liisa, Johanna Louise, David Robert. BS, U. Wash., 1956; MS, Carnegie Inst. Tech., 1960, PhD, 1962. Instr. physics Carnegie Inst. Tech., 1961-63; research asso. U. Ill., 1963-65, research asso. prof., 1965-66; asst. prof. U. Wash., Seattle, 1966-69, asso. prof., 1969-74, prof. physics, 1974-2000, prof. emeritus, 2001—. Vis. scholar State U. Groningen, Netherlands, 1972-73 Bassoonist, Seattle Symphony Orch., 1952-57; contbr. articles to profl. jours., books and encys AEC contract, 1967-77; NSF grantee, 1976-83; Dept. Energy grantee, 1983— Mem. AAAS, Am. Phys. Soc., Fedn. Am. Scientists, Sigma Xi, Sigma Phi Epsilon, Zeta Mu Tau. Achievements include first to treat electric quadrupole splitting theory in ferrous compounds, X-ray absorption fine structure studies of materials at high pressure and original guasicrystal tilings. Office: U Wash Dept Physics Seattle WA 98195-0001 E-mail: ingalls@phys.washington.edu.

INGALSBE, WILLIAM JAMES, lawyer; b. Guam, June 5, 1947; came to U.S., 1953; s. Wilbur and Erma I.; m. Heidi Marie Freed, June 21, 1969; 1 child, James. BA, Calif. State U., San Diego, 1969; JD, Southwestern U., 1975. Bar: Calif., 1975, U.S. Ct. Appeals (9th cir.) 1984, U.S. Dist. Ct. (cen. and so. dist.) Calif. 1976, U.S. Dist. Ct. (no. dist.) Calif. 1984, U.S. Claims Ct. 1979. Assoc. Spray, Gould & Bowers, L.A., 1975-76; ptnr. Monteleone & McCrory, L.A., Calif., 1976—. Editor-in-chief: Southwestern U. Law Rev., 1974. Vol. investigative atty. State Bar Calif., L.A., 1986. Mem. Assoc. Gen. Contractors Calif., L.A. County Bar Assn. (judge pro tem mcpl. ts. com. 1984-86, vol. atty. client rels. com. 1984-90). Avocations: fishing, golf, photography. Office: # 130 450 W 4th St Santa Ana CA 92701-4562 E-mail: ingalsbe@mmlawyers.com.

INGBAR, MARY LEE, economist; b. N.Y.C., May 18, 1926; d. Lee Adam Gimbel and Edward C. and Ruth (Prince) Mack; m. Sidney H. Ingbar, May 28, 1950; children: David H., Eric E., Jonathan. SB in Econs. cum laude, Radcliffe Coll., 1946, AM in Econs., 1948, PhD in Econs., 1953; MPH cum laude, Harvard, 1956. Corrector dept. econs. Harvard U., 1949-50, Tufts U., 1949; rsch. assoc. Grad. Sch. Pub. Adminstrn. Harvard U., Cambridge, Mass., 1961-66; assoc. prof. health econs. in residence U. Calif., San Francisco, 1972-75; prin. rsch. assoc. in preventive and social medicine Harvard Med. Sch., Boston, 1976—80, prin. rsch. assoc. in social medicine and health policy, 1980-85, prin. assoc. in social medicine and health policy, 1985—; prof. family and community medicine U. Mass. Med. Sch., Worcester, 1977-82. Prin. rsch. assoc. in medicine, Beth Israel Hosp., Boston, 1976-88; vis. prof. health econs. The Amos Tuck Sch. of Bus. Adminstrn. at Dartmouth Coll. and Dartmouth Med. Sch., 1976-77; project dir. Innovative Methods of Pricing Ambulatory Care Treatment for Patients with Hypertension/U.S. Dept. Health Human Svcs. grant, 1980-82; cons. various cos. including WaterTest Corp., Manchester, N.H., 1982-88, Software Craftsmen, Inc., Boston, 1982-84; bd. dirs. WaterTest Corp.; pres. IFF, Inc., 1989—; lectr. in field, others. Editorial bd. Medical Care Jour., 1977-79; contbr. chpts. to books, articles to profl. jours. Overseer Peter Bent Brigham Hosp., 1976-84; trustee Brigham and Women's Hosp., 1984-86. Fellow: APHA (chmn. med. care sect. 1978—79, governing coun. 1974—76, 1985—88, 1991—93); mem.: AAAS, N.Y. Acad. Scis., Internat. Health Econs. Assn., Assn. Univ. Programs in Health Adminstrn., Assn. Tchrs. of Preventive Medicine, Am. Assn. World Health, Inst. Ops. Rsch. and Mgmt. Scis., Mass. Pub. Health Assn., Acad. Health, Am. Hosp. Assn., Am. Econ. Assn., Am. Med. Informatics, Phi Beta Kappa (Iota chpt. of Mass.). Home and Office: 9 Follen St Cambridge MA 02138-3502

INGE, MILTON THOMAS, American literature and culture educator, author; b. Newport News, Va., Mar. 18, 1936; s. Clyde Elmo and Bernice Lucille (Jackson) I.; m. Betty Jean Meredith, 1958 (div. 1977); 1 child, Scott Thomas; m. Tonette Long Bond, 1982 (div. 1991); 1 stepchild, Michael Gordon Bond; m. Donaria Romeiro Carvalho, 1998. BA, Randolph-Macon Coll., 1959; MA, Vanderbilt U., 1960, PhD, 1964. Instr. English Vanderbilt U., 1962-64; asst. prof. Am. thought and lang. Mich. State U., 1964-68, assoc. prof., 1968-69; assoc. prof. English Va. Commonwealth U., Richmond, 1969-73, prof., 1973-80, chmn. dept. English, 1974-80; prof., chmn. dept. English, Clemson U., S.C., 1980-84; resident scholar in Am. studies USIA, Washington, 1982-84; Blackwell prof. English and humanities Randolph-Macon Coll., Ashland, Va., 1984—. Reader English Composition Test Coll. Entrance Exam Bd., 1967, 69, 77, 80; Va. Cultural Laureate, 92; dir. USIA Summer Inst. in Am. Studies, 1993—95; liberal studies disting. scholar-in-residence U. Louisville, 2003. Author: Donald Davidson: Essay and Bibliography, 1965, (with T.D. Young) Donald Davidson, 1971, The American Comic Book, 1985, Comics in the Classroom, 1989, Great American Comics: 100 Years of Cartoon Art, 1990, Comics as Culture, 1990, Faulkner, Sut, and Other Southerners, 1992, Perspectives on American Culture: Essays on Humor, Literature, and the Popular Arts, 1994, Anything Can Happen in a Comic Strip: Centennial Reflections on an American Art Form, 1995; editor: (books) Sut Lovingood's Yarns, 1966, 2d edit. 1987, High Times and Hard Times, 1967, Agrarianism in American Literature, 1969, A.B. Longstreet, 1969, Faulkner: A Rose for Emily, 1970, Wm. Byrd of Westover, 1970, Studies in Light in August, 1971, Frontier Humorists: Critical Views, 1975, Ellen Glasgow: Centennial Essays, 1976,(with J. Bryer and M. Duke) Black American Writers: Bibliographic Essays, 2 vols., 1978, Handbook of American Popular Culture, Vol. I, 1978, Vol. II, 1980, Vol. III, 1981, 3 vols. rev. and expanded edits., 1989, Concise Histories of American Popular Culture, 1982, (with E.E. MacDonald) James Branch Cabell: Centennial Essays, 1983, (with J. Bryer and M. Duke) American Women Writers: Bibliographical Essays, 1983, Huck Finn Among the Critics: A Centennial Selection, 1984, rev. edit., 1985, Truman Capote: Conversations, 1987, Naming the Rose: Essays on Umberto Eco's "The Name of the Rose", 1988, Handbook of American Popular Literature, 1988, A Nineteenth Century American Reader, 1988, The Comics, 1991, (with Sergei Chakovsky) Russian Eyes on American Literature, 1992, Dark Laughter: The Satiric Art of Oliver W. Harrington, 1993, Why I Left America and Other Essays of Oliver W. Harrington, 1993, William Faulkner: The Contemporary Reviews, 1994, (with James E. Caron) Sut Lovingood's Nat'ral Born Yarnspinner: Essays on George Washington Harris, 1996, Mark Twain's A Connecticut Yankee in King Arthur's Court, 1997, The Achievement of William Faulkner: A Centennial Tribute, 1998; Conversations with William Faulkner, 1999, "Co. Aytch," or a Side Show of the Big Show and Other Sketches by Samuel R. Watkins, 1999, Charles M. Schulz: Conversations, 2000, (with Ed Piacentino) The Humor of the Old South, 2001, (with Dennis Hall) Greenwood Guide to American Popular Culture, 4 vols., 2002; editor jours. Resources for American Literary Study, 1971-79, American Humor: An Interdisciplinary Newsletter, 1974-79; gen. editor Greenwood Press Bio-Bibliographies and Reference Guides in Popular Culture, Cambridge U. Press Am. Critical Archives, U. Press Miss. Studies in Popular Culture; book reviewer: Nashville Tenneseean, Richmond Times-Dispatch. Bd. dirs. Friends of Richmond Pub. Libary; bd. dirs. San Francisco Acad. Comic Art, James Br. Cabell Libr. Assocs., Va. Commonwealth U., Edgar Allen Poe Mus. Recipient Bd. Govs. award Am. Cultural Assn., 1999; fellow So. Fellowship Fund, 1959-62, Newberry Libr., 1987, Va. Found. Humanities, 1987, 93; grantee Fulbright-Hays, 1967-68, 71, 79, 88, 94, Mich. State U., 1965, 66, 68, Am. Philos. Soc., 1970, Clemson U., 1981, NEH, 1986, 91, 92; recipient Disting. Alumnus award Randolph-Macon Coll., 1995. Mem. MLA (hon. life, del. assembly 1976-78, 2001-03, chmn. elections com. 1980), South Atlantic MLA (program com. 1982-85, chmn. 1986, v.p. 1987, pres. 1988-89), Am. Studies Assn., Popular Culture Assn., Am. Humor Studies Assn. (pres. 1978, 88, Charlie award 1996), Soc. Study So. Lit. (exec. coun. 1971-73, 78-80, 86-88), Melville Soc., Ellen Glasgow Soc. (exec. coun. 1974-84, pres. 1987-88), Mus. Cartoon Art (nominating com. Hall of Fame 1975-95), European Assn. Am. Studies, So. Studies Forum (founder, exec. coun. 1988—), Popular Culture Assn. in South (v.p. 1987-88, pres. 1988-89), Mark Twain Cir. (chmn. nominating com. 1987-88), Mark Twain Cir. Am. (hon.), Cosmos Club, Phi Beta Kappa, Omicron Delta Kappa, Pi Delta Epsilon, Lambda Chi Alpha. Home: PO Box 129 Ashland VA 23005-0129 E-mail: tinge@rmc.edu.

INGE, WALTER HERNDON, writer; b. Mobile, Ala., July 24, 1933; s. Walter Herndon and Gratia (Seaman) Inge; m. Margaret Jane Leigh, Jan. 25, 1956 (dec. Mar. 1989); children: Gratia Harrison, Leigh Vaughan; m. Barbara Griffith Brady, June 19, 1999. BS in Biology, U. Ala., 1955; MA in Physiology, U. Calif., Berkeley, 1965, PhD in Physiology, 1972. Commd. USAF, 1955—76, advanced through grades to lt. col., ret., 1976; asst. prof. physiology USAF Acad., Colorado Springs, Colo., 1965—67; dir. engrng. and biotech. European Office, Aerospace Rsch., London, 1971—75; rsch. physiologist Wright-Patterson AFB, Dayton, 1975—77; asst. prof. physiology Boston U., 1977—82; rsch. assoc. Emory U. Sch. Medicine, Atlanta, 1982—87; prof., chair dept. physiology St. George U. Sch. Medicine, Grenada, West Indies, 1987—88; sci. writer Atlanta, 1988—. Acad. cons. Natick Labs., Mass., 1965—66. Contbr. Anglican Church. Avocations: skiing, hiking, mycology, amateur theatrics. Home and Office: 205 Windy Acres Rd Cleveland GA 30528

INGELFINGER, JULIE R. physician, researcher; d. Shirley C. Rich; m. Peter W. McDavitt, Sept. 3, 2000; 3 children. BA, Harvard U., 1964; MD, Albert Einstein Coll. of Medicine, Bronx, 1968. Lic. pediats. Am. Bd. of Pediat., 1973, subboard pediat. nephrology Am. Bd. of Pediat., 1974. Chief pediat. nephrology Mass. Gen. Hosp., 1994—2001, co-chief pediat. nephrology, 1989—94, sr. cons. pediat. nephrology, 2001—; prof. pediat. Harvard Med. Sch., Boston, 1999—. Pres. Am. Soc. of Pediat. Nephrology, 1994—95. Author: (book) Coping with Prednisone, (text) Pediatric Hypertension, (textbook, multiple edits.) Current Pediatric Therapy, over 150 rsch. papers; dep. editor New Eng. Jour. Medicine, 2001—. Chair, med. adv. bd. Nat. Kidney Found. of MA, RI, NH, VT, 2002; bd. trustees Spring Lake Ranch, Cuttingsville, Vt., 2001—. Multiple NIH and Found. Grants, NIH, and other agencies, 1980—. Mem.: Internat. Pediat. Nephrology Assn., Am. Soc. of Pediat. Nephrology (pres., coun. 1988—95), Women in Nephrology (coun. 1990), Soc. for Pediat. Rsch., Am. Pediat. Soc., Am. Soc. of Nephrology. Achievements include research in papers concerning the renin-angiotensin system in normal physiology, in development, and in disease. Avocations: piano, writing, hiking.

INGELHART, LOUIS EDWARD, journalism educator, retired; b. Minco, Okla., Jan. 19, 1920; s. Louis C. and Estella Lorinda (Burns) I.; m. Margaret Jeanette Wade, Nov. 24, 1948 (dec.); children: Sharon Margaret, James Louis. AA, Mesa Coll., 1940; BA, Colo. No. U., 1942, MA, 1947; PhD, Mo. U., 1953. Tchr. English Fruita (Colo.) Union H.S., 1946; instr. English Colo. No. U., Greeley, 1946-47; instr. journalism, dir. pub. rels. Wayne (Nebr.) State U., 1947-50; instr. journalism Stephens Coll., Columbus, Mo., 1952-53; dir. pub. info., prof. journalism Ball State U., Muncie, Ind., 1953-83, dir. student publs., chmn. dept. journalism, 1953-83, ret., 1983. Mem. exec. bd. Student Press Law Ctr., 1990-97, bd. dirs., life mem. adv. coun., 2000. Author: Freedom For the College Student Press, 1985, Press Law and Press Freedoms for High School Publications, 1986, Press Freedoms, 1987, What Americans Have Said About Freedom of Expression, 1993, Student Publications, 1993, Press and Speech

Freedoms in America 1619-1995, 1997, Press and Speech Freedoms in the World From Antiquity Until 1998, 1998, Mrs. Presidents, Logan's Front Porch, Jealousy's Double Jeopardy, 21st Century Almanack, The Ax and the Green Angel, Literature of Liberty, Ascension, Play Acting History; co-author: Public Relations Problems, 1951, Journey Toward Freedom, 1994; writer short stories, plays, novels, commentaries and essays; contbr. numerous articles to profl. jours. Staff sgt. USAF, 1942-46. Recipient Pioneer award Nat. Scholastic Press Assn., 1970, Journalism Achievement award Dow Jones Newspaper Fund, 1983, Silver Medal award Muncie Am. Advt. Fedn., 1986, Hugh Hefner First Amendment award Playboy Mag., 1989, Disting. Svc. award C.C. Journalism Assn., 1986; named Outstanding Alumnus Mesa State Coll., 1985, named Segamore of New Wabash by gov. Ind., 2000; Ingelhart First Amendment fund established by Coll. Media Advisors, 2001; Ingelhart Freedom of Press Fund Established by Coll. Media Advisors, 2002. Mem. AAUP, Soc. Profl. Journalists (First Amendment award 1990, named to Hall of Fame Ind. chpt.), Coll. Media Advisers (Noel Ross Streader award 1981, named Outstanding Adviser Student Newspaper 1969, Louis E. Ingelhart First Amendment award 1984, named to Hall of Fame 1994), Ind. Assoc. Press Mng. Editors Assn. (life), Assn. for Edn. in Journalism, Am. Fedn. Tchrs., Assn. for Edn. in Journalism and Mass Communications (spl. citations secondary edn. divsn. 1984), Ind. H.S. Press Assn. (life, Louis Ingelhart Svc. award 1985), Columbia Scholastic Press Advisers Assn. (life, Golden Crown award 1975, Gold Key award 1972), Quill and Scroll (hon.), Ball State U. Alumni Assn. (life), First Amendment Congress (v.p. 1980-97, exec. bd. dirs.), Journalism Edn. Assn. (Carl Towley award 1972), U. No. Colo. Alumni Assn. (Trail Blazer award 1983), Phi Delta Kappa (Hardy Disting. Svc. award 1991). Mem. Ch. Disciples Of Christ. Avocation: writing. Home: 615 N Tyrone Dr Muncie IN 47304-3141 Fax: 765-285-7997.

INGELS, JACK EDWARD, horticulture educator; b. Indpls., Mar. 28, 1942; s. Carl Eugene and Mary Louise (Fultz) I. BS, Purdue U., 1964; MS, Rutgers U., 1966; postgrad., Ball State U., 1968-70. Rsch. asst. Rutgers U., New Brunswick, N.J., 1964-66; prof. SUNY, Cobleskill, 1966-89, disting. teaching prof., 1990—. Hort. cons. J.C. Penney Corp., N.Y.C., 1966-69; landscape designer, 1966—; hort. and/or landscape cons. numerous small cos., 1970—; pres. J. Ingels Assoc., 1991—. Author: Landscaping: Principles and Practices, 6th edit., 2003, Ornamental Horticulture: Science, Operations and Management, 3d edit., 2000. Chmn. Cobleskill Restoration and Devel., Inc., 1991—, bd. dirs., 1988—; pres. Timothy Murphy Gourmet Soc., 1989—; mem. Schoharie County Coun. on Arts, Cobleskill, Albany Inst. of History and Art; bd. dirs. Cobleskill Partnership, 1996—. Named one of top ten landscape educators in Am., Landscape Mgmt. mag., 1995. Mem. Associated Landscape Contractors Am., Northeastern N.Y. Nursery Assn., Genesee-Finger Lakes Nursery Assn., Univ. Club (Albany, N.Y.), Moose, Elks. Avocations: gourmet cooking, landscape garden history, travel. Home: 139 Jay St Cobleskill NY 12043 Office: SUNY Horticulture Dept Cobleskill NY 12043 *To teach is a privilege that permits me to touch lives. To teach well is my obligation.*

INGELS, MARTY, theatrical agent, television and motion picture production executive; b. Bklyn., Mar. 9, 1936; s. Jacob and Minnie (Crown) Ingerman; m. Jean Maire Frassinelli, Aug. 3, 1960 (div. 1969); m. Shirley Jones, 1977. Ed., Erasmus High Sch., 1951-53, Forest Hills High Sch., 1953-55. Founder Ingels Inc., 1975—; formed Stoneypoint Prodns., 1981; TV and motion picture producer U.S. and Abroad; mgr. of Shirley Jones. Star: Dickens and Fenster series, ABC-TV, 1964; co-star: Pruitts of Southampton, 1968-69; films include Armored Command, 1962, Horizontal Lieutenant, 1965, Busy Body, 1967, Ladies Man, 1966, If It's Tuesday This Must Be Belgium, 1970, Wild and Wonderful, 1965, Guide for a Married Man, 1968; numerous TV appearances. Active various charity drives. Achievements include Owning the world's largest celebrity brokerage service, 1974; widely noted as the Henry Kissinger of Madison Avenue. Office: Network Prodns 4531 Noeline Way Encino CA 91436

INGELSON, BRIAN CHARLES, music educator, director; s. Ed and Jean Gladys Dora Ingelson; m. Beverley Faye Iles, Aug. 4, 1990; children: Sean Talbot Anderson, Matthew Ernest, William Brian. BA, U. of Calgary, 1984; MEd, U. of Mo., 1990. Cert. tchr. State of Calif., 2001, Province of Alta., 1985. Band dir. Calgary (Can.) Bd. of Edn., 1985—89, 1990—94; supr. student tchrs. U. of Nev., Las Vegas, 1994—95; prof. of music C.C. of So. Nev., Las Vegas, 1994—95; dir. of bands Palm Springs (Calif.) HS., 1995—. Condr. Sydney (Australia) Music Festival, 1997, Brianzza (Italy) Bandistico Internat., 1998, Disneyland Paris, Paris, 1998; prof. music Coll. of the Desert, Palm Desert, Calif., 1996—99. Condr.: Spirit of The Sands. Edn. liason Palm Springs (Calif.) Cmty. Concerts, 2001. Named Oustanding Music Dir.- Westside Story, Desert Theater League, 2001; recipient Alta. Achievement award in Arts, Province of Alta., 1988, Tchr. of the Yr. award, Soroptimist Internat., 1997, Congl. Cert. of Recognition award, US Congress, 1998, Wal- Mart Tchr. of the Yr. award, Cathedral City Wal-Mart, 2000, Congl. Cert. of Recognition, US Congress, 2000; scholar, U. of Mo., Columbia, 1989—90. Mem.: Music Educators Nat. Conf. Office: Palm Springs High School 2401 East Baristo Rd Palm Springs CA 92262 Home Fax: 760-360-5288; Office Fax: 760-778-0417. Personal E-mail: bband@gte.net. E-mail: bcingelson@psusd.k12.ca.us.

INGERMAN, PETER ZILAHY, systems analyst, consultant; b. N.Y.C., Dec. 9, 1934; s. Charles Stryker and Ernestine (Leigh) I.; m. Carol Mary Pasquale, Dec. 19, 1970 (div. May 1980); m. Colleen Frances McGaffey, Sept. 13, 1996. AB, U. Pa., 1958, MSEE, 1963; PhD, Greenwich U., 1991. CLU; cert. data processor, computer programmer, sys. profl., emergency med. technician. Rsch. investigator U. Pa., Phila., 1958-63; tech. dir. programming rsch. Westinghouse, Balt., 1963-65; mgr. RCA, Cherry Hill, N.J., 1965-72; sr. staff cons. Equitable Life Assurance Soc. of U.S., N.Y.C., 1972-77; ind. computer cons. Willingboro, N.J., 1977—. Adj. prof. computer sci. Pratt Inst. Tech., 1968-73; mem. working groups Internat. Fedn. Info. Processing, 1962— ; rep. Conf. Data Systems Langs., 1967-71; Am. Nat. Standards Inst., 1960-69; bd. dirs. Phila. Health Plan, Inc., 1975-77; Crossroads Runaway Program, Inc., 1981-82; Compliance, Inc., 1989—, Providence House, 1991-94, vice chair, 1991-94, peer reviewer, Open-Source Encyc., 2000—. Author: A Syntax-Oriented Translator, 1966, Russian transl., 1969; contbr. articles to profl. jours.; patentee electronic circuits. Bd. dirs. Providence Ho., 1991—94, vice chair, 1991—94; mem. Willingboro Emergency Squad, 1982—90, 2002—, bd. officers, 1986—89, 2003—; bd. dirs. Crossroads Runaway Program, Inc., 1981—82, Compliance, Inc., 1989—. Fellow Brit. Computer Soc. (life); mem. IEEE (life sr.), AAAS, Assn. Computing Machinery, Data Processing Mgmt. Assn., Am. Cryptogram Assn., Brit. Engring. Coun. (chartered info. sys. practioner, chartered info. sys. engr., chartered engr.), Independent Computer Cons. Assn. (treas. 1999-01), Sigma Xi (life), Am. Guild Organists (co-dean S.W. Jersey chpt. 1997-98, dean 1998-99, treas. 1999—), N.J. Acad. Scis., Mensa, Triple Nine Soc., Assn. Former Intelligence Officers, Upsilon Pi Epsilon. Achievements include patents for electronic circuits. Office: 40 Needlepoint Ln Willingboro NJ 08046-1997

INGERSOLL, ANDREW PERRY, planetary science educator; b. Chgo., Jan. 2, 1940; s. Jeremiah Crary and Minneola (Perry) I.; m. Sarah Morin, Aug. 27, 1961; children: Jeremiah, Ruth Ingersoll Wood, Marion Ingersoll Quinones, Minneola, George. BA, Amherst Coll., 1960; PhD, Harvard U., 1965. Rsch. fellow Harvard U., Cambridge, Mass., 1965-66; asst. prof. planetary sci. Calif. Inst. Tech., Pasadena, 1966-71, assoc. prof., 1971-76, prof., 1976—2003, Earle C. Anthony prof. planetary sci., 2003—. Mem. staff summer study program Woods Hole (Mass.) Oceanographic Inst., 1965, 70-73, 76, 80, 92; prin. investigator Pioneer Saturn Infrared Radiometer Team, NASA; mem. Voyager Imaging Team, NASA, Cassini Imaging Team; interdisciplinary scientist, Mars Global Surveyor Project, Galileo Project, NASA. Bd. trustees Poly. Sch., Pasadena. Fellow AAAS, Am. Geophys. Union, Am. Acad. Arts and Scis.; mem. Am. Astron. Soc. (vice-chmn. div. planetary sci. 1988-89, chmn. 1989-90). Office: Calif Inst Tech Dept Planetary Sci 150 21 Pasadena CA 91125-0001

INGERSOLL, MARYANN E. PATTERSON, health educator, holistic nurse; b. Durham, NC, Aug. 22, 1951; d. Hubert Clifton Jr. and Elizabeth R. (Fox) Patterson; m. Dennis Scott Ingersoll, Dec. 20, 1975; children: Christopher Scott, Elizabeth Patterson. BSN, U. N.C., 1973; MN in Parent and Child Health Nursing, La. State U., 1985; secondary vocat. health occupation cert., U. Houston, 1994. RN, N.C. Staff RN intermediate neonatal care nursing Tex. Children's/St. Luke's Hosp., Houston, 1975-76; pediat. staff nurse Meml. Pediat., Houston, 1976-79; clin. staff nurse Inwood Pediat., Houston, 1979-80; instr. med. terminology Phillips Jr. Coll., New Orleans, 1981-83; founder, dir. Parents Plus Parenting Ctr., New Orleans, 1985-86; substitute tchr., RN Humble (Tex.) Ind. Sch. Dist., 1986-90; nursing instr. No. Harris C.C., Humble, 1990-91; health occupations edn. instr. New Caney (Tex.) Ind. Sch. Dist., 1991-99; ret., 1999. Adv. bd. mem. tech. prep. program No. Harris C.C., Humble, 1992—, adv. bd. mem. ADN program, 1995-96; bd. mem. New Horizons, New Caney, Tex., 1994-95; adv. bd. mem. respiratory care program No. Harris C.C./Kingwood Coll., 1995-96. Tchr., mem. PTSA-New Caney H.S., 1992—97; mem. KW Athletic Boosters, Kingwood, 1992—97, Parents of Cheerleaders Club; fundraiser, dir. Thesbians Kingwood H.S. Dept. Drama, 1995—96; mem., vol. docent Houston Fine Arts Mus.; mem., vol. Tex. Children's Hosp., Houston, Dorrell Martin Dance Fusion, KUHF-NPR, Houston. Mem. Sigma Theta Tau, Alpha Delta Pi (scholarship award 1972). Avocations: travel, reading, yoga, sailing. Home: 1111 Hermann Dr 6-C Houston TX 77004 E-mail: mpi082251@aol.com.

INGERSOLL, PAUL MILLS, banker; b. Phila., Apr. 13, 1928; s. John H.W. and Frances Paul (Mills) I.; m. Eleanor S. Koehler, Oct. 6, 1951; children: Eleanor Ingersoll Sylvestro, Rita W., Frances M. BA, Princeton U., 1950. With Provident Nat. Bank, Phila., 1963-78, v.p. adminstrn. and exec. mgmt., 1969, sr. v.p. retail banking div., 1969-73, pres., chief adminstrv. officer, 1973-78. Pres., bd. dirs. Beaver Mgmt. Corp.; bd. dirs. Rittenhouse Trust Co.; cons. Christie, Manson & Woods Internat., Inc. Trustee Emeritus Drexel U., Bryn Mawr (Pa.) Hosp. 1st lt. AUS, 1950-52. Recipient Human Relations award Am. Jewish Com., 1973 Mem. Merion Cricket Club, State in Schuylkill, The Cts. Democrat. Episcopalian.

INGERSOLL, RICHARD KING, lawyer; b. Algoma, Wis., Aug. 13, 1944; s. Robert Clive and Bernice Eleanore (Koehn) I.; m. Caroline Soi-Keu Yee, Aug. 31, 1968; children: Kristin Paula Juk-Yee, Karin Eleanor Juk-Ling. BBA, U. Mich., 1966; JD, U. Calif.-Berkeley, Berkeley, 1969. Bar: Ill. 1969, Hawaii 1973. Asst. prof. U. Ill.-Champaign, Champaign, 1969-70; assoc. Sidley & Austin, Chgo., 1970-73; ptnr. Rush, Moore, Craven, Kim & Stricklin, Honolulu, 1973-88, Gelber, Gelber, Ingersoll & Klevansky, Honolulu, 1989—. Spkr. tax law seminars. Author various law materials. Mem. ABA (taxation, bus. and internat. law coms.), Waialae Country Club (sec.). Home: 944 Waiholo St Honolulu HI 96821-1226 E-mail: ringersoll@ggikf.com.

INGERSOLL, TED MERIAM, mail services executive, retired advertising executive; b. Cleve., Oct. 3, 1939; s. Edmund Meriam and Helen (Storer) I.; m. Jean M. McCutcheon, June 30, 1962; children: Karen Marie, Kristen James, Kimberley Sue. BFA, Kent State U., 1962. V.p., acct. exec. The Marschalk Co., Cleve., 1969-73; v.p., mgmt. supr. Tracy-Locke Advt., Denver and Dallas, 1973-81; exec. v.p. First Columbia Fin. Corp., Denver, 1981-84; dir. Mason Best Co., Dallas, 1984-87; pres. Richards/Ingersoll, Dallas, 1987-90; exec. v.p. Valentine Radford Advt., Dallas and Kansas City, Mo., 1991—2002, ret., 2002; pres. Cedar Creek Postal Svcs., LLC, 2003—. Bd. dirs., adv. bd. Bryan's House, Dallas, 1987—; bd. dirs. Communities in Schs., Dallas, 1994—; owner, mgr., pres. Cedar Creek Postal Svcs.; LLC, Glen Barrel City, Tex. Capt. USAF, 1962-68. Republican. Presbyterian. Avocations: snowskiing, golfing, music. Home: 3525 Turtle Creek Blvd Apt 5B Dallas TX 75219-5515 E-mail: ted.ingersoll@sbcglobal.net.

INGERSOLL, WILLIAM BOLEY, lawyer, real estate developer; b. Washington, Sept. 21, 1938; s. William Brown and Loraine (Boley) I.; m. Carolyn Grace Potter, Sept. 8, 1963; children: William Brett, Courtney Lynn, Wayne Brandon, Dana Lee. BS, Brigham Young U., 1964; JD, Cath. U. Am., 1968. Bar: Va. 1968, D.C. 1969. Atty. Office of Corp. Counsel D.C., 1967-69, Office Gen. Counsel HUD, 1969-70; ptnr. Fried, Klewans, Ingersoll & Bloch, Washington, 1970-72; pres. Ingersoll and Bloch Chartered, Washington, 1972—; of counsel Holland & Knight, Washington, 1998—. Mng. ptnr. JC Assocs. Real Estate Devel., Washington, 1973—; gen. counsel Am. Resort Devel. Assn.; lectr. in field. Co-editor-in-chief Land Devel. Law Reporter, Land Trends, 1973—, The Digest of State Land Sales, 1976—, Time Sharing Law Reporter, 1980—, D.C. Real Estate Reporter, 1982—, Real Estate Opportunity Report, 1986; contbr. in field. Bd. dirs. Nat. Timesharing Coun., 1981—; mem. Garrison Presdl. Commn., 1984; mem. bd. adv. J. Ruben Clark Law Sch., 1987-93, chmn., 1991-93; bishop McLean (Va.) Ward, LDS Ch.; mem. nat. adv. com. Inside Real Estate, 1985—. Mem. ABA, FBA, D.C. Bar Assn., Va. Bar Assn., Va. Assn. Trial Lawyers, Land Devel. Inst. (vice chmn.), Brigham Young U. Alumni Assn. (bd. dirs. 1984-92), Order of Coif, Univ. Club Washington. Home: 713 Potomac Knolls Dr Mc Lean VA 22102-1421 also: Holland & Knight Ste 100 2099 Pennsylvania Ave NW Washington DC 20006-1816 E-mail: wingerso@hklaw.com.

INGERSON, NANCY NINA MOORE, special education educator; b. Springfield, Ill., Sept. 10, 1940; d. Irvin Lysle and Dorothe Nina (Spencer) Moore; m. Paul Gates Ingerson, Aug. 13, 1966 (divorced); children: Paul G., Gregory M. BA in English Lit., U. Ill., 1963. Cert. secondary edn. educator, cert. spl. edn. educator. Sec., adminstrv. asst. Elec. Engring. Rsch. Lab. U. Ill., Urbana, 1958-66; adminstrv. asst. Hughes Aircraft Space and Comm., El Segundo, Calif., 1988-92; tchr. spl. edn. Narbonne H.S. L.A. Unified Sch. Dist., Harbor City, Calif., 1994—, social club chmn., 1996, 97, 99—, social club co-chmn., 2000—, mem. leadership coun., 1999—, chmn. dept. spl. edn., 2001—03. Independent. Lutheran. Avocations: porcelain doll making, tile painting, print making, drawing. Home: 3602 W Estates Ln Unit 103 Rolling Hills Estates CA 90274

INGHAM, KENNETH LEROY, III, systems programmer, consultant; b. Hunter AFB, Ga., May 3, 1962; s. Kenneth LeRoy and Patricia Jane (Kirk) Ingham. BS in Computer Sci. cum laude, U. N.Mex., 1985, MS in Computer Sci., 1994. Student engring. trainee space projects div. NASA Ames Research Ctr. Project Tech. Br., Moffett Field, Calif., 1981-82; student cons. U. N.Mex. Computing Ctr., Albuquerque, 1980-85; from systems programmer I to systems programmer II U. N.Mex. Computer and Info. Resources and Tech. Ctr., Albuquerque, 1985-91. Cons. Med. Graphics, Albuquerque, DemoGraFX, Innovative Computing, Sandia Nat. Labs., Applied Rsch. Assocs., N.Mex. Technet; instr. Bernalillo County Data Processing, Albuquerque, Usenix, Tech. Exch. Co., Southwest Cyberport, SkillBridge. Author: Unix Tool Building, 1991. Mem. Assn. for Computing Machinery (1st Pl. award local programming contest U. N.Mex. Chpt. 1986), Usenix, UniForum. Home and Office: 1601 Rita Dr NE Albuquerque NM 87106-1127

INGHAM, NORMAN WILLIAM, Russian literature educator, genealogist; b. Holyoke, Mass., Dec. 31, 1934; s. Earl Morris and Gladys May (Rust) I. AB, Middlebury Coll. in German and Russian cum laude, 1957; postgrad. Slavic philology, Free U. Berlin, 1957-58; MA in Russian lang. and lit., U. Mich., 1959; postgrad. in Russian lang. and lit., Leningrad (USSR) State U., 1961-62; PhD in Slavic langs. and lit., Harvard U., 1963. Cert. genealogist. Postdoctoral researcher Czechoslovak Acad. Scis., Prague, Czechoslovakia, 1963-64; asst. prof. dept Slavic langs. and lits. Ind. U., Bloomington, 1964-65; asst. prof. Harvard U., Cambridge, Mass., 1965-70, lectr., 1970-71; assoc. prof. U. Chgo., 1971-82, prof., 1982—, chmn. dept., 1977-83, dir. Eastern Europe and USSR lang. and area ctr., 1978-91. Mem. Am. Com. Slavists, 1977-83; mem. com. Slavic and Ea. European studies U. Chgo., 1979-91, chmn., 1982-91, also other coms.; dir. Ctr. for East European and Russian/Eurasian Studies, 1991-96; rep. internat. Rsch. and Exch. Bd.; cert. genealogist, 1994—. Author: E.T.A. Hoffman's Reception in Russia, 1974; editor: Church and Culture in Old Russia, 1991; co-editor: (with Joachim T. Baer) Mnemozina: Studia litteraria russica in honorem Vsevolod Setchkarev; mem. editorial bd. Slavic and East European Jour., 1978-87, adv. bd., 1987-89; assoc. editor Byzantine Studies, 1973-81; contbg. editor The Am. Genealogist, 1995—; contbr. and translator articles and book revs. Fulbright fellow, 1957-58, vis. fellow Dumbarton Oaks Ctr. for Byzantine Studies, 1972-73. Mem. Am. Assn. Advancement Slavic Studies (rep. coun. on mem. instns. 1985-96, area rep. nat. adv. com. for Ea. European lang. programs 1985-96), Am. Assn. Tchrs. Slavic and East European Langs., Early Slavic Studies Assn. (v.p. 1993-95, pres. 1995-97), Chgo. Consortium for Slavic and East European Studies (v.p. 1982-84, 98, pres. 1984-86, 98-2000, exec. coun. 1992-94), Phi Beta Kappa. Office: U Chgo Slavic Dept 1130 E 59th St Chicago IL 60637-1539 E-mail: ningham@uchicago.edu.

INGHRAM, MARK GORDON, physicist, educator; b. Livingston, Mont., Nov. 13, 1919; s. Mark Gordon and Luella Gallagher (McNay) I.; m. Evelyn Mae Dyckman, May 12, 1946; children: Cheryl Ann, Mark Gordon III. BA, Olivet Coll., 1939; PhD, U. Chgo., 1947. Physicist Manhattan Project, 1942-45; sr. physicist Argonne Nat. Lab., 1945-47; mem. faculty U. Chgo., 1947—, successively instr., asst. prof., assoc. prof., prof., Samuel K. Allison Disting. Service prof. physics, 1969-85, emeritus, 1985—, chmn. dept. physics, 1959-70, acting dir. Inst. for Study of Metals, 1960-61, asso. dean div. of phys. scis., 1964-71, master Phys. Sci. Coll. div., 1981-85, assoc. dean div. phys. sci., 1981-85, assoc. dean Coll., 1981-85. Mem. com. nuclear geophysics Nat. Acad. Sci., 1953-60, mem. com. sci. and pub. policy, 1966-69, mem. com. on exploration of moon and planets, 1958-61 Asso. editor: Jour. Chem. Physics, 1957-60; editorial bd.: Rev. Sci. Instruments, 1958-61; author articles in sci. jours. Fellow Am. Phys. Soc., Am. Acad. Arts and Scis.; mem. Nat. Acad. Scis. (J. Lawrence Smith medal 1957), AAAS. Home: 3077 N Lakeshore Dr Holland MI 49424-6022

INGIS, GAIL, interior designer, educator, writer, photographer, artist; b. Nov. 1, 1935; d. Bernard and Claire Gerber; m. Thomas H. Claus; children: Linda, Richard, Paul. Student, CUNY, 1953; grad. in interior architecture-design, N.Y. Sch. Interior Design, 1973, BFA, 1980; postgrad., Pratt Inst., N.J. Ins. Tech., Parsons Sch. Design. Prin. Ingis Design Assocs., Woodcliff Lake, N.J., Fairfield, Conn., 1970—. Adj. prof. U. Bridgeport, Conn., 2001—, U. New Haven, 2002—. Exhibitions include Agora Gallery SOHO, N.Y.C. Troop leader U.S. Girl Scouts, N.Y.C. and Woodcliff Lake, 1964—69; bd. trustees The Lockwood Mathews Mansion Mus., Norwalk, Conn. Recipient Watercolor Painting award, Wall St. Gallery, 1997, Cooper Lighting award, 23d Ann. Nat. Lighting Competition, 1999. Mem.: AIA (profl. affiliate), Westport Arts Ctr., Wilton Arts Coun., Rowayton Art Assn., Milford Arts Coun., Lyme Art Assn., New Haven Arts League, Shoreline Alliance for Arts, Guilford Art League, Madison Art Soc., Interior Design Educators Coun., Illuminating Engring. Soc. N.Am., Am. Soc. Interior Designers (admissions com. N.J. chpt. 1978, edn. chmn. 1978—86, co-chmn. pro-licensing com. 1984—86, bd. dirs. 1985—97, com. legis. for interior designers 1988—90, edn. chmn. 1994—95, bd. dirs. Conn. chpt. 1996—97, editor newsletter 1996—2002, Svc. award 1978, 1982—87), U.S. Profl. Tennis Assn. (cert. instr.), Westport Arts League. Home and Office: 200 Old Black Rock Tpke Fairfield CT 06825-

INGLE, JAMES CHESNEY, JR., geology educator; b. Los Angeles, Nov. 6, 1935; s. James Chesney and Florence Adelaide (Geldart) I.; m. Fredricka Ann Bornholdt, June 14, 1958; 1 child, Douglas James BS in Geology, U. So. Calif., 1959, MS in Geology, 1962, PhD in Geology, 1966. Registered geologist, Calif. Research assoc. Univ. So. Calif., 1961-65; vis. scholar Tohoku U., Sendai, Japan, 1966-67; asst., assoc. to full prof. Stanford U., Calif., 1968—, W.M. Keck prof. earth scis., 1984—, chmn. dept. geology, 1982-86. Co-chief scientist Leg 31 Deep Sea Drilling Project, 1973, co-chief scientist Leg 128 Ocean Drilling Program, 1989; geologist U.S. Geol. Survey W.A.E. 1978-81 Author: Movement of Beach Sand, 1966; contbr. articles to profl. jours. Recipient W.A. Tarr award Sigma Gamma Epsilon, 1958; named Disting. lectr. Am. Assn. Petroleum Geologists, 1986-87, Joint Oceanographic Institutions, 1991; A.I. Leverson award Am. Assn. Petroleum Geologists, 1988. Fellow Geol. Soc. Am., Calif. Acad. Scis.; mem. Cushman Found. (bd. dirs. 1984-91), Soc. Profl. Paleontologists and Mineralogists (Pacific sect. 1958—, pres. 1993-94), Am. Geophys. Union. E-mail: ingle@pangea.stanford.edu.

INGLE, MARTI ANNETTE, protective services official, educator; b. Waynesville, N.C., Apr. 3, 1972; d. William Carroll Ingle, Shirley Grooms Ingle. Student, East Coast Bible Coll., 1987—89; EMT-paramedic cert., Haywood C.C., Clyde, NC, 1993, tech. rescue and fire fighting, 1996; degree culinary arts and scis., Alaska Vocat. Tech. Coll., Seward, AK, 2000—01. Cert. emergency rescue technician 1996; tech. rescue instr., swiftwater rescue technician II 1997, haz mat ops. 1994, sr. fire investigations 1999, emergency boat ops. 1999, personal watercraft rescue 1999, PALS 1991, ACLS 1992, advanced trauma life support 1991, pediat. emergencies for prehospital providers 2001, tchr. Alaska, 2001. EMT-paramedic Haywood County Emergency Med. Svcs., Waynesville, NC, 1991—2002; EMS/tech. rescue instr. Haywood C.C., Clyde, NC, 1994—2002; EMS evaluator State of N.C., Raleigh, 1994—2002; EMS/tech. rescue instr. Blue Ridge C.C., Hendersonville, NC, 1995—2002, Tri-County C.C., Murphy, NC, 1996—2002, Southwestern C.C., Sylva, NC, 1998—2002; EMS/fire/rescue instr. Alaska Vocat. Tech. Coll., Seward, Alaska, 2001—. Mem.: N.C. Assn. Paramedics, N.C. EMS and Rescue Assn., N.C. Assn. Fire Svc. Instrs., Haywood County Rescue Squad (life; 1st lt. and sgt. 1994—99). Avocations: travel, white-water rafting, cooking, reading, mountain biking. Home: 151 Children St Waynesville NC 28786 Office: 215 N Main St Waynesville NC 28786 Personal E-mail: rafty981@yahoo.com.

INGLE, ROBERT D. newspaper editor, newspaper executive; b. Sioux City, Iowa, Apr. 29, 1939; s. Walter J. and Thelma L (McCoy) I.; m. Martha N. Nelson, Sept. 12, 1964 (div. 1984); 1 child, Julia L.; m. Sandra R. Reed, Mar. 2, 1985 BA in Journalism and Polit. Sci., U. Iowa, 1962. Various positions Miami Herald, 1962-75, asst. mng. editor, 1975-77, mng. editor, 1977-81; exec. editor San Jose (Calif.) Mercury News, 1981-93, pres., exec. editor, 1993-95; v.p. Knight-Ridder Inc., San Jose, Calif., 1995-99; pres. Knight-Ridder Ventures, San Jose, Calif., 1999—. Pres. Calif. First Amendment Coalition, 1990-92. Mem. AP Mng. Editors Assn., Am. Soc. Newspaper Editors Office: Knight Ridder New Media 50 W San Fernando St Ste 1200 San Jose CA 95113-2436

INGLE, SUD RANGANATH, management consultant; b. Pune, India, Oct. 6, 1942; Came to U.S., 1965; s. Ranganath V. and Sita R. I.; m. Neelima Kulkarni Ingle, June 21, 1970; children: Geeta, Vinita. B in Engring., Coll. Engring., Pune, 1964; MS in Indsl. Engring., Purdue U., 1966; MBA, U. Wis., Oshkosh, 1972. Quality control engr. Giddings and Lewis, Fond du Lac, Wis., 1966-70, Mercury Marine, Fond du Lac, 1970-77, gen. mgr., 1977-82; pres. Quality Circles Services, Fond du Lac, 1982—. Cons., trainer in field; assoc. prof. bus. Marian Coll. Fond du Lac, Wis., 1987—, initiator of Quality Productivity Mgmt. degree program, 1988, co-initiator MS program in Quality Values and Leadership, 1991. Author: Quality Circles Master Guide, 1982, Quality Circles in Service Industries, 1983, In Search of Perfection, 1985, (video programs and workbooks) Implementing ISO 9000 Standards Series, Organizational Quality Improvement, Implementing Quality Circles. Mem. Fond du Lac Art Council, 1970; local rep. Fox Valley India Soc., Appleton, Wis. 1979. Mem. Internat. Assn. Quality Control (founding), Am. Soc. Quality Control. Home: 318 Pheasant Ct Fond Du Lac WI 54935-5425 Office: PO Box 812 Fond Du Lac WI 54936-0812

INGLEFIELD, JOSEPH T., JR., allergist, immunologist, pediatrician; b. Duquesne, Pa., Apr. 29, 1930; MD, U. Rochester, 1957. Diplomate Am. Bd. Allergy & Immunology, Am. Bd. Pediatrics. Intern William Beaumont Army Hosp., El Paso, Tex., 1957-58; resident Tripler Army Hosp., Honolulu, 1958-60; fellow in pediatrics and allergies Children's Hosp., Washington, 1969-72; with Fairfax Hosp., Falls Church, Va. Mem. AMA, MSV, Am. Acad. Pediatrics, Assn. Am. Physicians, North Va. Pediatric Soc. Office: 107 N Virginia Ave Falls Church VA 22046-3324 Fax: (703) 532-1984. E-mail: dratopyst@aol.com.

INGLEHART, RONALD FRANKLIN, political science educator; b. Milw., Sept. 5, 1934; s. Gerald Almon and Helen Clara (Krippene) I.; m. Babette Feinberg, Aug. 16, 1963 (div. Sept. 1968); children: Elizabeth Lynn, Rachel Jennifer; m. Marita Rohr Rosch, May 5, 1986; children: Ronald Charles, Marita Helen. BA, Northwestern U., 1956; MA, U. Chgo., 1962, PhD, 1967. Asst. prof. U. Mich., Ann Arbor, 1967-71, assoc. prof., 1971-76, prof. polit. sci., 1977—, program dir. Inst. for Social Rsch., 1984—. Vis. prof. U. Mannheim, Germany, U. Geneva, U. Kyoto, Japan, U. Kobe, Japan, Free U., Berlin, Leiden U., U. Rome, U. Minas Gerais; mem. adv. coun. Berlin Sci. Ctr., 1992—, Ctr. for Polit. Studies, Ann Arbor, 1995—. Author: The Silent Revolution, 1977, Culture Shift, 1990, Modernization and Postmodernization, 1997, Human Values and Beliefs, 1998, Rising Tide? Gender Equality in Global Perspective, 2003, Human Values and Social Change, 2003; mem. editl. bd. seven scholarly jours. Gender, Islam and Democracy, 2003. Co-founder Euro-Barometer Surveys, Brussels, 1974—; pres. World Values Surveys Hdqrs., Stockholm, Sweden, 1988—. Mem. Internat. Soc. for Polit. Psychology, Internat. Polit. Sci. Assn.,

Am. Polit. Sci. Assn., Midwest Polit. Sci. Assn. Avocation: writing childrens stories. Home: 2626 Geddes Ave Ann Arbor MI 48104-2715 Office: Inst for Social Rsch 426 Thompson St Ann Arbor MI 48106-1248 E-mail: rfi@umich.edu.

INGLES, JOSEPH LEGRAND, social services administrator, political science educator; b. June 15, 1939; s. Vernal Willard and Helen Josephine (Graziano) Ingles; m. Hazel Jeanette Palmer, Aug. 18, 1962; children: Sally Van Dyke, Christine Walker, Joette Smith, Robert, Michael. BS, Brigham Young U., 1964; PhD, U. Mo., 1968. Rsch. asst. U. Mo., Columbia, 1967-68; grant policy specialist HEW, Washington, 1970-72; asst. prof. govt. and politics U. Md., College Park, 1968-75; dir. human resources Wasatch Front Regional Coun., Bountiful, Utah, 1975-77; utility consumer adv. Com. on Consumer Svc., Utah, 1977-93; medicaid mgr., third party liability and health Utah Dept. Human Svcs., Salt Lake City, 1993-94; child support mgr. Intake,Locate and Orders Office Recovery Svcs., Dept. Human Svcs., Salt Lake City, 1994-96, computer software trainer, 1996—. Spec faculty mem family and consumer studies Univ Utah, 1995; consult Ellingson Kilpack Assocs, Salt Lake City, 1972, Bonneville Research Corp, Santa Monica, Calif., 1971, US Dept Commerce, 1970; spec faculty mem Salt Lake Ctr Brigham Young Univ, 1988—94. Mem W Bountiful City Coun, 1982—88. Fellow, NDEA, 1964—67; grantee, Univ Md, 1969. Fellow: Am Soc Pub Admin (fellowship 1970—71); mem.: Nat Asn State Utility Consumer Advs (mem gas comt 1983—93), Nat Asn Regulatory Utility Comnrs (staff subcom on consumer affairs 1982—93), Snowbird Iron Blosam Lodge (chmn budget and fin comt 1987—96). Mem. Lds Ch. Home: 1485 N 1100 W Woods Cross UT 84087-1828 E-mail: Jingles@HS.State.UT.US.

INGLESI, NOREEN MARY, music educator, poet, composer; b. Providence, June 14, 1952; d. Anthony John and Mary (Marsella) Inglesi. A of Fine Arts/Music, C.C. of R.I., 1990; MusB, U. R.I., 1994, M in Music Edn., 1997. Cert. music tchr. grades PreK-12 pub. sch. Pvt. tchr. Robert's Music, Warwick, RI, 1994-95; tchr. music and chorus Warwick Sch. Dept., 1995, Scituate (R.I.) Pub. Sch., 1995—; grad. asst. U. R.I., 1995-97; tchr. music North Providence Sch. Dept., 1997—; instr. music C.C. of R.I., 1997—. Composer, arranger Andreau Marc Pub. Co., NY; composer, singer for performance group Double Helix; composer music for fall events Habitat for Humanity, 2003; composer original music Shakespeare's Comedy of Errors, Merchant of Venice Colonial Theatre, 2002—03. Author: (poetry) Stockpiled Passions, 1993; composer: Somalia, 1994, March of the Exalted, 1995, Children's Song Cycle, 1996, Symphony #2: Wonder s of Nature, 1999, (poetry CD) Somalia, 1995, Digital Mystery Tour, Dance of the Firefly, 1998; contbr. concert revs. to jours. and newspapers; performer: (CD) Where the Rivers Bend, 2001, CD, duet for flute and harp. Singer C.C. R.I. Chorus, Warwick, 1990—95, peer tutor; singer Feminist Chorus, Providence, 1990—94; orchestral piece performed by Culver Chamber Music Series, 1998, 1999; avante-garde arrangement of nursery rhymes performed by Insight Quartet, Italy, 1999. Recipient award, Am. Tuberculosis Soc., 1968, recognition, Billboard Nat. Songcontest, 1994—95, Composers Guild, 1994—96, honorable mention, Providence Jour. Bul. Poetry Contest, 1995, award, Nat. Endowmnet Arts, 2001; grantee, R.I. State Coun. Arts Nature Conservancy; scholar All Am., 1995. Mem.: TAXI, R.I. Songwriters Assn., R.I. Music Educators Assn. (pub. rels. mgr. 1995—96), R.I. Poetry Soc., Assn. Author/Composers, Nat. Educators Assn., Nat. Choral Soc., Phi Kappa Lambda, Phi Kappa Phi. Avocations: tennis, writing short stories, painting, swimming. E-mail: trid@aol.com.

INGLIS, ROBERT D. (BOB INGLIS), former congressman, lawyer; b. Oct. 11, 1959; m. Mary Anne Williams, Aug. 7, 1982; children: Robert D. Jr., Mary Ashton, Anne McCullough, Mabel Andrews, Sara Meade. AB summa cum laude in Polit. Sci., Duke U., 1981; JD, U. Va. Sch. Law, 1984. Atty. Leatherwood, Walker, Todd & Mann P.C., Greenville, S.C., 1986-92, 99—; mem. 103rd-105th Congresses from 4th S.C. dist., Washington, D.C., 1993-98; mem. Budget/Judiciary com. Washington, 1993-98. Chmn. 4th Congl. Dist. South Carolinians to Limit Congl. Terms; mem. Leadership Greenville Class XVI; loaned exec. Greenville County United Way, 1987; mem. exec. com. Greenville County Rep. Party; mem. exec. com. First Monday in Greenville. Mem. S.C. Bar Assn., Greenville County Bar Assn., Phi Beta Kappa. Office: PO Box 87 Greenville SC 29602 0087 E mail: binglis@lwtm.com.

INGLIS, WILLIAM DARLING, internist, health facility administrator; b. Columbus, Ohio, Aug. 12, 1931; s. John Cockins and Helen (Morgan) I.; m. Laura Hammer, June 5, 1955 (dec. Jan. 1974); children: Ruth Anne Inglis, William Darling Inglis IV; m. Suzanne Smith, May 7, 1977; 1 child, Andrew Scott Inglis. BA, Washington & Jefferson Coll., 1953; MD, Jefferson Med. Coll., 1957. Diplomate Am. Bd. Internal Medicine, Am. Bd. Pulmonary Medicine, Am. Bd. Palliative Medicine. Intern Meth. Episcopal Hosp., Phila., 1957-58; resident in internal medicine Jefferson Med. Coll., Phila., 1958-59, Walter Reed Army Hosp., Washington, 1962-65; commd. U.S. Army, 1959, advanced through grades to lt. col., 1966, ret., 1968; instr., fellow in pulmonary disease U. Louisville, 1968-69; ptnr. W. F. Millhon Med. Clinic, Columbus, Ohio, 1969-94; med. dir. hospice Riverside Meth. Hosp., Columbus, Ohio, 1994—2002, med. dir. home care, 1996—; med. dir. Mind/Body Inst., Columbus, Ohio, 1994-96. Clin. assoc. prof. Ohio State U., Columbus, 1969—; chmn. pulmonary sect., Riverside Meth. Hosps., Columbus, 1969-83, chmn. dept. medicine, 1983-86, pres. med. staff, 1988-89. Chmn. health svcs. United Cmty. Coun., Columbus, 1970-72; vol. physician Columbus Med. Assn. Free Clinic, 1994—, Columbus Hospice, 1978-85; trustee Washington and Jefferson Coll., Washington, Pa., 1985-89. Decorated U.S. Army Commendation medal; recipient Disting. Educator award Coll. Medicine and Pub. Health, Ohio State U., 1999. Fellow ACP (laureate), Am. Coll. Chest Physicians; mem. AMA, Nat. Hospice and Palliative Care Orgn. (ethics com. 1999-2002), Am. Acad. Hospice & Palliative Medicine, Med. Forum (pres. 1983). Presbyterian. Avocation: running. Home: 9167 Moors Pl N Dublin OH 43017-8220 Office: Hospice at Riverside/Grant 3595 Olentangy River Rd Columbus OH 43214-4034 E-mail: inglisw@ohiohealth.com.

INGOLD, CATHERINE WHITE, academic administrator; b. Columbia, S.C., Mar. 15, 1949; d. Hiram Hutchison and Annelle (Stover) White; m. Wesley Thomas Ingold, June 13, 1970; 1 child, Thomas Bradford Hutchison. Student, U. Paris-Sorbonne, 1969; BS in French with honors, Hollins Coll., 1970; MA in Romance Langs., U. Va., 1972, PhD in French, 1979; DHum honoris causa, Francis Marion U., Florence, S.C., 1992. Assoc. prof. romance langs. Gallaudet U., Washington, 1973-88, dir. hons. program, 1980-85, dean arts and scis., 1985-86, provost, v.p. acad. affairs, 1986-88; pres. Am. U. of Paris, 1988-92, Curry Coll., Milton, Mass., 1992-96. Dep. dir. Nat. Fgn. Lang. Ctr. Johns Hopkins U., 1996—2000, U. Md., 2000—. Recipient Prix Morot-Sir de Langue et Littérature françaises (Hollins). Mem. MLA, Nat. Collegiate Honors Coun., Lychnos Soc. (U.Va.), Phi Beta Kappa. Episcopalian. Home: 2015 N Brandywine St Arlington VA 22207-2200 Office: Nat Fgn Lang Ctr 1029 Vermont Ave NW Washington DC 20005-3517 E-mail: cwingold@nflc.org.

INGOLD, KEITH USHERWOOD, chemist, educator; b. Leeds, Eng., May 31, 1929; s. Christopher Kelk and Edith (Usherwood) I.; m. Carmen Cairine Hodgkin, Apr. 7, 1956; children: Christopher Frank (dec.), John Hilary, Diana Hilda. BSc with honors in Chemistry, Univ. Coll., London, 1949; DPhil, Oxford (Eng.) U., 1951; DSc (hon.), U. Guelph, 1985; LLD (hon.), Mt. Allison U., 1987; DSc (hon.), St. Andrews U., Scotland, 1989, Carleton U., 1992, McMaster U., 1995; LLD (hon.), Dalhousie U., 1996; Laurea Honoris Causa in Biology, U. Ancona, Italy, 1999. Postdoctoral fellow NRC Can., Ottawa, 1951-53, rsch. officer, 1955-77, assoc. dir. chemistry, 1977-90, disting. rsch. scientist, 1990—. Adj. prof. U. Guelph, Ont., Can., 1985-87, Brunel U., U.K., 1983-94, Carleton U. Ottawa, Can., 1991—, St. Andrews U., U.K., 1997—; postdoctoral fellow U. B.C., 1953-55; vis. scientist Chevron Rsch. Co., Richmond, Calif., 1966, Univ. Coll., London, 1969, 72, Ford Motor Co., 1971, Esso Rsch. and Engring. Co., Linden, N.J., 1973, U. Western Ont., 1975, 1993, Iowa State U., 1975, U. Bologna, Italy, 1975, 93, U. Adelaide, Australia, 1979, U. Grenoble, France, 1983, Australian Nat. U., 1987, 99, U. Freiburg, Germany, 1990, 91, U. Essen, Germany, 1990, U. Dusseldorf, Germany, 1991, U. Leiden, The Netherlands, 1992, 93, U. St. Andrews, Scotland, 1998. Decorated Order of Can., 1995; recipient Can. Silver Jubilee medal, 1977, Queen Elizbeth II Golden Jubilee medal, 2002, Humboldt Sr. Rsch. Fellowship award, Germany, 1989, Veris award, 1989, Lansdown Visitor award U. Victoria, B.C., 1990, Mangini prize U. Bologna, 1990, Izaak Walton Killam Meml. prize Can. Coun., 1992, Gold medal for sci. and engring. Natural Scis. and Engring. Coun. Can., 1998; Carnegie fellow U. St. Andrews, Scotland, 1977; vis. fellow Japan Soc. for Promotion of Sci., 1982, Italian Nat. Rsch. Coun., 1983; Nat. Sci. Coun. Republic China lectr., 1992. Fellow Royal Soc. Can. (treas. 1979-81, Centennial medal 1982, Henry Marshall Tory medal 1985), Royal Soc. (London, Davy medal 1990, Royal medal 2000), Chem. Inst. Can. (medal 1981, Syntex award for phys. organic chemistry 1983), Univ. Coll. (London), Royal Soc. Edinburgh (hon.); mem. Am. Chem. Soc. (award petroleum chemistry 1968, Pauling award 1988, Arthur C. Cope scholar 1992, James Flack Norris award phys. organic chemistry 1993), Chem. Soc. (award kinetics and mechanism 1978), Can. Soc. Chem. (v.p. 1985-87, pres. 1987-88, Alfred Bader award in organic chemistry 1989), Royal Soc. Chemistry (Ingold lectr. 1990). Achievements include research papers on free radical chemistry. Home: 72 Ryeburn Dr Ottawa ON Canada K1V 1H5 Office: Nat Rsch Coun of Can Ottawa ON Canada K1A 0R6 E-mail: keith.ingold@nrc.ca.

INGOLFSSON, THORSTEINN, diplomat; Permanent rep. to NATO Govt. of Iceland, Brussels, 1994-98, permanent rep. to UN N.Y.C., 1998—; amb. of Iceland to Cuba, 2001—; amb. of Iceland to Barbados, 2002—; amb. of Iceland to Jamaica, 2003—. Office: Permanent Mission Iceland to UN 800 3rd Ave Fl 36 New York NY 10022-7604

INGOLFSSON-FASSBIND, URSULA G. music educator; b. Zurich, Switzerland, Dec. 22, 1943; arrived in U.S., 1980; d. Franz Bernardin Fassbind and Gertrud M. Schmucki; m. Ketill Ingolfsson; children: Katla Soffia, Judith, Mirjam, Bera Bjorg. Nat. tchrs. diploma, Conservatory Zurich, 1964, soloist diploma, 1967; postgrad., U. Ariz., 1968—70. Tchg. asst. Conservatory Zurich, 1966—68; with Reykjavik (Iceland) Music Coll., 1970—79, Settlement Music Sch., Phila., 1987—2000; founder, dir., tchr., performer Leopold Mozart Acad. and Franz Fassbind Found., Phila., 2001—. Founder, dir. The Leopold Mozart Chamber Music Concerts, 2002—. Grantee Excellency in Tchg. grant, Wilmington (Del.) Piano Co., 2003. Mem.: Am. Composers Guild, Music Tchr. Nat. Assn. Democrat. Avocations: painting, gardening. Home and Office: Leopold Mozart Acad 4833 Pulaski Ave Philadelphia PA 19144

INGRAHAM, EDWARD CLARKE, JR., retired foreign service officer; b. Mineola, N.Y., Feb. 2, 1922; s. Edward Clarke and Dorothy Hathaway (Sutton) I.; m. Susan Hartman, Jan. 25, 1947; children: John Edward, James William, Elizabeth Ann Ingraham Reed. BA, Dartmouth Coll., 1943; postgrad., Cornell U., 1957-58. Editorial asst. Moody's Investors Service, N.Y.C., 1946-47; joined U.S. Fgn. Service, 1947; vice consul Cochabamba, Bolivia, 1947-48; 3d sec. embassy La Paz, Bolivia, 1948-50; vice consul Hong Kong, 1950-51, Perth, Australia, 1951-54; consul Madras, India, 1954-56; 2d sec. embassy Djakarta, Indonesia, 1958-60; officer charge Australia-New Zealand affairs State Dept., 1961-62, officer charge Indonesian affairs, 1962-65; assigned Nat. War Coll., 1965-66; chief of embassy polit. sect. Rangoon, Burma, 1966-69; dep. dir. research and analysis for East Asia, State Dept., 1969-71; polit. counselor embassy Islamabad, Pakistan, 1971-74; dir. Office of Indonesian, Malaysian and Singapore Affairs, State Dept., Washington, 1974-77; dep. chief mission Am. embassy, Singapore, 1977-79; diplomat in residence Lake Forest (Ill.) Coll., 1979-80; ret., 1980; freedom of info. advisor U.S. Dept. State, 1980-95. Mem. U.S. del. ANZUS council meeting, Canberra, Australia, 1962, Intergovtl. Group on Indonesia, Amsterdam, Netherlands, 1975, 77 Served with USAAF, 1943-45, ETO. Mem. Am. Fgn. Service Assn. Address: 7700 Sebago Rd Bethesda MD 20817-4844 E-mail: edingrdham@aol.com.

INGRAHAM, JOHN WRIGHT, banker; b. Evanston, Ill., Nov. 10, 1930; s. Harold Gillette and Mildred (Wright) I.; m. Barbara Gaye Barker, Nov. 8, 1967; children: Kimberly, Elizabeth, Scott AB, Harvard U., 1952, MBA, 1957; postgrad., NYU Grad. Sch. Bus., 1963-68. Jr. lending positions Citicorp, N.Y.C., 1957-66, sr. lending positions, 1966-70, head instl. recovery mgmt., 1970-78, dep. chmn., credit policy com., 1979-92, sr. v.p. oversight N.Am lending, 1979-84, sr. v.p., mem. credit policy com. for Latin Am. and investment banks, 1985-88, sr. v.p., mem. credit policy for global pvt. bank, 1989-92; sr. v.p., line risk mgr. for global pvt. bank Dynamo M Fund, Nassau, Bahamas, 1993-99; sr. v.p., sector risk mgr. Citigroup Global Asset Mgmt., Travelers Life and Annunity and Pvt. Banking, N.Y.C., 2000—. Bd. dirs. Dynamo M Fund, Nassau, Bahamas; past bd. dirs. Ark. Best Corp., Ft. Smith, Sprague Techs., Inc. Greenwich, Conn.; chmn. audit com. Presto Industries, Houston, 1986-88; vice chmn. bd. Penn Cen. Corp., Cin., 1978-84, chmn. fin. com., 1982-91, past bd. dirs.; rep. banking industry before coms. and hearings U.S. Ho. Reps., U.S. Senate, 1976-78; mem. N.Y. Crime Stoppers, N.Y.C. Police Found., 1993—. Trustee Noble and Greenough Sch., Dedham, Mass., 1987-94; mem. bus. adv. coun. to dean Grad. Sch. Bus., U. Ark, Fayetteville, 1985-95; mem. com. for Asia rsch. HArvard U. John King Fairbanks Ctr., Cambridge, Mass., 1993—. Lt. USN, 1952-55, Korea. Mem. Fin. Acctg. Standards Bd. (task force 1974-81), Robert Morris Assocs. (bd. dirs. 1972-75, Disting. Svc. award 1978), Union Club (N.Y.), Piping Rock (Locust Valley, L.I.), Gulfstream Bath and Tennis Club (Fla.), Ocean Club (Fla.), Harvard Club N.Y., St. Andrews Soc. State of N.Y., Everglades Club (Palm Beach, Fla.). Republican. Christian Scientist. E-mail: john.ingraham@citigroup.com.

INGRAHAM, JOSEPH EDWIN, financial officer; b. New Orleans, Oct. 29, 1946; s. Joseph Francis and Dorothy Margaret (Treiber) I.; m. Jeanne Arlene Galouye, July 18, 1970; children: Barbara Jeanne, Ashley Elizabeth, Joseph Francis II. BBA, Loyola U., New Orleans, 1969. CPA, La. Acct. Shell Oil Co., New Orleans and Houston, 1969-73; sr. acct. Peat, Marwick, New Orleans, 1973-76, Bourgeois, Bennett, Thokey & Hickey, New Orleans, 1976-77, Alexander Grant, New Orleans, 1977-79; treas. Bergeron Industries, New Orleans, 1979-83; exec. dir. fin. svcs. Archdiocese of New Orleans, 1983-2000; CFO Diocese Amarillo, Tex., 2000—. Staff sgt. USMCR, 1963-71. Republican. Roman Catholic. Office: Diocese Amarillo PO Box 5644 Amarillo TX 79117-5644 E-mail: jingraham@amarillodiocese.org., joe1029@swbell.net.

INGRAM, CECIL D. accountant, state legislator; b. Blackfoot, Idaho, Dec. 27, 1932; s. Orval Otto and Mary Marjorie (Evans) I.; m. Lois Ann Glenn, Dec. 28, 1952; children: Cynthia, William, Christopher. BBA, U. Oreg., 1962. Contr. transp. & distbn. divsn. Boise (Idaho) Cascade Corp., 1962-91; mem. Idaho Senate, Dist. 16, Boise, 1993—. Capt. U.S. Army, 1953-58, Korea. Mem. Masons, Mountain States Tumor Inst., Golf for Charity, Morrison Ctr., W Idaho Fair Bd., Salvation Army, United Way, Recreation Unlimited, Junior Achievement, Idaho Education Alliance for Science. Republican. Baptist. Home: 7025 El Caballo Dr Boise ID 83704-7320 Office: State Capitol PO Box 83720 Boise ID 83720-3720

INGRAM, CHARLES CLARK, JR., energy company executive; b. Dec. 10, 1916; s. Charles Clark and Winnie (Edwards) I.; m. Maxine Waterbury, Jan. 29, 1939; children: James C., Jack R. BS, U. Okla., 1940; LLD, Oral Roberts U., 1983. Registered profl. engr., Okla. With Oneok Inc., Tulsa, 1940—, pres., 1966-71, CEO, 1966-81, chmn., 1966-87, chmn. emeritus, 1987—. Former chmn. bd. trustees Frontiers of Sci. Found. of Okla., Inc., 1973-74; former adv. bd. Downtown Tulsa Unlimited; former bd. govs. Am. Citizenship Ctr., Oklahoma City; mem. pres.'s bd. visitors, chmn. Tulsa Engring. Coun., U. Okla. Maj. AUS, WWII, 1941-46. Named to Okla. Hall of fame, 1982. Mem. AIME, Am. Assn. Petroleum Geologists, Am. Gas Assn. (chmn. 1979-80), So. Gas Assn. (past pres.), Engrs. Soc. Tulsa, Okla. State C. of C. (pres. 1981), Oklahoma City C. of C., Tulsa C. of C., Nat. Alliance Businessmen (chmn. Ea. Okla. and Tulsa 1973-74), Propeller Club U.S., Summit Club, So. Hills Country Club (gov., past pres.), Cedar Ridge Country Club (Tulsa), Masons, Sigma Tau, Sigma Gamma Epsilon. Baptist. Office: Oneok Inc 100 W 5th St PO Box 871 Tulsa OK 74102-0871

INGRAM, DAVID B. entertainment company executive; b. Dec. 13, 1962; m. Sarah LeBrun; 1 child, Henry LeBrun. BA in History cum laude, Duke U., 1985; MBA in Mktg., Vanderbilt U., 1989. Dir. rsch. Duke U. Capital Campaign Office, Durham, N.C., 1985-87, dir., found. Young Alumni for The Capital Campaign, 1986-87; asst. to treas. Ingram Industries, Inc., Nashville, 1989-91; dir. sales Ingram Entertainment Inc., La Vergne, Tenn., 1991-92, asst. v.p. sales, 1992-93, v.p. major accounts, 1993-94, pres., COO, 1994—96. Chmn. bd. visitors The Duke Primate Ctr., 1987—; bd. dirs. Montgomery Bell Acad. Mem. Video Software Dealers Assn. (nat. bd. dirs.), Belle Meade Country Club, Golf Club Tenn., Caves Valley Golf Club, Green Spring Valley Hunt Club, Delta Tau Delta. Avocations: golf, cycling, running, tennis, hunting, reading, investments. Office: Ingram Entertainment Inc Two Ingram Blvd La Vergne TN 37089*

INGRAM, DENNY OUZTS, JR., lawyer, educator; b. Kirbyville, Tex., Mar. 23, 1929; s. Denny Ouzts and Grace Bertha (Smith) I.; m. Ann Elizabeth Rees, July 11, 1952; children: Scott Rees, Stuart Tillman. BA, U. Tex., 1955, JD with honors, 1957. Bar: Tex. 1956, N.Mex. 1967, Utah 1968. Editor Kirbyville Banner, 1949-50; mem. Tex. Ho. of Reps., 1951-52; assoc. Graves, Dougherty, Gee and Hearon (and predecessors), Austin, Tex., 1957, 59-60, partner, 1961-66; asst. prof. law U. Tex., 1957-59, U. N.Mex., 1966-67; prof. U. Utah, 1968-77; ptnr. McGinnis, Lochridge, and Kilgore, Austin, 1977-90, of counsel, 1991—; prof. law Tex. Wesleyan U. Sch. Law, 1991—. Vis. prof. U. Calif., Davis, 1973-74, U. Tex., summers 1968, 75, U. San Diego, 1993; research fellow Southwestern Legal Found., lectr. in field Contbr. numerous articles to law revs., chpts. to books; assoc. note editor: Tex. Law Rev., 1956-57. Research dir. Utah Constn. Revision Com., 1969-71, 73-74. Served with U.S. Army, 1951-54. Fellow Am. Coll. Trust and Estate Counsel, Am. Coll. Tax Counsel, Tex. Bar Found.; mem. ABA, Am. Law Inst. (life), Tex. Bar Assn., Utah Bar Assn., N.Mex. Bar Assn., Chancellors, Order of Coif, Phi Delta Phi. Democrat. Episcopalian. Home: 4055 Hildring Dr E Fort Worth TX 76109-4712 Office: Tex Wesleyan U Sch Law 1515 Commerce St Fort Worth TX 76102-6572

INGRAM, DOUGLAS HOWARD, psychoanalyst; b. N.Y.C., Feb. 8, 1943; s. Sidney David and Sylvia I.; m. Nancy Sue Reiner, Dec. 26, 1976; children: Alexander Isaac, Benjamin Zachary. AB, Columbia Coll., 1964; MD, NYU, 1968. Diplomate Am. Bd. Psychiatry and Neurology. Pvt. practice, N.Y.C., 1972—; med. dir. Karen Horney Clinic, N.Y.C., 1979-83; clin. prof. psychiatry N.Y. Med. Coll., Valhalla, N.Y., 1998—. Editor-in-chief Am. Jour. Psychoanalysis, 1991-00, Jour. Am. Acad. Psychoanalysis, 2002—. Fellow Am. Acad. Psychoanalysis (pres. 1997-98); mem. Assn. for Advancement of Psychoanalysis (pres. 1981-82), Am. Inst. Psychoanalysts (dean 1997-99). Office: 4 E 89th St New York NY 10128-0636

INGRAM, GEORGE, business executive; b. Montclair, N.J., Dec. 10, 1920; s. George and Frances Elizabeth (Watts) I.; m. Olive May Holtz, Feb. 15, 1947 (dec. Dec. 1999); children: Patricia (Mrs. S. K. Bone), George III (dec.), Sara, John. BS, Yale U., 1942; MS, Stevens Inst. Tech., 1948. Registered profl. indsl. engr., Pa. Indsl. engr. RCA, 1942-45; cons. mgmt. engr. Stevenson, Jordan & Harrison, Inc., N.Y.C., 1945-51; controller Riegel Paper Corp., 1951-57, Raytheon Co., Lexington, Mass., 1957-60, v.p., 1960-61, v.p. fin., 1961-63, sr. v.p., dir., 1963-68; sr. v.p. Champion Internat., Inc., N.Y.C., 1968-69, exec. v.p., 1969-72, dir., 1968-72; pres., chief exec. officer, dir. Reed Ingram Corp., N.Y.C., 1972-77, cons., 1977-83. Pres. Dionis Corp., Nantucket, Mass., 1977-87; chmn. bd., dir. Deerfield Splty. Papers, Inc., 1973-77, Oneida Packaging Products, Inc., 1973-77, Canadian Glassine Co., Ltd., 1973-77; chmn., sec., dir. Arctos Corp., Quaker Hill, Conn., 1980-86; pres., treas., dir. Fitchburg Engring. Corp., Mass., 1980-86; dir. M/A Com, Inc., Burlington, Mass., 1968-91. Trustee Coll. of Wooster, Ohio, 1970-88. Mem. ASME, Fin. Execs. Inst. (past pres. Boston; past chmn. nat. com. securities and exchanges regulation), Wellesley Coll. Club, Phi Gamma Delta. Republican. Episcopalian. Home and Office: Apt M-205 865 Central Ave Needham MA 02492-1344

INGRAM, GEORGE CONLEY, lawyer, judge; b. Dublin, Ga., Sept. 27, 1930; s. George Conley and Nancy Averett (Whitehurst) I.; m. Sylvia Williams, July 26, 1952; children: Sylvia Lark, Nancy Randolph, George Conley. AB, Emory U., 1949, LL.B., 1951. Bar: Ga. 1952. City atty. City of Smyrna, Ga., 1958-64, City of Kennesaw, Ga., 1964; judge Cobb County Juvenile Ct., 1960-64, Superior Ct., Cobb Jud. Cir., 1964-68; justice Supreme Ct. Ga., 1973-77; spl. asst. atty. gen. State of Ga., 1979-86; ptnr. Alston & Bird, Atlanta, 1977-98; sr. judge State of Ga., 1998—. Staff, faculty Judge Advocate Gen. Sch. U.S. Army U. Va., 1952-54. Former trustee Agnes Scott Coll., Kennesaw Coll. Found., Emory U.; trustee Cobb Cmty. Found., The Eleventh Cir. Hist. Soc. Inc.; emeritus mem. Emory Law Sch. Coun.; past pres. Cobb County YMCA, Cobb Landmarks Soc.; former chmn. ofcl. bd. 1st Meth. Ch. of Marietta, trustee. 1st lt. JAGC, USAR, 1952-54. Recipient Emory U. medal and Disting. Svc. award Kennesaw Mountain Jaycees, 1961, Ga. Jaycees, 1961, Emory Law Sch. Alumni Assn., 1985; Disting. Citizen award City of Marietta, Ga., 1973; Len Gilbert Leadership award Cobb County C. of C., 1985; Cobb County Citizen of Yr. award, 1990, hon. life mem. Ga. PTA. Fellow Am. Bar Assn. Found., Am. Coll. Trial Lawyers, Internat. Soc. Barristers, Am. Acad. Appellate Lawyers, Marietta-Cobb Mus. Art; mem. ABA, Am. Law Inst., State Bar Ga. (Tradition of Excellence award 1987), Cobb and Atlanta Bar Assns., Lawyers Club of Atlanta, Old War Horse Lawyers Club, Cobb County C. of C. (Pub. Svc. award 1970, Turner award in family law 2002) Georgian Club (bd. mem., founding chmn.), Rotary (award for vocat. excellence 1999), Order of Coif (hon.), Phi Delta Phi, Omicron Delta Kappa. Methodist. Home: 540 Hickory Dr Marietta GA 30064-3602

INGRAM, HELEN MOYER, political science educator; b. Denver, July 12, 1937; d. Oliver Weldon and Hazel Margaret (Wickard) Hill; m. W. David Laird; children from by previous marriage: Mrill, Maia, Seth. BA, Oberlin Coll., 1959; PhD, Columbia U., 1967. Lectr., asst. prof. polit. sci. U. N.Mex., 1962-69; with Nat. Water Commn., Washington, 1969-72; assoc. prof. polit. sci. U. Ariz., Tucson, 1972-77, prof. polit. sci., 1979-96; dir. Udall Ctr. Studies Pub. Policy, 1988-96; Warmington chair Sch. Social Ecology U. Calif., Irvine, 1995—. Author: (with Dean Mann) Why Policies Succeed of Fail, 1980, (with Nancy Laney and John McCain) A Policy Approach to Representation: Lessons from the Four Corners States, 1980, (with Martin, Laney and Griffin) Saving Water in a Desert City, 1984, (with Brown) Water and Poverty in the Southwest, 1987, Water Politics: Continuity and Change, 1990, (with Nancy Laney and David Gillilan) Divided Waters: Divided Waters: Bridging the U.S.-Mexico Border, 1995, (with Ann Schneider) Policy Design for Democracy, 1997; editor: (with Rathgeb Smith) Public Policy for Democracy, 1993, (with Joachim Blatter) Reflections on Water, 2001; book rev. editor Am. Polit. Sci. Rev., 1987-92. Sr. fellow Resources for Future, Washington 1977-79. Mem. Policy Studies Orgn. (pres. 1985), Am. Polit. Sci. Assn. (coun., treas. 1985-87), Western Polit. Sci. Assn. (past pres., v.p.). Home: 4749 E San Francisco Blvd Tucson AZ 85712-1238

INGRAM, JAMES CARLTON, economist, educator; b. Roanoke, Ala., Jan. 11, 1922; s. John Henry and Isabelle (Shanks) I.; m. Alice Jane Graham, May 1, 1948; children: Deborah, Susan, Melissa. BS, U. Ala., 1942; A.M., Stanford, 1947; PhD (Social Sci. Research Council fellow), Cornell U., 1952. Research analyst Indsl. Indemnity Ins. Co., San Francisco, 1947-48; successively asst. prof., assoc. prof., prof. econs. U. N.C., Chapel Hill, 1952—; dean U. N.C. (Grad. Sch.), 1966-69; vis. mem. London Sch. Econs., 1963-64; vis. prof. Thammasat U., Bangkok, Thailand, 1969-71; guest scholar Brookings Instn., 1976; disting. vis. prof. Johns Hopkins U. Bologna Ctr., 1984; vis. prof. Hopkins-Nanjing China Ctr., 1988. Author: Economic Change in Thailand Since 1850, rev. edit, 1971, Regional Payments Mechanisms, 1962, International Economic Problems, 1966, 3d edit., 1978, International Economics, 1983, 3d edit., 1993; Mng. editor: So. Econ. Jour, 1961-65. Served with AUS, 1942-46. Ford Found. fellow, 1963-64 Mem. Am. Econ. Assn., So. Econ. Assn. (mem. exec. com., pres. 1972-73) Home: 1012 Highland Woods Rd Chapel Hill NC 27517-4410 E-mail: jcingram@email.unc.edu.

INGRAM, JONATHAN HALL, music educator; b. Columbia, S.C., June 23, 1976; s. John Martin and Barbara Brazell Ingram. BA in Music Edn., U. of S.C., 1999. Band dir. Dutch Fork M.S., Irmo, 1999—. Mem. Orch., First Bapt. Ch., Columbia. Home: 524 Athena Dr Columbia SC 29223-5437

INGRAM, JUDITH ELIZABETH, writer, counselor; b. Alameda, Calif., May 6, 1951; d. William Ralph and Elizabeth (Lelis) Madler; m. Frank David Ingram, Sept. 4, 1971; 1 child, Melanie Anne. AA, Chabot Coll., Hayward, Calif., 1972; BS in Biology summa cum laude, Calif. State U., Hayward, 1978; MA in Counseling, St. Mary's Coll. of Calif., Moraga, 1996. Tech. writer Tech. Writing Svcs., Dublin, Calif., 1990-93; counselor trainee Valley Christian Counseling, Dublin, 1995-96, counselor, dir. devel., 1996-97. Mem.: ACA, Writer's Internat. Network/Writer's Inter-Age Network, Soc. Tech. Comm., Assn. for Spiritual, Ethical and Religious Values in Counseling, Am. Assn. Christian Counselors, We. Assn. Counselor Edn. and Supervision (bd. officer, newsletter editor). Presbyterian. Avocations: writing, desktop publishing and computer graphic designing, reading psychology, philosophy and women's issues. Home: 8724 Augusta Ct Dublin CA 94568-1063 E-mail: jingramtws@aol.com.

INGRAM, KENNETH FRANK, retired state supreme court justice; b. Ashland, Ala., July 7, 1929; s. Earnest Frank and Alta Mary (Allen) I.; m. Judith Louise Brown, Sept. 3, 1954; children: Jennifer Lynn Ingram Malone, Kenneth Frank Jr. BS, Auburn U., 1951; LLB, Jones Law Sch., 1963. Bar: Ala. 1963, U.S. Dist. Ct. (no. dist.) Ala. 1965, U.S. Dist. Ct. (mid. dist.) Ala. 1966. City councilman City of Ashland, Ala., 1956-58; mem. Ho. of Reps., Ala., 1958-66; presiding judge 18th Jud. Cir. Ct., Ala., 1968-87; judge Ala. Ct. Civil Appeals, Montgomery, 1987-89, presiding judge, 1989-91; assoc. justice Ala. Supreme Ct., Montgomery, 1991-97. Mem., chmn. Ala. Jud. Inquiry Commn., 1979-87. Contbr. articles on jud. ethics to profl. pubs. With USMC, 1952-54. Mem. Ala. Bar Assn., Masons. Democrat. Methodist. Avocations: woodworking, metal-crafting, tennis, swimming. Home: 264 1st St N PO Box 729 Ashland AL 36251-0729

INGRAM, LIONEL ROWAN, JR., manangement consultant; b. Anniston, Ala., Dec. 14, 1939; s. Lionel Rowan and Lida James (Scales) R.; m. Katharine Booth Margeson, June 15, 1963; children: Sarah Elizabeth, Katharine Kerr, Ian Lionel Henry. BS, U.S. Mil. Acad., 1963; MA in Pub. Adminstrn., Harvard U., 1966, MA in Polit. Economy and Govt., 1967, PhD, 1995. Commd. 2d lt. U.S. Army, 1963, advanced through grades to col., 1985; bn. comdr. tank bn. 3d Inf. Divsn., Kitzengen, Germany, 1979-81; ret., 1993; chief divsn. tng. and maintenance mgmt. tng. program 3d Infantry Divsn., Wurzburg, Germany, 1981-82; dep. dir. policy and plans divsn. U.S. Mission to NATO, Brussels, 1982-87; acad. dir. NATO course Nat. Def. U., Washington, 1987-88; mil. attache Def. Intelligence Agy., Copenhagen, Vilnius, Lithuania, 1989-93; mgmt. cons., 1995—. Pres. North Atlantic Devel. & Cons., 1996; advisor West Point Admissions; prof. polit. sci. U. N.H., Manchester and Durham, 1997—. Author: The Major Factors Influencing Allied Decisions Regarding the Allocation of Resources to NATO's Defense, 1995. Pres. PTA Brussels Am. Sch., 1987-89; mem. sch. adv. bd. Rygaards Internat. Sch., Copenhagen, 1991-93; vice chair Town Planning Bd., Exeter, N.H., 1998-2000, chair, 2000-02, selectman, 2002--; chmn. stewardship com. Christ Episcopal Ch., Exeter, 1995-98; bd. dirs. New Eng. Coun. for Orgnl. Effectiveness, 1997-98. Decorated knight comdr. Order of Danneborg (Denmark); Legion of Merit, Bronze Star with V. Fellow NSF; mem. Internat. Inst. Strategic Studies, Exeter C. of C. (chmn. edn. com. 1997-00), N.H. Coun. World Affairs, Portsmouth Athenaeum, Strawbery Banke Hist. Assn., 101st Airborne Assn., Rotary (bd. dirs. 1997-98, dist. chmn. 1998—, Youth Leadership Award), Phi Kappa Phi. Avocations: back-packing, cross-country skiing, reading, collecting stamps from german-speaking countries, collecting model soldiers. Home and Office: 22 Juniper Ridge Rd Exeter NH 03833-4409 E-mail: lionelingram@attbi.com.

INGRAM, MARTHA RIVERS, company executive; b. Charleston, SC, Aug. 20, 1935; m. E. Bronson Ingram (dec. 1995), Oct. 4, 1958; children: Orrin Henry III, John Rivers, David Bronson, Robin. BA in History, Vassar Coll., 1957. V.p., pub. affairs Ingram Industries Inc., Nashville, 1979—95, mem., bd. directors, 1981—, chmn. bd. dirs., 1995—. Bd. dirs. Baxter Internat., Weyerhaeuser Co., Ashley Hall, Vassar Coll., Harpeth Hall Sch., Ingram Micro Inc.; mem. adv. bd. Kennedy Ctr. for Performing Arts, Washington. Chmn. Tenn. Bicentennial Commn., 1996; bd. dirs. Tenn. Performing Arts Ctr., Nashville Ballet, Nashville Opera, Nashville Inst. for Arts, Nashville Symphony, Nashville Cmty. Found.; past chmn. United Way's Alexis de Tocqueville Soc.; founder, bd. dirs. Tenn. Repertory Theater; chmn. bd. trustees Vanderbilt U., 1999-. Mem. Nashville Area C. of C. Office: Ingram Industries Inc One Belle Mead Pl 4400 Harding Rd Nashville TN 37205-2244*

INGRAM, ORRIN HENRY, II, transportation executive; Grad., Vanderbilt U., 1982. With Ingram Industries Inc., Nashville, 1982—, co-pres., 1995—99, pres., CEO, 1999—; chmn. Ingram Barge Co., Nashville. Bd. dirs. Boys and Girls Club Mid. Tenn., Friends of Warner Pks., Vanderbilt Cancer Ctr., Bapt. Hosp. Corp.; bd. govs., chmn. U.S. Polo Assn. Office: Ingram Industries Inc 1 Belle Mead Pl 4400 Harding Rd Nashville TN 37205-2244*

INGRAM, RICHARD THOMAS, educational association executive; b. McKeesport, Pa., Sept. 29, 1941; s. Henry Stephen and Jean Catherine (Lis) I.; m. Mollie Mangan Brown, Apr. 6, 1968; children: Kirsten Collins, David Thomas. BS, Indiana U. Pa., 1963; MEd, U. Pitts., 1964; EdD, U. Md., 1969. High sch. tchr. Monroeville (Pa.) Sch. Dist., 1963-64; dir. psychometric svcs. U. Md., College Park, 1965-69; adj. instr. U. So. Calif., 1976, U. Va., 1971-79; program assoc. Assn. Governing Bds. of Univs. and Colls., Washington, 1971-74, exec. dir., 1974-78, exec. v.p., 1978-92, pres., 1992—. Dir. United Educators Ins. Risk Retention Group, Inc., Washington, 1988-99, Am. Coun. on Edn., 1995-96; adv. commr. Edn. Commn. of States, Denver, 1985-95; trustee Dickinson Coll., Pa., 1995-2002. Editor, author: Governing Public Colleges and Universities, 1993, Governing Independent Colleges and Universities, 1993. Trustee U. Charleston, W.Va., 1980-89, Connelly Sch. of Holy Child, Potomac, Md., 1987-93. Capt. U.S. Army, 1969-71, Vietnam. Recipient Disting. Alumni award Ind. U. Pa., 1992, Outstanding Alumnus Citation, Pa. Coll. Alumni Assn., 1994, Coll. Edn. Alumni Assn. award U. Md., 1996. Mem. Am. Assn. Higher Edn., Cosmos Club, Phi Delta Kappa. Democrat. Avocations: skiing, camping, fly fishing. Home: 12017 Gregerscroft Rd Potomac MD 20854-2148 Office: Assn Governing Bds Univ and Colls 1 Dupont Cir NW Ste 400 Washington DC 20036-1136

INGRAM, ROBERT A. pharmaceuticals company executive; b. 1942; BSBA, Ea. Ill. U., 1965. Sales rep. Merrell Dow Pharms., sales mgr., v.p. pub. affairs; v.p. govt. affairs Merck & Co., 1985, pres. Merck Frosst Can. Inc., 1988-90; exec. v.p. adminstrv. and regulatory affairs Glaxo Inc., 1990, exec. v.p., 1993, pres., COO, 1993, pres., CEO, 1994, chmn., 1999; CEO Glaxo Wellcome plc, England, 1997; pres., COO Pharm. Ops. GlaxoSmithKline, England, 2001—. Bd. dirs. Wachovia Corp. Office: GlaxoSmithKline plc 980 Great West Rd Brentford, Middlesex TW8 9 G S England

INGRAM, SAMUEL WILLIAM, JR., lawyer; b. Utica, N.Y., Mar. 20, 1933; s. Samuel William and Mary Elizabeth (Rosen) I.; m. Jane Austin Stokes, Sept. 30, 1961; children: Victoria, William BS, Vanderbilt U., 1954; LLB, Columbia U., 1960. Bar: N.Y. 1960. Assoc. Sullivan & Cromwell, N.Y.C., 1960-67; assoc. Shea Gallop Climenko & Gould, N.Y.C., 1967-68; ptnr. Shea & Gould and predecessors, N.Y.C., 1968-89, Ingram, Yuzek, Gainen, Carroll & Bertolotti LLP, N.Y.C., 1989—. Bd. dirs. Legal Aid Soc., N.Y.C., 1974-86, sec., 1978-86; trustee Green Mountain Valley Sch., Waitsfield, Vt., 1984-87. Served to 1st lt. USMC, 1954-57 Mem. ABA, N.Y. State Bar Assn., Assn. of Bar of City of N.Y. Avocation: athletic and outdoor activities. Home: 332 Long Ridge Rd Pound Ridge NY 10576-2005 Office: Ingram Yuzek Gainen Carroll & Bertolotti LLP 250 Park Ave Ste 600 New York NY 10177-0699 E-mail: singram@ingramllp.com.

INGRAM, SHIRLEY JEAN, social worker; b. Louisville, Oct. 22, 1946; BA in Social Sci., U. Hawaii, Pearl City, 1979; MSW, Fla. State U., 1982. Diplomate AM. bd. Social Work; lic. social worker, Ala.; qualified clin. social worker, Md.; registered play therapist/supr. Case mgr. Geriatric Residential Treatment Ctr., Crestview, Fla., 1982-84; case mgmt. supr. Okaloosa Guidance Ctr., Fort Walton Beach, Fla., 1984-86; family counselor Harbor Oaks Hosp., Fort Walton Beach, 1986-87; pvt. practice Fort Walton Beach, 1987-95; social worker USAF Family Advocacy Office, Hurlburt Field, Fla., 1995—2001; exec. dir. ct.-apptd. juvenile advocates program Madison County Courthouse, Huntsville, Ala., 2001—. Quality assurance bd. dirs. State Dept. Human Svcs., Madison County, Ala. Mem. Mental Health Assn. Okaloosa County (sec. bd. dirs. 1988—, mem. adv. bd. dirs. Area Agy. on Aging, chmn. adv. bd. dirs., Okaloosa County Area Agy. on Aging, pres.), NASW, Long Term Care Ombudsman Coun., AAUW, Sertoma. Home: 13884 Catawba Cir Athens AL 35611-6860 Office: Madison County Courthouse 100 Northside Sq Huntsville AL 35801

INGRASSIA, ANTHONY FRANK, human resource specialist; b. Middletown, NY, Sept. 22, 1926; s. Joseph and Mary (Dina) I.; m. Eleanor Mae Birkholz, Aug. 9, 1952; children: Michael, Mary, Steve, Laura, Anne, Jane, Lisa, Timothy. BA, U.Wis., 1948. Sports writer Milw. Sentinel, 1948-62; exec. v.p. Milw. Newspaper Guild, 1952-62; asst. dir. Dist. Coun. 48 Am. Fedn. State, County, Mcpl. Employees, AFL-CIO, Milw., 1962-64; labor rels. specialist, labor rels. dir. US P.O. Dept., Washington, 1964-69; dir. office labor-mgmt. rels. US CSC, Washington, 1970-78; asst. dir. labor-mgmt. rels. US Office Pers. Mgmt., Washington, 1979-82, asst. dir. agy. compliance and evaluation, 1982-86, dep. assoc. dir. pers. sys. and oversight, 1986-90, chmn. fed. prevailing rate adv. com., 1990-96; vice chmn., acting chmn. Fed. Salary Coun., Washington, 1992-95, vice chmn., 1995-2000. US del. ILO Pub. Employee Conf., Geneva, 1975-77, 86; spkr. seminar on collective bargaining U. Tel Aviv, 1979; cons. civil svc. reform Govt. Hungary and Poland, Budapest and Warsaw, 1991; cons. civil svc. Govt. of Saudi Arabia, Riyahd, 1986. Vol. Arlington (Va.) Food Assistance Ctr., 1992-97, Hospice, 1996-2002; ombudsman No. Va. Long Term Care Program, 1999-2003. Recipient presdl. rank awards Disting. Govt. Exec., 1980, Meritorious Govt. Exec., 1988. Mem. Soc. Fed. Labor Rels. Profl. (outstanding contbn. to fed. labor rels. award 1983-87), KC. Roman Catholic. Avocations: gardening, golf. Home: 12206 Cathedral Dr Lake Ridge VA 22192

INGUI, NICOLLE EILEEN, journalist; b. Ridgewood, NJ, Apr. 7, 1976; d. Leonard Anthony and Eileen Margaret Ingui. BS, U. Colo., 1998. Prodn. asst. NBC, N.Y.C., 1998; prodr. KUSA, Denver, 1998—99, WTSP, St. Petersburg, Fla., 1999—2000. Mem. Colo. Inst. for Leadership Tng., Denver; del. Emerging Leaders Forum, Colo., 1997. Mem.: Soc. Profl. Journalists, Sons of Italy. Roman Catholic. Avocations: theater, dancing, music, hiking. Home: 659 E Phillips Dr S Littleton CO 80122

INGWERSEN, MARTIN LEWIS, shipyard executive; b. Sandusky, Ohio, Nov. 5, 1919; s. John Christian and Irene Catherine (Hinkey) I.; m. Blanche Robinson, Apr. 26, 1947; children: Brenda, Richard Charles, Martin Lewis. BS, U. Notre Dame, 1941; postgrad., Western Res. U., 1941, Princeton U., 1943. Asst. to hull supt. Gt. Lakes Engring. Works, Ashtabula, Ohio, 1941-43, asst. supt., 1946-49; supt. plant Am. Ship Bldg. Co., Buffalo, 1948-50; mgr. plant Toledo, 1950-52, Lorain, Ohio, 1952-53; v.p. ops., 1954-58; v.p., works mgr. Ingalls Shipbldg. Corp., Pascagoula, Miss., 1958-65, v.p. ops., 1965-67; pres. Md. Shipbldg. and Drydock Co., Balt., 1967-68; exec. v.p. Lockheed Shipbldg. Co., Seattle, 1968-73; pres. Lockheed Shipbldg. and Constrn. Co., Seattle, 1973-76, exec. v.p. office of pres., 1976-86, trustee, 1973-86; cons. shipbldg. and ship repair, 1986—. Bd. dirs. Puget Sound Bridge and Dry Dock Co., Seattle, Colby Crane & Mfg. Inc., Seattle. Served to lt. USNR, 1943-46. Mem. Am. Bur. Shipping, Soc. Naval Architects and Marine Engrs., Am. Soc. Naval Engrs., Navy League, Propeller Club U.S., Notre Dame Club of Vero Beach. Roman Catholic. Home and Office: 910 Turtle Cove Ln #201 Vero Beach FL 32963 E-mail: mingwersen@aol.com.

INGWERSON, JOHN C. music educator; b. Albany, NY, Mar. 20, 1949; s. Clyde Ingwerson; m. Dar Mead, July 25, 1975. Mus D, U. Ariz., 1996. Instr. No. Ariz. U., Flagstaff, Ariz., 1982—85, U. Arizona, Tucson, 1988—89, Hinds C.C., Raymond, Miss., 1989—. Mem.: Guitar Found. of Am. Office: Hinds Cmty Coll PO Box 1100 Raymond MS 39154-1100 Office Fax: 601-857-3458. E-mail: jcingwerson@hindscc.edu.

INHOFE, JAMES M. senator; b. Des Moines, Nov. 17, 1934; m. Kay Kirkpatrik; children: Jim, Perry, Molly, Katy. BA, U. Tulsa, 1973. Pres. Quaker Life Ins. Co.; mem. Okla. Ho. Reps., 1966-69, Okla. State Senate, 1969-77; mayor City of Tulsa, 1978-84; mem. 1st Dist. Okla. Ho. of Reps., 1987-94; U.S. senator from Okla., 1995—; mem. armed svcs. com., intelligence com.; mem. environment and pub. works com. Served with U.S. Army, 1955-56. Republican. Office: 453 Russell Senate Bldg Washington DC 20510-0001 E-mail: jim_inhofe@inhofe.senate.gov.*

INIGO, RAFAEL MADRIGAL, retired electrical engineering educator; b. Madrid, June 18, 1932; arrived in U.S., 1963; s. Rafael G. and Francisca V. (Madrigal) I.; m. Eliana Soto, Apr. 29, 1961; children: C. Paulina, Alvaro A. Ing. El., U.T.F. Santa Maria, Val Chile, 1957; MSEE, U. Va., 1965, DSc in EE, 1966. Registered profl. engr., Va. Elec. engr. Branden Coppe Co., Coya, Chile, 1957-61; asst. prof. elec. engring. U.T.F. Santa Maria, Valparaiso, Chile, 1961-66; prof. elec. engring. UT Santa Maria, Valparaiso, 1966-68; assoc. prof. elec. engring. Va. Mil. Inst., Lexington, 1968-74, prof. elec. engring., 1974-78; assoc. prof. elec. engring U. Va., Charlottesville, 1978-85, prof. elec. engring., 1986-97, prof. emeritus, 1997—. Invited prof. U. Deusto, Spain, 1981, 83, 93, U. Seville, Spain, 1988, Rovira Virgil U., Tarragona, Spain, 2000. Author: Teoria de Circuitos, 1977, Vision por Computador, 1986, Robots Industriales Manipuladores, 2002; contbr. articles to profl. jours. Helen Wessel fellow U. Va., 1959, AID fellow U.S. Govt., 1963; Fulbright scholar U. Tech. Nat. Faculty Cordoba, Argentina, 1997. Avocations: photography, canoeing. Office: U Va Thornton Hall Dept Elec Engring Charlottesville VA 22903-6073 E-mail: rafainigo@earthlink.net.

INK, DWIGHT A. government agency administrator; b. Des Moines, Sept. 9, 1922; s. Dwight P. and Edna (Craun) I.; m. Margaret Child, Aug. 31, 1948; children: Stephen, Bruce, Lawrence, Barbara, Lauri; m. Dona A. Wolf, Feb. 14, 1981. BS, Iowa State U., 1947; MA, U. Minn., 1951. Budget and personnel officer City of Fargo (N.D.), 1948-50; chief mcpl. water sect. Bur. Reclamation Dept. Interior, Bismark, N.D., 1950-51; chief reports and statistics br. Savannah River Ops. Office AEC, Oak Ridge, 1952-55, exec. asst. to chmn. Washington, 1958-59, asst. gen. mgr., 1959-66; 1st asst. sec. for adminstrn. HUD, Washington, 1966-69; asst. dir. for exec. mgmt. Office of Mgmt. and Budget, Washington, 1969-73; dep. adminstr., acting adminstr. GSA, Washington, 1973-76, acting adminstr., Mar.-July 1985; exec. dir., pres. personnel project mgmt. CSC, Washington, May-Nov. 1977; v.p. Nat. Consumer Coop. Bank, Washington, 1980-81, U.S. Synthetic Fuels Corp., Washington, 1982-84; ind. cons. McManis and Assocs., Washington, 1984-85; asst. adminstr. AID, Washington. 1985-88; pres. Inst. of Pub. Adminstrn., N.Y.C., 1988-93, pres. emeritus, 1994—. Exec. dir. Alaska Reconstrn. Commn.; pres. Am. Consortium Internat. Pub. Adminstrn., 1980-83; adminstr. Cmty. Svcs. Adminstrn., 1981; chmn. White House Task Force on Edn., 1965; bd. dirs. N.Am. Mgmt. Coun., 1989-93; vice chair nat. adv. bd. Ctr. Study of Presidency. Chmn. Charter Commn. S.C., 1955; mem. exec. com. Ga.- Carolina Council Boy Scouts Am., 1954-55. Served to capt. USAR, 1942-58. Recipient Arthur Fleming award as one of the 10 Outstanding Young Men in Govt. U.S. C. of C., 1961, Disting. Svc. award AEC, 1966, Outstanding Achievement awards U. Minn., 1969, Iowa State U., 1986, Disting. Svc. award GSA, 1975, Outstanding Leadership award Assn. Govt. Accts., 1976, Commrs. award for Disting. Svc., CSC, Pub. Adminstr. of Yr. award Brigham Young U., 1978. Mem. Am. Pub. Works Assn. (bd. dirs.), Am. Soc. Pub. Adminstrn. (pres. 1978-79), Nat. Civil Service League (bd. dirs., career service award 1966), Pub. Adminstrn. Service (bd. dirs.), Nat. Acad. Pub. Adminstrn. (trustee), Internat. Inst. Adminstrv. Sci. (v.p. 1980-86), Coun. on Fgn. Rels., Delta Sigma Rho, Phi Kappa Phi. Home: #1115 19385 Cypress Ridge Ter Lansdowne VA 20176-5171

INKELES, ALEX, sociology educator; b. Bklyn., Mar. 4, 1920; s. Meyer and Ray (Gewer) K.; m. Bernadette Mary Kane, Jan. 31, 1942; 1 child, Ann Elizabeth BA, Cornell U., 1941, MA, 1946; postgrad., Washington Sch. Psychiatry, 1943-46; PhD, Columbia U., 1949; student, Boston Psychoanalytic Inst., 1957-59; A.M. (hon.), Harvard U., 1957; prof. honoris causa, Faculdade Candido Mendez, Rio de Janerio, 1969, Faculdade Candido Mendez, 2002. Social sci. research analyst Dept. State and OSS, 1942-46; cons. program evaluation br., internat. broadcasting div. Dept. State, 1949-51; instr. social relations Harvard U., Cambridge, Mass., 1948, lectr., 1948-57, prof. sociology, 1957-71, dir. studies social relations Russian Research Ctr., dir. studies social aspects econ. devel. Ctr. Internat. Affairs, 1963-71, research assoc., 1971-79; Margaret Jacks prof. edn., prof. sociology Stanford U., Calif., 1971-78, prof. sociology, 1978-90; sr. fellow Hoover Inst., 1978—; prof. emeritus, 1990—. Mem. exec. com. behavioral sci. div. NRC, 1968-75; lectr. Nihon U., Japan, 1985. Author: Public Opinion in Soviet Russia, 1950 (Kappa Tau Alpha award 1950, Grant Squires prize Columbia 1955); with R. Bauer, C. Kluckhohn) How the Soviet System Works, 1956, (with R. Bauer) The Soviet Citizen, 1959, Soviet Society (edited with H.K. Geiger), 1961, What is Sociology?, 1964, Readings on Modern Sociology, 1965, Social Change in Soviet Russia, 1968, (with D.H. Smith) Becoming Modern, 1974 (Hadley Cantril award 1974), Exploring Individual Modernity, 1983; editor: (with Masamichi Sasaki) Comparing Nations and Cultures, 1996, National Character: A Psychosocial Perspective, 1997, One World Emerging? Convergence and Divergence in Industrial Societies, 1998; editor-in-chief Ann. Rev. Sociology, 1971-79; editl. cons. Internat. Rev. Cross Cultural Studies; editl. bd. Ethos, Jour. Soc. Psychol. Anthropology, 1978; editor Founds. Modern Sociology Series; adv. editor in sociology to Little, Brown & Co.; contbr. articles to profl. jours. Recipient Cooley Mead award for Disting. Contbn. in Social Psychology, 1982; fellow Ctr. Advanced Study Behavioral Sci., 1955, Founds. Fund Research Psychiatry, 1957-60, Social Scis. Research Council, 1959, Russell Sage Found., 1966, 85, Fulbright Found., 1977, Guggenheim Found., 1978, Bernard van Leer Jerusalem Found., 1979, Rockefeller Found., 1982, Eisenhower Assn., Taiwan, 1984; NAS Disting. Scholar Exchange, China, 1983; grantee Internat. Rsch. and Exchs. Bd., 1989, NSF, 1989. Fellow AAAS (co-chmn. western ctr. 1984-87, chmn. Talcott Parsons award com. 1988-93), Am. Philos. Soc., APA; mem. NIMH, Nat. Inst. Aging (monitoring com. health retirement survey 1990—), Nat. Acad. Scis. (corr. human rights com. 1986-88, mem. com. on scholarly comms. with People's Republic of China, chmn. panel on social sci. and humanities, NRC panel on issues in democratization 1991-92), Am. Sociol. Soc. (coun. 1961-664, v.p. 1975-76), Ea. Sociol. Soc. (pres. 1961-62), World Assn. Pub. Opinion Rsch., Am. Assn. Pub. Opinion Rsch., Inter-Am. Soc. Psychology, Sociol. Rsch. Assn. (exec. com. 1975-79, pres. 1979), Soc. for Study Social Problems. Home: 1001 Hamilton Ave Palo Alto CA 94301-2215 Office: Stanford U Hoover Instn Stanford CA 94305 E-mail: inkeles@hoover.stanford.edu.

INKLEY, JOHN JAMES, JR., lawyer; b. St. Louis, Nov. 7, 1945; s. John James Sr. and Morjorie Jane (Kenna) I.; m. Catherine Ann Mattingly, Apr. 13, 1971; children: Caroline Marie, John James III. BSIE, St. Louis U., 1967, JD, 1970; LLM in Taxation, Washington U., St. Louis, 1976. Bar: Mo. 1970, U.S. Dist. Ct. (we. dist.) Mo. 1970, U.S. Dist. Ct. (ea. dist.) Mo. 1975, U.S. Tax Ct. 1975, U.S. Supreme Ct. 1975. Assoc. Padberg, Raack, McSweeney & Slater, St. Louis, 1970-73; ptnr. Summer, Hanlon, Summer, MacDonald & Nouss, St. Louis, 1973-81; city atty. City of Town and Country, Mo., 1979-84, spl. counsel, 1984-88; ptnr. Hanlon, Nouss, Inkley & Coughlin, St. Louis, 1981-83; ptnr., chmn. banking and real estate dept. Suelthaus & Kaplan, St. Louis, 1983-91; ptnr. Armstrong Teasdale LLP (and predecessor firm), St. Louis, 1991—; co-chmn. bus. svcs. group, 1993-2000; exec. com., 1994—. Mem. ABA, Mo. Bar Assn., Bar Assn. Met. St. Louis. Roman Catholic. Home: 35 Muirfield Ln Saint Louis MO 63141-7382 Office: Armstrong Teasdale LLP 1 Metropolitan Sq Ste 2600 Saint Louis MO 63102-2740

INKLEY, SCOTT RUSSELL, JR., state agency administrator; b. Cleve., Mar. 22, 1952; s. Scott Russell Sr. and Josephine (Newcomer) I.; m. Roxanne Munn, Aug. 21, 1982; children: Scott Russell III, Jonathan Welsh, Katherine Chisholm. Certificat d'assiduete, U. Grenoble, France, 1969; BA, Coll. of Wooster, 1974; cert. completion drug studies inst., Ohio State U., 1975; MA, George Washington U., 1979; postgrad., U. S.C., 1979. Specialist edn. Solon (Ohio) Mental Health Ctr., 1974-76; analyst research S.C. Ho. of Reps., Columbia, 1979-82, analyst research and dir. research, Joint Bond Rev. Com., 1981-91, dir. research Ways and Means Com., 1982-91, dir. Policy Devel. and Evaluation Com., 1992, dep. dir. state budget and control bd., 1992-95; dir. S.C. Bus. Gateway, 1995—. Mem. higher edn. funding adv. com., Columbia, 1984-91; advisor State Exec. Mgmt. Tng., Columbia, 1986-91. Lectr., facilitator S.C. Youth Leadership, 1984-91. Named one of Outstanding Young Men Am., 1985. Mem. Nat. Assn. State Budget Officers (exec. com. 1983-91), Fiscal Affairs and Govt. Ops. Assn., So. Legis. Conf., Nat. Conf. State Legislators, Internat. Platform Assn., Order of Palmetto. Home: 1025 Lawhorn Rd Blythewood SC 29016-8982 Office: 1201 Main St Ste 420 Columbia SC 29201-3230 E-mail: inkley@infoave.net.

INLOW, EDGAR BURKE, political science educator; b. Forest Grove, Oreg., Dec. 14, 1915; s. Harvey Edgar and Eva Lou (Skaggs) I.; m. Louise Maurer, Oct. 21, 1971; children by previous marriage: Rush, Morgan (Mrs. George Douglas), Gerd, Brand, Shane. AB, Wash. State U., 1937; MA, U. Calif., 1939; PhD, Johns Hopkins U., 1949; postgrad., Gen. Theol. Sem., N.Y.C., 1950. Instr. Princeton U., 1947-49; ordained to ministry Episcopal Ch., 1950; parish priest, 1950-57; non-stipendiary priest, 1957-81; ret., 1981; U.S. Dept. of Defense Mil. Asst Inst., Washington, 1957-61; prof. polit. sci. U. Calgary, Alta., Can., 1961-81, chmn. dept., 1961-71, prof. emeritus, 1981—. Project dir. Royal Commn. Health Svcs. Can., 1963—64; cons. Civil Svc. Commn. Can., 1963; vis. prof. Vanderbilt U., Nashville, 1964—65; lectr. St. Paul's U., Japan, 1954, McMaster U., Hamilton, Ont., 1968, U. Tehran, Iran, 1970, U. Pahlavi, Iran, 1970. Author: The Patent Grant, 1949, Studies in Canon Law, 1957, The Health Grant Program in Canada, 1963, The Divine Right of Persian Kings, 1967, ShahanShah, The Monarchy of Iran, 1979; contbr. articles to profl. jours. Served with U.S. Army, 1941—45. Recipient Appreciation cert. Def. Dept., 1961, citation His Imperial Majesty Iran, 1967; Social Sci. Rsch. Coun. fellow; Can. Coun. fellow. Mem. Brit. Inst. Persian Studies, SAR (nat. committeeman, pres. Seattle chpt.), Royal Soc. for Asian Affairs (hon. sec. for Can. 1971-81, Phi Beta Kappa. Address: 2340 Magnolia Blvd W Seattle WA 98199-3813

INLOW, RUSH OSBORNE, chemist; b. Seattle, July 10, 1944; s. Edgar Burke and Marigale (Osborne) I.; m. Gloria Elisa Duran, June 7, 1980. BS, U. Wash., 1966; PhD, Vanderbilt U., 1975. Chemist, sect. chief U.S. Dept. Energy, New Brunswick Lab., Argonne, Ill., 1975-78; chief nuclear safeguards br. Cruise missile sys., 1983-84; program mgr. Navy strategic sys., 1984-85; dir. weapon programs divsn., 1985-88; dir. prodn. ops. divsn., 1988-90; asst. mgr. safeguards and security, 1990-94; asst. mgr. nat. def. programs, 1994-96; dep. mgr., 1996-2000; prin. mem. tech. staff Sandia Nat. Labs., 2000—. Apptd. Fed. Sr. Exec. Svc., 1985. Served with USN, 1966-71. Tenn. Eastman fellow, 1974-75; recipient Pres. Meritorious Exec. awrd The White House, Pres. Clinton, 1994. Mem. Am. Chem. Soc., Sigma Xi. Republican. Episcopalian. E-mail: roinlow@sandia.gov.

INMAN, BOBBY RAY, educator, investor, former electronics executive; b. Rhonesboro, Tex., Apr. 4, 1931; s. Herman H. and Mertie F. (Hinson) I.; m. Nancy Carolyn Russo, June 14, 1958; children: Thomas, William. BA, U. Tex., 1950; grad., Nat. War Coll., 1972. Commd. ensign U.S. Navy, 1952, advanced through grades to adm., 1981; asst. naval attache Stockholm, 1965-67; exec. asst., sr. aide to vice chief naval ops. Washington, 1972-73; asst. chief staff intelligence on staff comdr. in chief U.S. Pacific Fleet, 1973-74; dir. Naval intelligence Dept. Navy, Washington, 1974-76; vice dir. Def. Intelligence Agy., 1976-77; dir. Nat. Security Agy., Ft. Meade, Md., 1977-81; dep. dir. CIA, 1981-82; chmn., pres., chief exec. officer Microelectronics and Computer Tech. Corp., Austin, Tex., 1983-86; chmn. bd., chief exec. officer Westmark Systems, Inc., Austin, 1986-89; pvt. investor Austin, 1990—; prof., Lyndon B. Johnson Centennial chair in nat. policy U. Tex. Decorated Def. D.S.M., Navy D.S.M., Legion of Merit, Def. Superior Service medal, Meritorious Service medal, Nat. Security medal, Joint Services Commendation medal. Office: 701 Brazos St Ste 500 Austin TX 78701-3232

INMAN, DANIEL JOHN, mechanical engineer, educator; b. Shawano, Wis., May 10, 1947; s. Glen and Wilma (Sidebotham) I.; m. Catherine Little, Sept. 18, 1982; children: Jennifer W., Angela W., Daniel J. BS, Grand Valley State, Allendale, Mich., 1970; MAT, Mich. State U., 1975, PhD, 1980. Instr. physics Grand Rapids (Mich.) Ednl. Park, 1970-76; tech. staff Bell Labs., Whippany, N.J., 1978; rsch. asst. Mich. State U., East Lansing, 1976-79, 79-80, instr., 1978-79; prof. SUNY, Buffalo, 1980; chmn. U. Buffalo, 1989-92; Samuel Herrick prof. engring., sci., mechanics Va. Tech., 1992-97, dir. Ctr. for Intelligent Material Sys. and Structures, 1997—, Goodson prof. mech. engring. Dir. Mech. Sys. Lab., Buffalo, 1984; adj. prof. Brown U., Providence, 1986; cons. Kistler Instrument Corp., Amherst, N.Y., 1985-90, Kodak, 1990-93; bd. visitors Army Rsch. Office, 1995-97; cons. United Techs. Rsch. Ctr., 1995—, Los Alamos Nat. Labs., 2000—. Author: Vibration: Control Stability and Measurement, 1988, 90, Eng Vibration, 1994, 96, 2d edit., 2000, Statics, 1998, Dynamics, 1998; assoc. editor SEM Jour. of Theoretical and Exptl. Modal Analysis, 1986, Mechanics of Structures and Machines, Jour. Intelligent Material Sys. and Structures, 1992—, Jour. Smart Materials and Structures, 1993—2000; editor Jour. Intelligent Material Sys. and Structures, Shock and Vibration, Shock and Vibration Digest. Presdl. Young Investigator NSF, 1984-89. Fellow ASME (chair Buffalo sect. 1986-87, assoc. editor Vibration, Acoustics, Stress and Reliability in Design, 1984-89, Jour. Applied Mechanics, tech. editor Jour. Vibration and Acoustics 1990-2000, Disting. Lectr. 1995—; Adaptive Structure award 2000), AIAA, Am. Acad. Mechs. Internat. Inst. for Acoustics and Vibration. Home: 3545 Deer Run Rd Blacksburg VA 24060-9091 Office: Va Tech Inst Dept Mech Engring Blacksburg VA 24061-0261

INMAN, EDWARD SALISBURY, III, former secretary of state, secondary school educator; b. Warwick, R.I., Aug. 11, 1960; s. Edward Salisbury Jr. and Evelyn (Godek) I.; m. Kelly Ann O'Shea, July 23, 1994; 2 children, Sarah Elizabeth, Hannah M. BA in Polit. Sci., R.I. Coll., 1983, BA in Social Sci., 1988. Tchr. Cranston (R.I.) Sch. Dept., 1987—; mem. Gen. Assembly, Provi-

dence, 1993—2001, chair water resources joint com., 1993—2001, dep. speaker pro tem, 1993—2001; sec. of state State of R.I., 2001—03. Founding mem. Coventry/East Greenwich Hockey Team, 1985—, now chmn. Coventry Alliance scholar, 1978, Polish Nat. Alliance scholar, 1978. Democrat. Avocations: tennis, golf, basketball. E-mail: einman@sec.state.ri.us.

INMAN, HARRY ANSEL, lawyer; b. Rochester, NY, Aug. 2, 1924; s. William Horace and Margaret (Crossette) Inman; m. Margaret Blackard, June 11, 1949 (div. July 1980); children: William H., Jennifer, David; m. Linda Cosby, Sept. 1980 (div. Dec. 1990). BA, MIT, 1943; student, Harvard U., 1948; LLB, U. Va., 1951. Bar: NY 1952, DC 1953, US Claims Ct. 1958, US Ct. Internat. Trade 1967, US Supreme Ct. 1958. Assoc. Sutherland, Linowitz & Williams, Rochester, 1952—53, Lord, Day & Lord, Washington, 1953—58; pvt. practice, 1958—59, 1964; ptnr. Wyatt, Saltzstein & Inman, 1959—63; counsel, ptnr. Patton, Boggs & Blow and predecessor firm, 1965—; affiliate Ortiz & Inman, Mexico City, 1962—68, Escobar, Antolinos, Ortiz & Inman, 1969—75; rep. to Sec. State's Adv. Com. on Pvt. Internat. Law, 1973; internat. advisor Creel, Garcia-Cuellar & Muggenburg, Mexico City, 1975—; observer final meeting Palme Commn., Stockholm, 1989. Contbr. articles. 1st lt. USAAF, 1943—46. Mem.: Procedural Aspects Internat. Law and Inst., Fed. Bar Assn., Washington Inst. Fgn. Affairs, Bar Assn. DC, Inter-Am. Bar Assn., Am. Law Inst., Am. Fgn. Law Soc., Am. Soc. Internat. Law, ABA, PTO, Univ. Club, Angler's Club, Harvard Club, Yale Club, Gibson Island Club, Met. Club. also: 4242 E West Hwy Bethesda MD 20815-5934 Office: Patton Boggs & Blow 1300 19th St NW Ste 260 Washington DC 20036-1609

INMAN, JAMES RUSSELL, claims consultant; b. Tucson, Ariz., May 24, 1936; s. Claude Colbert and Myra Eugenia (Langdon) Inman; m. Charleen M. Bowman Inman, Feb. 22, 1964 (div. 1977); m. Margaret Williams Kendrick, Apr. 26, 1996 (dec. Feb. 2002). Student, Pomona Coll., Claremont, Calif., 1954-60. Supr. res. dept. Honnold Libr. Claremont Coll., 1959-60; supr. casualty claims CNA Ins., L.A., 1961-70; asst. mgr., asbestos specialist, head entertainment claims Firemen's Fund, L.A., Beverly Hills, 1970—83; pres. Wilnor Corp., L.A., 1982—. Claims auditor dirs. and officers claims Harbor/Continental Ins., L.A., 1984-86; claims mgr. Advent Mgmt., L.A., 1987, Completion Bond Co., Century City, Calif., 1988; asst. to pres., claims specialist Am. Multiline Corp., L.A., 1988-92; sr. claims specialist Reliance Ins. Co., Glendale, Calif., 1992-94; expert witness in entertainment claims field. Mem. First Century Families: Calif.; mem. com. Baldwin Hills Dam Disaster, 1968-72; pres. Alcohol Info. Ctr., LA, 1983-85; pres.'s exec. coun., Woodbury U.; concours mem. Petersen Automotive Mus., others. Mem. LA Athletic Club, Wilshire Country Club, Sloane Club (London), Mercedes Benz Club Am., Classic Car Club Am., Rotary Internat. Avocations: classic cars, american and english silver. Home: 623 S Arden Blvd Los Angeles CA 90005-3814

INMAN, JEAN A. political party official; Chmn. Mass. Rep. Party, Boston, 2002—. Office: Mass Republican Party Ste 309 27 Water St Wakefield MA 01880-3038

INMAN, JOHN JEFFREY, finance educator; b. Indpls., Feb. 3, 1956; s. John Junior and Janice Virginia Inman; m. Sandra Renee Vaughan, May 28, 1983; children: Michael John, David Alexander. BS in Mech. Engring., Gen. Motors Inst., 1979; MBA, Ind. U., 1982; PhD, U. of Tex., 1990. Prodn. foreman Gen. Motors, Indpls., 1979—81; distbn. specialist Tex. Instruments, Dallas, 1982—88; asst. prof. U. of So. Calif., L.A., 1991—94; assoc. prof. of mktg. U. of Wis., Madison, Wis., 1994—2000; prof. of mktg. Katz Grad. Sch. of Bus. U. Pitts., 2000—. V.p. policy bd. Jour. Consumer Rsch., Madison, 1998—. Mem. editl. bd.: Jour. Retailing, 1999, Jour. Consumer Rsch., 1999—, Jour. Mktg., 2000—; contbr. articles to profl. jours. Mem.: Soc. for Consumer Psychology, Am. Econ. Assn., INFORMS, Am. Mktg. Assn., Assn. for Consumer Rsch. Office: University of Pittsburgh 356 Mervis Hall Pittsburgh PA 15260 Office Fax: 412-648-1693. Personal E-mail: jinman@katz.pitt.edu.

INMAN, LARRY JOE, basketball coach; b. Summer County, Tenn., Jan. 3, 1948; m. Bobby Gene Follis; children: Jody, Latrice, Tiffany. BS, Austin Peay State U., Clarksville, Tenn., 1970; M, Tenn. State U., 1977. Head coach basketball Gallatin (Tenn.) H.S., 1970-73, Mt. Juliet (Tenn.) H.S., 1973-78; head coach women's basketball Mid. Tenn. State U., Murfreesboro, 1978-86, Ea. Ky. U., Richmond, 1987—. Named Coach of Yr., Ohio Valley Conf., 1979—80, 1982—83, 1984—85, 1990—91, 1994—95, 1996—97, 2001, Man of Yr., 2001. Mem. Womans Basketball Coaches Assn. Office: Eastern Ky U Womens Athletic Dept Lancaster Ave Richmond KY 40475

INMAN, MARIANNE ELIZABETH, college administrator; b. Berwyn, Ill., Jan. 9, 1943; d. Miles V. and Bessee M. (Hejtmanek), Plzak; m. David P. Inman; Aug 1, 1964. BA, Purdue U., 1964; AM, Ind. U., 1967; PhD, U. Tex., 1978. Dir. Comml. Div. World Instruction and Translation, Inc., Arlington, Va., 1969-71; program staff mem. Ctr. for Applied Linguistics, Arlington, 1972-73; lectr. in French No. Va. Community Coll., Bailey's Crossroads, 1973; faculty mem., linguistic researcher Tehran (Iran) U., 1973-75; intern mgmt. edn. rsch. & devel. S.W Ednl. Devel. Lab., Austin, Tex., 1977-78; asst. prof., program dir. Southwestern U., Georgetown, Tex., 1978; dir. English lang. inst. Alaska Pacific U., Anchorage, 1980-87, chairperson all-U. requirements, 1984-88, assoc. dean acad. affairs, 1988-90; v.p. dean of coll. Northland Coll., Ashland, Wis., 1990-95; pres. Ctrl. Meth. Coll., Fayette, Mo., 1995—. Contbr. Pres. Commn. Foreign Lang. and Internat. Studies, Washington, 1978-79; manuscript evaluator The Modern Lang. Jour., Columbus, Ohio, 1979-84; cons. Anchorage Sch. Dist., 1984-90; cons., evaluator N. Cen. Assn. Colls. and Schs., Chgo., 1990—; mem. dean's task force Coun. on Ind. Colls., 1993-95; pres. Ind. Colls. and Univs. Mo., 1996-2000. Co-author: English for Medical Students, 1976; co-author and editor: English for Science and Engineering Students, 1977; contbr. articles to profl. jours. Treas. Alaska Humanities Forum, Anchorage, 1982-87; mem. Anchorage Matanuska-Susitna Borough Pvt. Industry Coun., 1983-86; mem. Sister Cities Commn., Anchorage, 1984-90; mem. Multicultural Edn. Adv. Bd., Anchorage, 1987-90; with speakers bur. Wis. Humanities Com., 1992-95, Mcpl. Libr. Bd., 1993-95; active Mo. Humanities Coun., 1997—; bd. dirs. Mo. Colls. Fund, Ind. Colls. and Univs. of Mo.; mem. bd. Great Rivers Coun. Boy Scouts Am., 1996—. Named Fellow of Grad. Sch., U. Tex. Austin, 1977-78, Nat. Teaching Fellow, Alaska Pacific U., Anchorage, 1980-81; recipient Pub. Svc. award Sister Cities Commn., Anchorage, 1987, Kellogg Found. Nat. fellowship, Battle Creek, Mich., 1988-91. Mem. League of Women Voters, Nat. Assn. Women in Edn., Am. Assn. for Higher Edn., Am. Coun on Teaching of Foreign Langs., Tchrs. of English to Speakers of Other Langs., Nat. Coun. Tchrs. of English, Alpha Chi, Alpha Lambda Delta, Delta Rho Kappa, Gold Peppers, Kappa Delta Pi, Mortar Bd., Omicron Delta Kappa, Phi Kappa Phi, Pi Delta Phi, Pi Lambda Theta, Sigma Delta Pi, Sigma Epsilon Pi, Sigma Kappa. Avocations: community theater, hiking, camping, fishing. Office: Ctrl Meth Coll 411 CMC Sq Fayette MO 65248-1198 E mail: minman@cmc.edu.

INMAN, ROBERT ANTHONY, writer; b. San Francisco, June 13, 1931; s. Verne Thomson and Irene Cootey Inman; m. Joan Marshall, June 18, 1958 (div. Apr. 1, 1985); children: Jeffrey Thornton, Michael Verne. BA with Gt. Distinction, Stanford U., Calif., 1952; at, U. of Vienna, Austria, 1952—54, Free U. of Berlin, 1956—57; MA, U. Wash., Seattle, 1959. Tchg. asst. U. Wash., Seattle, 1957—59, lectr., 1960—62; dir. pub. info. The Denver Post, 1965—71; aquisitions supr. Am. Inst. of Aeronautics and Astronautics, NYC, 1982—84, mng. editor jours, 1985—87; field ops supr. U.S. Bur. of the Census, 1990; freelance editor, cons. San Francisco, 1999—. Author: (novels) The Torturer's Horse, 1965, The Blood Endures, 1981. With MI corps U.S. Army, 1954—56. Grantee Fulbright scholar, US Dept. of State, 1952—53, 1953—54. Home and Office: 720 Gough St San Francisco CA 94102

INMAN, STEPHEN EUGENE, finance officer; b. Lawrence, Kans., Oct. 1, 1943; s. Arthur Eugene and Eunice Margaret (Hults) I.; m. Deborah Renée Southern, Dec. 18, 1987; 1 child, Alexandra Renée. BA in Polit. Sci., U. Del., 1965; MA in Polit. Sci., U. Kans., 1975. Commd. 2d lt. U.S. Army, 1965; advanced through grades to col., 1985; ret., 1992; sr. v.p. bus. ops., CFO, MPRI, Inc., Alexandria, 1992—. Bd. dirs. Helping Angels, Inc. Mem. Assn. U.S. Army, U.S. Army War Coll. Assn. Office: MPRI Inc 1201 E Abingdon Dr Ste 425 Alexandria VA 22314-1493

INMAN, WILLIAM PETER, lawyer; b. Cleve., June 29, 1936; s. James B. and Lillian (Frances) I.; m. Judith A. Clay, Feb. 5, 1994; children: William Peter, Elizabeth, David. Student, Miami U., 1954-55; BA, Ohio State U., 1958; JD, Case Western Res. U., 1960, MBA, 1966. Bar: Ohio 1960, Tex. 1985. Tax accountant U.S. Steel Corp., Cleve., 1960-63; asso. trust counsel Central Nat. Bank of Cleve., 1963-66; atty. Sherwin-Williams Co., Cleve., 1966-67, tax counsel, 1967, mgr. tax dept., 1967-68, corporate dir. taxes, 1968-69, asst. sec., dir. taxes, 1969-71, sec., dir. taxes, 1971-75, v.p., sec., asst. treas., 1975-78, v.p., treas., chief fin. officer, 1978-80; v.p. fin., chief fin. officer RTE Corp., Waukesha, Wis., 1980-83; fin. cons. Houston, 1983-85; corp. sec., gen. counsel Mera Bank, Phoenix, 1985-88; gen. counsel CADTEL Sys. Inc., Phoenix, 1988-95, Ariz. Bus. Assocs., L.L.C., Phoenix, 1995—. Mem. Greater Cleve. Growth Assn., 1969-80; Trustee Ohio Pub. Expenditure Council, 1969-80, v.p., 1970-73, pres., 1973-75, chmn. bd., 1975-77. Mem. Am. Soc. Corp. Secs., Fin. Execs. Inst., Cleve. Treasurers Club, N.A.M., Ohio Mfrs. Assn., Am., Ohio, Greater Cleve., Tex., Maricopa County, Ariz. bar assns., Estate Planning Council of Cleve., Tax Execs. Inst., Phi Delta Phi, Beta Gamma Sigma, Beta Alpha Psi. Home: 10333 E Pine Valley Dr Scottsdale AZ 85255-1700 Office: 1600 W Monroe 9th Fl Phoenix AZ 85007

INNES, KENNETH FREDERICK, III, lawyer; b. San Francisco, May 15, 1950; s. Kenneth F. Jr. and Jean I.; m. Patricia Ann Graboyes, May 12, 1973; children: Kenneth F. IV, Julia Christine. BA, San Francisco State U., 1972, JD, 1984. Bar: Calif. 1984, U.S. Dist. Ct. (no. dist.) Calif. 1987, U.S. Dist. Ct. (ea. dist.) Calif. 1988. Tchr. secondary schs., Red Bluff, Calif., 1973-74; postal clk. U.S. Postal Svc., Vallejo, Calif., 1977-84, postal insp. Denver, 1984-87; regional atty. U.S. Postal Inspection Svc., Memphis, 1987-90, fin. auditor, 1990-92, regional atty. San Francisco, 1992—. Capt. USMCR, 1974-77. Mem. ABA, Calif. Bar Assn., Mensa, Elks. Democrat. Roman Catholic. Home: 157 Heartwood Ct Vallejo CA 94591-5638 Office: US Postal Insp Svc PO Box 882528 San Francisco CA 94188-2528

INNES, LAURA, actress; b. Pontiac, Mich., Aug. 16, 1959; BA in Theater, Northwestern U. Appeared in local and nat. plays, including A Streetcar Named Desire, Edmund, Two Shakespearean Actors, Our Town, Three Sisters; appeared in TV series, including Wings, My So-Called Life, Party of Five, Brooklyn Bridge, Louis, ER, 1995— (also dir. episodes); dir. episodes of The West Wing, Presidio Med; TV films include And the Band Played On, 1993, See Jane Run, 1995, Just Like Dad, 1995, The Price of a Broken Heart, 1999, Taking Back Our Town, 2001; appeared in feature film Deep Impact, 1998, Can't Stop Dancing, 1999. Office: Dan Buchwald & Assoc 9229 Sunset Blvd Ste 710 West Hollywood CA 90069

INNES, WILLIAM B. chemist, consultant; b. Cambria, Calif., Mar. 8, 1913; s. Murray Innes and Katherine Dorsch; m. Dorothy V. Rundle, Aug. 7, 1938; children: Robert A., Walter R., Gordon, Roger W. BS, U. Calif., Berkeley, 1937; MS, U. Iowa, Iowa City, 1939, PhD, 1941. Rsch. chemist Champion Paper & Fibre Co., Hamilton, Ohio, 1941—42, Am. Cyanamid, Paper Chems., Stamford, Conn., 1942—43; rsch. scientist Manhattan Project Columbia U., N.Y.C., 1943—45; rsch. chemist Am. Cyanamid, Petroleum Chems., Stamford, Conn., 1945—57, group leader, 1957—61, rsch. assoc., 1961—67; pres. Purad Inc., Upland, Calif., 1965—95; ret., 1995. Panel leader CRC Com. Hydrocarbon Analysis, various, 1960—64. Contbr. articles to profl. jours. Mem.: AAAS, Am. Chem. Soc. (treas. San Gorgonio sect. 1967—70, v.p. 1967—70). Achievements include research in smog instrumentation and on the relation of NO emissions to photochemical smog; Work relating to the surface area and structure of absorbents and catalysts; invention of thermocatalytic instruments for smog-related components; co-developer of flame ionization hydrocarbon analyzer; catalysts related to petroleum refining; Titration pore volume method. Avocations: tennis, fishing, stock market. Home: 724 Kilbourne Dr Upland CA 91784 Home Fax: 909-985-4452. Personal E-mail: wmbinnes@netscape.net.

INNES-BROWN, GEORGETTE MEYER, real estate broker, insurance broker; b. Wilmington, Del., Mar. 20, 1918; d. George and Flora Sue (Saunders) Meyer; m. Andrew T. Innes, Jr., Nov. 26, 1947 (dec.); m. Roy Glen Brown, Jr., Mar. 6, 1991. Grad. Real Estate Law, theory, Conveyancing and Practice, Phila. Bd. Realtors Sch., 1945; grad. Fire, Marine, Casualty Ins., North Phila. Realty Bd. Sch., 1946; cert. appraiser, Villanova Coll., 1974. Lic. realtor, Pa., ins. broker and appraiser, Phila. Ins. broker, realtor, Phila., 1945—; ins. broker, 1946—; also appraiser. Residential and single family home builder, Bucks County, Pa., Princeton, N.J., 1955-61. Mem., spkr. Juniata Pk. Civic Assn., Phila., 1984. Recipient Knights Legion award Italian-Am. Press, 1971. Mem. Nat. Assn. Realtors (sec.-treas. and v.p. chpt. 1975-80), Am. Bus. Women's Assn. (chpt. v.p. 1971, Businesswoman of Yr. 1971), Phila. Women's Realty Assn. (pres. bd. govs. 1949-85, pres. 1949-51, Woman of Yr. 1972-73), Phila. Bd. Realtors (v.p. residential divsn. 1975), North Phila. Realty Bd. (v.p. 1975, 76, pres. 1977, Gustav A. Wick award 1979), Del. Coun. Realty Bds. (sec. 1974), Real Estate Multiple Listing Burs. (treas. 1972-76), Sigma Lambda Soc. (chpt. pres. 1948). Avocations: golf, dancing, gardening, cooking, embroidery. Home: 1162 SW Walnut Ter Boca Raton FL 33486-5565

INNIS, PAULINE, writer, publishing company executive; b. Devon, England; came to U.S., 1954; m. Walter Deane Innis, Aug. 1, 1959. Attended, U. Manchester, U. London. Author: Hurricane Fighters, 1962, Ernestine or the Pig in the Potting Shed, 1963 (paperback 1992), The Wild Swans Fly, 1964, The Ice Bird, 1965, Wind of the Pampas, 1967, Fire from the Fountains, 1968, Astronumerology, 1971, Gold in the Blue Ridge, 1973, 2d edit., 1980, reprinted 1995, My Trails (transl. from French), 1975, Prayer and Power in the Capital, 1982, The Secret Gardens of Watergate, 1987, Attention: A Quick Guide to Armed Services, 1988, Desert Storm Dairy, 1991, The Nursing Home Companion, 1993, Bridge Across the Seas, 1995, The Gospel of Joseph, 1998, I've Smashed the Devil's Window, 1999; co-author: Protocol, 1977. Bd. dirs. Washington Goodwill Industries Guild, 1962-66; membership chmn. Welcome to Washington Club, 1961-64; co-chmn. Internat. Workshop Capital Spkr.'s Club, 1961-64; pres. Children's Book Guild, 1967-68; dir. Ednl. Commn., bd. dirs. Internat. Conf. Women Writers and Journalists, Nat. Arboretum, 1992-96; criminal justice com. D.C. Commn. on Status of Women; founder vol. program D.C. Women's Detention Ctr.; chmn. women's com. Washington Opera, 1977-79; mem. Liaison Com. Med. Edn., 1979-85; nat. trustee Med. Coll. Pa., 1980—; mem. Edn. Commn. for Fgn. Med. Grads., 1986-97. Named Hoosier Woman of Yr., 1966. Mem. Soc. Women Geographers, Authors League, Smithsonian Assocs. (women's bd.), English-Speaking Union, Spanish-Portuguese Group D.C. (pres. 1965-66), Br. Inst. U.S., Am. Newspaper Women's Club (pres. 1971-73), Internat. Soc. Poets (disting.), Sulgrave Club, Internat. Clubs (co-chair 1997), Venerable Order St. John Jerusalem (comdr.), Internat. Neighbors Club. Home: 2700 Virginia Ave NW Washington DC 20037-1908

INNIS, ROY EMILE ALFREDO, organization executive; b. St. Croix, V.I., June 6, 1934; s. Alexander and Georgianna (Thomas) I.; m. Doris Valdena Funnye, Feb. 13, 1965; children: Roy Jr. (dec.), Alexander (dec.), Cedric, Patricia, Corinne, Kwame, Niger, Kimathi Mugabe. Student, CCNY, 1953-58. Chem. technician Vick Chem. Co., 1961-63; research asst. cardiovascular research labs. Montefiore Hosp., 1963-67; mem. CORE, 1963—, edn. chmn. Harlem group, 1964-68, chmn., 1965-68, 2d nat. vice chmn., 1967-68, asso. nat. dir., 1968, nat. dir., 1968-70, nat. chmn., nat. dir., 1970-82, nat. chmn., 1982—; founder and chmn. CORE Cmty. Sch., Bronx, N.Y., 1977. Exec. dir. Harlem Commonwealth Council, 1967-68; 1st ofcl. N.Am. del. Orgn. African Unity, Ethiopia, 1973, Uganda, 1975 Contbr.: chpt. to The Endless Crisis, 1973, Black Economic Development, 1970; pub.: chpt. to Profiles in Black, 1976. Served with AUS, 1950-52. Research fellow Met. Applied Research Center, 1967 Office: 817 Broadway New York NY 10003-4709

INNISS-BREWER, YVONNE, nurse, insurance company administrator; b. Sanicholas, Aruba, Netherlands Antilles, Mar. 10, 1948; came to U.S., 1975. d. William Conrad and Ruby Marion (Edwards) I. BS in Human Services, N.H. Coll., 1984, MS in Urban Studies, So. Conn. State U., 1986; Lic. Practical Nurse, John Radcliffe Sch. of Nursing, Oxford, Eng., 1969; MALS, Wesleyan U., 1990. Asst. charge nurse Churchill Hosp., Oxford, Eng., 1970-73; claims reviewer Aetna Life and Casualty, Hartford, Conn., 1975-77; lic. processor Hartford Steam Boiler, 1977-79, supr. claim services, 1979-82, mktg. asst., 1982-87, 88, exec. asst., 1988—. Mem Wadsworth Atheneum, Hartford, 1986—; mem. town com. A Conn. Party, 1992-93, sec., 1990-92. Mem. Internat. Platform Assn. Anglican. Office: Hartford Steam Boiler Inspection and Ins Co One State St Hartford CT 06012-3001 Home: 21 Regency Dr # 6 Bloomfield CT 06002 E-mail: yvonne.inniss-brewer@hsb.com.

INNMON, ARLENE KATHERINE (TARA INNMON), artist, dancer, writer, storyteller, minister, healer; b. Mpls., Oct. 28, 1950; d. Morris Jentof and Hulda Cecilia (Levine) Bangsund; children: Carl David, Erica Arlene. BS in Occupl. Therapy, U. Minn., 1973; student in Writing, Hamline U., 2000—. Activities dir. Mother of Perpetual Health Home, Brownsville, Tex., 1973-74; occupl. therapist Corpus Christi Meml. Med. Ctr., Corpus Christi, Tex., 1975—76, Mpls. Soc. for Blind, 1976-81, Grand Ave. Rest Home, Mpls., 1985-87, Tara's Healing Arts, 2000—. One-woman shows include Gus Lucky's Gallery, Mpls., 1987, Paul Whitney Larsen Gallery, St. Paul, 1998, Mayday Cafe, 1999, Anodyne Coffeehouse, 1999, Faribault, 2001, Betseys Back Porch, Mpls., 2002; group exhbns. include Art of Eye I, 1985—, II (multi-yr. traveling exhibits), 1998—, Katherine Nash Gallery, Mpls., 1994, Art and Soul Festival, San Francisco, 1999, Rose Resnick Lighthouse Show-Insights (Outstanding Artist award), San Francisco, 2002, Waterfall Gallery, Mpls., 2002; represented in permanent collections St. Paul Company, Sister Kenney Inst., pvt. collectors.n, Minn. Mem. Minn. Chpt. Abortion Rights, Mpls., 1981. Recipient 1st pl. award drawing, Sister Kenny Internat. Show, Mpls., 1988, People's Choice award bronze, 1990, Artist Appreciation award, Very Spl. Arts, Mpls., 1997, Jaehny award, 1998, 1st pl. award, Artists Beyond Disabilities, Long Beach, Calif., 1997, Docent award, Pa. Acad. Fine Arts, 1999, Sister Kenny Encouragement award, 1999, 2000, 2002, 2003, Best of Show award, Schenectady, N.Y., 2000, Outstanding Artist Insights, San Francisco, 2002, 2d pl. award, Art First, Princeton, N.J., 2003, Hon. Mention award, Insights, Louisville, 2003. Mem. SASE, The Loft. Avocations: dancing, reading. Home: 2016 27th Ave S Minneapolis MN 55406-1108

INNS, HARRY DOUGLAS ELLIS, retired optometrist; b. Tryconnel, Ont., Can., June 4, 1922; s. Thomas Henry and Eleanor (Ellis) I.; children from previous marriage: Susan Elizabeth, Douglas Michael; m. Helen Lynne Mitchell. Student, U. Toronto, 1946-48; grad, Ont. Coll. Optometry, 1950, OD, 1958. Practice optometry specialzing in contact lenses, Brantford, Ont., 1963-98. Contbr. articles to profl. jours.; patentee Inns extension disc to facilitate corneal measurements. Served to lt. RCAF, 1941-45. Fellow: Heraldry Soc. Can. (bd. dirs.), Royal Soc. Health, Assn. Contact Lens Practitioners Eng., Am. Acad. Optometry; mem.: Am. Contact Lens Specialists (sec.), Am. Optometric Assn., Can. Pub. Health Assn., Nat. Eye Rsch. Found., Better Vision Inst., Ont. Assn. Optometrists (Edn. Program award 1976, Contact Lens Program award 1978, Internat. Lecture award 1979, Appreciation award 1980, Dist. Svc. award 1981), Internat. Optometric and Optical League, Can. Assn. Optometrists, Ont. Optometrical Assn., Internat. Soc. Contact Lens Specialists (congress chmn.), RCAF Assn., Waterloo Alumni Assn., Royal Can. Mil. Int., Monarchist League Can., 78th Fraser Highlanders (maj.), Brantford C. of C., Kiwanis, Anglican Men's Club, Beta Sigma Kappa. Home: 67 Tutela Heights Brantford ON Canada N3T 1A4 E-mail: innsport@kwic.com.

INOUÉ, SHINYA, microscopy and cell biology scientist, educator; b. London, Jan. 5, 1921; came to US, 1948, naturalized, 1989; s. Kojiro and Hideko I.; m. Sylvia McCandless, July 18, 1952; children: Heather C., Jonathan H., Christopher W., Stephen K., Theodore D. Rigakushi, Tokyo U., 1944; MA, Princeton U., 1950, PhD, 1951; MA (hon.), Dartmouth Coll., 1959, U. Pa., 1966. Instr. U. Wash. Med. Sch., Seattle, 1951-53; asst. prof. Tokyo Met. U., 1953-54; rsch. assoc., assoc. prof. U. Rochester, NY, 1954-59; instr. Marine Biol. Lab., Woods Hole, Mass., 1961—, NATO Summer Sch., Cannes, Stressa, Szeged, 1967, 70, 75; prof., chmn. Dartmouth Med. Sch., Hanover, NH, 1959-66, U. Pa., Phila., 1966-89; disting. scientist Marine Biol. Lab., Woods Hole, 1980—. Cons. Am. Optical Co., 1954-60, NSF, 1962-65, NIH, 1965-70, Hamamatsu Photonics K.K., Hamamatsu City, Japan, 1988-2002, Nikon Corp., Tokyo, 1994—, Olympus Optical Co. Ltd., Tokyo, 1994-2001, Yokogawa Elec. Corp., Tokyo, 1997—, AutoQuant Imaging Inc., Watervliet, NY, 2000-, Universal Imaging Corp., Downington, Pa., 1984-2002; bd. dir., 1987-2002, Author: Video Microscopy, 2d edit., 1997; co editor: Molecules and Cell Movement, 1975; contbr. articles to profl. jours.; : mem. editl. bd. several sci. jours., ad hoc reviewer, advisor on sci. and tech. NSF, NIH, many Univ., founds. Trustee Marine Biol. Lab., 1970-77, 81-85, 92-96, mem. sci. coun., 1993-98. Recipient Rosenstiel award Brandeis U., 1988, Brown-Hazen award State of NY, 1988; Guggenheim Found. fellow, 1971-72; cancer rsch. scholar Am. Cancer Soc., NYC, 1955-58. Fellow Am. Acad. Arts and Scis., Royal Microscopial Soc. (hon.); mem. NAS, Biophys. Soc. (coun. 1968-71), Soc. Gen. Physiologists (coun., pres. 1962-65, 69-70), Am. Soc. Cell Biology (coun. 1970-73, E.B. Wilson award 1992), Optical Soc. Am., Microscopy Soc. Am. (Disting. Scientist award 1995), N.Y. Microscopical Soc. (Ernst Abbe award 1997). Achievements include 4 patents in optics. Avocations: reading, photography. Home: 40 Shore St Falmouth MA 02540-3146 Office: Marine Biol Lab 7 M B L St Woods Hole MA 02543-1015

INOUE, SUSUMU, medical educator; b. Kurashiki, Okayama, Japan, Mar. 23, 1940; came to U.S., 1966; married; children: Lisa, Hajime, Anne, Kenji. BS, Okayama (Japan) U., 1960, MD, 1964. Intern Yokosuka (Japan) Naval Hosp., 1964-65; resident Pediats. Children's Hosp. Mich., Detroit, 1966-68; dir. pediat. hematology, oncology Hurley Med. Ctr., Flint, Mich., 1987—, asst. dir. pediat. residency, 1987—; prof. pediats. Mich. State U., East Lansing, 1987; clin. prof. pediat. Wayne State U., Detroit, 1996—. Mem. Am. Soc. Hematology, Am. Soc. Clin. Oncology, Am. Soc. Pediat. Hematology, Oncology, Internat. Soc. Exptl. Hematology, Soc. Pediat. Rsch. Office: Hurley Med Ctr One Hurley Plz Flint MI 48503 E-mail: sinoue1@hurleymc.com.

INOUYE, DANIEL KEN, senator; b. Honolulu, Sept. 7, 1924; s. Hyotaro and Kame Imananga; m. Margaret Shinobu Awamura, June 12, 1949; 1 child, Daniel Ken. AB, U. Hawaii, 1950; JD, George Washington U., 1952. Bar: Hawaii 1953. Dep. pub. prosecutor, Honolulu, 1953-54; pvt. practice, 1954—; mem. Hawaii Territorial Ho. of Reps., 1954-58, Hawaii Territorial Senate, 1958-59, U.S. House of Reps., 1959—62; senator from Hawaii U.S. Senate (now 106th Congress), 1962—; mem. Senate Armed Svcs. Com., 1963—71; sec. Senate Dem. Conf., 1978-88; chmn. Dem. Steering Com., Senate Appropriations Com., 1971—; chmn. subcom. def., mem. Commerce Com., 1969—77; chmn. Senate Select Com. on Intelligence, 1976—79; ranking mem. subcom. budget authorizations Select Com. on Intelligence, 1979-84; chmn. Select Com. Indian Affairs, 1989—94, vice-chmn., 1990—; mem. Select Com. on Presdl. Campaign Activities, 1973-74; chmn. Sen. select com. Secret Mil. Assistance to Iran and Nicaraguan Opposition, 1987. Ranking minority mem. Appropriations subcom. on Def., Commerce, Sci., & Transp. subcom. on surface transp. & merchant marine; mem. Indian Affairs Com., Rules & Adminstrn. Com. Joint Com. on the Libr. & Congl. Intern Program, Dem. Steering & Coordination Com., Joint Com. on Printing; mem. Senate Watergate Com., 1973-74; sr. counselor Kissinger Commn., 1984; chmn. Senate Dem. Ctrl. Am. Study Group, 1984. Author: Journey to Washington. Active YMCA, Boy Scouts Am. Keynoter; temporary chmn. Dem. Nat. Conv., 1968, rules com. chmn., 1980, co-chmn. conv., 1984. Pvt. to capt. AUS, 1943-47. Decorated Medal of Honor, D.S.C., Bronze Star, Purple Heart with cluster; decorated Grand Cordon of the Order of the Rising Sun, Govt. Japan, 2000; named 1 of 10 Outstanding Young Men of Yr. U.S. Jr. C. of C., 1960; recipient Splendid Am. award Thomas A. Dooley Found., 1967 Golden Plate award Am. Acad. Achievement, 1968, Spirit of Hope award USO, 1999, Advocacy Conf. Congl. award Nat. Breast Cancer Coalition, 2002, Friend of Coast award Am. Coastal Coalition, 2002, Doughboy award U.S. Army, 2002, Sonny Montgomery award Nat. Guard Bur., 2003; Daniel K. Inouye Bldg. of Walter Reed Army Inst. Rsch., Naval Med. Rsch. Ctr., Bethesda, Md. dedicated in his honor, 2001; Hart-Dole-Inouye Fed. Ctr., Battle Creek, Mich. named in his honor, 2003. Mem. DAV (past comdr. Hawaii), Honolulu C. of C., Am. Legion (Nat. Comdr.'s award 1973) Clubs: Lion. (Hawaii), 442d Veterans (Hawaii). Democrat. Methodist. Home: 469 Ena Rd Honolulu HI 96815-1749 Office: US Senate 722 Hart Senate Bldg Washington DC 20510-0001

INOUYE, LORRAINE R. state legislator; b. Hilo, HI, June 22, 1940; m. Vernon Inouye; children: Ronald Jitchaku, Jay Kitchaku, Marcia Johansen. Mgr. Orchid Island Hotel, 1967-75; sales mgr. Hilo Hawaiian Hotel, Hilo and Kona Lagoon Hotels, 1975-86; pres. Aloha Blooms, Inc., 1998—; mem. Hawaii Senate, Dist. 1, Honolulu, 1998—; chair econ. devel. com. Hawaii Senate, Honolulu, mem. commerce and consumer protection com., mem. transp. and

intergovtl. affairs com. Mayor County of Hawaii, 1990-92; mem. Hawaii County Coun., 1984-90, Hawaii County Planning Commn., 1974-79; dir. Girl Scout Coun. Hawaii, 1995X; charter mem. Ho'okumu, North Hawaii Cmty. Hosp., 1991X. Mem. Rotary Club of Hilo. Democrat. Office: State Capitol 415 S Beretania St Rm 201 Honolulu HI 96813-2407*

INOUYE, SHARON K. physician, educator; b. Santa Monica, Calif., June 2, 1957; d. Mitsuo and Lily Ann Inouye; m. Stephen L. Helfand, Aug. 14, 1983; children: Benjamin, Joshua, Jordan. BA cum laude, Pomona Coll., 1977; MD, U. Calif., San Francisco, 1981; MPH with distinction, Yale U., 1989. Diplomate Am. Bd. Internal Medicine, Am. Bd. Geriatric Medicine, Nat. Bd. Med. Examiners. Intern in internal medicine U. Calif.-San Francisco/Moffit Hosps., 1981-82; resident in internal medicine Harvard-Beth Israel Hosp., Boston, 1982-83, U. Calif.-San Francisco Primary Care Program, 1983-84, adminstrv. chief resident, 1984; postdoctoral fellow in gen. internal medicine Stanford (Calif.) U. Sch. Medicine, 1984-85; attending physician divsn. gen. internal medicine VA Med. Ctr., Palo Alto, Calif., 1984-85, asst. dir. geriatric evaluation unit, attending physician West Haven, Conn., 1985-87; attending physician Adler Geriatric Assessment Ctr. Yale-New Haven Hosp., 1987—, asst. med. dir. continuing care unit, 1989—; asst. prof. medicine Yale U. Sch. Medicine, New Haven, 1986-87, 89-94, assoc. prof. medicine, 1994—; assoc. prof., 1999—; assoc. clin. prof. Yale U. Sch. Nursing, 1998-99, tenured assoc. prof., 1999—2002, prof. medicine, 2002—. Instr. Stanford U. Sch. Medicine, 1984-85; postdoctoral fellow Robert Wood Johnson Clin. Scholars Program, Yale U. Sch. Medicine, 1987-89; asst. dir. geriatric evaluation unit VA Med. Ctr., West Haven, Conn., 1985-87; vis. prof. Camp Hill Med. Ctr., Dalhousie U., Halivax, N.S., Can., 1995, Dartmouth-Hitchcock Med. Ctr., 1995, U. Pa., 1995, Mt. Sinai Med. Ctr., 1997, Can. Acad. Geriatric Psychiatry, McGill U., 1997; lectr., cons. in field. Mem. editl. bd. Am. Jour. Medicine, 1997—; reviewer various jours. in field; contbr. more than 80 articles to profl. jours., chpts. to books. MacArthur Rsch. Program on Successful Aging Scholar, 1989-91, Dana Found. Faculty scholar, 1989-92; recipient rsch. award Conn. Cmty. Care Inc., 1998, Donaghue Investigator award Donaghue Med. Rsch. Found., 1998—, Midcareer award Nat. inst. Aging, 1999—. Mem. ACP, Am. Fedn. Aging Rsch. (grantee 1989), Am. Fedn. Clin. Rsch., Am. Geriatrics Soc. (editl. bd. jour. 1995—, New Investigator award 1993, Clin. Investigator award for outstanding sci. achievement 1998), Am. Med. Women's Assn. (citation for scholastic achievement 1981), Gerontol. Soc. Am., Soc. Gen. Internal Medicine, Am. Soc. Clin. Investigation, Mortar Board Honor Soc., Phi Beta Kappa, Alpha Omega Alpha. Avocations: reading, piano, rollerblading, hiking. Office: Yale U Sch Medicine Dept Internal Medicine 20 York St # T-15 New Haven CT 06504-8900

INSALACO-DE NIGRIS, ANNA MARIA THERESA, middle school educator; b. N.Y.C., Oct. 18, 1947; d. Salvatore and Rosaria (Colletti) Insalaco; m. Michael Peter De Nigris, July 12, 1969; children: Jenniffer Ann, Tamara Alicia. BA in English and Langs., CCNY, 1969; MA in English Linguistics, George Mason U., 1988; postgrad., U. Va. Cert. endorsement in Adminstrn. and Supervision U. Va., 2002, English secondary tchr. Va. Tchr. Spanish and core subjects St. John's, Rubidoux, Calif., 1969-70; ESL specialist Sunset Hills Elem. Sch., San Diego, 1980; tchr. Sunrise Acres Elem. Sch., Las Vegas, Nev., 1984-85; tchr. 1st grade Talent House Pvt. Elem. Sch., Fairfax, Va., 1987-88; tchr. ESL Hammond Jr. High Sch., Alexandria, Va., 1988-90, Washington Irving Intermediate Sch., Springfield, Va., 1990-91; tchr. ESL 6th grade Ellen Glassgow Mid. Sch., Alexandria, 1991-92; tchr. ESL and English 7th grade Cooper Mid. Sch., McLean, Va., 1992-93; tchr. ESL Poe Mid. Sch., Annandale, Va., 1993-94; tchr. ESL and social studies Longfellow Mid. Sch., Falls Church, Va., 1994-95; tchr. ESL Herndon (Va.) Mid. Sch., 1995—; summer sch. asst. prin. Longfellow Mid. Sch., 2002. Tchr. adult ESL George Mason H.S., Falls Church, Va., 1988—89; chmn. for multicultural forum Coun. for Applied R&D George Mason U., 1990—94; mem. steering com., faculty adv. com. Herndon Mid. Sch., 1995—, program sponsor Reach for Tomorrow; coach for Krasnow Inst. George Mason U., 2000—; mem. sch. adoption com. Va. Dept. Transp., 1991, human rels. com., 1990—96, ESL Portfolio Assessment com., 1993—98; sch.-based mem. for minority achievement in prin.'s cabinet F.C. Hammond Jr. H.S., Alexandria, 1989—90; mem. Continuing Edn. Bd. Fairfax County, 1998—; co-chair WATESOL Secondary Interest Group, 1998—99, chair, 1999—2001; presenter in field. Vol. Family Svcs., Wright Patterson AFB, Ohio, 1971-72, ARC, Ohio and S.C., 1971-73; leader Girl Scouts U.S., 1980-87; Fairfax Edn. Assn. scholarship sponsor. Mem. Va. Edn. Assn. (del. 1990—), Nat. Assn. Bilingual Edn., ESL Multi-Cultural Conv. (presenter, facilitator 1989, socio-polit. concerns immigrant rights advocate 1995—), Tchrs. ESL, Washington Tchrs. ESL, Calif. Tchrs. ESL, Va. Assn. Tchrs. English, Fairfax Edn. Assn. (sch. rep., del. Va. Edn. Assn. and NEA), Italian-Am. Caucus (v.p. 1997-2000, pres. 2000—). Roman Catholic. Avocations: writing, reading, politics, helping others. Home: 8814 Hayload Ct Springfield VA 22153-1213 E-mail: denigris@erols.com., annamaria.denigris@fcps.edu.

INSANA, ARTHUR GERARD, writer, director; s. Arthur Joseph and Adelia Insana. Mng. editor On Location Mag., Hollywood, Calif., 1982—83, Shape Mag., Woodland Hills, Calif., 1986; pres./creative dir. CopyWrite Comm., Northridge, Calif., 1986—; writer/prodr. HilanaVision Prodns., Northridge, 1984—86. Dir.(prodr.): (audiodrama) Star Wars: Dark Empire; prodr.(dir.): (business audio) The Message of the Markets, (spiritual audio) Maximize the Moment, (audiobook) Gump & Co., (audiodrama) A Dragon Lover's Treasury of the Fantastic, (audio documentary) Mysteries of the Unknown: The Powers of Healing, Mysteries of the Unknown: Mystic Places; dir.(prodr.): (audiodrama) Star Wars: Dark Empire II; prodr.(dir.): Star Wars: Dark Lords of the Sith, Johnny Mnemonic, (audiobook) The Celestine Vision, (audiodrama) Star Wars: Dark Empire - The Collectors' Edition, The Midnight Club, (audiobook) Rich Kid, Smart Kid (Audie award, 2002, 2003), (business audio) Jack: Straight from the Gut; contbr. Mem.: Audio Publishers Assn. (assoc.). Personal E-mail: art.insana@verizon.net.

INSARDI, NINA ELIZABETH, benefits administrator; b. Port Chester, N.Y., Dec. 8, 1960; d. Albert Charles and Dorothy Elizabeth (Adis) I. BA in English magna cum laude, U. Richmond, 1982. Cert. employee benefits specialist. From exec. sec. to assoc. dir. benefits comm. CBS Inc., N.Y.C., 1984-97; dir. health benefits CBS, N.Y.C., 1998—2000, dir. health and welfare benefits, 2003—; dir. health benefits Viacom Inc., N.Y.C., 2000—02. Tutor Literacy Vols. of Am., Westchester, N.Y., 1989-94; fundraising vol. U. Richmond, N.Y. Alumni Chpt., 1993-97; election dist. leader Rye (N.Y.) Dem. Com., 1992-2001. Mem. Phi Beta Kappa. Democrat. Presbyterian. Avocations: travel, reading, camping. Office: CBS 51 W 52nd St New York NY 10019 E-mail: ninsardi@cbs.com.

INSCHO, JEAN ANDERSON, social worker, landscape designer; b. Camden, NJ, Oct. 31, 1936; d. George Myrick and Alfrida Elizabeth (Anderson) Hewitt; m. James Ronald Inscho, June 4, 1955 (div. Mar. 1982); children: James Ronald Jr., Cynthia Ann, Michael Merrick. BA, Fla. Atlantic U., 1971; MA in Coll. Teaching, Auburn U., 1974, postgrad., 1998-99. Instr. So. Union State Jr. Coll., Wadley, Ala., 1973-75; social worker Jefferson County Dept. Human Resources, Birmingham, Ala., 1976-77, Shelby County Dept. Human Resources, Columbiana, Ala., 1977-78, Houston County Dept. Human Resources, Dothan, Ala., 1978-98. Adj. instr. Troy State U., Dothan, 1984-97. Bd. dir., v.p. Adolescent Resource Ctr., 1992-93, sec., 1993-95; mem. Alzheimer's Assn. EPDA fellow Auburn U., 1973, 74. Mem.: Am. Horticultural Therapy Assn. (Ga.-Ala. chpt.), Wiregrass Master Gardeners (pres. 1994—95), Ala. Master Gardeners Assn. (bd. dir., sec. 2003—, sec. 2003), Dist. 7 State Employees Assn. (polit. action com. rep. 1994—98), Ala. State Employees Assn. (bd. dir.), Am. Daffodil Soc. Episcopalian. Avocations: gardening, needlecrafts, church activities.

INSEL, MICHAEL S. lawyer; b. N.Y.C., Apr. 19, 1947; s. Ralph David and Lillian Ruth (Solomon) I.; married; 1 child, Louis Leo. BA, Duke U., 1969; JD, NYU, 1973. Bar: N.Y. 1974, Fla. 1984. Assoc. Kelley Drye & Warren, N.Y.C., 1973-82, ptnr., 1982—; pres. French Am. Vintners LLC. Bd. dirs. Kobrand Corp., N.Y.C., Maison Louis Jadot, S.A., Beaune, France, L & L, S.A., Boe, France, Western Wine Svcs., Inc., North Bergen, N.J., Taittinger C.C.U.C., Reims, France, Kobrand Found., N.Y.C., The Kopf Family Found., Inc., St. Francis Vineyards, Sonoma, Calif., Domaine Carneros, Napa, Calif.; chmn. Goodwill Industries, Astoria, N.Y.; trustee Elsie del Fierro Charitable Trust, N.Y.C., 1985—, Barbara Bell Cumming Found., N.Y.C., 1991—. Mem.: ABA, Fla. Bar Assn., NY State Bar Assn. Avocations: sailing, golf, opera. Office: Kelley Drye & Warren 101 Park Ave Fl 30 New York NY 10178-0062

INSEL, THOMAS R. federal agency administrator, psychiatrist; BA, MD, Boston U. Intern Berkshire Med. Ctr., Pittsfield, Mass.; resident Langley Porter Neuropsychiatric Inst., U. Calif., San Francisco; several sci. rsch. positions NIMH, 1979—94; prof. psychiatry, dir. Yerkes Regional Primate Rsch. Ctr. Emory U., Atlanta, 1994—2002; dir. NIMH, 2002—. Fellow: Am. Coll. Neuropsychopharmacology. Office: NIMH 6001 Executive Blvd Rm 8235 Bethesda MD 20892

INSELMAN, LAURA SUE, pediatrician, educator; b. Bklyn., Nov. 2, 1944; d. Alexander M. and Rae (Bloom) Inselman. BA, Barnard Coll., 1966; MD, Med. Coll. Pa., 1970. Diplomate Am. Bd. Pediatrics, Am. Bd. Pediatric Pulmonology. Intern and resident St. Lukes Hosp. Ctr., N.Y.C., 1970-73; fellow in pediatric pulmonary disease Babies Hosp., N.Y.C., 1973-76; chief pediatric pulmonary divsn. Interfaith Med. Ctr., Bklyn., 1976-81, Newington Con. Children's Hosp., 1987-92; pulmunologist, med. dir. dept. respiratory care duPont Hosp. for Children, Wilmington, Del., 1992-99, med. dir. pulmonary function lab., 1992—. Asst. prof. pediatrics Cornell U. Med. Coll., N.Y.C., 1981-86; asst. clin. prof. pediatrics, Yale U. Sch. Medicine, New Haven, 1987-92; asst. prof. pediatrics, U. Conn. Health Ctr., Farmington, 1987-92; assoc. prof. pediatrics, Jefferson Med. Coll. Thomas Jefferson U. Hosp., Phila., 1992—; mem. staff Good Samaritan Hosp., West Islip, N.Y., 1982-87. Bd. dirs. Am. Lung Assn. Nassau-Suffolk, East Meadow, N.Y., 1983-86, Del., 1992—. Fellow Am. Acad. Pediatrics, Am. Coll. Chest Physicians; mem. Am. Thoracic Soc., Am. Fedn. Med. Rsch., N.Y. Acad. Medicine, Harvey Soc., Soc. Pediatric Rsch. Office: DuPont Hospital for Children 1600 Rockland Rd Wilmington DE 19803-3607 E-mail: linselm@nemours.org.

INSLEE, JAY R. congressman; b. Seattle, Feb. 9, 1951; s. Frank and Adele Inslee; m. Trudi Anne Inslee, Aug. 27, 1972; children: Jack, Connor, Joe. BA in Econs., U. Wash., 1973; JD magna cum laude, Willamette U., 1976. Atty. Peters, Fowler & Inslee, Selah, Wash., 1976-92; mem. from 14th dist. Wash. State Ho. of Reps., 1988-92; mem. from the 4th Dist. State of Wash. U.S. Congress, 1993-95; atty. Gordon, Thomas, Honeywell, Malanca, Peterson and Daheim, Seattle, 1995-96; regional dir., region 10 U.S. Dept. Health & Human Svcs., Seattle, 1997-98; mem. U.S. Congress from 1st Wash. dist., 1999—; resources com., fin. svcs. com.; banking and fin. svcs. com. U.S. Ho. Reps., 1999—. Charter mem. Hoopaholics1988—. Democrat. Office: US Ho Reps 308 Cannon Ho Office Bldg Washington DC 20515-4701*

INSLER, STANLEY, philologist, educator; b. N.Y.C., June 23, 1937; AB, Columbia Coll., 1957; postgrad., U. Tubingen, 1960-62; PhD, Yale U., 1963. Mem. faculty Grad. Sch., Yale U., 1963—, now prof. Sanskrit and comparative philology. Cons. NEH Contbr. numerous articles on ancient langs. and lits. of India and Iran to profl. publs; translator Songs of Zarathustra. Recipient fellowships Ford Found., fellowships Woodrow Wilson Found., fellowships Yale U. Mem.: Societe Asiatique, Assn. Française des Sanskritists, Royal Asiatic Soc. Gt. Brit. and Ireland, Philological Soc., Cambridge, Eng., Deutsche Morgenlandische Gesellschaft, Am. Oriental Soc. (pres., fin. dir.), Am. Acad. Arts and Scis. Office: Yale U Dept Linguistics Box 208236 New Haven CT 06520-8236 E-mail: insler-stanley@yale.edu.

INTEMANN, ROBERT LOUIS, physics educator, researcher; b. North Bergen, N.J., Feb. 23, 1938; s. Joseph Louis and Mildred Henrietta (Wood) I.; m. Marguerite Carmela DiNonno, Aug. 22, 1964; 1 child, Peter Michael. BE, Stevens Inst. Tech., 1959, MS, 1961, PhD, 1964. Asst. prof. physics Temple U., Phila., 1964-73, assoc. prof. physics, 1973-84, prof., 1984—, chmn. dept., 1985-90, asst. dean Coll. Arts and Scis., 1971-81, assoc. dean Coll. Sci. and Tech., 2001—; 20795432. Vis. scientist Atomic Energy Research Establishment, Harwell, Eng., 1970. Contbr. articles on rsch in theoretical atomic physics. Mem. AAUP, Am. Phys. Soc., Am. Assn. Physics Tchrs., AAAS, Sigma Xi. Avocations: skiing, tennis, photography, travel. Home: 209 Roberts Ave Glenside PA 19038-4108 Office: Temple U Dept Physics Philadelphia PA 19122

INTILLI, SHARON MARIE, television director, small business owner; b. Amsterdam, N.Y., Aug. 11, 1950; d. Francisco Joseph Intilli and Virginia Eleanor (Tallman) Monaco. Cert., Paralegal Inst., 1973; BA in Psychology, Fordham U., 1995. Group assoc. editor Matthew Bender & Co., N.Y.C., 1974-77; prodn. sec. 20/20 program, ABC, N.Y.C., 1977-78, prodn. assoc., 1979-80, program prodn. asst., 1980-82; legal contract adminstr. ABC Sports, N.Y.C., 1978-79, dir., assoc. dir. for freelance projects, 1984-87; staff assoc. dir. ABC Television Network, N.Y.C., 1982-98; freelance assoc. dir., 1998—. Owner GreenBeing, Inc. Contbg. editor Bender's Forms of Discovery, Vols. 15 & 16, 1975. Active Bd. Health, Hillsdale, N.J., 1989-95. Recipient Outstanding Individual Achievement cert. Nat. Acad. TV Arts & Scis., 1980-81. Mem. Dirs. Guild of Am. Avocations: writing, photography, cooking, baking, singing. Office: 310 W 91st St # 3 New York NY 10024 E-mail: greenbe@worldnet.att.net. *I believe that, if we are to "make a difference" in our lives and in the lives of others, it is of utmost importance to push past our fears and insecurities and self-centeredness and envision what speaking up or reaching out might actually accomplish. Then visualize doing nothing and think about what that might mean. Your course will be clear.*

INTRATER, CHERYL WATSON WAYLOR, career management consultant; b. Montreal, Que., Can., Sept. 8, 1943; naturalized, 1978; d. Alan Douglas and Jean Mary (Hughes) Watson; m. Donald L. Intrater, Nov. 11, 1990. BBA, Ga. State U., 1980. CPCU. Instr. ins. DeKalb Coll., Clarkston, Ga., 1978-79; mgr. divsn. Kemper Group, 1979-85; owner Ins. Support Svcs., Inc., Overland Park, Kans., 1986-91; v.p. Fortune and Co. Risk Mgrs., Inc., Overland Park, 1987—94. Owner Career Trend, Overland Park, 1994-97; v.p. orgnl. devel. and outplacement, ptnr., prin., career mgmt. cons. Alexander, Hoyt & Assocs., Overland Park, 1997-2001; owner Career Sys., Overland Park, Kans., 2001-; sr. cons. CSG Ptnrs. Inc., Overland Park, 2001-; dir. Career Mgmt. Svcs., Jewish Vocat. Svc., Overland Park, Kans., 2002—; adv. coun. Johnson County C.C. Ins. Inst., Overland Park, 1990—; lectr. in field. Mem. Ctrl. Exchange, 1998—. Mem. Nat. Assn. Ins. Women (named Region V Ins. Profl. of Yr. 1992, cert. profl. ins. woman, Outstanding Mem. of Yr. 1992), Assn. of Career Profls. Internat. of Kansas City (charter mem. 2001, pres. 2002), CPCU Soc. (Kansas City chpt.). Republican. Avocations: fitness training, reading, traveling.

INTRATOR, ORNA, statistician, educator, health services researcher; b. Tel Aviv, Dec. 1, 1960; came to U.S., 1986; d. Uri and Esther Kroch; m. Nathan Intrator; 2 children. BSc, Tel Aviv U., 1986; ScM, Brown U., 1988, PhD, 1991. Teaching asst. Brown U., Providence, 1986-90, rsch. asst., 1990-91, vis. asst. prof., 1991-92, asst. prof. rsch. dept cmty. health Ctr. for Gerontology and Health Care Rsch., 2000—; lectr., dir. lab. statis. cons. Hebrew U., 1993—99. Mem.: Am. Gerontol. Soc., Am. Statis. Soc., Sigma Chi. Address: 496 Morris Ave Providence RI 02906

INTRAVAIA, TONI, dance educator, journal editor; b. Covington, Ky., Oct. 11, 1922; d. Marion William Uhlschmidt and Mary Theresa Hellse; widowed; 1 child: Paul Joseph. BFA, W.Va. U., 1951; MS in Dance, Wis. U.; DMA in Dance, NYU. Cert. tchr. in dance notation. Dance asst. Nat. Music Camp, Interlochen, Mich., 1943-51; dir. dance workshop, Morgantown, W.Va., 1950-63, Carbondale, Ill., 1963—; artist in residence So. Ill. U., Carbondale, 1963-65, asst. in dance notation, 1965—. Dance cons. W.Va. U., Morgantown, Conn. Coll. Summer Sch. Dance, New London, dance notator human sys. rsch. com. So. Ill. U., Carbondale, 1960s, cons. biology dept. labanotator, guest lectr. fgn. lang. dept.; tchr. festivals and insts. Ohio, N.J., Pa., Mass., Calif., Utah, Va., Ill. and Colo., 1971-99; charter mem. NMC Concert Dance, Wichita Civic Ballet, TCU Ballet Co.; mem. Orchesis, Wis. U., W.Va. U. Author: And We Have Danced, Vol. II, 1982; co-author: (with Elizabeth Sherbon) On the Count of One, 1982; contbr. articles to profl. jours.; dir. numerous dance scores. Fundraiser Am. Cancer Soc., Jackson County, 1973—; treas., chmn. Youth Concerts, Carbondale, 1964—; mem. Pres.'s Coun. So. Ill. U. Found., 1994; dir. Children's Ballet Theater, Carbondale; active Arts Celebration, Carbondale, Arts Edn. Festival, So. Ill. U.; dir. religious edn. St. Francis Xavier, 1973—. Paul Harris fellow Rotary Club, Carbondale, 2000; recipient Cecchetti Coun. of Am. award Mich. U., 1966, Super Svc. award Lincoln Jr. H.S., Carbondale, 1977-78, 25 Yr. award Sacred Dance Guild Jour., Interlochen Day award, 1987, Unsung Hero award, 1987, Lay Leader in Edn. award Phi Delta Kappa, 1988, cert. appreciation Carbondale Cmty. Svc., 1994, Musical Tribute SIU, Carbondale, 2000; named to Hall of Fame Carbondale Elem. Sch. Dist. 95, 1989, Hon. Mayor, City of Carbondale, 1994. Mem. Dance Notation Bur. Inc., Internat. Double Reed Soc., Ill. Fedn. Music Clubs (treas. 1994—), Sacred Dance Guild (editor jour.), Am. Dance Guild, Meml. Hosp. Guild, Internat. Conf. Kinetography Laban (treas. 1990—), SIU Maga Mus., Carbondale Cmty. H.S. Music Boosters (life), St. Anthony Guild, St. Francis Xavier Women's Club, Morning Etude Club, So. Ill. U. Women's Club. Roman Catholic. Avocation: reading.

INTRIERE, ANTHONY DONALD, retired internist, gastroenterologist; b. Greenwich, Conn., May 9, 1920; s. Rocco and Angelina (Belcastro) I.; m. Carol A. Yarmey, Aug. 1, 1945; children: Sherry Shoemaker, Michael, Nancy M., Lisa A. MD, U. Mich., 1944. Intern New Rochelle (NY.) Hosp., 1944-45; pvt. practice Greenwich, 1947-53, Olney, Ill., 1956-61, Granite City, Ill., 1961—74, San Diego, 1974; fellow in internal medicine Cleve. Clinic, 1953-55; fellow in gastroenterology Lahey Clinic, Boston, 1955-56; ret., 1974. Capt. M.C., U.S. Army, 1945-47. Fellow Am. Coll. Gastroenterology (assoc.); mem. AMA, ACP (assoc.), Am. Soc. Internal Medicine, 50 Yr. Club Ill. Med. Soc. Home: 9981 Caminito Chirimolla San Diego CA 92131-2001 E-mail: tintriere@aol.com.

INTRILIGATOR, DEVRIE SHAPIRO, physicist; b. N.Y.C. d. Carl and Lillian Shapiro; m. Michael Intriligator; children: Kenneth, James, William, Robert. BS in Physics, MIT, 1962, MS, 1964; PhD in Planetary and Space Physics, UCLA, 1967. NRC-NASA rsch. assoc. NASA, Ames, Calif., 1967-69; rsch. fellow in physics Calif. Inst. Tech., Pasadena, 1969-72, vis. assoc., 1972-73; asst. prof. U. So. Calif., 1972-80; mem. Space Scis. Ctr., 1978-83; sr. rsch. physicist Carmel Rsch. Ctr., Santa Monica, Calif., 1979—; dir. Space Plasma Lab., 1980—. Cons. NASA, NOAA, Jet Propulsion Lab.; chmn. NAS-NRC com. on solar-terrestrial rsch., 1983-86, exec. com. bd. atmospheric sci. and climate, 1983-86, geophysics study com., 1983-86; U.S. nat. rep. Sci. Com. on Solar-Terrestrial Physics, 1983-86; mem. adv. com. NSF Divsn. Atmospheric Sci. Co-editor: Exploration of the Outer Solar System, 1976; contbr. articles to profl. jours. Recipient 3 Achievement awards NASA, Calif. Resolution of Commendation, 1982. Mem. AAAS, Am. Phys. Soc., Am. Geophys. Union, Cosmos Club. Achievements include being a participant Pioneer 10/11 missions to outer planets; Pioneer Venus Orbiter, Pioneers 6, 7, 8 and 9 heliocentric missions. Home: 140 Foxtail Dr Santa Monica CA 90402-2048 Office: Carmel Rsch Ctr PO Box 1732 Santa Monica CA 90406-1732

INTRILIGATOR, MARC STEVEN, lawyer; b. Oceanside, N.Y., July 14, 1952; s. Alan and Sally (Jacobs) I.; m. Roxann Kathleen Hoff, Aug. 28, 1977; children: Seth Adam, Joshua Ross, David Benjamin. BA, SUNY, Binghamton, 1974; JD, Boston U., 1977. Bar: N.Y. 1978. Assoc. Dreyer and Traub, N.Y.C., 1977-83, assoc. ptnr., 1984-85, sr. ptnr., 1985-96; of counsel Fischbein Badillo Wagner Harding, N.Y.C., 1996—. Projects editor: Boston U. law rev., 1976-77. Past pres. Croton Jewish Ctr., Highlands Country Club. Mem. ABA, Assn. Bar City N.Y., The Country Club at Lake MacGregor, Tau Epsilon Phi. Office: Fischbein Badillo Wagner Harding 909 3rd Ave New York NY 10022-4731 E-mail: mintrili@fbwhlaw.com.

INTRILIGATOR, MICHAEL DAVID, economist, educator; b. N.Y.C., Feb. 5, 1938; s. Allan and Sally Intriligator; m. Devrie Shapiro; children: Kenneth, James, William, Robert. SB in Econs., MIT, 1959; MA, Yale U., 1960; PhD, MIT, 1963. Asst. prof. econs. UCLA, 1963—66, assoc. prof., 1968—72, prof., 1972—, prof. dept. polit. sci., 1981—, prof. dept. policy studies, 1994—, dir. Ctr. Internat. and Strategic Affairs, 1982—92, 2000—02; dir. Jacob Marschak Interdisciplinary Coll., 1977—; dir. Burkle Ctr. Internat. Rels., 2000—02. Cons. Inst. Def. Analysis, 1974—77, ACDA, 1968, Rand Corp., 1962—65; sr. fellow Milken Inst., 1998—. Author: Mathematical Optimization and Economic Theory, 1971; author: (with Ronald Bodkin and Cheng Hsiao) Econometric Models, Techniques, and Applications, 1996; author: (with others) A Forecasting and Policy Simulation Model of the Health Care Sector, 1979; mem. adv. editl. bd.: Math. Social Scis., 1983—; editor (assoc. editor): Jour. Optimization Theory and Applications, 1979—91, Conflict Mgmt. and Peace Sci., 1980—; co-editor: (series) Handbook sin Economics, 1980—, Advanced Textbooks in Economics, 1972—; editor (with Kenneth J. Arrow): (book) Handbook of Mathematical Economics, 3 vols., 1981—85; editor: (with Zvi Griliches) Handbook of Econometrics, 3 vols., 1983—86; editor: (with B. Brodie and R. Kolkowicz) National Security and International Stability, 1983; editor: (with H. A. Jacobsen) East-West Conflict: Elite Perceptions and Political Opinions, 1988; editor: numerous others; contbr. articles to profl. jours. Recipient Disting. Tchg. award, UCLA, 1966, Warren C. Scoville Disting. Tchg. award, 1976, 1979, 1982, 1984; fellow Woodrow Wilson, 1959—60, MIT, 1960—61, Ford, 1967—68. Fellow: AAAS, Econometric Soc.; mem.: Russian Acad. Sci., Coun. Fgn. Rels., Internat. Inst. Strategic Studies. Office: UCLA Dept Econs Los Angeles CA 90095-0001 Business E-Mail: intriligator@econ.ucla.edu.

INUI, THOMAS SPENCER, physician, educator; b. Balt., July 10, 1943; s. Frank Kazuo and Beulah Mae (Sheetz) Inui; m. Nancy Stowe, June 14, 1969; 1 child, Tazo Stowe. BA, Haverford Coll., 1965; MD, Johns Hopkins U., 1969, ScM, 1973. Diplomate Am. Bd. Internal Medicine. Intern Johns Hopkins Hosp., Balt., 1969—70, resident in internal medicine, 1970—73; clin. scholar Johns Hopkins U., Balt., 1971—73, chief resident, instr., 1973—74; chief of medicine USPHS Indian Hosp., Albuquerque, 1974—76; chief gen. medicine, dir. health svc. rsch. Seattle VA Med. Ctr., 1976—86; dir. Robert Wood Johnson clin. scholars program U. Wash., Seattle, 1977—92, prof. dept. medicine and health svcs., 1985—92, head div. gen. internal medicine, 1986—92; prof., chmn. of dept. ambulatory care and prevention Harvard Med. Sch. and Harvard Pilgrim Health Care, Boston, 1992—2000; pres., CEO Fetzer Inst., 2000—01, Regenstrief Inst., Indianapolis, 2002—. Scholar-in-residence Assn. Am. Med. Coll., 2002. Contbr. articles to profl. publs. Surgeon USPHS, 1974—76. Fellow: ACP; mem.: APHA (mem. coun. 1988—90), Inst. Medicine, Soc. Tchrs. Family Medicine, Assn. Health Svcs. Rsch., Am. Fedn. Med. Rsch., Soc. Gen. Internal Medicine (pres. 1988—89, mem. coun. 1983—89), Alpha Omega Alpha, Phi Beta Kappa. Office: Regenstrief Institute 1050 Wishard Blvd RG-6 Indianapolis IN 46202 E-mail: tinui@iupui.edu.

INVERSO, MARLENE JOY, optometrist; b. Los Angeles, May 10, 1942; d. Elmer Encel Wood and Sally Marie (Sample) Hirons; m. John S. Inverso, Dec. 16, 1962; 1 child, Christopher Edward. BA, Calif. State U., Northridge, 1964; MS, SUNY, Potsdam, 1975; OD, Pacific U., 1981. Cert. doctor optometry, Wash., Oreg. English tchr. Chatsworth (Calif.) High Sch., 1964-68, Nelson A. Boylen Second Sch., Toronto, Ont., Can., 1968-70, Gouverneur (N.Y.) Jr.-Sr. High Sch., 1970-74, 76-77; reading resource room tchr. Parishville (N.Y.) Hopkinton Sch., 1974-75; optometrist and vision therapist Am. Family Vision Clinics, Olympia, Wash., 1982—. Coord. Lng. Disability Clin. SUNY, summers, 1975-77; mem. adv. com. Sunshine House St. Peter Hosp., Olympia, 1984-86, Pacific U. Coll. Optometry, Forest Grove, Oreg. 1986. Contbr. articles to profl. jours. Mem. Altrusa Svc. Club, Olympia, 1982-86; tchr. Ch. Living Water, Olympia, 1983-88, Olympia-Lacey Ch. of God, 1989—, sec. women's bd., 1990; bd. advisors Crisis Pregnancy Ctr., Olympia, 1987-89; den mother Cub Scouts Am. Pack 202, Lacey, Wash., 1987-88; vol. World Vision Countertop ptnr., 1986-97. Fellow Coll. Optometrists in Optometric Devel.; mem. Am. Optometric Assn. (sec. 1983-84), Assn. Children and Adults with Learning Disabilities, Optometric Extension Program, Sigma Xi, Beta Sigma Kappa. Avocations: bible study, professional speaking, training, and teaching. Home: 4336 Libby Rd NE Olympia WA 98506-2555

INVERSO, PETER A. state legislator; b. Trenton, N.J., Dec. 24, 1938; m. Geraldine Gonos, 1962; children: Donna Maria, Marylyn, Susan, Anthony, Diana. BS, Rider U., 1960. CPA, CGFM. Freeholder Mercer County, N.J., 1981-83, 87-89; mem. N.J. Senate, Dist. 14, Trenton, 1991—. Ptnr. Druker, Rahl and Fein. Address: 3625 Quakerbridge Rd Hamilton NJ 08619-1207*

INZANA, BARBARA ANN, professional musician, educator; b. Milw., Mar. 21, 1939; d. Joseph Lindsley and Marie Julia (Haerter) Raynor; m. John Thomas Inzana, June 19, 1965; children: Carolyn Marie, JoAnn Marian. BMus in Edn., Violin, Ind. U., 1961, MMus in Theory, 1969. Music tchr. Deerfield (Ill.) Pub. Schs., 1961—63; grad. teaching asst. theory dept. Ind. U. Music Sch., Bloomington, 1963—65; tchr. music St. James Elem. Sch., Falls Church, Va.,

1975—82, St. Mary's Elem. Sch., Alexandria, Va., 1982—83; master tchr. music George Washington U., Washington, 1983—91; choir dir., soloist Nativity Ch., Burke, Va., 1986—91; music dir. Burke Presbyn. Ch., 1992—2002; substitute tchr. Fairfax County (Va.) Schs., 2002—. Pvt. instr. voice, violin, viola, piano, composition and theory, Falls Church, Va.; vocal cons. St. Phillips Ch., Falls Church, 1990—91; poster presenter Nat. Voice Found., 2001. Pub. Washerwoman's Holiday for intermediate string orch., 1997, He Is Born, the Holy One, soprano/alto, flute and piano. Mem. AFTRA, SAG, Am. Guild Mus. Artists, Am. String Tchrs. Assn., N.Am. Bluebird Assn., Ind. U. Alumni Assn. (life). Home: 403 W Rosemary Ln Falls Church VA 22046-3847

INZANO, KAREN LEE, advertising agency executive; b. Cleve., July 27, 1946; d. William and Edith (Fisher) Phipps; children: Thomas, Laura, Sharon. Student, Litschert Sch. of Comml. Art, Cleve., 1970-72. Pres., founder AK Graphics Inc., Lakewood, Colo., 1973—2001; exec. dir. Rocky Mt. Coal Mining Inst., 2000—. Instr. advt. and small bus. Red Rocks C.C., 1983-90, mem. mktg. adv. bd., 1986-88. Chmn. Ch. Adminstrv. Bd., audio, visual adv. bd., 1995-97, Red Rocks, C.C.; active caucus Colo. Rep. Com., 1980, Green Mountain Homeowners, Lakewood, 1980-84; sr. v.p. Lakewood on Parade, 1985-86; bd. dirs. Lakewood Sister Cities Internat., 1980-89, Lakewood Civic Found., 1986-94; vol. Children's Advocacy Ctr., 1994-97vol. tchr. Children's Ct. Sch., Jefferson County; mem. D.A.'s Adv. Bd., 1992-94. Named State Champion of Free Enterprise Salesman With A Purpose, 1985; recipient Disting. Svc. award Sister Cities Internat., 1984. Mem. Jefferson County C. of C. (bd. dirs. 1980-90, chmn. bd. 1988-89, Small Bus. Person of Yr. 1982), Denver Advt. Fedn. Typographers Internat. Assn., Mac Users Group # 2, Edn. 200 #3, Woman Bus. Owners, Colo. Soc. Assn. Execs., Colo. Mining Assn. Avocations: tennis, travel, golf. Home and Office: 8057 S Yukon Way Littleton CO 80128-5510 Office: 8057 S Yukon Way Littleton CO 80128-5510 E-mail: mail@rmcml.org.

INZETTA, MARK STEPHEN, lawyer; b. N.Y.C., Apr. 14, 1956; s. James William and Rose Delores (Cirnigliaro) I.; m. Sharon Inzetta; children: Michelle, Margot, Mallory. BBA summa cum laude, U. Cin., 1977; JD, U. Akron, 1980. Bar: Ohio 1980, U.S. Dist. Ct. (no. dist.) Ohio 1980. Legal intern City of Canton, Ohio, 1979-80; assoc. W.J. Ross Co., LPA, Canton, 1980-84; v.p., asst. gen. counsel Wendy's Internat. Inc., Columbus, Ohio, 1984—. Instr. real estate law Stark Tech. Coll., Canton, 1983. Case and comment editor: Akron Law Rev., 1979-80. Bd. dirs. Brookside Village Civic Assn., 1985—87, treas., 1986—87; bd. dirs. Ct. Apptd. Spl. Advocates of Franklin County, Ohio, Dublin Cmty. Counselling Ctr.; legis. dir. Children's and Parents' Rights Assn., 1996—97, chmn., 1997—, State of Ohio Child Support Guidelines Commn., 1995—97, 1999—2001; treas. State of Ohio Task Force on Family Law and Children, 1998—2001; asst. coach Worthington Kilbourne H.S. Varsity Girls Lacrosse Team, 2002; chmn. campaign Earle Wise Appellate Judge, North Canton, Ohio, 1982; instr. religious edn. St. Peter's Cath. Ch. Recipient Am. Jurisprudence award Lawyers Coop. Pub. Co., 1978, Dir. of Yr. award North Canton Jaycees, 1982, Presdl. award of honor, 1984, Dist. Dir. award of honor Ohio Jaycees, 1984, Vol. of Yr. award Children's Rights Coun., 2001. Mem. ABA, Ohio Bar Assn., North Canton Jaycees (bd. dirs. 1981-82, v.p. 1982-83, pres. 1983-84), North Canton C. of C. (bd. dirs. 1983-84). Roman Catholic. Home: 295 Weatherburn Ct Powell OH 43065 Office: Wendy's Internat Inc 4288 W Dublin Granville Rd Dublin OH 43017-1442 E-mail: mark_inzetta@wendys.com.

IOANES, JOYCE, lawyer, social worker; b. Washington, Feb. 23, 1944; d. Raymond Andrew and Irma Elizabeth (Blazo) I. BA in French Lit., Dunbarton Coll., 1965; MS in Psychiat. Social Work, Simmons Coll., 1971; JD cum laude, Suffolk U., 1983. Bar: R.I. 1983, U.S. Cts. 1984, Mass. 1985; cert. Acad. Cert. Social Workers, 1978. Social caseworker R.I. Dept. Social and Rehab. Svcs., Cranston, Providence, 1968-74, casework supr. Cranston, Johnston, 1974-77; therapist Northwestern Mental Health Clinic, Greenville, R.I., 1974-75, Washington County Mental Health Clinic, Charlestown, R.I., 1977-79; mental health profl. R.I. Mental Health Advs. Office, Cranston, 1977—, atty., 1983—; sole practice law Jamestown, 1983—. Field instr. R.I. Coll., Roger Williams Coll., 1975-77, Providence Coll., 1975-81; mem. Gov.'s Task Force Community Placement of Geriatric Patients, 1977-81. Recipient Am. Jurisprudence award, 1980-81, R.I. Cmty. Person of Yr. award, 1993. Mem. ABA, Nat. Assn. Social Workers, Mass. Bar Assn., R.I. Bar Assn. Avocations: bicycling, gardening. Home: 78 Columbia Ave Jamestown RI 02835-1345 Office: RI Mental Health Cottage 405 Cranston RI 02920

IOANNOV, GEORGE N. gastroenterologist, researcher; b. Nicosia, Cyprus, Apr. 23, 1970; s. Nikolas G. and Georgia C. Ioannov; m. Jannicke Tvedt, May 5, 2000; 1 child, Nikolas. BA, Oxford U., 1993, MD, 1996; MS, U. Wash., 2002. Resident Oxford U. Hosp., England, 1996—97, Duke U. Med. Ctr., Durham, NC, 1997—2000; fellow U. Wash., Seattle, 2002—03. Contbr. articles to profl. jours. Sgt. U.S. Army, 1988—90. Fellow, VA Med. Ctr., Seattle, 2000—01; scholar Hobson Meml. scholar, Oxford U., 1973—76. Mem.: Am. Soc. Gastroent., Am. Gastroent. Assn. Avocations: literature, exercise, travel. Home: 3805 SW Admiral Way Seattle WA 98126 Office: Seattle VA Med Ctr 1660 S Columbian Way MS 152 Seattle WA 98108

IODICE, ARTHUR ALFONSO, biochemist; b. Rome, N.Y., Nov. 7, 1928; s. Gaetano and Loretta (Pace) Iodice. AB, Columbia U., 1950; PhD, SUNY, Syracuse, 1958. Postdoctoral fellow U. Calif., Berkeley, 1958-60, rsch. assoc., 1960-62, Inst. Muscle Disease, N.Y.C., 1962-65, asst. mem., 1965-69, assoc. mem., 1969-74; rsch. scientist Masonic Med. Rsch. Lab., Utica, N.Y., 1975—. Contbr. articles to profl. jours. Jane Coffin Childs Meml. Fund med. rsch., postdoctoral fellow U. Calif., 1958-60. Mem. AAAS, Electrophysiol. Soc., Am. Heart Assn., N.Y. Acad. Scis. Home: PO Box 663 Rome NY 13442-0663 Office: Masonic Med Rsch Lab 2150 Bleecker St Utica NY 13501-1738

IOFFE, GRIGORY, geography educator, researcher; b. Moscow, Oct. 21, 1951; s. Victor and Raisa I.; m. Yelena Kulagina, May 12, 1979; children: Mikhail, Nataliya. MA in Geography, Moscow State U., 1974; PhD in Geography, USSR Acad. Scis., 1980. Rsch. assoc. Inst. Rural Constrn. & Physical Planning, Moscow, 1974-80, Inst. Geography, USSR Acad. Scis., Moscow, 1980-88, dept. chair, 1988-89; asst. prof. geography Radford (Va.) U., 1990-94, assoc. prof. geography, 1994-00, full prof. geography, 2000—. Cons. com. on population NAS, Washington, 1994. Author: Agriculture in Non-Chernozem Zone, 1990; co-author: Continuity and Change in Rural Russia, 1997; co-editor: Population Under Duress: Geodemography of Post-Soviet Russia, 1999; ; co-author: The Environs of Russian Cities, 2000; mem. editl. bd. Columbia Gazeteer of the World, N.Y.C., 1998, Eurasian Geography and Economics, 2002—. Recipient Nat. Coun. for Soviet and East European Rsch., Washington 1995, 97, 99, NSF, 2002. Mem.: Am. Assn. Advancement Slavic Studies, Assn. Am. Geographers.

IONA, MARIO, retired physics educator; b. Berlin, June 17, 1917; came to U.S., 1941, naturalized, 1948; s. Mario G.V. and Dorothee (Berendes) I.; m. Nancy Mossman, Aug. 31, 1949; children: Steven, Ann. PhD, U. Vienna, Austria, 1939; postgrad., U. Uppsala, Sweden, 1939-41. Research asst., instr. U. Chgo., 1941-46; from asst. prof. to prof. physics U. Denver, 1946-85, prof. emeritus, 1985—; coord. High Altitude Labs., Mt. Evans and Echo Lake, Colo., 1946-82; cons. pvt. practice Denver, 1985—. Cons. Denver Schs., 1962-65, 84, Jefferson County Schs., Golden, Colo., 1973, Adams County Sch. Dist. 12, Northglenn, Colo., 1985, Internat. Orgn. for Standardization, tech. adv. group TC 12, 1990—; vis. prof. U. No. Colo., 1971; specialist U. Saugar, India, 1966; cons. in field. Assoc. editor: Physics Tchr., 1962-65, column editor, 1970-2000. Treas., sec., pres. Group Health Assn., Denver, 1952-66. Fellow AAAS; mem. Am. Phys. Soc., Am. Assn. Physics Tchrs. (chmn. com. on SI units and metric edn. 1987-91, Disting. Svc. citation 1971, Millikan Lecture award 1986), Colo.-Wyo. Acad. Sci. (pres. 1974-75), Nat. Sci. Tchrs. Assn., AAUP. Home: 2333 S Columbine St Denver CO 80210-5421 Office: U Denver Dept Physics & Astronomy Denver CO 80208-2238

IONASCU, ILEANA, mathematician, educator; b. Bucharest, Romania, Apr. 23, 1961; d. Alexandru and Ecaterina-Eugenia Ionascu. BS in Math., U. Bucharest, Romania, 1984, MS in Math., 1985; PhD in Math., U. New Hamsphire, 1994. H.s. tchr., Tirgoviste, Romania, 1985—87; jr. rschr. Math. Inst. of Romanian Acad. Scis., Bucharest, 1987—90; tchg. asst., lectr. U. N.H., Durham, 1990—94; fellow, lectr. U. Waterloo, Canada, 1994—96; lectr. U. Tex., Austin, 1996—98; vis. asst. prof. Ursinus Coll., Collegeville, Pa., 1998—99; asst. prof. Houston Bapt. U., 1999—. Mem.: Math. Assn. Am. Office: Houston Baptist Univ 7502 Fondren Rd Houston TX 77074 E-mail: iionascu@hbu.edu.

IONESCU TULCEA, CASSIUS, research mathematician, educator; b. Bucharest, Rumania, Oct. 14, 1923; naturalized, 1967; s. Ioan and Ana (Caselli) Ionescu Tulcea. MS, U. Bucarest, 1946; PhD, Yale, 1959. Mem. faculty U. Bucarest, 1946-57, assoc. prof., 1952-57; research assoc. Yale U., 1957-59, vis. lectr., 1959-61; assoc. prof. U. Pa., 1961-64; prof. U. Ill., Urbana, 1964-66, Northwestern U., Evanston, Ill., 1966-90, prof. emeritus, 1990—. Author: Hilbert Spaces (in Rumanian), 1956, A Book on Casino Craps, 1980, A Book on Casino Blackjack, 1982; co-author: Probability Calculus (in Rumanian), 1956, Calculus, 1968, An Introduction to Calculus, 1969, Honors Calculus, 1970, Topics in the Theory of Liftings, 1969, Sets, 1971, Topology, 1971, A Book on Casino Gambling, 1976; contbr. articles to profl. jours. Recipient Asachi prize Rumanian Acad., 1957. Office: Northwestern U 2033 Sheridan Rd Evanston IL 60208-0830

IOPPOLO, FRANK S., JR., lawyer; b. Rockville Centre, N.Y., Nov. 13, 1966; s. Frank S. and Carmela L. (Marrone) I. BA, Wake Forest U., 1988; JD, Fordham U., 1991. Bar: Fla. 1991, U.S. Dist. Ct. (mid. dist.) Fla. 1991, D.C. 1992, N.Y. 1992, U.S. Dist. Ct. (so. dist.) Fla. 1992, U.S. Supreme Ct. 1995. Assoc. Baker & Hostetler, Orlando, Fla., 1991-96; shareholder Greenberg Traurig, Orlando, 1996—. Bd. regents Leadership Fla., 1995-96, 97-98; chmn. bd. Ronald McDonald House Ctrl. Fla., 2002—; bd. dirs. Assoc. Marine Insts., Inc., 1995-97; pres., chmn. bd. Bay Point of Bay Hill Property Owners Assn., Inc., Orlando, 1994-96; bd. dirs. Seminole C.C. Found., 2002—. Mem. ABA, Fla. Bar Assn., Orange County Bar Assn., N.Y. State Bar Assn., D.C. Bar Assn., Wake Forest U. Alumni Assn. Ctrl. Fla. (pres. 1995-98), Seminole County, C. of C. (gen. counsel, 2001—), Seminole Coll. Found. (bd. dirs. 2001—). Avocations: sailing, snow and water skiing, reading, fishing, target shooting. Office: Greenberg Traurig Ste 650 450 S Orange Ave Orlando FL 32801-2316

IORIO, DOMINICK ANTHONY, philosophy educator, dean; b. Trenton, NJ, Sept. 13, 1931; s. Salvatore Iorio and Josephine D'Angelo; m. Stella M. Paterno, Jan. 26, 1957; children: Stephen, Michele. AB, Seton Hall U., 1955; AM, Fordham U., 1960, PhD, 1966. Asst. prof. Trenton Jr. Coll., 1957-65; from asst. prof. to assoc. prof. Rider Coll., Lawrenceville, N.J., 1965-90, dep. chair philosophy, 1969-73, prof., 1990-97, dean Coll. Liberal Arts and Sci., 1973-97, dean, prof. philosophy emeritus, 1997—. Cons. Thomas Edison State Coll., Trenton, 1983-00; chair bd. advisors Holy Ghost Prep., Cornwell, Pa., 1982-85; cons. program rev. N.J. Dept. Higher Edn., Trenton, 1975-79. Author: (book) Aristotelians of Renaissance Italy, 1991; co-editor: (book) The Holocaust: Lessons for the Third Generation, 1997; editor, transl.: (book) Malebranche: Dialogue Between a Christian Philosopher and a Chinese Philosopher, 1980. Elected mem. Bd. Freeholders, Mercer County, N.J., 1971-73; commr. Park Commn., Mercer County, 1974-81; chmn. N.J. Edn. Adv. Com., Trenton, 1982-86. Specialist 3d class U.S. Army, 1955-56. Recipient Cor Ad Cor Loquitor medal Newman Movement, 1964, Disting. Svc. award Gov.'s Edn. Adv. Com., 1986, Enrico Fermi Fedn. award, 1974. Mem. Internat. Soc. Christian Scholars, Am. Philos. Assn., Am. Cath. Philos. Assn., Renaissance Soc. Am., Soc. Europeene de Culture, Assn. for Philosophy of Edn. (dir.). Republican. Roman Catholic. Avocations: philately, numismatics, traveling. Home: 201 Berwyn Pl Lawrenceville NJ 08648-3607 E-mail: ioriotesc@earthlink.net.

IORIO, JOHN EMIL, retired education educator; b. Bklyn., Dec. 20, 1932; s. Frederick and Helen (Grandillo) I.; m. Helen Capobianco, Dec. 20, 1958; children: Frederick Joseph, John Richard. BS in Polit Sci., Manhattan Coll., 1954; MS in Elem. Edn., Bklyn. Coll., 1967; profl. diploma Adminstrn./Supervision, Fordham U., 1984. Cert. elem. tchr., adminstr., prin. supt. N.Y.S., N.Y.C. Elem. tchr. N.Y.C., 1965-72; adminstrv. asst. P.S. 214K, Dist. 19, N.Y.C., 1972-74, asst. prin., 1974-75; adminstr. Office of Fed. and State Reimbursable Programs, N.Y.C., 1975-76; asst. prin. Ps. 153Q, Dist. 24, N.Y.C., 1976; asst. prin., head of sch. PS 128Q Dist. 24, Queens, N.Y., 1976-79, prin., 1979-87; community supt. Dist. 24, Queens, 1987-90. Adj. prof. Fordham U., 1991; presenter at many ednl. confs. and workshops. 1983-90. Contbr. articles to profl. jours. Recipient Builder of Brotherhood award, Nat. Conf. Christians and Jews, 1981, Arts in Edn. Programs award, Young Audiences of N.Y., 1989, Project Innovation Spl. Merit award, Education mag., 1990, others; named Educator of Yr. Assn. Tchrs. of N.Y., 1988; grantee Nat. Endowment for Humanities, 1981. Home: 155-57 Bridgeton St Howard Beach NY 11414-2809

IOSEBASHVILI, ALEXANDER, research scientist, educator; b. Tbilisi, Georgia, Russia, Jan. 26, 1965; came to U.S., 1978; s. Otar and Rachael (Krikhel) I. DSc, NYU, 1991. Rsch. sci. Exxon-Mobil Co., N.Y.C. Hon. prof. sci. NYU, 1993. Organizer internat. collaboration for unity of scis. and their orgns. for helping humanity; mem. Am. Mus. Natural History, Nat. Geog. Soc., N.Y. Pub. Libr., Am. Liver Found., Chem. Horzon Found./AIChE. Recipient Cert. Excellence and Honor for Achievements in Sci.; Nobel prize for significant achievements and contbn. to worldwide humanity, Am. medal of Honor, Am. Biographical Inst., 2002, 03, Internat. Peace Prize, 2002, Congl. medal of excellence, Am. Biographical Inst., 2003, Presdl. Seal of Honor award Am. Biog. Inst., 2003; named to World order of Sci.-Edn.-Culture, 2002. Mem. AAAS, N.Y. Acad. Sci., Am. Psychol. Soc., Mus. Nat. History, Acad. Polit. Scis., Astron. Soc. of Pacific, Drs. of World, People's Med. Soc., Smithsonian Inst. Jewish. Achievements include research in important postulated scientific information scientific material in different spheres; analysis and discovering scientific problems of a crime; explanation and postulation mathematically, physico-philosophically and cosmologically of the questions regarding the interpretation of connection and nucleus, issues of classification of transformation of conception ONE into conception TWO; investigation of corruption, basically medical, especially in mental health system, dimining the death penalty and protection of the citizens, young women and young people, field of physico-atomic-cybernetical systems, initiative of pragmatic role of young females in participating in the moral medicine. Home: 99 05 63rd Dr Apt 9 V Rego Park NY 11374

IOVEL, ALLA, music educator, writer, pianist; arrived in U.S., 1999; d. Michael Shteinberg and Klara Gerlorina; m. Lev Iovel, Dec. 30, 1969; 1 child, Aleksandr. MusB in music theory, Music Coll., Leningrad, Russia, 1969; M in Music Edn., Leningrad State Conservatory, Russia, 1975. Cert. music edn. Pedagogical Inst., Ukraine, 1970. Tchr. piano Bloomfield Coll. Author: (textbook) Instrnl. Points and Methods on Theory of Harmony for Musical Educators, 1993, Lugansk State Coll. of Music, 1999; contbr. chapters to books, articles to profl. jours. Named to Golden Cir. of Tchrs., A.G. De Grado Found., 2001, 2002. Mem.: Music Tchrs. Nat. Assn., Piano Tchr. Soc. of Am. (High Honor Tchrs. award 2001, 2002), The Leschetizky Assn. Achievements include research in technical analysis of musical styles. Avocation: gardening. Home: 4 Lyons Place East Hanover NJ 07936

IOVINE, JIMMY, recording industry executive; b. Bklyn., 1953; s. Jimmy Iovine Sr.. Former engr. The Record Plant, N.Y.C.; ind. prodr., co-head Interscope Records, 1991—. Office: c/o Interscope Comm 10900 Wilshire Blvd Ste 1230 Los Angeles CA 90024-6532

IPPEN, ERICH PETER, electrical engineer, educator, physicist; b. Fountain Hill, Pa., Mar. 29, 1940; s. Arthur Thomas and Elisabeth Anne (Wagenplatz) I.; m. Dorothea Ellen Swensen, Sept. 24, 1966; children: Erich Peter, Jason Timothy. S.B., MIT, 1962; MS, U. Calif.-Berkeley, 1965, PhD, 1968. Mem. tech. staff Bell Labs., Holmdel, N.J., 1968-80; vis. prof. MIT, Cambridge, 1977-78, prof. elec. engring., 1980—, Elihu Thomson prof. elec. engring., 1987—, prof. physics, 1996—. Cons. Bell Labs., 1981-2000, Allied Corp., Mt. Bethel, N.J., 1982-90, MIT Lincoln Lab., 1999—. Contbr. articles to profl. jours.; patentee in field. Recipient Edward Longstreth medal Franklin Inst., 1982, Harold E. Edgerton award Soc. Photo-Optical Instrumentation Engrs., 1989, John Scott award City of Phila., 1991, Disting. Engring. Alumnus award U. Calif., Berkeley, 2000, MIT Killian award, 2001. Fellow Am. Acad. Arts and Scis., Optical Soc. Am. (R.W. Wood prize 1981), IEEE (Morris E. Leeds award 1983, Quantum Elecs. award 1997), Am. Phys. Soc. (Arthur L. Schawlow prize 1997); mem. NAS, NAE, Sigma Xi. Home: 156 School St Belmont MA 02478-3516 Office: MIT 77 Massachusetts Ave Cambridge MA 02139-4307 E-mail: ippen@mit.edu.

IPPOLITO, CHRISTOPHE, language educator; Diplome Études Approfondies, U. Paris IV, 1986; M in French, U. Paris III, 1992; PhD in French, Columbia U., 1998. French lectr. U. East Asia, Macau, China, 1988—90; French instr. Acad. Versailles, France, 1990—92; tchg. asst., instr. Columbia U., N.Y.C., 1993—98, acting adminstr. French House, 1996—98; vis. asst. prof. French Hamilton Coll., Clinton, NY, 1998—99, Amherst (Mass.) Coll., 1999—2001, Dickinson Coll., Carlisle, Pa., 2001—03; asst. prof. French U. Pacific, Stockton, Calif., 2003—. Author: Narrative Memory in Flaubert's Works, 2001; contbr. articles to profl. jours. Fellow Rsch., French and Egyptian Govts., 1986—88, Pres.', Columbia U., 1993—98; grantee Faculty Rsch., Amherst Coll., 1999. Mem.: MLA, Am. Coun. on Tchg. of Fgn. Langs., Women in French. Office: Univ Pacific Dept Modern Lang and Lit 3601 Pacific Ave Stockton CA 95211

IPPOLITO, MARIA F. psychologist, educator; b. Chgo., June 29, 1950; d. Robert Phillip and Florence Marie Ippolito; m. James Zarembski, Apr. 1993 (div. 1994). BA in English Lit., Knox Coll., 1972; postgrad., Northwestern U., 1985—88; MA in Psychology, Bowling Green State U., 1993, PhD in Psychology, 1998. Vis. prof. Bowling Green (Ohio) State U., 1999—2000; asst. prof. U. Alaska, Anchorage, 2000—. Presenter in field. Contbr. articles to profl. jours. Bd. mem. Child Care Connection, Inc., Anchorage, 2000—01, sec. bd. dirs., 2001—. Mem.: APA (divsn. 2 tchg. of psychology, divsn. 10 psychology and the arts), Soc. for the Social Studies of Sci., Soc. for Lit. and Sci., Internat. Soc. for the History of Behavioral and Social Scis., Cognitive Sci. Soc., Am. Psychol. Soc. Office: Univ Alaska Anchorage 3211 Providence Dr Anchorage AK 99508

IQBAL, TARIQ, physics educator, researcher; b. Wahcantt, Punjab, Pakistan, Nov. 6, 1950; s. Mohammad and Sakina (Bibi) Sharif; m. Ghazala Nasreen, June 8, 1979; 3 children. BSc, Punjab U., 1971; MSc in Physics, Quaid-e-Azam U., Pakistan, 1975; PhD in Exptl. Condensed Matter Physics, Brunel U., Eng., 1980. Microsoft Cert. Profl, 2000, Microsoft Cert. Sys. Engr., 2000. Lectr. in physics Islamia U., Pakistan, 1975-80, asst. prof. physics, 1980 87; rsch. assoc. Rutgers U., New Brunswick, N.J., 1987-93; assoc. prof. applied physics Ghulam Ishaq Khan Inst. Engring. Scis. and Tech., Pakistan, 1993-97; cons. Info. Tech., West Palm Beach, Fla., 1998-99; computer specialist West Palm Beach, Fla., 1999-2001; sys. adminstr. City of Riviera Beach, Fla., 2001—. Adj. faculty Middlesex County Coll., N.J., 1991-93; vis. faculty Fla. State U., summer 1997. Contbr. articles to Thin Films, Electronics Letters, Optics Letters, Jour. Materials Rsch., others. Sec. Pak Am. League, N.J., 1990-92. Merit scholar Quaid-e-Azam U., 1973-75; Edn. Ministry scholar, Pakistan, 1977-80; NASA/Am. Soc. Engring. Edn. Summer Faculty fellow Jet Propulsion Lab. of Calif. Inst. Tech., 1996. Mem. Am. Phys. Soc., Materials Rsch. Soc., Internat. Soc. for Optical Engring. Avocations: reading, sports. Address: 3917 Kenas St West Palm Beach FL 33403 E-mail: tiq786@hotmail.com.

IQBAL, ZAFAR, biochemist, neurochemist; b. Lucknow, India, July 12, 1946; came to U.S., 1972, naturalized, 1979; s. Shujaat Ali and Saleha (Begum) Siddiqui. Cert. proficiency in French, Lucknow U., 1965; PhD, All India Inst. Med. Scis., New Delhi, 1971. Jr. research fellow Council Sci. and Indsl. Research, India, 1963-66, research fellow, 1967-68; research scholar Directorate Gen. Health Services, India, 1966-67; asst. research officer Indian Council Med. Research, 1968-71; research assoc. in physiology, investigator Ind. U. Sch. Medicine, Indpls., 1972-82, asst. prof. med. biophysics, 1977-82, asst. prof. biochemistry, 1979-82; asst. prof. neurology and neurosci. Northwestern U. Sch. Medicine, Chgo., 1982-85; assoc. prof. pharmacology Chgo. Med. Sch., 1985-88; assoc. prof. neurology Northwestern U. Inst. for Neuroscience, Chgo., 1989-95; adj. prof. neurology and neurosci. Northwestern U. Med. Sch., 1995—; mem. Northwestern U. Ctr. Devel. Biology, Chgo., 1989—; health sci. specialist VA Cen. Office Med. Rsch. Svc., Washington, 1995—. Contbg. author: Macromolecules in Storage and Transfer of Biological Information, 1969, Macromolecules and Behavior, 1972, Growth and Development of the Brain, 1975, Mechanism, Regulation and Special Function of Protein Synthesis in the Brain, 1977, Peripheral Neuropathies, 1978, Neurochemistry and Clinical Neurology, 1980, Calcium-Binding Proteins, 1980, Axoplasmic Transport, 1981, Calcium and Cell Function, 1982; editor: Axoplasmic Transport, 1986, Recent Progress in Polyamine Research, 1986, The Physiology of Polyamines, 1987; mem. editorial bd. Neurochem. Rsch.; contbr. articles to profl. jours. Bd. dirs. India Cultural Coord. Cmty. Rsch. grantee NIH, 1973-77, Muscular Dystrophy Assn. Am., 1975-77, 94-97, Am. Cancer Soc., 1979-80, NSF, 1981, 84, Juvenile Diabetes Found., 1981, Am. Diabetes Assn., 1980; recipient internat. travel award NSF, 1984, Fidia Rsch. Found. award, 1987, UN Devel. Program Internat. Expert award, 1987, 93, award Am. Soc. for Biochemistry and Molecular Biology, 1994. Mem. AAAS, Am. Physiol. Soc., Indian Acad. Neuroscis., Soc. Biol. Chemists (India), Internat. Brain Rsch. Orgn., Internat. Soc. Neurochemistry (award 1994), Soc. Neurosci., Am. Soc. Neurochemistry, Ind. Acad. Sci. (chmn. cell biology 1982-83), N.Y. Acad. Scis., Biophys. Soc., Soc. Exptl. Biology and Medicine, Assn. Scientists of Indian Origin Am. (counselor 1986—), Ameer Khusro Soc. Am. (v.p.), Lucknow U. Alumni Assn., Lucknow Rschrs. Assn. in Am., All-Indian Inst. of Med. Scis. Assn., Assn. of Communal Harmony in Asia, Orgn. of Univ. Communal Harmony. Home: 19105 Warrior Brook Dr Germantown MD 20874 E-mail: iqbzaf@mail.va.gov., raabta@erols.com.

IQBAL, ZAFAR MOHD, cancer researcher, biochemist, pharmacologist, toxicologist, consultant, molecular biologist; b. Hyderabad, India, Dec. 12, 1938; came to U.S., 1965, naturalized, 1973; s. M.A. and Haleemunissa (Begum) Rahim. BSc, Osmania U., 1958, MSc, 1962; PhD, U. Md., 1970. Diplomate Am. Bd. Forensic Medicine, Am. Bd. Forensic Examiners. Fellow in molecular pharmacology Nat. Cancer Inst./NIH, Bethesda, Md., 1971-74; asst. prof. pharmacology Case Western Res. U., Cleve., 1974-76; assoc. dir. ERC programs in occupational toxicology U. Ill. Med. Ctr., Chgo., 1980-81, assoc. prof. microbiology, 1977-80, assoc. prof. occupational medicine and environ. health, 1976-93, assoc. prof. preventive medicine, 1982-93; faculty grad. coll. U. Ill., Chgo., 1977-93, dir. Carcinogenesis Labs., 1983-93, chair recombinant DNA instnl. com., 1982-93; chair HIV hazards in rsch. com. U. Ill. Grad. Coll. Faculty, Chgo., 1976-93; dir. Toxicology-Cancer, Chgo., 1987—; affiliate Lurie Cancer Ctr. Northwestern U., Chgo., 1996—. Cons. in field to OSHA, 1980-81, Clements Assocs., 1976-79, Expert Resources, 1982—, Ill. Cancer Coun., 1981-82, Toxicology Cancer, 1987—; lectr. continuing edn.; grant reviewer study sects. NIH; program project reviewer Nat. Cancer Inst., 2000; merit grant reviewer VA, 1981-82; mem. tech. bd. panel Gt. Lakes Protection Fund, 1989—; participant profl. confs.; NSF-Coun. Sci. and Indsl. Rsch. exch. scientist, 1981; sponsor, trainer India-U.S. exch. scientists NSF, 1985-86; peer reviewer: (jours.) Sci., Cancer Rsch., Jour. Biochem., Toxicology, Carcinogenesis, others, also books and films; spl. advisor RRL (India) Dirs., 1980-86; mem. U.S. AID's-Asia Environ. Partnership and Environ Tech. Network Asia, 1994—, Environ. and Tech. Network Asia-Latin Am. Program, 1996—; chair recombinant DNA com. U. Ill., Chgo., 1983-93; contbr. WHO Internat. Agy. for Rsch. Cancer, Tallinn, 1975, Budapest, 1979, Tokyo, 1981, Banff, 1983; mem. exec. bd. sci. and tech. advs. Am. Bd. Forensic Exams., 1997—. Author, editor: Molecular Mechanisms of Toxic Response; Pancreatic Carcinogenesis Mechanisms; editor Jour. Molecular Toxicology and Carcinogenesis; mem. editorial adv. bd. Forensic Examiner, 1995—; exec. bd. sci. and tech. advisors Am. Bd. Forensic Examiners, 1996—; contbr. more than 60 articles to profl. jours. NSF-CSIR exch. scientist, 1981; sponsor, trainer India-U.S. Exch. Scientists, NSF, 1985-86; spl. advisor RRL (India) Dirs., 1980—; pres. Rahim Meml. Found., 1995—. Fellow Coun. Sci. and Indsl. Rsch., India, 1963-65; Fogarty Internat. fellow Nat. Cancer Inst., NIH, 1970-71, staff fellow, 1971-74; grantee Nat. Cancer Inst./NIH, Nat. Inst. Occupational Safety and Health, EPA, State of Ill., 1974-93. Fellow Am. Coll. Forensic Examiners (life, diplomate, bd. cert. forensic medicine, editl. bd. advisors 1995—); mem. AAAS, Am. Assn. Cancer Rsch., Am. Pancreatic Assn., N.Y. Acad. Scis., Am. Chem. Soc., Soc. Toxicology, Am. Coll. Toxicology, Nat. Registry of Forensic Examiners, B.E.S.T. N.Am., Registry Global World Leaders, Soc. Toxicology (molecular biology, carcinogenesis and mechanism splty. sects.), NIHAA, Sigma Xi. Office: Toxicology-Cancer PO Box 60267 Chicago IL 60660-0267

IRAKI, WAITHAKA NJUGUNA, educator, journalist; b. Shamata, Kenya, Aug. 28, 1968; s. Barnabas Njuguna Iraki and Hannah Wangari Njuguna. BEd in Sci., Kenyatta U., Nairobi, 1991, MEd, 1996; MBA, U. Nairobi, 1996; postgrad., Jackson State U., 2001—. Lectr. U. Nairobi, 1997—2003. Assoc. cons. Midway Securities Internat., Nairobi, 1997—98. Contbr. newspapers on social/econ. issues. Mem. bd. govs. H.S., Kaheho, Kenya, 1999—2001. Named Best Lectr., Mgmt. Sci. Students Assn., 1998; recipient prize, Price Waterhouse, 1997; scholar, Kenyatta U., 1991, U. Nairobi, 1995, Fulbright, U.S. Dept. State, 2001. Mem.: Acad. Mgmt., Am. Econ. Assn. Avocations: journalism, photography, travel, poetry. Home: Apt 3 1108 Fairmont Ave Jackson MS 39204 Office: Jackson State Univ 1400 Jr Lynch St Jackson MS 39217 Personal E-mail: xniraki@yahoo.com. E-mail: waithaka.n.iraki@ccaix.jsums.edu.

IRANI, RAY R. oil, gas and chemical company executive; b. Beirut, Jan. 15, 1935; came to U.S., 1953, naturalized, 1956; s. Rida and Naz I.; children: Glenn R., Lillian M., Martin R. BS in Chemistry, Am. U. Beirut, 1953; PhD in Phys. Chemistry, U. So. Calif., 1957. Rsch. scientist, then sr. rsch. scientist Monsanto Co., 1957-67; assoc. dir. new products, then dir. research Diamond Shamrock Corp., 1967-73; with Olin Corp., 1973-83, pres. chems. group, 1978-80, corp. pres., dir., 1980-83, COO, 1981-83; chmn. Occidental Petroleum Corp. subs. Occidental Chem. Corp., Dallas, 1983-94; CEO Occidental Petroleum Corp., subs. Occidental Chem. Corp., Dallas, 1983-91; chmn. Can. Occidental Petroleum Corp. Ltd., Calgary, 1987-99; exec. v.p. Occidental Petroleum Corp., L.A., 1983-84, pres., COO, 1984-91, pres., 1991-96, chmn., CEO, 1991—, also bd. dirs. Bd. dirs. Am. Petroleum Inst., Oxy Oil and Gas USA Inc., Occidental Oil and Gas Corp., Occidental Petroleum Investment Corp., Cedars Bank, Kaufman and Broad Home Corp., Jonsson Cancer Ctr. Found./UCLA. Author: Particle Size; also author papers in field; numerous patents in field. Vice chmn. Am. U. Beirut; trustee U. So. Calif., St. John's Hosp. and Health Ctr. Found., Natural History Mus. Los Angeles County; bd. govs. Los Angeles Town Hall, Los Angeles World Affairs Coun. Mem. Nat. Petroleum Coun., Am. Inst. Chemists, Am. Chem. Soc., Sci. Rsch. Soc. Am., Indsl. Rsch. Inst., The Conf. Bd., The CEO Roundtable, Nat. Assn. Mfrs. (bd. dirs.), Am. Petroleum Inst. (bd. dirs.), U.S.-Russia Bus. Coun. Office: 10889 Wilshire Blvd Los Angeles CA 90024-4201

IRBE, ARTURS, professional hockey player; b. Riga, Latvia, Feb. 2, 1967; Hockey player Sharks, 1991-96, Stars, 1996-97, Canucks, 1997-98; goalie Carolina Hurricanes, Morrisville, NC, 1998—. Office: Carolina Hurricanes 1400 Edwards Mill Rd Raleigh NC 27607-3624

IRBY, HOLT, lawyer; b. Dodge City, Kans., July 4, 1937; s. Jerry M. and Virgie (Lorean) I.; m. LaVerne Smith, May 27, 1956; children: Joseph, Kathy, Kay, Karon, James. BA, Tex. Tech. U., 1959; JD, U. Tex., 1962. Bar: Tex. 1962, U.S. Dist. Ct. (no. dist.) Tex. 1963. Asst. city atty. City of Lubbock, Tex., 1962-63; assoc. Hugh Anderson, Lubbock, 1963-66; gen. counsel, sec. Merc. Fin. Corp., Dallas, 1966-69; gen. counsel, v.p. Ward Food Restaurants, inc., Dallas, 1969-71; pvt. practice, Garland, Tex., 1971—. Mem. lawyer referal com. State Bar Tex., 1977, 78. Mem. bd. deacons First Bapt. Ch., Garland, 1979-90, chmn., 1976-77; bd. dirs. Garland Assistance Program, 1980, Habitat for Humanity of Greater Garland, Inc., 1997-2001, Dallas Life Found., 1980-90, Toler Children's Cmty., 1983-85; bd. dirs. Garland Civic Theatre, 1986—, pres., 1990-91, 92-93, v.p., 1991-92; mem. Garland Drug Task Force, 1990; deacon South Garland Bapt. Ch., 1992—, chmn., 1993-94, 98-99, 2002-03. Mem. Tex. Trial Lawyers Assn., Tex. Assn. Bank Counsel, Tex. Bar Assn., Garland Bar Assn. (bd. dirs. 1986-96, sec. 1992-93, v.p. 1993-94, pres. 1995-96), Dallas Bar Assn., Praetor Legal Frat. (named outstanding mem. 1962), Lubbock Jaycees (dir. 1963-65), Kiwanis (dir. 1973-74). Office: Bank of Am Tower 705 W Avenue B Ste 404 Garland TX 75040-6241

IRBY, ROSALYN BRYSON, molecular biologist, researcher; b. Columbia, Mo. d. Marion Ritchie and Jane Kalips Bryson; m. George Samuel Irby, Dec. 29, 1971; children: Gretchen Elizabeth, Benjamin Amburn, Geoffrey Samuel;1 child, Melissa Jane Reynolds. PhD, U of So. Fla., Tampa, FL, 1988—94; BS, Duke U, Durham, NC, 1968—71. Asst. prof. H. Lee Moffitt Cancer Ctr & Res Inst, Tampa, Fla., 1998—; post doctoral H. Lee Moffitt Cancer Ctr., Tampa, Fla., 1994—98. Instr. U of So. Fla., Tampa, Fla., 1996—97. Leader G S of Am., Fla., 1980—92. Fellow Postdoctoral Fellowship, Am. Heart Assn., 1994—96, Am. Cancer Soc., 1997—98; grantee Rsch. Grant, Am. Cancer Soc./ Moffitt Cancer Ctr., 2001—. Mem.: Am. Assn. for Cancer Rsch. Achievements include patents pending for Discovery and devel. of a mutation in the SRC oncogene. Avocations: skiing, golf.

IREDALE, EUGENE GERALD, lawyer; b. Louisville, Nov. 16, 1951; children: Danielle, Jake. BA in History and Sociology, Columbia Coll., N.Y.C., 1973; JD, Harvard U., 1976. Bar: Mass. 1977, Calif. 1977. Atty. Fed. Defenders of San Diego, 1977-82, chief trial atty., 1982-83; prin. Law Offices of E. G. Iredale, San Diego, 1983—. Editor: Defending a Federal Criminal Case, 1980-83. Instr. Nat. Coll. for Criminal Def., Houston and Macon, Ga., 1979—. Mem. Nat. Assn. Criminal Def. Lawyers, Calif. Attys. for Criminal Justice, Criminal Def. Lawyers Club. Democrat. Office: 105 W F St Fl 4 San Diego CA 92101-6087 E-mail: iredale@aol.com.

IRELAN, ROBERT WITHERS, retired metal products executive; b. Takoma Park, Md., Mar. 10, 1937; s. Charles Morris and Julia Mae (McKenzie) I.; m. Barbara Lucille Mitchell, Mar. 21, 1959; children: Robert Withers Jr., Jonathan M. BS, U. Md., 1960. Copy reader, copy editor Wall St. Jour., Washington, 1960-66; assoc. editor Nation's Bus. Mag., Washington, 1966-68; pub. rels. rep. Kaiser Industries Corp., Oakland, Calif., 1968-70; exec. asst. to chmn. Kaiser Affiliated Cos., Oakland, 1970-79; mgr. corp. rels. Kaiser Aluminum & Chem. Corp., Oakland, 1979-82, midwest regional v.p. pub. affairs Ravenswood, W.Va., 1982-85, corp. v.p. pub. rels. Oakland, 1985-97, ret., 1997; corp. v.p. pub. rels. Maxxam Inc., Houston, 1990-99; ret., 1999. Vis. lectr. dept. comm. U. of the Pacific, Stockton, Calif., 2001-02. Co-editor: Lessons of Leadership, 1967. Mem. U. Md. Alumni Assn., Rancho Murieta Country Club. Democrat. Lutheran. Avocations: golf, travel, theatre, sports, reading. Home: 6798 Terreno Dr Rancho Murieta CA 95683 E-mail: golfbob@calweb.com.

IRELAND, FAITH, state supreme court justice; b. Seattle, 1942; d. Carl and Janice Enyeart; m. Chuck Norem. BA, U. Wash.; JD, Willamette U., 1969; M in Taxation with honors, Golden Gate U. Past assoc. McCune, Godfrey and Emerick, Seattle; pvt. practice Pioneer Square, Wash., 1974; judge King County Superior Ct., 1984—98; justice Wash. Supreme Ct., 1998—. Past dean Washington Jud. Coll.; past mem. Bd. Ct. Edn. Served on numerous civic and charitable bds.; past pro-bono atty. Georgetown Dental Clin.; past bd. dirs. Puget Sound Big Sisters, Inc.; founding mem. Wing Luke Asian Mus., 1967—, past pres., past bd. dirs.; bd. dirs. Youth and Fitness Found., 1998. Named Judge of Yr., Washington State Trial Lawyer's Assn., Man of Yr. for efforts in founding Wing Luke Asian Mus.; recipient Disting. Svc. award, Nat. Leadership Inst. Jud. Edn., 1998. Mem.: Superior Ct. Judges Assn. (past bd. dirs., pres. 1996—97, vice chair bd. dirs. jud. adminstrn. 1996—98), Wash. State Trial Lawyer's Assn. (past chair bd. dirs.), Washington Women Lawyer's (founding mem., Pres.'s award, Vanguard award), Rotary (bd. dirs. Seattle No. 4 1998), Rainer Valley Hist. Soc. (life; founding mem.). Office: Washington Supreme Ct 415 12th St W PO Box 40929 Olympia WA 98504-0929*

IRELAND, HERBERT ORIN, retired engineering educator; b. Buckley, Ill., June 12, 1919; s. Harvey Glenn and Anna Estella (Perkinson) I.; m. Mary Leota Austin, Mar. 1, 1941; children: Orin Lee, Marin Fae, Jeanne Lu. BS, U. Ill., 1941, MS, 1947, PhD, 1955. From research asst. to prof. civil engring. U. Ill., Urbana, 1946-79, emeritus, 1979—. Cons. soil mechanics and found. engring., 1946—. Contbr.: sect. to Structural Engineering Handbook, 1968; also articles profl. jours. Served from 2d lt. to maj., C.E. AUS, 1941-46. Fellow Am. Soc. C.E., Geol. Soc. Am.; mem. Am. Ry. Engring. Assn., Sigma Xi, Tau Beta Pi, Chi Epsilon. Methodist. Home: 1132 E Township Road 209 Gilman IL 60938-6114 E-mail: oireland@netzero.net.

IRELAND, KATHY, actor, apparel designer; b. Glendale, Calif., 1962; d. John and Barbara Ireland; m. Greg Olsen, 1988; children: Erik, Lily. CEO, chief designer Kathy Ireland Worldwide. Appearances in Sports Illustrated's Ann. Swimsuit Issues, 25th Anniversary Show Swimsuit Edit., Kathy Ireland LPGA Championship, ESPN, 2001; films include: Alien from L.A., 1988, Necessary Roughness, 1991, Mom and Dad Save the World, 1992, National Lampoon's Loaded Weapon I, 1993, The Player, Mr. Destiny, Amore, Backfire; TV films include Beauty and the Bandit, 1994, Danger Island, 1994, Miami Hustle, 1995, Gridlock, 1996, Once Upon A Christmas, 2000, Twice Upon A Christmas, 2001; TV appearances include: Down the Shore, The Edge, Tales from the Crypt, Without a Clue, Grand, Charles in Charge, Perry Mason, Boy Meets World, Melrose Place, The Watcher, Deadly Games, Sabrina the Teenage Witch, Suddenly Susan, Gun, Cosby, Touched by an Angel, Pensacola, For Your Love, Strong Medicine. Office: 5th Fl 1900 Avenue of the Stars Los Angeles CA 90067-4301

IRELAND, LINDA ANN, internist; b. Somers Point, N.J., July 29, 1971; d. Kenneth Bruce and Mary Ann Ireland. BS in Biology, Elizabethtown (Pa.) Coll., 1994; MD, Phila. (Pa.) Coll. Osteopathic Medicine, 1998. Diplomate Am. Bd. Internal Medicine. Fellow in cardiology Miriam Hosp. Brown U., Providence, 1998—. Tchr. Brown U., 2003—. Recipient Stephen A. Ronner award, Lehigh Valley Hosp., 2001. Fellow: Am. Coll. Cardiology. Methodist. Avocations: skiing, bicycling, kayaking, backpacking. Home: PO Box 194 Swansea MA 02777

IRELAND, PATRICIA, not-for-profit developer; b. Oak Park, Ill., Oct. 19, 1945; d. James Ireland and Joan Filipek; m. James Humble, 1968. BA, U. Tennessee, 1966; JD, U. Miami Law Sch., 1975. Flight attendant Pan Am. World Airlines, 1967-75; ptnr. Stearns, Weaver, Miller, Weissler, Alhadeff & Sitterson, Miami; nat. exec. v.p. NOW, 1987—91, pres., 1991—2001; initiator Global Feminist Conf.; rep. NOW; of counsel Katz, Kutter, Alderman, Bryant & Yon, 2001—03; CEO YWCA of the USA, Washington, 2003—. Author: What Women Want, 1996; contbr. law rev. Univ. Miami Law Sch. Office: YWCA 1015 18th St NW Washington DC 20036

IRELAND, PATRICK, artist; b. Ireland, 1935; came to U.S., 1957; Studio: 15 W 67th St New York NY 10023-6226

IRELAND, RODERICK L., state supreme court justice; m. Alice Alexander. Bachelor's degree, Lincoln U., 1966; Master's degree, Harvard U.; JD, Columbia U., 1969; PhD, Northeastern U., 1998. Assoc. justice Mass. Supreme Jud. Ct., 1997—. Judge Boston Juvenile Ct., 1977, 90, Mass. Appeals Ct., 1990-97. Mem. Eliot Congregational Ch. Office: Mass Supreme Jud Ct Pemberton Square 1300 New Courthouse Boston MA 02108-1701*

IRELAND, TIMOTHY, media consultant; s. Richard W. and Charlotte Ann I.; m. Robin Nancy Uris, Jan. 2, 1998; children: Madeleine Rose, Claire Tapley. BA, Swarthmore Coll., Swarthmore, PA, 1987. Maritime reporter The Courier-Post, Cherry Hill, NJ, 1988—89; govt./politics reporter The Trentonian, Trenton, NJ, 1989—90; investigative reporter The Courier-Post, Cherry Hill, NJ, 1990—92; polit./govt. reporter NY Daily News, N.Y.C., 1993—95; media rels. mgr. Bell Atlantic (Verizon), Newark, 1995—98; vp mktg./media rels. VFIM, Valley Forge, Pa., 1998—2003. Media cons. Rep. Com. of Pa., Harrisburg, Pa., 2000; campaign press sec. Hafer for Treas., Harrisburg, 2000; freelance journalist. Contbr. (book review) The Weekly Standard, (breakfast table) Slate Magazine, 2000, (opinion pieces) Politicspa.com. Republican. Roman Catholic.

IRENAS, JOSEPH ERON, judge, director; b. Newark, July 13, 1940; s. Zachary and Bessie (Shain) Irenas; m. Nancy Harriet Jacknow, Jan. 1, 1962; children: Amy Ruth, Edward Eron. AB, Princeton U., 1962; JD cum laude, Harvard U., 1965; postgrad., NYU Sch. Law, 1967-70. Bar: N.J. 1965, N.Y. 1982. Law sec. to justice N.J. Supreme Ct., 1965-66; assoc. McCarter & English, Newark, 1966-71, ptnr., 1972-92; judge U.S. Dist. Ct. N.J., 1992—. Trustee Hamilton Investment Trust, Elizabeth, NJ, 1980—83; mem. N.J. Supreme Ct. Dist. Ethics Com., 1984—86, vice chmn., 1986; adj. prof. law Rutgers Sch. Law, Camden, 1985—86, Camden, 1988—97, Camden, 1999—2002, N.J. Bd. Bar Examiners, 1986—88. Contbr. Chmn. bd. trustees United Hosps. of Newark, 1982—83; trustee United Hosps. Found., 1985—92, United Way Essex County, 1988—92, treas., 1990—92. Fellow: Am. Bar Found., Royal Chartered Inst. Arbitrators (London); mem.: ABA, Camden County Bar Assn., N.J. Bar Assn., Am. Law Inst., Union League Club, Nassau Club. Republican. Jewish. Office: Mitchell H Cohen US Courthouse One John F Gerry Plaza PO Box 2097 Camden NJ 08101-2097

IRENE, EUGENE ARTHUR, physical chemistry and materials science educator, researcher; b. Bklyn., Oct. 22, 1941; s. Louis Gene and Rose (Benvenuto) I.; m. Mary Ann Felice, July 18, 1964; children: Michael, Christina. BS, Manhattan Coll., 1963; PhD, Rensselaer Poly. Inst., 1972. Rsch. asst. Rensselaer Poly. Inst., Troy, N.Y., 1969-72; mem. rsch. staff IBM Thomas J. Watson Resource Ctr., Yorktown Heights, N.Y., 1972-82; prof. U. N.C., Chapel Hill, 1982—. Vice chmn. chemistry dept. U. N.C., 1987-90. Contbr. over 200 articles to profl. jours. Capt. USAF, 1963-69, Vietnam. Decorated Bronze Star; recipient NASA Sky Lab. award NASA, 1974, Invention award IBM Corp., 1974, 76. Fellow Am. Vacuum Soc.; mem. Electrochem. Soc. (Callinan award 1988), Materials Rsch. Soc. Roman Catholic. Home: 1143 Pebble Creek Crossing Durham NC 27713 Office: U NC Dept Chemistry Cb 3290 Chapel Hill NC 27599-3290 E-mail: gene_irene@unc.edu.

IREY, CHARLOTTE YORK, dance educator; b. Oklahoma City, Apr. 29, 1918; d. Charles William and Annie Charlotte (Upsher) York; m. Eugene Floyd Irey, June 10, 1942; 1 child, Susan Gail. BS with honors., U. Wis., 1940. Instr. dance Stephens Coll., Columbia, Mo., 1940-43; prof. dance U. Colo., Boulder, 1945-88, chmn. dance divsn., dept. theatre and dance, 1973-88; sole practice Indpls., 1976—. Author: (with Frances Bascom) Costume Cues, 1952. Recipient Robert L. Steans award U. Colo., Boulder, 1973, Thomas Jefferson award, 1980; Charlotte York Irey Studio/Theatre at U. Colo., Boulder named in her honor, 1984. Mem. Nat. Dance Assn. (pres. 1975-76, Scholar of Yr. 1982-83, Heritage honoree 1990), AAHPERD, Am. Coll. Dance Festival, Coun. Dance Adminstrs., Congress Dance Rsch., Am. Dance Guild. Episcopalian.

IRICK, BRETT D, manufacturing engineer; b. Mount Gilead, Ohio, Apr. 18, 1963; s. Carl M. and Anne E. Irick. BS in Mech. Engring., Ohio State U., 1985; MBA, U. of Mich., 1993. Mfg. engr. Ford Motor Co. - Vehicle Ops., Dearborn, 1985—95; mfg. leader/engring. Ford Motor Co. - Ranger Plant Vehicle Team, Edison, NJ, 1995—98; engring. supv./final assembly engring. Ford Motor Co. - Vehicle Ops., Dearborn, Mich., 1998—2000; supt. - plant engring. Ford Motor Co - Dearborn Frame Plant, 2000—01, new model mgr., 2001—. Adv. bd. to trustees NJIT, Newark, 1996—98. Gt registrar Cougar Club of Am., Mt. Airy, Md., 1988—2003; dir. Pk. Gate Condo Assoc, Edison, NJ, 1996—98; v.p. Fairlane East (east townhouses), Dearborn, Mich., 2001. Recipient Gold Award, Cougar Club of Am., 1997, Hon. Life Membership, 1989. Mem.: Soc. of Automotive Engineers, ASME, Am. Numis. Assn. (life), No. Calif. Cougar Club, Cascade Cougar Club, Tau Beta Pi. Mem. Methodist Ch. Avocations: automotive restoration, coin collecting, home improvement, travel. Home: 2 Brookwood Ln Dearborn MI 48120 Office: Ford Motor Co - Dearborn Frame Plant 3001 Miller Rd Dearborn MI 48121-1496 E-mail: birick@ford.com.

IRIE, PHILIP SHINAZO, physician, scientist; b. Osaka, Japan, Aug. 25, 1920; came to U.S., 1957; s. Rokuro and Taneko (Watanabe) I.; m. Masako Hinoue, May 29, 1969; children: Hanna Yoko, Robert Eiichi. BS, Daishi Coll., Kanazawa, Japan, 1942; MD, Osaka Imperial U., 1945; ScD, Osaka City U., 1961. Rsch. fellow Mt. Sinai Hosp., Chgo., 1957-58, Hahnemann Med. Coll., Phila., 1958-60, Sloan-Kettering Cancer Inst., N.Y.C., 1960-61, N.Y. Med. Coll., N.Y.C., 1969-70, mem. faculty, 1971—; rsch. fellow Mt. Sinai Med. Sch., NYU, N.Y.C., 1967-69, mem. faculty, 1972—. Contbr. articles to profl. jours. Recipient Physician Recognition award AMA, 1969, Ministry award Dept. Health and Pub. Welfare, Japan, 1992, Disting. Svc. award Yomiuri Newspaper, 1992. Mem. N.Y. State Med. Soc. (50 Yr. Svc. citation), N.Y. County Med. Soc., Mt. Sinai Med. Sch. Alumni Coun. Achievements include exploration of diuretic to control hypertension prolonging human life; diuretic and antihypertensive activity of luminous substance 3-aminophthalhydrazide; anticancer activity of some Latices and Luciferin. Office: 11035 71st Ave Forest Hills New York NY 11375-4560

IRISH, LEON EUGENE, lawyer, educator, non-profit organization executive; b. Superior, Wis., June 19, 1938; s. Edward Eugene and Phyllis Ione (Johnson) I.; m. Karla W. Simon; children: Stephen T., Jessica L., Thomas A., Emily A. BA in History, Stanford U., 1960; JD, U. Mich., 1964; D.Phil in Law, Oxford (Eng.) U., 1973. Law clk. to Assoc. Justice U.S. Supreme Ct. Byron R. White, 1967; cons. Office Fgn. Direct Investments, Dept. Commerce, 1967-68; spl. rep. sec. def. 7th session 3d UN Conf. Law of Sea; mem. Caplin & Drysdale, chartered, Washington, 1968-85; prof. law U. Mich. Law Sch., Ann Arbor, 1985-88; ptnr. Jones, Day, Reavis & Pogue, Washington, 1988-93; v.p., sr. counsel Aetna Life and Casualty Co., Hartford, Conn., 1993-95; pres., chmn. Internat. Ctr. Not-for-Profit Law, Washington, 1992—2002; pres., CEO United Way Internat., Alexandria, Va., 1996; sr. legal cons. World Bank, 1997—2001. Adj. prof. Georgetown U. Law Ctr., 1975-85; regent Am. Coll. Tax Counsel, 1986-89; mem. IRS Commr.'s Adv. Group, 1987; bd. dirs., sec. Vols. Tech. Assistance, 1978-, Found. for Devel. of Polish Agr. 1988-; vis. fellow World Bank, 1995-96; vis. prof. law Temple U., 2002-2003. Contbr. articles to legal jours. Mem. ABA, D.C. Bar Assn., Am. Law Inst., Am. Coll. Tax Counsel, Coun. on Fgn. Rels. Am. Coll. Employee Benefits Coun. Democrat. Home: 304 Kyle Rd Crownsville MD 21032-1843 E-mail: leon.Irish@temple.edu.

IRISH, THOMAS JUDSON, retired plastic surgeon; b. Forest City, Iowa, May 23, 1936; m. Sandra Rudolph. BS, Iowa State Coll., 1958; MD, State U. of Iowa, 1962. Intern King County Hosp. (now Harborview Hosp.), Seattle, 1962-63; pvt. practice Forest City, Iowa, 1963-66; resident in gen. surgery U. Colo. Med. Ctr., Denver, 1966-70; resident in plastic surgery Norfolk Gen. Hosp. & Kings Daughters Children's Hosp., Va., 1970-72; pvt. practice Plastic Surgeons NW, Tacoma, 1972—2003; med. dir. Franciscan Wound Care Ctr.; ret., 2003. Fellow in plastic surgery Canniesburn Hosp., Glasgow, Scotland, 1971. Fellow ACS; mem. Am. Soc. Plastic and Reconstructive Surgery, Alpha Omega Alpha.

IRIYE, AKIRA, historian, educator; b. Tokyo, Oct. 20, 1934; s. Keishiro and Naoko (Tsukamoto) I.; m. Mitsuko Maeda, May 14, 1960; children: Keiko, Masumi. BA, Haverford Coll., 1957; PhD, Harvard U., 1961. Instr. in history Harvard U., Cambridge, Mass., 1961-64, lectr. in history, 1964-66; asst. prof. history U. Calif., Santa Cruz, 1966-68, assoc. prof. U. Rochester, 1968-69, U. Chgo., 1969-71, prof., 1971-89, disting. service prof., 1983-89, chmn. dept. history, 1979-85; prof. history Harvard U., 1989—91, Charles Warren prof. history, 1991—, chmn. dept. history, 2002—. Vis. prof. Ecole des Hautes Etudes en Sciences Sociales, Paris, 1986-87, London Sch. Econs., 1992. Author: books, including After Imperialism, 1965, Across the Pacific, 1967, Pacific Estrangement, 1972, The Cold War in Asia, 1974, Power and Culture, 1981, The Origins of the Second World War in Asia and the Pacific, 1987, China and Japan, 1992, The Globalizing of America, 1993, Cultural Internationalism and World Order, 1997, Japan and the Wider World, 1997, Global Community, 2002; editor: The Chinese and the Japanese, 1980, other books. John Simon Guggenheim fellow, 1974-75 Mem. Am. Hist. Assn. (pres. 1988), Am. Acad. Arts and Scis., Orgn. Am. Historians, Soc. Historians Am. Fgn. Relations (pres. 1978) Office: Harvard U Dept History Cambridge MA 02138

IRIZARRY, ESTELLE DIANE, foreign language educator, writer, editor; b. Paterson, N.J., Nov. 13, 1937; d. Morris Jerome and Ceil Pearl (Schwartz) Roses; m. Manuel Antonio, Dec. 14, 1963; children: Michael Carl, Steven Edward, Nelson Paul. BA, Montclair State U., 1959; MA, Rutgers U., 1963; PhD in Philosophy, The George Washington U., 1970. Tchr. Glen Rock (N.J.) H.S., 1958-60, Ramapo (N.J.) Regional H.S., 1960-63; instr. U. P.R., Rio Piedras, 1963-66, Howard U., Washington, 1966-68, George Washington U., Washington, 1968-70; prof. Georgetown U., Washington, 1970—. Editor Spanish sect. Humanities Computing Yearbook, Oxford, U.K., 1988, Hispania, 1993-2000. Author: Escritores-pintores españoles, 1990, Estudios Sobre Rafael Dieste, 1992, Informática y Literatura, 1997. Recipient Tomas Barros Essay prize, La Coruna, Spain, 1990, Spanish Cross of the Civil Order of Alphonse the Sage, 1998; grantee Quincentennial grant, P.R. Com. for the Quincentenary, 1989. Mem. Am. Assn. Tchrs. Spanish and Portuguese, N.Am. Acad. of the Spanish Lang., Royal Spanish Acad. (corr.), Sigma Delta Pi. Avocations: writing, painting, literary computing. Home: 1600 N Oak St Apt 1615 Arlington VA 22209-2758

IRIZARRY, FRANCISCO ARMANDO, information systems executive, lawyer; b. San Juan, P.R., Feb. 7, 1962; s. Francisco Irizarry Cancel and Gloria Gonzalez; m. Kathleen Gladys Ryan, May 23, 1987; 1 child, Kevin. BA cum laude, U. Dayton, 1984, JD, 1987. Bar: Ohio 1988. Assoc. Rieser & Marx, Dayton, Ohio, 1988-90; mgr. content devel. and ops. NEXIS, Lexis-Nexis, Dayton, 1998-99, mgr. product devel. N.Am. legal market, 1999-2001; mgr. product devel. N. Am. legal market, 2001—. Trustee, treas., chmn. fin. com. CityFolk, Dayton, 1999—. Mem. Ohio State Bar Assn., Dayton Bar Assn., Phi Alpha Delta, Pi Sigma Alpha. Roman Catholic. Home: 5524 Hearthside Ct Dayton OH 45424-5231 Office: Lexis Nexis 9443 Springboro Pike Miamisburg OH 45342-4425 Fax: 937-865-1999. E-mail: francisco.irizarry@lexisnexis.com.

IRIZARRY-YUNQUE, CARLOS JUAN, lawyer, educator; b. Sabana Grande, P.R., June 24, 1922; s. Luis Manuel and Isabel (Yunque) Irizarry-Y.; m. Georgina Ortiz, Nov. 23, 1996; 1 dau., Lida Isis Irizarry Egele. BA, U. P.R., 1943, LL.B., 1949. Bar: P.R. Supreme Ct 1949, U.S. Circuit Ct 1952, U.S. Supreme Ct 1962. Legal advisor Dept. of Agr. and Commerce of P.R., San Juan, 1949-50, P.R. Police Dept., San Juan, 1950-53; asst. dist. atty. Ponce, P.R., 1953-56; prof. law Cath. U. of P.R., Ponce, 1966-73; assoc. justice of Supreme Ct. of P.R., San Juan, 1973-86; prof. law Interam. U. P.R., San Juan, 1986—. Author: Responsabilidad Civil Extracontractual, 1996, Responsabilidad Civil Extracontractual, 5th edit., 2000. Served with U.S. Army, 1943-46, 50-52. Mem. ABA, Inter Am. Bar Assn., P.R. Bar Assn., Am. Legion, Phi Alpha Delta. Clubs: Lions. Roman Catholic. Office: InterAm U Sch of Law 85 Federico Costa San Juan PR 00918 E-mail: iriyun@prtc.net.

IRLBECK, AMBER ROSE, journalist, scriptwriter; b. Amarillo, Tex., Oct. 15, 1976; d. Paul Louis and Connie Sue Irlbeck; m. Adam Robert Lewis, Jan. 10, 2001. degree in English, degree in Journalism, Tex. Tech U. Reporter Tulia (Tex.) Sentinel, La Ventana Yearbook, Lubbock, Tex.; online reporter Lubbock Online Network, Tex., online content editor; freelance writer LUbbock Avalanche Jour., Tex. Screenwriter, editor: films When Jesus Was Born, 2000; composer: Livin' My Life, 1994—95; author: (poetry) Muse of My Soul, 2001. Song leader United Meth. Ch., New Deal, Tex., 2001. Mem.: Soc. Profl. Journalists. Avocations: poetry, music. Home: 16 Fannin Dr Tulia TX 79088

IRONS, GEORGE VERNON, JR., cardiologist; b. Roanoke, Ala., Oct. 21, 1931; s. George Vernon Sr. and Velma (Wright) I.; m. Peggy Garner, June 5, 1956 (div. 1985); children: David Michael Irons, Dwight Garner Irons; m. Linda Johnson, May 24, 1986; children: Tracy Umstead Hildreth, Chad Scott Umstead. BS, Samford U., 1952; MD, U. Ala., Birmingham, 1956. Diplomate Am. Bd. Internal Medicine, Am. Bd. Cardiovas. Medicine. Intern Barnes Hosp., St. Louis, 1956-57; fellow in pathology U. Chgo., 1960-61, resident in internal medicine, 1961-63, fellow in gastroenterology, 1963-64; fellow in cardiology Duke U., Durham, N.C., 1964-66; cons. in cardiology Fayetteville (N.C.) VA Hosp., 1964-66; cardiologist, chmn. dept. cardiology Nalle Clinic, Charlotte, N.C., 1966-88; pres. Mid-Carolina Cardiology, Charlotte, 1988-92, cardiologist, 1988—. Capt. USAF, 1956-60. Exchange Club scholar, 1949, 52; recipient John R. Mott award Samford U., 1952. Fellow ACP, Am. Coll. Cardiology; mem. Alpha Epsilon Delta, Alpha Omega Alpha. Republican. Baptist. Avocations: skiing, boating, tennis. Office: Mid-Carolina Cardiology 1718 E 4th St Ste 501 Charlotte NC 28204-3288

IRONS, ISIE IONA, retired nursing administrator; b. Rixford, Pa., Oct. 26, 1934; d. William Ellis and Catherine (Fitzgerald) Irons. Grad. RN, Buffalo Gen. Hosp., 1955; BSN, U. Buffalo, 1959; MPH, U. N.C., 1962. OPD clin. dir. Buffalo Gen. Hosp.; nursing supr. N.Y. Telephone, Buffalo; asst. staff mgr., nursing mgr. So. Bell, Atlanta, asst. staff mgr. Recipient Best Bedside Nursing award, 1955. Home: 6435 Windsor Trace Dr Norcross GA 30092-2376

IRONS, JEREMY JOHN, actor; b. Cowes, Eng., Sept. 19, 1948; s. Paul Dugan and Barbara Anne (Sharpe) Irons; m. Sinead Moira Cusack, Mar. 28, 1978; children: Samuel James, Maximilian Paul. Performer (stage): John the

Baptist in Godspell, 1973, Mick in The Caretaker, 1974, Petruchio in The Taming of the Shrew, 1975, Harry Thunder in Wild Oats, 1976—77, 1986, James Jameson in Rear Column, 1978, The Real Thing, 1984 (Tony award, 1984), Richard II, Leontes in Winter's Tale, The Rover; performer: (film) Nijinsky, 1979, The French Lieutenant's Woman, 1981, Betrayal, 1982, Moonlighting, 1982, The Wild Duck, 1983, Swann in Love, 1983, The Mission, 1985, Chorus of Disapproval, 1988, Australia, 1988, Dead Ringers, 1988 (Best Actor N.Y. Film Critics' Circle, 1988), Danny, the Champion of the World, 1989, Reversal of Fortune, 1990 (Acad. award for Best Actor, 1991, Golden Globe for Best Actor, 1991), Kafka, 1991, Waterland, 1992, Damage, 1992, M. Butterfly, 1993, The House of the Spirits, 1994, The Lion King (voice), Die Hard with a Vengeance, 1995, Stealing Beauty, 1996, Lolita, 1997, The Chinese Box, 1997, Man in the Iron Mask, 1998, Dungeons and Dragons, 2000, Fourth Angel, 2000, And Now Ladies and Gentlemen, 2001, Callas Forever, 2001, Last Call, 2001; performer: (TV) Alex Hepburn in The Captain's Doll, 1982, Charles Ryder in Brideshead Revisited, 1980—81, Tales from Hollywood, 1992, Longitude, 1999. Decorated Legion d'Honneur France. Address: Hutton Mgmt 4 Old Manor Close Askett Bucks HP27 9NA England

IRONS, SPENCER ERNEST, lawyer; b. Chgo., Sept. 15, 1917; s. Ernest Edward and Gertrude Bertwhistle (Thompson) I.; m. Betty M. Chesnut, Jan. 16, 1954; children: Janet L., Nancy G., Edward S. AB, U. Chgo., 1938; JD, U. Mich., 1941. Bar: Ill. 1941, U.S. Dist. Ct. (no. dist.) Ill. 1953, U.S. Supreme Ct. 1962. Assoc. Holmes, Dixon, Knouff & Potter, Chgo., 1946-50, McKinney, Carlson, Leaton & Smalley, Chgo., 1950-54, ptnr., 1955-58; sr. atty. Brunswick Corp., Skokie, Ill., 1959-82; pvt. practice Flossmoor, Ill., 1983-92; ret., 1992. Mem. bd. editors U. Mich. Law Rev., 1939-41. Mem. bd. trustees Flossmoor Pub. Library, 1959-61; mem. Chgo. Crime Commn., 1954-82. Lt. col. U.S. Army, 1941-46, 61-62. Mem. ABA, Ill. Bar Assn., Chgo. Bar Assn. (bd. of mgrs. 1954-56), Law Club. Republican. Unitarian Universalist. Home: 2020 Plymouth Ln Northbrook IL 60062-6064

IRONS, WILLIAM GEORGE, anthropology educator; b. Garrett, Ind., Dec. 25, 1933; s. George Randall and Eva Aileen (Veazey) I.; m. Marjorie Sue Rogasner, Nov. 4, 1972; children— Julia Rogasner, Marybeth Rogasner BA, U. Mich., 1960, MA, 1963, PhD, 1969; postgrad., London Sch. Econs., 1964-65. With Army C.E., 1956-58; asst. prof. social relations Johns Hopkins U., 1969-74; asst. prof. anthropology Pa. State U., 1974-78; assoc. prof. anthropology Northwestern U., Evanston, Ill., 1978-83, prof., 1983—. Cons. Nat. Geog. Soc., NSF, AAAS, Social Sci. Research Council, Time-Life Books, U. Wash. Press, Random House, Worth Pubs., Rutgers U. Press, U. Tex. Press, Pelenum Press, Oxford U. Press, Cornell U. Press. Author: Perspectives on Nomadism, 1972, The Yomut Turkmen, 1975, Evolutionary Biology and Human Social Behavior, 1979, Adaptation and Human Behavior, 2000; mem. bd. editors Evolution and Human Behavior. With AUS, 1954-56. Recipient Lifetime Achievement award Commn. on Nomadic Peoples, Internat. Union Anthropol. and Ethnological Scis.; grantee NSF, 1973, 76, 83, 85, 86, Ford Found., 1974, Harry Frank Guggenheim Found., 1976. Fellow AAAS, Am. Anthrop. Assn.; mem. Assocs. in Current Anthropology, Human Behavior and Evolution Soc. (pres. 2001—03), Internat. Soc. Human Ethology, Internat. Soc. for Behavioral Ecology, Ctr. for Advanced Studies in Religion and Sci., Inst. for Religion in an Age of Sci., Phi Kappa Phi. Achievements include research on Turkmen of Iran, human behavioral ecology, evolutionary ethics. Home: 2604 Payne St Evanston IL 60201-2133 Office: Northwestern U Dept Anthropology 1810 Hinman Ave Evanston IL 60208-0809 E-mail: w-irons@northwestern.edu.

IRONS, WILLIAM V. state legislator; b. Providence, May 11, 1943; s. Milton H. and Harriet Viall I.; m. Mary Durand, 1968; children: Joan, Sarah, Katherine. BS, U. N.H., 1966; CLU, Amer. Coll., 1978. CLU. Civil engr. Green Engring., Boston, 1967-68, BIF Industries, Providence, 1968-72; ins. agt. Jack Awde, CLU Ins. Agy., Providence, 1972-81; owner Irons & Assocs. Ins. Agy., Warwick, R.I., 1981—; mem. R.I. Senate, Dist. 39, Providence, 1983—, pres., 2003—. Labor com., chmn. corp. com.; farmer Gov. Energy Coordinating Coun. Sponsor Rumford Little League; former chmn. Newman YMCA, 1980-81; mem. Am. Cancer Soc., R.I. State Dem. Com., 1976-80, East Providence Dem. City Com., 1980—, Dem. Ward Com., 1980—. Sgt. R.I. Army Nat. Guard, 1966-72. Mem. Am. Soc. CLU, R.I. Life Underwriters Assn. (past pres.), Rumford Lions Club. Roman Catholic. Address: PO Box 16210 Rumford RI 02916-0696*

IRSAY, JAMES STEVEN, professional football team owner; b. Lincolnwood, Ill., June 13, 1959; s. Robert Irsay and Harriet Pogerzelski; m. Margaret Mary Coyle, Aug. 2, 1980; children: Carlie Margaret, Casey Coyle, Kalen. B in Broadcast Journalism, So. Meth. U., 1982. With Balt. Colts., from early 1970's; owner, CEO Indpls. Colts, 1997—. Bd. dirs. Noble Ind. Composer, performer single Hoosier Heartland, 1985, single and video Go Colts, 1985, Colors, 1990. Bd. dirs. United Way Ctrl. Ind.; dir. Greater Indpls. Progress Com. Avocations: weight lifting, guitar, songwriting. Office: Indpls Colts 7001 W 56th St Indianapolis IN 46254-9725 also: Indianapolis Colts PO Box 535000 Indianapolis IN 46253

IRTZ, FREDERICK G., II, lawyer; b. Ft. Knox, Ky., Aug. 23, 1944; married; children: Kimberly, Fred III, Andrew. BS in Commerce, Eastern Ky. U., 1968; JD, U. Louisville, 1973. Bar: Ky. 1973, U.S. Dist. Ct. (we. dist.) Ky. 1974, U.S. Ct. Appeals (6th cir.) 1974, U.S. Tax Ct. 1975, U.S. Supreme Ct. 1977, U.S. Dist. Ct. (ea. dist.) Ky. 1979, Calif. 1981, U.S. Ct. Claims 1998. Atty IRS, Louisville, 1974-78; sole practice Lexington, Ky., 1978—. Speaker U. Ky. Estate Planning Seminar, Ky. Bar Assn., U. Ky. Agrl. Law Seminar, No. Ky. Soc. CPAs, Louisville Estate Planning Coun., Lexington Soc. MBAs, Fayette County Bar Assn. Chmn. Dist. Internat. Youth Exch., 1985, legal staff Oleika Temple, atty., chmn. budget com.; pres. Oleika Brass Band, 1982; bd. dirs. Ctrl. Ky. Youth Orchs. Lt. Col. U.S. Army Reserve ret. 1994. Decorated Bronze Star; named one of Outstanding Young Men Am., 1977; recipient Svc. award 4-H, 1987. Mem. Bluegrass Estate Planning Council (pres. 1978, speaker 1978, 83), ABA taxation, real property, and probate sect.), Ky. Bar Assn. (taxation sect., chair 1995-96), Fayette County Bar Assn. Lodges: Lions (pres. Bluegrass Breakfast club 1981-82, Lion of Yr. 1984). Home and Office: PO Box 22777 Lexington KY 40522-2777 Fax: 859-252-3692.

IRVIN, CHARLES LESLIE, lawyer; b. Corpus Christi, Tex., Mar. 2, 1935; s. Joseph and Louise (Frelon) I.; m. Shirley Jean Smith, Feb. 8, 1964; children— Kimberley Antoinette, Jonathan Charles. B.A., Tex. So. U., 1961, LL.B., 1964. Bar: Tex. 1964, U.S. Dist. Ct. (so. dist.) Tex. 1973, U.S. Dist. Ct. (ea. dist.) Tex. 1973, U.S. Supreme Ct. 1971, U.S. Ct. Appeals (9th cir.) 1982. Atty. U.S. Dept. Labor, Kansas City, Mo., 1964-67, Chgo., 1964-73; atty. Texaco, Inc., Chgo., 1973-74, Houston, 1974-79, Harrison, N.Y., 1979-81, sr. atty., Houston, 1981-88; divsn. atty., Midland, Tex., 1988, Denver, 1989-93, regional atty., mng. atty. adminstrn., Harrison, 1993-94, pvt. practice, Conroe, Tex., 1994—. Sgt. U.S. Army, 1955-58. Mem. Tex. Bar Assn., Tex. Bar Found., Houston Lawyers Assn. Congregationalist. Home: 314 Cochran St Conroe TX 77301 2559

IRVIN, GEORGE LEE, III, surgeon; b. Winston-Salem, N.C., Mar. 22, 1931; s. George Lee Irvin, Jr. and Virginia Lasater Irvin; m. Mary Frances Gibbs, Dec. 30, 1966; children: Lee, Catherine. BS, Davidson Coll., 1953—2003; MD, U. of N.C., 1957. Cert. Am. Bd. of Surgery, 1964. Prof. surgery U. of Miami, 1976—. Chief endocrine surgery U. of Miami, Dept. of Surgery. Sr. investigator (surgical rsch.) numerous peer reviewed pub. articles. Comdr. NIH, 1963—65. Recipient Commendation award, Dept. of Veterans Affairs, 1994. Fellow: ACS (fla. chpt. pres. 1998—99); mem.: Nathan A. Womack Surg. Soc. (pres. 1987—89), Am. Assn. of Endocrine Surgeons (pres. 1998—99), So. Surg. Assn. (2d v.p. 1980—81), Am. Surg. Assn. Achievements include development of Intraoperative hormone essays for clinical use. Office: Daughtry Family Dept of Surgery PO Box 016310 (M875) Miami FL 33101-6310 Office Fax: 305-243-4221.

IRVIN, HELEN ADCOCK, interior designer; b. Oxford, N.C., Mar. 31, 1939; d. Joseph Solomon and Virginia Daniel Adcock; m. John Lafayette Irvin, Aug. 30, 1959 (div. June 1974); children: Dorothy Anne, John Lafayette Jr., Helen A. Student, U. N.C., Greensboro, 1957. Owner, pres. Helen Irvin Interior Design, Greensboro, N.C., 1985—. Pres. Greensboro Opera Co., Greensboro. Mem. Greensboro Preservation Soc., Greensboro Symphony Guild, Capital City Club, High Hopes Garden Club, Kirkwood Garden Club, Symposium Book Club, Greensboro City Club. Republican. Presbyterian. Avocations: bridge, gardening. Home and Office: 1901 Pembroke Rd Greensboro NC 27408

IRVIN, MICHAEL JEROME, professional football player; b. Ft. Lauderdale, Fla., Mar. 5, 1966; BA in Bus. Mgmt., U. Miami, 1988. Wide receiver Dallas Cowboys, 1988—2000. Player Pro Bowl, 1991—95, Super Bowl XXVII, 1992, Super Bowl XXVIII, 1993, Super Bowl XXX, 1995. Played in Pro Bowl, 1991-95; named wide receiver The Sporting News NFL All-Pro team, 1991; named outstanding Player of Pro Bowl, 1991. Led league in receiving yards, 1991; played in Super Bowl XXVII, 1992, XXVIII, 1993, XXX, 1995. Office: Dallas Cowboys One Cowboys Pky Irving TX 75063

IRVIN, MICHAEL P. lawyer; b. Ft. Worth, Apr. 29, 1950; BA, U. Tex., 1972; JD, U. Houston, 1975. Bar: Tex. 1975. Ptnr. Fulbright & Jaworski L.L.P., Houston. Mem. ABA, Houston Bar Assn., State Bar Tex., Phi Delta Phi, Order of the Barons. Office: Fulbright & Jaworski LLP 1301 Mckinney St Ste 5100 Houston TX 77010-3031

IRVIN, ROBERT JULIAN, lawyer; b. Balt., Oct. 1, 1948; s. Julian Rowe and Gloria Virginia (Johnson) I.; m. Norma Ann Walsh, May 9, 1981; children— Catharine Leigh. B.A., U. Fla., 1970; J.D., U. Va., 1974. Bar: Fla. 1974. Assoc. Mahoney Hadlow & Adams, Miami and Jacksonville, Fla., 1974-76; assoc. Steel Hector & Davis, Miami, 1976-80, ptnr., 1980-87, chief exec. officer Collier Fin. Holding Co., Miami and Naples, 1987—. Bd. dirs. Internat. Ctr. Fla., Miami, 1984-86, chmn. investment in Fla. com., 1983-86; mem. Fla. Atty. Gen.'s Study Commn. on Money Laundering, Miami, 1983-84. Mem. Am. Land Title Assn. (mem. lenders' counsel group 1984—), Fla. Bar (mem. exec. council real property, probate and trust law sect. 1980-87, chmn. fgn. investment in real estate 1980-84, chmn. real estate investments by pension trusts 1984-87, real property sect. liaison to fgn. tax adv. com. tax sect. 1984). Republican. Episcopalian. Club: Coral Gables Country (Fla.). Home: 2843 S Bayshore Dr Apt P4D Miami FL 33133-6024 Office: Collier Fin Holding Co 3003 Tamiami Trl N Naples FL 34103-2714

IRVINE, HELEN ISABEL BECRAFT, interior designer; b. Washington Grove, Md., Oct. 16, 1934; d. Henry Willard and Grace Isabel (Coffman) Becraft; m. Harry Winfree Irvine, Jr., Nov. 26, 1958; 1 child, Carol Susan. Cert., Parsons Sch. Design, 1955; BS, NYU, 1957. With Craft Shop, Gaithersburg, Md., 1946—, prin., 1982—; salesman Becraft Realty, Gaithersburg, 1955—. Mem. Am. Inst. Interior Designers (bd. dirs.), Md. Sheep Breeders Assn., Mid Am. Appraisers Assn., Montgomery County Bd. Realtors, Nat. Early Am. Glass Club, Md. Hist. Soc. Lodges: Soroptimist. Democrat. Methodist. Home: 9510 Walker Rd Gaithersburg MD 20877 Office: Craft Shop 405 S Frederick Ave Gaithersburg MD 20877-2326

IRVINE, JOHN ALEXANDER, lawyer; b. Sault Ste. Marie, Ont., Can., Mar. 10, 1947; s. Alexander and Ruth Catherine (Woolrich) I.; children from previous marriage: John Alexander, Allison Brooks; m. Lynda Kaye Myska Jenkins, May 24, 1981; children: James Woolrich, William Myska. BS, Auburn U., 1969; JD, Memphis State U., 1972. Bar: Tenn. 1972, Ohio 1982, Tex. 1985. Law clk. U.S. Dist. Ct. (we. dist.) Tenn., 1972-73; asst. dist. atty. gen. 15th Jud. Cir. Tenn., 1973-78; assoc. Glankler, Brown, Gilliland, Chase, Robinson and Raines, Memphis, 1978-81; asst. gen. counsel Mead Corp., Dayton, Ohio, 1981-84; ptnr. Porter & Clements, Houston, 1984-87; prin. Boyer, Norton & Blair, 1987-89; ptnr. Thelen, Marrin, Johnson & Bridges, 1989-94, mng. ptnr. Houston office, mem. mgmt. com., 1991-94; ptnr. Porter & Hodges, L.L.P., 1995—, chmn. litig. practice group, 2002—, mem. mgmt. com., 2000—02. Bd. dirs. Make-A-Wish Found. Tex. Gulf Coast, 1985-86. Fellow Tex. Bar Found. (sustaining life; chair Region 4 nominating com. 2000), Houston Bar Found. (sustaining life); mem. ABA (vice chmn. com. corp. counsel, litig. sect. 1989-91, co-chmn. intellectual properties litig. com. 1996-99, co-chmn. trial practice com. 2000—), Internat. Assn. Def. Counsel, Am. Arbitration Assn. (bd. arbitrators), Nat. Assn. Securities Dealers (bd. arbitrators), Tex. Bar Assn., Tenn. Bar Assn., Fed. Bar Assn. (treas. 1997-98, v.p. 1998-99, pres.-elect 1999-2000, pres. 2000—), Memphis Bar Assn. (YLS, bd. dirs. 1976, treas. 1977), Ohio Bar Assn., Houston Bar Assn., Coll. State Bar Tex., Memphis State U. Law Sch. Alumnae Assn. (pres. 1975-76, 77-78), 5th Cir. Ct. Appeals Bar Assn., U.S. C. of C. (coun. on antitrust policy 1983—), Phoenix Club of Memphis (bd. dirs. 1977-79), Def. Rsch. Inst., Champions Golf Club, Houston Met. Racquet Club, Briar Club. Republican. Presbyterian. Avocations: sports, travel, reading.

IRVINE, PETER BENNINGTON, clergyman; b. Chattanooga, June 8, 1951; s. James Bennington and Susan (Chambliss) I.; m. Angela Cowan, Mar. 5, 1983; stepchildren: John Clark Rumble, Laura Rumble O'Connell. BA, U. Tenn., 1974, JD, 1979; postgrad., Bread Loaf Sch. of English, 1981-82. Bar: Tenn. 1979, Pa. 1983. Assoc. Chambliss, Bahner, Crutchfield, Gaston & Irvine, Chattanooga, 1979-81; copy editor Chattanooga Times, 1981-82; grant writer, researcher Seton Hill Coll., Greensburg, Pa., 1983-86, dir. devel., 1986-89; assoc. dir. planned giving U. Pitts., 1989-92, dir. planned giving, 1992-95; dir. devel. and univ. rels. Pa. State U., McKeesport, 1996-99; seminarian St. Brendan's Episcopal Ch., 2000—; oblate Order of Julian of Norwich, 2000—. Bd. dirs. Pitts. Camerata, 2000—. Mem. Nat. Soc. Fundraising Execs., Pitts. Planned Giving Coun. (pres. 1992-93). Episcopalian. Avocations: reading, canoeing, cross-country skiing, music, theatre. Home: 235 Foxhurst Dr Pittsburgh PA 15238-1817 Office: U Pitts 500 N Craig St Pittsburgh PA 15213-1103 E-mail: pbirvine@home.com.

IRVINE, REED JOHN, media critic, corporation executive; b. Salt Lake City, Sept. 29, 1922; s. William John and Edna (May) I.; m. Kay Araki, Aug. 14, 1948; 1 son, Donald. AB, U. Utah, 1942; postgrad., U. Colo., 1943-44, U. Wash., 1949; M.Litt., Oxford U., Eng., 1951. With Gen. Hdqrs. of Allied Occupation of Japan, Tokyo, 1946-48; economist bd. govs. Fed. Res. System, Washington, 1951-63, adviser internat. fin., 1963-77; chmn. bd. Accuracy in Media, Inc., Washington, 1971—; editor AIM Report; syndicated columnist, radio commentator. Chmn. Accuracy in Academia, 1985— Author: Media Mischief and Misdeeds, 1984; co-author: (with Cliff Kincaid) Profiles of Deception, 1990, (with Joseph C. Goulden and Cliff Kincaid) The News Manipulators, 1993. Dir. Council Def. of Freedom, Washington, 1970— . Served with USNR, 1942-43, USMC, 1943-46, PTO; to capt. USMCR, 1944-46. Recipient George Washington medal Freedom Found., 1980, Ethics in Journalism award World Media Assn., 1987. Mem. Phi Beta Kappa Mem. Lds Ch. Office: Accuracy in Media Inc 4455 Connecticut Ave NW # 330 Washington DC 20008-2328 E-mail: reed@aim.org.

IRVINE, ROSE LORETTA ABERNETHY, retired communications educator, consultant; b. Kingston, N.Y., Nov. 14, 1924; d. William Francis and Julia A.; m. Robert Tate Irvine Jr., Dec. 18, 1965 (dec. June 1968). BA, Coll. St. Rose, 1945; MA, Columbia U., 1946; PhD, Northwestern U., 1964. Tchr. English, Kingston H.S., 1946-47; tchr. English and speech Croton-Harmon H.S., Croton-on-Hudson, NY, 1947-49; instr. speech SUNY, New Paltz, 1949-53, asst. prof. New Platz, 1953-57, assoc. prof., 1957-64, prof. speech communication, 1964-85, prof. emeritus, 1985—. Guest prof. Yon Sei U., Seoul, 1970; U.S. del. U.S. Bi-Nat. Conf., Manila, 1976; adv. bd. Rondout Nat. Bank Norstar (now Fleet Bank), 1973-85; U. Chancellor's adv. bd. SUNY Senate, Albany, 1974-80; guest prof. Celtic lore Princess Grace Libr., Monaco, 1987; mem. faculty sr. rsch. partnership program SUNY, Albany, 1999—; cons., rschr., writer, 1985—; presenter in field. Contbr. articles to Speech Tchr., Ednl. Forum, Readers Theatre, others; writer, performer hist. scripts. Active Nat. Jr. League, Kingston, 1958-90; dir. Puppet Theater for Srs., N.Y., 1982-83; bd. trustees Friends of the Senate House State Hist. Site, Kingston, 1996-99, pres. 1999; bd. Ulster County adv. coun. to Office for Aging, 1998—, v.p., 2000—, pres. 2001—; mem. Gov. Pataki's Adv. Coun. Aging Svcs., 2000—; allocations com. United Way, Ulster County, 1998-2000; mem. Cornell Coop. Extension Program Com., 2003--. Honor Tuition scholar Coll. St. Rose, Albany, N.Y., 1941; named Outstanding Educator of Am., 1971. Mem. AAUW (liaison SUNY New Paltz 1966-85), Speech Comm. Assn. (mem. legis assembly 1967-68, emeritus), N.Y. State Speech Assn. (emeritus), Zeta Phi Eta, Delta Kappa Gamma, Kappa Delta Pi, Pi Lambda Theta. Roman Catholic. Avocations: historic preservation, historic research "John Vanderlyn Holters from Paris", golf, swimming, travel, local history. Home: 105 Lounsbury Pl Kingston NY 12401-5231 Office: SUNY Communications Dept New Paltz NY 12561

IRVINE, VERNON BRUCE, accounting educator, administrator; b. Regina, Sask., Can., May 31, 1943; s. Joseph Vern and Anna Francis (Philip) I.; m. Marilyn Ann Craik, Apr. 29, 1967; children: Lee-Ann, Cameron, Sandra. B in Commerce, U. Sask., 1965; MBA, U. Chgo., 1967; PhD, U. Minn., 1977. Cert. mgmt. acct. Rschr. Sask. Royal Commn. on Taxation, Regina, 1964; lectr. acctg. Coll. Commerce, U. Sask., Saskatoon, 1967-69, asst. prof., 1969-74, assoc. prof., 1974-79, prof., 1979—. Head dept. acctg., 1981-84; profl. program lectr. Inst. Chartered Accts., Regina, 1982-84, Soc. Mgmt. Accts., Saskatoon, 1982-84, 94-95. Co-author: A Practical Approach to the Appraisal of Capital Expenditures, 1981; Intermediate Accounting, Can. edi., 1982, 6th edit., 2001; contbr. articles to acctg. jours. Bd. dirs. Big Sisters of Sask., 1987-90. Grantee John Wiley & Sons, Ltd., 1981, 85, 87, 88, 92, 93, 96, 98, 2001, Soc. Mgmt. Accts. Can., 1979, Pres.'s Fund, U. Sask., 1978, Nelson Can. grantee, 1990. Fellow Soc. Mgmt. Accts. Can. (bd. dirs. 1979-82, 85 87, 89-92, chmn. Nat. Edn. Svcs. com.); mem. Can. Acad. Acctg. Assn. (pres. 1994-95, pres.-elect 1993-94, sec. 1992-93, exec. com., chmn. mem. com. 1989-91), Internat. Acctg. Stds. Com. (Can. rep.1984-87, 96-97), Internat. Fedn. Accts. Coun. (tech. advisor 1988-90), Soc. of Mgmt. Accts. of Sask. (pres. 1980-81), Sutherland Curling Club (treas. 1979-83), Saskatoon Golf and Country Club (bd. dirs. 1988-90). Home: 45 Cantlon Crescent Saskatoon SK Canada S7J 2T2 Office: U Sask Commerce Bldg 25 Campus Dr Saskatoon SK Canada S7N 5A7 E-mail: irvine@commerce.usask.ca.

IRVINE, WILLIAM BURRISS, management consultant; b. Wheeling, W.Va., July 20, 1925; s. Russell Drake and Elizabeth (Carney) I.; m. Allen Claywell; children: William, Mary, Edward. BA in Econs., Cornell U., 1949. V.p. Basil L. Smith Sys., Phila., 1949-66; pres. Pa. Graphic Arts, Inc., Phila., 1966-78, Classified Devel. Corp., Bryn Mawr, Pa., 1978—. Pres. Victor O'Neil Studios divsn. Herff Jones, Inc., N.Y.C., 1972-75; trustee Cornell Delta Phi Ednl. Found., N.Y., 1985; bd. dirs. Main Line Sch. Night, 1998. Author: Treasury of College Humor, 1947. Mem. St. Elmo Club of Phila., St. Elmo Club of N.Y., Lake White Club, Delta Phi (sec. 1960-62). Republican. Roman Catholic. E-mail: classdev@zoomnet.net.

IRVING, A. MARSHALL, retired marine engineer; b. Waterbury, Md., Apr. 10, 1929; s. Walter Reid and Gertrude Elizabeth (Bennett) I.; m. Arline Doris Timmermann, July 19, 1952; children: Marshall Reid, William Anderson, Laurie Anne, Pamela Leigh. BS in Marine Engring., U.S. Merchant Marine Acad., Kings Point, N.Y., 1951; MS in Mgmt. Engring., L.I. U., 1969. Registered profl. engr. N.Y. Marine engr. U.S. Lines Co., N.Y.C., 1951-52; design engr. Sikorsky Aircraft, Bridgeport, Conn., 1953; project engr. to quality control engr. mgr. Dayton T. Brown Inc., Bohemia, N.Y., 1953-72; main engines officer USS Intrepid, N.Y.C., 1954-56; gen. mgr. Cougar Inc., Chgo., 1972-73; adminstrv. law judge N.Y. State Dept. Environ. Conservation, Stony Brook, 1973-89; litigation cons. Mineola, N.Y., 1983—; environ. assoc. Town of Huntington, Long Island, 1992-94; retired, 1994. Subcom. chmn. and sec. Am. Nat. Stds. Inst. Z90, N.Y.C., 1968-90; dir., sec. Snell Meml. Found., St. James, N.Y., 1983-92. Designer prototype weapons delivery system for naval aircraft, 1968. Trustee, dir. Setauket Neighborhood House, 1975—. Mem. ASTM, NSPE, Am. Soc. Safety Engrs. Republican. Episcopalian. Avocations: boating, scuba diving, skiing, target shooting, antiquarian horology. Home: 48 Mud Rd Setauket NY 11733-2233

IRVING, DONALD C. English educator; b. Watseka, Ill, Mar. 11, 1938; s. Carl Richard and Magdalene Louise (Martin) I.; m. Janet Kay O'Neal, June 27, 1964 (div. Nov. 1993); children: Kathleen, Michael. BA, U. Ill., 1960; MA, So. Ill. U., 1962; PhD, Ind. U., 1969. Instr. English Ctrl. Mo. State U., Warrensburg, 1962-64; from instr. to prof. emeritus of English and Am. Studies Grinnell Coll., Iowa, 1968—2003, assoc. dean faculty, 1983-88, chmn. Am. studies, 1974-76, 84-86, chmn. English dept., 1972-74, 90-92, dir. off-campus studies, 1983-88. Mem. initial planning com. DARE, Grinnell, 1980-82. Office: Grinnell Coll Dept English/Am Studies PO Box C-7 Grinnell IA 50112-0805

IRVING, GEORGE STEVEN, actor; b. Springfield, Mass., Nov. 1, 1922; s. Abraham and Rebecca (Sack) Shelasky; m. Maria Karnilova, Oct. 17, 1948; children: Alexander, Katherine. Student, Leland Powers Sch. of Theatre, Boston, 1941. Actor (on Broadway) play, Oklahoma, 1943, Lady in the Dark, 1943, Call Me Mister, 1946, Along Fifth Avenue, 1949, Gentlemen Prefer Blondes, 1949, Two's Company, 1952, Me and Juliet, 1953, Can-Can, 1954, Bells Are Ringing, 1957, The Beggar's Opera, 1957, The Good Soup, 1957, Irma La Douce, 1960, Romulus, 1962, Bravo Giovanni, 1962, Seidman and Son, 1962, Tovarich, 1963, A Murderer Among Us, 1964, Alfie, 1964, Anya, 1965, Galileo, 1967, The Happy Time, 1968, Promenade, 1969, An Evening With Richard Nixon, 1972 (Drama Desk award), Irene, 1973 (Tony award for best supporting actor 1973), On Your Toes, 1983, Me and My Girl, 1986, Cinderella, The Merry Widow, N.Y. City Opera, 1994; stock and touring prodns.

IRVING, GEORGE WASHINGTON, III, veterinarian, research director, small business executive; b. N.Y.C., Apr. 25, 1940; s. George Washington Jr. and Frances (Connell) I.; m. Alice Marie Graves, Dec. 21, 1968; 1 child, George Washington IV. BS, U. Md., 1962; DVM, Purdue U., 1965; MS, Tex. A&M U., 1970. Diplomate Am. Coll. Lab. Animal Medicine, Am. Coll. Vet. Preventive Medicine. Commd. 1st lt. USAF, 1966, advanced through ranks to col., 1984; base veterinarian Niagara Falls Internat. Airport, N.Y., 1966, 388th Tactical Fighter Wing, Korat, Thailand, 1966-67; base veterinarian Wilford Hall USAF Med. Ctr., Lackland AFB, Tex., 1968; asst. chief vet. edn. br. USAF Sch. Aerospace Medicine, San Antonio, 1970-75; chief div. lab. animal medicine Armed Forces Inst. Pathology, Washington, 1976-79; grad. Armed Forces Staff Coll., 1975-76, Air War Coll., 1977; program mgr. Air Force Office Sci. Rsch., Bolling AFB, D.C., 1979-82, dir. life sci., 1982-83; USAF liaison U.S. Army Med. R & D Command, Ft. Detrick, Md., 1983-84, dir. med. chem. def. rsch. program, 1984-87; cons. to surgeon gen. USAF, Washington, 1983-95; dir. Armed Forces Radiobiology Rsch. Inst., Bethesda, Md., 1987-91; staff dir. Human Systems Ctr., Brooks AFB, Tex., 1991-94, vice comdr., 1994-95, dir. re-engring., 1995-96; ret. USAF, 1996; v.p. Conceptual MindWorks, Inc., 1996—, v.p. sci. and tech. support svcs. Instr. grad. rsch. program NIH, Bethesda, 1976-85; merit rev. VA, Washington, 1978-84; cons. Stunkard, Miller Assocs., Bowie, Md., 1976-79. Editor: Selected Topics in Laboratory Animal Medicine, 15 vols., 1971-75; contbr. articles to jours. and chpts. to books; editor: Contemporary Topics in Laboratory Animal Sciences, 1995-97. Vice-minister Secular Franciscan Order, Holy Name Province, 1989-91; min. Tex. Dist., Sacred Heart Province, 1992-94, Los Tres Compañeros/The 3 Companions Region, 1994-98. Decorated Legion of Merit, Def. Superior Svc. medal. Fellow Aerospace Med. Assn.; mem. AVMA, Assn. Mil. Surgeons of U.S. (McCallam award 1988), D.C. Vet. Med. Assn. (pres. 1982), Am. Assn. for Lab. Animal Sci. (pres. nat. capital area br. 1981-82, v.p. 1998, pres. 1999), San Antonio Life Scis. Assn. (sec.), Brooks Aerospace Found. (treas.), Brooks Heritage Found., Brooks AFB Rod and Gun Club (pres. 1973-74). Republican. Roman Catholic. Office: Conceptual MindWorks Inc 4318 Woodcock Dr Ste 210 San Antonio TX 78228-1316 E-mail: girving@teamcmi.com.

IRVING, GITTE NIELSEN, secondary education educator; b. Copenhagen, Nov. 5, 1954; came to U.S., 1976; d. Sven Aage and Aase (Espersen) Nielsen; m. Richard Frederick Irving, June 5, 1976; children: Erik Christian, Emilie Jessica. BA, U. Iceland, Reykjavik, 1976; MEd, Lesley Coll., 1977. Cert. elem. tchr., spl. edn. tchr., Mass.; cert. by Mass. Gen. Hosp. in use of Orton-Gillingham strategies for remediation of dyslexia, 1989. Spl. edn. aide Brookline (Mass.) Pub. Schs., 1977-78; spl. edn. tchr. Ashland (Mass.) Pub. Schs., 1978-81, Greater Lawrence Ednl. Collaborative, Andover, Mass., 1981-82; owner, dir. Comprehensive Academics, Inc., Winchester, Mass., 1983—. Tutor The Rivers Sch., Weston, Mass., 1998—; mem. early edn. planning Winchester Pub. Schs., 1986; com. missions and social concerns United Meth. Ch., Winchester, 1987, co-chair, 1988-91; adv. coun. Spl. Edn. Parents, Winchester, 1985-2001; mem. com. on sch. configurations, subcom. to Sch. Com., Winchester, 1991-92; spkr. European League of Mid. Level Edn. Ann. Conf., Amsterdam, The Netherlands, 1996. Editor spl. edn. presch. newsletter, 1985-86; guest columnist Winchester Star, 1986. V.p. Neighborhood Coop. Nursery Sch., Winchester, 1988-90; mem. sch. improvement coun. Muraco Elem. Sch., Winchester, 1993-95. Avocations: furniture refinishing, knitting and needlework, gardening. Home: 12 Stone Ave Winchester MA 01890-1332 Office: Comprehensive Acads 573 Main St Winchester MA 01890-2900

IRVING, JACK HOWARD, technical consultant; b. Cleve., Dec. 31, 1920; s. William M. and Lottie (Green) I.; m. Florence Friedman, Feb. 1, 1948; children: Paul Howard, Karen Joy, Michael William. BS, Calif. Inst. Tech., 1942; MA, Princeton U., 1948; PhD in Physics, Princeton, 1965. Mem. staff radiation lab. MIT, Cambridge, 1942-45; asst. physics Princeton (N.J.) U., 1946-48; fellow chemistry Calif. Inst. Tech., 1948-49; head systems planning and analysis dept. research and devel. labs. Hughes Aircraft Co., 1949-54; head spl. devices dept. Ramo-Wooldridge Corp., 1954-55, head intelligence systems dept., 1955-56, spl. asst. to exec. v.p., 1956-57, spl. asst. to pres. space tech. labs., 1957-58; corp. staff sci. Thompson Ramo-Wooldridge, Inc., 1958-60; asst. dir. Advanced Systems Planning div. Space Tech. Labs., Inc., 1960; v.p., gen. mgr. systems research and planning div. Aerospace Corp., El Segundo, Calif., 1960-63, v.p. corp. planning, 1965-72, v.p., gen. mgr. environment and urban div., 1972-75; tech. cons. and product devel. Jack H. Irving Assocs., Los Angeles, 1976—; vice chmn. Cabintaxi Corp., 1983-99; mgr. Applied Rsch. & Tech., 1994—. Aerospace vis. fellow Princeton, 1963-65; mem. com. on interplay of engrng. with biology and medicine Nat. Acad. Engrng., 1967-73; chmn., dir. Med. Systems Tech. Services, Inc., 1968-80; dir. Commuter Transp. Services Inc., 1974-87, mem. exec. com., 1974-79, treas., 1975-78, mem. audit com., 1979-90, chmn., 1979-84. Co-author, editor (textbook): Fundamentals of Personal Rapid Transit, 1978; contbr. articles to tech. publs. Asso. fellow Am. Inst. Aeros. and Astronautics; mem. Advanced Transit Assn., Am. Phys. Soc., Sigma Xi. Achievements include directing study fire control systems, logical design and programming first airborne digital computer, Minuteman ballistic missile, comm. satellites, personal rapid transit; inventor highly efficient rotary positive displacement pumps, compressors and expanders and their application to water distribution, air conditioning and refrigeration, and engines, including power generation and automobile engines. Home: 13202 Jonesboro Pl Los Angeles CA 90049-3643 E-mail: apprestek@brandx.net.

IRVING, JEFFREY ALAN, management consultant, educator, lawyer; b. N.Y.C., May 20, 1947; s. Herbert and Florence (Rapoport) I.; m. Maureen Pickett, July 20, 1988; children: Tara, Michael. BSBA cum laude, U. Denver, 1969; JD U. Okla., 1973; MBA with honors, Harvard U., 1980. Bar: N.Y. 1974, U.S. Dist. Ct. (ea. and so. dists.) N.Y. 1975, U.S. Ct. Appeals (2d cir.) 1975, U.S. Supreme Ct. 1978. Legal intern Legal Aid Soc., Norman, Okla., 1972-73; assoc. Pincus, Hutner, Seeman & Hasen, N.Y.C., 1973-74; exec. v.p., gen. counsel Global Sysco divsn. Sysco Corp., Garden City, N.Y., 1974-91; pres. food svcs. divsn. Seabrook Bros. and Sons. Inc., 1991-92. Founder, mng. dir. cons. firm, Great Neck N.Y.; mem. faculty Hofstra U. Coll. Bus. Administrn. Editor Human Rights Rsch. Coun. Jour., 1972-73; contbr. articles to Inc. mag., Food Svc. Distbr. mag. Bd. dirs. L.I. chpt. March of Dimes, 1975-91. Mem. Bar N.Y., Nassau County Bar Assn. (ethics com. 1974-80), Freight Users Assn. N.Y. (pres. 1978, bd. dirs. 1975-92). Republican. Avocations: tennis, sailing. Home: 195 Laurel Lane Syosset NY 11791 E-mail: icgnewyork@att.net.

IRVING, JOHN WINSLOW, writer; b. Exeter, N.H., Mar. 2, 1942; s. Colin F.N. and Frances (Winslow) I.; m. Shyla Leary, Aug. 20, 1964 (div. 1981); children: Colin, Brendan; m. Janet Turnbull, June 6, 1987; 1 child, Everett. Student, U. Pitts., 1961-62, U. Vienna, 1963-64; BA, U. N.H., 1965; M.F.A., U. Iowa, 1967. Asst. wrestling coach Phillips Exeter Acad., 1964-65; asst. prof. English Windham Coll., 1967-69, 70-72, Mt. Holyoke Coll., 1975-78; writer-in-residence U. Iowa, 1972-75; with Bread Loaf Writer's Conf., 1976, Brandeis U., 1978-79; asst. wrestling coach Northfield Mt. Hermon Sch., 1981-83, Fessenden Sch., 1984-86; head wrestling coach Vermont Acad., 1987-89. Author: (novels) Setting Free the Bears, 1969, The Water-Method Man, 1972, The 158-Pound Marriage, 1974, The World According to Garp, 1978, The Hotel New Hampshire, 1981, The Cider House Rules, 1985 (Academy award for best adapted screenplay 2000), A Prayer for Owen Meany, 1989, A Son of the Circus, 1994, A Widow for One Year, 1998, The Fourth Hand, 2001, others, (collection of short stories and essays) Trying to Save Piggy Sneed, 1996, My Movie Business (a memoir), 1999; contbr. short stories and revs. to other publs. Rockefeller Found. grantee, 1971-72; Nat. Endowment for Arts fellow, 1974-75, Guggenheim fellow, 1976-77; inducted into Nat. Wrestling Hall of Fame, 1992, Am. Acad. of Arts and Letters, 2001.

IRVING, ROBERT CHURCHILL, retired quality assurance professional, manufacturing company executive; b. Waltham, Mass., Sept. 15, 1928; s. Frederick Charles and Emily Alvina (Churchill) I.; children: Robert F., John W. AS, Franklin Inst. of Boston, 1965; cert. of profl. achievement, Northeastern U., 1975. Sr. draftsman Mason-Neilan, Boston, 1948-54; mgr. design svcs. Kinney Vacuum Co., Gen. Signal Corp., Boston, 1955-69; mgr. engring. svcs. Sturtevant div. Westinghouse Electric Corp., Hyde Park, Mass., 1969-81, supr. quality assurance, 1981-84; mgr. engring. svcs. Am. Davidson, Inc., Hyde Park, Mass., 1984-87, mgr. quality control, 1987-89; mgr. quality assurance Howden Sirocco, Inc., 1989-94; ret., 1994. Served with U.S.. Army, 1946-48. Mem. Am. Soc. for Quality Control, Am. Legion. Home: 11 Linda Ave Brockton MA 02301-3129

IRWIN, BONNIE D. English language educator, researcher; b. Chgo., Aug. 19, 1959; d. Robert E. and Martha R. Irwin; m. Ned S. Huston, Aug. 6, 1994. AB, U. Calif., Berkeley, 1981, MA, 1983, PhD, 1991. Adj. asst. prof. Iowa State U., Ames, 1991-94; prof. English, Ea. Ill. U., Charleston, 1994—. Contbr. articles to profl. jours., chpts. to books. Dissertation fellow AAUW, 1989; summer seminar grantee NEH, 1992, 97, summer rsch. grantee, 1995. Mem. MLA, Am. Folklore Soc. Office: Ea Ill U 600 Lincoln Ave Charleston IL 61920 E-mail: bdirwin@eiu.edu.

IRWIN, BYRON, management executive; b. Pottstown, Pa., June 25, 1941; s. Ronald and Gertrude (Gilbert) I.; divorced; children: Bart, Mark, Mila, Erik. BA, Drew U., 1966; MBA, George Washington U., 1968. Assoc. dir. Thomas Jefferson U. Hosp., Phila., 1971-78; pres., CEO, United Health Svcs., Binghamton, N.Y., 1978-83, Alta Bates Corp., Berkeley, Calif., 1983-84; dir. APM, N.Y.C., 1984-94; v.p. IBM, Hawthorne, N.Y., 1994-97; ptnr. Ernst & Young, LLP, N.Y.C., 1997-99; chmn., CEO Slotfinder.com, 2000—. Bd. dirs. Pocono Health Sys., 2001--; mem. adv. bd. Liberty Mut. Ins. Co., 1978-83, Binghamton SUNY Grad. Mgmt. Coun., 1978-83; speaker in field, 1980—. Contbr. numerous articles to profl. jours. Chmn. code com. N.Y. State Hosp. Rev and Planning Coun., Albany, N.Y., 1978-83; mem. adv. coun. Bd. Coop. Edn. Svc., Binghamton, 1978-83. Rsch. grantee Hartford Found., 1981-82. Mem. Am. Coll. Healthcare Execs., Am. Hosp. Assn., Am. Mgmt. Assn., Hosp. Assn. N.Y. (bd. dirs.). Avocations: skiing, hiking, tennis, racquetball.

IRWIN, GERALD PORT, physician; b. Muncie, Ind., July 11, 1945; s. Francis Inlow and Helen Marcella (Morgan) I.; m. Martha Sue Vincent, Mar. 10, 1946; 1 child, Tamara Suzette. AB in Biol. Sci., Ind. U., 1968; MD, Ind. U., Indpls., 1972. Diplomate Am. Bd. Family Physicians. Intern and resident Ball Meml. Hosp., Muncie, Ind., 1972-73; pvt. practice Alexandria, Ind., 1973—. Med. dir. Richland Twp. Fire Dept., Anderson. Mem. AMA (Physician Recognition award 1992-95, 98-2001), Am. Acad. Family Physicians,Ind. State Med. Assn., Ind. Assn. Family Physicians, Lions, Elks. Methodist. Avocations: computers, backpacking. Office: PO Box 124 Alexandria IN 46001-0124

IRWIN, GERMAINE, information technology executive; b. Camden, NJ, Oct. 17, 1969; d. Joseph Irwin, Sr.; m. William Kruse III, Nov. 17, 2001; 1 child, Devon Schley. BA, Ind. U., 1995; MBA, U. Phoenix, 2003. Pc, network specialist Pk. Pl. Entertainment, Atlantic City, 1994—2000; project leader MIS City of Santa Fe, 2000—01; bus. analyst web devel. Pk. Pl. Entertainment, Atlantic City, 2001—. Student mentor MentorNet, San Jose, Calif., 2002—03. Mem.: AAUW, ALA (chairperson 2002—03), Ind. Univ. Alumni Assn. (pres. 2002—03). Home: 2714 Evergreen Court Mays Landing NJ 08330 Office: Park Place Entertainment Park Place & the Boardwalk Atlantic City NJ 08401 Home Fax: 609-340-1511. Personal E-mail: girwin@alumni.indiana.edu.

IRWIN, GLENN WARD, JR., medical educator, physician, university official; b. Roachdale, Ind., July 18, 1920; s. Glenn Ward and Elsie (Browning) I.; m. Marianna Ashby; children: Ann Graybill Irwin Warden, William Browning, Elizabeth Ashby Irwin Schiffli. BS, Ind. U., Bloomington, 1942; MD, Ind. U., Indpls., 1944; LLD (hon.), Ind. U., 1986, Marian Coll., 1987. Diplomate: Am. Bd. Internal Medicine. Intern Meth. Hosp., Indpls., 1944-45; resident in internal medicine Ind. U. Med. Ctr., Indpls., 1945-46, 48-50; mem. faculty Ind. U., Indpls., 1950—, instr., asst. prof. then assoc. prof., 1950-61, prof. medicine, 1961-86, prof. emeritus, 1986, dean Sch. Medicine, 1965-73, dean emeritus, 1986, v.p., 1974-86; chancellor Ind. U.-Purdue U., Indpls., 1973-74, chancellor emeritus, 1989. Sr. assoc. Ind. U. Found. Bd. dirs. Goodwill Industries of Ctrl. Ind., Indpls., Greater Indpls. Progress Com., Greater Indpls. YMCA, Walther Med. Rsch. Inst., Walther Oncology Ctr., Indpls. Health Inst., Eiteljorg Mus. Western Art and the Am. Indian; elder 2d Presbyn. Ch. Served to capt. M.C. U.S. Army, 1946-48. Recipient Disting. Alumnus award Ind. U. Sch. Medicine, 1972, Otis R. Bowen Physician County Service award, Benjamin Harrison award, Ind. Acad. award; named Sagamore of the Wabash, Gov. of Ind., 1961, 79, 86. Fellow ACP (gov. for Ind. 1964-70); mem. AMA, Ind. State Med. Assn., Marion County Med. Soc., Ind. Soc. of Chgo., 500 Festival Assn., James Whitcomb Riley Meml. Assn. (bd. govs. 1986—), Newcomen Soc., Sigma Xi, Alpha Omega Alpha, Beta Gamma Sigma, Sigma Theta Tau. Clubs: Columbia (Indpls.), Contemporary (Indpls.), Meridian Hills Country, Skyline (bd. dirs.). Lodges: Masons (33 degree), Rotary. Home: 8025 N Illinois St Indianapolis IN 46260-2938 Office: Ind U-Purdue U at Indpls 1120 South Dr Indianapolis IN 46202-5135 E-mail: drglenni@aol.com.

IRWIN, HALE S. professional golfer; b. Joplin, Mo., June 3, 1945; s. Hale S. and Mabel M. (Philipps) I.; m. Sally Jean Stahlhuth, Sept. 14, 1968; children: Becky, Steven. BS in Marketing, U. Colo., 1968. Profl. golfer, 1968—; tour dir. PGA Am., 1978-79, v.p., 1979; joined Sr. PGA, 1995—. State chmn. Mo. Easter Seal campaign, 1977. Winner Heritage Classic, 1971, 73, 94, Piccadilly World Match Play, 1974-75, U.S. Open Championship, 1974, 79, 90, Western Open, 1975, Atlanta Golf Classic, 1975, 77, Glen Campbell-L.A., 1976, Fla. Citrus, 1976, Hall of Fame Classic, 1977, Australian PGA, 1978, South African PGA, 1979, World Cup, 1979, Hawaiian Open, 1981, Buick Open, 1981, 90, Bridgestone Classic Japan, 1981, Brazilian Open, 1982, Inverrary Classic, 1982, Bing Crosby Pro-Am., 1984, Meml. Tournament, 1983, 85, Bahamas Classic, 1986, Fila Classic, 1987, MCI Heritage Golf Classic, 1994, Ameritech Sr. Open, 1995, 98, Vantage Championship 1995, 97, Am. Express Invitational 1996, PGA Srs.' Championship, 1996, 97, 98, Mastercard Championship, 1997, LG Championship, 1997, Las Vegas Sr. Classic, 1997, 98, Burnet Sr. Classic, 1997-99, BankBoston Classic, 1997, 98, Boone Valley Classic, 1997, 99, Hyatt Regency Maui Kaanapali Classic, 1997, Toshiba Sr. Classic, 1998, U.S. Sr. Open, 1998, Energizer Sr. Tour Championship, 1998, Nationwide Championship, 1999, 2000. Mem. Phi Gamma Delta. Republican. Presbyterian. Achievements include tour victories Heritage Classic, 1971, 73, 94, U.S. Open, 1974, 79, Western Open, 1975, Atlanta Golf Classic, 1975, 77, Glen Campbell-Los Angeles, 1976, Fla. Citrus, 1976, Hall of Fame Classic, 1977, Hawaiian Open, 1981, Buick Open, 1981, Inverrary Classic, 1982, Bing Crosby Pro-Am, 1984, Meml. Tournament, 1983, 85, Bahamas Classic, 1986. Office: Golf Svcs Inc 9909 Clayton Rd Ste 209A Saint Louis MO 63124-1120 also: Sr PGA Tour 112 TPC Blvd Ponte Vedra Beach FL 32082-3046

IRWIN, HEATHER MAY, minister, interior designer; b. Troy, N.Y., Feb. 19, 1949; d. Richard Jay and Helen Irma I. Student, SUNY, 1969, New Sch. Contemporary Radio, 1979, Interior Design Soc., 1984. Ordained pastor Dave Robinson Ministries, Family Prayer Ctr., Tulsa, Okla., 2002. Reporter Capital Newspaper Group, Albany, N.Y., 1969-73; freelance writer Insight Mag., Latham, N.Y., 1973-76; owner, pub. The Daily Woman, Watervliet, N.Y., 1976-79; interior designer Mayfair Home Furnishings, Albany, 1980-85; owner, pres. Wingate House of Design, Albany, 1985—91; owner Creations Interior Design Firm, 1992—. Pres. Woman's Counseling Collective, Albany, 1977, Mission Vision Assn., Inc., 1997—; mem. New Hope for Life Ch., Nassau, NY, 1999—2003. Mem. Interior Design Soc. (pres. ea. N.Y. chpt. 1986-88). Clubs: Ecology (Mechecsville, N.Y.) (v.p. 1971). Avocations: swimming, tennis, reading, painting. Home: 49 Hillcrest Rd Latham NY 12110-4135

IRWIN, JENNIFER VOGEL, education educator; b. Westminster, Md., Jan. 29, 1973; d. David Leonard Vogel and LaVerne Duff; m. Jonathan Francis Irwin, July 18, 1998; 1 child, Samantha Jean. BA in Psychology, St. Mary's Coll. of Md., St. Mary's City, Md., 1995; M in Edn., Loyola Coll., Balt., Md., 2000; PhD in Edn., Am. U., Washington D.C., 2003. Reading specialist K-12 Md. State Dept. of Edn., 2000. Elem. sch. tchr. Balt. County Pub. Schs., Baltimore, Md., 1996—2001; asst. prof. edn. Anne Arundel C.C., Arnold, Md., 2001—. Advisor Student Edn. Assn. Anne Arundel C.C., 2001—. Mem.: ASCD, Internat. Reading Assn. Avocations: travel, biking, crafts, fitness. Office: Anne Arundel C C 101 College Pkwy Arnold MD 21012 Office Fax: 410-777-4401. E-mail: jvirwin@aacc.edu.

IRWIN, JOHN DAVID, electrical engineering educator; b. Mpls., Aug. 9, 1939; s. Arthur Fowle and Virginia I.; m. Patricia Edith Watson, Aug. 26, 1961; children: Geri Marie, John David, Laura Lynne. BEE, Auburn U., Ala., 1961; MS, U. Tenn., 1962, PhD, 1967. Mem. tech. staff Bell Labs., Holmdel, N.J., 1967-68; supr. Bell Labs, Holmdel, N.J., 1968-69; asst. prof. elec. engring. Auburn U., 1969-72, assoc. prof., 1972-73, assoc. prof., head dept., 1973-76, prof., head dept., 1976—, Earle C. Williams Eminent Scholar and dept. head, 1993—; pres. Southeastern Ctr. for Elec. Engring. Edn., Orlando, Fla., 1983-84. Author: (with Nelson and Carroll) Introduction to Computer Logic, 1975, Industrial Noise and Vibration Control, 1979, (with E.R. Graf) Basic Engineering Circuit Analysis, 1984, 7th edit., 2001, (with V.P. Nelson, H.T. Nagle, B.D. Carroll, J.D. Irwin) Digital Logic Circuit Analysis and Design, 1995, (with D.V. Kerns) Introduction to Electrical Engineering, 1995, On Becoming An Engineer, 1997; editor-in-chief The Industrial Electronics Handbook, 1997, Emerging Multimedia Computer Communication Technologies. Recipient Disting. Educator award. 2000; named Am. Soc. Engring. Edn.-Electrical and Computer Engring. Disting. Educator. Fellow IEEE (editor jour. Indsl. Electronics 1982-83, Centennial medal 1984, IEEE-Indsl. Electronics Soc. A.H. Hornfeck Svc. award 1986, IEEE Region III Outstanding Educator award 1989), Am. Soc. Engring. Edn. (Disting. Educator award 2001); mem. IEEE Edn. Soc. (pres. 1989-90, IEEE-Indsl. Electronics Soc. Achievement award 1991, IEEE Edn. Soc. award 1991, IEEE Edn. Soc./Soc. McGraw Hill Jacob Millman award 1993, Undergrad. Tchg. award 1998, Third Millennium medal 2000, Richard M. Emberson award, 2000). Roman Catholic. Home: PO Box 2740 Auburn AL 36831-2740 Office: Auburn U Dept Engring Auburn AL 36849

IRWIN, JOHN ROBERT, oil and gas drilling executive; b. Melbourne, Australia, July 24, 1945; came to U.S., 1969; s. Robert L. and Daisy O. I.; m. Margo E. Mayon, 1979; children: Joshua R., Elizabeth J. BE with honors, Melbourne U., M Engring. Sci., 1969; MS in Indsl. Adminstrn., Purdue U., 1970; AMP, Harvard Bus. Sch., 1990. Registered profl. engr., Australia. With Kerr-McGee Corp., 1970-72; ops. and mgmt. positions Transworld Drilling Co. (sub. Kerr-McGee Corp.), 1972-75; mgr. ops. Transworld Drilling Co., Sharjah, Nigeria and La., 1975-79, Atwood Oceanics, Inc., Houston, 1979-80, gen. mgr., 1980, v.p., 1980-88, exec. v.p., 1988-92; pres., CEO, 1992—. Bd. dirs. Atwood Oceanics, Inc., Offshore Tech. Conf.; chmn. Internat. Assn. Drilling Contractors, 2000. Fellow: Inst. Engrs. Australia. Avocations: reading, history, Australian Rules football. Office: Atwood Oceanics Inc PO Box 218350 Houston TX 77218-8350

IRWIN, JOHN THOMAS, humanities educator, educator; b. Houston, Apr. 24, 1940; s. William Henry and Marguerite Harriet (Hunsaker) I.; m. Laura Elizabeth Scott, Sept. 23, 1978 (div. 1991); m. Meme Amosso, May 29, 1993. BA, U. St. Thomas, 1962; MA, Rice U., PhD, 1970. Supr. public affairs library NASA Manned Spacecraft Center, Houston, 1966-7; asst. prof. English, Johns Hopkins U., 1970-74, prof. writing seminars, 1977—, Decker prof. in humanities, 1984—, chmn., 1977-96; editor Ga. Rev., U. Ga., 1974-77. Author: Doubling and Incest/Repetition and Revenge, 1975, expanded edit., 1995, The Heisenberg Variations, 1976, American Hieroglyphics, 1980, The Mystery to a Solution, 1994, Just Let Me Say This About That, 1998; editor: Johns Hopkins Press Fiction and Poetry series, 1978—; mem. editl. bd. Poe Studies, Ariz. Quar.; contbr. articles to profl. jours. Served with USNR, 1963-66. Recipient John Gardner medal Rice U., 1970, Christian Gauss prize, 1994, Scaglione prize for comparative lit., 1994; Danforth fellow, 1962, Guggenheim fellow, 1991. Mem.: Tudor and Stuart Club, F. Scott Fitzgerald Soc., Faulkner Soc., Poe Studies Assn. (v.p. 1995—97), Assn. Lit. Scholars and Critics. Home: 5313 Springlake Way Baltimore MD 21212-3413 Office: Johns Hopkins U Writing Seminars Gilman 135 Baltimore MD 21218

IRWIN, JOHN WESLEY, publisher; b. Toronto, Ont., Can., July 11, 1937; s. John Coverdale Watson and Annie Elizabeth (Hiltz) I.; m. Marjorie Eleanor Gray, Dec. 16, 1961; children— John Joseph, Marjorie Elizabeth, Peter David Gordon, Andrew James Gray. BA with honours, U. Toronto, 1959; LLD honoris causa, McMaster U., 1999. Tchr., 1959-60; pres. Book Soc. Can. Ltd. (ednl. books), Agincourt, Ont., 1960-83, Irwin Pub. Inc., 1983-89, Ednl. Project Resources Can. Ltd., Willowdale, Canada, 1994—96, Scripture Union-Can., 1997—. Chmn. bd. trustees McMaster Div. Coll., Hamilton, Ont., 1988-99. Recipient Canadian Confedn. medal, 1967 Mem. Assn. Canadian Pubs. (treas. 1977), Canadian Edn. Assn., Can. Copyright Inst. (gov. 1970-77, 81-99), Inter-Varsity Christian Fellowship Can. (dir. 1973—2003, chmn. 1979-91), Canadian Feed the Children (chmn. 1992-95), Peiromai Club (Toronto), Empire Club. Anglican. Home: 81 Bayview Ridge Willowdale ON Canada M2L 1E3 Office: 1885 Clements Rd Unit 226 Pickering ON Canada L1W 3U4 E-mail: john_w_irwin@compuserve.com.

IRWIN, KENNY, professional race car driver; b. Indpls., Aug. 5, 1969; Named Raybestos Rookie of Yr. award, 1998, NASCAR Craftsman Truck Series Rookie of Yr., 1996, USAC Stoops Freightliner Sprint Car Series Rookie of Yr., 1993. Achievements include 7 wins USAC Stoops Freightliner Sprint Car Series, 1993; finished 2d in points USAC Silver Crown Series, 1996; 5 full seasons USAC Skoal Nat. Midget Series, including 8 wins, 20 2d-place, 59 top-5, 87 top-10, 1996 championship; NASCAR Craftsman Truck Series, 1997—, including 2 wins Metro Dade-Homestead Motorsports Complex, Tex. Motor Speedway, 10th-place finish in series point standings. Avocations: golf, pool.

IRWIN, KERRI LYNNE, pharmacist, writer, small business owner; b. Salinas, Calif., Nov. 10, 1959; d. Leslie Morris Rosenblatt and Marilyn Phyllis Kent; m. George William Irwin, Jan. 14, 1983 (div. July 26, 2003); children: Jennifer Jae, Race Christopher. BS, Oreg. State, Corvallis, 1984. Registered pharmacist Oreg. Pharmacist Patrick's Pharmacy, Bend, Oreg., 1984—87, Ctrl. Oreg. Dist. Hosp., Redmond, 1987—89, Rite Aid, Bend, 1989—92, St. Charles Med. Ctr., Bend, 1992—2003; home care I.V. and Sisters Drug Store, 2003—. Owner Mountain View Bed and Breakfast. Author: (book) What's for Dinner? No Problem!, 2001. Avocations: painting, mountain biking, water-skiing, hiking, gardening. Home: 65705 W Hwy 20 Bend OR 97701

IRWIN, LINDA BELMORE, public relations/marketing consultant; b. Portland, Oreg., Apr. 29, 1950; d. Calvin C. and Dorothy B. (Belmore) Harper; m. Michael Hugh Irwin, June 24, 1989. Student, Portland State U., 1968-72. With Hyatt Regency, New Orleans, 1975-78; catering Hyatt Regency-Capitol Hill, Washington, 1978-80; dir. catering Hyatt, Anaheim, Calif., 1978-80; mgr. Dockside Yacht Sales, Annapolis, Md., 1981-85; dir. sales and mktg. Loew's Hotel, 1985-86; dir. mktg. Annapolis Marriot, 1986-88; ind. mktg. cons. Washington, Dallas, Cin. and Loudoun County, Va., 1988—. Amb. State of Md., Annapolis, 1986-88; mktg. chair Tourism Coun. Annapolis and Anne Arundel County; curricula advisor Anne Arundel C.C.; mem. fund raising com. Ch. Circle Beautification Trust; chair of comm., 2002—, chair of fellowship, 2002—03; officer St. Peters Episc. Ch., 2002—, program dir. stewardship com., 2003—; sec.-treas. Mt. Calvary Guild, 2003—; vol. Nat. Day Prayer, Habitat for Humanity, Loudoun Family Fest, Passion Play; media rep. Loudoun County. Mem. Nat. Banquet mgrs. Guild (founder L.A. chpt.), Nat. Assn. Female Execs. (area dir. 1985—), Annapolis C. of C. (ambassador 1985-88), Greater Washington Soc. of Assn. Execs., Anne Arundel Trade Coun., Md. Tourism Coun. (adv. bd.), Internat. Platform Assn. Republican. Episcopalian. Avocations: calligraphy, sailing, travel, literature, ballet. E-mail: mirwin@megapipe.net.

IRWIN, MARK, writer, educator; b. Faribault, Minn., Apr. 9, 1953; s. William Thomas and Mary Lou Irwin. BA, Case Western Res. U., 1974, PhD, 1982; MFA, U. Iowa, 1980. Assoc. prof. Cleve. Inst. Art, 1985-90; asst. prof. Ft. Lewis Coll., Durango, Colo., 1990-92; vis. poet U. Denver, 1992-93, Ohio U., Athens, 1993-94, U. Colo., Boulder, 1997-2000. Translator: Ardis Anthology of Eastern European Poetry, 1982, New Directions, 46, 1982, Notebook of Shadows (Philippe Denis), 1982, Ask the Circle to Forgive You (Nichita Staescu), 1983; author: (poems) The Halo of Desire, 1987, Against the Meanwhile, 1989, Quick, Now, Always, 1996, White City, 1999; editor: Museum Pieces; contbr. poems to periodicals. Recipient Nation/Discovery award, 1984, Pushcart prize, 1994-95, 97-98, 2003-, Colo. Recognition Lit. award, 1996, Colo. Book award, 2000; Traveling fellow Wright-Plaisance, 1977; Fulbright Traveling fellow, 1981; Individual fellow Ohio Arts Coun., 1985-86; fellow Helene Wurlitzer Found., 1988; grantee Lilly Found., 1989, NEA fellowship, 1993. Avocations: hiking, wildlife preservation, animal protection. Home: 3875 S Cherokee St Englewood CO 80110-3511

IRWIN, MELINDA LIGGETT, healthcare educator, researcher; b. Framingham, Mass., July 7, 1970; d. Donald and Rebecca Carroll Irwin; m. Mark Scott Ellis, July 21, 2001. PhD, U. SC., 1999; BS, Coll. of William and Mary, 1992; MS, U. NC, 1994; MPH, U. Wash., 2001. Postdoctoral rsch. fellow Fred Hutchinson Cancer Rsch. Ctr., Seattle, 1999—2001; asst. prof. Yale U., New Haven, 2001—. Prof. Yale U., New Haven, 2001—, rschr., 2001—. Recipient Doctoral Achievement award, U. SC., 1999. Achievements include research in Effect Of Exercise On Improving Breast Cancer Risk And Prognosis; Effect of exercise on visceral adipose tissue; Improving assessment of physical activity in epidemiologic studies. Home: 8 Northgate Rd Westport CT 06880 Office: Yale Univ 60 College Str PO Box 208034 New Haven CT 06520-8034 Home Fax: 203-785-6279; Office Fax: 203-785-6279. Personal E-mail: melinda.irwin@yale.edu. E-mail: melinda.irwin@yale.edu.

IRWIN, MILDRED LORINE WARRICK, library consultant, civic worker; b. Kellerton, Iowa, June 21, 1917; d. Webie Arthur and Bonnie Lorine (Hyatt) DeVries; m. Carl Wesley Warrick, Feb. 11, 1937 (dec. June 1983); children: Carl Dwayne, Arthur Will; m. John B. Irwin, Feb. 1, 1994 (dec. Apr. 10, 1997). BS in Edn., Drake U., 1959; M of Librarianship, Kans. State Tchrs. Coll., 1970. Cert. tchr., libr., Iowa. Elem. tchr. Monroe Ctr. Rural Sch., Kellerton, Iowa, 1935-37, Denham Rural Sch., Grand River, Iowa, 1945-48, Grand River Ind. Sch., 1948-52, Woodmansee Rural Sch., Decatur, Iowa, 1952-55, Centennial Rural Sch., Decatur, 1955-56; elem. tchr., acting libr. Cen. Decatur Sch., Leon, Iowa, 1956-71, media libr. jr. and sr. high sch., 1971-79; libr. Northminster Presbyn. Ch., Tucson, 1984-93, advisor, 1994—. Media resource instr. Graceland Coll., Lamoni, Iowa, 1971-72; lit. dir. S.W. Iowa Assn. Classroom Tchrs., 1965-69; instr. workshop Tucson Mall, Ariz., 2002, 03. Editor (media packet) Mini History and Quilt Blocks, 1976, Grandma Lori's Nourishing Nuggets for Body and Soul, 1985, As I Recall (Loren Drake), 1989, Foland Family Supplement III, 1983; author: (with Quentin Oiler) Van Der Vlugt Family Record, 1976; compiler, editor Abigail Specials, 1991, Abigail Assemblage, 1996; compiler Tribute to Ferm Mills 1911-1992, 1992; co-editor: (with Dorothy Heitlinger) Milestones and Touchstones, 1993, Musings From the Heart, 1999; compiler Musical Ministry, 2002; contbr. articles to publs. Leader Grand River 4-H Club for Girls, 1954-58; sec. South Ctrl. Iowa Quarter Horse Assn., Chariton, 1967-68; chmn. Decatur County Dems., 1981-83, del., 1970-83; pianist Salvation Army Amphi League of Mercy Rhythm Noters, 1984-90; pianist, dir. Joymakers, 1990—; Sunday Sch. tchr. Decatur United Meth. Ch., 1945-54, 80-83, lay speaker, 1981-83, dir. vacation Bible sch., 1982, 83. Named Classroom Tchr. of Iowa Classrom Tchrs. Assn., 1962, Woman of Yr., Leon Bus. and Profl. Women, 1978, Northminster Presbyn. Ch. Women, 1990; named to Internat. Profl. and Bus. Women Hall of Fame for outstanding achievements in field of edn. and libr. sci., 1995; English and reading grantee Nat. Dept. Edn., 1966. Mem. NEA (life), AAUW (chmn. Tucson creative writing/cultural interests 1986-87, 89-93, historian, 1994—, Honoree award for ednl. found. programs Tucson br., Svc. award 1991), Internat. Reading Assn. (pres. Clarke-Ringgold-Decatur chpts. 1967-68), Cen. Cmty. Tchrs. Assn. (pres. 1961-62), Pima County Ret. Tchrs. Assn. (pres. 1989-90), Decatur County Assn. (pres. 1961-63), Decatur County Ret. Tchrs. Assn. (historian 1980-83), Iowa Edn. Assn. (life), Presbyn. Women (hon. life 1990—), Luth. Ch. Libr. Assn. (historian Tucson area chpt. 1991-92, v.p. 1993-94, pres. 1994-95), Delta Kappa Gamma (pres. Iowa Beta XI chpt. 1974-76, sec. 1984-85, historian Ariz. Alpha Gamma chpt. 1986-89). Democrat. Presbyterian. Avocations: walking, computing, horseback riding, reading, writing. Home: 2879 E Presidio Rd Tucson AZ 85716-1539

IRWIN, MIRIAM DIANNE OWEN, book publisher, writer; b. Columbus, Ohio, June 14, 1930; d. John Milton and Miriam Faith (Studebaker) Owen; m. Kenneth John Irwin, June 5, 1960; 1 child, Christopher Owen. BS in Home Econs., Ohio State U., 1952, postgrad. in bus. adminstrn., 1961-62. Editl. asst. Am. Home Mag., N.Y.C., 1953-56; salesman Owen Realty, Dayton, Ohio, 1957-58, Clevenger Realty, Phoenix, 1958-59; home economist Columbus and

So. Ohio Electric Co., 1959-60; pub. Mosaic Press, Cin., 1977—. Owner Bibelot Bindery, 1987—. Author: Lute and Lyre, 1977, Forty is Fine, 1977, Miriam Mouse's Survival Manual, 1977, Miriam Mouse's Costume Collection, 1977, Miriam Mouse's Marrige Contract, 1977, Miriam Mouse, Rock Hound, 1977, Silver Bindings, 1983; editor: Tribute to the Arts, 1984, Chunging, 1996; contbg. author Publisher's Favorite, 1988; illustrator: Corals of Pennekamp, 1979. Daytime crew chief Wyoming Life Squad, Ohio, 1966-71. Recipient Norman Forgue award, 2000. Mem. Studebaker Family Nat. Assn. (archivist 2000—, bd.dirs. 2003—), Miniature Book Soc. (past bd. dirs., chairperson 1987-89). Presbyterian. Avocation: book collecting. Home and Office: 358 Oliver Rd Cincinnati OH 45215-2615 E-mail: mirwin@cinci.rr.com.

IRWIN, PAUL GARFIELD, minister, social services executive; b. Brantford, Ont., Can., Apr. 3, 1937; arrived in U.S., 1956; s. Wesley G. and Evelyn (Shelby) Irwin; m. Jean Rose Hathaway, Sept. 5, 1960; children: Christopher, Jonathan, Craig. BA, Roberts Wesleyan U., N.Y., 1960; MDiv, Colgate Rochester Theol. Sem., 1964; STM, Boston U., 1967; LLD (hon.), Rio Grande Coll., Ohio, 1981. Ordained to ministry United Meth. Ch., 1962. Pastor chs. in Boston, 1962—. V.p. Human Soc. U.S., Washington, 1976—92, pres., CEO, 1992—; v.p. Nat. Assn. Advancement Humane and Environ. Edn., 1980—; pres. World Soc. Protection Animals, London, 1984—. Mem.: Am. Bible Soc. (bd. dirs. 1985—), Asia Soc. (bd. dirs.). Office: Humane Soc US 2100 L St NW Washington DC 20037-1596

IRWIN, PETER JOHN, orthopaedic surgeon; b. East St. Louis, Ill., July 7, 1934; s. Peter and Anne (Sokalski) Iwasyszyn; m. Kathryn Swanson, June 15, 1960; children: Kathryn Linda, Mary Elizabeth, Amy Marie, Kenneth John, James Patrick. BS in Biology, St. Louis U., 1955, MD, 1959. Diplomate Am. Bd. Orthopaedic Surgery, Am. Bd. Forensic Medicine. Intern Creighton Meml. St. Joseph Hosp., Omaha, 1959-60; resident in orthopaedic surgery U. Ark. Med. Ctr., Little Rock, 1961-65, tchg. staff, 1965-97; pvt. practice Fort Smith, Ark., 1965-97; mem. staff St. Edward Mercy Med. Ctr., 1965-97; retired, 1997. Mem. staff Sparks Regional Med. Ctr., 1965-97, chief of staff, 1979, bd. dirs., 1980-87; ret. 1998. Lt. comdr. M.C., USN, 1966-68. Fellow ACS, Am. Acad. Orthopaedic Surgeons (councillor 1983-89); mem. AMA, So. Med. Assn., Sebastian County Med. Soc. (pres. 1997), Ark. Orthopaedic Assn. (pres. 1976-77), Mid-Am. Orthopaedic Assn. (founding mem., pres. 1993-94), Clin. Orthopaedic Soc., Inc., Mid-Ctrl. States Orthopaedic Soc. (pres. 1979-80), So. Orthopaedic Assn., Am. Orthopaedic Soc. for Sports Medicine, Am. Soc. Sports Medicine, Ark. Hand Club.

IRWIN, PETER LLOYD, biochemist, microbiologist; b. Dallas, July 13, 1957; s. Aubrey Donovan Irwin and Frances Kathryn Chaney. BA in Biology/Botany cum laude, U. Tex., 1974; MS in Plant Sci., Tex. A&M U., 1977; PhD in Plant Sci., Mich. State U., 1981. Plant physiologist plant sci. lab. USDA Agrl. Rsch. Svc. Eastern Regional Rsch. Ctr., Wyndmoor, Pa., 1981—95, sr. scientist, chimist, microbiologist, 1995—. Contbr. articles to profl. jours.; ad hoc reviewer Macromolecules, Carbohydrate Rsch., Jour. Carbohydrate Chemistry, Jour. Food Sci., Jour. Food Microstructure, Jour. Nutritional Biochemistry; invited reviewer Jour. Agrl. and Food Chemistry. Recipient Arthur S. Flemming award Washington Jr. C. of C., 1989; bronze medal Fed. Exec. Bd. Phila. Fed. Exec. Bd., 1994. Fellow Am. Inst. Chemists; mem. ACS, Biophysical Soc., Sigma Xi, Gamma sigma Delta, Phi Sigma. Independent. Episcopalian. Avocations: mathematics, classical civilizations, history. Home: 400 Burton Rd Oreland PA 19075-2204 Office: USDA Agrl Rsch Svc Microbial Biophysics and Residue Chem Lab Ea Regional Rsch Ctr 600 E Mermaid Ln Wyndmoor PA 19038-8551

IRWIN, PHILIP DONNAN, lawyer; b. Madison, Wis., Sept. 6, 1933; s. Constant Louis and Isabel Dorothy (Elfving) I.; m. Sandra L. McMahan, Sept. 14, 1985; children: Jane Donnan, James Haycraft, Victoria Wisnom, Philip Donnan Jr. BA, U. Wyo., 1954; LLB, Stanford U., 1957. Bar: Wyo. 1957, Calif. 1958. Assoc. O'Melveny & Myers, L.A., 1957-65, ptnr., 1965-2000, of counsel, 2000—. Mem. planning com. Inst. Fed. Taxation of U. So. Calif. Law Ctr., 1976—, chairperson, 1995-98; spkr. legal seminars. Contbr. articles legal jours. Trustee Mackenzie Found., Los Angeles, 1969— . Recipient Dana Latham Meml. Lifetime Achievement award, LA County Bar Assn. (Taxation Sect.), 2002. Mem.: Calif. Club (L.A.). Republican. Episcopalian. Office: O'Melveny & Myers 400 S Hope St Rm 1853 Los Angeles CA 90071-2899 E-mail: pirwin@omm.com.

IRWIN, R. ROBERT, lawyer; b. Denver, July 27, 1933; s. Royal Robert and Mildred Mary (Wilson) Irwin; m. Sue Ann Scott, Dec. 16, 1956; children: Lori, Stacy, Kristi, Amy. Student, U. Colo., 1951-54; BS in Law, U. Denver, 1955, LLB, 1957. Bar: Colo. 1957, Wyo. 1967. Asst. atty. gen. State of Colo., 1958-66; asst. divsn. atty. Mobil Oil Corp., Casper, Wyo., 1966-70; prin. atty. No. Natural Gas Co., Omaha, 1970-72; sr. atty., asst. sec. Coastal Oil & Gas Corp., Denver, 1972-83; ptnr. Baker & Hostetler, 1983-87; pvt. practice Denver, 1987—. Mem.: Rocky Mountain Oil and Gas Assn., Colo. Bar Assn., Denver Law Club, Los Verdes Golf Club. Republican. Office: 650 S Alton Way Apt 4D Denver CO 80247-1669

IRWIN, RICHARD DENNIS, electrical engineering educator; b. Albany, Ga., Mar. 27, 1958; s. Vernon Hugh and Martha Lucille (Carson) I.; m. Charlotte Anita Yancey, Mar. 8, 1981; children: Katherine Virginia, Thomas Ralph, Elizabeth Martha. BSEE, Miss. State U., Starkville, 1980; MS, Miss. State U., 1983; PhD, Miss. State U., Starkville, 1986. Registered profl. engr., Ohio. Instr. Miss. State U., 1983-86; assoc. sr. staff engr. Control Dynamics Co., Huntsville, Ala., 1986-87; asst. prof. Ohio U., Athens, 1987-90, assoc. prof., 1990-96, prof., 1996—, chair Sch. EECS, 1997—2002, Grad. chair, 1993—97, Thomas prof. engring., 2001—02; pres. Austral Engring. and Software, Inc.; dean and moss prof. of engring. tech. Russ Coll. of Engring. and Tech., Athens, 2002—. Cons. Control Dynamics Co., Huntsville, 1988, Systran, Dayton, Ohio, 1991, Wright State U., Dayton, 1990-92, Nichols Rsch., Huntsville, 1992; mem. steering com. Southeastern Symposium on Sys. Theory, 1988—, gen. chmn., 1994. Contbr. articles to Jour. Guidance, Control, Dynamics, Jour., Astron. Sci., Jour. Materials Engring. and Performance, Jour. Optimal Control and Applications, others. Recipient Outstanding Achievement award Ohio Soc. Profl. Engrs., 1989, Russ Rsch. award, 1993, Outstanding Mgmt. award NASA, 2001, Outstanding Project Mgmt. award NASA, 2002; NASA faculty fellow, 1988, 89, 90; grantee NASA, 1988-95, Dept. Edn., 1999—. Mem. IEEE (sr.), AIAA (sr.), Am. Astron. Soc., Am. Soc. Engring. Edn., Internat. Fedn. for Automatic Control (aerospace tech. com. 2000—, vice chair 2002--), Sigma Xi, Phi Kappa Phi, Tau Beta Pi, Eta Kappa Nu. Democrat. Achievements include development of frequency domain system identificaiton techniques for flexible systems; demonstration of control system design using experimental data models, first Internet accessible flexible structures control lab. Office: Ohio U Stocker 151 Athens OH 45701

IRWIN, ROBERT JAMES ARMSTRONG, investment company executive; b. Buffalo, June 27, 1927; s. Robert J.A. and Dorothy (McLean) I.; m. Donna Henwood, Sept. 10, 1966; children: William Baird, Elaine Mitchell, Elizabeth Flora, Robert J.A. IV, Ronald Henwood, Derrick Millet. BA, Colgate U., 1949; postgrad., U. Buffalo, 1949-50, Babson Inst. Finance, Wellesley, Mass., 1952-53. With Marine Trust Co. Western N.Y., Buffalo, 1958-66; v.p. Marine Midland Banks, Inc., N.Y.C., 1966-69, sr. v.p., 1969-71; exec. v.p. Dreyfus-Marine Midland Mgmt. Corp., 1970-72; sr. exec. v.p. Niagara Share Corp., Buffalo, 1972-74, pres., 1974-92, chief exec. officer, 1988-92, also bd. dirs.; chmn. bd., treas. ASA Ltd., 1993—. Bd. dirs. Boys Club of Western N.Y., 1953; adv. bd. Hauptman Woodward Med. Rsch. Inst., 1975—; trustee Baird Found., 1965—, Old Ft. Niagara Assn., 1986—, Ridley Coll. Scholarship Fund, Inc., James H. Cummings Found., 1978—, Libr. Found. Buffalo & Erie County, N.Y. State Hist. Assn.; trustee, treas. St. Barnabas Coll. Fund Inc. Mem. Saturn Club, Buffalo Canoe, Royal Canadian Yacht (Toronto), Univ. (N.Y.C.). Home: 6 Saint Andrews Walk Buffalo NY 14222-2010 Office: 11 Summer St Buffalo NY 14209-1210

IRWIN, STANLEY ROY, music educator, singer, conductor; b. Henderson, Tex., Jan. 23, 1941; s. Forrest Herbert and Hazel Marie (Gray) Irwin; m. Jane Parker, June 14, 1969; 1 child, Mark Alexander. BA, Baylor U., 1963; B Ch. Music, Southwestern Bapt. Theol. Sem., 1966; MusM, Southern Meth. U., 1969; MusD, Ind. U., 1988; diploma, Internat. Opera Ctr., 1974. Instr. music, choir dir. Simpson Coll., Indianola, Iowa, 1971-73; profl. singer Zurich Opera, Switzerland, 1973-75; prof. voice, dir. choirs Sch. Music DePauw U., Greencastle, Ind., 1975—. Profl. singer Indpls. Symphony Orch., 1978-79, 83, 85, Manhattan Philharmonic, N.Y., 1988, The Philharmonia Orch. of London, 1988, Martinuu Philharmonic, 1995, Indpls. Chamber Orch., 1996, 97, PBS, 1982, 91, NPR 1983, 85, Ill. Pub. Radio, 1982, 87, 91, WQXR, N.Y., 1988, Carnegie Hall, 1987, 96, Avery Fisher Hall, Lincoln Ctr., 1988, Barbican Hall, London, 1988, Dvorak Hall, Prague, 1995, Konzerthaus, Vienna, 1995, Indpls. Festival Orch., 1993, rec. (CD Gothic), 1993, (CD) Irwin Sings Gershwin, 1999; condr. various concerts Kennedy Ctr., 1979, Lincoln Ctr., 1984, Music Ctr., L.A., 1986, Carnegie Hall, 1990, 94, 98, White House, 1990, Honolulu Acad. of Arts, 1996, 2002, New Eng. Symphonic Ensemble, 1998, St. Peter's Basilica, Rome, St. Mark's Basilica, Venice, Italy, 2000, Cathedral, Florence, 2000; contbr. articles to profl. jours Bd. dirs. DePauw Choir, Greencastle, 1977—. Grantee DePauw U., 1983, 1987, John W. and Janice B. Fisher Fund, 1990. Mem. Nat. Assn. Tchrs. Singing, Am. Choral Dirs. Assn., AAUP, Pi Kappa Lambda (pres. Omicron chpt. 1986—). Avocations: golf, biking. Home: 522 E Washington St Greencastle IN 46135-1723 Office: DePauw Univ Sch Music Performing Arts Ctr 121E Greencastle IN 46135

ISAAC, LARRY W. sociologist, educator; b. Clevel., June 12, 1949; s. William E. Isaac and Lillie B. Ramsey; m. Judith A. Keller, May 1, 1969; children: Shayne A., Rachael N. BS in Indsl. Mgmt., U. Akron, 1971, MA in Sociology, 1974; PhD in Sociology, Ind. U., 1979. Assoc. instr. U. Akron, Ohio, 1973—74, Ind. U., Bloomington, 1977; asst. prof. to prof. Fla. State U., Tallahassee, 1978—2001, Mildred and Claude Pepper dist. prof., 2001—. Mem. editl. bd.: Am. Sociol. Rev., 1982—84, Am. Jour. Sociol., 1987—89, guest editor: Hist. Methods, 1997; contbr. articles. Mem. Oxford Round Table, England, 2003. Recipient Barrington Moore award, Am. Sociol. Assn., 1990; fellow, Nat. Inst. Mental Health, 1975—77; Rsch. grant, NEH, 2000. Mem.: So. Sociol. Soc. (exec. com. 1998—2000, v.p. 1999—2000). Office: Fla State Univ 516 Bellamy Bldy Tallahassee FL 32306 E-mail: lisaac@coss.fsu.edu.

ISAAC, STEVEN RICHARD, communications executive; b. Utica, N.Y., Dec. 19, 1947; s. Anthony Richard and Camille Cecilia (Potaro) I.; m. Martha Cash, Oct. 9, 1982; children: Charles Wesley, Spencer Anthony. BA in English, U. Buffalo, 1969; MS in Comm., Syracuse U., 1973; postgrad. in bus. adminstrn. program, Fordham U., 1978. Prin. Media Design Assocs., N.Y.C., 1973-75; dir. multimedia products The Am. Mgmt. Assn., N.Y.C., 1975-78; ptnr. Tng. by Design, Inc., N.Y.C., 1978-79; founder, chmn. and chief exec. officer Martin Direct, Inc. (formerly The Stenrich Group Inc.), N.Y.C., 1979-96; founder, CEO Martin Interactive, 1995-96; bd. dirs., exec. v.p., COO, The Martin Agy., 1996; pres. mktg. group Cadmus Comm. Corp., Richmond, Va., 1996-97, exec. v.p., 1997-99; CEO DMW Worldwide, 2000—02; exec. v.p. DIMAC Holdings, 2000—02; mng. dir. Interactive Mktg. Inst., Grad. Sch. Bus. Va. Commonwealth U., Richmond, 2002—. Author: Words for Phone: Writing Winning Telephone Scripts; contbr. articles to profl. jours. Mem. cmty. adv. bd. 1st Capital Bank; bd. dirs. Shady Grove YMCA. Mem. Direct Mktg. Assn., Richmond Ad Club, Commonwealth Club. Methodist.

ISAAC, WALTER LON, psychology educator; b. Seattle, May 31, 1956; s. Walter and Dorothy Jane (Emerson) I.; m. Susan Victoria Wells. BS, U. Ga., 1978; MA, U. Ky., 1983; postgrad., U. Ga., 1988-89, PhD, U. Ky., 1989. Advanced EMT Athens Gen. Hosp., 1977-79; teaching asst., rsch. asst. U. Ky., Lexington, 1979-87, instr. gifted student program, 1985, 87; instr. evening classes U. Ga., Athens, 1988, temp. asst. prof., 1989; asst. prof. psychology, mem. grad. faculty East Tenn. State U., Johnson City, 1989-98; assoc. prof. psychology Ga. Coll. and State U., Milledgeville, 1998—, tenure, 2002. Councilor for Coun. on Undergrad. Rsch, 1999—; reviewer McGraw-Hill Pub. Co., Cambridge, Mass., 1990—. Contbg. author: Aging and Recovery of Function, 1984; contbr. articles to profl. jours. Bd. dirs. Upper East Tenn. Sci. Fair, Inc., 1992-98; advisor to honor socs. Gamma Beta Phi, 1994-97, Psi Chi, 1999—. Mem. Am. Psychol. Soc., Southeastern Psychol. Assn., Soc. for Neurosci., Coun. on Undergrad. Rsch. (coun. 1999), Sigma Xi (grantee 1987). Avocations: stained glass, photography, canoeing. Home: 286 Old Plantation Trail Milledgeville GA 31061

ISAAC, WILLIAM MICHAEL, investment firm executive, former government official; b. Bryan, Ohio, Dec. 21, 1943; s. Charles R. and Ruth L. (Hallberg) I.; m. Carma Sue Dunbar, Aug. 15, 1965 (div. 1993); m. Christine Verney, Nov. 16, 1997; children: David M., Stephanie A., Lennon G., Quinn V. BS, Miami U. Oxford, Ohio, 1966; LL.D. (hon.), Miami U. Oxford, 1984; JD summa cum laude, Ohio State U., 1969. Bar: Wis. 1969, Ky. 1974, D.C. 1986. Mem. firm. Foley & Lardner, Milw., 1969-74; v.p., gen. counsel, sec. First Ky. Nat. Corp., Louisville, 1974-78; chmn. FDIC, Washington, 1978-85; ptnr. Arnold & Porter, Washington, 1985-93; chmn. The Secura Group, Washington, 1985—, Secura Burnett Co. LLC, San Fransisco, 1992—; mem. Depository Instns. Deregulation Com., 1981-85, Bush Task Group, 1982-85; chmn. Fed. Fin. Instns. Exam. Council, 1983-85. Bd. dirs. MPS Group, Inc., Jacksonville, 2000—, Am. Express Centurion Bank, Salt Lake City. Co-author: Bank Holding Companies: A Practical Guide to Bank Acquisitions and Mergers, 1972; contbr. articles on banking to profl. jours. Mem. nat. coun. Coll. Law, Ohio State U., Columbus, 1980—; mem. bus. adv. coun. Miami U., Oxford, Ohio, 1982—; trustee Miami U. Found., 1988-96; bd. dirs. Ohio State U. Found., The Cmty. Found. of Sarasato County; chmn. Goodwill Found.; trea. Goodwill Ind. Mem. ABA, Wis. Bar Assn., Ky. Bar Assn., Fed. Nat. Mortgage Assn. (adv. bd. 1989-90). Republican. Office: The Secura Group 7799 Leesburg Pike Ste 800N Falls Church VA 22043-2413 E-mail: billisaac@comcast.net.

ISAAC, YVONNE RENEE, construction company executive; b. Cleve., Apr. 13, 1948; d. Leon Warren and Vernice Leona (Hallom) I.; m. Harold E. Rhynie, Dec. 30, 1984. BA, Sarah Lawrence Coll., 1970; MS, Rensselaer Poly. Inst., 1973, Bklyn. Poly. Inst., 1976. Market rschr. GE Co., Phila., 1971-72; cons., planner SPA/Redco (subs. Perkins & Will), Chgo., 1972-75; sr. assoc. Perkins & Will, N.Y.C., 1975-76, project mgr., 1978-81; supply assoc. Mobil Oil Corp., N.Y.C., 1976-78; project mgr. Ehrenkrantz Group, P.C., N.Y.C., 1981-84; asst. dir. Met. Transp. Authority, N.Y.C., 1984-86; group dir. N.Y.C. Health & Hosps. Corp., N.Y.C., 1986-92; v.p. McDevitt Street Bovis, Atlanta, 1992-96; v.p., dir. profl. svcs. Bovis Constrn. Corp., Atlanta, 1996-98, sr. v.p., 1998—. Vis. assoc. prof. Pratt Inst., Bklyn., 1977; asst. prof. Columbia U. Grad. Sch. Architecture and Planning, N.Y.C., 1977-78. Mem. games adv. team Atlanta Paralympic Orgn. Com., 1995-96; bd. dirs. Girl Scout Coun. NW Ga., 1999—, exec. com., 2000—. Mem. Nat. Assn. for Equal Opportunity in Edn. (corp. advisory com.). Democrat. Home: 2333 Scarlett Walk Stone Mountain GA 30087-1106 Office: Bovis Lend Lease Ste 600 5909 Peachtree Dunwoody Rd NE 600 Atlanta GA 30328-8102

ISAAC NASH, EVA MAE, educator; b. Natchitoches Parish, La., July 24, 1936; d. Earfus Will Nash and Dollie Mae (Edward) Johnson; m. Will Isaac Jr., July 1, 1961 (dec. May 1970). BA, San Francisco State U., 1974, MS in Edn., MS in Counseling, San Francisco State U., 1979; PhD, Walden U., 1985; diploma (hon.), St. Labre Indian Sch., 1990. Nurse's aide Protestant Episcopal Home, San Francisco, 1957-61; desk clk. Fort Ord (Calif.) Post Exchange, 1961-63; practical nurse Monterey (Calif.) Hosp., 1963-64; tchr. San Francisco Unified Schs., 1974, counselor, instr. City Coll. San Francisco, 1978-79; tchr. Oakland (Calif.) Unified Sch. Dist., 1974—. Pres. sch. adv. coun., Oakland, 1977-78, faculty adv. coun., 1992-93; advt. writer City Coll., San Francisco, 1978; instr. vocat. skill tng., Garfield Sch., Oakland, 1980-81; pub. speaker various ednl. insts. and chs., Oakland, San Francisco, 1982—; lectr. San Jose State U., 1993; creator Language Arts-Step By Step program E. Morris Cox Elem. Sch., Oakland, 1995, 96; author, presenter material in field. Author video tape Hunger: An Assassin in the Classroom, 1993-94. Recipient Community Svc. award Black Caucus of Calif. Assn. Counseling and Devel., 1988, Cert. of Recognition, 1990; named Citizen of the Day, Sta. KABL, 1988. Mem. ASCD, Internat. Reading Assn., Nat. Assn. Female Execs., Am. Personnel and Guidance Assn., Calif. Personnel and Guidance Assn., Internat. Platform Assn. (Hall Fame 1989, Profl. Speaking cert. 1993), Phi Delta Kappa. Democrat. Avocations: travel, hiking, tennis, music, dancing. Office: Oakland Unified Sch Dist 1025 2nd Ave Oakland CA 94606-2296

ISAACS, ANDREA, editor, publisher, dancer, choreographer, former educator; b. Chgo., July 16, 1952; d. William H. and Sally (Shapiro) I. BFA, U. Ill., 1975; MA, U. Iowa, 1985. Cert. secondary tchr. Founder, artistic dir., pres. Moving Images Dance Co., Chgo. and Troy, N.Y., 1976-94; artist-in-residence Ill. Arts Council, Chgo., 1978-86; dance dir. Emma Willard Sch., Troy, 1986-94; founder, tchr. phys. intelligence U.S., Italy, France, Eng., Can.; founder Phys. Intelligence, Inc. Presenter Internat. Enneagram Assn. Confs., Balt., 1997, Denver, 1998, Toronto, 1999, San Francisco, 2000. Choreographer Village, 1985, Travelers, 1986, Dancing with a Foot in Two Worlds, 1988, Sacred Dream, 1989, Raven, 1990, Borrowed Ledges, Cocoon and Trinity, 1992, Avalon, 1992, Awakening, 1992, No Slack for You, 1993, Walking to the Falls, 1993, Northern Lights, 1993, Red Sea, 1994, Don't Worry Be Happy, 1994; editor: Enneagram Monthly, 1994—; pub. Enneagram Monthly, 1994—, founder EnneaMotion; author: Buddhist Six Realms of Being and the Enneagram, 1995, Movement as a Bridge Between Thought and Feeling, 1995, Using EnneaMotion to Explore the Nine Types, 1995, Experiencing the Types through EnneaMotion, 1995, Enneagram Demographic and the MBTI, 1996, Setting the Record Straight, 1996, EnneaMotion, 1997, Out of the Abyss: A Creative Journey of Self-Discovery, 1997, Frogs, Neuron Pathways and EnneaMotion, 1998, EnneaMotion-Transformation Through Movement, 1999, Beyond Type: Transformation Through Movement, 1999, EnneaMotion: The Somatic Enneagram, 2000, Conversation with Sandra Maitri, 2001, Physical Intelligence and Will, 2003. Ill. Arts Coun. fellow, 1980; Ill. Arts Coun. grantee, 1978-86; recipient N.Y. State Arts Decentralization awards, 1988, 89, 90, 92, 93. Mem. Dance Alliance (chmn. 1987—), Chgo. Dance Arts Coalition. Avocations: bookbinding, horses, biking, swimming, poetry. Home and Office: 117 Sweetmilk Creek Rd Troy NY 12180-9105 E-mail: andreais@earthlink.net .

ISAACS, DIANE SCHARFELD, English educator; b. Washington, Nov. 11, 1939; d. Arthur William Sharfeld and Lucille Speer Smith; m. Stephen D. Isaacs, June 8, 1963 (dissolved 2000); children: Deborah, David, Sharon; m. Jay L. Halio, May 26, 2002. BA with honors, Smith Coll., 1961; MA, Stanford U., 1972; EdD, Columbia U., 1982. Cert. tchr. English K-12, Social Studies, 7-12, prin., N.Y., N.J. Tchr. English, George Mason H.S., Falls Church, Va., 1963-65, Woodrow Wilson H.S., Washington, 1966-71; tchr. English and social studies Fieldston Sch., Riverdale, N.Y., 1971-74; tchr. English, Sidwell Friends Sch., Washington, 1974-78; asst. prof. Afro-Am. studies U. Minn., Mpls., 1978-83; vice prin. humanities Tenafly Bd. Edn., Tenafly, N.J., 1985-87; assoc. prof. Fordham U., Bronx, 1983-99; chmn. English dept. Nyack (N.Y.) Pub. Schs., 1987-93; coord. English grades 6-12 Manhasset (N.Y.) Pub. Schs., 1993-95; English dept. chair Wayne Hills, N.J., 1997-99; ret. Reader A.P. lit. U. Del., 2002; tchr. English U. Md., G.W.U., Am. U., 2000—. Sec., treas. adminstrv. unit dist. dept. chairs, 1998—, class meml. chair Smith Coll., 1991-2001, class sec. Nat. Cathedral Sch., 1957—; mem. Westchester Holocaust Commn. Recipient Yavner award N.Y. State Bd. of Regents, 1991. Mem. MLA, ASCD, Nat. Coun Tchrs. English (exec. com.), Conf on English Leadership, Am. Studies Assn. Avocations: theatre, black memorabilia, travel, folk art. Home: 8 Country Hills Dr Newark DE 19711 E-mail: dsipst@aol.com.

ISAACS, GERALD WILLIAM, retired agricultural engineering educator, consultant; b. Crawfordsville, Ind., Sept. 3, 1927; s. William Paul and Verna Ethel (Johnson) I.; m. Phyllis Joyce Seaton, Aug. 22, 1948; children: Joyce Irene (dec.), David Gerald, Donald Phillip, Joseph Lee (dec.), Susan Verna, Linda Kay. BSEE, Purdue U., 1947, MSEE, 1949; PhD in Agrl. Engring., Mich. State U., 1954. Registered profl. engr., Fla. Grad. asst. agrl. engring. dept. agrl. engring. Mich. State U., E. Lansing, 1952-54; instr. agrl. engring. Dept. Argl. Engring, Purdue U., W. Lafayette, Ind., 1948-52, from asst. prof. agrl. engring to prof. agrl. engring., 1954-1964, prof., head dept. argl. engring., 1964-81; prof., chmn. dept. agrl. engring. U. Fla., Gainesville, 1981-91, prof. emeritus, 1991—. Cons. engr. various mfg. and legal firms, 1958—. Contbr. articles to profl. jours. Recipient Massey Ferguson Gold medal Am. Soc. Agrl. Engrs., 1991, Silver medal Max Eyth Gesselschaft, Germany, 1979. Mem. Polish Acad. Sci., Rotary Internat. (dir. 1976-78, Paul Harris fellow 1993), Am. Soc. Agrl. Engrs. (nat. pres. 1982-83), Soc. German Engrs. (hon. corr. mem.) Lutheran. Avocations: photography, travel, music. Office: U Fla Dept Agrl and Biol Engring Frazier Rogers Hall Gainesville FL 32611

ISAACS, HAROLD, history educator; b. Newark, Dec. 19, 1936; s. Albert Lewis and Bertha (Wohl) I.; m. Doris Carol Mack, Apr. 25, 1974. BS in History, U. Ala., University, 1958, MA in History, 1960, PhD in History, 1968. Grad. tchg. fellow in history U. Ala., University, 1959-62; instr. in history Memphis State U., 1962-65; asst. prof. history Ga. Southwestern State U., Americus, 1965-70, assoc. prof. history, 1970-79, prof. history, 1979—. Bd. dirs. World Communities Theater, bd. advs. Ency. Developing World; scholar cons. Jimmy Carter Residency Program. Author: Jimmy Carter's Peanut Brigade, 1977; founder, editor Jour. of Third World Studies, 1984—. Advisor Young Dems., Ga. Southwestern State U., 1965-80, chmn. faculty capital campaign, 2003; founder, coord. Third World in Perspective Program Seminar Series, 1981—; coord. Black Leaders Lecture Series, 1981. Recipient Tchr. of Yr. award Alpha Phi Alpha, 1982, Outstanding Svc. award Americus Early Bird Civitan Club, 1983, Outstanding Historian and Humanitarian award SABU, 1994, Presdl. Citation for Disting. Svc., 1995, Outstanding Svc. to African Am. and Third World Studies SABU 1996-97, 1997, All-Africa award African Studies and Rsch. Forum, 2001. Mem. Assn. Third World Studies, Inc. (founder, pres., exec. dir., 1983-91, treas. 1983-97, proceedings editor 2002—, Presdl. award 1992, Harold Isaacs award). Democrat. Jewish. Home: 180 Lakeshore Dr Americus GA 31719-8233 Office: Ga Southwestern State U Dept History & Polit Sci 800 Wheatley St Americus GA 31709

ISAACS, JOHN T. research scientist; b. Balt., May 1, 1949; s. James Pershing and Arlene Wolfgang Isaacs; m. Sarah Dixon Isaacs, June 4, 1971; children: Katelin Patricia, Sarah Elizabeth, William James. BA, Johns Hopkins U., 1971; PhD, Emory U., 1978. Postdoctoral fellow Johns Hopkins U. Sch. Medicine, Balt., 1977—80, asst. prof., 1980—86, assoc. prof., 1986—93, full prof., 1993—, co-dir. divsn. exptl. therapeutics, 1998—, dir. cellular and molecular med. grad. program, 1999—2002. Mem. exptl. therapeutics study sect. NIH, Washington, 1989—93; cons. Cephalon, Inc., West Chester, Pa., 1995—; mem. Sci. Advocacy Bd., West Chester, 2001—. Editor-in-chief: The Prostate, 2000—, mem. editl. bd.: Cancer Rsch., 1987—95, 1995—, Clin. Cancer Rsch., 1994—, Jour. Clin. Endocrine, 1997—2001. Recipient CapCURE Rsch. award, Assn. for Cure of Cancer Prostate, Santa Monica, Calif., 1993—2001, Idea award, Dept. of Def., Washington, 1997—; grantee, NIH, Washington, 1981—. Mem.: AAAS, Am. Assn. for Lab. Animal Sci., Endocrine Soc., Am. Assn. Cancer Rsch., Soc. for Basic Biol. Urology Rsch., Am. Urol. Assn. (assoc.). Avocations: tennis, bicycling, backpacking. Home: 13638 Poplar Hill Rd Phoenix MD 21131 Office: Johns Hopkins Univ Sch Medicine 1650 Orleans St Baltimore MD 21231

ISAACS, KENNETH S(IDNEY), psychoanalyst, educator; b. Mpls., Apr. 7, 1920; s. Mark William and Sophia (Rai) I.; m. Ruth Elizabeth Johnson, Feb. 21, 1951 (dec. 1967); m. Adele Rella Bodroghy, May 17, 1969; children: Jonathan, James; stepchildren: John, Curtis, Peter and Edward Meissner. BA, U. Minn., 1944; PhD, U. Chgo., 1956; postgrad., Inst. Psychoanalysis, 1957-63. Intern Worcester State Hosp., Mass., 1947-48; trainee VA Mental Hygiene Clinic, Chgo., 1948-50; chief psychologist outpatient clinic system Ill. Dept. Pub. Welfare, 1949-56; research assoc., assoc. prof. U. Ill. Med. Sch., Chgo., 1956-63; practice psychoanalysis Evanston, Ill., 1960—. Supr. psychiat. residency program Evanston Hosp., Northwestern U., 1972-81, Northwestern Meml. Hosp.; pres. Chgo. Ctr. Psychoanalytic Psychology, 1984-87; cons. to schs., hosps., clinics, pvt. practitioners and industry; sr. cons. Beta Consulting Ltd.; pres. Kenisa Drilling Co., 1982-93, Kenisa Securities Co., 1982-93, Kenisa Oil Co., 1982-95. Author: Again with Feeling, 1989, Uses of Emotion, 1998, (syndicated newspaper column) A Psychologist's Notebook; contbr. articles to profl. publs. Served with AUS, 1943-45, ETO. Mem.: Chgo. Psychoanalytic Soc., Am. Bd. Profl. Psychology (bd. trustees 1994—2001), Am. Bd. Psychoanalysis (chair bd. dirs.), APA (bd. dirs. divsn. pschoanalysis), AAAS, Sigma Xi. E-mail: isaacs@storm.cncoffice.com.

ISAACS, MICHAEL BURTON, lawyer; b. Mar. 22, 1947; s. Richard and Bailey (Levine) I.; m. Mindy Isaacs, June 27, 1993; 1 stepchild, Tara Sousa. AB, U. Rochester, 1969; JD, Boston Coll., 1974. Bar: Mass. 1974, U.S. Dist. Ct. Mass. 1975, U.S. Ct. Appeals (D.C. cir.) 1975, D.C. 1979, U.S. Ct. Appeals (9th cir.) 1979, R.I. 1988. Staff atty. Mass. Cable TV Commn., Boston, 1974-75; gen. counsel, 1975-78; asst. gen. counsel Nat. Cable TV Assn., Washington, 1978-80; dir. planning and govt. affairs Colony Communications Inc., Providence, 1980-82; sole practice L.A., 1982-84; dir. corp. devel. Providence Jour. Co., L.A., 1984-87, also. dir. devel., regulatory and legal affairs, 1987-92; dir.

govt. affairs and pub. policy, 1992-94; v.p. govt. affairs and pub. policy, 1994-97; v.p. govt. & corp. rels., 1997; v.p. devel. Bresnan Comm., White Plains, N.Y., 1998-2000; atty., govt. pub. rels. cons. East Greenwich, RI, 2000—. External com. on telecomm. and higher edn. R.I. Bd. Govs. for Higher Edn., 1995; panelist at profl. convs. Bd. dirs. Jewish Srs. Agy., 2000—, Jewish Fedn. R.I., 2001—; mem. fin. bd. Town of East Greenwich, R.I., chair, 2001—; mem. R.I. Pub. Telecomms. Authority, 2001—. Mem. R.I. Bar Assn., Nat. Cable TV Assn. (utility rels. 1980-81, state-local coms. 1990, 94—), D.C. Bar Assn., Found for Cmty. Svc. Cable TV (bd. dirs. 1985-87), Fed. Comm. Bar Assn., New Eng. Cable TV Assn. (bd. dirs. 1981), Calif. Cable TV Assn. (bd. dirs. 1985-87), So. Calif. Cable TV Assn. (bd. dirs., v.p. 1986), City of L.A. Cable Operators Assn. (pres. 1986-87), Cellular Telecomm. Industry Assn. (legis. com. 1988-90), Cable Telecom. Assn. (bd. dirs.). Republican. Jewish.

ISAACS, NEIL D. literature educator; b. N.Y.C., Aug. 21, 1931; m. Ellen Lichtman, May 19, 1985; 4 children. AB in Comparitive Lit. and Philosophy, Dartmouth Coll., 1953; AM in English Lang. and Lit., U. Calif., Berkeley, Calif., 1956; PhD in English Lang. and Lit., Brown U., 1959; MSW, U. Md., 1989. LCSW 1993. Tchg. asst. Brown U., 1957—58, tchg. assoc., 1958—59; instr. CCNY, 1959—62, asst. prof., 1962—63, U. Tenn., Knoxville, Tenn., 1963—65, assoc. prof., 1965—71; prof. English U. Md., Coll. Pk., Md., 1971—2000, prof. emeritus, 2000—. Vis. asst. prof. U. Conn., Waterbury, Conn., 1964; mem. instnl. rev. bd. NIMH, 2001—; mem. adv. bd. Art Gliner Ctr. for Humor Studies, 1999—. Author: Structural Principles in Old English Poetry, 1968, Eudora Welty, 1969, Fiction inot Film: A Walk in the Spring Rain, 1970, All the Moves: A History of College Basketball, 1975, Checking Back: A History of N.H.L. Hockey, 1977, Covering the Spread, 1978, Jock Culture, U.S.A., 1978, Sports Illustrated Basketball, 1981, All the Moves: A History of College Basketball, 1984, Grace Paley: A Study of the Short Fiction, 1990, The Great Molinas: A Novel, 1992, Innocence and Wonder: Baseball through the Eyes of Batboys, 1994, Batboys and the World of Baseball, 1995, Vintage NBA Basketball: The Pioneer Era, 1996, The Miller Masks: A Novel in Stories, 2000, You Bet Your Life: The Burdens of Gambling, 2001; contbg. editor: Breeder's Cup Mag., 1984—, Sportsfan Mag., 2000—; editor: Approaches to the Short Story, 1963, Tennessee Studies in Literature, 1966, Tolkien and the Critics, 1968, The Sporting Spirit: Athletes in Literature and Life, 1977, Tolkien: New Critical Perspectives, 1981, The Unknown Constellations, 1995; mem. editl. bd.: Literature/Film Quarterly, 1973—88; contbr. chapters to books, columns in newspapers, articles to profl. jours. Office: Univ Maryland College Park MD

ISAACS, RICHARD B. investigative and protective services professional; b. Evanston, Ill., Nov. 12, 1942; s. Harry Columbus and Natalie I.; m. Catherine Anne Nicodemo, Oct. 25, 1980 (div. 1994). BA, NYU, 1964; MA, Columbia U., 1975. Cert. CPP. V.p. Blackstone & West, Inc., Phila., 1967-69; indsl. photographer N.Y.C., 1970-76; programmer STSC, Inc., N.Y.C., 1976-81; pres. Blackstone & West, Inc., N.Y.C., 1981-89; prin., sr. v.p. The Lubrinco Group, Inc., N.Y.C., 1989-2001. Dir. ASR Instrs. Coun., Arlington, Tex., 1983-2001. Author: (book) The Seven Steps to Personal Safety, 1993, rev. 1998; editor: The Bus. Security e-Jour., 1998-2001; others. Vol. Peace Corps, Colombia, 1964-66. Mem. Am. Soc. Law Enforcement Trainers (mem. security com. 1999-2001), Tactical Response Assn., Soc. Competitive Intelligence Profls., Internat. Assn. Counterterroism and Security Profls. Avocations: poetry, translating, flying, 50-meter free pistol, Aikido. Office: The Lubrinco Group Inc 215 Park Ave S Ste 711 New York NY 10003-1603 E-mail: rbisaacs@lubrinco.com.

ISAACS, ROBERT, conductor, director; b. Washington, DC, June 19, 1969; s. Arnold Robinson and Kathleen Taylor Isaacs. AB magna cum laude, Harvard U., 1992; MFA, Columbia U., 2002. Dir. choral music Garrison Forest Sch., Owings Mills, Md., 1993—97; assoc. condr. Nat. Youth Choir of Gt. Britain, Manchester, England, 1993—99; dir. choral activities Manhattan Sch. of Music, NYC, 2000—. Conductor (cd) Robert L. de Pearsall and Charles Wood: Madrigals and Partsongs. Fellow Benjamin Trustman Travelling fellowship, Harvard U., 1992-1993. Achievements include first to first countertenor ever admitted to the World Youth Choir. Office: Manhattan Sch of Music 120 Claremont Ave New York NY 10027 Office Fax: 212-749-5471. E-mail: ri30@hotmail.com.

ISAACS, ROBERT CHARLES, retired lawyer; b. July 16, 1919; s. David and Elsie (Weiss) I.; m. Doris Frances Shapiro, Nov. 20, 1943 (dec. 1982); 1 child, Leigh Richard; m. Mary Lou Anderson, Dec. 12, 1986. BA cum laude, NYU, 1941, JD, 1943. Bar: N.Y. 1943. Dep. asst. atty. gen. N.Y. State Dept. Law, Albany, 1943, spl. asst. atty. gen., 1946; ptnr. Nordlinger Riegelman Benetar, N.Y.C., 1946-71, Aranow Brodsky Bohlinger Benetar & Einhorn, N.Y.C., 1972-79, Benetar Isaacs Bernstein & Schair, N.Y.C., 1979-88. Mem. Lebanon (N.H.) Zoning Bd. Adjustment, 1988—; adj. prof. law St. John's U. Sch. Law, N.Y.C., 1961-72; mem. panel mediators and fact finders N.Y. State Pub. Employment Rels. Bd., 1968-88. Contbr. articles to profl. publs. Capt. U.S. Army, 1943-45, 51. Mem. ABA, ASCAP, Am. Arbitration Assn. (mem. panel arbitrators 1988), N.Y.C. Bar Assn., NYU Law Review Alumni Assn. Home: 5 Village Green West Lebanon NH 03784-1506

ISAACS, ROGER DAVID, public relations executive; b. Boston, Oct. 23, 1925; s. Raphael and Agnes (Wolfstein) I.; m. Joyce R. Wexler, Oct. 23, 1949; children: Gillian, Jan. Student, U. Wis., 1943; AB, Bard Coll., 1949. With Pub. Rels. Bd., Inc., Chgo., 1948—, account supr., 1948-51, ptnr., 1951-60, exec. v.p., 1960-66, pres., 1966-75, chmn., pres., 1975-86; chmn. PRB, a Needham Porter Novelli Co., Chgo.; exec. v.p., gen. mgr. Doremus Porter Novelli, Chgo., 1986-89; sr. counselor Porter/Novelli, Chgo., 1989-91, The Fin. Rels. Bd., Inc., Chgo., 1991—. Bd. dirs. North Bank, Chgo. Past bd. dirs. Anti-Defamation League Chgo., Jewish Family and Cmty. Svc., Sr. ctrs. Met. Chgo., Highland Park Hosp., Met. Crusade of Mercy, Suburban Fine Arts Ctr., Asthma and Allergy Found., Spertus Coll.; cmty. adv. bd. Sta. WBEZ; bd. dirs. Chgo. Crime Commn.; libr. vis. com. Spertus Inst. With AUS, 1943-45. Decorated Purple Heart. Mem. Pub. Rels. Soc. Am. (accredited), Met. Club, Publicity Club Chgo. Home: 1045 Hillcrest Rd Glencoe IL 60022-1215 E-mail: joroisaacs@aol.com.

ISAACS, S. TED, engineering executive; b. Louisville, July 13, 1914; s. Max and Rose (Kaplan) Isaacs; m. Ann Fabe, June 7, 1939 (dec. 2001); children: Marjorie McKelvey Isaacs, Susan Freund Isaacs. ChE, U. Cin., 1936, AS, 1944. Registered profl. engr., Ohio, cert. sr. grade fluid power tech. Instrument engr. Std. Oil Co. Ohio, Latonia, Ky., 1936-41; instrumentation mgr. Wright Aero. Corp., Lockland, Ohio, 1941-45; sr. process engr. Drackett Co., Cin., 1945-48; engr. control sys. H. K. Ferguson Co., Cleve., 1948; pres. Isaacs Co., Cin., 1948-86; mng. gen ptnr., pres. artist mgmt. divsn. AFTI Sys., Cin., 1986—. V.p. sales, pres. Indsl. Engring. Corp., Louisville, 1951—55. Author: (novella) Executive Sweets, 1999, Executive Sweets, rev., 2000, (poetry, illustration) Purple and Gold, 2002, A Guide to the Perplexed, 2002; columnist: B-Right-On, 1999—2001; contbr. articles to profl. jours., monthly column; author: (CD rec. poem) Moderation. Chmn. energy com. City Environ. Task Force, Cin., 1970—72; personal reader Cin. Radio Reading Svc., 1990—96; sponsor ann. tennis tournament Technion Israel Inst. Tech., Haifa, 1999—; sponsor ann. prize paper contest U. Cin. Coll. Engring. Mem.: Am. Technion Soc. (bd. dirs. Midwest region 2003—), Metric Assn. (v.p. 1962—65), Fluid Power Soc., Assn. Engrs. and Archs. Israel, Engring. Soc. Cin. (life; pres. jr. chpt. 1947—48), Instrumental Soc. Am. (sr.; local bd. dirs. 1946—47), U. Cin. Baldwin Soc., Nat. Assn. R.R. Passengers, U. Cin. Herman Schneider Lagacy Soc., Ohio Assn. R.R. Passengers, Sierra Club, Cin. Hatikva Investment Club (pres. 1991—93, v.p. rsch. 1994—99), Cephalo-Caudad Investment Club (pres. 1992—93). Democrat. Jewish. Avocations: swimming, bridge, spectator sports, music, art. Home and Office: AFTI Systems 4650 E Galbraith Rd Apt 311 Cincinnati OH 45236-2794 Fax: (513) 984-6015. E-mail: tisaacs@zoomtown.com.

ISAACS, SUSAN, novelist, screenwriter; b. Bklyn., Dec. 7, 1943; d. Morton and Helen (Asher) I.; m. Elkan Abramowitz, Aug. 11, 1968; children: Andrew, Elizabeth. Student, Queens Coll., 1965, DHL (hon.), 1996; LittD (hon.), Dowling Coll., 1988. From editorial asst. to sr. editor Seventeen mag., N.Y.C., 1965-70; freelance writer, 1970-76. Author: Compromising Positions, 1978, Close Relations, 1980, Almost Paradise, 1984, Shining Through, 1988, Magic Hour, 1991, After All These Years, 1993, Lily White, 1996, Red, White and Blue, 1998, Brave Dames and Wimpettes: What Women Are Really Doing on Page and Screen, 1999, Long Time No See, 2001; screenwriter Compromising Positions, 1985; screenwriter, co-producer Hello Again, 1987. Trustee Queens Coll. Found.; bd. dirs. North Shore Child and Family Guidance Assn; adv. bd. Nassau County Coalition Against Domestic Violence; bd. trustees Walt Whitman Birthplace Assn. Recipient Writers for Writers award Poets and Writers, 1996, The John Steinbeck award, 1999. Mem. PEN, Mystery Writers Am. (pres. 2001-02), Nat. Book Critic Circle, Poets and Writers (bd. dirs. 1994—, chmn. 1998—), Authors Guild, Internat. Assn. Crime Writers, Feminists for Free Expression, Creative Coalition, Am. Soc. Journalists and Authors. Jewish.

ISAACS-BRIGHT, SUSAN VIRGINIA KIRKPATRICK, research librarian, public speaker, advocate; b. West Point, Miss., Oct. 28, 1949; d. William Robert and Sara Rebecca I.; m. Wayne Milford Roberts, 1970 (div. 1979); children: David Wayne, Julie Andrea; m. Stephen Dewitt Bright, 1989. BS, U. S.C., 1971, MLS, 1974, EdD, 1997. Libr. tech. asst. U. S.C., Aiken, S.C., 1972-73; assoc. prof. libr. sci, asst. libr. pub. svcs., 1974-86; libr. Aiken Tech. Coll., 1986-90; mgr. tech. info. ctr. Westinghouse Savannah River Co, Aiken, 1990-96, sr. libr., libr. supr., 1996—. Mem. Aiken County Pub. Libr. Adv. Bd., 1996—; facilitator ALA learning disabilities workshop at Aiken County Pub. Libr., 1997. Author: (play) This Promise Is Unto You, 1997; (dissertation) Learning Disabilities: An Adult Discovery, 1997; editor (newsletter) The Libr. Connection, 1990-96. Mem. Pres. Regan's Project Serve, 1982; chairperson MIdland Valley Libr. Fund Dr., Langley, S.C., 1989-90; bd. trustees Aiken County Pub. Libr., 1997—. Cert. trainer Dept. Energy's Tng. Accreditation Tng. Bd., 1993, 95. Mem. AAUW (nominee young scholars U. S.C. 1979), Spl. Libr. Assn., S.C. Libr. Assn. (many offices including pres. 1981-84, Presidential Gavel award 1984), Ctrl. Savannah River Area Libr Assn. (chair mem. com. 1980-81, mem. grants-in-aid com., scholarship winner 1972), Learning Disabilities Assn. S.C. (bd. dirs. 2002—). Avocations: piano, singing, writing, fishing. Home: 1824 Lundee Dr Aiken SC 29803-5706 Office: Westinghouse Savannah River Co Libr Bldg 773-A Aiken SC 19808 E-mail: svisaacs@aol.com.

ISAACSON, ALLEN IRA, lawyer; b. N.Y.C., Nov. 10, 1938; s. Bernard and Sylvia Isaacson; m. Dena Mishkoff, Mar. 8, 1970; 1 child, David Andrew. AB, Princeton U., 1960; LLB, Yale U., 1963; postgrad., U. Melbourne, Australia, 1963-64; LLM in Taxation, NYU, 1973. Bar: N.Y. 1966. Assoc. Fried, Frank, Harris, Shriver & Jacobson, N.Y.C., 1966-70, ptnr., 1970—. Bd. dirs. FR Holdings, Inc. Fulbright fellow, 1963-64 Mem. ABA, N.Y. State Bar Assn., Assn. of Bar of City of N.Y. Home: 15 W 81st St New York NY 10024-6022 Office: Fried Frank Harris Shriver & Jacobson 1 New York Plz Fl 22 New York NY 10004-1980 E-mail: allen.isaacson@ffhsj.com.

ISAACSON, ARLINE LEVINE, food association administrator; b. Jan. 28, 1946; d. Harry and Sally (Fogelman) Levine; m. Leslie Robert Isaacson, Oct. 31, 1964 (div. July 1970); 1 child, Eric Michael. AAS in Hotel and Restaurant Mgmt., N.Y.C. Tech. Coll., 1983. Mgr. restaurant and lounge Holiday Inn, N.Y.C., 1982-83; mgr. Astors St. Regis Hotel, N.Y.C., 1983-84; mgr. banquet and conf. Mariner 15 Conf. Ctr., N.Y.C., 1984-85; dir. banquets, confs. and sales Sardi's Restaurant Corp., N.Y.C., 1985-87; dir. catering sales Days Inn Hotel, N.Y.C., 1987-91; mgr. catering sales St. Moritz on the Park Hotel, N.Y.C., 1991-92; dir. catering Roosevelt Hotel, N.Y.C., 1992-93; mgr. catering sales Sheraton Park Ave., N.Y.C., 1993-94; exec. dir. Wharton Bus. Sch. Alumni Assn., N.Y.C., 1997—. Dem. vol. Koch Re-election Campaign, N.Y.C., 1985. Mem. Food and Beverage Mgrs. Assn. (sec. 1984-88, 91, exec. dir. 1995—), Roundtable for Women in Food Svc. (treas. 1986-87), Meeting Planners Internat., Soc. Incentive Travel, Hotel Sales and Mktg. Assn., Internat. Food Svc. Execs., N.Y.C. Tech. Coll. Alumni Assn. (bd. dirs., v.p. 1986-87). Jewish. Avocations: dancing, travel, theatre, gourmet cooking. Home: 1836 E 18th St Brooklyn NY 11229-2965 Office: Wharton Club of NY PO Box 297-006 Brooklyn NY 11229-7006

ISAACSON, DEAN LEROY, statistician; b. St. Cloud, Minn., Apr. 10, 1941; married. BS, Macalester Coll., 1963; MS, U. Minn., 1966, PhD, 1968. Asst. prof. math. and stats. Iowa State U., Ames, 1968, assoc. prof. math. and stats., 1972, prof. math. and stats., 1976—84, prof. stats., 1984—, acting dir. statis. lab, head of stats., 1984-86, dir. statis. lab., head stats., 1986—2002. Author book on Markov Chains; contbr. numerous articles to profl. jours. Fellow Am. Statis. Assn.; mem. Inst. of Math. Stats. Office: Iowa State U Sci and Tech Statis Lab 102 Snedecor Hl Ames IA 50011-0001 E-mail: dli@iastate.edu.

ISAACSON, EDITH L. civic leader; b. N.Y.C., Jan. 18, 1920; d. I.A. and Bertha (Evans) Lipsig; m. Selian Hebald; children: Anne Mandelbaum, Selian Jr.; m. William J. Isaacson. Student, Radcliffe Coll., 1936-39, 41; LLB, St. Lawrence U., 1943. Pres. Forest Knolls Corp., N.Y.C., 1960-95, Norman Homes Corp., N.Y.C., 1968-95. Bd. govs. Medford Leas Residents Assn., 1990-92, v.p., 1991-92. Author biographies Am. artists; writer club handbooks. Fellow Pierpont Morgan Libr., N.Y.C.; mem. Carnegie Coun. Ethics Internat. Affairs, founders com. Am. Symphony Orch., N.Y., 1962; nat. sec. Women's Am. Orgn. Rehab. through Tng., 1950; trustee Allergy Found. Am.; bd. govs. Medford Leas Residents Assn., 1991; mem. Res. Fund Com., 1992-2000. Mem. Radcliffe Coll. Alumnae Assn. (chmn. clubs 1966), Harvard Clyb (N.Y.C.), Cosmopolitan Club (N.Y.C.) (bd. govs. 1987-2000), Radcliffe Club (pres. Washington 1969, N.Y.C. 1959, 63, bd. sponsors 1974-2000).

ISAACSON, JEFFREY ALAN, think-tank executive, physicist; s. David Gerald and Alice Christine Isaacson; m. Elizabeth Anne Mendelsohn; children: Zachary, Danielle. BS, Columbia U., 1982; MSE, Princeton U., 1984; PhD, MIT, 1991. U.S. Dept. Energy grad. fellow Princeton (N.J.) Plasma Physics Lab., 1982—84; U.S. Dept. of Energy practicum fellow Lawrence Livermore Nat. Lab., Livermore, Calif., 1984; managerial and rsch. positions RAND Corp., Santa Monica, Calif., 1991—99, v.p. nat. security rsch., 2000—. Contbr. articles to profl. jours. and publs. LCDR USNR, 2001—. Mem.: Am. Soc. Naval Engrs., Am. Phys. Soc. Office: RAND Corp 1200 S Hayes St Arlington VA 22202 Business E-Mail: jai@rand.org.

ISAACSON, JULANNE R. social worker, retired; b. Vicksburg, Miss., Dec. 3, 1924; d. Julian Soloan and Clara (Kahn) Rose; m. William Haspel Jr., Dec. 9, 1944; children: Katherine Clair, Judith Odette, Thomas William; m. Irwin Isaacson Jr., Apr. 18, 1987. BA, Newcomb Coll., 1945; MSW, Tulane U., 1965. Cert. social worker, La. Caseworker, supr. Family Svc. Soc., New Orleans, 1965-71; field instr. sch. social work Tulane U., New Orleans, 1968-73; field instr. sch. social welfare La. State U., Baton Rouge, 1969-75; exec. dir. Travelers' Aid Soc., New Orleans, 1971-73, Jewish Family Svc., New Orleans, 1973-94; mem. clin. faculty dept. psychiatry La. State U. Med. Sch., New Orleans, 1980-94. Docent New Orleans Mus. of Art. Recipient Nat. Coun. Jewish Women's Hannah Solomon award for cmty. leadership and commitment, 1994. Mem. NASW (Social Worker of Yr. 1977, Lifetime Achievement award 1993, chair com. on inquiry adjudicating ethics violations com.), Phi Beta Kappa. Democrat. Jewish. Avocations: painting, reading, writing in journal. Home: 3504 Napoleon Ave New Orleans LA 70125-4844

ISAACSON, KEITH BRYAN, gynecologist, medical researcher; b. Atlanta, Ga., Apr. 30, 1957; m. Jennifer Ann Hall, Feb. 14, 1987. MD, Med. Coll. of GA, Augusta, GA, 1979—83. Medical dipomate Ga., 1983. Dir., minimally invasive gyn surgery Newton Wellesley Hosp., Newton, Mass., 2001—; dir, reproductive endocrinology Mass. Gen. Hosp., Boston, Mass., 1993—2001. Recipient Golden Hysteroscope award, AAGL, 1999 and 2001. Office: Newton Wellesley Hosp 2014 Washington St 2 W Newton MA 02462 Office Fax: 617-243-5029. Personal E-mail: kisaacson@partners.org. E-mail: kisaacson@partners.org.

ISAACSON, MELVIN STUART, library director; b. N.Y.C., Apr. 12, 1949; s. Max and Ida (Savitsky) I.; m. Shelley Allyn Thielle, Apr. 3, 1976; 1 child, Scott Brandon. BA in English, Bklyn. Coll., 1972; MLS, Pratt Inst., 1973. Cataloger Yeshiva Univ., N.Y.C., 1973-76, John Jay Coll. of Criminal Justice, N.Y.C., 1976-77; head cataloger Pace Univ., N.Y.C., 1977-81; head of original monographs cataloging Columbia Univ., N.Y.C., 1982-87; head of cataloging Columbia Univ., Health Sci. Libr., N.Y.C., 1987; libr. dir. Pace Univ., N.Y.C., 1988-94; assoc. dir. librs. N.Y.C. Pace U., 1994—98, assoc. univ. libr., 1998—. Mem. ALA, Archons of Collophon, N.Y. Tech. Svcs. Librs. (sec., treas. 1983-84, membership/social chair 1984-85), Assn. Coll. and Rsch. Librs. N.Y., Westchester Acad. Libr. Dirs. Orgn., Beta Phi Mu. Avocations: theater, travel, swimming, physical fitness, reading. Home: 1415 Milford Ter Teaneck NJ 07666-2248 Office: Pace U Henry Birnbaum Libr Pace Plz New York NY 10038

ISAACSON, MILTON STANLEY (JIM ISAACSON), research and development company executive, engineer; b. Dayton, Ohio, Apr. 23, 1932; s. Max and Sylvia Mariam (Kirsin) I.; m. Joan Sue Koor, Sept. 4, 1955; children: Julie Fay, Jill Ellen, Jan Lynn. BSEE, Ohio State U., 1955. Registered profl. engr., Ohio. Successively design engr., mgr. quality control, div. mgr., dir. R & D Globe Industries, Dayton, 1957-70; pres. Nu-Tech Industries, Inc., Trotwood, Ohio, 1970—. Officer, bd. dirs. Food Svcs., Dayton, 1970-95. Patentee brushless DC motors and medical devices. Bd. dirs. Grace House Sexual Abuse Resource Ctr., Dayton, 1985—, pres., 1985-89; bd. dirs. Temple Israel Found., 1987-90, pres., 1990; v.p. Jewish Fedn. Greater Dayton, 1984—; bd. dirs. Big Bros./Big Sisters of Greater Dayton, 1965-95, pres., 1978-79; bd. dirs. Old Time Newsies, 1969—, pres., 1991-92. 1st lt. USAF, 1955-57. Recipient Dr. Alan F. Wasserman Leadership award Jewish Fedn. Dayton, 1972, Boss of the Yr. award Nat. Trail chpt. Am. Bus. Womens Assn., 1975, Outstanding Pub. Svc. award Sta. WKEF, Dayton, 1979, Outstanding Svc. award Big Bros./Big Sisters of Greater Dayton, 1977, 88, 304 Cmty. svc. award, 2002, Hon. Judge Carl D. Kessler Meml. award The Grace House, 1991. Mem. IEEE, Rotary (pres. Trotwood club 1989, sec. 1993—), Eta Kappa Nu. Avocations: fishing, traveling. Office: Nu-Tech Industries Inc 5905 Wolf Creek Pike Dayton OH 45426-2439

ISAACSON, ROBERT LEE, psychology educator, researcher; b. Detroit, Sept. 26, 1928; s. Emil Alfred and Evelyn (Johnson) I.; m. Susan Doherty, Dec. 16, 1956 (div. 1972); children— Gunnar, Lars, Mary Ingrid, Mary Christina; m. Ann W. Braden, Dec. 31, 1974; stepchildren— Richard, Milly Braden AB in Psychology, U. Mich., 1950, MS in Psychology, 1954, PhD in Psychology, 1958. Co-dir. U. Fla. Ctr. for Neurobiol. Sci., Gainesville, 1970-78; grad. research prof. U. Fla., Gainesville, 1977-78; disting. prof. psychology SUNY, Binghamton, 1978—, dir. Ctr. for Neurobehavioral Sci., 1978-88, Bartle prof., 1998—; prof. U. Cordoba, 2002; hon. prof. Nat. Univ. Cordoba, Argentina, 2000. Author: Limbic System, 2d edit., 1982; editor: (with others) Expression of Knowledge, 1982, The Hippocampus, vols. 3-4, 1986, The Vulnerable Brain and Environmental Risks, vols. 1-2, 1992, vol. 3, 1994. Pres. Alachua County Assn. for Retarded Children, Gainesville, 1973-75; chmn. dist. III Human Rights Advocacy Com., Gainesville, 1975-77. Served with USN, 1950-53, Korea Holloway fellow U.S. Navy, 1946-50; grantee NSF, NIH, U.S. Army Surgeon Gen. Fellow APA, AAAS; mem. Internat. Behavioral Neurosci. Soc. (councilor 1991-95, pres. 1999, Myers Lifetime Achievement award 2002), Soc. for Neurosci. (pres. con. N.Y. chpt. 1982-84), Assn. Neurosci. Depts. Programs, Am. Physiol. Soc., Sec. Health Rehab. Svcs. State of Fla. (mem. Blue Ribbon com. 1976). Office: Binghamton Univ Dept Psychology Binghamton NY 13902-6000 E-mail: isaacson@binghamton.edu.

ISAAK, G. EUGENE, lawyer; b. Bismarck, N.D., Nov. 23, 1937; s. G. C. and Caroline (Jassman) I.; m. Elizabeth Baquet, Aug. 3, 1968; children: Jason E., Melissa E. BS, BA, U. N.D., 1959, JD, 1961; LLM in Taxation, NYU, 1962. Bar: N.D. 1961, Ariz. 1963, U.S. Dist. Ct. Ariz. 1963, U.S. Ct. Appeals (9th cir.) 1965, U.S. Supreme Ct. 1965; CPA, Ariz. Assoc. Dunseath, Stubbs & Burch, Tucson, 1962-73, Haralson, Miller, Pitt & McAnally, P.C., Tucson, 1973—. Chmn. U. Ariz. Sch. Law Probate workshop, 1982. Asst. nat. legal officer CAP, 1976—; pres., bd. dirs. Pima County Parklands Found., 1994—. Fellow Am. Coll. Trust and Estate Counsel; mem. ABA, Ariz. Bar Assn. (probate and trust sect. com. 1985-90, 96-2000), Pima County Bar Assn., Am. Brittany Club (nat. bd. dirs. 1982-87, legal counsel 1988—). Republican. Lutheran. Office: Haralson, Miller Pitt & McAnally PC One S Church Ave Ste 900 Tucson AZ 85701-1620

ISAAK, ROBERT ALLEN, international management and political economy educator, writer; b. Akron, Colo., Sept. 2, 1945; s. Robert Deets and Marge Allen Isaak; m. Gudrun Kamm, Jan. 29, 1966; children: Sonya, Andrew Jay. BA in English Lit., Stanford U., 1966; MA in Internat. Rels., San Jose (Calif.) State U., 1967; PhD in Politics, NYU, 1971. Instr. internat. affairs New Sch. Social Rsch., N.Y.C., 1968—69; asst. prof. polit. sci. SUNY, Purchase, 1973, Fordham U., Bronx, NY, 1969—75; sr. rsch. assoc. Inst. Western Europe and Inst. on Internat. Change Columbia U., N.Y.C., 1975—78; assoc. prof. comparative polit. economy Johns Hopkins Sch. Advanced Internat. Studies, Bologna, Italy, 1978—81; prof. internat. mgmt. Pace U., White Plains, NY, 1975—78, 1981—. Cross-cultural cons. on European countries and U.S. Prudential Internat. and Global Intercultural, N.Y.C., 1992—96, 1997—; vis. prof. ecol. theory, Fulbright sr. scholar U. Heidelberg, Germany, 1996—97; vis. prof. globalization and new economy Grande École de Commerce, Grenoble, France, 2001, 02, vis. prof. global economy, Sophia Antipolis, France, 03. Author (with Ralph Hummel): Politics for Human Beings, 1975, 2d edit., 1980; author: Individuals and World Politics, 1975, 2d edit., 1981, American Democracy and World Power, 1977, European Politics, 1980; author: (with Wilhelm Hankel) Modern Inflation, 1982; author: (with Ralph Hummel) The Real American Politics, 1986; author: Managing World Economic Change, 1991, 3d edit., 2000, Green Logic: Ecopreneurship, Theory and Ethics, 1998. Facilitator bus. blueprints Yonkers (N.Y.) Homeless Shelter, 1994. Named sr. rsch. grantee, Fulbright Commn., 1996—97; recipient scholar medal for impact of books on social sci., Pi Gamma Mu, 1990, award for innovation in bus. edn., Mid. Atlantic Assn. Colls. Bus. Adminstrn., 1992. Avocations: poetry, tennis, skiing, guitar, painting. Office: Pace U Grad Ctr 1 Martine Ave White Plains NY 10606

ISABELLA, MARK DOUGLAS, management consultant; b. Phillipi, W.Va., Apr. 5, 1962; s. Thomas and Delores (Stockett) I.; m. Elizabeth Ann Bennett, Oct. 8, 1988. AA, Fairmont State Coll., 1982, BS, 1984; MA, Marshall U., 1993. From info. rep. to adminstrv. asst. W.Va. Dept. Human Svcs., Charleston, 1985-89; from sr. personnel specialist to sr. devel. cons. W.Va. Divsn. Personnel, Charleston, 1989—. Owner Isabella & Assocs., Charleston, 1996—. Mem. ASTD, Internat. Personnel Mgmt. Assn., Internat. Soc. for Performance Improvement, N.Am. Simulation and Gaming Assn. Roman Catholic. Office: WVa Divsn Personnel 1900 Kanawha Blvd E Bldg 6 Charleston WV 25305-0009

ISABELLA, MARY MARGARET, lawyer; b. Pitts., Oct. 16, 1947; d. Sebastian C. and Joanna C. (dec.) (Ferris) I. BS in Biology, Duquesne U., 1969; cert. med. technologist, Mercy Hosp., Pitts., 1970; JD, Duquesne U., 1975. Bar: Pa. 1976, U.S. Dist Ct. (we. dist.) Pa. 1976, U.S. Supreme Ct., 1982. Sole practice, Pitts., 1977—. Instr. Wheeling (W.Va.) Coll., 1978-80. Mem. coun. Brentwood Whitehall Assn., Pitts., 1984-90; bd. dirs. Dukes Ct., Duquesne U.; bd. govs. Law Alumni Assn., treas., 1993, sec., 1994-95; sec., treas. Brentwood Bus. Owners' Assn., 2001—. Mem. ABA (vice chair sole practice sect., 1994-2001), Pa. Bar Assn., Allegheny County Bar Assn., Delta Theta Phi (past asst. dist. chancellor). Lodges: Italian Sons and Daughters of Am. (trustee local chpt.). Republican. Roman Catholic. Office: 4101 Brownsville Rd Bldg 200 Pittsburgh PA 15227-3336 E-mail: mmiesq@juno.com.

ISABELLE, BEATRICE MARGARET, artist; b. Phila., Dec. 8, 1930; d. Renaud Joseph Isabelle, Carmela Didio; m. Sven Fritz Carstens, Jan. 1953 (div. Jan. 1977); children: Jana C. Young, Kai Bruce Carstens, Dane Fritz Carstens; m. Robert Dean Graves, Sept. 6, 1984. AA L.A. City Coll., 1973; BA, Calif. State U., L.A., 1975, MA, 1979. Cert. tchr. K-9 Calif., bilingual/cross cultural specialist pre-K-12, adult, cmty. coll. ethnic studies. Tchr. Hobart St. Elem. Sch., L.A., 1971—73, McDonnell Ave. Sch., L.A., 1973—76, Albion St. Elem. Sch., L.A., Calif., 1976—85, Dolores St. Elem. Sch., L.A., Calif., 1985—91; ret., 1991. Exhibitions include Huntington Beach Art Ctr., 1995, 1999, 2000, 2001, 2001, 2002, Golden West Coll. Art Gallery, 1997, 1998, 1999, 2000, 2001, 2002, Guggenheim Gallery, Chapman U., 2001. Vol. mental health svcs., Amigas Program L.A. Unified Sch. Dist., 1967—69; vol. Chicano field work EPIC, 1978; vol. youth facility MacLaren Hall, 1978. Recipient Award for Marine Edn. Program, Sch. Edn., U. So. Calif., 1981, award for theatre, Herald Examiner, 1982, Children's Theatre, 1983, Sculpture award, Orange County Artists, 2000, Orange Art Assn., 2001; scholar Scholarship award, Orange County Fine Arts, 2001. Mem.: Kappa Delta Pi, Psi Chi. Avocations: travel, reading, painting, sculpting, flying. Home: 6941 Cumberland Dr Huntington Beach CA 92647

ISABLE, ALISHA, elementary school educator; d. Anthony and Antoinette I.. BS in Elem. Edn., Morgan State U., Balt., 1999. Std. Profl. Cert. Md. State Dept. of Edn., 1999. Tchr. 3rd grade math. Balt. City Pub. Schs., Balt., 1999—2002, tchr. grade 4, 2002—. Master tchr. Morgan State U., Balt.,

2003—; founder pvt. tutoring svc.; creator website for students, 2000—01. Home: 2305 Tarelton Ln Parkville MD 21234 Office: Balt City Pub Schs 5201 Loch Raven Blvd Baltimore MD 21239 Personal E-mail: abisable@yahoo.com.

ISACOFF, MARK, psychologist; b. Bklyn., Mar. 2, 1953; s. David and Hannah (Zwirn) I.; m. Mindy Schwartzman, Aug. 28, 1977; children: Adam, Amy. BA in Psychology, Bklyn. Coll., 1975, MS of Edn. in Sch. Psychology, advanced cert. in sch. psychology, Bklyn. Coll., 1977; advanced tng. clin. biofeedback, Inst. for Psychosomatic Rsch., 1982; PhD, Hofstra U., 1987. Diplomate Am. Bd. Psychol. Specialites in Clin. Psychology; nationally cert. sch. psychology; lic. psychologist, N.Y. Cons. psychologist N.Y.C. Bd. Edn., 1977, 78-80; adj. asst. prof. Queens Coll., CUNY, 1978-79; psychol. counselor Bklyn. Coll., CUNY, 1978-79, adj. lectr. sch. edn. and grad. studies, 1979-80, adj. lectr. dept. psychology, 1979-81; staff psychologist Howard Beach Child Guidance and Family Counseling Ctr., Queens, 1979-90; psychologist Kings County Hosp. Ctr., Bklyn., 1980-86, dir. treatment in child psychiatry, 1982-86, clin. adminstrn. dir. Program for Adolescent Devel., 1986—. Clin. instr. psychiatry SUNY Downstate Med. Ctr., 1980-83, clin. asst. prof. psychiatry, 1983—; adj. asst. prof. Kingsborough C.C./CUNY, 2001—. Contbr. articles to profl. jours. Pres. Assn. of Sch. Psychologists Bklyn. Coll., 1976-77. Fellow Am. Orthopsychiat. Assn., Am. Bd. Psychotherapists and Psychodiagnosticians (diplomate); mem. APA, Am. Coll. Forensic Examiners, Nat. Assn. Sch. Psychologists, Bklyn. Psychol. Assn. (bd. dirs. 1978-86), Bklyn. Coll. Alumni Assn. (bd. dirs. 1974-84), Nat. Assn. Watch and Clock Collectors, Soc. Am. Magicians, Internat. Soc. Study of Dissociation. Office: Kings County Hosp Ctr 451 Clarkson Ave Brooklyn NY 11203-2097 E-mail: misacoff@yahoo.com.

ISACOFF, RICHARD IRWIN, banker, lawyer; b. New Haven, Sept. 7, 1950; s. Paul and Doris (Tashman) I.; m. Bette Ann Francesconi, May 2, 1970; 1 child, Kira Lyn. Student Clark U., 1968-70; B.A., Western New Eng. Coll., 1972, J.D., 1977. Bar: Mass. 1977, U.S. Dist. Ct. Mass. 1978. Trust officer 3d Nat. Bank, Springfield, Mass., 1973-77, v.p. human resources, 1977-80; dir. human resources, corporate sec. Aspen Systems, Corp., Rockville, Md., 1980-82; sr. v.p., dir. corporate staff, corporate sec. Provident Bank Md., Balt., 1982— ; instr. U. Mass., Amherst, part time 1976; sole practice, Springfield, part time 1977-80. Mem. allocations com. United Way Pioneer Valley, 1977-80; mem. fin. com. PBS-WGBY TV, Springfield. Mem. ABA. Office: Provident Bank Md 114 E Lexington St Baltimore MD 21202-1746

ISAF, FRED THOMAS, lawyer; b. Jacksonville, NC, Nov. 18, 1950; s. Thomas Fred and Rowanda (Maloof) I.; m. June J. Jeffcoat, Aug. 18, 1973; children: Julie, Thomas, Christa. BA, Duke U., 1972; JD, Emory U., 1975, LLM in Taxation, 1978. Bar: Ga. 1975. Ptnr. Peterson, Young, Self & Asselin, Atlanta, 1980-86; shareholder Roberts and Isaf, PC, Atlanta, 1986-94, Roberts, Isaf & Summers, PC, Atlanta, 1994-99; ptnr. McGuire Woods LLP, Atlanta, 1999—. Contbr. article to profl. jour. Dir. Pinecrest Acad., 1995—2002. Mem.: State Bar Ga., Cherokee Town and Country Club (sec. 1993, bd. dirs. 1994—2000, v.p. 1997, pres. 1998—99), Order of Barristers, Order of the Coif. Office: McGuire Woods Ste 2100 1170 Peachtree St Atlanta GA 30309 E-mail: fisaf@mcguirewoods.com.

ISAKI, LUCY POWER SLYNGSTAD, lawyer; b. Jersey City, Oct. 21, 1945; d. Charles Edward and Ann Mary (Power) Slyngstad; m. Paul S. Isaki, Aug. 26, 1967. BA summa cum laude, Seattle U., 1973; JD cum laude, U. Puget Sound, 1977. Bar: Wash. 1977. Case worker San Joaquin County Welfare, Stockton, Calif., 1968-70, Alameda County Welfare, Oakland, Calif., 1971-73; legal intern King County Prosecutor's Office, 1976-77; law clk. to hon. Justice Hamilton Wash. Supreme Ct., 1977-78; ptnr. Bogle & Gates, Seattle, 1978-99, mem. exec. com., 1990-94; sr. asst. atty. gen. State of Wash., 1999—. Cons. Region X, HHS, 1975; chair Atty. Gen. Gregoire's Task Force on Alternative Dispute Resolution, 1993-94. Bd. dirs. King County Family Svcs., Seattle, 1982-84, Wash. State Coun. Crime and Delinquency, 1981, Northwest Kidney Ctr., 2001—, vice chair 2003—; vice chair bd. trustees N.W. Kidny Ctr., 2003—; treas. Mother's Against Violence in America, 1994; trustee emeritus U. Puget Sound, 1985—, Seattle Youth Symphony, 1995, Ea. Wash. U., 1998-99; chmn. law sch. bd. visitors Seattle U., 1984-96; trustee Legal Found., Wash., 1992-95, sec. bd. dirs. 1993, v.p. bd. dirs. 1994, pres. 1995. Dean's scholar U. Puget Sound, 1976-77; recipient Disting. Law Grad. award U. Puget Sound, 1984, Majis award Seattle U., 1997. Mem. Wash. Women Lawyers (pres. Seattle-King County chpt. 1982), ABA (del. ABA Ho. of Dels., 1995-97), Wash. State Bar Assn. (bd. govs. 2000-03), King County Bar Assn. (sec. 1986-87, trustee 1987-90, treas. 1995-97, 1st v.p. 1998, pres. 1999-2000), Wash. Women Lawyers (v.p. 1984), King County Bar Found. (trustee 1987-90), U. Puget Sound Law Alumni Soc. (pres. 1979). Democrat. Office: Atty Gens Office 900 4th Ave Ste 2000 Seattle WA 98164-1076 E-mail: lucyi@atg.wa.gov.

ISAKOFF, SHELDON ERWIN, chemical engineer; b. Bklyn., May 25, 1925; s. Harry and Rebecca I.; m. Anita Ginsburg, Aug. 18, 1946; 1 son, Peter D. BS, Columbia U., 1945, MS, 1947, PhD, 1952. Guest fellow Brookhaven Nat. Lab., Upton, N.Y., 1949-50; with E.I. duPont de Nemours & Co., Inc., Wilmington, Del., 1951-90, dir. engring. research and devel., 1975-90, ret., 1990. Mem. Nat. Materials Adv. Bd., 1980-82; adj. prof. Columbia U., 1990—; trustee, United Engring. Trust, 1992-98, pres., 1995-97. Vice chair bd. Chem. Heritage Found., 1992-94, chair, 1995-98. With USNR, 1943-46. Recipient Egleston medal Columbia U., 1994, Alumni medal, 1996. Fellow AIChE (past dir., Founders award 1980, Inst. lectr. 1984, materials divsn. award 1986, v.p., pres.-elect 1989, pres. 1990, Thomas H. Chilton award, Wilmington sect. 1994, Mgmt. Divsn. award 1997, Van Antwerpen award 1997), AAAS; mem. NAE, Am. Chem. Soc., Sigma Xi, Tau Beta Phi, Phi Lambda Upsilon. Home: 102 Center Mill Rd Chadds Ford PA 19317-9212 E-mail: isakoffshe@aol.com.

ISAKOVIC, ABDEL, physicist, researcher; b. Stolac, Herzegovina, Bosnia-Herzegovina, Dec. 4, 1971; arrived in U.S., 1998; s. Smajo Isakovic and Fadila Culic. BSc, U. Sarajevo, Bosnia-Herzegovina, 1995; MSc, U. Minn., 2000, postgrad. Rsch. asst. U. Minn., Mpls., 1999—. Tchg. asst. U. Sarajevo, 1996—98, U. Minn., 1998—99. Fellow SpinTechI fellow, Strategic Analysis Inc., 2001, 3M Sci. and Engring. fellow, U. Minn., 2002—03. Mem.: AAAS, Bosnian Phys. Soc. (v.p. 1997—98), Soc. Indsl. Applied Math., Materials Rsch. Soc., Am. Phys. Soc. Achievements include research in magnetic anisotropy in ferromagnet/semiconductor hetersostructures; feasibility of transport of spin polarized carriers from semiconductors into ferromagnet; injection of spin polarized electrons from ferromagnet into semiconductor. Avocations: travel, archaeology, history, basketball. Office: Sch Physics and Astronomy 116 Church St SE Minneapolis MN 55455 Personal E-mail: isakovic@physics.umn.edu. E-mail: isakovic@physics.umn.edu.

ISAKSEN, ROBERT L. retired bishop; b. Bklyn. m. Beverly Sievertsen; children: Elisabeth, Lois. BA, Concordia Coll., Moorhead, Minn., 1957; MDiv, Luther Sem., St. Paul, 1961; STM, N.Y. Theol. Sem., 1971; DD (hon.), Upsala Coll., 1990. Ordained to ministry Am. Luth. Ch., 1961. Vicar St. Timothy Luth. Ch., Chgo., 1960; pastor Bethlehem, Bronx, N.Y., 1961-62, St. Peters, Bronx, 1962-68, Bethlehem, Baldwin, N.Y., 1972-81; Bronx Luth. coord. Planning Assn. of Bronx Luth. Chs., 1968-72; mission dir. Am. Luth. Ch., 1981-87; bishop New Eng. Synod Evang. Luth. Ch. in Am., Worcester, Mass., 1987-2000, ret.; interim pastor Stavanger Internat. Ch., Stavanger, Norway, 2003. Vis. prof. Yale Divinity Sch., 2001; adv. bishop to Bd. for Outreach, Evang. Luth. Ch. in Am., 1988-91, adv. bishop to Ch. Coun., 1992-97; chair Boston Ch. Leaders Covenant, 1995-96; pres. New Eng. Conf. Ch. Leaders, 1993. Bd. dirs. Luth. Immigration and Refugee Svcs., N.Y.C., 1983-87. Mem., Hendrick Hudson Male Chorus, 2002-. Lutheran. Home: 175 Ashley Hill Rd Brainard NY 12024 E-mail: pisak@cs.com.

ISAKSON, JOHNNY, congressman; b. Atlanta, Georgia, Dec. 28, 1944; m. Dianne Isakson; 3 children. BBA, U. Ga., 1966. Businessman, Atlanta; mem. U.S. Congress from 6th Ga. dist., 1999—, Georgia H. of Reps., 1976—90, Georgia St. Senate, 1993—96; vchmn. 21st century competitiveness subcom. Mem. Edn. and the Workforce, Transp. and Infrastructure coms. Winner spl. election to succeed Rep. Newt Gingrich, who resigned, 1999; represented Cobb County in the Ga. legislature 17 yrs.; Rep. candidate for gov. of Ga., 1990, Rep. primary candidate for U.S. Senate, 1996; Sunday sch. tchr. Mt. Zion Meth. Ch., 1978—. Republican. Office: US Ho Reps 132 Canon House Office Bldg Washington DC 20515-1006*

ISAKSON, PETER C. pharmaceutical executive; s. Andrew and Lucille Gale Isakson; m. Helen C Hamman, May 5, 1984; children: Matthew H, Sara H. BS, Weber State Coll., 1968—72; PhD, Wash. U., 1972. Asst./assoc. prof. U. of Va. Med. Sch., Charlottesville, Va., 1982—91; sr. fellow/vice pres. Pharmacia, Peapack, NJ, 1991—. Recipient Queeny award, Monsanto, 2000, Discoverer's award, Pharm. Manufacturer's of Am., 2002. Mem.: Am. Soc. of Pharmacology and Exptl. Therapeutics, Am. Assn. of Immunologists. Achievements include discovered and brought to the market Celebrex. Avocations: golf, bicycling, skiing. Office Fax: 973-644-9691. Personal E-mail: pisakson@optonline.net.

ISAMAN, FRANCIS E. engineering executive, researcher; b. Lewiston, Idaho, Jan. 18, 1930; s. Harry Franklin Isaman and Verde Mae Gossett; m. Virginia Anne Morris, Aug. 5, 1956; 1 child, Scott A. BA in Physics, U. Utah, 1951; MS in Bus., San Fernando Valley State U., 1968. Engr. Hughes Aircraft Co., Culver City, Calif., 1954—57, Statham Instruments Co., L.A., 1957—59; pres., co-founder Pacific Telemetry Sys., Culver City, 1959—63; engr. Rocketdyne divsn. N.A. Aviation, Canoga Park, Calif., 1964—65; pres., founder Technomerix (formerly Celtic Inc. Inc.), Granada Hills, Calif., 1965— . Providing Christian ministry to incarcerated persons and employment to gang members. Cpl. U.S. Army, 1952—54. Republican. Office Fax: 818-360-7986. E-mail: celind@verizon.net.

ISARD, PHILLIP ISAAC, medical nutritionist, consultant; b. L.A., May 18, 1949; s. Henry and Claris (Kaufman) I.; m. Pennel Donoher, May 20, 1977 (div. June 1990). BS in Biochemistry, Temple U., 1971; D Holistic Health, Am. Holistic Coll. Nutrition, Birmingham, Ala., 1992; DSc, Clayton Coll., Birmingham, 1994. Cert. med. nutritionist, N.Y. Rsch. asst. dept. exptl. surgery Hahnemann Hosp., Phila., 1967-72, rsch. assoc. dept. surg. rsch., 1968-72; chief small animal surgery Biokinetics Rsch. Lab., Temple U., Phila., 1969-74; rsch. assoc. dept. pharm. rsch. Med. Coll. Pa., Phila., 1974-81; medico-legal rschr. Med-Leg Rsch. Assocs., Huntingdon Valley, Pa., 1981-95; med. nutritionist Northumberland Valley Nutrition, Bethayres, Pa., 1992—; cons. Med. Nutritional Cons. NED, Huntington Valley, 1994—. Tchr. various cmty. colls., Phila., 1990—; nutrition cons. free clinic Nutrition Ptnrs., Bethayres, Pa., 1991—. Contbr. articles to profl. jours. Vol. Pennypack Watershed Assn., Willow Grove, Pa., 1970—; tchr. emergency com. Pa. Amateur Radio Club, Huntingdon Valley, 1990—. Rsch. grantee NSF, NIH, Def. Advanced Rsch. Projects Agy., 1967-74. Unitarian-Universalist. Achievements include research on muscle hypertrophy more efficient than cytologic hyperplasia in augmenting muscle physiologic parameters concerned with work requiring maximal O2 uptake and utilization. Home and Office: Med Nutricon NED 567 Hoyt Rd Huntingdon Valley PA 19006-8101 E-mail: wf3w@juno.com.

ISARD, WALTER, economics educator; b. Phila., Apr. 19, 1919; m. Caroline Berliner, July, 1943; children: Peter, Susan, Toni, Michael, Scott A., Roberta J., Anni K., Arthur. AB, Temple U., 1939; MA, Harvard U., 1941, PhD, 1943; postgrad., U. Chgo., 1941-42; degree (hon.), Poznan Acad. Econs., 1976, Erasmus U., 1978, U. Karlsruhe, 1979, Umea U., 1980, U. Ill., 1982, Binghamton U., 1997, U. Geneva, 2002. Lectr., rsch. assoc. Harvard U., 1949-53, vis. prof., 1965-70; assoc. prof. regional econs. MIT, 1953-56, assoc. dir. sect. urban and regional studies, 1953-55, dir., 1955-56; prof. econs. U. Pa., Phila., 1956-79; past chmn. dept. regional sci., chmn. dept. peace sci.; prof. Cornell U., 1979—. Vis. prof. regional sci. Yale U., 1960-61; exec. sec. Peace Rsch. Soc. (Internat.), 1955; cons. Resources for Future; hon. prof. U. Peking, 1993—, Northwestern U., China, 1993—; co-chair ECAAR, 1996, trustee, 2001—. Author: Atomic Power, An Economic and Social Analysis, 1952, Location and Space-Economy, 1956, Municipal Costs and Revenues, 1957, Methods of Regional Analysis, 1960, General Theory, 1969, Spatial Dynamics and Optimal Space-Time Development, 1979, Conflict Analysis and Practical Conflict Management, 1983, Arms Races, Arms Control and Conflict Analysis, 1988, Understanding Conflict and Science of Peace, 1992, Commonalities in Art, Science and Religion, 1997, Methods of Interregional and Regional Analysis, 1998, History of Regional Science and the Regional Science Association, International, 2003; editor: Regional Sci. Studies series, Peace Econs., Peace Sci. and Pub. Policy. Fellow AAAS, World Acad. Art and Sci. (pres. 1977-81), Am. Acad. Art and Sci., Am. Geog. Soc.; mem. NAS, Regional Sci. Assn. (pres., Founders medal 1978), Am. Econ. Assn., Econometric Soc., Assn. Am. Geographers, Peace Sci. Soc. (pres. 1998), August Lösch Ring, Phi Beta Kappa. Home: 3218 Garrett Rd Drexel Hill PA 19026-2912 Office: Cornell U Uris Hall Bldg 436 Ithaca NY 14853-7601

ISAY, DAVID AVRAM, writer, radio producer; b. New Haven, Conn., Dec. 5, 1965; s. Richard Alexander and Jane (Franzblau) I. BA, NYU, 1987. Pub. radio producer Sound Portrait Prodns., N.Y.C., 1988—. Author: Holding On, 1996; co-author: Our America, 1997, Flophouse, 2000; producer radio documentaries, 1988—. Recipient Peabody award, U. Ga., 1992, 96, 2000, 2002, Robert F. Kennedy Journalism award, RFK Found., Washington, 1995, 96; Guggenheim fellow, 1994, MacArthur fellow, 2000. Office: Sound Portraits Prodns Inc 176 Grand St Fl 3 New York NY 10013-3786 E-mail: dave@soundportraits.org.

ISAY, RICHARD ALEXANDER, psychiatrist; b. Pitts. s. Milton and Jeanette (Myers) I.; children: David, Joshua. AB, Haverford Coll., 1952-56; MD, U. Rochester, 1957-61; postgrad. psychoanalysis, Western New England Inst., New Haven, 1968-73. Cert. in psychiatry, 1969, psychoanalysis, 1974. Resident in psychiatry Yale U., New Haven, 1962-65; pvt. practice psychiatry and psychoanalysis, 1967—; asst. clin. prof. psychiatry Yale U. Sch. Medicine, New Haven, 1967-75, assoc. clin. prof. psychiatry, 1975-81, Cornell U. Med. Coll., N.Y.C., 1981—; mem. faculty Ctr. for Psychoanalytic Tng. and Rsch., Columbia U., N.Y.C., 1981—; assoc. clin. prof. psychiatry Cornell U. Med. Coll., N.Y.C., 1981-88, clin. prof. psychiatry, 1989—. Pres. Western New England Psychoanalytic Soc., New Haven, 1979-81. Assoc. editor: Models of the Mind, Their Relationship to Clinical Work, 1985; author: Being Homosexual: Gay Men and Their Development, 1989, Becoming Gay: The Journey to Self-Acceptance, 1996; contbr. articles to profl. jours. Bd. dirs. Nat. Lesbian and Gay Health Assn., 1987-97, v.p., 1992-97; bd. dirs. Hetrick Martin Inst., 1992-95. Lt. comdr. USN, 1965-67. Fellow Am. Psychiat. Assn. (disting. life, mem. gay, lesbian and bisexual issues com. 1987-93, chmn. 1991-93), Am. Psychoanalytic Assn. (cert., chmn. program com. 1981-84), Internat. Psycho-Analytical Assn. (chmn. Am. program com. 1979-81), Phi Beta Kappa. Office: 55 East End Ave New York NY 10028-7928

ISAYEV, AVRAAM ISAYEVICH, polymer engineer, educator; b. Privolnoe, Azerbaijan, Russia, Oct. 17, 1942; s. Isai S. and Basia Isayev; m. Lubov M. Dadasheva, July 26, 1969; 1 child, Daniela. MSChemE, Azerbaijan Inst. Oil & Chem., Baku, 1964; PhD in Polymer Engring., USSR Acad. Scis., Moscow, 1970; MS in Applied Maths., Inst. Electronic Machine Bldg., Moscow, 1975. Rsch. assoc. State Rsch. Inst. Nitrogen Industries, Severodonetsk, Russia, 1965—66; predoctoral Inst. of Petrochem. Synthesis Russia Acad. Sci., Moscow, 1967—69, rsch. assoc., 1970—76; sr. rsch. fellow Israel Inst. Tech., Haifa, 1977—78; sr. rsch. assoc. Cornell U., Ithaca, NY, 1979—83; assoc. prof. Inst. Polymer Engring., U. Akron, Ohio, 1983—87, prof., 1987—2001, dir. mold tech., 1987—, disting. prof., 2001—. Guest prof. U. Aachen, Germany, 1986, U. Linz, Austria, 1993, Kyoto Inst. Technology, Japan, 1996, Inst. Polymer Rsch., Dresden, Germany, 1997, U. San Carlos, Brazil, 1997; expert on plastics processing technologies, Malaysia, 1995. Editor: Injectioon Compression Molding Fund, 1987, Modelling of Polymer Processing, 1991, Liquid Crystalline Polymer Systems Technological Advances, 1996; contbr. articles. Expert witness U.S. Ho. of Reps., Washington, 1988; expert U.S. Army Rsch. Office, 1991; rev. panel NSF, Washington, 1991, 94, 2000-01. NASA fellow, 1985; recipient Laureate of Young Scientists USSR Acad. Scis., 1970, Cert. of Appreciation, U. Akron Bd. Trustees, 1988, 93, Outstanding Rschr. award U. Akron Alumni Assn., 1996, Silver medal The Inst. Materials, London, 1997, Vinogradov prize G. V. Vinogradov Soc. Rheology, Moscow, 2000, Omnova Solutions Signature Univ. award, Akron, 2000; named Disting. Corp. Inventor, Am. Soc. Patent Holders, 1995. Mem. Am. Chem. Soc. (Melvin Mooney Disting. Tech. award rubber divsn. 1999), N.Y. Acad. Scis., Soc. Plastics Engrs. (Cert. of Recognition 1994), Polymer Processing Soc. (treas. 1989-91), Soc. Rheology. Jewish. Achievements include 22 patents for Self-Reinforced Composites, Devulcanization of Rubbers and Decrosslinking of Crosslinked Plastics, in-situ copolymerization in polymer blends, multi-layer conductive and nonconductive polymers; fundamental research in polymer and composite processing. Office: U Akron Inst Polymer Engring 260 S Forge St Akron OH 44325-0301 E-mail: aisayev@uakron.edu.

ISBELL, DAVID BRADFORD, lawyer, educator; b. New Haven, Feb. 18, 1929; s. Percy Ernest and Dorothy Mae (Crabb) I.; m. Florence Bachrach, July 21, 1971; children: Christopher Pascal, Virginia Anne, Nicholas Bradford. BA, Yale U., 1949, LLB, 1956. Bar: Conn., 1956, D.C. 1957. Assoc. Covington & Burling, Washington, 1957-59, 61-65, ptnr., 1965-98, sr. counsel, 1998—; asst staff dir. U.S. Commn. on Civil Rights, Washington, 1959-61. Lectr. Sch. Law U. Va., 1962—, Georgetown U. Law Ctr., 1996—. Bd. dirs. ACLU, 1965-92; chmn. exec. bd. Vets. Consortium Pro Bono Program, 1992—. 2nd lt. U.S. Army, 1951-53. Mem.: ABA (mem. ho. dels. 1986—96, chmn. com. on ethics & profl. responsibility 1991—94), D.C. Bar (gov. 1978—82, pres. 1983—84), Cosmos Club. Home: 3709 Bradley Ln Bethesda MD 20815-4256 Office: Covington & Burling 1201 Pennsylvania Ave NW Washington DC 20004 E-mail: disbell@cov.com.

ISBELL, ROBERT, writer; b. Anderson, S.C., Nov. 26, 1923; s. Henry Pope and Aileen Annette (Dixon) I.; m. Frances Griffin, Apr. 19, 1953; children: Lyn, Andrea, Eden. AB in Journalism, U. S.C., 1948. Mng. editor Florence (S.C.) Morning News, 1950-53; v.p. Bankers Trust of S.C., Columbia, 1963-68, sr. v.p., 1972-76, exec. v.p., 1976-86; pres. Robert Isbell & Co. Inc., Banner Elk, N.C., 1986-93. Sr. v.p. S.C. Nat. bank, Columbia, 1969-71; mem. faculty Sch. Banking of South, La. State U., summers, 1971-72. Author: Atlanta: A City of Neighborhoods, 1993, The Last Chivaree, 1996, The Keepers, 1999. Served with AUS, 1943-46, PTO. Recipient Silver medal Am. Advt. Fedn., 1966, Thomas Wolfe Lit. award, 1996, Willie Parker Peace History Book award, 1997; inducted into Lambda Chi Alpha Hall of Fame, 1997. Episcopalian. Home: 369 Fairforest Dr Rutherfordton NC 28139

ISBERG, REUBEN ALBERT, radio communications engineer; b. Chugwater, Wyo., Dec. 11, 1913; s. Albert Gust and Laura Carolina (Thun) I.; m. Dorothe Louise Hall, Feb. 23, 1936; children: Jon Lewis, Barbara Louise Isberg Johnson, Edward Russel. AB in Phys. Sci., U. No. Colo., 1935. Registered profl. engr., Calif. Radio and TV engr. W2XBS/WNBT-NBC, N.Y.C., 1939-42; electronic devel. engr. div. war rsch. Columbia U., Mineola, N.Y., 1942-46; chief engr. KRON-TV, San Francisco, 1946-52; ind. cons. TV engr. various locations, 1952-54; sr. engr. Ampex Corp., Redwood City, Calif., 1954-60; statewide communications engr. U. Calif., Berkeley, 1960-67; ind. cons. radio communications engr. Berkley, 1967—. Chair sub-com. for FM radio stereo standards NSRC, Washington,1 960-61; mem. com. for establishing 2500 MHz instrnl. TV svc., FCC, 1965-67. Contbr. to profl. publs. Named Honored Alumnus, U. No. Colo., 1993. Fellow IEEE (chair awards com. vehicular tech. soc. 1984-90, Avant Garde medal and cert. 1991), Audio Engring. Soc., Soc. Motion Picture and TV Engrs., Radio Club Am.; mem. Acoustical Soc. Am., Soc. Cable TV Engrs., Inst. Radio Engrs. (chair San Francisco sect. 1951). Republican. Congregationalist. Achievements include work on guided radio communications in subways, mines, ships and buildings, U.S. and Can. patents for tunnel distributed antenna system with signal taps coupling approximately the same amount of energy. Home: Apt 115 32100 SW French Prairie Dr Wilsonville OR 97070-7471 E-mail: r.isberg@att.net.

ISBISTER, JAMES DAVID, pharmaceutical business executive; b. Mt. Clemens, Mich., Mar. 31, 1937; s. Russell Lowell and Clara (Wild) I.; m. Jenefir Diane Wilkinson, July 23, 1960; children: Wendy Jill Kalavritinos, Kirstin Ann Hammond. BA cum laude, U. Mich., 1958; postgrad., Princeton; postgrad. (Woodrow Wilson fellow), 1958-59; MA (scholar), George Washington U., 1966. Asst. to asst. sec. adminstrn. HEW, Washington, 1963-65; exec. officer Nat. Library Medicine, Bethesda, 1965-67, NIMH, Rockville, Md., 1967-70, dep. dir., 1970-73; vis. academic London Sch. Econs., 1973-74; dir. U.S. Alcohol, Drug Abuse and Mental Health Adminstrn., 1974-77; v.p. Orkand Corp., 1977-78; assoc. dir. Internat. Comm. Agy., 1978-80; exec. Washington rep. Blue Cross/Blue Shield Assn., 1980-82, sr. v.p., 1982-86, Consol. Healthcare, Inc., 1986-89; pres. Combined Technologies, Inc., 1987-89; pres., CEO Pharmavene Inc., 1990-97, chmn., 1995-97; vice-chmn. Shire Labs., 1997-98; chmn. Advancis Pharmaceutical Corp., 1999—. Bd. dirs. Delsys Pharm. Corp., Flagstar Bancorp., Tackson Ltd., chmn.; chmn. Nat. Adv. Mental Health Council, 1974-75, Nat. Adv. Coun. on Alcohol Abuse and Alcoholism, 1974-75, Internat. Conf. on Prevention, 1976; v.p. U.S. Com. Study Internat. Health Care, 1972-74; com. on substance abuse Inst. Medicine, NAS, 1987-90, com. on clin. practice guidelines, 1990-92, com. on dental edn., 1992-97. Editorial adv. bd.: Mental Health Digest, 1970-72, Adminstrn. in Mental Health, 1972-75. Mem. budget com. Washington Met. Health and Welfare Council, 1965-70; bd. dirs. Bedford Springs Festival for the Performing Arts, 1983-87 . Served with USAF, 1959-60, 61-62. Episcopalian. Home: 9521 Accord Dr Rockville MD 20854-4302 Office: Advancis Pharm Corp 942 Clopper Rd Gaithersburg MD 20854

ISBISTER, JENEFIR DIANE WILKINSON, microbiologist, researcher, educator, consultant; b. Rahway, N.J., June 4, 1936; d. Edwin Guy and Alvira Marie (Andrews) Wilkinson; m. James David Isbister, July 23, 1960; children: Wendy Jill Isbister Kalavritinos, Kirstin Ann Isbister Hammond. BS, Newberry (S.C.) Coll., 1957; MS in Med. Tech., Jefferson Med. Sch., Phila., 1958; PhD in Microbiology, U. Md., 1977. Med. technologist Princeton (N.J.) Hosp., 1958-60; instr. med. tech. sch. George Washington U., Washington, 1960-62, rsch. asst., 1976-77; rsch. microbiologist Environ. Biospherics, Inc., Rockville, 1978-80; group leader environ. microbiology dept. Atlantic Rsch. Corp., Alexandria, Va., 1980-89; pvt. practice cons. microbiologist Potomac, Md., 1989—; sr. tech. advisor ARCTECH, Inc., Chantilly, Va., 1989-92. Adj. prof. George Mason U., 1988-92, rsch. prof., 1992—; cons. Orkand Corp., Silver Spring, Md., 1979-80, U.S. DOE, Pitts., 1988-89, Advancis Pharm., Gaithersburg, Md., 2001—. Contbr. to book, articles to profl. jours. Sci. fair judge Montgomery and Fairfax County Schs., Md. and Va., 1975—; bd. dirs. Bedford (Pa.) Springs Music Festival, 1984-89. Va.-Carolina Chem. Corp. scholar, 1953; recipient Congl. High Tech. award Congl. Caucus for Sci. and Tech., 1985. Mem. ASTM (vice chair 1983-92, 99-2002), Am. Soc. for Microbiology, Am. Soc. for Clin. Pathologists, Cosmos Club, Phi Kappa Phi, Phi Sigma, Chi Beta Phi. Episcopalian. Avocations: reading, music, tennis, restoring old houses and furniture. Home: 9521 Accord Dr Rockville MD 20854-4302 Office: George Mason U Rm 303E Prince William II 10900 University Blvd Manassas VA 20110 E-mail: jisbiste@osf1.gmu.edu.

ISBRANDT, LESTER REINHARDT, pharmaceutical executive; b. Chgo., Jan. 29, 1946; s. Reinhardt and Renata Selma Isbrandt; m. Pamela Diane Conner; children: Derek, Michelle. BS, No. Ill. U., 1967; PhD, Mich. State U., 1972. Rsch. chemist Gulf Oil Co., Pitts., 1972—73; sect. head Procter and Gamble Co., Cin., 1973—84; v.p. Carter Wallace Inc., N.Y.C., 1884—1987, Bristol-Myers Squibb Co., N.Y.C., 1987—94, Warner Lambert Co., Morris Plains, NJ, 1994—98; founder and pres. Rhinotech Inc., New Hope, Pa., 1998—. Dir. New Hope Hist. Soc., New Hope, Pa., 2001—. Home: 2 Kingswoods Dr New Hope PA 18938 Office: Rhinotech Inc 2 Kingswoods Dr New Hope PA 18938 Business E-Mail: rhinotech@comcast.net.

ISCOE, IRA, psychology educator; b. N.Y.C., Feb. 1, 1921; s. Samuel and Anna (Leff) I.; m. Louise Koches, July 29, 1951; children: Craig, Neil, Ellen. BA, Sir George William's Coll., 1942; attended, McGill U., 1942; MA, UCLA, 1949, PhD, 1951. From asst. prof. psychology to assoc. prof. psychology U. Tex., Austin, 1951-61, prof. psychology, 1961—, dir. Inst. Human Devel., 1978-96, Ashbel Smith prof. psychology, 1986-96, Ashbel Smith prof. emeritus, 1996—. Dir. counseling ctr. U. Tex., Austin, 1968-78, Plan II Honors Program, 1981-86; disting. vis. scientist NIMH, Rockville, Md., 1978-79; cons. VA Hosp., Dallas, San Antonio, Temple, Tex., 1958—, NIMH, Washington, 1961—. Author: Coping, Adaptation, & Lifestyle, 1975; editor: Community Psychology in Transition, 1977, Social & Psychological Problems of Women, 1984. Pres. Human Opportunities Corp., Austin, 1964-67; chair Child Care Commn., Austin, 1986-92; mem. Com. Mental Health of Children, Tex., 1989-92; chair Com. Cmty. Care of Severly Mentally Ill, Austin, 1987-90; vol. psychol. svcs. Staff sgt. US Army, 1942-46, PTO. Decorated Bronze Medal; Gerontology Rsch. grantee Hogg Found. Mental Health, 1983-88, Child Abuse and Neglect Rsch. grantee Children's Bur., 1984-87. Fellow APA (bd. profl. affairs 1978-82, Disting. Svc. award 1980, rep. coun. 1964-67, 82-85, pres. divsn. cmty. psychology); mem. Tex. Psychol. Assn. (pres. 1967) SW Psychol. Assn. (pres. 1968). Democrat. Jewish. Avocations: hiking, cooking. Home: 3300 Greenlee Dr Austin TX 78703-1528 Office: U Tex Austin Psychology Dept Seay Bldg 108 Deky Keeton Austin TX 78712 Fax: 512-476-0504. E-mail: Iscoe@psy.utexas.edu.

ISDALE, CHARLES EDWIN, chemical engineer; b. DeQuincy, La., Mar. 10, 1942; s. Vester Edwin and Katherine Gwendolyn (Wincey) I.; m. Lucille Brown, Aug. 26, 1962; children: Charles Edwin Jr., Jennifer Denise Hunt, Amberly Lauren. BSChemE, La. State U., 1965; MBA, So. Ill. U., 1978. Registered profl. engr., Ill., La. Chem. engr. Firestone Synthetic Rubber, Lake Charles, La., 1965-69, A.E. Staley Mfg. Co., Decatur, Ill., 1969-72; dir. engring. and maintenance VIOBIN Corp., Monticello, Ill., 1972-80; pres. Control Enterprises, Inc., Savoy, Ill., 1980-95, College Station, Tex., 1995-97; sr. lectr. dept. chem. engring. Tex. A&M U., College Station, 1998—. Cons. Nabisco Brands, East Hanover, N.J., 1984—, Clorox, Jackson, Miss., 1987—, Alpharma, Chicago Heights, Ill., 1987—, Chinook Group, Sombra, Ont., Can., 1987—. Active Cornerstone Ch., College Station, Tex. Mem. AIChE (sect. chmn. 1972-73), Instrument Soc. of Am. (Man of Yr. 1986). Achievements include design of a configurable multivariate control method, a method for removal of solvent to low ppm levels from enzymes, design of a batch wheat germ oil extraction plant, design of an animal gland extraction plant; patents on processing beef lung for production of heparin. Home: 715 Canterbury Dr College Station TX 77845 Office: Tex A&M U Chem Engring Dept MS3122 College Station TX 77843-3122 E-mail: charles@isdale.com., c-isdale@tamu.edu.

ISDANER, LAWRENCE ARTHUR, accountant; b. Phila., June 6, 1934; s. Irving and Frances (Ford) I.; m. Audrey Goldstein, Apr. 4, 1957; children: Scott Alan, Bart Matthew. BS, U. Pa., 1956. CPA, Pa. Founder, mem. Isdaner & Co. LLC, CPAs, Bala Cynwyd, Pa., 1967—. Founding dir., chmn. bd. Allegiance Bank of N.Am., 1998—. Author: Army Industrial Fund and Cost Accounting Manual, 1958. Bd. dirs. Golden Slipper Club, Phila., 1974—, pres., 1977; internat. bd. dirs. Pop Warner Little Scholars, Phila., 1992—; mem. investment adv. bd. The Curtis Inst. Music. With U.S. Army, 1957-59. Mem. AICPA, Pa. Inst. CPAs, Germantown Cricket Club, Desert Mountain Club, Kiwanis. Avocation: tennis. Home: 1720 Balsam Ln Villanova PA 19085-1802 Office: Three Bala Plz Ste 501 West Bala Cynwyd PA 19004-3484 E-mail: lai@isdanerllc.com.

ISELE, WILLIAM PAUL, lawyer; b. Sept. 8, 1949; s. Francis Joseph and Anna Mae (Hauser) I.; m. Linda Hean Bender, May 1, 1976; children: William Nicholas, Christopher Paul, David Francis. BA in Philosophy, Cath. U. Am., 1971; MA in Philosophy, 1972; JD, Georgetown U., 1975. Bar: Va. 1975, Ill. 1976, U.S. Dist. Ct. (no. dist.) Ill. 1976, U.S. Dist. Ct. N.J. 1976; N.J. 1977, U.S. Supreme Ct. 1986, N.Y. 1989. Asst. dir. health law div. AMA, Chgo., 1976-81; assoc. Gross & Novak, East Brunswick, N.J., 1981-84; ptnr., 1985-88; of counsel Carella, Byrne, Bain & Gilfillan, Roseland, N.J., 1989; prin. Kern, Augustine, Conroy & Isele, P.C., Bridgewater, 1989-92; pvt. practice law, 1992-98; gen. counsel Office of Ombudsman for the Institutionalized Elderly, 1998-2000, N.J. Ombudsman for the Institutionalized Elderly, 2000—. Instr. So. Ill. U. Regional Healh Edn. Programs, Springfield, 1980-81; adj. prof. Seton Hall U. Law Sch., 1987-91. Cubmaster Pack 33, Boy Scouts Am., 1987—. Author: Confidentiality of Medical Records in N.J., 1983, The Hospital Medical Staff, 1984, Medical Society of New Jersey Model Medical Staff Bylaws, 1990, Under Oath: Tips for Testifying, 1994; contbr. articles to profl. jours. Mem. ABA, N.J. State Bar Assn. (chmn. health and hosp. law sect. 1989-91), Nat. Health Lawyers Assn., Am. Acad. Hosp. Attys., N.J. Soc. Hosp. Attys., Middlesex County Bar Assn., Cath. Lawyers Guild (trustee Metuchen diocese 1989-91), Nat. Assn. Pastoral Musicians (treas. Metuchen chpt. N.J. 1981-87). Home: 313 Brook Dr Milltown NJ 08850-1405 Office: PO Box 807 Trenton NJ 08625 E-mail: wisele@doh.state.nj.us.

ISELIN, DONALD GROTE, civil engineering and management consultant; b. Racine, Wis., Sept. 5, 1922; s. Harry Paul and Rose Ellen (Grote) I.; m. Jacqueline Myers, June 9, 1945; children— Donna Iselin Broom, Michael D., Madeline M. BS, U.S. Naval Acad., Annapolis, 1945; M.C.E., Rensselaer Poly. Inst., 1948; cert. in advanced mgmt. program, Harvard U., 1971. Registered profl. engr., D.C. Commd. ensign U.S. Navy, 1945, advanced through grades to rear adm., 1971, dep. chief civil engrs., 1973-76, chief civil engrs., 1977-81; ret., 1981; group v.p. Kaiser Engrs., Oakland, Calif., 1981-85. Decorated Legion of Merit (4); recipient Stephen Decatur award Navy League, 1968, Alumnus Engr. award Marquette U., 1980, Disting. Svc. medal Pres. U.S., 1981. Fellow Soc. Am. Mil. Engrs. (pres. 1978-79); mem. NAE, ASCE, NSPE, AIA (hon.). Republican. Roman Catholic. Home: 2695 Sycamore Canyon Rd Santa Barbara CA 93108-1913

ISELIN, JOHN JAY, foundation president; b. Greenville, S.C., Dec. 8, 1933; s. William Jay and Fannie Harrington (Humphreys) I.; m. Josephine Lea Barnes, Sept. 8, 1956; children: William Jay II, Benjamin Barnes, Josephine Lea, Fannie I. Minot, Alison Jay Russell. AB, Harvard U., 1956, PhD, 1965; BA, Corpus Christi Coll., U. Cambridge, Eng., 1958, MA, 1963; hon. degree, Adelphi U., L.I. U., Lander Coll. Rsch. fellow Brookings Inst., Washington, 1960-61; sr. writer Congl. Quar., Washington, 1961; corr.-editor Newsweek mag., 1962-65, sr. editor nat. affairs, 1965-69; v.p., pub. Harper & Row Publs. Inc., N.Y.C., 1969-71; pres., trustee Ednl. Broadcasting Corp., Channel 13, sta. WNET, N.Y.C., 1971-87; pres. The Cooper Union for the Advancement of Sci. and Art, N.Y.C., 1988-2000; pres. and dir. Marconi Internat. Fellowship Found., 2000—. Adj. prof. Columbia U., 2000—. Mem. bd. overseers Harvard U., 1970-76; mem. Acad. Polit. Sci., mem. Nat. Geog. Soc., Josiah Macy Jr. Found., Ventures in Edn.; Waterford Inst.; mem. Cathedral of St. John the Divine, N.Y. State Archives Inst. Recipient Disting. Citizen award trustees SUNY. Mem. Coun. on Fgn. Rels., Century Club, Harvard Club of N.Y.C. Office: Marconi Foundation 500 Mudd Hall Columbia Univ New York NY 10027 Home: Apt C606 200 E 66th St New York NY 10021-9185 E-mail: jji9@columbia.edu.

ISELY, HENRY PHILIP, association executive, integrative engineer, writer, educator; b. Montezuma, Kans., Oct. 16, 1915; s. James Walter and Jessie M. (Owen) I; m. Margaret Ann Sheesley, June 12, 1948 (dec. 1997); children: Zephyr, LaRock, Lark, Robin, Kemper, Heather Capri; m. Jelica Kungulovska, 2001. Student, South Oreg. Jr. Coll., Ashland, 1934-35, Antioch Coll., Yellow Springs, Ohio, 1935-37. Organizer Action for World Fedn., 1946-50, N.Am. Coun. for People's World Conv., 1954-58, World Com. for World Constl. Conv., 1958, sec. gen., 1959-66, World Constn. and Parliment Assn., Lakewood, Colo., 1966—; organizer worldwide prep. confs. World Constnl. Convention, 1963, 66, 67, 1st session People's World Parliament and World Constl. Conv., Switzerland, 1968; editor assn, jour. Across Frontiers, 1959—; co-organizer Emergency Coun. World Trustees, 1971, World Constituent Assembly, Innsbruck, Austria, 1977, Colombo, Sri Lanka, 1978-79, Troia, Portugal, 1991; organizer Provisional World Parliament 1st session, Brighton, Eng., 1982, 2nd Session, New Delhi, India, 1985, 3d Session, Miami Beach, Fla., 1987; mem. parliament, 1982—. Sec. Working Commn. to Draft World Constn., 1971-77, pres. World Svc. Trust, 1972-78; co-founder Builder Found., Vitamin Cottages, 1955—, (chmn. bd. dir s., 1985—), pres. Earth Rescue Corps., 1984-90, sec.-treas. Grad. Sch. World Problems, 1984-99, pres., 1999—, cabinet mem. Provisional World Govt., 1987—, pres. World Govt. Funding Corp., 1986—, Emergency Earth Rescue Adminstrn., 1995—, co-organizer Global Ratification and Elections Network, 1991— (sec. 1992—), prin. organizer 4th session Provisional World Parliament, Barcelona, Spain, 1996, 5th session, Malta, 2000, organizer first More Oxygen for the World conf., San Antonio, 1998; prof. world problems Grad. Sch. World Problems, 1990—; organizer Com. Five Global Expositions, 2001—. Author: The People Must Write the Peace, 1950, A Call to All Peoples and All National Governments of the Earth, 1961, Outline for the Debate and Drafting of a World Constitution, 1967, Strategy for Reclaiming Earth for Humanity, 1969, Call to a World Constituent Assembly, 1974, Proposal for Immediate Action by an Emergency Council of World Trustees, 1971, Call to A Provisional World Parliament, 1981, People Who Want Peace Must Take Charge of World Affairs, 1982, Plan for Emergency Earth Rescue Administration, 1985, Plan for Earth Finance Credit Corporation, 1987, Climate Crisis, 1989, Technological Breakthroughs for A Global Energy Network, 1991, Bill of Particulars: Why the U.N. Must Be Replaced, 1994, Manifesto for the Inauguration of World Government, 1994, Call to the Fourth Session of the Provisional World Parliament, 1995, Fifth Session, 1997, Critique of the Report of the Commission on Global Governance, 1995, Using Crtedit Careds and Electronic Accountin to Initiate New Global Accounting, Credit and Finance System, 1996, Double Jeopardy and the Phytoplankton Project, 1997, The Fallacy of Treating Labor as a Commodity, 2000, The Immediate Economic Benefits of World Government, 2000, The First Fifteen Global Ministries of World Government, 2002; co-author, editor: A Constitution for the Federation of Earth, 1974, rev. edit., 1991, also author several other world legis. measures adopted at Provisional World Parliament, 1968-96; co-author: Plan for Collaboration in World Constituent Assembly, 1991, Creator treatment for screen drama History Hangs by a Thread, 1993; designer: prefab modular panel sys. constrn., master plan Guacamaya project, Costa Rica; planner five world fairs, five sessions World Parliament, 2000. Candidate for U.S. Congress, 1958. Recipient hon. rsch. doctorate in edn., 1989, Honor award Internat Assn. Educators for World Peace, 1975, Ghandi medal, 1977, Honor award Internat Soc. Universalism, 1993. Mem. ACLU, Am. Acad. Polit. Sci., Fellowship of Reconciliation, World Union, World Federalist Assn., World Future Soc., Earth Island Inst., Populatin Reference Bur., Earth Action, People's Congress, Life Ext. Found., Interfaith Alliance, Internat. Assn. for Hydrogen Energy, Friends of Earth, Wilderness Soc., Solar Energy Soc., Sierra Club, Amnesty Internat., World Resources Inst., Human Rights Watch, Nat. Nutritional Foods Assn., Environ. Def. Fund, Greenpeace, Ctr. for Study of Democratic Instns., War Resistors League, Audubon Soc., Worldwatch Inst., Internat. Assn. Constl. Law, Earth Regeneration Soc., Zero Population Growth, Cancr Control Soc., Mt. Vernon Country Club, Lakewood Country Club. Socialist. Home: Lookout Mountain 241 Zephyr Ave Golden CO 80401-9589 Office: 8800 W 14th Ave Lakewood CO 80215-4817 Fax: 303-237-7685, 303-526-7933. E-mail: wcparliament@uswest.net.

ISEMAN, JOSEPH SEEMAN, lawyer; b. N.Y.C., May 29, 1916; s. Percy Reginald and Edith Helene (Seeman) I.; m. June Lorraine Bang, Dec. 10, 1966; children: Peter A., Frederick J., Ellen M.; stepchildren: Anne Hamilton, Susan E. Hamilton, William C. Hamilton. BA magna cum laude, Harvard U., 1937; LLB, Yale U., 1941; LHD (hon.), Am. U. of Paris, 1997. Bar: N.Y. State 1941, D.C. 1970, France, 1986. Investigator, clk. Comml. Factors Corp., 1937-38; atty. WPB, 1941-42; mng. dir. Iranian Airways Corp., 1946; assoc. Chadbourne, Wallace, Parke & Whiteside, N.Y.C., 1946-50, Paul, Weiss, Rifkind, Wharton & Garrison, N.Y.C., 1950-53, ptnr., 1954-86, counsel, 1987—. Counsel Charles F. Kettering Found., 1965-84. Author: A Perfect Sympathy, 1937; contbr. articles to profl. jours. Trustee Bennington Coll., 1969—81, acting pres., 1976; bd. dirs. Acad. for Ednl. Devel., Safe Horizon, 1980—, also chmn.; bd. dirs. The Hastings Ctr., 1999—, Am. U., Paris, 1987—2000, also vice chmn. Capt. USAF, 1942—46. Woodrow Wilson vis. fellow Coll. William and Mary, 1977, Ripon Coll., 1979, Rollins Coll., 1980, De Pauw U., 1980, Fisk U., 1981, Albright Coll., 1982, Hood Coll., 1983, Southwestern U., 1984. Mem. ABA, N.Y. State Bar Assn., Assn. of Bar of City of N.Y., Century Assn., Coveleigh Club, Phi Beta Kappa. Democrat. Office: 1285 6th Ave Rm 2828 New York NY 10019-6064

ISEMINGER, GARY HUDSON, philosophy educator; b. Middleboro, Mass., Mar. 3, 1937; s. Boyd Austin and Harriet Herring (Hudson); m. Andrea Louise Grove, Dec. 18, 1965; children: Andrew, Ellen. BA, Wesleyan U., 1958; MA, Yale U., 1960, PhD, 1961. Instr. philosophy Yale U., 1961-62, Carleton Coll., Northfield, Minn., 1962-63, asst. prof., 1963-68, assoc. prof., 1968-73, prof., 1973-94, William H. Laird prof. philosophy and liberal arts, 1994—2002, Stephen R. Lewis, Jr. prof. philosophy and liberal learning, 2002—. Vis. fellow Kings Coll., London, 1966, U. Lancaster, 1991; chair student-faculty adminstrn. com. Carleton Coll., 1970-71, dept. philosophy, 1972-75, 86-89, 98—, ednl. policy com., 1973-74, English dept. rev. com., 1973-74, com. Lucas Lectrs. in Arts, 1977-81, presdl. inauguration, 1987, edn. dept. rev. task force, 1988, Am. studies program rev. com., 1992, mem. tenure and devel. rev. com., 1985-87, Coll. Coun., 1987, Coll. Marshall, 2001—; acad. vis. London Sch. Econs., 1971; vis. prof. philosophy U. Minn., 1979, Mayo Med. Sch., 1986, 87, U. Lancaster, 1994, Trinity Coll. Dublin, 2000, Lingnan U., Hong Kong, 2003; Belgum meml. lectr. St. Olaf Coll., 1997; panelist divsn. fellowships NEH, 1980, 91; commentator Minn. Pub. Radio, 1981; dir. London arts program Associated Colls. Midwest, 1982; cons. Harvard U. Press, Univ. Calif. Press, Prentice-Hall, Cornell U. Press, Holt, Rinehart and Winston, Vanderbilt U. Press, Jour. Aesthetics and Art Criticism, Dialogue, Notre Dame Jour. Formal Logic, Jour. of Philosophy and Phenomenological Rsch., Inquiry; external reviewer, evaluator various philosophy depts.; presenter in field. Author: An Introduction to Deductive Logic, 1968, Logic and Philosophy: Selected Readings, 1968, 2d edit., 1980, Knowledge and Argument, 1984, Intention and Interpretation, 1992; mem. editl. bd. Am. Philos. Quar., 1989-92, Jour. of Aesthetics and Art Criticism, 1993—; contbr. articles, revs. to profl. jours. Mem. Minn. Humanities Commn., 1984-90, chair 1988-89 Grantee NSF Coun. Philos. Studies, 1968, Bush Found., 1983, Sloan Found. 1984, Faculty Devel. Endowment, 1989, 94, 2000, NEH, 1990, 91; recipient summer stipend NEH, 1971, 78, Disting. Alumnus award Wesleyan U., 1993; Woodrow Wilson fellow, 1958, fellow Univ. Coll., London, 1975, 78, Inst. Adv. Studies in the Humanities, U. Edinburgh, 1985; vis. scholar Cambridge U., 1996, York U., 2002. Mem. AAUP (pres. Carleton chpt. 1967-68), Am. Philos. Assn. (program com. western divsn. 1982, task force on the philosophy major 1989-90, program com. ctrl. divsn. 1991, chmn. com. on tchg. philosophy 1993-96, com. to award Matchette prize in philosophy 1993-95, bd. officers 1993-96), Am. Soc. Aesthetics (trustee 1996-99), Minn. Philos. Soc. (pres. 1978-79), Phi Beta Kappa (pres. Carleton chpt. 1968-69). Avocations: classical percussion, jazz vibraphone, choral singing. Office: Carleton College One North College St Northfield MN 55057-4002 E-mail: giseming@carleton.edu.

ISENBERG, ABRAHAM CHARLES, shoe manufacturing company executive; b. Lynn, Mass., Feb. 24, 1914; s. Louis and Alice (Lown) I.; m. Thelma F. Sisenwine, Oct. 30, 1938; children: Gerald, Lee Carol, Edward. BS, Wharton Sch., U. Pa., 1935. Cert. paralegal vol., county ct. mediator, lic. mediator, Fla. With Consol. Nat. Shoe Corp., Norwood, Mass., 1935—, exec. v.p., 1967-68, pres., CEO, 1968-72, chmn. bd., treas., 1972-74. Vice chmn. shoe divsn. Greater Boston area Combined Jewish Philanthropies, 1968—. Bd. dirs. New Eng. Anti-Defamation League of B'nai B'rith. Mem. Two Ten Assocs. (bd. dirs. 1956—, v.p. 1969—), Am. Footwear Assn. (bd. dirs. 1968, regional v.p. 1970—), Am. Footwear Inst. (trustee 1970-74), Boston Boot and Shoe Club (exec. com. 1967—, v.p. 1969, pres. 1973), Brandeis U. Men's Assocs. (bd. dirs. 1966—), Beta Sigma Rho. Clubs: Hebrew Rehab. Ctr. Men's (bd. dirs. 1970-72), B'nai B'rith (bd. dirs. 1979—). Home: 920 Riverview Dr SE Rio Rancho NM 87124 E-mail: abethelma@webtv.net. *I have found that being honest and ethical with those I associated with in business or community affairs was the most rewarding behavior I could follow. I realize that some who act entirely contrary to these principles appear to be very successful, but I would not want success on those terms.*

ISENBERG, HENRY DAVID, microbiology educator; b. Giessen, Germany, Mar. 9, 1922; came to U.S., 1937, naturalized, 1943; s. Gerson and Flora (Gruenebaum) I.; m. Lila S. Grossman, Feb. 15, 1948; children— Ina Pepi Isenberg Stein, Gerald Alan. BS, CCNY, 1947; MA, Bklyn. Coll., 1951; PhD, St. Johns U., 1959. Diplomate Am. Bd. Med. Microbiology (chmn. 1976-79, Disting. Svc. award 1994). Asst. dir. Angrist Labs., 1947-54; chief microbiology L.I. Jewish Med. Ctr., New Hyde Park, NY, 1954-97, chief emeritus, cons., 1997—2002, chief emeritus microbiology (pathology), dir. infection control (medicine), 2002—; cons. clin. microbiology Mt. Sinai Med. Ctr., 1997—2001; cons. Univs. Space Rsch. Assn., 1998—; asst. clin. prof. orthopedic surgery SUNY Downstate Med. Ctr., Bklyn., 1963-68, assoc. clin. prof. orthopedic surgery, 1968-71, professorial lectr. orthopedic surgery, 1971-89. Prof. clin. pathology SUNY Health Sci. Ctr., Stony Brook, 1970-89; clin. prof. microbiology and immunology U. South Fla. Sch. Medicine, 1982-87; prof. lab. medicine Albert Einstein Coll. Medicine, 1989-96, prof. pathology, 1996—; cons. in microbiology NASA, 1990—; professorial lectr. pathology Mt. Sinai Sch. Medicine, 1998-2001. Editor Jour. Clin. Microbiology, 1974-79, editor-in-chief, 1979-89; editor CRC Critical Revs. in Microbiology, 1978-81; editor in chief: CRC Forum in Bacteriology; sect. editor Manual of Clin. Microbiology, 4th edit.; editor: Manual of Clinical Microbiology, 5th edit.; editor-in-chief Clinical Microbiology Procedures Handbook, 1991-2002, 2d edit. 2000—, Essential Procedures in Clinical Microbiology, 1997-2002; mem. editl. bd. Applied Microbiology, 1969-74; contbr. numerous articles to profl. jours. and books; patentee in field. Served with U.S. Army, 1943-45. Named Microbiologist of Yr. Lab World Mag., 1978; recipient Kimble awrd, 1980; Profl. Recognition award Am. Bd. Microbiology/Am. Acad. Microbiology, 1994. Fellow Am. Acad. Microbiology (bd. govs.), N.Y. Acad. Scis., Am. Inst. Chemists, Infectious Disease Soc. Am., N.Y. Acad. Medicine; mem AAAS, Am. Soc. Microbiology (Becton-Dickinson award 1979, Alexander C. Sonnenwirth Meml. Lectr. award 1989, Disting. Svc. award N.Y. br. 1991, nat. 1996, hon. mem. 1999), Harvey Soc., Sigma Xi. Jewish. Home: 26922D Grand Central Pky Floral Park NY 11005-1010 Office: LI Jewish Med Ctr New Hyde Park NY 11040 E-mail: isenberg@lij.edu.

ISENBERG, HOWARD LEE, manufacturing company executive; b. Chgo., Dec. 21, 1936; children: Suzanne, Marc, Alan. BS, U. Pa., 1958. CPA, Ill. V.p. Conley Electronics, Chgo., 1960-63, Barr Co. div. Pittway Corp., Niles, Ill., 1963-68, pres. Barr Co. div., 1969-92; v.p. Pittway Corp., Niles, Ill., 1970-92, CCL Custom Mfg. (acquired Barr Co. in 1992), 1992—. Vice chmn., trustee Lake Forest (Ill.) Acad., 1986-98; trustee Providence-St. Mel H.S., Chgo., 1994—; chmn. The Barr Fund, 1993—. Home: 325 Oak Creek Dr Wheeling IL 60090-6741 Office: CCL Custom Mfg 6133 N River Rd Ste 800 Rosemont IL 60018-5175 E-mail: hisenberg@cclcustom.com.

ISENBERG, JAMES ALLEN, mathematics and physics researcher, educator; b. Boston, Mar. 14, 1951; s. Paul Charles and Ruth Selma (Schultz) I AB, Princeton U., 1973; PhD, U. Md., 1979. Postdoctoral fellow U. Waterloo, Ontario, Can., 1979-80, U. Calif., Berkeley, 1980-82; asst. prof. math. U. Oreg., Eugene, 1982-87, assoc. prof. math., 1987-93, prof. math., 1993—. Vis. asst. prof. Rice U., Houston, 1983-84, U. Minn., Mpls., 1985; vis. rsch. fellow U. Paris, France, 1986, Ctr. Math. Analysis, Canberra, Australia, 1988, Inst. for Theoretical Physics U. Calif., Santa Barbara, 1993, 99, 2003, Erwin Schrodinger Inst., Vienna, Austria, 1994, 95; vis. prof. U. Calif. San Diego, La Jolla, 1989, 2003; disting. vis. prof. U. Tours, France, 1996; vis. prof. Stanford U., 2002, Calif. Inst. Tech., 2003; conf. organizer Pacific Gravity Meeting, 1985—. Editor: Mathematics in General Relativity, 1988, Safaris in Spacetime, 2003; sci. columnist Brownsville Times; contbr. articles to profl. jours. Prospective student interviewer Princeton U., Eugene, 1974—; bd. mem. Brownsville City Libr.; mem. Brownsvillle Planning Commn. Grantee NSF 1983—, Ctr. Nat. Rsch. Sci., Paris, 1986. Fellow Am. Phys. Soc. (chair top group for gravitation), mem. Am. Math. Soc., Soc. Gen. Relativity & Gravitation. Achievements include research on long time behavior of solutions of Einstein's equations, solutions of Einstein constraints, twistor representation of solutions of the Yang Mills equations; use of heat equations to study the relationship between geometry and topology. Home: 717 Amelia Ave Brownsville OR 97327-2226 Office: Univ Oregon Dept Math Eugene OR 97405

ISENBERG, NORBERT, chemist, educator; b. Saarbruecken, Germany, June 17, 1923; came to U.S., 1938; s. Sally and Erna Isenberg; m. Edith Dorothy Sternheim, Nov. 23, 1950; children: Ralph Marvin, Mark Allan, Jon Franklin, Lori Beth. BA, Columbia U., 1948, MA, 1950; PhD, Rensselaer Poly. Inst., 1963. Tchg. asst. Columbia U., N.Y.C., 1949-50; instr. chemistry Skidmore Coll., 1950-54, asst. prof., 1954-63, assoc. prof., 1963-64; postdoctoral fellow U. Wis., Madison, 1963-64, asst. prof. Kenosha, 1964-66, assoc. prof., 1966-69, prof. Parkside/Kenosha, 1969-90, prof. emeritus chemistry, 1990—. Vis. prof. U. Wis., Madison, 1971-72; cons. Am. Motors Co., Kenosha, 1974, 78. Contbr. articles to profl. jours. Pres. Jewish Welfare Coun., Racine, Wis., 1986—; chairperson Adult Edn. Com., Racine, 1976, 84—. Cpl. U.S. Army, 1943-46. Named to Southeastern Wis. Educators Hall of Fame, 1992; grantee Smith Kline and French, 1957-59, NIH, 1957-62, NSF, 1958-61, Am. Cancer Soc., 1963-64. Fellow AAAS; mem. AAUP, Am. Chem. Assn., B'nai B'rith (pres. Kalman Klein Lodge, Racine, Wis. 1973). Avocations: music (piano), reading, history, art, travel. Home: 4118 Pennington Ln Racine WI 53403

ISENBERG, STEVEN LAWRENCE, retired publishing executive; b. Detroit, Oct. 19, 1940; s. A.G. Jerry and Lucille (Potaschnik) Isenberg; m. Barbara Lee Levy, Nov. 26, 1967; 1 child, Christopher Michael. BA in English, U. Calif., Berkeley, 1962; BA in English Lang. and Lit., Oxford (Eng.) U., 1964, MA, 1966; JD, Yale U., 1976; DHL (hon.), Adelphi U., 2000. Bar: N.Y. 1976. Asst. to dir. Bur. Budget, N.Y.C., 1967—68; chief staff, asst. to mayor Office of Mayor, N.Y.C., 1969—73; litigator Breed, Abbott and Morgan, N.Y.C., 1976—82; asst. to pub. Newsday, L.I., NY, 1982—83; pub., CEO So. Conn. Newspapers, Stamford, 1983—86; assoc. pub. Newsday, N.Y. Newsday, N.Y.C., 1986—90; pub. Sports, Inc., N.Y.C., 1987—88; exec. v.p. mktg. L.A. Times, 1991—92; deputy pub. Newsday/N.Y. Newsday, Melville, 1992—95; pub. N.Y. Newsday, 1994—95. Reuters fellow Green Coll., Oxford, 1997; vis. prof. U. Calif., Berkeley, 1996; chmn. bd. trustees Adelphi U., Garden City, NY, 1997—2001, pres. ad interim, 1999—2000, chmn. emeritus, 2001—; lectr. Yale Coll., 1999; vis. scholar, lectr. The New Sch., 1999; vis. prof. humanities Polytechnic U., Bklyn., 2000; Batten prof. pub. policy Davidson (N.C.) Coll., 2001; adj. prof. humanities U. Tex., Austin. Pres. adv. bd. U. Calif. Coll. Letters and Scis., Berkeley; chmn. bd. trustees Adelphi U., L.I.; bd. dirs. Franklin & Eleanor Roosevelt Inst.; mem. presdl. campaign staff Robert F. Kennedy, 1968, John V. Lindsay, 1972; bd. dirs. Mcpl. Arts Soc., Com. to Protect Journalists. Mem.: Coun. Fgn. Affairs, Century Assn., Yale Club. Democrat. Jewish. Home: Apt 3N 151 Central Park W New York NY 10023-1514

ISENHOWER, NELSON NOLAN, anesthesiologist; b. Newton, N.C., Feb. 9, 1948; s. Homer Hallard and Genevieve Elizabeth (Caldwell) I.; m. Rebecca Sue Wilson, Sept. 18, 1976; children: Lori Suzanne, Matthew Wilson. BS cum laude, Wake Forest U., 1970; MD, Bowman Gray Sch. Medicine, 1974. Diplomate Am. Bd. Anesthesiology. Commd. 2d lt. M.C., U.S. Army, 1970, advanced through grades to lt. col., 1983; intern Walter Reed Army Med. Ctr., Washington, 1974-75, resident in anesthesiology, 1975-78; mem. anesthesiology tchg. staff Brooke Army Med. Ctr., Fort Sam Houston, Tex., 1978-79, asst. chief anesthesiology, 1979-80, chief anesthesiology and operative svcs., dir. anesthesiology residency tng., 1980-83; cons. in anesthesiology U.S. Army Health Svcs. Command, 1980-83. Staff anesthesiologist Winchester Med. Ctr. (Va.), 1983—, chmn. dept. anesthesiology, 1987-89, 2nd v.p. med. staff, 1995, 1st v.p., 1996, pres., 1997; med. dir. Surgi-Ctr. Winchester, 1998—. Contbr. articles to profl. jours. Fellow Am. Coll. Anesthesiology; mem. AMA, Med. Soc. Va., No. Va. Med. soc., Am. Soc. Anesthesiology, So. Soc. Anesthesia, Internat. Anesthesia Rsch. Soc., Am. Soc. Reg. Anesthesia, Va. Anesthesiology Soc., Soc. Ambulatory Anesthesia. Republican. Baptist. Office: Winchester Anesthesiologists Inc 878 Fox Dr Winchester VA 22603-2807 E-mail: Nisenho@winanes.com.

ISERSON, KENNETH VICTOR, emergency medicine educator, bioethicist, author; b. Washington, Apr. 8, 1949; s. Isadore I. and Edith (Swedlow) I.; m. Mary Lou Sherk, June 16, 1973. BS, U. Md., 1971, MD, 1975; MBA, U. Phoenix, 1987. Diplomate Am. Bd. Emergency Medicine, Nat. Bd. Med. Examiners. Intern surgery Mayo Clinic, Rochester, Minn., 1975; resident emergency medicine Cin. Gen. Hosp., 1976-78; capt. USAF, 1978-80; chmn. emergency dept. Tex. A&M Coll. Medicine, Temple, 1980-81; asst. prof. surgery U. Ariz. Coll. Medicine, Tucson, 1981-84, residency dir. emergency medicine, 1981-91, assoc. prof. surgery, 1984-92; dir. Ariz. Bioethics Program U. Ariz., Tucson, 1991—, prof. surgery, 1992—2001; prof. emergency medicine U. Ariz. Coll. Medicine, Tucson, 2001—. Pres. Iserson Assocs. Ltd., Tucson, 1984—; vis. scholar Ctr. Clin. Med. Ethics U. Chgo., Pritzker Sch. Medicine, 1990-91. Author: Iserson's Getting Into a Residency: A Guide for Medical Students, 1988, 6th edit., 2003, Death to Dust: What Happens to Dead Bodies?, 1994, 2d edit., 2001, Non-Standard Medical Electives in the U.S. and Canada, 1997, 2d edit., 1998, Get Into Medical School! A Guide for the Perplexed, 1997, Grave Words: Notifying Survivors About Sudden Unexpected Death, 1999, (video and slide sets) The Gravest Words, 2000, Demon Doctors: Physicians as Serial Killers, 2002; sr. editor: Ethics in Emergency Medicine, 1986, 2d edit., 1995; mem. editl. bd. Cambridge Quar., 1991—, Jour. Emergency Medicine, 1985—; contbr. sci. articles to profl. jours. Med. dir. So. Ariz. Rescue Assn., Pima County, 1983—. Capt. USAF, 1978-80. Fellow Am. Coll. Emergency Physicians: mem. AMA, Med. Soc. U.S. and Mex. (treas. 2002-2003, v.p. 2003—), Soc. Acad. Emergency Medicine (pres. 1984-85, chmn. AMA rels. com. 1989—), Wilderness Med. Soc. (bd. dirs. 1987-91). E-mail: kvi@u.arizona.edu.

ISGETT, JOHN, auto dealership executive; b. Charleston, S.C., Apr. 10, 1969; m. Donna C. Isgett, Apr. 26, 1996; children: Sarah Caroline, John Thomas III. Grad. h.s., Hanahan, S.C. Paramedic Dorchester County Emergency Med. Svc., Summerville, S.C.; paramedic/flight Roper Hosp./Lifelink, Charleston; v.p. ops. Burdette Chevrolet, Darlington, S.C., 1996-2000; pres. Raceway Ford, Darlington, 2000—, Raceway Chevy, Pontiac, Buick & GMC, Lake City, S.C., 2000—, Raceway Chrysler Jeep Dodge, Hartsville, SC, 2002. Home: 103 Nez Perce St Darlington SC 29532-4237 Office: Raceway Ford 701 S Hwy 52 Bypass PO

Box 531 Darlington SC 29540 also: Raceway Chevy Pontiac Buick & GMC 410 W Main St PO Box 279 Lake City SC 29560 also: Raceway Chrysler Jeep Dodge PO Box 820 900 E Hwy 151 Hartsville SC 29550

ISH, DANIEL RUSSELL, law educator, academic administrator; b. Loon Lake, Sask., Can., Aug. 28, 1946; s. Leme Jay and Obeline Delia (Sicotte) I.; m. Diane Maureen Cote, Sept. 2, 1967 (div. 1970); m. Bonnie Jeanne Bolger, Dec. 22, 1970; children: Jason Bolger, Rachel Bolger. LLB, BA, U. Sask., 1970; LLM, Osgoode Hall Law Sch., Toronto, Ont., Can., 1974. Bar: Alta. 1971, Sask. 1979; called to Queen's Counsel, 1991. Lawyer H. Lloyd MacKay, Banff, Alta., 1970-71; asst. prof. law McGill U., Montreal, Que., Can., 1972-75; assoc. prof. U. Sask., Saskatoon, 1975-80, prof. law, 1980—, asst. dean law, 1977-78, dean, 1982-88, 96-97, 2002—; dir. Ctr. for Study of Cooperatives, 1989-95; Fulbright fellow Stanford U., 1995-96. Author: The Taxation of Canadian Co-operatives, 1975, The Law of Canadian Co-operatives, 1981, Co-operatives in Principle and Practice, 1992, Legal Responsibilities of Directors and Officers in Canadian Cooperation, 1996. Pres. Univ. Credit Union, Saskatoon, 1979-80. Mem. Law Found. Sask. (trustee 1982-88, 2002—), Law Soc. Sask. (bencher 1982-88, 2002—). Avocations: skiing, running. Office: U Sask Coll Law Saskatoon SK Canada S7N 5A6

ISHAK, KAMAL GEORGE, pathologist, consultant, pathologist, researcher, pathologist, educator; b. Atbara, Sudan, Mar. 2, 1928; arrived in U.S., 1957; s. George Ishak and Widad Matouk; m. Beatrice Winifred Boulton, 1959 (dec. 1970); children: Leila, Margaret. MD, Cairo U., 1951; PhD, Baylor U., 1963. Cert. anatomic and clin. pathology Am. Bd. Pathology, lic. W.Va. Fulbright scholar U.S. Naval Med. Rsch., Cairo, 1955—56; resident pathology Bapt. Meml. Hosp., San Antonio, 1957—59, Baylor U. Med. Ctr., Dallas, 1959—61; staff pathologist Armed Forces Inst. Pathology, Washington, 1963—65, chief hepatic and pediat. br., 1965—74, chmn. dept. hepatic pathology, 1974—90, chmn. dept. hepatic and gastrointestinal pathology, 1990—. Profl. lectr. Mount Sinai Sch. Medicine, 1985—; clin. prof. pathology Uniformed Svcs. U. for Health Scis., Bethesda, Md., 1996—. Author, editor: Neoplasms of the Liver, 1987, Clinical and Pathological Correlations in Liver Disease, 1998, Pathology of the Liver, 2001; co-author: Tumors of the Liver, 2001. Recipient Presdl. Rank award, Meritorious Exec., Sr. Exec. Svc., 1987, 2001, Disting. Svc. award, Am. Assn. for Study of Liver Diseases, Pres.'s award, U.S./Can. Acad. of Pathology, 2003. Fellow: Am. Soc. Clin. Pathologists, Royal Coll. Pathologists (hon.); mem.: European Assn. for the Study of Liver Diseases, Am. Soc. for the Study of Liver Diseases. Avocations: Middle East cooking, nature photography. Office: Armed Forcest Inst Pathology Washington DC 20306-6000

ISHAM, MARK, composer, jazz musician; b. N.Y.C., Sept. 7, 1951; s. Howard Fuller and Patricia (Hammond) I.; m. Donna Linson, Feb. 24, 1990. Film scores include: Never Cry Wolf, 1983, : Mrs. Soffel, 1984, The Times of Harvey Milk, 1984, Country, 1984, Trouble in Mind, 1985, The Hitcher, 1986, Made in Heaven, 1987, The Moderns, 1988, The Beast, 1988, Everybody Wins, 1990, Love at Large, 1990, Reversal of Fortune, 1990, Mortal Thoughts, 1991, Crooked Hearts, 1991, Point Break, 1991, Little Man Tate, 1991, Billy Bathgate, 1991, Cool World, 1992, A Midnight Clear, 1992, Of Mice and Men, 1992, The Public Eye, 1992, A River Runs Through It, 1992, Sketch Artist, 1992, Nowhere to Run, 1993, Fire in the Sky, 1993, Made in America, 1993, Short Cuts, 1993, Hidden Hawaii, 1994, Romeo is Bleeding, 1994, The Getaway, 1994, Quiz Show, 1994, Mrs. Parker and the Vicious Circle, 1994, Nell, 1994, Losing Isiah, 1995, The Net, 1995, Home for the Holidays, 1995, Last Dance, 1996, Gotti, 1996, Fly Away Home, 1996, Night Falls on Manhattan, 1997, Afterglow, 1997, The Education of Little Tree, 1997, Kiss the Girls, 1997, Blade, 1998, The Gingerbread Man, 1998, At First Sight, 1999, Free Money, 1999, October Sky, 1999, Body Shots, 1999, Galapagos, 1999, Varsity Blues, 1999, Rules of Engagement, 2000, Save the Last Dance, 2001, Impostor, 2001, Hardball, 2001, Don't Say a Word, 2001, Life as a House, 2001, The Majestic, 2001, TV themes include: Chicago Hope, : EZ Streets, recs. include: (solo) Vapor Drawings, 1983, : Castalia, 1988, Tibet, 1989, Mark Isham, 1991, Blue Sun, 1995, (with Charles Jankel): Charles Jankel, (with Tom Fogerty): Deal It Out, (with America): View From the Ground, (with Van Morrison): Live at the Belfast Opera House, : Into the Music, Inarticulate Speech of the Heart, Common One, Beautiful Vision, (with Art Lande): Story of Baku, : Eccentricities of Earl Dant, Rubisa Patrol, Desert Marauders, We Begin, (with Group 87): Group 87, : A Career in Dada Processing, (with the Rolling Stones): Voodoo Lounge, (with Bruce Springsteen): Human Touch, (with Willie Nelson): Across the Borderline, (with Toots Thielmans): Toots, Film Music. Office: Earle Tones Music Inc 23679 Calabasas Rd #522 Calabasas CA 91302

ISHAQ, MOUSA HANNA, materials engineer; b. Aboud, Jordan, Dec. 30, 1951; came to U.S., 1977; s. Hanna Yacoub and Salma Azar Ishaq; m. Kristin M. Peterson, Jan. 14, 1978; 1 child, John P. BS in Engring., Am. U., Cairo, 1977. Jr. engr. IBM, Essex Junction, Vt., 1978, assoc. engr., 1978-82, sr. assoc. engr., scientist, 1982-85, staff engr., scientist, 1985-87, adv. engr., scientist devel., 1987-97, sr. engr., scientist devel., 1997—. Tech. transfer rev. bd. IBM, 1998—. Inventor in field. Pres. Burlington-Bethlehem-Arad Sister City Project, Burlington, Vt., 1995—, task force, 1991; adv. bd. U.S./Arab Children's Artwork Exch., Burlington, 1991-94; mem. Vermonters for Peace in the Middle East, Vergennes, Vt., 1985—, Resettlement Coordinating Coun. for Cambodian Refugees, Burlington, 1983-85. Democrat. Lutheran. Avocations: travel, gardening, reading, swimming, fishing. Home: PO Box 341 Essex Junction VT 05453-0341 Office: IBM 1000 River St Essex Junction VT 05452-4299

ISHIGAKI, MILES MITSURN, musician, educator; b. Honolulu, Oct. 4, 1956; s. Edwin Mitsuo and Susanne Sadako Ishigaki; m. Teresa Ann Mendes, May 27, 2000; 1 child, Madison Masako. B in Mus. Edn., MusB in Performance, U. No. Colo., 1978; MusM in Performance, Colo. State U., 1980; MusD in Performance, U. Okla., 1988. Prof. music Calif. State U., Fresno, 1987—. Dir. West Coast Clarinet Congress, Fresno, 2000—. Mem.: Nat. Assn. Coll. Wind & Percussion Instrn. (chair 1988—), Internat. Clarinet Assn. (Yamaha Artist Clinician 1994—, Rico Grand Concert Artist 2000—). Office: Calif State U Dept Music 2380 E Keats Ave Fresno CA 93740-8023

ISHIHARA, BRYAN K. operations research analyst; b. Honolulu, Nov. 19, 1959; s. Morris S. and Mary K. Ishihara. BA in Bus. Adminstrn., BA in Math., U. Wash., 1981; MBA in Mgmt., Golden Gate U., San Francisco, 1983; MS in Ops. Rsch., Air Force Inst. Tech., Dayton, Ohio, 1985. Commd. USAF, 1981—2002, advanced through grades to lt. col., sci. analyst, 1981—2002; ops. rsch. analyst Northrop Grumman Info. Tech., Honolulu, 2002—. Decorated Meritorious Svc. medal USAF. Mem.: Air Force Assn., Assn. Old Crows, Omega Rho. Avocation: golf. Home: 1176 Ala Napunani St Honolulu HI 96818

ISHIHARA, TSUYOSHI, humanities educator; b. Tokyo, June 29, 1971; s. Shigeru and Yukiko Ishihara; m. Noriko Ishihara, July 30, 1996. BA in English Lit., Waseda U., Tokyo, 1994; MA in Am. Studies, Doshisha U., Kyoto, Japan, 1996; PhD in Am. Studies, U. Tex., 2003. Rsch. asst. Doshisha U., Kyoto, 1995—96; tchg. asst. Kyoto U., 1996—97; instr. Otemon Gakuin U., Osaka, Japan, 2003—. Participan Yale-China Am. Studies Seminar, New Haven, 1998. Contbr. Recipient Dr. Robert Grunden Meml. award, Am. Studies, U. Tex., 2002; scholar Ambassadorial scholar, Rotary Found., 1999; Fulbright scholar, 1999. Avocations: reading, bicycling, travel, camping. Home: 2-16-3 Takamatsu Nerima Tokyo 179-0075 Japan Office: Otemon Gakuin Univ 2-1-15 Nishi-Ai Ibaraki Osaka 567-8502 Japan

ISHII, AKIRA, medical parasitologist, malariologist, allergologist; b. Kochi, Japan, July 11, 1937; s. Katsuhiko and Fusae Ishii; m. Fuyuko Ishii, Mar. 20, 1968; children: Ken, Shin. MD, U. Tokyo, 1964, D Med. Sci., 1969; MSc, U. London, 1970. Cert. malaria advanced epidemiology. Rsch. assoc. Inst. Infectious Disease, U. Tokyo, 1969-74; asst. prof. Toyko Med. and Dental U., 1974-78, Inst. Med. Sci., U. Tokyo, 1978-79; prof. Miyazaki (Japan) Med. Coll., 1979-84, Okayama (Japan) U. Med. Sch., 1984-90; dir. dept. parasitology NIH, Tokyo, 1990-95; prof. Jichi Med. Sch., 1995—2003, prof. emeritus, 2003—. Com. mem. Japanese Internat. Coop. Agy., Tokyo, 1978—89; panel mem. U.S.-Japan Coop. Med. Program Parasitic Diseases, 1991—95, China-Japan Parasitology Seminar. Mem. editl. bd.: Japanese Jour. Tropical Medicine, Protozool. Rsch., Allergology Internat. Fellow: Royal Soc. Tropical Medicine and Hygiene, Am. Soc. Tropical Medicine and Hygiene; mem.: German-Japan Assn. for Protozoan Diseases (coun.), Japan Assn. Pub. Health, Japanese Soc. Internat. Health (pres., councilor, mem. exec. bd.), Japanese Soc. Infectious Disease (councilor), Japanese Soc. Allergologists (councilor), Japanese Soc. Med. Ent. Zoology (councilor, Soc. prize), Japanese Soc. Tropical Medicine (councilor), Japanese Soc. Parasitology (councilor, Koizumi prize). Avocations: mountain trips, golf, tennis. Home: 1-14-11 Matsubara Setagayaku Tokyo 156-0043 Japan

ISHII, CLYDE HIDEO, plastic surgeon; b. Lihue, Hawaii, Mar. 29, 1952; MD, Jefferson Med. Coll., 1978. Diplomate Am. Bd. Surgery, Am. Bd. Plastic Surgery. Past chief plastic surgery Queens Med. Ctr., Honolulu, asst. chief of surgery; chief plastic surgery Shriners Hosp., Honolulu, 1993—. Office: 1329 Lusitana St Ste 304 Honolulu HI 96813-2412

ISHII, YOSHINORI, environmental science educator; b. Tokyo, Mar. 14, 1933; s. Kichijiro and Kei Ishii; m. Hiroko Hisamune, Nov. 24, 1963; children: Yutaka, Makoto, Akira. BS, U. Tokyo, 1955, ED, 1977. Exploration geophysicist Teikoku Oil Co., Tokyo, 1955; rsch. geophysicist Japan Petroleum Exploration Co., Tokyo, 1955-67, sr. geophysicist, 1970-71, Japan Nat. Oil Corp., Tokyo, 1967-70; assoc. prof. geophysics U. Tokyo, 1971-78, prof. geophysics, 1978-93, prof. emeritus, 1993—; dep. dir. gen. Nat. Inst. Environ. Studies, Ibaraki, Japan, 1994-96, dir. gen., 1996-98; prof. Toyama U. Internat. Studies, 2000—. Mem. Sci. Coun. of Japan, Tokyo, 1988-91. Author: Introduction to Remote Sensing, 1981, Geophysical Engineering, 1988, Energy and Global Environmental Problems, 1995, Environmental Studies for Citizens, 2001, co-author several books; contbr. numerous articles to profl. jours. Mem. Engring. Acad. Japan, Soc. Exploration Geophysicists of Japan (pres. 1984-85, 1988-89, Best Paper award, Tokyo, 1976), Remote Sensing Soc. Japan, (v.p. 1981-88, pres. 1990-92), Japanese Assn. for Petroleum Tech. (v.p. 1982-86), Soc. Environ. Sci. Japan, Japan Soc. of Water Environment. Avocations: golf, computer. Home: 8-2-14 Hisagi, Zushi Kanagawa 249-0001 Japan Office: Toyama U Internat Studies Oyama-cho Kami-Niikawa-Gun Toyama 930-1292 Japan E-mail: tikyuu@qa2.so-net.ne.jp.

ISHIKAWA-FULLMER, JANET SATOMI, psychologist, educator; b. Hilo, Hawaii, Oct. 17, 1925; d. Shinichi and Onao (Kurisu) Saito; m. Calvin Y. Ishikawa, Aug. 15, 1950; 1 child, James A.; m. Daniel W. Fullmer, June 11, 1980. B of Edn., U. Hawaii, 1950, MEd, 1967, MEd, 1969, PhD, 1976. Diplomate Am. Acad. Pain Mgmt. Prof. Honolulu Bus. Coll., 1953-59; prof., counselor Kapiolani Community Coll., Honolulu, 1959-73; prof., dir. counseling Honolulu Community Coll., 1973-74, dean of students, 1974-77; psychologist, pres., treas. Human Resources Devel. Ctr., Inc., Honolulu, 1977—. Cons. United Specialties Co., Tokyo, 1979, Grambling (La.) State U., 1980, 81, Filipino Immigrants in Kalihi, Honolulu, 1979-84, Legis. Ref. Bur., Honolulu, 1984-85, Honolulu Police Dept., 1985; co-founder Waianae (Hawaii) Child and Family Ctr., 1979-92. Co-author: Family Therapy Dictionary, 1991, Manabu: The Diagnosis and Treatment of a Japanese Boy with a Visual Anomaly, 1991; contbr. articles to profl. jours. Commr. Bd. Psychology, Honolulu, 1979-85; co-founder Kilohana United Meth. Ch. and Family Ctr., 1993—. Mem. APA, ACA, Hawaii Psychol. Assn., Pi Lambda Theta (sec. 1967-68, v.p. 1968-69, pres. 1969-70, 96-98), Delta Kappa Gamma (sec., v.p. scholarship 1975, Outstanding Educator award 1975, Thomas Jefferson award 1993, Francis E. Clark award 1993). Avocations: jogging, tennis, dancing. Home: 154 Maono Pl Honolulu HI 96821-2529 Office: Human Resources Devel Ctr 1750 Kalakaua Ave Apt 809 Honolulu HI 96826-3725

ISHIMARU, AKIRA, electrical engineering educator; b. Fukuoka, Japan, Mar. 16, 1928; came to U.S., 1952; s. Shigezo and Yumi I.; m. Yuko Kaneda, Nov. 21, 1956; children: John, Jane, James, Joyce. BSEE, U. Tokyo, 1951; PhD, U. Wash., 1958. Registered profl. engr., Wash. Engr. Electro-Tech. Lab, Tokyo, 1951-52; tech. staff Bell Telephone Lab, Holmdel, N.J., 1956; asst. prof. U. Wash., Seattle, 1958-61, assoc. prof., 1961-65, prof. elec. engring., 1965-98, prof. emeritus, 1998—. Vis. assoc. prof. U. Calif., Berkeley, 1963-64; cons. Jet Propulsion Lab., Pasadena, Calif., 1964—, The Boeing Co., Seattle, 1984—. Author: Wave Propagation & Scattering in Random Media, 1978, Electromagnetic Wave Propagation, Radiation and Scattering, 1991; editor: Radio Science, 1982; founding editor Waves in Random Media, U.K., 1990. Recipient Faculty Achievement award Burlington Resources, 1990; Boeing Martin professorship, 1993. Fellow IEEE (editl. bd., Region VI Achievement award 1968, Centennial medal 1984, Antennas and Propagation Disting. Achievement award 1995, Heinrich Hertz medal 1999), IEEE Geosci. and Remote Sensing (Disting. Achievement award 1998, Third Millennium medal 2000), Acoustical Soc. Am., Optical Soc. Am. (assoc. editor jour. 1983), Inst. Physics U.K. (chartered physicist); mem. NAE, Internat. Union Radio Sci. (chmn. commn. B, John Howard Dellinger Gold medal 1999). Home: 2913 165th Pl NE Bellevue WA 98008-2137 Office: U Wash Dept Elec Engring PO Box 352500 Seattle WA 98195-2500 E-mail: ishimaru@ee.washington.edu.

ISHIZUKA, NOBUHISA, lawyer; b. N.Y.C., Dec. 29, 1960; s. Haruhisa and Ayako (Osawa) I.; m. Marcia Tsao-Ming Teng; children: Megumi, Midori. BA in East Asian Studies, Columbia U., 1982, JD, 1986; cert. of study, U. Tokyo, 1988. Bar: N.Y., D.C. Fgn. legal cons. Kashiwagi Sogo Law Office, Tokyo, 1986-87; atty. White & Case, Tokyo, 1987-88, N.Y.C., 1988-94, Morgan, Lewis & Bockius LLP, N.Y.C., 1994-96, ptnr., 1996-2000, Tokyo, 1999—, Skadden, Arps, Slate, Meagher & Flom LLP, Tokyo, 2000—; registered fgn. legal cons. Gaikokuho Jimu Bengoshi, 1999—. Legal counsel Ea. U.S. Kendo Fedn., N.Y.C., 1988—94; sec. JSR Am., Inc., Cin., 1988—, NGK, U.S.A. Inc., N.Y.C., 1992—, Teletechno, Inc., 1993—98. Sr. editor Columbia Law Rev., 1984-86. Mem. Phillips Acad. (Andover) Alumni Coun., 1998—2002. Japan Found. scholar, 1982-83; mem. U.S. Nat. Team-Kendo, 1982. Mem. ABA, N.Y.C. Bar Assn., N.Y. Athletic Club, Japanese Am. Assn. (mem. planning com. 1994-95, dir. 1995—, chmn. music scholarship com. 1995-99), Brit. Olympic Assn.-U.S. (N.Y. com. 1994-96), Sky Club, Dai-Ichi Tokyo Bar Assn. Avocation: rowing. Home: Belle Saison Hiroo 401 3-4-6 Shibuya-ku Tokyo 150-0012 Japan Office: Skadden Arps Slate Meagher & Flom LLP Izumi Garden Tower 1-6-1 Roppongi Minato-Ku Tokyo 106-6021 Japan E-mail: nishizuk@skadden.com.

ISIDORO, EDITH ANNETTE, horticulturist; b. Albuquerque, Oct. 14, 1957; d. Robert Joseph and Marion Elizabeth (Miller) I. BS in Horticulture, N.Mex. State U., 1981, MS in Horticulture, 1984; postgrad., U. Nev., Reno, 1992—. Range conservationist Soil Conservation Service, Estancia, Grants, N.Mex., 1980-82; lab. aide N.Mex. State U. Dept. Horticulture, Las Cruces, 1982, 83-84; technician N.Mex. State U. Coop. Extension Service, Las Cruces, 1983-84, county agrl. extension agt., 1985; area extension agt. U. Nev., Reno, Fallon, 1985—; hay tester Nev. Agrl. Services, Fallon, 1988-92; owner wholesale greenhouse Garden of Edith, 1996—. Mem. AAUW, Am. Soc. Hort. Sci., Am. Horticulture Soc., Am. Botany Soc., Am. Horticulture Therapy Assn., Alpha Zeta, Pi Alpha Psi. Avocations: hiking, gardening, church choir, macramé, flute. Home: 3900 Sheckler Rd Fallon NV 89406-8202 Office: Churchill County Coop Extension 1450 Mclean Rd Fallon NV 89406-8880

ISIK, MURAT, agricultural economist, researcher; b. Ankara, Turkey, Oct. 26, 1971; s. Burhan and Nevreste Isik. BS, Ankara U., 1993; MS, U. Ill., 1997, PhD, 2001. Postdoctoral rsch. assoc. Miss. State U., Starkville, 2001—02; assoc. scientist Iowa State U., Ames, 2002—03; asst. prof. U. Idaho, Moscow, 2003—. Contbr. articles to profl. jours. Mem.: Assn. Environ. and Resource Economists, We. Agrl. Econs. Assn., Am. Agrl. Econs. Assn. Office: Univ Idaho PO Box 442334 Moscow ID 83844 E-mail: misik@iastate.edu.

ISIK, TELA MAE, obstetrical/gynecological nurse practitioner; b. Springfield, Mo., Sept. 25, 1944; d. Vincent James and Ella Mae (Boyd) Rinaldi; m. Ahmet Ozer Isik, Apr. 5, 1973; children: Deniz James, Suzan Michelle. Diploma, Presbyn. U. Hosp. Sch. Nursing, 1966; BSN, Tex. Christian U., 1984; MPA, Troy State U., 1987. RN, Pa., Tex. Staff nurse John J. Kane Hosp., Pitts., 1966-70; commd. 2d lt. USAF, 1970, advanced through grades to maj., served in various locations, 1970-90; asst. charge nurse Obs. USAF Hosp., Wiesbaden, 1976-77; ob.-gyn. nurse practitioner USAF, Ellsworth AFB, S.D., 1978-82, Carswell AFB, Tex., 1982, Incirlik Air Base, Turkey, 1984-87, RAF, Lakenheath, U.K., 1987-90; ret. USAF, 1990; ob.-gyn. nurse practitioner Ft. Worth Pub. Health Dept., 1990-92, Tarrant County Hosp. Dist., 1992-2000, North Tex. Affiliated Med. Group, 2000—. Mem.: Uniformed Nurse Practitioner Assn., Tex. Nurses' Assn., AWHONN, ANA, Sigma Theta Tau. Avocations: reading, running, gardening. Home: 564 Greenway Dr Saginaw TX 76179-1154 Office: JPS Health Network Health Ctr for Women 3308 Deen Rd Fort Worth TX 76106-6524

ISIK, UGUR, neurologist; b. Diyarbakir, Turkey, June 22, 1969; s. Hasan and Methiye Isik. MD, Marmara U. Sch. of Medicine, Istanbul, Turkey, 1985—92. Resident, pediat. Marmara U. Sch. of Medicine, 1994—99; resident, pediat. neurology U. of N. C., Chapel Hill, 1999—2003; fellowship, pediat. epilepsy Wash. U. Sch. of Med., St. Louis, Mo., 2002—03. Author: (articles) Clin. Pediat., 2001, Pediat. Pulmonology, 2001, Pediat. Neurology, 2002. Mem.: Am. Acad. of Neurology. Avocations: cooking, reading, travel. Office: St Louis Children's Hosp One Children's Pl Saint Louis MO 63110

ISKANDAR, BERMANS JAMIL, pediatric neurosurgeon; b. Beirut, June 6, 1963; came to U.S., 1982; s. Jamil Bermans and Mona I. BA, Calif. State U., Northridge, 1985; MD, U. Pa., 1989. Surg. intern Boston U., 1989-90; resident Duke U., Durham, N.C., 1990-96; dir. pediatric & functional neurosurgery U. Wis., Madison, 1997—. Pediatric neurosurgery fellow Children's Hosp., Birmingham, Ala., 1996-97. Mem. AMA, Am. Assn. Neurol. Surgeons, Congress Neurol. Surgeons, Alpha Omega Alpha, Phi Kappa Phi. Office: U Wis Hosp 600 Highland Ave Ste K4/832 Madison WI 53792-0001

ISKO, IRVING D. corporate executive; b. N.Y.C., Nov. 26, 1927; s. Harry and Rose (Lehman) I.; m. June Alter, June 7, 1959 (dec. July 1980); children—Laura, Steven; m. Kathe Jados Truschke, Aug. 28, 1981; 1 child, Susan. BA, Cornell U., 1947; LL.B., Harvard U., 1950; LL.M. in Taxation, NYU, 1953. Bar: N.Y. bar 1950. Asso. firm Schlesinger & Berliner, N.Y.C., 1951-54; gen. practice law N.Y.C., 1954-56; v.p. Philipp Bros., Inc., 1956; v.p. minerals and chems. Philipp Corp., 1960; v.p. Engelhard Minerals & Chem. Corp., 1967—, sr. v.p., gen. counsel, 1972, exec. v.p., 1976—78, dir., 1978—, dep. chmn. bd., mem. exec. com., 1978—; pres., chief exec. officer, dir. Engelhard Corp., 1981-84. Chmn. Mendham Borough Zoning Bd., N.J., 1980-94; trustee Mendham Free Pub. Library, 1984-94; mem. chemistry com. Lehigh U., 1980; pres. The Isko Found., 1983—. Mem. ABA, Harvard U. Law Sch. Alumni Assn., Mendham Golf and Tennis Club.

ISLA, EXU REIDEMER QUERO, corrections professional, lawyer, author; b. Villasis, Pangasinan, The Philippines, May 30, 1941; camd to U.S., 1990; s. Francisco Lopez and Rosenda (Quero) I.; m. Carmen Rosales Isla, June 7, 1970; children: Mary, Christian, John, Imelda, Theresa, Francis. AA, U. Pangasinan, 1960, edn. degree, 1965, postgrad., 1970-72, 80-81, JD, 1985; BA, U. of East, Manila, 1963; bus. adminstrn. degree, Arellano U., The Philippines, 1969; legal asst. diploma, Internat. Corr. Schs., 1969. Instr. social studies U. Pangasinan, 1964-68, 69-72; cmty. devel. worker Presdl. Arms Cmty. Devel., The Philippines, 1968-69; tchr. social studies Manila Pub. Schs., 1968-69; tng. officer Capital Planning Corp., The Philippines, 1971-74; regional tng. officer Bur. Lands, The Philippines, 1974-79; provincial manpower devel. officer Nat. Manpower, Philippines, 1979-87; election registrar Commn. on Elections, The Philippines, 1987-89; legal asst. Nat. Bur. Investigation, The Philippines, 1989-90; probation officer Gary (Ind.) City Ct., 1991—; journalist Gary and N.W. Ind. INFO, 2001—. Rural devel. cons. Presdl. Office for Devel., The Philippines, 1978-81; youth devel. cons. Youth Movement in Barrios, The Philippines, 1978-86; quizzer for cert. exam., 2000. Columnist North Tribune and Ilocos Times, The Philippines, 1974 87, Weekly Express, The Philippines, 1987-89. Presdl. asst. for Province of Abra, Presdl. Regional Office for Devel. Regional Mgmt. Staff, 1978-81; regional sec. Rural Adv. Bd., The Philippines, 1978-81. Recipient provincial award Pangasinan-Dagupan City YMCA, nat. award Nat. YMCA, The Philippines, 1965, Found. for Youth Devel. in The Philippines, award of recognition Ministry Pub. Info., Ilocos Region, 1980, Pangasinan State U., 1981, Provincial Agr. Office Pangasinan, 1984, Mcpl. Coun. Urdaneta, Pangasinan, 1989, Outstanding Adminstr. award KC, The Philippines, 1982, Outstanding Parent award U. Pangasinan H.S., Dagupan City, 1989, Lew Wallace H.S., Gary, 1994. Mem. Am. Probation and Parole Assn., Am. Correctional Assn., Ind. Correctional Assn., Philippine Profl. Assn. (officer 1991—), Internat. Inst. N.W. Ind. (officer 1991—). Home: 5066 Pennsylvania St Gary IN 46409-2738 Office: Gary City Ct 1301 Broadway Gary IN 46407-1326

ISLAM, A.K.M. ANWARUL, civil engineer, consultant; b. Munshigonj, Dhaka, Bangladesh, July 1, 1968; s. Abdul Awal Mallik and Razia Sultana; m. Tamanna E Kabir Chowdhury, Oct. 15, 1992; children: Bisshoy Anwar, Ikra Anwar. MS, Fla. State U., 2000. Registered profl. engr., Fla., 2002. Lab. engr. Hyundai Engring. Co., Tangail, Bangladesh, 1995—97; tech. officer Pub. Works Dept., Singapore, 1997—98; structural engr. Post, Buckley, Schuh & Jernigan, Inc., Tallahassee, 2000—. Mem.: ASCE. Office: Post Buckley Schuh & Jernigan Inc 1901 Commonwealth Ln Tallahassee FL 32303 E-mail: aislam@pbsj.com.

ISLAM, FARHAD FUAD, electronics and computer research engineer; b. Rochford, United Kingdom, Oct. 5, 1961; s. Serajul and Gulenoor (Begum) I.; m. Rumaiya, Nov. 18, 1991. BSc in Engring., Bangladesh U., 1986, MSEE, 1988; PhDEE, Kyoto U., 1993. Lectr. Bangladesh U. of Engring./Tech., Dhaka, 1986-88, asst. prof., 1988-89; fellow Nippon Telegraph and Telephone Co. R&D Labs., Tokyo, 1993-95; rsch. engr. Hewlett Packard Labs., Tokyo, 1995-97, Canon Rsch. Labs., Sydney, 1997-2001, Mitsubishi Electronics USA, 2001—03, Renesas Tech. USA, Durham, NC, 2003—. Monbusho scholar Ministry of Edn., Sci. and Culture, 1989-93. Mem. IEEE, Inst. Electronics, Info. and Comm. Engrs. Japan, Inst. of Engrs. Australia. Avocations: sports, music, travel. Office: Renesas Tech Inc USA Design Engring Ctr-East 2635 Meridian Pky Durham NC 27713

ISLAM, MUHAMMAD AZADUL, physicist, educator, researcher; b. Bogra, Bangladesh, Dec. 23, 1951; came to U.S., 1975; s. Muhammad Mohsin Ali and Amena Khatun; m. Aziza Gole Afroz, July 24, 1987; children: Crescent Mamnun, Cosmo Hasibul. BSc with honors, Dhaka U., Bangladesh, 1974; MS, U. Ala., 1977; MPhil, Columbia U., 1979, PhD, 1981. Tchg. asst. U. Ala., Tuscaloosa, 1975-77; faculty fellow, then head tchg. asst. Columbia U., N.Y.C., 1977-79; grad. rsch. asst. Columbia Radiation Labs., N.Y.C., 1979-81; postdoctoral fellow Joint Inst. Lab. Astrophysics, U. Colo., Boulder, 1981-83; asst. prof. San Diego State U., 1983-85; asst. prof. physics SUNY, Potsdam, 1985-89, assoc. prof., 1989-97, prof., 1997—, chmn. dept., 1999—2000. NEH vis. scholar Columbia U., N.Y.C., 1993; vis. scholar MIT Cambridge, 1993, Ctr. for Astrophysics Harvard U., 1995. Author: Test Yourself Physics, 1999, Beyond Ordinary Light, 2003; contbr. articles to profl. publs. Talent and merit scholar Comilla Bd. Edn. Mem. AAAS, United Univ. Profs., N.Y. State United Tchrs., Am. Fedn. Tchrs., Islamic Soc. N.Am. (trustee Potsdam chpt. 1990—), N.Y. Acad. Scis., Am. Phys. Soc., Sigma Xi, Sigma Pi Sigma. Avocations: reading, travel, intellectual history of islamic civilisation. Home: 6 Poplar St Potsdam NY 13676-2113 Office: SUNY Dept Physics Potsdam NY 13676 E-mail: islamma@potsdam.edu.

ISLAM, NAUSHAD S. pharmacist, government agency administrator; b. Dhaka, Bangladesh, Dec. 21, 1961; arrived in U.S., 1989; s. A.H.M. Rafiqul and Hosne Ara Islam; m. Hasina Islam, July 9, 1990; children: Shadman, Nafisa, Safwan. BS pharmacy, Dhaka Univ., Dhaka, Bangladesh, 1986, MS pharmacy, 1988, Long Island Univ., Brooklyn, N.Y., 1992, MS pharmacy, 1999. Formulation scientist Dupont Pharm., Garden City, NY, 1994—97; sr. assoc. regulatory Schein Pharm., Cherry Hill, NJ, 1997—99; sr. scientist regulatory Solvay Pharm., Atlanta, 1999—2000; mgr. regulatory Schering-Plough Pharm., kenilworth, NJ, 2000—02; assoc. dir. regulatory Sankyo Pharm., Edison, NJ, 2002—. Adj. asst. prof. Long Island Univ. Sch. of Pharmacy, Brooklyn, NY, 2003—. Mem.: Am. Assn. of Pharm. Scientist, Bangladesh-Am. Pharm. (exec. bd. 1994—). Avocations: music, gardening, soccer. Home: 24 Spaniel Ct Kendall Park NJ 08824 Office: Sankyo Pharm 399 Thornall St Edison NJ 08837

ISLEY, ALEXANDER MAX, graphic designer, lecturer; b. Durham, N.C., Nov. 16, 1961; Max and Jane (Skinner) I. BED, N.C. State U., 1983; BFA, Cooper Union, 1984. Designer M & Co., N.Y.C., 1984-87; art dir. Spy Mag., N.Y.C., 1987-88; pres. Alexander Isley Inc., N.Y.C., 1988-93. Art dir. Archaeology mag., N.Y.C., 1988—, Forbes FYI Mag., N.Y.C., 1990—; design dir. Nickelodeon Mag., N.Y.C., 1993—; lectr. various graphic design orgns., 1984—. Recipient Herb Lubalin Meml. award Art Dirs. Club N.Y., 1984, more

than 200 awards for design and art direction; work is in permanent design collection Smithsonian Instn.; Nat. Endowment for Arts fellow, 1984. Mem. Am. Ctr. Design, Am. Inst. Graphic Arts, Soc. Pub. Designers, Soc. Environ. Graphic Designers, Alliance Graphique Internat. Office: Alexander Isley Inc 9 Brookside Pl Redding CT 06896-3204 E-mail: alex@alexanderisley.com.

ISMACH, ARNOLD HARVEY, retired journalism educator; b. N.Y.C., Dec. 28, 1930; s. Louis and Augusta (Lacher) I.; m. Judy Daniels, June 20, 1959 (div. 1975); children: Richard, Theresa. BA, U. Okla., 1951; MA, UCLA, 1970; PhD, U. Wash., 1975. News editor Union-Bulletin, Walla Walla, Wash., 1954-56; reporter, editor Sun-Telegram, San Bernardino, Calif., 1956-69; prof. journalism U. Minn., Mpls., 1973-85; dean journalism U. Oreg., Eugene, 1985-94, prof. journalism, 1994-97. Cons. Pub. Rels. Ctr., L.A., 1970-75; pres. Comm. Rsch. Ctr., Mpls., 1973-85. Co-author: New Strategies, 1976, Enduring Issues, 1978, Reporting Processes, 1981. Pres. Planned Parenthood S.W. Oreg., 1998-99; dir. ACLU Oreg., 1994-2001. Sgt. U.S. Army, 1951-54. Mem. Soc. Profl. Journalists, Assn. for Edn. in Journalism. Democrat. Avocation: photography. E-mail: aismach@ballmer.uoregon.edu.

ISMAEL, JENANN T. philosopher, educator; b. Spokane, Wash. d. Tareq and Jacqueline S. Ismael. BA, Reed Coll., 1989; MA, Princeton U., 1993, PhD, 1996. Mellon Found. post-doctoral fellow Stanford U., Calif., 1996—98; prof. U. Ariz., Tucson, 1998—. Mem.: Philosophy Sci. Assn., Am. Philos. Assn. Office: Dept Philosophy U Ariz Tucson AZ 85721

ISMAIL, ABU ZAFAR MOHAMED, physics educator, researcher, consultant; b. Keymore, India, Oct. 9, 1930; arrived in U.S., 1982; s. Abulkhair Mohamed and Zakiya Yusuf; children: Atif Zafar, Khurram Zafar, Faiza N. Zafar, Mona S. Zafar. MSc, Panjab U., Lahore, Pakistan, 1952, MA, 1954; BA with Honours, Cambridge (Eng.) U., 1958; DPhil in Elem. Particle Physics, Oxford (Eng.) U., 1964. Tchr. St. Mary's High Sch., Sukkur, Pakistan, 1952-53; instr. Mumtaz Coll., Khairpur Mirs, Pakistan, 1954-56; lectr., sr. lectr. Sind U., Hyderabad, Pakistan, 1958-65, assoc. prof., 1965-71, prof., 1971-72, Tripoli (Libya) U., 1972-82; prof. physics Daemen Coll., Amherst, N.Y., 1983—. Cons. Sci. First Inc., Buffalo, 1991—. Contbr. articles on high energy nuclear physics to profl. jours. Scholar Pakistan Ministry Edn., 1953; fellow Colombo PLan, 1960. Mem. Am. Assn. Physics Tchrs., Inst. Physics U.K., N.Y. Acad. Scis. Republican. Avocations: photography, writing fiction, stamp and book collecting. Home: 130 Breezewood Common East Amherst NY 14051-1425 Office: Daemen Coll 4380 Main St Amherst NY 14226-3592 E-mail: zismail@daemen.edu.

ISMAIL, MOURAD EL-HOUSSIENY, mathematician, educator, researcher; b. Cairo, Apr. 27, 1944; came to U.S., 1974; s. El-Houssieny Mahmoud Ismail and Aisha Mourad El-Shourbagy; m. Thanaa Mohamad Rashed, July 17, 1969. BS, Cairo U., 1964; MS, U. Alberta, Edmonton, 1969, PhD, 1974. Instr. Cairo U., Giza, Egypt, 1964-74; tchg. asst. U. Alberta, 1968-74; asst. scientist U. Wis., Madison, 1974-75; rschr., lectr. U. Toronto, Ont., Can., 1975-76; asst. prof. McMaster U., Hamilton, Ont., Can., 1976-81; asst. to assoc. prof. Ariz. State U., Tempe, 1979-89; prof. math. U. South Fla., Tampa, 1988—. Editor: Mathmatical Analysis, 1995, Special Sunctions, q-series, 1997, q-series from a Contemporary Perspective, 2000, Special Functions, 2000; editl. bd. Jour. of Approximation Theory, 2000—, Constructive Approximation, 1988—, The Ramanujan Jour., 1986—; editor (series) Cambridge U. Press, 1993-2000. Rsch. grant Rsch. Coun. of Can., 1977-82, NSF, 1978—, Nat. Security Agy., 1997—, Collaborative and Conf. grant NSF, 1990—. Mem. Am. Math. Soc., Math. Assn. of Am., Can. Math. Soc., Soc. for Indsl. and Applied Math. Avocations: reading, swimming. Office: U South Fla Dept Math Tampa FL 33620 E-mail: ismail@math.usf.edu.

ISMAIL, NUHAD, medical educator; b. Beirut, July 14, 1952; came to U.S., 1985; s. Mohammed Ismail and Fatima Ghosn; m. Mary Alice O'Conner, Sept. 8, 1984; children: Dani, Rami, Jana. BS, Am. U. Beirut, 1974, MD, 1978. Diplomate Am. Bd. Medicine, Am. Bd. Nephrology. Cons. internist ARAMCO, Dahran, 1980-81; internist, instr. medicine Am. U. Med. Ctr., Beirut, 1981-83; gen. practitioner King Khalid Mil. City, Hafar, 1988—2001; assoc. prof. medicine Vanderbilt U., Nashville, 2001—; cons. nephrologist, head sect. nephrology, dir. hemodialysis unit King Faisal Specialist Hosp and Rsch. Ctr., Riyadh, Saudi Arabia, 2001—. Author: Type II Diabetic Nephropathy, 1999; co-editor: Updated Textbook: Clinical Neph, Dialysis, Transplantation, 1999; assoc. editor: Clin. Nephrology, 1999; mem. editl. bd. Kidney Jour., 1994—; contbr. articles to profl. jours. Mem. Am. Soc. Nephrology, Nat. Kidney Found., Internat. Soc. Nephrology. Avocations: travel, poetry, calligraphy, swimming. Office: King Faisal Specialist Hosp PO Box 3354 Riyadh 11211 Saudi Arabia E-mail: ismail@kfshrc.edu.com.

ISMAIL, RAGHIB (ROCKET ISMAIL), professional football player; b. Newark, Nov. 18, 1969; Student, U. Notre Dame. With Toronto Argonauts, 1991-93, L.A. Raiders, 1993-97; wide receiver Carolina Panthers, 1999, Dallas Cowboys, 1999—. Achievements include being the NCAA Indoor Sprinting Champ. Office: Dallas Cowboys 2401 E Airport Freeway Irving TX 75063

ISMAIL, YAHIA HASSAN, dentist, educator; b. Egypt, Jan. 20, 1938; came to U.S., 1961; s. Hassan Kareem and Horia (Soloman) I.; m. Launa Lutz, Sept. 5, 1968; children: Alan Kareem, Zane Ziad. DDS, Cairo U., 1959; MS, U. Pitts., 1965, DMD, PhD, U. Pitts., 1973. Instr. Dental Sch. Cairo U., 1959-62; asst. prof. prosthodontics U. Pitts., 1962-68, assoc. prof., 1968-70, prof., 1970—, dir. prosthodontic grad. program, 1970—, chmn. dept. prosthodontics, 1973—; dir. acad. affaris, internat. affairs and grad. edn. Dental Medicine, U. Pitts., 1995—2001. Vis. prof., Paris and Marseille, France, Cairo and Alexandria, Egypt, European U., Brussels; mem. staff VA Hosp., Montefiore Hosp., Univ. Med. Ctr. Hosp., St. Margaret's Hosp. Contbr. articles to profl. jours., textbooks. Bd. dirs. Ridgewood Civic Assn., 1969-73; cubmaster Allegheny Trails council Boy Scouts Am.; coach Youth Soccer League Allegheny County. Recipient Chancellor's Pub. Svc. award, 1995. Fellow Internat. Coll. Dentists, Am. Coll. Dentists, Am. Coll. Prosthodontics, Royal Soc. Medicine, Am. Coll. Oral Implantologists, Internat. Congress Oral Implantologists, Am. Acad. Implant Prosthodontics (pres. elect 1989-90, pres. 1990-92); mem. ADA, Internat. Assn. Dentofacial Abnormalities (bd. dirs., sec., treas. 1973-77), Internat. Congress Oral Implantologists (v.p. 1985-86, pres. 1988-89), Am. Prosthodontic Soc. (internat. circuite courses humanities citation), Pa. Prosthodontic Assn. (past pres.), Prosthodontic Soc. Western Pa. (past pres.), Dental Soc. Western Pa. (bd. dirs.), Am. Coll. Oral Implantologists (pres. 1984-86), Am. Coll. Prosthodontists, Am. Assn. Dental Schs., Internat. Assn. Dental Rsch., Royal Coll. Physicians, Univ. Club, Omicron Kappa Upsilon. Republican. Office: U Pittsburgh Sch Dental Med Pittsburgh PA 15261-0001 *Talk about ideas and philosophies rather than other people.*

ISOGAI, MASAHARU, international business consultant, former women's apparel executive; b. 1939; AMP, Harvard U., 1985. With Ogiya, 1958-76, Jusco Co. Ltd., 1976-88; exec. v.p., gen. mgr. Jusco USA, Inc., 1988-96, sr. advisor, 1996-99; dir. Talbots, 1993-99; chmn. Revman, 1994-99; ret., 1999. Mem. Japanese Youth Goodwill Mission to U.S., 1964. Mem. Japanese Am. Assn. N.Y. (bd. dirs.), Assn. for Better N.Y. (hon. mem. exec. com., spl. amb. from Japan). Home: 220 E 65th St Apt 17M New York NY 10021-6626 E-mail: misogainy@bigplanet.com.

ISOM, KEVIN, writer; s. David L. and Tommie F. Isom. BA, Vanderbilt U., 1987; JD, Emory U., 1991. Bar: Ga. 1991. Author: Tongue in Cheek and Other Places, 2000, It Only Hurts When I Polka, 2001, short stories. Harold Stirling Vanderbilt scholar, Vanderbilt U. Mem.: GAPAC (mem. polit. com. 1994—95), Out of Emory (chair 1995—96), Human Rights Campaign.

ISOM, LLOYD WARREN, management consultant; b. Arkansas City, Kans., Feb. 9, 1928; s. Loyd Denver and Cora Louvina (Messner) I.; m. Marjorie Louise Ghramm, Aug. 30, 1950 (dec. Mar. 1984); m. Rita McClain, June 9, 1989; children: Cynthia Louise, John Warren. BS, Drake U., 1952. CLU. Pres., dir. First Security Group, Milw., 1965-68; v.p. mktg. Liberty Life, Greenville, S.C., 1968-71; pres., dir. Am. Health & Life, Balt., 1971-75, Pierce Nat. Life, L.A., 1975-77, Continental Life & Acc. Ins. Co., Boise, 1978-80; pres., owner Ins. Mgmt., Inc., Boise, 1980-82; v.p. Am. Gen. Corp., Houston, 1982-88; pres., dir. Sierra Health and Life Ins. Co., Las Vegas, 1988-90; mgmt. cons., ins. mgmt. and mktg. Las Vegas, 1990—. Bd. dirs. Sierra Health & Life, Las Vegas; chmn. adv. bd. for risk and ins. mgmt. U. Nev., Las Vegas, 1995-96. Chmn. project 90 Coll. of Idaho, 1980—. With USN, 1946-48. Mem. Am. Coll. Life Underwriters. Republican. Presbyterian. Avocations: golf, swimming, spectator sports.

ISOM, VIRGINIA ANNETTE VEAZEY, retired nursing educator; b. Tallapoosa County, Ala, Nov. 19, 1936; d. Jimmy L. and Bessie (Pearson) Veazey; m. William G. Isom, May 1959; children: William Gary, Marleah, James Leland. BSN, Tuskegee Inst., 1959; MSN, Syracuse U., 1974; PhD, Howard U., 1997. Cert. in nursing adminstrn. Am. Nurses' Credentialing Ctr.; cert. med.-surg. nursing. Asst. prof. med. surg. nursing Howard U. Coll. Nursing, Washington, 1975-86; edn. and tng. quality assurance coord. Howard U., Washington, 1986-87; patient care coord. Howard U. Hosp., Washington, 1987-88, coord. for spl. projects, 1988-90; prof. nursing Prince George's C.C., Largo, Md., 1992—2003; ret., 2003. Contbr. articles to profl. jour. Mem. ANA (cert. clin. specialist med. surg. nursing), Nat. League Nursing, Acad. Med. Surg. Nurses, Md. Nurses' Assn. Home: 534 Round Table Dr Fort Washington MD 20744-5638 E-mail: visom97@aol.com.

ISQUITH, FRED TAYLOR, lawyer; b. N.Y.C., June 6, 1947; s. Stanley and Rita (Hoskwith) I.; m. Susan Nora Goldberg, May 23, 1976: children: Fred, Rebecca. BA, CUNY, 1968; JD, Columbia U., 1971. Bar: N.Y. 1972, D.C. 1976, U.S. Dist. Ct. (so. and ea. dists.) N.Y. 1975, U.S. Dist. Ct. (no. dist.) N.Y. 1988, U.S. Dist. Ct. (we. dist.) Mich. 1992, U.S. Dist. Ct. Ariz. 1994, U.S. Dist. Ct. (ctrl. dist.) Ill. 1996, U.S. Ct. Appeals (2d cir.) 1975, U.S. Ct. Appeals (8th cir.) 1985, U.S. Ct. Appeals (3d cir.) 1986, U.S. Ct. Appeals (4th cir.) 1990, U.S. Supreme Ct. 1983, U.S. Dist. Ct. Colo. 1999, U.S. Dist. Ct. Nebr. 2000, U.S. Ct. Appeals (1st cir.) 2000. Assoc. Fulbright & Jaworski, N.Y.C., 1971-75, Kaye Scholer et al, N.Y.C., 1975-80; ptnr. Wolf Haldenstein Adler Freeman & Herz, N.Y.C., 1980—. Bd. dirs. 103 East 84th St. Corp., N.Y.C., Sheinkopf, Ltd.; lectr. Am. Conf. Inst., N.Y. State Bar Assn., N.Y. County Bar Assn., others; mediator Supreme Ct. State N.Y. County N.Y. Comml. Divsn.; arbitrator Am. Arbitration Assn.; lectr. in field. Author: An Introduction to Securities Arbitration, 1994, Real Estate Exit Strategies, 1994, Fundamental Strategies in Securities Litigation, 2000, Federal Civil Practice, 2000; A Scalpel in Your Hand Litigation As a Tool for Informing Responsible Corporate Guidance, 2002, Anatomy of a Deposition: Preparation for a Deposition in a Complex Finacial Case, 2002, The Seven Year Itch: A Survey of Experience Under the 1995 Amendments to the Security Laws, 2003; editor, weekly columnist The Class Act. Mem. devel. com. Friends Sem., N.Y.C., 1998—; clk., mem. vestry St. Thomas Ch. Fifth Ave., N.Y.C., 2002—. Mem. ABA (mem. internet com. anti-trust law sect.), NASCAT (pres.), N.Y. State Bar Assn. (coms. on securities and legis., arbitrator securities industry disputes sect.), N.Y. County Lawyers Assn. (chmn. bus. torts), D.C. Bar Assn., Assn. of Bar of City of N.Y. (Fed. Cts. com.), Bklyn. Bar Assn. (civil practice law and rules com., legis. com. and fed. cts. com.), Columbia Club. Office: Wolf Haldenstein Adler Freeman & Herz 270 Madison Ave New York NY 10016-0601

ISRAEL, BARRY JOHN, lawyer; b. Rockford, Ill., Mar. 14, 1946; s. Robert John and Bettie Jane (Erickson) I.; childn: Alison, Ashley, Brenna. BA, U. So. Calif., L.A., 1968; JD, George Washington U., 1974. Bar: Calif. 1975, D.C. 1976, U.S. Supreme Ct. 1978, U.S. Dist. Ct. Mariana Islands 1985. Assoc. Clifford & Warnke, Washington, 1975-83; ptnr. Stovall, Spradlin, Armstrong & Israel, Washington, 1983-86, Dorsey & Whitney, Washington, 1988-92, Stroock, Stroock & Lavan, Washington, 1992-95. Spl. counsel, pres. Federated States of Micronesia, 1982-84; spl. asst. atty. gen. Territory Guam, 1990-95; chmn. bd. Danao Internt. Holdings Co., Ltd.; bd. dirs. Kebar Inc., Jadora Ltd., Millenium Inst. of Lang. and Training, Voyages d' ICI. Author: (guides) Advance Adjusting Assoc. Investment Guides to the Federated States of Micronesia and the Republic of the Marshall Islands, 1989. 1st lt. U.S. Army, 1969-72. Democrat. Avocations: travel, tennis. Home: 1101 Luneta Plaza Santa Barbara CA 93109 also: The Royal Place II 6-6/429 #6/294 Soi Mahadle Kluang 2 Rajadaun Rd Lumpuri, Patumwan Bangkok 10330 Thailand E-mail: barryjon@aol.com.

ISRAEL, DAVID, journalist, screenwriter, producer; b. NYC, Mar. 17, 1951; s. Hyman and Edith Oringer I.; m. Lindy De Koven, Aug. 8, 1987. BS in Journalism, Northwestern U., 1973. Reporter Chgo. Daily News, 1973-75; columnist Washington Star, 1975-78, Chgo. Tribune, 1978-81, Los Angeles Herald Examiner, Los Angeles, Calif., 1981-84; chmn., pres. Big Prodn., Inc., Los Angeles, Calif.; prod., writer OCC Prodn., Los Angeles, Calif., 1985-88; exec. prodr., writer Lorimar TV, LA, 1988-92, Paramount Pictures, Hollywood, Calif., 1992-93; writer, exec. prodr. Stephen J. Cannell Prod., Inc., Hollywood, Calif., 1993-95. Dir. office of Pres., Los Angeles Olympic Organizing Com., 1984; exec. prodr. House of Frankenstein, NBC, Universal, 1997, exec. prodr. Mutiny, NBC, 1999, Y2K, NBC, 1999, Tremors, SciFi, 2002--. Supervising prodr., writer: A Comedy Salute to Baseball, NBC, 1985; supervising prodr., writer: Fast Copy, NBC, 1985-86; co-creator, supervising prodr.: Crimes of the Century, 1987-88; co-exec. prodr., writer: Midnight Caller, NBC, Lorimar TV, 1988-91, The Untouchables, Paramount TV, 1992-93; exec. prodr., writer: Jake Lassiter: Justice on the Bayou, NBC, Stephen J. Cannell Prodn., 1995; exec. prodr., writer: Pandora's Clock, NBC, Citadel Entertainment, 1996; consulting prodr., writer, Turks, CBS Studios, USA, 1998-99; coord. prodr. Monday Night Football, ABC Sports, 2000-01. Mem. AFTRA, Writers Guild Am., Chgo. Athletic Assn. Office: c/o Jared Levine Barnes Morris Klein mark Yorn Barnes&Livine Guggenheim Felker & Levine 1424 Second St Santa Monica CA 90401

ISRAEL, JAMES RAY, psychiatrist; b. Asheville, N.C., Dec. 4, 1936; s. Frank Ray and Katherine Evelyn (Wilson) I.; m. Barbara Daawn McLain, Apr. 14, 1958; children: Katherine Dawn Israel McCall, Mitchell Ray. BA, Berea Coll., 1959; MD, Wake Forst Med. Sch., 1963. Diplomate Am. Bd. Psychiatry and Neurology; lic. physician, N.C. Owner Forsyth Psychiat. Offices, Winston-Salem, NC, 1964—2001; staff physician Broughton State Hosp., Morganton, NC, 1964—65; ptnr. Lillington (N.C.) Med. Clinic, 1965-73; resident in psychiatry Wake Forest/Bapt. Med. Ctr., Winston-Salem, N.C., 1973-75, chief resident in psychiatry, 1975-76; from asst. to assoc. prof. psychiatry Bowman Gray Sch. Medicine/Wake Forest U., Winston-Salem, 1986-94; ptnr. Forsyth Psychiat. Assocs., Winston-Salem, 1986-94. Acting med. dir. Davidson County Mental Health Ctr., Lexington, N.C., 1976-80; dir. med. tchg. Charter Hosp., Winston-Salem, 1984; assoc. clin. prof. psychiatry Wake Forest U., 2000—; part-time psychiatrist Wake Forest U. Bapt. Med. Ctr., 2001—. Contbr. articles to profl. jours. Active Hartnett County Bd. Health, Lillington, N.C., 1968-72; vice chair Hartnett County Bd. Edn., Lillington, 1970; chmn. Red Cross Blood Drive Hartnett County, Lillington, 1968-69; host family Sister Cities Program, Winston-Salem, 1976. Maj. U.S. Army Res., 1965-72. Recipient Outstanding Svc. award Davidson County Mental Health, 1982, Tchg. Excellence award Bowman Gray Sch. medicine, 1983, others. Fellow So. Psychiat. Assn.; mem. AMA, Forsyth County Med. Soc., Forsyth County Psychiat. Soc., So. Med. Soc. Democrat. Methodist. Avocations: gardening, genealogy, north carolina history, travel, landscaping. Home: 2750 S Stratford Rd Winston Salem NC 27103-6924 Office: 2750 S Stratford Rd Winston Salem NC 27103-6924 E-mail: rayisrael36@hotmail.com.

ISRAEL, JEROLD HARVEY, law educator; b. Cleveland, Ohio, June 14, 1934; s. Harry and Florence S. (Schoenfeld) I.; m. Tanya M. Boyarsky, Sept. 28, 1959; children— Lewis, Laurie, Daniel BBA, Western Res. U., 1956; LLB, Yale U., 1959. Bar: Ohio 1959, Mich. 1967. Law clk. to Justice Potter Stewart U.S. Supreme Ct., Washington, 1959-61; asst. prof. Law Sch. U. Mich., Ann Arbor, 1961-64, assoc. prof., 1964-67, prof., 1967-96, Alene and Allan F. Smith prof., 1983-96, prof. emeritus, 1996—; Ed Rood Eminent Scholar in trial advocacy and procedure U. Fla. Coll. Law, Gainesville, 1993—. Exec. sec. Mich. Law Revision Commn., 1972-92; co-reporter Uniform Rules of Criminal Procedure, Nat. Conf. Commrs. Uniform State Laws; Alene and Allen F. Smith prof. emeritus U. Mich., Ann Arbor, 1996—. Co-author: Criminal Procedure Treatise, 1999, Criminal Procedure Hornbook, 2000, Modern Criminal Procedure, 2002, Criminal Procedure and the Constitution, 2002, White Collar Crime, 1996. Office: U Fla Law Sch Gainesville FL 32611-2038

ISRAEL, JOAN, social worker; b. Bklyn., July 19, 1943; d. Joseph Israel and Irene (Solon) Kansey; 1 child, Ariel Naomi Janesh. BA, Bklyn. Coll., 1965; MSW, U. Mich., 1974. Lic. clin. social worker, Nev. Social worker Alameda County Welfare Dept., Oakland, Calif., 1965-72; group therapist Pacific Ctr. for Human Growth, Berkeley, Calif., 1975-77; individual and group therapist, bd. dir. Bi-Ctr., San Francisco, 1976-78; clin. social worker, supr. Audrey L. Smith Devel. Ctr., San Francisco, 1977-78; psychiat. social worker South Nev. Adult Mental Health Dept., Las Vegas, 1978-84, part-time clin. social worker, 1988—; pvt. practice clin. social worker Las Vegas, 1984—. Contbr. articles to profl. publs. Organizer Drug/Alcohol Abuse Task Force, Las Vegas, 1983-84, Task Force on AIDS, Las Vegas, 1985-86. Mem. NASW (chair nominating com. 1978-80, 82-84, sec. 1984-86, chair com. on inquiry 1988—, legis. chair 1982-84, diplomate clin. social work), Sierra Club. Democrat. Jewish. Avocations: hiking, singing, opera, science fiction, dance. E-mail: israeljoan@wgbtv. Office: Ste 120 7200 Cathedral Rock Dr Las Vegas NV 89128

ISRAEL, KAY FRANK, communications educator; b. Shanghai, Jan. 20, 1946; came to the U.S., 1948; s. Ernest and Hildegard Israel; m. Judith Ann Feldman, Nov. 20, 1974; children: Joshua, Kerry. BS, U. Utah, 1968; MS, Boston U., 1973; PhD, MIT, 1984. Lectr. Boston U. Sch. Pub. Comm., 1975-83; asst. prof. comm. Ithaca (N.Y.) Coll., 1985-90; assoc. prof. comm. R.I. Coll., Providence, 1991—. Rsch. fellow MIT, Cambridge, 1975-76. Contbr. articles to profl. jours. Del. Dem. Party, County and State Convs., 1968-74; press sec. Greener for City Commn., Salt Lake City, 1973; campaign dir. Howe for Congress Com., Salt Lake City, 1974; mem. State Dem. Convention Platform and Logistics Coms., Salt Lake City, 1974; legis. aide Congressman Allan T. Howe, Washington, 1974-75; campaign dir. Harrington for Mayor, Newton, Mass., 1977; bd. dirs. United Way Tompkins County, Ithaca, N.Y., 1989-91, R.I. Ad Club, Providence, 1996-98; mem. pub. rels. and mktg. subcom. Boys and Girls Clubs R.I., Providence, 1992-93. With USN, 1968-72. Recipient Bell Ringer award Publicity Club New Eng., 1994. Mem. Pub. Rels. Soc. Am. (Cert. of Recognition 1987, 88, 89, 90, Pres.'s Citation 1987), Am. Polit. Sci. Assn., Am. Polit. Items Collectors. Office: RI Coll 600 Mt Pleasant Providence RI 02908 E-mail: kisrael@ric.edu.

ISRAEL, LESLEY LOWE, political scientist, consultant; b. Phila., July 21, 1938; d. Herman Albert and Florence (Segal) Lowe; m. Fred Israel, Dec. 18, 1960; children: Herman Allen, Sanford Lawrence. BA, Smith Coll., 1959. Dir. media advance Humphrey for Pres., Washington, 1967-68, dir. politic. intelligence, 1972; dir. scheduling Bayh for Pres., Washington, 1971; spl. asst. Jackson for Pres., Washington, 1975-76; coord. nat. labor Kennedy for Pres., Washington, 1979-80; sr. v.p. Kamber Group, Washington, 1981-87; pres., CEO Politics, Inc., Washington, 1987-95. Mem. nat. commn. ADL, 1991—94, mem. nat. exec. commn., 1994—; v.p. Nat. Conf. Soviet Jewry, 1990—; dir. Internat. Found. Election Sys., 1997—; pres. Jewish Cmty. Ctr. Greater Washington, Rockeville, Md., 1981—83; internat. election monitor and coord., 1995—; chmn. Washington regional bd. ADL, 1991—94; mem. Nat. Dem. Club, 1986—; sr. election officer Orgn. Security and Coop. Europe, Bosnia-Herzegovina, 1996; internat. election monitor U.S. Dept. State, 1997—; mem. Dem. Charter Commn., 1982—83, Dem. Del. Selection Commn., 1983—84, Dem. Site Selection Com., 1989—90, 1990—; bd. mgrs. Adas Israel Synagogue, 1981—83; former chmn. Washington bd. Friends Tel Aviv U. Named one of 100 Most Powerful Women, Washington mag., 1990; recipient Spl. Svc. award, Jewish Cmty. Ctr., 1984. Jewish. Home: PO Box 69 Royal Oak MD 21662-0069

ISRAEL, MARGIE OLANOFF, psychotherapist; b. Atlantic City, Apr. 30, 1927; d. Herman and Mary (Salter) Olanoff; m. Allan Edward Israel, Sept. 20, 1953; 1 child, Janet. Student U. Miami, 1945-46, 50, Am. Acad. Dramatic Arts, 1946-47; BA in Psychology cum laude, Hunter Coll., 1970; MSW with honors in fieldwork, Hunter Sch. Social Work, 1972; psychoanalytic tng. N.Y. Soc. Freudian Psychologists, 1965-70, Manhattan Ctr. for Advanced Psychoanalytic Studies, 1972-74, 76. Bd. cert. diplomate in clin. social work Am. Bd. Examiners of Clin. Social Workers. Celebrity interviewer Lunchin' with Marge radio show Sta. WFPG, Atlantic City, 1947-48; co-host Steel Pier Midnight radio show, 1949; publicity writer Hy Gardner Astor Hotel, N.Y.C., 1948; writer theatrical interviews Miami (Fla.) Daily News, 1950-51; sec. to exec. dir. Hebrew Old Age Ctr., Atlantic City, 1951-55; sec. to dir. TV-films and radio Nat. Office, Am. Cancer Soc., N.Y.C., 1959-66, asst. to dir. TV-films and radio,1966-70; social worker Bellevue Hosp., N.Y.C., 1972-76; field instr. socialworkN.Y. U., 1975-76; pvt. practice psychotherapy, N.Y.C., 1973—, Providence, 1991—, Wilmington, N.C., 1996—. Mental health disaster vol. Cape Fear N.C. chpt. Red Cross, 1997—. Fellow N.Y. State Soc. Clin. Social Work, Am. Orthopsychiat. Assn.; mem. NASW (diplomate), Nat. Fedn. Socs. Clin. Social Work (com. on psychoanalysis), Acad. Cert. Social Workers, N.Y. Acad. Scis. AAAS, Psi Chi. Home and Office: 5711 Andover Rd Wilmington NC 28403-3409

ISRAEL, MARTIN HENRY, astrophysicist, educator, academic administrator; b. Chgo., Jan. 12, 1941; s. Herman and Anna Catherine I.; m. Margaret Ellen Mitouer, June 20, 1965; children: Elisa, Samuel. SB, U. Chgo., 1962; PhD, Calif. Inst. Tech., 1969. Asst. prof. physics Washington U., St. Louis, 1968-72, assoc. prof., 1972-75, prof., 1975—, assoc. dir. McDonnell Ctr. for Space Scis., 1982-87, acting dean faculty arts and scis., 1987-88, dean faculty, 1988-94, vice chancellor, 1994-95, vice chancellor acad. planning, 1995-97. Mem. com. on space astronomy and astrophysics NRC, 1976-79; mem. High Energy Astrophysics Mgmt. Ops. Working Group NASA, 1976-84, co-chair Cosmic Ray Program Working Group, 1980-87, mem. space and earth scis. adv. com., 1985-88, chair Particle Astrophysics Magnet Facility Definition Team, 1985-87, mem. astrophysics coun., 1986-87, prin. investigator Heavy Nuclei Expt. High Energy Astronomy Obs., 1971-89, mem. structure and evolution of the universe subcom., 1996-99, chair ACCESS steering com., 1998-2000, mem. Space Sta. Utilization adv. subcom., 1998-2002, mem. GSFC Space Sci. vis. com., 1997-2001, chair, 2000-01; mem. GSFC Ctr. Dir.'s Vis. Com., 2000-01; chair Space Sci. Working Group, Assn. Am. Univs., 1983-85; chair nat. organizing com. 19th Internat. Cosmic Ray Conf., 1985, 1982-85; participant NASA Office Space Sci. Strategic Planning Workshop, 2002. Contbr. articles on cosmic ray astrophysics and observation of elemental and isotopic composition of cosmic rays to profl. jours. Recipient Exceptional Sci. Achievement award NASA, 1980; Sloan Found. fellow, 1970. Fellow Am. Phys. Soc. (chair astrophysics divsn. 1980-81); mem. Am. Astron. Soc. (mem. exec. com. high energy astrophysics divsn. 1982-84), AAUP, AAAS. Home: 2 Valley View Pl Saint Louis MO 63124-1810 Office: Washington U Campus Box 1105 1 Brookings Dr Saint Louis MO 63130-4899 E-mail: mhi@wuphys.wustl.edu.

ISRAEL, PAUL NEAL, computer design engineer, writer; b. Balt., Apr. 22, 1959; s. Sheldon Leonard and Sheila Lee (Goldmacher) I. BS in EECS, U. Calif., Berkeley, 1981. Project mgr. computer sci. dept. U. Calif., Berkeley, 1981-82; design engr. Electronic Signature Lock Corp., Berkeley, 1983; staff engr. Qantel Bus. Systems, Hayward, Calif., 1983-89; sr. hardware design engr. SBE, Inc., Concord, Calif., 1989-90; engring. contractor Renegade Systems, Sunnyvale, Calif., 1990-92; prin. engr. Unisys Corp., San Jose, Calif., 1992-95, NVsys, San Jose, 1995—. Patentee for avoiding instability in computer logic, method for cycle request with quick termination without waiting for the cycle to reach the destination by storing information in queue. Mem.: IEEE, Assn. Computing Machinery, Sierra Club. Avocations: model railroading, writing, sports, science fiction, fencing. Office: NVsys 1101 S Winchester Blvd Ste 297 San Jose CA 95128 E-mail: israel@hamster.org.

ISRAEL, ROBERT ALLAN, statistician; b. N.Y.C., Mar. 30, 1933; s. John J. and Ray (Sladkus) I.; m. Barbara Diane Johnston, Jan. 26, 1953; children: John, Richard, Deborah, Pamela, James, Michael. BA, Hofstra Coll., 1954; MS, Columbia U., 1957. Med. analyst Md. State Health Dept., Balt., 1959-63, chief div. statis. rsch., 1963-66; chief mortality stats. br. Nat. Ctr. for Health Stats., Washington, 1966-68, dir. div. vital stats., 1968-72, assoc. dir. for ops., 1972-75, dep. dir., 1975-92, assoc. dir. for internat. stats., 1992-95, ret., 1995. Head WHO collaborating ctr. for disease classification for North Am., 1975-95, ret., 1995; dep. exec. dir. Internat. Inst. for Vital Registration and Statistics, 1997—. Co-author: The Methods and Materials of Demography, 1973; co-editor: Encyclopedia of Biostatistics, 1997. Recipient Superior Svc. award U.S. Pub. Health Svc., 1972, 79, scholarship N.Y. State Bd. Regents, 1950-54, fellowship U.S. Public Health Svc., 1956-58, Special Recognition award Asst. Sec. for Health. Fellow APHA (stats. sect. award 1986), Am. Statis. Assn.; mem. Internat. Statis. Inst., Internat. Assn. Ofcl. Stats. Home: 16910 E Laney Ct Fountain Hills AZ 85268

ISRAEL, SCOTT MICHAEL, lawyer; b. Milw., Oct. 22, 1955; s. Phillip David and Bella Dawn (Rubin) Israel. BBA, U. Wis., 1977; JD, Marquette U., 1980. Bar: Wis. 1980, U.S. Dist. Ct. (ea. and we. dists.) Wis. 1980. Atty. Rausch, Sturm, Israel & Hornik, S.C., Milw., 1980—. V.p. Milw. Kollel, Inc., Beth Hamedrosh Hagodel Cemetery Assn. Mem.: State Bar Wis., Comml. Law League Am., Phi Eta Sigma. Jewish. Office: Rausch Sturm Israel Hornik SC 2448 South 102nd Street Suite 210 Milwaukee WI 53227 E-mail: Sisrael@wiscollect.com.

ISRAEL, STEVE, congressman; b. Brooklyn, N.Y., May 30, 1958; s. Howard and Madeline Israel; m. Randi Elkins, June 5, 1983; children: Carly, Elana. BA, George Washington U., 1982. Congl. aide U.S. Congress, Washington, 1979-83; consultant Steve Israel Assoc., Huntington, N.Y., 1985—; asst. county exec. County of Suffolk, Hauppauge, N.Y., 1988-92; town councilman Town of Huntington, 1993-2000; exec. dir. Inst. on the Holocaust and Law, Huntington, 1998-2000; mem. U.S. Congress from 2d N.Y. dist., Washington, 2001—; mem. fin. svcs. com., sci. com. Author/editor: Great Jewish Speeches, 1994. Founder Ctr. for Prejudice Reduction, Great Neck, N.Y., 1990; dir. Pederson-Krag Ctr., Huntington, 1996; founder, dir. L.I. Fgn. Affairs Forum, Mingola, N.Y., 1998. Life mem. NAACP; assoc. mem. Sons of Italy. Democrat. Jewish. Avocations: writing, historical rsch. Office: US Ho of Reps 18 W Carver St Huntington NY 11743-3322 also: US Ho of Reps 429 Cannon HOB Washington DC 20515 E-mail: israel@li.net.*

ISRAEL, WERNER, physics educator; b. Berlin, Oct. 4, 1931; s. Arthur and Marie (Kappauf) I.; m. Inge Margulies, Jan. 26, 1958; children: Mark Abraham, Pia Lee B.Sc., U. Cape Town, 1951, M.Sc., 1954; PhD, Trinity Coll., Dublin, 1960; D.Sc. (hon.), Queen's U., Kingston, Ont., 1987; Docteur honoris causa, U. Francois Rabelais, France, 1994; DSc (hon.), U. Victoria, B.C., Can., 1999. Asst. prof. physics U. Alta., 1958-68, prof., 1968-85, Univ. prof., 1985-96; adj. prof. dept. physics and astronomy U. Victoria, B.C., Can., 1996—; hon. prof. dept. physics and astronomy U. B.C., B.C. Sherman Fairchild disting. scholar Calif. Inst. Tech., 1974-75; vis. prof. Dublin Inst. Advanced Studies, 1966-68, U. Cambridge, 1975-76, Institut Henri Poincare, 1976-77, U. Berne, 1980, Kyoto U., 1986, 98; vis. fellow Gonville and Caius Coll., Cambridge, 1985; fellow Can. Inst. for Advanced Rsch., 1986—. Editor: Relativity, Astrophysics and Cosmology, 1973; co-editor: General Relativity, An Einstein Centenary Survey, 1979, 300 Years of Gravitation, 1987 Decorated officer Order of Can.; recipient Izaak Walton Killiam meml. prize, 1984, Joint medal in math. physics Ctr. de Recherche Math./Can. Assn. Physicists, 1995, Tomalla Found. for Gravitational Rsch. prize, 1996. Fellow Royal Soc. Can., Royal Soc. (London); mem. Can. Assn. Physicists (medal of Achievement in Physics 1981), Internat. Soc. Gen. Relativity and Gravitation (pres. 1997-01). Jewish. Office: U Victoria Dept Physics Astronomy Victoria BC Canada V8W 3P6 E-mail: israel@uvic.ca.

ISRAELACHVILI, JACOB NISSIM, chemical engineer; b. Tel Aviv, Aug. 19, 1944; came to U.S., 1986; s. Haim Israelachvili and Hela (Noma) Galili; m. Karina Haglund, Sept. 14, 1971; children: Josefin, Daniela. BA, U. Cambridge, 1968, MA & PhD, 1972. Prof. U. Calif., Santa Barbara, 1986—. V.p. Internat. Assn. Colloid & Interface Scientists, 1986-89. Author: Intermolecular and Surface Forces, 1985, 2d edit., 1991; contbr. rsch. articles to profl. pubs. Fellow Australian Nat. U., Canberra, 1974-86, Rsch. fellow U. Stockholm, Sweden, 1972-74; recipient Matthew Flinders medal, 1986. Fellow Royal Soc. London, Australian Acad. Sci.; mem. AIChE (award 1991), Nat. Acad. of Engring. (fgn. assoc. 1996), Alpha Chi Sigma. E-mail: jacob@engineering.ucsb.edu.

ISRAELIEVITCH, JACQUES H. violinist, conductor; b. Cannes, France, May 6, 1948; came to U.S., 1965, naturalized, 1976; s. Isidore and Simone (David) I.; m. Gail Ivy Bass, Aug. 27, 1972 (div. 1985); children: David James, Michael Benjamin, Joshua Alexander; m. Gabrielle Rubin, Dec. 22, 1985. Performer's cert., Ind. U., 1968. Mem. faculty Am. Conservatory Music, Chgo., 1974—78; co-founder Camarata Soc. Chgo., 1974; artist in residence Webster U., 1978—88; mem. New Arts Trio, 1998—; prof. violin Chautauqua Instn., 1999—. Asst. concertmaster Chgo. Symphony Orch., 1972—78, concertmaster St. Louis Symphony Orch., 1978—88, Toronto Symphony Orch., 1988—; performer: solo appearances with orchs. and in recital, —; founder Chgo. Pops Orch., 1975—; performer: world premier The Darkly Splendid Earth, The Lonely Traveller, 1991—; recorded (12 solo CDs including) Suite Hebraique, 1995—, Suite Francaise, 1997—, The Romance and Rhapsody of Max Bruch, 1997—. Decorated chevalier Order of Arts and Letters (France); recipient 1st prize Paris Conservatory Music, 1964; named winner Paganini Internat. Competition, Italy, 1965, Alumnus of Yr. Ind. U., 1973 Mem. Am. Fedn. Musicians, Soc. Am. Musicians. Clubs: Arts of Chgo. Office: Toronto Symphony Orch 212 King St W Ste 550 Toronto ON Canada MH5 1K5

ISRAELOV, RHODA, financial planner, writer, entrepreneur; b. Pitts., May 20, 1940; d. Joseph and Fannie (Friedman) Kreinen; divorced; children: Jerome, Arthur, Russ. BS in Hebrew Edn., Herzlia Hebrew Tchrs. Coll., N.Y.C., 1961; BA in English Lang. and Lit., U. Mo., Kansas City, 1965; MS, Coll. Fin. Planning, 1991. CFP, CLU. Hebrew tchr. various schs., 1961-79; ins. agt. Conn. Mut. Life, Indpls., 1979-81; fin. planner, 1st v.p. investments Smith Barney, Inc., Indpls., 1981—. Instr. for mut. fund licensing exams. Pathfinder Securities Sch., Indpls., 1983-87; cons. channel 6 News, 1984-85. Contbr. columns in newspapers, ; regular guest (Radio show) WTUX Radio, 1990—94. Recipient Gold Medal award Personal Selling Power, 1987; named Bus. Woman of Yr., Network of Women in Bus., 1986. Mem. Fin. Planning Assn., Nat. Assn. Life Underwriters, Women's Life Underwriters Conf. (founder), Soc. Fin. Svc. Profls., Nat. Coun. Jewish Women, Nat. Assn. Profl. Saleswomen, Nat. Spkrs. Assn. (pres. Ind. chpt. 1986-87, treas. 1984), Registry Fin. Planning Practitioners, Toastmasters (chpt. ednl. v.p. 1985-86), Soroptimists (bd. dirs.), Ctrl. Ind. Mensa. Avocations: piano, folk, square, folk and ballroom dancing, theatre. Office: Smith Barney Bank One Center Tower 111 Monument Cir Ste 3100 Indianapolis IN 46204-5193 E-mail: israelov@yahoo.com., rhoda.israelov@rssmb.com.

ISRAELS, LYONEL GARRY, hematologist, medical educator; b. Regina, Sask., Can., July 31, 1926; s. Simon and Sarah (Girtle) I.; m. Esther Hornstein, June 3, 1950; children: Sara, Jared. BA, U. Sask., 1946; MD, U. Man., 1949, MScawd, 1950, DSc (hon.), 1999. Intern Winnipeg Gen. Hosp., 1948-49; resident internal medicine and hematology Salt Lake County Hosp., 1950-52; fellow in hematology Kantonsspital, Zurich, 1952-53; dept. biochemistry U. Man., 1953-55, asst. prof. biochemistry, 1955-59, asst. prof. medicine, 1959-62, assoc. prof. medicine, 1962-66, prof. medicine, 1966—. Disting. prof., 1983—, acting head dept. medicine, 1977-79. Dir. Manitoba Inst. Cell Biology, 1970-73, sr. scientist, 1992—; exec. dir. Manitoba Cancer Treatment and Rsch. Found., 1973-92, 93—; attending physician Health Sci. Centre; mem. Med. Rsch. Coun. Can., 1973-75; chmn. Manitoba Health Rsch. Coun., 1980-87; mem. sci. coun. Internat. Agy. Cancer Rsch., 1989-93, chmn., 1992-93. Contbr. articles on biochem. and immunol. aspects of blood, blood forming organs and cancer to sci. jours. Recipient Humanitarian award, St. Boniface Hosp., Chancellor's award, U. of Manitoba, 2003. Fellow RCPC; mem. Am. Soc. Clin. Investigation, Can. Soc. Clin. Investigation (pres. 1968), Royal Coll. Physicians and Surgeons Can., Can. Hematol. Soc. (pres. 1972-74), Nat. Cancer Inst. Can. (pres. 1976-78), Manitoba Order of Buffalo Hunt. Decorated Order of Can.; L.G. Israels chair in hematology at Ben Gurion U. in his honor, 1996. Home: 502 South Dr Winnipeg MB Canada R3T 0B1 Office: 675 McDermot Ave Winnipeg MB Canada R3E 0V9 E-mail: lisraels@cc.umanitoba.ca.

ISRAELSKY, ROBERTA SCHWARTZ, speech pathologist, audiologist; b. N.Y.C., July 19, 1954; d. Julian H. and Sylvia (Fenster) Schwartz; m. Brad Richard Israelsky, June 24, 1984; children: Erica, Evan. BA, Temple U., 1976; MA, Hahnemann Med. Coll., 1977, Trenton State, 1978. Speech/language pathologist W Deptford Twp Sch., W. Deptford, N.J., 1978-81, Sunny Day Autistic Sch., Cherry Hill, N.J., 1981-83; adj. prof. sign lang., voice and articulation Glassboro St. Coll., Glassboro, N.J., 1982-89; speech, sign lang. pathologist and diagnostician Camden Co. Educ. Serv. Comm., Stratford, N.J., 1983-88; pvt. practice Voorhees, N.J., 1983—; prof. speech Camden County Coll., Blackwood, N.J., 1989—; speech/lang. pathologist Gloucester City Schs., 1990-94; speech/lang. specialist Mt. Holly Schs., Mt. Holly, N.J., 1994—. Adult supr. B'nai B'rith Girls, Cherry Hill, 1975-77; cons. Sign Lang. Assn. N.J., 1983. Author, Hearing and Publication, Consumer Guide to Hearing Aids, 1978. V.p. ORT, Cherry Hill, 1986-89, Women Tech. Soc., 1988-89, Hadassah, 1985-89. Mem. Am. Speech, Lang., Hearing Assn. (cert. clin. competence), N.J. Speech, Lang. Hearing Assn., TripCounty Speech, Lang., Hearing Assn. Democrat. Jewish. Avocations: singing, acting. Home and Office: 425 Hialeah Dr Cherry Hill NJ 08002-2037

ISRAILI, ZAFAR HASAN, scientist, clinical pharmacologist, educator; b. Moradabad, India, July 2, 1934; came to U.S., 1961, naturalized, 1977; s. Siddiq Hasan and Zahida Khatun I.; m. Sally Jean Smith, Oct. 24, 1970; children: Shahnaz Joy, Taj Hasan, Rana Shereen. BSc, Aligarh M. U., 1951, MSc (Merit scholar), 1953; PhD, U. Kans., 1968. Lectr. chemistry Aligarh M. U., 1953-54, sr. rsch. scholar, 1954-57; rsch. asst., jr. sci. officer AEC India, 1957-61; rsch. assoc. U. Kans., 1968-69; sr. rsch. chemist Alza Corp., Lawrence, Kans., 1969-70; asst. prof. medicine and chemistry Emory U., Atlanta, 1970-75, assoc. prof. chemistry, 1975-78, assoc. prof. medicine, 1975—, prof. chemistry, 1978—. Rsch. pharmacologist Atlanta VA Med. Ctr., Decatur, 1979-87; mem. sci. staff Grady Hosp., Atlanta, 1974—. Editor Ethnicity and Disease, 1997—; assoc. editor Drug Metabolism Revs., 1974—; mem. editl. bd. Drug Devel. Rsch., 1979—; mem. editl. com. Archives Venezuelan Pharm. Ter., 1983—, Am. Jour. Ther., 2003-; contbr. numerous articles to profl. jours., chpts. to books. Recipient Asia Found. award, 1962; Merck Sharpe & Dohm grantee, 1977, 85, 87, NIH grantee, 1978-83, VA grantee, 1979-87, Am. Heart Assn. grantee, 1989-91. Mem. Am. Soc. Clin. Pharmacology and Therapeutics, Am. Soc. Pharmacology and Exptl. Therapeutics, Soc. Exptl. Biology and Medicine, Am. Assn. Cancer Rsch., Am. Aging Assn., Am. Chem. Soc., Am. Soc. Hypertension, Chem. Soc. London, Internat. Soc. for Study Xenobiotics, Interam. Soc. Clin. Pharm. Therapeutics (pres.-elect 1997-2000, pres. 2000—), Internat. Soc. on Hypertension in Blacks, Am. Heart Assn., Sigma Xi, Rho Chi, Phi Lambda Upsilon. Moslem. Home: 3567 Cloudland Dr Stone Mountain GA 30083-4005 Office: Emory Univ Sch Medicine Dept Medicine 69 Jesse Hill Jr Dr Atlanta GA 30303-2607 E-mail: zisrail@emory.edu.

ISSA, AMALIA MARY, medical educator, researcher; b. May 11, 1966; d. Emile Issa and Clemence Samandar; m. William J. Foster. BSc, Concordia U., Montreal, Can., 1988; MSc, McGill U., Montreal, Can., 1991, PhD, 1998; cert., Harvard U., 2001. Rsch. assoc. McGill U., Montreal, 1998—2000; bioethicist clin. trials com. Montreal Gen. Hosp., 1998—2000; fellow Harvard Med. Sch., Boston, 2000—01; clin. ethics cons. Meml. Med. Ctr., Springfield, Ill., 2001—; asst. prof. So. Ill. U. Sch. Medicine, 2001—. Commr. for pub. hearing panel Synod of the Roman Cath. Archdiocese of Montreal, 1996; vis. scientist U. Toronto, Canada, 1999; mem. clin. ethics consultation svc. Ctr. for Clin. Ethics, Toronto, 1999; mem. ethics task force Mass. Gen. Hosp., Boston, 2000—01, cons. optimum care com., 2000—01; founder Montreal Bioethics and Catholicism Group, 2000; cons. clin. ethics ctr. Meml. Med. Ctr., 2001—. Manuscript reviewer: Jour. Am. Geriatrics Soc., 2002—; contbr. chapters to books, articles to profl. jours. Recipient Hoechst-Marion-Roussel Can. award for rsch., 1994—96; grantee, Alzheimer Soc. Can., 1998—2000, Fonds de la recherche en santé du Québec, 1999—2002. Mem.: Inst. for Theol. Encounter with Sci. and Tech. (founder), Soc. for Neurosci. (founder), Internat. Brain Rsch. Orgn. (founder), Can. Bioethics Soc. (founder), Cath. Health Assn. Can. (founder), Can. Christian Bioethicists Network (founder), Nat. Cath. Bioethics Ctr. (mem. task group certification program in Cath. Health Care Ethics 2001—02), Am. Soc. for Bioethics and Humanities. Avocations: fencing, model-building, hiking.

ISSA, DARRELL E. congressman; b. Cleveland, Ohio, Nov. 1, 1953; m. Kathy; 1 child: William. BA, Siena Heights U., 1976. Founder, pres-CEO Directed Electronics, Vista, Calif., 1982—99; mem. Congress, Calif., 48th dist., 2001—. Mem. House com. on Internat. Rels., House Judiciary com., House com. on Small Bus. Co-chair Calif. Civic Rights Initiative, 1996; served in Army. Recipient Inc. Magazine's Entreprenuer Yr. award, 1994, Ellis Island Medal of Honor. Past chmn. Consumer Electronics Assn., former govr. Electronic Indus. Alliance; dir. Bus.-Industry Political Action com., San Diego Econ. Devel. Assn., Greater San Diego County Chamber of Commerce; past pres. Am. Task Force for Lebanon; served bd. trustees Siena Heights U. Republican. Office: 211 Cannon House Office Bldg Washington DC 20515-0549*

ISSA, JEAN-PIERRE J, education educator, medical educator; m. Fadia Issa; children: Yasmine, Marielle. MD, The Am. U. of Beirut, 1987. Internal Medicine Md., 1990, Medical Oncology Md., 1993. Instr. of oncology The Johns Hopkins Oncology Ctr., Baltimore, 1994—95, asst. prof. of oncology, 1995—99; assoc. prof. The U. of Tex. M.D. Anderson Cancer Ctr., 1999—. Recipient Young Investigator award, Am. Soc. of Clin. Oncology, 1995, Outstanding Resident award, The Good Samaritan Hosp., 1990; several rsch. grants, NIH/Nat. Cancer Inst., 1986—2003, Colon Cancer Prevention Program Project grant, 2000—, grant, Am. Cancer Soc., 1999—2001, Leukemia Soc. of Am., 1997—2000, Kimmel scholar, Kimmel Found., 1997—99, scholar, Sidney Kimmel Found. for Cancer Rsch., 1997, 2001. Achievements include patents pending for methylated CpG island amplification; identification of the APO-B, CACNA1G, CDX2, EGFR, FBN1, GPR37, HSPA6, IQGAP2, KL, PAR2, PITX2, PTCH, SDC1, and SDC4 genes as differentially methylated in cancer, aging tissues & age-related disease. Office: University of Texas MD Anderson Cancer 1515 Holcombe Blvd Unit 428 Houston TX 77030 Office Fax: 713-745-2261. E-mail: jissa@mdanderson.org.

ISSARI, M(OHAMMAD) ALI, film producer, writer, consultant; b. Esfahan, Iran; s. Abbas Bek and Qamar (Soltan) I.; m. Joan Gura Aamodt, 1958; children: Scheherezade, Katayoun, Roxana. BA, U. Tehran, Iran, 1963; MA, U. So. Calif., 1968; PhD, 1979. Films officer Brit. Embassy, Brit. Council Joint Film Div., Tehran, 1944-50; asst. motion picture officer USIS, Tehran, 1950-65; cons. to various Iranian Govt. ministries on film and TV devels., 1950-77; liaison officer Am. and Iranian govt. ofcls., 1950-65; prof. cinema Coll. Communication Arts and Scis. Mich. State U., East Lansing, 1969-81, also dir. instructional film and multimedia prodn., 1969-78; mass media cons., 1981—; pres. Multimedia Prodn. Svcs., Thousand Oaks, Calif., 1989—. Film, public relations adviser to Iranian Oil Operating Cos. in, Iran, 1963-65; spl. cons. on edn. and instructional TV Saudi Arabian Ministry of Info., 1972; tchr. Persian lang. Iran-Am. Soc., Tehran, 1949-59; introduced audio-visual edn. in Iran, 1951; established first film festivals in Iran, 1949. Producer, dir. over 1000 instructional and documentary films, 1956-78; freelance film reporter: Telenews, UPI, CBS Iran, 1959-61; project dir., exec. producer: Ancient Iran Film Series, 1974-78; dir. film prodn. workshops, Cranbrook Inst., Detroit, 1973-74; author: A Picture of Persia, 1977, (with Doris A. Paul) What is Cinema Vérité?, 1979, Cinema in Iran, 1900-1979, 1989; contbr. articles on ednl. comm. and audio-visual instrn. to periodicals and profl. jours. Founder, exec. sec. Youth Orgn. of Iran, 1951-52; v.p. Rugby Football Fedn., Iran, 1952-53, pres., 1954-55. Decorated Order of Magnum Cap Ord: S.F. Danaie M. Sigillum (Denmark), Order of Cavalieres (Italy), Order of Oranje Nassau (The Netherlands), Orders of Kooshesh and Pas (Iran), Order of Esteghlal (Jordan), Order of Ordinis Sancti Silvestri Papae (Pope John 23d); recipient Meritorious Honor award USIA, 1965, Golden Eagle award Couns. for Internat. Non-Theatrical Events, 1975. Mem. Anglo-Iranian Dramatic Soc. (bd. dirs. 1943-50), Mich. Film Assn. (co-founder 1972, bd. dirs. 1972-73), Mid. East Studies Assn., N.Am. Soc. Motion Picture and TV Engrs. (life), Ancient Studies Inst. Inc. (co-founder, pres. 1991, 97-98), House of Iran, Inc. (co-founder, pres. 1990—), Delta Kappa Alpha (v.p. 1967). Fax: 805-498-0550. *Man will achieve his goals through honesty, hard work and perseverence. The goals worth pursuing are in the service of mankind.*

ISSELBACHER, KURT JULIUS, physician; b. Wirges, Germany, Sept. 12, 1925; arrived in U.S., 1936, naturalized, 1945; s. Albert and Flori (Strauss) Isselbacher; m. Rhoda Solin, June 22, 1955; children: Lisa, Karen, Jody, Eric. AB, Harvard U., 1946, MD cum laude, 1950; ScD (hon.), Northwestern U., 2001. Intern, then resident Mass. Gen. Hosp., Boston, 1950—53, chief gastrointestinal unit, 1957—89, chmn. com. rsch., 1967, dir. Cancer Ctr., 1987—2003, dir. emeritus, 2003—; investigator NIH, 1953—56; prof. medicine Harvard Med. Sch., 1966—, chmn. exec. com. depts. medicine, 1968—97, Mallinckrodt prof. medicine, 1972—97, disting. Mallinckrodt prof. medicine, 1998—, chmn. univ. cancer com., 1972—87. Mem. governing bd. NRC, 1987—90; mem. sci. bd. FDA, 1993; acad. liaison Novartis Biomed. Rsch. Inst., 2002—; editor Harrison's-on-line, 1999—. Editor-in-chief (Harrison): Principles of Internal Medicine, 1976, 1991—99. Recipient award for disting. achievement in nutrition, Bristol-Myers Squibb, 1991, Sci. Bd. FDA, 1993—97, Tree of Life award, Jewish Nat. Fund, 2001. Fellow: ACP (John Phillips award for disting. achievement in clin. medicine 1989); mem.: NAS (chmn. food and nutrition bd. 1983—88, mem. exec. com., mem. coun. 1987—90, chmn. com. on risk assessment of hazardous air pollutants 1991—94), Assn. Am. Physicians (pres. 1977—78, pres. 1977-78, Kober medal 2001 2001), Am. Gastroenterology Assn. (pres. 1974—75, Julius Friedenwald medal for outstanding achievement in gastroenterology 1985), Am. Acad. Arts and Scis. Achievements include research in molecular and genetic changes in malignant cells metastasis and colon cancer. Home: 20 Nobscot Rd Newton MA 02459-1323 Office: Cancer Ctr Mass Gen Hosp 139 13th St Charlestown MA 02129-2023

ISSELBACHER, RHODA SOLIN, lawyer; b. Springfield, Mass., June 12, 1932; d. Jay Zachary and Theo L. (Michelman) S.; m. Kurt J. Isselbacher, June 22, 1955; children: Lisa Isselbacher-Ramirez (dec.), Karen Isselbacher-Epstein, Jody Isselbacher-Coukos, Eric M. BA, Cornell U., 1954; JD, Harvard U., 1959. Bar: Mass. 1960, U.S. Dist. Ct. Mass. 1984. Assoc. firm Melvin Dangel, Boston, 1960-67, Sherin & Lodgen, Boston, 1965-67, Pollock & Katz, Boston, 1967-70; ptnr. firm Epstein, King & Isselbacher, Boston, 1971-91, gen. counsel Dana-Farber Cancer Inst., Boston, 1979-89; pvt. practice law Newton Centre, Mass., 1989-91; of counsel Edwards and Angell, Boston, 1991-92; legal counsel Mass. Gen. Hosp. Svc. League, 1969-85; legal cons. Children's Sch. of Sci., Woods Hole, Mass., 1969—. Cons. med. programming WGBH-TV, 1972-73. Alderman, Woods Hole, Mass., 1968; chmn. Newton United Fund, Mass., 1961; trustee Beaver Country Day Sch., 1975-77. Mem. Mass. Bar Assn., Boston Bar Assn., Mass. Health Lawyers Assn. Home and Office: 20 Nobscot Rd Newton MA 02459-1323 E-mail: isselbacher@helix.mgh.harvard.edu.

ISSELHARD, DONALD EDWARD, dentist; b. Belleville, Ill., Apr. 11, 1941; s. Bertram Joseph and Margaret Eda (Dobbins) I.; m. Annette Scanaliato, Mar. 1, 1980; children: Kerstin, Nissa, Michele, Tara. Student, St. Louis U., 1959-62; BS in Dentistry, U. Ill., Chgo., 1970, DDS, 1966; MBA, Maryville U., 1994. Gen. practice dentistry, Clayton, Mo., 1967-70, Creve Coeur, Mo., 1970—. Assoc. instr. Forest Park C.C., St. Louis, 1973-77; asst. prof. Washington U., St. Louis, 1975-77; lectr. Continuing Edn. Ctrs. Am., 1977-79; pres. Tempo Condo. Investment Corp., 1994—, Strategic Empowerment Inc., 1994, Fortune Tempo Med. Condominium Assn., Inc., 1995—. Author: (with others) Anatomy of Orofacial Structures, 1977, 7th edit., 2003; contbg. author Comprehensive Rev. of Dental Hygiene, 1986. Fellow Acad. Gen. Dentistry Dentistry Internat., Masters Acad. Gen. Dentistry; mem. ADA, Mo. Acad. Gen. Dentistry (v.p. 1996, pres. 1997-99), Greater St. Louis Dental Assn., Gateway Practice Devel. Assn. (pres. 1986 90). Home: 17726 Drummer Ln Chesterfield MO 63005-4223 Office: 12401 Olive Blvd Saint Louis MO 63141-5448 E-mail: disselhard@aol.com.

ISSERMAN, NANCY, political scientist, researcher; b. St. Louis, Feb. 19, 1951; d. Ferdinand and Marilyn Landis Isserman; m. Joel Horwitz, Sept. 6, 1982; children: Rachel, Sima, Michael, Gabriel. BA with spl. honors, U. Chgo., 1972; MSW, Washington U., St. Louis, 1973; MPhil, CUNY, 1982, postgrad. Asst. dir. Am. Jewish Com., Chgo., 1984-91; exec. dir. Com. on Decent Unbiased Campaign Tactics, Chgo., 1985-91; assoc. dir. Feinstein Ctr. for Am. Jewish History Temple U., Phila., 1992—; assoc. rsch. project dir. Coun. for Relationships, Phila., 1993—. Mem. adv. bd. Chgo. Panel on Pub. Sch. Policy and Fin., 1985-91. Editor: The Tribal Basis of American Life, 1998; author booklet Status of Jewish Professional Women in Jewish Organizations, 1994. V.p. PTO Torah Acad., Ardmore, Pa., 1994-2000; program head Cong. Beth HaMedrosh, Phila., 1995-2000. Fellow Wachs Spitzer in trauma studies, Coun. for Relationships, 2001. Mem. Assn. Jewish Studies. Avocations: gardening, reading, aerobic and cardiovascular exercise.

ISSHIKI, MASAYUKI, sociologist, educator, dean; b. Suzuka, Japan, Oct. 21, 1950; s. Mikio Isshiki and Michiko Isshiki-Fujii; m. Miwa Terada, Dec. 28, 1988. BA in Sociology, Sussex Coll., 1980, D in Sociology, 1986. V.p. Sanas Corp., Yokkaichi, Japan, 1980-83; rsch. scientist Triad PCL, Hong Kong, 1986-91; ptnr. Triad Cons., Suzuka, Japan, 1991-93; prof. Suzuka Internat. U., 1994—, dean grad. sch., 2002—. Author: Economic Development in Southeast Asia, 1991, Development of Bamboo, 1992, U.S. Watch, 1995—. Avocations: skiing, farming. Home and Office: Rm C-101 15-11 Minami-Ejima Suzuka Mie 510-0235 Japan E-mail: misshiki@mecha.ne.jp.

ISSLER, HARRY, lawyer; b. Cologne, Germany, Nov. 14, 1935; came to U.S., 1937; s. Max and Fanny (Grunbaum) I.; m. Doris Helen Lukow, June 1, 1958; children: Adriane P. Schorr, M. Valerie Priestley, Stephanie L. Beck. BS, U. Wis., 1955; JD, Cornell U., 1958. Bar: N.Y. 1958, U.S. Supreme Ct. 1962, U.S. Ct. Mil. Appeals 1967, U.S. Dist. Ct. (so. and ea. dists.) N.Y. 1960, U.S. Customs Ct. 1964, U.S. Tax Ct. 1964; cert. specialist in civil trial advocacy Nat. Bo. Trial Advocacy. Assoc. Wing & Wing, N.Y.C., 1958-60; assoc. Fuchsberg & Fuchsberg, N.Y.C., 1960-62; ptnr. Issler & Fein, N.Y.C., 1963-68, Shaw, Issler & Rosenberg, N.Y.C., 1968-70; pvt. practice N.Y.C., 1970-79; ptnr. Issler & Scrage, P.C., N.Y.C., 1980-99; sr. ptnr. The Law Firm of Harry Issler PLLC, N.Y.C., 1999—. Arbitrator Civil Ct., N.Y. County, 1979-91; hearing officer N.Y. State Tax Appeals, 1975-77, Supreme Ct. of N.Y., N.Y. County Med. Malpractice Panel, 1980-91; judge advocate N.Y. State; mem. neutral evaluator mediation panel Supreme Ct., N.Y. County, 1997—; charter mem. Trial Lawyers Care, Inc. Book reviewer: NY Law Jour., 2001—. Trustee N.Y. State Mil. Ednl. Found., 1997-2000; exec. v.p. Sutton Area Cmty., Inc., 2000—; v.p. 50 Sutton Pl. South Owners, Inc., 2002-03; pres. 50 Sutton Pl. South Owners Corp., 2003--. With U.S. Army, 1958-59, N.Y. Army N.G., 1963-88, ret. brig. gen., 1988. Ford Found. scholar, 1951-55. Mem. ABA, N.Y. State Bar Assn., Assn. of Bar of City of N.Y., Am. Trial Lawyers Assn., N.Y. State Trial Lawyers Assn., 42d Infantry Divsn. Officers Club (N.Y.C.pres. 1979-80), Officers Club (U.S. Mcht. Marine Acad.), 42d Infantry Rainbow Divsn. Assn. (pres. 1989), Phi Alpha Delta, Pi Lambda Phi (Omega chpt. pres. 1953-54). Home: 50 Sutton Pl S New York NY 10022-4167 Office: 110 E 59th St 29th Fl New York NY 10022 E-mail: harryissler@lawyer.com.

ISTEL, JACQUES ANDRE, mayor; b. Paris, Jan. 28, 1929; came to U.S., 1940, naturalized, 1951; s. Andre and Yvonne Mathilde Cremieux I.; m. Felicia Juliana Lee, June 14, 1973; 1 dau. by previous marriage, Claudia Yvonne. AB, Princeton, 1949. Stock analyst Andre Istel & Co., N.Y.C., 1950, 55; pres. Parachutes Inc., Orange, Mass., 1957-87, Intramgmt. Inc., N.Y.C., 1962-80; chmn. Pilot Knob Corp., 1982—; mayor Town of Felicity, Calif., 1986—; curator Ctrl. Point for Memories, Calif., 1992—. Pres. VI World Parachuting Championships, 1962; capt. U.S. Parachuting team, 1956, master of sports, USSR, 1956, capt., team leader, 1958; chmn. Mass. Parachuting Commn., 1961-62; life hon. pres. Internat. Parachuting Commn., Fedn. Aero. Internat., 1965— ; chmn. Hall of Fame of Parachuting, 1973—, Imp. Co. water commn. 1997—; founder Nat. Collegiate Parachuting League, 1957, World Commemorative Ctr., 1993; co-leader Nat. Geog. Soc. Vilcabamba Expdn., 1964. Author: Coe the Good Dragon at the Center of the World, 1985, Coe le Bon Dragon au Centre du Monde, 1985; editor in granite Museum Walls, 2001—; contbr. articles to encys., profl. jours.; patentee in field. Trustee Inst. for Man and Sci., 1975-82; bd. dirs. Marine Corps Scholarship Found., 1975 85. Served with USMC, 1952-54; lt. col. Res. Recipient Leo Stevens award, 1958, Diplome Paul Tissandier, 1969; named Chevalier de la Legion D'Honneur, 2003; world record holder for parachuting, 1961 Mem. Nat. Aero. Assn. (bd. dirs. 1965-68), Fedn. Internat. des Centres (pres. 1990—), Cercle de l'Union Interalliée (Paris), Marine Corps Res. Officers Assn., DAV (life), Racquet and Tennis Club (N.Y.C.), Princeton Club (N.Y.C.). Home: Northview Felicity CA 92283 also: 10 rue Galilée 75116 Paris France Office: 1 Center Of The World Plz Felicity CA 92283-7777 E-mail: ctrworld@aol.com.

ISTOCK, VERNE GEORGE, retired banker; b. Sept. 20, 1940; BA in Econs., U. Mich., 1962, MBA in Fin., 1963. Credit analyst trainee NBD Bancorp, Inc., Detroit, 1963—66, group head, 1971-77, head U.S. divsn., 1977-82, sr. v.p., 1979-82, exec. v.p., 1982-85, vice chmn., dir., 1985-93, chmn., CEO, 1994-95, also bd. dirs.; chmn. NBD Bank; pres., CEO First Chgo. NBD Corp., Chgo., 1995-98, chmn., 1996-98; chmn. bd. Bank One Corp., Chgo., 1999—2000, pres., 2000; ret., 2000. Bd. dirs. Kelly Svcs. Inc., Masco Corp., Rockwell Automation, Inc. Bd. dirs. Chgo. Coun. Fgn. Rels., Chgo. Crime Commn. Mem. U. Mich. Alumni Assn. (past pres., lifetime dir.), Bankers Roundtable (past

dir.), Econ. Club Chgo. (past dir.), Mich. Bus. Roundtable (past bd. dirs.), Comml. Club of Chgo., Econ. Club Detroit (past dir.), Ill. Bus. Roundtable (past dir.). Office: Bank One Corp 1 Bank One Plz Chicago IL 60670-0001 E-mail: verne_istock@bankone.com.

ISTOOK, ERNEST JAMES, JR., (JIM ISTOOK), congressman, lawyer; b. Fort Worth, Tex., Feb. 11, 1950; s. Ernest James and Dessie Cordelia Lyne I.; m. Judy Lee Bills, 1973; children: Amy, Butch, Chad, Diana, Emily. BA, Baylor U., 1971; JD, Oklahoma City U. Sch. Law, 1976. Reporter, State Capitol Stas. KOMA-TV, Oklahoma City, 1972—73, WKY-Radio, Oklahoma City, 1973—76; dir. Okla. Alcoholic Beverage Control Bd., 1977-78; legal counsel Okla. Gov. David Boren, 1978; dir. Warr Acres/Putnati City C. of C., 1982-86; councilman City of Warr Acres, Okla., 1982-86; atty. Istook & Assocs., 1983-93; mem. Okla. Ho. of Reps., 1986—92, U.S. Congress from 5th Okla. dist., Washington, 1993—; mem. appropriations com. Bd. dirs. Met. Libr. System, 1982-86, chmn., 1985-86 Named Taxpayer Friend of Yr., 1991, One of Ten best Legislators, 1992. Mem. Kappa Nu. Republican. Mem. Lds Ch. Office: US Ho Reps 2404 Rayburn HOB Office House Members Washington DC 20515-3605*

ISZARD, CALVIN OSCAR, JR., television production executive, public relations manager, former county freeholder; b. Millville, N.J., Nov. 20, 1943; s. Calvin Oscar Sr. Iszard and Margaret N. (Gardella) Pedulla; m. Nancy A. Jesuele, June 27, 1967 (div. 1973); m. Judith Ann Koons, Sept. 26, 1975 (div. June 2000); children: Barbara, Lisa, Jonathan. BA, Rowan U., 1966; MA, 1968. Adminstrv. asst. Tri-state Instructional Broadcasting, Phila., 1968-69; news producer, newscaster TV Sta. WHYY-TV-12, Phila., 1969-70; producer, dir. N.J. Pub. Network, Trenton, 1970-75, exec. producer, 1975-80; program mgr. Sta. WWAC-TV, Atlantic City, 1980-81; pres. Original Video, Inc., Trenton, 1981-84; facilities mgr. Bell Atlantic Corp. TV, Phila., 1984-95; staff mgr. Bell Atlantic External Affairs, Newark, 1995-2000; dir. external affairs Verizon Comms., Trenton, 2000—. Producer broadcast, corp. and home video programs, 1970-84; performer, narrator various freelance prodns., N.Y.C. and Phila., 1981-85. Host, producer TV series Atlantic City Tonight, 1981; exec. producer nat. PBS series Shepherd's Pie, 1975. Mem. coun. East Windsor (N.J.) Mcpl. Govt., 1988-91, dep. mayor, 1989-90; mem. adv. bd. East Windsor Community Edn. Adv. Coun., 1986-90; Rep. candidate for N.J. Gen. Assembly, 1989; elected Mercer County Freeholder, 1992-94, pres. bd. dirs., 1994, chairperson Mercer County (N.J.) Workforce Investment Bd., Literacy subcom.; pres. bd. dirs. Magnet Theatre Co., Trenton, N.J., 1998—, pres., 2001; mem. N.J. Transit Adv. Com.; mem. N.J. State Libr. Adv. Coun., 2002--. U. Pa. grantee, 1966; Ea. Ednl. Network grantee, 1975; recipient Best TV News Feature award Nat. Press Club, 1981, Achievement of Excellence award Bell Atlantic, 1991. Mem. N.J. Cable User's Assn. (pres. 1985-90), Mercer County Regional C. of C. (bd. dirs.), Mercer County Coll. Found. Republican. Methodist. Avocations: community service, travel, photography. Office: Verizon Comms NJ 1490 Prospect St Trenton NJ 08638 E-mail: coi322@aol.com., cajuin.iszard@verizon.com.

ITABASHI, HIDEO HENRY, neuropathologist; b. Los Angeles, July 7, 1926; s. Masakichi and Mitsuko (Kobayashi) I.; m. Yoko Osawa, Feb. 3, 1952; children: Mark Masa, Helen Yoko. AB, Boston U., 1949; postgrad., Yale U., 1949-50; MD, Boston U., 1954. Diplomate: in neuropathology Am. Bd. Pathology. Intern U. Mich. Hosp., Ann Arbor, 1954-55, resident in neurology, 1955-58; assoc. rsch. neurologist U. Calif., San Francisco, 1958-60, asst. clin. prof., 1964-65; asst. neuropathologist Langley Porter Neuropsychiat. Inst., San Francisco, 1960-65; cons. Neuropathologist San Francisco Gen. Hosp., 1964-65; assoc. prof. neurology, pathology U. Mich. Med. Sch., Ann Arbor, 1968-71; prof.-in-residence pathology and neurology UCLA, 1975-93, prof. emeritus, 1993—, acting vice chair dept. pathology Sch. Medicine; acting chair pathology Harbor-UCLA Med. Ctr., 1990-91; cons. neuropathology dept., chief med. examiner-coroner Los Angeles County, L.A., 1977—. Cons. VA Hosp., Sepulveda, Calif., 1977-92; spl. fellow in neuropathology Nat. Inst. Neurol. Diseases and Blindness, 1958-60. Contbr. numerous articles on neurol. disorders to med jours. Mem. Am. Assn. Neuropathologists, Am. Acad. Forensic Scis., Am. Acad. Neurology. Office: County LA Dept Coroner 1104 N Mission Rd Los Angeles CA 90033

ITAKETO, UMANA THOMPSON, systems and control engineer; b. Edem Aya, Ikot Abasi Akwa Ibom State, Nigeria, Oct. 30, 1959; s. Thompson Itaketo Umana and Dina Thompson Itaketo; m. Ima Umana Essiet, Dec. 26, 1995. Diploma with distinction, Petroleum Tng. Inst., Warri, Nigeria, 1979; B Engring. with honors, U. Tech., Enugu, Nigeria, 1985; M Engring., U. Nigeria, Nsukka, Nigeria, 1989; PhD, Fed. U. Tech., Owerri, Nigeria, 1999. Indsl. attachee Nigerian Agip Oil Co., Pt. Harcourt, Nigeria, 1978, Mobil Oil Co., Eket, Nigeria, 1983; univ. lectr. U. Nigeria, Nsukka, 1986—87; instrumentation engr. ExxonMobil Corp., 1987—. Instrumentation engr., 1991—. Author: The Design and Implementation of Interface Level Controller, 1985, Investigation into Various Controller Types/Tuning Methods for Improved Systems Response, 1988, State-Space/Matrix System Approaches in the Analysis and Control of Time Delays in Control Loops, 1995 (Coren Regd. 1992), The Development of Optimal Control Strategy for the Control of Non-Linear Systems Under Dynamic States, 1998, The Development of Performance Criterion for Optimal Control Studies on Non-Linear Systems, 1998, The Method of Isoclines In Determining the Stability of Non-Linear Systems Under Dynamic States, 1999, Application of Lyapunov's Second Method in the Stability Analysis of Oil/Gas Separation Process, 1998, Application of Isocline Plots of Non-Linear Systems for Aircraft Stability Under Dynamic States, 1999, The Stability of Non-Linear Systems Under Dynamic States, 1999, The Control of 2nd Order Non-linear Systems by a Proportional-plus-Integral-plus Derivative (PID) Controller, 1999, The Design and Installation of a Dissipation Array System for Lightning Prevention, 1999; contbr. articles to profl. jours.; reviewer ASME Jours. Active Nat. Youth Svc. Corp., 1985-86. Acad. scholar Cross River State Govt., 1980, Mobil Producing Nigeria, 1980, Fed. Govt. Nigeria, 1986, award Nigerian U. Engring. Students Assn., 2000. Mem. IEEE, Instrument Soc. Am., Internat. Fedn. Automatic Control, Nigerian Soc. Engrs., Coun. Registered Engrs. Nigeria (registered profl. engr.). Methodist. Avocations: football, chess, art, running, high-jumping. Office: ExxonMobil Prodn Co Kellog Tower Ste 854 601 Jefferson St Houston TX 77002

ITANO, HARVEY AKIO, biochemistry educator; b. Sacramento, Nov. 3, 1920; s. Masao and Sumako (Nakahara) I.; m. Rose Nakako Sakemi, Nov. 5, 1949; children: Wayne Masao, Glenn Harvey, David George. BS, U. Calif., Berkeley, 1942; MD, St. Louis U., 1945; PhD, Calif. Inst. Tech., 1950; DSc (hon.), St. Louis U., 1987. Intern City of Detroit Receiving Hosp., 1945-46; commd. officer USPHS, Bethesda, Md., 1950-70, advanced through grades to chief, sect. on chem. genetics, Nat. Inst. Arthritis and Metabolic Diseases, NIH, 1962-70, mem. hematology study sect., NIH, 1959-63, research fellow then sr. research fellow, Calif. Inst. Tech. Pasadena, 1950-54; prof. Dept. Pathology U. Calif. San Diego, La Jolla, 1970-88, prof. emeritus, 1988—. Vis. prof. Osaka (Japan) U., 1961-62, U. Chgo., 1965, U. Calif., San Francsico, 1967; cons. sickle cell anemia, mem. hematology study sect. 1953-63, various sickle cell anemia rev. coms., 1970-81, NIH, Bethesda. Editor: (with Linus Pauling) Molecular Structure and Biological Specificity, 1957; contbr. articles to profl. jours. George Minot lectr., AMA, 1955; Japan Soc. for Promotion of Sci. fellow, Okayama U., 1983-84. Mem. AAAS, NAS, Am. Acad. Arts and Scis., Am. Chem. Soc. (Eli Lilly award in Biol. Chemistry 1954), Am. Soc. Biochemistry and Molecular Biology, Am. Soc. Hematology, Internat. Soc. Hematology, Phi Beta Kappa, Sigma Xi, Alpha Omega Alpha. Office: U Calif Dept Pathology 9500 Gilman Dr La Jolla CA 92093-0506

ITKIN, DAVID, music director, conductor; MusB, MusM, Eastman Sch. Music; Mus D, Ind. U. Music dir. Kingsport Symphony Orch., 1991-94, Birmingham Opera Theater, 1991-94; assoc. condr. Ala. Symphony Orch., 1988-93; music dir., condr. Ark. Symphony Orch., Little Rock, 1993—; music dir., cond. Lake Forest Symphony Orch., 1997—. Guest condr. San Diego Symphony, Seoul Philharm., Colo. Symphony, Huntsville Symphony, State of Ala. Ballet, Waterloo-Cedar Falls Symphony, Charleston (S.C.) Symphony; artistic dir., condr. Lucius Woods Festival Concerts, Shanghai Broadcast Symphony, Delaware Symphony, New Hampshire Symphony, Indpls. Chamber Orch., Balt. Chamber Orch. Office: Ark Symphony Orch PO Box 7328 Little Rock AR 72217-7328

ITKIN, IVAN, nuclear scientist, applied mathematician; b. N.Y.C., Mar. 29, 1936; s. Abraham Aaron and Eda (Kreger) I.; m. Judith Ann Weiss, Aug. 19, 1962 (div. 1975); children: Marc Eric, Laurie Rachel; m. Joyce Lee Hudak, July 12, 1975; 1 child, Max Eugene. BSChemE, Poly. Inst., Bklyn., 1956; M in Nuclear Engring., NYU, 1957; PhD in Math., U. Pitts., 1964; D of Pub. Svc. (hon.), Chatham Coll., 1994. Assoc. scientist Bettis Atomic Power Lab. Westinghouse Electric Corp., Pitts., 1957-59, scientist, 1959-64, sr. scientist, 1964-71, fellow scientist, 1971-73; mem. Pa. Ho. of Reps., Harrisburg, 1973-98; dir. Office Civilian Radioactive Waste Mgmt. U.S. Dept. Energy, Washington, 1999-2001. Majority caucus chmn. Pa. Ho. of Reps., 1982-90, majority whip, 1990-92, majority leader, 1993-94, Democratic whip, 1995-98; Dem. nominee for Pa. gov., 1998; chmn. sci., tech., and resource planning com. Nat. Conf. State Legislators, Denver, 1988; del. Dem. Nat. Conv., 1984, 96; U.S. presdl. elector, 1992, 96. Election judge 19th Dist., 14th Ward, Pa., 1966-68; chmn. 14th Ward Dem. Com., Pitts., 1970-72. Recipient Keystone award Alcoholism and Addiction Assn., 1983, Award of Appreciation, Nat. Fedn. Blind, 1983, Disting. Svc. award Pa. Coll. Optometry, 1986; named House Mem. of Yr., Pa. Jewish Coalition, 1983. Mem. ACLU, Am. Nuclear Soc., Am. Jewish Congress, B'nai B'rith. Home: 6954 Reynolds St Pittsburgh PA 15208-2612 Fax: 412-363-7442. E-mail: iitkin@msn.com.

ITNYRE, JACQUELINE HARRIET, systems analyst; b. Camden, N.J., May 13, 1941; d. John Harold and Harriet Geraldine (Rankine) Bruynell; m. Thomas James Itnyre, Oct. 13, 1968 (dec. 1978); children: Beth Thierry, John. AS in Engring., Mercer County Coll., 1961; BA in Liberal Studies, San Jose State U., 1980, MLS, 1981. Media ctr. mgr. Milpitas (Calif.) Unified Sch. Dist., 1975-81; tech. libr. Lockheed Missiles and Space Co., Sunnyvale, Calif., 1981, programmer, 1982-83, with ground support Challenger-Space Lab 2 Palo Alto, Calif., 1984-85; systems mgr. gen. clin. rsch. ctr. Stanford (Calif.) U. Med. Sch., 1985-87, computing systems specialist divsn. epidemiology, 1988-96, local network adminstr. cancer biology rsch. labs., 1996-99; ind. contractor sys. and networking cons., web page designer, microarray data analyst, 1999—. Edna B. Anthony scholar San Jose State U., 1981. Mem. Assn. for Computing Machinery, ALA, Sierra Club. Avocations: cycling, travel, sewing, drawing, genealogy. Home: 1775 Southwood Dr San Luis Obispo CA 93401-6031 E-mail: jitnyre@charter.net.

ITO, CARL SUSUMU, computer engineer; b. Merced, Calfi., Dec. 12, 1959; s. Frank Fumi and Machiko Ito; m. Andrea Rene Spector, Nov. 1, 1985; children: Kevin, Lauren. BA, Pomona Coll., 1982; MS, Calif. State U., 1989. Computer programmer Unisys, San Diego, 1982-89; tchr. San Diego City C.C., 1991-94; sr. computer systems engr. DRS Techs., San Diego, 1989—. Nation chief YMCA Indian Guides, San Diego, 1991—94. Democrat. Avocations: piano, gardening. Home: 5864 Carnegie St San Diego CA 92122 Office: 2535 Camino Del Rio S Ste 300 San Diego CA 92108-3757 Fax: 858-587-0013. E-mail: itocs@icstf.navy.mil.

ITO, KEN, state representative; b. Honolulu, Apr. 29, 1944; m. Joyce Kitagawa; 1 child, Kendra Ito-Mizota. BE, U. of Hawaii, 1970. Tech. resource tchr., 1987—94; pub. sch. tchr., 1970—87; state rep., 1994—. Mem. arts in pub. places com. Ben Parker Elem. Sch.; mem. Castle HS Alumni and Cmty. Assn., Kane'ohe Bus. Group, Kane'ohe Cmty. Family Ctr., Kane'ohe Elem. Sch. Neighborhood Bd. #30, 1989—93, Soto Mission to Hawaii, Dem. Party of Hawaii; del. State Dem. Conv., 1990—92; sec., treas. Dist. Party. With USAF, 1962—66. Recipient Vet. Hon. Discharge, USAF, 1966. Mem.: Vets. of Fgn. Wars (pub. rels. officer), Honolulu Japanese C. of C., Hong Kong Bus. Assn., Kahaluu Lions Club. Democrat. Office: State Capital Rm 420 415 S Beretania St Honolulu HI 96813 Fax: 808-586-8474. E-mail: repito@Capitol.hawaii.gov.*

ITO, LANCE ALLAN, judge; b. LA, Aug. 2, 1950; s. Jim and Toshi Ito; m. Margaret York. BA cum laude, UCLA, 1972; JD, U. Calif., Berkeley, 1975. Bar: Calif. 1976. Civil atty., 1975—77; dep. dist. atty. gang unit, complaints divsn., organized crime unit LA County Dist. Attys. Office, 1977—87; judge LA County Mcpl. Ct., 1987—89, Superior Ct. Calif., LA County, 1989—. Vice chair Calif. Task Force on Youth Gang Violence, 1986, 89, Calif. Task Force on Victims Rights, 1988. Named Trial Judge of Yr., LA County Bar Assn., 1992. Mem.: Japanese-Am. Bar Assn., LA County Bar Assn., Calif. Judges Assn. (bd. dirs., mem. Calif. coun. on criminal justice). Democrat. Office: Criminal Cts Bldg 210 W Temple St Los Angeles CA 90012-3210

ITO, NOBORU, electric power industry executive; b. Qindao, Santon, China, Dec. 17, 1921; s. Eisho and Raiko (Watanabe) I.; m. Sachiko Tsuchiya (dec. Nov. 1978); children: Junko, Kyoko. B degree, Tohoku U., Sendai, 1946, D degree, 1973. Engr. Toyo Comm. Co., Kawasaki, 1946-50, Oi Electric Co., Tokyo, 1950-57, chief rschr. Yokohama, 1964-69, dir., 1970-83, cons., 1984-91; pres. Leo-B Corp., Yokohama, 1992—. Scientist Tokyo U., 1960-63, 89-91; lectr. Yamagata U., 1982-83; scientist U. So. Calif., L.A., 1985-86. Recipient invention prize Japan Inst. Invention, 1982, dir. prize Sci. and Tech. Agy. of Japan, 1982, yellow ribbon prize Japan Govt., 1984. Mem. IEEE (sr.), N.Y. Acad. Scis., Japan Phys. Soc., Japan Merits Club. Avocations: learning foreign languages, car trips. Office: Leo-B Corp R1012 6-13-53 Kikuna Kohokuku Yokohama 222 Japan

ITO, YOICHIRO, pathologist; b. Dec. 22, 1928; came to U.S., 1968, naturalized, 1978; s. Taichi and Ai (Kubota) I.; m. Ryoko Tanioka, Dec. 23, 1963; children: Koichi, Shin. MD, Osaka City U., 1958. Rotating intern U.S. Yokosuka (Japan) Naval Hosp., 1958-59; resident in pathology Cleve. Met. Gen. Hosp., 1959-61, Michael Reese Hosp., Chgo., 1961-63; instr. physiology Osaka City U. Med. Sch., 1963-68; vis. scientist Nat. Heart, Lung and Blood Inst., NIH, Bethesda, Md., 1968-78, med. officer, 1978—. Recipient 1st pl. award ann. sci. rsch. presentation at Cleve. Met. Gen. Hosp., 1960, Tech. Excellence award for devel. blood cell separator, 1979; Fulbright exch. scholar, 1959-63; WHO rsch. travel fund grantee Nat. Inst. Med. Rsch., London, 1968. Mem. N.Y. Acad. Scis., Kenshinkai. Achievements include research on innovation in separation sci., including continuous development of countercurrent chromatography, cell separation methods; initiated and developed countercurrent chromatography; patentee coil planet centrifuge, rotating-seal-free flow-through centrifuge, pH-zone-refining countercurrent chromatography, centrifugal precipitation chromatography. Office: NIH Bldg 50 Rm 3334 9000 Rockville Pike Bethesda MD 20892-8014 E-mail: itoy@nhlbi.nih.gov.

ITOH, TATSUO, engineering educator; b. Tokyo, May 5, 1940; s. Yohnosuke and Kimi (Okamoto) I.; m. Seiko Fukumori, June 16, 1969; children: Akihiro, Eiko. BS, Yokohama Nat. U., Japan, 1964, MS, 1966; PhD, U. Ill., 1969. Registered profl. engr., Tex. Research assoc. U. Ill., Urbana, 1969-71, research asst. prof., 1971-76; sr. research engr. Stanford Research Inst., Menlo Park, Calif., 1976-77; assoc. prof. U. Ky., Lexington, 1977-78, U. Tex., Austin, 1978-81, prof., 1981-90, Hayden Head prof., 1983-90; prof.and TRW endowed chair UCLA, 1991—. Guest rschr. AEG-Telefunken, Ulm, Fed. Republic of Germany, 1979; vis. prof. Def. Acad. Japan, 1991, U. Leeds, Eng., 1994—; hon. vis. prof. Nanjing Inst. Tech., China; hon. prof. Beijing Aeronautical and Astron. U., China, 1995—; adj. rsch. officer Comms. Rsch. Lab., Ministry of Post and Telecom., Japan, 1994; cons. Tex. Instruments, Dallas, 1979, Hughes Aircraft. Guest editor: Transactions, 1981; inventor millimeter-wave line, 1975, quasi-optical mixer, 1982, non-contact TD, 1995, high-power photo detector, 1995. Recipient Engring. Found. faculty awards, 1980-81, Billy and Claude Hocott Disting. Rsch. award, 1988, Disting. Alumnus award U. Ill., 1990, Shida award Min. of Post and Telecom., Japan, 1998, Japan Microwave prize Asia-Pacific Microwave Conf., 1998. Fellow IEEE (Millennium medal 2000, MTT Disting. Microwave Educator award 2000), Nat. Acad. Engring.; mem. Microwave Theory and Techniques Soc. (hon. life; editor 1983-85, pres. 1990, jour. editor Microwave and Guided Wave Letters 1991-94), Internat. Sci. Radio Union (chmn. USNC commn. D 1988-90, chmn. commn. D 1993-96, long range planning com. 1996—), Inst. Electronics and Comm. Engrs., Nat. Acad. Engring. Office: UCLA Dept Elec Engring Los Angeles CA 90095-0001 Home: 12 Eastfield Dr Rolling Hills CA 90274-5226 E-mail: itoh@ee.ucla.edu.

ITOH, WILLIAM H. former ambassador; b. Tokyo, May 30, 1943; m. Melinda White; children: Charlotte, Caroline. BA in Social Science, MA in History, Anthropology, U. N.Mex., 1971. Sec. tchr. Albuquerque Pub. Schs., 1967-68; asst. prof. history Calif. State U., Humboldt, 1972-73; U.S. Dept. State staff asst. and exec. officer Bur. Congressional Rels., 1975-76, congressional rels. office, 1980-83; country officer for Japan Bur. East Asian and Pacific Affairs, 1978-80, spl. asst., 1983-84, Office of Under Sec. for Pol. Affairs, 1984-86; consular and pol. officer U.S. Embassy, London, 1976-78; U.S. consul gen. Western Australia, Perth, 1986-90; dep. exec. sec. and acting exec. sec. Dept. State, 1991-93; exec. sec. Nat. Security Council White House, Washington, 1993-95; amb. to Kingdom of Thailand U.S. Dept. of State, 1995-98. Vis. prof. Kenan-Flager Bus. Sch., U. N.C., Chapel Hill. Logistics officer USAF, 1967-69. Address: 2782 N Wakefield St Arlington VA 22207-4152 E-mail: witoh@kenan.org.

ITTLESON, H(ENRY) ANTHONY, foundation executive; b. June 23, 1937; s. Henry and Nancy (Strauss) I.; m. Marianne Sundby, Feb. 6, 1961 (dec.); children: Henry Philip, Christina Bee, Stephanie. BA, Brown U., 1960. Credit adminstr. The CIT Group Inc., N.Y.C., 1961-68, v.p. Equipment Financing subs., 1968-70, asst. to pres., 1970-71, v.p. mktg., 1971-78, v.p. financing div., 1978-81, exec. v.p., 1981-92, exec. spl. projects, 1988-92; chmn. Travent Ltd., 1987-97; chmn., pres. Ittleson Found., 1973—. Chmn., pres. Ittleson Found., 1973—. Trustee Brown U.; trustee S.C. Aquarium. Mem. World Wildlife Fund (marine leadership com. and nat. coun.), Brown U. Club, Regency Whist Club, Deepdale Golf Club, Meadow Club, Nat. Golf. Links of Am., L.I. Wyandanch Club (Eastport, N.Y.), Shinnecock Hills Golf Club, Brays Island (S.C.), Cordillera Golf Club (Colo.), Loch Lomond Golf Club, Phi Gamma Delta. Home: Poco Sabo Plantation 1185 Poco Sabo Ln Green Pond SC 29446

ITTNER, HELEN LOUISE, entrepreneur; b. Saginaw, Mich., June 12, 1935; d. David Harvey and Helen (Austin) Jones; m. Frederick E. Ittner; children: David (dec.), Philip. BA, St. Mary's Coll., 1981. Pres. H.L.I. Enterprises, Inc., Moraga, Calif., 1988—. Mem. Moraga Sch. Bd., 1981-85, pres., 1984-85; bd. dirs. Hospice of Contra Costa, 1990-94, Hearst Castle Preservation Found., 1992-99; directress Altar Guild, St. Stephen's Episcopal Ch., 1993-95, vestry, 2000—, sr. warden, 2002-03; breast cancer adv. U. Calif. San Francisco Spl. Projects of Rsch. Excellence, 1997—; mem. Climb Against the Odds, Mt. Fuji, 2000. Mem. AAUW (Disting. Woman award 1991). Republican. Episcopalian. Home: 1858 School St Moraga CA 94556-1729

ITUAH, MARTINS O. pharmacist; b. Lagos, Nigeria, June 23, 1958; s. Napoleon and Felicia Ituah; m. Jannifer Ituah; children: Martins Jr., Linner, Roberto. MSc in Pharm. Scis., Pyatigorsk (USSR) Inst. Pharmacy, 1986; PharmD, Tex. South U., 1997. Grad. tchg. asst. Tex. South U. Coll. Pharm., Houston; resident Mid Mich. Med. Ctr., Midland, 1997—98; clin. coord. Del Sol Med. Ctr., El Paso, 1998, mgr. pharmacy, 1999, dir. pharmacy, 2000—. Cons., spkr. Key Pharm./Cor Therapeutics, 1998, Pfizer Pharm. Inc., 2000; spkr. Wyeth Pharm., 2000. Mem.: ASHP, Nigerian Pharm. Assn. (pub. rels. officer), Tex. South U. Alumni. Avocations: soccer, Ping Pong, Karate, films, travel. Office: Del Sol Med Ctr 10301 Gateway W El Paso TX 79925

ITURBIDE, GRACIELA, photographer; b. Mexico City, May 16; married, 1962; children: Manuel, Claudia, Mauricio. Student, U. Nat. Autanoma Mexico, 1969—72. Asst. Manuel Breva. Exhibitions include Galeria José Clemence Orosco, Mexico City, 1975, Midtown Y Gallery, N.Y.C., 1976, Centre Georges Pompldeu, Paris, 1982. Recipient prize, UN Internat. Labor Orgn., 1986, W. Eugene Smith award, 1987; Consejo Mexicano de Fotografia grantee, 1983, Guggenheim Found. grantee, 1987. Mem.: Mexican Coun. Photography (founding mem.). Home: c/o Cityscape Assocs 32 E Colorado Blvd Pasadena CA 91105

ITZKOFF, NORMAN JAY, lawyer; b. N.Y.C., Oct. 9, 1940; s. Louis and Rose Itzkoff; divorced; 1 child, Francesca Sandra. BS with distinction, U. Buffalo, 1961; LLB cum laude, Columbia U., 1965. Bar: N.Y. 1965, U.S. Dist. Ct. (so. and ea. dists.) N.Y. 1967, U.S. Ct. Appeals (2d cir.) 1967, U.S. Supreme Ct. 1971. Law clk. to judge U.S. Dist. Ct. (so. dist.) N.Y., N.Y.C., 1965-66; assoc. Cravath, Swaine & Moore, N.Y.C., 1966-74, Rosenman & Colin, N.Y.C., 1974-76, ptnr., 1976-86; sr. litigation counsel Siemens Corp., N.Y.C., 1988-93; cons., arbitrator and mediator, 1994—. Gen. counsel Assn. Internat. Photography Art Dealers Inc., N.Y.C., 1981-91. Editor: Dealing with Damages, 1983, Columbia U. Law Rev., 1963-65. Mem. adv. bd. Catskill Ctr. for Photography, Woodstock, N.Y., 1982-87; chmn. adv. bd. Ctr. for Photography at Woodstock, 1987-88. Harlan Fiske Stone scholar. Mem. ABA (jud. adminstrn. div. lawyers conf., com. on jud. qualification and selection, com. jud.compensation, sect. of litigation, com. corp. counsel), Fed. Bar Coun., N.Y. State Bar Assn. (alt. dispute resolution com., antitrust law sect., mem. coms. on court adminstrn. and practice and procedure, comml. and fed. litigation sect., com. on corp. counsel, entertainment arts and sports law sect., com. on fine arts, internat. law and practice sect. coms. internat. dispute resolution and subcom. arbitration, mcpl. law sect., profl. discipline com., trial lawyers sect., com. on fed. cts., com. on litigation mgmt. and econs.), Assn. Bar City N.Y. (alternative dispute resolution com., profl. discipline com., adv. bd. demonstration observation com., com. on nuclear tech. and law, com. on art law, liaison art law com., chmn. subcom. on state legislation 1983-84, Am. Arbitration Assn. (panel), Ctr. Pub. Resources (com. on disputes with distbrs., dealers and franchisees), Columbia Club, Westchester Rugby Club (N.Y.C.), Beta Gamma Sigma. Avocations: fine art photography, running. Home and Office: 2600 Netherland Ave New York NY 10463-4801

ITZKOWITZ, NORMAN, history educator; b. N.Y.C., May 6, 1931; s. Jack and Gussie (Schmier) I.; m. Leonore Krauss, June 13, 1954; children: Jay Noah, Karen Lisa. BA magna cum laude, CCNY, 1953; MA, Princeton U., 1956, PhD, 1959. Instr. depts. history and Oriental studies Princeton U., 1958-61, asst. prof. Oriental studies, 1961-66, assoc. prof. Near Eastern studies, 1966-73, prof., 1973—, master Wilson Coll., 1975-89. Vis. prof. CCNY, summer 1959, Tchrs. Coll., Columbia U., 1964, N.Y. U., 1969, 72, 74, Hebrew U., Jerusalem, 1970, U. B.C., summer 1971 Author: (with V. Volkan and A. Dod) Richard Nixon: A Psychobiography, 1997, Ottoman Empire and Islamic Tradition, 1980, (with V. Volkan) The Immortal Atatürk, 1984 Ford Found. fellow, 1954-59; HEW, SSRC, Littauer Found. fellow, 1970, 74 Mem. Am. Hist. Assn., Am. Oriental Soc. Jewish. Office: Princeton U 108 Jones Dr Princeton NJ 08540 *The goal of life is to be a mensch, a decent human being.*

IVAN, FRANCIS M. sales executive, writer; b. Greeley, Colo., Dec. 14, 1926; s. Godfrey A. and Esther Ann Ivan; m. Joan Carol Waidtlaw, May 27, 1962; 1 child, Kathleen. At, Jones Real Estate Coll., Denver, 1971—73. Lic. real estate broker Colo., Nev. Ptnr. Oldsmobile franchise, Burlingame, Calif., 1959—71, gen. mgr., 1959—71; owner and broker Money Land Co., Denver, 1971—84; owner and COO Pacific Equipment Brokers, San Diego, 1981—84; indsl. broker Reno (Nev.) Realty, 1993—. Mem. Bd. of Realtors, Denver, 1971—84. Author: (books) Why Not?, 2002, Who Knows?, 2002. With USN, 1943—47, PTO. Republican. Avocations: skiing, golf. Home and Office: Apt 73 800 Redfield Pkwy Reno NV 89509-6529

IVANCHENKO, LAUREN MARGARET DOWD, pharmaceutical executive; b. West Orange, N.J., Mar. 20, 1958; d. Bernard Peter and Virginia (Morsell) Dowd; m. John Ivanchenko, Aug. 12, 1990; 1 child, Liana Katherine. BS in Psycho.-Biology, Albright Coll., 1980; postgrad., Rutger's U., 1991—92; MBA, St. Joseph's U., 2002. Sales Bourroughs Wellcome Co., Rsch. Triangle Pk., NC, 1981—84, acct. mgr. med. ctr., 1984—96; therapeutic area specialist Glaxo Wellcome, Inc., 1996—2000; sr. exec. clin. specialist Glaxo Smith Kline, Inc., 2000—. Mem.: Am. Epilepsy Soc., N.J. Epilepsy Soc. (mem. profl. adv. bd. 2001—), Nat. Exch. Club, Beta Gamma Sigma, Phi Delta Sigma. Avocations: piano, reading.

IVANETICH, RICHARD JOHN, information technology executive; b. San Francisco, Feb. 12, 1941; s. John Henry and Catherine Madeline Ivanetich; m. Leonida Louise Bertone; children: Karina, Kenneth. BS Chemistry, U. Calif., Berkeley, 1963; PhD Physics, Harvard U., 1969. Asst. prof. physics Harvard U., Cambridge, Mass., 1969—74; rsch. staff mem. Inst. Def. Analyses, Alexandria, Va., 1975—84, asst. dir., sys. evaluation divsn., 1984—90, dir., computer and software engring. divsn., 1990—2002, Inst. fellow, 2003—. Mem. Naval Studies Bd., NRC, Washington, 1998—, Info. Sci. and Tech. Study Group, Def. Advanced Rsch. Projects Agy. (DARPA), Arlington, Va., 1990—. Mem.: Computer Soc., IEEE (IEEE), Assn. for Computing Machinery. Office: Inst Def Analyses 4850 Mark Center Dr Alexandria VA 22311

IVANICK, CAROL W. TRENCHER, lawyer; b. Springfield, Mass., Mar. 6, 1939; d. Joseph George and Daisy Wolf; m. Michael Ira Trencher, July 30, 1960 (div. Feb. 1984); children: Christopher, Daniel, Deborah; m. Peter Alan Ivanick (div. 1998). BA, Wellesley Coll., 1959; JD, Yale U., 1962. Bar: N.Y. 1963. Assoc. Cleary, Gottlieb et al, N.Y.C., 1962-67; ptnr. Dewey, Ballantine LLP, N.Y.C., 1976—. Chmn. adv. com. Pension Benefit Guaranty Corp., Washington, 1978-80; visiting lectr. Yale Law Sch., New Haven, Conn., 1978-79, 82-83. Avocations: ceramics, bowling, tennis. Home: 110 Riverside Dr New York NY 10024-3715 Office: Dewey Ballantine 1301 Avenue Of The Americas New York NY 10019-6022

IVANIER, PAUL, steel products manufacturing company executive; b. Cernauti, Romania, Oct. 12, 1932; s. Isin and Fancia Ivanier; m. Lily Neilinger, June 13, 1954; children: Shirley Retter, Janet Neuman-Ellis, Philip., McGill U., 1957; PhD (hon.), Ben-Gurion U. With Ivaco Inc. (formerly Sivaco Wire and Nail Co.), Montreal, v.p. ops., exec. v.p., 1969-76, pres., chief exec. officer, dir., 1976—. Bd. dirs. Ivacan Inc., Docap Corp. Grand patron Montreal Mus. Fine Arts; former bd. govs. U. Montreal, Concordia U., Royal Victoria Hosp. Corp.; internat. bd. govs. Ben Gurion U.; bd. dirs. Weizmann Inst. Scis., Med. Rsch. Found. Jewish Gen. Hosp. Decorated Order of Can. Mem. Can. Steel Producers Assn. (bd. dirs. past vice chmn.), Can. Steel Trade and Employment Congress (bd. dirs., founder), Club des Entrepreneurs/Conseil du Patronat du Quebec (Laureate 1989), Elmridge Golf and Country Club, Mt. Royal Club. Office: Ivaco Inc 770 rue Sherbrooke St W Montreal QC Canada H3A 1G1

IVANKOVICH, ANTHONY D. anesthesiologist, educator; b. Debeljaca, Yugoslavia, Mar. 25, 1939; came to U.S., 1965; m. Olga Ivankovich. MD, U. Zagreb, Croatia, 1963. Lic. physician, Ill.; diplomate Am. Bd. Anesthesiology. Resident in internal medicine County Hosp. Nunberg, Fed. Republic Germany, 1963-65; rotating intern Edgewater Hosp., Chgo., 1966; resident in anesthesiology U. of Chgo. Hosps., 1967-68; asst. prof. anesthesiology Stritch Sch. Medicine Loyola U., Maywood, Ill., 1970-71; instr. anesthesiology Pritzker Sch. Medicine U. Chgo., 1969, assoc. prof. anesthesiology, 1972-74; faculy Sch. Medicine Cook County Postgrad., Chgo., 1975—; prof. anesthesiology Rush Med. Coll. Rush-Presbyn. St. Luke's Med. Ctr., Chgo., 1980—, dir. Rush Pain Ctr., chmn. anesthesiology, 1980—. Attending anesthesiologist Stritch Sch. Medicine, Loyola U., Chgo., 1970-71, lectr. in anesthesiology, 1971-81; cons. anesthesiology Suburban TB Sanatorium, Hinsdale, Ill., 1970-71, Shriner's Hosp. for Crippled Children, Chgo., 1977-82; attending anesthesiology Michael Reese Med. Ctr., Chgo., 1971-74; chief oper. rm. svcs. 801st Gen. Hosp., USAR, Lincolnwood, Ill., 1971-73, chief surgery, 1973 74, assoc. chief profl. svcs., 1974-76; dir. anesthesia rsch. Michael Reese Med. Ctr., Chgo., 1971-74; chmn. anesthesiology Ill. Masonic Med. Ctr., Chgo., 1974-80, Rush-Presbyn.-St. Luke's Med. Ctr., Chgo., 1980—, chmn. coun. surg. chmn. divsn. surg. scis. and svcs., 1992-94, dir. Surg. Hosp., assoc. v.p., 1993—, dir. Women & Children's Hosp., assoc. v.p., 1994—; assoc. examiner Am. Bd. Anesthesiology, 1978; presenter in field. Author: (books) Nitroprusside and Other Short-Acting Hypotensive Agents, 1978, (book chpts. with others) Perspective in High Frequency Ventilation, 1983, Current Controversies in Thoracic Surgery, 1986, Anesthesia and ENT Surgery, 1987, Liposomes as Drug Carriers, 1987, Effective Hemostasis in Cardiac Surgery, 1988, Adjuncts to Cancer Therapy, 1989, Advances in Anesthesia, 1990, Cardiothoracic and Vascular Anesthesia Update, 1991, Cardiothoracic and Vascular Anesthesia Update, 1991, Clinical Anesthesia, 1992, Clinical Anesthesia Updates, 1992, Liposomes in Drug Delivery, 1992; contbr. articles and abstracts to profl. jours. Fellow Am. Coll. Anesthesiologists; mem. AMA, Internat. Assn. for Study of Pain, Internat. Anesthesia Rsch. Soc., Am. Soc. Anesthesiologists, Am. Heart Assn., Am. Coll. Chest Physicians, Am. Pain Soc., Pan Am. Med. Assn., Soc. for Intravenous Anesthesia, Ill. Med. Soc., Ill. Soc. Anesthesiologists, Soc. Neurosurg. Anesthesia and Neurologic Supporting Care, Midwest Pain Soc., Chgo. Med. Soc., Chgo. Soc. Anesthesiologists, Inst. of Medicine of Chgo., Chgo. Heart Assn., Sigma Xi. Office: Rush-Presbyn-St Luke's Med Ctr Dept Anesthesiology 1653 W Congress Pkwy Chicago IL 60612-3833

IVANOV, ALEXANDER V. biochemist, researcher; b. Grodno, Belarus, Nov. 1, 1970; came to U.S., 1995; s. Valerii V. and Elena M. Ivanov; m. Asya V. Grinberg. MS, Grodno State U., 1992; PhD, Med. Coll. Ohio, 2000. Substitute tchr. chemistry, biology Secondary Sch. # 10, Grodno, 1989-91; rsch. asst. Belozersky Inst. Physico-Chem. Biology Moscow State U., 1992-95; fellow Med. Coll. Ohio, Toledo, 2000—02, asst. prof. pharmacology, 2003—. Contbr. articles to profl. jours. Winner Belarus round All-USSR Student Biology Olympiad, Ministry of Edn., 1991. Mem. AAAS, Am. Biophys. Soc. Avocations: classical music, piano, tennis, travel. Office: Med Coll Ohio 3035 Arlington Ave Toledo OH 43614-5804 E-mail: aivanov@mco.edu.

IVANOV, ANATOLI F. education educator; s. Odarka A. Ivanova and Fedir Y. Ivanov; m. Elena G. Galkina, June 24, 1984; children: Irina A. Ivanova, Sergey A. PhD, Inst. of Math., Kiev, Ukraine, 1983. Rsch. assoc. U. of Ballarat, Australia, 1998—2002; prof. Pa. State U., Wilkes-Barre, 1994—. Author around 100 rsch. articles, papers and pubs. Rsch. Scholarships, AvH Stiftung (Germany), JSPS (Japan), 1985, 1990, 1997, 1998, 2001. Mem.: Am. Math. Soc. (assoc.). Office: Pa State Univ PO Box PSU Lehman PA 18627 Office Fax: 570-674-9072. E-mail: afi1@psu.edu.

IVANOV, EUGENE, geneticist, researcher; b. Tallinn, Estonia, Aug. 16, 1954; s. Leonid Ivanov and Tatjana Ivanova; m. Tatiana Bembel, July 3, 1986; children: Anton, Sasha. PhD, U. of St.Petersburg, Russia, 1976. Sr. rsch. assoc. Brandeis U., Waltham, Mass., 1992—95; sr. scientist and group leader Transkaryotic Therapies, Inc., Cambridge, Mass., 1995—. Fellow, Med. Rsch. Counsel, 1991. Mem.: AAAS (corr.). R-Liberal. Achievements include patents pending for methods to improve homologous recombination in mammalina cells. Avocation: winter swimming. Home: 390 East Foxboro St Sharon MA 02067 Office: Transkaryotic Therapies Inc 700 Main St Cambridge MA 02139 Office Fax: 617-613-4014. Personal E-mail: eivanov@aol.com. E-mail: eivanov@tktx.com.

IVANOV, KOSTADIN NIKOLOV, educator; b. Dimitrovgrad, Bulgaria; s. Nikola Kostov Ivanov and Velichka Vangelova Ivanova; children: Mira Ivanova, Emil. PhD, Bulgarian Acad. Scis., Sofia, 1990. Cert. nuc. engr., Bulgaria. Rsch. assoc. Pa. State U., University Park, 1996—97, asst. prof., 1997—99, assoc. prof., 1999—. Mem.: Am. Nuc. Soc. Home: 540 Westview Ave State College PA 16803 Office: Pa State U 230 Reber Bldg University Park PA 16802 Office Fax: 814-865-8499. Business E-Mail: kni1@psu.edu.

IVANOV, LYUBEN DIMITROV, naval architecture researcher, educator; b. Varna, Bulgaria, Apr. 14, 1941; came to U.S., 1991; s. Dimitar Dimov and Petra Christova (Grozdeva) I.; m. Svetlana Zekova, Aug. 14, 1965 (div. July 1977); children: Ognyan, Iskra; m. Irina Radeva, Aug. 18, 1977; stepchildren: Ivelin, Michaela. Diploma for Naval Architecture, Higher Naval Sch., Varna, Bulgaria, 1964; PhD, Leningrad Shipbuilding Inst., USSR, 1970. Chartered engr., U.K. Designer Inst. for Shipbuilding, Varna, 1964-66; asst. Tech. Univ., Varna, 1966, reader, head of dept., 1970-74, vice-dean for rsch., 1975-76, vice-dean for continuing edn., 1985-86, dean of faculty of shipbuilding, 1987-89, reader on ship structures, 1989-91; sr. engr. Am. Bur. Shipping, N.Y.C., 1991—. Vis. researcher Univ. Newcastle upon Tyne, U.K., 1974-75; dep. dirs. Inst. for Shipbuilding, Varna, 1986-87, mng. dir. 1987-89; v.p. Bulgarian Shipbuilding Corp., Varna, 1987-88. Mem. editorial bd. Marine Structures Jour., 1988-93. Founder, sec. Union of Bulgarian Scientists in Shipbuilding, Varna, 1982. Recipient badge of Honor, Presidium of the Union of Bulgarian Scientists, Sofia, 1984. Mem. Royal Instn. Naval Architects/U.K. (mem. internat. standing com. practical design of ships and mobile units symposium 1987-93), Soc. Naval Architects and Marine Engrs. Achievements include research in application of probabilistic methods in ship structures design and analysis. Home: 12 Brentwood Oaks Ct The Woodlands TX 77381-2525 Office: Am Bur Shipping ABS Plaza 16855 Northchase Dr Houston TX 77060-6006 Fax: 281-877-5820. E-mail: livanov@eagle.org.

IVANOVITCH, MICHAEL S. economist; b. Cetinje, Yugoslavia, Sept. 9, 1939; children: Alexandra, Nicholas, Alexander. Diploma in Law, U. Belgrade, Yugoslavia, 1961; MBA, Columbia U., 1972, M of Philosophy, 1976, PhD, 1977. Rsch. assoc. Columbia U. Inst. on Western Europe, N.Y.C., 1977-78; prof. Columbia U. Grad. Sch. Bus., N.Y.C., 1978-88; internat. economist Fed. Res. Bank of N.Y., N.Y.C., 1978-79; prin. adminstr., sr. economist Orgn. for Econ. Cooperation and Devel., Paris, 1979-89; pres. MSI Global, Inc., N.Y.C. and Paris, 1989—. Adj. prof. Columbia U.; advisor Groupe Arnault, Paris, 2000—, The Yasuda Life Ins. Co., London and Tokyo, 1990—, The Meiji Life Ins. Co., Tokyo, 1991—, Merrill Lynch, 1996—, Orix Corp., Tokyo, 1996—, ANZ Bank, 1997—, Sumitomo Trust & Banking Corp., 1997—. Democrat. Russian Orthodox. Avocation: music. Office: MSI Global Inc 340 W 57th St New York NY 10019-3706 E-mail: economics@msiglobal.com.

IVANY, ROBERT RUDOLPH, military officer, historian; b. Wels, Austria, Feb. 4, 1947; came to U.S., 1950; s. George Robert and Eva (Baranyai) I.; m. Marianne O'Donnell, July 29, 1973; children: Christopher, Mark, Julianne, Brian. BS, U.S. Mil. Acad., 1969; MA, U. Wis., 1976, PhD, 1980; postgrad., Army War Coll., 1989. Commd. 2d lt. U.S. Army, 1969, advanced through grades to lt. col., 1986; assoc. prof. dept. history U.S. Mil. Acad., West Point, N.Y., 1976-79; ops. officer 2d Squadron, 2d Armored Cav., Fed. Republic Germany, 1979-81; staff officer War Plans div. Pentagon, Washington, 1983; mil. aide to Pres. White House, Washington, 1984-86; comdr. 1st Squadron, 3d Armored Cav., Ft. Bliss, Tex., 1986-88; Student Army War Coll., 1989—. Decorated Superior Svc. medal, Legion of Merit, Bronze Star, Meritorious Svc. medal. Mem. U.S. Armor Assn. Avocations: reading; writing.

IVENS, MARY SUE, microbiologist, mycologist; b. Maryville, Tenn., Aug. 23, 1929; d. McPherson Joseph and Sarah Lillie (Hensley) Ivens. BS, East Tenn. State U., 1949; MS NIH rsch. trainee, Tulane U. Sch. Medicine, 1963; PhD, La. State U. Sch. Medicine, 1966; postgrad., Emory U. Sch. Medicine. Diplomate Am. Bd. Microbiology. Dir. microbiol. and mycol. labs. Lewis-Gate Hosp., Roanoke, Va., 1953—56; rsch. mycologist Ctrs. Disease Control, Atlanta, 1957—60; rsch. assoc. La. State U. Sch. Medicine, New Orleans, 1963—66; instr. medicine La. State U., 1966—72, instr. microbiology, 1966—72, clin. prof., 1972—. Dir. micology lab. La. State U. Sch. Medicine, 1963—72, lectr. sch. dentistry, 1968—70; assoc. prof. natural scis. Dillard U., New Orleans, 1972—; assoc. Marine Biol. Lab., Woods Hole, Mass., 1978—; cons. in field. Contbr. articles to profl. jours. Commr. conf. on ctr. Mycotic sera WHO, 1969; mem. La. assn. def. counsel expert witness bank, 1985—; bd. dirs. La. coun. Girl Scouts US, Cmty Relationships Greater New Orleans, Zoning Bd. River Ridge, La.; mem. exec. bd. River Ridge Civic Assn., 1982—98, sec., 1982—84; chmn. pers. bd. Riverside Bapt. Ch., River Ridge; dir. outreach First Bapt. Ch., New Orleans, 1989—97; chmn. gold medal award com. Sigma Xi, 1978. Recipient Rosicrucian Humanitarian award, 1981; fellow Macy, MBL, 1978—79; grantee NSF, NIH. Mem.: Nat. Inst. Sci., AAAS, Am. Soc. Microbiology (Nat. com. on membership 1983—87), Med. Mycological Soc. Am., Internat. Soc. Human and Animal Mycology, Sigma Xi. Office: Dillard U Div Natural Sci New Orleans LA 70122 Home: 809 Prestwick Dr Maryville TN 37803-6757

IVERACH, ROBERT JOHN, lawyer; b. Edmonton, Alta., Can., Dec. 13, 1947; s. David W. and Margaret L. (Ranton) I.; m. Susan Anne Long, May 6, 1977; children: Robert J., Michelle A. BA, U. Calgary, 1969; LLB, U. Alta., 1970; LLM, London Sch. Econs., 1971. Bar: Alta. 1972. Student, atty., Ballem, McDill & MacInnes, Calgary, Alta., 1971-74; ptnr. Fenerty & Co., Calgary, 1974-78; founding ptnr. Bell, Felesky & Iverach, Calgary, 1978— ; bd. dirs. Maxx Petroleum Ltd. Co-author: Canadian Income Tax Tips and Traps, 1979. Bd. dirs. Alta. Law Found., 1976-78. Viscount Bennett scholar, 1970. Mem. Law Soc. Alta., Can. Bar Assn. Progressive Conservative. Mem. United Ch. Can. Clubs: Ranchmen's, Petroleum, Glencoe (Calgary). Office: 350 7th Ave SW Suite 3400 Calgary AB Canada T2P 3N9

IVERIUS, PER-HENRIK, physician, biochemist, educator; b. Stockholm, Sept. 26, 1942; s. Karl Gösta and Märta Kristina (Engelbert) I. B in Med. Sci., U. Uppsala, Sweden, 1963, PhD in Med. Biochemistry, 1971, MD, 1975. Diplomate Am. Bd. Internal Medicine, Am. Bd. Endocrinology and Metabolism. Intern, resident Emmanuel Hosp., Portland, 1978-80; asst. prof. med. biochemistry U. Uppsala, 1972-74; sr. research fellow U. Wash., Seattle, 1980-82, acting instr. medicine, 1982-85; mem. staff VA Med. Ctr. and U. Utah Hosp., Salt Lake City, 1985-2000; asst. prof. medicine U. Utah, Salt Lake City, 1985-92, assoc. prof. medicine, 1992-2000; vis. scientist U. Joseph Fourier, Grenoble, France, 2000-01. Contbr. articles to profl. jours. Recipient Research Career Devel. award Swedish Med. Research Council, 1971-74; fellow Arthritis Found., 1975-78. Mem. ACP, Am. Diabetes Assn., Endocrine Soc. Office: Endokrint Centrum St Gorans Sjukhus St Goransplan 1 S-11281 Stockholm Sweden

IVERS, DONALD LOUIS, judge; b. San Diego, May 6, 1941; s. Grant Perrin and Margaret (Ware) I. BA, U. N.Mex., 1963; JD, Am. U., 1971. Bar: U.S. Dist. Ct. (D.C. 1972), U.S. Ct. Appeals (D.C. cir.) 1972, U.S. Ct. Mil. Appeals 1972, U.S. Supreme Ct. 1975. Assoc. Brault, Graham, Scott, Brault, Washington, 1972-78; chief counsel Republican Nat. Com., Washington, 1978-81; gen. counsel 1980 Rep. Nat. Conv. Site Selection Com., 1979-80; chief counsel Fed. Hwy. Adminstrn., U.S. Dept. Transp., 1981-85; counselor to sec., chmn. sec.'s safety rev. task force U.S. Dept. Transp., 1984-85; gen. counsel VA, 1985-89; acting gen. counsel U.S. Dept. Vet. Affairs, 1989-90, asst. to the sec., 1990; judge U.S. Ct. Appeals Vet. Claims, 1990—. Capt. U.S. Army, 1963-68, Vietnam, lt. col. Res., ret. Office: US Ct Appeals Vet Claims 625 Indiana Ave NW Washington DC 20004-2923

IVERSEN, LESLIE LARS, pharmaceutical executive; BA, U. Cambridge, 1961, PhD, 1964. V.p. neurosci. rsch. ctr. Merck, Sharpe & Dohme, 1983—95; founder Panos Therapeutics; prof. pharmacology Royal Postgraduate Med. Sch. Hammersmith Hosp., London; chmn. ACADIA Pharmaceuticals Inc., San Diego, 1998—. Vis. prof. dept. pharmacology U. Oxford, Oxford, England; dir. Med. Rsch. Coun. Neuropharmacology Unit, Cambridge, England, 1970—83. Contbr. articles over 350 to profl. jours. Fellow: Royal Soc. London; mem.: Nat. Acad. Sci. (assoc.). Office: ACADIA Pharmaceuticals 3911 Sorrento Valley Blvd San Diego CA 92121

IVERSON, ALLEN, basketball player; b. Hampton, Va., June 7, 1975; Grad., Georgetown U., 1996. Basketball player Phila. 76ers, 1996—. Named AP First Team All-Am., 1994, Big East Conf. Defensive Player of Yr., 1995—96, NBA Rookie of Month, Apr., Nov., 1997, MVP Schick Rookie game, 1997, Schick Rookie of Yr., 1997. Avocations: drawing, reading. Office: Philadelphia 76ers First Union Ctr 3601 S Broad St Ste 4 Philadelphia PA 19148-5287

IVERSON, JEFFREY G. music educator, director; b. Ada, Minn., Jan. 4, 1960; s. Gerald A. and Mildred T. Iverson; m. Katharine C. Hed; children: Rebekah K., Kirstin A., Lynnea C., Jenessa G. BA, Concordia Coll., 1978—82; MA, St. Cloud State. Music Edn. (K-12) Minn., 1982. Dir. of music Leeds Pub. Sch., ND, 1982—83, Climax Pub. Sch., Minn., 1983—88; dir. of bands Staples Motley H.S., Minn., 1988—. Sect. leader Staples Area Men's Chorus, Minn., 1988—2002. Recipient Exemplary Music Program, Minn. Music Educators, 1991. Mem.: Minn. Edn. Assn. (assoc.), Minn. Music Educators Assn. (assoc.), Assoc. Male Chorus of Am. (assoc.), Minn. Band Dir. Nat. Assn. (assoc.), NEA (assoc.). D-Conservative. Lutheran. Avocations: golf, walking, camping, sports, music. Home: 1424 8th St NE Staples MN 56479 Office: Staples Motley HS 401 Centennial Ln Staples MN 56479

IVERSON, JOHN WILFRED, educator; b. Brookings, S.D., Nov. 17, 1950; s. Marvin W. I. and Viola Gebhart. BS, S.D. State U., 1973. Tchr. 7th & 8th grade sci. Brookings Pub. Schs., 1973-75, tchr. 9th & 10th grade sci., 1975-77, tchr. 6th grade sci., 1977-94, tchr. 8th grade math. & algebra, 1995—. Coach middle sch. basketball Brookings Pub. Sch., 1973—, coach high sch. track, 1975-80, 87—. Roman Catholic. Avocations: fishing, running, reading, restoring old cars. Home: 604 3d St Brookings SD 57006 Office: George Mickelson Mid Sch 1801 12th St S Brookings SD 57006-5411

IVERSON, KRISTINE ANN, federal agency administrator; b. Elgin, Ill, Aug. 15, 1953; d. Theodore Clarence and Vivian (Schumaker) I. BA, DePauw U., Greencastle, Ind., 1975; MA, George Mason U., 1985; postgrad., Va. Poly. Inst. and State U., 1978. Legis. aide Rep. John B. Conlan, Washington, 1975-76; legis. asst. Sen. Orrin G. Hatch, Washington, 1977-81, sr. policy advisor, 1993-94, legis. dir., 1995—; employment policy dir. Senate Labor and Human Resources Com., Washington, 1981-88, minority staff dir., 1988-92; asst. sec. Congl. intergov. affairs US Dept. Labor, Washington, 2001—. Cons. Reagan-Bush Transition, 1980 Pres. The Ron Freeman Chorale, Arlington, Va., 1987-2000; steering com. George Mason U. Tech. Forum, 1983; del. 11th Dist. Rep. Conv., Fairfax, Va., 1992; mem. DePauw U. Alumni Bd., Greencastle, Ind., 1993-99; mem. Bd. of Visitors 2000-03. Recipient Young Alumni award DePauw U., Greencastle, 1993, John C. Stennis Congrl. fellow, 1999-2000. Mem. Alpha Omicron Pi;mem. The Falls Ch. (Episcopal). Republican. Avocations: music, sports. Office: US Dept Labor Congressional Intergovt Affairs 200 Constitution Ave NW Washington DC 20210 Office Fax: 202-693-4641.

IVERSON, LOUIS ROBERT, research ecologist; b. Jamestown, N.D., June 25, 1954; s. Norris Vernon and Virginia Iverson; m. Margaret Grace Saethre, May 6, 1978; children: Heather Renee, Aaron Louis. PhD, U. N.D., Grand Forks, 1981. Rsch. ecologist Ill. Natural History Survey, Champaign, 1982—92, USDA Forest Svc., Delaware, Ohio, 1992—. Adj. prof. Ohio State U., Columbus, 1993—. Ch. leader St. Mark's Luth. Ch., Delaware, 1993. Mem.: U.S.-Internat. Assn. for Landscape Ecology (pres., treas., program chair 1993—98, Disting. Landscape Ecologist award 2002), Ecol. Soc. of Am. (life), Sigma Xi (life). Lutheran. Achievements include research in Potential distribution of tree species following climate change; development of Integrated Moisture Index; research in GIS modeling of ecological trends. Avocations: bicycling, travel, squash, gardening. Office: USDA Forest Svc 359 Main Rd Delaware OH 43015

IVERSON, PETER JAMES, historian, educator; b. Whittier, Calif, Apr. 4, 1944; s. William James and Adelaide Veronica (Schmitt) I.; m. Kaaren Teresa Gonsoulin, Mar. 7, 1983; children: Erika, Jens, Tim, Scott. BA in History, Carleton Coll., 1967; MA in History, U. Wis., 1969, PhD in History, 1975. Vis. asst. prof. Ariz. State U., Tempe, Ariz., 1975-76; from asst. prof to prof. U. Wyo., Laramie, Wyo., 1976-86; coord. divsn. social and behavioral scis. Ariz. State U., Phoenix, 1986-88, prof. history Tempe, Ariz., 1988—, regents prof. history, 2000—. Panelist, reviewer Nat. Endowment Humanities, Washington, 1986—; vis. prof. Carleton Coll., 1991. Author: The Navajos: A Critical Bibliography, 1976, The Navajo Nation, 1981, Carlos Montezuma, 1982, The Navajos, 1990, When Indians Became Cowboys: Native Peoples and Cattle Ranching in the American West, 1994, Barry Goldwater: Native Arizonan, 1997, We Are Still Here: American Indians in the 20th Century, 1998, Riders of the West: Portraits From Indian Rodeo, 1999, Diné: A History of the Navajos, 2002; co-editor: Indians in American History, 1998; editor: The Plains Indians of the 20th Century, 1985, For Our Navajo People: Din+248 Letters, Speeches, and Petitions, 1900-1960, 2002; co-editor: Major Problems in American Indian History, 1994, 2d edit., 2001; assoc. editor The Historian, 1990-95; editl. bd. Pacific Hist. Rev., 1986-88, Jour. Ariz. History, 1987-89, Social Sci. Jour., 1988-96, Montana: The Magazine of Western History, 1993—, Western Historical Quarterly, 2000-02. Acting dir. McNickle Ctr. for History of Am. Indian, Newberry Libr., 1994-95, mem. adv. bd., 1993-2003; bd. dir. Ariz. Humanities Coun., 1993-99; chmn. Wyo. Coun. Humanities, 1981-82; mem. Heard Mus., Phoenix, 1986—, Desert Bot. Garden, Phoenix, 1986—. Recipient Chief Manuelito Appreciation award Navajo Nation, 1984, Disting. Achievement award Carleton Coll. Alumni Assn., 1992, Lifetime Achievement award Am. Indian Hist. Assn., 1999, Him-Dak Eco-Mus. Svc. award Ak-Chin Indian Cmty., 2001; Western Writers of Am. Spur Award, 2002 for best book on 20th century west; Newberry Libr. fellow, Chgo., 1973-74, Nat. Endowment Humanities fellow, 1982-83, Leadership fellow Kellogg Found., Battle Creek, Mich., 1982-85, NEH fellow, 1999-2000, Guggenheim Found. fellow, 1999-2000; Disting. Pub. scholar, Ariz. Humanities Coun., 1999. Mem. Am. Soc. Ethnohistory (coun. 1991-93, chmn. program com. 1994, chmn. prize com. 1987), Western Social Sci. Assn. (pres. 1988-89), Orgn. Am. Historians, Western History Assn. (chmn. prize com. 1991, co-chmn. program com. 1995, coun. 1995-98), pres. elect, 2003-2004. Office: Ariz State U Dept History Tempe AZ 85287-2501 E-mail: peter.iverson@asu.edu.

IVERSON, RICHARD MATTHEW, earth scientist; b. Albert Lea, Minn., Nov. 1, 1954; s. Roger Duane and Ona Lee Elsie (Whitman) I. BS, Iowa State U., 1977; MS, Stanford U., 1980, MS, 1981, PhD, 1984. Hydrologist U.S. Geol. Survey, Vancouver, Wash., 1984—. Chief debris-flow flume, Blue River, Oreg. Fellow: Geol. Soc. Am. (E.B. Burwell award 1991, Kirk Bryan award 2001); mem.: AAAS, Am. Geophys. Union (erosion and sedimentation com. 1986—), Mazamas Mountaineers club (Portland, Oreg.). Achievements include discovery of dynamic pore-pressure fluctuations in rapidly shearing granular materials. Office: # 100 1300 SE Cardinal Ct Vancouver WA 98683-9589 E-mail: riverson@usgs.gov.

IVERSON, ROBERT LOUIS, JR., internist, physician; b. Borden, Ind., Sept. 3, 1944; s. Robert L. and Agnes Maxine (Knight) I.; m. Elsa Maschmeyer, Sept. 3, 1967 (div. 1982); children: Nathan, Kirsten; m. Deborah A. Budd, June 16, 1984 (dec. May 1996); children: Richard, Colin; m. Amy M. Neidert, May 9, 1998. Student, Wabash Coll., 1962-64; BA, Ind. U., 1970, MD, 1974, Intern, 1974-75. Diplomate Am. Bd. Internal Med., diplomate in critical care medicine, Am. Bd. Internal Med. Intern Ind. U., Indpls., 1974-75; resident (internal med.) Methodist Hosp., Indpls, 1975-77; co-dir. critical care, mem. tchg. staff dept. medicine Meth. Hosp., Indpls., 1977-84; fellow in critical care med. U. So. Calif. Shock Rsch. Unit, Ctr. for Critically Ill, L.A., 1977; vis. lectr. U. So. Calif., L.A., 1977; co-dir. critical care, teaching staff, Dept. of Med. Methodist Hosp., Indpls, 1977-84; asst. prof. medicine Wayne State U., Detroit, 1984-96, assoc. prof. clin. medicine, 1996-2000; dir. med. affairs Hutzel Hosp., Detroit, 1996-97, vice chief med. staff, 1995-97, dir. ICU, 1986-2000, chief critical care medicine, 1988-2000; chief critical care svcs. Vassar Bros. Hosp., Poughkeepsie, NY, 2000—02. Mem. bd. Rudgate Neighborhood Assocs., Bloomfield Hills, Mich. 1996-98; mem. physician leadership coun. Detroit Med. Ctr., 1996-2000; participant Ind. Malpractice Rev. Panels, 1981-85; chief med. officer Oakland County (Mich.) Sheriff's Dept., 1997-2000, tactical med. officer Spl. Response Team (SWAT), 1997-2000. Author: (with others) Respiratory Care of the Neurosurgical Patient, 1983, Septic Shock in Critical Care Clinics, 1988; established adminstrv. core curriculum for intensivists Critical Care Clinics, 1993; contbr. abstracts and articles to profl. jours. Med. advisor to Ind. Coun. Emergency Response Teams, 1980-85, mem. Ind. Symphonic Choir, 1970-84, trustee, 1983-84; hon. dep. sheriff Marion County Sheriff's Dept., 1982-84; bd. dirs. City of Bloomfield Hills, Mich., Rudgate Neighborhood Assn., 1996-98. With U.S. Army, 1964-67, Vietnam. Fellow ACP, Am. Coll. Chest Physicians; mem. AMA, Soc. Critical Care Medicine, Am. Coll. Physician Execs., Wayne County Med. Soc. (elected del. 1990-91), Phi Beta Kappa. Avocations: music, shortwave radio communications, sailing, astronomy, astrophotography. Home: 5421 Ashley Pkwy Sarasota FL 34241

IVERSON, THOMAS EDWIN, retired academic administrator, mathematician, educator; b. Hamilton, Mont., June 4, 1938; s. Andrew Ivar and Helen Ruth (Wagar) I.; m. Doris Diane Douglass, June 12, 1960; children: Paul, Philip, Mark. BA, Westmont Coll., 1960; MA, Wash. U., 1964; PhD, Claremont Graduate Sch., 1975. Math. instr. Pitzer Coll., Claremont, Calif., 1970-74; asst. prof. math. Seattle Pacific U., 1974-76; interim dean Ctrl. Coll., Pella, Iowa, 1993-94, prof. math. and computer sci., 1976—2002, interim pres., 1997-98, provost, sr. v.p., 1998—2002; ret., 2002. Vis. prof. math. and computer sci. Moi U., Kenya, East Africa, 1988-89. Bd. dirs. Pella Cmty. Found., 1998—, On with Life, Ankeny, Iowa, 2000—. Republican. Mem. Reformed Ch. Am. Avocation: ranch in montana. Office: Ctrl Coll 812 University Pella IA 50219 E-mail: iversont@central.edu.

IVERSON, THOMAS JOHN, economist, educator; b. Sioux Falls, S.D., Nov. 1, 1951; s. Robert Welton and Joan Elizabeth Iverson; 1 child, Sarah Whitaker. PhD, U. Tex., Austin, 1980. Assoc. prof. econs. Ky. State U., Frankfort, 1980—88; prof. econs. U. Guam, Mangilao, 1988—. CEO Tom Iverson & Assocs., Mangilao, 1988—. Contbr. articles and book revs. to profl. jours. Home: Box 5209 Mangilao GU 96923 Office: Marc 303 Univ Dr Mangilao GU 96923 Personal E-mail: tiverson@uog9.uog.edu.

IVERSON, WAYNE DAHL, landscape architect, consultant; b. Mt. Horeb, Wis., Oct. 27, 1931; s. Inman Oliver and Anna Mathilda (Dahl) I.; m. Barbara Ruth Lusk, May 17, 1958; children: David, Ann, Caroline. BS, U. Wis., 1955, MS, 1956. Landscape architect Nat. Pk. Svc., San Francisco, 1956-58, Inyo Nat. Forest, Bishop, Calif., 1958-66; regional landscape architect, So. region U.S. Forest Svc., Atlanta, 1966-67, Calif. region, 1967-86; prin. Scenic Resource Mgmt., Sedona, Ariz., 1987—. Author: (handbook) National Forest Landscape Management, (with others) Landscape Assessment, 1975, (with others) Ameri-

can Landscape Architecture, 1989. Mem. bd. adjustment City of Sedona, 1989; mem. pks. and recreation com. Coconino County, Flagstaff, Ariz., 1989-97; bd. dirs. Keep Sedona Beautiful, Inc., 1988-97. Cpl. U.S. Army, 1952-54, Korea. Recipient 1st Alumni award Landscape Architecture dept., U. Wis., Madison, 1981, Award of Excellence, Nat. Soc. for Pk. Resources, 1982, Presdl. Design award Nat. Endowment for Arts, 1984, 1st Arthur Hawthorne Carhart award U.S. Forest Svc., 1992. Fellow Am. Soc. Landscape Architects. Avocations: hiking, travel, photography, nature study, genealogy. E-mail: wiversrm@sedona.net.

IVES, EDWARD DAWSON, folklore educator; b. White Plains, N.Y., Sept. 4, 1925; s. Warren Livingston and Millicent Clarissa (Dawson) I.; m. Barbara Ann Herrel, Sept. 8, 1951; children— Stephen John, Nathaniel Edward, Sarah Ruth AB, Hamilton Coll., 1948; MA, Columbia U., 1950; PhD, Ind. U., 1962; LLD, U. P.E.I., 1986; DLitt, Meml. U., Newfoundland, 1996. Instr. English Ill. Coll., Jacksonville, 1950-53; lectr. CCNY, 1953-54; instr. English U. Maine, Orono, 1955-62, asst. prof., 1962-64, assoc. prof., 1964-69, prof. folklore, 1969-99, chmn. anthropology dept., 1983-89; dir. Northeast Archives Folklore and Oral History, 1971-99, Maine Folklife Ctr., 1992-99, emeritus, 1999—. Author: Larry Gorman: The Man Who Made the Songs, 1964, reprinted 1993, Lawrence Doyle: The Farmer-Poet of Prince Edward Island, 1971, Joe Scott: The Woodsman-Songmaker, 1978, The Tape Recorded Interview, 1980, reprinted 1995, George Magoon and the Down East Game War, 1988, reprinted 1993, Folksongs of New Brunswick, 1989; (with Bruce Jackson) The World Observed, 1996, The Bonny Earl of Murray, 1997, Drive Dull Care Away, 1999. Served with USMC, 1943-46 Guggenheim fellow, 1965—66. Fellow Am. Folklore Soc.; mem. Oral History Assn. Home: 1392 River Rd Bucksport ME 04416-9708 E-mail: sandy.ives@umit.maine.edu.

IVES, J. ATWOOD, financial executive; b. Atlanta, May 1, 1936; s. Stephen Bradshaw and Ellen (Atwood) I.; m. Elizabeth Saalfield; children: Ian, Anna, Benjamin. BA in Econs., Yale U., 1959; MBA, Stanford U., 1961; AMP, Harvard U., 1975. CPA, Calif. Acct. Price, Waterhouse & Co., San Francisco, 1961-64; fin. analyst Textron, Inc., Providence, 1964-66; ptnr., v.p. Paine Webber Jackson & Curtis, 1966-74; dir. Gen. Cinema Corp., Chestnut Hill, Mass., 1970-92, sr. v.p. fin., CFO, 1974-83, exec. v.p., CFO, 1983-84, vice-chmn., CFO, 1985-91, mem. office of chmn., 1983-91; vice-chmn., CFO The Neiman Marcus Group, Inc., 1987-91, also bd. dirs.; chmn., CEO Eastern Enterprises, 1991-2000. Trustee Ea. Enterprises, Weston, Mass., 1989-2000; dir. or trustee of 136 mut. funds advised by Mass. Fin. Svcs. Co., 1992—; corp. adv. bd. Carroll Sch. of Mgmt., Boston Coll.; bd. dirs. KeySpan Corp. Trustee Mus. Fine Arts, Boston; bd. dirs. United Way of Mass. Bay; mem. bd. overseers WGBH Edn. Found.; pres. Becon Hill Village. With U.S. Army, 1961-62. Recipient award Haskins and Sells Found., 1961 Home: 17 W Cedar St Boston MA 02108-1211

IVES, JOHN MILTON, retired engineer; b. Bayonne, N.J., Mar. 26, 1943; s. John Milton and Mary J. (Sharkey) I.; m. Dorothy Mae Davis, Nov. 27, 1971; children: RoseMae, Michael John. BS in Engring., Ariz. State U., 1969; MS, U. So. Calif., 1980. Enlisted USAF, 1964, commd. 2nd lt., 1969; advanced through grades to capt. USAFR, 1978, advanced through grade to maj., 1983; electronics engr. weapons lab. USAF, Albuquerque, 1969-73, software engr. Rome (N.Y.) Air Devel. Ctr., 1973-78, computer systems analyst weapons lab., 1978-87, gen. engr. Space Tech. Ctr., 1987—91, ret., 1991. Part-time instr. Albuquerque Tech. Vocat. Inst. (T-VI), 1991—; contract worker, 1991—95; sys. analyst dept. labor State N.Mex., 1995—. Contbr. articles to profl. jours. Leader Boy Scouts Am., Rio Rancho, N.Mex., Cibola Little League, Rio Rancho, Sunset Little Legue, Rio Rancho; referee Rio Rancho Youth Soccer. Mem. IEEE. Lodges: KC. Roman Catholic. Avocations: bowling, guitar music, fishing. Home: 1660 Borealis Ave SE Rio Rancho NM 87124-2804

IVES, SAMUEL CLIFTON, minister; b. Farmington, Maine, Nov. 13, 1937; s. Alfred H. and Alice (Smith) I.; m. Jane Petherbridge, June 6, 1959; children: Bonnie, Stephen, Jonathan. BA, U. Maine, 1960; STB, Boston U., 1963, D of Ministry, 1983. Pastor Cape Elizabeth (Maine) United Meth. Ch., 1962-68, First United Meth. Ch., Bangor, Maine, 1968-73; dir. Maine Conf. Coun. on Ministries, Winthrop, Maine, 1973-77; sr. pastor Waterville (Maine) United Meth. Ch., 1977-86; dist. supt. So. Dist. United Meth. Ch., Portland, Maine, 1986-92; elected bishop United Meth. Ch., assigned to W.Va., Charleston, 1992—. Del. Gen. Conf. United Meth. Ch., 1972, 76, 80, 84, 88, 92; exec. com. Maine Coun. Chs., 1981-92; pres. Appalachian Devel. com., 1996-2000; v.p. W.Va. Coun. of Chs., 1996-2000. Mem. Gen. Bd. Discipleship United Meth. Ch., 1984-92, pres. Gen. Commn. on Religion and Race, 1996-2000; pres. Gen. Bd. Ch. and Soc., 2000—. Mem. Assn. Couples for Marriage Enrichment (cert. leader and trainer 1979—). Mem. United Methodist Ch. Home: 1804 Shadybrook Rd Charleston WV 25314-2268 E-mail: wvarea@aol.com.

IVES, STEPHEN BRADSHAW, JR., retired lawyer; b. N.Y.C., Oct. 6, 1924; AB, Harvard U., 1948; LLB, Yale U., 1951. Bar: R.I. 1952, D.C. 1970, U.S. Supreme Ct. 1960. Assoc. Hinckley, Allen, Salisbury & Parsons, Providence, 1952-57, ptnr., 1957-61; exec. asst. to adminstr. AID, Washington, 1961-62, dir. Office Korea Affairs, 1962-64, dir. Office East Asian Affairs, 1964-66, assoc. asst. adminstr. Far East, 1966-67, dept. asst. adminstr. East Asia, 1967-68, gen. counsel, 1968-70; ptnr. Wald, Harkrader and Ross, Washington, 1970-87; of counsel Pepper, Hamilton & Scheetz, 1987-95. Mem. R.I. Mechanics Lien Law Commn., R.I. Commn. Interstate Coop. Bd. dirs. Providence Community Fund, Children's Friend and Svc. R.I.; mem. U.S. del. U.S.-USSR Comml. Commn., 1975; dir. Bus. Coun. S.E. Europe, 1977-95, vice. chmn. 1991-95. Mem. ABA, D.C. Bar Assn. (chmn. div. internat. law and transactions 1976-77), R.I. Bar Assn. (past mem. exec. com.), Washington Fgn. Law Soc. (past pres.), Am. Soc. Internat. Law, Am. Arbitration Assn. (panel), Order of Coif, Phi Beta Kappa. Home: 3508 Macomb St NW Washington DC 20016-3162

IVESTER, JOY GODSHALL, educational administrator; b. Greenville, S.C., Dec. 1, 1972; d. Wayne Coleman and Jessie Ella (Jones) G. BA cum laude, Clemson U., 1995; MEd, Vanderbilt U., 1996. Cert. tchr. mild, moderate, severe, profound, educable mental, and trainable mental disabilities, S.C. Rsch. asst., grad. asst. Vanderbilt U., Nashville, 1995-96; tchr., employment specialist Greenville H.S., 1996-97; regional transition coord. S.C. Sys. Change Grant, Columbia, 1997; project coord. S.C. Transition System Change Grant, 1998—2003, S.C. and La. Cmty. Devel. Project, 2002—; program coord. U. SC Ctr. for Disabilities Resources. Mem. alternative diploma devel. bd., alternative assessment com. S.C. Dept. Edn.; mem. Peabody Coll. curriculum com. Vanderbilt U., Nashville, 1996—97; mem. Davidson county transition com., 1996—97; mem. S.C. transition adv. bd. State S.C., Columbia, 1997—, bd. mem. S.E. regional rep., internat. divsn. on career devel. and transition nominations com.; mem. Greenville Transp. Coalition, 2002—. Contbr. articles to profl. jours. Mem. Abbeville Recreation Coalition. Profl. scholar Vanderbilt U., Nashville, 1995-96. Mem. Coun. for Exceptional Children, Divsn. on Mental Retardation and Developmental Disabilities, Divsn. on Career Devel. and Transition. Episcopalian. Avocations: cooking, exercising, tennis, reading. Office: U of SC Sch of Medicine CDR Columbia SC 29208-0001 E-mail: ivesterj@cdd.sc.edu.

IVESTER, MELVIN DOUGLAS, retired beverage company executive; b. New Holland, Ga., Mar. 26, 1947; s. Howard Edward and Ada Mae (Pass) Ivester; m. Victoria Kay Grindle, Mar. 20, 1969. BBA cum laude, U. Ga., 1969. Acct. Ernst & Ernst, Atlanta, 1969—75; mgr. Ernst & Whinney, Atlanta, 1975—79; asst. contr., dir. corp. auditing The Coca-Cola Co., Atlanta, 1979—91, v.p., contr., 1981—83, sr. v.p. fin., 1983—84, sr. v.p., CFO, 1985—89; pres. European Cmty. Group, 1980—90, Coca-Cola USA, 1990—91, Coca-Cola N.Am. Group, 1991—93, prin. oper. officer, 1993—94, pres., COO, 1994—97, also bd. dirs., chmn., CEO, 1997—2000, ret., 2000; pres. Deer Run Investments LLC, 2001—. Bd. dirs. Georgia Pacific Corp., Sun Trust, Inc., S One Corp.; trustee, dir. U. Ga. Found.

IVEY, ELIZABETH S. retired physicist, educator; b. Schenectady, N.Y., Apr. 21, 1935; married, 1957 (div.), remarried, 1982; 5 children. BS in Physics, Simmons Coll., 1957; MA in Teaching, Harvard U., 1959; PhD in Mech. Engring. Acoustics, U. Mass., 1976. Prof. physics Simmons Coll., 1958-59, Bucknell U., 1960-63, Colo. State U., Ft. Collins, 1964-68, assoc. dean faculty, 1982-85, Louise Wolff Kahn prof., from 1985; prof. physics Smith Coll., 1969-90, chmn. dept. physics, 1983-90; provost Macalester Coll., St. Paul, 1990-95, U. Hartford, West Hartford, Conn., 1995-2000, provost emerita, 2000—. Vis. prof. Yale U., 1982. Bd. dirs. Minn. Inst. Talented Youth, 1990-95, World Press Inst., 1990-93, St. Paul Area United Way, 1990-95, Assn. Women Sci., 2001—; bd. trustees Hartford Coll. Women, 1995—, Mitchell Coll. 2003-; corporator Simmons Coll., 2000—. Recipient Woman Engr. award Soc. Women Engrs., 1988. Fellow AAAS; mem. Acoustical Soc. Am., Am. Assn. Physics Tchrs., Assn. Women in Sci. (pres.-elect 2003-04, pres. 2004—). Home: 25 High Wood Rd Bloomfield CT 06002 E-mail: ivey@hartford.edu.

IVEY, JAMES FREDERICK, JR., physician, health facility administrator; b. Orlando, Fla., Apr. 30, 1939; s. James Frederick and Naomi Nell (Milner) I.; m. Nancy Joan Martin, Aug. 5, 1961; children: Mary Nell, James Thomas, John Mark, Samuel Service, Daniel Dominic. BS in Biology, Duke U., U. Fla., 1960; MD, Emory U., 1964. Diplomate Am. Bd. Family Practice with cert. of added qualifications in geriatrics; FAA sr. aeromed. examiner. Intern Duval Med. Ctr., Jacksonville, Fla., 1964-65; resident Emory U./VA Hosps., Atlanta, 1965-66; physician Clermont, Fla., 1968-69; pvt. practice Palmer, Alaska, 1969-74; owner, physician Valley Med. Ctr., Inc., Palmer, 1974-91; staff physician Lakeside Med. Ctr. & Family Care, Lakeland, Fla., 1991-92; pvt. practice Lakeland, 1992-95; staff physician Polk Gen. Hosp., Bartow, Fla., 1995-96, Family First Med. Ctrs., Gainesville, Fla., 1996; med. dir. Trenton Med. Ctr., Fla., 1996—2001; physician for jails. Gilchrist, Levy and Dixie counties, 2001—; physician Alachua County Regional Juvenile Detention Ctr., 2001—03, Marion County Regional Juvenile Detention Ctr., 2001—03. Med. dir. Palmer (Alaska) Pioneer Home, 1979—91, Nugens' Ranch, Wasilla, Alaska, 1983—91, Starting Point, Inc., Wasilla, 1989—91, Arbors at Lakeland Nursing Home, 1992—96; courtesy clin. asst. prof. dept. cmty. health and family medicine U. Fla. Sch. Medicine. Former med. dir., co-founder Mat-Su Coun. Prevention of Alcoholism and Drug Abuse, Wasilla, Alaska, past chmn. bd. dirs.; elder and lay preacher United Presbyn. Ch., USA; mem. Trinity United Meth. Ch. Capt. USAF, 1966—68. Mem. Am. Acad. Family Physicians (pres. Alaska chpt. 1976), Christian Med. and Dental Soc., Alpha Tau Omega, Phi Kappa Phi, Phi Chi. Republican. Avocations: golf, music, cosmology, history, philosophy. Home: 6120 NW 35th Terr Gainesville FL 32653 Office: Trenton Med Ctr Inc PO Box 640 911 S Main St Trenton FL 32693-3239

IVEY, JOHN KEMMERER, lawyer; b. Ft. Worth, Aug. 31, 1961; s. Jack Lyndon Ivey and Catherine (Kemmerer) Harward; m. Kristy; children: Cameron, Alex. BBA in Fin., U. Tex., 1983, JD, 1985; grad., Nat. Inst. Trial Advocacy, 1989, Spence Trial Lawyer Coll., 1998. Bar: Tex. 1986, U.S. Dist. Ct. (no. dist.) Tex. 1986, U.S. Dist. Ct. (ea. dist.) Tex. 1988, U.S. Dist. Ct. (so. and we. dists.) Tex. 1989, U.S. Dist. Ct. (ea. dist.) Ark. 1987, U.S. Dist. Ct. Minn. 1990, U.S. Ct. Appeals (5th and 11th cirs.) 1987, Bd. Cert. Personal Inj. Trial Law Tex. Bd. Legal Specialization (1994), Coll. of The State Bar of Tex., 1995—. With Kraft & Assocs. PC, 1999—. Dir. and lectr. seminars Video Software Dealer's Assn., 1990, 91. Contbr. articles to profl. jours. Mem. State Bar Tex., ATLA, Tex. Trial Lawyers Assn., Dallas Trial Lawyers Assn. (Atticus Finch award 2001), Christ Epis. Ch., Plano, Tex. Home: 4125 Westmoreland Dr Plano TX 75093-3868 Office: 2777 N Stemmons Fwy Dallas TX 75207-2277 E-mail: jkivey@kraftlaw.com.

IVEY, MICHAEL WAYNE, mortgage broker; b. Albany, Ga., Nov. 27, 1964; s. Samuel Warlick and Barbara Ann (Norton) I. BBA, U. Ga., 1986. Cert. mortgage broker. Mortgage broker First So. Mortgage, Atlanta, 1986-87, Fed. Savs. Bank, Atlanta, 1987-88, Paragon Mortgage Corp., Atlanta, 1988-94; regional v.p. Mortgage.com, Atlanta, 1994-97; CEO, pres., cert. mortgage broker Capital City Mortgage Corp., Atlanta, 1997—. Bd. dirs. Powers Ridge Office Park, 1998—, Govs. Ridge Office Park, 2003—, Marietta Tree Keepers, 2003—; pres. bd. dirs. Ctr. for Children and Young Adults, 2003—, chmn., 2003. Mem. Cobb C. of C. (Leadership Cobb Class 1996-97, Ernest Barrett award, Hon. Comdrs. 1998), Marietta Kiwanis. Methodist. Home: 4682 Dudley Ln NW Atlanta GA 30327-3331 Office: Capital City Mortgage Corp Bldg 7 Ste 200 1827 Powers Ferry Rd NW Atlanta GA 30339-5621

IVEY, STEPHEN DAVID, lawyer; b. Glen Ridge, N.J., Jan. 15, 1953; s. Henry Franklin and Sylvia (Berg) I. BA in History, Polit. Sci., Pa. State U., 1975; JD, Georgetown U., 1978. Bar: Pa. 1978, U.S. Dist. Ct. (ea. dist.) Pa. 1979, U.S. Ct. Appeals (3d cir.) 1979, U.S. Supreme Ct. 1982, U.S. Ct. Appeals (fed. cir.) 1984. Law clk. to judge Supreme Ct. Pa., Phila., 1978-81; pvt. practice Phila., 1981—. Office: 325 S 16th St Philadelphia PA 19102-4936

IVEY, TOM DEXTER, cardiac surgeon; b. Dodgeville, Wis., May 22, 1945; m. Marianne Ivey; children: Bert, Brook. BS, U. Wis., 1967, postgrad., 1967-68, MD with honors, 1970. Acting instr. surgery U. Wash. Sch. Medicine, Seattle, 1975-77, asst. prof. divsn. cardiothoracic surgery, 1977-81, assoc. prof. dept. surgery, 1982-87, chief divsn. cardiothoracic surgery, 1982-88, prof. divsn. cardiothoracic surgery, 1987; prof. surgery U. Cin., 1988—. Attending in cardiac surgery Univ. Hosp.-Harborview and Children's Hosp., Seattle, 1977-88; chief divsn. thoracic and cardiovasc. surgery U. Cin. Hosp., 1988—; trustee Assoc. Univ Physicians, Seattle, 1985. Contbr. chpts. to books. Served with USPHS, 1971-75. Mem. Alpha Omega Alpha, Phi Eta Sigma, Phi Kappa Phi. Office: 2123 Auburn Ave Ste 238 Cincinnati OH 45219-2906

IVEY, WILLIAM HAMILTON, communications consultant; b. Newport News, Va., July 11, 1951; s. Henry Reese and Margaret Vaughan (Farmer) I.; m. Frances Katrina Parks, May 14, 1977; children: Jennifer Elizabeth, Martha Katrina. BA in Comms., U. Ctrl. Fla., 1973. Prodn. mgr. Internal Comms. Sys., Atlanta, 1974-77, v.p., 1977-79; pres. Bill Ivey & Co., Atlanta, 1979—. Mem. exec. bd. Ministries United for Svc. and Tng., Inc., Marietta, Ga., 1996—. Episcopalian. Home and Office: 3281 Turtle Lake Dr Marietta GA 30067-5020

IVEZAJ, VIKTOR N. auditor, consultant; b. Weissenburg, Germany, Jan. 24, 1972; came to U.S., 1973; s. Nikolla and Pashka Ivezaj. BA, Oakland U., 1994; MA, U. Detroit-Mercy, 1998; postgrad., Wayne State U., 1999—. Jud. clk. Wayne County Cir. Ct., Detroit, 1993; dir. cmty. svc. Oakland County Cir. Ct., Pontiac, Mich., 1993-94; law clk. Driggers Schultz & Herbst, P.C., Troy, Mich., 1994-97, Kupelian Ormond & Magy, P.C., Southfield, Mich., 1997-99; recruiter U.S. Dept. Commerce, Sterling Heights, Mich., 1998-99; cons., auditor Perry Johnson, Inc., Southfield, 1999—2002; adj. prof. polit. sci. Baker Coll., Clinton Twp., Mich., 2003—. Lectr., mem. Inter-Univ. Ctr., Dubrovnik, Croatia, 2000-01. Mem. internat. editl. bd. Internat. Jour. Albanian Studies, 1998. Mem.: Am. Polit. Sci. Assn., Acad. Polit. Sci., Automotive Industry Action Group, Phi Beta Delta. Democrat. Roman Catholic. Avocations: collecting literature novels, wine collecting, physical fitness, tutoring in civic literacy. E-mail: vivezaj@pji.com.

IVIE, EVAN LEON, computer science educator; b. May 15, 1931; s. Horace Leon and Ruth (Ashby) Ivie; m. Betty Jo Beck, Mar. 29, 1957; children: Dynette, Mark, Joseph, Robert, Ann, Rebecca, John, James, Mette, Emily, Peter. BS, BES, Brigham Young U., 1956; MS, Stanford U., 1957; PhD, MIT, 1966. Instr. MIT, Cambridge, 1960—66; mem. tech. staff Bell Labs., Murray Hill, NJ, 1966—79; prof. computer sci. Brigham Young U., Provo, Utah, 1979—; pres. Ivie Computer Corp., Provo, 1979—; dir. Joseph Smith Acad., Nauvoo, Ill., 2003—. Expert witness on computers for 12 lawsuits, 1983—; instr., dir. Joseph Smith Acad., Ill., 2002—. Leader Boy Scouts Am., 1954—83; mem. Warren Sch. Bd., NJ, 1975—78; developer Pioneer Ancestral Past, Utah Sesquicentennial, 1997. 1st lt. USAF, 1957—60. Recipient Fulbright scholarship, Kiev Poly. Inst., Ukraine, 1992—93; fellow, Stanford U., 1956—57. Mem.: IEEE (sr.), Assn. Computing Machinery. Republican. Mem. Lds Ch. Achievements include invention of Data Base Computers, 1972; Programmer's Workbench, 1975; Electronic Yellow pages, 1978; Reader's Workbench, 1984. Home: 1131 Dover Dr Provo UT 84604-5255 Office: Brigham Young U Provo UT 84602 also: 145 Wells St Rm 30 Nauvoo IL 62354 E-mail: evan@cs.byu.edu., evan@ivies.org.

IVINS, MARCIA S. astronaut; b. Balt., Apr. 15, 1951; d. Joseph L. Ivins. BS in Aerospace Engring., U. Colo., 1973. Lic. pilot. Engr. NASA Johnson Space Ctr., Houston, 1974—80; flight engr. Shuttle Tng., Aircraft, Aircraft Ops., Houston, 1980—; co-pilot NASA Adminstrv. Aircraft, Houston, 1980—. Mem. Exptl. Aircraft Assn., 99's, Internat. Aerobatic Club. Achievements include over 6000 flight hours in civilian and NASA aaircraft, 5 space missions, 1, 318 hours in space. Avocations: flying, reading, baking. Office: Astronauts Office NASA Johnson Space Ctr Houston TX 77058

IVORY, BENNIE, editor; b. Hot Springs, Ark., June 19, 1951; Mng. editor Clarion-Ledger, Miss., 1989—93; exec. editor Florida Today, 1993—95, The News Journal, Del., 1995—97; exec. editor, v.p. news group The Courier-Journal, Louisville, 1997—. Office: The Courier Journal 525 W Broadway Louisville KY 40202-2137 Mailing: Courier Journal PO Box 740031 Louisville KY 40201-7431*

IVORY, JAMES FRANCIS, film director; b. Berkeley, Calif., June 7, 1928; s. Edward Patrick and Hallie Millicent (DeLoney) Ivory. BFA, U. Oreg., 1951; MA in Cinema, U. So. Calif., 1957. Ptnr. Merchant-Ivory Prodns., N.Y.C., 1963—. Dir.(films): Venice: Theme and Variations, 1957, The Sword and the Flute, 1959, The Householder, 1963, The Delhi Way, 1964, Shakespeare Wallah, 1965, The Guru, 1969, Bombay Talkie, 1970, Adventures of a Brown Man in Search of Civilization, 1971, Savages, 1972, Autobiography of a Princess, 1975, The Wild Party, 1975, Roseland, 1977, Hullabaloo over Georgie and Bonnie's Pictures, 1978, The Europeans, 1979, The Five Forty Eight, 1979, Jane Austen in Manhattan, 1980, Quartet, 1981, Heat and Dust, 1983, The Bostonians, 1984, A Room with a View, 1986 (Acad. Award nominee for best dir.), Maurice, 1987 (Silver Lion shared award with Ermanno Olmi for best dir. Venice Film Festival 1987), Slaves of New York, 1989, Mr. and Mrs. Bridge, 1990, Howards End, 1992 (Acad. Award nominee for best dir., Cannes Internat. Film Festival 45th Anniversary Prize), The Remains of the Day, 1993 (Academy award nominee, Best dir. 1993), Jefferson in Paris, 1995, Surviving Picasso, 1996, A Soldier's Daughter Never Cries, 1998, The Golden Bowl, 2000, (sets and costumes) Handel's Apollo e Dafne Maggio Musicale, Florence, 1997; contbr. articles to profl. jours.; dir.:. Cpl. U.S. Army, 1953—55. Recipient Comdr. des Arts et Lettres (France), 1996, 1996; Guggenheim fellow, 1973. Mem.: Dirs. Guild Am. (D.W. Griffith award 1995). Democrat. Roman Catholic. Office: Merchant-Ivory Prodns 250 W 57th St Ste 1824/5 New York NY 10107-1913 E-mail: contact@merchantivory.com.

IVORY, MING MARIE, political scientist; b. Tokyo, Aug. 28, 1949; d. T. Austin and E. Virginia (Christine) I. BS, Tufts U., 1971; MA, U. Pa., 1973; PhD, MIT, 1986. Rsch. asst. Smithsonian Inst., Washington, summer 1970, 71; faculty assoc. Hampshire Coll., Amherst, Mass., 1973-75; profl. asst. NSF, Washington, 1975; sci. reporter Sta. WVHY-FM, Phila., 1976; profl. asst. Office of Sci. Advisor World Bank, Washington, 1977; cons. Internat. Sci. & Tech. Inst., Washington, 1978-79; sci. policy specialist U.S. Agy. for Internat. Devel., Washington, 1979-80, environ. protection specialist, 1980-85; asst. prof. Creighton U., Omaha, 1986-92. Vis. asst. prof. Madison Inst. James Madison U., Harrisonburg, Va., 1992-95; assoc. prof. Coll. Integrated Sci. and Tech., 1995—; coord. policy and stds. Commonwealth Info. Security Ctr., 2001-; cons. Bd. on Sci. and Tech. for Internat. Devel. NRC, 1992, Carnegie Corp., 1996. Del. Mass. Govs. Conf. on Librs. and Info. Svcs., 1978; elected del. White House Conf. on Librs. and Info. Svcs., 1979. Mem. Am. Polit. Sci. Assn., Soc. for Internat. Devel., Soc. for Social Studies of Sci. Democrat. Unitarian Universalist. Avocations: graphic arts, hiking. Home: 3155 Flint Ave Harrisonburg VA 22801-4732 Office: James Madison U Coll Integrated Sci & Tech Harrisonburg VA 22807-0001 E-mail: ivorymx@jmu.edu.

IVORY, PATRICK J. physician assistant; b. Bklyn., Dec. 29, 1950; s. Peter Francis Ivory and Margaret Mary Fitzgerald; m. Mary Kay Dennis, Oct. 2, 1971 (div. Aug. 1984); children: Craig, Brandon; m. Teresa Ann Dunn, Jan. 3, 1985; children: Sean, Amanda. Certificate, George Washington U., 1981, BS, 1983; MPAS, U. Nebr., 1998. Cert. physician asst. Hosp. corpsman, physician asst. USN, 1968-90, ret., 1990; physician asst. Emergency Physicians Inc., Jacksonville, Fla., 1990-93, Nittany Valley Rehab. Hosp., Pleasant Gap, Pa., 1993-94, Pa. State Geisinger Health Sys., Philipsburg, 1994—2002, mid level provider coord. western region, 1996—2002; asst. prof. physician asst. program Lock Haven (Pa.) U., 2002—. Adv. bd. P.A. program Phila. Coll. Osteo. Medicine, 1998—; instr. Loch Haven (Pa.) U., 1997—, Pa. Coll. Tech., Williamsport, 1997—; lectr. George Washington U., Washington, 1984—. Fellow Am. Acad. Physician Assts. (bd. dirs. 1981-90), Naval Assn. Physician Assts.; mem. Pa. Soc. Physician Assts. (bd. dirs., pres. 2003—), Vets. Caucus (bd. dirs. 1998-2000). Republican. Roman Catholic. Avocations: camping, auto repair, computers. Home: 33 Fay Circle Port Matilda PA 16870 Office: Lock Haven U Lock Haven PA 17745 E-mail: pivory@lhup.edu.

IVRY, ALFRED LYON, history of Jewish and Islamic philosophy educator; b. Bklyn., Jan. 14, 1935; s. Morris and Belle (Malamud) I.; m. Joann Saltzman, June 15, 1958; children: Rebecca, Jonathan, Sara Beth, Jessica. BA, Bklyn. Coll., 1957; MA, Brandeis U., 1958, PhD, 1963; D.Phil., Oxford (Eng.) U., 1971. From asst. prof. to assoc. prof. Cornell U., Ithaca, N.Y., 1967-74; prof. Ohio State U., Columbus, 1974-76; prof. Sch. Near Eastern and Judaic Studies Brandeis U., Waltham, Mass., 1976-89, Walter S. Hilborn prof. Mid. Eastern Studies, 1977-89; Skirball prof. Hebrew and Judaic studies NYU, N.Y.C., 1989—, prof. Mid. East studies, 1989—. Co-chmn. Colloquium in Medieval Philosophy, Boston, 1977-81, 84-89; chmn. Colloquium in Medieval Philosophy NYU, 1990-2000; dir. NYU Medieval and Renaissance Ctr., 2002—. Mem. editl. bd. Univ. Press of New Eng., 1982, 84, 86; editor: (translator) Al-Kindi's Metaphysics, 1974, Moses of Narbonne: Perfection of the Soul, 1977, Alexander Altmann: The Meaning of Jewish Existence, 1991, Averroes' Middle Commentary on Aristotles De anima, 1994, English-Arabic edit., 2002. Trustee Boston Hebrew Coll., 1981-87, adj. prof., 1983-90. Fulbright fellow, 1963-65, 72, 1982-83; grantee NEH, 1978-79, 80-81 Fellow Am. Oriental Soc., Am. Philos. Assn., Assn. for Jewish Studies (bd. dirs. 1971-74), Medieval Acad. Am., Soc. Medieval and Renaissance Philosophy (bd. dirs. 1985-90, v.p. 1993-94, pres. 1995-96), Am. Acad. for Jewish Rsch. (bd. dirs. 1989-2000). Jewish.

IVRY, DAVID, diplomat; b. Gedera, Israel, 1934; m. Ofra Ivry; three children. BS in Aero. Engring., Technion U., 1977. Chief rep. U.S.-Israel Strategic Dialogue, 1986-88; dir.-gen. Ministry Def., 1986-96; prin. asst. Min. Def. for Strategic Affairs, 1996-99; nat. security advisor, head Nat. Security Coun., 1999-2000; Israel's amb. to U.S. Washington, 2000—02. Head Inter-Ministerial Steering Com. on Arms Control, 1986-96; lead Israel's del. Multilateral Working Group on Arms Control and Regional Security, 1986-96. Bd. dirs. El-Al, 1978-82, Israel Aircraft Industries, 1982-92; bd. govs. Technion U., Haifa, 1987—. Maj. gen., comdr. Israel Air Force, 1977-82. Decorated Legion of Merit, USAF; recipient Disting. Svc. Order award Govt. Singapore, Amitai Distinction award for ethical adminstrn. and conduct State of Israel. Office: Embassy of Israel 3514 International Dr NW Washington DC 20008-3099 Fax: 202-364-5423. E-mail: ask@israelemb.org.

IVY, BENJAMIN FRANKLIN, III, financial and real estate investment advisor; b. Bremerton, Wash., May 18, 1936; s. Edward Byron Ivy and Ada Josephine (Anderson) Steele; m. Karen Yvonne Thompson, July 14, 1961 (div. June 1979); children: Britt Annemarie Ivy, Zenah Blair; m. Emily Cecile Rawlins, Apr. 18, 1982 (div. June 1992); m. Catherine Elaine Bracken, May 23, 2000. BME, Cornell U., 1959; MBA, Stanford U., 1961. CFP. Purchasing agent U. Calif., Berkeley, 1960-62; contract adminstr. Lockheed Missiles and Space div., Sunnyvale, Calif., 1962-64; asst. to pres. Tridea subsidiary McDonnell Douglas, Pasadena, Calif., 1964-68; v.p. Mitchum, Jones & Templeton, Inc., Palo Alto, Calif., 1968-74, Paine Webber, Palo Alto, 1974; pres. Morgan Investment Svcs., Inc., Palo Alto, 1974-84; v.p. Morgan, Olmstead, Kennedy & Gardner, Inc., 1974-84; pres., chmn. Ivy Fin. Enterprises, Inc., Palo Alto, 1984—; pres. Ivy Fin. Svcs., Palo Alto. V.p. and registered prin. Assoc. Group, Inc. subs. Pacific Life, L.A., 1984—, dir., 1994-98, Cert. Fin. Planner, 1989—. Founder, former dir. Found. to Eliminate the Nat. Debt, Palo Alto, 1992. Mem. Internat. Assn. Fin. Planners (charter, bd. dirs. 1972-73), Pacific Exch. (assoc.), Cornell U. Alumni Assn., Stanford Alumni Assn. (life), Stanford Bus. Sch. Alumni Assn. (life), Sharon Heights Golf and Country Club, Masons, Elks, Kappa Sigma. Avocations: golf, tennis, poetry, opera, international travel. Office: Ivy Fin Enterprises Inc 525 University Ave Fl 6 Palo Alto CA 94301-1903 E-mail: ifsinc@aol.com.

IVY, BERRYNELL BAKER, critical care nurse; b. Shreveport, La., June 24, 1954; d. Berry William and Zilphia Margaret (Nix) Baker; m. Kenneth James Ivy, Sr.,Apr. 17, 1988. ADN, Northwestern State U., 1981. RN, La., Tex., Nev.; cert. BLS, ACLS; cert. CCRN. Charge nurse Doctors Hosp., Shreveport, La., 1982-85; staff nurse ICU Schumpert Med. Ctr., Shreveport, La., 1985-88, Bayshore Med. Ctr., Pasadena, Tex., 1988-89, asst. head nurse ICU, 1989-92; staff nurse/charge nurse ICU Bossier Med. Ctr., Bossier City,

La., 1993-99, U. Tex. Med. Ctr., Galveston, 1999—2001; staff RN neuro-ICU Sunrise Med. Ctr., Las Vegas, 2001—. Mem. AACN, Nat. League Nurses, Am. Assn. Neurosci. Nurses, Soc. Critical Care Medicine. Avocations: raising boxers, sports, travel. Home: 900 Desert Inn Rd # 227 Las Vegas NV 89109 E-mail: ken-berrynell-ivy@msn.com.

IVY, CONWAY GAYLE, paint company executive; b. Houston, July 8, 1941; s. John Smith and Caro (Gayle) I.; m. Diane Ellen Cole, May 25, 1973; children: Brice McPherson, Elizabeth Cole. Student, U. Chgo., 1959-62, MBA, 1968; MA in Econs., 1972, postgrad., 1973-74; BS in Natural Scis., Shimer Coll., 1964; postgrad., U. Tex., 1964-65. Geol. asst. John S. Ivy, Houston, 1965-72; securities analyst Halsey Stuart & Co. and successor Bache & Co., Chgo., 1974-75; dir. corp. planning Gould Inc., Rolling Meadows, Ill., 1975-79; v.p. corp. planning and devel. Sherwin-Williams Co., Cleve., 1979-88; v.p., treas., 1989-92; v.p. corp. planning and devel., 1992—. Pres. Ivy Minerals Inc., Boise, Idaho, 1978—. Author numerous analytincal reports on brokerage industry. Trustee Michelson-Morley Centennial Celebration, 1987, Cleve. Inst. Music, 1983-94, treas., 1987-90, vice chmn., 1990-94. Mem. Am. Econs. Assn., Soc. Mining and Metallurgy and Exploration, am. Inst. Mining Engrs., Houston Club, Phi Gamma Delta. Republican. Office: 101 Prospect Ave NW Cleveland OH 44115-1093

IVY, EDWARD JOSEPH, plastic surgeon; b. Jan. 23, 1958; MD, Georgetown U., 1985. Diplomate Am. Bd. Surgery, Am. Bd. Plastic Surgery. Resident in surgery Mayo Clinic, Rochester, Minn., 1985-90, fellow in plastic surgery, 1990-92; fellow in aesthetic surgery Manhattan (N.Y.) Eye, Ear and Throat Hosp., 1992-93; pvt. practice plastic surgery San Francisco, 1993—98; entrepreneur, 1999—. Office: 450 Ferguson Dr Mountain View CA 94043

IVY, JACQUELINE M. interior architect; b. Summit, N.J., May 9, 1970; d. Edward Lee and Alice Mearns Ivy. BS in Arch., U. Va., Charlottesville, 1993; MS in Environ. Design and Arch., Yale U., New Haven, Conn., 1999. Intern coord. Peggy Guggenheim Collection, Venice, Italy, 1993—94; dir. pub. programs Josef & Anni Albers Found., Bethany, Conn., 1995—2002; design facilitator Anthropologie/Urban Outfitters, Phila., 2002—. Advisor Alliance for Arch., New Haven, 1996—2002; bd. dirs. New Haven Preservation Trust, 1999—, Guilford Handcraft Ctr., Conn., 2000—. Contbr. articles to profl. jours. Everitt Meeks fellowship, Yale U., 1999. Mem.: Yale Club of N.Y.C. Home: 59 Grove Beach Rd South Westbrook CT 06498 Office: Anthropologie 235 S 17th St Philadelphia PA 19603 E-mail: jackieivy@aol.com.

IVY, JOHN L. medical educator, researcher; b. Portsmouth, Va., Dec. 26, 1946; BS in Phys. Edn., Old Dominion U., 1970; MA in Exercise Physiology, U. Md., 1974, PhD in Exercise Physiology, 1976. Tchr. phys. edn. and sci. Thomas Eaton Jr. H.S., Hampton, Va., 1970; biology and physiology tchr., asst. football coach, head golf coach Kecoughtan H.S., Hampton, Va., 1971—73; asst. prof. biokinetics rsch. lab. dept. phys. edn. Temple U., Phila., 1976—77; rsch. assoc. Human Performance Lab., Ball State U., Muncie, Ind., 1976—77; postdoctoral fellow dept. preventive medicine Washington U. Sch. Medicine, St. Louis, 1978—80; asst. prof. dept. phys. edn. Coll. Health and Sch. Medicine dept. pharmacology U. S.C., Columbia, 1980—82; asst. prof. dept. kinesiology and health edn. Coll. Edn. U. Tex., Austin, 1982—84, assoc. prof. dept. kinesiology and health edn. Coll. Edn., 1984—89, prof., dir. exercise scis. labs. dept. kinesiology and health edn. Coll. Edn. and divsn. pharmacology Coll. Pharmacy, 1989—, Margie Gurley Seay Centennial prof., 1998—, chmn. dept. kinesiology and health edn., 1999—. Cons. clin. diabetes and nutrition sect. NIH, Phoenix, 1985—87; cons. com. mil. nutrition rsch. U.S. Army, 1987—88; mem. adv. bd. performance team Women's Athletic Dept. U. Tex., 1988—94; cons. Sports and Cardiovasc. Nutritionists, 1989—92, outside mem. long range planning com., 1989—90; cons. Shaklee U.S., Inc., 1988—93; mem. adv. bd. Q Health Club, 1994—96; cons. U.S. Olympic Com. Sports Medicine com. nutrition, 1992—94; mem. com. mil. nutrition and rsch. rev. panel NAS, 1995—99. Contbr. articles to profl. jours., chapters to books; jour. reviewer Am. Jour. Physiology, Endocrinology and Metabolism, 1993—2001, Jour. Optimal Nutrition, 1993—96, Diabetes, 1987—88, Internat. Jour. Sports Nutrition, 1995—, sect. editor physiology Rsch. Quar. for Exercise and Sport, 1988—91, mem. editl. bd. Medicine and Sci. in Sports and Exercise, 1987—2001, Am. Jour. Physiology, 1995—2001, Internat. Jour. Sport Nutrition, 1997—, reviewer Jour. Applied Physiology, Am. Jour. Physiology, Medicine and Sci. in Sports and Exercise, Internat. Jour. of Sports Medicine, Rsch. Quar., Am. Jour. Clin. Nutrition, Diabetes, Jour. Clin. Investiagation, Internat. Jour. Sports Nutrition, presenter in field. Recipient Nat. Rsch. Svc. award, NIH, 1978—80; grantee, Tex. Heart Assn., Ross Products, Pfizer, Inc., Shaklee U.S., Inc., U.S. Olympic Rsch. Com. Fellow: Am. Acad. Kinesiology Phys. Edn., Am. Coll. Sports Medicine (midwest chpt. 1977—79, southeast chpt. 1980—82, Tex. chpt. bd. trustees 1985—86, bd. trustees rep. for basic and applied sci. 1986—89, ambassador 1986—90, Tex. chpt. exec. dir. 1986—91, organizer, chair symosium diabetes and exercise I regulation of muscle 1988, organizer, chair symposium diabetes and exercise I regulation of muscl 1988, mem. rsch. rev. com. 1991—95, Tex. chpt. bd. trustees 1992—95); mem.: Am. Soc. Clin. Nutrition, Inc., Am. Inst. Nutrition, Am. Diabetes Assn. (mem. nutrition scis. and metabolism coun. 1991—93, mem. exercise coun. 1991—93, sec. exercise coun. 1991—93, program chair exercise coun. 1993, organizer, chair symposium role of exercise and phys. activity in the 1992, organizer, chair symposium exercise through the ages 1994, grantee 1996, rsch. award 1996), Am. Physiol. Soc., Sigma Xi, Phi Epsilon Kappa. Office: U Tex Dept Kinesiology 822 E BEL Austin TX 78712 E-mail: johnivy@mail.utexas.edu.

IVY, RICHARD F. retired minister; b. Boston, Apr. 27, 1928; s. Earl Arnett and Dorothy Ellen (Whitmarsh) I.; m. Hatsuko (Lily) Kanazawa, May 28, 1954; children: J. Timothy, Rose Ann Ivy Cogan. BA in Govt. Adminstrn., Coll. William and Mary, Newport News, Va., 1975. Ordained minister. Commd. U.S. Army, Japan, 1946—66, 1946—66; pastor Shadygrove Bapt. Ch., Figure Five, Ark., 1953—54. Author: (biography) Abraham Eustis: Artillery General, 1993. Organizer Dandy Citizens Assn., Inc., York County, Va., 1983, pres.; chair Yorktown Tercentenary Celebration, York County, 1990—91, York County Hist. Com., 1988—93. Recipient Comdr. award for civilian svc., Dept. of Army, 1983, County Pts. of Light, Nat. Assn. Counties, 1991, Outstanding Vol., York County, 1991. Mem.: Ft. Eustis Hist. and Archeol. Assn. (pres. 1993—97), Peninsula Caged Bird Soc. (chmn. 1983—), Bird Clubs of Va. (adminstrn. coord. 1983—), Bird Clubs Am. (dir. edn. and mgmt. 1994—, chair). Baptist. Avocations: breeding exotic birds, publishing education. Office: PCBS BCV or BCA PO Box 2005 Yorktown VA 23692

IVY, ROBERT ADAMS, JR., architect, editor-in-chief; b. Columbus, Miss. m. Holly Ivy; children: Virginia Edmunds, Robert Adams, Benjamin Ledyard. BA cum laude, U. South, 1969; BArch, Tulane U., 1976. Consulting arch., Columbus, 1981-96; editor-in-chief Archtl. Record Mag., N.Y.C., 1996—. Author: Fay Jones: Architect, 1991; editor Architecture South mag., 1993 96; prodr., screenwriter (documentary film) 1,000 Homes. Pres. Greater Columbus, 1987-89; co-founder Greater Columbus Learning Ctr., Inc.; trustee Columbus-Lowndes Libr., 1984—, chmn., 1987, 91; vestry mem. St. Paul's Episcopal Ch., Columbus, 1985 87; adv. bd. The Dwelling Pl., Ctr. for So. Culture, 1993—; commr. U.S. Pavilion Biennale di Venezia, 2002. Lt. USNR, 1970-73. Fellow AIA (bd. dirs. 1993-96), Philippine Inst. Archs.; mem. Am. Architecture Found. (bd. regents 1993-96), Miss. Inst. of Arts and Letters (bd. dirs. 1993—), Inst. Urban Design, Rembrandt Club. Office: Archtl Record 2 Penn Plz New York NY 10121-0101

IWAI, WILFRED KIYOSHI, lawyer; b. Honolulu, Aug. 21, 1941; s. Charles Kazuo and Michiko (Sakimoto) I.; m. Judy Tomiko Yoshimoto, Mar. 1, 1963; children: Kyle K., Tiffany Seiko. BS in Bus., U. Colo., 1963, JD, 1966. Bar: Hawaii 1966, Colo. 1966, U.S. Dist. Ct. Hawaii 1966, U.S. Ct. Appeals (9th cir.) 1966. Dep. corp. counsel State of Hawaii, Honolulu, 1966-71; assoc. Kashiwa & Kanazawa, Honolulu, 1971-75; ptnr. Kashiwa, Iwai, Motooka & Goto, Honolulu, 1975-82, Iwai & Morris, Honolulu, 1982—2001; pvt. practice Wilfred K. Iwai Atty. at Law, A Law Corp., Honolulu, 2002—. Mem. ABA, Hawaii Bar Assn., Assn. Trial Lawyers Am., Bldg. Industry Assn., Bldg. Owners & Mgrs. Assn. Hawaii. Clubs: Draftsmen's (Honolulu) (pres.). Office: PO Box 61392 Honolulu HI 96839

IWAMOTO, RALPH SHIGETO, artist; b. Honolulu, Sept. 13, 1927; s. Shigeo and Hatsu (Hibi) I.; m. Kathleen M. Zimmerman, Nov. 23, 1963. Student, Bklyn. C.C., 1949-51, Art Students League, 1948-49, 51-53. One-man shows at Regina Gallery, N.Y.C., 1955, Gima Gallery, Honolulu, 1956, Columbia (S.C.) Mus. Art, 1959, Watson Gallery, Elmira (N.Y.) Coll., 1968, Westbeth Gallery, N.Y.C., 1973, 74, SCAF Gallery, Sharon, Conn., 1986, St. Mary's Coll., St. Mary's City, Md., 1989; exhibited in group shows at Hui Nani Artists, Honolulu, 1948, Honolulu Art Assn., 1948, Honolulu Acad. Arts, 1948, Creative Gallery, N.Y.C., 1953, Contemporary Arts Gallery, 1955, Riverside Mus., 1956, Butler Inst. Am. Art, Youngstown, Ohio, 1957, 62, 71, Chrysler Mus. Art, Provincetown, Mass., 1958, Allegheny Coll., Meadville, Pa., 1958, Pa. Acad. Fine Arts, Phila., 1958, Detroit Inst. Arts, 1958, Art USA 58, N.Y.C., 1958, Whitney Mus. Am. Art, 1958-59, Kaymar Gallery, 1964, Western Mich. U., Kalamazoo, 1966, Clara Josephs Gallery, N.Y.C., 1967, 68, 69, Westbeth Gallery, 1970, 76, 81, 85, 92, 99-2002, Paterson State Coll., Paterson, N.J., 1976, Org. Ind. Artists, Bologna, Italy, 1978, Project Studio P.S. 1, Long Island City, N.Y., 1978, Poppy Johnson Gallery, N.Y.C., 1978, Japanese-Am. Hall, N.Y.C., 1979, Betty Parsons Gallery, 1979, 80 Washington Square Ea. Gallery, 1980, Bergen County Cmty. Mus., Paramus, N.J., 1983, Newark Mus., 1983, Kenkeleba Gallery, N.Y.C., 1985, Nassau C.C., Garden City, N.Y., 1986, Contemporary Artists Guild, GSA Gallery, N.Y.C., 1986, Contemporary Mus., Honolulu, 1990, Wadsworth Atheneum, Hartford, Conn., 1991, Zimmerli Art Mus., Rutgers U., New Brunswick, N.J., 1997, Taipei Gallery, N.Y.C., 1997, Chgo. Cultural Ctr., 1997, Japanese Am. Nat. Mus., L.A., 1997, Bedford Gallery, Walnut Creek, Calif., 1998, Taipei Fine Arts Mus., Taiwan, 1998, Kaohsiung Mus., Taipei, 1998, Inokuma Mus. Contemporary Art, Kochi, Japan, 1999, Fukuoka Art Mus., Kyushu, 1999, Senshu Mus. Art, Akita, Japan, 1999, Gallery One Twenty Eight, N.Y.C., 2001-03, Gary Snyder Fine art, 2002, New Britain Mus. of American Art, 2003; represented in permanent collections at Butler Inst. Am. Art, Youngstown, Ohio, Sheldon Swope Art Gallery, Terre Haute, Ind., Herbert Johnson Mus./Cornell U., Ithaca, N.Y., State Found. on Culture and Arts, Honolulu, Thurston Twigg-Smith Collection/Contemporary Arts Mus., Honolulu, Honolulu Advertiser Publ. Collection, Honolulu, St. Mary's Coll. Gallery, St. Mary's City, Md., Wadsworth Atheneum, Hartford, Conn., Zimmerli Mus./Rutgers U., New Brunswick, N.J., Japanese Cultural Ctr. of Hawaii, Honolulu, others, also pvt. collections. With U.S. Army, 1946-48. Recipient Purchase prize Butler Inst. Am. Art, 1957; John Hay Whitney Found. fellow, 1958; Adolph and Esther Gottlieb Found. grantee, 1987; Pollock/Krasner Found. grantee, 2002. Mem. N.Y. Artists Equity. Home: 463 West St Apt A1110 New York NY 10014-2040

IWAN, LORI E. lawyer; b. Chgo., Jan. 17, 1958; BA in Fin. with distinction, U. Ill., 1980, JD, 1983. Bar: Ill. 1983. Ptnr. Iwan, Cray, Huber, Horstman & VanAusdal LLC, Chgo. Dean FDCC Litigation Mgmt. Coll., 2003—. Author internet column Lori's Links, 1997—. Mem. Fedn. Def. and Corp. Counsel (bd. dirs., v.p., tech. sect. vice-chair, task force 1998, product liability chair 1999-2001, program chair 2002), Def. Rsch. Inst. (Law Inst. 1999-2001, trial tactics and techniques steering com. 1996-97, co-editor newsletter 1996-97, Internet rsch. subcom. chair 1998, CLE co-chair ann. meeting 1999—), Lawyers Club Chgo. (bd. dirs.). Office: Iwan Cray Huber Horstman & VanAusdal LLC 29 N Wacker Dr Ste 500 Chicago IL 60606-3203 Fax: 312-332-8451. E-mail: lei@iwancray.com.

IWASAKI, IWAO, engineering educator; b. Tokyo, Feb. 6, 1929; arrived in U.S., 1950; s. Kuramatsu and Ichiko (Ishihara) I.; m. Junko Ikegami, 1972. Student, U. Tokyo, 1948-50; BS, U. Minn., 1951, MS, 1953; Sc.D., MIT, 1957; D.Eng., Tohoku U., 1961; DEng (hon.), Colo. Sch. Mines, 2001. Asst. prof. U. Minn., Mpls., 1957-59, assoc. prof., 1963-66, prof., 1966-91, sr. rsch. assoc., endowed Taconite chair, 1999—. Rsch. engr. Nippon Steel Corp., Tokyo, 1959-63; tech. counselor Ctrl. Rsch. Inst. Mitsubishi Materials Corp., Omiya, Japan, 1991-99; adj. lectr. Waseda U., Tokyo, 1992-99. Contbr. articles to profl. jours. Mem. AIME (Antoine M. Gaudin award 1981, Arthur F. Taggart award 1981, 2003, Robert H. Richards award 1986), NAE (fgn. assoc.), Mining and Material Processing Inst. Japan, Resources Processing Soc. Japan, Soc. Mining Engrs. (Disting. mem.), Sigma Xi, Tau Beta Pi. Home: 3-16-2 Todoroki Setagaya-ku Tokyo 158-0082 Japan Office: Coleraine Minerals Rsch Lab U Minn Duluth One Gayley Ave Coleraine MN 55722 E-mail: iiwasaki@nrri.umn.edu.

IWASAKI, TETSUYA, engineering educator; b. Shibukawa, Gumma, Japan, Sept. 29, 1964; d. Tadashi and Mitsue Iwasaki; m. Junko Ito, June 8, 1991; children: Yota, Momo. BS, Tokyo Inst. Tech., 1987, MS, 1990; PhD, Purdue U., 1993. Postdoctoral rschr. Purdue U., West Lafayette, Ind., 1994-95; rsch. assoc. Tokyo Inst. Tech., 1995-96, asst. prof., 1996-97, assoc. prof., 1997-2000; asst. prof. U. Va., Charlottesville, 2000—02, assoc. prof., 2002—. Author: LMI and Control, 1997, A Unified Algebraic Approach to Linear Control Design, 1998. Recipient SICE Pioneer Prize, 2002, NSF Career Award, 2003; grantee, Ministry of Edn., 1995—99, NSF, 2002—, NIH, 2002—. Mem.: ASME, IEEE (sr.), Soc. Instrument and Control Engrs. Avocations: camping, skiing, boomerang. Office: Univ Va Mech & Aero Engring PO Box 400746 Charlottesville VA 22904-4746

IWASAWA, ISOO (FRANCIS IWASAWA), accountant, management consultant; b. Yokohama, Kanagawa, Japan, Jan. 9, 1936; d. Matasaku (Joseph) Ninomiya and Haruno (Ann); m. Kinuko (Kay) Sato, Mar. 15, 1963; children: Isoaki, Lisa, Chiharu, Leo. BSc, St. Martin's Coll., Olympia, Wash., 1960; postgrad., U. Wash., 1960-61, Georgetown U., 1961. CPA, Wash. Prin. Ernst & Whiney, Hong Kong, 1984-86; ptnr. Arthur Young, Hong Kong, 1986-89; mng. dir. Asahi Iwasawa & Assocs. Mgmt. Cons. Ltd., Hong Kong, 1989—. Bd. trustees St. Martin's Coll., Olympia, Wash., 2001—. Avocations: gardening, sailing, golfing. Office: China Resources Bldg FL 43 No 26 Harbour Rd Rm 4303 Wanchai Hong Kong

IX, ROBERT EDWARD, food company executive; b. Woodcliffe, N.J., Oct. 15, 1929; s. William Edward and Helen Elizabeth (Gorman) I.; m. Mildred Gilmore, June 27, 1959; children: Helen Adele, Alesia Gilmore, Robert Owens Gilmore, Julia Ryan, Christopher Prouty. AB, Princeton U., 1951; MBA, Wharton Grad. Sch., U. Pa., 1956; LL.D. (hon.), Marymount Coll., 1978, Sacred Heart U., Conn., 1984. Mgmt. cons. Arthur D. Little Inc., Cambridge, Mass., 1956-64; mktg. dir. Browne-Vintners Co., Distillers Corp.-Seagrams Ltd., N.Y.C., 1964-66; v.p. mktg. Schweppes (USA) Ltd., N.Y.C., 1966-68, pres., 1968; pres., chief exec. officer Cadbury Schweppes Inc., Stamford, Conn., 1970-78; chmn., chief exec. officer Am. region Cadbury Schweppes P.L.C., 1976-86. Bd. dirs. Cadbury Schweppes P.L.C., London, N.E. Bancorp Inc., Union Trust Co., New Eng. Frozen Foods, Inc., Am. Thread Co., Binney & Smith Inc., Royal Doulton Co. Inc., Loctite Corp., Health Waters Inc., O'Shaughnessy Funds, Inc. Trustee Marymount Coll., also chmn.; trustee Greenwich (Conn.) Acad., Trinity Pawling Sch. (N.Y.); mem. adv. council N.Y. Med. Coll., Valhalla, N.Y. Served to lt. comdr. USNR, 1951 55. Decorated Knight Sovereign Mil. Order Malta. Mem. Young President's Orgn., World Bus. Coun., Chief Execs. Forum, SW Area Commerce and Industry Assn. Conn. (dir. 1970-80, chmn. bd. 1976-77), Def. Orientation Conf. Assn. (dir.), Grocery Mfrs. Am. (dir. 1981-85), U.S. Navy League (dir. Conn.), Univ. Club (N.Y.C.), Belle Haven Club (Greenwich), Greenwich Country Club, Landmark Club (Stamford, chmn. bd. govs.). Roman Catholic. E-mail: cbix@webtv.net.

IYENGAR, JAGANNATHAN VIJAY, computer scientist, educator; arrived in U.S., 1979; s. Krishna Vijayaraghavan and Padma Desikachavi; m. Jayashree J. Iyengar, Jan. 29, 1979; children: Jayanth J., Janani J. DSc, Indian Inst. Sci., 1976; PhD, Indian Inst. Mgmt., 1979; M Bus Info. Sys., Ga. State U., 1981, PhD, 1989. Tech. support specialist, info. systems analyst Atlanta Gas Light Co., 1981—88; vis. asst. prof. John Carroll U., Cleve., 1990—93; assoc. prof. dir. MIS programs Jackson (Miss.) State U., 1993—2000; assoc. prof. MIS U. Wis., Whitewater, 2000—03, prof. MIS, 2003—. Contbr. articles to profl. jours. Capt. Indian Army Res., 1963—68. Grantee, NASA/Am. Soc. Engring. Edn., 2000, 2001, 2002. Mem.: Western Decision Scis. Inst., Am. Soc. Computing, Decision Sci. Inst. (paper awards). Republican. Avocations: tennis, hiking, basketball, aviation. Home: 209 N Westfield Rd Madison WI 53717 Office: U Wis 800 W Main St Whitewater WI 53190 Fax: 262-472-5733. E-mail: jiyengar@juno.com.

IYENGAR, RAMCHANDRA, retired surgeon; b. Bombay, 1935; MD, Calcutta Med. Coll., 1959. Diplomate Am. Bd. Surgery. Intern Stamford Hosp., 1977-78; resident in gen. surgery St. Vincent's Med. Ctr., Bridgeport, Conn., 1978-82, attending staff, 1983-99; ret., 1999. Fellow ACS, Royal Coll. Surgeons England.

IYER, RENGANATHAN GANESAN, mathematician; b. India, Feb. 8, 1960; s. Ganesan Venkataraman and Sita Ganesan; m. Anuradha Vedantham, May 12, 1991; children: Sumun S, Pranav G. BSc, Pune U., Pune, India, 1980, MSc, 1982; PhD, MIT, 1991. Asst. prof. math. Richard Stockton Coll. of NJ., Pomona, 1991—96, assoc. prof. math., 1996—. Grantee NSF, 1996—98, 1999—2002. Hindu. Avocations: travel, cooking, magic and mathematics. Office: Richard Stockton Coll NJ Jimmie Leeds Rd Pomona NJ 08240 E-mail: iyerr@stockton.edu.

IYER, SEEMA, chemist; b. Mumbai, India, Dec. 29, 1974; d. Shyam and Varsha Mudholkar; m. Venkatraman Iyer, May 20, 1999. BS, U. Bombay, India, 1996; MS, U. Pacific, 1998; PhD, Purdue U., 2001. Registered Pharmacist Maharashtra State Pharmacy Coun., India. Grad. tchg. asst. U. of the Pacific, Stockton, Calif., 1996—98; grad. rsch., tchg. asst. Purdue U., West Lafayette, Ind., 1998—2001; sr. rsch. chemist Albany Molecular Rsch., Inc., NY, 2002—. Author: (jour.) VACCINE, Pharm. Devel. And Tech., (proceedings) 18th Pharm. Tech. Conf. Recipient Albert and Anna Kienly award for excellence in tchg., Purdue U., 2000; Merit scholar, Premier Automobiles, Mumbai, India. Mem.: Indian Pharm. Assn., Am. Assn. Of Pharm. Scientists, Rho Chi. Home: 24 Hollandale Ln Apt A Clifton Park NY 12065 Office: Albany Molecular Rsch Inc 21 Corporate Cir PO Box 15098 Albany NY 12212 Office Fax: 518-464-0289. Personal E-mail: siyer29@yahoo.com. E-mail: seema.iyer@albmolecular.com.

IZADI, BABACK A. engineering educator; PhD, Ohio State U., 1995. Sr. prof. Devry U., Columbus, Ohio, 1982—98; asst. prof. SUNY, New Paltz, NY, 1998—. Mem.: IEEE, Eta Kappa Nu. Office: SUNY 75 S Manheim Blvd New Paltz NY 12561 Home Fax: ; Office Fax: 845-257-3730. Personal E-mail: bai@engr.newpaltz.edu. Business E-Mail: bai@engr.newpaltz.edu.

IZANT, ROBERT JAMES, JR., pediatric surgeon; b. Cleve., Feb. 4, 1921; s. Robert James and Grace (Goulder) I.; m. Virginia Lincoln Root, Sept. 27, 1947; children: Jonathan G. II, Mary Root, Timothy Holman. AB cum laude, Amherst Coll., 1943; MD, Western Res. U., 1946. Diplomate: Am. Bd. Surgery, Am. Bd. Pediatric Surgery. Resident in surgery U. Hosp., Cleve., 1946 52; resident in pediatric surgery Boston Children's Med. Center, 1952-55; asst. prof. pediatric surgery Ohio State U., 1955-58; prof., dir. pediatric surgery and pediatrics Case Western Res.U., 1958-90, prof. emeritus pediatric surgery and pediatrics, 1990—. Dir. div. pediatric surgery Univ. Hosps. Cleve., Rainbow Babies and Children's Hosp.; also MetroHealth Ctr. Hosp., 1958-86; mem. adv. bd. Ohio State Services for Children with Med. Handicaps, 1957—. Co-author: The Surgical Neonate; contbr. articles to profl. jours. Bd. dirs. alumni Western Res. Acad. Served to lt. (j.g.) M.C. USNR, 1947-49. Fellow ACS, Am. Acad. Pediatrics; mem. Central Surg. Assn., Am. Assn. Surgery of Trauma, AMA, Am. Bd. Surgery, Cleve. Surg. Soc. (pres. 1971-72), Cleve. Acad. Medcine (dir. 1971-74), Am. Trauma Soc. (founding mem.), Teratology Soc., Lilliputian Surg. Soc., No. Ohio Pediatric Soc., Brit. Assn. Pediatric Surgery, Pediatric Surgery Biology Club, Am. Pediatric Surg. Assn. (founding mem., pres. 1987-88), Western Res. U. Sch. Medicine Alumni Assn. (pres. 1961-62, bd. dirs. 2002—), Am. Burn Assn., Tavern Club (bd. dirs. 2000—), Sigma Xi, Alpha Omega Alpha, Nu Sigma Nu, Delta Kappa Epsilon. Home: 2275 Harcourt Dr Cleveland Heights OH 44106-4614 Office: Rainbow Babies and Childrens Hosp University Cir Cleveland OH 44106 Fax: (216) 795-4278. E-mail: rizant@adelphia.net.

IZARD, JOHN, lawyer; b. Hartford, Conn., Mar. 4, 1923; s. John and Elizabeth (Andrews) I.; m. Mary Bailey, apr. 16, 1955; children: Sarah Izard Pariseau, John Jr., David Bailey. BS, Yale U., 1945; LLB, U. Va., 1949. Bar: Ga. 1950. Assoc. King & Spalding, Atlanta, 1949-52, ptnr., 1952-90. Mem. Adminstrv. Conf. U.S., Washington, 1978-82. Author, pub.: A Traveler's Table, 2002; editor-in-chief Va. Law Rev., 1948; contbr. articles to legal periodicals. Mem. Nat. Com. To Study Antitrust Laws and Procedures, Washington, 1978; trustee Episcopal Media Ctr., Atlanta, 1988—, chmn., 1992-96; trustee U. Va. Law Sch. Found., Charlottesville, 1974-97. Lt. (j.g.) USNR, 1944-46, PTO. Mem. ABA (chmn. antitrust sect. 1974-75), Ga. Bar Assn. (chmn. antitrust sect. 1969-71), Atlanta Legal Aid Soc. (pres. 1960), Lawyers Club Atlanta, Capital City Club (bd. dirs. 1976-79), Peachtree Golf Club, Piedmont Driving Club. Democrat. Episcopalian. Home: 4061 Glen Devon Dr NW Atlanta GA 30327-3613 Office: King & Spalding 191 Peachtree St NE Ste 3900 Atlanta GA 30303-1740

IZAURRALDE, ROBERTO CÉSAR, science educator, researcher; b. Paraná, Argentina, Nov. 5, 1948; s. Hermenegildo Roberto Izaurralde and Elida Nahir Pelayo; m. María Cristina Quiroga Jakas, Oct. 11, 1972; children: Octavio Rafael, María Renée, Bernarda María, Arthur Benjamin. Agronomist Engr., Nat. U. of Córdoba, 1967—72; MS, Kans. State U., 1980—81, PhD, 1982—84. Asst. prof. Nat. U. of Córdoba, Argentina, 1976—86; grad. rsch. asst. Kans. State U., 1982—84; rsch. assoc. U. of Alta., Edmonton, Canada, 1986—90, asst. / assoc. prof., 1990—97; staff scientist Pacific NW Nat. Lab., Washington, 1997—2001, Joint Global Change Rsch. Inst., Coll. Pk., Md.; adj. prof. U. of Md., Coll. Pk., Md., 2002—. Exec. sec. Córdoba U. Exptl. Farm, 1978—80; faculty coun. mem. Nat. U. of Córdoba, 1986—86; cons. Greenhouse Gas Emissions Consortium, Edmonton, Canada, 1995; exec. com. mem. Consortium for Agrl. Soils Mitigation of Greenhouse Gases, Coll. Pk., Md., 2001—; rsch. leader Carbon Sequestration in Terrestrial Ecosystems Rsch. Ctr., Coll. Pk., Md., 2002—. Fellowship, Fulbright Program, 1980—81. Mem.: Am. Assoc. for the Advancement of Sci., Soil Sci. Soc. of Am., Am. Soc. of Agronomy. Achievements include research in sustainable agricultural production; simulation modeling of anhydrous ammonia retention in soil; simulation modeling of biogeochemical cycles; simulation modeling of climate change impacts on agriculture, water resources and ecosystems; leadership in developing soil carbon sequestration as a tool to mitigate global warming. Avocations: classical music, bicycling. Office: Joint Global Change Rsch Inst 8400 Baltimore Ave Ste 201 College Park MD 20740-2496 Office Fax: 301-314-6760. E-mail: cesar.izaurralde@pnl.gov.

IZENSTARK, JOSEPH LOUIS, retired radiologist, physician, educator; b. Chgo., Mar. 29, 1919; s. Paul and Flora (Berger) I.; m. Elizabeth Kaplan, June 25, 1944; 1 child, Susan Rebecca. BA, U. Calif., Berkeley, 1948; MD, U. Calif., San Francisco, 1951. Diplomate Am. Bd. Radiology, Am. Bd. Nuc. Medicine. Intern USPHS, Chgo., 1951-52; resident Kern Gen. Hosp., Bakersfield, Calif., 1952-53; resident in radiology Cedars of Lebanon Hosp., L.A., 1955-56; chief radiology resident Los Angeles County Harbor Gen. Hosp., Torrance, Calif., 1957-58; practice medicine Inglewood, Calif., 1953-55; practice radiology Bakersfield, 1971-99; dir. radiology Imperial Hosp., Inglewood, 1959-60; asst. prof. radiology Tulane U., 1960-62, assoc. prof., 1963; assoc. prof. radiology Emory U., 1963-67, dir. nuc. medicine, 1963-67; prof. radiology U. So. Calif., 1969-72; prof. health scis. Bakersfield State Coll., 1973-83; ret., 1999. Chief nuc. medicine Cedars of Lebanon Hosp., 1968-71; med. dir. edn. Bakersfield Meml. Hosp., 1983-87; spl. cons. radiol. health USPHS, Calif. Bur. Radiol. Health, U.S. Army; mem. La. Atomic Energy Adv. Coun.; dir. nuc. medicine Crawford W. Long Meml. Hosp.; mem. USPHS Commn. on Radiation Exposure Evaluation, Med. Bd. Calif., 1982-91. Author: Anatomy and Physiology for X-ray Technicians, 1961; contbr. articles to profl. jours. With AUS, 1941-45. Recipient Cert. of Merit, City of New Orleans, 1962, Physician of Yr. award Bakersfield Meml. Hosp., 1988, Outstanding Physician Contbns. to Medicine award Calif. State Assembly, 1992. Fellow Am. Cancer Soc., Am. Coll. Radiology; mem. Soc. Nuclear Medicine (pres. So. Calif. chpt. 1976), So. Valley Radiol. Soc. (pres. 1975), Kern County Med. Soc. (pres. 1978). *Set your goal in a definite clear outline taking each step one at a time, as if climbing a ladder. Think about your goals; don't talk about them. Concentrate your abilities, your studies, your friends while denying yourself luxuries. Make your own decisions; stick by them. Don't have regrets. Be honest, sincere, and dedicated without regard to time. Finally, don't give up the fight— stick to your goal.*

IZLAR, ROBERT LEE, forester; b. Waycross, Ga., Dec. 5, 1949; s. Durham Wright and Marion Ethel (Odom) I.; m. Janice Elaine Bullard, Aug. 10, 1974; children: Olivia Frances Tate, Durham Joel Poinsett. BS in Forest Resources, U. Ga., 1971, M Forest Resources, 1972; MBA, Ga. So. U., 1977; grad. Inst. for Orgn. Mgmt., U. Del., 1989; grad., MP officer basic course, 1972, Mil. Intel. offcr. adv. course, 1986; grad. with hons., Army Command/Gen. Staff Coll., 1989; grad., USAF War Coll., 1999. Registered forester, Ga. Teaching fellow U. Ga., Athens, 1971-72; dist. mgr. Brunswick Pulp Land Co., Woodbine, Ga., 1974-78; div. forester Am. Pulpwood Assn., Jackson, Miss., 1978-84; exec. v.p. Miss. Forestry Assn., Jackson, 1984-87; exec. dir. Ga. Forestry Assn., Atlanta, 1987-98; dir. Ctr. for Forest Bus., Warnell Sch. Forest Resources, U. Ga., 1998—; forest history cons. U. Miss. Ctr. for Study So. Culture, U.S. State Dept. Del. IX World Forestry Cong., Mexico City, 1986, 7th Am. Forestry Congress., 1996; Weyerhaeuser Disting. vis. lectr. Sch. Forestry and Environ. Studies Yale U., 1993; adj. prof. forest policy Joseph W. Jones Ecol. Rsch. Ctr.; mem. U. Ga.-NSF Long-Term Okefenokee Swamp Ecol. Rsch. Team; cons. history of Okefenokee Swamp Sta. WQED-TV/Nat. Geog. Soc., Turner Adventure Learning, The Carter Ctr., No. Light Prodns., U.S. Dept. Interior Fish and Wildlife Svc., GPTV Success Track; adv. bd. ForestExpress, 2000—02; continuing forest resource edn. coun. U. Ga., 1990—98; cons. in field. Contbr. articles to profl. jours. and revs., chpts. to books. Mem. Gov.'s Rivercare 2000 Commn., bd. dirs. U. Ga. Young Alumni Coun., 1978-81; lt. col. aide-de-camp to Govs. of Ga., Tenn., Ala. and La.; bd. trustees Ga. Forestry Found., 1992-98, sec. 1992-96, treas., 1997-98; Hon. Citizen of Tex., Ark. Traveller Commn. 1st lt. U.S. Army, 1972-74, Korea; col. Res., 1982—. Named Outstanding Young Alumnus, U. Ga., 1986, Forest Conservationist of Yr., Ga. Wildlife Fedn., 1998, Sr. officer of Yr., Selective Svc. Sys. Region II, 1998, Hon. Order Ky. Cols.; named to, Ga. Foresters Hall of Fame, 1997; recipient cert. appreciation, Strategic Air Commd., 1986, Appreciation award, Forest Landowners Assn., 1989, Aghon award, 1996, Agrl. award, U.S. Cong. Saxby Chambliss Ga., 1997, Wise Owl award, Ga. Forestry Assn., 1998, Forestry Commn. Appreciation award, 1999, Draper Ctr. medal, 2002; fellow, NSF, 1972; Blue Key Dorsey scholar, 1972. Mem.: SCV, SAR, Soc. Ga. Archaeology (bd. dirs. 2000—04), Miss. Forestry Assn., Ga. Forestry Assn. (Ga. divsn. hall of fame selection com. 1994—97, chair 2002—03), Vietnam Vets Am., Mil. Order Fgn. Wars U.S.A., Mil. Order World Wars, Res. Officers Assn., Mil. Order of Stars and Bars, Tall Timbers Rsch. Sta., Internat. Soc. Tropical Foresters, Orgn. Tropical Studies, Commonwealth Forestry Assn. (hon. sec. 1977—2002), Soc. Am. Foresters (Ga. divsn. pres. 1995, chpt. bd. dirs. 2003—, cert. forester), Nat. Coun. Forestry Assn. Execs. (pres. 1991—92), Jewish Nat. Fund (tree of life com. 1987—89), Demosthenian Lit. Soc., Army and Navy Union, Greater Okefenokee Assn. Landowners (Ga. chpt.), Huguenot Soc. S.C., Sphinx Club (faculy adv.), Shriners, Scottish Rite, Jayhole Club (pres. 1993), Commerce Club, Gridiron Club, Commandery Knights Templar, Old Guard of the Gate City Guard, York Rite, Hospitaler Order St. John of Jerusalem, Commandery Knights Templar, Sapelo Island Nat. Estuarine (rsch. res. adv. com. 1994—99), Blue Key (faculty advisor), Lodge of Mil. Rsch., Omicron Delta Kappa, Pi Gamma Nu, Phi Beta Delta, Phi Kappa Phi, Alpha Mu Epsilon, Alpha Phi Omega, Alpha Zeta, Gamma Sigma Delta, Xi Sigma Pi (pres. 1971—72, faculty advisor), Sigma Xi, U. Ga. Alumni Soc. (v.p. 1981—83, 1993—96, 1998—2002, bd. dirs.), Warnell Sch. Forest Resources Alumni Soc. (pres. 1994, Disting. Alumnus 1997). Episcopalian. Avocations: writing, woodworking.

IZMAILOV, ALEXANDER F. physicist, mathematician, researcher; b. Zelenodolsk, USSR, May 17, 1959; came to US, 1990; s. Farid Sh. and Kira M.; m. Lina S. Zeldovich, Sept. 17, 1989 (div. Jan. 1995). BS,MS in Theoret. Physics with honors, Kazan (USSR) U., 1981; PhD in Theoret. and Mathemat. Physics, USSR Acad. Scis., Moscow, 1986. Sr. rsch. scientist USSR Supreme Attestation Bd., 1987. Head Lab. Math. Simulation of Enhanced Oil Recovery, Ministry of Oil and Gas Industry, Moscow, 1981-90; rsch. scientist Lebedev Phys. Inst. USSR Acad. Scis., Moscow, 1986-89; rsch. prof. Poly. U., Bklyn., 1991-2001; v.p. Spear, Leeds & Kellogg, 2000—. Contbr. 45 articles to profl. jours. Grantee NASA, 1995, 97, 98, NSF, 1998, 2000; recipient 2nd prize USSR Competition in Theoret. Physics among undergrads., 1978. Mem. Am. Crystallographic Assn., Sigma Xi. Democrat. Avocations: stamp collecting, surrealistic art, rare history books and documents on ussr. Home: 735 Avenue W Apt 5N Brooklyn NY 11223-5555 E-mail: a1exizm@yahoo.com.

IZRAILEV, SERGEI, research scientist; b. Russia, 1971; s. Felix M. Izrailev, Nina Izraileva; married. BS Applied Physics and Math., Moscow Inst. Physics and Tech., 1991, MS Chem. Physics, 1993; PhD Physics, M Computer Sci., U. Ill., 1998. Rsch. scientist 3-Dimensional Pharms., Exton, Pa., 1998—2001, prin. rsch. scientist, 2001—. Software developer Beckman Inst. Advanced Sci. and Tech., Urbana, 1996—98. Contbr. Molecular visualization software, articles to profl. jours. Mem.: Am. Chem. Soc. Office: 3-Dimensional Pharms 8 Clarke Drive Cranbury NJ 08512 Business E-Mail: sizraile@prdus.jnj.com.

IZUCHUKWU, JOHN IFEANYICHUKWU, industrial engineer, mechanical engineer; b. Uke, Nigeria, May 6, 1955; arrived in US, 1976; s. Michael Chike and Cecilia Obiageli (Ikeakor) I.; m. Michele Anthea Palmer, July 22, 1989; children: Michael, John, Joseph. BS in Indsl. Enring., U. Portland, Oreg., 1980, MS in Mech. Engring., 1984; PhD in Indsl. Engring., Northeastern U., 1994; MBA, Northwestern U., 2002. Base mgr. OEM Mfg., Digital Equipment Corp., Portland, Oreg., 1980-85; computer-aided software engring. mgr. Digital Equipment Corp., Marlboro, Mass., 1985-87, mgr. mech. design automation, 1987, mgr. concurrent engring. and application ctr. for tech. Rochester, N.Y., 1989-91, group mgr. aerospace product strategy Marlboro, 1991-93, worldwide strategy mgr., integrated product devel., 1993-95; team leader, R & D Ethicon Endo-Surgery, Inc., Cin., 1995-98; sr. dir. global rsch., devel. and engring. Mallinckrodt, Inc., St. Charles, Mo., 1998-2001; pres., CEO VITALTECH, Inc., 2001—; CEO Core Devices, Inc., 2001—. Adj. prof. decision scis. Babson Coll., Wellesley, Mass., 1994—95, St. Louis U., 2001—, U. Mo., Rolla. Contbr. articles to engring. jours., including Jour. Mfg. Sci. and Engring.; patentee in field. Mem. ASME, Inst. Indsl. Engring. (sr. mem.). Home: 18002 Pine Canyon Ct Wildwood MO 63005-4938 Office: Mallinckrodt Inc PO Box 5840 Saint Louis MO 63134-0840 E-mail: jizuchukwu@aol.com.

IZZI, JOHN, educator, author; b. Providence, Dec. 31, 1931; s. Joseph and Elizabeth (Kinney) I.; m. Barbara Ann Freethy, Dec. 18, 1954; children: Kathleen, Donna, James; m. Patricia Margaret Crowley, Aug. 27, 1979; children: John, Matthew, Jessica. BA, Providence Coll., 1953; MEd, R.I. Coll., 1965; postgrad. (NSF grantee), U. Vt., 1959, 60, 63, Seton Hall U., 1961, Yale U., 1966; doctoral candidate (NSF grantee), Boston U., 1968—70. Tchr. LaSalle Acad., Providence, 1955-58, Warren (R.I.) H.S., 1958-60, Warwick (R.I.) Vets. H.S., 1960-62, Pilgrim H.S., Warwick, 1962—66, 1999—2001, head math. dept., 1968-72, 1968—72, Seekonk (Mass.) H.S., 1966-67; state supr. math. Mass. Dept. Edn., 1967-68; head math. dept. Toll Gate HS, Warwick, 1972—88, 2001—02; coord. secondary sch. R.I. Hosp., 1988-89; tchr. math. and sci. Westport (Mass.) H.S., 1989-91, math. adviser, biology/sci. tchr.; adj. faculty Bristol C.C., Mass., 1992-94. Pres. Smallstate Co., Warwick, 1975—; prin. Warwick Adult Edn., 1987-88; ext. lectr. U. R.I., 1976—: math. coach Toll Gate Acad. Decathlon State Champions, 1985, New Eng. Math. League Divsn. Champions, 1989-90; dir. Prep. Inst., Warwick, Math. Edn. Svc., Providence, 1965-66, Toll Gate Metrication Project, Warwick, 1972-73; creator 1st federally funded sch. metrication project in U.S., 1972, Izzi Metric Slide Chart, 1974, Izzi Decimal Notation, 1974; dir. Smallstate Math. Inst., Warwick, 1989-90, Smallstate Scholarship Svc., Warwick, 1991-93; pres. Smallstate Pub., 1994-96; advisor Am. Security Coun., 1973-79; pres. P & J Izzi Assocs., Warwick, 1997-99; metrication cons. Nat. Coun. Tchrs. Math., 1973—, computer software reviewer, textbook reviewer, 1981-88; adj. faculty C.C. R.I., 1981-85, Bristol C.C., Mass., 1992-94; metrication cons. State Depts. Edn., New England, Pa. and NY, 1977-80. Textbook reviewer AAAS, 1968-74; book reviewer Phi Delta Kappan, 1974-76; author: Metrication, American Style, 1974, Looking at the Metric System, 1977, Adult Metric Guide, 1977, Basic Metric Competency Test, 1977, My Irish, Voices of America, 1991; editl. adviser New Eng. Math. Jour., 1982-85; contbr. articles to various publs. Mem. Mass. Gov.'s Hwy. Safety Act Com., 1967-68. With U.S. Army, 1953-55. Recipient Disting. Achievement award Ednl. Press Assn. Am., 1974; named Best Math. Tchr. in Am., Ky. Ednl. TV, 1990. Mem. ASCD, NEA, Am. Fedn. Tchrs., Nat. Coun. Tchrs. Math., Am. Assn. Sch. Adminstrs. Metric Assn., Assn. Tchrs. Math. in New Eng., New Eng. Regional Metric Assn. (edn. commr. 1976-80), Mass. Dept. Edn. Assn. (v.p. 1967-68). Home: 243 Greenwood Ave Warwick RI 02886-2015 E-mail: johnizzi@aol.com.

IZZO, FRANCESCO, musicologist; b. Bologna, Italy, June 7, 1967; s. Alberto Izzo and Marialuisa Agnetti. PhD, NYU, NY, 1998—2003; MA, NYU, New York, 1996—98; BA, U of Rome La Sapienza, Rome, Italy, 1988—93. Assoc. dir. Am. Inst. for Verdi Studies at NYU, New York, NY, 2002—; adj. faculty NYU, New York, NY, 1999. Editor: (book) Ottocento e oltre: Scritti in onore di Raoul Meloncelli; author: (article) Verdi's Un giorno di regno: Two Newly-Discovered Movements and Some Questions of Genre, in _Acta Musicologica_ 73, Rachmaninoff in Italy: Criticism - Influence - Performance, in _Studies in Music from the Univ. of Western Ontario_ 15. Mem.: Am. Musicological Soc. Office: NYU- Music Dept 24 Waverly Pl Rm 268 New York NY 10003 E-mail: francesco.izzo@nyu.edu.

IZZO, HERBERT JOHN, language and linguistics educator, researcher; b. Saginaw, Mich., July 17, 1928; s. Joseph Anthony and Eleanor Bertha (Karau) I.; m. Barbara Suzanne McLaughlin, Sept. 22, 1958 (div); children: Victoria Sue Gutierrez, Alexander John, Sylvia Rachel Hunter, Daniel Stanley; m. Olga Frances Koutna, Dec. 30, 1989. *The family's pedagogical vocation began in 1913 when 19-year-old Eleanor, daughter of German immigrant farmers, taught her first class in a one-room school in Elkton, Michigan. Her son and two of her grandchildren followed in her footsteps: Alex is a professor of mathematics and Vicky an elementary teacher like her grandmother. When Dr. Olga Koutna became Mrs. Izzo, the Izzo teaching tradition merged with an older one; for Olga's grandfather Jan was a teacher in Moravia when Eleanor was a child, and Olga's father Otakar was a professor of chemistry at the University of Brno.* BA in Spanish, U. Mich., 1950, MA in Spanish and Italian, 1951, BS in Chemistry, 1953, PhD in Linguistics, 1965. Chargé de cours Huê (Vietnam) U., 1958-59; instr. Spanish U. Ariz., Tucson, 1960-61; instr. Spanish and linguistics Stanford (Calif.) U., 1961-64; asst. prof. Spanish San Jose (Calif.) State U., 1964-68; from assoc. to prof. linguistics U. Calgary, Alberta, Can., 1968-88, prof. emeritus, 1988—. Vis. asst. prof. fgn. langs. Mansfield (Pa.) State Coll., 1957; vis. prof. Romance linguistics U. Mich., Ann Arbor, 1977-78, 93-94; vis. prof. linguistics U. Bucharest, Romania, 1975-76; vis. prof. Italian, Stanford U., 1990-91; vis. scholar U. Mich., 1997—; adv. bd. Quaderni d'Italianistica, Can., 1979—. Author: Tuscan and Etruscan, 1972; editor: The Sixth LACUS Forum, 1980, Italic and Romance, 1985; editor for linguistics Am. Jour. Italian Studies, 1988-2002; translator Lost Papers of Ludwig von Mises, 1998-2001, Italian Dialect Studies of Carl L. Fernow, 2003. Bd. dirs. Fathers Alberta, Calgary, 1986-87. Grad. fellow U. N.Mex., 1953, Award for Advanced Study, Am. Coun. Learned Socs., 1963, Fulbright-Hays award U.S. Dept. State, 1966, 75. Mem. Am. Assn. Italian Studies, Linguistic Assn. Can. and U.S. (conf. organizer 1978), N.Am. Assn. for History of Lang. Scis. (v.p. 1977-80), Am. Assn. Tchrs. Italian (life), Linguistic Soc. Am. (life), Am. Classical League, Am. Assn. Tchrs. of Spanish and Portuguese (life), Can. Soc. Italian Studies (nominating com. 1977-78, adv. bd. 1974-80), Internat. Soc. Phonetic Scis., Nat. Assn. Scholars, Phi Beta Kappa, Phi Kappa Phil. Avocations: music, history, running. Home: 2515 Deake Ave Ann Arbor MI 48108-1330 E-mail: hizzo@umich.edu.

IZZO, THOMAS, college basketball coach; b. Iron Mountain, Mich., Jan. 30, 1955; m. Lupe Izzo; 1 child, Raquel. Grad., No. Mich. U., 1977. Head coach Ishpeming (Mich.) H.S., 1977-79; asst. coach No. Mich. U., 1979-83; with Mich. State U., East Lansing, 1983—, head coach Spartans, 1995—. Named to No. Mich. U. Hall of Fame, 1990, Upper Peninsula Hall of Fame, 1998. Office: Mich State U Athletic Dept 222 Breslin Ctr Jensen Fieldhouse East Lansing MI 48824

JABARA, MICHAEL DEAN, technology and business development entrepreneur; b. Sioux Falls, S.D., Oct. 26, 1952; s. James M. and Jean Marie (Swiden) J.; m. Gundula Beate Dietz, Aug. 26, 1984; children: James Michael, Jenna Mariel. Student, Mich. Tech. U., 1970-72; BSBA, U. Calif., Berkeley, 1974; MBA, Pepperdine U., 1979. Mgr. original Sprint project team So. Pacific Communications Corp., 1976-78; network product mgr. ROLM Corp., 1978-81; cons. McGraw Hill Co., Hamburg (Fed. Republic of Germany) and London, 1982-83; founder, CEO Friend Techs. Inc. (merger VoiceCom Systems, Inc., acquired by Premiere Techs., Inc. 1997), San Francisco, 1984-88; pres. VoiceCom Ventures, San Francisco, 1988-93; mng. dir. Telecom, EMS Group Ltd., London, 1993-95; owner Jabara & Co. LLC (now called Red Rock Ptnrs., Ltd.), Nev., 1993—; chmn. bd., COO Bingo Card Minder Corp., Stateline, Nev., 1996; owner TOIR LLC, Glenbrook, 1998-99, NewHoldings, LLC, Las Vegas, 2000—; CEO, chmn. bd. iTruckers, Inc., 2000—. COO Bingo Card Minder Corp., Stateline, Nev., 1996. Patentee in field. Bd. dirs. Tahoe-Douglas C. of C.; chmn. Tahoe Citizens Com., 1995-2000. Mem.: Mich. Tech Alumni Assn., U. Calif. Berkeley Bus. Alumni, Pepperdine Bus. Alumni, Las Vegas Jaguar Club. Avocations: classic cars, flying. Office: Red Rock Partners Ltd 7th Flr 3800 Howard Hughes Pkwy Las Vegas NV 89109 Office Fax: 702-784-0681. Business E-Mail: mjabara@redrockpartners.com.

JABBARI, BAHMAN, neurologist, educator; b. ZanJan, Iran, Jan. 22, 1942; came to U.S., 1968; s. Taghi Jabbari and Fatemeh Golzar-Jabbari; m. Fattaneh Tavassoli, Dec. 30, 1949. Undergrad. MD programs, Tehran (Iran) Med. Sch., MD, 1966. Diplomate Am. Bd. Psychiatry and Neurology with added qualification in clin. neurophysiology; licensed MD in Md., D.C. Intern Martland Med. Ctr., Newark, 1968-69; resident in neurology Albany (N.Y.) Med. Ctr., 1969-72; fellow Tulan Med. Sch., New Orleans, 1972-73, asst. prof., 1974-76; from assoc. prof. neurology to prof., chair Uniformed Svcs. U., Bethesda, Md., 1978-98, prof., chair neurology, 1998—. Adj. prof. George Washington U., Wash., 1985—, Georgetown U., Wash., 1986—; dir. clin. neurophysiology Walter Reed Army Med. Ctr., Wash., 1977—2000. Col. U.S. Army, 1986—. Recipient VA Superior Performance award. Mem. Internat. Movement Disorder Soc., Am. Epilepsy Soc., Am. Acad. Neurology, Am. Neurological Assn., Am. Soc. Clin. Neurophysiology, Royal Soc. Medicine. Office: Dept Neurology USUHS 4301 Jones Bridge Rd Bethesda MD 20814-4712 E-mail: bjabbari@mxa.usuhs.mil.

JABBOUR, GEORGETTE N. linguist, educator; b. Safita, Syria, Feb. 17, 1944; arrived in U.S., 1996; d. Nicolas Jabbour and Sefma Kussa. PhD in Applied Linguistics, U. Birmingham, Eng., 1997. Instr. higher edn. Damascus (Syria) U., 1980—93; asst. prof. N.Y. Inst. Tech., Old Westburg, NY, 1998—. Contbr. chapters to books. Mem.: AAUW (editor North Shore Br. Bull. 2002), Am. Assn. for Applied Corpus Linguistics, Am. Assn. for Applied Linguistics. Republican. Greek Orthodox. Achievements include research in computer assisted language learning. Avocations: writing, poetry, swimming. Home: Apt D 329 Main St Roslyn NY 11576-2165 Office: NY Inst Tech PO Box 8000 Old Westbury NY 11568

JABBOUR, NABIL MILAD, ophthalmologist; b. Beirut, Nov. 11, 1955; came to U.S., 1979; s. Milad S. and Rose J. (Hatem) J.; m. Nina R. Khalifé, Aug. 19, 1979; children: Noel, Jad. BSc, Am. U. Beirut, 1976, MD, 1980. Lic. physician W.Va. Intern in internal medicine Am. U. Beirut, 1979-80, resident dept. ophthalmology, 1980-83; fellow Retina Assocs./Mass. Eye & Ear Infirmary Eye Rsch. Inst. Harvard Med. Sch., Boston, 1983-85, chief fellow, 1984-85; asst. prof. ophthalmology W.Va. U., Morgantown, 1985-89, assoc. prof. ophthalmology, 1989-91; founder, owner Mid-Atlantic Retina Consultations, Morgantown, 1991—. Dir. retina and vitreous svc. W.Va. U., Morgantown, 1987-91, chmn. med. student edn. com., 1989-91, mem. biomed. rsch. support com., 1988-91; pres. ForSight Found., 1991—; chmn. med. records com. W.Va. U. Hosp., 1990-91, mem. patient care rev. com., 1990-91; educator, lectr., presenter in field. Contbr. numerous articles to profl. jours.; creator videotape Jabbour-Nutter Diathermy System Transconjunctival and Transscleral Diathermy; inventor in field. Pres. Parents' Assn. Alliance Christian Sch., 1988-89, bd. dirs., 1989—, pres. bd. dirs., 1991-93; pres. Homeowners' Assn. Willow Wick, 1989-90; chmn. W.Va. Diabetes Eye Coun., 1990-9; mem. W.Va. Diabetes Control Coun., 1990—; pres., trustee Trinity H.S., Morgantown, 1995—; v.p., trustee H.O.M.E., Houston, 1994—. Fellow ACS; mem. Am. Acad. Ophthalmology (honor award 2001), W.Va. Acad. Ophthalmology, Schepens Internat. Soc. (founding), Vitreous Soc., Sigma Xi. Achievements include development of Iris Speculum for open sky vitrectomy, vitreoretinal dissection set, high viscosity contact lens for vitreous surgery, transscleral diathermy electrode, diathermy return path, illuminated dissection spatula for vitrectomy, suction tip with soft guard, irrigation/aspiration manual set, illuminated wide angle contact lens for vitrectomy, right-angled infusion cannula. Office: Mid-Atlantic Retina Consultations Inc 3120 Collins Ferry Rd Morgantown WV 26505-3305

JABBUR, RAMZI J. management consultant; b. Beirut, Mar. 9, 1937; arrived in U.S., 1958; s. Jibrail S. and Asma Jabbur; 1 child from previous marriage, James R. BS, Am. U. Beirut, 1958; MS, Stanford U., 1960, PhD, 1963. Asst. prof. physics CUNY, NYC, 1967—70; dir. mgmt. sci. BBDO, NYC, 1970—74; dir. corp. planning W.R. Grace and Co., NYC, 1974—79; prin. and pres. Jabbur Assoc. Mgmt. Cons., NYC, 1980—. Contbr. articles to profl. jours. Home: 1380 Riverside Dr 5H New York NY 10033 Office: Jabbur Associates Ste 5H 1380 Riverside Dr New York NY 10033

JABERG, EUGENE CARL, theology educator, administrator; b. Linton, Ind., Mar. 27, 1927; s. Elmer Charles and Hilda Carolyn (Stuckmann) J.; m. Miriam Marie Priebe; children: Scott Christian, Beth Amy, David Edward. BA, Lakeland Coll., 1948; BD, Mission House Theol. Sem., 1954; MA, U. Wis., 1959, PhD, 1968. Ordained to ministry, United Ch. of Christ, 1959. U.S. army corr., 1949—50; staff announcer WKOW-TV, Madison, Wis., 1955-58, 67-68, WHBL, Sheboygan, 1943—56, WHA, Wis. U. Sta., 1957—58, KTCA=TV, Mpls., 1968—80; minister Pilgrim Congl. Ch., Madison, 1956-57; assoc. prof. speech Mission House Theol. Sem., Plymouth, Wis., 1958-62; asst. prof. communications United Theol. Sem., New Brighton, Minn., 1962-76, prof. communications, 1976-91, dir. admissions, 1984-87, dir. MDiv program, 1988-90, prof. emeritus, 1991—, acting dir. Masters programs, 1997-99. Bus. ptnr. Dimension 3 Media Svcs., Mpls., 1988-90; coord. spl. projects CTV North Suburbs Cable Access, 1991-2002; vis. scholar Cambridge U., Eng. Author, editor: A History of Lakeland-Mission House, 1962; author: The Video Pencil, 1980; contbr. articles, revs. to various publs.; producer films, videotapes. Artistic dir. Interfaith Players, Mpls., 1965-73; TV prodr., moderator Town Meeting of Twin Cities, Mpls., 1967-70; prodr., writer, host various radio and TV series, Mpls., 1970-89; mem. Ctr. Urban Encounter, Mpls., 1972-74, New Brighton Human Rights Commn., 1975-77; bd. mem. office comm. United Ch. Christ, N.Y.C., 1975-81; mem. North Suburban Sys. Cable Access Commn., 1986-91. Kaltenborn Radio scholar, 1957; grantee Assn. Theol. Sems., 1983; recipient Minn. Community TV award, 1993, Judges Choice award Alliance of Cmty. Media, 1999; named into Gallery of Distinction Lakeland Coll., 1996—; named to Sta. CTV-15 Hall of Fame, Roseville, Minn., 1998. Mem. Religious Speech Communication Assn. (co-chmn. 1972-74), World Assn. Christian Communication. Democrat. Avocations: travel, hiking, spectator sports, film. Home: 1601 Innsbruck Dr Minneapolis MN 55432-6046 Office: United Theol Sem 3000 5th St NW Saint Paul MN 55112-2507 E-mail: ecjaberg@aol.com.

JABINE, THOMAS BOYD, statistical consultant; b. Bklyn., N.Y., Jan. 26, 1925; s. Thomas and Emma Boyd Jabine; m. Marian Smith, Apr. 29, 1950; children: Thomas P., William T., Angie, Leslie N. BS Maths., MS Econs. and Sci., Mass. Inst. Tech., 1949. Various positions U.S. Bur. Census, Washington, 1949—69, chief stats. rsch. divsn., 1969—73; chief math. statistician Social Security Adminstrn., Washington, 1973—79; stats. policy expert Energy Info. Adminstrn., Washington, 1979—80; stats. cons. Self-employed, Washington, 1980—. Editor: Human Rights and Statistics: Getting the Record Straight, 1992; author: (govt. report) Survey of Income and Program Participation Quality Profile, 1990. Pres. Washington Stats. Soc., 1978—79. With USN, 1943—45. Fellow: Am. Stats. Assn. (chair com. privacy and confidentiality 1986, chair com. on sci. freedom and human rights 1981—84, mem. com. profl. ethics 2000—); mem.: Internat. Stats. Inst. Avocations: tennis, flute, constructor of cryptic crossword puzzles. Personal E-mail: tjabine@nas.edu.

JABLON, ELAINE, education consultant; b. N.Y.C., Dec. 8, 1950; d. James and Frances (Augone) Georgallas; m. Steven Ira Jablon, June 23, 1976. AA in Early Childhood Edn., Marjorie Webster Jr. Coll., Washington, 1971; BEd in Elem. Edn., U. Miami, 1973, MEd in Learning Disabilities, 1974. Tchr. Broward County Pub. Schs., Ft. Lauderdale, Fla., 1974-76, Orange County Pub. Schs., Orlando, Fla., 1976-77, substitute tchr., 1977-82, Osceola County (Fla.) Pub. Schs., 1977-82; cons. edn. cen. Fla., 1977—. Counselor youth diversion program, Orlando, 1978-80. Vol. Jack Eckerd for Fla. Gov., Kissimmee, 1977-78; info. rep. Epilepsy Found. of Am., Osceola, 1980-87. Mem. AAUW (chairwoman), ASCD, Am. Bus. Women's Assn. (edn. chairwoman 1980-82), Fla. ASDC, Fla. Network for Family and Parent Edn. (founding mem.), Assn. Early Childhood Edn. Internat., The Fla. Ctr. for Children and Youth, Council Exceptional Children -- Early Childhood Divsn. and Learning Disabilities Divsn., Learning Disabilities Assn., Fla. Fedn. Council for Learning Disabilities (writing com.), Learning Disabilities Assn., U. Miami Alumni Assn. Cen. Fla., Kissimmee Bus. and Profl. Women's Club (pres. 1985-86, v.p. 1986—, recipient citation). Lodges: Sons of Italy of Orlando (trustee 1978-80), Sons of Italy of Osceola County (trustee 1988). Avocations: walking, swimming, reading. Office: 808 Hastings Dr Kissimmee FL 34744-5804

JABLONSKI, JAMES ARTHUR, lawyer; b. Sheboygan, Wis., Nov. 12, 1942; s. John Alfred and Dena (Kaat) J. BBA, U. Wis., 1965, JD, 1968. Bar: Wis. 1968, Calif. 1969, U.S. Ct. Appeals (7th cir) 1969, U.S. Supreme Ct. 1974, Colo. 1976, U.S. Ct. Appeals (8th and 10th cirs.) 1976. Assoc. Pillsbury, Madison & Sutro, San Francisco, 1969-72; asst. prof. law Washington U., St. Louis, 1972-76; ptnr. Gorsuch Kirgis L.L.C., Denver, 1976—. Mem. Colo. Bar Assn., Wis. Bar Assn. (bd. govs. 1990-92), Denver Bar Assn. Clubs: Pinehurst Country (Denver). Democrat. Office: Gorsuch Kirgis Tower 1 1515 Arapahoe St Ste 1000 Denver CO 80202-2120

JABLONSKI, ROBERT LEO, architect; b. Chgo., Mar. 28, 1926; s. Leo Frank and Rose (Domian) J. BS, U. Ill., 1950. Lic. architect Nat. Coun. Archtl. Registration Bd., 1965. Chief planner Nat. Council YMCA, Chgo., 1957-64; assoc. univ. architect U. Ill., Chgo., 1964-69; coordinator architect U. Chgo., 1969-70; dir. bldg. program City of Chgo., 1970—2003; prin. Robert Jablonski Mgmt. Svcs., Arch., ALA, Chgo., 1988—. Served with U.S. Army, 1940-46, ETO. Mem.: ALA. Roman Catholic. Avocations: tennis, swimming.

JABLONSKY, STEPHEN, music educator, composer, artist, writer; b. N.Y.C., Dec. 5, 1941; s. Benjamin and Adelaide (Robinson) J.; m. Roberta Nusim, Aug. 29, 1965 (div. Jan. 1999); m. Tina Sophia Ostrander, May 23, 2003. BA, CCNY, 1962; postgrad., Harvard U., 1962-63; MA, NYU, 1964, PhD, 1973; postgrad., Bridgeport U., 1982-83; composition studies with Mark Brunswick, Leon Kirchner, Paul Turok, Pierre Boulez. Cert. music tchr., N.Y. Music tchr. N.Y.C. Bd. Edn., 1965—68; asst. dir. Lake Bryn Mawr Camp, Honesdale, Pa., 1968—70; assoc. prof. music theory & composition, humanities CCNY, N.Y.C., 1964—, chmn. music dept., 2002—. Cons. Lifetime Learning Systems, Fairfield, Conn., 1978-90; editor-in-chief The Work and Family Pub. Group, 1993-94; chief fin. officer, dir. computer svcs. Youth Mktg. Internat., 1994-98; v.p. The Weiner Nusim Found., 1997-2001; conducting fellow Nat. Orchestral Assn., N.Y.C., 1973-76; bd. dirs. Musigraphics, Inc., Easton, Conn., 1975-80; profl. artist/graphic designer, 1968—; cons. Youth Mktg. Internat., 1999—, CBS Camera III, 1975-76, Exxon/Affiliate Artists Conducting Program, 1976, Finalist All-Conn. Art Show, the Stamford Mus., 1990-91, All-Conn. Art Show, The Discovery Mus., 1991; contbg. editor Youth Media Internat., 1999-2001; contbr. articles to profl. jours. NEA fellow, 1975, N.Y. State Regents Teaching fellow, 1962; recipient Founders Day award NYU, 1974. Mem. AAUP, ASCAP, Internat. Trumpet Guild, Stamford Art Assn., New Canaan Soc. for the Arts, Profl. Staff Congress, Coll. Music Soc., Soc. Music Theory, Phi Mu Alpha Sinfonia, Alpha Epsilon Pi. Avocations: tennis, reading, art collector, philanthropy. Home: 1255 Westover Rd Stamford CT 06902-1037 Office: CCNY 138th St And Convent Ave New York NY 10031

JABRE, ANTHONY, neurosurgeon, educator; b. Mar. 28, 1953; MD, French Faculty Medicine, Lebanon, 1978. Neurosurgery resident U. Cin. Med. Ctr., 1978-85; neurosurgery fellow U. London, Queen Square, 1984-85, U. Zurich, Switzerland, 1985; asst. prof. neurosurgery Boston U., 1993-00; assoc. prof. neurosurg. Boston Univ., Boston, 2000—. Contbr. articles to med. jours. Office: Boston U Med Ctr 720 Harrison Ave Ste 710 Boston MA 02118-2334

JABRE, EDDY-MARCO, architect; b. Beirut, July 10, 1948; came to U.S., 1986; s. Farid and Lody (Abourizk) J.; m. Ifrandate Alame, Oct. 12, 1974; children: Moune, Joe, Marc. Architect DPLG, Ecole Nationale Superieure Des Beaux Arts, Paris, 1975; urban planner, Universite Paris XII, Vincennes, 1976. Ptnr. Atelier D'Etudes Raspail, Paris, 1975-78; dir. F.S.K., Riyadh, Saudi Arabia, 1978-80; sr. ptnr., pres. Copreco, Riyadh, Saudi Arabia, 1980-86; pres.

Nedcorp, Winchester, Mass., 1986—, Maine Nedcorp, Winchester, 1987—, Atrium Custom Homes, Winchester, 1987—. Avocations: swimming, reading, traveling. Office: Atrium Custom Homes PO Box 368 Winchester MA 01890-0468

JABRE, JOE F. neurologist, electromyographer; b. Beirut, Jan. 5, 1947; came to U.S., 1972; s. Farid Y. and Lody (Abou-Rizk) J.; m. Helen A. Perry, Oct. 6, 1974; children: Frederick, Monique, Christopher. B.Math., Christian Bros. Coll., Beirut, 1964; MD with honors, French Faculty Medicine, Beirut, 1972. Diplomate Am. Bd. Psychiatry and Neurology, Am. Bd. electrodiagnostic Medicine. Intern Boston City Hosp., 1972-73; resident Case Western Res. U., Cleve., 1973-77; fellow Cleve. Clinic Found., 1977-78; asst. prof. neurology La. State U. Med. Ctr., New Orleans, 1978-82; attending neurologist Med. Ctr. East New Orleans, 1982-83; assoc. prof. neurology Boston U., 1983—, dir. electromyography, 1983—, rsch. assoc. neuromuscular rsch. ctr., 1985—; attending neurologist Boston VA Med. Ctr., 1983—, co-chief Harvard-Boston U. Neurology Svc., 2000—. Invited guest lectr. numerous countries, 1989—. Author: EMG Manual, 1983. Fellow Am. Assn. Electrodiagnostic Medicine; mem. Am. Lebanese Med. Assn. (pres. 1994), Société de Neurophysiologie Clinique de Langue Française. Office: Boston VA Med Ctr 150 S Huntington Ave Boston MA 02130-4817

JABS, ARTHUR DEAN, JR., plastic surgeon; b. Monterey Park, Calif., Dec. 21, 1953; s. Arthur Dean and Janet Louise Jabs; m. Leslie Bowman, May 31, 1975 (div. June 1999); children: Hilary, Connor; m. Rebecca Pugh, June 1, 2002. BA, U. So. Calif., 1975; PhD, U. Ill., Chgo., 1980; MD, Rush Coll. of Medicine, Chgo., 1984. Diplomate Am. Bd. Plastic Surgery, Nat. Bd. Med. Examiners. Resident in gen. surgery St. Vincent's Hosp., N.Y.C., 1984-87; fellow in plastic surgery Columbia Presbyn. Med. Ctr., N.Y.C., 1987-89; staff surgeon Walter Reed Army Med. Ctr., Washington, 1989-92; pvt. practice specializing in cosmetic plastic surgery Bethesda, Md., 1992—. Clin. assoc. prof. surgery Uniformed Svcs. U. Health Scis., Bethesda, 1992—, U. Conn., 1993-96; attending surgeon Suburban Hosp., Bethesda, Fairfax Hosp., Falls Church, Va., 1997—, Charlotte Hungerford Hosp., Torrington, Conn., 1992-97, Winsted (Conn.) Meml. Hosp., 1992-96; attending surgeon dept. plastic surgery Walter Reed Army Med. Ctr., Washington, 1989-92; cons. plastic surgery NIH, Bethesda, 1991-92; presenter. Contbr. articles to profl. jours. Maj. U.S. Army Med. Corp., 1989-92. Fellow ACS, Am. Soc. Plastic Surgeons, Am. Soc. Aesthetic Plastic Surg., Northeastern Soc. Plastic and Reconstructive Surgeons; mem. Nat. Capital Soc. Plastic Surgeons. Avocations: tennis, wing shooting, skiing. Office: Cosmetic Surgery Assocs 10215 Fernwood Rd Ste 280 Bethesda MD 20817-1114 E-mail: jabs@cosmeticplastics.com.

JABS, CAROLYN RUTH, writer; b. Cleve., Nov. 3, 1950; d. Gerhardt A. and Esther R. (Poggemeier) Jabs; m. David L. Zamichow, June 30, 1982; children: Bert Zamichow, Jessie Zamichow, Zachary Zamichow. BA, Wittenberg U. Freelance writer, 1977—. Author: Re/Uses, 1982, The Heirloom Gardener, 1983; contbg. editor: Family PC Mag.; contbr. articles to consumer publs. Mem.: AAUW, Nat. Writers Union, Auditory Verbal Internat., Am. Soc. Journalists and Authors. Avocations: book clubs, bicycling, gardening. E-mail: crjabs@aol.com.

JABS, DOUGLAS ALAN, ophthalmology educator, researcher; b. Hartford, Conn., Oct. 2, 1951; m. Ethylin Wang, 1977; 1 child, Alexandra Wang. AB, Dartmouth Coll., 1973; MD, Johns Hopkins U., 1977, MS in Bus., 1999, MBA, 2000. Diplomate Am. Bd. Ophthalmology, Am. Bd. Internal Medicine, Nat. Bd. Med. Examiners. Intern Cornell-N.Y. Med. Ctr., N.Y.C., 1977-78; resident in ophthalmology Johns Hopkins Hosp., Balt., 1978-81, resident in internal medicine, 1981-83; fellow in rheumatology Johns Hopkins Med. Instns., Balt., 1983-84; asst. prof. ophthalmology Johns Hopkins U. Sch. Medicine, Balt., 1984-88, assoc. prof., 1988-93, asst. prof. medicine, 1987-89, assoc. prof., 1989-93, prof. ophthalmology and medicine, 1993—, prof. epidemiology, 2002—. Cons. FDA, Rockville, Md., 1994-2000. Recipient Sr. Scientist award, Rsch. to Prevent Blindness, 2002; Ethel Baxter-Sjogren Syndrome Found., 1995, Lew R. Wasserman merit award, Rsch. To Prevent Blindness, 1997; Olga Keith Weiss scholar award Rsch. to Prevent Blindness, 1991. Fellow Am. Acad. Ophthalmology, Am. Coll. Rheumatology; mem. Am. Uveitis Soc. Office: Johns Hopkins U Wilmer Eye Inst 550 N Broadway Ste 700 Baltimore MD 21205-2008

JABS, ETHYLIN WANG, human genetics physician, scientist, educator; b. Boston, Oct. 15, 1952; d. Shih Yi and Chun Lien (Chi) Wang; m. Douglas Alan Jabs, June 4, 1977; 1 child, Alexandra. BS, Johns Hopkins U., 1974, MD, 1977. Diplomate Am. Bd. Med. Genetics, Md. Bd. Med. Examiners, Am. Bd. Pediat.; lic. Clin. Cytogenetics, Clin. Genetics, Molecular Genetics. Intern The N.Y. Hosp. Cornell Med. Ctr., N.Y.C., 1977-78; from resident pediat. to prof. Johns Hopkins Hosp., Balt., 1978—98, Dr. Frank V. Sutland prof. pediatric genetics, 1998—, dir. Ctr. Craniofacial Devel. and Disorders, 1994—2002, dir. Internat. Coll. Genetic Rsch. Tng. program, 2002—. Collaborator Ctr. d'Etude du Polymorphisme Human Collaborator, 1989—; rsch. adv. Treacher Collins Syndrome Found., 1989-91; adv. com. cons. Nat. Inst. Dental Rsch., 1992; mem. adv. bd. NIH Deafness & Other Comm. Disorders, 1994, others; mem. adv. group on coordinating rare diseases rsch. NIH, 1997—; mem. NIHGR genome study sect., 1996-99; mem. bd. sci. counselors NIDCR, 2000--. Editor (ad hoc) Gene; editl. bd. mem. Jour. Craniofacial Genetics and Devel. Biology, 1995-2001; assoc. editor Genetics in Medicine, 1998—; cons. editor Pediatric Rsch., 1999—; reviewer Am. Jour. Human Genetics, Chromosoma, Cytogenetic and Cell Genetics, Gene, Genomics, Human Genetics, Human Molecular Genetics, Jour. Biol. Chemistry, Jour. Clin. Investigation, Procs. NAS, USA, Nature Genetics, Nucleic Acids Rsch., Somatic Cell and Molecular Genetics, Am. Jour. Med. Genetics, Molecular Medicine, others; lectr. and rschr. in field; contbr. articles to profl. jours., chpts. to books. Stetler Rsch. fellow 1981-83; Instnl. Rsch. grantee, 1985-86, Basil O'Connor Starter Rsch. grantee March of Dimes Defects Found., 1985-87; recipient New Investigator award NIH, 1984-87, Clinician-Scientist award Johns Hopkins U., 1986-88, NIH R01s, P50, P60 and D43 grantee, 1986—. Mem. AAAS, AMA, Am. Soc. Clin. Investigation, Am. Soc. Human Genetics, Am. Chinese Geneticist Assn. (nominating com. chmn. 1989, bd. dirs. 1993, pres. 1996-97), Am. Cleft Palate-Craniofacial Assn., Am. Coll. Med. Genetics, Human Genome Orgn., Soc. Pediatric Rsch., Soc. Craniofacial Genetics (pres. 1996-98), Chromosome Segregation and Aneuploidy Internat. Network, Am. Acad. Pediat. (sect. on genetics and birth defects), Coun. Med. Genetics Orgns. Office: Johns Hopkins Hosp CMSC 10-04 600 N Wolfe St Baltimore MD 21287-3914

JABS, JENNIFER, financial planner; b. Bristol, Conn., Sept. 22; d. Arthur Gustav and Frances Mary (Demma) J. BA, U. Hartford, 1976; MA, Trinity Coll., 1993. Cert. history, consumer interviewer, real estate.; cert. in dental radiation health and safety. Asst. mgr. Credit Bureau of Bristol, 1976-85; credit investigator, analyst Bristol Savings Bank, 1986-88; v.p. ops. and fins., oral maxillofacial surg. asst. O.M.S. Assocs., Bristol, 1986-2000, Dr. Steven Hunter, 2000—. Organ procurer for dental rsch., U. Zurich, 1988-2000; presenter Trinity Coll. Lecture Series, Hartford, Conn., 1990. Organizer, author of article Plainville (Conn.) Pub. Schs., 1985; reviewer of religious edn. St. Joseph Ch., Bristol, 1987, com. mem. 1986—; vol. Bristol Civic Theater, 1990-92; participant NASA Town Meet, 1992. Mem. Am. Classical League, Classical Assn. New Eng. (cert. classical humanities 1991), Am. Inst. Archaeology, Am. Dental Assts. Assn., Conn. Dental Assts. Assn., Trinity Club. Democrat. Roman Catholic. Avocations: swimming, hiking, arts and crafts, travel, astronomy.

JACCACI, AUGUST THAYER, JR., architect, educator; b. N.Y.C., Mar. 9, 1937; s. August Thayer and Helen Jenkins Jaccaci; m. Robin Charboneau Middleton, June 28, 1963 (div. June 1982); children: Anthony, Alexander; m. Joanne Karen Hobbs, Oct. 28, 1999. BA, Harvard Coll., 1960, MA in Tchg., 1964; MFA, R.I. Sch. Design, 1965. Tchr., coach Rutland (Vt.) H.S., 1960—61; admissions officer, coach Harvard Coll., Cambridge, Mass., 1961—63; admissions officer, tchr. R.I. Sch. Design, Providence, 1963—65; tchr., coach Phillips Acad. Andover, Mass., 1965—68; arts adminstr., lectr. Boston Coll., Newton, 1968—75; adminstr., coach Lawrence Acad., Groton, Mass., 1976—78; tchr. Burke Mountain Acad., East Burke, Vt., 1983—85; social arch. Unity Scholars, New Gloucester, Maine, 1998—2003. Pres. Metamatrix Assoc., Thetford, Vt., 1978; founder Am. Ctr. Creativity & Innovation, New Gloucester, 2003; ski coach, team capt. FIS World Ski Championships, Vail, Colo., 1989; guest lectr. Stanford Bus. Sch.; cons. Motorola, Fannie Mae, Pillsbury, AT&T, P.W. Minor, Micromentor, Chase Manhattan Bank, J.C. Penney, Polaroid, Vt. Agy. Human Svcs., Arthur Anderson, Xerox, Vol. Hosp. Assn. Am., Toronto Dominion Bank, No. Telecom, Canada, IMD, Europe, Credit Suisse, Europe, Brit. Petroleum, Europe; spkr. in field nat. and internat. Represented in permanent collections, Addison Gallery Am. Art; author: CEO: Chief Evolutionary Officer, 1999, General Periodicity, 2000. Candidate for gov., Vt., 1992, 1994. Recipient Svc. to Humanity Award, PW Minor Co., 2000, Earl award, Religious Futurist, 2002. Mem.: World Future Soc. (pres. Boston chpt. 1975), Creative Edn. Found. (tchr. 1972—2003, Leadership, Svc. and Commitment award 1990). Avocations: skiing, rowing, hiking. Home: 626 Penney Rd New Gloucester ME 04260 Fax: 207-926-3970. E-mail: unityscholars@earthlink.net.

JACCARD, JERRY-LOUIS, music educator, translator; b. Pasadena, Calif., Feb. 19, 1944; s. F.L. Jack and Dolly R. Jaccard; m. Alma Lemmon. B in Music Edn., U. Ariz., 1965; M in Music Edn., Holy Names Coll., 1976; EdD, U. Mass., 1995. Music specialist Kayenta (Ariz.) Pub. Schs., 1969-73, Show Low (Ariz.) Pub. Schs., 1973-80; dir. Kodaly Musical Tng. Inst., Inc. Hartt Sch. Music, U. Hartford, West Hartford, Conn., 1980-83; music specialist West Hartford Pub. Schs., 1982-93; assoc. prof. music Brigham Young U., Provo, Utah, 1993—. Cons. Waterford Sch. Provo City Schs., Utah; presenter in field. Co-author: The Complete Musician-Violin Book One, 2003; revision editor: Joy Through the Magic of Music, 1999; contbr. chpt. to book. Vol. music and curriculum specialist Provo City Schs., 1994—. Rsch. grantee Ford Found., Rockefeller Found., Swiss-Am. Cultural Exchange Coun.; recipient Outstanding Vol. Golden Apple award Provo Town Coun. PTA, 2000. Mem. Internat. Kodaly Soc. (v.p.), Orgn. Am. Kodaly Educators (past western divsn. pres., past nat. chair rsch. and publs., mem. editl. bd.), Fondation de la Famille Jaccard (life), Soc. Liszt-Kodály de España, Assn. Internat. d'Education Musicale Willems (bd. dirs.), Internat. Kodály Soc. (mem. editl. bd.), English Folk Dance and Song Soc. Mem. Lds Ch. Avocations: travel, family history, languages, gardening, collecting folk art. Office: Brigham Young Univ C-582 HFAC Sch Music Provo UT 84601 Fax: 801-422-0532. E-mail: jljaccard@byugate.byu.edu.

JACHE, ALBERT WILLIAM, retired chemistry educator, scientist; b. Manchester, N.H., Nov. 5, 1924; s. William Frederick and Esther (Ruemely) J.; m. Lucy Ellen Hauslein, June 14, 1948; children: Ann Gail, Ellen Ruth, Philip William, Heidi Verena. BS, U. N.H., 1948, MS, 1950; PhD, U. Wash., 1952. Sr. chemist Air Reduction Co., Murray Hill, N.J., 1952-53; rsch. assoc. dept. physics Duke U., 1953-55; asst. prof. dept. chemistry Tex. A&M U., College Station, 1955-58, assoc. prof., 1958-61; cons. Ozark Mahoning Co., Tulsa, 1960-61, assoc. rsch. dir., 1961-64; sr. rsch. assoc. Olin Mathieson Chem. Corp. (now Olin Corp.), New Haven, 1964-67, sect. mgr., 1965-67, cons., 1967-75; prof. chemistry Marquette U., Milw., 1967-90, prof. emeritus, 1990—, chmn. chem. dept., 1967-72, dean Grad. Sch., 1972-77, assoc. acad. v.p. for health scis., 1974-77, assoc. v.p.-acad. affairs, 1977-85; scientist-in-residence Argonne (Ill.) Nat. Lab., 1985-86, scientist, 1991-96, temporary appointment, 1991-96; with ChemLab, 2000—. Program coordination com. Med. Center S.E. Wis.; lectr. U. Tulsa, 1963-64, New Haven Coll., 1967; cons. Allied Chem. Corp., 1977-78, 2000-; salt panel com. remediation buried and tank wastes NAS/NRC, 1996-97. Trustee Milw. Sci. Ednl. Found.; pres. Milw. Sci. Ednl. Trust, 1973—; trustee Argonne Univs. Assn., 1977-80; chmn. Assn. Grad. Schs. in Cath. Univs., 1973-75; mem. AUA nuclear engring. edn. com. U. Chgo, 1977-89, chmn., 1984, sec., 1989; double bass player River Cities Symphony Orch., 1997-2001, Evergreen Comty. Orch., 1994—, Evergreen String Ensemble, 1994-2000, Marietta Chamber Orch., 1994-97. With AUS, 1942-46. Fellow AAAS, Am. Inst. Chemists; mem. Am. Chem. Soc. (chmn.-elect, program chmn. div. fluorine chemistry 1981, chmn. div. fluorine chemistry 1982), Sigma Xi, Omicron Kappa Upsilon, Alpha Sigma Nu. Achievements include research and numerous patents in the area of inorganic fluorine chemistry with emphasis on anhydrous hydrogen fluoride as a solvent or reaction medium and Hypofluorite chemistry. Home and Office: 301 Ohio St Marietta OH 45750-3139

JACHNA, JOSEPH DAVID, photographer, educator; b. Chgo., Sept. 12, 1935; m. Virginia Kemper, 1962; children: Timothy, Heidi, Jody. BS in Art Edn., Inst. Design, Ill. Inst. Tech., 1958, MS in Photography, 1961. Part-time photographic asst. Derwin Studio Darkroom, Chgo., 1953-54; photo-technician Eastman Kodak Labs., Chgo., 1954; photographer's asst. DeSort Studio, Chgo., 1956-58; free-lance photographer Chgo., 1961—; instr. photography Inst. Design, Ill. Inst. Tech., Chgo., 1961—69; assoc. prof. U. Ill., Chgo., 1969—75, prof., 1976—2001, prof. emeritus, 2001—. One-man shows include Art Inst. Chgo., 1961, St. Mary's Coll., Notre Dame, Ind., 1963, U. Ill., Chgo., 1965, 77, Lightfall Gallery Art Ctr., Evanston, Ill., 1970, U. Wis., Milw., 1970, Ctr. for Photog. Studies, Louisville, 1974, Nikon Photog. Salon, Tokyo, 1974, Afterimage Gallery, Dallas, 1975, Visual Studies Workshop Gallery, Rochester, N.Y., 1979, Chgo. Ctr. for Contemporary Photography, 1980, Focus Gallery, San Francisco, 1981, Photogenesis, Albuquerque, 1983, Andover (Mass.) Gallery, 1984, Chgo. State U., 1985, Tweed Mus. Art, Duluth, Minn., 1986, Gallery 954, Chgo., 1993, State of Ill. Galleries, Chgo., Lockport and Springfield, 1994, Fermilab, Batavia, Ill., 1995, Stephen Daiter Gallery, Chgo., 2000; exhibited in group shows at Art Inst. Chgo, 1963, 83, MIT, Cambridge, 1968, Walker Art Ctr., Mpls., 1973, 89, Renaissance Soc. Gallery U. Chgo., 1975, Mus. Contemporary Art, Chgo., 1977, 96—, Mus. Art RISD, Providence, 1978, Carpenter Ctr. Visual Arts, Harvard U., Cambridge, 1981, Nexus, Atlanta, 1983, Nat. Mus. Art., Washington, 1984, San Francisco Mus. Modern Art, 1985, Internat. Ctr. Photography, Tucson, 1992, Gallery 312, Chgo., 1996, Stockholm Subway, Sweden, 1999, Hyde Park Art Ctr., Chgo., 2001, Stephen Daiter Gallery, Chgo., 2002, 2003, Taken by Design: Photography at the Inst. of Design, 1937-1971, 2002; represented in permanent collections, Mus. Modern Art, N.Y.C., Internat. Mus. Photography, George Eastman House, Rochester, N.Y., MIT, San Francisco Mus. Modern Art, Mpls. Inst. Arts, Art Inst. Chgo., Ctr. Photog. Studies, Louisville, Ctr. for Creative Photography, U. Ariz., Tucson. Ferguson Found. grantee, 1973, Nat. Endowment for Arts grantee, 1976, Ill. Arts Council, 1979; Guggenheim fellow, 1980. Home: 5707 W 89 Pl Oak Lawn IL 60453-1225 E-mail: iceman@uic.edu.

JACINTO, GEORGE ANTHONY, social worker, counselor, educator, consultant; b. Gilroy, Calif., Dec. 21, 1949; s. George Peter and Isabelle Agnes (Joseph) J. BS in Criminology-Corrections, Calif. State U., Fresno, 1974; postgrad., Wash. Theol. Union, 1975, U. Wis., 1980, Boise State U., 1981; MEd in Guidance and Counseling Svcs., Albertson Coll. of Idaho, 1982; MSW in Clin. Social Work, Fla. State U., 1990; postgrad., Barry U. lic. clin. social worker. Youth min. Ch. St. Michael, Olympia, Wash., 1976-77; dir. youth ministry St. James Congregation, Franklin, Wis., 1977-80; diocesan youth dir. Cath. Diocese of Boise, Idaho, 1980-83; dir. religious edn. St. Andrew Ch., Orlando, Fla., 1983-84; vocat. rehab. counselor DLES State of Fla., Orlando, 1984-88, vocat. rehab. cons., 1988-89; social worker Fla. Hosp./Rebound, Orlando, 1989-91; vocat. program specialist Fla. Hosp. Med. Ctr., Orlando, 1991-92; mental health specialist Orange County Cmty. Corrections Dept., Orlando, 1992-96; adj. faculty Fla. State Univ. Sch. Social Work, Orlando, 1994-95, U. Ctrl. Fla., Orlando, 1994-96; clin. instr. Sch. Social Work, 1996—. Part-time home health social worker Olsten Health Svcs., Winter Park, Fla., 1991-92; fair hearings officer Orange County Dept. of Social Svcs. Orlando, 1991-92; founder Am. Life Planning Assocs., Orlando, 1985—; social worker, career and life planning cons., youth programming cons. Active diversion program Union St. Ctr., Olympia, Wash.; campaign leader for children's toys Indo-China Refugee Relief, Milw.; mem. adv. cmty. agys. concerned with youth issues; chair Dept. of Social Work Adv. Coun. U. Ctrl. Fla., 1991-92. Mem. NASW (chair Ctrl. Fla. unit 1990-92, bd. dirs. Fla. chpt. 1990-92, Nat. HIV task force Fla. chpt. liaison, ctrl. unit social worker of yr. 1993, del. assembly 1993, 96, 99), World Future Soc., Inst. Noetic Scis. Home: PO Box 533154 Orlando FL 32853-3154 Office: U Ctrl Fla Sch Social Work PO Box 163358 Orlando FL 32816-3358 E-mail: gjacinto@mail.ucf.edu.

JACK, DIXIE LYNN, software consultant, social worker; b. Orlando, Fla., Apr. 7, 1943; d. Alex and Dorothy Ellen (Dixon) J. BA, U. Wash., 1965; AA, Highline C.C., Des Moines, 1971. Tchr. Archdioces, Burien, Wash., 1968-70, Tukwila (Wash.) Sch. Dist., 1970-75; fin. svcs. technician Dept. Welfare, Seattle, 1982-84; social worker, supr. Dept. Children and Family Svcs., Everett, Wash., 1984-94; user support/tng. mgr. Lockheed Martin, Hartford, Conn., 1995-97; computer based tng. mgr. Am. Mgmt. Sys., Manchester, Conn., 1997; implementation, bus. process cons. Ctr. for Support of Families, Chevy Chase, Md., 1998; documentation specialist Amber Systems Inc., Bloomfield Hills, Mich., 1999—2002; implementation site coord. RCM Techs., 2002—. Cons. Juvenile Justice, Supreme Ct., Seattle, 1988-95. Mem. Assn. Univ. Women, Scarab Club, Birmingham-Bloomfield Arts Assn. Home: 836 Golf Dr Apt 302 Pontiac MI 48341

JACK, JANIS GRAHAM, judge; b. 1946; RN, St. Thomas Sch. Nursing, 1969; BA, U. Balt., 1974; JD summa cum laude, South Tex. Coll., 1981. Pvt. practice, Corpus Christi, Tex., 1981-94; judge U.S. Dist. Ct. (so. dist.) Tex., Corpus Christi, 1994—. Jud. mem. The Maritime Law Assn. U.S. Mem. ABA, Fed. Judges Assn., Fifth Cir. Dist. Judges Assn., Nat. Assn. Women Judges, Tex. Bar Found., State Bar Tex., The Philos. Soc. Tex., Order of Lytae, Phi Alpha Delta. Office: US Dist Ct 1133 N Shoreline Blvd Corpus Christi TX 78401

JACK, NANCY RAYFORD, supplemental resource company executive, consultant; b. Hughes Springs, Tex., June 23, 1939; d. Vernon Lacy and Virginia Ernestine (Turner) Rayford; m. Kermit E. Hundley, Dec. 19, 1979; 1 child by previous marriage, James Bradford Jack, III. Cert. in bus. adminstrn., Keller Grad. Sch. Mgmt., 1980; cert. in acctg., Harper Coll., 1972, cert. in corp. law and tax law, paralegal, 1973. Sr. sec. Gould, Inc., Rolling Meadows, Ill., 1971-73, staff asst., 1973-74, asst. sec., 1974-77, corp. sec., 1977-89, v.p., 1985-89; pres. The Corp. Ofcl. Sec., Wheaton, Ill., 1989-92, Corp. Minutes and More, Wheaton, 1992-99; assoc. dir. The Bus. Owners' Trustee, The Woodlands, Tex., 1999—. Recipient cert. of leadership YWCA Met. Chgo., 1975 Mem.: Kingwood Country Club, Beta Sigma Phi. Home and Office: 162 Linton Downs Pl The Woodlands TX 77382-1692

JACK, PATRICIA ANN, assistant principal; b. Little Rock, Ark. d. Levi and Leanna Johnson; m. Sherwin Jack, June 29, 1980; 1 child, Alese. Master's Adminstrn., Mercy Coll., Manhattan, NY, 2000; Master's Reading, Syracuse U., Syracuse, NY, 1996; BS, Oakwood Coll., Huntsville, AL, 1979. Asst. prin. Bd. of Edn., Brooklyn, NY, 2000—, dist. staff developer, 1999—2000, math/reading staff developer, 1996—99, mentor educator, 1994—96, spl. edn. educator, 1992—94, pre-kindergarten educator Syracuse, NY, 1988—92, grade 4 educator Benton Harbor, Mich., 1983—88. John hopkin's liason Bd. of Edn., Brooklyn, NY, 1996—99, cons. educator, 1994—96, co-chair school-wide program, 1992—94. Recipient Tchr. of the Yr., State of NY and State of Mich., Tchr. of the Yr., Spl. Edn. PS 306, Bklyn., and Benton Harbor, Mich. Avocations: reading, travel, history, antiques, doll collecting.

JACKAMEIT, KEVIN CHARLES, information scientist; b. Harrisonburg, Va., Aug. 25, 1973; s. Bonnie Scott Thompson. BS in Stats., Va. Poly. Inst. and State U., Blacksburg, 1996; MBA in Info. and Decision Support Systems, Va. Poly. Inst. and State U., 2000. Data processing technician (mos 251a) Va. Army N.G., Manassas, Va., 1990—; cost analyst / tech. mgr. Tecolote Rsch., Inc., Lexington Park, Md., 1996—. Mem.: Am. Statis. Assn., Soc. of Cost Estimation and Analysis. Home: 6939 Aidan Way King George VA 22485 Office: Tecolote Research Inc 22299 Exploration Dr Lexington Park MD 20653 Office Fax: 301-866-9049. Personal E-mail: kjackameit@tecolote.com. E-mail: kjackameit@tecolote.com.

JACKEL, LAWRENCE, publishing company executive; b. N.Y.C., July 25; s. Solomon and Sylvia (Fisher) J.; m. Ellen Jane Koons, Sept. 29, 1985; children: Kenneth Isaac, Molly Laurie, Sarah Kate. BBA, CCNY, 1961, MBA, 1966. Acct. Aviquipo, Inc., N.Y.C., 1961-62; fin. exec. Litton Industries, N.Y.C., 1962-68; group controller Alloys Unltd., Inc., N.Y.C., 1968 69; v.p. fin. Litton Ednl. Pub., Inc., N.Y.C., 1969-72, 1969-72, pres. Delmar Pubs. div. Albany, N.Y., 1973-80, 1973-80, exec. v.p., pres. N.Y.C., 1976-80; owner, pres. Tab Books Inc., 1980-90, 1980-90; group v.p. McGraw Hill, Blue Ridge Summit, Pa., 1990-92; pres. Jackel Group Inc.-Cons. and Pubs., Venice, Fla., 1992-93; vice chmn., CEO, owner Lectorum Publs., Inc., N.Y.C., 1993-96; chmn. Promotional Sales Books LLC, N.Y.C., 1996—. Mem. Univ. Club. Democrat. Jewish. Home: 7702 Cherry Laurel Ct Sarasota FL 34241 E-mail: Jackelpub@cs.com.

JACKEL, STEPHANIE DECK, publisher, editor, publishing executive; b. Salt Lake City, Jan. 4, 1938; d. Arthur Clarence Deck, Mary Winnifred Willey Deck; m. Martin Stewart Jackel; m. John Mason Churchill (div.); 1 child, Ethan Churchill;1 child, Amanda Churchill Casillas. BA, Stanford U., Palo Alto, Calif., 1960. Writer/prodr. Utah State Bd. of Edn., Salt Lake City, 1972—76; exec. dir. Utah Heritage Found., Salt Lake City, 1971—86, Preservation Maryland, Balt., 1986—88, Hist. Savannah Found., Savannah, Ga., 1988—97; pres. The Oglethorpe Press, Savannah, 1997—. Proprietor Printer's Ink, Savannah, 1999—. Prodr.: (film) Out of Sticks and Stones, 1973, City of the Great Salt Lake, 1975. Pres. Downtown Neighborhood Assn., Savannah, 1999—, Downtown Garden Club, Savannah, 1997—99; bd. dirs.. Chatham-Savannah Citizen Advocacy, Savannah, 1990—96; chmn. Nat. Alliance of Statewide Preservation Orgns., 1987—88; pres. Nat. Coun.of Preservation Execs., 1988—90; bd. advisors Nat. Trust for Historic Preservation, Washington, 1978—86; bd. dirs. Preservation Action, Washington, 1974—97; mem. citizens adv. com. Chatham Urban Transp. Study Commn., Savannah, 1998—2002; mem. urban design com. Savannah Devel. and Renewal Authority, Savannah, 1993; mem. Utah State Cultural and Historic Sites Rev. Com., Salt Lake City, 1979—86. Recipient Cert. of Appreciation, AIA (Ga. chpt.), 1996, Heritage Citation, Utah Heritage Found., 1986, Merit award, AIA (Utah chpt.), 1976. Home: 312 Habersham St Savannah GA 31401 Office: The Oglethorpe Press 326 Bull St Savannah GA 31401

JACKENDOFF, RAY SAUL, linguistics educator; b. Chgo., Jan. 23, 1945; s. Nathaniel and Elaine Muriel (Flanders) J.; m. Hildy Dvorak; children: Amy Sarah, Beth Liana. BA, Swarthmore Coll., 1965; PhD, MIT, 1969. Instr. UCLA, 1969-70; asst. prof. linguistics Brandeis U., Waltham, Mass., 1971-73, assoc. prof., 1973-79, prof., 1979—, chmn. linguistics and cognitive sci., 1979-92. Author: Semantic Interpretation in Generative Grammar, 1972 (Arts Humanities award Coun. Grad. Schs. in U.S. 1974), X-Bar Syntax: A Study of Phrase Structure, 1977, Semantics and Cognition, 1983, (with F. Lerdahl) A Generative Theory of Tonal Music, 1983, Consciousness and the Computational Mind, 1987, Semantic Structures, 1990, Languages of the Mind, 1992, Patterns in the Mind, 1993, The Architecture of the Language Faculty, 1997, Foundations of Language, 2002; mem. editl. bd. Music Perception, Cognitive Sci., Studia Linguistica, Natural Lang. and Linguistic Theory, Trends in Cognitive Scis. Soloist Boston Pops Orch., 1980 Guggenheim fellow, 1993-94, fellow Wissenschaftskolleg zu Berlin, 1999-2000. Mem. Linguistic Soc. Am. (exec. com. 1996-99, 2002-05 pres 2003), Soc. for Philosophy and Psychology (pres. 1990-91), Am. Acad. Arts and Scis. Jewish. Home: 79 Goden St Belmont MA 02478-2934 Office: Brandeis U Program Linguistics and Cognitive Sci Waltham MA 02454

JACKER, CORINNE LITVIN, playwright, writer; b. Chgo., June 29, 1933; d. Thomas Henry and Theresa (Bellak) Litvin. Student, Stanford U., 1950-52; BS, Northwestern U., 1954, MA, 1955, postgrad., 1955-56. Editor Liberal Arts Press, 1959-60, Macmillan Co., 1960-63, Scribner's, 1963-65; story editor Sta. WNET-TV, N.Y.C., 1969-71, CBS-TV, N.Y.C., 1972-74; instr. playwrighting NYU, 1976-78; vis. prof. playwriting Yale U., 1979-81. Adj. prof. Princeton U., 1986, 88, Columbia U., 1988-99, Breadloaf Sch. of English, 1988, NYU, 1990-91, U. Ga., 1995—; sci. cons. Benton Project for Broadcasting, U. Chgo., 1988-90. Exec. story editor, head writer (TV series) Best of Families, PBS, N.Y.C., 1975-77; head writer (TV series) Another World, 1981-82; author: Man, Memory, and Machines, 1964 (N.Y. Pub. Library 50 Best Books of Yr. 1964), Window on the Unknown, 1966 (AAAS 50 Best Books of Yr. 1966), A Little History of Cocoa, 1966, The Black Flag of Anarchy, 1968 (Pubs. Weekly 25 Best Books of Yr. 1968), The Biological Revolution, 1971, The Chocolate Bar Bust, 1994; playwright: The Scientific Method, 1970, Seditious Acts, 1970, Travellers, 1973, Breakfast, Lunch, & Dinner, 1975, Bits and Pieces, 1975 (Obie award 1975), Harry Outside, 1975 (Obie award 1975), Night Thoughts & Terminal, 1976, Other People's Tables, 1976, My Life, 1977, After the Season, 1978, Later, 1979, Domestic Issues, 1981, In Place, 1982, Songs from Distant Lands, 1985, (adaptation) Hedda Gabbler, 1989, The Island, 1991, (adaptation) The Three Sisters, 1992, In the Dark, 1993, Light, 1993, Getting Home, 1994, A New Life, 1995, The Promised Land, 1995, The Machine Age, 1996, Parties, 2000, The Showman's Daughter; TV writer, including: 3 episodes Actors' Choice, NET, 1970 (Emmy citation 1970), Virginia Woolf: The Moment Whole, NET, 1972 (CINE Golden Eagle award 1972); story editor: 4 episode series Benjamin Franklin, CBS, 1974 (Emmy citation 1974); The Adams Chronicles,

1975 (Peabody award 1975); Bicentennial Minutes, 1975, Loose Change, 1978, 3 episode series, NBC, 1978, 3 episodes of Best of Families, NET, 1978, The Jilting of Granny Weatherall, NET, 1980, Night Thoughts and Terminal BBC, 1978, Overdrawn at the Memory Bank, NET, 1983 (Rotterdam Film Festival, Am. Film Inst. Video Feature Film Festival). Rockefeller Found. grantee, 1979-80; residency Villa Serbelloni, Bellagio, Italy, 1987. Mem. Dramatists Guild, Writers Guild Am. East, PEN Home and Office: 110 W 86th St New York NY 10024-4049

JACKIW, ROMAN, physicist, educator; b. Lublinec, Poland, Nov. 8, 1939; came to U.S., 1949; s. Nicholas and Zenobia (Kostyk) J.; m. So-Young Pi, Sept. 4, 1981; children: Simone Ahlborn, Nicholas, Stefan Pi. BA, Swarthmore Coll., 1961; PhD, Cornell U., 1966; Doctorate (hon.), U. Uppsala, Sweden, 2000, U. Torino, Italy, 2000, Bogolyubov Inst., Kiev, Ukraine, 2003. Jr. fellow Harvard Soc. of Fellows, Cambridge, Mass., 1966-69; from asst. prof. to Jerrold Zacharias prof. physics MIT, Cambridge, 1969—. Vis. prof. Rockefeller U., N.Y.C., 1977-78, U. Calif., L.A., Santa Barbara, 1980, Columbia U., N.Y.C., 1989-90. Contbr. over 150 articles to profl. jours. Alfred P. Sloan fellow Sloan Found., 1969-71, J.S. Guggenheim fellow Guggenheim Found., 1977-78; recipient Dannie Heineman prize in math. physics Am. Phys. Soc., 1995, Dirac medal and prize Internat. Ctr. for Theoretical Physics, Trieste, Italy, 1998. Fellow Am. Acad. of Arts and Scis., Am. Phys. Soc.; mem. NAS, Nat. Acad. Scis. Ukraine (fgn. mem.). Achievements include research on fundamental processes in nature. Office: MIT 6-320 77 Massachusetts Ave Cambridge MA 02139-4307 E-mail: jackiw@lns.mit.edu.

JACKLE, KAREN DEE, real estate company executive; b. Santa Ana, Calif., June 26, 1945; d. Franklin Suits and Dorothy (Miller) Todd; m. Paul Herman Jackle, Oct. 12, 1968; children: Lara Irene, Julie Maureen. BA in History, Calif. State U., Long Beach, 1967. Elem. tchr. L.A. City Schs., 1967-68; social worker Los Angeles Dept. Pub. Social Svcs., 1968-70; with Seablue Pools, Harare, 1970; co-owner, property mgr., appraiser Paul Jackle & Assocs., Inc., Huntington Beach, Calif., 1971—; property mgr., appraiser Paul Jackle & Assocs., Huntington Beach, Calif., 1973-86, property developer, mgr., 1986—; pres. June Coast Corp., 1993—. Vice chmn. Huntington Beach Human Rels. Task Force, 1997—2002, chmn. events, 1997; block rep. H. Seacliff Homeowners Assn.; mem. Huntington Beach Infrastructure Com., 1998—. Recipient Achievement award, Orange County Human Rels. Task Force, 1998. Mem.: AAUW (mentoring program 1990—94, chmn. edn. found. 1991—92, chmn. membership com. 1992—94, pres. 1995—97, pub. policy 1997—, program v.p. 2000—01, state program com. 2001—03, pres. 2002—03, Huntington Beach chpt., state comm. com. 2003—, Nat. Assn. Businesswomen Remarkable Women award 2001), Sister City Club (chmn. 2003—). Avocations: aerobics, walking, theater, reading, travel. Office: 18652 Florida St Ste 300 Huntington Beach CA 92648-6069 E-mail: karjac@apcx.net.

JACKLEY, MICHAEL DANO, lawyer; b. Balt., Oct. 1, 1942; s. Francis Dano and Jean Diantha (Dietz) J.; m. Mary Margaret Mixer, July 5, 1977 (div.); children: Megan, Dano Mixer, Jackley; m. Karen Klare Blocher, Oct. 5, 1987. BA, U. Md., 1965, JD, 1970; LLM in Corp. Law with highest honors, George Washington U., 1977. Bar: D.C., Md. 1971, U.S. Tax Ct. 1973. Assoc. Williams, Brown, Eklund & Baldwin, Washington, 1971-74, Smith, Joseph, Greenwald & Laake and predecessor forms, Hyattsville, Md., 1974-77; prin. Joseph, Greenwald & Laake, PA, 1977—. Mem. Select Com. to Redraft D.C. Corp. Statute, 1977-86; tchr. Paralegal Inst., 1977-80; mem. peer rev. com. Md. Atty. Grievance Commn., 2001—. Adv. bd. Prince George's County Mental Health Assn., 1978-99. Key Delta Theta Phi scholar, 1970. Mem. ABA, Md. State Bar Assn., Prince George's County Bar Assn., DC Bar Assn. Democrat. Unitarian Universalist. Address: 6404 Ivy Ln Ste 400 Greenbelt MD 20770-1407 Personal E-mail: mdjackley@aol.com. Business E-Mail: mjackley@jgllaw.com.

JACKLIN, WILLIAM THOMAS, retired county official, educator; b. Chgo., Dec. 26, 1940; s. Robert Theodore and Florence Carrie (Dombrow) J.; m. Bonnie Joy Winquist; 1 child, Laura Carrie. BS, Roosevelt U., 1967; MS in Bus. Edn., Ind. U., 1968. Cert. fraud examiner, govt. fin. mgr. Assoc. instr. Ind. U., 1967-69; V.p. DuPage Corp., Lombard, Ill., 1970-73; inst. bus. Coll. DuPage, Glen Ellyn, Ill., 1969-77; chief dep. auditor DuPage County, 1973, county auditor, 1973-2000. V.p. DuPage County Employees Credit Union, 1978-79, pres., 1979-80; fiscal officer DuPage Met. Enforcement Group, 1987-94; exec. bd. Midwestern Intergovtl. Audit Forum, 1991-2000; bd. dirs. Franciscan Ministries, Inc., 1992-97, DuPage Heritage Gallery, Lombard Historical Commn., 1995-2000; pres. DuPage Heritage Gallery, 1997—. Announcer CRIS Radio for the Blind. Mem. Ill. Prairie Path; sec. York Twp. Rep. Orgn., 1978-80; treas. Highland Hills Assn., 1975-78; chmn. DuPage County com. Gerald R. Ford presdl. campaign, 1976; alt. del. 1992 Rep. Nat. Conv.; mem. fin. mgmt. project com. Ill. Dept. Commerce and Cmty. Affairs, 1980-82, bd. dirs. Lombard Hist. Soc., v.p., 1983-87, pres., 1987-91. Mem. Assn. Cert. Fraud Examiners, Nat. Assn. Local Govt. Auditors, Inst. Internal Auditors (govt. and pub. affairs com. 1976-82), Ill. Assn. County Auditors (sec.-treas. 1976-78, v.p. 1978-80, pres. 1980-84, treas. 1986-2000), Assn. Govt. Accts., Ind. Soc. of Chgo., Phi Delta Kappa. Lodges: Masons (sec. 1979-80). Christian Scientist. Home: 4908 Linscott Downers Grove IL 60515-3537 E-mail: billjacklin@earthlink.net.

JACKMAN, HUGH, actor; b. Sydney, NSW, Australia, Oct. 12, 1968; s. Chris Jackman; m. Deborra-Lee Furness, Feb. 1996; 1 child, Oscar Maximilian. BA, U. Tech., Sydney; student, Actor's Ctr., Sydney, Western Australian Acad. Performing Arts, Perth. Actor: (TV series) Correlli, 1995, Snowy River: The McGregor Saga, 1993; (films) Hey Mr. Producer, 1998; (TV series) Halifax f.p: Afraid of the Dark, 1998; (films) Paperback Hero, 1999, Erskineville Kings, 1999; (TV series) Oklahoma!, 1999; (films) X-Men, 2000, Someone Like You, 2001, Swordfish, 2001, Kate & Leopold, 2001, Standing Room Only, 2002, X2, 2003. Address: Endeavor Talent Agy 10th Fl 9701 Wilshire Blvd Bell CA 90201*

JACKMAN, JAMES DAVID, lawyer; b. Stubenville, Ohio, Aug. 13, 1960; s. Merle M. and Sarah L. Jackman; m. Lorraine P. Jackman, Apr. 30, 1988; children: Joshua A., Jeremy S. BS in Acctg., U. Akron, 1982; JD, Nova Southeastern U., 1985. Bar: Fla. 1985, Ohio 1990; cert. Am. Bd. Certification Consumer Bankruptcy. Pvt. practice law, pres., Bradenton, Fla., 1986—. Coach YMCA Youth Sports, Bradenton, 1994—. Mem. Kiwanis (com. chmn. 1990—), Masonic Lodge, Shriners. Avocations: football, basketball, youth sports coaching, movies, family activities.

JACKMAN, JAY M. psychiatrist; b. Bklyn., June 4, 1939; s. James Jeremiah and Dora (Emmer) J.; m. Judith Gail Meisels, Nov. 23, 1963 (div. Sept. 1987); children: Tenaya, Rashi, Jason Scott; m. Myra Hoffenberg Strober, Oct. 21, 1990. BA, Columbia U., 1960; MD, Harvard U., 1964; JD, U. Calif., San Francisco, Hastings Coll. Law, 1999. Diplomate Am. Bd. Psychiatry and Neurology; subsplty. cert. forensic psychiatry . Rotating intern San Francisco County Gen. Hosp., 1965; psychiat. resident Stanford U., 1969; asst. dir. cmty. psychiatry Mt. Zion Hosp., San Francisco, 1969-70; dir. drug treatment programs Westside Cmty. Mental Health Ctr., San Francisco, 1970-74; pvt. practice San Francisco, 1969-74; dir. Lanakila Clinic Kalihi-Palama Cmty. Mental Health Ctr., Honolulu, 1974-75; pvt. practice specializing in forensic psychiatry, Honolulu, 1975-90, Stanford, Calif., 1990—. Cons. Salvation Army Addiction Treatment Facility, Honolulu, 1974-81; chmn. Task Force on Drugs, Nat. Coun. Community Mental Health Ctrs., 1971-75; chmn. no. sect. Calif. Assn. Methodone Programs, 1973-74. Contbr. articles on substance abuse to profl. jours. Trustee Foothill-DeAnza C.C. Bd., 1993-98; active Mayor's Adv. Com. on Drug Abuse, Honolulu, 1975-77. Mem. Am. Psychiat. Assn. (commn. on drugs 1973-77), Am. Acad. Psychiatry and Law, Am. Coll. Forensic Psychiatrists, No. Calif. Psychiat. Soc., Calif. Attys. for Criminal Justice. Democrat. Jewish. Avocations: backpacking, hiking, dancing, scuba diving, beach walking. Fax: 650-213-8544. E-mail: jmjackman@aol.com.

JACKMAN, LEVON MERCHANT O'DAY, artist; b. Elgin, Ill., Sept. 8, 1924; d. Charles Henry and Althea May (Evans) Merchant; m. Daniel James O'Day, Nov. 8, 1947 (div. Jan. 1980); m. Warren Adams Jackman, Feb. 23, 1985. BA, Purdue U., 1946. Artistic dir., pres. Rivertrace Galleries, Galena, Ill., 1980-96; mem. Gallery 4, Fargo, N.D. Judge Coll. Hill Arts Festival, Cedar Rapids, Iowa. Exhibited in group shows at Pallette & Chisel Gallery, Galena, 1998, Rocco Buda Gallery, Dubuque, Iowa, 1998—, Spring St. Gallery, 2002—, Studio Work Gallery, Elizabeth, Ill., 2001—02, Main Gallery, Dubuque, Iowa, 2003, one-woman shows include Monroe (Wis.) Art Ctr., 2002, Univ. of Dubuque, 1998. Leader art elderhostel Galena Arts and Recreation Ctr., 1998. Mem. Ill. Arts Alliance, Episcopal Arts Coun. (bd. dirs. 1997—), Chgo. Art Inst., Chgo. Artists Coalition, Galena Artist Guild (Artist of the Yr. 1996). Avocations: gardening, traveling, opera, choir. Home and Office: 14 Talisman Trce Galena IL 61036-9354 E-mail: wjackman@galenalink.net.

JACKMAN, LLOYD MILES, chemistry educator; b. Goolwa, Australia, Apr. 1, 1926; came to U.S., 1967; s. Charles Stuart and Florence Olive (Green) J.; m. Marie Alma Sandow, 1950; children— Richard Miles, Donald Charles, Andrew Thorpe. BSc, U. Adelaide, Australia, 1945, BSc with honors, 1946, MSc, 1948, PhD, 1951. Asst. lectr. organic chemistry Imperial Coll., London, Eng., 1952, lectr., 1953; reader U. London, 1961-62; prof., head dept. organic chemistry U. Melbourne, Australia, 1962-67; prof. chemistry Pa. State U., 1967-91, prof. emeritus, 1992—. Author: Applications of NMR in Organic Chemistry. Beit fellow U. London, 1951-52; NSF sr. fgn. fellow, 1965; Guggenheim fellow, 1973-74; Wilsmore fellow chemistry, Melbourne, Australia; recipient Humboldt award, Fed. Republic Germany, 1977, 89. Fellow AAAS, Chem. Soc. London, Am. Chem. Soc., Royal Australian Chem. Inst. Home: 710 Glenn Rd State College PA 16803-3414 Office: 152 Davey Lab University Park PA 16802-6300 E-mail: lmj@psu.edu.

JACKMAN, ROBERT ALAN, retail executive; b. N.Y.C., Mar. 22, 1939; s. Joseph and Kate Queenie (Silverman) J.; m. Lois Wiederschall, June 10, 1962; children: Jennifer Sharon, Deborah Lynn. BS, U. Bridgeport, 1961. Dir. sales Mattel Inc., Hawthorne, Calif., 1963-75; sr. v.p. mktg. and sales Tyco Industries Inc., Moorestown, N.J., 1975-78; gen. mgr. Aurora Products Inc., Stamford, Conn., 1978-80; ptnr. Scott Lancaster Jackman Mills Atha, Westport, Conn., 1980-83; pres., chief exec. officer Leisure Dynamics Inc. div. Coleco Industries, Westport, 1983-86; with Oak Tree Publs., San Diego, 1983-87; exec. v.p. Coleco Industries Inc., West Hartford, Conn., 1986-88; gen. mgr. Tomy Am., Inc., Southport, Conn., 1988-90, also bd. dirs.; owner Yes I Can, 1990—. Cons. Harvard U. Bus. Sch. Club, N.Y.C., 1984. Patentee in field. With USAR, 1961-62. Recipient Disting. Alumni award U. Bridgeport (Conn.), 1986. Mem. U. Bridgeport Mktg. Coun., Mission Hills Country Club (Rancho Mirage, Calif.). Avocations: tennis, music, reading. Home: 8 Vin Elegante Rancho Mirage CA 92270-1969 Office: 35 325 Date Palm Dr Ste 131 Cathedral City CA 92234-7031

JACKOBOICE, SANDRA KAY, artist; b. Detroit, July 22, 1936; d. Virgil Ellsworth and Lucille Elizabeth LeSeur; m. Edward James Jackoboice, Jan. 11, 1958; children: E. Michael, Timothy Jon. BA, Aquinas Coll., Grand Rapids, Mich., 1989. Co-owner Fashion Plate, Grand Rapids, 1975-79; wardrobe cons. Steketees, Grand Rapids, 1980-82; owner Color Plus, Grand Rapids, 1983—. One-woman shows include FMB, Lowell, 1993, 1995, City Hall, Bielsko-Biala, Poland, 1995, Terryberry Gallery, Grand Rapids, 1997, Frederick Meijer Gardens, 1998, exhibited in group shows at Bot. Images Exhbn., Lansing, Mich., Artist Alliance Group Shows, represented by, Grand Gallery, Grand Rapids, Art Encounter Galleries, Las Vegas, Tamarack Gallery, Naples, Fla.; featured in Artists' Photo Reference Book, Pastel Artist Internat. mag., others. Mem. Jr. League, Grand Rapids, 1962—96, Downtown Mgmt. Bd., Grand Rapids, 1993—96, Grand Rapids Parking Commn., 1993—96; bd. dirs. Arts Coun. Greater Grand Rapids, 1997—2000. Recipient awards for art work. Mem.: S.W. Fla. Pastel Soc. (founder, advisor to bd. dirs. 2002—), Internat. Assn. Pastel Socs. (publicity chair 2001—, bd. dirs. 2003), Pastel Soc. Am., Am. Soc. Bot. Artists, Grand Valley Artists, Artists Alliance, Great Lakes Pastel Soc. (pres. 1997—2001, advisor to bd. dirs. 2002—, co-founder). Republican. Avocations: travel, art, tennis, golf. Office: Color Plus PO Box 6775 Grand Rapids MI 49516-6775

JACKOBS, MIRIAM ANN, dietitian; b. Sioux City, Iowa, Apr. 8, 1940; d. Abraham and Mary (Wadedo) Kaled; m. John Joseph Jackobs, Aug. 28, 1965; children: Mark James, Daniel Michael, Thomas Vincent. Student, St. Louis U., 1963; BS, Briar Cliff Coll., 1963; MS, Iowa State U., 1965; MA in Religion, Athenaeum of Ohio, Cin., 1995. Lic. in dietetics, Ohio. Instr. nutrition Ariz. State U., Tempe, 1965-67, Willoughby (Ohio) Eastlake Sch., 1967-69; clinical dietitian Migrant Clinic of Seneca County, Tiffin, Ohio, 1969-75; nutrition instr. Heidelberg Coll., Tiffin, 1969-75; founder, cons. dietitian Nutrition Cons. Svcs., 1974-94; oncology dietitian Hall Radiation Ctr., Cedar Rapids, 1983-87; nutrition instr. Mt. Mercy & Coe Colls., Cedar Rapids, 1976-87; clinical dietitian The Brethren's Home, Greenville, Ohio, 1987-89; dir. dietary dept. Washington Manor Retirement Ctr., Centerville, Ohio, 1989-90. Instr. Kettering (Ohio) Adult Sch., 1988-90, Mt. St. Joseph Coll., 1989—; adj. asst. prof. Wilmington Coll., 1990—; owner, cons. Spectrum Consulting, 1994—. Author: (book) Food Prep Manual, 1968, Diet Manual, 1988, rev. edit., 1992, 97; contbr. articles on nutrition to prof. jours. Com. chmn. LWV, Ohio and Iowa, 1970-82; fund raising chmn. PTA, Cedar Rapids, 1984-86; unit leader dist. coun. Boy Scouts Am., 1973-88; organizer Greenville Summer Symphony, Ohio, 1988. Recipient Silver Beaver award Boy Scouts Am., Alumni Svc. award Briarcliff U., 1971 St. George award Archdiocese Dubuque, 1985, Ohio Dietetic Assn. Mem. Merit award, 1998; Gen. Foods Found. fellow Iowa State U., 1965; Dole Leadership grantee, 1992. Mem. Am. Dietetic Assn., Ohio Dietetic Assn. (merit award), Ohio Cons. Dietitions (newsletter editor 1988-95, 2001—03, chair 1995-96, 2000-01), Greater Cin. Dietetic Assn. (coun. on practice chair elect 1997-98, 2000—, chair 1998-2000, pres. 1999-2000, 2002—, newsletter editor 1990-2003, grantee 1997), Greater Cin. Cons. Dietitians (newsletter editor 1991, health care facilities sec./chair-elect 1997-98, chair 1998-99, disting. mem. award), Cons. Dieticians, SCAN Practice Group, Hunger Malnutrition Dietetics Practice Group (newsletter editor 1996-98, treas. 1998-00), Cedar Rapids Youth Orch., Coe Woman (pres. 1977-78). Roman Catholic. Avocations: music, marathoning, race walking, travel, art. Home and Office: Spectrum Cons 4291 Flagstone Dr Mason OH 45040-8432 E-mail: m.jackobs@prodigy.net.

JACKS, BRUCE WILLIAM, civil engineer; b. Sacramento, Apr. 15, 1947; s. Arnold Bruce and Nelda Amelia (Schroeder) J.; m. Norah M. Nolan, Dec. 18, 1971; children: Brian, Aiden, Gregory, Darren. BSCE, U. Calif.-Davis, 1969. Asst. engr. Bechtel Corp., San Francisco, 1969-72; engring. estimator Teichert Constrn. Co., Woodland, Calif., 1972-74; contract. adminstr. Wismer & Becker, Sacramento, 1975-76; engring. mgr. Mackay & Somps Civil Engrs., Roseville, Calif., 1976—. With U.S. Army, 1970-76. Republican. Home: 6 Amherst Pl Woodland CA 95695-5168 Office: Mackay & Somps Civil Engrs Ste 100 1552 Eureka Rd Roseville CA 95678

JACKS, DAVID CLINTON, urologist; b. Pine Bluff, Ark., Aug. 22, 1950; s. William Ray and Jane Ella (Johnston) J.; children: Bradley, Blake. BS in Chemistry and Biology, U. Ark., 1972; MD, U. of Ark. Med. Scis., 1976. Pres. Ark. Caduceas Club, Little Rock, 1987-88, Jefferson County Med. Soc., Pine Bluff, 1986-88; state councillor So. Med. Assn., Birmingham, Ala., 1990-95; pres. Ark. Urologic Soc., 1995-97; chief of staff Jefferson Regional Med. Ctr., 1999—. Bd. dirs. Ark. Lithotripsy; mem. Ark. State Med. Bd., 1992—. Bd. dirs. Fifty for Future, Pine Bluff, 1988-91. Fellow ACS; mem. Am. Urol. Assn. (rep. South Ctrl. sect.). Office: South Ark Urology 4303 S Mulberry St Pine Bluff AR 71603-7017

JACKS, SIDNEY, engineer; b. St. Louis, Aug. 1924; s. Mike and Minnie Jacks; m. July 1952. B in Mech. Engring., Purdue U., 1947; M in Engring., St. Louis U., 1970. Registered profl. engr., Mo. Consulting engr. Ross & Baruzini, St. Louis, 1968-69; indsl. engr. Sidney Jacks Assoc., LLC, St. Louis, 1969—. Active East-West Gateway Housing Task Force, St. Louis, 1970-73. With USN, 1944-46. Mem. NSPE. Address: PO Box 11492 Saint Louis MO 63105-0292 Home and Office: Sidney Jacks Assocs LLC 368 N Hanley Rd Saint Louis MO 63130-4004

JACKSON, ALLEN KEITH, retired museum administrator; b. Rocky Ford, Colo., July 22, 1932; s. Monford L. and Leliah Jean (Hipp) Jackson; m. Barbara May Hollard, June 13, 1954; children: Cary Vincent, Deborah Kay, Edward Keith, Fredrick James. BA, U. Denver, 1954; postgrad., Cambridge (Eng.) U., 1955; Th.M. (Elizabeth Iliff Warren fellow), Iliff Sch. Theology, 1958; PhD, Emory U., 1960. Instr. sociology Emory U., 1958-60; chaplain, asst. prof. religion and sociology Morningside Coll., Sioux City, Iowa, 1960-62, dean coll., 1962-67; pres. Huntingdon Coll., Montgomery, Ala., 1968-93; dir. Idaho Mus. Natural History, Idaho State U., Pocatello, 1993—98; exec. dir. Nat. Heritage Ctr., 1998—2002; ret., 2002—. Past pres. Montgomery Area United Appeal. Fulbright scholar, Cambridge U., 1955, honor fellow, Emory U., 1960. Mem.: Ala. Coun. Advancement Pvt. Colls. (pres. 1975—81), Ala. Assn. Ind. Colls. and Univs. (pres. 1969—71), Rotary, Phi Kappa Phi, Beta Theta Pi, Omicron Delta Kappa, Phi Beta Kappa. Home: 633 W Mcnabb Rd Inkom ID 83245-1502 *A worthy aim it seems to me, is to seek the Truth and to share the truths you find.*

JACKSON, ALPHONSO, federal agency administrator; b. Marshall, Tex., Sept. 9, 1946; s. Arthur and Henriette (Green) J.; m. Marcia A. Clark-Jackson, June 18, 1988; children: Annette Watkins, Lesley Jackson. BS, Truman State U., 1968, MA, 1969; JD, Washington U., St. Louis, 1973. Dir., cons. svcs. Laventhol & Horwath, St. Louis, 1982-87; CEO Dept. of Pub. and Assisted Housing, Washington, 1987-89; pres. and CEO Housing Authority/City of Dallas, 1989-96; dep. secy. U.S. Dept H.U.D., Washington, 2001—. Bd. dirs. Zale-Lipshy Hosp., Dallas, 1992, Truman State U., 1995, Tex. So. U., 1998, Children's Med. Ctr., Dallas, 1994; chmn. Gen. Svcs. Commn. State of Tex., Austin, 1998. Recipient Chmn.'s award Nat. Boys and Girls Clubs of Am., 1997. Fellow The Aspen Inst. Avocations: jogging, tennis, reading. Office: US Dept HUD Dep Secy 451 7th St SW Washington DC 20410-1047

JACKSON, ANDREW PRESTON, library director; b. Bklyn., Jan. 28, 1947; s. Walter Luther Sr. and Bessie (Lindsey) J. BS, CUNY, 1990, MLS, 1996; pub. librs. profl. cert., SUNY. Asst. supr. pers. processing unit Human Resources Adminstrn. Agy. Child Devel. Pers. Dept., N.Y.C., 1968-70, coord. pers. svcs., 1970-76; customer rels. mgr., contracts mgr. Robinson Chevrolet, Novato, Calif., 1976-79; office mgr. Sesame Press, Inc., N.Y.C., 1979-80; exec. dir. Langston Hughes Cmty. Libr. and Cultural Ctr., Corona, N.Y., 1980—. Lectr. Black history, N.Y.C., 1986—; cons. evaluating Black heritage collections; adj. lectr. York Coll., CUNY, 2001—. Author: Queens Notes: A Work In Progress, Facts About the Forgotten borough of Queens New York, (foreword) African American Almanac, 9th edit., 2003; contbg. author: Handbook of Black Librarianship; contbr. articles to profl. jours. Chmn. social svcs. adv. coun. Cmty. Planning Bd. Areas 3 and 5, 1984—87; treas. No. Blvd. Mchts. Assn., Corona, 1985—99; mem. York Coll. Cmty. Adv. Coun., 1997—, N.Y. State Freedom Trails Commn., Queens Underground RR Com., 1997—; bd. trustees The Renaissance Charter Sch., 1999—; convenor Churchman's fellowship Corona Congl. Ch., 1987—89; mem. nat. adv. bd. CDF Langston Hughes Libr., 2001—; mem. cmty. adv. bd. Elmhurst (NY) Hosp. Ctr., 1983—97; bd. dirs. York Coll. Alumni Inc., Jamaica, NY, 1990—93, 1996—99; vice chair cmty. adv. bd. Otis Bantum Correctional Ctr., N.Y.C. Dept. Corrections, Rikers Island, NY, 1990—95. Sgt. USAF, 1964—68, Vietnam. Decorated Bronze Star; named Man of Yr., Nat. Assn. Negro Bus. & Profl. Women's Club, Inc., 1991, Ombudsman award, 1982, East Elmhurst Alumni Inc. Hall of Fame, 1998; recipient Cmty. Svc. award East Elmhurst Track Club, 1986, Tabernacle Cmty. C.M.E. Ch., Nat. Assn. Univ. Women (north shore br.), Cmty. award East Elmhurst-Corona Civic Assn., 1989, Outstanding Leadership in Queens award Queens Fedn. of Churches, 1988, Cert. of Appreciation Kiwanis, 1991, Cmty. Svc. award Minority Mgmt. Assn., N.Y.C., 1992, Cert. of Recognition August Martin H.S., 1992, Gov.'s award African-Americans of Distinction, N.Y. State Gov., 1994, Disting. Grad. award Nat. Assn. Equal Opportunity in Higher Edn., 1994, Cert. of Honor, Queens Borough Pres., 1994, Giving It Back, award W.C. Bryant H.S., 1995, Youth Devel. award 115th Police Precinct Coun., 1994, Recognition award N.Y. State Atty. Gen., 2002; Disting. Alumni award York Coll. Alumni Assn., Inc., 1996, Fufilling The Dream award CBS-TV, 1996, Scroll of Honor, 4W Circle of Arts and Enterprise, 1996, Cmty. Svc. award Nat. Coun. Negro Women, 1997, Cmty. Svc. award Elmcor Alumni Assn., 1998, Cmty. Svc. award Concerned African-Am. of Flushing, 1998, Lamplighter award Queens Borough Pub. Libr., 1999, Cmty. Svc. award N.Y. Fire Dept. African Heritage Soc., 2000, Outstanding Contbns. award Combined Treasury Dept., 2001, Appreciation award Grace Episc. Ch., 2001, Cmty. Person of Yr. award Delta Beta Zeta, 2001, Cmty. Activist award United for Progress Dem. Club, Cmty. Svc. award Corona Congl. Ch., 2002, Cultural award Key Women of Am., 2002, Cmty. Leader of Yr. award Alpha Kappa Alpha, 2003. Mem. NAACP (life), ALA, ALA Black Libr. Caucus (exec. bd. 1999—, Libr. Advocacy award 1999, Libr. Outreach award 1999, v.p., pres.-elect black caucus 2002—), Pub. Librs. Assn., Libr. Adminstrn. and Mgmt. Assn., N.Y. Black Librs. Caucus, N.Y. Libr. Assn. Avocations: speaking with youth, reading. Home: 25-14 97th St East Elmhurst NY 11369-1923 Office: Queens Borough Pub Libr Langston Hughes Comm Libr 100-01 Northern Blvd Corona NY 11368-1038

JACKSON, ANNE (ANNE JACKSON WALLACH), actress; b. Allegheny, Pa., Sept. 3, 1926; d. John Ivan and Stella Germaine (Murray) J.; m. Eli Wallach, Mar. 5, 1948; children: Peter, Roberta, Katherine. studied with Sanford Meisner and Herbert Berghof at Neighborhood Playhouse, with Lee Strassberg at Actor's Studio. Profl. debut: Cherry Orchard; mem. Am. Repertory Co.; Broadway plays include: Summer and Smoke, Oh, Men! Oh, Women!, Middle of the Night, Major Barbara, Rhinoceros, Luv, Waltz of the Toreadors, Diary of Anne Frank, 1978, Twice Around the Park, 1982-83, Nest of the Woodgrouse, 1984, Café Crown, 1989, Love Letters, 1991-92, Lost in Yonkers, 1992, In Person, 1993, The Flowering Peach, 1994, off-Broadway plays: Tennessee Williams Remembered, 1999, Mr. Peter's Connection, 1998, Down the Garden Path; London stage performances of The Typists, The Tigers, 1966; film appearances include: So Young, So Bad, 1950, Secret Life of an American Wife, 1968, Dirty Dingus McGee, 1970, Lovers and Other Strangers, 1970, The Shining, 1980, Sam's Son, 1985, Funny About Love, 1992, Folks, 1992, Johnnie Twennies, 1998, Something Sweet, 2000; TV appearances include: 84 Charing Cross Road, Private Battle, Everything's Relative, 1987, Law & Order, 1997, Education of Max Bickford, 2002; TV films: Family Man, Golda I and II, Out on a Limb, Baby M, 1988, The Rescuers: The Lady on the Bicycle, 1997; author: (autobiography) Early Stages, 1979. Recipient Obie award. Office: care Paradigm 200 W 57th St Ste 900 New York NY 10019-3211

JACKSON, BENJAMIN TAYLOR, retired surgeon, educator, medical facility administrator; b. Jacksonville, Fla., Apr. 28, 1929; s. Julian Harold and Helen Louise (Blasingame) J.; m. Alda Jean Davis, June 18, 1953; children: Benjamin Taylor Jr., Jean Leigh, Kimberly Louise, Jillian Davis. MD, Duke U., 1954; MS, Brown U., 1982. Diplomate Am. Bd. Surgery. Instr. Med. Coll. of Va., Richmond, 1963-64; asst. prof. Boston U. Sch. Medicine, 1964-67, assoc. prof., 1967-75, prof., 1975-80; vis. surgeon U. Hosp., Boston, 1975-80; prof. Brown U. Sch. Medicine, Providence, 1980-97, prof. in surgery emeritus, 1997—; chief surg. svc. VA Med. Ctr., Providence, 1980-97, cons. in surgery, 1997—; prof. surgery, rschr. Brown U., Providence, 1999—2002. Contbr. articles to profl. jours. Capt. U.S. Army, 1955-57. Mem. ACS, Soc. Univ. Surgeons, Soc. for Gynecologic Investigation. Methodist. Home: 11 October Ln Weston MA 02493-1724 Office: VA Med Ctr Davis Pk Providence RI 02908 E-mail: jackson.benjamin@providence.va.gov.

JACKSON, BETTY EILEEN, music and elementary school educator; b. Denver, Oct. 9, 1925; d. James Bowen and Fannie (Shelton) J. MusB, U. Colo., 1948, MusM, 1949, MusB in Edn., 1963; postgrad., Ind. U., 1952-55, Hochschule fur Musik, Munich, 1955-56. Cert. educator Colo., Calif. Tchr., accompanist, tchr. H.L. Davis Vocal Studios, Denver, 1949-52; tchg. assoc. Ind. U., Bloomington, 1952-53, U. Colo., Boulder, 1961-63, vis. lectr., summers 1963-69; tchr. Fontana (Calif.) Unified Sch. Dist., 1963—2002; pvt. studio, 1966—. Lectr. in music Calif. State U., San Bernardino, 1967-76; performer, accompanist, music dir. numerous musical cos. including performer, music dir. Fontana Mummers, 1980—, Riverside Cmty. Players, Calif., 1984—; performer Rialto Cmty. Theatre, Calif., 1983—; head visual and performing arts com. Cypress Elem. Sch., 1988-92. Performances include numerous operas, musical comedies and oratorios, Cen. City Opera, Denver Grand Opera, Univ. Colo., Ind. Univ. Opera Theater (leading mezzo), 3 tours of Fed. Rep. Germany, 1956-58; oratorio soloist in Ind., Ky., Colo., and Calif., West End Opera (lead roles), Riverside Opera (lead roles). Judge Inland Theatre League, Riverside, 1983-92; mem. San Bernardino Cultural Task Force, 1981-83; bd. dirs. Riverside-San Bernardino Counties Met. Auditions, 1988—; mem. adv. bd. Riverside Concert Opera, 1990-95. Fulbright grantee, Munich, 1955-56; named outstanding performer Inland Theatre League, 1982-84; recipient Outstanding Reading Tchr. award, 1990, Tchr. of Yr. nominations, 1990, 91, hon. svc. award, 1992. Mem. AAUW (bd. dirs., cultural chair 1983-86), NEA, Nat. Assn. Tchrs. Singing (exec. bd. 1985-89), Internat. Reading Assn., Music Educators Nat. Conf., Calif. Tchrs. Assn., Calif. Elem. Educators Assn., Fontana Tchrs. Assn.,

Music Tchrs. Assn., Arrowhead Reading Coun., San Bernardino Valley Concert Assn. (bd. dirs. 1977-83), Internat. Platform Assn., Nat. Assn. Preservation and Perpetuation of Storytelling, Order Eastern Star, Kappa Kappa Iota (v.p. 1982-83), Sigma Alpha Iota (life), Chi Omega. Avocations: community theater and opera, travel, collecting hummels and plates. Home: PO Box 885 Rialto CA 92377-0885

JACKSON, BEVERLEY JOY JACOBSON, columnist, lecturer; b. L.A., Nov. 20, 1928; d. Phillip and Dorothy Jacobson; m. Robert David Jackson (div. Aug. 1964); 1 child, Tracey Dee. Student, U. So. Calif., UCLA, UCLA. Daily columnist Santa Barbara (Calif.) News Press, 1968-92, Santa Barbara Independent, 1992—94; internat. lectr., 2003. Nat. lectr. Santa Barbara History, History of China Recreated, Chinese Footbinding, Shoes for Bound Feet, China Today; free lance writer, fgn. corr. Author: Dolls and Doll Houses of Spain, 1970; (with others) I'm Just Wild About Harry, 1979, Spendid Slippers: A Thousand Years of an Erotic Tradition, 1997, Ladder to the Clouds-Intrigues and Traditions of Chinese Rank, 1999, King Fisher Blue, 2002. Bd. dirs. Santa Barbara br. Am. Cancer Soc., 1963-92; art mus. coun. L.A. Mus. Art, 1959-96, costume coun., 1983-92; docent L.A. Mus. Art, 1962-64; exec. bd. Channel City Club, 1969-2003; adv. bd. Storyteller Sch. Homeless Children, Santa Barbara Hist. Soc. Mus., Coun. of Christmas Cheer, Women's Shelter Bldg., Direct Relief Internat., Nat. Coun. Drug and Alcohol Abuse, Santa Barbara Choral Soc., Am. Oceans Campaign, Hospice Santa Barbara, 1981-92, Stop AIDS Coun., Arthritis Found.; bd. dirs. So. Calif. Com. for Shakespear's Globe Theatre, Friends of U. Calif. Libr., Santa Barbara; chmn. Santa Barbara Com. for Visit Queen Elizabeth II, 1982—; founder costume guild Santa Barbara Hist. Soc.; curator Chinese collections Santa Barbara Hist. Mus.; hon. bd. Santa Barbara Salvation Army, Ensemble Theatre Santa Barbara. Mem. Commanderie Bordeaux de San Francisco. Home: PO Box 5118 Santa Barbara CA 93150-5118 E-mail: bevjack@silcom.com.

JACKSON, BEVERLY ROBERSON, state agency administrator, consultant; b. Kansas City, Mo., Mar. 9, 1950; d. Augustus William and Ora Cooper Roberson; m. David James Jackson, July 5, 1975; children: David Jr., Timothy. BA, Colo. Woman's Coll., 1971; MEd, Columbia U., 1975, EdD, 1978. Cert. tchr. nursery, K-12, trainer. Dir. pub. policy Zero to Three-Nat. Ctr., Washington, 1991—96; head start state collaboration dir. D.C. Govt., 1997—. Ind. ednl. cons. various univs., 1977—. Contbr. Fellow, Nat. Govs.' Assn., 2001—02. Mem.: Delta Sigma Theta. Office: Office of Early Childhood Devel 717 14th St NW Ste 450 Washington DC 20005

JACKSON, BILLY MORROW, artist, retired art educator; b. Kansas City, Mo., Feb. 23, 1926; s. Alonzo David and Opal May (Morrow) J.; m. Blanche Mary Trice, June 12, 1949 (div. Jan. 1988); children: Lon Allan, Robin Jackson Todd, Aron Drew, Sylvia Marie; m. Siti Mariah, Feb. 1988. BFA, Washington U., St. Louis, 1949; MFA, U. Ill., 1954. Prof. art U. Ill., Champaign, 1954-87, ret., 1987. One man show Jane Haslem Gallery, Washington, 1990; represented in permanent collections at Smithsonian Inst., Washington, Nat. Gallery of Art, Washington, NASA Archives, Washington, Union League Club Chgo., Boston Pub. Libr., Met. Mus. Art, N.Y.C., Mus. of Legion of Honor, San Francisco, Libr. of Congress, Washington, Springfield (Mo.) Art Mus., Conn. Acad. of Fine Arts, Hartford, Artist's Guild, St. Louis, Phila., Free Libr., Evansville (Ind.) Mus. of Arts & Scis., Joslyn Art Mus., Omaha, Norfolk Mus., Omaha, Reading (Pa.) Pub. Libr. and Art Gallery, Lakeview Ctr. of Art, Peoria, Ill., Butler Inst. Am. Art, Youngstown, Ohio, Civic Ctr. Art Collection, Springfield, Ill., N.Y. Hilton, N.Y.C., Ill. State Mus., Springfield, World Book Ency., Chgo., Rockefeller Ctr., Dulin Gallery of Art, Knoxville, Tenn., Swope Mus., Terre Haute, Ind., Bur. of Peclamation, Washington, EPA, Washington, Krannert Art Mus., U. Ill., Champaign, Wichita (Kans.) Art Mus., Gov.'s State Coll., Park Forest South, Ill., Champaign Nat. Bank, Parkland Coll., Champaign, Sheldon Meml. Gallery of Art, U. Nebr., Lincoln, Busey First Nat. Bank, Champaign, 1st Nat. Bank, Champaign, Swanlund Bldg., Bechmann Inst., U. Ill., Champaign, Keday (Malaysia) State Mus.Nelson-Atkins Mus. Art, Kansas City, Mo., R.I. Sch. Art and Design, Providence; commd. mural state Capitol Bldg., Springfield, Ill., Mara Inst. of Tech., Malaysia, Ill. Sch. for Deaf, Jacksonville, Quincy (Ill.) Vet. Hosp. and Home, Carle Hosp. Edn. Bldg., Urbana, Ill., Mural Agr. Libr., U. Ill., Champaign, mural Ill. State Police, Champaign, 2002, mural U. Ill., Champaign, 2003; subject of book Billy Morrow Jackson: Interpretations ot Time and Light (Howard E. Wooden), 1990, In Our Time, 1997, Krannert Art Mus., Champaign, Ill. Pvt. USMC, 1944—46, Okinawa. Democrat. Home: 706 W White St Champaign IL 61820-4706

JACKSON, BOBBY RAND, minister; b. Wilson, N.C., Dec. 14, 1931; s. Joel John and Bessie Francis (Mayo) J.; m. Martha Jane Ketteman, May 30, 1953; children: Stephen Rand, Philip Wayne. BA, Free Will Baptist Bible Coll., Nashville, 1954; MA, Bob Jones U., Greenville, S.C., 1955. Ordained to ministry Free Will Baptists Ch., 1951, evangelist, 1955—; asst. moderator Nat. Assn. Free Will Baptists, Nashville, 1972-77, moderator, 1978-87, mem. exec. com., 1972-87, chmn. exec. com., 1978-87, presiding officer of gen. bd., 1978-87. Author: Messages That Matter, 1960, Six Steps to Successful Living, 1962, Awakening in the Wilderness, 1965, Beyond the Stars, 1966; soloist: record albums Softly and Tenderly, 1968, Then Sings My Soul, 1969, Fill My Cup, Lord, 1970, My God and I, 1978, Songs from Two Generations, 1985 Mem. Free Will Baptist Bible Coll. Alumni Assn., Bob Jones U. Alumni Assn. Home: 1412 E 14th St Greenville NC 27858-4734 E-mail: bjea@greenvillenc.com.

JACKSON, BRUCE, cultural studies educator, writer, photographer; b. Brooklyn, May 21, 1936; s. Irving and Julia Blanche J.; m. Diane Christian, Sept. 22, 1973; children: Michael, Jessica, Rachel. BA, Rutgers U., Newark, 1960; MA, Ind. U., Bloomington, 1963. Assoc. prof. English and comparative lit. SUNY, Buffalo, 1968—71, prof. comparative lit., 1971—81, prof. English, 1971—90, dir. Ctr. Studies in Am. Culture, 1972—, SUNY Disting. prof., 1990, Samuel P. Capen prof. of Am. culture, 1997—. Exec. dir. Documentary Rsch., Inc., Buffalo, 1978—2000; trustee Am. Folklife Ctr., Libr. of Congress, Washington, 1984—89, chmn., 1988—89; dir. Market Arcade Film and Arts Ctr., Buffalo, 2000—; editor, publ. Buffalo Report, Buffalo, 2002—. Author: In the Life: Versions of the Criminal Experience, 1969, Wake Up Dead Man: Afro-American Worksongs from Texas Prisons, 1972, (book of essays) Disorderly Conduct, 1969, Get Your Ass in the Water and Swim Like Me: Narrative Poetry from Black Oral Tradition, 1974, (novel) The Programmer, 1979, A Thief's Primer, 1987, Fieldwork, 1987, Law and Disorder: Criminal Justice in America, 1985, Rainbow Freeware, 1986, Get the Money and Shoot: The DRI Guide to Funding Documentary Films, 1986, A User's Guide: Freeware, Shareware, and Public Domain Software, 1988; co-author: Death Row, 1980, Doing Drugs, 1983, rev. edit., 1986; editor: (essays) Folklore and Society, 1966, The Negro and His Folklore in 19th Century Periodicals, 1967, Your Father's Not Coming Home Any More, 1981, (book of essays) Feminism and Folklore, 1987, Teaching Folklore, 2nd ed., 1989, Jour. Am. Folklore, 1986—90; co-editor: The World Observed: Reflections on the Fieldwork Process, 1996, The Centennial Index: 100 Years of Journal of American Folklore, 1988, (annotated bibliography), 1977; author, photographer (book of text and photographs) Killing Time: Life in the Arkansas Penitentiary, 1977; prodr.: (films) Services Rendered, 1979; dir., editor (films) Death Row, 1979, co-prodr., co-dir., editor Robert Creeley: Willy's Reading, 1982, William August May, 1982, Out of Order, 1983, co-prodr., co-dir., editor, cinematographer Creeley, 1988; prodr.: (CD) Wake Up Dead Man (Grammy nomination, 1974); contbr. articles. Adv. bd. N.Y. Commn. on Correction Minimum Standards, Albany, NY, 1976—77; dir., then trustee Newport Folk Found., N.Y.C., NY, 1965—2000; mem., nat. coun. Inst. Am. West, Sun Valley, Idaho, 1976—81; bd. of governors N.Y. Found. Arts, 1989—93. Pfc USMC, 1953. Named chevalier, L'Order Arts et Lettres, France, 2002; grantee, Nat. Endowment for the Arts, 1979; fellow, Woodrow Wilson Found., 1960, Harvard Soc. of Fellows, 1963-1967, John Simon Guggenheim Found., 1971, grantee, Baldy Ctr. Law and Soc., 1972, 1992, Am. Philos. Soc., 1972, 1992, NEH, 1978, 1981, 1984, NEA, 1979, Fund for Investigative Journalism, 1979, Am. Film Inst., 1979. Mem.: Societe des Auteurs et Compositeurs Dramatiques. Democrat. Home: 96 Rumsey Rd Buffalo NY 14209 Office: SUNY 306 Clemens Hall Buffalo NY 14260 Personal E-mail: bjackson@buffalo.edu. E-mail: bjackson@buffalo.edu.

JACKSON, CARMAULT BENJAMIN, JR., physician; b. Newton, Mass., Apr. 19, 1924; s. Carmault Benjamin and Mabel (Robbins) Jackson; m. Lynda D. Shaneman; children: Carmault Benjamin III, Thomas J., Molly Ann. MD, U. Pa., 1952. Intern Hosp. of U. Pa., 1952—53, resident, 1953—56; internal medicine specialist U.S. Air Force, NASA Space Task Group, 1958—61; practice medicine specializing in internal medicine San Antonio, 1961—76; assoc. dir., assoc. prof. medicine M.D. Anderson Hosp. and Tumor Inst., Houston, 1977—79. Adminstr. Met. Gen. Hosp., San Antonio; med. adv. H.B. Zachry Co., San Antonio, Tower Life Ins. Co.; vice chmn. Tex. Health Coord. Coun. Served with U.S. Army, 1942—45, served with USAF, 1956—61. Decorated Purple Heart with 2 oak leaf clusters. Mem.: AMA, Inst. Medicine NAS, Bexar County (Tex.) Med. Soc., Am. Occupl. Medicine Assn., Am. Soc. Internal Medicine, Tex. Acad. Internal Medicine, Tex. Soc. Internal Medicine, Tex. Med. Assn., So. Med. Assn. Died Aug. 6, 2001.

JACKSON, CARNEY BRAND, veterinarian; s. Charles E. and Ina G. Jackson; m. Beth L. Leonard, May 17, 1975; children: Mark L., Luke E. DVM, Okla. State U., 1977. Diplomate Am. Coll. of Vet. Preventive Medicine, 1990, Am. Coll. of Vet. Pathologists, 1992. Asst. dir. pathology and vet. medicine WIL Rsch. Labs., Ashland, Ohio, 1996—2001; assoc. prof. U. of Ky., Lexington, Ky., 2001—, vet. pathologist, 2001—. Chief pathobiology divsn. Clin. Investigations, Wilford Hall Med. Ctr. Lackland AFB, San Antonio, 1993—95; chief anatomic pathology sect. Comparative Pathology Br., Vet. Sciences Divsn., Armstrong Lab. Brooks AFB, San Antonio, 1992—93; staff pathologist US Army Med. Rsch. Inst. of Infectious Diseases Ft. Detrick, Frederick, Md., 1988—92. Deacon Christian Missionary Alliance, Richmond, Ky. Lt col N.G. USAF, 1997—. Mem.: AVMA, Am. Coll. of Vet. Pathologists. Avocations: amateur radion, writing poetry. Office: UK Livestock Disease Diagnostic Center 1429 Newtown Pike Lexington KY 40511-1280 Office Fax: 859-255-1624. Personal E-mail: cjackson@uky.edu. E-mail: cjackson@uky.edu.

JACKSON, CHARLES IAN, writer, consultant; b. Keighley, Yorkshire, Eng., Feb. 11, 1935; s. Harry Sydney and Nellie (Crabtree) J.; m. Margaret Cochrane Storrie, July 10, 1963 (div. 1987); 1 child, Janet Clare Louise; m. Merlyn Hayward Farina (Martin), Aug. 16, 2001. BA, London U., 1956; MS, McGill U., 1959, PhD, 1961. Lectr. in geography London Sch. Econ., 1959-69; head econ. geography sect. Can. Dept. Energy, Mines and Resources, Ottawa, Ont., 1969-71; dir. planning and priorities Ministry of State for Urban Affairs, Ottawa, Ont., Can., 1972-78; sr. econ. affairs officer UN Econ. Commn. Europe, Geneva, Switzerland, 1978-81; exec. dir. Sigma Xi, New Haven, Ct., 1981-87. Cons. water resources UN Econ. Commn. Europe, 1966-67; cons. German Marshall Fund U.S., 1975-77, Ford Found., 1977, Environment Can., 1994-95; rsch. dir. Can. Ho. of Commons Standing Com. on Environment, 1991-92; dir. Chreod Ltd., 1993-97; assoc. fellow Timothy Dwight Coll., Yale U. Translator tech. lit. from French; editor Letters from the 49th Parallel 1857-73, 2000, The Arctic Journals of William Scoresby the Younger 1888-1813, 2003, and other books in field; author: Does Anyone Read Lake Hazen?, 2002, articles on history, resource mgmt. and geography; co-author Great Lakes: Great Legacy?, 1990; columnist (monthly mag.) Notes from Ptolemy, 1969-99. Dir. Found. Preservation of Capt. Cook's Ships., 1999—. Recipient Darton prize Royal Meteorol. Soc., 1962; recipient Evan Durbin prize Inst. Econ. Affairs, 1964 Mem. Hakluyt Soc. (council 1967-69), Champlain Soc., Soc. for History of Discoveries, Quinnipiack Club (New Haven), E-mail: ian_jackson@compuserve.com.

JACKSON, CHARLES WAYNE, food products executive, former telecommunications industry executive; b. Louisville, June 3, 1930, s. Wayne O. and Geneva Drake J.; m. Sallie I. Lambert, June 21, 1952 (div. Feb. 1980); m. Elizabeth J. Soptic, June 1, 1979; children: Thomas, Carol E., Charles N. BEE, Ga. Inst. Tech., 1952. Student engr. AT&T, Cin., 1954-55, dist. plant engr. Jacksonville, Fla., 1955-56, comml. rep to acctg. asst. Atlanta, 1956-59, transmission systems engr. to plant design engr. Kansas City, 1963-66; project mgr. to dir. major project Western Elec. Co., N.Y.C., 1966-69; engr. dir. TWX coord. to bus. relations dir. AT&T, N.Y.C., 1969-75; dir. pvt. lines rates Long Lines Co., Somerset, N.J., 1975, dir. pvt. lines rates to dir. planning Bedminster, N.J., 1975-81; dir. data prog. svcs. to dir. svc. devel. mktg. dept. AT&T, Bedminster, 1981-87; cons. pvt. practice Brandenburg, Ky., 1987-90; v.p. H&R Block Franchise, 1990-92; owner Squire Taber Apple Orchard, 1992—. V.p. Echo Enterprises, Inc., 1991—. 1st. lt. U.S. Army, 1952-54. Mem. Ky. State Horticulture Soc. (v.p., dir.), Elks. Methodist. Avocations: photography, horticulture. Home and Office: 1194 Adkins Rd Rineyville KY 40162-9722

JACKSON, CYNTHIA L. lawyer; b. Houston, May 6, 1954; BA, Stanford U., 1976; JD, U. Tex., 1979. Bar: Tex. 1979, Calif. 1980. Mem. Heller, Ehrman, White & McAuliffe, Palo Alto, Calif., 1983—, Baker & McKenzie, Palo Alto, 2000—. Mem. ABA. Office: Baker & McKenzie 660 Hansen Way Palo Alto CA 94304-1044

JACKSON, CYNTHIA WILLIFORD, special education educator; b. Mobile, Ala., Oct. 30, 1949; d. Gerald Dee and Mary Evelyn (Johnson) W.; m. Alan P. Jackson, Aug. 18, 1973; 1 child, Julie Lynette. BS in Elem. Edn., John Brown U., 1971; MS in Spl. Edn., U. Ctrl. Ark., 1972; EdD, U. Ala., 1998. Cert. tchr., Ala. Resource tchr. Decatur (Ark.) Elem. Sch., 1972-73, Montgomery (Ala.) County Sch. System, 1973-75, Birmingham (Ala.) City Schs., 1976-80; instr. Horizons Program-UAB, Birmingham, 1992-94; rsch. asst., adj. U. Ala., Tuscaloosa, 1995-98, asst. prof., 1998-99, State U. West Ga., Carrollton, 1999—2002; ednl. evaluator Douglas County Sch. Sys., 2002—. Pvt. cons. Auburn (Ala.) City Schs., 1989-91; psychometrist, Montgomery, 1975-76. Author: (with others) Profile of Commitment, 1995; contbr. chpt. to Mental Retardation, 5th edit.; contbr. articles to profl. jours. Mem. Coun. for Exceptional Children, Kappa Delta Pi, Phi Delta Kappa. Baptist. Avocations: reading, needlepoint, walking. Home: 2520 Gold Hill Ct Villa Rica GA 30180-8458 Office: Fairplay Middle Sch 8309 Hwy 166 Douglasville GA 30135 E-mail: drcindyj@yahoo.com.

JACKSON, DARNELL, judge; b. Saginaw, Mich., Feb. 2, 1955; s. Roosevelt and Annie Lois (Pratt) J.; m. Yvonne Kay Givens, July 29, 1978; children: Brandon Darnell, Elliott Stephen. BA, Wayne State U., 1977, JD, 1981; AA, Kalamazoo C.C., 1993. Office mgr., shift supr. Wayne State U., Detroit, 1979-81; mng. ptnr. Allan & Jackson, P.C., Saginaw, 1983-85; asst. city atty. Saginaw City Atty.'s Office, 1985-86; asst. prosecuting atty. Saginaw County Prosecutor's, Saginaw, 1986-89; assoc. Braun, Kendrick, Finkbeiner et al, Saginaw, 1989-90; instr. Paralegal Inst. Delta Coll., University Center, Mich., 1986, instr. Northeastern Basic Police Acad., 1991-96; dep. chief asst. prosecuting atty. Saginaw County Prosecutor's Office, 1990-93; adminstrv. dep. chief of police Saginaw Police Dept., 1993-96; dir. Office of Drug Control Policy State of Mich., Lansing, 1996-2001; dist. ct. judge 70th Jud. Dist. Ct., Saginaw, Mich., 2001—. Mem. Drug Edn. Adv. Com., Lansing, Mich., 1996-2001, DARE Policy Adv. Bd., Lansing, 1996-2001, Mich. Dispute Resolution, Saginaw, 1989-92, Sen. Cisky Adv. Com., Saginaw, 1992-94; co-chair Partnership for Drug Free Mich., 1997-2001; speaker in field. Bd. dirs. United Way of Saginaw County, 1996, Westchester Village/Essex Manor, 1994-96, Saginaw County Child Abuse and Neglect Coun., 1994-96, Mr. Rogers Say No to Drugs Program, 1991-95; mem. Saginaw Valley Sate U. Multicultural Adv. Com., 1991-96; adv. bd. Saginaw St. Mary's Hosp., 1991-94, State Sen. Jon Cisky Minority Affairs Adv. Com., 1992-94. Recipient award for Profl. Excellence, FBI/Saginaw County Gang Crime Task Force, 1995, Frederick Douglass award for Community Svc., Mich. State Legis., 1991, award for Effort in War on Drugs, Saginaw Police Dept. Spl. Ops. Unit, 1989, Spl. Tribute for Community Svc., Mich. State Legis., 1985, Comm. Svc. awards Wayne State Univ. Free Legal Aid Clin, 1980-81. Mem. Mich. Bar Assn., Saginaw County Bar Assn., Fraternal Order of Police, Internat. Assn. of Chiefs of Police, Mich. Assn. of Chiefs of Police, Nat. Orgn. of Black Law Enforcement Execs. Office: State of Mich Saginaw County Ct Ho Saginaw MI 48602

JACKSON, DAVID ALONZO, retired newspaper editor; b. Litchfield, Ill., Oct. 7, 1924; s. David Winchester and Maude Abbot (McEwen) J.; m. Mina Jean Miller, Feb. 18, 1950 (dec. July 1998); children: Anne, David M., Jennifer E., Jeffrey A.; m. Martha Ann McHenry Cassity, Aug. 1, 1999. Student, Tex. A&M U., 1943, Pasadena Jr. Coll., 1943; BA, Ill. Coll., 1949. Apprentice printer Litchfield News-Herald, 1946, mgr. classified advt., 1949-58, advt. mgr., 1958-74, editor, 1974-89; columnist Break Time, 1979—. Mem. Montgomery County Bd., 1994—; past mem. Litchfield Postal Adv. Com.; trustee Litchfield Carnegie Pub. Libr., 1957-95, pres. 1959-92, 93-95; v.p., sec. Lewis and Clark Libr. Sys., Edwardsville, Ill., 1965-71, 77-83, 86; chmn. Litchfield Fire and Police Commn., 1985-95; bd. dirs. Bottomley-Ruffing-Schalk Baseball Mus., 1997-2002; dir. Corr Cemetery, Carlinville, Ill., Elmwood Cemetery, Litchfield. With Corps Mil. Police U.S. Army, 1943—46, with Corps Mil. Police U.S. Army, 1950. Recipient Dedicated Leadership plaque Ill. Coll., 1984, Disting. Citizen award, 1986, County Master Citizen award Montgomery County Fair Bd., 1987, Spl. Mayoral award City of Litchfield, 1987, Civic Activities award Litchfield Rotary Club, 1987, Statesman of the Yr., Litchfield C. of C., 1990; So. Ill. U. Journalism Hall of Fame, 1996, Studs Terkel Humanities Svc. award, Ill. Humanities Coun., 2000. Mem. Ill. Hist. Soc., Montgomery County Geneal. Soc. (pres. 1990-91, 92-95), Ill. Coll. Alumni Assn. (sec. 1977-83, nat. pres. 1984), Ill. Geneal. Soc., Macoupin County (Ill.) Geneal. Soc., Iredell County (N.C.) Geneal. Soc., VFW, Moose, Am. Legion (mem. Litchfield sesquicentennial history book com.). Republican. Methodist. Home: 910 N Monroe St Litchfield IL 62056-1541 E-mail: davidajackson@webtv.net. *Every man has to do what he has to do.*

JACKSON, DAVID D. state legislator; b. Topeka, Nov. 7, 1946; m. Annette Sorber; children: Chad, Traci. BS cum laude, Kans. State U., 1968. Housing mgmt. specialist HUD, 1971-83; v.p. Midwest Mgmt., Inc., 1983-85; pres. Jackson's Greenhouse & Garden Ctr., Inc., 1985—; mem. Kans. State Senate, 2000—. Adv. bd. Cmty. Nat. Bank, 2003—. Bd. dirs. Seaman Unified Sch. Dist. 345 Sch. Bd., 1983-95, Kona Billfisher Owners Assn., 2002—; pres. Sunrise Optimist Club North Topeka, 1985-86, North Topeka on the Move, Inc., 1997—; comdr. Sons Am. Legion Post 400, 1985-86; clk. Soldier Twp. Bd., 1994—; v.p. North Topeka Bus. Alliance, 1998-2000; active Neighborhood Element Adv. Com. to the Topeka Shawnee County Consol. Plan for 2025, 1999, Capitol Area Planning Coun., 2003. Mem.: Greater Topeka C. of C. (bd. dirs. 2003—). Republican. Lutheran. Home: 2815 NE Rockaway Trail Topeka KS 66617 Office: State Capitol Rm 5135-B Topeka KS 66612 Fax: 785-233-6348. E-mail: hort68@netzero.net.

JACKSON, DAVID HUNTSMAN, retired cardiologist; b. Tuscaloosa, Ala., July 17, 1937; s. Ashel Linc and Merle (Baxter) J.; m. Sara Wyatt, June 12, 1960; children: Susan Elizabeth, Sara Lynne. BS, U. Ala., 1959; MD, Med. Coll. Ala., 1963. Diplomate Am. Bd. Internal Medicine, Am. Bd. Cardiovasc. Disease; lic. MD, Ala. Intern Med. Coll. of Ala., 1964; resident in internal medicine Harvard U. Med. Svcs.-Boston City Hosp., 1967-69; fellow in cardiovasc. disease U. Ala., Birmingham, 1969-71; asst. prof. cardiology U. Ala. Sch. Medicine, Birmingham, 1971-74; practice medicine specializing in cardiology Birmingham; ret., 2001. Mem. staff Univ. of Ala. Hosps. and Clinics, 1971-74, Bessemer Caraway Hosp., 1974-76, 83-2001, Brookwood Med. Ctr., 1974—, Healthsouth Med. Ctr., 1976—, Shelby Med. Ctr., 1984-2001, Montclair Bapt. Med. Ctr., 1985-2001, Princeton Bapt. Med. Ctr., 1985-2001, St. Vincent's Hosp., 1986—; chmn. exec. com. Bessemer Carraway Med. Ctr., also bd. dirs. 1975; chief of cardiology Brookwood Med. Ctr., 1981-84, vice chmn. dept. medicine, 1984-85. Contbr. articles to sci. and profl. jours. Lt. USN, 1964-67. Fellow: ACP, Coun. on Clin. Cardiology, Am. Coll. Chest Physicians, Am. Coll. Cardiology; mem.: AMA, Am. Soc. Nuclear Cardiology (founding), Am. Soc. Echocardiography, Birmingham Acad. Medicine, Birmingham Soc. Internists, Med. Assn. of State of Ala., Jefferson County Med. Soc., So. Med. Assn., Laennec Soc., Ballistocardiography Rsch. Soc. (editor procs. 1971), Am. Heart Assn., Ala. Heart Assn. (bd. dirs. 1975). Avocations: reading, fishing, fitness.

JACKSON, DAVID LEE, insurance company executive; b. Youngstown, Ohio, Dec. 3, 1946; s. Harold Truman and Helene Irene (DeVoe) J.; m. Lauren Janine Hite, May 27, 1977. BA, Malone Coll., 1968; MA, Kent State U., 1975. Br. mgr. Boebinger Realtors, Alliance, Ohio, 1975-80; real estate broker, pres. D.L. Jackson Agy., Inc., Alliance and Canton, Ohio, 1980-92; agt. Nationwide Ins., Alliance, Ohio, 1993—. Mem. Alliance Area Bd. Realtors (pres. 1982), Canton-Massillon Bd. Realtors, Rotary. Republican. Avocation: golf. Home and Office: 5337 Cherokee Ave NW North Canton OH 44720-6841

JACKSON, DAVID WILLIAMS, music educator; b. St. Joseph, Mo., Aug. 26, 1951; s. Levell Lavon Jackson and Eleanor (Williams) Weller; m. Dana Marie Obenauer, Nov. 2, 1951. BS Vocal Music Edn., Mo. Western State Coll., 1975. Cert. Tchr. Mo., 1975. Music edn. grades 6-12 Dixon R-1 Schools, Dixon, Mo., 1995—; tchr. Gainesville Pub. Schools, Gainesville, Mo., 1993—95. Dir. music Second Presbyn. Ch., St. Joseph, Mo., 1993; soloist, substitute choir dir. First Presbyn. Ch., Columbia, Mo., 1984—92; tin man in Wizard of Oz Pulaski County Fine Arts Assn., Waynesville, Mo., 1998; singer St. Joseph Cmty. Chorus and Cmty. Chorus Chamber Singers, St. Joseph, Mo., 1993. Music Scholarship, Mo. Western State Coll., 1969—75. Mem.: Mo. State Tchrs. Assn., Mo. Choral Dirs. Assn., Am. Choral Dirs. Assn., Music Educators Nat. Conf. Avocations: hunting, fishing, canoeing, camping, outdoors. Home: PO Box 63 Dixon MO 65459 Office: Dixon R-1 Schools Drawer A Dixon MO 65459

JACKSON, DEAN MICHAEL, broadcaster, writer; b. Auburn, Ind., Aug. 13, 1968; s. Robert Lloyd and Mary Jean (Dickerhoof) J. BA in Comm., Huntington (Ind.) Coll., 1991; postgrad., Purdue U. Freelance writer, Harlan, Ind., 1985—; utility announcer WBCL Radio, Ft. Wayne, Ind., 1989-91; staff reporter Evening-Star, Auburn, 1992-93; play-by play sportscaster WAYT-AM/WWIP-FM, Wabash, 1992-94; sports clk. Jour.-Gazette, Ft. Wayne, 1992-94; play-by-play sportscaster/on-air announcer WIFF AM/FM TV, Auburn, 1994-95; pub. address announcer Ft. Wayne Wizards Baseball, 1996; play-by-play sportscaster WLNB Radio, Ligonier, Ind., 1996-97; contbg. writer Fellowship of Christian Athletes, Sports Spectrum Mag., Kansas City, Mo., 1996—; on-air announcer WLAB Radio, Ft. Wayne, 1997-98; contbg. writer Angola (Ind.) Herald-Rep., 1998—; corr. Times-Union, Warsaw, Ind., 2000—; news and sports dir. Travis Broadcasting, LLC (WGL-AM, WCKZ-FM, WYLT, WXTW-FM, WNHT-FM), Ft. Wayne, 2001—; play-by-play announcer Taylor U., Huntington Coll., 2000—. Contbr. AP, ESPN Radio, Sporting News Radio, Network Ind.; pub. address announcer U. St. Francis, 2000—; play-by-play Ind.-Purdue Ft. Wayne, 2002—, Ft. Wayne Freedom Football, 2003—. Republican. Avocations: computers, speaking, reading, documentaries, writing. Home: 18105 Allen Rd Harlan IN 46743 E-mail: djackson@mailcity.com.

JACKSON, DENNIS KENT, military career officer; b. Cheyenne, Wyo., Nov. 16, 1946; BA, U. Wyo., 1968; MBA, Fla. Inst. Tech., 1980; grad., Command and Gen. Staff Coll., Def. Sys. Mgmt. Coll., Indsl. Coll. Armed Forces. Commd. 2nd lt. U.S. Army, 1969, advanced through grades to maj. gen., 1998, with 1st Bn., 37th Armor, 1st Armored Divsn., 1969-72, comdr. 707th Maintenance Bn., 7th Inf. Divsn., Divsn. G4, spl. asst. to Chief of Staff of Army, Dept. Army Hdqrs., comdr. 25th Inf. Divsn. Support Command, 1992-94, exec. officer to commdg. gen. U.S. Army Materiel Command; dir. logistics, engring. and security assistance (J4) U.S. Pacific Command; comdr. 19th Theater Army Area Command U.S. Army, Taegu, Korea, comdr. Ordnance Ctrs. and Schs., 30th Chief of Ordnance, 1998-2000, dir. logistics and engring. U.S. Ctrl. Command, 2000—. Decorated Army Achievement medal with oak leaf cluster, Army Commendation medal with two oak leaf clusters, Meritorious Svc. medal with four oak leaf clusters, Bronze Star, Legion of Merit with three oak leaf clusters, Def. Superior Svc. medal, Disting. Svc. medal. Office: Hdqs Ctrl Command MacDill AFB 7115 South Boundary Blvd Tampa FL 33621-5101 E-mail: jacksodk@centcom.mil., DennisKJackson@aol.com.

JACKSON, DONALD FRANK, organizational development consultant; b. Dallas, Aug. 2, 1941; s. Carter Vaden and Eliose Lovelady Jackson; children: Donald Frank II, Taylor, Shawna, Eric. BS, Ariz. State U., 1969. Rsch. mgr. Phoenix Newspapers, Inc., 1959-70; exec. dir. Cmty. Orgn. for Drug Abuse Control, Phoenix, 1970-72; pres. Don Jackson & Assocs., Phoenix, 1972-77, Don Jackson Co., Phoenix, 1977-95; mng. dir. Don Jackson Co. Ltd., Peterborough, Eng., 1995; pres. Leadership Edge Internat., 1995—. Total Quality Mgmt. cons. ST Microelectronics, Geneva, 1980—; quality leadership, teambldg. cons. USPHS, Indian Health Svcs., Rockville, Md., 1985—; cons., trainer Helenic Mgmt. Assn., Athens, 1988—; team bldg. cons. Ariz. Dept. Pub. Safety, Phoenix, 1979—; human resource mgmt. cons. S-T U., Roussett, France, 1995—. Author: Self-Management System, 1985, Performance Appraisal Implementation, 1988, People Power, 1990, (transl. 8 langs.), Total Quality Management, A Latch-Cascade Initiative, 1992, (transl. 8 langs.), Advanced Leadership for Total Quality Management, 1993, Advanced Problem Solving, 1994 (transl. 8 langs.), Responsibility Charting-Improving Communications in Lateral Organizations, 1994, (transl. 8 langs.) Trustee Phoenix Union H.S. Dist., 1969-74, Verde Valley (Ariz.) Pvt. Sch., 1974-75; bd. dirs. Phoenix

Execs. Club, 1977; mem. Ariz. State Bd. for Pvt. Post-Secondary Edn., 1995-97. Recipient Liberty Bell award Maricopa County Bar Assn., Phoenix, 1969, Disting. Svc. award Maricopa County Med. Soc., Phoenix, 1970; named Outstanding Young Man of Ariz. Phoenix Jaycees, 1971. Mem.: Am. Soc. Quality Control, Phoenix C. of C., Masons. Avocations: golf, bicycling. Office: PO Box 15202 Scottsdale AZ 85267-5202 E-mail: leadershipedge@msn.com.

JACKSON, DONALD WILSON, political science educator, lawyer; b. Houston, Tex., May 15, 1938; s. Enoch Wilson and Ozella Rae J.; m. Joanne Shea, Apr. 20, 1985; children: Daniel Wilson, Michael Oden. BA, So. Meth. U., Dallas, 1959; JD, So. Meth. U., 1962; PhD in Polit. Sci., U. Wis., Madison, 1972. Bar: Tex. 1962, Supreme Ct. 75. Assoc. Storey, Armstrong & Steger, Dallas, 1962—67; instr. polit. sci. So. Meth. U., 1967—68; asst. prof. polit. sci. Idaho State U., Pocatello, Idaho, 1970—74; jud. fellow Supreme Ct. U.S., Washington, 1974—75; Herman Brown prof. polit. sci. Tex. Christian U., Ft. Worth, 1975—. Author: An Introduction to Political Analysis: The Theory and Practice of Allocation, 1978, Even the Children of Strangers: Equality Under the U.S. Constitution, 1992 (Oustanding Book on Human Rights, Gustavus Myers Center for Human Rights, 1993), The United Kingdom Confronts the European Convention on Human Rights, 1997; editor: Presidential Leadership and Civil Rights Policy, 1995; co-editor: Comparative Judicial Review and Public Policy, 1992. Bd. dirs. ACLU, N.Y.C., 2000—01, Quaker United Nat. Com., N.Y.C., 1997—2000; mem. adv. bd. Am. United for Separation of Ch. and State, Washington, 1995—2001; bd. dirs. Tex. affil. ACLU, Austin, 1992—2001. Named Outstanding Prof. in North Tex., N. Tex. Assn. Phi Beta Kappa, 1984, Tex. Piper Prof., Minnie Stevens Piper Found., 2003; recipient Citizenship Participation: Bill of Rights award, Tarrant County LWV, 1995, Silver Spur award, Planned Parenthood of North Tex., 1997. Mem.: We. Polit. Sci. Assn., Internat. Polit. Sci. Assn. (sec.-treas. 1997—2000, mem. rsch. com. comparative jud. studies), Am. Judicature Soc., Am. Polit. Sci. Assn. (sec. treas. law and cts. sect. 1996—99), Phi Beta Kappa. Avocations: backpacking, golf. Office: Tex Christian U TCU Box 297021 Fort Worth TX 76129-0001 Home Fax: 817-377-4368; Office Fax: 817-257-7397. Personal E-mail: jackson12@mindspring.com. Business E-Mail: d.w.jackson@tcu.edu.

JACKSON, DONNA ANN, musician, piano instructor; b. Houston, Sept. 25, 1951; d. Gerald Averitt and Mary Patricia (Helton) Brewer. Student, Baylor U., 1969-71, U. Tex., 1971-72; MusB, Mont. State U., 1978; M Liberal Arts, Houston Bapt. U., 1990. Pianist, vocal coach Intermountain Opera Co., Bozeman, Mont., 1978-79; staff pianist Mont. State U., Bozeman, 1977-79; owner, operator Starnote Music, Brenham & Houston, 1981—; instr. piano Blinn Coll., Brenham, Tex., 1987-90; adminstr. devel. dept. Houston Grand Opera, Houston, 1991-93; organist Reid Meml. Meth. Ch., 1993-95. Creator, producer radio program Radio Central Artsguide, weekly, 1981-88. Organist, Brenham Presbyn. Ch., 1984-87; bd. dirs. Brenham Fine Arts League, 1984-87, Arts Coun. Washington County, Brenham, 1984-89; entertainment dir. Brenham Downtown Assn., 1987-88. Recipient Bronze medal Internat. Piano Recording Competition, 1985; Arts Achievement award Arts Coun. Washington County, 1989. Mem. Music Tchrs. Nat. Assn., Tex. Music Tchrs. Assn., Brenham Area Music Tchrs. Assn. (bd. dirs. 1984-90), Mensa. Democrat. Presbyterian. Avocations: baseball, opera, musical theater. Mailing: 1143 Peachford Ln Houston TX 77062

JACKSON, DONNA CARDAMONE, music educator; b. Utica, NY, Nov. 16, 1937; d. Angelo Joseph and Mary Christine Cardamone; m. David Lee Jackson, May 24, 1977; 1 child, Anna Lee. BA, Wells Coll., Aurora, NY, 1959; MA, Harvard U., 1964, PhD, 1972. Prof. of music U. of Minn., 1969—. Mem. edit. bd. Jour. of the Am. Musicological Soc., Phil., Pa., 1995—98. Author: (book) The Canzone Villanesca alla Napolitana, 1981; editor: Adrian Willaert and His Cir., 1978, Orlando di Lasso: Canzoni Villanesche, 1991. Recipient Fulbright award, US Govt., Bologna, Italy, 1966—67; grantee, Am. Coun. of Learned Societies. Mem.: Renaissance Soc. of Am., Società Italiana di Musicologia, Am. Musicological Soc. (coun. sec.). Avocations: gardening, golf. Home: 2159 Folwell Ave Falcon Heights MN 55108 Office: U of Minn Sch of Music 2106 Fourth St S Minneapolis MN 55455-0437

JACKSON, DONNA E. legal secretary, administrative assistant; b. Washington, June 18, 1958; Cert. in secretarial scis., 1978. Mem. legal/adminstrv. support staff law firm, Washington, 1988—. Author: (cmty. newsletter) A Royal Priesthood A Chosen Generation, 1997. Vol. Nat. Coun. Negro Women, Washington, 2000. African Methodist Episcopalian/Baptist. Avocations: poetry, reading, sewing, mentoring. Personal E-mail: Essenceofroyalty@yahoo.com. *The quality of life is increased by none other than the love and life of another.*

JACKSON, DONNIE RAY, electrical engineer, researcher; b. Baughman, Ky., Feb. 16, 1956; s. Arnold Jackson and Loretta Wumbles-Jackson; m. Mary Louise Lisanby, Oct. 6, 1979 (div. 1986); 1 child, Misty Dawn. Student, Ivy Tech. Coll., Sellersburg, Ind., Layfete Sch. Radio, Calif.; grad., Cleve. Inst. Elec. Elec. tech. R.F. Micro Svc., Charlestown, Ind., 1977—84, Baughman, Ky., 1984—2003. Engr. rschr. SFG Rsch. Ltd., Baughman, 1996—2003. Contbr. articles. Recipient Golden Poets award, 1989. Protesant. Achievements include invention of stationary field generator. Avocations: amatuer radio, astronomy, guitar, fishing, archery. Office: SFG RSch Ltd 2056 Turkey Creek Baughman KY 40911

JACKSON, EARL, JR., medical technologist, retired; b. Paris, Ky., Sept. 4, 1938; s. Earl Sr. and Margaret Elizabeth (Cummins) J. BA, Ky. State U., 1960; postgrad., U. Paris, 1978. Clin. rsch. coord. Harvard U., Boston, 1962-64; chem. devel. specialist Electro-Power Pacs, Corp., Cambridge, Mass., 1964-67; sr. rsch. tech. Mass. Gen. Hosp., Boston, 1967-81, med. tech. specialist, 1981-95; ret., 1995. Contbr. articles to profl. jours. Named to, Hall of Fame of Disting. Alumni, Ky. State U., 2002. Mem.: N.E. Assn. for Microbiology and Infectious Disease, Am. Soc. Clin. Microbiology, Am. Assn. Clin. Chemistry, N.Y. Acad. Sciences, AAAS, Boston Mus. of Fine Arts, N.Y. Met. Mus. of Art. Democrat. Home: 501 Fenwick Dr San Antonio TX 78239-2532 E-mail: EJR29@aol.com.

JACKSON, EDGAR B., JR., medical educator; b. Rison, Ark., May 30, 1935; m. Thelma Jackson, 1957; children: Gary, David, Michael, Laura. BA, Case Western Res. U., 1962, MD, 1966. Intern Cleve. Met. Gen. Hosps., Cleve., 1966—67, chief resident medicine, 1969—70; from sr. instr. medicine to asst. prof. to asst. clin. prof. Case Western Res. U., Cleve., 1970—83, assoc. clin. prof., 1983—86, clin. prof. medicine, 1986—, asst. dean, 1971—74, asst. prof. cmty. medicine, 1974—79; chief of staff, sr. v.p. for clin. affairs Univ. Hosps. of Cleve.; asst. prof. cmty. health Case Western Res. U., Cleve., 1977—88. Contbr. numerous articles to profl. jours. With U.S. Army, 1959—61. Named Carnegie Common Wealth Clin. scholar, 1970—72. Mem.: APHA, Am. Sickle Cell Anemia Assn. Inc. Office: Univ Hosp 11100 Euclid Ave Cleveland OH 44106-1736

JACKSON, ELIJAH, JR., communication executive; m. Delesia Renee, 1995; children: Mercedes Alexis, Elijah Elias. AA in Gen. Studies and Broadcasting, Ricks Coll., Rexburg, Idaho, 1982; AA in Theatre, AA in Speech Comm., Brigham Young U., Hawaii, 1984; BA in Comm., U. Hawaii, Manoa, 1987; postgrad., U. Southwestern La., Lafayette, Polk C.C., Winter Haven, Fla.; LLM in Taxation, U. Hawaii, Manoa. 1988; D of Juridicial Sci. in Taxation, Washington Sch. Law, Sandy, Utah, 1999; DSc in Taxation, Washington Inst. Grad. Studies. Tng. Prog. by Federal Mogul Corp., 1998; entrepreneurship tng., Hawaii C. of C., Honolulu, 1987; Bus. Etiquette and Protocol, U. of Hawaii Manoa, 1986; Fin. Mgmt. for Closely held Bus., Bank of Hawaii, 1985; Eng. Tech., Tampa Tech. Inst., 1981. Editor Oceanic Cablevision, Am. TV Corp., Time Warner Inc., Honolulu TV Com. Corp.; pvt. practice radio and TV project budget mgr., prodr., dir, videographer; legal rschr., legis. aide Com. on Consumer Protection and Commerce State of Hawaii Legislature; CEO Jackson Program, 10 years, Jackson Pacific Joint Venture, 10 years, Jackson Instructional TV Sys., 10 years; trustee, fiduciary, promoter JBS Inc. Parent Corp., Hawaii, Fla.; CEO, pres., promoter Jackson Family Limited Partnership, Ltd., 13 years, Jackson Family Limited Trust, 13 years, JBS Inc. Parent Corp., 13 years, Elijah Jackson, Jr., Inc., 13 years; CEO, pres., chmn., promoter Delesia Renee Jackson Inc., 13 years; legal rschr., legislative aide State of Hawaii, 13th Legislature Com. on Consumer Protection and Commerce, Hawaii, 1 year; intern field prod., videographer, ABC affiliate, KITV channel 4, 1 year; graphic design, photography, cons. video system design Sony and CMX videos, 2 years; with Washington Inst. Grad. Studies Grad. Tax Program, Sandy, Utah. Trustee, pres. Jackson Internat. Mgmt. Limited, Nassau, Bahamas; assoc. mgr. trainee Discount Auto Parts, Inc.; sales assoc. Anderson News Co., Lakeland, Fla., Tampa, Fla., Knoxville, Tenn; legal rschr., real estate rschr., paralegal JBS Mgmt. and Properties, JBS Land and Water Entertainment and Sports; pres., CEO, trustee, financer, ptnr., tax matter person, nominee, residual interest holder, promoter Jackson Family Limited Partnership, Ltd., Jackson Family Limited Trust, JBS Inc. Parent Corp., Jackson Broadcasting Sys., Inc., JBC Inc. Lead Corp. of Fla. Divsn., Jackson Broadcasting Co., Inc., Elijah Jackson, Inc., Jr., Inc., Jackson Enterprises, Inc., Jackson Commodity Credit Corp., Cashland Inc., Jackson Internat. Telecom. Corp., Jackson, Inc., Jackson Internat. Fin. Corp., others; chmn. bd. Elias, Elisha and Elisabeth Jackson Inc., JBS Mgmt. Corp., Jackson Entertainment Svcs., Inc., EJJ Productions Inc.; pres., CEO JBS Inc., 1986—. Radio/TV project budget mgr., prod., dir., videographer; editor for Oceanic Cablevision a/k/a Amer. TV Corp. a/k/a Time Warner Inc. d/b/a Honolulu TV Comm. Corp. Corp. sec., trustee, mem. Paul A. Diggs Cmty. Devel. Corp., et al; pres., CEO Jackson Merit Nat. and Internat. Scholarship Fund and Found., 1986—. Recipient cert. of appreciation VFW, 1998, 99. Mem. ABA, Amer. Payroll Assn. Office: Elijah Jackson Trust and Inc PO Box 92895 Lakeland FL 33804-2895 also: Wash Inst Grad Studies 2268 Newcastle Dr Sandy UT 84093-1743 Fax: 863-686-4659.

JACKSON, ELIZABETH RIDDLE, writer, translator, educator; b. Boston, May 13, 1926; m. Matthew Casey and Katharine (Kerr) Riddle; m. Gabriel Jackson, Dec. 1949 (div. Sept. 1969); children: Katharine, Rachel. BA, Reed Coll., 1947; MA, Wellesley Coll., 1959; Doctorat de l'Université, Sorbonne U., Paris, 1963. Statistician Nat. Bur. Econ. Rsch., N.Y.C., 1947-48; tchr. math. Putney (Vt.) Sch., 1948-49; tutor French Goddard Coll., Plainsfield, Vt., 1953-55; lectr. in French Knox Coll., Galesburg, Ill., 1963-65; assoc. humanities U. Calif. San Diego, La Jolla, 1965-66; prof. French San Diego State U., 1969-87. Cons. Toronto U. Press, PMLA; mem. rev. panel NEH, Washington, 1977; mem. screening com. Fulbright Study Abroad, 1981-92, Oreg. Shakespeare Festival. Author: L'Evolution de la Mémoire Involontaire dans l'oeuvre de Marcel Proust, 1966, Worlds Apart: Structural Parallels in the Poetry of Paul Valéry, Saint-John Perse, Benjamin Péret and René Char, 1976, Secrets Observateurs...: la Poésie d'André Chénier, 1993; translator: A Marvelous World: Poems by Benjamin Péret, 1985, Meidosems (by Henry Michaux), 1993. Grantee French Govt., 1960-61, Fulbright Found., 1960-61, Ctr. Nat. Rsch. Sci., France, 1965. Mem. Amnesty Internat., So. Oreg. Learning in Retirement. Avocations: music, hiking. Home: 1200 Mira Mar Ave Apt 616 Medford OR 97504-8554

JACKSON, ERIC ALLEN, philatelist; b. Long Beach, Calif., Jan. 3, 1955; s. Allen Joseph and Janice Meredith (Lyen) J.; m. Theresa Kathleen Strauss Jackson, Mar. 21, 1975 (div. Jan. 1997); children: Amy Marie, Jared Brady, Luke Allen; m. Tamara Jane Kaufman, July 18, 2002. Student, Chapman Coll., Orange, Calif., 1973-75. Owner pvt. practice, Anaheim, Calif., 1973-81; cons. William C. Tatham Stamp Co., Whittier, Calif., 1979-81; owner Whittier (Calif.) Philatelic Svcs., 1981-87; pvt. practice Herndon, Va., 1987-88, Leesport, Pa., 1988—. Expert com. The Philatelic Found., N.Y.C., 1979—, Am. Philatelic Soc., State College, Pa., 1979—, Profl. Stamp Expertising, Newport Beach, Calif., 1987—; bd. dirs., v.p. Am. Revenue Assn., Rockford, Iowa, 1980—, pres., 2001—; cons. Scott Pub. Co., Sidney, Ohio, 1980—. Contbr. articles to profl. jours. Mem. Am. Stamp Dealers Assn. (bd. dirs. 1998—), Am. Philatelic Soc., Am. Revenue Assn., Collectors Club of N.Y., Revenue Soc. Great Britain, Berks County C. of C., Berks County Hist. Soc., Nat. Trust for Historic Preservation. Republican. Avocations: antiques, baseball, fishing. Home: 1922 Clydesdale Dr Mohrsville PA 19541-8888 Office: Eric Jackson Co PO Box 728 Schoolside Pla Ste A-1 Leesport PA 19533-0728 E-mail: eric@revenuer.com.

JACKSON, EUGENE BERNARD, librarian, educator; b. Frankfort, Ind., June 18, 1915; s. John Herman and Goldie Belle (Michael) J.; m. Ruth Lillian Whitlock, Aug. 6, 1941. BS with distinction, Purdue U., 1937; BS in Libr. Sci. with honors, U. Ill., 1938, MA, 1942; LHD (hon.), Purdue U., 1994. Asst. engring. library U. Ill., 1938-40; asst. charge newspaper div. U. Ill. Library, 1940-41; documents librarian U. Ala., 1941-42; with tech. dept. Detroit Pub. Library, 1942-46; chief reference library Wright Field, Ohio; chief library sect. Central Air Documents Office, Dayton, Ohio, 1946-49; chief research information sect. Research and Devel. Command, Q.M.C., Washington, 1949-50; chief div. aero. intelligence NACA, 1950-52, chief div. research information, 1952-56; head library dept. research labs. Gen. Motors Corp., Warren, Mich., 1956-65, chmn. corp. com. tech. lit., 1959-65; dir. information retrieval and library services IBM Corp., Armonk, New York, 1965-71; library cons. in automation, Grad. Sch. Library Sci. U. Tex., Austin, 1971-72, prof. library sci., 1971-85, prof. emeritus, 1985—; mem. chancellors coun. The U. Tex. Sys., 1996—. V.p. Engring. Index, Inc., 1967-68, pres., 1968-73; also dir. Attendee Gordon Research Confs. on Sci. Information, N.H., 1964— ; vis. summer lectr. U. Mich., 1965, U. Ill., 1968; mem. task force United Engring. Info. System, 1966; cons.; U.S. mem. documentation com., adv. group aero. research and devel. NATO, Paris, France, 1953-61, chmn., 1955-56, dep. chmn., chmn. elect., 1960-61; McBee lectr. Simmons Coll., Boston, 1956; ofcl. U.S. del. gen. assemblies Fedn. International de Documentation, Tokyo, 1967, The Hague, 1968, Buenos Aires, 1970, Budapest, 1972, chmn. U.S. nat. com., 1970-72 Author: (with Ruth L. Jackson) Industrial Information Systems, 1978; editor: Special Librarianship, a New Reader, 1980; contbr. articles to profl. jours., chpts. to books. Mem. tech. adv. com. Macomb County (Mich.) Planning Commn. Served with AUS, 1943-46. Named Pioneer in Info. Sci., Chem. Heritage Found., 1998. Mem. Spl. Libraries Assn. (pres. 1962-63), A.L.A., Am. Soc. Info. Scis., AIAA (sec. Mich. 1964-65), Assn. Records Mgrs. and Adminstrs. Protestant Episcopalian (vestryman, lic. lay reader). Home: 5715 Mesa Dr Apt 303 Austin TX 78731

JACKSON, FRANCIS JOSEPH, research and development company executive; b. Providence, May 23, 1932; s. Francis Joseph and Mary Elizabeth (Ryan) J.; m. Mary Veronica Brennan, Sept. 1, 1956 (div. Mar. 1983); children: Mary Cecilia, Paul Francis, Thomas Edward.; m. Nancy M. McMahon, May 21, 1983. BS magna cum laude, Providence Coll., 1954; Sc.M., Brown U., 1957, PhD, 1960. Rsch. assoc. Brown U., 1959-60; sr. scientist Bolt Beranek & Newman Inc., Cambridge, Mass., 1960-68, divsn. v.p., 1968-77, v.p., 1977-79, sr. v.p., 1979-98, cons., 1998-99. Adj. prof. Cath. U., 1973-77. Contbr. articles to profl. jours. Recipient Personal Achievement award Providence Coll., 1989, 75th Diamond Jubilee award Providence Coll., 1992. Fellow Acoustical Soc. Am.; mem. IEEE (sr.), Am. Inst. Physics, Cosmos, Winchester Country Club (bd. dirs. 1992-94), Delta Epsilon Sigma. Home and Office: 14A Plato Ter Winchester MA 01890-2229

JACKSON, FRED LESTER, retired civil engineer; b. San Bernardino, Calif., June 24, 1922; s. Fred Orin and Gertrude Lorena (Graham) J.; m. Alice Louise Williams, Dec. 15, 1945; children: Francis William, Alan Thomas, Lorene Ann. BA, San Bernardino Valley Jr. Coll., 1942; BS, U. Calif., Berkeley, 1944; Cert. in Mgmt., U. Calif., L.A., 1966. Surveyor, constrn. engr. Calif. Div. Hwys., Bishop, 1944-46, chief survey party San Bernardino, 1946-50, dist. adv. planning engr., 1950-65; dist. design engr. Caltrans, San Bernardino, 1966-73, dist. constrn. engr., 1974, asst. design engr. Sacramento, 1975-79, br. chief hdqrs. design, 1980-84; ret., 1984. Recipient Cert. of Appreciation, Calif. Senate, 1984. Mem. ASCE (life). Mem. Christian Ch. (Disciples Of Christ). Avocations: woodworking, gardening, fishing, boating. Home: 8844 Bold Ruler Way Fair Oaks CA 95628-6417

JACKSON, GARY DEAN, lawyer; b. Dallas, Sept. 13, 1935; s. Troy Byrl and Leslie Evelyn (Sitton) J.; m. Gloria Ann Galouye, Dec. 22, 1957; children: David MacArthur, Daniel Marshall. BA in Govt., So. Meth. U., 1957; JD, Baylor U., 1961; grad., U.S. Army War Coll., 1979. Bar: Tex. 1961, U.S. Ct. Mil. Appeals 1968, U.S. Supreme Ct. 1968, U.S. Dist. Ct. (no., so., ea., we. dists.) Tex., U.S. Dist. Ct. (no. dist.) Ala., U.S. Dist. Ct. (ea. and we. dists.) Ark., 1988, U.S. Dist. Ct. (no. dist.) Iowa, 1999, U.S. Army Ct. Rev., 1975, U.S. Ct. Claims, U.S. Ct. Appeals (1st, 3d, 4th, 5th, 7th, 8th, 9th, 10th, fed. cirs.). Budget examiner Tex. Legis. Budget Bd., 1957-59; ptnr. Pace, Jarvis & Jackson, Tyler, Tex., 1961-66; mcpl. judge Arlington, Tex., 1966-69; spl. asst. Dept. of Justice, Washington, 1969-74; ptnr. Colvin & Jackson, Dallas, 1974-78, Jackson Jenkins & Rowton, Dallas, 1978-81, Jackson, Jackson & Loving, 1982-83, Jackson, Jackson, Loving & Gutman, 1984-86, Jackson, Loving & Kindred, 1986-92; pvt. practice Jackson Law Offices, P.C., Lindale, Tex., 1992—. Instr. in bus. law Tyler Jr. Coll., 1962-65, fraud seminars, 1972—. Contbr. articles to legal jours. Pres. Smith County Rep. Men's Club, 1965; counselor Baylor U. Law Sch., 1974; chmn. Lindale Area Water Devel. Com.; vice chmn. exec. com. Upper Sabine Water Alliance; voting mem. Region Water Planning Group "D" (NE Tex.). Recipient Commendations Dir. FBI, 1971, 72, Atty. Gen. U.S., 1971, also others. Mem. ABA, So. Meth. U. Alumni Assn., Baylor U. Law Sch. Alumni Assn., Mil. Order World Wars, Civil Affairs Assn., Army Res. Assn., Baylor Law Rev. Former Editors (pres. 1979), Masons, Scottish Rite, Delta Theta Phi. Republican. Baptist. Home: PO Box 2229 Lindale TX 75771-2229 Office: 15001 CR 472 PO Box 1210 Lindale TX 75771-1210 Fax: 903-882-8868. E-mail: jlo@lcii.net.

JACKSON, GARY LEE, military analyst; b. Houston, Tex., Sept. 15, 1947; s. Charles Andrew and Ruth Willma (Tew) Jackson; m. Meridel May Pettyjohn, Apr. 3, 1973; children: Gary Lee II, Thomas Jonathan. BA cum laude in polit. sci., Trinity U., 1965—69; PhD in govt., Georgetown U., 1969—85. Cert. Information Systems Security Professional (CISSP) Internat. Info. Systems Security Certification Consortium, 2002. Sr. info. security systems engr. Sci. Applications Internat. Corp., Herndon, Va., 1997—2002; homeland security cons. Northrop Grumman Corp., Alexandria, Va., 2002—03. Fellow in polit.-mil. studies Ctr. for Strategic and Internat. Studies, Washington, 1995—96. Asst. troop scoutmaster Boy Scouts of Am., Derwood, Md., 1989—91. Maj. U.S. Army, 1974—94, Ariz., Germany, Tex., Md., Va. Decorated Legion of Merit U.S. Army, Army Commendation medal U.S. Army, U.S. Army. Mem.: World Future Soc., Armed Forces Comm. and Electronics Assn. (assoc.), Mil. Officers Assn. of Am. (assoc.), Assn. of the U.S. Army (assoc.), Am. Polit. Sci. Assn. (assoc.), Inst. for Ops. Rsch. and Mgmt. Sciences (assoc.), NRA (assoc.), The Am. Legion (assoc.), VFW (assoc.). Conservative. Christian. Achievements include U.S. Army project director to develop air and land combat-intelligence communications theater-strategic level; theater exploitation study system computer model. Avocations: football, camping, watch collecting, book collecting. Home: 17336 Founders Mill Dr Derwood MD 20855 Office: Northrop Grumman Corp 6940 South Kings Hwy Ste 210 Alexandria VA 22310 Personal E-mail: jacksondoc@yahoo.com. E-mail: gjackson@northropgrumman.com.

JACKSON, GEORGE LYMAN, retired nuclear medicine physician; b. Arlington, Mass., Dec. 17, 1923; s. William and Alice (Tenney) J.; m. Alyce Verne Yeager, Sept. 7, 1946; children: Scott Douglas, Carole Elizabeth, Diane Priscilla, Richard Lee. BS cum laude, Franklin and Marshall Coll., 1944; MD, U. Pa., 1948. Diplomate: Am. Bd. Internal Medicine, Am. Bd. Nuclear Medicine. Intern Hosp. U. Pa., 1948-49, resident, 1949-52; practice medicine specializing in internal medicine Harrisburg, Pa., 1952-63; dir. med. edn., acting med. dir. Harrisburg Hosp., 1963-68, dir. undergrad. fellowships, 1968-69, head sect. nuclear medicine, 1965-75, med. dir. dept. nuclear medicine, 1975-89. Asst. prof. medicine Hahnemann Med. Coll., 1963-68, assoc. prof., 1968-70; clin. assoc. prof. M.S. Hershey Med. Centre, Pa. State U., 1970-76, clin. prof., 1976-90; dir. Harrisburg Hosp. Sch. Nuclear Medicine Tech.; adj. faculty Harrisburg Area Community Coll., Millersville State Coll.; cons., chmn. med. adv. com. Lebanon (Pa.) VA Hosp., 1968-75; nuclear medicine adv. Pa. Dept. Edn., Pa. Med. Soc., Pa. Blue Shield. Author, pub.: Of Thee I Sing, 1993, The Eclectic Club of Harrisburg, 1997; contbr. articles to profl. jours. Mem. Cen. Dauphin Sch. Bd., 1971-73; bd. dirs. Bethesda Mission, Harrisburg Hosp. Med. Edn. and Rsch. Found.; bd. dirs. New Hope Ministries, 1987-93, pres. 1988-93; chmn. archives and collections com. No. York County Hist. and Preservation Soc., 1998-2000. With USNR, 1942-45. Fellow ACP (govs. com. for coll. affairs 1969-76, gov. 1976-80, laureate 1985), Soc. Nuclear Medicine, Am. Coll. Nuclear Physicians (bd. regents), Am. Coll. Nuclear Medicine; mem. Am. Thyroid Assn., Pa. Soc. Internal Medicine (past pres.; chmn. liaison com.), Pa. Coll. Nuclear Medicine (pres.), Joint Rev. Com. Nuclear Medicine Tech., Phi Beta Kappa, Alpha Omega Alpha. Lutheran. Home: 22 N Baltimore St Dillsburg PA 17019-1210 *The efforts of my adult life have been directed primarily at three priorities— family, profession, church. Success in achieving any of these is a consequence of a combination of providence, help from others and personal attributes. Help from others involves, principally, my family (in its largest sense) and of these my wife is most important. She is a source of understanding, wise counsel, inspiration, support and balance. My associates help significantly by their dedication, industry and responsibility. Personal attributes are hard work, absolute honesty, religious belief, and a conviction that the only justification for my professional life is to help the sick patients whom I am privileged to serve.*

JACKSON, GEORGE MARK, writer, photographer; b. Atlanta, Aug. 27, 1952; s. George Marshall and Kathleen (Keating) J. BA, U. Ala., 1976; MA, U. Ctrl. Fla., 1988. Film critic Metro Mag., Bham, Ala., 1978-79, S. Side News, Orlando, Fla., 1979; lit. critic Sentinel Star (Orlando Sentinel), 1979-81; freelance writer, hist. rschr., 1981—. Author: (novel) (under pseudonym Kano Shinichi) Ninja-Men of IGA, 1989; contbr. Ft. Pierce Tribune, 1999-2002; contbr. articles and photography to mags. Mem. Friendship Force Treasure Coast (editor newsletter 1991). Home and Office: 2043 SE Isabell Rd Port Saint Lucie FL 34952-8865 E-mail: mjacks81@bellsouth.net.

JACKSON, GERALDINE, entrepreneur; b. Barnesville, Ga., Oct. 30, 1934; d. Charles Brown and Christine (Maddox) J.; 1 child, Prentiss Andrew. Nurses aide Grady Hosp., Atlanta, 1953—54; mail handler U.S. Post Office, Cicero, Ill., 1966-70; sec., tour guide Walgreens Lab., Chgo., 1970-74; credit clk. Sterling Jewelers, Atlanta, 1974-2000; sec. Willie A. Watkins Funeral Home, Atlanta, 2000—. Mem. Nat. Law Enforcement Officer Meml. Fund; assoc. mem. presdl. task force Rep. Nat. Com.; active Sacred Heart League. Mem. AARP, DAV, NAACP, Nat. Assn. Police Orgn., Internat. Assn. Chief Police, Ga. Sheriff's Assn., Nat. Right to Life. Democrat. Home: 1890 Myrtle Dr SW Apt 422 Atlanta GA 30311-4954

JACKSON, GILCHRIST L. surgeon; b. Dayton, Ohio, Sept. 30, 1948; s. William Hughes Jr. and Margaret Langhorne (Alexander) J.; m. Katina Ballantyne, Nov. 28, 1970; children: Marina, Alex, Scott, George. BA, Vanderbilt U., 1970; MD, U. Louisville, 1974. Fellow U. Tex. M.D. Anderson Cancer Ctr., Houston, 1979-80, faculty, 1980-81; active staff Kelsey-Seybold Clinic, Houston, 1981—, chief surgery, 2001—, chief of surgery, mem. exec. bd., 2001—. Active staff St. Luke's Episcopal Hosp., Houston, 1981—, Meth. Hosp., Houston, 1981-2001, VA Hosp., Houston, 1981-83, Ben Taub Hosp., Houston, 1981—; courtesy staff Tex. Children's Hosp., Houston, 1981—; mem. dir. Crump Cancer Ctr., Houston, 1984-95, Kelsey-Seybold Cancer Program, 1994—; prin. investigator Tex. Cmty. Oncology Network, Nat. Surg. Adjuvant Breast and Bowel Project, 1986-95. Contbr. articles to profl. jours. Active Mus. Fine Arts, Houston, 1995; bd. dirs. West Univ. Little League, Houston, 1990, 1991. Mem.: ACS (state chmn. cancer physician liaison program Commn. on Cancer 1998—2002), Thyroid Soc. Am., Am. Cancer Soc. (v.p. 1985—87, pres. 1987—89). Republican. Presbyterian. Avocations: golf, tennis, fishing, travel, bicycling. Office: Kelsey Seybold Clinic Dept Surgery 2727 W Holcombe Blvd Houston TX 77025-1669

JACKSON, GRACE LOUISE, education educator, writer; b. Killeen, Tex., Mar. 20, 1937; d. Robert King Allen and Mattie Gertrude Darter; m. Donny Ray Jackson, Dec. 27, 1969. BS in Edn., S.W. Tex. State U., 1957, MA, 1959; EdD, U. Wyo., 1965. Cert. elem. classroom tchr. Tex., 1957, supr. Tex., 1973. Fourth grade classroom tchr. Brazosport Ind. Sch. Dist., Freeport, Tex., 1957—60; third grade tchr., u. instr. U. Wyo., Laramie, 1960—63, prof. curriculum and instrn., 1978—95; asst./assoc. prof. U. North Tex., Denton, 1965—70; remedial reading specialist Austin (Tex.) Ind. Sch. Dist., 1971—76. Reading/lang. arts cons. various sch. districts, Wyo. Author: (children's picture book) Grandpa Had a Windmill, Grandma Had a Churn, 1977, Over on the River, 1980, (juvenile novel) Gone To Texas: Adventure or Bust!, 2003. Mem.: Soc. Children's Book Writers and Illustrators. Avocations: travel, genealogy, gardening, reading, walking.

JACKSON, GREGORY WAYNE, orthodontist; b. Chgo., Sept. 4, 1950; s. Wayne Eldon and Marilyn Frances (Anderson) J.; m. Nora Ann Echtner, Mar. 17, 1973; children: Eric, David. Student, U. Ill., 1968-70; DDS with honors, U. Ill., Chgo., 1974; MSD, U. Wash., 1978. Practice dentistry specializing in orthodontics, Chgo., 1978—. Instr. orthodontic dept. U. Ill. Coll. Dentistry, Chgo., 1978-81. Coach Little League Baseball, Oak Brook, Ill., 1986-89. Served to lt. USN, 1974-76. Mem. ADA, Ill. State Dental Soc., Chgo. Dental

Soc., Am. Assn. Orthodontists, Midwestern Soc. Orthodontists, Ill. Soc. Orthodontists, Omicron Kappa Upsilon. Evangelical. Avocations: golf, tennis, skiing. Office: 6435 S Pulaski Rd Chicago IL 60629-5148

JACKSON, GUIDA MYRL, writer, magazine editor, book editor, publisher; b. Clarendon, Tex., Aug. 30; d. James Hurley and Ina (Benson) Miller; m. Prentice Lamar Jackson (div. Jan. 1986); children: Jeffrey Allen, William Andrew, James Tucker, Annabeth Broomall Davis; m. William Hervey Laufer, Feb. 14, 1986. BA, Tex. Tech U.; MA, Calif. State U., Dominguez Hills, 1986; PhD, Greenwich U., Hilo, Hawaii, 1990. Tchr. secondary sch. English, Houston Ind. Sch. Dist., 1951-53, Ft. Worth Ind. Sch. Dist., 1953-54; pvt. tchr. music, freelance writer, Houston, 1956-71; editor newsletter Tex. Soc. Anesthesiologists, Austin, 1972-80; editor-in-chief Tex. Country mag., Houston, 1976-78; mng. editor Touchstone, lit. mag., Houston, 1976—. Contbg. editor Houston Town and Country mag., 1975—76; book editor Arte Publico, 1987—88; editor, pub. Panther Creek Press, 1999—; lectr. English U. Houston, 1986—95; instr. Montgomery Coll., 1996—; freelance writer, Houston, The Woodlands, Tex., 1978—. Author: (novels) Passing Through, 1979, A Common Valor, 1980, (play) The Lamentable Affair of the Vicar's Wife, 1989, (biog. reference) Women Who Ruled, 1990 (best reference lists award Libr. Jour. and Sch. Libr. Jour. 1990), (nonfiction) Virginia Diaspora, 1992, Virginia Diaspora CD-ROM, 2001, (lit. reference) Encyclopedia of Traditional Epic, 1994 (best reference list award ALA), (lit. reference) Traditional Epics: A Literary Companion, 1995, Encyclopedia of Literary Epics, 1996, (play) Showdown at Nosegay Cottage, 1997, (play) The Man From Tegucigalpa, 1998, (reference) Women Rulers Throughout the Ages, 1999, (play) Julia is Peculiar; editor: (anthologies) Heart to Hearth, 1989, African Women Write, 1990, Fall From Innocence, Memoirs of the Great Depression, 1998, (nonfiction) Legacy of the Texas Plains, 1994, Through the Cumberland Gap, 1995. Mem.: Houston Writers Consortium, Writers' Forum, Montgomery Lit. Arts Coun., Dramatists Guild, Woodland Writers Guild, Houston Writers Guild, PEN Ctr. West, Women in Comm. Avocations: music, gardening, poetry. Office: Panther Creek Press PO Box 130233 Spring TX 77373-0233 E-mail: panthercreek3@hotmail.com.

JACKSON, HAROLD, journalist; b. Birmingham, AL, Aug. 14, 1953; s. Lewis and Janye (Wilson) J.; m. Denice Estell Pledger, Apr. 30, 1977; children: Annette Michelle, Dennis Jerome. BS in Journalism and Polit. Sci., Baker U., 1975. Reporter Birmingham Post-Herald, Ala., 1975-80, UPI, Birmingham, Ala., 1980-83, state news editor, 1983-85; asst. nat. editor Phila. Inquirer, 1985-86; asst. city editor Birmingham News, Ala., 1986-87, editorial writer, 1987-94; editl. page writer The Balt. Sun, 1994-99; commentary editor Phila. Inquirer, 1999—. Journalist-in-residence Loyola Coll., Balt., 1997-98. Trustee Baker U., 1997—. Recipient Pulitzer Prize for editorial writing, 1991. Mem. Nat. Assn. Black Journalists (Journalist of Yr. award 1991), Birmingham Assn. Black Journalists (pres. 1987-90), Soc. Profl. Journalists (Green Eyeshade award 1989), Phila. Assn. Black Journalists. Presbyterian. Avocations: reading, aerobic exercise. Home: 57 Fox Hollow Ln Sewell NJ 08080-3139 Office: 400 N Broad St Philadelphia PA 19130-4015

JACKSON, HARRY ANDREW, artist; b. Chgo., Apr. 18, 1924; s. Harry Shapiro and Ellen Grace Jackson; m. Theodora Rehard DuBois, 1946 (div.); m. Grace Hartigan, 1948 (div.); m. Claire Rodgers, 1950 (dec.); m. Joan Hunt, 1951 (div.); m. Sarah Mason, Sept. 10, 1962 (div.); children: Matthew, Molly; m. Tina Lear, Aug. 11, 1973 (div.); children: Jesse, Luke, Chloe. Diploma, H.S., 1945; LLD (hon.), U. Wyo., 1986. Founder fine art foundry, Camaiore, Italy, 1964—, Harry Jackson Studios, Italy, 1965—; CEO Harry Jackson Studios (formerly Wyo. Foundry Studios, Inc.), Cody, Wyo., 1971—; founder Western Arts Found., 1974—; foundry ptnr. Jackson-Mariani Fine Art Foundry, Camaiore, Italy, 1985-98; founder Harry Jackson Art Mus., Cody, Wyo., 1994. Author: Lost Wax Bronze Casting, 1972, New York School Abstract Expressionists, 2000; one man exhbns. include Ninth St. Show, N.Y.C., 1951, Tibor de Nagy Gallery, N.Y.C., 1952, 53, Martha Jackson Gallery, N.Y.C., 1956, M. Knoedler & Co., N.Y.C., 1960, Amon Carter Mus., Fort Worth, 1961, 68, Kennedy Galleries, N.Y.C., 1964, 68, Smithsonian Instn., Washington, 1964, Whitney Gallery Western Art, Cody, 1964, 81, Mont. Hist. Soc., 1964, NAD, 1965, 68, Nat. Cowboy Hall of Fame, Oklahoma City, 1966, XVII Mostra Internazionale d'Arte, Premio del Fiorino, Florence, Italy, 1966, Pennational Artists Ann., Pa., 1967, Mostra de Arte Moderna, Convento di S. Lazzaro, Camaiore, 1968, Am. Artists Profl. League, N.Y., 1968, Cowboy Artists Am., 1971-76, S.W. Mus., L.A., 1979, Smith Gallery, N.Y.C., 1981, 85; major retrospective exhbns. include Buffalo Bill Hist. Ctr., 1981, Palm Springs Desert Mus., 1981, Mpls. Inst. Art, 1982, Camaiore, Italy, 1985, Met. Mus. Art, N.Y.C., 1987; represented in permanent collections Met. Mus. Art, NAD, Nat. Mus. Am. Art, Nat. Portrait Gallery, Washington, Her Majesty Queen Elizabeth II, Sandringam Castle, Eng., Am. Mus. of Gt. Britain, Bath, Eng., U.S. State Dept., Washington, Lyndon Baines Johnson Meml. Libr., Austin, Tex., Ronald Reagan Meml. Libr., Santa Barbara, Calif., Whitney Gallery Western Art, Plains Indian Mus., Buffalo Bill Hist. Ctr., Cody, Wyo., Wadsworth Atheneum, Hartford, Conn., Alberta Glenbow Mus., Calgary, Can., Univ. So. Calif., Stanford (Calif.) Univ., Love Libr. Univ. Nebr., Lincoln, Portsmouth (R.I.) Abbey, S.W. Mus., Gene Autrey Mus., L.A., Nat. Cowboy Hall of Fame, Oklahoma City, Gilcrease Mus., Tulsa, Fort Pitts Mus., Pitts., Amon Carter Mus., Pro Rodeo Cowboy Hall of Fame, Colorado Springs, Colo., Eiteljorg Mus., Indpls., Shelburne (Vt.) Mus., Columbus (Ga.) Mus. Arts & Scis., Oreg. Hist. Soc., Portland, Salt Lake City Art Ctr., Norfolk (Nebr.) Arts Ctr., Aspen (Colo.) Art Mus., Woolaroc Mus., Bartlesville, Okla., U. Wyo. Art Mus., Laramie, Mont. Hist. Soc., Helena, Norton Mus., Shreveport, La., Columbia U., N.Y.C., Trout Gallery Dickinson Coll., Carlisle, Pa., Ctrl. Wyo. Coll., Riverton, N.W. C.C., Powell, Wyo., Baylor Sch., Chattanooga, Orme Sch., Mayer, Ariz., others; commd. works include (sculpture) William R. Coe Commn., 1959, 60, Fort Pitt Mus., 1964, 73, Plains Indian Mus., Cody, Wyo., Ctrl. Wyo. Coll., Riverton, 1978, 81, Piazza della Chiesa, Capezzano, Pianore, Italy, 1985, Great Western Savs. & Loan, Santa Barbara, Calif., 1985, John Wayne monumental sculpture Beverly Hills, Calif, 1981, 84, (portrait busts) Met. Mus. Trustees, C. Douglas Dillon, 1985, 87, (portrait) "John Wayne" TIME cover, Aug. 8, 1969 (Nat. Best Cover Art award Am. Inst. Graphic Arts 1969), (paintings) Whitney Gallery Western Art, Cody, 1960, 66, (mural) R.K. Mellon. Served with USMC, 1942-45. Decorated Purple Heart with gold star; recipient Gold medal NAD, 1968; grantee Fulbright, 1954, Italian Govt., 1956, 57. Fellow NAD (academician), RISD, Nat. Acad. Western Art, Nat. Sculpture Soc., Am. Artists League; mem. Bohemian Club (San Francisco). Office: PO Box 2836 Cody WY 82414-2836 also: Via Monteggiori 55040 Camaiore Lucca Italy Fax: 307-587-6362. E-mail: njackson@wyoming.com.

JACKSON, HARVEY HARDAWAY, III, history educator, columnist; b. Fort Riley, Kans., Feb. 25, 1943; s. Harvey Hardaway Jackson, Jr. and Elizabeth Waite Jackson; m. Suzanne Brown, May 31, 1959; children: Kelly Jackson Roberts, William Blackwell, Anna Elizabeth. PhD, U. Ga., 1973. Instr. of history South Fla. Jr. Coll., Avon Park, Fla., 1966—70; prof., chair Clayton State Coll., Morrow, Ga., 1973—90, Jacksonville (Ala.) State U., 1990—. Mem. editl. bd. The Anniston (Ala.) Star, 2002—. Contbr. articles to profl. publs. (Milo B. Howard Jr. award, 1991). Rev. bd. for nat. hist. register Ala. Hist. Commn., Montgomery, Ala., 1995—2001. Mem.: Ala. Assn. Historians (pres. 2000—01). Home: 407 Rocky Ridge Rd NE Jacksonville AL 36265 Office: Jacksonville State U Jacksonville AL 36265 Personal E-mail: hjackson@jsucc.jsu.edu.

JACKSON, HEATHER, secondary school educator; b. Kingston, Jamaica, Jan. 21, 1972; d. Balfoe and Beryl Jackson. BA, William Paterson U., 1991, MEd, 1998; EdD, Seton Hall U., 2003. Cert. secondary sch english tchr. NJ, student personnel svc. NJ, supervisor NJ. Subs. tchr. Paterson Bd. Edn., 1996—97, tchr., 1997—2000; kindergarten tchr. East Orange-Little Phil. Sch., 1997—99; adminstr. Seton Hall U., South Orange, 1999—2000. Adj. prof. William Paterson U., Wayne, NJ, 1998—99. Mem.: Paterson Edn. Assn., N.J. Edn. Assn., Kappa Delta Pi. Avocations: writing, physical fitness, reading.

JACKSON, HERB, artist, educator; b. Raleigh, NC, Aug. 16, 1945; s. Walter H. and Virginia (Rogers) Jackson; m. Laura Dudley Grosch, June 9, 1967; children: Leif, Ulysses. BA, Davidson Coll., 1967; postgrad., Philips Universität; M.F.A., U. N.C., 1970. William H. Williamson Prof. Art Davidson Coll., NC, 1969—, chmn. dept. art, 1977-94; dir. Art Gallery, 1974-95; mem. artist adv. bd. Mint Mus. Art, Charlotte, NC, 1979-85. Bd. adv. Light Factory, Charlotte, 1990—, NC Dance Theater, NC, 1998. One-man shows include: Mint Mus. Art, Charlotte, 1973, U. Nev., Reno, 1973, Rahr Mus., Manitowoc, Wis., 1973, Jane Haslem Gallery, Washington, 1974, Nielsen Gallery, Boston, 1974, Impressions Gallery, Boston, 1975, 81, Hahn Gallery, Phila., 1976, Dryden Gallery, Charlotte, 1976, Van Straaten Gallery, Chgo., 1977, Frances Aronson Gallery, Atlanta, 1978, NC Mus. Art, Raleigh, 1979, Rowe Gallery, U. NC, Charlotte, 1979, Southeastern Center for Contemporary Art, Winston-Salem, NC, 1981, Phyllis Weil Gallery, NYC, 1981, 83, 85, 87, 88, 90, Princeton Gallery Fine Art, 1982, 83, Oxford Gallery (Eng.), 1982, DBR Gallery, Cleve., 1983, 84, Mint Mus. Art, Charlotte, NC, 1983, Springfield Mus. Art (Mo.), 1983, Asheville Mus. Art (NC), 1983, Nat. Acad. Scis., Washington, 1983, Cheekwood Art Ctr., Nashville, 1983, Reading Art Mus. (Pa.), 1984, Gulbenkian Found., Lisbon, Portugal, 1984, Huntsville Mus. Art (Ala.), 1984, Jerald Melberg Gallery, Charlotte, NC, 1984, 85, 87, 88, 90, 92, 93, 94, 96, 97, 98, 99, Fay Gold Gallery, Atlanta, 1986, 88, 92, Cumberland Gallery, Nashville, 1987, 96, Judy Youens Gallery, Houston, 1988, Peden Gallery, Raleigh, NC, 1988, 92, 93, Asheville (NC) Mus. Art, 1988, Allene Lapides Gallery, Santa Fe, 1989-90, Maurine Littleton Gallery, Washington, 1990, Hickory (NC) Mus. Art, 1993, St. Johns Mus. Art, Wilmington, NC, 1993, Bi-Nat. Cultural Ctr., Arequipa, Peru, 1994, parchman Stremmel Gallery, San Antonio, Tex., 1995-2001, Somerhill Gallery, Chapel Hill, NC, 1995, 98, Christa Faut Gallery, Cornelius, NC, 1996, 97, 99, 2000, 02, 03, La. Tech. U., Ruston, 1999, Lmar Dodd Art Ctr., La Grange, Ga., 1999, Greenville (NC) Mus. Art, 2000, Les Yeux du Monde, Charlottesville, Va., 2001, GSI Fine Art, Cleve., 2001, Fayetteville (NC) Mus. Art, 2002; numerous group shows, 1962—, latest being Internat. Print Biennale, Bradford, Eng., 1979, Mint Mus., Charlotte, 1979, 81, Southeastern Center Contemporary Art, Winston-Salem, 1979, Internat. São Paulo (Brazil) Bienal, 1979, Spring Mills Ann. Competition, Lancaster, SC, 1980, Weatherspoon Gallery, Greensboro, NC, 1980, Impressions Gallery, Boston, 1980, Associated Am. Artists, Phila., 1980, Am. Acad. and Inst. Arts and Letters, NYC, 1981, 1987, Bklyn. Mus. Art, 1981, World's Fair, Knoxville, Tenn., 1982, Davos, Switzerland, 1983, Palazzo Venezia, Rome, 1984, Miss. Mus. Art, 1984, U. Denver, 1984, Albuequerque Mus. Art, 1985, Fla. State U., 1985, St. John's Mus. Art, Wilmington, NC, 1986, U. Tex., San Antonio, 1987, Contemporary Arts Ctr. New Orlean, 1988, Kunstsammlungen der Veste Coburg, Fed. Republic Germany, 1988, Lorenzelli Fine Art, Milan, 1989, Exhbn. Hall of Union of Moscow Artists, Moscow, 1989, Samuel P. Harn Mus., Gainesville, Fla., 1990, New Orleans Mus. Art, 1995, Shanxia Govt. Art Gallery, Xian, China, 1996, Morris Mus. Art, Augusta, Ga., 1997, Mus. Del Vidrio, Monterey, Mex., 1999, Vanessa Suchar Fine Arts, London, Eng., 2000, Thomas McCormick Gallery, Chgo., 2002; represented in permanent collections: Balt. Mus. Art, Phila. Mus. Art, Victoria and Albert Mus., London, Whitney Mus. Art, NYC, Mpls. Inst. Arts, Nat. Acad. Sci., Washington, Indpls. Mus. Art, Bklyn. Mus., USIA, Japan, U. Wis., Sheboygan, Yale U., New Haven, Mus. Fine Arts, Boston, NY Public Library, Library of Congress, Washington, Mint Mus., Charlotte, So. Ill. U., Edwardsville, Kalamazoo Inst. Arts, Mus. Fine Arts, Springfield, Mass., Utah Mus., Salt Lake City, U. Nebr., Lincoln, U. Calif., Riverside, Minn. Mus. Art, St. Paul, Brit. Mus., London, others. Fellow Southeastern Ctr. for Contemporary Art Southeastern Seven, 1981, N.C. Visual Arts, 1984, Nat. Endowment for Arts and So. Arts Fedn., 1986; recipient N.C. award, 1999, Love of Tchg. award Hunter-Hamilton, 2003. Mem. Coll. Art Assn., So. Graphics Council, Charlotte Artists Coalition (dir. 1980-81), Mecklenberg-Charlotte Arts and Sci. Council (dir. 1977-79), Southeastern Coll. Art Conf. Home: PO Box 10 Davidson NC 28036-0010 Office: PO Box 7117 Davidson NC 28035-7117 Fax: 704 894-2691. E-mail: hejackson@davidson.edu. *The artist's integrity is all he truly has, after all the trends, fads, and movements have faded into history. I try to make art which will stand as a personal statement.*

JACKSON, HERMOINE PRESTINE, psychologist; b. Wilmington, Del., Mar. 11, 1945; d. Herman Preston Sr. and Ella Brooks Jackson. BA, Elizabethtown (Pa.) Coll., 1967; MA, Ohio State U., 1979, PhD, 1991. Tchr. Wilmington (Del.) pub. sch. sys., 1967-68, Phila. Pub. Sch. Sys., 1968-74; psychologist Midland (Mich.) Hosp., 1979-81, Cen. Mich. U., Mt. Pleasant, 1979-81, West Seneca (N.Y.) Devel. Ctr., 1981-90, N.Y. State Div. for Youth Buffalo Residential Ctr., 1990-94, Tryon Girls Ctr., 1994, Va. Dept. Juvenile Justice, Beaumont, 1994-97, Bon Air, 1997—2002, Bermuda Dept. Corrections, St. George, 2002—. Mem. admissions/discharge com. St. Augustine Ctr., Buffalo, 1983-90. Co-author test manual: Manual of Assessment Instruments for the MR/DD Population, 1978. Mem. Planning Coun., Buffalo, 1989-94. Named Outstanding Instr., Ctrl. Mich. U., 1981. Mem. APA, Am. Assn. on Mental Retardation, Psychol. Assn. Western N.Y., Coalition of 100 Black Women (corr. sec. 1988-91). Office: Bermuda Dept Corrections 31 Ferry Rd Saint Georges GE 01 Bermuda

JACKSON, IVOR, endocrinologist, educator; b. Glasgow, Scotland; s. Louis and Gertrude Jackson; m. Barbara Weiss, Apr. 26, 1972; children: Heather Rochelle, Amanda Ruth. MB ChB, Glasgow U., 1960; MA ad eundem, Brown U., 1985. Bd. cert. internal medicine, endocrinology. From asst. prof. to assoc. prof. to prof. medicine Tufts U. Sch. Medicine, Boston, 1974-84; prof. medicine Brown U. Sch. Medicine, Providence, 1984—; dir. divsn. endocrinology Brown Univ. Sch. Medicine and R.I. Hosp., Providence, 1984—2000; physician Endocrine Treatment Ctrs., Inc., Providence, 2003—; staff physician R.I. Hosp. Editor: Pituitary Adenoma, 1980, Thyrotropin--Releasing Hormone, 1989; contbr. articles and revs. to profl. jours. including Endocrinology, Sci., The Pituitary Gland. Fellow ACP, Royal Coll. Physicians; mem. Am. Soc. Clin. Investigation, Am. Thyroid Assn. (bd. dirs. 1988-92), Endocrine Soc., Assn. Am. Physicians, Endocrine Soc. of Republic of China (hon.). Achievements include isolation of thyrotropin-releasing hormone in mammalian brain. Office: Endocrine Treatment Center 51 Silver Spring St Providence RI 02904-4971

JACKSON, J. EDWARD, retired statistician; b. Rochester, N.Y., Jan. 12, 1925; s. James Arthur Jackson and Laura Hitchcock; m. Suzanne Montgomery, June 24, 1947; children: James, Janice, Judith. BA, U. Rochester, 1947; MA, U. N.C., 1949; PhD, Va. Poly. Inst., 1960. Statistician Eastman Kodak Co., Rochester, 1948—57; asst. process engr. Hercules Powder Co., Radford, Va., 1957—58; asst. prof. Va. Poly. Inst., Blacksburg, 1958—59; statistician Eastman Kodak Co., Rochester, 1959—85; pvt. cons. Self Employed, Rochester, 1985—90; ret., 1990—. Author: (book) A User's Guide to Principal Components, 1991. Pvt. first class U.S. Army, 1943—45, Various. Decorated Purple Heart; recipient Hunter Award, Am. Soc. for Quality Control, 1994. Fellow: Am. Soc. for Quality (various), Am. Statis. Assn. (various). Avocation: music, local history, railroad history, genealogy. Home: 16 Kettering Dr Rochester NY 14612 Personal E-mail: stmathstat@aol.com.

JACKSON, JAMES F. nuclear engineer, educator; b. Ogden, Utah, Aug. 15, 1939; s. Allyn Boyd and Virginia (Dixon) J.; m. Joan Borger, Aug. 25, 1960; children: James D., Bret A., Tracy L., Wendy L. BS, U. Utah, 1961; MS, MIT, 1962; PhD, UCLA, 1969. Rsch. engr. Atomics Internat., L.A., 1962066; nuclear engr. Argonne Nat. Lab., Idaho Falls, Idaho, 1969-72, group leader Argonne, Ill., 1972-74; assoc. prof. Brigham Young U., Provo, Utah, 1974-76, adj. prof., 1998—; cons. Los Alamos (N.Mex.) Nat. Lab., 1974-76, group/div. leader, 1976-82, dep. assoc. dir., 1979-81, div. leader, 1983-84, assoc. dir., 1984-86, dep. dir., 1986-98, staff mem., 1998-99, cons., 1999—. Contbr. articles to jours. in field. Mem. exec. bd. Community Devel. Com., Los Alamos, 1989-93; bd. dirs. Los Alamos Citizens Against Substance Abuse, 1989-93. Recipient E.O. Lawrence award Dept. Energy, Washington, 1983. Mem. NAE, Am. Nuclear Soc. (safety div. 1967—, exec. com. 1977-80), Tau Beta Pi. Republican. Mem. Lds Ch. Avocations: history, motorsports, photography. Home: 536 Sheffield Dr Provo UT 84604-5666 Office: Los Alamos Nat Lab Ofc Dir Los Alamos NM 87545-0001 E-mail: jackson538@attbi.com., jackson-james-f@lanl.gov.

JACKSON, JAMES KINSEY, lawyer; b. Savoy, Tex., Sept. 12, 1940; s. Jack Boem and Rosely (Edwards) J.; m. Carol Elizabeth Hudgins, Aug. 17, 1963; children— Janet, Joan. Student Wake Forest U., 1959; B.B.A., So. Meth. U., 1963; 1963; LL.B., U. Tex., 1966. Bar: Tex. 1966, D.C. 1970. Atty. office of chief counsel IRS, Washington, 1966-70; assoc. Steptoe & Johnson, Washington, 1971-75; ptnr. Pepper, Hamilton & Scheetz, Washington, 1975-77, Baker & Hostetler, Washington, 1978-80; v.p., asst. sec. Riddell, Fox, Holroyd & Jackson, P.C., Washington, 1980— . Mem. D.C. Bar, State Bar Tex., ABA (mem. taxation sect.). Contbr. articles to profl. jours. Office: Bishop Liberman Cook Et Al 1200 17th St NW Ste 600 Washington DC 20036-3013

JACKSON, JAMES LEWIS PERDUE, II, entertainment company executive; b. Chattanooga, May 29, 1946; s. James Oliver and Nellie Mae (Perdue) J.; 1 foster child, Abner Isaias Quinones. AA, Long Beach (Calif.) City Coll., 1972, Riverside (Calif.) City Coll., 1974; cert., Am. Bus. Inst., 1989. Cert. tax audit rep. IRS. Head designer, owner Jai et' Cie Haute Couture, L.A., 1983—; head artist and image devel. Platinum Gold Prodns., L.A., 1990-94; CEO, owner TOJA Entertainment Group, N.Y.C., L.A., 1990—; exec. v.p. Leg Records, L.A., 1995-96; food and beverage mgr. Gershwin Hotel, N.Y.C., 1997-98; ptnr. The LeBlanc Group, N.Y.C., 1997-98. West Coast mng. editor Twin Cities Exec. Mag., L.A., 1991-93; prodr. Three Points of Light Prodns., N.Y.C., 1996-99; costume designer Zipper Films, N.Y.C., 1997; author (screenplay) The Mary Wells Story, 1998; exec. prodr. The Tennis Shoe Cowboy, 1999, The Pink Triangle, 1999. Sustaining mem. Rep. Nat. Com., L.A., 1983; active N.Y. Black Rep. Coun., N.Y.C., 1999. With USN, 1964-69. Mem. Motown Alumni Assn. (exec. dir. N.Y.C. chpt.). Republican. Avocations: horse back riding, snow skiing, modern dance, opera, ballet. Office: TOJA Entertainment Group PO Box 1075 New York NY 10037-0994 Fax: 212-368-0485. E-mail: Jai2cool@aol.com., TOJAEntGrp@aol.com.

JACKSON, JAMES SIDNEY, psychology educator; b. Detroit, July 30, 1944; s. Pete James and Johnnie Mae (Wilson) J. BS, Mich. State U., 1966; MA, U. Toledo, 1970; PhD, Wayne State U., 1972. Probation counselor Lucas County Juvenile Ct., Toledo, Ohio, 1967-68; tchg. and rsch. asst. Wayne State U., Detroit, 1968-71; from asst. prof. to prof. psychology U. Mich., Ann Arbor, 1971—, faculty assoc. Rsch. Ctr. Group Dynamics, 1971—, dir. Rsch. Ctr. Group Dynamics, 1996—, rsch. scientist, 1986—, faculty assoc. Inst. Gerontology, 1976—, faculty assoc. Ctr. Afro-Am. and African Studies, 1982—, dir. Ctr. Afro-Am. and African Studies, 1998—, assoc. dean Rackham Sch. Grad. Studies, 1987-92, prof. pub. health, 1990—, dir. program for rsch. on Black Ams., 1976—, Daniel Katz Disting. Univ. prof. psychology, 1995—, Daniel Katz Collegiate prof., 1994-95; Hill Disting. vis. prof. U. Minn., 1995. Chair sociol. psychology tng. program U. Mich., 1980-86, 93-96; cons. Emergency Sch. Aid Project, 1973-74, Commn. on Equal Opportunity in Psychology, 1970, Project to Provide Psychol. Svcs. to Head Start Programs, 1973-74, European Econ. Commn. Project on Racism, Xenophobia and Immigration, 1989—; mem. com. on aging and com. on status of Black Ams., panel on race, ethnicity and health in later life, Nat. Acad. of Scis., NAS; mem. com. on African Am. Population Year 2000 and 2010 U.S. Census Bur.; mem. nat. adv. com. Boston Mus. Sci., 1998—; mem. Nat. Adv. Coun. on Aging, NIH, 1996-99; mem. bd. sci. counselors, Nat. Inst. Aging; invited rschr. Ecole des Hautes Etudes en Scis. Sociales, Paris, 1992—; disting. lectr. gerontology UCLA, 1992; mem. steering com. Nat. Acad. Aging Soc., 1995—. Author: The Black American Elderly: Research on Physical and Psychosocial Health, 1988, African American Elderly, 2d edit., 1997, (with Gurin P., Hatchett S.) Hope and Independence: Blacks Response to Electoral and Party Politics, 1989, Life in Black America, 1991, (with Chatters L., Taylor R.) Aging in Black America, 1993, (with H. Neighbors) Mental Health in Black America, 1996, (with R. Taylor and L. Clatters) Family Life in Black America, 1997; editor: New Directions: African Americans in a Diversifying Nation, 2000; editl. cons. Jour. Behavioral and Social Scientists; editl. bd. Jour. Gerontology, Applied Social Psychology Ann., Psychol. Bull., Jour. Social Issues; cons. editor Psychology and Aging; contbr. articles to profl. jours. Bd. dirs. Pub. Commn. on Mental Health, Ronald McDonald House, Ann Arbor, 1993—; bd. trustees Greenhills Sch., Ann Arbor, 1997-2003, v.p., 2002-03. Recipient Disting. Faculty Svc. award U. Mich., 1976, Harold R. Johnson Diversity Svc. award U. Mich., 2000; Urban Studies fellow Wayne State U., 1969-70; NSF fellow, 1969; Sr. Postdoctoral fellow Groupe d'Études et de Recherches sur la Science, École des Hautes Études en Sciences Sociales, 1986-87; Sr. Ford Found. Minority Postdoctoral fellow, 1986-87; Fogarty Sr. Internat. fellow, 1993-94; Robert W. Kleemeier award for rsch., Gerontol. Soc. Am. Fellow APA (divs. 9-20, policy and planning bd., fin. com. 1984-86, award for early contbns. 1983, Tenth Anniversary Peace and Social Justice award Soc. for the Study of Peace, Conflict and Violence, Peace Psychology divsn. 2000, com. on internat. relations, 1999-02, cahir 2001-02, Disting. Career Contbns. ro Rsch. award Divsn. 45, 2001), Am. Psychol. Soc., Gerontol. Soc. Am. (task force on minority issues in gerontology, chmn. 1988-92, anr. sci. conv. program com.); mem. AAAS (chair-elect sect. social, econ. and polit. scis.), Assn. Advancement of Psychology (trustee 1973-89, chmn. 1978-80), Inst. of Medicine, Nat. Acad. of Scis., Black Students Psychol. Assn. (nat. chmn. 1970-71), Assn. Black Psychologists (nat. chmn. 1972-73), Soc. Psychol. Study of Social Issues, World Future Soc., Assn. Behavioral and Social Scientists, Gerontol. Soc. Am. (chair behavioral and social scis. sect. 1997-98), Internat. Platform Assn., NIMH (nat. mental health coun. 1989-93, panel on equal access com. on instl. cooperation 1989-92), Psi Chi, Alpha Phi Alpha. Home: 340 Orchard Hills Dr Ann Arbor MI 48104-1832 Office: U Mich 5110 Inst Social Rsch 426 Thompson St Ann Arbor MI 48104-2321

JACKSON, JANE W. interior designer; b. Asheville, N.C., Aug. 5, 1944; d. James and Willie Mae (Stoner) Harris; m. Bruce G. Jackson; children: Yvette, Scott. Student, Boston U., 1964; BA, Leslie Coll., 1967; postgrad., Artisan Sch. Interior Design, 1980-82. Tchr. Montessori, Brookline, Mass., 1969-72; interior designer, owner Nettle Creek Shop, Honolulu, 1980-88; owner Wellesley Interiors, Honolulu, 1988—. Active Mayor's Com. for Small Bus., Honolulu, 1984. Mem. Honolulu Club. Democrat. Office: Wellesley Interiors PO Box 1622 Kaneohe HI 96744-1622

JACKSON, JANET DAMITA, singer, dancer; b. Gary, Ind., June 16, 1966; d. Joseph and Katherine J.; m. James DeBarge, 1984 (div. 1985). Albums include Janet Jackson, Dream Street, 1984, Control, 1986, Rhythm Nation 1814, 1991, janet, 1993, Design of a Decade, The Velvet Rope, 1997, All For You, 2001 (Grammy award for best dance recording, 2002); actress (TV series) Good Times, 1977, A New Kind of Family, Diff'rent Strokes, Fame; (films) Poetic Justice, 1993 (Academy award nomination Best Original Song 1993), Nutty Professor II, 2000. Recipient 6 Am. Music awards, 1987, 1988, 1991, 5 Grammy nominations, MTV Video Vanguard award, 1990, Grammy award, Best R&B song 1994 for "That's the Way Love Goes" with Terry Lewis and James Harris III; MTV Best Female Video for "If". Office: Creative Artists Agency 9830 Wilshire Blvd Beverly Hills CA 90212-1825*

JACKSON, JEFFERY M. information technology executive; BS Econ., Govt., Dartmouth Coll.; MS Mgmt., Northwestern U. From sr. fin. analyst to v.p., controller Am. Airlines, 1984—88; from sr. v.p., CFO Sabre Inc., Southlake, Tex., 1998, exec. v.p., CFO, 2002—. Mem. bd. dirs. Travelocity.com, 2002—. Office: 3150 Sabre Dr Southlake TX 76092

JACKSON, JERLANDO F.L. education educator; s. Dorothy Jean and Jerry Jackson. Mus B in Edn., U. of So. Miss., 1996; MEd, Auburn U., Ala., 1997; PhD, Iowa State U., 2000. Cert. Pub. Mgmt. Iowa State U., 1999. Asst. to the dean Iowa State U., Ames, 1998—2000; prof. U. of Wis. Madison, 2000—. Rsch. Grant, Nat. Assn. for Student Pers. Administrs., 2003. Mem.: Kappa Alpha Psi Frat., Inc. (life; pres. 2002—03). Achievements include research in Influence of race on position attainment and length of employment for acad. administrs. in higher and postsecondary edn. Office: U of Wis-Madison 1025 W Johnson St Madison WI 53706 Office Fax: 608-365-3135. E-mail: jjackson@education.wisc.edu.

JACKSON, JESSE L., JR., congressman; b. Greenville, S.C., Mar. 11, 1965; m. Sandra Jackson. BS, N.C A&T U., 1987; MA, Chgo. Theol. Sem., 1990; JD, U. Ill., 1993. Natl. field dir. The Rainbow Coalition, 1993—95; mem. U.S. Congress from 2d Ill. dist., Washington, 1996, mem. house appropriations com., 1997—. Democrat. Baptist. Office: US Ho of Reps 313 Cannon Office Bldg Washington DC 20515-1302*

JACKSON, JIMMY LEE, commissioner; b. Floydada, Tex., Mar. 20, 1939; s. Vernon Lester and Vivian (Inez) J.; m. Sue Ellen Jackson, June 6, 1959; children: Stephen Bradley, Deborah LeAnne. BA, U. N. Tex., Denton, 1962. Orgnl. dir. Dallas County Rep. Party, 1965-69; ptnr. Jackson-Terry Ins. Agy., Dallas, 1970-73; exec. dir. Dallas County Rep. Party, 1972-74; county commr. Dallas County, 1974—. Bd. mem. Tex. commn. on Jail Standards, Austin, 1999—; chmn., vice chmn. Nat. Assn. Counties Large Urban County Caucus, Washington, 1995, 96; chmn. Nat. Assn. Counties Deferred Compensation Adv. Com., Washington, 2002; mem., vice chmn. Nat. Assn. Counties Transp. and Telecomms. Policy Steering Com., Washington, 1995-2000. Exec. bd. North Ctrl. Tex. Coun. of Govts., Arlington, 1992-99, 2002; bd. mem., chmn. Dallas

Ctrl. Appraisal Dist., 1988-95; bd. mem. Tex. Assn. Regional Couns., 1996-99; mem., chmn. N. Ctrl. Tex. Coun. of Govts. Regional Transp. Coun., 1983-96; chmn. Tex. Conf. of Urban Counties, 1981; mem. Congressional Dist. Rep. Nat. Delegate Selection Com., 1992, 96; del. Rep. Nat. Conv., 1992; arrangements chmn., 1986, congressional and senatorial dist. caucus chmn., 1990, 92, 94, 96, Rep. State Conv.; pres. Irving Rep. Club, 1979, Rep. Assembly, 1986-87, Metrocrest Rep. Club, 1991-92. Republican. Avocations: fishing, travel. Office: Dallas County Rd and Bridge Dist 1 2311 Joe Field Rd Dallas TX 75229-3328 E-mail: jjackson@dallascounty.org.

JACKSON, JOHN HOWARD, lawyer, educator; b. Kansas City, Mo., Apr. 6, 1932; s. Howard Clifford and Lucile (Deischer) J.; m. Joan Leland, Dec. 16, 1962; children: Jeannette, Lee Ann, Michelle. AB, Princeton U., 1954; JD, U. Mich., 1959. Bar: Wis. 1959, Mo. 1959, Calif. 1964, Mich. 1970. Pvt. practice law, Milw., 1959-61; assoc. prof., prof. law U. Calif., 1961-66; prof. law U. Mich., 1966-97; univ. prof. law Georgetown U., Washington, 1998—, dir. Inst. of Internat. Econ. Law. On leave gen. counsel U.S. Office Spl. Trade Rep., 1973-74, acting deputy spl. rep. for trade, 1974; vis. prof. U. Brussels, 1975-76; vis. fellow Inst. for Internat. Econs., Washington, 1983; Hessel E. Yntema prof. law U. Mich., 1983-97, assoc. v.p. acad. affairs, 1988-89; disting. vis. prof. law Georgetown Law Ctr., Washington, 1986-87, 93; Ford Found. cons. legal edn., vis. prof. U. Delhi, India, 1968-69; Hersch Lauterpacht Meml. lectr. Cambridge (Eng.) U., 2002. Author: World Trade and the Law of GATT, 1969, Contract Law in Modern Society, 1973, 2d edit., 1980, Legal Problems of International Economic Relations, 1977, 4th edit. (with William Davey and Alan Sykes), 2002; (with Jean-Victor Louis and Mitsuo Matsushita) Implementing the Tokyo Round, 1984; (with Edwin Vermulst) Anti-Dumping Law & Practice: Comparative Study, 1989; The World Trading System, 1989, 2d edit., 1997, Restructuring the GATT System, 1990; (with Alan Sykes) Implementing the Urugauy Round, 1997, World Trade Organization, 1998, The Jurisprudence of GATT and the WTO, 2000; editor-in-chief Jour. Internat. Econ. Law; bd. editors: Am. Jour. Internat. Law, Jour. Law and Policy in Internat. Bus., others; contbr. articles to profl. jours. With M.I. U.S. Army, 1954-56. Recipient Wolfgang Friedman Memorial award Columbia U., 1992; Rockefeller Found. fellow for study European community law Brussels, 1975-76 Mem. ABA, Am. Soc. Internat. Law (v.p. 1990 92), Am. Law Inst., Council Fgn. Relations, Phi Beta Kappa, Order of Coif. Office: Georgetown U Law Ctr 600 New Jersey Ave NW Washington DC 20001-2022

JACKSON, JOHN CHARLES, retired secondary education educator, writer; b. Columbus, Ohio, Mar. 12, 1939; s. John Franklin and Mari Jane (Lusch) J.; m. Carol Nancy Tiggelbeck, June 24, 1990. Tchr. social studies Buckeye Local Sch., West Mansfield, Ohio, 1961-62, Grandview Heights (Ohio) City Schs., 1962-91; ret., 1991. Cooperating tchr. Project Bus. program Jr. Achievement, Grandview, 1984-91. Recipient Career Tchr. award Ohio State U. Coll. Edn. Alumni Soc., 1995; Martha Holden Jennings Found. scholar, 1968-69. Mem. Ohio Ret. Tchrs. Assn. (life), Franklin County Ret. Tchrs. Assn. (life), Ohio State U. Alumni Assn. (life), Am. Mensa Ltd. Republican. Methodist. Avocations: reading, tennis, college football. Home: 5741 Aspendale Dr Columbus OH 43235-7506

JACKSON, J(OHN) DAVID, physicist, educator; b. London, Ont., Can., Jan. 19, 1925; came to U.S., 1957, naturalized, 1988; s. Walter David and Lillian Margaret Jackson; m. Barbara Cook, June 26, 1949; children: Ian, Nan, Maureen, Mark. BS in Physics and Math., U. Western Ont., 1946, DSc (hon.), 1989; PhD in Physics, MIT, 1949. Rsch. assoc. dept. physics MIT, Cambridge, 1949; from asst. prof. to assoc. prof. math. McGill U., Montreal, Que., Can., 1950-57; from assoc. prof. to prof. physics U. Ill., Urbana, 1957-67; prof. U. Calif., Berkeley, 1967-92, dept. chair, 1978-81, prof. emeritus, 1993—. Vis. fellow Cambridge (Eng.) U., 1970; acting head theory group Fermilab, Batavia, Ill., 1972-73; head physics divsn. Lawrence Berkeley Lab., 1982-84; dep. dir. SSC Cen. Design Group, Berkeley, 1985-87; vis. sr. rsch. fellow Oxford (Eng.) U., 1988-89; mem. vis. com. Argonne Nat. Lab., CERN, SSC Lab., Stanford Linear Accelerator Ctr., others. Author: Physics of Elementary Particles, 1958, Classical Electrodynamics, 1962, rev. edit., 1975, 3d edit., 1998, Mathematics for Quantum Mechanics, 1962; also numerous articles; editor Ann. Rev. Nuclear and Particle Sci., 1977-93. J. S. Guggenheim Found. fellow, 1956-57, Ford Found. fellow, 1963-64. Fellow Am. Phys. Soc.; mem. NAS (elected 1990), Am. Acad. Arts and Scis. (elected 1989), ACLU (life). Avocations: mountain hiking, swimming, scientific bibliophily. Address: U Calif Berkeley Dept Physics Berkeley CA 94720-7300

JACKSON, JOHN EDWARD, educator, logistician, retired naval officer; b. Rapid City, S.D., Feb. 11, 1949; s. William Edward Joseph and Bettye Davis (Williams) J.; m. Valerie Lee McGilton, June 5, 1971; children: Gina Marie, Brian Howard. BA in Univ. Studies, U. N.Mex., 1971; MEd, Providence Coll., 1976; MS in Mgmt., Salve Regina U., 1983, cert. of advanced grad. studies, 1998; grad. mgmt. devel. program, Harvard U., 1997. Commd. USN, 1971, advanced through grades to capt., ret., 1998; disbursing officer USS Hunley AS-31, Charleston, S.C., 1972-74; food svc. officer Naval Edn. and Tng. Ctr., Newport, R.I., 1974-76; supply officer USS Joseph Strauss DDG-16, Pearl Harbor, Hawaii, 1976-78; data processing dept. dir. Nava. Supply Ctr., Pearl Harbor, 1978-80; prof. Ctr. Continuing Edn. U.S. Naval War Coll., Newport, 1980-83, prof. dept. nat. security decision-making, 1994-96, dean Coll. Continuing Edn., 1996—, assoc. dean for Distance Education, 2000—, dir. devel. and long range planning, 2002—; divsn. dir. Navy Fleet Material Support Office, Mechanicsburg, Pa., 1983-86; curricular officer U.S. Naval Postgrad. Sch., Monterey, Calif., 1986-90; supply officer USS Sierra AD-18, Charleston, 1990-92; exec. officer Naval Supply Ctr., Charleston, 1992-94; mil. chair logistics Naval War Coll., Newport, RI, 1994—. Speechwriter USN, 1978—. Former editor-in-chief newsletter The Oakleaf; editor: Logistics Leadership Series; contbr. articles to profl. jours. Mem. Soc. Logistics Engrs., Navy Supply Corps Assn. (bd. dirs. 1983-96, pres. 1994-96), Naval War Coll. Found., U.S. Naval Inst. (liaison officer). Home: 7 Mast Ct Middletown RI 02842-7212

JACKSON, JOHN HOLLIS, JR., lawyer; b. Mongomery, Ala., Aug. 21, 1941; s. John Hollis and Erma (Edgeworth) J.; m. Rebecca Mullins, May 27, 1967; 1 child, John Hollis III. AB, U. Ala., 1963, JD, 1966. Bar: Ala. 1966, U.S. Dist. Ct. (no. dist.) Ala. 1969, U.S. Ct. Appeals (11th cir.) 1993. Pvt. practice, Clanton, Ala., 1967—. County atty. Chilton County Commn., Clanton, 1969—; mcpl. judge Clanton, 1971-99, city atty., 1999—; dir. First Nat. Bank, Clanton, 1974-83; mem. adv. bd. Colonial Bank, Clanton, 1983—; mcpl. judge, Jemison, Ala., 1984—. Bd. dirs. Chilton-Shelby Mental Health Bd., Calera, Ala., 1974-83, pres., 1974-79; mem. State Dem. Exec. Com., Birmingham, Ala., 1974-98, County Dem. Exec. Com., Chilton County, 1982-94; del. Dem. Nat. Conv., N.Y.C., 1976. 1st lt. U.S. Army, 1966-67. Mem. Ala. Young Lawyers Sect. (exec. com. 1969-70), Chilton County Bar Assn. (pres. 1969, 74), Ala. State Bar Assn. (bd. bar commrs. 1984-87, 93-99, chmn. adv. com. to bd. bar examiners 1986-87, 19th cir. indigent def. commn. 1983—, chmn. disciplinary panel II 1997-99), Kiwanis, Phi Alpha Delta. Democrat. Methodist. Home: Samaria Rd Clanton AL 35045 Office: PO Box 1818 500 2nd Ave S Clanton AL 35046-1818

JACKSON, JOHN WYANT, medical products executive; b. Corpus Christi, May 25, 1944; s. Donald LeGarde and Marion (McNulty) J; m. Susan Gager, Sept. 6, 1969; children: Alexandra C., Kimberly F., Donald M., Jennifer L. BA, Yale U., 1967; MBA, INSEAD, Fontainbleau, France, 1971; diploma, Institut de Sci. Politique, Paris, 1966. With Merck & Co., Rahway, N.J., 1971-78; dir. med. products Far East Am. Cyanamid Co., Wayne, N.J., 1978-79, dir. med. products Americas and Far East, 1979-81, v.p. Americas and Far East, 1981-83, v.p. internat., 1983-86, pres. med. device divsn., 1986-91; pres. Gemini Med., Warren, N.J., 1991-96; chmn., CEO Celgene Corp., Warren, N.J., 1996—. Dir. U.S.-ROC Econ. Council, Crystal Lake, Ill., 1982-85; chmn. Biotech. Coun. N.J. Mem. Yale Devel. Bd.; bd. dirs. Gordonstoun Am. Found. Served to 1st lt. USMCR, 1967-70. Decorated Navy Commendation medal; decorated Purple Heart Mem. Soc. Paper Money Collectors. Republican. Episcopalian. Office: Celgene Corp Warren NJ 07059

JACKSON, JULIAN ELLIS, food company executive; b. Perry, Fla., Oct. 24, 1913; s. Eddie H. and Eva M. (Reid) J.; m. Laurana H. Filson, Oct. 6, 1956; children: Julian Ellis, Eddie King, Robert Allen, Victor Pharis, Julian Ellis IV, Lester Mitchell. Grad., Andrew Jackson High Sch., Jacksonville, Fla., 1931; DSc (hon.), Jones Coll., 1982. With Great Atlantic & Pacific Stores, 1931—43; pres. Jax Meat Co., 1943—58, Jackson's Minit Markets, Inc., 1958—69, Julian Jackson Investment Co., 1955—, Lil' Champ Food Stores, Inc., 1971—98. Co-owner Jackson-Cowart Realty Co., 1955-97; dir. Fla. Nat. Bank, Jacksonville, Arlington. Past pres. United Cerebral Palsy, Jacksonville; chmn. Jacksonville Boxing Commn., 1952-71; pres. Gator Bowl Assn., 1957, Fla. Baseball League, 1958-60; Bd. dirs. Palmdale Med. Center, Police Athletic League, Jacksonville, Jacksonville Marine Inst., Jones Coll., Jacksonville. Recipient Top Mgmt. award Sales and Mktg. Execs. Jacksonville, 1968; named Super Market Man of Yr., 1960, One of Top 100 Athletes of Jacksonville in Past 100 Yrs., 1999; elected to Fla. Food Inst. Hall of Fame, 1994. Mem. Fla. Super Market Assn. (pres. 1950-59, elected to Fla. Sports Hall of Fame 1994), Fraternal Order of Police, Sportsman Club, Univ. Club (Jacksonville), Univ. Country Club, River Club, Ponte Vedra Club, Masons, Shriners. Home: 7987 Hollyridge Rd Jacksonville FL 32256-7110 Office: Julian Jackson Investment Co 8535 Baymeadows Rd Ste 25 Jacksonville FL 32256-7445

JACKSON, KATHERINE CHURCH, former elementary school educator, reading educator; b. Phila., Apr. 26, 1925; d. John Edward and Katherine Darlington (Short) C.; m. James Kermit Jackson, Dec. 20, 1953; children: James Kermit, Quentin Winfield, Karen J. White. BS in Edn., Cheyney (Pa.) State Tchrs. Coll., 1946; MEd, Temple U., 1951; DEdin Adminstrn., Nova U., 1981. Cert. elem. sch. tchr., supr., prin., Pa. Elem. tchr. Pub. Schs., Oxford, N. Glenside, Pa., 1946-54, collaborator lang. arts, t.v. tchr. Phila., 1956-67, asst. dir., tng. specialist office of sch. vols., 1967-70, dist. supr., dir. reading, 1970-77, elem. prin., 1971-82; asst. prof. Lincoln U., Pa., 1986-87, reading and writing specialist, 1986-2000, ret., 2000. Prodr., photographer: (slide presentation) Parents Help With Reading, 1965; writer, prodr. (t.v. series, script) Reading Inservice for Teachers, 1965; creator, prodr., photographer (slide presentation) PL-142 Works for the Handicapped, 1980. Pres. bd. YWCA, West Chester, Pa., 1984-89; bd. dirs. Cmty. Ctr., West Chester, 1984-91. Recipient Profl. award Bus. and Profl. Women, 1966, Cmty. and Club Svc. award Keystone Federated Women's Club, 1989, Spirit of YWCA, YWCA of Greater West Chester, 1990, Cmty. Svc. award West Chester Black Student Union, 1994 Mem. AAUW, Fanny J. Coppin Federated Women's Club (chpt. pres. 1984—), Bus. Profl. Women (pres. Phila. chpt. 1965-69). Democrat. Episcopalian. Avocations: reading, singing, opera. Home: PO Box 663 Westtown PA 19395-0663

JACKSON, KEITH, law educator; b. Birmingham, Ala., Mar. 12, 1969; s. James W. and Jean E. Jackson; m. Tricia Dawkins, Aug. 5, 2000. BS in Bus. Adminstrn., U. Ala., Tuscaloosa, 1991; JD, Emory U., 1995. Bar: Ga. 1995, Ala. 1999. Atty. King & Spalding, Atlanta, 1995—96, Hendrick & Hunter, LLC, Atlanta, 1996—99; prof. Birmingham Sch. Law, 2000—. Mem.: Atlanta Coun. Young Lawyers (dir. 1998—99), Birmingham Bar Assn., Ala. Trial Lawyers Assn. Republican. Office: Riley & Jackson PC 1744 Oxmoor Rd Birmingham AL 35209

JACKSON, KENNETH ARTHUR, physicist, researcher; b. Connaught, Ont., Can., Oct. 23, 1930; s. Arthur and Susanna (Vatcher) J.; m. Jacqueline Della Olyan, June 20, 1952 (div.); children: Stacy Margaret, Meredith Suzanne, Stuart Keith; m. Camilla M. Maruszewski, June 21, 1980 (div.). BS, U. Toronto, 1952, MS, 1953; PhD, Harvard U., 1956. Postdoctoral fellow Harvard U., Cambridge, Mass., 1956-58, asst. prof. metallurgy, 1958-62; mem. tech. staff Bell Labs., Murray Hill, N.J., 1962-67, head material physics research dept., 1967-81, head optical materials research dept., 1981-89; prof. materials sci. and engring. U. Ariz., 1989—. Lectr. Welch. Found., 1970, 85; mem. research adv. panel Air Force Office Sci. Research, 1976-82, space application bd. Nat. Acad. Sci., 1974-82. Editor-in-chief Optical Materials, 1999—; contbr. articles to profl. jours.; patentee in field. Recipient Mathewson Gold medal AIME, 1966, Crystal growth award AACG, 1993, Frank prize IOCG, 1998, TMS Chalmers award, 2003. Fellow AAAS, The Metall. Soc.-AIME, Am. Phys. Soc.; mem. Internat. Orgn. Crystal Growth (treas. 1978-86, Frank prize 1998), Am. Assn. Crystal Growth (pres. 1968-75, coun., award 1993), Materials Rsch. Soc. (v.p. 1975-77, pres. 1977-78, coun.), Am. Soc. Metals, Engring. Coun. for Profl. Devel. (mem. coun.), Fedn. Materials Soc. (trustee). Office: U Ariz 4715 E Ft Lowell Rd Tucson AZ 85712-1201 E-mail: kaj@aml.arizona.edu.

JACKSON, KENNETH TERRY, historian, administrator; b. Memphis, July 27, 1939; s. Kenneth Gordon and Elizabeth Owen (Willins) J.; m. Barbara Ann Bruce, Aug. 25, 1962; children: Kevan Parish, Kenneth Gordon (dec.). BA magna cum laude, U. Memphis, 1961; MA, U. Chgo., 1963, PhD, 1966. Asst. prof. history Columbia U., N.Y.C., 1968-71, assoc. prof., 1971-76, prof., 1976-87, Mellon prof., 1987-90, Barzun prof., 1990—, chmn. dept. history, 1994-97. Vis. prof. Princeton (N.J.) U., 1973-74, George Washington U., 1982-83, UCLA, 1986-87; chair Bradley Commn. on History in Schs., 1987-90; chair Nat. Coun. for History Edn., Inc., 1990-92. Author: The Ku Klux Klan in the City, 1967, Crabgrass Frontier, 1985 (Bancroft prize 1986, Francis Parkman prize 1986), Silent Cities: The Evolution of the American Cemetery, 1989; co-editor: cities in American History, 1972; editor-in-chief Dictionary of American Biography, 1991-95, Scribner's Encyclopedia of American Lives, 1996—; editor Encyclopedia of New York City, 1995; gen. editor Columbia History of Urban Life, 30 vols., 1980—; co-editor American Vistas, 1971, 7th edit., 1995, Empire City: New York Through the Centuries, 2002. Trustee Nat. Coun. Hist. Edn., 1990—, South St. Seaport Mus., 1989—2001, Transp. Alternatives, 1995—97, Skyscraper Mus., 1996—2001, N.Y. Hist. Soc., 1996—, vice chmn., 1998—2001, pres., CEO, 2001—; trustee N.Y. State Hist. Assn., 1996—, Henry Luce Found., 2002—, Regional Plan Assn., 2003—; vestryman Trinity Ch. Wall St., 1997—. Capt. USAF, 1965—68. Recipient Mark Van Doren Tchg. award Columbia U., 1989, Outstanding Alumni award U. Memphis, 1989, Great Tchr. award Soc. Columbia Grads. 1999; fellow Woodrow Wilson Found., 1961-62, Guggenheim Found., 1983-84; sr. fellow NEH, 1979-80. Mem. Soc. Am. Historians (pres. 1998-2000), Orgn. Am. Historians (pres. 2000-2001), Am. Hist. Assn., Urban Hist. Assn. (pres. 1994-95), Century Assn. Episcopalian. Avocations: skiing, tennis, basketball. Home: 44 Kitchel Rd Mount Kisco NY 10549-4516 Office: Columbia U Dept History 603 Fayerweather Hall New York NY 10027

JACKSON, KENNETH WILLIAM, research scientist, educator; b. Shipley, Yorkshire, Eng., Feb. 11, 1944; s. Albert Edward and Winifred (Mason) J.; m. Pauline Robinson, Apr. 10, 1971; 1 child, Paul Jonathan. MSc, Imperial Coll., London, 1970, PhD, 1972. Rsch. scientist N.Y. State Dept. Health, Albany, 1972-77; sr. lectr. Sheffield (Eng.) City Polytechnic, 1977-84; prof. U. Sask., Saskatoon, 1984-87; rsch. scientist, prof. N.Y. State Dept. Health, SUNY, Albany, 1987—; chair dept. environ. health and toxicology SUNY, Albany, 1997-2000. Contbr. articles to profl. jours. Fellow Royal Soc. Chemistry. Avocation: certified alpine ski instructor. Office: NY State Dept Health PO Box 509 Albany NY 12201-0509 E-mail: jackson@wadsworth.org.

JACKSON, KINGSBURY TEMPLE, educational contract consultant; b. Newton, Mass., May 15, 1917; s. Ralph Temple and Elizabeth Mesarole (Rhodes) J.; m. June Stewart Cooper, July 29, 1950 (dec. Feb. 1976). BS, MIT, 1940; postgrad., NYU, 1949-51; MS, U. Ala., 1964, U. So. Calif., 1969, Pepperdine U., 1975. Registered profl. engr., Calif., Ala. Commd. 2d lt. U.S. Army, 1940, advanced through grades to lt. col., 1961, ret., 1965; comdr. U.S. Army Depot, also Camp Mercer, Korea, 1957-58; project officer, indsl. project dir. U.S. Army Saturn Space Vehicle Program and Pershing Missile System, 1959-61; dir. U.S. Army Missile Command Engring. Documentation Ctr., Redstone Arsenal, Ala., 1962-63; program coordinator NATO-Hawk Missile System, 1963-65; prin. contracting officer, chief European procurement U.S. Army Ordnance, 1964-65; lectr. mgmt. and engring. Grad. Sch., U. So. Calif., L.A., 1965-69; contractual relations supr. L.A. Bd. Edn., 1969-82; pres. Contract Consultants, L.A., 1982—, K.T. Jackson, Gen. Contractors, L.A., 1991—. Author: Engineering documentation Systems Development: Department of Defense and NASA, 1963, Aerospace Propellants and Chemicals: The Manager's Approach, 1968 Vice pres., mem. bd. dirs. Kingsbury Properties Ltd.; corp. sec., bd. dirs. The Concert Singers, Inc. Mem.: Am. Soc. Automotive Engrs. (rep. to Aerospace gen. stds. divsn. 1962—65), Am. Ordinance Assn. (mem. exec. bd. prodn. technique divsn.,Army rep.to engring. doc. sect. 1962—65), Am. Soc. Mil. Comptrs, Am. Soc. Indsl. Engrs., Nat. Space Soc., Aircraft Owners and Pilots Assn., Calif. Assn. Bus. Ofcls., Ret. Officers Assn. (life), Internat. Assn. Sch. Bus. Ofcls.(emeritus), The Concert Singers Inc., The Planetary Soc., A&E Flying Club, MIT Club (So and No. Calif.). Home and Office: Ste C302 3400 Paul Sweet Rd Santa Cruz CA 95065-1541 E-mail: kingtemp@aol.com.

JACKSON, KIRK ALLAN, music educator, director; b. St. Louis, Mo., Aug. 15, 1950; s. Herbert Earl and Gertrude George (Lichty) Jackson; m. Candine Lee Cagan, Nov. 24, 1991. AA Degree, Jefferson Coll., Hillsboro, Mo., 1970; MusB Edn., U.Mo., Kansas City, 1973; MusM Edn., U.Mo., St. Louis, 1998. Cert. Tchr. Music Mo., 1973. Music dir. - performer Dinner Playhouse, Inc., Kansas City, Mo., 1972—74, The Magic If, San Diego, 1974—75; music dir. - vocalist New Christy Minstrels, L.A., 1976—80; vocal music tchr. Simi Valley (Calif.) H.S., Calif., 1982—92, Dunklin R-5 Sch. Dist., Herculaneum, Mo., 1993—98, Ladue Sch. Dist., St. Louis, 1998—2001, Grandview R-2 Sch. Dist., Hillsboro, Mo., 2001—02, Dunklin R-5 Sch. Dist., Herculaneum, Mo., 2002—. Contemporary worship music dir. Webster Hills United Meth. Ch., Webster Groves, Mo., 2000—. Performer, (albums) Carmina Burana, 1992 (Grammy award, 1992). Mem. chorus St. Louis Symphony, 1992—97. Mem.: So. Calif. Vocal Assn. (v.p. 1984—88), Mo. Music Educators Assn. (dist. v.p. 1998—99), Mo. State Teachers Assn. (local pres. 1998—99), Music Educators Nat. Conf., Am. Choral Directors Assn. Methodist. Avocations: history, travel. Home: 1102 Crystal Heights Rd Crystal City MO 63019-1412 Office: Dunklin R-5 Sch Dist 277 Barclay St Herculaneum MO 63048

JACKSON, LAIRD GRAY, physician, educator; b. Seattle, Oct. 10, 1930; BA, Pomona Coll., 1951; MD, U. Cin., 1955. Diplomate Am. Bd. Internal Medicine, Am. Bd. Med. Genetics (bd. dirs.). Rotating gen. intern Sacramento County (Calif.) Hosp., 1955-56; resident in internal medicine Jefferson Med. Coll., Phila., 1959-61, NIH postdoctoral fellow med. oncology, 1961-62, instr. medicine, 1962-64, asst. prof. medicine, 1964-66, assoc. prof., 1966-69, assoc. prof. medicine, pediatrics and ob-gyn, 1969-78, prof., 1978—, dir. div. med. genetics, 1969-98. Founder, bd. dirs., treas. Am. Coll. Med. Genetics, 1991-95. Mem. editorial bd. Am. Jour. Med. Genetics, Prenatal Diagnosis, Repository of Human Chromosomal Variants. Capt. USAF, 1956-59. Leukemia Soc. fellow, 1963-65, Leukemia Soc. scholar 1965-70. Fellow ACP; mem. Am. Soc. Human Genetics (social issues com. 1976-80, bd. dirs.), Soc. Pediatric Rsch. Home and Office: 245 N 15th St Philadelphia PA 19102-1192 E-mail: lgj25@drexel.edu.

JACKSON, LARRY ARTOPE, retired college president; b. Florence, S.C., Feb. 7, 1925; s. Arthur Edward and Rosa (Gilbert) J.; m. Barbara Attwood, June 27, 1953; children: Elizabeth Jackson Eble, Arthur Edward, Barbara Jackson Allen, Charles Rhett. AB, Wofford Coll., 1947, DLitt (hon.), 1976; MDiv, Union Theol. Sem., 1953; MA, U. Pacific, 1973, DD (hon.), 1961; D in Humanities (hon.), Clemson U., 1991. Ordained to ministry United Meth. Ch., 1953; minister chs., 1953-59; prin. Santiago (Chile) Coll., 1959-64; provost Callison Coll. of U. Pacific, Stockton, Calif., 1964-70; v.p. for adminstrn. U. Evansville, 1970-73; pres. Lander Univ. (formerly Lander Coll.), Greenwood, S.C., 1973-92, ret., 1992. Vis. fellow Wolfson Coll., Cambridge U., 1985; appointed by Gov. to serve as mem. S.C. Commn. on Higher Edn., 2000—. Mem. Fulbright Commn. for Chile, 1961-64; mem. Commn. on Black Colls. Related to the Meth. Ch., 1973-76. With USAAF, 1943-45; with Am. Friends Svc. Com., 1948-49. Decorated Air medal with 2 oak leaf clusters. Mem. Rotary. Democrat. Home: 604 Cambridge Ave W Greenwood SC 29649-1967 Office: Lander Univ 301 Stanley Ave Greenwood SC 29649-2045 *Love is the law of life and it is by striving to live under the rule of this law that we find authenticity.*

JACKSON, LARRY C. publishing executive; b. Austin, Tex., Apr. 14, 1944; s. Laurence C. and Mary Ruth (McAngus) J.; m. Susan Blackburn, Dec. 15, 1966; children: Laurence III, Deborah Jackson McClure, Edward. BA in Journalism, U. Tex., 1968. City editor Arlington (Tex.) Daily News, 1967-69; City editor Laredo (Tex.) Times, 1969-71; mng. editor Henderson (Tex.) Daily News, 1971-72; gen. mgr. Austin Citizen, 1972-73; publ. Round Rock (Tex.) Leader, 1973-84, Pecos (Tex.) Enterprise, 1984-87, Corona (Calif.)-Norco Independent, 1987-91; editor, gen. mgr. Wharton (Tex.) Journal-Spectator, 1991—; v.p. River Pubs., Inc., 1994—. Charter pres. YMCA, Round Rock, Tex., 1981; mem. City Charter Commn., Round Rock, 1977; chmn. U.S. Bicentennial Commn., Round Rock, 1975-76; pres. Round Rock C. of C., 1975; bd. dirs. Tex. Newspaper Found., 1994—; mem. City Beautification Commn., Wharton, Tex., 1999—; life mem. Disciples of Christ Hist. Soc.; bd. dirs. Wharton County His. Mus., 2000—. Paul Harris fellow Rotary Internat. Found., 1995; named Citizen of Yr. Round Rock C. of C., 1984. Mem. Nat. Newspaper Assn. (Tex. state chair 2001—), Tex. Press Assn. (pres. 1998-99), South Tex. Press Assn. (pres. 1996), Rotary (pres. Wharton 1994-95), Wharton C. of C. (chmn. bd. 2001-02, Citizen of Yr. 2003). Republican. Mem. Ch. of Christ. Avocations: tchg. Bible class, playing Oboe, travelling by train. Home: 1203 N Fulton St Wharton TX 77488-3129 Office: Wharton Journal-Spectator 115 W Burleson St Wharton TX 77488-5003

JACKSON, LAUREN, professional basketball player; b. Australia, May 11, 1981; Profl. basketball player Seattle Storm, 2001—. Mem. Gems team Jr. World Championships, 1997; mem. WNBL Championship team, 2000. Named 3d internat. player selected 1st overall 5 yr. history, WNBA, 1 of 3 Australian players chosen in 1st round, All-Star Five Selection, WNBL, 2000, League's Most Valuable Player, WNBA, 2000, res. Western Conf. team, WNBA All-Star Game, Orlando, 2001, All-Star Five Selection, WNBL, 2001, First Round Draft Pick, WNBA, 2001, res. All-Star Team, 2001; recipient Olympics Silver medalist, 2000. Office: Seattle Sonics and Storm 351 Elliott Ave W Ste 500 Seattle WA 98119 E-mail: StormFans@sonics-storm.com.

JACKSON, LAWRENCE P. education educator; b. Balt., Md., June 12, 1968; s. Nathaniel and Verna M. Jackson; m. Regine Ostine, June 23, 2001. PhD, Stanford Univ., Palo Alto, Calif., 1997. Asst. prof. Howard Univ., Washington, 1997—2002, assoc. prof., 2002; asst. prof. Emory Coll., Atlanta, 2002—03, assoc. prof., 2003—. Author: Ralph Ellison: Emergence of Genius, 2002. Recipient faculty rsch., Nat. Endowment for Humanities, 2002; postdoctoral fellowship, Ford Found. Nat. Rsch. Coun., 1999—2000. Mem.: Am. Studies Assn., Modern Language Assn. Avocations: carpentry, music, writing. Office: Emory Coll Dept of English Callaway Bldg Atlanta GA 30322

JACKSON, LINDA B. social worker; b. N.Y.C., Feb. 16, 1956; d. Willie Chelsea Jackson, Fannie Mae Jackson; children: Athena Johnson, Alethea, Althea, Walter. BSW, Mercy Coll., 1986; FDC tng., Cornell U., 2002. Social worker Peekskill City Sch. Dist., Peekskill, NY, 1987—. Author: Poetry From the Soul; author: (poetry) Titanic, 2001 (Pres.'s award). Recipient Famous Poets award, 2002, Shakespeare trophy of excellence, Poet of Yr. medalliion, 2002. Mem.: Poetry Soc. Am. Avocation: writing. Home: 218 N James St Apt 4 Peekskill NY 10566-2848

JACKSON, LOLA HIRDLER, art educator; b. Faribault, Minn., Mar. 2, 1942; d. Earl Arthur and Marian Barbara (Pavek) Hirdler; children: Carilyn, Cherilyn, Marc. BS in Art Edn., Mankato State U., 1972, MA, 1975. Cert. tchr. Instr. art YWCA, Mankato, 1968-70; art instr. Mankato Area Vocat. Tech. Inst., 1971-72; pres., tchr., art dir. Jackson Studios, Mankato, 1969-78; art tchr. New Richland (Minn.) High Sch., Mankato (Minn.) State U., 1973-74; pres. Lola Ltd. Lt'ee Art Distbn., N.C., 1976—; tchr. art Lincoln Sch. Math. and Sci. Tech., Greensboro, N.C., 1988-90, chmn. dept., 1988, 89-90; tchr., chmn. art dept. Shallotte Mid. Sch., 1990—; instr. art Brunswick C.C., Supply, N.C., 1990-92; co-owner, pres. Jackson Carpenter Galleries, Ltd., Little River, S.C., 1997-99. Staff artist The Reporter, 1970-73; pres., bd. dirs. Fine Arts Inc., Gallery 500, Mankato, 1972-75. Bd. mem. Mankato Area Found., 1976-83. Recipient award Busch Found. Minn. Arts Coun., Nat. Endowment Arts, 1974. Mem. Profl. Pictures Framers Assn., N.C. Assn. of Edn. Republican. Roman Catholic. Avocations: stamp collecting, botany, birdwatching, biking, ballroom dancing.

JACKSON, M. LEIGH, analyst programmer, fine art photographer, graphic designer; b. Indpls., Sept. 26, 1946; s. Milton Lovelace and Anna Elizabeth (Robinson) J.; m. Elizabeth Anne Marshall, Sept. 26, 1981. BFA, Acad. Art Coll., San Francisco, 1983. Analyst programmer Crocker Bank, San Francisco, 1974-78; sr. analyst programmer Genasys Systems, San Francisco, 1978-79; pvt. practice, cons., 1979-83; sr. systems engr. Integral Systems, Walnut Creek, Calif., 1983-86; cons. GTE Govt. Systems, Mountain View, Calif., 1987-88; sr. cons. Deltam Systems, San Mateo, Calif., 1988—; propr., prin. Square Peg Graphics, Oakland, Calif., 1992—. With USN, 1965-69. Democrat. Roman Catholic. Home: 3256 Wyman St Oakland CA 94619-3434 Office: Square Peg Graphics 3256 Wyman St Oakland CA 94619-3434 E-mail: jakjackson@earthlink.net.

JACKSON, MARJORIE, musician; b. Oakland, Calif. d. Arthur Leslie and Mabel (Gohrman) Jackson. BA, MA cum laude, U. Calif., Berkeley; EdD, Columbia U., 1962; postgrad., Julliard Sch. Music, U. Denver, 1963. Instr. woodwind instruments Columbia U., N.Y.C., 1960-62; asst. dean women U. Fla., Gainesville, 1963-66; dean students Hollins (Va.) Coll., 1966-67; dean, assoc. prof. music Hobart and William Smith Colls., Geneva, N.Y., 1967-69; dean women Boise (Idaho) State U., 1969-72; freelance musician, 1972—. Oboist various symphonies, operas including Pitts. Symphony, Portland Symphony, Chautauqua Symphony, Louisville Orch., Met. Opera; faculty U. Louisville. Touring oboist: Martha Graham Dance Group, Gershwin Festival, (shows) Carmen Jones, Song of Norway, My Fair Lady. Mem. Am. Personnel and Guidance Assn., Nat. Assn. Student Personnel Adminstrs., Internat. Platform Assn., Nat. Assn. Women Deans and Counselors, Alpha Mu, Kappa Delta Pi, Alpha Lambda Delta, Beta Sigma Omicron. Clubs: Chautauqua Womens; Etude (Berkeley, Calif.). Home and Office: 100 Bay Pl Apt 911 Oakland CA 94610

JACKSON, MARK JAMES, engineering educator; b. Widnes, Lancashire, England, Feb. 14, 1967; arrived in U.S., 2001; s. George and Monica Mary Jackson; m. Joanne Lesly Pinnington, July 20, 1990. MA, U. of Cambridge, 1998; MS in Engring., Liverpool (Eng.) U., 1991, PhD, 1995. Chartered engr., Engring. Coun., UK, 1998. Mech. plant engr. I.C.I. Pharmaceuticals, Macclesfield, England, 1988—89, Anglo Blackwells, Widnes, England, 1990—91; tech. mgr. St. Gobain Abrasives Group Unicorn Internat., Gloucester, England, 1992—97; rsch. fellow U. of Cambridge, England, 1997—98; lectr. U. of Liverpool, 1998—2002; prof. of engring. Tenn. Technol. U., Cookeville, Tenn., 2002—. Chief tech. officer Vitrified Technologies Inc., Kans.City, 2002—; cons. tech. mgr. St. Gobain Abrasives Group Unicorn Internat., Gloucester, 1997—99; cons. engr. MIJA Ltd., Cambridge, 1997—2000. Contbr. chapters to books, articles to profl. jours. Councillor Halton Borough Coun., Widnes, 2001—02. Recipient prize, Imperial Chem. Industries, 1986; fellow, U. of Cambridge, 1997—98; scholar, Royal Acad. of Engring., 2000, Royal Soc. of London, 2000, Engring. and Phys. Scis. Rsch. Coun., 1992—95. Fellow: Liverpool (Eng.) and North Wales Materials Soc. (hon. sec. 1998—2002), Cambridge (Eng.) Philos. Soc. (life), Liverpool (Eng.) Athenaeum; mem.: ASME, Am. Soc. of Materials, Inst. of Materials, Minerals, and Mining, Instn. of Mech. Engrs. (scholar 1990). Labor. Mem. Ch.Of England. Achievements include design of manufacturing processes at the micro and nanoscale. Avocations: running, reading, travel, history, debating. Office: Tennessee Technological University POBox 5014 Cookeville TN 38505-0001 Office Fax: 931-372-6340. E-mail: mjackson@tntech.edu.

JACKSON, M.(ARVIN) DENNIS, journalism educator, writer; b. Jackson, Miss., June 30, 1945; s. Roy Dennis and Margie Emma (Cade) Jackson; m. Anna Jean Ferrell, Aug. 26, 1997. BA, Belhaven Coll., Jackson, Miss., 1967; MA, U. Ark., 1970, PhD in English, 1978. From asst. to assoc. prof. English U. Del., Newark, 1978—92, prof. English, 1992—, dir. journalism program, 1995—2003. Seminar dir. Bulgarian Mass Media Devel. Program, U.S. Info. Agy., Sofia, Bulgaria, 1994—95; mem. seminar faculty Nat. Writers Workshop, 1991—. Author: (book) A Programmed Study of Accelerated Reading Skills, 1975; mng. editor (jour.) Irish Renaissance Ann., 1980—83; editor: (jour.) The D.H. Lawrence Review, 1984—94; assoc. editor (book) D.H. Lawrence: An Annotated Bibliography of Writings About Him, Vol. I, 1982, D.H. Lawrence: An Annotated Bibliography of Writings About Him, Vol. II, 1985; co-editor: (book) D.H. Lawrence's "Lady", 1985, Critical Essays on D.H. Lawrence, 1988, D.H. Lawrence's Literary Inheritors, 1991, Editing D.H. Lawrence: New Versions of a Modern Author, 1995, The Journalist's Craft, 2002. Recipient Nat. Teaching Award, Poynter Inst. Media Studies, 1982, Harry T. Moore Disting. Scholar Award for Lifetime Achievement in D.H. Lawrence Studies, D.H. Lawrence Soc. N.Am., 1999, College of Arts and Science Outstanding Advisement Award, U. Del., 2000; fellow Gannett Teaching Fellowship, Assn. Edn. Journalism, 1981, Nat. Endowment for the Humanities, 1999. Mem.: Modern Language Assn., D.H. Lawrence Soc. N.Am. (sec.-treas. 1979—82, pres. 1985—86), Conf. of Editors of Learned Jours., Nat. Assn. Black Journalists (assoc.), Phi Beta Kappa. Democrat. Home: 814 Bradford Ln Newark DE 19711 Office: U Del Dept English 212 Memorial Newark DE 19716 Office Fax: 302-831-1585. E-mail: djackson@udel.edu.

JACKSON, MARY ELLEN, librarian, consultant; b. Oshkosh, Wis., Nov. 20, 1949; d. Lawrence Herbert and Jeanette Lucille Marten; m. Alan Robert Jackson, Sept. 11, 1971. BA, Carroll Coll., Waukesha, Wis., 1971; MLS, Drexel U., 1974. Libr. searching dept. U. Pa. Libr., Phila., 1973-74, head Rosengarten res., 1974-77, head serials dept., 1977-78; head interlibr. loan dept. U. Pa. Librs., Phila., 1978-93; access and delivery svcs. cons. Assn. Rsch. Librs., Washington, 1993-98; sr. program officer Access Svc., 1998—2003, dir. collections and access programs, 2003—. Cons., spkr. in field; adv. bd. Inst. for Sci. Info., Phila., 1993—96; dir. N.Am. Coordinating Com. on Japanese Libr. Resources, 1998—99; adv. bd. Ingenta Libr., 2001—02; governing bd. Internat. Fedn. Libr. Assoc., 2001—03. Author: Measuring the Performance of Interlibrary Loan Ops. in North Amer. Rsch. and Acad. Libraries, 1998, Interlibrary Loan/Resource Sharing Systems, 2000 ; editor: AMS Studies in Interlibrary Loan, Document Delivery, Access Svcs., and Resource Sharing (ILL/DD), 2000; editor 5 books, Rsch. Access Through New Technology, 1989, RLG Shared Resources Manual, 1992, Advances in Preservation and Access, 1992, Uses of Document Delivery Svc., 1994, Manging Resource Sharing in the Electronic Age, 1996; contbr. over 100 articles to profl. jour. Recipient cert. of merit Pa. Libr. Assn., 1993. Mem. ALA (Amer. Library Assn., various offices 1978—), Safari Club Internat., Beta Phi Mu. Avocation: sewing. Office: Assn Rsch Librs 21 Dupont Cir NW Ste 800 Washington DC 20036-1118

JACKSON, MARY JANE MCHALE FLICKINGER, principal; b. Cleve., Feb. 23, 1938; d. Thomas William Flickinger and Margaret Julia (Lydon) Flickinger Nichols; m. Robert Lowell Jackson, June 27, 1959; children: Julia Anna Jackson Somers, Patricia Lauck, Margaret Jacqueline Jackson Tyler. BS in Speech, St. Louis U., 1959; postgrad., U. Copenhagen, 1961-62; MS in Spl. Edn., Southern Ill. U., 1965; EdD, George Washington U., 1977. Cert. tchr. Md. 1972. Tchr. Ritenour Sch. Dist., Overland, Mo., 1959-60; tutor Spl. Sch. Dist. Handicapped, St. Louis, 1960-61; tchr. Rugaards Franske Skole, Copenhagen, Denmark, 1961-62; substitute tchr., primary tchr. St. Louis and Ladue, Mo., 1962-65; tchr. L.A. City Schs., 1966-67, Woodlin Elem. Sch., Silver Spring, Md., 1967-68; various teaching positions, 1968-71, 73-81; asst. prin. Ritchie Park Elem. Sch., Rockville, Md., 1971-73, various supr. positions, 1974-79; asst. prin. Stephen Knolls Sch., Kensington, Md., 1981-88, prin., 1988-97; adj. prof., supr. spl. edn. student tchrs. Trinity Coll., 1997—. V.p. Concerned Citizens Exceptional Edn., Washington, 1968-70; surrogate parent Assn. Retarded Citizens, Washington. Bd. dirs. Archdiocesan of Washington, 1986-91; pres. Bd. Edn., Washington, 1990-91; bd. dirs. United Cerebral Palsy, Montgomery County, 1992—; presenter Young Adult Insts. Internat. Conf., 1994. Recipient Lisa Kane award, 1964; Fulbright scholar, Russia, 2002. Mem. Wash. Hearing Soc. (bd. dirs. 1969-81), Coun. Exceptional Children (exec. bd., pres. Montgomery county chpt. 1992-93, polit. action coord. for Md. fedn. 1993, exec. com. divsn. of internat. spl. edn. and svcs. 1993), Alexander Graham Bell Assn. (pub. rels. com. 1979—), Rotary (pres. Wheaton-Kensington club 2000-2001), AAUW (v.p. for programs 2003—, Kenington/Rockville br., Md.), Roman Catholic. Home: 9900 Georgia Ave Apt T 11 Silver Spring MD 20902-5241 E-mail: jacksonjb@aol.com.

JACKSON, MARY L. health services executive; b. Phila., June 25, 1938; d. John Francis and Helen Catherine (Peranteau) Martin; m. Howard Clark Jackson III, Dec. 17, 1954; children: Michael, Mark, Brian, Bert. Student, Bucks County C.C., 1977-83. Asst. mgr. retail divsn. Sears Roebuck & Co., Bensalem, Pa., 1972-77; educator, adminstr., dir. Trevos Behavior Modification Program, Pa., 1975—, leadership tng. workshops, 1979—. Participant rsch. studies in field; salesman Makefield Real Estate, Morrisville, Pa., 1977-78; mortgage fin. cons. Tom Dunphy Real Estate, Feasterville, Pa., 1978-81; weight loss cons., Hulmeville, Pa., 1984—, also TV and radio appearances on behavior modification for weight loss and maintenance. Co-author: The Official Calorie Book; pub., columnist monthly newsletter The Modifier, 1977—; pub. several studies in weight loss field; pub. co-author multi-studies in field. Recipient Chapel of Four Chaplain award, 1977. Mem. Assn. Advancement Behavior Therapy, Bucks County Bd. Realtors, Hulmeville Hist. Soc. (founder, charter mem.). Democrat. Presbyterian. Avocations: reading, classical music, speed walking, knitting, fishing. Home: 218 Main St Hulmeville PA 19047-5635

JACKSON, MELBOURNE LESLIE, chemical engineering educator and administrator, consultant; b. Wisdom, Mont., Sept. 27, 1915; s. James R. and Adeline (Mallon) J.; m. Elizabeth Clara Ford, Apr. 2, 1944; children: Gary Leslie, Linda Mary, Laurie Elizabeth, Nancy Ruth. BSChemE, Mont. State U., 1941, D in Engring. (hon.), 1980; PhDChemE, U. Minn., 1948. Registered profl. engr., Wash., Idaho. Instr. chem. engring. U. Minn., Mpls., 1944-48; from asst. prof. to assoc. prof. U. Colo., Boulder, 1948-50; head process devel. U.S. Naval Ordnance Test Sta., China Lake, Calif., 1950-53; prof. U. Idaho, Moscow, 1953-65, 70-80, head dept. chem. engring., 1953-65, dean grad. sch., 1965-70, dean Coll. Engring., 1973, 78-80, 83. Cons. numerous corps. including James River Corp.; pres. U. Idaho Fed. Credit Union, Moscow, 1972-74. Patentee aeration/flotation devices, 1978, 80; contbr. articles to profl. jours. Chmn. Idaho Air Pollution Control Commn., Boise, 1959-72; chmn., trustee Moscow Sch. Dist., 1957-63. Fellow Am. Inst. Chem. Engrs; mem. Am. Chem. Soc., Am. Soc. Engring. Edn., Sigma Xi. Methodist. Avocations: boating, photography. Address: 532 Eisenhower Moscow ID 83843-9596 E-mail: mlj@uidaho.edu.

JACKSON, MICHAEL J. automotive retail company executive; Technician Mercedes Benz dealership, Cherry Hill, N.J., mng. ptnr. Euro Motorcars, Bethesda, Md.; dist. mgr. Mercedes-Benz N.Am.; sr. mktg. exec. Mercedes-Benz USA, Inc., pres., CEO, responsible for N.Am. bus., until 1999; CEO AutoNation, Inc., Ft. Lauderdale, Fla., 1999—. Former chmn. Mercedes-Benz Nat. Dealer Coun. Recipient All-Star Dealer award Sports Illustrated, 1990; mem. automotive execs. Dream Team, Automotive News, 2 times; recognized mem. of Mktg. 100, Advt. Age, 4 times. Office: AutoNation Inc 110 SE 6th St Fort Lauderdale FL 33301-5000

JACKSON, MICHAEL JOHN, retired physiologist, association executive; b. Walton-on-Thames, Eng., Apr. 12, 1938; came to U.S., 1967; s. Leslie William and Mable Maud (Rudd) J.; m. Beryl Ann Tidy, Aug. 20, 1960. B.Sc. with 1st class honors, U. London, 1963; Ph.D, U. Sheffield, Eng., 1966. Lectr. physiology U. Sheffield, 1965-67; asst. prof. George Washington U., Washington, 1967-71, assoc. prof., 1971-77, prof., 1977-90, assoc. dean, 1985-89, dean, 1989-90; exec. dir. Fedn. Am. Soc. Exptl. Biology, 1990-99. Guest investigator Nat. Inst. Arthritis, Metabolism and Digestive Disease, NIH, 1975-76; cons. USPHS, NIH, 1978, 81, 83, VA, 1978-81 Assoc. editor, Am. Jour. Physiology, 1979-85; contbr. articles to profl. jours. Recipient NIAMDD Research Career Devel. award., 1972-77 Mem. Physiol. Soc. (London), Am. Physiol. Soc., Coun. Eng. Sci. Soc. Execs., Am. Men Women Sci. (mem. adminstrv. bd.), Am. Soc. Assoc. Execs. Home: 1302 Forest Crk Sunset Beach NC 28468-4463 Office: 9650 Rockville Pike Bethesda MD 20814-3998

JACKSON, MICHAEL JOSEPH, singer; b. Gary, Ind., Aug. 29, 1958; s. Joseph Walter and Katherine Esther (Scruse) Jackson; 3 children. Student pvt. sch.; LHD (hon.), Fisk U., 1988. Lead singer Jackson-Five (later called The Jacksons), from 1969; performer (on numerous) TV series; recs. for Epic Records, performed at Queen Elizabeth's Silver Jubilee, May 1977, appeared in (films) The Wiz, 1978, Moonwalker, 1988, Dangerous the short film, 1993, (TV series) The Jacksons, 1976—77, albums with Jackson-Five include Diana Ross Presents the Jackson Five, 1969, ABC, Jackson Five Christmas Album, Third Album, 1970, Goin' Back to Indiana, Greatest Hits, Maybe Tomorrow, 1971, Looking Through the Windows, 1972, Farewell My Summer, Get it Together, Skywriter, 1973, Dancing Machine, 1974, Moving Violation, 1975, Joyful Jukebox Music, 1976, Boogie, 1980, albums with The Jacksons include The Jacksons, 1976, Goin' Places, 1977, Destiny, 1978, Triumph, 1980, The Jacksons Live, 1981, Victory, 1984, solo albums include Got To Be There, Ben, 1972, Music and Me, 1973, Forever Michael, The Best of Michael Jackson, 1975, Off the Wall, 1979, Thriller (listed in Guiness Book of World Records as most successful LP in rec. history), 1982, Bad, 1987, Dangerous, 1991, HIStory: Past, Present and Future, Book 1, 1995, Blood on the Dance Floor: HIStory in the Mix, 1997, Invincible, 2001, narrator E.T.: The Extra Terrestrial storybook, 1982, videos include We Are The World, 1990, Black or White, 1991, Leave Me Alone, 1993, leader of Jacksons U.S. tour, 1984; author: (autobiography) Moonwalk, 1988, Dancing the Dream Poems and Reflections, 1992. Named Best Male Artist, MTV-Europe, 1996, Favorite Male Artist Pop-Rock, Am. Music awards, 1996, Artist of a Generation, Brit. Awards., 1996, World's Best Selling R&B Male Artist, World's Best Selling Pop Male R&B Artist, World's Best Selling Male Rec. Artist, World's Best Selling Am. Male Artist, 1997, Jackson Five Induction in the Rock'n Roll Hall of Fame; recipient gold and platinum record awards, Grammy awards for Record of the Yr., (Beat It), Album of Yr. (Thriller), Pop vocal performer (Thriller), Rock vocal performer (Thriller), World's Best Selling Album of All Time (Thriller), Rock vocal performer for song Beat It, Rhythm and Blues vocal performance (Billie Jean), New rhythm and blues song (Billie Jean), Children's field for narration of E.T., The Innovator's award, Inst. for Musical Arts, 1996, Living Legend award for Best Video for Leave Me Alone, 1993, Cable Ace award, Performance in a Music Special or Series, 1994, World Music award, 1996.*

JACKSON, MICHAEL P. federal agency administrator; married; 1 child. BA, U. Houston; PhD in Govt. with distinction, Georgetown U., 1985. Reported to sec. edn. Pres. Reagan adminstrn.; spl. asst. to Pres. George H.W. Bush for cabinet liaison; COO IMS transp. sys. and svcs. Lockheed Martin; sr. v.p., counselor to pres. Am. Trucking Assn., 1993—97; chief of staff to sec. transp. U.S. Dept. Transp., dep. sec., 2001—. Rschr. Am. Enterprise Inst.; instr. polit. sci. U. Ga., Georgetown U. Republican. Office: US Dept Transp Office of Sec 400 7th St SW Washington DC 20590-0001

JACKSON, MICK, film director, producer; b. Aveley, Essex, Eng., Nov. 4, 1943; m. Hilary Henson. BA in Electronics with honors, U. Southampton, Eng.; postgrad. degree in drama, U. Bristol, Eng. Motion picture and T.V. dir., prodr. Prodr., dir. (TV films) Threads, 1985, The Race for the Double Helix, 1987, Life Story, 1987, (TV series) Connections, 1979, The Practice, 1997, Strange World, 1999; (films) That's Life, 2000; dir. (films) Chattahoochee, 1990, L.A. Story, 1991, The Bodyguard, 1992, Clean Slate, 1994, Volcano, 1997, Josiah's Canon, 1999, others; (TV movies) The Ascent of Man, 1973, A Guide to Armageddon, 1983, Yuri Nosenko, KGB, 1986, Indictment: The McMartin Trial, 1995 (Dir.'s Guild of America award, 1995), Tuesdays With Morrie, 1999 (Dir.'s Guild of America award, 1999), others; prodr. (TV show) The Age of Uncertainty, 1977. Office: ICM c/o Martha Lutrell 8942 Wilshire Blvd Beverly Hills CA 90211-1934

JACKSON, MILES MERRILL, retired university dean; b. Richmond, Va., Apr. 28, 1929; s. Miles Merrill and Thelma Eugertha (Manning) J.; m. Bernice Olivia Roane, Jan. 7, 1954; children: Miles Merrill III, Marsha, Muriel, Melia. BA in English, Va. Union U., 1955; MS, Drexel U., 1956; postgrad., Ind. U., 1961, 64; PhD, Syracuse U., 1974. Br. libr. Free Libr., 1955-58; acting libr. C.P. Huntington Meml. Libr., Hampton (Va.) U., 1958-59, libr., 1959-62, asst. prof. libr. sci., 1958-62; territorial libr. Am. Samoa, 1962-64; chief libr. Trevor Arnett Libr., Atlanta U., 1964-69; also lectr. Sch. Libr. Sci.; assoc. prof. State U. N.Y., Geneseo, 1969-75; prof. U. Hawaii, 1975—, dean, 1983-95, chmn. interdisciplinary program in communication and info. scis., 1985-89; cons. in field, 1995—. Fulbright lectr. U. Tehran, Iran, 1968-69; libr., cons. Fiji, Samoa, Papua New Guinea, Micronesia, USIA India, 1993, Pakistan, 1985, Nat. Libr. Edn., 1996, Govt. Am. Samoa, 1997, Hawaii Pub. Libr. Found., 1986-2000; chmn. bd. Hawaii Lit., Inc., 1985-88; commr. Hawaii Libr. Commn., 1996-97. Editor: A Bibliography of Materials on Negro History and Culture for Young People, 1968, Comparative and International Librarianship, 1971, International Handbook of Contemporary Developments in Librarianship, 1981, Pacific Island Studies: Review of the Literature, 1986, Linkages Over Space and Time, 1993, And They Came: A Brief History of Blacks in Hawaii, 2001; mem. editl. bd. Internat. Jour. Info. Mgmt., Internat. Libr. Rev., 1982-87; founder, editor Pacific Info. and Libr. Svcs. Newsletter; contbr. articles to profl. jours.; book reviewer. Bd. dirs. Cen. YMCA, 1986-94, Hawaii Gov.'s Coun. on Literacy, 1986-96, Hawaii ACLU, 1990-94, office holder in Dem. party of Hawaii, 1992—. With USNR, 1946-48. Recipient Outstanding Alumnus award Va. Union U., 1987; Rsch. grantee Am. Philos. Soc., 1966; Coun. on Libr. Resources fellow, 1970, vis. fellow Republic of China, 1986; Harold Lancour fgn. travel awardee Beta Phi Mu, 1976 Mem. ALA (chmn. Internat. Rels. Roundtable 1988-89), Assn. for Libr. and Info. Sci. Edn. (pres. 1989-90), Coll. Lang. Assn. (hon. mention poetry 1954, 2d prize award short story 1955) Democrat.

JACKSON, MILLARD IRVING, JR., lawyer, banker; b. Phila., June 19, 1939; s. Millard Irving and Marion (Bennett) J.; A.B., Duke U., 1961; LL.B., U. N.C., 1964; m. Marilynn Louise White, June 15, 1963; children— Michael Howard, David Alan. Admitted to N.C. bar, 1964; mem. trust dept. 1st Citizens Bank & Trust Co., Raleigh, N.C., 1964-66; asst. v.p. Provident Nat. Bank, Phila., 1966-76; v.p., dir. tax and estate planning Janney Montgomery Scott, Inc., Phila., 1976— . Mem. N.C. Bar Assn., S.E. Conn. Estate and Tax Planning Council, Internat. Assn. Fin. Planners. Republican. Presbyterian. Home: 850 Lewis Ln Bryn Mawr PA 19010-1206

JACKSON, MORTON BARROWS, lawyer; b. Devil's Lake, N.D., July 17, 1921; s. Anson Blake and Marjorie Barrows (Hill) J.; m. Nancy Abrams, Nov. 11, 1948 (div. 1956); children— Elizabeth Finch, Margaret Barrows Jackson McKay; m. Nancy Cooke Veitch de Herrera, May 5, 1962 (div. 1975); m. Marilyn Taylor Savage, Dec. 27, 1975 (div. 1988); m. Rosemarie Donner, Sept. 2, 1989. Student Harvard U., 1938-40; J.D., U. So. Calif., 1948. Bar: Calif. 1949. Assoc. Bledsoe, Cathcart, Boyd, Eliot & Curfman, and predecessors, San Francisco, 1948-51; assoc. Hill, Farrer & Burrill, Los Angeles, 1959-64, ptnr., 1964-68; ptnr. Jackson & Goodstein, Los Angeles, 1968-77; ptnr. Macdonald, Halsted & Laybourne, Los Angeles, 1978-88, Baker & McKenzie, 1988—, v.p. Intercontinental Engring. Corp., Bangkok, Thailand, 1951-54; exec. asst. to dir. Intergovtl. Com. for European Migration, Geneva, Switzerland, 1954-58, regional commr. Immigration and Naturalization Service, U.S. Dept. Justice, Richmond, Va., 1958-59; polit. editor, news commentator radio sta. KMPC, Los Angeles, 1960-78; host pub. affairs program TV sta. KTLA, Los Angeles, 1966-68. Bd. editors U. So. Calif. Law Rev., 1947-48. Bd. dirs., counsel Am. Youth Symphony; founding mem. bd. dirs. Los Angeles Chamber Orch., 1968-86, pres., 1977-79; bd. dirs. Los Angeles Master Chorale, 1978-88, Oreg. Bach Festival, 1981-88; bd. dirs., chmn. Thomas Jefferson Research Ctr., 1974-86; exec. sec. Western Region Assistance Fund of Met. Opera Nat. Council, 1975-87; trustee Reason Found., 1968—. Served to lt. comdr. USNR, 1941-46, PTO. Decorated D.F.C., Air medal with 5 oak leaf clusters; recipient Fourth Estate award Am. Legion, 1965; Agnes Underwood Freedom of Info. award Women in Communications. Mem. Los Angeles County Bar Assn., ABA (Silver Gavel awards 1964, 66), Fed. Bar Assn. (pres. Los Angeles chpt. 1969-70), Assn. Bus. Trial Lawyers, State Bar Calif., Los Angeles World Affairs Council, Town Hall, U. So. Calif. Alumni Assn., Order of Coif, Legion Lex (bd. dirs. 1967-70), Phi Delta Phi. Clubs: Harvard (So. Calif.), Met. (N.Y.C.), Los Angeles Athletic. Office: Baker & McKenzie 777 S Figueroa 37th Fl Los Angeles CA 90017

JACKSON, NAGLE, stage director, playwright; b. Seattle, Apr. 28, 1936; s. Paul Joseph and Gertrude (Dunn) J.; m. Sandra L. Suter, Sept. 15, 1963; children: Rebecca J., Hillary J. BA, Whitman Coll., 1958, LittD (hon.), 1995. Resident dir. Am. Conservatory Theatre, San Francisco, 1967-70; artistic dir. Milw. Repertory Theatre, 1970-76, McCarter Theatre, Princeton, NJ, 1979-90; stage dir. N.J. Opera Festival, Lawrenceville, 1985-91; currently assoc. artist Denver Center Theatre Co., Denver; prin. dir. Santa Fe Shakespeare Co. Guest dir. Gorky Theatre, Leningrad, 1988, Trøndelag Teatre, Trondheim, Norway, 1990. Playwright: At This Evening's Performance, 1985, Opera Comique, 1988, They Shoot Horses, Don't They?-The Musical (book and lyrics), 1992, This Day and Age, 1994, The Quick-Change Room, 1995, Moliere Plays Paris, 1996, A Hotel on Marvin Gardens, 2002, Taking Leave, 2002. Fulbright fellow, Paris, 1958; recipient Prize Onassis Found. Internat. Playwrights Competition for "The Elevation of Thieves", 1997. Mem. Soc. Stage Dirs. & Choreographers, The Dramatists Guild. E-mail: naglejackson@att.net.

JACKSON, NANCY GERTRUDE, federal government librarian; b. Ft. Wayne, Ind., Apr. 23, 1943; d. Clyde White and Margaret Edythe (McClung) J. B.A. magna cum laude, Concord Coll., 1965; M.S. in L.S., U. N.C., 1967; M.A., George Washington U., 1973. Asst., Concord Coll. Library, Athens, W.Va., 1961-65, U. N.C. Art Library, Chapel Hill, 1965-67; descriptive cataloguer Library of Congress, Washington, 1967-80, head post-cataloging, 1980-83, head English lang. sect. 5, 1981, publ. quality control analyst, 1984-86, head editorial sect. I Nat. Union Catalog, 1986-90, head post-cataloging, 1991-99; ret., 1999. Vol. tutor Job Corps, YWCA, Washington, 1972; vol. Ctr. for Environ. Edn., 1979-80. Mem. ALA, D.C. Library Assn., Library of Congress Profl. Assn. (newsletter editor 1975), Beta Phi Mu. Democrat. Presbyterian. Home: 2907 S Dinwiddie St Arlington VA 22206-1405

JACKSON, NANCY LEE, geography educator; b. Weymouth, Mass, Aug. 28, 1956; d. Sherwood Walter and Barbara Rose (Croker) J.. BA, Clark U., 1978; MS, Antioch/New Eng. Grad. Sch., 1986; PhD, Rutgers U., 1992. Field advisor Rural Cmty. Assistance, Rural Housing Improvement, Inc., Winchendon, Mass., 1979-80, asst. dir., 1980-81, dir., 1981-83; exec. dir. Rural New Eng., Inc., Waldboro, Maine, 1983-87; rsch. asst., IMCS Rutgers U., New Brunswick, N.J., 1987-92; asst. prof. N.J. Inst. of Tech., Newark, 1992-97, assoc. prof., 1997—, dir. Ctr. for Policy Studies, 1995-98, dir. grad. program in environ. policy studies, 1999—. Author: Environment Preservation an dPollution Prevention, 1997; Jour. Coastal Rsch., 2000—, assoc. editor: Estuaries, 2001—; contbr. articles to profl. jours. Mem. Planning Bd. Waldboro, 1984-87; bd. dirs. Coastal Econ. Devel. Corp., Bath, Maine, 1986-87, Rural New Eng., Inc., Waldoboro, 1982. Grantee, Ford Found., 1984—87, HHS, 1986—87, NATO, 1995—98, NOAA N.J. Sea Grant, 1995—98, 2000—01, 2002—, Deutscher Akademischer Austauschdienst, 1999, Nature Conservancy, 2002, Nat. Geog. Soc., 2002. Mem. Am. Geog. Soc., Assn. Am. Geographers, Coastal and Marine Specialty Group (bd. dirs. 1994-96). Office: NJ Inst Tech University Heights Newark NJ 07102

JACKSON, NANCY MORRISON, architect; b. Pitts., Aug. 15, 1922; d. Robert Kirk and Marcella Genevieve (Pfendler) Morrison; m. George Clark Jackson, Aug. 25, 1945; children: Ellen Jackson Rudy, Robert Clark, Mary Jackson Porter. BArch, Carnegie Mellon U., 1946. Arch. Prack & Prack, Pitts., 1942, Kaiser, Neal & Reid, Pitts., 1943—44, Marks & Simboli, Pitts., 1947, Edward C. Rook, Syracuse, NY, 1958, Austin-Mead, Hartford, Conn., 1967—70, Kane Farrel White, 1970—72; pvt. practice Farmington, Conn., 1972—78; gen. svcs. adminstrn. Washington, 1978—. Mem. Nat. Archtl. Accrediting Bd.; citations U.S. State Dept. Mem. admissions coun. Carnegie Mellon U.; mem. Cath. Family Svcs., Commn. for Ecumenical Affairs, Conn. Mem.: AIA (Masterspec rev. com.), Am. Arbitration Assn. (constrn. industry arbitrator), Conn. Soc. Arch. Bd., Arts Club of Washington, Kappa Alpha Theta. Roman Catholic. Home: 1307-3 E Abingdon Dr Alexandria VA 22314

JACKSON, NEAL A. lawyer; b. Raleigh, N.C., Sept. 6, 1943; s. Irvine L. and Dorothy A. Jackson; m. Louise M. Reggia (div. 1994); children: Adrienne, Kimberly; m. Sandra Willett, 1995. AB, U. N.C., 1965; JD, Georgetown U., 1968. Bar: D.C. 1968, Md. 1979. Pvt. practice, Washington, 1970—96; v.p. for legal affairs, gen. counsel & sec. Nat. Pub. Radio, Inc., 1996—. Mem.: ABA, Univ. Club, Edgemoor Club (pres. 1984—85). Home: 3408 Reservoir Rd NW Washington DC 20007-2328 Office: Nat Pub Radio Inc 635 Massachusetts Ave NW Washington DC 20001-3753

JACKSON, NONA ARMOUR, writer, illustrator; b. Denison, Tex., Sept. 22, 1939; d. Thomas Jefferson and Novella Mae (Binion) A.; m. R.L. Jackson, Jr., Apr. 16, 1966. Supr., illustrator Diaper Jeans, Inc., Denison, 1959-62; clothing pattern maker, designer Srader's Sportswear, Denison, 1963-65; receptionist Glad Tidings Ch., Sherman, Tex., 1981-84, pastor elderly ministry, 1984-87; author Pottsboro, Tex., 1987—. Spkr. in field. Author, illustrator, photographer: The Cotton Mill! Can Anything Good Come from There? Vol. I-IX, 1995, Industries 1873-1981, Vol. I, 1995, Churches 1906-1991, vol. II 1995, Schools 1890-1964, vol. III, 1995, Golden Rule Independent School Extra-Curricular Activities, vol. IV, 1995, Cotton Mill Community, vol. V, 1995, The People: A Biography in Three Volumes, Vols. VI-VIII, 1995, Associates, Vol. IX, Index, Vols. VI-IX, 1995, Vol. X, 2001, Addenda, 1998-2001; author, illustrator: Pioneers of North West Grayson County, Texas Mid to Late 19th Century and Early 20th Century: Delaware Bend, Red Branch/Prairie Valley, Rock Creek with Some Dexter, Texas Data, 1996, Pioneers of Central Grayson County, Texas Mid to Late 19th Century and Early 20th Century: Cherrymound and Ambrose, 1996, Pioneers of Central Grayson County, Texas Mid to Late 19th Century and Early 20th Century: Cedar Community, 1996, Pioneers of South East Grayson County, Texas Mid to Late, 19th Century and Early 20th Century: Pilot Grove, 1996, Series 1 (4000 B.C.-A.D. 1607) The Overseas Connection, Big Oaks from Little Trees Grow, vols. I-III, 2000, Series 2 (A.D. 1607-A.D.

1837) Immigrant & Colonial Ancestors, vols. IV-VIII, 2000, Series 3 (A.D. 1937-A.D. 1987) A Grayson County, Texas Epic-One Hundred and Fifty Years, vols. IX-XV, 2000, Series 4 (A.D. 1855-A.D. 1991), Twentieth Century-Big Oaks-Precious Memories, vols. XVI-XVII, 2000, Series 5-10 The Collective Works of Nona Jackson vols. XVIII-XXXIX, 2000, Series 11, Jesus or Die!, Father, Son & Holy Ghost, Obedience, and Walking With God, vols. XL-XLII, 2000, Yummy, Yummy, Sweets for the Tummy, 2002, Pass the Taters Please, 2002, Me, Myself & I, 2002, My Split Apart, vol. 59, 2002, The Final Chapter-Part I, The Cotton Mill! Can Anything Good Come From There?, 2002, Addenda-Part II, Nona's Family Update: The Last Report, vol. 60, 2002; contbr. articles and photographs to publs. Sec., treas., young people's supt. Sunnyside Bapt. Ch., Denison, 1963-65; Sunday sch. tchr. Glad Tidings Ch., Sherman, 1978-83; tour guide, hostess Grayson County Frontier Village, Inc., Denison, 1978-97; active Adopt a Nursing Home, Tex. Dept. Human Resources, 1999— Mem. Grayson County Humane Soc., Nat. Audubon Soc., Nat. Trust Hist. Preservation, Libr. Congress Assoc. (charter). Republican. Avocations: guitar, art, nature, theology, genealogy. Home: Unit 1 109 Houston Ave Pottsboro TX 75076-3031

JACKSON, PATIENCE KENNEY, grants adminstrator, library consultant; b. Pitts., Mar. 9, 1943; d. William James and Jane (Endsley) Kenney; m. Thad Alwill Jackson, Apr. 24, 1965; children: Rebecca Jackson Wright, Elizabeth Endsley. BA, Middlebury Coll., 1964; MLS, U. Pitts., 1965. Libr. U.S. Army Spl. Svcs., Pirmasens, Germany, 1966-67; head libr. Peters Twp. Libr., McMurray, Pa., 1967-68; rsch. libr. E.I. DuPont de Nemours, Wilmington, Del., 1968-72; field interviewer, New Eng. supr. Inst. Survey Rsch., Temple U., Phila., 1973-79; cataloger, reference libr. Daniel Webster Coll., Nashua, NH, 1977—79, libr. dir., 1979—88; libr. bldg. cons. Mass. Bd. Libr. Commns., 1988—. Cons. Franklin Mint, Inc., Franklin Ctr., Pa., 1972, Digital Equipment Corp., Merrimack, N.H., 1979-80, Wang Inst., Tyngsboro, Mass., 1981; bldg. cons. for pub. librs. in N.H., R.I., Vt., Maine and N.Y. Mem. ALA, Mass. Libr. Assn. Home: 7 Howard Rd Maynard MA 01754-1555 Office: Mass Bd Libr Comms 648 Beacon St Boston MA 02215-2013 Personal E-mail: Thadaj@aol.com. Business E-Mail: patience.jackson@state.ma.us.

JACKSON, PATRICK JOSEPH, real estate company officer; b. Minn., Mar. 31, 1942; s. Paul Arthur and Lucille Margaret (Cummings) J.; m. Barbara Ann Simpson, July 19, 1964 (div. Apr. 1980); children: Laura Kathleen, Katherine Lucille; m. Shirley Ann Wellman, Sept. 12, 1982 (div. Oct. 1998); m. Kath Jo Holm, Sept. 9, 2001, 1 child, Liza Ann Holm. BS, Portland State U., 1968. Bank loan officer First Nat. Bank of Oreg., Portland, 1964-68; credit mgr. Meier & Frank Corp., Portland, 1968-70; agt., mgr. Aetna Life, San Jose, Calif., 1970-75; dist. mgr. Calif. Casualty, San Jose, 1975-78; gen. agt. Great So. Life, San Jose, 1978-82; account agt., agy. owner Allstate Ins., San Jose, 1982—2001; assoc. Home Realty, 2001—; pres. Delta Direct Enterprises, Sequim, Wash., 2001—. Instr. Santa Clara (Calif.) U., 1974-76. Author: (monograph) The Affairs of, 1978; newspaper columnist, 1978-82. Mem. ins. subcom. Calif. State Senate, 1978; officer Los Gatos (Calif.) Police Res., 1970-78, treas., 1974-78; mem. Sch. Site Coun., Saratoga, Calif., 1978-80; mem. City Coun., Discovery Bay, Calif., 1991-95, mayor, 1993-94. Named Man of Yr., Los Gatos Youth Unltd., 1978. Mem. San Jose Life Underwriters (bd. dirs. 1974-76), No. Calif. Tollycraft Assn. (sec. 1995-97), Sequim Bay Yacht Club. Republican. Lutheran. Avocations: boating, fishing, shooting, reading. Office: Delta Direct Enterprises 325 E Washington St #106 Sequim WA 98382 E-mail: pjackson@olypen.com.

JACKSON, PAUL HOWARD, minister; b. Topeka, Nov. 10, 1952; s. Dwight Stover and Janice Ilona (Woeltje) J.; m. Elizabeth Ann McGhghy, July 23, 1977; children: Christopher, Jeremy, Catherine, Johanna, Caleb. BA, Washburn U., 1973; MLS, Emporia State U., 1974; MDiv, Concordia Sem., Clayton, Mo., 1979; postgrad., Ind. U., 1993-96; STM, Concordia Theol. Sem., Ft. Wayne, Ind., 1995. Ordained to ministry Luth. Ch.-Mo. Synod, 1979. Pastor St. Paul's Luth. Ch., Wakefield, Nebr., 1979-81, 1st Trinity Luth. Ch., Wayne, Nebr., 1979-81; libr., tchr. Luth. High. Sch. Indpls., 1981-82; libr., prof. St. John's Coll., Winfield, Kans., 1982-85; libr. Winfield (Kans.) Pub. Library, 1985-88; pastor 1st Luth. Ch., Pond Creek, Okla., 1986-88; libr. Concordia Theol. Sem., Ft. Wayne, Ind., 1988-96; multimedia prodr. Concordia Publ. House, St. Louis, 1996-2000; pastor St. Paul Luth. Ch., Texhoma, Okla., 2000—. Adj. prof. Concordia U. Wis., Mequon, 1995-2000; facilitator Pst-Seminary Applied Learning and Support, LCMS Com. on Ministerial Growth and Support. Prodr. W3 Word Witness Worship, 1998-2000, Concordia Self-Study CD-ROM, Concordia Electronic Theological Libr., Luther's Works on CD-ROM; content editor Christian Cyclopedia, Internet Version; contbr. articles to religious jours. Bd. dirs. Trinity Ch. S.E. Asian Mission, Winfield, 1984-86, Wash. Luth. Sch. Assn., 1997-98, v.p. 1997-98; co-chair Winfield Com. for Commemorating the Bicentennial of the Constn., Winfield, 1987-88; chmn. Coalition for Purchase and Renovation, St. John's Coll., Winfield, 1988; sec., treas. exec. com. Area 3 Libr. Svc. Authority, Ft. Wayne, 1990-93; organizer Texhoma Christmas Effort, 2000-02. Mem. Rotary Internat. (treas. Texhoma chpt. 2002—), Phi Kappa Phi, Mu Alpha Pi. Republican. Home: RR 1 Box 114F Texhoma OK 73949-9730 Office: St Paul Luth Ch PO Box 465 Texhoma OK 73949 E-mail: stpaul@ptsi.net. *All that I am I owe to my Lord and Savior Jesus Christ. What he has done through his life, death, and resurrection far exceeds anything we will ever accomplish.*

JACKSON, PETER, film director; b. Pukerua Bay, New Zealand, Oct. 31, 1961; m. Frances Walsh, 1987; 2 children. Grad.(hon.), Massey U., 2001. Owner WingNut Films, Weta Ltd., Three Foot Six, Nat. Film Unit, New Zealand, 1998. Dir.: (films) The Valley, 1976, (and prodr.) Braindead, 1987, (and writer) Bad Taste, 1987, (and prodr., writer) Meet the Feebles, 1989, (and screenplay) Braindead, aka Dead Alive, 1992, (and screenplay, co-prodr.) Heavenly Creatures, 1994, (and prodr., writer) aka Just the Feebles (USA), 1995, (and writer, prodr.) The Frighteners, 1996, aka Robert Zemeckis Presents: The Frighteners (USA), 1996, aka Frighteners (UK), 1997, (and writer, exec. prodr.): Forgotten Silver, 1995, (and screenplay, prodr.): (films) Lord of the Rings: The Fellowship of the Ring, 2001 (Nat. Bd. Rev. award for spl. achievement, 2001, Southea. Film Critics Assn. award best dir., best adapted screenplay, 2001, Las Vegas Film Critics Soc. award best dir., 2001, Fla. Film Critics Cir. award best dir., 2001, Am. Film Inst. award movie of yr., 2001, Golden Satellite award best motion picture, 2001, BAFTA award best film, David Lean award best achievement in direction, 2002), (and screenplay, exec. prodr.) Lord of the Rings: The Two Towers, 2002 (Las Vegas Film Critics award best dir., 2002, Online Film Critics Soc. award best dir., 2002, Dallas-Ft. Worth Film Critics award best dir., 2002); writer, prodr. : Jack Brown Genius, 1994. Office: c/o Ken Kamins Internat Creative Mgmt Inc 8942 Wilshire Blvd Beverly Hills CA 90211 also: WingNut Films Ltd PO Box 15 208 Miramar Wellington New Zealand*

JACKSON, PHILIP DOUGLAS, professional basketball coach; b. Deer Lodge, Mont., Sept. 17, 1945; m. June; 5 children. Grad., North Dakota, 1967. Basketball player N.Y. Knicks, 1967-78, N.J. Nets, 1978-80, asst. coach, 1980-82; head coach Albany Patrons (Cen. Basketball Assn.), 1982-87; asst. coach Chicago Bulls, 1987-89, head coach, 1989-98, Los Angeles Lakers, Los Angeles, 1999-. Mem. NBA Championship Team, 1970, 73; coach NBA championship team, 1991, 92, 93,96; named Coach of Yr., NBA, 1996. Office: Los Angeles Lakers PO Box 10 3900 W Manchester Blvd Inglewood CA 90306

JACKSON, PHILIP IRVING, literature educator, writer; m. Doris Lorie Jackson, Aug. 14, 1993; children: Brian, Jessica. BA, U. of Fla., Gainesville, 1995; MA, U. Ctrl. Fla., 2003. Professional Educator State of Fla., 1998, Teacher of Gifted Students State of Fla., 2002, Pacesetter Educator Coll. Bd., 1999. Tchr. Titusville H.S., Fla., 1996—. Adj. prof. Berv C.C. Contbr. articles. Mem.: MLA (assoc.). Green Party. Achievements include Conference speaker, Georgia State University; Recognized by Students as a Teacher of Excellence, Titusville High; Coached Golf team to District and Conference Championships. Avocations: golf, sailing. Office: Titusville HS 150 Terrier Trail Titusville FL 32780

JACKSON, RANDY, information technology executive; b. Oct. 16, 1944; s. James D. and Carmen (Brown) J.; m. Valerie Verne Crooks, April 10, 1999; children: Gail Lynn, Neil Allen. BS in Information Tech., U. Phoenix, 2001. Master cert. netware engr. Pres. Restaurant Technologies, El Segundo, Calif., 1981-88; dir. MIS, Gregory's Restaurants, Anaheim, Calif., 1988-90; ops. mgr. Tricare Inc., Irvine, Calif., 1990-92; dir. tech. Sun Health Corp., Sun City, Ariz., 1992—2001; chief info. officer City of Surprise, Ariz., 2001—. Contbr. articles to mags. Del. Ariz. Dem. Nat. Conv., N.Y.C., 1976, del. Utah, 1972. Mem. Networking Profl. Assn. (nat. orgn. chair bd. dirs. 1996, chair univ. rels. 1993-94, local chpt. pres. 1994), Health Info. Mgmt. Sys. SOc. (sr.). Avocation: photography. Home: 15843 N 135th Dr Surprise AZ 85374-5329 Office: City of Surprise 12425 W Bell Rd Surprise AZ 85374 E-mail: randy.jackson@surpriseaz.com.

JACKSON, RAYMOND A. federal judge; b. 1949; BA, Norfolk State U., 1970; JD, U. Va., 1973. Capt. U.S. Army JAGC, 1973-77; asst. U.S. atty. Ea. Dist. Va., Norfolk, 1977-93, chief criminal divsn., civil divsn., exec. asst.; judge U.S. Dist. Ct. (ea. dist.) Va., Norfolk, 1993—. Mem. jud. conf. U.S. Ct. Appeals (4th cir.); adj. faculty Marshall Wythe Sch. of Law, Coll. of William and Mary, 1978—93. Active Day Care and Child Devel. Ctr., Tidewater, 1980—86; mem. exec. com. Va. State Bar, 1991—93; bd. dirs. Peninsula Legal Aid Ctr., 1977. Col. Res. USAR, ret. 1998. Fellow: Va. Bar Found.; mem.: U.S. Judicial Conf. Com. Adminstrn. Magistrate Judge Sys., Va. Law Found., Am. Inn Ct. (Hoffman-l'Anson chpt. pres. 2000—02), South Hampton Rds. Bar Assn., Norfolk-Portsmouth Bar Assn., Old Dominion Bar Assn. (pres. 1984—86), U.S. Dist. Judges Assn. Office: 600 Granby St Norfolk VA 23510-1915

JACKSON, RAYMOND CARL, cytogeneticist; b. Medora, Ind., May 7, 1928; s. Thornton Comadore and Flossie Oliva (Booker) J.; m. T. June Snyder, Oct. 24, 1947; children: Jeffrey Wayne, Rebecca June. AB, Ind. U., 1952, AM, 1953; PhD, Purdue U., 1955. Instr. to asst. prof. U. N.Mex., Albuquerque, 1955-58; asst. prof. of Botany U. Kans., Lawrence, 1958-60, assoc. prof. of Botany, 1961-64, prof. of Botany, 1964-71, prof. and chmn. Botany, 1969-71; prof. and chmn. biol. scis. Tex. Tech U., Lubbock, 1971-78, Horn prof. of Biol. Scis., 1990—. Chmn. interdepartmental PhD Program in Genetics, U. Kans., chmn. dept. Botany, U. Kans., 1969-71; speaker and presenter in field. Contbr. numerous articles to profl. jours. Staff sgt. USAF, 1946-49. Mem. Genetics Soc. Am., Genetics Soc. of Can., Soc. for the Study of Evolution, Botanical Soc. of Am. (BSA Merit award 1992), Am. Soc. Plant Taxonomists, Internat. Orgn. of Plant Biosystematists, Delta Phi Alpha, Sigma Xi, Phi Sigma. Republican. Achievements include research in pairing control genes and their comparative effects at the diploid and polyploid levels; genetics, cytogenetics, and gametic selection in Haplopappus gracilis, cytogenetics of diploid Triticum species. Home: 7922A Aberdeen Ave Lubbock TX 79424-2808 Office: Dept Biol Scis Tex Tech Univ Lubbock TX 79409 Fax: 806-742-2963. E-mail: ray.c.jackson@ttu.edu.

JACKSON, REGGIE (REGINALD MARTINEZ JACKSON), former professional baseball player; b. Wyncote, Pa., May 18, 1946; s. Martinez Jackson; m. Juanita Jackson. Student, Ariz. State U. Outfielder Kansas City, then Oakland Athletics, 1967-75, Balt. Orioles, 1976, N.Y. Yankees, 1977-81; outfielder, designated hitter Calif. Angels, 1982-86, Oakland Athletics, 1987, advisor, 1988-93, N.Y. Yankees, 1993—. Mem. Am. League All-Star Team, 1969, 71-75, 77-82, 84; former commentator ABC Sports Author: (with Bill Libby) Reggie, 1975, (with Joel Cohen) Inside Hitting, 1975; appearances include (film), The Naked Gun, 1988. Inductee Baseball Hall of Fame, 1993; named Most Valuable Player Am. League, 1973, The Sporting News Major League Player of Year, 1973; Named to The Sporting News Am. League All-Star Team, 1969, 73, 75, 76, 80. Office: care Matt Merola 185 E 85th St Apt 18G New York NY 10028-2146 also: care NY Yankees Yankee Stadium 161st St and River Ave Bronx NY 10451

JACKSON, REGINALD SHERMAN, JR., lawyer, educator; b. Oct. 8, 1946; s. Reginald Sherman and Frances (Holland) J.; m. Joanne Marie Warren, Aug. 31, 1968; children: Reginald Sherman III, Michael W., Adam H. BA, Ohio State U., 1968, JD, 1971. Bar: Ohio 1971, U.S. Supreme Ct. 1976; cert. civil trial advocate Nat. Bd. Trial Advocacy. Mem. Fuller, Henry, Hodge Snyder, Toledo, 1971-76; asst. U.S. atty. no. dist. Ohio U.S. Dept. Justice, 1976-78; ptnr. Connelly, Jackson & Collier, Toledo, 1978—. Adj. prof. trial practice U. Toledo Coll. Law, 1976-89. Fellow Am. Bar Found., Ohio State Bar Found. (trustee 1998—), Toledo Bar Found. (pres. 1993-98); mem. ABA (ho. of dels. 1996-99, 2001—, exec. com. nat. caucus state bars, litig. sect.), Am. Bd. Trial Advocates, Ohio State Bar Assn. (pres. 2000-01), Toledo Bar Assn. (pres. 1989-90), Toledo Golf Hall of Fame (founder), Toledo Country Club (trustee 1981-93, pres. 1991-93), Rotary (trustee 1994-96, 1st v.p.). Home: 2907 River Rd Maumee OH 43537-3740 Office: Connelly Jackson & Collier 405 Madison Ave Ste 1600 Toledo OH 43604-1226 E-mail: rjackson@gcjc-law.com.

JACKSON, RENÉE BERNADETTE, English language educator; b. York, Pa., July 20, 1954; d. William Brice and Helen Elizabeth (Webb) J.; 1 child, Karla Janine. BA in Comm., Pa. State Harrisburg, Middletown, 1995, MA in Humanities, 1997; postgrad., Temple U., 1997—. Newsroom intern, journalist Harrisburg Patriot News, 1995; newsroom intern, corr. York (Pa.) Daily Record, 1995-96; rsch. asst. for coord. Master's Humanities Program Pa. State Harrisburg, Middletown, 1995-97; adj. prof. Harrisburg Area C.C., 1997; tchg. asst. African-Am. studies Temple U., Phila., 1997, rsch. asst. broadcasting, telecom. and mass media dept., 1998; adj. English prof. C.C. of Phila., 1999—; GMAT essay evaluator Educl. Testing Svc., Princeton, N.J., 1998—. Mem. AAUW, Assn. for Edn. in Journalism and Mass Comm., Am. Journalism Historians Assn., Nat. Assn. Black Journalists, Assn. for the Study of Afro-Am. Life and History, Assn. Black Women Historians, Soc. Profl. Journalists, Middle-Atlantic Popular Culture Conf. (exec. bd. mem., mem. planning com.). Avocations: historical writing projects, composing piano music, travel. Home: 107 Shelbourne Dr York PA 17403-3821

JACKSON, RENEE LEONE, lawyer; b. Winter Park, Fla., Sept. 26, 1966; m. J. David Jackson, Dec. 10, 1994; stepchildren: Ian, Kelsey; 1 child, Jalen. AA, Bethany Lutheran Coll., 1986; BS with high honors, U. Fla., 1988; JD magna cum laude, U. Minn. Law Sch., 1991. Lawyer Dorsey & Whitney, Mpls., 1991-93, Larkin, Hoffman, Daly & Lindgren, Bloomington, Minn., 1993—2001, Fulbright & Jaworski, Mpls., 2001—. Bd. dirs. Bloomington Cmty. Found., 1996—. Recipient Order of the Coif. Mem. ABA. Lutheran. Office: Fulbright & Jaworski LLP Ste 4850 225 S 6th St Minneapolis MN 55402

JACKSON, RHONDA, telecommunications professional, poet; b. N.Y.C. d. William Aaron and Emmeline Jackson; m. Ronald Anthony Nurse. AAS, Berkeley Coll., 1995; BA, NYU, 1998. Telecom. tech. assoc. Bell Atlantic, N.Y.C., 1980—; pres. Poetress Music, Fresh Meadows, N.Y., 1997—. Exec. dir. Excelsior Multicultural Inst., St. Albans, N.Y., 1997—; amb. People to People, Spokane, Wash., 2000—. Author: The Best Poems of 1997, 1997 (Editors Choice award 1997), Daybreak on the Land, 1997 (Editors Choice award 1997), The Line, 1998, Quiet Moments, 1999. Big sister Big Bros., Big Sisters, N.Y.C., 1997; bd. mem. Internat. Ambs., Raleigh, N.C., 1999; events coord. City Harvest, N.Y.C., 1999; tutor English and math. Literacy Ptnrs., N.Y.C., 2000; sec.-gen. United Cultural Conv., 2001; pres. Ophelia DeVore Alumni Performing Co., 2001; del. Nat. Writers Assn., 2001. Recipient Outstanding Achievement in Poetry, Famous Poets Soc., Ashland, Oreg., 1999, Pres. award for lit. excellence Nat. Authors Registry, Ohio, 2000, Diamond Homer trophy, 1999, Internat. Peace prize United Cultural Conv., 2002; named Poet of Yr., Famous Poets Soc., Ashland, 2000; inductee Internat. Poetry Hall of Fame, Internat. Soc. Poets, Owings Mills, Md., 1998; honored as one of 500 Living Legends in the World, 2002. Mem. NARAS, Nat. Writers Union, Assn. for Telecom. Execs., Songwriters Guild Am., Nat. Acad. Am. Poets, Internat. Biog. Assn. (life patron 2001). Home: PO Box 650136 Fresh Meadows NY 11365

JACKSON, RICHARD JOSEPH, epidemiologist, public health physician, educator; b. Newark, Oct. 23, 1945; s. Robert Joseph Jackson and Dorothy C. (Devine) Connolly; m. Joan M. Guilford, June 21, 1975; children: Brendan, Devin, Galen. AB in Biology, St. Peter's Coll., Jersey City, 1969; M in Med. Sci., Rutgers Med. Sch., 1971; MD, U. Calif. San Francisco, San Francisco, 1973; MPH in Epidemiology, U. Calif. Berkeley, Berkeley, 1979. Diplomate Am. Bd. Pediatrics, Am. Bd. Preventive Medicine; lic. physician, Calif. Intern, resident U. Calif., San Francisco, 1973-74, 77-78, resident San Francisco Gen. Hosp., 1974-75; officer Epidemic Intelligence Svc. U.S. Pub. Health Svc., Albany, N.Y., 1975-77; spl. epidemiologist World Health Orgn., Bihar State, India, 1976; med. officer Epidemiol. Studies Sect. Calif. State Dept. Health Svcs., Berkeley, 1979-88, acting chief Office Environ. Health Hazard Aassessment Sacramento, 1988-90, chief hazard identification and risk assessment br. Berkeley, 1990-91; chief hazard identification and risk assessment br. office environ. health hazard assessment Calif. EPA, Berkeley, 1991-92; chief divsn. communicable disease control Calif. State Dept. Health Svcs., 1992-94; dir. Nat. Ctr. Environ. Health, Ctrs. Disease Control and Prevention, Atlanta, 1994—. Adj. lectr. U. Calif. San Francisco, 1980—, asst. clin. prof., 1986—; adj. prof. Emory U. Rollins Sch. Pub. Health, 1998—. Lt. comdr. USPHS, 1975-77. Office: Nat Ctr Environ Health Ctrs Disease Control (F-29) 4770 Buford Hwy Atlanta GA 30341-3724 E-mail: RJJackson@cdc.gov.

JACKSON, RICHARD MONTGOMERY, former airline executive; b. Jacksonville, Fla., Dec. 9, 1920; s. William Kenneth and Katharine (Mitchell) J.; m. Martha Eustis Turner, Sept. 12, 1942; children: Richard Montgomery, Susanne (Mrs. Jeffrey Miller), William Mitchell. B.Sc., Harvard, 1942. With Am. Airlines, Inc., 1945-58; asso. L.S. Rockefeller, 1958-60; with Seaboard World Airlines, Inc., Jamaica, N.Y., 1960-80, pres., chmn. bd., 1960-80; chmn. exec. com. Flying Tiger Line, Jamaica, N.Y., 1980-81. Bd. govs., chmn. The Internat. Air Cargo Assn. Trustee Village of Lloyd Harbor, N.Y., 1960-68; pres. Lloyd Harbor Sch. Bd., 1957-58; trustee, pres. African Wildlife Found.; bd. govs. Huntington (N.Y.) Hosp., 1960-74. Lt. cmmdr. USNR, WWII. Mem.: Piping Rock (Locust Valley, N.Y.); Jupiter Island (Hobe Sound, Fla.); Wings (N.Y.C.); Cold Spring Harbor Beach Club (N.Y.). Home: 273 Southdown Rd Lloyd Harbor Huntington NY 11743

JACKSON, RICHARD PERRY, secondary school educator; b. Chgo., Sept. 7, 1950; s. Charles and Genevieve Jackson. BA, Midland Coll., 1974; MA, Chgo. State U., 1999. Basketball and track coach Emerson Sch. Dist. 152, 1974—79; phys. edn. instr. Harvey Sch. Dist. 152, 1974—97; varisty football and basketball coach Thornton High Sch., 1979—83; site supr. and program dir. Holmes Elem. Sch., 1993—95; pks. dept. chairperson of phys. edn. Sch. Dist 147, 2000—; adminstrv. asst. Rosa L. Park, 2001—, chair dept. phys. edn. Mem.: Tri County Official Assn., South Suburban Officals Assoc., Ctrl. Officals Assoc., Met. Officals Assoc., Am. Fed. Police, Fraternal Order of Police. Avocations: stepping, swimming, jogging, sports, music. Office: Rosa Parks Mid Sch 14700 Robey Ave Harvey IL 60426-1526

JACKSON, ROBBI JO, agricultural products company executive, lawyer; b. Nampa, Idaho, Apr. 12, 1959; d. William R. Jackson and Marilyn K. Samp Jackson Nunez. BS in Fin., U. Colo., Boulder and Denver, 1981; JD, U. Denver, 1987, LLM in Taxation, 1990. Bar: Colo. Asst. office mgr. Jerome Karsh & Co., Denver, 1982; office mgr. Almirall & Assocs., Englewood, Colo., 1983-84; assoc. Moye, Giles, O'Keefe, Vermeire & Gorrell, Denver, 1989-90, Holme Roberts & Owen, Denver, 1990-92; in-house gen. counsel Cmty. Corrections Svcs., Denver, 1992-96; CEO Enviro Cons. Svc., LLC, Lakewood, Colo., 1996—. Mem. staff Adminstrv. Law Rev., Denver, 1985, editor, 1985, mng. editor, 1986-87; co-author course of study materials; presenter in field. Mem. fin. com. Mile-High chpt. ARC, Denver, 1990-92; food delivery person Vols. of Am., Meals-on-Wheels, Denver, 1990-92. Recipient scholarships. Mem.: ABA, Colo. Bar Assn. (chmn. ethics com. 2003—). Republican. Avocations: running marathons and other races, biking, hiking, swimming, piano and organ playing.

JACKSON, ROBERT HOWARD, food company executive, scientist; b. Pitts., Jan. 3, 1932; s. Robert and Anna J.; m. Betty Jean Jackson, June 15, 1957; 1 child, Jay Michael. BS, Penn. State Univ., 1953, MS, 1955; PhD, Mich. State Univ., 1959. Asst. prof. Univ. Mass., Amherst, 1955-57; group leader R.J. Reynolds Industries, Winston-Salem, N.C., 1961-64; tech. dir. Lehigh Valley Dairies, Allentown, Pa., 1964-68; v.p. ops. Marriott Corp., Washington, 1968-79; pres.,COO Marshall Foods, Inc., Marshall, Minn., 1979-82; pres., CEO Nutrisearch Co., Cin., 1982-85; CEO Bioproducts Internat., Inc., Sarasota, Fla., 1985—. Bd. dirs. IDEP, LLC, Chgo., JJ Group, Inc., Chgo.; mem. adv. bd. Einstein Medical, Inc., LaJolla, Calif., 1995-96; dir. bus. devel. Quest Internat. (Unilever), Sydney, Australia, 1991-94. Contbr. articles to profl. jours. With U.S. Army, 1959-61. Mem. Inst. of Food Tech., Soc. Sigma Xi, Food Industry Assocs., Am. Men of Sci. Republican. Episcopalian. Avocations: physical fitness, golf, fishing, bass violinist. E-mail: jubilance@worldnet.att.net.

JACKSON, ROBERT KEITH, manufacturing company executive; b. South Bend, Ind., Apr. 20, 1943; s. Orval Russell and Dorothy Alice (Gailey) J.; m. Cheryl Dee Bronkhorst, Nov. 6, 1965; children: Jennifer Lynn, Stephen Robert. BS, Western Mich. U., 1966; MBA, Vanderbilt U., 1987. Vocat. tchr. Warren (Mich.) Consol. Schs., 1967-68; mfg. engr. Eaton Corp., Kalamazoo, 1968-77, gen. supt., 1977, Kings Mountain, N.C., 1977-80; plant mgr. Eaton Ltd., Manchester, Eng., 1980-84, Eaton Corp., Shelbyville, Tenn., 1984-91, mgr. mfg. and quality assurance Truck Components Ops. Kalamazoo, 1991-93, plant mgr. Humboldt, Tenn., 1993-96, ops. specialist, 1996-97; gen. mgr. Eaton Truck and Bus. Components (Shanghai) Co., Ltd., 1997—2001. Mem. adv. coun. indsl. studies Mid. Tenn. State U., Murfreesboro, 1985-91, Sch. Bus., 1990-91; mem. machine tool tech. adv. com. Jackson (Tenn.) State C.C., 1994-96; mem. devel. com. U. Tenn. at Martin, mem. mech. engring. adv. bd., 1995-96. Trustee Eaton Pub. Policy Assn., Cleve., 1985-89. Mem. Tenn. Assn. Bus. (bd. dirs. 1989-91), Rotary, Elks, KC. Republican. Roman Catholic. Home: 640 Dogwood Dr Monteagle TN 37356-2010 Office: Wai Gao Qiao Free Trd Zone 388 Ai Du Rd Pu Dong Shanghai 200131 China

JACKSON, ROBERT WILLIAM, utility company executive, retired; b. Beaumont, Tex., June 22, 1930; s. Robert and Elizabeth (Watler) J.; m. Theta Ann Watt, Aug. 14, 1959; 1 child, Robert W. Jr. BBA, U. Tex.; MBA, U. Ill. With Gulf States Utilities Co., Beaumont, Tex., 1955-79, sec., chief fin. officer, 1972-74, sec., treas., chief fin. officer, 1974-75, v.p. fin., chief fin. officer, sec., 1975-79, Cen. Ill. Pub. Svc. Co., Springfield, 1979-80, sr. v.p. fin., chief fin. officer, corp. sec., 1980-95, also bd. dirs.; pres., chief exec. officer CIPSCO Investment Co., Springfield, 1990-95, also bd. dirs.; sr. v.p. CIPSCO Inc., Springfield, 1990, also bd. dirs.; ret., 1995. Bd. dirs. 1st Bank of Ill. Co., Springfield, 1st Nat. Bank Springfield, Sangamon State U. Found.; bd. govs. Econs. Am. Mem. bus. adv. coun. U. Ill.; bd. dirs. Springfield Symphony Orch., United Way of Sangamon County; adv. bd. St. John's Hosp., Springfield. Served with U.S. Army, 1953-55. Mem. Am. Soc. Corp. Secs., Fin. Execs. Inst., Edison Electric Inst. (fin. exec. com.). Methodist.

JACKSON, RONALD L., II, communications educator; b. Cin., Aug. 4, 1970; s. Ronald Lee, Sr. and Sharon Marie (Prather) J.; m. Bereatha Ellynne Gould, June 2, 1995; children: Niyah S., Niles. BA, U. Cin., 1991, MA, 1993; PhD, Howard U., 1996, NYU, 2001. Guest lectr. U. Ga., 1997, Howard U., 1998, Rutgers, 1998, Truman State U., 1999, Wake Forest U., 2000, U. Tex., 2002, U. Ala., 2002. Author: Negotiation of Cultural Identity, 1999, Think About It: The question book for those curious about race and self-discovery, 2000, (with Michael Hecht and Sidney Ribeau) African American Communications, 2003, Understanding African American Rhetoric, 2003; contbr. articles to profl. jours. Recipient All Am. Scholar award, 1995. Mem. Nat. Comm. Assn. (chmn. black caucus 1999, Black Caucus Pioneering Leader award 2000), Ea. Comm. Assn. (chmn. internat. divsn. 1999, chmn. voices of diversity divsn. 2000, Everett Lee Hunt award for excellence in scholarship 2000, Franklyn S. Haiman award for disting. scholarship in freedom of expression, 2001), Nat. Assn. African Ams., Pa. Black Conf. Highter Edn., Omega Psi Phi (chpt. founder) Avocations: tennis, table tennis, racquetball, poetry writing, travel. Office: Pa State U 234 Sparks Bldg University Park PA 16802-5201 E-mail: rlj6@psu.edu.

JACKSON, ROSA M. educator; b. Columbia, S.C., Dec. 8, 1943; d. Alvin Jr. and Rosa Lee (Reese) Oree; m. Olin D. Jackson, June 14, 1969; children: Zandra Lalita, Delin Jawaski. BA, Benedict Coll., 1966; MEd, S.C. State U., Orangeburg, 1981. Cert. tchr. Tchr. 1st grade Richmond County Bd. Edn., Augusta, Ga.; tchr. 2nd grade McDuffie County Bd. Edn., Thomson, Ga.; tchr. 5th grade Lancaster County Bd. Edn., Kershaw; tchr. 2nd grade Richmond County Bd. Edn., Augusta, Ga. Mem. Richmond County Schs. Leadership Team. Sci. tchr. in residence. Mem. GAE, RCAE, NEA, Nat. Sci. Tchrs Assn., Ga. Sci. Tchrs. Assn., GA Staff Devel. Coun., Assn. for Multicultural Sci. Edn. Home: 3003 Bramble Wood Trl Augusta GA 30909-4105

JACKSON, ROY, chemical engineering educator; b. Manchester, Eng., Oct. 6, 1931; married 1957; 2 children. BA, Cambridge U., 1954, MA, 1958; DSc chem. engr., U. Edinburgh, 1968. Lectr. chem. engr. U. Edinburgh, 1961-64, reader, 1964-68; prof. Rice U., 1968-77, U. Houston, 1977-82; prof. chem. engr.

Princeton U., 1982-98, emeritus prof., 1998—. Fellow Royal Soc. London; mem. Am. Inst Chem. Engrs. Office: Princeton U Dept Chem Engring Princeton NJ 08544-0001 E-mail: rjackson@always-online.com.

JACKSON, SAMUEL L. actor; b. Washington, Dec. 21, 1948; m. LaTanya Richardson; 1 child, Zoe. Performances include: (TV series) Movin' On, 1972, Ghostwriter, 1992; (TV movies) The Trial of the Moke, 1978, Uncle Tom's Cabin, 1987, Common Ground, 1990, Dead and Alive: The Race for Gus Farace, 1991, Simple Justice, 1993, Assault at West Point, 1994, Against the Wall, 1994; (films) Together for Days, 1972, Ragtime, 1981, Eddie Murphy Raw, 1987, Coming to America, 1988, School Daze, 1988, (voiceover) Mystery Train, 1989, Do The Right Thing, 1989, Sea of Love, 1989, A Shock to the System, 1990, Def by Temptation, 1990, Betsy's Wedding, 1990, Mo' Better Blues, 1990, The Exorcist III, 1990, Goodfellas, 1990, Return of Superfly, 1990, Jungle Fever, 1991 (Best Actor award Cannes International Film Festival), Strictly Business, 1991, Juice, 1992, White Sands, 1992, Patriot Games, 1992, Johnny Suede, 1992, Jumpin' at the Boneyard, 1992, Fathers and Sons, 1992, National Lampoon's Loaded Weapon 1, 1993, Amos & Andrew, 1993, Menace II Society, 1993, Jurassic Park, 1993, True Romance, 1993, Hail Caesar, 1994, Fresh, 1994, Hail Caesar, 1994, The New Age, 1994, Pulp Fiction, 1994, Losing Isiah, 1995, Kiss of Death, 1995, Fluke, 1995, Die Hard With a Vengeance, 1995, The Great White Hype, 1996, Trees Lounge, 1996, The Search for One Eye Jimmy, 1996, A Time to Kill, 1996, The Long Kiss Goodnight, 1996, 187, 1997, Jackie Brown, 1997, Hard Eight, 1997, Eve's Bayou, 1997, Sphere, 1998, Out of Sight, 1998, The Negotiator, 1998, Rules of Engagement, 1999, Mefisto in Onyx, 1999, Star Wars Episode I: The Phantom Menace, 1999, Deep Blue Sea, 1999, Shaft, 2000, Unbreakable, 2000, Changing Lanes, 2002, Star Wars: Episode II - Attack of the Clones, 2002, XXX, 2002, Basic, 2003, S.W.A.T., 2003.*

JACKSON, SHARON SUE, music educator; b. Robinson, Ill., Nov. 26, 1962; d. Myrl William and Ellen Marie (Wright) Jackson. BS in music edn., Ind. State U., 1984, MS in mus. edn., 1986. Adj. percussion instr. Vincennes U., 1986—88; adj. percussion techniques instr. St. Mary of the Woods Coll., 1988; adj. percussion instr. Lincoln Trail Coll., Robinson, Ill., 1988—90; asst. prof. of music/asst. dir. of bands Vincennes U., 1988—89, asst. prof. of music/dir. of bands, 1989—94; vis. asst. prof. of music Ind. State U., 1990—; assoc. prof. of music/dir. of bands Vincennes U., 1994—. Percussion instr./staff mem. Vincennes-Lincoln H.S., Ind., South Knox H.S., Vincennes, Ind.; percussionist Philharmonia A Vent (profl. wind ensemble), Terre Haute, Ind., Vincennes U. Faculty Jazz Ensemble, Vincennes, Ind., Terre Haute Symphony Orch., Ind.; percussion instr./staff mem. Fountain Ctrl. H.S., Veedersburg, Ind.; instr./staff mem. Gt. Lakes Music Camp. Performer/clinician (2002 mtna national convention) George Crumb's Macrocosmos III - Music for a Summer Evening. Mem. Caribbean Consort Steel Drum Band, Terre Haute, Ind. Recipient Exemplary Svc. Award, Vincennes U., 2002, Five Yr. Svc. Award, Gt. Lakes Music Camp, 1995. Mem.: North Am. Steel Band Assn., Am. Fedn. of Musicians, Women Band Directors Internat., Ind. Bandmasters Assn., Percussive Arts Soc. (Ind. chpt. past sec.-treas. 2002—), Ind. Music Educators Assn., Music Educators Nat. Conf. (vu collegiate menc chpt. founder and faculty advisor), Knox County Music Directors Assn. (life), Pi Kappa Lambda, Sigma Alpha Iota (life). Republican. Methodist. Avocations: travel, sports. Office: Vincennes University 1002 N First St Vincennes IN 47591 Office Fax: 812-888-5531. E-mail: sjackson@indian.vinu.edu.

JACKSON, SHIRLEY ANN, academic administrator, physicist; b. Washington DC; d. George Hiter and Beatrice (Cosby) J.; m. Morris A. Washington; 1 son, Alan. B.S. in Physics, M.I.T., 1968, Ph.D., 1973; DSc (hon.) Bloomfield Coll., 1991, Fairleigh Dickinson U., 1993, hon. degree Dr Laws, Villanova, PA, 1996; Research asso. Fermi Nat. Accelerator Lab., Batavia, Ill., 1973-74, 75-76; vis. scientist European Orgn. for Nuclear Research, Geneva, 1974-75; mem. tech. staff AT&T Bell Labs., Murray Hill, N.J., 1976-91; visitor Stanford Linear Accelerator Center, 1976, Aspen Ctr. for Physics, 1976, 77; prof. physics Rutgers U., Piscataway, NJ, 1991-95; chairperson Nuclear Reg. Commn., 1995-99, U.S. rep to Gen. Conference of Internat. Atomic Energy, 1995-99; pres. Rensselaer Poly. Inst., 1999-; mem. com. edn. and employment women in sci. and engring. Nat. Rsch. Coun., 1980—; cons. NSF, 1977, Nat. Rsch. Coun., 1977-1991; dir. N.J. Resources Corp., Pub. Service Enterprise Group, PSE&G. Mem. ednl. council M.I.T., 1976-80, Internat. Nuclear Regulators Assn., 1997-99, trustee, 1975-85, 1987—; trustee Lincoln U. (Pa.), 1980—, Rutgers U., 1986—; mem. N.J. Commn. on Sci. and Tech.; mem. Com. Status of Women in Physics, 1986-88. Recipient Candace award Nat. Coalition 100 Black Women, Salute to Policy Makers award Exec. Women of N.J., 1986, Black Achievers in Industry award Harlem YMCA, 1986, N.J. Gov.'s award, 1993; Martin Marietta Corp. scholar, 1964-68; Prince Hall Grand Masons scholar, 1964-68; NSF trainee, 1968-71; Ford Found. fellow, 1971-73; grantee, 1974-75; Martin Marietta Corp. grad. fellow, 1972-73; mem. Assn. for Advancement of Science, (com. on sci., freedom and responsibility), Fellow, Am. Phys. Soc. (mem. com. on status of women in physics 1986—); Fellow, Am. Acad. Arts & Sci, mem. N.Y. Acad. Scis., Nat. Inst. Sci., Nat. Soc. Black Physicists (pres. 1979—), MIT Alumni Assn. (v.p. 1986—), Sigma Xi, Delta Sigma Theta. Editorial adv. bd. Jour. Sci. Tech. and Human Values, 1982— ; contbr. numerous articles to physics jours. Office: 110 8th St Troy NY 12180-3590*

JACKSON, SHIRLEY ANN, sociology educator; b. Buffalo, N.Y. d. Joseph Robert Jackson and Shirley Ann Brown. BA, Wayne State U., 1984; MA, U. Calif., Santa Barbara, 1990, PhD, 2000. Asst. prof. ethnic studies Bowling Green (Ohio) State U., 1996—98; asst. prof. sociology So. Conn. State U., New Haven, 1998—2003, assoc. prof. sociology, 2003—. Chair dept. of sociology So. Conn. State U., New Haven, 2001—. Author: A New Perspective: An Introduction to Sociology, 2002. Named Minority Scholar-in-Residence, Wellesley Coll., 1995—96; recipient Summer fellowship for tchg. history of the So. Civil Rights Movement, Harvard U., NEH, 1997, Summer Multicultural Tchg. fellowship, Tufts U., 1996, African Am. ABD Summer fellowship, U. of Ky., 1995, Grad. Rsch. Mentorship Program fellowship, U. of Calif., Santa Barbara, 1991—92. Mem.: New Eng. Sociol. Assn. (pres. 2003—), Sociologists for Women in Soc., Soc. for the Study of Social Problems, Assn. of Black Sociologists, Am. Sociol. Assn. (chair sect. on racial and ethnic minorities 2002—03). Achievements include research in race and ethnicity, social movements, gender, and urban/community. Office: So Conn State U 501 Crescent St New Haven CT 06515 Office Fax: 203-392-7087. E-mail: jacksons1@southernct.edu.

JACKSON, STANLEY EDWARD, retired special education educator; b. Washington, Sept. 3, 1918; s. Eugene Edward and Inez Christine (Booth) Jackson. BS, Miner Tchrs. Coll., Washington, 1939; MA, Columbia U., 1947, profl. diploma, 1948, EdD, 1958; postgrad., Johns Hopkins U., Peabody Inst. Elem. tchr. DC Pub. Schs., 1940-58, elem. sch. prin., 1958-66, dir. spl. edn., 1966-72; gov.-at-large Coun. Exceptional Children, Reston, Va., 1971-72, asst. exec. dir., membership, 1972-82; ret., 1982. Lectr. Cath. U., Washington, 1965—66, asst. prof. edn., 1967; instr. DC Tchrs. Coll., 1971—72, initiator Tchr. Aide Program Spl. Edn. Classes, 1968; founder Juvenile Decency Corps Uplift House, 1964; co-planner Mamie D. Lee Sch. Mentally Retarded, 1968. Author: School Organization for the Mentally Retarded, 1973, Educational Strategies and Services for Exceptional Children, 1976. Pres. Area K Bd. Commrs. Youth Coun., Washington, 1959—65; founder UPLIFT Cmty. House, Washington, 1963, pres. Chpt. 49, 1962—64, 1st pres. Fedn. 524, 1965—66; bd. dirs. Found. Exceptional Children, 1978. With U.S. Army, 1941—45, WWII. Decorated 4 Battles Stars; named Stanley E. Jackson Scholarship in his honor, Peabody Pres., Johns Hopkins U., 1988, Found. for Exceptional Children, 1980, Philanthropic Honor Roll, George Washington U., 1949—2001; recipient Yes I Care award, Found. for Exceptional Children, 1992, Plaque for Outstanding Svc., Commr. Coun., Washington, 1963, Outstanding Ret. Tchr. award, Jr. Citizens Corps, 1979, Stanley E. Jackson Spl. Edn. award established in his honor, Bd. Edn. D.C. Pub. Schs., 1973, Cert. of Appreciation, Nat. Fedn. Blind, 2001. Mem.: NAACP, AAUP, NEA, Dept. Elem. Sch. Prins., Coun. Exceptional Children, DC Congress Parents and Tchrs., Johns Hopkins Assoc. Program, Urban Legaue, AMVETS, Phi Delta Kappa, Kappa Delta Pi. Avocations: music, numismatics, writing, philanthropy. Home: Apt 703 One E University Pky Baltimore MD 21218

JACKSON, STEPHEN ERIC, public speaker, life strategist; b. Seymour, Ind., July 9, 1946; s. Ralph Marshall Jackson and Dolly Katherine (Britt) Tudor; m. Cheryl Jane Hallman, June 23, 1967 (div. 1985); children: Kirstina Leigh, Brandi Annette; m. Margaret Ann Skelton, Oct. 17, 1986 (div. 1989); m. Candy Sandler Clinard, Sept. 30, 1995. BA in Sociology, N. Tex. State U., 1976; grad., Tex. Law Enforcement Inst., 1991; MPA, U. North Tex., 1993. Lic. mediator, 1996. Police officer, sgt. Denton (Tex.) Police Dept., 1970-81; customer svc. mgr. Amerace Corp., Denton, 1981-83; dir. police and traffic svcs. U. North Tex., Denton, 1983-98; ptnr. Pathways Ednl. Corp., Irving, Tex., 1998—2001; pres. Pathways Life Mgmt. Seminars, Irving, 1999-2001; founder, pres. Life Strategies Inst. Tex., Ft. Worth, 2001—. Adj. faculty applied econs. U. North Tex., 2000—; public speaker, life mgmt. coord, v.p. Denton County Chiefs of Police, 1986-94. Contbr. articles to profl. jours. Precinct chmn. Denton County Rep. Party, 1982-85; mem. Pub. Transp. Task Force, Denton, 1989; chmn. steering com. Leadership Denton, 1990-95, 95-97, Leadership Denton Alumni Assn., 1991—; mem. parking com. Main St. Denton, Inter-Assn. Task Force on Alcohol and Other Substance Abuse Issues, 1995-97, local assoc. Nat. Coalition Bldg. Inst., 1990—; del./panelist White House Conf. on Hate Crimes, 1997. Mem. Internat. Assn. Campus Law Enforcement Adminstrs. (v.p. 1995-96, pres. elect 1996-97, pres. 1997-98), Tex.-N.Mex. Assn. Coll. and Univ. Police Depts. (Pres.'s award 1985, treas. 1993-96, Adminstr. of Yr. 1993), Internat. Assn. Chiefs of Police. Avocations: golf, tennis. Office: Life Strategies Inst Tex Ste 283 6387B Camp Bowie Fort Worth TX 76116

JACKSON, STEVEN DONALD, English educator; b. Columbus, Ohio, Sept. 2, 1949; s. Alfred Donald and Ruth Eleanor (Junk) J. BS, Ohio State U., 1971, MA, 1982. Staff libr. Ohio State U., Columbus, 1969-70; tchr. dept. chair Madison Plains Schs., London, Ohio, 1971—. Bd. trustees Madison Plains Scholarship Found., 1986—, Centry Village Hist. Site, 1996—. Mem. Nat. Coun. Tchrs. English, Ohio Edn. Assn., Madison Plains Edn. Assn., Ohio State Alumni Assn. Republican. Methodist. Avocations: gardening, genealogy, naval history. Home: 4283 Kelnor Dr Grove City OH 43123-2942

JACKSON, SUSANNE LEORA, retired creative placement firm executive; b. Rochester, N.Y., June 9, 1934; d. Daniel T. and Gertrude (Grantham) Sheriff; m. David K. Jackson, Mar. 12, 1954; children: Jonnie Sheehan, Jaynette Kettler. Student, Santa Fe Sch. Art, 1952-53, Midwestern U., 1953-55. Supr. ANR Prodn. Co., Houston, 1976-83; v.p. Robinhawk Drafting & Design, Houston, 1983-85; pres., CEO, chmn. bd. Houston Creative Connections, 1985-99; ret., 2000. Advt. & mktg. dir. Geotech Assn., Houston, 1989-90; past pres. Am. Inst. Design & Drafting, 1984-86; CEO NMASS Comm., 1998, Full Svc. Advt. Agy., 1996-99, Houston Tech. Connections, 1996-99, Outsource and Tech. Placement, 1996-99, Houston Creative Svcs., 1998-99, MicroTeach; bd. dirs. HyperDynamics. Design cons.: (mag.) Urbane, 1989-94. Mem. Mus. Fine Arts, Houston, 1988—2002, Greater Houston Partnership, 1989—98; mem. com. for advt. U. Houston-Math and Sci. Dept., 1999—; mem. nat. steering com. Women's Input Com., Houston Women Bus. Coun., 1999; bd. dirs. Literacy Advance, 1993—, pres. bd., 1999; bd. dirs. Women's Input Com., Houston Women Bus. Coun. Recipient Nat. Multimedia award Am. Advt. Fedn., 1999, also regional award. Mem. NAFE, Houston Advt. Fedn. (Silver and Merit awards 1989, Merit award 1990, Bronze award 1991, 2 Bronze awards 1992, 2 Gold and 4 Merit awards 1992, Gold and Bronze awards 1995, 3 Addys for Interactive 1999, 3 Gold Addys for Multimedia, Nat. Addy award 1999, Houston's Top Women Bus. Owners award 1995, 96, 97, 98, Top Tex. Bus. Women Owner award 1997), Greater Heights C. of C. (bd. dirs. 1994—, vice-chmn. 1996), Galleria C. of C., Rotary (treas. 1992, pres.-elect 1993, pres. 1994), U.S. C. of C. (Blue Chip Enterprise award 1993), Heights C. of C. (chairwoman Women in Action 1997); finalist Ernst & Young Entrepreneur of the Yr., 1998. Republican. Episcopalian. Avocations: oil painting, fishing, cooking. Studio: Las Animas Studio 4501 Brookwoods Houston TX 77092

JACKSON, THEODORE MARSHALL, retired oil company executive; b. Beaumont, Tex., Oct. 18, 1928; s. Robert and Mary Louise (Watler) J.; m. Maria Pierracou-Dobrowolska Countess de Wernicki de Vladis la Goda, June 19, 1954; 1 child, Mark Andrew. BBA in Engring, U. Tex., Austin, 1951. V.p., sec.-treas. Purvin & Gertz, Inc., Dallas, 1955-71; v.p. treasury and strategic planning New Eng. Petroleum Corp., N.Y.C., 1971-75; v.p. fin. Crown Central Petroleum Corp., Balt., 1975-83, sr. v.p., chief fin. officer, 1984-91, also bd. dirs. Bd. dirs., treas. Bd. of Child Care; emeriti gov. Wesley Theol. Sem. Lt. USNR, 1952-55. Mem. Beta Gamma Sigma, Delta Tau Delta. Republican. Methodist. Home: 8 Wythe Ct Glen Arm MD 21057-9134 E-mail: tmjack8@comcast.net.

JACKSON, THOMAS FRANCIS, III, lawyer; b. Memphis, Oct. 21, 1940; s. Thomas Francis and Sarah Elizabeth (Farris) J.; children: Thomas Francis, Wythe Macrae Bogy. Grad., The Taft Sch.; BA, Rhodes Coll., 1962; LLB, George Washington U., 1967. Bar: Tenn. 1967, U.S. Supreme Ct. 1974. Law clk. to chief judge U.S. Dist. Ct. Western Dist. Tenn., 1967-68; with Armstrong, Allen PLLC, Memphis, 1968-72, Lawler, Humphreys PLLC, Memphis, 1972-83; pvt. practice Memphis, 1983—. Lt. USNR, 1962-67. Mem. ABA, Tenn. Bar Assn., Memphis Bar Assn. Episcopalian. Home: 232 S Highland St Memphis TN 38111-4540 Office: PO Box 111221 Memphis TN 38111-1221 Fax: 901-324-6997. E-mail: tfj@lawtenn.com.

JACKSON, THOMAS GENE, lawyer; b. N.Y.C., Mar. 9, 1949; s. Alan Clark and Clare Seena (Werther) J.; m. Beatrice Lafrance Korab, June 11, 1972; children: Sarah Ann, Alan Edward. AB magna cum laude in English, Dartmouth Coll., 1971; JD, U. Va., 1974. Bar: N.Y. 1975, U.S. Dist. Ct. (so. and ea. dists.) N.Y. 1975, U.S. Ct. Appeals (2d cir.) 1975, U.S. Ct. Appeals (5th cir.) 1978, U.S. Supreme Ct. 1978, U.S. Ct. Appeals (D.C. cir.) 1986. Editor The Rsch. Group, Charlottesville, Va., 1973-74; assoc. Phillips Nizer Benjamin Krim & Ballon LLP, N.Y.C., 1974-82; ptnr. Phillips Nizer LLP, N.Y.C., 1982—. Mem. fed. bar coun. com. 2d Cir. Cts., 1997-2000, chmn. subcom. on tech. in the cts., 1997-2000. Mem. Village of Irvington Cable TV Adv. Com., N.Y., 1979-91, 95—, chmn. franchise renewal com., 1991-95; sec. Village of Irvington Environ. Conservation Bd., 1983-87, chmn., 1987—; mem. Dartmouth Coll. Alumni Coun., 1986-89. Mem.: ABA (sect. antitrust law, mergers and acquisitions com.), Assn. Bar City N.Y. (antitrust and trade regulation com. 1988—92, mergers acquisitions and joint ventures subcom. 1991—92), Am. Arbitration Assn. (comml. tribunal 1986—, panel of arbitrators), Dartmouth Coll. Class Secs. Assn. (v.p. 1984—85, pres. 1985—86), Dartmouth Club Westchester (sec. 1984—87, pres. 1987—90), Dartmouth Coll. Club Officers Assn. (exec. com. 1988—91). Home: 32 Hamilton Rd Irvington NY 10533-2311 Office: Phillips Nizer LLP 666 5th Ave New York NY 10103-0084

JACKSON, THOMAS HUMPHREY, academic administrator, lawyer; b. Kalamazoo, June 20, 1950; s. William Humphrey and Louise Longstreth (Cone) Jackson; m. Bonnie Eileen Gelb; children: Richard, Steven. BA, Williams Coll., 1972; JD, Yale U., 1975. Bar: N.Y. 1976, Calif. 1979. Law clk. to judge U.S. Dist. Ct. N.Y., 1975—76; law clk. to justice U.S. Supreme Ct., Washington, 1976—77; asst. prof., assoc. prof. to prof. Stanford U. Law Sch., Calif., 1977—86; prof. Harvard U. Law Sch., Cambridge, Mass., 1986—88; dean Sch. Law, U. Va., Charlottesville, 1988—91, v.p., provost, 1991—93; pres. U. Rochester, NY, 1994—. Assoc. Heller, Ehrman, White & McAliffe, San Francisco, 1979—81, spl. counsel, 1981—86. Co-author: Secured Transactions, 1982, Secured Transactions, 3d edit., 2000, Bankruptcy, 1985, Bankruptcy, 3d edit., 2000; author: Logic and Limits of Bankruptcy Law, 1986; mem. editl. bd.: The Found. Press, Inc. Trustee George Eastman House. Office: University of Rochester 240 Wallis Hall Rochester NY 14627-0011

JACKSON, THOMAS O. real estate appraiser, urban planner; BA in Polit. Sci. with honors, U. South Fla., 1975; MA in Polit. Sci., Ohio State U., 1979; M in Regional Planning, U. N.C., 1984; PhD in Urban and Regional Sci., Tex. A&M U., 2000. Cert. gen. real estate appraiser, Tex., Fla. Planning dir. City of West Melbourne, Fla., 1978-80; cmty. assistance cons. Fla. Dept. Cmty. Affairs, Tallahassee, 1983-84; sr. rsch. assoc. Econ. Rsch. Svcs., Inc., Tallahassee, 1984-86; project mgr. BHR Planning Group, Inc., Jacksonville, Fla., 1986-87, sr. cons., devel. econ. group Reynolds, Smith and Hills, Inc., Jacksonville, 1987-92; sr. project mgr. Harland Bartholomew & Assocs., Inc., Jacksonville, 1992-93; pres. Planning Rsch. Svcs., Inc., Jacksonville, 1993-94; dir. fin. adv. svcs. Coopers & Lybrand LLP, Houston, 1994-98; sr. cons. Entrix, Inc., Houston, 1998-99; pres. Real Property Analytics, Inc., Bryan, Tex., 2000—. Lectr. Coll. Architecture Tex. A&M U., College Station, 1998-99, lectr. Coll. Bus., 2002—; expert witness, presenter in field. Contbr. articles to profl. jours. Dissertation Rsch. grantee NSF, 1999; Dissertation fellow Lincoln Inst. Land Policy, 1999. Mem. Am. Planning Assn. (bd. dirs. 1993-94, chair legis. com. 1993-94), Am. Real Estate Urban Econ. Assn., Am. Real Estate Soc., Counselors Real Estate (membership devel. com. 1997, edn. com. 1997, pub. policy com. 1997-99, ethics profl. practice com. 1998—), Appraisal Inst. (ethics counseling com. 1995-97, mem. task group 1999—), Appraisal Found. (mem. appraisal stds. bd. 2001—), Am. Inst. Cert. Planners, Urban Land Inst. (assoc., reviewer 1993), Houston Assn. Realtors, Omicron Delta Kappa, Phi Kappa Phi, Pi Sigma Alpha, Themis. Office: Real Property Analytics Inc 1904 Streamside Way Bryan TX 77807-2715 Fax: 979-779-2493. E-mail: tomjackson@real-analytics.com.

JACKSON, THOMAS PENFIELD, federal judge; b. Washington, Jan. 10, 1937; s. Thomas Searing and May Elizabeth (Jacobs) J. AB in Govt., Dartmouth Coll., 1958; LLB, Harvard U., 1964. Bar: D.C., Md., U.S. Supreme Ct. 1970. Assoc., ptnr. Jackson & Campbell, P.C., Washington, 1964-82; U.S. dist. judge U.S. Dist. Ct. D.C., Washington, 1982—. Vestryman All Saints' Episcopal Ch., Washington, 1969-75; trustee Gallaudet U., Washington, 1985-99, St. Marys Coll., Md., 2001—. Lt. (j.g.) USN, 1958-61. Fellow Am. Coll. Trial Lawyers; mem. ABA, Bar Assn. D.C. (pres. 1982-83), Rotary. Clubs: Chevy Chase, Metropolitan, Lawyers', Barristers. Republican. Office: US Dist Ct US Courthouse 3rd & Constitution Ave NW Washington DC 20001

JACKSON, VALERIE PASCUZZI, radiologist, educator; b. Oakland, Calif., Aug. 25, 1952; d. Chris A. Pascuzzi and Janice (Mayne) Pacuzzi; 1 child, Price Arthur III. AB, Ind. U., 1974, MD, 1978. Diplomate Am. Bd. Radiology. Intern, resident in diagnostic radiology Ind. U. Med. Ctr., 1978-82; from asst. prof. radiology to prof. radiology Ind. U. Sch. Medicine, Indpls., 1982-94, John A. Campbell prof. radiology, 1994—. Dir. residency program in radiology Ind. U. Sch. Medicine, 1994—2003, interim chair dept. radiology, 2003—; trustee Am. Bd. Radiology. Contbr. over 50 articles to profl. jours., chpts. to books. Fellow: Soc. Breast Imaging (pres. 1990—92), Am. Coll. Radiology (bd. chancellors, chair 3 coms., pres. 2002—03); mem.: AMA, Radiol. Soc. N.Am., Am. Roentgen Ray Soc., Am. Inst. Ultrasound in Medicine, Alpha Omega Alpha. Office: Indiana U Sch Med Dept Rad 550 N Univ Blvd Rm 0663 Indianapolis IN 46202-2859

JACKSON, W. BRUCE, ophthalmology educator, researcher; b. Peterborough, Ont., Can., May 2, 1943; s. William Herbert and Marjorie Powell (Robinson) J.; m. Mary Lou Sparrow, May 13, 1967; children: David, Julie Alicia. MD, U. Western Ont., 1967. Diplomate Am. Bd. Ophthalmology. Intern Royal Victoria Hosp., Montreal, Que., 1967-68, resident in ophthalmology, 1968-72; prof., chmn. dept. ophthalmology McGill U., Que., 1987-91; prof., chmn. dept. ophthalmology, dir Eye Inst. U. Ottawa, 1991—. Fellow Royal Coll. Physicians and Surgeons. Avocations: skiing, swimming, tennis, golf. Office: U Ottawa Eye Inst 501 Smyth Ottawa ON Canada K1H 8L6 E-mail: bjackson@ottawahospital.on.ca.

JACKSON, WANDA BRITTON, educator; b. Marshall, Tex., Jan. 21, 1954; d. Arthur Britton, Sr. and Nuthel (Sparks) Britton; children: Giles Lee, Henry Olden Jr. BS in Social Sci. Composite, Wiley Coll., 1975; MS in Edn., Tex. So. U., 1981. Cert. social sci. composite Tex. Edn. Agy., mid-mgmt. supt. Tex. Edn. Agy. Tchr. Houston Ind. Sch. Dist., 1975—. Instr. South Dist. Houston Ind. Sch. Dist., 1992—94, yearbook sponsor Evan E. Worthing H.S., 1995—, instr. Crispus Attucks Mid. Sch., 1991—92, instr. Albert L. Thomas Mid. Sch., 1975—91, 1994—95. Active MacGregor Place Civic Club; active voter registration Harris County. Recipient Outstanding Texan award in the field edn., Tex. Book Legis. Caucus, 1991. Mem.: NEA, Houston Tchrs. Assn., Tex. State Tchrs. Assn., Iota Phi Lambda (pres. Beta Pi chpt. 1991—95, 2nd v.p. Beta Pi chpt.). Baptist. Avocations: cooking, swimming, travel. Home: 5119 Stuyvesant Ln Houston TX 77021

JACKSON, WENDY S. LEWIS, social worker; b. Grand Rapids, Mich., May 9, 1965; d. Thomas James and Karen Susan (Kinard) L. BA, U. Mich., 1987, MSW, 1989. Investigator def. D.C. Pub. Defender Officer, Washington, 1985; program asst. Detroit Urban League, 1989; coord. housing Ann Arbor (Mich.) Housing Commn., 1989-90; sr. assoc. United Way, Grand Rapids, 1990-93; program coord. The Grand Rapids Found., 1993-94, program dir., 1994—. Mgr. database Kent County Emergency Needs Task Force, Grand Rapids, 1990—, editor, 1990—; sec. Kent County Emergency Food Subcom., Grand Rapids, 1990—; mem. Kent County Domestic Violence Coordinating Com., Grand Rapids, 1990—; mem. pub. affairs com. Mich. League for Human Svcs., Lansing, 1990—; adj. prof. Grand Valley State U. Sch. of Social Work, 1994—. Contbr. articles to profl. jours. Vol. Blodgett Meml. Med. Ctr., Grand Rapids, 1982—; mem. task force Citizens League, Grand Rapids, 1990—; mem. pub. affairs task force United Way, Lansing, 1990—. Recipient Leadership award Kiwanis Club, 1983; Old Kent Bank and Trust scholar, 1983-87; Am. Marshall Meml. fellow, German Marshall Fund of U.S., 2001. Mem. NASW, Nat. Assn. Black Social Workers, U. Mich. Social Work Govs. (bd. mem. 1991—), U. Mich. Alumni Assn., Women's Leadership Coun., Urban League. Democrat. Episcopalian. Avocations: tennis, racquetball, photography, travel. Home: 16534 Huntington Rd Detroit MI 48219-4072 Office: The Grand Rapids Found 209-C Waters Bldg 161 Ottawa Ave NW Ste 209C Grand Rapids MI 49503-2757

JACKSON, WILLIAM DAVID, research executive; b. Edinburgh, Scotland, May 20, 1927; came to U.S., 1955, naturalized, 1968; s. Joseph and Margaret (Johnston) Jackson; m. Eleanor Burdeshaw; children from previous marriage: Margaret Eleanor, David Foster. B.Sc., U. Glasgow, Scotland, 1947, PhD, 1960; postgrad., U. Strathclyde, Glasgow, 1948. Apprentice English Electric Co., Stafford, 1945-47; research asst. elec. engring. dept. U. Strathclyde, Glasgow, 1948-51; lectr. elec. engring. U. Manchester, Eng., 1951-55, 57-58; vis. lectr. dept. elec. engring. MIT, 1955-57, asst. prof., 1958-62, assoc. prof., 1962-66, lectr. elec. engring., 1968-73; vis. prof. Tech. U., Berlin, Germany, 1966; prof. elec. engring., dept. energy engring. U. Ill., Chgo., 1966-67; prin. research scientist, dir. tech. edn. Avco-Everett Research Lab., Everett, Mass., 1967-72; prof. elec. engring. U. Tenn. Space Inst., Tullahoma, 1972-73; mgr. Electric Power Research Inst., Palo Alto, Calif., 1973-74; mgr. office coal research Interior Dept., Washington, 1974-75; dir. magnetohydrodynamic div. ERDA, Washington, 1975-77; dir. tech. analysis div. Office Energy Research, Dept. Energy, Washington, 1977-79; pres. Energy Cons., Inc., 1979-84, HMJ Corp., 1982—. Professorial lectr. George Washington U., 1979—91, vis. prof., 1986—87, adj. prof., 1991—; cons. numerous indsl. firms and govt. agencies, 1948—; bd. dirs. Hexogon Inc., prodn. v.p., 1999—2001; bd. dirs. Clean Energy Combustion, Inc., 2001—; mem. Internat. Magnetohydrodynamic Liaison Group, 1966—, chmn., 1969—74, sec., 1986—2002; coord. coop. program magnetohydrodynamic power generation U.S.-USSR, 1974—79; mem. numerous govt. and internat. coms. and panels. Editor: Electricity From MHD, 1968; editorial bd.: Internat. Jour. Elec. Engring. Edn, 1962-70; editor-in-chief Magnetohydrodynamics: An Internat. Jour., 1987-92. U.K. Fulbright scholar, 1955-57 Fellow Instn. Elec. Engrs. (past com. sec., chmn.), IEEE (sec.-treas. prof. group biomed. electronics Boston sect. 1962-63, energy devel. subcom. 1973—, chmn. 1988-98, energy devel. and power gen. com. 1986-99, mem. steering com. intersoc. energy conversion engring. conf. 1988—, conf. program chair 1989, conf. gen. chair 1996, 2002), ASME (past chmn. adv. energy systems divn., energy com. 1986-90), AIAA (assoc.; Energy Sys. award 1995); mem. AAUP, AAAS, Am. Phys. Soc., Am. Soc. Engring. Edn., Sigma Xi. Office: 2814 Jutland Rd Kensington MD 20895-2840

JACKSON, WILLIAM LAWRENCE (LARRY JACKSON), radio station executive; b. Boston, May 29, 1954; s. William N. and Jean N. Jackson; m. Sharolyn Jackson. BA in Communications, Freed-Hardeman Coll., 1976; MusB in Voice, U. Miss., 1977, MusM in Composition, 1980; postgrad., U. Miss., U. So. Miss., 1980-85. Instr. music Faulkner U., Montgomery, 1978-79, East Cen. Jr. Coll., Decatur, Miss., 1981-82; program dir. Sta. KAMU-FM/Tex. A&M U., College Station, 1985-86, mgr., 1986-94; coord. K-State Radio Network, Kans. State. U., 1994—. Named one of Outstanding Young Men in Am., 1979, 82. Mem. Ch. of Christ. Avocations: spectator sports, music, reading. Office: K-State Radio Network Kans State U 20 Mccain Auditorium Manhattan KS 66506-4701 E-mail: ljackson@ksu.edu.

JACKSON, WILLIAM RICHARD, entrepreneur; b. Nampa, Idaho, Aug. 23, 1936; s. Richard W. and Josie P. (Mulder) J.; m. Marilyn Kay Samp, June 10, 1956 (div. 1975); children: James Lee, Robbi Jo, Jolynn Kay. BA in Secondary Edn., N.W. Nazarene Coll., Nampa, 1957; MA in Secondary Edn. Adminstrn., U. No. Colo., 1961; EdM, U. Denver, 1964, PhD in Higher Edn. Adminstrn. and Rsch., 1991; PhD in, Stanford U., 1991. Owner, operator Janitorial Svc., Walla Walla, Wash., 1950-54; account mgr., collection contractor Montgomery Ward, Walla Walla, Wash., 1953-57; exec. ins. dir. edn. svcs. Idaho Sch. Employment, Boise, 1957-58; sch. tchr., football coach Humanities, Speech & Art, Caldwell, Idaho, 1958-60; tchr. psychology and econs. Englewood (Colo.) Sch. Dist., 1961-64; dir. student coun. Brook Forest Leadership Inst., Evergreen, Colo., 1961-64; co-owner, operator Jackson Bros. Investments, Englewood, 1970-84; co-owner, pres. Internat. Bell Mus., Inc., Evergreen, 1978-86; pres. Jackson Bros. Industries, Evergreen, 1984—, Jackson Internat., Inc., Evergreen, 1984—. Chmn. bd. Petro Silver, Inc., Denver, 1979-83; rsch. cons. in agr., toxic waste remediation and hyperbaric oxygenation medicine; sr. cons. Envrion. Health Found., San Francisco; mem. staff Southwest Rsch. Inst., San Antonio, Tex. Co-author: Brook Forest Leadership Curriculum, 1964, Disciplining Curriculum, 1978; author: Hyperbaric Oxygenation Effects on the Cognitive Function of Memory, Barter, The History, Mystery and Mastery of Mutual Exchange, Humic, Fulvic and Micorbial Balance: Organic Soil Conditioning, Environmental Care & Share, 1995, The Arthritis, Osteoporosis and Silica Link, The Calcium Deception, Fabulous Fulvic Electrolyte, 1995. Co-founder Benevolent Brotherhood Found., Denver, 1971—; bd. dirs. Ch. of the Nazarene, past chmn. bd. edn. Grantee Denver Presbyn. Med. Ctr., 1991, Hyperbaric Oxygen Therapy System, San Diego, 1991, Denver, 1991; recipient 1st Pl. Nat. Self-Publishing award Writer's Digest, 1993. Mem. Internat. Found. Hyperbaric Medicine, Undersea and Hyperbaric Med. Soc. (rsch. cons. 1990—), Stanford U. Alumni Assn., Phi Delta Kappa. Republican. Avocation: bartering. Office: Jackson Internat Rsch Ctr PO Box 1749 Evergreen CO 80437-1749 E-mail: wirjak@jps.net.

JACKSON, WILLIAM VERNON, library science and Latin American studies educator; b. Chgo., May 26, 1926; s. William Olof and Lillian (Scharenberg) J. BA summa cum laude, Northwestern U., 1945; MA, Harvard U., 1948, PhD, 1952; MS in L.S, U. Ill., 1951; Diploma honoris causa, U. Central Venezuela, 1968. Tchr. York Community High Sch., Elmhurst, Ill., 1946-47; teaching fellow Harvard U., 1948-50; spl. recruit Libr. of Congress, 1951-52; libr., asst. prof. libr. sci. U. Ill., Urbana, 1952-58, assoc. prof., 1958-62, U. Wis., Madison, 1963-65, faculty rsch. fellow, summers, 1963, 64; prof. libr. sci., dir. internat. libr. info. ctr. U. Pitts., 1966-70; prof. libr. sci. George Peabody Coll. for Tchrs., 1970-76; prof. Spanish and Portuguese Vanderbilt U., Nashville, 1970-76; prof. libr. sci. U. Tex. at Austin, 1976-86, prof. emeritus, 1986—, assoc. Inst. Latin Am. Studies, 1976—. Vis. lectr. U. Minn. Library Sch., summers 1954-56, Columbia U. Sch. Library Service, summers 1960, 90, Syracuse U. Sch. Libr. Sci., summer 1962, Simmons Coll. Sch. Libr. Sci., summer, 1974, 75, Coll. Librarianship, Aberystwyth, Wales, summer 1977, U. Zulia, Maracaibo, Venezuela, summer 1980, Dominican U. Libr. Sci., summers 1981-84, 86, 89-98, 2000, 02, Pratt Inst. Sch. Info. & Libr. Sci., summers 1995-98, Coll. of St. Catherine, summer 1999, 2001, L.I. U. Palmer Sch. Libr. and Info. Sci., summer 2001; vis. prof. Inter-Am. Libr. Sch., U. Antioquia, Medellín, Colombia, 1960, 68, adviser internat. exec. coun., 1961-63; cons. State Dept., 1956, 59, 61, 62, 67, 77, 2002, 2003; Regional AID Office for Ctrl.Am. and Panama, 1965-66, AID Mission to Brazil, 1967-72, AID Mission to Colombia, 1970-71, USIA, 1979-80, 85, 87, 89-92, 94-2000, OAS, 1970-71; Coun. Rectors Brazilian Univs., 1972; cons. rsch. librs. N.Y. Pub. Libr., 1965-70, Hispanic Found., Library Congress, Washington, 1964-65; Fulbright research scholar, France, 1956-57; Fulbright lectr. U. Córdoba (Argentina), 1958, adviser, 1970; adviser U. San Marcos, Peru, 1962, 75; external examiner U. West Indies, Jamaica, 1974-78; cons. Bibliothèque Nationale, France, 1979, 81-87; official rep. 350th anniversary Harvard U., 1986, Libr. of Congress Bicentennial, 2000; lectr. and researcher various librs. and univs. in Australia, Europe, Egypt, Singapore, Turkey, Latin Am. and U.S., 1987—; sr. fellow Dominican U., 1989—; Windsor lectr., U. Ill., 1990; vis. prof. faculty philosophy and letters U. Buenos Aires, 1991; dir. various activities on the Quin centennial and librs. in Latin Am., 1992; adv. U. Francisco Marroquín, Guatemala, 1992—; U. del Norte, Barranquilla, Colombia, 1993; various univs. and librs. in El Salvador, 1994—, Nat. Libr. and Archives Sch., Mexico City, 1995; lectr. Assn. Ecuatoriana de Bibliotecarios, 1998, Assn. Colombiana de Bibliotecarios, 1998, libr. sch. Univ. Costa Rica, 2003; advisor Francisco Marroquin Found., 2002--; pres. Coun. Books and Libs. in L.Am., 1993—; lectr. abroad for Centennial, N.Y. Pub. Libr., 1995-96. *Jackson has long specialized in library development in Latin America, as well as in Latin American collections in the United States. He has made over 90 trips to all parts of the region as consultant to the U.S. government and to many institutions and associations, lecturer, visiting professor and participant in professional meetings. He has written many books, reports, articles, and reviews. In addition, Jackson has studied and written on important American and foreign research libraries. He continues to lecture on higher education, Latin America, and libraries and to give seminars on international librarianship and great libraries and their collections.* Author: Basic Library Techniques, 1955, A Handbook of American Library Resources, 1955, 2d edit., 1962, Studies in Library Resources, 1958, The Foundation Grants Program, 1959, The Libraries of the Associated Colleges of the Midwest, 1960, Aspects of Librarianship in Latin America, 1962, second series, 1992, Library Guide for Brazilian Studies, 1964, The National Textbook Program and Libraries in Brazil, 1967, Resources of Research Libraries, 1969, Steps Toward the Future Development of a National Plan for Library Services in Colombia, 1971, Catalog of Brazilian Acquisitions of Library of Congress, 1964-74, 1977, Resources for Brazilian Studies at the Bibliothèque Nationale, 1980, Library Resources of Harvard University, 1986, Las Megabibliotecas, una Bibliografía Comentada, 1993, Resources of Research Libraries: A Bibliographical Guide to Printed Material, 1998; editor: U. Ill. Library Sch. Assn. News Letter, 1954-56, Assn. Coll. Research Libraries Monographs, 1961-66, Latin Am. Collections, 1974, Reference Publications in Latin American Studies, 1977—92, Library and Information Science Education in the Americas: Present and Future, 1981, Library and Information Science in France: A 1983 Overview, 1984, Doce Bibliotecarios Latinoamericanos, 1992; mem. editorial staff Libr. Trends, 1958-62, Ency. Libr. and Info. Sci., 1971-90, Jour. Libr. History, 1976-88, Internat. Jour. Revs. in Libr. and Info. Sci., 1985-88; assoc. editor World Librs., 1990-99; contbr. articles to profl. jours. and encys. Mem. ALA (chmn. internat. relations round table 1965-66, trustee endowment funds 1977-86), Ill. Library Assn., Assn. Library and Info. Sci. Edn., Bibliog. Soc. Am., Assn. Coll. and Research Libraries, MLA, Am. Assn. Tchrs. Spanish and Portuguese, Theatre Library Assn., Conf. on Latin Am. History, Latin Am. Studies Assn., Sem. on Acquisition Latin Am. Library Materials (pres. 1977-78), Assn. Caribbean Univ. and Research Libraries, Asociación Paceña de Bibliotecarios (hon.; La Paz, Bolivia), Phi Beta Kappa, Beta Phi Mu (pres. 1955-56), Phi Sigma Iota, Sigma Delta Pi (hon.), Phi Lambda Beta (hon.) Clubs: Harvard (Chgo.), Caxton (Chgo.). Home: 196 W Kathleen Dr Park Ridge IL 60068-2618 Office: U Tex Sch Info SZB 564 Austin TX 78712-1276

JACKSON, YOCONTALIE ANN, entertainment company executive; b. Camden, N.J., Nov. 8, 1957; d. James Washington and Rosalie Jackson; m. Stanley Leo Jackson; children: Amanda, Kirby. BA, Rutgers U., 1982; MA, So. N.H. U., 1997. Cert.: (paralegal). Paralegal Penn Mutual Life Ins., Phila., 1980—86; divsn. dir. developmental planning City of Camden, NJ, 1988—; CEO East Coast Entertainment Group, Camden, 1991—, Jackson & Assocs., Lindenwold, NJ, 1993—. Bd. dirs. Eleon Dance Co., Phila., 1989—. Prodr.(writer): (recording) Church Folk, 2001; performer (recording) He's Everything to Me, 1993, Anyway You Bless Me, 1995; exec. prodr.(writer): (live recording) An Evening of Elegance with Connie Jackson. Bd. dirs. Friends of Creative Arts, Camden, 2001—, Camden Bd. Edn., 1996, v.p., 1997. Named to Hall of Fame, Woodrow Wilson H.S., Camden, 1998; recipient Image award, Found. 2000, 1996. Mem.: Nat. Alliance of Mkt. Developers. Baptist. Avocations: tennis, basketball, jogging, ping pong, chess. Home: 28 Wright Ave Lindenwold NJ 08021

JACKSON-ELMOORE, CYNTHIA, dean, educator; BSChemE, U. of Del., 1988; MPA, U. of So. Calif., 1992, PhD in Pub. Adminstrn., 1990. Process engr. Corning Asahi Video Products, State Coll., Pa., 1988—89; intern City of LA, 1992—93; instr., tchg. asst., academic advisor U. of So. Calif., LA, 1991—94; asst. prof. Mich. State U., East Lansing, 1994—2002, assoc. prof., 2002—, acting asst. dean - urban affairs programs, 2002—. Exec. bd. mem. Mich. Capital Area Chpt., ASPA, Lansing, Mich., 1995—96; cons. W. K. Kellogg Found., Battlecreek, Mich., 1997—2000; co-dir., program in urban politics and policy Mich. State U., East Lansing, 1998—; bd. editors Jour. of Pub. Affairs Edn., Washington, 1998—; mem. faculty bd. of advisors Cmty. Econ. Devel. Program, Mich. State U., East Lansing, 2002—. Editor: (book) Nonprofits in Urban America, (journal symposium) The Role of Nonprofits in Urban Communities; contbr. edited vol. Recipient Hon. Mention, Ann. Dissertation Competition, Nat. Assn. of Schs. of Pub. Affairs and Adminstrn., 1994, Jeffrey Pressman award, Policy Studies Orgn., 2002; fellow Lilly Endowment Tchg. Fellowship, Mich. State U., 1999—2001; grantee, W.K. Kellogg Found., 1996—98; Doctoral Fellow, Sch. of Pub. Adminstrn., U. of So. Calif., 1990—93. Mem.: Assn. for Pub. Policy Analysis and Mgmt., Assn. for Rsch. on Nonprofit and Voluntary Action, ASPA (exec. com., sect. on mgmt. sci. and policy analysis 1997—2000), Am. Polit. Sci. Assn. (exec. coun. mem., sect. on pub. adminstrn. 1995—98), Influencing State Policy, Urban Affairs Assn. Office: Mich State U 242 Baker Hall East Lansing MI 48872

JACKSON LEE, SHEILA, congresswoman; b. Queens, N.Y., Jan. 12, 1950; m. Elwyn C. Lee; 2 children. BS, Yale U.; JD, U. Va. Sr. counsel select com. on assassinations U.S. Ho. of Reps., 1977; trial atty. Fulbright and Jaworski, 1978-80; sr. atty. United Energy Resources, Inc., 1980; assoc. judge Houston Mcpl. Ct., 1987-89; mem. Houston City Coun., 1990-94, U.S. Congress from 18th Tex. dist., 1995—; mem. judiciary com., sci. com.; ranking dem. subcom. immigration and claims, mem. crime subcom. Democrat. Office: US House Reps 2435 Rayburn Ho Office Bldg Washington DC 20515-4318*

JACKSON-TKAC, STEPHANIE ANN, nurse; b. Thomasville, N.C., Jan. 2, 1960; d. Ellis Wade and Nancy (Myers) J. BSN, East Carolina U., 1982. RN, cert. case mgr., infusion nurse. Staff nurse Pitt County Meml. Hosp., Greenville, N.C., 1981-83, N.C. Bapt. Hosp., Winston-Salem, N.C., 1983-87, Duke U. Med. Ctr., Durham, N.C., 1987-91, Rex Hosp., Raleigh, 1991—92; nurse clinician Health Infusion, Morrisville, 1992—95, Coram Health Care (formerly Health Infusion), Morrisville, 1992—94, infusion care mgr. Goldsboro and Kinston brs., 1995-96; with Chartwell S.E., 1996-97; per diem case mgr. Columbia Home Care, Raleigh, N.C.; home health per diem clin. nurse U. N.C., Chapel Hill; collections spec. Am. Red Cross; case mgr. Killette and Assocs., Inc., 1999—. Mem.: Infusion Nurses Soc., Case Mgr. Soc. Am. Republican.

JACOB, BERNARD MICHEL, architect; b. Paris; arrived in U.S., 1950, naturalized; s. Paul and Therese (Abase) J.; m. Rosamond Gale Tryon; children: Clara, Paul. Diploma in architecture, Cooper Union; BArch, U. Minn. Registered architect, Minn. Sr. designer Ellerbe Assocs., St. Paul; head design Grover Dimond & Assocs., St. Paul; co-founder Team 70 Architects, St. Paul, 1970—, pres., 1977—83, Bernard Jacob Architects Ltd., Mpls., 1983—. Mem. constrn. panel Am. Arbitration Assn., 1973— ; lectr. Sch. Architecture, U. Minn., Mpls., 1982— Editor: Architecture Minn. Mag., Minn. Soc. Architects, 1970-80; archtl. criticism columnist: Mpls. Star and Tribune, 1980-83, Corp. Report Mag., 1983; reviewer: (archtl. books) Choice Mag.; co-author: Skyway Typology/Mpls., Pocket Architecture/A Walking Guide to the Architecture Downtown Mpls. and St. Paul, 2d. rev. edit., 1988, Letters to Palladio, 1999. Founding chmn. Heritage Preservation Commn., St. Paul; past mem. St. Paul Planning Bd.; apptd. mem. Minn. State Designer Selection Bd., 1987-90; bd. dirs. Winslow House, 1995-97; chmn. archtl. subcom. Minn. Gov.'s Residence Coun., 1996-99. Fellow: AIA. Office: Bernard Jacob Architects Ltd 412 Foshay Tower 821 Marquette Ave Minneapolis MN 55402-2915 E-mail: palladio@skypoint.com.

JACOB, BRUCE ROBERT, law educator; b. Chgo., Mar. 26, 1935; s. Edward Carl and Elsie Berthe (Hartmann) J.; m. Ann Wear, Sept. 8, 1962; children: Bruce Ledley, Lee Ann, Brian Edward. BA, Fla. State U., 1957; JD, Stetson U., 1959; LLM, Northwestern U., 1965; SJD, Harvard U., 1980; LLM in Taxation, U. Fla., 1995. Bar: Fla. 1959, Ill. 1965, Mass. 1970, Ohio 1972. Asst. atty. gen. State of Fla., 1960-62; assoc. Holland, Bevis & Smith, Bartow, Fla., 1962-64; asst. to assoc. prof. Emory U. Sch. Law, 1965-69; rsch. assoc. Ctr. for Criminal Justice, Harvard Law Sch., 1969-70; staff atty. Cmty. Legal Assistance Office, Cambridge, Mass., 1970-71; assoc. prof. Coll. Law, Ohio State U., 1971-73, prof., dir. clin. programs, 1973-78; dean, prof. Mercer U. Law Sch., Macon, Ga., 1978-81; v.p., dean, prof. Stetson U. Coll. Law, St. Petersburg, Fla., 1981-94, dean emeritus and prof., 1994—. Contbr. articles to profl. jours. Mem. Fla. Bar, Sigma Chi. Democrat. Home: 1946 Coffee Pot Blvd NE Saint Petersburg FL 33704-4632 Office: Stetson U Coll Law 1401 61st St S Saint Petersburg FL 33707-3246 E-mail: jacob@law.stetson.edu.

JACOB, ELLIS, entertainment company executive; b. Calcutta, India, Oct. 5, 1953; arrived in Can., 1969; s. Raymond and Tryphosa Jacob; m. Sharyn Orzech, July 2, 1978; children: Lauren, Resa. B Commerce, McGill U., Montreal, Que., Can., 1974; M Bus., York U., Toronto, Ont., Can., 1976. Chartered acct., Ont., Que.; cert. mgmt. acct., Ont. Various fin. positions Ford Motor Co., 1977-80; contr. Motorola Can. Ltd., Toronto, Canada, 1981—87; v.p., corp. contr. Cineplex Odeon Corp., Toronto, 1987—88, sr. v.p., 1989, exec. v.p., CFO, 1989—97; exec. v.p., COO, Cineplex Odeon Can., Toronto, 1997—98; head integration Alliance Atlantis Comm. Inc., Toronto, 1998; CEO Galaxy Entertainment Inc., Toronto, 1998—. Bd. dirs. Alliance Atlantis Comm. Inc. Mem. Inst. Chartered Accts., Inst. Mgmt. Accts. Office: Galaxy Entertainment Inc 1303 Yonge St Ste 300 Toronto ON Canada M4T 2Y9 Fax: 416-935-1323. E-mail: ejacob@galaxycinemas.com.

JACOB, FRANÇOIS, biologist, educator; b. Nancy, France, June 17, 1920; s. Simon and Therese (Franck) Jacob; m. Lysiane Bloch, Nov. 27, 1947 (dec. 1984); children: Pierre, Laurent, Odile, Henri; m. Geneviève Barrier, 1999. MD, Faculty of Medicine, Paris, 1947; D.Sc., Faculty of Scis., Paris, 1954; D.Sc. (hon.), U. Chgo., 1965; Dr honoris causa, various univs. Asst. Pasteur Inst., 1950—56, head dept. cellular genetics, 1960—92, pres., 1982—88; prof. cellular genetics Coll. of France, 1964—92; prof. emeritus Coll. of France and Inst. Pasteur, 1992—. Author: (books) The Logic of Life, 1970, The Possible and the Actual, 1981, The Statue Within, 1987, Of Flies, Mice and Men, 1997. Recipient Charles Leopold Mayer prize, 1962, Nobel prize in physiology and medicine (with A. Lwoff and J. Monod), 1965. Mem.: Royal Acad. Scis. Madrid, Acad. Scis. Hungary, Académie Royale de Médecine de Belgique, Royal Soc. (London), Am. Philos Soc., Nat. Acad. Scis. (U.S.), Am. Acad. Arts and Scis. (fgn. mem.), Royal Danish Acad. Scis. and Letters (fgn. mem.), Académie Française Paris, Académie des Sciences (Paris). Achievements include research in on genetics bacterial cells and viruses; contbr. to mechanisms of information transfer (messenger RNA) and genetic basis of regulatory circuits, early stages of the mouse embryo. Office: Pasteur Inst 25 Rue du Dr Roux 75724 Paris Cedex 15 France

JACOB, MARVIN EUGENE, lawyer; b. N.Y.C., Feb. 4, 1935; s. Sam Jacob and Ann (Garfinkel) Law; m. Atara Binnun, Mar. 27, 1960; children: Shalom J., Aviva, Asher. BA, Bklyn. Coll., 1961; JD cum laude, N.Y. Law Sch., 1964. Bar: N.Y. 1964, U.S. Supreme Ct. 1967. Assoc. regional adminstr. SEC, N.Y.C., 1964-79; ptnr. Weil, Gotshal & Manges, N.Y.C., 1979—. Adj. prof. law N.Y. Law Sch., 1975—. Editor: Restructurings, 1993, Reorganizing Failing Businesses, 1999. Mem. ABA, N.Y. State Bar Assn. Office: Weil Gotshal & Manges 767 5th Ave Fl 29 New York NY 10153-0023

JACOB, PAUL BERNARD, JR., electrical engineering educator; b. Columbus, Miss., June 9, 1922; s. Paul Bernard and Sarah Dorsey (Jamison) J.; m. Mildred Evelyn Hammack, Aug. 20, 1946; children: William Boswell, Paul Bernard, III. BS in Elec. Engring., Miss. State U., 1944; MS, Northwestern U., 1948. Registered profl. engr., Miss. Engr., Tenn. Eastman Corp., Oak Ridge, 1944-46; mem. faculty Miss. State U., 1946-88, prof. elec. engring., 1956-88, prof. emeritus, 1988—, assoc. head dept., 1962-88, Paul B. Jacob high voltage lab. and endowed prof. chair elec. and computer engring. dept. Cons. in field; mem. steering com. Internat. Symposium on High Voltage Engring., 1987—. Author articles on high voltage engring. Recipient Alumnus of Yr. award Miss. State U., 1987, UOP Tech. award Instrument Soc. Am., 1988 Mem. IEEE (life), Power Engring. Soc. (chmn. com., Com. Disting. Svc. award), Am. Soc. Engring. Edn., Sigma Xi, Tau Beta Pi, Eta Kappa Nu (bd. dir. 1962-63, nat. v.p. 1982-83, nat. pres. 1983-84), Phi Kappa Phi, Sigma Alpha Epsilon (bd. dirs. 1961-69, nat. pres. 1969-71, Disting. Svc. award 1975, Highest Effort award for profl. accomplishments 1986, Merit Key award, Order of the True Gentleman 1994), Omicron Delta Kappa. Clubs: Rotary (past pres. Starkville, Miss.). Baptist. Home and Office: 102 Kenswick Ct Starkville MS 39759-9493 E-mail: pbj@ece.msstate.edu.

JACOB, PETER JAMES, obstetrician-gynecologist; b. N.Y.C., Apr. 17, 1946; BA in Biology, SUNY, 1969; MD, U. Zurich, 1976. Intern Hahnemann Med. Coll., Phila., 1976-77, resident ob-gyn., 1977-80; ob-gyn. So. Calif. Permanente Group Kaiser Hosp., Panorama City, Calif., 1980—. Fellow ACOG; mem. L.A. Ob-Gyn. Soc., Am. Assn. Gynecol. Laparoscopists, L.A. Acad. Medicine. Office: Kaiser Hosp So Calif Permanente Group 13652 Cantara St Panorama City CA 91402-5423

JACOB, ROBERT JOSEPH KASSEL, computer scientist, educator; b. Nov. 11, 1950; s. Ezekiel Joseph and Ethel Charlotte (Behr) Jacob; m. Kathryn Ann Allamong, June 9, 1973; children: Charlotte Allamong, Anne Elizabeth. BA, Johns Hopkins U., 1973, MSE, 1974, PhD, 1976. Tchg. asst., rsch. asst. Johns Hopkins U., Balt., 1972—76; computer scientist Naval Rsch. Lab., Washington, 1977—94; assoc. prof., lectr. George Washington U., Washington, 1978—94; assoc. prof. Tufts U., Medford, Mass., 1994—. Vis. prof. media lab. MIT, Cambridge, Mass., 2000—01. Assoc. editor: ACM Trans on Computer-Human Interaction, 1992—; contbr. chpts. to books, articles to profl. publs. Fellow, Johns Hopkins U., 1973—75. Mem.: IEEE, Human Factors Soc., Assn. Computing Machinery (vice chmn. Spl. Interest Group Computer-Human Interaction 2001—, recognition of svc. award 1999). Jewish. Avocations: sailing, piano, designing electronic organs. Home: 30 Valleyfield St Lexington MA 02421-7908 Office: Tufts U Dept Computer Sci Medford MA 02155

JACOB, ROSAMOND TRYON, librarian; b. Mpls., May 20, 1928; d. Philip Dorn and Rachel Chase (Denison) Tryon; m. Bernard Michel Jacob, Feb. 17, 1951; children: Clara, Paul. BA summa cum laude, Smith Coll., 1949; MA in Libr. Sci., U. Minn., 1974. Sec. Thames & Hudson Pubs., N.Y.C., 1950-51, Columbia Law Sch., N.Y.C., 1952-54, U. Minn., Mpls., 1955-59; libr. St. Paul Pub. Libr., 1976—98, ret. Coun. mem. Depository Libr. Coun. to Pub. Printer, Washington, 1985-88. Co-author: Minnesota State Documents: A Guide for Depository Libraries, 1984; author: (newsletter) Documents/Classified, 1980-96; editor: (newsletter) DOCSOUP, 1980-90. Mem. St. Paul LWV, 1965—. Mem. ALA (Bernadine Abbott Hoduski Founder award govt. documents roundtable divsn. 1994), Minn. Libr. Assn. (Disting. Achievement award 1990).

JACOB, STANLEY WALLACE, surgeon, educator; b. Phila., 1924; s. Abraham and Belle (Shulman) J.; m. Marilyn Peters; 1 son, Stephen; m. Beverly Swarts; children: Jeffrey, Darren, Robert; m. Gail Brandis; 1 dau., Elyse. MD cum laude, Ohio State U., 1948. Diplomate: Am. Bd. Surgery. Intern Beth Israel Hosp., Boston, 1948-49, resident surgery, 1949-52, 54-56; chief resident surg. service Harvard Med. Sch., 1956-57, instr., 1958-59; asso. vis. surgeon Boston City Hosp., 1958-59; Kemper Found. research scholar A.C.S., 1957-60; asst. prof. surgery U. Oreg. Med. Sch., Portland, 1959-66, asso. prof., 1966—; Gerlinger prof. surgery Oreg. Health Scis. U., 1981—. Author: Structure and Function in Man, 5th edit, 1982, Laboratory Guide for Structure and Function in Man, 1982, Dimethyl Sulfoxide Basic Concepts, 1971, Biological Actions of DMSO, 1975, Elements of Anatomy and Physiology, 1989; contbr. to: Ency. Brit. Served to capt. M.C. AUS, 1952-54; col. Res. ret. Recipient Gov.'s award Outstanding N.W. Scientist, 1965; 1st pl. German Sci. award, 1960; Markle scholar med. scis., 1960 Mem. Phi Beta Kappa, Sigma Xi, Alpha Omega Alpha. Achievements include co-discovery of therapeutic usefulness of dimethyl sulfoxide and MSM. Home: 1055 SW Westwood Ct Portland OR 97201-2708 Office: Oreg Health Scis U Dept Surgery 3181 SW Sam Jackson Park Rd Portland OR 97201-3011 E-mail: jacobs@ohsu.edu.

JACOB, SUSAN MARIE, nurse; b. New Brunswick, N.J., Dec. 30, 1961; BSN, U. Del., 1984. RN, La.; cert. pediat. nurse, cert. home health nurse, cert. coding specialist, cert. procedural coder. Staff/charge nurse Tex. Children's Hosp., Houston, 1984-90; patient care coord. Lakeview Home Health, Covington, La., 1994-96; dir. nursing Trinity Home Health, New Orleans, 1996-98; coder Children's Hosp., New Orleans, 1998-99; auditor Ochsner Clinic, New Orleans, 1999—. Mem. Am. Acad. Profl. Coders, Am. Health Info. Mgmt., Nat. Assn. Health Care Quality. Home: 854 Cross Gates Blvd Slidell LA 70461-4104

JACOB, WALTER CHARLES, lawyer; b. Rockville Centre, N.Y., May 18, 1945; s. Andrew Geza Jacob and Julia Rose Davidis; m. Jennie Ann, Aug. 5, 1972 (div. mar. 1983); children: Wendy Ann, Todd Andrew; m. Avelina Sharpless Jacob, Apr. 16, 1983; 1 child, Allison Elizabeth. BA, Roanoke Coll., 1968; JD, Washington & Lee U., 1971. Assoc. Hall, Monahan, Engle, Mahan & Mitchell, Leesburg, Va., 1971-76, ptnr., 1976-81; prin. Walter C.Jacob, P.C., Leesburg, Va., 1981—. Mem. Rep. Senatorial Inner Cir., Washington, 2000. Mem. Am. Trial Lawyers Assn., Va. Trial Lawyers Assn., Loudoun County Bar Assn. Roman Catholic. Avocations: boating, travel, physical fitness. Home: 4 Thorton Ct Sterling VA 20165 Office: Walter C Jacob PC PO Box 66 Leesburg VA 20178 E-mail: waltercjacobpc@aol.com.

JACOBEY, JOHN ARTHUR, III, surgeon, educator; b. Albuquerque, Oct. 27, 1929; s. John Arthur Jr. and Zelma Mae (Wolfe) Jacobey Mann. AB, Dartmouth Coll., 1951; postgrad., U. Colo., 1951-53; MD, Harvard U., 1956. Diplomate Am. Bd. Surgery, Am. Bd. Thoracic Surgery. Intern Jefferson Davis Hosp., Baylor U., Houston, 1956-57; resident Boston City Hosp., 1957-58, Dartmouth Med. Ctr., Hanover, N.H., 1958-59, Peter Bent Brigham Hosp., 1962-63, St. Mary's Hosp., London, 1963-64, Baylor Affiliated Hosp., Houston, 1964-65; rsch. fellow Harvard Med. Sch., 1959-62; pvt. practice medicine specializing in cardiovascular and thoracic surgery Denver, 1965-71, 72-76; staff surgeon Cheyenne (Wyo.) VA Med. Ctr., 1971-72; asst. prof. clin. surgery SUNY, Stony Brook, 1977-83; pvt. practice medicine specializing in cardiovascular and thoracic surgery Dover, N.J., 1984-92; active cardiothoracic surg. staff Robert Wood Johnson U. Hosp., New Brunswick, N.J., 1992—. Clin. instr. surgery U. Colo., Denver, 1965-69; clin. assoc. prof. surgery U. Medicine and Dentistry of N.J., Robert Wood Johnson Med. Sch., New Brunswick, 1984—; leader internat. cardiothoracic surg. delegation to China, Citizen Amb. Program of People to People Internat., 1994; prin. investigator treatment of acute coronary occlusion in patients with cardiogenic shock using cannula counter pulsation IRB sponsored at U. Medicine and Dentistry N.J.-Robert Wood Johnson Med. Sch., 2002—. Prin. investigator, author publs. on cannula counterpulsation, superior mediastinal exploration. Lay reader, chalice bearer Episcopal Ch., Manhasset, N.Y., 1976-83, Mountain Lakes, N.J., 1984-90, Westfield, N.J., 1990—. Fellow Am. Coll. Chest Physicians; mem. AMA, Soc. Thoracic Surgeons, Am. Thoracic Soc., N.J. Soc. Thoracic Surgeons, N.Y. Soc. Thoracic Surgery, N.J. Acad. Medicine, Am. Heart Assn., N.J. Med. Soc., Mass. Med. Soc., Harvard Club (Boston), Univ. Club (Denver), Dartmouth Club Suburban N.J. (pres. 1986-88), Westfield Glee Club (pres. 2001—). Republican. Avocations: skiing, sailing, tennis, golf. Office: 800 Forest Ave 15B Westfield NJ 07090-4377 E-mail: jacobey@earthlink.net.

JACOBI, FREDRICK THOMAS, newspaper publisher; b. Neenah, Wis., July 10, 1953; s. H. Paul and Patricia Mary (Steele) J.; m. Kim Lee Muenchow, Aug. 23, 1980; children: James Paul, Steven Thomas. AA in Bus., U. South Fla., 1973; BBA in Fin., Mktg., U. Wis., 1976; MBA in Mktg., U. Wis., Whitewater, 1980. Cert. newspaper circulation. City dist. mgr. Madison (Wis.) Newspapers Inc., 1977-79, city circulation mgr., 1979-80, circulation mgr., 1980-81, mktg. mgr., 1981-82, circulation dir., 1982-85, Gannett Co., Inc., Reno, Nev., 1985-88, regional circulation dir. Arlington, Va., 1988-90; pub., pres. Wausau (Wis.) Daily Herald, Gannett Co., Inc., 1990-92, Springfield (Mo.) News-Leader, 1993-96; v.p. Midwest region Gannett Co., Inc., 1993-96; pub., pres. Ft. Myers (Fla.) News-Press, 1996-2000, Rockford (Ill.) Register-Star, 2000—. Bd. dir. Coun. of 100, Rockford Coll., Inland Press Found.; com. chmn. Sales and Mktg. Exec., Madison, Ill., 1985. Editor Circulation-Central States, 1985. Program chmn. Jr. Achievement of Nev., Reno, 1987—88; pres. Springfield Bus. and Devel. Corp., 1996; bd. dir. Ozarks Press Assn., Make A Wish Mo., Horizon Econ. Devel., 1997—2000, Lee County Pub. Schs. Found., 1997—2000. Mem.: Newspaper Assn. Am., Inland Press Assn., Ill. Press Assn., Young Pres.'s Orgn., The Exec. Com., Rotary. Republican. Roman Catholic. Avocations: micro-computers, running, gardening. Office: Rockford Register Star 99 E State St Rockford IL 61104

JACOBI, JAN DE GREEFF, school administrator; b. N.Y.C., Oct. 26, 1944; s. Edwin George Jacobi and Marjorie (de Greeff) Litchfield; m. Virginia Powell Newton, July 26, 1986; children: Edwin, Marjorie, Peter. BA, Stanford U., 1967; MA, Columbia U., 1976. Asst. headmaster, English tchr. The Harvey Sch., Katonah, N.Y., 1973-82; head lower sch. St. Louis Country Day Sch., 1982-93; head mid. sch. Mary Inst. and St. Louis Country Day Sch., 1993—. Avocations: gardening, stargazing, golf. Home: 86 Aberdeen Pl Saint Louis MO 63105-2273 Office: Mary Inst and St Louis Country Day School 101 N Warson Rd Saint Louis MO 63124-1399

JACOBI, JOHN ALBERT, lawyer, engineer; b. Columbus, Ohio, June 28, 1947; s. James Henry and Annabelle Marie (Koenig) J.; m. Jane Alice Rohrer, Aug. 26, 1967; children: Jill Ann, James Andrew. BSME with honors, Rose-Hulman Inst. Tech., 1969; MS in Indsl. Engring., Tex. A&M U., 1970; JD, U. Mo., Kansas City, 1975. Bar: Mo. 1976, Tex. 1979, Fla. 1980, U.S. Patent and Trademark Office 1982, U.S. Supreme Ct. 1985; registered profl. engr., Mo., Tex., Fla. Civilian gen. engr. Red River Army Depot, Texarkana, Tex., 1969 71; indsl. engr. U.S. Army Aviation Sys. Command, St. Louis, 1971-72; chief engr. Lake City Army Ammunition Plant, Independence, Mo., 1973-78; from mgr. environ. affairs to atty. Tenneco, Inc., Houston, 1978-84, mgr. remediation, 1989-91; gen. atty. Tenn. Gas Transmission, Houston, 1985 88; mgr. tech. svcs. Tenneco Gas Transp., Houston, 1988-89; prin. Ecology and Environment, Inc., Houston, 1991-92; v.p., sr. cons. Woodward-Clyde Cons., Houston, 1992, v.p., 1993-97; pvt. practice Houston, 1995-96; chief bur. health Tex. Dept. Health, 1996-2000; gen. mgr. legal affairs Intercontinental Terminals Co., Houston, 2000—01. Phys. scientist Office Dir. Army Rsch., Pentagon, fall 1977; tech. dir. Harding Lawson Assocs., Houston, 1994-95; presdl. exch. exec. Tenneco Inc. Fed. Credit Union, 1978-79. Rsch. grantee Olin, 1968. Mem. ABA, NRA (life) Tex. Bar Assn., Fla. Bar Assn., Exptl. Aircraft Assn., Blue Springs Jaycees (bd. dirs. 1975-77, 1st v.p. 1977), Aircraft Owners and Pilots Assn., Blue Key, Tauy Beta Pi, Pi Tau Sigma, Alpha Pi Mu, Alpha Tau Omega. E-mail: jjacobi@iterm.com.

JACOBI, PETER PAUL, journalism educator, author; b. Berlin, Mar. 15, 1930; came to U.S., 1938, naturalized, 1944; s. Paul A. and Liesbeth (Kron) J.; m. Harriet Ackley, Dec. 8, 1956 (div. 1979); children: Keith Peter, John Wyn. BS in Journalism, Northwestern U., 1952, MS, 1953. Mem. journalism faculty Northwestern U., Evanston, Ill., 1955-81, profl. lectr., 1955-63, asst. prof., 1963-66, assoc. prof., 1966-69, prof. journalism, 1969-81, assoc. dean, 1966-74; communications cons. N.Y.C., 1980-84, Bloomington, Ind., 1985—; prof. journalism Ind. U., Bloomington, 1985-99, prof. emeritus, 1999—. News assignment editor, newscaster, theatre and music reporter NBC, Chgo., 1955-61; news editor ABC, Chgo., 1951-53; radio commentator on music and opera, 1958-65; theatre and film critic Sta. WTTW, Chgo., 1964-74, arts critic, 1975-77; theatre and film critic Hollister Newspapers Suburban Chgo., 1963-70; music columnist Chicagoan mag., 1973-74; script cons. Goodman Theater, Chgo., 1973-75; syndicated commentator on arts and media N.Am. Radio Alliance, 1978-80; arts corr. Christian Sci. Monitor, 1956-81; music critic, columnist Bloomington (Ind.) Herald-Times, 1985—; columnist Arts Indiana, 1987-2001, Editors Only, 1994—, Editor's Workshop, 1995-98. Author: Writing with Style, The News Story and the Feature, 1982, The Messiah Book-The Life and Times of G.F. Handel's Greatest Hit, 1982, (with Jack Hilton) Straight Talk about Videoconferencing, 1986, The Magazine Article: How to Think It, Plan It, Write It, 1991, (with others) From Budapest to Bloomington, Janos Starker and the Hungarian Cello Tradition, 1999; contbg. essayist Lyric Opera Companion, 1991; editor Chgo. Lyric Opera News, 1958-61, Music Mag./Musical Courier, Chgo., 1961-62; contbr. articles on writing to Folio, Ragan Report, other mags., articles on arts to Sat. Rev., Chgo. Daily News, N.Y. Times, Highlights for Children, World Book, others. Mem. AAUP, NATAS, Assn. Edn. in Journalism, Soc. Profl. Journalists, Ind. Arts Commn. (chmn. 1990-93), Arts Midwest, Bloomington Cmty. Arts Commn. Home: 3003 N Browncliff Ln Bloomington IN 47408-1317 Office: Ind U Sch Journalism Bloomington IN 47405

JACOBI, SANDRA E. molecular biologist, researcher; b. Charleston, S.C., Aug. 6, 1954; d. Lewis P. Long; m. Mark A. Jacobi, Nov. 18, 1955; children: Catherine R., Aaron C., Jessica R., Jason R. BS in Biology and BA in Chemistry, U. of Ark., Little Rock, 1990, ADN, 1998. RN. Rsch. asst. U. Ark. Med. Ctr., Little Rock, 1990—; staff nurse St. Vincent Hosp., Little Rock, 1998—. Travel nurse Fastaff, Denver, 2001—. Mem.: Phi Kappa Phi (hon.). Democrat-Npl. Catholic. Avocations: camping, travel. Office: University of ARK for Medical Sciences 4301 W Markham St Slot 750 Little Rock AR 72205 Home Fax: 501-296-1469; Office Fax: 501-296-1469. E-mail: jacobisandrae@uams.edu.

JACOBI, WILLIAM MALLETT, nuclear engineer, consultant; b. Elizabeth, N.J., Apr. 27, 1930; s. Roy H. and Lenore E. (Mallett) J.; m. Maureen Sullivan, Feb. 23, 1963; children: John, Karen, Paul, Michele. BSChemE, Syracuse U., 1951, PhD in Chem. Engring., 1955; MSChemE, U. Del., 1953. Project mgr. Clinch River Breeder Reactor Plant, Oak Ridge, Tenn., 1973-78; gen. mgr. Westinghouse Nuclear Tech. div., Pitts., 1979-81, Westinghouse Nuclear Fuel div., Pitts., 1981-84; v.p. Westinghouse Advanced Power Systems, Pitts., 1984-87; pres. Westinghouse Hanford Co., Richland, Wash., 1987-88; v.p. govt. ops. Westinghouse Electric Co., Pitts., 1988-91; pvt. practice Monroeville, Pa., 1991—. Sci. and tech. adv. com. mem. Argonne (Ill.) Nat. Lab., 1980-83; laser exec. rev. com. mem. Lawrence Livermore (Calif.) Nat. Lab., 1990-92. Active bishop's adv. com. Cath. Diocese of Pitts., 1990-92; panel mem. Nat. Rsch. Coun., 1992-93. Mem. Am. Nuc. Soc., Nat. Rsch. Coun. (sub-panel nuc. waste transmutation 1991-95), Greensburg Country Club, Alpha Chi Sigma. Republican. Home and Office: 119 Mt Vernon Dr Monroeville PA 15146-4815

JACOBOWITZ, CHANA M. cultural organization administrator; b. Bklyn., July 21, 1977; d. Shmuel Lustig and Dori Greenberg; m. Eliyahr Jocobowitz. MSW, Wurzweiller Sch. Social Work, NYC, 2002; BA in psychology, Touro Coll., Bklyn., 1998. Grant writer Universal Comm., Monsey, NY, 1996—98; site dir. Storefront Jewish Cmty. Ctr., Bklyn., 1998—2002; dir. govt. affairs Beth Madrash Goroha, Lakewood, NJ, 2002—. Recipient Nat. Merit Scholarship, 1996—98. Mem.: NJ Assn. of Fin. Aid Admstrs., Ea. Assn. of Fin. Aid Admstrs.

JACOBOWITZ, DAVID MEYER, pharmacologist; b. Bklyn., July 15, 1931; s. Louis and Anna Jacobowitz. BS, CCNY, 1953; MS, Ohio State U., 1958, PhD, 1962. Cert. pharmacologist. Postdoctoral fellow U. Pa. Sch. Medicine, Phila., 1962-63, assoc., 1963-67, asst. prof., 1967-70, assoc. prof., 1970-71; chief sect. on histopharmacology NIH, Bethesda, Md., 1971—; adj. prof. anatomy, physiology, and genetics Uniform Svcs. U., Bethesda, 2000. Contbr. articles to profl. jours. Cpl. U.S. Army, 1955. Recipient Career Devel. award NIH, 1967. Mem. Am. Soc. Pharmacology and Exptl. Therapeutics, Am. Coll. Neuropsychopharmacology, Neurosci. Soc., Neurochemistry Soc., Am. Soc. Cell Biology, Am. Assn. Anatomists. Avocation: wood turner. Office: Uniform Svcs U Anatomy Physiol & Genetics 4301 Jones Bridge Rd Bethesda MD 20814-4712 E-mail: dwj@helix.nih.gov.

JACOBOWITZ, ELLEN SUE, museum and temple curator, administrator; b. Detroit, Feb. 21, 1948; d. Theodore Mark and Lois Clairesse (Levy) Jacobowitz. BA, U. Mich., 1969, MA, 1970; postgrad. in art history, Bryn Mawr Coll., 1976-83; postgrad., Wharton Sch., 1997. Curator Phila. Mus. Art, 1972-90; administr. Cranbrook Inst. Sci., Bloomfield Hills, Mich., 1991-94; adminstr. Temple Emanu-El, Oak Park, Mich., 1995-96. Cons. ArtServe Mich., 1997; primary caregiver, 1998—. Author: The Prints of Lucas Van Leyden, 1983, American Graphics, 1860-1940, 1982. Treas. Sat. Luncheon Club, 1995—96, pres., 1999—2000; active Leadership Oakland, Detroit Inst. Arts; bd. dirs. Nat. Coun. Jewish Women, Detroit, 1990—91, Print Coun. Am., Balt., Netherlands Am. Amity Trust, Washington, 1982—84, Mich. Mus. Assn., 1993—94. Mem.: Detroit Inst of Arts, U. Mich. Alumni Assn., Am. Jud. Com. Avocations: cooking, gardening, reading, art, sports.

JACOBOWITZ, GLENN ROBERT, vascular surgeon; b. N.Y.C., Jan. 26, 1963; s. Walter Erwin and Suzanne Jacobowitz; m. Marilyn Forman; children: Bryan, Lauren. BA, Princeton U., 1985; MD, NYU, 1989. Diplomate Nat. Bd. Med. Examiners 1990, Am. Bd. Surgery with subspecialty in vascular surgery 1996. Asst. prof. surgery NYU, 1996—; attending surgeon vascular surgery NYU Med. Ctr., 1996—, Bellevue Hosp., N.Y.C., 1996—; chief vascular surgery Manhattan VA Hosp., N.Y.C., 1998—. Dir. vascular lab. NYU Med. Ctr., 1997—. Fellow: ACS; mem.: Soc. Vascular Surgery, Am. Assn. of Vascular Surgery, Phi Beta Kappa, Alpha Omega Alpha. Avocation: Tennis, . Office: NYU Vascular Assocs 530 First Ave Ste 6-F New York NY 10016 Office Fax: 212-263-7722. Business E-Mail: glenn.jacobowitz@msnyuhealth.org.

JACOBOWITZ, HAROLD SAUL, lawyer, b. N.Y.C., Aug. 26, 1950, s. William and Miriam (Spector) J.; m. Estrella B. Rivera, Oct. 26, 1972. BA, CUNY, 1972; JD, Rutgers U., 1977. Bar: N.Y. 1977, U.S. Dist. Ct. (so. dist.) N.Y. 1978, U.S. Dist. Ct. (ea. dist.) N.Y. 1978. Assoc. Goldman & Heffernan, N.Y.C., 1977-78; assoc. Zola & Zola, N.Y.C., 1978-79, Goldberg & Lysaght, N.Y.C., 1979-82; from atty. of record to cons. Am. Internat. Group (Jacobowitz, Spessard, Garfinkel & Lesman), N.Y.C., 1982—2001, cons., 2002—. Arbitration panel U.S. Dist. Ct. (ea. dist.) N.Y. Mem. ABA, N.Y. State Bar Assn., Assn. Bar City N.Y., N.Y. County Lawyers Assn., Assn. Trial Lawyers N.Y.C. (bd. dirs.). Office: Am Internat Group 70 Pine St New York NY 10270-0002 E-mail: harold.jacobowitz@aig.com.

JACOBS, AMELIA CAROL, orthodontist; b. Louisville, Oct. 9, 1952; d. Clarence Patterson and Jane (Williams) J.; m. William H. Clark, Jr.; children: Stephanie Jacobs Mattingly, Barton Jacobs Mattingly. BS, Ky. Wesleyan Coll., 1974; DMD, U. Louisville, 1980, cert. in orthodontics, 1982. Registered Ky. Bd. of Dentistry. Orthodontist, owner, Louisville, 1982—; clin. asst. prof. U. Louisville, 1982-88. Mem. ADA, Am. Assn. Orthdontists, Ky. Dental Assn., Ky. Assn. Orthodontists, Ky. Assn. Women Dentists (pres. 1982—), 80's Ortho Club (pres. 1982—), Phi Kappa Phi, Omicron Kappa Upsilon. Republican. Presbyterian. Avocations: saddle seat equitation, sewing, parenting, reading, crocheting. Office: Dr Amelia C Jacobs 4816 Greenwood Rd Louisville KY 40258-3634 E-mail: ameliajacobs@netscape.net.

JACOBS, ANDREW F. mortgage company executive; V.p., control, treasurer Capstead Mortgage Corp., Dallas, 1989—91, sr. v.p., control, treasurer, 1991—98, sec., 1992—98, exec. v.p., asset & liability, 1998, exec. v.p., finance, treasurer, sec., 1998—99, CFO, sr. v.p., finance, 1998—2003, sec., 2000—03, pres., CEO, 2003—. Office: Capstead Mortgage Corp 8401 N Central Expressway Ste 800 Dallas TX 75225-4410*

JACOBS, ANDREW ROBERT, lawyer; b. Newark, Sept. 18, 1946; s. Seymour B. and Pearle (Flaschen) J.; m. Yardana Steinberg, July 10, 1976; 1 child, Suzanne Michal. BA with high honors, Rutgers U., 1968; JD, Columbia U., 1971. Bar: N.J. 1971, D.C. 1976, U.S. Dist. Ct. N.J. 1971, U.S. Ct. of Appeals (3rd cir.) 1974, U.S. Supreme Ct. 1979, U.S. Dist. Ct. (ea. and so. Dists.) N.Y. 1980, N.Y. 1980, Pa. 1981, U.S. Ct. Appeals (2nd cir.) 1984, U.S. Claims Ct. 1986. Law clk. to chief judge U.S. Dist. Ct., Newark, 1971-72; asst. U.S. atty. U.S. Atty.'s Office, Newark, 1972-76; assoc. Cole Berman & Belsky, Rochelle Park, N.J., 1976, Lanigan O'Connell Jacobs & Chazin, Basking Ridge, N.J. and N.Y.C., 1977-78, ptnr., 1979-82; asst. U.S. atty., chief spl. pros., dep. chief criminal div. U.S. Atty.'s Office (ea. dist.), N.Y., 1983-85; ptnr. Horowitz & Jacobs, Hackensack, N.J. and N.Y.C., 1985-89, Gern, Dunetz, Davison & Weinstein, Roseland, N.J. and N.Y.C., 1990-93, Fitzsimmons Ringle & Jacobs, Newark, N.J., Hackensack, N.J. and N.Y.C., 1993-2000, Epstein, Fitzsimmons, Brown, Gioia, Jacobs and Sprouls, P.C., Chatham, Newark, Hackensack, N.Y.C., 2000—. Faculty Practicing Law Inst., N.Y.C., 1980-82; legal writing instr. N.Y. Law Sch., 1981-82; master Justice William J. Brennan, Jr. Inns of Ct., 1995—. Trustee N.J. YM-YWHA Camps, Fairfield, NJ, Milford, Pa., 1985—, pres., 2001—; trustee Congregation Shomrei Emunah, Montclair, NJ, 1985—96; pres. Rutgers Coll. Alumni Class 1968. Capt. U.S. Army, 1997. Harlan Fiske Stone scholar; recipient U.S. Dept. Justice Spl. commendation award, 1973, 75, U.S. Dept. Treasury ATF cert. of Appreciation, 1976, Jerome Michael prize for Excellence in Trial Advocacy Columbia U. Mem.: ATLA, ABA, Assn. Fed. Bar N.J., Essex County Bar Assn., Bergen County Bar Assn., Morris County Bar Assn., Assn. Criminal Def. Lawyers N.J., N.Y. State Trial Lawyers Assn., N.Y. County Lawyers Assn. (fed. cts. com.), N.J. State Bar Assn., Soc. Loyal Sons and Daus. of Rugers Coll. (elected), Phi Beta Kappa. Home: 47 Haller Dr Cedar Grove NJ 07009 Office: Epstein Fitzsimmons Brown Gioia Jacobs & Sprouls PC Box 901 245 Green Village Rd Chatham NJ 07928 also: 83 Maiden Ln 13th Fl New York NY 10038 also: 2 University Plz Ste 18 Hackensack NJ 07601-6202 also: 50 Park Pl Ste 903 Newark NJ 07102 Fax: 973-593-0179. E-mail: ajacobs@epsteinfitz.com.

JACOBS, ANN ELIZABETH, lawyer; b. Lima, Ohio, July 28, 1950; d. Warren Charles and Virginia Elizabeth (Lewis) J.; m. Mark S. Bush, Nov. 26, 1988; 1 child, Whitney Elizabeth. BA, George Washington U., 1972; JD, Cath. U., 1976. Bar: Ohio 1977, Calif. 1977, U.S. Ct. Appeals (D.C. cir.) 1980, U.S. Dist. Ct. (no. dist.) Ohio 1982, S.C. 2000. Asst. atty. gen. State of Ohio, Columbus, 1977-78; trial atty. EEOC of Ohio, Miami, Fla., 1978-80; sole practice Lima, 1980—. Bd. dirs. Allen County Blackhoof Area Legal Svcs. Assn., Marimor Industries, Inc., Lima. Pres., legal liaison Shawnee Sch. Dist. Bd. Edn., 2002-03; fundraiser Lima Symphony Orch., 1985, pres. legis. liaison, 2002-03; trustee Lima Art Assn., YWCA; bd. dirs. Sr. Citizens; mem. bd. elders Market St. Presbyn. Ch., chairperson mission comm., 2001. Recipient Recognition award US Naval Air Sta., Jacksonville, Fla., 1979. Mem. LWV, Ohio Bar Assn., Calif. Bar Assn., D.C. Bar Assn., Allen County Bar Assn. (chmn. juvenile ct. com. 1993). Avocations: sailing, golf, reading. Home: 1529 Shawnee Rd Lima OH 45805-3801 Office: Jacobs & Von der Embse 558 W Spring St Lima OH 45801-4728

JACOBS, ARNOLD STEPHEN, lawyer; b. N.Y.C., Feb. 26, 1940; s. Charles Edwin and Harriet (Flug) J.; m. Ellen Margaret Kheel, June 10, 1962; children: Beryl Kheel, Arnold Stephen Jr. BME, Cornell U., 1961, MBA, 1963, LLB with distinction, 1964. Bar: N.Y. 1964. Assoc. Hughes, Hubbard & Reed, N.Y.C., 1964-65, 1967-71; ptnr. Shea & Gould, N.Y.C., 1971-94, Proskauer Rose LLP, N.Y.C., 1994—. Adj. prof. N.Y. Law Sch., 1977-91. Author: The Impact of Rule 10b-5, 3 vols., 1974, Litigation and Practice Under Rule 10b-5, 6 vols., 1981—2001, Manual of Corporate Forms for Securities Practice, 4 vols., 1981—, Opinion Letters in Securities Matters: Text-Clause-Law, 3 vols., 1980—, Section 16 of the Securities Exchange Act, 2 vols., 1989—, Disclosure and Remedies Under the Securities Laws, 6 vols., 2002—; contbr. articles. Capt. U.S. Army, 1965-67, Korea. Mem. N.Y. State Bar Assn., Assn. of Bar of City of N.Y. (chmn. securities regulation com. 1982-86), Harmonie Club (N.Y.C.). Home: 108 E 82nd St Apt 7A New York NY 10028-1136 Office: Proskauer Rose LLP 1585 Broadway New York NY 10036-8299 E-mail: ajacobs@proskauer.com.

JACOBS, ARTHUR DIETRICH, educator, researcher, health services executive; b. Bklyn., Feb. 4, 1933; s. Lambert Dietrich and Paula Sophia (Knissel) Jacobs; m. Viva Jane Sims, Mar. 24, 1952; children: Archie(dec.), David L., Dwayne C., Dianna K. Hatfield. BBA, Ariz. State U., 1962, MBA, 1966. Enlisted USAF, 1951, commd. 2d lt., 1962, advanced through grades to maj., 1972, ret., 1973; indsl. engr. Motorola, Phoenix, 1973-74; mgmt. cons. State of Ariz., 1974-76, Productivity Internat., Tempe, Ariz., 1976-79; faculty assoc. Coll. Bus. Adminstrn. Ariz. State U., Tempe, 1977-94, sr. lectr., 1995, ret., 1996. Productivity advisor Scottsdale Meml. Health Svcs. Co., Ariz., 1979—84; rschr. U.S. Internment of European-Am. Aliens and Citizens of European Ancestry during World War II. Author: (book) The Prison Called Hohenasperg: An American Boy Betrayed by His Government During World War II, 1999; editor, pub.: Freedom of Information Times; co-editor: The World War Two Experience - The Interment of German-Americans, Documents, vol. IV (now in spl. collections of USAF Acad.); contbr. Bd. dirs. United Way of Tempe, 1979—85. Recipient Meritorious Svc. award, Coll. Ozarks, Mo., 2000. Mem.: Ops. Rsch. Soc. Am., Inst. Indsl. Engrs. (pres.ctrl. Ariz. chpt. 1984—85), Am. Soc. Quality Control, Ariz. State U. Alumni Assn. (bd. dirs. 1973—79), Optimist (life), Delta Sigma Pi, Beta Gamma Sigma, Sigma Iota Epsilon. Achievements include research in the special collections of the United States Air Force Academy. E-mail: adjacobs@foitimes.com.

JACOBS, CARL EUGENE, printing company official; b. Ft. Wayne, Ind., Nov. 28, 1942; s. Earl Oscar and Marguerite Louise (Unger) J.; m. Linda Maureen Peralta, Sept. 6, 1974; children: Brett, Kim, Kris. BS in Edn., Ball State U., 1965, MA in Speech, 1970. Tchr. Ft. Wayne Community Schs., 1965-70; instr., sports info. dir., dir. news bur. Ft. Hays (Kans.) State U., 1970-73; dir. pubs. Nat. Collegiate Athletic Assn., Mission, Kans., 1973-77; v.p. sales, mktg. The Lowell Press, Kansas City, Mo., 1977-94; dir. internat. sales Constable-Hodgins Printing Co., Kansas City, Kans., 1994-96; v.p. mktg. Richardson Printing, Inc., Kansas City, Mo., 1996—. Mem. prepress tech. adv. com. Penn Valley C.C., 1998—; bd. dirs. Greater Kans. City People to People, 2002—03, pres., 2003—. Trustee Kansas City Conservatory of Music, 1983-94; bd. dirs. Genesis Sch., Kansas City, 1987; ruling elder, mem. session Southridge Presbyn. Ch., Roeland Park, Kans., 1985-87, 89-91. Mem. Internat. Assn. Bus. Communicators (hon. life chpt. and dist., chpt. pres. 1978, internat. v.p., bd. dirs. 1981, trustee rsch. found. 1990-93), Kiwanis (bd. dirs., v.p. Downtown Kansas City Mo. club 1988-90, pres. 1991-92, Kiwanian of Yr. award 1994, 96), Kansas City Advt. Club. Republican. Avocations: sports, reading, writing. Home: 5720 Willow Pl Parkville MO 64152-6131

JACOBS, CHARLES NATHAN, editor, writer; b. Paterson, N.J., July 11, 1930; s. Samuel I. and Beatrice J. (Levine) J.; m. Joan Stearns Weiss, May 30, 1953 (div. 1979); children: Julie Gail, JoDee Winger; m. Rosalind H. Eigenfeld, Feb. 21, 1987. BA in Humanities, Columbia Coll., 1952; MS in Journalism, Columbia U., 1953. Reporter N.Y. Jour. Am., N.Y.C., 1950-53; owner Jacobs Dept. Store, Paterson, 1955-80; pub. Alameda Newspaper Group, San Francisco, 1985 87, Garden State Newspapers, Passaic, NJ, 1985 87; pvt. practice editl. cons. Woodcliff Lake, NJ, 1988—90; editor FOCUS Mag., Totowa, N.J., 1990-92; pres., pvt. practice editl. cons. CJ Enterprises, Woodcliff Lake, 1992—; editor Travel World Internat., 2000—02; travel editor That's Life Mag., 2002. Author: The Business of Writing, 1996, (novel) Blood Bond, 2002. Dep. mayor Paterson, 1966-70; campaign mgr. Kramer for Mayor, Paterson, 1966, 70, 74, 78. Sgt. U.S. Army, 1953-55. Recipient Disting. Svc. award Jaycees, Paterson, 1966, Nat. Vol. award Lane Bryant/U.S. Govt., Washington, 1969, various awards Soc. Profl. Journalists, N.Am. Travel Journalists Assn. Mem. N.Am. Travel Journalists Assn. (award winner), N.J. Press Club (award winner), Working Press Assn. (award winner), East West News Bur. (award winner). Jewish. Avocations: skiing, golf, reading, gardening. Home and Office: CJ Enterprises 16 Pinecrest Dr Woodcliff Lake NJ 07677-8220 E-mail: jac391@aol.com.

JACOBS, CHARLES P. lawyer; b. Buffalo, Apr. 2, 1950; s. Phillip Roblin and Joyce Marilyn (Schwab) J.; m. Jill Lang, June 10, 1973; children— Eliza, Lauren. B.A. in History, U. Pa., 1972; J.D., SUNY-Buffalo, 1975. Bar: N.Y. 1976, U.S. Dist. Ct. (we. dist.) N.Y. 1976. Assoc. firm Moot & Sprague, Buffalo, 1975-80; v.p., gen. counsel Envirogas, Inc., Hamburg, N.Y., 1980-84; former assoc. Saperston, Day Lustig, Gallick, Kirschner & Gaglione, P.C., Buffalo; now with Nixon, Hargrave, Devans & Doyle, Buffalo. Mem. ABA, N.Y. State Bar Assn., Erie County Bar Assn. Club: Buffalo Tennis and Squash. Office: Nixon Hargrave Devans & Doyle 1600 Empire Tower Buffalo NY 14202-3716

JACOBS, DAVID ERNEST, federal agency administrator; married; 2 children. BA in Polit. Sci., Antioch Coll., 1973; BS in Environ. Health, Oakland U., 1983; MS in Tech. and Sci. Policy, Ga. Inst. Tech., 1988; PhD in Environ. Engring., Kennedy Western U., 1998. Cert. indsl. hygienist. Teaching asst. quantitative analytical chemistry Oakland U., 1982, lectr., coord. qualitative analytical chemistry, 1983; chemist Nat. Stds. tech. Inc., 1983; environ. rsch. scientist Ga. Inst. Tech., 1983-87, dir. Ga. State Employee Hazardous Chems. Tng. Program, 1987-88, dir. So. Lead-Based Paint Tng. Consortium, 1989-92; dep. dir. Nat. Ctr. for Lead-Safe Housing, 1992-95. Bd. dirs. Nat. Lead Abatement Coun., 1993-95. Author: (Pres.'s task force report) Childhood Lead Poisoning Prevention; contbr. articles to profl. jours. Recipient Spl. Commendation, Dept. Justice, 1999. Mem. APHA, Am. Indsl. Hygiene Assn. (chmn. social concerns com. 1991, nat. nominating com. 1990-92, Ga. sect. sec. 1988, pres. 1989), Am. Acad. Indsl. Hygiene. Office: US Dept HUD Office Healthy Homes & Lead Hazard Contr 451 7th St SW P3202 Washington DC 20410-0001 E-mail: david_e._jacobs@hud.gov.

JACOBS, DAVID RICHARD, endocrinologist; b. N.Y.C., Jan. 5, 1931; s. Martin A. and Gertrude (Fagenson) J.; m. Pamela Neumann, May 11, 1957; children: Teresa E. Jacobs, Wendy J. Lipstein. AB, Oberlin (Ohio) Coll., 1951; MD, Western Res. U., 1956. Diplomate Am. Bd. Internal Medicine, Am. Bd. Endocrinology and Metabolism. Rotating intern Lenox Hill Hosp., N.Y.C., 1956-57; asst. resident, fellow in medicine Mount Sinai Hosp., N.Y.C., 1957-59, fellow in endocrinology, 1959-60, rsch. asst. in medicine, 1962-68, asst. attending physician in endocrinology, 1968-74, assoc. attending physician in endocrinology, 1974-95; instr. in medicine Mount Sinai Sch. Medicine, 1966-68, asst. clin prof. medicine, 1968-95; clin. assoc. prof. medicine NYU Sch. of Medicine, N.Y.C., 1994-97; clin. prof. medicine NYU Sch. Medicine, 1997—; attending physician in medicine Lenox Hill Hosp., N.Y.C., 1979—, chief endocrinology and metabolism sect., 1978—. Adj. assoc. attending in medicine Mount Sinai Hosp., N.Y.C., 1995—; adj. asst. clin. prof. medicine Mount Sinai Sch. of Medicine, 1995—; elected sr. rep. to med. bd. Lenox Hill Hosp., N.Y.C., 1989-91; sec. to med. bd. and mem. bd. trustees, 1990-91; cons. in endocrinology Am. Acad. of Ophthalmology and Otolaryngology, 1965-75, instr. endocrinology ann. meetings, 1965-78; lectr. in field. Contbr. articles to profl. jours. Capt. U.S. Army, 1960-62. Recipient Award of Merit Am. Acad. Ophthalmology and Otolaryngology, 1975. Fellow ACP; mem. AMA, Am. Fedn. for Med. Rsch., The Endocrine Soc., Am. Soc. for Bone and Mineral Rsch., N.Y. County Med. Soc., Med. Soc. State of N.Y. Avocations: music, tennis, travel. Office: 240 E 82d St New York NY 10028

JACOBS, DEBORAH L. librarian; b. L.A., Feb. 28, 1952; d. Morton Daniel and Adrienne (Rimmel) J.; m. Brian Brogan, Mar. 29, 1982 (div. 1985); 1 child, Jacob Brogan. BA in Govt., Mills Coll., 1974; MLS, U. Oreg., 1975. Children's libr. Deschutes Libr., Bend, Oreg., 1976-77; extension svcs. libr. Sacramento (Calif.) City Libr., 1977-78; libr., libr. dir. Corvallis (Oreg.)-Benton Pub. Libr., 1978-97; city libr. Seattle Pub. Libr., 1997—. Treas. Freedom to Read Found., Chicago, 1994-98. Bd. dirs. Northwest Sch., Seattle, Boys & Girls Club, Corvallis, 1993-97; chair Commn. Children & Families, Corvallis, 1992-97; sec., bd. dirs. da Vinci Days, Corvallis, 1993-97. Named libr. of yr. Libr. Jour., 1995, pub. employee of yr. Mcpl. League King Couny, Seattle, 1999, leader of yr. City of Seattle Mgmt. Assn., 1999, Governing Mag.Pub., Ofcl. of the Year, 2001. Mem. Am. Libr. Assn. (co-chair presdl. initiative 1997-99, v.p. Leroy-Merritt F und. 1998—, intellectual freedom champion 1995), Oreg. Libr. Assn. (pres. 1992-93), Wash. State Women's Forum, Wash. Libr. Assn., Bertelsmann Founds. Internat. Network Pub. Librs., Rotary. Democrat. Jewish. Avocations: baking, gardening, running, pottery. Office: Seattle Pub Libr 800 Pike St Seattle WA 98101-3922

JACOBS, DENNIS, federal judge; b. N.Y.C., Feb. 28, 1944; s. Harry N. and Rose J.; m. Judith Weissman. BA, Queens Coll., 1964; MA, NYU, 1965, JD, 1973. Atty. Simpson Thacher & Bartlett, N.Y.C., 1973-92; judge U.S. Ct. Appeals (2d cir.), N.Y.C., 1992—. Office: US Ct Appeals US Courthouse 40 Foley Sq Rm 1904 New York NY 10007-1502*

JACOBS, DENNY, state legislator; b. Moline, Ill., Nov. 8, 1937; s. Oral G. and Caroline Harroun (Pinkerton) J.; m. Mary Ellen Duffy, June 10, 1955; children: Patricia, Denise, Elizabeth, Michael, J.P., Tory. BA, Augustana Coll., 1959. Co-owner J & J Music, 1966-82; mktg. dir. Group W Cable, 1985-86; mayor East Moline, Ill., 1973—; mem. Ill. State Senate, 1986—. Vice chmn. transp. com., mem. agr., conservation, energy and environment com., chmn. citizens coun. econ. devel., chmn. intergovt. com. Ill. State Senate. Mem. Moose, Elks (Disting. Citizen award 1986), Eagles, KC. Address: 3511 8th St East Moline IL 61244-3521 Also: 606 19th St Moline IL 61265-2142*

JACOBS, DONALD P. dean emeritus, banking and finance educator; b. Chgo., June 22, 1927; s. David and Bertha (Novod) J.; children: Elizabeth, Ann, David; m. Dinah Nemeroff, May 28, 1978. BA, Roosevelt Coll., 1949; MA, Columbia U., 1951, PhD, 1956. Mem. research staff Nat. Bur. Econ. Research, 1952-57; instr. Coll. City N.Y., 1955-57; mem. faculty to Morrison prof. fin. Northwestern U. Grad. Sch. Mgmt., 1970-78, chmn. dept., 1969-75, dean, 1975—, Gaylord Freeman Disting. prof. banking, 1978—. Bd. dirs. CDW Corp., Hartmarx Corp., Prologis Corp., Terex Corp., Conf. Savs. and Residential Financing; co-dir. fin. studies Presdl. Commn. Fin. Structure and Regulation, 1970-71; sr. economist banking and currency comm. U.S. Ho. of Reps., 1963-64. Editor proc.: Conf. Savs. and Residential Financing, 1967, 68, 69; contbr. articles to profl. jours. Served with USNR, 1945-46. Ford Found. fellow,

1959-60, 63-64 Mem. Am. Econ. Assn., Am. Statis. Assn., Am. Fin. Assn., Econometrics Soc., Inst. Mgmt. Sci. Home: 617 Milburn St Evanston IL 60201-2407 Office: Northwestern Univ J L Kellogg Grad Sch Mgmt 2001 Sheridan Rd Evanston IL 60208-0814

JACOBS, EDWARD HAROLD, psychologist; b. N.Y.C., Aug. 4, 1953; s. Erwin and Rita Lillian (Finkel) J.; m. Vicki Dawn Touster, Oct. 30, 1983; children: Rebecca, Joshua. AB, Vassar Coll., 1975; MA, Temple U., 1977, PhD, 1981. Lic. pscyhologist, N.H.; lic. psychologist, Mass. Clni. fellow in psychology dept. psychiatry Harvard Med. Sch., Boston, 1979-80; psychologist Cambridge (Mass.) Guidance Ctr., 1981-82, East Boston (Mass.)-Winthrop Counseling Ctr., 1982-86; pvt. practice Cambridge, Mass., 1982-87, Londonderry, N.H., 1987—. Clin. cons. N.E. Rehab., Salem, N.H., 1984-87, New Eng. Neurol. Assocs., North Andover, 1984-87; mem. pub. info. com. Mass. Psychol. Assn., Boston, 1985-87; clin. instr. in psychology dept. psychiatry Harvard Med. Sch., Boston, 1989-93; founder, dir. Learning Resource Ctr., Londonderry, 1989—; profl. adv. bd. Stateline chpt. Children and Adults with Attention Deficit Disorder, 1993-98. Author: Fathering the ADHD Child: A Book for Fathers, Mothers and Professionals, 1998, ADHD: Helping Parents Help Their Children, 2000; consulting editor, book rev. bd. Am. Jour. Psychotherapy, 1993—; mem. editl. bd. Learning Disabilities: A Contemporary Jour. Bd. dirs. The Robert Frost Sch., Derry, N.H., 1987-88, Derry (N.H.) Vis. Nurses Assn., 1987-90; chmn. Southeastern Child Adv. Team, Derry, 1987; bd. dirs., campaign chmn. Derry (N.H.)-Londerderry-Timberlane United Way, 1995—, Heritage United Way, 2002. Mem. APA, Nat. Register Healthsvc. Providers in Psychology, Nat. Registry Cert. Group Psychotherapists, N.H. Psychol. Assn., Mass. Assn. for Psychoanalytic Psychology. Office: 12 Parmenter Rd Londonderry NH 03053-3280 E-mail: EHJPsych@aol.com.

JACOBS, ELEANOR, art consultant, retired art administrator; b. N.Y.C., July 25, 1929; d. Samuel and Mary (Praw) Cohen; m. Raymond Jacobs, Dec. 29, 1955; children: Susan, Laura. BA, NYU, 1979. Co-founder, v.p. The Earth Shoe Co., N.Y.C., 1969-79; art adminstr. Print Dept., Sotheby's, N.Y.C., 1980-81; exec. asst. Care, N.Y.C., 1982-84; exec. adminstr. Hirschl & Adler Galleries, N.Y.C., 1984-93. Art cons. Recipient Founders Day award NYU, N.Y.C., 1978; Artists fellow, 1985—. Mem. Nat. Arts Club (gov. 1989-97, exhbns. com. 1984—, curatorial com. 1990—, founder, editor exhibiting artists newsletter 1987—, admissions com. 1995—), Nat. Trust for Hist. Preservation, Artists Fellowship, 1985, Dutch Treat Club. Avocations: tennis, travel, art cons.

JACOBS, EUGENE GARDNER, JR., psychiatrist, psychotherapist, educator; b. Providence, Jan. 3, 1926; s. E. Gardner and Edna Jacobs; m. Alice L. Smith, Apr. 12, 1951 (div. 1980); children: Susan, Nancy, John, Peter. AB, Yale U., 1948; MD, U. Pa., 1952. Diplomate Am. Bd. Psychiatry and Neurology. Intern Pa. Hosp., Phila., 1952-53; resident Neurol. Inst. NY, NYC, 1953-54; rsch. fellow Columbia U., NYC, 1954-55; resident NY State Psychiat. Inst., Columbia Presbyn. Hosp., NYC, 1955-58; pvt. practice Phila., 1958—; cons. psychiatrist Pa. Hosp., 1997—2002, hon. psychiatrist, 2002—. Staff psychiatrist Inst. Pa. Hosp., Phila., 1958—62; clin. asst. prof. U. Pa., 1970—81; chief psychiatrist Student Health Svc., Temple U., Phila., 1973—77; sr. attending psychiatrist Inst. Pa. Hosp., Phila., 1974—97; chief dept. psychiatry Phila. Naval Hosp., 1981—85; clin. assoc. prof. MLP Hahnemann U., Phila., 1981—98; clin. asst. prof. U. Pa., 1997—; adj. clin. assoc. prof. MLP Hahnemann U., Phila., 1998—. Capt. USNR. Fellow: Am. Psychiat. Assn. (life); mem.: Phila. Psychiat. Soc., Am. Psychoanalytic Assn., Psychoanalytic Ctr. Phila. Home and Office: 5400 Wissahickon Ave Philadelphia PA 19144-5223 Fax: 215-842-0571.

JACOBS, FRANCIS ALBIN, biochemist, educator; b. Mpls., Feb. 23, 1918; s. Anthony and Agnes Ann (Stejskal) J.; m. Dorothy Caldwell, June 5, 1953; children: Christopher, Gregory, Paula, Margaret, John. BS, Regis Coll., Denver, 1939; postgrad, U. Denver, 1939-41; Fellow in Biochemistry, St. Louis U., 1941-49, PhD, 1949. Postdoctoral fellow Nat. Cancer Inst., Bethesda, Md., 1949-51; instr. physiol. chemistry U. Pitts. Sch. Medicine, 1951-52, asst. prof., 1952-54; asst. prof. biochemistry U. N.D. Sch. Medicine, Grand Forks, 1954-56, asso. prof., 1956-64, prof., 1964-87, prof. emeritus, 1987—. Dir., research supr. Nat. Sci. Research Participation Program in Biochemistry, 1959-63; advisor directorate for sci. edn. NSF. Contbr. articles to profl. jours. Mem. bishop's pastoral council Diocese of Fargo, N.D., 1979-86. Fellow AAAS, N.D. Acad. Sci. (editor 1967, 68); mem. Am. Soc. for Biochemistry and Molecular Biology, Am. Soc. for Nutritional Scis., Soc. Exptl. Biology and Medicine, Am. Chem. Soc. (chmn. Red River valley sect. 1971), AAAS, AMA, Sigma Xi (pres. chpt. 1965-66, Faculty award for Outstanding Sci. Resch. U. N.D. chpt. 1982, cert. of recognition 1987), Alpha Sigma Nu, Phi Lambda Upsilon, Phi Rho Sigma. Home: 1525 Robertson Ct Grand Forks ND 58201-7303 Office: U ND Sch Medicine Dept Biochemistry and Molecular Biology Grand Forks ND 58202 E-mail: fjacobs@medicine.nodak.edu. *In teaching and research I find that it is indeed a way of life. Have faith in yourself and your creator. Do what is right, and seek what is true.*

JACOBS, GEORGE, broadcast engineering consulting company executive; b. N.Y.C., July 16, 1924; s. Benjamin and Henrietta (Myerson) J.; m. Beatrice Gregerman, May 27, 1947; children: Michele Jacobs Gordon, Joy Jacobs Kirschbaum. BEE, Pratt Inst., 1949; MSEE, U. Md., 1960. Registered profl. engr., Md., D.C. Govt. exec. Voice of America, USIA, 1949-76; bd. Internat. Broadcasting, Washington, 1976-80; pres. George Jacobs & Assocs., Inc., Silver Spring, Md., 1980—. Commr. Commn. Broadcasting to Cuba, 1983; mem. U.S. Del. major ITU Comm. Confs., 1949-92; sr. advisor to chmn. U.S. Del. ITU Conf. on High Frequency Broadcasting, 1984, 87. Co-author: The Shortwave Propagation Handbook, 1976, 80, rev. edit., 1995; also articles. 2d lt. USAF, 1943-46. Decorated Air medal, 1945; recipient Marconi Gold medal engring. achievement Radio Club of Am., 1977, Superior Honor award U.S. Govt., 1976, Outstanding Performance award 1980; Presdl. Commn. Pres. U.S., 1983; Jack Poppele Broadcast Honor award, 1992, Radio Engring. Achievement award Nat. Assn. Broadcasters, 1997; named to CQ Radio Hall of Fame, 2001. Fellow IEEE, Radio Club of Am.; mem. Assn. Fed. Comms. Cons. Engrs. Avocations: amateur radio, philately, traveling. Office: George Jacobs & Assocs Inc 8701 Georgia Ave Silver Spring MD 20910-3713 Fax: 301-587-8801. E-mail: gja@gjainc.com.

JACOBS, GEORGE BRAUN, neurosurgeon; b. Poland, Jan. 9, 1934; naturalized U.S. citizen, 1954; s. Maurice and Lena J.; m. Rosanne Wille, 1980; children: Leigh, Steven, Alec. Jeffrey. Student, NYU, 1952-54; MD, SUNY, Syracuse, 1958; postgrad. in general surgery, Bronx Mcpl. Hosp., 1958-59; postgrad. in neurological surgery, Albert Einstein Coll. of Medicine, 1959-64. Cert. airline transport pilot, flight instr., sr. aviation med. examiner, FAA accident counselor. Attending neurosurgeon Hackensack (N.J.) Med. Ctr., 1965-86, sr. attending neurosurgeon, 1986—, chief neurosurgery sect., 1981-86; attending surgeon Holy Name Hosp., Teaneck, N.J., 1965, chief neurosurgery, 1976-81, 90-94; chief sect. neurosurgery Hackensack (N.J.) U. Med. Ctr., 1970-86; chief spine surgery Hackensack U. Med. Ctr., 1986—; chmn. dept. neurosurgery, chief spine surgery Hackensack (N.J.) U. Med. Ctr., 1986—; dir. spine svcs. Montefiore Med. Ctr. Albert Einstein Coll. Medicine, Bronx, 1992-93; prof. neurological surgery U. Pitts. Sch. Medicine, 1993-94; dir. spine ctr., spine surgery U. Pitts., 1993-94; prof. neurosurgery U. Medicine and Dentistry of N.J., Newark, 1994—. Vis. prof. neurosurgery, U. Saigon, Vietnam, 1965-66; clin. asst. prof. neurosurgery, N.J. Coll. Medicine, Newark, 1970-73; asst. prof. clin. neurosurgery, Albert Einstein Coll. Medicine, 1973-75; assoc. prof. clin. neurosurgery, 1975-89; prof. clin. neurosurgery, 1989-92, prof. neurosurgery, 1992-93; spkr. numerous convs./cons. in field. Author: (novel) A Simple Twist of Fate, (textbooks) Medical Malpractice: A Guide to Medical Issues, 1986, Textbook of Operatives Spine Surgery, 1999; contbr. numerous articles to profl. jours. and publs. Fellow U.S. Public Health Svc., 1959-60; bd. trustees Lehman Coll. Art Gallery, 1986-87; bd. dirs. Hackensack U. Med. Ctr. Found., 1997—, gov. bd. govs., 1979—; mem. Hillcrest Found. Bd., 1980—; bd. dirs. Lehman Coll. Art Gallery, 1986-87. Decorated Army Commendation medal for Vietnam Svc., 1966; Disting. Svc. cert. of Merit Bd. of Chosen Freeholders of Bergen County, 1971. Fellow USPHS, Am. Coll. Surgeons, Am. Coll. Angiology, Internat. Coll. Angiology, Internat. Coll. Surgeons, Scoliosis Rsch. Soc., Cervical Spine Rsch. Soc., N.Am. Spine Soc.; mem. AMA, Internat. Soc. Pediatric Neurosurgery, Internat. Health Policy and Mgmt. Inst., Am. Pain Soc., Am. Assn. Neurol. Surgeons (chmn. liaison com. 1976-78), Bergen County Med. Soc. (trustee 1976, mem. judicial com. 1977-82, chmn. legis. com. 1980), Congress of Neurol. Surgeons, Assn. of Mil. Surgeons of U.S., N.Y. Soc. Neurosurgery, Acad. Medicine N.J., N.J. Neurosurg. Soc. (mem. exec. com. 1973, chmn. peer review com., 1974, pres. 1989-90), Fla. Med. Assn., Fla. Physicians Assn., Soc. Surgeons of N.J., Med. Soc. N.J., San Francisco Neurosurg. Soc. (corr.), others. Avocations: golf, aviation, boating, cooking gourmet. : PO Box 4148 South Hackensack NJ 07606

JACOBS, GRACE GAINES, retired gerontologist, adult education educator; b. Mpls., Aug. 29, 1919; d. Abe S. and Ruth (Justman) Gaines; m. Michael M. Jacobs, Mar. 30, 1943; children: Laurence Bruce, Yana Arlene, Robert Marc. AA, Santa Monica City Coll., 1969; BA in Anthropology, Calif. State U., Northridge, 1971, MA in Ednl. Psychology, 1973. Owner, editor, pub. Publicraft Assocs., Detroit, 1948-50; instr. adult edn. L.A. City Schs., 1974-80. Writer: (handbook) Teaching Older Adults, 1978. Nat. program chair Gray Panthers, Phila. and Washington, 1982-84, mem. nat steering com., 1978-86; host Speaking of Seniors radio program KPFK-Pacifica, L.A., 1976-85; mem. Consumer Action Bd., San Francisco, 1988-93; mem. Pacific Bell Intelligent Network Task Force, San Francisco, 1984-87; mem. housing adv. com. City of Santa Cruz, Calif., 1984-90; obtained funding and site for startup SeniorNet Computer Ctr., Santa Cruz, 1989. Mem. Am. Soc. Aging, AAUW, LWV (chair 2 yr. study on nat health Santa Cruz, Calif., 1993-95), Geneal. Soc., Lifelong Learners Univ. Santa Cruz (pres. 1993-94). Democrat. Avocations: writing, family history.

JACOBS, GREGG ARTHUR, oceanographer, researcher; b. Denver, Apr. 10, 1964; s. Isaac and Shaaron Valeria Jacobs; m. Mary Beth Bradford, Mar. 4, 1964. BS, U. Colo., 1986, PhD, 1991; MS, Oreg. State U., 1988. EIT. Oceanographer Naval Rsch. Lab., Stennis Space Center, Miss., 1992—. Adj. faculty mem. U. So. Miss., Hattisburg, 1994—, U. Colo., Boulder, 2001—; principle investigator Naval Rsch. Lab., Stennis Space Center, 1995—. Contbr. articles to profl. jours. Achievements include research in decadal-scale trans-Pacific propagation and warming effects of El Nino anomaly; Yellow and East China Seas response to winds and currents; coastal wave generation in the Bohai Bay and propagation along the Chinese coast; sea surface height variations in the Yellow and East China Seas; the global structure of the annual and semi annual sea surface height variability from Geosat altimeter data; patents for consistent combination of altimeter data from multiple satellites; system for predicting wind-driven setup or setdown in continental shelf region. Home: 140 Rue Royal Slidell LA 70461 Office: Naval Research Laboratory Code 7323 Stennis Space Center MS 39529 Office Fax: 228-688-4759. Personal E-mail: ga_jacobs@hotmail.com. E-mail: jacobs@nrlssc.navy.mil.

JACOBS, GRETCHEN HUNTLEY, psychiatrist; b. N.Y.C., July 20, 1941; d. L. Gordon and Gertrude Mary (Eberz) La Pointe; m. Michael Edward Jacobs, Dec. 26, 1965 (div.); children: Dylan Huntley, Danielle La Pointe. BS, Fordham U., N.Y.C., 1963; MD, SUNY, Bklyn., 1968. Diplomate Am. Bd. Psychiatry and Neurology, Am. Bd. Child and Adolescent Psychiatry. Pediatric intern St. Luke's Hosp., N.Y.C., 1968—69; psychiatry resident George Washington U. Hosp., Washington, 1969—71; child psychiatry resident Beth Israel Hosp., Boston, 1972—73, McLean Hosp. Children's Ctr., Waltham, 1973—74; coord. health and human devel. Martha's Vinyard Sch. Sys., 1974—80; pvt. practice adult and adolescent/child psychiatry, 1974—; asst. clin. prof. child psychiatry Tufts U. Med. Sch., Boston, 1974—. Contbr. articles to profl. jours. Cons. Mass. Dept. Pub. Health Svcs. to Multi-Handicapped Children, 1974-75; bd. dirs. Mass. Dept. Social Svcs., 1979-83; founding mem., clin. dir. Vineyard Child Assault Prevention Project, 1986, Com. on Rural Child Psychiatry, 1988-92; active Hospice of Martha's Vineyard, Coun. for Young Children. Mem. AMA, NAACP, LWV, Am. Psychiat. Assn., New England Coun. Child and Adolescent Psychiatry, Am. Acad. Child and Adolescent Psychiatry, Mass. Med. Soc., Rotary Internat. Avocations: music, dancing, travel, sailing, theater, basketball. Home and Office: Tashmoo Farm RR 1 Box 600 Vineyard Haven MA 02568-9733

JACOBS, HAROLD ROBERT, mechanical engineering educator, practitioner; b. Portland, Oreg., Nov. 19, 1936; s. Harold Henry and Catherine Mae (Gill) J.; m. Georgene Kirkpatrick, Aug. 26, 1961; children: Sara Catherine, Harold Robert, Kenneth Patrick. BS cum laude, U. Portland, 1958; MS in Mech. Engring., Wash. State U., 1961; PhD in Mech. Engring., Ohio State U., 1965. Registered profl engr., Utah, Wash. Engr. GE, San Jose, Calif., Hanford, Wash., 1958-59, 60; instr. dept. mech. engring. Wash. State U., Pullman, 1959-61; rsch. engr. aerospace divsn. Boeing Co., Seattle, 1961-62, 63; instr. mech engring. Ohio State U., Columbus, 1963-64; mem. tech. staff Aerospace Corp., San Bernadino, Calif., 1964-67; prof. dept. mech. engring. U. Utah, Salt Lake City, 1967-69, from asst. prof. to assoc prof., 1969-74, chmn. fluid mechanics divsn. Coll. Engring., 1974-79, prof. mech. engring., 1974-84, chmn. applied mechanics divsn., 1977-84, chmn. dept. civil engring., 1978-79, assoc. dean rsch., 1981-84; prof. mech engring., head dept. Pa. State U., University Park, 1984-94, prof. emeritus, 1994—. Dean Coll. Engring., prof. mech. engring. Colo. State U., Ft. Collins, 1994-99; chief engr. CEEMS, Bothell, Wash., 1999—; mem. summer faculty Sandia Nat. Labs., Livermore, Calif., 1981; vis. prof. U. Strathclyde, Glasgow, Scotland, 1976-77; vis. prof. Imperial Coll., U. London, summer 1992; affiliate prof. mech. engring., U. Wash., Seattle, 1999—; cons. numerous corps. Mem. internat. adv. bd. Russian Jour. Engring. Thermophysics, 1991—; contbr. numerous articles to profl. jours.; patentee in field; reviewer numerous jours. Ohio State U. fellow, 1962-63. Assoc. fellow AIAA (assoc. adv. coun. Utah sect. 1971-77, treas. 1972-73, chmn. 1974-75, Engr. of Yr. award 1973, numerous coms.); fellow ASME (chmn. gen. papers, coordinating com. heat transfer divsn., chmn. com. on heat transfer in mfg. and material processing 1991-94, mem. numerous coms., tech. editor Jour Heat Transfer 1986-92); mem. ASEE, Am. Inst. Chem. Engrs. (dir. thermal systems divsn. 1994-96, dir. 1994-96, 2d vice chair 1998-99, 1st vice chair 1999-2000, chair 2000-2001, past chair 2001-02), Sigma Xi (Ohio State Outstanding Engring. Alumnus 1991). Office: CEEMS 8045 Toma Ln Clinton WA 98236 E-mail: geokir2@whidbey.com.

JACOBS, HARRY ALLAN, JR., investment firm executive; b. N.Y.C., June 28, 1921; s. Harry Allan and Elsie (Wolf) J.; m. Marie Stevens, Dec. 31, 1942 (dec. Sept. 1991); childrren: Nancy Jacobs Haneman, Harry Allan III; m. Joannie Patterson, Apr. 18, 1997. BA, Dartmouth Coll., 1942. With Bache Group Inc. (now Prudential-Bache Securities, Inc.), N.Y.C., 1946—, from ptnr. to chmn., 1956-86, sr. dir. investment supervisory group, 1987—. Bd. govs. N.Y. Stock Exch., 1969-72. Former trustee Trudeau Inst., Lake Placid, N.Y.; past dir. Dem. Nat. Com., Ctr. Nat. Policy; past chmn. Dem. Bus. Council. 1st lt. USAAF, 1942-45. Mem. Assn. Stock Exch. Firms (past com. chmn., mem. exec. com.), Investment Bankers Assn. (past gov., chmn. pub. rels. com.), Investment Assn. N.Y. (past pres.), Bond Club N.Y. (past gov., sec.), City Midday Club, Univ. Club, Econ. Club, N.Y. Stock Exch. Luncheon Club, Ardsley Country Club (N.Y.), Lake Placid Club (N.Y.). Clubs: Wall Street, Univ., Econ., N.Y. Stock Exchange Luncheon (N.Y.C.); Ardsley (N.Y.) Country; Lake Placid (N.Y.). Office: Prudential Securities Inc 1 New York Plz Fl 34 New York NY 10004-1901

JACOBS, HARRY MILBURN, JR., advertising executive; b. July 23, 1928; s. Harry Milburn and Nina (Gibbs) J.; m. Barbara Ann Mills; children: Kathryn, Christopher, Letitia. Student, East Carolina U., 1947-49; BFA, Corcoran Coll. Design, 1951. Art dir. The Hecht Co., Washington, 1951-53, Bradham & Co., Greensboro, N.C., 1953-54, sr. art dir., 1956-59; assoc. art dir. Cargill, Wilson & Acree, Richmond, Va., 1959-61, creative dir. Charlotte, N.C., 1961-68, corp. creative dir. Atlanta, 1969-74, pres., 1970-74, Martin Agy., Richmond, Va., 1977-83, vice-chmn., 1983-86, chmn. bd., 1986—, CEO, 1989, chmn. emeritus, 1997. Scoutmaster Boy Scouts Am., 1956-58, mem. exec. coun. Robert E. Lee coun., 1987-89; bd. visitors Sch. Journalism, U. N.C., Chapel Hill, Va. Commonwealth U. Found.; bd. overseers Corcoran Coll. of Design, Washington; bd. dirs. Meml. Guidance Clinic, Richmond Children's Mus., Marymount Park, Goodwill Industries, Richmond Sch. Ballet, Virginians in Support of Guard and Res., Downtown Presents; bd. dirs. exec. com. Richmond Renaissance, bd. dirs. exec. com. Tryon Palace Comm. With U.S. Army, 1954-56. Recipient numerous advt. awards; named Advt. Man of Yr. Silver medal Am. Advt. Fedn., 1972; named to Top 100 Creative People, 1972, 75, 81, Best Men in Advt., McCall's Mag., 1992; elected to Va. Comms. Hall of Fame, 1986, N.C. Advt. Hall of Fame, 1991, One Club Creative Hallof Fame, N.Y., 2001; named one of Nation's Top Advt. Leaders, Wall St. Jour., 1989. Mem. One Club Art & Copy N.Y., Art Dirs. Club of N.Y., Commonwealth Club, Capital Club. Republican. Office: Martin Agy One Shockoe Plaza Richmond VA 23219-4132 E-mail: hjacobs2@cox.net.

JACOBS, HARVEY S. lawyer; b. Bradley Beach, N.J., 1958; s. Joseph and Leatrice J.; m. Marcia E. Clarke; 2 children. BBA in Acctg., George Washington U., 1980; JD, Bklyn. Law Sch., 1983. Bar: N.Y. 1984, D.C. 1985, Md. 1995. Assoc. Graham & James (merger Austrian, Lance & Stewart and Graham & James), N.Y.C., 1984-87, Mudge Rose Guthrie Alexander & Ferdon, N.Y.C., 1987-88, Ginsburg Feldman & Bress, Washington, 1988-89; ptnr. Joyce & Jacobs, Washington, 1989-2000; mng. dir. Jacobs & Assocs., Attys. at Law, Washington, 2000—. Internet corr. ABC-TV World News Now; gen. counsel stress-free settlements. Author: A Business and Legal Guide to Global E-Commerce; editor: D.C. Bar Practice Manual; contbr. articles on Internet and real estate to Wired Unique Homes, Dist. Lawyer mags., Internet: Legal and Business Aspects, Small Bus. News, Georgetowner. Mem. ABA (sect. on bus. law), D.C. Bar Assn. (steering com. of real estate, housing and land use sect., former chair real property transactions subcom.), George Washington U. Sch. Govt. and Bus. Alumni Assn. (pres. 1986-88), Balt.-Washington Venture Group, Kiwanis (dir.). Office: Jacobs & Assocs Atty at Law Ste 800 2300 M St NW Washington DC 20037-4924 E-mail: jacobs@internet-law-firm.com.

JACOBS, IRWIN LAWRENCE, diversified corporate executive; b. Mpls., July 15, 1941; s. Samuel and Rose H. Jacobs; m. Alexandra Light, Aug. 26, 1962; children: Mark, Sheila, Melinda, Randi, Trisha. Student pub. schs. Chmn. Genmar Holdings, Inc., Mpls.; chmn. bd. Genmar Industries, Inc., Mpls.; chmn. Jacobs Trading Co., Mpls.; pres., CEO Jacobs Investors, Inc., Mpls.; pres. Jacobs Realty II, Inc., Mpls., 1993—, Jacobs Mgmt. Corp., 1983—, Gateway S/B, Inc., 1993—; chmn. Watkins Inc., Winona, Minn., Operation Bass, Inc., Gilbersville, Ky., 1996—, FLW Tour, Inc., Mpls., 1996—. Mem.: Mpls., Lafayette Country, Oakridge Country. Office: Genmar Holdings Inc 2900 IDS Ctr 80 S 8th St Minneapolis MN 55402-2100

JACOBS, IRWIN MARK, communications executive; b. New Bedford, Mass., Oct. 18, 1933; B in Elec. Engring., Cornell U., 1956; MS, MIT, 1957, ScD, 1959. Rsch. asst. in elec. engring. MIT, Cambridge, Mass., 1958-59, from asst. to assoc. prof., 1959-66; from assoc. to prof. info. and computer sci. U. Calif., San Diego, 1966-72; pres. Linkabit Corp., 1968-85; chmn. & CEO Qualcomm Inc., San Diego, 1985—. Cons. Applied Rsch. Lab. Sylvania Elect. Products, Inc., 1959—, Lincoln Lab. MIT, 1961-62, Indsl. Tchg. Mpls. Honeywell, Inc., 1963, Bolt Beranek & Newman, Inc., 1965; NASA resident rsch. fellow Jet Propulsion Lab., 1964-65; chmn. sci. adv. group Def. Comm. Agy. and Engring. Adv. Coun. U. Calif. Recipient Biann award, 1980, Excel award Am. Electronics Assn., 1989, Nat. Tech. medal U.S. Dept. Commerce Tech. Adminstrn., 1994. Fellow IEEE; mem. NAE, Assn. Computing Machinery, Sigma Xi. Office: Qualcomm Inc 5775 Morehouse Dr San Diego CA 92121-1714 also: 10185 Mckellar Ct San Diego CA 92121-4233

JACOBS, JAMES PAUL, retired insurance executive; b. Augusta, Ark., May 14, 1930; s. James Leonard and Ida Lee (Taylor) J.; m. Joan Gillum, Aug. 18, 1956; 2 children: LeAnn J. Alvarez, Caryl Lynn Watson. Student, Louis A. Allen Mgmt., 1970; Assoc. in mgmt., Ins. Inst. of Am., 1971. Underwriter trainee Ins. Co. of N. Am., Phila., 1954-55, underwriter Richmond, Va., 1955-58, supervising underwriter, 1958-64, underwriting mgr., 1964-68, Detroit, 1968-71; casualty mgr. Montgomery & Collins, Inc., L.A., 1971-73; ptnr. Tabb Brockenbrough & Ragland, Richmond, Va., 1973-1995, ret., 1995. Mem. agts. adv. coun. Comml. Union Ins. Co., Boston, Gt. Am. Ins. Co. Cin., Cigna Cos. Phila., Pa. Mfrs. Assn. Ins. Co., Phila., ITT Hartford, Conn., Jonathan Trumbell Assocs., Md. Ins. Group Agts. Forum, U.S. Fidelity and Guaranty Co.; bd. dirs. "All Industry" Va. "I" Day Corp., Richmond; instr. U. Richmond, 1965-78. Contbr. articles to profl. jours. Active in Colonial Williamsburg Assocs., Friends of Kennedy Ctr., Smithsonian Assocs.; bd. dirs. Daily Planet, Richmond (non-profit orgn. for aiding the homeless), pres., 1995-97. Capt. USMC, 1951-54. Mem. CPCU (bd. dirs. 1979-82, regional v.p. 1981, chpt. officer 1976-79). Republican. Methodist. Avocation: sports fan. *Strive to exceed expectations in your every endeavor.*

JACOBS, JEFFREY LEE, lawyer, education network company executive; b. Boston, Jan. 20, 1951; s. Philip and Millicent T. (Katz) J.; m. Deborah R. Rath, June 7, 1981; children: Alison, Hannah. BA, U. Pa., 1973; MPA, U. So. Calif., 1979; JD, Pace U., 1985. Bar: Conn. 1985, N.Y. 1988. Asst. to comptroller gen. U.S. Gen. Acctg. Office, Washington, 1976-80; sr. rsch. assoc. Nat. Acad. Pub. Adminstrn., Washington, 1980-83; dir. of seminars Prentice Hall, Clifton, N.J., 1985-87; pres. Profl. Edn. Network, Inc., Westport, Conn., 1987—. Lectr. Ga. Tax Inst., Ohio Fed. Tax Inst.; adj. prof. Quinnipiac Coll., Univ. New Haven; cons. SmartPros Ltd. Co-author: GAO: Government Accountability, 1979; producer, writer TV series The CPA Report, 1988-91; producer, writer radio series Legal Practice Alert, 1990—. Trustee Westport Pub. Libr. Mem. ABA (taxation sect.), Acad. Legal Studies in Bus. Home: 16 Janson Dr Westport CT 06880-2568 Office: SmartPros Ltd 12 Skyline Dr Hawthorne NY 10532-2133 E-mail: jeffjacobs@aol.com.

JACOBS, JEREMY M. diversified holding company executive, hockey team owner; b. Jan. 21, 1940; m. Margaret Jane Davis; 6 children. DHL (hon.), Canisius Coll.; BA, SUNY, Buffalo; grad. advancement mgmt. program, Harvard U. Chmn., CEO Del North Cos., Buffalo, 1968—; former owner Cin. Royals Basketball team; owner, gov. Boston Bruins, NHL, 1975—; owner, gov. Boston Garden, now Fleet Ctr., 1975—. Active United Way, NCCJ, Joint Ctr. for Polit. and Econ. Studies, Internat. Tennis Hall of Fame. Mem, U.S. Travel & Tourism Promotion adv. bd., 2003-. Office: Del North Company Inc 40 Fountain Plz Buffalo NY 14202-2229 also: 1 Fleetcenter Pl Ste 250 Boston MA 02114-1390*

JACOBS, JIM, actor, playwright, composer, lyricist; b. Chgo., Oct. 7, 1942; m. Diane Rita Gomez, June 5, 1965 (div. 1974); 1 child, Kristine; m. Denise Nettleton, Apr. 29, 1978 (div. 2003). Student, Chgo. City Coll., 1962-63. Appeared in over 50 cmty. and profl. theatre prodns. including Until the Monkey Comes, 1966, Take Me Along, 1967, Flora, The Red Menace, 1968, Entertaining Mr. Sloane, 1969, The Serpent, 1969, Don't Drink the Water, 1970, Jimmy Shine, 1970, all Chgo., No Place to Be Somebody, nat. touring co., 1971, on Broadway, 1971, The Magnolia Club, Chgo., 1975, The Local Stigmatic, Chgo., 1976; dir. The Ruffian on the Stair, Chgo., 1975; actor: (films) Medium Cool, 1969, Love in a Taxi, 1976, (TV series) Open All Night, 1982; author, lyricist, composer: (with Warren Casey) Grease, Broadway, 1972-80, (Tony award nomination 1972, Grammy award nomination 1972), London-West End, 1973, 77, motion picture, 1979, (revival) Grease, London, 1993— (Olivier award nomination), (revival) Broadway, 1994-98 (Tony award nomination), Grease On Ice (Am. Ice Show Tour), 1998—; author: (with Warren Casey) Island of Lost Coeds, 1979; (with Jim Weston) Bats in the Belfry, 1982; (with Jim Weston) Remember the Night, 1988. Recipient Humanitarian of Yr. award Young Adult Inst., N.Y.C., 1992. Mem. Dramatists Guild, Authors League Am., ASCAP, Actors Equity Assn., Screen Actors Guild., AFTRA Office: care Ronald Taft PC 18 W 55th St New York NY 10019-5315

JACOBS, JOHN E. lawyer; b. Detroit, Feb. 13, 1947; s. Morton and Gilberta (Jewell) J.; m. Gilda Gail Zalenko, June 6, 1971; children: Rachel H., Jessica E. BA, Mich. State U., 1968; JD, U. Mich., 1971. Bar: Mich. 1971, U.S. Dist. Ct. (ea. dist.) Mich. 1971, U.S. Ct. Appeals (6th cir.) 1984, U.S. Dist. Ct. (we. dist.) Mich. 1997. Assoc. Butzel, Levin, Winston & Quint, Detroit, 1971-76, ptnr., 1976-81; shareholder Mason, Steinhardt, Jacobs, Perlman & Pesick, P.C., Southfield, Mich., 1981-2000, DKW Law Group, P.C., Southfield, 2000—02, Maddin, Hauser, Wartell, Roth & Heller, P.C., 2002—. Contbr. articles to profl. jours. Pres. Jewish Family Svc., Southfield, 1991-93, Temple Emanu-El, Oak Park, Mich., 1995-97. Mem. ABA (mem. consumer fin. svcs. com. 1978—), Jewish Fedn. Met. Detroit (bd. govs. 1997—, mem. exec. com. 1998-99, 2002—). Democrat. Avocations: golfing, bicycling. Home: 8353 Hendrie Blvd Huntington Woods MI 48070-1613 Office: Maddin Hauser Wartell Roth & Heller PC Third Fl Essex Ctr 28400 Northwestern Hwy Southfield MI 48034

JACOBS, JOHN PATRICK, lawyer; b. Chgo., Oct. 27, 1945; s. Anthony N. and Bessie (Montgomery) J.; m. Linda I. Grams, Oct. 6, 1973; 1 child, Christine Margaret. BA cum laude, U. Detroit, 1967, JD magna cum laude, 1970. Bar: Mich. 1970, U.S. Dist. Ct. Mich (ea. dist.) 1970, U.S. Ct. Appeals (6th cir.) 1974, U.S. Supreme Ct. 1978, U.S. Ct. Appeals (D.C. cir.) 1988, U.S. Ct. Appeals (4th cir.) 2001. Law clk. to chief judge Mich. Ct. Appeals, Detroit, 1970-71; assoc., then ptnr. Plunkett & Cooney P.C., Detroit, 1972-92, also bd. dirs.; founding ptnr., prin. mem. O'Leary, O'Leary, Jacobs, Mattson, Perry & Mason P.C., Southfield, Mich., 1992-99; prin., owner John P. Jacobs, P.C., 1999—. Investigator Atty. Grievance Com., Detroit, 1975-84; mem. hearing panel Atty. Discipline Bd., Detroit, 1984-87, 94—; adj. prof. law Sch. Law, U. Detroit, 1983-84, faculty advisor, 1984-89, Pres.'s Cabinet, 1982—; elected rep. State Bar Rep. Assembly, Lansing, Mich., 1980-82, 91-92, 93-96; fellow Mich. State Bar Found., 1990-98; treas., mem. steering com. Mich. Bench-Bar Appellate Conf. Com., 1994—; apptd. mem. Mich. Supreme Ct. Com. on Appellate Fees, 1990; spl. mediator appellate negotiation program Mich. Ct. Appeals, 1995—; mem. exec. com. Mich. Appellate Bench-Bar Conf. Found., 1996—; appellate counsel to State Bar of Mich., mem. profl. ethics com., 1998, mem. multi-disciplinary practice com., 1999. Bd. editors Mich. Lawyers Weekly. Bd. dirs. Boysville of Mich., Clinton, 1988-95, 99—, chmn. pub. policy com., 1993-95, pub. policy liaison, 1999—; apptd. mem. State Bar Mich. Blue Ribbon Com. Improving Def. Counsel-Insurer Rels., 1998-99. Named Mgsr. Malloy Cath. Lawyer of Yr., Archdiocese of Detroit, 2001; recipient Robert E. Dice Med. Malpractice Def. Atty. award, Mich. Physicians, 1986; fellow Reginald Heber Smith fellow, 1971—72. Fellow Am. Acad. Appellate Lawyers, Mich. Std. Jury Instn. (subcom. employment law 1984-87); mem. ABA (litigation sect., appellate subcom., torts and ins. practice), Internat. Assn. Def. Counsel (v.p., amicus curiae com., med. and legal malpractice coms., product liability com.), Fedn. Ins. and Corp. Counsel, Mich. Def. Trial Counsel (chmn. amicus curiae com. 1986-88, chmn. future planning com., bd. dirs. 1989—, treas. 1993-94, sec. 1994-95, v.p. 1995-96, program chair 1990, 94, 95, pres., 1996-97), Def. Rsch. Inst. (state rep. 1997-98, Outstanding Performance Citation 1997, nat. appellate com. steering com. 1997—), Cath. Lawyers Soc. (bd. dirs. 1988-98, emeritus dir. 1998—, pres. 1994-95), Supreme Ct. U.S. Hist. Soc., Supreme Ct. Mich. Hist. Soc., Democrat. Roman Catholic. Avocations: collecting antique law books, film. Office: The Dime Bldg 719 Griswold Ste 600 Detroit MI 48226

JACOBS, JONATHAN A. philosopher, educator; b. Stamford, Conn., Nov. 28, 1955; s. N. J. and S. M. Jacobs; m. Nancy L. Pruitt; children: Nathan, Daniel. BA, Wesleyan U., Middletown, Conn., 1977; PhD, U. Pa., 1983. Prof. Philosophy Colgate U., Hamilton, NY. Vis. prof. U. Edinburgh, Scotland, 1999; hon. lectr. U. St. Andrews, Scotland, 2000. Author: Practical Realism and Moral Psychology, 1995, A Philosopher's Compass, 2001, Choosing Character, 2001, Dimensions of Moral Theory, 2002. Rsch. fellow, Earhart Found., 1999, 2001, 2003. Mem.: So. Soc. for Phliosophy and Psychology, Brit. Soc. for Ethical Theory, Am. Philos. Assn., Clare Hall Cambridge U. (life). Office: Colgate U Dept Philosophy and Religion Hamilton NY 13346 E-mail: JJacobs@mail.colgate.edu.

JACOBS, JOSEPH JAMES, lawyer, communications company executive; b. Toronto, Ont., Can., Mar. 18, 1925; came to U.S., 1925; s. Sidney and Hildred Veronica (Greenberg) J.; m. Carole Evelyn Bent, Jan. 22, 1946 (div. 1972); children— Carole Lynn Urgenson, Joseph James III; m. Edna Mae Meincke, Jan. 5, 1973. J.D., Tulane U., 1950. Bar: La. 1950, N.Y. 1951, U.S. Dist. Ct. (so. dist.) N.Y. 1953, U.S. Ct. Mil. Appeals 1953, U.S. Ct. Appeals (2d cir.) 1977, U.S. Ct. Appeals (D.C. cir.) 1980. Assoc. Proskauer, Rose, Goetz & Mendelsohn, N.Y.C., 1950-53; asst. gen. counsel, asst. to pres. Am. Broadcasting Co., N.Y.C., 1954-60; gen. atty. Metromedia, Inc., N.Y.C., 1960-61; dir. program and talent negotiations United Artists TV, Inc., 1961-66; atty. United Artists Corp., N.Y.C., 1966-69; v.p., counsel United Artists Broadcasting, Inc., N.Y.C., 1969-71; gen. atty. ITT World Commd. Inc., N.Y.C., 1972-74; v.p., legal dir. ITT Commd. Ops. and Info. Svcs. Group (formerly U.S. Tel. & Tel. Corp.), N.Y.C. and Secaucus, N.J., 1974-83, ITT Comms. and Info. Svcs., Inc., Secaucus, 1983-87; v.p., gen. counsel U.S. Transmission Systems, Inc., Secaucus, 1984-87, ITT World Comms. Inc., Secaucus, 1984-87; of counsel Seyfarth, Shaw, Fairweathr & Geraldson, N.Y.C., 1988-89; v.p., gen. counsel Graphic Scanning Corp., Englewood, N.J., 1989-91; v.p., gen. counsel Ram/BSE, L.P., Woodbridge, N.J., 1992; pvt. practice, Wainscott, N.Y., 1992-95. Bd. editors Tulane Law Rev., 1949, asst. editor-in-chief, 1950; cons. 1996—. Served with parachute inf. U.S. Army, 1943-46, ETO, PTO, to maj. USAFR ret. Mem. Order of Coif. Republican. Jewish. Office: 6380 Sweet Maple Ln Boca Raton FL 33433-1933

JACOBS, JOSEPH JOHN, engineering company executive; b. June 13, 1916; s. Joseph and Afiffie (Forzley) J.; m. Violet Jabara, June 14, 1942; children: Margaret, Linda, Valerie. BS in Chem. Engring, Poly. Inst. N.Y., Bklyn., 1937, MS, 1939, PhD, 1942. Registered profl. engr., N.Y., N.J., La., Calif. Chem. engr. Autoxygen, Inc., N.Y.C., 1939-42; sr. chem. engr. Merck & Co., Rahway, N.J., 1942-44; v.p., tech. dir. Chemurgic Corp., Richmond, Calif., 1944-47; pres. Jacobs Engring. Co., Pasadena, Calif., 1947-74; chmn. bd., CEO Jacobs Engring. Group Inc., Pasadena, 1974-92, chmn. bd., 1992—. Prin. ptnr. Calif. Tech. Ptnrs.; bd. dirs. Cedars Bank. Contbr. tech. articles to profl. jours. Trustee Poly. U. N.Y., Harvey Mudd Coll.; mem. Assocs. Calif. Inst. Tech.; bd. dirs. Inst. Contemporary Studies, Calif.; bd. visitors Anderson Sch., UCLA. Recipient Herbert Hoover medal United Engring. Socs., 1983 Fellow AIChE, Am. Inst. Chemists, Inst. for Advancement Engring.; mem. AAAS, Nat. Acad. Engring., Am. Chem. Soc., L.A. C. of C., Pasadena C. of C., Annandale Golf Club, Sigma Xi, Phi Lambda Upsilon. Office: Jacobs Engring Group Inc 1111 S Arroyo Pkwy Pasadena CA 91105-3254

JACOBS, JULIAN I. federal judge; b. Balt., Aug. 13, 1937; s. Sidney and Bernice (Kellman) J.; m. Donna Buffenstein; children: Richard S., Jennifer K. BA, U. Md., 1958, JD, 1960; LL.M., Georgetown U., 1965. Bar: Md., 1960. Atty. chief counsel's office IRS, Washington, 1961-65, trial atty. regional counsel's office Buffalo, 1965-67; assoc. Weinberg & Green, Balt., 1967-69, Hoffberger & Hollander, Balt., 1969-72, Gordon Feinblatt Rothman Hoffberger & Hollander, Balt., 1972-74, ptnr., 1974-84; judge U.S. Tax Ct., Washington, 1984—. Chmn. study commn. Md. Tax Ct., 1978-79, mem. rules com., 1980; mem. spl. study group Md. Gen. Assembly, 1980; adj. prof. grad. tax program U. Balt., 1991-93; adj. prof. law, U. San Diego, 2001; adj. prof. grad. tax program, U. Denver, 2001—. Mem.: U Md. Law Rev. Bd. Mem. Md. State Bar Assn. (past chmn. taxation sect.), Balt. City Bar Assn. (past chmn. tax legis. subcom.). Office: US Tax Ct 400 2nd St NW Washington DC 20217-0002

JACOBS, KAREN LOUISE, medical technologist; b. Kingston, N.Y., May 7, 1943; d. William Charles and Vera Elizabeth (Kelly) J. BS in Applied Tech., Empire State Coll., 1976; MS in Pub. Svc. Adminstrn., Russell Sage Coll., 1982. Sr. lab. tech., hosp. lab. supr. City of Kingston Labs., 1962-68; sr. rsch. asst. Dudley Obs., Albany, N.Y., 1972-75; lab. adminstr. Albany Med. Coll., 1976-99, faculty, 1982-97; tchr. environ. edn. Five Rivers Environ. Edn. Ctr., Delmar, NY, 1999—; tchr. natural sci. Heldeberg Workshop. Guest lectr. Sage Coll.; coord. complex labs. JCAHO regulations, 1997; infection control com. and subcoms. on AIDS mgmt. and human immunodeficiency virus universal precautions Albany Med. Ctr. Infection Control, 1987-97, accreditation regulatory oversight com.; pvt. piano tchr. Albany Acad. for Boys, 1999—; accompanist Siena Coll./Cmty. Chorale; accompanist Colonie Sr. Citizens. Bd. dirs. chpt. Leukemia Soc. Am., 1983-87; judge sci. and tech. summer issue on excellence in Am. U.S. News and World Report; vol. asst. naturalist Five Rivers Environ. Ctr. Mem. Clin. Lab. Mgmt. Assn. (del. citizen amb. program to China 1989), Am. Soc. Clin. Pathologists, Earthwatch, Nat. Speleological Soc., Hudsonia (bd. dirs. 1995), Adirondack Mountain Club. Home: 50 Meadowbrook Dr Apt 149 Slingerlands NY 12159-2146

JACOBS, KENNETH A. composer, educator; b. Sept. 13, 1948; s. Harvey C. Jacobs; children: Jennifer, Michael, David, Sarah. BA, N.Mex. State U., 1969, MusM, 1970; DMA, U. Tex., 1975. Prof. N.Mex. Western U., 1971, U. Tenn., 1974—. Composer: (orch.) Caravans, Symphony #1, Symphony #2-Gypsy Nights, Symphony #3, Symphony #4-Wonderland's Gifts, Concerto for violin and orch., flute concerto-Angels Speak No Words, clarinet concerto-Imaginings on the Wind; (wind ensemble) Again Wild Spring; (soprano and string trio) Midsummer Vocalise; (string quartet) Canopy of Dreams; (computer synthesized tape) Saffron, Elena, Woman on the Dunes, Little Birds, Second Touch, The Sun Gatherer; (ballet) Magic of the Rainbow Man, Secret World, Spirit Dances; (piano) Windows to Three, Treasures of a Captured Sun, Tracing Infinity, Ring of Gold, Portraits; (woodwinds) Bookends, While Children Sleep; (brass quintet) Ambassadors of Fortune; (choir and keyboard) Letters of Love, Five Biblical Songs, In His Hand; (voice and percussion) The Pine Planters; (trumpet) Through the Hourglass; (horn) Night Covers All, Rivulet, Snowman; (tuba) Mountain Mischief; (viola) Drifter's Heart; (oboe) Sand Castles; (flute) Legends, Jenny's Delight, Indian Summer; (clarinet) Fragments Torn From the Heart; (string bass) Anxious Arrivals; (alto sax) The Wind at the Top of the Hill; (bassoon) Twilight Voices; (songs) Bow to Your Partner, And You Hold Me, Gestures in the Face of Time, others; (multimedia with photography) Private Obsessions, Savanna Afternoon; (multimedia with synchronized artwork projections) Passage to Honor House, Draw Down the Dark Moon, Celestial Illusions, A Model, Winter Strategy, Walk in Many Lands, Scenes from the Earth; guest artist numerous orgns.; commns. Balt. Sch. Arts, DeReggi Interarts Ensemble, U. Tenn. Orch., U. Tenn. Bicentennial, Tenn. Music Tchrs. Assn.; contbr. articles to jours. U. Tenn. grantee; recipient Disting. Composer award Tenn. Music Tchrs. Assn., 1988, 95, Bergen Festival, 1996, S.A.I./Cath. U. award, 1998, Brown U. Choral prize, 1982, Tex. Music Edn. Assn. award, 1974, CCNY award, 1985, Internat. New Music Composers Competition, 1988, Tenn. Composer Competition award, 1988, others. Mem. Broadcast Music Inc., Coll. Music Soc., Soc. of Composers, Southeastern Composers League, Phi Kappa Phi, Pi Kappa Lambda. Home: 1229 Westbury Rd Knoxville TN 37922-8010

JACOBS, LAURA, probation/parole officer; b. N.Y.C., Oct. 17, 1959; d. Peter Leopold Jacobs and Nancy Jane (Norris) Robinson. BS, York Coll. of Pa., 1979; paralegal cert., Pa. State U., 1987. Cert. ct. reporting network evaluator; cert. Better Bus. Bur. arbitrator. Proprietor The Frame Shop, York, 1982-83; crisis intervention counselor York County Mental Health Ctr., York, 1981-84; probation/parole officer York County Probation Dept., 1984—. CRN evaluator New Insights, York, 1988—. Mem., former chair DUI Adv. Coun., York, 1986-2003, chair criminal justice com., 1988-2003; vol. mediator Mediation Svcs. for Conflict Resolution, York, 1996—, bd. dirs., 1996-99; vol. arbitrator Better Bus. Bur., Lancaster, Pa., 1997-99; mem. tng. com. Mediation Svcs. for Conflict Resolution, York, 1996-99; mem. York County DUI Spkr.'s Bur. Home: 24 S Hartley St York PA 17404-3702 Office: York County Probation Dept 100 W Market St York PA 17401-1332 E-mail: inj1@netzero.net.

JACOBS, LESLIE WILLIAM, lawyer; b. Akron, Ohio, Dec. 5, 1944; s. Leslie Wilson and Louise Francis (Walker) J.; m. Laurie Hutchinson, July 12, 1962; children— Leslie James, Andrew Wilson, Walker Fulton. Student, Denison U., 1962-63; BS, Northwestern U., 1965; JD, Harvard U., 1968. Bar: Ohio 1968, D.C. 1980, U.S. Supreme Ct. 1971, Brussels 1996. Law clk. to Chief Justice Kingsley A. Taft Ohio Supreme Ct., 1968-69; assoc. Thompson, Hine and Flory, Cleve., 1969-76, ptnr., 1976—, chmn. antitrust, internat. and regulatory area, 1988-99; chmn. bus. regulation and trade dept. Thompson Hine LLP and predecessor, Cleve., 1999—. Lectr. conf. bd. Ohio Legal Ctr. Insts., Ohio State Bar Assn. Antitrust and Corp. Counsel Insts., Fed. Bar Assn., ABA, Canadian Inst., Internat. Assn. Young Lawyers, others; mem. Ohio Bd. Bar Examiners, 1990-94. Contbr. articles to profl. jours. Chmn. EconomicsAmerica, 1990-93; mem. vis. com. Case Western Res. U. Sch. Law, 1985-91; trustee, mem. exec. com. The Holden Arboretum; mem. Leadership Cleve., 1988. Lt. comdr. USNR, 1967-79. Fellow Am. Bar Found. (life), Ohio State Bar Found. (life, trustee 1985-87, Ritter award 1997); mem. ABA (ho. dels. 1986—, antitrust law sect. coun. 1985-88, officer 1991-97, state del. 1995-2001, nominating com. 1995-2001, bd. gov. 2001—, task force on corp. liability), Ohio State Bar Assn. (pres. 1987, Ohio Bar medal 1990), Cleve. Bar Assn. (chmn. jud. selection com. 1982, trustee 1983-85), Am. Law Inst., 6th Cir. Jud. Conf. (life), Nat. Conf. Bar Pres., Harvard Club (N.Y.C.), Chagrin Valley Hunt Club, Union Club (Cleve.), Castalia Trout Club. Republican. Presbyterian. Office: Thompson Hine LLP 3900 Key Ctr 127 Public Sq Cleveland OH 44114-1291

JACOBS, LINDA JOAN, educator; b. Balt., Mar. 25, 1941; d. Bernard and Freda (Statter) White; m. Martin H. Jacobs, Aug. 3, 1963. BA, U. Md., 1962, MA, 1965, EdD, 1971. Tchr. Baltimore County Pub. Schs., Towson, Md., 1962-64, resource supr., 1967-68; research teaching asst. U. Md., College Park, 1964-67, asst. prof. spl. edn., 1968-71, undergrad. program coordinator, 1971-73; dir. spl. edn. Anne Arundel County Bd. Edn., Annapolis, Md., 1974-77; asst. supt. Md. State Dept. Edn., Balt., 1977-79; dir. Harbour Sch.-Am Innovative Learning Ctr., Annapolis, 1979-89, The Harbour Sch., Annapolis, 1990—. Sec. bd. dirs. Bernard White & Co., Pikesville, Md., 1979-89, Harbour Sch., Balt.; cons. to over 125 sch. dists. throughout U.S., 1971—; presenter Internat. Coun. for Exceptional Children Conf., 1989, 90, 91. Author: (books) Every Child an Individual, 1987, The Fourth R - Behavin' Right, 1991, 1998, 1999, 2001, 2003. Mem. Gov.'s Commn. on Funding for Spl. Edn., Annapolis, 1975, Gov.'s Adv. Com. on Handicapped, Annapolis, 1977, Com. to Re-elect Lamb, Anne Arundel, Md., 1986. Recipient Gov.'s Citation for 25 Yrs. Service to the Handicapped, 1987. Mem. Assn. Retarded Citizens, Council for Exceptional Children (Md. state pres. 1970-72), Assn. for Children with Learning Disabilities (advisor 1979—), Kappa Delta Pi. Democrat. Jewish. Avocation: photography. Home: 8808 Sonya Rd Randallstown MD 21133-4016 Office: Harbour Sch 1277 Green Holly Dr Annapolis MD 21401-4676

JACOBS, LINDA ROTROFF, elementary school educator; b. Peebles, Ohio, June 10, 1942; d. Joseph Harold Rotroff and Mary Lucille (Peterson) Rotroff Nixon; m. Donald Eugene Jacobs, Nov. 29, 1968; 1 child, Donald Brett. BS in Edn., Ohio State U., 1963; MA in Edn., U. Cin., 1968; postgrad., U. Cin., Miami U., Xavier U., 1968—, Coll. Mt. St. Joseph, 1968—. Cert. tchr., Ohio. Tchr. K-8 Forest Hills Bd. Edn., Cin., 1963-74, 77—; tchr. kindergarten Chillicothe (Ohio) Bd. Edn., 1974-77; tchr. reading adult edn. Cin., 1975; tchr. kindergarten Mercer Elem. Forest Hills, Cin., 1977—, tchr. pupil enrichment program, 1997—. Cooperating tchr. student tchrs. Ohio U., U. Cin., No. Ky. U., 1965—; tchr. summer sch. 4th-7th grades math./lang. arts, Cin., 1964-68, kindergarten and 1st grade Forest Hills, Cin., 1978-82; tchr. rep. Head Start, Chillicothe, 1975-77; kindergarten coord. Forest Hills and Hamilton County, Cin., 1965-70, 83-85; mem. supt.'s coun. Forest Hills, Cin., 1979, 82, 88; tchr. rep. PTA, Cin., 1967, 73, 82, 89; facilitator Forest Hills Summer Sch., 1993-96, 97-99; master tchr./advisor entry tchrs. Forest Hills, 1993—; career mentor Ashford-McCarthy Resources, Inc., 1993-94; coord. early entrance screening Hamilton County, 1994, 95, faculty mem. Intervention Based Multifactored Evaluation Com., 1994, 95, mem. Collaboration Team for Inclusion of Spl. Children, 1994, 95; mem. responsive classroom team, 1996-97; mem. steering com. accelerated schs., 1997-98, mem. diversity cadre Accelerated Schs., Great Aspirations pilot program Mercer Elem. Sch., mem. profl. devel. cadre, 1999-2000. Author: Getting Ready for Kindergarten, 1978, Parenting Tips, 1982, Intervention Assistance Team Handbook, 1992 Cons. Women Helping Women, Cin., 1989. Recipient Ohio State U. Scarlet and Gray award, 1995; named Hamilton County Tchr. of Yr., 1965, Educator of Yr., Anderson Hills C. of C., 2000. Mem. NEA, Nat. PTA (rep.) Tchrs. Applying Whole Lang., Ohio Edn. Assn. (del. 1965), Southwestern Ohio Edn. Assn., Forest Hills Educators Assn. (sec. 1964-68, Martha Holden Jennings scholar 1976-77), DAR, Ohio State U. Alumni Club of Clermont County (sec. 1995—), Anderson Hills Hist. Soc., Forest Hills Ret. Staff Assn., Hamilton County Ret. Tchrs. Assn., Police Officers Hall of Fame (hon.), Clermont County Herb Soc., Alpha Kappa Delta (sec. 1975—). Mem. Ch. of Christ. Avocations: interior decorating, writing stories/poems, music, landscaping, reading.

JACOBS, MARIAN, advertising agency owner; b. Stockton, Calif., Sept. 11, 1927; d. Paul and Rose (Sallah) J. AA, Stockton Coll. With Bottarini Advt., Stockton, 1948-50; pvt. practice Stockton, 1950-64; with Olympius Advt., Stockton, 1964-78; pvt. practice Stockton, 1978—. Pres. Stockton Advt. Club, 1954, Venture Club, Stockton, 1955; founder Stockton Advt. and Mktg. Club, 1981. Founder Stockton Arts Comms., 1976; co-founder Sunflower Entertainment for Institutionalized, 1976, Women Execs., Stockton, 1978; founding dir. Pixie Woods, Stockton; bd. dir. Goodwill Industries, St. Mary's Dining Room, Alan Short Gallery; mem. Calif. Coun. for the Humanities, 1994-95. Paul Harris fellow Rotary Club, 1994; recipient Woman of Achievement award San Joaquin County Women's Coun., Stockton, 1976, Achievement award San Joaquin Delta Coll., Stockton, 1978, Friend of Edn. award Calif. Tchrs. Assn., Stockton, 1988, Stanley McCaffrey Disting. Svc. award, U. of the Pacific, Stockton, 1988, Athena award for Businesswoman of Yr. Greater Stockton C. of C., 1989, Role Model award Tierra del Oro Girl Scouts U.S., 1989, Heart of Gold award Dameron Hosp. Found., 2000; named Stocktonian of the Yr. Stockton Bd. of Realtors, 1978, Outstanding Citizen Calif. State Senate & Assembly, 1978, Woman of Yr. State of Calif. Assembly, 2002, Woman of Achievement Kaiser-Permanente Womens Wellness Conf., 2002, Disting. Alumni Vol., Univ. of the Pacific, 2003; the Marian Jacobs Literary Forum was established in her honor. Republican. Roman Catholic. Avocations: art, photography. Home and Office: 4350 Mallard Creek Cir Stockton CA 95207-5205

JACOBS, MARY SHARRON, librarian; b. Endicott, N.Y., June 19, 1947; d. John Arnold and Evelyn Grace Jacobs; student U. Buffalo, 1965-68, M.L.S., SUNY, Geneseo, 1971, D in Naturopathy, Clayton Sch. Natural Healing, 1996. Dir., David A. Howe Public Library, Wellsville, N.Y., 1972— . Practitioner of alternative health modalities including polarity balancing. Librarian, Sovereign Grace Ch., 1978-85, coordinator women's activities, 1980-87, trustee, 1983, PCA com., 1992-97, Sunday Sch. tchr., 2002. Mem. Allegany County Library Assn. (v.p. 1981-83), N.Y. State Library Assn. Republican. Office: 155 N Main St Wellsville NY 14895-1149 E-mail: wel_mary@stls.org.

JACOBS, MICHAEL MOISES, aerospace engineer, consultant; b. Miami, Fla., June 21, 1950; s. Michael and Adeline Delores (D'Alessandro) Jacobs; m. Gloria Rose Benis, Mar. 1, 1980; children: Nicole Michelle, Amber Marie, Michael Matthew. BS in Physics & Math., U. Miami, 1972, MS in Physics, 1973, PhD in Physics, 1975. Cert. tchr. Calif., 1976. Scientist Sci. Applications Inc., Atlanta, 1976; engr. RBF & Assoc., Newport Beach, Calif., 1976—77; tchr. Orange Coast Coll., Costa Mesa, Calif., 1976—79; aerospace engr. Rockwell Internat., Seal Beach, Calif., 1977—80, Aerospace Corp., El Segundo, Calif., 1980—. Contbr. articles to profl. jours. Elder Presbyn. Ch., Mission Viejo, Calif., 1995—97; bd. dir. Little League Baseball, Lake Forest, Calif., 1996—2001. Recipient awards, USAF, 1991, 1992, 1996, Aerospace Corp., 1992; grantee Rsch. grant, NSF, 1975. Avocations: coaching baseball, guitar, running. Home: 21761 Eveningside Lane Lake Forest CA 92630 Office: The Aerospace Corp 2350 E El Segundo Blvd El Segundo CA 90245-4609

JACOBS, MICHAEL ROY, microbiologist, researcher; arrived in U.S., 1979; s. Philip and Ruth Joan Jacobs; m. Gretta Hazel Jacobs; children: Erica Yvonne, Kevin Bryan, Paul Daniel, David Andrew. MB, BChir, U. Witwatersrand, Johannesburg, 1971, Diploma in Tropical Medicine and Hygiene, 1974, Diploma in Pub. Health, 1976, PhD, 1978. Fellow faculty pathology Coll. Medicine South Africa, 1977, diplomate in Pub. Health and Med. Microbiology Am. Bd. Med. Microbiology, 1980. Microbiologist South African Inst. for Med. Rsch., Johannesburg, 1977—79; dir. clin. microbiology U. Hosps. Cleve., 1979—; asst. prof. dept. pathology Case Western Res. U., Cleve., 1979—86, assoc. prof. dept. pathology, 1986—93, prof. dept. pathology, 1993—. Com. mem. Drug Resistant Streptococcus Pneumoniae Therapeutic Working Group, Atlanta, 1977—2000; com. mem. sinusitis guidelines com. Sinus and Allergy Health Partnership, Washington, 1998—2000. Contbr. chapters to books, articles to profl. jours. Mem.: Am. Soc. for Microbiology, Infectious Disease Soc. Am., Royal Coll. Pathologists. Achievements include discovery of first strains of Streptococcus pneumoniae resistant to multiple groups of antimicrobial agents in South Africa in 1978; development of treatment guidelines for acute otitis media; treatment guidelines for community acquired pneumonia; treatment guidelines for acute bacterial rhinosinusitis; research in antimicrobial susceptibility of resppiratory tract pathogens. Office: Case Western Reserve Univ/Univ Hospitals 11100 Euclid Ave Cleveland OH 44106

JACOBS, NORMAN G(ABRIEL), sociologist, educator; b. N.Y.C., Feb. 28, 1924; s. Joseph and Beatrice (Esserman) J.; m. Margaret Alice Ayres, Aug. 20, 1956; children: Laurie, Charles. BS, CCNY, 1943; AM, Harvard U., 1950, PhD, 1951. Sociologist natural resources sect. SCAP, Tokyo, 1945-46; lectr. Taiwan Normal U., 1955-57; researcher Am. U., 1957-59; community devel. adviser AID, Shiraz, Iran, 1959-61; from asst. prof. to prof. sociology U. Kans., Lawrence, 1962-65; prof. sociology and Asian studies U. Ill., Urbana, 1965-90, prof. emeritus, 1990—; adj. prof. East Asian studies Dickinson Coll., Carlisle, Pa., 1990—. Fulbright prof., Thailand, 1965-66; sr. research scholar Korean Inst. Buddhist Studies, 1975; exchange prof. Keio U., Tokyo, 1968-69 Author: The Origin of Modern Capitalism and Eastern Asia, 1958, 81, Sociology of Development, 1966, Modernization without Development, 1972, The Korean Road to Modernization and Development, 1985, Patrimonial Interpretation of Indian Society, 1989, A Collectors' Manual of the Stationery and Collateral Matieral of Allied and Japanese Prisoners of War and Civilian Internees During the Great Pacific War, 1942-46, 2000, also articles; co-author: Japanese Coinage, 1953, 72. With AUS, 1943-46. Mem.: Dai Nippon Soc. of The Netherlands, Internat. Soc. for Japanese Philately. Theravada Buddhist. Home: 233 Walnut St Carlisle PA 17013-3734 Office: Dickinson Coll Dept East Asian Studies Carlisle PA 17013

JACOBS, NORMAN JOSEPH, publishing company executive; b. Chgo., Oct. 28, 1932; s. Herman and Tillie (Chapman) J.; m. Jeri Kolber Rose, Jan. 2, 1977; 1 son, Barry Herman; children by previous marriage— Carey, Murray, Dale. BS in Mktg, U. Ill., 1954. Display salesman Chgo. Daily News, 1954-57; dist. mgr. Davidson Pub. Co., Chgo., 1957-62; v.p. Press-Tech, Inc., Evanston, Ill., 1962-69; pres. Century Pub. Co., Evanston, 1969—. Bd. dirs. Chgo. Bulls. Bd. dirs. United Cerebral Palsey Chgo. Served with USNR, 1951-59. Mem. B'nai B'rith, Birchwood Tennis Club, Alpha Delta Sigma, Tau Epsilon Phi. Jewish. Office: Century Pub Co 990 Grove St 4th Fl Evanston IL 60201-6510

JACOBS, NOVA, scriptwriter, filmmaker; b. Victorville, Calif., Feb. 19, 1975; d. Peter and Linnah Jacobs. BFA, U. of Wash., 1998; MFA in Cinema, TV, U. So. Calif., 2002. Dir., dir.: (films) Box, (Ofcl. Selection, Palm Springs Internat. Film Festival, 1999); writer, writer: (films) Schrodinger's Cat. Fellow Alfred P. Sloan Found. award, 2001—02; scholar Jack Nicholson Writing scholar, 2001—02.

JACOBS, PAUL, lawyer; b. N.Y.C., Sept. 29, 1946; s. William R. and Sylvia (Wanshel) J.; m. Lisette Simon, Oct. 10, 1979; children: Alexia, Caroline. BA, Colgate U., 1967; JD, Columbia U., 1971. Bar: N.Y. 1971, U.S. Dist. Ct. (so. dist.) N.Y. 1971. Assoc. Reavis & McGrath, N.Y.C., 1971-78, ptnr., 1978-89, Fulbright & Jaworski, N.Y.C., 1989-96, sr. ptnr., 1996—. Mem. adv. com. Grace Ventures Corp., Cupertino, Calif., 1988-98, Euro-Am.-I C.V., San Bruno, Calif., 1988-98; sec. Zygo Corp., Middlefield, Conn., 1992—. Mem. N.Y. Bar Assn., N.Y.C. Bar Assn., Phi Beta Kappa, The University Club. Office: Fulbright & Jaworski 666 5th Ave Fl 31 New York NY 10103-0001 E-mail: p.jacobs@fulbright.com.

JACOBS, PAUL ALAN, lawyer; b. Boston, June 5, 1940; s. Samuel and Sarah (Rodman) J.; m. Carole Ruth Greenstein, Aug. 28, 1962; children: Steven N., Cheryl R., David F., Craig A. BA in Econs. magna cum laude, Tufts U., 1960; JD magna cum laude, U. Denver, 1968. Bar: Colo. 1968, U.S. Dist. Ct. Colo. 1968. Personnel officer First Nat. Bank Denver, 1964-68; assoc. Holme Roberts & Owen, Denver, 1968-73, sr. ptnr., 1973-93; exec. v.p., gen. counsel Colo. Rockies profl. baseball orgn., Denver, 1991-95; ptnr. Jacobs Chase Frick Kleinkopf & Kelley, Denver, 1995—. Bd. dirs. Anti-Defamation League B'nai B'rith, Denver, 1987-95, Colo. Sports Hall of Fame, 2000—, Am. Jewish Com., 2002-. Served to 1st lt. USAF, 1960-63. Mem. ABA, Denver Bar Assn., Colo. Bar Assn. Jewish. Avocations: skiing, racquetball. Home: 4041 S Narcissus Way Denver CO 80237-2025 Office: Independence Plz 1050 17th St Ste 1500 Denver CO 80265-2078 E-mail: pjacobs@jcfkk.com.

JACOBS, PAUL E. communications executive; PhD in Elec. Engring, U. Calif., Berkeley, 1989. Engring. positions Qualcomm, 1990—95, exec. v.p.; pres. Qualcomm Wireless & Internet Group, San Diego. CEO QCP Inc. (subsidiary of Qualcomm). Office: Corp Hdqs Qualcomm Inc 5775 Morehouse Dr San Diego CA 92121 Office Fax: 858-658-2100.

JACOBS, PAUL ELLIOT, lawyer; b. Sioux City, Iowa, Feb. 11, 1946; s. Leonard D. and Ruth (Jelenk) J.; m. Renee M. Glennon, Mar. 4, 1972; children: Sarah, Andrew, Ian. BA, Northwestern U., 1968; JD, Santa Clara U., 1971. Bar: Calif. 1972. Dept. dist. atty. Santa Clara County Dist. Atty., San Jose, Calif., 1972-76; ptnr. Beauzay, Hammer, Ezgar, Bledsoe & Sprenkle, San Jose, Calif., 1976-85, Hammer & Jacobs, San Jose, Calif., 1985—. Lectr. CEB, ABA, San Diego County Bar Assn., Santa Clara County Bar Assn., Calif. Family Law Reports. Contbr. articles on family law to profl. jours. Planning commr., City of

Saratoga, Calif., 1992-94, mem. city coun., 1994-98, mayor, City of Saratoga, 1995-96; chmn. Santa Clara County Hist. Heritage Commn., 1977-80, San Jose Hist. Mus. Assn., 1977-80. Fellow Am. Acad. Matrimonial Lawyers (treas. No. Calif. chpt. 1983-85); mem. Santa Clara County Bar Assn. (chmn. family law com. 1981, 82), State Bar Calif. (lectr. family law sect., family law adv. commn. 1981-86, chmn. 1985-86). E-mail: PaulJ@hammerandjacobs.com.

JACOBS, RALPH, JR., artist; b. El Centro, Calif., May 22, 1940; s. Ralph and Julia Vahe (Kirkorian) J. Paintings appeared in: Prize Winning Art (3 awards), 1964, 65, 66, and New Woman Mag., 1975; one man shows and exhbns. Villa Montalvo, Calif., Stanford Rsch. Inst., Calif., Fresno Art Ctr., Calif., de Young Meml. Mus., Calif., Rosicrucian Mus., Calif., Cunningham Meml. Gallery, Calif., 40th Ann. Nat. Art Exhibit, Utah, Nat. Exhbn. Coun. of Am. Artists Socs., N.Y.C., Am. Artists Profl. League Show, Armenian Allied Arts, Calif., Monterey Peninsula Mus. Art, Calif. Recipient 1st place award Statewide Ann. Santa Cruz Art League Gallery, 1963, 64; 2nd place award Soc. Western Artists Ann. M.H. de Young Mus., 1964; A.E. Klumpkey Meml. award, 1965. Address: PO Box 5906 Carmel CA 93921-5906

JACOBS, RANDALL BRIAN, lawyer; b. N.Y.C., July 8, 1951; s. John and Evelyn Jacobs; 1 child, Jillian. BA, Coll. of Idaho, 1972; JD, U. West L.A., 1978. Bar: Calif., D.C., Wis. Lawyer B. Randall Jacobs Law Corp., Brentwood, Calif., 1978—; real estate broker Morgan Reed & Co., Brentwood, 1979—; pvt. investigator Randy Brian Assocs., Brentwood, 1976—. Reserve deputy sheriff, L.A. County Sheriff, L.A., 1979—. Mem. NRA, Internat. Defensive Pistol Assn. (life), U.S. Practical Shooting Assn. (life), Shom Rim Soc., Calif. Rifle and Pistol Assn., Calif. Police Pistol Assn., Mensa, Masons, Shriners. Office: 654 N Sepulveda Blvd # 17 Los Angeles CA 90049-2169

JACOBS, RANDALL SCOTT DAVID, lawyer; b. Sept. 6, 1944; s. Irving and Lea Sylvia (Kerner) Jacobs; m. Jill Barbara Weiss, June 20, 1981; children: Evan, Todd. BSBA, NYU, 1967, LLM in Corp. Law, 1971; JD, Temple U., 1970. Bar: N.Y. 1977, U.S. Dist. Ct. (ea. dist.) N.Y. 1979, U.S. Dist. Ct. (so. dist.) N.Y. 1979, U.S. Ct. Appeals (2d cir.) 1980, U.S. Supreme Ct. 1980. Assoc. Coudert Brothers, N.Y.C., NY, 1968; with Comml. Coverage Corp., N.Y.C., 1971—78; assoc. Levy, Tandet, Sohn and Loft, N.Y.C., 1978—82; of counsel Harvis and Zeichner, N.Y.C., 1982—84; ptnr. Rich, Krinsly, Dorman & Jacobs, P.C., N.Y.C., 1984—91, Mintz and Fraade, PC, N.Y.C., 1991—94, Brahm Investments, Inc., N.Y.C., 1995—96, Recap. Ptnrs., LLC, N.Y.C., 1996—2000, FMG Acquisitions Fund, LLC, N.Y.C., 2000—, Turnaround Capital, LLC, 2003—. Mem. staff Temple Law Quarterly Law Rev., 1969—70. Mem.: Assn. of Bar of City of N.Y., N.Y. State Bar Assn., ABA. Office: 67 Wall St Ste 1901 New York NY 10005

JACOBS, RICHARD ALAN, management consultant; b. Portland, Maine, Aug. 16, 1934; s. Harry Gordon and Bernice (Levine) J.; m. Nancy Dean, Feb. 8, 1958; children: Karen, Alison. BS, MIT, 1956; MBA, Roosevelt U., Chgo., 1979. Mgr. engring. Mobil Chem., Macedon, N.Y., 1956-60; plant mgr. Champion Internat., Ft. Wayne, Ind., 1960-63; v.p. Quester Corp., Toledo, 1963-66; sr. v.p A. T. Kearney, Inc., Chgo., 1966-96; mgmt. cons. Supply, N.C., 1996—. Author: Production Control, 1970, Systems Management, 1978. Trustee Village of Northbrook, Ill., 1980-84; trustee MIT, Cambridge, Mass., 1993—, dir. alumni bd., 1980—, chmn. alumni fund, 1987-89. 1st lt. U.S. Army, 1957-58. Mem. Soc. Plastics Engrs. (pres., bd. dirs. 1976-77), MIT Alumni Assn. (pres. 1992, 93-94), MIT of Chgo. Club (bd. dirs. 1977—). Home and Office: 3375 Channelside Dr SW Supply NC 28462-2106 E-mail: dickjacobs@alum.mit.edu.

JACOBS, RICHARD DEARBORN, consulting engineering company executive; b. Detroit, July 6, 1920; s. Richard Dearborn and Mattie Phoebe (Cobleigh) J.; divorced; children: Richard, Margaret, Paul, Linden. BS, U. Mich., 1944. Registered profl. engr., Ill., Mich., Wis., Miss. Engr. Detroit Diesel Engine divsn. Gen. Motors, 1946-51; mgr. indsl. and marine engine divsn. Reo Motors, Inc., Lansing, Mich., 1951-54; chief engr. Kennedy Marine Engine Co., Biloxi, Miss., 1955-59; marine sales mgr. Nordberg Mfg. Co., Milw., 1959-69, Fairbanks Morse Engine divsn. Colt Industries, Beloit, Wis., 1969-81; pres. R.D. Jacobs & Assocs., cons. engrs., naval arch. & marine engrs., Roscoe, Ill., 1981—. With AUS, 1944-46. Mem. ASTM, Soc. Naval Archs. and Marine Engrs. (chmn. sect. 1979-80), Soc. Automotive Engrs., Am. Soc. Naval Engrs., Soc. Am. Mil. Engrs., Navy League U.S., Propeller Club U.S., Masons. Unitarian Universalist. Office: 11405 Main St Roscoe IL 61073-9569

JACOBS, RICHARD JAMES, banker, educator; b. Jamaica, N.Y., Sept. 27, 1941; s. John Beck and Doris Marie (Lewin) J.; m. Jean Anita McIntosh, Aug. 29, 1964; children: Kristine Anne, John McIntosh. BA, Muhlenberg Coll., 1963; MBA, U. Pa., 1965. With Gulf Oil, 1965-72, fin. mgr., 1970-71, mktg. advisor Pitts., 1971-72; v.p. mktg. and ops. Finnegans, Inc., Chevy Chase, Md., 1972-73; dir. planning Geico Ins. Co., Chevy Chase, 1973-76; v.p., gen. mgr. G.H. Realty, Annapolis, Md., 1976-78; asst. v.p. mktg. Md. Nat. Bank, Balt., 1978-80, v.p. mktg., 1980-86, sr. v.p. mktg., 1986-88, sr. v.p. wholesale support, 1988-90; chmn., CEO Bottom Line Co., Balt., Md., 1990—. Instr. mktg. Md. Banking Sch., Annapolis, 1988-2001; exec. dir. Wholesale Traders Group, 1981-83; prof. mktg. Johns Hopkins U., Balt., 1990-92. Coord. United Way, Balt., 1979; pres. Amberley Community Assn., Annapolis, 1980; off season job coord. Balt. Colts., 1982. Mem. Bank Mktg. Assn. (adv. coun. 1988-89), Mktg. Info. Group, Mchts. Club, Center Club, Fleet Reserve Club. Roman Catholic. Avocations: boating, fishing, cooking, travel. Home: 59 Fox Dr Ocean View DE 19970 Office: Bottom Line Co 1 E Lexington St Baltimore MD 21202-1701 E-mail: blcjake@aol.com.

JACOBS, ROBERT ALAN, lawyer; b. Waco, Tex., June 23, 1937; s. Abe and Ruth (Englander) J.; m. Sue C. Braunstein, Aug. 22, 1961; children: Jacqueline Anne, Michelle Keri. BBA, U. Tex., 1957; LLB cum laude, NYU, 1960, LLM in Taxation, 1963. Bar: N.Y. 1961. Assoc. Greenbaum, Wolff & Ernst, N.Y.C., 1961-63; asst. br. chief, chief counsel IRS, Washington, 1963-67; assoc. Paul, Weiss, Rifkind, Wharton & Garrison, N.Y.C., 1967-69; sr. tax mem. Milgrim Thomajan Jacobs & Lee PC, N.Y.C., 1969-87; tax ptnr. Milbank, Tweed, Hadley & McCloy, LLP, N.Y.C., 1987—2002, cons. ptnr., 2002—; head low income tax clinic Benjamin A. Cardozo Sch. Law, 2002; underwriting dir. Gulf Ins. Group, 2002—. Adj. prof. law NYU, 1976-85; vis. sr. lectr. taxation, U. Calif. Davis, 1977; spl. counsel to sec. treas., Washington, 1965-67. Note and comment editor NYU Law Rev.; contbr. articles to profl. jours. Mem. adv. group Senate Fin. Com. Staff on Subchpt. C. Revision, 1983-85; arbitrator Civil Ct. City of N.Y., 1972—; bd. dirs. Community Action Legal Svcs., 1978-82, MFY Legal Svcs., 1991-98, N.Y. County Lawyers, 1990-93. With U.S. Army, 1960-61, 61-62. Root-Tilden scholar; recipient commendation medal U.S. Army. Mem. ABA (tax sect., asst. sec. 1987-88, chmn. com. corp. stockholder relationships 1983-85, chmn. task force on pass-through entities 1986-88), Am. Law Inst., Tax Forum (chmn. 1989-2001), Am. Coll. Tax Counsel, N.Y. State Bar Assn. (tax sect., exec. com. 1980—, chair 2001), Tax Club (chmn. 1987-88). Office: Milbank Tweed Hadley & McCloy LLP 1 Chase Manhattan Plz Fl 47 New York NY 10005-1413 E-mail: rjacobs@milbank.com., rajacobs@gulfins.com.

JACOBS, ROBERT COOPER, political scientist, consultant; b. N.Y.C., Jan. 23, 1939; s. Max and Paula (Glotzer) J.; m. Barbara Linda Lax (div.); children: Michael, Deborah; m. Mollie Jenks Edson (div.); children: Elliot, Madeleine, Eleanor. AB, CCNY, 1959; AM, Columbia U., 1961, PhD, 1970. Instr. Colby Coll., Waterville, Maine, 1965-68, asst. prof., 1968-70; from asst. prof. to prof. Cen. Wash. U., Ellensburg, 1970—, dir. law and justice, 1974-88, prof., 1982—2002, prof. emeritus, 2002—. Vis. prof. criminal justice Temple U., 1988-89. Contbr. articles to profl. jours. and encyclopedias. Mem. Kittitas County Juvenile Accountability Bd., Ellensburg, 1975-79; trustee Ellensburg Pub. Libr., 1994—, chmn., 1996, 2000; mem. Wash. State Pistol Team. N.Y. State Regents scholar, 1955-59; State of N.Y. teaching fellow, 1962-63. Mem. Am. Polit. Sci. Assn., Wash. Assn. Criminal Justice Educators (past pres.), Supreme Ct. Hist. Soc. Democrat. Avocations: computers, hiking, target shooting. Home: 707 E 7th Ave Ellensburg WA 98926-3214 Office: Ctrl Wash U Dept Polit Sci Ellensburg WA 98926 E-mail: jacobsr@cwu.edu.

JACOBS, ROLAND WILLIAM, psychiatrist; b. Bklyn., Nov. 1, 1952; s. Stanley Jacobs and Rita Jameson; m. Patricia Lynn Traynor, Sept. 20, 1989; 1 child, Bryce Traynor. BA in Zoology, Rutgers U., 1975; MD, U. N.J., 1979. Diplomate Am. Bd. of Psychiatry and Neurology, 1985, geriatric psychiatry Am. Bd. of Psychiatry and Neurology, 1992, Am. Bd. of Forensic Medicine, 1999. Intern and resident in psychology UCLA, Sepulveda (Calif.) VA Med. Ctr., 1979—83; med. dir. geriatric psychiatry Northridge Hosp., Sherman Way Campus, Van Nuys, Calif., 1986—93; med. dir. Pacific Shores Hosp., Oxnard, Calif., 1993—97; med. dir. ctr. for geriatric psychiatry Encino-Tarzana Med. Ctr., Calif., 1997—99; med. dir. Pine Grove Hosp., Canoga Park, Calif., 1999—2002; pvt. practice Taos, N.Mex., 2002—. Rsch. psychiatrist UCLA Sch. of Medicine, 1987—92, asst. clin. prof., 1988—93; psychiatric cons. Granada Hills (Calif.) Cmty. Hosp., 1994—, Motion Picture and TV Fund, Woodland Hills, Calif., 1999—. Contbr. chapters to books, articles. Mem. L.A. County Older Adult Task Force, L.A., Calif., 1986—87; civil surgeon Immigration and Naturalization Svcs., L.A., 1997—2002; bd. dirs. L.A. County Alzheimer's Assn., L.A., 1992—99, mem. med. and sci. adv. bd., 1990—2002; participant, gerontology think tank Calif. State U., Northridge, 1997—2002. Named America's Top Psychiatrists, Consumers' Rsch. Coun. of Am., 2002—03; recipient Profl. Cmty. Svc. award, Bernardi Multipurpose Sr. Ctr., 1990, Congl. Award for Outstanding Svc. to Cmty., Howard L. Berman, U.S. Congressman, 1990, Cert. of Appreciation, Barbara Boxer, U.S. Senator, 1996, Commendation, County of LA, 1996; fellow, NIMH, 1983—85. Mem.: L.A. County Bar Assn. (spl. masters referee 1996), Am. Soc. Clin. Psychopharmacology, Soc. Neurosci., Am. Soc. Aging, Internat. Psychogeriatric Assn., Am. Assn. Geriatric Psychiatry, Am. Neuropsychiatric Assn., Brit. Brain Rsch. Assn. (hon.), European Brain and Behavior Soc. (hon.). D-Liberal. Achievements include development of first older adult community outreach and referral resource in the San Fernando Valley; guidelines for pharmacological treatment of behavior and mood in dementia; design of designed and implimented three inpatient and partial hospitalization programs in Los Angeles and Ventura Counties; research in neuropathology of the nucleus basalis in Alzheimer's disease; elemental analysis of aluminum in Alzheimer's disease; low field strength magnetic resonance imaging of Alzheimer's and other dementing illnesses. Avocations: photography, alpine skiing. Home: PO Box 535 Arroyo Seco NM 87514 Office: 156 Cerrito-Colorado Rd Valdez NM 87580 Personal E-mail: rolandjacobs@starband.net.

JACOBS, ROLLY WARREN, judge; b. Nashville, Aug. 26, 1946; s. William Clinton Jr. and Eleanor Olive (Warren) J.; m. Karen Lee Ponist, Sept. 16, 1972; children: Collin Wayne, Tyler Warren. BA in Econs., Washington & Lee U., 1968; JD, U. S.C., 1974. Bar: S.C. 1975, U.S. Dist. Ct. for S.C. 1975. Assoc. Carl R. Reasonover, Camden, S.C., 1975-77; ptnr. Reasonover & Jacobs, Camden, S.C., 1977-80; pvt. practice law Camden, S.C., 1980-99; judge family ct. 5th Jud. Cir., S.C., 1999—. Asst. city judge Mcpl. Ct., Camden, 1976-77; master in equity S.C. Jud. Sys., Camden, 1978-99; mem. Jud. Coun. for S.C., Columbia, 1989-2000; mem. fee dispute panel S.C. Bar Assn., 1986-93. Bd. dirs. ARC, Camden, 1976-78, Am. Cancer Soc., Camden, 1976-78, United Way, Camden, 1978-82; active Boy Scouts Am., Camden, 1984-96. Capt. U.S. Army, 1968-72. Recipient Dist. Award of Merit Indian Waters Coun. Boy Scouts Am., 1991; named Scouting Family of Yr., 1990. Mem. ABA, VFW, S.C. Bar Assn., Am. Legion, Res. Officers Assn., Elks. Methodist. Home: 418 Lafayette Way Camden SC 29020-1642 Office: Kershaw County Courthouse PO Box 664 Camden SC 29020-0664

JACOBS, RUTH HARRIET, poet, playwright, sociologist, gerontologist; b. Boston, Nov. 15, 1924; d. Samuel J. Miller and Jane G. (Miller); m. Neal Jacobs, Aug. 1948 (div.); children: Eli, Edith. BS, Boston U, 1964; Ph.D, Brandeis U., 1969. Reporter, feature writer Herald-Traveler, Boston, 1943-49; tchr. Mass. Bay Community Coll., Northeastern U., 1961-69; prof. sociology Boston U., 1969-82; prof., chmn. dept. sociology Clark U., Worcester, Mass., 1982-87; rsch. scholar Ctr. for Rsch. on Women Wellesley Coll., Mass., 1985—; prof. human svcs. Springfield Coll., Manchester, N.H., 1988—; lectr. Regis Coll., Weston, Mass., 1989—2002. Vis. prof. Coll. William and Mary, 1990; vis. rsch. scholar Five Colls. Women's Rsch. Ctr., Mount Holyoke Coll., 1992; spkr. in field. Author: Life After Youth: Female, Forty, What Next, 1979, Button, Button, Who Has the Button, 1983, rev. edit., 1996, (manual) Older Women Surviving and Thriving, 1987, Out of Their Mouths, 1988, Be an Outrageous Older Woman: A.R.A.S.P., 1991, rev. edit., 1993, 2d rev. edit., 1997, We Speak for Peace: An Anthology, 1993, Women Who Touched My Life: A Memoir, 1996, The ABC's of Aging: Mother Ruth Rhymes for Ageing, Sageing and Rageing, 2000; co-author: Re-Engagement in Late Life: Re-Employment and Re-Marriage, 1979, (Play) Coming Into Eighty, 2003; contbr. articles to profl. jours., chpts. to books, poetry to anthologies and mags. NIMH grantee, 1972-75; Faculty fellow NSF, 1977-78; recipient Dewing Peace award, Pendle Hill, Walingford, Pa., 1993 Mem.: New Eng. Sociol. Assn. (v.p. 1976, Pioneer award 1993, Athena award for mentoring 1998). Mem. Soc. Of Friends. Home and Office: 75 High Ledge Ave Wellesley MA 02482-1042

JACOBS, SHELDON, investment advisor; b. Milw., Jan. 29, 1931; s. Bert and Ruth Jacobs; m. Lisbeth C. Jacobs, Feb. 29, 1964; children: Roy, Julie DePree. BS, U. Nebr., 1952; MS, NYU, 1955. Mgr. audience measurements Sta. ABC-TV, N.Y.C., 1957-70; dir. sta. rsch. NBC-TV, N.Y.C., 1970-79; editor, pub. The No-Load Fund Investor, Ardsley, N.Y., 1979—; founder The BJ Group (now Gen. Electric Pvt. Access Group), Scarsdale, 1986—. Mem. adv. panel Boardroom Reports, Greenwich, Conn., 1992—. Author: Put Money In Your Pocket, 1974; author, editor, pub.: Handbook for No-Load Fund Investors, 1981-2000, Sheldon Jacobs' Guide to Successful No-Load Fund Investing, 1995, 98. Bd. dirs. Westchester C.C. Found., Valhalla, N.Y., 1999. Capt. U.S. Army, 1952-54, Korea. Avocation: art collecting. Office: No Load Fund Investor 410 Saw Mill River Rd Ardsley NY 10502

JACOBS, STEPHEN LOUIS, lawyer; b. Staples, Minn., June 22, 1953; s. James P. and Gertrude G. (Willis) J.; m. Sue E. Bell, June 14, 1975; 2 children. BA, St. John's U., 1975; JD, William Mitchell Coll. of Law, St. Paul, 1979. Bar: Minn. 1979, U.S. Dist. Ct. Minn. 1979. Assoc. Bertie, Bettenburg & Strong, St. Paul, 1979-84; ptnr. Bertie, Bettenberg, Jacobs & Bettenburg, St. Paul, 1984-89; pvt. practice law St. Paul, 1989—. Mem. Minn. Bar Assn., Kiwanis (pres. St. Paul-Midway chpt. 1987-88, 97-98, bd. dirs. 1984-2003). Roman Catholic. Office: 190 Midtown Commons 2334 University Ave W Saint Paul MN 55114-1802

JACOBS, SUSAN S. ambassador; b. Detroit, Jan. 1945; m. Barry Jacobs; 3 children. BA in Polit. Sci., U. Mich.; postgrad., George Washington Univ. Various former positions in Caracas, Tel Aviv, New Delhi and San Salvador U.S. Dept. of State; former dep. asst. sec. for global affairs Bur. of Legis. Affairs, Washington; U.S. amb. to Papua New Guinea, 2000—. Office: DOS Amb 4240 Port Moresby Pl Washington DC 20521*

JACOBS, THEODORE JOSEPH, psychiatrist, educator; b. July 3, 1931; AB, Yale U., 1953; MD, U. Chgo., 1957. Clin. prof. psychiatry Albert Einstein Coll. Medicine, Bronx, N.Y., 1985—; tng. and supervising analyst N.Y. Psychoanalytic Inst., N.Y.C., 1985—, NYU Psychoanalytic Inst., N.Y.C., 1985—. Clin. prof. psychiatry Sch. Medicine NYU, 1990. Author: The Use of the Self: Countertransference and Communication in the Analytic Situation, 1991; co-editor: On Beginning an Analysis, 1991. Mem. Assn. for Child Psychoanalyis (pres. 1996-98). Address: 46 Walworth Ave Scarsdale NY 10583-1430 also: 170 E 77th St New York NY 10021-1912 E-mail: theojmd@aol.com.

JACOBS, THOMAS PRICE, internal medicine educator; b. N.Y.C., June 13, 1942; s. Thomas Price and Anne Snowden (Brennan) J.; m. Janice Marie Carmody, Feb. 24, 1968; children: Kevin, Michael, Timothy, Jennifer, Brian. AB, Amherst Coll., 1964; MD, Johns Hopkins U., 1968. Diplomate in internal medicine and endocrinology Am. Bd. Internal Medicine. Resident in medicine Presbyn. Hosp., N.Y.C., 1968-70, 72-73; fellow in endocrinology U. Wash., Seattle, 1973-75; asst. prof. clin. medicine Columbia U., N.Y.C., 1975-81, assoc. prof., 1981-93, prof., 1993—. Examiner Physician for Human Rights. Contbr. articles to med. jours. Pres. Tenafly (N.J.) Jr. Soccer League, 1989-2003; trustee Am. U. Beirut, 1996—. Maj. M.C., U.S. Army, 1970-72, Vietnam. Fellow ACP; mem. Am. Soc. for Bone and Mineral Rsch., Endocrine Soc., Pituitary Soc., Phi Beta Kappa, Sigma Xi, pres. Tennis Club,N.J., Soccer League, 1989-2003. Home: 66 Magnolia Ave Tenafly NJ 07670-2121 Office: Columbia-Presbyn Med Ctr 161 Fort Washington Ave New York NY 10032-3713

JACOBS, TIMOTHY ANDREW, epidemiologist, international health consultant, medical missionary; b. St. Petersburg, Fla., Nov. 5, 1944; s. W. Andrew and Virginia (Ott) J.; m. Carolyn Martin, Nov. 4, 1972; 1 child, Jenny Thuy Ha. BSN, U. Fla., 1970; MS, PNP, U. Utah, 1976; PhD, Internat. Inst. Advanced Studies, 1979; C.T.M., Liverpool (Eng.) Sch. Tropical Medicine, 1982; cert. hosp. epidemiology, U. Iowa, 1985; MPH, Yale U., 1991; cert. in internat. (Spanish) living, Sch. Internat. Tng., Brattleboro, Vt., 1984. Nat. design and media cons. Nat. Assn. Pediatric Nurse Assocs. and Practitioners, Cherry Hill, N.J., 1977-83; asst. prof., co-coord. community health nursing U. N.D., Grand Forks, 1980; vol. epidemiologist, pub. health specialist Vinh Children's Hosp., Vinh City, Vietnam, 1989; pediatric staff nurse I U. Fla. Pediatric Svc., Shands Teaching Hosp., Gainesville, 1970; instr. pediatric nursing U. Utah Coll. Nursing, Salt Lake City, 1976-77; pvt. cons. Internat. Cmty. Health and Epidemiology, New Haven, 1990-94; med. supr., health svcs. mgr. Brown & Root Logcap Med. Clinic, Port-au-Prince, Haiti, 1994-95; med. tech. proposal cons. UN, Rwanda, Angola, 1995; specialist Home Health Care, Tampa, Fla., 1996—. Vol. pub. health scientist, cons. Hanoi (Vietnam) Sch. Pub. Health; cons. epidemiologist Vinh and Huong Son, Vietnam, 1993; internat. edn. cons. U. Am., New Orleans, 1994; cons. infectious disease epidemiology, consulate of Nicaragua, Miami, Health for Health Svcs. Hurricane Mitch, 1998; cons. Christian Haitian Outreach Clinics and Orphanages, Jeremie and Mariani, Haiti, 1998—; pediatric clin. planner and designer, Carrafour, Haiti, 2002; principal designer Ambulatory Primary Care Clinic, Mariani, Haiti, 2002. Contbg. editor Episource, 1991, 97, Resources in Epidemiology; contbr. articles to profl. jours.; contbr. to poetry jours.; anthologies Daybreak on the Land, 1997, Audiotape Sounds of Poetry, 1997, Archive of the Vietnam Conflict, Personal Papers Collection, 1999. Donor, contbr. Asian Family and Cmty. Empowerment Ctr., St. Petersburg, Fla., Caribbean Mercy, Mercy Ships, Garden Valley, Tex., 2001, Love a Child Orphanage and Med. Clinic, Fond Parisien, Haiti, 2001-02. Capt. Nurse Corps, U.S. Army, 1968-73, Vietnam. Recipient Cert. of Achievement in HIV-AIDS Edn., AIDS Project, New Haven, Conn., 1994, Editor's Choice award for outstanding achievement in poetry Nat. Libr. Poetry, 1997. Fellow Royal Soc. Tropical Medicine and Hygiene (London), Am. Biog. Inst. (advisor, rsch. adv. bd.); mem. AMA, VFW, Am. Legion, Vietnam Vets. Am., Nat. Assn. Pediatric Nurse Assocs. and Practitioners (com. dir. graphics & logos mil. chpt., former chmn. nat. art and exhibits subcom., former mem. pub. rels. com., Cert. Recognition 1983), Am. Pub. Health Assn. (epidemiology sect., internat. healthsect., mem. caucus pub. health and faith cmty.), Internat. Assn. Med. Assistance to Travellers, Fla. Pub. Health Assn., Nat. Adolescent Health Promotion Network, Assn. Mil. Surgeons U.S., Ret. Army Nurse Corps Assn., Liverpool Tropical Sch. Assn. (Eng.), Assn. Yale Alumni in Pub. Health, Consortium for Internat. Nursing Edn., Rsch. & Practice, U.S.-Vietnam Friendship Assn., Doctorate Assn. N.Y. Educators, Fleet Marine Force Corpsman Assn. (former Conn. rep., charter mem.), U.S. Navy Corpsmen United Assn., Am. Assn. Navy Hosp. Corpsmen, U.S. Army (Vietnam) 24th Evacuation Hosp. Assn. (com. asv. reunion 1993), Vets. Vietnam Restoration Project, U.S. Com. Scientific Cooperation with Vietnam, N.Y. Acad. of Sci., Walter Reed Army Med. Ctr. Soc. (charter), Spl. Ops. Med. Assn., Soaring Soc. Am., Tampa Bay Soaring Soc. (student pvt. pilot), Sigma Xi, Sigma Theta Tau (charter mem. Gamma Rho chpt.), Phi Kappa Phi. Avocation: flying. Home: 11333 Calgary Cir Tampa FL 33624-4804 E-mail: epidoc91@tampabay.rr.com.

JACOBS, TIMOTHY LESTER, sociologist, educator, genealogist; b. Quincy, Mass., May 28, 1948; s. Raymond Halford Jacobs and Sylvia Dearborn Baker; children: Star Cecile Hansen, Thorin Elessar, Travis Dean Harris Baker, Tyler Alden Nathaniel, Andrew Timothy Lester. AA in Liberal Arts, Mohegan C.C., Norwich, CT, 1982; BA in Anthropology, Sociology and Linguistics, MA in Anthropology, Wesleyan U., 1985; PhD in Anthropology, U. Conn., 2002. Assoc. prof. sociology and anthropology Naugatuck Valley C.C., Waterbury, Conn., 1985—. Recipient Tchg. Excellence award, NEASC, 2000, Meritorious Svc. award, Order of the Founders and Patriots of Am., 2002; fellow Etherington fellow, Wesleyan U., 1982—85. Fellow: Conn. Profl. Genealogists Coun.; mem.: SAR (chpt. registrar 2001—02), Am. Anthrop. Assn., St. George's Soc. of NY, Conn. Geneal. Soc., Watson Clan Assn., The Kelsey Kindred, Soc. of Sons of Colonial New Eng., Descendants of Loyalists and Patriots of the Am. Revolution, Soc. of the War of 1812 (state registrar 2002—02), Mil. Order of the World Wars, Sons & Daughters of the First Settlers of Newbury, MA, Descendants of Founders of Ancient Windsor, Descendants of Founders of Norwich, Conn., Descendants of Founders of Saybrook, North Am. Manx Assn., Nat. Huguenot Soc., Descendants of the Founders of Hartford, Conn. (genealogist 2002—02), Descendants of the Colonial Clergy (life), Mil. Order of the Crusades (life), Order of the Crown of Charlemagne (life), Flagon & Trencher (life), Descendants of Colonial Physicians and Chirurgiens (life), Descendants of Washington's Army at Valley Forge (life), Descendants of Early Quakers (life), Sons & Daughters of Colonial and Antebellum Bench & Bar (life), Presdl. Families of Am. (life), Order of Indian Wars of the U.S. (life), Order of Descendants of Colonial Governors (life), Baronial Order of the Magna Charta (life), Order of Descendants of Pirates and Privateers (life; founder, pres., genealogist 2001—02), Descendants of Knights of the Garter (life), Roger Williams Family Assn. (life), Order of the Founders and Patriots of Am. (life; state registrar 2001—02, Meritorious Svc. award 2002), Am. Rifle Assn. (life), Winthrop Soc. (life; pres. 1999—2002), Sons of Union Veterans of the Civil War (assoc.), Scotch-Irish Soc. of the U.S.A., Naval Order of the US, Soc. of Colonial Wars, Descendants of Whaling Masters, St. Andrew's Soc. of Conn., Murray Clan Assn., New Eng. Hist. Geneal. Soc., Friends of Godfrey Libr., Soc. of Mayflower Descendants, Phi Beta Kappa (life). Republican. Office: Naugatuck Valley C C Chase Pkwy Waterbury CT 06708 Personal E-mail: tjacobs@mail.wesleyan.edu.

JACOBS, TRAVIS BEAL, historian, educator; b. N.Y.C., Apr. 22, 1936; s. Albert Charles and Loretta Field (Beal) J.; m. Eleanor Morison (div. 1982); children: Travis Beal, Holmes Morison. AB, Princeton U., 1958; MA, Columbia U., 1960, PhD, 1971. Mem. faculty Middlebury Coll. (Vt.), 1965—, prof. history, 1978-92, Fletcher D. Proctor prof. Am. history, 1992—, chmn. dept. history, 1976-88, 91-95. Editor: Middlebury College General Catalogue: Bicentennial Edition, 2000; co-editor: Navigating The Rapids, 1918-1971, From the Papers of Adolf A. Berle, 1973, Eisenhower at Columbia, 2001, America and the Winter War, 1939-1941, 1981. Cons. 20th Century Fund, 1972-73; bd. dirs. Psi Upsilon Found., 1971-98, hon., 1998—; trustee Sheldon Mus., 1984-90, 95-2001, pres., 1987-90; pres. Chappaquiddick Island Assn., 1983-86; participant Eisenhower Centennial Programs, 1990. Earhart fellow, 1989-90, 95-96. Mem. Am. Hist. Assn., Ctr. for Study of Presidency, Orgn. Am. Historians, Soc. Historians Fgn. Rels., Vt. Hist. Soc., Princeton Club (N.Y.C.). Episcopalian. Home: 1104 Vt Route 125 Bridport VT 05734-9756 Office: Dept Hist Middlebury Coll Middlebury VT 05753 E-mail: tjacobs@middlebury.edu.

JACOBS, WALTER DARNELL, political scientist, educator; b. Lone Wolf, Okla., Mar. 11, 1922; s. John Clayton and Patience Caroline (Goodlander) J.; m. Mary Anderson Stout, Oct. 27, 1978; 1 child, Sara Downs. BS, Columbia U., 1955, MA, 1956, PhD in Pub. Law, 1961. Commd. 2d lt. U.S. Army, 1943, advanced through grades to col., 1964; exch. specialist Libr. Congress, Washington, 1957-59; rsch. specialist Spl. Ops. Rsch. Office, Washington, 1959-61; asst. prof. then prof. U. Md., College Park, 1961-65, assoc. prof., 1965-68, prof., 1968-81. European adv. coun. Dept. State. Author: Modern Governments, 3d edit., 1966, Frunze, The Soviet Clausewitz, 1969, Terrorism in South Africa, 1973, At the Sharp Edge in Africa, 1974, Bewitched Anteater, 1976, African Turmoil and American Interests, 1976, The Flaw in the CAD, 1998; contbr. articles to profl. jours. Chmn. Charleston (S.C.) Rep. Party, 1995-97. Mem. SAR, Am. Africal Affairs Assn. (chmn. 1971-78), Washington Friends Antibolshevik Block Nations, World Peace Soc. (dir. 1967-81), Am. Mil. Inst., Am. Polit. Sci. Assn. Def. Orientation Conf. Assn. (dir. 1971-74), Mukumburu Surf Club, Delta Kappa Epsilon, Pi Sigma Alpha. Home: 62 Smith St Charleston SC 29401-1330 E-mail: darnell62@aol.com.

JACOBS, WENDELL EARLY, JR., lawyer; b. Detroit, Nov. 15, 1945; s. Wendell E. and Mildred P. (Horton) J.; m. Elaine M. Lott (div.); children: Wendell Early III, Damon R. BFA, Denison U., 1969; JD, Wayne State U., 1972. Bar: Mich. 1972, U.S. Dist. Ct. (ea. dist.) Mich. 1973, Fla. 1974. Asst.

prosecutor Jackson County, Mich., 1973-76; ptnr. Jacobs & Engle, Jackson, 1977—. Mem. Mich. Coun. on Crime and Delinquency. Mem. Nat. Assn. Criminal Def. Lawyers, Criminal Def. Attys. Mich., Jackson County Bar Assn., Eagles Club, Grotto Club, Elks. Avocations: paddleball, motorcycling. Home: 9281 Greenwood Rd Grass Lake MI 49240-9590 Office: Jacobs & Engle 1104 W Michigan Ave Jackson MI 49202-4123

JACOBS, WENDY, editor, writer, translator; b. Conn. d. Gerald and Eileen Jacobs. BA, U. Conn., 1974; postgrad., Norwich U. (now Vt. Coll.), 1974, Ind. U., 1975, U. Toronto, 1979. Mem. editl. dept. Plenum Pub., N.Y.C., 1974-77; editor Macmillan Pub., Toronto, Ont., Can., 1978-79; cons., writer, editor Bus., Govt., Pub., Toronto, 1980-91, Bus., Acad., Pub., New Orleans, 1991—. Faculty mem. ann. lit. festival, mem. editl. staff, bd. dirs. Faulkner Soc., New Orleans, 1992—. Office: 3508 Robert St New Orleans LA 70125-4808

JACOBS, WILLIAM FREDRIC, physician; b. Chgo., Aug. 11, 1938; s. Fred Emmit and Allie Elizabeth Jacobs; m. Gail Ayers, April 26, 1988; children: Allison, Jennifer. BA, U. Tex., 1960; MD, U. Tex., GAlveston, 1965. Diplomate in internal medicine and cardiovascular disease Am. Bd. Internal Medicine; diplomate Nat. Bd. Med. Examiners. Clin. asst. prof. internal medicine Georgetown U. Hosp., Washington, 1970-97, co-dir. cardiology exercise lab., 1970-79; assoc. prof. internal medicine, divsn. cardiology U. Tex. Med. Br., Galveston, 1997—, dir. cardiology clinics and med. edn., 1997—. Contbr. articles to profl. jours. Fellow ACP, Am. Coll. Cardiology. Avocations: tennis, boating, pistol shooting. Office: U Tex Med Br 301 University Blvd Galveston TX 77555-0553 E-mail: bjacobs@utmb.edu.

JACOBS, WILLIAM PAUL, botanist, educator; b. Boston, May 25, 1919; s. Vincent H. and Elizabeth (Kennedy) J.; m. Jane Shaw, Mar. 12, 1949; children: Mark, Anne. AB magna cum laude, Harvard U., 1942, PhD, 1946. Research assoc. biology Harvard U., 1946-47; jr. prize fellow Harvard Soc. Fellows, 1947-48; faculty Princeton, 1948—, prof. biology, 1962-89, prof. emeritus, 1989—, W.L. Schultz prof. biology, 1969. Mem. com. innovation lab. study Biol. Scis. Curriculum Study, 1959-64; vis. prof. U. Calif.-Berkeley, 1953, U. Oxford, 1962, U. Lausanne, 1967, U. Colo., 1972, U. Bristol (Eng.), 1980 Author: (with C.E. LaMotte) Regulation in Plants by Hormones, 1964, Plant Hormones and Plant Development, 1979; contbr. articles to sci. publs. Served with M.C. AUS, 1942-44. Recipient Morrison prize, N.Y. Acad. Scis., 1951, Medal, Brno Agrl. U., 1994; fellow Sheldon Travelling fellow, 1944, Lalor fellow, 1950—51, Sr. Postdoctoral fellow, NSF, 1957, Faculty fellow, 1962, Guggenheim fellow, 1967. Mem. Soc. Study Devel. and Growth (pres. 1960-61), Bot. Soc. Am. (Dimond prize 1974), Am. Soc. Plant Physiologists (editorial bd. 1968-72, Barnes award for lifetime achievement 1998), Phycological Soc. Am., Internat. Soc. Plant Morphologists, Internat. Phycological Soc., Internat. Plant Growth Substances Assn. Home: 64 Maclean Cir Princeton NJ 08540-5621 Office: Princeton U Dept Molecular Biology Princeton NJ 08544-0001 E-mail: wpjacobs@princeton.edu.

JACOBS-CAREY, SHEILA L. immunologist; b. N.Y.C., Oct. 10, 1939; d. Max and Rosalind Lehrhaupt; m. Richard D. Jacobs, 1961 (div. 1980); children: Marcy G. Little, Sharon L. Jacobs; m. Robert R. Carey, Apr. 21, 1985. BS, Carnegie Inst. Tech., Pitts., 1961; MS, L.I. U., Bklyn., 1964; PhD, Columbia U., N.Y.C., 1968. Instr. SUNY-Downstate Med. Ctr., Bklyn., 1968—71; rsch. asst. CUNY/Lehman Coll., Bronx, 1972—76; rsch. assoc. prof. N.Y. Med. Coll., Valhalla, NY, 1976—81; assoc. prof. Wagner Coll., S.I., NY, 1981—82; sr./prin. scientist Schering-Plough Corp., Bloomfield, NJ, 1982—85; leader Schering-Plough Rsch. Inst., Kenilworth, NJ, 1985—. Lectr. in field. Contbr. Mem.: AAAS, Internat. Soc. for Interferon and Cytokine Rsch., Am. Chem. Soc., Audobon Soc., Phi Sigma, Phi Kappa Phi, Sigma Xi. Avocations: reading, snorkeling, cooking. Home: 52 Ivy Pl Wayne NJ 07470 Office: Schering-Plough Rsch Inst 1011 Morris Ave Union NJ 07083

JACOBSEN, BRENDA, internist, emergency physician; b. Minden, Nebr., Sept. 4, 1962; d. Delbert James and Donna Joyce (Ottun) J.; m. Ralph Hansen. BSN, Pensacola Christian Coll., Fla., 1984; BS, U. West Fla., Pensacola, 1991; D in Osteopathic Medicine, U. Health Scis. Coll. Osteopathic Medicine, 1996. Cert. BLS; ACLS, ATLS, PALS. Intern Oakland Gen. Hosp., Madison Heights, Mich.; resident South Pointe Hosp. CCF, Warrensville Heights, Ohio. Mem.: Escambia County Med. Assn., Fla. Med. Assn., Christian Med. Dental Assn., Am. Coll. Osteo. Internists, Am. Osteo. Assn., Am. Coll. of Emergency Physicians, Alpha Epsilon Delta.

JACOBSEN, DIANE D. business executive and foreign policy specialist; b. N.Y.C., Sept. 21, 1944; d. A. Leonard and Lizette DeMell; m. Thomas H. Jacobsen, June 15, 1985 (dec. July 20, 2002). Bachelors Degree, CUNY, 1965; M in Liberal Arts, Washington U., 1995, M in Internat. Affairs, 1999, PhD in Internat. Affairs, 2003. Sr. exec. Internat. Bus. Machine, Armonk, N.Y., 1965-86; sr. v.p. Bapt. Health Ins., Jacksonville, Fla., 1987-88; pres., CEO Dependable Ins. Group, Jacksonville, 1988-91; pres. DeMell Group, Clayton, Mo., 1991—. Sponsor conflict resolution seminars Ctr. for Internat. Understanding, St. Louis, 1995-2000; adv. dir. internat. leadership program Washington U., St. Louis, 1998-2000. Commr. St. Louis Art Mus., 1992-2000; bd. mem. Children's Hosp., St. Louis, 1992-94, Repertory Theater, Webster Grove, Mo., 1992-95. Mem. Women's Fgn. Policy Group. Avocations: woodworking, swimming, cycling.

JACOBSEN, GERALD BERNHARDT, biochemist; b. Spokane, Wash., Nov. 25, 1939; s. Hans Bernhardt and Mabel Grace (Swope) J.; m. Sally-Ann Heimbigner, June 7, 1961 (div. 1976); children: Claire Elise, Hans Edward; m. Jean Eva Robinson, Dec. 5, 1976. BA, Whitman Coll., 1961; MS, Purdue U., 1965, PhD, 1970. Postdoctoral fellow Oreg. State U., Corvallis, 1970-73; rsch. chemist Lamb-Weston, Inc., Portland, Oreg., 1973-85, sr. rsch. chemist, 1985—. Presenter at profl. confs. Contbr. articles to profl. jours. Grantee NSF, 1960; NIH grad. fellow, 1965; Herman Frasch postdoctoral fellow Oreg. State U., 1970. Mem. AAAS, Am. Oil Chemists Soc., Am. Chemistry Soc., Assn. Ofcl. Analytical Chemists, Sigma Xi. Achievements include patents for Process for Making A Starch Coated Product, Coated Potato Product Process. Home: 1204 Knollwood Ct Richland WA 99352-9448 Office: Lamb Weston Tech Ctr 2005 Saint St Richland WA 99352-5306 E-mail: jjjazz@aol.com., jerry.jacobsen@lambweston.com.

JACOBSEN, HUGH NEWELL, architect; b. Grand Rapids, Mich., Mar. 11, 1929; s. John Edwall and Lucy Ellen (Newell) J.; m. Robin Kearney, Dec. 27, 1952; children: John Edwall, Matthew Christian, Simon Townsend. BA, U. Md., 1951; B.Arch., M.Arch., Yale, 1955; cert., Archtl. Asso. Sch. Architecture, London, Eng., 1954; L.H.D. (hon.), Gettysburg Coll., 1974, Bradford Coll., 1990; DFA (hon.), U. Md., 1993. Architect with Philip Johnson, New Canaan, Conn., 1955, Keyes, Lethbridge & Condon, Washington, 1957-58; prin. Hugh Newell Jacobsen, FAIA, Washington, 1958—. Lectr. univs.; vis. prof. U. Cairo, Egypt, 1970 Editor: A Guide to the Architecture of Washington, D.C., 1965; prin. works include U.S. Embassy, Paris, addition to U.S. Capital, two Smithsonian Mus. (renovations), So. Vt. Art Ctr. Mem. adv. bd. Internat. Hassan Fathy Inst.; trustee Corcoran Gallery Art, 1973-81, Washington Gallery Modern Art, 1965-69, Washington Theater Club, 1965-72. Served with USAF, 1955-57. John Fitzgerald Kennedy Meml. fellow New Zealand Govt., 1971, Silver medal for distinction in design Tau Sigma Delta, 1981; named to Hall of Fame U. Md., 2000. Fellow AIA (Centennial award 1996, nat. AIA honor awards 1969, 74, 78, 80, 85, 88, numerous AIA chpt. awards, 20 Archtl. Record awards, Outstanding Learning Disabled Achiever award 1990, others); mem. NAD (elected), Cosmos Club (Washington), Century Assn., Yale Club (N.Y.C.). Office: 2529 P St NW Washington DC 20007-3024

JACOBSEN, JEFFREY RICHARD, music educator; b. Dickinson, ND, July 30, 1952; s. Richard Lee and Hope Melba Jacobsen; m. Michele R. Barta, Aug. 16, 1974; 1 child, Nicolai Lee. BS in Music Edn., Mayville State U., 1974; M in Mus. Edn., U. ND, 1982; PhD in Music Edn., U. No. Colo., 1986; Postdoc. in Conducting, Northwestern U., 2001, U. SC., 1996—97; Post Doctoral Study in Conducting, U. of Iowa, Iowa City, IA, 1996—2002, Cleve. Inst. of Music, Cleveland, OH, 1998—98. Asst. dir. chamber orch., jazz ensemble U. ND, 1981—82; condr. orch., dir. jazz ensemble, jazz combo, assoc. dir. jazz studies program U. No. Colo., 1982—84; dir. orch. and jazz ensemble Boulder Valley Pub. Schs., 1984—94; orch. dir. Blue Valley Sch. Dist., 1994—2001; artistic dir., condr. youth symphony Kansas City Philharm. East Orch., 1995—2001; artistic dir., founding condr. Blue Valley Chamber Orch., Overland Park, Kans., 1996—2001; artistic dir., condr. Orch. of the Pines, Nacogdoches, Tex., 2001—; dir. orch. activities Stephen F. Austin State U., Nacogdoches, Tex., 2001—. Artistic dir. Youth Symphony Kansas City, 1995—2001; prin. bassist Liberty (Mo.) Symphony Orch., Liberty, 1996—2001; bassist Mahler Fest. Orch., Boulder, Colo., 1999—; prin. bassist Puccini Fest., Kansas City, 1999—, Rapides Symphony, Alexandria, La., 2001. Musician (bassist): (rec.) Hot IV, 1985 (Nomination for Grammy in Jazz Category). Mem. Boulder Musician's Union, Boulder, Colo., 1988—94. Recipient Outstanding Orch. Dir., Kans. Orch. Directors Assn., 2000-2001, Mary Taylor Award for Excellence in Classroom Tchg., Boulder Valley Schools, 1991-1992, Guest Condr., ND All State Orch. Festival, 2001, Region 21/4 Tex. Music Educators Assn., 2001, Region 7 Tex. Music Educators Assn., 2002. Mem.: Tex. Music Educators Assn., Tex. Orch. Dirs Assn., Nat. Sch. Orch. Assn. (divsn. chmn. 1986—88), Am. String Tchrs. Assn., Music Educators Nat. Conf., Internat. Soc. of Bassists, Am. Symphony Orch. League, Conductor's Guild. Avocations: racquetball, bicycling, fly fishing, chess. Home: 337 County Rd Nacogdoches TX 75965-2221 Office: Stephen F Austin State University Department of Music Nacogdoches TX 75962-3043 Office Fax: 936-468-5810. Personal E-mail: jjacobsen@sfasu.edu. E-mail: jjacobsen@sfasu.edu.

JACOBSEN, JON ANTHONY, bank officer, lawyer; b. Omaha, Mar. 20, 1961; s. Robert Stanley and Joyce Ann (Hingtgen) Jacobsen; m. Debra Jean Slavin, Feb. 6, 1980; children: Gerard Christopher, Peter James, Jamie Marie. BSBA, Creighton U., 1983; JD, U. Iowa, 1988. Bar: Nebr. 1989, Dist. Nebr. (admitted to practice U.S. Dist. Ct.) 1989, Dist. Nebr. (admitted to practice U.S. Ct. Appeals (8th cir.)) 1989. Mgmt. info. cons. Arthur Andersen & Co., Omaha, 1983—85; pres. Prosthetic Designs, Inc., Davenport, Iowa, 1988—89; assoc. Sherrets & Smith, Omaha, 1989—90; campaign coord. Staskiewicz for Congress, Omaha, 1990; state coord. Assn. Nebr. Cmnty. Action Agencies, Lincoln, Nebr., 1990—91; exec. v.p., finance devel. Sportsworld Complex Co., Omaha, 1990—91; asst. dir. Creighton U., Omaha, 1991—95; mgr. South Pacific Tranquility IcePlex, LLC, Omaha, 1995—2000; v.p., gen. counsel South Pacific Tranquility Inc., Omaha, 1995—2000; sr. mgnt. rep. First Nat. Bk. of Omaha, Omaha, 2000—01, trust officer, 2001—. Adj. instr. Nebr. Coll. Bus., Omaha, 1999—2001. Contbr. articles. Vol. George W.Bush for President Campaign, 1995. Named Family of the Year, Knights of Columbus, 1995; recipient Nat. Forensic League Degree of Distinction award. Mem.: Pack 100, Omaha Boy Scouts of Am., Devel. Stewardship Ctr., Omaha Bar Assn., Nebr. State Bar Assn., Nebr. Fed. of Catholic Sch. Parents, Knights of Columbus, Optimist Club, Beta Gamma Sigma, Alpha Sigma Nu. Republican. Roman Catholic. Avocations: golf, swimming, Reagan and modern US pres., John Ford-John Wayne film study, Ellis Peters' Brother Cadfael mystery series. Home: 2506 So 46th Ave Omaha NE 68106 Office: First nat Bk of Omaha 1620 Dodge St Stop 1071 Omaha NE 68197 Office Fax: 402-633-3366. E-mail: jjacobsen@fnni.com.

JACOBSEN, LAREN, programmer, analyst; b. Salt Lake City, June 15, 1937; s. Joseph Smith and Marian (Thomas) J.; m. Audrey Bartlett, July 29, 1970 (div.); children: Andrea, Cecily, Julian. BS, U. Utah, 1963. Programmer IBM, 1963-70; sys. programmer Xerox Computer Svcs., 1970-79; pres. Prescient Investment Co., 1975-82; sr. sys. analyst Quotron Sys., L.A., 1979-86; programmer, analyst Gt. Western Bank, 1987-92; word processing adminstr. Intex Svcs, Inc., Montebello, Calif., 1993-99; data processing specialist ACC Info. Svcs., L.A., 2000—. Cons. in field. With USAR, 1961. Mem.: Am. Guild Organists (dean San Jose chpt. 1966—67), Mensa. Home: PO Box 91174 Los Angeles CA 90009-1174 E-mail: larenj@yahoo.com.

JACOBSEN, MAGDALENA GRETCHEN, former mediator, former federal agency executive; b. N.Y.C., July 26, 1940; d. Carl J. and Helen Jacobsen; m. Bruce Donald Henricus, Dec. 20, 1986. Cert. labor studies, AFL-CIO, 1971; cert. labor studies, bargaining and arbitration, Harvard U., 1973; cert. indsl. rels., U. Calif., San Francisco; 1975; BS, U. San Francisco, 1987; MS, Golden Gate U., 1989. Sec. CBS TV, Hollywood, Calif., 1962-65; flight attendant Continental Airlines, L.A., 1965-69, mgr. labor rels., 1972-76; local union official, sec.-treas. steward and stewardess divsn. ALPA, Washington, 1966-72; commr. Fed. Mediation and Conciliation Svcs., San Francisco, 1976-89, Portland, Oreg., 1992-93; dir. employee rels. City and County of San Francisco, 1989-92; bd. Nat. Mediation Bd., Washington, 1993—2002; active past pres. Industrial Relations Research Assn., Champagne, Ill., 2002—. Mem. Indsl. Rels. Rsch. Assn. (mem. exec. bd. 1980—, pres. San Francisco chpt. 1985-87, Portland chpt. 1992, D.C. chpt. 1997-98, nat. pres.-elect, 2000, pres. 2001). Avocations: golf, swimming, poetry, short-story writing. Office: Industrial Relations Research Assn U Illinois 504 E Armory Ave Rm 121 Champaign IL 61820 Fax: 217-265-5130. E-mail: jacobsen@nmb.gov.

JACOBSEN, RAYMOND ALFRED, JR., lawyer; b. Wilmington, Del., Dec. 14, 1949; s. Raymond Alfred and Margaret (Walters) J.; m. Marilyn Perry, Aug. 4, 1973; 1 child, Hunter Perry. BA, U. Del., 1971; JD, Georgetown U., 1975. Bar: D.C. 1975, U.S. Supreme Ct. 1982. From assoc. to ptnr. Howrey & Simon, Washington, 1975-97; dir. antitrust/trade regulation group McDermott, Will & Emery, Washington, 1997-, ptnr., 1997—, head regulatory and govt. affairs dept. and mem. mgmt. com. Adj. prof. internat. anti-trust law Am. U. Law Sch. Spl. projects editor Law & Policy in International Business, 1974-75. Served to capt. U.S. Army, 1975. Mem. ABA (antitrust law sect., litigation sect., internat. law sect., pub. contract law sect.), D.C. Bar Assn., U.S. Supreme Ct. Bar Assn., City Club (Washington), Army and Navy Country Club. Republican. Home: 4205 Maple Tree Ct Alexandria VA 22304-1035 Office: McDermott Will & Emery 600 13th St NW Fl 12 Washington DC 20005-3096 E-mail: rayjacobsen@mwe.com.

JACOBSEN, RICHARD T. mechanical engineering educator; b. Pocatello, Idaho, Nov. 12, 1941; s. Thorleif (dec.), and Edith Emily (Gladwin) J. dec.); m. Vicki Belle Hopkins, July 16, 1959 (div. Mar. 1973); children: Pamela Sue, Richard T, Eric Ernest; m. Bonnie Lee Stewart, Oct. 19, 1973; 1 child, Jay Michael; stepchild: Erik David Lustig. BSME, U. Idaho, 1963, MSME, 1965; PhD in Engring. Sci., Wash. State U., 1972. Registered profl. engr., Idaho. Instr. U. Idaho, 1964-66, asst. prof. mech. engring., 1966-72, assoc. prof., 1972-77, prof., 1977—, chmn. dept. mech. engring., 1980-85, assoc. dean engring., 1985-90, assoc. dir. Ctr. for Applied Thermodynamic Studies, 1975-86, dir., 1986-99, dean engring., 1990-99; dep. lab. dir., chief scientist Idaho Nat. Engring. Environ. Lab. Bechtel BWXT Idaho LLC, Idaho Falls, 1999-2001, assoc. lab. dir. strategic mgmt., chief scientist, 2001—03, chief scientist, 2003—, assoc. lab. dir. energy and environ. sci., 2003—. Guest rschr. Nat. Inst. Standards Tech., 1979, 86, 99; mem. annex 18 thermophys. properties environ. acceptable refrigerants com. Internat. Energy Agy., 1991-98; mem. nat. adv. coun. Fed. Lab. Consortium for Tech. Transfer, 2002—, Idaho State U. Coll. of Engring., 2000—. Author: International Union of Pure and Applied Chemistry, Nitrogen International Thermodynamic Tables of the Fluid State 6, 1979; Oxygen-International Thermodynamic Tables of the Fluid State-9, 1987, Ethylene-International Thermodynamic Tables of the Fluid State-10, 1988, ASHRAE Thermodynamic Properties of Refrigerants (2 vols.), 1986, (monograph series) Thermodynamic Properties of Cryogenic Fluids, 1997; numerous reports on thermodynamic properties of fluids, 1971— ; contbr. articles to profl. jours. Recipient Outstanding Engr. award Idaho State U., 2002; NSF sci. faculty fellow, 1968-69; NSF rsch. and travel grantee, 1976-83; Nat. Inst. Standards and Tech. grantee, 1974-91, 95-98, Gas Rsch. Inst. grantee, 1986-91, 1992-98, Dept. Energy grantee, 1991-95. Fellow ASME (faculty advisor 1972-75, 78-84, chmn. region VIII dept. heads com. 1983-85, honors and awards chmn. 1985-91, K-7 tech. com. thermophys. properties 1985—, chmn. 1986-89, 92-95, 2001—, rsch. tech. com. on water and steam in thermal power systems, 1988—, gen. awards com. 1985-91, chmn. 1988-91, com. on honors 1988-99, vice chmn. 1995-99, mem. bd. on profl. practice and ethics, 1991—, v.p. profl. practice 1998-2001, Inland Empire Sect. Engr. of Yr. award 1999), N.W. Coll. and Univ. Assn. for Sci. (bd. dirs. 1990-93), Idaho Rsch. Found. (bd. dirs. 1991-99, 2000—), Soc. Automotive Engrs. (Ralph R. Teetor Edn. award, Detroit 1968), ASHRAE (co-recipient Best Tech. Paper award 1984), Sigma Xi, Tau Beta Pi, Phi Kappa Phi (Disting. Faculty award 1989). Office: Idaho Nat Engring Environ Lab Bechtel BWXT Idaho LLC PO Box 1625 Idaho Falls ID 83415-0001 E-mail: jacor@inel.gov.

JACOBSEN, THEODORE H. (TED H. JACOBSEN), labor union administrator, secondary school educator; b. N.Y.C., July 27, 1933; BS, Fordham U., 1955; postgrad., Hunter Coll., 1957-80, NYU, 1957-80, Columbia U., 1957-80. Cert. HS English tchr. N.Y.C. Tchr. N.Y.C. Bd. Edn. (on leave), 1957-86; editor Labor News and Trade Union Handbook N.Y.C. Ctrl. Labor Coun., AFL-CIO, N.Y.C., 1986—. Mem. exec. bd. Jewish Labor Com., N.Y.C., 1977—, Workers Def. League, N.Y.C., 1986—, Am. Labor ORT, N.Y.C., 1986—; regional v.p. Union Label and Svc. Trades Dept., NY, 1980—96; mem. adv. bd. Harry Van Arsdale Jr. Coll. Labor Studies, Empire State Coll., N.Y.C., 1986—; mem. adv. coun. occupation edn. N.Y.C. Bd. Edn., 1986—, vice chmn., 1989—; bd. dirs. Nat. Ethnic Coalition Orgns., Inc.; mem. bd. govs. Forum; sec. N.Y.C. Ctrl. Labor Coun. AFL-CIO. Mem. Cmty. Bd. 8, N.Y.C., 1987—93; mem. N.Y.C. Sch. to Work regional coun. Regional Planning Assn.; mem. exec. bd. Friends A. Philip Randolph Campus HS City Coll., 1990—; bd. dirs. Cath. Interracial Coun., 1987—, United Way N.Y., 1988—95, Coun. Environ., N.Y.C., 1988—95, Italian Acad. Found., Nat. Ethnic Coalition Orgns., Inc., Italic Studies Inst.; trustee Italian Hosp. Soc., ARC Greater N.Y., 1989—2001, Italian Hosp. Soc.; mem. exec. bd. Workman's Cir. Home-Geriatric Ctr., 1986—89, treas., 1989—; sec. Robert F. Wagner Labor Archives NYU, N.Y.C., 1986—; mem. bd. advisors Transition Ctr., N.Y.C. Bd. Edn., 1991, Svc. Area Planning Group, 1991; mem. Naval War Coll. Found., 1989—; mem. N.Y. State coastal mgmt. adv. com. N.Y. Harbor Maritime Industry, 1988—; charter mem. Battle Normandy Found., 1988—; chmn. N.Y. Trade Union Com. Histadrut, 1992—; mem. Asian Pacific Am. Labor Alliance; life mem. Workmen's Cir. Arbeter Ring; patron N.Y.C. Met. Opera. Decorated knight Order of Merit (Italy), knight officer Order Sts. Maurice and Lazarus, comdr. Order Merity Savoy; named Man of the Yr., Jewish Heritage Com. and Educators chpt., 1990, Educator of the Yr., Assn. Tchrs. N.Y., 1986, June 23, 1993 Theodore 'Ted' jacobsen Day, Queens Borough Pres.; recipient Cope awards, N.Y. State United Tchrs., 1975, 1978, Best Newsletter award, 1974, 1975, 1979, 1980, 1981, Spl. award educators chpt., Jewish Labor Com., 1986, Roberto Clemente award, Nat. Assn. P.R. Civil Rights, 1988, 75th Anniversary Cert. of Appreciation, U.S. Dept. Labor, 1988, Hurricane Hugo Disaster Relief citation, ARC, 1991, Good Scout award, Greater N.Y. Couns. Boy Scouts Am., 1992, Spl. Recognition award, Hispanic Labor Com., 1992, Leadership Svc. Recognition award, United Way N.Y.C., 1992, Consumer Merit award, N.Y. Consumer Assembly, 1992, Torch of Hope award, Pride Judea, 1993, Congl. Ellis Island medal Honor, 1993, N.Y.C. Coun. citation, 1993, Coalition Labor Union Women award, 1994, John LaFarge award interracial justice, Cath. Interracial Coun. N.Y., 1995, N.Y.C. Nova Ancora Job Tng. Program award of appreciation, N.Y.C. Dept. Probation, 1995, Disting. Svc. award, Internat. Brotherhood Elec. Workers, Local 3, J divsn., 1996, Robert Briscoe award, Emerald Isle Immigration Ctr., 1996, George Meany award, Greater N.Y. Couns. Boy Scouts Am., 1999. Mem.: NAACP (80th Anniversary Exempler award 1991, golden life heritage), NATAS (bd. govs. N.Y. chpt.), AFTRA, Nat. Italian-Am. Found., TV and Radio Working Press Assn., Internat. Platform Assn., Jewish Heritage Com., Black Trade Unionists Leadership Com., Coalition Labor Union Women, Internat. Labor Commn. Assn., Cath. Tchrs. Assn., Jewish Tchrs. Assn., United Fedn. Tchrs. (mem. P.M. staff 1973—, editor newsletter, chpt. chmn. 1974—86, Eli Trachtenberg award 1966, 1974, 1977, 1981, Albert Lee Smallheiser citation 1976), Acotr's Fund (life), Citizens Commn. African Union, United African Congress (mem. coun. elders, mem. adv. bd.), Lower East Side Tenement (hon. commr. 1992—), U.S. Naval Inst., Irish-Am. Studies Com., Irish-Am. Heritage Mus., U.S. Holocaust Meml. Mus. (charter), Asia Soc., Elks, B'nai B'rith (trustee 1989—96, bd. dirs. Adelstein Family Project HOPE Found. Housing Elderly 1992—), Order Sons Italy Am., Loyal League Yiddish Sons Erin (hon.). Avocations: theater, opera, travel. Office: NYC Cen Labor Coun AFL-CIO 386 Park Ave S New York NY 10016-8804 E-mail: thjnycusa@aol.com.

JACOBSEN, THOMAS WARREN, retired archaeologist, educator, freelance journalist; b. Mankato, Minn., Mar. 18, 1935; s. Maurice and Effie (Jensen) J.; m. Kathryn Jane Anderson, Aug. 18, 1956 (dec. June 1978); children: Mark Thomas, Kirsten; m. Susan K. Lehr, Aug. 1, 1981 (div. Dec. 1991); m. Sharyn Anne Elmquist, Jan. 18, 1997. BA, St. Olaf Coll., 1957; MA, U. Minn., 1960; postgrad., Am. Sch. Classical Studies, Athens, Greece, 1962-63; PhD, U. Pa., 1964. Asst. prof. classics, classical archeology Vanderbilt U., 1964-66; asst. prof. Ind. U., 1966-68, assoc. prof., 1968-75, prof., 1975-92; prof. emeritus, 1992—; chmn. dept. classical studies Ind. U., 1975-78, dir. program in classical archaeology, 1970-85. Staff mem. excavations, Porto Cheli, Greece, 1962, 65, 66, field dir., 1967, dir. excavations at Franchthi Cave, Greece, 1967-96, staff excavations, Kea, Greece, 1963; du Pont spl. rsch. fellow Am. Sch. Classical Studies Athens, 1980-81; vis. scholar Tulane U., 1992—. Gen. editor Excavations at Franchthi Cave, Greece, 1985-96; mem. editorial bd. Archaeology, 1988-92. Served with AUS, 1957. Fulbright scholar Greece, 1962-63; Olivia James fellow Archeol. Inst. Am., Greece, 1968-69; Am. Council Learned Socs. fellow, 1973-74; NSF postdoctoral fellow, 1973-74; Am. Philos. Soc. grantee, 1973-74 Mem. Internat. Clarinet Assn., Archaeol. Inst. Am. (Charles Eliot Norton Meml. lectr. spring 1988), Am. Shc. Classical Studies (mng. com., emeritus), Hellenic Numismatic Soc. Lutheran. Home: 3970 Laurel St New Orleans LA 70115-1364 Office: Tulane U Dept Classical Studies New Orleans LA 70118 E-mail: twj@tulane.edu.

JACOBSEN, VAN PAUL, lawyer; b. Olivia, Minn., Nov. 26, 1954; s. Ivan Robert and Nola Ruth Jacobsen; children: Natalie, Evan. BS, U. Minn., 1977, JD, 1982. Bar: Minn. 1982, U.S. Dist. Ct. Minn. 1986, U.S. Supreme Ct. 1997. Law clk. Dakota County Atty.'s Office, Hastings, Minn., 1980-82; asst. county atty. Renville County, Olivia, Minn., 1982-84; assoc. Simmons, Hunt & Jacobsen, Olivia, Minn., 1985-87, Steward, Perry, Mahler & Bird, Rochester, Minn., 1985-87; ptnr. Bird and Jacobsen, Rochester, Minn., 1987—. Vol. Legal Assistance of Olmsted County, Rochester, 1985—; mem. social concerns com. 1st Presbyn. Ch., Rochester, 1997—; bd. dirs. Vol. Connection, Rochester, 1990-92. Mem. Minn. Trial Lawyers Assn., Minn. State Bar Assn., Nat. Orgn. Social Security Claimant's Reps., Minn. Arabian Horse Assn., Internat. Arabian Horse Assn. Home: 628 73rd St NW Rochester MN 55901-5509 Office: Bird and Jacobsen 305 Ironwood Sq 300 3rd Ave SE Rochester MN 55904-4619 E-mail: vpjacobsen@aol.com.

JACOBSON, ALBERT HERMAN, JR., industrial and systems engineer, educator; b. St. Paul, Minn., Oct. 27, 1917; s. Albert Herman and Gertrude Jacobson; m. Elaine Swanson, June 1960; children: Keith, Paul. BS Indsl. Engring./Adminstrn. cum laude, Yale U., 1939; SM Bus. and Engring. Mgmt., MIT, 1952; MS in Applied Physics, U. Rochester, 1954; PhD in Indsl. and Mgmt. Engring., Stanford U., 1976. Registered profl. engr., Calif. Pers. asst. Yale U., New Haven, Conn., 1939-40; indsl. engr. in electronics Radio Corp. of Am., Camden, N.J., 1940-43; prodn. officer USN BuORD, 1943-44; RINSMAT USN Colonial Radio Corp. (Sylvania), Buffalo, 1944-45; INSORD USN Eastman Kodak Co., Rochester, N.Y., 1945-46; chief engr., dir. quality control Naval Ordnance Office, Rochester, N.Y., 1946-57; staff engr. Space Satellite Program Eastman Kodak Co., Rochester, 1957-59; assoc. dean Coll. Engring. and Architecture Pa. State U., University Park, Pa., 1959-61; v.p., gen. mgr. to pres. Knapic Electro-Physics Inc., Palo Alto, Calif., 1961-62; prof. of indsl. and systems engring. Coll. of Engring. San Jose State U., 1962—, co-founder, coord. Cybernetic Systems grad. program, 1968-88. Cons. in field. Lockheed, Motorola, Santa Fe R.R., 20th Century Fox, Alcan-Aluminium Corp., Banner Container, Sci. Mgmt. Corp., No. Telecom, Siliconix, others. Author: Military and Civilian Personnel in Naval Administration, 1952, Railroad Consolidations and Transportation Policy, 1975; editor: Design and Engineering of Production Systems, 1984; contbr. articles to profl. jours. Mem., chmn. Pers. Commn. City of Mountain View, Calif., 1968-78; troop chmn., scoutmaster, mem. Stanford Area Coun. Boy Scouts of Am., Palo Alto, 1970-83; chmn. Campus Luth. Coun. San Jose State U., 1981-86; mem. Santa Clara Valley Luth. Parish Coun., 1991—; pres. N.Y. State Young Adults Coun. YMCA, 1954-55. Lt. comdr. USNR. Recipient commendation USN, 1946; Alfred P. Sloan fellow Program Exec. Devel. MIT, 1951-52, NSF fellow, Stanford U., 1965-66; recipient Scouters Key and Award of Merit Stanford Coun. Boy Scouts Am., 1976. Mem. Am. Soc. Engring. Edn., Inst. Indsl. Engrs., Am. Prodn. and Inventory Control Soc. (bd. dirs. 1975—), Masons, Sigma Xi, Tau Beta Pi. Lutheran. Avocations: orchestra and choir, swimming, tennis, skiing, photography. Home: 1864 Limetree Ln Mountain View CA 94040-4019 Office: San Jose State U Coll Engring 1 Washington Sq San Jose CA 95192-0001

JACOBSON, ALLEN HOWARD, economist; b. N.Y.C., July 5, 1939; s. Jack Joseph and Mary (Laxman) J.; m. Gladys Cecile Safier, Sept. 20, 1970; children: Gennifer Ann, Allison Lindsay. BA, NYU, 1962, postgrad., 1965. Lic.

acct. exec. in securities bus., real estate agt., gen. securities prin.; lic. broker/dealer in securities bus. Economist Lional D. Edie & Inc., N.Y.C., 1966-69; sr. economist U.S. Trust Co., N.Y.C., 1969-79; ptnr. Washington Analysis Corp., 1979-87; v.p. NatWest Markets, Washington, 1988-95; sr. v.p. HSBC Securities, Inc., 1995-99; ptnr. Washington Analysis Corp., 1999—. Mem. Nat. Economists Club (v.p. 1982-83, 91-92, bd. govs. 1992-93), Nat. Assn. Bus. Economists (coun. nat. chpt. 1985-86), Washington Assn. Money Mgrs., Montgomery County Assn. Realtors, Lakewood Club, Norbeck Club (bd. dirs. 1981-82). Avocations: tennis, aerobics, real estate, golf, dancing. Home: 13140 Brushwood Way Potomac MD 20854-1025 Office: Washington Analysis Corp 1120 Connecticut Ave NW Ste 400 Washington DC 20036-3939 E-mail: ajacobson@washingtonanalysis.com.

JACOBSON, ANNETTE MOFF, chemical engineer; b. Latrobe, Pa., May 6, 1957; d. Charles James Jr. and Mary Agnes (Antinori) Moff; m. Donald Bruce Jacobson, Aug. 22, 1981; children: Jennifer Lynn, Amanda Rose. BSChE, Carnegie Mellon U., 1979, PhD in Chem. Engring., 1988. Chem. engr. PPG Inds., Inc., Pitts., 1979-81, sr. rsch. engr., 1981-85; assoc. dir. colloids, polymers & surface program Carnegie Mellon U., Pitts., 1988-89, lectr. in chem. engring., 1988-95, sr. lectr. chem. engring., 1996-2001, outreach dir. data storage systems ctr., 1999-2001, prin. lectr. chem. engring., 2001—. Workshop lectr. in field. Inventor in field. Amoco Found. fellow, 1986-88, Carnegie Mellon U. Women's Clan scholar, 1978-79, Babcock & Wilcox scholar Carnegie Mellon U., 1977-79; recipient G.D. Parfitt award Chem. Engring. Student Group, 1987. Mem. AIChE, Am. Chem. Soc., Internat. Assn. Colloid and Interface Scientists, Sigma Xi (corr. sec. 1994-99, v.p. 1996-98). Avocations: gardening, reading, hiking.

JACOBSON, ANTONE GARDNER, zoology educator; b. nr. Salt Lake City, May 22, 1929; s. Rufus Ingman and Marvell (Gardner) J.; m. Jacqueline James, July 26, 1962; children: Lauren, Eric. AB, Harvard U., 1951; PhD, Stanford U., 1955. Mem. faculty dept. zoology U. Tex., Austin, 1957—, assoc. prof., 1961-68, prof., 1968-97, prof. emeritus, 1997—; instr. Marine Biol. Lab., Woods Hole, Mass., 1969-70. Contbr. articles to profl. jours. Harvard Nat. scholar, 1947-51, Henry Newell Honors scholar, 1951-55. Mdm. Internat. Soc. Devel. Biologists, Soc. Devel. Biology, Am. Soc. Zoologists, Am. Assn. Anatomists, Sigma Xi. Home: 201 Skyline Dr Austin TX 78746-3610 Office: Univ Tex MCDB Pat Labs Austin TX 78712 E-mail: antone@mail.utexas.edu.

JACOBSON, ARLAND DEAN, religion educator; b. Mitchell, S.D., Sept. 25, 1941; s. Olaf Johannes and Ruth Amelia (Gjesdal) J. m. Wilhelmine Treadwell, Aug. 15, 1964; children: Erik Eugene, Karin Inga. BA, Augustana Coll., 1963; student, Div. Sch., U. Chgo., 1964-65; BD, Luther Theol. Sem., St. Paul, 1967; PhD, Claremont Grad. Sch., 1978. Ordained to ministry Evang. Luth. Ch. Am., 1967. Pastor Scranton (N.D.) Luth. Parish, 1967-71, St. Paul Luth. Ch., Humboldt, S.D., 1974-76; vis. prof. Loyola Marymount U., L.A., 1978-79; asst. prof. Concordia Coll., Moorhead, Minn., 1979-83; exec. dir. CHARIS Ecumenical Ctr. and Fargo-Moorhead Communiversity, Moorhead, 1983—. Chair bd. Great Plains Inst. Theology, Bismarck, N.D., 1969-71; mem. Faith and Order Commn., Minn. Coun. Chs., Mpls., 1985-92. Author: Wisdom Christology in Q, 1978, The First Gospel, 1991, Ecumenical Shared Ministry in the United Methodist Church, 1995, A Journey into our Christian Past, 1999; also numerous articles and revs. Chair conf. planning com. Internat. Coalition for Land-Water Stewardship in the Red River Basin, Moorhead, 1983-85, chair edn. com., 1985-87. Scholar Luth. Theol. Sem., 1966, scholar in residence Inst. for Ecumenical and Cultural Rsch., 1990, Harvard Inst. Mgmt. Lifelong Learning, 1992, Tantur Ecumenical Inst., Jerusalem, 1997; Bush fellow, 1992. Mem. Soc. Bibl. Lit., Cath. Bibl. Assn., Soc. for Advancement Continuing Edn. for Ministry (sec. 1996—), The Jesus Seminar, Westar Inst., Jazz Arts Group (bd. mem. 1995—). Home: PO Box 6 Moorhead MN 56561-0006 Office: Concordia Coll Charis Ecumenical Ctr Moorhead MN 56562-0001 E-mail: jacobson@cord.edu.

JACOBSON, BARRY STEPHEN, lawyer, judge; b. Bklyn., Mar. 30, 1955; s. Morris and Sally (Ballaban) J.; m. Andrea Jacobson; children: Faith Blair, Matthew Aaron Jacobson. Cert. in drama, Sch. of Performing Arts, N.Y.C., 1973; BA, CUNY, 1977, MA, 1980; JD, Bklyn. Sch. Law, 1980. Bar: N.Y., 1981, U.S. Dist. Ct. (ea. and so. dists.) N.Y. 1981, U.S. Dist. Ct. (we. and no. dists.) N.Y., 1988, U.S. Dist. Ct. D.C., 1988, U.S. Ct. Appeals (2d cir.) 1981, U.S. Ct. Appeals (fed. and D.C. cirs.) 1988, U.S. Supreme Ct. 1984, U.S. Ct. Claims, 1985, U.S. Tax Ct. 1988 and others. Sole practice, Bklyn., 1981; asst. corp. counsel N.Y.C. Law Dept., Bklyn., 1981-84; asst. dist. atty. Borough of Queens, Kew Gardens, N.Y., 1984-85; judge adminstrv. law N.Y. Dept. Motor Vehicles, Bklyn., 1985-86, 87-92; assoc. counsel N.Y. State Dept. Health, N.Y.C., 1986; arbitrator N.Y.C. Small Claims Ct., 1986-91; pvt. practice Bklyn., 1992—. Gen. counsel Amersfort Flatlands Devel. Corp., Bklyn., 1981-82; arbitrator N.Y.C. Civil Ct. 1987-92; adminstrv. law judge N.Y.C. Parking Violators Bur., 1987-93; mem. Indigent Defenders Appeal Panel, 1988-96; sr. adminstrv. law judge N.Y.C. Parking Violation Bur., 1989-93; leader Nat. Jud. Coll., N.Y. Mem. Roosevelt Dem. Party, Bklyn., 1984-95, mem. adv. bd., 1989-92, treas., 1990-92; active Kings Hwy. Dem. Party, Bklyn., 1982-95, Dem. com. 1986-95; active King's County Young Dems., 1985-86; gen. counsel Bklyn. Coll. Hillel, Bklyn. Coll. Student Govts., 1980-90, also advisor; treas. local div. dept. mtr. vehicles pub. employees fedn. AFL-CIO; coun. ldr. div. #255 Pub. Employee's Fedn., 1989-92, conv. del. 1989, 90, 91; chmn. Bklyn. Traffic Employee Assistance Prog., 1989-92. Named one of Outstanding Young Men Am., 1983, 85, 86, 87, 88. Mem. ABA (judicial sect., spl. const. judges traffic cts. com.), Am. Judges Assn. (hwy. safety com.), Bklyn. Bar Found. (trustee, bd. dirs.), Am. Arbitration Assn. (forums 1988—), Am. Judicature Soc., Assn. Adminstrv. Law Judges (pres.), N.Y. State Dept. Motor Vehicles (v.p.), N.Y. State Adminstrv. Law Judges Assn. (pres. bd. dirs. parking violation com., v.p.), N.Y. State Bar Assn. (pres. for DMV, spl. com. juvenile justice, adminstrv. law jud. coms., jud. adminstrn. com.), Bklyn. Bar Assn. (family ct. com., chmn. young lawyers sect., trustee 1991, chmn. adminstrn. law com.), N.Y. County Lawyers Assn. (family Ct. Com.), Bklyn. Coll. Alumni Assn. (gen. counsel student govt. affiliate 1983-92, bd. dirs. 1985-92), Jaycees, B'nai B'rith, Hillel (bd. dirs. 1983-91, gen. counsel 1987-91), many others. Jewish. Avocations: motorcycling, drama, theatre, target shooting, flying. Home: 342 Coleridge Ln Jericho NY 11753-2605 Office: 26 Court St Ste 810 Brooklyn NY 11242-1108 E-mail: ticklaw@aol.com.

JACOBSON, BERNARD, lawyer; b. Hartford, Conn., Feb. 27, 1930; s. Samuel Barnard and Lillian Jacobson; m. Florence Ellen Greenberg, Oct. 7, 1956; children: Daniel John, Alice Lash, Nancy Jacobson-Penn. AB, Amherst Coll., 1951; LLB, Columbia U., 1954. Bar: Conn. 1955, Fla. 1957, U.S. Dist. Ct. (so. dist.) Fla. 1957, U.S. Ct. Appeals (11th cir.) 1961. Pvt. practice, Miami, Fla., 1957-68; ptnr. Fine, Jacobson, Miami, Fla., 1968-94, Holland & Knight LLP, Miami, Fla., 1994—2002, Akerman Senterfitt, Miami, 2002—. Pres., CEO Rep. Mortgage Investors, Miami, 1973-81; presenter in field. Contbr. articles to profl. jours. Chmn. Fla. Congl. Partnership, Miami, 1987; vice chmn. Greater Miami C. of C., 1988-92. With U.S. Army Counter Intelligence Corps, 1955-57. Mem. ABA, Fla. Bar Assn. Avocations: tennis, boating, skiing. Office: Akerman Senterfitt One SE 3d Ave Ste 2800 Miami FL 33131 E-mail: bjacobson@akerman.com.

JACOBSON, BONNIE BROWN, energy consulting company executive, statistician, writer, researcher; b. Annapolis, Md., Feb. 15, 1952; d. Albert Robert and Ruth Marie (Puhak) Brown. BS cum laude, LaRoche Coll., Pitts., 1974; MS, U. Pitts., 1976. Rsch. assoc. Squibb Inst. Med. Rsch., Princeton, N.J., 1976-78; assoc. statistician N.E. Utilities Svc. Co., Hartford, Conn., 1978-80, statistician, 1980-82, sr. statistician, 1982-83, mgr. consumer rsch., 1983-87, corp. statistician, 1987-89; project mgr. energy div. ICF Kaiser Engrs., Fairfax, Va., 1989-91; v.p., 1991-92, AUS Conss., Phila., 1992-94; owner/cons. Energy Access, Maple Glen, Pa., 1995—. Microgravity rschr. KC-105 Mission 89-2, NASA, 1989; chmn. Space Access, Inc., 1989-90; cons. stats., Hartford, 1976-89; adviser Electric Power Rsch. Inst., Palo Alto, Calif., 1978-89; evaluation prin. investigator Conn. Low Income Weatherization Conservation Program, 1988-92; rsch. plan developer Conn. Energy Assistance Study Project, Hartford, 1983-84. Rsch scholar U. Pitts., 1974-76. Mem. NAFE, Am. Statis. Assn., Am. Mktg. Assn., Electric Utility Market Rsch. Coun. Avocations: golf, skiing, tennis, racquetball, reading. Home and Office: Energy Access 1804 Hood Ln Maple Glen PA 19002-6104 E-mail: energybbj@aol.com., energyaccweb@aol.com.

JACOBSON, CAROLE RENEE, lawyer, educator; b. N.Y.C., Feb. 10, 1935; d. Daniel and Sally (Leader) Gold; m. David S. Jacobson, Jan. 28, 1962; 3 children. BS with honors, U. Pa., 1956; MA English with honors, Columbia U., 1957; JD, Rutgers U., 1979. Bar: Pa. 1980, Fla. 1982, N.J. 1983; cert. English tchr., N.J. Tchr. Manhasset (L.I., N.Y.) High Sch., 1958-62, Westfield (N.J.) High Sch., 1962; dir. social services South Brunswick (N.J.) High Sch., 1976; sr. counsel N.J. Casino Control Commn., Atlantic City, 1981—. Editor N.J. Voter, 1974-75. Elected Hunterdon (N.J.) Cen. Regional Bd. Edn., 1983, 86, 89-92, v.p., 1986-87, pres. 1987-88; mem. Raritan Twp. (N.J.) Bd. Adjustment, 1979-82, vice chmn., 1981; Hunterdon County freeholder candidate, 1975; chmn. legis. subcom. State Consumer Affairs Adv. Com., 1976-82; mem. N.J. State bd. LWV, 1974-75, pres. Hunterdon County, 1972-74, Plainfield, 1968-70; pres. Vol. Bur. Hunterdon County, 1974-76; trustee Hunterdon County Housing Council, 1972-76; mem. Citizens Housing Corp. Raritan Twp. 1971-72; chmn. Hunterdon County Coalition Better Pub. Schs., 1971-72; mem. State Adv. Commn. on the Status of Women, 1991-94. Recipient resolution of appreciation Bd. Adjustment, Raritan Twp., 1982. Home: 1 Pinewood Ct Flemington NJ 08822-4909 Office: Arcade Bldg Tennessee Ave & Boardwalk Atlantic City NJ 08401

JACOBSON, CHARLES EDWARD, JR., urologist; b. Nov. 11, 1910; BS, Trinity Coll., Hartford, Conn., 1931; MD, Cornell U., 1935; MS, U. Minn., 1941. Retired from career as urologist. Mem. numerous nat. and internat. med. socs. Home: 45 Wyllys St Manchester CT 06040-5613

JACOBSON, CLAIRE E. music therapist; b. N.Y.C., Sept. 28, 1929; d. Philip and Sophie Winkler; children: Sandra, Jerry; m. Marvin Roth, Mar. 6, 1994. BA in Psychology, Fla. Internat. U., 1976, postgrad., 1993—; diploma, Nat. Guild Piano Tchrs., 1948. Music dir. Jewish Cmty. Ctr., Miami, Fla., 1979—; music therapist Dade County Schs., Miami, 1980—. Performer, therapist for the elderly, Miami Beach, Fla., 1979—; bd. dirs. Caravel Homeowners Assn., Miami, 1980—. Mem. Hadassah, Sierra Club, B'nai B'rith, Golden Key, Psi Chi, Phi Kappa Phi. Jewish. Avocations: piano, singing, writing. Home: 6741 SW 91st Ave Miami FL 33173-2423 E-mail: cjnyfl@aol.com.

JACOBSON, DAVID EDWARD, lawyer; b. Port Chester, N.Y., May 17, 1949; s. Robert Herzel and Ruth Doris (Rosenzweig) J.; m. Debra Ann Denkensohn, Aug. 10, 1973; 1 child, Andrew. BA in Econs., U. Rochester, 1971; JD, SUNY, Buffalo, 1974; LLM in Taxation, Georgetown U., 1977. Bar: N.Y. 1975, D.C. 1976, U.S. Tax Ct. 1982, U.S. Ct. Appeals (fed. cir.) 1983. Atty.-advisor Office of Chief Counsel, IRS, Washington, 1974-79; tax counsel com. on fin. U.S. Senate, Washington, 1979-81; assoc. firm Thelen Reid & Priest LLP, Washington, 1981-86, ptnr., 1986—. Mem. Partnership Coun., 2001—. Vol. Income Tax Assistance, Arlington, Va., 1977-81; treas. Overlook Townhouse Homeowners Assn., Arlington. Mem. ABA (mem. tax sect. 1982—, vice chmn. regulated utilities com. 1988-90, chmn. 1990-92), N.Y. State Bar Assn. Office: Thelen Reid & Priest LLP 701 Pennsylvania Ave NW Ste 800 Washington DC 20004-2608 E-mail: djacobson@thelenreid.com.

JACOBSON, DENNIS JOHN, lawyer; b. Racine, Wis., June 1, 1953; s. Donald Lee and Donna Marie (Andress) J.; m. Debra Jean Tully, Dec. 21, 1981; 1 child, Rebecca Michelle. BA, Western State Coll., Gunnison, Colo., 1975; JD, U. Denver, 1978. Bar: Colo. 1978, U.S. Dist. Ct. Colo. 1978, U.S. Ct. Appeals (10th cir.) 1987. Dep. dist. atty. 1st Jud. Dist. Colo., Golden, 1978-81; assoc. Polidori, Rasmussen & Gerome, Lakewood, Colo., 1981-83; ptnr. Polidori, Gerome, Franklin & Jacobson, Lakewood, 1983-99; solo practice, 2000—. Lectr. Colo. Law Enforcement Tng. Acad., Golden, 1979-89; adj. prof. bus. law Colo. Christian U., 2002–. Co-author: DUI Manual State of Colorado, 1981. Cen. com. Jefferson County Rep. Com., Colo., 1986-88. Mem. ABA, Colo. Bar Assn. (bd. govs. 1988-90, v.p. 1990-91), 1st Jud. Dist. Bar Assn. Colo. (pres. 1987-88, contbr. to newsletter 1985-97, Outstanding Young Lawyer award 1983, Merit award 1998). Avocations: instrumental and vocal music, sports, scuba diving. Office: 333 S Alison Pkwy #300 Lakewood CO 80226

JACOBSON, DORANNE, photographer; b. Ann Arbor, Mich., Jan. 28, 1940; d. Russell Everett and Dorothy Louise Novy Wilson; m. Jerome Jacobson, June 16, 1963; children: Laurie Grace Sarah, Joshua Robert Russell. Student, U. London, 1959-60; BA, U. Mich., 1961; PhD, Columbia U., 1970. Lectr. CCNY, N.Y.C., 1969-70; rsch., seminar assoc. Columbia U., N.Y.C., 1970—; dir. Internat. Images, Springfield, Ill., 1980—. Cons. Am. Mus. Natural History, N.Y.C., 1978-80; cons., editor UNICEF, N.Y.C., 1981-88; lectr. Inst. for Asian Studies, N.Y.C., 1987-97; acad. study leader Am. Mus. Natural History, N.Y.C., Smithsonian Instn., Washington, 1991—. Author: India: Land of Dreams and Fantasy, 1992, The Civil War in Art: A Visual Odyssey, 1996; co-author (with S. Wadley): Women in India: Two Perspectives, 1998, 2 other books; contbr. articles to profl. jours., numerous photographs to mags. Grantee Woodrow Wilson Found., 1961-62, NDFL, 1961-64, NIMH, 1964-68, AMNH Ogden Mills, 1972-73, NEH, 1977-78, Am. Coun. Learned Socs., 1971-72, 78-79, Am. Inst. Indian Studies, 1974-75, 78-79, Smithsonian Instn., 1985. Fellow Am. Anthropol. Assn.; mem. AAUW, Assn. Asian Studies, Soc. Women Geographers, Editl. Photographers Group. Avocation: international travel. Home: 2617 Clifton Dr Springfield IL 62704-4233 E-mail: dj232@columbia.edu.

JACOBSON, EARL JAMES, lawyer, investment banker; b. Chgo, May 10, 1940; s. Benjamin L. and Mary (Urman) J.; children: Joan, John. BA, U. Ill., 1961; MBA, U. Chgo., 1963; JD, Loyola U., Chgo., 1980. Bar: Ill. 1980, US Dist. Ct. (no. dist.) Ill. 1980, US Ct. Internat. Trade 1980, US Ct. Customs and Patent Appeals 1980, US Tax Ct. 1985, US Supreme Ct. 1985. Indsl. salesman Honeywell, Xerox, Chgo., 1964-67; dir. mktg. Mastech Computer, Chgo., 1967-71, Datronic Rental Co., Chgo., 1971-81; v.p. Dearborn Computer Co., Pk. Ridge, Ill., 1981-82; sr. syndication officer Seattle 1st Nat. Bank, Schaumburg, Ill., 1982-83; v.p. fin. and syndication Hartford Fin. Svc., Inverness, Ill., 1983-85; v.p. corp. fin. and corp. counsel Lease Investment Corp., Chgo., 1985-86; dir. equity placement CIS Corp., Syracuse, NY, 1986-87; pres. Mid Tech Funding, 1987-89, Smith Wilson Acceptance Corp., 1989—92; regional mgr. valuation rsch. Deloitte & Touche, Chgo., 1992—97, regional mgr., 1997—99; funding mgr. Internat. Profit Assoc., Buffalo, 1999-2000; dir. corp. fin. dept. Am. Fin. Mgmt., Inc., Arlington Heights, Ill., 2000—. Dir., gen. counsel Info. Sys., Arlington Heights, 1st Securities, Inc., Chgo., Citifirst, Inc., Chgo. Served with USAF, 1963-69. With USAF, 1963—69. Mem. ABA, Nat. Assn. Securities Dealers, Equipment Syndication Assn., Ill. State Bar Assn., Chgo. Bar Assn. Club: 20 Plus (Chgo.) (pres. 1980-82). Home: 4200 W Lake Ave Apt A102 Glenview IL 60025-7402

JACOBSON, EDWARD (JULIAN EDWARD JACOBSON), lawyer; b. Chgo., Mar. 18, 1922; s. Lewis Frederick and Pearl (Hoffman) J. BA magna cum laude, Carleton Coll., 1942; Baker Scholar with Distinction, Harvard Bus. Sch., 1943; JD with honors, U. Ariz., 1946; DHL (hon.), Carleton Coll., 1994, Ariz. State U., 1995. Bar: Ariz. 1947, U.S. Dist. Ct. Ariz. 1947, U.S. Ct. Appeals (9th cir.) 1956, U.S. Supreme Ct. 1963. Law clk. to presiding justice Ariz. Supreme Ct., Phoenix, 1947-48; asst. atty. gen. Ariz. Atty. Gen.'s Office, Phoenix, 1948-50; ptnr. Snell and Wilmer, Phoenix, 1950-89, of counsel, 1990—. Author: The Art of Turned Wood Bowls, 1985. Pres. Civic Ctr. Mgmt. Bd., 1960-90, Phoenix Art Mus., 1974-76, Heard Mus., 1962-64, Phoenix Cmty. Coun., 1960-62, Family Svc. Phoenix; mem. Ariz. Commn. on Arts, 1979-88; bd. visitors Coll. Law U. Ariz., Tucson, 1978-80. Recipient Man of Yr. award Phoenix Advt. Club, 1974, Disting. Achievement award Ariz. State U. Law Sch., 1976, Disting. Achievement award Ariz. State U. Coll. Fine Arts, 1982, Gov.'s Arts award State of Ariz., 1983, Centennial Presdl. medal Ariz. State U., 1985, Visionary award Valley Leadership Alumni Assn., 1990, Historymaker award The Hist. League of Ariz. Hist. Soc., 1993. Fellow Ariz. Bar Found. (founding bd. mem. 1980, Walter E. Craig award 1995); mem. ABA, Ariz. Bar Assn., Maricopa County Bar Assn., Law Soc. Ariz. State U. (pres. 1974-75), Am. Judicare Soc., University Club, Phoenix Country Club. Home: 2201 N Central Ave Phoenix AZ 85004-1417 Office: Snell & Wilmer One Arizona Ctr Phoenix AZ 85004-0001 E-mail: bjacobson@swlaw.com.

JACOBSON, EUGENE DONALD, educator, administrator, researcher; b. Bridgeport, Conn., Feb. 19, 1930; s. Morris and Mary (Mendelsohn) J.; m. Laura Kathryn Osborn, June 9, 1973; children from previous marriage: Laura Ellen, Susan Ruth, Morris David, Daniel Frederick, Miriam Louise. BA, Wesleyan U., 1951; MD, U. Vt., 1955; MS, SUNY-Syracuse, 1960; DrMed (hon.), Jagiellonian U., 1996. Assoc. prof. UCLA Sch. Medicine, 1965-66; prof., chmn. U. Okla. Sch. Medicine, Okla. City, 1966-71, U. Tex. Med. Sch., Houston, 1971-77; vice dean Coll. Medicine U. Cin., 1977-85; dean Sch. Medicine, U. Kans., Kansas City, 1985-88; dean Sch. Medicine, U. Colo., Denver, 1988-90, prof., 1990-99, acting head divsn. gastroenterology, 1994, prof. emeritus, 1999—. Cons. NIH, Bethesda, Md., 1968-72, mem. nat. digestive adv. bd., 1985-87; chmn. Nat. Commn., U.S. Congress, Washington, 1977-79; cons. Upjohn Co., Kalamazoo, 1970-87, G. D. Searle and Co., Chgo., 1984-85 Contbr. 320 articles to profl. jours. Served to maj. U.S. Army, 1956-64 NIH Rsch. grantee, 1967-97. Fellow ACP; mem. AMA (ho. of dels. 1991—), Am. Soc. Clin. Investigation, Assn. Am. Physicians, Am. Physiol. Soc., Am. Gastroenterol. Assn. (pres. 1989-90, Friedenwald medal 1998), Am. Digestive Health Found. (bd. dirs. vice chair 1995-98).

JACOBSON, FRANK JOEL, cultural organization administrator; b. Phila., Sept. 14, 1948; s. Leonard and June Anette (Groff) J.; m. Stephanie Lou Savage, July 5, 1970; children: Aaron Jeffery, Adam Michael, Ashley Celeste. BA, U. Wis., 1970; MFA, Boston U., 1973. Mng. dir. Mont. Repertory Theater, Missoula, Mo., 1973-75; asst. prof. drama U. Mont., Missoula, 1973-75; program dir. Western States Arts Found., Denver, 1975-77, dir. programs, 1977-78, gen. mgr. budget/planning, 1978-79; exec. dir. Arvada (Colo.) Ctr. for the Arts & Humanities, 1979-85; dir. theatres and arenas City & County of Denver, 1985-87; pres., CEO Scottsdale (Ariz.) Cultural Coun., 1987—. Bd. dirs. Met. Denver Arts Alliance, pres., 1979-85, Rocky Mountain Arts Consortium, pres., 1979-80. Contbr. articles to profl. jours. Mem. panel theater program Nat. Endowment for the Arts, Washington, 1990-92; bd. dirs. Scottsdale Focus, 1988-93, 93-97, Arizonans for Cultural Devel., 1992-97; bd. dirs. Scottsdale Edn. Found., 1994-99, chmn., 1994-96; bd. dirs. Scottsdale Convention and Visitors Bur., 2001—. Mem.: Assn. for Performing Arts Presenters (bd. dirs. 1984—87), Rocky Mountain Theatre Assn. (bd. dirs., pres. 1976—78), Mont. State Theatre Assn. (bd. dirs., pres. 1974—75), Am. Theatre Assn. (bd. dirs. 1976—78), Scottsdale C. of C. (bd. dirs. 2001—). Office: Scottsdale Cultural Council 7380 E 2nd St Scottsdale AZ 85251-5604

JACOBSON, GARY STEVEN, lawyer; b. Holyoke, Mass., Sept. 4, 1951; s. Rudolph Milton and Frederika Helena (Vanderryn) J.; m. Sharon W. Turkish, June 16, 1974; children: Lowell Daniel, Lee Stuart. BA cum laude, Wesleyan U., Middletown, Conn., 1973; JD, Northwestern U., 1976. Bar: Conn. 1976, N.Y. 1977, N.J. 1977, U.S. Ct. Appeals (3d cir.) 1981, U.S. Ct. Appeals (2d cir.) 1996. Investigative atty. N.Y. State Commn. on Jud. Conduct, N.Y.C., 1976-77; spl. asst. atty. gen. Office Spl. State Prosecutor, N.Y.C., 1977-79; assoc. Hofheimer, Gartlir, Gottlieb & Gross, N.Y.C., 1979-80, Kleinberg, Moroney, Masterson & Schachter, Millburn, N.J., 1980-85, ptnr., 1986-90; of counsel Kelley Drye & Warren, N.Y.C., 1990-91, ptnr., 1992-96, Farer Siegal Fersko, Westfield, NJ, 1996-98; bankruptcy trustee Panel Chpt. 7, 1997—; mem. Gary S. Jacobson, LLC, Mountainside, Springfield, 1998—2002; of counsel Herold and Haines, Warren, NJ, 2002—. Co-author: Commercial Litigation in New York State Courts, 1995; editor: Judicial Discipline Reporter, 1976. Republican. Jewish. Home: 99 Susan Dr Chatham NJ 07928-1055 Office: Herold and Haines PA 25 Independence Blvd Warren NJ 07059-6747 Address: Gary S Jacobsen LLC PO Box 697 468 Morris Ave Springfield NJ 07081-0697

JACOBSON, GERALD, orthodontist; b. Phila., Mar. 15, 1937; s. Simon Louis and Bess (Kirsh) J.; m. Marlene Pechter, Dec. 22, 1963; children: Alicia Sue and Andrew David. BA, Muhlenberg Coll., 1957; DDS, Temple U., 1961; postgrad., U. Pa., 1964. cert. orthodontics, 1964. Orthodontist Atrium Med. Dental Ctr., Cherry Hill, N.J., 1965—; attending dentist Thomas Jefferson U. Hosp., Phila., 1965-78; staff J.F.K. U. Med. Ctr., Cherry Hill, 76—; assoc. prof. of orthodontics Temple U. Sch. Dentistry, Phila., 1986—. Lectr. U. Pa. Sch. Dentistry, Phila., 1968-72; adj. faculty lectr. Camden County Coll., Blackwood, N.J., 1972-98, Camden County Tech. Inst., Berlin, N.J., 1972-97. Mem. alumni bd. dirs. Temple U. Sch. Dentistry, 1992-. Capt. USAF, Robins AFB, 1961-63. Mem. ADA, Am. Assn. Orthodontists, Mid. Atlantic Soc. Orthodontists, N.J. Assn. Orthodontists, N.J. Dental Assn., So. Dental Soc, Temple U. Dental Alumni (bd. dirs. 1992—), Greater Phila. Soc. Orthodontists (bd. dirs. 1990-96, pres. 1994-95), U. Pa. Orthodontic Alumni Assn. (pres. 1978-79), Alpha Omega (pres. 1974-75), Omicron Kappa Upsilon Nat. HOn. Dental Fraternity. Avocations: photography, painting, music, sports, travel. Office: Atrium Med-Dental Ctr 1910 Route 70 E Cherry Hill NJ 08003-2123

JACOBSON, GILBERT H. lawyer, director; b. Memphis, Feb. 6, 1956; s. Irvin and Edith (Shainberg) J.; m. Shauna Brown, Aug. 23, 1983; children: Yisroel, Esther, Nechama, Mordechai, Avrohom, Doniel. BBA, Memphis State U., 1980; JD, Touro Coll. Sch. Law, Huntington, N.Y., 1983. Bar: N.Y. 1984, Tenn. 1985, Colo. 1986. Tax cons. Rooney, Pace, Inc., N.Y.C., 1983-84; chief fin. officer Denton Mills, Inc., New Albany, Miss., 1984-85; endowment cons. Coun. of Jewish Fedns., N.Y.C., 1986-90, assoc. dir. endowment devel., 1990-92, assoc. dir. planned giving and found. rels., 1992-95; dir. Endowment Found. UJA Fedn. Bergen County, River Edge, N.J., 1995-99; assoc. exec. dir. planned giving and endowments UJA-Fedn. N.Y., N.Y.C., 1999—2002; mng. dir. Stellar Fin., 2002—. Contbr. articles to profl. jours. Founding pres. Torah Comty. Project, Denver, 1985-86; officer Congregation Adas Israel, Passaic, N.J., 1987-99. Carmi Schwartz fellow Coun. Jewish Fedns., 1993. Mem. N.Y. State Bar Assn. Avocation: talmudic study. Office: Stellar Fin Inc 3 Landmark Ctr East Stroudsburg PA 18301 E-mail: gjacobson@stellarfinancial.org.

JACOBSON, HELEN GUGENHEIM (MRS. DAVID JACOBSON), civic worker; b. San Antonio; d. Jac Elton and Rosetta (Dreyfus) Gugenheim; m. David Jacobson, Nov. 6, 1938; children: Liz Helenchild, Dottie J. Miller. BA, Hollins U. With news and spl. events staff NBC, N.Y.C., 1933-38; 1st v.p. San Antonio Bexar County coun. Girl Scouts U.S.A., 1957-63; Tex. state rep. UNICEF, 1964-69; bd. dirs. U.S. com. UNICEF, 1970-80, hon. bd. dirs., 1980—. Bd. dirs. Nat. Fedn. Temple Sisterhoods, 1973-77, Temple Beth-El Sisterhood, Youth Alternatives, Inc., Child Guidance Ctr., chmn. bd., 1960-63; bd. dirs. Sunshine Cottage Sch. for Deaf Children, chmn. bd. 1952-54; pres. Cmty. Welfare Coun., 1968-70; pres. bd. trustees San Antonio Pub. Libr., 1957-61; trustee Nat. Coun. Crime and Delinquency, 1964-70, San Antonio Mus. Assn., 1964-73; bd. dirs. Cancer Therapy and Rsch. Ctr. South Tex., 1974—, sec. 1977-83; pres. S.W. region Tex. Coalition for Juvenile Justice, 1977-79; chmn. Mayor's Commn. on Status of Women, 1972-74; del. White House Conf. on Children, 1970; mem. Commn. on Social Action of Reform Judaism, 1973-77; chmn. Foster Grandparent project Bexar County Hosp. Dist., 1968-69; sec. Nat. Assembly for Social Policy and Devel., 1969-74; pres. women's com. Ecumenical Ctr. for Religion and Health, 1975-77; chmn. criminal justice planning com. Alamo Area Coun. of Govts., 1975-77, 1987-88; mem. Tex. Internat. Women's Yr. Coordinating Com., 1977; co-chmn. San Antonio chpt. NCCJ, 1980-84; chmn. United Negro Coll. Fund Campaign, 1983, 84; sec. nat. bd. Avance, Inc., 1991-93; trustee Target 90/Goals for San Antonio, 1986-90; hon. mem. bd. dirs. Witte Mus., 1994—. Recipient Headliner award for civic work San Antonio chpt. Women in Comms., 1958, Nat. Humanitarian award B'nai B'rith, 1975, City of Peace award, 1991; named Vol. Woman of Yr. Express-News, 1959, Spl. Svc. award Tex. Soc. Psychiat. Physicians, 1994; honoree San Antonio chpt. NCCJ, 1970, Nat. Jewish Hosp., 1978; inductee San Antonio Women's Hall of Fame, 1986, others. Mem. Nat. Coun. Jewish Women (Hannah G. Solomon award 1979), Internat. Women's Forum, San Antonio 100, Argyle Club. Home: 207 Beechwood Ln San Antonio TX 78216-7345

JACOBSON, HERBERT LEONARD, licensing executive; b. N.Y.C., Mar. 22, 1940; s. David and Lena (Goldberg) J.; m. Beverly Goldman, Nov. 23, 1961; children: Julie Ellen, Joel Howard. BS in E.E., U. R.I., 1961; LL.B., Bklyn. Law Sch., 1965; LL.M., NYU, 1970. Bar: N.Y. 1965, N.J. 1972. Planning engr. Am. Electric Power, 1961-66; patent atty. RCA Corp., 1966-74, counsel, 1974-79, dir. licensing, 1979-83, staff v.p., 1983-86; exec. v.p. GE and RCA Licensing Mgmt. Operation, Inc., 1986-98, GE Licensing, 1999-2000. Home: 7322 Floranada Way Delray Beach FL 33446-2371

JACOBSON, HOWARD, classics educator; b. Bronx, N.Y., Aug. 21, 1940; s. David and Jeannette (Signer) J.; m. Elaine Z. Finkelstein, June 10, 1965; children: Michael Noam, Daniel Benjamin, Joel Avram, David Moses. BA, Columbia U., 1962, PhD, 1967; MA, U. Chgo., 1963. Instr. Greek and Latin Columbia U., 1966-68; asst. prof. classics U. Ill., 1968-73, assoc. prof., 1973-80, prof., 1980—; Lady Davis vis. prof. Hebrew U., Jerusalem, winter 1983. Mem. Inst. for Advanced Study, Princeton, N.J., 1993-94. Author: Ovid's

Heroides, 1974, The Exagoge of Ezekiel, 1983, A Commentary on Pseudo-Philo's Liber Antiquitatum Biblicarum (2 vols.), 1996; editor for Latin studies: Illinois Classical Studies Supplements. Nat. Endowment for Humanities fellow, 1971-72, 89; assoc. Ctr. for Advanced Study, U. Ill., 1983-84, spring 1994. Mem. Am. Philol. Assn. (Charles J. Goodwin Merit award 1985), Corr. assoc. Forum on Israel Studies CUNY; Phi Beta Kappa. Jewish. Office: Dept Classics 4090 Foreign Languages Bldg 707 S Mathews Ave Urbana IL 61801-3625

JACOBSON, HOWARD NEWMAN, obstetrics and gynecology educator, researcher; b. St. Paul, Aug. 13, 1923; s. Irvin Oliver and Nora Henrietta (Olson) J.; m. Barbara Jane Dinger, Aug. 20,1961. BSc in Medicine, Northwestern U., Chgo., 1947, BM, 1950, MD, 1951. Intern Presbyn. Hosp., Chgo., 1950-51, resident in ob-gyn, 1951-52; fellow, rsch. fellow in obstetrics, mem. family clinic Harvard Sch. Pub. Health, Boston, 1952-55; resident Boston Lying-In Hosp. and Free Hosp. for Women, Brookline, Mass., 1955-58; obstetrician, physiologist Lab. Neuroanat. Scis., Nat. Inst. Nervous Disease and Blindness, NIH, Bethesda, Md., 1958-60; instr., asst. prof. Harvard Med. Sch., Boston, 1960-65; assoc. prof. U. Calif., San Francisco, Berkeley, 1965-69; dir. Macy program Med. Sch. Harvard U., 1969-74; prof. dept. cmty. medicine Coll. Medicine and Dentistry NJ, Piscataway, NJ, 1974-78; dir. Inst. Nutrition, clin. prof. U. NC, Chapel Hill, 1978-88; rsch. prof. Coll. Pub. Health U. So. Fla., 1988—2003; prof. dept. ob-gyn U. South Fla. Med. Sch., Tampa, 1990-96, facilitator spl. programs Health Sci. Ctr., 1996—2003. Cons. Children's Bur., HEW, Washington, 1964-73, GAO, Washington, 1974-83, AMA, 1980-82, 88—; mem. food and nutrition bd. NRC/NAS, Washington, 1971-74; prof. dept. biology and Sch. Home Econs., U. N.C., Greensboro, 1978-88, Ellen Swallow Richards lectr., 1978; cons. pregnancy and nutrition study U. Minn., Mpls., 1979—; adj. prof. dept. food, nutrition and instn. mgmt. East Carolina U. Sch. Home Econs., Greenville, 1981-88; mem. nutrition grad. faculty N.C. State U., Raleigh, 1979-88. Contbr. over 130 articles and abstracts to FMA Today, Jour. Nurse-Midwifery, Clin. Nutrition, Contemporary Internal Medicine, Food and Nutrition News, Nutrition Today, New Eng. Jour. Medicine, chpt. to books. Panel vice chmn. White House Conf. on Food, Nutrition and Health, Washington, 1969; chmn. Quality of Life Conf., Mass. Med. Soc., Boston, 1972; mem. hunger com. Episcopal Ch. S.W. Fla., 1990-94; mem. Fla. Health Start Initiative working Group, 1991—. Lt. (j.g.) USNR, 1943-46, PTO. Recipient Agnes Higgins award March of Dimes and APHA, 1987; recipient Career Devel. award NIH, 1963-65. Fellow Am. Coll. Ob-Gyn (assoc.); mem. Am. Soc. Clin. Nutrition, Am. Physiol. Soc., Mass. Med. Soc. (chmn. commn. 1972-74), Fla. Pub. Health Assn. (chmn. sect. 1990-91), Am. Dietetic Assn. (hon.). Democrat. Achievements include co-develop. of guides for clin. nutrition studies, portable ultrasound for body composition; co-determination of nature of cardiovasc. changes at birth; co-intro. of computer assisted methodology in nutrition; co-initiation of modern nutrition standards for healthy pregnancy. Office: U South Fla Coll Pub Health 13201 Bruce B Downs Blvd Tampa FL 33612-3805

JACOBSON, ISHIER, retired utility executive; b. Worcester, Mass., June 21, 1922; s. Aaron and Mollie (Mallor) J.; m. Maria Bohm, Dec. 18, 1948; children: Joanna M., Jonathan B., Paula R. BA, Clark U., 1946; MSME, Harvard U., 1947, LLB, 1951. Bar: Conn. 1951. Asst. to pres., gen. counsel Connor Engring. Corp., Danbury, Conn., 1951-53; with Citizens Utilities Co., Stamford, Conn., 1954-90, exec. v.p., 1970, pres., chief oper. officer, 1970-81, pres., chief exec. officer, 1981-90, also dir. Chmn. bd. dirs. Silver Hill Hosp., New Canaan, Conn. Served to lt. USNR, 1942-46. Home: 326 Four Brooks Rd Stamford CT 06903-4605

JACOBSON, JAMES BASSETT, insurance executive; b. San Francisco, Nov. 16, 1922; s. James Peter and Bertha (Bassett) J.; m. Janice Isabel Meilstrup, Aug. 29, 1949; children: Steven Blair, Karen Christine, Richard Barlow. BS, UCLA, 1947; postgrad., U. Pa., 1947-48; MBA, U. So. Calif., 1954. CLU. With Prudential Ins. Co. Am., various cities, 1948-83, v.p. group pension mktg. Newark, 1967-70, sr. v.p. in charge group ins., 1970-73, pres., western ops. L.A., 1973-83; exec. v.p. CalFed Inc. and Calif. Fed. Savs. & Loan Assn., L.A., 1983-87; chmn., chief exec. officer Beneficial Standard Life Ins. Co., L.A., 1987-88, chmn. bd. dirs., 1984-88. Chmn. bd. dirs. Bonneville Internat. Corp., Salt Lake City; bd. dirs. Deseret Trust Co., Salt Lake City, Deseret Trust Co. of Calif., L.A., Galorath, Inc., El Segundo, Calif. Author: An Analysis of Group Creditors Insurance, 1954. V.p. L.A. Philharmonic Assn., 1977-83, bd. dirs., 1975-83; vice chmn. Community TV So. Calif. L.A., 1983, bd. dirs., 1979 83; chmn. bd. dirs. Orthopaedic Hosp., L.A., 1981-84, trustee, 1980-84; chmn. bd. L.A. Ballet, 1974-79, bd. dirs., 1974-83; mem. Calif. Round Table, 1981-83; bd. dirs. Dance Gallery, L.A., 1988-92, NCCJ L.A. Region, 1987-95, co-chair, 1994-96; chmn. bd. trustees Criminal Justice Legal Found., 1993-95, bd. trustees 1990—, Sacramento; bd. dirs. v.p. L.A. Area coun. Boy Scouts Am., 1980-85, others. With U.S. Army, 1943-46, 2d lt. res., 1951. Recipient Silver Beaver award Boy Scouts Am., 1984, Cmty. Svc. award UCLA Alumni Assn., 1985. Mem. Am. Coll. CLUs, Calif. C. of C. (bd. dirs. 1974-83), L.A. C. of C. (bd. dirs. 1981-83), Calif. Club, Lochinvars Club (pres. 1981-84).

JACOBSON, JAMES LAMMA, JR., data processing company executive; b. Washington, May 19, 1946; s. James Lamma Jacobson Sr. and Hazel Virginia (Howard) Jacobson Tatelman; m. Dayle Barbara Jackson, Dec. 30, 1972; children: Julie, Christie, Jennie. BBA, Drexel U., 1969. Systems engr. IBM Corp., Arlington, Va., 1969-70, mktg. rep., 1970-74, mktg. instr. Atlanta, 1975-76, mktg. mgr. Akron, Ohio, 1977-79; founder, pres. Jacore Techs., Inc., Atlanta, 1979-84, chmn., 1985—; exec. cons. Mainline Info. Systems, Tallahassee, 1991-92; pres. Jacobson & Horne, Inc., Tallahassee, 1992—; chmn. JSS Enterprises, 1996—. Chmn. JSS Enterprises, 1996—. Chmn. Vida Nueva of North Fla.; pres. Faith Chapel. Mem. Ch. of God. Avocations: tennis, hunting, fishing. Home and Office: 8 Farnum St Augusta ME 04330-7234

JACOBSON, JEANNE MCKEE, humanities educator, writer; b. New Brunswick, NJ, Oct. 26, 1931; d. Edward Price and Jean Sheppard McKee; m. John H. Jacobson; children: John E., Jean K. Pokrzywka, Jennie, James G. BA, Swarthmore Coll., 1953; MS, SUNY, Brockport, 1973; PhD, SUNY, Albany, 1981. Gen. studies prin. Hebrew Acad. Capital Dist., Albany, N.Y., 1980-87; adj. faculty SUNY-Albany, Coll. St. Rose, 1983-87; from asst. to assoc. prof. Western Mich. U., Kalamazoo, 1987-95, interim dept. chair, 1993-95; adj. prof. Hope Coll., Holland, Mich., 1995-99; rsch. fellow A.C. Van Raalte Inst., Holland, 1995—2003, rsch. fellow emeritus, 2003—. Author (with others): Albertus C. Van Raalte: Dutch Leader & American Patriot, 1996, A Dream Fulfilled, 1997; author: (textbook) Content Area Reading: Integration with the Language Arts, 1998, Detecta-Crostics: Puzzles of Mystery, 2003; editor: Reading Horizons, 1988—95; assoc. editor: Drood Rev. of Mystery, 1989—. Active majority coun. EMILY's List. Democrat. Presbyterian. Avocations: reading, creating puzzles. Home and Office: 1521 S Lakeshore Dr Sarasota FL 34231-3405 E-mail: jacobsonj@hope.edu.

JACOBSON, JEFFREY E. lawyer, consultant; b. NYC, Aug. 19, 1956; s. Murray and Adele (Ebert) J.; m. Linda Moel, Aug. 11, 1984; children: Justin Myles, Sari Amanda. BA, Fordham U., 1976; JD, N.Y. Law Sch., 1980. Bar: N.Y. 1982, D.C. 1982, U.S. Tax Ct. 1982, U.S. Ct. Internat. Trade 1982, U.S. Dist. Ct. (so. and ea. dists.) N.Y. 1982, U.S. Ct. Appeals (2nd cir.) 1988, U.S. Supreme Ct. 1988. Assoc. SESAC, Inc., N.Y.C., 1980-82; sole practice N.Y.C. and D.C., 1982-85; sr. ptnr. Jacobson & Colfin, P.C., N.Y.C., Washington, L.I., 1985-90, mng. mem., 1991—; exec. v.p., sec. Fifth Ave. Media, Ltd., N.Y.C., 1995—; assoc. prof. Five Towns Coll., N.Y., 1999—. Asst. mgr. Embassy Theatre, N.Y.C., 1975, Victoria Theatre, N.Y.C., 1975; asst. Theatre Confections, Inc., N.Y.C., 1975; mgr. Criterion Theatre, N.Y.C., 1976; mgr., sec. Squirrels Prodns. Ltd., N.Y.C., 1976-88; pres. Aldous Demian Prodns., Ltd., N.Y.C., 1980-82; spkr. in field. Mem. editl. bd. Mealey's Intellectual Property Litigation Law Report, 1992-93; contbr. articles to profl. jours.; music and internat. promotion mgmt., 1984-85; columnist IMPS Jour., 1990-95; featured columnist Replication News Medialine, 1998-2002. Mem. Rep. candidate assembly; v.p. Pelham Pkwy., 1983-88; entertainment arbitrator Am. Arbitration Assn., N.Y.C., 1984-95; counsel Pelham Pkwy. Block Assn., Inc., 1991; panelist Mid-Am. Music Conf., Detroit, 1993, Black Radio Exclusive, Econs. of Music, 1993; league lawyer Hewlett-Woodmere Little League, 1994-2000; planning bd. Inc. Village of Hewlett Harbor, 2001—. Recipient Cert. of Merit Bronx House, 1973, Nathan Burkan award ASCAP, 1980, Plaque of Appreciation, Am. Arbitration Assn., 1985; named Most Admired Men and Women of Yr., 1993, Two Thousand Notable Am. Men, 1993-95, Man of Yr., 1996. Mem. ABA (chmn. subcom. on satellites, chmn. subcom. on copyright compliance, chmn. subcom. on copyright renewal, patent trademark, copyright law sect., forum com. on entertainment and sports law sects., spl. com. on corp. practice 1992-97, sub. com. on broadcasting and music industry, forum com. on comm. law, young lawyer's divsn., vice chmn. 1992-94, patent, trademark, intellectual property sect. exec. com., 1992-93, media law com., young lawyers divsn., founder Urban Intellectual Property Law seminars 1993-95, dir., 1993-95, spl. com. on atty. opinions 1994—, spl. com. on internet 1997—, chmn. subcom. on internat. copyright 2002-03, com. on databases, com. on atty./client opinions, spl. com. internet usage, internat. trademark treaties & laws com. 2002—, ethics and profl. responsibility com.), Assn. Bar City N.Y. (entertainment law com. 1992-95, 2001—, trademark law com. 1997-2000), Copyright Soc. USA (com. on Bicentennial of copyright, mem. editl. bd. Jour. of Copyright Soc. 1991-93, 97—, trustee 2001—, exec. com. 2002—, co-chmn. website com. 2002—), Nat. Acad. Rec. Arts and Scis. (edn. com., columnist N.Y. chpt. newsletter 1997-2000), Rock and Roll Hall of Fame and Mus. (founding mem.), Internat. Assn. Entertainment Lawyers, B'nai B'rith (v.p. 1988-91), Order of the Arrow Brotherhood, Sephardic Jewish Brotherhood Am., Masons (officer 1997-2000, planning bd. Village of Hewlett Harbor 2001—), Audubon Soc. Inc., Phi Delta Phi. Jewish. Avocations: music, photography, swimming, stereo equipment, traveling. Office: Jacobson & Colfin PC 19 W 21st St New York NY 10010-6805 also: 1208 W Broadway Hewlett NY 11557 E-mail: jejesq@aol.com., jeff@thefirm.com.

JACOBSON, JEROLD DENNIS, lawyer; b. N.Y.C., Oct. 12, 1940; s. Sidney and Lillian D. (Fink) J.; m.Gertraude M.J. Holle-Suppa, May 4, 1998; children: Diana, Lisa, Pamela. AB, U. Vt., 1962; JD, Cornell U., 1965; LLM in Labor Law, N.Y. U., 1966. Bar: N.Y. 1966, U.S. Dist. Ct. (so. and ea. dists.) N.Y. 1968, U.S. Dist. Ct. (no. dist.) N.Y. 1981, U.S. Ct. Appeals (2d cir.) 1979, U.S. Ct. Appeals (5th cir.), 1980, U.S. Ct. Appeals (11th cir.) 1981, U.S. Supreme Ct. 1982. Assoc. to gen. counsel ILGWU, AFL-CIO, N.Y.C., 1966-69; assoc. Rains, Rogrebin and Scher, N.Y.C. and Mineola, N.Y., 1969-70, Guggenheimer & Untermyer, N.Y.C., 1970-74, ptnr., 1975-85, Summit, Rovins & Feldsman, N.Y.C., 1986-89, Patterson, Belknap, Webb & Tyler, N.Y.C., 1989-91, Proskauer Rose LLP, N.Y.C., 1991—. Lectr. in labor and employment relations law Practising Law Inst., Am. Soc. Law and Medicine, Profl. Edn. Systems, Inc. Contbr. articles to prolf. jours. Bd. dirs. Nassau County chpt. N.Y. State Civil Liberties Union; mem. adv. bd. U. Vt. Holocaust Study Ctr., U. Vt. Coll. Arts and Scis.; bd. dirs. Harlem Day Charter Sch. Mem. ABA, Legal Aid Soc., Am. Arbitration Assn., Am. Acad. Hosp. Attys., N.Y. State Bar Assn. (lectr). Office: Proskauer Rose LLP 1585 Broadway Fl 20 New York NY 10036-8299 E-mail: jjacobson@proskauer.com.

JACOBSON, JERRY IRVING, biophysicist, theoretical physicist; b. Bklyn., Jan. 25, 1946; s. Saul Lane and Miriam (Cassin) J.; m. Debra Maria Delso, Aug. 18, 1975; children: Solomon, Jacqueline, Faith, Maria. BA, Bklyn. Coll., 1963-66; DDS, DMD, Temple U., 1970; PhD, CUNY, 1983; PhD in Medicine, Bundel Khand U., 2002. Oral surgeon Tremont Med. Group, Bronx, N.Y., 1972-73, University Ave. Med. Group, Bronx, N.Y., 1973-77; pvt. practice Westchester and New City, N.Y., 1972—; pres. Perspectivism Found., Jupiter, Fla., 1980—, Inst. Theoretical Physics & Advanced Studies for Biophys., Jupiter, 1985—, Alzheimers Rsch. Found., Jupiter, 1990—, Jacobson Resonance Inc., Jupiter, 1991—, Magneto Therapeutics Mfg., Inc., 1994—, Jacobson Resonance Machines Inc., 1995—; prof. rsch., founding dir. microgravity and electromagnetics Inst. Molecular Medicine, U. Calif., Irvine, 1996; CEO, pres. Pioneer Svcs. Internat., Ltd., Deerfield Beach, Fla., 1996—; chmn. dept. applied med. physics and neuromagnetics Nat. Med. and Rsch. Inst., Boca Raton, Fla., 1997—; pres. Pioneer Svcs. Internat. Ltd., Juno Beach, Fla., 1996; chmn. bd., CEO Jacobson Resonance Enterprises, Inc., Juno Beach, Fla., 1998—, chmn. bd., pres., CEO Boco Raton, Fla., 1998—2000, also dir. R&D, dir. sci. and tech., chmn. bd., pres., CEO Boynton Beach, 2000—. Spkr. in field. Contbr. articles to profl. jours.; holder med. and plasma physics and agricultural patents and dental patents in U.S. and 80 other countries. Served to capt. Army Dental Corps, 1970-72. Mem. Am. Phys. Soc., Bioelectromagnetics Soc., European Bioelectromagnetics Soc., Italian Assn. Biomed. Physics, Internat. Assn. Biologically Closed Electric Circuits (mem. internat. adv. bd.). Avocations: oil painting, musical composition, fiction writing, philosophy. Home and Office: 2006 Mainsail Cir Jupiter FL 33477-1418

JACOBSON, KENNETH MARK, journalist, writer, editor; b. Madison, Wis., Sept. 30, 1949; s. Norman and Jean Charlotte (Pines) J. BA, U. Calif., Berkeley, 1973. Sports writer Berkeley Daily Gazette, 1965-67, 69-72; reporter AP, Amsterdam, The Netherlands, 1973-75; corr. McGraw-Hill World News, Paris, 1975-78; freelance journalist, writer Amsterdam, Paris, Berlin, Frankfurt, Vienna, Antwerp, Boston, 1978-85; assoc. editor Metals Week (McGraw-Hill, Inc.), N.Y.C., 1985-86, sr. editor, 1986-88, mng. editor, 1988-89, editor-in-chief, 1990-91; freelance journalist, writer N.Y.C., Santiago, Chile, 1991-93; editor New Tech. Week, Washington, 1993-98; writer Washington and Annapolis, Md., 1998—. Author: Joodse Ontmoetingen, 1993, Embattled Selves: An Investigation into the Nature of Identity through Oral Histories of Holocaust Survivors, 1994; translator: The Children of Izieu: A Human Tragedy, 1985. Recipient fellowship Meml. Found. for Jewish Culture, 1982-83, Citation, Nat. Press Club Newsletter Journalism Awards, 1989. Mem. Phi Beta Kappa. Democrat. Jewish. Avocations: languages (dutch, french, german, italian, spanish), sailing, fishing. E-mail: kenjacobson@hotmail.com.

JACOBSON, LAWRENCE SEYMOUR, television executive producer; b. Waterbury, Conn. children: Marlo, Amy. BA, U. Conn. Exec. producer Jim Ameche Prodns.; exec. east coast prodn. Am. Internat. Pictures, 1977-80; pres. Grosso-Jacobson Entertainment Corp., N.Y.C., 1980; exec vp and cfo Fox Inc., Beverly Hills, CA, 1997. Assoc. prodr. Children's Theatre WNBC, N.Y.C., 1961, Emmy Awards NBC, 1962, Connie Francis Spl. ABC, 1963; exec. prodr. Jim Ameche Prodns., 1963-65, Carlton Fredricks Program ABC, 1966-67, Water World, 1971-75, The Racers, 1974-79, Miss Am. Teenager Pageant, 1977-79, Daytime Star, 1979, Comeback, 1979-80, Baker's Dozen, 1981-82, (CBS) Night Heat, 1983-88 (Gemini award Best Dramatic TV series 1986, 87, TV Guide award Most Popular program, Can., 1986, 87), (CBS) Trackdown, 1984, (CBS) Hot Shots, 1985, (CBS) Out of the Darkness, 1985 (Christopher award), (CBS) Diamonds, 1985-87, Gunfighters, 1987, Cop Talk, 1989, (NBC) True Blue, 1989-90, (NBC) Family for Joe, 1989-90, (USA) Counterstrike, 1990-93, (CBS) Top Cops, 1990-94, (ABC) Bellevue Emergency, 1991, (NBC) Secret Service, 1992, (CBS) Gangsters, 1992, (ABC) Police File, 1992, Juvenile Justice, 1994, (CBS) Remember Me, 1995, (CBS) While My Pretty One Slept, 1996, (USA) The Big Easy, 1996-98, (CBS) Let Me Call You Sweetheart, 1997, (Pax) Haven't We Met Before, 2002, (Pax) All Around the Town, 2002, (HBO) Judgement Day, 2002. Mem. N.Y.C. Film, Theatre and Broadcasting Adv. Coun. (mayor's 1983-90). Office: Grosso-Jacobson Entertainment 767 3rd Ave New York NY 10017-2023 also: Fox Inc PO Box 900 Beverly Hills CA 90213-0900

JACOBSON, LESLIE SARI, biologist, educator; b. N.Y.C., May 22, 1933; d. William and Gussie (Mintz) Goldberg; m. Homer Jacobson, Aug. 18, 1957 (div. Dec. 1995); children: Guy Joseph, Ethan Samuel. BS, Bklyn. Coll., 1954, MA, 1955; postgrad., Columbia U., 1956; postgrad. (NIH fellow), Calif. Inst. Tech., 1960; PhD, NYU, 1962. Instr. dept. biology Bklyn. Coll., 1954-57; prof. biology L.I. Coll. Nursing, Bklyn., 1963-74, dean Grad. Sch., 1973-74; asst. prof. biology Long Island U., Bklyn., 1963; fellow dept. chemistry Bklyn. Coll., 1961-63, prof. health sci., 1974—, dean Sch. Gen. Studies and Continuing Higher Edn., 1974-80, dean Grad. Studies and Continuing Higher Edn., 1980-82, dean Grad. Studies, 1980-88, dean Grad. Studies and Rsch., 1988-89, prof. dept. health and nutritions scis., 1989—, chair dept. health and nutrition sci., 2003—, exec. dir. Applied Scis. Inst., 1994-95, Koppelman prof., 1995-97; acting v.p. Rsch. Found. CUNY, N.Y.C., 1998—2000. Chair Brooklyn Coll. Dept. Health And Nutrition Sci., 2003-2006; nat. program chmn. Assn. Continuing Higher Edn., 1978, nat. bd. dirs., 1978-81, pres.-elect, 1980-81, pres., 1981-82; bd. dirs. Center for Labor and Mgmt., N.Y.; dir. N.Y. Regional Cabinet Adult Continuing Edn., 1982—; mem. adv. com. on minorities Coun. Grad. Schs., 1987-90, svcs. com. Grad. Record Exam. Bd., 1990-93, chmn. Acad. policy com. all-univ. senate CUNY, 1992-98; exec. com. univ. com. rsch. awards, CUNY, 1994, vice chmn. com. rsch. awards, 1995-97, co-chair univ. com. rsch. awards, 1996-97; bd. dirs. Hyperion Capital Mgt.; invited spkr. at nat. meetings Issues in Higher Edn.; founder Inst. Ret. Profls. and Execs., Bklyn. Coll., 1976. V.p. Alpha Sigma Lambda Found., 1983-88; v.p. Mapleton Midwood Cmty. Health Bd. Inc., 1990—; v.p. B'nai B'rith Hillel JACY Assn., 1986-93; exec. mem. Hillel of N.Y., 1986-97; bd. dirs. Meth. Hosp., 1989—; v.p. Am. Lung Assn. of Bklyn.; mem. exec. com. Am. Lung Assn., 1996; pres.-elect Am. Lung Assn. City of N.Y., 2002; mem. Nat. Coun. Am. Lung Assn., 2001-. Recipient Founders Day award NYU, 1961, N.Y. Outstanding Adult Educator award, N.Y.C., 1978, Nat. Merit award, Assn. Continuing Higher Edn., 1984, Leadership award, 1986, Citation for svc. to cmty. N.Y.C. Coun., 1987, Citation for excellence in edn. Bklyn. Boro Pres., 1987, Citation for outstanding svc. to cmty. N.Y. State Assembly, 1987, N.Y. State Senate, 1987, Disting. Preventive Health Leadership award Am. Lung Assn. Bklyn., 1999. Mem. Sigma Xi, Alpha Sigma Lambda (nat. pres. 1978-80) Achievements include rsch. and publs. in bacterial virology and endocrine physiology, and on issues in higher edn. Office: Bklyn Coll CUNY Dept Health Nutritional Sci Bedford Ave & Ave H Brooklyn NY 11210 E-mail: jacobson@brooklyn.cuny.edu.

JACOBSON, LESTER BARRY, cardiologist; b. New Haven, Conn., Oct. 17, 1941; children: Reuben Bruce, Eli Aaron. AB, Clark U., 1963; MD, U. Chgo., 1967. Diplomate Am. Bd. Internal Medicine; Am. Bd. Cardiovascular Disease. Asst. chief cardiology svc. USPHS, San Francisco, 1972-74; dir. coronary unit U. Calif. Med. Ctr., San Francisco, 1974-75; staff cardiologist Pacific Med. Ctr., San Francisco, 1975-79; cardiologist, dir. cardiovascular edn. and tchg. Kaiser Found. Hosp., San Francisco, 1979-83; cardiologist in pvt. practice San Francisco, 1983—. Author: (textbooks) Arrhythmias: Case Studies, 1979, Cardiac Pacing: Principles and Case Studies, 1981. Fellow ACP, Am. Coll. of Cardiology, Am. Heart Assn. (coun. on clin. cardiology). Office: Calif Pacific Med Ctr 2340 Clay St Rm 226 San Francisco CA 94115-1932 Fax: 415-923-3564.

JACOBSON, LLOYD ELDRED, retired dentist; b. Madison, Minn., Mar. 9, 1923; s. Jacob Elton and Hilda Emily (Larson) J.; m. Ruth Solveig Skinsnes, Jan. 26, 1945; children: Rolf, Kathryn, Heidi. Student, St. Olaf Coll., 1943-44, 46-47, U. Chgo., 1945-46; DDS, U. Minn., 1951. Gen. practice dentistry, Kenyon, Minn., 1951-91; ret., 1991. Chmn. Am. Luth. Ch. Coun., Mpls., 1972-74; vol. World Brotherhood Exch., Bumbuli, Tanzania, 1965; treas. Kenyon Sch. Bd., 1958-60, Kenyon Devel. Corp., 1955-60. 1st lt. 14th Aif Force (Flying Tigers), USAAF, 1943-45, CBI. Recipient Outstanding Alumni award St. Olaf Coll., 1972, Disting. Alumni award U. Minn. Sch. Dentistry, 1987. Mem. Minn. Dental Assn. (treas. 1980-86), S.E. Dist. Dental Soc. (pres. 1979-80, sec.-treas. 1976-79), Rice County Dental Soc. (pres. 1969). Lodges: Lions (pres. Kenyon club 1952-54, dist. sec.-treas. 1974, Citizen of Yr. award 1986). Republican. Avocations: wood working, golf, stamp collecting. Home: 521 Spring St Kenyon MN 55946-1242 E-mail: rughnjake@aol.com.

JACOBSON, MARC PETER, art educator, educator; b. Madison, Wis., Aug. 21, 1954; s. James August and Marilyn Joan (LaBrec) J.; m. Nicala Marie Aiello, May 16, 1996 (div. Sept. 1999). BFA, U. Wis., 1976, MFA, 1985. Instr. Milw. Inst. Art and Design, 1985-90, U. Wis., Milw., 1985-89; asst. prof. fine arts Herron Sch. Art, Indpls., 1993-98; assoc. prof. fine arts Herron Sch. of Art, Indpls., 1998 . Vis. asst. prof. found. studies Herron Sch. Art., Indpls., 1990-93; co-juror regional competition Midwest Mus. Am. Art, Elkhart, Ind., 1999. One-man shows include Jan Cicero Gallery, Chgo., 1993, Quincy (Ill.) Art Ctr., 1996, Ruschman Gallery, Indpls., 2000, Columbia (Mo.) Coll., 2001, Indpls. Mus. Art, 2001; exhibited in group shows at Valdosta State U., 1997 (hon. mention), Fla. State U., 1997, U. Bridgeport, 1998 (hon. mention), Embassy of France, Washington, 1998, Sioux City Art Ctr., Iowa, 1999 (hon. mention), John A. Cade Ctr. Fine Art, Anne Arundel C.C., Arnold, Md., 2000, Allentown (Pa.) Art Mus., 2000, Charles Allis Art Mus., Milw., 2002, Allen Sheppard Gallery, N.Y.C., 2002, DePauw U., Greencastle, Ind., 2003; work represented in Painting as a Language, 2000. Active Found. in Art, Theory and Edn., 1996—. Recipient Tchg. Excellence award Herron Sch. Art, 1997; Individual Artist grantee Ind. Arts Commn., 1995; Arts Coun. Indpls. creative renewal fellow, 2001. Mem. Coll. Art Assn. Avocations: tennis, saxophone, classical and jazz music. Home: 5867 Broadway St Indianapolis IN 46220-2503 Office: Herron Sch Art 1701 N Pennsylvania St Indianapolis IN 46202-1472 E-mail: mjacobso@iupui.edu.

JACOBSON, MARCUS J. retired mechanical engineer; b. Houston, May 2, 1930; s. Max and Bessie Jacobson; m. Judith Sandra Tearle, Sept. 15, 1965; children: Mitzi, Barry. BA, Rice U., Houston, 1951; BSME, Rice U., 1952, MS in Mech. Engring., 1954; PhD in Engring., UCLA, 1965. Design engr. Douglas Missiles and Space Divsn., Culver City, Calif., 1952; instr., asst. prof. Rice U., Houston, 1952—62; dynamics engr. Lockheed Calif. Co., Burbank, 1963—64; prin. engr. Northrop Grumman Corp., Hawthorne, Calif., 1964—95; ret., 1995. Contbr. V.p., then pres. bd. edn. Inglewood Unified Sch. Dist., Inglewood, Calif., 1973—77. Fellow: AIAA (assoc.); mem.: Marina del Rey B'nai B'rith (newsletter editor 2001—03), Tau Beta Pi. Avocation: bridge. Home: 5337 Holt Ave Los Angeles CA 90056

JACOBSON, MARIAN SLUTZ, lawyer; b. Cin., Nov. 10, 1945; d. Leonard Doering and Emily Dana (Wells) Slutz; m. Fruman Jacobson, Sept. 21, 1975; 1 child, Lisa Wells. BA cum laude, Ohio Wesleyan U., 1967; JD, U. Chgo., 1972. Bar: Ill. 1972, U.S. Dist. Ct. (no. dist.) Ill. 1972, U.S. Ct. Appeals (7th cir.) 1973. Assoc. Sonnenschein Nath & Rosenthal, Chgo., 1972-79, ptnr., 1979—. Vis. com. U. Chgo. Law Sch., 1992-94. Mem. ABA, Chgo. Coun. Lawyers. Office: Sonnenschein Nath & Rosenthal 233 S Wacker Dr Ste 8000 Chicago IL 60606-6491 E-mail: msj@sonnenschein.com.

JACOBSON, MARK ANDREW, epidemiologist, educator, physician; b. Kans. City, Mo., May 14, 1949; BA, U. Calif., Berkeley, 1971; MD, U. of Calif., San Francisco, Calif., 1981. Diplomate Infectious Diseases Soc. of Am., 1986. Intern then resident Kaiser Found. Hosp., Oakland, Calif., 1981—84; prof. of medicine U. of Calif., San Francisco, 1986—. Dir. Ctr. for AIDS Rsch. Clin. Core U. Calif., 1994—. Author: AIDS Clinical Review, 1989—2001. Chmn. ACTG Complications of HIV Rsch. Agenda Com. NIH, Washington, 1998—2000. Achievements include development of therapies for AIDS-related complications. Office: University of California San Francisco Ward 84 995 Potrero San Francisco CA 94110

JACOBSON, MICHAEL FARADAY, consumer advocate, writer; b. Chgo., July 29, 1943; s. Larry and Janet (Siegel) J.; m. Donna Ruth Lenhoff; 1 child, Sonya. BA, U. Chgo., 1965; postgrad., U. Calif., San Diego, 1965-67; PhD, MIT, 1969. Research assoc. Salk Inst. for Biol. Studies, 1970-71; cons. Ctr. for Study of Responsive Law, 1970-71; co-founder, exec. dir. Ctr. for Sci. in the Pub. Interest, Washington, 1971—. Founder Ctr. for Study Commercialism, 1990. Author: Nutrition Scoreboard, 1975, Eater's Digest, 1972, The Complete Eater's Digest and Nutrition Scoreboard, 1986; (with others) The Booze Merchants, 1983, Salt: The Brand Name Guide to Sodium, 1983, The Changing American Diet, 1983, The Fast Food Guide, 1986, 2d edit., 1991, Marketing Booze to Blacks, 1987, Tainted Booze, 1987, Marketing Disease to Hispanics, 1989, Kitchen Fun for Kids, 1991, Safe Food, 1991; co-editor: Food for People Not for Profit, 1975, Cooking With the Stars, 1992, What Are We Feeding Our Kids?, 1994, Marketing Madness: A Survival Guide for a Consumer Society, 1995, Restaurant Confidential 2002. Originator, nat. coord. Food Day, 1975-77. Office: Ctr for Sci in the Pub Interest 1875 Connecticut Ave NW Ste 300 Washington DC 20009-5736

JACOBSON, MURRAY M. chemical engineer; b. Boston, Jan. 2, 1915; s. Robert H. and Charlotte (Moses) J.; m. Madelyn Ruth Marder, June 28, 1962; stepchildren: Marc, Paul, Richard. BS, Tufts U., 1935; postgrad., MIT, 1948. Engr. GE, Lynn, Mass., 1940; chem. engr. Watertown (Mass.) Arsenal Labs., 1940-54, chief chem. metallurgy lab., 1955-56, chief materials scis. lab., 1957-62; dep. chief materials engring. div. Army Materials Rsch. Agy., Watertown, 1963-66; chief prototype lab. Army Materials and Mechanics Rsch. ctr., Watertown, 1967-69, chief materials test div., 1970-74; tech. mgr. Jacon Industries, Boston, 1975-90, materials engring. cons., 1975—. Mem. Com. on Corrosion, U.S. War Adv. Com., 1942-45; invited panelist Nat. Acad. Scis., 1976-79. Recipient Cert. of Commendation U.S. War Dept., 1945. Mem. ASM, Am. Chem. Soc., Nat. Assn. Corrosion Engrs. (Boston chpt. chmn. 1954-55). Home: 285 Clark Rd Brookline MA 02445-5847

JACOBSON, NORMAN L. retired agricultural educator, researcher; b. Eau Claire, Wis., Sept. 11, 1918; s. Frank R. and Elma E. (Baker) J.; m. Gertrude A. Neff, Aug. 24, 1943; children: Gary, Judy. BS, U. Wis., 1940; MS, Iowa State U., 1941, PhD, 1947. Asst. prof. animal sci. Iowa State U., Ames, 1947-49, assoc. prof., 1949-53, prof., 1953, Disting. prof. agr., 1963-89, assoc. dean Grad. Coll., 1973-88, assoc. v.p. rsch., 1979-88, assoc. provost, 1988-89, dean Grad. Coll., 1988-89, emeritus disting. prof. agr., 1989—, interim chair Dept. Food Sci. and Human Nutrition, 1990-92. Contbr. articles to profl. jours., chpts. to books. Served to lt. USN, 1942-46, ETO, PTO. Fellow AAAS, Soc. for Nutritional Scis., Am. Soc. Animal Sci. (Morrison award 1970), Am. Dairy Sci. Assn. (pres. 1972-73, Am. Feed Mfrs. Assn. award 1955, Borden award 1960, award of honor 1978, Disting. Svc. award 1989). Presbyterian. Home: 2200 Hamilton Drive Apt 302 Ames IA 50014-8274 Office: Iowa State U 313 Kildee Hl Ames IA 50011-3150 E-mail: nljacob@iastate.edu.

JACOBSON, PETER A. lawyer; s. Arthur V. and Teresa (Cesare) J. BA, Union Coll., 1966; JD, Albany Law Sch., 1969. Bar: N.Y. 1971, U.S. Dist. Ct. (we. dist.) N.Y. 1971, U.S. Ct. Appeals (2d cir.). Spl. agt. FBI, Rochester, N.Y., 1969-76; asst. dist. atty. Monroe County Dist. Atty.'s Office, Rochester, 1976-85; ptnr. Trevett, Lenweaver & Salzer, P.C., Rochester, 1985—. Mem. N.Y. State Bar Assn. Home: 222 Fairhaven Rd Rochester NY 14610-2203 Office: Trevett Lenweaver & Salzer PC 2 State St Ste 1000 Rochester NY 14614

JACOBSON, PETER LARS, neurologist, educator; b. Englewood, N.J., Feb. 17, 1951; s. George Pershing and Mona (Friedman) J.; m. Karen Joy Frenkel, June 11, 1972; children: Kersten Jenny, Lars Edward II. BA summa cum laude, Princeton U., 1973; MD, Washington U., 1977. Chief resident in neurology U. N.C. Hosp., Chapel Hill, 1980-81; fellow in electro-encephalography Mayo Clinic, Rochester, Minn., 1981-82; pres. Pinehurst (N.C.) Neurology, P.A., 1982—; clin. prof. neurology U. N.C., Chapel Hill, 1982—, adj. prof. journalism, 1990—. Chmn. dept. neurology Moore Regional Hosp., Pinehurst, 1985-87. Columnist The Pilot, 1989—. Trustee The O'Neal Sch., Southern Pines, N.C., 1992—. Recipient Lange Med. Book prize Washington U., 1976, Samson F. Wennerman award in surgery, 1977, Cert. of Appreciation, State of N.C., 1987; Mosby scholar, 1977. Fellow Am. Acad. Neurology, Am. EEG Soc.; mem. N.C. Neurol. Soc. (pres. 1990-91), Am. Med. Writers Assn., Alpha Omega Alpha, Phi Beta Kappa. Avocations: running, writing. Office: Carolina Headache & Pain Ctr PA PO Box 920 Aberdeen NC 28315-0920

JACOBSON, PHILLIP LEE, architect, educator; b. Santa Monica, Calif., Aug. 27, 1928; s. Allen Wilhelm and Greta Percy (Rohde) J.; m. Effie Laurel Galbraith, Nov. 6, 1954; children: Rolf Wilhelm, Christina Lee, Erik Mackenzie. B. Archtl. Engring. with honors, Wash. State U., 1952; postgrad. (Fulbright scholar), U. Liverpool, Eng., 1952-53; M.Arch., Finnish Inst. Tech., Helsinki, 1969. Field supr. Gerald C. Field Architect, 1950; designer, draftsman John Maloney Architect, 1951, 53-55; designer, project mgr. Young, Richardson, Carleton & Detlie Architects, 1955-56; designer, project architect John Carl Warnecke Architect, San Francisco, 1956-58; ptnr., design dir. TRA, Seattle, 1958-92; prof. architecture and urban design and planning Coll. Architecture and Urban Planning, U. Wash., Seattle, 1962—2000. Author: Housing and Industrialization in Finland, 1969, The Evolving Architectural Design Process, 1969; contbr. articles to profl. jours.; major archtl. works include Aerospace Research Lab., U. Wash., Seattle, 1969, McCarty Residence Hall, 1960, Highway Adminstrn. Bldg., Olympia, Wash., 1970, Sea-Tac Internat. Airport, 1972, Issaquah (Wash.) High Sch., 1962, State Office Bldg. 2, Olympia, 1976, Sealaska Corporate Hdqrs. Bldg., Juneau, Alaska, 1977, Group Health Hosp., Seattle, 1973, Metro Shelter Program, Seattle, 1977, N.W. Trek Wildlife Preserve, 1976, Rocky Reach/Rock Island Recreation Plan, 1974, master plan mouth of Columbia River, 1976, U. Wash. Biol. Sci. Bldg., 1981, Wegner Hall, Wash. State U., 1982, Wash. Conv. Ctr., 1988, King County Aquatics Ctr., 1990, Albuquerque Airport, 1989, U. Wash. Health Scis. H Wing, 1993. Mem. Seattle Planning and Redevel. Council, 1959-69, v.p., 1966-67; mem. Seattle Landmark Preservation Bd., 1976-81; trustee Pilchuck Sch., 1982-2001, Northwest Trek Found., 1987-94, AIA/Seattle Archtl. Found., 1986-92. With U.S. Army, 1946-47. Fulbright-Hays Sr. Rsch. fellow Finland, 1968-69; named to Order of White Rose Govt. of Finland, 1985; recipient Silver plaque Finnish Soc. Architects, 1992; recipient numerous design awards. Fellow AIA (pres. Wash. state Council 1965, dir. Seattle chpt. 1970-73, sr. council 1970—, Seattle chpt. medal 1994); mem. Am. Inst. Cert. Planners, Phi Kappa Phi, Tau Beta Pi, Tau Sigma Delta, Scarab, Sigma Tau (outstanding alumnus 1967). Home: PO Box 45368 Seattle WA 98145-0368 Office: U Wash PO Box 355720 Seattle WA 98195-5720

JACOBSON, RAYMOND EARL, electronics company entrepreneur and executive; b. St. Paul, May 25, 1922; s. Albert H. and Gertrude W. (Anderson) J.; m. Margaret Maxine Meadows, Dec. 22, 1959 (div. 1986); children: Michael David, Karl Raymond, Christopher Eric. BE with high honors, prize for excellence in mech. engring., Yale U., 1944; MBA with distinction, Harvard U., 1948; BA in Econ. (Rhodes Scholar), Oxford U., 1950, MA, 1954. Asst. to gen. mgr. PRD Electronics, Inc., Bklyn., 1951-55; sales mgr. Curtiss-Wright Electronics Divsn., Carlstadt, N.J., 1955-57; dir. mktg. TRW Computers Co., L.A., 1957-60; v.p. ops. Electro-Sci. Investors, Dallas, 1960-63; pres. Whitehall Electronics, Inc., Dallas, 1961-63, dir., 1961-63; chmn. bd. Gen. Electronic Control, Inc., Mpls., 1961-63, Staco, Inc., Dayton, Ohio, 1961-63; pres. Maxson Electronics Corp., Gt. River, N.Y., 1963-64, Jacobson Assocs., San Jose, Calif., 1964-67; co-founder, pres., chmn., CEO Anderson Jacobson, Inc., San Jose, Calif., 1967-88. Chmn. Anderson Jacobson, SA, Paris, 1974-88, Anderson Jacobson, Ltd., London, 1975-85, Anderson Jacobson Can., Ltd./Ltée, Toronto, 1975-85, Anderson Jacobson, GmbH, Cologne, 1978-83, CXR Corp., San Jose, 1988-94; bd. dirs. Tamar Electronics, Inc., L.A., Rawco Instruments, Inc., Dallas, 1960-63, Micro Radionics, Inc., L.A., 1964-67, ComputerMan USA, Inc., Reno, 1997—; lectr. engring., UCLA, 1958-60, lectr. bus. adminstrn. U. Calif. Berkeley, 1965-66; mem. underwriting Lloyd's London, 1975-96. Eagle Scout Boy Scouts Am., 1935, committeeman, 1968-80. Lt. (j.g.) USNR, 1943-46. Mem. Assn. Am. Rhodes Scholars, Harvard Bus. Sch. Assn., Oxford Soc., Yale Class of 1944 (exec. com.), Oxford Brasenose Soc., Courtside Tennis Club, Seascape Swim and Racquet Club, Sigma Xi, Tau Beta Pi. Republican. Lutheran. Home: 543 Elk River Ct Reno NV 89511

JACOBSON, RICHARD JOSEPH, lawyer; b. Ft. Benning, Ga., July 12, 1943; s. Harold Gordon and Ruth Fern (Enenstein) J.; m. Judy Josephine Dunbar, Sept. 17, 1966; 1 child, David Dunbar. AB, Harvard U., 1965, PhD, 1970; JD, U. Va., 1977. Bar: Ill. 1977, Va. 1977, D.C. 1979, U.S. Dist. Ct. (no. dist.) 1977, U.S. Ct. Appeals (7th cir.) 1991. Asst. prof. English U. Va., Charlottesville, 1970-74; assoc. Keck, Mahin & Cate, Chgo., 1977-83, ptnr., 1984-96; prin. Flaherty & Jacobson, P.C., Chgo., 1996—. Author: Hawthorne's Conception of the Creative Process, 1965; contbr. articles to profl. jours. Pres. North Park Condominium assn., Chgo., 1978-80. Woodrow Wilson Nat. fellow, 1965. Mem. Va. State Bar Assn., D.C. Bar Assn., Chgo. Bar Assn. (chmn. com. preventing atty. malpractice 2000-2001), Assn. Profl. Responsibility Lawyers, Cliff Dwellers Club, Lawyers Club Chgo., Chgo. Literary Club. Home: 850 W Adams St Apt 3D Chicago IL 60607-3088 Office: Flaherty & Jacobson PC 134 N Lasalle St Ste 1600 Chicago IL 60602-1108 E-mail: rjacobson@fljlaw.com.

JACOBSON, ROBERT ANDREW, chemistry educator; b. Waterbury, Conn., Feb. 16, 1932; s. Carl Andrew and Mary Catherine (O'Donnell) J.; m. Margaret Ann McMahan, May 26, 1962; children: Robert Edward, Cheryl Ann BA, U. Conn., 1954; PhD, U. Minn., 1959. Instr. Princeton U., N.J., 1959-62, asst. prof., 1962-64; assoc. prof. Iowa State U., Ames, 1964-69, full prof., 1969-99, asst. dean Scis. and Humanities, 1982-85, prof. emeritus, 1999—. Chemist Ames Lab, Iowa, 1964-69, sr. chemist, 1969-99. Contbr. articles to profl. jours. Recipient Wilkinson Teaching award Iowa State U., Ames, 1974, 91. Mem. Am. Chem. Soc., Am. Crystallographic Assn. (chmn. apparatus and standards com. 1982-83) Avocations: gardening, painting. Home: 2732 Thompson Dr Ames IA 50010-4759 Office: Iowa State U 1271 Gilman Ames IA 50011-3111 E-mail: raj@ameslab.gov.

JACOBSON, SANDRA W. lawyer; b. Bklyn., Feb. 1, 1930; d. Elias and Anna (Goldstein) Weinstein; m. Irving Jacobson, July 31, 1955; 1 child, Bonnie Nancy. BA, Vassar Coll., 1951; LLB, Yale U., 1954. Bar: N.Y. 1955, U.S. Supreme Ct. 1960, U.S. Dist. Ct. (so., ea. dists.) N.Y. 1972, U.S. Ct. Appeals (2nd cir.) 1975. Ptnr. Mulligan, Jacobson & Langenus, N.Y.C., 1964-88, Hall, McNicol, Hamilton & Clark, N.Y.C., 1988-92; sole practitioner N.Y.C., 1992—2003; atty. NY Sisters Place Legal Counsel Ctr., 2003—. Lectr. in family law. Contbr. articles to profl. jours. and chpts. to books. Mem.: ABA (family law sect.), Internat. Acad. Matrimonial Lawyers, Westchester Women's Bar Assn., Ind. Jud. Screening Panel, Com. to Improve Availability of Legal Svcs., Am. Acad. Matrimonial Lawyers (bd. mgrs. N.Y. chpt. 1987—89, 1991—93, chair lawyer specialization com. 1999—2000, bd. mgrs. N.Y. chpt., 1995-98, 2000-2002, v.p., 1998-2000, 2002-), Westchester County Bar Assn., Assn. of Bar of City of N.Y. (com. women in the cts. 1986—96, sec. 1987—90, state cts. of superior juridiction 1987—90, women in the profession 1989—92, chair 1990—93, chmn. 1990—93, judiciary 1995—99, family law 1999—2000, com. matrimonial law, 1984-87, 2001-, chmn. 1990-98), Women's Bar Assn. of State of N.Y. (chair cts. com. 1987—88, CLE com. 1998—99, by-laws 1999—2001, co-chair amicus com. 2002—, matrimonial com., co-chmn. 1987-89, co-chair task force on ct. reogrn.), N.Y. Women's Bar Assn. (matrimonial and family law com. 1984—2000, chmn. 1986—88, jud. screening com. 1987—88, pres. 1989—90, ethics commn. 1990—), N.Y. State Bar Assn. (co-chair lawyer specialization 1999—, family law sect., legis. and exec. com.), Phi Beta Kappa. Office: NY Sisters Place 2 Lyon Pl Ste 300 White Plains NY 10601

JACOBSON, SIDNEY, editor; b. N.Y.C., Oct. 20, 1929; s. Reuben and Beatrice (Edelman) J.; m. Ruth Allison, July 4, 1957 (div. Feb. 1975); children: Seth, Kathy Battat; m. Maggi Silverstein, Feb. 26, 1975. BA, NYU, 1950. Exec. editor Harvey Comics, N.Y.C., 1952-83, Marvel Comics, N.Y.C., 1983-89; v.p., editor in chief Harvey Comics Entertainment, L.A., 1989—. Author: Streets of Gold, 1985, Another Time, 1989, Pistol: The Story of Pete Reiser, 2003; writer (comic books) Captain Israel, 1972, The Black Comic Book, 1973, (TV animation series) Johnny Cypher in Dimension Zero, 1975, (TV series) Felix the Cat, 1982, (monthly) You Can't Do That in Comics, 1986; lyricist various popular songs. Mem. Am. Soc. Composers, Authors and Pubs., Am. Guild Authors and Composers, Authors Guild. Home: 11740 Wilshire Blvd Los Angeles CA 90025 Office: Harvey Comics Entertainment 11835 W Olympic Blvd Los Angeles CA 90064-5001

JACOBSON, SUSAN BOGEN, psychotherapist; b. Far Rockaway, N.Y., June 19, 1957; d. Paul and Blanche (Itzkowitz) Bogen; m. Adam Hartley Jacobson. BS in Bus. Adminstrn., SUNY, Albany, 1977; MS in Mental Health Counseling, Nova U., Ft. Lauderdale, Fla., 1992. Nat. cert. counselor; lic. mental health counselor, Fla. Pvt. pactice psychotherapist, Boca Raton, Fla., 1992—; instr. CCM Partnerships, Inc., Delray Beach, Fla., 1995—. Officer Coun. for Marriage Preservation and Divorce Resolution, Boca Raton, 1995; mem. 15th Judicial Cir. Ctl Arbitration Com. for Fla. Bar, 1999-2000. Bd. dirs. Aid for Victims of Domestic Assault, 1998. Mem.: ACA. Avocations: golf, boating, gourmet cooking. Office: 1498 W Palmetto Park Rd Ste 498 Boca Raton FL 33486

JACOBSON, SVERRE THEODORE, retired minister; b. Loreburn, Sask., Can., Sept. 20, 1922; s. Sverre and Aline Tomina (Joel) J.; m. Phyllis Lorraine Sylte, Sept. 14, 1948; children— Katherine Ann, Paul Theodore. BA, U. Sask., 1946; BD, Luther Theol. Sem., Sask., 1947; postgrad., Luther Theol. Sem., St. Paul, Minn., 1952-53; ThD, Princeton Theol. Sem., 1959. Ordained to ministry Evang. Luth. Ch., 1947. Pastor, Lomond, Alta., 1947-53; lectr. Luther Theol. Sem., Saskatoon, Sask., 1956-57; pastor Torquay, Sask., 1958-63; asst. to pres. Evang. Luth. Ch. Can., Saskatoon, 1963-70, pres., 1970-85. Interim parish pastor Calgary, Alta., Saskatoon, Weyburn, Elbow and Loreburn, Sask., 1987-98; lectr. Luth. Theol. Sem., Saskatoon, 1987-88. Evangelist Lutheran Ch. Of Can. Home: 53 Moxon Crescent Saskatoon SK Canada S7H 3B8

JACOBUS, CHARLES JOSEPH, lawyer, title company executive, writer; b. Ponca City, Okla., Aug. 21, 1947; s. David William and Louise Graham (Johnson) J.; m. Heather Jeanne Jones, June 6, 1970; children: Mary Helen, Charles J. Jr. BS, U. Houston, 1970, JD, 1973. Bar: Tex. 1973; cert. specialist residential and commerical real estate law Tex. Bd. Legal Specialization. Pvt. practice, Houston, 1973-75; staff counsel Tenneco Realty, Inc., Houston, 1975-78, v.p., gen. counsel, 1979—83; chief legal counsel Speedy Muffler King, Deerfield, 1978-79; v.p. Commerce Title Co., Houston, 1983-85; sr. v.p. Charter Title Co., Houston, 1986—; ptnr. Jacobus & Melamed PC, Houston, 1988-97; shareholder Jenkens & Gilchrist, Houston, 1998-99; pvt. practice Bellaire, Tex., 1999—. Adv. dir. Prosperity Bank, Houston; adj. faculty Tex. A&M U., 1986-90; adj. prof. U. Houston Law Ctr., Houston C.C., Champions Sch. Real Estate; instr. advanced real estate law State Bar Tex., mem. coun. real estate probate and trust law section, course dir., 1990, Tex. Land Title Assn. Sch. Author: Real Estate Law, 2d edit., 1996, Texas Real Estate, 8th edit., 2001, 9th edit., 2004; co-author: Mastering Real Estate Titles and Title Insurance in Texas, 1996, Georgia Real Estate, 1995, Ohio Real Estate, 2d edit., 1990, Calif. Real Estate, 1989, Keeping Current with Texas Real Estate, updated annually, Real Estate Principles, 9th edit., 2001, Real Estate, An Introduction to the Profession, 9th edit., 2001, Texas Title Insurance, updated annually, Texas Real Estate Brokerage and the Law of Agency, 2002; co-author: Real Estate Brokerage Law and Practice; editor: Building Blocks of a Commercial Transaction, 1992, Building Blocks of a Residential Real Estate Transaction, 1994, Texas Real Estate Law Deskbook, 1995; editor-in-chief Tex. Forms Manual. Chmn. Planning and Zoning Commn., Bellaire, Tex., 1976-77; bd. dirs. Tax Increment Fin. Dist., Bellaire, 1984-91; chmn. task force on edn. Tex. Real Estate Commn.; chmn. profl. adv. com. dept. urban and regional planning Tex. A&M U., 1988-89; 1st asst. scoutmaster Boy Scout World Jamboree, Holland, 1995, scoutmaster, Chile, 1999; scoutmaster Nat. Boy Scout Jamboree, 1997, 1st asst. scoutmaster, 2001; mayor City of Bellaire, 1998-2000; sec.-treas. Harris County Mayors and Coun. Assn. 1999. Recipient Peggy Hayes Tchg. Excellence award TLTA, 1993, Don Roose award of excellence in real estate edn., 2001. Mem. ABA (acquisitions editor books and pubs. com. 1994-2001, chmn. brokers and brokerage com. 1986-93), Internat. Wine Food Soc. (host Houston chpt. 1993-94), Am. Coll. Real Estate Lawyers, Nat. Assn. Corp. Real Estate Execs. (chpt. v.p.), Am. Land Devel. Assn. (bd. dirs.), Tex. Land Title Assn. (chmn. forms manual com., TREC earnest money contract task force), Tex. Land Title Inst. (chmn. 2001), State Bar Tex. (mem. coun. of real estate, probate and trust law sect. 2002—), Tex. Real Estate Tchrs. Assn. (Outstanding Real Estate Educator 1986), Houston Real Estate Lawyers Coun., Real Estate Educator's Assn. (pres. 1987-88, Real Estate Educator of Yr. 1986, 2000), Houston Bar Assn. (chmn. real estate sect. 1987-88), Bellaire/S.W. Houston C. of C. (Outstanding Businessman of Yr. 1990, chmn. Tex. Real Estate Commns. Edn. Task Force, 1999-2000), U. Tex. Mortgage Lending Inst. (faculty), U. Houston Law Alumni Assn. (bd. dirs.). Universal Order Knights of Vine (master barrister Houston chpt.), Rotary, Les Amis Escoffier. Republican. Roman Catholic. Home: 5223 Pine St Bellaire TX 77401-4820 Office: Ste 615 6750 West Loop S Bellaire TX 77401-4525 E-mail: chuck@chuckjacobus.com.

JACOBUS, GEORGE ANTHONY BODLEY (ANTON JACOBUS), investment banker; b. Bournemouth, Hampshire, England, Nov. 22, 1938; s. Marcus Henry Kyril and Diana (Longstaff) J.; m. Lilia Wyszkowski, 1960 (div. 1971); children: Andrew Hamilton Oscar Longstaff Jacobus, Susana Elizabeth; m. Julia Grimani Watson, 1973; 1 child, Thomas Edmund Grimani Bodley. MMSA extra cert., H.M.S. Conway Naval Coll., Anglesea, Eng., 1955; BSc, BA, Boston U., 1963; postgrad., Oxford U. Sch. Mgmt, 1978. With Oppenheimer Consultants/A D Little Inc., Boston and Caracas, 1966-70; with Coopers & Lybrand, London, 1970-78, Rank Orgn. PLC, London, 1978-86; investment banker Financiere Indosuez/Banque Indosuez, London and Paris, 1986-91; mng. dir. Financiere Indosuez, London, 1987-91; dep. head Joint Investment and Adv. Svc., 1992-96. Dir. fin. and funding Game Conservancy Trust, Fordingbridge, Hampshire, U.K.; sec. Habitat Rsch. Trust, Allerton Rsch. and Ednl. Trust; dir. Game Conservancy Ltd., U.K. Sci. Rsch. Coun. Internal Audit Svc.; spl. advisor European Commn.-Poland and Hungary Adv. and Rsch. Exec. Programme, Bulgaria, 1992-93; chmn. European Synchrontron Radiation Facility, Audit Commn. Fellow Inst. Fin. Accts., Inst. Internal Auditors, Brit. Inst. Mgmt.; mem. Assn. Internat. des Etudiants en Scis. Economiques et Commerciales (internat. sr., life), Aldershot Beagles, The Naval Club, Rallye de Fontainebleau, Glyn Celyn Beagles. Home and Office: Stockley Cross Staunton-on-Arrow Herefordshire HR6 9LD England E-mail: antonjacobus@onetel.com.

JACOBY, ANNE CATHERINE, supervisory nurse; b. Lincoln, Nebr., July 5, 1950; d. Billy Burton and Arleen Mae (Heinz) Michael; m. Jonathon L. Jacoby; children: Melissa Anne, Matthew David. BSN, U. Nebr. Coll. Nursing, 1972; postgrad., The Meth. Hosp., 1980; MSN, U. Nebr. Coll. Nursing, 1982; PhD in Nursing, Tex. Woman's U., 1988. CCRN, ACLS. Staff nurse med. ICU U. Nebr. Hosp., Omaha, 1972-74; staff nurse coronary care, ICU Immanuel Med. Ctr., Omaha, 1974-77; staff nurse coronary care Tufts New England Med. Ctr., Boston, 1978-79; staff nurse respiratory ICU Mass. Gen. Hosp., Boston, 1977-79; asst. prof. Tex. Woman's U. Coll. Nursing, Dallas, 1988-89; coord. pulmonary rehab. program Presbyn. Hosp. Dallas, 1989-90, staff nurse coronary care, 1987-92; supr. nurse rsch. Presbyn. Hosp. Dallas Inst. Exercise and Environ. Medicine, 1992-93; supr. nurse Smith Nursing Svc., Dallas, 1993-96; chair spl. programs Rivier Coll. Sch. Nursing and Health Scis., Nashua, N.H., 1997-99, mem. faculty, 1999—2000; v.p. Stone Giant Cons., LLP, 2000—. Contbr. articles to profl. jours. Named Notable Woman Tex., Young Community Leaders Am. Mem. ANA, AACN, Am. Heart Assn., Sigma Theta Tau.

JACOBY, ERIKA, social worker; b. Miskolc, Hungary, May 1, 1928; came to U.S. 1949; d. Jeno and Malvina (Salamonovits) Engel; m. Emil Jacoby, Sept. 24, 1950; children: Jonathan D., Benjamin M., Michael D. BA, Calif. State U., Northridge, 1971; MSW, U. So. Calif., L.A., 1975. Tchr. Adat Ari El Religious Sch., North Hollywood, Calif., 1961-73; tchr./counselor Camp Ramah, Ojai, Calif., summers 1961-72; clin. social worker Family Svc. of L.A., Van Nuys, 1975-80; psychiatric social worker Kaiser Psychiatry, Van Nuys, 1980—; clin. social worker in pvt. practice North Hollywood, Calif., 1975—; ret., 1997. Lectr. in field; conductor workshops in field. Contbr. articles to profl. jours. Mem. Nat. Assn. Social Workers, Common Cause, Hadassah, Amnesty Internat., Adat Ari El. Democrat. Jewish. Avocations: reading, biking, music, arts.

JACOBY, HENRY DONNAN, economist, educator; b. Dallas, June 25, 1935; s. Henry Harris and Margaret Cameron (Miller) J.; m. Martha Hughes Jacoby, Apr. 4, 1959; children— Daniel Donnan, Caroline Hughes. BS in Mech. Engring, U. Tex., Austin, 1957; PhD in Econ, Harvard U., 1967. Systems analyst Tudor Engring. Co., San Francisco, 1959-61; economist Harvard Devel. Adv. Service, Argentina Project, 1963-65; asst. prof. dept. econs. Harvard U., Cambridge, Mass., 1965-69; assoc. prof. polit. economy John F. Kennedy Sch. Govt., 1969-73; prof. mgmt. MIT, Cambridge, 1973—, William. F. Pounds prof. mgmt., 1991—2001, chmn. faculty, 1988-91; dir. global change program, 1991—; dir. Center for Energy Policy Research, 1978-83; vis. scholar London Bus. Sch., 1983-84. Chmn. Mass. Gov.'s Emergy Energy Tech. Adv. Com., 1973-74; mem. Nat. Petroleum Coun., 1975-83. Author: (with F.S. Brooman) Macroeconomics, 1970, (with R. Dorfman and H.A. Thomas, Jr.) Models for Managing Regional Water Quality, 1973, (with J.D. Steinbruner) Clearing The Air, 1973, Analysis of Investment in Electric Power, 1979, (with R. deLucia) Energy Planning for Developing Countries, 1982, (with R.L. Gordon and M.B. Zimmerman) Energy: Markets and Regulation, 1987. Served with USN, 1957-59. Mem. Am. Econ. Assn., Tau Beta Pi. Democrat. Episcopalian. Office: MIT Sloan Sch of Mgmt 50 Memorial Dr Cambridge MA 02142-1347

JACOBY, IRVING, physician; b. N.Y.C., Sept. 30, 1947; s. Philip Aaron and Sylvia Jacoby; m. Sara Kay Vartanian; children: James Tyler, Kathryn Aaryn. BS magna cum laude, U. Miami, Coral Gables, Fla., 1969; MD, Johns Hopkins U., 1973. Diplomate Am. Bd. Internal Medicine, Am. Bd. Infectious Diseases, Am. Bd. Emergency Medicine, Am. Bd. Preventive Medicine (undersea and hyperbaric medicine). Intern Boston City Hosp., 1973-74, resident in medicine, 1974-75, chief resident, 1978-79; resident in medicine Peter Bent Brigham Hosp., Boston, 1975-76, fellow in infectious diseases, 1976-78; asst. dir. emergency med. svcs. U. Mass. Med. Ctr., Worcester, 1979-84; asst. dir. dept. emergency med. U. Calif. Med. Ctr., San Diego, 1984—, assoc. prof. med. surgery, 1988-94, hosp. dir. for emergency preparedness and response, 2003—; prof. med. surgery, 1994—. Disaster control officer, assoc. dir. Hyperbaric Med. Ctr., 1985—; vis. physician, cons. infectious diseases Soroka Med. Ctr., Ben Gurion U., Beer-Sheva, Israel, 1980; flight physician New Eng. Life Flight, Worcester, 1982-84, Life Flight Aeromed. Program U. Calif., 1984-87. Sect. editor for disaster medicine Jour. Emergency Medicine; assoc. editor Undersea and Hyperbaric Medicine, 1996-2002. Comdr. Disaster Med. Assistance Team CA-4, 1991—. Fellow ACP, Am. Coll. Emergency Physicians; mem. Am. Soc. Microbiology, Infectious Diseases Soc. Am., Nat. Assn. Disaster Med. Assistance Teams (vice chair 1999, chmn. 2000-01), Soc. Acad. Emergency Medicine, Undersea and Hyperbaric Med. Soc., World Assn. for Disaster and Emergency Medicine, Disaster Emergency Response Assn., Johns Hopkins Med. and Surg. Assn., Iron Arrow Leadership Soc., Omicron Delta Kappa, Phi Kappa Phi, Alpha Epsilon Delta, Phi Eta Sigma. Office: U Calif Med Ctr 200 W Arbor Dr San Diego CA 92103-8676

JACOBY, JACOB, consumer psychology educator; b. Bklyn., Feb. 17, 1940; s. David and Frances (Berman) Jacoby; m. Francine Crystal Jacoby (div.); children: Robin Ann, Jonathan Scott; m. Renée Berkowitz; 1 child, Dana Eve. BA, Bklyn. Coll., 1961, MS, 1963; PhD, Mich. State U., 1966. Prof. consumer behavior Purdue U., West Lafayette, Ind., 1968-81, NYU, 1981—. Cons. DuPont, Gen. Electric Co., Gen. Motors Co., Am. Assn. Adv. Agys., Procter and Gamble, Standard Oil, U.S. Senate, FTC, FDA, others Author: Brand Loyalty, 1978, Miscomprehension of Televised Communication, 1980, The Comprehension and Miscomprehension of Print Communications, 1987. Served to 1st lt. USAF, 1965-68 Recipient Outstanding Contbn. to Advt. award Am. Acad. Advt., 1991, Disting. Sci. Contbn. award Soc. for Consumer Psychology, 1996. Fellow APA (pres. divsn. 23 1973-74, Disting. Sci. Rsch. award 1995), Assn. for Consumer Rsch. (pres. 1975); mem. Am. Mktg. Assn. (H.H. Maynard award 1978), Am. Assn. Pub. Opinion Rsch., Advt. Ednl. Found. (bd. dirs.). Jewish. Office: NYU 44 W 4th St New York NY 10012-1106 E-mail: JJacoby@stern.nyu.edu.

JACOBY, NEIL HERMAN, JR., astronautic engineer, consultant; b. Chgo., Oct. 20, 1940; s. Neil Herman and Clair (Gruhn) J. BA in Astronomy, UCLA, 1965, MS in Engring., 1969. Sci. guide Griffith Obs., L.A., summer 1962; comuter program cons. UCLA Western Data Processing Ctr., 1966-67; tchg. asst. in astrodynamics UCLA Sch. Engring. and Applied Sci., summer 1968; staff scientist Computer Scis. Corp., L.A., 1972-76; sys. analyst Sys. Devel. corp., Santa Monica, Calif., 1977-81; cons. in astrodynamics, astronautics L.A., 1981—. Ind. property mgr., L.A., 1979—. Contbr. articles to sci. and profl. jours. bd. dirs. Westwood Homeowners Assn., L.A., 1981—. Named to Hall of Fame, Internat. Biographical Ctr.; recipient Internat. Diploma of Honor Am. Order of Excellence, 500 founders of the 21st. Century, IBC Presidential Seal of Honor, American Biographical Institute. Mem. AIAA, AAAS, Am. Astronautical Soc. (sr.), Am. Biograph. Inst., N.Y. Acad. Sci., Internat. Biog. Assn. (Cert. of Merit), Planetary Soc., Alpha Gamma Sigma. Achievements include development of time series for rapid and accurate missile trajectory deterimination and an orbit determination method using 5 observations; a novel method of non-co-planer orbital transfer for a geocentric satellite; determined that 3 observations of right ascension and declination of a comet are substantially better than 5 observations in determining a comet's orbit because of very high eccentricity of its orbit; development of of an original solution to determine productions of closest approaches of near earth objects; an accurate, rapid and novel numerical integration method for predicting orbits of potentially hazardous asteroids, including perturbations of all planets in our solar system. Home and Office: 1434 Midvale Ave Los Angeles CA 90024-5406 E-mail: njacoby@prodigy.net.

JACOBY, RICHARD ALLEN, pathologist, dermatologist; b. Rochester, N.Y., June 27, 1950; s. Marvin and Florence J.; m. Christine Marie Jacoby, Mar. 25, 1984; children: Benjamin, Joanna. BA, NYU, 1972; MD, Jefferson Med. Coll., 1976. Diplomate Am. Bd. Pathology, Am. Bd. Dermatology, Am. Bd. Dermatopathology. Intern and resident in pathology Lankenau Hosp., Phila., 1976-79; resident and tchg. asst. in pathology NYU, N.Y.C., 1979-80; fellow in dermatopathology NYU Med. Ctr., N.Y.C., 1980-81; resident in dermatology Skin and Cancer Hosp.-Temple U. Health Scis., Phila., 1981-84; dir. dermatopathology Hahneman U., Phila., 1984-88, interim chmn. dermatology, 1986-88; dir. dermatopathology Jefferson Med. Coll., Phila., 1988-97; pres. Inst. for Dermatopathology, Phila., 1997-2000; chief med. officer PathSOURCE, N.Y.C., 1998-2000, Inform Dx, Nashville, 2000-2001; regional mng. dir. Ameripath Phila., Conshohocken, Pa., 2001—. Cons., dermatopathologist Melanoma Program-Jefferson Med. Coll., Phila., 1988-93. Asst. editor Dermatopathology-Practical and Conceptual, 1995-99. Mem. AMA, Am. Acad. Dermatology, Am. Soc. Dermatopathology, Internat. Soc. Dermatopathology, Phila. Dermatologic Soc. Avocation: golf. Home: 118 Muirfield Ct Moorestown NJ 08057 Office: Ameripath Phila 20 Ash St Conshohocken PA 19428

JACOBY, ROBERT HAROLD, management consulting executive; b. N.Y.C., June 9, 1942; s. Harold and Ruth (Johnson) J. BA in Econs., Dartmouth Coll., 1964; MA in Polit. Philosophy, Columbia U., 1998, MPhil, 2001. Cert. mgmt. cons. Prin. Albert Ramond & Assocs. Inc., Chgo., 1968-75; pres. Systemetrics Internat. Inc., Indpls., 1975-77; v.p. Theodore Barry & Assocs., London, 1977-82; ptnr. Deloitte & Touche, N.Y.C., 1982—85; pres. R.H. Jacoby & Assocs. Inc., N.Y.C., 1985—. Contbr. articles to profl. jours. Mem. Acad. Mgmt., Am. Econ. Assn., Am. Water Works Assn., Nat. Assn. Corp. Dirs., Am. Gas Assn., Strategic Mgmt. Soc., Am. Arbitration Assn. (comml. arbitrator 1982—), The Strategic Leadership Forum. Office: RH Jacoby & Assoc Inc 355 South End Ave New York NY 10280-1005

JACOBY, TAMAR, journalist, author; b. N.Y.C., Nov. 28, 1954; d. Irving and Alberta (Smith) J. Grad., UN Internat. Sch., N.Y.C., 1972; BA, Yale U., 1976. Writer, editor Hudson Rsch. Europe, Paris, 1976-77; editorial staff N.Y. Rev. Books, 1977-81; dep. editor Op-Ed Page N.Y. Times, 1981-87; sr. writer Newsweek, N.Y.C., 1987-89, justice editor, 1988-89; self employed author, 1989—. Lectr. Yale U., New Haven, Conn., 1986-90; instr. The New Sch. for Social Rsch., N.Y.C., 1991; vis. prof. The Cooper Union for Advancment of Sci. and Art, 1998. Author: Someone Else's House: America's Unfinished Struggle for Integration, 1998; editor: Reinventing the Melting Pot: The New Immigrants and What It Means To Be American, 2004; contbr. articles to Fgn. Affairs, The Weekly Std., New Republic, Commentary. Dir. N.Y. Civil Rights Coalition. Fellow Nat. Endowment for the Humanitites, 1992, Alicia Patterson journalism fellow, 1990, Manhattan Inst. for Policy Rsch. sr. fellow. Mem. Coun. Fgn. Rels. Home: 78 Hawthorne Pl Montclair NJ 07042-2604

JACOBY, THOMAS S. cultural organization administrator; b. Konigsberg, Fed. Republic Germany, May 13, 1935; came to U.S., 1939; s. Berthold and Anni (Pfingst) J.; m. Adrienne Zacansky, Apr. 14, 1962; children: Michael, Melissa. BS in Edn., West Chester U., 1958; EdM, Temple U., 1961. Cert. health, phys. edn. tchr. Tchr. Sch. Dist. of Phila., 1958-69, dept. head, athletic dir., 1969-71, supr. health and phys. edn., 1971-90, curriculum coord. phys. edn. and athletics, 1990-93, adminstrv. asst. to regional supt., 1993-95, adminstrv. asst. student svcs., 1995-97, dir. svcs. to students with disabilities, 1997-99; ednl. cons., 1999-2000; exec. dir. Phila. Reads, 2000—. Adj. asst. prof. Temple U., Phila., 1976—; cons. Tech. Adv. Svc. for Attys., Blue Bell, Pa., 1977—; bd. dirs. Lake Owego Camp for Boys, Greeley, Pa. Author: (pamphlets) Physical Education for the Bicentennial, 1976, Street Games of Philadelphia, 1985; contbg. editor: Unique Games and Sports Around the World, 2001. Pres. Phila. Coun. B'nai B'rith, Phila., 1985, Jewish Cmty. Rels. Coun., 1998-2000, co-chmn. edn. com. Jewish Coun. on Pub. Affairs, 2001—. Mem. AAHPERD (2003 conv. mgr., Honor award 2002), Pa. State Assn. Health, Phys. Edn., Recreation and Dance (pres. 1980, conv. mgr. 1975, 79, exhibits mgr. Ea. Dist. 1988-92, pres. elect Ea. Dist. 1993, pres. Ea. Dist. 1994, Profl. Honor awards 1973, 90, Elmer B. Cottrell award 1984), ASTM, ASCD, Am. Assn. Sch. Adminstrs., Am. Camping Assn., Phi Delta Kappa. E-mail: T.Jacoby@verizon.net.

JACOBY, WILLIAM JEROME, JR., internist, retired military officer; b. Mt. Carmel, Pa., Aug. 9, 1925; s. William Jerome and Florence Marie (White) J.; m. Joeann J. Powroznick, May 5, 1956; children: William Jerome, Teresa Marie. AB, Emory U., 1946; MD, Jefferson Med. Coll., 1950. Diplomate Am. Bd. Internal Medicine. Commd. lt. (j.g.) M.C., USN, 1950, advanced through grades to rear adm., 1972, intern Jefferson Med. Coll. Hosp., Phila., 1950-51, resident in internal medicine, 1951-52, 55-56; Am. Heart Assn. fellow, 1956-57; chmn. dept. medicine U.S. Naval Hosps., 1964-69, Phila., 1969-72; chmn. dept. medicine, dir. edn. and rsch. Nat. Naval Med. Ctr., Bethesda, Md., 1972-75; comdg. officer Naval Regional Med. Ctr., Portsmouth, Va., 1975-78; dir. med. svcs. VA Cen. Office, Washington, 1978-80, dep. chief med. dir., 1980-83. Assoc. clin. prof. Jefferson Med. Coll., 1969—; prof. medicine George Washington U. Med. Sch., 1972, Eastern Va. Sch. Medicine, Norfolk, 1976-78; mem. adv. coun. Nat. Heart, Lung and Blood Inst., NIH, 1972-75. Contbr. articles to profl. jours. Decorated Legion of Merit, Meritorious Svc. medal. Fellow ACP (Laureate award 1996); mem. Assn. Mil. Surgeons (Founders medal 1974), Alpha Omega Alpha, Phi Beta Pi. Roman Catholic. Home: 737 E Tazewells Way Williamsburg VA 23185-6521

JACOCKS, MAC ALEXANDER, surgeon; b. Greensboro, N.C., 1950; MD, U. Okla., 1977. Diplomate Am. Bd. Surgery, Am. Bd. Gen. Vascular Surgery. Intern U. Okla. Health Sci. Ctr., Oklahoma City, 1977-78, resident in surgery, 1978-82; fellow in cardiol. rsch. Harvard Med. Sch., Boston, 1979-80; surgeon U. Hosp., Oklahoma City; prof. surgery U. Okla. Health Sci. Ctr. Fellow ACS; mem. AMA, Am. Assn. of Vascular Surgery, Western Vascular Soc. Office: U Okla Dept Surgery 920 Stanton L Young Blvd PO Box 26901 Oklahoma City OK 73126-0901

JACONETTY, THOMAS ANTHONY, lawyer; b. Chgo., May 21, 1953; s. George Bernard and Mary Jane (Sgarioto) J.; m. Judith Hamill; 1 child, Nicole Alicia. AB in History and Polit. Sci. summa cum laude with honors, Loyola U., Chgo., 1975; JD, Northwestern U., 1978. Bar: Ill. 1978, U.S. Dist. Ct. (no. dist.) Ill. 1978, U.S. Ct. Appeals (7th cir.) 1979; cert. rev. appraiser. Adminstrv. asst. Chgo. Dept. Aviation, 1979; asst. corp. counsel Chgo. Dept. Law, 1980; asst. to commr. Cook County Bd. Tax Appeals, Chgo., 1981-83, dep. commr., 1983-87, commr., 1988-89, chief dep. commr., 1989—; sole practice Chgo. Lectr. Ill. Inst. for Continuing Legal Edn.; lectr. and presenter Lorman Edn. Svcs., Lincoln Inst. Land Policy, Internat. Assn. of Assessing Officers, Chgo. Chpt. of Appraisal Inst., Commerce Clearing House Ill. State Tax Reports Nat. Bus. Inst. Asst. editor, indexer: Corwin on the Constitution, 1981; author book chpts.; editor: Issues Confronting Properties Affected by Contamination or Environmental Problems, 2002, Valuation of Subsidized Housing, 2003; contbr. articles to profl. jours., property tax policies and adminstr. practices, Can., U.S., 2000. Mem. Cook County Dem. Orgn.; pres., bd. dirs. Polish and Am. Citizens Club, 1981—; pres. Italian Am. Cath. Assn., Chgo., 1981—; mem. Old Timers' Baseball Assn., Art Inst. Chgo., Channel 11-PBS, Mus. Sci. and Industry, Ill. Spl. Olympics, Nat. Trust Hist. Preservation, Libr. of Congress, Ill. Alzheimer's Assn., Civic Fedn. Tax Com.; mem. planning com. Nat. Conf. State Tax Judges, 1999—, chair 2002—. Mem. ABA, Ill. Bar Assn. (mem. assembly 1988-91, 92-94, state and local taxation sect. coun. and several subcoms., chmn. 1994-95, vice chmn. 1993-94, ad hoc and 4 separate civic fedn. coms. on property tax reform, 1994-96, 2000-2001), Chgo. Bar Assn. (chmn. election law com.), Internat. Assn. Assessing Officers (arbitrator cir. ct. Cook County, 1990-97, various sects., legal coms., chmn. nat. legal com. 1995-2002, Donohoo Essay award, 1996), Justinian Soc. Italian Lawyers, Northwestern Law Sch. Alumni Assn., Loyola U. Alumni Assn., Pi Sigma Alpha, Alpha Sigma Nu. Avocations: travel, reading. Office: Cook County Bd of Review 118 N Clark St Ste 601 Chicago IL 60602-1311

JACOVIDES, LINOS JACOVOU, electrical engineer, researcher; b. Paphos, Cyprus, May 10, 1940; s. Jacovos and Zoe (Evangelides) Jacovides; m. Katie McNamee; children: James, Michael, Christina, Julia. BS, U. Glasgow, Scotland, 1961, MS, 1962; PhD, U. London, 1965. Sr. rsch. engr. Def. Rsch. Labs. GM, Calif., 1965-67; sr. rsch. engr. elec. engring. GM Rsch. Labs., Warren, Mich., 1967-76, dept. rsch. engr. elec. engring. dept., 1975-85, asst. dept. head elec. engring. dept., 1985-87, prin. rsch. engr., 1987-88, head elec. and electronics dept., 1988-98; dir. Delphi Rsch. Labs., Warren, 1999—, Shelby Township, Mich., 1999—. Editor: Electric Vehicles, 1981; contbr. articles to profl. jours. Fellow: IEEE; mem.: Soc. Automotive Engrs., Industry Applications Soc. of IEEE (pres. 1990). Home: 154 Touraine Rd Grosse Pointe Farms MI 48236-3322 Office: M/C 483 478 103 51786 Shelby Pky Shelby Township MI 48315-1786 E-mail: linos@aol.com., linos.jacovides@delphi.com.

JACOX, ADA KATHRYN, nurse, educator; b. Centreville, Mich. d. Leo H. and Lilian (Gilbert) Jacox. BS in Nursing Edn., Columbia U., 1959; MS in Child Psychiat. Nursing, Wayne State U., 1965; PhD in Sociology, Case Western Res. U., 1969. RN. Dir. nursing Children's Hosp.-Northville State Hosp., Mich., 1961—63; assoc. prof., then prof. Coll. Nursing Univ. Iowa, Iowa City, 1969—76; prof., assoc. dean Sch. Nursing U. Colo., Denver, 1976—80; prof., dir. rsch. ctr. sch. nursing U. Md., Balt., 1980—90, dir. ctr. for health policy rsch., 1988—90; prof. sch. nursing, Independence Found. chair health policy Johns Hopkins U., Balt., 1990—95; prof., assoc. dean for rsch. Coll. Nursing Wayne State, Detroit, 1996. Co-chmn. panels to develop clin. guidelines for pain mgmt. U.S. Agy. for Health Care Policy and Rsch., 1990—94; chair AIDS study sect. NIH, 1990—92. Co-author: Organizing for Independent Nursing Practice, 1977 (named Book of Yr., Am. Jour. Nursing), A Process Measure for Primary Care: The Nurse Practitioner Rating Form, 1981 (named Book of Yr., Am. Jour. Nursing); editor: Pain: A Sourcebook for Nurses, 1977 (named Book of Yr., Am. Jour. Nursing). Recipient Disting. Achievement in Nursing Rsch. and Scholarship, Alumni Assn., Columbia U. Tchrs. Coll., 1975, Disting. award for spl. achievement, Nat. Coalition for Cancer Survivorship, 1994, Cameo award for rsch. excellence, Sigma Theta Tau, 1996, Rozella Schlotfeldt Leadership award, MAIN, 1997; fellow Carver fellow, U. Iowa, 1972. Fellow: Am. Acad. Nursing; mem.: Wayne State U. Alumni Assn. (Disting. Alumni award 1994), Inst. of Medicine, NAS (com. on nat. needs for biomed. and rsch. pers. 1984—87), Am. Acad. Nursing, Am. Health Quality Assn. (bd. dirs. 1998—2001), Am. Pain Soc. (chair clin. practice guidelines com. 1995—2000, bd. dirs. 1999—2001), Am. Nurses Found. (pres. 1982—85), AMA (mem. health policy agenda work group 1983—86), ANA (dir. 1978—82, 1st v.p. 1982—84). Office: Wayne State U Coll Nursing 5557 Cass Ave Detroit MI 48202-3615

JACOX, JOHN WILLIAM, retired mechanical engineer and consulting company executive; b. Pitts., Dec. 12, 1938; s. John Sherman and Grace Edna (Herbster) J.; 1 child, Brian Erik; m. Roma Jankauskaite, Sept. 3, 1993. BSME in Indsl. Mgmt., Carnegie Mellon U., 1962, BS in Mech. Engring., 1962. Mfg. engr. Nuclear Fuel div. Westinghouse Elec. Co., Pitts., 1962-64; rsch. engr. Continental Can Co. Metal R&D Ctr., Pitts., 1964-65; data processing sales engr. IBM, Pitts., 1965-66; mktg. mgr. nuclear products MSA Internat., Pitts., 1966-72; v.p. Nuclear Cons. Svcs., Inc., Columbus, Ohio, 1973-84; v.p. NUCON Internat., 1981-84; bd. dirs. NUCON Europe Ltd., London, 1981—; pres. Jacox Assocs., Inc., 1984-2001; ret., 2001; cons., lectr. Nat. Ctr. for Rsch. in Vocat. Edn., 1978-84 ; author, presenter, session chmn. DOE/Harvard U. Nuclear Air Cleaning Confs., 1974—; lectr. Harvard U. Sch. Pub. Health Air Cleaning Lab., 1986—; co-chmn. program subcom. Tech. Alliance Cen. Ohio, 1984-85, vice-chmn., chmn.-elect dir. subcom., 1986-87, chmn. bd. trustees, 1986; tech. transfer com. Dayton Area Tech. Network; program com. World Trade Devel. Club; mem. legis. svcs. com. coop. edn. adv. com. Otterbein Coll., 1978-82; industry advisor Franklin U. Grad. Sch. Bus., 1994—. Mem. NRA (patron), ASHRAE (standards com. 3.2 and 9.4), ASTM (chmn. F-21), ASME (code com. nuclear air and gas treatment, main exec. com., chmn. subcom. field test procedures), Am. Nuclear Soc. (pub. info. com.), N.Y. Acad. Scis. (life), Ohio Acad. Sci. (life), Am. Nat. Stds. Inst., Internat. Soc. Nuc. Air Treatment Techs. (co-founder, officer), Columbus Area C. of C. (tech. roundtable 1983), Air Force Assn. (life), Mensa, Sun Bunch (pres. 1980-81), Dayton Area Tech. Network (subcom. on tech. transfer), Tech. Transfer Soc. Office: PO Box 29720 Columbus OH 43229 0720 Home: 4471 Summit Rd Pataskala OH 43062-8880

JACOX, MARILYN ESTHER, chemist; b. Utica, NY, Apr. 26, 1929; d. Grant Burlingame and Mary Elizabeth (Dunn) J. BA, Syracuse U., 1951; PhD, Cornell U., 1956; ScD (hon.), Syracuse U., 1993. Postdoctoral rsch. assoc. U. NC, Chapel Hill, NC, 1956-58; fellow in fundamental rsch. Mellon Inst., Pitts., 1958-62; rsch. chemist Nat. Bur. Std., Washington, 1962—; fellow Nat. Bur. Std. (now Nat. Inst. Std. and Tech.), Gaithersburg, Md., 1986-95, sci. emeritus, 1996—. Mem. editorial bd. Revs. Chem. Intermediates, 1984-89, Jour. Chem. Physics, 1989-91; contbr. numerous articles to profl. jours. Recipient gold medal U.S. Dept. Commerce, 1970, Fed. Women's award, 1973, Lippincott award, 1989, Hillebrand prize Chem. Soc. Washington, 1990, WISE lifetime achievement award, 1991, E. Bright Wilson award in Spectroscopy, Am. Chem. Soc., 2003. Fellow AAAS, Am. Phys. Soc., Washington Acad. Scis. (Phys. Sci. award 1968); mem. Am. Chem. Soc., Exec. Women in Govt. (sec. 1981, vice-chmn. 1982), Inter-Am. Photochemical Soc. (exec. com. 1978-79), Sigma Xi (pres. elect NBS chpt. 1987-88, pres. 1988-89). Office: Nat Inst Standards & Tech Optical Technology Division Gaithersburg MD 20899-8441 E-mail: marilyn.jacox@nist.gov.

JACQUENEY, STEPHANIE A(LICE), lawyer; b. Freeport, N.Y. d. Theodore and Mona (Graubart) J. BS, Cornell U., 1979; MPA, JD, Syracuse U., 1982. Bar: N.Y. 1983, U.S. Dist. Ct. (so. and ea. dists.) N.Y. 1983. Law clk. to U.S. atty. U.S. Dist. Ct. (No. Dist.) N.Y., Syracuse, 1981-82; assoc. Olwine, Connelly, Chase, O'Donnell & Weyer, N.Y.C., 1982-84, Cadwalader, Wickersham & Taft, N.Y.C., 1984-87; asst. counsel Manhattan Cable TV, Inc., N.Y.C., 1987-89, gen. counsel, 1989-90, v.p., gen. counsel, 1990-92; v.p. legal dept. Time Warner Cable of N.Y.C., 1992-94; dir. bus. affairs Radio City Prodns., N.Y.C., 1994-97, sr. dir. bus. affairs, 1997—; v.p. legal and bus. affairs Madison Square Garden, N.Y.C., 1999—. Mem. ABA, N.Y. State Bar Assn., Assn. of Bar of City of N.Y. (com. on arbitration 1984-88, com. on copyright and intellectual property 1996-99), N.Y. County Lawyers Assn. Office: Radio City Entertainment Madison Square Garden 2 Penn Plz Fl 14 New York NY 10121-0101

JACQUES, JOSEPH HOWARD, human resources professional; b. Washington, Jan. 17, 1944; s. Howard Francis and Mary Gertrude Jacques; m. Jeanann Jacques, Aug. 5, 1967; children: Jeffrey, Joanna, Jonathan, Jennifer, Jean Marie. BA, Belmont Abbey Coll., 1966; JD, Emory U., 1969. Bar: (D.C.) 1969, (N.C.) 1971. Newsboy Washington Star, 1954-56, Washington Post, 1956-62; letter carrier U.S. Post Office, Washington, Atlanta, 1961—69; benefits dept. staff R.J. Reynolds Industries, Winston-Salem, N.C., 1970-75; mgr. compensation and benefits Ala. Bancorp., Birmingham, 1975-77; human resources dir. Potomac Ctr., Hagerstown, Md., 1978—. Bd. dirs. Hospice Washington County, Hagerstown, 2000-03, United Way of Washington County, Hagerstown, 2000-02. Republican. Roman Catholic. Home: 13510 Paradise Dr Hagerstown MD 21742-2420 Office: Potomac Ctr 1380 Marshall St Hagerstown MD 21740 E-mail: jockojacques@hotmail.com.

JACQUES, JOSEPH WILLIAM, investment advisor; b. Stroudsburg, Pa., Sept. 26, 1953; s. Joseph Francis and Millie C. (Dave) J.; m. Joy Lynn Turner, Dec. 28, 1974; children: Jeffrey, Justin, Joelle, Jeremy. AA in Acctg., Northampton Community Coll., 1973; BS in Acctg., Bloomsburg U., 1974. CPA, Md.; registerd fin. planner master, Md., investment advisor, Md. Auditor U.S. Gen. Acctg. Office, Washington, 1975-82; pres. Coord. Fin. Svcs., Ltd., Bethesda, Md., 1982-84, Joseph W. Jacques, CPA, PA, Rockville, Md., 1985—. Registered rep. Jacques Fin., LLC, 1990—. Contbr. articles to profl. jours. Pres. Avery Forest Homeowners Assn., Rockville, 1989-90. Mem. Nat. Assn. Life Underwriters, Internat. Assn. Registered Fin. Planners, Internat. Assn. Fin. Planners, Md. Assn. CPA's. Republican. Roman Catholic. Avocations: tennis, golf, children. Home and Office: 15430 Avery Rd Rockville MD 20855-1711

JACQUES, RAOUL THOMAS, lawyer; b. Milw., Aug. 7, 1934; s. Arthur Francis and Maude (Mayotte) J.; m. Alice C. Jacques, June 15, 1957 (div. Oct. 1973); children: Marian, Stephen; m. Diana Lynn Hunt, Dec. 20, 1975 (div. Nov. 1983); children: Carina, Michelle, Emilie, Ashley; m. tutsie Silapalikit-Porn, apr. 5, 1987. BS, Marquette U., 1957; LLB, U. Ariz., 1959. Bar: Ariz. 1959, U.S. Dist. Ct. Ariz. 1971. From trust officer to v.p. TransAm. Title (Ariz.), Tucson and Phoenix, 1959-65, 67—; ptnr. MacLean & Jacques, Phoenix, 1965-67; bd. dirs. Land Registrations Inc., Phoenix, Del Webb Corp. Real Estate Adv. Bd. Republican. Roman Catholic. Home: PO Box 7296 Phoenix AZ 85011 7296 Office: MacLean & Jacques 40 E Virginia Ave Phoenix AZ 85004-1122

JACQUESSON, ALAIN L. librarian; b. Geneva, Nov. 3, 1946; s. Guy and Elisabeth (Giddey) J.; m. Marie-Jose Chanez, Feb. 8, 1975; children: Severine, Mathieu. Responsable Ecole de bibliothecaires, Geneva, 1978—81; project chief U. Geneva, 1981—88; dir. Bibliothèques Municipales, Geneva, 1988—93, Bibliothèque Publique et Universitaire, Geneva, 1993—. Mem. ALA, Assn. of Swiss Librs., Assn. French Librs., Am. Soc. Info. Sci. Office: Bibliotheque Publique Univ Parc des Bastions 1211 Geneva 4 Switzerland Fax: (022) 418-28-01. E-mail: alain.jacquesson@bpu.ville-ge.ch.

JACQUETTE, YVONNE HELENE, artist; b. Pitts., Dec. 15, 1934; Student, R.I. Sch. Design, 1952-56; studies with John Frazier, Robert Hamilton, Herman Cherry, Robert Roche. Instr. Moore Coll. Art, Phila., 1972; instr. painting, vis. artist U. Pa., 1972-76, 79-82, instr. Grad. Sch. Fine Arts, 1979-84; instr. Parsons Sch. Design, 1975-78; instr. painting Pa. Acad. Fine Arts Grad. Sch., 1991—. Vis. artist Nova Scotia Coll. Art, 1974; artist in residence Harvard U., 1995; represented by DC Moore Gallery, N.Y.C., Mary Ryan Gallery (Prints) N.Y.C.; instr. in field. One-woman shows include St. Louis Art Mus., 1983-84, Berggruen Gallery, San Francisco, 1984, Yuracho Seibu-Takanawa Art, Tokyo, 1985, Brooke Alexander Inc., 10 shows 1974-88, 90, 92, 95, N.Y. Mus. Art, Bowdoin Coll. Mus. Art, Maine, 1986, D.C. Moore Gallery, 1997, 2000, 2003, Mary Ryan Gallery, 1997, Huntington (W.Va.) Mus., 1997, Mention: Retrospective, Cantor Arts Ctr., Stanford (Calif.) U., 2002, Colby Coll. Mus., Waterville, Maine, 2002, Utah Mus., Salt Lake City, 2002, Hudson River Mus., Yonkers, NY, 2003; 2-person show Mary Ryan Gallery, 1997; exhibited at Rutgers U. Art Gallery, 1972, Whitney Mus. Art, 1972, N.Y. Cultural Ctr. and U.S. Travelling Show, 1972-73, Internat. Biennial, Tokyo, 1974, Art Inst. Chgo., 1975, Mus. Modern Art, N.Y., 1981-82, Weatherspoon Gallery, N.C., Met. Mus. Art, Mus. Modern Art, Whitney Mus. Am. Art, N.Y., Colby Coll. Mus., Library Congress, Washington, Staatliche Mus., Berlin, Carnegie Inst. Mus. Art, Pitts., Am. Acad. Inst. Arts and Letters, N.Y.; prin. works include painting in oil N. Cen. Bronx Hosp., 1973, five color lithograph Horace Mann Sch., Riverdale, N.Y., 1974, mural for Fed. Bldg. and Post Office, Bangor Maine, 1979-82; prints commissioned by Provincetown Fine Arts Workcenter, 1992, Zimmerli Mus. Rutgers, 1993, Bus. Com. for the Arts, 1994; illustrator Country Rush, Adventures in Poetry, 1982, Aerial, Eyelight Press, 1981, Fast Lanes, 1984; film (with Rudy Burckhardt) Night Fantasies, 1992; set designer Sch. Hardknocks, Dance Theatre Workshop, N.Y.C. and nat. tour, 1989; print commd. by Cleve. Print Club, 1999. Recipient Nat. Acad. Painters award, 1998; Guggenheim Meml. Found. grantee, 1997-98. Mem.: Am. Acad. Arts and Letters (Painting award 1990), Artists Equity Assn., Nat. Acad. (Painting award 1998, Print award 1999). Office: 50 W 29th St New York NY 10001-4227

JACZKOWSKI, FRANK STANISLAUS, retired civil engineer; b. Cleve., May 28, 1935; s. Frank Alexander and Rachel (Bielawski) J. BSCE, Case Inst. Tech., 1957. Registered prof. engr., Ohio. Designer, detailer Howard, Needles, Tammen and Bergendoff, Cleve., 1957-61, design engr., 1961-68, project design engr., 1968-71, sr. structural engr., 1971-97. Office: HNTB Corp 55 Erieview Plz Cleveland OH 44114

JADLOW, JOSEPH MARTIN, economics educator; b. Nevada, Mo., Oct. 27, 1942; s. Joseph Martin and Polly Jene (Yancey) J.; m. Janice Lynn Wickstead; children: Joanna, Jennifer. BA, Cen. Mo. State, 1964, MA, 1965; PhD, U. Va., 1970. Asst. prof. Okla. State U., Stillwater, 1968-72, assoc. prof., 1972-76, prof. econs., 1976—, head dept. econs., 1993-99. Cons. numerous law firms. Contbr. articles to profl. jours. Mem. Am. Econ. Assn., So. Econ. Assn. (sec.-treas. 1977—), Lions (pres. 1991-92, bd. dirs. 1985-93). Republican. Methodist. Avocations: sports, jogging, old time radio shows. Office: Coll Bus Adminstrn Okla State U Stillwater OK 74078-0001

JADOT, JEAN LAMBERT OCTAVE, clergyman; b. Brussels, Nov. 23, 1909; s. Lambert Paul and Gabrielle Marie (Flanneau) J. D.Philosophie Thomiste, U. Catholique Louvain, Belgium, 1930. Ordained priest Roman Catholic Ch., 1934, consecrated bishop, 1968; parish asst., 1934-39; nat. chaplain Jeunesse Etudiante Catholique, 1939-45; chaplain Ecole Royale Militaire, 1945-52; chief chaplain Force Publique Belgian Congo, 1952-60; nat. dir. Propagation of Faith for Belgium, 1960-68; apostolic pro nuncio Thailand; also apostolic del., 1968-71; apostolic pro nuncio in Cameroun and Gabon, also apostolic del. Laos, Malaysia, Singapore, 1971-73; apostolic del. to U.S.A., 1973-80; permanent observer of Holy See to OAS, 1978-80. Pro pres. Secretariat for Non Christians at Vatican, 1980-84; titular arch-bishop of, Zuri, 1968 Served as chaplain Belgian Army, 1945-52. Decorated Order Leopold. Roman Catholic. Address: Val des Seigneurs 32-82 1150 Brussels Belgium E-mail: jjadot@swing.be.

JADVAR, HOSSEIN, nuclear medicine physician, biomedical engineer; b. Tehran, Iran, Apr. 6, 1961; arrived in U.S., 1978, naturalized, 1995; s. Ramezan Ali and Fatemeh (Afzal) Jadvar; m. Mojgan Maher, 1995; 1 child, Donya S. BS, Iowa State U., Ames, 1982; MS, U. Wis., Madison, 1984, U. Mich., Ann Arbor, 1986, PhD, 1988; MD, U. Chgo., 1993. Diplomate Am. Bd. Nuc. Medicine, cert. Bd. Nuc. Cardiology. Rsch. asst. dept. human oncology U. Wis., Madison, 1983-84; rsch. asst. dept. elec. engring. U. Mich., Ann Arbor, 1984-88; sr. rsch. engr. Arzco Med. Electronics, Inc., Chgo., 1988-89; sr. rsch. assoc. Pritzker Inst., Ill. Inst. Tech., Chgo., 1989-92; med. intern U. Calif., San Francisco, 1993-94; resident in radiology Stanford (Calif.) U., 1994-96, resident in nuclear medicine, 1996-98, chief resident in nucelar medicine, 1997-98; clin. fellow in radiology (positron emission tomography) Harvard Med. Sch., Boston, 1998-99; asst. prof. radiology and biomed. engring. U. So. Calif., L.A., 1999—, vis. assoc. in bioengring. Calif. Inst. Tech., Pasadena, 2001—; fellow in clin. effectiveness program Sch. Pub. Health Harvard U., 2003. Reviewer study sect. small bus innovative rsch. program NIH, 1989; session chmn. IEEE/EMBS Ann. Conf., Seattle, 1989. Contbr. articles to profl. jours., chapters to books. Recipient Resident Rsch. award, NIH, 1994; grantee, Am. Cancer Soc., The Wright Found. Fellow: Am. Coll. Nuc. Medicine (faculty New Orleans 2000, faculty Tampa 2001, faculty Scottsdale 2002, faculty San Antonio 2003); mem.: IEEE, Soc. for Molecular Imaging, L.A. Radiol. Soc. (faculty 2002), Calif. Med. Assn. (nuc. med. sci. com. 2002—), Computers in Cardiology (local organizing com. 1990), Acad. Molecular Imaging, Soc. Nuc. Medicine (Tetalman Young Investigator award 2000, seed grant award 2000), Radiol. Soc. N.Am. (Resident Rsch. award 1997, seed grant award 2002), Am. Coll. Nuc. Physicians (Resident Rsch. award 1998), Eta Kappa Nu, Sigma Xi, Tau Beta Pi. Achievements include patents for for esophgeal catheters and method and apparatus for detection of posterior ischemia. Home: 1125 Medford Rd Pasadena CA 91107-1703 Office: U So Calif Divsn Nuc Medicine Dept Radiology Keck Sch Medicine 1200 N State St GNH 5250 Los Angeles CA 90033 E-mail: jadvar@usc.edu.

JAEGER, ALVIN A. (AL JAEGER), secretary of state; b. Beulah, N.D., 1943; m. Naomi Berg, 1969 (dec. 1979), m. Kathy Grangaard Anderson, 1986; children: Todd, Stacy, Heidi. Grad., Bismarck State Coll., 1963, Dickinson State U., 1966; postgrad., U. N.D., 1968, Mont. State U., 1970. Tchr. Killdeer High Sch., 1966-69, Kenmare High Sch., 1969-71; with Mobil Oil Corp., 1971-73; real estate broker, 1973-93; sec. of state State of N.D., 1993—. Active Charity Luth. Ch. With N.D. Army N.G. Named Realtor of Yr. Mem. Nat. Assn. Secs. State (exec. com., com. chmn.), Fargo-Moorhead Area Assn. Realtors (mem. coms. edn., profl. stds., bylaws, multiple listing svc.), N.D. Assn. Realtors (past chairperson state bylaws), Bismarck Kiwanis Club. Office: Sec of State Dept 108 600 E Boulevard Ave Bismarck ND 58505-0500

JAEGER, KENNETH JOHN, music educator; b. Rockford, Ill., Nov. 17, 1953; s. Kenneth and Arlene Jesse Jaeger; m. Dana Ann Thomas, Aug. 13, 1977; children: Jillian Marie, Brittany Jean. BMus, Ariz. State U., 1976; MS in Fine Arts, So. Oreg. State Coll., 1995. Cert. tchr. Ariz., 1977, music adjudicator Ariz., 1999. Band dir., tchr. Tolleson Union H.S., Ariz., 1977—91; band dir., tchr., dept. chair Westview H.S., Avondale, Ariz., 1989—. Contbr. Prin. guest condr. City of Glendale, Ariz., 2001; playing mem., band mgr. Summer Band, Glendale, 1996—. Recipient Excellence in Edn. award, Tolleson Union H.S. Dist., 1997. Mem.: Nat. Fedn. of Interscholastic Music Assn., Nat. Assn. for Music Edn., Ariz. Music Educators Assn. (v.p. h.s. activities 1999—2001, pres.-elect 2001—03, pres. 2003—, George C. Wilson Leadership award 2001). Office: Westview High sch 10850 W Garden Lakes Pkwy Avondale AZ 85323

JAEGER, LESLIE GORDON, university administrator; b. Southport, Eng., Jan. 28, 1926; s. Henry M. and Beatrice A. (Highton) J.; m. Annie Sylvia Dyson, Apr. 3, 1948; children: Valerie Ann, Hilary Frances.; m. Kathleen Grant, July 24, 1981. BA, Cambridge U., 1946, MA, 1950; PhD, London U., 1955, DSc, 1986; DEng (hon), Carlton U., 1991, Meml. U., 1994, Tech. U. of N.S., 1995. With W.P. Thompson & Co., Liverpool, Eng., 1948-50, Renold Ltd., Manchester, Eng., 1950-52; mem. faculty Univ. Coll. of Khartoum, 1952-56; Univ. lectr. Cambridge (Eng.) U., 1956-62; prof. civil engring. and applied mechanics McGill U., Montreal, Que., Can., 1962-64, 66-70; Regius prof. engring. U. Edinburgh, Scotland, 1964-66; dean Coll. Engring., U. N.B., Fredericton, 1970-75, acting v.p., 1972-73; acad. v.p. Acadia U., Wolfville, N.S., Can., 1975-80; spl. asst. to pres. Tech. U. N.S., Halifax, 1980-85, v.p. rsch., 1986-93; emeritus rsch. prof. tech. U. N.S., 1993—. Cons. structural engring. Expo '67, Rolls Royce Ltd., Adjeleian & Assos., Ottawa, and others. Author: (with A.W. Hendry) The Analysis of Grid Frameworks and Related Structures, 2nd edit, 1968, Elementary Theory of Elastic Plates, 1962, Cartesian Tensors in Engineering Science, 1964, (with B. Bakht) Bridge Analysis Simplified, 1985, (with B Bakht) Bridge Analysis by Micro Computing, 1988, (with A.A. Mufti and B. Bakht) Bridge Superstructures, New Developments, 1996; contbr. numerous rsch. papers to profl. jours. Mem. Cambridge City Coun., 1961-62; mem. Nat.

Coun. Liberal Party U.K., 1960-62; mem. bd. govs. Magdalene Coll., Cambridge, 1959-62. With Royal Navy, 1945-48. Decorated Order of Can., 2002; recipient Telford premium Instn. Civil Engrs., 1959, Nat. Rsch. Coun. Can. rsch. grantee, 1962-92, A.B. Sanderson award Can. Soc. Civil Engring., 1983; Gzowski medal Engring. Inst. Can., 1985, cert. of merit Indian Insts. of Engrs., 1989, Assoc. Profl. Engrs. N.S. Engring. award, 1992, P.L. Pratley award, 1993, Julian C. Smith medal Engring. Insts. Can., 1996, Nova award Constrn. Innovation Forum, Mich., 2000. Fellow Royal Soc. Edinburgh, Can. Acad. Engring., Engring. Inst. Can., Can. Soc. for Civil Engring. (pres. 1992-93); mem. Mason Club (N.S.). Office: Dalhousie U 1340 Barrington St Halifax NS Canada B3J 1Y9 E-mail: Leslie.Jaeger@ns.sympatico.ca.

JAEGER, MARC JULIUS, physiology educator, researcher; b. Berne, Switzerland, Apr. 4, 1929; came to U.S., 1970; s. Francis K. and Jeanne (Perrin) J.; m. Frances Dick, Dec. 1960 (div. 1972); children: Dominic, Olivia; m. Ina Claire Burlingham-Forbes, June 23, 1973. BA, Gymnasium, Berne, 1948; MD, U. Berne, 1954. Diplomate Swiss Bd. Pulmonary Diseases. Resident, fellow U. Hosp. of Berne, 1954-63; asst. prof. U. Fribourg, Switzerland, 1963-69; assoc. prof. U. Fla. Coll. Medicine, Gainesville, 1970-76, prof., 1976—2000, prof. emeritus, 2000—. Contbr. over 50 articles to profl. jours., including those on the separation of gases and isotopes such as U235 and deuterium. Democrat. Achievements include 6 patents for a Method of Separating Solutes and Gases, for a method to Transport Large Amounts of Heat without Coolant and on ventilation of spaces, filled with granules, which have only one opening; research in mechanics of breathing, deep sea diving, air pollution and its effects on the lungs, smoking and its effects on the lungs. Home: 5915 SW 36th Way Gainesville FL 32608-5150 Office: U Fla Coll Medicine Gainesville FL 32610 E-mail: mjaeger@phys.med.ufl.edu.

JAEGER, PATSY ELAINE, retired secondary education educator, artist; b. Douglas, Ariz., Mar. 18, 1936; d. Thomas Conrad and Cora Maxine Forbes; m. John Walter Jaeger, Aug. 26, 1956 (div. Feb. 1984); children: Sherilee Jaeger Zigan, John Everett. BA in Fine Arts, Chapman U., 1961; MA in Art History, Calif. State U., L.A., 1970; MA in Edn. Adminstrn., San Francisco State U., 1988. Life gen. secondary credential life gen. jr. h.s. spl. secondry credential, spl. secondary art credential, preliminary adminstrv. credential, Calif. Tchr. adult edn. oil painting Novato Unified Sch. Dis., 1973—78; tchr. art, chmn. fine arts dept. Torrance (Calif.) H.S., 1962-71; tchr. art and math., chmn. art dept. San Jose Jr. H.S., Novato, Calif., 1974—79; tchr. art and English, chmn. site coun. Hill Jr. H.S., Novato, 1979-83; tchr. English, San Marin H.S., Novato, 1983-95, leadership tchr., 1995-96, tchr. art, 1996-98; semi-ret., 1998; specialist tobacco use edn. Marin County Office Edn., 2000—03. Chmn. site rev. team Novato Unified Sch. Dist., 1981; specialist tobacco use edn. Marin County Office Edn., 2000-03. Set designer Cavalleria Rusticana, 1981; cover designer Dimensions III, 1987, also contbr. articles. Coord. cmty. vol. program Hill Jr. H.S., 1981-83; mem. Lydia Circle, United Meth. Women, 1999—. Recipient pub. svc. award U.S. Postal Svc., Torrance, 1968, Tchr. of Yr. award Parent-Tchr.-Student Assn. Hill Jr. H.S., 1983, Extra Step award Marin Spl. Edn. Adv. Com., 1996. Mem. Nat. Mus. Women in Arts (charter), Fine Arts Mus. San Francisco. Republican. Avocations: book illustration, painting, gardening, singing. Home: 40 Brown Dr Novato CA 94947-7404

JAEGER, RICHARD CHARLES, electrical engineer, educator, science center director; b. N.Y.C., Sept. 2, 1944; s. O. Fred and Mary Jane (Shatzer) J.; m. Joan Carol Hill, Dec. 28, 1964; children: Peter, Stephanie. BSEE with high honors, M in Elec. Engring., U. Fla., 1966, PhD in Elec. Engring., 1969. Staff engr. IBM Corp., Boca Raton, Fla., 1969—72, adv. engr., 1972-74, 77-79, rsch. staff Yorktown Heights, NY, 1974—76; assoc. prof. Auburn (Ala.) U., 1979—82, prof. elec. engring. dept., 1982—90, alumni prof., 1983—88, disting. prof., 1990—; dir. Ala. Microelectronics Ctr., Auburn, 1984—2000, interim dir. wireless egnring., 2001—. Program com. Internat. Solid State Circuits Conf., San Francisco and N.Y.C., 1978-93, program vice-chmn., 1992, program chmn., 1993; program co-chmn. Internat. VLSI Cirs. Symposium, Kyoto, Japan, 1989, conf. chmn., Honolulu, 1990, exec. comm. chair, 2000—. Author: Introduction to Microelectronic Fabrication, 1988, 2d edit., 2002, Microelectronic Circuit Design, 1997, 2d edit., 2003, Computerized Circuit Analysis Using SPICE Programs, 1997; editor: IEEE Jour. Solid State Cirs., 1995-98; contbr. over 200 articles to profl. jours.; patentee in field. Grantee NSF, Semicondr. Rsch. Corp., Dept. Def., Ala. Rsch. Inst. Fellow IEEE, Solid State Cirs. Coun. IEEE (pres. 1990-91, v.p. 1988-89, sec. 1984-87); mem. Computer Soc. IEEE (bd. govs. 1985-86, Outstanding Contbn. award 1984, Golden Core award 1996), IEEE Solid-State Cirs. Soc. (adcom mem. 1996—, Outstanding Contbn. award 1998, Millenium medal 2000). Home: 711 Jennifer Dr Auburn AL 36830-7116 Office: Auburn U Elec and Computer Engring 200 Broun Hall Auburn AL 36849-5201 E-mail: jaeger@eng.auburn.edu.

JAEGER, ROBERT JOSEPH, medical supplies professional; b. Evanston, Ill., July 24, 1932; s. Robert Joseph and Margaret Ann (Blameuser) J.; m. Carolyn, June 27, 1956; children: Matthew, Mark, David, Robert, Steven. Grad., Alexian Bros. Sch. Nursing, 1953; Cert. phys. therapy, Mayo Clinic, 1955; BSN, DePaul U., 1969, MBA, 1974; grad., Commd. and Gen. Staff Coll., Air War Coll. RN; registered phys. therapist. With Am. Hosp. Supply, Evanston, 1957-61, Aloe Med., St. Louis, 1962-66; salesman Burrows Co., Wheeling, Ill., 1966-95, v.p. product mgmt., 1995—. Pres. Northbrook (Ill.) Civic Found., 1980; bd. dirs. Northbrook Libr., 1979-85; trustee Village of Northbrook, 1985—; past pres. Northbrook Fourth of July Assn.; tchr. St. Norberts Cath. Ch.; coach Northbrook Little League; vol. YMCA, Boy Scouts Am., others. Col. ANC USAR, ret. Mem.: AMSUS, DePaul U. Nursing Alumni Assn. (past pres.), Res. Officers Assn., Am. Legion (life). Republican. Roman Catholic. Home: 1266 Church St Northbrook IL 60062-4502 E-mail: reggiebob@aol.com., bjaeger@burrowsco.com.

JAENEN, CORNELIUS JOHN, history educator, consultant; b. Cannington Manor, Can., Feb. 21, 1927; m. Ina May Turner Jaenen. MA, U. Manitoba, Winnipeg, Can., 1950; BEd, U. Manitoba, Can., 1958; PhD, U. Ottawa, Can., 1963; LLD, U. Winnipeg, Can., 1981. Diplome de fin d'etudes, Bordeaux, France. Housemaster Ravenscourt Sch., Winnipeg, Can., 1949-52; instr. Imperial Ethiopian Govt., Addis Ababa, 1952-55; tchr. City if Winnipeg Schs., 1955-58; asst. prof. Meml. U., St. John's, Can., 1958-59; asst. full prof. United Coll., Winnipeg, Can., 1959-67; prof. U. Ottawa, Can., 1967-92, emeritus prof., 1992—. Founding pres. Canadian Ethnic Studies Assn., 1971-73; pres. French Colonial Hist. Soc., 1986-88, Canadian Hist. Assn., 1988-89; chmn. Ethnic Histories Panel, Sec. of State, Can., 1971-86. Author: Friend and Foe, 1976 (Sainte-Marie prize, 1974), The Role of the Church in New France, 1976, The French Regime in the Upper Country of Canada, 1996' author, editor: Les Franco-Ontariens, 1993 (Legault prize, 1993), The Apostles' Doctrine and Fellowship: A Documentary History, 2003; contbr. chpts. to books and essays to jours. Mem. Manitoba Adv. Com. on Bilingualism, Winnipeg, 1963-65, Canadian Consultative Com. on Multiculturalism, Ottawa, 1973-76, Ontario Coun. on Grad. Studies, Toronto, 1973-76; cons. Canadian Mus. Civilization, Ottawa, 1991-2001, Coun. Hist. Found., 2000—. Decorated officer Order of Leopold II; recipient Ronsard medal Govt. France, 1947, Gold medal in Edn., U. Man., 1958. Fellow Royal Soc. Can. (sec. 1999—, J.B. Tyrrell medal 1994), Order of Leopold II (officer 2000). Home: 9 Elma St Gloucester ON Canada K1T 3W8 Office: Dept History University of Ottawa Ottawa ON Canada K1N 6N5 Fax: (613) 562-5995. E-mail: history@uottawa.ca.

JAFAR, JAFAR JEWAD, neurosurgeon, educator; b. Beirut, June 2, 1949; came to U.S., 1976; s. Jewad and Rahiba (Fakhoury) J.; m. Scheherazade Al-Abed, Oct. 9, 1978; children: Layla, Neda, Nadia. Student, Pahlavi U., Shiraz, Iran, 1967-70, MD, 1976. Diplomate Am. Bd. Neurol. Surgery. Intern Pahlavi U. Hosps., 1975-76; resident in basic surgery U. Chgo. Hosps. and Clinics, 1976-77; resident in neurol. surgery U. Chgo., 1977-82; chief resident in neurol. surgery, hon. asst. house physician The Nat. Hosp. for Nervous Diseases, London, 1980; chief resident in neurol. surgery U. Chgo., 1981-82; asst. prof. neurosurgery U. Ill., Chgo., 1982-87, assoc. prof. neurosurgery, 1988-89, dir. stroke rsch. lab., dept. neurosurgery, 1982-89, dir. cerebral blood flow lab., dept. neurosurgery, 1982-89; assoc. prof. neurosurgery NYU, 1989—2000, prof. neurosurgery, 2000—. Chief neurosurgery svc. Westside VA Med. Ctr., Chgo., 1982—; dir. cerebrovascular surgery NYU, 1989—. Contbr. articles on neurosurgery to profl. jours. Pahlavi U. Sch. Medicine scholar, 1970-75. Mem. Am. Assn. Neurol. Surgeons (cerebrovascular surgery sect.), Congress Neurol. Surgeons, Chgo. Neurol. Soc., Cen. Neurosurg. Soc. Office: NYU Med Ctr 530 1st Ave New York NY 10016-6402 E-mail: jafar.jafar@med.nyu.edu.

JAFEK, BRUCE WILLIAM, otolaryngologist, educator; b. Berwyn, Ill., Mar. 4, 1941; s. Robert William and Viola Mabel (Newstrom) J.; m. Mary Bell Kirkpatrick, Sept. 1, 1962; children: Lynette A., Robert K., Timothy B., Britta C., Kayla E., Kristen M. BS, Coe Coll., 1962; postgrad., U. Omaha, 1962; MD, UCLA, 1966. Instr. dept. otology/laryngology Johns Hopkins Sch. Medicine, Balt., 1971-73; asst. prof. dept. otolaryngology U. Pa. Med. Sch., Phila., 1973-76; prof., dept. chmn. dept. otolaryngology/head and neck surgery U. Colo. Med. Sch., Denver, 1976-98, prof., 1998—. Served with USPHS, 1971-73. Recipient Fowler award Triologic Soc., 1983, Cottle award Am. Rhinol. Soc., 1991. Mem. Triologic Soc. (west region v.p. 1999), Am. Acad. Otolaryngology/Head and Neck Surgery. Republican. Mem. Lds Ch. Office: U Colo Health Sci Ctr 4200 E 9th Ave # B-205 Denver CO 80220-3706 E-mail: bruce.jafek@uchsc.edu.

JAFFA, AYAD A. medical educator, medical researcher; Student, Brunel Tech. Coll., Bristol, Eng., 1975—77; BSc in Biol. Chemistry with honors, U. Essex, Colchester, Eng., 1980, PhD in Biol. Chemistry, 1984. Postdoctoral fellow dept. medicine Med. U. S.C., Charleston, 1984—86, rsch. assoc. dept. medicine, 1986—89, asst. prof. medicine dept. medicine, endocrinology-diabetes-metabolism divsn., 1989—96, asst. prof. pharmacology dept. cell and molecular pharmacology and exptl. therapeutics, 1990—96, mem. grad. faculty, 1991—, assoc. prof. medicine dept. medicine, divsn. endocrinology-diabetes-med. genetics, 1996—, assoc. prof. pharmacology dept. cell and molecular pharmacology and exptl. therapeutics, 1996—. Mem. rsch. com. endocrinology-diabetes-med. genetics divsn. Med. U. S.C., Charleston, 1986—; grant reviewer Med. U. Rsch. Com. VA; vis. prof. Cath. U. of Chile, Santiago, 1996; lectr. in field. Manuscript reviewer: Am. Jour. Physiology, Kidney Internat., Life Scis., Jour. Pharmacology and Exptl. Therapeutics, Diabetes; contbr. articles to profl. jours. Recipient FIRST award, 1995; grantee, Med. U. S.C., 1991—92, 1992—93, 1995—96, VA, 1993—, NIH, 1995—. Mem.: Am. Fedn. Clin. Rsch. (Henry Christian award 1995), Am. Diabetes Assn. (exec. mem. fund raising com. S.C. affiliate 1992—96, bd. dirs. 1995—, Rsch. and Devel. award 1990, John A. Colwell award 1992, Rsch. award 1996). Achievements include research in pathogenesis of diabetic nephropathy, mechanisms of progressive renal disease, renal kallikrein-kinin system, kallikrein and renin gene regulation and expression, growth factors and signal transductio. Office: Med U SC Dept Medicine Divsn Endocrinology 171 Ashley Ave Charleston SC 29425-0001

JAFFE, ALAN STEVEN, lawyer; b. Portland, Maine, Nov. 11, 1939; s. Herman and Rose (Simon) J.; m. Elizabeth L. Reiss, Nov. 3, 1943; children: David, Robert, Richard. BS cum laude, Cornell U., 1961; LLB cum laude, Columbia U., 1964. Bar: N.Y. 1964. Assoc. Poletti, Freiden, Prashker and Gartner, N.Y.C., 1964-65; asst. chief counsel N.Y.C. Anti-Poverty Program, 1965-66; ptnr. Proskauer Rose LLP, N.Y.C., 1966—, chmn., 1999—. Bd. dirs. Lincoln Savs. Bank, N.Y.C., 1984-92. Editor Columbia Law Rev., 1962-64. Bd. dirs., v.p. Coun. Jewish Fedns. N.Am., N.Y.C., 1992-99, Jewish Cmty. Rels. Coun., N.Y., 1987-91; bd. dirs., mem. exec. com. Beth Israel Med. Ctr., 1995—, Am. Jewish Joint Distbn. Com., 1991—; bd. govs. Jewish Agy. for Israel, 1999-2001; pres. Altro Health and Rehab. Svcs., Inc., N.Y.C., 1983-86, pres. UJA Fedn. of N.Y., 1992-95, bd. dirs. 1980—, chmn. bd. domestic affairs, 1988-91; bd. dirs. N.Y.C. Coalition for Homeless, 1995-98; mem. N.Y.C. Sports Devel. Corp., 1995-98; bd. dirs. Am. Jewish Com., 2002—, chmn. Nat. Legal Com., 2002—. Office: Proskauer Rose LLP 1585 Broadway Fl 27 New York NY 10036-8299

JAFFE, ALLAN S. cardiologist, educator; b. July 8, 1944; MD, U. Md., 1973. Inter Washington U. Sch. Medicine, St. Louis, 1973—74, resident, 1974—76, fellow in cardiology, 1976—78, from asst. prof. to prof. medicine, 1978—95; prof., chief cardiovascular divsn. SUNY Health Sci. Ctr., Syracuse, 1995—99; prof. med. Mayo Med. Sch., 1999—. Contbr. over 350 articles to profl. jours. Office: 200 1st St SW Rochester MN 55905-0001 E-mail: jaffe.allan@mayo.edu.

JAFFE, ARTHUR MICHAEL, physicist, mathematician, educator; b. N.Y.C., Dec. 22, 1937; s. Henry and Clarisse Jaffe; m. Nora Frances Crow, July 24, 1971; 1 child, Margaret Collins; m. Sarah Robbins Warren, Sept. 12, 1992. AB, Princeton U., 1959; BA, Cambridge U., 1961; PhD, Princeton U., 1966; MA, Harvard U., 1970. Acting asst. prof. math. Stanford U., 1966-67; asst. prof. physics Harvard U., Cambridge, Mass., 1967-69, assoc. prof., 1969-70, prof. physics, 1970-77, prof. math. physics, 1977-85, Landon T. Clay prof. math. and theoretical sci., 1985—, chmn. dept. math., 1987-90. Rsch. fellow Princeton U., 1965—66, vis. prof. math. physics, 1971; rsch. fellow Stanford Linear Accelerator Ctr., 1966—67; mem. Inst. for Advanced Study, 1967; vis. prof. Eidgenössische Technische Hochschule, Zurich, 1968, Rockefeller U., 1977, U. Rome, 1993, Boston U., 2001; Porter lectr. Rice U., 1982; Hahn lectr. Yale U., 1985; Hendrik lectr. Math. Assn. Am., 1985; mem. pres.'s com. Nat. Medal of Sci., 1997—2002, acting chair, 2001—02; mem. sci. bd. Santa Fe Inst., 1998—; founding mem. and pres. Clay Math. Inst., 1998—2002; bd. dirs. Internat. Math. Olympiad 2001, 1998—, Inst. Schs. of the Future, 2001—. Author: Vortices and Monopoles, 1980, Quantum Physics, 1981, 87, Quantum Field Theory and Statistical Mechanics, Expositions, 1985, Constructive Quantum Field Theory, 1985; assoc. editor Jour. Math. Physics, 1970-72; mem. editl. coun. Annals of Physics, 1975-77, asst. editor, 1977-2002; editor Communications Math. Physics, 1976-2000, chief editor, 1979-2000; mem. adv. bd. Letters in Math. Physics, 1975—; editor Progress in Physics, 1979-86, Selecta Mathematica Sovetica, 1980—, Revs. in Mathematical Physics, 1990; contbr. articles to profl. jours. Alfred P. Sloan Found. fellow, 1968-70; Guggenheim Found. fellow, 1977-78, 92; award Math. and Phys. Scis., N.Y. Acad. Sci., 1979; Dannie Heineman prize for Math. Physics, 1980; NSF fellow, 1961-64; NAS Air Force Office Sci. Rsch. fellow, 1965-67. Fellow AAAS (chair math. section, 2001), Am. Phys. Soc., Am. Acad. Arts and Scis.; mem. U.S. Nat. Acad. Scis., Am. Math. Soc. (exec. com. of coun. 1991-95, pres. 1997-98), Internat. Assn. Math. Physics (pres. 1991-96), Coun. of Scientific Soc. Pres. (chmn. 2000), Joint Policy Bd. for Math. (chair 1998). Home: 27 Lancaster St Cambridge MA 02140-2837 E-mail: jaffe@math.harvard.edu.

JAFFE, BERNARD MICHAEL, surgeon, department chairman; b. N.Y.C. s. Abner I. and Sylvia (Rothman) J.; m. Marlene Lambert, June 4, 1961; children: Mark Allen, Debra Lynn. BA, U. Rochester, 1961; MD, NYU, 1964. Diplomate Am. Bd. Surgery (dir. 1982-88, sr. dir. 1988—, exec. com. 1987-88, rep. to Am. Bd. Med. Specialists 1986-89). Asst. prof. surgery Washington U., St. Louis, 1971-75, asso. prof., 1975-77, prof., 1977-79; prof., chmn. dept. surgery SUNY Health Sci. Ctr at Bklyn., 1979-92, vice-chmn. dept. surgery, chief div. surg. rsch., 1992-2000; prof. surgery Tulane U., New Orleans, 2000—. Author: (with Behrman) Methods of Hormone Radioimmunoassay, 1980; editor in chief Surgical Rounds, 1989—. Served to lt. col. USAF, 1972-74. James IV traveling surg. fellow. Mem. ACS, Assn. Acad. Surgery (pres. 1978-79), Soc. Univ. Surgeons (sec. 1979-82, pres. 1983-84), Am. Surg. Assn., Soc. Clin. Surgery, Surg. Biol. Club I (sec. 1982-85), Am. Soc. Clin. Investigation, Soc. for Surgery Alimentary Tract (pres. 1987-88), So. Surg. Assn., Halsted Soc., Transplant Soc., Soc. for Surg. Oncology, Soc. Exptl. Biology (med. councillor 2002—), Phi Beta Kappa, Alpha Omega Alpha. Office: Tulane Univ Med Ctr 1430 Tulane Ave New Orleans LA 70112-2699

JAFFE, DONALD NOLAN, lawyer; b. East Cleveland, Ohio, Feb. 20, 1938; s. David Baer and Vivian (Kramer) J.; m. Sandra Lois Katz, Aug. 11, 1963; children: Deborah Susan, Charles Edward. AB, Case Western Res. U., 1959, JD, 1961. Bar: Ohio. Law clk. U.S. Ct. Appeals (6th cir.), Cleve., 1962-64; asst. law dir. City of Cleveland Heights, Ohio, 1964-66; trust officer Union Commerce Bank, Cleve., 1966-69; asst. U.S. atty. Dept. Justice, Cleve., 1969-72; sole practice law Cleve., 1972-82; of counsel Persky, Shapiro & Arnoff Co., LPA, Cleve., 1982—. Acting judge Cleveland Heights, Mcpl. Ct., 1972-75, Shaker Heights Mcpl. Ct., Ohio, 1982-94; arbitrator Am. Arbitration Assn., Ohio State Employment Rels. Bd., Cuyahoga County Common Pleas Ct., BBB; hearing officer Ohio Dept. Edn. Author article in field. Councilman City of Cleveland Heights, 1976; mem. Gallon Club, ARC, Cleve., 1978; pres. No. Ohio coun. Am. Jewish Congress, 1972; trustee Jewish Family Svc. Assn. Cleve. With USAR, 1961—74, brig. gen., dep. comdr. Ohio Mil. Res., 1986—. Fellow Ohio State Bar Found.; mem. Ohio State Bar Assn. (coun. of dels. 1984-92, 93—, bd. govs. labor and employment law sect.), Cleve. Bar Assn., Ripcon Club, Tau Epsilon Rho (supreme recorder 1979, pres. Cleve. grad. chpt. 1971), Delta Sigma Rho, Pi Sigma Alpha, Kappa Kappa Psi. Avocations: tennis, swimming, jogging, chess, aerobics. Home: 2 Nantucket Ct Cleveland OH 44122-7535 Office: Persky Shapiro & Arnoff 50 Public Sq 1410 Terminal Tower Cleveland OH 44113 E-mail: djaffelaw@aol.com.

JAFFE, ELAINE SARKIN, pathologist; b. N.Y.C., Aug. 27, 1943; d. David and Mona (Shane) Sarkin; m. Michael Evan Jaffe, July 22, 1967; children: Gregory, Caleb. AB, Cornell U., 1965; MD, U. Pa., 1969. Cert. Am. Bd. Pathology. Intern in pathology Georgetown U. Hosp., 1969; resident anatomic pathology Clin. Ctr. NIH, Bethesda, Md., 1970-72; sr. investigator lab. pathology Nat. Cancer Inst., NIH, Bethesda, Md., 1974-80, chief hematopathology sect. lab. pathology, 1980—, dep. chief lab. pathology, 1982—; chief pathology anatomy dept., clin. ctr. NIH, Bethesda, 1982—. Med. dir. USPHS, 1970—2000. Assoc. editor: Cancer Rsch.; mem. editl. bd. Am. Jour. Pathology, Blood; mem. editl. bd.: Clin. Lymphoma; Am. Jour. Surg. Pathology; editor: Surgical Pathology of the Lymph Nodes and Related Organs, 1984, 2d edit., 1996, WHO Classification of Hematopoietic and Lymphoid Neoplasms, 2001; contbr. articles to New Eng. Jour. Medicine, Blood. Decorated Commendation medal, Meritorious Svc. medal, Outstanding Svc. medal; recipient Fred W. Stewart award, Meml. Sloan Kettering Cancer Ctr., 2002. Mem. Am. Soc. Hematology (exec. coun. 1988-91), U.S.-Can. Acad. Pathology (pres. 1998-99), Am. Soc. Investigative Pathology (Meritorious awards), Soc. for Hematopathology (adv. bd.). Office: NCI NIH Lab of Pathology 10 Center Dr MSC-1500 Bethesda MD 20892-1500

JAFFE, ERIC ALLEN, physician, educator, researcher; b. N.Y.C., Apr. 7, 1942; s. Robert Irving and Ruth (Stern) J.; m. Barbara Ruth Little, Feb. 25, 1971; children: Matthew, Alison. Student, Cornell U., 1959-62; MD, SUNY, Bklyn., 1966. Intern then resident Kings County Hosp., Bklyn., 1966-68; resident N.Y. Hosp., N.Y.C., 1968-70, fellow divsn. hematology, 1970-72; instr. medicine Cornell U. Med. Coll., N.Y.C., 1972-73, asst. prof., 1973-77, assoc. prof., 1977-82, prof., 1982-96, adj. prof., 1996—; chmn. dept. of medicine Interfaith Med. Ctr., 1996—; prof. medicine SUNY Downstate Med. Ctr., Bklyn., 1997—. Editor: The Biology of Endothelial Cells, 1984. Recipient Young Scientist award Passano Found., Balt., 1977. Mem. Am. Soc. Clin. Investigation, Assn. Am. Physicians. Achievements include development of method of culturing endothelial cells. Office: Dept Medicine Interfaith Med Ctr 1545 Atlantic Ave Brooklyn NY 11213 E-mail: ejaffe@interfaithmedical.com.

JAFFÉ, ERNST RICHARD, medical educator and administrator; b. Chgo., Jan. 4, 1925; s. Richard Hermann and Berta (Kohn) J.; m. Anne Jane Sylvestre, Aug. 5, 1950; children: Stephanie Anne Green, Richard Sheridan Jaffé. BS, U. Chgo., 1945, MD, MS in Pathology, U. Chgo., 1948; DHL (hon.), Yeshiva U., 1987. Diplomate Am. Bd. Internal Medicine, Hematology, Nat. Bd. Med. Examiners; lic. physician, N.Y. Intern Med. Presbyn. Hosp., N.Y.C., 1948-50, resident, 1953-55; postdoctoral fellow Albert Einstein Coll. of Medicine, Bronx, NY, 1955-57, instr., asst. prof., 1957-62, assoc. prof., 1962-69, prof. medicine, 1969-84, acting dean, 1972-74, 83-84, sr. assoc. dean, 1974-83, 84-91, disting. univ. prof. medicine, 1984-92, disting. univ. prof. medicine emeritus, 1992—. Mem. hematology study sect. Nat. Inst. Health, Bethesda, Md., 1972-82, Hirschl Sci. Adv. Com. I.T. Hirschl Trust, N.Y.C., 1974-92, N.Y. Community Trust Blood Disease Panel, N.Y.C., 1978-97; dir. Belfer Inst. for Advanced Biomed. Studies, 1978-92. Co-editor Seminars in Hematology, 1968-2000, co-editor emeritus, 2000—; editor-in-chief Blood, 1975-77; contbr. articles to profl. jours. Nat. bd. govs. ARC, Washington, 1984-90, chmn. blood svcs. com., 1988-90; bd. dirs. Nat. Marrow Donor Program, 1987-2000; bd. dirs. Henry M. and Lillian Stratton Found., 1985-96, pres., 1989-96; trustee Bergen Cmty. Regional Blood Ctr., 1997-2000 . With U.S. Army, 1944-46; capt. USAF, 1951-53. Named Career Scientist, Health Rsch. Coun.; recipient Charles R. Drew award ARC, 1990. Fellow Internat. Soc. Hematology (counselor 1980-88, v.p. 1984-88, historian 1990—); mem. Am. Soc. Hematology (pres. 1983, historian 1993—, Outstanding Svc. award 1998), Assn. Am. Physicians, Am. Fedn. Clin. Rsch., Am. Soc. Clin. Investigation, Am. Physiol. Soc., Assn. Am. Med. Colls. (emeritus), Coun. Acad. Socs. (adminstrv. bd. 1985-90, chmn. 1989), N.Y. Soc. Study Blood (pres. 1978-80), Soc. for Exptl. Biology and Medicine (pres. 1993-95, past pres. 1995-97), U. Chgo. Alumni Assn. (Profl. Achievement citation 1992), U. Chgo. Med. Alumni Assn. (Disting. Svc. award 1981), Phi Beta Kappa, Sigma Xi, Alpha Omega Alpha. Lutheran. Avocations: philately, photography, reading. Office: Albert Einstein Coll Medicine 1300 Morris Park Ave Bronx NY 10461-1926 E-mail: ejaffe@pol.net. *Nothing is more satisfying than to have done a good job and to have earned the affection of your colleagues. However, wife and children are paramount!!*

JAFFE, EVAN, rabbi; b. Balt., Jan. 3, 1953; s. Marvin and Carolyn J.; m. Phyllis Lerner, June 6, 1982; children: Jordana Tatiana, Atara. BA, Columbia U., 1982; MA, Jewish Theol. Sem. Am., N.Y.C., 1987; postgrad., U. Pa., 2002. Ordained rabbi, 1987. Rabbi Flemington (N.J.) Jewish Cmty. Ctr., 1987—. Chaplain Hunterdon Devel. Ctr., Clinton, N.J., 1990—, Greenbrook (N.J.) Regional Ctr., 1992—, Edna Mahon Correctional Ctr., Clinton, 1998—, Hagedorn Geriatric Ctr., Glen Gardner, N.J., 1990-96; pres. Women's Crisis Svcs., Flemington, 1994-95, hon. bd. mem.; bd. dirs. Jewish Family Svcs., Somerville, N.J., 1996—; pres. Hebrew Free Loan Assn. of Somerset, Hunterdon and Warren Counties, NJ, 1994--; v.p. Open Rd., 1999--. Author: Illustrated Dictionary of Ballet, 1980. Avocations: jogging, playing recorder, skiing. Home: 51 Coppermine Vlg Flemington NJ 08822-1570 E-mail: fjcc@blast.net.

JAFFE, F. FILMORE, lawyer, retired judge; b. Chgo., May 4, 1918; s. Jacob Isadore and Goldie (Rabinowitz) J.; m. Mary Main, Nov. 7, 1942; children: Jo Anne, Jay. Student, Southwestern U., 1936-39; JD, Pacific Coast U., 1940. Bar: Calif. 1945, U.S. Supreme Ct. 1964. Practiced law, Los Angeles, 1945-91; ptnr. Bernard & Jaffe, Los Angeles, 1947-74, Jaffe & Jaffe, Los Angeles, 1975-91; apptd. referee Superior Ct. of Los Angeles County, 1991-97, apptd. judge pro tem, 1991-97; ret., 1997; atty. in pvt. practice, 1997—. Mem. L.A. Traffic Commn., 1947-48; arbitrator Am. Arbitration Assn., 1968-91; chmn. pro bono com. Superior Ct. Calif., County of Los Angeles, 1980-86; lectr. on paternity; chair family law indigent paternity panel L.A. County Supr. Ct., 2001—. Served to capt. inf. AUS, 1942-45. Decorated Purple Heart, Croix de Guerre with Silver Star, Bronze Star with oak leaf cluster; honored Human Rights Commn. Los Angeles, Los Angeles County Bd. Suprs.; recipient Pro Bono award State Bar Calif., commendation State Bar Calif., 1983. Mem. ABA, Los Angeles County Bar (honored by family law sect. 1983), Los Angeles Criminal Ct. Bar Assn. (charter mem.), U.S. Supreme Ct. Bar Assn., Masons, Shriners Office: 433 N Camden Dr Ste 400 Beverly Hills CA 90210-4408 E-mail: filmorejaffe@earthlink.net.

JAFFE, HAROLD W. federal agency administrator; b. Newton, Mass. AB, U. Calif., Berkeley; MD, UCLA. Clin. rsch. investigator, venereal disease control program CDC, Atlanta, epidemic intelligence svc. officer, chief, AIDS epidemiology program, deputy dir. for sci., HIV/AIDS program, dir. AIDS/HIV program, head, HIV, STD and TB lab., acting dir., Nat. Ctr. for HIV, STD and TB prevention, 2001—. Office: 1600 Clifton Rd NE E07 Atlanta GA 30333

JAFFE, HERB, retired newspaper editor, columnist; b. Newark, Oct. 12, 1932; s. Frank and Adele (Weiner) J.; m. Francine Lozowick, Mar. 30, 1958; children: Steven, Michael. BA in History, Rutgers U., 1954; LLD (hon.), Seton Hall U., 1990. Reporter Newark Star-Ledger, 1954-64, night city editor, 1964-67, legal affairs and investigative writer, 1967-88, op-edit. columnist, 1973-95, legal affairs editor, 1988-95; mem. civil justice reform act adv. com. U.S. Dist. Ct. N.J., 1994-95. Adj. asst. prof. journalism NYU, N.Y.C., 1969-74; TV news commentator Sta. WWOR, Channel 9, Secaucus, N.J., 1976-84; mem. N.J. Supreme Ct. Media Rels. Com., Trenton, N.J., 1978-95. Author: Pro Bono Law, 1972 (ABA Cert. Merit award), Liability Crisis, 1987 (ABA Cert. Merit award). With U.S. Army, 1954-55. Recipient Journalism award N.J. State Bar Assn., 1971-78, Scripps-Howard Found. Journalism award, 1974, Nat. Gold Bell award Am. Mental Health Assn., 1975; inductee Rutgers U. Hall of Disting. Alumni, 1991. Mem. N.J. Press Assn. (1st place award for enterprise reporting 1981, 1st place award for investigative reporting 1983), N.J. Alliance for Action (Achievement award 1989), B'nai B'rith (Man of Yr. award Linden N.J. chpt. 1984). Jewish. Avocations: golf, hiking, swimming. Home: 10713 Dover Creek Ave Las Vegas NV 89134-5250

JAFFE, HOWARD LAWRENCE, rabbi; b. N.Y.C., Nov. 7, 1955; s. Nathaniel Herbert and Eleanor Georgine (Arkow) J. BA, CUNY, 1978; MA in Hebrew Lit., Hebrew Union Coll.-Jewish Inst. Religion, 1981. Ordained rabb. 1983. Asst. rabbi Temple Israel, Mpls., 1983-85, assoc. rabbi, 1985-88; rabbi Mountain Jewish Comty. Ctr., Warren, NJ, 1988—2000, Temple Har Shalom (formerly Mountain Jewish Comty. Ctr.). Chmn. Watchung Hills Ministry Assn., Warren, 1988—90; chmn. privilege card com. Union Am. Hebrew Congregation, 1989—93; trustee United Israel Appeal, N.Y.C., 1989—91; sr. rabbi Temple Isaiah, Lexington, Mass.; vice-chair Union Am. Hebrew Congregation Commn. on Outreach and Syngogue Cmty. Vice-chair UAHC Jr. and Sr. youth com.; mem. N.Am. bd. WUPJ; co-chair UAHC-CCAR Commn. on Synagogue Affiliation; Bd. dirs. Jewish Family Svcs., Sommerville, 1990, Somerset Coun. Alcoholism, Sommerville, NJ, 1990. Mem. Ctrl. Conf. Am. Rabbs, NJ Assn. Reform Rabbis (pres.), co-chair Lexington Intrfaith Clergy Assn. Office: Temple Isaiah 55 Lincoln St Lexington MA 02421 E-mail: rabbijaffe@templeisaiah.net.

JAFFE, ISRAELI ARRON, internist, rheumatologist, educator; b. N.Y.C., Dec. 21, 1927; s. Max and Esther Jaffe; m. Judith Snyder; children: Naomi, Audrey, Caroline. BA, NYU, 1947; MD, Columbia U., 1950. Diplomate Am. Bd. Internal Medicine 1974, Am. Bd. Rheumatology. Intern Presbyn. Hosp., 1950—52; resident NIH, Bethesda, Md., 1952—54; instr. medicine Georgetown U., Washington, 1953—55; from assoc. prof. to prof. medicine N.Y. Med. Coll., 1960—78; prof. clin. medicine Columbia U., N.Y.C., 1978—. Surgeon USPHS, 1953—2000. Fellow: Am. Coll. Physicians; mem.: Am. Coll. Rheumatology (master). Republican. Jewish. Achievements include discovery of d.penicillamine treatment for rheumatoid arthritis. Home: 130 E End Ave New York NY 10008 Office: 161 Fort Washington Ave New York NY 10022

JAFFE, JEFF HUGH, retired food products executive; b. Washington, Dec. 25, 1920; s. Henry A. Jaffe and Mildred (Loewenberg) Auslander; m. Natalie Rubin, Dec. 31, 1945; children: Bonita Jaffe Berens, Holly Anne. BS in Archtl. Engring., Va. Poly. Inst. and State U., 1943. Chmn. bd. dirs., pres. The Chunky Corp. (now Ward Candy, Inc.), 1950-69; pres., CEO candy, chocolate and biscuit group Ward Foods Inc., 1969-71, pres., COO, 1971-72; also bd. dirs. Ward Foods, Inc., 1972-74; chmn. bd. dirs., pres. Schutter Candy Co., 1958-67, Klotz Confection Co., 1960-67; pres., CEO The Schrafft Candy Co., 1974-78; v.p. consumer products group Gulf and Western Industries, 1974-78; pres., CEO Bernan Foods, Inc., 1980-85, ret., 1985. Bd. dirs. Cmty. Nat. Bank of S.I., N.Y., Ward Foods, Inc., Ward Candy Co., Oxford Energy Co.; guest lectr. Harvard Bus. Sch., 1970-84. Bd. dirs., nat. treas. Young Pres.'s Orgn., Woodmere Acad., Martin County (Fla.) Libr. Found.; bd. dirs. Village Hewlett Bay Park. Mem. Assn. Mfrs. of Confectionery and Chocolate (past chmn.), Candy Execs. Club, Property Owners Assn. (Sailfish Point, Fla., pres., chmn. transition com., chmn. emeritus, CEO). Home: 6500 SE Harbor Cir Stuart FL 34996-1952

JAFFE, KATHARINE WEISMAN, retired librarian; b. Cambridge, Mass., Apr. 27, 1927; d. Maurice and Esther (Feinberg) W.; m. Myron I. Jaffe, Dec. 18, 1949; children: Stephen Philip, Jane Elizabeth J. Martin, Samuel Morris. AB in Am. Civilization, Colby Coll., 1948, MS in Libr. Sci., Simmons Coll., 1952. Asst. children's libr. Boston Pub. Libr., 1948-51; libr. Mishkan Tefila Synagogue, Newton, Mass., 1955-58, Temple Emmanuel, Newton, 1958-59; reserve libr. Brandeis U., Waltham, Mass., 1960-62; reference libr., archives libr., rare books libr. Boston Coll., 1963-75; vol. libr. and archives libr. Berkshire Hist. Soc., Pittsfield, Mass., 1994-96; chairperson Friends of Libr., New Marlborough, Mass., 1978-94. Libr. rep. to design referenc and Atrium New Libr. Boston Coll., 1973-75; founding chair bookstore Brandeis Women's Com., Noami Lodge, 1950-75; book group leader, organizer, 1955-75; voter edn. chair South and Ctrl. Berkshire chpt. LWV, 1994-96, 97-2001, pres. 1996-97, mem. governing bd.; docent Edith Wharton Home, Mount Lenox, 1988-92; class sec. Colby '48, 1993-98, class agt., 2000—; assoc. editor New Marlborough Hist. Soc. Pictorial Hist. New Marlborough, 2001, sec. New Marlborough Hist. Soc., 2002—; co-v.p., 2002—; founder Knowledgable Voter Participation acad. rsch/comms. voter enhancement project, 2003—. Jewish. Avocations: reading mysteries and U.S. and international politics, travel. Home: PO Box 113 Mill River MA 01244

JAFFE, LOUISE, English language educator, creative writer; b. Bronx, NY, May 17, 1936; d. Joseph and Anna (Movitz) Neuwirth; m. Steven Jaffe, Aug. 26, 1962 (div. 1975); 1 child, Aaron Lawrence; m. Leo Gerber, 1993. BA, Queens Coll., 1956; MA, Hunter Coll., 1959; PhD, U. Nebr., 1965; MFA, Bklyn. Coll., 1991. From instr. to prof. English Kingsborough C.C., Bklyn., 1965-95, prof. emerita, 1995—. Author: Hyacinths and Biscuits, 1985, Wisdom Revisited, 1987, Light Breaks, 1995, The Great Horned Owl's Proclamation and Other Hoots, 1997; author numerous poems and fiction stories; mem. editl. bd. Cmty. Review CUNY, 1984—. Recipient First prize N.Y. Poetry Forum, 1980, First prize, First honorable mention Shelley Soc. N.Y., 1983-84, others. Mem.: Am. Mensa. Democrat. Jewish. Avocations: creative writing, scrabble, crossword puzzles., people watching, poetry. Home: 2411 E 3rd St Brooklyn NY 11223-5357 Office: Kingsborough Cmty Coll Oriental Blvd Brooklyn NY 11235-4906 E-mail: athena9x@aol.com.

JAFFE, MARCIA WEISSMAN, elementary education educator; b. Bklyn., June 23, 1934; d. Adolph and Marigold (Bush) Weissman; m. Stanley Jaffe, Nov. 23, 1957; children: David, Andrew, Steven. BA, Bklyn. Coll., 1956; MA, John Carroll U., 1977. Tchr. 3d grade E. Meadow (N.Y.) Sch. Dist.; 6th grade tchr., race rels. advisor Shaker Heights (Ohio) Bd. Edn. Founder, adviser student group race rels. S.G.O.R.R, 1983—. Recipient Gov.'s award, Nat. Sch. Bd., Martin Luther King award City of Shaker Heights. Address: 2729 Rochester Rd Cleveland OH 44122-2166

JAFFE, MARK M. lawyer; b. Paterson, N.J., Sept. 18, 1941; s. Irving and Bertha (Margolis) J.; m. June A. Fisher, June 19, 1977. BS in Econs., U. Pa., 1962; JD, Columbia U., 1985. Bar: N.J. 1965, La. 1968, N.Y. 1970, U.S. Dist. Ct. (ea. dist.) N.Y., U.S. Ct. Mil. Appeals, U.S. Ct. Appeals (2d and 5th cirs.), U.S. Dist. Ct. N.J., U.S. Supreme Ct. Assoc. Hill, Betts & Nash, LLP, N.Y.C., 1969-72; ptnr. Hill, Betts & Nash, N.Y.C., 1972—. Lt. USCGR, 1965-68. Mem. ABA, N.J. Bar Assn., La. Bar Assn., Assn. of Bar of City of N.Y., Am. Judicature Soc., Maritime Law Soc. Home: 377 Rector Pl New York NY 10280-1432 Office: Hill Betts & Nash 99 Park Ave New York NY 10016

JAFFE, MARVIN EUGENE, pharmaceutical company executive, neurologist; b. Phila., July 16, 1936; s. William Reuben and Ida Dorothy (Weiner) U.; m. Joan Sheila Fineman; children: Jonathan, Matthew, Ondria, Joshua. BS, Temple U., 1956; MD, Jefferson U., 1960. Diplomate Am. Bd. Psychiatry and Neurology. Intern Womack Army Hosp., Ft. Bragg, N.C., 1960-61; resident Jefferson Med. Coll., Phila., 1964-67; neurologist Phila. Gen. Hosp., 1967-70, rsch. physician Merck Sharp & Dohme Rsch. Labs., West Point, Pa., 1970-78, v.p., 1978-87, sr. v.p., 1987-88; pres. R.W. Johnson Pharm. Rsch. Inst., 1988-94; assoc. prof. Jefferson Med. Coll., Phila., 1982—98. Med. adv. Wilson's Disease Adv. Bd., N.Y.C., 1984-98; bd. dirs. Royal Soc. Medicine Found., 1990—, v.p. 1992-95, pres., 1995-98; bd. dirs. Celltech Group P.L.C., Vernalis Group, P.L.C., Immunomedics, Inc., Allos Therapeutics; mem. vis. com. Whitaker Coll., MIT, 1997-2002. Contbr. articles to profl. jours. Capt. U.S. Army, 1960-64, Germany. Fellow Am. Acad. Neurology, Am. Heart Assn. (stroke coun.); mem. Alpers Soc. for Clin. Neurology (sec., treas. 1982-88), Pharm. Mfrs. Assn. (steering com. 1983-94, chmn. 1993-94), Am. Physician's Fellowship (nat. dir. 1980—).

JAFFE, MELVIN, securities company executive; b. N.Y.C., May 20, 1919; s. Benjamin and Zelda (Karp) J.; m. Muriel Hamptman, June 9, 1941 (dec. Mar. 1984); children: Marcy, Meredith; m. Suzanne MacMillan, Jan. 20, 1985; children: Cynthia Johnson, Katie Marsico. BS in Edn., Bucknell U., 1940. Pres. Benjamin jaffe & Son Inc., Bklyn., 1946-68; sr. v.p. investments Morgan Stanley Dean Witter Reynolds, Garden City, NY, 1969—. Pres. Lions Internat., Blkyn., 1965. Staff sgt. U.S. Army, 1942-45, ETO. Mem. Am. Legion (Post 304), Masons. Jewish. Home: 374 Golfview Rd Ste 505C North Palm Beach FL 33408 Home (Summer): Apt 505 374 Golfview Rd North Palm Beach FL 33408-3566

JAFFE, MORRIS EDWARD, insurance executive; b. Bklyn., Apr. 23, 1947; s. Eugene Netter and Sabina (Sensor) J.; m. Laurie F. Lucas, Feb. 14, 1986; children by previous marriage: Shelley Lynne Jaffe Venincasa, James Edward. Student, U. Miami, Fla., 1965-67; BS in Math., U. Md., 1970. CLU, ChFC, CFP (investment advisor rep., resident ins. advisor), LUTC. Sales, ops. mgr. Levitz Furniture, Rockville, Md., 1972-75; agt. and sales mgr. Metro. Life Ins. Co., Camp Springs, Md., 1975-86; ptnr., ind. ins. agt. Price, Williams, Jaffe & Assocs., Brandywine, Md., 1986-88; ind. ins. agt. So. Md. Ins. Agy., Brandywine, Md., 1988-96; propr. Jaffe Assocs., Brandywine, 1996—. Mem. pres.'s conf. Metro. Life, Camp Springs, Md., 1977, leader's conf., 1975, 76, 78, 80, pres.'s adv. coun., 1978. Treas., v.p. Gwynn Park High Sch. Parent-Tchr.-Student Assn., Brandywine, 1987-92; mem. Prince Georges Mental Health Assn., Largo, Md., 1988-91, 96—; mem. Regional Inst. for Children and Adolescents-So. Md. Citizens Adv. Bd., Cheltenham, 1988-2002, chmn., 1989-96; mem., treas. Friends of RICA, Cheltenham, 1988—; sponsor Boy Scouts Am. Mem.: Life Underwriters PAC (state treas. 1987—90), Soc. Fin. Svc. Profls., Nat. Assn. Ins. and Fin. Advisers of Prince Georges (dir. 1977—99, sec. 1981—82, treas. 1982—85, pres. 1985—86, state committeeman 1986—99, Agt. of Yr. 1984), Nat. Assn. Ins. and Fin. Advisors of Md. (dir. 1985—, sec./treas. 1999—2000, v.p. 2000—01, pres.-elect 2001—02, pres. 2002—03, immediate past pres. 2003—, named Outstanding Local Pres. 1986, elected to Hall of Fame 1997), Nat. Assn. Ins. and Fin. Advisors (voting del. to nat. coun. 1986, 2002). Office: Jaffe Assocs PO Box 230 Brandywine MD 20613-0230 E-mail: ed.jaffe@verizon.net.

JAFFE, MURRAY SHERWOOD, retired surgeon; b. Sept. 29, 1926; s. Lester A. and Rosa (Shor) J.; m. Margery Blum, Mar. 26, 1951; children— Emily, Margaret, Dan BS, MD, U. Cin., 1948. Diplomate Am. Bd. Surgery. Intern Barnes Hosp., St. Louis, 1948-49; resident Cin. Gen. Hosp., 1949-50, 52-56, Cin. VA Hosp., 1949-50, 52-56, Dayton VA Hosp., Ohio, 1949-50, 52-56; practice medicine specializing in surgery Cin., 1958-98; asst. chief surgery VA Hosp., Cin., 1958-82; pres. med. staff Jewish Hosp., Cin., 1978-80; pres. Medco Peer Rev., 1981-84; retired surgeon, 1996; assoc. clin. prof. surgery emeritus U. Cin. Pres. Ohio div. Am. Cancer Soc., 1970-71. Served with USN, 1945, 50-52 Mem. ACS, Cin. Surg. Soc., U. Cin. Grad. Surg. Soc., Shriners, Phi Beta Kappa, Alpha Omega Alpha Republican. Jewish. Home: 56 Tradd St Charleston SC 29401-2540 E-mail: jaffems@dycon.com.

JAFFE, ROBERT BENTON, obstetrician, gynecologist, reproductive endocrinologist; b. Detroit, Feb. 18, 1933; s. Jacob and Shirley (Robins) J.; m. Evelyn Grossman, Aug. 29, 1954; children: Glenn, Terri. MS, U. Colo., 1966; MD, U. Mich., 1957. Intern U. Colo. Med. Ctr., Denver, 1957-58, resident, 1959-63; asst. prof. Ob-Gyn. U. Mich. Med. Ctr., 1964-68, assoc. prof., 1968-72, prof., 1972-74, dir. steroid rsch. unit, 1964-74; prof. U. Calif., San Francisco, 1974—, chmn. dept. ob-gyn and reproductive scis., 1974-96, dir. reproductive endocrinology ctr., ctr. reproductive scis., 1977-2000. Mem. nat. adv. council, mem. human embryology and devel. and reproductive biology study sect. Nat. Inst. Child Health and Human Devel.; bd. dirs. Population Resource Center. Author: Reproductive Endocrinology: Physiology, Pathophysiology and Clinical Management, 1978, 4th edit., 1999, Prolactin, 1981, The Peripartal Period, 1985; contbr. numerous articles to profl. jours.; mem. editorial bd. Jour. Clin. Endocrinology and Metabolism, 1971-75, Fertility and Sterility, 1972-78; editor-in-chief Obstetric and Gynecologic Survey, 1991—. Josiah Macy Found. faculty fellow, 1967 70, 81; USPHS postdoctoral fellow, 1958-59, 63-64; Rockefeller Found. grantee, 1974-78 ; Andrew Mellon Found. grantee, 1978-81 Mem. Endocrine Soc. (coun. 1985-86, sec.-treas. 1994-99), Soc. Gynecologic Investigation (pres. 1975-76, Pres.'s Disting. Scientist award 1993, Pres.'s Mentorship award 2000), Perinatal Rsch. Soc. (pres. 1973-74), Am. Coll. Obstetricians and Gynecologists (awards), Assn. Am. Physicians, Inst. Medicine Nat. Acad. Scis., Royal Coll. Obstetricians and Gynaecologists, The Hormone Found. (pres. 1999—). Democrat. Jewish. Home: 90 Mt Tiburon Rd Belvedere Tiburon CA 94920-1512 Office: U Calif Med Sch OB Gyn & Reproductive Sci San Francisco CA 94143-0556

JAFFE, ROBERT STANLEY, lawyer; b. Walla Walla, Wash., May 16, 1946; BA, U. Wash., 1968, JD, 1972. Bar: Wash. 1972. Ptnr. Preston Gates & Ellis, L.L.P., Seattle, 1986—. Mem. ABA (mem. corp., banking and bus. law sect., mem. small bus. com. 1982-92), Order of Coif. Office: Preston Gates & Ellis LLP Bank Am Tower 701 5th Ave Ste 5000 Seattle WA 98104-7078

JAFFE, RUSSELL MERRITT, pathologist, research director; b. Albany, N.Y., Jan. 1, 1947; AB cum laude, MD with honors, PhD in Biochemistry, Boston U., 1972. Diplomate Am. Bd. Pathology (clin., chem.), Nat. Bd. Med. Examiners. Med. intern Boston U. Med. Ctr., 1972-73; resident in clin. pathology NIH, Bethesda, Md., 1973-75, sr. staff physician clin. pathology dept., 1973-79, chief resident tng. program clin. chemistry sect., 1976-79; fellow health rsch., practice, policy devel. Health Studies Collegium, 1979—; dir. ELISA/ACT Biotech., Sterling, Va., 1987—, Princeton BioCenter, 1989-92. Prin. faculty Oriental Med. Strategy in Western Med. Practice, HSC, N.Y.C., 1980-85. Assoc. editor The New Physician, 1971-72, sr. assoc. editor, 1972-73. Bd. govs. Light Found., 1980-99. Comdr. USPHS, 1973-79. Recipient Nat. Rsch. award Am. Acad. Med. Preventics, 1979, J.D. Lane award USPHS, 1975, Excellence in Rsch. award Mead Johnson, 1969, Man of Yr. award Hillel Found., 1967. Fellow Am. Coll. Nutrition, Am. In-Vitro Allergy/Immunology Soc., Am. Soc. Clin. Pathologists; mem. APHA, Am. Assn. Clin. Chemists. Achievements include patent in field. Home: 300 Amwell Rd Hopewell NJ 08525-3116 Office: ELISA/ACT Biotech 14 Pidgeon Hill Dr Ste 300 Sterling VA 20165-6133

JAFFE, SIGMUND, chemist, educator; b. New Haven, Mar. 1, 1921; s. Morris and Rose (Blosveren) J.; m. Elaine Leventhal, Aug. 25, 1946; children—Matthew Lee, Paul Jonathan. AB with high distinction in Chemistry, Wesleyan U., Middletown, Conn., 1949; PhD, Iowa State U., 1953. Research in rare earths Ames (Iowa) Lab., 1949-53; research in carbides, metal and high temperature inorganic reactions, research labs. Air Reduction Corp., 1953-58; prof. chemistry Calif. State U. at Los Angeles, 1958-86, prof. emeritus, 1986—, chmn. dept., 1958-64, part-time prof., 1986—. Vis. prof. Queen Mary Coll., U. London, 1978-79; Research solid propellant fuel systems, 1958-60; photochemistry and gas phase kinetics Jet Propulsion Lab., Calif. Inst. Tech., Pasadena, Calif., 1960-64; NIH fellow Wiezmann Inst. Sci., Israel, 1964-65, vis. prof., 1971-72 Contbr. articles to profl. jours. Served with USNR, 1942-46. Named Outstanding prof. Calif. State U. at Los Angeles, 1973-74 Mem. Am. Chem. Soc., Sigma Xi, Phi Beta Kappa, Phi Lambda Upsilon, Phi Kappa Phi. Home: 14107 Village 14 Camarillo CA 93012-7013 Office: Calif State U Dept Chemistry Los Angeles CA 90032

JAFFE, STEVEN ALAN, real estate investor and management executive; b. Boston, Feb. 21, 1948; s. Barney and Beatrice Lillian Jaffe; m. Barbara Stein, Apr. 15 1973; children: Melissa Beth, Amanda Lauren, Samantha Joanna. BA, U. Wis., 1970, postgrad., 1971-72; JD, Bklyn. Law Sch., 1975. Bar: N.Y. 1976. Exec. v.p. S/A Assocs., Garden City, N.Y., 1977-88, Winstar Inc., N.Y.C., 1989-91; pres. The Eastern Way, Ltd., Tucson, 1989—, The New Group, Ltd., Tucson, 1990—, The New Group (Ariz.) Ltd., 1991—. Judge entrepreneurship competition U. Ariz. Sch. Bus., Tucson, 1994, 95. Mem. Pima County Rsch. Real Estate Coun., Roosevelt Rough Riders. Avocation: horseback trail riding. Home: 3730 E Sumo Septimo Tucson AZ 85718 Office: The Eastern Way Ltd 1810 E Blackridge #312 Tucson AZ 85719

JAFFEE, ANNETTE WILLIAMS, novelist; b. Abilene, Tex., Jan. 10, 1945; d. Jules Henry and Evelyn June (Witensky) Williams; m. Dwight M. Jaffee, Aug. 16, 1964 (div. May 1991); children: Jonathan, Elizabeth. BS, Boston U., 1966. Author: Adult Education, 1981, Recent History, 1988, The Dangerous Age, 1998. N.J. Arts Coun. grantee State of N.J., 1985 86, Geraldine Dodge fellow Yaddo, 1991. Mem. PEN.

JAFFEE, KAY, musician, musicologist; b. Lansing, Mich., Dec. 31, 1937; d. Fred Hodgson and Mary Beulah (Rabuck) Cross; m. Michael Jaffee, July 24, 1961. BA, U. Mich., 1959; MA, NYU, 1965, PhD, 2001. Assoc. dir., founding mem. The Waverly Consort, N.Y.C., 1964—. Mem. adv. bd. Jour. Musicology, 1982-2001. Debut Carnegie Recital Hall, 1966; performer on Renaissance wind and keyboard instruments, harps, psalteries, and percussion instruments; tours include N.Am., 1967—, also Gt. Britain and L.Am.; appeared at Casals Festival, 1981, 83, Madeira Bach Festival, 1981, Hong Kong Festival, 1988, Caramoor Festival, also TV appearances; 14 recs. with Waverly Consort for CBS Masterworks, Angel/EMI and WAVE Records; contbr. articles and revs. to profl. jours. Recipient Disting. Alumni award NYU Grad. Sch. Arts and Sci., 1990, Howard Mayor Brown award Early Music Am., 2000, Am. Eagle award Nat. Music Coun., 2003. Mem. Am. Musicological Soc. Home: PO Box 386 Patterson NY 12563-0386

JAFFE-NOTIER, PETER ANDREW, secondary education educator; b. Holland, Mich., Apr. 9, 1947; s. M. Robert and Ann Jean (Jackson) Notier; m. Vicki Janet Westbrook, Aug. 11, 1971 (div. 1982); children: Andrew Wright Notier, Matthew Westbrook Notier, Timothy Jackson Notier; m. Tamara Jane Jaffe, July 11, 1986; children: Zachary Hayden, Claire Emanuelle. AB cum laude, Dartmouth Coll., 1969; MA, Harvard U., 1972. Cert. secondary tchr. English tchr. Lyons Twp. High Sch., La Grange, Ill., 1973—; English instr. U. Ill., Urbana-Champaign, Ill., 1983-84. Sponsor LION sch. newspaper, LaGrange, Ill., 1986-97, Menagerie sch. mag., LaGrange, 1986 95; coord. Discovery Ctr., 1991-94. Tchr. Peace Corps, Kingdom of Tonga, 1969-71; mem. chair Lyons Twp. Youth Commn., LaGrange, 1975-81; mem., pres. Irving Park Community Food Pantry, Chgo., 1985-88; bd. dirs. Irving Park Homeless Shelter, Chgo., 1986-90; mem. Chgo. Sanctuary Alliance, Chgo., 1984-88; mem. Oak Park Farmer's Market Commn., 1990-94. Named Outstanding Young Man in Am. Jaycees, 1971, Outstanding Secondary Tchr. U. Chgo., 1980-82, 86; recipient Community Svc. award Chgo. Fedn. Community Coms., 1975, Gold Crown award Columbia Scholastic Press Assn., 1987-95, Presdl. Scholars' Tchr. Recognition award U.S. Dept. Edn., 2003. Mem. NEA, Nat. Coun. Tchrs. of English, Assn. for Supervision and Curriculum Devel. Mem. Reformed Ch. in Am. Avocations: sailing, cross-country skiing, gardening, woodworking. Office: Lyons Twp High Sch 100 S Brainard Ave La Grange IL 60525 E-mail: pnotier@lths.net.

JAFFESON, RICHARD CHARLES, association executive administrator; b. Rochester, N.Y., May 6, 1947; BA cum laude, U. Akron, Ohio, 1969; MA, U. Akron, 1971; postgrad., U. Cin., 1971-72. Sr. environ. planner Md.-Nat. Capital Park Planning Commn., Silver Spring, Md., 1972-78; coordinator council progs. Am. Planning Assn., Washington, 1978-82; dir. sci. and tech. Ctr. for Profl. Devel., U. Md., College Park, 1982-90; dir. edn. RBA, 1990-93; exec. dir. Nat. Certification Commn., Chevy Chase, Md., 1993—. Ind. rsch. supr. Smithsonian Instn., Bombay Nat. Hist. Soc., 1973-76; exec. dir. Nat. Women's Baseball Hall of Fame, 1998—. Author: Cert. Program Devel. Guide, 1994; creator, editor (mo. bull.) Capital Capsule, 1983-88; creator, prodr. (weekly tape) Event and Employment Recording, 1984-92; exec. editor Capital Comments newsletter, 1985-86; author: Silver Spring Success: An Interactice History of Silver Spring Maryland, 1995, 6th edit., 2003, Certification Commentary, vol. 1, 1996; editor, author (monthly Nat. Cert. Commn. news) Certification Comm., 1993—; author, pub. (weekly Nat. Women's Baseball news) Fame Forum, 1998—; contbr. articles to profl. jours. Mem. Am. Planning Assn. (chpt. v.p. 1978-80, 84-86, Disting. Svc. award 1977, 84, 87, 97), Assn. Am. Geographers (pres. 1976-77, 2002-03, mgr. award fund 1982—, Disting. Svc. award 1983), Am. Econ. Devel. Coun. (dir. basic econ. devel. course 1984-90, bd. regents 1989-91), Am. Inst. Cert. Planners. Avocations: physical fitness, baseball, wildlife. E-mail: certification@usa.com., hallfame@usa.com.

JAFREE, MOHAMMED JAWAID IQBAL See GEOFFREY, IQBAL

JAGACINSKI, CAROLYN MARY, psychology educator; b. Orange, N.J., Apr. 12, 1949; d. Theodore Edward and Eleanor Constance (Thys) Jagacinski; m. Richard Justus Schweickert, Dec. 27, 1980; children: Patrick, Kenneth. AB with honors in psychology, Bucknell U., 1971; MA in Psychology, U. Mich., 1975, PhD in Psychology and Edn., 1978. Rsch. assoc. U. Mich., Ann Arbor, 1978-79, Purdue U., West Lafayette, Ind., 1979-80, vis. asst. prof., 1980-83, rsch. psychologist, 1983-86, vis. lectr., 1986-88, asst. dean, 1988-89, asst. prof. psychology, 1988-94, assoc. prof., 1994—. Contbr. articles to profl. jours. U. Mich. predoctoral fellow, 1977-78, dissertation grantee, 1977-78; Exxon Edn. Found. grantee, 1983-84. Mem. APA, Midwestern Psychol. Assn., Soc. for Judgment and Decision Making, Am. Ednl. Rsch. Assn., Psychonomic Soc., Sigma Xi, Psi Chi. Avocations: tennis, reading. Office: Purdue Univ Dept Psychol Scis West Lafayette IN 47907

JAGENDORF, ANDRÉ TRIDON, plant physiologist; b. N.Y.C., Oct. 21, 1926; s. Moritz Adolph and Sophie Sheba (Sokolsky) J.; m. Jean Elizabeth Whitenack, June 12, 1952; children: Suzanne E., Judith C., Daniel Z.S. BA, Cornell U., 1948; PhD, Yale U., 1951. Merck postdoctoral fellow UCLA, 1951-53; from asst. prof. to prof. Johns Hopkins U., 1953-66; prof. plant physiology Cornell U., Ithaca, N.Y., 1966—, Liberty H. Bailey prof. plant physiology, 1981-96, Liberty H. Bailey prof. emeritus, 1997—. Author papers, revs. in field. Recipient Outstanding Young Scientist award Md. Acad. Sci., 1961, Kettering Rsch. award, 1963; Weizmann fellow, 1962 Fellow Am. Acad. Arts and Scis., AAAS; mem. NAS, Am. Soc. Plant Physiologists (hon., life, pres. 1967, C.F. Kettering award in photosynthesis, 1978, Charles Reid Barnes award 1989), Am. Soc Biol. Chemists, Am. Soc. Photobiology (councilor 1980), Soc. Gen. Physiologists, Am. Soc. Cell Biology, Japanese Soc. Plant Physiologists. Jewish. Office: Cornell U Plant Biology Dept Plant Sci Bldg Ithaca NY 14853 E-mail: atj1@cornell.edu.

JAGER, MARK ALAN, publishing executive, writer; b. Cadillac, Mich., Feb. 19, 1965; s. Les A. and Carole Nadine Jager; m. Deana Sue Jager, Aug. 26, 1995; children: Emili Shea, Madelein Carole, Mark Daniel. AA, Northwestern Mich. Coll., 1991; A in Journalism, Ferris State U., 1994. Pres. Zosma Publs., Marion, Mich., 1995—. Author: Mystic Michigan, Mystic Michigander, Tripping America the Fantastic. Office: Zosma Publications PO Box 284 Marion MI 49665

JAGER, MERLE LEROY, aerospace engineer; b. Eugene, Oreg., Sept. 22, 1942; s. Earl Christian and Alma Marie (Jensen) J.; m. Shannon Kay Jacobsen, Mar. 18, 1967; children: Holly, Peter, Melanie, Marissa BS in Mech. Engring., Oreg. State U., 1965; MS in Aeronautical Engring., U. So. Calif., 1967. Aerodynamicist Lockheed-Calif. Co., Burbank, 1965-68; rsch. engr. The Boeing Co., Seattle, 1968-70; aerodynamics engr. Gates Learjet Corp., Torrance, Calif., 1970; project engr. Irvin Industries, Inc., Gardena, Calif., 1971-73; aerodynamics engr. Northrop Corp., Hawthorne, Calif., 1973-91, mgr. flight mechanics Pico Rivera, Calif., 1991-95; aerodynamics mgr. McDonnell Douglas Corp., Long Beach, Calif., 1995—. Patentee in field. Treas. Goldenwest Assn., Westminster, Calif., 1976-78; tribal chief YMCA Indian Princesses Program, Huntington Beach, Calif., 1986-87; bishopric counselor Mormon Ch., Westminster, 1986-95. Mem. AIAA, Tau Beta Pi, Pi Tau Sigma, Sigma Tau. Republican. Home: 6771 Findley Cir Huntington Beach CA 92648-3075 Office: McDonnell Douglas Corp Long Beach CA 90810

JAGERMAN, DAVID LEWIS, mathematician; b. N.Y.C., Ny., Aug. 27, 1923; s. Morris and Helen (Bader) J.; m. Adrienne Israel, Sept. 8, 1951; children: Diane Tharp, Barbara Magic, Laurie Sutter. BEE, Cooper Union, N.Y.C., 1949; MS in Math., NYU, N.Y.C., 1954, PhD in Math., 1962. Jr. engr. Reeves Instrument Corp., N.Y.C., 1951-55; staff scientist Stavid Engring., Plainfield, N.J., 1955-59; design specialist Convair, San Diego, 1957-59; sr. math. staff cons. System Devel. Corp., Santa Monica, Calif., 1959-63; math. cons. disting. mem. technical staff AT&T Bell Labs., Holmdel, N.J., 1963-89; math. cons. NEC USA, Princeton, N.J., 1989—. Tchr. indsl. math. St. Peters Coll., 1968-73; prof. math. Stevens Inst. Tech., 1967-75, prof. elec. engring. and computer sci., 1984-90; prof. math. Fairleigh Dickinson U., Rutherford, N.J., 1958-67. Cpl. AC U.S. Army, 1942-45. Mem. IEEE (sr.). Achievements include research in stochastic models, queueing systems and teletraffic analysis. Office: RUTCOR Rutgers Ctr Ops Rsch PO Box 5062 New Brunswick NJ 08903-5062

JAGGER, JANINE, epidemiologist; BA, Moravian Coll., 1972; MPH, U. Pitts., 1974; PhD in Epidemiology, U. Va., 1987. Rsch. assoc. Yale U., 1978; faculty medicine U. Va., 1979—; founder Internat. Healthcare Worker Safety Ctr., 1994—. Cons. in field. Founder, editor-in-chief: Advances Exposure Prevention. Named MedTech Hero, Advanced Med. Tech. Assn., 2001; recipient Disting. Inventor award, Intellectual Property Owners Inc., 1988; fellow MacArthur Found. fellow, 2002. Achievements include development of IPINet surveillance system; patents in field. Office: Internat Health Care Worker Safety Ctr PO Box 800764 Charlottesville VA 22908-0764*

JAGGER, MICK (MICHAEL PHILIP JAGGER), singer, musician; b. Dartford, Kent, Eng., July 26, 1943; s. Joe and Eva Jagger; m. Bianca Perez Morena de Macias, May 12, 1971 (div. Nov. 1979); children: Jade, Karis; m. Jerry Hall, Nov. 21, 1990 (div. 1999); children: Elizabeth Scarlett, James Leroy Augustine, Georgia May Ayeesha, Gabriel Luke Beauregard. Student, London Sch. Econs., 1962-64. Mem., lead singer occasional guitarist Rolling Stones, 1962—, tours (of Europe) 1970, 73, 76, 82, 90, 95, 98, 2002, (of U.S.) 1966, 69, 72, 75, 78, 81, 89, 94, 97, 99, 2002, (of Australia), 1973, Europe and Japan, 1990, film appearances include Performance, 1969, Ned Kelly, Gimmie Shelter, Sympathy for the Devil, 1970, Ladies and Gentlemen, The Rolling Stones, 1974, Let's Spend the Night Together, 1983, Freejack, 1992, Bent, 1997, The Man From Elysian Fields, 2001; composer (with Keith Richards): (I Can't Get No) Satisfaction, Brown Sugar, Honky Tonk Woman, Jumpin' Jack Flash, Sympathy for the Devil, Get Off My Cloud, Paint it Black, 2000 Light Years from Home, Star Star, Have You Seen Your Mother, Baby (Standing in the Shadows), Mother's Little Helper, Ruby Tuesday, Lady Jane, The Citadel, You Can't Always Get What You Want, Fool to Cry, Start Me Up, She's So Cold, As Tears Go By, Wild Horses; albums with Rolling Stones include England's Newest Hitmakers: The Rolling Stones, 12 x 5, 1964, The Rolling Stones, Now!, December's Children (And Everybody's), Out of Our Heads, 1965, Aftermath, Big Hits, High Tide, & Green Grass, 1966, Between the Buttons, Flowers, Got Live If You Want It, Their Satanic Majesties Request, 1967, Beggars Banquet, 1968, Let it Bleed, Through the Past, Darkly, 1969, Get Yer Ya Yas Out, 1970, Stone Age, Gimme Shelter, Hot Rocks 1964-1971, Jamming with Edward, Milestones, Sticky Fingers, 1971, Exile on Main Street, 1972, No Stone Unturned, More Hot Rocks (Big Hits and Fazed Cookies), Goat's Head Soup, 1973, It's Only Rock and Roll, 1974, Metamorphosis, Rolled Gold, Made in the Shade, 1975, Black and Blue, 1976, Love You Live, 1977, Some Girls, 1978, Emotional Rescue, 1980, Sucking in the Seventies, Tatoo You, 1981, Still Life, 1982, Under Cover, 1983, Rewind (1971-1984), 1984, Dirty Work, 1986, Steel Wheels (also co-producer), Flashpoint, 1991, Voodoo Lounge, 1994 (Grammy award Best Rock Album, 1994), Striped, 1995, Rock and Roll Circus, 1996, Bridges to Babylon, 1997, No Security, 1999, Forty Licks, 2002, solo albums She's The Boss, 1985, Primitive Cool, 1987, Wandering Spirit, 1993; Goddess in the Doorway, 2001; solo singles include Just Another Night of You, Let's Work, (with David Bowie) Dancin' in the Streets; prodr.(films): Enigma, 2001. Named to Rock and Roll Hall of Fame, 1989. Office: Virgin Records 338 N Foothill Rd Beverly Hills CA 90210-3611*

JAGIELSKA, JANINA, retired librarian; b. Kruszewo, Poland, Dec. 27, 1938; d. Kazimierz and Anna (Witkowska) Zawadzki; m. Jozef Jagielski, Sept. 27, 1959; children: Wojciech, Malgorzata. MSc, Inst. Libr. and Info. Sci., Lublin, Poland, 1978. Head Pub. Commune Libr., Maly Plock, Poland, 1963-65, Pub. Dist. Libr., Kolno, Poland, 1965-75; head of lending dept. Warsaw (Poland) Pub. Libr., 1976-82, dep. dir., 1983-91, dir., 1992—2003; retired. Supr. Bibliography of Warsaw Public Library, vol. 1, 1998, Bibliography of Warsaw Public Library, vol. 2, 1999. Mem.: Polish Librs. Assn. (vice chmn. br. bd. 1985—89, sec. br. bd. 1979—85, gen. sec. main bd. 1993—2001). Roman Catholic. Avocations: literature, travel, theatre, hand-knitting. Home: Mala 2 05-075 Wesola Poland Office: Biblioteka Pub m St Warszawy ul Koszykowa 26 00950 Warsaw Poland

JAGLOM, ANDRE RICHARD, lawyer; b. N.Y.C., Dec. 23, 1953; s. Jacob and Irene (Moore) J.; m. Janet R. Stampfl, Apr. 12, 1980; children: Peter Stampfl Jaglom, Wendy Stampfl Jaglom. BS in Mgmt., BS in Physics, MIT, 1974; JD, Harvard U., 1977. Bar: N.Y. 1978, U.S. Dist. Ct. (so. and ea. dists.) N.Y. 1978, U.S. Supreme Ct. 1982, U.S. Ct. Appeals (2d cir.) 1987. Assoc. Paul, Weiss, Rifkind, Wharton & Garrison, N.Y.C., 1977-84; mng. ptnr. Stecher Jaglom & Prutzman LLP, N.Y.C., 1984-2000; ptnr. Tannenbaum Helpern Syracuse & Hirschtritt LLP, N.Y.C., 2000—. Bd. dirs. Cmty. Fund of Bronxville, Eastchester and Tuckahoe, Inc., 1988-94; lectr. law and the culinary bus. French Culinary Inst.-Cornell Sch. Hotel Adminstrn., 2002—. Computer mktg. and distbn. editor Computer Law Reporter, 1984-90; Am. Law Inst. ABA course of study on product distbn. and mktg., mem. faculty 1983—, chmn., 1987—; contbr. article to law jours.; contbr chpt. to Legal Checklists, 1988—. Trustee bd. edn. Bronxville Union Free Sch. Dist., 1997-2001. Mem. NY State Bar Assn., Bar Assn. City N.Y. (computer law com. 1986-89, sec. 1990-94, com. on tech. and practice of law 1993-96), Am. Inst. Wine and Food (bd. dirs. N.Y. chpt. 1991-99, treas. 1992-99, adv. bd. 2000—). Office: 900 3d Ave New York NY 10022-4728

JAGLOM, HENRY DAVID, actor, director, writer; b. London, Jan. 26, 1941; s. Simon M. and Marie (Stadthagen) J.; m. Victoria Foyt, 1991. Pres. Rainbow Film Co., Los Angeles, Jagfilms, Inc., Los Angeles, Rainbow Releasing, Los Angeles. Writer, dir. (films) A Safe Place, 1971 (selected for N.Y. Film Festival 1971), Tracks (selected for Cannes Film Festival 1976), Sitting Ducks, 1980 (selected for Cannes Film Festival), Can She Bake a Cherry Pie?, 1983 (selected for Berlin Film Festival 1983); actor, writer, dir. (films) Always (But Not Forever), 1985, Someone to Love, 1987 (selected for Cannes Film Festival), New Year's Day, 1989 (selected for Venice Film Festival 1989), Eating (selected for Deauville Film Festival 1990), Venice/Venice, 1991 (selected for AFI/L.A. Film Festival), BabyFever, 1993, Last Summer in The Hamptons, 1995 (selected for London Film Festival, AFI/L.A. Film Festival), Déjà Vu, 1998, Festival in Cannes, 2002; presenter Hearts and Minds, 1973 (Acad. award best documentary 1973); writer, dir. Shopping, 2003. Office: Rainbow Film Co 9165 W Sunset Blvd West Hollywood CA 90069-3129 E-mail: rainbow@rainbowfilms.com.

JAGNOW, DAVID HENRY, petroleum geologist; b. Dubuque, Iowa, Nov. 24, 1947; s. Albert August and Ardath Helen (Goettsch) J.; remarried Lara LaVonne Jordan, Aug. 7, 1999; children: Daniel David, Robert Carl, Beth Laura. BA in Geology, U. Iowa, 1970; MS in Geology, U. N.Mex., 1977. Exploration geologist Shell Oil Co., Houston, 1973-77; staff geologist Energy Reserves Group, Denver, 1977-78; exploration mgr. Donald C. Slawson Oil Prodr., Oklahoma City, 1978-82; cons. geologist pvt. practice, Edmond, Okla., 1982-87, Los Alamos, N.Mex., 1987-99, Albuquerque, 1999—; venture capitalist Venture Capital Info., Edmond, 1986-87, Los Alamos, 1987-99, Albuquerque, 1999-2001; conservation chair Nat. Speleological Soc., 1995-2000; dir. Project Underground VA, 1995—; pres. Summa Energy Corp., San Francisco, 2002—. Mem. caves and karst task force Bur. Land Mgmt., Carlsbad, N.Mex., 1991-93, Guadalupe caverns geology panel Nat. Park Svc., Carlsbad, 1993. Author: Cavern Development in the Guadalupe Mountains, 1979, Stories From Stones, 1992; mem. adv. bd. Jour. Cave and Karst Studies, 1998-2001. Conservation chair, chair Pajarito Grotto, Los Alamos, 1998-2000. Recipient Gov.'s Dist. Svc. award Gov. Iowa, 1970, W.A. Tarr award Sigma Gamma Epsilon, 1970, Lowden prize Geology U. Iowa, 1970. Fellow Nat. Speleological Soc. (Conservation award 1995, Outstanding Svc. award 2001); mem. Am. Assn. Petroleum Geologists, N.Mex. Entrepreneurs Assn. (bd. dirs. 1988-89), Cave Rsch. Found. (chief scientist 1988-89), Omicron Delta Kappa. Lutheran. Avocations: caving, hiking, rock collecting, cave science, reading. Office: Summa Energy Corp PO Box 93398 Albuquerque NM 87199-3398 E-mail: David@Jagnow.com.

JAGODA, BARRY LIONEL, writer, media adviser, communications consultant; b. Youngstown, Ohio, Feb. 5, 1944; s. Saul S. and Anne (Fradin) J. BA, U. Tex., 1966; MS, Columbia U., 1967. Writer, editor NBC News, Washington, N.Y.C., 1967-69; producer CBS News, N.Y.C., 1969-75; partner Houston, Ritz, Cohen, Jagoda, N.Y.C., 1975; TV advisor Jimmy Carter presdl. campaign, 1976; spl. asst. to the Pres., Washington, 1977-79, cons., 1979-80; pres. Am. Info. Exchange, 1980—; dir. news and pub. affairs George Washington U., 1983-87; v.p. Stackig, Sanderson and White Advt. and Pub. Rels., 1988-93, Shandwick Pub. Affairs, Washington, 1993-97, IMPAC Corp., 1997-2001; dir. comms. U. Calif., San Diego, 2003—. Recipient Emmy award as producer CBS news special, Watergate 1974. Chmn. bd. dirs. Friends of Raoul Wallenberg Found., 1989-96. Ford Found. fellow, 1967 Mem. Nat. Bus. Travel Assn., Sigma Delta Chi. Home: 9302 La Jolla Farms Rd La Jolla CA 92037-2901 Office: Univ Calif 9500 Gilman Drive San Diego CA 92093 E-mail: bjagoda@ucsd.edu.

JAGODA, ROBERT EUGENE, writer, retired communications executive; b. Kansas City, Mo., Nov. 18, 1923; m. Kitty Kuhne Jagoda, Apr. 8, 1948; 1 child, Eric. BS, Northwestern U., 1949. Copy editor Chgo. Tribune, 1946—48; freelance writer, photographer, sch. tchr. Hart, Mich., 1949—53; mem. advt./comm. staff Union Carbide, Cleve. and N.Y.C., 1953—60; speechwriter, comm. mgr. IBM, White Plains, NY, 1960—86; freelance speechwriter, advt., pub. rels. cons. N.Y.C., 1986—. Author: A Friend in Deed, 1976 (prin. selection of Mystery Guild, 1977), Nobody Wants My Resume, 1980, Senzi: A Woman to Remember, 2001. Pres. Ulster County SPCA, Kingston, NY, 1990—95, Ulster County Arts Coun., Kingston, 1980—83; vice chair state adv. com. U.S. Commn. on Civil Rights, NY, 1978—82. Sgt. infantry U.S. Army, 1943—45, ETO. Decorated Purple Heart, Bronze Star; recipient Presdl. Unit citation, Combat Infantry award. Mem.: IBM Quarter Century Club, Ex-Prisoners of War. Democrat. Unitarian Universalist. Avocations: writing, reading, photography, baseball. Home: 547 Lucas Ave Ext Kingston NY 12401-8215 E-mail: jrejji@msn.com.

JAGODZINSKI, RUTH CLARK, retired nursing administrator; b. N.Y.C., Feb. 24, 1938; d. John Kirkland and Ruth Fishwick Clark; m. Thomas John Jagodzinski, Nov. 1962 (div. 1974); children: Christine Ruth, James Clark. Diploma, Roosevelt Hosp. Sch. Nursing, 1959. RN, Nev., N.Y. Head nurse drug/alcohol detox Sunrise Hosp., Las Vegas, Nev., 1973-75; program coord. careunit North Las Vegas (Nev.) Hosp., 1975-77; co-owner, adminstr. Sunrise Home Health, Las Vegas, 1983-89; dir. pers. PRN Home Health, Las Vegas, 1990-91; dir. home health svcs. Med. Pers. Pool, Las Vegas, 1990-92; dir. profl. svc. Olsten Kimberly Quality Care, Las Vegas, 1992-95; adminstr. Valley Home Health, Las Vegas, 1995-97; regional dir. ops. Integrated Health Mgmt. Svcs., Brunswick, Ga., 1997-98; ind. cons., 1998-99; intake mgr. Gentiva Health Svcs. (formerly Olsten Health Svcs.), Las Vegas, 1999—2002, ret., 2002. Mem. Nev. State Cert. Bd. Substance Abuse Counselors and Program Adminstrs., 1976-86, 90-97, pres., 1980-86. Mem. Nev. Gov.'s Adv. Bd. for Alcohol and Drugs; bd. dirs. We Care Found., 1974—; trustee Community Referral Svcs., 1975-80; bd. dirs. Alcohol Program So. Nev., 1975-85; mem. In-Home Care Svcs. Clark County, 1978-83; bd. dirs. So. Nev. Girls Clubs, 1984-86; mem. adv. bd. Nathan Adelson Hospice, Las Vegas, 1977-89; chmn. nursing subcom. profl. ednn. div. So. Nev. chpt. Am. Cancer Soc., 1989-90, mem. Nev. Bd. Com. on Occupational Excellence, 1989-90. Recipient Community Svc. award Alcohol Program So. Nev., 1978, Svc. award We Care Found., 1989. Mem. Home Health Care Assns. Nev. (life, v.p. 1984-86, 91-95, pres. 1995-98, Svc. award 1999). Home: 4573 Royal Ridge Way Las Vegas NV 89103-5034

JAGR, JAROMIR, professional hockey player; b. Kladno, Czechoslavakia, Feb. 15, 1972; Profl. hockey player Poldi Kladno, 1988—90, Pitts. Penguins, 1990—. Named to Czechoslavakian League All-Star Team, 1989—90, Sporting News and NHL All-Star 1st Teams, 1994—95; recipient Art Ross Trophy, 1994—95. Office: WA Capitals MCI Ctr 601 F St NW Washington DC 20001

JAHANGIR, Z(ULFIQUAR) M(UHAMMED) G(OLAM) SARWAR, molecular biologist, educator; b. Manohardi, Bangladesh, Feb. 1, 1954; came to U.S., 1985, permanent resident, 1994; s. Mohammed Golam and Pari Banu (Ali) Sattar; m. Anjuman Ara Rahman, Aug. 21, 1982; children: Arthee Eileen, Arnab Zabid. BSc in Fisheries with honors, Bangladesh Agrl. U., 1977; MSc in Indsl. Fisheries, U. Cochin, India, 1980; PhD in Molecular biology, CUNY, 1994. Teaching fellow Bangladesh Agrl. U., Mymensingh, 1977-80, lectr., 1980-82, asst. prof., 1982; teaching asst. U. Alta., Edmonton, Can., 1982-85; grad. fellow Bklyn. Coll., CUNY, 1985-89, adj. lectr., 1985-93; rsch. scientist Rsch. Found., CUNY, Bklyn., 1994-95; asst. prof. molecular biology Richard Stockton Coll. N.J., Pomona, 1995-2000; asst. prof. molecular genetics Wabash Coll., Crawfordsville, Ind., 2000—; adj. asst. prof. biology Coll. of Staten Isle., CUNY, 2002—; sr. sci. tech. CSI, CUNY, 2002—. Vis. asst. prof. molecular genetics Wabash Coll., Ind., 2000—01; vis. asst. prof. Bklyn. Coll. of CUNY, 2001—; adj. asst. prof. Kingsborough CUNY, 2001—; rsch. assoc. Undersea Rsch. Found., Inc., NJ, 2000—02; coord. Tech. Transfer Conv. 2000, Atlantic City; adj. asst. prof. biology Coll. S.I. CUNY, 2002—, sr. sci. technologist Coll. S.I., 2002. NOAA grantee, 1993-95, 2000-01; Nat. Marine Fisheries Svc. grantee, 2000-01. Mem. AAAS, Am. Soc. Ichthyologists and Herpetologists, Am. Fisheries Soc., Am. Soc. Zoologists, Assn. Bangladesh Chem. and Biol. Soc. N.Am. (v.p.), Bangladesh Assn. Agrl. Scientists Am. (pres. 1996-97), Bangladesh Devel. Initiative, Bangladesh Soc. Inc. N.Y., Nat. Geog. Soc., The Genetics Soc. Am., N.Y. Acad. Scis., Soc. Sys. Biologists, Bangladesh Assn Agrl. Scientists in Am. (pres. 1996-98), Sigma Xi. Achievements include development of molecularly tagged lake sturgeon through genetic engineering. Office: Richard Stockton Coll NJ Biology/NAMS Jim Leeds Rd Pomona NJ 08240-0195

JAHANMIR, SAID, materials scientist, mechanical engineer; b. Mar. 18, 1950; married; 2 children. BSME, U. Wash., 1971; MSME, MIT, 1973, PhD in Mech. Engring., 1976. Instr. mech. engring. MIT, 1975-76; lectr. mech. engring. U. Calif., 1976-77; asst. prof. Sibley Sch. Mech. & Aerospace Engring. Cornell U., 1977-80; sr. staff engr. Exxon Rsch. and Engring. Co., 1980-85; program dir. tribology program NSF, 1985-87; group leader Nat. Inst. Stds. & Tech., 1987—2002; pres., CEO Miti Heart Corp., Gaithersburg, Md., 2002—. Adj. prof. mech. engring. U. Md., 1987-96; adj. prof. U. Del., 1997—; presenter in field. Author: Tribology in Manufacturing Processes, 1994, Friction and Wear of Ceramics, 1994, Machining of Ceramics and Composites, 1999; exec. editor Machining Sci. and Tech. Jour.; contbr. articles to profl. jours., chpts. to books; patentee in field. Mem.: ASME (v.p. rsch. 2001—, chair tribology divsn. 1997—99, bd. rsch. and tech. devel. 1995—98, assoc. editor 1990—93, tribology divsn. exec. com. 1988—90, others, Disting. Svc. award, Mayo D. Hersey award 2001), Am. Soc. for Artificial Internal Organs, Soc. Tribologists and Lubrication Engrs. (fellows com. 1993—99, edn. com. 1987—95, ceramics and composites com. founding chmn. 1987—89, ann. meeting program com. 1987—91, lubrication fundamentals com. 1986—87, Internat. award). Office: Miti Heart Corp PO Box 83610 Gaithersburg MD 20883 E-mail: sjahanmir@mitiheart.com.

JAHIEL, RENE INO, physician; b. Boulogne, Seine, France, Mar. 29, 1928; s. Richard and Cecile (Lwovsky) J.; m. Deborah Berg, May 8, 1955; children: Abigail, Richard, Beth. BA, NYU, 1946; MD, SUNY (Downstate Med. Coll.), Bklyn., 1950; PhD, Columbia U., 1957. Intern Montefiore Hosp., N.Y.C., 1950-51; resident Mt. Sinai Hosp., N.Y.C., 1951—52, fellow in virology, 1952-55; exptl. immunologist Nat. Jewish Hosp., Denver, 1957-59; asst. attending pathologist, exptl. pathology Mt. Sinai Hosp., 1959-61; asst. prof. pub. health Cornell U. Med. Coll., N.Y.C., N.Y., 1961-66; rsch. assoc. prof. preventive medicine NYU, N.Y.C., 1967-70, rsch. prof., 1970-76, rsch. prof. medicine, Sch. Medicine, 1976-88. Cons. health svcs. rsch., policy and planning, 1989—; adj. prof. health svcs., rsch. and policy New Sch. for Social Rsch., 1991-96; dean faculty of sci. and pub. health, Ecole Libre des Hautes Etudes of N.Y., 1991-94, v.p. scis., 1994—; vis. prof. dept. cmty. medicine and healthcare, U. Conn. Health Ctr., 1995-98, lectr., 1999—; pres. Internat. Health Policy Rsch. Corp., Hartford, Conn., 1995—; med. dir. Southbury (Conn.) Tng. Sch., 1993-95; med. cons. State of Conn. Dept. Mental Retardation, 1996-97; tchr. met. leadership program, U. Coll., NYU, 1969-73; physician Assn. for Help for Retarded Children, 1982-88, Young Adult Inst., 1984-89, Assn. for Children with Retarded Mental Devel., 1988-93; cons. Nat. Ctr. for Health Svcs. Rsch., 1983-85; bd. dirs. N.Y. Scientists Com. Pub. Info., 1974-79, Physicians Forum, 1975-84; cons. Yale U Primary Care Tng. Program at Waterbury (Conn.) Hosp., 2000—. Author sci. rsch. articles on tissue culture, virology, interferon, preventive medicine, health policy, health svcs. rsch., homelessness, sociology of knowledge: editor: Homelessness: A Prevention-Oriented Approach, 1992. Mem. interferon adv. com. Am. Cancer Soc., 1984-93; mem. nat. bd. Com. for Nat. Health Svc., 1976-79, coalition, 1980-85. Lt. USNR, 1955-57. Grantee USPHS, 1966-79. Mem. APHA (chmn. com. health svcs. rsch. 1980-87, Med. Care sect. award 1985, governing coun. 1983-85, 99—, chmn. homelessness study group 1984-90, chmn. policy com. caucus on disablement 1989-92, founding chmn. caucus on homelessness 1990-91, chmn. membership com. spl. interest group on disability 1993-97, chair 1998-99, edn. bd. 2000-2001), Internat. Assn. Health Policy (bd. dirs. 1998-2000), Physicians for Social Responsibility, Internat. Soc. Sys. Sci. Health Care, Assn. Health Svcs. Rsch. (Spl. Recognition award 1986), World Assn. for Psychosocial Rehab. (chmn. com. on mental handicaps 1992-94), founding mem. Internat. Soc. for Equity in Health. Home and Office: Unit 729 250 Main St Hartford CT 06106-1875 E-mail: jahiel@nso2.uchc.edu.

JAHN, GARY ROBERT, foreign language educator; b. Mpls., Sept. 29, 1943; s. Robert Gerhardt and Katherine Joann (Johnson) J.; m. Kathryn Justine Raynoha, Aug. 26, 1968 (div. Dec. 1982); children: Thomas, Phillip, Helen; m. Sandra Anne Martin, Mar. 10, 1984; children: Katherine, Nathaniel. BA cum laude, U. Minn., 1965; MA, U. Wis., 1968, PhD, 1971. Asst. prof. St. Olaf Coll., Northfield, Minn., 1971-72; asst. prof. SUNY, Buffalo, 1972-77, U. Minn., Mpls., 1977-81, assoc. prof., 1982—97, prof., 1998—. Editor Slavic and East European Jour., 1988-93. Author: Russian Conjugation and Declension, 1990, The Death of Ivan Ilich: An Interpretation, 1993, The Death of Ivan Ilich: A Critical Companion, 1998, Electronic Russian, 2002; author articles on Russian lit. and lang. tchg. tech. Mem. Am. Assn. for the Advancement of Slavic Studies, Am. Assn. Tchrs. of Slavic and East European Langs. (exec. coun. 1988-93). Office: U Minn Inst Linguistics ESL and Slavic Langs 214 Nolte Ctr Minneapolis MN 55455

JAHN, KIRSTIN N. lawyer; b. Buffalo; d. Elmer A. and Marilyn A. Jahn. BBA, U. Mass.; JD, U. Buffalo, 1992. Bar: N.Y. 1992, Nev. 1996, Colo. 1998. Pvt. practice, N.Y.C.

JAHNG, JUNGJOO, information technology educator; b. Euisung, Kyungbook, South Korea, Feb. 9, 1967; arrived in U.S., 1995; s. Sungyoon Jahng and Soonjah Kim; m. Heeyoung Sin, Jan. 22, 1994; children: Edward Wookjin, Anna Sahee. BA, Seoul Nat. U., 1989, MBA, 1991; PhD, U. Wis., Milw., 2000. Info. tech. cons. Samil Coopers & Lybrand, Seoul, 1991; info. tech. specialist Samsung SDS, Seoul, 1992—95; asst. prof. Rensselaer Poly. Inst., Troy, NY, 2000—. Contbr. articles to profl. jours. Mem.: Assn. for Info. Sys., Beta Gamma Sigma. Office: Rensselaer Poly Inst Lally Sch Mgmt and Tech 110 8th St Troy NY 12180 Office Fax: 518-276-8661.

JAHNS, JEFFREY, lawyer; b. Chgo., July 6, 1946; s. Maxim G. and Josephine Barbara (Czernek) J.; m. Jill Metcoff, Sept. 8, 1973; children: Anna Hope, Claire Martine, Elizabeth Grace. AB, Villanova U., 1968; JD, U. Chgo., 1971. Bar: Ill. 1971, U.S. Dist. Ct. (no. dist.) Ill. 1971, U.S. Ct. Appeals (7th cir.) 1973, U.S. Supreme Ct. 1974. Assoc. Roan & Grossman, Chgo., 1971-77, ptnr., 1977-81, Seyfarth Shaw, Chgo., 1981—. Mem. tax mgmt. adv. bd. Bur. Nat. Affairs, Washington, 1981--. Co-author: Corporate Acquisition Debt Interest Deduction, 1973; contbr. numerous articles to legal publs., chpts. to books. Trustee, chmn. Chgo. Architecture Found., 1982—; bd. dirs. Prairie Ave. House Mus., 1995-98; trustee, treas. Graham Found., 1998—. Ctr. for Urban Studies fellow U. Chgo., 1969-71. Mem. ABA, Chgo. Bar Assn. (chmn. various coms.), Internat. Coun. Shopping Ctrs., Mid-Day Club, Econ. Club Chgo., Lambda Alpha. Office: Seyfarth Shaw 55 E Monroe St Ste 4200 Chicago IL 60603-5863

JAIN, HIMANSHU, materials science engineering educator; b. Mainpuri, India, Jan. 20, 1955; came to U.S., 1974; s. Chandra Kumar and Kusuma Devi Jain; m. Sweety Agrawal, Feb. 14, 1990; children: Isha Himani, Raina Himani. MS, Banaras U., Varanasi, India, 1972; M of Tech., Indian Inst. Tech., Kanpur, India, 1974; D of Engring. Sci., Columbia U., 1979. Postdoctoral appointee Argonne (Ill.) Nat. Lab., 1980-82; assoc. scientist Brookhaven Nat. Lab., Upton, N.Y., 1982-85; T.L. Diamond Chair prof. material sci. and engring. Lehigh U., Bethlehem, Pa., 1985—. Vis. scientist Indian Inst. Tech., Kanpur, 1985; Fulbright lectr., rschr. U. Cambridge, Eng., 1998, U. Aberdeen, Scotland, 1998. Editor: Current Trends in the Science and Technology of Glass, 1989, Atomic Migration and Defects in Materials, 1991, Diffusion in Amorphous Materials, 1994, Practical Implications of Glass Structure, 1997; contbr. more than 170 articles to profl. jours. Recipient Zachariasen award for Outstanding Contbn. to Glass Sci., 1997; Humboldt fellow U. Dortmund, Germany, 1991-92. Fellow Am. Ceramic Soc. (chmn. Lehigh Valley chpt. 1990); mem. Ceramic Ednl. Coun., Internat. XAFS Soc., Materials Rsch. Soc., The Metals, Minerals and Materials Soc. Achievements include patents for electro-optic polymers; discovery of anomalous isotope mass effect and window effect in a glass; demonstration of feasibility of unoccupied volume in a glass and of radiation enhanced sintering in a ceramic. Office: Lehigh U 5 W Packer Ave Bethlehem PA 18015-3001

JAIN, NEMI CHAND, chemist, coating scientist, educator; b. Kota, Rajasthan, India, Oct. 15, 1951; came to U.S., 1983, naturalized, 1993; s. Chand Mal and Raj Devi (Nopra) J.; m. Shashi Bala Jain, Jan. 29, 1981; children: Nimisha, Seema. BSc, U. Rajasthan, 1971, MSc, 1973, PhD, 1978; postgrad., N.D. State U., 1990, McCorne Rsch. Inst., 1994, Baldwin-Wallace Coll., 1996. Lectr. chemistry Nat. Coun. of Edn. Rsch. Tng., Ajmer, India, 1976-77; asst. prof. U. Delhi, 1977-83; postdoctoral rsch. assoc. U. Va., Charlottesville, 1983-85; rsch. assoc./assoc. lab. dir. Colo. State U., Ft. Collins, 1985-89; rsch. scientist/team leader Sherwin-Williams Co., Chgo., 1989-96, sr. scientist, 1996—, sr. scientist, team leader Warrensville Heights, Ohio, 2000—. Advisor Harry Truman Coll., Chgo., 1999; cons. and lectr. in field. Developer waterborne coatings; developer coating test course Sherwin-Williams U., 1995; contbr. chpt. to book, numerous articles to profl. jours. Judge, Chgo. Sci. Fair, 1992, 95, 97, 98, 99, 2000, Competitive Leadership, Profl. Mgmt. Assn., 1997, 98, 1st Responder/Indsl. Med. Tech., 1995—, U. No. Colo, 1989, Am. Chem. Soc. H.S. Edn. Com., 1996—; grand awards judge Intel Internat. Sci. and Engrs. Fair, Cleve., 2003. CSIR fellow, 1973-76, Sardar Patel U. fellow, 1972, Lucknow U. tchr. fellow, 1979; recipient Disting. Nat. award for study abroad Govt. of India, 1983-85, State Govt. Rajasthan merit scholar, 1967-73, Bill Welch Excellence award Automotive Finishes, 2001. Fellow Am. Inst. Chemists; mem. ASTM, Am. Chem. Soc. (mem. h.s. edn. com. 1996-97), Internat. Union Pure and Applied Chemistry, ASM Internat., Sigma Xi. Jain. Avocations: reading, walking, cooking, travel, computer, gardening. Office: Sherwin Williams Co 4440 Warrensville Center Rd Warrensville Heights OH 44128 Home: 2199 Autumn Run Wooster OH 44691-1596 Fax: (216) 332-8670. E-mail: ncjain@sherwin.com.

JAIN, PIYARE LAL, physics educator; b. Punjab, India, Dec. 11, 1921; came to U.S., 1949; naturalized, 1961; s. Labh Ch and Maya (Devi) J.; m. Sulakshana Dhawan, Feb. 15, 1966. BA, Punjab U., 1944, MA, 1948; PhD, Mich. State U., 1954. Research asso. chemistry dept. U. Minn., 1953-54; instr. physics dept. State U. N.Y., Buffalo, 1954-59, asst. prof., 1959-61, assoc. prof., 1961-67, prof., 1967—. Research asso. U. Chgo., 1959-60, Lawrence Radiation Lab., Berkeley, Calif.; vis. prof., Bristol, Eng., 1961-62, U. Wash., Seattle, summer 1960; Fulbright vis. prof. Rajasthan U., India, 1965-66; Sci. adviser Am. embassy AID, New Delhi, India, summer 1966 Recipient Excellence award State of N.Y. and United Univ. Professions, Hind Ratten award Govt. of India, 1994. Fellow Am. Phys. Soc. Achievements include rsch. in sold state physics, electron and nulcear magnetic reesonance, cosmic radiation and high energy physics, relativistic heavy ion physics. Home: 223 Surrey Run Buffalo NY 14221-3363 Office: Suny At Buffalo Buffalo NY 14260-0001

JAIN, RAJ, engineering educator; b. Satna, India, Aug. 17, 1951; came to U.S., 1974; s. Shanti Lal and Sulochana Devi Jain; m. Neelu Hathishah; children: Sameer, Amit. B of Engring., A.P.S. U., Rewa, India, 1972; M of Engring., Indian Inst. of Sci., 1974; PhD, Harvard U., 1978. Sr. engr. Digital Equipment Corp., Maynard, Mass., 1978-80, prin. engr. Hudson, Mass., 1980-82, cons. engr. Littleton, Mass., 1983-90, sr. cons. engr., 1991-94; prof. Ohio State U., Columbus, 1994-2000; chief tech. officer, co-founder Nayna Networks, Milpitas, Calif., 2000—. Bd. tech. adv. Teradiant Networks, San Jose, Calif., Corona Networks, Millpitas, Calif., Avatar Networks, Freemont, Calif., Rhonet Sys., Columbus, Ohio; spkr. in field. Author: Control Theoretic Formulation of Operating Systems Resource Management, 1979, The Art of Computer Systems Performance Analysis, 1991 (award 1992), FDDI Handbook: High-Speed Networking with Fiber and Other Media, 1994; patentee in field. Sec. Jain Ctr. of Greater Boston, Wellesley, Mass., 1978-84. Fellow IEEE, Assn. Computing Machinery. Home: 19886 Bonnie Ridge Way Saratoga CA 95070-5010 Office: Nayna Networks 180 Rose Orchard Way San Jose CA 95134 E-mail: jain@acm.org.

JAIN, VIJAY K. electrical engineer, educator; m. Urmil Jain; children: Rashi, Ruchi, Anita. PhD, Mich. State U., 1964. Assoc. prof. Fla. State U., Tallahassee, 1968—72, U. South Fla., Tampa, 1972—76, prof., 1976—95, dir. Ctr. Digital Computational Video, 1986—, disting. prof., 1995—, dir. Ctr. Commn. Signal Processing, 1999; program dir. NSF, Arlington, Va., 2001—02. Contbr. articles to profl. jours. Scholar Askounes-Ashford Disting scholar, USF, 1996. Achievements include research in pencil of functions approach, nonlinear VLSI cell, OWSS wireless technology, ECG measurement through liquid media, TESH network; large-scale VLSI/USLI/WSI reconfigurable architectures for

signal/image processing and general computing; development of digital signal processing; image processing; digital comm; computational video comm; large area VLSI/ULSI/WSI; sys. on a chip. Office: University of South FLorida 4202 E Fowler Avenue Tampa FL 33620

JAISWAL, DINESH KUMAR, pharmaceutical scientist, educator; b. Howrah, India, Mar. 5, 1947; came to U.S., 1983; s. Jagadish Prasad and Phool Kumari Jaiswal; m. Manju Jaiswal, Feb. 10, 1971; children: Rahul, Kunal. BS in Pharmacy, Banaras Hindu U., Varanasi, India, 1970, MS in Pharmacy, 1972, PhD in Pharmacy, 1978. Assoc. prof. Banaras Hindu U., 1973-75, 78-83; chemist Phoenix Lab., Hicksville, N.Y., 1983-84; sr. chemist Superpharm, Islip, N.Y., 1984-86; mgr. Quad Pharm., Indpls., 1986-90; sr. devel. pharmacist GAF Chem. Co., Wayne, Ind., 1990-93; prin. scientist Mova Pharm., Caguas, P.R., 1993-96, Forest Labs., Inwood, N.Y., 1996—. Contbr. articles to profl. jours., including Jour. Pharm. Scis., PHarm. Rsch., USA, Pharmatech/Manchester. Jr. rsch. fellow UGC, New Delhi, India, 1975, sr. rsch. fellow, 1976, rsch. assoc., 1977. Mem. Am. Assn. Pharm. Scientists, Parenteral Drug Assn. and Controlled Release Soc. Achievements include patent for pharmacuetical tablet with PVP having enhanced drug dissolution rate. Home: 6 Sunflower Ct Holtsville NY 11742-2520 Office: 48 Mall Dr Commack NY 11725

JAITE, GAIL ANN, music educator; b. Painesville, Ohio, Mar. 11, 1953; d. Gail Clarence King and Barbara Mary Safick; m. Charles E. Jaite, Jr., Mar. 22, 2003. BA, Hiram Coll., 1975. Music tchr. Jordak Elem. Sch., Middlefield, Ohio, 1975—; prin., owner Tall Pines Dog Tng., 2002—. Instr. dog agility Kenston Cmty. Edn., Auburn, Ohio, 2000—; dir. tri-sch. honors band Cardinal Schs., Middlefield, 1984—. Active in cmty. theatre; soloist Geauga County hunger task force. Mem.: Music Educators Nat. Conf., Northeastern Ohio Edn. Assn. (leader workshops), Ohio Music Edn. Assn., LELRC Dog Club, Northeastern Ohio Dog Club (pres.), Buckeye Retriever Club, Delta Kappa Gamma. Home: 13769 Old State Rd Middlefield OH 44062

JAKAB, IRENE, psychiatrist; b. Oradea, Rumania; came to U.S., 1961, naturalized, 1966; d. Odon and Rosa A. (Riedl) J. MD, Ferencz József U., Kolozsvar, Hungary, 1944; lic. in psychology, pedagogy, philosophy cum laude, Hungarian U., Cluj, Rumania, 1947; PhD summa cum laude, Pazmany Peter U., Budapest, 1948; Dr honoris causa, U. Besançon, France, 1982, U. Pécs, Hungary, 1999. Diplomate Am. Bd. Psychiatry, Am. Bd. Pediatric Neuropsychology. Rotating intern Ferencz József U., 1943-44; resident in psychiatry Univ. Hosp., Kolozsvar, 1944-47, resident in neurology, 1947-50; resident internal medicine Univ. Hosp. for Internal Medicine, Pécs, Hungary, 1950-51; chief physician Univ. Hosp. for Neurology and Psychiatry, Pécs, 1951-59; staff neuropathol. rsch. lab. Neurol. Univ. Clinic, Zurich, 1959-61; sect. chief Kans. Neurol. Inst., Topeka, 1961-63; dir. rsch. and edn., 1966; resident psychiatry Topeka State Hosp., 1963-66; asst. psychiatrist McLean Hosp., Belmont, Mass., 1966-67, assoc. psychiatrist, 1967-74; prof. psychiatry U. Pitts. Med. Sch., 1974-89, prof. emerita, 1989—, co-dir. med. student edn. in psychiatry, 1981-89. Dir. John Merck Program, 1974-81; mem. faculty dept. psychiatry Med. Sch., Pecs, 1951-59; asst. Univ. Hosp. Neurology, Zurich, 1959-61; assoc. psychiatry Harvard U., Boston, 1966-69, asst. prof. psychiatry, 1969-74, program dir. grad course mental retardation, 1970-87; lectr. psychiatry, 1974—; mem. Am. Bd. Pediatric Neuropsychiatry, editor in chief newsletter. Author: Dessins et Peintures des Aliénés, 1956, Zeichnungen und Gemälde der Geisteskranken, 1956, Pictorial Expression in Psychiatry, 1998; editor: Psychiatry and Art, 1968, Art Interpretation and Art Therapy, 1969, Conscious and Unconscious Expressive Art, 1971, Transcultural Aspects of Psychiatric Art, 1975; co-editor: Dynamische Psychiatrie, 1974; mem. editl. bd. Confinia Psychiatrica, 1975-99; contbr. articles to profl. jours. Recipient 1st prize Benjamin Rush Gold medal award for sci. exhibit, 1980, Bronze Chris plaque Columbus Film Festival, 1980, Leadership award Am. Assn. on Mental Deficiency, 1980; Menninger Sch. Psychiatry fellow, Topeka, 1963-66. Mem. AMA, Am. Psychol. Assn., Am. Psychiat. Assn., Société Medico Psychologique de Paris, Internat. Rorschach Soc., N.Y. Acad. Scis., Internat. Soc. Psychopathology of Expression (v.p. 1959—), Am. Soc. Psychopathology of Expression (chmn. 1965—, Ernst Kris Gold Medal award 1988), Royal Soc. of Medicine (overseas fellow), Internat. Soc. Child Psychiatry and Allied Professions, Internat. Assn. Knowledge Engrs. (v.p. for medicine 1988-95), Deutschsprachige Gesellschaft für Psychopathologie des Ausdruckes (hon. Prinzhorn prize 1967), Hungarian Psychiat. Assn. (hon. 1992), World Psychiat. Assn. (co-chmn. sect. on mass and media and mental health, co-chmn. sect. on psychopathology of expression). Home and Office: 74 Lawton St Brookline MA 02446-5801

JAKES, JOHN, author; b. Chgo., Mar. 31, 1932; s. John Adrian and Bertha (Retz) J.; m. Rachel Ann Payne, June 15, 1951; children: Andrea, Ellen, John Michael, Victoria. AB, DePauw U., 1953, LittD (hon.), 1977; MA, Ohio State U., 1954; LLD (hon.), Wright State U., 1976; LHD (hon.), Winthrop Coll., 1985, U. S.C., 1993, Ohio State U., 1996. With advt. dept. Abbott Labs., 1954-60; with creative dept. various advt. agencies, 1960-69; creative dir. Dancer Fitzgerald Sample Co., Dayton, Ohio, 1969-70. Rsch. fellow dept. history U. S.C., 1989. Author: The Texans Ride North, 1952, A Night for Treason, 1956, Murder He Says, 1958, When the Star Kings Die, 1967, Master of the Dark Gate, 1970, The Kent Family Chronicles: The Bastard, 1974, The Rebels, 1975, The Seekers, 1975, The Furies, 1976, The Titans, 1976, The Warriors, 1977, The Lawless, 1978, The Americans, 1980, North and South Trilogy: North and South, 1982, Love and War, 1984, Heaven and Hell, 1987, California Gold, 1989, Homeland, 1993, In the Big Country, 1993, American Dreams, 1998, On Secret Service, 2000, Charleston, 2002, (juvenile) Susanna of the Alamo, 1986, (musical) Great Expectations - The Musical, 1999; co-editor anthology: New Trails, 1994; editor: (anthology) A Century of Great Western Stories, 2000. Trustee DePauw U. Recipient Ohio Gov.'s award, 1977, ann. lit. award Friends of Rochester Pub. Libr., 1983, Citizen-Celebrity award for libr. advocacy White House Conf. on Librs., 1995, Disting. Alumni award Ohio State U. Coll. Humanities, 1995, Western Heritage Lit. award Nat. Cowboy Hall of Fame, 1995, Profl. Achievement award Ohio State U. Alumni Assn., 1997, Career Achievement award S.C. Humanities Coun., 1998, Cooper medal Thomas Cooper Libr., U. S.C., 2002. Mem. S.C. Acad. Authors, Western Writers Am., Dramatists Guild, Authors Guild, PEN, Writers Guild of Am. (East), Century Assn. Office: care Rembar & Curtis Attys 19 W 44th St New York NY 10036-5902 E-mail: jjfiction@aol.com.

JAKES, WILLIAM CHESTER, electrical engineer; b. Milw., May 15, 1922; s. William Chester and Eleanor (Knight) J.; m. Mary Elizabeth Bristle, Sept. 3, 1948; children: Robert, Elizabeth. BS in Elec. Engring., Northwestern U., 1944, MS in Elec. Engring, 1947, PhD, 1949. With Bell Tel. Labs., Inc. (various locations), 1949-87, head radio transmission research dept., 1963-71; dir. Radio Transmission Lab., North Andover, Mass., 1971-87. Mem. sci. adv. bd. Voice of Am., 1957-58 Contbr. articles to profl. jours.; patentee antennas and comm. systems. With USN, 1944-46. Ph.D. (hon.) Iowa Wesleyan U., 1961; recipient Alumni Merit award Northwestern U., 1962 Fellow IEEE (Paper award 1971, co-recipient Alexander Graham Bell medal 1987); mem. Eta Kappa Nu, Pi Mu Epsilon. Home: 58 Wild Rose Dr Andover MA 01810-4620 *Intense dedication to physics and engineering with constant desire for understanding and intellectual honesty, plus the enjoyment of working with others, have been my guiding principles.*

JAKEWAY, EDWIN WILLIAM, lawyer; b. Flint, Mich., Dec. 12, 1936; s. Edwin William and Lucille (Hodge) J.; m. Suzanne Henry, June 23, 1963; children: Craig Edwin, Morgan Henry, Sally Pamela, Brooke Song. AA, Flint C.C., 1957; BA, Eastern Mich. U., 1958; JD, Detroit Coll. Law, 1961; DCL, Mich. State U., 1993, LLD (hon.). Bar: Mich. 1961, U.S. Dist. Ct. (ea. dist.) Mich. 1961, U.S. Ct. Appeals (6th cir.) 1986, U.S. Supreme Ct. 1993; diplomate Nat. Bd. Trial Advocacy. Assoc. Ransom & Fazenbaker, Flint, 1961-62; asst. pros. atty. County of Genesee, Flint, 1962-63; assoc. Neal, Keil & Jakeway, Flint, 1964-68; pvt. practice Grand Blanc, Mich., 1968—; atty. Jakeway, Jakeway & Jakeway P.C. Contbr. articles to profl. jours. Trustee Detroit Coll. Law, 1981-94. With Mich. NG, 1955-63. Kiwanis scholar, 1958-61. Mem. ABA, ATLA, Mich. Bar Assn., Mich. Trial Lawyers Assn., Genesee County Bar Assn. Presbyterian. Avocation: fly fishing. Office: 8161 S Saginaw St # G Grand Blanc MI 48439-1825

JAKLE, KENNETH RICHARD, broadcasting executive; b. Effingham, Ill., Aug. 7, 1942; s. Kenneth Dean amd Kaythryn Joan (Loy) J.; m. Sharon S. James, Jan. 12, 1980; children by previous marriage: Ann Elizabeth, Joellen Kaythryn, Richard Edward. BS in Comm., U. Ill., 1964. Sales mgr. Sta. WKEI, Kewanee, Ill., 1964-65; gen. mgr. Sta. WCRA, Effingham, 1965-66; mng. owner Sta. WRMN-AM-FM, Elgin, Ill., 1966-74, pres., 1974—, Sta. WJKL, Elgin, 1974—, Sta. WBIG, Aurora, Ill., 1994—, Radio Shopping Show, Inc. V.p., dir. Clinton (Ill.) Daily Jour. and Pub., 1979—; pres. Sta. KSHP, Las Vegas, 1996—; chmn. bd., pres. Las Vegas Radio Co., Inc., 2002—, Big Broadcasting Co., Inc., 2002—, Elgin Broadcasting Co., Inc., Las Vegas Radio Land Co., Inc.; bd. dirs. First Ill. Valley Bank & Trust Co., San Jose Tri-County Bank, First Cmty. Bank. Bd. mgrs., Sherman Hosp., Elgin, chmn. 1993-2001; chmn. Sherman Health Sys., 2001—, chmn. Elgin Econ. Devel. Commn., 1975-77; pres. Elgin YMCA, 1972-73; bd. dirs. Elgin Symphony Orch., Elgin Downtowner, Easter Seal Assn., Upper Kane County Heart Assn., Larkin Home for Children, Salvation Army; bd. dirs. Elgin Devel. Corp., treas.; chmn. bd., pres. Sherman West Ct. Nusing Home; savs. bond chmn. Kane County, 1982-83; founding mem. Elgin Ctr. City Redevel. Corp., bd. dirs., 1991—; mem. Dennis Hastert Fin. Com., 1989—. With USNG, 1964-66. Recipient Disting. Svc. award Jaycees, 1969. Mem. Nat. Assn. Broadcasters, Nat. Radio Broadcasters Assn., Ill. Broadcasters Assn., Elgin Hist. Soc. (dir.), Greater Elgin C. of C. (1st v.p., exec. com. 1985—, pres. 1988—), Nat. Spkrs. Assn. (bd. dirs. exec. com. 1999—), Profl. Spkrs. of Ill. (bd. dirs., pres. 1995-96, recipient Chicagoland Comms. and Leadership award 1995, cert. speaking profl. designation 1999), Rotary (pres. Elgin chpt. 1976-77), Masons, Shriners. Avocation: commercial pilot with multi engine and instrument rating. Home: 9N874 Koshare Cir Elgin IL 60123-8422 Office: Stas WRMN/WJKL 14 Douglas Ave Elgin IL 60120-5546

JAKOBE, VIRGINIA ELLIS, retired educator; b. Molino, Mo., Sept. 10, 1922; d. Clyde William and Lucy (Baker) Ellis; m. Henry George Jakobe Sr., Feb. 23, 1963; 1 child, Henry George. BS, NE Mo. State U., 1946; MA, Columbia U., 1960. Cert. elem. art tchr., Mo., N.Y. Tchr. Ellis Sch., Molino, 1941-43; tchr. art and English Marceline Sch., Mo., 1943-44; remedial tchr. Berkley Sch., Mo., 1944-46; tchr. elem. art Maplewood Sch., Mo., 1946-54, Univ. City Schs., Mo., 1954-63, Saranac Lake (N.Y.) Cent. Schs., 1970-90. Editor Show Me Art, 1962-64; originator The Children's Art Exhibit Saranac Lake Cen. Sch., 1970—. Pres. Saranac Lake./N.Y. PTA., 1968-69, St. Louis County Art Tchrs. Assn., 1954-55. Mem. N.Y. State Art Tchrs. Assn., Paint and Palette Artists Assn., Delta Kappa Gamma (sec.). Republican. Episcopalian. Home: 12 Rockledge Rd Saranac Lake NY 12983-1928

JAKOBSSON, NAOMI D. state representative; b. Somerville, NJ, Sept. 28, 1941; m. Eric Jakobsson. BA, Univ. of Ill., 1977, MA, 1979. State Rep. House of Rep., Dist. 103, Ill., 2002—; instr. Univ. of Ill., 1980—84; recorder of deeds Champaign County, 1984—. Candidate Ill. State House of Rep., dist. 103, Ill., 2002. Mem.: Gov. Accountability & Streamlining, Elections & Campaign Reform, Habitat for Humanity of Champaign County (bd. mem.), Internat. Assoc. of Clerks, Recorders, Election Officials & Treas., Ill. Assoc. of County Clerks & Recorders, Univ. YWCA (exec. dir., Champaign), State Gov. Admin., Higher Ed., Develop. Disabilities - Mental II, appropriations - Higher Ed., Appropriations Comm.- Elem. & Secondary Ed. Democrat. Office: Capitol 284-S Stratton Office Bldg Springfield IL 62706 also: District 206 N Randolph Suite 120 Champaign IL 61820*

JAKOPEC, CARL THOMAS, pharmaceutical company executive; b. Chgo., May 31, 1945; s. Charles George and Lillian (Seps) J.; m. Elizabeth Todd Dunlap, Aug. 23, 1969 (div. Sept. 1976); m. Carol Coon Jakopec, Jan. 7, 1977; children: Kimberly Jo, Jeffery Allyn. BS in Pharmacy, Drake U., 1969. Registered pharmacist, Iowa. Chief pharmacy Walgreen Drug Co., Des Moines, 1969-77; owner Greeley (Colo.) Pharmacy Corp., 1977-81; mgr. govt. sales Marion Labs., Inc., Kansas City, Mo., 1981-95; dir. govt. sales Forest Labs., Inc., N.Y.C., 1996—. Mem. nat. commn. on the future of Drake U., 1988, mem. nat. adv. bd. coll. pharmacy, 1997—. Bd. dirs. Little League Baseball, Greeley, 1977-84. Mem. Am. Soc. Cons. Pharmacists, Am. Pharm. Assn., Am. Soc. Health Sys. Pharmacists, Sports Car Club Am. (bd. dirs. 1991-92), Ferrari Club Am. Avocations: officiating auto racing, travel, grandchildren, golf. Home and Office: Forest Labs Inc 4033 Highland Castle Ct Las Vegas NV 89129-3664

JAKSA, DAVID MICHAEL, wireless network company official; b. Oct. 14, 1946; BSEE, Rose Hulman Inst. Tech., 1968; MBA, U. Iowa, 1982. Mgr. gen. comm. bus. Rockwell Internat., Cedar Rapids, Iowa, 1976-87, dir. satellite bus. Richardson, Tex., Santa Ana, Calif., 1987-91, dir. bus. devel. Richardson, 1991-98; gen. mgr. wireless DSL, Nortel Networks, Dallas, 1998—2002; pres., CEO David M. Jaksa Bus. Cons., 2002—. Home: 626 Torrey Pines Ln Garland TX 75044-4112 E-mail: dave.jaksa@verizon.net.

JAKUB, KATHLEEN ANN, medical/surgical nurse; b. Pitts., June 9, 1947; d. Michael E. and Mary Ellen (Kirchner) J. Diploma, St. Francis Med. Ctr., 1968; BA in Sociology, BA Adminstrn. Justice, U. Pitts., 1979, BSN, 1992; MS in Profl. Leadership, Carlow Coll., 1996. Cert. intermediate care nurse, trauma nurse, otorhinolarnygology and head-neck nurse. Staff nurse phys. rehab. St. Francis Med. Ctr., Pitts., 1968—70; staff nurse-orthopedics-plastics U. Pitts. Med. Ctr., 1970-75; staff nurse head/neck and ophthalmology, 1975—88; patient care mgr. med. and surg. unit U. Pitts. Med. Ctr., 1988—96, case mgr. neurosurgery dept., 1996—99, case mgr. performance improvement dept., 1999—2001; mgr. quality improvement U. Pitts. Cancer Ctrs., 2001—03; triage nurse, outpatient dept. Hillman Cancer Ctr., 2003—. Nursing rep. radiation safety com. U. Pitts. Med. Ctr. Mem. Soc. Head and Neck Nurses, Am. Trauma Soc. Home: 4372 Winterburn Ave Pittsburgh PA 15207-1185 E-mail: jakubk@msx.upmc.edu.

JAKUBAUSKAS, EDWARD BENEDICT, college president; b. Waterbury, Conn., Apr. 14, 1930; s. Constantine and Barbara (Narstis) J.; m. Ruth Friz, Aug. 29, 1959; children— Carol, Marilyn, Mark, Eric. BA, U. Conn., 1952, MA, 1954; PhD, U. Wis., 1961. Economist FPC, 1956, Dept. Labor, 1956-58; instr. U. Wis., 1961-62, asst. prof. econs., 1962-63; asst. prof. Iowa State U., 1963-65, assoc. prof., 1965-66, prof., 1966-71; dean U. Wyo., 1971-76, prof. econs., 1971-79, v.p. acad. affairs, 1976-79; pres. SUNY, Geneseo, 1979-88, Cen. Mich. U., Mt. Pleasant, 1988-92; cons. in higher edn., 1992—. Author: Manpower Economics, 1971. Served with U.S. Army, 1954-56. Mem. Am. Assn. State Univs. and Colls. Mem. United Chs. of Christ.

JAKUBOWSKY, FRANK RAYMOND, religious writer; b. Belfield, N.D., Oct. 11, 1931; s. William and Catherine (O'bach) J. Student, U. N.D., 1950-52. Chemist Sherwin Williams Paint Co., Emeryville, Calif., 1958-85; pres. Bold Books, Oakland, Calif., 1978—. Editor Spiritfest, Berkeley, Calif., 1997—. Author: Creation, 1978, Jesus Was a Leo, 1979, The Psychological Patterns of Jesus Christ, 1982, The Creative Theory of the Universe, 1983, Caldecott, 1985, Frank on a Farm, 1988, Lake Merritt, 1988, Thank God, I Am Alive, 1989, Whitman Revisted, 1989, Spiritual Symbols for the Astrology of the Soul, 1990, This New World; Birth: Sept. 8, 1958, 1990, Perceptive Types, 1993, Father Figure Frank's Stories, 1996, Inspiration Stories, 1998, Universal Mind, 1998, Big Bang Goes Puff, 1999. Pfc. U.S. Army, 1952-54. Mem. Urantia Fellowship, Inst. Noetic Scis., Nat. Coun. Geocosmic Rsch. Roman Catholic. Avocation: writing songs for children on fraimba. Home: 1565 Madison St Apt 308 Oakland CA 94612-4511

JALAL, IBRAHIM MOHAMMAD, pharmaceutical executive; b. Jaffa, Palestine, July 8, 1943; arrived in Jordan, 1948; s. M. I. and Bahiyyah (Rous) J.; m. Nadia S. Tahboub, July 30, 1973; children: Diana, Rania, Shadia, Saba. BS in Pharmacy, U. Alexandria, Egypt, 1967; MSc in Pharmacy, Phila. Coll. Pharmacy & Sci., Pa., 1972; PhD in Pharmacy, U. Wis., Madison, 1978. Prodn. mgr. Arab Pharms., Sult, Jordan, 1967-70, 72-73; teaching asst. U. Wis., 1973-74, rsch. asst., 1974-78; group leader Riker Labs. subs. 3M Ctr., St. Paul, 1978-79; tech. vp. Hikma Internats., Amman, Jordan, 1979—. Adj. prof. U. Jordan, 1981-84; mem. com. on MSc exam Yarmouk U., Irbid, Jordan, 1982—; tech. cons. Ministry of Health, Amman, 1987-89. Contbr. articles to profl. jours. Mem. Am. Assn. Pharm. Scientists, Jordan Pharm. Assn. Home: PO Box 925554 Amman Jordan Office: Hikma Pharms PO Box 182400 Amman Jordan

JALALI, BEHNAZ, psychiatrist, educator; b. Mashad, Iran, Jan. 26, 1944; came to U.S., 1968; d. Badiolah and Bahieh (Shahidi) Samimy; m. Mehrdad Jalali, Sept. 18, 1968. MD, Tehran (Iran) U., 1968. Rotating intern Burlington County Meml. Hosp., Mt. Holly, N.J., 1968 69; resident in psychiatry U. Md. Hosp., Balt., 1970-73; asst. prof. psychiatry dept. psychiatry Sch. Medicine Rutgers U., Piscataway, N.J., 1973-76, Yale U., New Haven, Conn., 1976-81, assoc. clin. prof. psychiatry, 1981-85; assoc. clin. prof. psychiatry dept. psychiatry UCLA, 1985-94, clin. prof. psychiatry dept. psychiatry Sch. Medicine, 1994—. Dir. psychotherapy Sch. Medicine Rutgers U., Piscataway, 1973-76; dir. family therapy unit dept. psychiatry Yale U., New Haven, 1976-85; chief clin. med. svcs. Mental Health Clinic, 1987-96; coord. med. student edn. in psychiatry West L.A. VA Hosp., 1985—; dir. family therapy clinic W.Va. VA Hosp., 1991—, co-leader Schozophrenia Clinic, Mental Health Clinic, West Los Angeles VA Med. Ctr., 1996—. Author: (with others) Ethnicity and Family Therapy, 1982, Clinical Guidlines in Cross-Cultural Mental Health, 1988; contbr. articles to profl. jours. Fellow Am. Psychiatric Assn., Am. Orthopsychiatry Assn., Am. Assn. Social Psychiatry; mem. Am. Family Therapy Assn., So. Calif. Psychiatric Assn. (chair com. for women 1992), World Fedn. Mental Health. Avocations: photography, hiking, cinema, painting. Home: 1203 Roberto Ln Los Angeles CA 90077-2304 Office: UCLA Dept Psychiatry West LA VA Med Ctr B116aa Los Angeles CA 90073-1003

JALBERT, JANELLE JENNIFER, financial consultant, educator; d. Gerald Edward and Linda S. Jalbert. AA, Pasadena City Coll., 1995; BA (cum laude), Calif. State U, Northridge, 1998; student, Nat. U. Chartered retire plans specialist. Tchr. Sun Valley (Calif.) Mid. Sch., 1999—2000, New Ave. Ednl. Ctr., Monterey Park, Calif., 2000—02; owner, educator J-Bear Ednl. Enterprises, Monrovia, Calif., 2001—; prin., owner Jalbert-Thomason Photography, Arcadia, Calif., 2003—. Bd. dirs. Delta Dimensions, 2003—; cons. Hondiat Inc., Arcadia, Calif., 1994—; presenter in field. Author: Success Skills, 2001. Fundraiser, mem. crew Calif. AIDS Ride 4 &5, LA, 1997—98; ptnr. Life in the Word, Fenton, Mo., 2001, World Changers Ministries, College Park, Ga., 2001, Jesse Duplants Ministries, New Orleans, 2002—; ptnr. Aaron's Army TD Jakes Ministries, Dallas, 2003—. Grantee Ednl. award, Sunshine Brooks Found., 1994, Sushine Brooks Found., 1995, John Glyes Ednl. Fund, 1997; scholar Collegiate Honor scholar, Nat. U., 2002. Mem.: Jr. C. of C. (com. Kasukabe, Japan Visitath 1999), Soroptimist Internat. (Youth Citizenship award 1991), Blue Key (bd. dirs. 1996—98, Cmty. Svc. award 1996), Omicron Delta Kappa (pres. 1997—98), Alpha Gamma Sigma (chair fundraising 1994—95), Sigma Kappa Alumnae (1st v.p. membership 2003—). Avocations: travel, languages, wine, marine activities, photography. Office: Waddell & Reed 150 S Los Robles 880 Pasadena CA 91101

JALENAK, PEGGY EICHENBAUM, volunteer; b. Little Rock, Oct. 14, 1935; d. E. Charles and Helen Lockwood Eichenbaum; m. Leo Richard Jalenak, Jr., Aug. 28, 1955; children: Laurie J. Williamson, Terri J. Mendelson, Jan J. Ordway, E. Charles. Commr., vice chair Tenn. Art Commn., Nashville, 1975—80; bd. dirs., exec. com. Tennesseans for the Arts, Nashville, 1981—85; bd. dirs. Tenn. State Mus. Found., Nashville, 1994—2003. Bd. dirs. Nat. Found. Jewish Culture, N.Y.C., 1999—; former bd. dirs. Ballet Memphis, Theatre Memphis, Memphis Arts Coun.; former bd. dirs., sec., treas. Opera Memphis; bd. dirs. Memphis Jewish Fedn., 1997—; bd. dirs., past pres., sec. Memphis Jewish Hist. Soc. Memphis & Mid South, 1998 ; bd. dirs. Temple Israel Mus., 2001—, Bornblum Solomon Schechter Sch., 2002—; adv. bd. Judaic studies program U. Memphis, 2000—. Named Tenn. Arts Amb., Tenn. Arts Commn., 1985. Home: 6025 River Oaks Rd Memphis TN 38120

JALILI, NADER, mechanical engineer, educator; b. Tehran, Iran, Oct. 26, 1970; came to U.S., 1995; s. Ahmad and Delnaz (Doulat Abadi) J.; m. Jaleh Esmailzadeh, Dec. 5, 1993; children: Paneed Fatemeh, Pouya Mohammad. BSc with 1st class honors, Sharif U. tech., Tehran, 1992, MSc with 1st class honors, 1995; PhD, U. Conn., 1998. Design cons. Iranian truck Mfg., Tehran, 1992-93; tchg. asst. Sharif U. Tech., Tehran, 1993-95; design engr. Iranian Crane Mfg., Tehran, 1993-95; lectr. Azad U. Karaj, Iran, 1994-95; design cons. Indsl. Mixers Mfg. Co., Esfehan, Iran, 1994-95; rsch. asst. U. Conn., Storrs, 1995-98; vis. asst. prof. dept. mech. engring. No. Ill. U., DeKalb, 1999-2000; asst. prof. mech. engring. Clemson (S.C.) U., 2000—. Computer cons. Sharif U. Tech., 1993-94, U. Conn., 1997-98. Contbr. articles to profl. jours. U. Conn. scholar fellow, 1995-98; recipient Career award NSF, 2003. Mem. ASME, IEEE. Moslem. Avocations: volleyball, running, soccer. Home: 811 Issaqueena Terr # 1908 Central SC 29630 E-mail: jalili@clemson.edu.

JALURIA, YOGESH, mechanical engineering educator; b. Nabha, Punjab, India, Sept. 8, 1949; came to U.S., 1970; s. Jagdishwar and Maya J.; m. Anuradha Malhotra, Sept. 9, 1975; children: Pratik, Aseem, Ankur. BS, Indian Inst. Tech., Delhi, 1970; MS, Cornell U., 1972, PhD, 1974. Mem. tech. staff Bell Labs., Princeton, NJ, 1974-76; asst. prof. Indian Inst. Tech., Kanpur, 1976-80, Rutgers U., New Brunswick, NJ, 1980-82, assoc. prof., 1982-85, prof. of mech. engring., 1985-91, prof. II, disting. prof., 1991—2001, Bd. Govs. prof., 2001—. Cons. David Sarnoff Lab., SRI, Princeton, 1989-90, Steel Authority, Ranchi, India, 1977-80, others; mem. NSF grants rev. panel, other panels, 1996-98; NSF vis. scientist Indian Inst. Tech., 1988-89; lectr. in field; participant workshop on natural convection NSF, Colo., 1982, Indo-Australian Solar Energy Workshop, New Delhi, 1978, others; assoc. tech. editor J. Heat Transfer, 1993-99; mng. editor Computational Mechanics, 1994-99, co-editor, 2000—; spkr. in field; editor, CRC Book Series in Computational Techniques and Applications. Author: Natural Convection Heat and Mass Transfer, 1980; co-author: Computational Heat Transfer, 1986, 2d edit., 2003, Buoyancy Induced Flows, 1988, Computer Methods for Engineering, 1988, Design and Optimization of Thermal Systems, 1998; contbr. chpts. to books: Natural Convection, 1985, Handbook of Single-Phase Convective Heat Transfer, 1987, Energy Storage Systems, 1989, Handbook of Fire Protection, 1995, numerous others; contbr. more than 300 articles and papers to profl. jours. and confs. including Rev. Sci. Instrum., Jour. Heat Transfer, Jour. Thermophysics Heat Transfer, Numerical Heat Transfer, Jour. Fluid Mech., Jour. Numerical Meth. Engring.; mem. numerous editorial bds. including mem. editorial adv. bd. Numerical Heat Transfer, 1987—; mem. editorial bd. Internat. Jour. Numerical Meth. Heat and Flow, 1990—; reviewer including Applied Mechanics Rev., Jour. Fluid Mechanics, Jour. Heat Transfer, Jour. Solar Energy Engring.; referee numerous articles. NATO Disting. lectr., 1984, 88; recipient cert. of recognition Dept. of Commerce, 1982, Disting. Alumni award IIT, 1994, Max Jakob Meml. award ASME/AIChE, 2002. Fellow ASME (chmn. nat. heat transfer conf., coord. com. 1991-92, exec. com. heat transfer divsn. 1998—, Heat Transfer Mem. award 1995, Worcester Reed Warner medal 1999, Freeman scholar 2000), Am. Phys. Soc., Combustion Inst., India Assn. of East Brunswick (pres. 1985, 91, 94-96), Cornell India Assn. (v.p. 1972-73). Democrat. Hindu. Achievements include patents for Methods and apparatus for heating articles, for Methods and apparatus for avoiding undesirable deposits in crystal growing operations; copyrighted computer software in materials processing and electronics cooling; research in thermal processing of materials, fires, computational heat transfer, natural convection, cooling of electronic equipment and environmental flows, flows rising above finite heated bodies, interaction of buoyant flows with surfaces, buoyant jet flows, mixed convection in enclosures, heat removal from heated elements on a vertical surface, thermal stratification and heat rejection problems, solar energy storage in salt-gradient solar ponds, numerical and experimental simulation of thermal processes in manufacturing systems, computer aided design of thermal systems, knowledge based design methodology, and enclosure fire growth processes. Office: Rutgers U Mech Engring Dept New Brunswick NJ 08903 E-mail: jaluria@jove.rutgers.edu.

JAMAR, STEVEN DWIGHT, law educator; b. Ishpeming, Mich., May 11, 1953; s. Dwight W. and Lorraine (Persgard) J.; m. Shelley June Von Hagen-Jamar, May 19, 1979; children: Alexander S., Eric D. BA, Carleton Coll., 1975; JD cum laude, Hamline U., 1979; LLM with distinction, Georgetown U., 1994. Bar: Minn. 1979, D.C. 1993, U.S. Supreme Ct. 1985. Jud. clk. Minn. Supreme Ct., St. Paul, 1979-80; pvt. practice law Minn., 1980—89; prof. law U. Balt., 1989-90; prof. Sch. Law, Howard U., Washington, 1991—, dir. legal rsch. and writing program, 1990—2002; assoc. dir. Inst. Intellectual Property and Social Justice, 2003—. Cons. on Environ. Legal Info. Sys. project NASA, 1998-2002; cons. on Global Legal Info. Network to Law Libr. of Congress, 1999—. Co-author: Essential Lawyering Skills: Interviewing, Counseling, Negotiation, and Persuasive Fact Analysis, 1999; contbr. articles to profl. jours. Rsch. fellow Law Libr. Congress, 2000-01. Mem. ABA, ACLU, Legal Writing Inst. (pres.

1997-98), Am. Soc. Internat. Law, Amnesty Internat., Assn. Legal Writing Dirs., Sierra Club. Avocations: canoe camping, soccer, go, photography, guitar. Office: Howard U Sch Law 2900 Van Ness St NW Washington DC 20008-1106

JAMES, ALLIX BLEDSOE, retired university president; b. Marshall, Tex., Dec. 17, 1922; s. Samuel Horace and Tannie Etta (Judkins) James; m. Sue Nickens, Feb. 14, 1945; children: Alvan Bosworth, Portia Veann. AB, Va. Union U., 1944, MDiv, 1946; ThM, Union Theol. Sem. Va., 1949, ThD, 1957; postgrad., Boston U., summer 1951, Pa. State U., summer 1957; LLD, U. Richmond, 1970; DD, St. Paul's Coll., 1980. Ordained to ministry Bapt. Ch., 1942. Moderator No. Neck Bapt. Assn., 1950-52; minister Union Zion Bapt. Ch., Gloucester, Va., 1944-53, Mt. Zion Bapt. Ch., Downings, Va., 1945-57, 3d Union Bapt. Ch., King William, Va., 1953-70; dean students Va. Union U., Richmond, 1950-57, dean Sch. Theology, 1957-70, Henderson-Griffith prof. pastoral theology, v.p., 1960-70, pres., 1970-79, pres. emeritus, 1979-85, 93—, chancellor, 1985-93. Author: Calling a Pastor in a Baptist Church, Threescore and Ten Plus-the Pilgrimage of an African-American Educator, 1922-, 1997; contbg. editor: The Continuing Quest, 1970. Chmn. Richmond City Planning Commn., 1969—75; dir. Va. Electric and Power Co., Dominion Resources, Inc., Consol bank and Trust Co.; mem. Commn. on Ch. Family Fin. Planning; mem. scholarship selection com. Philip Morris, Inc.; mem. Mayor's Commn. on Human Rels., 1963—65; pres. Norrell Sch. PTA, 1963—65; mem. exec. com. Ctrl. Va. Ednl. TV; mem. Richmond Independence Bicentennial Commn., Richmond Downtown econ. and Devel. Commn.; co-chmn. Northside Cmty. assn., 1964—68; chmn. Univ. Ctr. in Va.; mem. State Bd. Edn. Va., 1975—85, pres., 1980—82; bd. dirs. NCCJ, Va. Inst. Pastoral Care, Task Force for Renewal Urban Strategy and Tng., Richmond chpt. ARC, 1974—75, Better Richmond, Inc., Richmond Downtown Devel. Unltd., Am. Coun. on Edn., 1970—72, Richmond renaissance, Inc., Met. Richmond Leadership; mem. adv. bd. Inst. for Bus. and Cmty. Devel. U. Richmond; bd. fellows Interpreters House, Lake Janaluska, NC; trustee Richmond Meml. Hosp., Nat. Assn. for Equal Opportunity in Edn., v.p.; pres. Richmond Gold Bowl Sponsors, Inc., Nat. Conf. Richmond and Jews, Inc., 1987—90; nat. co-chair Nat. Conf. Christians and Jews, Inc., 1994; chmn. bd. dirs. Cosol. Bank and Trust Co., chmn./bd. dirs., 2001—. Named Citizen of Yr., Astoria Beneficial Club, 1971, Univ. chapel named Allix B. James Chapel in his honor, 1992; recipient Disting. Svc. award, Links, Inc., 1971, Ednl. Achievement award, 1985, Good Govt. award, Richmond First Club, 1985, Brotherhood award, NCCJ, 1975, Mozelle E. Manuel Outstanding Svc. award, Met. Bus. League, 1991, Exemplary Vision award, Fullwood Foods, Inc., 1992, Flame Bearers Edn. award, United Negro Coll. Fund, 1997, Citizen of Yr., Omega Psi Phi, 1972, Strong Men and Women Excellence in Leadership 2000 series award, Va./N.C. Power, 2000, Disting. Cmty. Svc. award, Sigma Pi Phi, 2003. Mem.: Clergy Assn. Richmond Area (pres.), Bapt. Gen. Conv. Va. (exec. bd.), Soc. for Advancement Continuing Edn. for Mins. (exec. bd.), Am. Bapt. Conv. (pres. coun. on theol. edn. 1969—72), Am. Assn. Theol. Schs. (pres. 1970—72), Greater Richmond C. of C. (bd. dirs.), Kiwanis (honoree Richmond area Appreciation Dinner 1993), Alpha Phi Alpha (Achievement award 1981, 1985), Alpha Kappa Mu. Office: Va Union U 1500 N Lombardy St Richmond VA 23220-1784

JAMES, ALTON EVERETTE, JR., radiologist; b. Oxford, NC, Aug. 22, 1938; s. Pattie Royster; children: Everette III, Jeannette, Elizabeth. AB, U. N.C., 1959; MD, Duke U., 1963; MSc, Johns Hopkins Sch. Pub. Health, 1971. Diplomate Am. Bd. Radiology, 1969. Fellow Harvard Med. Sch., Boston, 1966—69; from asst. to prof. radiology Johns Hopkins Med. Sch., Balt., 1969—74; dir. rsch. radiology Johns Hopkins Hosp., Balt., 1969—74; fellow Royal Soc. Medicine, London, 1974—75; chmn. dept. radiology and radiol. sciences Vanderbilt U. Sch. Medicine, Nashville, 1975—92; founder Vanderbilt Ctr. Med. Imaging Rsch., 1978—; pres. Am. Roentgen Ray Soc., 1994—95, N.C. State U. Sch. Vet. Medicine Found., Raleigh, NC, 1996—98. Vis. scientist Nat. Cancer Inst., 1992—93, NIH, 1992—93; sr. program officer NAS, 1993—94; clin. prof. Georgetown U., 1994—, U. N.C., 1996—; adj. prof., chair emeritus Vanderbilt U. Sch. Medicine, Nashville, 1994—; lectr. Johns Hopkins Med. Sch., Balt., 1993—; bd. visitors U. N.C., 1980; deans coun. Johns Hopkins Bloomberg Sch. Pub. Health, 2002—; founder Russell Morgan Fund, Johns Hopkins, 2002. Author 24 textbooks; contbr. 500 articles to profl. jours. Spl. advisor sci. tech. Office Gov. NC, Raleigh, 1994—96; pres. Assn. Univ. Radiology, 1989, Soc. Chairs Radiology Dept., 1981—, Am. Roentgen Ray Soc., 1992; mem. bd. Duke U. Med. Sch., 1986—94. Capt. U.S. Army, 1964—66. NRC/NAS Picker fellow, 1969-71, Royal Soc. Medicine Hon. fellow, 1974-75. Mem.: Am. Roentgen Ray Soc. (Gold medal 2003), Assn. U. Radiologists (Gold medal 2003), Nat. Coun. Radiation Protection, Bd. NC Sch. Vet. Med. (pres. 1997—98), NIH Conjoint Com. Radiology, Can. Radiol. Soc. (hon.), Pres.'s Club (John Hopkins U.), Chancellors Club (U. N.C.), Davidson Club, Preservation N.C. Bd. Coun., Alpha Omega Alpha. Avocations: writing, 19th and 20th century American art, folk art, pottery, tennis. Home: 205 New Castle Pl Chapel Hill NC 27517 Office: St James Place 205 New Castle Place Chapel Hill NC 27514 Home Fax: 919-942-0347. Personal E-mail: everette@nc.rr.com.

JAMES, ANTHONY F. social worker; b. Somerville, N.J., July 2, 1948; s. John Anthony and Margaret Grover James; m. Deborah Elizabeth Williams, Sept. 16, 1989; 1 child, Michael White;1 child, Yareeva Jennings. BA in Polit. Sci., Rutgers U., 1969, postgrad. Employment specialist Somerset County Employment and Placement/C.E.T.A., 1975—82, N.J. Assn. on Correction/Morrow Project, New Brunswick, NJ, 1982—85; family counselor, program dir. Urban League of Union County/Youth Partnership Program, 1985—87; program dir. Grant Ave. Cmty. Ctr., Plainfield, NJ, 1987—90; salesmen Global Auto Mall, North Plainfield, NJ, 1990—93, Sansone Auto Galleria, Avenel, NJ, 1990—93; optional customer rep. Am. Comm. Network, Pitts., 1993—. Avocations: photography, karate instructor, physical fitness. Home: 6062 Lafayette Ave Somerset NJ 08873

JAMES, BRUCE RICHARD, information specialist; b. Cleve., Oct. 19, 1942; s. George R. and Dorothy B. (Watson) J.; m. Jo Ann Osborn, Feb. 5, 1966 (div. Feb. 1982); children: Michael, Jeffrey, Stephen; m. Nora Ellen Thomas, May 11, 1985. BS, Rochester (N.Y.) Inst. Tech., 1964. V.p. Keller-Crescent Co., Evansville, Ind., 1964-70; v.p. Cardinal Co., San Francisco, 1970-73; pres., CEO Uniplan Corp., San Francisco, 1973-83, Electrographic Corp., San Francisco, 1983-93; chmn., CEO Barclays Law Pubs., San Francisco, 1986-94; pres., CEO Nev. New-Tech, Inc., Incline Village, Nev., 1993—; pub. printer of the U.S., 2002—. Mem. dean's adv. coun. U. Nev. Las Vegas Boyd Sch. of Law, 1999-2002; bd. dirs. BIPAC, Washington, 1999-2002; chmn. bd. dirs. Polish-Am. Print Co., Warsaw, 1990-93; pres. Printing Industries of Calif., 1989-91; mem. dean's adv. bd. U. Nev.-Las Vegas Boyd Sch. of Law, 1999=2002; pub. printer, CEO U.S. Govt. Printing Office, 2002—. Candidate U.S. Senate, 1997-98; chmn. bd. trustees Rochester Inst. Tech., 1993—; chair emeritus bd. trustees Sierra Nev. Coll., Incline Village, 1997—; mem. Bd. of Equalization, Reno, 1995-97; trustee U. Nev. Desert Rsch. Inst., 1999-2002; dir. Nev. Test Site Devel. Corp., 1999-2002, Western Folklife Ctr., Elko, Nev., 1999-2002; bd. dirs. Cmty. Found. Western Nev., 1999-2002; fin. chmn. Nev. Rep. Party, 2000-2002. Commencement spkr. Rochester Inst. Tech., 1998, Alumnus of Yr., 1997; recipient Silver Beaver award Boys Scouts Am., 1992. Mem.: Nat. Fedn. Independent Businesses, Printing Industries of Am. (chair congl. roundtable), Alexis de Tocqueville Soc. (Nev. state chmn. 1999—), World Trade Club San Francisco, Las Vegas C. of C., Internat. Wine and Food Soc., Confrerie de la Chaine des Rotisseurs, Stirling Club (Las Vegas), Genesse Valley Club (Rochester N.Y.). Republican. Episcopalian. Office: Office of Pub Printer US Govt Printing Office Washington DC 20401

JAMES, CAROL LEE, communications executive; b. Farmington, Minn., Aug. 30, 1947; d. Clayton Roger and Jane Ellen (Bowe) Christian; m. Michael D. Moss, Jan. 27, 1996. BA, U. Minn., 1968. Asst. editor Miller Pub., Mpls., 1968-70; mng. editor Midland Coops. (now Land O'Lakes, Inc.), 1970-79; dir. publs., pub. affairs Farm Credit Svcs., St. Paul, 1979-81; v.p. Nat. Coop. Bus. Assn. and Coop. Devel. Found., 1981-84; sr. cons. assoc. Food Sys. Assocs., Washington, 1984-98; prin. Carol James Comm., Alexandria, Va., 1984—. Founder and co-owner Restoration Restaurants, St. Paul, 1975-78; researcher Andrew J. Volstead Mus., 1979. Author: Strengthening People to People Development into the 1990's, 1988, A Guide to Debt for Development, 1989, Spanning Boundaries: Rethinking Community, Competitiveness, and Cooperation, 1995; co-author: Toward a New Consensus on Public/Private Approaches to International Development, 1988, Insuring Development Through Popular-Based Insurance, 1991, editor: Finding Co-ops., 1984; Washington editor and co-pub. Dairy Profit Weekly, 1989-99. V.p. and gen. mgr. St. Paul Cable Coop., 1979-81; bd. dirs. Fairfax Cable Assn., Merrifield, Va., 1983-91, Greenbelt Co-op., Inc., Savage, Md., 1989-91, Nat. Coop. Bus. Assn., 1992-94, DPW Pub., Inc., Mpls., 1993-99. Recipient Co-op. Comm. award Nat. Coordinating Com. for Oct., Washington, 1983. Mem. Co-operative Comm. Assn. (past pres., Michael A. Graznak award), Nat. Press Club. Home and Office: 1000 N Vail St Alexandria VA 22304-1939

JAMES, CHARLES E., JR., lawyer; b. Pontiac, Mich., Sept. 19, 1948; BA, Occidental Coll., 1970; JD with high distinction, U. Ariz. Bar: Ariz. 1973. Ptnr. Gust Rosenfeld, Phoenix, 1979—86, Snell & Wilmer, Phoenix, 1992—99, Squire, Sanders and Dempsey, Phoenix, 2000—, Chapman and Cutler, Phoenix, 1986—92. Mem. ABA, Nat. Assn. Bond Lawyers. Office: Squire Sanders & Dempsey 40 N Central Ave Ste 2700 Phoenix AZ 85004-4498 E-mail: cjames@ssd.com.

JAMES, CHARLES FRANKLIN, JR., engineering educator, educator; b. Des Arc, Mo., July 16, 1931; s. Charles Franklin and Beulah Frances (Kyte) J.; m. Mollie Keeler, May 18, 1974; children: Thomas Elisha, Matthew Jeremiah. BS, Purdue U., 1958, MS, 1960, PhD, 1963. Registered profl. engr., Wis. Sr. indsl. engr. McDonnel Aircraft Co., 1963; asst. prof. U. R.I., 1963-66, prof., chmn. dept. indsl. engring., 1967-82, co-founder, mem Robotics Rsch. Ctr., 1980-83; C. Paul Stocker prof. engring. Ohio U., Athens, 1982-83; dean Coll. Engring. and Applied Sci., U. Wis.-Milw., 1984-95; v.p. academics Milw. Sch. of Engring., 1995-2000; ret., 2000. Cons. Asian Productivity Orgn.; arbitrator Fed. Mediation and Conciliation Service, Am. Arbitration Assn.; bd. dirs. Badger Meter Co., Milw. Contbr. articles to profl. jours. With USAF, 1951-55. Recipient Silver medal Tech. U. Budapest, Hungary, 1989. Mem. NSPE, ASME, Wis. Soc. Profl. Engrs. (pres. Milw. chpt. 1993-94, Outstanding Profl. Engr. in Edn. 1993, state-wide treas. 1994-96), Inst. Indsl. Engrs., Am. Soc. Engring. Edn., Soc. Mfg. Engrs., Am. Foundrymen's Soc., Engrs. and Scis. of Milw. (bd. dirs. 1988-95, v.p. 1991-93, pres.-elect 1993-94, pres. 1994-95).

JAMES, CLARITY (CAROLINE FAYE JAMES), mezzo-soprano, b. Wheatland, Wyo., Apr. 27, 1945; d. Ralph Everett and Gladys Charlotte (Johnson) J. Mus.B., U. Wyo., 1964; Mus.M., Ind. U., 1967. Cert. instr. Radiance Technique. Prof. voice Radford (Va.) U., 1990—. Asst. prof. voice U. Iowa, Iowa City, 1968-72 Debut in opera as Madame Flora in: The Medium, St. Paul Opera, 1971; also sang role with Houston Grand Opera, 1972, Opera Theatre St. Louis, 1976, Augusta (Ga.) Opera Co., 1976; N.Y.C. Opera debut as Baroness in: The Young Lord, 1973; N.Y.C. Opera debut as Widow Begbick in Mahogonny, Opera Co. of Boston, 1973; created role Mother Rainey in: The Sweet Bye and Bye, 1973; Mrs. G. in: Captain Jinks, 1976; Mrs. Cratchit in A Christmas Carol (Musgrave), 1979; created Mrs. Doc in world premiere of A Quiet Place (Leonard Bernstein), Houston, 1983; debut Chgo. Lyric Opera, 1983, Vienna Staatsoper, 1986, National Symphony, 1986, Phila. Orch., 1986; numerous appearances with opera cos. throughout U.S. and fgn. countries including, Dallas Civic Opera, Cin. Opera Co., Netherlands Opera, Amsterdam, Florentine Opera. Rec. artist. Martha Baird Rockefeller grantee, Corbett Found. grantee, 1968; Met. Opera Assn. grantee; recipient Lillian Garabedian award Santa Fe Opera, 1967, Exemplary Alumni award U. Wyo., 1994; named Young Artist Nat. Fedn. Music Clubs, 1972. Office: Radford U Dept Music Radford VA 24142 E-mail: cjames@radford.edu.

JAMES, DANIEL, III, military officer; BA in Psychology, U. Ariz., Tucson, 1968; grad., Air Commd. Staff Coll., 1981. Commd. 2d lt. Air Nat. Guard, 1968, advanced through grades to lt. gen., 2002—, dir., 2002—. Chmn. Greater Austin Quality Coun., 1998—99. Decorated Legion of Merit, Dissing. Flying Cross with oak leaf cluster, Air medal with six oak leaf clusters, Air Force Commendation medal, Air Force Achievement medal, Vietnam Gallantry Cross with palm; recipient Garvey-Woodson award, Black United Fund Tex., 1995, Outstanding Svc. award, Tex. STARBASE, 1995—96, Benjamin D. Foulois First Flight award, Air Force Assn. Tex., 1997, Cmty. Svc. award, Ctrl. Tex. Combined Fed. Campaign, 1997—98, Honored Patriot award, Selective Svc. Sys., 1998—99, Mil. Svc. commendation, Joint Session Tex. Legis., 1999, Palmetto Patriot award, SC, 1999. Office: Nat Guard Bur 1411 Jeff Davis Hwy Arlington VA 22202*

JAMES, DAVID LEE, lawyer, international advisor, author; b. Chgo., Aug. 23, 1933; s. Roy L. and Ethel (Wells) J.; m. Sheila Feagley, May 26, 1962; children: Pamela, James, Winifred, Paul, Brian, Adam. AB, Harvard U., 1955; JD, U. Chgo., 1960; grad. exec. program, Stanford U., 1979. Bar: N.Y. 1961, N.J. 1967, Hawaii 1976, Ill. 1987. With various law firms, N.Y.C., 1960-67; counsel and asst. gen. counsel, asst. sec. Texasgulf Inc., 1967-75; gen. counsel, sec. Dillingham Corp., Honolulu, 1975-77, v.p., gen. counsel, sec., 1977-84, v.p. legal affairs, sec. San Francisco, 1984-85; asst. gen. counsel, asst. sec. Crown Zellerbach Corp., San Francisco, 1985-86; sr. ptnr., sr. corp. atty. Arnstein & Lehr, Chgo., 1987-90, of counsel, 1990-96; chmn. bus. programs East-West Ctr., Honolulu, 1990-92; chief of party and sr. law devel. advisor USAID and Govt. of Indonesia, Jakarta, Indonesia, 1992-93; pres. Bus. Strategies Internat., San Francisco, Calif., 1993—, www.bsicorp.net, San Francisco, 1993—. Hon. consul of Malaysia, Hawaii, 1977-84; adv. bd. Internat. and Comparative Law Ctr., Southwestern Legal Found., Dallas, 1976-91; adv. com. Law of Sea Inst., Honolulu, 1977-84; lectr. in law Stanford U. Sch. Law, 1996-98. Author: Doing Business in Asia, 1993, The Executive Guide to Asia-Pacific Communications, 1995; contbg. editor TheFeature.com; contbr. various articles on bus. and legal subjects. Bd. dirs. Chgo. Chamber Orch., 1988-90, pres. 1989-90, Jr. Achievement Hawaii, 1976-84, Hawaii Opera Theatre, 1981-84, Friends of East-West Ctr., 1982-84; mem. Morristown (N.J.) Bd. Edn., 1967-68. Served to lt. (j.g.) USNR, 1955-57. Mem. Outrigger Canoe Club (Honolulu), Harvard Club (N.Y.C.). Office: Bus Strategies Internat 425 Market St Ste 2200 San Francisco CA 94105-2434 E-mail: djames@bsicorp.net.

JAMES, EDGERRIN, football player; b. Aug. 1, 1978; Football player Indpls. Colts, 1999—. Guest spkr. DARE prog. various schools; founder Edgerrin James Found. Named All-Pro 1st Team Assoc. Press, Coll. and Pro Football Newsweekly, Football Digest, Pro Football Weekly, Sporting News, USA Today, All AFC Team Football News, Pro Football Weekly, NFL All Rookie Team Coll. and Pro Football Newsweekly, Football Digest, Football News, Pro Football Weekly. Achievements include NFL rushing title, 1999, Pro Bowl player, 1999. Office: Indpls Colts PO Box 535000 Indianapolis IN 46253 also: 7001 West 56th Street Indianapolis IN 46254

JAMES, ELIZABETH JOAN PLOGSTED, pediatrician, educator; b. Jefferson City, Mo., Jan. 15, 1939; d. Joseph Matthew Plogsted and Maxie Pearl (Manford) Plogsted Acuff; m. Ronald Carney James, Aug. 25, 1962; children: Susan Elizabeth, Jason Michael. BS in Chemistry, Lincoln U., 1960; MD, U. Mo., 1965. Diplomate Am. Bd. Pediat., Am. Bd. Neonatal-Perinatal Medicine. Resident in pediat. U. Mo. Hosps. & Clinics, Columbia, 1965-68, fellow in neonatology, 1968-69, dir. neonatal-perinatal medicine Children's Hosp., 1971—; fellow in neonatal-perinatal medicine U. Colo. Hosps., Denver, 1969-71; from asst. to assoc. prof. pediatrics and obstetrics sch. medicine U. Mo., 1971-83, prof. child health and obstetrics, 1983—. Dir. pediatric edn. program dept. child health sch. medicine U. Mo., Columbia, 1989-98. Mem. editl. bd. Mo. Medicine, 1983—; contbr. chpts. to books and articles to profl. jours. Fellow Am. Acad. Pediat. (sect. neonatal-perinatal medicine); mem. Mo. State Med. Assn., Boone County Med. Soc., Alpha Omega Alpha. Roman Catholic. Avocations: classical music, bicycling, herb gardening. Office: U Mo Hosps & Clinics Childrens Hosp 1 Hospital Dr Columbia MO 65201-5276 E-mail: jamese@health.missouri.edu.

JAMES, ESTELLE, economist, educator; b. Bronx, NY, Dec. 1, 1935; d. Abraham and Lee (Zeichner) Dinerstein; m. Ralph James (div. 1971); children: Deborah, David; m. Harry Lazer, June 27, 1971 (dec. 1994). BS, Cornell U., 1956; PhD, MIT, 1961. Lectr., econs. dept. U. Calif., Berkeley, 1964-65; acting asst. prof. Stanford U., 1965-67; assoc. prof. SUNY, Stony Brook, 1967-72, prof., 1972-94, provost, div. Social and Behavioral Sci., 1975-79, chmn. dept., 1982-86. Vis. scholar Yale U., Australian Nat. U., Tel Aviv U., Brookings Inst., others; cons. World Bank, Washington, 1986—91, sr. economist, 1991—94, lead economist, 1994—2000, cons., 2000—; vis. fellow Urban Inst., Washington, 2002—. Author: (book) Hoffa and the Teamsters, 1964, The Nonprofit Sector in Market Economies, 1986, Pub. Policy and Pvt. Ed. in Japan, 1988, The Nonprofit Sector in Internat. Perspective, 1989, Averting the Old Age Crisis, 1994, The Gender Impact of Pension Reform, 2003; contbr. articles to profl. jour. Recipient Fulbright award, 1979; fellow, Woodrow Wilsont Internat. Ctr., Washington, 1981—82, Netherlands Inst. Advanced Study, 1986—87, U.S. Dept. Edn., 1988, Sec. of Navy, 1990, AAUW, Soc. Sci. Rsch. Coun.; grantee Rsch., Spencer Found., USAID, NEH, Exxon Edn. Found., NSF. Mem.: Am. Econs. Assn. E-mail: ejames@estellejames.com.

JAMES, FOB, JR., (FORREST HOOD JAMES), former governor; b. Lanett, Ala., Sept. 15, 1934; s. Forrest Hood Sr. and Rebecca (Ellington) J.; m. Bobbie Mae Mooney; children: Forrest Hood III, Timothy E., Patrick F. BSCE, Auburn U., 1955. Mem. Montreal Alouettes, Ont., Can., 1956-57; constrn. supt. Ala., 1958-62; founder, chmn. bd. Diversified Products Corp., 1962-78; gov. State of Ala., 1978-82, 96-99; CEO Coastal Erosion Control, Inc., Escambia County Environ. Corp. Active Cystic Fibrosis Found., Boy Scouts Am., Ala. Saftey Coun., Jr. Achievement, Future Farmers Am. Served as lt. U.S. Army, 1957-58. Mem. Young Pres.'s Orgn., Ala. Road Builders Assn. (hon. life), Am. Legion, Spade Honor Soc., Alpha Sigma Epsilon. Republican.

JAMES, FRANCIS EDWARD, JR., investment counselor; b. Woodville, Miss., Jan. 5, 1931; s. Francis Edwin and Ruth (Phillips) J.; m. Iris Senn, Nov. 3, 1952; children: Francis III, Barry, David. BS, La. State U., 1951; MS, Rensselaer Poly. Inst., 1966, PhD, 1967. Commd. 2d lt. USAF, 1950, advanced through grades to col., 1972; prof. mgmt. and statistics, chmn. dept quantitative studies Air Force Inst. Tech., Wright Patterson AFB, 1967-71, dir. grad. edn. div. mgmt. programs, 1972-74; ret. USAF, 1974; pres. James Investment Rsch., Inc., Alpha, Ohio, 1972—. Cons. math. modeling. Author: A Matrix Solution for the General Linear Regression Model; contbr. articles to profl. jours. Bd. dirs. James Capital Alliance, Inc. Decorated Legion of Merit, D.F.C., Air medal, Joint Services Commendation medal, Meritorious Service medal; recipient Outstanding Acad. Achievement award Rensselaer Poly. Inst., 1965, first Alumni Fellow appointment Rensselaer Poly. Inst. Mem. Am. Statis. Assn., Mil. Ops. Research Soc., Am. Fin. Assn., Investment Counsel Assn. Am., Mktg. Technicians Assn., Soc. Logistics Engring. (Eckles award 1973, tech. chmn.), Sigma Iota Epsilon, Epsilon Delta Sigma. Lodges: Masons, Rotary. Home: 2604 Lantz Rd Dayton OH 45434-6627 Office: James Investment Rsch Inc PO Box 8 Alpha OH 45301-0008 *To come up with an outstanding idea is brilliance. To put that idea into action is real genius.*

JAMES, FRANCIS MARSHALL, III, anesthesiologist; b. Phila., Pa., Dec. 22, 1935; MD, Hahnemann U., 1961. Intern Phila. Gen. Hosp., Phila., 1961—62; resident Hosp. U. Pa., Phila., 1964—67, attending anesthesiologist, 1967—68, NC Bapt. Hosp., Winston-Salem, 1968—2000; assoc. dean grad. med. edn. Wake Forest U., NC, 1999-2000, faculty Sch. Medicine, 1968—2000, chair dept. anesthesiology, 1983—98, prof. emeritus, 2001—. Dir. Am. Bd. Anesthesiology, 1988-2000, pres., 1999-2000. Office: Wake Forest U Sch Medicine Dept Anesthesiology Medical Ctr Blvd Winston Salem NC 27157-1009 E-mail: fjames@wfubmc.edu.

JAMES, GARY DOUGLAS, biological anthropologist, educator, researcher; b. Norwich, Conn., Dec. 6, 1954; s. Godfrey Merchant and Joan (McIlwaine) J.; m. Kathleen Louise Wilson, July 28, 1979. BA, Wake Forest U., 1976; MA, Pa. State U., 1980, PhD, 1984. Part-time instr. Pa. State U., University Park, 1982-84; postdoctoral assoc. Cornell U. Med. Coll., N.Y.C., 1984-86; from asst. prof. to assoc. rsch. prof. physiology in medicine and biophysics Med. Coll. Cornell U., NYC, 1991—98; rsch. prof. Decker Sch. Nursing, SUNY, Binghamton, 1998—, dir. inst. for primary and preventive health care, 1999—, adj. prof. anthropology, 1999—2003, prof. anthropology, 2003—. Adj. prof. dept. psychology SUNY, Binghampton, NY, 2000—. Contbr. chpt. to book, articles to profl. jours. Recipient New Investigator Rsch. award NIH, 1986, Internat. Man of the Yr. award Internat. Biog. Ctr., 1993; NIH postdoctoral trainee, 1984. Fellow Human Biol. Assn. (sec.-treas. 1992-96, exec. com. 1996-2000), Soc. Behavioral Medicine; mem. AAAS, Am. Assn. Phys. Anthropologists, Internat. Platform Assn., Soc. for Study Social Biology, Am. Soc. Hypertension, Am. Anthrop. Assn., Am. Dermatologlyphics Assn. (exec. com. 1996-98, sec. 1998-99, editor newsletter 2001—, pres.-elect/pres. 2002—), The Harvey Soc. Lutheran. Office: Decker Sch of Nursing Binghamton Univ SUNY Box 6000 Binghamton NY 13902-6000 E-mail: gdjames@binghamton.edu.

JAMES, GENEVA BEHRENS, secondary school educator; b. Marietta, Minn., Mar. 23, 1942; d. Siegfried and Dora (Schoenrock) Behrens; m. Howard James, Aug. 2, 1963; children: Scott, Dawn. BS, Mankato State U., 1963. Tchr. English Minn. High Schs., 1964-65; instr. acctg. adult continuing edn. Bellevue, Nebr., 1971-75; dir. adult basic edn. ctr., 1974-91; vol. coord. Adult Basic Edn. Ctr., Bellevue, 1983-91; instr. secondary schs. Bellevue, 1980-2000; instr. computer literacy, 1984-91; instr. pilot computer program, 1987-88; advanced placement eng. instr., 1999-2000. Seminar presenter Nebr. State Adult Edn. Assn., 1986, Commn. on Adult Basic Edn., 1987; mem. review bd. English Curriculum Textbook Selection Com. for 10-yr. curriculum, 1996—, Bellevue (Nebr.) Pub. Schs. Computer Utilization Com., 1992—; mem. adv. bd. adult edn., 1993—; mem. student mgmt. team Bellevue West H.S., 1995, mem. disciplinary curriculum team, 1995; developed Jr. Career Project Grade 11, 1998; chmn. North Ctrl. Accreditation Team, 1996, advanced placement instr., 1999-2000; mem. indsl. internship Work Keys-Perkins Grant, 1996; continuing edn. instr. Met. C.C., Omaha, 1999, instr. Advanced Placement English, 1999-2000; noncredit class instr. Met. C.C., 1999—. Reader, Radio TAlking Books. Mem. exec. com. Boy Scouts Am., 1974-80; mem. met. cmty. PLUS task force, 1986-88; vol. Adminstrv. Offices Fontenelle Nature Assn., 2000—, Radio Talking Books, Omaha, 2000—, Durham We. Heritage Mus. Recipient indsl. internship 1997, Careers 2000, scholarship 1998. Mem.: PEC (bd. dirs. 1998—2000), NEA, AAUW, Nat. Coun. Tchrs. English (profl. edn. coun. 1998—2000), Bellevue Edn. Assn. (bldg. rep. 1997, nat. honor soc. selection com. 1996, dist. scholarship selection com. 1996—2000, exec. bd. 1998—2000), Adult and Continuing Edn. Assn. Nebr., Nat. Assn. Pub. and Continuing Adult Edn., WHAR Investment Club (pres.), Alpha Delta Kappa (chmn. scholarship com. 1985—86, 1991—2000, pres. 2002—, state legis. chair 2000—). Republican. Lutheran. Home: 5004 Lakeside Dr Papillion NE 68133-4715 E-mail: genjames@aol.com.

JAMES, GEORGE BARKER, II, investment executive; b. Haverhill, Mass., May 25, 1937; s. Paul Withington and Ruth (Burns) J.; m. Beverly A. Burch, Sept. 22, 1962; children: Alexander, Christopher, Geoffrey, Matthew. AB, Harvard U., 1959; MBA, Stanford U., 1962. Fiscal dir. E.G. & G. Inc., Bedford, Mass., 1963-67; fin. exec. Am. Brands Inc., N.Y.C., 1967-69; v.p. Pepsico, Inc., N.Y.C., 1969-72; sr. v.p., chief fin. officer Arcata Corp., Menlo Park, Calif., 1972-82; exec. v.p. Crown Zellerbach Corp., San Francisco, 1982-85; sr. v.p., chief fin. officer Levi Strauss & Co., San Francisco, 1985-98. Bd. dirs. Pacific States Industries, Inc., Clayton Group Inc., Crown Vantage Corp (chmn.), Dresdner RCM Capital Corp, Sharper Image, Inc., Callious Software Inc., Canned Foods Inc.; dir. Il Fornaio Restaurants. Author: Industrial Development in the Ohio Valley, 1962. Mem. Andover (Mass.) Town Com., 1965-67; mem. Select Congl. Com. on World Hunger; mem. adv. coun. Calif. State Employees Pension Fund; chmn. bd. dirs. Towle Trust Fund; trustee Nat. Corp. Fund for the Dance, Cate Sch., Levi Strauss Found., Stern Grove Festival Assn., Zellerbach Family Fund, San Francisco Ballet Assn., Com. for Econ. Devel.; bd. dirs. Stanford U. Hosp., Calif. Pacific Med. Ctr. KQED; vice-chmn. World Affairs Coun.; mem. San Francisco Com. on Fgn. Rels. With AUS, 1960-61. Mem. Pacific Union Club, Bohemian Club, Menlo Circus Club, Harvard Club, N.Y. Athletic Club. Home: 207 Walnut St San Francisco CA 94118-2012 Office: Crown Vantage Inc 4445 Lakeforest Dr Ste 700 Cincinnati OH 45242

JAMES, GERARD LUZ AMWUR, II, former lieutenant governor; b. Christainsted, St. Croix, Mar. 18, 1953; m. Lisa Ann C. James; children: Jenee', Gerard III, Jenelle, Jalani. BA, Howard U., 1975; diploma, Am. Acad. McAllister Inst. Funeral Svc., 1982. Lic. Funeral Dir. N.Y., Comml. Pilot Cert. Sen. V.I. Legislature, 1992—99; lt. gov. U.S. V.I., 1999—2003; chmn. Banking Bd., 1999—2003; commr. V.I. Divsn. Banking and Ins., 1999—2003. Apprentice Crowe's Funeral Home, Queens, NY; pres. James Meml. Funeral Home, Inc., 1983—92. Mem. Holy Cross Cath. Ch. 2nd lt. U.S. Army, 1975—79, capt. USMC, 1979—81. Mem.: Nat. Conf. Lt. Govs. (exec. com.), Aircraft Owners and Pilots Assn., N.Y. State Funeral Dirs. Assn., Nat. Funeral Dirs. Assn., Nat. Funeral Dirs. and Morticians Assn., Omega Psi Phi. Democrat. Mailing: PO Box 224605 Christiansted VI 00822-4605*

JAMES, GORDON, III, lawyer; b. Montclair, N.J., Feb. 24, 1947; s. Ernest Gordon Jr. and Betty (Wackerman) J.; m. Adelia Louise Medlin (div. Sept. 1989); children: Deidre Leigh, Diana Catherine, Gordon Daniel; m. Yolanda Trapana. BS, U. Tenn., 1969; JD, Vanderbilt U., 1972. Bar: Fla. 1972, U.S. Dist. Ct. (so. dist.) Fla. 1972, D.C. 1973, U.S. Ct. Appeals (11th cir.) 1980, U.S. Dist. Ct. (mid. dist.) Fla. 1985, U.S. Dist. Ct. (no. dist.) Fla. 1986, U.S. Supreme Ct. 1988. Assoc. Bradford, Williams, Kimbrell, et al, Miami, Fla., 1972-76; ptnr. Druck, Grimmett, Norman, Weaver, Scherer, Ft. Lauderdale, Fla., 1976-77, Druck, Grimmett, Scherer, James, Ft. Lauderdale, 1977-78, Grimmett, Scherer, James, Ft. Lauderdale, 1978-79, Conrad, Scherer, James & Jenne, Ft. Lauderdale, 1979-95, Heinrich Gordon Hargrove Weihe & James, Ft. Lauderdale, 1995—. Eucharistic lay minister, All Saints Episcopal Ch., 1991—; Gueardian Ad LIet Program Broward County, 1995-. Capt. USAR, 1969-77. Mem. ABA, Fla. Bar Assn. (vice chmn. civil rule of procedure com. 1990-91), Nat. Assn. R.R. Counsel, Am. Bd. Trial Advs. (cert., Ft. Lauderdale chpt. pres. 1998), Def. Rsch. Inst., Fla. Def. Lawyers (pres. 1991-92). Republican. Avocations: fishing, snow skiing, scuba diving, physical and aerobics exercise. Office: Heinrich Gordon Hargrove Weihe & James 500 E Broward Blvd Fort Lauderdale FL 33394-3000 E-mail: jamesiii@heinrichgordon.com.

JAMES, H. NEAL, video, record, movie producer, director; b. Commerce, Ga., Oct. 10, 1952; s. Carl and Viola (Thomas) J. Student, Gainesville Jr. Coll., 1972-73, U. Ga., 1973-74. Pres. Neal James Orgn., Inc., Athens, Ga., 1979—, Cottage Blue Music BMI, Nashville, 1986—, Prodns. Unlimited, Nashville, 1987—; v.p. Video Zine Enterprises Inc., Athens, 1987—. Pres. 3d Coast Video Promotions, Nashville, Neal James Music BMI, Hidden Cove Music ASCAP, Millennium II Prodns., Neal James Prodns. Featured songwriter The Nashville Network, 1987; produced projects featuring George Jones, Willie Nelson, Hank Cochran, Dottie West, Merle Haggard, Vern Gosdin, Johnny Paycheck, Steve Cropper, The Tams, REM, Bruce Springsteen, Shondells, David Allen Coe. Recipient 16 nominations for songwriting Country Music Assn., 1984, 85, 87, Producer of Yr. award, 1993, Dir. of Yr. award, Lifetime Achievement award Ho. Reps., Ga., Masters award, 2000. Mem. Am. Fedn. Musician, Music Video Assn., Nat. Entertainment Journalists Assn., Nat. Acad. Rec. Arts and Scis., Country Music Assn., Broadcast Music Inc. Avocations: sports cars, real estate, flying, sailing, scuba diving. Home and Office: PO Box 121626 Nashville TN 37212-1626

JAMES, HELEN ANN, plastic surgeon; b. Palmerston North, New Zealand, May 5, 1940; came to U.S., 1977; d. George Headley and Betty Beatrice (McDonald) J.; married (dec. Apr. 1993). MB, ChB, U. Otago, Dunedin, New Zealand, 1964; Fellow, Royal Coll. Surgeons, London, England, 1972. Diplomate Am. Bd. Plastic Surgery. Internship Palmerston North Hosp., New Zealand, 1965-66; residency plastic surgery Brd Earn Hosp., Perthshire, England, 1973-74, St. Lukes Hosp., Bradford, England, 1975-77; fellow plastic surgery Mount Sinai Med. Ctr., Miami Beach, 1977-79; residency plastic surgery N.C. Meml. Med. Ctr., Chapel Hill, 1979-81; St. Joseph Hosp., Bellingham, Wash.; pvt. practice Bellingham, Wash. Mem. AMA, Am. Soc. Plastic and Reconstructive Surgeons, Am. Soc. Aesthetic Plastic Surgeons, Wash. State Med. Assn. Avocations: tennis, birding, cycling. Office: 3001 Squalicum Pkwy Ste 5 Bellingham WA 98225-1930

JAMES, HELEN FOSTER, education director; b. San Diego, Sept. 3, 1951; d. Seth Charles and Naomi Charlene; m. Robert Paul James, May 25, 1987. BA, San Diego State U., 1973, MEd, 1980; DEd, No. Ariz. U., 1990. Cert. adminstrv. svcs., libr. svcs., C.C. credential, elem. credential. Elem. tchr. Jamul (Calif.) Sch. Dist., 1978-82; media specialist San Diego (Calif.) County Office Edn., 1982-89; coord. libr. media svcs. Santee (Calif.) Sch. Dist., 1989-96, San Diego State U., 1996—. Publs. adv. bd. Ednl Horizons, Bloomington, Ind., 1988-92; adv. bd. mem. Sch. Book Fairs, St. Petersburg, Fla., 1993-95; com. mem. Calif. Young Reader Medal Com., Calif., 1994-98; mem. Carnegie Com., 2001-02. Author: Across the Generations, 1997, Day Adventures, 2003. Adv. cons. San Diego (Calif.) Children's Mus., 1982-94; bd. mem. Carlsbad (Calif.) Children's Mus., 1994-96. Fellow Calif. State U. L.A., 1986. Mem. Internat. Reading Assn., Calif. Tchrs. English, Soc. Children's Book Writer's and Illustrators, Greater San Diego Reading Assn. (pres. 1985-86, bd. mem., award of excellence 1993), Pi Lambda Theta (com. mem., Anna Tracey Meml. award 1993). Avocations: hiking, camping, backpacking. Home and Office: 3818 Riviera Dr Apt 1 San Diego CA 92109-6307

JAMES, HENRY THOMAS, former foundation executive, educator; b. Ferryville, Wis., May 19, 1915; s. Harry T. and Alice (Morgan) J.; . Vienna Lewis, June 6, 1939; children: Angelyn Alice (Mrs. Richard J. Grillo), Henry Thomas, Jennifer Lewis (Mrs. Timothy J. Regan), Mary Ellen (Mrs. Robert S. Lewis), Elizabeth Elinor (Mrs. Betty Folliard), Arthur Earl. BS, Wis. State U., 1938; Ph.M., U. Wis., 1939; PhD, U. Chgo., 1958. High sch. tchr., Barron, Wis., 1939-42; supervising prin. Woodville, Wis., 1942-43; counselor U. Wis., Madison, 1946; supt. schs. Augusta, Wis., 1946-49, Whitewater, Wis., 1949-50; asst. supt. pub. instrn., 1950-54; lectr. U. Mich., 1954; asso. dir. Midwest Adminstrn. Center, asst. prof., asso. prof., dir. field services U. Chgo. Sch. Edn., 1954-58; prof. Stanford Sch. Edn., 1958-70, dean, 1966-70; pres. Spencer Found., Chgo., 1970-85, pres. emeritus, 1985—. Cons. in field, 1954—, dir. studies sch. bds. and state sch. finance systems, 1954—; mem. N.Y. Fleischmann Commn., 1969-72, Presdl. Task Force on Edn., 1968, 80; adviser subcom. efficiency and innovation in edn. Com. Econ. Devel.; study dir. The Nation's Report Card, 1986-87; series editor various pub. cos.; chmn. vis. com. Ednl. Testing Svc., 1989-90. Sr. author: School Revenue Systems in Five States, 1961, Wealth, Expenditures and Decision-Making for Education, 1963, Determinants of Educational Expenditures in Large Cities of the United States, 1966, The New Cult of Efficiency and Education, 1969; Editor: Boardmanship, 1961; Editorial adv. bd.: Edn. and Urban Society, 1968—, Contemporary Edn. Rev., 1982—; Contbr. articles to profl. jours. Served to lt. USNR, 1943-46. Recipient Distinguished Service award Nat. Assn. State Bds. Edn., 1973, Viterbo Coll. award for service to higher edn., 1975, Outstanding Service award Am. Edn. Fin. Assn., 1988. Mem. Am. Ednl. Research Assn. (chmn. nominating com. 1964-65, cons. editor jour. 1964-70, program chmn. 1968), Am. Assn. Sch. Adminstrs., AAAS, Nat. Acad. Edn., Univ. Council Ednl. Adminstrn., Chgo. Com., Council on Fgn. Relations, Phi Delta Kappa (bd. editorial cons. 1974-85). Presbyterian. Home: Knollwood Village 1047 Village Sq Altoona WI 54720-2558

JAMES, HERMAN DELANO, college administrator; b. St. Thomas, V.I., Feb. 25, 1943; s. Henry and Frances (Smith) J.; m. Marie Nannie Gray, Feb. 25, 1964; children— Renee, Sybil, Sidney BS, Tuskegee Inst., 1965; MA, St. John's U., N.Y.C., 1967; PhD, U. Pitts., 1972; LLD (hon.), Tuskagee U., 1996. Asst. prof. U. Mass., Boston, 1973-78, assoc. provost, 1975-77, asst. chancellor, 1977-78; vice provost Calif. State U.-Northridge, 1978-82; v.p. Rowan Coll. N.J., 1982-84; pres. Rowan U., Glassboro, 1984-98, pres. emeritus, disting. prof., 1998—. Bd. dirs. Mid. States Assn., S. Jersey Industries. Contbr. articles to profl. jours. Bd. dirs. Gloucester County (N.J.) United Way; mem. transition team for gov.-elect James Florio, N.J. NIH fellow, 1968-71; recipient Outstanding Achiever award Boston YMCA, 1977, Outstanding Contbr. award Nat. Ctr. for Deafness, 1982, Civic award Cherry Hill Minority Civic Assn., N.J., 1985; Tosney award, Amer. Assn. of Univ. Admin., 1994. Mem. Am. Assn. Higher Edn., Am. Sociol. Assn., N.J. C. of C. (bd. dirs.). Avocation: basketball. Home: 6 Brownstone Blvd Kirkwood Voorhees NJ 08043-3450 Office: Rowan U 201 Mullica Hill Rd Glassboro NJ 08028-1702

JAMES, JANIS LYNNE, b. Houston, Apr. 25, 1962; d. Bobby J. and Judith M. (Jennings) J. BA, U. Houston, 1985; MSW, U. Denver, 1992; MDiv, Iliff Sch. Theology, Denver, 1993. Avocations: vocal and instrumental music, sports.

JAMES, JEANNETTE ADELINE, state legislator, accountant; b. Maquoketa, Iowa, Nov. 19, 1929; d. Forest Claude and Winona Adeline (Meyers) Nims; m. James Arthur James, Feb. 16, 1948; children: James Arthur Jr., Jeannette, Alice Marie. Student, Merritt Davis Sch. Commerce, Salem, Oreg., 1956 57. Payroll supr. Gen. Foods Corp., Woodburn, Oreg., 1956-66; cost acctg., inventory control clk. Pacific Fence & Wire Co., Portland, Oreg., 1966-67, office mgr., 1968-69; substitute rural carrier U.S. Post Office, Woodburn, 1967-68; owner, mgr., acct. and tax preparer James Bus. Svc., Goldendale, Wash., 1969-75, Anchorage, 1975-77, Fairbanks, Alaska, 1977—; co-owner, mgr. Jolly Acres Motel, North Pole, Alaska, 1987—; mem. Alaska Ho. of Reps., Juneau, 1993—2003; chmn. House State Affairs, 1995-2000, jud. com., 1998 2002; vice chmn. Legis. Coun., 1995-96; chmn. joint com. Adminstrv. Regulation Rev., 1997-98, ho. majority leader, 2001—02. Cert. workshop and seminar leader, 1989-91; instr. workshop Comm. Dynamics, 1988. Vice chmn. Klickitat County Dems., Goldendale, 1970-74; bd. dirs. Mus. and Art Inst., Anchorage, 1976-80; pres. Anchorage Internat. Art Inst., 1976-78; chmn. platting bd. Fairbanks North Star Borough, 1980-84, mem. Planning Commn., 1984-87; treas., vice chmn. 18th Dist. Reps., North Pole, Alaska, 1984-92; mem. City of North Pole Econ. Devel. Com., 1992-93. Named Legislator of Yr., Alaska Farm Bur., 1994, Alaska Outdoor Coun., 2000, Juneau Empire, 2002, Guardian of Small Bus., Nat. Fedn. Ind. Bus., 1998, Friend of Psycology, 2001; recipient Defender of Freedom award, NRA, 1994, Friend of Municipalities award, Alaska Mcpl. League, 1996, Courage in Preserving Equal Access award, Alaska chpt. Safari Club Internat., 2000, Cmty. Svc. award, Arctic Alliance for People, 2001. Mem. Internat. Tgn. in Comm. (Alaska State winner speech contest 1981, 86), North Pole C. of C., Emblem Club, Rotary (treas. North Pole 1990), Eagles, Women of Moose. Presbyterian. Avocations: bowling, dolls, children. Home: 3068 Badger Rd North Pole AK 99705-6117 E-mail: jamesjeannette@gci.net.

JAMES, JOYCE MARIE, lawyer; b. Cin., Oct. 23, 1951; d. James Andrew and June Eleanor Connelly; m. Daniel K. James; children; Sarah Marie, Susan Barbara. Student, Shimer Coll., 1968-70; BA, U. Minn., 1974; JD cum laude, William Mitchell Coll. Law, 1979. Bar: Minn. 1979, U.S. Dist. Ct. Minn. 1979. Law clk. to presiding justice Minn. Dist. Ct., Stillwater, 1977-79; assoc. Dorsey & Whitney, Mpls., 1979-83, MacIntosh & Commers, Mpls., 1983-84; trust officer U.S. Bancorp, Mpls., 1984-90, v.p. personal trust, 1991-95, v.p. compliance, 1995—2002, v.p. regional personal trust spl. matters, 2002—, v.p. trust, 2003—. Adj. prof. William Mitchell Coll. Law, 1995-96. Chmn. legal advice clinics, Mpls., 1985-86, religious edn. com. Risen Saviour Ch., 2002-03; mem. ann. fund com. William Mitchell Coll. Law, 1999-2001, co-chair, 2000. Mem. ABA (task force legal fin. planning, significant new devels. in probate and trust law com.), YWCA (deferred giving com. 1986), Minn. State Bar Assn. (probate and trust law sect., chmn. community rels. com. 1984-87, pub affairs com. 1987-88, vice chair elder law sect. 1991-92, chmn. legis. subcom. 2001-2003), Minn. Women Lawyers Assn. (pres. 1984-85), Minn. Womens Fund (deferred giving com. 1985), Hennepin and Ramsey County Bar Assn. Avocations: golf, piano, biking, scripting.

JAMES, KATHRYN A. secondary education educator; b. Springfield, Mo., Aug. 1, 1925; d. Joseph Fred and Sybil Mae (Rogers) Giboney; m. Charles Elwyn James, Jan. 24, 1948 (wid. May 1999); children: Kathryne Janette, Jacquelyn Annette, Charles Roger. BSEd, S.W. Mo. State Tchrs. Coll., Springfield, 1945; MA, U. Mo., 1955; postgrad., U. Va., 1968. Life-term tchg. cert. in art, design, and home econs.; tchg. certs. in 6 states. Art supr. Mountain Grove (Mo.) Pub. Schs., 1945-47; art instr. Moberly (Mo.) Jr. Coll., 1947-49, Exptl. Sch., Springfield, Mo., 1949-54; art and home econs. instr. Ashland (Ky.) Pub. Schs., 1954-59; intinerant art tchr. Boyd County (Ky.) Pub. Schs., 1960-63; tchr. U. Ky., Lexington, 1963-65; art inst. Fairfax Pub. Schs., Va., 1965-68; art tchr. Terre Haute (Ind.) Pub. Schs., 1968-73, Springfield (Mo.) Pub. Schs., 1973-87. Judge sewing contests Singer Sewing Machine Co., Ashland, 1957-59, tchr. sewing classes pub. schs., adult evening and pub. sch. art classes, Ashland, 1956-58, Springfield, 1982-83. Author curriculum/art dept. Ashland and Terre Haute schs., 1955, 67-68; designer/banner constructor: Richard Ghephardt, Springfield, 1987. Campaigner Mo. State Legislators, Springfield, 1980-81, others. Recipient Gov.'s award Hon. Order of Ky. Cols., Lexington, 1965. Mem. Ky. Cols., Nat. DAR (flag chmn. 1991—, art awards 1995-97). Methodist. Avocations: china painting, interior decorating, freelance art work. Home: 1019 Joanne Dr Webb City MO 64870-1778 E-mail: jameswood@joplin.com.

JAMES, KAY COLES, federal agency administrator; b. Portsmouth, Va., June 1, 1949; d. Susie Armistead Coles; m. Charles Everett James; children: Charles Jr., Elizabeth, Robert III. BS, Hampton (Va.) Inst., 1971. Traffic svc. advisor C&P Telephone, Roanoke, Va., 1971-72, group supr., 1973, force mgr., 1974; conf. coord. devel. disabilities project State of Va., Richmond, 1978-79; asst. to housing coord. Housing Opportunities Made Equal, Richmond, 1980-81, dir. community edn. and devel., 1981-83; personnel dir. Cir. City Stores, Beltsville, Md., 1983-85; dir. pub. affairs Nat. Right to Life Com., Washington, 1985-88; asst. sec. pub. affairs Dept. Health and Human Svcs., Washington, 1989—90; assoc. dir. Office of Nat. Drug Control Policy, 1991—93; sr. v.p. Family Rsch. Coun., 1993—94; sec. Health and Human Resources Dept., Richmond, Va., 1994—96; dean Sch. of Govt. Regent U., 1996—99; sr. fellow of the Citizenship Project Heritage Found., 1999—2001; dir. O.P.M., Washington, 2001—. Pres. Black Ams. for Life, Washington, D.C., 1985-88; asst. sec. pub. affairs HHS Office of the Sec., Washington, D.C., 1989—; mem. White House Com. on Children, Washington, D.C., 1988, White House Task Force on Blacks, Washington, D.C., 1988, Nat. Coalition on Pro-Family Issues, Washington, D.C., 1988; co-founder Nat. Family Inst., Washington, D.C., 1987; chair, Nat. Gambling Impact Study Com., 1999-2001. Contbr. numerous articles to jours. and newspapers. Republican. Presbyterian. Avocations: reading, walking, cooking. Office: OPM Off of Dir Theodore Roosevelt Bldg 1900 E St NW Washington DC 20415-1000 Office Fax: 202-606-2577.

JAMES, KAY LOUISE, management consultant, healthcare executive; b. Little Rock, Feb. 13, 1948; d. Charles Robert and Mary Virginia (Morgan) J. BA, Vanderbilt U., 1970; MBA, U. Chgo., 1986. Diplomate Am. Coll. Healthcare Execs.; CPA, Ill., Mo. Mgr. Wallace Community Mental Health Ctr., Nashville, 1973-78; sr. cons. Ernst & Whinney, Washington, 1978-79, Chgo., 1979-81, mgr., 1981-84; dir. Am. Hosp. Supply Corp., Evanston, Ill., 1984-85; mgr. Am. Hosp. Supply Fin. Corp., Evanston, 1985-86; sr. mgr. KPMG Peat Marwick, Kansas City, Mo., 1986-89, ptnr., 1989-92, Katz, James & Assocs., Inc., Plymouth Meeting, Pa., 1992-93; pres. James Mgmt. Assocs., Inc., Nashville, 1994—; CEO U.S. Med. Minds, 2000—02; pres. TAB Nashville, 2001—. Spkr. mgmt. and entrepreneurial topics various grad. programs and profl. assns. Mem. AICPA. Democrat. Avocation: tennis. Office: TAB Nashville 3200 West End Ave Ste 500 Nashville TN 37203-1322

JAMES, L. WARD, medical/surgical nurse, consultant; b. Atlanta, Dec. 14, 1946; s. Linton James and Virginia Ward; m. Catherine James (dec. Aug. 1994). Assocs. Degree, Mesa (Ariz.) C.C., 1995. RN Ariz. RN various orgns., Phoenix, 1995—2001; founder, spkr. Nat. Assn. Ind. Nurses, Tempe, Ariz., 2001—. Author: Pocket Guide to Independent Nursing, 2001. Mem.: Masons. Democrat. Avocations: flying, gliding. Office: Nat Assn Indp Nurses 1125 E Broadway Rd #116 Tempe AZ 85282

JAMES, LOUIS MEREDITH, personnel executive; b. St. Augustine, Fla., June 12, 1941; s. Claire Meredith and Katherine Louise (Colson) J.; m. Karen Lee Libby, Nov. 25, 1966 (div. Mar. 1974); children: Michelle Lee, Kevin Meredith; m. Antoinette Frances Guerrero, Dec. 23, 1978; 1 child, Aaron Teague. BA, U. Minn., 1964. Personnel mgr. Army & Air Force Exch. Svc., worldwide, 1967-77; salary and wage specialist Dept. Def. Wage Staff, Rosslyn, Va., 1977-82; dep. chief Dept. Def. Wage Divsn. NAF Br., Arlington, Va., 1982-98, ret., 1998. Commr. Transp. Safety Commn., Vienna, Va., 1986-98, vice chair, 1992-93, chair, 1993-96; mem. Bd. Zoning Appeals, Vienna, 1998-99; mem. Fairfax/Falls Ch. Cmty. Svcs. Bd.; pres. nonprofit corp. Families United for Non-Profit Residences Fund, Housing for Developmentally Disadvantaged. With U.S. Army, 1965, Vietnam. Decorated Purple Heart. Mem. DAV (life), VFW (life), Vietnam Vets. Am. (life mem., local chpt. state coun. and nat. com., bd. dirs., v.p., pres. 1987—, Nat. Mem. of Yr. 1995), Mil. Order of Purple Heart (life), U.S. Army Officer Candidate Sch. Assn. (life), Lions (v.p., bd. dirs., chmn. membership com. Vienna chpt.), Ruritans, Masons. Republican. Presbyterian. Avocations: fishing, sports, classical music, reading. E-mail: bgard1vet.shentel.net. Home: PO Box 581 Basye VA 22810-0581

JAMES, MARIE MOODY, clergywoman, musician, vocal music educator; b. Chgo., Jan. 23, 1928; d. Frank and Mary (Portis) Moody; m. Johnnie James, May 25, 1968. B Music Edn., Chgo. Music Coll., 1949; postgrad., U. Ill., Champaign-Urbana, 1952, 72, Moody Bible Inst., Chgo., 1963-64; MusM, Roosevelt U., 1969, MA, 1976; DD, Internat. Bible Inst. and Sem., Plymouth, Fla., 1985; postgrad., Trinity Evang. Div. Sch., Deerfield, Ill., 1995; DRE, Logos Grad. Sch., 1995. Key punch operator Dept. Treasury, Chgo., 1950-52; tchr. Posen-Robbins Bd. Edn., Robbins, Ill., 1952-59; tchr. vocal music Englewood High Sch., Chgo., 1964-84; music counselor Head Start, Chgo., 1965-66. Exec. dir. House of Love DayCare, 1983, 88, Mary P. Moody Christian Acad., 1989, supt., 1989; dir. Handbell Choir for Srs. Maple Park United Meth. Ch., 1988-92; bd. dirs. Van Moody Sch. Music, Chgo. Composer, arranger choral music: Hide Me, 1963, Christmas Time, 1980, Come With Us, Our God Will Do Thee Good, 1986, The Indiana House, 1987, Behold, I Will Do a New Thing, 1989, Mary P. Moody Christian Academy School Song 1989, Glory and Honor, 1992. Organist Allen Temple A.M.E. Ch., 1941-45; asst. organist Choppin A.M.E. Ch., 1945-49; organist-dir. Progressive Ch. of God in Christ, Maywood, Ill., 1950-60; missionary Child Evangelism Fellowship, Chgo., 1955-63; unit leader YWCA, New Buffalo, Mich., 1956-58; min. of music God's House of All Nations, Chgo., 1960-80; pastor God's House of Love, Prayer and Deliverance, Robbins, 1982—; chmn. Frank and Mary Moody Scholarship Com., 1984—; dir. music Christian Women's Outtreach Ministry, 1984-88; mem. Robbins Community Coun., 1987-88; camp counselor Abraham Lincoln Ctr., 1951-53. Coppin A.M.E. Ch. scholar, 1946; recipient Humanitarian award God's House of Love, Prayer and Deliverance, 1992, Disting. Leadership award God First Ministries, 2002. Mem. Music Educators Nat. Conf., Good News Club (tchr. 1987-90, Robbins, Ill.). Home: 8154 S Indiana Ave Chicago IL 60619-4712

JAMES, MARILYN SHAW, secondary education educator, social service worker; b. Chgo., Apr. 6, 1926; d. Harry and Louise A. (Milkey) Shaw; m. Eugene Nelson James, June 17, 1950; children: Jim, Mark, Katherine, Caroline. BS, Carthage Coll., 1947; MA, U. Iowa, 1954. Tchr. home econs. Highland Park (Ill.) High Sch., 1947-50, Hampshire (Ill.) High Sch., 1950-51; instr. home econs. No. Ill. U., DeKalb, 1963-65; tchr. Winkie Bear, Sycamore, Ill., 1970-71; sub. tchr. DeKalb and Sycamore Sch. Dists., 1969—, Hinckley-Big Rock, Ill., 1973-80; homemaker coord. Family Svc. Agy., DeKalb, 1980-88, ret. V.p. Kishwaukee Symphony Assocs., 1988—90, pres., 1990; mem. Adv. Com. on Elder Concerns, 1991—, chmn., 1996—97; moderator First Congl. Ch., DeKalb, 1983—84; bd. dirs. Stage Coach Players, DeKalb, 1988—90, 2001—, stage mgr., 1954—; bd. dirs. Family Svc. Agy., DeKalb, 1971—79. Named Stage Coacher of Yr., Stage Coach Players, 1990. Mem. AAUW (v.p. scholar 1980, 90, 93, 94, 95, 96), LWV (legis. chair 1983), DeKalb County Home Economists, DeKalb Drama Club (pres. 1986-87), Univ. Women's Club (pres. 1991), Family Svc. Aux. (pres. 1998—), DeKalb Women's Club (bd. dirs.), Thursday Arts Lit. Club (pres. 1998—). Democrat. Home: 212 Tilton Park Dr Dekalb IL 60115-1942

JAMES, MARION RAY, magazine founder, editor; b. Bellmont, Ill., Dec. 6, 1940; s. Francis Miller and Lorraine A. (Wylie) J.; m. Janet Sue Tennis, June 16, 1960; children: Jeffrey Glenn, David Ray, Daniel Scott, Cheryl Lynne. BS, Oakland City Coll., Ind., 1964; MS, St. Francis Coll., Fort Wayne, Ind., 1978. Sports and city editor Daily Clarion, Princeton, Ind., 1963-65; English tchr. Jac-Cen-Del H.S., Osgood, Ind., 1965-66; indsl. editor Whirlpool Corp., Evansville and LaPorte, Ind., 1966-68, Magnavox Govt. and Indsl. Electronics Co., Fort Wayne, 1968-79; editor, pub., founder Bowhunter mag., Fort Wayne, Ind., 1971-88, editor-in-chief Kalispell, Mont., 1989-2001, editor emeritus, 2001—. Instr. Purdue U., Ft. Wayne, Ind., 1980-88. Author: Bowhunting for Whitetail and Mule Deer, 1975, Successful Bowhunting, 1985, My Place, 1991, The Bowhunter's Handbook, 1997, Of Blind Pigs and Big Bucks, 2002; editor: Pope and Young Book of Bowhunting Records, 1975, 93, 99, Bowhunting Adventures, 1977. Recipient Best Editorial award United Community Svc. Publs., 1970-72; named Alumnus of Yr., Oakland City Coll., 1982; named to Hall of Fame, Mt. Carmel High Sch., Ill., 1983, Archery Hall of Fame, 2003. Mem. Outdoor Writers Assn. Am. (Excellence in Craft Lifetime Achievement award 1999), Ft. Wayne Assn. Bus. Editors (pres. 1975-76, Ft. Wayne Bus. Editor of Yr. award 1969), Toastmasters (Able Toastmaster award), Alpha Phi Gamma, Alpha Psi Omega, Mu Tau Kappa Home: PO Box 1509 2011 Ridgecrest Dr Whitefish MT 59937-1509 E-mail: mrjames@cyberport.net. *Read! Being a good reader is the key to good thinking. Develop and expand your mind through active use of the printed word and you will discover a wide world of unlimited possibilities - and ultimate success that comes with self-discovery.*

JAMES, MARK OLOV, education educator; b. Jamestown, N.D., Oct. 10, 1954; s. Robert Louis and Joan Dee (Lillie) James; m. Choon Huay Chua, June 30, 1978; children: Robert, Mark, Jeremy, Daniel, Tiffany. BA, Brigham Young U., Laie, Hawaii, 1979; MA, Brigham Young U., 1981; PhD, U. Hawaii, 1996. From English instr. to assoc. prof. Brigham Young U. Hawaii Campus, Laie, 1981-92; dir. study program Tchrs. English to Speakers Other Lang., Laie, 1992—. Author: (book) Beyond Words, 1989. Pres. fgn. lang. instrn. com. Laie Elem. Sch., 1991—95, assoc. dean lang. and linguistics, 1997—. U.S. Dept. Edn. fellow, 1990—91. Mem.: TESOL (editor 1992—, TESL reporter), Internat. Assn. World Englishes (charter). Mem. Lds Ch. Office: Brigham Young Univ PO Box 1834 Laie HI 96762 E-mail: jamesm@byuh.edu.

JAMES, MARY LEE, human resources specialist, retired; b. West Plains, Mo., May 6, 1949; d. James W. and Wanda (Ray) Brown; m. William Edward James, Feb. 6, 1971; children: William Alexander James, John Douglas James. BS in Edn., U. Mo., 1971. Tchr. South San Antonio Ind. Sch. Dist., 1971-72, Harrisonville (Mo.) Cass R-IX Sch. Dist., 1972-75; human resources mgr. Cass County Publ. Co., Harrisonville, 1977-2000, ret., 2000. Exec. dir. Cass Med. Ctr. Found., Harrisonville, 1990-93, v.p., 1996-2000. With Harrisonville Park Bd., 1988-2000; mem. Belton-Ozanam Southland Coop. Adv. Bd., Belton, 1993—; v.p. Congl. Award Coun. Mo., Kansas City, 1993—; sec. 17th Jud. Cir. Ct. Apptd. Spl. Advocates, Warrensburg, 1996—; trustee U. Columbia Jefferson Club U. Mo., 1997—, Bd. Curators U. Mo., 1999—, v.p., 2003. Democrat. Methodist. Avocations: golf, gardening, reading. Home: 902 Bird Ave Harrisonville MO 64701

JAMES, MARY SPENCER, nursing home health administrator; b. London, Ont., Can., July 10, 1949; d. Richard Spencer and Helen Frances (Winterbottom) James; m. Robert Peter Owler, Oct. 4, 1969 (div. June 25, 1975). AA, Norwich U., 1969; Nursing Diploma, Toronto (Ont.) Gen. Hosp., 1973; BA in Psychology, U. Vt., 1975. RN, Calif. Staff nurse Toronto Gen. Hosp., 1973—77, Stanford (Calif.) U. Hosp., 1977—81, B.C. Children's Hosp., Vancouver, 1981—83; sr. staff nurse King Abdul Aziz Mil. Hosp., Tabuk, Saudi Arabia, 1983—84, Charter Med. Ltd./Tawam Hosp., Al Ain, Abu Dhabi, United Arab Emirates, 1984—87; nurse Dubai Petroleum Co., United Arab Emirates, 1987—88; nursing dir. Ygia Polyclinic, Limassol, Cyprus, 1988—89; nurse Stat Travelers, Inc., L.A., 1990—91; staff nurse Lucile Salter Packard Children's Hosp. at Stanford, Palo Alto, Calif., 1991—92; case mgr. H.S.S.I. Home Care and Olsten Healthcare, Milbrae and San Francisco, 1992-93; nursing dir. CHS Home Health Agy., San Francisco, 1993—94; liaison nurse coord., pvt. duty supr. United Nursing Internat., San Francisco, 1994—95; nursing supr. Staff Builders Home Care Svcs., Santa Rosa, Calif., 1995; part-time home health coord. Sun Plus Home Health Svcs., Petaluma, Calif., 1995—; part-time case mgr. Kentfield (Calif.) Rehab. Hosp. Part-time case mgr. Kentfield (Calif.) Rehab. Hosp., 2001—. Avocations: aerobics, weight training, hiking, reading. Home: 54 Creek Ct Cotati CA 94931 5122

JAMES, MICHAEL THAMES, information technology executive, consultant; b. Gulfport, Miss., Feb. 16, 1949; s. William Denning and Christell (Cruthirds) J.; m. Debra Lynn Bryant, May 21, 1983; children: William Bryant, Shelley Christine. BS, U.S. Naval Acad., 1971; MS, U. So. Calif., 1978. Commd. ensign USN, 1971, advanced through grades to lt., 1975, resigned, 1978; mktg. rep. IBM, South Bend, Ind., 1978-79; cons. Price Waterhouse, Houston, 1979-85; internal cons. Shell Oil, Houston, 1985-86; mgr. systems devel. & support Carolina Power & Light, Raleigh, 1986-91; v.p. Sprint Kansas City, 1991-93; ptnr. KPMG Peat Marwick, Dallas, 1994-96; prin. Scott, Madden & Assocs., Dallas, 1996-98; CEO James Cons. Group, Plano, Tex., 1998—. Guest lectr. N.C. State U., 1989-91; mem. adv. bd. So. Meth. U. Cox Sch. Bus., 1997—. Mem. computer studies adv. bd. Meredith Coll., 1987-91; adv. bd. Kansas City Met. Spl. Olympics, 1993; mem. industry steering com. Sch. Bus., U. Kans., 1993-94. Mem. Inst. Mgmt. Cons. (sec.-treas. Houston chpt. 1984-85), U.S. Naval Acad. Alumni Assn. (sec.-treas. Triangle area chpt. 1987-91), Stonebriar Country Club, Texoma Sailing Club. Republican. Presbyterian. Avocations: golf, tennis, sailing. Home: 4525 Emerson Dr Plano TX 75093-7226 E-mail: mikejames@jamesconsultinggroup.com.

JAMES, MILTON GARNET, economist; b. Guyana, Jan. 27, 1937; came to U.S., 1969, naturalized, 1976; s. Reginald Montgomery and Caroline Elizabeth J.; m. Joyce Fernandes, July 31, 1960; children: Milton Garnet, Michael, Mark. BS, U. London, 1964; MBA, St. John's U., N.Y., 1972; PhD, U. London, 1973.

Instr. econs. Baruch Coll. CUNY, 1972-74; asst. prof. mktg. Ramapo Coll., N.J., 1974-77; cons. econs. N.Y.C., 1978—. Chmn. Guyanese Cmty. Coun., U.S., 1976—; mem. N.Y.C. Bd. Edn., 1987—99. Recipient Pub. Svc. award Guyanese Cmty. Coun., 1982. Mem. Am. Econs. Assn., Caribbean Studies Assn., Masons. Episcopalian. Achievements include research in economic development, econometric forecasting, monetary and fiscal policies. Home: 649 E 23rd St Brooklyn NY 11210-1127 E-mail: jamesmilton11@aol.com.

JAMES, MURIEL MARSHALL, writer, lecturer, psychotherapist; b. Berkeley, Calif., Feb. 14, 1917; d. John Albert and Hazel (Knowles) Marshall; m. Paul Wesley James (div.); children: Ann, Duncan, John. BA with honors, U. Calif., Berkeley, 1956; MDiv, DDiv, Ch. Divinity Sch. Pacific, 1957, 2000; EdD, U. Calif., 1964. Lic. family psycho therapist, Calif. Instr., coord. ARC, San Francisco, 1941-43; safety inspector Kaiser Shipyards, Richmond, Calif., 1943-44; tchr. Oakland (Calif.) Pub. Schs., 1948-52; min. Orinda (Calif.) Cmty. Ch., 1957-59; dean Laymen's Sch. Religion, Berkeley, Calif., 1959-68; instr. U. Calif. Ext., Berkeley, 1966-69; dir., therapist Oasis Edn. & Treatment Ctr., Lafayette, Calif., 1968-73; psychotherapist pvt. practice, Lafayette, Calif., 1969—. Lectr. James Inst., Lafayette, 1969—. Author, co-author: Born to Win: Transactional Analysis with Gestalt Experiments, 1971, Winning with People: Group Exercises in Transactional Analysis, 1973, Born to Love: Transactional Analysis in the Church, 1973, Transactional Analysis for Moms and Dads: What Do You Do With Them Now That You've Got Them?, 1974, The Power at the Bottom of the Well, 1974, The OK Boss, 1975, The People Book: Transcational Analysis for Students, 1975, The Heart of Friendship, 1976, Techniques for Psychotherapists and Counselors, 1977, A New Self: Self Therapy with Transactional Analysis, 1977, Marriage is for Loving, 1979, Breaking Free: Self-Reparenting for a New Self, 1981, Winning Ways in Health Care, 1981, It's Never Too Late to Be Happy, 1985, expanded edit. 2002, The Better Boss in Multicultural Organizations, 1991, Hearts on Fire: Romance and Achievement in the Lives of Great Women, 1991, Passion for Life: Psychology and the Human Spirit, 1991, Religious Liberty on Trial: Hanserd Knollys, Early Baptist Hero, 1997, Perspectives in Transactional Analysis, 1998; contbr. chpts. to books, articles to profl. jours. Named to Internat. Educators Hall of Fame, 2000. Mem. Interat. Transactional Analysis Assn. (pres. 1980-82). Avocations: friends, family, travel, teaching, creating new books. Address: PO Box 356 Lafayette CA 94549-0356 Fax: 925-256-8527.

JAMES, NEWELL E. music educator, musician; b. Covington, Ky., Dec. 2, 1956; s. D. Clayton and Erlene Downs James; m. Janie Redden, June 17, 1989; 1 child, Katie. M Music Edn., Miss. State U., 1982. Band dir. Caddo Pub. Schools, Shreveport, La., 1991—. Mem. New Dimensions Brass Quintet, Shreveport, La., 1995—; initial incorporator Dist. 8 Band Directors Assn., Shreveport, La.; first dir. Shreveport Met. Concert Band, Shreveport. Mem. group study exch. team Rotary Club, Shreveport, 1987. Mem.: Music Educators Nat. Conf., Phi Delta Kappa, Phi Kappa Phi. Home: 1604 Captain Shreve Dr Shreveport LA 71105

JAMES, P(HYLLIS) D(OROTHY) (BARONESS JAMES OF HOLLAND PARK OF SOUTHWOLD IN COUNTY OF SUFFOLK), author; b. Oxford, Eng., Aug. 3, 1920; d. Sidney Victor and Dorothy May Amelia (Hone) J.; m. Connor Bantry White, 1941 (dec. 1964); children: Clare Bantry, Jane Bantry. Student Brit. schs.; LittD (hons.), U. Buckingham (Eng.), 1992, U. Hertfordshire (Eng.), 1994, U. Glasgow (Scotland), 1995, Durham U., 1998, Portsmouth U., 1999; DLitt, U. London, 1993; D, U. Essex, Eng., 1996. Adminstr. Nat. Health Service, 1949-68; apptd. prin. Civil Svc. Home Office, 1968; prin. Police Dept., 1968-72, Criminal Policy Dept., 1972-79. Author: Cover Her Face, 1962, A Mind to Murder, 1963, Unnatural Causes, 1967, Shroud for a Nightingale, 1971; (with T.A. Critchley) The Maul and the Pear Tree, 1971; An Unsuitable Job for a Woman, 1972, The Black Tower, 1975, Death of an Expert Witness, 1977, Innocent Blood, 1980, The Skull Beneath the Skin, 1982, (play) A Private Treason, 1985, A Taste for Death, 1986, Devices and Desires, 1989, The Children of Men, 1992, Original Sin, 1994, A Certain Justice, 1997, Time to be in Earnest, 1999, Death in Holy Orders, 2001, The Murder Room, 2003. Gov. BBC, 1988-93; bd. dirs. Brit. Coun., 1988-93; bd. dirs., chair lit. adv. panel Arts Coun. Gt. Britain, 1988-92. Decorated Order Brit. Empire, 1983; created life peer (Baroness) of U.K., 1991; assoc. fellow Downing Coll., Cambridge, 1986, hon. fellow, 2000; hon. fellow St. Hilda's Coll., Oxford, 1996, Girton Coll., Cambridge, 2000; recipient Grandmaster award Mystery Writers of Am., 1999. Fellow Royal Soc. Lit., Royal Soc. Arts; mem. Soc. of Authors (chmn. 1984-86, pres. 1997—), Detection Club. Office: Greene & Heaton Ltd 37 Goldhawk Rd London W12 8QQ England

JAMES, ROBERT GREGORY, investment company executive; b. Ord, Nebr., Apr. 2, 1925; s. Ernest C. and Cora Gregory James; m. Ardis Butler James, Dec. 22, 1949; children: Robert Jr., Catherine, Ralph. BS, Northwestern U., 1946; MBA, Harvard U., 1948, PhD, 1953. CPA Tex., N.Y. Asst. prof. MIT, Cambridge, 1950—53; br. chief CIA, Washington, 1954—57; economist Continental Oil Co., Houston, 1957—59; pres. marine transport co. Mobil Oil, N.Y.C., 1959—64; v.p. Mobil Oil Co., N.Y.C., 1965—69; pres. Enterprise Asset Mgmt., Inc., N.Y.C., 1969—. Bd. dirs. Ctr. for Def. Info., Washington, 1981—, Citizens Exch. Coun., N.Y.C., NY, 1985—, Human Rights Watch-Europe and Ctrl. Asia, N.Y.C., NY, 1990—, Human Rights in China, N.Y.C., NY, 1992—. Rear admiral USNR, 1943—81, PTO. Decorated Legion of Merit USN. Presbyterian. Avocations: quilt collecting, skiing. Office: Enterprise Asset Mgmt Inc Ste 1200 475 Fifth Ave New York NY 10017

JAMES, RONALD J. lawyer; b. Apr. 8, 1937; s. Raymond Babe and Jennie May (Smith) J.; m. Vivian Thelma, June 1961 (div. Sept. 1969); m. Patricia O'Donnell, Oct. 31, 1970; children: Ronald Jr., Kevin, Shannon, Kelly, Catlin. BA, U. Mo., 1959; JD, Am. U., 1966; MA, So. Ill. U., 1971. Bar: Iowa 1966, Ohio 1977, U.S. Supreme Ct. 1972. Legis. aide U.S. Congress, Washington, 1963-64; dir. City of Waterloo, Iowa, 1966-67; asst. county atty. Black Hawk County, Iowa, 1967-69; spl. asst. to counselor to Pres. The White House, Washington, 1970-71; trial atty. Dept. Transp., Washington, 1971-72; asst. gen. counsel EEOC, Chgo., 1972-75; adminstr. wage and hour divsn. Dept. Labor, Washington, 1975-77; ptnr. Squire, Sanders & Dempsey, Cleve., 1977—; chief human resources capital officer and asst. sec. Dept. of Homeland Def. 1st lt. U.S. Army, 1960-63. Avocations: soccer, skiing, african-american history, buffalo soldiers. Office: Squire Sanders & Dempsey LLP 4900 Key Tower Cleveland OH 44114 E-mail: rjames@ssd.com.

JAMES, RUBY MAY, retired librarian; b. Tucson, Ariz., Nov. 13, 1924; d. Theophil Frederic and Etelka Eva (Blumberg) Buehrer; m. Hubert R. James, Apr. 7, 1945; 1 child, Judith M. Victor. BA, U. Ariz., 1946, MEd, 1976; student, U. Iowa. Cert. elem. libr. Tchr. Tucson Unified Sch. Dist., 1947-48, elem. libr., 1974-89; ret. Recipient YMCA Svc. to Children award; Edn. Enrichment grantee. Mem. Pi Lambda Theta, Alpha Delta Kappa, Delta Kappa Gamma.

JAMES, SHARPE, mayor, state legislator; b. Jacksonville, Fla., Feb. 20, 1936; m. Mary Mattison; 3 children. Grad., Montclair State Coll.; M, Springfield Coll.; student, Washington State U., Columbia U., Rutgers U.; LLD (hon.), Montclair State U., 1988; PhD (hon.), DrewU., 1991. Former mem. faculty Essex County Coll., Newark, from 1968, then prof.; mayor City of Newark, 1986—; mem. N.J. Senate, Dist. 29, Trenton, 1999—; comm. N.J. State Redevelopment Authority, 1995—. Mem. Newark City Council, 1970-86; bd. trustees U.S. Conf. Mayors, v.p. N.J. chpt. Served with AUS. Named Mayor of Yr., N.J. Conf. Mayors, 2001, The Most Valuable Pub. Ofcl., City and State Mag.; named to N.J. Elected Officials Hall of Fame, 1999; recipient Arts Leadership award, U.S. Conf. Mayors and Ams. for the Arts, 2002. Democrat. Avocation: tennis. Office: 50 Park Place Suite 1535 Newark NJ 07102*

JAMES, SHERMAN ATHONIA, social epidemiologist, educator; b. Hartsville, S.C., Oct. 25, 1943; s. Jerome and Helen Genese (Bachus) J.; m. Vera Lucia Moura; children: Sherman Alexander, Scott Anthony. AB, Talladega Coll., 1964; PhD, Washington U., 1973. Prof. epidemiology U. N.C., Chapel Hill, 1973-89, U. Mich., Ann Arbor, 1989—, assoc. dean acad. affairs Sch. Pub. Health. Cons. NIMH, NIH, Bethesda, Md., 1979-83, Nat. Heart, Lung and Blood Inst., 1985—, Nat. Inst. Environ. Health Sci., 1990—; cons. NAS, Washington, 1994—. Contbr. articles to profl. jours. Capt. USAF, 1964-69. Fellow Soc. of Fellows, U. Mich., 1993—. Fellow Am. Heart Assn., Acad. Behavioral Medicine Rsch., Soc. Behavioral Medicine, Am. Coll. Epidemiology; mem. Am. Men and Women of Sci. Inst. Medicine. Avocations: travel, photography, tennis, nature walks. Office: Univ Mich 109 Observatory St Ann Arbor MI 48109-2029

JAMES, SUNIL, aerospace engineer; b. Kottayam, India, June 30, 1968; s. Kureekottil Pothen and Philly J.; m. Archana, Apr. 21, 2000. B Tech., Indian Inst. Tech., Kanpur, 1990; MS, SUNY Buffalo, 1994, PhD, 1998. Scientist Vikram Sarabhai Space Ctr., Trivandrum, India, 1990-92; rsch. asst. SUNY, Buffalo, 1992-98; sr. rsch. engr. Rolls-Royce, Indianapolis, 1998—. Contbr. articles to profl. jours. Mem. AIAA (2nd place AIAA Tech. Paper Competition 1995), Am. Phys. Soc. Office: Rolls-Royce Speed Code T-14 2001 S Tibbs Ave Indianapolis IN 46241

JAMES, THOMAS LARRY, chemistry educator; b. North Platte, Nebr., Sept. 8, 1944; s. James Jennings and Guinevere (Richards) J.; m. Olga Schmidlin; children: Marc, Tristan. BS, U. N.M., 1965; PhD, U. Wis., 1969. Research chemist Celanese Chem. Co., Corpus Christi, Tex., 1969-71; NIH postdoctorate fellow U. Pa., Phila., 1971-73; prof. chem., pharmaceutical chemistry and radiology U. Calif., San Francisco, 1973—, chair dept. pharm. chemistry, 1995—, dir. Magnetic Resonance Lab., 1975. Author: NMR in Biochemistry, 1975; editor: Biomedical NMR, 1984, Methods in Enzymology, 1989, 4th edit., 2001; mem. editl. bd. Jour. Magnetic Resonance, Jour. Biomolecular NMR, Magnetic Resonance Imaging; editor FEBS Letters; contbr. articles to profl. jours. Mem. Internat. Soc. Magnetic Resonance, Am. Biophys. Soc., Am. Chem. Soc., Am. Biochem. Soc., Soc. Magnetic Resonance in Medicine, Phi Beta Kappa, Phi Kappa Phi, Kappa Mu Epsilon. Mem. Cmty. Of Christ. Avocations: skiing, kayaking, travel, photography. Office: U Calif Mission Bay Genentech Hall San Francisco CA 94143-2280 E-mail: james@pollack.ucsf.edu.

JAMES, THOMAS NAUM, cardiologist, educator; b. Amory, Miss., Oct. 24, 1925; s. Naum and Kata J.; m. Gleaves Elizabeth Tynes, June 22, 1948; children: Thomas Mark, Terrence Fenner, Peter Naum. BS, Tulane U., 1946, MD, 1949. Diplomate Am. Bd. Internal Medicine (mem. bd. govs. 1982-88), Bd. Cardiovasc. Diseases (bd. dirs. 1972-78). Intern Henry Ford Hosp., Detroit, 1949-50, resident in internal medicine and cardiology, 1950-53, staff, 1959-68; instr. medicine Tulane U., New Orleans, 1955-58, asst. prof., 1959; prof. medicine U. Ala. Med. Ctr., Birmingham, 1968-87, prof. pathology, 1968-73, assoc. prof. physiology and biophysics, 1969-73, dir. Cardiovasc. Rsch. and Tng. Ctr., 1970-77, chmn. dept. medicine, dir. divsn. cardiovasc. disease, 1973-81, Mary Gertrude Waters prof. cardiology, 1976-87, Disting. prof., 1981-87; prof. medicine, prof. pathology U. Tex. Med. Br., Galveston, 1987—, pres., 1987-97, dir. WHO Cardiovasc. Ctr., 1988-98, Thomas N. and Gleaves T. James disting. chair cardiol. scis., 1997—. U. Tex. Med. Br., Galveston, 1997—; physician-in-chief U. Ala. Hosps., 1973-81; mem. adv. coun. Nat. Heart Lung and Blood Inst., 1975-79; pres. 10th World Congress Cardiology, 1986; mem. cardiology del. invited by Chinese Med. Assn. to China, 1978; Campbell orator Queens U., Belfast, No. Ireland, 1982; Mikamo lectr. Japan Circulation Soc., 1982; Sir Thomas Lewis lectr. Brit. Cardiac Soc., 1983, Einthoven lectr. U. Leiden, The Netherlands, 1993, Bailey K. Ashford lectr. U. P.R., 1995; hon. lectr. U. Padua, 1998. Author: Anatomy of the Coronary Arteries, 1961, The Etiology of Myocardial Infarction, 1963; Mem. editl. bd. Circulation, 1966-83, Am. Jour. Cardiology, 1968-82, Am. Heart Jour, 1976-79; contbr. articles to profl. jours. Capt. M.C. U.S. Army, 1953-55. Recipient Sesquicentennial Medal of Honor Paul Tulane Coll. Tulane U., 1997, 50-year Lifetime Achievement award Tulane Med. Alumni Assn., 1999, James B. Herrick award, Am. Heart Assn., 1999. Fellow ACP (gov. Ala. 1975-79, master 1983); mem. AMA, Am. Clin. and Climatological Assn. (v.p. 1992-93, councillor 1992-93), Assn. Am. Physicians, Am. Soc. Clin. Investigation, Assn. Univ. Cardiologists (pres. 1978-79), Am. Heart Assn. (pres. 1979-80, Herrick award Coun. on Clin. Cardiology 1999), Am. Coll. Cardiology (v.p. 1970-71, trustee 1970-71, 76-81, First Disting. Scientist award 1982, chmn. publs. com. 1994-97), Am. Soc. Pharmacology and Exptl. Therapeutics, Soc. Exptl. Biology of Medicine, Am. Coll. Chest Physicians, Ctrl. Soc. Clin. Rsch., Internat. Soc. and Fedn. Cardiology (pres. 1983-84), WHO (expert adv. panel on cardiovascular diseases 1988-97), So. Soc. Clin. Investigation, Am. Fedn. Clin. Rsch., Ala. Acad. Honor. Philos. Soc. Tex., Phi Beta Kappa, Sigma Xi, Omicron Delta Kappa, Alpha Omega Alpha, Alpha Tau Omega, Phi Chi. Clubs: Cosmos, Mountain Brook, Galveston Artillery. Presbyterian. Office: U Tex Med Br 301 University Blvd Galveston TX 77555-0175

JAMES, TIMOTHY DALE, music educator; b. Martinsville, Ind., Feb. 18, 1957; s. Ralph Dale and Janice May James; m. Susan Caroline McCollum, July 28, 1984; 1 child, Megan Elizabeth. MS in Music Edn., U. of Ill., Urbana/Champaign, IL, 1982—85; B.M.E. (Tchg. Area) in Music Edn., Ind. U., Bloomington, IN, 1975—80. Life Indiana Teachers License Ind. Dept. of Edn., 1985. Choral dir. Fountain Ctrl. Jr.-Sr. H.S., Veedersburg, Ind., 1980—83, Knox H.S. and Mid. Sch., Knox, Ind., 1983—84; choral dir./assistand band Monrovia Jr./Sr. H.S., Monrovia, Ind., 1984—87; choral dir. Martinsville H.S., Martinsville, Ind., 1987—. Choral dir. First United Meth. Ch., Martinsville, Ind., 1997—, Monrovia Christian Ch., Monriovia, Ind., 1986—96; counselor Interlochen Nat. Music Camp, Interlochen, Mich., 1979—80. Music coord. Veterans Meml. Found., Martinsville, Ind., 2002. Mem.: Music Educators Nat. Conf., Ind. Choral Directors Assn. (life), Am. Choral Directors Assn. (life), U.S. Chess Fedn., Ind. U. Alumni Assn. (life). Home: 80 Tulip Drive Martinsville IN 46151 Office: Martinsville High School 1360 East Gray St Martinsville IN 46151 Personal E-mail: tjames@scican.net. E-mail: tjames@scican.net.

JAMES, TRACEY FAYE, screenwriter; b. Wilmington, Ohio, Feb. 4, 1963; d. James Whitney and Lydia Wanell (Wethington) James. Student, Art Instrn. Schs., 1980, Arlington Career Ctr., 1985. Freelance screenwriter, San Antonio, 1981—; sports photographer No. Va. Sun, Arlington, Va., 1988. Author (screenplays): Nights of Terror, 1987, Dark Lords, 1991, Diamond Run, 1996, At the Hands of Mercy, 1997, A Lesson in Murder, 1999. Recipient award for patriotic svc. U.S. Treasury, 1981. Republican. Episcopalian. Avocations: writing, drawing, bowling, movies, music.

JAMES, VIRGINIA LYNN, contracts executive; b. March AFB, Calif., Feb. 6, 1952; d. John Edward and Azelle Virginia (Morrill) Anderson; children: Raymond Edward, Jerry Glenn James Jr. Student, Sinclair C.C., 1981-83, U. Tex., San Antonio, 1980, Redlands U., 1986, San Diego State U., 1994. With specialized contracting USAF, Wright-Patterson AFB, Ohio, 1973-77, with logistics contracting Kelly AFB, Tex., 1977-81, contract specialist Wright-Patterson AFB, Ohio, 1981-84; spl. asst. Peace Log, Tehran, Iran, 1977; acting chief of contracts cruise missile program Gen. Dynamics/Convair, San Diego, 1984-86; contracts mgr. VERAC, Inc., San Diego, 1986-90, Gen. Dynamics, San Diego, 1990-92; mgr. contracts Scientific-Atlanta, San Diego, 1992-93; dir. contracts GreyStone, San Diego, 1993-95; dist. constn. mgr. OHM, San Diego, 1995-98; v.p. contract and procurement MWH Ams., Inc., Louisville, 1998—. Cons. Gen. Dynamics, San Diego, 1985, Efratrom, 1986. Mem.: NAFE, Nat. Contract Mgmt. Assn., Nat. Mgmt. Assn. Republican. Office: Montgomery Watson Ste 101 9401 Williamsburg Plz Louisville KY 40222 E-mail: ginger.james@mw.com.

JAMES, WAYNE EDWARD, electronic engineer; b. Racine, Wis., Apr. 2, 1950; s. Ronald Dean James and Arlene Joyce (Mickelsen) Dawson; m. Edith Yvonne Cone, Apr. 6, 1997; children: Terry Scott, Kevin Arthur. BS in Electronic Engring. Tech., U. So. Colo., 1976; MS in Computer Sci., Colo. U., 1996. Electronic technician Lawrence Livermore (Calif.) Nat. Lab., 1976-80, Inmos Corp., Colorado Springs, Colo., 1980-86, CAD engr., 1986-87, United Techs. Microelectronics Ctr., Colorado Springs, 1988-97, ASIC engr., 1997—. Sec.-treas. Stratmoor Hills Vol. Fire Dept., Colorado Springs, 1983, 84, lt., 1985, capt., 1986. Served with USN, 1968-72. Named Fireman of Yr., Stratmoor Hills Vol. Fire Dept., 1983. Lutheran. Office: Aeroflex UTMC 4350 Centennial Blvd Colorado Springs CO 80907-3778

JAMES, WILLIAM RAMSAY, cable television executive; b. South Bend, Ind., Oct. 6, 1933; s. William Stubbs and Rose (Ramsay) J.; m. Jane Mehrer, Dec. 29, 1955; children: William Harold, Martha Courtney Quay. BS in Mech. Engring., Princeton U., 1955; MBA, Harvard U., 1960. CPA, Mich. Plant mgr. N. A. Woodworth Co., Ferndale, Mich., 1960-62; ptnr. Touche Ross & Co., Detroit, 1962-69; v.p., gen. mgr. Sta. WJR, Detroit, 1969-80; exec. v.p. Capital Cities Communications, N.Y.C., 1980-86, pres. Cable TV div. Bloomfield Hills, Mich., 1980-86; pres. James Communications Inc., 1986-87; mng. ptnr. James Communications Ptnrs., Bloomfield Hills, 1988—. Trustee, treas. William Beaumont Hosp., Royal Oak, Mich. 1st lt. USAF, 1956-58. Mem. AICPA, Mich. Assn. CPAs, AAA Mich. (bd. dirs.), Country Club (Bloomfield Hills, Mich.), Orchard Lake (Mich.) Country Club, Lost Tree Club (Palm Beach, Fla.), Everglades Club (Palm Beach). Republican. Episcopalian. Office: James Communications Ptnrs 38710 Woodward Ave Bloomfield Hills MI 48304-2851

JAMES, WILLIAM W. financial consultant; b. Oct. 12, 1931; s. Will and Clyde (Cowdrey) James; m. Carol Ann Muenter, June 17, 1967; children: Sarah James Banks, David William. AB, Harvard U., 1953. Cert. trust and fin. advisor. Asst. to dir. overseas divsn. Becton Dickinson & Co., Rutherford, NJ, 1956-59; stockbroker Merrill Lynch, Pierce, Fenner & Smith, Inc., St. Louis, 1959-62; with trust divsn. Boatmen's Nat. Bank, St. Louis, 1962-90, v.p. in charge estate planning, sr. v.p., 1972-90; sr. v.p. Boatmen's Trust Co., St. Louis, 1989-96, fin., trust mktg. cons., 1996—. Mem. gift and bequest coun. Barnes Hosp., St. Louis, 1963—67, St. Louis U., 1972—78; dir. Mark Twain Summer Inst., St. Louis, 1987—92. With U.S. Army, 1953—55. Mem.: Am. Inst. Banking, Mo. Bankers Assn., Estate Planning Coun. St. Louis, Harvard Alumni Assn. (bd. dirs. 1987—90), Noonday Club (St. Louis), Mo. Athletic Club, Harvard Faculty Club (Cambridge, Mass.), Harvard Club St. Louis (pres. 1972—73). Republican. Home: 1415 Michele Dr Saint Louis MO 63122-1404

JAMESON, J(AMES) LARRY, chemical company executive; b. Elizabethtown, Ky., 1937; s. William Kendrick and Ruth Helen (Krause) J.; m. Mary Louise Wojcik, June 26, 1965; children: Renee, Jennifer, Julie. BA in Math., Bellarmine Coll., 1959; BS in Chem. Engring., U. Detroit, 1963, MBA, 1970. Tech. mgr. automotive products Rinshed Mason et Cie, Paris, 1965-69; ops. mgr. vinyl coated fabrics Inmont Corp., Toledo, 1969-75, v.p., gen. mgr. European ops. London, 1975-79, v.p., gen. mgr. automotive finishes products Detroit, 1979-83, sr. v.p. worldwide automotive, 1983-86; pres. Coatings & Colorants div. BASF, Clifton, N.J., 1986-93; pres., CEO Pirelli Cable Corp., Florham Park, N.J., 1993-96, v.p. Ferro Chem. Corp., Cleve., 1996—. Mem. Soc. Automotive Engrs., Orchard Lake Country Club, The Country Club. Avocations: golf, tennis, skiing, hunting. Home: 17181 Hidden Point Dr Chagrin Falls OH 44023-2001 Office: Ferro Corp 1000 Lakeside Ave E Cleveland OH 44114-1147

JAMESON, PATRICIA MARIAN, government agency administrator; b. Pitts., Mar. 17, 1945; d. Vernon L. and Dorothy Leam (Wilson) J. BA, Northwestern U., 1967; MA, Ohio State U., 1969. With HUD, 1970-2000, project mgr., 1976-77, acting dir. housing mgmt., 1978, dep. area mgr. Milw. Area Office, 1978-85, acting area mgr., 1979-80, 82, regional dir. adminstrn. Chgo. Regional Office, 1985-95, dir. adminstrv. svc. ctr., 1995-2000, ret., 2000. Vol. ARC, Sierra Club; active Denver World Affairs Coun., Internat. Inst. for Edn.; vol. Habitat for Humanity; vol. tax aide program AARP. Recipient Quality Performance award HUD, 1973, 75, 80, Outstanding Performance award, 1980, 85, 87, 88, 90, 91, 92, 94, 96, 97, 98, 99, 2000, Disting. Svc. award 1992, 2000, Secs. award for Supervisory Excellence, 1998. Mem. NAFE, Fed. Execs. Inst. Alumni Assn., Phi Beta Kappa, Pi Sigma Alpha.

JAMESON, PAUL WRIGHT, lawyer, consultant; b. Evanston, Ill., July 13, 1951; s. John Hulbert Jameson and Barbara Broadhurst Adler; m. Carol Graham Graham, May 5, 1984; children: Nora Elizabeth, Morgan Wright. BA, U. Pitts., 1973, MA, 1976; JD, Georgetown U., 1979. Bar: D.C. 1979. Assoc. Stewart & Stewart, Washington, 1979—84; atty. Schagrin Assocs., Washington, 1985—2001, Hale and Dorr, LLP, Washington, 1991—2002; pres. Jameson Internat., Vienna, Va., 2002—. Mem.: No. Va. Tech. Coun. (biomedtech com., internat. com. 2000). Democrat. Avocations: rock climbing, wine tasting. Home Fax: n/a. Personal E-mail: paul@jameson-international.com.

JAMESON, PAULA ANN, lawyer; b. New Orleans, Feb. 19, 1945; d. Paul Henry and Virginia Lee (Powell) Bailey; children: Paul Andrew, Peter Carver. BA, La. State U., 1966; JD, U. Tex., 1969. Bar: Tex. 1969, D.C. 1970, U.S. Dist. Ct. D.C. 1970, U.S. Ct. Appeals (D.C. cir.) 1972, Va. 1973, U.S. Supreme Ct. 1973, U.S. Dist. Ct. (ea. dist.) Va. 1976, U.S. Ct. Appeals (4th cir.) 1976, N.Y. 1978, U.S. Ct. Appeals (5th cir.) 1978, U.S. Ct. Appeals (2d cir.) 1985. Asst. corp. counsel D.C. Corp. Counsel's Office, 1970-73; sr. asst. county atty. Fairfax County Atty.'s Office, Fairfax, Va., 1973-77; atty. Dow Jones & Co., Inc., N.Y.C., 1977-79, ho. counsel, 1979-81, asst. to chmn. bd., 1981-83, ho. counsel, dir. legal dept., 1983-86; sr. v.p., gen. counsel, corp. sec. PBS, Alexandria, Va., 1986-98; ptnr. Arter & Hadden, Washington, 1998-2000; v.p., gen. counsel Gibson Guitar Corp., Nashville, 2000-01; pres. Jameson Legal & Cons. Svcs., McLean, Va., 2000—03; exec. v.p., COO Children's Def. Fund., Washington, 2003—. Mem.: Copyright Soc. (past trustee), D.C. Bar Assn., Fed. Comms. Bar Assn. Democrat. Roman Catholic. E-mail: paulajameson@att.net

JAMESON, SANFORD CHANDLER, education educator; b. Toronto, Ohio, Feb. 12, 1932; s. Sanford Frank and Dorothy Lee (Robinson) J.; m. Joan Sheridan, June 29, 1963; children: Jennifer Joan, Julie Jo. BS, Miami U., Oxford, Ohio, 1954; MA, Case Western Res. U., 1960. Asst. dir. admission Case Western Res. U., Cleve., 1957-60; assoc. dir. admissions Carleton Coll., Northfield, Minn., 1960-63; asst. regional dir. Coll. Entrance Exam. Bd., Evanston, Ill., 1963-66, asst. dir. internat. edn. Ctrl. Office N.Y.C., 1966-69, assoc. for internat. edn., 1969-71, dir. internat. edn. Washington, 1971-94, dir. emeritus, 1994—. Chmn. Nat. Coun. Evaluation Fgn. Ednl. Credentials, 1974-78, active, 1964-94; chmn. Alliance for Internat. Ednl. Exch., 1986-88, active, 1980-94; mem. Internat. Sch. Svc., 1974-81, 83-90, 2001—, chmn., 1988-90, Author, editor workshop reports in field. Lt. USNR, 1954-57. Recipient cert. of appreciation, U.S. Dept. State, 1992. Mem. SAR, Nat. Assn. Coll. Admission Counselors, NAFSA: Assn. Internat. Educators (life, mem., bd. dirs., chmn. admissin sect., pres. 1976-77), Am. Assn. Collegiate Registrars and Admission Officers (cert. of appreciation 1995), Soc. Mayflower Descs., Md. Mayflower Soc. (bd. dirs. 1997—, Soc. of Cincinnati (docent Anderson House), Masons (32d degree), Shriners, Sigma Alpha Epsilon. Presbyterian (elder). Home and Office: 4948 Sentinel Dr Bethesda MD 20816-1239

JAMES-STRAND, NANCY LEABHARD, advertising executive; b. Oak Park, Ill., July 30, 1943; d. Arthur Ferdinand and Virginia Stella (Albertelli) Leabhard; m. Jack William Strand, July 1, 1971. Student, U. Madrid, 1963-64; BA in Teaching Spanish, U. Ill., 1965. With advt. sales Chgo. Tribune, 1968-69; asst. mgr. Nationwide Advt., Chgo., 1969-78, regional mgr., 1978—. Home: 140 S Grove Ave Oak Park IL 60302-2806 Office: Nationwide Advt 35 E Wacker Dr Chicago IL 60601-2103

JAMGOCHIAN, VICTORIA, interior designer; b. Richmond, Va., Apr. 18, 1922; d. John A. and Azniv (Marsevonian) Jamgochian. BS in Psychology, Coll. William and Mary, 1946; cert. interior design and architecture, Parsons Sch. Design, N.Y.C., France, Italy, 1955. Cert. comml., residential and office interior designer. Asst. interior designer McMillen, Inc., N.Y.C., 1955-56, Lord and Taylor, N.Y.C., 1956-57; interior designer J. Frank Jones Interiors, Richmond, 1957-61, Miller & Rhoads, Richmond, 1961-67, Thalhimer's Indsl. Design, Richmond, 1967-79; exec. dir. design Chasen's Bus. Interiors, Richmond, 1979—2001. Hospitality, 1967; projects pub. in Interiors Mag., 1968; Interiors Mag., 1969, Va. Record, 1971; interior designer (prin. works) Country Club of Va., The Woman's Club, Richmond, Va., Busch Gardens Hospitality Ctr., Williamsburg, Va., Pres.'s House, U. Richmond, Va., Richmond Meml. Hosp., Va. Bapt. Hosp., Lynchburg, Engineer's Club, Richmond, Rotunda Club, Timme Plaza Motor Inn (now Hilton Hotel), Wilmington, N.C., Ctrl. Nat. Bank (Now Wachovia), Richmond, Va., Chemtreat, Inc., Richmond, Cascades Restaurant and Meeting Center, Williamsburg Motor House, Colonial Williamsburg, Inc., Williamsburg, Va. Mem.: William and Mary Alumni Soc., Kappa Delta. Avocations: tennis, travel, horseback riding, piano. Home: 211 Sleepy Hollow Rd Richmond VA 23229-7153

JAMIESON, GRAHAM A. biochemist, organization official; b. Wellington, New Zealand, Aug. 14, 1929; came to U.S., 1956; s. Andrew Wilson and Nan (Graham) J.; m. Barbara MacLachlan, Feb. 20, 1960; 1 child, Brian. BSc, U. Otago, 1949; MSc with first class honors in Organic Chemistry, U. New Zealand, 1951; PhD Lister Inst. Preventive Medicine, U. London, 1954, DSc,

1972. Research fellow dept. biochemistry Cornell U., N.Y.C., 1956; research biochemist Am. Nat. Red Cross, Bethesda, Md., 1961-64, asst. dir. research, 1964-69, dir. research, 1969-78, assoc. dir. blood services, 1978-84, sr. scientist, 1984—. Vis. scientist NIH, 1957-61, mem. exptl. hematology study sect., 1978-84; lectr. biochemistry Georgetown U., Washington, 1961, professorial lectr., 1966-74, adj. prof., 1974-96; Winzler Meml. lectr. U. Fla., 1975; mem. adv. com. on blood preservation and substitutes U.S. Army Med. Rsch. and Devel. Command, 1980-92, chmn., 1981-92; vis. prof. U. Sao Paulo, Brazil, 1992, U. Barcelona, Spain, 1993. Editor: (with T.J. Greenwalt) Red Cell Membrane-Structure and Function, 1969, Formation and Destruction of Blood Cells, 1970, Glycoproteins of Blood Cells and Plasma, 1971, The Human Red Cell In Vitro, 1974, Transmissible Disease and Blood Transfusion, 1975, Trace Components of Plasma-Isolation and Clinical Significance, 1976, The Granulocyte: Function and Clinical Utilization, 1977, The Blood Platelet in Transfusion Therapy, 1978, (with D.M. Robinson) Mammalian Cell Membranes, Vol. I, 1978—, Generalizations and Methodology, Vol. II, 1978—, The Diversity of Membranes, Vol. III, 1978—, Surface Membranes of Specific Cell Types, Vol. IV, 1978—, Membranes and Cellular Functions, Vol. V, 1978—, Responses of Plasma Membranes; Interaction of Platelets and Tumor Cells, 1982, Platelet Membrane Receptors: Molecular Biology Immunology, Biochemistry and Pathology, 1988; mem. editorial bds. Thrombosis Rsch., 1978-81, Thrombosis Haemostas, 1989—, Internat. Jour. Hematology, 1989—, Blood, 1996—; contbr. articles to profl. jours. Sir George Grey scholar U. New Zealand., 1951, U. Otago 50; John Edmond fellow. Fellow AAAS; mem. Am. Soc. Biol. Chemists, Am. Chem. Soc., Biochem. Soc. (London), Internat. Soc. Thrombosis and Hemostasis (Shirley Johnson award 1997), N.Y. Acad. Scis., Am. Heart Assn. (exec. com., council on thrombosis), Am. Soc. Hematology, Soc. Exptl. Biology and Medicine, Soc. for Complex Carbohydrates (exec. com.) Home: 5622 Johnson Ave Bethesda MD 20817-3504 Office: Am Nat Red Cross 15601 Crabbs Branch Way Rockville MD 20855-2736

JAMIESON, JAMES BRADSHAW, foundation administrator; b. L.A., June 10, 1931; s. Charles Cameron and Ruth (Bradshaw) J.; m. Perry McNaughton, Dec. 27, 1959; children: Jeffrey McNaughton, Dalton Charles. AA, Citrus Coll., 1950; BA, Claremont Men's Coll., 1955; MA, Claremont Grad. Sch., 1958; PhD, Brown U., 1966. Assoc. prof. polit. studies Pitzer Coll. and Claremont Grad. Sch., 1968-75; rsch. polit. scientist UCLA, 1972-73; v.p. for devel. Pitzer Coll., 1968-72, v.p., 1973-78, prof. polit. studies, 1975-83, exec. v.p., 1979-83, acting pres., 1978-79; prof. govt. Claremont Grad. Sch., 1975-87; v.p. for rsch. Claremont McKenna Coll., 1983-87; exec. dir. Found. for Performing Art Ctr., San Luis Obispo, Calif., 1987-96; pres. SLO Capers, San Luis Obispo, Calif., 1997—. Commr. Calif. Postsecondary Edn. Commn., Sacramento, 1987-92; dir. Global Village, Seattle, 1989-95; resident cons. Centennial Celebration Calif. Politech. State U., Obispo, Calif., 2000-02. Contbr. articles to profl. jours. Staff, sec. Ctrl. Coast Performing Arts Ctr. Commn., San Luis Obispo, 1993-95. Sgt. USAF, 1950-52. Fellow Brown U., 1960, 63, tchg. fellow, 1962, fellow Resources for the Future, 1964; rsch. grantee U.S. Dept. Interior, 1972-73; recipient Cal Poly U Pres.' Arts award, 1999. Mem. Santa Lucia Flyfishers (bd. dirs. 1988—), Trout Unltd. (bd. dirs. Calif. coun. 1989-94, bd. dirs. nat. bd. 1986-90), Marine's Meml. Club. Avocations: flyfishing, tennis, restoring vintage automobiles. Office: SLO Capers PO Box 12843 San Luis Obispo CA 93406-2843

JAMIESON, JOHN EDWARD, JR., social services administrator, minister, bioethicist; b. Philadelphia, Pa., Mar. 5, 1945; s. John Edward and Frances (Hayes) J.; m. Marilyn T. Haws, June 8, 1968; children: Douglas Stuart, Heather Lynn, Mark Stuart. BA, U. Pa., 1967; MDiv, Ref. Episcopal Sem., Phila., 1970; PhD, Christian Bible Coll., Rocky Mount, N.C., 1990. Ordained to ministry Ref. Episcopal Ch., 1970, Bapt. Ch., 1978. Pastor Trinity Ref. Episcopal Ch., Phila., 1970-73, St. Mark's Ref. Episcopal Ch., Miami, Fla., 1973-75, Hammonton (N.J.) Bapt. Ch., 1978-81; supr. Nepaug Christian Acad., New Hartford, Conn., 1976-78; coord. ops. emergency med. svcs. div. AID Ambulance Svc., Atlantic City, 1982-83; paramedic mobile ICU, West Jersey Health, Camden, N.J., 1983-88; dir. pastoral care Atlantic City Med. Ctr., 1988—. Pastor Grace Bible Chapel, Ocean City, N.J., 1988-95; min. pastoral care Cornerstone Ministries, Ocean City, 2000-02; vice chmn. instnl. med. ethics com. Atlantic City Med. Ctr., 1988-96, co-chair, 1996—. Editor Bibl. Bioethics, 1990. Chaplain Somers Point (N.J.) Vol. Rescue Squad, 1987-96, Ocean City Fire Dept., 1995—; bd. dirs. Atlantic County unit Am. Cancer Soc., Absecon, N.J., 1988-90, program coord. Cansurmount support program, 1988-90; bd. trustees Ctrl. Ocean City Union Chapel; exec. v.p. Reformed Bible Inst. Delaware Valley, 2000-01. Mem. Am. Assn. Christian Counselors, So. Jersey Ethics Alliance, Internat. Critical Incident Stress Found., Am. Acad. Experts in Traumatic Stress (bd. cert. expert), Fedn. Fire Chaplains. Republican. Avocations: travel, photography, reading. Office: Atlantic City Med Ctr 1925 Pacific Ave Atlantic City NJ 08401-6713 *When we concentrate our thoughts on that which is true, noble, right, pure, lovely, admirable and excellent we are lifted above the drudgery of life and open ourselves to the possibility of true greatness.*

JAMIESON, LELAND, retired career management consultant; b. Miami, Fla., July 12, 1935; s. Leland Shattuck and Ellen (Tansel) J.; m. Gretchen Kimball, June 22, 1957; children: Eric Kimball, Heidi Peek. BD, Episcopal Theol. Sch., 1960; BA, U. N.C., 1957. Asst. min. St. Michael's Episcopal Ch., Raleigh, N.C., 1960-63; asst. dir. program Episcopal Diocese of N.C., Raleigh, 1963-66, asst. mgr., 1966-68, assoc. mgr., 1968-78; mng. dir. Horace Bushnell Meml. Hall Corp., Hartford, Conn., 1978-85; assoc. Coordinating Fin. Planning, Farmington, Conn., 1986-91; sr. cons. ExecuPower, Inc., Farmington, Conn., 1991-92; sr. advisor Bernard Haldane Assocs., Hartford, Conn., 1992-94; prin. Jamieson Assocs., West Hartford, Conn., 1994-98; prin. search cons. Matthews & Stephens Assocs., Rocky Hill, Conn., 1998-2000. Faculty mem. Conn. Re-employment Workshops, Hartford, 1993-96. Author: Finding Hidden Jobs, 1997, Black-eyed Susans, 1999; author weekly newspaper column, 1992-96. Dir. Conn. Halfway House, Hartford, 1973-75, Farmingham C. of C., 1986-89. Mem. Internat. Assn. Career Mgmt. Profls. (founder, 1st pres. Hartford Region chpt.), Phi Beta Kappa. Avocations: poetry, classical music, reading. Home: 24 Birchwood Rd East Hampton CT 06424-1312 E-mail: leejamieson@erols.com.

JAMIESON, MICHAEL LAWRENCE, lawyer; b. Coral Gables, Fla., Mar. 2, 1940; s. Warren Thomas and Ruth Amelia (Gallman) J.; children: Ann Layton, Thomas Howard; m. Elizabeth Marie Peeples, Dec. 31, 1992. BA in English, U. Fla., 1961, JD with honors, 1964. Bar: Fla. 1964, U.S. Dist. Ct. (mid. dist.) Fla. 1964, D.C. 1998, N.Y. 1999. Teaching asst. U. Fla., 1964; law clk. U.S. Ct. Appeals (5th cir.), 1964-65; assoc. Holland & Knight LLP and predecessor firms, Tampa, Fla., 1965-69; ptnr. Holland & Knight and predecessor firms, Tampa, Fla., 1969—, chmn. bus. law dept., 1992—. Editor-in-chief U. Fla. Law Rev., 1963 Trustee Law Ctr. U. Fla., chmn. bd. dirs., 1986-88; bd. dirs., chmn. Bus. Com. for the Arts Inc., 1989-90; trustee Tampa Bay Performing Arts Ctr. Inc., 1989—, chmn. devel. coun., 1990-91; trustee Cmty. Found. Greater Tampa, 1990-97; chmn. devel. com. Fla. C. of C. Found., 1992-95; mem. Tampa Leadership Conf., Golden Triangle Civic Assn. Recipient Gertrude Brick Law Rev. award, 1963 Fellow Am. Bar Found.; mem. ABA (mem. com on corp. laws, mem. com. on fed. regulation of securities), Am. Law Inst., Hillsborough County Bar Assn., Greater Tampa C. of C. (mem. bd. govs. 1988-91), Com. 100 (mem. policy bd. 1989-92, trustee 1998—), Univ. Club, Tampa Club (bd. dirs. 1985-89, pres. 1987-88), The Down Town Assn., Order of Coif, Phi Kappa Phi. E-mail: mjamieso@hklaw.com.

JAMIESON, STUART WILLIAM, surgeon, educator; b. Bulawayo, Rhodesia, July 30, 1947; came to U.S., 1977; MB, BS, U. London, 1971. Intern St. Mary's Hosp., London, 1971; resident St. Mary's Hosp., Northwick Park Hosp., Brompton Hosp., London, 1972-77; asst. prof. Stanford U., Calif., 1980-83, assoc. prof., 1983-86; prof., head cardiac surgery U. Minn., Mpls., 1986-89, U. Calif., San Diego, 1989—. Dir. Minn. Heart and Lung Inst., Mpls., 1986-89; pres. Calif. Heart and Lung Inst., San Diego, 1991-95. Co-author: Heart and Heart-Lung Transplantation, 1989, editor: Heart Surgery, 1987; contbr. over 600 papers to med. jours. Recipient Brit. Heart Found. Fellowship award, 1978, Irvine H. Page award Am. Heart Found., 1979, Silver medal Danish Surg. Soc., 1986. Fellow ACS, Royal Coll. Surgeons, Royal Soc. Medicine, Am. Coll. Chest Physicians, Am. Coll. Cardiology; mem. Royal Coll. Physicians (licentiate), Internat. Soc. for Heart Transplantation (pres. 1986-88), Calif. Heart and Lung Inst. (pres. 1991—), Internat. Soc. Cardiothoracic Surgery (pres. 2003-). Office: U Calif Divsn Cardiothoracic Surgery 200 W Arbor Dr San Diego CA 92103-8892

JAMIESON, T. JOHN, writer, English language educator; b. Detroit, Mar. 12, 1956; s. Theodore and Mary Kelleher Jamieson; m. Mary Mulvihill, Dec. 27, 1979. BA in English, Oakland U., 1976; MA in English, Northwestern U., 1985; MDiv, Nashotah House Theol. Sem., 1992; postgrad., Calvin Theol. Sem., 1993-95. Ordained priest Episcopal Ch., 1992, renounced ministry, 1993. Curate St. Paul's Ch., Muskegon, Mich., 1992; interim curate Parish All Saints Ashmont, Boston, 1993; English tchr. Muskegon Heights (Mich.) H.S., 1997; adj. instr. English Grand Valley State U., Allendale, Mich., 1998. Chpt. chmn. Prayer Book Soc., Chgo., 1986-91. Contbr. chpts. to books and articles to profl. jours. Richard Weaver fellow Intercollegiate Studies Inst., 1982-83, Marguerite Eyer Wilbur fellow Marguerite Eyer Wilbur Found., 1985. Mem. Prismatic Club Detroit. Am. Political Sci. Assn., Eric Voegelin Soc. Roman Catholic. Avocations: roller coaster riding, fencing. Home: 1478 Leahy St Muskegon MI 49442 E-mail: jamiesoj@aol.com.

JAMIN, MATTHEW DANIEL, lawyer, magistrate judge; b. New Brunswick, N.J., Nov. 29, 1947; s. Matthew Bernard and Frances Marie (Newburg) J.; m. Christine Frances Bjorkman, June 28, 1969; children: Rebecca, Erica. BA, Colgate U., 1969; JD, Harvard U., 1974. Bar: Alaska 1974, U.S. Dist. Ct. Alaska 1974, U.S. Ct. Appeals (9th cir.) 1980. Staff atty. Alaska Legal Svcs., Anchorage, 1974-75, supervising atty. Kodiak, Alaska, 1975-81; contract atty. Pub. Defender's Office State of Alaska, Kodiak, 1976-82; prin. Matthew D. Jamin, Atty., Kodiak, 1982; ptnr. Jamin & Bolger, Kodiak, 1982-85, Jamin, Ebell, Bolger & Gentry, Kodiak, 1985-97; part-time magistrate judge U.S. Cts., Kodiak, 1984—; shareholder Jamin, Ebell, Schmitt & Mason, Kodiak, 1998—. Part-time instr. U. Alaska Kodiak Coll., 1975—; active Theshold Svcs., Inc., Kodiak, 1985—, pres., 1985-92, 95-96, 99-2000. Mem. Alaska Bar Assn. (Professionalism award 1988), Kodiak Bar Assn. Office: US Dist Ct 323 Carolyn Ave Kodiak AK 99615-6348 E-mail: matt@jesmkod.com.

JAMISON, DANIEL OLIVER, lawyer; b. Fresno, Calif., Nov. 28, 1952; s. Oliver Morton and Margaret (Ratcliffe) J.; m. Debra Suzanne Parent, May 23, 1981; 1 child, Holly Elizabeth. Student, Claremont Men's Coll., 1970-72; BA in Philosophy, U. Calif., Berkeley, 1974; JD, U. Calif., Davis, 1977. Bar: Calif. 1977, U.S. Dist. Ct. (ea. dist.) Calif. 1977, U.S. Dist. Ct. (no. dist.) Calif. 1982, U.S. Ct. Appeals (9th cir.) 1987. Law clk. to judge M.D. Crocker U.S. Dist. Ct. (ea. dist.) Calif., Fresno, 1977-78; assoc. Stammer, McKnight, Barnum & Bailey, Fresno, 1978-83, ptnr., 1983-95; shareholder Sagaser, Franson, Jamison & Jones (formerly Sagaser, Hansen, Franson & Jamison), 1995—99; pvt. practice Law Offices of Daniel O. Jamison, P.C., Fresno, 1999—. Vol. atty. Calif. H.S., Fresno, 1983-87, 89-94; mem. Assocs. of Valley Children's Hosp., Fresno, 1980-81; co-chmn. Fresno County Law Day, 1995-96; panelist for CEB Selected Issues in Employment Discrimination and Wrongful Discharge Litigation; panelist on indigent care Calif. Soc. for Healthcare Attys.; panelist Lorman Edn. Svcs. on Health Care Corp. and Physician Compliance Programs in Calif., Pres' Circle, Bulldog Found., Calif. State U., Fresno; sustaining mem. Fresno Met. Mus., corp. mem. Comty. Med. Found.; mem. Fresno Hist. Soc., Fresno City and County Conv. and Visitor's Bur. Mem. ABA, Fed. Bar Assn., No. Calif. Assn. Def. Counsel, Fresno County Bar Assn. (spkr.), Fresno County C. of C., Calif. C. of C., East Dist. Hist. Soc. (charter mem.), 9th Jud. Cir. Hist. Soc., Calif. Soc. for Healthcare Attys., Am. Health Lawyers Assn. Republican. Avocations: golf, aerobics. Office: 2445 Capitol St Ste 150 Fresno CA 93721-2224 E-mail: dojamison@jamisonpc.com.

JAMISON, DARLENE, geriatrics nurse; b. St. Louis, Mo., July 10, 1957; d. Earline Mosby; m. Oscar B. Jamison, Oct. 1986; children: Tanalecia Quanalette, Ron Elliot Powell. LPN, St. Louis Coll. Health Careers, 1998. Lic. practical nurse Oak Knoll Nursing Home, Ferguson, Mo., 2000—. Owner Art Designs & More gallery, St. Louis, 2003—. Author: Poetry of Life, 2001, Poetry of Understanding, 2002; Quezema by Dr. Belayneh Abate. Avocations: fishing, writing, art, camping, cooking. Office: Art Designs and More 3024 N Lindbergh Blvd Saint Ann MO 63074

JAMISON, DEAN TECUMSEH, economist; b. Springfield, Mo., Oct. 10, 1943; s. Marshall Verdine and Mary Dell (Temple) J.; m. Joanne Leslie, Sept. 14, 1971 (div. 1995); children: Julian C., Eliot A., Leslie S.; m. Kin Bing Wu, Jan. 19, 1997. AB in Philosophy, Stanford U., 1966, MS in Engring. Sci., 1967; PhD in Econs., Harvard U., 1970. Asst. prof. grad. sch. bus. Stanford U., Palo Alto, Calif., 1970-73; economist World Bank, Washington, 1976-88, dir., 1992-93, advisor, 1993-98; dir. Ctr. for Pacific Rim Studies UCLA, 1993-2000, prof. Sch. Pub. Health, Grad. Sch. Edn. and Info. Studies, 1988—; dir. econs. adv. svc. WHO, Geneva, 1998-2000; fellow Fogarty Internat. Ctr., NIH, 2001—. Chmn. ad hoc com. on health R&D for developing countries WHO, Geneva, 1996-97; bd. trustees Drug Strategies, 1994—; chmn. bd. on global health Inst. Medicine NAS, 2000—; mem. adv. bd. Inst. Human Virology, 2001—. Author (with L. J. Lau): Farmer Education and Farm Efficiency, 1982, Disease Control Priorities in Developing Countries, 1993, World Bank World Development Report 1993: Investing in Health, 1993, WHO World Health Report 1999: Making a Difference, 1999; cons. editor AERA Ency. Rsch., 6th edit., 1992. Fellow Woodrow Wilson Found., 1967, NSF, 1968, Bill and Melinda Gates Found. fellow, 2001. Mem. Inst. Medicine Nat. Acad. Scis. Avocation: tennis. Office: Fogarty Internat Ctr NIH 16 Center Dr MSC 6705 Bethesda MD 20892-6705 Fax: (310) 206-4018. E-mail: jamisond@mail.nih.gov.

JAMISON, ELYWN PAUL, secondary education educator; b. Sandstone, Minn., Mar. 26, 1939; s. Ross Charles and Deloris J.; m. Marilyn Ruth Thomason, July 27, 1962; children: Alexia Marie, Melissa Ann, Lial Nathan. BA, U. No. Colo., Greeley, 1967, MA, 1969. Cert. tchr., Iowa. Secondary tchr. Sinclair Jr. High, Englewood, Colo., 1967-69, Newton (Iowa) Cmty. Sch. Dist., 1969-98. Mem. negotiations com. Newton Cmty. Edn. Assn., 1983-85. Served as Airman 2d class Airforce, West Germany 1961-64. Adult Sun. sch. tchr. Cmty. Heights Alliance Ch., Newton, 1999; mem. gov. bd., 1988-91, chmn. bd. dirs. 1992. Mem.: Gideon's Internat. Avocations: hunting, fishing, building, traveling, placing personal worker new testaments. Home: 6736 S 28th Ave E Newton IA 50208-8128

JAMISON, FRANK RAYMOND, independent video producer, retired communications educator; b. Independence, Mo., Mar. 25, 1938; s. Eldon Verl and Pauline Francis (Mericle) J.; m. Paula Ann Wissing; children: Diana Cherie, Thomas Marshall, Noel Avery. BA, U. Mo., Kansas City, 1960; MS, Syracuse U., 1962; Edn. Specialist, U. No. Colo., 1967. Continuity dir. Sta. WEAR, Syracuse, N.Y., 1961; sales svc. dir. Sta. KCMO-TV, Kansas City, Mo., 1961-62; founder, gen. mgr. Sta. KUNC-FM, U. No. Colo., Greeley, 1966-67, dir. radio and TV, 1962-67; mgr. TV svcs. Western Mich. U., Kalamazoo, 1967-84, head media svcs., 1984—91, prof. instnl. media, 1977—2001, mgr. video distbn., 1991-2001, prof. emeritus, 2000—; founder, gen. mgr. Edu CABLE, Kalamazoo, 1989-2001; head audiovisual svcs. King Faisal Specialist Hosp. and Rsch. Ctr., Riyadh, Saudi Arabia, 1977-79; founding ptnr. Lotus Media, Kalamazoo, 1997—. Bd. dirs. Allegis Credit Union, vice chair, 1999—; mem. nat. conv. com. Assn. for Ednl. Comms. and Tech., Washington, 1992; mem. internat. adv. senate Amity Bus. Sch., New Delhi, 1995—; mem. internat. adv. coun. The Interstate Traveler Project, 2002—; mem. adv. bd. Mother's Trust/Mother's Pl., Ganges, Mich., 1998—2001; bd. dirs. Cmty. (Cable) Access Ctr. Exec. prodr. TV series Every Child a Wanted Child, 1983 (Cable Ace award 1984); prodr. TV series Poets in Their Time, 1977-79 (Ohio State award 1980); assoc. prodr. radio program Where Are We?, 1969 (Armstrong award 1970); TV prodr. 12th World Scout Jamboree, 1967 (Silver Anvil award). Bd. dirs. New Vic Theatricals, Inc., 1978—82, Art Coun. Greater Kalamazoo, 1978—82; faculty advisor Students for a Free Tibet, 1995—2001; mem. S.W. Mich. Coun., Boy Scouts Am., 1967—70, 1992—95; founding chair U.S. Postal Svc. Customer Adv. Coun., 1994—98; nat. sec. Alliance for Cmty. Media, 1986, bd. dirs., 1984—87. Sgt. USAR, 1956—62. Recipient Philo T. Farnsworth award, Nat. Fedn. Local Cable Programming, 1984, Hometown U.S. A. award, 1985, Network Founder award, SCOLA TV Network, 1990, 50 Yr. Vet. award, Boy Scouts Am., 1996, Videographer award of excellence for human rights programming, 1997, Videographer award of distinction for creativity, 1999, Communicator award of distinction for ethnic understanding, 2002; various grants for acad. projects. Mem.: AAUP, Am. Mensa Ltd., Buddhist Assn. S.W. Mich. (pres. 1990—99, bd. dirs. 1990—, treas. 2001—02, pres. 2002—), Buddhadharma Soc. (faculty advisor 1991—2001), West Mich. Men's Coun. (sec. bd. dirs. 1994—96), Arabian Philatelic Assn., Am. Philatelic Soc. (life). Avocations: philately, videography, international travel, racquetball. Home and Office: Lotus Media 2906 Memory Ln Kalamazoo MI 49006-5535 E-mail: frank.jamison@wmich.edu.

JAMISON, HARRISON CLYDE, oil company executive, retired; b. St. Louis, Jan. 15, 1925; s. William Clyde and Katherine Maurice (Fitzgerald) J.; m. Beverly Joy Johnson, June 26, 1946; children: Susan, David, Leslie, Daniel, Dale, Nancy, Sara BA cum laude, UCLA. Geologist Richfield Oil Corp., Bakersfield, Calif., 1950-52, Olympia, Wash., 1952-55, L.A., 1955-60, regional exploration supr., 1961-65; Alaska dist. mgr. Atlantic Richfield Co., Anchorage, 1966-69, Alaska coord. Dallas, 1969-70; mgr. govt. rels. Alyeska Pipeline Svc. Co., 1971-72; chief geologist ARCO Oil & Gas Co., Dallas, 1973-80, v.p. dist. mgr. Denver, 1981; pres. ARCO Exploration Co., Dallas, 1981-85; sr. v.p. Atlantic Richfield Co., L.A., 1981-85. Contbr. articles to profl. jours. Former bd. dirs. Tex. Rsch. League, Austin, Dallas Citizens Coun., Mex. Am. Legal Def. and Edn. Fund, Resolution Seismic Svcs. Inc., Wilmington, Del., ARCO Alaska Inc., Thomas Wilson Dibblee Jr. Geol. Found., Hospice of Bend. Fellow Geol. Soc. Am. (former chmn. bd. dirs., trustees GSA Found. 1986-88); mem. Am. Assn. Petroleum Geologists, N.W. Energy Assn. Home and Office: 37615 S Stoney Cliff Ct Tucson AZ 85739-1412

JAMISON, JAMES MARK, cell biologist; b. Warren, Ohio, July 12, 1951; s. James William and Dorothy Mildred (Mocella) J.; m. Cheryl Louise Burgess, Sept. 5, 1992; children: Miguel, Rachel. BSEd, Kent State U., 1973, MS in Ecology, 1981, PhD in Cell Biology, 1986. Postdoctoral fellow N.E. Ohio U. Coll. of Medicine, Rootstown, Ohio, 1986-89; rsch. and forensic scientist Gennan Corp., Akron, Ohio, 1989-91; instr. of microscopic anatomy N.E. Ohio U. Coll. of Medicine, Rootstown, 1992-95, rsch. asst, prof. of microbiology, immunology, 1995-96, rsch. asst., prof. of urology, 1997—. Contbg. author: Progress in Molecular and Subcellular Biology, 1994. Com. chmn. Pack 3274 Cub Scout Pack, Stow, Ohio, 1996-98; dist. tng. chmn. Moecomdws Dist. Cub Scouts, Akron, 1997-2000; scoutmaster Stow, 1998-2002. Grantee Summa Health System Found., Akron, 1991—, NATO Internat. Coll. Rsch., Brussels, 1994-96, Am. Inst. for Cancer Rsch., Washington, 1998-2000, Hess, Roth, Kaminsky and Maxon Urol. Rsch. Found., Erie, Pa., 1997-99. Mem. Am. Assn. of Anatomists, Am. Soc. for Cell Biology, Electron Microscopy Soc. Am., Internat. Soc. for Interferon Rsch., Am. Soc. Pharmacognosy, Soc. for Basic Urologic Rsch. Office: Dept Urology Neoucom 4209 SR 44 PO Box 95 Rootstown OH 44272-0095

JAMISON, JAYNE, magazine publisher; Grad., Penn. St. U., 1978. Advertising dir. American Health, pub.; group pub., parenthood group Gruner & Jahr USA Pub., N.Y.C., 1994—97; pub. v.p. Redbook, 1997—2003; pub., v.p. Seventeen, 2003—. Office: Seventeen Mag 1440 Broadway 13th Fl New York NY 10018*

JAMISON, JOHN CALLISON, business educator, investment banker; b. Lafayette, Ind., July 12, 1934; s. John Ruger and Sara (Callison) J.; m. Carol Ann Sansone, July 7, 1979; children: Kelly Elizabeth Supplee, Deborah Louise Jamison. BS in Indsl. Econs., Purdue U., 1956; MBA, Harvard U., 1961. Assoc. Goldman, Sachs & Co., N.Y.C., 1961-69, ptnr., 1969-82, ltd. ptnr., 1983—99; dean Sch. Bus. Adminstrn., John N. Dalton prof. bus. adminstrn. Coll. William and Mary, Williamsburg, Va., 1983-90; pres. bd., CEO The Mariners' Mus., Newport News, Va., 1991-93, trustee, 1991—; pres. Williamsburg Cmty. Trust, 2001—. Bd. dirs. Hershey Foods Corp., Pa., Williamsburg Winery, Va. Bd. govs. Purdue Found., West Lafayette, Ind., 1979-83; bd. dirs. Theatre Devel. Fund, N.Y.C., 1979-83; mem. corp. Hurricane Island Outward Bound Sch., Rockland, Maine, 1983-95; mem. vis. com. Harvard Grad. Sch. Edn., 1983-89. Lt. USN, 1956-59, PTO. Recipient Old Master award Purdue U., 1977; recipient Sagamore of Wabash award Gov. of Ind., 1982 Mem. Rotary, Beta Gamma Sigma Episcopalian. E-mail: mallardee@aol.com.

JAMISON, JUDITH, dancer; b. Phila., May 10, 1943; d. John Jamison. Student, Fisk U., Phila., Phila. Dance Acad. (now U. of Arts); studied with, Anthony Tudor, John Hines, Delores Brown, John Jones, Joan Kerr, Madame Swaboda. Dancer Alvin Alley's Am. Dance Theatre, N.Y.C., 1965-80; artistic dir. Alvin Ailey's Am. Dance Theatre, N.Y.C., 1990—; dancer, choreographer touring U.S., Europe, Asia, S.Am., Africa, 1980—; formerly with Maurice Hines Dance Sch., N.Y.C.; founder Jamison Project, 1988-91. Vis. disting. prof. U. Arts; guest assoc. artistic dir. 30th ann. tour Alvin Ailey's Am. Dance Theatre, 1990—; guest appearances Harkness Ballet, Am. Ballet Theatre, San Francisco Ballet, Dallas Ballet. Dancer debut Agnes DeMille's The Four Marys, 1965, (Broadway plays) Joseph's Legend, Vienna Opera, Le Spectre de la Rose, Brussels, Paris, N.Y.C., Maskela Language, 1969, Cry, 1971, Choral Dance, 1971, Mary Lou's Mass, 1971, The Lark Ascending, 1972, The Mooche, 1975, Passage, 1978, (Broadway plays) Sophisticated Ladies, 1980, choreographer Divining Hymn for Alvin Ailey Am. Dance Theatre, works for Maurice Bejart, Dancers Unltd., Dallas, Washington Ballet, Jennifer Muller/The Works, Alvin Ailey Repertory Ensemble, Ballet Nuevo Mundo de Caracas, Riverside for Alvin Ailey Am. Dance Theatre, (Operas) Boito's Mefistofele, Opera Co. Phila.; author: Dancing Spirit, 1993. Recipient Dance Mag. award, 1972, Key to City, N.Y.C., 1976, Spirit of Achievement award Nat. Women's Divsn., Yeshiva U. Albert Einstein Coll. Medicine, 1992, Golden Plate award, Am. Acad. Achievement, 1993. Address: Alvin Ailey Am Dance Theater 211 W 61st St Fl 3 New York NY 10023-7832

JAMISON, KAY, psychologist; BA, MA, UCLA, 1971, CPhil, 1973, PhD, 1975. Asst. UCLA, 1974—87, assoc. prof. of psychiatry, 1974—87; prof. psychiatry Sch. Medicine Johns Hopkins U., Balt., 1987—. Hon. prof. English U. St. Andrews, Scotland. Author: (book) Touched With Fire: Manic-Depressive Illness and the Artistic Temperament, 1993 (Most Outstanding Book in biomed. sci. Am. Assn. Pubs., 1990), An Unquiet Mind, 1995 (NY Times Bestseller), Night Falls Fast: Understanding Suicide, 1999; contbr. articles to profl. jours. Named Hero of Medicine, Time mag.; named one of Best Drs. in U.S., five chosen for pub. TV series Great Minds of Medicine; recipient William Styron award, Nat. Mental Health Assn., 1995, Rsch. award, Am. Suicide Found., 1996, Leadership award, Cmty. Mental Health, 1999; fellow MacArthur fellow, 2001. Office: Johns Hopkins Hosp Dept Psychiatry Meyer 3-181 Psychiatry 600 North Wolfe St Baltimore MD 21287

JAMISON, MARGARET RUTH, psychotherapist, freelance/self-employed writer; b. Salt Lake City, Utah, Dec. 13, 1937; d. Lee McLain and Judith Carver (French) White; m. Alan Rosenthall Koch, Feb. 25, 1956 (div. Nov. 6, 1965); children: Michael Andrew Koch, David Alan Koch, Jeffery Bryan Koch. BA, U of WA, Seattle, WA, 1970, MEd, 1976; PhD, Columbia Pacific U, San Rafael, CA, 1985. Cert. LMFT Health Professions Quality Assurance Divsn./WA. Internat. Cert. Intergrative Body Psycother. Pacific NW Inst. of Integrative Body Psychother.; grief counselor Assoc. for Death Edn. & Coun. Clin. assoc. Crisis Clinic, Seattle, 1966—68; ed. dir. Neighborhood House Child Care Svc., Seattle, 1970—71; instr. Seattle Ctrl. Comm. Coll., Seattle, 1971—76; dir. Umbrella Comm. Svc., Port Angeles, Wash., 1983; emergency svc. coord. Clallam-Jefferson Comm. Action Prog., Port Angeles, Wash., 1986; facilitator Home Health & Hospice, Jefferson Gen. Hosp., Port Townsend, Wash., 1991—98; pvt. practice K-C Coun., Port Townsend, Wash., 1986—2002. Cons./trainer Hospice of Whatcom County, Bellingham, Wash., 1985—92; cons. Port Angeles Sch. Dist., Port Angeles, Wash., 1988—93; cons./trainer HIV/AIDS Clallam County Pub. Health Dept., Port Angeles, Wash., 1991. Author: (article) RN Mag., 1985, (essay) Our Turn, Our Time, 2000, Midlife Clarity, 2002. Treas. Friends for the Ctr. for Urban Studies, Seattle, 1970—72; mem. Jefferson County Critical Incident Stress Debriefer, Port Townsend, Wash., 1996—99, 2002, Seattle Urban League, Seattle, 1963—65. Grantee fund for improvement of Post-secondary ed., Seattle Ctrl. Comm. Coll., 1973—74, Advanced Instl. Devel. Project, 1974—75; scholar Profl. women in Ed., U of Wash., 1968. Mem.: Internat. Critical Incident Stress Found., Am. Red Cross, Assoc. for Death Ed. & Coun. Achievements include co-founder of Hospice of Clallam County; founder of Hospice of San Juan County; coordinator of Survivors of Suicide. Avocations: hiking, sailing, kayaking, cross-country, piano. Home: Ms Margaret Jamison PO Box 1815 Port Townsend WA 98368 Office: K-C Counseling 1025 Garfield Street Port Townsend WA 98368

JAMISON, RICHARD MELVIN, virologist, educator; b. Rayne, La., Oct. 28, 1938; s. Melvin Linwood and Lina Katharine (Muller) J.; children: Richard Wilhelm, Diane Elizabeth, Bonnie Alyssa. MS (USPHS fellow), Baylor U. Coll. Medicine, 1962, PhD, 1966. Diplomate Am. Bd. Med. Molecular Microbiology (trustee 1983-89, 92-99). Rsch. assoc. Oak Ridge Nat. Lab., 1966-67; asst. prof. U. Colo. Med. Ctr., Denver, 1967-70; virologist La. State U. Med. Ctr., Shreveport, 1970—, prof. microbiology and immunology, 1978—, prof. pediatrics, 1987—, pres. gen. faculty, 1992-93; editor Cumitechs, Am. Soc. Microbiology, 1998—. Cons. Al Fateh U., Socialist People's Libyan Arab Jamahiriya. Vice pres. Shreveport Civic Opera Assn., 1977-79. Fellow Am. Acad. Microbiology; mem. AAAS, Am. Soc. Microbiology, Pan Am. Soc. Clin. Virology, Shreveport Orchid Soc. (pres. 1987-89, treas. 1992-94, v.p. 1995-97, 2000-02). Achievements include research in host-virus interactions and picornaviruses, diagnostic and clinical virology. Home: 8602 Rampart Pl Shreveport LA 71106 Office: PO Box 33932 Shreveport LA 71130-3932

JAMISON, ROGER W. pianist, piano educator; b. Marion, Ohio, June 18, 1937; s. Harold Theodore and Martha Louise (Haas) J.; m. Caroline R. Hansley, Jan. 26, 1957; children: Lisa Renee, Eric Karl. BS, Ohio State U., 1959, MA (scholar), 1961; postgrad. Oberlin Conservatory, Oakland U.; student George Haddad, Columbus, Ohio, Mischa Kottler, Detroit. Piano faculty mem. Detroit Conservatory of Music, 1964-68, Cranbrook Schs., Bloomfield Hills, Mich., 1981-84; performer in one-man mus. presentation Spirits of Great Composers, 1979—; dir. music Birmingham Temple, Farmington Hills, Mich., 1984-95; soloist Brunch with Bach series Detroit Inst. Arts., Detroit Symphony Orch.'s Internat. Brahms Festival; regular soloist Christ Ch., Cranbrook, 1982-95; concert tour of Eng., 1991; condr. All Ohio Piano Ensemble, 1997; cons. Royal Oak Arts Council; adjudicator Am. Coll. Musicians. Mem. Nat. Guild of Piano Tchrs. (past pres. Oakland-Macomb chpt.) Address: 173 W Heffner St Delaware OH 43015-1258

JAMISON, WARREN, writer, lecturer, publisher; s. Robert William J.; m. Kitty Sue Wilkerson, Oct. 7, 1961; children: Cynthia Sue, Brian Erik. Co-author: (with Danielle Kennedy) How to List and Sell Real Estate in the 21st Century, 2002; (with Ed McMahon) Ed McMahon's Superselling, 1989, (Literary Guild Selection); (with others) Screw: The Truth About Walpole Prison by the Guard Who Lived It, 1989, (Conservative Book Club Selection), (with Brian Jamison and Josh Gold) Electronic Selling: 23 Steps to E-Selling Profits, 1997; editor: (books) Ed McMahon's The Art of Public Speaking, 1986, How to Master the Art of Selling, Tom Hopkins, 1980, 2d rev. edition, 1982, The Official Guide to Success, 1983, Tom Hopkins, Guide to Greatness in Sales, Tom Hopkins, 1992, Toughness Training for Life, Dr. James E. Loehr, 1993, The New Toughness Training for Sports, Dr. James E Loehr, 1994, The Anti-Diet Book, Jack Groppel, 1995. Mem. Authors Guild, Am. Soc. Journalists and Authors. Home and Office: 1667 SW Fifth St Gresham OR 97080-6722 E-mail: w@jamison.org.

JAMMAL, JOSEPH JAMIL, cardiologist; b. Damascus, Syria, 1951; Degree, Coll. Pérès Lazaristes, Damascus; MD, Damascus U., 1974. Intern D.C. Gen. Hosp., Washington, 1976-77, resident in internal medicine, 1977-79; fellow in cardiology Albany Med. Ctr.-VA Hosp., 1979-81; staff Sutter Roseville Med. Ctr., Sutter Meml. Hosp., Sacramento. Fellow Am. Coll. Cardiology. Office: 2 Medical Plaza Dr Ste 165 Roseville CA 95661-3038

JAMMALAMADAKA, PAPA RAO, molecular biologist; b. Pedamiram, Andhra Pra, India, Aug. 10, 1952; came to U.S., 1986; s. Lakshmi Narasimha Murty and Venkata Satyavati Jammalamadaka; m. Srilakshmi S.P.P. Jammalamadaka, May 3, 1986; 1 child, Sai Teja. MSc, Madurai Kamaraj U., Madurai, 1976; MPhil, U. Hyderabad, 1979, PhD, 1985. Postdoctoral fellow Wayne State U., Detroit, 1986-89, Victoria U. of Wellington, N.Z., 1989-91; sr. postdoctoral fellow Waite Agrl. Rsch. Inst., Adelaide, South Australia, 1991-94; postdoctoral fellow Med. Coll. Ga., Augusta, 1995-99; sr. rsch. scientist Wayne State U., Detroit, 1999—. Contbr. articles to profl. jours. Avocations: reading, meditation, international travel. Office: Wayne State U Immunology and Microbiol 540 E Canfield Rm 7233 Detroit MI 48201 Home: 24467 Bethany Way Novi MI 48375-2821 E-mail: pjammala@hotmail.com.

JAMMALAMADAKA, VIJAYA LAKSHMI, environmental specialist; b. Pachmarhi, India, Mar. 30, 1953; came to U.S., 1972; d. Pillalamarri Ramakrishna Murthy and P. Sati Tulasi; m. Sreenivasa Rao Jammalamadaka, July 1, 1972; children: Arvind Kumar, Aruna Rani. BSc in Biology, Chemistry and Physics, Maharani's Coll., Jaipur, India, 1972; MS in Environ. Sci., Ind. U., 1975. Cert. Am. Inst. Cert. Planners. Environ. scientist HDR Svcs., Santa Barbara, Calif., 1977-81; environ. planner II divsn. Environ. Rev. County Resource Mgmt., Santa Barbara, 1988-89, energy planner III energy divsn., 1989-90; adminstrv. svcs. officer V ACT Planning Dept., Canberra, Australia, 1990; air quality specialist Air Pollution Control Dist., Santa Barbara, 1992—. Trustee Leadership Santa Barbara County, 1995-99; mem. steering com. East Side Study Group, Santa Barbara, 1995; bd. dirs. Sustainability Project Santa Barbara, Cmty. Environ. Coun., 2000—. Mem. Nat. Assn. Environ. Profls. (bd. dirs. Calif. chpt. 1999-2001), Assn. Environ. Profls., Am. Planning Assn., Toastmasters (bd. dirs. Whine and Dine Advanced Club 2002). Democrat. Avocations: travel, facilitation. Office: County Air Pollution Control Dist 26 Castilian Dr # B-23 Goleta CA 93117-3027

JAMPEL, ROBERT STEVEN, ophthalmologist, educator; b. N.Y.C., Nov. 3, 1926; s. Carl Edward and Frances (Hirschman) J.; m. Joan I. Myers, Oct. 2, 1952; children— Henry, Delia, James, Emily. AB, Columbia U., N.Y.C., 1946, MD, 1950; MS, U. Mich., Ann Arbor, 1957, PhD, 1958. Assoc. in ophthalmology Columbia U., N.Y.C., 1962-69, asst. prof. ophthalmology, 1969-70; prof., chmn. ophthalmology Wayne State U., Detroit, 1970—, dir. Kresge Eye Inst., 1970—. Served to lt. USN, 1952-54 Mem. Am. Acad. Ophthalmology, Assn. Research in Vision, Assn. Univ. Profs. Ophthalmology, Acad. Neurology. Home: 4363 Barchester Dr Bloomfield Hills MI 48302-2116 Office: Hutzel Hosp 4717 St Antoine St Detroit MI 48201-1423

JAMPOLE, MICHAEL, music educator, composer; b. NYC, Jan. 12, 1953; s. Sidney and Anita Prager Jampole; m. Jane Hutten, Dec. 30, 1979; 1 child, Jaime Kikpole. MusB in Edn., Northwestern U., 1973; MS in Edn., No. Ill. U., 1983. Music Teaching, grades K-12 State of Ill., 1973, Classroom Teaching, grades K-9 State of Ill., 1984. Band dir. Wilmette (Ill.) Pub. Schools, 1974—, chair dept. music, 1995—; band dir. Rockford (Ill.) Pub. Schools, Rockford, 1973. Condr., musician, Beach Park, Ill., 1969—; composer, arranger, Beach Park, 1970—; clinician, lectr., Beach Park, 1995—. Contbr. Vol. Northwestern U. Sch. of Music, Evanston, Ill., 1993—2002; mem. Waukegan (Ill.) Mcpl. Band; vol. Unity Ch. of Kenosha and Racine, Wis. Mem.: NEA, Ill. Edn. Assn., Am. Sch. Band Dirs. Assn., Music Educators Nat. Conf., Ill. Music Educators Assn. (Outstanding Music Educator 2000), Northwestern U. Marching Band Alumni. Democrat. Avocations: guitar, singing, computers. Office: Wilmette Public Schools 569 Hunter Road Wilmette IL 60091 Home Fax: 847-256-0083; Office Fax: 847-256-0083. Personal E-mail: jampolem@nttc.org. E-mail: jampolem@nttc.org.

JAMRICH, JOHN XAVIER, retired university administrator; b. Muskegon Heights, Mich., June 12, 1920; s. John and Mary (Mudry) J.; m. June Ann Hrupka, June 26, 1944; children: June Ann, Marna Mary, Barbara Sue. Student, Milw. State Tchrs. Coll., 1939-40, Ripon Coll., 1940-42; BS, U. Chgo., 1942-43; MS, Marquette U., 1946-48; PhD, Northwestern U., 1951; LHD (hon.), No. Mich. U., 1968. Instr. math. Marquette U., 1946-48; asst. instr. math. U. Wis., 1948-49; asst. dean men Northwestern U., 1949-51; dean students Coe Coll., Cedar Rapids, Iowa, 1951-55; dean faculty, prof. math. Doane Coll., Crete, Nebr., 1955-57; assoc. dir. Legis. Survey Higher Edn. in Mich., 1957-58; prof. higher edn., dir. Center for Study Higher Edn., Mich. State U., 1957-63, assoc. dean Coll. Edn., prof. higher edn., 1963-68; pres. No. Mich. U., 1968-83, adj. prof., 1983—. Cons.-examiner N. Central Assn. Colls. and Secondary Schs., 1962— ; cons. in field, 1959— ; Ford Found. cons. for devel. U. Nigeria, 1964; cons. higher edn. Govt. of Thailand, 1967; dir. Lake Superior & Ishpeming R.R.; chmn. Nat. Adv. Council Fin. Aid to Students, 1975 Author numerous articles in field; co-author several books; piano and vocal music composer. Bd. dirs. Mich. Joint Council on Econ. Edn., 1977— ; trustee Marquette (Mich.) Gen. Hosp.; bd. dirs. Bay Cliff Health Camp, Marquette; mem. Mich. Council for Arts, 1969-73. Served to capt. USAAF, 1942-46. Decorated Order Lion Finland; recipient City of Peace award (Israel), World War II Victory medal Russian Govt., 1997, Disting. Svc. medal U.S. Dept. Army, 1983. Mem. Newcomen Soc. N.Am. Home: 13971 Croton Ct Jacksonville FL 32224

JAMSHIDIPOUR, YOUSEF, bank executive, economist, financial advisor; b. Arak, Iran, July 7, 1935; came to U.S., 1991; s. Hossein and Kobra (Sohrabi) J.; m. Aghdas Jalaifar, 1938; children: Ramin, Lily, Katia. BA, Tehran U., 1959, MBA, 1961; MA, The Am. U., 1963; MPA, Harvard U., 1973; postgrad., U. Mich., U. Colo. Dir. gen. Bank Markazi Iran, Tehran, 1963-76; v.p. Iranian Inst. of Banking, Tehran, 1973-78; exec. v.p., mem. exec. bd. Bank Melli Iran, Tehran, 1976-80; exec. v.p. D.M.I., Geneva, Switzerland, 1981-88; sr. fin. advisor Hill Samuel Investment Svc., London, 1988-91; fin. cons. 1st Affiliated Securities, Irvine, Calif., 1991-93; fin. planner IDS Fin. Svcs., Irvine, 1993-95; sr. financial advisor Am. Express Fin. Advisors Inc., Irvine, 1995—. Lectr. U. Tehran, 1973-78. Contbr. articles to profl. jours. Office: Am Express Fin Advisors 2 Park Plz Irvine CA 92614-8561

JAN, CHWU-CHING HWANG, environmental chemistry consultant; b. Taipei, Taiwan, July 10, 1956; d. Chau-Ching and Hsiu-Mei (Lin) Huang; m. Deng-Yang Jan; 1 child, Avery. BS, Nat. Cheng-Kung U., 1978; MBA, U. Chgo., 1995; PhD, Ohio State U., 1986. Rsch. asst. Nat. Sci. Found., Taipei, Taiwan, 1978-79; lab. mgr. Nat. Tsing Hua U., Hsinchu, Taiwan, 1979-81; sr. rsch. chemist UOP, Des Plaines, Ill., 1986-92; cons. IRIS DC Inc., Elk Grove Village, Ill., pres., 1993—. Ptnr. Russian Investment Solutions, L.P., Chgo., 1998—; advisor technology CASDAY Co., Ltd., Hsinchu, Taiwan, 1993—. Contbr. articles to profl. jours. including Jour. Electro.-analytical Chem., Interfacial Electrochem., Analytical Chemistry. Mem.: Am. Chem. Soc. (Internat. Student grant 1985). Achievements include patents for hydrotreating processes for organic and halogenerated organic feedsocks containing undesirable olefinic and/or halogen components and/or organic materials, process for decomposing peroxide impurities in a tertiary butyl alcohol feedstock. Office: IRIS DC Inc 1644 Von Braun Trl Elk Grove Village IL 60007-3100 E-mail: dyccjan@aol.com.

JAN, GEORGE POKUNG, political science educator; b. Peking, Jan. 6, 1925; came to U.S., 1955; s. Yunan and Tehchieh (Lee) J.; m. Norma Yingchiang Wen, Sept. 28, 1946; children: Gregory, David, Daniel. BA, Nat. Chengchi U., Nanking, China, 1949; MA, So. Ill. U., 1956; PhD, NYU, 1960. Various positions including editor newspaper/mag., tchr., writer, dean, 1949-55; instr. Chinese NYU, N.Y.C., 1959-60; asst. prof. polit. sci. No. Ill. U., DeKalb, 1961; asst. to full prof. of govt. U. S.D., Vermillion, 1961-68, dir. Summer Inst. for Asian Studies, 1964-66; prof. polit. sci. U. Toledo, 1968-93, prof. emeritus, 1993—, chmn. Asian studies program, 1970-93, dir. Inst. for Asian Studies, 1990-93; pres. Am. Inst. Tech., Toledo, 1993-00. Vis. prof. polit. sci. Beijing U., China, 1988; hon. rsch. fellow Rsch. Ctr. for Contemporary China, Beijing U., 1988—; adviser to China U. Geol. Scis., Beijing, 1993—; hon. chmn. bd. Second H.S., Wenzhou Tchr's. Coll., China, 2000—. Author: The Chinese Commune Experiment, 1964, A Practical English Grammar for Junior Middle Schools, 1953, A Study of English Words, 1955, How to Do Business with China, 1994, Introduction to Political Science, 2000, others; editor: Government of Communist China, 1966, The International Politics of Asia, 1969, China Bus. Newsletter, 1993-98, International Relations of Asia, 1998, Political Development of China, 1998; bd. editors Asian Profile Jour., 1983-86, Jour. Econs. and Internat. Rels., 1986—, The New World of Politics, 1991—; contbr. articles to profl. jours., ency. and books. Pres. Chinese Assn. Greater Toledo, 1983-84; bd. dirs. Toledo Coun. on World Affairs, 1969-76; chmn. keynote session, Symposium on Chinese Ams. in the 1990s, Detroit, 1987; hon. chmn. bd. Second H.S. Wenzhou Tchrs. Coll., 2000—. Recipient Outstanding Svc. award The Internat. Inst. of Greater Toledo, 1983, teaching grants Asia Found., Japan Soc., 1964, 65, 66, rsch. grants U. Toledo, U. S.D., U. Mich., U. Chgo. numerous years, Significant Contribution award Pacific Cultural Found., Republic of China, 1988; named Hon. Rsch. Fellow, Rsch. Ctr. for Contemporary China, Beijing U., 1988, others. Mem. AAUP, Am. Polit. Sci. Assn., Midwest Polit. Sci. Assn., Assn. Asian Studies, Ohio Chinese Acad. and Profl. Assn. (bd. dirs. 1991—, pres. 1994-95), Mich. Chinese Acad. and Profl. Assn. (outstanding leadership award 1992), Am. Assn. Chinese Studies, Internat. Studies Assn., Ohio Internat. Edn. Assn. (chmn. planning and program com. 1976-77), Chinese Acad. and Profl. Assn. of Mid-Am. (bd. dirs. 1986-89), Am. Biog. Inst., Inc. (rsch. bd. advisors 1996—), Internat. Biog. Ctr. (hon. adv. coun.), Phi Beta Kappa, Pi Sigma Alpha, Phi Kappa Phi, Pi Gamma Mu, Phi Beta Delta. Avocations: gardening, photography, travel, swimming, chess. Home: 3041 Valley View Dr Toledo OH 43615-2237 E-mail: aitje@aol.com.

JANA, SADHAN C, education educator, researcher; s. Surendra Nath and Snehalata Jana; m. Soma Dasadhikari, Dec. 11, 1987; children: Subhra Jyoti, Sanhita. B, U. of Calcutta, 1983—86; M, Indian Inst. of Tech., 1986—88; PhD, Northwestern U., 1991—93. Postdoctoral fellow CUNY, 1993—94; sr. engr. Gen. Electric Rsch. Ctr., Schenectady, NY, 1994—98; asst. prof. U. Akron, 1998—. Mem. summer faculty NASA Glenn Rsch. Ctr., Cleve., 1999—99; rsch. asst. U. Mass., Amherst, 1988—91, Northwestern U., Evanston, Ill., 1991—93. Named Disting. Young Alumnus, U. of Calcutta, 2001; recipient NSF Career award, 2002—, Gold medal, U. of Calcutta, 1986; Nat. Merit scholar, Govt. of India, 1977—86, NASA/OAI Summer Faculty fellowship, NASA Glenn Rsch. Ctr., 1999. Mem.: Polymer Processing Soc. (assoc.), Am. Chem. Soc. (assoc.), Soc. Plastics Engrs. (assoc.). Achievements include patents for process for multi-layer polymeric articles with surface conductivity; on process for making composite materials with thermoplastic and thermosetting polymers; on process for shear isolation of rubber latex particles without chemicals; on design of single extrusion screws for immiscible polymer blends. Office: U Akron 250 S Forge St Akron OH 44325-0301 Office Fax: 330-258-2339.

JANACEK, BEDRICH, organist; b. Prague, Czech Republic, May 18, 1920; s. Bedrich Frantisek and Marie (Rausova) Janacek; m. Elisabet Wentz, Jan. 1, 1951; 1 child, Fredrik. Soloist examination in organ idem, State Conservatory of Music, Prague, 1942, master class for organ, 1945—46, diploma ex., 1946; Choir Master degree, Royal High Music Sch., Stockholm, 1961. Organist various concerts, Europe, U.S.A., 1942—; including Royal Festival Hall, London; other concert halls in Eng., Belgium, Czech Republic, Germany, Hungary, Italy, Sweden; also soloist with orchs.; also recs.; tchr. organ State Conservatory of Music, Prague, 1946—48; parish musician Cathedral Parish, Lund, Sweden, 1965—85. Composer: organ compositions and choral works including 2 cantatas with orch., compositions for brass and organ. Decorated Comdr. of Merit Ordo Militaris et Hospitalaris Sancti Lasari Hierosolymitani; recipient City of Lund Cultural prize, 1980, 1988, Royal Distinction Litteris et Artibus, Stockholm, 1993. Home: Kyrkogatan 17 S 222 22 Lund Sweden

JANAK, PETER HAROLD, automotive company executive; b. Detroit; BS in Aerospace Engring., Miss. State U., 1963; grad. exec. program, Stanford U., 1994. Rsch. fluid amplifiers dept. aerospace engring. Miss. State U., State College, 1962—63; propulsion engr. space disvn. Chrysler Corp., New Orleans, 1963—65; from sr. engr. to chief performance analysis sect. Teledyne-Brown Engring., Hunstville, Ala., 1965—68; head propulsion tech. sect. TRW Def. and Space Sys. Group, Houston, 1968—71, mgr. surveillance sys. engring. McLean, Va., 1972—78, mgr. signal processing sys. dept., 1978—79, mgr. SURTASS engring., 1979—80, mgr. undersea surveillance projects and combat sys., 1980—83, mgr. def. sys. ops. Fairfax, Va., 1987—90, mgr. tax modernization program, 1990—92, dep. gen. mgr. divsn. info svcs., 1992—94, v.p., gen. mgr. divsn. info. svcs., 1994—95; mgr. propulsion sys. dept. Technologieforschung, GmbH, Stuttgart, Germany, 1971—72; v.p., dep. gen. mgr. ea. divsn. PRC Sys. Svcs., McLean, 1983—84, pres., gen. mgr. divsn. sys. engring. and analysis, 1984—87; v.p., chief info. officer TRW Inc., Cleve., 1995—98; chief info. officer Delphi Automotive Sys., Troy, Mich., 1998—99; v.p., chief info. officer Delphi Corp., Troy, 1999—. Mem. external rsch. adv. bd. Miss. State U. Mem.: IEEE, Conf. Bd., Working Coun. Chief Info. Officers, Soc. Automotive Engrs., Soc. Mfg. Engrs. Office: Delphi Corp 5725 Delphi Dr Troy MI 48098-2815

JANAK, ROBERT LOUIS, foreign language educator; b. Schulenburg, Tex., Jan. 7, 1945; s. Josef Peter and Edna Petrolina (Kubos) J. BA in History, Lamar U., Beaumont, Tex., 1966; Fulbright Fellowship, Babes-Bolyai U., Cluj, Romania, 1966; MA in History, U. Kans., Lawrence, 1969. Cert. history and Spanish tchr., Tex. Spanish tchr. Hebert H.S., Beaumont, Tex., 1970-82, West Brook H.S., Beaumont, Tex., 1982—; creator of Czech exhibit Inst. Texan Cultures, San Antonio, 1999-2001. Fgn. lang. dept. chmn. Hebert H.S., 1972-80, West Brook H.S., 1984-90, Beaumont, Tex.; tchr. leader People to People Friendship Caravan, Soviet Union, 1989; co-chmn. Site-Based Decision Making Com., Beaumont, Tex., 1992-93. Columnist Cesky Hlas, 1996-03; contbr. articles to profl. jours. Del. County Dem. Conv., Jefferson County, Tex., 1980, 84, 88, 90; campus campaign coord. United Way, Beaumont, Tex., 1987-2002; adv. coun. Czech Cultural Ctr., Houston, 1996; leader of student group Masaryk U., Brno, Czechslovakia, 1990. Named Honorary Citizen Town Coun., Trojanovice, Czech Rep., 1992, Tex. Regional Tchr. of Yr., Texas Edn. Agy., 1992; recipient Good Apple Award Parent Tchr. Assn., Beaumont, Tex., 1989, Mirabeau B. Lamar award South Park Lodge 1320 A.F.&A.M., Beaumont, Tex., 1989. Mem. Czech Heritage Soc. Tex. (trustee 1988-03, pres. 1982-83, 92-93), Czechoslovak Soc. Arts and Scis., Tex. State Tchrs. Assn., PTA Assn. (treas. 1979-81, historian 1982-85). Democrat. Methodist. Avocations: tombstone inscriptions, genealogy, local history. Home: 545 Threadneedle St Beaumont TX 77705-2415 Office: West Brook High Sch 8750 Phelan Blvd Beaumont TX 77706-5199

JANARDAN, KONANUR GUNDAPPASETTY, mathematics and statistics educator; U.S. citizen; m. Aru Janardan; 3 children. BSc in Stats. and Math., U. Mysore, 1956, MSc in Indsl. Stats., 1957; MA in Maths., Pa. State U., 1968, PhD in Math. Stats., 1970. Instr. in stats. Pa. State U., University Park, 1969-70; asst. prof. Montclaire State Coll., Upper Montclaire, N.J., 1970-71; assoc. prof. math. systems Sangamon State U., Springfield, Ill., 1971-80, dir. statis. lab. and tech. svcs., 1973-77, chmn. dept. math. systems, 1977-80, prof. math. systems, 1980-83; prof. stats., dir. math. scis. cons. div. math. scis. N.D. State U., 1983-86, dir., prof. stats., 1985-86; prof. stats. dept. maths. Ea. Mich. U., Ypsilanti, 1986—. Vis. prof. stats. dept. maths. and stats. U. Pitts., 1980-81; vis. prof. to Dr. Sir. M. Visvesvaraya chair U Mysore, India, 1993-94, cons. Div. Water Pollution Control, Ill. EPA, Springfield, 1972-83, Div. Air Pollution Control, 1973; rsch. for Ill. Econ. and Fiscal Commn., 1973; statis. cons. So. Ill. U., 1974; cons. Ill. Dept. Pub. Aid, 1975, Ill. Inst. Natural Resources, Chgo., 1978, Lockheed Engring. & Mgmt. Svcs. Co., Las Vegas, Nev., 1982, Northern Great Plains Rsch. Ctr., Mandan, N.D., 1983-86, Red River Valley Potato Rsch. Lab., East Grand Forks, 1983-88, Metabolism and Radiation Rsch. Lab. USDA Agr. Svc., Fargo, N.D., 1983-86, U.S. Constrn. Engring. and Rsch. Lab. Dept. Army, Champaign, Ill., 1985-86, EPRI of Detroit Edison, 1989-92, cons. to BBK-Financial, turnaround & crisis mngmnt., 1994. Assoc. editor, Communications in Statistics, 1995—, Reviewer Am. Statistician, Jour. Am. Statis. Assn., Sankhya, Can. Jour. Stats., Communications in Stats., BioSci., Statis. Distbns. in Sci. Work, Jour. Statis. Planning and Inference, Statis. and Probability Letters; reviewer stats. WEST Pub. Co., McMillan Pub. Co., PWS-Kent Pub. Co.; contbr. numerous articles to profl. jours. Maharaja's Coll. scholar, Mysore, 1956, U. Mysore scholar, 1957; recipient Vsyya Tyaga Bhushan award Karnataka Arya Vysya Mahashabha Charitable Trust, 1997. Fellow Inst. Combinatorics and Applications; mem. Biometric Soc., Am. Statis. Assn. (founding sec., v.p. cen. Ill. chpt. 1977-78, sec. elect 1978-79, 81-82, pres. elect 1979-81, com. minorities in statis. 1984-87), Am. Water Works Assn. (nat. standards com., 1984-87). Home: 3056 Cedarbrook Rd Ann Arbor MI 48105-3403 Office: Ea Mich U 504N Pray Harrold Hall Ypsilanti MI 48197-2210 E-mail: KGJanardan@comcast.net.

JANAVARAS, BASIL JOHN, business educator, consultant; b. Corinth, Corinth, Greece, Nov. 1, 1943; came to U.S., 1962; s. John Basil and Loukia Demetra (Tzakona) J.; m. Linda Mae Larson, Aug. 19, 1972; children: Loukia Linda, John Basil (dec.). BA, Minot State U., 1967; MS, U. N.D., 1969; EdD, No. Ill. U., 1974. Bus. instr. Mankato (Minn.) State U., 1969-72, asst. prof., 1974-76, assoc. prof., 1977-80, prof., 1980—; dir. Internat. Bus. Inst., Mankato, 1986-89, chairperson, dir., 1986-91; pres., CEO Ianavaras & Assocs. Internat., Inc., 1990—; dir. internat. bus. studies U. St. Thomas, St. Paul, 1992—. Pres. Odyssey Gift Shops, Mankato, 1978-94; dir. Internat. Bus. Exec. Program, St. Paul, 1988—, Minn. State U. Sys., Vienna, Austria, 1990-92. Author: Student Guide to International Business, 1988, Student Resource Manual, 1992, Global Marketing Management System, 1998; contbr. articles to profl. jours. Grantee Mankato State U., 1988-89, U.S. Dept. Edn., 1988-90, So. Minn. Initiative Fund, 1988-90. Mem. Acad. Internat. Bus., Minn. World Trade Week (bd. dirs. 1983—, pres. 1989), Minn. Dist. Export Coun., Minn. World Trade Assn. Home: 27 Capri Dr Mankato MN 56001-4119 Office: Minn State U Mankato 150 Morris Hall Mankato MN 56001-6044 E-mail: basil.janavaras@mnsu.edu.

JANC, JOHN J. language educator; b. Blue Island, Ill., July 24, 1945; BA in French Lang. and Lit., English Lang. and Lit., U. Wis., Eau Claire, 1967; MA in French Lang. and Lit., U. Mich., 1968; MA in Comparative Lit., U. Wis., 1974, PhD in French Lang. and Lit., 1981; diplôme de méthodologie audio-visuelle, U. Poitiers, France, 1975; Doctorat, U. La Sorbonne Nouvelle, Paris, 1977; diplôme supérieur de Français des Affaires, C. of C. and Industry Paris, 1981. Instr. French St. Benedict Coll., Ferdinand, Ind., 1968—69, U. Wis. Stout, Menomonie, 1969—72; lectr. English CAREL, Royan, France, 1972—74; prof. French Minn. State U., Mankato, 1979—. Spkr. numerous workshops and seminars; tester Internat. Baccalaureate Exam, Mpls., St. Paul and Owatonna, Minn., 1990—95. Author: (edit. critique) Les Deux Trouvailles de Gallus, 1983, (series) Que se passe-t-il en France in Minn. Lang. Rev., 1987—, (edit. critique) Victor Hugo: Torquemada, 1989, Faisons des progrès: Manuel de conversation, 1997, (edit. critique) Victor Hugo: Hernani, 2001; contbr. articles to profl. jours., papers to profl. confs. Decorated Chevalier dans l'Ordre des Palmes Académiques French Govt.; named CASE Univ. Prof. of Yr., State of Minn., 1988; grantee, U. Wis., Madison, 1976, Minn. State U., 1980, 1982, 1987, 2000, NEH, 1990; Woodrow Wilson fellow, 1967—68, E.B. Fred fellow, U. Wis., Madison, 1976—77, Fulbright fellow, 1976—77. Mem.: Ctrl. States Conf. (pub. rels. com. 1990—91, pub. awareness com. 1991—92, leadership mentor 1996—97, state svcs. com. 1997—98, grants and fiscal devel. com. 1998—2002, bd. dirs. 2000—01, rev. bd. ann. report 2001—03, leadership program 2002, awards and scholarships com. 2002, bd. dirs. 2002—03, local chair ann. conf. 2003), Am. Assn. Tchrs. French (Minn. chpt., pres. 2001—03), Minn. Coun. Tchg. Langs. and Cultures (v.p. 1987—90, co-chair fall conf. 1990, chair fall conf. 1991, pres. 1991—92, exhibits chair fall conf. 1991—, co-chair fall conf. 1992, campus coord. French lang. contest 1994—96, advt. editor Minn. Lang. Rev. 1997—, Emma Birkmaier award 1994), Soc. des Etudes Romantiques et Dix-Neuvièmistes, Am. Coun. Tchg. Fgn. Langs., Assn. des Amis de Victor Hugo, Sigma Tau Delta, Pi Delta Phi, Phi Kappa Phi, Kappa Delta Pi, Alpha Mu Gamma. Office: Minn State U AH 227 Mankato MN 56001

JANCZAK, ANDREW ANTHONY, executive; b. Buenos Aires, Feb. 20, 1950; came to U.S., 1955; s. Zygmunt and Gertrude (Sierocki) J.; m. Helen Mary Gimber, Jan. 27, 1973; children: Andrew S., Jeanette M. BS in Aerospace Engring., Polytech. Inst. Bklyn., 1972, MS in Mgmt., 1976. Mktg. dir. Telsonic/Trescott, Inc., L.I. City, N.Y., 1973-76; pres. Belzona, Inc., Uniondale, N.Y., 1976-83; pres., owner Molecular Systems, Inc., Edgewood, N.Y., 1983-90; pres. Enecon Corp., Bethpage, N.Y., 1990—. Patentee in field. Avocations: golf, boating. Office: Enecon Corp 700 Hicksville Rd Ste 110 Bethpage NY 11714-3496

JANDES, KENNETH MICHAEL, superintendent of schools; b. Berwyn, Ill., Aug. 6, 1943; s. George Jerry and Dorothea Frieda Clara (Grabow) J.; m. RoseMary Patricia Klingebiel, June 18, 1966; children: Michael Jon, Kenneth Mark. BS in Edn., Ill. State U., 1966; MEd, Loyola U., Chgo., 1972; EdD, No. Ill. U., 1984. Cert. tchr., chief sch. bus. official, gen. adminstrv., supt., Ill. Math. tchr. Brook Park Sch., LaGrange Park, Ill., 1966-69, sci. tchr., 1969-74, acting prin., 1972-74; prin. Waterman Sch., South Holland, Ill., 1974-79, Berger-Vandenberg Sch., Dolton, Ill., 1979-95; supt. Lincoln Sch. Dist. # 156, Calumet City, Ill., 1995—2001, Ridgeland Sch. Dist. # 122, Oak Lawn, Ill., 2001—. Chmn. dept. applied saxophone Am. Conservatory Music, Chgo., 1968-78 ; owner, operator Midwest Music Mart, Riverside, Ill., 1968-73; primary sci. cons. Instructor Mag., Dansville, N.Y., 1969-73; adj. prof. Govs. State U., University Park, Ill., 1985—; performing saxophonist Ken Jandes Dance Orch., Andy Tecson Jazz Ensemble. Composer of numerous choral, band, and orchestral works, 1961—; contbr. articles to profl. jours. Bd. dirs. Cmty. Family Svc. and Mental Health Ctr. La Grange, 1968-74; pres. bd. dirs. ECHO Spl. Edn. Coop., 1999-2001; bd. dirs. Thornton Fractional Area Ednl. Coop., v.p., 1998-99; mem. bd. supts. AERO Spl. Edn. Coop., 2001--; mem. com., treas. Boy Scouts Am., Woodridge, 1985-96; baseball coach Woodridges Athletic Assn., 1980-89; active com. on youth traffic safety Ill. Sec. of State, 1987-91;

chmn. Thornton Twp. Regional Action Planning Project, 1996-99; mem. chancel choir St. Luke Presbyn. Ch., Downers Grove, Ill., 1976—, elder, 1980-86, 92-98. Named one of Outstanding Young Men Am. Jaycees, 1970. Mem. ASCD, Am. Assn. Sch. Adminstrs. (Nat. award 1986), Ill. Assn. Sch. Adminstrs., Ill. Assn. Sch. Bus. Ofcls., Ill. Congress Parents and Tchrs. (hon. life), South Cook County Elem. Sch. Supt.'s Assn. (pres. 1997-98), Calumet City C. of C., Bus. Assocs. Calumet City, MENSA, Lions, Kappa Delta Pi, Phi Mu Alpha Sinfonia, Phi Delta Kappa. Avocations: astronomy, tennis, mathematics, computers, scientific reading, wine and fine dining. Home: 6671 Wheatfield St Woodridge IL 60517-1715 Office: Ridgeland Sch Dist 122 6500 W 95th St Oak Lawn IL 60453

JANDL, HENRY ANTHONY, architect, educator; b. Spokane, July 17, 1910; s. Paul and Marie (Zitterbart) J.; m. Gertrude Ward, June 4, 1940 (dec. 1976); children: Margaret M., H. Ward (dec.); m. Nancy Crater, Oct. 2, 1976. Student, Fontainebleau (France) Sch. Fine Arts, 1933; B.Arch., M.Arch., Carnegie Inst. Tech., 1935; M.F.A. in Architecture, Princeton U., 1937; postgrad., Ecole des Beaux Arts, Paris, 1937-39. Faculty Princeton, 1940-43, 45—, prof. architecture, 1957-75, prof. emeritus, 1975—; acting dir. Princeton (Sch. Architecture), 1964; exec. officer Princeton (Sch. Architecture and Urban Planning), 1968-74; plant engr. Corning Glass Works, N.Y., 1943-45; pvt. practice architecture, 1943—. Vis. critic U. Va., 1957; cons. architect; cons. on phys. facilities to comdg. gen., Fort Monmouth, N.J., 1966-67; archtl. cons. art and architecture com. Diocese of Trenton. Mem., vice chmn. bd. Environ. Design Rev. for Princeton Twp.; bd. trustee CB Wellness Found., 2000—. John Stewardson fellow, 1933; Whitney Warren fellow, 1937; Recipient Princeton prize, 1935; honor award for design of Princeton Borough Hall N.J. chpt. AIA, 1966 Fellow AIA (pres. Capitol chpt. N.J. 1961-62, James River chpt. 1978—, Coll. of Fellows 1971—, AIA Sch. medal 1937); mem. Assn. Collegiate Sch. Architecture, Assn. Princeton Grad. Alumni, Nat. Inst. Archtl. Edn., Alpha Rho Chi (medal for excellence 1935), Phi Kappa Phi, Tau Sigma Delta. Clubs: Kennebunk River. Republican. Home: 4311 Coventry Rd Richmond VA 23221-3213 also: 229 Island Beach Rd Wells ME 04090-4418

JANECEK, LENORE ELAINE, insurance specialist, consultant; b. May 2, 1944; d. Morris and Florence (Bear) Picker; m. John Janecek, Sept. 12, 1964; children: Frank, Michael. MAJ in Speech Comms., Northeastern Ill. U., 1972; postgrad., U. Notre Dame, 1979-80; MBA, Columbia Pacific U., 1982; cert. in C. of C. mgmt., U. Colo., 1982. Adminstrv. asst., exec. dir. Ill. Mcpl. Regirement Fund, Chgo.; pres., owner Secretarial Office Svcs., Chgo., 1976-78; founder, pres. Lincolnwood (Ill.) C. of C. and Industry, 1978-85; pres. Lenore E. Janecek & Assocs., Lincolnwood, 1985—. Rep. 10th dist. U.S. C. of C., 1978—; appointee Health Care Reform Task Force, 1992—; apptd. by Pres. Bill Clinton Selective Svc. Bd., 1993—; apptd. by Gov. Jim Edgar Ill. Health Care Cost Containment Coun., 1994—; mem. adv. bd. Women Healthcare Execs. Network, Chgo. Artists Coalition, Ill. Lincoln Scholars Series Program, Leadership Ill. Author: Health Insurance: A Guide for Artists, Consultants, Entrepreneurs and Other Self-Employed, 1993. Mem. mktg. bd. Niles Twp. Sheltered Workshop; pres. Lincolnwood Sch. Dist. 74 Sch. Bd. Caucus; bd. dirs., officer, founder Ill. Fraternal Order Police Aux.; bd. dirs., officer Lincolnwood Girl's Softball League, PTA; bd. dirs. United Way, 1982-83; mem. sch. curriculum com. Lincolnwood Bd. Edn.; apptd. by Pres. Reagan to Selective Svc. Bd., 1983; pres. United Way Skokie Valley, Ill., 1989; pres., founder Leadership Ill., 1992—, Twp. Coord. and Health Care advisor, Gov. Jim Edgar, Ill., 1990—; founder, pres. Save the Patient, 2001. Talent scholar Northeastern Ill. U., 1972; Ill. Assn. C. of C. Execs. scholar, 1979-80; named Disting. Grad. of Yr. Nat. Honor Soc., 1985; chosen one of Top 100 Women Leaders in Am., 1988; recipient Outstanding Women in Healthcare Mgmt. award Women Health Exec. Network, 1994. Mem. Hadassah. Office: 980 N Michigan Ave # 1400 Chicago IL 60611-7500 E-mail: ljanecek@aol.com., ljainsurance@aol.com.

JANES, BRANDON CHAISON, lawyer; b. Uvalde, Tex., Oct. 9, 1951; s. Brandon Chaison and Phyllis (Collins) J.; children: Margaret, Michael, Brandon. BBA, Baylor U., 1972; JD, U. Tex., 1976. Bar: Tex. 1976, U.S. Dist. Ct. (we. dist.) Tex. 1978, U.S. Tax Ct. 1981, U.S. Ct. Appeals (5th cir.) 1981, U.S. Supreme Ct. 1981. Assoc., then ptnr. Grambling & Mounce, El Paso, Tex., 1976-80; ptnr. Small, Craig & Werkenthin, Austin, Tex., 1981-97, Akin, Gump, Strauss, Haver & Feld, Austin, Tex., 1997—. Contbr. articles to profl. jours. Mem. ABA (taxation sect.), State Bar Tex., Tex. Soc. CPAs. Home: 901 Forest View Dr Austin TX 78746-4521 Office: Akin Gump Strauss Haver & Feld 816 Congress Ave Ste 1900 Austin TX 78701-4042 E-mail: bjanes@akingump.com.

JANES, CLARENCE HARRISON, JR., music educator; b. Birmingham, Ala., Mar. 9, 1960; s. Clarence Harrison and Betty Louise Janes. MusB, Samford U., 1982, M in Music Edn., 1985; ednl. specialist, U. Ala., Birmingham, 1992. Cert. class AA vocal/gen. music Ala., class AA principalship Ala., class A supr. Ala. Gen. music educator Mountain Brook E(Ala.) Elem., 1982—83; choral music educator W. A. Berry H.S., Birmingham, 1983—85; gen. music educator Lee Elem., Birmingham, 1988—95; choral music educator, fine arts dept. chair Huffman H.S., Birmingham, 1995—. Vol. Children's Hosp. Ala., Birmingham, 1990—2002. Finalist Southeastern Regional finalist, Nat. Assn. Tchrs. Singing, 1979, State finalist Ala., 1979. Mem.: Music Educator's Nat. Conf., Am. Choral Dirs. Assn. Anglican. Avocation: golf. Home: 5327 Whisper Wood Dr Hoover AL 35226 Office: Huffman High School 950 Springville Rd Birmingham AL 35205 Personal E-mail: chipsinger@aol.com.

JANES, JOSEPH W. library and information science educator; b. Oneida, NY, Oct. 22, 1962; s. Donald L. and Jeannette M Janes; life ptnr. Janette Hartley. AB in Math., Syracuse U., 1982, MLS, 1983, PhD Info. Transfer, 1989. Asst. prof. U. Mich., Ann Arbor, 1989—97; dir. Internet Pub. Libr., Ann Arbor, Mich., 1995—99; asst. prof. U. Wash., Seattle, 1999—2003, assoc. prof., 2003—. Author: Internet Public Library Handbook, 1999, Online Retrieval: A Dialogue of Theory and Practice, 1999, The Internet Searcher's Handbook, 1996, Introduction to Reference in the Digital Age, 2003. Rsch. grantee, Libr. Congress, 2000, Andrew W. Mellon Found., 1996, U.S. Dept. Edn., 1993, Online Computer Libr. Ctr., 2003. Mem.: ALA, Am. Soc. for Info. Sci. and Tech. Office: U Wash Info Sch Box 352840 Seattle WA 98195

JANES, ROBERT ROY, museum executive, archaeologist, museum consultant; b. Rochester, Minn., Apr. 23, 1948; m. Priscilla Bickel; children: Erica Helen, Peter Bickel. Student, Lawrence U., 1966—68, BA in Anthropology cum laude, 1970; student, U. of the Ams., Mexico City, 1968, U. Calif., Berkeley, 1968—69; PhD in Archaeology, U. Calgary, Alta., Can., 1976. Postdoctoral fellow Arctic Inst. N.Am., U. Calgary, 1981-82; founding dir. Prince of Wales No. Heritage Centre, Yellowknife, N.W.T., 1976-86, project dir. Dealy Island Archaeol. and Conservation Project, 1977-82; founding exec. dir. Sci. Inst. of N.W.T.; sci. advisor Govt. of N.W.T., Yellowknife, 1986-89; exec. dir., pres., CEO Glenbow Mus. Art Gallery Libr. and Archives, Calgary, 1989-2000; fellow Glenbow-Alta. Inst., 2000—. Mus./heritage cons., 2000—; adj. prof. archaeology U. Calgary, 1990—. Author: Preserving Diversity-Ethnoarchaeological Perspectives on Culture Change in the Western Canadian Subarctic, 1991, Museums and the Paradox of Change, 1995, 2d edit., 1997; author: (with others) The Arctic Institute of North America Technical Paper No. 28, 1983; author manuscripts, monographs; contbr. articles to profl. jours. Mem. First Nations/CMA Task Force on Mus. and First Peoples, 1989-92, Banff, Kootenay and Yoho Nat. Pks. Devel. Adv. Bd.; mem. nat. adv. bd. Ctr. for Cultural Mgmt., U. Waterloo, chair, 2003; chair bd. dirs. Friends of Banff Nat. Pk., 2003; vice-chair bd. dirs. Biosphere Inst. of Bow Valley, 2003. Recipient Nat. Parks Centennial award Environ. Can., 1985, Can. Studies Writing award Assn. Can. Studies, 1989, Disting. Alumni award Alumni Assn. of U. Calgary, 1989, L.R. Briggs Disting. Achievement award Lawrence U., 1991, Queen Elizabeth II Golden Jubilee Commemorative medal 2003; Can. Coun. doctoral fellow, 1973-76; rsch. grantee Govt. of Can., 1974, Social Scis. and Humanities Rsch. Coun. Can., 1988-89. Fellow Arctic Inst. N.Am. (bd. dirs. 1983-90, vice chmn. bd. 1985-89, hon. rsch. assoc. 1983-84, chmn. priorities and planning com. 1983-84, exec. com. 1984-86, assoc. editor Arctic jour. 1987-97), Can. Mus. Assn. (hon. life, cert. accreditation 1982, Outstanding award in Mus. Mgmt., Outstanding Achievement award for publ. 1996), Am. Anthrop. Assn. (fgn. fellow); mem. Can. Archaeol. Assn. (v.p. 1980-82, pres. 1984-86, co-chmn. fed. heritage policy com. 1986-88), Can. Art Mus. Dirs. Orgn. (mem.-at-large bd. dirs. 1992-95), Alta. Mus. Assn. (moderator seminars 1990, Merit award 1992, Merit award for Museums and the Paradox of Change 1996), Assn. Cultural Execs. (bd. dirs. 1999--2002, ACE award for Can. Cultural Mgmt. 1998), Sigma Xi. Home: 104 Prendergast Pl Canmore AB Canada T1W 2N5

JANES, WILLIAM SARGENT, real estate corporation executive; b. Cambridge, Mass., Mar. 24, 1953; s. G. Sargent and Ann (Brown) J.; m. Alice Maxine Rowley, June 19, 1982; children: Pack Sargent, Maxine Cotton. BA, Bowdoin Coll., 1976. Sr. sales cons. Coldwell Banker, Washington, 1976-84; ptnr. Lincoln Property Co., Washington, 1984-89; pres. Rock Creek Ptnrs., Inc., Washington, 1990—; prin. RMB Realty, Washington, 1990—. Bd. dirs. Am. Skiing Co., Brazos Advisors, Brazos Fund L.P., CapStar Hotel Co.. Carr Real Estate Svcs., DaVinci Advisors Max/FW, L.L.C., The Mendik Co., Inc., MeriStar Hospitality Corp., MeriStar Investments Ptnrs., L.P., Paragon Group, Inc. Tristee Bpwdpom Coll., Washington Nat. Cathedral Found.; mem. circles bd. Kennedy Ctr. Mem. NAREIT, SIOR, Urban Land Inst. Home: PO Box 1204 Middleburg VA 20118-1204 Office: RMB Realty Inc 1133 Connecticut Ave NW Washington DC 20036-4305

JANEWAY, RICHARD, university official; b. LA, Feb. 12, 1933; s. VanZandt and Grace Eleanor (Bell) J.; m. Katherine Esmond Pillsbury, Dec. 23, 1955; children: Susan Kent, David VanZandt, Elizabeth Anne. AB, Colgate U., 1954; MD, U. Pa., 1958. Diplomate Am. Bd. Psychiatry and Neurology. Intern Hosp. U. Pa., 1958—59; resident N.C. Baptist Hosp., Winston-Salem, 1963—66; mem. faculty Bowman Gray Sch. Medicine (now Wake Forest U. Sch. Medicine), Winston-Salem, 1966—; prof. neurology Wake Forest U., Winston-Salem, 1971—2003, prof. medicine and mgmt., 1997—2003, prof. emeritus, 2003—, dir. Cerebral Vascular Rsch. Ctr., Bowman Gray Sch. Medicine, 1969—71; dean Bowman Gray Sch. Medicine, Wake Forest U., Winston-Salem, 1971—85, exec. dean, 1985—94, v.p. health affairs, 1983—90, exec. v.p. health affairs, 1990—97. Exec. com. So. Nat. Bank, Winston-Salem, N.C., 1982-92; exec. com. BB&T Corp., chmn. exec. com. 2001-03; nat. adv. coun. regional med. programs HEW, 1974-77; mem.-at-large Nat. Bd. Med. Examiners, 1979-87; mem. N.C. Joint Conf. Com. on Med. Care, Inc., 1983-2003; mem. N.C. Inst. Medicine. Active Winston-Salem Forsyth County Bd. Edn., 1970-73; bd. dirs. Nat. Assn. for Biomed. Rsch., 1993-96; Ams. for Med. Progress, Inc., 1993-97, Winston-Salem Found., 1994-2002, chmn., 1997, 98; trustee Colgate U., 1988-95, Winston-Salem State U., 1991-95. Capt. USAF, 1959—63. USPHS fellow, 1956; Markle scholar, 1968-73 Fellow: ACP, Am. Heart Assn. (coun. on stroke), Am. Acad. Neurology; mem.: AMA, Soc. Med. Adminstrs., Greater Winston-Salem C. of C. (bd. dirs. 1985—89, 1991—95, chmn. 1992), Inst. Medicine of NAS, Am. Clin. and Climatol. Assn., Assn. Am. Med. Colls. (exec. coun. 1977—86, mem. accreditation coun. on grad med. edn. 1981—85, chmn. coun. of deans 1982—83, exec. com. 1982—86, chmn. 1984—85), Am. Neurol. Assn., Rotary (dir. 1977—80, v.p. 1981—82, pres. 1982—83), Alpha Omega Alpha, Sigma Xi, Phi Beta Kappa. E-mail: rjaneway@triad.rr.com.

JANG, RICHARD WAYSON, radiologist, educator; b. San Jose, Calif., 1932; MD, U. Calif., San Francisco, 1956. Diplomate Am. Bd. Radiology. Intern San Francisco Gen. Hosp., 1956-57; resident in pathology VA Hosp., Oakland, Calif., 1959-60; resident in radiology U. Minn., 1960-64; med. dir. radiology Brookside Hosp., San Pablo, Calif., 1992-96; instr. radiology U. Calif., San Francisco, 1964—; pvt. practice Calif., 1966; mem. staff Doctors Med. Ctr. of San Pablo, Calif. Mem. AMA, East Bay Radiol. Soc., Alameda-Contra Costa Med. Assn., Am. Coll. Radiology, Calif. Med. Assn., Calif. Radiological Soc., San Francisco Bay Radiol. Soc.

JANG, SONG-HYON, management consultant; b. Wonju, Kangwondo, Korea, Oct. 27, 1939; s. Ki-Hun and Ki-Ja (Chae) J.; m. Phil-Bok, Oct. 9, 1972; children: Jean-Hee, Sae-Hee. BA, Chungang U., 1965; MBA, L.I. U., 1970. Asst. to pres. Chungang U., Seoul, Korea, 1965-68; adminstrv. asst. Korean Mission to UN, N.Y.C., 1970-71; resident rep. Sandoz, Ltd.-Korea, Seoul, 1971-81; lectr. Sogang U., Seoul, 1972-84; exec. v.p. Korea McNeil, Ltd., Seoul, 1983-84; pres. Schering Korea, Ltd., Seoul, 1983-84, S.H. Jang & Assocs., Inc., Seoul, 1984—. Auditor Bus. World Svcs. Ad Agy., Seoul, 1988-90, J. Walter Thompson Korea, Ltd., 1993—. Author: Foreign Investment Guide to Korea, 1986, The Key to Successful Business in Korea, 1988, Pursuing Successful Second Career, 1998. Mem.: Royal Asiatic Soc. (counselor 2003—), Korea Swiss Assn. (pres. 1995—), Korea Exec. Search Cons. Assn. (pres. 2000—01), Swiss-Korean Bus. Coun. (chmn. 2003—), Korea-German Chamber (bd. dirs. 2002—), Am. C. of C. in Korea (gov. 1995—97), Internat. Pub. Rels. Assn., IMD Alumni Assn. (chpt. pres. 1985—), Rotary (pres. Seoul chpt. 1993—94). Office: SH Jang & Assocs Inc Yorji Dreamville 701 275-1 Yonjidong Chongro-Ku 110-470 Seoul Republic of Korea E-mail: shjanda@chollian.net.

JANG, YOUNG-IL, research scientist, consultant; BS summa cum laude, Seoul Nat. U., 1991, MS, 1995; PhD, MIT, 1999. Rsch. asst. Seoul Nat. U., 1993—95; rschr. Korea Electronics Tech. Inst., Seoul, 1995; rsch. asst. MIT, Cambridge, Mass., 1995—99, postdoctoral assoc., 1999—2000; rsch. staff mem. Oak Ridge (Tenn.) Nat. Lab., 2000—. Sci. adv. com. Korea Inst. Sci. and Tech. Info., 2001—. Contbr. articles to profl. jours. Fellow Eugene P. Wigner fellow, Oak Ridge Nat. Lab., 2000—02, Acad. Excellence fellow, Korean Ministry of Edn., 1995; scholar, Seoul Nat. U., 1988—91. Fellow: Global Network of Korean Scientists and Engrs. (chief info. officer 2000—02); mem.: Korean Am. Scientists and Engrs. Assn. (sec. Tenn. chpt. 2003—), Electrochem. Soc., Materials Rsch. Soc., Am. Ceramic Soc., Am. Chem. Soc., Sigma Xi. Achievements include invention of polymer electrolyte, intercalation compounds, and electrodes for batteries; research in mass transport and thermodynamic properties of lithium intercalation compounds; energy storage and conversion technologies. Office: Oak Ridge Nat Lab PO Box 2008 Mail Stop 6030 Oak Ridge TN 37831-6030

JANGER, RICHARD KENNETH, lawyer; b. Chgo., Oct. 31, 1936; s. Max and Myrtle J.; m. Lois Lieberman, Dec. 20, 1959; children: Seth, Joanna, Lee. BS, Northwestern U., 1958, JD, 1961. CPA Ill. Assoc. McDermott Will & Emery, Chgo., 1962-64; ptnr. Levenfeld, Eisenberg, Janger & Glassberg, Chgo., 1964-98, Eisenberg & Janger, Chgo., 1999—. With U.S. Army, 1961. Mem. ABA, Chgo. Bar Assn. Home: 250 Cedar Ave Highland Park IL 60035-4138 Office: Eisenberg & Janger 77 W Wacker Dr Fl 46 Chicago IL 60601-1635 E-mail: rkj@eisenberg-janger.com.

JANI, BINOY R. ophthalmologist, surgeon; Diplomate Am. Bd. of Ophthalmology. Clin. instr. for lion's club charity eye clinic; clin. instr. Lion's Club Charity Eye Clinic; pvt. practice Eye Consultants of No. Va., Springfield, Va., 2001—.

JANI, SUSHMA NIRANJAN, pediatric psychiatrist; b. Gwalior, Madhya, Pradesh, India, Sept. 26, 1959; came to U.S., 1983; d. Kirty Ambalal and Purnima Kirty (Bhatt) Dave; m. Niranjan Natwerial Jani, Mar. 30, 1983; children: Suni Jani, Raja Jani, Roma Jani. Intern Sci., Mithibai Coll., Bombay, India; MB, BS, B.J. Med. Coll., Ahmedabad, India; MD in Adult Psychiatry, Ind. U., 1984; MD in Child Psychiatry, Johns Hopkins U., 1987. Diplomate Am. Bd. Psychiatry and Neurology, sub-bd. Child Psychiatry, Am. Bd. Pediat., Am. Bd. Forensic Examiners. Pediat. emergency physician Mercey Hosp., Balt., 1997—99; child psychiatrist Johns Hopkins Univ. Hosp., Balt.; asst. clin. prof., mem. faculty dept. pediats. and psychiatry Georgetown U. Med. Ctr., Balt., assoc. prof. pediat. and psychiatry; assoc. prof. psychiatry Georgetown U.; med. dir. Chesapeake network Devereux Found., Md., Va., W.Va., Washington and Del., 1998-99; med. dir. Riverside Hosp., Washington, 1999—; pediat. emergency physician Howard County Hosp., 1999—. Chief cons. psychiatrist Balt. Detention Ctr., 1988-89, cons. psychiatrist Vets. Hosp., Indpls., 1986-87. Vol. Radha-Krishna Leprosy Camp, Bombay, 1981-83. Mem. AMA, Am. Acad. Child & Adolescent Psychiatry, Am. Psychiatry Assn., Md. Psychiat. Soc., Columbia Assn., India Assn., Am. Acad. Podiatrics. Hindu. Avocations: reading, knitting, sewing, letter-writing. Home: 10485 Owen Brown Rd Columbia MD 21044-3835 Office: Riverside Hosp 4460 Macarthur Blvd NW Washington DC 20007-2516

JANIAK, ANTHONY RICHARD, JR., investment banker; b. Pitts., Sept. 21, 1946; s. Anthony R. and Ann Theresa Janiak; m. Anne Marie McDevitt, Aug. 23, 1969; children: Brian Richard, Carolyn Marie. BS, Pa. State U., 1968; MBA, U. Chgo., 1970. Assoc. Smith Barney & Co., N.Y.C., 1970-74; v.p. Smith Barney Internat., Tokyo, 1974-77, Smith Barney, Harris Upham & Co., N.Y.C., 1977-78, mng. dir., 1980—; v.p. Smith Barney, Harris Upham Internat., Paris, 1978-80; mng. dir., dir. internat. Smith Barney Inc., N.Y.C., 1995-98; mng. dir. Salomon, Smith Barney, N.Y.C., 1998—. Bd. dirs. Global Wrap Cons. Group, Tokyo, Soditic Fin., Geneva, Fubon Securities, Taipei, Taiwan; chmn. bd. dirs. Genesis Energy LLC, 1999-2002; mem. adv. com. bus. coun. UN, 1984-90, N.Y.C.; mem. task force on fin. svcs. U.S.-Japan Businessmen's Coun., 1982-83; mem. adv. com. on pub. affairs Japan Soc., N.Y.C., 1986-88; mem. emerging markets adv. com. SEC, 1991-93; exch. ofcl. Am. Stock Exch., 1992—, NASDAQ listing com., 1999-2000. Bd. dirs. Town and Village Civic Club of Scarsdale, 1992-95, 98-2001, A Better Chance, 2003—; trustee Scarsdale Hist. Soc., 1999-2001. Republican. Roman Catholic. Avocations: tennis, coin collecting, music, golf. Home: 172 Woodbrook Rd White Plains NY 10605 Office: Salomon Smith Barney 388 Greenwich St New York NY 10013-2339 E-mail: a.richard.janiak@ssmb.com.

JANIAK, JANE MARIE, librarian; b. Bklyn., Jan. 10, 1947; d. Charles Joseph and Jane Rosalie (Michalski) J. BA, Fordham U., 1968; MLS, Columbia U., N.Y.C., 1970. Sr. info. technologist Shell Oil Co., N.Y.C. and Houston, 1968-71; libr. Caltex Petroleum, N.Y.C., 1971-72; chief libr. Port Authority of N.Y. & N.J., N.Y.C., 1972-95. Mem. Spl. Librs. Assn.

JANIAN, PAULETTE, lawyer; b. Selma, Calif., Oct. 21, 1946; d. Charles and Alice (De Kozan) J.; children: Dennis-Paul, Matthew, Denise, Nicholas. BA, Fresno State U., 1968; JD, Hastings Coll. Law, 1971. Bar: Calif. 1972, U.S. Dist. Ct. (ea. dist.) Calif. 1972. Ptnr. Shepard, Shepard & Janian, Selma, Calif., 1971—; city atty. City of Selma, 1974-83; judge pro tem Fresno County Superior Ct., Calif., 1973. Mem. Fresno County Bar Assn. (sec. 1975, chmn. family law sect. 1995-96), Order of Ea. Star. Mem. Armenian Apostolic Ch. Home: 3190 S Fowler Ave Fresno CA 93725-9328 Office: Shepard Shepard & Janian PO Box 407 1814 E Front St Selma CA 93662-0407 E-mail: pjanian@pacbell.net.

JANICAK, PHILIP GREGORY, psychiatry educator, researcher; b. Chgo., Aug. 2, 1946; s. Edward and Josephine (Raskauskas) J.; m. Mary Judith Cray, Oct. 16, 1976; 1 child, Matthew Cray. BS in Psychology with honors, Loyola U., Chgo., 1969, MD, 1973. Diplomate Am. Bd. Psychiatry and Neurology. Asst. clin. prof. dept. psychiatry Loyola U., Maywood, Ill., 1976-78; research assoc. U. Chgo., 1979-81; asst. prof. U. Ill., Chgo., 1982-85, assoc. prof., 1986-92, prof., 1992—. Chief rsch. unit Ill. State Psychiat. Inst., Chgo., 1984-96; med. dir. psychiat. clin. rsch. ctr. U. Ill., 1996—. First author: Principles and Practice of Psychopharmacotherapy, 1993, 3d edit., 2001. NIMH grant co-investigator, 1986, 91, 93; NIMH grant prin. investigator, 1990; NIH grant assoc. program dir. 2000. Fellow Am. Psychiat. Assn. (disting. fellow). Roman Catholic. Avocation: voice. E-mail: pjanicak@psych.uic.edu.

JANICH, DANIEL NICHOLAS, lawyer; b. Chgo., Aug. 8, 1952; s. Nicholas and Antoinette (Colasurdo) J. BA with honors, Marian Coll., 1974; JD, John Marshall Law Sch., 1978; LLM in Taxation, DePaul U., 1986. Bar: Ill. 1978, U.S. Dist. Ct (no. dist.) Ill. 1978, U.S. Ct. Appeals (7th cir.) 1980, U.S.Tax Ct. 1986, U.S. Supreme Ct. 1990. Mem. legal dept. Liberty Mutual Ins. Co., Chgo., 1978-84; instr. law DePaul U., Chgo., 1984-85; assoc. O'Keefe, Ashenden, Lyons & Ward, Chgo., 1985-87, Nisen & Elliott, Chgo., 1987-88, Chadwell & Kayser Ltd., Chgo., 1988-90, Masuda, Funai, Eifert & Mitchell, Ltd., Chgo., 1991-97, Altheimer & Gray, Chgo., 1997-98, Freeborn & Peters, Chgo., 1999—. Contbr. articles to profl. jours. Mem. ABA, Chgo. Bar Assn., Ill. State Bar Assn., Am. Arbitration Assn., Delta Theta Phi. Roman Catholic. Home: 1575 Sandpebble Dr Wheeling IL 60090-5920 Office: Apt 348 1575 Sandpebble Dr Wheeling IL 60090-5920 E-mail: djanich@freebornpeters.com.

JANICKI, ROBERT STEPHEN, retired pharmaceutical company executive; b. Manette, Wash., Dec. 7, 1934; s. Stephen Walter and Elizabeth Caroline (Gorman) J.; m. I. Jane Betcher, Aug. 18, 1956; children: Robert, Beth, David. BS, Grove City Coll., 1956; MD, Temple U., 1961. Diplomate Nat. Bd. Med. Examiners. Intern U.S. Naval Hosp., Phila., 1961-62; resident in occupl. medicine USN, 1962-63; assoc. dir. clin. rsch. Dow Pharms., Indpls., 1966-68; assoc. med. dir. Neisler divsn. Union Carbide Corp., Sterling Forest, N.Y., 1968-69; assoc. med. dir. regulatory affairs Abbott Labs., North Chicago, Ill., 1969-70, dir. clin. rsch. pharm. products divsn., 1970-71, v.p. med. affairs pharm. products divsn., 1971-79, v.p. research pharm. products divsn., 1979-83, corp. v.p. R & D pharm. products divsn., 1983-89, sr. v.p., 1989-90. Bd. dirs. Sunpharm Corp., Jacksonville, Fla., Afferon Corp., Wayne, Pa.; cons. New Drug Devel. Contbr. articles profl. to jours. Trustee Grove City (Pa.) Coll., 1995-99. Lt. comdr. M.C.,USN, 1961-66. Fellow Am. Coll. Clin. Pharm.; mem. Am. Soc. Clin. Pharmacology and Therapeutics, Sigma Xi, Alpha Omega Alpha. Home: 138 Anchor Dr Vero Beach FL 32963-2941

JANICOT, DANIEL CLAUDE EMMANUEL, foundation administrator; b. Neuilly Sur Seine, France, May 20, 1948; s. Francois-Xavier and Antoinette (Mauxion) J.; previously married to Monique Bibal; children: Laetitia, Mathilde; m. Catherine Lachenal; 1 child, Thomas. Law Degree, Faculte de Droit de Paris, 1972; Grad. Degree, Inst. D'Etudes Politiques, Paris, 1971; Postgrad. Degree, Ecole Nationale D'Adminstrn., Paris, 1975. Auditor State Coun., Paris, 1975—, dep. sec.-gen., 1978-82, maitre des requetes, 1979; maitre de confs. Inst. D'Etudes Politiques, 1976-78, Ecole Nationale des Ponts et Chausees, Paris, 1977-78; gen. rapporteur Commn. D'Acces Aux Documents Adminstrn., Paris, 1979; v.p. Nat. Libr., Paris, 1981; maitre de seminaire Ecole Nationale D'Adminstrn., Paris, 1982-93; dir. exec. office of dir. gen. UNESCO, Paris, 1991-94, asst. dir. gen., 1994—. State councillor, State Coun., Paris, 1995—. Author: (book) La Cooperation Internationale. Bd. dirs. Pompidou Ctr. Libr., Paris, 1979; del. gen. Union Centrale des Arts Decoratifs, Paris, 1982-86, Am. Ctr., Paris, 1980-90; chmn. bd. dirs. Ctr. Nat. d'art contemporain, Grenoble, 1995; vice-chmn. bd. dirs. Inst. franÇais de gestion, 1996—. Chevalier Ordre Nat. du Merite, France, 1988, Ordre Nat. Des Arts et Des Lettres, France, 1985, Chevalier Ordre Nat. Légion d'Honneur, 1999 Home: 6 Rue Casimir Perier Paris 75007 France Office: Conseil d'Etat Palais Royal 75100 Paris France

JANIGA-PERKINS, CONSTANCE GABRIELLE, language educator; d. Edward John and Margaret (Mihalovic) Janiga; m. Michael Allen Perkins, Mar. 8, 1992; 1 child, Gabrielle Janiga Perkins. PhD, Ind. U., 1987; BA Spanish maj., Douglass Coll., 1977. Assoc. prof. of hispanic lang. and lit. Modern Languages and Classics, Tuscaloosa, Ala., 1987—; asst. prof. Spanish SUNY, Oswego, 1986—87. Co-editor (with Dr. Heitor Martins): (critical edition) Dialogo Entre o Deus Momo e o Censor. VII Anuario do Museu da Inconfidencia e do Grupo de Museus e Casas Historicas de Minas Gerais. Brasilia: Ministerio da Educacao e Cultura, 1985.; contbr. critical articles, studies to profl. publs. V.p. Univ. Pl. Sch. PTA, 1999—2003; active Girl Scouts U.S. Fellow, NEH, 1991, 1992; grantee, Fulbright Found., 1983, U.S. Dept. Edn./Fulbright Found., 1995—97, 1986; Fulbright Rsch./Tchg. grantee, Costa Rica, 1991, Arts & Sciences Tchg. fellow, Coll. of Arts and Scis., 1997—2001. Mem.: South Ea. Coun. on L.Am. Studies, South Ea. MLA, Nat. Fulbright Assn., Parent Tchr. Assn., Phi Beta Kappa, Sigma Delta Pi, Sigma Beta Delta. Office: Modern Langs and Classics BB Comer 200 Tuscaloosa AL 35487-0246 Home Fax: 205-348-2042; Office Fax: 205-348-2042. Personal E-mail: cjaniga@bama.ua.edu. E-mail: cjaniga@bama.ua.edu.

JANIGIAN, BRUCE JASPER, lawyer, educator; b. San Francisco, Oct. 21, 1950; s. Michael D. Janigian and Stella (Minasian) Amerian; m. Susan Elizabeth Frye, Oct. 4, 1986; children: Alan Michael, Alison Elizabeth. AB, U. Calif., Berkeley, 1972; JD, U. Calif., San Francisco, 1975; LLM, George Washington U., 1982. Bar: Calif. 1975, U.S. Supreme Ct. 1979, D.C. 1981. Dir. Hastings Rsch. Svcs., Inc., San Francisco, 1973-75; judge adv. in Spain, 1976-78; commr. U.S. Navy and Marine Corps Ct. Mil. Rev., 1978-79; atty. advisor AID U.S. State Dept., Washington, 1979-84; dep. dir., gen. counsel Calif. Employment Devel. Dept., Sacramento, 1984-89; Fulbright scholar, vis. prof. law U. Salzburg, Austria, 1989-90; chmn. Calif. Agrl. Labor Rels. Bd., 1990-95; v.p. Europe, resident dir. Salzburg (Austria) Seminar, 1995-96; U.S. legate European Acad. Scis. and Art, 1996—; Rapporteur, World Economic Forum, 1996; of counsel Weintraub Genshlea Chediak Sproul, Sacramento, 1998—2001; pvt. practice Sacramento, 2001—; adviser European-Am. C. of C., 2003—. Prof. McGeorge Sch. Law, U. Pacific, Sacramento, 1986—, Inst. on

Internat. Legal Studies, Salzburg, summer 1987, London Inst. on Comml. Law, summers 1989, 92-93; vis. scholar Hoover Inst. War, Revolution and Peace, Stanford U., 1991-92; dir. Vienna-Budapest East/West Trade Inst., 1993; vis. prof. law U. Salzburg, 1995-96, prof. internat. bus. mgmt., Golden Gate U., 1998—. Editor: Financing International Trade and Development, 1986-87, 89, International Business Transactions, 1989, 92, International Trade Law, 1993-94. Coord. fund raiser March of Dimes, Sacramento, 1987; adviser European-Am. C. of C., 2003—. Capt. USNR, JAGC, 1976-79, mem. Res. Fulbright scholar, 1989-90; decorated Navy Achievement medal; recipient USAID Meritorious Honor award, Faculty of Yr. award Golden Gate U., 2001. Mem.: Am. Soc. of Internat. Law, Austro-Am. Soc., World Art Forum (v.p. 1996), European Acad. Scis. and Art (U.S. Legate 1996—), Pub. Internat. Law and Policy Group, Anthony M. Kennedy Am. Inn of Ct. (barrister 1998—2001), Sacramento Bar Assn. (exec. com. taxation sect. 1988—89, chair internat. law sect. 1999—2002), D.C. Bar Assn., Calif. Bar Assn., Marine Meml. Assn., Navy League (gen. counsel 1997—), Naval Res. Officers Assn. (life), Knights of Vartan, Sacramento Capitol Club (dir. 1999—2001), Comstock Club (bd. dirs. 1998—99), Sacramento Met C. of C. (award for program cntbns. and cmty. enrichment 1989), Rotary (chair, internat. found. com. 1999—2002), Fulbright Assoc. (life), Phi Beta Kappa. Avocations: cross-country skiing, tennis, bicycling. Home: 1631 12th Ave Sacramento CA 95818-4146 Office: 400 Capitol Mall Ste 900 Sacramento CA 95814-4407 Business E-Mail: law@janigian.com.

JANIKOWSKI, STANLEY M. retired tax specialist, advocate; b. Reading, Pa., Aug. 26, 1930; s. Stanley A. and Cecelia E. Janikowski; m. Zosia B. Mieczkowski, July 19, 1952; children: Monica, Rebecca, Jan. BS in Econs., Albright Coll., 1952; MBA, U. Chgo., 1953. Cert. corp. tax exec. Tax Exec. Inst. Sr. auditor Price Waterhouse, Phila., 1955—60; mgr. tax acctg. The Budd Co., Phila., 1960—71; corp. tax mgr. Bendix Corp., Southfield, Mich., 1971—82, Hammermill Paper, Erie, Pa., 1983—89. U.S. Army auditor Audit Agy., Mpls., 1954—55; pres. Mgmt. Club Bendix Ctr. Am. Mgmt. Assn., Southfield, Mich., 1978—81; mem. taxpayer svc. IRS, Erie, 1995—99. Pres. Erie County Diabetes Assn., 1991—93; grass roots and congl. dist. elections team coord. AARP, Erie, 2000—03; sr. issues coord. United Way, Erie, 2002—03; bd. mem. Congl. Action to Lift With Love, 1998—2003; v.p. parish coun. St. Julia's Ch., 2002—03. With U.S. Army, 1953—55. Fellow, U. Chgo. Grad. Sch. Bus., 1952—53; James McKinsey scholar, 1953. Avocations: golf, fishing, walking, bicycling, bowling. Home: 1401 Central Dr Erie PA 16505

JANIS, CONRAD, actor, jazz musician, art dealer, film producer, director; b. N.Y.C. s. Sidney and Harriet J.; children: Christopher, Carin; m. Maria Grimm, Nov. 30, 1987. Appeared in numerous Broadway plays including Junior Miss, 1942, Dark of the Moon, 1945, The Next Half Hour, 1945, The Brass Ring, 1951 (World Theater award), Time Out for Ginger, 1952, Visit to a Small Planet, 1957, Sunday in New York, 1961, Marathon '33, 1963, The Front Page, 1969, Same Time Next Year, 1975-76; films include Snafu, 1945, Margie, 1946, That Hagen Girl, 1947, Let's Rock, 1958, Airport '75, The Duchess and the Dirtwater Fox, 1976, The Buddy Holly Story, 1977, Roseland, 1977, Oh, God! Book II, 1979, Nothing in Common, 1987, Sonny Boy, 1987, Mr. Saturday Night, 1992, The Gods Must Be Crazy III, 1992; star, dir. The Feminine Touch, 1995, The Cable Guy, 1995, Addams Family Reunion, 1998; actor, dir. The November Conspiracy, 1996; appeared in over 350 major network TV shows including Suspense, 1950, Highway to Heaven, 1986, Golden Girls, 1987, 89, Murder, She Wrote, 1988, 91, Baywatch, 1996, The New Rockford Files, 1997, Frasier, 1997, 2000, 02, Diagnosis Murder, 1998, (recurring role) Family Law, 1999-2000; numerous TV movies including Miracle on 34th Street, 1973, The Virginia Hill Story, 1974, The Magnificent Magnet of Santa Mesa, 1977, The Gossip Columnist, 1984, The Red Light Sting, 1984, Asimov's Probe, 1987, Caddie Woodlawn, 1988, Time After Time, 2002; TV series include I Bonino, Quark, Mork and Mindy, 1978-82; spokesperson TV series on modern art, Appreciating Art, 1991; leader jazz group, 1951—; TV appearances with Johnny Carson, Diana Shore, Mike Douglas, The Late Show with Ross Schaeffer, David Letterman Show, spls. include Burt Convy, Juke Box Hits, Jerry Lewis Telethons, others; appeared in major jazz clubs throughout US, jazz festivals, Monterey, Calif., Palm Springs, Calif., Sacramento, L.A. Classic and many others, concerts at N.Y. Carnegie Hall, Town Hall, Phila. Acad. Music, Nugget Jazz Festival, Playboy Jazz Festival, 1997, others; jazz trombonist with various artists including Roy Eldredge, Coleman Hawkins, Buddy Rich, Bobby Hackett, Hot Lips Page, Wild Bill Davison; leader Beverly Hills Unlisted Jazz Band, 1978— (subject of PBS spl. titled That's A Plenty 1981), The Tuxedo Junction, (PBS spl.) This Joint is Jumpin, 1997; writer, producer, star: (with others) (video spl.) This Joint Is Jumpin', 1997, numerous recs. for many jazz labels; co-owner. Sidney Janis Gallery, N.Y.C.; co-founder with Maria Grimm, producer Golden Era Pictures (co. now titled MiraCon Pictures), 1988—. Recipient Theatre World award, 1952; named to Playboy Jazz Poll, 1960, 61; Silver Theatre award, 1950 Mem. AFTRA, Acad. Motion Picture Arts and Scis., Actors Equity Assn., Screen Actors Guild, Am. Fedn. Musicians, Aftra. Clubs: Nautico (Bilbao, Spain), Bohemian Club (San Francisco). Fax: (310) 273-0180. E-mail: traid43@aol.com.

JANIS, F. TIMOTHY, technology company executive; b. Chgo., Apr. 11, 1940; s. Fabian M. and Phyllis (Underwood) Janiszewski; m. Kathryn Dickey; children: Mark David, Paul Joseph, Melissa Ann. BS in Chemistry, Wichita State U., 1962, MS in Chemistry, 1963; PhD in Chemistry, Ill. Inst. Tech., 1968. Asst., then assoc. prof. chemistry Ill. Benedictine Coll., Lisle, Ill., 1969-74; asst. acad. dean Franklin (Ind.) Coll., 1974-77; divn. dir. Indpls. Ctr. for Advanced Rsch., 1977-92; founder and pres. ARAC, Inc., Franklin, Ind., 1992—. Cons. Argonne (Ill.) Nat. Lab., 1968-74, Office Pers. Mgmt., Denver, 1988-94; mem. adv. bd. R&D Enterprise Asia Pacific, 1999. Co-author: Moving R&D to Marketplace, 1993, rev. edit., 1995, 25 publs. on tech. transfer; internat. editor Tech. Bus. Mag., 1998-2000. Mem. Lisle Cmty. High Sch. Bd., 1970-72; bd. dirs. Near North Devel. Corp., Indpls., 1990-94. Named Sagamore of the Wabash, Gov. of State of Ind., 1990. Mem. Tech. Transfer Soc. (treas., pres. 1990-92, exec. dir. 1993-96). Roman Catholic. Avocations: golf, reading, sightseeing, grandchildren. Office: 604 Davis Dr Franklin IN 46131-7682 Fax: (317) 738-3980. E-mail: tjanis@aracinc.com.

JANIS, MICHAEL JON, molecular biologist, entrepreneur; b. Meadville, Pa., June 6, 1970; s. Richard Joseph and Kathleen Ann (Conlin) J. BS in Biology, Northeastern U., 1994; MS in Biochemistry, Johns Hopkins U., 2001; postgrad. in Molecular Biology and Biochemistry, UCLA, 2001—. Cert. in emergency disaster response ARC. Biochem. technologist intern Ciba-Corning Diagnostics, Medfield, Mass., 1991-92; rsch. perfusion intern dept. cardiothoracic surgery Boston U. Hosp., 1992-93; founder, pres. Structural Design Concepts, Boston, 1994-96; molecular rsch. assoc. Geron Corp., Menlo Park, Calif., 1996-99; founder, pres. MOLECULIM, Menlo Park, Calif., 2001; assoc. scientist, molecular rschr. Affymetrix, Inc., Santa Clara, Calif., 1999—. Patentee in field. Vol. ARC, Palo Alto, Calif., 1999-2001. Mem.: Am. Chem. Soc., Am. Assn. Cancer Rsch. (assoc.). Avocations: rowing, sculling, music, mountaineering, skiing. Home: 610 London St San Francisco CA 94112 Office: Affymetrix Inc 3380 Central Expressway Santa Clara CA 95051 E-mail: mjanis@chem.ucla.edu.

JANIS, MICHEL, pathology educator; b. Tighina, Romania, Mar. 30, 1926; s. Leon and Maria (Imas) J.; m. Rosamond Pomerantz, Dec. 24, 1953; children—Juliane, Marc, Lynn. Student Med. Inst., Samarcand, USSR, 1942-45; M.D., Sorbonne, Paris, 1952. Diplomate Am. Bd. Pathology. Intern Bklyn. Jewish Hosp., 1954-55; resident Bronx Municipal Hosp. Ctr. (N.Y.), 1955-56; fellow National Cancer Inst., Columbia Presbyterian Med. Ctr., N.Y., N.Y., 1958-59; assoc. pathologist St. Elizabeth's Hosp., Elizabeth, N.J., 1959-60; asst. attending Bronx Mcpl. Hosp. Ctr. 1960, attending, 1961—2000, dir. tumor registry, 1973-80; instr. Albert Einstein Coll. Medicine, 1960, asst. prof. pathology, 1961-67, assoc. prof., 1967-78, prof., 1978-84, vis. prof., 1984—; attending Bronx-Lebanon Hosp. Ctr., 1982-87, dir. dept. pathology, 1982-84; dir. dept. pathology Westchester Sq. Med. Ctr., Bronx, 1982-97; cons. Letchworth Village Hosp., Thiells, N.Y., Rockland County Med. Examiner's Office, Pomona, N.Y.; mem. pulmonary pathology panel Eastern Coop. Oncology Group, Madison, N.Y., 1976-90. Contbr. chpt. to book, articles to profl. jours. Trustee, Temple Beth Shalom, Hastings-on-Hudson, N.Y., 1969. Served as capt. M.C., U.S. Army, 1956-58. Health Rsch. Coun. N.Y. grantee, 1962. Mem. Internat. Acad. Pathology (hon.), N.Y. Path. Soc., N.Y. State Soc. Pathologists, Arthur Purdy Stout Soc. Surg. Pathologists, Internat. Assn. Study of Lung Cancer, Pathologists Club N.Y. (sec. 1978-80, v.p. 1980-82, pres. 1982-84). Democrat. Jewish. Home: 4 Floral Dr Hastings On Hudson NY 10706-1202 Office: 2475 Saint Raymonds Ave Bronx NY 10461-3124

JANISCHEWSKYJ, WASYL, electrical engineering educator; b. Prague, Czechoslovakia, Jan. 21, 1925; s. Ivan and Hanna (Ravych) J.; m. Emilia Miszczuk; children: Roxolana, Marko. Student, Tech. U. Hannover, Fed. Republic of Germany, 1948-50; B of Applied Sci., U. Toronto, 1952, M of Applied Sci., 1954; Hon. Doctor, Natl. Tech. U. of Ukraine Polytechnical Inst., Kyiv, 1998. Registered profl. engr., Ont. Testing engr. Moloney Electric Co., Toronto, Can., summer 1952; demonstrator/instr. U. Toronto, 1952-55, lectr. to prof., 1959-90, prof. emertius, 1990—, asst. dept. head elec. engring., 1964-70, assoc. dean faculty of applied sci. and engring., 1978-82; elec. engr. Aluminium Labs., Kingston, Ont., 1955-59; elect. engr. NRC, Ottawa, Ont., Can., summer 1961, Ont. Hydro, Toronto, Can., summers 1962-65. Contbr. over 100 articles to profl. jours. Fellow IEEE; mem. Am. Soc. for Engring. Edn., Internat. Elec. Commn., Internat. Conf. on Large High Vol. Elec. Systems, Can. Elec. Assn., Assn. Profl. Engrs. Ont., Taras Shevchenko Sci. Soc., Ukrainian Free Acad. Scis. Mem. Ukranian Orthodox Ch. Home: 65 Humbercrest Blvd Toronto ON Canada M6S 4K6 Office: Univ Toronto Dept Elec/Computer Engring Toronto ON Canada M5S 3G4 E-mail: janisch@ecf.utoronto.ca.

JANITSCHEK, HANS, journalist; b. Vienna, Nov. 6, 1934; s. Norbert J and Grete Helene Janitschek; m. Elfriede Gerda Ruisinger Janitschek, Aug. 6, 1959; children: Stefan Patrick, Angela Judith. BA, Haverford coll., Haverford, PA, 1953—54; MA, U. of Vienna, Vienna, Austria, 1955—57. Staff corr. United Press, Vienna, 1955—57, Reuter's, Vienna, 1958—59; fgn. editor Express Newspaper, Vienna, 1960—62; vice consul Austrian Govt., New York, NY, 1963—64; sec. gen. Socialist Internat., London, 1965—76. Chmn./pres. Earth Soc. Found., New York, NY, 1992; pres. Un Soc. Of Writers &Art, New York, NY, 1988. Author: (book) Mario Soares, Portrait, Oscar Arias, Pursuit Of Peace, Hans Dichand, Biography. Mem. Dutch Treat Club, New York, NY, 1979, Met. Club, New York, NY, 1979. Roman Catholic. Office: Swan Books Box 953 Pine Plains NY 12567 Office Fax: 518-398-6012.

JANJIGIAN, VAHAN, equity research director, editor; b. Aden, Yemen, Aug. 16, 1956; came to U.S., 1960; s. Papken Vahan Janjigian and Anahis (Der Bedrossian) Odabashian; m. Nooné Gandjumian, Apr. 17, 1993; children: Lori Anais, Luciné Nooné, Lily Tatyana. BS, Villanova (Pa.) U., 1978; MBA in Mgmt. Sci., Va. Tech. U., 1982, PhD in Fin., 1985. Chartered fin. analyst. Sales rep. Unimet, Inc., Blacksburg, Va., 1979, traffic mgr., 1979-80; rsch. asst. Va. Tech. U., Blacksburg, 1980-85; asst. prof. U. Del., Newark, 1985-90, Northeastern U., Boston, 1990-97; equity rsch. dir., editor Forbes, Inc., N.Y.C., 1997—. Vis. prof. Am. U. Armenia, Yerevan, 1992, Boston Coll., Chestnut Hill, 1996-97. Contbr. articles to profl. jours. Mem. Am. Fin. Assn., N.Y. Soc. Security Analysts, Assn. for Investment Mgmt. and Rsch. Avocations: running, investing, reading, photography. Office: Forbes Inc 60 5th Ave New York NY 10011-8882 E-mail: vjanjigian@forbes.com.

JANKE, JOHN ERIC, secondary educator; b. Longview, Wash., Mar. 30, 1960; s. John Charles and Rose Kathryn (Albertson) J. AA, Lower Columbia Coll., 1982; BA in History, Ctrl. Wash. U., 1984, MEd, 1999; BA in Edn., Western Wash. U., 1986. Cert. tchr., Wash. Jr. sch. high tchr. Bd. Edn., Kelso, Wash., 1986-94, jr. high tchr. Longview, 1986-94, Spannaway, Wash., 1994-2000. Named Alumni of Yr. Ctrl. Wash. U., 1997. Mem. NEA, Wash. Edn. Assn., Kelso Edn. Assn. Avocations: golfing, stamp collecting, pool. Home: 912 Elizabeth St Kelso WA 98626-2817 E-mail: johnjanke@yahoo.com.

JANKE, KENNETH, investment consultant; b. Ft. William, Ont., Can., May 13, 1934; s. Adolf Earthman and Julianna (Dika) J.; m. Sally Mildred Roach, June 29, 1957; children: Kenneth Stuart, Laura Lynn, Julie Ann. Student, Mich. State U., 1952-56. Asst. mgr. Household Fin. Co., Detroit, 1958—60; gen. mgr. Nat. Assn. Investors, Royal Oak, Mich., 1960—76, pres., CEO, 1976—2002, chmn., CEO, 2002—. Bd. dirs. Investment Edn. Inst., Royal Oak, pres. 1995-2002, chmn., 2002—; bd. dirs. World Fedn. Investors, Brussels, pres., 1995—. Author: Ask Mr. Naic, 1982, Golf Is A Funny Game (But It Wasn't Meant To Be), 1992, Starting and Running a Profitable Investment Club, 1996; co-author: Wit and Wisdom of Golf, 1997; columnist mag. Better Investing. Chmn. Mich. Golf Hall of Fame, Lake Orion; pres. Am. Cancer Soc.-Oakland Country, Southfield, Mich., 1974-75; pres., bd. dirs. NAIC Growth Fund, Royal Oak; bd. dirs. AFLAC, Inc., Columbus, Ga.; bd. advisors Mich. PGA, West Bloomfield. With U.S. Army, 1956-58, ETO. Recipient Disting. Svc. award Investment Edn. Inst., 1972, Founder award Am. Cancer Soc., 1970; inductee Dearborn Sports Hall of Fame, Mich., 2002. Fellow Fin. Analysts Soc. Detroit (pres. 1984—), Fin. Analysts Fedn.; mem. Nat. Investor Rels. Inst. (pres. Detroit 1985—), Western Golf Assn. (bd. dirs., pres.), Indianwood Golf and Country Club (Lake Orion), Renaissance Club (Detroit), NFL Alumni (Lauderdale, Fla.), Scalawag's Country club (Mt. Clemens, Mich.), Masons. Republican. Episcopalian. Avocations: golf, golf collecting. Home: 4305 W Maple Rd Bloomfield Hills MI 48301-2901 Office: Nat Assn Investors Corp 711 W 13 Mile Rd Madison Heights MI 48071-1806

JANKE, RONALD ROBERT, lawyer; b. Milw., Mar. 2, 1947; s. Robert Erwin and Elaine Patricia (Wilken) J.; m. Mary Ann Burg, July 3, 1971; children—Jennifer, William, Emily. B.A. cum laude, Wittenberg U., 1969; J.D. with distinction, Duke U., 1974. Bar: Ohio 1974. Assoc. Jones Day, Cleve., 1974-83, ptnr., 1984—. Served with U.S. Army, 1970-71, Vietnam. Mem. ABA (chmn. environ. control com. 1980-83), Ohio Bar Assn., Greater Cleve. Bar Assn., Environ. Law Inst. Office: Jones Day N Point 901 Lakeside Ave E Cleveland OH 44114-1190

JANKLOW, MORTON LLOYD, lawyer, literary agent; b. N.Y.C., May 30, 1930; s. Maurice and Lillian (Levantin) J.; m. Linda Mervyn LeRoy, Nov. 27, 1960; children: Angela LeRoy, Lucas Warner. AB, Syracuse U., 1950; JD, Columbia U., 1953. Bar: NY 1953, DC 1961, U.S. Dist. Ct. (so. and ea. dists) NY, U.S. Ct. Appeals (2d cir.), U.S. Supreme Ct. Chmn., CEO Morton L. Janklow Assocs., Inc., 1977-89; of counsel Janklow & Ashley, LLP, N.Y.C., 1989—; sr. ptnr. Janklow & Nesbit Assocs., 1989—. Trustee Managed Accts. Svcs., PaineWebber PACE funds, 1996-2003; chmn. Janklow & Nesbit (U.K.); bd. dirs. Revlon, Inc., 1997-2000, Orbis Comm., Inc., N.Y.C., 1986-89; bd. dirs., mem. finance com. McCaffrey & McCall, Inc., N.Y.C., 1962-87; chmn. exec. com. Harvey Group, Inc., N.Y.C., 1968-71, Cable Funding Corp., N.Y.C., 1971-73; mem. exec. com. Sloan Commn. Cable Comm., 1970-71, Andrew Wellington Cordier fellow Columbia U. Sch. Internat. Affairs; vis. lectr. Radcliffe Coll., Columbia U. Law Sch., NYU; bus. and fin. adv. bd. NYU Press and NYU Sch. Arts, 1977—; donor, founder Morton L. Janklow Professorship of Lit. and Artistic Property, Columbia U. Sch. Law; life mem., Harlan Fiske Stone fellow of Columbia U. Law Sch.; founder Morton L. Janklow Program for Advocacy in the Arts, Columbia U. Law Sch.; mem. dean's coun. Columbia U. Law Sch., 1992—. Bd. dirs., exec. com., devel. chmn. City Center Music and Drama, 1971-75; bd. dirs. Film Soc., Lincoln Ctr., 1972-75, Am. Cinematheque, 1971-75; bd. govs. Jewish Mus., 1969-75; dir., chmn. Janklow Found.; trustee Mr. and Mrs. Harry M. Warner Found., 1965—, Sidney Sheldon Found.; mem. Council of Friends, Whitney Mus. Am. Art, 1973-82, also mem. com. on paintings and sculptures; ad hoc com. on pub. and merchandising activities Met. Mus. Art; bd. advisors Princeton U. Art. Mus., 1984-89; mem. adv. bd. Guggenheim Mus., 1980-86; adv. council Sch. Arts, NYU; mem. Ind. Com. on Arts Policy; bd. advisors Columbia U. Jour. Art and the Law; assn. of fellows Pierpoint Morgan Libr., N.Y.C.. Served with AUS, 1953-55. Decorated chevalier l'Ordre des Arts et des Lettres de la Republique Française. Mem. ABA, N.Y. Bar Assn., Assn. of Bar of City of N.Y. (membership com. 1967—), N.Y. County Lawyers Assn., Fed. Comms. Bar Assn., Am. Judicature Soc., Coun. on Fgn. Rels., Com. on the Rsch. Librs., N.Y. Pub. Libr: chmn. Arthur Ross Book award Jury. Office: 445 Park Ave New York NY 10022-2606 E-mail: mjanklow@janklow.com.

JANKLOW, WILLIAM JOHN, congressman, former governor; b. Chgo., Sept. 13, 1939; s. Arthur W. and LouElla Bernice (Gulbranson) J.; m. Mary Dean Thom, Sept. 3, 1960; children— Russell, Pam, Shonna. BSBA, U. S.D., 1964, JD, 1966. Bar: S.D. bar 1966, U.S. Supreme Ct. bar 1970. Staff atty. S.D. Legal Services, 1966-67, directing atty., chief officer, 1967-72; chief trial atty. S.D. Atty. Gen's. Office, Pierre, 1973-74, atty. gen., 1975-78; gov. SD, 1979—87, 1995—2003; U.S. Repr. from S.D., 2003—. Lectr. in field Bd. dirs. Nat. Legal Services Corp. Served with USMC, 1956-59. Recipient Nat. award for legal excellence and skill Nat. Legal Aid and Defenders Assn., 1968 Mem. Nat. Assn. Attys. Gen., Am., S.D. trial lawyers assns., Am. Judicature Soc. Republican. Lutheran. Office: 1504 Longworth HOB Washington DC 20515-4101*

JANKO, ALBERT BELA, physician; b. Budapest, Hungary, Jan. 21, 1934; came to U.S., 1957; MD, UCLA, 1959; student, U. Budapest Sch. of Medicine, 1952-56. Diplomate Am. Bd. Ob-gyn. Intern Cin. Gen. Hosp., U. Cin. Coll. Medicine, 1959-60; resident Stanford Med. Ctr., Palo Alto, Calif., 1963-66; with Cmty Hosp., Monterey Peninsula, Calif.; dir. medicine Monterey Osteoporosis Prevention Med. Clinic, 1986—. Clin. assoc. prof. emeritus Stanford Med. Ctr. Mem. Am. Coll. Ob-gyn., Am. Coll. Surgeons, Am. Soc. Reproductive Medicine, Calif. Med. Assn., Assn. Profs. Ob/Gyn (life). Office: 503 Aguajito Rd Carmel CA 93923

JANKO, JAMES ANTHONY, writer, educator; b. La Salle, Ill. s. John George and Lorraine Janko; m. Chanpidor Uong, Oct. 16, 2000. MA(hon.), San Francisco State U., 1989—93. Author: (fiction) Mirrors (Ilinois Arts Coun. Award for Fiction, 2002).

JANKO, MAY, graphic artist; b. N.Y.C., Feb. 27, 1926; d. Jacob and Clara (Schupler) J. BA, Hunter Coll., 1946, MA, 1952; student, Art Students League, 1949-53. Tchr. art N.Y.C. Pub. Schs., 1953-58; textile designer DNE Walter & Co., N.Y.C., 1958-63, Old Deerfield, N.Y.C., 1963-68, M. Lowenstein Corp., N.Y.C., 1968-84. Exhibited in group shows: Libr. of Congress, Washington, 1956, 63, American Prints Today, 1959, Whitney Mus. Am. Art, N.Y.C., 1959, Pa. Acad., Phila., 1959, Bklyn. Mus., 1960, Taipei (Taiwan) Nat. Mus., 1984, 90, 92, Bronx Mus. Arts, 1989, Krasdale Satellite Gallery of Bronx Mus. Arts, 1989, Salmugundi: 13th Ann. Exhbn., 1990; represented in permanent collections: Met. Mus. Art, N.Y.C., Rockefeller Collection, N.Y.C., Cin. Mus. Art, Nat. Gallery, Washington. Recipient Achievement award Hunter Coll., 1959, Arts award Louis Comfort Tiffany Found., 1959, Leo Meissner award NAD, N.Y.C., 1984, I.B. Markell award in graphics Audubon Artists, N.Y.C., 1961, Daniel Serra y Navas Meml. award, 1994, Art Students League N.Y. Graphics award, 1995, Mem. Soc. Am. Graphic Artists (life; mem. coun. 1977, Henry B. Shope award 1954, Graphic Chem. award 1985), Boston Printmakers, Am. Color Print Soc., Art Students League (life).

JANKO, RICHARD CHARLES MURRAY, humanities educator; b. Weston Underwood, Eng., May 30, 1955; arrived in U.S., 1982; s. Charles Arthur Janko and Helen Murray; m. Michele Ann Hannoosh, May 26, 1984. BA with 1st class honors in Classics, Cambridge U., Eng., 1976; MA, PhD in Classics, Cambridge U., 1980. Temp. lectr. U. St. Andrews, Scotland, 1978—79; rsch. fellow Trinity Coll., Cambridge, 1979—82; asst. prof. Columbia U., N.Y.C., 1982—87; prof. classics UCLA, 1987—94; prof. greek Univ. Coll. London, 1995—2002; prof. and chair classical studies U. Mich., Ann Arbor, 2003—. Editor Ayios Stephanos Excavations, 1989—; co-dir. Philodemus Translation Project, 1992—. Author: (book) Homer, Hesiod and the Hymns, 1982, Aristotle on Comedy, 1984, Aristotle: Poetics, 1987, The Iliad: A Commentary, Vol. IV, 1992, Philodemus: On Poems Book I, 2000 (Mommsen prize, 2002, Goodwin award, 2002). Guggenheim Found. fellow, 1986—87, Nat. Humanities Ctr. fellow, 1990. Avocation: walking. Office: Univ of Michigan Dept Classical Studies Ann Arbor MI 48109

JANKOVIC, JOSEPH, neurologist, educator, scientist; b. Teplice, Czechoslovakia, Mar. 1, 1948; came to U.S., 1965; m. Cathy Sue Inselberg, May 26, 1973; children: Jason, Daniel, Zachary. MD, U. Ariz., 1973. Diplomate Am. Bd. Neurology. Med. intern Baylor Coll. Medicine, Houston, 1973-74, asst. prof. neurology, 1977-84, assoc. prof., 1984-88, prof., 1988—; resident in neurology Columbia U., N.Y.C., 1974-76, chief resident in neurology, 1976-77. Dir. Parkinson's Disease Ctr. and Movement Disorder Clinic, Houston, 1977—; sr. attending physician Meth. Hosp., Houston, 1988—. Author over 500 articles and book chpts. in field; editor/co-editor 16 med. books; mem. editorial bd. jours. Movement Disorders, Clin. Neuropharmacology, Neurology Jour., Jour. Neurology Psychiatry. Chmn. sci. adv. bd. Blepharospasm Rsch. Found.; mem. adv. bd. Dystonia Med. Rsch. Found., Internat. Tremor Found., Tourette's Syndrome Med. Adv. Bd. Grantee disease rsch. founds., pharmaceutical cos., NIH Fellow Am. Acad. Neurology; mem. AMA, Am. Neurol. Assn., Soc. for Neurosci., Movement Disorders Soc. (pres.-elect 1991-94, pres. 1994-96). Avocations: tennis, family activities, music. Office: Baylor Coll Medicine 6550 Fannin St Ste 1801 Houston TX 77030-2744

JANKOWSKA, MARIA ANNA, librarian, educator; b. Jarocin, Poland, Aug. 12, 1952; d. Tadeusz and Aleksandra (Ruszkowska) Nocun; m. Piotr L. Jankowski, Jan. 14, 1978; children: Pawel Pat, Marta Maja. MA, Sch. Econs., Poznan, Poland, 1975, PhD, 1983; M Libr. Info. Sci., U. Calif., Berkeley, 1989. Rsch. and tchg. asst. Sch. Econs., Poznan, 1976-83, asst. prof., 1983-85; catalog libr., asst. prof. U. Idaho, Moscow, 1989-94, network resources libr., assoc. prof., 1995—, prof., 2001—. Author: Electronic Guide to Polish Research and University Libraries, 1996, Idaho Geospatial Data Center, 1998; founding editor Green Libr. Jour., 1991-94; gen. editor Electronic Green Jour., 1994—. Recipient Movers and Shakers award Libr. Jour., 2002; guest scholar Smithsonian Inst., Woodrow Wilson Internat. Ctr., Washington, 1985; fellow U Calif., Berkeley Sch. Libr. and Info. Studies, 1989; grantee Rsch. Coun. Grant, U. Idaho, 1990, 95, 2001, Internat. Rsch. and Exchs. Bd., Washington, 1995, 96. Mem. ALA (chair task force on environ. 1993-95, 98—), Idaho Libr. Assn., Beta Phi Mu. Office: U Idaho Libr Rayburn St Moscow ID 83844-0001 Fax: (208) 885-6817. E-mail: majanko@uidaho.edu.

JANKOWSKI, CHRISTOPHER JAMES, anesthesiologist, educator; s. Richard Leon and Karen Marie Jankowski; m. Janine Marie Yanisch, Aug. 13, 1988; 1 child, Maria Christina. MD, U. of Rochester, 1993; BM, Lawrence U., Wis., 1984. Diplomate Am. Bd. of Anesthesiology, 1999. Cons.physician Mayo Clinic and Found., Rochester, Minn., 1997—; asst. prof. of anesthesiology Mayo Med. Sch., Minn., 2000—03. Grantee Rsch. Starter Grant, Found. for Anesthesia Edn. and Rsch., 2002—; scholar Marvin J. Hoffman Scholarship, U. of Rochester Sch. of Medicine and Dentistry, 1989—93. Mem.: Soc. for Advancement of Geriatric Anesthesiology, Am. Geriatrics Soc., Minn. Med. Assn., Internat. Anesthesia Rsch. Soc., Am. Soc. Anesthesiol., AMA, Alpha Omega Alpha. Office: Mayo Clinic 200 First Street SW Rochester MN 55905

JANKOWSKI, JEFFERY J. developmental psychology educator; b. Toledo, Aug. 18, 1962; m. Katherine R. (Bennett) J. BA, U. Toledo, 1985, MA, 1989, PhD, 1992. Adj. instr. U. Toledo, 1989-92; postdoctoral fellow Albert Einstein Coll. Medicine, Bronx, N.Y., 1992-95, asst. prof. devel. psychology, 1995—; postdoctoral fellow NIH, 1992-95. Cons. Harvard Sch. Pub. Health, Chgo., 1995, Columbia U. Sch. Pub. Health, N.Y.C., 1998—. Contbr. articles to sci. jours., including Jour. Exptl. Child Psychology, Child Devel., Devel. Psychology. Postdoctoral fellow NIH, 1992. Mem. APA, Am. Psychol. Soc., Soc. for Rsch. in Child Devel., Internat. Soc. for Infant Studies. Avocations: reading, woodworking, gardening, weightlifting. Office: Albert Einstein Coll Medicine Kennedy Ctr 1300 Morris Park Ave Bronx NY 10461 E-mail: jankowsk@aecom.yu.edu.

JANKOWSKI, THEODORE ANDREW, artist; b. New Brunswick, N.J., Dec. 14, 1946; s. Theodore Andrew and Lois (Amarescu) J.; m. Rebecca Buck, July 23, 1983; 1 child, Tito Henry. Student, McMurrough Sch. Art, Indialantic, Fla., 1956-58, 74-75, R.I. Sch. Design, 1972, Cape Sch. of Art, Provincetown, Mass., 1975-76, 79-87, Cen. Fla. U., 1976-77. One-man shows include Eye of Horus Gallery, Provincetown, 1985; exhibited in group shows at Provincetown Art Assn. Mus., 1984, Bethlehem (Pa.) City Hall, 1988, Michael Ingbar Gallery, N.Y.C., 1988, 91; represented in permanent collections at State Mus. at Palace of Peter the Gt., Leningrad, USSR, Mishkan Olemanut Mus. Art, Israel, Novosibirsk (Russia) Picture Gallery, CIGNA Mus., Phila., Johns Hopkins U., Balt., Hiroshima Peace Meml. Mus., Hiroshima Japan - Hunter Mus. of Am. Art, Chattanooga, Holyoke (Mass.) Mus. Art, McGill U., Montreal, Que., Can., Downey (Calif.) Mus. Art, Ark. Art Ctr., Little Rock, Muzeum Niepoldlegosi,

Warsaw, Poland, Nat. Mus. Bosnia, Sarajevo, Yad Vashem The Holocaust Martyrs and Heroes Art Mus., Jerusalem, Beloit Coll. Wright Mus. ARt, Pradd Sch. Design, N.Y.C., Mt. Holyoke Coll. Art Mus., others. Home: PO Box 791 Kapaau HI 96755-0791

JANNE D'OTHEE, BERTRAND M. radiologist, researcher; b. Verviers, Belgium, June 27, 1966; s. Charles Janne d'Othee and Anne Dessain. MD, Cath. U. Louvain, Belgium, 1992. Cert. radiologist, Belgium. Clin. fellow in interventional radiology U. Med. Ctr., Toulouse, 1997—98, attending interventional radiologist, 1998—99; rschr. in interventional radiology Dartmouth Coll., Lebanon, NH, 1999—2000; attending interventional radiologist Beth Israel Deaconess Med. Ctr., Boston, 2001—. Contbr. articles to profl. jours. Mem. Am. Heart Assn. (coun. on cardiovasc. radiology), Am. Assn. Univ. Radiologists, Cardiovasc. and Interventional Radiology Soc. Europe, French Soc. Radiology (grantee 1999). Office: Beth Israel Deaconess Med Ctr Dept Radiology CC308 Boston MA 02215

JANNETTA, PETER JOSEPH, neurosurgeon, educator; b. Phila., Apr. 5, 1932; s. Samuel and Frances (Alfano) J.; m. Diana R. Jannetta, Sept. 9, 1989; children: Susan, Carol, Joanne, Peter, Elizabeth, S. Michael. AB, U. Pa., 1953, MD, 1957. Diplomate Am. Bd. Surgery, Am. Bd. Neurol. Surgery. Intern Hosp. U. Pa., 1957-58, resident in surgery, 1958-63; resident in neurosurgery, asso. UCLA Center for Health Scis., 1963-66; asst. instr. U. Pa., 1958-62, instr., 1960-63, instr. surgery, 1962-63; assoc. prof., chmn. surgery La. State U., 1966-71, prof., chmn. neurosurgery, 1971; prof. neurosurgery U. Pitts., 1971-76, Francis Sergeant Cheever Disting. prof., 1976-98, chmn. dept. neurol. surgery, 1976-2000, dir. divsn. neurol. surgery, 1973-2000; active staff Presbyn.-Univ. Hosp., Pitts., Children's Hosp. Pitts.; sr. attending staff Montefiore Hosp., Pitts.; sr. cons. VA Hosp., Pitts.; prof., vice chmn. dept. neurosurgery Allegheny Gen. Hosp. Sec. of health Commonwealth of Pa., 1995-96. Co-editor: The Cranial Nerves, 1981, Trigeminal Neuralgia, 1990; contbr. numerous articles to profl. jours. Mem. A.C.S., AMA, AAAS, Am. Surg. Assn., Allegheny County, Pa. med. socs., Assn. Academic Surgery, Am. Assn. Neurol. Surgeons, Congress Neurol. Surgeons, Fellowship Acad. Neurosurgeons, Internat. Assn. Study Pain, Internat. Soc. Pediatric Neurosurgery, Mid-Atlantic, Pa., Pitts. neurosurg. socs., N.Y. Acad. Scis., Pitts. Acad. Medicine, Pitts. Surg. Soc., Ravdin-Rhoads Surg. Soc., Research Soc. Neurol. Surgeons, Soc. Critical Care Medicine, Soc. Neurol. Surgeons, Soc. Neurosci., Soc. Neurosurg. Anesthesia and Neurol. Supportive Care. Office: Allegheny Gen Hosp Dept Neurosurgery 420 E North Ave Ste 302 Pittsburgh PA 15212

JANNEY, ALLISON, actress; b. Dayton, Ohio, Nov. 19, 1960; BA, Kenyon Coll.; pvt. studies in acting, Neighborhood Playhouse, N.Y.C. Appeared in feature films: Big Night, 1996, Private Parts, 1997, Primary Colors, 1998, Six Days, Seven Nights, 1998, The Ice Storm, 1997, Celebrity, 1998, 10 Things I Hate About You, 1999, Drop Dead Gorgeous, 1999, Nurse Betty, 2000, American Beauty, 1999, Leaving Drew, 2000, Finding Nemo (voiceover), 2003, How to Deal, 2003; plays (on Broadway) A View From The Bridge (Tony award nominee 1998, Outer Critics Circle award,Drama Desk award); appearances on TV: The West Wing (role C.J. Gregg), 1999—, A Girl Thing (TV mini), 2000 Recipient Outstanding Featured Actress in a Play for "A View From the Bridge", Drama Desk Award, 1998, Outstanding Supporting Actress in a Drama Series for "The West Wing", Emmy Award, 1999, 2000, Best Actress in a Television Series Drama for "The West Wing", Golden Satellite, 2000, Best Ensemble Cast Performance for "The West Wing", 2000, Outstanding Female Actor in a Drama Series for "The West Wing", The Actor Awards, 2000, Outstanding Ensemble in a Drama Series for "The West Wing", 2000, Outstanding Supporting Actress in a Drama Series for "The West Wing", Emmy Awards, 2001, Outstanding Female Actor in a Drama Series for "The West Wing", The Actor Awards, 2001, Outstanding Ensemble in a Drama Series for "The West Wing", 2001, Outstanding Female Actress in a Drama Series for "The West Wing", Emmy Awards, 2002. Office: John Wells Prodns Warner Bros TV Rm 204 4000 Warner Blvd Bldg 133 Burbank CA 91522-0001

JANNEY, DELLANN, accountant, educator; b. Quincy, Ill., Sept. 1, 1965; d. Harlan G. and Virgilee A. (Cochran) Balk; m. Jeffrey L. Janney, May 7, 1988; children: Lauren L., Alexis A. BS in Acctg., Culver-Stockton Coll., 1987; MBA, Western Ill. U., 1990; D in Mgmt., Webster U., 1998. CPA Ill. Gen. acctg. analyst Sheller-Globe Corp., Keokuk, Iowa, 1987-88; corp. acct. Quincy Newspapers Inc., 1988-89; acctg. instr. John Wood CC, Quincy, 1989-92; assoc. prof. acctg. Culver-Stockton Coll., Canton, Mo., 1992—. Mem. pres.'s long-range planning com. Culver-Stockton Coll., Canton, 1994—2000; mem. Canton R-V Bus. and Tech. Adv. Bd., 1999—; treas., trustee Canton Pub. Libr., 1990—2000; treas., bd. dirs. Sun-N-Surf Swim Club, 1988—99. Mem.: Inst. Mgmt. Accts. Home: 8 Janney Cir Canton MO 63435-1274 Office: Culver-Stockton Coll 1 College Hl Canton MO 63435-1257

JANNEY, DONALD WAYNE, lawyer; b. Clinton, N.C., Jan. 9, 1952; s. Wayne Columbus and Bernice (Talley) J.; m. Sydney Louise Rhame, May 28, 1977; children: Taylor Columbus, Camden St. Clair. BA, Furman U., 1974; JD, U. Va., 1978. Bar: Ga. 1978, U.S. Dist. Ct. (no. dist.) Ga. 1978, U.S. Ct. Appeals (11th cir.) 1982. Assoc. Troutman Sanders, Atlanta, 1978-85; ptnr. Troutman Sanders and predecessor firm, Atlanta, 1985—. Bd. dirs. State YMCA Ga., Atlanta, 1980-91. Mem. ABA, Ga. Bar Assn., Atlanta Bar Assn., Lawyers Club Atlanta, Phi Beta Kappa. Baptist. Home: 705 E Morningside Dr Atlanta GA 30324-5220 Office: Troutman Sanders Ste 5200 600 Peachtree St NE Atlanta GA 30308-2216 E-mail: donald.janney@troutmansanders.com.

JANNEY, KAY PRINT, retired theatre arts educator, theatre director; b. Cleve., June 22, 1938; d. Walter James and Zenza Mae (Williams) Print; m. Frederick George Janney, Feb. 6, 1960; children: Brooke Hopkins, Eric Matthew, Catherine Marie. BA cum laude, Case Western Res. U., 1959, MA, 1962. Copywriter Howard Marks Advt., Cleve., 1958-59; tchr. Speech, drama and English South-Euclid (Ohio) Lyndhurst Pub. Schs., South Euclid, 1960-61, Lakewood (Ohio) Pub. Schs., 1961-62; tchr. speech and drama, dept. head Berea (Ohio) High Sch., 1962-65; instr. in communication scis. U. Conn., Storrs, 1966-70, instr. in communication and dramatic arts Avery Point and Groton, 1971-74, asst. prof. communication and dramatic arts, 1975-80, assoc. prof. communication and dramatic arts, 1981-89, prof. dramatic arts, 1990-97, prof. emeritus, 1997—. Author: (monographs) A Bibliography on the Mask, 1989, Masks: The Power of Transformation-Put a New Face on Your Curriculum, 1989, Scriptsearch, 1988; book reviewer Speech Communication Teacher, 1990, Black Like My Soul Is Black (Michael Bradford), 1994-95; dir. (theatre prodns.) Mother Hicks, 1992, The Hide 'N Seek Odyssey of Madeline Gimple, 1991, The Angel With The Broken Wing, 1990, In A Room Somewhere, 1990, others; contbr. articles to profl. jours. Adjudicator Cmty. Theatre Coun., New London County, Conn., 1977, 93-97, chair of judges, 1987-89; adjudicator Mass. Drama Guild, 1986-93, Conn. Drama Assn., 1989. Named to Parma City (Ohio) Schs. Hall of Fame. Mem. AAUW, Am. Alliance for Theatre and Edn. (co-chair, founder mid./jr. H.S. program com. 1972—, chair membership com. 1989, bd. dirs. 1988-91, chair conv. 1993), New Eng. Theatre Conf. (chair children's theatre divsn. 1986-89, judge John Gassner Meml. Playwriting Contest 1989-95, v.p. nat. conf. 1993, coll. fellows 1993—), Conn. Alliance for Arts, Ballard Inst., Mus. of Puppetry (chair 1995-2003), Assitej. Republican. Congregationalist. Avocations: music, needlework, travel, cross-cultural exchange.

JANNEY, OLIVER JAMES, lawyer, plastics and semiconductor company executive; b. N.Y.C., Feb. 11, 1946; s. Walter Coggeshall and Helen Jennings (James) Janney; m. Suzanne Elizabeth Lenz, June 21, 1969; children: Elizabeth Flower, Oliver Burr. BA cum laude, Yale U., 1967; JD, Harvard U., 1970. Bar: Mass. 1970, N.Y. 1971, Fla. 1991. With Walston & Co., Inc., N.Y.C., 19770-73, asst. v.p., 1971-73; assoc. Cleary Gottlieb, Steen & Hamilton, N.Y.C., 1973-76; with RKO Gen., Inc., N.Y.C., 1976-90, asst. sec., 1977-85, asst. gen. atty., 1978-82, asst. gen. counsel, 1982-85, sec., gen. counsel, 1985-89; exec. v.p., gen. counsel, sec. Uniroyal Tech. Corp., Sarasota, Fla., 1990—. 1st lt. USAR, 1969—77. Mem.: ABA, Assn. Bar of City of N.Y., N.Y. State Bar Assn., Am. Corp. Counsel Assn., Sleepy Hollow Country Club Scarborough. Republican. Home: 1684 Peregrine Point Dr Sarasota FL 34231-2331 Office: Uniroyal Tech Corp 3401 Cragmont Dr Tampa FL 33619

JANNEY, SALLY BAGGS, civic worker; b. Long County, Ga., Aug. 27, 1936; d. Albert Hall and Thelma Christine (Swindell) Baggs; m. John David Janney, Nov. 17, 1962; children: John David II, Karen Janney Rhodes. Student, Draughons Coll., 1954-55, Armstrong Jr. Coll., Savannah, 1955-57, U. Ga., 1957-59. Adminstrv. asst. to chief profl. svcs. U.S. Army Hosp., Ft. Stewart, Ga., 1956-62; cons. Leggett Dept. Store, Beckley, W.Va., 1980-85, dir. White Gloves and Party Manners program, 1983-89; mgr. Touch of Gold, Beckley, 1990-98. Editor The West Virginia Clubwoman mag., 1986-88. Publicity dir. W.Va. Sports Festival, 1970-74; mem. recreation commn. City of Oak Hill, 1972-80; chmn. LGA White Oak Country Club, 1980-81, 88-90, 99-02; cub scout den mother; past pres. Oak Hill Grade Sch. PTA; mem. altar guild, worship com., United Meth. Women, Margaret Stimson Fellowship Oak Hill United Meth. Ch. Mem. Am. Optometric Assn. (mem. congress com. 1984-92), Aux. to Am. Optometric Assn. (pres. 1983-84), Oak Hill Jr. Woman's Club (pres. 1966-68, Woman of Yr. 1970-71), Woodland Oaks Garden Club (pres. 1975-79, 99-01), Oak Hill Civic League, Fayette Study Club (pres. 1986 88), Aux. to W.Va. Optometric Assn. (pres. 1978-79, 83-84, treas.), W.Va. Garden Club (life), Beautification Commn., City of Oak Hill, 2002—, Aux. to So. Coun. Optometrists (pres. 1981-82), Am. Found. for Vision Awareness (life). Methodist. Avocations: golf, bridge, travel. Home: 2020 Edgewood Dr Oak Hill WV 25901-2074

JANNEY, STUART SYMINGTON, III, investment company executive; b. Balt., Aug. 30, 1948; s. Stuart Symington and Barbara (Phipps) J.; m. Lynn Mary Buchheit, Oct. 28, 1975; children: Emily, Matthew. BA, U. N.C., 1970; JD, U. Md., 1973. Bar: Md. 1973. Legis. asst. Sen. Charles Mathias U.S. Senate, Washington, 1973-75, fgn. policy asst. Sen. Howard Baker, 1976-77; spl. asst. U.S. Sec. State U.S. State Dept., Washington, 1975-76; ptnr. Niles, Barton & Wilmer, Balt., 1977-86; mng. dir. Alex Brown & Sons, Balt., 1986-94; head Brown Asset Mgmt., Balt., 1986-93; chmn. bd. Bessemer Trust Co., N.Y.C., 1994—, Bessemer Securities Corp., N.Y.C., 1994—. Bd. dirs. Md. Million, Inc., Essex Internat., Inc., 1995-98. Bd. dirs. Johns Hopkins U., Balt., 1995—, vice chmn., 1995-2002; chmn. bd. dirs. Applied Physics Lab., 1991—, Md. Zool. Soc., Balt., 1979—; bd. dirs. Md. Horsebreeders, 1991-98, Breeders Cup Ltd.; chmn. Thoroughbred Owners and Breeders Am.; bd. dirs., Keeneland Assoc., sec. Nat. Audubon Soc., N.Y.C., 1982-92; steward Jockey Club U.S. Mem.: NY Racing Assn. Office: Bessemer Trust Co 630 5th Ave New York NY 10111-0100

JANNING, JOHN LOUIS, research scientist, consultant; b. Dayton, Ohio, Mar. 30, 1928; s. Eugene Alois and Frieda Marie (Kessen) J.; m. Dolores Mary Nartker, Nov. 29, 1952; children: Kathleen, Janet, Theresa, Lawrence, Thomas, Richard, Jacqueline. Electronic technician U. Dayton, 1956-58; cons. engr. NCR Corp., Dayton, 1958-88; liquid crystal display cons. JLJ, Inc., Dayton, 1988—. Contbr. articles to profl. jours.; numerous patents in high tech. field including implantable med. devices; inventor thermal printing wafer, plasma displays, field emission displays and LCDs. With inf. U.S. Army, 1950-52. Recipient Outstanding Profl. Achievement award Affiliate Socs. Coun. Engring. and Sci. Found. Dayton, 1982; inducted into Dayton Walk-of-Fame, 2001. Mem.: IEEE (sr.), Inventors Coun. Dayton, Soc. for Info. Display, Engrs. Club Dayton. Roman Catholic. Avocations: computer, bridge, chess, public speaking. Home and Office: 332 Vindale Dr Dayton OH 45440-3364 also: Lab at 4656 Wilmington Pike Dayton OH 45440 E-mail: janning@compuserve.com.

JANNINI, RALPH HUMBERT, III, electronics executive; b. Boston, Dec. 30, 1932; s. Humbert P. and Marian H. (Roman) J.; m. Pauline T. Occhinto, Feb. 16, 1957; children: Ralph H. IV, Mark L., Lisa M. BS in Acctg., Bentley Coll., 1957. CPA, Mass. Auditor New Eng. Electric System, Westboro, Mass., 1957-68, mgr. rates and statistics, 1968-73; asst. to pres. Gas Inc.-Colonial, Lowell, Mass., 1973-76; v.p. Colonial Gas Co., Lowell, 1976-87; pres. James Millen Electronics, Malden, Mass., 1988—. Cons. Antennas Etc., Andover, Mass., 1980—; prin. Unadilla/Reyco/InLine Products, 1986—, Andover Book and Collaborative, 1995—. Served with U.S. Army, 1952-53, Korea. Republican. Roman Catholic. Office: James Millen Electronics 87 Belmont St North Andover MA 01845-2304

JANNOTTI, GENE PATRICK, business consultant, telecommunications professional; b. Newburgh, N.Y., Oct. 10, 1946; s. Pellegrino and Anne J. BS in Math., Siena Coll., 1968; MA in Math., St. John's U., 1970; MS in Bus. Policy, Columbia U., 1981. Cert. sys. profl. Asst. programmer N.Y. Tel., N.Y.C., 1971-72, computer ops. mgr., 1973-80, staff mgr., 1980-84; programmer Bell Labs., Greensboro, N.C., 1972-73; dist. mgr. Bell Comm. Rsch., Piscataway, N.J., 1984-87; staff dir. NYNEX Corp. Comm., N.Y.C., 1987-89, NYNEX Videoteleconferencing, N.Y.C., 1989-91; dir. ops. NYNEX Computer Ops., Pearl River, N.Y., 1991; dir. NYNEX Software Devel., N.Y.C., 1992-95; founder, pres. LCA, Llewellyn Cons. Assocs., Westfield, N.J., 1995-98; dir. Computer Scis. Corp., 1998—; founder Unique Cruise and Travel, 2000—, prin., owner, 2000—. Capt. USAR, 1968-74. Mem. Data Processing Mgmt. Assn. (bd. dirs. N.Y. chpt. 1980-84, exec. v.p. 1984), Project Mgmt. Inst., Germania Corinthian Union Lodge # 11, Free and Accepted Masons. Roman Catholic. Avocations: travel, gardening, photography. Home and Office: PO Box 2458 Westfield NJ 07091-2458 E-mail: GENEJ@homemail.com., gjanott@csc.com.

JANNUZI, EUGENE FREDRIC, retired manufacturing executive; b. Beaver Falls, Pa., Nov. 9, 1915; s. Raphael and Teresa Anita (Silvester) J.; m. Margaret Anna Moltrup, Feb. 10, 1945. *During Navy service in World War II, Mr. Jannuzi was the Commanding Officer of Landing Craft Infantry in invasions of Sicily, Salerno, Normandy and Southern France. Mother and father, Italian immigrants, met in their teens in the United States and raised twelve children, the first born in 1900. Father-in-law J.T. Moltrup was one of the founders and first president of Moltrup Steel Products Company in Beaver Falls, Pennsylvania. The company has a national reputation for producing cold finished steel bars for industry where close-tolerance specifications are essential. Wife's cousin Merle Moltrup, a pioneer aviator, flew some of the first air mail in the 1920s.* BS, Geneva Coll., Beaver Falls, 1936; MEd, U. Pitts., 1941. Sci. tchr. Beaver Falls Sch. Dist., 1936-42; reporter Pitts. Post-Gazette, 1946-51; asst. dir. pub. rels. & advtg. Jones & Laughlin Steel Corp., Pitts., 1951-66; chmn., pres. Moltrup Steel Products Co., Beaver Falls, 1966-89; ret., 1989. Author: (novel) Bright Star, 1997. Mem. Beaver County Planning Commn., 1966-89; past trustee Geneva Coll.; past dir. Am. Iron & Steel Inst.; elder 1st Presbyn. Ch., Beaver Falls. Lt. USN, 1942-46 ETO. Recipient Others award Salvation Army, Beaver Falls, 1993. Mem. Pitts. Press Club, Rotary (pres. Beaver Falls club 1972-73), Am. Legion (life). Republican. Avocations: tennis, golf, writing, speaking. Home: 308 7th St Patterson Hts Beaver Falls PA 15010-3234

JANNUZI, F. TOMASSON, economics educator; b. Pitts., Apr. 23, 1934; s. Frank Humbert and Angela Mary (Tomasson) J.; m. Barbara Lucille Gallagher, Sept. 15, 1957; children: Buell Tomasson, Frank Sampson. AB, Dartmouth Coll., 1955; PhD in Econ., U. London, 1958. Field rep. for So. Asia, E. Africa Found. For Youth and Student Affairs, N.Y.C., 1959-61; asst. rep. The Asia Found., N.Y.C., 1961-62, program officer for So. Asia div. San Francisco, 1962-65, asst. rep. for India, 1965-68; vis. lectr. in econs. U. Tex., Austin, 1968-72, dir. at the Ctr. for Asian Studies, Nat. Resource Ctr. for So. Asia, 1972-86, assoc. prof. of econs., 1973-79, prof. of econs. and Asian studies, 1979-98, assoc. chmn. dept. econs., 1995-97, prof. emeritus econs., 1998—. Pres. Asia Rsch. Assoc. Inc., Austin, Tex., 1985-99; vis. fellow Internat. Devel. Ctr. U. Oxford, Eng., 1989-92; sr. assoc. mem. St. Antony's Coll. Oxford, 1989; vis scholar Ctr. for South Asian Studies, U. Va., 1999—; cons. USAID, Dept. State, Def. Intelligence Coll., The World Bank, 1973—. Author: Agrarian Crisis in India: The Case of Bihar, 1974, India in Transition: Issues of Political Economy in a Plural Society, 1988; India's Persistent Dilemma: The Political Economy of Agrarian Reform, 1994; co-author: (with James T. Peach) The Agrarian Structure of Bangladesh, 1980; contbr. articles to various books, monographs, reports. Dir. Austin Coun. on Fgn. Affairs Inc., Tex., 1987-98; mem. Inst. of Current World Affairs, Hanover, N.H., 1987—; trustee Am. Inst. of Indian Studies, Chgo., 1973-87, chmn. 1979-81. Fellow Ford Found.; mem. Phi Beta Kappa. Democrat. Avocation: travel. Home: 1835 Mountainside Dr Blacksburg VA 24060-9203 E-mail: ftjannuzi@msn.com.

JANO, GHASSAN, oncologist, hematologist; b. Damascus, Syria, Mar. 17, 1959; came to U.S., 1986; s. Mazhar Jano and Souhyla Al-Ashraf; married; 3 children. MD, Damascus U., 1983. Diplomate Am. Bd. Internal Medicine, 1991, Am. Bd. Hematology, 1997, Am. Bd. Med. Oncology, 1997. Internal medicine physician U. Newcastle, Eng., 1981-83, U. London, 1983-84; hematology rschr. U. Ill., Chgo., 1987-88, fellow in hematology/oncology, 1991-94; intern, resident in internal medicine Louis Weiss Meml. Hosp. U. Chgo., 1988-91; oncologist/hematologist Hammond Clinic, Munster, Ind., 1994—. Asst. prof. medicine U. Ill., Chgo. Mem. Ind. Med. Soc. Home: 8712 Aintree Ln Burr Ridge IL 60527-8389 Office: Premier Hematology Oncology 929 Ridge Rd Ste 5 Munster IN 46321 E-mail: g.jano@attbi.com.

JANOS, JAMES See VENTURA, JESSE

JANOS, JAMES DONALD, security and safety consultant; b. Martins Ferry, Ohio, Apr. 29, 1949; s. James and Susie Janos; m. Janet L. Smith, Feb. 2, 1980; children: Janelle N., Justin K. AAS in Indsl. Security, W.Va. No. C.C., 1987; BA in Criminal Justice BOR, West Liberty State Coll., 1987; MS in Safety Mgmt., W.Va. U., 1995. Security cons. Diebold Inc., Wheeling, W.Va., 1979-80, Day and Night Security, Wheeling, 1981-83; broadcast engr. Sta. WOMP Radio, Bellaire, Ohio, 1983-86; electronics cons. Bethany (W.Va.) Coll., 1987-89; safety intern Vandenberg AFB, Lompoc, Calif., 1990; broadcast engr. Sta. WKWK-Radio Inc., Wheeling, 1991—96, sports broadcaster, 1991—96. Broadcast engring. cons., Bridgeport, Ohio, 1990—. Vol. disaster svcs. ARC, Wheeling, 1990; libr. asst. OCPL, Wheeling, 1996—; comms. officer Ohio County CAP. With USN, 1975—78, with USAF, 1967—74. Master Mason; mem. Am. Soc. Safety Engrs., Nat. Assn. Radio and Telecommunications Engrs. Avocations: photography, research investigation, amateur astronomy. Home and Office: 400 Jacquette St Bridgeport OH 43912-1012 E-mail: jamesdjanos@comcast.net.

JANOSKI, HENRY VALENTINE, investment advisor, former banker; b. Nanticoke, Pa., Feb. 14, 1933; s. Bruce and Marie (Rozmarek) J.; m. Rita Rosemary Ruane, Sept. 27, 1980; children: Maria, Elizabeth. BA magna cum laude, Yale U., 1955; MBA, U. Pa., 1960. CFA. Sr. credit analyst Nat Bank Detroit, 1960-63; asst. cashier First Nat. Bank, Wilkes-Barre, Pa., 1963-65; sr. v.p. Northeastern Bank, Scranton, Pa., 1965-80; investment counselor, fin. planner Clarks Summit, Pa., 1980-92; realtor assoc., 1992; chief trust investment officer Penn Security Bank and Trust Co., Scranton, 1992—2001, sr. investment officer Linden Asset Mgmt., Inc., Scranton, 2002—. Instr. fin. Marywood Coll., Scranton, 1983. Bd. dirs. Cmty. Med. Ctr., Scranton, 1974-97, asst. treas., 1976-91; bd. dirs. Emergency Med. Svcs. Northeastern Pa., Pittston, 1976—, pres., 1985-87; bd. dirs. Polish Am. Congress No. Pa. divsn., Scranton, 1972—, v.p., 1972-89, pres., 1989—; bd. dirs. Ethics Inst. N.E. Pa., Dallas, 1991-96; bd. dirs., treas. Keystone chpt. Am. Heart Assn., Scranton, 1968-74; chmn. Campaign for Yale U., Northeastern Pa., 1976-78; incorporating dir. Lackawanna County U.S. Constn. Bicentennial Commn., 1987-88; treas. Grove St. Home Sch. Assn., Clarks Summit, 1987-90; lectr. Christ the King Ch., Dunmore, 1982-87, Our Lady of the Snows Ch., Clarks Summit, 1987—, Ch. of St. Benedict, Newton Twp., 1991—; allocations vol. United Way, 1988-91, 2002--. 1st lt. AUS, 1955-57. Recipient Assn. U.S. Army award, 1954, Disting. Mil. Student award, 1955, Am. Legion award, 1947, 51, Cert. Leadership Lackawanna, 1989. Mem. Fin. Analysts Phila., Fin. Analysts Fedn., Inst. Chartered Fin. Analysts (chartered fin. analyst), Assn. for Investment Mgmt. and Rsch., Estate Planning Coun. Northeastern Pa., Experiment in Internat. Living (France), Le Cercle Francais (treas. 1994—), Ecologia/Ekologiya, Wyo. Hist. and Geol. Soc., Greater Scranton C. of C., Esperanto League for N.Am., Universala Esperanto Asocio, Friends of Poland of Lackawanna County, Polish Nat. Alliance, Polish Falcons Am., Polish Am. Hist. Assn., Kosciuszko Found., Assn. Yale Alumni (rep. 1988-91), Aircraft Owners and Pilots Assn., Schultzville Airport Pilots Assn., Westmoreland Club (Wilkes-Barre), Scranton Club, Yale Club of Northeastern Pa. (sec. 1985-88, alumni sch. com. interviewed applicants 1965-98), U. Pa. Club (Lackawanna County), Leadership Lackawanna Alumni Assn., Phi Beta Kappa. Republican. Roman Catholic. Avocations: travel, languages. Home: 107 Carteret Dr Clarks Summit PA 18411-1009 Office: Linden Asset Mgmt Inc 507 Linden St Ste 101 Scranton PA 18503

JANOSKI, REGINA JANE, nursing educator; b. Norristown, Pa., May 7, 1948; d. Warren T. and Anna M. (Evanik) Dewees; m. John M. Janoski, Aug. 16, 1969; 1 child, Ian C. Diploma, Lankenau Hosp. Sch. Nursing, Phila., 1969; BSN magna cum laude, Eastern Coll., St. David's, Pa., 1987; MSN, Villanova U., 1990. RN, Pa.; cert. med.-surg. nurse. Staff nurse med./surg. Sacred Heart Hosp. and Rehab. Ctr., Norristown, 1969-71, head nurse med./surg., 1972-77, clin. coord. rehab. and med./surg., 1978-83; med.-surg. nursing instr. West Chester (Pa.) U., 1993-96; nursing instr. Montgomery County C.C., Blue Bell, Pa., 1996-2000, asst. prof. nursing, 2000—. Adj. faculty, clin. instr. cmty. health Eastern Coll., St. Davids, Pa., 1990; wound and skin clinician Osteo. Med. Ctr., Phila., 1990-93. Recipient Profl. Nurse Traineeship award, 1989-90. Mem. Sigma Theta Tau. E-mail: rjanoski@mc3.edu.

JANOSKO, RUDOLPH E. M. psychiatrist; b. Munhall, Pa., Apr. 30, 1930; s. Rudolph E. and Anne (Gerek) J.; m. Audrey M. Nemeth, May 18, 1932; children: Beth, Gwen, Ellen. BS, U. Pitts., 1952, MD, 1956. Cert. in psychiatry Am. Bd. Psychiatry and Neurology. Intern Easton (Pa.) Hosp., 1956-57; resident in psychiatry U. Pitts., 1957-59, 61-62; instr. psychiatry U. Pitts. Sch. Medicine, 1962-65; lectr. U. Pitts. Dept. Spl. Edn., Grad. Sch., 1966-70; clin. asst. prof. psychiatry U. Pitts. Sch. Medicine, 1965-75; mem. attending staff Presbyn.-Univ. Hosp., Pitts., 1962—; faculty Pitts. Psychoanalytic Inst., 1970—; clin. assoc. prof. psychiatry U. Pitts. Sch. Medicine, 1975—; tng. and supervising analyst Am. Psychoanalytic Assn., Pitts. Psychoanalytic Inst., 1979—; pres. Pitts. Psychoanalytic Ctr., 1981-83; dir. Pitts. Psychoanalytic Inst., 1985-86. Med. dir. Family Svcs. of Western Pa., Pitts., 1988-99; cons. Greater Pitts. Guild for Blind, Bridgeville, Pa., 1964—, Social Security Adminstrn., HHS, Pitts., 1979—, Pitts. Pastoral Inst., 1999—. Author in field. Capt. USAF, 1959-61. Recipient Meritorious Distinction award Greater Pitts. Guild for Blind, 1967, Outstanding Tchr. award Western Psychiat. Inst., 1981. Fellow Am Psychiat. Assn. (disting. life); mem. Am. Psychoanalytic Assn., Pitts. Acad. Medicine, Pitts. Psychoanalytic Soc. (pres. 1983-85), AMA. Republican. Roman Catholic. Avocation: running. Home: 2534 Mt Royal Rd Pittsburgh PA 15217-2542 Office: 161 N Dithridge St Pittsburgh PA 15213-2646

JANOVER, ROBERT H. lawyer; b. NYC, Aug. 17, 1930; s. Cyrus J. and Lillian D. (Horwitz) J.; m. Mary Elizabeth McMahon, Oct. 23, 1966; 1 child, Laura Lockwood. BA, Princeton U., 1952; postgrad., U. Vienna, 1956; JD, Harvard U., 1957. Bar: N.Y. 1957, U.S. Supreme Ct. 1961, D.C. 1966, Mich. 1973. Practice law, N.Y.C., 1957-65; cons. Office of Edn., HEW, Washington, 1965; legis. atty. Office of Gen. Counsel, HEW, Washington, 1965-66; asst. gen. atty. Mgmt. Assistance Inc., N.Y.C., 1966-71; atty. Ford Motor Credit Co., Dearborn, Mich., 1971-74; mem. firm Freud, Markus, Slavin, Toohey & Galgan, Troy, Mich., 1974-79; pvt. practice Detroit, 1979-82, Bloomfield Hills, Mich., 1982—. Contbr. articles to profl. jours. Bd. dirs. Oakland Citizens League, 1976—96, v.p., 1976—79, 1979—96; bd. dirs. Civic Searchlight, Inc., 1976—96. 1st lt. arty. U.S. Army, 1952—54, Korea. Mem.: ABA, Harvard Law Sch. Assoc., Am. Inns Ct. (master of the bench 1996—99), Assn Bar of City of N.Y., Bar Assn. D.C., Detroit Met. Bar Assn., N.Y. State Bar, Mich. State Bar, Soc. 3d Inf. Divsn., Harvard Club (N.Y.C.), Nassau Club (Princeton, N.J.), Princeton Club of N.Y., Princeton Club of Mich. (pres. 1991—92). Home: 685 Ardmoor Dr Bloomfield Hills MI 48301-2415 Office: 100 W Long Lake Rd Ste 200 Bloomfield Hills MI 48304-2774 E-mail: rjanover@aol.com.

JANOW, CHRIS, mechanical engineer; b. N.Y.C., Apr. 22, 1953; s. John and Angie (Bizzios) Janow. BME, CCNY, 1975, MME, 1980. Mech. engr. Fuze Devel. and Engr. Directorate, Picatinny Arsenal, N.J., 1975-80; mech. engr. nuclear and fuze div. Large Caliber Weapons System Lab, Picatinny Arsenal, 1980-84; mech. engr. fuze div. Armament Engring. Directorate, Picatinny Arsenal, 1984-85; systems engr. battlefield mgmt. br., fire control div. Fire Support Armaments Ctr., Picatinny Arsenal, 1985-87; program mgmt. engr. AUS Office of Product Mgr. for Fuzes, Picatinny Arsenal, 1987-88, gen. engr. and assoc. product mgr. for close combat, 1988-94; assoc. dir. U.S. Army Fuze Mgmt. Office, 1994—. Exec. sec. Fuze Engring. Standardization Working Group, Dept. Def., 1983—85; organizer numerous confs.; tech. cons. U.S. Army Fuze Safety Rev. Bd., 1987—; U.S. prin. rep. NATO AC/310 Subgroup II (Fuzes), 1994—2003, NATO AC/326 Subgroup II (Initiation Systems), 2003—. V.p. Greek Orthodox Youth Am., St. Spyridon Ch., N.Y.C., 1974—75.

Mem.: Nat. Def. Indsl. Assn., Pi Tau Sigma. Avocations: travel, working out, model making, stamp collecting, golf. Home: 34 Hilltop Ter Bloomingdale NJ 07403-1510 E-mail: cjanow@pica.army.mil.

JANOW, LYDIA FRANCES, meeting planner; b. N.Y.C., Dec. 2, 1957; d. John and Angie (Bizzios) J. BA cum laude, CCNY, 1978; grad., CBS Div. Publ., 1984. Cert. meeting planner. Exec. sec. Family Weekly Mag., N.Y.C., 1978-81, asst. mdse. mgr., 1981-83; spl. events mgr. Family Weekly/USA Weekend, N.Y.C., 1983-86; mgr. meetings & events Mag. Pubs. Assn., N.Y.C., 1986-88; conv. svcs. mgr., sales & catering mgr. Sheraton Heights Hotel, Hasbrouck Heights, N.J., 1989-91; conf. mgr. Aviation Week Group McGraw Hill Inc., N.Y.C., 1991-93, dir. tradeshows and confs., 1993—. Editor: Newsletter Heights Hotel, 1991; contbr. articles to profl. jours. Camp counselor, Hellenic-Am. Neighborhood Action Com., N.Y.C., 1974-78; tchr., Sunday sch., St. Spyridon Ch., N.Y.C., 1974-80. Mem. Internat. Assn. Exhibit Mgrs., Meeting Planners Internat., Assn. Trade Show Exhibitors, Internation Assn. for Exposition Mgmt., Exhibit Mgrs. and Conf. Organizers. Greek Orthodox. Avocations: photography, sports, reading. Home: 29 Levitt Ave Bergenfield NJ 07621-1904

JANOWER, MURRAY L. radiologist, consultant; b. Detroit, Oct. 28, 1934; m. Linda Janower; 3 children. Student, U. Detroit, 1952-54; MD, Wayne State U., 1958. Diplomate Am. Bd. Radiology. Radiologist Mass. Gen. Hosp., Boston, 1964-71; radiologist-in-chief St. Vincent Hosp., Worcester, Mass., 1971-2000; radiol. cons., 2001—. Author: Administration of Radiology Departments, 1971, Radiology of the Colon, 1981; contbr. over 90 articles to med. jours. Bd. dirs. Boston Guild for Hard of Hearing, 1981-85, Newton (Mass.) Art Ctr., 1986-90. Maj. USPHS, 1960-62. Mem. AMA, Am. Coll. Radiology (vice speaker, speaker, bd. chancellors, pres. 1996), New Eng. Roentgen Ray Soc. (treas., pres. 1979), Mass. Med. Soc., Mass. Radiol. Soc., (treas., pres. 1981, assoc. program dirs. radiology pres. 2000). E-mail: janower@yahoo.com.

JANOWITZ, JAMES ARNOLD, lawyer; b. N.Y.C., Sept. 2, 1946; s. Arnold and Erna (Frankel) J.; m. Katherine Eva Sborovy, Aug. 6, 1967; children: Jessie Elizabeth, William Aaron. BA, Haverford Coll., 1967; JD, NYU, 1971. Bar: N.Y. 1972, U.S. Dist Ct. (so. dist.) N.Y. 1972. Tchr. St. David's Sch., N.Y.C., 1968-72; assoc. Guzik & Boukstein, N.Y.C., 1972-73, Reavis & McGrath, N.Y.C., 1973-74, Pryor, Cashman & Sherman, N.Y.C., 1974-76; ptnr. Pryor, Cashman, Sherman & Flynn, N.Y.C., 1977—. Adj. prof. Cardozo Law Sch., Yeshiva U., N.Y.C., 1992; bd. dirs. Avenue Entertainment, 1986-99. Editor NYU Jour. Internat. Law and Politics, 1970-71. Mem. N.Y. State Bar Assn., Assn. of Bar of City of N.Y. Office: Pryor Cashman Sherman & Flynn 410 Park Ave Fl 10 New York NY 10022-4407

JANOWSKI, KARYN ANN, artist; b. Milw., Aug. 15, 1958; d. Robert Arthur and Evelyn Rose (Spanbauer) J. BS in Art, U. Wis., 1984. Dir., founder Warehouse Studio for Visual Artists and Musicians, Madison, 1984-86, 88-89. Tchg. asst. art therapy seminar U. Wis., 1983; gallery assoc. San Francisco Women Artists Gallery, 1990-91; fine art expert Eppraisals.com, 2000-01. Muralist Whitewater (Wis.) Hist. Soc., 1980, Mifflin St. Cmty. Coop Mural, Madison, 1987; contbr. pubs. American Artists, an Illustrated Survey of Leading Contemporaries, The California Art Rev., Art Comm. Internat. Curated Collection I; scenic artist: The Wind in the Willows; collections include Microsoft Image Archive, Tralfamadore Coop, Archive of Wis. Regional Primate Rsch. Ctr., Pfizer Corp., N.Y.C., Dynamic Resources, Soc. of Haight-Ashbury Charade, San Francisco, Niels and Faith Ingwersen, Jeff Scott Olson, Esq, Hadji Rahimipour, Madeline and Bernie Sakmar, L.A.; exhbns. include: Wis. Ctr., Madison, Firehouse 7, DAS Club, The Cannery Bldg., San Francisco, L.A. Mcpl. Art Gallery, Advocate Gallery, L.A., Circle Elephant Art, L.A., Southampton Cultural Ctr., Hofstra Mus., L.I., Chgo. Mus. Contemporary Art; contbr. Dictionary Internat. Biography, Cambridge, Eng. Mem. L.A. Cultural Affairs Slide Registry, 1996—, Artists Space, N.Y.C. Democrat. Avocations: antiques, music, nature, antique rugs. Home and Office: 1775 N Orange Dr Apt 202 Los Angeles CA 90028-4334 E-mail: paintstudio@earthlink.net.

JANOWSKI, THADDEUS MARIAN, architect; b. Cracow, Poland, Aug. 16, 1923; came to U.S., 1960, naturalized, 1972; s. Stanislaw and Maria (Kijak) J.; m. Zofia K. Owinski, Apr. 19, 1949 (div.); 1 child, Barbara Margaret MCP in Architecture, Poly. Acad., Cracow, 1949; MArch, U. Ill., 1962; PhD (hon.), Inst. Three Dimensional Perception, 1987. Chief architect Miastoprojekt Cracow, 1949-58; chief cons. So. Poland K.U.A., Warsaw, 1958-60; lectr. Poly Acad. Cracow, 1947-50, 1958-60; instr. U. Ill., 1960-62; assoc. prof. U. Man., Can., 1962-65, Iowa State U., Ames, 1965-71; prof. Syracuse U., N.Y., 1971—; proprietor, dir. Mus. Archtl. Graphics Internat., 1994—. Pres. Inst. Three Dimensional Perception, Inc., 1985; chief arch. for Saudi royal family estates, Ga., 1983-89; prin., dir. Mus. Archtl. Graphics Internat., 1991—; chmn. hon. doctorates com. Syracuse U. Senate, 1978-81. Numerous exhbns. in U.S. and Europe, 1949—; built over 6 million sq. ft. constrn. comms. include Interstate Farm Devel., Des Moines, 1967, Settlement of town houses, East Des Moines, 1969. Co-author: Sacred Art in Poland, 1955; The Urban Scale, 1968. Patentee in field. Recipient numerous prizes nat. or internat. competitions including prize Polish Embassy bldg., Peking, China, 1955, 1st prize Polish Pavillion, Brussels, Belgium, 1956, 1st prize astronomy obs. and planetarium Warsaw, 1956, award exptl. bldg., Moscow, 1959, 1st prize sch. bldgs., Poland, 1960, prize Red Rock Hill Devel., San Francisco, 1961, 2d prize campus, Dublin, Ireland, 1964, 1st prize Olympic Stadium, Banff, Can., 1962, 2d and 3rd prizes fall out shelters Office Civil Defense, 1964, 2d prize, 1966; 1st prize Bicentennial medal Iowa, 1972; 1st prize for U.S. Stamp Copernicus Quincentennial; 1st prize and commn. for monument commemorating victims of Katyn Massacre, Toronto, 1979, Syracuse, N.Y., 1985. Fellow World-Wide Acad. Scholars New Zealand, Intercontinental Biographical Assn. (U.K.); mem. Assn. Polish Architects, Assn. Painters, Sculptors and Artists in Poland, Assn. Scientists Hist. Armament, Canadian Assn. U. Tchrs., NRA, Am. Legion. Address: 575 Reynolds Bend Rd SE Rome GA 30161-2546 *On our beautiful planet, architecture is one of the necessary evils. It is a sensor of society's cultural level, therefore the architect determines the dignity of environment by restraint, simplicity, honesty, obviousness, and antiexhibitionism.*

JANSEN, ANGELA BING, artist, educator; b. N.Y.C., Aug. 17, 1929; d. Lester and Jean Bing; m. Gunther Jansen, Mar. 8, 1956; children— Edmund, Douglas. BA, Bklyn. Coll., 1951; MA, NYU, 1953; student, Bklyn. Mus. Art Sch., 1947-50, Atelier 17, N.Y.C., 1950-52. Tchr. art, public schs., N.Y.C., 1954-60. One-man shows: Madison (Wis.) Art Center, 1977, Gimpel & Weitzenhoffer, N.Y.C., 1974, 78, group shows: Bklyn. Mus., 1950, 70, 76, Library of Congress, Washington, 1969, 71, Ljubljana Internat. Print Biennale, Yugoslavia, 1971, 73, 75, 77, Venice Biennale, 1972, Internat. Exhbn. Drawing, Rejeka, Yugoslavia, 1972 (award), Internat. Print Biennale, Cracow, Poland, 1978; represented in permanent collections: Mus. Modern Art, N.Y.C., Met. Mus. Art, N.Y.C., N.Y. Pub. Library, Art Inst. Chgo., Tate Gallery, London, Victoria and Abert Mus., London, Bibliotheque Nationale, Paris, Bklyn. Mus., Phila. Mus. Art, Fonds d'Art Contemporain, Centre de Recherche et d'Etude de la Sculpture Contemporaine, Mauberge, France, Musée du Petit Format, Couvin, Belgium, Bklyn. Mus., Francine Tyler Art Forum, summer, 1979. Nat. Endowment for Arts grantee, 1974-75

JANSEN, DANIEL ERVIN, former professional speedskater, marketing professional, former Olympic athlete; b. Milw., June 17, 1965; s. Harry William and Geraldine (Grajek) J.; m. Robin Wicker, Apr. 28, 1990 (div.); children: Jane Danielle, Olivia Renee. Student, U. Wis., Milw., 1986, 87, 89. Speed skater U.S. Olympic Com., Colorado Springs, Colo., 1984—; pro tour speedskater, 1994—; sports mktg. profl. Miller Brewing Co., Milw., 1988—. Overall World Cup Champion Internat. Skating Union, 1986, 87, 92, 93, 94, World Sprint Champion, 1988, 94; recipient Gold medal for 1000m men's speedskating Lillehammer Winter Olympic Games, 1994. Roman Catholic. Achievements include setting world record for 1000m race in 12.43 seconds, Lillehammer Winter Olympic Games, 1994.

JANSEN, DONALD ORVILLE, lawyer; b. Odessa, Tex., Nov. 17, 1939; s. Orville Charles and Dolores Elizabeth (Olps) J.; m. E. Janice Law; children: Donald Orville, Lauren, Christine, David, Margaret BBA magna cum laude, Loyola U., New Orleans, 1961, JD cum laude, 1963; LLM, Georgetown U., 1966. Bar: La. 1963, Tex. 1965. Ptnr. Fulbright and Jaworski, Houston, 1966—. Served to capt. JAGC, U.S. Army, 1963-66 Mem. ABA, Fed. Bar Assn. State Bar Tex., La. Bar Assn., Am. Coll. Trust and Estate Counsel Roman Catholic. Home: 5212 Sagesquare St Houston TX 77056-7041 Office: Fulbright & Jaworski 1301 Mckinney St Ste 5100 Houston TX 77010-3031

JANSEN, G. THOMAS, dermatologist; b. Manitowoc, Wis., July 16, 1926; s. Gerald M. and Sarah (Grady) J.; m. Frances Bovick, Sept. 6, 1952; children: Mark, Kurt, Anne, Drew, Fran. BS, U. Wis., Madison, 1948, MD, 1950. Diplomate: Am. Bd. Dermatology (pres. 1985-86). Intern Med. Coll. of Va., 1950-51; resident in dermatology U. Wis., 1953-54, U. Mich., 1954-56; practice medicine specializing in dermatology Little Rock, 1956—; pres. Little Rock Dermatology Clinic, 1968—. Mem. faculty U. Ark. Med. Center, 1956—, prof. dermatology, 1965—, chmn. dept., 1965-82; mem. staff Doctors Hosp., U. Ark. Hosp., St. Vincent Infirmary, Bapt. Hosp.; pres. Am. Dermatology Found., 1980-81 Served as officer M.C. USNR, 1951-54. Recipient Disting. Svc. award, Am. Bd. Dermatologists, 1987, Finnerud award, 1996, Alumni citation, U. Wis. Med. Sch., 2002. Mem. AMA, Am. Dermatol. Assn. (pres. 1993), Am. Acad. Dermatology (asst. sec.-treas. 1980-83, sec.-treas. 1983-85, pres.-elect 1987, pres. 1988, hon. 1991, Master in Dermatology 1991, Everett C. Fox Lectureship award 1995, Gold medal 1997), Soc. Investigative Dermatology, Nat. Program Dermatology, Am. Coll. Chemosurgery, So. Med. Assn. (pres. 1976-77, Disting. Svc. award 1991), Ark. Med. Soc., Ark. Dermatol. Soc., Pulaski County Med. Soc., Alpha Omega Alpha. Roman Catholic. Home: 6601 Pleasant Pl Little Rock AR 72205-2868 Office: 500 S University Ave Ste 501 Little Rock AR 72205-5307

JANSEN, JOHN CARL, recording producer and engineer; b. Boston, Oct. 3, 1947; s. Carl John and Lily (Sandbeck) J. Student, U. Conn., 1965-66, 68-69, Sch. Visual Arts, 1969-70. Guitar player, Conn. and N.Y., 1965-70; rec. engr. Electric Lady Studios, N.Y.C., 1970-72; freelance producer, engr. Eng., 1972-73; chief engr. Ramport Studios, London, 1974-76; producer, engr. John Jansen Prodns., Upper Montclair, N.J., 1976—; owner, mgr. Zak Comm., multimedia prodn. co., Upper Montclair, 1996—. Cons. engr. House Music Studios, West Orange, N.J., 1983—. With U.S. Army, 1966-68, Vietnam. Recipient 25 gold and platinum records Rec. Industry Assn. Mem. Nat. Acad. Recording Arts and Scis. Avocations: song writing, tennis, golf.

JANSEN, KATHLEEN MARY, librarian; b. San Francisco, Oct., 24, 1951; d. Wilfred Hugh and Margaret (Jack) Craig; m. Robert Lawrence Jansen, Oct. 8, 1978; children: Heather Margaret, Sarah Elizabeth. AA, Allan Hancock Coll., 1971; BA, U. Calif., Riverside, 1973; MLS, San Jose State U., 1976. Children's librarian Ottumwa (Iowa) Pub. Library, 1977; reference librarian Lake County Library, Lakeport, Calif., 1977-79, county librarian, 1979—. Deacon Kelseyville Presbyn. Ch., Kelseyville, Calif., 1984-87, 2001—. Mem. Calif. County Librarians Assn. Democrat. Office: Lake County Library 1425 N High St Lakeport CA 95453-3857

JANSEN, KEVIN P. biology educator; s. Paul H. and Juanita F. Jansen. PhD, U. South Fla., 2001. Asst. prof. biology U. of Va. Coll. at Wise, 2000—. Vis. asst. prof. biology Eckerd Coll., St. Petersburg, Fla., 1998—2000. Grad. Tchg. asst., S.W. Mo. State U., 1991—93, U. South Fla., 1993—98, Rsch. grantee, Fla. Fish and Wildlife Commn. Nongame Wildlife Program, 1997—2000. Mem.: Beta Beta Beta. Achievements include research in ecology and evolution of reptiles and amphibians in Central and North America. Office: U Va's Coll at Wise 1 College Ave Wise VA 24293

JANSEN, MICHAEL JOHN, healthcare executive; b. Swannanoa, N.C., July 24, 1945; s. Edward John and Mary Bernadette (Haughian) J.; m. Roxanne Shellenberger, June 27, 1970 (div. May 1992); m. Linda Kathryn Hughes, Aug. 21, 1993; children: Kathryn Anne, Victoria Elizabeth. BS in BA, U. S.C., 1967; M. Health Adminstrn., Duke U., 1976. Adminstrv. asst. Watts Hosp., Durham, N.C., 1976-77; asst. dir. Durham County Gen. Hosp., 1977-80; asst. adminstr. St. Joseph's Hosp., Atlanta, 1980-83, sr. v.p., COO, 1983-89; group v.p. SunHealth, Charlotte, N.C., 1989-90; sr. assoc. adminstr., COO Cape Fear Valley Med. Ctr., Fayetteville, N.C., 1991-2001; CEO MedAccom, Research Triangle Park, NC, 2001—03; adminstr. Breezewood Family Healthcare, Fayetteville, NC, 2003—. Bd. dirs. St. Joseph's Hosp., Atlanta, 1985-89, Fayetteville Symphony Orch., 1993-95, United Way of Cumberland County, Fayetteville, 1993-95; chmn. bd. dirs. Shared Svcs. for So. Hosps., Atlanta, 1986-87. Capt. USAF, 1967-72, Col. USAFR, 1990-96. Recipient Falcon award/Spaatz award Civil Air Patrol, 1967. Fellow Am. Coll. Healthcare Execs. Office: Breezewood Family Healthcare PA PO Box 87448 Fayetteville NC 28304

JANSEN, RAYMOND A., JR., newspaper publishing executive; Former pub., CEO, Hartford (Conn.) Courant; pub., CEO, pres. Newsday, Melville, NY, 1994—; exec. v.p. Times Mirror, L.A., 1999—2000; sr. v.p. Tribune Publ., 2000—. Office: Newsday Inc 235 Pinelawn Rd Melville NY 11747-4250

JANSEN, ROBERT BRUCE, consulting civil engineer; b. Spokane, Wash., Dec. 14, 1922; s. George Martin and Pearl Margaret (Kent) J.; m. Barbara Mae Courtney, Sept. 18, 1943. BSCE, U. Denver, 1949; MSCE, U. So. Calif., 1955. Registered profl. engr., Calif., Colo., Wash. Chief Calif. Div. Dam Safety, Sacramento, 1965-68; chief of ops. Calif. Dept. Water Resources, Sacramento, 1968-71, dep. dir., 1971-75, chief design and constrn., 1975-77; asst. commr. U.S. Bur. Reclamation, Denver, 1977-80; cons. civil engr., 1980—. Cons. TVA, Chattanooga, 1981—, So. Calif. Edison Co., Rosemead, 1982—2002, Pacific Gas and Electric, San Francisco, 1982—93, Hydro-Quebec, Montreal, 1986—98, Ala. Power Co., Birmingham, 1986—, Ga. Power Co., 1989—94. Author: Dams and Public Safety, 1983; editor: Safety of Existing Dams, 1983; co-author: Development of Dam Engineering in the United States, 1988; editor and co-author: Advanced Dam Engineering for Design, Construction, and Rehabilitation, 1988. Mem. U.S. Soc.on Dams (chmn.1979-81), ASCE, NAE (elected). Home and Office: 509 Briar Rd Bellingham WA 98225-7811

JANSEN, VIRGINIA, art historian, educator; d. Frederick H. and Marian Brindle Miller; m. George Jansen, June 14, 1966. AB in German Lang. and Lit., Smith Coll., 1964; postgrad., Freie U., Berlin, 1964—65; MA in History of Art, U. Calif., Berkeley, 1967, postgrad., 1968—72, PhD in History of Art, 1975. Tchg. asst. Französisches Gymnasium, Berlin, 1964—65; assoc. curator Montreal Mus. Fine Arts, Canada, 1967—68; instr. divsn. fine arts Foothill Coll., Los Altos Hills, Calif., 1972—73; lectr. dept. fine arts U. Santa Clara, Calif., 1973—75; asst. prof. U. Calif., Santa Cruz, 1975—83, assoc. prof., 1983—93, prof. art history, 1993—. Vis. lectr. dept. design U. Calif., Davis, 1972; presenter in field. Contbr. articles to profl. jours. Mem.: Medieval Assn. of the Pacific (coun. mem. 1999—2002, mem. nominating com. 2001—02), Assn. Villard de Honnecourt for the Interdisciplinary Study of Medieval Tech., Sci. and Art, Vernacular Arch. Group, Brit. Archaeol. Assn., Archeology Soc. France, Internat. Ctr. Medieval Art (mem. nominating com. 1983, bd. dirs. 1987—90, chair state discipline com. 1990—96, bd. dirs. 1992—95), Medieval Acad. Am. (medieval acad. reprint texts com. 1999—), Coll. Art Assn., Soc. Archtl. Historians (bd. dirs. 1998—2001, chair founders award com. 2000—01, nominating com. 1999—2000). Office: Cowell Coll Univ Calif 1156 High St Santa Cruz CA 95064

JANSMA, THEODORE JOHN, JR., psychologist; b. Phila., Apr. 17, 1943; s. Theodore John and Ruth Virginia (Gezon) J.; m. Jo Bernadette Battiston, June 28, 1969; children: Theodore John III, Christopher Paul. BA, Calvin Coll., Grand Rapids, Mich., 1965; MA, Mich. State U., 1967; PhD, Ill. Inst. Tech., 1971. Lic. psychologist, Mich., Ill.; diplomate clin. hypnotherapy. Mental health intern I, II Chgo. State Hosp., 1966-69; mental health counselor II Charles F. Read Zone Ctr., Chgo., 1970-71; dir. Project Talk, Chgo., 1970-71; psychologist III Charles F. Read Zone Ctr., Chgo., 1971-72; staff psychologist Pine Rest Christian Hosp., Grand Rapids, 1972-80, dir. psychology dept., 1977-80; assoc. clin. prof. Coll. Human Medicine Mich. State U., 1976-84; pvt. practice, 1980—. Diplomate Am. Coll. Forensic Examiners. Author: Becoming Kate, 1990. Bd. dirs. Ada (Mich.) Christian Sch. Assn., 1990-96, Ada Christian Sch. Found., 1990-96, pres., 1995, 96. Mem. Am. Psychol. Assn., Mich. Psychol. Assn., Grand Rapids Area Psychol. Assn., Soc. for Clinic. and Experimental Hypnosis, Internat. Soc. for Study of Dissociation, Internat. Coun. Psychologists, Nat. Bd. for Cert. Clin. Hypnotherapists. Avocations: carpentry, boating, travel, painting. Home: 1669 River Oaks Dr SE Ada MI 49301-9353 Office: 3330 Claystone St SE Grand Rapids MI 49546-7716

JANSON, BARBARA JEAN, publisher; b. Mason City, Iowa, Mar. 7, 1942; d. Harley Arnold and Helen Victoria (Henrickson) J.; m. W. John Shallenberger, Feb. 24, 1963 (div. Sept. 1980); children: Mona, Ann; m. John Batty Henderson, Sept. 8, 1984 (div. 1990); m. Arthur R. Hilsinger, Aug. 31, 1997. BS in Math., Iowa State U., 1965; MS in Math., Trinity Coll., 1970; MBA, U. R.I., 1982. Cert. math. tchr., Iowa, N.Y., Conn. Math. tchr. Pub. High Schs., Avon, Farmington, Bloomfield, Conn., 1966-68, Ulster Acad., Kingston, N.Y., 1971-73; math. instr. Ulster County Community Coll., Kingston, 1973; math. editor Houghton Mifflin Co., Boston, 1974-77; math. instr. Bristol County Community Coll., Fall River, Mass., 1977-78; asst. dir. editorial Am. Math. Soc., Providence, 1978-81, dir. of publ., 1982-85; founder, pres. Janson Publs., Inc. (purchased by Tribune Edn. Group), Providence and Dedham, Mass., 1985-96; pres. Janson Publs., Inc., Dedham, 1996-98; pub. cons. Everyday Learning/Tribune Edn. Group, 1996-98; pres. Janson Assocs., Dedham, 1996—. Mem. expert panel materials devel. ref. NSF, 1996-99; rep. sci. publ. com. Am. Heart Assn., 1986-90; mem. R.I. State Adv. Commn. on Librs.; mem. R.I. Legis. Commn. for Math. and Sci. Edn., 1991; mem. adv. com. R.I. State Systemic Initiative in Math. and Sci., 1993-94; Mass. state adv. bd. Math. & Sci. Edn., 2000—. Editor: Scholarly Publishing: Managing Today, Planning for Tomorrow, 1986. Bd. dirs. Planned Parenthood of R.I., Providence, 1986-87, First Parish Unitarian Ch., Beverly, Mass., 1975-76; mem. steering com. Am. Math. Project, Berkeley, Calif., 1986-92; mem. oversight com. Resources Math. Reform Ednl. Devel. Ctr., Newton, Mass.; adv. mem. R.I. State Coun. on Librs. Recipient Mortar Bd. award Iowa State U., 1965. Mem. AAAS, LWV, Soc. for Scholarly Publishing (bd. dirs. 1986-90, chair ann. meeting 1985), N.Y. Acad. Sci., Am. Math. Soc., Math. Assn. Am., Nat. Coun. Tchrs. Math., Assn. Am. Publishers (jours. com. 1982-85), Nat. Assn. Women Bus. Owners. Unitarian Universalist. Home and Office: 8 Jackson Pond Rd Dedham MA 02026-5524

JANSON, PATRICK, singer, actor, conductor, educator; b. Cleve., Oct. 10, 1967; s. Robert L. and Gloria Ann (Dominguez) J.; m. Christine Marie Fondaw, June 8, 1991; children, Emma Susanne, Madison Ann. MusB, Baldwin-Wallace Coll., 1990. Singer, actor, dir., mus. dir., condr. various theatres and opera cos., 1990—, tchr. music St. Joseph Acad., Cleve., 1990-91, 98—, Univ. Sch., Hunting Valley, Ohio, 1991-92; tchr. Perry-Mansfield Performing Arts Camp, Steamboat Springs, Colo., summer 1993, 95, Usdan Ctr. for the Creative and Performing Arts, L.I., N.Y., summer 1998. Prodn. asst. Broadway musical The Life. Recipient 1st pl. prize Profl. Artists Devel. Competition, 1990. Mem. Actors Equity Assn., Alpha Sigma Phi (pres. interfraternity coun. 1988-89, pres. chpt. 1989-90). Address: 1097 Plainfield Rd Cleveland OH 44121-2533 E-mail: pjanson02@aol.com.

JANSON, RICHARD ANTHONY, plastic surgeon; b. Passaic, N.J., Nov. 30, 1945; m. Mary Ann Janson, 1971; children: Sarah, Matthew. BA, Rice U., 1967; MD, Med. Coll. Wis., 1971. Diplomate Am. Bd. Plastic Surgery. Intern St. Joseph Hosp., Denver, 1971-72, resident in gen. surgery, 1972-76; resident in plastic surgery U. Tex. Med. Branch, Galveston, 1976-79; pvt. practice Grand Junction, Colo., 1979—. Fellow ACS, Am. Soc. Plastic & Reconstructive Surgeons; mem. Colo. Soc. Plastic & Reconstructive Surgeons. Office: 1120 Wellington Ave Grand Junction CO 81501-6129

JANSONS, MARISS, orchestra conductor; b. Riga, Latvia, USSR, Jan. 14, 1943; s. Arvid and Erhayda Jansons; 1 child, Ilona. Diploma, Leningrad Conservatory, Vienna Conservatory. 2d condr. Leningrad Philharm. Orch., USSR, 1973—, assoc. prin. condr., 1985—96; music dir. Oslo Philharm. Orch., Norway, 1979—2002; prof. of conducting St. Petersburg Conservatoire, 1991—. Prin. guest condr. BBC Welsh Orch., Cardiff, 1984-88; prin. guest condr. London Philharm., 1992-97; guest condr. Berlin Philharm. Orch., Vienna Philharm. Orch., Royal Concert Gebouw, Amsterdam, also major symphony orchs. in Great Britain, U.S., Can.; music dir. Pitts. Symphony Orch., 1997-2003, Bavarian Radio Symphony Orch., 2003-. Condr. various recordings with Chandos Records, 1984-86, EMI/Angel Records, 1986—, exclusive artist EMI, 1991—. Recipient Royal Norwegian Order of Merit from His Majesty the King of Norway, 1988, with grade Comdr. with Star, 1995; named Artist of the Soviet Union, 1991, EMI Artist of Yr., 1996. Address: IMG Artists 616 Chiswick High Rd London W4 5RX England Office: Pittsburgh Symphony Orchestra Heinz Hall 600 Penn Ave Ste 1 Pittsburgh PA 15222-3259

JANSSEN, JAMES ROBERT, consulting software engineer; b. Frederick, Md., June 14, 1959; s. Robert James and Kathryn Doris (Randolph) J.; m. Deborah June Dellwo, Mar. 15, 1986 (div. Sept. 20, 1988). BSEE, Stanford U., 1981, MSEE, 1982. Simulation technician Varian Assocs., Palo Alto, Calif., 1981; hardware design engr. Fairchild Test Systems, San Jose, Calif., 1982-86, Factron Test Systems, Latham, N.Y., 1986-87; software, sys. designer Schlumberger Technologies Labs., Palo Alto, 1988; software engr. Photon Dynamics, Inc., San Jose, 1989-90, ADAC Labs., Milpitas, Calif., 1990-92, software, system designer Aalborg, Denmark, 1992, Milpitas, 1992-94; consulting software engr. self-employed, Sunnyvale, Calif., 1994-96; mem. tech. staff Netscape Comms. Corp., Mountain View, Calif., 1996-99, Am. Online Inc., Mountain View, 1999-2001; pres., founder MouseMine, Inc., Scotts Valley, Calif., 2001—03. Pres., founder Digital Studio Systems, Inc., Sunnyvale, 1990-93. Patentee multiple timing signal generator. Civic vol. City of Sunnyvale, 1993. Mem. Tau Beta Pi. Avocations: motocross racing, auto race driving, auto race spectating, composing and recording pop music, piano. Home and Office: 721 Wolverine Way Scotts Valley CA 95066-2923 E-mail: jimj@ihwy.com. *I know enough to know how little I know.*

JANSSEN, MICHAEL ALLEN, astronomer; b. Boise, Idaho, Sept. 30, 1937; s. Winfred Stuart and Glenys (Bassett) J.; m. Elizabeth Goodspeed Fredrick (div. Sept. 1974); children: Aaron Michael, Elizabeth Goodspeed; 1 stepson, Daniel Benbenisty; m. Saundra Zena Sutton, June 4, 1979. BA, U. Calif., Berkeley, 1963, PhD, 1972. Physicist Lawrence Radiation Lab., Livermore, Calif., 1963-67; rsch. asst. U. Calif., Berkeley, 1971-72; resident rsch. assoc. NRC, Jet Propulsion Lab., Pasadena, Calif., 1972-74, sr. scientist, 1974-76, mem. tech. staff, 1976-96, group supr., 1989-91, sect. mgr., 1991-93, lead scientist, astrophysics, 1994-97, sr. mem. tech. staff, 1996—, asst. mgr. divsn. earth and space scis., 1997—2002, prin. scientist, 2002—. Editor: Atmospheric Remote Sensing by Microwave Radiometry, 1993; contbr. more than 50 articles to profl. jours. Recipient Exceptional Sci. Achievement medal, NASA, 1992. Mem. Am. Astron. Soc., Internat. Union Radio Sci., Internat. Astron. Union, Am. Geophys. Union. Achievements include participation in discovery of cosmic background anisotropy. Office: Jet Propulsion Lab Mail Stop 169-506 4800 Oak Grove Dr Pasadena CA 91109-8001 E-mail: michael.a.janssen@jpl.nasa.gov.

JANSSEN, PETER ANTON, magazine editor and publisher; b. San Francisco, July 1, 1936; s. Clayton Robson and Florence Ethel (Mohr) Janssen; m. Kyra Oppermann, Dec. 28, 1958 (div. Nov. 1973); children: Katherine, Kristen; m. Karen Christine Cole, Jan. 20, 1974 (div. Mar. 1990); children: Peter Anton, Elizabeth; m. Renée Starring Cartwright, Mar. 7, 1992. BA in History, Stanford U., 1960; MA, Northwestern U., 1961. Edn. editor Time mag., N.Y.C., 1974-76; sr. editor Money, N.Y.C., 1977-78; editor-in-chief Parent's mag., N.Y.C., 1978, Us Mag., N.Y. Times Co., N.Y.C., 1979-80, Nation's Bus. mag., Washington, 1981, Motor Boating & Sailing Mag., N.Y.C., 1982-93, editor, pub., 1993-2000; editl. dir. Hearst Custom Pub., N.Y.C., 2000—. Adj. prof. U. Calif. Berkeley, 1972; cons. Dept. Transp. HEW, HHS. Contbr. With U.S. Army, 1956—58. Recipient Silver Gavel award, ABA, 1968. Mem.: Edn. Writers Assn. (pres. 1969—71, numerous awards 1965—70), Am. Soc. Mag. Editors, Am. Powerboat Assn., U.S. Yacht Racing Union, Overseas Press Club, Port Washington Yacht Club (Harbor Found. N.Y., Harbor Found. N.J.), N.Y. Yacht Club. Presbyterian. Avocations: sailing, boat racing, tennis, skiing. Home: 452 Meadowbrook Rd Fairfield CT 06824 Office: Hearst Custom Pub 250 W 55th St New York NY 10019-5201 E-mail: pjanssen@hearst.com.

JANSSEN-PELLATZ, EUNICE CHARLENE, healthcare facility administrator; b. Urania, La., Mar. 23, 1948; d. Luther Clarence and Eunice Bobby (Pendarvis) Smith. BS in Nursing, Humboldt State U., 1970; MS in Nursing, Calif. State U., Fresno, 1980. Dir. nurses, asst. adminstr., coord. patient care svcs. Mad River Community Hosp., Arcata, Calif.; nursing supr. Fresno (Calif.) Community Hosp.; emergency response coord. Humboldt County Pub. Health Dept. Mem. Am. Soc. Healthcare Risk Mgmt. Home: 824 Diamond Dr Arcata CA 95521-8212 E-mail: pellatz@humboldt1.com.

JANSSENS, JOE LEE, controller, consultant; b. Alpine, Tex., Apr. 13, 1964; s. Charles Louis Janssens and Sue Ellen (Cheairs) Ticknor; m. Diana Bookout, Sept. 9, 1995; children: Ryan, Stephanie. BBA in Fin., Tex. A&M U., 1986; BA in Spanish, U. Houston, 1996. CPA Tex., cert. mgmt. acct. Staff auditor Price Waterhouse, Houston, 1988-89; consol. acct. Energy Ventures, Inc., Houston, 1989-92; sr. internat. acct. Ashland Exploration, Inc., Houston, 1992-95; contr. Peak Svcs. USA Ltd., Texas City, Tex., 1996-97, Peak USA Energy Svcs., Ltd., Houston, 1997, Tube-Alloy Corp., Houston, 1997-98; fin. dir. Grant Prideco SA de C.V. Veracruz, Mexico, 1998-2000; fin. svcs. rep. IBM (formerly PriceWaterhouseCoopers), Houston, 2001—. Mem.: Inst. Mgmt. Accts. Roman Catholic. Avocations: western history, linguistics, scuba diving. Home: 7803 Braesdale Ln Houston TX 77071-1303 Office: 777 Eldridge Pkwy Ste 500 Houston TX 77079 E-mail: janssejl@bp.com.

JANSSON, JOHN PHILLIP, architect, consultant; b. Phila., Nov. 27, 1918; s. John A. and Isabelle (Ericson) Jansson; m. Ann C. Winter, Apr. 8, 1944 (div. Oct. 1970); children: Linda Ann, Lora Jean; m. Elizabeth Clow Peer, Jan. 21, 1978 (dec. May 1984). BArch, Pratt Inst., 1947; postgrad., SUNY, 1949. Registered arch., N.Y., lic. Nat. Coun. Archtl. Registration Bd.s. Architect various firms, 1949-54; pvt. practice architecture N.Y.C., 1949—; cons. mktg. products, materials and svcs. to bldg. and constrn. industry, 1949—; exec. v.p. Archtl. Aluminum Mfrs. Assn., N.Y.C., 1954-58; mgr. market devel. Olin-Metals Div., N.Y.C., 1958-62; dir. Pope, Evans & Robbins, cons. engrs., 1970-82; ptnr. Morris Ketchum, Jr. and Assocs., Archs., 1964-68; exec. dir. N.Y. State Coun. Architecture, 1968-73; associated, 1973-74; dir. Gruzen & Ptnrs., 1972-74; pres. Bldg. Constrn. Tech., 1975-78; v.p. Ehrenkrantz Group, 1974-82. Cons. N.Y. State Pure Waters Authority, 1968—69; chmn. N.Y. State Architecture-Constrn. Interagency Com., 1968—74; sec. N.Y. State Gov.'s Adv. Com. State Constrn. Programs, 1970—71; dir. U.S. trade mission leader to Nigeria Dept. of Commerce, 1981. Mem. N.Y. State Citizens Com. Pub. Schs., 1952—55; v.p. citizens adv. com. Housing Authority, Town of Oyster Bay, NY, 1966—68; bd. dirs. Bldg. Industry Data Adv. Coun., 1976—78, Park Ten Coop., 1981—82; instr. Outward Bound, Hurricane Island, Rockland, Maine, 1982—; media specialist Image Ctr. Am.'s Cup, 1987. Served to capt. USMCR, 1943—46. Mem.: AIA (mem. archs. govt. com. 1971—77), Soc. Mil. Engrs. Soc. N.Y.C., Am. Mgmt. Assn., Associated Coun. Arts, Nat. Trust Historic Preservation, Soc. Archtl. Historians, N.Y. State Assn. Archs. (dir.), N.Y. Bldg. Congress, Archtl. League N.Y., Nat. Inst. Bldg. Scis., BRAB Bldg. Rsch. Inst., Nat. Inst. Archtl. Edn., Constrn. Specialist Inst., Am. Arbitration Assn., Fleety Res. Assn., Victorian Soc. Am., Mus. Modern Art, U.S. Naval Acad. Officers and Faculty Club, Md. Capital Yacht Club (bd. dirs. 1993—94). Home: 6301 River Crescent Dr Annapolis MD 21401-7721

JANTZ, CYNTHIA MARIE, librarian; b. McKenzie, Tenn., Nov. 8, 1957; d. Willfred and Mary (Cantrell) J. AS, Vol. State Community Coll., 1977; BS, Bethel Coll., 1979; MLS, Vanderbilt U., 1988. Cert. tchr., Tenn. Tchr. Union Elem. Sch. Sumner County Bd. Edn., Gallatin, Tenn., 1979-82, English and reading tchr. T.W. Hunter Mid. Sch. Hendersonville, Tenn., 1982-90, libr. T.W. Hunter Middle Sch., 1990—. Cheerleading sponsor T.W. Hunter Mid. Sch., Hendersonville, 1983-90. Mem. choir St. Luke Cumberland Presbyn. Ch.; mem. Hendersonville Cmty. Singers, 1987—. Bob Hope Honor scholar, 1977-78, Hutchins scholar, 1978-79. Mem. NEA, ALA, Internat. Reading Assn. (local chpt.), Tenn. Edn. Assn., Sumner County Edn. Assn., Tenn. Assn. Mid. Schs., Gamma Beta Phi. Home: PO Box 156 Hendersonville TN 37077-0156 Office: TW Hunter Mid Sch 3140 Long Hollow Pike Hendersonville TN 37075-8781

JANTZEN, J(OHN) MARC, retired education educator; b. Hillsboro, Kans., July 30, 1908; s. John D. and Louise (Janzen) J.; m. Ruth Patton, June 9, 1935; children: John Marc, Myron Patton, Karen Louise. AB, Bethel Coll., Newton, Kans., 1934; A.M., U. Kans., 1937, PhD, 1940. Elementary sch. tchr., Marion County, Kans., 1927-30, Hillsboro, Kan., 1930-31; high sch. tchr., 1934-36; instr. sch. edn. U. Kans., 1936-40; asst. prof. Sch. Edn., U. of Pacific, Stockton, Calif., 1940-42, assoc. prof., 1942-44, prof., 1944-78, prof. emeritus, 1978—, also dean sch. edn., 1944-74, emeritus, 1974—, dir. summer sessions, 1940-72. Condr. overseas seminars; mem., chmn. commn. equal opportunities in edn. Calif. Dept. Edn., 1959-69; mem., chmn. Commn. Tchr. Edn. Calif. Tchrs. Assn., 1956-62; mem. Nat. Coun. for Accreditation Tchr. Edn., 1969-72. Bd. dirs. Ednl. Travel Inst., 1965-89. Recipient hon. svd. award Calif. Congress Parents and Tchrs., 1982, McCaffrey disting. Svc. award in recognition of leadership in higher edn., cmty. relationships and internat. svc. San Joaquin Delta Coll., 1996. Mem. NEA, Am. Edn. Rsch. Assn., Calif. Edn. Rsch. Assn. (past pres. 1954-55), Calif. Coun. for Edn. Tchrs., Calif. Assn. of Colls. for Tchr. Edn. (sec., treas. 1975-85), Rotary (Outstanding Rotarian of Yr. award North Stockton 1990, Paul Harris fellow 1980), Stockton Coun. PTA Found., Phi Delta Kappa. Methodist. Home: Folsom, Calif. *I maintain that my success in life is a result of multiple factors, among which the most important are a supportive home environment on a Kansas family farm; a wife who shared her husband's ambitions and supported him fully, often at considerable personal sacrifice; an attempt to serve others through a "power with" attitude rather than a "power over" struggle; and a conviction that one's life transcends the immediacy of the here and now.* Died Aug. 26, 2001; Stockton, Calif..

JANUARY, CRAIG TAYLOR, cardiologist, researcher; b. Iowa City, Iowa, Apr. 1, 1947; s. Lewis Edward and Virginia Eloise January; m. Marilyn Sheehey, Oct. 19, 1985; children: Kathleen Elaine, Anna Taylor. MD, PhD, U. of Iowa, 1976. Cert. internal medicine Am. Bd. of Internal Medicine, 1979, cardiovascular diseases Am. Bd. of Internal Medicine, 1981. Asst. prof. medicine U. of Chgo., 1982—89, assoc. prof. medicine, 1989—94; prof. medicine and physiology U. of Wis., 1995—. Chief of cardiology U. of Wis., Madison, 1995—97. Various roles Chgo. Am. Heart Assn., 1985—94. Rsch. grants, NIH and Am. Heart Assn., 1981—2002. Mem.: Cardiac Electrophysiology Soc. (v.p., pres. elect. 2002—). Achievements include research in Research in cardiac arrhythmias and sudden cardiac death mechanisms. Home: 3430 Crestwood Dr Madison WI 53705 Office: Univ of Wis 600 Highland Ave Madison WI 53792 Office Fax: 608-263-0405.

JANURA, JAN AROL, apparel manufacturing executive; b. Chgo., May 12, 1949; s. Cornel Harold Charles and Violet Mary Janura. BS, Colo. State U., 1971; MA, Fuller Theol. Sem., 1973; postgrad., Harvard Bus. Sch., 1997. Area dir. Young Life Campaign, Seattle, 1973-76; CEO, dir. Carol Anderson, Inc., L.A., 1977—; CFO Fresh Retail Chain, 1988—, Outdoor Videos Inc., 1988—; CEO Old Maui Brand, Rancho Dominguez, Calif., 2000—. Dir. Camp Anderson; pres. L.A. Electric Motorcar Co., 1979-80; prin., dir. Pheasant Hill Orchards, Connel, Washington; founder, CEO Old Maui Brand men's shirt co.; bd. dirs. C.A., Inc., catalog mfg. Nordstrom, Neiman Marcus, Coldwater Creek; founder Feather Chuckers Brand clothing, Carol Anderson's By Invitation; founder oldmaui.com, cabionline.com. Mem. Rep. Nat. Com., 1986, Rep. Presdl. Task Force, 1984-86; trustee Janura Libr., Glendale; founder Smiling Moose Lodge, Cameron, Mont. Weyerhaeuser fellow, 1972-73, Glendale Fellowship Found.; bd. dirs. Palos Verdes Found., We. Leadership Found., Starr Leadership Found., SW Leadership Found., NW Fellowship, Rivergate Fellowship, Crested Butte, Colo., Glendale (Calif.) Young Life Found. Fellowship, Oaks Christian H.S., Westlake, Calif.; commerce spkrs. Colo. State U., Fort. Collins, 2003. Recipeint Salesman of Yr. award, 1983, 84; Carpenteria fellow, 2002. Mem. Fly Fishermen Am. (life), Trout Unlimited (life), Henrys Fork Found., Calif. Trout, 11-99 Found. (life), Pvt. Aircraft Owners Assn., Beechcraft Owners' Club, Montana and Land Reliance, Friends of Montana Land Reliance, Mammoth Lakes Fly Fisherman, Young Pres.'s Orgn. (L.A. chpt., Beta Forum), World Pres. Orgn., Friends of Norris Theater, Snowcreek Athletic Club, L.A. Athletic Club, Wash. Athletic Club, N.Y. Athletic Club, Pres. Pointe Assn. (pres. 1991-96), Juniper Ridge Assn., Admirals Club (life), Solomon Hill Hunt Club, Scootney Farms Hunting Club, Ironwood Country Club, Fly Fisherman Club, Virginia Country Club (Long Beach, Calif.; winner 50th Intergalactic Golf Tournament 1999). Office: 18915 S Laurel Park Rd Rancho Dominguez CA 90220-6005 E-mail: jjanura@oldmaui.com.

JANUS, MARK DAVID, priest, psychologist, consultant; b. Rochester, N.Y., Mar. 31, 1953; s. Casimir Paul and Pearl Joan (Krajnik) J. BA magna cum laude, St. John Fisher Coll., Rochester, 1974; MA, Cath. U., Washington, 1978; PhD, U. Conn., 1992. Ordained priest Roman Cath. Ch., 1979. Clergy Cath. Info. Ctr., Grand Rapids, Mich., 1978-79, Paulist Ctr., Boston, 1979-83; dir. rsch. Covenant House, Boston, 1983-84; chaplain U. Conn., Storrs, 1984-89, lectr. clin. psychology, 1989-90; clinician U. Conn. Health Ctr., Storrs, 1990-91; faculty Ind. U. Med. Ctr., Indpls., 1991-92, Ohio State Coll. of Medicine, Columbus, 1992-98; pvt. practice Columbus, 1998—; chaplain Ohio State U., Columbus, 1998—. Cons. Children's Hosp. Sexual Abuse Team, Boston, 1979-84; rsch. cons. Covenant House, Toronto, Ont., Can., 1985-90; presenter on adolescent and child sexual abuse over 40 juried presentations. Author: (with others) Child Pornography & Sex Rings, 1984, Adolescent Runaways: Causes & Consequences, 1987, Running for Their Lives, 1995; contbr. articles to profl. jours.; appearances include Nightline, Can. radio and TV, numerous newspapers. Bd. dirs. Robert F. Kennedy Action Corps, Boston, 1982-2001, Madonna Hall, Marlborough, Mass., 1984-92; active Pastoral Care Com. Diocese of Norwich, Conn., 1988-92. Mem. APA, Missionary Soc. St. Paul The Apostle. Achievements include research on nature of physical and sexual abuse of homeless and runaway adolescents, on their experiences at home and on the streets, and the pastoral responses to the religious influences present in sexual abuse. Home: 98 W Lane Ave Columbus OH 43201-1021 Office: 1706 E Broad St Columbus OH 43203-2039

JANUS, TODD JEFFREY, neurologist, medical educator; b. Springfield, Ill., Oct. 25, 1955; s. Daniel John and Linda Lee Jaeger Janus; m. Margaret Ann Hawkins, Aug. 27, 1983; children: Marie Kathryn, Elizabeth Jane. BA, Drake U., 1977; PhD, Northwestern U., 1984; MD, Rush Med. Coll., 1986. Diplomate Am. Bd. Psychiatry and Neurology, Am. Bd. Clin. Pathologists. Intern in internal medicine U. Tex. Sch. of Medicine, Houston, 1986-87, resident in neurology, 1987-90; fellowship in neuro-oncology U. Tex./M.D. Anderson Cancer Ctr., Houston, 1990-92; asst. prof. dept. neurology U. Iowa Coll. Medicine, Iowa City, 1992-97; assoc. med. dir. Abbott Lab., Abbott Park, Ill., 1997—2000; asst. prof. Rush Med. Coll., Chgo., 1998—; staff physician No. Ind. Neurol. Inst. Dir. neuro-onolocy clinic U. Iowa Coll. Medicine, 1992-97; staff physician VA Med. Ctr., 1992-97. Contbr. articles to profl. jours. Recipient Eagle Scout Boy Scouts Am., 1968; recipient numerous grants. Mem. AMA, Am. Assn. for Cancer Rsch., Am. Acad. Neurology, Am. Chem. Soc., Am. Soc. for Clin. Oncology, Soc. for Neuro-Oncology. E-mail: tjanus@pol.net.

JANZEN, LEE, professional golfer; b. Austin, Minn., Aug. 28, 1964; Mem. Ryder Cup Team, 1993. Winner No. Telecom Open, 1992, Phoenix Open, 1993, U.S. Open, 1993, 98; Buick Classic, 1994; The Players Championship, 1995; Kemper Open, 1995; Sprint International, 1995. Office: Sports Link 545 Delaney Ave Ste 4 Orlando FL 32801-3866

JANZEN, NORINE MADELYN QUINLAN, medical technologist; b. Fond du Lac, Wis., Feb. 9, 1943; d. Joseph Wesley and Norma Edith (Gustin) Quinlan; m. Douglas Mac Arthur Janzen, July 18, 1970; 1 son, Justin James. BS, Marian Coll., 1965; med. technologist, St. Agnes Sch. Med. Tech., Fond du Lac, 1966; MA, Ctrl. Mich. U., 1980. Med. technologist Mayfair Med. Lab., Wauwatosa, Wis., 1966-69; supr. med. technologist Dr.'s Mason, Chamberlain, Franke, Klink & Kamper, Milw., 1969-76, Hartford-Parkview Clinic, Ltd., 1976-94; patient svc. ctrs. supr. Med. Sci. Labs., Wauwatosa, Wis., 1994-97, Poole Med. Tech. Med. Sci. Labs, 1997-98; clin. mgr. Planned Parenthood Wis., 1997-99; coord. health in bus. Hartford Parkview Clin., 1990-91, drug program coord., 1991-94; outreach coord. Cmty. Meml. Hosp., Menomonee Falls, Wis., 2000—. Co-chair joint mtg. Clin. Lab. Mgrs. Assn. and Wis. Assn. for Clin. Lab. Scientists, 1993-94. Coord. Warhawk Band Booster Uniform Project, 1997—99; mem. Dem. Nat. Com., 1973—; substitute poll worker Fond du Lac Dem. Com., 1964—65; post card ministry coord. Meth. Ch., 1996—2001, cmty. league youth col., recognition coord.; focus team leader Coll. Youth Ministries, Meth. Ch., 2000—; mem. Post Card Ministry Bd., 1998—2001; bd. dirs. Menomonee Falls Teen Ctr., 2000—. Mem.: AAUW (corr. sec. 1994—96, rec. sec. 1996—98, pub. policy chair 1998—2001, chair Evening of Literary Excellence 2001—02, pres. 2001—03, treas. 2003—, state, dist. 2 coord. 2003—), Southeastern Suprs. Group (co-chmn. 1976—77), Milw. Soc. Clin. Lab. Scientists (pres. 1971—72, bd. dirs. 1972—73, exec. sec. 1999—), Clin. Lab. Mgmt. Assn. (co-chair joint meeting 1993—94), Wis. Assn. Clin. Lab. Scientists (chmn. awards com. 1976—77, treas. 1977—81, dir. 1977—84, pres.-elect 1981—82, pres. 1982—83, chmn. awards com. 1984—85, dir. 1985—87, chmn. awards com. 1986—87, chair ann. meeting 1987—88, exec. sec. 1991—, Mem. of Yr. award 1982, 1995, numerous svc. awards), Nat. Soc. Clin. Lab. Scientists (awards com. chair 1984—87, 1988—91, nominations com. 1989—92), Am. Soc. Clin. Lab. Scientists (people to people clin. lab. scientist del. to People's Rep. China 1989, Mem. of Yr. award 1997), Warhawk Band Boosters (uniform fundraiser chair 1996—98, chair Trysting Place tent party fundraiser 1997—2000), Comms. of Wis. (chmn. 1977—79, originator), LWV, Cmty. League, Alpha Mu Tau, Alpha Delta Theta (nat. dist. chmn. 1967—69, nat. alumnae dir. 1969—71). Methodist. Home: N 98 W 17298 Dotty Way Germantown WI 53022-4618 Office: Cmty Meml Hosp W180 N 8085 Town Hall Rd Menomonee Falls WI 53051 E-mail: nmjanzen@aol.com.

JANZOW, WALTER THEOPHILUS, retired college administrator; b. Ada, Minn., Dec. 18, 1918; s. Frederick William and Emma (Wiegner) J.; m. Frances Enae Snider, June 4, 1944; children— Fred, Frank, Kathleen, Daniel. Student, Concordia Coll., 1935-37; BA, Concordia Sem., St. Louis, 1941, M. Div., 1944; MA, So. Ill. U., 1957; PhD, Nebr. U., 1970; D.D. (hon.), Concordia Sem., Springfield, Ill., 1965. Ordained to ministry Lutheran Ch., Mo. Synod, 1944; pastor Zion Luth. Ch., Mavie, Minn., 1944-45, Immanuel Luth. Ch., McIntosh, Minn., 1945-51, Murphysboro, Ill., 1951-59; prof. sociology Concordia Tchrs. Coll., Seward, Nebr., 1959-63, pres., 1963-77, dir. coll. relations, 1977-83; pres. Concordia Luth. Sem., Edmonton, Alta., Can., 1984-87. Pres. So. Ill. Dist. Luth. Ch. Mo. Synod, 1957-59 Editor: Issues in Christian Education, 1968-70, The Great Breakthrough, 1962; Contbr. articles to religious jours. Bd. dirs. State U. Nebr. Adv. Council, 1973-77. Mem. Am., Midwest Sociol. assns., Nebr. Assn. Ch. Colls. (pres. 1964-65), Nebr. Assn. Colls. and Univs. (pres. 1971-72), Soc. Sci. Study Religion, Luth. Acad. Scholarship, Luth. Human Relations Assn. Am. Home: 7515 Sherman St Lincoln NE 68506-4656 E-mail: tedjanzow@webtv.net.

JAO, MIEN, civil engineer educator; b. Nanto, Taiwan, May 30, 1963; s. Re-chang and Chung-Yin Jao; m. Wendy Chung; 1 child, Jonathan F. BS in Civil and Hydraulic Engring., Chung-Yuan U., 1985; M in Engring., Pa. State U., 1991, PhD in Civil Engring., 1995. Registered profl. engr., Tex., Pa., Va. Civil engr. Army of the Republic of China, Taiwan, 1985-87; project engr. Dept. of Transp., Taiwan, 1988-89; grad. asst. Pa. State U., University Park, 1990-94; project engr. GTS Techs. Inc., Fairfax, Va., 1995-98; asst. prof. Lamar U., Beaumont, Tex., 1998—2003, assoc. prof., 2003—. Contbr. articles to sci. and profl. jours. Recipient Gill Young Investigator award, Gill Found., 2000. Mem. ASCE, Phi Kappa Phi, Chi Epsilon, Nat. Civil Engring. Hon. Soc. (James M. Robbins Excellence-in-Teaching award 2003). Avocation: badminton. Office: Lamar U Dept Civil Engrng Beaumont TX 77710

JAQUA, RICHARD ALLEN, pathologist; b. Fort Dodge, Iowa, Apr. 15, 1938; s. John Franklin and Esther Constance (Rossing) J.; m. Mary Joanne Stewart, Dec. 29, 1969. BA magna cum laude, Yale U., 1960; MD, Harvard U., 1965. Diplomate: Am. Bd. Pathology, Am. Bd. Nuclear Medicine. Teaching fellow pathology Harvard Med. Sch., 1965-67; resident clin. pathology NIH, 1967-69; intern pathology Mass. Gen. Hosp., Boston, 1965-66, fellow tumor pathology Meml.-Sloane Kettering Cancer Center, N.Y.C., 1969-70; asst. prof. pathology U. S.D. Sch. Medicine, Vermillion, 1970-73, asso. prof., 1973-74, asso. prof., acting chmn. dept. lab. medicine, 1974-77, prof., chmn. dept. lab. medicine, 1977—2002, dir. Electron Microscopy Lab. and Clin. Virology Lab., 1979—2002; pathologist VA Hosp., Sioux Falls, SD, 1978—2002; physician Lab. Clin. Medicine, Sioux Falls, 1970—2002. Part-time prof. pathology Sch. Medicine U. S.D., 2003—. Served with USPHS, 1967-69. Recipient Outstanding Prof. awards U. S.D. Med. Students, 1971, 75, 77, 90; VA grantee, 1980-82. U. S.D. Faculty Recogition award, 1986. Fellow Coll. Am. Pathologists, Am. Soc. Clin. Pathologists; mem. Electron Microscopy Soc. Am., Am. Assn. Cancer Edn., AAAS, Internat. Acad. Pathology, Soc. Nuclear Medicine, Sigma Xi, Alpha Omega Alpha. Home: 27546 483rd Ave Canton SD 57013-5511 Office: USD Health Sci Ctr 1400 W 22nd St Sioux Falls SD 57105-1505 E-mail: rjaqua@usd.edu.

JAQUES, THOMAS FRANCIS, librarian; b. Crowley, La., Dec. 25, 1938; s. Robert E. and Frances (Broussard) J.; m. Trudy Seidel, May 16, 1964; children: Michael, Christopher. BSBA, U. Southwestern La., 1960; MS in Libr. Sci., La. State U., 1968. Cert. adminstrv. libr. La. Asst. libr. Rapides Parish Libr., Alexandria, La., 1968-73; asst. state libr. Miss. Libr. Commn., Jackson, 1973-75; state libr. State Libr. La., Baton Rouge, 1975—. Office: Office of State Library PO Box 131 Baton Rouge LA 70821-0131

JAQUITH, GEORGE OAKES, ophthalmologist; b. Caldwell, Idaho, July 29, 1916; s. Gail Belmont and Myrtle (Burch) J., m. Pearl Elizabeth Taylor, Nov. 30, 1939; children: Patricia Ann Jaquith Mueller, George, Michele Eugenie Jaquith Smith. BA, Coll. Idaho, 1938; MB, Northwestern U., 1942, MD, 1943. Intern Wesley Meml. Hosp., Chgo., 1942-43; resident opthalmology U.S. Naval Hosp., San Diego, 1946-48; pvt. practice medicine, specializing in opthalmology Brawley, Calif., 1948—. Pres. Pioneers Meml. Hosp. staff, Brawley, 1953, dir. exec. com. Calif. Med. Eye Coun., 1960—, v.p. Calif. Med. Eye Found., 1976—. Sponsor Anza coun. Boy Scouts Am., 1966—, Gold card holder Rep. Assocs., Imperial County, Calif., 1967-68, PTO. Served with USMC, USN, 1943-47 Mem. Imperial County (pres. 1961), Calif. Med. Assn. (del. 1961—), Nat., So. Calif. (dir. 1966—, chmn. med. adv. com. 1968-69), Soc. Prevention Blindness, Calif. Assn. Opthalmology (treas. 1976—), San Diego, L.A. Opthal. Socs., L.A. Rsch. Study Club, Nathan Smith Daivs Soc., Coll. Idaho Assocs., Am. Legion, VFW, Res. Officers Assn., Basenji Assn., Nat. Geneal. Soc., Cuyamaca Club (San Diego), Elks, Phi Beta Phi, Lambda Chi Alpha (Hall of Fame). Presbyterian (elder). Address: 665 Western Ave Brawley CA 92227-0511

JARAMILLO, CARLOS ALBERTO, civil engineer; b. Medellin, Colombia, Dec. 5, 1952; came to the U.S., 1986; s. Alberto and Maria Jaramillo; m. Celeste Jaramillo; children: Daniel J., Nicolas, Diego A. BCE, U. Nacional, Medellin, 1978; MS, U. Minn., 1980. Registered profl. engr., Wis., Colombia. Engr. Integral S.A., Medellin, 1977-79, sr. design engr., 1980-86; rsch. asst. St. Anthony Falls Lab., Mpls., 1979-80; civil engr. Mead & Hunt Inc., Madison, Wis., 1986-89; sr. geotech. engr. Harza Engring. Co., Chgo., 1989—2001, jr. ptnr., 1998—2001; sr. geotech. engr., ptnr. MWH Global, Chgo., 2001—. Prof. Escuela de Ingenieria de Antioquia, Medellin, 1981-86; designer numerous dams & underground structures. Cons. to public utilities, various countries 1994—; contbr. articles to profl. jours. Mem. ASCE (rock mechanics com.), U.S. Soc. on Dams, U.S. Nat. Soc. Soil Mechanics and Found. Engring., Phi Kappa Phi. Avocations: jogging, photography, philately, astronomy. Office: MWH Global Ste 1900 175 W Jackson Blvd Chicago IL 60604 Business E-Mail: carlos.a.jaramillo@mwhglobal.com.

JARAMILLO, MARI-LUCI, retired federal agency administrator; b. Las Vegas, N.Mex., June 19, 1928; BA magna cum laude, N.Mex. Highland U., 1955, MA with honors, 1959; PhD, U. N.Mex., 1970. Tchr., Albuquerque and Las Vegas, N.Mex., 1955-65; asst. prof. U. N.Mex., 1965-72, assoc. prof., chmn. dept. elem. edn., 1972-75, assoc. prof. edn., 1976-77, prof., 1977, spl. asst. to pres., 1981-82, assoc. dean Coll. Edn., 1982-85, v.p. for student affairs, 1985-87; amb. to Republic of Honduras U.S. Dept. State, 1977-80, dep. asst. sec. for Inter-Am. affairs, 1980-81; asst. v.p., dir. Ednl. Testing Service, Emeryville, Calif., 1987-93; dep. asst. sec. for Inter-Am. affairs Dept. Def., Washington, 1993-95. Bd. trustees Tomas Rivera Nat. Policy Ctr., Claremont (Calif.) Coll. Grad. Sch., 1985-93; minority recruiter Dept. State, Washington, 1990-2000; commr. Calif. Commn. of Post-Secondary Edn., Sacramento, 1990-93; active Coun. Am. Ambs., Washington, 1983—; bd. dirs. Latin Am. Scholarship Program for Am. Univs., Boston, Children's TV Workshop, N.Y.C.; cons. for curriculum, tchr. tng. and sch. reform, 1960—. Author: Madame Ambassador: The Shoe Maker's Daughter, 2002; contbr. articles to jours., chpts. to books. Bd. dirs. Internat. House, U. Calif., Berkeley, 1989-93; scholar panelist Nat. Latino Comm. Ctr., L.A., 1990—; active Bay area Network L.Am. Women, San Francisco, 1987-93. Decorated Order Francisco Morazan (Honduras), Order of Great Silver Cross (Honduras); recipient Cubberly award Stanford U., 1975, N.Mex. Disting. Svc. award, 1977, Anne Roe award Harvard U. Grad. Sch. Edn., 1986, PRIMERA award Mex. Am. Women's Nat. Assn., 1990; named Outstanding Chicana, 1975, Hon. Honduran Citizen, Govt. of Honduras, 1980, Disting. Woman of Yr., U. N.Mex. Alumni Assn., 1985, Disting. Hispanic lectr. Calif. State U. at Fullerton, 1988, Outstanding Hispanic Educator, 1988, Outstanding Leader in Edn. to Hispanic Cmty., 1991. Mem. Nat. Assn. Bilingual Edn., Latin Am. Assn., Am. Assn. Colls. for Tchr. Edn., Nat. Council La Raza. Home: 4829 Mesa Prieta Ct NW Albuquerque NM 87120-4620

JARANSON, JAMES M. psychiatrist, public health service officer; b. Thief River Falls, Minn., Oct. 2, 1947; s. John E. and Sylvia E. Jaranson. BA in English, Concordia Coll., Moorhead, Minn., 1969; MD, U. Minn., 1973, MA in Anthropology, 1976; M in Psychiat. Epidemiology, Harvard U., 1978. Diplomate Am. Bd. Psychiatry. Psychiat. cons. Indian Health Svc., Portland, Oreg., 1976—78, Pub. Health Svc., San Francisco, 1979—83; psychiatrist Regions Hosp., St. Paul, 1983—; dir. internat. mental health U. Minn. at Ramsey Med. Ctr., St. Paul, 1984—97; med. dir. Ctr. for Victims Torture, Mpls., 1989—2001; dir. cultural psychiatry U. Minn., Mpls., 1992—98, prin. investigator, refugee pop. study, 1998—. Bd. dirs. Soc. for Study of Psychiatry and Culture, Portland, Oreg.; mem. faculty dept. psychiatry and divsn. epidemiology U. Minn., Mpls., 1983—. Editor: Caring for Victims of Torture, 1998. Comdr. USPHS, 1979—83. Grantee, NIH, 1998—2003. Fellow: Am. Psychiat. Assn.; mem.: World Psychiat. Assn. (sect. officer, co-chair 1996—). Achievements include research in politically-motivated torture, refugee trauma and cultural psychiatry. Avocations: music, theater, bicycling. Home: 1950 Loras St #405 San Diego CA 92104 Office: Regions Hosp 640 Jackson St Saint Paul MN 55101 Fax: 651-254-1892. E-mail: jaran001@umn.edu.

JARBLUM, WILLIAM, lawyer; b. Havana, Cuba, Aug. 29, 1945; came to U.S., 1946; s. Richard S. and Dora F. (Nadel) J.; m. Susan P. Reich, May 24, 1970 (div. 1991); m. Loraine Gage Bassett, Jan. 4, 1992; children: Kimberly, Meredith. Student U. Va., 1962-64; B.A., C.W. Post Coll. of L.I.U., 1967; J.D., Georgetown U., 1970. Bar: N.Y. 1971, U.S. Dist. Ct. (so. and ea. dists.) N.Y. 1972. Assoc., Otterbourg, Steindler, Houston & Rosen, P.C., N.Y.C., 1970-71, Finley, Kumble, Underberg, Persky & Roth, P.C., N.Y.C., 1971-73; ptnr. Persky & Jarblum, P.C., N.Y.C., 1973-75, Fine, Tofel & Saxl, N.Y.C., 1975-77; sole practice, N.Y.C., 1977-79; ptnr. Jarblum Solomon & Fornari, P.C., N.Y.C., 1979-89, Phillips, Nizer, Benjamin, Krim & Ballon, N.Y.C., 1989-94, counsel, Buchalter, Nemer, Fields & Younger, N.Y.C. and L.A. Asst. regional dir. western states Citizens for Humphrey-Muskie, Washington, 1968. Mem. Assn. Bar City N.Y., N.Y. State Bar Assn., N.Y. County Bar Assn. (com. on securities and exchanges). Home: 6027 Sandhurst Ln # C Dallas TX 75206-4720 Office: Buchalter Nemer Fields & Younger 237 Park Ave New York NY 10017-3140 also: Buchalter Nemer Fields & Younger 601 S Figueroa St Los Angeles CA 90017-5704 also: 1583 Lindacrest Dr Beverly Hills CA 90210-2521

JARBOE, KENAN PATRICK, think-tank executive, researcher; b. Rogers City, Mich., Feb. 25, 1954; s. Louis and Mary Jarboe. BS in Engring., U. Mich., 1977, PhD, 1983. Asst. prof. U. Md., College Park, 1983—85; analyst Congl. Office Tech. Assessment, Washington, 1985—87; legis. asst. Senator Jeff Bingaman, Washington, 1987—90; mem. profl. staff US Senate Govtl. Affairs Com., Washington, 1989—90; chief economist US Senate Dem. Policy Com., Washington, 1990—92; mem. profl. staff US Senate Banking Com., Washington, 1992; sr. US strategist G7 Group, Inc., Washington, 1995—97; prin. Jarboe & Assocs., Washington, 1997—; pres. Athena Alliance, Washington, 1999—. Adj. prof. Georgetown U., Washington, 1994—. Steering com. Capitol Hill Bus. Improvement Dist., Washington, 2001; commr. Anc 6B, Washington, 1999—2003, chair, 2001—03; chair planning com. Capper Carrollsburg Cmty. Devel. Corp., Washington, 2002. Fellow Sr. fellow, Work and Tech. Inst., 1996—98. Home and Office: 911 E Capitol St SE Washington DC 20003

JARBOE, MARK ALAN, lawyer; b. Flint, Mich., Aug. 19, 1951; s. Lloyd Aloysius and Helen Elizabeth (Frey) J.; m. Patricia Kovel, Aug. 20, 1971; 1 child, Alexander. Student, No. Mich. U., 1968-69; AB with high distinction, U. Mich., 1972; JD magna cum laude, Harvard U., 1975. Bar: Minn. 1975, U.S. Dist. Ct. Minn. 1975, U.S. Ct. Appeals (8th cir.) 1975, U.S. Ct. Appeals (7th cir.) 1993. Law clk. to presiding justice Minn. State Ct., St. Paul, 1975-76; from assoc. to prin. Dorsey & Whitney LLP, Mpls., 1976-81, ptnr., 1982—. Lectr. U. Minn. Law Sch., Hamline U. Sch. Law. Contbr. articles to profl. jours. Pres. parish coun. Ch. of Christ the King, Mpls., 1981-83. Mem. Fed. Bar Assn., Native Am. Bar Assn., Minn. Am. Indian Bar Assn., Mensa, Phi Beta Kappa.

Republican. Roman Catholic. Home: 4816 W Lake Harriet Pky Minneapolis MN 55410-1903 Office: Dorsey & Whitney LLP 50 S 6th St Ste 1500 Minneapolis MN 55402-1498 E-mail: jarboe.mark@dorsey.com.

JARC, FRANK ROBERT, retail executive; b. Waukegan, Ill., Apr. 4, 1942; s. Frank Joseph and Edith Gertrude (Cankar) J.; m. MeRandy Jarc; 1 dau., Jennifer. BS in Indsl. Engring, U. Mich., 1964; MBA, Harvard U., 1967. Mgmt. trainee Mich. Bell Telephone Co., 1964; with regulatory proceedings dept. United Airlines, Chgo., 1966; fin. analyst Ford Motor Co., Dearborn, Mich., 1967, Freeport Minerals Co., N.Y.C., 1972-73; Fin. analyst Esmark, Inc., Chgo., 1973; controller subs. Swift Grocery Products Co., Chgo., 1973-75; fin. v.p. subs. Estech, Inc., Chgo., 1975-77; v.p. consumer products subs. Estech Gen. Chem. Co., Agrl. Chems. Corp., Chgo., 1977-80; exec. v.p., chief fin. officer Wilson Foods, Oklahoma City, 1980-87; sr. v.p., chief fin. officer United Airlines, Chgo., 1987; exec. v.p., chief fin. officer R.R. Donnelley Co., Chgo., 1987-95; exec. v.p., CFO Viking Office Products, L.A., 1996-99; sr. v.p. corp. devel. Office Depot, 1999—. Chmn. audit com. Brady Corp., 2000—. Bd. mgrs. YMCA. Capt. USAF, 1967-71. Mem. Evans Scholarship Alumni Assn., Chgo. Club, Execs. Club Chgo., Chgo. Commonwealth Club, Econ. Club. Home: 501 Oakwood # 3E Lake Forest IL 60045 Office: Office Depot 950 W 190th St Torrance CA 90502-1001

JARCHO, JUDITH LYNN, artist, art educator; b. Mpls., Mar. 24, 1944; d. Paul and Lillian (Garetz) Brazman; m. Michael Jarcho, Nov. 24, 1968; children: Jason M., Johanna Molly. BFA, Mpls. Coll. Art & Design, 1968; tchg. credential elem. and art edn., Coll. St. Rose, Albany, N.Y., 1975. Grades K-6 art tchr. Albany Sch. Dist., 1971-74; art tchr. Portrait Soc., La Jolla, Calif., 1996, San Digeto Art Assn., Del Mar, Calif., 1996, El Cajon (Calif.) Art Assn., 1997. Juror Del Mar Art Fair/Art Exhbn., 1995, El Cajon Art Assn. Annual Exhbn., 1996, San Diego Art Inst., 1998. Works exhibited San Diego Mus. Art, 1994, Rose-Hulman Inst. Tech., Terre Haute, Ind., 1994, Nat. Arts Club, N.Y.C., 1994, Poudre Valley Artist League, Denver, 1995, Tijuana (Mexico) Cultural Ctr., 1995, Hampton Classic, Bridgehampton, N.Y., 1995, Perry House Galleries, Old Town Alexandria, Va., 1995, Linda Joslin Gallery, La Jolla, Calif., 1995, Mpls. Found., 1996, Robert Mondavi Food & Wine Ctr., Orange County, Calif., 1996, The Parrish Art Mus., South Hampton, N.Y., 1996, San Diego Mus. Art, 1995-99, Univ. Club, San Diego, 1998. Philantropist Helen Woodward Animal Ctr., Rancho Santa Fe, Calif., 1996-98; past pres. San Diego Mus. of Art Artist Guild. Named Entrepreneur of Yr., Vishe Corp., San Diego, 1998, Best Canine Artist, Manhattan Guest mag., 2001, Overall Gold award ann. report competition League Am. Comm. Profls., 2001. E-mail: jjarcho@msn.com.

JARDETZKY, OLEG, medical educator, researcher; b. Yugoslavia, Feb. 11, 1929; came to U.S., 1949, naturalized, 1955; s. Wenceslas Sigismund and Tatiana (Taranovsky) J.; m. Erika Albensberg, July 21, 1975; children by previous marriage: Alexander, Theodore, Paul. BA, Macalester Coll., 1950, D.Sc. (hon.), 1974; MD, U. Minn., 1954, PhD (Am. Heart Assn. fellow), 1956; postgrad., U. Cambridge, Eng., 1965-66; LL.D. (hon.), Calif. Western U., 1978; MD (hon.), U. Graz, Austria, 1994; Doctorate (hon.), U. Aix-Marseille II, 1998. Research fellow U. Minn., 1954-56; NRC fellow Calif. Inst. Tech., 1956-57; asso. Harvard U., 1957-59, asst. prof. pharmacology, 1959-66; dir. biophysics and pharmacology Merck & Co., 1966-68, exec. dir., 1968-69; prof. Stanford U., 1969—, dir. Stanford Magnetic Resonance Lab., 1975-97, dir. NMR Center, Sch. Medicine, 1983-84; dir. emeritus Stanford Magnetic Resonance Lab., 1998—. Vis. fellow Merton Coll., Oxford (Eng.) U., 1976; cons., vis. prof., lectr. in field; chmn. Internat. Coun. on Magnetic Resonance in Biology, 1972-74; dir. Internat Sch. on Magnetic Resonance in Biology, Ettore Majorana Ctr., Sicily, 1993—; chmn. biotech. panel World Fedn. Scientists, 1998—. Contbr. articles to profl. jours.; mem. editorial bd. Jour. Theoretical Biology, 1961-88, Molecular Pharmacology, 1965-75, Jour. Medicinal Chemsitry, 1970-78, Biochimica Biophypica Acta, 1970-86, Revs. on Bioenergetics, 1972-89, Biomembrane Revs., 1972-80, Jour. Magnetic Resonance in Biology and Medicine, 1986—2000, Jour. Magnetic Resonance, 1993—2000. Recipient career devel. award USPHS, 1959-66, Kaiser award, 1973, Von Humboldt award, 1977, Pauling medal, 1984, Grand Gold Honor insignia (Austria), 1993, Founder's gold medal Internat. Coun. Magnetic Resonance in Biology, 1994, Prix Marianne Dessewffy Internat. Conf. of Genealogy and Heraldry, 1998; grantee NSF, 1957—, NIH, 1957—; travel fellow Am. Physiol. Soc., 1959. Fellow AAAS; mem. Am. Chem. Soc., Am. Soc. Biol. Chemistry and Molecular Biology, Biophys. Soc., Assn. Advanced Tech. in Biomed. Scis. (pres. 1981-88), Internat. Soc. Magnetic Resonance (chmn. divns. of biology and Medicine 1986-89), Phi Beta Kappa, Sigma Xi, Alpha Omega Alpha. Home: 950 Casanueva Pl Stanford CA 94305-1068 Office: Stanford U CCSR 269 Campus Dr Rm 3155-B Stanford CA 94305-5174 E-mail: jardetzky@stanford.edu.

JARDINE, MURRAY DONALD, political science educator; b. Regina, Sask., Can., Oct. 14, 1954; s. Donald James and Jean Borland Jardine. BS, U. Regina, 1977; BBA, Tex. Tech. U., 1983, MA, 1985; PhD, Duke U., 1992. Vis. asst. prof. polit. sci. La. State U., Baton Rouge, 1990-96; vis. asst. prof. State U. West Ga., Carrollton, 1996-97; asst. prof. polit. sci. Auburn (Ala.) U., 1997-99, assoc. prof., 1999—. Asst. dir. Eric Voegelin Inst., La. State U., 1991-95. Author: Speech and Political Practice, 1998; editor: Fundamental Issues in Political, Economic, and Social Theory, 1998; contbr. articles to profl. jours. Recipient Alpha Lambda Delta Freshman Honor Soc. award for superior instrn. freshman stuents, 1995, Pi Sigma Alpha Outstanding Polit. Sci. Prof. award, 2002. Mem. Am. Polit. Sci. Assn., Am. Acad. Religion, Rhetoric Soc. Am. Roman Catholic. Office: Auburn U Dept Polit Sci Auburn AL 36849-5208 E-mail: jardimu@mail.auburn.edu.

JARECKI, HENRY GEORGE, physician, financial executive; b. Stettin, Germany, Apr. 15, 1933; s. Max Jarecki and Gerda Kunstmann; m. Gloria Friedland, 1957; children: Andrew, Thomas, Eugene, Nicholas. MD, U. Heidelberg, Germany, 1957. Diplomate Am. Bd. Psychiatry and Neurology. Dir. Mocatta Metals Corp., N.Y.C., 1970-89, Mocatta & Goldsmid Ltd., London, 1973-89, Mocatta Hong Kong Ltd., 1975-89; chmn. Brody, White & Co. Inc., N.Y.C., 1971-95, Brody White Ltd, London, 1989-95, Guana Island Hotel Corp., British Virgin Islands, 1975—, Falconwood Corp., N.Y.C., 1976—, MovieFone, Inc., N.Y.C., 1989-99, PsychoGenics, Inc., Hawthorne, N.Y., 1998—. Asst. clin. prof. dept. psychiatry Sch. Medicine Yale U., New Haven, 1970—; gov. BVI Cmty. Coll., British Virgin Islands, 1989—; trustee Inst. Internat. Edn., 2000—; bd. dirs. Sotheby's Holdings, Inc., 2000—. Author: Modern Psychiatric Treatment, 1971; contbr. articles to profl. jours. Adv. coun. Princeton U., Yale U. Sch. Medicine Dept. Psychiatry, 1992—; trustee Am. Mus. Natural History, 1991-99; bd. dirs. Botanic Soc. Brit. V.I., 1986—, Chgo. Bd. Trade, 1993-96; internat. liaison com. Food Corps Program, 1987-95, Island Resources Found., Tortola, Brit. Virgin Is., 1988—. Mem. Nat. Futures Assn. (bd. dirs. 1979-93), Am. Psychiat. Assn. (Presdl. Commendation 1984). Office: Falconwood Corp 3rd Fl 565 5th Ave New York NY 10017-2413 E-mail: hj@jarecki.com.

JARECKIE, GRETCHEN KINSMAN FILLMORE, retired English language educator; b. Hanover, N.H., Apr. 19, 1927; d. Ernest George and Gretchen Mary (Kinsman) Fillmore; m. Stephen Barlow Jareckie, Aug. 10, 1959. BA cum laude, Syracuse U., 1949; MA, Mt. Holyoke Coll., 1968; Cert. of Advanced Grad. Study, Assumption Coll., 1982. English tchr. Jericho High Sch., Jericho Center, Vt., 1952-53, Meml. Jr. High Sch., Beverly, Mass., 1955-59, Utica (N.Y.) Free Acad., 1959-61, Wachusett Regional High Sch., Holden, Mass., 1961-67; English and music tchr. Brigham Acad., Bakersfield, Vt., 1953-54; asst. prof. English Anna Maria Coll., Paxton, Mass., 1968-74; instr. in English Framingham (Mass.) State Coll., 1974-80; ret., 1980. Author: To the Uttermost Parts of the Earth: Missionaries Who Went Out from Holden's First Congregational Church from 1818 to 1939, 1995. Mem. MLA, Worcester Mt. Holyoke Club. Democrat. Congregationalist. Avocations: music, research, writing. Home: 47 Mount View Dr Holden MA 01520-2137

JARECKIE, STEPHEN BARLOW, museum curator; b. Orange, N.J., Feb. 18, 1929; s. Eugene Albert and Doris Condit (Brittin) J.; m. Gretchen Kinsman Fillmore, Aug. 10, 1959. BA, Lehigh U., 1951; MA, Syracuse U., 1961. Installation asst. Munson-Williams-Proctor Inst., Utica, N.Y., 1955-60, edn. asst., 1960-61; registrar Worcester (Mass.) Art Mus., 1961-83, assoc. in photography, 1962-69, assoc. curator photography, 1969-73, curator photography, 1973-94, curator of photography emeritus, 1995—; photo. adv. Fitchburg (Mass.) Art Mus., 1996—. Author: WAM catalogue, The Early Republic: Consolidation of Revolutionary Goals, 1976, American Photography: 1840-1900, 1976, Photographers of the Weimar Republic, 1986; contbr. to catalogue, pamphlets, articles to mus. lit. With AUS, 1951-53. Guest Fed. Republic of Germany for study of republic's museums, 1967. Mem. U.S. Naval Inst. (assoc.) Episcopalian. Achievements include building scale model original bldgs., grounds of Proctor Inst., 1957-60. Home: 47 Mount View Dr Holden MA 01520-2137 Office: 185 Elm St Fitchburg MA 01420-7503

JARES, DANIEL JOHN, secondary school educator; b. Berwyn, Ill., Nov. 7, 1948; s. Laddie Joseph Jares and Ethel Jenny Hemmer. BA in Social Studies Edn., U. Ill., 1970; MAT, U. Fla., 1974. Tchr. social studies Addison Trail H.S., Addison, Ill., 1970—. Mem.: Nat. Coun. Social Studies. United Church Of Christ. Home: 1331 S Finley Rd # 407 Lombard IL 60148 Office: Addison Train High Sch 213 N Lombard Rd Addison IL 60101

JARLES, RUTH SEWELL, education educator; d. Nashville Clyde Sewell and Zetta Marie Hurt; m. Terry Waters Milligan, June 16, 1990; m. Marion Evert Jarles, Dec. 19, 1957 (div. Mar. 1980); children: Leslie Marie Murphy, Eva Colleen Wakeley, Brian Keith. AA, Western Okla. State Coll., 1976; BA magna cum laude, U. Colo., Colorado Springs, 1982; MDiv, U. Denver, 1985, PhD, 1993. Dir. Christian edn. Patrick Henry Village Army Chapel, Heidelberg, Germany, 1973—74; dir. curriculum Grace Child Devel. Ctr., Altus, Okla., 1976—77; dir. Christian edn. First Congl. Ch., Colorado Springs, Colo., 1980—84; asst. to the dir. joint PhD program U. Denver, Iliff Sch. Theology, 1991—92; adj. faculty, tchg. or rsch. asst. U. Denver, Iliff Sch. Theology, Front Range and Auraria C.C., 1983—98; asst. materials sci. br. Nat. Renewable Energy Lab., Golden, Colo., 1994—95; exec. dir. Colo. Libr. Assn., Denver, 1995—98; gen. edn. faculty Art Inst. Colo., Denver, 1998—. Seminar leader Gender Differences in Comm. in the Workplace; session convenor, panel mem. Women in Religion. Contbr. articles to profl. jours. Student senate Iliff Sch. Theology, Denver, 1984—86; mentor students cmty. svc. projects Art Inst. Colo., Denver, 1997—2002; chair/mem. South Africa task force, race and religion com., women's com. Iliff Sch.Theology, Denver, 1984—92; mem. publs. com. Colo. Women's Agenda, Denver, 1993—95; chair/mem. edn., fin., adminstrv. bd., music and fine arts, peace with justice coms. Trinity United Meth. Ch., Denver, 1984—92; mem. exec. com. Nat. Renewable Energy Lab. Women's Network, Golden, 1994—95; active Art Inst. Colo. christmas project Denver Safe Ho., 2001—02. Recipient E. Craig Brandenburg award, United Meth. Ch.; scholar Ea. Star Tng. awards for Religious Leadership, The Grand Chpt. Colo., Order Ea. Star, 1984—86; Oliver Read Whitley scholar, Iliff Sch. Theology, Seminarian scholar, Ctr. for Biblic Studies, Jerusalem, Israel, Ga. Harkness scholar, United Meth. Ch. Mem.: AAUW, Denver Art Mus., Nat. Women's History Mus., Nat. Mus. for Women in the Arts. Home: 2457 Ingalls St Edgewater CO 80214 Office: Art Inst Colo 1200 Lincoln St Denver CO 80203

JARMA, DONNA MARIE, secondary education educator; b. Portsmouth, Va., Aug. 31, 1949; d. Harry A. Sr. and Dreau M. (Schaedel) J. AA, Temple (Tex.) Jr. Coll., 1969; BA, U. Mary-Hardin Baylor, 1971; MA, Tex. Woman's U., 1990, PhD, 2003. Tchr. English and Spanish Troy H.S., 1971—77, Howe H.S., 1977—2002. Mem. campus improvement com., Howe Ind. Sch. Dist., 1995-96, mem. curriculum com., 1993; instr. English Grayson County Coll.; instr. Tex A&M U., Commerce, Tex. Contbr. articles to The Leaflet and Inland, English in Tex. Lector and Cath. Christian Doctrine, St. Mary's Cath. Ch., Sherman, Tex., 1988—. Named Tchr. of the Yr., Region 10, Tex. Edn. Assn., 1999, Tchr. of Yr. Wal-Mart, 2000. Mem. NCTE (presenter 1999), Tex. Coun. Tchrs. English (presenter 1994-2003, English and Lang. Arts Educator of Yr. 1998-99), Tex. Gifted/Talented (presenter, Austin, 1993-97). Roman Catholic. Avocations: writing, music, book collecting, bicycling, computers. Home: 2300 W Taylor St Sherman TX 75092-2765 E-mail: djarm@texoma.net.

JARMIE, NELSON, physicist, consultant; b. Santa Monica, Calif., Mar. 24, 1928; s. Louis and Ruth (Wydman) J. BS, Calif. Inst. Tech., 1948; PhD, U. Calif., Berkeley, 1953. Staff mem. Los Alamos Sci. Lab., 1953-97. Co-founder Pajarito Ski Area, 1957; Los Alamos Sci. Lab. cons. for Dept. Energy regulatory compliance; vis. prof. U. Calif., Santa Barbara, 1960; adj. prof. U. N.Mex., 1957-71; mem. adv. coun. Los Alamos Grad. Ctr., 1958-88; participant Vis. Scientist Program, 1965-71; field mycologist Nat. Park Svc., 1991-98; rsch. on nuclear and particle physics, astrophysics and mycology; cons. for conduct of ops. and quality assurance fed. regulations; taxonomist of macromycetes cons., 1997—. Contbr. numerous articles to sci. jours. and mags.; rsch. in nuclear and particle physics, astrophysics and taxonomic mycology. Mem. Econ. Devel. Council Los Alamos County, N.Mex., 1968. Recipient Disting. Performance award Los Alamos Nat. Lab., 1986. Fellow AAAS, Am. Phys. Soc.; mem. Mycol. Soc. Am., N.Am. Mycol. Soc., Am. Assn. Physics Tchrs., Sigma Xi, Tau Beta Pi. Achievements include research in light-nuclei energy levels; 3-body breakup, nucleon-nucleus scattering, astrophysical reactions; kinematic codes, straggling calculations and infrared laser diagnostics; fundamental properties of antimatter; field surveys of macromycetes.

JARMOLOWICZ, C. RENEE, artist, art educator; b. Detroit, Apr. 27, 1951; d. Russell Richard Bauer and Coramae (Isgrig) Brodeur; m. John Arthur Jarmolowicz, Aug. 20, 1977; children: Monica Joy, Luke Edward. BA, Siena Heights U., Adrian, Mich., 1974; attended, Mich. State U., East Lansing, 1977. High sch. art instr. Marlette (Mich) Cmty. Schs., 1975-79; art instr. Cros-Lex Cmty. Edn., Croswell, Mich., 1982-83, 85-86; elem. art instr. St. Edward on the Lake Sch., Lakeport, Mich., 1985-86; elem. art instr. Sts. Peter and Paul Sch., Ruth, Mich., 1990-92; elem. art. cons. for spl. gifted consortium Huron Cty. Intermediate Sch. Dist., Bad Axe, Mich., 1991; pvt. art instr. Our Lady of Lake Huron Sch., Harbor Beach, Mich., 1992-95, Hummingbird's Quill Calligraphy & Design Studio, Deckerville, Mich., 1992-96; instr. Valley Scribes, Midland, Mich., 1997, Mich. Assn. Calligraphers, Royal Oak, 1994—; instr., adj. faculty St. Clair Cty. Cmty. Coll., Port Huron, Mich., 1995—2003; owner, artist Hummingbird's Quill Calligraphy & Design Studio, Deckerville, Mich., 1991—2002, Artist Alcove, Deckerville, 2003—; facilitator drawing galleries program Detroit Inst. Arts, 2003—. Spkr., demonstrator Vis. Artist's Day, Ling Elem. Sch., Hemlock, Mich., 1994, Sororian Club, Deckerville, 1996, Mich. State U. Ext., 4-H Visual Arts and Crafts Workshop, Kettunen Ctr., Tustin, Mich., 1998, Kerrytown Dist. Bookfest, Ann Arbor, Mich., 2003; vol. instr. Assn. Calligraphic Arts & Speedball Arts Products Co.; instr. We. Res. Calligraphers, Cleve., 2000, 21st Internat. Gathering of Lettering Artists, Boston, 2001, Hollander's Sch. Book & Paper Arts, Ann Arbor, Mich., 2002—, New Orleans So. Arts Assn., 2003. Artist: (letter arts-mixed media with calligraphy) Rites of Passage, 1996 (First prize 1996, Juror's Acknowledgement 1996), Untitled, 1997, (Juror's award 1997), (handmade manuscript book-mixed media with calligraphy) Friendship Garden, 1997 (Juror's award 1997, Merit award 1997), Homage to the Creator I - Litany of Trees, 1998 (First place 1998), (handmade book-mixed media) Woods, 1998 (Best of Show 1998), Earth Woman, 1999 (second place 1999), Act of Contrition, 1999 (Best of Mixed Media 1999). Election inspector Marion Twp. Election Bd., Deckerville, 1992—2002, election inspector, chair, 1996—2000. Recipient Second Place award Port Sanilac Art in the Park VIII, 1997, First Place award Lexington Fine Arts Fair, 1997, Internat. Art Fest, 1997, 3d place award Port Sanilac Art in the Park X, 1999, 2d place award Arts Expo, 2000; Marjorie H. Pavelich Calligraphy Study grant, 2000. Mem. Mich. Assn. Calligraphers (chair 20th anniversary com. 1997), Assn. for the Calligraphic Arts, Port Sanilac Fine Arts Assn., Valley Scribes, Detroit Artists Market, Detroit Inst. Arts. Studio: Artist Alcove 4150 Mills Rd Deckerville MI 48427-9390

JARMON, LAWRENCE, developmental communications educator; b. L.A., Nov. 7, 1946; s. Robert and Movella (Young) J. Student, Harbor C.C., Wilmington, Calif., 1966; BA in Phys. Edn., Calif. State U., 1969; MS in Phys. Edn., U. Wash., 1972; EdD in Edn. Adminstrn., Wash. State U., 1975; MA in Adminstrn. Health and Safety, Calif. State U., L.A., 1988. Cert. alcohol and drug problems specialist. Athletic dir., instr. dept. phys. edn. L.A. SW Coll., 1975—86, agy. dir. summer program for disadvantaged youth, 1975—94, asst. dean instruction, 1976, project adminstr. NCAA, 1977—79; instr. health edn. Golden West Coll., Huntington Beach, Calif., 1978; instr. dept. English Calif. State U., L.A., 1986; instr. dept. edn. Nat. U., L.A., 1986-88; prof. devel. comm. L.A. S.W. Coll., 1988—, staff devel. coord., dir. nat. youth sports program, 1992-96, dir. coll. recruitment and cmty. rels., 1997-99, supr. Learning Resource Ctr., 1997—, v.p. to pres. student svcs., 2000—01; spl. asst. to exec. dir. facilities, planning and devel. W. L.A. Coll., Culver City, Calif., 2001—02, dean student svcs., 2002—. Author numerous booklets, manuscripts and manuals on sports programs and edn. qualifications and policies. Bd. dirs. Black Edn. Commn., L.A. Unified Sch. Dist., Calif. State U., L.A. Alumni Assn., Involvement for Young Achievers, L.A., L.A. Police Dept. Football Centurions, Paradise Ch. Found., Inc., L.A., Pop Warner Little Scholars, Inc., Phila.; employee assistance program liaison officer L.A. Cmty. Dist.; asst. exe. dirs. Cmty. Coll. Dist., 2001-. Named one of Outstanding Young Men of Am., 1980, 81. Mem. AHHPERD, Am. Alliance Health Edn., Am. Assn. Sch. Adminstrs., Calif. State U. Alumni Assn., U. Wash. Alumni Assn., Wash. State U. Alumni Assn., Calif. Assn. Health, Calif. C.C. Chief Student Svc. Adminstrs. Assn., Phys. Edn. and Recreation, Calif. State Athletic Dirs. Assn., L.A. Jr. C. of C., Nat. Interscholastic Athletic Adminstrs. Assn., Phi Delta Kappa, Kappa Alpha Psi. Office: West LA Coll 9000 Overland Ave Culver City CA 90230-3519 Fax: 310-287-4327. E-mail: jarmonl@wlac.edu.

JARMUSCH, JIM, director, actor; b. Akron, Ohio; Actor: (films) American Autobahn, 1984, Straight to Hell, 1987, Helsinki Napoli All Night Long, 1987, Leningrad Cowboys Go to America, 1989, The Golden Boat, 1990, In The Soup, 1992, Iron Horsemen, 1994, Tigrero: A Film That Was Never Made, 1994, Blue in the Face, 1995, Typewriter, the Rifle & the Movie Camera, 1996, Cannes Man, 1996, Sling Blade, 1996, Divine Trash, 1998, (TV series) Fishing With John, 1991, American Cinema, 1994; writer, dir., editor, prodr., composer: Permanent Vacation, 1982 (Joseph von Sternberg prize Mannheim, Internat. Critics prize Figueira da Foz, Portugal 1981); dir., writer, editor: Stranger Than Paradise, 1984 (Camera D'Or Cannes Film Festival 1984, Best Picture of Yr. Nat. Soc. Film Critics 1984); dir., writer: Down By Law, 1986 (Best Film award Locarno, Best Fgn. Film Norway, Denmark and Israel), Mystery Train, 1989 (Highest Artistic Achievement prize Cannes Film Festival), Dead Man, 1995 (World Premiere Cannes Film Festival 1995, Felix award Best Non-European Film 1996, Best Cinematography award N.Y. Critics Cir. 1996); dir., writer, prodr.: Ghost Dog: The Way of the Samurai, 1999; dir., co-writer: Coffee and Cigarettes (Somewhere in California), 1993 (Golden Palm Cannes Film Festival 1993); exec. prodr.: When Pigs Fly, 1993; dir., cinematographer: Year of the Horse, 1997; cinematographer: You Are Not I, 1981; dir., writer, prodr.: Night on Earth, 1991 (Grand award Best Feature Film Houston Internat. Film Festival 1992, Ind. Spirit award Best Cinematography 1993); dir.: Coffee and Cigarettes, 1986, Coffee and Cigarettes (Memphis version), 1989.

JARNAGAN, HARRY WILLIAM, JR., project manager; b. Cedar Rapids, Iowa, Nov. 7, 1953; s. Harry William and Virginia Lillian (Grusy) J.; m. Anne Therese Tompkins, June 7, 1975; children: Douglas William, Michael Patrick, Marianne Virginia. BS, U.S. Mil. Acad., 1975; M of Engring., Tex. A&M, 1984. Registered profl. engr., Tex. Project mgr. Dunbar & Dickson, Inc., Clute, Tex., 1980-83, 84-85; grad. tchg. asst. Tex. A&M U., Coll. Sta., 1983-84; cost. engr. Bechtel Power Corp., Houston, 1985-87; project control engr. Tenn. Valley Authority, 1987-88, Fluor-Daniel, Inc., Rochester, NY, 1988-90, MK-Ferguson Co., Oak Ridge, Tenn., 1990-95; mgr. Avlis project controls U.S. Enrichment Corp., Livermore, Calif., 1995-97; western region project controls mgr. Internat. Tech. Corp., Pleasanton, Calif., 1997-98; project mgr. Hatch Mott McDonald, San Jose, Calif., 1998—. Capt. U.S. Army, 1975-80. Mem.: Am. Assn. Cost Engrs. (pres.), Tau Beta Pi. Lutheran. Avocations: running, weight lifting, sky diving. Home: 875 Henderson Way Tracy CA 95376-8944 Office: Hatch Mott McDonald 3825 Hopyary Rd Ste 240 Pleasanton CA 94588-3232 E-mail: harry.jarnagan@vta.org.

JARNECKE, ROY WILLIAM, clinical psychologist; b. Hammond, Ind., Oct. 9, 1949; s. William Grover and Eileen Colma (Dempsey) J.; m. Barbara Jane Roop Jarnecke, Sept. 11, 1972; children: Erica, Jennifer, Rachel, Andrew. BS, Ball State U., Muncie, Ind., 1971; MA, Miami U., Oxford, Ohio, 1974, PhD, 1979. Lic. clin. psychologist, Va. Bd. Psychology. Coord. adolescent inpatient svcs. Regional Mental Health Ctr., Kokomo, Ind., 1977-81; regional coord. Middle Peninsula Northern Neck Counseling Ctr., Warsaw, Va., 1981-84; clin. psychologist Counseling and Psychol. Assocs., Fredericksburg, 1984-96; adjunct faculty Mary Washington Coll., Fredericksburg, Va., 1987—; clin. psychologist Behavioral Healthcare of Fredericksburg, Va., 1996—. Bd. dirs. Serenity Home, Fredericksburg, 1985-89, 94-98, Fredericksburg Personal Counseling Svc., 1986-91; bd. dirs., v.p., treas. Rappahannock Mediation Ctr., Fredericksburg, 1989-94; adminstrv. dir. Counseling and Psychol. Assocs., Fredericksburg, 1984-96. Author: Student Guide to Child Development, 1973, Student Guide to Human Development 3rd edit., 1972, 4th edit., 1974; contbr. articles to profl. jours. Soccer coach Stafford (Va.) Recreational Soccer League, 1987—98; psychol. cons. Big Brothers./Big Sisters, 1991—; actice in cmty. theatre; bd. dirs. Stagedoor Prodns., 2001—; elder, clk. of session The Presbyn. Ch., Fredericksburg, 1989—92. Recipient Faulkner award Big Bros. Big Sisters, Fredericksburg, 1994, Profl. Svc. award Mental Heath Assn. Fredericksburg, 2002. Mem. APA, Va. Acad. Clin. Psychology, Va. Psychol. Assn. Presbyterian. Avocations: singing, basketball, softball, civil war history, genealogy. Home: 11 Fairfax Cir Fredericksburg VA 22405-2914 Office: Behavioral Healthcare of Fredericksburg 312 Progress St Ste 200 Fredericksburg VA 22401-3356 E-mail: rjarneck@netzero.com.

JAROFF, LEON MORTON, magazine editor; b. Detroit, Feb. 27, 1927; s. Abraham and Ruth (Rockita) J.; m. Claire Lynn Fox, Aug. 15, 1954 (div. Nov. 1975); children: Peter, Jill, Susan, Nicholas, Jennifer; m. Mary Katherine Moran, Jan. 10, 1976. BS in Elec. Engring. and Math., U. Mich., 1950. Writer Materials and Methods Mag., N.Y.C., 1950-51; researcher, reporter, corr. Life Mag., N.Y.C., Detroit, Chgo., 1951-58; corr., assoc. editor, sr. editor Time Mag., N.Y.C., Detroit, Chgo., 1958-79, scis. editor N.Y.C., 1985-87, contbr., 1988—; founder, mng. editor Discover Mag., N.Y.C., 1980-84. Co-chair bd. for student publs. U. Mich., 1992-98; cons. Internat. Astron. Union's Working Group on Near-Earth Objects. Author: The New Genetics, 1991, also 44 Time mag. cover stories. Trustee Neurosci. Rsch. Found., La Jolla, Calif.; bd. dirs. Rogosin Inst., N.Y.C.; mem. Coun. Media Integrity, 2001-. With USN, 1944-45. Recipient Robert S. Ball Meml. award Aviation Space Writers Assn., 1978, Excellence award, 1989; Sci. Writing award AAAS/Westinghouse Corp., 1978, Sci. Writing award Am. Inst. Physics/U.S. Steel Corp., 1976, 82, 83; Asteroid 7829 Jaroff named in his honor. Fellow AAAS, Com. for Sci. Investigation of Claims of the Paranormal; mem. Am. Soc. Mag. Editors (exec. com. 1984-85), Am. Inst. Physics (adv. com. 1982—). Jewish. Avocations: tennis, computers, chess. Home: PO Box 1080 East Hampton NY 11937-0901 Office: Time Mag Time & Life Bldg 1271 Avenue Of The Americas New York NY 10020-1300 E-mail: neonleo@aol.com.

JARON, DOV, biomedical engineer, educator; b. Tel Aviv, Oct. 29, 1935; came to U.S., 1958, naturalized, 1972; s. Meir and Sara (Levit) Yarovsky; m. Brooke E. Boberg, Sept. 16, 1978; children: Shulamit, Tamara. BS magna cum laude, U. Denver, 1961; PhD, U. Pa., 1967. Sr. research asso. Maimonides Med. Center, Bklyn., 1967-70; dir. surg. research Sinai Hosp. of Detroit, 1970-73; asso. prof. elec. engring. U. R.I., Kingston, 1973-77, prof., 1977-79, coordinator biomed. engring., 1973-79; prof. biomend. engring. and sci. Drexel U., Phila., 1979—, dir. Biomed. Engring. and Sci. Inst., 1979-96. Calhoun disting. prof., 1998—; vis. prof. elec. engring. Rutgers U., New Brunswick, N.J., 1968-73; adj. prof. biomed. engring. Wayne State U., 1971-73; adj. prof. physiology Temple U. Sch. Medicine, 1980—; adj. prof. radiology Jefferson Med. Coll., 1983—; dir. Div. Biol. and Critical Systems, NSF, 1991-93; assoc. dir. Nat. Ctr. Rsch. Resources, dir. biomedical tech. NIH, 1996-98. Contbr. articles to sci. jours. NSF, NIH, Office Naval Research, pvt. founds. research grantee. Fellow AAAS, IEEE, Am. Inst. for Med. and Biol. Engring.; mem. AAUP, Internat. Fedn. for Med. and Biol. Engring. (pres. 2000-2003), Biomed. Engring. Soc., Am. Soc. for Engring. Edn., Assn. for Advancement Med. Instrumentation, Internat. Soc. Artificial Organs, Am. Soc. for Artificial Internal Organs, Biophys. Soc., N.Y. Acad. Scis., Engring. in Medicine and Biology of IEEE (pres. 1986-87), Sigma Xi, Tau Beta Pi, Eta Kappa Nu. Achievements include research of cardiac assist devices, cardiovascular dynamics and modeling, biomed. instrumentation. Home: 122 Bethlehem Pike Philadelphia PA 19118-2815 Office: Drexel U Sch Biomed Engring Sch and Health Systems 32nd and Chestnut St Philadelphia PA 19104 E-mail: dov.jaron@drexel.edu.

JAROS, ROBERT JAMES, information technology executive; b. Port Reading, NJ, June 30, 1939; s. Michael and Marian (Kurta) J.; children: Marian Reilly, Jennifer, Christina Student, Rutgers U., 1957-65. With Prudential Ins. Co., Newark, 1957-77; sr. sys. analyst, project leader Ins. Svcs. Office, N.Y.C., 1977-81; project mgr. Shearson Lehman Bros. Inc., N.Y.C., 1981-88; cons. G &

J Assocs., Middletown, NJ, 1988—; commn. Middletown Housing Authority, 1995—. Trustee, v.p. Lin-Mid Corp., 1997—. Mem. Middletown Twp. Transp. Com., 1988—; mem., past pres. Rolling Knolls Civic Assn.; mem. U.S. Power Squadron, Watchung Power Squadron; Rep. County committeeman, Monmouth County, 1989-2001. With USAR, 1962-68. Fellow Life Mgmt Inst. Soc. of Greater N.Y.; mem. Am. Soc. CLU's, Am. Legion. Roman Catholic. Home and Office: Apt 624 2 Oakdale Dr Middletown NJ 07748 E-mail: robertjjaros@aol.com.

JAROSH, COLLEEN MARIE, educator, mediator, consultant; b. Cresco, Iowa, July 4, 1951; d. Raymond James and Marjorie Ester (Burr) McGee; m. Kenneth Charles Jarosh, July 21, 1979; children: Michael, Rebecca. ADN, N.E. Iowa Tech. Inst., Calmar, 1974; BSN, Upper Iowa U., Fayette, 1980; MAE in Edn., U. No. Iowa, Cedar Falls, 1984. RN, Iowa. Nurse Schoitz Meml. Hosp., Waterloo, Iowa, 1974-76, USPHS, Tuba City, Ariz., 1976-77, Phoenix Indian Med. Ctr., 1977-78, Palmar Meml. Hosp., West Union, Iowa, 1978-79; instr. N.E. Iowa Tech. Inst., 1979; sch. nurse Upper Iowa U., 1979, adj. instr., 1979-83; writer, co-editor newsletter Dept. Human Svcs., Waterloo, 1994-98; ednl. cons. Janesville, Iowa, 1980—. Mediator Child Welfare, 1998—. Vol. St. Mary's ch., Waverly, Iowa, 1994—; support group leader Luth. Social Svcs., Waterloo, 1994. Mem. Rosary Soc., Iowa Foster Adoptive Parents Assn (bd. dirs.), Acad. Family Mediators. Avocations: special needs adoption, prairie restoration, tree planting, reading. Office: Colleen Jarosh Ednl Cons 9405 Taylor Rd Janesville IA 50647-1124

JAROSKI-GRAF, JILL ANN, biology educator, writer, dental hygienist; b. Rhinelander, Wis., Apr. 23, 1956; d. Raymond John and Ann Mae (Juday) Jaroski; m. Stephen Edward Graf, June 25, 1994; 1 child, Savannah. AA in Dental Hygiene, Madison Area Tech. Coll., 1980; BS in Dental Hygiene, post secondary tchg. cert., Marquette Univ., 1988; MS in Anatomy and Microbiology, U. Wis., Stout, 1990. Founding tchr. biology, limnology and life sci. Conserve Sch., Land O'Lakes, Wis., 2000—; assoc. prof. biology and forensic sci. Mount Senario Coll., Ladysmith, Wis., 1989-2000; chief dep. coroner Rusk County, 1993—2000. Author: Dental Charting: A Standard Approach, 2000. Recipient Disting. Alumni award in Dental Hygiene, Marquette Univ., 2001. Fellow Am. Coll. Forensic Examiners. Avocations: cross-country skiing, kayaking, canoeing, biking, fishing. Office: Conserve Sch 5400 N Black Oak Lake Rd Land O Lakes WI 54540

JARPE, GEOFFREY PELLAS, lawyer; b. Milw., Aug. 2, 1945; s. Gunnar E. and Laura Johnson (Camp) J.; m. Lezlie J. Myhra, Aug. 10, 1968; children: Nathan M., Rachel K., Joseph S. BA, U. Mich., 1967, JD, 1969. Bar: Minn. 1970, U.S. Dist. Ct. Minn. 1973, U.S. Ct. Appeals (8th cir.), 1973, U.S. Dist. Ct. (ea. dist.) Mich. 1982, U.S. Dist. Ct. (ea. dist.) Wis. 1987, U.S. Claims Ct. 1990, Wis. 1989, U.S. Dist. Ct. (we. dist.) Wis., 1995, U.S. Supreme Ct. 1990; cert. Nat. Bd. Trial Advocacy. Spl. asst atty. gen. State of Minn., St. Paul, 1970-72; assoc. Maun & Simon, St. Paul, 1972-78, ptnr., 1978-2000, Maslon Edelman Borman & Brand, Mpls., 2001—. Mem. ABA, Minn. State Bar Assn. (cert. civil trial specialist, civil litigation sect.), Hennepin County Bar Assn., U. Mich. Club (pres. Twin Cities chpt. 1985-87), Am. Bd. Trial Adv. Lutheran. Office: Maslon Edelman Borman & Brand 3300 Wells Fargo Ctr 90 S 7th St Minneapolis MN 55402-4140

JARQUE URIBE, CARLOS, former federal official; b. Mexico City, Oct. 18, 1954; Actuary Degree, U. Anáhuac, 1976; diploma, M in Econs. and Polit. Sci., London Sch. Econs.; postgrad., U. Oslo; PhD in Econs., Nat. U. Australia; postgrad., Harvard U. Pres. Nat. Inst. for Stats., Geography and Informatics; gen. dir. stats. Dept. Programming and Budget; pres. Interdeptmental Pub. Fin. Com.; gen. dir. Internat. Stats. Inst.; world pres. UN Stats. Commn.; pres. UN Cartographic Conf.; sec. of social develop. Govt. of Mexico, 1999—2000; project mgr. sustainable develop. Inter-Amer. Develop. Bank, 2001—. Tech. sec. Nat. Devel. Plan, 1995-2000; vis. prof. Harvard U. Contbr. articles to profl. jours. Recipient Nat. Sci. and Tech. award, Nat. Actuaries' award, Benito Juárez medal of merit, Henri Willen Methorst medal, Adolf Quetelet medal. Office: 1300 New York Ave NW Washington DC 20577

JARRARD, LEONARD EVERETT, psychologist, educator; b. Waco, Tex., Oct. 23, 1930; s. Thomas Ivan and Levis Everett (Lasswell) J.; m. Janet Grier Shoop, Aug. 16, 1958; children: Alice Grier, David Frazier, Hugh Everett. BA, Baylor U., Waco, 1955; MS, Carnegie Inst. Tech., Pitts., 1957, PhD, 1959. Asst. to asso. prof. psychology Washington and Lee U., 1959-66; assoc. prof. to prof. psychology Carnegie-Mellon U., 1966-71; Robert L. Telford prof. psychology Washington and Lee U., Lexington, Va., 1971-2001, prof. emeritus, 2001—. Vis. lectr., prof. exptl. psychology U. Oxford, Eng., 1975-76; interim assoc. prof. anatomy U. Fla., 1965-66; acad. visitor Inst. Psychiatry, U. London, 1988-89. Editor: Cognitive Processes of Nonhuman Primates, 1971; cons. editor: Jour. Comparative and Physiol. Psychology, 1970-75, Behavioral Neurosci. Psychology, 1995-2001. Served with USAF, 1952-54. Fellow AAAS, APA, APS; mem. Soc. for Neurosci., Psychonomics Soc., Va. Acad. Sci. So. Soc. Philosophy and Psychology, Phi Beta Kappa, Omicron Delta Kappa, Sigma Xi. Home: RR 5 Box 1067 Lexington VA 24450-9805 Office: Washington and Lee U Dept Psychology Lexington VA 24450

JARRARD, MARILYN MAE, nursing consultant, nursing researcher; b. York, Nebr., July 13, 1939; d. Frederick Albert and Esther Marie (Kollmann) Elze; m. William John Jarrard (div.); children: Rebecca Ann, Melissa Linn. Diploma in nursing, Luth. Sch. Nursing, Sioux City, Iowa, 1959. RN Iowa, Fla., cert. nutritional support nurse. Staff nurse U. Iowa Hosps. and Clinics, Iowa City, 1959-60, 69-70, minimal care charge nurse, 1971-74, staff nurse medical oncology, 1974-75, hyperalimentation nurse, 1975-79; staff nurse VA Hosp., Iowa City, 1960-65; charge nurse Offutt Air Base Hosp., Omaha, 1965-66; hyperalimentation nurse clinician Northwestern Meml. Hosp., Chgo., 1979-81; nutritional support nurse, team coord. Leila Hosp. and Health Ctr., Battle Creek, Mich., 1981-87; clin. specialist wound care Smith & Nephew Perry, Massillon, Ohio, 1987-89; clin. specialist-I.V. Smith & Nephew, Inc. Wound Mgmt. Divsn., Largo, Fla., 1989—2001; freelance nurse cons. Saint Petersburg, Fla., 2001—. Cons., rschr. in field. Contbr. articles to profl. jours. With USNG, 1976—79. Mem.: Infusion Nurses Soc., Am. Soc. Parenteral and Enteral Nutrition (nursing faculty 1977), Oncology Nursing, Soc. Healthcare Epidemiology Am., Assn. Profls. Infection Control and Epidemiology, Inc., Nat. Assn. Vascular Access Networks. Home: 701 53d Terr N Saint Petersburg FL 33703

JARRELL, CHARLES MICHAEL, bishop; b. Opelousas, La., May 15, 1940; Student, Immaculata Minor Sem., Cath. U. Ordained priest Roman Cath. Ch. 1967, bishop 1993. Bishop Diocese of Houma (La.)-Thibodaux, 1993—2002, Diocese of Lafayette, La., 2002—.

JARRELL, IRIS BONDS, elementary school educator, business executive; b. Winston-Salem, N.C., May 25, 1942; d. Ira and Annie Gertrude (Vandiver) Bonds; m. Tommy Dorsey Martin, Feb. 13, 1965; 1 child, Carlos Miguel; m. 2d, Clyde Rickey Jarrell, June 25, 1983; stepchildren: Tamara, Cris, Kimberly. Student, U. N.C., Greensboro, 1960-61, 68-69, student, 1974-75, Salem Coll., 1976; BS in Edn., Winston-Salem State U., 1983; M in Elem. Edn., Gardner-Webb Coll., 1992. Cert. tchr., N.C. Tchr. Rutledge Coll., Winston-Salem, 1982-84; owner, mgr. Rainbow's End Consignment Shop, Winston-Salem, 1983-85; tchr. elem. edn. Winston-Salem/Forsyth County Sch. Svcs., 1985-96; dir. Knollwood Bapt. Pre-Sch., 1996-97; tchr. gifted/talented students Winston-Salem/Forsyth County Schs., 1998; tchr. Clemmons Elem. Sch., 1998—. Contbr. poetry to mags. Mem. Assn. of Couples for Marriage Enrichment, Winston-Salem, 1985-86; mem. Winston-Salem Symphony Chorale; mem. Planned Parenthood. Mem. NOW, Internat. Reading Assn., N.C. Assn. Adult Edn., Forsyth Assn. Classroom Tchrs., World Wildlife Fund, Greenpeace, KlanWatch. Democrat. Baptist. Avocations: singing, writing, sewing, gardening, reading. Home: 101 Cheswyck Ln Winston Salem NC 27104-2905 E-mail: ijarrell@bellsouth.net.

JARRELL, STEPHEN BROOKS, economics educator; b. Huntsville, Ala., Jan. 10, 1949; s. Lawson E. and Elizabeth E. (Absher) J.; children: Jennifer, Jason, Sara, Shane. BS in Math., U. Ala., Tuscaloosa, 1971; MS in Econs., Purdue U., 1972, PhD in Econs., 1978. Prof. econs. Western Ky. U., Bowling Green, 1975-88, U. Mont., Air Force Inst. Tech. MBA Program, Great Falls, 1980-81, Western Carolina U., Cullowhee, N.C., 1988-- Interim head of dept. econs. and fin. Western Carolina U., 1994-95. Author: Basic Business Statistics, 1988, Basic Statistics, 1994; contbr. articles to profl. jours. Mem. Phi Beta Kappa, Omicron Delta Epsilon, Pi Mu Epsilon. Office: Dept Mgmt and Internat Bus Western Carolina Univ Cullowhee NC 28723

JARRELL, WESLEY MICHAEL, environmental scientist, educator; b. Forest Grove, Oreg., May 23, 1948; s. Burl Omer and Edith LaVerne (Sahnow) J.; m. Leslie Rose Cooperband; children: Benjamin George, Emily Theresa. BA, Stanford U., 1970; MS, Oreg. State U., 1974, PhD, 1976. Asst. prof. soil sci. U. Calif., Riverside, 1976-83, assoc. prof., 1983-88, Oreg. Grad. Inst., Portland, 1988-91, prof., 1991-99, head dept., 1992-94; sr. scientist U. Wis., Madison, 2001—02; prof., head natural resources and environ. scis. U. Ill., Champaign, 2003—. Internat. cons. Contbr. articles to profl. jours. Home: 4410 N Lincoln Ave Champaign IL 61822 Office: U Ill Dept Natural Resources and Environ Scis Urbana-Champaign IL 61801 E-mail: wjarrell@uiuc.edu.

JARRETT, ALEXIS, insurance agent, lawyer; b. Independence, Kans., July 2, 1948; d. Robert Patterson and Betty June (Johnson) Jarrett. BS, U. Minn., Duluth, 1970; postgrad., U. Mo., 1974—77; JD, John Marshall Law Sch., 2001. Lic. property and casualty ins. Ind., life and health ins. Ind., cert. Life Underwriting Tng. Coun.; coach Minn. Tchr. Esko (Minn.) Pub. Schs., 1970-74; asst. dir. athletics, head coach basketball, softball, track U. Mo., Columbia, 1974-77; pvt. practice Schererville, Ind., 1984—; pres., CEO INFINITE Sports and Entertainment, Inc., 2002—. Women's basketball and softball color analyst Regional Radio Sports, N.W. Ind., 1992—94; with Moot Ct. Coun., 1999; jud. extern Cir. Ct. Cook County, Chgo., 1999; coord. Women's Sports Info. Dept., U. Mo., 1974—77; v.p. legal affairs Nat. Assn. State Farm Agts., Inc., 1997—2000; contract advisor NFL Players Assn., 2002—, Women's Nat. Basketball Players Assn., 2002—, CFL Players Assn., 2003—. Contbr. articles to newspapers. Sponsor Lake County (Ind.) HS Girls Basketball Banquet, 1989—99; bd. dirs. Samaritan Counseling Ctr. N.W. Ind., pres., 1994; bd. dirs. VNA Found., sec.-treas., 1994; celebrity Am. Heart Assn. Celebrity Dinner; v.p. S.W. Lake divsn. Am. Heart Assn., 1992—94; mem. bd. advisors Basketball Hall of Fame, 1999—; bd. dirs. Boys and Girls Club N.W. Ind.; mem. adv. bd. indsl. rsch. liaison program Ind. U., Bloomington, 1990—96. Recipient Individual with Vision award, Ind. HS Athletic Assn., 1996. Mem.: ABA (entertainment and sports law forum, labor and law com., ins. law com., sports law subcom.), Sports Lawyers Assn., Chgo. Bar Assn. (labor and employment law com., ins. law com., immigration law com., health law com.), Ind. State Med. Assn. Alliance (chair media rels. 1990—91, treas. 1992—93, chair media rels. 1993—94), Am. Bus. Women's Assn. (pres. New Image chpt. 1983, Woman of the Yr. 1983), Lake County Med. Soc. Alliance (pres. 1992—94), Nat. Life Underwriters (bd. dirs. N.W. Ind. chpt. 1995, 1996, 1997). Address: 2330 Wicker Blvd Schererville IN 46375-2810

JARRETT, ALFRED A. social policy analyst; b. Kalangba, West Africa, Dec. 7, 1950; AA, Muscatine C.C., 1974; BA, U. Ill., 1977, MA, 1979; PhD, Ohio State U., 1984. Peer counselor, tchg. asst. U. Ill., Springfield, 1977-79; family therapist, clin. coord. Sangamon County Youth Svc. Bur., Springfield, 1979-80; grad. rsch. tchg. assoc. Ohio State U., Columbus, 1980-83; adult protective svc. program specialist Tex. Dept. Human Svcs., Dallas, 1987; adj. asst. prof. social work U. Tex., Arlington, 1987-89; founder, dir. Internat. Ctr. on Ethnicity and Gender, Arlington, 1989-91; from asst. prof. to dir., assoc. prof. social work Paul Quinn Coll., Dallas, 1989-93; interim dir., coord. social adminstrn, policy & planning Ala. A&M U., Huntsville, 1993—. Policy analyst, social planner, internat. cons., 1983—. Author: Curriculum Design for Ethnic Minority Males, 1992, A Case Management Training Guide for Social Practitioners, 1993, The Rationale for Africa's Retrogression: Militarization and Tribalism, 1994, The Underdevelopment of Africa: Colonialism, Neo-Colonialism and Socialism, 1995, Strategies and Techniques for Building Community Coalitions, 1996, Strategies and Techniques of Grant Writing, 1999; co-author: Social Issues Impacting Ethnic Minorities and Gender: Intervention Strategies for Social Practitioners, 1990; editor: The Impact of Macro Social Systems on Ethnic Minorities in the U.S.A., 1999; contbr. articles to profl. jours., chpts. to books. Bd. dirs. Children First. Mem. Coun. Social Work Edn., Phi Alpha, Phi Beta Delta. Office: PO Box 645 Normal AL 35762-0645

JARRETT, CYNTHIA S. accountant; b. Tenn. m. Michael Ward Jarrett. BS, U. Tenn., Martin, 1973, MBA, 1980. Dir. budget and human res. U. Tenn., Martin, 1974-83; bus. mgr. Dyersburg State C.C., Dyersburg, Tenn., 1983-90; v.p. for bus. affairs U. Montevallo, Ala., 1990—. Bd. dirs., treas. Leadership Shelby County, 1998—. Mem. Montevallo Rotary Club (pres., v.p., sec., treas. 1993—). Office: Univ of Montevallo Station 6010 Montevallo AL 35115 E-mail: jarrettc@montevallo.edu.

JARRETT, DALE, race car driver; b. Conover, N.C., Nov. 26, 1956; m. Kelley Jarrett; children: Jason, Natalee, Karsyn. Named winner, Daytona 500, 1993, 1996, 2000, Mello Yello 500, 1994, Miller 500, 1995, Coca-Cola 600, 1996, Goodwrench 400, 1996, Brickyard 400, 1996, 1999, Pa. 500, 1997, Goody's Headache Powder 500, 1997, Exide NASCAR 400, 1997, VAW-GM 500, 1997, Dura-Lube 500, 1997, Transouth Fin. 500, 1997, 1998, MBNA Platinum 400, 1998, Winston 500, 1998, Pontiac Excitement 400, 1999, KMart 400, 1999, Pepsi 400, 1999. Office: DAJ Racing Inc PO Box 564 Conover NC 28613-0564 also: c/o Robert Yates Racing 115 S Dwelle St Charlotte NC 28208-2929

JARRETT, JEFFREY D. federal agency administrator; Bur. dir. Pa. Dept. Environ. Protection, dep. sec. for mineral resources and mgmt.; dep. asst. dir. program ops. Office Surface Mining; dir. Surface Mining Reclamation and Enforcement U.S. Dept. Interior, Washington, 2002—. Office: US Dept Interior Surface Mining Reclamation & Enforcement 1951 Constitution Ave NW Washington DC 20240

JARRETT, KEITH, pianist, composer; b. Allentown, Pa., May 8, 1945; Student, Berklee Sch. Music, 1963. Pianist with groups led by Art Blakey, 1965, Charles Lloyd, 1966-69, Miles Davis, 1970-71; rec. with group led by Art Blakey: Buttercorn Lady, 1966; recs. with groups led by Charles Lloyd: Dreamweaver, Forest Flower, In Europe, The Flowering, 1966, Love In (Live at Fillmore), Journey Within, Live in the Soviet Union, 1967, Soundtrack, 1968; recs. with groups led by Miles Davis: Miles Davis at Fillmore, Live—, Evil, Get Up With It, Directions, 1970; soloist, leader of own groups, 1969—; recs. as leader of own groups or as solo artist: Life Between The Exit Signs, 1967, Restoration Ruin, Somewhere Before, 1968, Gary Burton/Keith Jarrett, 1971, Mourning of a Star, Birth, El Juicio, Ruta and Daitya, Expectations, Facing You, 1971, Fort Yawuh, In The Light, Solo Concerts Bremen & Lausanne, 1973, Treasure Island, Belonging, Luminessence, Death and the Flower, Backhand, 1974, The Koln Concert, Mysteries, Shades, Bob-Be, Byablue, Arbour Zena, 1975, Survivors' Suite, Eyes of The Heart, Staircase, Hymns/Spheres, Sun Bear Concerts, 1976, My Song, 1977, Personal Mountains, Nude Ants, Moth and The Flame, 1979, The Celestial Hawk, Sacred Hymns, Invocations, 1980, Concerts Bregenz and Munich, 1981, Standards Volumes 1 & 2, Changes, 1983, Spirits, Standards Live, 1985, Still Live, Book of Ways, 1986, Dark Intervals, Changeless, 1987, Paris Concert, 1988, Tribute, 1989, Standards In Norway, 1989, The Cure, 1990, Vienna Concert, Bye Bye Black Bird, 1991, At the Dear Head Inn, 1992, Bridge of Light, 1993, At The Blue Note (6 CD set, 1994), La Scala, 1995, Tokyo '96; also recorded with Airto, Freddie Hubbard, Marion Williams, Kenny Wheeler, Gary Peacock, Charlie Haden, Paul Motian; classical recs. include J. S. Bach—Well Tempered Clavier Book 1 (piano), 1987, Book 2 (harpsichord), 1991, Goldberg Variations (harpsichord), 1989, French Suites (harpsichord), 1991, Handel Keyboard Suites, 1993, (with Michala Petri) Handel—Sonatas for Recorder and Continuo, 1990, Bach— Sonatas for Flute and Harpsicord, 1992, (with Dennis Russell Davies/Stuggart Chamber Orch.) Mozart Piano Concerto No. 21, 23, 27, Lou Harrison—Piano Concerto and Suite for violin, piano and orch., 1988, Alan Hohvaness—Lousadzak, 1989, (with Gidon Kremer) Arvo Part—Fratres, 1983, Shostakovich—24 Preludes and Fugues, Opus 87, 1991; (with Kim Kashkashian) Bach Sonatas for Viola da Gamba, 1991; concert soloist with San Francisco Symphony, Phila. Orch., Boston Symphony Orch., Am. Composers Orch., St. Paul and English Chamber Orch., Rochester and Bklyn. Philharm.; subject of biography: Keith Jarrett: The Man and His Music (Ian Carr), 1991. Decorated officier de L'Ordre des Arts et des Lettres (France); recipient Guggenheim award, 1972, Grand Prix du Disque, Govt. of France, 1972, Prix du Pres. de la Republique (France), 1991; recs. nominated for Grammy award, 1974, 86, 88, 92, 98; recs. named Record of Yr., Time mag., Downbeat mag., Stereo Rev., 1974, N.Y. Times, 1975, 92, Rolling Stone mag., 1976, CD Rev., 1992, Downbeat, 1996; named Pianist/Artist of Yr., Downbeat mag., 1974, 75, 94, 96, 97, 98, Keyboard mag., 1976, 82, 91, Swing Jour. (Japan), 1980, 86, 87, 89, 91, 93, 94, 95, 96; 1st improvising musician to perform Met. Opera, N.Y.C., 1978, Vienna State Opera, 1991, La Scala, Milan, 1995. Mem. Royal Swedish Acad. Music.

JARRETT, MARK PAUL, rheumatologist, medical administrator; b. Bklyn., Dec. 29, 1949; s. Irving and Claire Jarrett; m. Michele Jonas, Aug. 15, 1974; children: Matthew, Nicole, Tyler. BS, Muhlenberg Coll., 1971; MD, NYU, 1975; MBA, Wagner Coll., 1994. Bd. cert. Am. Bd. Internal Medicine, Am. Bd. Rheumatology, Am. Bd. Geriatrics, Am. Bd. Quality Assurance and Utilization Rev. Physicians. Intern in internal medicine Montefiore Hosp., Bronx, 1975; resident in internal medicine, 1976—78; rheumatology fellow Montefiore Hosp./Albert Einstein Coll. Medicine, 1978-80; asst. prof. medicine Northwestern U. Med. Sch., Chgo., 1980-82; dir. rheumatology S.I. U. Hosp., 1982-98; sr. med. dir. Care Mgmt. Group Greater N.Y., Lake Success, N.Y., 1999-2000, pres., 2000-2001; chief med. officer S.I. Univ. Hosp., 2001—. Clin. asst. prof. medicine SUNY Health Scis. Ctr.-Downstate, Bklyn., 1982—. Bd. dirs. Cmty. Cable TV, S.I., 2000-2001, Physician Health Svcs. N.Y., N.Y.C., 1998-2001. Fellow ACP, Am. Coll. Rheumatology; mem. AMA, Am. Fedn. Rsch., Am. Geriatrics Soc., Am. Mgmt. Assn., Chief Med. Officers Soc., Richmond County Med. Soc. (pres. 1990), Phi Beta Kappa. Avocations: travel, gourmet food. Office: Staten Island Univ Hosp 475 Seaview Ave Staten Island NY 10305 E-mail: mjarrett@si.rr.com.

JARRETT, NOEL, chemical engineer, researcher; b. Long Eaton, Eng., Nov. 17, 1921; came to U.S., 1926, naturalized, 1942; s. John Richard and Lena Eliza (Hexter) J.; m. Violet E. Dipner, Sept. 24, 1949; children: Robert, Kenneth, James, Thomas. BS in Chem. Engring, U. Pitts., 1949; MS in Chem. Engring, U. Mich., 1951. Lubrication sales engr. Freedom-Valvoline Co., Freedom, Pa., 1949-50; rsch. engr., group leader, asst. chief Alcoa Labs., Aluminum Co. Am., 1951-65, chief div. process metallurgy, 1965-69, asst. dir. metal prodn. labs., 1969-81, tech. dir. smelting rsch. and devel., 1981-82, tech. dir. chem. engring. rsch. and devel., 1982-87; ret., 1987; prin. Noel Jarrett Assocs. Patentee smelting, melting and purification of alumninum. Served with U.S. Army, 1942-45. Fellow Am. Soc. Metals; mem. NAE, Am. Isnt. Chem. Engrs., Minerals, Metals and Materials Soc., VFW, Am. Legion, Masons, Elks, Sigma Xi. Episcopalian. Home and Office: 149 Jefferson Dr New Kensington PA 15068-3127 *I have found that the one who performs the tasks immediately at hand so well that his work cannot be ignored will reap society's rewards without asking.*

JARRETT, POLLY HAWKINS, secondary education educator, retired; b. Columbia, S.C., May 6, 1929; d. William Harold and Ann Beatrice (Carson) Hawkins; m. Nov. 21, 1953 (dec. Aug. 1984); children: William Guy Jr., Henry Carson. Student, Montreat Coll., 1947-49; BS in Secondary Edn., Longwood Coll., 1951. Tchr. 7th grade McDowell County Schs., Marion, N.C., 1951-52; tchr. 8th grade Marion City Schs., 1952-53, Burke County Schs., Morganton, N.C., 1954-56; tchr. 7th grade Wake County Schs., Raleigh, N.C., 1956-58, Durham (N.C.) County Schs., 1958-59; tchr. 7th and 8th grade Raleigh City and Wake County Schs., Raleigh, 1959-79; tchr. social studies Wake County Pub. Schs., Raleigh, 1979-90, ret., 1990. Adv. bd. State Employees Credit Union, Raleigh, 1988-92, 94-00. Mem. United Daus. of the Confederacy (chpt. pres. 1978-81, 91-96, divsn. historian 1981-83, dist. VI dir. 1983-85, divsn. chaplain 1986-90, divns. parliamentarian 1994-96, chmn. bd. trustees 1990-91), Delta Kappa Gamma (chpt. pres. 1988-90, regional dir. 1990-92, state 2d v.p. 1997-99, chmn. N.C. divsn. State Conv. 2001, mem. steering com. 2003), Kappa Delta Pi, Pi Delta Epsilon, Pi Gamma Mu. Democrat. Methodist. Avocations: travel, growing roses, reading, pets. Home: 3405 White Oak Rd Raleigh NC 27609-7620

JARROW, ROBERT ALAN, economics and finance educator, consultant; b. Hackensack, N.Y., June 16, 1952; s. Benjamin Charles and Irene Elizabeth (Kozniewski) Jaworowski; m. Gail Dian Goundry; children: Kyle, Tate, Heather. BA, Duke U., 1974; MBA, Dartmouth Coll., 1976; PhD, MIT, 1979. Prof. fin. and econs. Cornell U., Ithaca, N.Y., 1979—. Cons. Bank of Am., San Francisco, 1987-89, Merrill Lynch, 1994, Kamakura Corp., 1995—, FDIC, 2003. Author: Option Pricing, 1983, Finance Theory, 1988, Modelling Fixed Income Securities and Interest Rate Options, 1996, 2d revised edit., 2002, Derivative Securities, 1996, 2000; contbr. articles; assoc. editor: Rev. Derivatives Rsch., 1997—, Rev. Futures Markets, 1987—; editor: Math. Fin., 2002; co-editor: Jour. Derivatives, 1999—2002. Recipient Pomerance prize Chgo. Bd. Options Exch., 1982; named Fin. Engr. Yr., 1997. Mem. Am. Fin. Assn., Econ. Soc., Ops. Rsch. Soc., Soc. for Promotion Econ. Theory, Math. Assn. Am. Avocations: jogging, soccer, Karate. Office: Cornell U Sage Hall Ithaca NY 14853

JARUGULA, VENKATESWAR RAO, medical researcher; b. Pandillapally, India, Mar. 30, 1964; arrived in U.S., 1991; s. Koteswara Rao and Tirupathamma Jarugula; m. Rupa Latha Injam, Aug. 30, 1967; children: Praneeth, Sahithi. BS, Kakatiya U., 1986, MS, 1989; PhD, U. Ga., 1996. Asst. prof. Coll. Pharmacy Howard U., Washington, 1996—97; rev. scientist FDA, Rockville, Md., 1997—. Contbr. Mem.: Am. Assn. Pharm. Scientists (abstract screening com. 2000—). Achievements include research in pharmacokinetics and biotransformation of novel anti cancer Drodrugs of 5-Fluoeouracil; a novel boron delivering compound being investigated for Boron Neutron Capture Therapy in Brain Tumor Treatment. Office: FDA 5600 Fishers Ln Rockville MD 20857

JARVI, NEEME, conductor; b. Tallinn, Estonia, June 7, 1937; arrived in U.S., 1980; s. August and Elss Jarvi; m. Liilia Jarvi, Sept. 2, 1961; children: Paavo, Kristjan, Maarika. Diploma in Music and Conducting, St. Petersburg (USSR) State Conservatorium, 1960; hon. doctorate, U. Aberdeen, Scotland, Music Conservatory of Talinn, Estonia, Gothenberg (Sweden) U., U. Mich. Condr. Estonian Radio Symphony Orch., 1960-63, chief condr., 1963-76, Estonian State Opera, 1963-76, Estonian State Symphony, 1976-80; prin. condr. Gothenburg (Sweden) Symphony Orch., 1982—; prin. condr., music dir., condr. laureate Royal Scottish Orch., Glasgow, 1984-88; music dir. Detroit Symphony Orch., 1990—. Prin. guest condr. Birmingham Symphony Orch., England, 1980—83; guest condr. N.Y. Philharm. Orch., Boston Symphony Orch., Phila. Orch., Chgo. Symphony, Royal Concertgebow, Amsterdam, Philharmonia London, London Symphony, Scandinavian Orch., Met. Opera House, N.Y.C. Decorated Knight Comdr. North Star Order Sweden; recipient 1st prize in conducting, Accademia Nazionale di Santa Cecilia, 1971.*

JARVI, PAAVO, conductor; b. Tallinn, Estonia, 1963;, U.S., 1980; Studied at, Curtis Inst. of Music, Los Angeles Philharm. Inst. Prin. guest condr. Royal Stockholm Philharm., City of Birmingham, Eng.; condr. Cin. Symphony Orch., 2001—. Condr. UBS Verbier Youth Orch. (summer series); artistic adv. Estonian Nat. Symphony Orch., 2002—. Named Editor's Choice, Feb. 2003 edit. of Gramophone; recipient Kultuurkapital award, Estonian Min. of Culture. Office: CSO Administrative Offices Music Hall 1241 Elm St Cincinnati OH 45202

JARVI, SUSAN I. research scientist, educator; b. Mass. BS, Fitchburg State U., 1983; MS, U. Mass., 1986; PhD, No. Ill. U., 1989. Rsch. fellow Beckman Rsch. Inst., City of Hope Nat. Med. Ctr., Duarte, Calif., 1990—93, Smithsonian Instn., Washington, 1993—96; assoc. scientist USGS-BRD, Hawaii Volcanoes Nat. Pk., Hawaii, 1995—; asst. prof. U. Hawaii, Hilo, 2000—. Contbr. articles. Smithson Rsch. fellow, Smithsonian Instn., 1993, Rsch. grant, USGS-BRD, 1993—98, NSF, 2001—, U. Hawaii, 2002. Office: Univ Hawaii 200 W Kawili St Hilo HI 96720 Office Fax: 808-974-7693. E-mail: jarvi@hawaii.edu.

JARVIK, LISSY F. psychiatrist; b. The Hague, Netherlands; m. Murray F. Jarvik, Dec. 19, 1954; children: Laurence A., Jeffrey G. AB cum laude, Hunter Coll., N.Y.C.; MA, PhD, Columbia U.; MD, Western Res. U. Diplomate Am. Bd. Pediat. From rsch. asst. to psychiatrist II N.Y. State Psychiat. Inst., N.Y.C.; rotating intern Mt. Sinai Hosp., N.Y.C.; resident in pediatrics Babies Hosp., Columbia Presbyn. Med. Ctr., Vanderbilt Clinic, N.Y.C.; resident in psychiatry N.Y. State Psychiat. Inst., N.Y.C., 1965-68; asst. attending, then attending psychiatrist Vanderbilt Clinic, 1962-72; from rsch. assoc. to assoc. prof. Columbia U. Coll. Phys. and Surg., 1956-72; chief psychogenetic unit West Los

Angeles VA Med. Ctr., 1970-82, chief psychogeriatric unit, 1982-87; prof. psychiatry UCLA Med. Sch., 1982-94, prof. emeritus, 1994—. M.S. McLeod vis. prof. U. Adelaide, Australia, 1981; vis. prof. Australian Postgrad. Med. Found., 1981; Disting. Physician Dept. VA, 1987-93, emeritus, 1993—; dir. UPBEAT program, 1991-99, dir. GETSMART program, 1993-99; cons. in field, mem. numerous task forces. Mem. editl. bd. profl. jours.; founding co-editor Alzheimer Disease and Associated Disorders--An Internat. Jour.; contbr. over 300 articles to profl. jours. Recipient R. Thornton Wilson award, 1967, Woman in Sci. award UCLA, 1981, Group Research award Assn. for Specialists in Group Work, 1984, Research award Alzheimer Disease and Related Disorders Assn., L.A. chpt., 1985, Jack Weinberg Memorial award Am. Psychiatric Assn., 1986, Robert W. Kleemeier award Gerontol. Soc. of Am., 1986, Edward B. Allen award Am. Geriatrics Soc., 1986, Disting. Scientific Achievement award Calif. State Psychol. Assn., 1987, Irving S. Wright award Am. Fedn. for Aging Rsch., 1988, William C. Menninger Meml. award ACP, 1993, Svc. to Psychogeriat. award Internat. Psychogeriat. Assn., 1995, C. Charles Burlingame award The Inst. Living, 1998; named Woman of Achievement, Women's Equality Day, 1980, Woman of Yr., AAUW, Santa Monica, 1985; named to Hunter Coll. Alumni Assn. Hall of Fame, 1991; Foundation fellow Ctr. for Advanced Study in Behavioral Scis., 1988-89. Fellow AAAS, Gerontol. Soc. Am. (Joseph T. Freeman award 1996), Am. Geriatric Soc., Internat. Soc. Twin Studies, Am. Acad. Pediatrics, Am. Psychol. Assn. (div. pres.); mem. Am. Med. Womens Assn., Am. Soc. Human Genetics, Am. Psychopath Assn., Am. Aging Assn., Am. Soc. on Aging, Behavior Genetics Assn., Internat. Assn. Gerontology, Am. Psychiat. Assn. (Disting. Psychiatrist Lectr. 1996), Am. Assn. for Geriat. Psychiatry (past pres., Founders award 1990-91, Sr. Investigator award, 1993, Pfizer Pioneer in Geriatric Psychiatry award 2000), Internat. Psychogeriat. Assn., N.Y. Acad. Scis., West Coast Coll. Biol. Psychiatry, World Psychiat. Assn., Sigma Xi. Office: 760 Westwood Plz Los Angeles CA 90095-1759 also: VA Med Ctr 11301 Wilshire Blvd # 11L Los Angeles CA 90073-1003 E-mail: ljarvik@ucla.edu.

JARVIK, ROBERT K. biomedical research scientist; b. Midland, Mich., May 11, 1946; m. Marilyn vos Savant, 1987. BA, Syracuse U., 1968, DSc (hon.), 1983; MA, NYU, 1971; MD, U. Utah, 1976; Dr sc (hon.), Hahnemann U., 1985. Rsch. asst. Div. Artificial Organs U. Utah, Salt Lake City, 1971-76, asst. dir. exptl. labs. Div. Artificial Organs, 1976-82, asst. rsch. prof. surgery, 1979-87; pres. Symbion, Inc., Salt Lake City, 1981-87, Jarvik Rsch., Inc., N.Y.C., 1987—; mem. nat. selection panel NASA Tchr. in Space Project, Washington, 1985. Sect. editor Internat. Jour. Artificial Organs, 1979-88; inventor repeating hemostatic clip instruments and cartridges, total artificial hearts powered by electrohydraulic energy; patentee in field. Named Inventor of Yr. Intellectual Property Owners, 1983, named John W. Hyatt award Soc. Plastics Engrs., 1983; recipient Golden Plate Am. Acad. Achievement, 1983, Gold Heart award Utah Heart Assn., 1983, Nat. Hero award, 1992. Mem. Am. Soc. Artificial Internal Organs Home: 1 COLUMBUS PL New York NY 10019-8200

JARVIN, LINDA, research scientist; b. Stockholm, Mar. 7, 1971; arrived in US, 1998; d. Sigvard and Marianne Jarvin; m. Marco Lubrano Scorpaniello, July 7, 2001. PhD in Psychology, U. Paris 5, 1999. Assoc. Yale U., New Haven, 1998—99, assoc. rsch. scientist, 2000—. Assoc. dir. Yale U. Pace Ctr., New Haven, 2001—. Contbr. articles to profl. jours., chpts. to books. Mem.: APA, Am. Ednl. Rsch. Assn. Office: Yale Univ Pace Ctr 340 Edwards St New Haven CT 06520

JARVIS, DAPHNE ELOISE, laboratory administrator; b. Lithia, Fla., Feb. 18, 1945; d. Grady Edwin and Vera Eloise (Smith) Smith; m. Hubert E. Jarvis, Aug. 1, 1964; 1 child, Jessica Ellen. BS, Blue Mountain Coll., 1966; MA, Spalding U., 1972. Cert. med. technologist with specialist in blood bank. Med. technologist St. Anthony's Hosp., Louisville, 1968-69, Clark County Meml. Hosp., Jeffersonville, Ind., 1969-73; asst. to edn. coord. ARC, Washington, 1973-75; dir. Grace Bapt. Ch. Sch., Bryans Rd., Md., 1978-83; sect. chief blood bank Physicians Meml. Hosp., LaPlata, Md., 1975-76, 83-84; supr. donor blood labs. Southwest Fla. Blood Bank, Tampa, 1984-87, dir., 1987-89; asst. dir. tech. svcs. Ark. Region ARC, Little Rock, 1989-93, dir. tech. svcs./hosp. svcs. Ark. Regional Blood Svcs., 1993-95; mfg. team leader Lifeblood-Midsouth Regional Blood Ctr., Memphis, 1995-2000, tech. mgr., 2000—. Lectr. UAMS Sch. Med. Tech., Little Rock, 1989-95. Children's leader Ingram Blvd Bapt. Ch., West Memphis, Ark., 1995—. Mem. Am. Assn. Blood Banks, Am. Soc. Quality, South Ctr. Assn. Blood Banks (membership com. 1989-95). Office: Lifeblood Midsouth Reg Blood Ctr 1040 Madison Ave Memphis TN 38104-2198

JARVIS, DAVID ALAN, engineer; b. Oak Hill, W.Va., May 9, 1959; s. August Christopher and Sylvia Marie (Holliday) J. BSCE, W.Va. Inst. Tech., 1981, M of Engring., 1987. Process engr. FMC Corp., South Charleston, W.Va., 1981-85; project engr. Maxon Corp., Muncie, Ind., 1987—2003, sr. product engr., 2003—. Inventor, patentee in field. Active Jr. Achievement, Muncie, 1988—. Mem. Tau Beta Pi. Democrat. Roman Catholic. Avocations: golf, travel, bowling, gardening, music. Home: 3901 S Beacon St Muncie IN 47302-5848 Office: Maxon Corp 201 E 18th St PO Box 2068 Muncie IN 47302 E-mail: chemicale3@hotmai.com., djarvis@maxoncorp.com.

JARVIS, DEBRA JEAN, fire chief, consultant; b. Indpls., June 1, 1953; d. George and Phyllis Joyce (DeHart) Bretzlaff; m. Greg A. Jarvis, Nov. 19, 1994. AS in Fire Sci., Ind. U., Kokomo, 1982; BS in Mgmt., Ind. Wesleyan U., 1988; Exec. Fire Officer, Nat. Fire Acad., 1996; MA in Leadership Studies, Lewis U., 2000. Firefighter, EMT Pike Twp. Fire Dept., Indpls., 1978-81, station officer, 1981-84, battalion chief, 1984-90; divsn. chief Lawrence Twp. Fire Dept., Indpls., 1990-95; fire chief Homewood (Ill.) Fire Dept., 1995-97, Oakbrook (Ill.) Fire Dept., 1997—. Trustee Women in the Fire Svc., 1989-92; cons., spkr., 1981—; contractor Inst. Pub. Safety Personnel, Inc., Indpls., 1994—. Contbr. articles in field. Precinct inspector, Ind. Election Bd., Indpls., 1990-95; small gp. leader Living Springs Cmty. Ch., Homewood, Ill., 1996—; firefighter-training dir. Worth Twp. Vol. Fire Dept., Whitestown, Ind., 1986-90. Named Firefighter of Yr., Homewood (Ill.) C. of C., 1996, Forum Series honoree Girls, Inc., Indpls., 1992. Mem. Dupage County Chiefs Assn., Internat. Assn. Fire Chiefs, Internat. Soc. Fire Svc. Instrs., Ill. Fire Chiefs. Avocations: photography, flower arranging. Home: 1530 190th St Homewood IL 60430-4007

JARVIS, DONALD BERTRAM, judge; b. Newark, N.J., Dec. 14, 1928; s. Benjamin and Esther (Golden) J.; m. Rosalind C. Chodorcove, June 13, 1954; children: Nancie, Brian, Joanne. BA, Rutgers U., 1949; JD, Stanford U., 1952. Bar: Calif. 1953. Law clk. to justice John W. Shenk Calif. Supreme Ct., 1953-54; assoc. Erskine, Erskine & Tulley, 1955, Aaron N. Cohen, 1955-56; law clk. Dist. Ct. Appeal, 1956; assoc. Carl Hoppe, 1956-57; adminstrv. law judge Calif. Pub. Utilities Commn., San Francisco, 1957-91, U.S. Dept. of Labor, San Francisco, 1992—. Mem. exec. com. Nat. Conf. Adminstrv. Law Judges, 1986-88, sec. 1988-89, vice-chair, 1990-91, chair-elect, 1991-92, chair 1992-93; pres. Calif. Adminstrv. Law Judges Coun., 1978-84; mem. faculty Nat. Jud. Coll., U. Nev., 1977, 78, 80; mem. U.S. Bd. of Alien Labor Cert. Appeals, 1995—. Chmn. pack Boy Scouts Am., 1967-69, chmn. troop 1972; class chmn. Stanford Law Sch. Fund, 1959, mem. nat. com., 1963-65; dir. Forest Hill Assn., 1970-71; patron San Francisco Opera. Served to col. USAF Res., 1949-79. Decorated Legion of Merit. Mem. ABA (mem. ho. of dels. 1993-99, vice chair jud. divsn. 1997-98, chair elect 1998-99, chair 1999-2000), State Bar Calif., Bar Assn. San Francisco, Calif. Conf. Pub. Utility Counsel (pres. 1980-81), Air Force Assn., Res. Officers Assn., Ret. Officers Assn., San Francisco Gem and Mineral Soc., Stanford Alumni Assn., Rutgers Alumni Assn., Phi Beta Kappa (pres. No. Calif. 1973-74), Tau Kappa Alpha, Pi Alpha Theta, Phi Alpha Delta. Home: 530 Dewey Blvd San Francisco CA 94116-1427 Office: 50 Fremont St San Francisco CA 94105-2230

JARVIS, ELBERT, II, (JAY JARVIS), employee benefits specialist; b. Washington, N.C., Sept. 20, 1944; s. Elbert J. Sr. and Laura F. (Lilley) J.; m. Anita Kleinfeld, Nov. 28, 1968 (div. Nov. 1983); 1 child, Elbert J. III; m. Audrey H. Liebross, July 28, 1991; 1 child, Benjamin Grover. A of Bus. Adminstrn., No. Va. C.C., 1972; BSBA, George Mason U., 1974. Sales mgr. Baumgarten Co., Washington, 1970-71; sales rep. Mass Mut., Washington, 1974-84; pres. The Pers. Dept., Inc., Annandale, Va., 1983—2001, Jarvis Consulting Ltd., 2001—. Founder No. Va. Group Health Alliance, No. Va. C. of C., 1998. Editor: (student handbook) Focal Point, 1973, Beth El Temple 1995-97, bd. dirs. Directory chair, 1990, 91, 92, 94, web master, 1999-2000, fund chair, 2000—; v.p. Brotherhood, 1999—. Scoutmaster, Webelos leader Boy Scouts Am., Clifton and Arlington, Va., 1970-71, 85-86; mem. county com., state del. Arlington Rep. Party, 1975-85; pres., sec. Arlington Jaycees, 1980-82; pres., bd. dirs. Lafayette Village Cmty. Assn., Annandale, Va., 1994-95; bd. dirs. Beth El Hebrew Congregation, v.p. 2000-01, 1st v.p. Brotherhood Beth El, 1999-2001, Brotherhood pres., 2001-2003, webmaster, 1999-2000, chmn. permanent endowment fund, 2000—, v.p., treas. 2003—; bd. dirs. Annadale Sq. Office Condominium, 1999. Mem. Am. Compensation Assn., Health Underwriters Assn. (sec. No. Va. chpt. 1996-97), Washington chpt. Cert. Employee Benefit Specialists (assoc.), Arlington C. of C. (chmn. comms. com. 1983, bd. dirs. 1988-92, 92-94, chmn. sml. bus. coun. 1990, 92, chmn. expo com. 1991, chmn. awards and small bus. week 1994, Disting. Svc. awards 1989), Soc. Employee Benefits Profls., Alexandria C. of C. (mem. advantage program com. 1993-96), Fairfax County C. of C. (vice chmn. small bus. awards 1993-94, mem. team captain 1996), Northern Va. C. of C. (founder, bd. chair 1998—), Lafayette Village Comm. Assn. (pres.). Jewish. Avocations: canoeing, camping, photography. Home: 7828 Ashley Glen Rd Annandale VA 22003-1556 Office: Jarvis Cons Ltd PO Box 1650 Annandale VA 22003 E-mail: jay@jarvisconsulting.org.

JARVIS, GILBERT ANDREW, humanities educator, writer; b. Chelsea, Mass., Feb. 13, 1941; s. Vernon Owen and Angeline M. (Burkard) J.; m. Carol Jean Ganter, Jan. 26, 1963; children: Vicki Lynn, Mark Christopher. BA, St. Norbert Coll., De Pere, Wis., 1963; MA, Purdue U., 1965, PhD, 1970. Prof. Ohio State U., Columbus, 1970-95, chmn. humanities edn., 1980-83, assoc. chmn. dept. ednl. theory and practice, 1983-87, chmn. dept. ednl. studies, 1987-95, dir. ESL programs, 1994-2000, chmn. prof. emeritus, 1995—. Cons. Internat. Edn. Program, U.S. Dept. Edn., Washington, 1977-84, many schs., agys. and pub. cos. Author: Et Vous?, 1983, 86, 89; Invitation, 1979, 2d edit., 1984, 3d edit., 1988, 4th edit., 1993, Y tu?, 1986, 2d edit., 1988, Connaitre et se connaitre, 3d edit., 1986, Invitation Essentials, 1991, 2d edit., 1995, Invitation au monde francophone, 2000; editor: The Challenge for Excellence, 1984; mem. editl. bd. Modern Lang. Jour., 1979-86; adv. bd. Can. Modern lang. Rev., 1982—. Mem. Am. Coun. Tchg. Fgn. Langs. (editor Rev. Fgn. Lang. Edn. 1974, 75, 76, 77), Phi Delta Kappa. Avocations: travel, photography. Home: 8337 Evangeline Dr Columbus OH 43235-1136

JARVIS, IRENE, retired medical/surgical nurse; b. Bronx, Ny, Aug. 24, 1924; d. John Henry and Ella Harrison Jarvis; 1 child, Yvonne Marie Johnson. MA, BA, Bklyn Coll., Brooklyn, NY, 1978. RN NY State Edn. Dept., 1950. Child abuse expert NYC Dept. of Human Resouces, New York, NY, 1973—92; hosp. investigator NYC Dept. of Hospitals, New York, NY, 1960—73; head nurse Cumberland Hosp., New York, NY, 1950—59. Adventist. Avocations: travel, reading.

JARVIS, LINDA MARIE, music director, music educator; b. Minneapolis, Minn., Oct. 17, 1954; d. Lyle Dayton and Edna Walker Bergseth; children: Kathryn, Paul. BA Music Edn., Augsburg Coll., 1976. Organist/choir dir. Mt. Olivet Luth. Ch., Minneapolis, Minn., 1977—87; music tchr. Hopkins Pub. Schools, Minnetonka, Minn., 1992—; dir. of music ministry St. Philip the Deacon Luth. Ch., Plymouth, Minn., 1996—; freelance performer and instr. Minneapolis, Minn. Repertoire and stds. chmn. Am. Choral Dirs. Assn. of Minn., Eden Prairie, Minn., 2000—. Singer: (choral workshop) Carnegie Hall, 2000. Mem.: Am. Guild Organists, Am. Choral Dirs. Assn. Lutheran. Avocations: hiking, skiing, travel. Home: 7288 Bren Ln Eden Prairie MN 55346 Office: Hopkins N Jr HS 10700 Cedar Lake Rd Minnetonka MN 55305

JARVIS, MARY GRACE, principal; Prin. Smoky Hill H.S., Aurora, Colo., 1988—2003, Cherokee Trail H.S., 2003—. Recipient Blue Ribbon Sch. award, 1990—91, Micken Found. Nat. Edn. award, 1993, NASSP/MetLife Nat. Prin. of the Year, 1996. Office: Cherokee Trail High Sch 25901 E Arapahoe Rd Aurora CO 80016*

JARVIS, PETER R. lawyer; b. N.Y.C., July 19, 1950; BA in Econs. magna cum laude, Harvard U., 1972; MA in Econs., JD, Yale U., 1976. Bar: Oreg. 1976, U.S. Dist. Ct. Oreg. 1976, U.S. Ct. Appeals (9th cir.) 1977, Wash. 1983, U.S. Dist. Ct. (we. dist.) Wash. 1983, U.S. Dist. Ct. (ea. dist.) Wash. 1985, U.S. Tax Ct. 1991. Mem. Stoel Rives LLP, Portland, Oreg. Author: (with others) Oregon Rules of Professional Responsibility (updated annually); editor, author: (with others) The Ethical Oregon Lawyer, 1991, 98; ethics columnists: Oregon Law Jour.; spkr. on legal ethics issues. Mem. ALI (Harrison Tweed Spl. Merit award 1993), Oreg. State Bar (former mem. legal ethics com., Pres.'s Membership Svcs. award 1991), Wash. State Bar (mem. profl. conduct com.), Phi Beta Kappa. Office: Stoel Rives LLP 900 SW 5th Ave Ste 2600 Portland OR 97204-1268

JARVIS, RICHARD S. academic administrator; b. Nottingham, Eng., Feb. 13, 1949; came to U.S., 1974; s. John Leslie and Mary Margaret (Dodman) J.; m. Marilou Thompson, Nov. 7, 1986; stepchildren: Kimberly Nipko, Christopher Healey. BA in Geography, Cambridge (Eng.) U., 1970, MA, 1974, PhD in Geography, 1975. Lectr. Durham (Eng.) U., 1973-74; assoc. prof. SUNY, Buffalo, 1975-87, asst. to pres., 1986-87, v.p. acad. Fredonia, 1987-90, prof. geoscis., 1987-90; vice provost SUNY Sys., Albany, 1990-94; chancellor Univ. and C.C. Sys. Nev., Reno and Las Vegas, 1994-99, U.S. Open U., Aurora, Colo., 1999—2002, Oreg. U. Sys., 2002—. Mem. adv. bd. Bechtel Nev., Las Vegas, 1995-97, NTS Devel. Corp., Las Vegas, 1997. Editor: River Networks, 1983; contbr. articles to profl. jours. Trustee United Way, Reno, 1996-99, EDAWN, Reno, 1996-99. Office: Oreg Univ Sys PO Box 751 Portland OR 97207 E-mail: richard_jarvis@ous.edu.

JARVIS, ROBERT MARK, law educator; b. NYC, Oct. 17, 1959; s. Rubin and Ute (Hacklander) J.; m. Judith Anne Mellman, Mar. 3, 1989. BA, Northwestern U., 1980; JD, U. Pa., 1983; LLM, NYU, 1986. Bar: N.Y. 1984, Fla. 1990. Assoc. Haight Gardner Poor & Havens, N.Y.C., 1983-85, Baker & McKenzie, N.Y.C., 1985-87; asst. prof. law ctr. Nova Southeastern U., Ft. Lauderdale, Fla., 1987-90, assoc. prof., 1990-92, prof., 1992—. Chmn. bd. dirs. Miami Maritime Arbitration Bd., 1993-94; vice chmn. bd. dirs. Miami Internat. Arbitration and Mediation Inst., 1993-94; mem. adv. bd. Carolina Acad. Press, 1996—, Sports Law Reporter, 2000—, hospitalitylawyer.com, 2000—. Co-author: AIDS: Cases and Materials, 1989, 3d edit, 2002, AIDS Law in a Nutshell, 1991, 2d edit., 1996, Notary Law and Practice: Cases and Materials, 1997, Travel Law: Cases and Materials, 1998, Sports Law: Cases and Materials, 1999, Art and Museum Law: Cases and Materials, 2002, Gaming Law: Cases and Materials, 2003; author: Careers in Admiralty and Maritime Law, 1993, An Admiralty Law Anthology, 1995; editor: Maritime Arbitration, 1999, Law of Cruise Ships, 2000; co-editor: Prime Time Law: Fictional Television as Legal Narrative, 1998, Bush v. Gore: The Fight for Florida's Vote, 2001, Amicus Humoriae: An Anthology of Legal Humor, 2003; mem. editl. bd. Washington Lawyer, 1988-94, Jour. Maritime Law and Commerce, 1990-92, 2001—, assoc. editor, 1993-95, editor, 1996-2000, Maritime Law Reporter, 1991-99, Hospitality Law, 1999-2001; adv. bd. Transnat. Lawyer, 1991—, World Arbitration and Mediation Report, 1990—, U. San Francisco Maritime Law Jour., 1992-95, 2002—; contbg. editor Preview U.S. Supreme Ct. Cases, 1990-95, 99-2002. Mem.: ABA (vice chmn. admiralty law com. young lawyers divsn. 1992—93, chair 1993—94), Phi Delta Phi (province pres. 1989—91, coun. 1991—93), Assn. Am. Law Schs. (chmn.-elect maritime law sect. 1991—93, chmn. 1993—94), Maritime Law Assn. U.S., Fla. Bar Assn. (admiralty law com. 1988—95, vice chmn. 1991—92, chmn. 1992—93, exec. coun. internat. law sect. 1992—96), Acacia, Northwestern U. Club South Fla. (v.p. 1992—93, pres. 1993—95), Phi Beta Kappa. Democrat. Jewish. Avocations: theatre, running. Office: Nova Southeastern U Law Ctr 3305 College Ave Fort Lauderdale FL 33314-7721 Business E-Mail: jarvisb@nsu.law.nova.edu.

JARVIS, TYLER J. mathematician; b. Salt Lake City, July 29, 1966; s. Donald Karl and Janelle Leona (Jamison) J.; m. Heidi (Baumann). BS, Brigham Young Univ., Provo, UT., 1989, MS, 1990; MA, Princeton Univ., 1992, PhD, 1994. Asst. prof. Miss. State U., Starkville, 1994-96, Brigham Young Univ., Provo, Utah, 1996—2001, assoc. prof., 2001—. Bd. dir. Meyer and Liechty Corp., Lindon, Utah. Contbg. author Orbifolds in Mathematics and Physics, 2002. Recipient Career Award NSF, 1995-98; Grad. fellow Nat. Def. Sci. and Engring., 1990-93; Presdl. scholar Brigham Young U., Provo, 1984-89. Mem. Am. Math. Soc. Mem. Lds Ch. Office: Dept of Math Brigham Young Univ Provo UT 84602

JARVIS, WILLIAM ROBERT, epidemiologist, educator; b. Oakland, Calif., June 2, 1948; s. John James and Mattie Belle (Steele) J.; m. Janine M. Jason, July 4, 1982; children: Danielle Kristin, Ashley Alana. BS in Psychology with honors, U. Calif., Davis, 1970; MD, U. Tex., Houston, 1974. Intern U. Tex. Med. Ctr., Houston, 1974-75; resident in pediat. Children's Hosp., L.A., 1975-77; pediatric infectious disease fellow Toronto Hosp. for Sick Children, 1977-78; fellow pediat. infectious diseases, virology, public health Yale U. Sch. Med., 1978-80; commd. med. officer USPHS, 1980, advanced through grades to capt., 1990; asst. chief Nat. Nosocomial Infections Surveillance Systems Ctrs. for Disease Control, Atlanta, 1981-90, asst. chief epidemiology br., 1984-87, chief epidemiology br. hosp. infections program, 1987-91, chief investigation, prevention br. hosp. infections program, 1991-2000, acting dir. hosp. infections program, 1996-98, assoc. dir. program devel. Divsn. Healthcare Quality Promotion, 2001—02; pres. Shea, 2001—02; dir. Office Extramural Rsch. Nat. Ctr. for Infectious Diseases, Atlanta, 2002—. Asst. prof. pediat. infectious disease and immunology Emory U., Atlanta, 1985-96, assoc. prof., 1996—; asst. prof. Rollins Sch. Pub. Health, 1999—. Contbr. Mem. Infectious Diseases Soc. Am., Am. Soc. Microbiology, Soc. Hosp. Epidemiologists, Sigma Xi. Roman Catholic. Avocations: stock market, gardening, tennis, travel. Home: 827 W Ponce De Leon Ave Decatur GA 30030-2859 Office: Ctrs Disease Control and Prevention Office Extramural Rsch-Nat Ctr Infectiou 1600 Clifton Mailstop C-19 Atlanta GA 30333 E-mail: wrj1@cdc.gov.

JARZEN, DAVID MACARTHUR, research scientist; b. Cleve., Oct. 19, 1941; s. Leonard Donald Jarzen and Lucille Katherine MacArthur; m. Susan Althea Klein, Nov. 24, 1962; children: Thomas, Robert. BS, Kent (Ohio) State U., 1967, MA, 1969; PhD, U. Toronto, 1973. Curator fossil plants Nat. Mus. of Can., Ottawa, Ont., Can., 1973-85, rsch. scientist, 1985-90; palynologist, rsch. scientist Canadian Mus. of Nature, Ottawa, 1990-96; coord. mus. ops. Fla. Mus. of Natural History, Gainesville, 1997—2002; dir. global edn. Selby Bot. Gardens, Sarasota, Fla., 2002—03. Acting dir. Can. Mus. of Nature, Ottawa, 1980-81. Author book; contbr. articles to profl. jours. Fellow Nat. Explorer's Club; mem. Am. Assn. of Stratigraphic Palynologists (pres. elect 2001), Internat. Freelance Photographers, Orgn. for Tropical Studies, Inc., Rainforest Conservation Soc. of Queensland, Bot. Soc. of Am. (paleobotany sect), World Conservation Union, Palynological and Palaeobotanical Assn. of Australasia, Internat. Fedn. of Palynological Socs. (sec., treas. 1984-89), Internat. Fedn. of Palynological Socs. (v.p. 1992-96, councillor 1988-96), Can. Assn. of Palynologists (pres. 1980-81, pres.-elect 1979-80), St. John's Coll., Ohio Acad. of Sci., Assn. for Tropical Botany, Fla. Acad. Scis. Mailing: PO Box 1136 Sarasota FL 34230 E-mail: aquilapollenites@sigmazi.org.

JASCHIK, SCOTT P. editor; b. Boston, May 8, 1963; s. Nathan L. and Suzanne (Melin) J. BA, Cornell U., 1985. Asst. editor Chronicle of Higher Edn., Washington, 1985-88, sr. editor, 1988-92, assoc. mng. editor, 1992-96, dep. mng. editor, 1996-98, mng. editor, 1998-99, editor, 1999—. Mem. Am. Soc. Mag. Editors, Investigative Reporters and Editors, Edn. Writers Assn. Office: Chronicle of Higher Edn 1255 23d St NW Washington DC 20037 E-mail: scott.jaschik@chronicle.com.

JASCOURT, HUGH D. lawyer, arbitrator, mediator; b. Phila., Mar. 25, 1935; s. Jacquard A. and Gladys Mae (Bregen) J.; m. Resa B. Zall, Nov. 28, 1963; children: Stephen, Leigh. AB, U. Pa., 1956; JD, Wayne State U., 1960. Bar: Mich. 1961, U.S. Supreme Ct. 1965, D.C. 1967. Atty. advisor U.S. Dept. Labor, Washington, 1960-64; asst. dir. employee-mgmt. rels. Am. Fedn. Govt. Employees, Washington, 1964-65; atty. advisor Nat. Labor Rels. Bd., Washington, 1965-66; exec. dir. Fed. Bar Assn., Washington, 1966-67; house counsel Am. Fedn. of State, County, & Mcpl. Employees, Washington, 1967-69; sr. labor-law counsel Bd. of Gov. Fed. Reserve Bd., Washington, 1969-72; dir. Pub. Employment Rels. Rsch. Inst., Washington, 1972-74; asst. solicitor U.S. Dept. of Interior, Washington, 1974-82; sr. labor-law counsel U.S. Dept. Commerce, Washington, 1982-90; pres. Agency for Dispute Resolutions and Synergistic Rels., Greenbelt, Md., 1991—. Lectr. George Washington U. Law Sch., Washington, 1970—75; chmn. unfair labor practice panel Prince George County Employee Rels. Bd., Upper Marlboro, Md., 1972—83; mem. Greenbelt (Md.) Employee Rels. Bd., 1977—, chair, 2002—; panel mem. Fed. Mediation and Conciliation Svc., Nat. Mediation Bd., Nat. Assn. Security Dealers, Libr. of Congress, D.C. PERB, Washington, N.J. PERC, N.J. Bd. Mediation, SSA-Am., Fedn. Govt. Employees; arbitrator/mediator, 1973—. Author, editor: Trends in Public Sector Labor Relations, 1973, Government Labor Relations, 1979; author: (with others) Labor Relations, 1978-82; Collective Bargaining, 1980; labor rels. editor Jour. Law and Edn., 1972-2001. Pres. Road Runners Club Am., 1962-66, Prince George's County (Md.) Fedn. of Recreational Couns., 1969, Prince George's County Coun. of PTAs, 1989-90; mem. Prince George's County Cmty. Adv. Coun., 1988—; coach U.S. track and field team AAU So. Games, Trinidad, 1964, Internat. Cross Country Championship, Morocco, 1966; v.p. Am. Running and Fitness Assn., 1968-84. Inductee Road Runners Club Am. Hall of Fame, 1986; initial inductee D.C. Road Runners Club Hall of Fame, 1994; named master ofcl. honoree Penn Relays, 2000. Fellow Coll. of Labor and Employment Lawyers; mem. ABA (com. on state and local labor employment and law, chmn. subcom. 1982—, co-chmn. com. on fed. svc. labor and employment law 1985-97, mem. mediation com., sect. on dispute resolution), ASPA, Soc. Fed. Labor Rels. Profls. (bd. dirs. 1992-93), Assn. for Conflict Resolution (charter mem., co-chair fed. workplace ADR com. 2002-), Indsl. Rels. Rsch. Assn., Internat. Pers. Mgmt. Assn., Am. Arbitration Assn., Md. Coun. on Dispute Resolution. Office: Agency Dispute Resolution & Synergistic Rels 18 Maplewood Ct Greenbelt MD 20770-1907 E-mail: hugh.d.jascourt@verizon.net.

JASEN, MATTHEW JOSEPH, lawyer, state justice; b. Buffalo, Dec. 13, 1915; s. Joseph John and Celina (Perlinski) Jasinski; m. Anastasia Gawinski, Oct. 4, 1943 (dec. Aug. 1970); children: Peter M., Mark M., Christine (Mrs. David K. Mac Leod), Carol Ann, (Mrs. J. David Sampson); m. Gertrude O'Connor Travers, Mar. 25, 1972 (dec. Nov. 1972); m. Grace Yungbluth Frauenheim, Aug. 31, 1973. BA, Canisius Coll., 1937; LLB, U. Buffalo, 1939; postgrad., Harvard U., 1944; LLD (hon.), Union U., 1980, N.Y. Law Sch., 1981. Bar: N.Y. 1940. Ptnr. firm Beyer, Jasen & Boland, Buffalo, 1940-43; pres. U.S. Security Rev. Bd., Wurttemberg-Baden, Germany, 1945-46; judge U.S. Mil. Govt. Ct., Heidelberg, Germany, 1946-49; sr. ptnr. firm Jasen, Manz, Johnson & Bayger, Buffalo, 1949-57; justice N.Y. Supreme Ct. (8th jud. dist.), 1957-67; judge N.Y. Ct. Appeals, 1968-85; U.S. Supreme Ct. spl. master S.C. v. U.S., 1987-88; spl. master Ill. vs. Ky. U.S. Supreme Ct., 1989-95; of counsel Moot & Sprague, Buffalo, 1986-90; counsel Jasen, Jasen & Sampson, P.C., Buffalo, 1990-99, Jasen & Jasen, P.C., Buffalo, 1999—. Mem. N.Y. State Jud. Screening Com., 1996—. Contbr. articles to profl. jours. Mem. council U. Buffalo, 1963-66; trustee Canisius Coll. Chair of Polish Culture, also, Nottingham Acad. Served to capt. AUS, 1943-46, ETO. Fellow Hilbert Coll.; recipient Disting. Alumnus award SUNY-Buffalo Sch. Law, 1969, Disting. Alumnus award Alumni Assn., 1976, Disting. Alumnus award Canisius Coll., 1978, Edwin F. Jaeckle award SUNY-Buffalo Sch. Law, 1982. Mem. Nat. Conf. Appellate Judges, State U. N.Y. at Buffalo Law Sch. Alumni Assn. (pres. 1964-65), Am., N.Y. State, Erie County bar assns., Am. Law Inst., Am. Judicature Soc., Lawyers Club Buffalo (pres. 1961-62), Nat. Advocates Club, Profl. Businessmen's Assn. Western N.Y. (pres. 1952), Phi Alpha Delta, DiGamma Soc. Roman Catholic (mem. Bishop's Bd. Govs., Buffalo diocese 1951—). Clubs: K.C. (4 deg.). Home: 26 Pine Ter Orchard Park NY 14127-3928 Office: Ste 700 69 Delaware Ave Buffalo NY 14202-3805 E-mail: jjatts@buffnet.net.

JASHEL, LARRY STEVEN (L. STEVEN ROSE), entrepreneur, media consultant; b. Dayton, Ohio, Jan. 21, 1950; s. Joseph John and Ruth Margarete (Race) J. Student, Harper Coll., Palatine, Ill., 1968-70. Pub.'s asst. Pub.'s Devel. Corp., Chgo., 1971-73; pub. rels. dir. Ill. Entertainer/Chgo. Star/Bankers' Guide, Chgo., 1973-76; v.p. Internat. Media Prodns., Inc., Chgo., 1976-78, Microdynamics Corp., Chgo., 1978-80; exec. v.p. Calif. Aqua Tech, Inc., The Solar Generation, L.A., 1980-82; pres., CEO Ra-Tel Comms. Corp., Ra-Tel Entertainment Corp./Cable Radio, Chgo., 1982-88; founder Steven Rose Prodns. and L.S. Jashel Assocs., Chgo., 1988-98; founder, CEO Spuppets, Ltd., 1996, Children's Cultural Network, 2000—; exec. dir. Superior Benefit Solutions, 1998-2000. TV producer, dir., writer Ind. Broadcasting, Chgo., 1982—; radio producer, on-air personality Nat. Pub. Radio, Chgo. and Washington, 1982—, WJRC-AM, Chgo., 1987-88; music producer for ind. rec. artists, Chgo., 1982—; cons. Corp. for Pub. Broadcasting, 1982—; speaker in field. Musician (singer and composer): 180 copyrighted songs; author: Song of a New

Age, 1990, A Bakers Dozen, 1995, (book and TV script) Lovestar--The Exciting Adventures, 1994—95; author: (prodr. and dir.) Spuppets (puppets in space), 1997; co-author: Morning Song, 1997; author: The Best Poems of 1997, (book) Planet Medieval, 1998, Mystic Blue and the Z-Generation, 2001, Beyond Dreams, 2002; musician: (musical acts) The Detours, Sudden, The Amboy Dukes, The Yellow Brick Road, J.J. Lee and the Radiants, 1964—72, Mystic Blues, 2002—; actor: (films) Sore Losers, 2001, Road to Perdition, 2002, Insanity, 2003—; author: (book) Discovery of Earf, 2003. Recipient Blue Ribbon Athlete award, Midwest Sports Assn., 1968, Film Festival award 1984, Am. Svc. award Am. Svc. Corp., 1988, Editor's Choice award Nat. Libr. Poetry, 1992, 97, Nat./Internat. award of Distinction for children's video and packaging, 1998, Videographer award, 1998, Telly award, 2000, Omni award, 2001; named delegation rep. to Presdl. Inaugaration Ball, Washington, 1980. Mem. ASCAP (award 1998-99, 2000), NARAS (Grammy awards 1982—), Nat. Assn. Pvt. Enterprise, Smithsonian Instn. (nat. assoc.), Nat. Cable TV Assn., Internat. Assn. Bus., Eckankar, Children's Entertainment Assn., Chgo. C. of C. Avocations: writing for children, bicycling, camping, hiking. Office: 15519B Keating Ave Oak Forest IL 60452-3616

JASIEWICZ, RONALD CLARENCE, anesthesiologist, educator; b. Suffern, N.Y., June 8, 1964; s. Clarence William and Adele Helen (Rucki) J. AAS in Sci. and Math., SUNY, Rockland, 1984; BS in Life Sci., N.Y. Inst. Tech., 1987; DO, N.Y. Coll. Osteo. Medicine, 1992; AAS in Emergency Med. Tech., SUNY, Rockland, 1993. Diplomate Am. Bd. Anesthesiology, Am. Osteo. Bd. Anesthesiology, Nat. Bd. Osteo. Med. Examiners. Unit asst. Good Samaritan Hosp., Suffern, 1980-87; paramedic Empress Ambulance Svc., Yonkers, N.Y., 1985-86, Nyack (N.Y.) E.M.S., 1986-87; intern in medicine and surgery Wilson Meml. Regional Med. Ctr., Johnson City, N.Y., 1992-93; asst. clin. instr. Stony Brook (N.Y.) Med. Sch., 1993-96; resident in anesthesiology Univ. Med. Ctr., 1993-96; fellow pediatric anesthesiology Children's Hosp. of Buffalo, 1996-97; clin. instr. Buffalo Med. Sch., 1996-97; pediatric anesthesiologist U. Med. Ctr. Stony Brook, N.Y., 1997—; asst. prof. anesthesiology SUNY Sch. Medicine, Stony Brook, 1997—. Mem. admission com. SUNY Stony Brook Med. Sch., 1998-2001, mem. cirriculum com., 2001-. Bd. mgrs., treas. Stonington at Port Jefferson-Condominium II, 1998—2001; bd. dirs. Stonington at Port Jefferson HOA, 1998—2001. Med. corps. USNR, 1998—. Am. Osteo. Coll. Anesthesiologists, Am. Osteo. Assn., Sigma Omicron. Roman Catholic. Avocations: downhill skiing, travel, kayaking, physical fitness, the arts. Office: U Med Ctr at Stony Brook Dept Pediatric Anes Stony Brook NY 11794-0001

JASINSKI-CALDWELL, MARY L. company executive; b. Chester, Pa., May 8, 1959; d. A. Robert and Helen M. Jasinski; m. William A. Caldwell, Aug. 4, 1990; children: Helaina M., Anna L. Student, student, Loyola Coll., Balt., 1980; AS, Goldey Beacom Coll., Wilmington, Del., 1982, BS, 1983. Registered orthotic fitter; cert. sr. pharmacy technician. Gen. mgr. pension plan City Pharmacy of Elkton (Md.), Inc., 1975-96, treas., 1987-96, jr. ptnr., 1994, v.p., 1996—; founder, pres. City Home Health Care, Inc., Elkton, 1997—. Disc jockey, promoter Garfield's Restaurant, Elkton; editl. writer local newspapers; pro-life columnist KC newsletter; nat. bd. advisors McKesson Drug Co., 2001—. Creator ednl. program PARTICIP.A.A.T.E. For Life. Advisor Cecil County Pregnancy Ctr., Cecil County Bd. Edn. Textbook Adoption Policy Com., 1995; pro-life educator City of Elkton, Inc.; bd. dirs. Cecil County chpt. ARC, 1996—2001, fin. devel. chmn., 2000—01; bd. dirs. Mission Am., Inc., Md. Right to Life, 1993—94, co-chair Cecil County chpt., 1993—94. Alpha Chi scholar, Lindback scholar; recipient J.W. Miller award, Outstanding Achievement in Excellence award K.C., 1994, Ralph and Eleanor Hicks Outstanding Vol. svc. award ARC, Cecil County, Md., 1999-2000; named Family of Yr., 1995; named to Honor Roll of Best 250 Independents in U.S., Drug Topics, 1992. Mem. NAFE, NRA, Am. Pharmacists Assn. (assoc.), Am. Mgmt. Assn., Nat. Fedn. Ind. Bus., Bd. Orthotic Cert., Am. Assn. Pharm. Technicians, Nat. Right to Life Com., Am. Life League, Internat. Platform Assn., Pro-Life Md., Christian Coalition, Cath. Alliance, Cecil County C. of C., Stopp Internat., Human Life Internat., Concerned Women for Am., Pharmacists for Life, Goldey Beacom Coll. Alumni Assn., Movement for a Better Am., Cath. League, Liberty Alliance, Epic Pharmacies, Inc., Susan B. Anthony List, Alpha Chi. Republican. Roman Catholic. Avocations: home improvement, gardening, social concerns, pro-life education, reading. Office: City Pharmacy Inc 723 N Bridge St Elkton MD 21921-5398 E-mail: citypharmacy@dol.net.

JASIORKOWSKI, ROBERT LEE, real estate broker, computer consultant; b. Milw., Nov. 17, 1954; s. Thomas Joseph and Alice Rosemary (Lee) J. BA, U. Wis., Milw., 1987. Dir. info. tech., real estate broker, property mgr. Nat. Realty Mgmt., Inc., Milw., 1990—. Real estate broker ERA Worth Realty, Inc., Glendale, Wis., 1991-94; computer cons. Hometrak Realty, Milw., 1986-90. Mem. Nat. Assn. Realtors, Nat. Assn. Real Estate Appraisers (cert.), U. Wis.-Milw. Alumni Assn. (life). Republican. Avocations: photography, astronomy. Home: 3561 S Honey Creek Dr Milwaukee WI 53220-1246 Office: Nat Realty Mgmt Inc 1155 Quail Ct Pewaukee WI 53072-3768 E-mail: rjasior@national-realty.net.

JASKIEWICZ, DAVID WALTER, optometrist; b. Beaver Falls, Pa., Aug. 28, 1956; s. Walter John and Edith Marie (Maljevec) J.; m. Cynthia Marie Frederick, Sept. 22, 1984; 1 child, Calista Marie Frederick-Jaskiewicz. BSME, U. Notre Dame, 1978; BS in Gen. Scis., Pa. Coll. Optometry, Phila., 1980, OD, 1983. Lic. optometrist, Pa. Assoc. Optometric Care, Aliquppa, Pa., 1983-85; assoc., jr. ptnr. Eye Care Assocs., Erie, Pa., 1985-88; assoc. Pearle Vision, Pitts., 1988-90; owner Valley Vision Ctr., Monaca, Pa., 1990-92; assoc. Walmart Vision Ctr., Monaca, 1992—. Chair optometric adv. bd. Walmart, 1994-96, optometrist bus. enhancement and solutions team, 2001—. Named Walmart Dr. of Yr., 2000. Mem. U. Notre Dame Sorin Soc. Roman Catholic. Avocations: swimming, biking, hiking, reading, music. Home: 340 Pinkerton Rd Wexford PA 15090-8678 Office: Rt 18 Monaca PA 15061

JASKOT, JOHN JOSEPH, retired insurance company executive; b. Allentown, Pa., Dec. 5, 1921; s. George W. and Anna (Kuzma) J.; m. Joyce Ranck, May 25, 1946; children: Lisa Anne, Philip Ross. Student, Muhlenberg Coll., Allentown, 1947-49; JD with honors, George Washington U., 1951, LL.M., 1953. Bar: D.C. 1951. Exec. v.p., gen. counsel, corp. sec. United Svcs. Life Ins. Co., Washington, 1953-88; v.p., legal counsel United Svcs. Gen. Life Co., 1968-87; v.p. Bankers Security Life Ins. Soc., 1985-88, also bd. dirs.; sec. Provident Life Ins. Co., 1983-86, United Olympic Life Ins. Co., 1984-86; sec., sr. v.p. USLICO Corp., 1984-88; ret., 1988. With USCGR, 1942-46, PTO. Mem. Am. Arbitration Assn. (arbitrator 1988—). Home: 15101 Interlachen Dr # 920 Silver Spring MD 20906-5620 *True success should only be measured by an individual's own assessment of his accomplishments.*

JASKOWSKI, TROY D, immunologist, researcher; b. Minneapolis, Minn., Jan. 17, 1968; s. John Edward Jaskowski and Betty Earline Teal; m. Maria Consuelo Fierro, Sept. 6, 1993; children: Milagros Lorenza, Marisa Athena. Microbiology, Weber State U., Ogden, UT, 1988—96; Clin. Lab. Sci., Chemistry, Weber State U., 1988—96. Rsch. specialist, immunology ARUP Inst., Salt Lake City, 1990—. Contbr. articles. Mem.: Assn. of Med. Lab. Immunologists (AMLI) (assoc.). Achievements include development of Serologic and Protein assays. Office: ARUP Inst 500 Chipeta Way Salt Lake City UT 84108 Office Fax: 801-584-5109. E-mail: jaskowtd@aruplab.com.

JASKULA, JANET, pediatrics nurse, educator; b. Chgo., Mar. 9, 1951; d. John J. and Katheryn O. (Cheatham) J. Diploma, Ill. Masonic Med. Ctr., Chgo., 1973; BSN cum laude, Sonoma State U., Rohnert Park, Calif., 1983; MS, U. Calif., San Francisco, 1986. Cert. pub. health nurse. Staff nurse Rush Med. Ctr., Chgo., 1973-75, Kentfield (Calif.) Hosp., 1976-78, R.K. Davies Hosp., San Francisco, 1978-80, Marin Gen. Hosp., Greenbrae, Calif., 1983-86; clin. nurse in pediatrics U. Calif., San Francisco, 1980-86, clin. nurse III, in pediatric surgery, 1986-94, asst. clin. prof. dept. family health care nursing; pediatric clin. instr. Coll. San Mateo, Calif., 1994-96; clin. specialist pediatric nephrology U. Calif., San Francisco, 1995—. Mem. ethics com. U. Calif., San Francisco, 2002—. Mem. ANA, Calif. Nurses Assn., U. Calif. San Francisco Nursing Alumni Assn., Sigma Theta Tau.

JASLOW, HOWARD, engineer; b. Bklyn., Jan. 5, 1935; s. Louis and Myrtle (Schneider) J.; m. Barbara Theodora Karney, June 9, 1956; children: Amy Lisa, Russell Todd, Kenneth Mark, Wayne Harris, Melinda Kay. B in Aeronautical Engring., Poly. Inst. Bklyn., 1956; MS in Physics, Adelphi U., 1963. Engr. N.Am. Aviation, L.A., 1956—58, Republic Aviation, Farmingdale, NY, 1958-61; chief engr. Colt Firearms, Jericho, N.Y., 1961-72; project engr. Oceanics Inc., Plainview, N.Y., 1972-76; mgr. rsch. & devel. Gould, Inc., Melville, N.Y., 1976-82; sr. rsch. engr. Norden Sys., Melville, 1983-84; dir. engring. ILC Data Device Corp., Bohemia, N.Y., 1984-87; sr. staff scientist Digital Signal Corp., Bohemia, 1987-91; pres. Innovative Algorithms, Smithtown, N.Y., 1991—. Mem. AIAA. Home: 22 Creekside Way Asheville NC 28804-1763 Office: Innovative Algorithms 22 Creekside Way Asheville NC 28804-1763 E-mail: innovalg@aol.com.

JASON, J. JULIE, money manager, author, lawyer; b. Owensboro, Ky. d. Richard and Grazina Pauliukonis; m. Marius J. Jason, Dec. 19, 1970; children: Ilona, Leila. BA, Baldwin-Wallace Coll., 1971; JD, Cleve. State U., 1974; LLM, Columbia U., 1975. Bar: Ohio 1974, N.Y. 1976, U.S. Dist Ct. (so. dist.) N.Y. 1976, U.S. Ct. Appeals (2d cir.) 1976, U.S. Supreme Ct. 1978. Pvt. practice, N.Y.C., 1974-78; asst. gen. counsel Paine Webber, N.Y.C., 1978 83; pres. P.W. Trust and Paine Webber Futures Mgmt. Co., N.Y.C., 1983-88; sr. fin. svcs. atty. Donovan, Leisure, Newton & Irvine, N.Y.C., 1988-89; co-founder, mng. dir. Jackson, Grant & Co., Stamford, Conn., 1989—. Arbitrator NYSE; mediator U.S. Bankruptcy Ct., 1997. Author: You and Your 401(K), 1996, The 401(K) Plan Handbook, 1997, Strategic Investing, 2001; columnist: 401-OK. Mem. ABA, AAUW (chair scholarship com. 1992-93), Nat. Assn. Securities Dealers (cert. arbitrator, cert. mediator), Am. Soc. Journalists & Authors, Investment Co. Inst. (sec. regulation com. 1978-83), The Corp. Bar, Columbia U. Alumni Club of Fairfield County (pres. 1993-94, chair pres.'s coun. 1994-96). Office: Jackson Grant & Co 1177 High Ridge Rd Stamford CT 06905-1203

JASPER, DORIS J. BERRY, nurse; b. Banner, Miss., Sept. 12, 1933; d. William Richard and Lena Martha (Gambill) Berry; m. Lyman W. Jasper, Jan. 8, 1949; children: Richard L., Lynn William. Student, Blytheville (Ark.) Sch. Nursing, 1949, Purdue U., Westville, Ind., 1979-80, Lake Mich. Coll., Benton Harbor, 1980—83. Staff nurse St. Anthony's Hosp., Michigan City, Ind., 1951-66; pvt. duty nurse Michigan City, 1962-68; emergency rm. nurse St. Anthony's Hosp., 1968-74; charge nurse, emergency rm. nurse Meml. Hosp., Michigan City, 1974-75; pvt. duty nurse Three Oaks, Mich., 1972-84, Michigan City, 1981-88; staff nurse Alpha Christiansan Registry, New Buffalo, Mich., 1988—; pvt. practice Three Oaks, 1989-90; owner, practitioner Jaspers Health Care, Three Oaks, 1991—; owner, mgr. D.J.'s Frolick Kennel. Pvt. practice No. Ind., So. Mich.; co-owner, mgr. grain farm. Med. missionary Chiadoc, El Paso, Tex., 2002. Mem. Bus. and Profl. Women's Club, Inc. (legis. chair dist. 2 1987-88, rec. sec. dist. 2, exec. bd. mem.), Mich. Fedn. Bus. Profl. Women USA (legis. chair dist. 9), New Buffalo Area Bus. Profl. Women (legis. chair), Tenn. Walking Horse Assn., Smithsonian Inst. Republican. Baptist. Avocations: reading, horseback riding, raising Tenn. walking horses, traveling, breeding trainer of Rottweiller dogs. Home and Office: 1883 Bethel Church Rd Camden TN 38320

JASPER, JOHN A. writer, lawyer; b. Latonia, Ky., Feb. 26, 1954; s. John A. and Adraw C. Jasper; m. Alexandra Powers Everhart; children: Caitlin, Taulbe. BA, North Ky. U., Highland Heights, KY, 1976; MA, U. of Cincinnati, Cincinnati, OH, 1979; JD, Antioch Law Sch., Washington, DC, 1982. Factory worker UPS, Cincinnati, Ohio, 1972—76; asst. city mgr. Covington, Ky., 1976—77; city mgr. Chevy Chase, Friendship Heights, Md., 1977—79; legis. asst. U.S. Senate Judiciary Commn., Washington, 1980—82; prosecutor State of Ky., Luoisville, 1983—88; sr. atty. US Govt., Washington, 1988—. Panelist Mystery Writers Conf., 2000—01, Va. Festival of the Book, 2000—01. Author: (novels) Sweet Poison of Misused Wine. Campaign mgmt. Ky. Governer race, Congress race, County Exec. race, Ky., 1983—87. Independent. Avocation: rugby. Home: 4101 Cathedral Avenue Washington DC 20016 Personal E-mail: jasperbook@aol.com.

JASPER, NORMAN HANS, engineer; b. Detmold, Germany, May 10, 1918; came to U.S., 1932; s. Friedrich and Hannah (Franzmeier) J.; m. Wilma L. Knief, Aug. 1940; children: Norma, Richard. BME, CCNY, 1941; MS, U. Md., 1952; Dr. Engring., Catholic U. Am., 1956. Naval architect Puget Sound Naval Shipyard, Bremerton, Wash., 1941-46; with David Taylor Model Basin U.S. Navy, Washington, 1946-61, spl asst. David Taylor Model Basin, 1960-61, tech. dir. R&D lab. Panama City, Fla., 1961-72, sci. adviser comdr. operational test evaluation force Norfolk, Va., 1972-73; pres. Lagoon Investment Co., Tallahassee, 1972—. Mem. U.S. Navy Anti-Submarine Warfare Coun., 1961-68. Author numerous tech. papers and reports. Sloan Inst. Advanced Engring. Studies fellow MIT, 1971-72; recipeint Disting. Civilian Svc. awards U.S. Navy Dept., Def. Dept., 1962. Fellow ASME; mem. Am. Soc. Naval Architects and Marine Engrs. (mem. tech. panels and coms.), Elks, Sigma Xi. Achievements include development of patented explosion-resistant ship design for minesweeping. Avocations: tennis, camping, travel, rare coin collecting, art collecting.

JASPER, SEYMOUR, lawyer; b. N.Y.C., May 15, 1919; s. Louis and Gussie (Levitch) J.; m. Geulah Eidelsberg, Nov. 24, 1940 (dec.); children: Michael, Ronald, Jeffrey, Idylia; m. Barbara Gray, Feb. 11, 1975. BS, NYU, 1939; JD, Columbia U., 1956. Bar: N.Y. 1956. Assoc. Young, Kaplan & Edelstein, N.Y.C., 1956-59; ptnr. Jasper, Sandler & Lipsay, N.Y.C., 1959-62; pvt. practice, N.Y.C., 1962—. With USN. Office: 115 E 87th St New York NY 10128-1136 E-mail: sey1@rcn.com.

JASPERSE, JOHN, performing company executive; Grad., Sarah Lawrence Coll., 1985. Artist dir. John Jasperse Co., N.Y.C. Choreographer Baryshnikov Dance Found. for White Oak's Dance Project, 1999—2000, Batsheva Dance Co., Tel Aviv, 1999—2000, Lyon Opera Ballet, 2002. Recipient Choreography prize, 3d Suzanne Dellal Internat. Dance Competition, Tel Aviv, 1996, 3 awards, Recontres Internaionales Choregraphiques de Bagnolet, 1996, Mouson award, Kunstlerhaus Mousonturm, Frankfort, Germany, 1997, Doris Duke award, 1998; fellow, N.Y. Found. Arts, 1988, 1994, NEA, 1992, 1994, 1995—96, John Simon Guggenheim Meml. Found., 1998, Scripps/ADF Primus-Tamaris, 1999. Home: 463 West St #214H New York NY 10014

JASPERSEN, FREDERICK ZARR, economist; b. Phila., Sept. 23, 1938; s. Frederick Franklin and Jean Lorraine (Zarr) J.; m. Margie C. Trainor, Oct. 10, 1965. BA in Internat. Relations, Dartmouth Coll., 1961; MA Peace Corps fellow, Ind. U., 1965, PhD in Econs., 1969. Mem. Peace Corps, Colombia, 1961-63; teaching asst. fellow Ind. U., Bloomington, 1961 65; Harvard U. econ. advisor Ministry Fin., Chile, 1968-69; economist Standard Oil N.J., N.Y.C., 1969-70, Am. Embassy Brazil, 1970-71; sr. economist World Bank, Washington, 1978-86, lead economist macroecon. adjustment policy and growth, 1987-91; chief devel. policy rsch. divsn. Inter-Am. Devel. Bank, Washington, 1991-95; sr. advisor Internat. Fin. Corp., Washington, 1995-98; dir. Latin Am. Inst. of Internat. Fin., Washington, 1999—. Lectr. econs. Chile, Brazil, Ind. U. Contbr. author: World Development Report, 1981, Adjustment Experience and Growth Prospects of the Semi-Industrial Countries, 1981; co-editor: Pathways to Growth: Comparing Latin America and East Asia, 1997. V.p. Sidwell Friends Sch. Alumni Assn., 1978-80. Ford Found. Latin Am. teaching fellow Fletcher Sch., Tufts U., 1967-68 Mem. Am. Econ. Assn., World Affairs Coun. Clubs: Dartmouth (Washington), Cosmos (Washington). Home: 5013 Randall Ln Bethesda MD 20816-1959 Office: Ste 8500 2000 Pennsylvania Ave NW Washington DC 20006-1852

JASPERSON, JOHN ARTHUR, public health service educator, consultant; b. Takoma Park, Md., Oct. 31, 1946; s. Robert Arthur Jasperson and Gwendolyn Miracle; m. Susan Margaret Jasperson, July 31, 1974 (div. Apr. 1, 1992); children: Cynthia Anne, David Russell. BS in Health Scis., Calif. State U., Chico, 1973; MPH in Nutrition, Loma Linda U., 1976, MPH in Health Edn., 1977. Pub. health educator S.W. Dist. Health Dept., Caldwell, Idaho, 1977—80; health edn. specialist Idaho Dept. Health and Welfare, Boise, Idaho, 1980—81; health educator Idaho Cancer Coord. Commn., Boise, 1981—84; dir. health edn. Sutter County Health Dept., Yuba City, Calif., 1985—88; health edn. cons. Calif. Dept. Health Svcs., Sacramento, 1988, HIV prevention trainer, 1988—. Bd. dirs. ARC, Yuba City, 1986—88; vol. United Way, Yuba City, 1987—88; chmn. sch. bd. SDA Elem. Sch., Caldwell, 1983—85; del. Canyon County Idaho Dem. Party, Boise, 1984. Mem.: APHA, Calif. Soc. Pub. Health, Calif. Pub. Health Assn., Harley Owners Group, Sierra Club, Moose. Democrat. Avocations: motorcycling, bicycling, hiking, swimming. Home: 1370 Dustin Townhouse 10 Yuba City CA 95993-2741 Office: Dept Health Svc AIDS 611 N 7th St Sacramento CA 95814

JASSO, GUILLERMINA, sociologist, educator; b. Laredo, Tex., July 22, 1942; d. José Jasso-Rodríguez and Guillermina de los Santos-Lozano. BA, Our Lady of the Lake Coll., 1962; MA, U. Notre Dame, 1970; PhD, Johns Hopkins U., 1974. Asst. prof. Barnard Coll. and Columbia U., N.Y.C., 1974-77; spl. asst. to commr. U.S. Immigration and Naturalization Svc., Washington, 1977-79; dir. rsch. U.S. Select Commn. on Immigration and Refugee Policy, Washington, 1979-80; asst. prof. U. Mich., Ann Arbor, 1980-82; assoc. prof. U. Minn., Mpls., 1982-86, prof., 1986-87; prof., dir. theory workshop U. Iowa, Iowa City, 1987-91; prof. NYU, N.Y.C., 1991—, dir. methods workshop, 1991-97. Mem. study sect. on social sci. and population NIH, 1991-95; mem. U.S. Com. for Internat. Inst. for Applied Sys. Analysis, 1993—; mem. various programs NSF, 1987-96, 98-99; panel on demographic and econ. impacts of immigration NAS, 1995-97; population rsch. subcom. Nat. Inst. Child Health and Human Devel., NIH, 1998-2002, adv. com. SBE Directorate, NSF, 2003—; vis. prof. Zentrum Umfragen, Methoden, und Analysen, Mannheim, Germany, 1995, U. Leipzig, Germany, 1996; core rsch. team bination study on migration between Mex. and US, U. Commn. on Immigration Reform, 1995-97; disting. alumni lectr. U. Notre Dame, 1987; pub. lectr. Our Lady of Lake U., 1989; disting. lectr. NSF, 2003. Author: The New Chosen People, 1990; mem. editl. bd. Social Justice Rsch., 1985—, Jour. Math. Sociology, 1985—, Rationality and Society, 1999—, European Sociological Review, 2001-, Internat. Jour. Computer Sociology, 2001-; dep. editor Am. Sociol. Rev., 1996-99; contbr. articles to profl. jours. Grantee Russell Sage Found., 1983-85, Rockefeller Found., 1985-86, NSF, 1994-97, 2000-2002, NIH, 1995-99, 2000-, PEW, 2001-; fellow Ctr. for Advanced Study in Behavioral Scis., Stanford, Calif., 1999-2000. Fellow Johns Hopkins Soc. Scholars; mem. Am. Sociol. Assn. (chair internat. migration sect. 1996-99, chair theory sect. 1996-99, chair rat. choice sect. 2000—, chair soc. psychol. sect. 2002-), Sociol. Rsch. Assn. Office: NYU Dept Sociology 269 Mercer St 4th Fl New York NY 10003-6633 E-mail: gj1@nyu.edu.

JASSO, WILLIAM GATTIS, public relations executive; b. Akron, Ohio, Mar. 2, 1953; s. Joseph and Jean E. (Gattis) J.; m. Jeanne Marie Taylor, Aug. 20, 1977; 1 child, Megan Elizabeth. BA in Comms., U. Akron; student Crisis Mgmt. Sch. and Advanced Pub. Affairs Sch., Fed. Emergency Mgmt. Agy.; student, Mich. State Sch. Bus., 1993; MS in Comms. Mgmt., Syracuse U. News dir. Sta. WHLO, Akron, 1972-81; news anchor, editor Sta. WNEO-TV, Northeast Ohio, 1978-81; govt. affairs mgr. Warner Cable Communications, Dublin, Ohio, 1981-83, corp. dir. pub. rels., 1983-85; v.p. communications Nat. Golf. Found., Jupiter, Fla., 1985-88; asst. to mayor City of Akron, 1988-94; dir. govt. affairs and media rels. Time Warner Cable of N.E. Ohio, Akron, 1994-95; dir. pub. affairs Time Warner Cable N.E. Ohio, 1995-96; v.p. pub. affairs, 1996—. Guest lectr. U. Akron, Kent State U., 1988—; pub. rels. chmn. Ohio Sports Fest, 1988-90; motivator Youth Motivation Task Force, Akron, 1989-2002; City of Akron liaison NEC World Series of Golf, 1988-94; nat. selection panel mem. Golf Digest 100 Best Golf Courses in U.S., 1987—; organizer 1st Golf Summit, Westchester C. of C., N.Y., 1986; producer nat. launch Time Warner Inc.'s Road Runner high-speed online svc., 1996. Editor: Golf Curriculum Kit, 1987, Golf Driving Range Manual, 1987, (mag.) GolfMarket Today, 1986-88, The Spirit of Akron, 1989; producer, reporter (documentary) John Lennon--Beatle Without A Country, 1975. Committeeman Great Trail coun. Boys Scouts Am., 1989 91; trustee Canton Cmty. Forum; mem. 1993-94 class Leadership Akron; bd. dirs. Akron Child Guidance Ctr., 1995-2000; mem. pub. affairs com. Akron Regional Devel. Bd. Recipient 6 awards AP, 1975-81, 8 awards Akron Press Club, 1974-81, 4 Image awards Ohio Cable TV Assn., 1994-99, Pinnacle award Gt. Lakes Cable Assn., 2003. Mem. Pub. Rels. Soc. Am. (accredited pres. Akron chpt. 1990-91, Presdl. Citation award 1993), Cable TV Pub. Affairs Assn. (bd. dirs. 2003—, 2 Beacon awards 1994-99). Avocations: golf, writing, public speaking, guitar. Office: Time Warner Cable NE Ohio 530 S Main St Ste 1751 Akron OH 44311-1090

JASSY, EVERETT LEWIS, lawyer; b. N.Y.C., Feb. 4, 1937; s. David H. and Florence A. (Pollak) J.; m. Margery Ellen Rose; children: Katherine Savitt Lennon, Andrew Ralph, Jonathan Scott. AB, Harvard U., 1957, JD, 1960. Bar: N.Y. 1960, D.C. 1975. Assoc. Dewey Ballantine, N.Y.C., 1960-68, ptnr., 1968—, chmn. mgmt. com., 1996—. Mem. ABA, N.Y. State Bar Assn., Assn. of Bar of City of N.Y., The Tax Club, Harmonie Club (bd. govs. 1999-2001), Fairview Country Club, Washington Athletic Club. Avocations: golf, travel. Home: 20 Tompkins Rd Scarsdale NY 10583-2838 Office: Dewey Ballantine LLP 1301 Avenue Of The Americas New York NY 10019-6022

JASTHI, SIVA RAMA KRISHNA, software professional, consultant; b. Guntur, India, June 8, 1965; s. Pullaiah and Drakshayani (Modukuri) J.; m. Bhaskarani Chennupati, Aug. 31, 1994; children: Tapan, Deepta. B Tech., Jawahrlal Nehru Tech. U., Anantapur, India, 1987; M Tech., P.S.G. Coll. Tech., Coimbatore, India, 1990; PhD, Indian Inst. Tech., New Delhi, 1994; CMII grad., Ariz. State U., 1999. Rsch. scholar Indian Inst. Tech., Delhi, 1990-93, sr. sci. officer, 1993-95; sr. software engr. Computervision India, Pune, 1995-96, Computervision Corp., Bedford, Mass., 1996-98; prin. software engr. Metaphase Tech. Inc., Arden Hills, Minn., 1998—2001, EDS, Arden Hills, 2001—. Mem. cmty. faculty Metro State U., Minn., 2001—; cons. Bharat Heavy Elecs. Ltd., Bhopal, India, 1993-95. Reviewer Computer and Indsl. Engring. jour.; contbr. articles to profl. jours. Mem. Indian Instn. Indsl. Engrs. (life), Instn. Engrs. India (life, Best Rsch. Paper award 1994), Indian Soc. Tech. Edn. (life). Avocations: net surfing, reading for kids, indoor games. Office: EDS PLM Solutions 4233 Lexington Ave N Ste 3290 Saint Paul MN 55126-6160 E-mail: sjasthi@msn.com., siva.jasthi@eds.com.

JASTROCH, LEONARD ANDREW, lawyer; b. Milw., Dec. 31, 1948; s. Edwin Francis and Frances Mary (Brodnan) J.; m. Bonnie Schmidt, Mar. 27, 1993; children: Nina Marie, Justin Mark. JD, Marquette U., 1972. Bar: Wis. 1973, U.S. Dist. Ct. (ea. and we. dists.) Wis. 1973, U.S. Supreme Ct. 1976, U.S. Tax Ct. 1982. Sole practice, Waukesha, Wis., 1973-77; sr. ptnr. Jastroch & LaBarge SC, Waukesha, 1978—. Adj. prof. bus. law Alverno Coll. Bd. dirs. Waukesha Family YMCA. Mem. Wis. Bar Assn., Waukesha Bar Assn., Milw. Bar Assn., Wis. Acad. Trial Lawyers, Assn. Trial Lawyers Am., ABA, Delta Theta Phi. Home: Hartland WI Office: Jastroch & LaBarge SC 640 W Moreland Blvd Waukesha WI 53188-2433

JASTROW, ROBERT, physicist, educator; b. N.Y.C., Sept. 7, 1925; s. Abraham and Marie (Greenfield) J. AB, Columbia, 1944, MA, 1945, PhD, 1948; post-doctoral fellow, Leiden U., 1948-49, Princeton Inst. Advanced Study, 1949-50, 53, U. Calif. at Berkeley, 1950-53; D.Sc. (hon.), Manhattan Coll., 1980, N.J. Inst. Tech., 1987. Asst. prof. Yale, 1953-54; cons. nuclear physics U.S. Naval Research Lab., Washington, 1958-62; head theoretical div. Goddard Space Flight Center NASA, 1958-61, chmn. lunar exploration com., 1959-60, mem. com., 1960-62; dir. Goddard Inst. Space Studies, N.Y.C., 1961-81; adj. prof. geology Columbia, 1961-81, dir. Summer Inst. Space Physics, 1962-70; adj. prof. astronomy Columbia (Summer Inst. Space Physics), 1977-82; adj. prof. earth sci. Dartmouth, 1973-92; pres. G.C. Marshall Inst., 1985, chair, 2002—; dir. Mt. Wilson Inst., 1991—. Author: The Evolution of Stars, Planets and Life, 1967, Astronomy: Fundamentals and Frontiers, 1972, Until the Sun Dies, 1977, God and the Astronomers, 1978, 2d edit., 1992, Red Giants-White Dwarfs, 1991, The Enchanted Loom, 1981, How To Make Nuclear Weapons Obsolete, 1985, Journey to the Stars, 1989; editor: Exploration of Space, 1960; co-editor: Jour. Atmospheric Scis., 1962-74, The Origin of the Solar System, 1963, The Venus Atmosphere, 1969. Recipient Medal of Excellence Columbia, 1962, Grad. Faculties Alumni award, 1967; Arthur S. Flemming award, 1965; medal for exceptional sci. achievement NASA, 1968 Fellow Am. Geophys. Union, AAAS, Am. Phys. Soc.; mem. Internat. Acad. Astronautics, Coun. Fgn. Rels., Leakey Found., Nat. Space Soc. (bd. govs.), Cosmos Club. Office: Mt Wilson Observatory Hale Solar Lab 740 Holladay Rd Pasadena CA 91106-4115 E-mail: jastrow@mtwilson.edu.

JASZCZAK, RONALD JACK, physicist, researcher, consultant; b. Chicago Heights, Ill., Aug. 23, 1942; s. Jacob and Julia (Gudowicz) J.; m. Nancy Jane Bober, Apr. 15, 1967; children: John, Monica. BS with highest honors, U. Fla., 1964, PhD, 1968. Staff physicist Oak Ridge Nat., 1969-71, AEC postdoctoral fellow, 1968-69; prin. rsch. scientist Searle Diagnostics, Inc., 1971-73, sr. prin.

rsch. scientist, 1973, rsch. group leader, 1973-77, chief scientist, 1977-79; assoc. prof. radiology Duke U. Med. Ctr., Durham, N.C., 1979-89, prof., 1989—, assoc. prof. biomed. engring., 1986-91, prof., 1992—. Rsch. prof. Inst. of Stats. and Decision Scis., 1992-93; founder, chmn. bd. dirs. Data Spectrum Corp., Hillsborough, N.C.; investigator Nat. Cancer Inst. Grant, 1983—, Dept. Energy Grant, 1989—. Contbr. articles to profl. jours.; patentee in field. Fellow NASA, 1964-67, U. Fla., 1967-68; RCA scholar, 1963-64. Fellow IEEE; mem. IEEE Nuc. and Plasma Scis. Soc. (pres. 1997-98), AAAS, Soc. Nuc. Medicine (Paul C. Aebersold award 2000), Am. Phys. Soc., Am. Assn. Physicists in Medicine, Soc. Photo-Optical Instrumentation Engrs., Sigma Xi, Phi Beta Kappa, Phi Kappa Phi, Tau Sigma, Sigma Pi Sigma. Office: Duke U Med Ctr Dumc 3949 Durham NC 27710-0001

JATINEN, JANE ELLEN, social worker, educator; b. Hackensack, N.J., Mar. 18, 1942; d. Richard and Catherine (Bell) Cochrane; m. Dennis Carl Jatinen, July 6, 1968 (div. Jan. 1975); 1 child, Andrew. BA in Sociology, Douglass Coll./Rutgers U., 1964; MSW, U. Mich., 1967. Lic. social worker, NC. Psychiat. social worker Community Svcs div. Calif. Dept. Welfare, L.A., 1967-70, Santa Barbara (Calif.) Community Mental Health Svcs., 1970-72; cons., counselor Social Advocates for Youth, Goleta, Calif., 1973-74; specialist, social work educator U. Tex. Sch. Social Work, Austin, 1975—98; socia. worker II Madison County Health Dept., NC, 1999—. Mem. family violence adv. com. Tex. Dept. Human Svcs., Austin, 1990-93. Parliamentarian PTSA bd. dirs. L.B.J. High Sch., Austin, 1989-91; mem. United Way of Tex. Grantee, Tex. Dept. Protective and Regulatory Svcs., 1984—97. Mem. NASW (legis. action com. Tex. chpt. 1988-91, del. nat. del. assembly 1989-92, steering com. 1989-98, Social Worker of Yr. award Austin unit 1994), Am. Assn. for Protection Children. Office: Madison County Health Dept Marshall NC

JATLOW, PETER I. pathologist, medical educator, researcher; b. New Brunswick, N.J., Feb. 12, 1936; s. Daniel and Anne (Davis) J.; m. Stephanie Bea Yager, Dec. 22, 1959; children— Allison, Julia BS, Union Coll., Schenectady, 1957; MD, SUNY Downstate Med. Ctr., Bklyn., 1961; MS (hon.), Yale U., 1976. Intern Montefiore Hosp., Bronx, N.Y., 1961-62; resident Yale-New Haven Hosp., 1962-66, asst. prof. lab. medicine Yale U., New Haven, 1968-73, assoc. prof. lab. medicine, 1973-76, prof. lab. medicine, 1976—, chmn. dept. lab. medicine, 1984—. Cons. FDA, Washington, 1978-82; mem. biomed. research rev. com. USPHS, Nat. Inst. Drug Abuse, Rockville, Md., 1982-86; mem. test material deve. subcom. FLEX Program Nat. Bd. Med. Exam., Philly, 1990-91. Editor: Methodology in Analytical Toxicology, vol. II, 1982; editorial bd. Clin. Chemistry, 1973-83, Selected methods in Clin. Chemistry, 1976-79, Jour. Analytical Toxicology, 1978-79, Therapeutic Drug Monitoring, 1979-86, 90—, Clinica Chimica Acta, 1984-90, Am. Jour. Clin. Pathology, 1988—; contbr. numerous articles to profl. jours. Served to surgeon USPHS, 1966-68 Recipient Irving Sunshine award in clin. toxicology Internat. Assn. Therapeutic Drug Monitoring and Toxicology, 1993. Fellow Coll. Am. Pathologists; mem. AAAS, Acad. Clin. Lab. Physicians and Scientists (pres. 1983-84, Gerald T. Evans award 1988), Am. Soc. Clin. Pathology, Am. Assn. Clin. Chemistry (award for outstanding contbns. to clin. chemistry in selected area of rsch. 1985, award for outstanding contbns. in edn. 1995). Home: 617 Saddle Ridge Rd Orange CT 06477-2024 Office: Yale U Sch Medicine Dept Lab Medicine 333 Cedar St Dept Lab New Haven CT 06510-3289

JAUDES, RICHARD EDWARD, lawyer; b. St. Louis, Feb. 22, 1943; s. Leo August Jr. and Dorothy Catherine (Schmidt) J.; m. Mary Kay Tansey, Sept. 22, 1967; children: Michele, Pamela. BS, St. Louis U., 1965, JD, 1968. Bar: Mo. Supreme Ct. 1968, U.S. Dist. Ct. (ea. dist.), Mo. 1973 U.S. Ct. Appeals (8th cir.) 1973, U.S. Supreme Ct. 1990. With Peper, Martin, Jensen, Maichel & Hetlage, St. Louis, 1973-97, mng. ptnr., 1990-93; lawyer, co-chair labor and employment practice group Thompson Coburn LLP, St. Louis, 1997—; mem. mgmt. com. Thompson Coburn, St. Louis, 1997—2000. Bd. dirs. Baldor Electric Co., 1999— Vol. Civic Entrepreneurs Orgn., St. Louis, 1990; vol. counsel St. Louis chpt. MS Soc., 1990—, exec. com. Lt. USN, 1968-73; comdr. USNR, ret. Office: Thompson Coburn LLP US Bank Plz Saint Louis MO 63101-1693 E-mail: rjaudes@thompsoncoburn.com.

JAUDES, WILLIAM E. retired lawyer; b. St. Louis, 1937; s. August William and Gertrude Johanna (Simon) J.; m. Carol Joan Hurtgen, June 30, 1961; children: Phyllis Anne, Richard William, Suzanne Louise. AB, U. Mo., 1958; JD, St. Louis U., 1962, MBA, 1969. Bar: Mo. 1962, Ill. 1964, U.S. Dist. Ct. (ea. dist.) Mo. 1962, U.S. Supreme Ct. 1966, U.S. Ct. Appeals (8th cir.) 1980. Atty. Union Electric Co., St. Louis, 1963-73, gen. atty., 1973-80, gen. counsel, 1980-85, v.p. gen. counsel, 1985-88. Author: introduction to Mo. Bar Assn. book, Adminstrative Law, 1979. Home: Saint Louis, Mo. Died July 23, 2001.

JAUDON, VALERIE, artist; b. Greenville, Miss., Aug. 6, 1945; d. Baize R. and Gladys E. (Hill) J.; m. Richard Kalina, Oct. 23, 1979. Student, Miss. State Coll. for Women, 1963-65, Memphis Acad. Art, 1965, U. of Americas, Mexico, 1966-67, St. Martins Sch. Art, London, 1968-69. One-woman shows of paintings include, Holly Solomon Gallery, N.Y.C., 1977-79, 81, Pa. Acad. Fine Arts, Phila., 1977, Galerie Bishofberger, Zurich, Switzerland, 1979, Galerie Hans Strelow, Dusseldorf, Fed. Republic Germany, 1980, Corcoran Gallery, Los Angeles, 1981, Sidney Janis Gallery, N.Y.C., 1983, 85, 86, 88, 90, 93, 96, Quadrat Mus., Bottrop, Fed. Republic Germany, 1983, Amerika Haus, Berlin, 1983, Dart Gallery, Chgo., 1983, Fay Gold Gallery, Atlanta, 1985, Macintosh/Drysdale Gallery, Washington, 1985, Barbara Scott Gallery, Bay Harbor Islands, Fla., 1994, Miss. Mus. Art, Jackson, 1996, Betsy Senior Gallery, N.Y.C., 1998, Stadel Mus., Frankfurt, Germany, 1999-2000, Von Lintel Gallery, N.Y.C., 2003; numerous group shows including, Mayor Gallery, London, 1979, Galerie Habermann, Cologne, Germany, 1979, Galerie Hans Strelow, Dusseldorf, 1979, Galerie Modern Art, Vienna, Austria, 1980, Mus. Modern Art, Oxford, Eng., 1980, Greenberg, Gallery, St. Louis, 1980, Sidney Janis Gallery, N.Y.C., 1980, San Francisco Art Inst., 1980, Mus. Modern Art, N.Y.C., 1980, Leo Castelli Gallery, N.Y.C., 1980, Thomas Segal Gallery, Boston, 1980, Venice (Italy) Biennale, 1980, Nat. Gallery of Art, Washington, 1980, Chgo. Art Inst., 1981, Mus. Fine Arts, Boston, 1982, Neuberger Mus., Purchase, N.Y., 1982, Hudson River Mus., Yonkers, N.Y., 1983, Berkshire Mus., Pittsfield, Mass., 1983, La Jolla Mus., Calif., 1983, Margo Leavin Gallery, Los Angeles, 1984, Bronx Mus., 1985, Am. Ctr., Paris, 1986, Dayton Art Inst., 1987, Cin. Art Mus., 1989, Tel Aviv Mus. Art, 1992, Robert McClain Gallery, Houston, 1996, Turner/Runyon Gallery, Dallas, 1997, Kunsthallen Brandts Kaledefabrik, Odense, Denmark, 2001, Angel Row Gallery, Nottingham, England, 2001, Porin Taidemuseo, Eteläranta, Finland, 2002, Von Lintel Gallery, N.Y.C., 2002; executed ceramic mural Equitable Bldg., N.Y.C., 1988, brick and granite plaza Police Plaza, N.Y.C., 1989; Blue Pools Courtyard Birmingham (Ala.) Mus. Art, 1993; mosaic floor Washington Nat. Airport, 1997; represented in permanent collections including Hirshhorn Mus., Washington, Mus. Modern Art, N.Y.C., Albright-Knox Art Gallery, Buffalo, N.Y., Fogg Art Mus., Cambridge, Mass.,Sammlung-Lugwig Mus., Aachen, Fed. Republic Germany, Dayton (Ohio) Art Inst., Nat. Museum of Women in the Arts, Washington, St. Louis Art Mus., Ludwig Mus., Budapest, Hungary, Miss. Mus. Art, Jackson. Recipient 1st prize award So. Contemporary Arts Festival, 1967, Art award Miss. Inst. Arts and Letters, 1981, 97, Excellence in Design award N.Y.C. Art Commn., 1988, civic Spirit award Women's City Club of N.Y., Merit award Am. Soc. Landscape Architects Ala. chpt., 1994; named Honored Artist from State of Miss. Nat. Mus. Women in Arts, Washington; N.Y. State CAPS grantee for graphics, 1980; Visual Arts Fellowship grant Nat. Endowment Arts, 1988; N.Y. Found. for Arts grantee in painting, 1992. Address: 795A Accabonac Rd East Hampton NY 11937-1807 E-mail: vjaudon@earthlink.net.

JAUREGUI, CONNIE LEE, internist; b. Cin., Apr. 3, 1962; d. James Harold and Joan Lee (Marston) S.; Luis Jauregui, Sept. 16, 2000. BS in Biology cum laude, U. Cin., 1984; MD with honors in Psychiatry, Med. Coll. Ohio, 1991. Histocompatibility technologist Hoxworth Blood Ctr., Cin., 1985-87; intern in internal medicine Pa. State U. Hershey Med. Ctr., 1991-92; resident in internal medicine Med. Coll. Ohio, Toledo, 1992-94; pvt. practice, Toledo, 1994—. Contbg. author: Diagnosis and Management of Bone Infections, 1995. Mem. AMA, Ohio Med. Assn., Toledo Acad. Medicine. Lutheran. Avocations: swimming, travel to exotic locations. Office: 7055 W Central Ave Toledo OH 43617

JAUREGUI, LUIS ERNESTO, physician, pharmacologist; b. La Paz, Bolivia, Oct. 13, 1945; s. Luis Ernesto and Bertha (Peredo) J.; children: Marie Christine, Elizabeth Ann, Mary Kathryn; m. Connie Jauregui, Sept. 16, 2000. BS, U. Geneva, 1969; MD, Wayne State U., 1972. Diplomate Am. Bd. Internal Medicine. Resident in internal medicine Hutzel Hosp., Detroit, 1975; fellow in infectious disease Detroit Med. Ctr., 1977; assoc. dir. med. edn., chief infectious diseases St. Vincent Mercy Med. Ctr., Toledo, 1977—. From asst. prof. to clin. prof. medicine and microbiology Med. Coll. Ohio, Toledo, 1977—; co-dir. Ctr. Applied Pharmacology St. Vincent Mercy Med. Ctr., U. Toledo, 1989—. Author: The New Generation of Quinolones, 1990, Temas de Salud Publica en el Neuvo contexto de la Salud Reproductiva, Antimicrobianos uso en Infectologia Clinica; editor, author: Diagnosis and Management of Bone Infections. Mem. Am. Coll. Physicians, AMA, Am. Soc. Microbiology, European Soc. Microbiology, Infectious Diseases Soc. Am., Internat. Soc. Chemotherapy. Avocations: opera, soccer. Office: St Vincent Med Ctr 2213 Cherry St Toledo OH 43608-2603

JAURON, DICK, professional football coach; b. Peoria, Ill., Oct. 7, 1950; m. Gail Jauron; children: Kacy, Amy. Degree in History, Yale U. Profl. football player Detroit Lions, 1973-77, Cin. Bengal, 1978-80; co-owner health and fitness ctr. Cin.; with Nautilus; secondary coach Buffalo Bills, 1985; defensive backs coach Green Bay Packers, 1986—94; defensive coord. Jacksonville Jaguars, 1995—98; head coach Chgo. Bears, 1999—. Active numerous charities. Named 1974 Pro Bowl selection. Avocation: golf. Office: care Chicago Bears Halas Hall at Conway Park 1000 Football Dr Lake Forest IL 60045-4829

JAUSLIN, JEAN-FRÉDÉRIC, library director; b. Neuchâtel, Switzerland, July 31, 1954; s. Emile and Yvonne (Guyot) J.; m. Carol Berthoud, Sept. 15, 1984; children: Jérôme, Pascal, Raphaël. Lic., Univ. Neuchâtel, 1978; PhD, Tech. U., Zurich, 1984. Sci. advisor Winterthur (Switzerland) Ins., 1984-85; head computer sci. dept. Neuchâteloise Ins., 1985-90; dir. Swiss Nat. Libr., Bern, 1990—. Mem.: Lions (pres. 1993—94). Office: Swiss Nat Libr Hallwylstr 15 3003 Bern Switzerland

JAUVTIS, ROBERT LLOYD, lawyer; b. Bklyn., Oct. 19, 1946; s. Louis and Betty (Slomiansky) J. B.A., U. Rochester, 1968; J.D., Albany Law Sch., 1973; LL.M. in Labor Law, NYU, 1976. Bar: N.Y. 1974, U.S. Ct. Appeals (2d cir.) 1975, U.S. Supreme Ct. 1980. Assoc. Vladeck, Waldman, Elias & Engelhard, P.C., N.Y.C., 1974-78; assoc. Epstein Becker & Green, P.C., N.Y.C., 1978-82, ptnr., 1982— ; moot ct. judge N.Y. Law Sch. Wagner Labor Law Competition, N.Y.C., 1980-82; lectr. Contbr. articles to legal jours. Served with USAR, 1969-74. Mem. ABA, N.Y. State Bar Assn., Assn. Bar City N.Y., Am. Soc. Personnel Adminstrn. (bd. dirs. met. N.Y. chpt. 1983-85). Office: Epstein Becker & Green PC 250 Park Ave Ste 1200 New York NY 10177-1211

JAVELLAS, INA JUNE, social worker; b. Pawhuska, Okla., June 15, 1934; d. Tom D. and Grace Elizabeth (Hyde) J. BA, U. Okla., 1956, MSW, 1958. Diplomate NASW in Clin. Social Work. From social work asst. to psychiat. social worker Griffin Meml. Hosp., Norman, Okla., 1957-62; social work supr. Enid (Okla.) State Sch., 1962-63, Vinita, Okla., 1963; psychiat. social worker Okla. State Dept. Mental Health, Tulsa, 1963-65, coord. cmty. mental health divsn., 1965-77, chief cmty. mental health planning and devel., 1977-78, dep. dir. cmty. mental health programs, 1978-79; pvt. practice Norman, Okla., 1979—. Cons., surveyor DHHS, Pub. Health Svcs., HCFA Psychiat. Facilities Survey Program, 1970—; cons. Okla. State Bd. Lic. Social Workers, 1989—. Vol. Project Heartland Okla. (Svcs. to Victims, Survivors, and Families of Apr. 19, 1995 Oklahoma City Bombing, 1999 Okla. Tornado), State Dept. Mental Health, 1995-97; pers. chair, bd. dirs. REST homeless day ctr., Oklahoma City, 1992-98; Oklahoma City downtown outreach com., bd. dirs. Cleveland County Mental Health Assn., Norman, 1993-95; chair bd. vis. Okla. Sch. Social Work, 2000—. Recipient Cert. Appreciation, Assoc. Cath. Charities, 1997, also Profl Devel. Nat. award; named to U. Okla. Sch. Social Work Hall of Honor, 1999. Mem. NASW (Okla. Social Worker of Yr. 1970, 96), Acad. Cert. Social Workers, Okla. Health and Welfare Assn. (life, Disting. Svc. award 1977), U. Okla. Alumnae Assn. (life), Phi Mu (life). Democrat. Episcopalian. Avocations: genealogy, travel, embroidery, football, reading. Home: 112 Crystal Bnd Norman OK 73069-8612

JAVID, MANUCHER J. retired neurosurgery educator; b. Tehran, Iran, Jan. 11, 1922; came to U.S., 1944, naturalized, 1957; s. Asdolah and Touba (Ahdiyeh) J.; m. Lida Emma Fabbri, Oct. 19, 1951; children— Roxane, Daria, Jeffrey, Claudia. MD, U. Ill., 1946. Diplomate: Am. Bd. Neurosurgery. Intern Augustana Hosp., Chgo., 1946-47, resident gen. surgery, 1947-48, resident neurosurgery, 1948-49; asst. in neuropathology Ill. Neuropsychiat. Inst., Chgo., 1948-49; fellow in neurosurgery Lahey Clinic, Boston, 1949; resident neurosurgery New Eng. Med. Center, Boston, 1950; clin. research fellow neurosurgery Mass. Gen. Hosp., Boston, 1950, asst. resident, 1951, sr. resident neurosurgery, 1952; teaching fellow in surgery Harvard, 1952; instr. Med. Sch. U. Wis., Madison, 1953-54, asst. prof., 1954-57, asso. prof., 1957-62, prof. neurosurgery, 1962-98, endowed named prof. neurol. surgery, 1998, emeritus prof., 1998—, chmn. dept. neurosurgery, 1963-95. Cons. neurosurgeon VA Hosp., Madison, 1956-98. Contbr. articles profl. jours. Mem. AMA, ACS, AAUP, AAAS, Soc. Neurol. Surgeons, Am. Assn. Neurol. Surgeons, Am. Assn. Med. Colls., Soc. for Neurosci., Central Neurosurg. Soc. (pres. 1964), Internat. Intradiscal Therapy Soc. (treas. 1987-90, pres.-elect 1990—, pres. 1991, hon. mem. 1999), N.Y. Acad. Scis., Xeiron, Sigma Xi, Phi Beta Pi, Alpha Omega Alpha.. Mem. Baha'i Faith. Club: Rotarian. Achievements include introduction of osmotherapy in neurosurgery and ophthalmology by the clin. use of urea for reduction intracranial and intraocular pressure. Home: 4750 Lafayette Dr Madison WI 53705-4865 E-mail: mjavid@facstaff.wisc.edu. *Since I was a small child, I wanted to be a doctor and help the sick. As I grew older, the Baha'i Faith, served as a guideline to achieve this goal. Its teachings have helped me to appreciate the oneness of God, the oneness of religion, the oneness of humanity, and the sanctity of life.*

JAVIER-DEJNEKA, AMELIA LUISA, accountant; arrived in U.S., 1964; d. Ladislao Walter Dejneka and Elena Angelica Gomba; m. Washington Javier, July 14, 1973 (dec. June 1985); children: Walter Daniel, Maria Elena. BBA, Fla. Internat. U., 1976; degree in Computer Programming, Miami Tech. Coll., 1986. Investor Atlantic Acct. & Investment, Miami, Fla., 1984—; acct., owner A&M Acct. & Mgmt., Miami, 1999—; designer, owner A&M Designer Gallery, Miami, 1999—; prin., owner A&M Profl. Svc., Miami, 2002—. Recipient Blue Ribbon award, Argentina Consulate & Com., 1995. Avocations: swimming, dancing, walking, travel. Home: 9449 Byron Ave Miami FL 33154

JAVITS, ERIC MOSES, lawyer, diplomat; b. N.Y.C., May 24, 1931; s. Benjamin Abraham and Lily Javits; m. Margaretha Espersson, May 24, 1979; children by previous marriage: Jocelyn Ingrid, Eric Moses. Student, Stanford U., 1948-49; AB, Columbia U., 1952, JD, 1955. Bar: N.Y. 1955, U.S. Supreme Ct. 1959. Temp. cons. Office Def. Moblzn., Washington, 1951; assoc. firm Javits & Javits, N.Y.C., 1955-58, mem. firm to ptnr., 1958-82; sr. ptnr. Javits, Robinson, Brog, Leinwand & Reich, P.C. (and successor firms), 1984-89; cons. to Dept. State, amb.-designate to Venezuela, 1989-90; sr. counsel Robinson, Brog, Leinwand, Reich, Genovese & Gluck, P.C. (and successor firms), 1993—2001; U.S. rep. and amb. to Conf. on Disarmament in Geneva, 2002—. Ind. gen. ptnr. ML Venture Ptnrs., 1982-96; spl. dep. to N.Y. Atty. Gen. Elections Frauds Bur., 1958-59; counsel N.Y. Senate Com. on Affairs of City N.Y., 1959; mem. N.Y.C. Commn. for Protocol, 1994-2001; bd. dirs. N.Y. State Conv. Ctr. Oper. Corp., 1995-2001; past dir. N.Y. Stock Exch., Am. Stock Exch., over the counter cos. Author: SOS New York, 1961. Mem. numerous charitable coms.; bd. govs. N.Y. Young Rep. Club, 1955-58, v.p., 1957-58, bd. advisers, 1958-64; trustee French Inst./Alliance Francaise, 1995-2001, Cardozo Law Sch., 1997-2001; mem. exec. com. Jacob K. Javits campaigns, 1954-80; mem. N.Y. Rep. County Com., 1960-64; mem. exec. com. Nat. Rep. Club, 1962-70; exec. sec. U.S. Paper Exporters Coun., Inc., 1964-72; mem. bd. Spain-U.S.A. C. of C., 1993-2001; chmn. emeritus Spanish Inst., N.Y.C.; bd. dirs. Fair Return League, Inc., pres., 1975—; chmn. Republican Eagles, 1999-2001. Decorated Order of Isabel La Catolica (Spain), 1981, 89; recipient Spanish Inst. Gold medal, 1994. Mem.: Nacoms, U. Club N.Y.C., Phi Alpha Delta, Beta Theta Pi, Phi Beta Kappa. Jewish. Office: US Mission Geneva C/D 11 Rte De Pregny 1292 Chambesy Switzerland

JAVITS, JOSHUA MOSES, lawyer; b. N.Y.C., Jan. 2, 1950; s. Jacob Koppel and Marian (Borris) J.; m. Sabina Paula Golding, May 25, 1985. BA, Yale U., 1972; JD, Georgetown U., 1978. Bar: D.C. 1979, Calif. 1983. Trial atty. NLRB, L.A., 1978-83; assoc. Mullholland & Hickey, Washington, 1983-85, Cades, Schutte, Fleming & Wright, Washington, 1985-87; arbitrator Washington, 1985-88; mem., chmn. Nat. Mediation Bd., Wshington, 1988-93; ptnr. Ford & Harrison, Washington, 1993—2001; arbitrator and mediator, 2001—. Mem. ABA, Indsl. Relations Rsch. Assn., Soc. Fed. Labor Relations Profls., Soc. Profls. in Dispute Resolution. Fax: 202-237-2050. E-mail: JJAVITS@aol.com.

JAVITT, JONATHAN C. physician, ophthalmologist, health information technologist; b. NYC, Nov. 7, 1956; s. Norman B. and Suzanne (Markovits) J.; m. Marcia C. Fishman, June 29, 1986; children: Zachary, Matthew, Gabrielle. AB with honors, Princeton U., 1978; MD, Cornell U., 1982; MPH, Harvard U., 1984. Diplomate Am. Bd. Ophthalmology. Intern Lenox Hill Hosp., N.Y.C., N.Y., 1982-83; resident Wills Eye Hosp., Phila., 1984-87; fellow Johns Hopkins Hosp., Balt., 1988-89; instr. Johns Hopkins U., 1987-90, asst. prof., 1990-99, prof., 1999—; asst. prof. Georgetown U., Washington, 1990-93, assoc. prof., 1993-96, prof. Sch. Medicine, prof. sch. Pub. Policy, 1996—; founder, chmn. Certitude, Inc., Mpls., 1994—; sr. v.p., nat. med. dir. United Health Care/Applied Health Care Informatics, Mpls., 1997-98; chmn. Health Directions LLC, Bethesda, 1998—; founder, pres., vice chmn. EMEDX, Inc., 1999—. Founder Coderyte, Inc., 2000; bd. dirs. Acad. Homeland Security; expert cons. Health Care Fin. Adminstrn., Balt., 1987—; spl. employee The White House Health Reform Task Force, Washington, 1992; cons. Nat. Eye Inst./NIH, 1990—, Nat. Inst. Diabetes Digestive and Kidney Disease/NIH, 1991—, Agy. for Health Care Policy Rsch., 1994—, The World Bank, Washington, 1993—, Swedish Coun. on Tech. Improvement, 1997, Japanese Min. of Health, 1993, Australia Min. of Health, 1994—; apptd. Pres.'s Info. Tech. Adv. Com., 2003—. *Dr. Javitt has more than 20 years of experience in health information technology, public health, pharmaceutical and medical device development, and clinical medicine. Presidential appointment to chair healthcare section of President's information Technology Policy. Extensive experience in design and implementation of information systems related to health care. Experience in design and pharmaceutical and medical device trials. More than 200 scientific books, chapters, articles, and abstracts related to outcomes research, health economics, information technology, and pharmacoeconomics. Clinical expertise in ophthalmology and glaucoma.* Sect. editor Archives of Ophthalmology, 1993—, Ophthalmology Times, 1993—; author more than 200 books, chpts., articles; patentee in field. Com. chair Nat. Health Policy Coun., Washington, 1992—; cmty. spkr. on health care The White House, 1992—; trustee Md. Rep. Party, 2000—; mem. campaign com. Bush for Pres., 2000; mem. Rep. Presdl. Roundtable; bd. dirs. Washington Jewish Fedn., Brookdale Inst., Am. Joint Distbn. Com.; active Johns Hopkins Pres.'s Club, Weill Cornell Med. Coll. Deans Cir., Rep. Senatorial Trust; fin. dir. Erlich for Gov., 2002. Recipient Cert. of Appreciation, USAF, 1991, Physician Scientist award Nat. Eye Inst., 1988; U.S. Presdl. Letter of Appreciation, 1993; Kellogg Found. fellow, 1983, sr. fellow Potomac Inst. for Policy Studies, 2001—; named guest of honor Japanese Glaucoma Soc., 1996, New England Ophthalmologic Soc., 1997. Fellow Am. Acad. Ophthalmology (Honor award 1990, Sr. Recognition award 2000), Am. Glaucoma Soc.; mem. AMA, AOPA, NBAA, Assn. for Rsch. in Vision and Ophthalmology, Assn. for Health Svc. Rsch., Am. Glaucoma Soc., Kehilath Jeshurun, Royal Ocean Racing Club, Princeton Club, Harvard Club, Cosmos Club. Avocations: sailing, aviation. Office: Health Directions LLC 4733 Bethesda Ave Ste 720 Bethesda MD 20814 E-mail: jjavitt@healthdirections.net.

JAVITT, NORMAN B. medical educator, researcher; b. N.Y.C., Mar. 9, 1928; s. Bernard and Zara (Hillman) Jakubovitz; m. Suzanne Markovits, June 5, 1955; children: Jonathan Chaim, Daniel Coleman, Joel Israel, Gail Hannah. AB cum laude, Syracuse U., 1947; PhD in Physiology, U. N.C., 1951; MD, Duke U., 1954. Diplomate Am. Bd. Internal Medicine; lic. physician, N.Y. Predoctoral fellow USPHS, Chapel Hill, N.C., 1949-51; intern Mt. Sinai Hosp., N.Y.C., 1954-55, asst. resident, 1957-58, chief resident, 1959-60, Sara Welt fellow in medicine, spl. USPHS, 1961-62; asst. physician, advanced fellow Am. Heart Assn. Vanderbilt Clinic, Columbia Coll. Physicians and Surgeons, N.Y.C., 1957-58; instr. dept. medicine NYU Sch. Medicine, 1962-64, asst. prof., 1964-68; assoc. prof. Cornell U.Med. Coll., N.Y.C., 1968-73, prof., 1973-83; assoc. attending physician N.Y. Hosp., N.Y.C., 1968-73, attending physician, 1973-83; prof. medicine, prof. pediatrics NYU Med. Ctr., N.Y.C., 1983—, dir. divsn. hepatic diseases, 1983-2000; guest investigator Nat. Inst. Child Health and Development, Nat. Insts. of Health, Bethesda, Md., 2000—; assoc. dir. clin. rsch. unit NYU Med. Ctr., N.Y.C., 1985-90. Cons. Meml. Sloan-Kettering Cancer Ctr., N.Y.C., 1970-83; vis. prof. Rockefeller U. Hosp., 1970-76; cons. medicine VA Hosp., Bklyn., 1977-83; chief divsn. gastroenterology Cornell-N.Y. Hosp. Med. Ctr., 1973-81, chief divsn. hepatic diseases, acting chief divsn. gastroenterology, 1981-83; cons. Tisch Hosp., NYU Med. Ctr., 1983—; mem. tng. grant study sect. Nat. Inst. Arthritis, Metabolic & Digestive Diseases, NIH, 1978-85; mem. steering com. Nat. Cooperative Gallstone Study, 1973-80, chmn. clin. mgmt. com., 1974-78; gen. medicine study Section A, NIH, 1976-80. Mem. editl. adv. bd. Hosp. Practice, 1969-93; assoc. editor Jour. Lipid Rsch., 1977-78, 86—, editl. bd., 1983—; author, editor 2 books; contbr. articles to profl. jours. Capt., M.C., U.S. Army, 1955-57. Fellow ACP; mem. Am. Physiol. Soc., Am. Soc. Pharmacology and Exptl. Therapeutics, Am. Fedn. Clin. Rsch., Am. Soc. Clin. Investigation, Am. Assn. Study of Liver Disease, Am. Gastroenterol. Assn., Am. Soc. Clin. Pharmacology and Therapeutics, Am. Soc. Biol. Chemists, Am. Pediatric Soc., Am. Soc. Parenteral and Enteral Nutrition, Harvey Soc., Sigma Xi, Alpha Omega Alpha. Jewish. Avocation: grandparenting. Home: 501 E 79th St New York NY 10021-0735 Office: NYU Med Ctr Divsn Hepatic Disease New York NY 10016 E-mail: norman.javitt@med.nyu.edu.

JAVORE, GARY WILLIAM, lawyer; b. San Antonio, Apr. 3, 1952; s. Fred Walter and Glennice Jean (Gilbert) J. BA, Kent (Ohio) State U., 1975; JD, Cleve. State U., 1978. Bar: Tex. 1978, U.S. Dist. Ct. (we. dist.) Tex. 1981, U.S. Ct. Appeals (5th cir.) 1981, U.S. Supreme Ct. 1981. Atty. Bexar County Legal Aid, San Antonio, 1979-81; prin. Johnson, Christopher, Javore & Cochran, San Antonio, 1981—. Author, speaker legal seminars. Mem. Leadership San Antonio Class XXIV. Fellow Tex. Bar Found., San Antonio Bar Found.; mem. San Antonio Trial Lawyers Assn. (bd. dirs. 1986—, treas. 1991, pres. 1993, Outstanding Young Lawyer award 1986), Greater San Antonio Builders Assn. (cons., exec. bd. 1990—, v.p. assoc. coun. 1993), Tex. Trial Lawyers Assn., Order of Barristers. Avocations: wood carving, tennis, scuba diving. Office: Johnson Christopher Javore & Cochran 5802 Northwest Expy San Antonio TX 78201-2851

JAW, ANDREW CHUNG-SHIANG, software analyst; b. Tainan, Taiwan, Feb. 10, 1953; came to U.S., 1978; s. Ping-Tsen and Pey-Yuh Jaw; m. Amy Chi, July 30, 1979; children: Andrew, Anfin, Audrey. BS in Mech. Engring., Tatung Inst. Tech., Taipei, Taiwan, 1974; MS in Metallurgical Engring., Poly. Inst. N.Y., 1981; MSEE, Syracuse U., 1987. Engr. Tatung Co., Taipei, Taiwan, 1976-78; sr. assoc. engr. IBM Corp., Endicott, NY, 1980-89, Rochester, Minn., 1990-91; software cons. A BOC Health Care Co., Madison, Wis., 1991-92; sr. software engr. A Rockwell Internat. Co., Milw., 1992-94; staff software assurance analyst ARDIS Co., Lincolnshire, Ill., 1994-96, lead tech. programmer analyst, 1996-98, Am. Mobile Satellite Corp., Lincolnshire, Ill., 1998-2000; sr. network mgmt. sys. engr. Motient Corp., Lincolnshire, Ill., 2000—. Adj. prof. info. sys. ITT Tech. Inst., Greenfield, Wis., 2003—. Patentee in field. Recipient Cert. of Merit, Assembly of the State of NY, 1985; rsch. fellow Poly. Inst. NY, 1979. Mem. IEEE Computer Soc. E-mail: andy.jaw@motient.com.

JAWIDZIK, EDWARD MARK, priest; b. New Brunswick, N.J., Apr. 25, 1954; s. Edward John and Phyllis Jean (Kaczmarek) Jawidzik. BA in Humanities, St. Mary's Sem.Coll., Balt., 1976; MDiv, Immaculate Conception Sem., Mahwah, N.J., 1980. Ordained priest Roman Catholic Church, 1981. Parochial vicar St. Mary of the Lake Ch., Lakewood, NJ, 1981—86; parochial vicar Our Lady Star of the Sea Ch., Long Branch, NJ, 1986—87, St. Ann's Ch., Keansburg, NJ, 1987—94; pastor Our Lady of Perpetual Help Ch., Highlands, NJ, 1994—95; parochial vicar St. Rose Ch., Belmar, NJ, 1995—2001, St. Robert Bellarmine Ch., Freehold, NJ, 2001—. Rep. for Bayshore Deanery Priest's Coun., Trenton, NJ, 1992—95; pro-life chaplain Monmouth County, NJ, 1995—; rep. for coastal Monmouth Deanery Priest's Coun., Trenton, NJ, 1995—2001. Mem Keansburg Alliance on Substance Abuse, 1987—94; Chap-

lain KC Bayside Coun., E. Keansburg, 1987—92, KC St Catharine's Coun., Spring Lake, NJ, 1999—2001. Recipient Proclamation of Acclaim (10th ann. ordination), Mayor and Borough Coun., Keansburg, N.J., 1991, Proclamation Mayor and Borough Coun. (for service to Keansburg residents, Keansburg, 1994. Mem.: Freehold Twp. Histl. Presevation Commn., Acton Inst. Study Religion and Liberty, Freehold Clergy Assn. Roman Catholic. Avocations: baseball, history, music. Home: 61 Woodstock Pl Freehold NJ 07728 Office: St Robert Bellarmine Ch 61 Georgia Rd Freehold NJ 07728 Office Fax: 732-409-3496.

JAWIN, ANN JULIANO, human resource specialist; b. Barnesboro, Pa. d. Santo and Benedetta (Vanchiere) Giuliano; m. Edward Henry Jawin; children: Ronald, Paul. BA, CUNY, 1943; PhD, St. John's U., 1976. Asst. personnel dir. Davis & Geck, N.Y.C., 1945-52; guidance counselor h.s. divsn. N.Y.C. Bd. Edn., 1962-86; dir. guidance Bramson Tech. Coll., N.Y.C., 1986-89; pres., founder Ann J. Jawin Assocs., N.Y.C., 1990—; founder, chair bd. dirs. Queen's Women's Ctr., Inc., N.Y.C., 1987—. Author: A Women's Guide to Career Preparation, 1979, Report on Sex Bias in N.Y. Public Schools, 1977, Where's the Money for College?, 1985. Founder, chair bd. dirs. Dougbay Manor Civic Assn., Douglaston, N.Y., 1966—; pres. Bay Terrace Cmty. Coun., Bayside, Queens, N.Y., 1955-66; N.Y. State Committeewoman N.Y. State Dem. Party. Recipient Susan B. Anthony award NOW, 1985, Ralph Bunche award UN Assn., 1996, vol. svc. award Mayor Rudolph Giuliani, N.Y.C., 1997, Citation of Merit Fernando Ferrer Bronx Borough Pres., 1998, Hall of Fame award Hunter Coll., 1993, Ralph Burche award, 1996; named Humanitarian of Yr. Dems. for New Politics, 1995, Hunter Coll. Hall of Fame, 1993. Mem. AAUW (Leadership award 2001), N.Y. State Guidance Assn., Ams. of Italian Heritage (founder, chair bd. dirs. 1987—, Woman of Yr. 1998, Disting. Leadership award 2002). Roman Catholic. Avocations: walking, reading, swimming, gardening. Office: Queen's Women's Ctr 12055 Queens Blvd Rm 325 Jamaica NY 11424-1015 E-mail: Qwomenstr@aol.com.

JAWORSKA, TAMARA, painter, tapestry maker; b. Archangel, Russia; arrived in Can., 1969; d. Antonio Jankowski; m. Tadeusz Jaworski, 1957; children: Ewa, Piotr. BFA in Painting, State Acad. Fine Arts, Lodz, Poland, 1950, MFA in Design and Weaving Art, 1952; M of Painting (hon.), Accademia Italia, 1982. From asst. prof. to sr. asst. prof., lectr. State Acad. Fine Arts, Poland, 1952-58. One-woman shows include State Gallery of Textiles, Lodz, 1965, State Gallery of Fine Arts,Warsaw, 1965, Pushkin Nat. Mus., Moscow, 1966, Fine Arts Mus., Plymouth, U.K., 1968, Scottish Woolen Gallery, Galashields, 1968, Richard Demarco Gallery, Edinburgh, Scotland, 1968, Rothman's Art Gallery, Stratford, 1970, Merton Gallery, Toronto, 1970, London Art Gallery, 1971, Glendon Art Gallery, Toronto, 1972, Nienkamper Art Gallery, Toronto, 1979, Art Gallery of Hamilton, 1980, Nat. Museums and Art Galleries in Spain, 1980-81, Can. Cultural Ctr., Paris, 1981, Galerie Inard, Paris, 1981, Munich Art Gallery, Germany, 1982, Galerie Inard, Toulouse, France, 1982, 91, Galerie Inard, Paris, 1984, 91, Leo Kamen Gallery, Toronto, 1987, 89, John B. Aird State Gallery, Toronto, 1992, Peak Gallery, Toronto, 1997, Solo Gallery, Toronto, 2003, also exhibits in France, Germany, Belgium, Switzerland, Luxembourg, U.K., Spain, Austria, Poland, Russia, Hungary, U.S., Mex., Can., Paris, Eng., Scotland, Holland, Austria, Spain, Moscow, Poland, Hungary, Can., U.S., others; group exhbns. include Warsaw and Lodz art galleries, Pushkin Mus., European Art Gallery, Moscow, Richard Demarco Gallery, Edinburgh, Fine Art Mus., Plymouth, Eng., Merton Gallery, Toronto, Hermitage Leningrad Mus., USSR, Nat. Art Gallery, Teheran, Mus. Modern Art, Mexico City, Art Gallery of Ont., RCA-Art 2000, Toronto and Stratford, 2000; exhibited tapestries at New Coll., Galerie Inard, Ctr. Nat. de la Tapisserie d'Abusson, Paris, later in Madrid, Barcelona, Valencia, San Sebastian, Paris, Munich, Zurich, others; works in permanent collections of Pushkin Nat. Mus., European Art Gallery, Moskau, Russia, Nat. Mus., Warsaw, Nat. Mus. of Textile Arts, Lodz, Poland, Nat. Mus. of Home Army, King City, Krakow, Poland, Galashields Art Inst., Scotland, Bank of Montreal, Toronto, Bell Can., Ottawa, Molson Canadian, Toronto, Mutual Ins. of Can., Toronto and many corp. and pvt. collections in Europe, Am., Mid. East; subject of articles in art books and mags. Apptd. to Order of Can. for outstanding achievements in creative arts, 1994; recipient Gold medal-Triennial di Milano, Interior Design and Architcture, Milan, 1957, award for excellence Wool Gathering, Montreal, 1974, Gold medal Academia Italia delle Arti, 1980, Gold Centaur, Academia Italia delle Arti, 1982, Gold medal and 1st prize Internat. Art Competition, N.Y.C., 1985, Commemorative medal Gov. Gen. Can., 1993, Highest Civilian Recognition for Achievements in Field of Creative Visual Arts, Order of Can., 1994, Golden Jubilee medal Her Majesty Elizabeth II, 2002. Fellow York Univ.; mem. Royal Can. Acad. Arts, Academia Italia delle Arti, Ontario Soc. Artists. Home: 49 Don River Blvd Toronto ON Canada M2N2M8 E-mail: tamtad@ica.net.

JAWORSKI, DOLORES DALEY, advanced nurse practitioner; b. Camden, N.J., Apr. 8, 1947; d. Joseph A. and Dolores Martha (Lane) Daley; m. Gary Lee Snyder, Dec. 28, 1968 (div.); children: Justin Conrad, Yvonne Kristen; m. Thomas Matthew Jaworski, Dec. 24, 1982. RN, St. Vincent Med. Ctr., 1968; AA, St. Petersburg Jr. Coll., 1992; BS in Health Arts, Coll. St. Francis, 1994; MN, U. South Fla., 1997. RN, Fla.; cert. emergency nurse, critical care nurse, advanced nurse practitioner; cert. TNCC. Mem. continuing edn. faculty Pinellas County (Fla.) Sch. System, 1977-84; cardiopulmonary specialist St. Anthony Hosp., St. Petersburg, Fla., 1984-89, emergency dept. educator, 1989-90, staff RN emergency, 1991-94, Northside Hosp., St. Petersburg, 1994—; family practice advanced nurse practitioner St. Petersburg/Dunedin, Fla., 1997—. Med. legal cons. County of Pinellas, 1990—. Mem. Am. Heart Assn. (nursing coun. Fla. affiliate 1980-91, health site com., 1990-92, Bronze award 1984, Gold award 1988). Avocations: sewing, clothing design, photography. Home: 6536 27th Way N Saint Petersburg FL 33702-6324

JAWORSKI, ERNEST G. retired biotechnologist; b. Mpls. m. Pauline Jaworski; children: Diane, David, Christopher. BS in Chemistry, U. Minn., 1948; MS in Biochemistry, Oreg. State U., 1950, PhD in Biochemistry, 1952. Ret. dir. biol. scis. Monsanto Co., St. Louis; scientist in residence St. Louis Sci. Ctr.; former interim dir. Donald Danforth Plant Sci. Ctr. Bd. dirs. Divergence. Recipient Nat. Medal Tech., 1998. Achievements include development of Assemblying and leading the team that developed the world's first practical system to introduce foreign genes into plants. Avocations: skiing, blue-water sailing, travel, science education.

JAY, CHARLES DOUGLAS, religion educator, college administrator, clergyman; b. Monticello, Ont., Can., Oct. 10, 1925; s. Charles Arthur and Luella Gertrude (McPherson) J.; m. Ruth Helen Crooker, Jan. 30, 1948; children—David, Ian, Garth BA, Victoria Coll., U. Toronto, Ont., 1946; MA, U. Toronto, Ont., 1948; M.Div., Emmanuel Coll., 1950; PhD, U. Edinburgh, 1952; D.D. (hon.), Queen's U., 1971, Wycliffe Coll., 1976, Regis Coll., 1980, U. St. Michael's Coll., 1983, Victoria U., 1999. Ordained to ministry United Ch. of Can., 1950. Lectr. dept. philosophy Queen's U., 1946-47; pastor Elk Lake-Matachewan Ch., Ont., 1952-54, Trafalgar-Sheridan Ch., Oakville, Ont., 1954-55; asst. prof. philosophy of religion and Christian ethics Emmanuel Coll. U Toronto, 1955-58, assoc. prof., 1958-63, prof. philosophy of religion and ethics, 1963-91, registrar, 1958-64, prin., 1981-90; prof. emeritus Emmanuel Coll., 1991—. Founding dir. Toronto Sch. Theology, 1969-80; R.P. McKay meml. lectr., various univs., colls. across Can., 1966-67; spl. lectr. Hankuk Theol. Sem., Seoul, Korea, 1978, Fed. Theol. Sem., Pietermaritzburg, Republic of South Africa, 1981, Union Sem., Manila and Nanjing Theol. Sem., Nanjing, People's Republic of China, 1991; mem. working group Dialogue with People of Living Faiths and Ideologies, World Council Chs., 1970-83; chmn. div. world outreach United Ch. of Can., 1975-82; mem. commn. on accreditation Am. Assn. Theol. Schs., 1962-68 Contbr. chpts. to various books Served with Can. Officers Tng. Corps, 1943-45, as chaplain Royal Can. Navy Res., 1956-59 Decorated Order of Can. Fellow Am. Theol. Schs., 1963. Mem. Assn. Theol. Schs. U.S. and Can. (v.p. 1976-78, pres. 1984-86), Can. Theol. Soc. Office: 75 Queen's Park Crescent Emmanuel Coll Toronto ON Canada M5S 1K7 E-mail: cdouglas.jay@utoronto.ca.

JAY, FRANK PETER, writer, lexicographer, educator; b. Bklyn., Feb. 12, 1922; s. Frank G. and Harriet Ann (Niffer) J.; m. Jayne Marie Charles, Aug. 15, 1947; children— Jennifer, Christopher, Alison, Angela, Jonathan, Melissa, Bryan, Nicole, Matthew. AB, Fordham U., 1943; MA, Columbia U., 1946. Mem. faculty Fordham U., 1946-92, prof. English, 1948-92; editor-in-chief reference books Funk & Wagnalls, N.Y.C., 1963-65, exec. editor, 1968-73; editor-in-chief reference books Reader's Digest, N.Y.C., 1965-66; editor-in-chief IEEE Dictionary, 1977, 84, 88. Author: Jack: The Story of a Pretty Good Donkey, 1970, also articles, short stories; editor-in-chief: The New Internat. Year Book, 1963, 64, 65, Internat. Everyman's Ency., 20 vols, 1970. Served with USAAF, 1942-43. Mem. Overseas Press Club (N.Y.C.), Princeton Club (N.Y.C.), Manhasset Bay Yacht Club, Kappa Delta Pi. Home: 3 Huntington Rd Port Washington NY 11050-3510

JAY, HARVEY H. dermatologist, educator, researcher; b. Jersey City, Oct. 24, 1944; s. Jack and Miriam Jay; m. Phyllis Scheinberg, Dec. 1, 1985; children: David, Laura, Rachel, Rebecca. AB, Columbia Coll., 1966; MD, NYU, 1970. Diplomate Am. Bd. Dermatology. Pvt. practice specializing in dermatology, NYC, 1974—; clin. asst. prof. dermatology Cornell Med. Coll., NYC, 1977—. Expert in pulsed-light epilight and photoderm treatment of unwanted hair, ingrown hairs, blood vessels, rosacea, leg veins, scars and brown spots. Capt. USAFR, 1971-76. Fellow Am. Acad. Dermatology, Am. Soc. for Laser Medicine and Surgery; mem. AMA, Med. Soc. of County of NY, NY State Med. Soc., NY State Dermatology Soc., Dermatology Soc. Greater NY Office: 45 E 62nd St New York NY 10021-8025

JAY, JERRY LEON, SR., retired publishing executive, industrial engineer; b. Jenkins, Mo., Mar. 22, 1951; s. George Henry and Mary Louisa J.; children: Jerry L. Jr., Drake Allen. Journeyman Seneca Controls, Fraser, Mich., 1978-81; maintenance mgr. Kent-Moore Corp., Detroit, 1981, S.R. of Tenn., Ripley, 1982-85; ret. Jerry L. Jay Publ., Verona, Mo., 1985. Author: Patent Applications Simplified, 1996; patentee pneumatic desedimentiation machine improvement, process and apparatus for separating plastics from contaminants, pneumatic desedimentation machine. Home: 16 E Delta St Aurora MO 65605

JAY, NORMA JOYCE, artist; b. Wichita, Kans., Nov. 11, 1925; d. Albert Hugh and Thelma Ree (Boyd) Braly; m. Laurence Eugene Jay, Sept. 2, 1949; children: Dana Denise, Allison Eden. Student, Wichita State U., 1946-49, Art Inst. Chgo., 1955-56, Calif. State Coll., 1963. Illustrator Boeing Aircraft, Wichita, 1949-51; co-owner Back Door Gallery, Laguna Beach, Calif., 1973-88. Guest artist Coos Art Mus., 2003. One-woman shows include Milcir Gallery, Tiburon, Calif., 1978, Newport Beach City Gallery, 1981; exhibited in group shows at Am. Soc. Marine Artists ann. exhbns., 1978-2001, Peabody Mus., Salem, Mass., 1981, Mystic Seaport Mus. Gallery, Conn., 1992-95, Grand Ctrl. Gallery, N.Y., 1979-84, The Back Door Gallery, Laguna Beach, 1973-88, Mariners' Mus., Newport News, Va., 1985-86, Nat. Heritage Gallery of Fine Art, Beverly Hills, Calif., 1988—, Md. Hist. Mus., 1989, Kirsten Gallery, Seattle, 1991-97, R.J. Schaefer Gallery Mystic (Conn.) Seaport Mus., 1992, Vallejo Gallery, Newport Beach, Calif., 1992, Caswell Gallery, Troutdale, Oreg., 1994-95, Columbia River Maritime Mus., Astoria, Oreg., 1994, Arnold Art Gallery, Newport, Conn., 1994, Mystic Internat. Exhbn., 1995, Lu Martin Galleries, Laguna Beach, 1996—, Frye Art Mus., Seattle, 1997, Cummer Mus. Art & Gardens, Jacksonville, Fla., 1997-98, Cape Mus. Fine Arts Inc., Dennis, Mass., 2001, Coos Art Mus., Coos Bay, Oreg., 2003, Newport Art Mus., R.I., 2003, Maine Maritime Mus., Bath, 2003; represented in permanent collections including James Irvine Found., Newport Beach, Niguel Art Assn., Laguna Niguel, Calif., Deloitte, Haskins & Sells, Costa Mesa, Calif., M.J. Brock & Sons Inc., North Hollywood, Calif., others. Recipient Best of Show award Ford Nat. Competition, 1961, First Pl. award Traditional Artists Exhbn., San Bernadino County Mus., 1976, artist award Chriswood Gallery Invitational Exhbn., Rancho California, Calif., 1973, Dirs. Choice award, People's Choice award Coos Art Mus. Marine Exhbn., 1996, featured guest artist, 1998, Coos Art Mus., 2003, 1st Pl. award Maritime Art Exhibit, Newport Harbor Nautical Mus., Newport Beach, 1998-99. Fellow Am. Soc. Marine Artists (charter); mem. Niguel Art Assn. (first pres. 1968, hon. life mem. 1978), Artists Equity, Am. Artists Profl. League. Democrat.

JAY, PETER AUGUSTUS, writer, farmer; b. N.Y.C., Nov. 27, 1940; s. Peter and Gertrude (McGinley) J.; m. Stephanie Gerard, Oct. 27, 1967 (div. Dec. 1972); m. Irna Moore, Dec. 28, 1973; children: William, Sarah. BA, Harvard U., 1962. Vol. Peace Corps, Peru, 1962-64; journalist The Aegis, Bel Air, Md., 1964-65, The Washington Post, 1965-73; columnist The Balt. Sun, 1974-98; owner, editor, pub. The Record, Havre de Grace, Md., 1973-89; family farm operator Havre de Grace, Md., 1988—. Nieman fellow Harvard U., 1972-73. Author, editor: Havre de Grace: An Informal History, 1986; contbr. articles to profl. publs. Recipient numerous awards. Avocations: farmer, horseman, professional charterboat captain. Office: 100 St John St PO Box 696 Havre De Grace MD 21078-0696 E-mail: pajay@juno.com.

JAY, WILLIAM WALTON, lawyer; b. N.Y.C., June 29, 1943; s. William Chauncy and Miriam Bell (Samuels) J.; widowed; children: William Robert, Michael Samuel. BA, Emory U., 1965; JD, U. Chgo., 1968; MS in Mgmt., Rensselaer Poly. Inst., 1984. Bar: Ill. 1968, Ariz. 1969, U.S. Dist. Ct. Ariz. 1969, Conn. 1985, N.Y. 1990. Atty. semiconductor products div. Motorola, Inc., Scottsdale, Ariz., 1968-71; pvt. practice, Phoenix, 1971-72; asst. atty. gen. State of Ariz., Phoenix, 1972-74; atty. Kaiser Engrs. div. Kaiser Industries Corp., 1974-75; counsel Naval Sea Systems Command, USN, Pascagoula, Miss., 1975-79; dep. counsel Elec. Boat Corp., Groton, Conn., 1979-99; pvt. practice Groton, 1999—. Chmn. Groton City Dem. Com.; mem. Groton Representative Town Meeting, Groton Town Dem. Com. Served with USN, 1961-65. Mem. ABA (pub. contracts sect.), State Bar Ariz., Nat. Contract Mgmt. Assn. (fellow, lectr., pres. Gulf Coast chpt. 1978, bd. dirs. Gulf Coast chpt. 1979, ctrl. Conn. chpt. 1987, cert. profl. contract mgr.), Shipbuilders Coun. Am. (contracts com. 1982—), Phi Beta Kappa, Pi Sigma Alpha, Phi Delta Phi, Beta Theta Pi. Lodges: Rotary, Lions. Presbyterian. Home: PO Box 30002 Las Cruces NM 88003-8002 Office: PO Box 30002 Las Cruces NM 88003-8002 E-mail: jayw4@prodigy.net., floridafats1@yahoo.com.

JAYABOSE, SOMASUNDARAM, pediatrician; b. Paramankurichi, Tamil Nadu, India, July 18, 1945; arrived in U.S., 1971; s. Somu and Kosalai Somasundaram; m. Nirmala Perumal, July 11, 1973; children: Sundar, Geetha. MBBS, Madurai Med. Coll., India, 1969. Diplomate Am. Bd. Pediat., Am. Bd. Pediat. Hematology-Oncology. Asst. prof. pediat. N.Y. Med. Coll., Valhalla, 1977—79; chief pediat. hematology-oncology N.Y. Med. Coll.-Westchester Med. Ctr., Valhalla, 1979—. Prof. pediat. N.Y. Med. Coll., 2002—; founder, med. dir. Children's Cancer Fund, Valhalla, 1993—. Contbr. chapters to books. Avocations: photography, travel. Office: NY Med Coll Munger Pavilion R110 Valhalla NY 10595 Office Fax: 914-594-4022. E-mail: S_Jayabose@nymc.edu.

JAYASEKARA, WIPUL P. engineer; b. Sri Lanka, 1968; came to U.S., 1987; BA, Pomona Coll., 1991; MS, Carnegie Mellon U., 1993, PhD, 1998. Adv. engr. Hitachi Corp., San Jose, Calif., 1998—. Contbr. articles to profl. jour. Mem. IEEE.

JAYE, DAVID ROBERT, JR., retired hospital administrator; b. Chgo., Aug. 15, 1930; s. David R. and Gertrude (Gibfried) J.; m. Mary Ann Scanlan, June 6, 1953; children— David, Jeffery, Kathleen. BS, Loyola U. at Chgo., 1952; M.H.A., Northwestern U., 1954. Adminstrv. asst. Chgo. Wesley Meml. Hosp., 1953-54; asst. adminstr. Sharon (Pa.) Gen. Hosp., 1957-60, St. Joseph Hosp., Joliet, Ill., 1960-65; adminstr. Sacred Heart Hosp., Allentown, Pa., 1965-69; pres., chief exec. officer St. Joseph's Hosp., Marshfield, Wis., 1969-90; cons. Marshfield, 1990—. Regional v.p. Sisters of Sorrowful Mother Ministry Corp., Milw., 1989-91; bd. dirs. Marshfield Savs. and Loan; cons. Marshfield, Wis., 1991—. Past pres. North Central Wis. Hosp. Council; mem. Wis. State Health Policy Council; bd. dirs. Wis. Blue Cross, Marshfield Devel. Corp., Health Care Ministry, Manitowoc, Wis., 1992—. Served as lt., Med. Service Corps USAF, 1954-57. Fellow Am. Coll. Hosp. Adminstrs. (coun. regents); mem. Am. Hosp. Assn. (coun. fed. rels., ho. of dels.), Cath. Hosp. Assn. (past trustee), Wis. Hosp. Assn. (past chmn. bd. trustees), Rotary, Elks, KC. Home and Office: 8925 W Minch Dr Minocqua WI 54548-9785

JAYNE, CYNTHIA ELIZABETH, psychologist; b. Pensacola, Fla., June 5, 1953; d. Gordon Howland and Joan (Rockwood) J. AB, Vassar Coll., 1974; MA, SUNY, Buffalo, 1978, PhD, 1983. Lic. psychologist, Pa. Instr. dept. psychiatry Temple U. Sch. Medicine, Phila., 1982-84, asst. prof., 1984-85, asst. dir. outpatient svcs., asst. dir. residency tng., 1982-85, clin. asst. prof., 1985—; pvt. practice psychology Phila., 1985—. Adj. prof. Chestnut Hill Coll., 1994—. Contbr. articles to profl. jours. Soc. for Sci. Study Sex scholar, 1981; Sigma Xi grantee, 1981, Kinsey Inst. Dissertation award, 1983. Mem. Ea. Psychol. Assn., Soc. for Sci. Study Sex (bd. dirs. 1984-86).

JAYNES, JAMES B. geneticist, educator; b. Waynesville, N.C., Mar. 11, 1953; s. James Bruce Jaynes and Mary Ellen Boone; m. Miki Fujioka, May 31, 1997; 1 child, Cristen Hemingway. PhD in Physics summa cum laude, U. Wash., 1980. Postdoctoral fellow U. Calif., San Francisco, 1988—91; assoc. prof. genetics Thomas Jefferson U., Phila., 1992—. Grantee rsch., NIH, 1994—2003, NSF, 1997—98, 1998—2001, 2001—. Mem.: AAAS, Genetics Soc. Am. Office: Thomas Jefferson U 1020 Locust St Room JAH-490 Philadelphia PA 19107

JAYNES, ROBERT HENRY, JR., retired military officer, b. Greeneville, Tenn., Feb. 6, 1948; s. Robert Henry and Della Mae (Broyles) J.; m. Peggy Jane Farmer, Dec. 24, 1981. BS, East Tenn. State U., 1970. Pilot 57th assault helicopter co. U.S. Army, Republic of Vietnam, 1972-73, advanced through grades to lt. col., 1988, co. commdr., 1976-78, aviation tng. developer/evaluator for dir. evaluation Ft. Rucker, Ala., 1978-80, battalion advisor Alaska NG Kotzebue, 1980-81, exec. officer recruiting battalion San Juan, P.R., 1981-84; officer-in-chg. Chief of Staff of Army's Allied Office Hall of Fame U.S. Army Command and Gen. Staff Coll., Ft. Leavenworth, Kans., 1984-85; exec. officer U.S. Army Space Initiatives Study U.S. Army Space Coun., Washington, 1985; student and staff group leader Command and Gen. Staff Coll. U.S. Army, Ft. Leavenworth, Kans., 1986-87; program mgr. U.S. Army enlistment incentives Office of Dep. Chief of Staff for Personnel/The Pentagon, Washington, 1988-93; ret. U.S. Army, 1993; mgr., dir. fed. programs Network Computing Devices, Bethesda, Md., 1993-95; bus. devel. mgr. Computer Assocs. Internat., Inc., Reston, Va., 1995-2000; v.p. A&T Systems Inc., Silver Spring, Md., 2000-2001; co-founder, exec. v.p. Link Mgmt. Group, Alexandria, Va., 2001—02; dir. fed. bus. devel. Steel Cloud Inc., Dulles, Va., 2002; founder, CEO Jaynes Assocs., Inc., Nokesville, Va., 2002; acct. exec. US Army Nextira One Fed. LLC, 2003—. Contbr. articles to profl. jours. Founding mem. Leavenworth Computer Coun., pres. 1986-87. Decorated Bronze Star and Legion of Merit. Mem. Assn. U.S. Army, Army Aviation Assn. Am. (v.p. mem. 1975-76, v.p. student affairs 1986-87), Recreational Equipment Assn., Scabbard & Blade, Pentagon Personal Computer User Group (founder, program chmn., vendor rep., newsletter editor 1987-89, chmn. 1989-91). Avocations: hunting, fishing, camping, computers, automobiles. Office: Jaynes Assocs Inc 13425 Bristow Rd Nokesville VA 20181-3227 E-mail: bobjaynes@comcast.net.

JAYSON, MELINDA GAYLE, lawyer; b. Dallas, Sept. 29, 1956; d. Robert and Louise Adelle (Jacobs) J. BA, U. Tex., 1977, JD, 1980. Bar: Tex. 1980, U.S. Dist. Ct. (no. dist.) Tex. 1980, U.S. Ct. Appeals (5th and 11th cirs.) 1981, U.S. Dist. Ct. (so. dist.) Tex. 1989, U.S. Ct. Appeals (8th cir.) 1990, U.S. Supreme Ct. 1991. Assoc. Akin, Gump, Strauss, Hauer & Feld, Dallas, 1980-86, ptnr., 1987-96, Melinda G. Jayson, P.C., 1996—; gen. counsel Hall Fin. Group, Dallas, 1999—. Comml. arbitrator, mem. regional adv. coun. Am. Arbitration Assn.; arbitrator, mediator N.Y. Stock Exch., NASD Regulation, Inc. and Dispute Solutions, Inc.; mediator U.S. EEO Commn., 1999-2000; arbitrator Nat. Arbitration Forum, 2000—. Named one of Outstanding Young Women Am., 1983. Mem. Tex. Bar Assn., Dallas Bar Assn., State Bar of Tex. (mem. dist. 6A grievance com. 1997-99, mem. professionalism enhancement com. 1997-99), Writers Clan. Office: Ste 2015 5445 Caruth Haven Ln Dallas TX 75225-8166 E-mail: ilsekramer@aol.com.

JEAN, PATRICIA ANNE, medical center administrator; b. Methuen, Mass., Sept. 15, 1946; Diploma in Nursing, Worcester (Mass.) City Hosp., 1967; BSN magna cum laude, U. Lowell (Mass.), 1984; MSN in Nursing Adminstrn., U. Mass., 1992. cert. critical care unit nurse. Nurse Boston City Hosp., 1967; staff nurse Holy Family Hosp. and Med. Ctr., Methuen, Mass., 1967-69, charge nurse ICU, 1969-70, asst. head nurse, 1970-83; nurse mgr. cardiac unit Holy Family Hosp. and Med. Ctr., Methuen, Mass., 1983-93; dir. cardiology Cath. Med. Ctr., Manchester, N.H., 1993-94, nurse mgr., 1993-94, dir. cardiology, 1994-95, Cath. Med. Ctr. and Elliott Hosp., Manchester, 1995-96; adminstr. cardiac svcs. Optima Healthcare, Manchester, 1996—. Contbr. articles to profl. jours. Mem. Am. Orgn. Nurse Execs. (affiliate), Am. Coll. Cardiovasc. Adminstrs., Am. Coll. Cardiovasc. Nurses, Am. Coll. Med. Adminstrs., U. Lowell Nursing Honor Soc., Sigma Theta Tau. Home: 412 Forest St Methuen MA 01844-1939

JEAN-LOUIS, GIRARDIN, psychologist, educator, researcher; b. Port-Au-Prince, Haiti, Dec. 7, 1967; s. Jean-Louis Girardin and Marie L. Beaugris. BA, CUNY, 1992, MA, 1997, PhD, 1997. Instr. CUNY, Staten Island, 1994-97; rsch. psychologist U. Calif., San Diego, 1997-2000; asst. prof. L.I. U., Bklyn., 2000—, SUNY, Bklyn., 2000—. Co-dir. sleep lab. Coll. L.I., 1994-97; clin. dir. Kingsbrook Jewish Med. Ctr., N.Y., 2000—. Contbr. articles to profl. jours. Postdoctoral fellow NIH-NHLBI, 1997. Mem. Am. Acad. Sleep Medicine (Trainee fellow 1997), Sleep Rsch. Soc. (Rsch. Merit award 1999). Avocations: music, hiking, reading, jogging. Office: SUNY Down State Med Ctr. Box 58 450 Clarkson Ave Brooklyn NY 11203 E-mail: jeanlouisg@yahoo.com.

JEANLOZ, ROGER WILLIAM, biochemist, educator; b. Berne, Switzerland, Nov. 3, 1917; came to U.S., 1947, naturalized, 1953; s. William M. and Rose (Poisat) J.; m. Dorothea A.H. de Passavant, Dec. 20, 1945; children: Patrick Marc (dec.), Claude-André, Raymond François, Danielle Renée, Sylvie Anne. Baccalaureate, Coll. Geneva, Switzerland, 1936; Chem.E., U. Geneva, 1941, D.Sc., 1943; A.M. (hon.), Harvard, 1961; D.Sc. (hon.), U. Paris, 1980. Research asso. U. Geneva, 1943-45, U. Basel, 1945-46; asst. U. Montreal, 1946-47; sr. research fellow NIH, 1947-48; sr. scientist Worcester Found. Exptl. Biology, 1948-51; asso. biochemist Mass. Gen. Hosp., Boston, 1951-61, biochemist, 1961—; research asso. Harvard Med. Sch., 1951-57, asso. organic chemistry, 1957-60, asst. prof. biol. chemistry, 1960-61, asso. prof., 1961-69, prof., 1969-88, emeritus prof. biol. chemistry and molecular pharmacology, 1988—. Mem. bd. tutors biochem. scis. Faculty Arts and Scis., Harvard U., 1960—; mem. study sect. physiol. chemistry div. research grants NIH, 1964-68, 69-70; mem. physiol. chemistry B. research study com. Am. Heart Assn., 1971-74. Author: (with Balazs) The Amino Sugars, 3 vols, 1965, (with Gregory) Glycoconjugate Research, 2 vols, 1979; Editor; Carbohydrate Research; editorial bd.: Connective Tissue Research, Molecular Biology, Biochemistry and Biophysics, Biochimie, Glycoconjugate Jour.; contbr. articles to profl. jours. Recipient medal Société de Chimie Biologique de France, 1960, medal U. Liege, 1964, Prix Jaubert U. Geneva, 1973, Stratton award Am. Friends of Switzerland, 1981, Alexander von Humboldt Sr. Scientist award, 1983; Guggenheim fellow, 1976-77. Fellow AAAS; mem. Am. Soc. Biol. Chemists, Am. Chem. Soc., Swiss Chem. Soc., Royal Chem. Soc. (London), French Biochem. Soc., Biochem. Soc., Soc. for Glycobiology, Am. Coll. Rheumatology. Home: 42 Ruthven Rd Newton MA 02458-2316 Fax: (617) 244-9161. E-mail: jeanloz@fas.harvard.edu.

JEANNE, ROBERT LAWRENCE, entomologist, educator; b. NYC, Jan. 14, 1942; s. Armand Lucien and Ruth (Stuber) Jeanne; m. Louise Grenville Bluhm, Sept. 18, 1976; children: Thomas Lucien, James McClure. BS in Biology, Denison U., 1964; postgrad., Justus-Liebig U., Giessen, Fed. Republic Germany, 1964-65; MA, Harvard U., 1968, PhD in Biology, 1971. Instr. biology U. Va., Charlottesville, 1970-71; asst. prof. biology Boston U., 1971-76; asst. prof. entomology U. Wis., Madison, 1976-79, assoc. prof., 1979-83, prof., 1983—. Rschr.: numerous publs. on social insects. Fellow Rotary Found., 1964—65, Guggenheim Meml., 1986—87; grantee NSF, 1972—. Mem.: Wis. Acad. Scis., Arts and Letters, Animal Behavior Soc., Internat. Union Study Social Insects (chmn. protempore, sec.-treas. 1979—80, pres. western hemisphere sect. 1981, assoc. editor insectes Sociaux 1986—2002), Assn. Tropical Biology, Phi Beta Kappa, Sigma Xi. Achievements include numerous discoveries relating to nest construction, nest architecture, commmunication, defense, caste polymorphism, polyethism, social organization, and life histories in social wasps. Office: U Wis Dept Entomology 1630 Linden Dr Madison WI 53706-1520 E-mail: jeanne@entomology.wisc.edu.

JEANNERET, PAUL RICHARD, management consultant; BA in Psychology, U. Va., 1962; MA in Psychology and Sociology, U. Fla., 1963; PhD in Indsl. and Orgnl. Psychology, Purdue U., 1969. From cons. to sr. cons. Lifson, Wilson, Ferguson & Winick, Inc., Houston, 1969-73; v.p. PAQ Svcs., Inc., 1972-90, pres., 1990—; prin. LWFW, Inc., Houston, 1974-76, mng. prin., 1977-81, Jeanneret & Assocs., Houston, 1982—. Grad. rsch. asst. Purdue U.,

1967-69; instr. physiol. and introductory psychology Old Dominion Coll., Norfolk, Va., 1965-67; adj. prof. psychology dept. U. Houston, 1982—. Cons. editor: Jour. Applied Psychology, 1989-94; panel editor: Pers. Psychology, 1994-98. Lt. (j.g.) USNR, 1964-67. Fellow APA (divsn. indsl. and orgnl. psychology, divsn. cons. psychology), Soc. Orgnl. Behavior; mem. Am. Compensation Assn., Soc. Indsl. and Orgnl. Psychology (elected officer 1995-98), Disting. Profl. Contbns. award 1990, M. Scott Myers award 2002), Tex. Indsl./Orgnl. Psychologists, Houston Area Indsl. and Orgnl. Psychologists (past exec. com.), Sigma Xi. Office: Jeanneret & Assocs Inc 601 Jefferson St Ste 3900 Houston TX 77002-7913

JEANNIOT, MICHEL ANDRE, lawyer; b. Montreal, Que., Apr. 16, 1958; s. Pierre J. Jeanniot and Mariette (Guay) Dean; m. Danielle Boisvert; 1 child, Caroline. DEC, Coll. Vieux Montreal, 1980; LLB, U. Quebec, 1983. Bar: Que. 1984. Assoc. Kaufman-Respitz, Montreal, 1985-88, ptnr., 1988, Gross-Pinsky, Montreal, 1989—. Spl. auditor Nat. Expo. on Housing, Montreal, 1990. Mem. Assn. Trial Lawyers Am. (comml. litigation divsn. 1987—), Can. Bar Assn., Richelieu Valley Golf & Country Club, ATLA. Home: 280 Place Beaulac Laprairie QC Canada J5R 4L6 Office: 2 Place Alexis Nihon # 1000 Montreal QC Canada H3Z 3C1 Fax: 514-933-0810. E-mail: mjeanniot@grosspinsky.com.

JEANSONNE, MARY SCANLAN, not for profit developer; b. Crowley, La. d. Howard Vincent and Lucy Duhon Scanlan; m. John Allen Jeansonne Jr., Dec. 28, 1966; children: Michelle Jeansonne Anderson, John Allen III. BA, St. Mary's Dominican Coll., New Orleans, 1967; M in Speech Pathology, U. La., 1977. Tchr. St. Mary's Dominican H.S., New Orleans, 1967-68; debate, speech coach LaGrange Sr. H.S., Lake Charles, La., 1968-70; nonprofit cons. Lafayette, La., 1981—. Treas. Lafayette Parish Bar Aux., 1977-78; bd. dirs. Jr. League Lafayette, 1979-85, pres., 1984-85; mem. adv. bd. Cath. Carmel Sch., Lafayette, 1983-85; bd. dirs. Family Tree Lafayette Parenting Ctr., 1983-84, Acadiana Arts Coun., 1983-84, Vermillionville Historic Found., Lafayette, 1993-96, Lafayette C. of C., 1993-99, La. Serve Commn., Lafayette, 1995-98; bd. dirs., sec. Big Bros. Big Sisters, Lafayette, 1985-89; pres. Vol. Ctr. Lafayette, 1987-88; bd. dirs. Leadership La., Baton Rouge, 1989-91, co-chair, 1994-96; sec. Solid Rock Found., Lafayette, 1990-91; chmn. La. Lottery, Baton Rouge, 1990-94; nominating chair area V Assn. Jr. Leagues, 1993-94; vice chair Lafayette Econ. Devel. Authority, 1999-2000; chmn. bd. dirs. Coun. Better La., Baton Rouge, 2000-01. Named Homecoming Parade Grand Marshall U. La., 1991. Roman Catholic. Avocations: travel, reading, movies.

JEAS, WILLIAM C. aerospace engineering executive, consultant; b. Worcester, Mass., June 9, 1938; m. Irene M. Merkle, June 18, 1961; 1 child, Dean W. BS, U.S. Naval Acad., 1961; MS, Air Force Inst. Tech., 1970. Commd. 2d lt. USAF, 1961, advanced through grades to col., 1980, various R & D, engring. and prodn. assignments, 1961-85, ret., 1986; COO, v.p. mktg. TE Products, Inc., Framingham, Mass., 1986-91. Bd. dirs. TE Consulting, Inc. Mem. IEEE (sr. mem.), AIAA (sr. mem.), SPIE, Armed Forces Comms. Electronics Assn., U.S. Naval Acad. Alumni Assn. Home: 87 Wesson Ter Northborough MA 01532-1955

JECH, THOMAS J. mathematics educator; b. Praha, Czechoslovakia, Jan. 29, 1944; came to U.S., 1969; s. Frantisek and Bozena (Mausová) J.; m. Paula B. Dragounová, Sept. 7, 1965; children: Pavel, Susanna. RNDr., Charles U., Prague, Czechoslovakia, 1966. Jr. fellow U. Bristol (England), 1968-69; assoc. prof. SUNY, Buffalo, 1969-74; prof. Pa. State U., University Park, 1974-2000, prof. emeritus, 2000—. Vis. assoc. prof. UCLA, 1970-71, vis. prof., 1981; vis. assoc. prof. Princeton (N.J.) U., 1972; vis. prof. Stanford (Calif.) U., 1974, U. Hawaii, 1984, Normal U., Beijing, 1987, U. Marie et Pierre Curie, Paris, 1989, Calif. Inst. of Tech., 1991; vis. fellow All Souls Coll., Oxford, Eng., 1988; vis. prof. U. Paris VII, 1990; visitor ETH, Zurich, Switzerland, 1989, Inst. of Advanced Study, Princeton U., 1973; fellow Ctr. for Theoretical Study, Prague, 2000—. Author six books; editor Annals Pure and Applied Logic, 1987—; contbr. about 100 articles to profl. jours. Grantee NSF, 1970-2000, U.S. Israel Binat. Sci. Found., 1984-86, 89-91, U.S. Japan Sci. Found., 1985-87, Fulbright Found., 1989, 96, Rockefeller Found., 1998; exch. scientist NAS, 1976, 87. Mem. Am. Math. Soc. (editor 1980-88), Assn. of Symbolic Logic. Office: CTS Jilska 1 Prague Czech Republic E-mail: jech@math.cas.cz.

JECKAVITCH, DAVID M. music educator; b. Ellwood City, Pa., Oct. 28, 1949; s. Brownie S. and Viola E. Jeckavitch; m. Mary H. Johnson, July 29, 1949; 1 child, Melissa M. BS in Music Edn., Ind. U. of Pa., 1971, MEd in Music Edn., 1974. Tchr. instrumental music United H.S., Armagh, Pa., 1971—72, Westmont Hilltop Sch. Dist., Johnstown, Pa., 1972—77, Ind. Area Sch. Dist., Indiana, Pa., 1977—. Bd. dirs. Ind. U. of PA Honors Band, Indiana, Pa.; pres. Carbaugh Svc. Scholarship Com., Indiana, Pa., 1982—. Mem. KC, Indiana, Pa., 1980, Civic Band, Johnstown, Pa., 1972. Recipient 25 years Outstanding Svc. Plaque, Ind. U. of Pa, Honors Band, 1998. Mem.: NEA, Music Educators Nat. Conf., Am. String Tchrs. Assn., Pa. Music Educators Assn. (sec.-treas. dist. VI), Pa. Music Educators Assn. (pres. dist. III 1971—72), Pa. State Educators Assn. Achievements include Co-founder of Indiana University of Pennsylvania Honors Band; Guest conductor for Music festivals; Adjudicator and judge parades. Avocations: gardening, travel, stocks and financial investing. Home: 114 Valley Rd Indiana PA 15701-3637 Personal E-mail: djeckavitch@adelphia.net.

JECKLIN, LOIS UNDERWOOD, art corporation executive, consultant; b. Manning, Iowa, Oct. 5, 1934; d. J.R. and Ruth O. (Austin) Underwood; m. Dirk C. Jecklin, June 24, 1955; children: Jennifer Anne, Ivan Peter. BA, State U. Iowa, 1992. Residency coord. Quad City Arts Coun., Rock Island, Ill., 1973-78; field rep. Affiliate Artists Inc., N.Y.C., 1975-77; mgr., artist in residence Deere & Co., Moline, Ill., 1977-80; dir. Vis. Artist Series, Davenport, Iowa, 1978-81; pres. Vis. Artists Inc., Davenport, 1981-88; pres., owner Jecklin Assocs., Davenport, 1988—. Asst. to exec. dir. Walter W. Naumburg Found., N.Y.C., 1990—; cons. writer's program St. Ambrose Coll., Davenport, 1981, 83, 85; mem. com. Iowa Arts Coun., Des Moines, 1983-84; panelist Chamber Music Am., N.Y.C., 1984, Pub. Art Conf., Cedar Rapids, Iowa, 1984; panelist, mem. com. Lt. Gov.'s Conf. on Iowa's Future, Des Moines, 1984. Trustee Davenport Mus. Art, 1975-98, hon. trustee, 1998—; trustee Nature Conservancy Iowa, 1987-88; steering com. Iowa Citizens for Arts, Des Moines, 1970-71; bd. dirs. Tri-City Symphony Orch. Assn., Davenport, 1968-83; founding mem. Urban Design Coun., HOME, City of Davenport Beautification Com., 1970-72; bd. govs. Mus. Arts & Design, NYC, 1995—; devel. coun. U. Iowa Mus. Art, 1996-2002. Recipient numerous awards Izaak Walton League, Davenport Art Gallery, Assn. for Retarded Citizens, Am. Heart Assn., Ill. Bur. corrections, many others; LaVernes Noyes scholar, 1953-55. Mem. Am. Symphony Orch. League, Crow Valley Golf Club, Outing Club, Rotary. Republican. Episcopalian. Home and Office: 2717 Nichols Ln Davenport IA 52803-3620 E-mail: jecklin@webtv.net.

JEDRZEJAS, MARK J. microbiologist, researcher; b. Bielsko-Biala, Poland, Sept. 17, 1961; came to U.S., 1989; BS/MS, Jagellonian U., Cracow, Poland, 1988; MS, Cleve. Clin. Foudn./Cleve. State U., 1991; PhD, Cleve. Clin. Found., Cleve. State U., 1993. Rsch. asst. Japellanien U., Cracow, 1988-89, Cleve. State U., 1990-92; postdoctoral fellow U. Ala., Birmingham, 1993-94, rsch. assoc., 1994-95, asst. prof., 1995—2001; assoc. scientist Children's Hosp. Oakland Rsch. Inst., 2001—. Office: Chldns Hosp Oakland Rsch Inst 5700 Martin Luther King Jr Way Oakland CA 94609 Office Fax: 510-450-7914. Business E-Mail: MJedrzejas@chori.org.

JEDZINIAK, LEE PETER, lawyer, educator, insurance company officer; b. Springfield, Mass., June 1, 1956; s. Leo Stanley and Helena (Ludwin) J. BA in Polit. Sci., The Citadel, 1978; JD, U. S.C., 1981. Bar: S.C. 1981, U.S. Dist. Ct. S.C. 1982, U.S. Ct. Appeals (4th cir.) 1982, U.S. Ct. Appeals (11th and D.C. cirs.) 1983, U.S. Ct. Appeals (3d, 5th and 10th cirs.) 1984, U.S. Tax Ct. 1985, U.S. Ct. Appeals (9th cir.) 1985, U.S. Supreme Ct. 1985. Law clk. to presiding judge 15th Jud. Cir. Ct., Conway, S.C., 1981-83; atty. consumer advs. office State of S.C., Columbia, 1983-85, staff counsel dept. ins., 1985-88, gen. counsel dept. ins., 1988-95, state dir. ins., 1995-99; v.p. compliance S.C. Farm Bur. Ins. Cos., West Columbia, 1999—. Profl. lectr. MPA and MBA depts. Golden Gate U., 1984-90, St. Leo Coll., 1990-93, Troy State U., 1991-2000. Mem. S.C. Bar Assn., Citadel Alumni Assn. Roman Catholic. Office: SC Farm Bur Ins Cos PO Box 2124 West Columbia SC 29171-2124 Fax: 803-794-8765. E-mail: ljedziniak@scfbins.com.

JEE, JAMES RODNEY, statistician; s. James and Jean Jee; m. Fern Jee; 1 child, Justin. BS, Miss. State U., 1977, MS, 1978; PhD, William Marsh Rice U., 1985. Engr. McDonnell Douglas Tech. Services, Clear Lake, Tex., 1978—81; mem. tech. staff Jet Propulsion Lab., Pasadena, Calif., 1985—94; sr. statistician Risk Data Corp., Irvine, Calif., 1994—98; sr. staff scientist HNC Software, Inc., Irvine, 1998—2002; mgr. analytic sci. Fair Isaac Corp., Irvine, 2003—. Contbr. articles to profl. jours. Mem.: Soc. for Indsl. and Applied Math., Am. Statis. Assn. (So. Calif. chpt. v.p. profl. affairs 1999—2000, So. Calif. chpt. pres. 2001—03). Home: 1944 E Puente Ave West Covina CA 91791 Personal E-mail: rodjee@earthlink.net.

JEE, JUSTIN SOONHO, government official; b. Pusan, Korea, June 29, 1951; came to U.S., 1976; s. Hanwoong and Boksoo (Park) J.; m. Ahyung Lee, May 2, 1976. BS, U. Korea, 1976; BS in Acctg., U. Minn., 1980; MBA, San Diego State U., 1984. CPA, Minn., Va.; cert. mgmt. acct.; cert. internal auditor. Tax acct. Midway Nat. Bank, St. Paul, 1981-83; fin. analyst Medical, Inc., Inver Grove Heights, Minn., 1984-87; sr. acct. Internat. Trade Adminstrn., Import Adminstrn., U.S. Dept. Commerce, Washington, 1987-90; sr. bus. devel. specialist Minority Bus. Devel. Agy., U.S. Dept. Commerce, Washington, 1990-96; sr. import compliance specialist import adminstrn. Internat. Trade Adminstrn. U.S. Dept. Commerce, Washington, 1996-98; auditor U.S. Internat. Trade Commn., Washington, 1998—. Cons. Bus. Devel. Ctr., San Diego, 1984. Mem. AICPA, Inst. Cert. Mgmt. Accts. (cert.). Avocations: classical music, poetry, attending performing arts, art exhbns. Home: 13804 Foggy Hills Ct Clifton VA 20124-2407 Office: US Internat Trade Commn 500 E St SW Washington DC 20024-2760

JEEP, JOHN MICHAEL, language educator; b. Quebec, Can., July 3, 1954; arrived in U.S., 1954; s. Charles W. and Winifred Jeep Jr.; m. Lynda Hoffman, Apr. 18, 1975; 1 child, Carina. MA, U. Münster, 1985; PhD in German Lang., U. Chgo., 1990. German lectr. U. Osnabrück, 1985-86, U. Münster, 1986; instr. of German Loyola U., Chgo., 1986-87, 90-91; German tchr. Lab. Schs. U. Chgo., 1987-90, 91; vis. prof. Miami U., Oxford, Ohio, 1992-93, asst. prof., 1993-98, assoc. prof., 1998—, dir. Intensive German Summer Program, German dept., 1993, 98, 00, dir. Austrian Scholars Program, 1997, 99, 01, assoc. developing faculty learning commns., 2001—; co-dir. Ohio Tchg. Enhancement Program, 1999—; dir. univ. tchg. and learning programs Millikin U., Decatur, Ill., 2001—03. Cons. Houghton-Mifflin Pub., Boston, 1995—96, Boston, 2000; reviewer grant proposals NEH, Washington, 1995—97; mem. adv. com. MLA Internat. Bibliography, 2001—. Author: (book) Alliterating World-Pairs in Old High German, 1995, Stabreimende Wortpaare bei Notker Labeo, 1987; bibliographer: Med. Feminist Index, 1997—; editor: Medieval Germany: An Encyclopedia, 2001; co-editor: (book) Das Hymelreich ist Gleich Einem Verborgen Schatz, 1987; contbr. articles to profl. jours.; reviewer: profl. jours. Grantee Summer Rsch., NEH, 1991, Doe Title III Strengthening Instn., Milikin U., 2002—02. Mem.: MLA (bibliographer Germanic studies 1992—), Ohio Coun. Libr. Humanities, Am. Assn. Tchrs. German, Soc. Germanic Philology (mem. exec. com.), German Studies Assn., Delta Phi Alpha (German hon. nat. officer). Avocations: sports, travel, reading. Office: Miami U GREAL Irvin Hall 134 400 E Spring St Oxford OH 45056-1859 E-mail: jeepjm@po.muohio.edu.

JEEVANANDAM, VALLUVAN, surgeon, educator; b. Tuticorin, Tamil Nadu, India, Aug. 20, 1960; s. Malayappa and Chellam Jeevanandam; m. Sheela Jambukesan, June 30, 1985; children: Veena, Vinesh. MD summa cum laude, Columbia U., 1984. Bd. cert. cardiothoracic surgery Am. Bd. Thoracic Surgery, 1993, bd. cert. surgery Am. Bd. Surgery, 1990. Assoc. prof. surgery Temple U., Phila., 1995—98, U. Chgo., 1998—2002, prof. surgery, 2002—. Dir. heart failure and transplantation Temple U., Phila., 1992—98; chief cardiothoracic surgery U. Chgo., 1998—, dir. heart transplantation and mech. devices, 1998—. Contbr. articles to profl. jours. John Jay scholar, Columbia U., 1977—80. Mem.: Soc. Heart Transplantation, Soc. Thoracic Surgeons, Am. Assn. Thoracic Surgery, Alpha Omega Alpha, Phi Beta Kappa. Independent. Hindu. Achievements include patents for laser heart revascularization. Avocations: tennis, photography. Office: Univ Chicago 5841 S Maryland Ave Chicago IL Personal E-mail: jeevan@uchicago.edu.

JEEVARAJAN, JUDITH A. chemist; b. Madras, India, June 6, 1964; arrived in U.S., 1988; d. Susei Kulandai and Mary Jaya Raja; m. Antony Susiah Jeevarajan, May 18, 1988; children: Jessie, Jerome, John. BS, Stella Maris Coll., 1984; MS, Loyola Coll., Madras, 1986, U. Notre Dame, 1991; PhD, U. Ala., 1996. Scientist Lynntech, Inc., College Station, Tex., 1996-97; postdoctoral rschr. Tex. A&M U., College Station, 1997; scientist Lockheed Martin Space Ops., Houston, 1998—. Contbr. articles to profl. jours. Recipient award, Dept. Def., USAF. Mem.: Electrochem. Soc. Roman Catholic. Avocations: reading, gardening, travel. Home: 15407 Pinenut Bay Ct Houston TX 77059 Office: Lockheed Martin 2101 Nasa Rd 1 MS EP5 Houston TX 77058

JEFFCOAT, CATHLEEN MERLE, musician, educator; b. Redcliffe, Queensland, Australia, Feb. 20, 1971; d. Norman Dingwall Jeffcoat. MusB, Western Australian Conservatorium of Music, Perth, Australia, 1992; Artists' Cert., Franz Liszt Music Acad., Budapest, Hungary, 1996; MusM, U. of Md., 1999, DMA, 2002. Violin tchr., Perth, Australia, 1989—93, Budapest, 1993—96; head of string dept. Servite Coll., Tuart Hill, 1989; violin tchr. St. Denis' Primary Sch., Tuart Hill, 1989, Carmel Primary Sch., Dianella, 1991—92; tchr. Am. Internat. Sch., Budapest, 1994—96; violin tchr. Perth, 1996—97; violin and viola tchr. College Park, Md., 1997—2002; violin faculty D.C. Youth Orch., Washington, 2001—02; violin, viola, and chamber music prof. Peabody Inst., Balt., 2002—; violin and viola tchr. Balt., 2002—. Programming asst. Clarice Smith Performing Arts Ctr., College Park, 2001—02; asst. to music dir. and artistic dir. Grand Teton Music Festival, Jackson Hole, Wyo., 2000—01; asst. coord. Nat. Orchestral Inst. and the William Kapell Internat. Piano Competition, College Park, 1997—98; asst. mgr. Nat. Orchestral Inst. and the U. of Md. Symphony Orch., College Park, 1999—2001; guest lectr. Western Australian Conservatorium of Music, Perth, 1995; guest prof. Franz Liszt Acad. Music, Budapest, 1995—96. Musician (violinist): Singapore Symphony Orch., tour to Malaysia, Germany and Switzerland, Bach Sinfonia, Grand Teton Music Festival Orch., Wyo., Alexandria Symphony Orch., West Australian Symphony Orch.; musician: (rank and file violinist); musician: (violinist) Hungarian Radio and TV Symphony Orch.; musician: (concert artist) solo and chamber music concerts, U.S., Hungary, Australia; asst. concertmaster: Chamber Orch. Am. Recipient Hungarian Govt. scholarship, Hungarian Ministry of Culture, 1993—96, Masonic scholarship, Grand Lodge of Western Australia, 1989, Returned Servicemen's Leagues scholarship, Returned Servicemen's League, Perth, 1989, Masonic scholarship, Grand Lodge of Western Australia, 1991, 1992. Mem.: Md. String Tchrs. Assn., Coll. Music Soc., Am. String Teachers Assn., D.C. Tchrs. Assn. (membership chair 2003—). Office: Peabody Inst 21 E Mount Vernon Pl Baltimore MD 21202

JEFFE, SIDNEY DAVID, automotive engineer; b. Chgo., May 6, 1927; s. J.I. Jeffe; children: Robert A., Leslie A. BSME with honors, Ill. Inst. Tech., 1950; MS in Automotive Engring. with honors, Chrysler Inst. Engring., 1952; postgrad., Carnegie-Mellon U., 1968. With Chrysler Corp., 1950-80, v.p. engring. and rsch., 1976-80; sr. v.p. ops. Sheller Globe Corp., Detroit, 1982-86; prof. mech. engring. Ohio State U., 1980-82; sr. v.p. internat. bus. and tech. devel. and implementation, head customer and govt. rels. activities Sheller Globe Corp., Detroit, 1986-90; v.p. internat. bus. and tech. devel. Mesnel S.A.-Schlegel Corp., Madison Heights, Mich., 1990-92; internat. bus. and tech. cons., expert witness, 1992—. Exec. dir. Transp. Rsch. Ctr. Ohio, E. Liberty; sec.-treas. Transp. Rsch. Bd. Ohio, 1980-82; sr. v.p. internat. bus. and tech. devel. United Tech. Engineered Sys. Divsn., 1990; bd. dirs. J.L. French Automotive Castings Inc.; engring. and bus. cons. Energy Conversion Devices, Inc., 2000—. Responsible for devel. Chrysler's first front-wheel drive cars-Omni, Horizon, K cars and Minivans, 1976-80; author papers in field. Served with AUS, 1945-47. Fellow Engring. Soc. Detroit, Soc. Automotive Engrs. (Russell Springer award 1957, Coll. Fellows 1985); mem. Tau Beta Pi (Outstanding New Mem. award 1948), Pi Tau Sigma (Outstanding New Mem. award 1949). Clubs: DC Ranch Country (Scottsdale, Ariz.), Orchard Lake Country, Detroit Athletic, Ren Cen. Unitarian Universalist. Home: 20405 N 93d Pl Scottsdale AZ 85255

JEFFERDS, WILLIAM JOHN, military advisor; b. Stockton, Calif., Sept. 26, 1929; s. Wallace Vincent and Margaret (Moreing) J.; m. Patricia Ann, Aug. 16, 1949; children: Jerilyn Ann, Janelle Kay, Mark Christian. BA, San Jose State U., 1952; EdD, U. Calif., Berkeley, 1966; grad., Harvard U., 1984. Cert. tchr., Calif. Advanced through grades to maj. gen., 1985; commd. U.S. Army, 1964-68; bn. comdr. 2/159 inf. bn., 1974-75; brigade comdr. 49th MP brigade, 1977-82; comdg. gen. 40th CA task force, 1979-82; comdg. gen. 40th mech. ifn. divsn., 1985-88; tchr. Alum Rock Sch. Dist., San Jose, Calif., 1952-56; asst. prin., 1956-58; prin., 1958-62; asst. supt., 1962-68; supt., 1968-87; comdr. Calif. Army Nat. Guard, Sacramento, 1987-89; spl. asst. chief nat. guard bur. Pentagon, Washington, 1990-2000; sr. mil. advisor Gov. of Calif. and dir. of office of mil. support, 2000—. Dir. Calif. Dept. Gen. Svcs., 2003—. Chmn. March of Dimes Walkathon, Santa Clara County, 1972. Decorated Legion of Merit, Disting. Svc. medal, Order of Calif. Mem. Nat. Guard Assn. U.S., Nat. Guard Assn. Calif. Republican. Roman Catholic. Home: 124 Gold Rock Ct Folsom CA 95630 E-mail: wjefferds@aol.com.

JEFFERIES, JOHN TREVOR, astrophysicist, observatory administrator; b. Kellerberrin, Australia, Apr. 2, 1925; came to U.S., 1956, naturalized, 1967; s. John and Vera (Healy) J.; m. Charmian Candy, Sept. 10, 1949; children: Stephen R., Helen C., Trevor R. MA, Cambridge (Eng.) U., 1949; DSc, U. Western Australia, Nedlands, 1962. Sr. research staff High Altitude Obs., Boulder, Colo., 1957-59, Sacramento Peak Obs., Sunspot, N.Mex., 1957-59; prof. adjoint U. Colo., Boulder, 1961-64; prof. physics and astronomy U. Hawaii, Honolulu, 1964-83, dir., Inst. Astronomy, 1967-83; dir. Nat. Optical Astronomy Obs., Tucson, 1983-87, astronomer, 1987-92. Cons. Nat. Bur. Stds., Boulder, 1960-62; disting. vis. scientist Jet Propulsion Lab., 1991-94. Author: (monograph) Spectral Line Formation, 1968; contbr. articles to profl. jours. Guggenheim fellow, 1970-71. Mem. Internat. Astron. Union, Am. Astron. Soc. Home: 1652 E Camino Cielo Tucson AZ 85718-1105 E-mail: jtjeff@concentric.net

JEFFERIES, MICHAEL JOHN, retired electrical engineer; b. London, Feb. 2, 1941; came to U.S., 1967; s. Charles William and Dorothy Eleanor (Bates) J.; m. Mary Ann Cenci, May 27, 1969; children: Carlyn, Kevin. B.Sc. in Elec. Engring., Nottingham U., 1963, PhD, 1967. With Gen. Electric Co., Schenectady, 1967-76, mgr. cryogenics br. corp. research and devel., 1976-77, mgr. elec. systems and tech. lab., 1977-80, R&D mgr. engring. physics labs., 1980-87; gen. mgr. tech. Gen. Electric Motors, Ft. Wayne, Ind., 1987-90; faculty elec. engring. tech. Purdue U., 1990-93; v.p. tech. and mfg. Carrier Corp., Syracuse, N.Y., 1993-95, ret. Contbr. articles to profl. jours. Fellow IEEE; mem. Instn. Elec. Engrs. (U.K.). Home: 4315 Hepatica Hill Rd Manlius NY 13104-8714

JEFFERIS, PAUL BRUCE, lawyer; b. Barnesville, Ohio, Jan. 11, 1952; s. Maurice D. and Ruth C. (Rinehart) J.; m. Shirley R. Zervos, Sept. 13, 1997; children: Paul M., Elaini Noel Zervos. BA, Ohio State U., 1977; JD, U. Akron, 1980. Bar: Ohio 1980. Asst. prosecutor Belmont County, St. Clairsville, Ohio, 1981-83; pvt. practice, Barnesville, 1983—. Bd. dirs. St. Clairsville Drug and Alcohol Coun., 1982—. With USN, 1975-77. Mem. ABA, Belmont County Bar Assn., Am. Legion, Moose. Roman Catholic. Avocations: reading, hunting. Office: 58884 Wright Rd Barnesville OH 43713-9799

JEFFERS, BEN, political organization executive; Chmn. La. Dem. Party, 1997—2003; now pres. Ben Jeffers, Inc. Office: Ben Jeffers Inc 301 E Blvd Baton Rouge LA 70802*

JEFFERS, DONALD E. retired insurance executive, consultant; b. Louisville, Ill., Aug. 21, 1925; s. Byron V. and Alice B. (Burgess) J.; m. Marion D. Benna, Aug. 14, 1948 (dec.); 1 son, Derek; m. Janice C. Smith, Apr. 21, 1979 (dec.). BS in Accountancy, U. Ill., 1948. C.P.A., Ill., D.C. Sr. acct. Coopers & Lybrand, CPAs, N.Y.C. and Chgo., 1948-56; asst. v.p. Continental Casualty Co., Chgo., 1956-64; dep. comptr. First Nat. Bank Boston, 1965-67; exec. v.p., treas. Interstate Nat. Corp., Chgo., 1967-74, pres., chief exec. officer, 1974-85, also dir.; chmn., dir. Interstate Ins. Group and Geo. F. Brown & Sons Inc.; chmn. Jeffers & Assocs., Inc., San Diego, 1985—86; ret., 1986. Former sec., dir. Ill. Ins. Info. Service; underwriting mem. Lloyd's London, 1977-99. Served with inf. AUS, 1943-45. Decorated Purple Heart. Mem. AICPA. Home: 3405 Florida St Apt 308 San Diego CA 92104

JEFFERS, IDA PEARLE, management consultant, volunteer; b. Houston, Tex., Sept. 5, 1935; d. Stanford Wilbur and Ida Pearle (Kinkead) Oberg; m. Samuel Lee Jeffers, Aug. 29, 1956; children: John Laurence (dec.), Julie Elizabeth Flynn, Melinda Leigh Hurley. Student, U. Colo., 1953-56; BA in History, U. N.Mex., 1957. Asst. to mayor City of Albuquerque, 1978, dir. capital improvements, 1979-81; pres. Orgn. Plus, 1988-98. Guest lectr. U. N.Mex. Albuquerque Pub. Sch., 1968-71. Chmn. Comprehensive Plan Rev., Bond Issue, various coms., Albuquerque, 1968-98; mem. Middle Rio Grand Coun. Govts., Albuquerque, 1972-74; mem. Environ. Planning Commn., Albuquerque, 1972-77, chmn. 1975-76; chmn. Citizen Adv. Group, Community Devel., Albuquerque, 1974-75; mem. Jr. League, Albuquerque, 1966-97, bd. dirs. 1970-76; mem. N. Mex. Architect, Engrs. Joint Practice Bd. 1978-85, chmn. 1983-85; treas. St. Mark's Episcopal Ch., 1983-86; pres. Eldorado High Sch. Parents, Albuquerque, 1985-86; pres. Regional Conservation Land Trust, Albuquerque, 1987-91; trustee Found., Study and Care of Organic Brain Damage, Houston, 1972-82, pres. 1982-94; mem. Urban Transp. Planning Policy Bd., 1972-74; founder, chair Friends of Sandia (N.Mex.) Sch., 1965-68, chmn. devel. pre-sch. bd., 1974; mentor Leadership Albuquerque, 1987-91; bd. dirs. Good Govt. Group, Albuquerque, 1988-92, treas. 1988-92; mem. Albuquerque Arts Alliance, 1988-91; mem. Albuquerque All Faiths, All Faith's Receiving Home Aux., 1964-68, sec. 1966, Jr. Women Club, 1963-66, Chaparral Coun. Girl Scouts leaders, 1971-73, selections chmn., 1973-74, Albuquerque Tutorial Coun., 1967-69; found. bd. Albuquerque Youth Symphony, 1995-97. Recipient Disting. Pub. Svc. award, State of N. Mex., 1975, Disting. Woman of N. Mex. award, N.Mex. Women's Polit. Caucus, 1976, Golden Talon award Eldorado High Sch., Albuquerque, 1985, Panhellenic Coun. Disting. Alumnae award 1979. Mem. Rotary, Delta Gamma (pres. 1963-67, chmn. collegiate adv. bd. 1968-71, Cable and Shield awards 1970, 77). Republican. Episcopalian. Avocations: gardening, sewing, skiing, music. E-mail: sljeffe@worldnet.att.net.

JEFFERS, JOHN WILLIAM, lawyer; b. N.Y.C., May 11, 1936; s. William Hicks and Thelma Leone (Seeger) J.; children: Michael D., Thomas W., James B., John P. AB cum laude, Harvard U., 1958; JD, U. Pa., 1964. Bar: Ohio, 1964, U.S. Dist. Ct. (no. dist.) Ohio 1965. Assoc. Rosenthal,Roesch, Buckman & McLandrich, Cleve., 1964-67, Weston, Hurd, Fallon, Paisley & Howley, Cleve., 1967-71, ptnr., 1971—. Capt. USMC. Mem. Ohio Assn. Civil Trial Attys. (chmn. med. malpractice com. 1987-94, exec. com. 1990-97), Cleve. Bar Assn. (past chmn. Cuyahoga County Common Pleas and Ct. Appeals com.). Avocations: travel, tennis, golf, bicycling. Office: Weston Hurd Fallon Paisley & Howley 2500 Terminal Tower Cleveland OH 44113

JEFFERS, MICHAEL BOGUE, lawyer; b. Wenatchee, Wash., July 10, 1940; s. Richard G. and Betty (Ball) J. BA, U. Wash., 1962, LLB, 1964; LLM in Taxation, NYU, 1970. Bar: Wash. 1964, N.Y. 1970, Calif. 1988. Ptnr. Hughes & Jeffers, Wenatchee, 1964-65, 68, Hill, Betts & Nash, N.Y.C., 1970-72, Battle Fowler, N.Y.C., 1973-88, Buchalter, Nemer, Fields & Younger, Newport Beach, Calif., 1988-89, Riordan & McKinzie, Costa Mesa, Calif., 1989-90, Phillips, Haglund, Haddan & Jeffers, Newport Beach, 1991-93, Jeffers, Shaff & Falk, LLP, Newport Beach, Calif., 1994—2002, Dechert LLP, Newport Beach, 2002—. Sec. Thornburg Mortgage Inc. Mem. ABA, Calif. Bar Assn., Orange County Bar Assn., Wash. State Bar Assn., U. Wash. Alumni Assn. (pres. Greater N.Y. chpt. 1972-88), Pacific Club, Nat. Wild Turkey Fedn., Ballet Pacifica, Explorers Club, Phi Gamma Delta. Office: Dechert LLP 4675 MacArthur Ct Ste 1400 Newport Beach CA 92660 E-mail: michael.jeffers@dechert.com.

JEFFERS, TRELLIE LEE JAMES, language educator, dean; b. Eatonton, Ga., Dec. 12, 1933; d. Charlie and Florence (Paschal) James; m. Lance F. Jeffers, May 26, 1959 (dec. July 1985); children: Valjeanne Jeffers Thompson,

Sidonie Jeffers Jones, Honorée F. BA, Spelman Coll., 1955; MA, Calif. State U., 1970; DA, Atlanta U., 1986. Cert. adminstrn. and supervision. Tchr. high schs., Ga., Ill., N.C., Fla., 1955-66; asst. prof. Calif. State U., Long Beach, 1969-71; freelance writer Carolina Times, Durham, N.C., 1979-82; coord. Learning Resource Ctr., chmn. Resource Ctr. Clark Coll., Atlanta, 1983-85; prof. English Talladega (Ala.) Coll., 1985—, dean divsn. humananities and fine arts, 1998—. Vis. lectr. N.C. Ctrl. U., Durham, 1975-81, chair English component acad. skills, 1977-78. Author: poems; contbr. article to book. Fellow NEH, 1988, 93. Mem. Libr. Congress, Coll. Lang. Assn., So. Conf. on African Am. Studies (mem. adv. bd. 1992, 99), Ala. League Advancement Edn., George Moses Horton Soc., Pi Lamda Theta, Kappa Delta Pi. Democrat. Roman Catholic. Avocations: sewing, creative writing, cooking, singing, gardening. Home: 219 Edgewood Ave Talladega AL 35160-3021 Office: Talladega Coll 627 Battle St W Talladega AL 35160-2354 E-mail: tjeffers@talladega.edu.

JEFFERSON, CHARLES E. state representative; b. Waco, Tex., Mar. 31, 1945; children: Carl Edward, Curtis Lamar, Charles Jr. Student, Paul Quinn Coll. Mem. Ill. Ho. of Reps., 2001—. Past v.p. United Way; mem. Winnebago County Bd. With U.S. Army. Mem.: Rockford Sportsmen Golf Assn. (past pres.), Lions (past pres.), Masons. Democrat. Office: 281-S Stratton Office Bldg Springfield IL 62706 Address: EJ Zeke Giorgi Ctr 200 S Wyman # 304 Rockford IL 61107*

JEFFERSON, JAMES WALTER, psychiatry educator; b. Mineola, N.Y., Aug. 14, 1937; s. Thomas Hutton and Alice (Withers) J.; m. Susan Mary Cole, June 25, 1965; children: Lara, Shawn, James C. BS, Bucknell U., 1958; MD, U. Wis., 1964. Cert. Am. Bd. Psychiatry and Neurology, Am. Bd. Internal Medicine. Asst. prof. psychiatry U. Wis. Med. Sch., Madison, 1974-78, assoc. prof., 1978-81, prof., 1981-92; disting. sr. scientist Dean Found. for Health, Rsch. and Edn., Madison, 1992-98; clin. prof. psychiatry U. Wis. Med. Sch., Madison, 1992—; disting. sr. scientist Madison Inst. Medicine, 1998—. Pres. Healthcare Tech. Sys., Madison, 1998—; co-dir. Lithium Info. Ctr., Madison, 1975—, Obsessive Compulsive Info. Ctr., Madison, 1990—; dir. Ctr. Affective Disorders, Madison, 1983-92. Co-author: Neuropsychiatric Features of Medical Disorders, 1981, Lithium Encyclopedia for Clinical Practice, 1983, 2nd edit., 1987, Depression and Its Treatment, 1984, 2nd edit., 1992, Anxiety and Its Treatment, 1986, Handbook of Medical Psychiatry, 1996. Served to maj. U.S. Army, 1968-71. Fellow ACP, Am. Psychiat. Assn.; mem. Collegium Internat. Neuropsychopharmacologium, Am. Soc. Clin. Psychopharmacology (nat. bd. trustees 1996—). Avocations: bicycling, travel. Office: Madison Inst Medicine 7617 Mineral Point Rd Madison WI 53717-1623 E-mail: jjefferson@healthtechsys.com.

JEFFERSON, JOSEPH MURRAY, banker; b. Heilwood, Pa., July 9, 1919; s. Ernest Maloy and Edith (Morris) J.; m. Mary Margaret Kerr, May 27, 1943 (dec. Mar. 1991); children: James Murray, Sharon Lee; m. Mary Jo Greenly, Dec. 11, 1999; 1 stepchild, Traci Romedy. BS, Waynesburg (Pa.) Coll., 1943; postgrad., Ind. U., 1949-51, Dartmouth Coll., 1963-64. Laborer Buckeye Coal Co., Nemacolin, Pa., 1936-41; sec. First Fed. S&L Assn., Waynesburg, Pa., 1945-52; exec. v.p., CEO Provident Fed. S&L Assn., Pitts., 1953-61; v.p. First Fed. S&L Assn. of Pitts., 1961-68; pres., CEO Washington (Pa.) Fed. Savs. Bank, 1968-86, dir. emeritus, 1995—; dir., vice chmn. Fed. Home Loan Bank of Pitts., 1986-91. Bd. dirs. Pa. Indsl. Devel. Agy., Harrisburg, 1963-64, Pa. Econ. League, Harrisburg, 1985-95, YMCA, Washington, 1968-85. With U.S. Army Aircorps, 1941-42, lt. USN, SubPac, 1943-46. Named to Pa. Cmty. Bankers Hall of Fame, 1992. Mem. U.S. S&L League (dir. exec. com. 1968-71), Pa. S&L League (pres. 1963-64), Masons (32 deg.), Lions (Melvin Jones fellow). Avocations: golf, public speaking. Home: 320 Olympia St Pittsburgh PA 15211-1367

JEFFERSON, KATHLEEN HENDERSON, retired secondary education educator; b. Pine Bluff, Ark., Sept. 20, 1928; d. Horace and Fannie Henderson; children: Ellen, Regina. BS in Chemistry, U. Ark., 1951; MEd in Maths. Edn., Tuskegee (Ala.) Inst., 1973. Cert. tchr., D.C., Ark. Tchr. Ark. Pub. Schs., Pine Bluff, 1952-78, U. Ark., Monticello, 1978-79, D.C. Pub. Schs., Washington, 1979—; chairperson maths. dept., tchr. Dunbar Sr. High Sch., Washington, 1982-96; ret., 1996. Adj. prof. U. D.C., 1997—. Mem. LWV, Pine Bluff, 1973-77, St. Francis De Sales Ch., Washington; vol. mathematics tutor, St. Francis De Sales Sch., 2000—. NSF fellow, 1960, Internat. Paper Co. fellow, 1970-73. Mem. ASCD, D.C. Coun. Tchrs. of Maths., D.C. Tchrs. Union Local, Delta Sigma Theta. Roman Catholic. Avocations: reading, swimming, chess.

JEFFERSON, KRISTIN MARIE, museum director; b. Tacoma, Jan. 15, 1947; d. Edward Harold and Helen Marie (Chandler) J. BA, Bard Coll., 1968; MFA, Hunter Coll., 1974; MPS Tisch Sch. Arts, NYU, 1999. Facilities adminstr. Sterling Inst., Washington, 1969-71; prof. art CUNY, 1971-79; art dealer N.Y.C., 1979—. Founding pres., exec. dir. Mus. of World Art, 1989—. Author: She-Images of Woman in Art, 1983, Magic in the Mind's Eye-Alchemy of Collecting, 1987; curator mus. quality art exhibits, 1982—; prodr. The Nanzetta Legacy, Choreography of Memory, When the Spirit Moves Shared Visions Prodn. Studio, 1997-99; assoc. prodr. Free to Dance, PBS-TV Series/Am. Masters; line prodr. AMC-TV documentary Hattie McDaniel; prodr., creative dir. Shared Visions Prodn. Studio, 1997—; coordinating prodr. Martha Graham Legacy Project, 2002.. Mem. pub. rels. staff Sotheby's benefit for Cath. Relief Svcs. to Benefit the Famine Victims of Ethiopia, 1985. Episcopalian. Home: 330 W 56th St New York NY 10019-4248

JEFFERSON, KURT WAYNE, political science educator; b. Macomb, Ill., Jan. 17, 1966; s. Robert Wayne and Sally Ann (Wallace) J.; m. Lori Jeanene Merriman, Aug. 8, 1992; children: Kelly Lynn, Megan Leigh, Nicole Layne. BA in Polit. Sci. magna cum laude, Western Ill. U., 1988; MA in Polit. Sci., U. Mo., 1989, PhD in Polit. Sci., 1993. Grad. tchg. asst. dept. polit. sci. U. Mo., Columbia, 1988-91, instr. dept. polit. sci., 1992; instr. dept. social and cultural studies Stephens Coll., Columbia, 1992-93; asst. prof. polit. sci. dept. polit. sci. Westminster Coll., Fulton, Mo., 1993-99, assoc. prof. polit. sci. dept. polit. sci., 1999—, chair dept. polit sci., 1999-2000, 2002—. Vis. asst. prof. dept. polit. sci. U. Mo., Columbia, summer, 1993; dir. Churchill Acad., Westminster Coll., Fulton, 1996—99; coord. leadership studies, 1997—; cons. U. Mo. Rsch. Bd., U. Mo. Sys., St. Louis, 1996; editl. adv. bd. Collegiate Press, Alta Loma, Calif., 1997—98. Contbr. articles to profl. jours.; author: Christianity's Impact on World Politics: Not by Might, nor by Power, 2002. Soccer coach Columbia Soccer League, 1993—94, 2001—02; prayer coord. Men Without Fear men's ministry, Columbia, 2002—; bd. dirs. Christian Chapel Assembly of God, Columbia, 2003—. Mem.: Brit.. Politics Group, Am. Polit. Sci. Assn. Avocations: bible reading, sports, banjo playing, reading. Home: 3701 Triple Crown Dr Columbia MO 65202-4849 Office: Westminster Coll 501 Westminster Ave Fulton MO 65251-1129 Fax: 573-592-5191. E-mail: jeferk@jaynet.wcmo.edu.

JEFFERSON, MARGO L. journalist; b. Chgo., Oct. 17, 1947; BA in English and Am. Lit. cum laude, Brandeis U., 1968; MS, Columbia U., 1971. Editor Newsweek, 1973—78; asst. prof. dept. journalism NYU, 1979—83, 1989—91; contbg. editor Vogue, 1984—89, 7 Days, 1984—89; lectr. Am. Lit., performing arts & criticism Columbia U., N.Y.C., 1991—93; critic culture desk The New York Times, 1993—95, Sunday theater critic, 1995—97, cultural corr., 1997—. Recipient Pulitzer Prize for criticism, 1995. Office: The New York Times 229 W 43rd St New York NY 10036-3959

JEFFERSON, RALPH HARVEY, international affairs consultant; b. Rochester, N.Y., Aug. 6, 1927; s. Charles Frederic and Mabel Florence (Thomas) J.; m. Jenny Chaapel Clark, Oct. 29, 1960; children: Edward Clark, Jenny Chaapel, Alexandra Victoria. BA, Yale U., 1949; LLB, Harvard U., 1952; cert., Inst. d'Etudes Politiques, Paris, 1956. Bar: N.Y. 1952. Treas. Harvard Legal Aid Bur., 1950-52; atty. Root, Ballantine, Harlan, Bushby and Palmer, N.Y.C., 1952-55; legal adviser to def. adviser U.S. Mission to NATO, Paris, 1960-63; atty. Office of Asst. Gen. Counsel, Office Sec. of Def., Washington, 1957-60, 63-66; acting spl. adviser for prisoner of war affairs Office of Asst. Sec. Def., Washington, 1970-71, dep. dir. in Europe-NATO Directorate, 1967-70, 72-78; civil dep. comdt., dir. studies NATO Def. Coll., Rome, 1978-82; dir. for NATO policy Office Asst. Sec. Def., Washington, 1982-88; sr. rsch. fellow Nat. Def. U., Washington, 1988-89; internat. affairs cons. Washington, 1994—. Bd. dirs. Chol Chol Found. for Human Devel. With USN. Mem. Diplomatic and Consular Officers Ret. (assoc.). Avocations: piano, tennis, sailing. Home and Office: 507 Epping Forest Rd Annapolis MD 21401-6562

JEFFERSON, SANDRA TRAYLOR, choreographer, ballet coach; b. Tarboro, N.C., Feb. 28, 1942; d. Charles Labon and Doris Vivian (Parker) Traylor; m. Milton Franklin Jefferson, July 2, 1960; children: Mark Franklin, Todd Christopher. Student, Parks Sch. Dance, Petersburg, Va., 1947-58, Sch. of the Richmond (Va.) Ballet, 1958-60; diploma, Julia Mildred Harper Sch. Dance, Richmond, 1960; studied with Robert David Brown, Sterling, Va., 1978-80. Soloist Ballet Impromptu, Richmond, 1958-60; freelance dance instr. Chantilly, Va., 1968-70; ballet coach Artistic Skating Club of Sterling, 1980; founder, dir. Ballet for Skaters, Manassas, Va., 1980-89; artistic dir., cons. in choreography No. Va. Artistic Skating Club, Manassas, 1986-89. Artistic dir. Skating Club of Manassas, 1989; founder, dir. Ballet for Skaters, Seabrook, Md., 1989-94; choreographer, ballet coach Nat. Capitol Dance and Figure Club, Seabrook and Washington, 1989-94; founder, dir. Ballet for Figure Skaters, Sterling, Va., 1993-94; students include nat. medalists in the U.S. and Can. and mems. Can. World Team, U.S. Olympic Sports Festival Team; freelance choreographer, ballet coach, Sterling, 1993—. Developer: Brosano Technique Vocabulary of Movement, 1986, Free Form Ballet, 1993; co-developer (artistic skating technique) Brosano Technique, 1981. Social dir. Jaycee-ettes, Winchester, Va., 1963—67. Recipient Achievement award Jaycee-ettes, 1963, 64, 65, 66, 67, U.S. S.E. Soc. Roller Skating Tchrs. Am. award, 1988, World Decoration of Excellence award Am. Biog. Inst., 1989. Mem.: Profl. Dance Tchrs. Assn. Methodist. Avocations: art, music. Home and Office: 507 S Maple Ct Sterling VA 20164-2710

JEFFERSON, WALLACE B. state supreme court justice; BA James Madison Coll., JD U. Tex. Cert.: Tex. Bd. Legal Specialization (in civil appellate law). With Groce, Locke & Hebdon, San Antonio, 1988—91; ptnr. Crofts, Callaway & Jefferson, San Antonio, 1991—2001; justice Supreme Ct. Tex., Austin, 2001—. Mem. bd. dirs. San Antonio Pub. Libr. Found., Alamo Area Big Bros./Big Sisters.; mem. edn. com. San Antonio Area Found. Mem.: San Antonio Bar Assn. (pres. 1998—99). Office: 201 W 14th St Austin TX 78701 also: PO Box 12248 Austin TX 78711*

JEFFERSON, WILLIAM J. (JEFF JEFFERSON), congressman; b. Lake Providence, La., Mar. 14, 1947; BA, Southern Univ., 1969; JD, Harvard U., 1972; LLM, Georgetown U, 1996. U.S. Ct. Appeals law clerk; ptnr. Jefferson, Bryan and Gray; legislative asst. to Sen. Johnston; state sen., 1981-90; mem. U.S. Congress from 2nd dist. La., 1991—. Mem. ways and means com., Dem. steering com., subcoms. select revenue and trade. Served AUS, Judge Advocate General Corps. Democrat. Office: US Ho of Reps 240 Cannon House Ofc Bldg Washington DC 20515-1802*

JEFFERY, GEOFFREY MARRON, medical parasitologist; b. Dundee, N.Y., May 13, 1919; s. Joseph Ewart and Augusta (Knapp) J.; m. Jane Wicker, Aug. 16, 1941; children: Janet A. Harrison, Thomas W., Sarah V. Houghton, Susan E. Tosh. AB, Hobart Coll., 1940; MA, Syracuse U., 1942; ScD, Johns Hopkins U., 1944; MPH, Yale U., 1961. Biol. aide health and safety dept. TVA, 1944; commd. officer USPHS, 1944, scientist dir., 1960; tech. aid. cons. malaria control in war areas TVA, 1944-45; assigned divsn. lab. svcs. Communicable Disease Ctr., 1945-46, charge br. lab. Sch. Tropical Medicine, 1946-47; asst. prof. biology U. Bridgeport, Conn., 1947-48; charge Malaria Rsch. Lab., NIH, Milledgeville, Ga., 1948-54; mem. staff Lab. Tropical Diseases-Lab. Parasite Chemotherapy, NIAID, NIH, Columbia, S.C., 1954-63, head sect. epidemiology, 1961-63; asst. chief Lab. Parasite Chemotherapy, NIAID, NIH, Bethesda, 1963-66, acting chief, 1966, chief, 1967-69, C.Am. Malaria Rsch. Sta., San Salvador, El Salvador, 1969-74; asst. dir. Bur. Tropical Diseases, Ctr. Disease Control, Atlanta, 1974-75; dir. vector biology and control div. Bur. Tropical Diseases, 1975-81; asst. dir. divsn. parasitic diseases Ctr. for Infectious Diseases, Ctrs. for Disease Control, 1982-84. Mem. expert adv. panel on malaria WHO, 1963—99; assoc. mem. commn. malaria Armed Forces Epidemiol. Bd., 1965-69, mem., 1969-73; Del. Internat. Congress Tropical Medicine and Malaria, Lisbon, 1958, Rio de Janeiro, 1963, Teheran, Iran, 1968; Del. Internat. Congress Parasitology, Rome, Italy, 1964, Washington, 1969; Del. Internat. Conf. on Protozoology, London, 1965, Latin Am. Congress Parasitology, Medellin, Colombia, 1973; mem. sci. group on chemotherapy of malaria WHO, Geneva, 1967, mem. sci. group on parasitology, Teheran, 1968; cons. on status of malaria in Africa AID, 1979; mem. sci. working group on applied field rsch. in malaria WHO, Geneva, 1979, mem. steering com., 1981-86; cons. on malaria U.S.-China Health Agreement, 1980; del. Asia and Pacific Conf. on Malaria, Honolulu, 1985; temp. advisor meetings WHO, Kuala Lumpur, 1981, Albuquerque, 1982, Nairobi, 1983, Bangkok, 1984; invited participant concerted action 1st plenary meeting on malaria modelling European Union, Tuebingen, Germany, 1998. Contbr. numerous articles to sci. jours. tropical medicine and parasitology. Recipient Pub. Health Svc. Commendation medal, 1966, Dept. Army cert. of appreciation patriotic civilian svc., 1973 Fellow Royal Soc. Tropical Medicine (local sec. 1984-89); mem. Am. Soc. Tropical Medicine and Hygiene (sec.-treas. 1961-67, v.p. 1971, pres. 1975, Bailey K. Ashford award 1959), Am. Soc. Parasitologists, Assn. Southea. Biologists (editor bull. 1959-60, exec. com. 1962-66), Tropical Medicine Assn. Washington, Southea. Soc. Parasitologists, S.C. Acad. Sci. (mem. council 1960, 62, Jefferson award 1952, 56, 60), Commd. Officers Assn. USPHS, Sigma Xi, Kappa Sigma. Presbyterian. Home: 1093 Blackshear Dr Decatur GA 30033-2612 Office: Center Disease Control Atlanta GA 30333 E-mail: gjeffery@worldnet.att.net.

JEFFERY, WILLIAM RICHARD, developmental biology educator, researcher; b. Chgo., June 9, 1944; s. William and Marjorie (Gross) J. BS, U. Ill., Chgo., 1967; PhD, U. Iowa, 1971. Rsch. assoc. U. Wis., Madison, 1971-72, Sch. Medicine, Tufts U., Boston, 1972-74; asst. prof. biophysics U. Houston, 1974-77; asst. prof. zoology U. Tex., Austin, 1977-80, assoc. prof., 1980-85, prof., 1985-87, J.F. Miescher Regents prof., 1987-90; prof. zoology U. Calif., Davis, 1990-93, prof. molecular and cellular biology, 1993-96; prof., head biology Pa. State U., University Park, 1997-99; prof., chair biology U. Md., College Park, 1999—. Co-dir. embryology course Marine Biology Lab., Woods Hole, Mass., 1983-87, active, 1975—. Mem. editl. bd. Devel., 1987-98, Jour. Exptl. Zoology, 1989—, Seminars in Devel. Biology, 1990-96, Seminars in Cell and Devel. Biology, 1997—, Biol. Bull., 1985-90, Cell Motility and the Cytoskeleton, 1985-86, Internat. Jour. Devel. Biology, 1989-2002, Animal Biology, 1991—, Internat. Rev. of Cytology, 1999—, Molecular Biol. Evolution, 2000—, Internat. Jour. Devel. Biology, 2002-; N.Am. editor Zygote, 1993-96 Fellow AAAS; mem. Am. Soc. Zoologists (divsn. chmn. 1988-90, Outstanding Svc. award 1990), Soc. Devel. Biologists (trustee 1987-89, 1995-97, pres. 1995-96), Am. Soc. Cell Biology, Sigma Xi. Home: 714 Tanley Rd Silver Spring MD 20904-2839 Office: Univ Md Dept Biology 1200 Bio Psych Bldg College Park MD 20742-0001 E-mail: wj33@umail.umd.edu.

JEFFORDS, JAMES MERRILL, senator; b. Rutland, Vt., May 11, 1934; s. Olin Merrill and Marion (Hausman) J.; m. Elizabeth Daley; children: Leonard Olin, Laura Louise. BS, Yale U., 1956; LLB, Harvard U., 1962. Bar: Vt. 1962. Law clk. to Judge Ernest Gibson Vt. Dist., 1962; ptnr. Bishop, Crowley & Jeffords, Rutland, 1963-66, Kenney, Carbine & Jeffords, Rutland, 1966-69; atty. gen. State of Vt., 1969-72; ptnr. George E. Rice, Jr. and James M. Jeffords, 1973-74; mem. 94th -100th Congresses from Vt.; mem. agr. com., ranking minority mem. edn. and labor com., chmn. environ. study conf., 1978-79; a founder Congl. solar coalition, mem. Congl. tourism caucus, mem. Nat. Commn. on Employment and Unemployment Stats., 1979-89; U.S. Senator from Vt., 1989—; ranking mem. environ. and pub. works, health, edn., labor and pensions com., vet. affairs com., fin. com. Mem. spl. com. on aging; mem. New Eng. Congl. Caucus, N.E.-Midwest Coalition; town agt. Shrewsbury, 1964-68, zoning adminstr., 1966-68, zoning adminstr., 1966-68; mem. Jud. Selection Bd., 1967-68; chmn. Hwy. Dept. Investigating Com., 1968; mem. Vt. Senate, 1967-68; chmn. environment and pub. works, health edn. labor and pensions com., vet. affairs com., fin. com. With USNR, 1956-59; capt. Res. (ret.). Mem. ABA, Vt. Bar Assn., Rutland County Bar Assn., Am. Judicature Soc. (dir. 1973-76), VFW, Lions, Elks. Independent. Congregationalist (Trustee). Office: US Senate 413 Dirksen Bldg Washington DC 20510-4503 E-mail: vermont@jeffords.senate.gov.

JEFFREDO, JOHN VICTOR, aerospace engineer, manufacturing company executive, inventor; b. LA, Nov. 5, 1927; s. John Edward and Pauline Matilda (Whitten) J., m. Elma Jean Nesmith (div. 1958); children: Joyce Jean Jeffredo Ryder, Michael John; m. Doris Louise Hinz, (div. 1980); children: John Victor, Louise Victoria Jeffredo-Warden; m. Gerda Adelheid Pillich, 1980. Grad. in aero. engring., Northrop U., 1949; AA in Machine Design, Pasadena City Coll., 1951; grad., Ordnance Sch. U.S. Army, 1951; postgrad. U. So. Calif., 1955—58, Palomar Coll., 1977—96; MBA, La Jolla U., 1980, PhD in Psychology, 1984. Design engr. Douglas Aircraft Co., Long Beach and Santa Monica, Calif., 1955-58; devel. engr. Honeywell Ordnance Corp., Duarte, Calif., 1958-62; cons. Honeywell Devel. Labs, Seattle, 1962-65; supr. mech. engring. dept. aerospace divsn. Control Data Corp., Pasadena, Calif., 1965-68; project engr. Cubic Corp., San Diego, 1968-70; supr. mech. engring. dept. Babcock Electronics Co., Costa Mesa, Calif., 1970-72; owner, operator Jeffredo Gunsight Co., Fallbrook, Calif., 1971-81; chief engr. Western Designs, Inc., Fallbrook, Calif., 1972-81, exec. dir., 1981-88, CEO, 1988-96, owner, operator, 1981-87, Western Design Concepts, Inc., 1987-94; exec. dir. JXJ, Inc., San Marcos, Calif., 1981-88, CEO, 1988—. Mgr. Jeffredo Gunsight divsn., 1981-94, chief engr. JXJ, Inc., 1987-92 (merger JXJ, Inc. and Western Design Concepts, Fallbrook, Calif.), prin. 1992—, owner, mgr., Energy Assocs., San Diego, 1982-86, pres. Jeffredo Internat., 1984-88, founder, CEO John-Victor Internat., San Marcos, Calif., Frankfurt, Fed. Rep. Germany, 1988-99, The Jeffredo Solution, Fallbrook, 1996—; pres., CEO, Maritime Shoshone, Inc., 2000-01, chmn., CEO, 2001—; engring. cons. Action Instruments Co., Inc., Gen. Dynamics, Alcyon Corp., Systems Exploration, Inc. (all San Diego), Hughes Aircraft Co., El Segundo, Allied-Bendix, San Marcos, Santa Barbara Rsch., Goleta, Calif.; bd. dirs. Indian World Corp., JXJ, Inc., John-Victor Internat.; owner, operator Maritime Shoshone, Inc., 2000—; chmn. bd. The Badger Creek Studio, Fallbrook, 1997—. Author: Gabrieleño, New Perspective on the Island Gabrielino, The Ocean People, Wildcatting, Then There Were None, 1999; contbr. articles to profl. jours. and mags.; guest editl. writer Town Hall, San Diego Union; narrator: (film) The Sacred Desert, 1994; spkr. in field; patentee agrl. frost control, vehicle off-road drive system, recoil absorbing system for firearms, telescope sight mounting system for firearms, breech mech. sporting firearm, elec. switch activating system, 37 others, others pending. Active San Diego County Border Tsk Force on Undocumented Aliens, 1979-80, 81-82, mgr., rep. Island Gabrieleno Group, NAGPRA repatriation project, 1995—, historian Maritime Shoshone, 1995—, spokesman Island Shoshone, 1995—; bd. dirs. Nat. Geographic Soc., 1968. With U.S. Army, 1951-53. Recipient Superior Svc. Commendation award U.S. Naval Ordnance Test Station, Pasadena, 1959. Mem. AIAA (sr.), NRA (life), Calif. Rifle and Pistol Assn. (life), Soc. Automotive Engrs., San Diego Zool. Soc., The Wilderness Soc., Catalina Island Conservancy, The Nature Conservancy, Clan Stewart Soc. Am., Ducks Unlimited, Pechanga Band of Luiseno Indians (life), Cova, Catalina Island Mus. Soc., The Planetary Soc., Soc. for Calif. Archaeology, Skeptics Soc., North County Scots. Avocations: chess, music, archaeology, painting, sculpting. Home: PO Box 387 Bonsall CA 92003-0387 also: PO Box 387 Bonsall CA 92003-0387

JEFFRESS, CHARLES H. retired art educator; b. San Francisco, May 21, 1920; s. Charles Howard and Mary O. Jeffress; m. Jane Jeffress, June 6, 1944; children: Jane H., Charles H. III, George W., John D. BA, La. Coll., 1971; MA, Stephen F. Austin State U., Nacogdoches, Tex., 1972, MFA, 1976. Cert. pilot, instr. Prof. La. Coll., Pineville, La., 1973, prof. art emeritus, 1985—. Instr., pilot Basic Flying Sch., Shaw AFB; instr. instrument Shaw AFB. Exhibitions include over 20 galleries, Represented in permanent collections. Nat. Guard, 1937—39, lt. col. USAF, 1940—80, China, 2nd. Lt. pilot Nat. Guard, 1943, 1st. Lt. pilot Nat. Guard, 1944, capt. Nat. Guard, 1946 reserves USAF, 1946, maj. reserves USAF, 1955, lt. col. reserves USAF, 1964. Recipient pair of Chinese airforce wings. Mem.: China-Burma-India Hump Pilots Assn., Daedalians. Republican. Methodist. Avocations: golf, fishing. Home: 1713 Simmons St Alexandria LA 71301

JEFFRESS, D. AMES, prosecutor; b. Lexington, Mass., Feb. 24, 1965; d. William Jorace Jr. and Judith Jones Jeffress; m. Christopher Reid Cooper, May 1, 1999. BA, Williams Coll., 1987; diploma, Free U., Berlin, 1989; JD, Yale U., 1992. Bar: Va. 1993, D.C. 1996. Law clk. to Hon. Gerhard Gesell, Washington, 1992-93; counsel U.S. Dept. Def., Washington, 1993-94; counsel to dep. atty. gen. U.S. Dept. Justice, Washington, 1994-96; asst. U.S. atty. Office of U.S. Atty., Washington, 1996—. Mem. Yale Law Sch. Assn. (pres. 1998—). Democrat. Avocation: running marathons. Home: 5405 Potomac Ave NW Washington DC 20016-2553

JEFFREY, FRANCIS, software developer, forecaster; b. Calif., 1950; BA in Computational Neurophysiology, U. Calif., Berkeley, 1972. Research assoc. U. Calif., San Diego, 1972-73; cons. Sci. Applications, Inc., La Jolla, Calif., 1973-75; entrepreneur Big Sur, Calif., 1973-77; cons. Alive Systems Info. Scis., San Francisco, 1978-87; founder, pres., chief exec. officer Alive Systems, Inc. and Elfnet, Inc., Malibu, Calif., 1987—. Cons. NASA & U.S. Def. Advanced Rsch. Projects Agy. Inst. for Advanced Computation, Sunnyvale, Calif., 1973-75, Human-Dolphin Found., 1980-82, 87-89, Esalen Inst., 1982-83; co-founder (with Sir. A.C. Clarke, R.W. Benster), Arthur C. Clarke Communicators, Palo Alto, Calif., 2000—; spkr. in field. Author: (with others) Handbook of States of Consciousness, 1986, John Lilly So Far, 1989, (with others) Voices from The Edge, 1995, Patent Cooperation Treaty International Publication WO 97/24663, 1997, Japanese edit., 1998, European Union edit., 1999, (with others) "Heathsea: diet for a big ocean, 2001; originator Malibu civic dolphin protection resolution, 1992, whales as living cultural resources resolution, 1994; designer com. co-piloting; creator symposium Radical Connectionism and the Visualization of Network Programs, 1999—; patentee in field. Co-founder New Forum, Monterey, Calif., 1984, Gt. Whales Found., San Francisco, 1986, chmn., CEO, Malibu (Calif.) Dolphin Recovery Ctr., 1996—; co-founder Big Sur chpt. L5 Nat. Space Soc.; creator Annual Malibu (Calif.) Symposium on Radical Connectionism and the Visualization of Network Programs, 1999—; mem. multi-author panel discussion series Techno 2000, Beyond 2000. Mem. AAAS, IEEE, Assn. for Computing Machinery, Am. Soc. for Cybernetics (founding, control sys. group), Amnesty Internat. (leadership group), Cousteau Soc. (life mem.). Achievements include patents for communication co-pilots, cellular network computing and communications, "Adverteasing" (trademark) for suspended resolution of hypertext links, Angel (trademark), and Elfnet (trademark). Home and Office: PO Box 6844 Malibu CA 90264-6844 Fax: 206-230-0313.

JEFFREY, J. JANN, artist, educator; b. Oklahoma City, Dec. 29, 1940; d. Albert Lee and Jessie Elizabeth (Leister) Lowther; children: September Jann, Heather, Jill Alistar; m. David Leroy Jeffrey, Aug. 21, 1988. BFA, U. Okla., 1963; MEd, U Ctrl. Okla., 1978; postgrad., U. Okla., 1985; postgrad. studies, Stephen F. Austin State Univ., 1995. Art instr. Bishop McGuiness High Sch., 1965-68, Okla. Sci. and Arts Found., 1969-71, Heritage Hall, 1974—90, Corrigan Camden High Sch., Corrigan, Tex., 1991—; adj. prof. art Rose State Jr. Coll., 1978-81, Oklahoma City Cmty. Coll., 1986-90, Angelina State Jr. Coll., 2003. One person show New York Internat. Gallery, 1995; one man exhibit Nacogdoches, Tex., 1993; collaborative exhibit Sante Fe, 1994; exhibited in shows at Okla. Festival of Arts, Oklahoma City, 1968, 69, 70, 72, Okla. Mus. of Art, 1969, 73, 75, 76, 77, Okla. Designer Craftsman Ann., Oklahoma City, 1977, 81, 83, 87, Art Educators Invitational, Oklahoma City, 1989, Arts Place II, Oklahoma City, 1989, 90, Kirkpatrick Ctr., Oklahoma City, 1988, 89, 90, Alliance for Visual Arts, Stillwater, Okla., 1990, Electronic Gallery, 1989, 90, Okla. Governor's Gallery, Oklahoma City, 1990, Nat. Ghost Town Hall of Fame Mus., Anaconda, Mont., 1990, Colo. Gallery Arts, Littleton, Colo., 1990, Leslie Powell Gallery, Lawton, Okla., 1990, 92, Duncan (Okla.) Juried Exhbn., 1992, Tex. Art Edn. Juried Electronic Gallery, 1992. Docent Chair Okla. Mus. Art, Oklahoma City, 1969-73, trustee, 1971-75; artist in residence, juror State Arts Coun., Oklahoma City, 1990; curator for state high sch. juried exhbn. Okla. Mus. Art, Oklahoma City, 1981-83. Recipient Quality Art Program award, 1980, Tchr. of Excellence award, 1987, Okla. Outstanding Art Educator, 1987, 1st place award for photograph Nat. Ghost Town Hall of Fame, 1990, Progressive Art Edn. State award, Okla., 1990. Mem. Nat. Art Edn. Assn. (State Assembly Governing bd.), Tex. Art Edn. Assn. Office: Corrigan/Camden High Sch 504 S Home St Corrigan TX 75939-2624

JEFFREY, JOHN ORVAL, lawyer; b. Portsmouth, Va., Aug. 6, 1963; s. Orval L. and Mary L. (Coakley) J. BA, U. Dayton (Ohio), 1985; diploma internat. legal studies, U. San Diego, Paris, 1987; JD, Southwestern U., L.A., 1988. Bar: Calif. 1988, U.S. Dist. Ct. (cen. dist.) Calif. 1988. Assoc. Shield & Smith, L.A., 1989-90, Hewitt, Kaldor & Prout, L.A., 1990-93; mgr. bus. and legal affairs fx subs. Fox TV; v.p. bus. and legal affairs AND Interactive; sr. counsel, dir. legal affairs Discovery Comms.; now exec. v.p. corp. strategy and gen. counsel

Live365.com. Campaign worker John Glenn Campaign for Pres., N.H., 1984; vol. Amnesty Internat. Mem. ABA (internat. law sect., litigation sect., entertainment/sports law sect.), Internat. Bar Assn., Los Angeles County Bar Assn. (mem. evaluation profl. standards com., mem. legis. activity com., mem. artists and the law com.), Phi Alpha Delta, Alpha Nu Omega. Democrat. Avocations: tennis, long distance running, french reading proficiency. Office: Live365 dot com 1291 E Hillsdale Blvd Ste 225 Foster City CA 94404

JEFFREY, ROBERT GEORGE, JR., industrial company executive; b. Bronx, N.Y., Oct. 2, 1933; s. Robert George and Ethel Ruth (Rohrbeck) J.; m. Linda L. Nardone; children: Diana, Christine, Jennifer, Joseph. BBA, Pace U., 1959; MBA, NYU, 1966. CPA, N.Y., N.J. Sr. acct. Deloitte & Touche, N.Y.C., 1959-65; asst. mgr. corp. acctg. Union Camp Corp., Wayne, N.J., 1965-66, asst. to comptr., 1966-69, mgr. corp. acctg., 1969-70, dir. fin. planning, 1970-72, corp. comptr., 1972-79; exec. v.p. Huntington Mgmt. Corp., 1980-82; v.p. fin. Rudco Industries Inc., 1982-84, sr. v.p., 1984-87; ptnr. R.G. Jeffrey, CPA, Wayne, 1987—. Adj. prof. taxation William Paterson U., 1993—; bd. dirs. The Corby Group. Trustee Wayne Twp. Bd. Edn., 1975-78. Served with USAF, 1952-56. Mem. AICPA, N.Y. State Soc. CPAs, N.J. Soc. CPAs (bd. dirs. Passaic County chpt.), Fin. Execs. Inst. Home: 28 Pelham Rd Wayne NJ 07470-2873 Office: 61 Berdan Ave Wayne NJ 07470-3229

JEFFREY, THERBER KENT, music educator; s. Marvin Kent and Linda Richardson Therber; m. Dawn Monuwella Therber, Dec. 29, 2001. MusB, U. Tenn., Knoxville, 1988. Band dir. Red band H.S. Hamilton County Dept. Edn., Chattanooga, 1999—2002; band dir. Armuchee H.S. Floyd County Ga. Dept. Edn., Rome, Ga., 2002. Bass trombonist Jericho Brass, Rome, 2000. Recipient Dir.'s award, performing arts consultants, Chgo., 2002. Mem.: Ga. Music Educator's Assn. (assoc.), Tenn. Music Edn. Assn. (assoc.), Phi Mu Alpha Sinonia (assoc.). Baptist. Avocations: gardening, music performance. Office: Armuchee HS 4203 Martha Berry Hwy NW Rome GA 37379 E-mail: bassbene1@att.net.

JEFFREY, TIMOTHY MICHAEL, film director; b. Detriot, Mich., May 28, 1949; BS, MA, Central Mich. U. Counselor Boysville of Mich., Macon, 1980—94; counselor, spkr.,writer The Jeffrey Porch Ltd., Ann Arbor, Mich., 1980—94; cons. Right Mgmt., 1985—95; actor numerous films & commercials, Mich., 1988—2000; film dir. Sept. Moon Prodn., Bloomfield, Mich., 2000—. Editor screenwriters and writers novels; author: (short stories) Milk Teeth, 2001, (plays) Parking at Bell Creek, 2001, (screenplays) You Are Here, 2003; exec. prodr.: (poetry) Boysville Poetry. Coach various sports. Office: PO Box 8351 Ann Arbor MI 48107

JEFFREYS, ARCELIA TAYLOR, education educator; b. Oxford, NC, Dec. 10, 1944; d. Irene Taylor Allen. BS, NC Ctrl. U., 1968, MS, 1970; EdD, U. NC, Greensboro, 1989. Instr., advisor Shaw U., Raleigh, NC, 1970—72; tchr., coach Wake County Pub. Schs., Raleigh, NC, 1972—83; supr. student tchrs. NC Ctrl. U., Durham, 1989—. Cons. Durham Pub. Sch. Tchrs., 1995—. Chmn. fund-raising ADA, Raleigh, NC, 1995—96. Fellow U. Coll. fellow, 2003; grantee Minorities Presence grantee, U. NC, 1984—87. Mem.: NCAHPERD (assoc.; com. mem. 2002—). Baptist. Avocations: golf, travel. Home: 1137 Shonele Lane Stem NC 27581 Office: North Carolina Central University 1801 Fayetteville Street Durham NC 27707-3129 Office Fax: 919-530-6156. Personal E-mail: ajeffreys16@aol.com. E-mail: ajeffrey@wpo.nccu.edu.

JEFFREYS, ELYSTAN GEOFFREY, geological engineer, petroleum consultant and appraiser, gemologist; b. Apr. 26, 1926; s. Geoffrey and Georgene Frances Theodora (Littell) J.; m. Pat Rumage, May 1, 1946 (div.); children: Jeri Lynn, David Powell; m. Peggi Villar, Feb. 28, 1975 (div. 2000); m. Sandra H. Garthwait, Aug. 5, 2002. Geol. Engr., Colo. Sch. Mines, 1951, grad. in Econ. Evaluation and Investment Decision Methods, 1972, 91. Registered profl. engr., Miss., land surveyor, Miss, profl. geologist, Ala.; cert. sr. appraiser of oil and gas properties Am. Soc. Appraisers. Ptnr. G. Jeffreys & Son, 1951-53, Jeffreys & Launius, 1953-55; pvt. practice petroleum exploration, 1954-77; exploration mgr. Arrowhead Exploration Co., Mobile and Brewton, Ala., 1977-83; cons. petroleum geologist and appraiser, 1964—. Pres., chmn. bd. dirs., CEO Major Oil Co., Jackson, Miss., 1961—84, v.p., 1984—98, The Jeffreys Co., Inc., Mobile, 1976—96, pres., CEO, 1996—2001; asst. mgr. Kee Energy Co., LLC, 1996—. Vestryman Trinity Episcopal Ch., Mobile, 1989-92, 94-96, sr. warden, 1991-92; bd. trustees The Appraisal Found., 1993-94. With 3d U.S. Army, 1944-46, ETO. Mem. Miss. Geol. Soc., Ala. Geol. Soc., New Orleans Geol. Soc. Am. Assn. Petroleum Geologists (50 Yr. Membership 2001), Gulf Coast Assn. Geol. Socs. (treas. 1960, Cert. of Svc. 1971), Soc. Petroleum Evaluation Engrs., Miss. Assn. Petroleum Landmen, Assn. Petroleum Landmen of Ala., Masons (32 degree), Shriners, Pi Kappa Alpha. Address: 115 Fairway Dr Daphne AL 36526-7401 Office Fax: 251-621-1630. E-mail: egjeffreys@aol.com.

JEFFREYS, REBECCA ELIZABETH, professional flutist; b. Glens Falls, N.Y., Dec. 7, 1966; d. William Alwyn Geoffrey and Sara Jane (Smock) Cormier; m. John Paul Jeffreys, May 27, 1989. BA, Crane Sch. Music, Potsdam, N.Y., 1989; MA, Cath. U. Am., 1993. Free-lance flutist, 1989—; master class tchr., 1989—; flutist Jeffreys and Miller Duo, Washington, 1992—98; pvt. music tchr. Holton-Arms Sch., 1996—99. Dir. Woodbridge Flute Choir, 1996-2002. Prodr.: (CD), 2000, 2002. Mem.: Flute Soc. Washington, Nat. Flute Assn. (chair local arrangements, presenter Nat Flute Conv. 2002). Avocations: gardening, travel.

JEFFRIES, DAVID HAMILTON, investment banker; b. Oxford, Eng., July 1, 1957; s. Graham H. and Elizabeth T. (Jones) J.; m. Elizabeth Hilary Willett, Aug. 23, 1980 (dec. 2001). BA magna cum laude, Haverford Coll., 1979; MA, Yale U., 1980, JD, 1984. Bar: NY 1985. Assoc. Sullivan & Cromwell, NYC, 1984-86, Lehman Bros., NYC, 1986-99, J.P. Morgan & Co., Inc., NYC, 1999—2001, ABN Amro, Inc., NYC, 2002—. Mem. Pelham C.C., Phi Beta Kappa. Office: ABN Amro Inc 55 E 52nd St New York NY 10055

JEFFRIES, JOHN WORTHINGTON, historian, educator; b. Oxford, Miss., Apr. 6, 1942; s. William Worthington and Mary Ruth (Franklin) J.; m. Renate Spitzer, June 13, 1964; children: Martha J. Crews, William W. BA, Harvard U., 1963; MPhil, Yale U., 1971, PhD, 1973. History instr. Princeton (N.J.) U., 1972-73; from asst. prof. to prof. history U. Md., Balt., 1973-91, prof., chair, 1992—. Cons. various presses and orgns. Author: Testing the Roosevelt Coalition, 1979, Wartime America, 1996, Encyclopedia of American History, vol. 8: 1929-1945, 2003; co-author: While Soldiers Fought, 1987; contbr. articles to profl. jours. Lt. USN, 1963-68. Mem. Am. Hist. Assn., Orgn. Am. Historians, Acad. Polit. Sci., Phi Beta Kappa. Home: 13 N Hilltop Rd Catonsville MD 21228-4818 Office: U Md Balt County Dept History Baltimore MD 21250 E-mail: jeffries@umbc.edu.

JEFFRIES, MCCHESNEY HILL, JR., lawyer; b. Atlanta, Dec. 25, 1954; s. McChesney Hill Sr. and Alice Elizabeth (Mitchell) J.; m. Virginia Lee Hartley, Aug. 2, 1980; children: Virginia Hartley, McChesney Hill III. BA with high distinction, U. Va., 1977, JD, 1980. Bar: Ga. 1980, U.S. Dist. Ct. (no. dist.) Ga. 1980, U.S. Ct. Appeals (11th cir.) 1980. Assoc. Hurt, Richardson, Garner, Todd & Cadenhead, Atlanta, 1980-85, Long, Aldridge & Norman, Atlanta, 1985-87, ptnr., 1988-95; ptnr., head Capital Markets Group, Alston & Bird, Atlanta, 1995—. Contbr. articles to profl. jours. Mem.: ABA, Atlanta Bar Assn. (founding dir. bus. and fin. law sect.), Ga. Bar Assn. (securities com.), Piedmont Driving Club (Atlanta). Presbyterian. Avocation: sports. Home: 4575 Jett Rd NW Atlanta GA 30327-4561 Office: Alston & Bird One Atlantic Ctr 1201 W Peachtree St Atlanta GA 30309-3424

JEFFRIES, MICHAEL S. apparel executive; b. 1945; m. Susan Jeffries; 1 child, Andrew. BA in Econs., Claremont Coll.; MBA, Columbia U. With Abraham and Straus, 1968; exec. v.p. merchandising Bullock's, 1980-83; pres., CEO Alcott & Andrews, 1983-89; exec. v.p. merchandising Paul Harris, 1990-92; pres., CEO Abercrombie & Fitch, Ohio, 1992—. Office: Abercrombie & Fitch 6301 Fitch Path New Albany OH 43054*

JEFFRIES, RICHARD HALEY, physician, broadcasting company executive; b. Harrisburg, Pa., June 7, 1941; s. Richard Lawrence and Jeanette Ruth (Haley) J.; 1 child, Richard Straley. BS, Pa. State U., 1963; DO, Kirksville Coll. Osteo. Medici, 1968. Diplomate Am. Coll. Osteo. Internists. Intern Cmty. Gen. Osteo. Hosp., Harrisburg, 1968-69, resident in internal medicine, 1969-72, attending staff dept. internal medicine, 1972—, dir. coronary and intensive care units, 1983-86, chmn. dept. medicine, 1986-98, v.p. med. staff, 1977-79, pres., chief of staff, 1979-82; pvt. practice Harrisburg, 1972—; founder, pres. Quaker State Broadcasting, Inc., WTPA-FM, Mechanicsburg, Pa., 1982-99; founder, sec. Midstate Comm., Inc., 1990-97; vice chmn. dept. medicine Pinnacle Health Sys., 1998—2002, chief internal medicine, 2000—, chmn. dept. medicine, 2002—. Sr. clin. instr. Phila. Coll. Osteo. Medicine, 1977-81, clin. asst. prof., 1981—; clin. asst. prof. Hahnemann Med. Coll., Phila., 1977—, N.Y. Coll. Osteo. Medicine, N.Y.C., 1981-84; adj. asst. prof. U. Osteo. Medicine and Health Scis., Des Moines, 1990—; regional clin. faculty Kirksville (Mo.) Coll. Osteo. Medicine, 1993; trustee Cmty. Gen. Osteo. Hosp., Harrisburg, 1979-84, mem. staff exec. com., 1974-84, 86-2000, chmn. staff exec. com., 1979-82; sr. flight surgeon FAA, 1975—; med. dir. Ecumenical Home of Harrisburg, Beverly Preferred Choice Hospice Program, Harrisburg, 1995—, Blue Ridge Haven East Nursing Home, Harrisburg. Contbr. articles to profl. jours. Chmn. fundraising dr. Dauphin County Retarded Citizens Assn., 1984; founding mem., bd. dirs., past pres. Dauphin Residences, Inc., 1974-81; mem. Allied Arts Fund, Physicians Divsn., 1992, 93, 94; alumni bd. Kirksville Coll. Osteo. Medicine, 1997—. Mem. Am. Osteo. Assn., Pa. Osteo Med. Assn., Am. Coll. Osteo. Internists, Am. Heart Assn. (bd. dirs. Sun Ctrl. Pa. chpt. 1976-79), Daguerreian Soc., Alpha Chi Sigma. Republican. Methodist. Avocations: photography, photographic collection, fly fishing, travel. Home: 516 Halyard Way Enola PA 17025 Office: Bronstein-Jeffries PA 4830 Londonderry Rd Harrisburg PA 17109-5207

JEFFRIES, ROBERT JOSEPH, retired engineer, educator, business executive; b. Norwalk, Conn., Jan. 6, 1923; s. Charles William and Christine (Jacobsen) J.; m. Anna Darling Cumming, Oct. 13, 1945; children: Christine Darling, Bruce Cumming. BS, U. Conn., 1944, MS, 1946; DEng, Johns Hopkins U., 1948. Engr. NACA, 1944-46; instr. Johns Hopkins U., 1946-48; research assoc. N.C. State Coll., 1948-49; assoc. prof. Mich. State U., 1949-54; tech. planning adviser Schlumberger Instrument Co., 1954-55; asst. to pres. Daystrom, Inc., 1955-57; pres., founder Data-Control System, Inc., 1957-66, chmn. bd., 1966-68; prof. U. Bridgeport, Conn., 1968-75, ret.; founder, dir. Ednl. & Tech. Cons., Inc., 1953-57. V.p., dir. TJB Resources Inc., 1972-88; dir. emeritus Evergreen Fund Family; v.p., founder Found. Instrumentation Edn. and Rsch., 1958-66; fellow-in-residence Edgar Cayce Found., Virginia Beach, Va., 1981-88; prof. Atlantic U., 1986-90. Editor Jour. Instrument Soc. Am., 1953-54; contbr. tech. papers. Trustee Am. Unitarian Assn., Cmty. Ch. Coll., Sun City Ctr., Tampa Bay Cmty. Found., SCC coun. Recipient Disting. Alumnus award U. Conn., Disting. Alumnus award John Hopkins U. Fellow NRC; mem. Instrument Soc. Am. (pres. 1957-58), Assn. Rsch. and Enlightenment (trustee), Conn. Commn. for Higher Edn. (vice chmn.), U. Conn. Engring. Alumni Assn. (pres. 1969-71), Sigma Xi, Tau Beta Pi, Eta Kappa Nu. Home: 1010 American Eagle Blvd Apt 502 Sun City Center FL 33573-5284

JEFFRIES, ROBIN, computer engineer; BA in Math. summa cum laude, U. Iowa, 1969; MA in Quantitative Psychology, U. Colo., 1977, PhD in Quantitative Psychology, 1978. Rsch. assoc. U. Colo., Boulder, Carnegie-Mellon U., 1983-93; mem. tech. staff Hewlett Packard Labs.; disting. engr. Sun Microsystems, Palo Alto, Calif., 1993—. Office: Sun Microsystems 17 Network Cir MPK 17-114 Menlo Park CA 94025

JEFFRIES, RUSSELL MORDEN, communications company official; b. Carmel, Calif., July 15, 1935; s. Herman M. and Louise (Morden) J.; m. Barbara Jean Borcovich, Nov. 24, 1962; 1 child, Lynne Louise. AA, Hartnell Coll., 1971. Sr. communications technician AT&T, Salinas, Calif., 1955-91. Mayor City of Salinas, 1987-91. Pres. El Gabilan Sch. PTA, Salinas, 1971-74, Salinas Valley Council PTA, 1975-76; mem. Salinas City Sch. Bd., 1975-81; mem. Salinas City Council, 1981-87; bd. dirs. Community Hosp. Salinas Found., 1987—, Salinas-Kushikino Sister City, 1987—, pres. 1992-93, John Steinbeck Ctr. Found., 1987-96, Food Bank for Monterey County, 1992-96; hon. bd. dirs. Monterey Film Festival, 1987-96, Calif. Rodeo Assn., 1987; mem. ctrl. bd. Calif. Regional Water Quality, 1992—; commr. Moss Landing Harbor, 1996. Recipient hon. service award PTA, Salinas, 1976; cert. of appreciation Calif. Dept. Edn., 1980, Salinas City Sch. Dist., 1981, Calif. Sch. Bds. Assn., 1981, Steinbeck Kiwanis, Salinas, 1987; named hon. mem. Filipino community Salinas Valley, 1988. Mem. Salinas C. of C., Native Sons Golden West, K.C., Rotary, Moose. Republican. Roman Catholic. Avocations: fishing, hunting, bowling, golf. Home: 204 E Curtis St Salinas CA 93906-2804

JEFFRIES, SEYMOUR BARNARD, lawyer; b. N.Y.C., Oct. 10, 1916; BBA, CUNY, N.Y., 1939; JD, Harvard U., 1948. Bar: N.Y. 1964. Prof., chmn. dept. bus. adminstrn., jurisprudence Bklyn Coll. Pharmacy, 1949-58; trade rels., legis. liason dir. Warner Lambert Pharm. Co., 1958-60; investment, legal cons. Investors Counsel Inc., N.Y.C., 1963-65; pres. Med. Securities Fund Inc., N.Y.C., 1963-65; adviser, dir., ofcl. negotiator govt. Israel Drug and Fine Chem. Indsl. Merger, 1962-70; pvt. practice, 1964—; gen. counsel Pre-Paid Prescription Svcs. Corp., 1966-68. Cons. Family Drugs N.Y.C. Health and Welfare Coun.; specialist, lectr. in health care law field; specialist med. care ethics; lectr. consumer law, corp. and internat. law. Contbr. articles to profl. jours; contbg. author: Remington's Practice of Pharmacy. Mem. ABA, Am. Nassau Bar Assn., (chmn. internat. law com. 1997, chmn. pre-paid legal svcs. com. 1974-76), Am. Phar. Assn., Trial Lawyers Assn. Nassau County, AAUP, Kings County Pharm. Assn.(Leadership plaque 1955). Home: Island and Ibsen Sts Woodmere NY 11598 Office: 809 Ibsen St PO Box 388 Woodmere NY 11598-0388 E-mail: Dr.Jeffries@worldnet.att.net.

JEGEN, SISTER CAROL FRANCES, religion educator; b. Chgo., Oct. 11, 1925; d. Julian Aloysius and Evelyn W. (Bostelmann) J. BS in History, St. Louis U., 1951; MA in Theology, Marquette U., 1958, PhD in Religious Studies, 1968; hon. degree, St. Mary of the Woods, Terra Haute, Ind., 1977. Elem. tchr. St. Francis Xavier Sch., St. Louis, 1947-51; secondary tchr. Holy Angels Sch., Milw., 1951-57; coll. tchr. Mundelein Coll., Chgo., 1957-91; prof. pastoral studies Loyola U., Chgo., 1991—. Adv. coun. U.S. Cath. Bishops, Washington, 1969-74; trustees Cath. Theol. Union, Chgo., 1974-84. Author: Jesus the Peace Maker, 1986, Restoring Our Friendship with God, 1989; co-author: (with Byron Sherwin) Thank God, 1989; editor: Mary According to Women, 1985. Participant Nat. Farm Worker Ministry, Fresno, Calif., 1977—; mem. Pax Christi, U.S.A., 1979—, Jane Addams Conf., Chgo., 1989. Recipient Loyola Civic award Loyola U., Chgo., 1981, Chgo. medallion for Excellence in Catechesis, 1996, Sor Juana award Hispanic Ministry, 2000; named one of 100 Women to Watch Today's Chgo. Woman, 1989. Mem. Cath. Theol. Soc. Am., Coll. Theology Soc., Cath.-Jewish Scholars Dialog, Liturgical Conf. Democrat. Roman Catholic. Avocations: music, gardening. Home: Wright Hall 6364 N Sheridan Rd Chicago IL 60660-1700 Office: Loyola U Inst Pastoral Studies 6525 N Sheridan Rd Chicago IL 60626-5385

JEGEN, LAWRENCE A., III, law educator; b. Chgo., Nov. 16, 1934; s. Lawrence A. and Katherine M. Jegen; children: Christine M., David L. BA, Beloit Coll., 1956; JD, U. Mich., 1959, MBA, 1960; LLM, NYU, 1963. Bar: Ill. 1959, U.S. Dist. Ct. (no. dist.) Ill. 1959, U.S. Dist. Ct. (so. dist.) Ind. 1962, Ind. 1966, U.S. Tax Ct. 1966, U.S. Ct. Appeals (7th cir.) 1980, U.S. Supreme Ct. 1980. Tax cons. Coopers & Lybrand, N.Y.C., 1960-62; asst. prof. law Ind. U., Indpls., 1962-64, assoc. prof., 1964-66, prof., 1966—, Thomas F. Sheehan prof. tax law and policy, 1982—, prof. philanthropic studies Ctr. Philanthropy, 1992—, external tax counsel, 1997—. Ind. U. rep. to Nat. Assn. Coll. and Univ. Attys.; co-founder Annual Tax Inst. for Colls. and Univs.; bar rev. lectr., vis. prof. in field; spl. counsel Ind. Dept. Revenue, 1963-65, Gov.'s Commn. on Med. Edn., 1970-72; mem. commr.'s adv. com. IRS, 1981-82; advisor Notre Dame Estate Planning Inst.; mem. Ind. Corp. Law Survey Commn.; state tax notes corr. for tax analysts; contbg. editor Inst. Bus. Planning's Tax Planning Svc.; bd. dirs., officer Ind. Continuing Legal Edn. Forum; 1st chmn. bd. dirs. Baccalaureate Edn. Sys. Trust of Ind.; mem. Ind. Gen. Assembly Study Commn.-Ind. Gen. Corp. Act; mem. Ind. Corps. Survey Commn., 1965—; commr. Nat. Conf. Uniform State Laws, 1981-91; dir. N.Am. Wildlife Assn., 1981-90. Author: Indiana Will and Trust Manual, 1967-95; Lifetime and Estate, Personal and Business Planning, 1987; Estate Planning and Administration in Indiana, 1979, numerous other books, articles, chpts. Chmn. bd. dirs. Ind. Bar Ednl. Sys. Tchrs., 1988-89; mem. adv. bd. Ind. U. Ctr. on Philanthropy. Named hon. sec. of state, State of Ind., 1967, 1980, hon. dep. atty. gen., 1968, hon. state treas., 1969, Ford fellow, 1963; recipient Spl Alumni Tch. award, Ind. U. Alumni Assn., 1970, 1976, 1980, 1985, Excellence in Taxation award for improvement tax adminstrn., State of Ind. Quality for Ind. Taxpayers, Inc., 1990, The Thomas Hart Benton Mural medallion, 1993, 3 Sagamore of the Wabash awards, State Ind., Internat. award, Assn. Continuing Legal Administrators for Excellence in Continuing Legal Edn., Ind. U. Most Outstanding Law Prof. award 6 times, Pres.'s Cir. Commemorative medallions Ind. U. Disting. Tchg. award. Fellow Am. Bar Found. (life), Am. Coll. Probate Counsel, Am. Coll. Tax Counsel; mem. ABA, FBA, Mid-West Inst. Estate and Tax Planning (adv. bd.), Ind. Bar Assn. (chmn. taxation sect. 1969-70, presdl. citation 1971), Indpls. Bar Assn. (Dr. Morton Finney Jr. Excellence in Legal Edn. award), Ind. Trial Lawyers Assn. (corp. taxation, estate taxation, state and local taxation). Office: Indiana Univ Sch Law 530 W New York St Indianapolis IN 46202-3225 E-mail: profjegen@aol.com.

JEGLIE, JILL A. urban planner; b. Cleve., June 29, 1958; d. Ronald George Jeglie and Jeanne Marie Feddor. BSBA in Gen. Mgmt., Fla. Atlantic U., 1982, MPA in Environ. Growth Mgmt., 1989. Office mgr./tech. support Paragon Software, Inc., Boca Raton, Fla., 1982-86; from rsch. asst. to rsch. assoc. Fla. Atlantic U.-Joint Ctr. for Environ. and Urban Problems, Ft. Lauderdale, Fla., 1986—90; from planner to sr. planner land use divsn. Tallahassee and Leon County Planning Dept., Fla., 1990—99; town planner Planning, Zoning and Bldg. Dept., Longboat Key, Fla., 1999—, planning, zoning, bldg. dir., 2001—. Mem. tech. adv. com. Sarasota-Manatee County Met. Planning Orgn.; mem. Manatee County Ad Hoc Transp. Com. Co-author: Review of Growth Management Environmental and Urban Issues Conference, 1987. Mem. Mayor's Com. on Race Rels., Tallahassee, 1998-99. Fellow in Environ. Growth Mgmt., Fla. Atlantic U., 1989. Mem.: Fla. Planning and Zoning Assn. (bd. dirs. S.W. Fla.), Am. Inst. Cert. Planners, Am. Planning Assn. Democrat. Office: Planning Zoning and Bldg 501 Bay Isles Rd Longboat Key FL 34228-3142

JEHLE, MICHAEL EDWARD, financial executive; b. Lawrence, Kans., Apr. 2, 1954; s. Edwin Paul and Catherine Claire (Cragoe) J.; m. Kimberly Ellen Davis, Aug. 4, 1979; children: Kathryn Anne, Christine Michelle. BS, S.W. Mo. State U., 1976; JD, Stanford U., 1979. Bar: Calif., Ill., Pa. Atty. The First Nat. Bank of Chgo., 1979-84, sr. atty., 1984-86; v.p., gen. counsel Equibank, Pitts., 1986-87, sr. v.p., gen. counsel, sec., 1987, Equimark Corp., Pitts., 1987-89, exec. v.p., chief fin. officer, 1989-90; pres. Strategic Adv. Group, Pitts., 1990-95, Strategic Healthcare Advisors, Pitts., 1993-95; dir. rsch. MED 3000 Group, Inc., Pitts., 1995-96; pres. THI Inc., Pitts., 1996—. Co-author: Sovereign Lending, 1984. Mem. ABA, Nat. Health Lawyers Assn., Healthcare Fin. Mgmt. Assn. Republican. Methodist. Avocation: wine collecting. Home: 411 Maple Ln Sewickley PA 15143-1021 Office: THI Inc 411 Maple Ln Sewickley PA 15143-1021

JEKEL, JAMES FRANKLIN, physician, public health educator; b. St. Louis, Oct. 14, 1934; s. Oscar Henry and Frances Sarah (Newell) J.; m. Janice Marilyn Clark, Aug. 30, 1958; children: Clifford R., Mark R., Linda F., Timothy W. AB, Wesleyan U., 1956; MD, Washington U., St. Louis, 1960; MPH, Yale U., 1965. House officer Hartford (Conn.) Hosp., 1960-62; epidemiologist Ctrs. for Disease Control, Atlanta, 1962-67; asst. prof. pub. health Yale U. Sch. Medicine, New Haven, 1967-71, assoc. prof., 1971-80, prof., 1980-97, prof. emeritus, 1997—, C.E.A. Winslow prof. pub. health, 1982-97, dir. residency program in gen. preventive medicine, 1975-93; asst. dir. Robert Wood Johnson Scholar Program Robert Wood Johnson Clin. Scholar Program, New Haven, 1976-95; dir. sect. preventive medicine and cmty. health Griffin Hosp., Derby, Conn., 1996—. Pres. Bd. Health Quinnipiack Valley Health Dist., Hamden, Conn., 1986-91. Lt. comdr. USPHS, 1962-67. Fulbright Faculty fellow The Bahamas, 1985-86; recipient various rsch. grants, 1968—. Fellow Am. Coll. Preventive Medicine, Am. Sci. Affiliation; mem. Am. Pub. Health Assn., Christian Med./Dental Soc. Presbyterian. Office: Griffin Hosp 130 Division St Derby CT 06418

JELALIAN, ALBERT V. electrical engineer; b. Bridgewater, Mass., June 30, 1933; s. Siragan and Zarouhi (Tanelian) J.; m. Mary B. Karoghlanian; children: Alan H., Leslie K. BSEE, Northeastern U., 1957. Reg. profl. engr., Mass. Engr. Raytheon Co., Lexington, Mass., 1957-81, mgr. electro-optics lab Sudbury, Mass., 1981-86, asst. dir., 1986-91, asst. mgr. equipment devel. labs. (electro optics), 1991-92; pres. Jelalian Sci. & Engring., Bedford, Mass., 1992—. Inventor: holds ten patents relating to aviation safety and mil. products; contbr. articles to profl. jours.; author: Laser Radar Systems, 1992; guest editor IEEE Procs. Spl. Issue on Laser Radar Sys., 1995-96. Recipient Recognition award NASA, Washington, 1974, Group Achievement award, 1975, Disting. Svc. award IRIS, 1993, Nat. Sci. and Tech. award IRIS, 1998; fellow Mil. Sensing Symposium. Mem. IEEE (sr.), Infrared Info. Symposium (vice chmn. active systems 1989-91, nat. chmn. 1991-93), Optical Soc. Am. Office: Jelalian Sci & Engring 3 Reeves Rd Bedford MA 01730-1334

JELEN, TED G. political scientist; b. Evergreen Park, Ill., Apr. 30, 1952; s. Thaddeus Andrew and Frances Jelen; m. Marthe Atwater Chandler, June 14, 1982; children: Christopher Michael Chandler, Robert Martin Chandler. BA, Knox Coll., Galesburg, Ill., 1970—74; PhD, Ohio State U., Columbus, 1974—79. Prof., polit. sci. Benedictine U., Lisle, Ill., 1981—97, U. Nev., Las Vegas, 1997—. Editor Jour. Sci. Study Religion, 1999—2003. Author: (book) Between Two Absolutes: Public Opinion and the Politics of Abortion, 1992, Public Atitudes Toward Church and State, 1995, A Wall of Separation? Debating Church-State Relations in the United States, 1998, To Serve God and Mammon, 2000; editor: Religion and Politics in Comparative Perspective, 2002. Mem.: Midwest Polit. Sci. Assn., Soc. for the Sci. Study of Religion, Am. Polit. Sci. Assn. Avocation: guitar. Office: Univ Nev 4505 Maryland Pkwy Las Vegas NV 81954-5029 Office Fax: 702-895-1065. E-mail: jelent@unlv.neveda.edu.

JELINCH, FRANK ANTHONY, lawyer; b. San Jose, Calif., July 22, 1943; s. Frank Anthony and Minnie Leona J.; m. Roberta Katherine Magi, Dec. 27, 1975; 1 child, Michelle. BA cum laude, San Jose Sate U., 1965; JD, U. Calif., Berkeley, 1968. Bar: Calif. 1969, U.S. Dist. Ct. (no. dist.) Calif. 1969, U.S. Supreme Ct. 1972. Ptnr. Jelinch & Rendler, Cupertino, Calif., 1980—. Instr. Lincoln U. Sch. Law, San Jose, 1980; founder Cupertino Nat. Bank. Chmn. San Francisco Shakespeare Festival, 1997-98, Terra Found., San Jose, 1980—; commr. Los Gatos Parks Commn., 1980-88, Cupertino Parks & Recreation, 1996—, chair, 1997, 2001; dir. state bd. Calif. Parks and Recreation Commrs. Assn.; commr. Cupertino Fine Arts Commn., 1990-94; chair Am. Heart Assn. Cardiac Fundraising Drive, 1996; pres. Los Gatos Friends of the Arts; bd. dirs. State Bd. parks Commrs., 2001—, Cupertino Cmty. Svcs. Bd., 2001—. Capt. U.S. Army, 1969-73, Command Judge Advocate, 1st Signal Brigade, USARV, 1971, legal officer Op. Homecoming (Vietnam returning POW's) 1973. Recipient Bronze Star, Oak Leaf Cluster, Army Commendation Medal (1st Oak Leaf Cluster), Vietnam. Mem. ABA (EEOC com.), Sunnyvale-Cupertino Bar Assn. (pres. 1990), Cupertino C. of C. (pres. 1998-99, del. trade delegation to Taiwan 2000), Santa Clara County Bar Assn. (gov. 1990), Calif. State Bar Assn., Santa Clara County Trial Lawyers Assn., U.S. Supreme Ct. Hist. Soc., Phi Alpha Theta, Pi Sigma Alpha. Office: Jelinch & Rendler 20863 Stevens Creek Blvd Cupertino CA 95014-2125

JELINEK, FREDERICK, electrical engineer, educator; b. Prague, Czechoslovakia, Apr. 18, 1932; arrived in U.S., 1949, naturalized, 1955; s. William and Trudy (Kocmanek) J.; m. Milena Tobolova, Feb. 4, 1961; children— Hannah, William. BS, MIT, 1956, MS, 1958, PhD, 1962; DS Math. and Physics (hon.), Charles U., Prague, 2001. Instr. MIT, Cambridge, 1959-62; lectr. Harvard U., Cambridge, 1962; asst. prof. Cornell U., Sch. Elec. Engring., Ithaca, N.Y., 1962-66, assoc. prof., 1966-72, prof., 1972-74; vis. scientist MIT, Lincoln Lab., 1964, 65, IBM, 1968-69; sr. mgr. continuous speech recognition IBM, T.J. Watson Research Center, Yorktown Heights, N.Y., 1972-93; prof., dir. Ctr. Lang. and Speech Processing Whiting Sch. Engring. Johns Hopkins U., Balt., 1993—. Author: Probabilistic Information Theory, 1968, Statistical Methods for Speech Recognition, 1998; contbr. articles to profl. jours. Chmn. Liberal Party, Ithaca, N.Y., 1970-72, mem. state exec. com., 1971-73. Recipient Outstanding Achievement in the Field of Speech Comm. European Speech Comm. Assn., 2000; named One of top 100 innovators in speech recognition by Tech. Mag., 1981. Fellow IEEE (life; pres. Info. Theory Group 1977, bd. govs. 1970-79, 81-86, Info. Theory Group best paper award 1971, Soc. award Signal Processing Soc. 1998, Golden Jubilee Paper award Info. Theory Soc. 1998, Third

Millennium medal 2000, Computer, Speech and Lang. paper award 2002). Office: Johns Hopkins U Ctr Lang and Speech Processing Barton Hall 3400 N Charles St Baltimore MD 21218 E-mail: jelinek@jhu.edu.

JELINEK, JOHN JOSEPH, public relations executive; b. San Pedro, Calif., Sept. 3, 1955; s. Joseph Francis and Patricia Valerie (Powers) J.; m. Christl Michele Schneider, June 1986 (div. July 1997). BA, Loyola U., 1977; MA, Loyola-Marymount U., 1983; postgrad., Syracuse U. Assoc. editor E-Go Enterprises, Sherman Oaks, Calif., 1976-77; advt. dir. Select Promotions, Irvine, Calif., 1977-78; editor SCORE Internat., Westlake Village, Calif., 1978-79; exec. editor Petersen Pub. Co., L.A., 1979-82, editor, 1982-85; pub. rels. account exec. Hill and Knowlton Inc., L.A., 1985-87; acct. supr. Freeman/McCue Pub. Rels., Newport Beach, Calif., 1987-88; account supr. tech. div. Fleishman Hillard Inc., L.A., 1988-89; rep. pub. affairs corp. news dept. Ford Motor Co., Dearborn, Mich., 1989-90; product info. mgr. Ford of Can., Oakville, 1990-92; car product devel., pub. affairs mgr. Ford Motor Co., Dearborn, Mich., 1993-96, product devel., pub. affairs mgr., 1996-98, dir. car strategy comm., 1998-2001, Ford brand comm. mgr., 2001—02; v.p. pub. affairs Ford of Can., Oakville, 2002—. Author: (with others) Consumer's Guide to 1978 Trucks, 1978, Consumer's Guide to 1980 Trucks, 1979, Complete Guide to Used Cars, 1981, How to Buy the Best Compact Truck, 1984; columnist Guns & Ammo Mag., 1980-84, Petersen's Hunting Mag., 1986-87. Capt. Calif. State Mil. Res. 1982-89. Recipient 1st place award Calif. Newspaper Pub. Assn., 1977 Mem. NRA (life), L.A. County Mus. Natural History-Automobile Collection Coun., Aircraft Owners and Pilots Assn., Nat. Aeronautical Assn., Detroit Inst. Art. Republican. Roman Catholic. Avocations: travel, flying, skiing, cooking. Office: Ford Motor Co Can The Canadian Rd Oakville Canada L6J 5E4 E-mail: jjelinek@ford.com.

JELINEK, JOSEF EMIL, dermatologist; b. Prague, Czechoslovakia, Feb. 12, 1928; came to U.S., 1958, naturalized, 1964; s. Frank and Olga (Frankl) J.; m. Vera Adrienne Schnitzer, June 19, 1960; children— David Frank, Paul William. M.B., BS, U. London, 1951; postgrad., U. London Postgrad. Sch., 1956, NYU, 1963—. Diplomate Am. Bd. Dermatology. Intern, house surgeon in orthopedics St. Mary's Hosp., London, 1951-52; house physician in internal medicine Harold Wood Hosp., Essex, Eng., 1952, Princess Beatrice Hosp., London, 1955; registrar in internal medicine Royal Victoria Hosp., Bournemouth, Eng., 1955-57, Dulwich Hosp., London, 1957-58; precepteeship in dermatology with Norman B. Kanof, N.Y.C., 1961-62; chief resident dermatology Bellevue Hosp., N.Y.C., 1962-63; chief resident Univ. Hosp., N.Y.C., 1963; cons. VA Hosp., N.Y.C., 1965—; asst. attending physician Bellevue Hosp., N.Y.C., 1965—; attending physician Univ. Hosp., N.Y.C., 1976—, chief skin and cancer unit, 1973; clin. prof. dermatology N.Y. U. Sch. Medicine, 1976—; practice medicine specializing in dermatology, 1963—. Cons. AMA Council on Drugs and the Dept. of Drugs, 1972. Author: The Skin in Diabetes, 1985; contbr. articles to profl. jours, also chpts. to textbooks. Served to flight lt. RAF, 1952-54. Fellow ACP, Am. Acad. Dermatology; mem. Atlantic Dermatologic Conf. (past chmn.), Dermatologic Soc. Greater N.Y. (past pres.), N.Y. Acad. Medicine (past chmn.), Manhattan Dermatol. Soc. (past pres.), Am. Folk Art Soc. (pres. 1986-91). Office: NYU Med Offices Ste 351 418 Lafayette St New York NY 10003-6947

JELINEK, VERA, university director; b. Kosice, Czechoslovakia, Dec. 16, 1935; came to U.S., 1947; d. Joseph and Margit (Lefkovits) Schnitzer; m. Josef E. Jelinek, June 19, 1960; children: David, Paul. BA in History, CUNY, 1956; MA, Johns Hopkins U., 1958; PhD in Modern European History, NYU, 1977; diploma, Sch. Advanced Internat. Study, Bologna, Italy. Translator Rockefeller Bros. Fund, N.Y.C., 1958-59; exec. dir. U.S. Youth Coun., N.Y.C., 1959-63; dir. internat. programs, social and natural scis. NYU, N.Y.C., 1985—, dir. Lillian Vernon Ctr. for Internat. Affairs, 2000—, dir. The Energy Forum, 2000—. Mem. adv. com. N.Y.C.-Budapest Sister City Program, 1991-94; prin. dir. pilot tng. program for new UN diplomats NYU, 1996-97. Author audio cassette: Before You Go-Italy, 1985. Mem. edn. com. Mus. Am. Folk Art, N.Y.C.; edn. co-chair The Am. Antiques Show, 2002. Recipient fellowship Ford Found., 1960, grant NYU Curriculum Challenge Fund, 1989, 90, 99, Phillip E. Frandson award Nat. Univ. Continuing Edn. Assn., 1991. Mem. Am. Folk Art Soc., Carnegie Coun. on Ethics and Internat. Affairs, Women's Fgn. Policy Group, Phi Beta Kappa. Democrat. Avocations: tennis, jogging, folk art, cooking, travel. Office: Lillian Vernon Ctr Internat Affairs 58 W 10th St New York NY 10011

JELKIN, JOHN LAMOINE, lawyer; b. Hildreth, Nebr., Dec. 24, 1952; s. Lamoine George and Verna Mae (DeJonge) J.; m. Diane Louise Davis, June 10, 1978; children: Jessica Jean, Jaclyn Jade. BA, Univ. Nebr., 1975; JD, U. Nebr., 1978. Bar: Nebr. 1978, U.S. Dist. Ct. Nebr. 1978. Assoc. Duncan & Duncan, Franklin, Nebr., 1978-81; ptnr. Duncan, Duncan & Jelkin, Franklin, 1981-87, Duncan, Duncan, Jelkin & Walker, Franklin, 1987—2003, Duncan, Duncan and Jolkin, 2003—. Bd. dirs. Nebr. Continuing Legal Edn., Inc., 1995—; sec.-treas. Hildreth Area Bus. Devel. Corp., 1983-88; dep. atty. Buffalo County, Kearney, Nebr., 1986. Vol. fireman; chmn. Franklin County Dems., 1984-98; dep. atty. Franklin County, Nebr.; seminar presenter, speaker NCLE, Inc., 1991, 92, 93 94, 98; mem. ch. council St. Peters Luth. Ch., Hildreth, Nebr., 1988, pres., 1989-90; vice-chmn. Trinity Luth. Ch. Endowment Fund, 2002—; pres. Hildreth Alumni Assn., 1990-95, Hildreth Cmty. Improvement Project, 1992-93; active Hildreth Industrial Devel. Com., 1995, chmn., 1997; bd. dirs. Franklin County Cmty. Found., 1995—, Nebr. Child Abuse Prevention Fund, 1996-2000. Mem. ABA (mem. real estate probate and trust sect.), Nebr. Bar Assn. (exec. com. real estate, probate and trust sect. 1992-94, chmn. 1994-95, real estate practice guidelines com. 1991—), Buffalo County Bar Assn., Nebr. Assn. Trial Attys., 10th Jud. Bar Assn. (pres. 1983-84, 98-99), Lions (bd. dirs. 1993—, v.p. 1982-85, pres. 1985-86, 2000-01). Republican. Lutheran. Office: Duncan Duncan & Jelkin PO Box 340 Hildreth NE 68947-0340 E-mail: jelkinlaw@mailcity.com.

JELKS, MARY LARSON, retired pediatrician; b. Galva, Ill., 1929; MD, U. Nebr., 1955. Diplomate Am. Bd. Pediats., Am. Bd. Allergy and Immunology. Intern Johns Hopkins Hosp., Balt., 1955-56, resident, 1956-57, 58-60, Grace-New Haven Hosp., 1957; fellow U. Fla. Tchg. Hosp., 1960-61; clin. asst. prof. U. South Fla.; ret.; active aerobiology, 1985—. Fellow Am. Acad. Allery and Immunology, Am. Acad. Pediats.; mem. AMA. Achievements include active research in aerobiology. Home: 1930 Clematis St Sarasota FL 34239-3813 E-mail: mjelks99@cs.com.

JELLEMA, JON, state legislator, educator; b. Bloomington, Ind., Dec. 7, 1943; s. William Harry and Frances (Peters) J.; m. Betsy Zevalkink; children: Frances, Kate, Jon R., Elizabeth. BA, Calvin Coll., 1966; MA, Mich. State U., 1972. Prof. Grand Valley State U., Allendale, Mich., 1972-94; asst. dean William James Coll., Grand Valley State U., Allendale, 1986-87; dir. liberal studies program Grand Valley State U., Allendale, 1988-89, chmn. English dept., 1989-91, prof. English dept., 1991-94; mem. Mich. Ho. of Reps., Lansing, 1994-2000; dean Arts and Humanities divsn. Grand Valley State U., Allendale, 2001—. Vice-chmn. appropriations com., vice chmn. subcom. on transp., chmn. joint capital outlay comm., chmn. policy comm., mem. edn. commn. states, mem. urban caucus. Pres. Grand Haven (Mich.) Pub. Sch. Bd., 1972-84; founder North Ottawa Cmty. Coalition. Mem. Assn. for Values in Higher Edn., Greater Grand Rapids Coun. for Arts, World Affairs Coun., Ottawa County United Way, Phi Kappa Phi. Avocations: sailing, skiing. Home: 510 Park Ave Grand Haven MI 49417-2107 Office: 290 LSH-GVSU Allendale MI 49401

JELLICO, NANCY ROSE, painter, sculptor; b. LaGrange, Ga., Sept. 22, 1939; d. James Davis and Mary Myrtle (Capley) Norris; m. John Anthony Jellico, Dec. 22, 1960 (div. 1981); children: Janice Lee, Carol Anne, Kenneth Alan; m. Glenn Howard Hildebrandt, May 2, 1987 (div. 1992). Diploma, Colo. Inst. Art, 1960. Registrar Colo. Inst. Art., Denver, 1961-64, instr., 1964-65. Group exhibits include Gene Autry Western Heritage Mus., L.A., 1994-95, Wyo. Meml. Pioneer Mus., Douglas, 1992-95, Tucson Mus. Art, 1991-94, Murisaki Gallery, Tokyo, 1992, Mus. Nebr. Art, Kearney, 2000, numerous others; commd. works include The Upjohn Co., Kalamazoo, 1983-90, St. Thomas Theol. Sem., Denver, 1985, 88, 90, Pro Rodeo Hall Fame & Mus. Am. Cowboy, Colorado Springs, 1983, Chadron State Coll., Nebr., 2001-02, illustrator featured articles numerous publs. including Art of the West mag., 1990, Equine Images mag., 1989, Cowboy Internat. mag., 1987, Southwest Art mag., 1986, Wild West mag., 1995. Mem. Will James Soc. Office: Jellico Studio Western Art 85558 479th Ave Amelia NE 68711-3233

JELLICORSE, JOHN LEE, communications and theatre educator; b. Bristol, Tenn., Nov. 1, 1937; s. Harold Lee and Kathleen (Nickels) J.; m. Lenah Mary Lawrence, July 21, 1961 (div. 1980); 1 child, Jennifer Lee; m. Delayna Maxine Jordan, June 28, 1992; 1 child, John Adam. AB, U. Tenn., 1959; PhD, Northwestern U., 1967. From instr. to assoc. prof. Northwestern U., Evanston, Ill., 1962-69; assoc. prof. U. Tenn., Knoxville, 1969-74; prof., head dept. communication and theatre U. N.C., Greensboro, 1974-88, dir. theatre divsn., 1988-90, dir. broadcasting/cinema divsn., 1990-91; dean Sch. Comm. Hong Kong Bapt. U., 1991-94; prof. U. N.C., Greensboro, 1994—2001, head dept. broadcasting and cinema, 2001—. Cons. Wroclaw Tech. U., Poland. Contbr. chpts. to books, articles to profl. jours. Recipient Outstanding Tchr. award Northwestern U., 1968; So. Fellowship Fund fellow, 1959-62. Mem. AEJMC, Assn. for Comm. Adminstrn., Am. Film Inst., Internat. Comm. Assn., Nat. Comm. Assn., Univ. Film and Video Assn. Office: U NC Greensboro 209 Brown PO Box 26170 Greensboro NC 27402-6170 E-mail: jljellic@uncg.edu.

JELLIFFE, ROGER WOODHAM, cardiologist, clinical pharmacologist; b. Cleve., Feb. 18, 1929; s. Russell Wesley and Rowena (Woodham) J.; m. Joyce Miller, June 12, 1954; children: Susan, Amy, Elizabeth, Peter. BA, Harvard U., 1950; MD, Columbia U., 1954. Diplomate Am. Bd. Internal Medicine, Am. Bd. Cardiovascular Disease. Intern Univ. Hosps., Cleve., 1954-56; also jr. asst. resident in medicine; Nat. Found. Infantile Paralysis exptl. medicine fellow Case Western Res. U., Cleve., 1956-58; staff physician in medicine VA Hosp., Cleve., 1958-60, resident in medicine, 1960-61; instr. medicine U. So. Calif. Sch. Medicine, L.A., 1961-63, asst. prof., 1963-67, assoc. prof., 1967-76, prof. medicine, 1976—. Developer Lab. Applied Pharmacokinetics, 1973—, The USC*PACK Computer Programs, 1973—; cons. Dynamic Scis., Inc., Van Nuys, Calif., 1976-93, Simes S.P.A., Milan, 1979-97, IVAC Corp., San Diego, 1983-88, Bionica, Sydney, Australia, 1987-94. Author: Fundamentals of Electrocardiography, 1990; cons. editor Am. Jour. Medicine, 1972-78, Current Prescribing, 1974-79, Am. Jour. Physiology, 1984-91, Computers in Biology and Medicine, 1994—, Therapeutic Drug Monitoring, 1995—; contbr. articles to profl. jours.; patentee in field. Advanced Rsch. fellow L.A. County Heart Assn., 1961-64; recipient Rsch. Achievement award Clin. Scis. Am. Assn. Pharm. Scis., 1997. Fellow ACP, Am. Coll. Med. Informatics, Am. Coll. Clin. Pharmacology, Am. Heart Assn. Coun. on Clin. Cardiology; mem. Am. Soc. Clin. Pharmacology and Therapeutics (chmn. pharmacometric sect. 1995-97), Am. Fedn. Clin. Rsch., Am. Med. Informatics Assn. Achievements include research on optimal mgmt. of drug therapy; development of computer programs for optimal mgmt. of drug therapy; population pharmacokinetic modeling; development of intelligent infusion devices; supercomputer resources for parametric and nonparametric population modeling; software for "multiple model" design of drug dosage regimens. Office: 2250 Alcazar St Rm CSC-134-B Los Angeles CA 90089-0107 E-mail: jelliffe@hsc.usc.edu.

JELLINEK, GEORGE, broadcast executive, writer, music educator; b. Budapest, Hungary, Dec. 22, 1919; came to U.S., 1941; s. Daniel and Jolan Jellinek; m. Hedy Dicker, July 29, 1942; 1 child, Nancy Berezin. Student, Lafayette Coll., 1943; MusD (hon.), L.I. U., 1984. Dir. program services SESAC, Inc., N.Y.C., 1955-64; rec. dir. Muzak, Inc., N.Y.C., 1964-68; music dir. Sta. WQXR, N.Y.C., 1968-84; asst. prof. music NYU, N.Y.C., 1976-91. Author: (biography) Callas, Portrait of a Prima Donna, 1960, 2d edit. 1986, (opera librettos) (music by Eugene Zador) The Magic Chair, 1966, The Scarlet Mill, 1968; contbg. editor: Stereo Rev. mag., 1958-74, Ovation mag., 1974-88; author: (book) History Through the Opera Glass, 1994; contbr. articles to the N.Y. Times, Musical America, The Opera Quar. Trustee Bagby Found. Served to 1st lt. M.I., U.S. Army, 1942-46. Recipient Maj. Armstrong Broadcast award, 1978, Ohio State award, 1978, Gabriel award, 1982, George Washington award Am. Hungarian Found., 1986, Gold medal Internat. Radio Festival, 1995, Grammy award, 1996. Mem. ASCAP, AFTRA. Office: Sta WQXR 122 5th Ave New York NY 10011-5605

JELLINEK, MICHAEL STEVEN, psychiatrist, pediatrician; b. N.Y.C., Sept. 30, 1948; s. Kurt and Kate (Jacoby) J.; m. Barbara A. Jellinek, June 14, 1970; children: David M., Abraham R., Isaiah T., Hanna R. BA, Columbia Coll., 1970; MD, Albert Einstein Coll. Medicine, 1973. Diplomate Nat. Bd. Med. Examiners, Am. Bd. Pediatrics; diplomate in psychiatry and child psychiatry Am. Bd. Psychiatry and Neurology. Instr. pediatrics Montefiore Hosp. & Med. Ctr., N.Y.C., 1976—79; chief child psychiat. svcs. Mass. Gen. Hosp., Boston, 1979—, asst. in pediat., 1979—81, asst. pediatrician, 1981—83, dir. outpatient psychiatry, 1984—93, assoc. pediatrician, 1984—86, assoc. psychiatrist, 1984—86, pediatrician, 1986—, psychiatrist, 1986—, asst. gen. dir. ambulatory svcs., 1992—, sr. v.p. ambulatory svcs., 1994—2001, sr. v.p. adminstrn., 1995—2001; pres. Newton Wellesley Hosp., 2001—; assoc. prof. psychiatry (pediatrics) Harvard U., Boston, 1987—96, prof. psychiatry and pediatrics, 1996—. Asst. instr. Columbia U., N.Y.C, 1970; cons. Shriner Burns Inst., Boston, 1979—. Dir. Camp Rainbow, Croton-on-Hudson, 1977-81. Fellow Am. Acad. Pediat., Am. Acad. Child Psychiatry (treas. 1991-93, Simon Wile award 1993); mem. Am. Pediat. Soc., Am. Psychiat. Soc. (Ittleson award 1999), Soc. Prof. Child Psychiatry, New Eng. Coun. Child Psychiatry. Democrat. Jewish. Avocations: running, soccer coach, carpentry. Home: 132 Pleasant St Newton MA 02459-1828 Office: Mass Gen Hosp Fruit St Bulfinch 351 Boston MA 02114

JELLINEK, MILES ANDREW, lawyer; b. Dec. 27, 1947; s. Alfred Marquis and Rena Elizabeth (Felberg) J.; m. Annabelle Francis O'Leary, Apr. 9, 1976; children: Beth Elise, Laura Anne. BA, U. Pa., 1969, JD, 1974. Bar: Pa. 1974, N.J. 1987. Law clk. Ct. Common Pleas, Phila., 1974-75; sr. mem. Cozen O'Connor, Phila., 1975—. Adj. instr. dept. legal studies Temple U., 2001—. Mem. Germantown Cricket Club (Phila.). Democrat. Jewish. Avocations: tennis, squash, golf, singing. Office: Cozen O'Connor 1900 Market St Philadelphia PA 19103-3527 E-mail: Mjellinek@cozen.com.

JELLINEK, ROGER, editor; b. Mexico City, Jan. 16, 1938; came to U.S., 1961; s. Frank Louis Mark and Marguerite Lilla Donne (Lewis) J.; m. Margherita DiCenzo, Dec. 22, 1963 (div. 1984); children: Andrew Mark, Claire; m. Eden-Lee Murray, 1984; 1 child, Everett Peter Murray. Student, Bryanston Sch., Dorset, Eng., 1951-56; MA, Cambridge U., Eng., 1961. Assoc. editor Random House, 1963-64; editor Walker & Co., N.Y.C., 1964—65, N.Y. Times Book Rev., N.Y.C., 1966—70, dep. editor, 1970—73; editor in chief Times Books, Quadrangle/N.Y. Times Book Co., N.Y.C., 1974—78, sr. editor, 1978—81, editor Lamont newsletter and yearbook Palisadee, 1981—91; pres. Clairemark, Ltd., 1981—, Jellinek & Murray Lit. Agy.; editl. dir. Inner Ocean Pub., Makawao, Hawaii, 2000—. Editor Atlantic Realm Project, 1983-93; editl. dir. Inner Ocean Pub., 2000—; pub. Hawaii map series. Pres. ArtMaps Ltd., 1996—. With Royal Marines, 1956-57; 2d lt. Brit. Intelligence Corps, 1957-58. Mellon fellow Yale U., 1961-63. Home and Office: 3623 Kumu St Honolulu HI 96822-1102

JELLOWS, TRACY PATRICK, software engineer; b. Quincy, Mass., Oct. 15, 1951; s. Henry David and Dorothy Margret (Joyce) J. BS in Physics, Bridgewater (Mass.) State Coll., 1981; postgrad., U. Mass., Boston, 1982. Software engr. Lotus Devel. Corp., Cambridge, Mass., 1984-85, sr. software engr., 1985-89, prin. engr. 1-2-3 Graphics, 1989-90; prin. engr. Edsun Labs., Waltham, Mass., 1990-91; prin. engr., cons. Saturn Software, Brockton, Mass., 1991-96; prin. engr. Thomson Fin. Svcs., Boston, 1996-98; cons. engr. Saturn Software, Brockton, Mass., 1998-2000; advising engr. Lotus Devel. Corp., Cambridge, Mass., 2000—. Mem. IEEE, Assn. Computing Machinery, Aircraft Owners and Pilots Assn., Mensa. Democrat. Roman Catholic. Avocations: music, computer software and hardware, boating, general aviation. Home: 15 Westview Dr Mansfield MA 02048-1042 E-mail: tjellows@attbi.com.

JELSMA, ELIZABETH BARBARA, music educator; b. Newark, N.J., Aug. 24, 1934; d. Joseph Augsdurfer and Clara Stiehl; m. Lawrence Franklin Jelsma, June 15, 1967 (div. Sept. 30, 1976); children: Deborah Lynn, Lawrence Frank, Elizabeth Louise, Mark Andrew. B of Music Edn., Northwestern U., 1959, MusM, 1961. Tchr. 1st grade Jenner Sch., Chgo.; tchr. music grades K-8, Yavapai Sch., Scottsdale, Ariz.; pvt. piano tchr. N.J., Ill. and Ariz. Judge piano Ariz. State U., Tempe, Ariz., 1962—63; accompanist Bach Madrigal Soc., Phoenix, 1964—66. Recipient various awards for solo performances. Republican. Roman Catholic. Avocations: reading, travel, swimming.

JELUS, SUSAN CRUM, writer, editor; b. Cin., Sept. 14, 1952; d. Robert Malcolm and Jean Moses Crum; m. Raymond Jelus, Aug. 1, 1975 (div. Dec. 1989). BA, Miami U., Oxford, Ohio, 1974. Continuity mgr. Sta. WLWT TV, Cin., 1975-77; traffic mgr. Sta. WCKY-WWEZ, Cin., 1977-79; advt. coord. Cintas Corp., Cin., 1979-80; audio-visual writer-prodr. Dayton, 1981-84; tech. writer Sinclair C.C., Dayton, 1984-86; sr. instrnl. developer The Reynolds & Reynolds Co., Dayton, 1986-95; publs./on-line help author Rsch. Computer Svcs., Dayton, 1995—; editor, pub. New Song Press, Dayton, 1995—. Editor: (lit. jour.) A New Song, 1996—; contbr. poetry to anthologies and lit. mags. Bd. dirs. Hist. Dist. Archtl. Rev. Bd., Germantown, Ohio, 1990-93; campaign tng. chairperson United Way, Dayton, 1987; dir. Jr. Handbell Choir, South Park United Meth. Ch., Dayton, 1995; dir. youth choir Centerville (Ohio) United Meth. Ch., 2000-01; dir. handchime choir Huffman Pl., 2002—. Recipient Commendation award for poetry Chester H. Jones Found., 1995, Award of Merit, Soc. for Tech. Comm., 1989. Mem. AAUW, Nat. Mus. for Women in the Arts, Soc. Tech. Comm. Democrat. Avocations: painting, acoustic guitar. Office: New Song Press PO Box 629 Dayton OH 45409-0629 E-mail: editor@newsongpress.com.

JEMELIAN, JOHN NAZAR, management consultant; b. N.Y.C., May 10, 1933; s. Nazar and Angel (Jizmejian) Jemelian; m. Rose Melkonian, Nov. 22, 1958; children: Sheri, Lori, Brian, Joni. BS, U. So. Calif., 1956. CPA Calif., 1961. Mgr. audit staff Price Waterhouse & Co., Los Angeles, 1958-64; treas. The Akron, Los Angeles, 1964-82, v.p. fin., 1976, exec. v.p., 1977-82; v.p., gen. mgr., dir. Acromil Corp., City of Industry, Calif., 1982-85; sr. v.p. fin. and adminstrn., chief fin. officer, sec., treas. World Vision Inc., 1985-98; pres. Claremont Facilities Corp., 1990—, Pasadena Resources Corp., 1990-94. Dir. D.I. Engring., Inc.; fin. advisor African Enterprises, 1966—68. Bd. dirs. Pasadena Christian Sch., 1965—67, 1969—70, treas., 1965—67; chmn. bd. Donor Automation, 1975—2001; trustee Haigazian Coll., Beirut, 1974—78; deacon Lake Ave. Congl. Ch., 1964—68, trustee, 1970—73, chmn. bd. trustees, 1972—73, chmn. ch. com., 1974; chmn. bd. Media Ministries, Inc., 1975—95; trustee Narramore Christian Found., 1976—93, Met. Ministries, 1979—80; chmn. Christian Bus. Men's Com., 1979—81, 1986—87, Sahag Mesrob Armenian Christian Sch., 1980—85; deacon, elder Ch. on the Way, 1980 95; chmn. bd. dirs. Armenian Gospel Mission, 1999—; bd. dirs. Forest Home Christian Conf. Ctr., 1972—75, 1978—81, 1984—88, 1992—95, 2001—. With F.A. U.S. Army. Named Boss of Yr. Beverly Hills chpt., Nat. Secs. Assn., 1970. Mem.: AICPA, Retail Contr. Assn. (dir. 1973—74), Calif. Soc. CPA, Toastmasters-Windjammers L.A. (pres. 1963), L.A. Athletic Club, Beta Gamma Sigma, Beta Alpha Psi, Delta Sigma Pi. Home: 261 Sharon Rd Arcadia CA 91007-8044 Office: PO Box 5051 Monrovia CA 91016-3198 Fax: 626-301-1128. E-mail: jjemelia@worldvision.org.

JEMISIN, NOAH, artist, educator; b. Birmingham, Ala., Apr. 7, 1943; s. Noah Sr. and Blanche (McDolle) J.; m. Janice Erlin Finklea, 1968 (div. 1977); 1 chld, Nora K. BS in Fine Arts, Ala. State U., Montgomery, 1966; MA, U. Iowa, 1972, MFA, 1974. Exec. dir., curator Bronx River Art Ctr. and Gallery, Bronx, N.Y., 1986-90; adj. prof. C.W. Post Coll./L.I. U., Brookville, N.Y., 1992-94; master artist City Arts, N.Y.C., 1994—; artist, cons. Charter Sch., Lansing, Mich., 1996—; master artist Arts Connection, N.Y.C., 1999; instr. El Puente Acad., Bklyn., 1995—. Adj. prof. Purchase Coll.-SUNY, 1999; mem. adv. bd. Bronx River Art Ctr. and Gallery, 1986-92; mem. panel N.Y. Found. for the Arts, N.Y.C., 1997; mem. 20th Century Art panel Met. Mus. Art, N.Y.C., 1986, 87; vis. artist Parsons Sch. Design, N.Y.C., 1985. Recipient award for sculpture Pollock-Krasner Found., 1997, award for painting, 1994, 2000; award for painting N.Y. Found. for the Arts, 1994; Arts Internat. travel grantee to West Africa, 1992, 95. Avocations: reading, running, film, music (jazz). Home: 315 Berry St Brooklyn NY 11211-5130

JEMISON, MAE CAROL, physician, engineer, entrepreneur, philanthropist, educator, former astronaut; b. Decatur, Ala., Oct. 17, 1956; d. Charlie and Dorothy (Green) J. BS in ChemE, BA in African-Am. Studies, Stanford U., 1977; MD, Cornell U., 1981. Physician Peace Corps, Sierra Leone, Western Africa, 1983—85; pvt. practice L.A.; mission specialist NASA, Houston, 1987—93, astronaut on space shuttle Endeavor, 1992; prof. Dartmouth Coll., 1995—2002; mem, bd. dirs. Scholastic Inc.; national sci. literary advocate Bayer Corp., 1995—. Founder, pres. BioSentient Corp., The Jemison Group, Inc., 1993—, The Earth We Share Internat. Sci. Camp; A.D. White prof.-at-large Cornell U.; founder, pres. The Dorothy Jemison Foundation for Excellence, 1994—; mem., bd. dirs. Scholastic, Inc.; national sci. literary advocate Bayer Corp., 1995—; bd. dirs. Valspar Corp., Kimberly-Clark Corp. Author: Find Where The Wind Goes, 2001; TV host Discovery Channel, World of Wonder, 1994—95. Mem.: NAS Inst. Medicine. Achievements include being first woman of color to fly in space. Office: Jemison Group Inc PO Box 591455 Houston TX 77259

JEMMOTT, LORETTA SWEET, nursing educator; BSN, Hampton Inst., 1978; MSN in Mental Health Nursing, U. Pa., 1982, PhD in Human Sexuality Edn., 1987. Asst. prof. nursing Rutgers U. Coll. of Nursing, Newark, 1987-93, assoc. prof. nursing, 1993-94; dir. Ctr. for AIDS Rsch. Columbia U. Sch. Nursing, N.Y.C., 1994-95; assoc. HIV Ctr. for Clin. & Behaviors Studies Columbia U. and N.Y. State Psychiatric Inst., N.Y.C., 1994—; vis. rsch. scholar dept. psychology Princeton U., NJ, 1995—; rsch. assoc. Population Studies Ctr. U. Pa., Phila., 1995—, assoc. prof. grad. sch. edn., 1995—, assoc. prof. nursing Ctr. for Urban Health Rsch., 1995—, dir. Ctr. for Urban Health Rsch. Sch. Nursing, 1996—. Contbr. articles to profl. pubs. Fellow Am. Acad. Nursing, 1992; recipient Outstanding Nursing Achievement and Rsch. award Concerned Black Nurses, 1989, Outstanding Service award, Rutgers Coll. Nursing, 1990, Gov. of N.J. Nurse Merit award in Advanced Nursing Practice, 1992, Outstanding Rsch. award Northern N.J. Black Nurses Assn., 1992, Congressional Merit award, 1995. Mem.: Inst. of Medicine, 1999-. Office: U Pa Ctr for Urban Health Rsch Philadelphia PA 19104 also: U Penn Sch of Nursing 420 Gaurdian Dr Rm 345 NEB Philadelphia PA 19104-6096 E-mail: jemmott@pobox.upenn.edu.

JEN, FRANK CHIFENG, finance and management educator; b. Shanghai, May 15, 1931; came to U.S., 1957; s. Seybold E. and Susan (Lin) J.; m. Daisy Chi, Aug. 26, 1962; children: Amy K., Wendy K., Edward K. BS, N. Central Coll., 1959; MBA, U. Wis., 1960, PhD, 1963. Asst. prof. finance SUNY, Buffalo, 1964-66, assoc. prof., 1966-68, prof., 1968-97, chmn. dept. fin., 1967-70, Mfrs. & Traders Trust Co.'s prof. banking/fin. to emeritus, 1972-97, 97—, Univ. rsch. scholar, 2002—, chmn. dept. fin., 1967-70, chmn. dept. operating analysis, 1970-77, dir. bank mgmt. inst. and advanced comml. lending program, 1977-97, co-dir., dir. China MBA program, 1984-91, univ. rsch. scholar, 2002—. Vis. prof. Dalian (China) U. Tech., 1980—; Am. dir. Consulting and Rsch. Ctr. Nat. Mgmt. Ctr., Dalian U. Tech., 1995—. Contbr. articles to profl. jours. Mem. Am. Fin. Assn., Am. Econ. Assn., Soc. Econ. and Fin. Mgmt. in China (pres. 1985-88), Pi Gamma Mu, Beta Gamma Sigma. Home: 287 Forestview Dr Buffalo NY 14221-1439 Office: SUNY Buffalo Sch Mgmt Jacobs Ctr Amherst NY 14260-0001 E-mail: frankjen@buffalo.edu.

JEN, JOSEPH JWU-SHAN, federal agency administrator; b. Chung King, Sichuan, China, May 8, 1939; arrived in U.S., 1962; s. H.C. and Lucia (Chang) J.; m. Salina Fond, Sept. 4, 1965; children: Joanne Pauline, Jeffrey Jay. BS, Nat. Taiwan U., 1960; MS, Wash. State U., 1964; PhD, U. Calif., Berkeley, 1969; MBA, So. Ill. U., 1986. Asst. prof. Clemson (S.C.) U., 1969-74; rsch. food technologist U.S. Dept. Agr., Beltsville, Md., 1975; assoc. prof. Clemson (S.C.) U., 1974-79, prof., 1979; assoc. prof. Mich. State U., East Lansing, 1979-80; mgr. Campbell Soup Co., Camden, N.J., 1980-83, dir., 1983-86; chmn. divsn. food sci. and tech. U. Ga., Athens, 1986-92; dean Coll. Agr. Calif. Poly. State U., San Luis Obispo, 1992—2001; under sec. rsch., edn. and econ. USDA, Washington, 2001—. Vis. prof. Nat. Taiwan U., 1976. Editor: Chemistry and Function of Pectin, 1986, Quality Factors of Fruits and Vegetables, 1989; contbr. articles to profl. jours. Recipient Cert. of Merit, Ministry of Econ. Affairs, Rep. of China, 1980, Ministry of Agr., Rep. of China, 1988, Disting. Educator award, NACTA, 1999, Grad. Alumni achievement award, Wash. State U., 2002. Fellow Inst. Food Technologists (chmn. fruits and vegetable products 1988-89); mem. Am. Chem. Soc., Chinese Am. Food Soc. (pres. 1977, Profl. Achievement award 1986), Sigma Xi. Achievements include first to hydropho-

bic chromatography in food enzyme research; development of high quality dehydrated vegetable pieces; establishment of teaching and research program in food processing in China and Taiwan; established innovative public/private partnership programs at Colif. Poly. State U. Office: USDA Research, Edn & Econ 1400 Independence Ave SW Washington DC 20250 Office Fax: 202-690-2842.

JENCKS, CHRISTOPHER SANDYS, public policy educator; b. Balt., Oct. 22, 1936; s. Francis Haynes and Elizabeth (Pleasants) J. BA, Harvard U., 1958, M.Ed., 1959; postgrad., London Sch. Econs., 1959-61; LL.D., Kalamazoo Coll., 1969; D.Litt., Columbia Coll., 1983. Assoc. editor New Republic mag., 1961-63; fellow Inst. Policy Studies, Washington, 1963-67; mem. faculty Harvard U., 1967-80, 96—, prof., 1973-80, 96—, Malcolm Wiener prof. social policy, 1998—; John D. MacArthur prof. sociology and urban affairs Northwestern U., Evanston, Ill., 1980-96; vis. prof. U. Chgo., 1994-95. Author: (with David Riesman) The Academic Revolution, 1968, (with others) Inequality, 1972, Who Gets Ahead?, 1979, (with Paul Peterson) The Urban Underclass, 1991, Rethinking Social Policy, 1992, The Homeless, 1994, (with Meredith Phillips) The Black-White Test Score Gap, 1998. Guggenheim fellow, 1967-68, 82-83, Inst. for Advanced Study fellow, 1985-86, Russell Sage Found. fellow, 1991-92, Ctr. for Advanced Study in Behavioral Scis., 1997-98, 2001-02. Mem.: Nat. Acad. Scis. Office: Harvard U Kennedy Sch Govt Cambridge MA 02138

JENDA, OVERTOUN MALANDULA, mathematician, educator, mathematician, researcher, dean; b. Mzimba, Malawi, Aug. 29, 1954; arrived in US, 1977; s. Gehazi Malandula Jenda and Tafwakose Kawamba; m. Claudine Arnold Longwe, Nov. 16, 1957; children: Overtoun Malandula Jr., Emily Temwa. BS, U. Malawi, Zomba, 1976; MA, U. Ky., 1978, PhD, 1981. Assoc. lectr. Chancellor Coll., Zomba, 1976—77, lectr., 1981—84, acting head math. dept., 1983—84, students warden, 1981—84; lectr. U. Botswana, Gaborone, Malawi, 1984—87; vis. asst. prof. U. Ky., Lexington, 1987—88; asst. prof. Auburn (Ala.) U., 1988—92, assoc. prof., 1992—97, prof., 1997—, dir., 1994—2000, acting head dept., 2001, assoc. dean, 2000—. Vis. prof. U. Waterloo, Ont., Canada, 2001—01. Co-author: (graduate and research textbook) Relative Homological Algebra, 2000; contbr. articles to profl. jours. Recipient Outstanding Achievement for Minorities award, Auburn U. Alumni Assn., 2001; AFGRAD fellow, African-American Inst., 1977—81. Mem.: Nat. Assn. Mathematicians, Am. Math. Soc., Math. Assn. Am., Nat. Geog. Soc. Democrat. Achievements include introduced Gorenstein injective, projective, and flat modules in Algebra; development of recruiting and retention programs at Auburn University. Avocations: travel, movies, reading, gardening. Home: 641 Elizabeth Dr Auburn AL 36830-7118 Office: Auburn Univ Dept Math Auburn AL 36849-5310 Office Fax: 334-844-4661. Personal E-mail: jendaov@auburn.edu. E-mail: jendaov@auburn.edu.

JENDEN, DONALD JAMES, pharmacologist, educator; b. Horsham, Sussex, Eng., Sept. 1, 1926; came to U.S., 1950, naturalized, 1958; s. William Herbert and Kathleen Mary (Harris) J.; m. Jean Ickeringill, Nov. 18, 1950; children: Tricia Jenden Billes, Peter Donald, Beverly Jean Jenden Riedlinger. BSc in Physiology with 1st class honours, Kings Coll. London, 1947; MB, BS with honours, U. London, 1950; PhD in Pharm. Chemistry (hon.), U. Uppsala, Sweden, 1980. Demonstrator pharmacology U. London, 1948-49; lectr. pharmacology U. Calif.-San Francisco, 1950-51, asst. prof. pharmacology, 1952-53; mem. faculty UCLA, 1953, assoc. prof., 1956-60, prof. pharmacology, 1960—, prof. pharmacology and biomath., 1967—, chmn. dept. pharmacology, 1968-89. Wellcome vis. prof. U. Ala., Birmingham, 1984; mem. brain research inst. UCLA, 1961—. Contbr. articles in field. Served to lt. comdr. M.C., USNR, 1954-58. USPHS Postdoctoral fellow, 1951-53, NSF Sr. Postdoctoral fellow; hon. research assoc. Univ. Coll., London, 1961-62; Fulbright Short-Term Sr. Scholar award, Australia, 1983; recipient Univ. Gold medal U. London, 1950. Fellow Am. Coll. Neuropsychopharmacology, West Coast Coll. Biol. Psychiatry (charter); mem. AAAS, Am. Soc. Pharmacology and Exptl. Therapeutics, Am. Physiol. Soc., Physiol. Soc. (London), Soc. Neurosci., Am. Chem. Soc., Western Pharmacology Soc. (pres. 1970), Assn. for Med. Sch. Pharmacology, Am. Soc. Neurochemistry, Internat. Union Pharmacology. Home: 3814 Castlerock Rd Malibu CA 90265-5625 E-mail: jenden@ucla.edu.

JENE, JOANNE, anesthesiologist; b. Portland, Oreg., June 15, 1935; d. John and Clara (Hoffmann) J. BA, Willamette U., 1957; MD, Oreg. Health and Scis. U., 1960. Diplomate Am. Bd. Anesthesiology. Intern Phila. Gen. Hosp., 1960-61; resident Oreg. Health and Scis. U., Portland, 1961-63; instr. dept. anesthesiology U. Calif., San Francisco, 1963-64; staff physician Legacy Emanuel Hosp., Portland, 1964—. Chmn. Bd. of Med. Exam., State of Oreg., 1991-92. Mem. Oreg. Women's Forum, Portland, 1990—, Mazama, Portland, 1964—, YWCA, Portland, 1991—; vol. Project HOPE; past pres. Project HOPE Alumni Assn.; bd. dirs. Found. for Med. Excellence, 1986-97, pres., 1996. Recipient Outstanding Alumni citation, Willamette U., 1968, Disting. Svc. award, Oreg. Soc. Anesthesiologists, 1999, Treasure of Emanuel award, Emanuel Hosp. Found., 2001, Dr. Citizen of Yr. award, Oreg. Med. Assn., 2001. Mem. Am. Soc. Anesthesiologists (bd. dirs. 1986-99, asst. sec. 1994-97, sec. 1997-99), Am. Coll. Physician Execs., Oreg. Soc. Anesthesiologists (past pres.), Oreg. Med. Assn., Multnomah County Med. Soc., City Club of Portland. Avocations: photography, travel, golf, cooking. Office: Oreg Anesthesiology Group 140 NW 14th # 300 Portland OR 97209 Fax: (503) 222-2828. E-mail: jenejo@aol.com.

JENEFSKY, JACK, wholesale company executive; b. Oct. 27, 1919; s. David and Anna (Saeks) Jenefsky; m. Beverly J. Mueller, Feb. 23, 1962; 1 child, Anna Elizabeth 1 stepchild, Cathryn Jean Mueller. BSBA, Ohio State U., 1941; postgrad., Harvard Bus. Sch., 1943; MA in Econs., U. Dayton, 1948. Surplus broker, Dayton, 1946—48; sales rep. Remington Rand-Univac, Dayton, 1949—56, mgr. AF acct., 1957—59, br. mgr. Dayton, 1960—61, regional mktg. cons. Midwest region, 1962—63; pres. Bowman Supply Co., Dayton, 1963—. Selection adv. bd. Air Force Acad., 3d congl. dist. chmn., 1974—82; chmn. 3d dist. screening bds. Mil. Acad., 1976—82; coord. Great Lakes region, res. assistance program CAP, 1970—73. From pvt. to capt. USAAF, 1942—46, CBI, maj. USAF, 1951—53, col. Res. Mem.: Miami Valley Mil. Affairs Assn. (trustee 1985—, pres. bd. trustees 1987—88), Nat. Sojourners (pres. Dayton 1961—62), Ohio State U. Alumni Assn. (pres. Montgomery County, Ohio 1959—60), Dayton Area C. of C. (chmn. spl. events com. 1970—72, chmn. rsch. com. on mil. affairs 1983—87), Air Force Assn. (comdr. Ohio wing 1957—58, 1958—59), Res. Officers Assn. (pres. Ohio dept. 1956—57, nat. coun. 1957—58, chmn. R&D com. 1961—62), Harvard Bus. Sch. Club Dayton (pres. 1961—62, chmn. selection com., Fed. Govt. Employee of Yr. 1991, 1992), Lions. Jewish. Home: 136 Briar Heath Cir Dayton OH 45415-2601 Office: Bowman Supply Co PO Box 1404 Dayton OH 45401-1404 E-mail: bowmansupply@att.net.

JENES, THEODORE GEORGE, JR., retired career officer; b. Portland, Oreg., Feb. 21, 1930; s. Theodore George and Mable Marie (Moon) Jenes; m. Beverly Lorraine Knutson, Jan. 29, 1953; children: Ted, Mark. BS, U. Ga., 1956; MS, Auburn U., 1969; grad., Army Command and Gen. Staff Coll., Armed Forces Staff Coll., Air War Coll.; LLD (hon.), U. Akron, 1986. Enlisted U.S. Army, 1951, commd. 2d lt., 1953, advanced through grades to lt. gen., 1984, various assignments, 1953-75; comdr. 3d Brigade, 2d Inf. Div., Republic of Korea, 1975-76, 172d Inf. Brigade, Ft. Richardson, Alaska, 1978-81; dep. commdg. gen. U.S. Army Tng. Ctr., Ft. Dix, N.J., 1976-78; comdr. 4th Inf. Div., Ft. Carson, Colo., 1982-84; dep. commdg. gen. U.S. Army Combined Arms Combat Devel. Activity, Ft. Leavenworth, Kans., 1981-82; comdg. gen. 3d U.S. Army, Ft. McPherson, Ga., 1984-87; commander U.S. Army Forces Ctrl. Command, Ft. McPherson, Ga., 1984-87; dep. comdg. gen. hdqrs. U.S. Army Forces Command, Ft. McPherson, Ga., 1984-87, ret., 1987; cons. Burdeshaw and Assocs., 1987-88; gen. mgr. Seattle Tennis Club, 1988-94. Decorated D.S.M., Legion of Merit, Bronze Star, Meritorious Service medal, Air medal, Army Commendation medal, Vietnamese Cross of Gallantry with Silver Star. Mem.: Am. Hellenic Ednl. Progressive Assn., Assn. U.S. Army, Rotary. United Methodist. Avocations: reading military history, golf. Home: 809 169th Pl SW Lynnwood WA 98037-3307 Fax: 425-745-8068.

JENG, HELENE WU, administrative librarian; b. Taipei, Taiwan, July 23, 1938; came to U.S., 1966; d. Shou-Li and Mei-Tze (Huang) Wu; m. Bih-Jing Jeng, Nov. 27, 1971; children: Henry David, Lana Keren. BA, Soochow U., Taipei, 1962; MLS, Appalachian State U., 1968. Asst. to dir. Nat. Sci. Mus., Taipei, 1962-64; pub. asst. Taiwan Power co., Taipei, 1964-66; head libr. Lancaster Extension/U. S.C., 1968-73, Villa Julie Coll., Balt., 1974-78; libr. Mt. Wilson State Hosp., Balt., 1978-81; reference libr. U.S. Army Med. Rsch. Inst., Edge, Md., 1981-83; adminstrv. libr. Md. Dept. of Planning, Balt., 1983—. Elder, Balt. Taiwanese Presbyn. Ch., Randallstown, Md., 1997; pres. Taiwanese Am. Assn., Balt. and Columbia, Md., 1986. Mem. ALA, Md. Libr. Assn. Republican. Avocations: reading, classical music, performing arts, travel, sightseeing. Home: 16 Woodholme Village Ct Pikesville MD 21208-1408 Office: Md Dept of Planning Libr 301 W Preston St Ste 1101 Baltimore MD 21201-2392

JENG, TZYY-WEN, biochemist, researcher; b. Taichung, Taiwan, Nov. 2, 1947; came to U.S., 1974; s. Ching-Po and Yu-Ju (Wong) J.; m. Kwan-Yee Sum; children: Howard L., Way A. BS, Nat. Taiwan U., Taipei, 1970; PhD, U. Calif., Berkeley, 1978. Rsch. assoc. U. Ariz., Tucson, 1979-84, rsch. asst. prof., 1984-86, rsch. specialist and rsch. asst. prof., 1986-88; sr. rsch. biochemist Abbott Labs., Abbott Park, Ill., 1988-90, rsch. investigator, 1991-92, assoc. rsch. fellow, 1992—. Author: Natural Toxins, 1980; contbr. articles to Jour. Molecular Biology. Wilhelm Bernard Fund grantee Internat. Congress on Electron Microscopy, 1982. Mem. N.Y. Acad. Scis. Achievements include patents in field. Office: Abbott Labs AP 20 100 Abbott Park Rd Apt 20 Abbott Park IL 60064-3502

JENIKE, MICHAEL ANDREW, psychiatrist, educator; b. Edinburgh, Scotland, May 8, 1945; m. Julie Ann Ryan; children: Lisa, Eric, Sara. BS, Tufts U., 1967; MS, U. Mass., 1969; MD, U. Okla., 1978. Intern U. Okla., Oklahoma City, 1978-79; resident in internal medicine Mass. Gen. Hosp., Boston, 1979-82; instr. dept. psychiatry Harvard U., Boston, 1982-83, from asst. prof. psychiatry to assoc. prof., 1983-94, prof., 1995—; assoc. chief of psychiatry Mass. Gen. Hosp., Boston, 1986—. Author: Handbook of Geriatric Psychopharmacology, 1985, Geriatric Psychiatry and Psychopharmacology: A Clinical Approach, 1989; editor: Obsessional Disorders, 1992; co-editor (with L. Baer and W.E. Minichiello): Obsessive-Compulsive Disorders: Theory and Management., 1986, 1990, Obsessive-Compulsive Disorders: Practical Management, 1998; co-editor: (with M. Asberg) Understanding Obsessive Compulsive Disorder, 1990; co-editor: (with S.E. Hyman) Manual of Clinical Problems in Psychiatry, 1990; contbr. articles to profl. jours. Capt. USAF, 1969-73, Vietnam. Dupont-Warren fellow Harvard U. Med. Sch., 1982. Mem. Am. Geriatrics Soc., Am. Psychiat. Assn., AMA, AAAS, Am. Assn. Geriatric Psychiatry, Alpha Omega Alpha. Avocations: swimming, running, basketball. Office: Mass Gen Hosp Dept Psychiatry 13th St Bldg 149 Fl 9 Charlestown MA 02129

JEN-JACOBSON, LINDA, biochemist, educator; b. Kunming, China, Oct. 29, 1941; PhD, U. Ill., 1967. Assoc. prof. U. Pitts., 1993—98, prof., 1998—. Rschr. U. Pitts., 1967—. Fellow: AAAS; mem.: Am. Soc. Biochemistry and Molecular Biology, Protein Soc., Biophys. Soc. Office: U Pitts Dept Biol Scis Pittsburgh PA 15217-1308 Fax: 412-624-4759. E-mail: ljen@pitt.edu.

JENKIN, JAMES THOMAS, videotape editor; b. Monclair, N.J., Apr. 28, 1964; s. David Alan and Dolores Ann (Hyland) J. Student, Raritan Valley Coll., Somerville, N.J., 1987-88; cert. advanced non-linear editing, Avid Sch. Forman Rising Sun Coatings, Flemington, N.J., 1985-89; with dept. videotape playback Picsonic Prodns., N.Y.C., 1989-91, videotape editor, 1991—; sr. editor program Headliners and Legends MSNBC, 1999—2002, sr. editor primetime unit, 2002—; pres. TBM Prodns., Hoboken, NJ. Pres. Thought Bubble Media. Contbr. articles to mags. Recipient various Telly awards, 1991, 92, 95, Communicator award, 1997, Videographer award, 1998, Silver medal NY Festival, 2001. Mem. Internat. TV Soc. Avocations: music composition, softball, tennis, movie research. E-mail: TBMedia@aol.com.

JENKINS, ALBERT FELTON, JR., lawyer; b. Madison, Ga., Jan. 18, 1941; s. A. Felton and Jimmie Lucille (Davis) J.; m. Julie Richardson Green, Apr. 16, 1966; children: A. Felton III, Emily Green, Alan Davis. AB, U. Ga., 1963, LLB, 1965. Bar: Ga. 1965, U.S. Dist. Ct. (no. dist.) Ga. 1965, U.S. Ct. Appeals GA. 1965, U.S. Ct. Appeals (4th cir.) 1981, U.S. Ct. Appeals (5th cir.) 1966, U.S. Ct. Appeals (11th cir.) 1981, U.S. Ct. Appeals (D.C. cir.) 1987, U.S. Supreme Ct. 1968. Assoc. King & Spalding, Atlanta, 1965-70, ptnr., 1971-92, ret. ptnr., 1992—. Chmn. bd. visitors U. Ga. Law Sch., Athens, 1974; mem. Gov.'s Appellate Jud. Selection Com., Atlanta, 1972-73, Gov.'s Jud. process Rev. Com., Atlanta, 1984-85, Ga. Joint Study Commn. on Revenue Structure, 1992-95, Ga. Agrl. Exposition Authority; dir. Dundee Mills, Inc., 1994-95. Co-author: (2 vol. treatise) Georgia Civil Procedure Forms-Practice, 1988. Sec. U. Ga. Bd. Trustees, 1979-85; chmn., pres. Atlanta Unit Am. Cancer Soc., 1982-83; trustee Atlanta Fulton Pub. Libr. Sys., 1995-97. Sgt. Air Nat. Guard, 1965-71. Fellow Am. Bar Found.; mem. State Bar of Ga. (pres. Young Lawyers 1972-73, bd. govs. 1983-91), Piedmont Driving Club (Atlanta), Phi Beta Kappa, Omicron Delta Kappa. Methodist. Office: King & Spalding 191 Peachtree St SW Ste 4100 Atlanta GA 30303-1763

JENKINS, ALEXANDER, III, business executive; b. Weymouth, Mass., Feb. 17, 1934; s. Alexander and Eva Gladys (Price) J.; m. Judith H. Switzer, Jan. 4, 1975; children: Alexander Tuxbury, Edith Garland, Charles Jordan. BS, Yale U., 1956; MBA, Harvard U., 1961. Rsch. asst. Harvard Bus. Sch., Boston, 1961-62; treas. Ocean Rsch. Equip., Inc., Falmouth, Mass., 1962-65, 77-78, Orion Rsch., Inc., Cambridge, Mass., 1962-70, exec. v.p., 1970-71; pvt. practice cons. Cambridge, Mass., 1971-79; v.p. Adcole, Cambridge, Mass., 1972-77; pres. Jenkins Trading Inc., Chelsea, Mass., 1973-91; prin. Sormani Calendars divsn., Chelsea, 1991—. Treas., dir. Pintek, Inc., 1979-81; div. mgr. Spectra Physics, 1980-81; pres., CEO Orion Rsch., Inc., Cambridge, 1981-88, chmn., chief exec. officer, 1988-89; pvt. cons., 1989—, treas. Jenkins Trading Inc. (dba Sormani Calendars) 1991—; bd. dirs. Reagecon Diagnostics Ltd. With USN, 1956-59. Episcopalian. Home: 37 Breakwater Dr Chelsea MA 02150-4024 Office: 121 Webster Ave Chelsea MA 02150 E-mail: sormani@mindspring.com.

JENKINS, ALICE MARIE, secondary school educator; b. Adair, Iowa, June 7, 1922; d. Charles Erwin Hall and Elizabeth Catherine Clarke Hall; m. Doyce Gwendon Pitts, June 27, 1943 (dec. Mar. 27, 1977); 1 child, Beverly Lou; m. Richard Jenkins, June 24, 1978. BA, Drake U., 1963. Tchr. rural and county schs., 1940—54, Linden (Iowa) Pub. Sch., 1954—55, Woodward (Iowa) State, 1955—60, 1971—93, Boone (Iowa) Pub. Sch., 1960—71, Woodward Cmty., 1993—. Mem.: VFW, Am. Legion Aux. (past pres.), Alpha Delta Kappa (past pres.). Democrat. Methodist. Avocations: cooking, reading, music. Office: Woodward-Granger HS 306 W 3rd St Woodward IA 50276-1033

JENKINS, ALYCE MITCHEM, secondary school educator, writer; b. Harvard, Ill., Nov. 3, 1935; d. John Foster and Queenie Black Mitchem; m. Reese Valmer Jenkins, Dec. 27, 1962; children: David William, Elizabeth Ann Jenkins Manfredi. BA, U. Colo., 1957; MS, U. Wis., 1961. Cert. tchr. Ill., Wis., Ohio, N.J. English tchr. Crystal Lake (Ill.) H.S., 1957—60; demonstration tchr. No. Ill. U., DeKalb, 1961—62; English, social studies tchr. H. Schenk Jr. H.S., Madison, Wis., 1962—66; homebound tchr. Cleve. Pub. Schs., 1971—76, 1977—78; tchr. social studies Laurel Sch., Shaker Heights, Ohio, 1977—78; English instr. Kean U., Union, NJ, 1980; social studies, English tchr. Middlesex (N.J.) H.S., 1980—85, 1993—94; freelance writer, 1985—. Founder, leader Rainbow Writers, Bridgewater, 1992—95. Author: Lost in a Blizzard, 2001; co-author: College Board Achievement: English Composition, 1988; contbr. over 100 articles to adult and juvenile periodicals. Founder, leader Connected Hearts Adoption Triad Support, North Plainfield, NJ, 1997—; instr., mentor Sisters Aftercare, Bridgewater, NJ, 2001—03; adv. bd. N.J. Adoption Resource Clearing House, 2003—; mem. Presbyn. Women, 1997—. Fellow Knapp Grad., U. Wis., 1960—61. Mem.: Bound Brook Writers, Soc. Children's Book Writers and Illustrators (award com., Mag. Merit awards 1999, Mag. Merit award 1996), Pi Lambda Theta, Kappa Delta Pi, Phi Beta Kappa. Democrat. Presbyterian. Avocations: genealogy, reading, gardening, correspondence, grandchildren. Home: 11 Clifton Ave New Brunswick NJ 08901 Personal E-mail: alycemj@aol.com.

JENKINS, ANTHONY CHARLES, correspondent; b. London, Apr. 13, 1956; came to U.S., 1986; s. Victor Silberstein and Anne Elizabeth Jenkins de Blanes; m. Jayne H. Tsuchiyama, Jan. 5, 1995; 1 child, Max. BA, Durham U., U.K., 1978. Sr. account exec. Internat. Mktg., London, 1980-82; Nicaragua corr. Guardian Newspaper, London, 1982-85, sr. corr. Central Am. and Caribbean, 1985-86; N.Y. corr. Expresso, Lisbon, Portugal, 1986-89, N.Am. bur. chief N.Y.C., NY, 1989—. Author: Nicaragua and the U.S.A. Years of Conflict, 1989, Nicaragua A Decade of Rebellion, 1991; contbr. articles to profl. jours. Pres. Durham Students' Union, 1978-79; gen. sec. Fgn. Corr. Assn., Nicaragua, 1984-86. Recipient Gazeta Prize, Journalists' Assn., Portugal, 1988. Fellow Ctr. Internat. Policy; mem. UN Corrs. Assn. (pres. 2003—). Avocations: skiing, sailing, flying. Office: Expresso Rm S-360 UN New York NY 10017

JENKINS, BILLIE BEASLEY, film company executive; b. Topeka, June 27, 1943; d. Arthur and Etta Mae Capelton; m. Rudolph Alan Jenkins, Nov. 1, 1935; 1 child, Tina Caprice. Student, Santa Monica City Coll., 1965-69. Exec. sec. to v.p. prodn. Screen Gems, L.A., 1969-72; exec. asst. Spelling/Goldberg Prodns., 1972-82; dir. adminstrn. The Leonard Co./Mandy Films, 1982-85, v.p., 1985-87; exec. asst. to pres. and chief oper. officer 20th Century Fox Film Corp., L.A., 1986-87, dir. adminstrn., 1987-90, dir. prodn. svcs. & resources Fox Motion Pictures div., 1990-92. Program coord. Am. Film Inst. Gary Hendler Minority Filmmakers Program, 1990-93; pres., CEO Masala Prodns., Inc., 1991—. Asst. to exec. producer: (films) War Games, 1984, Spacecamp, 1986; (movies for TV) Something about Amelia, 1984, Alex, The Life of a Child, 1985; (series) Paper Dolls, 1985, Cavanaughs, 1987, Charlie's Angels, Rookies, others; exec. prodn. cons. (documentary) The Good, The Bad, The Beautiful, 1995-96. Commr. L.A. City Cultural Heritage Commn., 1992-93. Named 1991 Woman of Excellence, Boy Scouts Am.; honored First African-Am. Women Pioneers of So. Calif. Top Ladies of Distinction City of Angels chpt. L.A., 1999. Mem.: Motivating Our Students Through Experience (mem. exec. bd.), Ind. FeatureProdns./West, Am. Film Inst., Black Women's Network, Women in Film Assn. (pres. 1991, 1992, advisor to exec. bd. 1993—95), Top Ladies of Distinctions. Avocations: photography, gardening, writing. E-mail: masalainc@aol.com.

JENKINS, BRENDA GWENETTA, early childhood and special education specialist; b. Durham, N.C., Aug. 11, 1949; d. Brinton Alfred and Ophelia Arden (Eaton) Jenkins. BS, Howard U., 1971, MEd, 1972; postgrad., Trinity Coll., Am. U., U. D.C., Marymount Coll., 1976—. Cert. tchr., Washington; cert. Advanced Grad. Studies Spl. Edn., aerobics instr., Nat. Dance Exercise Instr.'s Tng. Assn. Cheerleading coach Howard U., Washington, 1971-86; aerobics instr. D.C. Pub. Schs., Washington, 1982-97, tchr.; v.p. Nerdlihc Corp., Washington, 1985—; co-owner Fantasia Early Learning Acad., Washington, 1985-98; ptnr. Jenkins, Trapp-Dukes and Yates Partnership., Washington, 1984; instr. aerobics Washington Dept. Recreation, Washington, 1988-93; instr. You Fit, Inc. Nat. Children's Ctr. Washington, 1991-93, Anthony Bowen YMCA, Washington, 1992-93; instr. health, nutrition support Rockville, Md., 1992; instr., coach Maryvale PomPom/cheerleaders, Montgomery County, Md., 1992-94, asst. chmn. tchr. collabrative program, 1992-94, co-chair program com. tchr. collaborative, 1995-96; fitness instr. Oxedine Performing Arts Acad., Prince George's County, 1995-96; Goals 2000 English, lang. arts, history writer D.C. Pub. Schs., 1995-96. Aerobic instr. handicapped Coun. Exceptional Children, Washington, 1982, recreation svcs., City of Rockville, 1986—; developer My Spl. Friend program, 1984, BJ's Thinking Cap, 1991, Learning Creations, 1994, Girlfriends; bldg. rep. Washington Tchrs. Union AFT, AFL-CIO, 1987-89, 91-94, 1996, asst. bldg. rep., 1990-91, 94-95, bldg. rep. 1997—; supr. foster grandparent program Sharpe Health Sch., 1988—; trainer AIDS in Workplace, 1990, Early Childhood Substance Abuse Project Tng., 1992-93, Substance Abuse Prevention Edn., 1995, Metro Foster Grandparent Program, Washington, 1992-93; mem. preschool adv. bd. D.C. Pub. Schs., 1992-93, coordinating curriculum coun., 1994-96; master tchr. Coop. Tchr. Corp., 1993; curriculum writer, 1993; v.p. spl. edn. Washington Tchrs. Union Local 6, 1994--; stds. specialist, 1997—; presenter in field; del. 75th convention Am. Fed. Tchrs., 1998; mem. adv. bd. Supt.'s Tchr. Affairs, 1999; mem. Spl. Edn. State Adv. Panel, Washington, 1998-2000, D.C. Parent Tng. and Info. Ctr., ARC, Inc. Adv. Panel; exec. bd. dirs. Assembly of Petworth, 1998--; D.C. Pub. Schs. recruiter Nat. Alliance Black Sch. Educators, Nashville, 1999, resident mentor tchr., 1999--; mem. Disting. Educators Roundtable, 1998; presenter creative dance workshops Washington Srs. Wellness Ctr., 2003. Singer: 2000 Voices Lincoln Meml., 2000. Active D.C. Spl. Edn. State Adv., 1998, presenter AFT Civil, Human, Women's Rights Conf., 1998; Internat. Space Camp, Huntsville, Ala., 1998. Recipient Outstanding Svc. award Kappa Delta Pi, 1978, 79, 81, 82, 84, citation Washington Tchr. Union, 1985, State winner Elem. Level Nat. Citizenship Edn. Tchr.'s award Ladies Aux. VFW, Washington, 2002-03.; named DC Tchr. of Yr. Coun. Chief State Sch. Officers, 1998; grantee spl. edn. DC Pub. Sch. state office, 1993, Citibank, 1994; named to Hall of Fame Bison Found. Inc., Howard U., 1995; recipient Washington Post grants in the arts, 1999-2000, 2000-01, 01-02, Masonic Scottish Rite Educator excellence award, 2001, recipient Elem. Level Nat. Citizenship Edn. Tchr. award VFW, 2002-2003. Mem.: ASCD, Am. Fedn. Tchrs. (presiding officer WTU Spl. Educator and Svc. Provider Forums 1998—, tchr. speaker on Capitol Hill 1999, 2000, sch. to careers tchr. extern 2001, tchr. speaker on Capitol Hill 2001, DCPS new tchr. orientation trainer 2001, new tchr. coord. 2001—, DCPS new tchr. orientation trainer 2002, 2003, mem. 2000 voices at Lincoln Meml., Washington, D.C., Nat. State Tchrs. of Yr.), Coun. Exceptional Children, Howard Alumni Cheerleaders Assn. (co-founder 1977, pres. 1990—94, v.p. 1998—, Outstanding Recognition award 1984, Recognition award named Brenda G. Jenkins Outstanding Cheerleader award 1987), D.C. Parents and Friends of Children with Special Needs (bd. dirs., mem. critical ptnrs. group/supts. task force 2003), Kappa Delta Pi (convocation presenter, Balt. 1999, exec. com. Theta Alpha chpt.). Democrat. Avocations: alumni cheerleading, fashion design, cooking, dancing, poetry writing.

JENKINS, BRUCE STERLING, federal judge; b. Salt Lake City, Utah, May 27, 1927; s. Joseph and Bessie Pearl (Iverson) J.; m. Margaret Watkins, Sept. 19, 1952; children— Judith Margaret, David Bruce, Michael Glen, Carol Alice. BA with high honors, U. Utah, 1949, LLB, JD, U. Utah, 1952. Bar: Utah 1952, U.S. Dist. Ct. 1952, U.S. Supreme Ct. 1962, U.S. Circuit Ct. Appeals 1962. Pvt. practice, Salt Lake City, 1952-59; assoc. firm George McMillan, 1959-65; asst. atty. gen. State of Utah, 1952; dep. county atty. Salt Lake County, 1954-58; bankruptcy judge U.S. Dist. Ct., Utah, 1965-78, judge, 1978—, chief judge, 1984-93. Adj. prof. U. Utah, 1987-88, 95-99. Research, publs. in field; contbr. essays to Law jours.; bd. editors: Utah Law Rev, 1951-52. Mem. Utah Senate, 1959-65, minority leader, 1963, pres. senate, 1965, vice chmn. commn. on orgn. exec. br. of Utah Govt., 1965-66; Mem. adv. com. Utah Tech. Coll., 1967-72; mem. instl. council Utah State U., 1976. Served with USN, 1945-46. Named Alumnus of Yr. award Coll. Law Univ. Utah, 1985; recipient Admiration and Appreciation award Utah State Bar, 1995, Emeritus Merit of Honor award U. Utah Alumni Assn., 1997. Fellow Am. Bar Found.; mem. ABA, Am. Inn Ct., Utah State Bar Assn. (Judge of Yr. 1993), Salt Lake County Bar Assn., Fed. Bar Assn. (Disting. Svc. awrd Utah chpt. 1993), Order of Coif, Phi Beta Kappa, Phi Kappa Phi, Phi Eta Sigma, Phi Sigma Alpha, Tau Kappa Alpha. Democrat. Mem. Lds Ch. Office: US Dist Ct 462 US Courthouse 350 S Main St Salt Lake City UT 84101-2106

JENKINS, CHARLES H., JR., retail company executive; m. Dorothy Chao; children: Jennifer, Anthony. BBA in bus. adminstrn., Emory U., 1964, MBA in bus. adminstrn., 1965; PhD, Harvard Bus. Sch. Asst. to real estate v.p. Publix, 1969, v.p., 1974, exec. v.p., 1988, chmn. exec. com., 1990—2000, COO, 2000, CEO, 2001—. Pres. Lakeland C. of C. Mem.: Boston Symphony Orch. Bd. of Overseers. Office: Publix Super Markets Inc 3300 Airport Rd Lakeland FL 33811

JENKINS, CLARENCE WILLIAM, JR., academic administrator; b. Saginaw, Mich., June 29, 1949; s. Clarence William and Lillian Irene Jenkins; m. Ruth Ann Jenkins, June 10, 1972; children: Laura, Amanda, Jon, Paul. BS in Edn., Dr. Martin Luther Coll., 1971; MA in Edn., Coll. of St. Thomas, 1982; MA in English, Ctrl. Mich. U., 1985; PhD in English, U. Wis., Milw., 1996. English prof. St. Croix Luth. H.S., West St. Paul, 1975-82; recruitment dir. Mich. Luth. Sem., Saginaw, 1982-86; English prof. Wis. Luth. Coll., Milw., 1986-97, dir. devel., 1997—. Lectr. Hofstra U., N.Y.C., 1994, Baseball Hall of Fame, Cooperstown, N.Y., 1995, Soc. Am. Baseball Rschrs., San Francisco, 1997, Internat. Baseball Conf., Phoenix, 1998. Contbr. articles to profl. publs. Alderman City Coun., Wauwatosa, Wis., 1997—; mem. Housing Authority, Wauwatosa, 1997—. Named Mid-Mich. Volleyball Coach of Yr. Saginaw News, 1985, Lake Mich. Volleyball Coach of Yr. Lake Mich. Conf., 1989, 90, 92, 93; Dist. Coach of Yr. Nat. Assn. for Interscholastic Athletics, 1992, 93.

Mem. MLA, Soc. Am. Baseball Rschrs. Avocation: collecting baseball memorabilia. Office: Wis Luth Coll 8800 W Bluemound Rd Milwaukee WI 53226-4626 E-mail: clarence_jenkins@wlc.edu.

JENKINS, DARRELL LEE, librarian; b. Roswell, N.Mex., Aug. 12, 1949; s. Lindon C. and Joyce (King) J.; m. Susan Jenkins. BA, Ea. N.Mex. U., 1971; MLS, U. Okla., 1972; MA, N.Mex. State U., 1976. Asst. edn., psychology, gift libr. N.Mex. State U., Las Cruces, 1972—73, edn. psychology libr., 1973—74, asst. reference libr., 1974—75, asst. catalog libr., 1975—76, asst. serials libr., 1976—77, acting head reference dept., 1977; adminstrv. svcs. libr. So. Ill. U., Carbondale, 1977—82, dir. libr. svcs., 1982—91, head social scis. divsn., 1992—2001. Cons. U.S. Naval Base, So. Ill. U., Groton, Conn., 1985-91; chmn. bd. dirs. CEC Comm., Inc., 1997-99. Author: Specialty Positions in ARL Libraries, 1982; co-author: Library Development and Fund Raising Capabilities, 1988; contbr. articles to profl. jours. Mem. ALA (chmn. libr. orgn. mgmt. sect. 1985-86), Am. Soc Info. Sci., Assn. Christian Librs., Ill. Libr. Computer System Orgn. (pres. 1985-86), Phi Kappa Phi, Beta Phi Mu, Phi Alpha Theta (Outstanding Libr. award 2002), Republican. Mem. Ch. Assembly God. Avocations: tennis, swimming, biking.

JENKINS, DEBRA REID, artist; b. Grand Rapids, Mich., Mar. 24, 1955; d. Russell Eugene and Peggy Ann Reid; m. Garth Edmund Jenkins, Oct. 14, 1978. Student, Kendall Sch. Design, Grand Rapids, 1973-75, Aquinas Coll., 1978-90. Hand decorator Heckman Furniture, Grand Rapids, 1975-80, Widdicomb Furniture, Grand Rapids, 1978-79, LaBarge Mirrors, Holland, Mich., 1980-89; fine artist, illustrator Debra Reid Jenkins Studio, Grand Rapids, 1989-97, Lowell, Mich., 1997—. Illustrator: (books) I Wanted to Know All About God, 1993, I See the Moon, 1997, My Freedom Trip, 1998, Here is Christmas, 2000, Glory, 2001, (mags.) Babybug, 1998, Ladybug, 2001, 2002, 2003. Recipient Emerging Artist award Am. Artist Mag., 1995. Mem. Pastel Soc. Am. (signature mem.), Soc. Gilders, Am. Soc. Portrait Artists, Soc. Children's Book Writers and Illustrators. Avocations: Feldenkrais tai chi, religious philosophy, dog training, kayaking, canoeing. Home and Studio: Debra Reid Jenkins Studio 14200 Thompson Dr Lowell MI 49331

JENKINS, DONALD JOHN, museum administrator; b. Longview, Wash., May 3, 1931; s. John Peter and Louise Hazel (Pederson) J.; m. Mary Ella Bemis, June 29, 1956; children— Jennifer, Rebecca BA, U. Chgo., 1951, MA, 1970. Mus. asst. Portland (Oreg.) Art Mus., 1954-56, asst. curator, 1960-69, curator, 1974-75, dir., 1975-87, curator Asian art, 1987—, chief curator, 1998-2001; assoc. curator oriental art Art Inst. Chgo., 1969-74. Mem. gallery adv. com. Asia House Gallery, N.Y.C., 1977-91; application reviewer NEH, Washington, 1984-86; lectr. various museums and art orgns., 1969—. Author: (exhbn. catalogues) Ukiyo-e Prints and Paints, 1971, The Ledoux Heritage, 1973, Masterworks in Wood/China and Japan, 1976, Images of Changing World, 1983, The Floating World Revisited, 1993. Mem. Pittock Mansion Adv. Com., Portland, 1975-87, chmn., 1983-84; chmn. NW Regional China Coun., Portland, 1980-89; mem. art selection com. Performing Arts Ctr., Portland, 1983-89; bd. dirs. Classical Chinese Garden, Portland, 2000—. Recipient Uchiyama Susumu Meml. award Japan Ukiyo-e Soc., 1993, Order of Rising Sun with gold rays and rosette Japanese Govt., 1994, Flying Horse Cmty. Svc. award N.W. China Coun., 1996. Mem. Am. Assn. Mus., Soc. for Japanese Arts, Assn. Asian Studies, Ukiyo-e Soc. Am., Japan-Am. Soc. Oreg. (chmn. cultural affairs com. 1987-98), The Internat. House of Japan. Home: 16418 NW Rock Creek Rd Portland OR 97231-2406 Office: Portland Art Mus 1219 SW Park Ave Portland OR 97205-2486 E-mail: donald.jenkins@pam.org.

JENKINS, EDWARD BEYNON, research astronomer; b. San Francisco, Mar. 20, 1939; s. Francis Arthur and Henrietta Beynon (Smith) J.; m. Myrna Dean Stewart, June 29, 1963; children: Brian Francis, Eric Dean. AB, U. Calif., Davis, 1962; PhD, Cornell U., 1966. Rsch. assoc. Princeton (N.J.) U., 1966-67, mem. rsch. staff, 1967-73, rsch. astronomer, 1973-79, sr. rsch. astronomer, 1979—. Mem. mgmt. and ops. working group NASA, Washington, 1976-79, 88-91, mem. astrophysics subcom., 1992-93; mem. com. on space astronomy and astrophysics NAS, Washington, 1986-89; co-investigator Space Telescope Imaging Spectrograph, 1985—, Far Ultraviolet Spectroscopic Explorer, 1989—; prin. investigator Interstellar Medium Absorption Profile Spectrograph, 1980-2002. Contbr. numerous articles to Astrophys. Jour. Recipient Rsch. award Alexander von Humboldt Found., 1992-93. Mem. Am. Astron. Soc. (v.p. 1996-99), Internat. Astron. Union (pres. Commn. 44, 1988-91). Democrat. Unitarian Universalist. Office: Princeton U Obs Astronomy Dept Princeton NJ 08544-0001

JENKINS, ELAINE PARKER, secondary school educator; b. Charleston, S.C., Sept. 25, 1950; d. William Lucius and Nancy Stevenson (Beaty) Parker; m. Marshall Pinckney Sherard, Jr. (div.); children: Marshall Pinckney III, Jessica Parker; m. Howard Claude Jenkins, June 14, 1986; children: David Wayne, Kristen Michelle. BA in English and Edn., Presbyn. Coll., 1971; MS in Curriculum and INstrn., English Edn., NC State U., 2003. Tchr. English Blythewood (S.C.) Jr. H.S., 1972-74, McDuffie H.S., Anderson, S.C., 1976-78, G.B.S. Hale H.S., Raleigh, N.C., 1987-90, East Wake H.S., Wendell, N.C., 1990-95, So. Wayne H.S., Dudley, N.C., 1995-1997, Clayton (N.C.) H.S., 1997—2000, head English dept., 1997-99, leader sr. tchr. journalism, head dept., 1999-2000. Yearbook tchr. various secondary schs. Clayton Middle Sch., 2000-2001, Riverwood Mid. Sch., 2001—, lang. arts dept. chair, sch. improvement team chair, 2001-02, mentor, 2002. Bd. dirs. Faith Luth. Sch., Raleigh, 1995-97; tchr. Lord of Life Luth. Ch., 1986—, mem. choir, 1986-99, 2003—. Mem. Nat. Coun. of Tchrs. of English, Nat. Middle Sch. Assn., N.C. English Tchrs. Assn., N.C. Assn. Educators/NEA, N.C. Scholastic Media Assn. (v.p. yearbook divsn. 1998-99), Journalism Edn. Assn., Thomas Wolfe Soc. Home: 4612 Winterlochen Rd Raleigh NC 27603-3868 Office: Riverwood Mid Sch 204 Athletic Club Blvd Clayton NC 27520-2716 E-mail: epjteach1@aol.com.

JENKINS, ELLEN JANET (JAN JENKINS), historian, history educator; b. Austin, Tex., Sept. 11, 1952; d. Neal and Melissa (Harwell) J.; m. W.E. Whittaker, III, Aug. 18, 1972 (div. July 1982); 1 child: William Barry. BA, U. Tex., Dallas, 1977; MA, U. North Tex., 1983, PhD, 1992. Tchr. Garland (Tex.) Ind. Sch. Dist., 1977-81; tchg. fellow history U. North Tex., Denton, 1982-86; rsch. asst. Rsch. Laboratory Archeology and History of Art, Oxford U., Eng., 1984; asst. prof. history U. Ark., Monticello, 1992-97; from asst. prof. to assoc. prof. history, dir. U. Honors Ark. Tech. U., Russellville, 1997—2002, assoc. prof. history, 2002—. Fundraising, restoration St. Matthew's Ch., Harwell, Eng. 1981, 84; editl. bd. Drew County Hist. Jour., Monticello, 1994-96. Author: (with John M. Fletcher) The Harwell Trail, 1981; contbr. (book reviews) Teaching History, 1992-94; Great Lives from History: American Women, 1995, (essays) Encyclopedia of Propaganda, 1997, The Encyclopedia of Anglo-American Relations, 2002, (book revs.) Seventeenth Century News, 2002-03, Choice, 2002-03. Bd. dirs. Drew County Hist. Mus., Monticello, 1993-95; spkr. various civic orgns., Dallas, 1988-97, Monticello, 1992-97, Russellville, 1997-98. Rsch. grantee U. Ark., Monticello, 1993, 94, 96, Tchg. Project grantee Ark. Humanities Coun., Nat. Endowment for Humanities, 1995-96. Mem. Assn. St. Cross Coll. at Oxford U., Ark. Assn. Coll. History Tchrs., So. Hist. Assn., European Hist. sect. of So. Hist. Assn. (nominating com. 1998-2001), Phi Alpha Theta. Democrat. Office: Ark Tech U Social Scis and Philosophy WPN 267 Russellville AR 72801 E-mail: jan.jenkins@mail.atu.edu.

JENKINS, EVERETT WILBUR, JR., lawyer, author, historian; b. Oklahoma City, Nov. 28, 1953; s. Everett Wilbur and Lillie Bell (Ingram) J.; m. Monica Lynn Endsley, June 3, 1978 (sep. Dec. 31, 2000); children: Ryan, Camille, Jennifer, Cristina. BA cum laude, Amherst Coll., 1975; JD, U. Calif., Berkeley, 1978. Bar: Calif. 1979. Dep. county counsel Contra Costa County, Martinez, Calif., 1980-81; dep. city atty. City of Richmond, Calif., 1981-84, asst. city atty., 1984—; bd. atty. West County Agy., Richmond, 1981-90; authority atty. Solid Waste Mgmt. Authority West Contra Costa, Richmond, 1985-87, 88-91. Legal rep. tech. adv. com. Contra Costa County Solid Waste Commn., Martinez, Calif., 1986-87, pub. mem., 1987-88; adv. atty. West Contra Costa Transp. Adv. Com., San Pablo, 1994—; bd. atty. Richmond Housing Authority, 1992-99; bd. dirs. Contra Costa Co. Hazardous Materials Commn., Maritnez, 1987-88. Author: Pan-African Chronology, 1996, Pan-African Chronology II, 1998, Pan-African Chronology III, 2001, The Muslim Diaspora, 1999, The Muslim Diaspora, vol. 2, 2000, The Creation, 2003. Bd. dirs. YMCA of the East Bay, Oakland, 1996—; bd. dirs. West Contra Costa YMCA, Richmond, 1987—, chair program com., 1991-92, vice chair bd. dirs. 1992-96, chair bd. dirs., 1996-98, chair cmty. gifts campaign, 1992-94 (named Rita Davis Vol. of the Yr., 1993); umpire Little League Baseball, 1997—, ASA Softball, 1997—. Mem. ABA, State Bar Calif. (exec. bd. pub. law sect. exec. com. 1987-91, editor Pub. Law News 1988-91, liaison to bd. govs. 1991-92), Continuing Edn. Bar (joint adv. com. 1993-96), Contra Costa County Bar Assn., Charles Houston Bar Assn., Nat. Assn. Sports Officials. Independent. Office: City Atty's Office 1401 Marina Way South Richmond CA 94804-1654

JENKINS, FRANCES OWENS, retired small business owner; b. Leonard, Tex., Nov. 12, 1924; d. R. Melrose and Maureen (Durrett) Owens; m. William O. Jenkins (div. 1961); children: Steven O., Tamara. Student theatre arts, East Tex. State U., 1939-42, Ind. U., 1945-48, U. Tenn., 1954-56. Fashion model Rogers Modeling Agy., Boston, 1950-52, Rich's, Knoxville, Tenn., 1955-60; owner, instr. Arts Sch. Self-Improvement and Modeling, Knoxville, 1959-69; owner, pres. Fran Jenkins Boutique, Knoxville, 1964-95; ret., 1995. Cons. Miss Am. Pageant, Knoxville, 1958-66. Actress Carousel Theatre, Knoxville, 1955-58. Home: 8833 Cove Point Ln Knoxville TN 37922-6402 also: 71 Pelican Cir Panama City Beach FL 32413-7018

JENKINS, GEORGE L. lawyer, entrepreneur; b. Wheeling, W.Va., Jan. 30, 1940; s. George Addison and Mildred Irene (Liggett) J. AB magna cum laude, Kent State U., 1963; JD with honors, U. Mich., 1966. Bar: Ohio 1966. Assoc. Vorys, Sater, Seymour & Pease, Columbus, Ohio, 1966-71, ptnr., 1975—; 1st asst. atty. gen. State of Ohio, Columbus, 1971-75. Bd. dirs. Fleagane Enterprises, Inc., JMHS, Inc., Impex Logistics, Inc., Nat. Am. Logistics, Inc., ECNext, Inc., CP Techs., Inc. Mem. ABA, Ohio Bar Assn., Columbus Bar Assn. (chmn. various coms. 1966—), Columbus Athletic Club, Muirfield Country Club, Desert Mountain Club, others. Democrat. Methodist. Avocations: tennis, jogging, travel, reading, golf. Office: Vorys Sater Seymour & Pease PO Box 1008 52 E Gay St Columbus OH 43215-3161 E-mail: gljenkins@vssp.com.

JENKINS, HOWARD M. supermarket executive; b. 1951; MBA, Emory U. With Publix Supermarkets, Inc., Lakeland, Fla., 1966—, v.p. rsch., exec. v.p., 1976-90, CEO, 1990—2001, chmn. bd. dirs., 1990—. also: 1936 George Jenkins Blvd Lakeland FL 33815-3760

JENKINS, JAMES SHERWOOD, JR., pharmacologist; b. Franklin, Tenn., July 25, 1941; s. Jim S. and Martha A. Jenkins; m. Tina M. Fulks; children: Kenneth, Candice, Christina. BS, David Lipscomb U., 1962; Pharmacy degree, U. Tenn., 1965, PD, 1974; Cert. Geriatic Practice, U. Miss., 1987. Diplomate Am. Acad. Pain Mgmt.; lic. pharmacist, pharmacologist. Clin. practice, rsch., 1969—; pvt. rsch. in hypertension therapy and others, 1980—. Author: Roseville Art Pottery, vol. I, 1997, vol. II, 1998, vol. III, 1999, vol. IV, 2000, vol. V, 2003, A Preliminary Report, 1997; mem. editl. adv. bd. Am. Jour. Pain Mgmt.; contbr. articles to profl. jours. Holder over 40 world and U.S. aviation speed records. Fellow Am. Coll. Apothecaries; mem. Nat. Aeronautic Assn. (life), Phi Delta Chi. Office: Clin Pharmacology Cons PO Box 15113 Rio Rancho NM 87174-0113 E-mail: cpc2451@msn.com.

JENKINS, JEFFREY ERIC, theater critic, educator; b. Wichita, Kans., Aug. 5, 1954; s. Lenville Elmer and Helen Bea Etta Jenkins; m. Vivian Cary Jenkins, Nov. 11, 1992; stepchildren: Christopher J. Cary, Oliver M. Cary. BA magna cum laude, San Francisco State U., 1982; MFA, Carnegie Mellon U., 1985. Instr. drama NYU, N.Y.C., 1998—; mng. editor Theatre Topics, Balt., 1995-2000; assoc. editor, essayist Best Plays, Woodstock, Vt., 1999—2000, editor N.Y.C., 2000—; N.Y.-based theater critic Seattle Post-Intelligencer, 1996—. Vis. asst. prof. drama NYU, N.Y.C., 2000-2001, 02—03; judge Henry Hewes Design Awards, 1997—, chair, 2002—; mem. adv. com. Am. Theatre Wing, N.Y.C., 2002—; mem. adv. coun. William Inge Theatre Festival, 2002—; guest critic Prague (Czech Republic) Quadrennial, 1995, Gdansk (Poland) Shakespeare Festival, 1993; bd. dirs. Theater Hall of Fame, 2001-. Contbr.: (books) Companion to Twentieth Century Theatre, 2001, Back Stage Handbook for Performing Artists, 1995. With U.S. Army M.C., 1972-75. Mem. Internat. Assn. Theatre Critics, Am. Soc. for Theatre Rsch., Am. Theatre Critics Assn. (chmn. 1999-2001, exec. com. 1995-2001), Am. Theatre and Drama Soc. (bd. dirs. 2001-), Found. of Am. Theatre Critics Assn. (bd. dirs 1995-2001), Assn. for Theatre in Higher Edn., Literary Mgrs. and Dramaturgs of the Ams., N.Y. Drama Desk, William Inge Theatre Festival (adv. coun.2002—). E-mail: editor@bestplaysonline.com.

JENKINS, JERRY WAYNE, musician; b. Houston, Jan. 4, 1949; s. Troy and Virgie Nettie Jenkins; m. Regina Milligan Jenkins; 1 child, Jerry Wayne (dec.). Student, S.W. Bus. Coll., 1967—68, Tex. So. U., 1969. Mem. The TSU Toronadoes, 1967—71; mus. dir. L.J.F. Prodns., 1971—74; rd. shows musician/bandleader Archie Bell's rd. tours, 1975—79; A&R man Saba Records, 1979—81; entertainment dir., band leader The DollHouse Club, 1981—84; CEO J. Waine Prodns., Houston, 1984—; record prodr. Bulls Eye Blue Record, 1998—2000; A&R person The Firm Records, Houston, 2000—. Bassist: Archie Bell's prodn. of Tighten Up, prodr. albums for Buddy Ace, Joe "Guitar" Hughes: ; author: (autobiography) The Making of Black Diamond, Play the Music Toronadoes. With U.S. Army, 1969. Achievements include patents for in field; patents pending for Huddle Master. Home: 12506 Rubin St Houston TX 77047

JENKINS, JOHN EDWARD, JR., electronics executive, engineering educator; b. Charlotte, N.C., Aug. 14, 1937; s. John Edward and Ruby (Killian) J.; m. Leslie Blyth, Mar. 27, 1969; children: Isabel Margaret Jenkins Bader, Iain Edward. BSEE, Duke U., 1958; MBA, Harvard U., 1960; PhD, Edinburgh (Scotland) U., 1970. Registered profl. engr., N.C. Projects coord. Astra, Inc., Raleigh, N.C., 1960-63; ops. analyst Rsch. Triangle Inst., Rsch. Triangle Park, N.C., 1963-65; lectr. elec. engring. Edinburgh U., 1965-71, U. N.C., Charlotte, 1971—; v.p. Jenkins Electric Co., Charlotte, 1971-95, pres., 1995-2000. Chmn. engring. commn. Elec. Apparatus Svc. Assn., St. Louis 1988-90. Assoc. editor Electrical Insulation, 1990-96; contbr. chpt. to Handbook of Electric Motors, 1995; inventor, patentee in field. Mem. IEEE (sr., dir. 1975-76, Outstanding Engr. N.C. 1980). Republican. Presbyterian. Avocation: walking. Office: Jenkins Electric Co Inc 5933 Brookshire Blvd Charlotte NC 28216-3386 E-mail: ejenkins@jenkins.com.

JENKINS, JOHN SMITH, retired academic dean, lawyer; b. Pittston, Pa., Dec. 11, 1932; s. Walter Hershel and Mildred (Lewis) J.; m. Marilyn Lewis, Aug. 23, 1958; 1 child, John Smith Jr. BA, Lafayette Coll., Easton, Pa., 1954; JD with honors, George Washington U., 1961; MA, Am. U., 1967. Bar: Va. 1961, U.S. Ct. Appeals for the Armed Forces, 1964, U.S. Supreme Ct. 1982. Commd. ensign U.S. Navy, 1955, advanced through grades to rear admiral, 1978; stationed at naval communications sta. Pearl Harbor, Hawaii, 1955—56; duty on U.S.S. Rochester, 1956-57; with Bur. Naval Personnel, 1957-62; with Hdqrs. 1st Naval Dist. Boston, 1962-64; staff Office Navy JAG, 1964-65; staff Office Legis. Affairs, 1969-71; staff Office of Asst. Sec., 1971-73; spl. counsel to sec. Office of Sec., 1973-76; asst. civil law JAG, 1976-78; dep. JAG, 1978-80; JAG, 1980-82; asst. dean Nat. Law Ctr. George Washington U., Washington, 1982-86, assoc. dean, 1986-2000, sr. assoc. dean, 2000—01, sr. assoc. dean emeritus, 2001. Decorated D.S.M. Legion of Merit. Fellow Am. Bar Found.; mem. ABA (ho. of dels., chair standing com. on lawyers in the armed forces 1991-94, standing com. on delivery of legal svcs. 1997-2001, standing com. on legal assistance for mil. pers. 2001-), FBA, Judge Advs. Assn., Army and Navy Club (gov. 1988-98), George Washington U. Club. Episcopalian. Home: 5809 Helmsdale Ln Alexandria VA 22315-4138 E-mail: jsjmlj@aol.com.

JENKINS, JOHNIE NORTON, research geneticist, research administrator; b. Barton, Ark., Nov. 3, 1934; married, 1959; 2 children. BSA, U. Ark., 1956; MS, Purdue U., 1958, PhD in Genetics, 1960. Rsch. assoc. in agronomy U. Ill., Urbana, 1960-61; rsch. geneticist Agrl. Rsch. Svc., USDA, 1961-80, dir. Crop Sci. Rsch. Lab., 1980—. Prof. crop sci. and mem. grad. faculty Miss. State U., 1964—. Recipient Mobay Cotton Rsch. Recognition award, Verdant Crop Genetics award of yr., 2000. Fellow AAAS, Am. Soc. Agronomy, Crop Sci. Soc. Am. Achievements include research on host plant resistance to cotton insects and nematodes, investigations of basic causes of insect and nematode resistance in cotton plants and development of factors which will confer resistance. Office: USDA-ARS Crop Sci Rsch Lab PO Box 5367 Mississippi State MS 39762-5367

JENKINS, JUDITH ALEXANDER, bank consultant; b. Fort Sill, Okla., Oct. 14, 1940; d. James Buchanan and Gerry Lee (Gibbs) Permenter; m. Robert Miles Turner, Oct. 28, 1962 (div. 1972); m. Clarence Withers Alexander, Dec. 19, 1975 (div. Jan. 1987); m. David Claude Jenkins, Apr. 23, 1994. Student, U. Okla., 1958-59; BA in English, U. Tulsa, 1962; MBA, U. Okla., 1969; postgrad., U. St. Thomas, 1975-78. Asst. cashier So. Nat. Bank of Houston, 1971-73, asst. contr., 1973-74, asst. v.p. and asst. contr., 1974, v.p., contr., 1974-77, sr. v.p., contr., 1977-79; cons., 1979—. Mem. Beta Gamma Sigma, Gamma Phi Beta. Office: 16218 Wrangler Rd Rosharon TX 77583 E-mail: calikino@msn.com. *Learning, discipline, and independence are my goals and the major contributors to my success in business and personal life.*

JENKINS, KENNETH VINCENT, literature educator, writer; b. Elizabeth, N.J. s. Thomas Augustus and Rebecca Meredith (Williams) J.; 4 children. AB, MA, Columbia Coll.; postgrad., Columbia U. Tchr. South Side Sr. High Sch., Rockville Centre, N.Y., 1953-72, chmn. dept. English, 1965-72. Prof. English, Afro-Am. lit. Nassau Community Coll., Garden City, N.Y., 1972—, chmn. Afro Am. studies dept., 1975—, supr. adj. faculty, 1974-82; cons. in English, N.Y. State Dept. Edn., Albany, 1965-72; mem. Regents Question Com. in English, Albany, 1966-71; owner Black Books and Artifacts. Author: Teaching African Literature, 1960, Last Day in Church, 1965; contbr. revs., poems to profl. publs. Chmn. bd. dirs., founder Target Youth Ctrs., Inc., 1973-76, African-Am. Book Ctr., 1982—; mem. nat. bd. Pacifica Found., 1973-79, chmn., 1975-76, pres., 1976-78; bd. dirs. Sta. WBAI-FM, N.Y.C., 1972-85, Nassau County Youth Bd., 1976-2000, chmn., 1978-99, chair emeritus 1999—; mem. N.Y. Gov.'s Commn. on Youth, 1984-94; bd. dirs. L.I. Cmty. Found., 1989-98, N.Y. State Youth Support, Inc., 1990-93. Recipient cmty., county, state awards, M.L. King Award, Celebration Com. Nassau County, 1990, Special Svc. Award One Hundred Black Men, 1994, Nat. Coun. of Negro Women, Inc. Award, 2003; Pennington grantee, 1953. Mem. Afro-Am. Inst., Assn. Study of Afro-Am. Life and History, Mensa, Phi Delta Kappa, mem. bd. Schomburg Ctr., N.Y.C., 1990. Office: Nassau C C Garden City NY 11530 E-mail: jenkink@sunynassau.edu.

JENKINS, KEVIN GERARD, lawyer; b. Bronx, N.Y., Jan. 1, 1954; s. Kenneth Thomas and Marie Mary Jenkins; m. Janet Eugenia Jenkins; children: Lynn, Gina, Scott, Christopher. BA, Western Conn. State U., 1976; MA, New Sch. Social Rsch., 1978; JD, Bklyn. Law Sch., 1982; LLM, NYU, 1986. Bar: N.Y. 1983, N.J. 1985. Atty. Con Edison, N.Y.C., 1983-86, N.Y.C. Transit Authority, Bklyn., 1986-88; gen. counsel local 1-2 Utility Workers Union Am., N.Y.C., 1988—; atty. N.Y. State United Tchrs., N.Y.C., 2000—. Mem. ABA, ATLA, Acad. Polit. Sci., N.Y. State Bar Assn., N.Y. County Lawyers Assn. Democrat. Roman Catholic. Avocation: sports. Office: Utility Workers Union Am 5 West 37th St New York NY 10018

JENKINS, LEANN, government executive; b. Ponca City, Okla., June 30, 1958; d. Leon Odell Long and Mary Beth Spilman; m. Jeffrey Dee Jenkins, Feb. 29, 1976; children: Justin Miles, Jennifer Ann. BA, So. Nazarene U., Bethany, Okla., 1991. Exec. dir. Okla. Fed. Exec. Bd., Oklahoma City, 1994—. Bd. dirs. United Way, Oklahoma City, 2002—02, Oklahoma City Meml. Found., 1995—2002, Cmty. Coun. Ctrl. Okla., Oklahoma City, 1998—2002. Recipient Disting. EEO award, Dept. Air Force, 1989, Meritorious Civilian Svc., 1995, Exemplary Civilian Svc., 1996, Jack Niles medal of honor, 2000. Mem.: NAFE, Am. Soc. Pub. Adminstrn. (coun. mem. 1998—2002). Office: Okla Fed Exec Bd 215 Dean A McGee Ste 320 Oklahoma City OK 73102 Office Fax: 405-231-4165.

JENKINS, LOUIS (WOODY), television executive, state legislator; b. Baton Rouge, Jan. 3, 1947; s. Louis and Doris Laverne (Rowlett) J.; m. Diane Carole Aker, June 15, 1968; children: Margaret Ann, Elizabeth Ann, David Aker, Catherine Ann. BA in Journalism, La. State U., 1969, JD, 1972. Newsman Sta. WLCS, Baton Rouge, 1964-65; announcer Sta. WAFB-TV, Baton Rouge, 1965-66; pub., editor North Baton Rouge Jour., Baton Rouge, 1966-69; pres. Great Oaks Co., 1972—; CEO WBTR-TV. With KMNO-TV, Monroe, La., 1998—, WSTY-TV, Hammond, La., 1998—; mem. La. Ho. of Reps., Baton Rouge, 1972-2000, chmn. com. on labor, 1988-92; mem. Emerald Direct, Amway Corp., 1994-. Author: Declaration of Rights, Louisiana Constitution of 1974. Del. La. Constl. Conv., Baton Rouge, 1973-74; Pres. Reagan's adv. Com. for Trade Negotiations, 1982-84; exec. dir. Coun. for Nat. Policy, 1981-85, bd. dirs. 1990-99; founder, chmn. Friends of the Ams., 1984—; co-founder, chmn. Am. Legis. Exch. Coun., 1977-78; hon. chmn. La. delegation Rep. Nat. Conv., 1996; Rep. nominee U.S. Senate from La., 1996. Named Legislator of Yr., Nat. Taxpayers Union, 1978, Eagle Forum, 1990; recipient Outstanding Editorial Writing award La. Press Assn., 1969, Prodr. Best Local TV News Program in U.S. award Community Broadcasters Assn., 1992, Samuel Adams award Local Govt. Coun., 1999. Mem. Nat. Assn. TV Program Execs., Cmty. Broadcasters Assn. Office: WBTR-TV 914 N Foster Dr Baton Rouge LA 70806-1807

JENKINS, LOUISE SHERMAN, nursing researcher, educator; b. Normal, Ill., Jan. 19, 1943; d. Fred and Zylpha Louise (Garrett) Sherman; m. Gary L. Jenkins, Oct. 30, 1965 (div. July 1976). Diploma, Evanston Hosp. Sch. Nursing, 1963; BS, No. Ill. U., 1979; MS, U. Md., Balt., 1982, PhD, 1985. Asst. head nurse intensive care Cmty. Meml. Hosp., LaGrange, Ill., 1963-65; head nurse coronary care Luth. Gen. Hosp., Park Ridge, Ill., 1965-69; nurse clinician hemodialysis unit Evanston (Ill.) Hosp., 1969-74; head nurse Skokie (Ill.) Valley Cmty. Hosp., 1974-75; faculty dept. continuing edn. N.W. Cmty. Hosp., Arlington Heights, Ill., 1975-80; Walter Schoeder chair nursing rsch. U. Wis. Milw. Sch. Nursing and St. Luke's Med. Ctr., Milw., 1987-96; faculty Sch. Nursing U. Md., Balt., 1996—, acting dir. grad. studies, 1997-98, dir. grad. studies, 1998—2003. Mem. editl. bd. Jour. Cardiopulmonary Rehab., mem. rev. panel Am. Jour. Health Behavior, Nursing Rsch., Heart & Lung. Chair Am. Heart Assn., Milw., 1988—95, exec. bd. dirs. Wis. affiliate, 1995—96, fellow, 2001; chair Coun. Cardiovasc. Nursing, Dallas, 1995—97, fellow. Fellow, Am. Heart Assn., 2001; fellow, Clin. Nurse scholar, Robert Wood Johnson Found., U. Calif., San Francisco, 1985—87. Mem.: N.Am. Soc. Pacing and Electrophysiology, Coun. Nursing Rsch., Midwest Nursing Rsch. Soc. (gov. bd. 1993—95), Wis. Nurses Assn. (bd. dirs. 1988—90, Excellence in Nursing Rsch. award 1995), Am. Assn. Cardiovasc. and Pulmonary Rehab. (bd. dirs.-at-large 1993—95), Sigma Xi, Sigma Theta Tau. Office: Sch Nursing U Md 655 W Lombard St Baltimore MD 21201-1512 E-mail: jenkins@son.umaryland.edu.

JENKINS, LYNN M. state legislator; b. Topeka, June 10, 1963; m. Scott M. Jenkins; children: Hayley, Hayden. AA, Kans. State U., 1984; BS, Weber State Coll., 1985. CPA. CPA, 1985—; rep. Kans. State Ho. Reps., 1998—; mem. Kans. State Senate, 2000—, mem. gen. govt. budget com., ins. com., post audit com., govt. orgn. and elections com., taxation com. Mem. adv. bd. Ct. Apptd. Spl. Advocate; bd. dirs. YMCA Metro, Family Svc. and Guidance Ctr.; treas., bd. dirs. Prince of Peace Presch.; active Jay Snideler PTO, Susanna Wesley United Meth. Ch. Mem. Kans. Soc. CPAs. Republican. Methodist. Home: 5940 SW Clarion Ln Topeka KS 66610 Office: State Capitol Rm 460-E Topeka KS 66612 Fax: 785-271-6585.

JENKINS, MARSHALL, internet consultant, entrepreneur; b. Dayton, Ohio, Apr. 8, 1952; s. Bobbie Whitfield and Louise (Stafford) J.; m. Catherine Fogle. AA, Brevard C.C., Cocoa, Fla., 1972; BA, U. South Fla., 1975; MS, Fla. State U., 1978. Program analyst Planning Rsch. Corp., Cocoa Beach, Fla., 1978-81; assoc. engr. Martin Marietta Aerospace, Kennedy Space Ctr., Fla., 1982-83; project and product assurance engr. (mgmt. system analyst) Lockheed Space Ops. Co., Titusville, Fla., 1983-91; founder, owner Quaylor Comm., Melbourne, Fla., 1991-99; pres., mgr. Quaylor.Com LLC. Profl. internet website developer, mgmt. sys. cons. Vol. Spl. Olympics Dist. Competitions, Merritt Island, Fla., 1983. Mem. Am. Mgmt. Assn., Space Coast Seminole Boosters Inc. (pres. Melbourne, Fla. 1986-87, bd. dirs. 1987-88), Fla. State U. Seminole Boosters Inc. (Brevard County, Fla. area chmn. 1987-88), Fla. State U. Alumni Assn., Tau Kappa Epsilon. Republican. Methodist. Avocations: tennis, golf, travel. Home: 4365 Windover Way Melbourne FL 32934-8518

JENKINS, MELVIN LEMUEL, lawyer; b. Halifax, NC, Oct. 15, 1947; s. Solomon Green and Minerva (Long) Jenkins; m. Wanda Joyce Holly, May 20, 1972; children: Dawn, Shelley, Melvin, Holly Rae Ann. B.S., N.C. Agrl. and State U., 1969; J.D., U. Kans., 1972. Bar: Nebr. 1973, US. Dist. Ct. Nebr. 1973. Atty. Legal Aid Soc., Kansas City, Mo., 1972, HUD, Kansas City, Mo., 1972—73; regional atty. U.S. Commn. on Civil Rights, Kansas City, Mo., 1973—79, regional dir., 1979—2002; atty. Stennis and Assocs., Omaha,

2002—. Chmn. A.M. Roundtable, Kansas City, 1981—83; mem. Kansas City Human Relations Commn., 1980. Mem. Mo. Black Adoption Adv. Bd., Kansas City, 1981—; bd. dirs. Joan Davis Spl. Sch. Mem.: ACLU, ABA, Fed. Bar Assn., Nat. Bar Assn., Nebr. Bar Assn., Urban League, Masons (master mason for civil rights 1979). Mem. Ame Ch. Home: 8015 Sunset Cir Grandview MO 64030-1461 Office: 300 S 19th St Ste 216 Omaha NE 68102

JENKINS, MICHAEL GRADY, judge; b. Millen, Ga., Apr. 25, 1961; s. Solomon Leslie (Chuck) and Marjorie (McBride) J.; m. Yvonne M. Wiley, Apr. 28, 2001. BS, Ga. So. Coll., 1984; JD, John Marshall Law Sch., 2000. Newspaper reporter Statesboro (Ga.) Herald, 1985-87; ins. agt. Sylvania, Ga., 1987-93; chief magistrate judge Screven County, Sylvania, 1993—. Comml. timber prodr. Mem.: Rocky Branch Hunting Club (pres. 1997—), The Pinnacle Club, Sylvania Rotary (sec., v.p., pres.). Mem. Christian Ch. Avocations: competition body building, hunting, fishing. Office: Screven County Magistrate Ct PO Box 64 216 Mims Rd Sylvania GA 30467

JENKINS, PAMELA LYNN, music educator; b. Flint, Mich., Dec. 16, 1950; d. Thressabelle O'Dell -Jenkins and Edgar Raymond Jenkins; life ptnr. Patti-Jean Cousens, Sept. 23, 1987. MM, Ctrl. Mich. Univ., 1994—97. Cert. Piano Technician 1981. Instr. U. of Maine at Augusta, 1997—; piano technician Acoustic Piano tuning, Southport, Maine, 1974—; musician Boogie2Shooz, East Tawas, Mich. Mem.: North Am. Saxophone Alliance, Piano Technicians Guild (assoc.). Democrat-Npl. Siddha Yoga. Avocations: hiking, camping, boating. Home: Po Box 405 Southport ME 04576 Office: University of Maine at Augusta 46 University Dr Augusta ME 04330 Personal E-mail: pam@boogie2shooz.com. E-mail: pjenkins@maine.edu.

JENKINS, PAUL, artist; b. Kansas City, Mo., July 12, 1923; s. William Burris and Nadyne (Fellers) J.; m. Esther Ebenhoe, 1944 (div.); 1 child, Hilarie Paula; m. Alice Baber, 1964 (div.); m. Suzanne Donnelly, 1979. Student, Art Students League, N.Y.C., 1948-52; Hum.D., 1973, 96. Author: (plays) Strike the Puma, 1966; co-author: Observations of Michel Tapie, 1956, Shaman to the Prism Seen, 1987, Anatomy of a Cloud, 1983, Seven Aspects of Amadeus and the Others, 1992, Shaman to the Prism Moon, 1994, articles, (films) The Ivory Knife, 1965; exhibitions include Studio Paul Facchetti, Paris, 1954, Gimpel Weitzenhoffer Gallery, N.Y.C., Karl Flinker Gallery, Paris, Georges Fall Gallery, Galerie Patrice Trigano, Galerie Sapone, Nice, Gimpel Fils Gallery, London, Gallery Art Point, Tokyo, Martha Jackson Gallery, N.Y.C., Assoc. Am. Artists, NY, Galerie Proarta, Zurich, Chateau-Musée de Cagnes Sur Mer, Joseph Rickards Gallery, N.Y., one-man shows include Mus. Fine Arts, Houston, San Francisco Mus. Art, Palm Springs Desert Mus., Musée Picasso, Antibes, Mus. Nice, France, Hofstra Mus., Hempstead, N.Y., Butler Inst. Am. Art, Youngstown, Ohio, Basilica Palladiana Vicenza, Centre D'Art Contemporain Bouvet Ladubay, Saumur, Represented in permanent collections Mus. Modern Art, Whitney Mus., Guggenheim Mus., NY, Corcoran Gallery, Washington, Tate Gallery, London, Musee D'Art Moderne, Paris, Centre Georges Pompidou, Fondation Maeght, St-Paul-de-Vence, Musee Picasso, Antibes, Stedelijk Mus., Amsterdam, Netherlands, Mus. Western Art, Tokyo, exhibitions include Redfern Gallery, London. Served with USNR, 1943-45. Decorated Commandeur des Arts et Lettres France; recipient Silver medal Corcoran Gallery Art, 1967, Art Dir.'s award for Anatomy of a Cloud, 1984, Life Achievement award Butler Inst. Am. Art, 1997, medal City of Paris, 1997, Benjamin West Clinedinst medal Artists' Fellowship N.Y., 2000. Mem. Royal Cambrian Acad. (hon.; Wales), Nat. Acad. N.Y. (elected). Studio: Imago Terrae PO Box 6833 Yorkville Sta New York NY 10128

JENKINS, REESE V. historian, educator; b. Muncie, Ind., June 28, 1938; s. John Thomas and Vada Arline Fraze Jenkins; m. Alyce Jeanette Mitchem Jenkins, Dec. 27, 1962; children: David William, Elizabeth Ann Manfredi. BA, U. Rochester, 1960; MS, U. Wis., 1963, PhD, 1966. Tchr. history and math. Madison (Wis.) Ctrl. Univ. H.S., 1963—64; asst. prof. history No. Ill. U., Dekalb, 1966—67; from asst. to assoc. prof. history of sci. and tech. Case Western Res. U., Cleve., 1967—78; dir., editor Thomas A. Edison Papers Rutgers U., New Brunswick, NJ, 1978—95, prof. history, 1978—. Harvard-Newcomen Bus. History fellow Harvard U., Boston, 1969—70; vis. assoc. prof. history U. Rochester, NY, 1976—77; hist. cons. Eastman Kodak Co., Rochester, 1993, Fuji Photofilm Co., Ashagara, Japan, 1995—99; participant PBS-TV programs on Thomas Edison, 1979—95; prin., cons., participant PBS-TV Am. Experience: George Eastman, 2000—01. Author: Images & Enterprise, 1975 (award N.Y. Photo Soc., 1976, Choice award, 1976), Japanese edit., 1998; editor-in-chief Papers of Thomas A. Edison, Vols. 1-3, 1989—94 (award Assn. Am. Pubs., 1989), microfilm edit., 1985—95; contbr. articles to profl. jours.; mem. editl. bd.: N.J. History, 1980—. Trustee Wesley Found., Rutgers U., New Brunswick, 1984—90, chair, 1987—89. Recipient award of recognition, N.J. Hist. Commn., Trenton, 1991; grantee NSF, NEH, NEA, numerous others. Mem.: Soc. for History of Tech. (exec. coun. 1980—82, 1992—94, chair various coms. 1977—, Dexter prize 1978), Assn. for Documentary Editing (chair various coms. 1991—96, commendation 1996), History of Sci. Soc. (pres. Mid-West Junta 1978—79, coun. 1973—75). Democrat. Presbyterian. Avocations: reading, photographica, family history, women's collegiate basketball, walking. Home: 11 Clifton Ave New Brunswick NJ 08901-1503 Office: Dept History Rutgers U College Ave Campus New Brunswick NJ 08903-5059 Fax: 732-227-0608. Business E-Mail: reese638@aol.com.

JENKINS, RICHARD LEE, manufacturing company executive; b. Lynchburg, Va., July 20, 1931; s. Robert Julian and Beulah Vivian (Crews) J.; m. Doris E. Rucker, Dec. 24, 1958; children: Terena M., Richard C. BA, Lynchburg Coll., 1957; MBA, U. Mass., 1970. Various fin. mgmt. positions Gen. Electric Co., Lynchburg, Schenectady, N.Y., and Pittsfield, Mass., 1957-72; controller, mgr. Mfg. Transformer div. Allis-Chalmers, Pitts., 1972-75; gen. mgr. Indsl. Pump div. Allis-Chalmers, Cin., 1975-79; sr. v.p. Lynchburg Foundry, 1979-81; gen. mgr. service div. Siemens-Allis, Inc., Atlanta, 1981-84; sr. v.p. adminstrn. and internat. ops., chief fin. officer Diversified Products Corp., Opelika, Ala., 1984—. Treas., bd. dirs. Micah Corp. of Berkshire County, Pittsfield, 1968-72; bd. dirs. Va. Nat. Bank, Lynchburg, 1979-81. Auditor ARC, Pittsfield, 1966; bd. dirs., exec. on loan United Community Services, Pittsfield, 1972; campaign chmn. Piedmont Heart Assn., Lynchburg, 1980. Served with USN, 1950-54, Korea. Mem.: Cherokee Country (Atlanta), Saugahatchee Country (Opelika). Home: 2245 Springwood Dr Auburn AL 36830-7231 Office: Diversified Products Corp 309 Williamson Ave Opelika AL 36804-7313

JENKINS, ROBERT BERRYMAN, real estate developer; b. Evanston, Ill., Oct. 11, 1950; s. Clive Ridley and Genevieve (Brown) Crawford J.; m. Carol Lynn Kealey, Sept. 22, 1984; children: Paul Brown, Leighanne Kealey. BEE, Cornell U., 1972; postgrad., U. W. Fla., 1974. Cert. Profl. Solar Technology, 1984. Owner Fothergill's Outdoor Sportsman, Aspen, Colo., 1978-81; owner, engr. Sophisticated Solar, Aspen, 1983-85; owner/pres. Sandhill Devels., Gulf Breeze and Aspen, 1985—; owner, pres. Roaring Fork Liquors, Inc., Glenwood Springs, Colo., 1992-2000. Grad. Leadership Santa Rosa County, Fla., 1988-89. Recipient U.S. Dept. Energy Nat. Award for Energy Innovation, 1987, Gov.'s Energy award Fla. Gov., 1987; named Man of Yr., Gulf Breeze, 1991. Mem. Internat. Coun. Shopping Ctrs., Trout Unltd. (life). Republican. Methodist. Avocations: snowskiing, flyfishing, whitewater rafting. Address: PO Box 14 200 Doc Henry Rd Woody Creek CO 81656

JENKINS, ROBERT GORDON, retired air force officer, technology executive, government executive; b. Charlottesville, Va., Dec. 14, 1941; s. Charles Gordon and Rosa Lee (Berry) J.; m. Nicki Jean Mitchell, Aug., 1966; children: Lara Elizabeth, Christopher Scott. BS, Va. Poly. Inst. and State U., 1964; MS, W.Va. U., 1967. Commd. USAF, 1968—, advanced through grades to brig. gen., fighter pilot, 1968-75; comdr. 22d Tactical Fighter Squadron, Bitberg Air Base, Germany, 1981-82; asst. chief staff AOC Allied Air Forces Ctrl. Europe, Boerlink, Germany, 1982-84; dep. comdr. for ops. Tactical Air Warfare Ctr., Eglin AFB, Fla., 1984-85; comdr. Air Forces Iceland, Keflavik, 1985-87; vice comdr. 354 Tactical Fighter Wing, Myrtle Beach, S.C., 1987-88, comdr., 1988-90; dep. dir. gen. purposes forces HQ USAF, Pentagon, Washington, 1990-92, dep. dir. ops., 1992; comdr. 51st Fighter Wing, Osan Air Base, Korea, 1992-94; vice comdr. 7th Air Force, Osan Air Base, Korea, 1994-95; dir. logistics HQ Pacific Air Force, 1995-97; pres. Exco Techs. Inc., 1997-2000; dir. aviation mgmt. U.S. Dept. Energy, 2000—. Decorated Legion of Merit with cluster, DFC, 2 Meritorious Svc. medals, 12 Air medals, 2 Commendation medals, DFC with cluster, Disting. Svc. medal. Mem. Order of Daedalians. Home: 9853 Hidden Estates Cv Vienna VA 22181-6090 E-mail: RandNJenk@aol.com.

JENKINS, ROBERT NORMAN, reporter, editor; b. Washington, Oct. 22, 1943; s. Jack Julian and Mina Lorraine (Katz) J.; m. Dianne Ruth Lang, June 1966 (div. June 1973); children: Kirsten Rose, Joshua Matthew; m. Dianne Carol Dearmin, Dec. 14, 1974; children: Michael Robert, Ryan Robert. BA in Journalism, Mich. State U., 1965. Newspaper reporter Grand Rapids (Mich.) Press, 1965-67; newspaper reporter, editor Newsday, Garden City, N.Y., 1967-69, St. Petersburg (Fla.) Times, 1969—. Recipient 1st Place News Section Design, Fla. Soc. Newspaper Editors, 1974. Mem.: Soc. Am. Travel Writers (nat. v.p. 1999—2001, Lowell Thomas Travel award Gold 1996, 2000, Lowell Thomas Travel award Silver 1996, 1999, Lowell Thomas Travel award Bronze 1999, 2000, 2001, 2002), Hon. Coaches Mich. State U. Office: St Petersburg Times 490 1st Ave S Saint Petersburg FL 33701-4204 E-mail: jenkins@sptimes.com.

JENKINS, ROBERT ROWE, lawyer; b. Norwalk, Ohio, Aug. 8, 1933; s. Robert Leslie and Millie Leona (Rowe) J.; m. Francis Jean Cline, June 12, 1955 (div. July 1972); children: Diane Elaine, Katherine Eileen; m. Jean Dingus, July 9, 1972. Student, Lebanon Valley Coll., 1951-55; BS in Chemistry, Eastern Coll. (now U. Balt.), 1967; JD, U. Balt., 1975. Bar: Md. 1976, U.S. Dist. Ct. Md. 1976, U.S. Ct. Appeals (4th cir.) 1979, U.S. Supreme Ct. 1979. Atty. Social Security Adminstrn., Balt., 1975-76; trial atty. Nelson R. Kandel, Balt., 1976-77; sole practice Balt., 1977-81; ptnr. Jenkins Block & Mering, Balt., 1981—. Faculty continuing profl. edn. of lawyers Md. Inst., Balt., 1986—. Ruling elder Redeemer Presbyn. Ch., Presbyn. Ch. Am., Balt., 1982—. Served with U.S. Coast Guard, 1955-59. Mem. ABA, Md. Bar Assn., Balt. City Bar Assn., Assn. Trial Lawyers Am., Md. Trial Lawyers Assn., Christian Legal Soc., Nat. Orgn. Social Security Claimant's Rep. (exec. com.). Republican. Avocations: fishing, boating. Home: 1003 Travers St Cambridge MD 21613-1543 Office: Jenkins Block and Assoc PO Box 739 828 Airpax Rd Ste 300 Cambridge MD 21613 also: 33 W Franklin St Ste 102 Hagerstown MD 21740-4826 E-mail: rjenk5906@aol.com

JENKINS, RUBEN LEE, retired chemical company executive, lawyer; b. Beggs, Okla., Nov. 27, 1929; s. William Arnold and Myrtle (Kimble) J.; m. Sylvia Griffin, July 17, 1956; children: Amy, Kimble Lee, William Griffin. BA, U. Okla., 1952, LLB, 1956; LLM, NYU, 1959. Bar: Okla. 1956. Law clk. to presiding justice U.S. Dist. Ct. (we. dist.) Okla., Oklahoma City, 1956; clk. U.S. Ct., Oklahoma City, 1956-58; research asst. in internat. law NYU, N.Y.C., 1958-59; assoc. Allende & Brea, Buenos Aires, Argentina, 1959-60; exec. v.p., gen. counsel White Eagle Internat., Midland, Tex., 1960-65; v.p. corp. devel. Plough, Inc., Memphis, 1965-71, dir, 1970, sr. v.p. hdqrs., 1972-73, exec. v.p., 1973-76, pres., 1976-89; dir. Schering-Plough Corp., Madison, N.J., 1971-89, sr. v.p., 1976-80, exec. v.p., 1980-89. Bd. dirs. RFS Hotel Investors, Memphis. Bd. dirs. Chickasaw coun. Boy Scouts Am., Memphis; hon. trustee Memphis U. Sch. Capt. USMC, 1952-54. Mem. ABA, Tenn. Bar Assn., Okla. Bar Assn., Non-Prescription Drug Mfrs. Assn. (bd. dirs. 1976-89), Palm Beach Polo and Country Club. Methodist. Address: 2886 Winding Oaks Ln West Palm Beach FL 33414 E-mail: rljenkins1@aol.com.

JENKINS, SHERRY L. state accounting manager; b. San Diego, Aug. 2, 1956; children: Shannon D., Adam D. AAS, Oscar Rose Jr. Coll., Midwest City, Okla., 1978; BS in Acctg. and Fin., Harrington U., London, 1981, MBA, 2000; BS, Oklahoma City U., 1999. Cert. flexible compensation Employers Coun. on Flexible Compensation, 2002. Accounts specialist II State of Okla. - Employees Benefits Coun., Oklahoma City, 1996—99, FSA claim supr., 1999—2000, mgr. members accounts, 2000—. Recipient Govenor's Commendation award, State of Okla. - Gov,. Frank Keating, 2000. Mem.: Delta Mu Delta (assoc.; Zeta Omega chpt.), Alpha Sigma Lambda (assoc.; Omicron Chi). Office: OK Employees Benefits Council Ste 1200 200 N Harvey Oklahoma City OK 73102 Office Fax: 405-232-1729. E-mail: sjenkins@ebc.state.ok.us.

JENKINS, SPEIGHT, opera company executive, writer; b. Dallas, Jan. 31, 1937; s. Speight and Sara (Baird) J.; m. Linda Ann Sands, Sept. 6, 1966; children: Linda Leonie, Speight. BA, U. Tex.-Austin, 1957; LL.B., Columbia U., 1961; DMus (hon.), U. Puget Sound, 1992; HHD, Seattle U., 1992. News and reports editor Opera News, N.Y.C., 1967-73; music critic N.Y. Post, N.Y.C., 1973-81; TV host Live from the Met, Met. Opera, N.Y.C., 1981-83; gen. dir. Seattle Opera, 1983—. Classical music editor Record World, N.Y.C., 1973—81; contbg. editor Ovation Mag., N.Y.C., 1980—87. Served to capt. U.S. Army, 1961-66. Recipient Emmy award for Met. Opera telecast La Boheme TV Acad. Arts and Scis., 1982 Mem. Phi Beta Kappa Assocs. Presbyterian. Home: 903 Harvard Ave E Seattle WA 98102-4561 Office: Seattle Opera PO Box 9248 Seattle WA 98109-0248

JENKINS, THOMAS LLEWELLYN, physics educator; b. Cambridge, Mass., July 16, 1927; s. Francis A. and Henrietta (Smith) J.; m. Glen Pierce, July 8, 1951; children: Gale F., Phillip P., Matthew A., Sarah E. BA, Pomona Coll., 1950; PhD, Cornell U., 1956. Physicist Lawrence Radiation Lab., Livermore, Calif., 1955-60; faculty Case Western Res. U., Cleve., 1960—, prof. physics, 1968-94, prof. emeritus physics, 1994—. Sci. and Engring. Research Council fellow Southampton U., (Eng.), 1983 Mem. Am. Phys. Soc., AAAS, Phi Beta Kappa, Sigma Xi. Home: 869 Belwood Dr Cleveland OH 44143-3239 Office: Case Western Res Univ Physics Dept Cleveland OH 44106

JENKINS, TONY DEAN, salesman; b. Dallas, Jan. 26, 1961; s. Frank Jr. Jenkins and Leotha Hamilton; m. Adriana Rodriguez Jenkins, Aug. 6, 1983; children: Tony D. Jr., Benjamin D. BS, Dallas Bapt. U., 1983. Asst. mgr. Church's Chicken, Dallas, 1990-91; sales rep. Mut. of Omaha, Dallas, 1992-94; driver Schneider Nat., Greenbay, Wis., 1994-96; dispatcher Glazer's Wholesale, Dallas, 1996-99; spl. rep. George S. May Internat. Co., Park Ridge, Ill., 1999-2000; ind. sales rep. Dallas, 2000—; agt. Farmers Ins., Addison, Tex., 2002—. 1st lt. U.S. Army, 1984-87 Mem. Alpha Phi Alpha. Avocations: golf, tennis, jogging. Office: PO Box 380863 Duncanville TX 75138-0863 E-mail: JTDJenkins1@aol.com.

JENKINS, VIRGINIA, visual arts educator, artist; b. Bay City, Mich., Nov. 6, 1951; d. James George and Florence Virginia (Schultz) Jenkins; m. David T. Morrison, Aug. 31, 1974 (div. Aug. 1986). BFA, Mich. State U., 1973; MFA, U. Utah, 1975. Instr. Loretto Hts. Coll., Denver, 1982-85, Red Rocks C.C., Lakewood, Colo., 1987-88, U. No. Colo., Greeley, 1986-88, asst. prof. painting, 1988-92, assoc. prof. painting, 1992-96, prof. painting, 1996—, chair visual arts dept. Cons. Coral Gables (Fla.) Internat. Art Ctr., 1999; presenter in field. Exhibitor paintings at Tointon Gallery, Greeley, 1998, Edge Gallery, Denver, 1999. Mem.: Colo. Art Edn. Assn., Nat. Art Edn. Assn., Colo. Artists Registry, Coll. Art Assn. Home: 2680 S Vine St Denver CO 80210-5949 Office: U No Colo Dept Visual Arts Greeley CO 80639-0001

JENKINS, WILLIAM L. (BILL JENKINS), congressman; b. Detroit, Nov. 29, 1936; m. Mary Kathryn Myers; 4 children. BA Tenn. Tech. U., 1958, JD U. Tenn., 1961. Farmer, Rogersville; atty.; circuit ct. judge 3d jud. dist. State of Tenn., 1990-96; mem. 105th-108th Congress from 1st Tenn. Dist., Washington, 1997—. Former dir. Home Fed. Savs. and Loan, Tenn. Bd. dirs. TVA, 1972-78; mem. Tenn. Ho. of Reps., 1963-71, spkr. of House, 1969-71; commr. Tenn. Dept. Conservation; policy advisor energy and legis. issues to gov. State of Tenn.; chmn. Tenn. Heart Assn., Cancer Crusade. Mem. Hawkins County Farm Bur., Am. Legion, Masons. Republican. Baptist. Avocations: hunting, fishing. Office: US House of Reps 1207 Longworth House Office Bl Washington DC 20515-4201 also: PO Box 769 320 W Center St Kingsport TN 37660-3658

JENKINS, ZERETHA LENORE, publishing executive; b. Monroe, La., Jan. 10, 1959; d. Woodrow and Rosa Lee Jenkins. BA in Psychology, U. La., 1981; MFA in Dramatic Writing, NYU, 1990. CICM N.Y., ICM N.Y. Pres., CEO E.F.S. Enterprises, Inc., N.Y.C., 1994—; pres. E.F.S. Prodns., N.Y.C., 1998—. Bd. dirs. Washington Heights Home Health Care Program, N.Y.C., 1994—. Author: Walking by Faith: An Afro-American Trilogy, 1999; screenwriter: screenplays The Rape of Leila Meshki, 1998, author poetry, short stories. Named winner script category, Writer's Digest Ann. Writing Competition, 1990. Mem.: The Drama League, Am. Screenwriters Assn. Avocations: tennis, video games, piano, ice skating, jazz. Office: EFS Enterprises Inc Ste 6E 2844 Eighth Ave New York NY 10039

JENKINS-ANDERSON, BARBARA JEANNE, pathologist, educator; b. Chgo. d. Carlyle Fielding and Alyce Louise (Walker) Stewart; m. Sidney Bernard Jenkins, Sept. 22, 1951 (div. June 1970); children: Kevin Jenkins, Judy Kelly, Sharolyn Sanders, Marc Jenkins, Kayla French; m. Arthur Eugene Anderson, Sept. 30, 1972. BS, U. Mich., 1950; MD, Wayne State U., 1957. Diplomate Am. Bd. Pathology. Intern Providence Hosp., Detroit, 1958-59, resident in psychiatry, 1959-60; resident in pathology Henry Ford Hosp., 1961-62, U. Mich. Affiliated Program, 1962-65; staff pathologist Wayne County Hosp., 1966-70, Detroit Receiving Hosp., 1970-72; asst. prof. pathology Wayne State U. Med. Sch., Detroit, 1970—72, assoc. prof. pathology, 1973—; adminstrv. med. dir. Detroit Med. Ctr. Univ. Labs., Detroit, 1988—; chief pathology Detroit Receiving Hosp./Univ. Health Clinic, Detroit, 1990—. Instr. U. Mich., 1966-70. Recipient Leonard Sain award U. Mich., 1980. Mem. Alpha Omega Alpha. Avocations: golf, interior design. Office: DMC Univ Labs 4201 Saint Antoine St Detroit MI 48201-2153

JENKINS-BRADY, TERRI LYNN, publishing executive, journalist; b. Albuquerque, Sept. 19, 1952; d. Hubert Arnold Jenkins and Helen Hope Zumwalt; m. Timothy Daniel Brady, July 4, 2000; stepchildren: Cori Danielle Brady, Colt Mitchell Brady. Student, U. Albuquerque, 1971—75, U. N.Mex., 1976. Pub. rels./fund-raiser March of Dimes; asst. to editor Prime Time, Albuquerque, 1995—2000, columnist, 2000—02; editor Al Bowl Querque Times, Albuquerque, 2000; editor in chief, ptnr. Write Up The Road Pub., Kenton, Tenn., 2002—; retail sales rep., freelance writer, 1974—79. Co-author: Romancing the Road, 2002; editor: Driven 4 Profits, 2002; author, editor: newsletter Billy Beaver's Traveler, 2001—02. Mem. adv. bd. Hiland Sr. Ctr., Albuquerque, 1996—97; co-founder Further Up the Road scholarship Rotary Club, Union City, Tenn., 2002. Recipient Bronze and Silver medals, Imperial Soc. Tchrs. Ballroom Dance, 1981. Mem.: Small Pubs. Assn. N.Am., Writer's Ink. Avocations: travel, writing, designing wearable art, astrology, ballroom dancing. Office: Write Up The Road Pub PO Box 69 Kenton TN 38233-0069 E-mail: info@writeuptheroad.com.

JENKINS-OWEN, SHARON, land use planner; b. Bklyn. d. George F. and Dorothy P. Jenkins; m. David Owen, June 30, 1990. BA, U. Tenn., 1984; MPA, Fla. Gulf Coast U., 2001. Cert. Am. Inst. Cert. Planners, 1994. Planner City of Fort Myers, Fla., 1988-89, Lee County, Fort Myers, Fla., 1997-99; planning project mgr. WilsonMiller, Inc., Fort Myers, Fla., 1989-2001; mem. Gov.'s Affordable Housing Study Commn., 2002—. Dist. dir. Calusa chpt. Fla. Planning and Zoning Assn., Fort Myers, 1993-95; leadership Lee County grad. S.W. Fla. C. of C., 1996; mem. 1997 FAPA conf. steering com. Fla. chpt. Am. Planning Assn., Fort Myers, Fla., 1996-97, exec. com., sect. chairperson, 1996-97, chpt. del., 1996-98, local sect. profl. devel. officer, 1998-2000, continuing profl. devel. program mem., 2000-03; Calusa chpt. dir. Fla. Planning and Zoning Assn., Fort Myers, Fla., 1999-2001, Legis. Policy com., 1999-2001; chamber mem. Govt. Affairs subcom. Greater Fort Myers C. of C., Fla., 1999-2001; mem. real estate investment soc., Fort Myers, Fla., 2000-2001; land use subcom. mem. Smart Growth, Fort Myers, Fla., 2000-2001; bd. dirs. Econ. Devel. Coalition, Ft. Myers, 2000—. Recipient USAA Nat. award U.S. Achievement Acad., 2001. Mem.: Fla. Planning and Zoning Assn. (v.p. membership 2002—03). Office: WilsonMiller Inc 4571 Colonial Blvd Fort Myers FL 33912 Fax: 941-939-3412. E-mail: sjowen@wilsonmiller.com.

JENKS, DENNIS, publishing executive; Owner Osborne/Jenks Prodns., Wethersfield, Conn. Office: care Osborne/Jenks Prodns 936 Silas Deane Hwy Wethersfield CT 06109-4273

JENKS, GEORGE MILAN, retired lawyer; b. Dickinson, N.D., Feb. 26, 1933; s. John Leo and Mary Magdalene (Bleth) J.; m. Elaine Marjorie Ketterling, May 12, 1956; children: Gregory Martell, Jeffrey Michael. AS in Civil Engring., Multnomah Jr. Coll., 1958; BS, U. Oreg., 1960, MEd, 1961; JD, Lewis & Clark Coll., 1971. Bar: Oreg. 1972, U.S. Ct. Appeals, 1977, U.S. Supreme Ct. 1977. Assoc. Law Firm David Weinstein, Portland, Oreg., 1972-75; sr. ptnr. Jenks & Weinstein, P.C., Portland, 1975-98; ret., 1998. Lectr., instr. Bus. Law Inst., Portland, 1975-82; sec. Levesque & Assocs., Portland, 1985—; advisor ct. rules Multnomah County Dist. Ct. Contbr. articles to profl. jours. Pres. Milwaukie (Oreg.) Luth. Ch., 1973-75; bd. dirs. Luth. Family Svcs. Oreg. and S.W. Wash., 1975-82; chmn. bd. dirs. Milwaukie Luth. Found., 1975—. With U.S. Army, 1953-56. Mem. ABA, Oreg. State Bar Assn., Multnomah County Bar Assn., Clackamas County Bar Assn., Kiwanis. Republican. Avocations: fishing, clamming, crabbing, boating, gardening.

JENKS, GLENN ARNOLD, musician, educator; b. Boston; s. Edwin Hamilton Jenks and Nancy Arnold; m. Faith Perley Getchell, Sept. 17, 1981. MusB, Earlham Coll., 1969. Tchr. Maine Ctr. Inst., Pittsfield, 1970—71, Rivers Country Day Sch., Weston, Mass., 1971—73; performer Weston and Camden, Maine, 1973—75; performer, sideman, composer Camden, 1975—78; tchr., performer, composer, 1978—. Composer: more than 75 mus. works, including waltzes, lyric pieces and ragtime for piano, concerto for piano and orch., string quartet, sonata for violin and piano, vocal music, pop stylings; editor: (newsletter) Mid-Maine Rose Soc., 1991—92. Mem. bd. incorporators Bay Chamber Concerts, Rockport, Maine, 1991—; bd. dirs. Downeast Friends of Folk Arts, Camden, 1981—85, Merryspring Hort. Park, Camden, 1986—95. Recipient Hon. Mention, Woodrow Wilson Found., 1969. Mem.: Maine Composers Forum, Maine Music Tchrs. Assn. (commd. composer chmn. 1998—99), Am. Rose Soc. Democrat. Avocations: bird watching, gardening, lecturing on roses, hiking. Office: Bonnie Banks Prodns PO Box 811 Camden ME 04843

JENKS, THOMAS EDWARD, lawyer; b. Dayton, Ohio, May 31, 1929; s. Wilbur L. and Anastasia A. (Ahern) J.; m. Marianna Fischer, Nov. 10, 1961; children— Pamela (dec.), William, David, Christine, Daniel, Douglas Student, Miami U., Oxford, Ohio, 1947-50; JD cum laude, Ohio State U., 1953; hon. grad., U.S. Naval Sch. Justice, 1953. Bar: Ohio 1953, U.S. Dist. Ct. (so. dist.) Ohio 1961, U.S. Supreme Ct. 1971, U.S. Ct. Appeals (6th cir.) 1984. Pvt. practice, Dayton, 1955—; atty. Jenks, Pyper & Oxley, Dayton. Lectr. in field. Served to 1st lt. USMC, 1953-55 Fellow Am. Coll. Trial Lawyers (life), Am. Bar Found., Ohio Bar Found.; mem. ABA (ho. of dels. 1985-88), Dayton Bar Assn. (pres. 1978-79), Ohio Bar Assn. (bd. govs. litigation sect., 1990-98), Internat. Assn. Def. Counsel, Ohio Assn. Civil Trial Attys., Am. Bd. Trial Advs. (adv.), Kettering C. of C. (past pres.), Kettering Holiday at Home Found. (past pres.), Order of Coif, Dayton Lawyers Club (pres. 1999-2002), Optimist Club (past pres. Oakwood chpt.), Phi Delta Phi, Sigma Chi. Republican. Roman Catholic. Office: Jenks Pyper & Oxley Courthouse Plz SW 10 N Ludlow St Dayton OH 45402

JENKS, TOM, writer; b. Temple, Tex., Aug. 23, 1950; s. Edwin Riley and Ouida (Baxter) J.; m. Carol Louise Edgarian, Aug. 21, 1993; children: Richard, Anne Riley, Lucy Honor, Olivia Far. BA magna cum laude, U. Va., 1980; MFA, Columbia U., 1983. Contbg. editor Paris Rev., N.Y.C., 1980—; assoc. fiction editor Esquire mag., N.Y.C., 1983-85; sr. editor Scribners, N.Y.C., 1985-87; lit. editor GQ mag., N.Y.C., 1987-91; vis. lectr. Iowa Writer's Workshop, Iowa City, 1989; Hurst prof. Washington U., St. Louis, 1990; vis. prof. U. Calif., Davis, 1990-93. Editor Writer Nights Lincoln Ctr., N.Y.C., 1986-88. Author: Our Happiness, 1990; editor: Hemingway's The Garden of Eden, 1986, (with Raymond Carver) American Short Story Masterpieces, 1987, (with Carol Edgarian) The Writer's Life, 1997; pub., editor Narrative Mag., 2003—; contbr. articles to profl. jours. Mem. Poets Editors Novelists Am. E-mail: ti@narrativemagazine.com.

JENKS, WILLIAM ROBERT, music educator; b. Richlands, Va., Aug. 15, 1974; s. Maskel David and Linda Carroll Jenks; m. Angelica Joy Jones, June 10, 2000. BS in Edn., Concord Coll., Athens, W.Va., 1997. Cert. tchr. Va., W.Va. Ch. dir. of music Concord United Meth. Ch., Athens, W.Va., 1995—98; music/band tchr. West Iredell Mid. Sch. Iredell-Statesville Schs., Statesville, NC, 1998—99, dir. of bands Statesville H.S., 1998—99; ch. dir. of music Wesley Meml. United Meth. Ch., Statesville, 1998—99; assoc. dir. bands. Richland H.S. Tazewell

County Pub. Schs., Richlands, Va., 1999—2000, wrestling coach Richland H.S., 1999—2000, wrestling coach Graham H.S. Bluefield, W.Va., 2000—; ch. dir. music Bland St. United Meth. Ch., Bluefield, W.Va., 1999—2001; band/music tchr. Straley and Ceres Schs. Mercer County Pub. Schs., Princeton, W.Va., 2000—02; ch. dir. music Carr Meml. United Meth. Ch., Glenwood, W.Va., 2001—; dir. of bands Pocahontas H.S. Tazewell County Pub. Schs., Pocahontas, Va., 2002—03; band dir. Spanishburg Sch. Mercer County Pub. Schs., 2003—. Guest condr./clinician Mercer County Handbell/Choirchime Festival, Princeton, W.Va., 2000—02, Wyo. All-County H.S. Band, Pineville, W.Va., 2000; guest condr. Radford U. Wind Ensemble, Radford, Va., 2000, Princeton All-City Band, Princeton, W.Va., 2000—; guest clinician Capital H.S., Charleston, W.Va., 1995—. Bd. mem. W.Va. All-State Children's Chorus, Charleston, W.Va., 2001—02. Recipient Outstanding Jazz Performer, UNC-Charlotte, 1995, Outstanding Brass Soloist-Trombone, W.Va. Music Educator's Assn., 1995, 1996, Honors Competition Soloist, Concord Coll., 1996, Who's Who Among Coll. and U. Students, Marquis' Who's Who and Concord Coll., 1996; grantee Grant toward a performance given by The Montclaire String Quartet, W.Va. Commn. of the Arts, 2001; scholar Music Talent Scholarship, Concord Coll., 1992, Ella Holroyd Music Scholarship, 1994, Bill Caruth, Sr. Music Scholarship, 1996. Mem.: Internat. Assn. of Jazz Educators (assoc.), NEA (assoc.), Internat. Trombone Assn. (assoc.), Music Educator's Nat. Conf (assoc.), Phi Sigma Phi (life). Independent. United Methodist. Home: HC 71 Box 200 Bailey Hollow Road Princeton WV 24740 Office: Spanishburg Sch Spanishburg WV Personal E-mail: bobby_jenks@hotmail.com. E-mail: bobbyjenks@amateurwrestler.com.

JENKS-DAVIES, KATHRYN RYBURN, retired daycare provider and owner, civic worker; b. Lynchburg, Va., Oct. 9, 1916; d. Charles Arthur and Jessie Katherine (Moorman) Ryburn; m. Thomas Edgar Jenks Jr., Sept. 9, 1941 (dec. June 1975); children: Thomas Edgar III, Jessika, Timothy; m. Robert E. Davies, Dec. 27, 1986 (dec. Mar. 1996). BS, State Tchr. Coll., 1938; postgrad., Mary Washington Coll., 1947-48, U. Va., 1957-58, William and Mary Coll., 1967-68, Va. Commonwealth U., 1969-70. Elem. tchr. various schs., Grundy, Va., 1939-41; phys. therapist U.S. Army, Ft. Bragg, N.C., 1942, operator motor pool Ft. Still, Okla., 1943-44, occupational therapist Augusta, Ga., 1944-45; instr. phys. edn. King George (Va.) High Sch., 1947-48, Stafford (Va.) High Sch., 1949-50, substitute tchr., 1950-53; owner, dir. Kay's Kindergarten, Fredericksburg, Va., 1959-83; ret., 1983. Featured in Fredericksburg Times mag., The Free Lance-Star and Richmond Newspapers. Counselor Girl Scouts U.S.A., Grundy, Va., 1939-41; life mem. Kenmore Assn., 1949—; mem. Hist. Fredericksburg Found., Inc., 1953—, vol. Garden Week and Christmas Open House; mem. Mental Health Bd., 1978-84; founder Ford Franklin Found., 1968-78; mem. Fredericksburg Clean Cmty. Commn., 1987—; rep. United Way, Fredericksburg; instr. art ceramics Cmty. Ctr. Fredericksburg, 1950-80; bd. dirs. Miss Fredericksburg Fair Pageant, 1965-88; participant cmty. parades; coord. Fredericksburg Agrl. Fair 18th Century Craft People and Artisans, 1988-93, also others; bd. dirs. Antique Farm Implements, Gas and Steam Engines, 1989-93, Fredericksburg Fair, 1994-96; active State Fair of Va., 1981-95, Am. Heritage Showcase Endl. Reenactment Pioneer Farmstead, 1981-96. Recipient Virginia Ellison Vol. Svc. award Fredericksburg Clean Community Commn., 1976-87, Recognition of Svc. award, 1983-84, 1st, 2nd. and 3rd pl. trophies cmty. parades, awards radio Stas. WFLS and WFVA, 1949-89; honored by Kiwanians for travelogue for fund raiser, 1995—, vol. award, 1997. Mem. AAUW (advt. chmn. travelogue 1971-89, Donor Honoree award 1983, 98, bd. dirs. 1971-79), Lioness Club (bd. dir. 1968-87, Lioness Tamer 1984—, bd. dirs. 1996-97, Tongue Wagger 1985, 96—), Soroptimist Internat. Fredericksburg (life mem., sec. 1971-73, pres. 1973-75, bd. dirs. 1971-78, co-chmn. Soroptimist Travelogue 1991-93, First Class Pub. Recognition Trophy 1986, Women Helping Women award 1982, named 1 of 5 who have made a difference in cmty. 1994), Order of Eastern Star (hostess 1995, 96, 97, 98), Nat. League of Fredericksburg (bd. dir., Svc. Recognition Trophies 1963, 69, 80), Izaac Walton League (bd. dir. Dog Mart parade 1965-72). Republican. Episcopalian. Avocations: ceramics, drama, dancing, travel, golf. Home: 8 Blair Rd Fredericksburg VA 22405-3025

JENKS-JAY, NAN, environmentalist educator; b. Savana, Ill., Dec. 2, 1951; d. Philip Armstrong and Ruth Louise Jenks; m. Carl E. Phelps, Nov. 22, 2000; 1 child, Jessica E. Jay. BA in Biology, Kent (Ohio)State U., 1976; M in Environ. Studies, Yale U., New Haven, Conn., 1986. Field rschr. raptor breeding census Ohio Biol. Survey, Columbus, 1974—76; dir. Nantucket Island tern mgmt. and piping plover protection program summers Trustees of Reservations, Beverly, Mass., 1978—85; instr. environ. and life sci. dept. Berkshire C.C., Pittsfield, Mass., 1979—81; assoc. dir. environ. studies Williams Coll., Williamstown, Mass., 1981—94; Hedco endowed prof. in environ. studies, dir. environ. studies U. Redlands (Calif.), 1994—97; dir. environ. affairs and sr. lectr. Middlebury (Vt.) Coll., 1997—. Bd. of trustees The Nature Conservancy, VT Chpt., Montpelier, Vt., 1998—; external rev. com. environ. studies program Middlebury (Vt.) Coll., 1988, Bowdoin Coll., Brunswick, Maine, 1989, U. Vt., Burlington, 1996, Rowan U., Glassboro, NJ, 2001, Lewis and Clark Coll., Portland, Oreg., 2001, U. Alaska, Fairbanks, 2002; roundtable to design sustainable sci. ctr. for 2012 Project Kaleidoscope, Washington, 2003; avian and wetland specialist, internat. countryside stewardship exch. team Countryside Inst., Glastonbury, England, 1993; bd. trustees Shelburne (Vt.) Farms, 1999—; coun. of acad. advisors for environ. program's study New Eng. Bd. Higher Edn., Boston, 1992—94; environ. grad. student fellowship award com. Robert Switzer Found., Concord, NH, 1988—94. Mem. editl. adv. bd. Orion Nature Quarterly, 1990—98, Assn. Environ. Profls., 1994—2000, referee Jour. Field Ornithology, 1990—2000; contbr. articles, chapters to books. Com. mem. & chair ('83, '86) Williamstown Conservation Commn., Williamstown, Mass., 1979—86; exec. bd. mem. Mass. Dept. Environ. Mgmt., Boston, 1986—93, chair, 1989—93; adv. com. on natural resources and environment Senator Jane Swift, Boston, 1990—94; adv. com. we. Mass. Mass. Assn. of Conservation Commns., Amherst, 1988. Recipient Allen Morgan award for membership devel., Nat. Land Trust Alliance, 1994, EPA Environ. Merit award, 2003, Vermont Gov. Award for Environ. Excellence, 2003; grant Shared Instrn. Materials for Environ. Studies Programs, New Eng. Consortium Undergrad. Sci. Program, 1991, Sense of Place: defining the Character of a Rural New Eng. Cmty. grant, Mass. Found. for the Humanities, 1992—93, grant Environ. Design Studio: Collaborative Learning, Problem Solving and GIS Software, NEH/FIPSE, 1994—96, grant, U.S. EPA, 1996, Nathan Cummings Found., 1999—2001, grant Towards an Enhanced Environ. Studies Program, Andrew W. Mellon Found., 2000—03. Achievements include Founder NJJ regional land conservation organization, 1986; sustainable coll. strategic plan. Office: Middlebury College Farrell House Middlebury VT 05753 Office Fax: 802-443-2458. E-mail: jenksjay@middlebury.edu.

JENNERICH, EDWARD JOHN, university official and dean; b. Bklyn., Oct. 22, 1945; s. William James and Anna Johanna (Whicker) J.; m. Elaine Zaremba, May 27, 1972; children— Ethan Edward, Emily Elaine BA, Trenton State Coll., 1967; MSL.S., Drexel U., 1970; PhD, U. Pitts., 1974. Cert. tchr., learning resources specialist. Tchr. U.S. history Rahway High Sch., N.J., 1967-70; librarian Westinghouse High Sch., Pitts. Pub. Sch., 1970-74; adminstrv. intern U. Pitts, 1973; chmn. dept. library sci. Baylor U., Waco, Tex., 1974-83; dean Sch. Library Sci. So. Conn. State U., New Haven, 1983-84; v.p. acad. affairs Va. Intermont Coll., Bristol, 1984-87; grad. dean Seattle U., 1987-89; assoc. provost for acad. adminstrn., dean Grad. Sch., 1989-97; pres. Knowledge N.W. Inc., 1997—. Mem. rev. panel Fulbright Adminstrv. Exch., 1983-86. Co-author: University Administration in Great Britain, 1983, The Reference Interview as a Creative Art, 1987, 2d edit., 1997; contbr. articles to profl. jours. Bd. dirs. Waco Girls Club, Tex., 1977-83 Mem. ALA (office for libr. pers. resources 1980-82), Am. Assn. Univ. Adminstrs. (bd. dirs. 1980-82, 83-86, 89-93, 94—, v.p. 1996—, exec. com. 1982-87, chmn. overseas liaison com. 1982-87, Eileen Tosney Adminstrv. Excellence award 1985), Assn. for Coll. and Rsch. Librs. (exec. bd. dirs. 1984-88), Phi Delta Kappa. Republican. Episcopalian. Avocations: collecting and painting military miniatures, reading, travel, outdoor sports, sailing. Home: 6935 NE 164th St Kenmore WA 98028-4282

JENNERICH, ELAINE, librarian; b. New Castle, Pa., Apr. 17, 1947; d. C. Paul and Regina Anna (Wajert) Zaremba; m. Edward John Jennerich, May 27, 1972; children: Ethan Edward, Emily Elaine. AB, Syracuse U., 1968; MSLS, Drexel U., 1970; PhD, U. Pitts., 1974. Ref. libr. CarLow Coll., Pitts., 1971-74; head ref. svc. Baylor U., Waco, Tex., 1974-83; libr. bond investment Aetna Life and Casualty, Hartford, Conn., 1983-84; ref./media libr. Va. Intermont Coll., Bristol, Va., 1984-85; libr. dir. Emory & Henry Coll., Emory, Va., 1985-87; circulation libr. U. Wash., Seattle, 1988 89; constrn. coord. U. Wash. Librs., Seattle, 1989-91, staff devel. coord., 1991—. Co-author: Reference Interview As Creative Art, 1997. Mem. ALA, Phi Beta Mu, Chi Omega. Roman Catholic. Office: Univ of Washington Suzzallo Libr PO Box 352900 Seattle WA 98195-2900

JENNETT, SHIRLEY SHIMMICK, home care management executive, nurse; b. Jennings, Kans., May 1, 1937; d. William and Mabel C. (Mowry) Shimmick; m. Nelson K. Jennett, Aug. 20, 1960 (div. 1972); children: Jon W., Cheryl L.; m. Albert J. Kukral, Apr. 16, 1977 (div. 1990) Diploma, Rsch. Hosp. Sch. Nursing, Kansas City, Mo., 1958. RN, Mo., Colo., Tex., Ill. Staff nurse, head nurse Rsch. Hosp., 1958-60; head nurse Penrose Hosp., Colorado Springs, Colo., 1960-62, Hotel Dieu Hosp., El Paso, Tex., 1962-63; staff nurse Oak Park (Ill.) Hosp., 1963-64, NcNeal Hosp., Berwyn, Ill., 1964-65, St. Anthony Hosp., Denver, 1968-69; staff nurse, head nurse, nurse recruiter Luth. Hosp., Wheat Ridge, Colo., 1969-79; owner, mgr. Med. Placement Svcs., Lakewood, Colo., 1980-84; vol., primary care nurse, admissions coord., team mgr. Hospice of Metro Denver, 1984-88, dir. patient and family svcs., 1988, exec. dir., 1988-94; pres., profl. geriatric care mgr. Care Mgmt. & Resources, Inc., Denver, 1996—. Mem. NAFE, Nat. Women Bus. Owners Assn., Nat. Hospice Orgn. (bd. dirs. 1992-95, coun. former bd. mems. 1995—), Nat. Orgn. Profl. Geriatric Care Mgrs., Denver Bus. Women's Network. Mem. Ch. of Religious Sci. Avocations: reading, walking, golf. Office: Care Mgmt & Resources Inc 2055 S Oneida St Ste 150 Denver CO 80224-2435 E-mail: sjennett@earthnet.net.

JENNEWEIN, JAMES JOSEPH, architect; b. New Rochelle, N.Y., July 20, 1929; s. Carl Paul and Gina (Pirra) J.; m. Edith Joan Wilson, Nov. 28, 1953; children: James Christopher, Gina Louise, Donald Andrew, Jonathan Paul. BArch, Syracuse U., 1952. Fulbright scholar Stuttgart U. (Technische Hochschule), Federal Republic of Germany, 1955-56; draftsman McCoy & Blair Architects, White Plains, N.Y., 1956-57; designer Harrison & Abramovitz Architects, N.Y.C., 1957-60; prin./ptnr. Jennewein Architects, N.Y.C., 1961-62; prin. McElvy, Jennewein, Stefany & Howard, Architects, Tampa, Fla., 1962-84, Jennewein, Archtl. Planning, Tampa, 1984; prin., ptnr. Jennewein Schemmer and Assocs., Tampa, 1985-91; ptnr. Ruyle and Masters Plus Jennewein, Architects, P.A., Tampa, 1992—. Pres. Fla. State Bd. Architecture, 1969-72. Trustee Brookgreen Gardens, Murrells Inlet, S.C., 1983—; chmn. Gasparilla Art Show, Tampa, 1977, Tampa C. of C. Environ. Com., 1987; pres. Tampa Bay Art Ctr., 1975, Tampa Mus. Art, 1985. Lt. (j.g.) USN, 1952-55. Recipient House of Yr. award Archtl. Record, N.Y.C., 1963, Ybor Sta. P.O. award Hillsborough County Planning Commn., Tampa. 1989. Fellow AIA; mem. Fla. Assn. AIA (pres. 1985-86, Pullara award 1985), Fla. Cen. Chpt. AIA (pres. 1967-68, Honor medal 1985), Nat. Sculpture Soc. (allied profl.), Tampa Yacht Club, University Club, Ye Mystic Krewe of Gasparilla, Tampa. Republican. Episcopalian. Avocations: fishing, sailing. Home: 4710 W Clear Ave Tampa FL 33629-5512 Office: Ruyle and Masters Plus Jennewein Archs 3333 W Kennedy Blvd Ste 203 Tampa FL 33609-2959

JENNIGES, NATHANIEL JOHN, marketing professional; b. Springfield, Minn., June 10, 1976; s. Karen K. and Gregory L. Noble(Stepfather); m. Sarah Anne Stipher, June 16, 2001. BSEE, Rose-Hulman Inst. Tech., 1998. Mfg. process engr. Motorola CSG, Libertyville, Ill., 1997—98; process quality engr. Motorola PCS, Libertyville, Ill., 1998—99, product quality mgr., 1999—2001, tech. mktg. analyst, 2001—01, mktg. mgr., 2002—. Founder, bd. dirs. eKiwanis Chgo., 2001—. Achievements include patents pending for Methods of Using Presence Information in Mobile Devices. Avocations: travel, sports, computers. Home: Apt 202 1919 Country Dr Grayslake IL 60030 Office: Motorola Personal Communications Sector 600 North US Highway 45 Libertyville IL 60048 Personal E-mail: njenniges@earthlink.net. E-mail: nathan.jenniges@motorola.com.

JENNINGS, ALFRED HIGSON, JR., music educator, actor, singer; b. Danbury, Conn., Dec. 24, 1959; s. Alfred Higson and Linda (Keating) J. BS, U. Conn., 1982, MMus, 1984. Cert. profl. educator, Conn. Teaching asst., choral dept. U. Conn., Storrs, 1982-84; tchr. music Danbury Pub. Schs., 1985—; ptnr. Jennings Oil Co., 1999—. Asst. condr. Concert Choir/Chamber Singers, U. Conn., 1982-84, asst. dir. Annual Elizabethan Christmas Dinner Concert, 1983; musical dir. for theatrical prodns. Danbury High Sch., 1985-88; baritone soloist St. Matthew Episcopal Ch. Choir, Wilton, Conn., 1986—. Vocal dir. plays The Sound of Music, 1986, Camelot, 1988, Annie, 1990, others; actor in plays Godspell, 1985, South Pacific, 1987, Oklahoma!, 1988, You're a Good Man, Charlie Brown, 1988, Into the Woods, 1991, Assassins, 1992, Sweeney Todd, 2001, others; actor, in opera Amahl and the Night Visitors, 1998, 2000. Named Tchr. of Yr., South St. Elem. Sch., 1990, 97, Roberts Ave. Elem. Sch., 1997; recipient Project Redesign grant Danbury Pub. Schs., 1991-92, Exemplary Program award, Conn. Assn. Schs., 1997. Mem. NEA, Musicals at Richter, Inc. (sec. 1987-88, v.p. 1988-89, program editor 1991-94), Orff-Schulwerk Assn., Conn. Edn. Assn., Music Educators Nat. Conf., Conn. Music Educators Assn. Avocations: singing, conducting, theatre. Home: 8 Cipolla Ln Brookfield CT 06804-1511 Office: Danbury Pub Schs 63 Beaver Brook Rd Danbury CT 06810-6211 E-mail: ahj@aol.com.

JENNINGS, ALSTON, lawyer; b. West Helena, Ark., Oct. 30, 1917; s. Earp Franklin and Irma (Alston) J.; m. Dorothy Buie Jones, June 12, 1943; children: Alston, Eugene Franklin, Ann Buie. AB, Columbia U., 1938; JD, Northwestern U., 1941. Bar: Ark. 1941. Practiced law, Little Rock, 1947—; spl. agt. intelligence unit Treasury Dept., 1946; asso. Wright, Harrison, Lindsey & Upton, 1949-51, mem., 1951-60, Wright, Lindsey, Jennings, Lester & Shults, 1960-65, Wright, Lindsey & Jennings, 1965—. Mem. adv. bd. Salvation Army, Pulaski County. Served to lt. USNR, 1941-45. Fellow Am. Bar Found.; mem. ABA, Ark. Bar Assn., Pulaski County Bar Assn. (past pres.), Internat. Assn. Def. Counsel (pres. 1972-73), Am. Coll. Trial Lawyers (regent 1975-79, treas. 1979-80, pres.-elect 1980-81, pres. 1981-82) Home: 1801 Beechwood St Little Rock AR 72207-2001 Office: 200 W Capitol Ave Little Rock AR 72201-3605

JENNINGS, CHARLES ROBERT, educator; b. NYC, May 14, 1963; s. Norman Laurie and Nellie Mae (Lewis) J. BS, U. Md., 1986; MS, CUNY, 1990; MRP, Cornell U., 1994, PhD, 1996. Project mgr. Tridata Corp., Arlington, Va., 1988-91; asst. prof. pub. mgmt. John Jay Coll Criminal Justice, CUNY, NYC, 1997—2002; dep. commr. Pub. Safety, White Plains, NY, 2002—. Cons. in field. Chair, mem. Bd. Fire Commr., Ithaca, NY, 1993-96. Mem. Am. Statis. Assn., Nat. Fire Protection Assn., Regional Sci. Assn. Internat., Urban and Regional Info. Systems, Inst. Fire Engr. (assoc.). E-mail: cjennings@manitouinc.com.

JENNINGS, DEAN THOMAS, lawyer; b. Mar. 17, 1951; s. Paul Alyosis and Bonnie Mae; m. Kathleen Kay Kiefer, June 15, 1973; children: Matthew Thomas, Margaret Jo. BS in English, Iowa State U., 1973; JD, Creighton U., 1976. Bar: Iowa 1976, Nebr. 1982, U.S. Dist. Ct. (so. dist.) Iowa 1976. Tchr., coach Boone H.S., Iowa, 1972-73; ptnr. McGinn, McGinn, Jennings & Springer, Council Bluffs, Iowa, 1974—. Mem. ABA, Assn. Am. Trial Lawyers, Iowa Bar Assn., Nebr. Bar Assn. Office: McGinn McGinn Jennings & Springer 25 Main Pl Ste 500 Council Bluffs IA 51503 E-mail: mmjs@cbiowa.com.

JENNINGS, FREDERIC BEACH, JR., economist, saltwater flyfishing guide; b. Boston, Dec. 29, 1945; s. Frederic Beach III and Ellen (Osgood) J.; m. Lucille Candace Giglio, Aug. 15, 1975; children: Frederic Beach V, Thomas Chapin. BA magna cum laude, Harvard U., 1968; MA in Econs., Stanford U., 1980, PhD in Econs., 1985. Jr. medicare acct. Blue Cross-Blue Shield, Boston, 1968-69; ind. rsch. fellow Inst. Humane Studies, Menlo Park, Calif., 1969-71, 77-78; asst. mgr. Globe Bag Co., South Boston, 1972-73; rsch. asst. Charles River Assocs., Cambridge, Mass., 1973-74; rsch. and teaching fellow Stanford (Calif.) Dept. Econs., 1974-79; instr. econs. Tufts U., Medford, Mass., 1979-83; asst. prof. Bentley Coll., Waltham, Mass., 1985-87; sr. econ. cons. The Mac Rsch. Group, Cambridge, 1987-88, Charles River Assocs., Boston, 1988-91; sr. mgr. Econ. Analysis Group Office of Fed. Tax Svcs. Arthur Andersen & Co., Washington, 1991-92; pres. EconoLogistics, Ipswich, Mass., 1992—; owner Peak Dawn Anglers, Ipswich, 1996—; founder Ctr. Ecol. Econ. and Ethical Edn., Ipswich, 1998—. Chmn., rep. Stanford Grad. Student Coun., 1974-76; senator Stanford Student Senate, 1975-76; co-pres. Associated Students Stanford U., 1976-77; founder Stanford Grad. Students Assn., 1978-79, The Bentley Participants, Waltham, 1986-87, Full Circle Discussion Group Tufts U., Medford, 1981-84; resident assoc. Residential Edn., Stanford, 1978-79. Author: Democracy in Disarray, 1978, Mystical Tides, 1996, (paper) Value, Exchange and Profit, 1966, (essays) Academy, Society and Personal Growth, 1983, Whither Our Education?, 1983; co-author Greenpeace Study on Fisheries Mgmt., 1999. Mem. joint Greenpeace Study on Fisheries Mgmt., 1999. Mem. Am. Econ. Assn., Cliometrics Soc., Indsl. Orgn. Soc., Western Econ. Assn., Atlantic Econ. Soc., Kress Soc., Harvard Travellers Club, Rotary. Avocations: fly fishing, sailing, skiing, tennis, golf. Home: 261 Argilla Rd Ipswich MA 01938-2615 Office: EconoLogistics 59 Market St Ipswich MA 01938-2212 also: Peak Dawn Anglers PO Box 946 Ipswich MA 01938-0946 E-mail: Fbj@fohe.zzn.com.

JENNINGS, HENRY SMITH, III, cardiologist; b. Atlanta, May 16, 1951; s. Henry Smith Jr. and Elizabeth (Martin) J.; m. Polly Cooper; 1 child, Mary Bailey. BS summa cum laude, Davidson Coll., 1973; MD, Vanderbilt U., 1977. Diplomate Am. Bd. Internal Medicine, subspecialty cardiovascular diseases and interventional cardiology, Nat. Bd. Med. Examiners; lic. physician and surgeon, Tenn., Ky. Intern internal medicine Vanderbilt U. Affiliated Hosps., Nashville, 1977-78, resident internal medicine, 1978-80; fellow clin. cardiology divsn. cardiology dept. medicine Vanderbilt U., Nashville, 1980-82; clin. instr. medicine Vanderbilt U. Sch. Medicine, Nashville, 1982-89, asst. clin. prof. medicine, 1989-97, assoc. clin. prof. medicine, 1997—; med. dir. Cardiac Rehab. Ctr. St. Thomas Hosp., Nashville, 1984—2001, assoc. chief cardiac scis., 2001—. Mem. active staff St. Thomas Hosp., Nashville; affiliate staff Vanderbilt U. Med. Ctr., Nashville; mem. courtesy staff Centennial Med. Ctr., Nashville; mem. cons. staff Bapt. Hosp., Nashville. Contbr. articles to profl. jours. Bd. dirs. Heart Inst., St. Thomas Hosp., Nashvile, 1992-94, Tenn. Heart Inst., 1989-91. Justin Potter med. scholar Vanderbilt U. Sch. Medicine, Nashville, 1973-77. Fellow ACP, Am. Coll. Cardiology, Am. Coll. Chest Physicians, Coun. Clin. Cardiology Am. Heart Assn., Soc. Cardiac Angiography and Interventions; mem. AMA, Am. Assn. Cardiovasc. and Pulmonary Rehab., Internat. Soc. Heart Transplantation, Am. Heart Assn., So. Med. Assn., Tenn. Med. Assn., Nashville Acad. Medicine, Gottlieb Friesinger Soc. (pres.-elect 2001, pres. 2002). Methodist. Home: Northumberland 3 Castle Rising Nashville TN 37215-4126 Office: Saint Thomas Cardiology Cons PC 4230 Harding Pike Ste 530 Nashville TN 37205-2013 Fax: 615-292-2763. E-mail: hjennings@stcardiology.com.

JENNINGS, JACOB HILL, lawyer, director; b. Bishopville, SC, May 15, 1930; s. Henry Caldwell and Mary Green (Hill) Jennings; m. Jane Marie Hancock, Feb. 22, 1958; children: Jacob H., Rebeckah B. BA, Wofford Coll., 1950; LLB, U. SC, 1953. Bar: SC 1953, US Dist. Ct./SC 1955, US Supreme Ct. 1977. Ptnr. Jennings & Jennings, Bishopville, 1955; dir. Nat. Bank SC, Sumter, SC; mem. SC Legis., SC, 1958; bd. dir. Lee County Meml. Hosp., Bishopville, 1984. Editor: (Law Quar.) SC Law Quar., 1953. Lt. col. USAF, 1953—55. Mem.: So. Conf. Bar Pres., ABA, Am. Coll. Trial Lawyers, SC Bar (pres. 1984—85). Methodist. Office: Jennings & Jennings PA 1 Court House Sq Bishopville SC 29010-1600

JENNINGS, JAMES WILSON, JR., lawyer; b. Temple, Tex., Aug. 10, 1943; s. James W. and Mary Lee (Patton) J.; m. Anne Rita Moran, Aug. 9, 1969; children: Helene, Anne Conway, Mary. BA in English, Washington and Lee U., 1965, JD, 1972. Bar: Va. 1972, U.S. Dist. Ct. (we. dist.) Va. 1972, U.S. Ct. Appeals (4th cir.) 1980, U.S. Supreme Ct. 1991. Law clk. Supreme Ct. of Va., Richmond, 1972-73; ptnr. Woods, Rogers & Hazlegrove, Roanoke, Va., 1973—. Adj. prof. Washington and Lee Sch. of Law, 1999. Chmn. bd. editors Jour. Civil Litig., 1990-94, Mcpl. Liability Reporter, 1990-93, bd. editors Def. Coun. Jour.; contbr. articles to profl. jours. Co-chmn. drive for attys. United Way, 1975; chmn. fund drive for attys. Am. Cancer Soc., 1976; bd. dirs. Art Mus. of Western Va., 1990-96, v.p., 1995-96; bd. dirs. Opera Roanoke, 1988-96, pres., 1996; trustee Funds of Diocese of Southwestern Va.; v.p. Art Mus. of Western Va., 1995-96. Lt. (j.g.) USN, 1965-69. Fellow Va. Law Found., 1997. Mem. ABA, Nat. Assn. Ry. Trial Counsel, Am. Bd. Trial Advocates (pres. Va. chpt. 1995-96), Va. Bar Assn., Va. Assn. Def. Attys. (pres. 1988-89), Roanoke City Bar Assn. (medical-legal liaison com. 1990-94), Internat. Assn. Def. Counsel, Assn. Def. Trial Attys. (exec. coun. 1997-2003, pres. 2002), Def. Rsch. Inst. (bd. dirs. 2001-03, Exceptional Performance citation 1989), Assn. Internat. de Droit des Assurances, Downtown Roanoke Inc. (bd. dirs. 1981-89), Washington and Lee Alumni Assn. (bd. dirs. 1984-88), Roanoke Regional C. of C. (bd. dirs. 1989-93), Order of Coif, Roanoke Country Club (bd. govs.), Shenandoah Club. Episcopalian. Home: 2710 Rosalind Ave SW Roanoke VA 24014-2330 Office: Woods Rogers & Hazlegrove 10 S Jefferson St Ste 1400 Roanoke VA 24011-1331

JENNINGS, JERRY D. federal agency administrator; b. Flint, Mich., July 2, 1940; s. C. Oren and Retha S. (Wood) J.; m. Misako Sonoda, Oct. 10, 1976; children: Catherine, Victoria, Elizabeth. Student, Mott Community Coll., Flint, Mich., 1958-59, U. Mich., 1960; BS, Ea. Mich. U., 1961; student, John Jay Coll., CUNY, 1970-71, Harvard U., 1987. Intelligence officer CIA, Washington and S.E. Asia, 1965-68; spl. agt. FBI, Memphis, N.Y.C., 1968-72; spl. asst. to dir. Office Nat. Narcotics Intelligence Dept. Justice, Washington, 1972-73; staff mem. NSC, Washington, 1973-82; exec. dir. Office of Sci. and Tech. Policy and White House Sci. Coun., Washington, 1982-86; acting dir. Selective Svc. Sys., Washington, 1987, dep. dir., 1988—90; acting dir. Fed. Emergency Mgmt. Agy., Washington, 1990, dep. dir., 1991-92; chmn., chief exec. officer Phoenix Comm. and Rsch. Co., McLean, Va., 1993—2000; deputy asst. sec. def and dir. Def. POW/Missing Personnel Office, 2001—. Served to Capt. USMC, 1961-65. Mem.: SAR, VFW (life), Mil. Order Carabao, Am. Legion (life), Army and Navy Club (Washington). Baptist. Avocations: tennis, skiing, chess. Office: OASD Internat Security Affairs 2400 Defense Pentagon Washington DC 20301-2400

JENNINGS, JON PAUL, nonprofit foundation executive; b. Richmond, Ind., Oct. 2, 1962; s. Paul Nathan and Alice Belle Jennings. MPA, Harvard U., 2000. Scout, video coord. Boston Celtics, 1986-90, asst. coach, scouting coord., 1990-97; White House fellow The White House, Washington, 1997-98, sr. asst. to Cabinet Sec., 1998-99; acting asst. atty. gen. U.S. Dept. of Justice, Washington, 1999-2000; sr. advisor to Cabinet Sec., The White House, 2000-01; co-founder, pres. Team Harmony Found., Cambridge, Mass., 1993—. Winner NBA World Championship, 1986; named NBA All Star Coach, Boston Celtics, 1990-91, one of 10 Most Outstanding Young Leaders, Boston Jaycees, 1996. Roman Catholic. Avocations: flying, reading, basketball. Office: Team Harmony Found 401 Park Dr Boston MA 02215 Fax: 617-425-6300. E-mail: info@teamharmony.org., jennings@teamharmony.org.

JENNINGS, JOSEPH ASHBY, banker; b. Richmond, Va., Aug. 12, 1920; s. Joseph Ashby and Leone (Bishop) J.; m. Anne Barrow Hatcher, Oct. 29, 1960; children: Joseph Ashby III, Ashby Anne. BS, U. Richmond, 1949, DSc (hon.), 1980; grad. certificate, Stonier Grad. Sch. Banking, Rutgers U., 1952; LLD (hon.), Va. Union U., 1991. With United Va. Bank, Richmond, 1949-85, v.p., 1956-66, sr. v.p., 1966-67, exec. v.p., 1967-71, pres., 1971, chmn. bd., 1972-85; also dir.; vice chmn. bd. United Va. Bankshares, Inc., 1972-75, pres., 1975-76, chief adminstrv. officer, 1972-76, chmn. bd., chief exec. officer, 1976-85, chmn. bd., 1985-86. Served with USAAF, 1942-46. Mem. Fin. Analysts Fedn. (past exec. v.p., dir.), Phi Beta Kappa, Omicron Delta Kappa, Phi Delta Theta, Beta Gamma Sigma. Presbyterian.

JENNINGS, JULIANNE, cultural organization administrator; b. Providence, Mar. 13, 1961; d. James Jennings; m. Francis J. O'Brien Jr., Feb. 2, 1995 (div. 2002); children: Brian Coelho, Julia Coelho, Lily-Rae O'Brien. Student in Nursing, C.C. R.I., Warwick. Cons. R.I. Indian Coun., Providence. Cons. R.I. State Coun. Arts, R.I. Com. Humanities. Co-author: Understanding Algonquian Indian Words, 1996, A Massachusett Language Book, Vol. 1, 1998, Bringing Back Our Lost Language, 1999; author: Succotash, 1998; creator (audio cassette tape) Nokas-I Come From Her, 2000. Grantee R.I. Com. Humanities, 1996, R.I. Found., 1997, R.I. State Coun. Arts, 1998. Avocations: native american basket making, native american beading, native american singing, native american painting. Home and Office: 40 Haverford Rd Warwick RI 02886-1034

JENNINGS, LINDA STURGILL, volunteer; b. Norton, Va., July 16, 1952; d. Claude Clayborn and Beverly Jean (Pierson) Sturgill; m. Warner Craig Jennings, June 11, 1977; children: Warner Claybourne, William Cameron. BA in Elem. Edn., Va. Polytechnic Inst. and State U., 1974. Elem. tchr. Powhatan (Va.) County Sch. Dist., 1974-76, Alleghany County Sch. Dist., Covington, Va.,

1976-77, Normandy Sch. Dist., St. Louis, 1977-79, Aurora (Colo.) Pub. Schs., 1979-82. Active United Meth. Women, pres., Republican Women, treas., Friends of Powder River Symphony; trustee sch. bd. Converse County Sch. Dist., Douglas, Wyo., 1991-95; soccer coach Douglas Recreation, 1991-95; grant coord. Nat. Endowment of Arts; bd. dirs. Children's Devel. Svc. of Campbell Co. Named Disting. Sch. Bd. Mem., Wyo. Sch. Bd. Assn., 1995. Mem. AAUW, LWV, PEO. Avocations: reading, cooking, traveling, gardening, bridge. Home: 1100 Jason Ct Gillette WY 82718-6263

JENNINGS, LOUIS BROWN, retired humanities educator; b. Lancaster, S.C., May 5, 1917; s. Arthur Ewart and Selma Helms Jennings; m. Grace Irene Allen, May 24, 1943 (dec.); children: Carolyn Jennings Sautter, Sharon Jennings Moore. AB, Duke U., Durham, N.C., 1938; BD, Crozer Theology Sem., Chester, Pa., 1945; grad. studies, U. Pa., Phila., 1942—45; PhD, U. Chgo., 1964. Ordained minister United Ch. of Christ, 1956. From instr. to prof. Marshall U., Huntington, W.Va., 1948—79; assoc. prof. Ohio U., Portsmouth, 1961—69, prof. Ironton, 1965—72. Dept chmn. Marshall U., 1948—79. Co-author: (Book) Biography of Edgar Johnson Goodspeed, 1948; author: Biography of Shirley Jackson Case, 1949, The Function of Religion, 1978. Fellow Crozer Theol. Sem., 1947—48, Univ. of Chgo., 1947—48; grantee Ford Found. for Advancement of Edn., 1951—52. Democrat. United Ch.Of Christ. Avocation: walking. Home: 5822 Kirknewton Dr Salisbury MD 21804

JENNINGS, MARCELLA GRADY, rancher, investor; b. Springfield, Ill., Mar. 4, 1920; d. William Francis and Magdalene Mary (Spies) Grady; student pub. schs.; m. Leo J. Jennings, Dec. 16, 1950 (dec.). Pub. relations Econolite Corp., Los Angeles, 1958-61; v.p., asst. mgr. LJ Quarter Circle Ranch, Inc., Polson, Mont., 1961-73, pres., gen. mgr., owner, 1973— ; dir. Giselle's Travel Inc., Sacramento; fin. advisor to Allentown, Inc., Charlo, Mont.; sales cons. to Amie's Jumpin' Jacks and Jills, Garland, Tex. Investor. Mem. Internat. Charolais Assn., Los Angeles County Apt. Assn. Republican. Roman Catholic. Home and Office: 509 Mount Holyoke Ave Pacific Palisades CA 90272-4328

JENNINGS, MICHAEL C. engineer, designer, psychologist, consultant; b. Tulsa, Okla., Nov. 10, 1951; s. James Hollis and Dorothy Fay Jennings; m. Kriza Adora Matthews, May 24, 1975. BS in Exptl. Cognitive Psychology, Ctrl. State U., Wilberforce, Ohio, 1975; MA in Exptl. Cognitive Psychology, U. Dayton, Ohio, 1977; MS in Info. Sci., U. Pitts., 1994. Human factors engr. USAF, Dayton, 1985—90, tng. SPO, 1985—90; exec. adminstrv. asst. Nat. Dairy Bd., Arlington, Va., 1995—96; human factors cons. Prodigy Svcs. Corp., White Plains, NY, 1996—98; usability engr. Logical Design Solutions, NYC, 1998—99, ui designer, 1998—99; usability engr. Mar. First Inc., NYC, 1999—2001, info. arch., 1999—2001; human factors cons. Centrport Inc., Westport, Conn., 2001—02; usability arch. Virtumundo Inc., Kansas City, Mo., 2002—. Owner, CEO MiJen Prodns., Kansas City, Mo., 2003—. Contbr. articles to mags.;, performer recs., composer songs. Pub. rels. Nat. Intellectual Property Assn., 1990—91. With U.S. Army, 1969—71, Vietnam. Recipient Doty Engring Excellence award, Aero. Sys. Div. WPAFB, 1990. Mem.: Usability Profls. Assn., Psi Chi. Democrat. Bapt. Avocations: chess, tennis, songwriting, poetry, computer programming. Home: Apt 1103 803 W 48th St Kansas City MO 64112 Office: Virtumundo Inc Ste 500 4600 Madison Kansas City MO 64112 E-mail: mijenva@aol.com.

JENNINGS, NANCY ANN, retired elementary education educator; b. Bristow, Okla., July 11, 1932; d. John Linard and Charlie Estelle (Hooper) Stucker; m. Jerald Leon Jennings, June 4, 1951; children: Jan, Catherine Jennings Hackman, Elizabeth. BS, U. Okla., 1956; MS, Washburn U., Topeka, Kans., 1974. Cert. elem. tchr., Kans. Tchr. Whitson Grade Sch. Dist. 501, Topeka, 1970-75, Delia Grade Sch Dist. 321, St. Marys, Kans., 1978-79, Silver Lake (Kans.) Grade Sch. Dist. 372, 1979-85, ret., 1985. Mem. Kans. Hist. Soc. Mem. NEA (life), AAUW (bd. dirs.), DAR (regent Topeka chpt. 1989-91, sec.-treas. N.E. dist. Kans. 1992-95, chmn. pres.-gen.'s project state com. 1992-95, co-chair Kans. DAR geneal. records), Topeka Area Ret. Tchrs. Assn. (v.p. 1992-93), Internat. Reading Assn. (sec. 1983-84), Topeka Aux. Kans. Engring. Soc. (pres. 1987-88), Woman's Club (2d v.p. 1989-91), PEO Kans. (corr. sec. 1993—, guard 1994—, pres. 1995-97), Alpha Delta Kappa (pres. 1989-91), Kappa Delta Pi, Alpha Phi (2d v.p. 1989-90). Presbyterian. Avocations: genealogy, reading, sewing, gardening, bridge. Home: 11340 NW 13th St Topeka KS 66615-9620

JENNINGS, PAUL CHRISTIAN, civil engineering educator, academic administrator; b. Brigham City, Utah, May 21, 1936; s. Robert Webb and Elva S. (Simonsen) J.; m. Millicent Marie Bachman, Aug. 28, 1981; m. Barbara Elaine Morgan, Sept. 3, 1960 (div. 1981); children: Kathryn Diane, Margaret Ann. BSCE, Colo. State U., 1958; MSCE, Calif. Inst. Tech., 1960, PhD, 1963. Prof. civil engring., applied mechanics Calif. Inst. Tech., Pasadena, 1966—2002, chmn. divsn. engring., 1985-89, v.p., provost, 1989-95, acting v.p. for bus. and fin., 1995, 98-99, prof. emeritus, 2002—. Mem. faculty bd. Calif. Tech. Inst., 1974-76, steering com., 1974-76, chmn. nominating com., 1975, grad. studies com., 1978-80; cons. in field. Author: (with others) Earthquake Design Criteria. Contbr. numerous articles to profl. jours. 1st lt. USAF, 1963-66. Recipient Honor Alumnus award Colo. State U., 1992, Achievement in Academia award Coll. Engring., 1992; Erskine fellow U. Canterbury, New Zealand, 1970, 85. Fellow AAAS, New Zealand Soc. Earthquake Engring.; mem. ASCE (Walter Huber award 1973, Newmark medal 1992), Seismol. Soc. Am. (pres. 1980), Earthquake Engring. Rsch. Inst. (pres. 1981-83), Athenaeum Club. Avocations: fly fishing, hiking. Home: 640 S Grand Ave Pasadena CA 91105-2423 Office: Calif Inst Tech Mail Code 104-44 Pasadena CA 91125-0001 E-mail: pcjenn@caltech.edu.

JENNINGS, PETER CHARLES, television anchorman; b. Toronto, Ont., Can., July 29, 1938; s. Charles and Elizabeth (Osborne) J.; m. Valerie Godsoe (div.), Kati Marton (div.), Kayce Freed, 1997; children: Elizabeth, Christopher. Student, Trinity Coll. Sch., Port Hope, Ont., Carleton U., Ottawa, Ont.; LLD, Rider (N.J.) Coll. Began career with Sta. CFJR, Ont.; formerly with CBC, Montreal, Que., CJOH-TV, Ottawa; former parliamentary corr., network anchorman Canadian TV, Ottawa; network anchorman, nat. corr. ABC News, N.Y.C., 1964—; anchor ABC Evening News, 1965—68; London anchorman World News Tonight, 1978—83, anchorman, sr. editor, 1983—; also involved with prodn. numerous network documentaries.; anchorman Peter Jennings Reporting, 1990—; moderator news spls. for children; anchorman Capital to Capital; anchor TV series The AIDS Quarterly, PBS. Recipient 9 Emmy awards for news reporting, Alfred I. DuPont-Columbia U. award. Mem. Internat. Radio and TV Soc., Overseas Press Club (awards). Office: ABC Press Relations 47 W 66th St Fl 2 New York NY 10023-6201*

JENNINGS, RALPH HENRY, JR., physician; b. Benton, Ark., Mar. 12, 1940; s. Ralph Henry and Martha (Cate) J.; m. Rodney Antoinette Ward, Mar. 4, 1967; children: Ralph Henry III, Martha Lynn, Michael Ward. BS, U. Ark., Little Rock, 1962, MD, 1965. Diplomate Am. Bd. Ob-Gyn. Intern Grady Hosp., Atlanta, 1965-66; resident in ob-gyn. U. Ark Med. Ctr., Little Rock, 1966-67, 69-71; pvt. practice, Lakeland, Fla., 1971—. Contbr. articles to profl. jours.; presenter in field. Co-chair curriculum com. and adv. com. Polk County Bd. Edn. Sex Edn. Task Force, Lakeland, 1986-87. With USAF, 1967-69. Am. Cancer Soc. fellow, 1970-71. Fellow ACS, Am. Coll. Ob-Gyn., South Atlantic Assn. Ob-Gyn. (pres. 1996), So. Gynecol. and Obstet. Soc. (pres. 1996, coun. 1989-90), Southeastern Obstet. and Gynecol. Soc. (pres. 1991), So. Med. Assn. (sec. gynecol. sect. 1981-83, chair gynecol. sect. 1984-85, edn. coun. 1989); mem. Fla. Med. Soc., Fla. Ob-Gyn. Soc. Avocation: running. Home: 1634 Caldwell St Lakeland FL 33803-2403 Office: Watson Clinic LLP PO Box 95000 1600 Lakeland Hills Blvd Lakeland FL 33804-5000

JENNINGS, REBA MAXINE, retired critical care nurse; b. Gainesville, Mo., Oct. 28, 1936; d. William Claude and Osa Marie (Whillock) Loftis; m. Robert Wayne Jennings, Nov. 10, 1953; children: Sherry Anita, Robert Allen, Lalia Marie. Diploma, Burge Sch. Nursing, Springfield, Mo., 1983. ACLS, RN Mo. Med-surg. staff nurse AMI-Springfield Community Hosp., 1983-84; pvt. duty nurse Western Med. Svcs., Springfield, 1984; staff nurse in CCU, ICU, emergency dept. Tri-County Sisters of Mercy Hosp., Mansfield, Mo., 1984-85; cardiac telemetry staff nurse St. John's Regional Health Ctr., Springfield, 1985-93; nurse obs. unit Valley Hosp., Palmer, Alaska, 1993-94; nurse PCU Alaska Regional Hosp., Anchorage, 1994; PCU nurse Providence Alaska Med. Ctr., Anchorage, 1995-98; ret., 1998.

JENNINGS, RICHARD MILBURN, resort developer; b. Washington, Nov. 7, 1927; s. Maurice Edgar J. and Norma Milburn; m. Nini Bjonness, Mar. 21, 1964 (div. 1986); children: Lynn Urban, Stephanie, Jan. Student, Stanford U., 1944-46; BA, Ariz. State U., 1955; MA, Georgetown U., 1968, PhD in Govt., 1975. Commd. 2d lt. U.S. Army, 1947, advanced through grades to brigade comdr., 1969; asst. to Sec. of Def., 1971—72; retired U.S. Army, 1975; pres. Western Colo. Investments, Aspen, 1982-89; sr. v.p. Preferred Resorts, Aspen, 1989-95; pres. Western Resorts Internat., Aspen, 1995-98, chmn., 1998—2001. Author: U.S./Soviet Arms Competition, 1975; contbr. articles to profl. jours. Pres. Anderson Ranch Arts Ctr., Showmass Village, Colo., 1979-82; nat. coun. mem. Aspen Theater in the Park, 1997-99. Decorated Legion of Merit with oak leaf cluster, Korean Silver Star, Bronze Star with 3 oak leaf clusters, Air medal with 7 oak leaf clusters, Vietnamese Gallantry Cross. Mem. Nat. Assn. Realtors, Stanford Alumni Assn., Indian Wells Tennis Club, Maroon Creek Club. Avocations: writing, skiing, tennis. Home: 75852 Camino Cielo Indian Wells CA 92210 Office: Western Resorts Internat 1004 Vine St Aspen CO 81611

JENNINGS, ROBERT BURGESS, experimental pathologist, medical educator; b. Balt., Dec. 14, 1926; s. Burgess Hill and Etta (Crout) J.; m. Linda Lee Sheffield, June 28, 1952; children: Carol L., Mary G., John B., Anne E., James R. BS, Northwestern U., 1947, MS, B.M., 1949, MD, 1950. Diplomate Am. Bd. Pathology (trustee 1976-87, pres. 1986-87). Intern Passavant Meml. Hosp., Chgo., 1949-50, resident pathology, 1950-51; mem. faculty Northwestern U. Med. Sch., 1953-75, prof. pathology, 1963-75, Magerstadt prof. and chmn. pathology dept., 1969-75; prof., chmn. dept. pathology Duke U. Med. Sch., Durham, N.C., 1975-89, James B. Duke prof., 1980—. Vis. scientist Middlesex Hosp. Med. Sch., London, 1961-62; cons. VA Rsch. Hosp., Chgo.; mem. attending staff Northwestern Meml. Hosp., Chgo., 1963-75; mem. pathology A Study sect. USPHS, 1960-65; mem. clin. cardiology adv. com. NIH, 1976-80, mem. cardiovascular and renal study sect., 1992-95. Mem. editl. bd. Lab. Investigation, 1967-95, Archives Pathology, 1970-80, Jour. Molecular and Cellular Cardiology, 1972-89, Exptl. and Molecular Pathology, 1973-99, Circulation, 1988-91, 93-96, Circulation Rsch., 1976-82, Histopathology, 1977-92, Am. Jour. Pathology, 1983-92, Jour. Applied Cardiology, 1986-90, Cardiosci., 1990-95, Trends in Cardiovascular Medicine, 1991-92, Cardiovascular Pathology, 1991-95. Served as lt. (j.g.) USNR, 1951-53. Recipient Peter Harris award Internat. Soc. Heart Rsch., 1992, Disting. Achievement award Soc. Cardiovasc. Pathology, 1996; Markle scholar med. scis., 1958-63 Office: Duke U Med Ctr Dept Pathology Durham NC 27710-0001 E-mail: jenni004@mc.duke.edu.

JENNINGS, STEPHEN GRANT, academic administrator; b. Indpls., Dec. 6, 1946; s. Grant Orville and Helen Zura (MacDonald) J.; m. Sarah Ferguson, Apr. 26, 1969; children: Amy Jennings Bishop, Meredith Jennings Poole. BA, Trinity U., 1968; MS, Miami U., Oxford, Ohio, 1970; PhD, U. Ga., 1976; diploma in ednl. mgmt., Harvard U., 1982; LLD, Coll. Ozarks, Point Lookout, Mo., 1997; LHD, Simpson Coll., 1998. Asst. dean for resident life So. Meth. U., Dallas, 1970-73; asst. dir. housing U. Ga., Athens, 1973-76; assoc. dean students Tulane U., New Orleans, 1976-80; v.p. student svcs. Furman U., Greenville, S.C., 1980-83; pres. Coll. of Ozarks, Point Lookout, Mo., 1983-87, Simpson Coll., Indianola, Iowa, 1987-98, Oklahoma City U., 1998-2001, U. Evansville, Ind., 2001—. Instnl. cons. Am. Coll. in London, 1995; bd. dirs. Old Nat. Bank, Nat. Pub. Radio and TV (WNIN). Mem. Coun. Ind. Colls., Nat. Assn. Schs., Colls. and Univs. (bd. dirs. 1993—), Nat. Assn. Intercollegiate Athletics (coun. of pres. 1983-87), So. Assn. Colls. and Schs. (vis. teams 1982—), North Cen. Assn. Colls. and Schs. (vis. teams 1989—), So. Assn. Coll. Student Pers. (pres. 1983), Harvard U. Alumni Assn. (class rep.), Rotary, Evansville Club, Sigma Alpha Epsilon. Avocations: racquet sports, golf, reading. Office: U Evansville Office of President 1800 Lincoln Ave Evansville IN 47722-0001

JENNINGS, THOMAS PARKS, lawyer; b. Alexandria, Va., Nov. 16, 1947; s. George Christian and Ellen (Thompson) J.; m. Shelley Corrine Abernathy, Oct. 30, 1971; 1 child, Kathleen Eayre. BA in History, Wake Forest U., 1970; JD, U. Va., 1975. Bar: Va. 1975. Assoc. Lewis, Wilson, Lewis & Jones, Arlington, Va., 1975-78; atty. First Va. Banks, Inc., Falls Church, 1978-80, gen. counsel, 1980—, sec., 1993-99, sr. v.p., 1995—. Adj. prof. George Mason U. Sch. Law, Arlington, 1987-88. Trustee Arlington Cmty. Found., 1998—, treas., 2001—; dir. Rixey St. Found., Inc., 1997—; deacon Georgetown Presbyn. Ch., Washington, 1980-82, elder, 1983-85, 95-97, trustee, 1988-90, dir. Bd. Pensions, Presbyn. Ch. USA, 2001—. With U.S. Army, 1970-71. Mem. ABA, Am. Soc. Corp. Secs., Va. State Bar Assn., Va. Bankers Assn. (legal affairs com.), Fairfax County Bar Assn., Am. Corp. Counsel Assn., Washington Met. Area Corp. Counsel Assn. (bd. dirs. 1984-87). Avocations: bridge, kayaking. Office: First Va Banks Inc 6400 Arlington Blvd Ste 420 Falls Church VA 22042-2336

JENNINGS, TONI, lieutenant governor; b. Orlando, Fla., May 17, 1949; d. Jack C. and Margaret (Murphy) J. BA, Wesleyan Coll., Macon, Ga., 1971; postgrad., Rollins Coll., 1972-73. Pres. Jack Jennings and Sons, Inc., Gen. Contractors, Orlando, 1973—; mem. Fla. Ho. of Reps., 1976-80, Fla. Senate, 1980—2000, pres., 1996—2000; lt. gov. Florida, 2003—. Republican leader pro tempore, 1982-83, 85, 86, Rep. leader, 1984, 86-88. legis. del. Orange County, 1980-82, 86-88. Bd. dirs. Salvation Army; active Rep. Women's Federated Club of Winter Park, Orlando Women's Rep. Club Federated. Recipient Spl. Commendation award Fla. Restaurant Assn., 1979, Meritorious Svc. award Fla. Fedn. Humane Socs., 1979, Disting. Alumni awrd Wesleyan Coll., 1981, Freedom award Women for Responsible Legislation, 1982, Support of Law Enforcement award Fla. Sheriffs Assn., Outstanding Efforts award Tampa Missing Children Help Ctr., 1983, Outstanding Svc. award Grocers' Assn. Fla., 1983, Legis. award Fla., 1983, Legis. award Fla. Chiropractic Assn., 1983, 86, Appreciation award Fla. Med. Assn. and Physicians of Fla., 1983, 2d Ann. Frank J. Fahrenkopf, Jr. Outstanding State Minority Leader award, 1988, Ann. Legis. award for Leadership in Econ. Devel. Legislation award Fla. C. of C., 1987; named Legislator of Yr., Orange County Young Rep. Club, 1980-81. Mem. Orlando Area Bd. Realtors (Friend of Realtors award 1989), Builders and Contractors, Ctrl. Fla. Builders Exch., Delta Kappa Gamma, Phi Kappa Phi, Kappa Delta Epsilon. Office: Lt Gov The Capitol PL-05 Tallahassee FL 32399-0001*

JENNINGS, SISTER VIVIEN, English language educator; b. Jersey City; d. Eugene O. and Alice (Smith) J. BA, Caldwell Coll.; MA in English, Cath. U. Am.; MS in Telecommunications, Syracuse U.; PhD in English, Fordham U.; EdD (hon.), Providence Coll.; LittD (hon.), Caldwell Coll.; postgrad., Oxford (Eng.) U., 1994. Prof. English Caldwell Coll., 1960-69; major supr. Dominican Sisters-Caldwell, 1969-79; instr. broadcasting writing Syracuse U., 1979-80; with community affairs dept. Sta. WIXT TV, Syracuse, N.Y., 1980; dir. telecommunications Barry U., 1982-83; dir. pub. affairs Cath. Telecommunications Network Am., 1983-84; pres. Caldwell Coll., 1984-94, prof. English, 1995-99; prin. St. Dominic Acad., Jersey City, 1999—. Originator, designer campus TV studios Caldwell Coll., Barry U.; curriculum planner, coord. new grad.-level curriculum in telecommunications Barry U.; lectr. on ednl. and media issues. Producer: Centenary Journey, 1981, Advent Vesper Chorale, 1981, American Immigrant Church, 1982, Las Casas: Ministry of Presence, 1987; co-producer: The Boat People, 1980. Founder, dir. Children's TV Experience; founder Project Link Ednl. Ctr., Newark. Recipient Gov.'s Pride N.J. Albert Einstein award for edn., 1989. Office: St Dominic Acad 2572 Kennedy Blvd Jersey City NJ 07304-2107

JENNINGS, WILLBUR, musician, popular; Songwriter (with James Horner) "My Heart Will Go On" for movie Titanic, 1997 (Grammy award, 1999, Academy award Oscar, 1998, Golden Globe award, 1998, Golden Satellite award, 1998), (with Jack Nitzsche and Buffy Sainte-Marie) "Up Where We Belong" for movie Officer and a Gentleman, 1982 (Academy award Oscar, 1983, British Academy award BAFTA, 1984, Golden Glove award, 1983), (with Lalo Schifrin) "People Alone" for movie The Competition, 1980 (nominated for Oscar, 1981), (with James Horner) "Dreams to Dream" for movie An American Tale: Fievel Goes West, 1991 (nominated for Golden Globe award, 1992), (with Eric Clapton) "Tears in Heaven" for movie Rush, 1991 (nominated for Golden Globe award, 1992). Office: c/o BMI Writer/Publisher Relations 3rd Fl W 8730 W Sunset Blvd Los Angeles CA 90069-2210

JENNINGS, WIRT HOLMAN, JR., retired marketing executive; b. Newberry, S.C., Oct. 5, 1927; s. Wirt Holman and Dorothy Elizebeth (Suber) J.; m. Carrie Lucille Braswell, Oct. 26, 1947; children: Michael Earl, Martha Jane, Dorothy Elizebeth. BS in Math. and Chemistry, Newberry Coll., 1949; grad., Lynhurst U., 1958. Area rep. to mgr. T.A. Edison, Inc., West Orange, N.C., 1949-52; sales trainee Esso Std. Oil, N.J., Columbia, S.C., 1952-55, sales rep. Bennettsville, S.C., 1955-56; sales supr., asst. dist. mgr. Esso, Humble, Enco, Columbia, 1956-64, dist. mgr. Birmingham, Ala., 1964-67, project coord. Memphis, 1967-68; nat. project coord. Exxon Co. USA, Houston, 1968-75, innovative project coord. Charlotte, N.C., 1975-80, Memphis, 1980-83, Houston, 1983-85; pres. Mktg. Expeditors, Inc., Houston, 1985-93; councilman Newberry County Coun., 1997-2001. Co-founder, pres. Cayce/West Columbia (S.C.) Jaycees, 1956; pres. Ala. Petroleum Coun., Birmingham, 1966; pres. AARP, Newberry, 1997—; chmn. Rep. Party, Newberry, 1997—; mem. founding bd. dirs. Nat. Ins. Automotive Svc. Excellence, Washington, 1972-74; bd. trustees Newberry Coll., 2000—; bd. dirs. Houston Water and Sewer, 1971-75. With USN, 1945-46. Mem. Newberry Coll. Home Guard (commdr. 1997—), Columbia Exxon Annuitant Club (ex-officio, pres. 1998—). Avocations: fishing, hunting, golfing. Home: 51 Jennings Pt Prosperity SC 29127-8842 E-mail: jennings@scmail.com.

JENNISON, BRIAN (LESTER), environmental specialist; b. Chelsea, Mass., June 13, 1950; s. Lewis L. and Myra S. (Piper) J. BA, U. N.H., 1972; PhD, U. Calif., Berkeley, 1977; cert. hazardous materials mgr., U. Calif., Davis, 1986. Tchg., rsch. asst. U. Calif., Berkeley, 1972-77; staff rsch. assoc. Dept. of Molecular Biology, Berkeley, 1978-80; instr. dept. biology Calif. State U., Hayward, 1977; sr. biologist San Francisco Bay Marine Rsch. Ctr., Emeryville, Calif., 1980-81; inspector I Bay Area Air Quality Mgmt.Dist., San Francisco, 1981-83, inspector II, 1983-88; enforcement program specialist Bay Area Air Quality Mgmt. Dist., San Francisco, 1988-92; dir. air quality mgmt. divsn. Washoe County Dist. Health Dept., Reno, Nev., 1992-2000; dir. Lane Regional Air Pollution Authority, Springfield, Oreg., 2000—. Cons. U.S. Army Corps of Engrs., L.A., 1980, San Francisco, 1981; instr. U. Calif., Berkeley, 1990-93, Assoc. Bay Area Govs., 1990-92; adj. prof. U. Nev., Reno, 1994-2003. Contbr. articles to profl. jours. Harbor Br. Found. fellow, 1977-78. Mem.: AAAS, Assn. Local Air Pollution Control Officers (bd. dirs. 2001—), Air and Waste Mgmt. Assn. (chmn. Ea. Sierra chpt. 1994—96), Navy League U.S. (life), Rotary, Phi Beta Kappa. Avocations: railroad history, photography. Office: LRAPA 1010 Main St Springfield OR 97477-4879 E-mail: bljennison@earthlink.net., brian@lrapa.org.

JENNISON, RÓBIN L. former state legislator, lobbyist; s. Denise Jennison. Grad., Fort Hayes State U. Kans. state rep. Dist. 117, 1990—; spkr. Kans. House of Rep., 1999—2001; farmer, stockman, lobbyist Ruffin Properties, 2002—, Mem. Kans. Farm Bur., Kans. Livestock Assn., Kans. Wheat Growers Assn. Office: Ruffin Properties PO Box 17087 Wichita KS 67217

JENNY, CAROLE, physician, researcher; b. St. Louis, Mo., June 4, 1946; d. Vance Buescher and Alice Emelie Jenny; m. Thomas Allen Roesler, Mar. 16, 1974; children: Laura Alice Roesler, Amelia Martha Roesler. BA, U. of Mo., 1968; BMS, Dartmouth Med. Sch., 1970; MD, U. of Wash., 1972; MBA, Wharton Sch., U. of Pa, 1976. Pediatrics Am. Bd. of Pediat., NC, 1977. Prof. of pediat. Brown Med. Sch., Providence, 1996—; dir., child protection team Hasbro Children's Hosp., Providence. Com. on child abuse and neglect Am. Acad. of Pediat., Elk Grove Village, Ill. Mem. Am. Profl. Soc. on the Abuse of Children, Chgo., 1991—. Recipient Outstanding Svc. to Maltreated Children, Am. Acad. of Pediat., 1999, Ray Helfer award, Nat. Coalition of Children's Trust Funds, 2002. Achievements include research in child abuse, head trauma, sexual abuse. Office: Brown Medical School 593 Eddy St Potter-005 Providence RI 02903 E-mail: carole_jenny@brown.edu.

JENNY, FREDERIC YVES, economist, educator; b. Geneva, Sept. 29, 1943; s. Frederic Marc and Madeleine (Permezel) J.; m. Sarah Harrison Beers, Feb. 4, 1984. Student, Ecole Superieure des Scis. Econ. et Comml., Paris, 1966; PhD in Econs., Harvard U., 1975; Doctorat d'Etat, U. Paris, 1977; Dr. Honoris Causa, U. Wuhan, China, 1983. Prof. econs. ESSEC, Cergy-Pontoise, France, 1972—; rapporteur Commission de la Concurrence, Paris, 1980-85, rapporteur gen., 1985-86, Conseil de la Concurrence, Paris, 1987-93, vice-chmn., 1993—. Mem. conseil des ètudes Inst. Nat. de la Statistique et des Etudes Economiques, Paris, 1982-86; mem. Conseil Scientifique de l'Evaluation, Paris, 1990-96; chmn. competition law and policy com. Orgn. Econ. Cooperation and Devel., 1994—; chmn. com. in internat. trade and competition World Trade Orgn., 1997—. Co-author: Concentration et politique des Structures industrielles, 1975, L'Entreprise et les politiques de concurrence, 1976, Initiation a la theorie micio-economique, 1983. Decorated Officier Ordre Nat. du Mérite, 1999, Officier Ordre Nat. de la Légion d'Honneur, 2003. Avocations: photography, sailing. Office: Conseil de la Concurrence 11 rue de l'Echelle Paris 75001 France

JENRETTE, JOSEPH MALPHUS, III, radiation oncologist; b. Raleigh, Feb. 24, 1951; s. Joseph Malphus and Helen Bell (Broughton) J.; m. Elizabeth Chandler, Dec. 24, 1954; children: Emma Chandler, Elliott Broughton. BA, U. N.C., 1973; MD, Med. U. S.C., 1979. Diplomate Am. Bd. Radiology. Resident in radiation oncology Med. U. S.C., Charleston, 1979-83, instr. radiation oncology, 1983-86, asst. prof., 1986-89, assoc. prof., 1989—2003, prof. radiation oncology, 2003—, interim chmn. dept. radiation oncology, 2003—. Contbr. articles to profl. jours. Pres. S.C. divsn. Am. Cancer Soc., 1989-90; exec. com. Hollings Cancer Ctr., Charleston, 1990—; pres. Charleston Symphony Orch., 1990-92; pres., founder Over the Rainbow Arts, Charleston, 1988—; v.p. Am. Classical Homes Found., N.Y.C., 1993—, Charleston Preservation Soc., 1990-92; bd. dirs. The Cmty. Found., 1996-99; bd. trustees Ashley Hall Sch., 1996-98; bd. visitors Coll. of Charleston, 1997—. Recipient Carolopolis award Preservation Soc., 1989, Pace Leadership awardee Am. Cancer Soc., 1985, Danforth Leadership awardee Danforth Found., 1969. Mem.: AMA, Am. Soc. for Therapeutic Radiology and Oncology, Radiol. Soc. N.Am., S.C. Oncology Soc. (pres. 1992—93), Am. Coll. Radiation Oncology, S.C. Med. Soc., Skyview Club, Charleston Men's Book Club, Order of Holy Grail. Avocations: swimming, reading, fishing, travel, child rearing. Office: Medical University of SC Dept Radiation Oncology Charleston SC 29425

JENRETTE, THOMAS SHEPARD, JR., music educator, choral director; b. Roanoke, Va., Feb. 1, 1946; s. Thomas Shepard and Virginia Catherine (Harris) J. BA, U. N.C., 1968, MusM, 1970; D of Mus. Arts, U. Mich., 1976. Choral dir. Cummings High Sch., Burlington, N.C., 1969-72; dir. cultural arts Burlington (N.C.) City Schs., 1972-73; dir. choral activities S.W. State U., Marshall, Minn., 1976-79, East Tenn. State U., Johnson City, 1979—. Dir. music First Christian Ch., Johnson City, 1981-84, Covenant Presbyn. Ch., Johnson City, 1991—; dir. East Tenn. State U. Chorale European Tour, 1985, 98, 2001; guest condr. choral festival N.C. High Sch., Raleigh, 1987, 2002, Govs. Sch. for Arts, Murfreesboro, Tenn., 1987, Nat. Seminar of Intercollegiate Men's Choruses, Inc., 1992; guest condr. N.C. All-State Male Choir, 1997, All-East Tenn. H.S. Male Choir, 1998, Tenn. All-State H.S. Male Choir, 2001, S.C. All-State Male Choir, 2002, Ga. All-State H.S. male choir, 2003, Nat. Condrs. Conf., U. So. Miss., 2000; so. divsn. repertoire and stds. chair for male choirs Am. Choral Dirs. Assn., 1999—. Grantee East Tenn. State U., 1988, 90, 96, 99. Mem. Am. Choral Dirs. Assn. (life, conductor 1986, 88, 94, 2000, so. divsn. convs., 89, 99 nat. conv., so. divsn. repertoire and stds. chair for male choirs 1999—), Tenn. Music Educators Assn. (conductor state convs. 1990, 91, 94, 2000, dir. White House, Christmas 1989, 2001, Canticum Novum Festival, Caracas, Venezuela, 1996), Internat. Fedn. Choral Music, Nat. Assn. Tchrs. Singing, The Coll. Music Soc. (life), Music Educators Nat. Conf. (condr. so. divsn. conv. 1997), Phi Mu Alpha (hon.), Omicron Delta Kappa, Pi Kappa Lambda. Home: 2734 E Oakland Ave Apt C-25 Johnson City TN 37601-1887 E-mail: jenrette@etsu.edu.

JENSCH, CHARLES CAMPBELL, lawyer; b. St. Paul, Apr. 15, 1929; s. Charles C. Jensch and Dorothy Tilden Stoms; m. Helen Joan Alan, Jan. 26, 1957; children: Jeanne, Clifton, Diana, Charles, Marianne, Christine. AB cum laude, Williams Coll., 1950; JD, U. Mich., 1953. Bar: Ill. 1953, Minn. 1978; cert. real property law specialist. Assoc. Wilson & McIlvaine, Chgo., 1953-58; asst. sec. Story & Clark Piano Co., Chgo., 1958-60; v.p., asst. legal counsel A.E. Staley Mfg. Co., Decatur, Ill., 1960-69; exec. v.p., pres., sec. Sunstar Foods, Inc., Mpls., 1969-80; v.p., dir. Petersen, Tews & Squires, St. Paul, 1980-96; of counsel Krass Monroe, P.A., Mpls., 1998—. Mem. Minn. State Bar Assn., Barristers Club. Home: 197 Avon St S Saint Paul MN 55105-3319 Office: Krass Monroe PA Southpoint Office Ctr 1650 West 82nd St Ste 1100 Minneapolis MN 55431-1447 E-mail: CharlesJ@Krassmonroe.com.

JENSEN, ARTHUR ROBERT, psychology educator; b. San Diego, Aug. 24, 1923; s. Arthur Alfred and Linda (Schachtmayer) J.; m. Barbara Jane DeLarme, May 6, 1960; 1 child, Roberta Ann. BA, U. Calif., Berkeley, 1945; PhD, Columbia U., 1956. Asst. med. psychology U. Md., 1955-56; research fellow-Inst. Psychiatry U. London, 1956-58; prof. ednl. psychology U. Calif., Berkeley, 1958-94; prof. emeritus, 1994—. Author: Genetics and Education, 1972, Educability and Group Differences, 1973, Educational Differences, 1973, Bias in Mental Testing, 1979, Straight Talk about Mental Tests, 1981, The g Factor, 1998; contbr. to profl. jours., books. Guggenheim fellow, 1964-65, fellow Ctr. Advanced Study Behavioral Scis., 1966-67 Fellow AAAS, Am. Psychol. Assn., The Glaton Inst., Am. Psychol. Soc.; mem. Psychonomic Soc., Am. Soc. Human Genetics, Soc. for Social Biology, Behavior Genetics Assn., Psychometric Soc., Sigma Xi. Office: U Calif Sch Edn Berkeley CA 94720-0001

JENSEN, ARTHUR SEIGFRIED, consulting engineering physicist; b. Trenton, N.J., Dec. 24, 1917; s. Emil Anthony and Emma Anna (Lund) J.; m. Lillian Elizabeth Reed, Aug. 9, 1941; children: Deane Ellsworth, Alan Forrest, Nancy Lorraine. BS, U. Pa., 1938, MS, 1939, PhD in Physics, 1941; diploma in advanced engring., Westinghouse Sch. Applied Sci., 1972, diploma in computer sci., 1977. Registered profl. engr., Md. Research physicist U.S. Naval Research Labs., Washington, 1941; research physicist RCA Labs., Princeton, N.J., 1945-57; mgr. spl. electron devices Westinghouse Electronic Tube Div., Balt., 1957-65; sr. adv. physicist Electronics Systems Ctr., Balt., 1965-91; cons. physicist Westinghouse Electronic Systems Ctr., Balt., 1991-94; co-owner, chief engr. Jensen Cons. Engring., 1994—. Mem. Md. State Bd. Registration Profl. Engrs., 1979-86, vice chmn., 1983-86; cons. Nat. Acad. Sci., 1970 Contbr. articles to profl. jours.; 25 patents. Mem. Endowed Sons of Norway Found., Nancy Lorraine Jensen Meml. Scholarship Fund. Served to capt. USN, 1941-46, USNR, 1946-77, ret., 1977—. Hector Tyndale fellow, 1939, George Lieb Harrison fellow, 1940; recipient outstanding svc. award Engrs. Coun. Md., 1986, Gov.'s citation, 1986, Westinghouse spl. patent award, 1972; endowed Sons of Norway Found., Nancy Lorraine Jensen Meml. Scholarship Fund. Fellow IEEE (life), Washington Acad. Scis.; mem. AAAS, AIAA, Res. Officers Assn., Ret. Officers Assn., Naval Res. Assn., Am. Phys. Soc., Am. Assn. Physics Tchrs., Soc. Photo-Optical Instrumentation Engrs., Optical Soc. Am., N.Y. Acad. Scis., Md. Acad. Scis. (chmn. awards com.), Nat. Coun. Engring. Examiners (chmn. internat. rels. com.), Infrared Info. Symposium, Am. Legion, Fleet Res. Assn., Sons of Norway, Nat. Eagle Scout Assn., Vigil Honor Order of Arrow, Sigma Xi, Pi Mu Epsilon, Kappa Phi Kappa. Clubs: U.S. Naval Acad. Officers and Faculty. Achievements include patents in field. Home and Office: Chapel Gate 1104 Oak Crest Village 8820 Walther Blvd Parkville MD 21234-9022

JENSEN, CHRISTIAN EDWARD, family practice physician; b. Newark, July 7, 1933; s. Arnold Vang Jensen and Helen Marie Palme; m. Gail Lillian Baxter, Oct. 31, 1957; children: Christian J., Wendy Joy. BS, Rutgers U., 1954, MA, 1955; MD, Duke U., 1972; MPH, Med. Coll. Wis., 1989. Diplomate Am. Bd. Family Practice, Am. Bd. Preventive Medicine in Occupl. Medicine. Intern Naval Hosp., Portsmouth, Va., 1955-56; self-employed bus. exec. Middletown, N.J., 1957-65; pvt. practice specializing in family medicine Denton, Md., 1973-82; med. supr. E.I. DuPont de Nemours, inc., Seaford, Del., 1982-90; med. dir., pres. Delmarva Found. for Med. Care, Easton, Md., 1991-93, assoc. med. dir., 1998-99; dir. occupl. medicine U.S. Naval Acad., Annapolis, Md., 1993-97; med. dir. Western Integrity Ctr., 2000—. Author: Physicians of Caroline County Maryland, 1774-1984. Deacon Calvary Bapt. Ch., Denton, Md., 1976—. Capt. USNR, 1955-97. Fellow Am. Acad. Family Physicians, Am. Coll. Occupl. and Environ. Medicine, Am. Coll. Physician Execs. Home: 8950 Pealiquor Landing Rd Denton MD 21629-2317

JENSEN, CHRISTOPHER DOUGLAS, civil engineer; b. Alliance, Nebr., July 22, 1962; s. Roger August and Carolyn Joyce (Cole) J. BS in Civl Engring., U. Wyo., 1984. Profl. civl engr. Nev. 1990, Wyo. 1991, Nebr. 1991. Civil engr. Bennett-Carter and Assocs., Rock Springs, Wyo., 1985-89, G.C. Wallace, Inc., Las Vegas, Nev., 1989-91, Baker and Assocs., Torrington, Wyo., 1991—99, Natural Resources Conservation Svc., 1999—. Mem. Am. Soc. Civil Engrs., Nat. Soc. Profl. Engrs. (scholarship com. 1988). Republican. Lutheran. Home: 1914 4th Ave Scottsbluff NE 69361-2534 Office: 818 Ferdinand Plaza Ste C Scottsbluff NE 69361

JENSEN, CRAIG MARTIN, chemistry educator; b. Wenatchee, Wash., Apr. 13, 1955; s. James Sheridan and LaVonne Gay (Kinzenbach) J.; m. Janet Elizebeth Stevens, Nov. 11, 1979; children: Katherine, Steven. BS, U. Calif., Santa Barbara, 1979; PhD, UCLA, 1984. Cannery worker Wakefield Seafoods, Sandpoint, Alaska, 1975; chem. technician Occidental Rsch. Corp., Irvine, Calif., 1979-80; postdoctoral fellow U. Calif., San Diego, 1984-86; asst. prof. chemistry U. Hawaii, Honolulu, 1986-92, assoc. prof., 1992-97, prof., 1997—. Cons. HySorb Tech. Inc., Albuquerque, 1995-2001, New Materials Ctr., Osaka, Japan, 1998—, United Tech., Hartford, Conn. Contbr. over 65 articles to profl. jours. Recipient Rsch. Success Story award Hydrogen Tech. Adv. Panel of U.S. Dept. Energy, 1999. Mem. Am. Chem. Soc., Neutron Scattering Soc. Am., Internat. Energy Agy. (hydrogen storage expert 1997—). Achievements include patents in fields of homogeneous catalysis and hydrogen storage materials. Office: U Hawaii Dept Chemistry Honolulu HI 96822 Fax: 808-956-5908. E-mail: jensen@gold.chem.hawaii.edu.

JENSEN, DALE FINNLAY, accountant; b. Muenchwellier, Germany, Mar. 1, 1961; s. Charles F. and Barbara J. Jensen; children: Eric, Ryan. BS in Acctg., Ariz. State U., 1985. CPA, Ariz. Contr. Transp. Coop., Inc., Phoenix, 1983-85; mgr. Henry & Horne, P.L.C., Scottsdale, Ariz., 1985—. SScout leader Park 243 and Troop 343 Boy Scouts of Am., 1997—. Mem. AICPA, Ariz. Soc. CPA's, Ariz. State U. Alumni Assn., Pi Kappa Alpha (pres., sec.). Home: 15104 E Green Valley Rd Fountain Hills AZ 85268-1311 Office: Henry & Horne PLC 7098 E Cochise Rd Scottsdale AZ 85253-4517

JENSEN, DALLIN W. lawyer; b. Afton, Wyo., June 2, 1932; s. Louis J. and Nellie B. Jensen; m. Barbara J. Bassett, Mar. 22, 1958; children: Brad L., Julie N. BS, Brigham Young U., 1954; JD, U. Utah, 1960. Bar: Utah 1960, U.S. Dist. Ct. Utah 1962, U.S. Supreme Ct. 1971, U.S. Ct. Appeals (10th cir.) 1974, U.S. Ct. Appeals D.C. 1980. Asst. atty. gen. Utah Atty. Gen., Salt Lake City, 1960—83, solicitor gen., 1983—88; shareholder Parsons, Behle & Latimer, Salt Lake City, 1988—. Alt. commr. Upper Colo. River Commn., 1983—; mem. Colo. River Basin Salinity Adv. Coun., 1975—; commr. Utah Reclamation Mitigation and Conservation Commn., 2003—; spl. legal cons. Nat. Water Commn., Washington, 1971—73. Author (with Wells A. Hutchins): The Utah Law of Water Rights, 1965; mem. editl. bd. Rocky Mountain Mineral Law Found., 1983—85; contbr. articles on water law and water resource mgmt. to profl. jours. Served with U.S. Army, 1955—57. Mem. Lds Ch. Home: 3565 S 2175 E Salt Lake City UT 84109-2902 Office: PO Box 45898 Salt Lake City UT 84145-0898 E-mail: d.jensen@pblutah.com.

JENSEN, DENNIS LOWELL, lawyer; b. Erie, Pa., July 5, 1951; s. Lowell and Roberta (Umbaugh) J. Student, Cornell Coll., 1969-70; BA, Macalester Coll., 1973; JD, U.Houston, 1973. Bar: Tex. 1977, U.S. Dist. Ct. (so. dist.) Tex. 1978, Calif. 1981. Sole practice, Houston, 1977-78, asst. housing coordinator Santa Ana Housing Authority, Calif., 1979; polit. cons. Huntington Beach, Calif., 1980-81; legis. analyst Tosco Corp., Los Angeles, 1981-82; polit. cons. Lynn Wessell Co., 1982-83, George Young & Assocs., 1983-84; legis. aide Los Angeles City Councilman Ernani Bernardi, 1984-86; dep. atty. Los Angeles City Atty.'s Office, 1986-95; pvt. practice Huntington Beach, 1995—. Lectr. in field. Contbr. articles to profl. jours. Campaign mgr. for Congressman Tom Kindness, Hamilton, Ohio, 1978, Initiative to Abolish Inheritance Tax, Bakersfield, Calif., 1980; alumni admissions rep. Macalester Coll., 1984; mem. bd. dirs. Adult Day Svc. Orange County, 1998-; instr. Calif. State U. Extended Edn. programs gerontology and geriatric care mgmt., 1999-. Mem. Am. Assn. Polit. Cons., Nat. Acad. Elder Law Attys., Orange County Bar Assn. (vice chmn. elder law sect.), Order of Barons, Phi Delta Phi. Republican. Home: 18801 Gregory Ln Huntington Beach CA 92646-1921 Office: Dennis L Jensen Atty at Law 18377 Beach Blvd Ste 212 Huntington Beach CA 92648-1349

JENSEN, DENNIS MARK, marketing executive; b. Lawrence, Kans., Oct. 26, 1946; s. Keith E. and Betty M. (Gardner) J.; m. Wendalyn A. Dennis, Mar. 21, 1969 (div. Nov. 1987); 1 child, Michael Shawn; m. Mary Forbes Russell, Aug. 21, 1996; children: Russell Forbes, Kaisa Hathaway, Perry Mark. Student, Ind. State U., 1964, Ind. U., 1964-66; BA, Adrian Coll., 1968; MA, U. Fla., 1970; postgrad., U. Mo., 1970-71, 74-77. Teaching asst. English U. Fla., Gainesville, 1968-70; teaching asst. speech and dramatic art U. Mo., Columbia, 1970-71, 74-77; project analyst Pfizer Pharms., N.Y.C., 1977-80, mgr. communications devel., 1980-81; mgr. tech. com. Pfizer Inc., N.Y.C., 1981-86; mgr. profl. rels. Pfizer Internat., N.Y.C., 1986-89, sr. mgr. profl. rels., 1989-96, mktg. mgr., 1996—. Elder Pleasantville Presbyn. Ch., N.Y., 1981-83. With USN, 1971-74. Recipient tng. grants NIH, USPHS, Ind. U. Med. Ctr., 1964, Am. Cancer Soc. Adrian Coll., 1966. Mem. AAAS, Am. Soc. Microbiology. Methodist. Office: Pfizer Internat 235 E 42nd St New York NY 10017-5755

JENSEN, DICK LEROY, lawyer; b. Audubon, Iowa, Oct. 25, 1930; s. A.B. and Bernice (Fancher) J.; m. Nancy Wilson, June 30, 1956; children: Charles F., Sarah R. (dec.). LL.B., U. Iowa, 1954. Bar: Iowa 1954. Practice in, Audubon, Iowa, 1958-60; gen. counsel, sec. Walnut Grove Products, Co., Atlantic, Iowa, 1960-64; legal staff W.R. Grace & Co., Atlantic, 1964-66; gen. counsel, v.p., sec. Spencer Foods, Inc., Iowa, 1966-72, dir., 1968-72; mem. Dreher, Simpson and Jensen, Des Moines, 1972—. Notes and legis. editor: Iowa Law Rev, 1953-54. Pres. S.W. Iowa Mental Health Inst., 1964-66. Served to lt. USNR, 1955-58. Mem. Masons, Sigma Nu, Phi Delta Phi. Republican. Presbyterian. Home: 3901 River Oaks Dr Des Moines IA 50312-4638 Office: Dreher Simpson & Jensen The Equitable Bldg Ste 222 Des Moines IA 50309-3723 E-mail: djensen@dreherlaw.com.

JENSEN, DONALD NORMAN, diplomat, writer; b. San Francisco, Feb. 8, 1951; s. Thomas Christian Jensen and Alma Theresa Foppiano; m. Julienne Lambre, Nov. 3, 1984. BA, Columbia U., 1973; MA, Harvard U., 1977, PhD, 1979. Vis. asst. prof. govt. Cornell U., Ithaca, N.Y., 1979-80; rsch. assoc. Stanford (Calif.) U., 1980-84; fgn. svc. officer Dept. State, Washington, 1985-96; assoc. dir. broadcasting Radio Free Europe/Radio Liberty, Washington, 1996—2002, dir. comms., 2002—. Missile insp. On-Site Inspection Agy., Washington, 1988; monitor Russian Duma elections, Bryansk, 1993; dir. U. Md. in Moscow, 1994-95; former cons. PBS, Washington. Editor: School Days, Rule Days, 1983; contbg. author: Business and the State in Russia, 2000, The Power of Corruption, 2001, The Deadball Era: The National League; contbr. articles to profl. jours., including East European Jour. Constl. Law, Demokratizatsiya, Nat. Interest. Active alumni activities Columbia U., N.Y.C., 1974—. Mid-career fellow Harriman Inst., Columbia U., 1984. Mem. Soc. Am. Baseball Rsch., San Francisco Hist. Soc., Nat. Maritime Mus. Assn. Republican. Roman Catholic. Avocations: baseball history and writing, san francisco history, wine collecting, model railroading. Home: 3301 Coryell Ln Alexandria VA 22302 Office: Radio Free Europe/Radio Liberty Ste 1100 1201 Connecticut Ave Washington DC 20036 E-mail: jensend@rferl.org.

JENSEN, EDMUND PAUL, retired bank holding company executive; b. Oakland, Calif., Apr. 13, 1937; s. Edmund and Olive E. (Kessell) J.; m. Marilyn Norris, Nov. 14, 1959; children: Juliana L., Annika M. BA, U. Wash., 1959; postgrad., U. Santa Clara, Stanford U., 1981. Lic. real estate broker, Oreg., Calif. Mgr. fin. plan and evaluation Technicolor, Inc., Los Angeles, 1967-69; group v.p. Nat. Industries & Subs, Louisville, 1969-72; v.p. fin. Wedgewood Homes, Portland, 1972-74; various mgmt. positions U.S. Bancorp, Portland, 1974-83; pres., COO U.S. Bancorp, Inc., Portland, 1983-93; vice chmn., COO U.S. Bancorp, Inc., Portland, 1993-94; pres., CEO Visa Internat., 1994-99; ret., 1999. Bd. dirs. U.S. Nat. Bank of Oreg., U.S. Bank Washington. Chmn. United Way, 1986, N.W. Bus. Coalition, 1987; bd. dirs. Saturday Acad., Portland, 1984—, Visa U.S.A., Visa Internat., Marylhurst Coll., Oreg. Bus. Coun., Oreg. Downtown Devel. Assn., Oreg. Ind. Coll. Found., 1983—, treas., 1986—, chmn., 1988—; bd. dirs. Portland Art Mus., 1983—, vice chmn., 1989—. Mem. Portland C. of C. (bd. dirs. 1981—, chmn. 1987), Assn. Res. City Bankers, Assn. for Portland Progress (pres. 1988), Waverly Country Club, Multnomah Athletic Club, Arlington Club, Olympic Club.

JENSEN, ELOUISE HENRIE, volunteer; b. Manti, Utah, Jan. 20, 1932; d. Irven Lund and Orlene (Larsen) Henrie; m. Clayne R. Jensen, Mar. 14, 1952; children: Craig R., Michael H., Blake, Christian. Student, Brigham Young U., 1950—53, Utah State U., 1958—62. Housing bd. Brigham Young U. Women, 1972—82, pres., 1982, Utah Valley Symphony Guild, 1983—84. Mem.: Utah Valley Symphony Bd., US Tennis Assn., Ridge Tennis Club (tournament chmn. 1984), Riverside Country Club (pres. 1987—88, 2001—02), Etienne Club (pres. 1979), Cleafon Club (pres. 1981). Republican. Mem. Lds Ch. Office: 3131 N Cottonwood Ln Provo UT 84604-4497 E-mail: 3131@mstar2.net.

JENSEN, ELWOOD VERNON, biochemist; b. Fargo, N.D., Jan. 13, 1920; s. Eli A. and Vera (Morris) J.; m. Mary Welmoth Collette, June 17, 1941 (dec. Nov. 1982); children: Karen Collette, Thomas Eli; m. Hiltrud Herborg, Dec. 21, 1983 AB, Wittenberg U., 1940, DSc (hon.), 1963; PhD, U. Chgo., 1944; DSc (hon.), Acadia U., 1976, Med. Coll. Ohio, 1991; MD (hon.), U. Hamburg, 1994. Faculty U. Chgo., 1947-90, assoc. prof. biochemistry Ben May Inst. Cancer Rsch., 1954-60, prof., 1960-63, Am. Cancer Soc. rsch. prof. physiology, 1963-69, dir. Ben May Inst., 1969-82, dir. Biomed. Ctr. Population Research, 1972-75, prof. physiology, 1969-73, 77-84, prof. biophysics, 1973-84, prof. biochemistry, 1980-90, Charles B. Huggins disting. svc. prof., 1981-90, emeritus prof., 1990—; rsch. dir. Ludwig Inst. for Cancer Rsch., 1983-87; scholar-in-residence Fogarty Internat. Ctr. NIH, 1988, Cornell U. Med. Coll., 1990—91; prof. Inst. for Hormone and Fertility Rsch. U. Hamburg, Germany, 1992—97. Nobel vis. prof. Karolinska Inst., Huddinge, Sweden, 1998, STINT vis. scientist, 1998-99, prof. emeritus, 1999-2001; John and Gladys Strauss chair for cancer rsch. U. Cin., 2002-; vis. scientist NICHD/NIH, 2001; vis. prof. Max-Planck-Inst. for Biochemie, Munich, 1958; chemotherapy rev. bd. Nat. Cancer Inst., 1960-62, bd. sci. counselors, 1969-72; mem. Nat. Adv. Coun. Child Health and Human Devel., 1976-80; adv. com. biochemistry and chem. carcinogenesis Am. Cancer Soc., 1968-72, coun. for rsch. and clin. investigation, 1974-77; mem. assembly life scis. NRC, 1975-78; com. on sci., engring. and pub. policy Nat. Acad. Scis., 1981-82; rsch. adv. bd. Clin. Rsch. Inst. of Montreal, 1987-96, Klinik for Tumor Biologie, Freiburg, 1993-2002, Strang Cancer Prevention Ctr., 1994-98; cons. Rockefeller U. Hosp., 1990-92. Mem. editl. bd. Perspectives in Biology and Medicine, 1966—, Archives of Biochemistry and Biophysics, 1979-84, Biochemistry, 1969-72, Life Scis., 1973-78, Breast Cancer Rsch. and Treatment, 1980—, Endocrine-Related Cancer, 1994—, Jour. Biol. Markers, 1998—; assoc. editor: Jour. Steroid Biochemistry, 1974-94; contbr. articles to profl. jours. Recipient D.R. Edwards medal, 1970, La Madonnina prize, 1973, Pap award, 1975, prix Roussel, 1976, Nat. award Am. Cancer Soc., 1976, Gregory Pincus Meml. award, 1978, Gairdner Found. award, 1979, Lucy Wortham James award, 1980, Charles F. Kettering prize, 1980, Golden Plate award, 1980, Nat. Acad. Clin. Biochemistry award, 1981, Scientist of Yr. award Achievement Rewards for Coll. Scientists Found., 1981, Pharmacia award, 1982, Hubert H. Humphrey award, 1983, Rolf Luft medal, 1983, Renzo Grattarola medal, 1984, Fred C. Koch award, 1984, Axel Munthe award, 1985, Humboldt Sr. Rsch. prize, 1992, Joseph Bolivar DeLee award Chgo. Lying-In Hosp., 1995, Brinker Internat. award for breast cancer rsch., 2002; Guggenheim fellow, 1946-47. Mem. NAS (coun. 1981-84), AAAS (Amory prize 1977), Am. Soc. Biochemistry and Molecular Biology, Am. Chem. Soc., Am. Assn. Cancer Rsch. (G.H.A. Clowes award 1975, Dorothy P. Landon prize 2002), Endocrine Soc. (pres. 1980-81), Am. Gyn/Ob Soc. (hon.), St. Paul Surg. Soc. (hon.), EORTC Receptor and Biomarker Group (hon.), Honorable Order Ky. Cols. Office: U Cin Dept Cell Biology Vontz Ctr Molecular Studies 3125 Eden Ave Cincinnati OH 45267-0521

JENSEN, ERIK MICHAEL, law educator; b. Washington, Aug. 26, 1945; s. Wayne Ivan and Anna Elizabeth (Nelson) J.; m. Helen Burgin, May 4, 1981; 1 child, Addie. SB, MIT, 1967; MA, U. Chgo., 1972; JD, Cornell U., 1979. Bar: N.Y. 1980, U.S. Dist. Ct. (so. dist.) N.Y. 1983, U.S. Ct. Appeals 1983, U.S. Tax Ct. 1981. Law clk. to Hon. Monroe G. McKay, Salt Lake City, 1979-80; assoc. Sullivan & Cromwell, N.Y.C., 1980-83; from asst. prof. law to prof. Case Western Res. U., Cleve., 1983-98, David L. Brennan prof., 1998—. Vis. prof. Cornell U., 1999. Author: (with others) Federal Income Taxation of Oil and Gas Investments, 1989; co-editor Jour. Legal Edn., 1992-98. Adv. coun. Musical Arts Assn. Cleve. Orch., 1984-85. With U.S. Army, 1968-70. Mem. ABA, Cleve. Bar Assn., Am. Polit. Sci. Assn., Internat. Fiscal Assn., Nat. Tax Assn., Order of Coif (exec. com. 1994-2000). Home: 3215 Warrington Rd Cleveland OH 44120-3306 Office: Case Western Res U Sch Law 11075 East Blvd Cleveland OH 44106-7148 E-mail: emj@po.cwru.edu.

JENSEN, FRODE, III, lawyer; b. Denver, Colo., May 30, 1950; s. Frode and Camille McLean (Anderson) Jensen; m. Catherine Spotswood Hall, Aug. 6, 1980; children: Christian McLean, Catherine Spotswood Hall, Henry Carter. Grad., Phillips Acad.; BA, Williams Coll., 1972; JD, Columbia U., 1976. Bar: NY 1977, US Dist. Ct. (so. and ea. dist.)/NY 1979, Conn. 1985. Law clk. US Dist. Ct. Del., Wilmington, 1976—77; assoc. Davis Polk & Wardwell, NYC, 1978—83, Cummings & Lockwood, Stamford, Conn., 1983—85, ptnr., 1985—88, Winthrop, Stimson, Putnam & Roberts, Stamford, Conn., 1988—. Mem.: Conn. Bar Assn., Assn. of Bar of City of NY, ABA. Office: Winthrop Stimson Putnam & Roberts PO Box 6760 Stamford CT 06904-6760

JENSEN, GLORIA VERONICA, adult nurse practitioner; b. Montreal, Que., Can., Aug. 29, 1931; arrived in U.S., 1955; d. William Russell Boyd and Veronica Elizabeth Clarke; m. Joseph Edgar Jensen Jr., May 26, 1955 (div. June 11, 1989); children: William, Joanne, Neil, Christina, Karen. RN Calif.; lic. real estate agt. Calif. Nurse emer. rm. Royal Victoria Hosp., Montreal, 1953—55; postpartum nurse Good Samaritan Hosp., L.A., 1955—56; pvt. duty nurse Laguna Hills, Calif., 1988—91; relief work nurse Allergy and Asthma Assn., Mission Viego, Calif., 1992—99; nurse Saddleback Med. Group, Laguna Hills, 1998—. Vol. ARC, Subic Bay, Philippines, 1965—67, chmn. vols., 1965—67; mem. Valiant Women Mission Hosp., Mission Viejo, Calif. Mem.: Kiwanis. Republican. Roman Catholic. Avocations: opera, sewing, music, sailing. Home: 30922 Lucia Ln Laguna Beach CA 92677

JENSEN, HANNE MARGRETE, pathology educator; b. Copenhagen, Dec. 9, 1935; came to U.S., 1957; d. Niels Peter Evald and Else Signe Agnete (Rasmussen) Damgaard; m. July 21, 1957 (div. Apr. 1987); children: Peter Albert, Dorte Marie, Gordon Kristian, Sabrina Elisabeth. Student, U. Copenhagen, 1954-57; MD, U. Wash., 1961. Resident and fellow in pathology U. Wash., Seattle, 1963-68; asst. prof. dept. pathology U. Calif. Sch. Medicine, Davis, 1969-79, assoc. prof., 1979—2001, dir. transfusion svc., 1973—, prof., 2001—. McFarlane prof. exptl. medicine U. Glasgow, Scotland, 1983. Mem. No. Calif. Soc. for Electron Microscopy, U.S. and Can. Acad. of Pathology, Am. Cancer Soc., Am. SOc. Clin. Pathologists, Am. Assn. for Advancement of Sci., Am. Assn. of Blood Banks, Calif. Blood Bank System, People to People Internat., Internat. Platform Assn; fellow Pacific Coast Obstetrician and Gynecol. Soc., Coll. of Am. Pathologists. Office: U Calif Sch Medicine Dept Pathology Davis CA 95616

JENSEN, HANS WILLIAM, library director; b. Sept. 8, 1953; BA in Math, History, U. Wis., 1975, MALS, 1977. Asst. dir. Sun Prairie (Wis.) Pub. Libr., 1978-83; dir. Portage (Wis.) Pub. Libr., 1983—. Office: Portage Pub Libr 253 W Edgewater St Portage WI 53901-2117 E-mail: hjensen@scls.lib.wi.us.

JENSEN, HAROLD LEROY, medical liability insurance administrator, physician; b. Mpls., Aug. 17, 1926; s. Harold Hans and Nell Irene (Cameron) Jensen; m. Nancy Elizabeth Scharff, Sept. 9, 1950 (div. 1976); children: Eric Richard, Kris Ann, Beth Susan; m. Sandra Lee Steinel, Oct. 18, 1976. BS, U. Ill., 1950, MD, 1955. Intern Ill. Ctrl. Hosp., Chgo., 1955-56, resident, 1956-57; pvt. practice in internal medicine Ill., 1957—87; mem. staff Ingalls Meml. Hosp., Harvey, Ill., dir. continuing med. cdn., 1979-87, v.p. med. affairs, 1987-2000, cons. med. affairs, 2000—. Asst. clin. prof. medicine U. Ill.; guest lectr. Gov.'s State U., University Park, Ill.; bd. gov. ISMIE Mut. Ins. Co., 1986—. Mem. editl. bd.: Chgo. Healthcare, 1990—93; contbr. articles to profl. jours. Chmn. Med. Polit. Action Com., 1990—92; pres. bd. dirs. Homewood (Ill.) Pub. Libr., 1970—76; mem. policy bd. Cook County Healthcare Summit, 1990; chmn. Met. Chgo. Health Info. Network, 1995—2000. With U.S. Army, 1944—46. Mem.: AMA (del. 1983—95), Ill. Med. Physicians' Svc. Orgn. (bd. dirs. 1995—96), Am. Coll. Utilization Rev. Physicians (bd. dirs. 1985—89, cert.), ACP Execs., Chgo. Health Econ. Coun. (vice chmn. 1981—85), Ill. Med. Soc. (trustee 1983—86, sec., treas. 1986, chmn. bd. trustees 1988—90, treas. 1988—96), Chgo. Med. Soc. (pres. 1985—86), Flossmoor Country Club (pres. 1972—73). Republican. Office: ISMIE Mutual Ins Co 20 N Michigan Ave Chicago IL 60602-4811

JENSEN, HELENE WICKSTROM, retired nutritionist, educator; b. Carthage, Mo., Mar. 3, 1929; d. Frank Emil and Lois (Stroup) Wickstrom; m. Robert Gordon Jensen, Dec. 20, 1947; children: Gordon Lee, Jeffrey Alan. BS, U. Mo., 1951; MS, U. Conn., 1983; PhD, Century U., 1996. Registered dietitian; cert. dietitian/nutritionist. Dietitian-in-charge U. Mo., Columbia, 1952-56; therapeutic dietitian Windham Community Meml. Hosp., Willimantic, Conn., 1967, dir. food service, 1967-72; dir. sch. lunch program Windham Pub. Schs., Willimantic, 1963-66; lectr. U. Conn., Storrs, 1972-78, leader ednl. outreach program, 1979-92; ret., 1992. Recipient award Met. Life Ins. Co., 1985, Czajowski Nutrition award U. Conn., 1989, Disting. Alumna award U. Conn. Agr. and Natural Resources Alumni Assn., 1989. Mem. Am. Dietetic Assn. (presenter), Am. Sch. Food Svc. Assn. (exec. bd. 1989-91, presenter), Soc. Nutrition Edn., Conn. Sch. Food Svc. Assn. (com. mem.), Conn. Nutrition Coun. (presenter), Conn. Dietetic Assn. (presenter, Dietitian of Yr. 1987), Phi Kappa Phi, Gamma Sigma Delta. Home: 186 Chaffeeville Rd Storrs Mansfield CT 06268-2637

JENSEN, JAMES E. director congressional and government affairs; b. Santa Monica, Calif., Oct. 26, 1953; BA, U. Calif., Berkeley, 1976. Aid to Rep. Jim Lloyd, Calif., 1978-79; adjunct prof. Johns Hopkins U., 1978-79; aid to Senator Al Gore, 1980-87; dir. congressional pub. affairs Office of Tech. Assessment, Washington, 1987-95; dir. congressional, govt. affairs Nat. Acad. Scis., Washington, 1995—. Fellow Nat. Ctr. Atmospheric Rsch. Office: National Academy of Sciences 2101 Constitution Ave NW Washington DC 20418-0006

JENSEN, JAMES ROBERT, dentist, educator; b. Mpls., Mar. 17, 1922; s. Ernest William and Edith Ann (Norstedt) J.; m. Alvern Halverson, Mar. 24, 1945; children: Thomas, Mark, James, Elizabeth. BA, U. Minn., 1944, D.D.S., 1946, MS, 1950. Diplomate Am. Bd. Endodontics. Teaching asst. U. Minn., 1948-50, asst. prof., 1950-53, assoc. prof., 1953-57, prof., chmn. div. operative dentistry and endodontics, 1957-69, asst. dean acad. affairs, 1969-74, assoc. dean acad. affairs, 1974-90, chmn. dept. restorative scis., prof., dir. div. endodontics, 1990-92, prof. emeritus, 1992—. Cons. endodontics VA Hosp., Mpls.; team leader operative dentistry and endodontics Project Vietnam of AID; cons. dental health Pan Am. Health Orgn., WHO; curriculum cons. U. North Sumatra, Indonesia, 1986-87; mem. staff King Saud U., Riyadh, Saudi Arabia, 1987—, U. Autonoma, Neuva Leon, Mex., 1974—; postgrad. faculty U. Autonoma de Neuva Leon, Monterrey, Mex. Author: (with Thomas P. Serene and Fernando Sanchez) Fundamentos Clinicos de Endodoncia, 1977, (with Thomas P. Serene) Fundamentals of Clinical Endodontics, 8th edit., 1984, Japanese edit., Effective Dental Assisting, 7th edit., 1991; contbr. articles to profl. jours. Served with U.S. Army, 1943-44; as capt. Dental Corps, 1946-48; res. dental surgeon USPHS and Assn. Res. Officers. Fellow Am. Coll. Dentists, Internat. Colls. Dentists; mem. ADA, Minn. Dental Assn., Mpls. Dist. Dental Soc., Am. Assn. Endodontists. Home: 2167 Rosewood Ln N Saint Paul MN 55113-5324

JENSEN, JOLI, communications educator; b. Bad Kreuznach, Germany, Feb. 23, 1954; d. Donald D. and Janet (Kepner) J.; m. Craig Allan Walter, July 13, 1985; children: Charles William, Thomas Craig. BA in Psychology, U. Nebr., 1975; MA in Journalism, U. Ill., 1977, PhD in Communication, 1985. Asst. prof. U. Va., 1983-85, U. Tex., 1985-91; assoc. prof. U. Tulsa, 1991-2000, prof., 2000—. Writing cons. MCI/Worldcom, Okla., 1992—. Author: Redeeming Modernity, 1990, The Nashville Sound, 1998, Is Art Good For Us, 2002. Recipient univ. fellowship NEH, 1993, faculty tchg. grant U. Tulsa, 1992-98, faculty fellowship U. Tex., 1987. Office: Faculty of Communication U Tulsa Tulsa OK 74104 E-mail: joli-jensen@utulsa.edu.

JENSEN, LEO, artist; b. Montevideo, Minn., 1926; Student, Walker Art Ctr., Mpls., 1946—48. Solo exhbns. include: Creative Gallery, N.Y.C., 1953, Amel Gallery, N.Y.C., 1964, 65, Sakowitz Gallery, Houston, 1964, New Britain Mus. Am. Art, Conn., 1967, Arras Gallery, N.Y.C., 1976, Vorpal Gallery, N.Y.C., 1987, Mattatuck Mus., Waterbury, Conn., 1990, Childers Gallery, Ft. Lauderdale, Fla., 1992, Meisner Soho, N.Y., 1993, Chapel St. Gallery, New Haven, 1996; exhibited in group shows Mus. Modern Art, N.Y.C., U. New Haven, Milw. Art Ctr., Inst. Contemporary Art, Boston, Norfolk Mus., Yale Art Gallery, Palacio de Cristal, Madrid, Nat. Portrait Gallery, Washington, Chgo. Hist. Soc., Am. Mus. Natural History, N.Y.C., Baseball Hall of Fame, Cooperstown, N.Y.,

Mattatuck Mus., Conn., Butler Inst. Am. Art, Youngstown, Ohio, also other mus. in 64 countries; represented in pub. collections Gertrude Herbert Meml. Art Inst., Augusta, Ga., Rose Art Mus. Brandeis U., Phillip Morris, N.Y.C., Brown U. Gallery, Walkter Art Ctr., Mpls., U.S. Info. Agy., Washington, Conn. Savings Bank, Pepperidge Farms Baking Co., Achenbach Found., San Francisco, New Britain Mus. Am. Art., Mattatuch Mus., Sheraton Hotels, Spool Frog Bridge, Willimantic, Conn., Mark Twain Libr, Reading, Conn., Acad. Ednl. Devel., Washington, others, plus numerous pvt. collections. Scholar Walker Art Ctr., 1946-48. Home: PO Box 264 Ivoryton CT 06442-0264

JENSEN, LYNN EDWARD, retired medical association executive, economist; b. Rock Springs, Wyo., May 27, 1945; s. Glen and Helen (Anderson) J.; m. Carol Jean Lombard, June 10, 1967 (dec. Dec. 2001); children: Chelsea, Kara. BA, Idaho State U., 1967; PhD, U. Utah, 1979. Rsch. assoc. Dept. Commerce, Washington, 1967, U. Utah, 1971-74, Utah State Planning Office, 1971-74; economist AMA Rsch. Ctr., Chgo., 1974-75, dir., 1975-85; v.p. health policy AMA, Chgo., 1985-96, group v.p. strategic mgmt. and devel., 1996-97, COO, 1997-2000, interim exec. v.p., 1998, ret., 2000. Mem. Robert Wood Johnson Found. Adv. Com., Princeton, N.J., 1983-84, Johnson & Johnson Cmty. Health Program, 1985-88; health adv. com. GAO. Editor-in-chief Intermountain Econ. Rev., 1972-73; assoc. editor Jour. Bus. and Econ. Stats., 1981-85; contbr. articles to profl. jours. With U.S. Army, 1968-70. Mem. AMA, Assn. Am. Med. Soc. Execs., Am. Soc. Assn. Execs., Am. Econ. Assn., Nat. Assn. Bus. Economists. Presbyterian. Avocations: reading, computers, swimming, photography, biking.

JENSEN, MARGARET, real estate broker; b. Payson, Utah, Aug. 12, 1948; d. Basil D. Broadbent and V. Merlene Ellsworth; m. Don E. Jensen, Sept. 27, 1997; children: Chad, Troy, Kristin, Dean, Debbie, Sean, Julie. AS, Casper Coll., 1968; BS with distinction, Colo. State U., 1989, postgrad., 1990. Grad. Realtor Inst., CRB, CRS, EMT. Clk. Colo. 8th Jud. Dept., Loveland; owner, CEO Lil Rascals, Ft. Collins, 1980-96; real estate salesperson Hometown Advantage, Loveland, 1996, Century 21, Ft. Collins, 1996; pres. Home Sweet Home Realty, Inc., Ft. Collins, 1997—; owner Home Sweet Home Bakery, Inc., Home Sweet Home Knitted Creations, Inc. Rental cons. Ft. Collins, 1985-99; tax cons., Ft. Collins, 1975-90; family cons. Ft. Collins, 1990-97. Participant Miss Am. Pageant, 1968, Instr. ARC, Ft. Collins, 1976-85; tax preparer for VITA IRS, Ft. Collins, 1975-90; supr. trip to Russia People to People, 1990. Mem. Lions Club Internat., Mortar Bd., Golden Key Nat. Honor Soc., Colo. Assn. of Realtors, Nat. Assn. of Realtors, Omicron Nu, Alpha Gamma Delta, Phi Kappa Phi. Avocation: knitting hats for hospital patients and newborns. Home and Office: 2205 Stonecrest Dr Fort Collins CO 80521-1318 E-mail: buycolorado@aol.com.

JENSEN, MARK KEVIN, foreign language educator; b. Bethesda, Md., Aug. 13, 1951; s. Harold Boyd and Annabelle Bertha Jensen; m. Agnès Guichard, Dec. 20, 1976; 1 child, Gregory. BA, Princeton U., 1974; MA, U. Calif., Berkeley, 1983, PhD, 1989. Assoc. prof. French, Pacific Luth. U., Tacoma, 1989—, chair dept. lang. and lit., 2001—. Co-author: The Traveler in the Life and Works of George Sand, 1994, Mélanges sur l'oeuvre de Paul Bénichou, 1995, Mélodrames et romans noirs, 1750-1890, 2000; translator: Émile Zola's J'Accuse, 1992, Paul Bénichou's The Consecration of the Writer, 1999; contbr. articles to profl. jours. Pres. Cercle Français de Tacoma, 1993-95, 2002-03; co-founder United for Peace of Pierce County; co-founder, v.p. Anna Comstock Dinner Club and Literary Union, 1993—. Mem. MLA, AAUP, Am. Assn. Tchrs. French, Assn. Internat. des Etudes Françaises, Assn. des Amis D'Alfred de Vigny, Washington Assn. Fng. Lang. Tchrs., People for Peace, Justice, and Healing. Home: 3110 N 31st St Tacoma WA 98407-6411 Office: Pacific Luth U Dept Lang and Lit Tacoma WA 98447-0003 E-mail: jensenmk@plu.edu.

JENSEN, MARVIN ELI, retired agricultural engineer; b. Clay County, Minn., Dec. 23, 1926; s. John M. and Inga C. (Haugness) J.; m. Doris A. Lundberg, Sept. 4, 1947; children: Connie, Jeffrey, Eric. BS in Agr., N.D. State U., 1951, MS in Agrl. Engring., 1952, DSc (hon.), 1988; PhD in Civil Engring., Colo. State U., 1965. Instr., asst. prof. N.D. State U., Fargo, 1952-55; agrl. engr. Soil and Water Rsch. divsn. USDA, Bushland, Tex., 1955-58, head irrigation and drain sect. Ft. Collins, Colo., 1959-61, investigation leader Ft. Collins and Kimberly, Idaho, 1961-68; dir. Snake River Conservation Rsch. Ctr. Agrl. Rsch. Service USDA, Kimberly, 1969-78, nat. program leader Ft. Collins and Beltsville, Md., 1979-87; dir. Colo. Inst. for Irrigation Mgmt. Colo. State U., Ft. Collins, 1987—92; ret. Pres. Internat. Commn. Irrigation and Drainage, New Delhi, 1984-87. Editor: (monograph) Design and Operation of Farm Irrigation Systems, 1980; sr. editor: (manual) Evapotranspiration and Irrigation Water Requirements, 1990. Recipient Disting. Svc. award USDA, 1983, W.E. Morgan Alumni Achievement award, 1990, Disting. Svc. award Colo. State U., 1994; named to USDA-ARS Sci. Hall of Fame, 2000. Fellow Am. Soc. Agrl. Engrs. (tech. v.p. 1983-86, John Deere Gold medal 1982); mem. NAE, ASCE (hon., chmn. irrigation and drainage div. 1976-77, Tipton award 1982, Arid Lands Hydraulic Engring. award 1990, State-of-the-Art award, 1992). Avocations: golf, photography.

JENSEN, MICHAEL CHARLES, journalist, lecturer, author; s. Stanley Charles and Billie Jane (Cooke) J.; m. Jane Rice Woodruff, July 23, 1960; children: Heidi, Michael Charles Jr. AB, Harvard U., 1956; MS, Boston U., 1961. Reporter Boston Herald-Traveler, 1960-63, exec. fin. editor, 1963-64; reporter, editor N.Y. Times, N.Y.C., 1970-78; chief. fin. corr. NBC Nightly News, Today program, N.Y.C., 1978-2000. Lectr. in field. Author: The Financiers, 1976; contbg. author: Corporations and Their Critics, 1980; contbr.: articles to Saturday Rev., Harvard Bus. Rev. Served to lt. (j.g.) USNR, 1957-60. Recipient Page One award Newspaper Guild N.Y., 1973, Deadline Club award N.Y.C. profl. chpt. Sigma Delta Chi, 1976, media awards for econ. understanding, 1980, Janus awards for excellence in fin. broadcasting, 1981, 88, award for best news documentary San Francisco Film Festival, 1984, Gabriel awards Assn. Cath. Broadcasters, 1988, 89, 93, Disting. Alumnus award Boston U., 1989, EDI award Nat. Easter Seal Soc., 1991, Nat. News Emmy, 1993; named best econs. and bus. corr. in Am., TV Guide, 1988; named Luminary, 1999. Mem. Am. Soc. Bus. Press Editors (pres. N.Y. chpt. 1965-66), Am. Bus. Press (dir. 1967) Clubs: Harvard of N.Y. E-mail: mikejensencom@aol.com.

JENSEN, MICHAEL WAYNE, writer; b. Grand Rapids, Minn., Jan. 25, 1954; s. Lloyd Winfred and Helen Hyacinth Jensen. AAS, Itasca C.C., 1978; BA, U. Minn., 1988. Author: (novels and screenplays) Oaxacan Blue, 1985, When the Oak Falls, 1999, Running Far, 2000, Sun Dancer, 2003; author: (songwriter, rearranger) Red Sky at Night and Other Piano Solos, 1999. Fellow, Helene Wurlitzer Found., Blue Mountain, scholar, Charles K. Blandin Found., 1977, grantee, Minn. Arts Bd., 1997. Roman Catholic. Avocations: piano, guitar, reading, backpacking, skiing. Home: 21550 Mishawaka Rd Grand Rapids MN 55744

JENSEN, N. JEAN, special education educator, secondary school educator; 3 children. BS in Edn., U. Kans., 1968; MA in Spl. Edn., U. Kans., Regent's Center, 1990; MA in Edn., Avila U., 1992, postgrad. Cert. tchr. Mo., 2003. Elem. edn. tchr. Shawnee Mission (Kans.) Dist., 1968—76; tchr. English pub. H.S., 1970; early childhood edn. adminstr., state trainer pvt. schs., St. Charles, Mo., 1976—79; tchr. and curriculum developer pub. sch. sys., 1981—86; vocat. opportunity program designer pvt. high sch., 1986—95; spl. edn. tchr., 1987; studies in cultural diversity curriculum developer and tchr. pvt. high sch., 2001—03. Consulting tchr. and trainer Ozanam, Kansas City, 1990—98. Author: (poetry collection) Lifelong Loves Literary Sampler, (textbook) Job Readiness for the Exceptional Student. Webelos leader & merit badge counselor Boy Scouts Am., St. Charles, Mo., 1979—81, merit badge counselor Olathe, Kans., 1981—88; Sunday sch. tchr. middle sch. class Coll. Ch. of the Nazarene, Olathe, 1981—83. Grantee, U. Kans., 1987—89, Carl Perkins Vocat. Edn., U.S. Govt. and the state of Mo., 1989—96; scholar, State of Kans., 1986—87. Mem.: Coun. of the Exceptional Child (assoc.). Achievements include research in Correlations Between Substance Use and Attentional Deficits; The Use of Learning Strategies with Special Needs Vocational High School Students. Personal E-mail: edpsyched@aol.com.

JENSEN, NANCY DAGGETT, music educator; b. L.A., Sept. 10, 1942; d. Daniel Thomas and Louise Helen (Kuljian) Daggett; m. Sven Oxfeldt Jensen, Nov. 19, 1978; children: Lori, Brian. BA, San Jose State U., 1964, MA, 1967. Cert. master tchr. in music. Pvt. piano tchr., Los Altos, Calif., 1967—. Mem. Music Tchrs. Assn. of Calif. (pres. 1972-74, 82-83, 85-86, 93-94, state chmn. cert. of merit 1974-79), Calif. Assn. of Profl. Music Tchrs., Steinway Soc. (bd. dirs.).

JENSEN, PAUL EDWARD TYSON, business educator, consultant; b. New Orleans, Apr. 27, 1926; s. Paul Christian and Nena Laura (Robertson) J.; m. Jule Valerie Geisenhofer, Jan. 10, 1953; children: Christian, Elena, Constance. BS in Physics, Tulane U., 1947, BBA, 1949; MBA, Golden Gate U., 1976. Asst. mgr. Cuban Atlantic Sugar Co., Lugareño, Cuba, 1952-55; sr. engring. specialist GTE, Mountain View, Calif., 1955-82; sr. staff engr. TRW, Inc., Sunnyvale, Calif., 1982-92; dean Sch. of Bus., Northwestern Poly. U., Fremont, Calif., 1988—, also bd. trustees. Cons. geog. info. sys. TRW, Inc., Sunnyvale, 1993-94. Capt. USMCR, 1945-61, WWII, Korea. Fellow Soc. Tech. Comm. (assoc.); mem. IEEE (life, sr. mem.), Am. Phys. Soc., Internat. Soc. Computer Modeling and Simulation, World Future Soc., Assn. Old Crows. Presbyterian. Avocations: amateur radio, jogging, photography, travel. Home: 8033 Regency Dr Pleasanton CA 94588-3131 Office: Northwestern Poly U 117 Fourier Ave Fremont CA 94539-7482

JENSEN, PAUL ROLF, lawyer, real estate investor; b. San Francisco, Nov. 12, 1958; s. Rolf Levald and Ouida (Moore) J.; m. Pamela Balogh, Apr. 3, 1993; children: Peter John, David Christian Rolf, Stephen Paul Levald. AB, U. Calif., Berkeley, 1981; JD, Whittier Coll., 1990. Bar: Calif. 1991; lic. real estate broker Calif. Dept. Real Estate. Legis. dir. Am. Def. Inst., Washington, 1983-84; campaign advisor U.S. Senator Jeremiah Denton, Washington, 1984-86; assoc. atty. Elhai & McIntosh, Hacienda Heights, Calif., 1991; prin. atty. Jensen & Assocs., Newport Beach, Calif., 1992-95; ptnr. Jensen & McIntosh, Hacienda Heights, 1995—2000; gen. counsel Jensen Properties, LLC, Newport Beach, 1997—2000; sr. counsel U.S. Senate Com. on Environment and Pub. Works, Washington, 2001—. Mem. Federalist Soc. (pres. Duke Law Sch. chpt. 1990-91), Bahia Corinthian Yacht Club. Republican. Presbyterian. Avocations: sailing, antiquarian book collecting, travel, wine collecting, fishing. Home: 10304 E Hunter Valley Rd Vienna VA 22181-3012 Office: US Senate 415 Hart Senate Office Bldg Washington DC 20510

JENSEN, PHILIP BAILEY, urologist; b. Kingston-on-Thames, Surrey, Eng., Apr. 10, 1922; s. Axel P.C. and Mabel (Bailey) J.; m. D. Patricia Riley, Nov. 20, 1953; children: Frances, Charles, Richard. MB, BS, London U., 1952. Diplomate Am. Bd. Urology. House physician Middlesex Hosp., London, 1952-53, Cen. Middlesex Hosp., London, 1953, Royal No. Hosp., London, 1953-54; resident Greenwich (Conn.) Hosp., 1954-56, Columbia Presbyn. Med. Ctr., N.Y.C., 1956-59; pvt. practice Greenwich, 1959-75, Sharon, Conn., 1976—; attending physician Greenwich (Conn.) Hosp., 1959-75, United Hosp., Port Chester, N.Y., 1961-75, New Milford (Conn.) Hosp., 1977-93, attending physician emeritus, 1993—; attending physician Sharon (Conn.) Hosp., 1977-93, attending physician emeritus, 1993—. Instr. urology Coll. Physicians and Surgeons, Columbia U., N.Y.C., 1959-75. Lt. Royal Naval Vol. Res., 1941-46. Fellow ACS. Avocations: travel, golf. Home: PO Box 727 59 Hilltop Rd Sharon CT 06069-2131

JENSEN, REGINA BRUNHILD, psychotherapist; b. Bredstedt, Germany, Oct. 26, 1951; came to U.S., 1973; d. Karl Adolf and Hildegard (Weiss) Schlosser; m. Benny Hvitfelt Jensen, July 31, 1976; stepchildren: Anita, Lisa; 1 child, Rayna Maria, 1991. BS in Physiotherapy, Krankengymnastik Schule, Tuebingen, 1971; MA in Counseling Psychology, Vt. Coll., 1983; PhD Human Behavior, Ryokan Coll., 1984; PhD Clin. Psychology, Sierra U., 1987. Physiotherapist Urban Krankenhaus, Berlin, 1971-73; staff physiotherapist Werner & Beck Physical Therapy, Santa Maria, Calif., 1976-83; pvt. practice health cons. Santa Ynez, 1982—. Cons. Jensen Enterprises, Solvang, 1975—, Alexander & Jensen Assocs., L.A., 1983-85; adolescent crisis counselor Santa Ynez Valley High Sch., 1984-86; tutor, program coordinator Sierra U., Santa Monica, 1985—; dir. Inst. for Human Systems Integration, Santa Ynez, 1985—; founder, clin. dir., The Learning Ctr., 1987—. Author: Education for the Medical Consumer, 1983, To Liberate or to Enslave, 1985, How To Buy Back Your Soul, 1987; publisher Fully Alive Publs., 1988—; pub., founder Healing Art Expressions, 1987—; contbr. articles to profl. papers and jours. Mem. Calif. Assn. For Marriage and Family Therapists. Avocations: poetry writing, singing, dancing, nature walks, animals. Home and Office: 2880 Baseline Ave # B Santa Ynez CA 93460-9354

JENSEN, REUBEN ROLLAND, former automotive company executive; b. Ainsworth, Nebr., Dec. 22, 1921; s. Jens Christian and Amy Caroline (Boyer) J.; m. Janet A. McCann, Oct. 19, 1974; children: Shannon (Mrs. Roger Santora), Bruce. Student, U. Nebr., 1938-41. With Gen. Motors Corp., Detroit, 1946, jr. engr. Hydra-Matic div., 1965-67, gen. mgr. Hydra-Matic div., 1967-70, gen. mgr. Allison div., 1970-72, v.p., group exec., 1972-74, exec. v.p., 1974-84. Mem. adv. bd. Chem. Bank Internat., 1973-86. Served with USNR, 1943-45. Recipient Silver Beaver, Disting. Eagle, Silver Buffalo, Boy Scouts Am., 1973 Mem. Assn. U.S. Army, Navy League U.S., Am. Ordnance Assn., Quail Ridge Country Club (Boynton Beach, Fla.), Meadowbrook Country Club (Northville, Mich.), Masons. Home: 3609 Chinaberry Ter Boynton Beach FL 33436-4528 also: 18500 Sheldon Rd Northville MI 48167-9535

JENSEN, RICHARD ALLEN, mathematician, educator; b. Northfield, Minn., Nov. 11, 1941; s. Milford Carlton and Nora Otelia Jensen; m. Christine Ellen Reynolds, Apr. 17, 1972; children: Leif, Tryg, Bryn, Lars, Jens. AB, Princeton U., 1963; MA, U. Wis., 1964, PhD, 1969. Asst. prof. U. Miami, Coral Gables, Fla., 1969—72; instr. Normandale C.C., Bloomington, Minn., 1973—. Contbr. articles to profl. jours. Mem.: Math. Assn. Am. Home: 3 Walden Place Northfield MN 55057-1600 Office: Normandale Community College 9700 France Ave So Bloomington MN 55431

JENSEN, RICHARD CURRIE, lawyer; b. Flushing, N.Y., June 5, 1939; s. David T. and Isabel (Currie) J.; m. Leslie Dodge, Jan. 9, 1965; children: Tracy, Richard, David, Meredith, Lauren, Christopher. BS in Social Studies, Villanova U., 1961; JD, Fordham U., 1964. Bar: N.Y. 1965. Staff atty. Comml. Union Ins. Co., N.Y.C., 1965-67; ptnr. Morris, Duffy, Ivone & Jensen, N.Y.C., 1967-85, Ivone, Devine & Jensen, Lake Success, N.Y., 1985—. Mem. ABA, N.Y. State Bar Assn., Nassau County Bar Assn., Am. Soc. Law & Medicine, N.Y. State Med. Malpractice Defense Assn. Republican. Roman Catholic. Office: Ivone Devine & Jensen 2001 Marcus Ave Ste 100N New Hyde Park NY 11042-1024

JENSEN, RICHARD DENNIS, librarian; b. Payson, Utah, Oct. 20, 1944; s. Ruel Whiting and Ethel Josepha (Otte) J.; m. Maxine Swasey, Apr. 21, 1966; children: Shaun, Craig, Todd, Jana, Brad, Kristine, April, Lynne. BS in Zoology, Brigham Young U., 1971, MLS, 1976. From asst. sci. libr. to pub. svc. coord. Brigham Young U., Provo, Utah, 1971—2001, reference svc. coord., 2001—. Co-author: Agricultural and Animal Sciences Journals and Serials: An Analytical Guide, 1986, (indexes) Great Basin Naturalist, 50 Year Index, 1991, BYU Geology Studies, Cumulative Index, vol. 1-37, 1954-1991, 1992. Mem. Lds Ch. Avocations: farming, sports, camping. Office: Brigham Young U Libr Sci & Maps Dept 2324 HBLL Provo UT 84602-2734 E-mail: Richard_Jensen@byu.edu.

JENSEN, RICHARD JORG, biology educator; b. Sandusky, Ohio, Jan. 17, 1947; s. Aksel Carl and Margaret (Wolfe) J.; m. Faye Robertson, May 30, 1970. BS, Austin Peay State U., 1970, MS, 1972; PhD, Miami U., 1975. Asst. prof. Wright State U., 1975-79; prof. St. Mary's Coll., 1979—. Guest prof. U. Notre Dame, Ind., 1981—, dir. Greene-Nieuwland Herbarium, 1988—; sr. rsch. fellow Ctr. for Field Biology, Austin Peay State U., 1986-88; vis. scholar dept. botany Miami U., 1987; panelist systematic biology program NSF, 1983-87. Assoc. editor Am. Midland Naturalist, 1988—; mem. exec. com. Am. Midland Naturalist, 1989—; mem. editl. bd. Plant Systematics and Evolution, 1990-96; assoc. editor Systematic Botany, 1996-2000. Recipient Award for outstanding tchg. Wright State U., 1978, Maria Pieta award for outstanding tchg. St. Mary's Coll., 1997; named to Austin Peay State U. Acad. Hall of Fame, 1998; NSF grantee, 1973, 79, 85, 87, 95, Rsch. Corp. grantee, 1984, Eli Lilly grantee, 1990. Fellow: Ind. Acad. Sci. (co-chair program com. 1988, fellow com., biol. survey com., publ. com., grantee 1983, 1991); mem.: Internat. Oak Soc. (bd. dirs. 1997—, webmaster 2000—, membership chair 1997—), Soc. Systematic Biology, Internat. Assn. Plant Taxonomy, Bot. Soc. Am., Am. Soc. Plant Taxonomists (rsch. com. 1987—90, chmn. 1989—90, treas. 1991—96, coun. mem. at large 2000—, honors and awards com. 2000—, chair 2001, Disting. Svc. award 1996), Sigma Xi (grantee 1974). Democrat. Avocations: reading, computing, genealogy research. Home: 2044 Carrbridge Ct South Bend IN 46614-3514 Office: St Mary's Coll Dept Biology Notre Dame IN 46556 also: Greene-Nieuwland Herbarium Univ of Notre Dame Dept Biology Notre Dame IN 46556 E-mail: rjensen@saintmarys.edu., sparky0408@msn.com.

JENSEN, ROBERT GORDON, nutritionist, consultant; b. Carthage, Mo., Jan. 2, 1926; s. Wiggo England and Thelma Nancy (Judd) J.; m. Helene Catherine Wickstrom, Dec. 20, 1947; children: Gordon, Jeffrey. BS, U. Mo., 1950, MS, 1951, PhD, 1954. Instr. U. Mo., Columbia, 1954-55, asst. prof., 1955-56, U. Conn., Storrs, 1956-61, assoc. prof., 1961-66, prof., 1966-91, prof. emeritus, 1991—. Author, editor: Handbook of Milk Composition, 1995; contbr. over 200 articles to profl. jours. With USN, 1944-46, ETM. Fellow Am. Dairy Sci. Assn., 2000. Fellow: Am. Dairy Sci. Assn., Internat. Soc. Rsch. Human Milk Lactation (founding mem., 1st recipient Macy-Gyorgy award 1995); mem.: Am. Soc. Nutrition Sci., Am. Oil Chem. Soc. (Supelco-Nicholas Pelick award 1998). Home: 186 Chaffeeville Rd Storrs Mansfield CT 06268-2637 E-mail: rjensen@uconnvm.uconn.edu.

JENSEN, ROBERT TRAVIS, physician, educator, researcher; b. Minot, N.D., Mar. 19, 1926; s. John and Katherine N. (Arnold) J.; m. Rosemary Elizabeth McEachern; children: Janet, Katherine, Tova Marie. Student, Concordia Coll.; BA, Denison U., 1946; MD, U. Minn., 1949; Diploma in Tropical Medicine and Hygiene, London Sch. Hygiene and Tropical Medicine, 1958; MPH, Johns Hopkins U., 1967. Diplomate Am. Bd. Internal Medicine, Am. Bd. Preventive Medicine. Commd. capt., physician officer Med. Corps U.S. Army, Japan, Korea, 1950-51, advanced through grades to col., 1967, ret., 1976, physician officer Med. Corps., 1950-51, physician officer Brooke Army Hosp., Walter Reed Inst. Rsch., 1952-55, physician officer Ft. Meade Hosp., 1955-57, chief dept. pub. health Acad. Health Sci., 1971-76; missionary physician Luth. Ch., Tanzania, 1957-66; chief dept. health, edn. and welfare U.S. Civil Adminstrn., Okinawa, Ryuku Isls., 1969-71; supt. state chest hosps. Dept. Health State of Tex., San Antonio, 1977-82; assoc. prof. dept. family practice Health Scis. Ctr. U. Tex., San Antonio, 1983-97, ret., 1997; pvt. practice in internal medicine, 1997-98; ret., 1998. Lectr., cons. in field. Contbr. articles to med. jours. Decorated Silver Star, Bronze Star, Legion of Merit cluster. Fellow Am. Coll. Physicians, Am. Coll. Preventive Medicine; mem. Am. Soc. Tropical Medicine and Hygiene. Republican. Presbyterian. E-mail: drrtj@aol.com.

JENSEN, ROBERT TRYGVE, retired lawyer; b. Chgo., Sept. 16, 1922; s. James T. and Else (Uhlich) J.; m. Marjorie Rae Montgomery, Oct. 3, 1959 (div. June 1973); children: Robert Trygve, James Thomas, John Michael; m. Barbara Mae Wilson, Aug. 5, 1974. Student, U. N.C., 1943; LL.B., JD, BS, Northwestern U., 1949; LL.M., U. So. Calif., 1955. Bar: Calif. 1950. Asst. counsel Douglas Aircraft Co., Inc., 1950-52, 58-60, counsel El Segundo div., 1952-58; gen. counsel Aerospace Corp., El Segundo, 1960-84, asst. sec., 1961-67, sec., 1967-85. Founding mem. World Assn. Lawyers of World Peace Through Law Center. Served with AUS, 1942-46, PTO. Mem. Alpha Delta Phi, Phi Delta Phi. Fax: (310) 475-0445. E-mail: rtjsr@aol.com.

JENSEN, ROGER CHRISTIAN, industrial engineer; b. Brigham City, Utah, Nov. 7, 1945; s. Armour Anton and Jenny (Ray) J.; m. Marian Carol Potts, Nov. 26, 1975; 1 child, Lea Smith Jensen. BS, U. Utah, 1969; JD, No. Ky. State, 1974; MS in Engring., U. Mich., 1977; PhD, W.Va. U., 1989. Registered profl. engr., Ohio; cert. safety profl., profl. ergonomist. Indsl. hygiene engr. USPHS, Cin., 1969-76, rsch. indsl. engr. Morgantown, W.Va., 1977-78, br. chief divsn. safety rsch., 1978-83, rsch. indsl. engr., 1984-88, sr. indsl. engr., 1988-90, chief safety controls sect., 1990-91. Vis. ergonomist U. New South Wales, Sydney, 1991; sr. ergonomist UES, Inc., Dayton, Ohio, 1992-98, divsn. dir. applied sci. divsn., 1998-99; asst. prof. dept. safety and health Mont. Tech., 1999-2002, assoc. prof., 2002—. Author: Nursing & Back Injury, 1988. Mem. Human Factors and Ergonomics Soc., Am. Soc. Safety Engrs. Democrat. Home: 3002 Mammoth Dr Butte MT 59701-8008 E-mail: rjensen@mtech.edu.

JENSEN, ROY ANDREW, pathologist; b. Kansas City, Kans. s. George Jens and Lois Maxine (Eastland) J.; m. Linda Jo Clark, June 16, 1978; children: J. Andrew, Derek T., Brett H. AA, Neosho County C.C., 1978; BS, Pitts. State U., 1980; MD, Vanderbilt U., 1984. Surg. pathology fellow Vanderbilt U., Nashville, 1987-88, asst. prof. cell biology, pathology, 1991-96, assoc. prof., 1996—. Cons. VA Med. Ctr., Nashville, 1991—, Biofield Corp., Roswell, Ga., 1995-96, Cytometry Assocs., Brentwood, Tenn., 1996—. Cub scout, webelos leader Boy Scouts Am., Franklin, Tenn., 1994—. Grantee NIH, 1994—, rsch. grantee Susan G. Komen Found., 1996-97m cancer ctr. support grant. Mem. AAAS, Am. Assn. Cancer Rsch., Am. Soc. Investigative Pathology, U.S. Acad. Pathology, Canadian Acad. Pathology. Democrat. Presbyterian. Achievements include patent for neutralizing monoclonal antibody of PDGF receptor, method of detection and diagnosis of pre-invasive cancer, hepatocyte growth factor, a growth factor with broad spectrum activity for epithelial cells. Home: 2701 Longwood Ln Franklin TN 37069-7013 Office: Vanderbilt U Med Ctr 4918 Tvc Nashville TN 37232-0001 E-mail: roy.jensen@vanderbilt.edu.

JENSEN, SAM, lawyer; b. Blair, Nebr., Oct. 30, 1935; s. Soren K. and Frances (Beck) J.; m. Marilyn Heck, June 28, 1959 (div. Jan. 1987); children: Soren R., Eric, Dana; m. Carmen Patton, Apr. 7, 1990. BA, U. Nebr., 1957, JD, 1961. Bar: Nebr. 1961. Mem. Smith Bros., Lexington, Nebr., 1961-63, Swarr, May, Smith and Andersen, Omaha, 1963-83, Erickson & Sederstrom, P.C., Omaha, 1983—. Chmn. bd. dirs., v.p. bd. dirs. Omaha Public Power Dist., 1979-81; chmn. Nebr. Coordinating Commn. for Postsecondary Edn., 1976-78. Del. Nat. Rep. Conv., 1960, mem. Nebr. Rep. Ctrl. Com., 1968-70; mem. Regents Commn. Urban U., U. Nebr., Omaha, chmn. Task Force on Higher Edn.; mem. Hwy Commn. State of Nebr., 1989-95; vice chmn. Opera Omaha, 1992-95, v.p., 1994-96. Recipient Disting. Service award U. Nebr., 1981 Mem. Omaha Bar Assn. (past exec. com.), Nebr. Bar Assn. (chmn. com. public relations 1973-76), Am. Bar Assn., U. Nebr. Alumni Assn. (pres. 1976-78), Rotary Club, Omaha Club, Beta Theta Pi, Phi Delta Phi. Clubs: Rotary, Omaha, Racquet. Office: 1 Regency Westpointe 10330 Regency Parkway Dr Omaha NE 68114-3774 E-mail: sj@eslaw.com., Jensen@cox.net.

JENSEN, STEVEN RICHARD, radiologist, consultant; b. Green Bay, Wis., Mar. 14, 1951; s. Merton James and Joanne (Rouse) J.; m. Patricia Ann Jensen, June 22, 1974; children: Erica Leona, Brian Patrick, Amanda Joanna, Cassandra Leigh. Student, U. Wis., Eau Claire, 1969-72; MD, U. Wis., Madison, 1976. Diplomate Am. Bd. Radiology. Postgrad. fellow Mass. Gen. Hosp., Boston, 1980-81; instr. radiology Harvard Med. Sch., Boston, 1980-81; asst. clin. prof. U. Calif., San Francisco, 1981-84; ast. prof. U. Wis., Madison, 1984-86; radiologist Suburban Radiology Cons., Mpls., 1986—2001; with Cons. Radiologists, Mpls., 2002—. Radiology cons. Found. for Health Care Evaluation, Mpls., 1990—, Allina Health Sys., Mpls., 1996-2001; bd. dirs. Medlinks, Bloomington, Minn., 1997-2001; med. dir. radiology Mercy and Unity Hosps., Mpls., 1995-2001. Contbr. articles to profl. jours. Sec.-treas. North Oaks Homeowners, 1988-92; chair parish festival St. Odilia Ch., Shoreview, Minn., 1991-94. Served to lt. comdr. USN, 1976-84. Named Radiology Tchr. of Yr., U.S. Navy, 1984, U. Wis., 1986. Mem. Radiol. Soc. N.Am., Am Coll. Radiology, Soc. Cardiovascular Radiology, Minn. State Radiology Soc., North Oaks Golf Club (fin. com. 1993-97), Alpha Omega Alpha. Avocations: golf, bicycling, music, skiing, collecting vintage guitars. Office: Cons Radiologists 825 Nicollet Mall Minneapolis MN 55402- E-mail: jenss001@aol.com.

JENSEN, THEODORE W. language educator; b. Sacramento, Calif., Aug. 31, 1944; s. Joseph Blaine Jensen and Mary Irene James; m. Myrna Louise Simmons, May 20, 1967; children: Blaine Squires, Elizabeth Ann Gordon, Brenda Irene Huck. BA, U. Mont., 1966, MA, 1970; PhD, SUNY, Buffalo, 1976. Part-time lectr. Canisius Coll., Buffalo, 1972—73; part-time instr. Millard Fillmore Coll., Buffalo, 1973—74; prof. Ea. Mont. Coll., Billings, 1974—95; prof. Spanish Mont. State U. at Billings, 1995—. Sec. EMC Hispanic Student Scholarship Fund, 1984—86. Author (novel): Matamor; contbr. articles to profl. jours., chapters to books. Fundraiser and telephone bank Muscular Dystrophy Telethon, Billings, Mont., 1993—99; vol., Strawberry Festival Downtown Bus. Assn., Billings, Mont., 2000—03; vol., Festival of Trees Nat. Coun. for the Prevention of Child Abuse, Billings, Mont., 1993—2002; vol., Thanksgiving Dinners for the Needy Flakesgiving Campaign, KCTR radio, Billings, Mont.,

1996—2002; vol., South Park Mex. Fiestas Nuestra Senora de Guadalupe Ch., Billings, Mont., 1999—2002; vol., Christmas Parade City of Billings, Billings, Mont., 2002; vol. fundraiser and walker Relay for Life Against Cancer, Billings, Mont., 2001; vol., ASMSUB Children's Easter Egg Hunt Billings, Mont., 1997—2002; founding mem. North Rockies Hispanic Edn. Found., 1986—90; caller/fund raiser alumni phonathons Mont. State University-Billings, Billings, Mont., 1993—2002. 1st lt. U.S. Army, 1966—68, Vietnam. Decorated Bronze Star; recipient Chris Rosas award, Billings Latino Club, 1979; grantee, Xerox Corp., 1986, EMC Found., 1985, William Randolph Hearst Found., 1983, 1979, Rsch., Am. Coun. Learned Socs., 1978. Mem.: Mont. Assn. Lang. Tchrs. (assoc.; ex officio mem. exec. bd. 1997—2000, pres. 1978—79), Pacific Northest Coun. Langs. (assoc.), Am. Assn. Tchrs. Spanish and Portuguese (assoc.), Instituto Internacional de Literatura Iberoamericana (assoc.), VFW (assoc.), Am. Legion (assoc.), Alpha Mu Gamma (assoc.), Sigma Delta Pi (assoc.), Sigma Chi (assoc.). Home: 2225 Maple St Billings MT 59102 Office: Mont State U at Billings 1500 North 30th Billings MT 59101 Personal E-mail: fuzzybear3@imt.net.

JENSEN, THOMAS LEE, lawyer; b. Cin., Dec. 29, 1948; s. Carl and Martha Jensen; m. Nannette Curry; children: Natalie, Laura. Student, Cumberland Coll., 1972, No. Ky. U., 1978. Rep. State of Ky., 1985-96, Ky. Ho. of Reps.; minority floor leader, 1991-94; pvt. practice Jensen Cessna & Benge, London, Ky., 1978—. Active Just Say No to Drugs Program; del. Mexico for Am. Coun. Young Polit. Leaders; chmn. Laural County Rep. Com.; legal counsel Mem. Rep. Ho. of Reps., 1988; chmn. Ky. State Rep. Party; bd. dirs. Cumberland River Comprehensive Care. Mem. C. of C. (local bd. dirs.), Masons, Shriners. Republican. Presbyterian. Office: Jensen Cessna & Benge 303 S Main St London KY 40741-1906

JENSEN, WALTER EDWARD, lawyer, educator; b. Chgo., Oct. 20, 1937. AB, U. Colo., 1959; JD, Ind. U., 1962, MBA, 1964; PhD (Univ. fellow), Duke U., 1972. Bar: Ind. 1962, Ill. 1962, D.C. 1963, U.S. Tax Ct. 1982, U.S. Supreme Ct. 1967. Prof. bus. law U. Colo., Boulder, 1958-62; assoc. prof. Colo. State U., 1964-66, U. Conn., Storrs, 1966-67, Ill. State U., 1970-72; prof. bus. adminstrn. Va. Poly. Inst. and State U., beginning 1972, prof. fin., ins. and law, 1972-; with Inst. Advanced Legal Studies, U. London, 1983-84; prof. U.S. Air Force Grad. Mgmt. Program, Europe, 1977-78, 83-85; Duke U. legal rsch. awardee, rschr., Guyana, Trinidad and Tobago, 1967; vis. lectr. pub. internat. law U. Istanbul, 1988, Roberts Coll. U. Bosporous, Istanbul, Uludag U., Turkey, 1988; rschr. U. London Inst. Advanced Legal Studies, London Sch. Econs. and Inst. Commonwealth Studies, 1969, 71-74, 76; Ford Found. Rsch. fellow Ind. U., 1963-64; faculty rsch. fellow in econs. U. Tex., 1968; Bell Telephone fellow in econs. regulated pub. utilities U. Chgo., 1965. Recipient Dissertation Travel award Duke U. Grad. sch., 1968; Ind. U. fellow, 1963, 74, scholar, 1963-64. Mem. D.C. Bar Assn., Ill. Bar Assn., Ind. bar Assn., ABA, Am. Polit. sci. Assn., Am. Soc. Internat. Law, Am. Judicature Soc., Am. Bus. Law Assn., Alpha Kappa Psi, Phi Alpha Delta, Pi Gamma Mu, Pi Kappa Alpha, Beta Gamma Sigma. Contbr. articles to profl. pubs.; staff editor Am. Bus Law Jour., 1973— ; vice chmn. assoc. editor for adminstrv. law sect. young lawyers Barrister (Law Notes), 1975-83; book rev. and manuscript editor Justice System Jour; A Mgmt. Rev., 1975— ; staff editor Bus. Law Rev., 1975— . Home: 3358 Glade Creek Blvd 5 Roanoke VA 24012 Office: Va Poly Inst and State U Blacksburg VA 24060

JENSEN, WILLIAM POWELL, lawyer, educator; b. Newport, R.I., Apr. 4, 1963; s. William Marvin and Jean (Powell) J.; m. Robin R. Jensen. BS in Indsl. Engring., Tex. A&M U., 1985; JD, St. Mary's U., 1989. Bar: Tex. 1989. Equity participating assoc. Matthews and Assoc. LLP, Houston, 1989-96, Browning Bushman, Houston, 1997-99, Shook, Hardy & Bacon, Houston, 1999—. Bd. dirs. Magic Earth, Inc.; spkr. Tex. A&M U., College Station, 1993-97. Author: (with others) Punitive Damages, Modern Dictionary for the Legal Profession, 1993; contbr. articles to profl. jours. Youth counselor Chapelwood Meth. Ch., Houston, 1990-92; pres. Korean Martial Arts Acad., Houston, 1993-94. Mem. State Bar Tex., Am. Intellectual Property Law Assn., Houston Intellectual Property Law Assn. Avocations: martial arts, running. Office: Shook Hardy and Bacon 600 Travis # 1600 Houston TX 77002-2911 E-mail: wjensen@shb.com.

JENSEN-CARTER, PHILIP SCOTT, photographer, photographer; b. N.Y.C., Aug. 9, 1950; s. Jerry and Phoebe (Nortman) Carter; m. Lyndsay Jensen, Jan. 8, 1983. BFA, Md. Inst. Coll. Art, 1972; grad., Scarborough Sch. Studio mgr. George Hausman, Inc., N.Y.C., 1973-76; CEO Jensen-Carter Photographer, Bedford Hills, N.Y., 1976—. Mem. Advt. Club Westchester (Gold award of excellence 1990, 95, 96, 2000, 03, Silver award of excellence 1990, 95, 96, 97, 2003, Bronze award of excellence 1997), Women in Comm. (Clarion award Westchester chpt. 1997, 98, 99, Bronze and Silver awards 1997). Democrat. Avocations: golf, cycling, antiquing, restoration, traveling. Home: 33 Fairmount Rd Goldens Bridge NY 10526-1110 Office: Jensen-Carter Photographer PO Box 479 Bedford Hills NY 10507-0479

JENSEN-RUOPP, HELGA SPITKO, school program administrator, consultant; b. Kosterchan, May 24, 1946; came to US, 1954. d. George and Greta Maria Spitko; m. John Martin Jensen, June 9, 1968 (div. May 1984); children: John-Karl, Caroline, Michael, Heidi; m. James Martin Ruopp, Apr. 9, 1988. BA, Adelphi U., 1968, MA, 1970, We. Conn. State U., 1992; EdD, Columbia U., 1992, 2000. Biology tchr. Danbury (Conn.) High Sch., 1986-98; coord. K-12 sci. Danbury Pub. Schs., 1998—. Tchr. German German Lang. Sch. Danbury; adj. instr. Western Conn. State U., Danbury, 1993—, cons., 1998-2000; instr. Coop. Program for Superior High Sch. Students, 1993; scientist, tchr. drug metabolism Boehringer Ingelheim Pharm., 1989-90; ecologist Key Issues Inst.: Keystone Sci., 1997; mem. Goals 2000 Grant Implementation; presenter in field. Mem. Candlewood Lake Authority, Danbury, 1993. Fellow Conn. Sci. Tchrs. Assn., N.Y. Acad. Scis., Phi Delta Kappa, Kappa Delta Pi; mem. AAUW, Conn. Sci. Suprs. Assn., Assn. Supervision and Curriculum Devel. Lutheran. Avocations: excercising, walking, mountain biking, painting, sculpting. Office: Danbury Bd Edn Beaver Brook Rd Danbury CT 06810

JENSH, RONALD PAUL, anatomist, educator; b. NYC, June 14, 1938; s. Werner G. and Dorothy (Hensle) J.; m. Ruth Eleanor Dobson, Aug. 18, 1962; children: Victoria Lynn, Elizabeth Whitney BA, Bucknell U., 1960, MA, 1962; PhD, Jefferson Med. Coll., 1966. Instr. in anatomy Thomas Jefferson U., Phila., 1966—68, assoc. in radiology, 1966—68, asst. prof. radiology and anatomy, 1968—74, assoc. prof. radiology, 1968—92, assoc. prof. anatomy, 1968—74, prof. anatomy, 1982—94, vice chmn., 1984—94, prof. pathology, anatomy and cell biology, 1994—, assoc. prof. pediatrics, 1992—, chmn. curriculum com., 1987—93, head anatomy div. Coll. Allied Health Scis., 1975—88, co-dir. pre-doctoral tng. program, 1971—79, course coord. histology, 1988—. Staff Op. Concern Inc., Cherry Hill, N.J., 1970-72; cons. reproductive biology Bio-Search Inc., Argus Rsch. Lab. Inc., Ortho Rsch. Found. Contbr. articles to sci. jours. Task force com. on comm. S. Jersey Methodist Conf., 1974-80; chmn. Learning Resources Ctr., Haddonfield United Meth. Ch., NJ, 1976-79. Recipient Christian R. and Mary F. Lindback Found. Disting. Teaching award, 1978, Disting. Alumnus award, 1985, Faculty Achievement award Burlington Northern Found., 1989, Jefferson Med. Coll. Portrait, 1994, Award for Disting. Alumnus in a Chosen Profession, Bucknell U., 1997. Mem. AAAS, Am. Soc. Zoologists, N.Y. Acad. Scis., Teratology Soc. (treas. 1989-92), Behavioral Teratology Soc. (pres. 1985-86), Am. Assn. Anatomists, Soc. Am. Mus. Natural History, Inst. Social Ethics and Life Scis., Jefferson Med. Coll. Alumni Assn. (hon. life), Phi Beta Kappa, Sigma Xi, Psi Chi, Phi Sigma. Home: 230 E Park Ave Haddonfield NJ 08033-1835 Office: 562 Jefferson Alumni Hall 1020 Locust St Philadelphia PA 19107-6799 E-mail: ronald.jensh@jefferson.edu.

JENSON, HAL BROCKBANK, physician; b. Payson, Utah, Oct. 9, 1954; s. G. Rulon and Betty Ruth (Brockbank) J. BS summa cum laude, Brigham Young U., 1975, MS, 1977; MD, George Washington U., 1979. Diplomate Nat. Bd. Med. Examiners, Am. Bd. Pediatrics, 1985, Am. Bd. Pediatric Infectious Diseases, 1994. Resident in pediatrics Case-Western Res. U., Cleve., 1979-82, chief resident, 1982-83; fellow pediat. infectious diseases, epidemiology Yale U., New Haven, 1983-85, instr. pediatrics, epidemiology, 1985-86, asst. prof., 1986-90, asst. prof. cancer ctr., 1988-90; assoc. prof. pediatrics and microbiology U. Tex. Health Sci. Ctr., San Antonio, 1990-96, chief pediatric infectious diseases, 1990—2002, prof. pediatrics, microbiology, 1996—2002; chief infectious diseases Santa Rosa Children's Hosp., San Antonio, 1990—2002; prof. pediatrics and microbiology, chair dept. pediatrics, dir. Ctr. for Pediat. Rsch., Eastern Va. Med. Sch./Children's Hosp. of The King's Daus., Norfolk, 2002—; sr. v.p. for acad. affairs Children's Hosp. of the King's Daus., Norfolk, 2002—. Co-editor: (with R.E. Behrman and R.E. Kliegman) Nelson Textbook of Pediatrics, 2000, 03; co-editor: (with R.S. Baltimore) Pediatric Infectious Diseases, Principles and Practice, 1995, 2001; reviewer Jour. AMA, 1987—, Jour. Pediatrics, 1987—, Clin. Infectious Diseases, 1990—, Pediatrics, 1991—, others; contbr. articles to profl. jours. Recipient Physician Scientist award Nat. Inst. Allergy and Infectious Diseases NIH, 1985, Swebilius Cancer Rsch. Award Yale U. Sch. Medicine, 1986, 87. Fellow Pediatric Infectious Diseases Soc. (Outstanding Young Investigator award 1990), Am. Acad. Pediatrics; mem. Am. Soc. Microbiology, Am. Soc. Virology, Soc. Pediatric Rsch., Children's Oncology Group, Infectious Diseases Soc. Am., Am. Pediatric Soc., Internat. Assn. for Rsch. on Epstein-Bar Virus and Associated Disease, Va. Pediatric Soc. Avocations: recreational sports, scuba diving, camping. Office: Children's Hosp of The King's Daus 601 Children's Ln Norfolk VA 23507 Office Fax: 757-668-9766.

JENSON, JON EBERDT, association executive; b. Madison, Wis., Aug. 1, 1934; s. Theodore Joel and Gertrude Beatrice (Edberdt) J.; m. Jeannette Marie Hasman, May 1, 1976; children: James, Peter. BS, U. Wis., 1956; postgrad., Goethe U., Frankfort, Germany, 1956; diploma, U. Cologne, West Germany, 1957. From staff rep. to dir. mktg. and tech. svcs. Forging Industry Assn., Cleve., 1959-75; exec. v.p., sec. Am. Metal Stamping Assn., Cleve., 1975-80; pres. Precision Metalforming Assn., Independence, Ohio, 1980-2000, pres. emeritus, 2000—; interim dir. Precision Machined Products Assn., Brecksville, Ohio, 2001—02. Exec. dir., sec. Forging Industry Ednl. and Rsch. Found., Cleve., 1967-75; lectr. NYU, 1973-75; Ohio bd. advisors Liberty Mut. Ins. Co. Author: Forging Industry Handbook, 1966; editor: Metal Forming mag, 1975-90, pub. 1990-2000. Bd. regents Insts. Orgn. Mgmt., U.S. C. of C., 1977-83, vice chmn., 1982, chmn., 1983; mem. bd. regents Marycrest Sch., Independence, Ohio, 1979-86; bd. dirs. Cleve. Conv. and Visitors Bur., 1988; chmn. Consuming Industries Trade Action Coalition, 1999—; mem. U.S. adv. trade com. With USNR, 1958-59. Rotary Internat. fellow, 1956 Mem. Am. Soc. Assn. Execs. (cert. assn. exec.), Cleve. Soc. Assn. Execs., Rockwell Springs Trout Club, Capitol Hill Club. Home: 5700 Brookside Rd Cleveland OH 44131-6013 E-mail: jjenson@pma.org.

JENSON, PAULINE ALVINO, retired speech and hearing educator; b. Orange, N.J. m. Bernard A. Jenson; 1 child, Mark J. BS, Trenton State Coll., 1948; MA, Columbia U., 1950, PhD, 1969. Tchr. English and history Bordentown (N.J.) H.S., 1948-49; tchr. Lexington Sch. for Deaf, N.Y.C., 1950-51, with rsch. dept., 1969-70; tchr. N.J. Sch. for Deaf, West Trenton, 1951-56, 58-61, St. Mary's Sch. for Deaf, Buffalo, 1956-58; speech pathologist Hunterdon Med. Ctr., Flemington, N.J., 1959-60, dir. speech and hearing, 1960-62; asst. prof. Trenton (N.J.) State Coll., 1962-65; instr., lectr. Teacher's Coll., Columbia U., N.Y.C., 1966-69; prof. dept. speech pathology and audiology Trenton (N.J.) State Coll., 1970-95; Yrbk Dedica, 1978; prof. dept. lang. and comm. sci. Coll. N.J. (formerly Trenton State Coll.), 1995-98, chmn. dept., 1991-94, prof. emerita, 1998. Cons. Universal Films & Visual Arts, N.Y.C., 1968-70, State Agys. and Schs. for Handicapped, N.J., N.Y., 1976-98; evaluator Coun. on Edn. of Deaf, Washington, 1979-83. Author: (with others) Speech for the Deaf Child, 1971; inventor cueing system for deaf speakers, 1976; editor: (info. booklets) Topics, Princeton, N.J., 1980-86 Help line vol. N.J. Assn. for Children with Hearing Impairments, Princeton, 1973-95; co-author, cons. Senate Bills on Deafness, Trenton, 1979-98; commr. Legislative Commn. to Study Svcs. for Hearing Impaired Children, Trenton, 1988-90. Post Master's scholar U.S. Office Edn., Tchrs. Coll., Columbia U., 1965-66; grantee N.J. Dept. Edn., 1973, N.J. Dept. Human Svcs., 1992-96. Mem. N.J. Assn. for Children with Hearing Impairment (founder, exec. dir. 1973-95, Pauline Jenson award at The Coll. of N.J. named in her honor, 1996), N.J. Speech, Lang. and Hearing Assn. (life, Disting. Svc. award 1985, disting. clin. svc. award 1998), Am. Speech, Lang. and Hearing Assn. (cert., life). Avocation: bibliophily. Office: PO Box 1336 Princeton NJ 08542-1336

JENSON, RONALD ALLEN, religious executive, educator; b. Bremerton, Wash., Apr. 15, 1948; s. Robert C. and Maxine (Mitchell) J.; m. Mary Kunz, Dec. 27, 1969; children: Matthew Robert, Mary Rachael. BA in Speech Comms. cum laude, Lewis and Clark Coll., 1969; MDiv summa cum laude, We. Conservative Bapt. Sem., 1972, DMin, 1974. Ordained to ministry Ch. of The Saviour, 1976. Pastor Ch. of the Saviour, Wayne, Pa., 1973—79; pres. Ch. Dynamics, San Bernardino, Calif., 1978—79, Internat. Sch. Theology, San Bernardino, 1978—86; vice chancellor Internat. Christian Grad. U., San Bernardino, 1983—86; founder, chmn. High Ground, 1987—. Chmn. Future Achievement Internat., 1997—. Author: (book) How to Succeed the Biblical Way, 1981, Dynamics of Church Growth, 1981, Together We Can, 1982, Always Advancing, Always Planning, 1984, Kingdoms at War, 1996, The Bible in Business, 1990, Make a Life Not Just a Living, 1996, Life Maximizers, 1997, Fathers and Sons, 1998, Taking the Lead, 1998, Achieving Authentic Success, 2000. Mem. nat. exec. com. Reagan's Yr. of the Bible; mem. bd. govs. Coun. Nat. Policy. Named to Outstanding Young Men in Am., 1976. Mem. Am. Assn. Higher Edn. Home and Office: 12989 Abra Dr San Diego CA 92128-2326

JENSON, WILLIAM G. federal agency administrator; b. Hartford, Conn. BA in History, Hobart Coll., 1970; JD, Suffolk U., 1975. Bar: Mass. 1975. Atty. Office Gen. Counsel USDA, Washington, 1976-96, jud. officer, 1996—. Instr. USDA, 1980—, mem. grad. sch.'s paralegal com., 1987. Mil. intelligence specialist1970 U.S. Army, 1970—72, Vietnam. Mem.: ABA (vice chairperson adminstrv. law and regulatory practice-agr. sect. 1996—), Mass. Bar Assn. Office: Dept Agr Office Jud Officer S Bldg Rm 1449 Washington DC 20250-0001 E-mail: william.jenson@usda.gov.

JENSSEN, WARREN DONALD, microbiologist, consultant; b. Woodbridge, N.J., Aug. 23, 1942; s. Joseph and Lillian (Anderson) J.; m. Donna M. Larson; children: Kirsten E., Erik C. BA, Rutgers U., 1965, PhD, 1970; MS, Purdue U., 1966. Diplomate Am. Acad. Microbiology, Am. Bd. Bioanalysis. Tchg. fellow Purdue U., W. Lafayette, Ind., 1965-66; rsch. fellow Rutgers U., New Brunswick, N.J., 1966-70; postdoctoral fellow Rutgers Med. Sch., New Brunswick, N.J., 1983-84; rsch. fellow Robert Wood Johnson Med. Sch., 1984-87; adj. prof. Union County Coll., Cranford, N.J., 1969-70, asst. prof., 1970-74, assoc. prof., 1974-79, prof., 1979-85, sr. prof., 1985—; adj. prof. Kean Coll., Union, N.J., 1972-75. Clin. microbiology cons. JFK Med. Ctr., Edison, N.J., 1973-76, Raritan Bay Med. Ctr., Perth Amboy, N.J., 1976-98, VA Med. Ctr., Lyons, N.J., 1989-96; dir. health svcs. lab. Union County Coll., 1974-82; dir. Union County Pub. Health Lab., 1977-82; pub. health bacteriologist N.J. Dept. Environ. Protection, 1973—; assoc. med. staff Raritan Bay Med. Ctr., 1985—; clin. lab. dir. N.J. Bd. Med. Examiners, 1985—; adj. clin. instr. Robert Wood Johnson Med. Sch., 1985-91; adj. prof. biomed. careers program Univ. Medicine and Dentistry of N.J., 1999—2002; recycling coord., Califon, 1988-92, Hunterdon County Health Adv. Com., 1985-88, Hunterdon County Mcpl. Officers Assn., 1987-89. Contbr. articles to profl. jours. Den leader, asst. scoutmaster Boy Scouts Am., Califon, N.J., 1980-84; vice chmn. bd. Health, Califon, 1983-89; mem. Environ. Comm., Califon, 1985-89. Mem. Theobald Smith Soc., Am. Soc. Microbiology, N.J. Link for Microbiology (program chair 1983-85), AAUP (exec. bd. 1973-98). Achievements include antibiotic action on membrane-associated polyribosomes of Streptococcus faecalis, photoinduction of sporulation in Trichoderma viride, computerized compilation of antimicrobial susceptibility data, fatal septicemia due to CDC-DF2 in a splenectomized patient, a novel insertion of a resistance transposon in methicillin-resistant Staphylococcus aureus, prevalence of MLS resistance and erm gene classes among clinical strains of staphylococci and streptococci, molecular epidemiology of MLS resistance in staphylococcus aureus and coagulase-negative staphylococci. Home: 83 River Rd Califon NJ 07830-4371 Office: Union County Coll 1033 Springfield Ave Cranford NJ 07016-1528 E-mail: jenssen@ucc.edu.

JENTZ, GAYLORD ADAIR, law educator; b. Beloit, Wis., Aug. 7, 1931; s. Merlyn Adair and Delva (Mullen) Jentz; m. JoAnn Mary Hornung, Aug. 6, 1955; children: Katherine Ann, Gary Adair, Loretta Ann, Rory Adair. BA, U. Wis., 1953, JD, 1957, MBA, 1958. Bar: Wis. 1957. Pvt. practice law, Madison, 1957-58; from asst. prof. to assoc. prof. bus. law U. Okla., 1958-65; assoc. prof. U. Tex., Austin, 1965-68, prof., 1968-98, Herbert D. Kelleher prof. bus. law, 1982-98, prof. emeritus, 1998—, chmn. gen. bus. dept., 1968-74, 80-86. From vis. instr. to vis. prof. U. Wis. Law Sch., Wis., 1957—65. Author (with others): Texas Uniform Commercial Code, 1967; author: rev. edit., 1975; author: (with others) Business Law Text and Cases, 1968, Business Law Text, 1978, Legal Environment of Business, 1989, Texas Family Law, 7th edit., 1992, Business Law Today-Alternate Essentials Edition, 4th edit., 1997, Fundamentals of Business Law, 5th edit., 2002, West's Business Law: Text and Cases, 9th edit., 2004, West's Business Law: Alternate Edition, 9th edit., 2004, Law for E-Commerce, 2002, West's Business Law-Case Study Approach, 2003, Business Law Today-Interactive Text, 6th edit., 2003; dep. editor: Social Sci. Quar., 1966—82, mem. editl. bd.:, 1982—94, editor-in-chief: Am. Bus. Law Jour., 1969—74, adv. editor:, 1974—. With U.S. Army, 1953—55. Named to CBA Hall of Fame, 1999; recipient Outstanding Tchr. award, U. Tex. Coll. Bus., 1967, Jack G. Taylor Tchg. Excellence award, 1971, 1989, Joe D. Beasley Grad. Tchg. Excellence award, 1978, CBA Found. Adv. Coun. award, 1979, Grad. Bus. Coun. Outstanding Grad. Bus. Prof. award, 1980, James C. Scorboro Meml. award for outstanding leadership in banking edn., Colo. Grad. Sch. Banking, 1983, Utmost Outstanding Prof. award, 1989, CBA award for excellence in edn., 1994, Banking Leadership award, Western States Sch. Banking, 1995, Civitatis award, U. Tex., 1997. Mem.: So. Bus. Law Assn. (pres. 1967), Wis. Bar Assn., Tex. Assn. Coll. Tchrs. (pres. Austin chpt. 1967—68, mem. exec. com. 1979—80, state pres. 1971—72), Acad. Legal Studies Bus. (pres. 1971—72, mem. exec. com. 1989—94), Am. Arbitration Assn. (nat. panel 1966—96), Southwestern Fedn. Adminstrv. Disciples (v.p. 1979—80, pres. 1980—81), Phi Kappa Phi (pres. 1983—84), Omicron Delta Kappa. Home: 4106 N Hills Dr Austin TX 78731-2826 Office: U Tex MSIS Dept McCombs Sch Bus CBA 5 202 1 University S Austin TX 78712

JEON, BANG NAM, economist, researcher; b. Masan, Korea, Sept. 20, 1954; came to U.S., 1981; s. Soong Il and Kap Sun (Park) H.; m. Kyong Ae Shin, Aug. 8, 1981; children: Tae Whan (Ted), Mee Jung (Mimi), Mee Young (Michelle). BA, Seoul (Korea) Nat. U., 1977; MA, Ind. U., 1983, PhD, 1987. Economist Korea Exch. Bank, Seoul, 1977-81; cons. Hudson Inst., Indpls., 1986; asst. prof. econs. Rose-Hulman Inst. Tech., Terre Haute, Ind., 1987-88; from assoc. prof. to prof. econs. Drexel U., Phila., 1988—. Vis. rsch. fellow Ind. U., Bloomington, 1988; vis. prof. Soongsil U., Seoul, 2000, 02. Author: Factoring Financing, 1981. Dai-Han Ins. Group fellow, 1974-77; recipient Henry M. Oliver Meml. award Ind. U., 1987, Univ. Rsch. Scholar award Drexel U., 1992. Mem. Am. Econ. Assn., Am. Fin. Assn., Western Econ. Assn., Midwest Econ. Assn., Acad. Internat. Bus. Presbyterian. Avocation: tennis. Home: 135 Sheldrake Dr Paoli PA 19301-1242 Office: Drexel U 32D And Market St Philadelphia PA 19104 E-mail: jeonbana@drexel.edu.

JEPPESEN, ALAN KARL, lawyer; b. Nampa, Idaho, Dec. 19, 1941; s. Karl and Kleo B. Jeppesen; m. Jeanne Nelson Jeppesen, Aug. 20, 1965; children: Rebeca Rae Jeppesen Christensen, Amelia Anne Casaras, Kevin Karl, Erik Alan, Kristen Kaye. BA in English, U. Idaho, 1967; JD in Law, U. Utah, 1970. Bar: Utah 1970, U.S. Dist. Ct. Utah 1970. Assoc. Clyde & Pratt, Salt Lake City, 1970-75; atty. Tooele (Utah) City Corp., 1975-80; pvt. practice law Tooele, 1980-92; prosecutor Tooele County Atty., 1992—2001; atty., advisor Office of Hearhings and Appeals, Social Security Adminstrn., Salt Lake City, 2001—. Avocations: stained glass, photography. Home: 468 S 300 W Tooele UT 84074-2944 Office: Social Security Adminstrn Office Hearings and Appeals 57 W 2d S Salt Lake City UT 84101

JEPSEN, PETER LEE, court reporter; b. Virginia, Minn., Dec. 23, 1952; s. Peter Frederick and Delores Audrey (Sorenson) J.; m. Valerie Lynn Tow, Mar. 20, 1976; children: Sarah Jo, Jennifer Lynn, Elizabeth Ann. Student, St. Cloud State U., 1971, Mankato State U., 1972, Southwestern AVTI, Jackson, Minn., 1978. Registered profl. reporter; chartered shorthand reporter. Freelance ct. reporter Carney & Assocs., Rochester, Minn., 1978-79; ofcl. ct. reporter State of S.D., Sioux Falls, 1979-80; part owner, reporter Carney & Assocs., Rochester, 1980-83; realtime captioner Can. Captioning Devel. Agy., Toronto, Ont., 1984-85, mgr. live captioning services, 1985-87; captioning trainer and cons. XScribe Corp., San Diego, 1987-88, mgr. captioning products and services, 1988-91; dir. U.S. Senate Office of Captioning Svcs., Washington, 1991-92; v.p. U.S. Captioning, Inc., San Diego, 1992-93; dir. U.S. Senate Office Captioning Svcs., Washington, 1994—. Lutheran. Avocations: reading, music, writing. Office: St 54 The Capitol Washington DC 20510-0001

JEPSEN, THOMAS CHARLES, information technology professional, technology historian; b. Rockford, Ill., June 1, 1948; s. William White and Ruth M. Jepsen; m. Marsha Ann Hamman, June 7, 1969; 1 child, Hans. BA, U. Colo., 1986. Mem. tech. staff Fujitsu Network Comm., Raleigh, 1996-2000, strategic mktg. mgr., 2000-01; instr. NC State U., 2002. Scholar in residence Pa. Hist. and Mus. Commn., 2003. Author: My Sisters Telegraphic: Women in the Telegraph Office, 1846-1950, 2000, Distributed Storage Networks: Architecture, Protocols, and Management, 2003; programming langs. editor IT Professional Mag., Los Alamitos, Calif., 1999—; editor: Java in Telecommunications, 2001. Mem. IEEE, Assn. Computing Machinery, Soc. for Historians of the Gilded Age and Progressive Era, Nat. Coalition Ind. Scholars. Achievements include invention of method and apparatus for generating permanent connections using graphical user interface. Home: 515 Morgan Creek Rd Chapel Hill NC 27517-4931 E-mail: tjepsen@mindspring.com.

JEPSON, HANS GODFREY, investment company executive, director; b. Spencer, W.Va., July 24, 1936; s. Hans G. and Juanita Imogene (Shears) J.; m. Barbara Gayle Keller, Dec. 3, 1966. AB magna cum laude, Princeton U., 1958. Exec. editor Arnold Bernhard & Co., NYC, 1961—68; v.p., rsch. dir. Dominick & Dominick, Inc., NYC, 1968—70; dir., sr. v.p., rsch. dir. Alliance Capital Mgmt. Corp., NYC, 1970—76; exec. v.p., chief investment officer U.S. Trust Co. NY, NYC, 1976—80; pres. Valquest Assocs., Inc., NYC, 1980—, Lafayette Enterprises, Inc., NYC, 1983—, The Stanton Corp., Del., 1994—. Bd. dirs. J. Aron Charitable Found.; adv. coun. to pres. Am. Bible Soc. 2d lt. U.S. Army, 1958—59, capt. USAR, 1959—66. Mem. Assn. for Investment Mgmt. and Rsch., N.Y. Soc. Security Analysts, Dial, Elm and Cannon Club (Princeton, N.J.), Princeton Club (N.Y.C.), Econ. Club (N.Y.C.), La Boule New Yorkaise (N.Y.C.), Fedn. Petanque USA, Inc. Home: 11 5th Ave New York NY 10003-4342 Office: Lafayette Enterprises Inc 126 E 56th St Fl 23 New York NY 10022-3639

JEPSON, ROBERT SCOTT, JR., international investment banking specialist; b. Richmond, Va., July 20, 1942; m. Alice Finch Andrews, Dec. 28, 1964; children: Robert Scott, John Steven. BS, U. Richmond, 1964, M of Commerce, 1975; JD (hon.), Gonzaga U., 1986; DCS (hon.), U. Richmond, 1987; DH (hon.), Hamline U., 1988; LLD (hon.), Tusculum Coll., 1989, Ashland U., 1990, Elmhurst Coll., 1991; DSC in Bus. Adminstrn., Franklin U., 1996. With Va. Commonwealth Bankshares, Richmond, 1966-68; v.p. corp. fin. Birr Wilson & Co., Inc., San Francisco, 1968-69; pres. Calif. Capital Mgmt. Corp., Irvine, 1970-73; v.p., dir. corp. fin. Cantor Fitzgerald & Co., Beverly Hills, Calif., 1973-75; dir. corp. planning and devel. Campbell Industries, San Diego, 1975-77; v.p., mgr. merger and acquisition divsn. Continental Ill. Bank, Chgo., 1977-82; sr. v.p., group head U.S. Capital Markets Group, 1st Nat. Bank Chgo., 1982-83; chmn., CEO The Jepson Corp., Chgo., 1983-89, Jepson Assoc. Inc., Savannah, Ga., 1989—. Chmn. Jepson Vineyards Ltd., Ukiah, Calif., 1985—, Coburn Optical Industries Inc., Tulsa, 1992-98; chmn., CEO Kuhlman Corp., Savannah, Ga., 1993-99; bd. advisors Jepson Found., Chgo., 1988—; bd. dirs. Circuit City Stores, Inc., Richmond, Va., AGL Resources, Inc., Atlanta, Dominion Resources, Inc., Richmond, Va.; asst. prof. fin. Nat. U., 1976; lectr. U. Richmond, U. Chgo., Northwestern U., Kansas U., Luther Coll., Wake Forest U. Bd. trustees Gonzaga U., Spokane, Wash., 1982—86, Hamline U., St. Paul, 1987—92; bd. trustees, vice rector U. Richmond, 1992—95; mem. bd. advisors Franklin U., Columbus, 1996—; bd. dirs. Ga. Cancer Coalition, 2002—; bd. visitors Savannah Coll. of Art and Design, 2001—. 1st lt. U.S. Army, 1964—66. Recipient Citation Honor Founders medal Elmhurst Coll., Ill., 1994, Volunteerism and Philanthropy award Coun. Ind. Colls., 1997. Mem. Commonwealth Club (Richmond), Savannah Yacht Club, Oglethorpe Club (Savannah), Chatham Club (Savannah), Plantation Club (Savannah), Omicron Delta Kappa, Alpha Kappa Psi, Beta Gamma Sigma (Entrepreneur of Yr. medallion 1996), Phi Gamma Delta. Republican.

JERDEE, THOMAS HARLAN, business administration educator, organization psychology researcher and consultant; b. Mpls., Aug. 30, 1927; s. Thomas Elias and Agnes (Christensen) J.; m. Marian Alice Raether, July 26, 1953; children— William Hans, Robert Gustaf BA, Gustavus Adolphus Coll., 1950; MA, U. Minn., 1956, PhD, 1960. Asst. prof. bus. adminstrn. U. N.C., Chapel

Hill, 1959-63, assoc. prof., 1963-68, prof., 1968—. Prof. emritus U. N.C., Chapel Hill, 1991—. Co-author: Older Employees, 1985, Becoming Aware, 1976. With USN, 1952-54. Avocations: hiking, bicycling, canoeing, skiing. Home: 206 Spring Ln Chapel Hill NC 27514-3540 E-mail: ujerdr@mindspring.com.

JEREN, JOHN ANTHONY, JR., lawyer; b. Youngstown, Ohio, Feb. 23, 1946; s. John and Irene E. (Struharik) J.; m. Marjorie C. Barbarie, July 11, 1973; children: Lisa Ann, Christine Alicia, Suzanne Beth, John A. III. BS in Bus., Ohio State U., 1968; JD, Ohio No. U., 1973. Bar: Ohio 1973, U.S. Dist. Ct. (no. dist.) Ohio 1974. Ptnr. Wellman & Jeren Co., L.P.A., Youngstown, Ohio, 1977—91, Tablack, Wellman, Jeren, Hackett & Skoufatos Co., L.P.A., 1991—. Recipient Willis Soc. award Ohio No. U., 1974. Mem.: Ohio State Bar Assn. (chmn. workers compensation sect. 1994—95). Home: 8199 Burgess Lake Dr Youngstown OH 44514-2745 Office: Tablack Wellman Jeren Hackett & Skoufatos Co LPA 67 Westchester Dr Youngstown OH 44515-3902

JERESATY, ROBERT MICHEL, cardiologist, educator; b. Zahlé, Lebanon, Apr. 30, 1929; came to U.S., 1954; s. Michel S. and Annette M. (Braidi) J.; m. Catherine A. Namnoum, Nov. 7, 1959; children: Denise, Michael, Joseph, Nadine, Joanne., Oriental Coll., Zahlé, 1945-47; Baccalaureate, St. Joseph U., Beirut, 1949, MD, 1954. Diplomate Am. Bd. Internal Medicine, subsplty. Bd. Cardiovascular Diseases. Intern Springfield (Mass.) Hosp., 1954-55; resident in medicine Boston City Hosp., 1955-56; fellow in cardiology Columbia Presbyn. Med. Ctr., N.Y.C., 1956-57, 1957-58; resident in medicine St. Francis Hosp., Hartford, Conn., 1958-59; chief sect. cardiology St. Francis Hosp. and Med. Ctr., Hartford, 1959-94; from asst. prof. to assoc. prof. medicine U. Conn. Sch. Medicine, 1970-80, prof. medicine, 1980; sr. attending physician dept. medicine St. Francis Hosp. and Med. Ctr., Hartford, 1980, emeritus staff, cardiology chief, 2000—. Clin. instr. medicine Columbia U. Coll. Physicians and Surgeons, 1956-57, Harvard Med. Sch., 1957-58; from asst. vis. physician to assoc. vis. physician dept. medicine St. Francis Hosp. and Med. Ctr., Hartford, 1963-67, mem. exec. com. dept. medicine, 1980-83, mem. med. staff coun., 1982-85, chmn. rsch. com., 1967-83; med. dir. Hoffman Heart Inst. Conn., 1991-99; mem. exec. com. Combined Hosps. Fund, Hartford, Conn., 1982-84; rep. St. Francis Hosp. and Med. Ctr./Profl. Staff Coun. Capital Area Health Consortium. 1987-97; mem. adv. com. Donaghue Med. Rsch. Found., 1991-96; corporator St. Francis Hosp. and Med. Ctr., 1992; dir. Maximillian E. and Marion O. Hoffman Found., West Hartford. Fellow ACP, Am. Coll. Chest Physicians, Am. Coll. Cardiology (gov. for Conn. 1978-81, bd. extended learning 1983-84), Soc. for Cardiac Angiography and Interventions (charter), Coun. on Geriatric Cardiology; mem. Am. Heart Assn. (fellow coun. clin. cardiology 1969-99), Heart Assn. Greater Hartford (chmn. rsch. com. 1970-73), Conn. Heart Assn. (rsch. com. 1968-74), Hartford County Med Assn., Hartford Med. Soc. (chmn. program com. 1971-72). Home: 36 Lakeview Dr West Hartford CT 06117-1018 Office: St Francis Hosp & Med Ctr 114 Woodland St Hartford CT 06105-1208

JEREZ-FARRAN, CARLOS, language educator; b. Barcelona, Feb. 14, 1950; arrived in U.S., 1980; s. Baltasar Jerez-Soler and Josefa Farran-Mir. BA, Sheffield (Eng.) U., 1980; PhD, U. Mass., 1986. Asst. prof. U. Notre Dame, Ind., 1986—92, assoc. prof. Spanish, 1992—. Contbr. articles to profl. jours. Fellow, NEH, 1992. Mem.: MLA, Nanovic Inst. European Studies, Am. Assn. Tchrs. Spanish and Portuguese. Office: Dept Romance Languages Univ Notre Dame Notre Dame IN 46556 Home: 54213 Terrace Ln South Bend IN 46635

JERGENS, MARIBETH JOIE, school counselor; b. Cleve., May 3, 1945; d. Raymond Wenceslaus and Elsie Koryta J.; children: Annemarie Gurchik, Keith Robert Gurchik. Student, St. Joseph Acad., Cleve., 1959—63, U. Vienna, Austria, 1965; BS in Elem. Edn., Coll. Mt. St. Joseph on-the-Ohio, 1967; MEd in Ednl. Counseling, Cleve. State U., 1984; cert. in Ednl. Adminstrn., Akron U., 1988; postgrad. in edn. and clin. psychology, Kent State U., 1989—. Cert. elem., spl. edn. and adult edn. tchr., counselor. Coord. info. svcs. Halle Brothers, Cleve., 1961—67; tchr. North Olmstead (Ohio) City Schs., 1967-75; tchr. adult basic edn. Polaris Vocat. Sch., Berea, Ohio, 1977-78; tchr. adult edn., ESL Lakewood (Ohio) City Schs., 1978-79; tchr. 2d grade St. Rose Sch., Lakewood, 1979-80; tchr. learning disabled students, tutor Cleve. Pub. Schs. Watterson-Lake Elem. Sch., 1980-85; tutor handicapped Cleve. Christian Home, 1982-84; elem. sch. counselor, tchr. learning disabilites Cleve. Pub. Schs., A.B. Hart Mid. Sch., 1995-97; tchr. human devel. and learning Kent (Ohio) State U., 1997-98; sch. psychologist asst. PSI Assocs., Inc., 1998-99; tchr. Wade Park Sch. Cleve. Mcpl. Sch. Dist., 1999-2000; pvt. practice Rocky River Psychol. Svcs., Ohio, 1999—2003; intervention specialist Dike Montessori Magnet Sch., 2000-01. Counselor West Side Cmty. Mental Health Ctr., Cleve., 1983-84; sales mgr. Field Enterprises Inc., Cleve., 1975-77; fund raising spkr., vol. Cerebral Palsy Camp Rosemary Home for Children United Torch, Cleve., 1961-65; coordinated vol. svcs. area colls. Allen Halfway Ho., Cin., 1965-67; rschr. interventions children with guns and violence in Am. schs., 1998-99; elem. counselor Cleve. Pub. Schs. Adams-Rhodes Cluster, 1985-94; spkr. in field. Contbr. articles to newspapers. Vol. Fairview Gen. Hosp., Cleve., 1959-63, Cerebral Palsy Camp, 1959-63, Allen Halfway House for Children, Cin., 1963-67; co-founder Westshore Separated, Div. and Remarried Caths., Cleve., 1975-85; chair North Olmsted Jr. Women's Club; parish coun. St. Brendan Ch., North Olmstead, 1975-87, founder cath. separated and div. ministry, 1976-85, counselor; mem. com. Cleve. Symphony, Cleve. Art Mus.; summer civil rights activist to implement Fed. Ct. Order Desegregation, Ctrl. H.S., Little Rock, 1957, New Orleans, 1958, Mobile, Ala., 1959; active Am. Aeobics and Fitness Assn., Audobon Soc., Cleve. Natural History Mus., Cleve. Mus. Art, Dem. Party, Edgewater Yacht Club (NCSS), English-Speaking Union, Holden Arboretum, St. Malachi Cath. Ch., Cath. Ch. Spl. Commn. on Priests Sexual Abuse, 2002-03; mem. rev. bd. Cleve. Cath. Diocese, 2003--. Recipient Speaker's United Torch award United Way, Cleve., 1st Pl. prize in clothing design Stretch & Sew, 1975, 1st Pl. prize in needlepoint Framemakers Art, 1983, 1st Pl. in three interstate art contests, musical recording, singing with the Cleve. Symphony Orch., NCSS regatta. Mem. Am. Assn. Counseling and Devel., AAUW, Am. Assn. Marriage and Family Therapists, Am. Psychol. Assn., Assn. for Curriculum and Supervision, Am. Sch. Counselor Assn., N.E. Ohio Counselors Assn., Ohio Counselors Assn., Ohio Assn. Counseling and Devel., Coun. for Exceptional Children, Am. Sch. Counselor Assn., ASCD, Gestalt Inst., Audubon Soc., Cleve. Psychol. Assn., Cleve. Mus. Art, Cleve. Natural History Mus., Cleve. Tchrs. Union, Gestalt Inst., Am. Aerobics and Fitness Assn., Edgewater Yacht Club, English Speaking Union, Holden Arboretum, Pi Lambda Theta. Democrat. Avocations: aerobics, art, cycling, dancing, gardening. Home: 727 Tollis Pkwy Broadview Heights OH 44147

JERGER, EDWARD WILLIAM, mechanical engineer, university dean; b. Milw., Mar. 13, 1922; s. Nickolaus and Ann (Huber) J.; m. Dorothy Marie Post, Aug. 2, 1944 (dec. 1981); children: Betty Ann Murphy, Barbara Lee Smyth; m. Elizabeth Cordiner Sweitzer, Mar. 27, 1982. BS in Mech. Engring, Marquette U., 1946; MS, U. Wis., 1948; PhD, Iowa State U., 1951. Registered profl. engr., Iowa, Ind. Process engr. Wis. Malting Co., Manitowoc, 1946-47; asst. prof. mech. engring. Iowa State U., 1948-55; assoc. prof. mech. engring. U. Notre Dame, 1955-61, prof., head mech. engring., 1961-68, assoc. dean, 1968-82, prof. mech. engring., 1982-97, prof. emeritus, 1989—. Cons. U. Madre De Maestra Santiago, Dominican Republic, 1965-71 Bd. dirs. Beaufort County Schoolbook Found. Served with USAAF, 1943-46. Mem. ASME, Am. Soc. Engring. Edn., Nat. Soc. Profl. Engrs., Internat. Assn. Housing Sci. (dir.), Nat. Fire Protection Assn., Internat. Assn. Arson Investigators, Sigma Xi, Phi Kappa Phi, Pi Tau Sigma (nat. v.p. 1969-74, pres. 1974-78), Tau Beta Pi. Home: 4 Coburn Ct Okatie SC 29909-4560 Office: Univ Notre Dame Coll Engring Notre Dame IN 46556-5637 E-mail: profjerger@aol.com.

JERINS, EDGAR, artist, painter; b. Lincoln, Nebr., June 12, 1958; s. Gunars and Rita (Cepure) J. Grad., Pa. Acad. Fine Arts, 1980. One-man shows include Latvian Fgn. Art Mus., Riga, Latvia, 1992, Artists Coop. Gallery, Omaha, Nebr., 1996, Nat. Mus. Cath. Art and History, N.Y.C., 1997, Ark. Art Ctr., Little Rock, 2001, Tatistcheff Gallery, NYC, 2002, Frye Art Mus., Seattle, 2002, Mus. of Nebr. Art, 2003; represented by Tatistcheff Gallery, N.Y.C. Elizabeth Greenshields Found. grantee, 1980; recipient Scholastic Art Awards scholarship, 1976, Bergan prize Pa. Acad. Fine Arts, 1978, L.A. Bicentennial Student Competition award, 1981, Caroline Gibbons Granger Meml. award Pa. Acad. Fine Arts, 1987. Mem. Copley Soc. (Nathaniel Burwash Artist award 1997). Republican. Lutheran. Avocations: theatre, ballet. Home: 326 E 84th St Apt 4C New York NY 10028-4486

JERMIASON, JOHN LYNN, elementary school educator, farmer, rancher; b. Rochester, Minn, Jan. 9, 1958; s. Orlyn and Evelyn S. Jermiason; m. Ann M. Gebhardt, June 30, 1990. BA in Music, Psychology, St. Olaf Coll., 1981; AS in Agr., N.D. State U., 1982; BS in Edn., Minot State U., 1990. Sales rep. Century 21 Real Estate, Minot, ND, 1989; ind. farmer, rancher Minot, 1982—. Substitute elem. tchr. Minot Pub. Sch., 1993—. Prin. violist Minot Symphony Orch., 1983—, bd. dir., 1996—; mem. ch. coun. Augustana Luth. Ch., Minot, 1989-91; mem. No. Lights String Quartet. Mem.: Elks, Kappa Delta Pi, Phi Mu Alpha. Avocation: church choir. Home and Office: PO Box 452 Minot ND 58702-0452

JERMINI, ELLEN, educational administrator, philosopher; b. Krefeld, Germany, Aug. 25, 1939; came to U.S., 1986. d. Maximilian and Mathilde (Wachtberger) Wilms; m. Helios Jermini, 1961 (div. June 1989); children: Mariella Arnoldi, Diego Jermini. PhB, U. Healing, 1984, M in Healing Sci., 1985, PhD, 1986; PhB, U. Philosophy, 1992. Sec., Germany, Switzerland, 1962; pub. translator, 1984—; seminar organizer, 1983—; dir. U. Philosophy/European Found., 1986—; pres., also chmn. bd. dirs. U. Healing, Campo, Calif., 1986-99, 99—; pres. U. Philosophy, Campo, 1986—; abbot Absolute Monastery, Campo, 1986-99; chmn. bd. Regent. Editor: (newsletter in Italian) Absolute, (newsletter in German) Absolute. Spkr. various univs. and orgns. in Calif. and N.Y., 1989-99, St. Petersburg, Moscow, 1991, Africa, 1994, Egypt, 1995, various seminars and workshops, Ghana, Nigeria, Can., Bahamas, Europe, New Zealand, Australia, The Philippines, China. Mem. Toastmasters Internat. (Able Toastmaster, chmn. bd., mktg. dir.). Avocations: writing, skiing, swimming, playing tennis, flying. Home and Office: U Healing 1101 Far Valley Rd Campo CA 91906-3213

JERNIGAN, DONALD, hospital administrator; Exec. v.p. Adventist Health Sys./Sunbelt Health Care Corp., Orlando; v.p., chief exec. multistate hosp. divsn. Adventist; CEO, pres. Fla. Hosp. Ctr., 1999—. Office: 111 N Orlando Ave Winter Park FL 32789

JERNIGAN, HOWARD MAXWELL, JR., biochemistry educator, researcher; b. Winston-Salem, N.C., Apr. 13, 1943; s. Howard Maxwell and Ruth Roland (Ray) J.; m. Diane Moore, Mar. 1, 1968; 1 child, Paula Marie Jernigan Gordon. BS in Chemistry, W.Va. U., 1965; PhD in Biochemistry, U. N.C., 1970. From asst. prof. dept. biochemistry to prof. U. Tenn., Memphis, 1973—90, prof., 1990—, acting chair dept. molecular sci., 2002. Contbr. articles to sci. jours., including Exptl. Eye Rsch., Archives Biochemistry and Biophysics, Biochim. Biophys. Acta. Rsch. grantee NIH, 1979—. Mem. AAAS, Am. Soc. for Biochemistry and Molecular Biology, Assn. for Rsch. in Vision and Ophthalmology, Am. Chem. Soc., Internat. Soc. for Eye Rsch., Sigma Xi. Methodist. Avocation: breeding tropical fish. Office: U Tenn Dept Ophthalmology 956 Court Ave Ste B229 Memphis TN 38163-0001

JERNIGAN, JOHN LEE, lawyer; b. Atlanta, May 29, 1942; s. Alton Lee and Marian (Heidt) J.; m. Virginia McKinney; children: Lee Ashley, Frank McKinney. AB, Davidson Coll., 1964; JD, U. N.C., 1967. Bar: N.C. 1967. Assoc. Smith, Anderson, Blount, Dorsett, Mitchell & Jernigan, Raleigh, N.C., 1969-72, mng. ptnr., 1972—. Bd. adv. U. N.C. Banking Law Inst., U. N.C. Law Sch. Campaign for Carolina Law Steering Com. Bd. visitors Davidson (N.C.) Coll., 1986—; trustee Choate-Rosemary Hall, Wallingford, Conn., 1989-92. Capt. U.S. Army, 1967-69. Fellow N.C. Bar Found.; mem. N.C. Bar Assn. (chmn. bus. law sect. 1985-87, bd. govs. 1989-92, chmn. bar ctr. cabinet 1994-98, pres.-elect 1998-99, pres. 1999-2000), Wake County Bar Assn., Cardinal Club (bd. dirs.), So. Conf. Bar Pres., Nat. Conf. Bar Pres., Supreme Ct. Hist. Soc. Episcopalian. Office: PO Box 2611 Raleigh NC 27602-2611

JERNSTEDT, RICHARD DON, public relations executive; b. McMinnville, Oreg., Feb. 26, 1947; s. Don and Catherine (Anderson) Jernstedt; m. Jean Diane Woods, Dec. 28, 1969; children: Ty Parker, Tiffin Kay. BS, U. Oreg., 1969. Mgr. mktg. com. Container Corp. Am., Chgo., 1976—78; exec. v.p. Golin/Harris, Chgo., 1983—85, pres., 1988—91; CEO Golin/Harris Comm., Chgo., 1991—. Bd. dirs. Off the St. Club of Chgo., 1984; bd. govs. 410 Club, 1991—. Lt. (j.g.) USNR, 1968—72. Named Outstanding Jr., U. Oreg., 1968; recipient Golden Trumpet award, Publicity Club of Chgo. Mem.: Arthur Page Soc., Corp. Voice (bd. dirs.), Coun. Pub. Rels. Firms (bd. dirs., vice chmn.), Internat. Pub. Rels. Assn., Pub. Rels. Soc. Am. (Silver Anvil award 1986), Internat. Assn. Bus. Communicators. Republican. Presbyterian. Avocations: sports, music, photography, traveling.

JEROME, JOHN JAMES, lawyer; b. N.Y.C., Oct. 17, 1933; s. Eugene George and Gladys Odette (Conterno) J.; ; children by previous marriage: Christopher J., Jennifer T.; m. Maureen M. Murphy, Sept. 19, 1981; children: Mairin Ashling, Emily Campbell. BBA, St. John's U., N.Y.C., 1958, LLB, 1961. Bar: N.Y. 1962, U.S. Dist. Ct. (so. dist.) N.Y. 2d cir., 3d cir., U.S. Supreme Ct., U.S. Dist. Ct. (ea. dist.) N.Y. 1964. Assoc. Milbank, Tweed, Hadley & McCloy, N.Y.C., 1962-70, ptnr., 1970-98; pres. Jerome Advisors, LLC, N.Y.C., 1999—. Adj. prof. N.Y. Law Sch., 1978-81; lectr. Am. Law Inst., Corp. Strategies, Inc., N.Y. State Bar Assn., Nat. Law Jour., Oreg. Law Sch., Ky. Law Sch. With U.S. Army, 1954-57. Mem. ABA (program chmn.), N.Y. State Bar Assn., Assn. of Bar of City of N.Y. (chmn. com. on bankruptcy and corp. reorgn. 1990-93), Nat. Bankruptcy Conf. Clubs: N.Y. Athletic, Sharon and Norfolk Country. Home: 1165 5th Ave New York NY 10029-6931 Office: 80 Chambers St New York NY 10007

JEROME, JOSEPH WALTER, mathematics educator; b. Phila., June 7, 1939; s. Joseph Walter and Hermena Josephine (Ostertag) J.; m. Sara Tobin, July 2, 1999. BS in Physics, St. Joseph's U., 1961; MS, Purdue U., 1963, PhD, 1966. Vis. asst. prof. U. Wis., Madison, 1966-68; asst. prof. Case Western Res. U., Cleve., 1968-70; faculty Northwestern U., Evanston, Ill., 1970—, assoc. prof., 1972, prof. math., 1976—. Vis. fellow Oxford (Eng.) U., 1974—75; vis. prof. U. Tex., Austin, 1978—79, Rush Med. Coll., Chgo., 1994—97; cons. Bell Labs., NJ, 1981—87; vis. scientist, 1982—83; vis. scholar U. Chgo.1, 1985; mem. adv. panel Internat. Workshops on Computational Electronics, 1990—; reviewer in field. Author (with S. Fisher): Springer Lecture Series Math. 479, 1975, Approximation of Nonlinear Evolution Systems, 1983, Analysis of Charge Transport, 1995; mem. editl. bd.: Jour. Nonlinear Analysis, Jour. Computational Electronics; contbr. more than 110 articles to profl. jours. Br. Sci. Coun. sr. vis. fellow Oxford, 1974-75; NSF rsch. grantee, 1970—; recipient disting. alumnus award Purdue U. Sch. Sci., 1996. Mem. Am. Math. Soc., Soc. for Indsl. and Applied Math. Roman Catholic. Office: Northwestern U 2033 Sheridan Rd Evanston IL 60208-0830 E-mail: jwj@math.northwestern.edu.

JEROME, NORGE WINIFRED, nutritionist, anthropologist; b. Grenada, Nov. 3, 1930; arrived in U.S., 1956, naturalized, 1973; d. McManus Israel and Evelyn Mary (Grant) J. BS magna cum laude, Howard U., 1960; MS, U. Wis., 1962, PhD, 1967. Cert. nutrition specialist; fellow Am. Coll. Nutrition. Asst. prof. U. Kans. Med. Sch., Kansas City, 1967-72, asso. prof., 1972-78, prof., 1978-95, dir. cmty. nutrition divsn., 1981-95, prof. emerita, 1996—, interim assoc. dean minority affairs, 1996—98; dir. Office of Nutrition, AID, Washington, 1988-91; sr. rsch. fellow Univ. Ctr./AID, Washington, 1991-92. Mem. tech. adv. group The Nat. Ctr. for Minority Health; dir. ednl. resource centers U. Kans. Med. Center, 1974-77, head community nutrition labs., 1978-95; cons. Children's TV Workshop, 1974-77; chairperson adv. bd. Teenage Parents Center, 1971-75; mem. planning and budget council, children and family sers. United Community Services, 1971-80; mem. panel on nutrition edn. White House Conf. on Food, Nutrition and Health, 1969; mem. bd. dirs., health care com. Prime Health, 1976-79; bd. dirs. Council on Children, Media and Merchandising; mem. consumer edn. task force Mid-Am. Health Systems Agy., 1977-79; commr. N.Am. working group Commn. Anthropology Food and Food Habits, Internat. Union Anthrop. and Ethnol. Scis., 1979-80; chmn. com. nutritional anthropology Internat. Union Nutritional Scis., 1979-80; mem. lipid metabolism adv. com. NIH, 1978-80; mem. nat. adv. panel multi-media campaign to improve children's diet U.S. Dept. Agr., 1979-81; bd. advisers Am. Council on Sci. and Health, 1985-88. Sr. author: Nutritional Anthropology, 1980; asso. editor: Jour. Nutrition Edn, 1971-77; adv. council, 1977-80; editor: Nutritional Anthropology Communicator, 1974-77; editorial adv. bd.: Med. Anthropology: Cross Cultural Studies in Health and Illness, 1976-88; adv. bd.: Internat. Jour. Nutrition Planning, 1977-88, Nutrition and Cancer: An Internat. Jour, 1978—2000, Jour. Nutrition and Behavior, 1981-86; contbr. articles to profl. jours. Mem. com. man-food sys. NRC, 1980-83; bd. dirs. Kansas City Urban League, 1969-77, Crittenton Ctr., Kansas City, Mo., 1979-80; mem. awards com. in nutrition edn. Met. Life Found., 1983-85; pres. Assn. for Women in Devel., 1991-93; trustee U. Bridgeport, Conn., 1992—; trustee Child Health Found., 1992-2000, chmn. bd. dirs., 1996-98; v.p., bd. trustees U. Bridgeport, Conn., 1997—; bd. dirs. Black Health Care Coalition of Kansas City, 1993-2002, Johnson County (Kans.) Found. on Aging, 2001--; bd. dirs. Solar Cookers Internat., 1992-2000, pres., 1998, 99; mem. Commn. on Aging, Johnson County, Kans., 1997—. Decorated Dau. Brit. Empire.; recipient First Higuchi/Irvin Youngberg Research Achievement award U. Kans., 1982, Excellence in Academia award Inst. Caribbean Studies, 2002. Fellow Am. Soc. for Nutritional Scis., Am. Anthrop. Assn. (chairperson com. on nutritional anthropology 1974-77, founder com. nutritional anthropology 1974), Soc. Applied Anthropology, Am. Coll. Nutrition, Soc. Med. Anthropology, Am. Soc. Nutritional Scis., 1998; mem. Am. Public Health Assn. (food and nutrition council 1975-78, governing council 1982-85), Am. Inst. Nutrition (program com. 1983-86), Am. Soc. Clin. Nutrition, Am. Men and Women of Sci., Nat. Acad. Scis. (world food and nutrition study panel), N.Y. Acad. Scis., Inst. Food Technologists, Am. Dietetic Assn., Assn. for Women in Devel. (pres. 1991-93), Soc. Behavioral Medicine, Club of Rome (U.S. assoc.) Office: U of Kans Med Ctr 3901 Rainbow Blvd Kansas City KS 66160-7313 *Creative blending appears to have been the key for me— the melding of multiple traditions and styles, the melding of philosophies and strategies, and most importantly, the melding of ancient and modern thought and practices.*

JERRITTS, STEPHEN G. management consultant; b. New Brunswick, N.J., Sept. 14, 1925; s. Steve and Anna (Kovacs) J.; m. Audrey Virginia Smith, June 1948; children: Marsha Carol, Robert Stephen, Linda Ann; m. 2d, Ewa Elizabet Rydell-Vejlens, Nov. 5, 1966; 1 son, Carl Stephen. Student, Union Coll., 1943-44; B.M.E., Rensselaer Poly. Inst., 1947, MS Mgmt., 1948. With IBM, various locations, 1949—58, IBM World Trade, N.Y.C., 1958—67, Bull Gen. Electric divsn. Gen. Electric, France, 1967—70, merged into Honeywell Bull, 1970—74; v.p., mng. dir. Honeywell Info. Sys. Ltd., London, 1974—76; group v.p. Honeywell U.S. Info. Sys., Boston, 1977—80; pres., COO Honeywell Info. Sys., 1980—82; pres., CEO Lee Data Corp., 1983—85; with Storage Tech. Corp., 1985—88, pres., COO, 1985—87, vice-chmn., 1987—88; pres., CEO NBI Corp., 1988—92; cons., advisor Price Waterhouse and Wang Labs Creditors Comm., 1992—93; corp. sr. v.p., pres. Latin Am. Wang Labs., Inc., 1993—98. Interim CEO Zapotec Inc., 1999; bd. dirs. Honeywell, Inc., Storage Tech. Corp., NBI Corp., Latin Am. Wang Labs. Bd. dirs. Guthrie Theatre, 1980-83, Charles Babbage Inst., 1980-92, Minn. Orch., 1980-85; trustee Rensselaer Poly. Inst., 1980-85, mem. adv. bd. Lally Sch. Mgmt., 1994—, Rensselaer Poly. Inst. With USN, 1943-46, lt. USNR, 1946-57. Mem. Computer Bus. Equipment Mfrs. (dir. exec. com. 1979-82), Assoc. Industries Mass. (dir. 1978-80). Home and Office: 650 College Ave Boulder CO 80302-7136 Fax: 303-442-2140.

JERRYTONE, SAMUEL JOSEPH, financial broker; b. Pittston, Pa., Mar. 21, 1947; s. Sebastian and Susan Teresa (Chiampi) J.; children: Sandra, Cheryl, Samuel, Sebastian. Assoc. in Bus., Scranton (Pa.) Lackawanna Jr. Coll., 1966. Mgr. House of Jerrytone Beauty Salon, West Pittston, Pa., 1967-68; regional sales dir. United Republic Life Ins., Harrisburg, Pa., 1970-76; night instr. Wilkes-Barre (Pa.) Vo-Tech High Sch., 1976-78; spl. sales agt. Franklin Life Ins. Co., Wilkes-Barre, 1978-80; instr. Jerrytone Beauty Sch., Pittston, Pa., 1968-69, supr., 1969-95, pres., CEO, 1975, Jerrytone Tng. Ctrs., Pittston, 1989, Las Vegas, 1989; fin. broker Exec. Bus. Mgmt. and Property Svcs., 2001—. Prof. sch. evaluator Nat. Accrediting Com. Arts and Scis., 1974-95; mem. adv. craft com. Wiles-Barre Vo-Tech H.S., 1988. Mem. com. Rep. Presdl. Task Force, Washington, 1984, mem. parish coun. Guardian Angel Cathedral, Las Vegas, 1997. Mem. Pa. Hairdressers Assn., Nat. Accrediting Com. Cosmetology, Am. Coun. Cosmetology Educators, Masons (3d degree award 1983, 32d degree award Lodge Coun. chpt. consistory 1984), Shriners (Irem temple). Roman Catholic. Avocations: reading, golf, bowling, music, video filming. E-mail: s.jerrytone@att.net.

JERVIS, JANE LISE, college official, science historian; b. Newark, N.J., June 14, 1938; d. Ernest Robert and Helen Jenny (Roland) J.; m. Kenneth Albert Pruett, June 20, 1959 (div. 1974); children: Holly Jane Pruett, Cynthia Lorraine Pruett; m. Norman Joseph Chonacky, Dec. 26, 1981; children: Philip Joseph Chonacky, Joseph Norman Chonacky. AB, Radcliffe Coll., 1959; MA, Yale U., 1974, MPhil, 1975, PhD in History of Sci., 1978. Freelance sci. editor and writer, 1962-72; lectr. in history Rensselaer Poly. Inst., 1977-78; dean Davenport Coll., lectr. in history of sci. Yale U., 1978-82; dean students., assoc. prof. history Hamilton Coll., 1982-87; dean coll., lectr. in history Bowdoin Coll., 1988-92; pres. Evergreen State Coll., Olympia, Wash., 1992-2000. Cons. in field. Author: Cometary Theory in 15th Century Europe; contbr. articles to profl. jours.; book reviewer; presenter in field. Trustee Maine Hist. Assn., 1991-92, Stonehill Coll., 1996-02, Providence St. Peter's Hosp., 1997-2000; chair Maine selection com. Rhodes Scholarship Trust, 1990-92, chair N.W. selection com., 1992-93; commr. N.W. Assn. Schs. and Colls. Commn. on Colls., 1994-99. E-mail: jjervis99@comcast.net.

JERVIS, ROBERT, political science educator; b. N.Y.C., Apr. 30, 1940; s. Herman and Dorothy J.; m. Kathe Weil, June 19, 1967; children: Alexa, Lisa. BA, Oberlin Coll., 1962; MA, U. Calif.-Berkeley, 1963, PhD, 1967. Asst. prof. govt. Harvard U., 1968-73, assoc. prof., 1973-75; vis. assoc. prof. polit. sci. Yale U., 1974-75; prof. polit. sci. UCLA, 1975-80, Columbia U., N.Y.C., 1980—, Adlai E. Stevenson prof. of internat. rels., 1989—, chair exec. com. of faculty arts and scis., 1993-94, acting assoc. v.p. arts and scis. for planning, 1994-95. Lady Davis vis. prof. Hebrew U., Jerusalem, spring 1977 Author: Perception and Misperception in International Politics, 1976, The Illogic of American Nuclear Strategy, 1984, Psychology and Deterrence, 1985, The Logic of Images in International Relations, 2d edit., 1989, The Meaning of the Nuclear Revolution, 1989, System Efects: Complexity in Political and Social Life, 1997; editor: Perspectives on Deterrence, 1989, Dominoes and Bandwagons, 1990, Soviet American Relations after the Cold War, 1991, Coping with Complexity in the International System, 1992; contbr. articles to prof. jours. Guggenheim fellow, 1978-79; recipient Grawemeyer award Ideas Improving World Order, Nevitt Sanford Career Achievement award Internat. Soc. Polit. Psychology, 1992, Lionel Trilling award, 1998. Fellow AAAS; mem. Am. Polit. Sci. Assn. (v.p. 1988-89, pres. 2000-01, Best Book in Polit. Psychology award 1998), Internat. Studies Assn. (Security Studies award 1996), Coun. on Fgn. Rels. (fellow 1970-71). Democrat. Home: 1170 5th Ave New York NY 10029-6527 Office: Columbia U Dept Polit Sci New York NY 10027 E-mail: RLJ1@columbia.edu.

JESBERG, ROBERT OTTIS, JR., educational consultant, science educator; b. Springfield, Ill., Nov. 17, 1947; s. Robert O. Sr. and Catharine I. (Patton) J.; m. Ruth Marie Andreas, Aug. 21, 1971; children: Kate Debra, Amy Lyn. BA in Biology, Susquehanna U., 1969; MEd, Temple U., 1971, secondary prin. cert., 1974. Cert. secondary biology and gen. sci. tchr., secondary sch. prin. Sci. tchr. Centennial Schs., Warminster, Pa., 1969—, asst. prin., 1979, 85, 88; sci. cons. K'NEX Industries, Inc., Hatfield, Pa., 1994—; sci. coord. Centennial Schs., Warminster, Pa., 1996-98; mem. adv. com. Gov.'s Sci. Inst. Carnegie Mellon U., 1999—; cons. edn. K'nex Edn., Hatfield. Site dir., instr. Lawrence Hall of Sci., NSF Summer Insts., U. Calif., Berkeley, 1990-92; sci. cons. Singapore Am. Schs., 1993; dir. adult edn. Centennial Schs., Warminster, Pa., 1984-97, staff devel. trainer, 1985—; instr. Pa. Commonwealth Excellence in Sci. Tchg. Alliance, Franklin Inst. Mus., Phila., 1996—. Author: (with others) K'NEX Racer Energy Educator Guide, 1996, K'NEX Bridges Educator Guide, 1996. Elder Lenape Valley Presbyn. Ch., New Britain, Pa., 1988—. Recipient Outstanding Sci. Supr. in Pa. Pa. Sci. Suprs. Assn., 1989; named Outstanding Educator in Bucks County, Pa. Bucks County ASCD, 1987, Outstanding Contbn. and Svc. to Bucks County ASCD, 1987. Mem. Nat. Sci. Tchrs. Assn., Pa. Math/Sci. Eisenhower Consortium (chairperson 1997-98, 2003-), Bucks County Sci. Tchrs. Assn. (pres. 1992-99). Republican. Home: 116 Blue Jay Rd Chalfont PA 18914-3104 Office: K'Nex Edn 2990 Bergey Rd Hatfield PA 19440-0700

JESKE, CHARLES MATTHEW, lawyer; b. Bartlesville, Okla., July 16, 1964; s. Arnold Carl and Maudie Marie (Matthews) J.; m. Pamela Kay Paholek, May 20, 1989. BBA in Fin./Acctg., Tex. A&M U., 1986; JD, South Tex. Coll. Law, Houston, 1989. Bar: Tex. 1989, U.S. Dist. Ct. (so. dist.) Tex. 1990, U.S. Ct. Appeals (5th cir.) 1990. Briefing atty. 14th Dist. Ct. of Appeals Tex., Houston, 1989-90, 90-91; sr. assoc. atty. Renneker & Assocs., Houston, 1991-96; pvt. practice Jeske & Assocs. PLLC, Houston, 1996—, mng. ptnr., 1998—. Contractor, investment analyst Jeske Homes, Bryan, Tex., 1986—. Trustee, officer Meml. Hollow Citizens, Inc., Houston, 1994-96. Mem. ABA, Houston Bar Assn., Tex. A&M U. Former Students Assn., Phi Alpha Delta Alumni Assn. Republican. Lutheran. Avocations: photography, travel. Home and Office: 12407 Barryknoll Ln Houston TX 77024-4113 E-mail: cmjeske@usa.net.

JESKE, HOWARD LEIGH, retired life insurance company executive, lawyer; b. York, Nebr., Sept. 25, 1917; s. Charles W. and Sina (Hanna) J.; m. Bettyclaire Barton, Nov. 23, 1943; children: Vaughn C., Craig B., Lynn Ellen Braziel, Laurel Claire McFarland. AB, Cornell Coll., Mt. Vernon, Iowa, 1940; LL.B., McGeorge Coll. Law, Sacramento, 1951. Bar: Calif. 1951. Capt. USAAF, 1942-45. Mem. ABA, Calif. Bar Assn., Sutter Club (Sacramento). Republican. Home: 4035 Eagles Nest Auburn CA 95603-5922

JESKY, T. J. pharmaceutical products executive; b. Chgo., Feb. 15, 1947; s. Henry J. and Joan F. (Lalko) J. Student, Universidad de las Ams., Mex., 1964-65; BA Mktg. and Retailing, Bradley U., 1969. Field rep. Morton Norwich, Chgo., 1973-76, major account rep., 1976-79; Chgo. dist. mgr. Norwich Eaton Pharms., N.Y., 1979-80; N.Y.C. dist mgr. Norwich Eaton (A Procter & Gamble Co.), N.Y., 1980-83; mgr. Midwest and P.R. divsn. Norwich Eaton, Oak Brook, Ill., 1983-90; mgr. P.R. divsn. nat. accounts, mgr. nat. hosp. divsn. Procter & Gamble Pharms., Norwich, N.Y., 1990-93, mgr. divsn. Cin., 1994-95; pres., CEO Studebaker's, Inc., Scottsdale, Ariz., 1995-97, Ionosphere, Inc., Scottsdale, 1997-98, Barrington Labs., Inc., Las Vegas, 1998-2000; CEO Eaton Labs., Inc., Las Vegas, 2000—. Contbr. articles to profl. jours. Mem. Pharm. Mfr. Assn., Am. Mgmt. Assn., Nat. Pharm. Coun. Home: PO Box 8744 Scottsdale AZ 85252-8744

JESPERSEN, JOHN KRESTEN, librarian; b. Seattle, Wash., Feb. 11, 1946; s. Johannes Kresten and Josephine Mae Jespersen; m. Heather Bruce Pattison, June 14, 1986. BA, Providence Coll., 1969—73; AM, Brown U., 1973—77, PhD, 1977—84; MLIS, U. of R.I., 1998—2000. Vis. lectr. MIT, Dept. of Architecture, 1984, Yale U., Sch. of Architecture, 1984—88; vis. asst. prof. Mary Wash. Coll., 1986—87, The Coll. of William and Mary, 1987—88; asst. prof. S.W. Mo. State U., Springfield, 1988—89; lectr. in ornament Tech. U. of N.S., Sch. of Architecture, Halifax, 1989—90; reference libr. Curry Coll., Milton, Mass., 2001—02; evening reference libr. RISD, Providence, 2001—02; tech. services supr. Curry Coll., Milton, Mass., 2002—. Author (co-author): (exhibition) Rubenism; author: (jour.) Perspecta, 23, Crit 21. Scholar Samuel H. Kress Travel Fellowship, Samuel H. Kress Found., 1979. Mem.: ALA (assoc.), Beta Phi Mu. Avocations: guitar, silversmith. Office: Curry Coll 1071 Blue Hill Ave Milton MA 02186-2395 E-mail: kjespers@curry.edu.

JESPERSEN, ROBERT RANDOLPH, legal consultant; b. N.Y.C., June 17, 1936; s. Randolph Foyen and Marie (Larsen) J.; m. Shirley Dubber, Dec. 20, 1958; children: Robert Randolph Jr., Craig Christopher. AB, Columbia U., 1958, AM, 1964; JD, U. Houston, 1975; LLM, U. Tex., 1987. Bar: Tex. 1975, Ark. 1981, U.S. Supreme Ct., U.S. Ct. Appeals (5th and 8th cirs.), U.S. Dist. Ct. (so. dist.) Tex., U.S. Dist. Ct. (ea. dist.) Ark., U.S. Ct. Mil. Appeals. Pvt. practice law, 1975—. Moderator Am. Arbitration Assn. conf., Little Rock, 1987; asst. atty. gen. Tex., 1975-76; apprentice banker The Bank of N.Y., N.Y.C., 1964-66; mgmt. analyst U.S. Govt., Washington, 1961-62; hon. consul Kingdom of Lesotho, Jurisdiction of Tex., 1972-75; legal cons., 1995—; adj. prof. law U. Ark.-Little rock, 1987-91, prof. bus. law, 1980-95, prof. emeritus, 1995—; vis. prof. law U. Auckland, 1993; vis. sr. lectr. bus. law Massey U., N.Z., 1991; vis. disting. lectr. internat. bus. Calif. State U., Long Beach, 1987; vis. prof. bus. law U. Tex., Austin, 1987; part-time instr. Houston C.C., 1975-76; part-time tchg. fellow U. Houston, 1974-75; sr. advisor Assn. African Univs., Accra, Ghana, 1971-72; headmaster Kurisini Internat. Edn. Ctr., Dar-es-Salaam, Tanzania, 1969-71; dir. devel. African-Am. Inst., N.Y.C., 1967-69; assoc. dir. career svcs. Princeton U., 1966-67; asst. dir. univ. placement Columbia U., 1962-64. Co-author: Business Law: Comprehensive Edit., 1987, Business Law: Text and Cases, 1984, 8th edit., 1996, American Legal System, 1986; editor, contbr.: Industrial Laws, 1980; editl. bd. Jour. Legal Studies Edn., 1983-85, The Houston Lawyer, 1978-80; editor: Proc. of Internat. Legal Studies Assn. Ann. Mtg., 1988; contbr. numerous articles to profl. jours. 1st lt. USMC, 1958—61, col. res. USMC, 1961—88. Recipient Tchg. Excellence award Nat. Conf. of Acad. Bus. Adminstrn., 1993, Faculty Excellence award Coll. Bus. Adminstrn., U. Ark.-Little Rock, 1992; Sam M. Walton Free Enterprise fellow, 1995, Peace Rsch. fellow U. Auckland Ctr. for Peace Studies, 1992.. Mem. Nat. Assn. Scholars, The Federalist Soc. for Law and Pub. Policy Studies (lawyers divsn. Ark. chpt. dir. 1992-93, 94-95, pres. 1991-92), Am. Bus. Law Assn. (pres. 1988-89), So. Reg. Bus. Law Assn. (pres. 1983-84), Ark. Bar Assn. (mem. alternative dispute resolution com. 1987-88, 92-93, internat. law com. 1983-84), State Bar of Tex. (exec. com. mil. law sect. 1978-80), Southwestern Fedn. Adminstrv. Disciplines (bd. dirs. 1982-84), Internat. Consular Acad., Am. Arbitration Assn., Assn. Law Tchrs. G.B., Assn. of Attenders and Alumni of the Hague Acad. Internat. Law, Nat. Arbitration Forum, Order of Barristers, Order of Advocates, Golden Key, Beta Gamma Sigma (chpt. pres. 1985-86), Phi Kappa Phi (chpt. pres. 1984-85), Phi Alpha Delta, Alpha Kappa Psi, Alpha Phi Omega. Republican. Office: PO Box 33471 Pensacola FL 32508

JESSEE, DEBORAH WILLIAMS, nursing administrator; b. Washington, Nov. 7, 1959; d. Claude Hampton and Doris Lee (Collins) Williams; m. Dennis L. Jessee; 1 child, Kara Jo. AS, Bluefield (W.Va.) State Coll., 1988; LPN, Mercer County Voc. Tech. Ctr., Princeton, W.Va., 1986. Cert. critical care nurse, trauma nurse, clinician II, CPR instr., ACLS instr. Nurse extern Princeton (W.Va.) Cmty. Hosp., 1987-88; charge nurse CCU Bluefield (W.Va.) Regional Med. Ctr., 1988-95; clin. dir. skilled nursing unit Bluefield Regional Med. Ctr., 1995—. Mem.: W.Va. Orgn. Nurse Execs. Office: 500 Cherry St Bluefield WV 24701-3306 E-mail: djessee@brmc.org.

JESSEE, ROY MARK, lawyer; b. Kingsport, Tenn., Feb. 8, 1966; s. Roy Claude and Myrtle Delight (Robinette) J.; m. Cortney Wynn Williams, June 30, 1990. BA, King Coll., 1988; JD, U. Va., 1991. Bar: Va. 1991, U.S. Dist. Ct. (we. dist.) Va. 1992. Law clk. Ct. of Appeals of Va., Bristol, 1991-92; assoc. atty. Mullins, Thomason & Harris, Norton, Va., 1992-94; shareholder, prin., atty. Mullins, Thomason, Harris & Jessee, Norton, Va., 1995-98; shareholder, prin. Mullins, Harris & Jessee, Norton, Va., 1998—. Contbr. articles to legal jours. Chmn. Scott County Dem. Party, 1993-95, 95-97. Named one of Outstanding Young Men in Am., 1989. Mem. ABA, Wise County Bar Assn. (pres.-elect 1998, pres. 1999), Am. Judicature Soc., Va. Assn. Def. Attys. Democrat. Baptist. Avocations: running, weight lifting, reading, writing poetry. Home: 157 Fraley Ave Duffield VA 24244 Office: Mullins Harris & Jessee PO Box 1200 30 Seventh St Norton VA 24273

JESSEE, WILLIAM FLOYD, executive; b. Bristol, Va., Sept. 25, 1946; s. Floyd H. and Willie M. Haga J.; m Sarah King, Oct. 7, 1989; children: William Brian, Matthew Jacob, Christopher Larson. AB, Stanford U., 1968; MD, U. Calif., La Jolla, 1972. Lic. physician, Colo., Ill., Ky. Med. dir. Santa Clara Valley PSRO, San Jose, 1978-80; assoc. prof. U. N.C. Sch. Pub. Health, Chapel Hill, 1980-86; v.p. Joint Commn. Accreditation of Healthcare Orgns., Oakbrook Terrace, Ill., 1986-91, 93-94, Humana, Inc., Louisville, 1991-93; pres., CEO UNIVA Health Network, Louisville, 1994-96; v.p. AMA, Chgo., 1996-99; pres., CEO Med. Group Mgmt. Assn., Englewood, Colo., 1999—. Chmn. Commn. Profl. and Hosp. Activities, Ann Arbor, Mich., 1986—95; cons., tech. advisor WHO, Geneva, 1986, 90, 92; bd. dirs. Exempla Healthcare, Denver. Contbr. articles to profl. jours. Fellow: Am. Coll. Preventive Medicine, Am. Coll. Med. Quality (hon.); mem.: AMA, Am. Coll. Med. Practice Execs. Avocations: tennis, hiking, photography. Office: Med Group Mgmt Assn 104 Inverness Ter E Englewood CO 80112-5313 E-mail: wfj@mgma.com.

JESSELSON, ROBERT, musician, educator; b. N.Y.C., Nov. 4, 1949; m. Sara Schechter-Schoeman. Student, Staatliche Hochschule fuer Musik, Freiburg, Germany, 1976; MusM, Eastman Sch. Music, 1999; DMA, Rutgers U., 1990. Prof. U. S.C., Columbia, 1981—. Cellist Am. Arts Trio; dir. USC String Project, 1981—97; prin. cello S.C. Philharm. Orch., 1981—95, Orquesta-Sinfonica de Las Palmas, Spain, 1996—97; cello tchr. S.C. Governor's Sch. for the Arts, 1985—2002. Contbr. articles to profl. jours. Grantee, Merrill Lynch, 1996, Nord Found., 1997, Ctrl. Carolina Found., 1997, Lipscomb Found., 1997, Colonial Life, 1997, NationsBank, 1997, Bostik Found., 1998, Upton Found., 1998, Fund Improvement Secondary Edn., U.S. Dept. Edn. (FIPSE), 2000, 2001, Knight Found., 2001, Psaras Fund, 2002. Mem.: Am. Strings Tchrs. Assn. with Nat. Sch. Orch. Assn. (NSOA) (pres., bd. mem. 1998—), Music Tchrs. Nat. Assn., Music Educators Nat. Conv. (MENC), Pi Kappa Lamda. Office: School Music Univ SC Columbia SC 29208 Office Fax: 803-777-6508. Personal E-mail: rjesselson@mozart.sc.edu. E-mail: rjesselson@mozart.sc.edu.

JESSEN, CHRIS MICHAEL, music educator; b. Rolla, Mo., Nov. 25, 1972; s. Clark e. and Mary Ann (Knight) J. BS in Music Edn., Quincy (Ill.) U., 1995; MS in Ednl. Adminstrn., PhD in Ednl. Adminstrn., Columbia State U., Metairie, La., 1998. Lic. funeral dir. Dir. music Green Forest Sch., Salem, Mo., 1996—. Mem. NEA, Masons, (K.T.), Shriners, Royal Order of Scotland, Loyal Orange Instn., K.P. Democrat. Episcopalian. Home: RR 4 Box 466 Salem MO 65560-9224

JESSEN, DAVID WAYNE, accountant; b. Albuquerque, Jan. 13, 1950; s. Irving Matthew and Lucille Barbara (Huber) J.; m. Melissa Meyer, Oct. 4, 1975; children: Jennifer Leigh, Kimberly Paige. BBA in Acctg., U. N.Mex., 1972. CPA N.C., N.Mex., S.C. Staff acct. local CPA firm, Albuquerque, 1971-74, jr. ptnr., 1974-75; mgr. in charge Santa Fe office Ernst & Young, 1975-80, prin. in charge Santa Fe office, 1980-82, dir. taxes N.Mex. offices, 1980-86, tax ptnr. N.Mex. offices, 1984—, ptnr.-in-charge N.Mex. offices Raleigh, NC, 1987-89. Mem. Arthur Young Nat. Real Estate Com., 1988, mem. nat. hightech com., 1988-94; ptnr., dir. entrepreneurial svcs. Ernst & Young, Raleigh, 1989-2002, S.E. region dir. entrepreneurial svcs., 1992-94, dir. tax dept., 1995—, dir. tax entrepreneurial svcs., 1998-2003. Asst. scoutmaster Boy Scouts Am.; bd. dirs. St. Joseph Hosp. Health Care Found., 1986—87, N.C. Mus. Art Found., 1992—, treas., 1994—2001, Kiwanis Found. Eagle Scout, Bus. Friends Coun., N.C. Soc. to Prevent Blindness; chmn. pres.'s cir. Wake Med. Ctr. Found., 1996—2001, bd. dirs., 1997—, WakeMed, vice-chmn. fin. com., exec. com.; bd. dirs. Food Bank of N.C., 2001—, chmn. fin. com., treas.; mem. parents coun. U. N.C., Chapel Hill, 2000—03; mem. Ch. Congregation at Duke U. Chapel; treas. bd. dirs. N.C. Mus. Art, 2003—. Mem. AICPA (nat. com. small bus. taxation), Coun. for Entrepreneurial Devel. (treas. 1989-92, bd. dirs.), Nat. Assn. Accts. (Raleigh chpt., v.p., bd. dirs. 1989-91), N.Mex. Estate Planning Coun., N.Mex. Soc. CPAs (taxation com., pub. rels. com., v.p. Santa Fe chpt. 1980), N.C. Assn. CPAs, Santa Fe C. of C., Albuquerque C. of C., Raleigh C. of C., Santa Fe Jaycees, Albuquerque Jaycees, Elks, Kiwanis, West Raleigh Rotary, Alpha Kappa Psi. Home: 4921 Misty Oak Dr Raleigh NC 27613-6349

JESSEN, MICHAEL ERIK, surgeon, educator; b. Melita, Man., Can., May 26, 1958; came to U.S., 1986; s. Paul Erik and M. Isabelle (Spafford) J. Student, U. Man., Winnipeg, 1975-77, MD, 1981. Diplomate Nat. Bd. Med. Examiners, Am. Bd. Surgery, Am. Bd. Thoracic Surgery; cert. gen. surgery specialist, cardiovasc. and thoracic surgery specialist Royal Coll. Surgeons Can. Intern U. Man., 1981-82, resident in gen. surgery, 1982-86; rsch. fellow in surgery Duke U. Med. Ctr., Durham, N.C., 1986-88, resident in thoracic surgery, 1988-90; asst. prof. thoracic and cardiovasc. surgery U. Tex. Southwestern Med. Ctr., Dallas, 1991-95, assoc. prof., 1995-2000, prof., 2000—. Chief cardiothoracic surgery Dallas VA Med. Ctr., also dir. residency tng. program in thoracic surgery; presenter in field. Contbr. numerous articles and abstracts to publs. Isbister scholar, 1976, U. Manitoba Alumni scholar, 1976, Maxwell Rady scholar, 1977, Morton Stall scholar, 1977; faculty fellow U. Manitoba, Can. Heart Found. fellow, 1987; grantee Am. Heart Assn., 1987, 94, 96, 2002, Tex. Advanced Tech. Program, 1991, 94, 97, NIH, 1998. Fellow ACS, Royal Coll. Physicians and Surgeons Can., Am. Coll. Cardiology; mem. AMA, Am. Heart Assn. (coun. cardiovascular surgery), Am. Soc. for Artificial Internal Organs, Soc. Thoracic Surgeons, Soc. Univ. Surgeons, Am. Assn. for Thoracic Surgery, Internat. Soc. Magnetic Resonance in Medicine. Home: 4710 Bent Tree Ct Coppell TX 75019-6121 Office: U Tex Southwestern Med Ctr 5323 Harry Hines Blvd Dallas TX 75390-8879 E-mail: michael.jessen@utsouthwestern.edu.

JESSEPH, LINDA, process analyst; b. Wichita, Kans., May 14, 1954; d. Charles Peter Yaverski and Roberta Ann Pursell; m. Rodney Clarence Jesseph (div. Aug. 29, 1985); children: Christopher, Jaclyn. BS, Southwestern Coll., 1999; MA, Webster U., 2002. Libr. Bombardier, Wichita, 1995—99, process analyst, 1999—. Bd. mem. Human Svcs. Bd. Wichita City Coun., 1996—97. Mem.: Assn. for Children for the Enforcement of Support (coord. Kans. 1987—2000, chairperson 1998—99). Office: Bombardier One Learjet Way Wichita KS 67209

JESSEPH, STEVEN AUSTIN, career transition executive; b. Seattle, June 26, 1951; s. John Ervin and Marley Mary (Austin) J.; m. Bonnie Lynn Fogle, July 4, 1981; children: Jason Todd, Lane Nolan, Bethany Lynn, Blaire Ashley. BA in Psych., Otterbein Coll., 1973; MS in Corrections, Xavier U., 1977; postgrad., Ohio State U., 1979-81. Adminstrv. specialist Franklin County Welfare Dept., Columbus, Ohio, 1974; probation officer Franklin County Mcpl. Ct., Columbus, 1974-81; v.p. Promark Co., Cin., 1981-83; mgr. corp. outplacement Fox-Morris Assoc., Charlotte, N.C., 1983-86, v.p. career transition svcs., 1987-90, sr. v.p. nat. accts., 1991-92, sr. v.p. southeast region gen. mgr., 1992-94; dir. job replacement svcs. Sara Lee Corp., Chgo., 1994, exec. dir. job replacement svcs., 1994—, exec. dir. global workplace values and safety, 1997—. Contbr. articles to profl. jours. Chair internat. adv. group Worldwide Responsible Apparel Prodn. Program, 2000—; bd. dels. Nat. Safety Coun.; chair social responsibility com. Am. Apparel & Footware Assn. Avocations: golf, fishing, travel. Office: Sara Lee Corp Three First National Plz Chicago IL 60602

JESSER, BENN WAINWRIGHT, chemical engineering and construction company executive; b. N.Y.C., June 10, 1915; s. Edward Arthur and Vera Wainwright (Benn) J.; m. Alice Forster Abeel, July 3, 1939 (dec.); m. Dorothea Potter Coogan, Aug. 29, 1954 (div.); children: Wendy, Penny, Bonnie Benn, John, Dorothea.; m. Barbara Gill Jenter, June 6, 1982. BS in Chem. Engring, Princeton U., 1936, MS, 1941. Control engr. du Pont Co., Gibbstown, N.J., 1936-38; instr. Princeton U., 1938-42; v.p. ops. M.W. Kellogg, N.Y.C./London, 1942-71; pres. Hoechst-Uhde Corp., Englewood Cliffs, N.J., 1971-80, chem. engring. cons., 1980—. Contbr. articles to profl. jours. Chmn. bd. trustees Stoneleigh Burnham Sch.; bd. dirs. coun. Girl Scouts U.S.; trustee Saddle River Country Day Sch. Mem. Am. Inst. Chem. Engrs., ASME, Princeton Engring. Assn. (pres.), Class '36 Princeton (pres.), Com. Engring. Law, Princeton Alumni of Nantucket (pres.), Sigma Xi, Tau Beta Pi. Clubs: Sankaty Head Golf, Amelia Island Plantation, Nantucket Yacht, Fox Meadow Tennis; Princeton (N.Y.C.). Republican. Episcopalian. Home: 83 Sea Marsh Rd Amelia Island FL 32034-5040 *One of the most important characteristics for both happiness and success is enthusiasm. Enthusiasm is both contagious and catalytic. People around an enthusiastic person join in the enthusiasm for a project, a game or a trip. And enthusiasm has a catalytic effect in enhancing the chance of success of the event.*

JESSOR, RICHARD, psychologist, educator; b. Bklyn., Nov. 24, 1924; s. Thomas and Clara (Merkin) J.; m. Shirley Glasser, Sept. 27, 1948 (div. 1982); children: Kim, Tom; m. Jane Ava Menken, Nov. 13, 1992. Student, CCNY, 1941-43; BA, Yale U., 1946; MA, Columbia U., 1947; PhD, Ohio State U., 1951. Intern, clin. psychology trainee VA/Ohio State U., Columbus, 1947-50; asst. prof. psychology U. Colo., Boulder, 1951-56, assoc. prof., 1956-61, prof., 1961—, dir. rsch. program problem behavior Inst. Behavioral Sci., 1966-97, dir. Inst. Behavioral Sci., 1980—2001, dir. rsch. program on health behavior Inst. Behavioral Sci., 2001—. Dir. MacArthur Found. Rsch. Network on Successful Adolescent Devel. Among Youth in High Risk Settings, 1987-96; cons. Nat. Inst. on Drug Abuse, 1975-76, Nat. Inst. on Alcohol Abuse and Alcoholism, 1976-80, WHO, Geneva, 1976-80; cons. in field. Author: (with T.D. Graves, R.C. Hanson & S.L. Jessor) Society, Personality, and Deviant Behavior: A Study of a Tri-Ethnic Community, 1968, (with S.L. Jessor) Problem Behavior and Psychosocial Development: A Longitudinal Study of Youth, 1977, (with J.E. Donovan and F. Costa) Beyond Adolescence: Problem Behavior and Young Adult Development, 1991; co-editor: Contemporary Approaches to Cognition, 1957, Cognition, Personality and Clinical Psychology, 1967, Ethnography and Human Development: Context and Meaning in Social Inquiry, 1996; editor: New Perspectives on Adolescent Risk Behavior, 1998, Perspectives on Behavioral Science: the Colorado Lectures, 1991; cons. editor Jour. Cons. and Clin. Psychology, 1975-77, Cmty. Mental Health Jour., 1974-78, Alcohol Health and Rsch. World, 1981-90, Alcohol, Drugs and Driving, 1985-92, Adolescent Medicine: State of the Art Revs., 1989—; mem. editl. bd. Prevention Sci., 1999—; cons. editor Sociometry, 1964-66, assoc. editor, 1966-69; contbr. articles to profl. jours. Served with USMC, 1943-46, PTO. Decorated Purple Heart; Social Sci. Rsch. Coun. pre-doctoral fellow Ohio State and Yale U., 1950 51; Social Sci. Rsch. Coun. fellow Ohio State U., 1954, Social Sci. Rsch. Coun. postdoctoral fellow U. Calif.-Berkeley, 1956-57, NIMH spl. rsch. fellow Harvard-Florence Rsch. Project, Italy, 1965-66, Ctr. for Advanced Study in the Behavioral Scis. fellow Stanford U., 1995-96; recipient Faculty Rsch. Lectureship award U. Colo., 1981-82; Gallagher lectr. Soc. Adolescent Medicine, 1987. Fellow APA, Am. Psychol. Soc. (charter fellow); mem. Soc. for Psychol. Study of Social Issues, Soc. for Study of Social Problems. Avocations: mountain climbing, running marathons. Home: 1303 Marshall St Boulder CO 80302-5803 Office: U Colo Inst Behavioral Sci Cb 483 Boulder CO 80309-0001 E-mail: jessor@colorado.edu.

JESSUP, DWIGHT WILEY, academic administrator, educator; b. Iowa Falls, Iowa, Dec. 23, 1937; s. Dale Ernest and Florence Leota Jessup; m. Karin Marie Jessup, June 6, 1959; children: Randall David, Elisa Marie Case, Colleen Michele Inwards. BA, Bethel Coll., 1960; MA, U. Minn., 1965, PhD, 1978. Social sci. tchr. Minnehaha Acad., Mpls., 1961-63; asst. to dir. pub. affairs Bethel Coll., St. Paul, 1963-68, asst. prof., 1968-75, assoc. dean, assoc. prof., 1975-82, academic dean, prof. history and polit. sci., 1982-89; dean sch. arts and scis., prof. history and polit. sci. Biola U., La Mirada, Calif., 1989-93; v.p. for Academic Affairs and dean, prof. history and polit. sci. Taylor U., Upland, Ft. Wayne, Ind., 1993—. Author: Reaction and Accommodation: The U.S. Supreme Court and Political Conflict: 1809-1835; contbr. articles to profl. jours. Bd. dir. Bapt. Joint Com., Washington, 1987—; chair student acad. programs commn. Coun. for Christian Coll. and Univ., Washington, 1996-2003. Recipient Spurgeon award St. Paul Boy Scouts, 1981. Mem. Am. Assn. Higher Edn., Am. Polit. Sci. Assn., Am. Soc. for Legal History, Conf. on Faith and History, Org. of Am. Historians, Supreme Ct. Hist. Soc. Avocations: international travel, reading, wilderness camping, fine and performing arts, church activities. Office: Taylor U 236 W Reade Ave Upland IN 46989 E-mail: dwjessup@tayloru.edu.

JESSUP, EDWIN HARLEY, III, aerospace engineering executive; b. New Haven, Mar. 5, 1947; s. Edwin Harley Jr. and Patricia Ann (Potter) J.; m. Laura French Lally, May 22, 1975; children: Todd Benjamin, Brian Arthur. BS in Aerospace Engring., Brown U., 1968; MS in Aero. Engring., USAF Inst. Tech., Wright-Patterson AFB, Ohio, 1976. Commd. 2nd lt. USAF, 1968, advanced through grades to lt. col., 1992, pilot, 1968-75, program mgr. Wright-Patterson AFB, 1976-80, dir. tng. Loring AFB, Maine, 1980-84, dir. operational testing and evaluation Edwards AFB, Calif., 1984-90; ret., 1990; aerospace engring. mgr. Delex Sys., Inc., California, Md., 1991—. USAF Avionics Lab. rep. Joint Technical Coord. Group/Joint Munitions Effectiveness Manual, 1982-84. Named Project Engr. of Yr. Wright Aero. Labs., Wright-Patterson AFB, 1980. Mem. Air Force Assn., Order of Daedalians (chpt. adjutant 1984—), Ret. Officers Assn., Tau Beta Pi. Roman Catholic. Avocations: private piloting, sailing. Home: 2460 Abigail Ct Prince Frederick MD 20678-3382 Office: Delex Systems Inc 44425 Pecan Ct Ste 152 California MD 20619-2046 E-mail: ejessup@delex.com.

JESSUP, JAN AMIS, arts volunteer, writer; b. Chgo., Aug. 10, 1927; d. Herman Harvey and Anita (Lincoln) Sinako; m. Everett Orme Amis, Dec. 20, 1970 (dec. Nov. 1981), m. Joe Lee Jessup, Apr. 16, 1989. BA, U. Minn., 1948; postgrad., Rutgers U., 1969-70. Bd. dirs., mem. exec. com. Broward Ctr. Performing Arts Pacers, Ft. Lauderdale, Fla., 1985—88, pres., 1987—88; spkr. U. Internat. Bus., Beijing, 1985. Active not-for-profit orgns. including Girl Scouts U.S., Boy Scouts Am., Presbyn. Ch.; active beautification com., Lighthouse Point, Fla., 1978—89, sec., 1988—91; rep. to Fla. Art Orgns., 1987—88; bd. dirs. Archways, Ft. Lauderdale, 1987—91, Fla. Grand Opera, 1993—; trustee Miami City Ballet, 1991—94; adv. bd. Guild of the Palm Beaches, 1994—95; bd. govs. Fla. Philharm. Orch., 1981—98, v.p. representing all affiliates, 1985—87, 1992, 1994—96, exec. com., 1989—93, v.p. individual giving, 1991—92, Boca Raton bd. dirs., 1994—2002, chmn. affiliate com., 1994—95; mem. program com. Boca Raton Ctr. for Arts, 2002—; trustee Harid Conservatory, 1997 ; founding pres. Harid Guild, 1997—99. Mem.: Royal Dames Cancer Rsch. (trustee 1995—97), Gold Coast Jazz Soc. (bd. dirs. 1992—98, v.p. 1994—98), Royal Palm Dinner Theatre (bd. dirs. 1998—2000), The Opus Soc. (chmn. 1981—85, bd. dirs., mem. exec. com. 1981—96, pres. 1989—93), Am. Symphony Orch. League Vol. Coun. (sec. 1986—87, bd. dirs. 1986—92), Ft. Lauderdale Philharm. Soc. (bd. dirs. 1986—), Opera Soc. (sec. 1986—87, bd. dirs. 1986—, v.p. pub. rels. 1987—88), Am. Symphony Orch. League (v.p. 1987—88, vice chmn. 1989—90, pres. 1989—90, advisor 1990—91, assoc. Resource Devel. Inst. 1996—98, bd. dirs. 1998—, liaison and com. mem. Nat. Youth Orch. Festival 2000 Com. 2000—), Internat. Game Fish Assn. (adv. coun. 2001—), Nat. Soc. Arts and Letters, Centre For The Arts (program com. 2002—), Harid Conservatory of Music, Inc., Ocean Reef Club, Sea Grape Garden Club (past pres.), Royal Palm Yacht and Country Club Women's Club, Boca Raton Resort and Club. Republican. Avocations: music listening, boating, fishing, writing, bridge. Home: 133 Coconut Palm Rd Boca Raton FL 33432-7975 E-mail: janjessup@aol.com., amisj@bellsouth.net.

JESSUP, JOE LEE, business educator, management consultant; b. Cordele, Ga., June 23, 1913; s. Horace Andrew and Elizabeth (Wilson) J.; m. Janet Amis, Apr. 16, 1989. BS, U. Ala., 1936; MBA, Harvard U., 1941; LLD (hon.), Chung-Ang U., Seoul, Korea, 1964. Sales rep. Proctor & Gamble, 1937-40; liaison officer bur. pub. rels. U.S. War Dept., 1941; spl. asst. and exec. asst. Far Ea. div. and office exports Bd. Econ. Warfare, 1942-43; exec. officer to chief of staff Svcs. of Supply-Europian Theatre, 1943-44; exec. officer, office deptl. adminstrn. Dept. State, 1946; exec. sec. adminstr.'s adv. coun. War Assets Adminstrn., 1946-48; v.p. sales Airken, Capitol & Service Co., 1948-52; assoc. prof. bus. adminstrn. George Washington U., 1952, prof., 1952-77, prof. emeritus, 1977—, asst. dean Sch. Govt., 1951-60; pres. Jessup and Co., Ft. Lauderdale, Fla., 1957—2002. Bd. dirs. Giant Food, Inc., Washington, mem. audit com., 1971—75; bd. dirs. Hunter Assn. Labs., Fairfax, Va., mem. exec. com., 1966—69, exec. v.p., 1967, coord. Air Force Regources Mgmt. program, 1951—57; del. in edn. 10th Internat. Mgmt. Conf., Sao Paulo, Brazil, 1954, 11th Internat. Mgmt. Conf., Paris, 1957, 12th Internat. Mgmt. Conf., Sydney and Melbourne, Australia, 1960, 13th Internat. Mgmt. Conf., Rotterdam, The Netherlands, 1966, 14th Internat. Mgmt. Conf., Tokyo, 1969, 15th Internat. Mgmt. Conf., Munich, 1972; mem. Md. Econ. Devel. Adv. Commn., 1973—75. Mem. Civil Svc. Commn., Arlington County, Va., 1973—75; trustee Tng. Within Industry Found., Summit, NJ, 1954—58; mem. bd. overseers Lynn U., Boca Raton, Fla., 1991—2002; mem. adv. bd. Youth Automotive Tng. Ctr., Hollywood, Fla., 1993—; trustee Philharm. Orch., Fla., 1986—91; mem. nat. adv. coun. Ctr. Study of Presidency, 1974—99; mem. Atlanta regional panel selection of White House fellow, 1990—95, mem. Miami regional panel. Decorated Bronze Star; recipient cert. of appreciation Sec. of Air Force, 1957 Mem.: Royal Palm Yacht and Country Club, Univ. Club (Washington), Harvard Club (N.Y.C.). Home: 133 Coconut Palm Rd Boca Raton FL 33432-7975

JESSUP, PAUL FREDERICK, financial economist, educator; b. Evanston, Ill., Apr. 16, 1939; s. Paul S. and Gertrude (Strohmaier) J.; m. Johanna A.M. Friesen, June 27, 1970; children: Christine Marieke, Paul Charles Friesen. BS, Northwestern U., 1960, PhD, 1966; AM, Harvard U., 1963; BA, U. Oxford, Eng., 1963; MA, U. Oxford, 1983. Economist com. banking and currency U.S. Ho. of Reps., Washington, 1963-64; faculty U. Minn., Mpls., 1967-82, prof. fin., 1973-82; with Jessup & Co., Inc., St. Paul, 1982—; William Kahlert prof. mgmt. and econs. Hamline U., St. Paul, 1988—. Dir. Gerbill Inc.; Sabbatical prof. in residence Fed. Res. Bank, Mpls., 1973-74 Author: The Theory and Practice of Nonpar Banking, 1967, (with Roger B. Upson) Returns in Over-the-Counter Stock Markets, 1973, Competing for Stock Market Profits, 1974, Modern Bank Management: A Casebook, 1978, Modern Bank Management, 1980, Invest To Win: A Coach's Guide to Stocks, Bonds and Mutual Funds, 2001; editor: Innovations in Bank Management: Selected Readings, 1969; contbr. articles to profl. jours. Bd. dir. Assoc. of the James Ford Bell Libr. Mem. Midwest Fin. Assn. (past pres.) Clubs: Skylight (Mpls.); Univ. Club (Chgo.). Home: 1979 Shryer Ave W Saint Paul MN 55113-5414 Office: Hamline U 1536 Hewitt Ave Saint Paul MN 55104-1284

JESSUP, PHILIP CARYL, JR., b. Utica, N.Y., Aug. 30, 1926; s. Philip C. and Lois K. (Kellogg) J.; m. Dorothy A. Kerr, Jan. 15, 1951 (div.); children: Timothy, Nancy, Margaret; m. Helen I. Ibbitson, Jan.24, 1969; stepchildren: Genevieve, Lucinda, Francesca, Alexander. BA, Yale Coll., 1949; JD, Harvard U., 1952. Bar: N.Y. 1954. Atty. Whitman, Ransom & Coulson, N.Y.C., 1952-58; legal officer Internat. Nickel Co., Inc., N.Y.C., 1958-63; gen. solicitor internat. Inco Ltd., N.Y.C., 1963-68; chief legal officer, sec., dir. Inco Europe Ltd., London, 1968-72; pres., mng. dir. P.T. Internat. Nickel Indonesia, Jakarta, 1972-78; v.p., gen. counsel and sec. Inco Ltd., N.Y.C., Toronto, Can., 1978-84; sec., gen. counsel Nat. Gallery Art, Washington, 1985-2000. Dir. Biogen N.V., Geneva, 1981-85; chmn. bd. Inco Gulf, E.C., Bahrain, 1980-84; chmn. bd. Am. Friends Nat. Gallery Art Australia, N.Y.C., 2001—; bd. dirs. Norfolk Land Trust, Norfolk, Conn., 2002—, asst. treas., 2003—. Trustee Obor, Internat. Book Inst. Inc., Phila., 1978—2001, sec.-treas., 1989-96, chmn. bd., 1996-2001; mem. adv. commn. H.H. Humphrey Fellowship Program, 1984-89; trustee Asia Soc., 1991-99, sec., 1993-99, mem. adv. com. Washington Ctr., 1985-2000, chmn. adv. com., 1989-2000; pres. Friends of Hosp. for Sick Children, Toronto, 1985—; mem. Coun. on Fgn. Rels., N.Y.C., 1972—; pres. West Brooklyn Ind. Dems., 1956-58. Served to staff/sgt. C.E., U.S. Army, 1944-46. Mem. ABA, Assn. of Bar of City of N.Y., Century Assn. (N.Y.C.). Democrat. Home: 97 Gamefield Rd Norfolk CT 06058-1272

JESSUP, R. JUDD, health care executive; b. San Francisco, Oct. 15, 1947; s. R. Bruce and Adaline (Brown) J.; m. Jeanne (Bannash), Sept. 7, 1968 (div. Dec. 1987); children: Jarrett, Jody, Rik, Alycia; m. Charlene (Massei), May 19, 1990. BA, Knox Coll., 1969; MBA, U. Colo., Denver, 197l. Dir. mktg. svc. Blue Cross Blue Shield, Denver, 1972-78, dir. alt. delivery sys., 1978-80; pres. HMO Colo., Inc., Denver, 1980—87, Take Care Health Plan, Concord, Calif., 1987-94, Take Care, Inc., Concord, Calif., 1991-94; pres., HMO divsn. F. H. P. Internat., Fountain Valley, Calif., 1994-96; pvt. investor Calif., 1996—2002; CEO U. S. Labs, Irvine, Calif., 2002—. Bd. dir. Corvel Corp.; Novamed Eyecare Svc.; Pacific Dental Benefits; U.S. Labs, Inc.; chmn. Coast To Coast Wireless, Inc. Avocation: golf. Home: 30962 Via Serenidad Trabuco Canyon CA 92679-4002

JESSUP, WILLIAM EUGENE, lawyer; b. Macon, Ga., Aug. 7, 1952; s. Lauren Eugene and Katharine Kimbrough (Hosch) J. BA in English, Emory U., 1974, LLM in Taxation, 1980; JD, U. Ga., 1977. Bar: Ga. 1977, Tenn. 1981, La. 1986, U.S. Supreme Ct. 1982, U.S. Ct. Appeals (5th cir.) 1977, U.S. Ct. Appeals (6th cir.) 1982, U.S. Dist. Ct. (no. dist.) Ga. 1977, U.S. Dist. Ct. (mid. dist.) Tenn. 1981, U.S. Dist. Ct. (so. dist.) La. 1986, U.S. Dist. Ct. (ea. dist.) Tenn. 1999. Assoc. Waller Lansden Dortch & Davis, Nashville, 1981-82; pvt. practice Nashville, 1982-85; assoc. Monroe & Lemann, New Orleans, 1984-86; pvt. practice New Orleans, 1986-88, Atlanta, 1988-94. Contbr. articles to profl. jours. Mem. ABA, State Bar Ga., State Bar Tenn., State Bar La., Rotary, Phi Delta Phi, Alpha Tau Omega. Methodist. Avocations: golf, songwriting, college football, singing. Office: 737 Market St, Ste 309, PO Box 4926 Chattanooga TN 37405-0926

JESTER, JAMES VINCENT, opthalmology educator; b. Riverside, Calif., Sept. 7, 1950; s. Arthur Vincent and Alice Elizabeth (Coen) J.; m. Maureen Krieger, Dec. 18, 1977; children: Alexander, Bryan, Rebecca. BS in Biology, U. So. Calif., 1972, PhD in Exptl. Pathology, 1978. Spl. rsch. fellow Nat. Eye Inst., Bethesda, Md., 1982-83; asst. prof. ophthalmology Georgetown U., Washington, 1986-91; prof. ophthalmology U. Tex. Southwestern Med. Ctr., Dallas, 1991—; asst. prof. ophthalmology U. So. Calif., 1983—86. Contbg. editor jours. Investigative Ophthalmology and Visual Sci., 1986—, Current Eye Rsch., 1986—, Exptl. Eye Rsch., 1986—; mem. editl. bd. Cornea, 1988-96; contbr. over 180 articles to Lab. Sci., Ocular Surface and chpts. to profl. jours.; rsch. on corneal wound healing and refractive surgery. Mem. ad hoc sic. rev. Nat. Eye Inst., Bethesda, md., 1989-91. Recipient Rsch. award Fight for Sight, 1981, Rsch. Manpower award Rsch. to Prevent Blindess, 1986, Sr. Sci. Investigator award, 1994 & 2002; NIH grantee, 1983—. Mem. AAAS, Am. Soc. Cell Biology, Assn. Rsch. in Vision and Ophthalmology (program plan 1991-93). Avocations: hiking, fishing, cooking, civil war history. Home: 3240 Lovers Ln Dallas TX 75225-7626 Office: U Tex Southwestern Med Ctr 5323 Harry Hines Blvd Dallas TX 75390-9057

JESTER, WILLIAM DAVID, lawyer; b. Jacksonville, Fla., May 18, 1954; s. Harold Leon Jester and Betty Lee (Babb) Notestine; children: Joanna Megan, Zachary Kegan. BS, Troy (Ala.) State U., 1988; JD, U. Fla., 1991. Bar: Fla. 1991, Ala. 1998, U.S. Dist. Ct. (mid. dist.) Fla. 1991, U.S. Dist. Ct. (no. dist.) Fla. 1993, U.S. Dist. Ct. (so. dist.) Fla. 1996, U.S. Dist. Ct. (mid. dist.) Ala. 1998, U.S. Dist. Ct. (so. dist.) Ala. 1999, U.S. Ct. Appeals (11th cir.) 1998, U.S. Dist. Ct. (so. dist.) Ala. 1999. Assoc. Coker, Myers, Schickel, Cooper & Sorenson, PA, Jacksonville, Fla., 1991-93; ptnr. Boyes & Jester P.A., Gainesville, Fla., 1993-96; dir. Galloway Johnson Tompkins Burr Smith, PLC, Gulf Breeze, Fla., 1996—. Mem.: Ala.Trial Lawyers Assn., Inns of Ct., Escambia/Santa Rosa Bar Assn. Avocations: flying, golf, reading, snow skiing. Office: Ste 2 1101 Gulf Breeze Pky Gulf Breeze FL 32561-4891 E-mail: djester@gjtbs.com., wdjester@aol.com.

JESTIN, HEIMWARTH B. retired university administrator; b. Montreal, Quebec, Canada, Sept. 24, 1918; s. Emil Ernst and Rosa (Ege) J.; m. Catherine M. Townshend, Oct. 14, 1944; children— Loftus, Jennifer, Carolyn. BS, Central Conn. State Coll., 1947; MA, Yale, 1949, PhD, 1954. Head English dept., tchr. history Thomaston HS, Conn., 1947-50; prin. Canton HS, Collinsville, Conn., 1951-53; supt. schs. Canton, Conn., 1953-62; prof. philosophy and edn. Ctrl. Conn. State Coll., Conn., 1956-65, dean coll., 1965-67, v.p. acad. affairs, 1967-85; provost Conn. State U., Conn., 1985-87. Prof. U. Hartford, 1961-63. Author: Critical Experiences During the Early Years of Superintendency, 1955, The Canton Evaluation Plan, 1960, Role of the Superintendent of Schools in Connecticut, 1967, Ecology Holds Key to Man's Destiny, 1969, Well-Educated Barbarians, 1970, Higher Education Direction, 1971, Year Round Schooling Keyed to Modern Need, 1972, For a New State University System, 1977, They Know a Lot, But are They Educated?, 1977, Crucial Year for Higher Education, 1978, Enrollments Not Nose Diving, 1979, To Improve Higher Education, a Two-Tier University System, 1980, For a State University System, 1981; co-editor: The Connecticut Study of the Role of the Public School, 1960. Trustee Roaring Brook Nature Center; bd. mgr., life mem. Conn. PTA. Served with AUS, 1941-46. Decorated Order Brit. Empire. Mem. Conn. Council Sch. Coll. Rels. (hon.); PTO Home: Farmington, Conn. Died Aug. 4, 2000.

JESURUN, CARLOS ANTONIO, pediatrician, educator, neonatologist; b. San Antonio, Feb. 18, 1949; m. Nancy Nemeth; children: David, Cristina. BA, U. Mich., 1970; MD, Baylor U., 1973. Cert. med. mgmt. 2002. Resident in pediats. Wayne State U., Detroit, 1973-76; fellow in perinatal medicine Children's Hosp. Mich., Detroit, 1976-78; prof. Tex. Tech U. Health Scis. Ctr., El Paso, 1979—; chief med. staff Thomason Hosp., El Paso, 1988, 97. Rep. AMA Orgn. Med. Staff Sect., Chgo., 1994-2000. Dir. program com. March of Dimes, El Paso, 1997—2003; chmn. exec. subcom. Tex. Tech. U. Health Sci. Ctr., El Paso, 2002—03. Mem.: Tex. Perinatal Assn., Tex. Med. Assn. (perinatal health subcom. 2003). Avocations: walking, stamp collecting, dancing, travel, golf. Office: Tex Tech U 4800 Alberta Ave El Paso TX 79905-2709 E-mail: antonio.jesurun@ttuhsc.edu.

JESURUN, JOHN ALBERTO, playwright, director; s. Harold Mendez and Dolores Jesurun. BA, Phila. Coll. of Art, 1972; MA, Yale U., New Haven, Conn., 1974. Prof. Goethe U., Frankfurt, Germany, 1988, Justus-Liebig U., Giessen, Germany, 1998, Kyoto U. of Art and Design, Kyoto, 2002—03. Author: (plays) Deep Sleep (Obie Award, 1986), Chang in a Void Moon (Bessie Award, 1987), Snow, Shatterhand Massacree, Everything That Rises Must Converge, Philoktetes; author: (director) White Water, (screenplays) Black Maria, (plays) Faust/How I Rose. Fellow MacArthur Fellowship, MarArthur Found., 1996-2001, Rockefeller Playwright's Fellowship, Rockefeller Found., 1987, Guggenheim Fellowship, Guggenheim Found., 1990, NEA Playwright's Fellowship, NEA, 1988, NEA Visual Artist's Fellowship, 1988, Found. for Contemporary Performance Arts Fellowship, Found. for Contemporary Performance Arts, 1993, NY Found. for the Arts Performance Arts Fellowship, NY Found. for the Arts, 1988. Mem.: Dramatists' Guild.

JETER, DEREK SANDERSON, professional baseball player; b. Pequannock, N.J., June 26, 1974; Baseball player N.Y. Yankees, 1995—. Named Minor League Player of Yr., The Sporting News, 1994, Am. League Rookie of Yr., Baseball Writers Assn. of Am., 1996. Achievements include being a mem. of World Series Champions, 1996, 98, 99. Office: NY Yankees Yankee Stadium E 161st and River Ave Bronx NY 10451

JETER, HOWARD F. diplomat; b. Union, S.C., Mar. 6, 1947; m. Donice M. Jeter; 2 children. BA, Morehouse Coll.; MA, Columbia U., UCLA. Legis. intern Ga. Ho. Reps.; with Fgn. Svc.; with bur. oceans and internat. environ. and sci. affairs Dept. State, 1977-78; econ., comml. and consular officer Maputo, Mozambique, 1979-82; polit. officer Dar es Salaam, Tanzania, 1983-86; dep. dir. U.S. Liaison Office, Windhoek, Namibia, 1984; dep. chief of mission Maseru, Lesotho, 1987-88; charge d'affaires, 1989-90; dep. chief of mission Windhoek, 1990-93; amb. to Botswana Dept. State, 1993-96, spl. presdl. envoy to Liberia, 1997—99; amb. to Nigeria Lagos, 2001—. Recipient Superior Honor award, Sr. Performance award; Internat. fellow Columbia U., fellow Ford Found., Merrill Overseas Study-Travel fellow. Mem. Am. Fgn. Svc. Assn., Coun. Fgn. Rels., Phi Beta Kappa. Office: African Bur Dept Of State Washington DC 20520-0001 also: US Embassy 2 Eleke Crescent PO Box 554 Lagos Nigeria*

JETER, WAYBURN STEWART, retired microbiology educator, microbiologist; b. Cooper, Tex., Feb. 16, 1926; s. Joseph Plato and Beulah (Stewart) J.; m. Margaret Ann McDonald, May 30, 1947; children— Randall Mark, Monette Ann, Marcus Kent. BS, U. Okla., 1948, MS, 1949; PhD, U. Wis., 1950. Diplomate: Am. Bd. Microbiology. Mem. faculty U. Iowa, 1950-63, assoc. prof., 1958-63; prof. microbiology U. Ariz., Tucson, 1963-89, prof. microbiology emeritus, 1989—, prof. pharmacology and toxicology, 1983-91, prof. pharmacology and toxicology emeritus, 1991—, head dept. microbiology and med. tech., 1967-83, dir. lab. cellular immunology, 1976-91, dir. med. tech. program, 1976-79. Vis. prof. immunology and med. microbiology U. Fla., 1980; pres. Scientific Rels. Svcs., Inc., 1988—99. Contbr. articles profl. jours. Served with USNR, 1943-46. Fellow AAAS; mem. Am. Acad. Microbiology, Am. Assn. Immunologists, Ariz. Acad. Sci., Am. Soc. Microbiology (mem. council 1975-77), Soc. Exptl. Biology and Medicine, Sigma Xi. Democrat. Presbyterian. Home: 5140 N Via Sempreverde Tucson AZ 85750-5966 E-mail: wayjeter@aol.com.

JETLEY, KARUN, systems analyst, consultant; s. Baldev Krishan and Shobhna Jetley. BS, Houston Bapt. U., 1985—90; MBA, U. of Houston, 1990—92. Business Warehouse SAP/ Tex., 2000. Systems analyst effesoft, Houston, 1993—97; data arch. Reliant Energy, Houston, 1998—99; pres. effesoft, Houston, 2000—02; global data arch. BMC Software Inc., Houston, 2002—. Bd. mem. CMP Adv. Bd., Houston, 2002—. Mem.: Houston Advt. Fedn. (corr.). Achievements include first to creation of new product segment within software industry; effesoft Trademark; effesoft Suite - Copyright. Personal E-mail: knvrqut@aol.com.

JETT, BRENT W. astronaut, military officer; b. Pontiac, Mich., Oct. 5, 1958; m. Janet Leigh Lyon, 1992. BS in Aerospace Engring., U.S. Naval Acad., Annapolis, Md., 1981; MS in Aero. Engring., U.S. Naval Postgrad. Sch., Monerey, Calif., 1989. Commd. ensign USN, Annapolis, Md., 1981, advanced through grades to capt., 2002; naval aviator USN Fighter Squadrons 101 and 74, Naval Air Sta. Oceana, Va. Beach, 1983—86; student Naval Postgrad. Sch., Monterey, Calif., 1986—89; project test pilot USN Strike Aircraft Test Directorate, 1989—91; F-14B pilot USN USS Saratoga, 1991—92; astronaut USN Johnsoon Space Ctr., Houston, 1992—. Decorated Disting. Flying Cross USN, 3 space flight medals, Exceptional Svc. medal NASA. Mem.: Soc. Exptl. Test Pilots, U.S. Naval Acad. Alumni Assn., Assn. Space Explorers, Assn. Naval Aviation. Achievements include 3 space flights, 4000 flight hours in over 30 different aircraft and 450 carrier landings. Office: Asromaut Office NASA Johnson Space Ctr Houston TX 77058

JETT, DENNIS COLEMAN, foreign service officer; b. Waltham, Mass., June 26, 1945; s. Clifton H. and Helen (Driscoll) J.; children: Brian, Allison, Noa; m. Lynda Schuster, Dec. 31, 1989. BA, U. N.Mex., 1967, MA, 1969; PhD in Internat. Rels., U. Witwatersrand, 1998, postgrad. Political officer U.S. Embassy, Buenos Aires, Argentina; watch officer Operations Ctr. Dept. of State, Washington, 1975-76; economist Econ. Bureau Dept. of State, Washington, 1976-80; sci. attache U.S. Embassy, Tel Aviv, Israel, 1980-83, deputy chief of mission Lilongwe, Malawi, 1986-89, Monrovia, Liberia, 1989-91; exec. asst. to under sec. for polit. affairs Dept. of State, Washington, 1992-93; acting spl. asst. to the President Nat. Security Coun., Washington, 1993; amb. to Mozambique U.S. Embassy, Maputo, 1993-96, amb. to Peru Lima, 1996—. Lt. USNR, 1965-72. Recipient Disting. Honor award, 1991, Cobb award, 1999. Mem. Am. Fgn. Svc. Assn. (Christian A. Herter award 1995). Office: Am Embassy Lima Apo AA 34031

JETT, ERNEST CARROLL, b. Liberty, Tex., July 10, 1945; BA cum laude, Baylor U., 1967; MA, La. State U., 1969; JD, U. Tex., 1973. Bar: Tex. 1973, U.S. Dist. (so. dist.) Tex. 1979, U.S. Ct. Appeals (5th cir.) 1979, U.S. Supreme Ct. 1979, Mo. 1980. Mem. legal staff Cooper Industries, Inc., 1973-75, Tenneco, Inc., 1975-79; v.p., gen. counsel, sec. Leggett & Platt, Inc., Carthage, Mo., 1979—. Editor Tex. Internat. Law Jour. 1972-73. Mem. ABA, Am. Corp. Coun. Assn., Am. Soc. Corp. Secs., State Bar Tex., Mo. Bar Assn., Phi Alpha Theta, Alpha Chi, Phi Eta Sigma, Phi Delta Phi, Pi Gamma Mu. Office: Leggett & Platt Inc 1 Leggett Rd Carthage MO 64836-9649 E-mail: ernest.jett@leggett.com.

JETT, STEPHEN CLINTON, geography and textiles educator, researcher; b. Cleve., Oct. 12, 1938; s. Richard Scudder Jett and Miriam Ida (Horn) Greene; m. Mary Frances Manak, Aug. 7, 1971 (div. 1977); 1 child, Jennifer Frances; m. Lisa Sue Roberts, June 17, 1995. AB, Princeton U., 1960; postgrad., U. Ariz., 1962-63; PhD, Johns Hopkins U., 1964. Instr. geography Ohio State U., Columbus, 1963-64; asst. prof. geography U. Calif., Davis, 1964-72, assoc. prof., 1972-79, prof., 1979—2000, prof. textiles and clothing, 1996—2000, prof. emeritus geography and textiles and clothing, 2000—, chmn. geography, 1978-82, 87-89. Author: Navajo Wildlands, 1967 (1 of 50 Books of Yr., Am. Inst. Graphic Arts 1967, 1 of 20 Merit Award Books, Western Book Pubs. Assn. 1969), House of Three Turkeys, 1977, Navajo Architecture, 1981 (1 of Outstanding Acad. Books, Choice mag. ALA 1981), Navajo Placenames and Trails of the Canyon de Chelly System, Arizona, 2001, France, 2003; (monograph) Tourism in the Navajo Country, 1966; editor jour. Pre-Columbiana; contbr. numerous articles to profl. jours. and chpts. to books. Mem. Hist. and Landmarks Commn., Davis, 1969-73; vice chmn. Gen. Plan Noise Element Study Com., Davis, 1974-76, chmn. ad hoc citizens noise com., 1997-98; mem. exec. coun. Univ. Farms Unit Number 1 Neighborhood Assn., Davis, 1987-90. Fellow Am. Geog. Soc., Explorers Club; mem. AAAS, Assn. Am. Geographers (chair Am. Indian splty. group 1989-91), Soc. Am. Archaeology, Epigraphic Soc. (bd. dirs. 1996—), Inst. for Study of Am. Cultures (bd. dirs. 1996—), Found. Rsch. Ancient Maritime Explorations (bd. dirs., treas. 2002-). Avocations: travel, photography, textiles and other ethnographic arts, french language and culture. E-mail: scjett@hotmail.com.

JETTER, ARTHUR CARL, JR., insurance company executive; b. Omaha, Oct. 9, 1947; s. Arthur Carl and Virginia Ann (Turner) J.; m. Jennifer Ann Jochim, Mar. 30, 1974; children: Arthur Carl III, Sarah Ann. BBA, Dana Coll., 1974. Registered health underwriter; CFP, CLU; registered employee benefits cons.; FLMI. Sales rep. life ins. Guarantee Mut., Omaha, 1974-81; pres. Art Jetter & Co., Omaha, 1981—, Employers Mut. Acceptance Co., Omaha, 1981—. Capt., helicopter pilot inf. U.S. Army, 1968-72, Vietnam. Fellow Life Mgmt. Inst.; mem. CLU (cert., edn. chmn. Omaha chpt. 1984-91), Nat. Assn. Ind. Life Brokerage Agencies (chmn. 2000), Nat. Assn. Health Underwriters (pres. 1991-92, Gordon Meml. award 1995, Health Ins. Industry person of yr. 1995), Mass Mktg. Ins. Inst. (Person of Yr. award 1993). Republican. Lutheran. Home: 13624 Parker Cir Omaha NE 68154-3829 Office: Art Jetter and Co 11305 Chicago Cir Omaha NE 68154-2636 E-mail: art@jetter.com.

JETTER, FRANCES S. illustrator, educator, artist; b. Bklyn., N.Y., Dec. 20, 1951; d. Joseph L. and Rose Jetter; m. Irving Grunbaum, July 22, 1973. BFA, Parsons Sch. of Design, 1972. Contbg illustrator N.Y. Times, N.Y.C., 1976—; book jacket designer and illustrator Franklin Watts, N.Y.C., 1976—89; faculty mem. Sch. for Visual Arts, N.Y.C., 1979—; contbg illustrator Nation Mag., N.Y.C., 1979—, Time Mag., N.Y.C., 1980—, Wash. Post, Washington, 1981—. Illustrators' adv. panel Norman Rockwell Mus., Stockbridge, Mass., 2003—. One-woman shows include Broadway Windows, NYU, exhibitions include Davidson Galleries, Seattle, illustrated limited edit., The Fixer by Bernard Malamud, Taras Bulba and Other Tales (Nikolai Gogol); author: (book chpt.) The Education of an Illustrator; contbr. articles to mags.; Represented in permanent collections Detroit Inst. Arts, Grinell Coll., Fogg Art Mus., NY, NY Pub. Libr. Print Collection. Recipient Cert. of Merit, Soc. of Illustrators, 1983—88, Cert. of Design Excellence, Print Design Ann., 1986—89, Award of Excellence, Soc. of Newspaper Designers, 1981, Comm. Arts Illustration Ann., 1984, Cert. of Merit, Soc. of Illustrators, 1990, 1993, 1994, 2001, 2002, Cert. of Design Excellence, Print Design Ann., 1991, 1993, 1999, 2000, 2001, Award of Excellence, Soc. of Newspaper Designers, 1987—88, Comm. Arts Illustration Ann., 1985, 1992, 1995, 1997, 2000; NY Found. for the Arts Fellowship, 2003. Avocations: reading, walking, visiting museums, attending movies. Home: 390 West End Ave New York NY 10024 Office: 390 West End Ave New York NY 10024 Home Fax: 212-877-8528; Office Fax: 212-877-8528. Personal E-mail: fjetter@earthlink.net. E-mail: fjetter@earthlink.net.

JETTKE, HARRY JEROME, retired government official; b. Detroit, Jan. 2, 1925; s. Harry H. and Eugenia M. (Dziatkiewicz) J.; m. Josefina Suarez-Garcia, Oct. 22, 1948; 1 child, Joan Lillian Clark. BA, Wayne State U., 1961; grad., Civilian Police Acad., Westlake, Ohio, 1999. Cert. drug specialist FDA. Owner, operator Farmacia Virreyes/Farmacias Regina, Toluca, Mexico, 1948-55; intern pharmacist Cunningham Drug Stores, Detroit, 1955-63; drug specialist, product safety specialist FDA, Detroit, 1963-73; acting dir. for Cleve., U.S Consumer Pruduct Safety Commn., 1973-75, compliance officer, 1975-78, supr. investigations, 1978-82, regional compliance officer, 1982-83, sr. resident, 1983-90; ret., 1990. Served with Fin. Dept., U.S. Army, 1942-43. Mem. Am. Soc. for Quality Control (sr.; chmn. Cleve. sect. 1977-78, cert. quality technician, cert quality engr.), Asociacion Nacional Mexicana de Estadistica y Control de Calidad, Ohio Gun Collectors Assn., Cleve. Fed. Exec. Bd. (policy com.), Civilian Police Acad. Westlake Police Dept. Roman Catholic. Home: 25715 Yeoman Dr Cleveland OH 44145-4745

JETTON, GIRARD REUEL, JR., lawyer, retired oil company executive; b. Washington, Feb. 19, 1924; s. Girard Reuel and Hallie (Grimes) J.; m. Mera Riddell, Sept. 4, 1948 (dec. Dec. 1997); children: Mera Elizabeth, Robert Girard, James Thomas. BS in Engring., George Washington U., 1945, BA, 1947; JD, Harvard U., 1950. Bar: D.C. 1951, Md. 1959, Ohio 1960. Elec. engr. in rsch., 1944-45; patent atty., 1950-51; atty. IRS, Washington, 1951-54; trial atty. Dept. Justice, Washington, 1954-55; atty. then ptnr. McClure & McClure, Washington, 1955-60; with Marathon Oil Co., Findlay, Ohio, 1960-85, asst. to chmn. bd., 1969-73, corp. sec., 1973-85; pvt. practice Findlay, 1985—. With USNR, 1945-46. Mem. Bar Assn. D.C., Findlay/Hancock County Bar Assn., Met. Club (Washington). Home and Office: 170 Orchard Ln Findlay OH 45840-1130

JETZER, ALEXANDRE F. pharmaceutical executive; CEO Sandoz. Office: Sandoz Lichtstrasse 35 4002 Basel Switzerland

JEUB, MICHAEL LEONARD, financial consultant; b. Mpls., Mar. 2, 1943; s. Leonard M. and Florence J.; m. Alice Ann Linden (div. 1980); children: Christopher Michael, Annette Michelle; m. Julia Jean Stephenson, Feb. 4, 1983; children: Michael Leonard Jr., Robert. BS in Acctg., Calif. State Poly. U., 1966. CPA, Tex., Calif. Staff acct. Ernst & Whinney, L.A., 1966-70; CFO Internat. Clin. Lab., Inc., Nashville, 1970-85, pres. east, 1985-88; pres. August Enterprises, 1988-91; pres., COO, CFO MICA, San Diego, 1991-93; exec. v.p., CFO, treas. Nat. Health Labs., Inc., 1993-94; sr. v.p., CFO Jenny Craig Internat., 1994-2000; fin. cons. La Jolla, Calif., 2000—01; ptnr. Tatum CFO, 2000—; CFO, The Immune Response Loop, San Diego, 2002—. Office: 3878 Ruffin Rd Ste B La Jolla CA 92123 E-mail: MikeJeub@aol.com.

JEUNET, JEAN-PIERRE, film director; b. Roanne, Loire, France, Sept. 3, 1955; Dir., writer: Delicatessen, 1991 (Tokyo Gold award Tokyo Internat. Film Festival 1991, César awards best writing, best direction 1991, Catalonian Internat. Film Festival best dir. award and prize of Screenwriter's Critic and Writer's Catalan Assn. 1991; nominated BAFTA Film award Brit. Acad. Awards for Best Film not in the English Lang., 1991), La Cité des enfants perdus, 1995 (nominated Golden Palm, Cannes Film Festival, 1995, nominated Ind. Spirit award for Best Fgn. Film, 1996), Amelie, 2001 (ShoWest award, 2002, BAFTA best screenplay award, 2002); dir. L'Évasion, 1978, Le Manège, 1980 (César award best short animation film 1981), Le Bunker de la dernière rafale, 1981, Pas de repos pour Billy Brakko, 1984, Foutaises, 1989 (Golden Palm, Cannes Film Festival, best short film 1989), Alien: Resurrection, 1997 (nominated Saturn award Acad. Sci. Fiction, Horror and Fantasy Films, 1997), Ulysse 31, 1999. Office: c/o Artmedia 20, Avenue Rapp 75 007 Paris France

JEUNG, ALBERT, secondary school educator; b. N.Y.C. MusM, Calif. State U., Long Beach. Cert. K-12 tchr. Calif. Orch., health, phys. edn. tchr. Aliso Niguel H.S., Aliso Viejo, Calif., 1993—; music instr. Calif. State U., Long Beach, 1997—99; orch. dir. Santa Ana (Calif.) Coll., 2000—01, La Primavera Orch., Calif., 2000—. Dir. honor orch. Kern County H.S., Bakersfield, Calif., 2002; dir. honor orch Central Coast Mid. Sch., 2001, Yorba Linda/Placentia Unified Sch. Dist., Calif.; clinician, presenter in field. Recipient Toyota Internat. Tchr. Program award, Toyota Motor Sales, USA, 2000, Summer Tchr. fellowship, Northwestern U., Chgo., 1996. Mem.: Calif. Music Educators Assn. (state conf. presenter 2002), So. Calif. Sch. Band and Orch. Assn. (v.p. string edn. 2002, meritorious svc. award). Office: Aliso Niguel HS 28000 Terrace View Drive Aliso Viejo CA 92656

JEVTIC, MILOMIR, artist, sculptor; b. Valjevo, Yugoslavia; s. Sreten Jevtic and Milena Mitrovic; m. Ana Sonc, July 7, 1977; children: Damjan, Matija. MA in Art, U. Lubljana, Yugoslavia, 1973. Engr. artist Wausau (Wis.) Tile, 1995-96, Strescon Industries, Balt., 1997-98. Prin. works include sculpture Woodely Garden Pk., monument Reverend Matej Nemadovic, sculpture U. Student Housing Devel. Achievements include patent in method of casting materials using flexible resilient mold. Home: 1 Knoll Mist Ln Gaithersburg MD 20879 E-mail: jevticart@cs.com.

JEW, HENRY, pharmacist; b. Hong Kong, June 10, 1950; BS in Pharmacy, U. Ga., 1974. Preceptor to externship program So. Sch. of Pharmacy, U. Ga., 1974-78; researcher Brompton's Mixture, 1977-78; pharmacist VA Med Ctr, Decatur, Ga., 1984—89, VNS Inc., Atlanta, 1992—99, Kaiser Permanente, 2000—02.

JEWEL, (JEWEL KILCHER), folk singer, songwriter; b. Homer, Alaska, May 23, 1974; Past student, Interlochen Musical Acad., Mich. Albums include Pieces of You, 1995, Spirit, 1998, Joy: A Holiday Collection, 1999, This Way, 2001, 0304, 2003; (single) Who Will Save Your Soul, 1995, You Were Meant for Me, 1996; vocalist Craft, 1996, Crossroads, 1996, Wizard of Oz in Concert: Dreams Come True, 1995, Farm Aid, 1996 (TV), The Ghosts of Christmas Eve, 1999; Films include: Ride With the Devil, 1999; TV guest appearances include Holmes, 1999, Speakeasy, 1999. Author: A Night Without Armor, 1998, Chasing Down the Dawn, 2000. Office: care Atlantic Records 75 Rockefeller Plz New York NY 10019-6908*

JEWELEWICZ, RAPHAEL, obstetrician, gynecologist, educator; b. Nowogrodek, Poland, Dec. 26, 1932; came to U.S., 1963; s. Chaim and Chaia (Tawricki) J.; m. Ronnie Oved, July 3, 1955; children: Rachel, Dov, Daniel, Dory. MD, Hebrew U., Jerusalem, 1961. Cert. Am. Bd. Ob-gyn. 1971, 89, reproductive endocrinology, 1974. Intern Hadassah Hebrew U. Hosp., Jerusalem; resident NYU Med. Ctr., Bellevue Hosp., N.Y.C.; assoc. prof. ob-gyn. Columbia U., N.Y.C., 1975-92; prof. ob-gyn. SUNY, 1992—; chair. dept. ob-gyn. Memonides Medical Ctr., Bklyn. Bd. dirs. divsn. reproductive endocrinology Columbia U. Coll. Physicians and Surgeons, N.Y.C.; chmn. ob-gyn. Maimonides Med. Ctr.; prof. ob=gyn. SUNY, Bklyn. Author: Clinical Aspects of Cervical Incompetence, 1989, The Menstrual Cycle: Physiology, Reproductive Disorders and Infertility, 1993; editor ob-gyn. investigation: mem. editorial bd. several sci. jours.; contbr. over 100 articles to profl. jours. Mem. Am. Coll. Ob-gyn., Am. Coll. Surgeons, Am. Fertility Soc., Am. Gynecol. & Obstet. Soc.,

N.Y. Obstet. Soc., N.Y. Gynecol. Soc. (pres. 1994-95), Soc. for Gynecol. Jewish. Avocations: opera, ballet, theater, travel. Home: Church St Alpine NJ 07620 Office: Memonides Med Ctr Dept Ob-gyn 4802 10th Ave Brooklyn NY 11219-2844

JEWELL, FRANKLIN P. lawyer; b. Frankfort, Ky., Sept. 26, 1952; s. Wilbert Franklin and Lucille (Perry) J.; m. Rebecca Ann Wright, June 22, 1974; children: Brandon Neil, Amanda Wright. B.A., U. Ky., 1974; J.D., U. Louisville, 1977. Bar: Ky. 1977, U.S. Dist. Ct. (we. dist.) Ky. 1979, U.S. Dist. Ct. (ea.dist.) Ky. 1989. Interviewer, clk. Jefferson Dist. Pub. Defender, Louisville, 1975-77, staff atty., 1977-79, asst. chief juvenile div., 1979-82, chief trial atty. adult div., 1982-88; assoc. Popkin, Stern & Meyer, 1989—; speaker ednl. instns. and seminars. Mem. Kenwood Elem. PTA, Louisville, 1983-84, Parkland Elem. PTA, 1984-85, Klondike Elem. PTA, 1987-89; vice chmn. bd. Shawnee Christian Ch. Recipient awards for advocacy in felony cases, juvenile cases, capital trials, Jefferson Dist. Pub. Defender, 1977-88. Mem. Ky. Bar Assn. (continuing legal edn. award 1981), Louisville Bar Assn. (chmn. subcom. cir. ct. criminal def.), Phi Alpha Delta. Democrat. Office: 200 S 5th St Louisville KY 40202-3215

JEWELL, GEORGE BENSON, lawyer, educator, minister; b. Evanston, Ill., Mar. 26, 1944; s. Benson Murray and Ellen Louise (Mahle) J.; m. Pamela Elaine Peterson, Aug. 12, 1967; children: Jeffrey Benson, Brian Edward. BA, Beloit (Wis.) Coll., 1966; MDiv, Gordon-Conwell Theol. Sem., 1978; JD, Washington U., St. Louis, 1971. Bar: Ill. 1971, Mo. 1972, Mass. 1990, U.S. Dist. Ct. (ea. dist.) Mo. 1973, U.S. Dist. Ct. Mass. 1991, Ind. 1998. Trust adminstr. Ill. Nat. Bank, Springfield, 1971; corp. atty. Ralston Purina Co., St. Louis, 1971-75; assoc. pastor Westminster Presbyn. Ch., Bluefield, W.Va., 1978-81, sr. pastor Cape Girardeau, Mo., 1981-86, Evang. Free Ch., Cape Girardeau, 1986-88; pvt. practice Cape Girardeau, 1988-89; counsel, dir. gift planning, adj. assoc. prof. bus. law Gordon Coll., Wenham, Mass., 1989-97; dir. legal support svcs. Renaissance Inc., Carmel, Ind., 1997-98, v.p. legal support svcs., v.p. client svcs., 1998-99, v.p., sr. counsel, 1999—2002; v.p. Wachovia Trust Co., 2003—. Instr. in bus. law S.E. Mo. State U., Cape Girardeau, 1986; cons. Stone, McGhee, Feuchtenberger & Barringer, Bluefield, 1980-81; mng. editor Washington U. Law Quar. Author: Charitable Trusts; contbr. chpts. to Life Insurance Answer Book. Deacon Ctrl. Presbyn. Ch., St. Louis, 1974-75; scoutmaster Appalachian coun. Boy Scouts Am., Bluefield, 1979; bd. advisors Sta. KUGT, Cape Girardeau, 1988, Boston Rescue Mission, 1994-97; baccalaureate spkr. Ctrl. H.S., Cape Girardeau, 1988; workshop presenter Congress '93 and Congress '94, Boston; bd. dirs. Young Life of Cape Girardeau. Mem. ABA, Nat. Assn. Coll. and Univ. Attys. (ad hoc com. on income devel. 1990-91, ad hoc com. svcs. small colls. 1991-93, com. profl. devel., 1993-97), Nat. Assn. Estate Planners and Couns., Ind. State Bar Assn. (mem. probate rev. com. 1999-2002), Mass. Soc. Sons Am. Revolution, Boston Bar Assn. (coll. and univ. com., estate planning com.), Planned Giving Group of New Eng., Christian Fin. Advisors Network (founder), Mo. Bar Assn. (franchise tax subcom. corp. law and bus. orgn. coms.), Evang. Free Ch. Ministerial Assn., Sigma Alpha Epsilon. Avocations: swimming, tennis, sailing. Office: Wachovia Trust Co 3 Beaver Valley Rd Wilmington DE 19803 E-mail: george.jewell@wachovia.com.

JEWELL, GEORGE HIRAM, lawyer; b. Fort Worth, Jan. 9, 1922; s. George Hiram and Vera (Lee) J.; m. Betty Jefferis, July 21, 1944 (dec. Feb. 2000), children: Susan Jewell Cannon, Robert V., Nancy Jewell Wommack; m. Nancy Hart Glanville, May 19, 2001. BA, U. Tex., 1942, LLB, 1950. Bar: Tex. 1950. With Baker & Botts, LLP, Houston, 1950—; sr. ptnr. Baker & Botts, Houston, 1960-90, counsel, 1990—. Trustee Tex. Children's Hosp., Houston, 1977—, pres., 1982-83, chmn., 1984-86; bd. dirs. Schlumberger Found., N.Y.C., 1982-90. Lt. USNR, 1943-46, 50-53. Fellow Am. Coll. Tax Counsel, Am. Bar Foun.; mem. ABA, Houston Country Club, Coronado Club (pres. 1976-77), Old Baldy Club (chmn. 1993-98), Eldorado Country Club (pres. 1995-96), Blind Brook Club, Order of Coif, Phi Beta Kappa, Phi Delta Phi. Office: Baker Botts LLP 1 Shell Plz Houston TX 77002 Home: 1000 Uptown Park Blvd Houston TX 77056

JEWELL, PATRICK FRANK, retired surgeon; b. Detroit, Mar. 26, 1934; MD, U. Mich., 1958. Diplomate Am. Bd. Surgery. Intern Munson Hosp., Traverse City, Mich., 1958-59; resident in Surgery Northwestern U. Med. Ctr., Chgo., 1959-63; resident in Pediatric Surgery Children's Hosp., Detroit, 1964-65; ret. Fellow ACS, Am. Acad. Pediatrics; mem. Am. Pediatric Surg. Assn. E-mail: pfjewell@umich.edu.

JEWELL, SUSAN DIANE, wildlife biologist, writer; b. N.Y.C., Feb. 27, 1955; d. Howard Allen and Marian Anita Jewell. BS, U. Vt., 1977; MS, U. Conn., 1982. Cert. wildlife biologist, lic. pilot, cert. scuba diving. Biol. technician Savannah River Ecology Lab., Aiken, SC, 1984—86; rsch. biologist Nat. Audubon Soc., Tavernier, Fla., 1986—90; biologist Nat. Park Svc., Homestead, Fla., 1990—92; sr. biologist U.S. Fish and Wildlife Svc., Boynton Beach, Fla., 1992—98, biologist (for endangered species) Arlington, Va., 1998—2002. Assoc. editor Endangered Species Bull. U.S. Fish and Wildlife Svc., Arlington, 2001—, sci. advisor Birdscapes mag., 2001—, chair of fed./state com. for Everglades water quality, Boynton Beach, 1996—98. Author: (book) Exploring Wild South Florida, 1993, Exploring Wild Central Florida, 1995. Recipient hon. mention, Writer's Digest Writing Contest, 2001. Mem.: Soc. Environ. Journalists, Outdoor Writers Assn. Am. Achievements include discovery of insect species in Georgia not previously known to exist in that state. Office: US Fish and Wildlife Svc MS 420 4401 North Fairfax Dr Arlington VA 22203

JEWETT, GEORGE FREDERICK, JR., forest products company executive; b. Spokane, Wash., Apr. 10, 1927; s. George Frederick and Mary Pelton (Cooper) J.; m. Lucille Winifred McIntyre, July 11, 1953; children: Mary Elizabeth, George Frederick III. BA, Dartmouth Coll., 1950; MBA, Harvard U., 1952. Asst. sec., asst. treas. Potlatch Corp., 1955-62, v.p. adminstrn., 1962-68, corp. v.p. adminstrn., 1968-71, sr. v.p., 1972-77, vice chmn. bd. adminstrn., 1977-78, vice chmn., 1979-99, retired, 1999. Trustee Calif. Pacific Med. Found. Mem.: NY Yacht Club, Pacific Union Club, Bohemian Club, St. Francis Yacht Club. Home: 2990 Broadway St San Francisco CA 94115-1062 Office: 1 Maritime Plz Ste 1640 San Francisco CA 94111-3506

JEWETT, JOHN RHODES, real estate executive; b. Indpls., Nov. 21, 1922; s. Chester Aten and Grace (Rhodes) J.; m. Marybelle Bramhall, June 12, 1946; children: John R., Jane B. BA, DePauw U., 1944. Econ. research analyst Eli Lilly & Co., Indpls., 1946-48; with Pitman-Moore Co., Indpls., 1948-65, v.p., asst. to pres., 1959-65; with F.C. Tucker Co., Inc., Indpls., 1965—, v.p., 1978-98, Colliers Turley Martin Tucker, Indpls., 1998—. Pres. Market Sq. Arena, 1974-79, Ind. Pacers (profl. basketball team), 1977-79 Served with AUS, 1943-46. Mem. Met. Indpls. Bd. Realtors, Ind. Assn. Realtors, Nat. Assn. Realtors. Clubs: Meridian Hills Country, Kiwanis. Home: 8504 Bent Tree Ct Indianapolis IN 46260-2348 Office: 2500 One American Sq Indianapolis IN 46282

JEYAKUMAR, RAMANUJAM, physicist; b. Kovilpatti, India, Sept. 24, 1966; s. Venkataswamy Ramanujam and Ramanujam Sivagamy; m. Jeyakumar Ramaprabha, June 16, 1999. BSc in Physics, Madurai Kamaraj U., 1986, MSc in Physics, 1988; PhD in Physics, Nat. Phys. Lab., New Delhi, 1998. Tchr. G Venkataswamy Naidu Coll., Kovilpatti, India, 1989-90; rsch. fellow Ctrl. Electrochem. Rsch. Inst., Karaikudi, India, 1991-93; sr. rsch. fellow Nat. Phys. Lab., New Delhi, 1994-98, rsch. assoc., 1998-2000, Indira Gandhi Ctr. for Atomic Rsch., Kalpakkam, India, 2000; post doctoral fellow U. Waterloo, Canada, 2000—. Avocations: book reading, tv watching, playing chess, basketball. Office: U Waterloo Dept Elec Computer Engring Waterloo ON Canada N2L 3G1 Home: 304-270 Eiwo Ct Waterloo ON Canada N2K 3M6 E-mail: jkrnaidu@yahoo.com., rjayakum@ece.uwaterloo.ca

JEYAMITRA, DEVARAJ, physician; b. Mar. 26, 1944; MBBS, Madurai (India) Med. Coll., 1967. Dir. med. svc. Mid-Hudson Forensic Psychiat. Ctr., New Hampton, N.Y. Address: 42 Ryerson Rd New Hampton NY 10958-3411 E-mail: mhmddxj@gw.omh.state.ny.us.

JEYDEL, RICHARD K. lawyer; b. Livingston, N.J., Jan. 10, 1950; m. Ellen C. Ebert, Aug. 30, 1981; children: Patricia, Peter. AB, Sarah Lawrence Coll., 1972; JD, Harvard U., 1975. Bar: N.J. 1975, N.Y. 1983, U.S. Ct. Appeals (3d and 5th cirs.) 1983. Assoc. McCarter & English, Newark, 1976-79; corp. counsel Kanematsu-Gosho (USA), Inc., N.Y.C., 1979-85, v.p., gen. counsel, 1985-91; sr. v.p., sec., gen. counsel Kanematsu USA Inc., N.Y.C., 1991—. Past mem. ethics com. Supreme Ct. Dist. XIII; mem. panel of arbitrators and mediators, large complex case program arbitrator and pres. panel mediator Am. Arbitration Assn. Capt. U.S. Army, 1975-76. Mem. ABA, Am. Corp. Counsel Assn. (bd. dirs. 1996-2002), N.J. Bar Assn., N.J. Corp. Counsel Assn. (bd. dirs. 1986-90, 93—, past pres.), Am. Arbitration Assn. (panel arbitrators and mediators, bd. dirs. 1996—). Office: Kanematsu USA Inc 114 W 47th St Fl 23 New York NY 10036-1510 E-mail: rjeydel@kanematsuusa.com.

JEYNES, MARY KAY, college dean; b. Miami, Fla., Oct. 31, 1941; d. Nasrallah and Martha (Jabaly) Demetry; m. Paul Jeynes, Sept. 30, 1978.. BS, Fla. State U., 1963. Program dir. Orange County YMCA, Orlando, Fla., 1964-69, Ea. Queens YMCA, Belrose, N.Y., 1970-73, regional coord. N.Y. State Park and Recreation Commn., N.Y.C., 1974-77; dir. health, fitness and recreation YWCA of N.Y.C., 1978-79; dean continuing edn. and adult programs Marymount Manhattan Coll., N.Y.C., 1980—. Mem.: East Manhattan (N.Y.) C. of C. (pres. 1996—97, chmn. bd. dirs. 1998—2002). Office: Marymount Manhattan Coll 221 E 71st St New York NY 10021-4532

JEZIERSKI, JOHN VINCENT, historian, educator; b. Cleve., Apr. 5, 1943; s. John Anthony Jezierski, Mary Margaret Jezierski; m. Diane Joan Gross; children: Nathan Andrew, Caroline Elizabeth. AB Classics, John Carroll U., 1965; MA, Indiana U., 1967, PhD, 1971. Prof. history Saginaw Valley State U., University Center, Mich., 1971—. Vis. prof. Am. cultures Sikoku U., Tokushima, Japan, 1983—84. Author: Enterprising Images: The Goodridge Brothers, African American Photographers, 1847-1922, 2000 (Hist. Soc. Michigan, award of Merit in Pub., 2000), A Picture Perfect Family, The Goodridge Brothers, African American Photographers, 2000. Named Disting. Faculty, Mich. Assn. Governing Bds., 1983; recipient Franc A. Landee award for Excellence in Teaching, Saginaw Valley State U., 1981, Earl L. Warrick award Excellence in Rsch., 1999—2000, The Stuart D. and Vernice M. Gross award for lit., 2000—01, Tchg. fellow, Govt. Can., 1983, Summer Stipend, NEH, 1985; fellow, Govt. Can., 1986, Fletcher Jones fellow, The Huntington Libr., 1999, Colo. Endowment for the Humanities, 2003; scholar, Saginaw Valley State U. Faculty Assn., 1988. Office: Saginaw Valley State U 307 Brown Hall University Center MI 48710 Personal E-mail: jvjez@svsu.edu. Business E-Mail: jvjez@svsu.edu.

JEZL, BARBARA ANN, retired chemist, automation consultant; b. Pitts., June 7, 1947; d. James L. and Elizabeth (Bannister) J. BS in Chemistry, U. Del., 1969, PhD in Organic Chemistry, 1974. Jr. chemist Am. Cyanamid, Pearl River, N.Y., 1969-70; NSF postdoctoral assoc. U. Cin., 1974-76; inst. application specialist E.I. DuPont de Nemours & Co., Wilmington, Del., 1976-79, mem. computing staff, 1979-84, staff specialist, 1985-93, sr. rsch. chemist scientific computing divsn., 1993-99; ret., 1999. Author: Science, 1990; contbr. articles to profl. jours. Bd. dirs. Unitarian-Universalist Fellowship of Newark, 1981-85, pres., chmn. bd., 1986-87, 2002-, rep. Delaware Valley Area Coun., Phila., 1983-85, v.p. Fellowship of Newark, 1984-85. Mem. AAAS, IEEE Computer Soc., Am. Chem. Soc., Assn. for Computing Machinery, Macintosh Sci. and Tech. Assn. (bd. dirs., co-chmn. tech. adv. com. 1990-99, conf. co-chair eSEAM 97, Apple customer adv. bd. 1997—). Avocations: equestrian, agrarian, aviation. Home: 5448 W Pinehurst Dr Wilmington DE 19808-2619

JEZUIT, LESLIE JAMES, manufacturing company executive; b. Chgo., Nov. 4, 1945; s. Eugene and Tillie (Fleszewski) J.; m. Janet Diane Bushlus, Oct. 12, 1968; children— Douglas Blake, Kevin Lane BS in Mech. and Aerospace Engring., Ill. Inst. Tech., 1969, MBA, 1974. Mgr. engring. graphic systems group Rockwell Internat., Chgo., 1968-74, dir. comml. systems Cicero, Ill., 1974-75; v.p. mktg. and sales Mead Digital Systems, Dayton, Ohio, 1975-80; v.p. mktg. and sales Signal div. Fed. Signal Corp., University Park, Ill., 1980-81, pres. Signal div., 1981-85, v.p. corp. devel. Oak Brook, Ill., 1985-86; div. mgr. power distbn. div. Eaton Corp., Milw., 1986-87, gen. mgr. indsl. control and power distbn. div., 1987-88, v.p., 1988-91; pres., chief oper. officer Robertshaw Controls Co., Richmond, Va., 1991-95; pres., CEO, chmn. bd dirs. Quixote Inc., Chgo., 1995—; chmn. Transp. Mgmt. Techs., LLC, Chgo., 1998-2001, Quixote Corp., 2001. Instr. Keller Sch. Mgmt., Chgo., 1982-83 Patentee in field Active United Way, Chgo., 1983-85; mem. Chgo. Crime Commn.; bd. dirs. Better Bus. Bur. of Milw., 1986, United Performing Arts Found of Milw., 1986, Greater Milw. Com., 1991-92. Mem. Gas Appliance Mfrs. Assn. (bd. dirs. 1994-96), Will County Local Devel. Co. (v.p. 1984-85, Bus. Man of Yr. award 1985), South Suburban C. of C., Monee C. of C., Am. Highway Users Assn. (bd.dirs. 2001—). Clubs: Metropolitan (Chgo.). Republican. Avocations: boating, fishing, cross country skiing, photography. Home: 26576 Countryside Lake Dr Mundelein IL 60060-3342 Office: Quixote Inc 1 E Wacker Dr Chicago IL 60601-1802 E-mail: quixpres@msn.com.

JHABVALA, RUTH PRAWER, writer; b. Cologne, Germany, May 7, 1927; lived in India, 1951-75; came to U.S., 1975; d. Marcus and Eleonora (Cohn) Prawer; m. Cyrus S. H. Jhabvala, 1951; 3 children. MA, London U., 1951, DLitt (hon.), 1986, LHD (hon.), 1995, D Arts (hon.), 1996. Author: (novels) To Whom She Will, 1955, The Nature of Passion, 1956, Esmond in India, 1957, The Householder, 1960, Get Ready for Battle, 1962, A Backward Place, 1965, A New Dominion, 1972, Heat and Dust, 1975 (Booker award for fiction Nat. Book League 1975), In Search of Love and Beauty, 1983, Three Continents, 1987, Poet and Dancer, 1993, Shards of Memory, 1995; (short story collections) Like Birds, Like Fishes and Other Stories, 1964, A Stronger Climate: Nine Stories, 1968, An Experience of India, 1971, How I Became a Holy Mother and Other Stories, 1976, Out of India: Selected Stories, 1986, East Into Upper East, 1998; (film scripts) The Householder, 1963 (with James Ivory), Shakespeare Wallah, 1965 (with Ivory), The Guru, 1968, Bombay Talkie, 1970, Autobiography of a Princess, 1975, Roseland, 1977, Hullabaloo over Georgie and Bonnie's Pictures, 1978, The Europeans, 1979, Jane Austen in Manhattan, 1980, Quartet, 1981, Heat and Dust, 1983, The Bostonians, 1984, A Room With a View, 1986 (Writers Guild of Am. award for best adapted screeplay 1986, Acad. award for best adapted screenplay 1986), (with John Schlesinger) Madame Sousatzka, 1988, Mr. and Mrs. Bridge, 1990, Howards End, 1992 (Acad. award for best adapted screenplay 1992), Remains of the Day, 1993 (Acad. award nomination for best adapted screenplay 1993), Jefferson in Paris, 1995, Surviving Picasso, 1996, (with James Ivory) A Soldier's Daughter Never Cries, 1998, The Golden Bowl, 2000. Decorated comdr. Brit. Empire, Guggenheim fellow, 1976; Neil Gunn. Internat. fellow, 1979; MacArthur Found. fellow, 1984-89. Home: 400 E 52d St New York NY 10022-6404

JHIN, MICHAEL KONTIEN, health care executive; b. Hong Kong, Jan. 26, 1950; came to U.S., 1958; s. Paul Y and Monica P. Jhin. BSME, Rensselaer Poly. Inst., 1971; MBA, Boston U., 1974. Adminstrv. asst. St. Vincent Hosp., Worcester, Mass., 1974-76; asst. dir. Thomas Jefferson U. Hosp., Phila., 1976-79, assoc. dir., 1979-84; exec. dir., CEO, Temple U. Hosp., Phila., 1984-88; exec. v.p. Long Beach (Calif.) Meml. Health Sys., 1988-90; pres., CEO, St. Luke's Episcopal Hosp., Houston, 1990-2000; pres., CEO St. Luke's Episcopal Hosp. Health Sys., Houston, 1995—. Bd. dirs. Joint Commn. on Accreditation Healthcare Orgns. Bd. dirs. Greater Houston Partnership, 1999—, Alley Theatre, 1999-, Houston World Affairs Coun., 1998—, Jr. Achievement 1992-2000, Houston Forum, 1996—, Tex. Hosp. Assn., 1993-96, Tex. Heart Inst., 1998—, United Way Tex. Gulf Coast, 1999—, exec. com.; mem. Houston Hosp. Coun., 1991-96, chmn. bd., 1994-95. Fellow Am. Coll. Healthcare Execs., Rensselaer Alumni Assn. (pres. 1996-97, bd. dirs. 1991-98), Am. Hosp. Assn. (regional policy bd. 1992-95); mem. World Pres.'s Orgn. Office: St Luke's Episcopal Health Sys 6720 Bertner St Houston TX 77030-2604

JHINGRAN, ANUJA, oncologist, educator; b. India, Nov. 15, 1962; arrived in U.S., 1980; BA, Smith Coll., 1984; MD, Tex. Tech. U., 1988. Intern Baylor Coll. Medicine, Houston, resident in radiation oncology, 1993; radiation oncologist John Sealy Hosp., Galveston, Tex., 1993-95, Rosewood Med. Ctr., Houston, 1995-96, Columbia Spring Br. Hosp., Houston, 1995-96, Brazosport Hosp., Lake Jackson, Tex., 1995—, Columbia West Houston Hosp., 1996. Asst. prof., clin. dir. U. Tex. Med. Br., Galveston, 1993-95; asst. prof. U. Tex. MD Anderson Cancer Ctr., Houston, 1996—. Contbr. articles to profl. jours. Mem. AMA, Am. Radiol. Soc., Am. Assn. Women Radiologists, Am. Radium Soc., Am. Soc. Therapeutic Radiation Oncology, Tex. Med. Assn., Tex. Radiol. Soc. Office: UT MD Anderson Cancer Ctr Box 97 1515 Holcombe Blvd Houston TX 77030

JHUNJHUNWALA, JAGADISH S. retired urologist; b. Jan. 1, 1940; MD, Govt. Med. Coll., Nagpur, India, 1963; MS in gen. surgery, Grant Med. Coll., Bombay, India, 1967. Prof. urology Med. Coll. Ohio, Toledo, 1991—2001; pres. Associated Physicians of MCO, Toledo, 1994-96, chmn. bd., 1996-98; chief of staff Med. Coll. Hosp., Toledo, 1998—2002, emeritus prof., 2002—. Contbr. articles to profl. jours. Bd. trustees Nat. Kidney Found. N.W. Ohio, 1984—, Hindu Temple, Toledo, 1990—; med. dir. Life Connection Ohio, Toledo, 1987-94. Office: Dept Urology 3065 Arlington Ave Toledo OH 43614-2570 Home: 3840 Sulphur Spring Rd Toledo OH 43606-2324 E-mail: jjhunjhunwala1140@aol.com.

JI, QING, chemist, researcher; b. Yanji, Jilin, China, Mar. 1, 1964; s. Zhenwen Ji and Shuqin Cai; m. Liyuan Pei, Jan 6, 1990. PhD, U. Strathclyde, Glasgow, Scotland, 1994. Rsch. scientist Va. Tech., Blacksburg, 1995-2000; sr. chemist Henkel Loctite Corp., Industry, Calif., 2000—. Contbr. articles to profl. jours. Tech. co-op fellow Brit. Coun., 1988. Mem. ACS. Home: 422A S Orange Ave Monterey Park CA 91755 Office: Henkel Loctite Corp 15051 E Don Julian Rd City Of Industry CA 91746 Fax: (626) 336-0526.

JIA, WEITAO, dental products executive, researcher; b. Shanghai, May 14, 1959; s. Kexi Jia and Xianchai Cheng; m. Shari Xiafei Chang, Jan. 11, 1988; children: Irene, Ricky. Diploma in stomatology, Shanghai, China, 1981; MSc, NYU, 1988; PhD, Kennedy Western U., Thousand Oaks, Calif., 1999. Rsch. asst. Shanghai Second Med. U. Sch. Stomatology, 1981-87; rsch. asst., instr. NYU, N.Y.C., 1987-89; rschr. Jeneric/Pentron, Inc., Wallingford, Conn., 1989-95, mgr. composite R&D, 1995-97, dir. R&D, 1997-99, v.p. dental product R&D, 1999—2001; v.p. R&D, Pentron Clin. Techs., LLC, 2001—. Bd. dirs. CJ Multi Tech Enterprises, Inc. Wallingford, 1997—. Patentee in field. Mem. AAAS, Am. Assn. Dental Rsch., Acad. Dental Materials, Internat. Assn. Dental Rsch., N.Y. Acad. Scis. Office: Pentron Clin Techs LLC 125 N Plains Industrial Rd Wallingford CT 06492 Personal E-mail: weitaojia@hotmail.com. Business E-Mail: wjia@pentron.com.

JIALAL, ISHWARLAL, medical educator; b. Durban, Natal, South Africa, Oct. 13, 1953; B in Medicine, B in Surgery, U. Natal, South Africa, 1976, MD, 1983. Registered med. practitioner, specialist in chem. pathology South African Med. and Dental Coun., diplomate Royal Coll. Pathologists (Eng.), Am. Bd. Internal Medicine, Am. Bd. Clin. Chemistry. Intern in medicine and surgery King Edward VIII Hosp., U. Natal Med. Sch., Durban, South Africa, 1977, resident in endocrinology and metabolism divsn., 1978—82; resident dept. chem. pathology U. Natal, 1978—82, sr. lectr./specialist depts. medicine and chem. pathology, 1984—87; fellow divsn. diabetes and metabolism Harvard Med. Sch., E.P. Joslin Rsch. Lab., Joslin Diabetes Ctr., Boston, 1983—84; dir. clin. pathology R.K. Khan Hosp., U. Natal Med. Sch., 1984—87; assoc. prof./sr. specialist dept. chem. pathology and medicine U. Natal Med. Sch., 1987; sr. fellow divsn. metabolism, endocrinology and nutrition, dept. medicine U. Wash., Seattle, 1987—88; asst. prof. depts. clin. nutrition, internal medicine and pathology U. Tex. Southwestern Med. Ctr., Dallas, 1988—92, co-dir. Lipid Clinic, 1990—, assoc. prof. dept. pathology, internal medicine and clin. nutrition, 1992—, dir. clin. chemistry dept. pathology, 1992—, sr. investigator Ctr. Human Nutrition, 1992—, prof. internal medicine and pathology, 1997—, assoc. dir. divsn. clin. pathology, 1997—. Dir. divsn. clin. chemistry Parkland Meml. Hosp.; attending physician, co-dir. Lipid Disorders Clinic, Parkland Meml. and Aston Ambulatory Care Ctr.; attending physician endocrinology & metabolism Parkland Meml. and Zale Lipshy Hosps.; cons. chem. pathologist VA Med. Ctr., Dallas; vis. scientist dept. chem. pathology and metabolic disorders St. Thomas Hosp. Med. Sch., London, 1984; cons. chem. pathologist Dallas VA Med. Ctr., 1995—. Recipient Clin. Rsch. grant, Am. Diabetes Assn., 1996. Office: U Tex Southwestern Med Sch Dept Pathology 5323 Harry Hines Blvd # Cs3114 Dallas TX 75390-7208

JIANG, BAOMING, scientist; b. Qichun, Hubei, China, Mar. 17, 1962; came to U.S., 1985. s. Y. Jiang and Lan Lin; m. Gail Fang, Aug. 1987; children: Victoria, James. DVM, Cen. China Agrl. U., Wuhan, 1983; MS, Ohio State U., 1987, PhD, 1991. Postdoctoral fellow Emory U. Sch. Medicine, Atlanta, 1991-93; rsch. assoc. Nat. Rsch. Coun., NSF, Washington, 1993-94; sr. rsch. scientist Am. Home Products Co., Pearl River, N.Y., 1994-98; sr. staff fellow Ctrs. for Disease Control and Prevention, Atlanta, 1998—. Named Disting. Scientist, Immigration and Naturalization Svcs., 1992. Contbr. rsch. articles to profl. jours. Mem. Am. Soc. for Virology, Delta chpt. Phi Zeta. Avocations: sports, reading, gardening. Home: 4891 Miller Rd SW Lilburn GA 30047-5332 Office: NICD/Ctr Ctrs for Disease Control Viral Gastroenteritis Sect CMS G04 1600 Clifton Rd Atlanta GA 30333 Fax: (404) 639-3645. E-mail: bxj4@cdc.gov.

JIANG, CANWEN, genetic scientist, researcher; s. Mengyun Jiang and Xiaohua Zhang; m. Lan Du, Sept. 7, 1967; 1 child, Jennifer. PhD, Imperial Coll. of Sci., Tech., and Medicine, London, 1992; Postdoctoral Fellow, U. of Calif., Berkeley, 1992—94. Prin. scientist Genzyme Corp., Framingham, Mass., 2001—, sr. scientist, 1998—2001. Rsch. staff scientist Genzyme Corp., Mass., 1994—98. Author: (original rsch.) Cardiovascular biology (Outstanding Young Investigator Award, 1992); scientist (research) Rsch. and Devel. of Novel Therapy (v.p. for Rsch. Award, 1996). Mem.: Am. Soc. of Gene Therapy, Am. Heart Assn. Achievements include patents for Novel treatment for genetic disease; research in Original research articles in many journals including Science. Home: 2 Charina Rd Northboro MA 01532 Office: Genzyme Corp 31 New York Ave Framingham MA 01701

JIANG, HONG, information scientist; b. Beijing, Dec. 30, 1969; d. Zikang Jiang and Yuehua Fang; m. Xuefeng Wang. BA, Renmin U. of China, Beijing, 1996; MS in Biostats., U. Nebr., 2000. Statistician Tsinghua U., Beijing, 1991—96; rsch. asst. U. Nebr., Lincoln, 1999—2000; data analyst Douglas County Health Dept., Omaha, 2000—. Cons. on stats. and SAS programming U. Nebr., Lincoln, 1999—2000; cons. on database Douglas County Health Dept., 2000—; state immunization assessment coord. CDC and Prevention. Contbr. Mem.: Nat. Assn. for Pub. Health Stats. and Info. Sys., Am. Statis. Assn. Office: Douglas County Health Dept 1819 Farnam St Omaha NE 68183 E-mail: hjiang@co.douglas.ne.us.

JIANG, HONGXING, physics educator, researcher; s. Yulong Jiang and Zhen Xie; m. Jingyu Lin, Nov. 23, 1983; children: Frank, Andrew, Kelly. PhD, Syracuse U., 1981—86. Various edn. positions to assoc. prof. physics Kans. State U., Manhattan, Kans., 1993—98, prof. physics; dir. Kans. Advanced Semiconductor Coord. Lab., Manhattan, Kans., 1999—. Advisor PhD program; vis. scientist Sandia Nat. lab., Albuquerque. Author: (Teaching, Researching, invention) Micro-size light emitters, 2001. Grantee Research Grants, 1992—. Mem.: Materials Rsch. Soc., Internat. Optical Soc., Am. Phys. Soc. Office: Kansas State U Cardwell Hall Manhattan KS 66506 Office Fax: 785-532-5636. Business E-Mail: jiang@phys.ksu.edu.

JIANG, TAO, mathematician, educator; arrived in U.S., 1994; s. Chaoshi Jiang and Shugui Xia. PhD, U. of Ill., 2000. Asst. prof. Mich. Technol. U., Houghton, Mich., 2000—01, Miami U., Oxford, Ohio, 2001—. Spkr. at internat. and nat. profl. meetings. Contbr. more than 25 articles to profl. jours. Recipient Hohn-Nash award, U. of Ill. math. dept., 2000. Mem.: Phi Kappa Phi (hon.).

JIANG, WENXIN, statistician, researcher; b. Chang zhou, China, June 8, 1967; s. Yaoming and Yun (Xu) J. MS, Cornell U., 1995, PhD, 1996. Asst. prof. Northwestern U., Evanston, Ill., 1996—2002, assoc. prof., 2002—. Contbr. articles to profl. jours. Office: Northwestern U Dept Statistics 2006 Sheridan Rd Evanston IL 60208-0852 E-mail: wjiang@northwestern.edu.

JIANG, WILLIAM YUYING, business educator, consultant, researcher; b. Hengyang, Hunan Province, China, Jan. 18, 1955; s. Rongguang Jiang and Hongkang Lei; m. Leslie Rongqui Yi, Sept. 5, 1988; children: Cosmo Yi, Cordelia Yi. BA in English, Hunan Normail U., Changsha, China, 1981; MA in English Lexicology, Xiamen U., China, 1984; MA in Comparative Lit., U. Ill.,

1985, MS, 1986; MPhil in Bus., PhD in Bus., Columbia U., 1991. Asst. prof. San Jose State U., 1991—94, assoc. prof., 1994—97, prof., 1997—. Mng. dir. JS Cresvale Securities (US) Inc., Cupertino, Calif., 1999—2001; chancellor First Light Acad., Centreville, Va., 2002—. Translator: (novel) The Egoist, To Kill a Mockingbird; contbr. articles. Recipient Acad. Rsch. award, Chinese NSF, 1997, 2000; scholar, Pres. Fellowship, 1984—86, Columbia U., 1987, 1988, 1989, 1990; Marjorie Hope Nicolson scholar, 1987, Provost's Internat. scholar, San Jose State U., 2003. Mem.: Internat. Mgmt. Assn. Human Resource (chmn. mgmt. divsn. 1995—96), The Asian Am. Mfg. Assn., Chinese Economist Soc., Monte Jade Soc. Sci. and Tech., Indsl. Rels. Rsch. Assn., The Am. Econ. Assn., Assn. Chinese Profs. U.S. (dir. bd. 2001—03, dir. mem. 2001—03), Acad. Mgmt. (participation com. chair 1999—2002). Avocations: skiing, travel, foreign languages learning, reading. Home: 19901 La Mar Dr Cupertino CA 95014-3377 Office: San Jose State Univ One Washington Sq San Jose CA 95192-0070 Personal E-mail: jiang_w11@hotmail.com. E-mail: jiang_w@cob.sjsu.edu.

JIANG, YONG PING, research scientist; b. China, July 11, 1956; came to U.S., 1983; s. Hepei and Xudai J.; m. Xiao Fang, June 22, 1985; children: Alexandra, Barbara F. BS, Nanjing U., China, 1982; MS, Rutgers U., 1985, PhD, 1988. With Nat. Hosp., Arlington, Va., 1988-90; asst. prof. Temple Med. Sch., Phila., 1990-92; rsch. investigator U. Mich. Med. Ctr., Ann Arbor, 1992-95; assoc. scientist Harvard Med. Sch., Boston, 1995-98; CEO ABTEK, Inc., Malden, Mass., 1996—. Vice chmn. bd., pres. Bio-Pharm. Co., Beihan, China, 1996—. Patentee in field. Recipient rsch. award Am. Heart Assn., 1994-95. Mem. AAAS, Am. Assn. Hematology (rsch. award 1993). Avocations: fishing, music, travel. Office: ABTEK Inc 376 Washington St Malden MA 02148 E-mail: yjiang9999@aol.com.

JIBBEN, LAURA ANN, state agency administrator; b. Peoria, Ill., Oct. 1, 1949; d. Charles Otto and Dorothy Lee (Skaggs) Becker; m. Michael Eugene Hagan, July 7, 1967 (div. Apr. 1972); m. Louis C. Jibben, July 14, 1972. BA in Criminal Justice, Sangamon State U., 1984; MBA, Northwestern U., 1990. Asst. to chief of adminstrn. Ill. Dept. Corrections, Springfield, 1974-77, exec. asst. to dir., 1977-80, dep. dir., 1980-81; mgr. toll services Ill. Tollway Dept., Oak Brook, 1981-86; chief adminstrv. officer Regional Transp. Authority, Chgo., 1986-90, fund mgr. loss financing plan, 1987-90, also, chmn. pension trust, exec. dir., 1990-96; v.p., gen. mgr. MTA, Inc., Chgo., 1996-99; ptnr. Hanson Engrs., Inc., Oak Brook, Ill., 1999-2000; sr. project mgr., cons. mgmt. Alfred Benesch & Co., 2000—02, v.p., 2002—. Cons. labor studies Sangamon State U., Springfield, 1981; bd. dirs. Chgo. Found. for Women. Mem. surface tranps. adv. panel U. Ill., 1997—2000; apptd. mem. transp. adv. bd. City of Naperville, 1988—90; bd. dirs. Family Shelter Svcs., 1990—91; bd. dirs., chair devel. com. Govt. Assistance Program, 1997—2000, sec. bd., 1999; mem. surface transp. adv. panel U. Ill., 1997—2000; mem. nat. adv. bd. Women's Transp. Seminar, 1996—; mem. Peoria Women's Fund Grants Com., 2003; mem. traffic seminar Bradley Univ., 2002—03. Recipient Appreciation award VFW, Chgo., 1983, award Ill. State Toll Hwy. Authority, 1986; named Woman of Yr., Nat. Women's Transp. Seminar, 1991, AAUW, 1991. Mem. NAFE, Women's Transp. Seminar (Woman of Yr. award Chgo. chpt. 1991, Nat. Woman of Yr. 1991), Beta Sigma Phi (treas., v.p., corr. sec. Naperville and Easton, Ill. chpts.), Lambda Alpha. Avocations: reading, jogging, gardening, golf. Office: Alfred Benesch & Co 401 Main St Ste 1110 Peoria IL 61602-1241 E-mail: ljibben@benesch.com.

JIBSON, RANDALL WADE, geologist; b. San Jose, Calif., Apr. 17, 1956; s. Jay Robert and Myrtle Richins Jibson; m. Linda Sue Watts; children: Matthew, Daniel, Karen. BS, San Diego State U., 1980; MS, Stanford U., 1982, PhD, 1985. Geologist U.S. Geol. Survey, Menlo Park, Calif., 1983—85, Reston, Va., 1985—90, geomechanics rsch. coord., 1990—94, rsch. geologist, 1994—2002. Editor: (book) Geological Society of America Special Paper 236, 1989; contbr. articles to profl. jours. incl. Environ. and Engring. Geoscience (AEG Best Publ. Award, 1996), chapters to books. Mem.: Geol. Soc. of Am., Phi Kappa Phi. Church Of Jesus Christ Of Latter-Day Saints. Office: US Geological Survey Box 25046 MS 966 Denver Federal Center Denver CO 80225 Business E-Mail: jibson@usgs.gov.

JIE, MIN, mechanical engineering educator, researcher; b. Wuhan, Hubei, China, Nov. 29, 1963; s. Fangzuo Jie and Shizheng Han; m. Rong Xie, Sept. 13, 1966; 1 child, Meng. BS, U. Sci. and Tech. of China, 1985; MS, Peking U., 1988. Rsch. asst. Peking U., 1985-88; asst. prof. then assoc. prof. Huazhong U. Sci. and Tech., Wuhan, 1988-97; guest rschr. The Hong Kong Poly. U., 1997-98; rsch. asst. U. Mich., Dearborn, 1998—. Contbr. articles to profl. jours. Mem. Hubei Soc. Theoretical and Applied Mechs. (acad. sec. solid mechs. com. 1995-97), Am. Soc. Civil Engrs., Am. Soc. Mech. Engrs. Office: U Mich 4901 Evergreen Rd Dearborn MI 48128 Also: Apt 201 Bldg 22 8176 Brooke Park Dr Canton MI 48187 Home: # 201bld2 8176 Brooke Park Dr Canton MI 48187-5114 Fax: 313-593-3851. E-mail: mjie@umich.edu.

JIH, CHANG-SHIN, education educator; b. Taipei, Taiwan, R.O.C., Oct. 8, 1955; s. Tsung-Chung Jih and Yu-Tong Jih-Lea; m. Donna Ann Price, May 18, 2000; m. Wan-Li Ho, Dec. 25, 1983 (div. Sept. 1998); 1 child, Yeou-Rong. MPhil, Temple U., 1992. Instr. Chang-Taun U., Taipei, Taiwan, 1983—88, Temple U., 1989—94, Manor Coll., Pa., 1992—2000, Montgomery County Cmty., 1995—2002, Phila. C.C., 2002, Wan Inst. of Grad. Studies, 2002. Editor: (novels) Tao of Jesus, 1998, (Journal) Voice of Truth, 1983, News of Congress, 1978—81. Dir. K.M.P., Taipei, 1982—83. Lt. U.S. Army, 1983—85, Taiwan. Recipient Master of Martial Arts, Clinton Admin., 1998. Buddhist. Achievements include development of Founder of GoldenLight Center. Avocations: music, swimming, basketball, yoga, tai chi. Home: 8529 Rising Sun Ave #143 Philadelphia PA 19111 Office: Mauov College 700 Fox Chase Rd Jewkintown PA 19046

JIHA, JACQUES, economist; b. Port-au-Prince, Haiti, Apr. 4, 1958; came to U.S., 1979; s. Jacob Jiha and Mercilie Jerome; m. Marie Chantale Fulcher, Dec. 15, 1984; children: Christine Amanda, Kimberly. BA, Fordham U., 1985; MA, New Sch. Social Rsch., 1988, PhD, 1991. Prin. economist N.Y. State Assembly, Ways & Means Com., Albany, 1988-91; exec. dir. N.Y. State Legis. Tax Study Commn., Albany, 1992-94; chief economist office of the comptroller City of N.Y., 1994-97, deputy comptroller, 1997—2002; dep. comptroller Office of Comptroller Nassau County, 2002—. Contbr. articles to profl. jours. Mem. Am. Econ. Assn. Democrat. Avocations: reading, sports, beer making, cooking. Office: City of NY Office of Comptroller 1 Centre St Rm 510 New York NY 10007-1602

JILER, LINDA CERISE, retired fire and aviation program support specialist, fire emergency dispatcher, consultant, researcher, writer; b. Santa Monica, Calif., Dec. 30, 1956; d. Milton John "Jack" Jiler and Peggy Jean Williams. AA, Lassen Coll., 1979, Cert. Forestry Technician, 1980. Cert. Calif. Dept. Forestry and Fire Protection Fire Acad., 1990. Fire clk./firefighter-wildland Lassen Coll. Contract Crew, Susanville, Calif., 1976-77; forestry technician (fire) U.S. Forest Svc. Lassen Nat. Forest/Eagle Lake Ranger Dist./Bogard Ranger Sta., Susanville, Calif., 1977-80; dist. personnel technician U.S. Dept. Interior-Bur. Land Mgmt., Susanville Dist., Calif., 1981-86; pub. contact rep. U.S. Dept. Interior Bur. Land Mgmt. Susanville Dist., Susanville, Calif., 1986; wildland firefighter/dispatcher Lassen Coll. Contract Fire Crew, Susanville, Calif., 1986-87; fire, aviation program asst., lightning detection specialist U.S. Dept. Interior Bur. Land Mgmt., Calif. State Office, Sacramento, 1988-93; 9-1-1 interagy. fire dispatcher Calif. Dept. Forestry and Fire Protection, Camino, 1988-93; 9-1-1 interagency emergency commd. ctr. Calif. Dept. Forestry and Fire Protection, Camino Interagency Emergency Command Ctr., 1988-93; cons. info. svcs. Sacramento, 1993—. Speaker in field; pub. info. officer USDA-FS, U.S. Dept. Interior-Bur. Land Mgmt., CDF, 1983-93. Author: How to Get A Job with the Federal Government, 1983, rev. edit., 1985, 86, Injury and Claim Processing Manual, 1985, Demobilization Training Guide, 1985, Train-the Trainer Wildland Fire Timekeeping Procedures, 1985, (manual) California State Office SOP for Intelligence Gathering, 1987-88; co-author: (manual) California Interagency Mobilization Guide, 1988, Bur. of Land Management's State Policy for Handling of Burn Victims, 1988. Recipient Cert. of Appreciation, Lassen County Bd. Suprs., 1986, 87, Cert. of Appreciation and Cert. of Recognition for Outstanding Performance, U.S. Forest Svc. Pacific S.W. Region, 1987, Nat. Wildland Coord. Group award for Outstanding Performance, U.S. Forest Svc. Pacific N.W. Region and Wallow Whitman Nat. Forest, 1986, Superior Achievement and Profl. Contbns. award U.S. Dept. Agriculture Forest Svc. and U.S. Dept. Interior Bur. Land Mgmt., 1990; cert. Appreciation Eldorado Bd. Suprs. U.S. Forest Svc., 1992, Recognition award Oakland Athletics Baseball Club, 1987, Recognition award San Diego Padres Baseball Club, 1988. Mem. ACLU, Am. Soc. for Prevention of Cruelty to Animals, The Humane Soc. U.S., World Wildlife Fedn., Calif. State Employees Assn. (classification rep. 1989-93), Calif. Profl. Firefighters, Chronic Fatigue Immune Dysfunction Syndrome Assn. Am., Chronic Fatigue Immune Dysfunction Syndrome and Fibromyalgia Support Groups, Nat. Trust for Hist. Preservation, Nat. Conf. Incident Command System Fin. Officers, Nat. Australian Shepherd Club Am., Sigma Kappa (alumni past pres.), Sierra Club. Democrat. Avocations: australian shepherds, calligraphy, sociology studies, social justice, civil rights.

JILER, WILLIAM LAURENCE, publisher; b. Bridgeport, Conn., Oct. 16, 1925; s. Jacob and Sarah J.; m. Jan Gardner, Oct. 14, 1956; children: Wendy Jo, James Paul. BS, Bates Coll., Lewiston, Maine, 1948; postgrad., U. So. Calif., 1950. With E.R. Squibb & Co., New Brunswick, N.J., 1948-50; with Commodity Research Bur., Inc., N.Y.C., now Jersey City, 1950-64, 69-85, pres., 1969-85; with Standard & Poor's Corp., 1964-69, dir., 1964-69. Mem. econ. adv. com. Commodity Futures Trading Commn., 1975-76; founder, pres. Trendline Corp. Author: How Charts Can Help You in the Stock Market, 1962; assoc. editor: Commodity Year Book, 1951-80; created the CRB Commodity Futures Index Traded as a Futures Contract on the New York Futures Exchange. Served to 2d lt. USAAF, 1943-45. Mem. Nat. Assn. Bus. Economists, Market Technicians Assn., N.Y. Soc. Security Analysts. *Find a need and fulfill it to the best of your ability.*

JILHEWAR, ASHOK, gastroenterologist; b. Nanded, Maharashtra, India, Jan. 30, 1947; came to U.S., 1977; naturalized 1987; BS, Marathwada U., Aurangabad, India, 1970; MB, Marathwada U., 1970; MD, Govt. Med. Coll., Aurangabad, 1970. Diplomate Am. Bd. Internal Medicine, Am. Bd. Gastroenterology, Am. Bd. Geriatric Medicine, Am. Bd. Quality Assurance and Utilization Rev. Physicians. Rotatory intern Med. Coll. Hosp., Aurangabad, India, 1968-70; resident St. Luke's Hosp. and Royal infirmary, Huddersfeild, Bolton, Eng., 1970-72; med. registrar internal medicine Gen. Hosp., Sligo, Ireland, 1973-77; chief resident PG1 and internal medicine U. Health Scis.-Chgo. Med. Sch. and VA Hosp., 1977-79; clin. instr. U. Heath Scis.-Chgo. Med. Sch., 1978-79; fellow in gastroenterology Michael Reese Hosp., Chgo., 1980-81; mem. exec. com. Meth. Hosp., Chgo, 1985-90, chmn. dept. med., 1988-90; mem. staff dept. medicine Grant Hosp., Chgo., 1986—. Lectr. preventive and social medicine Med. Coll., Aurangabad, 1970; mem. exec. com. Meth. Hosp. Chgo., 1985-90, v.p. med. staff, 1987-88, treas., sec. 1985-87, chmn. dept. medicine, 1988-90; med. dir. approved homr for intermediace care nursing home, 1986-95; med. advisor Office Hearings and Appeals, HHS, 1985—; med. reviewer Ill. Med. Rev. Orgn., 1993—, Crescent Cmty. Found. for Med. Care, 1994—. Fellow Royal Coll. Physicians Can., Am. Coll. Internat. Physicians; mem. AMA, ACP, Am. Headache Soc., Am. Gastroenterol. Assn., Royal Coll. Physicians U.K., Royal Coll. Physicians Ireland, Ill. State Med. Assn., Chgo. Med. Soc. (PRO study com., fee mediation subcom. 1992). Office: North Park Stomach Clinic 5393 N Milwaukee Ave Chicago IL 60630-1251 E-mail: ajilhewar@hotmail.com.

JILLETTE, ARTHUR GEORGE, JR., school system administrator, educator; b. Malden, Mass., May 1, 1937; s. Arthur George and Esther Harriett (Peachey) J.; m. Janet Downs White, June 20, 1960 (div. 1973); 1 child, Joseph Arthur; m. Beatrice Miriam Ellis, May 3, 1975; children: Grace Harder, Andrew Hopkins, Timothy Hopkins. BS, Boston U., 1960, MRE, 1964; cert. in audio communicative disability, NYU, 1967. Cert. tchr., N.H., community coll. adminstr., Calif. Assoc. rsch. scientist NYU Deafness Rsch. Ctr., N.Y.C., 1965-67; cons. spl. edn. N.H. Dept. Edn., Concord, 1967-74, 85-88, 1997-99, acting dir. spl. edn., 1974-75; dir. planning and devel. N.H. Div. Vocat. Rehab., Concord, 1975-79; dean spl. svcs. N.H. Tech. Coll., Claremont, 1979-83, dean students, 1983-85; dir. spl. svcs. Sch. Admnstrv. Unit #43, Newport, NH, 1988—91, asst. supt. schs., 1991-94; dir. spl. svcs. Sch. Adminstrv. Unit 32, Lebanon, N.H., 1994-97; dir. spl. edn. Lyme N.H. Sch. Dist., 1999—2000; coord. spl. edn. svcs. Goshen-Lempster Coop. Sch. Dist., 2000—. Dir. Lake Sunapee Mediation Program, Newport, 1990—, pres., 1996—; mem. state adv. coun. Individuals with Disabilities Edn. Act., 1989-94; consumer mem. N.H. State Bd. Hearing Care Providers, 2001—; pres., dir. Sullivan County Rehab. Ctr., Claremont, 1980-83. Editor: Denominational Work With the Deaf, 1966. Moderator Town of Goshen, N.H., 1980—, planning bd. chmn., 1985-89, zoning bd. chmn., 1986-89; mem. Goshen-Lempster Coop. Sch. Bd., 1975-80, 95-2000, chmn., 1979-80, 97-2000; mem., sec. Newport Revitalization Com., 2002—. Social and Rehab. Svcs. fellow U.S. Dept. Edn., 1964-65. Mem. Nat. Stereoptician Assn., Nat. Assn. Watch and Clock Collectors, N.H. Assn. Spl. Edn. Adminstrs., Elks, Odd Fellow, Masons. Democrat. Mem. Soc. Of Friends. Avocations: house restoration, stereo photography, clock restoration, computers. Home: PO Box 1016 Goshen NH 03752-1016 Office: Sch Adminstrv Unit # 71 School Rd Lempster NH 03605

JIMBO, MASAHITO, medical educator; b. Tokyo, Jan. 26, 1960; came to U.S., 1993; s. Fujio and Mariko (Hashimoto) J.; m. Soh Mitsuko, July 4, 1984; children: Masaya, Chihiro. MD, Keio U. Sch. Medicine, Tokyo, 1985, PhD, 1994; MPH, U. N.C., 2000. Diplomate Am. Bd. Family Practice. Rotating intern Okinawa Chuba Hosp., Japan, 1985-86, resident in internal medicine, 1986-87, Keio Univ. Hosp., Tokyo, 1987-91, fellow in nephrology, 1991-93; resident in family practice Thomas Jefferson Univ. Hosp., Phila., 1993-96; staff physician First Health Family Care Ctrs., Troy, N.C., 1996-97, med. dir., 1997-99; asst. prof. family medicine Thomas Jefferson U., 1999—. Bd. dirs. Mid-Carolina Physician Orgn., Inc. Contbr. articles to profl. jours. Ministry Edn., Sci. & Culture grantee, Tokyo, 1993; fellow Japan-N.Am. Med. Excg. Found., Tokyo, 1993, Noguchi Med. Rsch. Inst., Phila., 1991. Mem. Am. Acad. Family Physicians, Am. Coll. Physicians, Japanese Soc. Internal Medicine, Japanese Soc. Ultrasound, Japanese Soc. Emergency Medicine. Roman Catholic. Avocations: running, skiing, cycling, reading. Home: 348 Manor Rd Lafayette Hill PA 19444-1741 Office: Thomas Jefferson Univ Dept Family Medicine 1015 Walnut St Ste 401 Philadelphia PA 19107-5005 E-mail: masahito.jimbo@jefferson.edu.

JIMENEZ, BETTIE EILEEN, retired small business owner; b. LaCygne, Kans., June 8, 1932; d. William Albert and Ruby Faye (Cline) Montee; m. William R. Bradley, Aug. 21, 1947 (dec. Sept. 1950); 1 child, Shirley; m. J.P. Jimenez, Feb. 20, 1951 (div. Nov. 1978); children: Pamela, Joe Jr., Robin Michelle. Student, Ft. Scott Jr. Coll., Paola, Kans., 1979-81. Reporter LaCygne Jour., 1943-45; union recorder I.L.G.W.U., Paola, 1956-57; mgr. Estes Metalcraft, Osawatomie, Kans., 1977-82; owner El Rey Tavern, Osawatomie, 1980-95; ret., 1995; with Estes Metalcraft, 2002—. Home: 516 Walnut Ave Osawatomie KS 66064-1254 E-mail: bjozks@idir.net.

JIMENEZ, CARLOS, Spanish language educator; b. Jerez, Andalusia, Spain, Aug. 16, 1963; arrived in U.S., 1987; s. Domingo Jimenez and Manuela Lopez; m. Mercedes Juliá, June 2, 1987. MA, Villanova U., 1990; PhD, U. Pa. Asst. prof. Spanish Cabrini Coll., Radnor, Pa., 1999—. Coord. study abroad Cabrini Coll., Radnor, 1999—, dir. study abroad program in Spain, 1999—. Author: (books) Aventura, 1993, Album, 2002; contbr. poetry to revs. Mem.: MLA, Asociacion de Licenciados y Doctores en Estados Unidos Espanoles, Am. Assn. Tchrs. of Spanish and Portuguese. Home: 1524 County Line Rd Bryn Mawr PA 19010 E-mail: jcjimenez@cabrini.edu.

JIMÉNEZ, CARMEN JULIA, language educator; d. Roberto Jiménez and Petra Pizarro; m. Angel D. Mejías, May 24, 1987; 1 child, Victor Cortés Herrera. BA, U. PR, 1987; MA, U. Utah, 1994; PhD, Pa. State U., 2002. Health educator Congreso Latinos Unidos, Phila., 1999—2000; lectr., asst. prof. U. Utah, Salt Lake City, 2000—01; asst. prof. Salisbury (Md.) U., 2001—. Tchg. asst. U. Utah, Salt Lake City, 1992—94; grad. asst. Pa. State U., University Park, 1994—98. Advisor Latino Students Assn. Salisbury U., 2001—03. Recipient Cert. of Recognition, The Puerto Rican Students Assn., 1995—97; fellow Sparks Dissertation fellow, Pa. State U., 1998; grantee, 1997. Mem.: MLA, Phi Sigma Iota. Avocations: reading, travel. Office: Salisbury Univ 1101 Camden Ave Salisbury MD 21801

JIMENEZ, EMMANUEL, economist; b. Manila, Philippines, Dec. 5, 1952; came to U.S., 1961; s. Privado Garcia and Imelda (Yatco) J.; children: Sara, Nicholas, Sebastian, Simon. BA with honors, McGill U., 1974; MA, U. Toronto, 1975; PhD, Brown U., 1980. Cons. The World Bank, Washington, 1978-84; assoc. prof. U. Western Ontario, London, Can., 1980-88; sr. economist, div. chief, dir. The World Bank, Washington, 1984—. Author: Pricing Policy in the Social Sectors, 1987; co-author: Financing Education in Developing Countries, 1986, Developing the Private Sector, 1989; contbr. articles to profl. jours. Allen Oliver Meml. fellow McGill U., 1974, fellow Brown U., 1975. Roman Catholic. Avocations: jogging, reading, bicycling, hiking. Office: The World Bank 1818 H St NW Washington DC 20433-0001

JIMÉNEZ, LEONARDO, popular accordionist; b. San Antonio, Mar. 11, 1939; Inducted International Music Hall of Fame, 2003. Accordionist with his own conjunto (group) mid-50s, recorded for many local labels with Anglo musician, Doug Sahm for Atlantic, 1972, appeared (documentaries) Les Blank/Chris Strachwitz, 1974, (films) True Stories: Chulas Fronteras, 1974, toured and recorded with Ry Cooder and Peter Rowan, mem. Tex. Tornados band, albums Entre Humo y Botellas, 1989, Un Mojado Sin Licencia, 1993, Flaco Jimenez, 1994, Ay Te Dejo En San Antonio, El Sonido de San Antonio, Flaco's Amigos, Y Su-Conjunto. Recipient Grammy award Best Mex.-Am. Performance, 1996, Grammy for Arhoolie LP: Ay Te Dejo En San Antonio, 1987, Grammy for best Tejano performance, 1999. Office: c/o Ideas Etc Mgmt PO Box 5727 San Antonio TX 78201-0727*

JIMENEZ, SERGIO A. internist, science educator, rheumatologist; b. Cuzco, Peru, Feb. 21, 1942; s. Julio Alexandre and Bertha Margarite (Astete) J. BS, Nat. U. San Marcos, Lima, Peru, 1959, MD, 1964; MS, U. Pa., 1984. Diplomate Am. Bd. Internal Medicine. Asst. prof. dept. medicine U. Pa., Phila., 1974-80, asst. prof. dept. orthop. surgery, 1978-80, assoc. prof. medicine and orthop. surgery, 1980-86, prof., 1986-87; prof. medicine, dir. rheumatology rsch. Thomas Jefferson U., Phila., 1987-92, prof. biochemistry and molecular biology, 1987—, dir. divsn. rheumatology, 1992—, Dorrance H. Hamilton prof. medicine, 1992—, vice chmn. rsch. dept. medicine, 1999—2003. Hon. adj. fellow Benjamin Franklin Inst., Phila., 1981—; chmn. med. adv. bd. Scleroderma Rsch. Found., Mid-Atlantic Chpt., 1979—; mem. rsch. scholarships com., Ea. Pa. chpt. Arthritis Found., 1981-84; mem. med./sci. bd. Scleroderma Fedn., 1994—; mem. Nat. Inst. Health Gen. Medicine A Study Sect., 1990-94, mem. spl. rev. com., 1995—; Nat. Inst. Health Peer Review Oversight Group, 1998—; bd. sci. councellors Nat. Inst. Arthritis Musculoskeletal Diseases, NIH, 1999—; acting chmn., bd. councellors Nat. Inst. Arthritis Musculoskeletal Diseases NIH, 2000-02; chmn. bd. scientific councellors Nat. Inst. Arthritis Musculoskeletal Disease, NIH, 2002—. Author over 270 articles to med. jours., 450 abstracts in procs. worldwide sci. jours., 90 editls., revs., and chpts. to jours. and books. Bd. dirs. Washington Square West Civic Assn., Phila., 1978-82, v.p., 1981-82, trustee, 1988—; mem. Phila. Hispanic C. of C., 1990—. Capt. Peruvian Army Res., 1964-65. Recipient Gerald P. Rodnan award for excellence in scleroderma rsch., U. Pitts., 1986, Joseph Lee Hollander award for excellence in rheumatology Ea. Pa. Arthritis Found., 2000; program project for rsch. on osteoarthritis, NIH, 1992—. Fellow Soc. for Molecular Medicine; mem. Am. Coll. Rheumatology, Am. Soc. Biol. Chemistry and Molecular Biology, Osteoarthritis Rsch. Soc. (exec. bd. 1994—, pres.-elect 1997-2000, pres. 2000-02), Internat. Soc. for Matrix Biology (founding mem.), Am. Soc. Matrix Biology. Republican. Roman Catholic. Avocations: fine arts, sculpture, opera, anthropology, archeology. Home: 900 Spruce St Philadelphia PA 19107-6131 Office: Thomas Jefferson Univ 233 S 10th St Ste 509 Philadelphia PA 19107-5541 E-mail: sergio.jimenez@jefferson.edu.

JIMÉNEZ-BELTRAN, DOMINGO, executive; b. Zaragoza, Spain, Apr. 2, 1944; s. Mariano and Maria Gloria (Beltran) J.; married; one child. Indsl. engr. Polytech U., Madrid, 1967; environ. engring. cons., 1968-82; exec. advisor Min. Pub., Works & Planning, 1983-85; deputy dir. gen. Internat. EU Rels., 1985-86; head divsn. health, phys. safety & quality Consumers Policy Svc., European Commn., 1987-91; dir.-gen. environ. policy Ministry Pub. Works, Transport and Environment, Spain, 1991-94; exec. dir. European Environ. Agy., Copenhagen, Denmark, 1994—. Contbr. articles to profl. jour. Office: EEA 6 Kongens Nytorv DK-1050 Copenhagen Denmark E-mail: domingo.jimenez@eea.eu.int.

JIMMAR, D'ANN, elementary education educator, fashion merchandiser; b. Leighton, Ala., Dec. 10, 1942; d. Harry D. Qualls and Lillian Jimmar. BS in Elem. Edn., Ala. A&M U., 1965, MS in Urban Studies, 1973; PhD in Higher Edn., Iowa State U., 1986. Elem. tchr. Limestone County Bd. Edn., Athens, Ala., 1966-68, Huntsville City Bd. Edn., Ala., 1968-71; instr. dept. cmty. planning and urban studies Ala. A&M U., Huntsville, Ala., 1973-78; rsch. asst. dept. sociology and anthropology Iowa State U., Ames, Iowa, 1978-79, rsch. aide, 1980-81, 82-83; ednl. aide, substitute tchr. Ames Cmty. Sch. Dist., Iowa, 1983-86; coord. practicums Nova U., Ft. Lauderdale, Fla., 1986-87; tchr. Downtown Adult Edn. Ctr., Ft. Lauderdale, Fla., 1987-88, Apollo Mid. Sch., Hollywood, Fla., 1988-89, Greenview Elem. Sch., Columbia, SC, 1989-91; dir. rsch. edn. NuWAE Ent., Houston, 1991-92; cosmetic cons., counter mgr. Elizabeth Arden Foley's/May Co., 1992-99; resource cons. RCI, Inc., Tex. So. U., 1999-2000; ed. cons. Houston, 2000—. Sec.-treas. Ames Tenant Landlord Svcs., 1982-83, bd. dirs. 1982-, 83, 84-85, chmn., 1984-85. Recipient svc. award Local Govt. Study Commn., Huntsville, 1972, Ms. Alumni award Ala. A&M U., 1978. Mem. ASCD, Ala. A&M U. Alumni Assn. (chaplain 1977-78), Phi Delta Kappa, Delta Sigma Theta. Home: 8001 W Tidwell Rd Apt 416 Houston TX 77040-5536

JIMMINK, GLENDA LEE, retired elementary school educator; b. Lamar, Colo., Feb. 13, 1935; d. Harold Dale and Ruth Grace (Ellenberger) Fasnacht; m. Gary Jimmink, Oct. 24, 1964 (div. 1984); 1 child, Erik Gerard. BA, U. LaVerne, Calif., 1955. Tchr. elem. grades Pomona (Calif.) Unified Sch. Dist., 1955-61, Palo Alto (Calif.) Unified Sch. Dist., 1961-65, San Rafael (Calif.) Sch. Dist., 1966-95; ret., 1995. Mem. curriculum coun. San Rafael Sch. Dist., 1983-90, 94-95, mentor tchr., 1989-90, mem. social studies steering com., 1990-95; charter mem. Marin County Curriculum Connection, 1991-95. Artist, pub. (calendar) Dry Creek Valley, 1987; author: World Geography Resource Handbook for Tchrs., 1990, others. Mem. Marin Arts Coun., San Rafael, 1988-95, Big Bros.-Big Sisters, San Rafael, 1986-93, Earthwatch, 1990—. Mem. Colored Pencil Soc. Am. (signature mem.), Mendocino Art Assn., Richmond Art Ctr., Sierra Club, Gualala Arts Assn., Nature Conservancy, Berkeley Art Ctr. Avocations: art, reading, horticulture, travel.

JIN, DI, economist; b. China, 1959; came to U.S., 1986; s. Jingde Jin and Jin Zhou; m. Zhen Wu, 1991; 1 child, Rubing Jin. BS, Shanghai Jiao Tong U., China, 1982; MMA, U. R.I., 1987, PhD, 1991. Asst. engr. China State Shipbuilding Corp., Beijing, 1982-86; rsch. asst. U. R.I., Kingston, 1987-91; rsch. fellow Woods Hole (Mass.) Oceanographic Inst., 1991-93, asst. scientist, 1993-97, assoc. scientist, 1997—. Cons. Nat. Rsch. Coun., Washington, 1993-94. Contbr. articles to profl. jours. Recipient Outstanding Social Sci. PhD Dissertation award Nat. Sea Grant Assn., 1992. Mem. Am. Econ. Assn., Assn. Environ. and Resource Economists, Am. Agr. Econs. Assn., Phi Kappa Phi. Office: Woods Hole Oceanographic In 5 School St Woods Hole MA 02543-1138

JIN, DOO JUNG, geophysicist, educator, researcher; b. Hadong, Kyong Nam, Korea (South), Aug. 6, 1942; arrived in U.S., 1969; s. Jae Ho Jin, Pil Ah Choe; m. Bong Ja Chin; children: Sungsoo, Sue Young, Hyewon. BS, Inha Inst.of Tech., Inchon, Korea, 1963; MS, Stanford U., 1971; PhD, So. Meth. U., 1979. Mem. technical staff Tex. Instruments, Inc., Dallas & Alexandria, Va., 1974—76; sr. geophysicist Texaco Houston Rsch. Ctr., Houston, 1979—85; consulting geophysicist Geoengring. Consultants, Houston, 1985—87; sr. staff scientist Chem-Nuclear Geotech, Inc., Grand Junction, Colo., 1987—91; consulting geoscientist Geoenvironmental Consultants, Grand Junction, 1991—92; instr. Columbia Basin Coll., Pasco, Wash., 1992—97; assoc. prof. chemistry and phys. sci. Northwest Coll.; mem. Nat. Environ. Justice Adv. Coun., 2003—. Reviewer Ground Water Pub. Co., Westerville, 1994—2001. Contbr. articles to profl. jours. Corp. Korean Army, 1964—66. Mem.: Am. Geophys. Union, Soc.of Exploration Geophysicists. Assemblies Of God. Avocation: hiking. Home: 5506 114th Ave NE Kirkland WA 98033 Office: Northwest College 5520 108th Ave NE Kirkland WA 98033 Office Fax: 425-889-7815. Business E-Mail: dj.jin@ncag.edu.

JIN, JIN YAN, science educator; b. Beijing, July 18, 1978; d. Haixing Yan and Ling Li; m. Feng Jin, Aug. 9, 2001. BS, Peking U., 1997; PhD, SUNY at Buffalo, 2003. Rsch. asst. Nat. Inst. of Pharm. R & D, Beijing, 1997—98; grad. rsch. asst. SUNY at Buffalo, Dept. of Pharm. Sciences, Amherst, NY, 1998—. Treas. U. at Buffalo, Am. Assn. of Pharm. Scientists Student Chpt., Amherst, NY, 1999—2000; sec. U. at Buffalo, Pharm. Sciences Grad. Student Assn., 1999—2000. Contbr. articles to profl. jours. Recipient The Mathematically Precocious Youth, Johns Hopkins U., 1991, The Li Zhende prize and a Hope-Star medal, Beijing No. Eight Mid. Sch., 1993, The Medicine and Pharmacy prize, Japanese Pharm. Corp. and the Internat. Exch. Ctr. of the Dept. of Pub. Health of China), 1995—96; Excellent Student Scholarship for Undergraduates, Peking U., 1994—95, 1996—97. Mem.: U. at Buffalo Pharm. Sciences Alumni Com., Am. Assn. of Pharm. Scientists. Home: 6598 Dysinger Rd apt 18 Lockport NY 14094 Office: State University of New York at Buffalo 528 Hochstetter Hall Amherst NY 14260

JIN, LI, education educator; s. Yongwei Jin and Jingfeng Wang; m. Jian Lai, Jan. 16, 1988; children: Bryan Bohan, Jonathan Junshen. PhD, U. of Tex. - Houston Health Sci. Ctr., 1994. Postdoctoral fellow Stanford U., Stanford, Calif., 1994—96, asst. prof. U. of Tex. - Houston Health Sci. Ctr., Houston, 1997—99, assoc. prof., 2000—01; prof. U. of Cin., Cincinnati, Ohio, 2001—; adj. prof. Fudan U., Shanghai, 1997—. Achievements include research in Human Population Genetics and Genetics of Complex Diseases. Office: Univ of Cincinnati 3223 Eden Ave Cincinnati OH 45267-0056 E-mail: li.jin@uc.edu.

JIN, XUECHENG, engineering researcher; b. Harbin, People's Republic China, May 28, 1966; came to U.S., 1995; s. Shixia Jin and Yicheng Liang; m. Shujie Zhao, Jan. 15, 1992; 1 child, Joy Qiu. Jin. B in Engring., Tsinghua U., Beijing, China, 1990; MSc, Stanford (Calif.) U., 1997, student, 1998—. Rsch. scholar Nat U. of Singapore, 1992-93; assoc. rsch. fellow Gintic Inst. of Mfg., Singapore, 1993-95; rschr. Stanford U., 1995—. Sr. tutor Nat. U. Singapore, 1995—. Contbr. articles to profl. publs.; inventor micromachined ultrasonic transducer fabrication. Recipient RWB Stephens prize Ultrasonic Internat., 1997, region 3.6.9. winner IEEE Engring. Medicine and Biology Soc., 1998, region 10 winner, 1994, Engring. Acoustics award Acoustic Soc. of Am., 1997. Mem. IEEE. Avocation: tennis. Office: Edwards L Ginzton Lab Stanford U Stanford CA 94305 Home: 2677 Waverly St Palo Alto CA 94306

JIN, YAN, university educator, researcher, consultant; b. Nanjing, Jiangsu Province, China, July 13, 1959; s. Zhen Jin, Qican Qian; m. Jannie Jiaying Wu; children: Emily, Jessica. Doctor of Engineering, University of Tokyo, Tokyo, Japan, 1985—88. Rsch. assoc. Stanford U., Palo Alto, Calif., 1991—94, sr. rsch. scientist, 1994—96; asst. prof. U. So. Calif., LA, 1996—99, assoc. prof., 1999—. Founder, v.p.l Vite Corp., Mountain View, Calif., 1996—, dir. bd., 1996—99; chief cons. Jinteck, Arcadia, 1994—; dir. IMPACT Lab. U. S.C., LA; tech. advisor ePM LLC, Austin, Tex., 2002—. Inventor Virtual Design Team - Organization Simulator, 1995; editor: Multimedia Technology for Collaborative Design and Manufacturing, 1997; author: Data Mining for Design and Manufacturing, 2001, Coordination Theory and Collaboration Technology, 2001, Universal Design Theory, 1998, Computational Organization Theory, 1993, (Conference publication) 5th World Multiconference on Systems, Cybernetics and Informatics, 2001; contbr. articles to profl. jours. and papers to confs. Recipient Faculty Career award, NSF, 1998, Rsch. award, Toyota Motor Corp., 1993—2002, Ford Motor Co., 1998, Best Paper award, 14th Internat. Conf. on design theory and methodolgy, 2002; Monbusho scholar, Ministry of Edn., Japan, 1983—88. Mem.: ASME, Am. Assn. Artificial Intelligence. Office: U So Calif 3650 McClintock Ave OHE-430 Los Angeles CA 90089-1453 Personal E-mail: yjin@usc.edu. Business E-Mail: yjin@usc.edu.

JIN, ZHONGHAI, physicist; b. Taihu, China, Jan. 26, 1963; arrived in U.S., 1990; s. Fu-You Jin and Tao-Mei Yin; m. Qingyu Chen, July 20, 1987; children: Pongyang, Lucy Ahren. BS, U. Sci. China, 1984; MS, Chinese Acad. Sci., Hefei, China, 1987; PhD, U. Alaska, 1995. Postdoctoral rschr. U. Alaska, Fairbanks, 1995-96, Scripss Inst. Oceanography, La Jolla, Calif., 1996-99; rsch. scientist U. Calif., San Diego, 1999—2000; sr. scientist AS&M, Inc., Hampton, Va., 2000—. Mem. Am. Geophys. Union, Am. Meteorol. Soc. Achievements include development of a coupled atmosphere-ocean radiative transfer model and its research applications. Avocations: basketball, soccer, music. Office: Ste 300 1 Enterprise Pky Hampton VA 23666

JINDRA, CHRISTINE, editor; b. Cleve., Sept. 18, 1947; d. Lad Joseph and Ann Frances (Makar) J.; m. Peter J. Junkin, Aug. 1, 1970 (div. Dec. 1987); children: William Patrick, Michael Lad. BS in Journalsim, Ohio State U., 1969. City reporter Buffalo News, 1969-70; metro reporter Plain Dealer, Cleve., 1970-82, assignment editor, nat. reporter, 1982-84, state editor, 1984-86, metro editor, 1986-88, feature editor, 1988-92, asst. mng. editor, 1992-2001, Sunday editor, 2001—. Mem. Women's Cmty. Found., Women's City Club. Avocations: skiing, gardening, traveling, cooking. Office: Plain Dealer 1801 Superior Ave E Cleveland OH 44114-2198

JING, NAIHUAN N. mathematician; b. Wuhan, China, Jan. 1962; s. Mu Jing and Shunxian Peng; m. Hui Gu, Nov. 0, 1963; children: Juliana H., Gloria E. MS, Wuhan U., Wuhan, China, 1984, Yale U., 1988, PhD, 1989. Mem. Inst. for Advanced Study, Princeton, 1989—90; asst. prof. U. Mich., Ann Arbor, 1990—92; from asst. prof. to assoc. prof. U. Kans., Lawrence, 1992—95; mem. Math. Sci. Res. Inst., Berkeley, Calif., 1999—99; assoc. prof. N.C. State U., Raleigh, 1996—2001, prof., 2001—. Recipient Chutian Scholar and Professorship awards, Hubei Edn. Commn., 2001-2006, Rsch. fellowship, Alexander von Humboldt Found., 2003. Mem.: Am. Math. Soc. Office: NC State Univ Box 8205 Raleigh NC 27695-8205

JINKINS, WM. MICHAEL, theology studies educator; b. Lufkin, Tex., Oct. 5, 1953; s. Arden L. and Rita B. (Fenley) Jinkins; m. Deborah Bradshaw, Sept. 27, 1975; children: Jeremy Michael, Jessica Michelle. BA, Howard Payne Univ., Brownwood, Tex., 1975; MDiv, Southwestern Sem., Fort Worth, Tex., 1979; DMin, Austin Presbyn. Sem., Austin, Tex., 1983; PhD, Univ. Aberdeen, Aberdeen, Scotland, 1990. Assoc. pastor St. Stephen's Presbyn. Ch., Irving, Tex., 1979—83; pastoral asst. Beechgrove Ch., Aberdeen, 1987—90; pastor Brenham Presbyn. (Tex.) Ch., 1990—93; prof pastoral theology Austin Presbyn. Theol. Sem., Austin, Tex., 1979—83. Author: The Church Faces Death, 1999, Invitation to Theology, 2001, Christianity, Tolerance & Pluralism, 2003. Grantee ATS Faculty Rsch. Grant, Assn. Theol. Studies, 1999, Oxford Fellowhip, Graduate Theol. Union, 1999. Mem.: Soc. for the Scientific Study of Religion, Soc. of Bibical Lit., Am. Acad. Religion. Presbyn. Office: Austin Presbyn Theol Sem 100 East 27th St Austin TX 78705

JINKS, ROBERT LARRY, retired newspaper publisher; b. Mt. Pleasant, Tex., Jan. 26, 1929; s. Leon Carlton and Mary (Cunnyngham) J.; m. Anne Claire van Ravesteyn, May 8, 1971; children by previous marriage: Laura Beth, Daniel Carlton, Beau Pottorff. BJ, U. Mo., 1950; MS, Columbia, 1956. News editor Muskogee (Okla.) Times-Democrat, 1950-51; reporter Greensboro (N.C.) Daily News, 1953-55; reporter, city editor Charlotte (N.C) Observer, 1956—60; mem. staff Miami (Fla.) Herald, 1960-77, mng. editor, 1966-72, exec. editor, 1972—76; editor, v.p. San Jose (Calif.) Mercury News, 1977-81; sr. v.p. news and ops. Knight-Ridder Corp., Miami, Fla., 1981-89; pub. San Jose (Calif.) Mercury News, 1989-94, ret., 1994. Pres. AP Mng. Editors, 1975—76, Fla. Soc. Newspaper Editors, 1975; bd. dirs. McClatchy Newspapers, Inc. With AUS, 1951-53. Named to 50th anniversary honors list Columbia Grad. Sch. Journalism, 1963, Disting. Grad., 1983; Disting. Grad. award U. Mo., 1990. Mem. Am. Soc. Newspaper Editors (dir. 1980-86).

JINNETT, ROBERT JEFFERSON, lawyer; b. Birmingham, Ala., May 9, 1949; s. Bryan Floyd Jr. and Elizabeth Coleman (Borders) J.; m. Doreen S. Ziff, Aug. 2, 1975 (div.); children: Brynn Leigh, Maren Alexandra. BA, Harvard U., 1971; JD, Cornell U., 1975. Bar: N.Y. 1976, U.S. Dist. Ct. (no. dist.) N.Y. 1976, U.S. Dist. Ct. (so. dist.) N.Y. 1978, U.S. Dist. Ct. (ea. dist.) N.Y. 1979, U.S. Supreme Ct. 1988; cert. info. sys. security profl.; Microsoft cert. profl. Law clk. N.Y. State Ct. Appeals, Albany, 1975-77; assoc. Rogers & Wells, N.Y.C., 1977-82, LeBoeuf, Lamb, Greene & MacRae, N.Y.C., 1983-85; ptnr. LeBoeuf, Lamb, Leiby & MacRae, N.Y.C., 1986-94, LeBoeuf, Lamb, Greene & MacRae, L.L.P., N.Y.C., 1994, of counsel, 1995—. Pres. LeBoeuf Computing Techs., LLC., N.Y.C., 1996—. Contbr. articles to profl. jours. Recipient 3d nat. prize Nathan Burkan Meml. Competition, ASCAP, 1974; German Acad. Exch. Svc. fellow U. Heidelberg, Germany, 1971-72. Mem. S.R., Jamestowne Soc. Republican. Episcopalian. Avocation: poetry. Office: LeBoeuf Lamb Greene MacRae 125 W 55th St New York NY 10019-5369 E-mail: Jinnett@llgm.com.

JINRIGHT, JOHN WILLIAM, music educator; b. Troy, Ala., Nov. 23, 1962; s. J.P. and Ruth Cardwell J. BA, Birmingham So. Coll., 1984; MSEd, Troy (Ala.) State U., 1992; PhD, Auburn (Ala.) U., 2003. With purchasing dept. Nuncie's Music, Birmingham, 1983-88; with mgmt. Bandstand Inc., Birmingham, 1988-90; sales rep. Capitol Music, Montgomery, Ala., 1990-91; tchr., instr. Troy State U., 1993—. Reviewer Multimedia Ednl. Resources for Learning and Online Tchg. music discipline team, 2000—. Contbr. articles to profl. jours. Mem. Soc. for the Preservation and Encouragement of Barbershop Quartet Singing in Am. (pres. Troy chpt. 2001), Contemporary A Cappella Soc. (amb. 2000—), Music Educator's Nat. Conf., Nat. Assn. of Profl. Band Instrument Repair Technicians, Ala. Arts Alliance, Tri-M Music Honor Soc., Lambda Chi Alpha, Omicron Delta Kappa. Avocations: a cappella singing, book collecting. Home: 3675 Banks Hwy Troy AL 36081 Office: Long Sch of Music Troy State U Troy AL 36082

JINRIGHT, NOAH FRANKLIN, vocational school educator, security executive; b. Banks, Alabama, Dec. 5, 1936; s. William Carroll and Ila Marie (Garrett) J.; m. Sarah Ann (Graham) Nickolson, Nov. 21, 1959 (div. Sept. 1974); children: Charlene M., Lisa A., Michael D.; m. Frances Lenora (Gaskins), June 11, 1978; children: Diana Carol, Jonathan Franklin. Cert. archtl. and mech. drafting, Columbus Tech., GA., 1971, CNC, 1983, cert. plate and pipe welder, 1984. Lic. ins. agt., Ga; cert. security officer. Operator scale Bibb Textiles, Columbus, Ga., 1954-56; operator press and share Columbus Iron Works, Columbus, Ga., 1957-58; ins. agt. Interstate Life, Columbus, Ga., 1958-61; operated winder, starter, generator Joe Hooten, Inc., Columbus, Ga., 1960; fireman City of Columbus, Columbus, Ga., 1960-66; ins. agt. Murray Meadows Ins. Agy., Columbus, Ga., 1960—67; advt. rep. Jinright Enterprises, Columbus, Ga., 1966; ins. agt. Security Life of Ga., Columbus, Ga., 1966; operator share and press Pascoe Steel, Columbus, Ga., 1966-67; machinist Goldens' Foundry and Machine Works, Columbus, Ga., 1967; carpenter, roofer Muscogee County Sch. Dist., Columbus, Ga., 1968-72, pattern maker Pekor Iron Works, Columbus, Ga., 1972-78; instr. metals tech. Spencer H.S., Columbus, Ga., 1978-91, Carver H.S., Columbus, Ga., 1991-94; security officer Sizemore Security Internat., 1994-95, 97-99; instr. metals tech. Kendrick H.S., Columbus, Ga., 1994-99; ret., 1999; security officer Sizemore Security Internat., 1999-2001, The Wackenhut Corp. Security Internat., 2001—03, Securitas Security Svc., USA, Inc., 2003—. Past mfg. rep. printing and advtg. specialties; cons. Voc. Tng. and Rsch. Inst., Seoul, Korea, 1989-90; instr., ptnr. with M. Davis; fire protection supr. 9311th A.F.Rescuer Squadron Columbus, Ga., (Tech. Sgt.). Contbg. articles to local newspapers. Sponsor Spencer H.S. AWS Club, 1979-81; exec. trainer Precision Metalforming Assn., 1996-99; past trustee Epworth United Meth. Ch., ch. usher; mem. Columbus Confederate Drill Team; adv. bd. Am. Biog. Inst., 1999—. Tech. sgt. USAFR, 1963-65. Recipient: Recruiting cert. USAF, 1991-92, Best Drilled Soldier Award Co. D., (three times) Nat. Guard; named top marksman (expert) in Co.D. 560th Armn. Engr. Bn. (48th divsn.), Bn. Champion, 1962; 3d Best in State Ga., 1962, (with Master Sgt. Davis, top NCO instr., staff sgt.); Top NCO instr., Master Sgt. in Bn. 1962; named Rschr. of the Yr., Am. Biog. Inst., 2001; Who's Who Worldwide, 1993; Sterling Who's Who, 1994; Who's Who Exec. Club, 1994-95; Who's Who in the South and Southwest, 1997-2002; IBC Internat. Biographical Ctr., Cambridge, Eng., 1998-99; Who's Who in Am., 1998; Who's Who in the World, 1998; Who's Who of the Yr., 1999; Contemporary Who's Who, 2003; Who's Who in Am. Biog., 2003; Who's Who in Fin. and Industry, 2002-03; Who's Who in Am. Educ., 2004-2005, Am. Biog. Inst. Bd. of Adv., 1999-; Am. Biog. Inst. Rschr. of the Yr., 2001. Mem. NEA, Internat. Soc. Welding Educators (1st symposium program adv. bd. mem.), Am. Foundry Soc., Am. Welding Soc. (adv. bd.), Vocat. Indsl. Clubs Am. (advisor, cert. of appreciation region VIII 1996), Trade and Indsl. Educators Ga. (mem. West Ga. Sch. to work-evaluation team 1994-99), Muscogee Edn. Assn., Ga. Assn. Educators, Ga. Vocat. Assn., Am. Vocat. Assn., Precision Metalforming Assn., Am. Foundrymen's Soc., Ga. Teacher's Union, So. Assn. Colls. and Schs., Ga. Assn. Educators, Methodist. Avocations: fishing, hunting, camping, model building, photography. Home: PO Box 63 Columbus GA 31902-0063 Office: 2040 Lee Rd 427 Phenix City AL 36867 Fax: 334-297-7545.

JIRAUCH, CHARLES W. lawyer; b. St. Louis, Apr. 27, 1944; m. Sally J. Costello, 1968 (div. Mar. 1977); m. Dana K. Bowen, 1980; children: Melissa, Mathew, Kathleen. BSEE, Washington U., 1966; JD, Georgetown U., 1970. Bar: Ill. 1971, Ariz. 1975, Nev. 1991, Calif. 1993, Colo. 1993, U.S. Patent Office 1970, U.S. Supreme Ct. 1978. Atty. Leydig, Voit & Mayer, Chgo., 1970-71, McDermott, Will & Emery, Chgo., 1971-75, Streich Lang, Phoenix, 1975-2000, Quarles & Brady Streich Lang, Phoenix, 2000—; examiner U.S. Patent Office, 1968—70. Bd. dirs. Valley Big Bros./Big Sisters, 1980-86, pres. bd. dirs., 1985-86; pres., bd. dirs. Valley Big Bros./Big Sisters Found., 1988-92; bd. advisors to dean Ariz. State U. Sch. Engring., 1998—; bd. dirs., gen. coun. Ariz. Bus. and Edn. Coalition, 2002—; mem. Ariz. Dem. Coun. Mem. ABA, Internat. Bar Assn., Calif. Bar Assn., Ariz. Bar Assn. and Found., Maricopa County Bar Assn. and Found. (tech. law sect. bd. dirs. 2000—, chmn. 2001—), Am. Judicature Soc., Am. Intellectual Property Law Assn., Ariz. Civil Liberties Union, Ariz. Software Tech. Coun.(bd. dirs. 2000-02), Am. Electronic Assn. (exec. com. Ariz. chpt. 1999—), Ariz. Tech. Coun. (bd. dirs. 2002—), Ariz. C. of C. (edn. and tech. comms. 2002—). Democrat. Roman Catholic. Office: Quarles & Brady Streich Lang 2 N Central Ave Fl 2 Phoenix AZ 85004-2345

JIROTKA, GEORGE M. lawyer; b. Berwyn, Ill., May 8, 1957; s. Zdenek F. and Jaromira (Kralovec) J. BA, Columbia U., 1979; MBA, U. Chgo., 1980; JD, U. Tex., 1983. Assoc. Annis, Mitchell, Cockey, Edward & Roehn, P.A., Tampa, Fla., 1984-86, Fowler White Boggs Banker, P.A., Tampa/Clearwater, Fla., 1986-91, ptnr./shareholder, 1991—. Chmn. mem. 6th judicial cir. nom. commn., 1999-2002. Commr./mayor Belleair Shore, Fla., 1986-98; chmn. Pinellas County (Fla.) Planning Coun., 1988-98; pres. Suncoast League of Municipalities, 1994—, dir.; dir. Fla. League of Cities, 1997-98; sec.-treas. Pinellas Suncoast Transit Authority, 1996-98, bd. dirs.; mem. Pinellas County Pub. Employee Rels. Commn., 1996—; trustee Pinellas Suncoast Fire & Rescue Dist. Firefighters Pension Trust, 1999—; mem. 2d jud. dist. nominations commn., 2002—. Mem. Gulf Beaches on Sand Key C. of C. (Outstand Cmty. Svc. award 1994). Rep. Roman Cath. Avocations: politics, fin. Office: Fowler White Boggs Banker PA 501 E Kennedy Blvd Ste 1700 Tampa FL 33602

JIROVEC, MARY ANN, music educator; b. Milw., Sept. 6, 1952; d. John Frank and Irene Doris (Spychalski) J. BFA, U. Wis., Milw., 1974, MS in Mus. Edn., 1978. Music tchr. grades 5-12 Harlem (Mont.) Pub. Schs., 1974-76; music tchr. grades 5-9 West Allis (Wis.) Sch. Dist., 1976-89, 91-93; O.M. summer ministry team Ukraine and Poland, 1992; music tchr. West Allis (Wis.) Sch. Dist., 1995—; overseas refugee worker Operation Mobilisation, Austria, Poland, Romania, Czech Republic, 1989-90, secondary English tchr. Szczecinek (Poland) Schs., 1994-95. Participant tchr. exch., Novosibirsk, Russia, 1996, Wales/Poland cultural exch. program, 1998. Music and drama teams, English workshops, Int. Messengers, Operation Mobilisation local Polish chs., Ukraine, Czech Republic, 1989—, Poland summer campaign coord., 1990; spl. ministry team leader, Yucatan, Mex., 1999, 2001; vacation bible sch. leader, 2001-02; coord., praise leader Milw. March for Jesus, 1992-94, 1996-2001. U. Wis. Grad. Music grantee, 1976-77. Mem.: Wis. Contemporary Music Forum (sec. 1977), Knighwind Ensemble, Delta Omicron (Wis. pres. 1973—74), Phi Kappa Phi. Avocations: international travel, cultural events, reading. Home: 3467 S 68th St Apt 2 Milwaukee WI 53219-4034

JISCHKE, MARTIN C. academic administrator; b. Chgo., Aug. 7, 1941; m. Patricia Fowler; children: Charles, Marian. BS in Physics with honors, Ill. Inst. Tech., 1963; MS in Aeronautics and Astronautics, MIT, 1964, PhD in Aeronautics and Astronautics, 1968. Engr. Rand Corp., Santa Monica, Calif., 1965; research engr. Battelle N.W. Lab., Richland, Washington, 1970; research fellow Donald W. Douglas Lab., Richland, 1971, Nat. Aeronautics and Space Adminstrn., Moffett Field, Calif., 1973; from asst. prof. to prof. aerospace, mech. and nuclear engring. U. Okla., 1968-75, prof., dir. Sch. Aerospace, Mech. and Nuclear Engring., 1977-81, interim pres., 1985, dean Coll. Engring., 1981-86, mem. various coms., 1985; White House fellow, spl. asst. to sec. of transp. U.S. Dept. Transp., Washington, 1975-76; chancellor U. Mo., Rolla, 1986-91; pres. Iowa State U., Ames, 1991-2000, Purdue U., 2000—. Bd. dirs. Kerr McGee Corp., Wabash Nat. Corp., Mo. Alliance for Sci., 1987-91, The Keystone Found., 1984-90, Mo. Corp. for Sci. and Tech., vice-chmn., 1990-91; participant Japanese Econ. Found. Vis. Leaders Program, 1983; mem. Gov.'s Coun. on Sci. and Tech. State of Okla., 1983-84, Gordon Rsch. Conf. on Geophysics; mem. planning com. for 80's Okla. State Regents for Higher Edn.; mem. organizing com. 14th Midwestern Mechanics Conf.; mem. adv. com. for engring. sci. NSF Engring. Directorate, 1985-88; mem. com. on statewide postsecondary telecomm. policy Mo. Coordinating Bd. for Higher Edn., 1987-91; chmn. Congrl. Aero. Adv. Com., 1987-89; sci. adviser to Gov. of Mo., 1990-91; mem. Am. Coun. on Edn. Com. on Math. and Sci., 1990-91. Contbr. articles and reports to profl. publs. Civilian aide Sec. of Army, State of Mo. East, 1987-91; bd. dirs. Bankers Trust, 1995—, Iowa Spl. Olympics, Am. Coun. on Edn., 1996—, Nat. Merit Scholarship Corp., 1997—; mem. Kellogg Commn. on the Future of State and Land-Grant U., 1995—, founding pres. Global Consortium of Higher Edn. and Rsch. for Agr., 1999. Recipient Ralph Teetor award Soc. Automotive Engrs., 1971, Brandon H. Griffith award U. Okla., U. Okla. Regents award for superior teaching, 1975, IIT Prof. Achievement award, 1992, Delta Tau Delta Achievement award, 1992, Engrs. Club St. Louis Achievement award, 1991, Dept. Army Outstanding Civilian Svc. medal, 1991; NASA fellow, 1966; NSF fellow, 1965; AEC/NORCUS summer faculty fellow, 1970-71, NASA/ASEE fellow, 1973. Fellow AAAS, AIAA (assoc., sec.-treas. Okla. chpt., vice chmn., chmn.); mem. ASME, AAUP (v.p., pres. Okla. chpt.), NSPE, Am. Phys. Soc., Am. Soc. Engring. Edn. (Centennial Medallion 1993), Nat. Assn. State Univs. and Land Grant Colls. (bd. dirs., chair 1997-98), Assn. Big Twelve Univs. (pres. 1994-96), Mo. Soc. Profl. Engrs., Rotary, Phi Beta Kappa, Tau Beta Pi, Sigma Xi, Pi Tau Sigma, Sigma Gamma Tau, Sigma Pi Sigma, Phi Eta Sigma. Home: 500 McCormick Rd West Lafayette IN 47906 Office: Purdue U Office of the Pres West Lafayette IN 47906

JIUYONG, SHI, judge; b. Zhejiang, China, Sept. 1926; BA in Govt. and Pub. Law, St. John's U., Shanghai, 1948; MA in Internat. Law, Columbia U., 1951, postgrad., 1951-54. Asst. rsch. fellow Internat. Law Inst. Internat. Rels., Beijing, 1956-58; sr. lectr., assoc. prof. Internat. Law Fgn. Affairs Coll., Beijing, 1958-64; rsch. fellow Internat. Law Inst. Internat. Law, Beijing, 1964-73, 73-80; tchr. Internat. Econ. Law Dept. Law Peking U., 1980-85; prof. Internat. Law Fgn. Affairs Coll., Beijing, 1984-93; prof. Law Fgn. Econ. Law Tng. Ctr. Min. Justice People's Republic China, Beijing, 1987-88; judge Internat. Ct. of Justice, The Hague, The Netherlands, 1994—, v.p., 2000—03, pres., 2003—. Adviser Chinese Soc. Internat. Law, Beijing, Chinese del. 35th session Gen. Assembly UN, China's Alt. Rep. Sixth Com. to 35th session, Chinese del. to 36th, 37, 38th sessions UN Gen. Assembly and China's del. Sixth Com. at same sessions, 1981-83; legal adviser Ministry Fgn. Affairs People's Republic China, 1980-93, Office Chinese Sr. Rep. Sino-Brit. Joint Liaison Group on Hong Kong plenary sessions, 1985-93, Chinese Ctr. Legal Consultancy, Beijing, 1989-93, Chinese del. 1980 Ann. Meeting Bd. Govs. Internat. Monetary Fund and Internat. Bank Reconstruction and Devel., del. Ministry Fin. People's Republic China Internat Bank Reconstruction and Devel., Chinese del. talks between Govt. China and Asian Devel. Bank, 1986, Chinese side Working Group Sino-Brit. Negotiations regarding Hong Kong, 1984, Chinese del. Disarmament Conf., 1991-92; del. Chinese del. to sessions Asian-African Legal Consultative Com., 1981, 83, 93, Chinese del. legal consultations between Ministry Fgn. Affairs of People's Republic China and Dept. State U.S. Am., 1983, 1984, Chinese del. negotiations between Govt. People's Republic China and Govt. U.S. Am. on Mut. Promotion and Protection of Investment Agreement, 1983, 1984; expert sr. legal experts meeting rev. Montevideo program, UN Environ. Program, Geneva, 1991, Nairobi, 1991; lectr. internat. fin. instns. Nat. Bureau Oceanography, People's Republic China, 1986, protection of private fgn. investment Hague Acad. Internat. Law Regional Program, Beijing, 1987, Grad. Inst. Internat. Studies, Geneva, 1988, autonomy in Internat. Law Sem. UN Office, Geneva, 1988, certain issues relating to legal status of Hong Kong Spl. Adminstrv. Region, internat. trade regulation, 1985-86, others; chmn. panel discussions new internat. econ. order Beijing Conf. Law of the World World Peace through Law, 1990; participant symposium internat. law arms control and disarmament, Geneva, 1991, Seminar Draft Code Crimes and internat. criminal jurisdiction, symposium on tchg., dissemination and rsch. internat. law in devel. countries, Beijing, 1992. Mem. Am. Soc. Internat. Law, Internat. Law Commn. (rep. to 45th session UN gen. Assembly 1990, 30th meeting of Asian-African Legal Consultative Conf. 1991, mem. 1987-93, rapporteur, 1988, chmn. 1990, lectr. 1991), Inst. Hong Kong Law Chinese Law Soc., Standing Com., Beijing Com., Eighth Ann. Com., Chinese People's Polit. Consultative Conf., Fgn. Econ. and Trade Arbitration Commn., China Coun. Promotion Internat. Trade, Steering Com. Office: Internat Ct of Justice Peace Palace 2517 KJ The Hague Netherlands

JIVETIN, ALEXANDER, geophysicist, educator; b. Tashkent, Uzbekistan, USSR, June 8, 1952; arrived in U.S., 1992; s. Anatoly Vasilievich and Anna Vasilievna Jivetin; m. Stella Gensirovskaia, Oct. 21, 1975; children: Sergey, Julia. M of Geophysics, Tashkent U., 1974; PhD in Geology and Minerology, Moscow Geoprospecting Inst., 1983. Sr. lab. technician Ctrl. Asia Inst. Geology and Mineral Resources, Tashkent, 1974-76; main engr. sci. dept. Uzbekistan Ministry of Geology, Tashkent, 1976-79; sr. rschr. Inst. of Oil and Gas Geology, Tashkent, 1979—92; pvt. tutor math., physics and earth sci. Bklyn., 1992-98; tchr. Ohr Eliezer Sch., Bklyn., 1998—. Acad. sec. govt. seismol. com., Tashkent, 1978—79; expert Ministry of Geology, 1984—92. Author: How Gods Dodged the Big Bang, or Is Life Preprogrammed?, Combined Anthropic Priciple; contbr. over 25 articles to profl. jours.; patent for lottery game methods. Organizer, pres. Nature Conservation Soc. Uzbekistan, 1986-92. Mem. N.Y. Acad. Scis. Office: Ohr Eliezer Sch 2115 Benson Ave Brooklyn NY 11214 E-mail: sciencestreamjivetin@hotmail.com.

JIVIDEN, JAMES CARL, educational administrator; b. L.A., Sept. 25, 1970; s. James Allan and Patrice J. BA with distinction, Ohio No. U., 1992, JD, 1995. Bar: Calif. Atty., San Francisco, 1995-97; tchr. social studies Matlock Acad., West Palm Beach, Fla., 1997-2000, asst. dir., 2000—. Ohio No. U. scholar, 1992-95, NEH scholar, 1999. Mem ABA, ASCD, State Bar Calif., $100,000 Club. Democrat. Office: Matlock Acad PO Box 19717 West Palm Beach FL 33416-9717

JO, HOJE, finance educator; b. Seoul, Korea, Jan. 23, 1954; came to U.S., 1980; s. Yong Chun and Kyung Hee (Lee) Cho; m. Sahie Kang, May 25, 1981; children: Hellen, Haesue. BA in Chinese Lit., Seoul Nat. U., 1977; MBA in Fin., SUNY, Buffalo, 1982; PhD in Fin., U. Fla., 1986. Asst. prof. U. N.Mex., Albuquerque, 1986-89; asst. prof. fin. Santa Clara (Calif.) U., 1990-96, assoc. prof. fin., 1996—. Contbr. articles to profl. jours. Vice-chmn. exec. bd. Silicon Valley Korean Sch., 1996-98. Recipient Competitive Rsch. award Chgo. Bd. Options Exchange, 1993, Outstanding Paper award Global Fin. Assn., 1994, Best Paper award, 1996, 2001, Iddo Sarnat award Jour. Banking and Fin., 1996, Best Paper award Pacific Basin Fin. Conf., 2000, Best Paper award, Korean Securities Assn., 2002. Mem. Korean Am. Fin. Assn. (regional dir. 1992-96, exec. bd. dirs. 1996—), Silicon Valley Korean C. of C. (presenter 1992, Profl. Man of Yr. 1992, 99). Methodist. Avocations: singing, swimming. Office: Santa Clara U 500 El Camino Real Santa Clara CA 95053-0001 Fax: (408) 554-4029. E-mail: hjo@.scu.edu.

JOACHIM, BRIGITTA GOLDEN, writer, advertising agency executive, media consultant; b. Berlin; d. Carl and Gisele (Zeisel) Golden; children: Nancy, Lynne, James. Student, Manhattan Sch. Mus., NYU, 1947-49; cert. TV workshop, Hofstra U., 1972, BA cum laude, 1973, MA with honors, 1976; postgrad., Columbia U., 1973-74. Cert. speech pathologist, N.Y. Election interviewer CBS News, N.Y.C., 1970; comm. specialist South Nassau Communities Hosp., Nassau County, N.Y., 1970-74, Assn. for Help Retarded Children, Brookville, N.Y., 1970-74, Beth Israel Hosp., N.Y.C., 1970-74; talent and rsch. coord. Am. Alive NBC-TV, N.Y.C., 1978-79; creative dir., writer Jim Sant Andrea Shows Producers, N.Y.C., 1979-82; pres., creative dir. Media for the XX's, N.Y.C., 1982—. Tchr. Hendrix St. Day Nursery; prof. media and comm. Touro Coll., N.Y.C., 1987—; media cons. Researcher Investigative News Group, N.Y.C., 1987—; judge radio and TV Internat. Clio awards, 1981—; media writer Writers Conf. to China, 1984; finalists judge Am. Film Festival, 1986-87; judge Internat. Film and Video Awards, 1987—, Cable Ace awards; blue ribbon panel Emmy awards, 1987—, Internat. Emmy awards, 1999. Editor ednl. film Mother and Child, 1976; scriptwriter The Chase is On, A Breed Apart, Women of Louisiana, Model of Tommorrow, Sexually Speaking, Stress,

1981-88, The New You (Physicians Med. Pub.), 1988; dir. Fitness Fables I, II & III with Tony Randall. Past pres. Westbury PTA, Old Westbury, N.Y.; active Lincoln Ctr. Theatre, Mus. Modern Art; host, sponsor fgn. students AFS; dir. Children's Video Project, 1990-91, Children's Media Project, 2000—. Mem. Brit. Acad. Film and TV Arts, Nat. Acad. TV Arts and Scis. (forum producer N.Y. chpt. 1978, mem. nominating com. bd. govs.), N.Y. Alumni Assn. (mem. Hofstra U. exec. bd.), N.Y. Women in Film and TV (bd. dirs. 1997-2000), Fgn. Press Assn., Cinema Club, Sigma Pi, Nat. Honor Soc. Jewish. Avocations: walking, music, theater, films, travel. Office: Media for the XXs 60 W 66th St Ste 20E New York NY 10023-6214 E-mail: BJMEDIAXX@aol.com.

JOANOU, PHILLIP, advertising executive; b. Phoenix, June 5, 1933; s. Paul and Alice (Lukken) J.; m. Michelle Mason, Aug. 18, 1956; children: Janet, Phillip, Jennifer, Kathleen. BS, U. Ariz., 1956; MA, N.Y. Acad. of Art, 1996. Exec. v.p. Galaxy Inc., Los Angeles, 1958-60; sr. account exec. Erwin Wasey Co., 1960-64; account supr. Dancer, Fitzgerald, Sample Co., Los Angeles, 1964-67; v.p. Grey Co., Los Angeles, 1966-68, Doyle, Dane & Bernbach Inc., Los Angeles, 1968-71; exec. v.p., dir. Nov. Group, N.Y.C. and Washington, 1971-72; pres., dir. Dailey & Assocs., L.A., 1973-83, chmn., chief exec. officer, 1984-95. Instr. mktg. U. So. Calif., 1975-76, dir. inst. advt. studies, 1976-77. Mem. Washington Com. to Re-elect Pres. Nixon, 1971-72; advisor Pres. Ford Election Com., 1976, Pres. Reagan Campaign, 1980; founder, dir. Partnership For A Drug Free Am.; pres. La Canada Ednl. Found. trustee Art Ctr Coll. Served to capt. USAR, 1957-58. Recipient Pvt. Sector Initiative award Pres. Reagan and Bush, 1987; named Advt. Leader of the West, Am. Advt. Fedn., 1992. Mem. Western States Advt. Assn. (dir. 1975—, pres. 1980-81, Advt. Man of Yr. 1983), Am. Assn. Advt. Agencies (gov. 1980-81, bd. dirs. 1981-83). Clubs: California. Republican. Episcopalian.

JOB, AMY GRACE, librarian, educator; b. Orange, N.J., Mar. 8, 1942; d. George Calvert and Amy Clark (Barret) Segear; m. Kenneth A. Job, Nov. 8, 1968; children: Karen, Annmarie, Kenneth Jr. BA, Montclair State Coll., 1964, MEd, 1978; MLS, Rutgers U., 1966; EdD, Seton Hall U., 1987. Cert. ednl. media specialist, N.J. Libr. Potsdam (N.Y.) State Coll., 1965-67, William Paterson U., Wayne, N.J., 1960—, instr., 1968—, Kean State Coll., Union, N.J., 1969-70. Cons. Pompton Lakes (N.J.) Schs., 1993, Pub. Schs., Paterson, 1992-94. Author: (with others) Selection Bibliography, 1994; co-author: Reference Work in School Libraries, 1996, School Library Media Specialist as Manager, 1997, Now What Do I Do?, 2001; contbr. articles to profl. jours. Mem. West Milford (N.J.) Bicentennial com. West Milford Hist. Soc., 1974-76, mem. 150th Celebration com., 1983-85. Recipient Disting. Svc. award, NJ Libr. Assn. Colls. and Univs., 1992, N.H. Hist. Day Outstanding Educator award, 2001. Mem. N.J. Libr. Assn. (chair coms. 1972—), ALA, Ednl. Med. Assn. (chair N.J. sect. 1980—). Avocations: reading, gardening. Home: 5 Navajo Trail West Milford NJ 07480-3609 E-mail: joba@wpunj.edu.

JOBE, ANN CONNOR, dean, educator; B Biology, Secondary Edn., Middlebury Coll.; RN, Col. St. Catherine, 1976; MSN Med.-Surg. Nursing/Edn., U. Minn., 1978; MD, U. Nevada, 1986. Asst. prof. dept. family medicine, asst. dean student affairs Sch. Medicine, assoc. dean student affairs, 1992—94, assoc. prof., 1993—97, assoc. dean student affairs, acad. programs, 1994—95, sr. assoc. dean, 1995—2001, prof., 1997—, asst. vice chancellor health scis., 1998—2001; instr. dept. family medicine East Carolina U.'s Brody Sch. Medicine, 1989; resident in family practice Fla. Hosp., Orlando; instr. nursing U. Nevada, Las Vegas, Nev.; nurse in neurosurgery U. Hosps., Minneapolis; interim vice chancellor health scis. East Carolina U., Greenville, NC, adj. clin. prof. Sch. Nursing, 1994—; dean Mercer U.-Sch. Medicine, 2001—. Spkr. in field. Contbr. articles to nat. jours. including Am. Jour. Clin. Nutrition, multimedia edn. projects, Family Medicine, Jour. Nutrition Edn., Acad. Medicine, Archives Family Medicine, Family Community Health. Founding bd. chmn. non-profit orgn. Common Ground Solutions. Grantee Nat. Cancer Inst., W.K. Kellogg Found., U.S. Dept. Health and Human Svs., Am. Acad. Family Physicians Found. . Office: 1400 Coleman Ave Macon GA 31207

JOBE, LARRY ALTON, financial company executive; b. Knox City, Tex., Jan. 12, 1940; s. Lloyd Alton and Georgia (Swift); m. Suzanne Marie Storch, Aug. 2, 1980; 1 dau., Jennifer Marie; children by previous marriage: Lorrie Aileen, Lezlie Amee, Lowell Alton, Lloyd Alan, Leland Austin, Llewyn. BBA, U. North Tex., 1961, postgrad., 1961-65. CPA, Tex. Joined Grant Thornton, Dallas, 1961, mgr., 1967-69, ptnr., 1968-69, mng. ptnr., mem. exec. com., 1973—, S.W. regional mng. ptnr., 1983-91; chmn. Legal Network, Inc., 1991—; pres. Nat. Corporate Network, 1997—; chmn. Ind. Bank Tex., 2002—; asst. sec. commerce Washington, 1969-72; v.p. fin. Dart Industries, 1972-73. Mem. acctg.adv. bd. U. North Tex., U. Tex.; bd. dirs. Ind. Nat. Bank. Contbr. articles to profl. jours. Bd. dirs. Dallas Citizens Coun., Eisenhower World Affairs Inst.; chmn. bd. trustees Dallas Theol. Sem.; mem. Chief Execs. Roundtable; chmn. bd. Dallas Alliance for Minority Enterprise, Dallas Minority Bus. Ctr., Profl. Devel. Inst. of U. North Tex.; mem. pres.'s coun. North Tex. State U. Recipient Excellence in Acctg. award Haskins and Sells Found., 1960; Outstanding Alumni award U. North Tex., 1965, Pres.' Svc. award, 1986; U.S. Interagy. Audit Tng. award, 1970, Outstanding Svc. award, 1st Place Author's award Fed. Govt. Accts. Assn., 1970. Mem. AICPA, Tex. Soc. CPAs, Fed. Govt. Accts. Assn., Dallas C. of C. (dir., vice chmn.), Blue Key, Phi Eta Sigma, Alpha Chi, Alpha Lambda Pi, Beta Alpha Psi. Office: 600 N Pearl St Ste 2100 Dallas TX 75201-2825 E-mail: ljobe@legaljobnet.com.

JOBS, STEVEN PAUL, computer company executive; b. Feb. 24, 1955; s. Paul J. and Clara J. Jobs; m. Laurene Powell, Mar. 18, 1991. Student, Reed Coll. With Hewlett-Packard, Palo Alto, Calif.; designer video games Atari Inc., 1974; co-founder Apple Computer Inc., Cupertino, Calif., chmn. bd., 1975—85; pres. NeXT, Inc., Redwood City, Calif., 1985—96, CEO; interim CEO Apple Computer, Cupertino, Calif., 1997—, now CEO, chmn. Chmn., CEO Pixar Animation Studios, 1986—. Recipient Nat. Medal Tech., presented by Pres. Ronald Reagan, Entrepreneur of the Decade award, Inc. Mag., Jefferson award for pub. svc. Achievements include co-designer (with Stephan Wozniak) Apple I Computer. Office: Pixar Animation Studios 1200 Park Ave Emeryville CA 94608-3677*

JOCHIM, MICHAEL ALLAN, archaeologist; b. St. Louis, May 31, 1945; s. Kenneth Erwin and Jean MacKenzie (Keith) J.; m. Amy Martha Waugh, Aug. 12, 1967; children: Michael Waugh, Katherine Elizabeth. BS, U. Mich., 1967, MA, 1971, PhD, 1975. Lectr. anthropology U. Calif., Santa Barbara, 1975-77, asst. prof., 1979-81, assoc. prof., 1981-87, prof., 1987—, dept. chmn., 1987-92; asst. prof. Queens Coll. CUNY, Flushing, 1977-79. Mem. archaeology rev. panel NSF, Washington, 1988-90. Author: Hunter-Gatherer Subsistence and Settlement, 1976, Strategies for Survival, 1981, A Hunter-Gatherer Landscape, 1998; editor (series) Interdisciplinary Contributions to Archaeology, 1987—; editor Am. Antiquity, 2004—. Chmn. Community Adv. Com. for Spl. Edn., Santa Barbara County, 1980-82. Grantee NEH, 1976, NSF, 1980, 81, 83, 89, 91, 94, 2002, Nat. Geog. Soc., 1987, 97, Wenner-Gren, 1999. Fellow Am. Anthrop. Assn.; mem. Soc. for Am. Archaeology, Sigma Xi. Office: U Calif Dept Anthropology Santa Barbara CA 93106 E-mail: jochim@anth.ucsb.edu.

JOCHNER, MICHELE MELINA, lawyer; b. Naperville, Ill., May 19, 1966; BA summa cum laude, Mundelein Coll., 1987; JD with honors, DePaul U., 1990, LLM in Taxation Law, 1992. Bar: Ill. 1990, U.S. Dist. Ct. (no. dist.) Ill. 1990, U.S. Ct. Appeals (7th cir.) 1996, U.S. Supreme Ct. 1996. Law clk. U.S. Securities & Exch. Commn., Chgo., 1989; legal rsch. asst. to prof. Marlene Nicholson DePaul U. Sch. Law, Chgo., 1989-91, legal rsch. asst. to assoc. dean Vincent Vitullo, 1989-91; law clk. extern U.S. Dist. Ct. (no. dist.) Ill., Chgo., 1989-90; judicial law clk. Cir. Ct. of Cook County, Chgo., 1991-92, staff atty., 1992-93, sr. staff atty., 1993-95, acting supr. legal rsch. divsn., 1995-96; staff atty. permanency project child protection divsn. Cir. Ct. Cook County, Chgo., 1996-97; jud. law clk. to Chief Justice Mary Ann G. McMorrow Ill. Supreme Ct., Chgo., 1997—. Adj. prof. law John Marshall Law Sch., Chgo., 1994—, DePaul U. Coll. Law, 1998—; mem. subcom. money transfers and adminstrv. regulations Ill. Supreme Ct., 1995—96; judge Herzog Moot Ct. Competition, 1997—; spkr. in field. Contbr. articles to profl. jours. Recipient Harold A. Shertz award, Film, Air & Package Carriers Conf., 1990. Fellow: Ill. Bar Found.; mem.: ABA, U.S. Supreme Ct. Hist. Soc., Chgo. Bar Assn. (Alliance for Women, mem. constitutional law com., judiciary com.), Fed. Bar Assn., Ill. Bar Assn. (elected assembly mem. 2000, bd. govs. 2002—, chair gen. practice sect. coun., chair continuing legal edn. subcom., fmr. mem. standing com. legal edn., admission and competence, mem. tradition of excellence award subcom., mem. bench and bar sect. coun., co-editor Bench and Bar Newsletter, mem. jud. evaluations com., Lincoln award 2d pl. 1994, Lincoln award 1st pl. 1996, Lincoln award 2d pl. 1997, Lincoln award 1st pl. 1999, Lincoln award 2d pl. 2000, Lincoln award 1st pl. 2002, 2001), planning com. 4th Annual Women Everywhere: Partners in Svc. Project, Order of Coif, Phi Sigma Tau, Kappa Gamma Pi. Avocation: writing fiction, non-fiction.

JOCHUM, JAMES J. federal agency administrator; BA in Polit. Sci. with high distinction, U. Iowa, 1987, JD, 1990. Atty. Foley & Lardner, Milwaukee, 1990—92; asst. v.p. Brenton Bank, Cedar Rapids, Iowa, 1992—94; internat. trade counsel Office of Sen. Charles E. Grassley, 1994—97, legis. dir., 1997—99; majority counsel U.S. Senate Banking Com.; sr. mgr. govt. rels. Accenture L.L.P., 2000—01; asst. sec. export adminstrn. U.S. Dept. Commerce, Washington, 2001—03, asst. sec., import adminstrn., 2003—. Mem.: Order of Coif. Republican. Office: Dept Commerce Import Adminstrn 14th St & Constitution Ave NW Rm 9099B Washington DC 20230*

JOCHUM, VERONICA, pianist; b. Berlin; d. Eugen and Maria (Montz) J.; m. Wilhelm V. von Moltke, Nov. 15, 1961. MusM, Staatliche Musikhochschule, Munich, 1955, Concert Diploma, 1957; pvt. study with, Edwin Fischer, Josef Benvenuti, 1958-59, Rudolf Serkin, Phila., 1959-61. Faculty Settlement Sch. Music, Phila., 1959-61, New Eng. Conservatory Music, Boston, 1965—, Berkshire Music Center, Tanglewood, 1974, Radcliffe Inst., Cambridge, Mass. Recs. with Laurel, Deutsche Grammophon, Philips, Golden Crest, Pro Arte, GM Recs., CRJ, Tahra recs., Tudor; Numerous tours, throughout N. and S. Am., Asia, Europe and, Africa; as soloist with world renowned orchs., including Boston Symphony, Balt. Symphony, London Philharmonic, Los Angeles Chamber Orch., London Symphony, Mpls. Symphony, Berlin, Hamburg and Munich Philharmonics, Bavarian and Bamberg Symphonies, Munich Chamber Orch., radio orchs. of Hamburg, Munich, and Frankfurt, Orch. Maggio Musicale, Florence, La Fenice Orch., Venice, RAI-Orch., Naples, Mozarteum Orch., Salzburg, Concertgebouw Orch., Amsterdam, The Hague Philharmonic, Venezuelan Symphony, Caracas, Jerusalem Symphony, others; appearances on radio and TV, recitals in more than 50 countries on 4 continents; participant, Marlboro Music Festival, Montreux Festival, Bregenz Festival, Mecklenburg Festival, Festival de Vallonie (Belgium), Tanglewood, En. Music Festival, Chambermusic East. Bd. mem. Berkshire Inst. Theology and the Arts. Recipient cross Order of Merit (Germany); Bunting fellow Harvard U., 1996-97. Office: New Eng Conservatory Music 290 Huntington Ave Boston MA 02115-5018

JOCK, PAUL F., II, lawyer; b. Indpls., Jan. 25, 1943; s. Paul F. and Alice (Sheehan) J.; m. Gail A. Webre, Sept. 16, 1967; children: Craig W., Nicole L. BBA, U. Notre Dame, 1965; JD, U. Chgo., 1970. Bar: Ill. 1970, N.Y. 1990. Ptnr. Kirkland & Ellis, Chgo. and N.Y.C., 1970-2001; v.p., gen. counsel GM Asset Mgmt., N.Y.C., 2000—. V.p. legal affairs Tribune Co., Chgo., 1981. Assoc. editor U. Chgo. Law Rev., 1969-70. Served to lt. USN, 1965-67. Mem. ABA, Chgo. Bar Assn., Assn. of the Bar of City of N.Y. Address: GM Asset Mgmt 767 Fifth Ave New York NY 10153 E-mail: paul.jock@gm.com.

JOCKUSCH, CARL GROOS, JR., mathematics educator; b. San Antonio, July 13, 1941; s. Carl Groos and Mary English (Dickson) J.; m. Elizabeth Ann Northrop, June 17, 1964; children— William, Elizabeth, Rebecca. Student, Vanderbilt U., 1959-60; BA with highest honors, Swarthmore Coll., 1963; PhD, M.I.T., 1966. Instr. Northeastern U., 1966-67; asst. prof. math. U. Ill., Urbana-Champaign, 1967-71, assoc. prof., 1971-75, prof., 1975—. Contbr. articles to profl. jours.; editor Jour. Symbolic Logic, 1974-75, Proc. Am. Math. Soc., 1997—. Mem. Assn. Symbolic Logic, Am. Math. Soc., Math. Assn. Am. Home: 704 E McHenry St Urbana IL 61801-6846 Office: Univ Ill Dept Math 1409 W Green St Urbana IL 61801-2943

JOEHL, RAYMOND JOSEPH, surgeon, educator; b. Alton, Ill., July 20, 1948; m. Julia Nelle Garrels, Aug. 28, 1970; children: Jacob, Samuel, Hillarie, Sarah, Claudia, Hannah. BA, U. Pa., 1970; MD, St. Louis U., 1974. Diplomate Am. Bd. Surgery. Resident in surgery Pa. State U., Hershey, 1974-79, rsch. fellow, 1979-80, from asst. to assoc. prof. surgery, 1980-85; from assoc. prof. to prof. surgery Northwestern U., Chgo., 1985-91, James R. Hines prof. surgery, 1993—2003; prof. surgery Loyola U., Maywood, Ill., 2003—. Chief divsn. gen. surgery and dir. residency in surgery, 1995-2000, attending surgeon Northwestern Meml. Hosp., VA Chgo. Health Care Sys.-Lakeside divsn., 1985-2003, Hershey Med. Ctr., 1980-85, Loyola U. Med. Ctr., Maywood, 2003—; chief surg. svc., VA Chgo.-Lakeside, 1987-95, 2001-03, Hines VA Hosp., Ill., 2003—. Fellow ACS, Am. Surg. Assn.; mem. Soc. Univ. Surgeons, Soc. for Surgery Alimentary Tract, Alpha Omega Alpha. Episcopalian. Avocations: children, advocate for disabled especially blind, teaching. Office: Loyola U Med Ctr Dept Surgery 2160 S 1st Ave Maywood IL 60153 Business E-Mail: raymond.joehl@med.va.gov.

JOEL, AMOS EDWARD, JR., telecommunications consultant; b. Phila., Mar. 12, 1918; s. Amos Edward and Anna (Potsdamer) J.; m. Rhoda Ethel Fenton (dec.); children: Jeffrey (dec.), Stephanie, Andrea. BEE, MIT, 1940, MEE, 1942. Registered profl. engr., N.Y. Mem. tech. staff Bell Tel. Labs., N.Y. and N.J., 1940-52, supr., 1952-54, dept. head, 1954-61, dir. Holmdel, N.J., 1961-67, cons., 1967-83, ret., 1983; cons., 1983—. Cons. AT&T Bell Comm. Rsch., GTE, IBM, Contel, Pacific Tel.; lectr. in field of switching sys. Author: Electronic Switching Central Office Systems of the World, 1976, Electronic Switching: Digital Central Office Systems of the World, 1982, History of Science and Technology in the Bell System-Switching Technology, 1982; author: (with others) Fundamentals of Digital Switching, 1983, 2d edit., 1990, Electronics, Computers and Telephone Switching, 1990, Future of the Central Office, 1991; contbr. articles to encys. and profl. jours.; holder more than 70 patents. Co-recipient Outstanding Patent award N.J. R & D Coun., 1972, Stuart Ballantine medal Franklin Inst., 1981, Centary prize Internat. Telecom. Union, 1983, Columbian medal City of Genoa, Italy, 1984, Kyoto prize in advanced tech., 1989, Nat. Med. of Tech., 1993; named N.J. Inventor of Yr., 1989. Fellow IEEE (life, co-recipient Alexander Graham Bell medal 1976, IEEE medal of honor 1992, nat. medal tech. 1993, 3d Millennium medal 2000), Am. Acad. Arts and Scis.; mem. NAE, AAAS, Comm. Soc. of IEEE (pres. 1973-75), Sigma Xi, Eta Kappa Nu (Karapetoff eminent members' award 2000). Avocations: organ and keyboard music, railroading. Home: Winchester Gardens One Turnberry Ct Maplewood NJ 07040-2423 E-mail: a.joel@ieee.org.

JOEL, RICHARD MARC, academic administrator, law educator, dean; b. NYC, Sept. 9, 1950; s. Avery Joel and Annette (Bloom) Ashwal; m. Esther Duora Ribner, Nov. 11, 1973; children: Penina, Avery, Arielle, Noam. BA, NYU, 1972, JD, 1975. Bar: N.Y. 1976, U.S. Dist. Ct. (ea. dist.) N.Y. 1976. Asst. dist. atty. Borough of Bronx, N.Y., 1975-78; dir. alumni affairs Yeshiva U., N.Y.C., 1978-80, asst. dean Cardozo Sch. Law, 1980-82, assoc. dean Cardozo Sch. Law, 1982—, adj. prof. law, 1985—, pres., 2002—. Sec. Hebrew Acad. Long Beach, N.Y., 1983—; bd. dirs. Jewish Community Council Oceanside, N.Y., 1977-81, Young Israel Oceanside, 1986—. Root-Tilden scholar NYU, 1972-75. Mem. ABA. Democrat. Jewish. Avocations: music, youth work. Home: 712 Hermleigh Rd Silver Spring MD 20902-1601 Office: Yeshiva U Cardozo Sch Law 55 5th Ave New York NY 10003-4301

JOEL, WILLIAM LEE, II, interior and lighting designer; b. Richmond, Va., Feb. 23, 1933; s. J. Alton and Dorothy Joel; m. Merry Pick, June 5, 1955; children: Taryn, Dana, Wendy, Holly. Student, R.I. Sch. Design, 1953-55; AB, Brown U., 1955; postgrad., N.Y. Sch. Interior Design, 1956, Pratt Inst., 1958-61. Cert. interior designer Commonwealth of Va. Draftsman Mills Denmark Inc., N.Y.C., 1957-58; with sales and interior design Lord & Taylor's Inc., N.Y.C., 1958-61; pres., interior designer Richmond (Va.) Art Co. Inc. Instr. Va. Commonwealth U. (formerly Richmond Profl. Inst.), 1963-67; set designer Barksdale Theatre, Hanover, Va., 1977-88; mem. adv. bd. interior design program Va. Poly. Inst and State U., 1986-90; speaker numerous orgns., radio and TV programs. Prin. works include Culpepper (Va.) Hosp., The Curles Neck Pl., Richmond, Dominion Nat. Bank, Richmond, Gary, Stoch, Walls offices, Richmond, Gov.'s Exec. Mansion, Commonwealth Va., 1976, Hello Inc., Richmond, Hill Bldg., Richmond, Hunter House Mus., Norfolk, Va., Richmond, Fredericksburg and Potomac R.R. Co. corp. hdqrs., Rolph Clark Stone Packaging Co. offices, Straub and Dalch office complex, Westminster Canterbury House, Richmond, Wickham Valentine House, Willow Oaks Country Club, Continental Cablevision, Richmond, St. Paul Episcopal Ch., Richmond, numerous residences; author: articles published bi-monthly in Rich Art website. Co-chmn. com. for cert. Va. Interior Designers, 1982-90; mem. Downtown Mktg. Com., chmn. subcom. Xmas Sound and Lighting, Richmond, 1988-91, mem. prodn. Richmond Forum sets and lighting design, 1989-95; bd. visitors Found. for Interior Design Edn. and Rsch., 1977-84, mem. accreditation com., 1984-88; mem. Va. Mus. Fine Arts, City of Richmond Christmas Candlelight Com., edn. com. Retail Mchts. Assn., 1980-85; mem. urban design com. Ctrl. Richmond Assn., 1993. 1st lt. USMC, 1952-57. Recipient award Va. Mus. Fine Arts, Richmond, 1970, Cert. Distinction, 1973; named contest winner Richmond Symphony Orch., 1975. Fellow Am. Soc. Interior Designers (cert., pres. Va. chpt. 1970-72, 80-81, mem. nat. bd. 1972-74, 76-77, regional v.p. 1976-77, nat. com. 1976); mem. Nat. Fire Protection Assn. Avocations: sailing, canoeing, electronics, sport cars. Home: 8905 Sierra Rd Richmond VA 23229-7828 Office: Richmond Art Co 500 E Main St Ste 600 Richmond VA 23219-2431

JOELSON, MARK RENÉ, lawyer; b. Paris, Oct. 23, 1934; came to U.S., 1941, naturalized, 1947; s. Michael and Helen (Streicher) J.; m. Anastasia Whelan, June 4, 1967; children: Helen, Daniel, Marisa. BA, Harvard U., 1955, LLB, 1958; diploma in law, Oxford U., Eng., 1962. Bar: D.C. 1958, U.S. Supreme Ct. 1959. Atty. U.S. Dept. Justice, Washington, 1958-63; assoc., then ptnr. Arent, Fox, Kintner, Plotkin & Kahn, Washington, 1963-80; ptnr. Wald, Harkrader & Ross, Washington, 1980-85, Morgan, Lewis & Bockius LLP, Washington, 1986-97; pvt. practice, 1998—. Mem. adv. com. internat. investment, tech. and devel. U.S. Dept. State, 1978-87; cons. UN Conf. Trade and Devel., 1977-79; adj. prof. Georgetown U., Washington; panelist N.Am. Free Trade Agreement, Am. Arbitration Assn., Nat. Arbitration Forum. Author (with Earl W. Kintner): An International Antitrust Primer, 1974; author: An International Antitrust Primer, 2d edit., 2001; editor (with others): Current Legal Aspects of Doing Business in the E.E.C., 1978; editor: Enterprise Law in the 80's, 1980, Joint Ventures in the United States, 1988. Fulbright scholar Oxford U., 1961-62. Mem. ABA (chmn. sect. internat. law and practice 1983-84, del. Internat. Bar Assn. coun. 1984-92), Internat. Bar Assn., Fed. Bar Assn. (pres. D.C. chpt. 1976-77), Washington Inst. Fgn. Affairs, Cosmos Club (Washington), Order of Brit. Empire. E-mail: joelsonmr@msn.com.

JOERGENSEN, JOHN P, librarian; b. Lynchburg, Va., July 27, 1961; s. Leo P and Nora L Joergensen; m. Patricia M Dwyer, Mar. 15, 1964; children: Lillian R, Magdalen J, Adele M, Leo J. J.D., Temple U., Phila., PA, 1989—92; MS LIS, Drexel U., Phila., PA, 1995—97; MA, Fordham U., Bronx, NY, 1983—85. Member of Bar: NJ 1992. Libr. Rutgers U. Sch. of Law, Camden, NJ, 1996—. Mem.: Am. Assn. of Law Libraries (chair, citation formats com. 2002—03), Beta Phi Mu. Achievements include first to Creator New Jersey Courts Publishing Project. Office: Rutgers Univ Sch of Law 215 North 5th St Camden NJ 08102 Office Fax: 856-225-6488. E-mail: jjoerg@camlaw.rutgers.edu.

JOERGENSEN, PER BAY, economist, insurance executive; b. Grinsted, Denmark, July 25, 1945; s. Johannes and Lilly (Nielsen) J.; 1 child, Jens Frederik Bay. BSc in Econs., Bus. Sch. of Copenhagen, 1973, MSc in Econs, 1975; exec. program for smaller cos., Stanford U., Calif., U.S., 1980, 91. Head of EDP dept. Mutual Health Ins. of Denmark, Copenhagen, 1972-76, asst. mgr., 1976-79; dir. Internat. Health Ins., Copenhagen, 1979-82; mng. dir. Internat. Health Insur., Copenhagen, 1982—. Pres. Folkeligt Oplysnings Forbund, Copenhagen, 1979-97. Pres. The Conservative Party, Copenhagen, 1981-91. Mem. Stanford Bus. Sch. Alumni (bd. dirs. 1981—). Lutheran. Office: Internat Health Ins 6-8 Palaegade DK-1261K Copenhagen Denmark E-mail: ihi@ihi.dk.

JOERN, CHARLES EDWARD, JR., lawyer; b. Oak Park, Ill., Apr. 27, 1951; s. Charles Edward and Eleanor Joern; m. Christine Mary Lake, July 28, 1973; children: Jessica, William, Marisa, Angela, Alexandra. BA, Knox Coll., 1973; M in Urban Affairs, U. Colo., 1976; JD, De Paul U., 1980. Bar: Ill. 1980, U.S. Dist. Ct. (no. dist.) Ill. 1980, U.S. Ct. Appeals (7th cir.) 1981, U.S. Supreme Ct. 1995. Asst. to planning cons. J.R. Crowley and Assocs., 1973-74; sys. analyst Aravada, Colo. Bldg. Inspection Divsn., U. Colo. sponsorship, 1974-75; student intern divsn. comprehensive health planning Colo. Dept. Health, 1976; law clk. Cook County Legal Assistance Found., Chgo., 1978; consumer fraud divsn. Office Ill. Atty. Gen., 1979-80; assoc. Pope, Ballard, Shepard & Fowle, Ltd., Chgo., 1980-94, Burke, Weaver & Prell, Chgo., 1994-2000, Holland & Knight, Chgo., 2000—. Panel atty. Chgo. Vol. Legal Svcs. Found. Bd. advisors N.C. Outward Bound Sch., Morgantown, 1983-99; bd. dirs. Richport YMCA, LaGrange, Ill., 1984—, chmn., 1990-93; village trustee LaGrange Park, 1997—. Fellow in pub. affairs U. Colo., 1979. Mem. ABA (litigation sect.), Ill. State Bar Assn., Chgo. Bar Assn. (chmn. child abuse and neglect com. 1985-86), Pi Alpha Alpha. Republican. Roman Catholic. Office: Holland & Knight LLC 131 S Dearborn Chicago IL 60603 E-mail: charles.joern@hklaw.com.

JOERRES, JEFFREY A. staffing company executive; BS, Marquette U. Various mgmt. positions IBM; v.p. sales and mtkg. ARI Network Svcs.; v.p. mktg. Manpower, Inc., Milw., from 1993, sr. v.p. European ops. and global account mgmt. and devel., until 1999, pres., CEO, 1999—, chmn., 2001—. Office: Manpower Inc 5301 N Ironwood Rd Milwaukee WI 53217-4982

JOERSZ, FRAN WOODMANSEE, secondary education educator; b. Bismarck, N.D., Apr. 29, 1954; d. Joe G. and Winnie (McGillic) Woodmansee; m. Jon D. Joersz; children: Brett, Ben, Courtney. Student, Bismarck State Coll., 1972; BA in Edn., U. Wyo., 1975. Tchr. 3rd grade Deer Trail (Colo.) Pub. Sch., 1975-76; tchr. 8th grade remedial reading Mandan (N.D.) Jr. High Sch., 1976-78; tchr. title I reading Saxvik St. Mary's Grade Sch., Bismarck, 1979; tchr. 8th grade devel. reading Wachter Jr. High Sch., Bismarck, 1979-81; tchr. 7th grade devel. reading written and oral communications Hughes Jr. High Sch., Bismarck, 1981—. Bd. dirs. Rape Victim Adv. Program; founding bd. dirs. Our Kids Need to Know; state bd. dirs. Make A Wish Found. Recipient Milken award, 1994. Mem. PEO, N.D. Edn. Assn. (Tchr. of Yr. 1991, Profl. Courage award 1994), Internat. Reading Assn., Nat. Assn. Student Activity Advisers. Avocations: walking, reading, volleyball, writing, traveling. Home: 520 N Mandan St Bismarck ND 58501-3748 Office: Hughes Mid Sch 500 Ash Coulee Dr Bismarck ND 58503

JOFEN, JEAN, foreign language educator; BA, Bklyn. Coll., 1943; MA, Brown U., 1945; PhD, Columbia U., 1960; MS, Yeshiva U., 1961. Cert. sch. psychologist, N.Y. Teaching fellow Brown U., 1943-44; lectr. adult edn. Bklyn. Coll., 1951-61; assoc. prof. Yeshiva U., N.Y.C., 1955-62; assoc. prof., chmn. dept. Germanic and Slavic langs. Bernard M. Baruch Coll., N.Y.C., 1962-77, prof., 1977—, chmn. dept. modern langs., 1977-83, chmn. dept. Germanic, Hebraic and Oriental langs., 1983—, bd. govs., 1973—. Mem. adv. bd. Jewish Studies CUNY, 1986; lectr., speaker various sci., civic and religious orgns. and socs. in U.S. and Europe; scholar abroad, Vienna, Austria, 1991. Author: A Linguistic Atlas of Eastern European Yiddish, 1964, rev. edit., 1967, Das letzte Geheimnis (in German), 1972, The Jewish Mystic in Kafka, 1987, (textbooks) Yiddish for Beginners, 1963, Yiddish Literature for Beginners, 1972, (with Y. Kerstein) Hebrew for Beginners, 1975, (with E. Mok) Chinese for Beginners, 1980; editor Elizabethan Concordance series: The Concordance of The Works of Christopher Marlowe, 1979, A Concordance to The Shakespeare Apocrypha, 3 Vols., 1987; Nat. Endowment for Humanities; assoc. editor Jour. Evolutionary Psychology; contbr. numerous articles to profl. jours. Recipient Nat. Jewish Culture Found. award, 1963, Kohut Found. award, 1966, Bernard M. Baruch Coll. medal for 35 yrs. svc., AAUW award, 1968, 69, others; fellow Inst. for Yiddish Lexicological Rsch. Inst., 1963—; grantee Ford Found., 1970, Population Coun. Rockefeller Inst., 1970-71, Rsch. Found. CUNY, 1985, Lucius N. Littauer Found., 1986, Austrian Fed. Ministry for Sci. and Rsch., 1991. Fellow Jewish Acad. Arts and Scis.; mem. Am. Assn. Tchrs. German, MLA, AAUP, Am. Assn. Profs. Yiddish (pres.), Am. Psychol. Assn., Marlowe Soc. Am. (founder 1975, pres. 1975-84, organizer 1st. Internat. Congress in Eng. 1983), Mich. Acad. Arts and Scis., Acad. Scis. and Humanities CUNY, Sigma Alpha. Address: 409 Avenue I Brooklyn NY 11230-2619

JOFFE, BARBARA LYNNE, computer management professional, computer artist; b. Bklyn., Apr. 12, 1951; d. Lester L. and Julia (Schuelke) J.; 1 child, Nichole. BA, U. Oreg., 1975; MFA, U. Mont., 1982. Cert. project mgr. IBM; cert. project mgmt. profl. Project Mgmt. Inst. Applications engr., software developer So. Pacific Transp., San Francisco, 1986-93; computer fine artist Barbara Joffe Assocs., San Francisco, Englewood, Colo., 1988—; instr. computer graphics Ohlone Coll., Fremont, Calif., 1990-91; adv. programmer,

project mgr.-client/server Integrated Sys. Solutions Corp./IBM Global Svcs. So. Pacific/Union Pacific Railroads, Denver, 1994-97; applications sys. mgr. IBM Global Svcs./CoBank, Greenwood Village, Colo., 1997-99; exec. project mgr. IBM/GM Web Hosting, 2000—01, IBM/Cendant, 2001—. Artwork included in exhibits at Calif. Crafts XIII, Crocker Art Mus., Sacramento, 1983, Rara Avis Gallery, Sacramento, 1984, Redding (Calif.) Mus. and Art Ctr., 1985, Euphrat Gallery, Cupertino, Calif., 1988, Computer Mus., Boston, 1989, Siggraph Traveling Art Shown, Europe and Australia, 1990, 91, 4th and 7th Nat. Computer Art Invitational, Cheney, Wash., 1991, 94, Visual Arts Mus., N.Y.C., 1994, 96, IBM Golden Circle, 1996. Recipient IBM Project Mgmt. Excellence award, 1998. Mem. Project Mgmt. Inst. (cert.), Assn. Computing Machinery. Avocations: art, gardening, hiking.

JOFFE, BENJAMIN, mechanical engineer, consultant; b. Riga, Latvia, Feb. 23, 1931; came to U.S., 1980, naturalized, 1985; s. Alexander and Mery (Levenson) J.; m. Frida Erenshteyn, Aug. 6, 1960; children: Alexander, Helena. ASME, Mech. Tech. Sch., Krasnoyarsk, USSR, 1951; BSME, Polytechnic Inst. Moscow, 1959; MSME, Polytechnic Inst. Riga, 1961; PhD, Acad. Scis., Riga, 1969; D in Physics honoris causa, Latvian Acad. Scis., 2000. Design engr. Electromachine Mfg. Corp., Riga, 1955-59, head engring. dept., 1959-62; sr. design engr. Acad. Scis., Riga, 1962-67; sr. scientist Inst. Physics, Riga, 1967-78; chief design engr. Main Design Bur., Riga, 1978-80; sr. design engr. Elec-Trol, Inc., Saugus, Calif., 1980-81; sr. design engr. VSI Aerospace divsn. Fairchild, Chatsworth, Calif., 1981-85; mech. engring. mgr. Am. Semiconductor Equipment Tech., Woodland Hills, Calif., 1985-90; mem. tech. staff Jet Propulsion Lab. Calif. Inst. Tech., Pasadena, 1991-97; staff scientist aerospace/comm. divsn. ITT, Ft. Wayne, Ind., 1997—2003. Presenter numerous papers and books in field. Author: Electromagnetic Identification and Orientation of Parts (EMAGO), 1976, (books) Inventions in Latvia in the Field of Technology and Means of Production of Apparatus and Machines, 1965, Inventions in Latvia: Production of Apparatus and Machines, 1971, Orientation of Parts by Electromagnetic Field, 1972, Inventions in Latvia: Elements of Automatics, Calculating and Control-Measuring Systems, 1973, Inventions in Latvia: Elements and Mechanisms of Apparatus and Machines, Technology and Means of Their Production, 1977, among others; contbr. articles to profl. jours. Recipient Honored Inventor award Latvian Republic, Riga, 1967, 1st prize Latvian Acad. Scis., 1972, Latvian State award in engring. scis., 1974, certs. of recognition NASA, 1996, 97, 2002. Mem. Planetary Soc. Republican. Achievements include more than 230 patents for discovery of physical and engineering basis for noncontact techniques of orientation, identification and assembly of parts by electromagnetic fields; mechanisms and machines design for semiconductive and spacecraft industries.

JOFFE, ROBERT DAVID, lawyer; b. N.Y.C., May 26, 1943; s. Joseph and Bertha (Pashkovsky) J.; children by prior marriage: Katherine, David; m. Virginia Ryan, June 20, 1981; stepchildren: Elizabeth DeHaas, Ryan DeHaas. AB, Harvard U., 1964, JD, 1967. Bar: N.Y. 1970, U.S. Dist. Ct. (so. and ea. dists.) N.Y. 1971, U.S. Ct. Appeals (2d cir.) 1972, U.S. Supreme Ct. 1973. Maxwell Sch. Africa Pub. Svc. fellow (funded by Ford Found.), Republic of Malawi, 1967-69; state counsel, 1968-69; assoc. Cravath, Swaine & Moore, N.Y.C., 1969-75; ptnr. Cravath, Swaine & Moore LLP, N.Y.C., 1975—, dep. presiding ptnr., 1998, presiding ptnr., 1999—. Apptd. to bd. dirs. by Pres. Clinton, Romanian Am. Enterprise Fund, 1994-2003. Bd. dirs. Lawyers Com. for Human Rights, The Jericho Project, 1985—97, Franklin Resources, 2003—; chair Harvard Law Sch. Nat. Fund, 1995—97, dean's adv. bd., 1997—; bd. dirs. Fiduciary Trust Co. Internat., 1999—, The After Sch. Corp. Mem. ABA, N.Y. Bar Assn., Assn. of Bar of the City of N.Y. (chmn. trade regulation com. 1980-83, exec. com. 1995-99, nominating com. 2001-02, v.p. 2003—), Coun. on Fgn. Rels., Human Rights Watch/Africa (adv. com.), Harvard Club, Century Assn. Home: 300 W End Ave Apt 13A New York NY 10023-8156 Office: Cravath Swaine & Moore LLP 825 8th Ave Fl 46 New York NY 10019-7475

JOFFE, RUSSELL T. dean; BS, U. Witwatersrand, Johannesburg, S. Africa, 1977. Diplomate Am. Bd. Psychiatry and Neurology, 1984. Intern Mount Sinai Hosp., Toronto, Canada; resident in psychiatry Royal Ottawa Hosp., U. Ottawa, McMaster U.; fellow NIH, Bethesda, Md., 1983—85; mem. dept. psychiatry U. Toronto; chair dept. psychiatry and behavioral neurosciences McMaster U., 1991—97, dean faculty of health scis.; dean U. Medicine and Dentistry N.J. - N.J. Med. Sch., 2001—. Mem. Expert Adv. Com. on Psychiatric Illness of U.S. Pharmacopoiea, 1990—. Contbr. of more than 250 articles in profl. jours.; author: more than 30 chpts. for med. textbooks about depression. Recipient Award of Excellence, Depressive and Manic Depressive Assn. Ont.; grantee of more than 50 rsch. grants. Fellow: Royal Coll. Physicians and Surgeons Can., Am. Psychiatric Assn. (Gold award for Academically Sponsored Programs). Office: 185 S Orange Ave Newark NJ 07103

JOGLAR, FRANCISCO, academic administrator; Dean U. P.R., Sch. Medicine, San Juan, 1999—. Office: A-878 Main Bldg PO Box 365067 San Juan PR 00936-5067 E-mail: fjoglar@rcm.upr.edu.

JOGLEKAR, PRAFULLA NARAYAN, information systems management educator, consultant; b. Dhulia, India, May 12, 1947; s. Narayan D. and Nirmala N. (Parchure) J.; m. Suvarna V. Lagu, Oct. 15, 1951; children: Aditya, Ajinkya. BSc, Nagpur (India) U., 1966; MBA, Indian Inst. Mgmt., Ahmedabad, India, 1968; MS, U. Pa., 1972, PhD, 1978; postgrad., U. Rochester, U. Minn., Ind. U. Staff analyst Dept. Atomic Energy, Bombay, India, 1968-69; systems analyst Voltas (PVT) Ltd., Bombay, 1969-70; mgmt. research analyst U. Pa., Phila., 1970-72; from instr. to full prof. La Salle U., Phila., 1972-87, chmn. mgmt. dept., 1973-77, 79-82, dir. applied research ctr., 1979-85, Lindback prof. bus. adminstrn., 1987-89, Lindback prof. prodn. and ops. mgmt., 1991—. Mgmt. cons. various pvt. firms, govt. agys., nonprofit orgns., Phila., 1972—; expert witness fed. court, Montreal, Can., 1985. Contbr. articles to profl. jours. and confs.; editor Varta, Indian Students Assn., Phila., 1975-76. Pres. Marathi Mandal, Phila., 1980-81; mem. People to People Systems Engring. Delegation, Peoples Republic China, 1986. Nat. Merit scholar Govt. of India, Nagpur and Ahmedabad, 1962-68, D.C.M. scholar Indian Inst. Mgmt., Ahmedabad, 1968; grantee La Salle U., 1977, 89, 80, 82, 87, 90, 92, 93, 96, 97, 98, 99; NASA/ASEE faculty summer fellow, 1993, 94, 2000, 01. Mem. Inst. Mgmt. Scis., Am. Mgmt. Assn., Nonprofit Mgmt. Assn. (bd. dirs. 1985-90), Beta Gamma Sigma. Hindu. Avocations: travel, bridge, puzzles. Home: 202 Lenape Ave Elkins Park PA 19027-3514 Office: La Salle U 1900 W Olney Ave Philadelphia PA 19141-1199 E-mail: joglekar@Lasalle.edu.

JOHANET, HENRY TERRY, sales executive; b. Chgo., June 29, 1964; s. Enrique Oscar and Marilyn Johanet; m. Flor Mary Camba, May 8, 1988; children: Ricky, Genevieve. BA, Northeastern Ill. U.; MBA in Mktg., DePaul U., Chgo., 2003. Fin. planner Met Life, N.Y.C., 1988—92; regional v.p. Vincam Human Resources, Coral Gables, Fla., 1992—96; dist. sales mgr. Novartis Pharms., East Hanover, NJ, 1997—. Chmn. exec. network Des Plaines C. of C., Ill., 1995—96. Mem.: Nat. Soc. Hispanic MBAs. Roman Catholic. Avocations: travel, cooking, sports.

JOHANN, ANNE DOROTHY, visual artist, painter, printmaker, graphic artist; b. North Tarrytown, N.Y., Feb. 24, 1957; d. John Thomas and Elizabeth Keay (Hamilton) Sekelsky; m. Thomas Richard Johann, Aug. 28, 1982. BFA with highest honors, Pratt Inst., 1980. Printer asst. Solo Press, Inc., N.Y.C., 1980—82; tchr. oil painting Croton-Cortlandt Ctr. for Arts, Cortlandt Manor, NY, 1994, 1995, 2001—, tchr. watercolor painting, 1998—, tchr. drawing, 2001—, bd. dirs. Open edit. print, The Old Mill as seen from the Charles Bridge, Prague, N.Y. Graphic Soc., 2001. Recipient award, N.Y. State Art Tchrs., 1975, residency grantee, Vt. Studio Ctr., Johnson, Vt., 2000, artist grantee, Vt. Studio Ctr., 2000, Award of Excellence, Manhattan Arts Internat. mag., 1999, Vasari Oil Colors award, Art of N.E. U.S.A., Silvermine Guild Galleries, New Canaan, Conn., 2000, Westchester Arts Coun. Mcpl. Challenge grant, CCCA/Town of Cortlandt, 2001—02. Mem.: Croton Coun. on Arts, N.Y. Artists Equity Assn., Nat. Assn. Women Arts (France Lieber Meml. award 2002), New Haven Paint and Clay Club (David T. Langrock Found. prize for landscape 2001, honorable mention active mems. exhibit 2001). Home: 316 Grand St Croton On Hudson NY 10520-3500 E-mail: johann@bestweb.net.

JOHANNES, JOHN ROLAND, political science educator, academic administrator; b. Milw., Dec. 15, 1943; s. Jerome Fridolin and Teresa (Stoiber) J.; m. Frances Virginia Slater, Aug. 5, 1967; children: Teresa, Michael, James. BS, Marquette U., 1966; AM, Harvard U., 1968, PhD, 1970. Asst. prof. polit. sci. Marquette U., Milw., 1970-75, assoc. prof., 1975-84, prof., 1984-95, chmn. dept. polit. sci., 1980-88, dean Coll. Arts and Scis., 1988-93; v.p. acad. affairs Villanova (Pa.) U., 1995—. Chmn. Bradley Inst. for Democracy and Pub. Values, 1988-93. Author: Policy Innovation in Congress, 1972, To Serve the People, 1984; co-editor and contbr. editor Money, Elections, and Democracy, 1990; contbr. articles to profl. jours. Am. Philos. Soc. grantee, 1978; Everett Dirksen Ctr. grantee, 1981, 82, NEH grantee, 1972. Mem. Am. Polit. Sci. Assn., Midwest Polit. Sci. Assn., So. Polit. Sci. Assn., Assn. Am. Colls. and Univs. Home: 840 Galer Dr Newtown Square PA 19073-3517 Office: Villanova U Office Acad Affairs 800 E Lancaster Ave Villanova PA 19085-1603 E-mail: john.johannes@villanova.edu.

JOHANNES, KAY L. insurance company executive; b. Milw., July 3, 1952; d. James Ben and Evelyn (Horne) J.; m. Thomas A. Rozek, June 13, 1972 (div. Oct. 1975); m. Alexander David Bub, Jan. 5, 1982; 1 child, David A. AAS in Visual Comm., Milw. Area Tech. Coll., 1972; BS in Instrnl. Tech., Rochester Inst. Tech., 1977. Audio visual tech. Nicolet H.S., Glendale, Wisc., 1972-75; visual designer, animator Pohlman Studios, Milw., 1977-79; designer multimedia AV Centrum AB, Stockholm, 1979-80; owner, prodr. Johannes, Milw., 1980-82; audio visual prodr. Photography Unltd., Milw., 1982-87; sr. salestrack specialist Northwe. Mut. Life Ins. Co., Milw., 1987—. Chair visual comm. adv. bd. Milw. Area Tech. Coll., 1990—. Vol. Big Brothers/Big Sisters, Ozaukee County, Wisc., 1978-91. Mem. order of Amaranth (royal matron), White Shrine Jerusalem (worthy high priestess). Methodist. Avocations: motorcycles, computer web design. Home: W4802 Knuth Rd Random Lake WI 53075 Office: Northwe Mut Fin Network 720 E Wisconsin Ave Milwaukee WI 53202 E-mail: kayj@myexcel.com.

JOHANNESSEN, JANET A. science educator; b. Orange, NJ, Sept. 7, 1953; d. Bernt F. and Esther M. Benson; m. Lloyd D. Johannessen, May 25, 1974; 1 child, Erik;1 child, Karen. AA in Biology, County Coll. of Morris, 1973; BS in Chemistry, Fairleigh Dickinson U., 1977, MS in Chemistry, 1983. Chemist, group leader Ashland Chem. Drew Divsn., Boonton, NJ, 1973—89; prof. chemistry and biology County Coll. of Morris, Randolph, NJ, 1989—. Author chemistry and biology lab. manuals. Mem. Emergency Planning Coun., Morris County. Mem.: Met. Assn. Coll. Biologists, NJ Edn. Assn., Am. Chem. Soc. Avocations: travel, reading. Office: County Coll of Morris 214 Center Grove Rd Randolph NJ 07869 E-mail: jjohannessen@ccm.edu.

JOHANNS, MICHAEL O. governor; b. Osage, Iowa, June 18, 1950; s. John Robert Sr. and Adeline Lucy (Royek) J.; m. Constance J. Weiss, June 10, 1972 (div. Dec. 1985); children: Justin Michael, Michaela Susan; m. Stephanie A. Suther, Dec. 24, 1986. BA, St. Mary's Coll., Winona, Minn., 1971; JD, Creighton U., 1974. Jud. law clk. Nebr. Supreme Ct., Lincoln, 1974-75; assoc. lawyer Cronin & Hannon, O'Neill, Nebr., 1975-76; ptnr. Office of Nelson Johanns, Lincoln, 1976-91; mayor City of Lincoln, 1991-98; gov. State of Nebr., 1999—. Mem. Lancaster County Bd., Lincoln, 1983-87; mem. City Coun. Lincoln, 1989-91. Mem. Nebr. Bar Assn. Republican. Roman Catholic. Avocations: skiing, biking, reading. Office: Office of Gov PO Box 94848 Lincoln NE 68509-4848 E-mail: mjohanns@notes.state.ne.us.

JOHANNSEN, CHRIS JAKOB, agronomist, educator, administrator; b. Randolph, Nebr., July 24, 1937; s. Jakob J. and Marie J. (Lorenzsen) J.; m. Joanne B. Rockwell, Aug. 16, 1959; children: Eric C., Peter J. BS, U. Nebr., Lincoln, 1959, MS, 1961; PhD, Purdue U., 1969. Program leader lab. for applications of remote sensing Purdue U., 1966-69, from asst. prof. to assoc. prof. agronomy, 1969-77, dir. ag data network, 1985-87, dir. lab. for applications of remote sensing, 1985—; prof. U. Mo., Columbia, 1977-84, dir. geogrpahic resources ctr., 1981-84; dir. Ag Data Network, Purdue U., 1985-87, Lab. for Applications of Remote Sensing, 1985—; prof. Purdue U., W. Lafayette, Ind., 1985—; dir. Nat. Resources Rsch. Inst., 1987-93, Environ. Scis. and Engring. Inst./Purdue U., West Lafayette, 1994-96. Vis. prof. U. Calif., Davis, 1980—81; cons. Lockheed Electronics, Houston, 1975—76, NOAA, Columbia, Mo., 1978—80, FAO UN, Nairobi, Kenya, 1983, 87, Rome, 87, U.S. Agy. Internat. Devel., Ea. Africa, 1983, USDA-Soil Conservation Svc., Washington, 1984—85, IBM, 1991, Ball Aerospace Corp., 1995, Space Imaging Inc., 1996—, Aventis CropSci. Inc., 1998—, RapidEye Corp., 2001—; pres. Ecologistics Ltd., 1996—2002, assoc., 2002—; vis. chief scientist Space Imaging Inc., 1996—97; adj. prof. Katholieke U. Leuven (Belgium). Pres. coun. St. Andrew's Luth. Ch., Columbia, 1975-77; asst. scoutmaster Boy Scouts Am., Gt. Rivers coun., Columbia, 1979-84, West Lafayette, 1985-91; pres. Purdue Luth. Ministry, 1989-95; apptd. mem. West Lafayette Redevel. Authority, 2001-2004. Recipient Tech. Innovation Rsch. award NASA, 1979, Disting. Svc. award Mo. Assn. Soil and Water Conservation Dists., 1982, Agr. Alumni Merit award U. Nebr., 1995. Fellow: Ind. Acad. Scis., Soil and Water Conservation Soc. (pres. 1982—83), Am. Soc. Agronomy, Soil Sci. Soc. Am., Am. Soc. Photogrammetry and Remote Sensing (Outstanding Svc. award 1992); mem.: Geosci. and Remote Sensing Soc. of IEEE, Internat. Union Soil Sci., World Assn. Soil and Water, Rotary (Lafayette chpt. bd. dirs. 1995—98), Epsilon Sigma Phi (Internat. award 2000). Home: 209 Cedar Hollow Ct West Lafayette IN 47906-1671 Office: Purdue Univ LARS/AGRY 500 Central Dr West Lafayette IN 47907-2022 E-mail: johan@purdue.edu.

JOHANNSEN, SONIA ALICIA, retired county official; b. Glasgow, Mont., Dec. 30, 1935; d. Rudolph H. and Maude Agnes (Millis) Skonord; m. H. Douglas Johannsen, June 5, 1954 (dec. Nov. 1977); children: Tara Lee, Jodi Jean; m. Edward J. Bunz, Jan. 11, 1980; stepchildren: Barbara Ann Bunz, Diane Marie Bunz, Susan Kay Bunz. Clk. City of LaPorte, Iowa, 1967-69, mayor, 1970-75; mem. Black Hawk County Bd. Supervisors, Waterloo, Iowa, 1977-88, 94-98; ret., 1998. Past pres. Village Aux., 1999—2000, treas., 2002—; pres. Village Found. Bd.; vice chair Black Hawk County Regional Planning Coun., 2001—; pres. Met. Transit Authority Black Hawk County, 2002—; treas. Black Hawk County Rep. Women; pres. 1st Dist. Rep. Women. Mem.: LWV (pres. 2001—03), Am. Legion Aux. Lutheran. Office: Apt 6209 1730 Village Pl Waterloo IA 50702-5843 Fax: 319-291-8522. E-mail: super_jo@cedarnet.org.

JOHANSEN, BARBARA B. social worker, consultant; b. N.Y.C. d. William R. and Kathleen D. (McGowan) Busse; m. John C. Johansen; children: Kathleen, Paul(dec.). BS, Fordham U., 1956, MSW, 1988; cert. in psychosocial Oncology, Meml. Sloan Kettering Med. Ctr, 1990. Lic. social worker Conn. Coord. family edn. Diocese Bridgeport, Conn., 1976-77; exec. dir. Change Pace Experiences, Inc., New Canaan, Conn., 1983-89; med. social worker Bridgeport Hosp., 1986-87, Greenwich (Conn.) Hosp., 1988-2000. Mem. adv. bd. Vol. Ctr., Stamford, Conn., 1986—94, Ctr. for Hope, Darien, Conn., 1990—; mem. com. Hole in the Wall Gang Fund, Inc., New Haven, 1989—94. Mem. social work com. Am. Cancer Soc. Fairfield County, Westport, Conn., 1988—96. Named Woman of Yr., AAUW New Canaan, 1992, recipient Make a Difference award, YWCA, 1986, Golden Rule award, J. C. Penney Co., Inc., 1986, Cmty. Leader award, Women in Mgmt. Inc., 1986, Lane W. Adams Excellence in Social Work award, Am. Cancer Soc., 1996. Mem.: NASW (diplomate in clin. social work), Assn. Oncology Social Workers. Avocations: reading, travel. Home: 23 Green Meadow Ln New Canaan CT 06840-6823

JOHANSEN, DAVID ALAN, musician, educator; b. Champaign, Ill., Sept. 4, 1958; s. Walter Henry and Mary Lou Johansen. MusB, Ft. Hays State U., 1976—80; MS in Music Edn., The U. of Ill., 1981—82; Mus D, The U. of Iowa, 1986—91. Dir. of vocal and instrumental music St. Thomas More Prep/Marian H.S., Hays, Kans., 1982—86; instr. of music St. Olaf Coll., Northfield, Minn., 1991—92; asst. prof. of music Western State Coll. of Colo., 1992—94; vis. asst. prof. of trombone studies The U. of Iowa, 1994—95; asst. prof. of music Western State Coll. of Colo., 1995—98; asst. prof. of low brass studies Southeastern La. U., 1998—. Prin. trombonist The Hays Symphony Orch., Kans., United States, 1982—86; second trombonist The Cedar Rapids Symphony Orch., Iowa, 1986—91, The Baton Rouge Symphony Orch., 1998—. Contbr. articles to profl. jours. Mem.: The Coll. Music Soc., The Internat. Trombone Assn., Phi Mu Alpha Sinfonia (faculty advisor 1999). Home: PO Box 1914 Natalbany LA 70451-1914 Office: Southeastern La U SLU Box 10815 Hammond LA 70402 Office Fax: 985-549-2892. Personal E-mail: dajohansen@i-55.com. E-mail: djohansen@selu.edu.

JOHANSEN, EIVIND HERBERT, special education services executive, former army officer; b. Charleston, S.C., Mar. 7, 1927; s. Andrew and Ruth Lee (Thames) J.; m. Dolores E. Klockmann, June 9, 1950; children: Chris Allen, Jane Elizabeth. BS, Tex. A&M U., 1950; MS, George Washington U., 1968; postgrad., Harvard U., 1955, Army Command and Gen. Staff Coll., 1963, Naval War Coll., 1968, Advanced Mgmt. Program, U. Pitts., 1971. Quartermaster officer U.S. Army, 1950-79, advanced through grades to lt. gen., 1977; strategic planner Office Joint Chiefs of Staff, 1968-69, group comdr., 1969-70; army dir. distbn., 1970-72; army dir. materiel, 1972-75; comdg. gen. Army Aviation Systems Command, St. Louis, 1975-77; army dep. chief staff for logistics Washington, 1977-79; ret., 1979; pres., CEO Nat. Industries for Severely Handicapped, Inc., 1979-92. Mem. exec. council, chmn. mgmt. improvement com. Fed. Exec. Bd., St. Louis, 1975-77; bd. advs. Am. Def. Preparedness Assn., St. Louis, 1975-77, tech. and mgmt. adv. bd., Washington, 1977-79; chmn. Army Logistics Policy Council, 1977-79; bd. advs. Army Logistic Mgmt. Coll., 1978-79, Army Mgmt. Engring. Coll., 1978-79 Contbr. articles to profl. jours. Mem. President's Com. for Purchase from Blind and Other Severely Handicapped, Washington, 1973-74, chmn., 1975; mem. President's Com. on Employment of Handicapped; bd. dirs., chmn. ind. ops. com. Mo. Goodwill Industries, 1975-77; chmn. youth program Jr. Achievement, St. Louis, 1975-77; sponsor Air Explorer Post, Boy Scouts Am., 1975-77; bd. dirs. Q.M. Found., 1979-88, 92-93. Decorated DSM, Legion of Merit with two oak leaf clusters, Bronze Star, numerous others; recipient Tex. A&M Disting. Alumnus award, 1985, Hall of Honor award Tex. A&M, 1997, Disting. Svc. award Nat. Industries for Severely Handicapped, 1992, Disting. Career award Nat. Assn. Rehab. Facilities, 1992; named to Quartermaster Hall of Fame, U.S. Army, 1992. Mem. Assn. U.S. Army (bd. advisors St. Louis 1975-77), Am. Helicopter Soc., Army Aviation Assn. Am., Ret. Officers Assn., Nat. Rehab. Assn., Tex. A&M Alumni Assn. Washington (exec. bd. 1974, 78-79, pres. 1975, bd. dirs. 1993-95), George Washington U. Alumni Assn., U. Pitts. Alumni Assn., Harvard U. Alumni Assn., Toastmasters. Home: 3084 Darby Rd Keswick VA 22947-2720

JOHANSEN, ERLING, retired dental educator and dean; b. Overhalla, Norway, Apr. 8, 1923; came to U.S., 1945; s. Trygve Vilmar and Jenny Marie (Gansmo) J.; m. Inger Marie Nordback, July 4, 1952; children: Erling Trygve, Erik Bjarne, Steven Douglas. DMD cum laude, Tufts U., 1949; PhD, U. Rochester, 1955; DSc (hon.), Athens (Greece) U., 1981; HHD (hon.), New Eng. Sch. Law, 1993. Eastman/Squibb fellow, dental rsch. Rochester (N.Y.) U., 1950-55, asst. prof. dentistry, 1955-58, assoc. prof. dentistry, 1958-61, prof. dental rsch., 1961-66, Welcher prof. dental rsch., 1966-78, chair dept. dentistry and dental rsch., 1955-78; prof. general dentistry Tufts U. Sch. Dental Medicine, Boston, 1979-95, acting chmn. oral health svc. dept., 1979-86, dean, 1979-95, dean emeritus, Disting. Prof. emeritus, 1995—. With Norwegian Armed Forces Dental Corps, 1949-50, Norwegian Pub. Health Svc., 1950; cons. Strong Meml. Hosp., Rochester, 1958-79, Eastman Dental Ctr., Rochester, 1967-78, Genesee Hosp., Rochester, 1967-78, Monroe Cmty. Hosp., Rochester, 1968-75; project supr. Rochester Neighborhood Health Ctr., 1965-70, Migrant Dental Program, Rochester, 1965-70; coord. dental program, U. Rochester Cancer Ctr., 1974-78; cons. Highland Hosp., 1975-78; numerous coms. and consultantships, including AMA Coun. on Drugs, USPHS, Bur. Environ. Health, Nat. Inst. Dental Rsch., King Abdulaziz U., Jeddah, Saudi Arabia, Ministry of Health, Kuwait, others; internat. lectr. and presenter in field. Contbr. articles to profl. jours.; editor Jour. Dental Edn., 1974-76, AAAS Symposium 11, 1979, AAAS Symposium on Oral Health of Elderly, 1987; patentee in field of remineralizing solution; reviewer, mem. editl. bds. various jours. Bd. dirs., chair, fundraising com., pres. Scandinavian Charitable, West Newton, Mass., 1995—, pres., 2003; Gavel lectureship com., Forsyth Inst., Boston, 1997—. Lt., Norwegian Army, 1949-50. Disting. Lectr. Pan Am. Health Orgn., WHO, 1973; Dr. Erling Johansen Endowed Professorship, Tufts U., 1994. Fellow AAAS (coun. mem. 1963-67, 72-77), Am. Coll. Dentists (chmn. We. N.Y. sect., New Eng. sect.), Internat. Coll. Dentists, Pierre Fauchard Dental Honor Soc.; mem. ADA (internat. com., 7th dist., N.Y., 1969-76, Coun. Scientific Rsch., N.Y., 1971-78; various coms. and task forces; presenter testimony U.S. Ho. of Reps. 1986), Am. Assn. Dental Schs. (chmn. sect. advanced edn. 1968-69, v.p. advanced edn. programs 1970-74, exec. com. 1970-74, adminstrv. bd. coun. deans 1989-93, chair 1992-93, various other coms. and subcoms.), Am. Assn. Dental Rsch. (sec.-treas., bd. dirs. 1976-79), Internat. Assn. Dental Rsch. (coun. mem. 1958-61, 69-76, bd. dirs. 1974-75, various coms. and subcoms.), Greater N.Y. Dental Soc. (Dr. Irving E. Gruber award 1998), Mass. Dental Soc. (rsch. awards com. 1980—), Dental Soc. Norway, Korean Dental Assn. (hon.), Tufts U. Alumni Assn. (Disting. Svc. award 1994), Sigma Xi, Omicron Kappa Upsilon. Avocations: fishing, skiing, photography, historical research. Home: 69 Windsor Rd Needham MA 02492-1440 Office: Tufts U Sch Dental Medicine One Kneeland St Boston MA 02111

JOHANSEN, KAREN LEE, retired sales executive; b. Sheldon, Iowa, Dec. 5, 1945; d. Alvin Anthony and Marjory Gertrude (Kuiper) Eich; m. Pete Brunsting, May 15, 1964 (div. Dec. 1983); children: Jeffrey Brunsting, Keri Wallenstein; m. Alan Brockberg, Oct. 30, 1988 (div. Apr. 1991); m. Alan Johansen, Aug. 21, 1993. Student, Sioux Valley Hosp. Sch. Nsg., 1963-65; grad., S.D. Police Acad., 1978; postgrad., Phoenix Paralegal Inst., 1981-82. Owner Redwood Steak House and Lounge, White, S.D., 1975-76; dep. sheriff Brookings (S.D.) County Sheriff's Office, 1978-79; clk. of ct. City of Gillette, Wyo., 1980-82; child support enforcement officer Campbell County, Gillette, 1982-84; jud. asst. Wyo. Dist. Ct., Sheridan, 1984-85; office mgr. Felt & Martin Law Firm, Billings, Mont., 1985-87; owner paralegal svcs. office, Pipestone, Minn., 1987-89; dist. agt. Prudential Ins. Co. Am., Pipestone, 1989-91, sales mgr. Austin, Minn., 1991-93; mgr. S.W. Minn. Prudential Ins. Co., Worthington, Minn., 1993-94; cons. Aanenson Agy., Inc., Fulda, Slayton, Minn., 1994-95; estate planner, agt. Farm Bur. Ins. Co., Slayton, Minn., 1994-96, Prudential Ins., Slayton, Minn., 1996-97; ret. Campaign to Re-Elect Andy Steensma, Pipestone, 1990; mem. Ihlen (Minn.) City Coun., 1990; chair Brookings Summer Art Festival, 1976-79, chair, 1977-79, chair entertainment, 1976. Mem. Nat. Assn. Life Underwriters, Nat. Assn. Security Dealers. Democrat. Avocations: reading, travel, animals. E-mail: haneyho@frontiernet.net.

JOHANSEN, ROBERT HENNY, horticulturist, geneticist; b. Grafton, ND, July 26, 1922; m. Donna Joan Mootz, Jan. 17, 1948; children: Robert, Ann, Gail, Brian. BS agr., North Dakota AC, Fargo, ND, 1949, MS, 1954, PhD horticulture, 1964. Prof. emeritus North Dakota State U, 1993. Asst. (horticulture) North Dakota State U, Fargo, ND, 1950, asst. prof., 1957, assoc. prof., 1960, prof., 1993. Cons. Calbee Co., Japan, 1984. Author: (articles) Valley Potato Grower, 1992, (article) Nat. Potato Breeding Report, 1982—83, ND State Seed Jour., 1962—85, Am. Potato Jour., 1957—65; contbr. ICSV6 USN, 1944—96, USS Anteom. Recipient 25 yr. of svc. to ND, Quarter Century Club, 1974, Canner Packer, 1975, Meritorious, Red River Valley Potato Growers, 1978, Harvest Bowl, 1979, Outstanding Svc, Potato Chip/Snack Food Assoc., 1984, Excellence in Rsch., Grower Mag., 1984, Meml., SD Hort. Soc., 1985, Agr. of the Yr., Alpha Zeta, 1985, Outstanding Svc, US Seed Potato Industry, 1986, Appreciation Day, Walhalla Potato Growers, 1987, Appreciation, High Plains Vegetable Growers, 1989—90, Pioneer of the Yr., NW Farm Mgr. Assoc., 1990, Appreciation, CA Potato Growers, 1991, Excellence in Horticulture, R.L. Wodarz, 1981, Disting. Svc., Prairie Potato Coun., 1992; grantee funding, Frito-Lay, Red River Valley Potato Growers Assoc., Simplot, Snack Food Assoc., U of CA, USDA-ARS. Mem.: Faculty Senate, NDSU Harvest Bowl Comm. (V chmn. 1985, chmn. 1974—79, V chmn. 1980—81), Red River Valley Potato Ext. Adv. Comm., Potato Crop Adv. Comm., NCR 150 Potato Processing Comm. (sec. 1984), Potato Assoc. of Am. (pres. 1970—71), Potato Assoc. of Am. (life), Univ. Athletic Comm. (sec. 1978—79), Elks, VFW, Am. Legion. Lutheran. Achievements include featured in 1980 issue of Binford's Guide; research in potato breeding; reducing sugar accumulation in potato clones; first to finding new potato varieties; research in virus resistance. Avocation: gardening. Home: Centralia, Wash. Died July 18, 1996.

JOHANSEN, ROBERT JOHN, electrical engineer; b. S.I., N.Y., Mar. 30, 1952; s. Odd Ingvold and Theresa Florence (Stanislawiszyn) J. Grad. h.s., Staten Island, N.Y., Staten Island, N.Y., 1970. Comm. technician AAT Electronics Corp., S.I., 1975-78; engr. ITT Mackay Corp., Elizabeth, N.J., 1978 85; product engr. Panasonic Co., Secaucus, N.J., 1985-94; cons. comm. systems S.I., N.Y., 1994-96; sr. tech. assoc. Lucent Technologies-Wireless Tech. Prodn. Ctr., Piscataway, N.J., 1997—; tech. staff Philips Consumer Comms.-Lucent Techs., 1998—; test engr. Motorola, Piscataway, N.J., 1999—. Cons. SRF Electronics, 2001—. Contbr. articles to profl. jours. Active People for Perot

Campaign, S.I., 1992, United We Stand Am., 1992. Mem. IEEE, Am. Amateur Radio League, S.I. Amateur Radio Assn. (pres. 1989-91, 2000—, mem. exec. coun.), Radio Club Am. Home and Office: 61 Burnside Ave Staten Island NY 10302-2302 E-mail: wb2srf@juno.com.

JOHANSEN, ROBERT JOSEPH, consulting actuary; b. N.Y.C., May 2, 1922; s. Irving Joseph and Margaret (McKee) J.; m. Mary Carroll Hayes, June 27, 1964; children: Mary Carroll, Robert Hayes, David McKee. BA, Manhattan Coll., 1943; MA, Columbia U., 1974. With Met. Life Ins. Co., N.Y.C., 1947-82, 3d v.p., 1964-68, 2d v.p., 1968-69, v.p. personal ins. adminstrn., 1969-70, v.p., 1970-72, v.p., actuary, 1972-82; cons. actuary, 1982—. Sec. Coun. Profl. Assns. on Fed. Stats., 1980-83, chmn., 1984; vice chmn. exec. com. Ins. Guaranty Corp. N.Y., 1974-82. Contbr. articles to profl. jours. Trustee Dominican Coll., Blauvelt, N.Y., 1970-87; former pres. Van Cortlandt Terr. Assn.; mem. Mayor's Com. for Cmty. Rels., Yonkers, N.Y., 1978-86. Served with USAAF, 1943-46. Fellow Soc. Actuaries (treas. 1980-83, gen. chmn. edn. and exam com. 1970-71, chaired com. that produced the 1983 Table A annuity valuation mortality table, mem. com. on rsch. mgmt. 1998-91, com. on experience studies 1988-91, com. on life ins. rsch. 1993—, chmn. 1997—, chmn. task force on mortality guarantees in variable products 1996—, developed Annuity 2000 valuation mortality table; mem. individual life ins. valuation mortality taskforce, 2000-2003, com. for internat. symposia on living to 100 and beyond, (chmn.) 2002-, com. on life ins. co. expenses, 2000-; mem. Am. Acad. Actuaries, Am. Statis. Assn., Internat. Actuarial Assn., N.Y. Actuaries Club (treas. 1978-81), Actuarial Studies in Non-Life Ins., N.Y. Acad. Scis. Roman Catholic. Office: Life Actuarial Svcs 56 Pershing Ave Yonkers NY 10705-3631 E-mail: rjjfsa@aol.com.

JOHANSON, DONALD CARL, physical anthropologist; b. Chgo., June 28, 1943; s. Carl Torsten and Sally Eugenia (Johnson) J.; 1 child, Tesfaye Meles. BA, U. Ill., 1966; MA, U. Chgo., 1970, PhD, 1974; DSc (hon.), John Carroll U., 1979; D.Sc. (hon.), Coll. of Wooster, 1985. Mem. dept. phys. anthropology Cleve. Mus. Natural History, 1972-81, curator, 1974-81; pres. Inst. Human Origins, Berkeley, Calif., 1981-97, dir. Tempe, Ariz., 1997—. Prof. anthropology Stanford U., 1983-89, Ariz. State U., 1997, Virginia M. Ullman chair human origins, 2000; adj. prof. Case Western Res. U., 1978-81, Kent State U., 1978-81. Co-author: (with M.A. Edey) Lucy: The Beginnings of Humankind, 1981 (Am. Book award 1982), Blueprints: Solving the Mystery of Evolution, 1989, (with James Shreeve) Lucy's Child: Discovering a Human Ancestor, 1989, (with Kevin O'Farrell) Journey from the Dawn: Life with the World's First Family, 1990, (with Lenora Johanson and Blake Edgar) Ancestors: In Search of Human Origins, 1994, (with Blake Edgar) From Lucy to Language, 1997, (with Giancarlo Ligabue) Ecce Homo, 1999; host PBS Natures Series; prodr. (film) Lucy in Disguise, 1982; host, narrator NOVA series In Search of Human Origins, 1994 (Emmy nomination 1995); contbr. numerous articles to profl. jours. Recipient Jared Potter Kirtland award for outstanding sci. achievement Cleve. Mus. Natural History, 1979, Profl. Achievement award U. Chgo., 1980, Gold Mercury Internat. ad personem award Ethiopia, 1982, Humanist Laureate award Acad. of Humanism, 1983, Disting. Svc. award Am. Humanist Assn., 1983, San Francisco Exploratorium award, 1986, Internat. Premio Fregene award, 1987, Alumni Achievement award U. Ill., 1995, Anthropology Media award Am. Anthropol. Assn., 1999, Webby award for best sci. web site becominghuman.org, 2002; named Endowed Chair Virginia Ullman Chair in Human Origins, Webby award Internat. Acad. Digital Arts and Scis., 2002; grantee Wenner-Gren Found., NSF, Nat. Geog. Soc., L.S.B. Leakey Found., Cleve. Found., George Gund Found., Roush Found. Fellow AAAS, Calif. Acad. Scis., Rochester (N.Y.) Mus., Royal Geog. Soc.; mem. Am. Assn. Phys. Anthropologists, Internat. Assn. Dental Rsch., Internat. Assn. Human Biologists, Am. Assn. Africanist Archaeologists, Soc. Vertebrate Paleontology, Soc. Study of Human Biology, Societe de l'Anthropologie de Paris, Centro Studi Ricerche Ligabue (Venice), Founders' Coun., Chgo. Field Mus. Natural History (hon.), Assn. Internationale pour l'etude de Paleontologie Humaine, Mus. Nat. d'Histoire Naturelle de Paris (corr.), Explorers Club (hon. dir.), Nat. Ctr. Sci. Edn. (supporting scientist). Office: Inst Human Origins Ariz State U PO Box 874101 Tempe AZ 85287-4101

JOHANSON, KNUT ARVID, JR., retired engineering executive; b. St. Augustine, Fla., Aug. 27, 1936; s. Knut Arvid and Constance Elinor (Harrison) J.; m. Eleanor Marie Friesen, Nov. 28, 1956; children: Michael James, David Bryan, Phillip Arvid. BSEE, Tex. A&I U., 1959; MSChemE, U. Houston, 1978. Registered profl. engr., La., Tex., Calif. Instrumentation engr. maintenance dept. Union Carbide Corp., Texas City, Tex., 1959-67, sr. control sys. engr. Taft, La., 1967-72, control sys. commissioning engr. UNIFOS plant Stenningsund, Sweden, 1971, group leader sys. engring. group Port Lavaca, Tex., 1973-90, prin. control sys. engr. Houston, 1990-2001. Control sys. mgr. EQUATE Joint Venture, Kuwait, 1994-96, control sys. mgr. Optimal Joint Venture, Malaysia, 1997, process standards mgr., 1998-2001; instr. LaMarque Ind. Sch. Dist., 1964-66, Victoria Coll., 1977. Contbr. articles to profl. jours. Served with U.S. Army, 1960-62. Fellow Instrument Soc. Am. (v.p., exec. bd. 1975-77, 85-87, Disting. Svc. award 1998, Disting. Fell. Grade, 1999). Baptist. Home and Office: 2010 Dowling Dr Richmond TX 77469-5114 E-mail: arvid@johanson.us.

JOHANSON, PATRICIA MAUREEN, artist, architect, park designer; b. N.Y.C., Sept. 8, 1940; d. Alvar Einar and Elizabeth (Deane) J.; m. E.C. Goossen (dec.); children: Alvar Deane, Gerrit Hull, Nathaniel James. Student, Bklyn. Mus. Art Sch., 1958, Art Students League, 1961; AB, Bennington Coll., 1962; MA, Hunter Coll., 1964; BS, BArch, City Coll. Sch. Architecture, 1977; DFA (hon.), Mass. Coll. of Art, 1995. Vis. prof. art SUNY-Albany, 1969; vis. artist MIT, 1974, Oberlin (Ohio) Coll., 1974, Alfred (N.Y.) U., 1974, West Tex. State U., 1988, Yale U., 1989, Mass. Coll. Art, Boston, 1994, Calif. State U., Monterey Bay, 1997, 99; Southworth lectr. Colby Coll., Waterville, Maine, 1981; cons. Mitchell-Giurgola Assocs., architects, N.Y.C., Phila., 1972—, Oikos, Seoul, South Korea, 1996, Yukong Ltd., Ulsan, South Korea, 1996, Seoul Devel. Inst., Seoul, 1999, Millenium Park, Seoul, 1999, Nat. Endowment for Arts, Washington, 1988, City of Petaluma, Calif., 1999, Carollo Engrs., 2001, The Murie Ctr., Moose, Wyo., 2001—; artist-in-residence N.Y. Found. for Arts, 1987—; del. Survival and the Arts, Sundance Inst., Utah, 1991; del. Global Forum Gen. Assembly, Kyoto, Japan, 1993, Art & Environ., Ankara, 1997, Year 2000 Symposium, Dumbarton Oaks, Washington, keynote spkr. Internat. Fedn. of Landscape Architects, Belem, Brazil, 2002, Art in Embassies program U.S. Dept. State; mem. grants selection com. NEA, 2000. Solo shows Tibor de Nagy Gallery, N.Y.C., 1967, SUNY at Albany, 1969, Montclair (N.J.) State Coll., 1974, Rosa Esman Gallery, N.Y.C., 1978, 79, 81, 83, Dallas Mus. Art, 1982, Philippe Bonnafont Gallery, San Francisco, 1984, New Arts Program, Kutztown, Pa., 1987, Albany Acad., 1987, Painted Bride Art Ctr., Phila., 1991; National Museum of Kenya, Nairobi, 1996—, Salina Art Ctr., Kans., 2001; retrospectives, Bennington Coll., 1973, 91, Twining Gallery, N.Y.C., 1987, Berkshire Mus., Pittsfield, Mass, 1987; group shows, Hudson River Mus., Yonkers, N.Y., 1964, Bennington Coll., 1964, 84, Stable Gallery, N.Y.C., 1966, Tibor de Nagy Gallery, N.Y.C., 1966, 68, Larry Aldrich Mus., Ridgefield, Conn., 1968, Mus. Modern Art, N.Y.C., 1968, Grand Palais, Paris, 1968, Kunsthaus Zurich, 1969, Tate Gallery, London, 1969, Vassar Coll., 1969, Finch Coll. Mus., 1971, Everson Mus., Syracuse, N.Y., 1971, Detroit Inst. Arts, 1973, MIT, 1974, 83, Casa Thomas Jefferson, Brasilia, Brazil, 1975, Pa. Acad. Fine Arts, Phila., 1975, Greenwich (Conn.) Library Art Gallery, 1977, Bklyn. Mus., 1977, 80, New Gallery Contemporary Art, Cleve., 1977, Cleve. State U., 1977, Cooper-Hewitt Mus., N.Y.C., 1978, Mus. Modern Art, N.Y.C., 1979, Berkshire Mus., Pittsfield, Mass., Newark Mus., 1979, Graham Gallery, N.Y.C., 1980, U. Mass., Amherst, 1980, Mus. Contemporary Art, Chgo., 1981, Sotheby-Parke Bernet, N.Y.C., 1980, Centro de Documentación de Arte Actual, Barcelona, Spain, 1980, 81, Galeria O'Patacón la Coruña, Spain, 1981, SUNY, Old Westbury, 1981, Rosa Esman Gallery, 1981, 82, 83, Miami U., 1981, Met. Mus. Art, N.Y.C., 1982, 83, Berkshire Mus., 1982, 86, Laumeier Sculpture Park, St. Louis, 1982, 93, 94, Teatro Contadino, Naples, 1982, Dallas Mus. Natural History, 1982, 93, Suzanne Gross Gallery, Phila., 1984, Harvard U., 1984, Stamford Mus., Conn., 1985, 89, Md. Inst. Art, 1985, Bard Coll., N.Y., 1985, 90, U. Calif., La Jolla, 1985, Ark. Art Ctr., Little Rock, 1985, Warwick Mus., R.I., 1985, Marisa Del Re Gallery, N.Y.C., 1986, Am. Acad. Arts and Letters, N.Y.C., 1986, Hunter Coll. Art Gallery, 1986, 91, 93, Stamford Mus., Ct., 1989, Albany Inst. History and Art, 1988, Kouros Gallery, N.Y., 1988, L.I. U., 1989, Blum-Helman Gallery, N.Y., 1989, Murray State U., Ky., 1989, N.Y. State Mus., 1989, Burchfield Art Ctr., Buffalo, 1990, Grand Rapids (Mich.) Art Mus., 1990, U. North Tex., Denton, 1990, Hofstra U. Art Mus., 1990, Salina (Kans.) Art Ctr., 1991, U. Houston, 1991, Crocker Art Mus., Sacramento, 1991, Laguna (Calif.) Art Mus., 1991, 94, Centro Insular de Cultura, Spain, 1991, San Jose State U., 1991, Nat. Theater, Brasilia, Brazil, 1992, Queens (N.Y.) Mus. of Art, 1992, Whatcom Mus., Bellingham, Washington, 1993, Calif. Crafts Mus., San Francisco, 1993, 94, Nat. Mus. of Fine Arts, Rio De Janeiro, 1993, La Defense, Paris, 1993, San Jose Mus. of Art, Calif., 1993, U. Pa., 1993, Salt Lake Art Ctr., Utah, 1993, Madison (Wis.) Art Ctr., 1993, La Virreina, Barcelona, Spain, 1994, Longwood Art Ctr., Va., 1994, De Cordova Mus., Mass., 1994, Ctr. for the Arts, Miami, 1994, Dahl Fine Arts Ctr., S.D., 1994, Gallery Nikko, Tokyo, 1994, 96, Soho 20 Gallery, N.Y.C., 1994, Internat. Sculpture Ctr., Washington, 1994, Pratt Manhattan Gallery, N.Y.C., 1994, Skidmore Coll., 1996, Brickbottom Gallery, Somerville, Mass., 1996, 2003, Michael Fuchs Gallery, Berlin, 1997, City Coll. N.Y., 1997, Gallery Route One, Point Reyes, Calif., 1999, The Presidio, San Francisco, 1999, Villa Medici, Rome, 2000, Mass. Coll. Art, 2000, French Cultural Svcs. Gallery, N.Y.C., 2000, Institut Francais D' Architecture, Paris, 2000, Contemporary Arts Ctr., Cin., 2002Mus. of Contemporary Art, L.A., 2003; represented in permanent collections, Detroit Inst. Arts, Dallas Mus. Art, Mus. Modern Art, Met. Mus. Art, N.Y.C., Nat. Mus. Women in Arts, Washington, Herbert F. Johnson Mus., Cornell U., Berkshire Mus., N.Y. State Council on Arts Film Collection, Syracuse, Storm King Art Ctr., Mountainville, N.Y., Crawford and Chester Sts. Park, Cleve., Oberlin Coll., Bennington Coll., Brandeis U., U. Mass., Amherst, also pvt. collections; films The Art of the Real, USIA, 1968, Stephen Long, CBS-TV, 1968, Patricia Johanson: Cyrus Field, 1974, The City Project: Cleveland, 1977, A Conversation with Patricia Johanson, Heritage Cablevision, 1985, Patricia Johanson, Berks (Pa.) Community TV, 1990, Patricia Johanson: The Leonhardt Lagoon, 1992, Patricia Johanson: A Sense of Place, 1992, Patricia Johanson: Multilevel Designs, Aesthetic, Ecological, Functional, Cedar Arts Forum, Iowa, 1994, Q&A with Patricia Johanson, PBS, 1998, Chicken Scratch with Patricia Johanson, Petaluma, California Cmty. TV, 1999, Johanson interview The Environment Show Nat. Pub. Radio, 2000; author: Art and Survival: Creative Solutions to Environmental Problems, 1992; works include park design, sculpture, ecological landscapes, street furniture, pavement designs, site planning for Consol. Edison Co., Yale U., Columbus East High Sch., Ind., House and Garden mag., Internat. Yr. of Child Commn., Fair Park Lagoon, Dallas, Corning Preserve, Albany, Cathedral Sq., Sacramento, Calif., Pelham Bay Pk., N.Y.C., Candlestick Pt. State Park, San Francisco, Umame Project, Brasilia, Brazil, Park for a Rainforest, Amazonas, Brazil, Nairobi River Park, Kenya, Ulsan Dragon Park, Ulsan, Korea, The Rocky Marciano Trail, Brockton, Mass., Millenium Park, Seoul, French Cultural Svcs. Garden, N.Y., South Ninth St. Corridor, Salina, Kans., Lakeville Water Recycling Facility and Tidal Wetlands Park, Petaluma, Calif., Pub. Art Master Plan, Rockland County, N.Y., 1990, Ecol. Master Plan Greater Boston Metropolitan Region, 1994—, Sugarhouse Pedestrial Crossing, Salt Lake City. Bd. dirs. New Arts Program, Pa., 1988—; bd. advisors Artists Representing Environ. Arts, Inc., N.Y.C., 1991—. Guggenheim fellow, 1970, 80, NEA fellow, 1975, Olesen fellow Bennington Coll., 1991; Adolph & Esther Gottlieb Found. grantee, 1998; recipient 1st prize Environ. Design Competition, Montclair State Coll., 1974, Internat. Womens Yr. award, 1976, Gold medal Acad. Italia delle Arti, Parma, 1979, Townsend Harris medal CCNY, 1994, Arts and Healing NEtwork award, 2003; named to Hunter Coll. Hall of Fame, 1987; named to Mepham H.S. Hall of Fame, 1998, Arts and Healing Network award, 2003. Mem. Global Forum Arts Group. Home: 179 Nickmush Rd Buskirk NY 12028-3202 E-mail: johansonsite@aol.com. *Let problems be your inspiration.*

JOHANSSON, ALICIA BARBARA, musician; b. Warsaw, May 21, 1941; d. Boleslaw Bielik and Halina Helena Napiorkowska; m. Evert Johansson, May 13, 1972 (div. 1978); m. Kjell Johansson, Jan. 2, 1980 (div. 1986); 1 child, Sandra; m. James McClung, Nov. 29, 1986 (div. 1995). *Daughter Sandra Lillian Johansson studies currently at the University of Colorado at Denver. She is listed in the National Dean's List honoring America's outstanding college students' 25th silver anniversary edition 2001-2002 volume III. Sandra is a member of Phi Theta Kappa, in the honors program and on the president's list. She is majoring in international affairs.* BA in Piano Solo, Conservatory of Warsaw, 1961, MA in Musical Sci., 1968; cert. organist, U. Stockholm, 1984. Radio anchor Polish Radio and TV, Warsaw, 1959—63; piano accompanist Royal Opera, Stockholm, 1973—78, Cramer and Cullberg Ballet, Stockholm, 1974—80, Opera Ballet Sch., Stockholm, 1973—86, various concerts, Stockholm, 1978—86, Cleve. Ballet, 1986—90, Colo. Ballet, Denver, 1990—2000; tchr. piano and organ various chs., Cleve. and Denver, 1987—; pvt. accompanist, tchr. Denver, 1990; organist Jefferson Ave. United Meth. Ch., Denver, 2003—, choir dir., 2003—. Organist Jefferson Ave United Meth. Ch., Denver, choir dir. Performer: numerous organ and piano concerts; composer ch. music, 1973—. Organizer Royal Opera and Ballet Club, Stockholm, 1975—86. Mem.: Music Tchrs. Assn., Am. Guild Organists, Musicians Union. Democrat. Avocations: investing, hiking, travel, nature. Home and Studio: 7165 S Gaylord St E-6 Littleton CO 80122 E-mail: Ajca80122@aol.com.

JOHANSSON, JOHN THOMAS, retired science educator; b. Fargo, N.D., Nov. 16, 1932; s. Hugo and Hazel May Johansson; m. Janet Ellen Bosworth, Dec. 27, 1956; children: Thomas, David. MS, N.D. State U., 1960; BA, Minn. State U., 1955, BS, 1954. Cert. tchr. Minn. Chmn. dept. sci. & biology Ind. Sch. Dist., Detroit Lakes, Minn., 1955—98. Mem.: NEA (life), Nat. Biology Tchrs. Assn., Minn. Edn. Assn. (life). Home: 1105 N Shore Dr Detroit Lakes MN 56501-4213 E-mail: jjohansson@lakesnet.net.

JOHANSSON, LENNART VALDEMAR, Swedish industrialist; b. Gothenburg, Oct. 3, 1921; s. Waldemar and Alma (Nordh) J.; m. Inger Hedberg, 1944; 3 children. AB, SKF, 1943; DTech (hon.), Chalmers U., 1979, Sarajevo U., 1983. Mng. of mfg., 1961; gen. mgr., 1966; dep. mng. dir., 1969; pres., group CEO, 1971-95; chair, 1985-92; hon. chair, 1992—. Recipient King of Sweden's medal, Finnish Order of the Lion John Ericsson medal, 1986. Avocations: sailing, swimming. Home: AB SKF SE-41550 Göteborg Sweden

JOHLIN, FREDERICK CARL, JR., medical educator; b. Ohio, Sept. 3, 1953; s. Frederick Carl Johlin, Sr.; m. Beverly Johlin; children: Cheryl, Eric. BS in Chemistry and Math., U. Toledo, 1976; MD, Med. Coll. Ohio, 1980. Resident Med. Coll. Ohio, Toledo, 1980—83; fellow gastroenterology U. Iowa Hosp. and Clinic, Iowa City, 1983—86, assoc. prof., 1986—. Recipient Fellowship award, Liver Found., 1984. Achievements include patents in field. Office: Univ Iowa Hosps & Clinics 200 Hawkins Dr Iowa City IA 52242

JOHN, CHRISTOPHER, congressman; b. Jan. 5, 1960; m. Payton Smith. BA, La. State U., 1982. Mem. La. Ho. of Reps., 1988—96, U.S. Congress from 7th La. dist., 1997—, mem. energy and commerce com. Democrat. Office: US House of Reps 403 Cannon House Off Bldg Washington DC 20515-0001 also: 800 Lafayette St Ste 1400 Lafayette LA 70501-6800 also: 1011 Lake Shore Dr Ste 306 Lake Charles LA 70601-9415*

JOHN, ELTON HERCULES (REGINALD KENNETH DWIGHT), musician; b. Pinner, Middlesex, Eng., Mar. 25, 1947; s. Stanley and Sheila Eileen (Farebrother) Dwight. Student, Royal Acad. Music, London, 1959-64. Singer, songwriter, musician, began playing piano, 1951, joined group Bluesology, 1965, appeared (films) Tommy, 1975, toured America 10 times, 1970—76; composer: (broadway musical) Aida, 2000 (Tony award for Best Original Score); composer, performer Empty Sky, 1969, Elton John, 1970, Tumbleweed Connection, 11.17.70, Friends, Madman Across The Water, 1971, Honky Chateau, 1972, Don't Shoot Me I'm Only The Piano Player, Goodbye Yellow Brick Road, 1973, Caribou, Greatest Hits, 1974, Empty Sky, Captain Fantastic and the Brown Dirt Cowboy, Rock of the Westies, 1975, Here and There, Blue Moves, 1976, Greatest Hits Vol. II, 1977, A Single Man, 1978, Victim of Love, 1979, 21 at 33, 1980, Jump Up, 1982, Hearts, 1984, Ice on Fire, 1985, Leather Jackets, Your Songs, 1986, Live in Australia, 1987, Reg Strikes Back, 1988, Sleeping with the Past, The Thom Bell Sessions, 1989, To Be Continued, 1990, The One, 1992, Duets, 1993, Made in England, 1995, Love Songs, 1996, The Big Picture, 1997, Elaborate Lives: The Legend of Aida, 1998—99, The Road to El Dorado, 2000, composer, performer singles Lady Samantha, 1969, From Denver to L.A., Take Me to the Pilot/Your Song, Border Song, 1970, Friends, Levon, 1971, Tiny Dancer, Rocket Man, Honky Cat, Crocodile Rock, 1972, Daniel, Saturday Night's Alright for Fightin', Goodbye Yellow Brick Road, Step into Xmas, 1973, Bennie and the Jets, Don't Let the Sun Go Down on Me, The Bitch Is Back, Lucy in the Sky with Diamonds, 1974, Philadelphia Freedom, Someone Saved My Life Tonight, Island Girl, 1975, I Feel like a Bullet (In the Gun of Robert Ford), Don't Go Breaking My Heart, Sorry Seems to Be the Hardest Word, 1976, Bite Your Lip (Get Up and Dance), 1977, Ego, 1978, Mama Can't Buy You Love, Victim of Love, Part-Time Love, Johnny B Goode, Little Jeannie, Song for Guy, Are You Ready for Love, 1979, Song for Guy, 1979, Little Jeannie/Conquer the Sun, Don't Ya Wanna Play This Game No More?, 1980, Chloe, 1981, Empty Garden (Hey Hey Johnny), Blue Eyes, 1982, I'm Still Standing, Kiss the Bride, I Guess That's Why They Call It the Blues, 1983, Sad Songs (Say So Much), Who Wears These Shoes, 1984, Wrap Her Up, Nikita, Heartache All Over the World, 1986, Candle in the Wind, 1987, I Don't Wanna Go on with You Like That, Town of Plenty, Candle in the Wind (live), A Word in Spanish, 1988, Healing Hands, 1989, You Gotta Love Someone, Easier to Walk Away, Don't Let the Sun Go Down on Me, 1991, The One, 1992, Believe, Made in England, 1995; composer (singer): (album) The Muse, 1999, The Road to El Dorado, 2000, One Night Only: The Greatest Hist Live, 2000, Songs From the West Coast, 2001; composer music (film) The Lion King, 1994 (Best Original Song Acad. award for Can You Feel the Love Tonight?). Established Elton John Aids Found., 1993—; Chmn. Watford Football Club, 1976—90, pres., 1990—. Named to Rock & Roll Hall of Fame, 1994; recipient Gold Discs for all albums composed, Best British Male Artist Brits award, 1991, Grammy award, 1981, Grammy Legend award, 2000. Achievements include played to over 2 million people across 4 continents, 1984, 86; first popular Western singer to perform in USSR, 1979. Address: Twentyfirst Artists Ltd 1 Blythe Rd London W14 OH9 England also: Ste 370 8900 Wilshire Blvd Beverly Hills CA 90211*

JOHN, FRANK HERBERT, JR., real estate appraiser, real estate investor, health products executive; b. Georgetown, Guyana, Mar. 4, 1961; s. Frank Herbert Clement and Doris Marian (Schofield Jones) J.; m. Barbara Jean Stewart, June 1989 (div. Dec. 1999); 1 child, Andre Nicholas John. BBA, Howard U., 1984. Lic. real estate appraiser. Intern IBM, NYC, 1983, account rep. Washington, 1984-92; pres. Washington Appraisal, 1993—, Global Health Tech., LLC, Wash., DC, 2002—. Bd. dirs. Concerned Black Men, Washington, 1990-93, chmn. internat. awareness program, 1990-93. Mem. Nat. Assn. Realtors, D.C. C. of C., Delta Sigma Pi, Beta Gamma Sigma. Baptist. Office: Washington Appraisal 601 Pennsylvania Ave NW Ste 900 Washington DC 20004-3615

JOHN, GERALD WARREN, hospital pharmacist, educator; b. Salem, Ohio, Feb. 16, 1947; s. Harold Elba and Ruth Springer (Pike) J.; m. Jean Ann Marie Orris, Nov. 5, 1977; children: Patrick Warren, Jeanette Lynn. BS in Pharmacy, Ohio No. U., 1970; MS, U. Md., 1974. Registered pharmacist, Ohio, S.C. Staff pharmacist North Columbiana County Cmty. Hosp., Salem, 1970-72; asst. resident in hosp. pharmacy U. Md. Hosp., Balt., 1972-73, sr. resident, 1973-74, chmn. patient care pharmacies, 1974-76; dir. pharmacy Ohio Valley Hosp., Steubenville, 1976-97; exec. dir. Tri-State Health Svcs., Inc., 1997—. Mem. adv. bd. Contemporary Pharmacy Practice, 1977-83; preceptor profl. externship program Ohio No. U. Sch. Pharmacy, 1977—; adj. clin. instr. practical experience program Duquesne U. Sch. Pharmacy, 1976—; dir. pharmacy Trinity Med. Ctr., Steubenville, 1997—. Columnist Weirton Daily Times, 1990-94. Trustee, v.p. Valley Hospice Inc., 1985-98, 2000—. Named Hosp. Pharmacist of Yr., Md. Soc. Hosp. Pharmacists, 1976, Outstanding Young Man of Am., U.S. Jaycees, 1977. Fellow Am. Soc. Con. Pharmacists; mem. Am. Soc. Hosp. Pharmacists, Ohio Soc. Hosp. Pharmacists, Jefferson County Acad. Pharmacy, Southeastern Ohio Soc. Hosp. Pharmacists (pres. 1985-87), Rho Chi, Phi Eta Sigma. Methodist. Avocation: wae kune do karate (black belt).

JOHN, HUGO HERMAN, natural resources educator; b. Natoma, Kans., Feb. 13, 1929; s. Lorenz Louis and Clara Marie (Doehrmann) J.; m. Prudence Patricia Shuck, Sept. 9, 1950; children: Patrick, Peter, Sarah. BS, U. Minn., 1959, MS, 1961, PhD, 1964. From asst. prof. to assoc. prof. Coll. Forestry U. Minn., St. Paul, 1964-69, prof., 1969-72; prof. Coll. Forestry, Wildlife and Range Scis., assoc. dean U. Idaho, Moscow, 1972-74; dean, prof. Sch. Natural Resources U. Vt., Burlington, 1974-83; dean Coll. Agriculture and Natural Resources, dir. Agrl. Expt. Sta. and Coop. Extension U. Conn., Storrs, 1983-87, prof. natural resources, 1987-94, prof. emeritus, 1994—. Forestry expert UN Food and Agr. Orgn., Puerto Cabezas, Nicaragua, 1965-66, Nat. Univ. Medellin, Colombia, 1969-71; cons. Taconic Found., N.Y.C., Internat. Paper Co., N.Y.C., 1981-84; sr. cons. UN Devel. Programme, Humane Soc. of U.S., 1993—; devel./planning cons. Internat. Exec. Svcs. Corps., Zimbabwe, 1996, Ukraine, 1998. Contbr. articles to profl. jours. Mem., treas. bd. dirs. Smokey House Project, Danby, Vt., 1976—; bd. dirs. Merek Forest Found., Rupert, Vt., 1980-83, Ea. States Expn., West Springfield, Mass, 1989—, mem. Conn. trustees, 1984—, chmn., 1989-94. With U.S. Army, 1950-52. Mem. Soc. Am. Foresters (chmn. accreditation com. 1981-84), Am. Forestry Assn. Avocations: gardening, woodworking. Home: Box 732 501 4th Ave SE Mapleton MN 56065-9782

JOHN, LEONARD KEITH, aerospace and mechanical engineer; b. Lahore, Pakistan, Apr. 10, 1949; arrived in Can., 1975; s. Edwin Kenneth William and Olive (Khairullah) J.; m. Yvonne Anna Lee-Anan, Dec. 20, 1980; children: Sarah Ashley, Jason William. Full tech. cert., Harrow Coll. Tech. and Art, Middlesex, Eng., 1971; BS with honors, Hendon Coll., London, 1975; M in Engring., U. Toronto, 1978. Chartered engr., U.K.; registered profl. engr., Ont.; lic. pvt. pilot, Can. Aero. engring. tng. Westland Helicopters Ltd., Hayes, England, 1965—70, R&D engr., 1970—71, devel. engr. Hendon, England, 0191—1975; sr. devel. engr. non-metallics Bombardier Aerospace de Havilland (formerly Boeing Can.), Downsview, Canada, 1975—80, chief advanced composites and nonmetallics, 1985—89, chief advanced composites and chem. tech., 1989—93, mgr. materials tech., 1993—2002, prin. engring. specialist, materials tech., 2002—. Pres. 620688 Ont. Inc., Toronto, 1985—; composité adv. bd. E.I. Du Pont de Nemours & Co., Inc., Wilmington, Del., 1985; cons. to Revenue Can. Taxation-Rsch. and Devel. Investment Tax Credit, 1987-88; lectr. continuing edn. course in advanced materials Faculty Applied Sci. and Engring., U. Toronto, 1989—; Disting. lectr. NASA, 1994; presenter in field. Contbr. articles to profl. jours.; patentee in field; violins exhibited Planete Composite, Bordeaux, France, 1985, Ont. Sci. Ctr., Toronto, 1988—, Sec. of State Exhibit, Bravo Can., Toronto, Quebec City and Vancouver, 1988, 40th Internat. Soc. for Advancement Material and Process Engring. Symposium and Exhbn., Anaheim, Calif., 1995—. Recipient Outstanding Svc. award Soc. for Advancement of Material and Process Engring., 1979; original violin deeded to Can. as a cultural gift and designated as being of Outstanding Significance and Nat. Importance. Fellow: Royal Aeronautic Soc. (UK), Inst. Mech. Engrs. (Eng., mem. aerospace industries divsn. 1984—); mem.: Assn. Profl. Engrs. Province Ont., Can. Aeronautics and Space Inst. (F.H. Baldwin award 1982). Mem. Ch. of England. Achievements include invention of graphite fibre violin and violin type musical instruments; life and achievements featured in a dedicated television program, part of documentary series on extraordinary men airing on global, prime and Men TV, syndicated in global markets, 2003-. Avocations: flying, travel, music. Home: 5037 Elderview Ct Mississauga ON Canada L5M 5A9 Fax: 905-828-6261.

JOHN, LEWIS GEORGE, political science educator; b. Waco, Tex., Nov. 25, 1936; s. Lewis Hervin and Margaret Reese J.; m. Annette Louise Church, June 3, 1961; children: Andrew Lewis, Christopher Donald. BA, Washington & Lee U., 1958; M in Pub. Affairs, Princeton U., 1961; PhD, Syracuse U., 1973. Asst. dean students, dir. fin. aid and placement Washington & Lee U., Lexington, Va., 1963-66, assoc. dean students, 1968-69, dean students, prof. politics and adminstrn., 1969-90, prof. politics and adminstrn., 1969—. Leader workshops and seminars, various colls., 1981-85; presenter symposia and confs. Contbr. articles to profl. jours. and chpts. to books. Chmn. Lexington Sch. Bd. 1979-80; pre-law adviser NCAA Faculty Athletics, 1993-2001, rep., 1998-2001 Served to 1st lt. US Army, 1961-63. Woodrow Wilson fellow Princeton U., 1959-60; Fulbright scholar U. Edinburgh, 1958-59. Mem. ASPA, Nat. Assn. Student Personnel Adminstrs. (bd. dirs. 1977-79, 87-89, region III exec. bd. 1980-85, chmn. career devel. and profl. standards div. 1987-89, Disting. Svc. award 1982), Va. Assn. Student Personnel Adminstrs. (pres. 1975, Outstanding Profl. award 1983), Am. Polit. Sci. Assn., Phi Beta Kappa, Beta Gamma Sigma, Omicron Delta Kappa (faculty sec. Washington and Lee chpt. 1987-90, 98-2001, faculty advisor 1990-98), Omicron Delta Epsilon, Pi Sigma Alpha. Democrat. Presbyterian. Avocation: sports. Home: 8 Edmondson Ave Lexington VA 24450-1904 Office: Washington & Lee U Williams Sch 101B Lexington VA 24450 E-mail: johnl@wlu.edu.

JOHN, MERTIS, JR., record company executive; b. Detroit, May 22, 1932; s. Mertis and Lillie G. (Robinson) J.; m. Essie M. Wincher, June 16, 1957; 1 child, Darryl E. AA, Wayne Coll., 1978; student, Marygrove Coll., 1999—2000. Songwriter King Records, Cin. and N.Y.C., 1955-67; founder Mertis Music Co., Detroit, 1962—; founder, pres. Meda Records, 1981—. Corr. mem. Broadcast Music Inc. Speaking from the Heart, 1996; author: My Life and My Experiences in the Entertainment World, 1999, poetry; co-prodr.: Inside Music, 1977; songwriter: This Is Your Day, 1996 (presented to Rock and Roll Hall of Fame, 1996); composer: over 300 songs. With U.S. Army, 1952—54, Korea. Recipient Golden Poet award World of Poetry, 1989, 90; inducted into the Rock and Roll Hall of Fame, 1996. Mem. Detroit Soc. Musicians and Entertainers (chmn. bd. dirs. 1984—), Nat. Acad. Rec. Arts and Scis., Am. Fedn. Musicians, Masons (32d degree). Baptist. Fax: 313-862-5882.

JOHN, RICHARD C. enterprise development organization executive; b. Milw., Mar. 17, 1950; s. Richard C. and Mary W. (Widrig) J.; m. Carolyn H. Flinn, June 2, 1973; children: Catherine M., Yuri G., Meredith C. BBA, U. Wis., 1972; MBA, Northwestern U., 1982. CPA. Supr. sr. acct. Price Waterhouse, N.Y.C., 1972-78; with Amoco Corp., Chgo., 1978-83; supr. fin. contr. Amoco Prodn. Co. Internat., Chgo., 1983-84; mgr. acctg. Amoco Oil Co., Chgo., 1984-85; staff dir. budgets Amoco Corp., Chgo., 1985-87; mgr. fin. & adminstrn. Amoco Chem. Co., Houston, 1987-89; contr. Amoco Performance Products, Atlanta, 1989-93; mgr. Amoco Corp., Chgo., 1993-96; v.p. fin. and adminstrn., CFO Opportunity Internat., Oak Brook, Ill., 1996—. Bd. dirs., treas. Opportunity Transformation Investments, Oak Brook, Opportunity Microcredit Fund, Oxford, Eng.; bd. dirs. Oportunidad Microfinanzas, Guadalajara, Mexico, 2003—. Bd. dirs., treas. Flagstaff Mission to the Navajos, 1996—; deacon 4th Presbyn. Ch., 1979-87; elder, treas. Clear Lake Presbyn. Ch., 1988-89; officer, mem. choir Johnson Ferry Bapt. Ch., 1990-93; missions com. small group leader, bd. dirs. Wheaton Bible Ch., 1994—, elder, 2003—. Mem. AICPA, Fin. Execs. Internat. Office: Opportunity Internat 2122 York Rd Oak Brook IL 60523-1930 E-mail: rjohn@opportunity.org.

JOHN, RICHARD RODDA, transportation executive; b. Berlin, Mar. 31, 1929; came to U.S., 1938; s. Richard R. and Margaret G. (Howard) J.; m. Suzanne L. Heckman, June 7, 1958; children: Richard Rodda, Margaret Louise, Robert Edward. BS in Engring. Physics magna cum laude, Princeton U., 1951, MSME, 1952, MS in Aero. Engring., 1953, PhD in Aero. Engring., 1957. Dir. Aerophysics lab. AVCO Corp., Wilmington, Mass., 1958-70, chief mech. engring. div., 1971-76, dir. Office Energy and Environment, 1976-82, dep. dir., chief scientist, 1982-89; dir. John A. Volpe Nat. Transp. Systems Ctr., Cambridge, Mass., 1990—. Mem. adv. com. on space power and electric propulsion, NASA, 1965-70, aero. engring. dept. adv. coun. Princeton U., 1972-78. Contbr. articles to profl. jours. Recipient Presdl. Meritorious Rank award, 1987, Presdl. Disting. Rank award from Pres. Bus., 1990, from Pres. Clinton, 2000; Howard C. Phillips fellow Princeton U., 1952, Guggenheim fellow, 1953. Mem. AIAA (assoc., chmn. electric propulsion com. 1965-70); Soc. Automotive Engrs. (rsch. exec. bd. 1978-85), Phi Beta Kappa, Sigma Xi. Congregationalist. Avocations: gardening, golf, 20th century print collecting, classical music. Home: 19 Saddle Club Rd Lexington MA 02420-2102 Office: Dept Transp John A Volpe Nat Transp Systems Ctr 55 Broadway-Kendall Sq Cambridge MA 02142

JOHN, RICKY, state official; b. Chaguanas, Trinidad, May 2, 1957; BSEE, N.J. Inst. Tech., 1981, MS in Mgmt., 1992; PhD in Engring. Mgmt., Kennedy-Western U., 2000. Space shuttle flight test engr. NASA, Kennedy Space Ctr., Fla., 1981-82; lectr. John Donaldson Tech. Inst., Trinidad, West Indies, 1982; systems engr. FAA, N.Y.C., 1983-84; adminstr. divsn. energy N.J. Bd. Pub. Utilities, Newark, 1985-96, tech. adviser, 1996—. Developer space shuttle tech. launch procedures, 1981. Judge and presenter of NASA award, North N.J. Regional Sci. Fair, 1993—; mem. edn. com. N.J. Martin Luther King, Jr. Commn., 1987-90. Named Energy Mgr. of Yr. N.J. Assn. Energy Engrs., 1994, N.J. Aviation Hall Fame; recipient Nat. Cert. of Recognition U.S. Dept. Energy, 1995. Mem. IEEE, N.J. Inst. Tech. Alumni Assn. (trustee 1991—, treas. 1994-96, v.p. pub. rels. 1996-98). Home: 350 Davis Ave Kearny NJ 07032-3558

JOHN, ROBERT MCCLINTOCK, lawyer; b. Phila., May 21, 1947; s. Lewis Timothy and Marie (McClintock) J.; m. Barbara Ann Weand, May 10, 1975; children: Jennifer, Ryan. BA, Villanova U., 1969, JD, 1972. Bar: Pa. 1972, U.S. Dist. Ct. (ea. dist.) Pa. 1973, U.S. Ct. of Appeals (3d cir.) 1998. Atty. Schneider, Nixon & John, Hatboro, Pa., 1972-74, ptnr., 1975-93, sole proprietor, 1993—. Scoutmaster Boy Scouts Am., Hatboro, 1972—, long range planning com., 1979; lectr. and student loan com. Hatboro-Horsham High Sch., 1972-95, co-chmn. Tip of the Hat Cavalcade of Bands, 1994, 95, 96; co-prs. Hatters for Music, 1997-99; prodr. multi media banquet show Marching Hatters, 1994-2000; mgr. Little League, Horsham, Pa., 1985-96, girls' sr. tournament coach, 1993; referee Hatboro-Horsham Youth Basketball Assn., 1990-91, mgr., 1991-94. Recipient award Hatboro-Horsham Sch. Bd., 1979, medal Hatboro YMCA Triathlon, 1983, Silver Beaver award Boy Scouts Am., 1981, Scoutmaster's award of Merit, 1989, Nat. God and Svc. award, 1991, Hatboro-Horsham H.S. Prin.'s Golden Apple award, 1997, Martin Luther King Humanitarian award Upper Moreland Mid. Sch., 1997, Cmty. Svc. award Borough of Hatboro, 2002, others; named to Hatboro-Horsham H.S. Hall of Fame, 2000. Mem. Pa. Bar Assn., Montgomery County Bar Assn., Greater Hatboro C. of C. (pres. 1983, Honored Citizen Svc. to Youth award 1984, judge advocate 1984—, chmn. awards com. and prod. multimedia awards ceremony biannual borough ball, 86, 89, 97, 99, 2001, 2003), Navy League (sec. southeastern Pa. coun. 1975-89, pres. 1989, S.E. Pa. Coun. Svc. to Youth and Community award 1990, Willow Grove naval Air Sta. svc. award 1986), Rotary (pres. 1984, Dist. Gov.'s Outstanding Pres.'s award 1984, host family foreign exch. students). Republican. Roman Catholic. Avocations: scouting, swimming, cycling, backpacking. Home: 83 Home Rd Hatboro PA 19040-1830 Office: Schneider Nixon & John 76 Byberry Ave # 698 Hatboro PA 19040-3419 E-mail: legalbeaglermj@juno.com.

JOHN, SARAH, physicist; b. Trivandrum, India, Feb. 18, 1953; arrived in U.S., 1981; d. Walliaveetil John and Sarah (Thomas) J. BSc, Univ. Coll., Trivandrum, India, 1971, MSc, 1973; MS, Coll. William and Mary, 1984, PhD, 1986. Tchg. asst. Coll. William and Mary, Williamsburg, Va., 1981-86; staff scientist Sci. & Tech. Corp., Hampton, Va., 1988-91, Vigyan, Inc., Hampton, Va., 1991-92; postdoctoral fellow N.Mex. State U., Las Cruces, 2001—02; rsch. assoc. U. Md., College Park, 2003—. Vis. asst. prof. U. Mo., Columbia, 1994—97. Contbr. articles to profl. jours. Nat. Sci. Talent Search awardee, India, 1968. Mem.: IEEE, Am. Phys. Soc. Achievements include development of a novel computational technique for quantum dynamics as a stochastic process and formulating a geometric model for nuclear absorption from microscopic theory; research in image processing and nonlinear optics.

JOHN, SELENA LATRICIA, systems analyst; b. Savannah, Ga., Feb. 18, 1972; d. Gloria W. John. B in Social Work, Savannah State Coll., 1995, MPA, Savannah State U., 1999. Med. social svcs. profl. Meml. Health U., Savannah, 1997-98; adolescent counselor Tidelands Cmty. Svc. Bd., Savannah, 1999; grad. intern. Chatham County Fin. Dept., Savannah, 1999; logistics acct. analyst Diamond Crystal Brands, Savannah, 1999—. Intern, vol. Boys and Girls Clubs of Am., Savannah, 1993-95; vol. ARC, 1998-99, campaign com. Mayor, Savannah, 1997; coord., organizer Voter Registration, Savannah, 1998-99; vol. Buckle-up Am., St. Joseph's Candler Hosp., Habitat for Humanity. Grad. Students scholar Ga. Regents Bd. Acad. Scholarship, 1998-99. Mem. NASW, Coalition Minority Pub. Adminstrs., Am. Soc. Pub. Adminstrs., Sigma Gamma Rho. Home: 1123 Darwin St Savannah GA 31415 Office: 3000 Tremont Rd Savannah GA 31405-1500 E-mail: slj1922@hotmail.com.

JOHN, SUSAN V. state representative; b. Nov. 20, 1957; BA, George Washington U.; JD, Syracuse U. Bar: N.Y. Assoc. Phillips, Lytle, Hitchcock, Huber and Blaine, 1983—; mem. N.Y. State Assembly, mem. jud. com., edn. com., also mem. energy com., libs. and edn. tech. com., chair labor com. Chair Legis. Commn. on Solid Waste Mgmt., 1995—97, Alcholism and Drug Abuse Com., 1997—99, Govtl. Ops. Com., 1999—2000; served on Joint Legis. Joint Budget Conf. Com. on Mental Health, 1998, Joint Budget Conf. Com. on Edn., 1999—2000. Chair Majority Steering Com.; serves on Judiciary, Edn., Energy, Libraries and Tech. and Social Svcs. Coms.; chair subcom. Pub. Sch. Violence. Mem. Greater Rochester Assn. Women Attys. Office: 274 Goodman St N Ste C-254 Rochester NY 14607-1154 also: NY State Assembly LOB Rm 522 Albany NY 12248-0001 E-mail: johns@assembly.state.ny.us.

JOHN, YVONNE MAREE, artist, designer; b. Leeton, N.S.W., Australia, Sept. 8, 1944; came to U.S., 1966; d. Percy Edward and Gladys May (Markham) Thomas; m. Michael Peter John, Aug. 20, 1966; children: Michael Christian, Stephen Edwin. AA in Interior Design, 1976. Artist: selected exhibits of work include: Royal Mus., Sydney, Australia, 1994, Ventura (Calif.) County Courthouse, Wash. Women in Art, Olympia, 1990, Timberland Libr., OLympia, 1990, Maska Internat. Gallery, Seattle, 1991 (cert. of excellence painting), Michael Stone Collection, Washington, D.C., 1992, Nat. Hdqtrs. Am. Soc. Interior Decorators, Washington, 1992, The Funding Ctr., Alexandria, Va., 1992, New Eng. Fine Arts Inst. Nat. Invitational Exhbn., Woburn, Mass., 1993, Mus. d'Art Moderne, Bordeaux, France, 1993, Abney Galleries, N.Y., 1993, Mus. Modern Art, Miami, Coral Gables, Fla., 1993, Hargus Unique Gallery, Pomona, Calif., UN Fourth World Conf. on Women, Beijing, China with Nat. Mus. of Women in Art, Washington, 1995, with Ariz. State U., World's Women on Line, 1995, on World Wide Web http://www.yvonnemaree. aussie.com.au, 1996, Gallery Bri Ontario, Can., 1996, Art Comm. Internat., Phila., 1996, V.I.P. Lobbies World Bank, Washington, 1996-97, World Fine Art, N.Y.C., 1997; permanent collections include Royal Mus. Sydney, Australia, O'Toole Collection, Melbourne, Victoria, Australia, Ronald Reagan Collection, Calif., Nat. Mus. Women in Arts, Washington, Patterson Collection, Mich., Witherow Collection, Washington, Samaniego Colllection, Calif. Recipient cash and cert. awards, Sydney, Australia, 1950s, ribbon awards Australian County Fairs, 1950s; 1st round winner Hathaway Competition, Ventura, Calif., 1970s Republican. Roman Catholic. Avocations: tennis, golf, swimming, reading, gardening. Office: Yvonne Maree Designs PO Box 2143 Olympia WA 98507-2143

JOHNA, SAMIR, surgeon; b. Baghdad, Iraq, Nov. 22, 1958; s. Denkha Johna and Doris Bercham; m. Layla Nano, Apr. 14, 1992; 1 child, Kristin Ishtar. M.B.Ch.B., Baghdad Coll. of Medicine, Iraq, 1983. Diplomate Am. Bd. Surgery ACS, 1999. Asst. prof. of surgery Loma Linda U. Sch. of Medicine, Loma Linda, Calif., 1999—; assoc. dir. for surg. residency program Loma Linda U. Med. Ctr., 2002—. Attending surgeon So. Calif. Permanente Med. Group, Fontana, Calif., 2002—. Contbr. Fellow: ACS; mem.: Assyrian Med. Soc. (founder). Home: 1616 W Olive Ave Redlands CA 92373 Office: Southern California Permanente Medical 9961 Sierra Ave Fontana CA 92335 Home Fax: 909-335-0323. Personal E-mail: s.johna@verizon.net.

JOHNOPOLOS, STEPHEN GARY, commission outreach representative; b. Chgo., Jan. 3, 1950; s. Alexander and Anna (Poncher) J. BS, De Paul U., 1973. Cons., writer music, advt., pub. rels., Saxton, Pa., 1972-83; program coord., grantsman Huntingdon County Commrs., Huntingdon, Pa., 1983-85, human svcs. dir., 1985-87; program dir., grantsman Employment & Tng., Inc., Huntingdon, 1988; commn. rep. So. Alleghenies Planning and Devel. Commn., Altoona, Pa., 1989—. Lectr. and spkr. in field of health and fitness. Author: Proposals and Grants: A Comprehensive Curriculum, 1987, One Branch, 1988, Writing Proposals That Sell, 1988. Pres. Tussey Mountain Sch. Dist., Saxton, 1984-85, Weatherization, Inc., Huntingdon, 1987, Employment and Tng. Inc., Huntingdon, 1987, Mental Health/Mental Retardation Citizens Adv. Bd., 1990-91. Recipient Past Pres. award of appreciation Weatherization Bd. Dirs., 1988, Tussey Mountain Sch. Dist., 1985, Tussey Mountain Jaycees, 1978, Poetry Award of Merit, 1989, Golden Poety award, 1989, Silver Poet award, 1990. Avocations: choreography, personal fitness tng, martial arts, national level jazz piano performer. Office: So Alleghenies Pl-Devel Com 541 58th St Altoona PA 16602-1158 E-mail: Sgjpno1@charter.net.

JOHN PAUL, HIS HOLINESS POPE, II, (KAROL JOZEF WOJTYLA), bishop of Rome; b. Wadowice, Poland, May 18, 1920; s. Karol and Emilia (Kaczorowska) W.. Student, Jagiellonian U., Krakow, 1937—39, ThD, 1949; studied in underground sem., Krakow, 1942—46; D in Ethics, Pontifical Angelicum U., Rome, 1948; Doctorate (hon.), J. Guttenberg U., Mainz, Fed. Republic Germany, 1977. Ordained priest Roman Cath. Ch., 1946. Pastor St. Florian's Parish, Krakow, 1948; student chaplain Jagiellonian U., 1949; prof. moral theology Krakow, 1953; prof. ethics, then chmn. dept. philosophy Cath. U. of Lublin, 1954—58, dir. ethics inst., 1956—58; aux. bishop of Krakow, 1958; archbishop of Krakow, 1964—78; great chancellor Pontifical Theol. Faculty, Krakow; created cardinal by Pope Paul VI, 1967; elected Pope, 1978; installed, 1978. Author: (book) Play Easter Vigil and Other Poems, 1979, Be Not Afraid: Pope John PaulII Speaks Out on His Life, His Beliefs, and His Inspiring Vision for Humanity, 1984, Blessed Are the Pure of Heart, 1988, On the Vocation and the Mission of the Lay Faithful in the Church and in the World, 1989, The Place Within: The Poetry of Pope John Paul II, 1994, Catechism of the Catholic Church, 1994, The Way to Christ: Spiritual Exercises, 1994, Love and Responsibility, 1995, The Gospel of Life (Evangelium Vitae), 1995, Crossing the Threshold of Hope, 1995, God, Father and Creator, 1996, Pope John Paul II: In My Own Words, 2002, Go in Peace: A Gift of Enduring Love, 2003, The Goldsmith's Shop, (books, poetry, plays, including) Love and Responsibility, 1960, The Acting Person, 1969, Foundations of Renewal, 1972, Sign of Contradiction, 1976, (encyclicals) The Redeemer of Man, 1979, On Human Work, 1981, The Apostles of the Slavs, 1985, The Lord, the Giver of Life, 1986, Redemptoris Mater, 1987, Sollicitudo Rei Socialis, 1987, Redemptoris Missio, 1990, Centesimus Annus, 1991, Veritatis Spendor, 1993, Evangelium Vitae, 1995, Ut Unum Sint, 1995, Fides et Ratio, 1998, Ecclesia de Eucharistia, 2003. Mem.: Polish Acad. Scis. Roman Catholic. Address: Palazzo Apostolico Vatican City 00120 Vatican City*

JOHNS, BEVERLEY ANNE HOLDEN, special education administrator; b. New Albany, Ind., Nov. 6, 1946; d. James Edward and Martha Edna (Scharf) Holden; m. Lonnie J. Johns, July 28, 1973. BS, Catherine Spalding Coll., 1968; MS, So. Ill. U., 1970; postgrad., Western Ill. U., 1973-74, 79-80, postgrad., 82, U. Ill., 1984-85. Cert. adminstr., tchr. Ill. Demonstration tchr. So. Ill. U., Carbondale, 1970-72; instr. MacMurray Coll., Jacksonville, Ill., 1977—79, 1990—93, 2002—03; intern Ill. State Bd. Edn., Springfield, 1981; program supr. Four Rivers Spl. Edn. Dist., Jacksonville, 1972—2003; learning and behavior cons., 2003—. Chair Ill. Spl. Edn.; conf. coord. Ill. Alliance, Champaign, 1982-94; lectr., cons. in field. Author: Report on Behavior Analysis in Education, 1972; author: (with V. Carr) Techniques for Managing Verbally and Physically Aggressive Students, 2002; author: (with V. Carr and C. Hoots) Reduction of School Violence: Alternatives to Suspension, 1997; author: (with B. Johns, E. Crowley & E. Guetzloe) Effective Curriculum for Students with Behavioral Disorders, 2002; author: (with J. Keenan) Techniques for Managing a Safe School, 1997; editor: Position Papers of Ill. Council for Exceptional Children, 1981; contbr. articles to profl. jours. Bd. dirs. Jacksonville Area Assn. Retarded Citizens, v.p., 1993-94, sec. 1996-99; govt. rels. chair Internat. Coun. Exceptional Children, 1984-87; fed. liason Ill. Adminstrs. Spl. Edn., 1985-86. So. Ill. U. fellow, 1968; resolution honoring Beverly H. Johns Internat. Coun. for Exceptional Children Conv., 1982; recipient Recognition cert. Ill. Atty. Gen., 1985, Outstanding Leadership award Internat. Coun. Exceptional Children, 2000; named Jacksonville Woman of Yr., Bus. and Profl. Women, 1988, Unsung Hero Jacksonville Jour.-courier, 1993. Mem. ASCD, Assn. Retarded Citizens (com. 1982-85), Ill. Coun. for Children with Behavioral Disorders (founder, past pres., pres. Ill. divsn. for learning disabilities 1991-92, Presdl. award 1985), Ill. Alliance for Exceptional Children (v.p. 1982-94), Learning Disabilities Assn. (bd. dirs., pres. 2000-03), Ill. Coun. Exceptional Children (past pres., chair govt. rels. com. 1982-95, 97-98, governing bd. 1984-95, Presdl. award 1983, Lifetime Achievement award 1989, First Lady 1993), Internat. Coun. for Children with Behavioral Disorders (pres. 1997), West Cen. Assn. for Citizens with Learning Disabilities (founder, com. chair 1997), Internat. Pioneer Press (editor CEC pioneer divsn., pres. internat. pioneers divsn.), Internat. Divsn. Learning Disabilities (exec. bd.), Delta Kappa Gamma (chpt. pres. 1988-90, state exec. bd. 1991—), Phi Delta Kappa. Roman Catholic. Avocation: world travel. Home: PO Box 340 Jacksonville IL 62651-0340 E-mail: bevjohns@juno.com.

JOHNS, ELIZABETH JANE HOBBS, educational administrator; b. Roanoke Rapids, N.C., July 18, 1941; d. Florence Eugene and Elizabeth Holt (Massey) Hobbs; m. Lewis Clarence Johns, Apr. 7, 1961; 1 child, Karen Anne Johns Cuccaro. AA with honors, Valencia Community Coll., 1984; BSBA with honors, Fla. So. Coll., 1988; MS in Mgmt., Fla. Inst. Tech., 1996. Med. receptionist Dr. Harold Knowles, Orlando, Fla., 1959—61; sec. Lockheed Martin, Orlando, 1961—77, edn. adminstr., 1977—, chair bd. credit union, 1987—97. Bd. dirs. Martin Marietta Fed. Credit Union; mem. diamond counsel Roy E. Crummer Grad. Sch. Bus., 1991—93. Mem. cmty. adv. bd. sch. continuing edn. Hamilton Holt Sch.; mem. continuing edn. coun. for women Valencia C.C., 1984—93. Named one of Outstanding Women in Bus., 1985, one of Top Ten Employees, Martin Marietta Aerospace, Orlando, 1983, one of Top 100, 1978. Mem. Am. Bus. Women's Assn., Valencia Community Coll. Alumni Assn. (bd. dirs. 1984-93), Orlando C. of C. (post secondary edn. task force), Phi Theta Kappa. Republican. Methodist. Avocations: cooking, boating, fishing. Office: Lockheed Martin Elec/Missil MP 147 5600 Sand Lake Rd Orlando FL 32819-8907 Address: 452 Songbird Way Apopka FL 32712 Home: 452 Songbird Way Apopka FL 32712-3709

JOHNS, EMERSON THOMAS, chemical company executive; b. Phila., June 24, 1947; s. Charles and Sophia (Milak) J.; m. Marlene Catherine Giorello, Oct. 9, 1971; children: Tracey, Jeffrey. BS in Acctg., Mt. St. Mary's Coll., 1969; MBA in Fin., Widener U., 1980. Auditor DuPont Co., Atlanta, Parlin, N.J., Wilmington, N.C., Beamont, Tex. and, Clinton, Iowa, 1969-77, fin. analyst internat. dept. Wilmington, Del., 1978-80, mgr. acctg. and internal controls, 1981-82; mgr. acctg. and bus. analysis dept., petrochems. dept. Savannah River plant Dupont Co., Aiken, S.C., 1983-85; mgr. adminstrv. svcs. atomic energy div. DuPont Co., Wilmington, 1986-89, mgr. govt. contracting fin. dept., 1989—; fin. mgr. engring. Engring. DuPont Fin., Wilmington, 1990; fin. mgr. integrated ops. DuPont Engring., Wilmington, 1992, global fin. mgr. ebgrubg, svcs, abd security, health and environment, 1994, global fin. mgr. Engring., Safety and Health Instrumentation Ctr., 1999—, CFO, ops. leader engring., safety, health and environ., corp. remediation and facilities svcs., 2002—. Instr. bus. edn. St. John the Beloved. Bd. dirs. St. Mary Help of Christians Sch., Aiken, 1985, chmn.-elect, 1986; bd. dirs. Foxchase Civic Assn., Aiken, 1986; advisor Jr. Achievement, Wilmington, 1987-90, in-sch. instr., 1989-90; mem. Christian formation St. John the Beloved, Wilmington, 1988-89, com. chmn., 1989-90; spl. funds solicitor United Way, 1995-2000. Mem. Constrn. Industry Inst. (bd. advisors, rsch. com. 1997-99, co-chmn. rsch. com. 2000, chmn. rsch. com. 2001, chmn. leveraged funding 2002), Foxchase Swim Club (pres. 1985). Roman Catholic. Avocations: golf, travel. Home: 1105 Kelly Dr Yeatman Estates Newark DE 19711 Office: DuPont Co GSB/ENGR 1007 Market St Wilmington DE 19898-0001 E-mail: emerson.t.johns-1@usa.dupont.com.

JOHNS, JANET SUSAN, physician; b. Chgo., July 18, 1941; d. Nicholas C. and Doris Ann (Douglas) J.; m. Harlan R. Bullard; children: George, Sam. AB, Ind. U., 1963, MD, 1966. Diplomate Am. Acad. Family Practice. Intern Meml. Hosp., South Bend, Ind. Home: 3510 Woodcliff Dr Lafayette IN 47905-8834 Office: Purdue U Student Health 1826 Push West Lafayette IN 47905

JOHNS, KAREN LOUISE, nurse, psychotherapist; b. Chgo., Jan. 21, 1942; d. John Leonard and Virginia Selma (Kliner) J. Diploma in Nursing, St. Elizabeth Hosp., Chgo., 1962; BSN, Loyola U., Chgo., 1967; MSN, Calif. State U., L.A., 1972; MA in Psychology, Immaculate Heart Coll., L.A., 1978. RN Calif., lic. marriage and family therapist, clin. specialist in psychiat./mental health nursing; registered poetry therapist. Staff nurse Luth. Gen. Hosp., Park Ridge, Ill., 1962-63; staff nurse, insvc. edn. coord. Holy Family Hosp., Des Plaines, Ill., 1963-67; instr. St. Vincent's Coll. of Nursing, L.A., 1967-72; assoc. prof. L.A. Valley Coll., Van Nuys, Calif., 1972-76; nurse Brotman Med. Ctr., Culver City, Calif., 1976-77, St. John's Hosp., Santa Monica, Calif., 1977-78, VA Med. Ctr., L.A., 1982—; counselor Kedren Cmty. Mental Health Ctr., L.A., 1980-81. Mem. Nat. Assn. Poetry Therapy (bd. dirs. 1989-91). Office: WLA VA Med Ctr 11301 Wilshire Blvd Los Angeles CA 90073-1003

JOHNS, LESLIE A. music educator; b. Winfield, Kans., July 7, 1966; d. Ray M. and Joyce M. Barkus; m. Lonnie R. Johns, Dec. 31, 1986; children: Jeremy, Garrett, Logan. AS in Bus. Adminstrn., No. Okla. Coll., Tonkawa, 1997; BS in Entertainment Bus., Oklahoma City U., 2000; MBA, Cameron U., Lawton, Okla., 2003. Musician, 1984—2000; instr. No. Okla. Coll., 2000—, asst. v.p. acad. affairs, 2000—02, dir. tutoring, 2002—. Composer: numerous songs. Pres., v.p. Parent Tchr. Orgn., Peckham Sch., 1990—92. Church Of Christ.

JOHNS, MARGARET BUSH, neuroendocrinologist, painter, researcher, educator; b. Boston, July 31, 1928; d. Ernest William Bush and Ellinor (Brennan) Gazik; m. D. Craig Johns, Jan. 15, 1953 (div. 1982); children: Katherine Adrian, Sara Elizabeth; m. H. Peter Stern, May 30, 1985. *Grandmother, Katharine T. Meagher Brennan, Milton, Massachusetts, educator, helped Saint Katharine Drexell, founder Sisters of the Blessed Sacrament, Philadelphia.1890's Grandfather, James Augustus Brennan, Athletic League, 1870s Baseball Hall of Fame, founded" Brennans" Philadelphia. played chamber music with Victor Herbert. Mother was a diarist. Stepfather, L. Martin Gazik LLD helped create Liberia's first map, 1954-56. Father, Ernest William Bush, DO, Still College Osteopathy, 1902, practiced Southern Pines, N.C., 1905-74. Daughters Katherine A. Johns, AIA, Old Chatham, N.Y., Sara Johns Griffen, President Olana Partnership Olana, Hudson, N.Y. Grandchildren Julia and Christopher Shaw, Emily and Stephen Griffen. Husband H. Peter Stern LLD, violinist and chairman of Storm King Art Center, Mountainville, N.Y., vice chairman World Monuments Fund, Vice chairman International Rescue Committee.* Student, George Washington U., 1945-47, NYU, 1951-53; BA, Hunter Coll., N.Y.C., 1971; PhD, Rutgers U., 1979. Postdoctoral NIH rsch. fellow Mt. Sinai Med. Sch., NYC, 1978-81; instr. dept. biol. sci. Hunter Coll., NYC, 1982-83; rsch. scientist NYU, NYC, 1985; ind. rschr. in neuroendocrinology Mountainville, NY, 1985—. Cons. Lederle Labs., 1984; reviewer NIH, NSF, 1982—. Contbr. articles to Nature, Endocrinology, Annals of N.Y. Acad. Sci. Vol. tutor non-English-speaking children N.Y. Pub. Sch. Sys., N.Y.C., 1964; vol. landscape coord. Neighbors United for Justice in Housing, Newburgh, N.Y., 1988—, vol. edn. cons. Harlem Valley Secure Ctr., Wingdale, N.Y., 1998—. Fellow: The Endocrine Soc. Democrat. Achievements include first to discover a function of the vomeronasal organ in mammalian physiology; discovered specific and saturable in vitro uptake of serotonin in gonadotrophs in the anterior pituitary of rats and humans and that Prozak blocks it completely; discovered reflex ovulation can be triggered by smell. Avocations: writing, gardening, travel. Home: 192 6th Ave New York NY 10013-1228 Office: PO Box 330 Mountainville NY 10953-0330

JOHNS, MICHAEL DOUGLAS, health care corporate executive, former federal official, writer, former federal government official; b. Allentown, Pa., Sept. 8, 1964; s. Glenn Franklin and Nancy Louise (Hummel) J.; m. Nicole Denise Miles, Sept. 30, 1995 (div. 1999); 1 child, Michael Douglas Jr. Student, Cambridge (Eng.) U., 1984; BBA in Econs., U. Miami, 1986. Editl. intern Nat. Journalism Ctr., Washington, 1983; Lyndon Baines Johnson intern Congressman Don Ritter, Washington, 1984; asst. editor Policy Rev. Mag., Washington, 1986-88; fgn. policy analyst The Heritage Found., Washington, 1988-91; spl. asst. to pres. Drew U., Madison, N.J., 1991-92; speechwriter to Pres. of U.S. The White House, Washington, 1992; speechwriter to U.S. Sec. Commerce U.S. Dept. Commerce, Washington, 1992-93; dir. rsch. Internat. Rep. Inst., Washington, 1993-94; mgr. corp. comm., sr. writer Eli Lilly and Co., Indpls., 1994-95; aide to U.S. Senator Olympia J. Snowe U.S. Senate, Washington, 1996-97; sr. assoc. S.R. Wojdak & Assocs., Phila., 1997-2000; v.p. Gentiva Health Svcs., Melville, NY, 2000—02. Fgn. policy group advisor Dole for Pres., Inc., Washington, 1996; sr. advisor to global devel. projects Internat. Rep. Inst., Kuwait, Turkey, other nations, 1993-94; guest polit. and pub. policy analyst MacNeil/Lehrer News Hour, C-SPAN, CNBC, PBS Nightly Bus. Report, Fox Morning News, Voice of Am., BBC, others; sr. mgmt. and mgr. mktg., comms. and investor rels. for Fortune 1000 health svcs. co., 2000-02; guest lectr. UN, Vassar Coll., U. N.C., Chapel Hill, others. Author: Seventy Years of Evil in the Soviet Union, 1988, U.S. and Africa Statistical Handbook, 1990, U.S. and Africa Statistical Handbook, 2d edit., 1991; co-author: Freedom in the World: The Annual Survey of Political Rights and Civil Liberties, 1993, Finding Our Roots, Facing Our Future: America in the 21st Century, 1997; contbg. editor: USSR Monitor newsletter, The Heritage Found., 1989—91; contbr. articles to Wall St. Jour., Christian Sci. Monitor, Nat. Rev., others. Active Luth. Ch. of the Holy Spirit, Emmaus, Pa. Recipient Century III Leadership award, Shell Oil Co., 1981, Svc. award, Kiwanis, 1982, Cert. appreciation, Spl. Olympics, 1983, award of appreciation, Lao Vets Am., 1995, numerous citations, Congl. Record, U.S. Congress, Web awards of Long Island, 2001. Mem.: Washington Ind. Writers, Bush/Quayle Alumni Assn., Reagan Alumni Assn., Pa. Assn. Govt. Rels., Nat. Journalism Ctr. Alumni Coun., Am. Assn. Homecare (pub. affairs com.), Am. Med. Writing Assn., Pub. Rels. Soc. Am., Internat. Assn. Bus.

Commnicators, Nat. Investor Rels. Inst., Assn. on Third World Affairs, Iron Arrow Honor Soc., Lambda Chi Alpha (Internat. Hall of Fame 1996). Republican. Lutheran. Home: 321 Avalon Court Dr Melville NY 11747 E-mail: mjohns8@aol.com.

JOHNS, RICHARD JAMES, physician, educator; b. Pendleton, Oreg., Aug. 19, 1925; s. James Shanard and Pearl (McKenna) Johns; m. Carol Greacen Johnson; children: Richard Clark, Robert Shanard, James Ashmore. BS, U. Oreg., 1947; MD, Johns Hopkins U., 1948. Diplomate Am. Bd. Internal Medicine. Intern Johns Hopkins Hosp., Balt., 1948—49, asst. resident, 1951—53, fellow in medicine, 1953—55, resident, 1955—56, instr., 1955—57, physician, 1956—, asst. prof., 1957—61, assoc. prof., 1961—66, asst. dean admissions, 1962—66, prof. medicine, 1966—, dir. subdept. biomed. engring., 1966—70, mem. adv. bd., prin. profl. staff Applied Physics Lab., 1967—, prof., dir. dept. biomed. engring., 1970—91, disting. svc. prof., 1991—. Bd. dirs. Sparton Corp. Bd. visitors Sch. Engring., Duke U., 1986—; chmn. adv. com. Divsnl. Health Scis. and Tech., Harvard-MIT, 1987—92; mem. com. sci., engring. and pub. policy NAS, 1988—90; mem. sci. adv. com. GM, 1991—97; sec., vice chmn., chmn. med. bd. Myasthenia Gravis Found.; trustee Am. Bd. Clin. Engring., pres., 1976—83; bd. dirs. Whitaker Found., 1991—94. Capt. M.C. U.S. Army, 1949—51. Fellow: Royal Soc. Medicine, Am. Inst. for Biol. and Med. Engring. (founding), AAAS, ACP; mem.: Inst. Medicine-NAS (coun. 1987—90), IEEE (pres. group on engring. in medicine and biology 1970—72), Biomed. Engring. Soc. (bd. dirs. 1972—75, pres. 1978—79), Assn. Am. Physicians, Am. Soc. Clin. Investigation, Am. Clin. and Climatol. Assn. (v.p. 1977—78, sec.-treas. 1979—85, pres. 1986—87), Sparton Corp. (dir. 2002—), Annapolis Yacht Club, Caduceus Club, Elkridge Club, Johns Hopkins Club (v.p. 1969—70), Peripatetic Club, Interurban Clin. Club (pres. 1980—81), Johns Hopkins Med. Soc. (pres. 1968—69), Tau Beta Pi, Nu Sigma Nu, Phi Kappa Psi, Alpha Omega Alpha, Sigma Xi. Home: 203 E Highfield Rd Baltimore MD 21218-1105 Office: Johns Hopkins U Sch Med 1830 E Monument St Ste 501 Baltimore MD 21287 E-mail: rjohns@jhmi.edu.

JOHNS, RICHARD SETH ELLIS, lawyer; b. Eugene, Oreg., Apr. 23, 1946; s. Frank Errol Jr. and Emily Elizabeth (Ellis) J.; m. Eleanor Lee Kuntz, Mar. 8, 1981. BA in English, U. Calif., Santa Barbara, 1968; JD, U. Calif., San Francisco, 1971. Bar: Calif. 1971, Ill. 1972. Instr. law U. Chgo., 1972-73; assoc. Atchison, Topeka & Santa Fe RR, Chgo., 1973-75, Furth, Fahrner, Bluemle & Mason, San Francisco, 1975-84; ptnr. Rubenstein, Bohachek & Johns, San Francisco, 1985-88, Kipperman & Johns, San Francisco, 1988—. Contbr. articles to Calif. Law Rev. Bd. dirs. Congregation Beth Shalom, San Francisco, 1982-92, Bay Area sect. Am. Jewish Com., 1984—, pres., 2003—; leader Family Policy Task Force, 1987-88; guest of Christian Dem. Union, Konrad Adenhauer Stiftung-German-Am. Jewish Exchange Program, Fed. Republic Germany, 1985; dir. Mus. of the City of San Francisco, 1996-97, v.p., 1997-2002, San Francisco Mus. and Hist. Soc., 2002—, The San Francisco Old Mint Task Force, 2001-02. 1st lt. U.S. Army, 1972-75. Mem. ABA, Calif. Bar Assn., Concordia-Argonaut Club, Ill. State Bar. Office: Kipperman & Johns 57 Post St Ste 604 San Francisco CA 94104-5023 E-mail: rsejohns@aol.com .

JOHNS, ROY (BUD JOHNS), publisher, writer; b. Detroit, July 9, 1929; s. Roy and Isabel Johns; m. Judith Spector Clancy, 1971 (dec. 1990); m. Frances Moreland, 1992. BA in English and Econs., Albion (Mich.) Coll., 1951. Various editorial positions Mich. and Calif. daily newspapers, 1942-60; bur. chief Fairchild Pubs., 1960-69; dir. corp. communications Levi Strauss & Co., 1969-81, corp. v.p., 1979-81; pres. Synergistic Press, Inc., San Francisco, 1968—. Bd. dirs. Applewood Books, Bedford, Mass., 1988—; founder, ptnr. Apple Tree Press, Flint, Mich., 1954-55; cons. on comms., pub., and related areas. Author: The Ombibulous Mr. Mencken, 1968, What is This Madness?, 1985; co-editor, author: Bastard in the Ragged Suit, 1977; scriptwriter, exec. producer: What is This Madness?, 1976; exec. producer: The Best You Can Be, 1979 (CINE Golden Eagle award 1980); editor: Old Dogs Remembered, 1993, paperback edit., 1999; free-lance writer numerous mag. articles. Mem. Nat. Coun. of Mus. of Am. Indian, N.Y.C., 1980-90; bd. dirs. The San Francisco Contemporary Music Players, 1981—, pres., 2000-01; bd. dirs. Greenbelt Alliance, San Francisco, 1982—, pres., 1990-95; bd. dirs. Save San Francisco Bay Assn., 1996-97, San Francisco Performing Arts Libr. and Mus., 1998=2001. Inventor sport of ride and tie racing, 1971. Home and Office: 3965 Sacramento St San Francisco CA 94118-1627 E-mail: goodreading@synergisticbooks.com.

JOHNS, TIMOTHY ROBERT, judge; b. Aberdeen, S.D., July 17, 1948; s. Frank Edward Johns and Helen Theresa Mock; m. LeAnn L. Thoresen, Nov. 25, 1978; children: Nicholas, Justin. BA, No. State U., 1970; JD, U. S.D., 1974. Dep. states atty. Butte County, S.D., 1974-75; atty. City of Nisland, S.D., 1974-75; pvt. practice Belle Fourche, S.D., 1974-75; magistrate State of S.D., Deadwood, 1975-89, cir. ct. judge, 1989—. Mem. S.D. Jud. Qualifications Commn., 1997—2001. Mem., pres. Deadwood-Lead (S.D.) Jaycees, 1978-85; bd. dirs. Adv. Coun. Black Hills coun. Boy Scouts Am., Northern Hills Adjustment Tng. Ctr., Spearfish, S.D., Northern Hills YMCA of Lead, State Bd. S.D. Spl. Olympics. Recipient Keyman award Deadwood-Lead Jaycees, 1982-83; named Outstanding Young Man of Am. Mem.: SD Judges Assn. (pres. 1995—96), Kiwanis (pres. 2001—02), KC. Roman Catholic. Avocations: reading, hunting, fishing, boating. Home: 110 S Main St Lead SD 57754-1541 Office: 4th Jud Cir Ct PO Box 626 78 Sherman St Deadwood SD 57732-1341

JOHNS, WARREN LEROI, lawyer; b. Nevada, Iowa, June 9, 1929; s. Varner Jay and Ruby Charlene (Morrison) J.; m. Elaine C. Magnuson, July 24, 1955 (div. June 1983); children: Richard Warren, Lynn Cherie Johns-Pence; m. Ruth Page Scott, Sept. 29, 1985. BA, La Sierra U., 1950; MA, Andrews U., 1951; JD, U. So. Calif., 1958. Bar: Calif. 1959, U.S. Dist. Ct. (cen. dist.) Calif. 1959,U.S. Supreme Ct. 1963, Md. 1976, D.C. 1976, U.S. Dist. Ct. Md. 1976, U.S. Dist. Ct. D.C. 1976, U.S. Tax Ct. 1976, U.S. Ct. Appeals (4th cir.) 1976, U.S. Ct. Appeals (10th cir.) 1977, U.S. Ct. Customs and Patent Appeals 1979. Gen. counsel So. Calif. Conf. Seventh-day Adventists, Glendale, 1959-63, Pacific Union Conf. Seventh-day Adventists, Glendale and Sacramento, 1964-69; pvt. practice Sacramento, 1969-75; gen. counsel Gen. Conf. Seventh-day Adventists, Washington, 1975-92, trustee; pvt. practice Brookeville, Md., 1992-98. Mem. adv. bd. Ctr. for Ch./State Studies, De Paul U. Chgo., 1987-93, spl. counsel to gen. conf., 1992-95; spl. counsel Adventist HealthCare Corp., Columbia Union HealthCare Corp., 1992-97. Author: Dateline Sunday USA, 1967, Ride to Glory, 1999; editor CreationDigest.com, 2001, Creation Equation Newsletter, 2002; founding editor JD, 1978-92. Chmn. bd. dirs., pres. Sacramento Area Econ. Opportunity Coun., 1974. Recipient Frank Yost award Ch. State Coun., Glendale, Alumnus of Achievement award Andrews U., 1981, Alumnus of Yr. award La Sierra U., 1994. Mem. AAAS, ABA (vice-chmn. com. on torts, non-profit, charitable and religious orgns., sect. of tort and ins. practice 1990-91). Democrat. Avocations: sports, photography, book collecting. Office: 21320 Georgia Ave Brookeville MD 20833-1132

JOHNSEN, EUGENE CARLYLE, mathematician and educator; b. Mpls., Jan. 27, 1932; s. Bernhardt Thorwald and Esther Elvira (Eklund) J.; m. Marjorie Marie Wacklin, Aug. 31, 1957. BChem, U. Minn., 1954; PhD, Ohio State U., 1961. NAS/NRC Rsch. Assoc. Nat. Bur. Stds., Washington, 1962-63; lectr. math. U. Calif., Santa Barbara, 1963-64, asst. prof., 1964-68, assoc. prof., 1968-74, prof., 1974-94, prof. emeritus, 1994—, dir. summer sessions, 1981-94, 94-97. Vis. lectr. in math. U. Mich., Ann Arbor, 1968-69; vis. scholar in sociology Harvard U., Cambridge, Mass., 1984-85; mathematician Sperry Rand, St. Paul, 1956, 57; instr. chem. and math. U. Minn., 1956-57; instr. math. Ohio State U., Columbus, 1962; organizer and co-organizer of math. social sci. confs.; reviewer NSF. Contbr. numerous articles to profl. jours.; referee numerous profl. jours.; mem. editl. bd. Jour. Math. Sociology. Mem. Los Angeles County Mus. Art, 1985—, L.A. Music Ctr. Opera League, 1986—; mem. Santa Barbara C. of C./U. Calif. Santa Barbara Bus. Adv. Com., 1979-84. Grantee USAFOSR, NSF, Dept. Edn.; Fulbright travel award fellow U. Tübingen, 1969; fellow NSF, 1959. Mem. AAAS, Am. Math. Soc., Math. Assn. Am., Am. Statis. Assn., Soc. Indsl. and Applied Math., Internat. Network for Social Network Analysis, Am. Sociol. Assn. (acting chair, then chair math. sociology sect. 1995-97), U. Calif. Santa Barbara Faculty Club, Channel City Club, Am.-Scandinavian Found., Sons of Norway (pres. Ivar Aasen Lodge 1999-2001, 03—), Phi Beta Kappa, Sigma Xi, Phi Lambda Upsilon, Pi Mu Epsilon, Alpha Chi Sigma. Avocations: music, opera, tennis, travel. Home: 1603 Paterna Rd Santa Barbara CA 93103-1826 Office: U Calif Dept Math Santa Barbara CA 93106-3080

JOHNSEN, KAREN K. marketing professional; b. Easton, Pa., June 28, 1939; d. Charles Edward and Gladys Swensen Kennedy; m. Henry Lehmann Johnsen, May 26, 1962; children: Erik Lehmann, Elisa Beth Johnsen Peters. BS in Bus. cum laude, Russell Sage Coll., Troy, N.Y., 1961; MS in Bus. Edn., SUNY, Albany, 1970. Cert. bus. tchr. N.Y., 1970. Sec., account svc. divsn. McCann-Erickson, Inc., N.Y.C., 1961—62; exec. asst. pub. relations Johnson & Johnson, New Brunswick, NJ, 1962—65; sec., staff writer investment divsn. Glens Falls Ins. Co., NY, 1965—66; exec. sec. to pres., sec.-treas. Glens Falls Portland Cement Co., 1966—69; fund raising, pub. relations, audience developer Lake George Opera Festival, Glens Falls, 1970—73; publicity dir. fund raising campaign Glens Falls YMCA; freelance writer, adminstrn./media/mktg. cons., 1974—; exec. asst., media dir., staff writer Kimberly Comm., Inc., Chatham, NJ, 1974—82; sales mgr. Lifelines Gifts & Cards, N.Y.C., 1982—84; entrepreneur mktg., sales and mgmt. KJ Assocs., 1985—. Club directory chmn., bull. editor Welcome Wagon Newcomers Club, Summit, NJ, 1974—75; charter sec. pub. relations Scotch Plains Assn. Concerning Environment, 1999—; former bd. dirs. Plainfield Symphony Soc.; sec. Lake George Opera Guild, 1970—73, Edvard Grieg Soc., 1996—2000; charter sec. adv. bd. Project 2000, Norwegian Immigration Assn., 1996—. Mem.: NAFE, AAUW (chpt. treas. 1972, comm. chmn. 1998—), Vesterheim Norwegian-Am. Mus., Am. Scandinavian Found., Scandinavian Am. Heritage Soc., Russell Sage Coll. Alumnae Assn. (class agt., alumnae admissions liaison 1995—, class reunion chair 2001, 2006), Vasa Order of Am. (past dist. sec., cultural leader, supr. children's clubs, N.J. dist., past sec., past chmn., cultural leader, supr. children's clubs local lodge), Order Ea. Star, Delta Pi Epsilon. Presbyterian. Avocations: skiing, singing, writing, folk-art painting. Home and Office: 109 Glenside Ave Scotch Plains NJ 07076

JOHNSEN, MAY ANN, artist, sculptor, graver; b. Port Chester, N.Y., May 12; d. Michael Colangelo and Mary Agnes (Visconti) Visconti; m. David Stanley May Johnsen, Nov. 6, 1940; 1 child, David Mark. Artist Silver Point Gallery, Brainard, N.Y. Exhibited national and internationally including. Hamilton Miniature Nat. Exhibit, Ohio (miniature marine award), World Miniature Art Exhbn., Tasmania, Australia, Silvermine Guild Artists Nat. Exhibition of New Canaan, Conn. (marine award), Nat. Marine Painter Internat. show Breverd Mus. Florid, Internat. Soc. Marine Painters show Heritage Plantation Mus., Sandwich, Mass., Miniature Soc. Painter Sculptors Internat. show, Fla., Miniature Soc. Painters Sculptors Gravers Internat. show, Ga., Miniature Soc. Painter Graders Scuptor N.C. Internat. show, Miniature Internat. show Painters Gravers Sculptors Ark., Harness Racing Art Exhibit, Lexington, Ky., Allegheny Internat. Miniature Painters show, Bluefield, W.Va., Nat. Miniature Show, South Port, N.C., Albany Inst. History and Art, Albuquerque Nat. exhibit, Bertrand Russel Peace Found., Gold Medal Competition for Distinguished Marine Art, Franklin Mint Gallery, Pa., Internat. Exhibit, Smithsonian Inst., Washington, Drawings Internat., Barcelona, Spain, Nat. Exhibit, Catherine Lorillard Wolf, N.Y.C., Mural Exhibit, Schuyler Sch., Albany, N.Y., others. Recipient Spl. Mariner award, Nassau, N.Y., two first prizes Columbia County Fair, Chatham, N.Y. Recipient 1st and 2d Pl. Watercolor awards, 2nd Pl. Graphic Silver Point award, Calvatone, Italy. Mem. Am. Soc. Miniature Painters of N.J., Soc. Marine Painters, Marine Painters Am., Miniature Painters, Sculptors and Gravers of Washington, D.C. (assoc.), N.J. Soc. Miniature, Graver, Sculptors, Painters, Washington D.C. Miniature Soc., Ohio Miniature Soc., Soc. Internat. Marine Painters, Wofld Fedn. Miniaturists. Roman Catholic. Home: Silver Point Gallery Box 5 Route 20 Brainard NY 12024 Office: Silver Point Gallery Rt 20 Box 5 Brainard NY 12024

JOHNSEN, NIELS WINCHESTER, ocean shipping company executive; b. New Orleans, May 9, 1922; s. Niels Frithjof and Julia Anita (Winchester) J.; m. Millicent Alva Mercer, Sept. 9, 1944; children: Niels Mercer, Ingrid Christina Johnsen Barrett, Gretchen Anita Johnsen Bryant Student, Tulane U., 1939-42. V.p. States Marine Lines, N.Y.C., 1946-56, Central Gulf Lines, Inc., N.Y.C., 1947-65, vice chmn., 1965-71, chmn., 1971-98, Internat. Shipholding Corp., N.Y.C., 1979—2003, dir., 1979—; chmn. Waterman Steamship Corp., N.Y.C., 1989-97. Dir. Reserve Fund, Inc., N.Y.C., 1970-97. Bd. mgrs. Seamens Ch. Inst., N.Y.C., 1974-90. Served to lt. (j.g.) U.S. Maritime Service, 1942-45 Recipient award Marine Soc., 1993, medal of honor Ellis Island, 1994, Internat. Hall of Fame award Maritime Assn., 1993; named CEO of the Yr., 1990, Bronze ward 2nd pl. Fin. World. Mem. Nat. Cargo Bus. (bd. dirs. 1970-96), Am. Bur. Shipping (bd. mgrs. 1967-92), Seamens Ch. Inst. (hon. bd. mem., Silver Bell award 1988, Admiral of the Ocean Sea award 1993), India House (bd. dirs. 1962-98), Rumson Country Club (pres. 1985), Seabright Beach Club. Republican. Presbyterian. Avocations: golf, skiing. Office: Internat Shipholding Corp 1 Whitehall St New York NY 10004-2109

JOHNSEN, WALTER CRAIG, security firm executive; b. N.Y.C., Dec. 15, 1950; s. Walter S. Johnsen and Therese L. Nissen; m. Wendy Ann Wilding Davies, July 14, 1990; 1 child, Walter. BS, Cornell U., 1973, MS in Eng., 1974; MBA, Columbia U., 1978. Gen. ptnr. First Century Partnerships, N.Y.C., 1981-85; v.p. Smith Barney, Harris Upham Venture Corp., 1978-85; mng. ptnr. Johnsen Securities, N.Y.C., 1985-95; pres. Acme United Corp., Fairfield, Conn., 1995—. Bd. dirs. Acme United Corp., Fairfield, Conn. Mem. St. Francis Yacht Club, Cornell Club, Westhampton Yacht Squadron, Mill Reef Club, Union Club. Office: Acme United Corp 1931 Black Rock Turnpike Fairfield CT 06432-4823

JOHNSON, ABIGAIL, investment company executive; BA in Art History, Hobart and William Smith Coll., 1984; MBA, Harvard U., 1988. Rsch. assoc. Booz, Allen and Hamilton; portfolio mgr. Fidelity Investments, Boston, 1988—, assoc. dir., 1994—, sr. v.p., 1998—, pres., 2001—. Bd. dirs. FMR Corp. Office: Fidelity Investments 82 Devonshire St Boston MA 02109-3605

JOHNSON, ADRIA ELAINE, financial analyst, accountant; b. Louisville, Ky., Apr. 13, 1971; d. William Phillip and Brenda Carole Swafford; children: Brenlie Elaine Rhodes, Kenneth Lafranzo Rhodes; m. John Edward Johnson, June 29, 2002. BS, Ball State U., 1994. Accountant Humana, Louisville, 1994—97, LG&E Energy Corp., Louisville, 1997—99; fin./mktg. analyst Brown & Williamson Tobacco Corp., Louisville, 1999—. Contbr. poems to various publs. Pres. Sanctuary Choir-5th Street Baptist Ch., Louisville, 1999—2001. Mem.: Nat. Black MBA Assn. Democrat. Baptist. Home: 12511 Bridgetown Pl Louisville KY 40245 Office: Brown and Williamson Tobacco Corp 401 South 4th St Ste 200 Louisville KY 40202

JOHNSON, ALAN M. optometric physician; BS in Chemistry summa cum laude, Mich. Tech. U., Houghton, 1990; BS in Vision Sci., Ferris State U., Big Rapids, Mich., 1993; Doctor of Optometry with highest distinction, Ferris State Coll. Optometry, Big Rapids, 1994. Postgrad. fellow in ocular disease and co-mgmt. Eye Inst. Utah, Salt Lake City, 1995, staff optometrist, 1995-97; optometric physician and profl. liaison Spokane (Wash.) Eye Clinic, 1997—. Mem. Am. Optometric Assn. (contact lens and low vision sects.). Avocations: running, cross country skiing, hiking. Office: Spokane Eye Clinic 427 S Bernard St Spokane WA 99204-2559

JOHNSON, ALBERT WESLEY, retired advisor on governance; b. Insinger, Sask., Can., Oct. 18, 1923; s. Thomas William and Louise Lillian (Croft) J.; m. Ruth Elinor Hardy, June 27, 1946; children: Andrew, Frances, Jane, Geoffrey. BA, U. Sask., 1942; MA, U. Toronto, Ont., Can., 1945; MPA (Littauer fellow), Harvard U., 1950, PhD (Littauer fellow), 1963; LLD (hon.), U. Regina, 1977, U. Sask., 1978, Mt. Allison U., 1982, Queen's U., 1992, Carleton U., 1999. Dep. provincial treas. Govt. of Sask., Regina, 1952-64; asst. dep. minister fin. Govt. of Can., Ottawa, Ont., 1964-68, econ. adviser to prime minister on constn., 1968-70, sec. treasury bd., 1970-73, dep. minister nat. welfare, 1973-75; pres. CBC, Ottawa, 1975-82; Skelton-Clark fellow Queens U., 1982-83; prof. polit. sci. U. Toronto, 1983-89; sr. fellow Can. Centre for Mgmt. Devel., Ottawa, 1989-91. Cons. on governance Internat. Monetary Fund, Indonesia, 1988, 91, S. Africa, 1992-99; chmn. task force on univ. programs, Sask., 1992-93. Contbr. articles to profl. publs.; editorial bd.: Can. Public Policy, 1974-75. Bd. dirs. Nat. Film Bd., 1970-82, U. Sask. Hosp., 1957-64; mem. Nat. Arts Centre, 1975-82; bd. govs. U. Sask., Saskatoon, 1952-63. Recipient Gold medal Profl. Inst. of Pub. Svc. of Can., 1975; decorated Companion of the Order of Can., 1997; A.W. Johnson Disting. Chair established Sask. Dept. Fin., 2000. Mem. Ottawa Polit. Economy Assn. (pres. 1969-70), Inst. Public Adminstrn. Can. (pres. 1962-63, Vanier medal 1976, nat. council 1951-69), Can. Polit. Sci. Assn. (exec. council 1963-64) Mem. United Ch. of Can. Fax: (613) 225-3313.

JOHNSON, ALBERTA CLARK, psychology educator; b. Chattanooga, Apr. 19, 1942; d. William Ross and Helen W. Clark; m. John Burlin Johnson, Mar. 12, 1965; children: Sonya K., Roxanne Johnson Dingman. BA, U. N.C., Greensboro, 1964; MS, U. Ariz., 1979, PhD, 1988. Cert. family life educator, Nat. Coun. Family Rels. Membership dir. Tucson Area Coun. Camp Fire, 1981-83; asst. dir. Ext. Winter Sch., Tucson, 1984-87; human devel. specialist U. Ariz. Coop. Ext. Svc., Tucson, 1983-87; assoc. faculty Pima C.C., Tucson, 1987-88; family life specialist U. Ariz. Coop. Ext. Svc., 1989-92, U. Ark. Coop. Ext. Svc., Little Rock, 1989-92; cons. Little Rock, 1992-93; asst. prof. psychology and edn. Floyd Coll., Rome, Ga., 1993-97, assoc. prof. psychology, 1997—2002, prof. psychology, 2002—. Sec., governing state bd. dirs. Parents Anonymous of Ariz., Phoenix, 1983-84; mem. Gov.'s Coun. on Children, Youth and Families, Phoenix, 1983-84; pres. bd. dirs. Pima County chpt. Parents Anonymous, Tucson, 1985-86; v.p. Women's Info. Network, Inc., Rome, 1997-99; bd. dirs. Ga. Breast Cancer Coalition, 2000—. Named Woman of Excellence, 1998, Women in Mgmt. and Greater Rome C. of C. Mem.: AAUP, APA, Coun. Tchrs. of Undergrad. Psychology, Am. Psychol. Soc., Nat. Coun. on Family Rels., Pi Lambda Theta, Kappa Omicron Nu, Psi Beta (v.p.). Avocations: photography, hiking, camping, reading. Office: Floyd Coll PO Box 1864 3175 Highway 27 N Rome GA 30162-1864 E-mail: ajohnson@floyd.edu.

JOHNSON, ALEX CLAUDIUS, English language educator; b. Freetown, Sierra Leone, Aug. 14, 1943; came to U.S., 1991; s. Eunice Angela (Thorpe) Johnson; m. Daphne Marvel Taylor; children: Marvin(dec.), Joyemi. BA in English Lang. and Lit. with honors, U. Durham, Eng., 1968; MA in English and Am. Lit., U. Kent, Canterbury, Eng., 1971; MPhil in Linguistics, U. Leeds, Eng., 1974; PhD in English, U. Ibadan, Nigeria, 1982. Tchr. various h.s., Freetown, Sierra Leone, 1968-69, 71-72; sr. lectr., lectr. English dept. Fourah Bay Coll., Sierra Leone, 1974-88, sr. lectr., acting head classics/philosophy dept., 1987-88, assoc. prof., head English dept., 1988-91; vis. prof. English lang. and Creole studies U. Bayreuth, Germany, 1982-84; vis. prof. S.C. State U., Orangeburg, 1991-92, prof., 1992. Acting vice prin. Fourah Bay Coll., summer 1989, 90, dean faculty of arts, 1989-91; cons. UNESCO, 1985-89; external assessor U. Cape Coast, Ghana, 1988. Contbr. articles to internat. profl. jours., papers to internat. confs. and symposia. Chief examiner West Africa Examinations Coun., Accra, Ghana, 1978-91, Inst. Edn., U. Sierra Leone, 1980-91; chair Nat. Primary Curriculum Revision Com., 1981. Mem. SAMLA, South Ea. Renaissance Conf., Coll. Lang. Assn., African Lit. Assn., West African Linguistic Soc. (sec., organizer 13th West African Langs. Congress, Freetown, 1978), West African MLA (exec. com. 1981-82). Episcopalian. Home: 767 Windmill Way Orangeburg SC 29118-2838 E-mail: johnsonac@scsu.edu.

JOHNSON, ALICE ELAINE, retired academic administrator; b. Janesville, Wis., Oct. 9, 1929; d. Floyd C. and Alma M. (Walthers) Chester; m. Richard C. Johnson, Sept. 25, 1948 (div. 1974); children: Randall S., Nile C., Linnea E. BA, U. Colo., 1968. Pres., administrator Pikes Peak Inst. Med. Tech., Colorado Springs, Colo., 1968-88. Mem. adv. com. to Colo. Commn. on Higher Edn., 1979-80, State Adv. Coun. on Pvt. Occupational Schs., Denver, 1978-86; mem. tech. adv. com. State Health Occupations, 1986-88; bd. dirs. All Souls Unitarian Ch., Colorado Springs, 1990-96, mem. celebration team, 1990-91, pres. bd. trustees, 1991-93. Mem. Colo. Pvt. Sch. Assn. (pres. 1981-82, bd. dirs. 1976-88, Outstanding Mem. 1978, 80), Phi Beta Kappa. Democrat. Unitarian Universalist. Avocations: writing, travel, reading. E-mail: oma1902@hotmail.com. *We must review and renew our committment, as a nation, to true freedom of religion, and resist current tendencies to mix church and state.*

JOHNSON, ALLEN FREDERICK, federal agency administrator; Grad., George Mason U.; Masters Degree, MBA, Stanford U. Chief agr. negotiator Office of the U.S. Trade Rep. Exec. Office of the Pres., Washington, 2001—; legis. aide Senator Charles Grassley. Exec. dir. Iowa Soybean Assn., 1988—91, Iowa Soybean Promotion Bd. Mem.: Nat. Oilseed Processors Assn. (pres.). Republican. Office: Exec Office of the Pres US Trade Rep 600 17th St NW Washington DC 20508-4801

JOHNSON, A(LYN) WILLIAM, chemistry educator, writer, researcher, consultant; b. Calgary, Alta, Can., Dec. 16, 1933; came to U.S., 1954, naturalized, 1981; s. Alyn C. and Irene (Johnston) J.; m. Joan Auger, July 26, 1956; children: Patricia, Nancy, Robert, Katherine. BS, U. Alta., 1954; PhD, Cornell U., 1957. Research fellow Mellon Inst., Pitts., 1957-60; asst., then asso. prof. chemistry U. N.D., 1960-65; asso. prof., chmn. dept. chemistry U. Sask. Regina, 1965-67; dean Grad. Sch., prof. chemistry U. N.D., Grand Forks, 1967-75, 77-88, dir. R & D, 1967-75, prof. chemistry, 1988-94, emeritus prof., 1995—. Vis. prof. U.S. Mil. Acad., West Point, N.Y., 1994-95, U. Mass., Amherst, 1989; dir. N.D. regional environ. assessment program N.D. Legis. Coun., Bismarck, 1975-77. Author: Ylid Chemistry, 1966, Ylides and Imines of Phosphorus, 1993, Invitation to Organic Chemistry, 1998, also over 50 articles to profl. jours. Fellow: AAAS, Chem. Inst. Can.; mem.: Am. Chem. Soc. (cons. C3S program), Rotary, Sigma Xi. Episcopalian. Home: 9 Tanyard Ln Bella Vista AR 72714-2450

JOHNSON, ANITA (MARY ANITA JOHNSON), physician, medical service administrator; b. Clarksburg, W.Va., Oct. 18, 1926; d. Paul F. and Mary Elizabeth (Harris) Johnson; m. Lawrence J. Ciessau, Aug. 22, 1959 (div. 1974); children: Matthew A., Susan E., Sharon L., Mark A.; m. Ralph Allen Fretwell, Dec. 18, 1976 (dec. Aug. 18, 2001). BS, North Tex. U., 1946; MD, Woman's Med. Coll. Pa., 1950. Intern Baylor U. Hosp., Dallas, 1950-51, resident, 1951-54; practice medicine specializing in internal medicine Dallas, 1954-58, Chgo., 1958—; instr. internal medicine Southwestern Med. Coll., U. Tex., Dallas, 1954-58; med. dir. YWCA, Dallas, 1955-58; physician for infant welfare Chgo. Bd. Health, 1960-63; house physician, emergency physician St. Mary of Nazareth Hosp. Ctr., Chgo., 1963-81, instr. nurses ICU, 1963-80, asst. cardiologist, 1963-86, sec. med. staff, 1974-75, treas. med. staff, 1980, pres. med. staff, 1982, 84; med. dir. Family Care Ctr., 1973-74, chief med. clinics, 1977-78, chmn. credentials com., 1982-92, chief internal medicine, 1983-92; clin. instr. medicine U. Health Scis., Chgo. Med. Sch., North Chicago, Ill., 1982-95; nat. med. dir. Nat. Cath. Soc. Foresters Ins. Co., Chgo., 1975-77. Chmn. ann. benefit com. St. Mary of Nazareth Hosp. Ctr., 1992; cons. internal medicine Lisbon VA Hosp., Dallas, 1955-56; lectr. to cmty. elem. sch. students on opportunities in health field, 1967—; gov. bd. St. Mary Nazareth Hosp. Ctr., 1991-94, life trustee, 1994—. Named Med. Woman of Yr., St. Mary of Nazareth Hosp. Ctr., 1973. Mem. ACP, AMA (del. hosp. med. staff sect. 1980-92), Ill. Soc. Internal Medicine (councillor 1990-93), Am. Soc. Internal Medicine, Am. Coll. Angiology, Am. Med. Women's Assn. (S.W. regional dir. 1955-58, nat. chmn. publicity and pub. rels. 1991-93, pres.-elect br. 2, 1981, 82, 89, 90, pres. 1983-85, 91-94, regional gov. Midwest sect. 1985-91, bd. dirs. 1985-91, 92-98, v.p. fin. 1997-98, cmty. svc. award 1991, nat. chmn. retirement issues com. 1993-2000, nat. pres.-elect 1998-99, Pres.'s Recognition award 1998, Bertha Van Hoosen Nat. award 1999, found. bd. dirs. 1999—), Ill. State Med. Soc. (trustee 1987-90, com. on CME accreditation 1987-96, coun. on pub. rels. on membership svcs 1992, govt. affairs com. 1991—, jud. panel mem. 2003-), Chgo. Med. Soc. (councillor 1980—, chmn. malpractice ins. com., del. to Ill. Med. Soc. 1981—, pres. Northside br. 1985-87, chmn. practice mgmt. com. 1990-93, nominating com., Midwest Clin. Conf. 1991—, Cook County jud. panel 1995-2000, chmn. sr. physicians com. 1997-99, chmn. subcom. continuing med. edn. 1997-98, chmn. presdl. ad hoc com. sr. physicians 1997-99, chmn. continuing med. edn. com. 1998—, chmn. election com. 2002—, created M. Anita Johnson award 1999—), Zeta Phi. Home and Office: 6226 Edgebrook Ln W Indianhead Park IL 60525-6983 *Learning to look beyond today has been one of the greatest lessons I've learned. Long term is what matters, whether one is talking about relationships, money or goals one sets for oneself.*

JOHNSON, ANITA ROCHELLE, mental health specialist; b. Nashville, Tenn., Nov. 5, 1960; d. Charlene and Prentice Nance; 1 child, Marcus Dionte. BS in Psychology, Mid. Tenn. State U., Murfreesboro, 1982. Author: (inspirational poetry) A Touch Of Spiritual Praise. Mem.: Alpha Kappa Alpha Inc. (life). Democrat-Npl. Home: 727 Work Dr Nashville TN 37207 Personal E-mail: nitapoet1@aol.com

JOHNSON, ANNE BRADSTREET, research physician, educator; b. Boston, Mar. 5, 1927; d. Stafford F. Johnson and Catherine (Tyler) Stadie; m. Jack Minkoff, June 19, 1948; children: Ellen Louise, Paul Andrew. BA, Cornell U., 1948, MD, 1951. Diplomate Am. Bd. Internal Medicine, Am. Bd. Anat. Pathology and Neuropathology. Rotating intern Mt. Sinai Hosp., Cleve., 1951-52, resident internal medicine, 1952-53, Cleve. City Hosp., 1953-54; fellow Univ. Hosp., 1954-55; pvt. practice internal medicine Cleve., 1955-57; from instr. to assoc. prof. Albert Einstein Coll. Medicine, Bronx, NY, 1962—2002, assoc. prof. dept. pathology, 1977, assoc. prof. dept. neurosci., 1980, prof. emeritus, 2002—. Contbr. articles to profl. jours. Grantee NIH, Nat. Multiple Sclerosis Soc., United Leukodystrophy Found., Alzheimer's Assn. Mem. AAAS, Am. Assn. Neuropathologists, Histochem. Soc., Coll. Am. Pathologists, Internat. Acad. Pathology, Soc. for Neurosci., N.Y. Acad. Scis. Office: Albert Einstein Coll Med Dept Pathology K 604 1300 Morris Park Ave Bronx NY 10461-1975 Home: 57 Ruxton Rd Great Neck NY 11023

JOHNSON, ANNE HALE, educational association administrator, director; b. Rochester, N.Y., Oct. 12, 1923; d. Ezra Andrews and Josephine (Booth) Hale; m. Arthur William Johnson, July 20, 1957; children: Joy Sanborn, Randall, Christiane Brooks (dec.). BA, Smith Coll., 1945; MA, Columbia U., 1952; MDiv, Union Theol. Sem., N.Y.C., 1956. Exec. dir. Rochester Assn. for the UN, 1946-49; asst. to dir. World Fedn. UN Assns./Internat. Student Movement for UN, Paris, 1950-51; exec. dir. Citizens for Ike, Rochester, 1951-52; midwest field rep. U.S. Com. for UNICEF, Chgo., 1953; dir. Christian edn. Swarthmore (Pa.) Presbyn. Ch., 1956-57; tchr. and coord. adult edn. issues Georgetown Presbyn. Ch., Washington, 1957-72, 85—; tchr. Old and New Testament courses Madeira Sch., McLean, Va., 1961-62. Spkr. in fields of fgn. policy, religious activities, women's issues. Contbr. articles to newspapers. Mem. bd. Union Theol. Sem., 1990—, chair, 1996—; mem. bd. Madeira Sch., 1993-97, Faith and Politics Inst., Washington, 1992—, Presbyn. Women, Washington, 1992-96; v.p. bd. The Living Pulpit, Bronx, N.Y., 1991—; sec.-treas. Safe Travel Am., Potomac, Md., 1987—; founding bd. mem. Rep. Coalition for Choice, Washington, 1989—, bd., 2002—; mem. Montgomery County Rep. Ctr. Com., 1994-2002; mem. steering com. Covenant Network of Presbyns., 1998, mem. adv. com., 2002; mem. Planned Parenthood Found., 1998—. Republican. Presbyterian. Home: 10600 Red Barn Ln Potomac MD 20854-1953

JOHNSON, ANNE STUCKLY, retired lawyer; b. Axtell, Tex., Jan. 8, 1921; d. Arnold Joseph and Angeline (Morris) Stuckly; m. Edward James Johnson, Oct. 9, 1943 (dec. 1967); children: Edward M., Ronald J., Dennis L., Shawn T., Rozlynn Jan, Anne J'lynn, Kevin J, Karal Ian, Donna Lynn. BA, Baylor U., 1940; MA in Econs., St. Mary's U., 1974, JD, 1980. Bar: Tex. 1980. Claims clk. Social Security Adminstrn., Amarillo, Tex., 1940-42; asst. chief divsn. pers. Pantex Ordnance Plant, Amarillo, Tex., 1942-43; chief divsn. pers. Cactus Ordnance Works, Dumas, Tex., 1943-44; citations unit supr. Gen. Hdqrs. Far East Command, Tokyo, 1950-51; v.p., treas. Drive-Safe Corp., San Antonio, 1967-69; counseling psychologist ARC, San Antonio, 1968-69, Divsn. Pers. Office, Ft. Sam Houston, 1969, pers. mgmt. specialist, 1969-77; pvt. practice Oliver B. Chamberlin Offices, San Antonio, 1981-86, San Antonio, 1987-93; ret., 1994. Active Am. Heart Assn., 1983—. Mem. ABA, San Antonio Bar Assn., Tex. Bar Assn., Am. Trial Lawyers Assn., Assn. Social Econs., Tex. Trial Lawyers Assn., Phi Alpha Delta, Pi Gamma Mu, Omicron Delta Epsilon. Home: 3714 Hunters Point San Antonio TX 78230

JOHNSON, ANTHONY O'LEARY (ANDY JOHNSON), meteorologist, consultant; b. Tampa, Fla., Apr. 19, 1957; s. Paul Bryan and Katie Hobbs (Nunez) J. BS in Meteorology, Fla. State U., 1979. Cert. cons. meteorologist. Courthouse runner Gregory, Cours, et. al., Tampa, 1977; water resources planner S.W. Fla. Water Mgmt. Dist., Brooksville, 1978; staff meteorologist Sta. WTVT-TV, Tampa, 1979-82, systems mgr., 1982-89, weather office mgr., 1989—. Meterol. cons. Gulf Coast Weather Svc.-Weather Vision, Tampa, 1979—; software devel. mgr. TTI Techs. Inc., Tampa, 1989-92; site coord. Space Sci. and Engring. Ctr. U. Wis., Madison, 1989—. Active capital improvements com. Plantation Homeowners Assn., Tampa, 1991; judge Hillsborough Regional Sci. Fair, Tampa, 1990, 91, 92, 96; fundraiser Dunedin Youth Guild, 1992, Northside Mental Health Hosp. Aux., 1993, 94, Children's Home, Pinellas Aux., 1993, 94, 95; vol. Sch. Enrichment Vols. in Edn. (SERVE), 1992. Mem. AAAS, Am. Meteorol Soc. (Seal of Approval for TV weathercasting 1982—, v.p. West Fla. chpt. 1984-85, pres. 1989-92, 94—), Internat. Platform Assn., Phi Beta Kappa, Pi Mu Epsilon, Chi Epsilon Pi. Republican. Achievements include development of quantitative predictive methods of energy delivery interruption in severe Florida freezes; research on temporal and spatial climatological anomalies on landfalling hurricanes in West Central Florida. Office: Sta WTVT-TV Weather Svc 3213 W Kennedy Blvd Tampa FL 33609-3006 Home: 3912 W Dale Ave Tampa FL 33609-4405 E-mail: AndyCCM@aol.com.

JOHNSON, ANTONIA AXSON, corporate executive; b. Sept. 6, 1943; d. Axel Axson and Antonia Johnson; m. P. Göran Ennerfelt; children: Alexandra Mörner, Caroline Mörner, Axel Mörner, Sophie Mörner. Student, Radcliffe Coll., 1963-64; MA in Psychology and Econs., U. Stockholm, 1971. With Nordstjernan AB, 1971-79, Axel Johnson AB, Stockholm, 1979—, chmn., 1982—. Chmn. bd. Axel Johnson Inc., Stamford, Conn., City Mission of Stockholm; bd. dirs. The Axel and Margaret Axson Johnson's Found.; bd.dirs. NCC Nordic Constrn. Co.; bd. dirs. World Childhood Found.; mem. IVA-Royal Swedish Acad. of Engring. Scis., Xerox Corp.; bd. dirs. Axfood AB, Nordstjernan AB, Axel Johnson Internat., Sweden. Named Profl. Woman of Yr., 1987, Fin. Woman of Yr., 1988; named # 1 of Am.'s Top 25 Women Bus. Owners, Nat. Found. for Women Bus. Owners and Working Woman, 1992, named # 4 of Am.'s Top 50 Women Bus. Owners, 1993. Office: Axel Johnson AB Villagatan 6 PO Box 26008 S-100 41 Stockholm Sweden also: Axel Johnson Inc 300 Atlantic St Stamford CT 06901-3522

JOHNSON, ARLENE LYTLE, government agency official; b. Pitts., Jan. 20, 1937; d. Willis and Minnie Lee (Blackman) Neal; children: Robin Gerome Lytle, Cheryl Rose Lytle Slye. Student, various profl. courses. Clk.-typist Pa. Dept. Revenue, Harrisburg, 1955; office sec. Akron (Ohio) Jewish Ctr., 1956-57; clk.-stenographer Pa. Employment Service, Pitts., 1960-61, Dept. Treasury, Washington, 1961; sec.-stenographer Dept. HEW, Washington, 1961-70; exec. sec. to dir. Bur. Cmty. Health Svcs., Health Svcs. Adminstrn., Dept. HEW, Rockville, Md., 1970-81; staff asst. to dep. asst. sec. for children and families Dept. HHS, 1981-93, staff asst. to asst. sec. for children and families, 1993—. Recipient Spl. Recognition award USPHS, 1991, Superior Svc. award Health Svcs. and Mental Health Adminstrn., 1973, Sustained Superior Svc. award HHS, 1984-90, 1991-2003, Spl. Recognition award Human Devel. Svcs. Adminstrn. for Children and Families, 1989, 91. Jehovah'S Witness. Home: 15609 Everglade Ln Unit 103 Bowie MD 20716-3270 Office: Rm 600 370 Lenfant Promenade SW Washington DC 20447-0001 E-mail: aljohnson@acf.hhs.gov.

JOHNSON, ARTHUR GILBERT, microbiology educator; b. Eveleth, Minn., Feb. 1, 1926; s. Arthur Gilbert and Selma (Niemi) J.; m. Mildred Louise Anderson, June 15, 1951; children: Susan, Sally, Gary, Peter. BA, U. Minn., 1950, M.Sc., 1951; PhD, U. Md., 1955. Biochemist Walter Reed Army Inst. Rsch., Washington, 1952-55; asst. prof. U. Mich., 1956-62, asso. prof., 1962-66, prof. microbiology, 1966-78; prof., head dept. med. microbiology/immunology U. Minn. Sch. Medicine, Duluth, 1978-99, prof. emeritus, 1999—. Mem. pre, postdoctoral and spl. fellowships study sect. NIH, 1968-70; mem. nat. adv. dental rsch. coun. NIH, 1972-75; mem. Nat. Bd. Med. Examiners, 1980-84; mem. bacteriology and mycology study sect. NIH, 1983-87, chmn., 1986-87; cons. microbiology. Editor Infection and Immunity, 1977-86. Served with US Merchant Marine, 1943-46. Mem. Am. Assn. Immunologists, Am. Soc. Microbiology, Infectious Diseases Soc. Am., Soc. Biol. Therapy, Immunocomprised Host Soc., Internat. Endotoxin Soc., Assn. Med. Sch. Microbiology and Immunology Chairs (pres. 1991-92). Achievements include research on immunology. Home: 209 Rockridge Cir Duluth MN 55804-1857 Office: U Minn Sch Medicine Dept Microbiology/Immunology Duluth MN 55812

JOHNSON, ARTHUR INGRAM, obstetrician and gynecologist; b. Goodman, Miss., Nov. 12, 1941; s. Arthur Patrick and Laurene Louise (Wright) J.; m. Drina Luz Villalobos; children: Anita, Anthony, Christos, Angela, Arthur. BS in Chemistry, Tougaloo (Miss.) Coll., 1962; MD, U. Mich., 1967; MPH, UCLA, 1975. Diplomate Am. Bd. Ob-Gyn. Intern Wayne County Gen. Hosp., Mich., 1967-68; resident UCLA, 1971-75; physician Ross Loos Med. Group, 1975-79; pvt. practice L.A., 1979—. Sec. med. staff Cedars Sinai Med. Ctr., L.A., 1991, treas., 1992, clin. chief of obstetrics, 1992, vice chief of staff, 1993-94, clin. chief ob-gyn., 1995-96, chief of staff, 1998-99; bd. dirs. Cedars Sinai Med. Sys., L.A., 1996—. Dir. L.A. Free Clinic, 1990-98, Hollywood Urban Project, L.A., 1995-96; trustee 1st Presbyn. Ch. of Hollywood, 1993-96; dir. Nat. Health Found., 1998 . Capt. USAF, 1968-70. Decorated Bronze Star medals (2). Fellow ACOG. Democrat. Avocations: reading, walking, skiing, bowling. Office: 8631 W 3rd St Ste 444 Los Angeles CA 90048-5908

JOHNSON, ARTHUR WILLIAM, JR., retired planetarium executive; b. Steubenville, Ohio, Jan. 8, 1949; s. Arthur William and Carol (Gilcrest) J. BMus, U. So. Calif., 1973. Lectr. Griffith Obs. and Planetarium, 1969-73; planetarium writer, lectr. Mt. San Antonio Coll. Planetarium, Walnut, Calif., 1970-73; dir. Fleischmann Planetarium U. Nev., Reno, 1973-2001; ret., 2001. Apptd. Nev. state coord. NSTA/NASA Space Sci. Student Involvement Program, 1994. Writer, prodr. films (with Donald G. Potter) Beautiful Nevada, 1978, Riches: The Story of Nevada Mining, 1984. Organist, choirmaster Trinity Episcopal Ch., Reno, 1980—; bd. dirs. Reno Chamber Orch. Assn., 1981-87, 1st v.p., 1984-85. Nev. Humanities Com., Inc. grantee, 1979-83. Mem. Am. Guild Organists (dean No. Nev. chpt. 1984-85, 96-99, 2002-), Assn. Anglican Musicians, Internat. Planetarium Soc., Cinema 360 (treas. 1985-90, pres. 1990-98), Pacific Planetarium Assn. (pres. 1980), Lions (pres. Reno Host Club 1991-92), Large Format Cinema Assn. (v.p. 1996-99). Republican. Episcopalian. E-mail: arthurj@unr.edu.

JOHNSON, BADRI NAHVI, sociology educator, real estate business owner; b. Tehran, Iran, Dec. 1, 1934; came to U.S., 1957; d. Ali Akbar and Monir Khazraii Nahvi; m. Floyd Milton Johnson, July 2, 1960; children: Rebecca, Nancy, Robert. BS, U. Minn., 1967, MA, 1969, PhD, 2001. Stenographer Curtis 1000, Inc., St. Paul, 1958-62; lab. instr. U. Minn., Mpls., 1966-69, teaching asst., 1969-72; chief exec. officer Real Estate Investment and Mgmt. Enterprise, St. Paul, 1969—; prof. emeritus sociology Anoka-Ramsey C.C., Coon Rapids, Minn., 1973—2003. Pub. speaker, bd. dirs., sponsor pub. radio KFAI, Mpls., 1989-93; established an endowed scholarship for women Anoka Ramsey C.C., 1991. Radio talk show host KCW, Brookline Parks, Minn., 1993. Organizer Iranian earthquake disaster relief, 1990; bd. dirs. dist. 7 Cmty. Coun., 1996-98. Recipient Earthquake Relief Orgn. citation Iranian Royal Household, 1968, Islamic Republic of Iran citation for organizing earthquake disaster relief, 1990. Mem.: NEA, Sociologists of Minn., Minn. Edn. Assn., Women's Leadership Forum, Nat. Social Scis. Assn., U. Minn. Alumni Assn. Avocations: world travel, classical and historical novels, exotic food, gardening. Home: 1726 Iowa Ave E Saint Paul MN 55106-1334 Office: Anoka-Ramsey Cmty Coll 11200 Mississippi Blvd NW Minneapolis MN 55433-3470 E-mail: john1800@tc.umn.edu.

JOHNSON, BARBARA ELAINE SPEARS, retired education educator; b. Chgo., May 24, 1932; d. William Everett and Sadie Mae (Fennoy) Spears; m. John Gilbert Johnson, July 29, 1967 (dec. Jan. 1985); children: Steven W., Jeri-Lynn Johnson Jackson. AB, U. Chgo., 1952; EdB, Chgo. Tchrs. Coll., 1954; EdM, Loyola U., Chgo., 1967; EdS, U. Ill., Chgo., 1982; MSEd in counseling, Chgo. State U., 1986. Tchr. Chgo. Pub. Schs., 1954-64, counselor, 1964-70; evening tchr. Chgo. Pub. High Schs., 1964-66; dir. resource skills City Colls. of Chgo., 1970-84, dir. audio visual, 1985-86, coordinator academic support ctr., 1986-87, prof. acad. support, 1988-93; prof. emeritus City Colls. of Chgo., 1993—. Faculty coun. City Colls. of Chgo., v.p. 1989-90, pres. 1990-91. Coordinator food ministry Cosmopolitan Community Ch., Chgo., 1983-90. Recipient Dedication to Youth award McCosh Sch. Council, 1985, citations of recognition Ill. Community Coll. Bd., 1982, 84. Fellow Ill. Com. Black Concerns in Higher Edn. (plaque 1984); mem. AARP (exec. bd. mem. 1997—, v.p. 2000), Ill. C.C. Faculty Assn. (life, exec. bd. 1979—, pres. 1981-82, plaque 1982), Ill. Assn. Personalized Learning Programs (exec. bd., treas. 1975-85, Outstanding Contbn. award 1985), U. Ill. Mothers Assn. (chair 1977-81), Ill. C.C. Annuitants Assn. (exec. bd. dirs. 1993—, pres. 1995-97), Sr. Friends, Alpha Kappa Alpha (50 yr. mem. award 2002). Home: 8610 S Vernon Ave Chicago IL 60619-6015

JOHNSON, BARBARA ELIZABETH, lawyer; b. Des Moines, Aug. 2, 1957; d. William Frederick and Dorothy Jane (Colvin) Spotz; m. Richard Gordon Johnson, Mar. 4, 1984. BS, Grove City (Pa.) Coll., 1979; JD, Coll. of William and Mary, 1984. Bar: Pa. 1984, U.S. Dist. Ct. (we. dist.) Pa. 1984, U.S. Ct. Appeals (3d and Fed. cirs.) 1984. Patent agt. NASA-Langley Rsch. Ctr., Hampton, Va., 1982-84; assoc. atty. The Webb Law Firm, Pitts., 1984-92, shareholder, dir., 1992—. Mng. dir. The Webb law Firm, 2001—; chmn. Obershenk Medallion Trust, Aspen Quality Care, Inc.; bd. dirs. Precision Staffing Svcs., Inc. Mem.: Pitts. Intellectual Property Law Assn. (pres. 2000—01), Am. Chem. Soc. (chmn. Pitts. sect. 1995), Pitts. Chemists Club. Republican. Avocations: piano, writing, baking, automobile repairing. Office: The Webb Law Firm 436 7th Ave Ste 700 Pittsburgh PA 15219-1827 E-mail: bjohnson@webblaw.com.

JOHNSON, BARBARA JANE, music educator; b. Bartow, Fla., Oct. 5, 1955; d. Robert Samuel and Betty Jane (Luttrell) J. BME, Fla. State U., 1977; MMus, Southwestern Bapt. Theol. Sem., Ft. Worth, 1982. Band dir. Haines City (Fla.) Jr. High, 1977-79, Bartow Jr. High, 1982-86; music/drama tchr. Amman Bapt. Sch., Jordan, 1987—. Acad. dir. Amman Bapt. Sch., 1996-97, properties dir., 1998-99; dir. cmty. choir YWCA, 1991-2001; tchr., advisor Nat. Music Conservatory, 1987—. Mem. Music Educators Nat. Conf., Fla. Music Educators Assn., Fla. Bandmasters Assn. Republican. Avocations: photography, snorkeling, fishing, travel, scuba diving. Home: PO Box 17093 111-95 Amman Jordan Office: Amman Bapt Sch PO Box 17033 111-95 Amman Jordan E-mail: maestro@go.com.jo.

JOHNSON, BARBARA JEAN, retired judge, lawyer; b. Detroit, Apr. 9, 1932; d. Clifford Clarence and Orma Cecile (Boring) Barnhouse; m. Ronald Mayo Johnson, June 24, 1965; 1 child, Belinda Etezad. BS, U. So. Calif., 1953, JD, 1970. Bar: Calif. 1971. Ptnr. Angela, Burford, Johnson & Tookay, Pasadena, Calif., 1970-77; judge L.A. Mcpl. Ct., 1977-81, L.A. Superior Ct., 1981-97; ret., 1997. Lectr. U. So. Calif. Law Sch. profl. program; adj. prof. Southwestern U. Law Sch. Recipient Ernestine Stahlhut award, 1981. Mem. Calif. Judges Assn., 1977-98, Nat. Assn. Women Judges, 1980-98, Calif. Women Lawyers Assn. (pres. 1976-77), Women Lawyers Assn. LA (pres. 1975-76), Christian Legal Soc. Home: 1000 Prospect Blvd Pasadena CA 91103-2810

JOHNSON, BARBARA JEAN, rehabilitation nurse, gerontology nurse; b. Pottsville, Pa., Sept. 14, 1948; d. Guy F. and Rachel S. (Schwenk) Boger; m. Ronald L. Johnson, Apr. 25, 1970; children: Jennifer E., Roxanne M. Diploma in nursing, Reading (Pa.) Sch., 1967. LPN, Pa. Pvt. duty nurse Health Care InCorp, Auburn, Pa., 1982-83; staff nurse med.-surg. unit St. Joseph's Hosp., Reading, 1967-69; staff nurse Visiting Nurse Assn. of Reading and Berks County, 1969-73; team leader skilled unit Laurel Living Ctr. (name now Laurel Ctr.), Hamburg, Pa., 1983—. Home: 1457 Summer Hill Rd Auburn PA 17922-9027

JOHNSON, BENJAMIN F., VI, economist, consultant; b. Kingston, N.Y., Sept. 17, 1952; s. Benjamin F. and Alice (Terry) J. BA in Econs., U. South Fla., 1974; MS in Econs., Fla. State U., 1977, PhD in Econs., 1982. Sr. utility analyst Office of Pub. Counsel, State of Fla., 1974-77; pres., cons. economist Ben Johnson Assocs., Inc., Tallahassee, Fla., 1977—. Contbr. articles to N.Y. Times, Pub. Utilities Fortnightly, profl. jours. Mem. Am. Econ. Assn. Office: 2252 Killearn Center Blvd Tallahassee FL 32309-3573

JOHNSON, BERNADINE, piano educator, composer; b. Melrose Park, Ill., Sept. 23, 1951; d. Henry Eugene and Dorothy Dean (Sutton) Wilhelm; m. Robert Eugene Johnson, June 17, 1972; children: Joshua David, Jeffrey Robert, Jonathan Brakefield. BA in Music Edn., Ind. Wesleyan U., Marion, 1974. Pvt. piano tchr., Fremont, Mich., 1976—; piano instr. Jordan Coll., Fremont, 1981, Blue Lake Fine Arts Camp, Twin Lake, Mich., 1982; accompanist Grand Valley State U., Allendale, Mich., 1989. Adjudicator Mich. State Solo and Ensemble Festival, 1990—. Arranger: (piano books) Christmas Hits for Piano, 1992, Student Messiah, 1993, Student Classics, 1994, Great Songs About God, 1996, In Praise of His Name, 2001; dir., creator Madrigal Singers, Fremont, 1985—; dir., actress Stage Door Players, Fremont, 1975-90; musician, dir. Ch. of the Living Christ, Fremont, 1976—; composer for Alfred Pub. Co. Mem. music enhancement com. Newaygo County Cmty. Svcs., Fremont, 1980—. Recipient Alumni award fine arts dept. Ind. Wesleyan U., Marion, 1992, Cultural Arts award Newaygo County Cmty. Svcs., 1998; named Woman in Leadership, Huntington Banks, Fremont, 1996. Mem. Nat. Music Tchrs. Assn., Mich. Music Tchrs. Assn., Piano Tchrs. Forum Grand Rapids. Republican. Mem. Reformed Ch. Home: 332 E Main St Fremont MI 49412-1324

JOHNSON, BERNETTE J. state supreme court justice; b. Ascension Parish, La. d. Frank Joshua Jr. and Olivia W. Johnson. BA, Spelman Coll., Atlanta, 1964; JD, La. State U., 1969. Bar: La. Law intern Civil Rights divsn. U.S. Dept. Justice; judge La. Civil Dist. Ct., 1984-94, chief judge, 1994; assoc. justice La. Supreme Ct., New Orleans, 1994—. Legal svc. atty. New Orleans Legal Asst. Corp. Bd. dirs. YMCA, New Orleans; chmn. bd. Learning Ctr., Great St. Stephen Full Gospel Bapt. Ch. Named Woman of Yr., LaBelle chpt. Am. Bus. Women's Assn., 1994. Office: Supreme Ct Bldg 301 Loyola Ave New Orleans LA 70112-1814*

JOHNSON, BETTY LOU, secondary education educator; b. Stockwell, Ind., Apr. 4, 1927; d. Paul Stanley Jones and Ethel Leona (Royer) J.; m. Kenneth Odell Johnson, Aug. 5, 1950; children: Cynthia Jo (Mrs. James P. Greaton), Gregory Alan. BS in Home Econs., Purdue U., 1948; postgrad., Northwood Inst. Culinary Arts, 1981, 83. Cert. home economist. Tchr. LaCrosse (Ind.) Jr.-Sr. High Sch., 1948-49, Wendell L. Willkie High Sch., Elwood, Ind., 1949 51, Thomas Carr Howe High Sch., Indpls., 1951-57; substitute tchr. Gt. Oaks Joint Vocat. Sch. Dist., Cin. Mem. AAUW, Am. Home Econs. Assn. (life), Ohio Home Econs. Assn. (life), John Purdue Club, Purdue Pres.'s Coun., Purdue U. Alumni Assn. (life), Gamma Sigma Delta. Home: Cincinnati, Ohio. Deceased.

JOHNSON, BETTY MARIE, retired nursing educator; b. Rockford, Ill., Mar. 5, 1931; d. Martin Henry and Hildur Marie (Tinberg) Johnson. Diploma, Swedish Am. Hosp., 1951; BSN, U. Minn., 1955; MSN, U. Colo., 1962; PhD, U. Wis., 1970. Staff nurse Swedish - Am. Hosp., Rockford, Ill., 1951-52, Swedish Hosp., Mpls., 1952-55; ednl. dir. Swedish - Am. Hosp., 1955-61; asst. prof. Case Western Reserve U., Cleve., 1962-66; acad. advisor U. Wis., Madison, 1969-70, asst. prof., 1970-74; dean, prof. U. S.C., Columbia, 1975-80; dir. continuing edn. project for deans Am. Assn. Colls. of Nursing, Washington, 1981-83; vis. prof. Med. Coll. Ga., Augusta, 1983-84, U. Utah, Salt Lake City, 1984; dir. essentials project Am. Assn. Colls. of Nursing, Washington, 1985-87; vis. prof. U. Va., Charlottesville, 1980-81, prof., acting assoc. dean, 1987-91, prof., dept. chmn. Coll. Wise, 1991—2000, prof. emeritus, 2001—. Site visitor nat. arthritis bd. NIH, Bethesda, Md., 1977—82; chair preliminary rev. panel Commn. on Collegiate Nursing Edn., 1997—98, task force to train evaluators, 1997, accreditation rev. com., 1997—2001, accreditation visitor, evaluation trainer, 1997—; bd. dirs. Southwest Va. Area Health Edn. Ctr.; adv. bd. SW Va. Grad. Med. Edn. Consortium; cons. in field. Contbr. bd. dirs. Hope House for Abused Women, Norton, Va., 1992—98. Recipient Cert. of Merit, U. S.C., 1980, Hero award, Quillen Health Care, 1996. Mem.: AAUW (pres. Norton chpt. 1997—98), Va. Assn. Colls. Nursing, Nat. League Nursing (accreditation site visitor 1977—80), Am. Assn. Higher Edn., Am. Assn. Univ. Adminstr., Pi Lambda Theta, Sigma Theta Tau. Home: 715 Tiffany Dr Gaithersburg MD 20878-1820 E-mail: bmj7q@uvawise.edu.

JOHNSON, BOB W. state senator; b. Little Rock, Ark., Oct. 23, 1963; Mem. for 31st dist. Ark. Ho. of Reps., Little Rock, 1984—99, spkr. of ho.; mem. Ark. State Senate, 2001—. Chair ALC/performance based budgeting subcom.; chair legis. facilities. Baptist. Office: PO Box 130 Morrilton AR 72110

JOHNSON, BOINE THEODORE, instruments company executive, mayor; b. N.Y.C., Dec. 17, 1931; s. Boine Theodore and Emma (Hall) J.; children: Boine Theodore III, Marc Ian, Jordan James, Jann Louise; m. Kathleen Piaggesi, July 11, 1992. BA cum laude, Williams Coll., 1953; MBA with high distinction (Baker scholar), Harvard, 1958. Instr. Harvard Bus. Sch., 1958-59; asst. to dir. corporate planning AMF Corp., N.Y.C., 1959-62; mgr. mgmt. cons. div. Commonwealth Services Inc., N.Y.C., 1962-66; mgr. corporate planning Gen. Electric Co., 1966-68; sr. v.p. corporate devel., gen. mgr. chem. div. Technicon Corp., Tarrytown, N.Y., 1968-79; v.p. Perkin Elmer Corp., Norwalk, Conn., 1979-81; v.p., gen. mgr. Capintec, Inc., Montvale, N.J., 1981-82; pres. Voland Corp., Hawthorne, N.Y., 1982-88; pres., chmn. Texture Techs. Corp., Scarsdale, N.Y., 1988—. Dir. Datamedic, Inc., Peoples Bank for Savs. of New Rochelle, Meditron, Inc. Trustee, mayor Village of Scarsdale, N.Y., 1971-77; bd. dirs., vice chmn. Westchester County Assn. Served to lt., C.E. USNR, 1953-56. Mem. Sci. Apparatus Makers Assn., Theta Delta Chi (trustee edn. found. 1968-72, pres. Founders' Corp. 1966-87, pres. grand lodge 1969-71), Williams Club, Amateur Comedy Club (N.Y.C.), Town Club (Scarsdale), St. Botolph Club (Boston). Republican. Presbyterian. Home and Office: 18 Fairview Rd Scarsdale NY 10583-2136

JOHNSON, BRAD, football player; b. Marietta, Ga., Sept. 13, 1968; m. Nikkie Johnson. Postgrad in phys. edn., Fla. State Univ. Quarterback Tampa Bay Buccaneers, 2001—, Wash. Redskins, 1999—2000, Minn. Vikings, 1992—98. Involved Muscular Dystrophy Assn., Children's Miracle Net., Children's Hosp., Toys for Tots. Achievements include one of the most accurate passers in NFL history. Office: Tampa Bay Buccaneers 1 Buccaneers Pl Tampa FL 33607-

JOHNSON, BRIAN KEITH, electrical engineering educator; b. Madison, Wis., Mar. 11, 1965; s. Alton Cornelius and Virginia Rae (Korener) Johnson; m. Elizabeth M. Williams, Jan. 3, 1998; children: Erica Pearl, Mark Macrae. BS, U. Wis., 1987, MS, 1989, PhD, 1992. Registered profl. engr., Wis., Idaho. Teaching asst. U. Wis., Madison, 1988, rsch. asst., 1988-92; engr. Lawrence Livermore Nat. Labs., Livermore, Calif., 1989; asst. prof. U. Idaho, Moscow, 1992-97, assoc. prof., 1997—. Instr. Coll. Engring. Tchg. Asst. Tng., U. Wis., Madison, 1988, Engring. profl. devel., 1992-98; co-advisor Iron Cross Leadership Soc., Madison, 1988-92, U. Idaho IEEE Student Chpt., 1995—; dir. Western Virtual Engring., 1996-99. Lodge chief Order of the Arrow, Boy Scouts Am., 1982-84, dir. Brownsea Double 2Course, Madison, 1987, advisor, 1990-92. Recipient Vigil Hon. Membership, Order of the Arrow, Boy Scouts Am., 1988, Leadership award, Exploring Boy Scouts Am., 1986, Outstanding Young Faculty award U. Idaho Coll. Engring., 1995. Mem. IEEE (chair working group on utility applications of supercondrs. 1999—, sec. IEEE working group on modeling and simulation of distributed resources, 2001—, mem. AdCom intelligent transp. systems coun., ITS coun.), Am. Soc. Engring. Edn., Internat. Coun. on Large Electric Sys. Lutheran. Avocations: cross country skiing, bicycling, backpacking. Office: U Idaho Dept Elec Engring Moscow ID 83844-0001

JOHNSON, BRUCE, engineering educator; b. Hawarden, Iowa, Sept. 4, 1932; s. York and Dorothy Ellen (DeBruce) J.; m. Dorothy Jane Rylander, Aug. 27, 1955; children: Sharon Hilgart, Kristen Aiken. BS in Mech. Engring., Iowa State U., 1955; MS in Mech. Engring., Purdue U., 1962, PhD, 1965. Instr. U.S. Naval Acad., Annapolis, Md., 1957-59, assoc. prof., 1964-70, project dir. model basin, 1968-76, prof., 1970-99, Naval Sea Systems Command prof. hydrodynamics, 1975-87, dir. Hydromechanics Lab., 1976-87, dir. ocean engring. program, 1996-99, dir. spl. projects hydromechanics lab., 2000—, prof. emeritus, 2001—. Instr. Purdue U., 1959-64; chmn. 18th Am. Towing Tank Conf., 1977, U.S. Rep. Info. Com. Internat. Towing Tank Conf., 1975-84, chmn. symbols and terminology group, 1985-99, editor, pub. ITTC Symbols and Terminology List, 1996—. Author: (with T. Gillmer) Introduction to Naval Architecture, 1982, (with D. Newman) Engineering Economic Analysis, 1994; editor: (with B. Nehrling) Proc. of 18th Am. Towing Tank Conf., 1977; contbr. articles to profl. publs. Trustee Bauman Bible Telecasts, 1970-93, fin. chmn., 1990-93; mem. Bowie State U. Found., 1995-97. Served with USN, 1955-59.

Recipient award for excellence in engring. teaching Western Electric Fund, 1971, Navy Meritorious Civilian Svc. award, 1994, 96, Navy Superior Civilian Svc. award, 1998, 00, Svc. Excellence award Naval Acad. Alumni Assn., 1998, Meritorious Pub. svc. award USCG, 2002; Ford Found. grantee, 1962-64. Fellow Soc. Naval Archs. and Marine Engrs. (chmn. Chesapeake Sailing Yacht Symposium 1985, 87, chmn. electronic media com. 2000—, exec. com. 2000—, chmn. fishing vessel ops. and safety panel 2001—); mem. ASME, Am. Soc. Naval Engrs. (chmn. scholarship com. 1983-89, nat. coun. 1986-88, 89-91), Md. Capital Yacht Club (bd. dirs. 1986-93, commodore 1992), Naval Acad. Sailing Squadron, Chesapeake Bay Yacht Racing Assn. (pres. 1990). Methodist. Achievements include rsch. in naval architecture, hydrodynamics. Home: 7101 Bay Front Dr Apt 523 Annapolis MD 21403 Office: Dept Naval Architecture and Ocean Engring US Naval Acad Annapolis MD 21402 E-mail: aronj@bellatlantic.net.

JOHNSON, BRUCE ALLAN, engineering executive; b. Lakeview, Mich., Sept. 12, 1965; s. Bruce Allan Johnson and Margaret (Hedrick) Henderson; m. Kimberly Catherine Sis, Sept. 1996; children: Lyndsy Brianna Autumn, Torin Allan. BJME, Mich. Technol. U., 1988; BS in Mech. Engring., Mich. Tech. U., 1995; BA in Internat. Bus., Kirkwood Coll., 1996; BSBA, Shelborne U., 2001. Project engr. Post Cereals, Battle Creek, Mich., 1988-90; sr. project engr. Sara Lee Corp., Zeeland, Mich., 1990-93; project mgr. Coastline Projects, Holland, Mich., 1993-96; dir. engring. R&D Conagra, Greeley, Colo., 1996-98; dir. advanced steel tech. Perceptron, Ft. Collins, Colo., 1998—2003; dir. sales, mktg. Merilab Inc., Englewood, Colo., 2003—. Holder 5 patents in field. Mem. JME, SAE, Am. Soc. Heating, Refrigeration, Air Conditioning Engring., Iron and Steel Soc., Am. Meat Inst. (bd. dirs. 1998—). Republican. Avocations: skiing, boating, scuba diving, racquetball, sand volleyball. Office: Perceptron 3307 S College Ste 313 Fort Collins CO 80525

JOHNSON, B(RUCE) CONNOR, biochemist, educator, consultant; b. Regina, Sask., Can., Apr. 28, 1911; came to U.S., 1937; s. Wilfred Connor and Edna Pearl (Young) J.; m. Elizabeth Marie Peterson, Sept. 1, 1940 (div.); children: Bruce Connor II, Peter Young, Stephen Paine, Elizabeth Carter (dec.), Christina Marie; m. Halina Victoria Bogdanska, Oct. 25, 1966; 1 child, Margaret Edna. BA in Chemistry, McMaster U., 1933, MA in Chemistry, 1934; PhD in Biochemistry, U. Wis., 1940. Chemist Can. Canners, Hamilton, Ont., 1934-37; DuPont fellow U. Ill., Urbana, 1940-42; rsch. biochemist Golden State Co., San Francisco, 1942-43; from asst. prof. to assoc. prof. U. Ill., Urbana, 1943-51, prof. biochemistry, 1951-65; prof., head dept. biochemistry and molecular biology U. Okla. Health Scis. Ctr., Oklahoma City, 1965-79, prof., 1979-82, prof. emeritus, 1982—; disting. career scientist Okla. Med. Rsch. Found., Oklahoma City, 1982—. Rsch. scientist Inst. de Chimie Biologique, U. Strasbourg, France, 1971; mem., head biochemistry sect. Okla. Med. Rsch. Found., Oklahoma City, 1966-73, head vitamins and nutrition rsch., 1973-81; rsch. scientist dept. pediats. Coll. Medicine, U. South Fla., St. Petersburg, 1985-87; mem. nutrition study sect. NIH, 1962-66; cons. Can. Sci. Svc., Winnipeg, Man. and Ottawa, Can., 1952, 64, Armour & C., Cen. Rsch. Labs., Chgo., 1957-63, Agrl. Rsch. Coun., Fedn. Rhodesia and Nyasaland, 1962, N.Mex. State U., Las Cruces, 1975, others; ofcl. U.S. del. Pres. Eisenhower's 2d Atoms for Peace Mission to S.Am., 1956, 2d UN Atoms for Peace Conf., Geneva, Switzerland, 1958, USAF, Dept. of Def. Symposium on Arctic Biology and Medicine, Fairbanks, Alaska, 1965, White House Conf. on Food and Nutrition, Washington, 1969, others; invited participant to numerous symposia including Gordon Conf. on Vitamins & Metabolism, New London, N.H., 1956, Workshop on Vitamin K Function, Internat. Nutrition Congress, San Diego, 1981, Internat. Conf. on Post-Translational Covalent Modification of Proteins for Function, Oklahoma City, 1982; U.S. State Dept. del. OEEC-Paris, 1958, SEAMEO, Jakarta, Indonesia, 1974. Author: Methods of Vitamin Determination, 1948; editor: Post-Translational Modifications of Proteins, 1983; contbr. chpts. to 25 books, 1955-86; mem. editl. bd.: Jour. Nutrition, 1966-70; mem. sci. adv. bd.: Nat. Vitamin Found., 1953-56; contbr. numerous papers on nutrition and biochemistry to profl. publs. Pres. 1st Unitarian Ch. Oklahoma City, 1972, Alliance Française d'Oklahoma City, 1980. Recipient Nutrition Coun. award Am. Feed Mfrs. Assn., 1960, Purkyne medal Czech Acad. Sci., 1969, Osborne and Mendel award Am. Inst. Nutrition, 1975; Guggenheim Found. fellow U. Reading, Eng., 1955, NSF sr. fellow Inst. de Chimie des Substances Naturelles, Nat. Ctr. Sci. Rsch., Gif-sur-Yvette, U. Paris, France, 1961-62, U. Uppsala, Sweden, 1962. Fellow: Am. Soc. Nutritional Scis.; mem.: Soc. Exptl. Biology and Medicine, Am.Chem. Soc., Am. Soc. Biochemistry and Molecular Biology, Biochem. Soc. (Gt. Britain), Endocrine Soc., Internat. Haemostasis and Thrombosis Soc., Am. Assn. Med. Colls., AAAS. Avocations: philately, ancient and world history, travel, canoeing. Office: Okla Med Rsch Found 825 NE 13th St Oklahoma City OK 73104-5005 Fax: (405) 271-3980. E-mail: connor-johnson@omrf.ouhsc.edu.

JOHNSON, BRUCE EDWARD HUMBLE, lawyer; b. Columbus, Ohio, Jan. 22, 1950; s. Hugo Edward and M. Alice (Humble) J.; m. Paige Robinson Miller, June 28, 1980; children: Marta Noble, Winslow Collins, Russell Scott. AB, Harvard U., 1972; JD, Yale U., 1977; MA, U. Cambridge, Eng., 1978. Bar: Wash. 1977, Calif. 1992. Atty. Davis Wright Tremaine LLP, Seattle, 1977—. Mem. oversight com. King County Gov. Access Channel, 1996—2001. Bd. dirs. Seattle Repertory Theatre, 1993—, pres., 1999-01; bd. dirs. Huntington's Dis. Soc. of Am., N.W. chpt., 2001—. Mem. ABA (tort and ins. practice sect., media law and defamation torts com. chair 1999-2000). Home: 711 W Kinnear Pl Seattle WA 98119-3621 Office: Davis Wright Tremaine LLP 2600 Century Sq 1501 4th Ave Seattle WA 98101-1688

JOHNSON, BRUCE MARVIN, English language educator; b. Chgo., Apr. 29, 1933; s. George A. and Elsie L. (Clausing) J.; m. Jean C. Kruger, June 29, 1957; 1 son, Abram. BA, U. Chgo., 1952, Northwestern U., 1954, MA, 1955, PhD, 1959. Instr. English U. Mich., 1958-62; asst. prof. English U. Rochester (N.Y.), 1962-68, assoc. prof., 1968-76, prof., 1976-92, prof. emeritus, 1992—, chmn. dept. English, 1981-84. Author: Conrad's Models of Mind, 1971, True Correspondence: A Phenomenology of Thomas Hardy's Novels, 1983. Sr. fellow NEH, 1974-75; fellow Guggenheim Found., 1977-78 Democrat. Home: Apt 407 16540 Heron Coach Way Fort Myers FL 33908-5523 Office: U Rochester Dept English Rochester NY 14627

JOHNSON, BRUCE ROSS, elementary education educator; b. La Porte, Ind., May 18, 1949; s. Egbert Johannes Daniel and Ruth Elvera (Johnson) J. BS, Ball State U., Muncie, Ind., 1971; ME, Valparaiso U., 1975; postgrad., Nat. Coll. Edn., Evanston, Ill., 1974, Beijing Normal U., 1988, Western Mich. U., U. Va., Ind. U. Purdue, Antioch U., Seattle, Calif State U. Cert. elem. sch. tchr., Ind. Vol. tchr. Peace Corps, St. Vincent, W.I., W.I., 1971-72; tchr. South Ctrl. Sch., Union Mills, Ind., 1972-76, 77—; tchr. gifted and talented Purdue U., 1995—, guest lectr. dept. edn., 1995—2002. Missionary tchr. Luth. Ch., Liberia, West Africa, 1976-77; vis. instr. U. London, 1974, U. Moscow, 1974, U. Paris, 1974; ednl. seminar China, 1988, Japan, 1990, Australia, 1993; guest lectr. dept. edn. Purdue U., 1995-2002. Contbr. articles to newspapers. Pres. People to People Internat., La Porte, Ind., 1981-83, trustee, Kansas City, Mo., 1983-88; bd. dirs. La Porte County Libr. Leasing Corp., 1988—; mem. ch. coun. Bethany Luth. Ch., La Porte, 1983-86, 90-93; LaPorte County Bicentennial Commn., 1975-76; v.p. Friends of La Porte County Libr., 1984-86, pres., 1986-88; chmn. books and coffee meet the author series LaPorte County Pub. Libr., 1985—; trustee La Porte County Hist. Soc., 1985-92, 94—; v.p. N.W. Ind. Geneal. Soc., 1981-82; pres. Cmty. Concert Assn., La Porte, 1984; mem. Pan Am. Games Com., 1986-87; mem. steering com. La Porte County Spelling Bee, 1979-91, chmn., 1981, 85, 90, 99; LaPorte County Leadership, Inc., 1986-87; chmn. Miss. Valley coun. People-to-People, 1983-88; mem. bicentennial com. Bill of Rights, 1989-90; bd. dirs. LaPorte Literacy Coalition, 1997—2002. Named one of Outstanding Young Men Am., 1985, State finalist NASA Tchr.-in-Space project, 1985; Ind. State Tchrs. Assn. scholarship, 1970, Dean Earl A. Johnson Outstanding Svc. award Ball State U., 1971; cert. of merit Ind. Dept. Edn., 1985. Mem. NEA (life), Ind. State Tchrs. Assn., Amateur Music Club (pres. 1982-83), Little Theater Club (bd. dirs. 1980-83, 89-92), Lions (pres. 2000-01, bd. dirs. 1983—), Phi Delta Kappa (life). Avocations: performing in musical theater, collecting foreign coins, traveling, gardening. Home: 2012 Village Rd LaPorte IN 46350-7874 Office: South Cen Community Schs 9808 S 600 W LaPorte IN 46382-9600

JOHNSON, BRYN K. academic administrator, consultant; s. Dallas M. Johnson and Wilhelmina J. Niblett. BA, U. of Va., 1997; MBA, Kogod Sch. of Bus., Am. U., Washington, DC, 2001. Sr. banker Wachovia Bank, NA, Fairfax, Va., 1997—99; asst. br. mgr., banking officer F&M Bank- Peoples, Warrenton, Va., 1999; sr. adminstrv. asst. Kogod Sch. of Bus., Am. U., Washington, 2000—01; mng. ptnr., cons. IDChange (Implementing Devel. Change), LLC, Fairfax, Va., 2001—02; asst. dir. ctr. for tchg. excellence Am. U., Washington, 2002—. Bd. dirs., treas., consulting Project Hope Internat., Annapolis, 2001—; cons. Ecnorrot, LLC, Reston, Va., 2003—. Mem.: AF & A Masons.

JOHNSON, C. NICHOLAS, dance company executive; b. Jan. 15, 1955; MFA in Dance/Drama, U. Ariz.; studied with, Stefan Niedzialkowski, Frank Hatchett, Richard Levi, De Marco, N.Y.C. Assoc. artistic dir. Goldston & Johnson Sch. of Mimes; chief officer Mid-Am. Dance Theatre, Wichita, Kans.; asst. prof., dir. dance, modern dance, jazz, mime Coll. Fine Arts Wichita State U. Freelance tchr., dir., choreographer and performer various U.S. ballet schs. and univs. Performer Marcel Marceau World Ctr. Mime, Invisible People Mime Theatre, Internat. Children's Theatre Festival, Hong Kong. Kans. Arts Commn. fellow, 1999. Office: Wichita State U Sch Performing Arts-Dance PO Box 101 Wichita KS 67260-0001 E-mail: johnson2@twsuvm.uc.twsu.edu.

JOHNSON, C. TERRY, lawyer; b. Bridgeport, Conn., Sept. 24, 1937; s. Clifford Gustave and Evelyn Florence (Terry) J.; m. Suzanne Frances Chichy, Aug. 24, 1985; children: Laura Elizabeth, Melissa Lynne, Clifford Terry. AB, Trinity Coll., 1960; LLD, Columbia U., 1963. Bar: Ohio 1964, U.S. Ct. Appeals (6th cir.) 1966, U.S. Dist. Ct. (so. dist.) Ohio 1970. Legal dep. probate ct. Montgomery County, Dayton, Ohio, 1964-67; head probate dept. Coolidge Wall & Wood, Dayton, 1967-79, Smith & Schnacke, Dayton, 1979-89, Thompson, Hine and Flory, Dayton, 1989-92; head estate planning and probate group Dayton office Porter, Wright, Morris & Arthur, Dayton, 1992—. Frequent lectr. on estate planning to various profl. orgns. Contbr. articles to profl. jours. Fellow Am. Coll. Trust and Estate Counsel; mem. Ohio Bar Assn. (bd. govs. estate planning, trust and probate law sect., chmn. 1993-95), Dayton Bar Assn. (chmn. probate com. 1992-94), Ohio State Bar Found. (trustee 1995-2000), Ohio CLE Inst. (trustee 1995-99, chair 1998-99), Dayton Legal Secs. Assn. (hon.), Dayton Bicycle Club. Home: 8307 Rhine Way Centerville OH 45458-3017 Office: Porter Wright Morris & Arthur 1 S Main St Ste 1600 Dayton OH 45402-2028 E-mail: ctjohnson@porterwright.com.

JOHNSON, CAGE SAUL, hematologist, educator; b. New Orleans, Mar. 31, 1941; s. Cage Spooner and Esther Georgianna (Saul) J.; m. Shirley Lee O'Neal, Feb. 22, 1968; children: Stephanie, Michelle. Student, Creighton U., 1958-61, MD, 1965. Intern U. Cin., 1965-66, resident, 1966-67, U. So. Calif., 1969-71, instr., 1971-74, asst. prof., 1974-80, assoc. prof., 1980-88, dir. Comprehensive Sickle Cell Ctr., 1991—, prof., 1988—. Chmn. adv. com. Calif. Dept. Health Svcs., Sacramento, 1977—; dir. Hemoglobinopathy Lab., L.A., 1976—; bd. dirs. Sicke Cell Self-Help Assn., L.A., 1982-86. Contbr. numerous articles to profl. jours. Dir. Sickle Cell Disease Rsch. Found., L.A., 1986-94; active Nat. Med. Fellowships, Inc., Chgo., 1979—; chmn. rev. com. NIH, Washington, 1986-91; chmn. adv. coun., 1995-97, mem. adv. coun., 1997-2002. Major U.S. Army, 1967-69, Vietnam. Fellow N.Y. Acad. Scis., Am. Coll. Angiology; mem. Am. Soc. Hematology, Am. Fedn. Clin. Rsch., Western Soc. Clin. Investigation, Internat. Soc. Biorheology, E.E. Just Soc. (sec.-treas. 1985-93, pres. 1994-95, sec. 1996—). Avocation: restoring antique automobiles. Office: 2025 Zonal Ave Los Angeles CA 90089-0110

JOHNSON, CANDICE ELAINE BROWN, pediatrics educator; b. Cin., Mar. 21, 1946; d. Paul Preston and Naomi Elizabeth Brown; m. Thomas Raymond Johnson, June 30, 1973; children: Andrea Eleanor, Erik Albert. BS, U. Mich., 1968; PhD Microbiology, Case Western Reserve U., 1973, MD, 1976. Diplomate Am. Bd. Pediat., 1981. Intern, resident in pediat. Rainbow Babies and Children's Hosp./Met. Gen. Hosp., Cleve., 1976-78; fellow in ambulatory pediatrics Met. Gen. Hosp., 1978-79; asst. prof. pediat. Case Western Res. U., Cleve., 1980-90, assoc. prof., 1990-97; prof. pediat. U. Colo., Denver, 1997—; pediatrician Children's Hosp., Denver, 1997—. Mem. rev. panel NIH, Washington, 1993; faculty sen. Case Western Res. U., 1988-91. Contbr. articles profl. jours. Mem. Am. Acad. Pediat., Pediat. Infectious Disease Soc., Soc. for Pediatric Rsch., So. Utah Wilderness Alliance, Sierra Club. Home: 2290 Locust St Denver CO 80207-3943 Office: Child Health Clinic B032 1056 E 19th Ave Denver CO 80218-1007 E-mail: johnson.candice@tchden.org.

JOHNSON, CARL FREDERICK, marriage and family therapist; b. July 18, 1947; BA in Psychology, Northwestern U., 1969; MA in Clin. Psychology, Ga. State U., 1975. Lic. marriage and family therapist, Ga. Grad. tchg. asst. Ga. State U., Atlanta, 1972-73; family therapist Bridge Family Ctr., Atlanta, 1973-80; pvt. practice The Family Workshop, Atlanta, 1979—. Adj. instr. Dekalb C.C., Clarkston, Ga., 1981-82; appointee Ga. Composite Bd. Profl. Counselors, Social Workers and Marriage and Family Therapists, 1985-93; exec. dir. Ga. Assn. Marriage and Family Therapy, Atlanta, 1997—. Contbr. articles to profl. jours. Fellow: Am. Assn. for Marriage and Family Therapy (Divsnl. Contbn. award 1993, Outstanding Contbn. to Marriage and Family Therapy award 2001); mem.: Assn. Marital and Family Therapy Regulatory Bds. (founder, pres. 1987—91, coord. devel. nat. licensing exam in marital and family therapy 1989—92), Ga. Assn. for Marriage and Family Therapy (chair legis. affairs com. 1980—85, 1993—95, Outstanding Contbn. award 1983, 1985, 1993, Lifetime Achievement/Disting. Svc. award 1996). Home: 751 N Parkwood Rd Decatur GA 30030-5023 Office: Family Workshop Ste 410 2957 Clairmont Rd NE Atlanta GA 30329-1647

JOHNSON, CARL RANDOLPH, chemist, educator; b. Charlottesville, Va., Apr. 28, 1937; BS, Med. Coll. Va., 1958; PhD in Chemistry, U. Ill., 1962. NSF rsch. fellow chemistry Harvard U., 1962; from asst. to prof. chemistry Wayne State U., Detroit, 1962—90, Disting. prof., 1990—2001, chair dept. chemistry, 1997—2001, Disting. prof. emeritus, 2002—. Humboldt sr. scientist, 1991; bd. dirs. Organic Syntheses, Inc. Mem. adv. bd.: Jour. Organic Chemistry, 1976—81. Alfred P. Sloan fellow, 1965-68. Mem. Am. Chem. Soc. (assoc. editor jour. 1984-89, Harry and Carol Mosher award 1992, Arthur C. Cope Sr. Scholar award 2002). Achievements include research in organic sulfur chemistry, especially sulfoxides and sulfoximines, exploratory synthetic chemistry, synthesis of compounds of potential medicinal activity, organometallic chemistry, synthesis of natural products, enzymes in synthesis. Office: Wayne State Univ Dept Chemistry Detroit MI 48202 E-mail: crj@chem.wayne.edu.

JOHNSON, CAROLE JEAN, b. Temple, Tex., June 5, 1959; d. Lloyd Melvin Johnson and Shirley Faye (Bruss) Druley; 1 child, James Adam. AA, NE Wis. Tech. Coll., 1988. Bookkeeper, sec. White House Music, Waukesha, Wis., 1976-77; acct. Lamplight Farms, Brookfield, Wis., 1979; prodn. clk. W.A. Krueger, Brookfield, Wis., 1979-80; data processing asst. Video Images, West Allis, Wis., 1980-85; adminstrn. asst. Jones Intercable, Brookfield, 1985; computer programmer Anamax Corp., Green Bay, Wis., 1988-89; quality assurance analyst Nielsen Mktg. Rsch., Green Bay, Wis., 1989; applications programmer N.E. Wis. Tech. Coll., Green Bay, 1990—95; programmer/analyst Fabry Glove & Mitten Co., Green Bay, 1995-96; tech. svcs. mgr. Technology Cons. Corp., Green Bay, 1996—2001; pres. Strategic Property Investments, Thornton, Colo., 2001—. Roman Catholic. Office: 4011 E 129th Way Thornton CO 80241

JOHNSON, CAROLE A. writer, artist; b. L.A., Calif., Nov. 19, 1952; d. Wilson Henry and Beverly Boswell Albertson; m. Alan Norman O'Kain, Apr. 1976 (div. Aug. 1984); m. Geary Francis Johnson, May 14, 1985. Student, San Diego State U., 1972; BA, UCLA, 1974; student, L.A. Sch. for Bus., 1974—76. Receptionist/sec. Kaufman & Broad Home Sys., L.A., 1974—76; mgr. for prodn. and sales Melles Griot Indsl. Lenses, New Port Beach, Calif., 1976—82; leasing sec. Santa Anita Devel. Corp, Newport Beach, Calif., 1982—84; law sec. Geary F. Johnson, Esq., Pacific Palisades, Calif., 1986—88; sec./receptionist MacGuard Security, Pacific Palisades, Calif., 1990—94. Author: (poetry in 22 anthologies) in Nat. Libr. Poetry (Best Elite Poets, 2000, 2001, 2002), (short stories) Tickled By Thunder (Yr.'s Best Fiction, 1997), of numerous editls., novels; writer: of numerous songs. Recipient Bronze medallion, Internat. Libr. of Poetry, Pres.'s award for Lit. Excellence, Iliad Press, Twelve Editor's Choice, Internat. Libr. of Poetry, Best Outstanding Poets, Amherst Soc., 1999, Outstanding Achievement in Poetry Silver award Cup. Mem.: Am. Screenwriters Assn., Songwriters Am., Internat. Soc. Poets, Newport Beach Jr. League Calif., UCLA Alumnus, Nat. Authors Registry, Nat. Charity League, Assistance League Calif., Nat. Home Gardening Club. Avocations: photography, needlework. Home: 6413 Firebrand St Los Angeles CA 90045-1208

JOHNSON, CAROLYN A. retired computer specialist; b. Macon, Ga., Oct. 5, 1941; d. Clair Warren and Leone (Powell) J. BA, U. Utah, 1964; MSA, George Washington U., 1973. Cert. data processor. Part-time sec. Navy Fed. Credit Union, Washington, 1960-64; sec. U. Minn., Mpls., 1964-67; computer specialist Dept. of Army, Washington, 1968-98; ret. E-mail: carolyn20003@aol.com.

JOHNSON, CAROLYN JEAN, retired law librarian; b. Beaver Dam, Wis., Nov. 7, 1938; d. Henry William and Bernice Mae (Haas) Krueger; m. Robert Edward Johnson, June 19, 1960; children: Eric Steven, Kristin Elizabeth. BS in Edn., Wartburg Coll., 1960. Tchr., various locations, 1960-64, Hennepin County Library, 1972-81; libr. 3M Tech. Libr., St. Paul, 1981-86; law libr. 3M Ctr. Law Libr., St. Paul, 1986-2000; ret., 2000. Mem. Am. Assn. Law Libraries, Minn. Assn. Law Libraries. Lutheran. Avocations: reading, walking, cooking.

JOHNSON, CAROLYN M. librarian, writer; b. Bklyn., Apr. 3, 1949; AA in Liberal Arts, Queensborough C.C., Bayside, N.Y., 1970; BA in English and Am. Lit., Hunter Coll., 1973; M Libr. and Info. Sci., St. John's U., Jamaica, NY, 1975, MA in English and Am. Lit., 1980. Cataloging libr. Pace U. Libr., N.Y.C., 1978—79, N.Y. Bot. Garden Libr., Bronx Park, NY, 1979—81; libr., web rschr., writer Greenwood Press, Westport, Conn., 1980—2002, Librs. Unltd. divsn. Greenwood Pub. Group, Westport, 2002—. Online libr., ednl. writer THE BOOK BAG on Am. Online, N.Y.C., 1996—2001; web site rschr., evaluator, site summary writer studyweb.com, San Diego, 1999—2000; web site evaluator Ctr. for Montessori Tchr. Edn., White Plains, NY, 1997—99. Author: Discovering Nature with Young People: An Annotated Bibliography and Selection Guide, 1987, Using Internet Primary Sources to Teach Critical Thinking Skills in the Sciences, 2003; contbr. articles to profl. jours., articles to lit. mags. Mem.: Soc. Children's Book Writers and Illustrators. Avocations: photography, reading, genealogy, classical music. E-mail: WriterLibr@aol.com.

JOHNSON, CARYN See GOLDBERG, WHOOPI

JOHNSON, CHANNEY, elementary school educator; b. Chgo., Ill., Dec. 2, 1963; d. Mary Hampton and Michael Edgar Johnson; 1 child, Christina Flowers. BA, Grinnell Coll.; MS, Barry U.; EdD, Fla. Internat. U. Fla. Educator's Certificate Fla., 1986. Tchr. Miami-Dade County Pub. Schools, Fla., 1985—92, Mus. of Sci., Miami, 1987—88; asst. prin. Miami-Dade County Pub. Schools, Fla., 1992—98, prin., 1998—; adj. prof. Fla. Internat. U., 2002—. Cons. Barry U.-Annenberg Challenge, Miami Shores, Fla., 2001. Multicultural recruitment Grinnell Coll., Grinnell, Iowa, 1987—2003; campaign worker DNC, Miami, Fla., 2000—02; voters' registration vol. NAACP, Miami-Dade, Fla., 2000—01; accreditation com. New Birth Bapt. Ch., Miami, Fla., 1997—99, charter sch. com., 2001—03. Recipient Prin. of the Yr. Nominee, Dade Counseling Assn., 1998—99, Asst. Prin. of the Yr., Region Finalist, Miami-Dade County Pub. Schools, 1997—98, Tchr. of the Yr., Ludlam Elem. Sch., 1989—90; Delores Auzenne fellow, Fla. Internat. U., 1993—97, Citibank Tchr. Mini-grant, Citibank Success Fund, 1987—88. Mem.: Magnet Schools of Am., United Way Leadership Cir. (assoc.). Achievements include research in comparative study of high-achieving and low-achieving African-American students in an urban setting. Avocation: calligraphy. Home: 1651 NE 115 St #33C Miami FL 33181 Office: Caribbean Elementary School (M-DCPS) 11990 SW 200 St Miami FL 33177 Personal E-mail: doc63chan@aol.com. E-mail: cjohnson1@dadeschools.net.

JOHNSON, CHARLES BARTLETT, mutual fund executive; b. Montclair, N.J., Jan. 6, 1933; s. Rupert Harris and Florence (Endler) J.; m. Ann Demarest Lutes, Mar. 26, 1955; children: Charles E., Holly, Sarah, Gregory, William, Jennifer, Mary (dec.). BA, Yale U., 1954. With R.H. Johnson & Co., N.Y.C., 1954-55; pres. Franklin Distbrs., Inc., 1957-97; chmn., CEO, Franklin Resources, Inc., 1969—. Bd. dirs. various Franklin and Templeton Mut. Funds; bd. govs. Investment Co. Inst., 1973-88. Trustee Crystal Springs Uplands Sch., 1984-92; bd. dirs. Peninsula Cmty. Found., 1986-96, San Francisco Symphony, 1984-2002; bd. overseers Hoover Instn., 1993—. 1st lt. U.S. Army, 1955—57. Mem. Nat. Assn. Securities Dirs. (bd. govs. 1990-92, 96-98, chmn. 1992), Commonwealth Club of Calif. (bd. dirs. 1995-97). Office: Franklin Resources Inc One Franklin Pkwy San Mateo CA 94403-1906

JOHNSON, CHARLES DANIEL, radiologist; b. Boise, Idaho, Oct. 7, 1952; m. Therese Ann Petsche; 1 child, Kristina. BS, Coll. Idaho, 1975; MD, Mayo Med. Sch., 1979; MS, U. Minn., 1984. Resident in internal medicine Mayo Clinic, Rochester, Minn., 1979-81, resident in diagnostic radiology, 1979-84, sr. assoc. cons., 1986-90, from asst. to prof. radiology, 1990-97, prof. radiology, 1997—; assoc. diagnostic radiology Duke U., Durham, NC, 1984-86. Cons. virtual colonoscopy Nat. Cancer Inst., 1995, 96; corp. advisor radiography and fluoroscopy equipment GE, 1991-96, 98; prin. investigator Am. Coll. Radiology Imaging Network, NIH, 2000-; head sect. GI radiology, 1991-99, head body MRI, 2001-2003. Grantee, NIH, 1997—. Mem. Am. Coll. Radiology (chair colon cancer con. 1996, 97), Am. Roentgen Ray Soc., Radiol. Soc. N.Am., Soc. Gastrointestinal Radiologist (Traveling Fellowship award 1997). Office: Mayo Clinic 200 1st St SW Rochester MN 55905-0002

JOHNSON, CHARLES FLOYD, television executive, producer; b. Camden, NJ, Feb. 12; s. Orange Maull and Bertha Ellen (Seagers) J.; m. Sandra Brashears, June 4, 1966 (div. 1971); m. Anne Burford, June 18, 1983; 1 child, Kristin. BA, Howard U., 1962, JD, 1965; student, U. Del., 1960. Bar: D.C., 1968. Atty., advisor US Copyright, Washington, 1967-70; assoc. Howard Berg Law Offices, Wilmington, Del., 1970-71; prodn. coordinator Universal TV, Universal City, Calif., 1971-74, assoc. producer The Rockford Files and Baa Baa Black Sheep, 1974-76, producer The Rockford Files, Simon and Simon (pilot), Hellinger's Law, 1976-80, supervising producer Magnum P.I., 1982-86, co-exec. producer Magnum P.I., 1986-88, exec. producer Revealing Evidence, 1990; producer Bret Maverick Warner Bros. TV, Burbank, Calif., 1981-82; prod. Voices of Our People (In Celebration of Black Poetry) Sta. KCET/Pub. Broadcasting Sys., LA, 1981-82; co-exec. prodr. B.L. Stryker Blue Period Prodn., LA, 1988-90; co-exec. prodr. JAG Paramount Studios, LA, 1996—. Vice chmn. Media Forum, LA, 1980-85; bd. dir. Comm. Bridge, LA, 1981-89. Author: (bull.) Copyright & Developing Countries, 1967; co-author: Black Women in Television, 1990; co-exec. producer Quantum Leap, 1992-93, JAG, 1996—, (pilot) First Monday, 2001; exec. producer The Rockford Files movies, 1993-96, co-exec. Prod. Nary CIS pilot and series, 2003. Bd. dir. Ind. Video and Filmmakers, 1985-90, Kwanza Found., 1985—, Crossroads Theatre Acad., 1990-98, Mediascope, 1994—, Santa Clarita Film Festival, 1997—. With US Army, 1965-67. Recipient Stony Brook Coll. Preparatory award, 1979, Howard U. Alumni Assn. award, 1982, 85, Outstanding, Achievement Minorities in Broadcasting Award, 2000. Mem.: SAG, AFTRA, Am. Film Inst., Prodrs. Guild Am. (treas. 1996—98, sec. 1998—2001), Caucus for Prodrs., Writers and Dirs., Acad. TV Arts and Scis. (student activities com., Emmy award 1978, 1981, 7 Emmy nominations), Writers Guild Am., Omega Psi Phi (chpt. treas. 1961—62). Democrat. Methodist. Avocations: bicycling, traveling. Office: Sunset Gower Studios 1438 N Gower St Bldg 35 4th Fl Los Angeles CA 90038

JOHNSON, CHARLES L., II, military officer; BSCE, USAF Acad., 1972; MS in Engring. Adminstrn. and Law, George Washington U., 1976; grad., Air Command and Staff Coll., 1986, Air War Coll., 1991, Def. Sys. Mgmt. Coll., 1993; grad. in Exec. Devel., U. Ill., 1995. Commd. 2d lt. USAF, 1972, advanced through grades to maj. gen., 1999; UH-1N/CH-3E instr. pilot, chief scheduling and tng. 89th Mil. Airlift Wing, Andrews AFB, Md., 1973-78; AB-212 instr. pilot Joint DOD Helicopter Tech. Asst. Field Team Royal Saudi Air Force, Taif Air Base, Saudi Arabia, 1978-79; C-141 flight examiner, chief pilot, chief current ops. 60th Mil. Airlift Wing, Travis AFB, Calif., 1980-83; chief spl. actions and studies group Airlift and Trainers Sys. Program Office, Wright-Patterson AFB, Ohio, 1983-85; chief C-17 program divsn. Mil. Airlift Command, Scott AFB, Ill., 1986-90; mil. asst. to asst. sec. of Air Force for acquisition The Pentagon, Washington, 1991-92; comdr. 97th Ops. Group 97th Air Mobility Wing, Altus AFB, Okla., 1992-93; dir. C-141 Sys. Program Office Warner Robins Air Logistics Ctr., Robins AFB, Ga., 1993-96; program dir. C-17 Sys. Program Office Aero. Sys. Ctr., Wright-Patterson AFB, Ohio, 1996-99; dir.

logistics, Hdqrs. Air Mobility Command Scott AFB, Ill., 1999; dir. plans and programs, Hdqrs. Air Mobility command, 1999-2000; comdr. Okla. City Air Logistics Ctr., Tinker AFB, Okla., 2000—. Decorated Legion of Merit with one oak leaf cluster, Meritorious Svc. medal with 5 oak leaf clusters. Office: Tinker AFB / AFMC 3001 Staff Dr Tinker AFB OK 73145-3306 E-mail: charles.johnson@tinker.af.mil.

JOHNSON, CHARLES LAVON, JR., clinical neuropsychologist, consultant; b. Raleigh, N.C., Aug. 31, 1954; s. Charles Lavon Sr. and Edna Louise (Schaaf) J.; m. Janet Andrews, June 23, 1990. BA, N.C. State U., 1976, MS in Sociology, 1979, MS in Psychology, 1983; PhD, Fielding Inst., Santa Barbara, Calif., 1989. Lic. practicing psychologist. Instr., sch. psychologist N.C. State U., Raleigh, 1983-84; contractual psychologist Wake County Pub. Sch. System, Raleigh, 1985-86; clin. psychology intern John Umstead Hosp., Butner, N.C., 1988, staff psychologist, 1989; cons. psychologist Springmoor Life Care Retirement Community, Raleigh, 1988-90; sr. psychologist Dorothea Dix Hosp., Raleigh, 1989-91; contractual psychologist Cumberland County Pub. Sch. System, Fayetteville, N.C., 1989-91; cons. psychologist Disability Determination Svcs., Raleigh, 1991—; pvt. practice, 1990—. Cons. clin. neuropsychologist Coastal Plan Hosp., Rocky Mount, 1991-93, Tenth Jud. Dist. Juvenile Ct., Raleigh, 1990-91, Dartmouth Clinic, Southern Pines, N.C., 1990-92), clin. instr. dept. psychiatry U. N.C. Sch. Medicine, Chapel Hill, 1990-94. Contbr. articles to profl. jours. Mem. West Raleigh Citizens Adv. Coun., Raleigh, 1985-90. Avocations: music, golf, antiques. Office: Disability Determination PO Box 243 Raleigh NC 27602-0243

JOHNSON, CHARLES LESLIE, aerospace physicist, consultant; b. Ashland, Ky., Mar. 1, 1962; s. Charles Leslie and June Mays (Gesling) J.; m. Carol Elaine Peck, May 7, 1988; children: Carl Stuart, Leslie Arlene. BA in Chemistry and Physics, Transylvania U., 1984; MS in Physics, Vanderbilt U., 1986; grad., Internat. Space U., 1991. Rsch. physicist Gen. Rsch. Corp., Huntsville, Ala., 1986-90; aerospace physicist NASA-Marshall Space Flight Ctr., Huntsville, 1990-98; mgr. Interstellar Propulsion Rsch. NASA, Huntsville, Ala., 1998-2000, mgr. In-Space Transp. Techs., 2000—. Cons. Gen. Rsch. Corp., Huntsville, 1990-91; co-chmn. space symposium Tech. and Bus. Exhbn. and Symposium, 1994; chmn. STEDTRAIN (Sci. Tech. Edn. and Tng.) symposium, 1995. Tech. cons.: (motion picture) Lost in Space, 1998; contbr. articles to profl. jours. Deacon 1st Christian Ch., Huntsville, 1989-91. Named Profl. of Yr., Huntsville Assn. Tech. Socs., 1998. Mem. AIAA (chmn. space programs and techs. conf., advanced techs. and applications symposium 1996), Nat. Space Soc., World Future Soc. (pres. North Ala. chpt. 1998-99, prin. investigator propulsive small expendable deployer space experiment 1998—), Am. Geophysical Union. Republican. E-mail: lesjohnsonastp@yahoo.com.

JOHNSON, CHARLES MINOR, physicist; b. Nashville, May 31, 1923; s. Charles Minor and Ida Louise (Robertson) J.; m. Kathryn White, Oct. 8, 1948 (div. Sept. 1964); 1 child, Jane; m. Anne Keech Aubrey, Oct. 4, 1964; 1 child, Steven. B Engring, Vanderbilt U., 1945; PhD in Physics, Duke U., 1951. Sr. rsch. assoc. in radiation lab. Johns Hopkins U., Balt., 1955-56; sect. mgr. Rsch. Divsn. ECI, Balt., 1956-60; dir. Emerson Rsch., Silver Spring, Md., 1960-61; sr. project mgr. IBM, Bethesda/Yorktown, Md./N.Y., 1961-86; chief scientist Dept. Army/Safeguard System, Arlington, Va., 1967-73; prin. scientist ANSER, Arlington, 1986-88, MITRE, Arlington, 1988—. Mem. scientific advisory group Joint Strategic Planning Staff, Omaha, 1971-79; adv. bd. Ga. Tech. Rsch. Inst., Atlanta, 1980-85. Contbg. author: Radar Handbook (Skolnik), 1970; contbr. articles to profl. jours. and publs.; patentee in field. Recipient Founder's medal Vanderbilt U., Nashville, 1945, Outstanding Scientific Contbn. award U.S. Army, Arlington, 1973. Mem. IEEE (sr., life), Am. Phys. Soc. Avocation: tennis. Office: MDA/POET 7100 Defense Pentagon Washington DC 20301

JOHNSON, CHARLES OWEN, retired lawyer; b. Monroe, La., Aug. 18, 1926; s. Clifford U. and Laura (Owen) Johnson. BA, Tulane U., 1946, JD, 1969; LLB, Harvard U., 1948; LLM, Columbia U., 1955. Bar: La. 1949. Pvt. practice, Monroe, 1949-50; mem. law editl. staff West Pub. Co., St. Paul, 1953; atty. Office of Chief Counsel, IRS, Washington, 1955-79, chief Ct. Appeals br. Tax Ct. divsn., 1968-79. Author: (book) The Geneology of Several Allied Families, 1961. With AUS, 1950—52. Fellow: Samuel Victor Constant Soc.; mem.: SCV, S.R. (past pres. D.C. soc.), SAR (past pres. D.C. soc.), FBA, Va. Hist. Soc., Miss. Hist. Soc., Nat. Gavel Soc. (past treas., past pres.), Nat. Lawyers Club, La. Bar Assn., St. Nicholas Soc. City of N.Y., Va. Geneal. Soc., St. David's Soc. N.Y., Round Table Club of New Orleans, Harvard Club of Boston, Army and Navy Club Washington, Order of Scions of Colonial Cavaliers 1640-1660 (gov., founding gov.), Soc. Cin., Mil. Order Stars and Bars (past judge adv. gen.), Soc. Desc. Jersey Settlers, Huguenot Soc. La. (past pres.), Huguenot Soc. S.C., Sons and Daus. of Pilgrims (past treas., 2d dep. gov. gen.), Royal Soc. St. George, St. Andrew's Soc. Washington, Sons Union Vets, Nat. Soc. Desc. Early Quakers (past nat. presiding clk.), Soc. Colonial New Eng. (past gov. gen. nat. soc.), Soc. of 1812 (past pres. D.C. soc.), Soc. Colonial Wars (past dep. gov. D.C. soc., lt. gov., gov.), The Hereditary Order of the Families of the Pres. and First Ladies of Am. (founding mem.), St. David's Soc. of N.Y., Nat. Soc. Sons and Daus. of Antebellum Planters 1607-1861 (past pres. gen.), Sons and Daus. Colonial and Antebellum Bench and Bar 1565-1861 (founding pres. gen. 1994—98, past pres. gen.), Order Descs. Colonial Physicians and Chirurgiens (past. pres. gen.), Order First Families R.I. and Providence Plantations 1636-1647 (past gov. gen.), Hereditary Order First Families of Mass. (registrar gen.), Order First Families Miss. 1699-1817 (gov. gen. 1967—69), Order Founders and Patriots of Am. (past gov. D.C. and La. soc.), First Families of Ga. (past chancellor gen.), Hereditary Order Descs. Colonial Govs. (past gov. gen.), Soc. Descs. Colonial Clergy (past chancellor gen.), Order Ams. of Armorial Ancestry (past pres.), Soc. Descs. Old Plymouth Colony, Jamestowne Soc., Sons and Daus. of Province and Republic of West Fla. 1763-1810 (past gov.), La. Colonials. Home: Apt 809S 2111 Jefferson Davis Hwy Arlington VA 22202-3121 Home (Winter): Patrician Condominiums Apt 223 3450 S Ocean Blvd Palm Beach FL 33480

JOHNSON, CHARLES RICK, lawyer; b. Burke, SD, July 29, 1942; s. George Fielding and Corinne J. Johnson; m. Frances Ellen Driscoll, 1965; children: Stephanie, Sarah, George, Charlie. JD, U. SD, 1966. Bar: SD 1966, US Dist. Ct./SD 1966, US Ct. Appeals (8th cir.) 1966, US Supreme Ct. 1976. Assoc. Johnson Law firm, 1966—69; ptnr. Johnson & Johnson, 1969—71; sr. ptnr. Johnson, Eklund & Davis, Gregory, SD, 1971; lectr. in field. Contbr. articles. Mem.: SD Trial Lawyers Assn. (pres. 1976—77), SD Bar Assn. (pres. 1984—85), Am. Assn. Criminal Def. Atty., Am. Bd. Criminal Lawyers, Am. Bd. Trial Advocates, Assn. Trial Lawyers Am., ABA, Three Fingers of Red Eye Soc. (Gregory, SD), Phi Beta Kappa. Republican. Episc. Office: State Bar SD 405 Main St Gregory SD 57533-1639

JOHNSON, CHARLES WILLIAM, state supreme court justice; b. Tacoma, Wash., Mar. 16, 1951; BA in Econs., U. Wash., 1973; JD, U. Puget Sound, 1976. Bar: Wash. 1977. Justice Wash. Supreme Ct., 1991—. Co-chair Wash. State Minority and Justice Commn. Mem. bd. dirs. Wash. Assn. Children and Parents; mem. vis. com. U. Wash. Sch. Social Work, bd. visitors Seattle U. Sch. Law; liaison ltd. practice bd., co-chair BJA subcom. on juc. svcs.; mem. Am. Inns of Ct., World Affairs Coun. Pierce County. Mem. Wash. State Bar Assn., Tacoma-Pierce County Bar Assn. (Liberty Bell award young lawyers sect. 1994). Avocations: sailing, downhill skiing, cycling. Office: Wash State Supreme Ct 415 12th St W PO Box 40929 Olympia WA 98504-0929*

JOHNSON, CHERYL ANN, judge; b. Aurora, Ill., Sept. 30, 1946; d. Ellsworth Tower and Vava Vieda (Munson) Johnson; m. Gregory William Lasley, May 27, 1989. BS, Ohio State U., 1968; MS, U. Ill., Urbana, 1970; JD, John Marshall Law Sch., Chgo., 1983. Bar: Tex. 1984, Ill. 1984, U.S. Ct. Appeals (7th cir.) 1986, U.S. Dist. Ct. (we. dist.) Tex. 1991, cert.: Tex. Bd. Legal Specialization (in criminal law). Jud. clk. U.S. Ct. Appeals for 5th Circuit, 1983-84; pvt. practice Austin, 1984-98; judge Tex. Ct. Criminal Appeals, Austin, 1999—. Tutor Literacy Austin, 1997—99; active El Buen Samaritano Episcopal Mission, 2001—. Mem.: State Bar Coll. Office: Tex Ct Criminal Appeals Capitol Sta PO Box 12308 Austin TX 78711-2308

JOHNSON, CHERYL ELIZABETH, writer, publisher, educator; b. Grand Rapids, Mich, Aug. 3, 1952; d. Thomas Joseph and Lutricia Pat (Jones) Devine; m. Robert Dwayne Johnson, Jan. 19, 1972; children: Cherie Elizabeth, Marianne Roxie. AA, Alvin C.C., Tex., 1975; BS in Elem. Edn. summa cum laude, U. Houston, 1977. Elem. tchr. Pearland Ind. Sch. Dist., Tex., 1977-78, Santa Fe Ind. Sch. Dist., Tex., 1978-81, Alvin Ind. Sch. Dist., 1981-83; ind. writer, tchr. Alvin, 2001—03; cons. Tex. Assessment of Knowledge Skills, Alvin, 2001—03, Tex. Primary Reading Inventory, 2001—03. Cons. Tex. Assessment Skills, Alvin, 1983—, Criterion-Referenced Assessment Program for Tex., US Nat. Assessment Ednl. Progress, Norm-Referenced Vol. Assessment Program for Am., Tex. State Bd. of Ed. approval First Class Program, Tex.; founder Devine Ednl. Corp., Cheryl E. Devine Found., Inc. Author: Kids Excel Standardized Test Help: Every Student a Success, Read It, Hear It, Do It series, Read to Graduate, Teens Excel, Grades PK-12, 1983-2003, Video on CD-ROM & DVD; creator Sounds Fishy, A Fun Phonics Game, Go Fish for Initial, Sounds the English Letters Say, 56 Playing-Card ABC Wildlife Deck for Preschoolers and all Emergent-Readers, 1996, Phonograms, All the sounds of the English Language Are Found Inside Animal Names, 2000, Sounds Fishy Deck II, 2000 (114 cards, also on videocassette and CD-ROM and DVD, 2003) presents double the Phonetics Bd. in Texas State of Ed., state hist. of Texas Ed. Agency textbook adaption, according to TEA Reviewer #1, exclusively State Approved Phonetics Tutor Video, now on CD-ROM in Reading First program textbook kit. Founder Cheryl E. Devine Found., Inc., 2000. Avocations: reading, swimming, aerobic dancing, writing. Home and Office: PO Box 1115 Alvin TX 77512-1115 E-mail: DevineEdu@pdq.net.

JOHNSON, CHRISTINE ANN, nurse; b. Omaha, Nebr., Aug. 23, 1951; d. Ralph James and Marlene (Marlenee) Matney; m. Timothy Carl Johnson, Aug. 1, 1970; children: Erik Carl, Christine Nicole. Cert. practical nurse, Met. Tech. Community Coll., 1973; BA cum laude, Creighton U., 1989. LPN, Nebr.; cert. pregnancy exercise instr.; cert. lactation cons. EKG technician Bishop Clarkson Meml. Hosp., Omaha, 1971-74, lic. practical nurse, 1978—, instr. pregnancy exercise, 1984-86, instr. sibling preparation, 1985-86, instr. breastfeeding, 1985-95; LPN Cons. in Cardiology, P.C., Omaha, 1974-78; lactation cons. Bergan Mercy Med. Ctr., Omaha, 1994—. Tchg. asst. dept. psychology, child psychology, adolescent psychology, devel. psychology Creighton U., 1987-88. Assoc. editor (cons.' corner) Jour. Human Lactation, 1994-96. Sec. United Meth. Women First United Meth. Ch., 1984-85, chmn. 1985-86; vol. Radio Talking Book, 1985; mem. Omaha Pub. Schs. Superintendent's Task Force on Human Growth and Devel., 1986, Project Linus, 1997—; vol. Paws for Friendship, 1997 2002, Dresses for Humanity Durham Western Heritage Mus., Omaha, 1999, Therapy Dogs, Inc., 2002—. Mem. Internat. Lactation Cons. Assn., Psi Chi. Methodist. Home: 4618 N 129th Ave Omaha NE 68164-1708 Office: Bergan Mercy Med Ctr 7500 Mercy Rd Omaha NE 68124-2319

JOHNSON, CHRISTOPHER LAYNE, computer scientist, researcher; s. Ronald and Marcella Johnson. BA in Computer Sci., Baylor U., Waco, Tex., 1989—93; PhD in Computer Sci., Northwestern U., Evanston, Ill., 1993—99. Engr. Honeywell Tech. Ctr., Minneapolis, Minn., 1999—2000; sr. artificial intelligence engr. The MITRE Corp., McLean, Va., 2000—. Mem. Georgetown U. Symphony Orch., Washington, 2001—03, Northwestern U. Philharmonic, Evanston, Ill., 1993—98. Fellow, NSF, 1993—96. Mem.: Mortar Bd. Soc., Upsilon Pi Epsilon Honor Soc. Avocations: music, films. Office: MITRE Corp 7515 Colshire Dr McLean VA 22102-7508

JOHNSON, CHRISTOPHER RAY, medicine, computer science, mathematics, and bioengineering educator; b. Kansas City, Kans., Jan. 17, 1960; s. Raymond Lee Johnson and Sherlie (Steffans) Baker; m. Katharine A. Coles, Nov. 25, 1989. BS, Wright State U., 1982; MS, U. Utah, 1984, PhD, 1990. Asst. prof. physics Westminster Coll., Salt Lake City, 1985-89, assoc. prof. U. Utah, Salt Lake City, 1996—, disting. prof. dept. computer sci., 2002—, dir. sch. computing, 2003—, dir. scientific computing and imaging inst. Adj. assoc. prof. math. U. Utah, Salt Lake City, 1996—, rsch. assoc., 1996. Fellow Presdl. Faculty fellow, NSF, 1995. Mem. Am. Phys. Soc., N.Y. Acad. Sci., Engrs. in Medicine and Biology. Avocations: piano, mountain biking, reading, cross country skiing. Office: Sci Inst 3490 MEB U Utah Salt Lake City UT 84112

JOHNSON, CLARENCE RAY, minister; b. Port Arthur, Tex., Jan. 31, 1943; s. Ervin Ray and Mina Frances (Cox) J.; m. Betty Olene Mears, Nov. 22, 1962; children: Gregory Clarence, Garemy Kevin, Darren Kendall, Sherry Lynn. Ordained to ministry Ch. of Christ, 1962. Min. Hwy. 29 Ch. of Christ, Liberty Hill, Tex., 1962-63, Jonestown Ch. of Christ, Leander, Tex., 1963-70, Springhill (La.) Ch. of Christ, 1970-75, La Porte (Tex.) Ch. of Christ, 1975-84, Exton (Pa.) Ch. of Christ, 1984-91, Shiloh Ch. of Christ, Mexia, Tex., 1991-97, Susquehanna Ch. of Christ, Marietta, Pa., 1997—. Tchr., counselor Sabinal (Tex.) Bible Camp, 1978-80. Author: (with others) Is It Lawful?, 1989, Psalms to Sing, 1995, series of tracts, 1983-94, series of Bible study work books, 1995-97; news editor Gospel Guardian, 1971-73; contbr. articles to profl. jours. Trustee Liberty Hill Ind. Sch. Dist., 1968-70; panel mem. life issues seminar La. State U. Med. Coll., Shreveport, 1973. Republican. Home and Office: 323 W High St Elizabethtown PA 17022-2141 E-mail: clarencejohnson@comcast.net. *Your child's first concepts of his heavenly Father are almost certain to be based on what he has seen, heard, and experienced at the hand of his physical father. May God help us strike that delicate balance between strictness and mercy, and provide a loving, secure atmosphere where our children may properly grow "in wisdom and stature, and in favor with God and men".*

JOHNSON, CLARENCE TRAYLOR, JR., state judge; b. Trenton, Fla., Aug. 16, 1929; s. Clarence Traylor and Jessie Granade (Wilson) J.; m. Shirley Ann Traxler, Aug. 30, 1957; children: James Waring, Robert Dale, Douglas Earl, Jan Elizabeth. BSBA, U. Fla., 1955, JD, 1958. Ptnr. Cone, Wagner, Nugent, Johnson, McKeown & Dell, West Palm Beach, Fla., 1958-71; sr. cir. ct. judge 18th Jud. Cir. of Fla., Brevard and Seminole Counties, 1971-92. Chmn. Fla. Conf. of Cir. Judges, 1990-91; mem. Fla. Bench Bar Commn., State of Fla., 1990-92; faculty Fla. Jud. Coll., 1988-90; mem. Fla. Fed.-State Jud. Coun., 1989-91, Jud. Coun. Fla., 1989-91. Pres. Jr. C. of C., Cocoa, Fla., 1963-64; chmn. bd. Cen. Brevard YMCA, Cocoa, 1965-66; pres. YMCA, Brevard County, 1968-71, Rotary, Cocoa, 1965-66; charter pres. Vassar B. Carlton Am. Inn of Ct., 1992-93. With USAF, 1950-54. Recipient Disting. Svc. award Cocoa Jaycees, 1965, Jud. Achievement award Acad. Fla. Trial Lawyers, 1987. Mem. ABA, Brevard County Bar Assn. (pres. 1969-70), The Fla. Bar (bd. govs. 1970-71). Lutheran. Avocation: fishing. Home: 600 Heron Dr Merritt Island FL 32952-4022

JOHNSON, CLARK CUMINGS, lawyer, educator; b. Traverse City, Mich., Nov. 19, 1940; s. Harold Eugene and Mary Delight (Cummings) Johnson; m. Kerry Jane Spencer, May 1, 1990; children: Asher, James, Christopher, Spencer, Sterling, Iris. BA, U. Mich., 1963; JD cum laude, Wayne State U., 1970, MS, 1985, PhD, 1990; LLD (hon.), Mich. State U., 2002. Bar: Mich. 1970, U.S. Dist. Ct. (ea. dist.) Mich. 1970, U.S. Supreme Ct. 1974. Asst. atty. gen., Mich., 1970—71; ptnr. Schmidt, Nahas, Coburn & Johnson, Mount Clemens, 1971—74; prof. law Mich. State U., 1974—, assoc. dean, 1984—85. Home: 1687 Quarton Rd Birmingham MI 48009-1037 Office: Mich State U 83 E Shaw Ln East Lansing MI 48824-1300 E-mail: johns938@msu.edu.

JOHNSON, CLARK EVERETTE, JR., judge; b. Jacksonville, Ala., Oct. 2, 1923; s. Clark Everette and Nora Lee (Kelley) J.; m. Arlene Washam, Feb. 23, 1952; children: David Terrel, Paul T., Clark Everette III. BS in Commerce, U. Ala., 1947, LLB, 1948. Bar: Ala. 1948. Pvt. practice, Albertville, Ala., 1948-71; asst. dist. atty. Marshall County, 1952-53; cir. judge 27th Jud. Cir., Marshall County, 1971-88. Tchr. Sunday sch. local Meth. ch., 1950—; candidate for Ala. Ho. of Reps., 1958, 62. With AUS, 1943-46. Decorated Purple Heart. Mem. Ala. Bar Assn., Marshall County Bar Assn. Home: 5 Wright Rd Albertville AL 35951-4130

JOHNSON, CLARKE COURTNEY, financial consultant, educator; b. Wisconsin Rapids, Wis., July 11, 1936; s. Julius and Esther (Larsen) L. BSEE, U. Wis., 1958; MSIM, Purdue U., 1962, PhD, 1972. Asst. prof., asst. dean U. Wis.-Milw., 1966-72; vis. prof. Boston U. Sch. Mgmt., 1973-75; assoc. prof., assoc. dean DePaul U. Coll. Commerce, Chgo., 1975-77; prof., dean Iona Coll. Sch. Bus., New Rochelle, N.Y., 1977-79; prof. fin. Pace U. Grad. Sch. Bus., N.Y.C., 1979-98, chmn. dept., 1985-98, chmn. faculty coun. Sch. Bus., 1996 98; ret., 1998; pres. C. Johnson and Assocs., 1998—. Cons. in field Contbr. articles to profl. jours. Served with USAF, 1958-61. Mem. Am. Fin. Assn., Am. Econs. Assn., Fin. Mgmt. Assn., Eta Kappa Nu, Beta Gamma Sigma. Home: 333 E 79th St Apt 20Y New York NY 10021-0961 Office: 333 E 79th St Apt 20Y New York NY 10021-0961 E-mail: ckcjohnson@aol.com.

JOHNSON, CLAUDIA ANDERSON, psychologist, Jungian analyst; b. Duluth, Minn., June 15, 1940; d. Carl Engwald and Irma Rose (Seymour) Anderson; m. Giles C. Upshur Jr.; children: Jean Marie, Julie Ann. BA summa cum laude, U. Minn., 1968; MA, U. Utah, 1971, PhD, 1974. Surveyor Joint Commn. on Accreditation of Hosps. Orgn., Chgo., 1978-80; pvt. practice Roanoke, Va., 1981-91, Richmond, Va., 1991-97, Woodbridge, Va., 1997—. Quality assurance coord. VA Med. Ctr., Salem, Va., 1980-85; asst. prof. Med. Coll. Va., 1992-2000. Mem. Inter Regional Soc. Jungian Analysts (candidate rep. 1996-97). Avocations: reading, gardening, writing, fishing. Home: 8470 Creek St Franktown VA 23354

JOHNSON, CLIFTON HERMAN, historian, archivist, former research center director; b. Griffin, Ga., Sept. 13, 1921; s. John and Pearl (Parrish) Johnson; m. Rosemary Brunst, Aug. 2, 1960; children: Charles, Robert, Virginia. Student, U. Conn., 1943—44; BA, U. N.C., 1948, PhD, 1959; MA, U. Chgo., 1949; postgrad., U. Wis., 1951. Tutor LeMoyne Coll., Memphis, 1950—53, asst. prof., 1953—56, prof., 1960—61, 1963—66; asst. prof. East Carolina Coll., 1958—59; asst. libr. and archivist Fisk U., 1961—63; exec. dir. Amistad Rsch. Ctr., New Orleans, 1966—92, emeritus, 1992. Author (with Carroll Barber): The American Negro: A Selected and Annotated Bibliography for High Schools and Junior Colleges, 1968; author: A Legacy of La Amistad: Some Twentieth Century Black Leaders, 1989, Abolitionism in the Antislavery Movement, 1997; editor: God Struck Me Dead: Religious Conversions and Experiences and Autobiographies of Ex-Slaves, 1969. Exec. bd. dirs. All Congregations Together, 1997—; bd. dirs. La. World Expn., 1980—82, Lillie Carroll Jackson Mus., 1978—89, Countee Cullen Found., 1981—87, Friends of Archives La., 1978—90, La. Folklife Commn., 1982—85, Ctr. for Black Music Rsch., 1986—, New Orleans Urban League, 1994—; cons. DreamWorks Prodns., 1997. With AUS, 1940—45. NEH fellow, 1994. Mem.: Nat. Assn. Human Rights Workers, Orgn. Am. Historians, Assn. for Study Negro Life and History, Soc. Am. Archivists, So. Hist. Assn. E-mail: clifton@peak.org.

JOHNSON, CONOR DEANE, mechanical engineer; b. Charlottesville, Va., Apr. 20, 1943; s. Randolph Holaday and Louise Anna (Deane) J.; m. Laura Teague Rogers, Dec. 20, 1966; children: William Drake, Catherine Teague. BS in Engring. Mechanics, Va. Poly. Inst., 1965; MS, Clemson U., 1967, PhD in Engring. Mechanics, 1969. Registered profl. engr., Calif. With Anamet Labs., Inc., 1973-82, sr. structural analyst, 1973-75, prin. engr. San Carlos, Calif., 1975-81, v.p., 1981-82; program mgr. Aerospace Structures Info. and Analysis Ctr., 1975-82; co-founder, pres. CSA Engring., Inc., Mountain View, Calif., 1982—. Tech. dir. damping conf., exec. com. N.Am. Conf. on Smart Materials and Structures. Contbr. articles to profl. jours.; patentee in field. Capt. USAF, 1969-73 Mem. AIAA (structural dynamics tech. com.), ASME (adaptive structures tech. com., structures and materials award 1981), N.Am. Smart Structures and Materials Conf. (mem. exec. com., tech. chmn. Damping confs. 1991, 93, 95, 96), Gourmet Cooking Club, Sigma Xi. Methodist. Home: 3408 Beresford Ave Belmont CA 94002-1302 Office: CSA Engring Inc 2565 Leghorn St Mountain View CA 94043-1613

JOHNSON, CORNELIUS RAYMOND, assistant city attorney; b. Waco, Tex., Jan. 20, 1963; s. Virgil O. Howard and Beatrice Farline Johnson; m. Gay Lanell Pasley (div. Dec. 1999). AA, Tarrant County Jr. Coll., 1990; BS, Tex. Christian U., 1991; JD, U. Tulsa, 1995. Bar: Okla. 1996, U.S. Ct. Appeals (10th cir.) 1996, U.S. Dist. Ct. (no. and ea. dists.) Okla. 1997, U.S. Dist. Ct. (we. dist.) Okla. 1998, U.S. Supreme Ct. 2000. Assoc. atty. Law Firm of Riggs, Abney, Tulsa, 1996-99; asst. city atty. Tulsa City Atty.'s Office, Tulsa, 1999—. Bd. dirs. Leadership Tulsa, 1999. Maj. USAR. Mem. ABA, Okla. Bar Assn., Spl. Forces Assn., 1st Calvalry Divsn. Assn., 1st Infantry Divsn. Assn., Internat. Churchill Soc., Nat. Black Prosecutors Assn. Democrat. Unitarian Universalist. Avocations: weight lifting, jogging, reading, cooking, horseback riding. Office: Tulsa City Attys Office 200 Civic Ctr Tulsa OK 74103-3856

JOHNSON, CORWIN WAGGONER, law educator; b. Hamlet, Ind., Oct. 5, 1917; s. Lonnie Edmund and Nora Lee (Drake) J.; m. July 24, 1942; m. Evelyn Banks; children: Kent Edmund, Kirk Allan. BA, U. Iowa, 1939, JD, 1941; postgrad. (Sterling fellow), Yale U. Law Sch., 1941, 46. Bar: Iowa 1941, Calif. 1946, Tex. 1957. Spl. agt. FBI, Dept. Justice, 1942-46; instr. in law U. Iowa, 1946-47; asst. prof. law U. Tex., Austin, 1947-49, asso. prof., 1949-54, prof., 1954—. Co-author: Cases and Materials on Property, 8th edit., 2002, Principles of Property, 3d rev. edit., 1989; contbr. articles to law revs. Mem. Austin Planning Commn., 1954-56. Mem. ABA, Tex. Bar Assn., Am. Law Inst., Order of Coif, Phi Beta Kappa. Democrat. Methodist. Home: 3425 Monte Vista Dr Austin TX 78731-5722 Office: U Tex Law Sch 727 E Dean Keeton St Austin TX 78705-3224 E-mail: cwjohnson@mail.law.utexas.edu.

JOHNSON, CRAIG M. real estate development executive; BS, U. Ill., 1975; MBA, DePaul U., 1977. Sr. v.p. cmty. devel. U.S. Home Corp., Houston, 1995—; v.p. cmty. devel. Lennar Corp., Miami, Fla.; pres. Strategic Techs., Inc., Miami, Fla., 2002—. Office: US Home Corp 10707 Clay Rd Houston TX 77041-5497 E-mail: johnsoncr@ushome.com.

JOHNSON, CRAIG N. banking consultant; b. Warren, Pa., Jan. 8, 1942; s. Norman Andrew and Edice (Rieder) J.; m. Sally Van Dusen, May 23, 1969; children: Maria Pepper, Anna Sergeant, Samantha Bennett. BS, U. Pa., 1963, MBA, 1968. Cert. mgmt. cons. Inst. Mgmt. Cons. Prin. William E. Hill & Co. Inc., N.Y.C., 1968-72; v.p. INA Properties, Phila., 1972-75; sr. prin. Hay Assocs., Phila., 1975-80; pres. Lavino Shipping Co., Phila., 1980-90; pres., dir. Maritrans Inc., Phila., 1990-93; mng. dir., adv. dir. Glenthorne Capital Inc., 1994; chmn. Blair Corp., 2003—. Bd. dirs. The Phila. Contributorship, Blair Corp., chmn., 2003—; bd. dirs. Chestnut Hill Healthcare, Cathedral Village. Mem. Com. of Seventy, Phila., 1975-97; bd. dirs. Acad. Natural Scis., Phila.; trustee Springside Sch., 1994-98; assoc. trustee U. Pa., 1990-96. Repubican. Episcopalian. E-mail: craig.johnson74@verizon.net..

JOHNSON, CRAIG THEODORE, portfolio manager; b. Chgo., Oct. 1, 1955; s. C. Theodore and Dorothy (Lind) J.; m. Dianne Lee Eggen, Oct. 12, 1985; children: Juliana, Kyle. BSBA, Drake U., 1977. Asst. mgr., asst. buyer Marshall Field & Co., Chgo., 1977-80; asst. mgr. Wickes Cos., Wheeling, Ill., 1980-82; salesman John Hancock, Des Plaines, Ill., 1982-83; portfolio mgr. Leonetti & Assocs., Inc., Buffalo Grove, Ill., 1983—. Mem. Nat. Assn. Investors, World Future Soc. Republican. Lutheran. Avocations: reading, sports, gardening, astronomy. Office: Leonetti & Assocs Inc 1130 W Lake Cook Rd Ste 300 Buffalo Grove IL 60089-1976 E-mail: cjohnson@leonettiassoc.com.

JOHNSON, CRANE, writer, lawyer; b. Bayard, Nebr., June 30, 1921; s. Carl Arthur and Pearl (Haskins) J. MA, U. So. Calif., 1948; postgrad., Stanford U., 1949; PhD, Case We. Res. U., 1960; LLB, N.Y. Law Sch., 1960; LLM, NYU, 1968. Bar: N.Y., 1962. Vol. legal aid lawyer. Author: Past Sixty, 1953, Thirty-Five One Act Plays, 1967, Presque Isle Village, 1995, Three Jacumba Tales, 1998, Ten Stories, 1999, Twelve Jacumba Tales, 1999, Jacumba Heidi, 2000, Buckboard to Jacumba, 2001, Mountain Springs Saga, 2002. U.S. rep. at ednl. confs. in London and Vienna. Served with AUS, WWII. Mem. N.Y. Bar Assn. Address: PO Box 158 Jacumba CA 91934-0158

JOHNSON, CRYSTAL ELAINE, psychologist, community activist, poet, writer, educator; b. Springfield, Mass., Apr. 5, 1967; d. Stephen Harris and Carole Rence Johnson. BS, U. Mass., 1990; MS, Northeastern U., Boston, 1998. Case mgr., social worker Dept. of Social Svcs., Boston, 1990—92; supr. sch.-based svcs. Boston Cmty. Ctrs., 1992—95; exec. dir. Positive EDGE, City of Cambridge, Mass., 1999—. Cons. Blackout Arts Collective, Boston, 2000—, Critical Breakdown-AFSC, Cambridge, 2001—. Author: Soul Sister's Diary, A Collection of Short Stories and Poems, 2003. Mem. Reaching All Youth Com., 2000—. Home: 35 Tonawanda St Dorchester MA 02124 E-mail: cristyluv_99@yahoo.com.

JOHNSON, CURTIS DEAN, historian, educator; b. Duluth, Minn., July 16, 1949; s. Henry Walter and Alice Irene Johnson; m. Lita Anna Krievans, June 26, 1982. BS, Moorhead State U., 1972; PhD, U. Minn., 1985. Tchr. Hillcrest Luth. Acad., Fergus Falls, Minn., 1972—77; asst. prof. history Mount St. Mary's Coll., Emmitsburg, Md., 1985—91, assoc. prof. history, 1991—. Author: (book)

Redeeming America: Evangelicals and the Road to Civil War, 1993, Islands of Holiness: Rural Religion in Upstate New York, 1790-1860, 1989. Office: Mount Saint Mary's College Dept History Emmitsburg MD 21727

JOHNSON, CURTIS LEE, publisher, editor, writer; b. Mpls., May 26, 1928; s. Hjalmar N. and Gladys (Goring) J.; m. Jo Ann Lekwa, June 30, 1950 (div. 1974); children: Mark Alan, Paula Catherine; m. Rochelle Miller Hickey, Jan. 11, 1975 (div. 1980); m. Betty Axelrod Fox, Aug. 28, 1982 (div. 1990). BA, U. Iowa, 1951, MA, 1952. Mag. and ency. editing and writing, Chgo., 1953-60; textbook and ednl. editing and writing, 1960-66; editor, pub. December Press, 1962—, pres., 1985—; free-lance editing and writing, 1966-72, 78—; mng. editor Aldine Pub. Co., 1972-73; v.p. St. Clair Press, 1973-77; sr. writer Bradford Exchange, 1978-81; mng. editor Regnery Gateway, 1981-82. Author: (with George Uskali) How to Restore Antique and Classic Cars, 1954; novels Hobbledehoy's Hero, 1959, Nobody's Perfect, 1973, Lace and a Bobbitt, 1976, The Morning Light, 1977, Song for Three Voices, 1984; The Mafia Manager, 1991, (with R. Craig Sautter) Wicked City Chicago, 1994, Thanksgiving in Vegas, 1995, 500 Years of Obscene...and Counting, 1997; editor: (with Jarvis Thurston) Stories from the Literary Magazines, 1970, Best Little Magazine Fiction, 1970, (with Alvin Greenberg), 1971, (with Jack Conroy) Writers in Revolt, 1973, (with Diane Kruchkow) Green Isle in the Sea, 1986, Who's Who in Writers, Editors & Poets, 1985-2000; essays The Forbidden Writings of Lee Wallek, 1978, (with R. Craig Sautter) A Small Book of Martyrs, 2003; also fiction, articles; cons. editor: Panache mag, 1967-76. Served with USN, 1946-53. Nat. Endowment Arts writing grantee, 1973, 81 Mem. Nat. Writers Union, Phi Beta Kappa, Club d'Ronde. Office: December Press PO Box 302 Highland Park IL 60035-0302

JOHNSON, CURTIS LILDON, drilling engineer; b. La Mesa, Tex., May 11, 1922; s. William Marion and Annie Mary (Pearson) J.; married Feb. 21, 1945; children: Sarah Ann, Rebecca Sue, Richard Curtis. BBA, U. Tex., 1949, JD, 1948. Agt. Bur. Internal Revenue, Corpus Christi, Tex., 1949-50; civil svc. dir. NAS Hosp., Corpus Christi, 1950-51; wire line operator Otis Pressure Control, Corpus Christi, 1951-52; directional driller Houston Oil Field Material Co., Corpus Christi, 1952-60, dist. svc. mgr. Alice, Tex., 1960-64; v.p. svcs. D&W Oil Tools, Corpus Christi, 1964-67; owner, pres. Target Directional Drilling and Petroleum Cons., Corpus Christi, 1967-79, 80-85; v.p., ops. mgr. Goldston Oil Co., Houston, 1979-80; pres. J.O. Resources Devel. Co., Corpus Christi, 1985-93; acct. mgr., sales rep. Multi-Shot (a BWWC Co.), Corpus Christi, 1993—2003; ret. Sgt. USAF, 1942-45, PTO. Recipient award Pres. of Tunisia, 1980. Mem. Soc. of Petroleum Engrs., Internat., Corpus Christi Am. Petroleum Inst., Victoria Am. Petroleum Inst., Masons. Democrat. Avocations: golf, hunting, sports officiating.

JOHNSON, CYNDA ANN, physician, educator; b. Girard, Kans., July 16, 1951; BA in Biology and German with honors, Stanford U., 1973; MD, UCLA, 1977; MBA, U. Mo., Kansas City, 1999. Diplomate Am. Bd. Family Medicine (bd. dirs., pres. 1999-2000). Tchg. fellow U. N.C., Chapel Hill, 1980-81; intern U. Kans. Med. Ctr., Kansas City, 1977-78, 1978-80, prof., acting chair dept. family medicine, 1998—99; prof., head dept. family medicine U. Iowa Coll. Medicine, Iowa City, 1999—. Mem. Am. Acad. Family Physicians, Soc. Tchrs. Family Medicine, Iowa Acad. Family Physicians, Iowa Med. Soc. Office: U Iowa Coll Medicine 200 Hawkins Dr 01286-D PFP Iowa City IA 52242-1097 E-mail: cynda-johnson@uiowa.edu.

JOHNSON, CYNTHIA L(E) M(AE), lawyer; b. Detroit, Mar. 1, 1952; d. Robert Alexander and Frances Esedell (Peeples) J.; children: Alexandra, Lauren Gayle. BA, U. Mich., 1973, MPH, 1975; JD cum laude, Mich. State U., 1984. Bar: Mich. 1984, U.S. Dist. Ct. (ea. dist.) 1984, U.S. Supreme Ct. 1989; cert. mediator and arbitrator. Health planning asst. Charles R. Drew Postgrad. Sch. Medicine, L.A., 1974; dep. project dir. Mich. Health Maintenance Orgn. Plans, Detroit, 1975; sr. health program analyst N.Y. Health and Hosps. Corp., N.Y.C., 1975-77; health care cons. UAW, Detroit, 1977-84; jud. law clk. Mich. Ct. Appeals, 1984-86, Mich. Supreme Ct., 1986-87; ptnr. now Clark Hill, PLC, Detroit, 1987-2000; shareholder Couzens, Lansky, et al, P.C., 2000—. Chpt. treas. Jack N Jill Am.; bd. dirs. Mich. Metro Girl Scouts Coun., Ronald McDonald House of Detroit. Mem. ABA, Mich. Bar Assn., Am. Arbitration Assn. (cert.), Detroit Bar Assn., Wolverine Bar Assn., Delta Sigma Theta. Office: Couzens Lansky etal PC Penobscot Bldg 645 Griswold St Ste 1300 Detroit MI 48226-3202 Office Fax: 313-967-0344. Business E-Mail: cynthia.johnson@couzens.com.

JOHNSON, CYRUS EDWIN, grain farmer, former food products executive; b. Alton, Ill., Feb. 18, 1929; s. Cyrus L. and Jennie C. (Keen) J.; m. Charlotte E. Johnson; children: Judie M., Renee B. BS, U. Ill., 1956, MA, 1959. Dist. traffic mgr. Ill. Bell Telephone Co., Chgo., 1970-71, dist. comml. mgr., 1971-73; v.p. social action Gen. Mills, Inc., Mpls., 1973-78, v.p. dir. corp. personnel, 1978-80, v.p. human resource environment, 1980-81, v.p., dir. facilities and services, 1981-91; grain farmer Alton, Ill., 1977-91. Dir. Ault, Inc., Mpls., Life-Span, Inc., Mpls. 1982-88. Bd. dirs. United Way Mpls. Area, 1975-86; active Nat. YMCA, 1973-79; mem. citizens adv. com. Mpls. Tech. Inst., 1981-84; mem. deans adv. council Coll. Bus., U. Ill., Chgo., 1981-84; past pres. Harvard U. Bus. Sch. Assn., Boston, 1978-79; mem. adv. coun. div. bus. Bethune-Cookman Coll.; bd. dirs. Greater Mpls. area Girl Scouts U.S., 1983-90, nat. bd. dirs., 1990-99; bd. dirs. W.Va. State Coll. Found., 1989-91. Served with U.S. Army, 1950-52. Recipient Old Masters Program award Purdue U., 1975; recipient Chgo. Defender Roundtable of Commerce award, 1963 Mem.: Rotary; Masons. Baptist.

JOHNSON, D'ELAINE ANN HERARD, artist, consultant; b. Puyallup, Wash., Mar. 19, 1932; d. Thomas Napoleon and Rosella Edna (Berry) Herard; m. John Lafayette Johnson, Dec. 22, 1956. BA in Art Edn., Ctrl. Wash. U., 1954; MFA in Painting, U. Wash., 1958, postgrad., 1975, U. London, 1975. Instr. art Seattle Pub. Schs., WA, 1954-78; instr. Mus. History and Industry, Seattle, 1954-56; art dir., instr. Martha Washington Sch. for Girls, Seattle, 1955-58; instr. art workshops Seattle Pub. Schs., WA, 1960-70; dir. Mt. Olympus Estate, Edmonds, WA, 1971. Cons. art groups, Wash. State, 1954—; lectr. Ctrl. Wash. State U. Seattle PTA, Creative Arts Assn., Everett, Everett C.C., Women's Caucus for Art, Seattle, Llubs Art Gallery d'Elaine, Edmonds, Wash., 1957-62, numerous others; pvt. art instr. Seattle, 1960-68; served as art juror for numerous shows; TV art instr., TV-9 U. Wash., 1968; lectr. in field. Exhibited in group shows: Seligman Gallery, Seattle, 1956, Woessner Gallery, Seattle, 1957, 58, Henry Art Gallery, Seattle, 1958, 62, 64, 65, 69, 72, 73, Seattle Art Mus., 1959, 65, 75, Mus. History and Industry, Seattle, 1959, 60, 63, 64, Wash. State Art Exhbns., Wenatchee, 1959, 60, 62, 67, Pacific N.W. Arts and Crafts Fair, Bellevue, 1959, 60, 72-78, Nova Scotia Art Mus., Halifax, 1960, 71, Seattle U., 1965, Nat. Art Gallery, Seattle, 1966—, Art Gallery Hawaii, Oahu, The Gallery, Maui, 1966-68, Park's Gallery, San Jose, Calif., 1967, 68, Park's Galleries, San Jose, San Francisco, Santa Barbara, Carmel, Newport Beach, Calif., 1967, 68, State Capitol Mus., Olympia, Wash., 1968-70, 74, 80, Diamond Head Gallery, Honolulu, 1968, 69, The Gallery Lahaina, Hawaii, 1969, Centennial Art Gallery, Halifax, N.S., 1970, Dartmouth Heritage Mus., Halifax, 1970, 71, Mt. St. Vincent U. Art Gallery, Halifax, 1970, Zwicker's Gallery, Halifax, 1970-73, Gallery 1667, Halifax, 1970-71, Avelles' Gallery, Creative Fine Arts Gallery, Vancouver, The Creative Eye Gallery, Friday Harbor, Wash., 1970, 134th St. Gallery, Halifax, 1971, Panaca Gallery, Bellevue, 1971, 73, Anacortes Arts and Crafts Fair, Wash., 1972, 76-78, Seattle Art Mus. Pavillion Sales Gallery, 1973-75, Meml. U., St. John's Nfld., 1974, Whatcom Mus. Bellingham, Wash., 1974, 75, 80, 82, Grand Gallery, Seattle, 1975, Mus. No. B.C., Maritime Mus., Vancouver, Frye Art Mus., Seattle, 1975, 76, 88, 89, 91, 92, Shoreline Mus. History, Wash., 1976-80,Wash. State Cousteau Soc., Seattle, 1980, U. Oreg., 1981, Edmonds Art Mus., Wash. 1984, 94, Missoula Art Mus., Mont., 1984, Gallery II, Phoenix, 1985, Newport Mus., Oreg., 1986, New Space Gallery, Seattle, 1987, The Viking Gallery, The Chrysalis Gallery, Bellingham, Wash., Art 54 Gallery, N.Y., Emory U., Atlanta, 1988,Prince George Art Gallery, B.C., 1989, Nordic Heritage Mus., Seattle, Rosicrucian Egyptian Mus., San Jose, 1990, King County Arts Commn. Gallery, St. Mark's Cathedral, Seattle, 1991, Kinsey Gallery, Seattle, 1992, Karshner Mus., Puyallup, Wash., 1994, 95, Ilwaco Heritage Mus., Wash., 1994, Northlight Gallery, Everett, Wash., Newmark Gallery, Seattle, 1995, Columbia River Maritime Mus., Astoria, Oreg., 1997, Bon Marché Gallery, Seattle, 1998. Founder Mt. Olympus Preserve for Arts, Edmonds, Wash., 1971, sponsor art events, 1971—; active Wash. Coalition Citizens with Disabilities. Elected to Wash. State Art Commn. Registry, Olympia, 1982; recipient numerous awards. Mem. Nat. Artist Equity, Internat. Soc. Artists, The Cousteau Soc., Creative Arts Assn., Am. Coun. for Arts, Nat. Women's Studies Assn., Nat. Mus. Women in Arts, Women's Caucus for Art, Assn. Am. Culture, Internat. Platform Assn., Nat. Pen Women., Retired Tchrs.' Assn., Kappa Delta Pi, Kappa Pi. Avocations: scuba diving, camping, travel, violin, writing. Home and Office: 16122 72nd Ave W Edmonds WA 98026-4517

JOHNSON, DALE GEDGE, pediatric surgeon; b. Salt Lake City, Sept. 27, 1930; s. Morris C. and Leah (Gedge) J.; m. Beverly Clark, Dec. 22, 1952; children: Pam, Paul, Charlotte, Peter. BS, U. Utah, 1953, MD, 1956. Diplomate Am. Bd. Surgery; cert. spl. competence pediatric surgery. Tech. asst. dept. anatomy Harvard U. Sch. of Medicine, Boston, 1957-58; investigator in exptl. surgery Walter Reed Army Inst., Washington, 1961-63; assoc. in rsch. surgery U. Pa., Phila., 1963-64, asst. prof. pediatric surgery, 1966-71; assoc. prof. surgery U. Utah Sch. of Medicine, Salt Lake City, 1971-76, assoc. prof. pediatrics, 1971-77, prof. surgery, 1976—, prof. pediatrics, 1977—; surgeon-in-chief Primary Children's Med. Ctr., Salt Lake City, 1971—. Trustee Primary Children's Med. Ctr., 1995—; vis. prof. Project Hope Med. Relief Project, Krakow, Poland, 1980, 81, 83, 88, 89; editorial cons. Pediatric Surgery Internat., 1986-93. Contbr. numerous articles to profl. jours. and 28 chpts. to med. textbooks; assoc. editor: Jour. of Pediatric Surgery, 1976-79, Clin. Pediatrics, 1980-84. Mem. Mormon Tabernacle Choir, Salt Lake City, 1971-80; bd. dirs. Salt Lake Repertory Orch., Salt Lake City, 1976-77, Am. Cancer Soc., 1972-78. Capt. U.S. Army Med. Corps, 1961-63. Named Outstanding Alumnus, Children's Hosp. of Phila., 1990; recipient Polish Order of Merit Silver medal, 1991, Sword of Hope award Am. Cancer Soc., 1991, Merit of Honor award U. Utah Alumni Assn., 1998. Fellow Am. Coll. Surgeons; surg. fellow Am. Acad. Pediatrics (recipient Arnold M. Salzberg Mentorship award 2002), Am. Surg. Assn., Soc. Univ. Surgeons, AMA, Brit. Assn. Pediatric Surgeons; mem. Pacific Assn. Pediatric Surgeons (pres. 1990-91), Am. Pediatric Surg. Assn. (sec. 1973-76, pres. 1985-86). Mem. Lds Ch. Avocations: history, biography, music, personal computers, skiing. Office: Primary Childrens Med Ctr Dept Ped Surg 100 N Medical Dr Ste 2600 Salt Lake City UT 84113-1103 E-mail: dale.johnson@utah.edu.

JOHNSON, DAN R. engineering executive; b. Torrance, Calif., Feb. 2, 1960, s. Warren B. and Shirley F. Johnson; m. Paula J. Johnson, May 12, 1986; children: Samantha J., Julia M. BS in Mech. Engring., U. Calif., Berkeley, 1982, MS in Mech. Engring., 1985. Dept. mgr. TRW Space & Tech., Redondo Beach, Calif., 1982—2000; dir. engring. Newport Corp., Irvine, Calif., 2000—01; chief engr. Northrup Grumman Space Tech., Redondo Beach, 2001—. Fellow, TRW, 1984—85. Mem.: ASME. Republican. Roman Catholic. Achievements include patents for 3-Axis Beam Waveguide Antenna; Capacitive Resolver; Large aperture precision gimbal. Office: Northrup Grumman Space Technology One Space Park Redondo Beach CA 90278 E-mail: dan.johnson@trw.com.

JOHNSON, DANETTE IFERT, communication educator; b. Olney, Md., Oct. 3, 1968; d. Norman Daniel and Anna Eileen (Norwood) I.; m. Steven Kent Johnson. BA, W.Va. Wesleyan Coll., Buckhannon, 1990; MA, Northwestern U., Evanston, Ill., 1992, PhD, 1994. Vis. instr. W.Va. Wesleyan Coll., Buckhannon, 1993-94, asst. prof. comm., 1995-2000, dir. forensics, 1995-98, assoc. prof. comm., 2000—; asst. prof. comm. Tex. Tech U., Lubbock, 1994-95. Contbr. articles to profl. jours.; mem. editl. rev. bd. Comm. Rsch. Reports, 1996—. Mem. choir 1st United Meth. Ch., Buckhannon, 1995—. Travel grantee Appalachian Coll. Assn., 1995-00; Salzburg Seminar fellow, 1998; recipient Top Paper award in interpersonal comm. Ea. Comm. Assn., 1995, 97, past pres. award Ea. Com. Assn., 2001. Mem. Nat. Comm. Assn., United Meth. Women, Ea. Comm. Assn. (life, chair interest group 1997-98, advt. mgr. 1998), Internat. Comm. Assn., Phi Kappa Phi (pres. 1996-98). Office: WVa Wesleyan Coll 59 College Ave Buckhannon WV 26201-2600

JOHNSON, DANIEL E. university educator, dean; b. Jamestown, N.Y., June 9, 1948; s. Arthur Johnson, Minnie T. Johnson; m. Margaret R. Ryan. Doctor of Education, University of Southern California, Los Angeles, California, 1983—88, Master of Science in Systems Management, 1974—77; Bachelor of Business Administration, Kent State University, Kent, Ohio, 1968—70; Associate in Applied Science, Jamestown Community College, Jamestown, New York, 1966—68. Lieutenant Colonel United States Air Force, Offutt AFB, NE, 1972—94; University Professor Embry-Riddle Aeronautical University, Offutt AFB, NE, 1994—2002. Mem.: Association of Old Crows, Air Force Association, Academy of Management, Papillion Lions Club. Home: 802 Bailey Dr Papillion NE 68046 Office: Embry-Riddle Aeronautical University 106 Peacekeeper, Dr STE 806 Offutt A F B NE 68113-3214 Office Fax: 402 292 3095. Personal E-mail: danieljohnsond@erau.edu.

JOHNSON, DANIEL MILO, sociology educator, university dean; b. Springfield, Ohio, June 10, 1940; s. Everett Milo and Hilda Mabel (Carder) J.; m. Carolyn Elaine Clark, Mar. 28, 1961; children: Darin Scott, Brenton Christopher. BA, Tex. Christian U., 1963, MA, 1965; PhD, U. Mo., 1973. Chair sociology, social scis. Blackburn Coll., Carlinville, Ill., 1970-73; assoc. prof. sociology and pub. affairs Sangamon State U., Springfield, Ill., 1973-78, prof., 1978-79; assoc. prof. sociology Va. Commonwealth U., Richmond, 1979-80, prof. sociology, 1980-91, chair sociology and anthropology, 1980-83, dir. survey rsch. lab., 1983-88, interim assoc. dean humanities and scis., 1987-88; prof. sociology, dean Sch. Community Svc., U. North Tex., Denton, 1990—. Cons. Collateral Communications, 1991, Evangel Coll., 1990, Richmond Urban Inst., 1988, City of Richmond, 1987. Co-author: Black Migration in America, 1981, Middle Size Cities of Illinois, 1980; contbr. articles to profl. jours. Grantee Gov.'s Employment and Tng. Dept., Va., 1987-88; recognized for Outstanding Svc. in Field of Population Population Action Coun., 1983. Mem. Am. Sociol. Assn., So. Sociol. Soc., Population Assn. Am., Urban Affairs Assn., Va. Sociol. Assn., Ill. Sociol. Assn. (pres. 1979-80).

JOHNSON, DARRYL NORMAN, ambassador; b. Chgo., 1938; m. Kathleen Desa Forance; 3 children. BA cum laude in English Literature, U. Wash., 1960. With Boeing Co., Seattle; fgn. svc. officer Dept. State, Bombay, 1966-68, Hong Kong, 1969-73, Moscow, 1974-77, Beijing, 1984-87, Warsaw, 1988-91, officer-in-charge Yugoslav affairs Washington, 1977-79, 1979-81, amb. to Lithuania, 1991—94, amb. to Thailand, 2001—; dep. asst. for East Asian and Pacific affairs Sec. of State, 2000—01; Pearson fellow Office Senator Claiborne Pell, Washington, 1981-82, spl. asst. to Under Sec. Polit. Affairs, 1982-84. Dir. Am. Inst., Taipei, Taiwan, 1996—99; dep. coord. for assistance to former Soviet Union, 1994—96; dep. dir. Bosnian Task Force, 1996; polit. adv. Chief Naval Ops., 1999—2000. Office: US Embassy 120-22 Wireless Rd Bangkok 10330 China*

JOHNSON, DAVID, medical administrator; Dir. divsn. oncology, hematology Vanderbilt Clinic, Nashville. Office: Vanderbilt U 777 Preston Research Bldg Hematology/Oncology Nashville TN 37232-6307

JOHNSON, DAVID (DAVID MAKENNA), writer; b. Detroit, Mich., Jan. 19, 1958; s. John Allen and Alice Camerl Johnson. Student, Wayne State U. Recipient Editor's Choice award, Internat. Libr. Poetry, 2000, Award of Recognition, 1998. Home: 23252 Park Pl Dr Southfield MI 48034

JOHNSON, DAVID ALLEN, singer, songwriter, investment advisor, minister; b. Indpls., Dec. 15, 1954; s. Eugene Robert and Vivian Claire (Moon) J. BA in English, Ind. U., 1977; cert., Columbia Sch. of Broadcasting, 1985. Ordained to ministry United Christian Ch., 1996. Founder, pres. Worldwide Assn. Disabled Entrepreneurs, Indpls., 1993—; Founder Global Access and Info. Network (GAIN), L.L.C., DAJ Consulting Co.; wealth mgmt. exec. Bayshore Bank and Trust. Singer, songwriter gospel and love songs; contbr. poems and articles to various pubs.; concert promoter in field. Named 2000 Poet of the Yr., Famous Poets Soc. Mem. MENSA, Internat.-Nat. Ctr. for Creativity, Toastmasters (pres. 2000-01—). Republican. Avocations: reading, writing, biblical rsch., basketball. Home and Office: 5958 Devington Rd Apt 1 Indianapolis IN 46226 E-mail: coffeecupguy@aol.com.

JOHNSON, DAVID ALLEN, music educator; b. Danville, Ill., Oct. 14, 1957; s. Harry David and Colletta Murray Johnson; m. Martha Smith Johnson, June 23, 1985; 1 child, Emma Louise. MusB, Western Ill. U., 1980; MA in secondary edn., Western Ky. U., 1988; EdD, U. Louisville, 2000. Band dir. Homer (Ill.) Ind. Schs., 1986—87; adj. instr. Campbellsville (Ky.) U., 1995—2000, Western Ky. U., Bowling Green, 1993—95; band dir. Cumberland Co. Schs., Burkesville, Ky., 1989—95; asst. prof. music edn. Iowa Wesleyan Coll., Mt. Pleasant, 2000—. Author: (dissertation) Devel. of Music Aptitude and effect on scholastic Achievement of 8 to 12 yr. olds, 2000 (Dean's Citation, 2000). Mem.: Percusive Arts Soc., Music Educators Nat. Assn. Republican. Methodist. Avocations: golf, composing music. Home: 511 E Washington Mount Pleasant IA 52641 Office: Iowa Wesleyan Coll 601 N Main Mount Pleasant IA 52641

JOHNSON, DAVID CHESTER, university chancellor, sociology educator; b. Jan. 21, 1933; s. Chester Laven and Olga Henriett (Resnick) J.; m. Jean Ann Lunnis, Sept. 10, 1955 (dec. 1996); children: Stephen, Andrew, Jennifer. BA, Gustavus Adolphus Coll., 1954; MA, U. Iowa, 1956, PhD, 1959; LLD, Luther Coll., 1993. Instr. to prof. sociology Luther Coll., Decorah, Iowa, 1957-69; dean arts and scis. East Stroudsburg (Pa.) U., 1969-76; v.p. acad. affairs St. Cloud (Minn.) State U., 1976-83; dean Gustavus Adolphus Coll., St. Peter, Minn., 1983-90; chancellor U. Minn., Morris, 1990-98; cons. to Scandinavian univs., 1999—. Leader of numerous hiking groups to Norwegian mountains. Mem. bd. Friends of Libr., U. Minn. Librs., 2003—. NSF sci. faculty fellow Inst. Social Rsch., Oslo, 1965-66, adminstrv. fellow Am. Coun. Edn., Luther Coll., 1968-69, Summer Leadership fellow Bush Found., Inst. Edn. Mgmt., Harvard U., 1981; Kennedy Swedish Fund grantee, 1976. Mem. Elder Learning Inst. U. Minn. (pres), U. Minn. Retirees Assn. (pres.), Am. Swedish Assn. Democrat. Lutheran. Home: 1235 Yale Pl Apt 1705 Minneapolis MN 55403-1948

JOHNSON, DAVID PAUL, music educator; b. Madison, Wis., Jan. 25, 1950; s. Paul Strepper and Shirley Johnson; m. Mary Lea Bowers, Aug. 21, 1971; children: Scott David, Kimberly Matie. BA Music Edn., U. Wis. Madison, 1972. Cert. Tchr. DPI Madison, Wis., 1972. Trip dir. YMCA, Madison, Wis., 1966—68; first sgt. Wis. N.G. Band, Madison, Wis., 1972—2002; adjudicator Wis. Sch. Music Assn., Madison, 1972—. Adjudicator Wis. Sch. Music Assn., Madison, Wis., 1975—. None (none) None (none, none). None none, None, None. 1sg Army N.G., 1972—2002, Madison, WI. Decorated Army Commendation Medal Wis. N.G. Mem.: Phi Beta Mu (assoc.; none, none none). Conservative. Catholic. Achievements include patents for None. Avocations: gardening, fishing, none, none, none. Home: 431 Fairview Dr Viroqua WI 54665 Office: Cashton Oublic Schools 540 Coe St Cashton WI 54619 Personal E-mail: johnsond@cashton.k12.wi.us. E-mail: johnsond@cashton.k12.wi.us.

JOHNSON, DAVID RAYMOND, lawyer; b. Bartlesville, Okla., Sept. 12, 1946; s. Lloyd Theodore and Mary Pauline (Auten) J.; m. Marion Frances Monroe, May 14, 1977; children: Marc, Meredith. BA, Tulane U., 1968; JD, U. Va., 1971. Bar: Tex. 1971, D.C. 1977, U.S. Dist. Ct. D.C. 1979, U.S. Ct. Appeals (D.C. cir.) 1981, U.S. Supreme Ct. 1982, U.S. Claims Ct. 1984. Assoc. Fulbright & Jaworski, Houston, 1971-72, Washington, 1974-78, ptnr., 1978-87; atty.-advisor Office of Gen. Counsel of Air Force, Washington, 1972-74; ptnr. Gibson, Dunn & Crutcher LLP, Washington, 1987—. Trustee Washington Episcopal Sch., 1991-93, McLean Sch. Md., 1994-96. Capt. USAF, 1972-74. Mem. D.C. Bar Assn., Phi Beta Kappa, Raven Soc., Order of Coif, Congressional Country Club. Office: Gibson Dunn & Crutcher LLP 1050 Connecticut Ave NW Ste 900 Washington DC 20036-5306

JOHNSON, DAVID REYNOLD, lawyer; b. Binghamton, N.Y., Aug. 8, 1945; s. Reynold Benjamin and Beatrice (Rashleigh) Johnson; m. Judith Harvey, Dec. 22, 1968; children: Bryan, Kathryn. BA, Yale U., 1967, JD, 1972; student, Univ. Coll., Oxford, Eng., 1967-68. Bar: DC 1973, U.S. Ct. Appeals (5th and 11th cirs.) 1973. Law clk. to Hon. Malcolm R. Wilkey U.S. Ct. of Appeals, Washington, 1972-73; ptnr. Wilmer, Cutler & Pickering, Washington, 1973—92, 1998—2002, counsel, 1993—95. Founding. pres., CEO, chmn. Counsel Connect; co-dir. Cyberspace Law Inst.; spkr., writer computerization of law and hypertext. Contbr. articles to profl. jours.

JOHNSON, DAVID SELLIE, civil engineer; b. Mpls., Apr. 10, 1935; s. Milton Edward and Helen M. (Sellie) J. BS, Mont. Coll. Mineral Sci. Tech., 1958. Registered profl. engr., Mont. Trainee Mont. Dept. Hwys., Helena, 1958-59, designer, 1959-66, asst. preconstrn. engr., 1966-68, regional engr., 1968-72, engring. specialities supr., 1972-89, preconstrn. chief, 1989-93, forensic engr., 1965—, traffic accident reconstructionist, 1978—; dir. mktg. Jacobs (Sverdrup) Civil, Inc., Helena, 1994—. Consulting engr., 1985—. Contbr. articles on hwy. safety to profl. jours. Adv. bd. mem. Helena Vocat.-Tech. Edn., 1972-73. Fellow Inst. Transp. Engrs. (expert witness coun.); mem. NSPE, Nat. Acad. Forensic Engrs. (diplomate), Mont. Soc. Profl. Engrs., Transp. Rsch. Bd. (geometric design com., tort liability com.), Wash. Assn. Tech. Accident Investigators, Corvette Club, Treasure State Club (pres. Helena 1972-78, sec. 1979-82), Shriners. Avocations: photography, sports car racing. Home and Office: 1921 E 6th Ave Helena MT 59601-4766

JOHNSON, DAVID WESLEY, lawyer; b. Rochester, N.Y., Mar. 13, 1933; BA, U. Rochester, 1954; LLB, Columbia U., 1959. Bar: N.Y. 1961, U.S. Dist. Ct. (so. dist.) N.Y. 1961, U.S. Dist. Ct. (no. dist.) N.Y. 1971. Counsel, sec., v.p. Textile Banking Co., N.Y.C., 1959-68; legis. counsel CIT Fin. Corp., N.Y.C., 1968-70; ptnr. Otterbourg, Steindler, Houston & Rosen, N.Y.C., 1970-71, Palmer & Johnson, Tupper Lake, N.Y., 1971-74; pvt. practice Tupper Lake, 1974—. Bd. dirs. Adirondack Cmty. Trust Trustee, chmn. bd. North Country C.C., Saranac Lake, N.Y., 1973-82; bd. dirs., pres. High Peaks Hospice, Inc., Saranac Lake, 1988-92; bd. dirs., v.p. Lake Placid (N.Y.) Ctr. for Arts, 1989—, Franklin County Children's Legal Svcs., Inc., pres., 1991—; trustee Nat. History Mus. of the Adirondacks, 1998—; bd. dirs. Adirondack Med. Ctr. Found., 2001—. Mem. Franklin County Bar Assn. (pres. 1979-81), N.Y. State Bar Assn., Lawyers Assn. Textile Industry (bd. dirs., sec.-treas. 1962-71), Assn. Comml. Fin. Attys. (bd. dirs., v.p. 1962-71). Office: 51 Lake St Tupper Lake NY 12986-1624 E-mail: jnglaw@adelphia.net.

JOHNSON, DAVID WILFRED, JR., ceramic scientist, researcher; b. Windber, Pa., Sept. 23, 1942; s. David W. Sr. and Vanessa J. (Shoff) Johnson; m. Bonnie Kay Respet, June 20, 1964; children: Analee J., Bradley D. BS in Ceramic Sci., Pa. State U., 1964, PhD in Ceramic Sci., 1968. Tech. staff Bell Tel. Labs., Murray Hill, N.J., 1968-83; supr. advanced ceramic processing AT&T Bell Labs., Murray Hill, 1983-88; dir. metallurgy and ceramics rsch. dept. Bell Labs Lucent Techs., Murray Hill, 1988-2000; dir. materials rsch. dept. Agere Sys., New Providence, NJ, 2001—02; editor Jour. of Am. Ceramic Soc., 2002—. Adj. prof. Stevens Inst. Tech., Hoboken, NJ, 1982—; Taylor lectr. Pa. State U., University Park, 1989. Contbr. articles to profl. jours. Chmn. Bedminster Twp. Zoning Bd. Adjustment, NJ, 1991—94, 1996—. Fellow: Am. Soc. Materials, Am. Ceramic Soc. (v.p. 1990—92, treas. 1992, pres. 1994, Ross Coffin Purdy award 1978, Fulrath award 1984, John Jeppson award 1998, Indsl. Rsch. prize 2000); mem.: Acad. Ceramics, Materials Rsch. Soc., NAE (adj. prof. 1993), AAAS. Achievements include patents in field; research in in ceramic powder processing as applied to ferrites, ceramic substrates, sol-gel silica glass and high temperature superconductors. E-mail: johnsond@stevens-tech.edu.

JOHNSON, DAVID WILLIS, former food products executive; b. Tumut, New South Wales, Australia, Aug. 7, 1932; arrived in U.S., 1976; s. Alfred Ernest and Eileen Melba (Burt) Johnson; m. Sylvia Raymonde Wells, Mar. 12, 1966; children: David Ashley Lawrence, Justin Christopher Kendall, Harley Alistair Kent. B in Econs., U. Sydney, Australia, 1954, diploma in Edn., 1955; MBA, U. Chgo., 1958. Exec. trainee Ford Motor Co., Geelong, Australia; mgmt. trainee Colgate-Palmolive, Sydney, 1959-60, product mgr., 1961, asst. to mng. dir., 1962, brands mgr., 1963, gen. products mgr., 1964-65, asst. gen. mgr., mktg. dir. Johannesburg, 1966, chmn., mng. dir., 1967-72; pres. Warner-Lambert/Parke Davis Asia, Hong Kong, 1973-76; pres. personal products divsn. Warner-Lambert Co., Morris Plains, NJ, 1977, pres. Am. Chicle Divsn., 1978, exec. v.p., gen mgr. Entenmann's div. Bay Shore, NY, 1979, pres. specialty foods group Morris Plains, 1980-81, v.p., 1980-82, pres., CEO Entenmann's divsn. Bay Shore, 1982; v.p. Gen. Foods Corp., White Plains, NY, 1982-87; exec. officer Entenmann's, Inc., Bay Shore, 1982-87; chmn., pres., CEO Gerber Products Co., Fremont, Mich., 1987-89, chmn., CEO, 1989-90; pres., CEO, dir. Campbell Soup Co., Camden, NJ, 1990-97, chmn. bd., 1993—, pres., CEO, 2000-2001. Bd. dirs. Colgate-Palmolive Co.; exec. mem. adv. bd. Donaldson, Lufkin & Jenrette Mcht. Banking Ptnrs.; mem. adv. coun. U. Notre Dame Coll. Bus. Adminstrn., U. Chgo. Grad. Sch. Bus. Named Dir. of Yr., Nat. Assn. Corp.

Dirs., 1997; recipient Disting. Alumnus award, U. Chgo., 1992. Mem.: Grocery Mfrs. Am. (past bd. dirs.), Nat. Food Products Assn. (past bd. dirs.), Am. Bakers Assn. (past. bd. dirs.). Office: Campbell Soup Co World Hdqrs Campbell Pl Camden NJ 08103

JOHNSON, DAVID WOLCOTT, psychologist, educator; b. Muncie, Ind., Feb. 7, 1940; s. Roger Winfield and Frances Elizabeth (Pierce) J.; m. Linda Mulholland, July 7, 1973; children: James, David, Catherine, Margaret, Jeremiah. BS, Ball State U., 1962; MA, Columbia U., 1964, EdD, 1966. Asst. prof. ednl. psychology U. Minn., Mpls., 1966-69, assoc. prof., 1969-73, prof., 1973—, Emma Birkmaier prof. in ednl. leadership, 1994—. Bd. dirs. Infrared Solutions, Inc.; orgnl. cons., psychotherapist. Author: Social Psychology of Education, 1970; (with Goodwin Watson) Social Psychology: Issues and Insights, 1972, Reaching Out, 1972, 8th edit., 2003, Contemporary Social Psychology, 1973; (with F. Johnson) Joining Together, 1975; (with D. Tjosvold) Porductive Conflict Management, 1983, Circles of Learning, 1984, 4th edit., 2002; (with R. Johnson) Learning Together and Alone, 1975, 5th edit., 1998, Human Relations and Your Career, 1978, 3d Edit., 1991, Educational Psychology, 1979, Structuring Cooperative Learning, 1987, Creative Conflict, 1987, Leading the Cooperative School, 1989, 2d edit., 1994, Cooperation and Competition: Theory and Research, 1989, Teaching Students to be Peacemakers, 1991, 3d edit., 1995, video, 1991, Learning Mathematics and Cooperative Learning, 1991, Creative Controversy, 1992, 3d edit., 1995, Positive Interdependence, 1992, (video) 1992, Meaningful and Manageable Assessment Through Cooperative Learning, 1996, Learning to Lead Teams, 1997, Human Relations: Valuing Diversity, 1999, Meaningful Assessment, 2002, Multicultural Education and Human Relations, 2002; (with R. Johnson, E. Holubec) Cooperative Learning, 1984, 7th edit., 1998, Cooperation in the Classroom, 1984, 7th edit., 1998, Advanced Cooperative Learning, 1988, 3d edit., 1998, Cooperative Learning: Increasing College Faculty Instructional Productivity, 1991, The Nuts and Bolts of Cooperative Learning, 1994, Academic Controversy, 1997; (with R. Johnson, K. Smith) Active Learning: Cooperative Learning in the College Classroom, 1991, 2d edit., 1998; editor Am. Ednl. Rsch. Jour., 1981-83; contbr. over 500 articles to profl. jours. and edited books. Bd. dirs. Walk-In Counseling Ctr., 1971-74. Recipient Gordon Allport award Soc. for Psychol. Study of Social Issues, 1981, Helen Plante award Am. Soc. Engring. Edn., 1984, Outstanding Rsch. award Am. Pers. and Guidance Assn., 1972, Nat. Coun. for the Social Studies Rsch. award, 1986, Outstanding Rsch. award AACD, 1988, award for Outstanding Contbn. Am. Edn. Minn. ASCD, 1990, Outstanding Alumni of Yr. award Ball State U., 1990, Rsch. and Practice award S.W. Ohio Planning Coun. for Insvc. Edn., 1990, Excellence in Tchg. award Dept. Def. Schs., Panama, 1994, Emma Birkmaier Prof. in Ednl. Leadership Coll. Edn. U. Minn., 1994-97. Fellow APA (Disting. Contbns. Applications of Psychology to Edn. and Tng. award 2003); mem. Am. Sociol. Assn., Am. Ednl. Rsch. Assn. (award for Outstanding Contbn. to Coop. Learning 1996, Disting. Scholar award 2001), Am. Mgmt. Assn., Am. Assn. for Counseling and Devel., Nat. Rsch. Coun. Home: 7208 Cornelia Dr Minneapolis MN 55435-4160 Office: U Minn 330 Burton Hall Minneapolis MN 55455 *Success is a combination of focus, perseverance, and pain-endurance.*

JOHNSON, DAVY L. protective services official, minister, writer; b. Feb. 23, 1950; s. Willie Thomas Johnson, Mary Johnson; m. Loretta Parker, Aug. 23, 1975; children: Rachel Leetta Johnson Benjamin, Aaron Lee. AA, BMCC, 1984; cert., Nat. Tax Tng. Sch., 1989; BA in Econs., Regents Coll., 1996; postgrad., Bklyn. Coll. Accts. payable specialist Citibank N.A., N.Y.C., 1970—82; shift supr. Credit Suisse First Boston, N.Y.C., 1984—95; sch. safety agt. N.Y. Police Dept., N.Y.C., 1997—; min. Evangelistic Ch. of Christ, Queens, NY, 1973—. Author: The Devil Light, 2001, Trilogy of Horror, 2001, And Down Will Come Baby, 2001, Chameloman, 2001; author: (short story) The Figure, Dream Leapers, Walkers; author: poet. Democrat. Avocations: reading, writing, bicycling, physical fitness. Home: 50-03 Broadway 1C Woodside NY 11377

JOHNSON, DENISE REINKA, state supreme court justice; b. Wyandotte, Mich., July 13, 1947; Student, Mich. State U., 1965-67; BA, Wayne State U., 1969; postgrad., Cath. U. of Am., 1971-72; JD with honors, U. Conn., 1974; LLM, U. Va., 1995. Bar: Conn. 1974, U.S. Dist. Ct. Conn. 1974, Vt. 1980, U.S. Ct. Appeals (2d cir.) 1983, U.S. Dist. Ct. Vt. 1986. Atty. New Haven (Conn.) Legal Assistance Assn., 1974-78; instr. legal writing Vt. Law Sch., South Royalton, 1978-79; clerk Blodgett & McCarren, Burlington, Vt., 1979-80; chief civil rights divsn. Atty. Gen.'s Office, State of Vt., 1980-82; chief pub. protection divsn. Atty. Gen.'s Office, Montpelier, Vt., 1982-88; pvt. practice Shrewsbury, Vt., 1988-90; assoc. justice Vt. Supreme Ct., Montpelier, 1990—. Chair Vt. Human Rights Commn., 1988-90. Mem. Am. Law Inst., Am. Judicature Soc. Office: Vt Supreme Ct 109 State St Montpelier VT 05609-0001

JOHNSON, DENNIS L. conductor, music educator; b. Grand Rapids, Mich., Feb. 17, 1946; s. Fay Arnold and Violet Marie Johnson; m. Renay M. Raymor; children: Erika Mehta, Reid. B in Music Edn., U. Mich., 1968; MusM, Mich. State U., 1981. Dir. ensembles Western Ill. U., Macomb, 1981—85; dir. bands and orch. Murray (Ky.) State U., 1985—. Musician, guest condr., clinician. Named Ky. Col., Ky. State Legislature, 1999. Mem.: Music Educators Nat. Conf., Coll. Band Dirs. Nat. Assn. (state chmn. 1998—2000), World Assn. for Symphonic Bands and Ensembles (pres. elect 2001, pres.), Am. Bandmasters Assn., Phi Beta Mu (Outstanding Contbr. to Music award 1999). Avocations: swimming, fishing. Home: 1552 Canterbury Murray KY 42071 Office: Murray State Univ Music Dept Murray KY 42071 Home Fax: 270-762-3965. Personal E-mail: dennis.johnson@murraystate.edu.

JOHNSON, DENNIS ROBERT, lawyer; b. Mpls., Aug. 1, 1946. BS in Bus., U. Minn., 1972, JD, 1975. Bar: Minn. 1975, U.S. Dist. Ct. Minn. 1975. Ptnr. Meshbesher & Spence, Ltd., Mpls., 1975—. Bd. dirs. Minn. Legal Advice Clinics, Mpls., 1978-82. 1st lt. U.S. Army, 1966-69, Vietnam. Mem. Minn. Trial Lawyers Assn. (bd. dirs. 1979—, chmn. legis. com. 1980-84, chmn. edn. com. 1984-86, exec. com. 1984, chmn. fin. com. 1986, treas. 1987, v.p. 1988-89, pres. 1989-90), Minn. State Bar Assn. (mem. med. legal com. 1982—), Assn. Trial Lawyers Am. (sustaining mem.), Cert. Civil Trial Specialists. Office: Meshbesher & Spence Ltd 1616 Park Ave Minneapolis MN 55404-1695

JOHNSON, DEWEY, JR., retired biochemist; b. Sapulpa, Okla., Sept. 23, 1926; s. Dewey and Maude (Hickey) Johnson; m. Patricia R. Rodgers, Feb. 14, 1953 (dec. Mar. 1997); children: Joseph D., Paul D., Mary Ann, Richard E.; m. Carol S. Martin, Sept. 25, 1999. BS, Colo. State U., 1950; MS, U. Conn., 1955; PhD, Rutgers State U., 1958. Nutritionist Limecrest Rsch. Lab., Newton, N.J., 1958-63; biochemist Equitable Life, N.Y.C., 1963-79, Met. Life, N.Y.C., 1980-90, disability underwriter, 1990-92; chemist EPA, Edison, NJ, 1993—2001; ret., 2001—. Contbr. Avocation: Avocations: gardening, woodworking. Home: 59 Dunnell Rd Maplewood NJ 07040-1333

JOHNSON, DEWEY E(DWARD), JR., dentist; b. Charleston, S.C., Mar. 19, 1935; s. Dewey Edward and Mabel (Momeier) Johnson. AB in Geology, U. N.C., 1957, DDS, 1961. Pvt. practice dentistry, Charleston, 1964-92; assoc. to Stanley H. Karesh, DDS Charleston, 1970-77; tech. market rschr., designer, 1970-90. Indsl. designer, various orgns., 1965, 75, 77, 88, 91, 92, 01. Served to lt. USNR, 1961-63. Mem. ADA, Royal Soc. Health, Charleston C. of C. (cruise ship com. 1969), Charleston Dental Soc., Hibernian Soc., Charleston Mus., Internat. Platform Assn., Charleston Libr. Soc., S.C. Hist. Soc., Gibbes Art Gallery, Preservation Soc. of Charleston, Navy League U.S., Optimist Club, Phi Kappa Sigma, Sigma Gamma Epsilon, Psi Omega. Achievements include various scientific and engineering designs; patentee in dental matrix device. Home: 112 Folly Road Blvd Charleston SC 29407-7509

JOHNSON, DIANA ATWOOD, business owner, innkeeper; b. Rochester, N.Y., Nov. 3, 1946; d. Edwin Havens and Barbara (Field) A.; m. Kenneth Durant Milne, June 10, 1967 (div. Apr. 1982); m. Howard Samuel Tooker, May 5, 1985 (div. Aug. 1994); m. John Samuel Johnson, June 2, 1996. BA, Skidmore Coll., 1968. Owner, innkeeper Old Lyme (Conn.) Inn, 1976-2001. Vice-chmn., bd. dirs. Maritime Bank & Trust, Essex, Conn., 1995-99; adv. bd. Webster Bank, 1999-2001; incorporator Lawrence Meml. Hosp., New London, Conn., 1990-95. Trustee Conn. River Mus., Essex, 1976-98, pres., 1989-94, chmn., 1994-96; trustee Lyme Hist. Soc., Old Lyme, 1985-87, Lyme Acad. Fine Arts, Old Lyme, 1980—, chmn. 1996—, treas., 1992-96; trustee Mystic Coast Travel and Leisure Coun., 1992—, chmn. 1994-96; bd. dirs. Conn. chpt. Nature Conservancy, 1994—, sec., 2001, chair govt. rels. com. 2001—; chmn. Town of Old Lyme Open Space Com., 1998-2000, mem., 1998—; mem. State of Conn. Natural Heritage, Open Space and Watershed Land Acquisition Rev. Bd., 1998—; mem. adv. bd. Norwich Navigators, 1995-99; dir. Southeastern Conn. Enterprise Region, 1995-2001; del. Rep. Nat. Conv., San Diego, 1996, chmn. Rep. Town Com., 2000-02, vice chmn., 1998-99; mem. Conn. Rep. Fin. Com., 1997-2003; state ctrl. committeewoman 20th Dist. Conn. Republican Party, 2001-03. Recipient Disting. Adv. for the Arts award Conn. Commn. on the Arts, 1999. Mem. Nat. Restaurant Assn., Conn. Restaurant Assn. (bd. dirs. 1991-93, 99-2001), Prof. Assn. Innkeepers, Gray Gables Croquet Club (founder), U.S. Croquet Assn. Republican. Presbyterian. Avocations: american antiques, antique house restoration, croquet. Home: 12 Tantummaheag Rd Old Lyme CT 06371-1137 Office: 75 Crystal Ave New London CT 06320 also: PO Box 787 Old Lyme CT 06371 E-mail: dianaajohnson@aol.com.

JOHNSON, DIANE, educator; b. Seattle, Sept. 1, 1942; BA in Edn., Cen. Wash. State U., 1965. Cert. tchr., Wash. Tchr adult basic edn., English as 2d lang. Author: All American Holocaust, 1995. Organizer injured workers' alliances. Avocations: musician, pets, gardening, travel, historical movies. Home and Office: Nat Coalition and Alaska Alliance Injured Workers PO Box 10975 Fairbanks AK 99710-0975 E-mail: Flutend@yahoo.com.

JOHNSON, DOLORES ESTELLE, shop owner, retired; b. Phila., Dec. 2, 1932; d. William Johnson Bellamy and Sadie Louise (Waddell) Messado; m. Edward Harding Johnson Jr., Aug. 29, 1953 (dec. Feb. 1981); children: Louise P., Edward A., Marie E., Michael G. Parking enforcement officer City of Phila. Police Dept., 1957—59; jeweler, owner LuBelle Jewelers, Phila., 1963—83; originator, owner, baker Pizzarama, Phila., 1965—67; armed guard Globe Security Corp., Phila., 1977—79; artist, jeweler, owner Piercing Eyes Indian Crafts, Phila., 1982—97; ret., 1997. Recipient Outstanding Cmty. Svc. award, Pepsi Cola Co., 1966, award, Chapel of the Four Chaplains for humanitarian works. Mem. United Am. Indians of Delaware Valley, Amerindian Soc. (v.p.), Atlantic City's Garden Ctr. Mus. Art (life). Episcopalian. Avocations: poetry, art, music, camping.

JOHNSON, DON EDWIN, lawyer; b. Decatur, Ill., Jan. 29, 1939; s. B. Edwin and Mary Louise (Pitzer) J.; m. Suzanne Curtis, Aug. 23, 1959; children: Jennifer, Marc Wade. BA cum laude, Millikin U., 1959; LLB, U. Ill., 1961, JD, 1968. Bar: Ill. 1961, U.S. Dist. Ct. (so. dist.) Ill. 1961, U.S. Tax Ct. 1986. Law clk. Ill. Supreme Ct., Springfield, 1961-63; assoc. Hohlt, House & DeMoss, Pinckneyville, Ill., 1961-66; ptnr. Johnson Seibert & Bigham, Pinckneyville, 1966—; state's atty. Perry County, Ill., Pinckneyville, 1968-72. Bd. dirs. 1st Nat. Bank, Pinckneyville, First Perry Bancorp, Pinckneyville. Contbr. articles to profl. jours. City atty. DuQuoin, Ill., 1965-68, Pinckneyville, 1983-2003; bd. dirs. Rend Lake Coll. Found., Ina, Ill., 1981-90; bd. visitors U. Ill. Coll. Law, 1984-88. Fellow Am. Coll. Trust and Estate Counsel, Am. Bar Found., Ill. Bar Found. (chmn. 1986-87); mem. Ill. State Bar Assn. (chmn. fed. tax sect. 1983-84, chmn. mineral law sect. 1984-86, 94-95, 96-97), Energy and Mineral Law Found. (trustee 1985—), Nat. Acad. Elder Law Attys., Pinckneyville C. of C. (pres. 1968), So. Ill. Golf Assn. (pres. 1997—), USGA (sectional affairs com. 1994—), Rotary (pres. 1966, 76), Scottish Rite, Shriners, Red Hawk Country Club, Crab Orchard Golf Club, Kelly Greens Golf and Country Club, Delta Sigma Phi. Republican. Presbyterian. Avocations: golf, travel, stamp and coin collecting. Home: 605 W South St Pinckneyville IL 62274-1236 Office: Johnson Seibert & Bigham One N Main St Pinckneyville IL 62274 Fax: 618-357-3314. E-mail: JSBAttorneys@Midamer.net.

JOHNSON, DONALD CLAY, librarian, curator; b. Clintonville, Wis., Aug. 19, 1940; s. Everett Clay and Gertrude Edna Dorthea (Learmann) J. BA, U. Wis., 1962, PhD, 1980; MA, U. Chgo., 1967. Curator S.E. Asia Collection Yale U., New Haven, 1967-70; head reference libr. No. Ariz. U., Flagstaff, 1971-72; asst. libr. reader svcs. Nat. U. Malaysia, Kuala Lumpur, 1972-74; head reader svcs. Coll. William and Mary, Williamsburg, Va., 1980-87; curator Ames Libr. South Asia, U. Minn., Mpls., 1987—. Author: Southeast Asia: A Bibliography, 1970, Guide to Reference Materials on Southeast Asia, 1970, Index to Southeast Asian Journals, 1982, Agile Hands and Creative Minds, a Bibliography of Textile Traditions in Afghanistan, Bangladesh, Bhutan, India, Nepal, Pakistan, and Sri Lanka, 2000, Wedding Dress Across Cultures, 2003. Scholar Ford Found., 1963-64; rsch. grantee Am. Inst. Indian Studies, 1989, 90, 94. Mem. ALA (life), Assn. for Asian Studies (editor Resources for Scholarship series 1997-98). Avocation: textiles in South and Southeast Asia. Office: U Minn Ames Libr South Asia 309 19th Ave S Minneapolis MN 55455-0438 E-mail: d-john4@tc.umn.edu.

JOHNSON, DONALD EDWARD, JR., lawyer; b. Denver, Sept. 24, 1942; s. Donald Edward and Miriam Bispham (Chester) J.; m. Charlotte Marie Hassett, Aug. 15, 1964; children: Julie Anna, Jenny Marie. Student, Lewis and Clark Coll., 1960-62; BA in History, U. Ariz., 1968; JD, U. Wyo., 1971. Bar: Wyo. 1971, Colo. 1971, U.S. Dist. Ct. Colo. and Wyo. 1971, U.S. Supreme Ct. 1978. Assoc. Hammond and Chilson, Loveland, Colo., 1971-72; dep. dist. atty. 8th Jud. Dist., Loveland and Fort Collins, Colo., 1972-80, chief dep. dist. atty., 1977-80; assoc. Allen, Rogers, Metcalf and Vahrenwald, Ft. Collins, 1980-82, ptnr., 1982—. Asst. city atty., prosecutor City of Loveland, 1971-72; asst. mcpl. judge, Loveland, 1972; instr. bus. law Ames Coll., 1972-74; lectr. Regional Homocide Sch., 1977. Author: Criminal Conspiracy—The Colorado District Attorney's Evidence Manual, 1976; student editor ABA Law Student Jour. Chmn. 45th Republican House Dist., 1977-82; mem. Colo. Rep. Central Com., 1980-85; mem. Loveland Open Space Adv. Bd., 1977-78; bd. dirs. Loveland United Way, 1977-84, pres., 1981-83; bd. dirs. Loveland Midget Athletic Assn., sec., 1974-78; mem. ctrl. com. Parlimentarian Larimer County Rep., 1992-96; mem. local adv. bd. McKee Med. Ctr., Loveland, 1992—, pres., 1995—; mem. adv. bd. Banner Health Sys., Colo., 1996—, pres., 1999-2002; mem. adv. bd. Cmty. Found. No. Colo., Loveland, 2003—; treas. 8th Jud. dist. Victims Assistance Law Enforcement Fund, 1990-96 (8th judicial dist.), mem. nominating commn., 1998—; mem. Larimer County Bench-Bar Commn., 1993-95. Served to sgt. USMC, 1966-68. Mem. ABA (Gold Key award 1970), Larimer County Bar Assn. (exec. com. 1990-2002, pres. 1995-96), Colo. Bar Assn. (bd. govs. 1997-2002), Colo. Trial Lawyers Assn. Episcopalian. Office: Allen Vahrenwald & Johnson LLC Key Bank Bldg 125 S Howes St 1100 Fort Collins CO 80521

JOHNSON, DONALD HARRY, JR., government official, educator; b. Chgo., May 30, 1950; s. Donald Harry and Dorothy Wright (Millard) J.; m. Kathryn Elizabeth Wiersum, June 24, 1972 (div. Aug. 1987); children: Eric Donald, Christine Melin. BA Elem. Edn. and History, Carthage Coll., Kenosha, Wis., 1972; postgrad., Harvard U., 1977, 2000; MA Higher Edn. Adminstrn., U. Mich., 1979, MA Polit. Sci., 1980, PhD, 1982; MA, Inst. (Fair Housing) John Marshall Law Sch., 1998, 99, John F. Kennedy Sch. Govt., 2000. Cert. tchr. K 8, social scis., Ill., Wis., Colo., V.I. Equal opportunity specialist/civil rights analyst U.S. Dept. HUD, Chgo., 1988—. Elem. edn. tchr. All Sts. and V.I. Pub. Schs., St. Thomas, 1972-75; commr. V.I. Athletic Assn., 1973-75; higher edn. adminstr. Carthage, Suomi Coll., Springfield (Ill.) Coll., U. Mich., 1975-83; dir. admissions Suomi Coll., 1977-78; adminstr. Disabled Student Newsletter, U. Mich., 1978-79; adminstrv. asst. Office of Minority Svcs., U. Mich., 1978-79, admissions officer U. Mich., 1979-81; dean coll. Springfield Coll., 1981-83; exec. coun. Ctrl. Ill. Fgn. Lang. Coll. Consortium, 1981-83, chmn. internat. studies group, 1981-83; cons. polit. candidates, Ann Arbor, Washington, Chgo., 1979—; polit. sci. prof. U. Mich., Lincolnland Coll., U. Ill.-Springfield, Coll. DuPage, Triton Coll., Elmhurst Coll., Aurora (Ill.) U., 1980-90; rsch. affiliate Caribbean Rsch. Inst., U. V.I., 1980-82; rsch. cons. Afro-Am. Thematic Project, U. Ill.-Springfield, 1983-85; chmn. HUD Disabled Employee Adv. Com., Chgo., 1988—, labor/mgmt. exec. com., 1996-98; cons. colls. and univs.; lectr. in field. Contbg. author: Theory and Practice of 3rd World Solidarity, 2001; guest commentator NBC Today, 1982, Nat. Pub. Radio, 1984; author, ERIC, Nat. Inst. Edn., Boulder, Colo., 1982; editor: Disabled Student Newletters, U. Mich., 1978-79. Disting. guest Embassy of Finland, Washington, 1995; candidate local sch. coun., Chgo., 1994; ednl. guest speaker Com. of Ill. State Bd. Edn., Chgo., 1994; mem. com. ACCESS LIVING, Chgo., 1991-99, ednl. com. C. of C., Springfield, 1982; disability trainer to pub. and pvt. sector individuals, 1978—. Named Disting. Young Alumnus award Carthage Coll., Kenosha, Wis., 1982; Rackham grantee U. Mich., 1980-82, others.; recipient HUD Superior Accomplishment award 1999. Mem. Am. Fedn. Govt. Employees (election chmn. 1991, exec. coun. 1997-99), Phi Alpha Theta. Lutheran. Avocations: freelance writing, bicycling, scuba diving. Home: 2206 W Morse Ave Chicago IL 60645-4820 Office: US Dept HUD 77 W Jackson Blvd Ste 2101 Chicago IL 60604-3511

JOHNSON, DONALD RAYMOND, lawyer; b. N.Y.C., June 26, 1960; s. Donald Francis and Jacqueline E. (Barnett) J. BA, Liberty U., 1982, MA, 1984; JD, Washington and Lee U., 1989; postgrad., Va. Polytech. Inst., Yale U., U. Va. Bar: Va. 1989, D.C. 1991, N.Y. 1995, U.S. Dist. Ct. (no., so., and ea. dists.) N.Y., U.S. Dist. Ct. (ea. and we. dists.) Va., U.S. Ct. Appeals (fed. cir.), U.S. Supreme Ct., U.S. Ct. Internat. Trade. Pvt. practice, Charlottesville, Va., 1989-96; dir., pres. Internat. Brokerage & Investment Co., Charlottesville, 1991-99; dir., v.p. Internat. Investment Svcs., Inc., Charlottesville, 1991-2000; pvt. practice N.Y.C., 1995—; pres. Real E.S. AG, 2003—. Bd. dirs. Excellence in Edn., Charlottesville, 1990-92, Heritage Soc., Charlottesville, 1990-92, World of Life Internat., 2000—; U.S. del. German-Am. Multiplicitorian Seminars, founder Mission, Inc., 2000—. Named one of Outstanding Young Men of Am., Alumnus of the Yr.; recipient numerous awards and honors for ednl., civic, and social activities. Mem. ABA, ATLA. Republican. Baptist. Avocations: running, sailing, tennis. Office: 90 Schermerhorn St Brooklyn NY 11201-5028 Fax: 801-340-1789. E-mail: drjohnson@att.net.

JOHNSON, DORIS ANN, educational administrator; b. Marinette, Wis., Dec. 4, 1950; d. Jerome Louis and Jean Fern (Henry) La Plant; m. Daniel Lee Leonard, June 10, 1972 (div. June 1987); children: Jeremiah Daniel, Erica Leigh, Wesley Cyril; m. Paul Robert Johnson, Oct. 21, 1989; stepchildren: Kindra Michelle, Tanya Mari. Student, U. Wis., Oshkosh, 1969-70; BA in Edn., U. Wis., Eau Claire, 1973; MS in Edn., U. Wis., Whitewater, 1975; postgrad., Oreg. State U., 1988. Reading specialist Brookfield (Wis.) Cen. High Sch., 1975-79; lead instr. N.E. Wis. Tech. Coll., Marinette, 1979-87; dir. adult basic edn. Umpqua C.C., Roseburg, Oreg., 1987-95, dir. developmental edn., 1995—2003, dir. grants, 2003—. Founding bd. dirs. Project Literacy, Umpqua Region, Roseburg, 1989-98; mem. adv. bd. Umpqua Cmty. Action Network, Roseburg, 1987-94; mem. State Dirs. of Adult Edn., Oreg., 1987-2002, vice chair, 1992-93, chair, 1993-94; dir. Title III grant, 2002; mem. Adminstrn. Assn., Roseburg, 1989—, chair, 1993-94, 94-95; bd. dirs. Greater Douglas United Way, 1994-2000; adv. bd. Oreg. Litaracy Line, 1994-96. Co-author literacy module Communication Skills, 1988; author ednl. curriculum. Founding mem., bd. dirs. St. Joseph Maternity Home, Roseburg, 1987-90; mem. Literacy Theater, Roseburg, 1988-95; mem. Project Leadership, Roseburg, 1988-89; mem. adv. bd. Oreg. Literacy Line, 1994-96; mem. Roseburg Valley Rep. Women, 1994-96. State legalizatoin assistance grantee Fed. Govt., 1988-93, homeless literacy grantee Fed. Govt., 1990-91, family literacy grantee Fed. Govt., 1991-93, intergenerational literacy grantee State of Oreg., 1991, literacy expansion grantee Fed. Govt., 1992-95, literacy outreach grantee Fed. Govt., 1992-2002, staff devel. spl. projects grantee Fed. Govt., 1992-93, Title III grantee Fed. Gov., 2002—. Fellow TESOL, Inst. Inst. Leadership Devel., Am. Assn. Adult and Continuing Edn., Oreg. Assn. Disabled Students, Oreg. Developmental Edn. Studies, Oreg. Assn. for Children with Learning Disabilities, Western Coll. Reading and Learning Assn., Am. Assn. Women in Coll. and Jr. Coll., Roseburg Valley Rep. Women, Altrusa Internat. Club of Roseburg (chair literacy com. 1993-97), Rep. Women. Republican. Lutheran. Avocations: peer counseling, reading, hiking, cooking, running support groups. Home: 761 Garden Grove Dr Roseburg OR 97470-9670 Office: Umpqua CC PO Box 967 Roseburg OR 97470-0226 E-mail: doris.johnson@umpqua.edu.

JOHNSON, DOROTHY CURFMAN, elementary education educator; b. Smithsburg, Md., Nov. 21, 1930; d. Paul Frank and Rhoda Pearl (Witmer) Curfman; m. Robert Nelson Johnson, Jan. 24, 1953 (div. Dec. 1965); children: Gregory Nelson, Eric Paul. Student, Gettysburg Coll., 1948-50, Waynesboro Bus. Coll., 1950, Broward C.C., Ft. Lauderdale, Fla., 1967; BS in Edn., Fla. Atlantic U., 1969, postgrad., 1975-76. Cert. tchr., Fla. Sec. to prodn. mgr. Westinghouse Elec. Corp., Sunbury, Pa., 1951-53; sec. to v.p., sales Metal Carbides Corp., Youngstown, Ohio, 1966; tchr. Sch. Bd. of Broward County, Ft. Lauderdale, Ohio, 1969-93, curriculum specialist, 1993-96. Masters in Edn. Prog., 1973-74, team coord. Sanders Park Elem., Pompano Beach, Fla., 1985-96; mem. North Area Adv. Bd., Pompano Beach, 1990-96; sec. Sanders Park PTA, Pompano Beach, 1994-96. Sec.-treas. Georgen Arms Bd. of Dirs., Pompano Beach, 1997—; dir. Georgen Arms Condo, Inc., Pompano Beach, 1974—; active Jr. League, Youngstown. Recipient Master Tchr. award State of Fla., 1981-82. Mem. Alpha Xi Delta. Lutheran. Home: 280 S Cypress Rd Apt 5 Pompano Beach FL 33060-7038

JOHNSON, DOROTHY PHYLLIS, retired counselor, art therapist; b. Kansas City, Mo., Sept. 13, 1925; d. Chris C. and Mabel T. (Gillum) Green; BA in Art, Ft. Hays. State U., 1975, MS in Guidance and Counseling, 1976, MA in Art, 1979; m. Herbert E. Johnson, May 11, 1945; children: Michael E., Gregory K. Art therapist High Plains Comprehensive Mental Health Assn., Hays, Kans., 1975-76; art therapist, mental health counselor Sunflower Mental Health Assn., Concordia, Kans., 1976-78, Pawnee Mental Health Svcs., 1978-91, co-dir. Project Togetherness, 1976-77, coord. partial hospitalization, 1978-82, outpatient therapist, 1982-91; pvt. practice, 1991-97, ret., 1997; dir. Swedish Am. State Bank, Courtland, Kans., 1960—, sec., 1973-77. Mem. Kans., Am. art therapy assns., Am. Mental Health Counselors Assn., Am. Counseling Assn., Kans. Counseling Assn., Assn. for Humanistic Psychologists, Assn. Transpersonal Psychologists, Assn. Specialists in Group Work, Phi Delta Kappa, Phi Kappa Phi. Contbr. articles to profl. jours. Home: PO Box 200 Courtland KS 66939-0200

JOHNSON, DOUG, advertising and public relations executive; b. Watertown, N.Y., Aug. 16, 1919; s. H. Douglas and Clare (Lane) J.; m. Geraldine Evans, Aug. 11, 1943; children: Andrew (dec.), Molly E., Faith D. Student pub. schs. Pres. Doug Johnson Assos. (pub. relations), Syracuse, N.Y., 1949-61, Barlow/Johnson, Inc. (advt. and pub. relations), Syracuse, 1961-80, Johnlow Corp., Fayetteville; chmn. bd. Nowak Barlow Johnson, Fayetteville, 1980-82; v.p. mktg. Edward Joy Co., Inc., Syracuse, 1982-84. Pres. 10 Co. Mktg.; dir. Agway Indemnity Ins. Co., Dewitt, N.Y., Key Bank of Central N.Y., Syracuse, Syracuse Baseball Club, Inc.; chmn. exec. com. Agway Ins. Co., Dewitt. Home sec. to congressman, 1949-65; bd. dirs., v.p. Community Gen. Hosp. Syracuse, N.Y. State Coll. Forestry Found.; bd. dirs., past pres. Syracuse Boys Club ; v.p. N.Y.C. Assoc. Artists; pres. L.W. Artists Assn., 1997-98; bd. dirs., past pres. USO of CNY, nat. bd. dirs., USO. Served with AUS, 1941-45. Decorated Purple Heart with 3 oak leaf clusters, Bronze Star, Combat Infantry Badge with Silver Star. Mem. Pub. Rels. Soc. Am. (cert. bus. communicator), Syracuse C. of C. (pres. 1968-69) Clubs: Century (gov.). Home and Office: 1444 Leisure World Mesa AZ 85206-2304 E-mail: dougjohnse@aol.com.

JOHNSON, DOUGLAS BLAIKIE, lawyer; b. Chgo., Sept. 13, 1952; s. Marvin Melrose and Anne Stuart (Campbell) J.; m. Pamela Jane Tomlinson, Aug. 1, 1975; children: Richard Aaron, Lauren Stuart, Diana Blaikie, Scott Nathaniel, Catherine Joan. BSME, U. Nebr., 1974; JD, Seton Hall U., 1980. Bar: Nebr. 1980, U.S. Dist. Ct. Nebr. 1980; registered profl. engr., Nebr., Ark. Project engr. DuPont, Cleve., 1974-75, Exxon Chems., Linden, N.J., 1975-78, cost engr., 1978-80; sr. engr. InterNorth, Inc., Omaha, 1980-82, market planner, 1982-84, corp. planner, 1984-85, bus. mgr., 1985-86; program mgr. Brunswick Corp., Lincoln, Nebr., 1987-95; product devel. mgr. Lincoln Composites, 1995-98, sr. bus. devel. mgr., 1999-2000, dir. oilfield products, 2000—02; mgr. Gen. Dynamics, 2003—. Mem. ABA, ATLA, Nebr. Bar Assn., Lincoln Bar Assn., Triangle, Sigma Tau, Pi Tau Sigma, Phi Eta Sigma. Republican. Presbyterian. Home: 4600 Birch Hollow Dr Lincoln NE 68516-5107 Office: Gen Dynamics 4300 Industrial Ave Lincoln NE 68504-1107 E-mail: djohnson@gdatp.com.

JOHNSON, DOUGLAS WELLS, lawyer; b. May 31, 1949; s. Robert Douglas and Mildred Irene (Fehr) J.; m. Kathryn Ann Hoberg, Oct. 18, 1980. BA, U. Denver, 1971, JD, 1974. Ptnr. Mellman, Mellman & Thorn, Denver, 1974-80; sr. atty. Amoco Corp., Chgo., 1980-91; mgr. real estate Amoco Oil Co., Chgo., 1991-94; sr. atty. Amoco Corp., Chgo., 1994-98; v.p. and chief counsel BP Pipelines N. Am., Warrenville, Ill., 1998—. U. Denver Alumni scholar, 1967-71. Mem. ABA, Ill. Bar Assn., D.C. Bar Assn., Chgo. Bar Assn., Kappa Delta Pi. Home: 3040 Indianwood Rd Wilmette IL 60091 Office: BP America Inc 4101 Winfield Rd Warrenville IL 60555

JOHNSON, DOUGLAS WILLIAM, physician, radiation oncologist; b. Westpoint, NY; s. Andrew Larson and Barbara Joan (Rosborough) J.; m. Susan Mary Friedman, July 23, 1977; children: Danielle, Michael. BS in Biology, Va. Polytechnic Inst., Blacksburg, Va., 1976; MD, Med. Coll. Va., Richmond, 1979. Chmn. radiation oncology David Grant USAF Med. Ctr., Travis AFB, Calif., 1983-87; ptnr. Fla. Radiation Oncology Group, Jacksonville, Fla., 1987—. Asst. prof. radiation-oncology Stanford Med. Ctr., Stanford U., Calif., 1983-87; asst. prof. oncology Mayo Clinic Med. Sch., Rochester, Minn., 1995—; fellow Am. Coll. Radiology, Phila., 1995. Patentee in field. Col. USAF, 1975—. Fellow Am. Coll. Radiology; mem. Am. Soc. Therapeutic Radiology & Oncology. Avocation: aviation. Office: Baptist Regional Cancer Ctr 1235 San Marco Blvd Ste 3 Jacksonville FL 32207-8560

JOHNSON, DUANE FADINAND, librarian; b. Brookville, Kans., Oct. 26, 1940; s. Orlando F. and Alice Mae (Halsey) J.; m. Ann Lynn Dolloff, Sept. 15, 1963 (dec. 1978); 1 dau., Marcia Kay (dec.). AB, Kans. Wesleyan U., 1964; MS, Fla. State U., 1966. Asst. librarian Salina Pub. Library, Kans., 1966-68; dir. Great Bend Pub. Library and Central Kans. Library System, Kans., 1968-72, Hutchinson Pub. Library and South Cen. Kans. Library System, Kans., 1972-82; state librarian Kans. State Library, Topeka, 1982—. Cons. Nat. Libr. Tanzania, 1996. Active Bd. Edn., US Dist. 313, 1977-82; del. White House Conf. on Libraries, 1979, 91. Mem. ALA (coun. mem., exec. bd. 1986-90), Kans. Library Assn. (pres. 1976), Mountain Plains Libr. Assn. (pres. 1986-87), Western Coun. State Librarians (pres. 1987, 2000), Beta Phi Mu Home: 2125 SE 36th St Topeka KS 66605-2411 Office: Kans State Library State Capitol Topeka KS 66612

JOHNSON, DUANE P. retired academic administrator, consultant; b. Wadena, Minn., Mar. 19, 1937; s. Julian C. and Lillian M. (Petri) J.; m. Mary E., Oct. 22, 1960; children: Michael D., Gregory P. BS, Iowa State U., 1959; MEd, Colo. State U., 1970. County extension agt. 4-H Oreg. State U., Gresham, 1959-70, ext. specialist 4-H and youth devel. Corvallis, 1970-80, state leader 4-H, 1980-94, prof. adult edn., ext. specialist program devel., 1994-2000; ednl. cons., 2000—; prof. emeritus Oreg. State U., 2001—. Cons. Nat. 4H Japanese Exch. Program, 2000—. Contbr. numerous articles to profl. jours. Recipient Am. Spirit award USAF Recruiting Svc., 1991. Mem. Nat. Assn. Ext. 4-H Agts. (Disting. Svc. award 1979), Assn. Vol. Adminstrn., ASCD, Oreg. State U. Ext. Assn., Epsilon Sigma Phi (we. regional v.p. 2003—, Disting. Svc. award 1995). E-mail: johnsodu@onid.orst.edu.

JOHNSON, DWAYNE DOUGLAS (THE ROCK), professional wrestler, actor; b. Hayward, Calif., May 2, 1972; s. Rocky and Ata Johnson; m. Dany Garcia, May 3, 1997. Grad., Freedom H.S., Bethleham, Pa. Actor: (TV) Saturday Night Live, That '70s Show, The Net; (films) The Mummy Returns, 2001. Achievements include World Wrestling Fedn. champion. Office: c/o WWF Titan Tower 1241 E Main St Stamford CT 06902

JOHNSON, DWIGHT ALAN, lawyer; b. Huntington, W.Va., Sept. 26, 1945; s. Oliver Frederick and Garnette (Taylor) J.; m. Bonny Libbey, Nov. 15, 1969; children: Claire L., Daniel F., Philip T. BA, Princeton U., 1968; JD, Yale U., 1974. Bar: Conn. 1975, D.C. 1975, U.S. Ct. Appeals (D.C. cir.) 1976. Assoc. Jones, Day, Reavis & Pogue, Washington, 1974-77, Murtha Cullina LLP, Hartford, Conn., 1977-80, ptnr., 1980—, chmn. exec. com., 1990-95. Bd. dirs. Phonon Corp., Simsbury, Conn. Sec., bd. dirs. Conn. Capitol Region Growth Coun., Hartford, 1992-97; bd. dirs. Conn. Sci. Mus., 1978-84, pres., 1982-83; bd. dirs. Parents Anonymous Conn., Inc., 1981-87, pres., 1983-85; bd. dirs. Tutu Found. Devel. and Relief South Africa, 1986-89, Lyme Disease Found., 1990-94; bd. dirs. Hartford Symphony Orch., 1991—, pres., 1994-96; trustee World Affairs Coun., 1998-2001, Conn. Energy Found., 1984-90, Conn. Policy Econ. Coun., 1996-98; bd. dirs. ARC of Greater Hartford Chpt., 2000--. With U.S. Army, 1968-71, Vietnam. Decorated Bronze Star. Mem. Conn. Bar Assn. (mem. exec. com. pub. utilities law sect. 1979—). Office: Murtha Cullina LLP City Pl 185 Asylum St Hartford CT 06103

JOHNSON, E. DIANE, librarian; b. Columbia, S.C., June 21, 1956; d. Clark R. and C. Estelle (Graham) J. BA magna cum laude, U. Wis., 1978; MA, U. Minn., 1980. Libr. Health Scis. Libr./Univ. Mo., Columbia, 1980-85, head info. svcs., 1986—. Designated instr. Med. Libr. Assn., 1990—; del. Citizen Ambassador Prog. Med. Librs. Delegation to China, 1989; active various clinics and workshops in field; others. Contbr. articles to profl. jours. Recipient grad. sch. tuition scholarship U. Minn., 1979, Libr. Sci. Acad. award U. Wis., Oshkosh, 1978, Ida and George Eliot prize Med. Libr. Assn., 1998, Estelle Brodman award Med. Libr. Assn., 1999, Hetzner award for excellence in acad. health sci. librarianship, 1999, others. Office: U Mo J Otto Lottes Health Scis Libr Columbia MO 65212-0001

JOHNSON, E. ERIC, insurance executive; b. Chgo., Feb. 7, 1927; s. Edwin Eric and Xenia Alice (Waisanen) J.; m. Elizabeth Dewar Brass, Sept. 3, 1949; children: Christal L. Johnson Neal, Craig R. BA, Stanford U., 1948. Dir. group annuities Equitable Life Assurance Soc., San Francisco, 1950-54, div. mgr. L.A., 1955-59; v.p. Johnson & Higgins of Calif., L.A., 1960-67, dir., 1968-87, chmn., 1986-87, TBG Fin., L.A., 1988—. Bd. dirs. Am. Mutual Fund; exec. v.p. Johnson & Higgins, N.Y.C., 1984-87, Law Environ. Group, Showscan Corp. Bd. dirs. Sta. KCET, pub. TV, L.A., 1977-95, chmn., 1992-94; mem. adv. bd. UCLA Med. Ctr., 1983—, chmn. 1995-97; bd. dirs. Jonsson Comprehensive Cancer Ctr., UCLA, 1985—, Stanford U. Grad Sch. Bus., 1986-91; trustee Nuclear Decommissioning Trust, Rosemead, Calif., 1986-94, Calif. State Dept. Mental Hygiene, Calif. Coun. for Econ. Edn. Mem. Calif. Club, L.A. Country Club, Vintage Club, Riviera Tennis Club, Links Club N.Y.C., Beach Club, So. Calif. Tennis Assn. (v.p.), Tehama Golf Club. Avocations: golf, tennis, contemporary art, spectator sports. Office: TBG Fin 2029 Century Park E Los Angeles CA 90067-2901

JOHNSON, E. PERRY, lawyer; b. Pa., 1943; BA, W. Va. U., 1965, JD, 1968. Bar: W. Va. 1968, D.C. 1981, Mo. 1983. Instr. Boston U. Sch. Law, 1973-74, asst. dir., 1977-79, bur. competition, exec. asst. to chmn., 1979, dep. dir., 1979-80, dir., 1980-81; ptnr. Bryan Cave, St. Louis. Vis. asst. prof. W. Va. U., 1972-73; adj. prof. St. Louis U. Sch. Law, 1985-86. With USN, 1968-72. Mem. ABA. Office: Bryan Cave 211 N Broadway Ste 3600 Saint Louis MO 63102-2733

JOHNSON, EARL, JR., judge, author; b. Watertown, SD, June 10, 1933; s. Earl Jerome and Doris Melissa (Schwartz) J.; m. Barbara Claire Yanow, Oct. 11, 1970; children: Kelly Ann, Earl Eric, Agaarn Yanovitch. BA in Econs., Northwestern U., 1955, LL.M., 1961; JD, U. Chgo., 1960. Bar: Ill. 1960, US Ct. Appeals (9th cir.) 1964, DC 1965, US Supreme Ct. 1966, Calif. 1972. Trial atty., organized crime sect. Dept. Justice, Washington, Miami, Fla. and Las Vegas, Nev., 1961-64; dep. dir. Neighborhood Legal Svc. Project, 1964-65, OEO Legal Svc. Program, 1965-66, dir., 1966-68; vis. scholar Ctr. for Study of Law and Soc. U. Calif., Berkeley, 1968-69; assoc. prof. U. So. Calif. Law Ctr., LA, 1969-75, dir. clin. programs, 1970-73, prof. law, 1976-82, dir. Program Study Dispute Resolution Policy, Social Sci. Rsch. Inst., 1975-82; assoc. justice Calif. Ct. Appeal, 1982—; co-dir. Access to Justice Project European U. Inst., 1975-79. Vis. scholar Inst. Comparative Law, U. Florence, Italy, 1973, 75; Robert H. Jackson lectr. Nat. Jud. Coll., 1980; adv. panel Legal Svc. Corp., 1976-80; legis. impact panel Nat. Acad. Sci., 1977-80; faculty Asian Workshop on Legal Svcs. to Poor, 1974; mem. Internat. Legal Ctr., Legal Svcs. in Developing Countries, 1972-75; founder, bd. mem. Action for Legal Rights, 1971-74; pres., trustee Western Ctr. on Law and Poverty, 1972-73, 76-80; v.p., chmn. exec. com. Calif. Rural Legal Assistance Corp., 1973-74; exec. com. Nat. Sr. Citizens Law Ctr., 1980-82; sec. Nat. Resource Ctr. for Consumers of Legal Svc., 1974-82; chair Nat. Equal Justice Libr. Com., 1989-92; pres., Consortium for Nat. Equal Justice Libr., Inc., 1992-95, bd. dir., 1995—; chair Calif. Access to Justice Working Group, 1993-96; mem. Calif. Commn. on Access to Justice, 1997—, co-chmn., 2002-03. Author: Justice and Reform: The Formative Years of the Am. Legal Svc. Program, 1974, 2d edit., 1978, Toward Equal Justice: A Comparative Study of Legal Aid in Modern Soc., 1975, Outside the Courts: A Survey of Diversion Alternatives in Civil Cases, 1977, Dispute Processing Strategies, 1978, Dispute Resolution in Am., 1985, Calif. Trial Guide, 8 vols., 1986, Tex. Trial Guide, 6 vols., 1989, NY Trial Guide, 5 vols., 1990, Fla. Civil Trial Guide, 5 vols., 1990, Ill. Civil Trial Guide, 5 vols., 1991, Fed. Trial Guide, 5 vols., 1992, Ind. Civil Trial Guide, 5 vols., 1992, Calif. Family Law Trial Guide, 5 vols., 1992, Pa. Civil Trial Guide, 5 vols., 1992, Mich. Trial Guide, 5 vols., 1993, NC Civil Trial Guide, 5 vols., 1993, Calif. Criminal Trial Guide, 3 vols., 1994; editor U. Chgo. Law Rev, 1960; mem. editl. bd. Jour. Law and Social Inquiry, 1987—; contbr. articles to books and periodicals. Bd. dir. Beverly Hills Bar Found., 1972-73, Nat. Legal Aid and Defenders Assn., 1987-91; trustee LA Legal Aid Found., 1969-71; mem. LA County Regional Planning Commn., 1980-81; bd. visitors U. San Diego Law Sch., 1983-86. Served with USNR, 1955-58. Recipient Dart award for acad. innovation U. So. Calif., 1971, Loren Miller Legal Svc. award Calif. State Bar, 1977, Appellate Justice of the Yr. award LA Trial Lawyers Assn., 1989, Outstanding Jud. Achievement award Calif. Trial Lawyers Assn., 1991, Legal Svc. Pioneer award LA Legal Aid Found., 1999; named So. Calif. Citizen of Week, 1978; Ford Found. fellow, 1960; Dept. State lectr., 1975; grantee Ford Found.; grantee Russell Sage Found.; grantee Law Enforcement Assistance Adminstrn.; grantee NSF. Fellow Am. Bar Found. (rsch. adv. com. 1996-2001, chair 1999-2002); mem. ABA (com. chmn. 1972-75, spl. com. resolution minor disputes 1976-83, coun. sect. of individual rights and responsibilities 1990-91, consortium on legal svc. and the pub. 1991-94), Calif. Bar Assn., LA Bar Assn. (neighborhood justice ctr. com. 1976-81), Law and Soc. Assn., Nat. Legal Aid and Defender's Assn. (bd. dir. 1968-74), Am. Acad. Polit. and Social Sci., Calif. Judges Assn. (appellate cts. com. 1983-87, 93-99, ethics com. 1985-89), Internat. Assn. Procedural Law, Internat. Legal Aid Group, 1999, Order of Coif. Democrat. Office: Ct Appeals Calif 2d Appellate Dist 300 S Spring St Los Angeles CA 90013-1230 E-mail: justej@aol.com. *I have profound faith in the power of ideas to shape American society and in the special significance of one fundamental concept— equal justice, in its full meaning.*

JOHNSON, EARLE BERTRAND, insurance executive; b. Otter Lake, Mich., May 3, 1914; s. Bert M. and Blanche (Sherman) J.; m. Frances Pierce, 1940 (dec.); children: Earle Bertrand (dec.), Victoria, Julia, Sheryl; m. Peggy Minch Rust, Apr. 30, 1972. BS, U. Fla., 1937, JD, 1940. With State Farm Ins. Cos., Bloomington, Ill., 1940-95, regional agy. dir., 1958-60, regional v.p., 1960-65, v.p., sec. State Farm Mut. Automobile Ins. Co., 1965-80, dir., 1967-88; sr. v.p., treas. State Farm County Mut. Ins. Co. Tex., 1965-80, treas., 1963-80; chmn. State Farm Life Ins. Co., 1970-86, dir., mem. exec. com., 1965-88. V.p., mem. exec. com. State Farm Fire & Casualty Co., 1965-80, dir., 1965-95; dir. State Farm Investment Mgmt. Corp., v.p., sec. State Farm Internat. Svcs., Inc., 1967-81; mem. exec. com. State Farm County Mut. Ins. Co. Tex., 1970-86. Mem. Agy. Officers Round Table (exec. coms.), Am., Fla. bar assns., Soc. Former FBI Agts., Life Ins. Mktg. and Research Assn. (dir. 1975-78), Life Underwriter Tng. Council (trustee 1974-77), Phi Alpha Delta, Phi Kappa Tau. Home: 59 N Country Club Pl Bloomington IL 61701-3450 Office: State Farm Life Ins Co One State Farm Plaza Bloomington IL 61701

JOHNSON, EARVIN See JOHNSON, MAGIC

JOHNSON, EDDIE BERNICE, congresswoman; b. Waco, Tex., Dec. 3, 1935; d. Lee Edward and Lillie Mae (White) J.; m. Lacy Kirk Johnson, July 5, 1956 (div. Oct. 1970); 1 child, Dawrence Kirk. Diploma in Nursing, St. Mary's Coll. of South Bend, 1955; BS in Nursing, Tex. Christian U., 1967; MPA, So. Meth. U., 1976; LLD (hon.), Bishop Coll., 1979, Jarvis Coll., 1979, Tex. Coll., 1989, Houston-Tillotson Coll., 1993, Paul Quinn Coll., 1993. Chief psychiat. nurse psychotherapist Vets. Hosp., Dallas, 1956-72; state rep. Tex. Ho. Reps. Dist. 33-0, Dallas, 1972-77; regional dir. HEW, Dallas, 1977-79, exec. asst. to adminstr. for primary health care policy Washington, 1979-81; v.p. Vis. Nurse Assn. of Tex., Dallas, 1981-87; mem. Tex. State Senate, dist. 23, 1986-93, U.S. Congress from 30th Tex. dist., Washington, 1993—, mem. sci., transp. and infrastructure coms.; chair Black caucus 107th U.S. Congress. Cons. div. urban affairs Zales Corp., Dallas, 1976-77; exec. asst. personnel div. Neiman-Marcus, Dallas, 1972-75; pres. Eddie Bernice Johnson & Assocs., Inc., Metroplex News, Dallas-Ft. Worth Airport. Bd. dirs. ARC. Recipient Citizenship award Nat. Conf. Christians and Jews, 1985; named an Outstanding Alumnus St. Mary's Coll. of Nursing, 1986. Mem. Alpha Kappa Alpha. Democrat. Office: US Ho of Reps 1511 Longworth HOB Washington DC 20515-4330

JOHNSON, EDGAR MCCARTHY, psychologist; b. Jacksonville, Fla., Oct. 29, 1941; s. James Mack Johnson and Dorothy (Vickers) Logue; m. Fatima Nunes, Sept. 9, 1967; children: Victoria C., David M. BS in Applied Psychology, Ga. Inst. Tech., 1964; MS in Exptl. Psychology, Tufts U., 1967, PhD in Exptl. Psychology, 1969. Rsch. psychologist U.S. Army Rsch. Inst., Alexandria, Va., 1970-78, chief human factors sect., 1978-80, dir. systems rsch. lab., 1980-82, tech. dir., 1982-93, dir., 1993—2002; chief psychologist U.S. Army, 1982—2002; mem. rsch. staff Inst. Def. Analyses, Alexandria, Va., 2002—. Served to capt. U.S. Army, 1968-70. NDEA fellow, 1965-67. Fellow APA, Am. Psychol. Soc., Human Factors and Ergonomics Soc., Washington Acad. Sci. (Sci. Achievement award 1980); mem. Cosmos Club (Washington), Sigma Xi. Home: 5315 Renaissance Ct Burke VA 22015-2194 Office: Inst for Def Analyses 4850 Mark Ctr Dr Alexandria VA 22311-1882 E-mail: emj1@sigmaxi.org., emjohnso@ida.org.

JOHNSON, EDNA SCOTT, English language educator, volunteer; b. Sioux Falls, S.D., Aug. 15, 1913; d. George Emil and Emma Erika (Pearson) Nelson; m. Preston William Scott, May 29, 1939 (dec. Apr. 1969); children: William Scott (dec. 1969), Gregory N. Scott; m. Merritt W. Johnson, Jan. 1, 1973 (dec. May 1978). BA, U. S.D., 1936. Cert. secondary tchr. English, French instr. Beresford (S.D.) High Sch., 1936-39. Pres. Hecla (S.D.) Sch. Bd., 1950-63, Assn. Sch. Bds., S.D., 1954-60, state pres. nat. exec. com.; state del. to White House Conf. on Edn., 1955; cons. Am. Social Hygiene Soc., 1956; exec. com. Gov.'s Lay Conf. Edn., S.D., 1962; mem. Landmarks Commn., S.D. Commn. for Jud. Change, 1975-84. Author: School Board Members Handbook, 1957, Brown County History, 1981, Bethlehem Lutheran Church History, 1984, (booklet) Railroads of Brown County, 1984; editor Brown County LWV Bull., 1991-92. Den mother Cub Scouts, 1951-61; leader Brown County Sch. Dist. Reorganization Bd., S.D., 1953-57; mem. devel. com. U. S.D., 1958-66; pres. Brown County Libr. Bd., 1958-77, S.D. PTA, 1960-62, state pres. nat. bd.; pres. Brown County Hist. Soc., 1986-88, Community Concerts Bd., chmn., Aberdeen, 1981-85; gen. chmn. Diamond Jubilee, Hecla, 1960-61, Declaration of Independence Celebration, Brown County, 1976, Brown County State Centennial Celebration, S.D., 1988-91; bd. dirs. Aberdeen United Way, 1983-84; sheriff Dakota Midlands Western Corral, pres. 1989-91; bd. pres. Dakotah Prairie Mus., 1954-59; mem. Bethlehem Luth. Ch. Choir. Recipient Outstanding Svc. award U. S.D., 1956, Outstanding Sch. Bd. Mem. award S.D. Sch. Bd. Assn., Sch. Bell award S.D. Sch. Bd. Assn., 1984, Svc. award S.D. State U., 1984; named First Lady of Aberdeen, 1984. Mem. AAUW (pres.), NEA, S.D. Edn. Assn., P.E.O., O.E.S., Aberdeen Area Arts Coun., Fedn. Women's Clubs, N.S.U. Faculty Wives, Aberdeen Area Geneal. Soc., LVW (pres. 1996-98), Sons of Norway, MC3 Club, Time Club, Chi Omega, Delta Kappa Gamma. Avocations: research and writing, reading, history, walking. Address: PO Box 1566 Aberdeen SD 57402-1566

JOHNSON, EDWARD CROSBY, III, financial company executive; b. Boston, June 29, 1930; s. Edward Crosby and Elsie (Johnson) J.; m. Elizabeth Bishop Hodges, Oct. 8, 1960; children: Abigail Pierrepont, Elizabeth Livingston, Edward Crosby. AB, Harvard U., 1954. With Fidelity Investments, Boston, 1957—, pres., chief exec. officer, 1972-77; chmn. bd., chief exec. officer parent co. FMR Corp., 1977—. Bd. dirs. Ctr. for Neurologic Diseases; hon. trustee Mus. Fine Arts, Boston. Served with AUS, 1954-56. Fellow Am. Acad. Arts and Scis.; mem. Mass. Hist. Soc. Office: Fidelity Investments 82 Devonshire St Boston MA 02109*

JOHNSON, EDWARD MICHAEL, lawyer, consultant; b. Waco, Tex., July 12, 1944; s. Edward James and Anne Margaret (Stuchly) J.; m. Yvonne Margaret Hill, May 7, 1977; children: Hilary Yvonne, Megan Joy, Michael David. BA in Polit. Sci., S.W. Tex. State U., 1967; JD, St. Mary's U., 1970. Bar: Tex. 1971, U.S. Dist. Ct. (we. and so. dist.) Tex. 1972, U.S. Ct. Claims, 1972, U.S. Supreme Ct. 1976. Asst. law libr. Bexar County Law Libr., 1968-69; briefing clk. Judge Preston H. Dial, Jr., 1969-70; briefing atty. U.S. Dist. Judge John H. Wood Jr., San Antonio, 1971-72; asst. U.S. atty. Dept. Justice, San Antonio, 1972-76; sole practice San Antonio, 1976-81; sr. atty. Wiley, Garwood, Hornbuckle, Higdon & Johnson, San Antonio, 1980-81; pres. McCabe Petroleum Corp., San Antonio, 1981; chmn. bd., CEO, gen. counsel Blue Chip Petroleum Corp., San Antonio, 1981-83; pres., gen. counsel Harvest Investments Corp., San Antonio, 1983-87, also dir.; gen. ptrn. Med. Mobility Ltd. IV, San Antonio, 1984-87; mgr. Med. Mobility Joint Venture, San Antonio, 1984-87; exec. cons. Advance Tax Representation, Inc., 1987-88; gen. ptrn. Harvest Venture Capital Ltd. I, San Antonio, 1986-87; pres., gen. counsel Blue Chip Securities Corp., San Antonio, 1984-87; rep. First Investors Corp., 1987-88; pres., CEO Johnson, Curney, Garcia, Wise & Farmer P.C., 1990-2000; Diamond direct distbr. Amway Corp., 1997—2000; mem. exec. com. EcoQuest Internat., 2002—. Host radio program The Christian Lawyer, 1990-91, TV program God's Army, 1990-98; mem. adv. bd. Red McCombs Galleria Imports, 1996-98, Network Mktg. Lifestyles Mag., 1999-2002, Hovey Motorcars, 1999—. Co-chmn. fund raising Am. Heart Assn., San Antonio, 1982-84; bd. dirs. Am. Cancer Soc., San Antonio, 1982-84; chmn. San Fernando Cathedral Endowment Fund, San Antonio, 1986; mem. Gideons Internat., San Antonio, 1982-86, mem. exec. bd. San Antonio Christian Schs., 1983-84, San Antonio Christian Legal Soc., 1991-2000, Fed. Bar Licensing Bd., 1976-78; bd. dirs. Tex. Bible Coll., 1984-87, Christian Businessmen's Com., San Antonio, 1981-88, Cornerstone Christian Schs., San Antonio, 1991-92, mem., spkr., pres. Med. Ctr. chpt. 1988-91, mem. Full Gospel Businessmen's Fellowship, 1981-92, pres. 1985-88, field rep., 1988-92; Rep. precinct chmn., 1988-89; bd. dirs. Assn. Spirit Filled Fellowships, 1991-93; pres. God's Army Internat. Found., Inc., 1990-92; gen. counsel, bd. dirs. Four Winds Ministries, Inc., 1992-93; scoutmaster Alamo area coun. Boy Scouts Am., San Antonio, 1973-74; founder, chmn. Christian Businessmen's Focus on the Family, San Antonio, 1984-85. Recipient spl. commendation Dept. Transp. 1973, Dept. Air Force HQ, ATC, 1974, Dept. Treasury, 1974; named Outstanding Asst. U.S. Atty. Dept. Justice, 1974-75, One of Outstanding Young Texans, 1976. Mem. Fed. Bar Assn. (pres. San Antonio chpt. 1975-76, v.p. 1973-74, sec. 1972-73, treas. 1971-72, Outstanding Chpt. Pres. award 1976), Tex. Bar Assn., San Antio Bar Assn. (spl. asst. to exec. dir. 1968-69). Republican. E-mail: edjohnson@ecoquestintl.com.

JOHNSON, ELAINE LUCILLE, artist, director; b. New Orleans, La., Oct. 1, 1957; d. Lionel Lloyd Johnson, Sr. and Lucille (Green) Johnson; children: Keva, Kima, Kori Richard. Attended, Univ. of New Orleans, N.O., La., 1977—79, St. Bernard Comm. Coll., Chalmette, La., 1984, Nunez Comm. Coll., 2002. Cert. Nurse aide, Nursing Home/ St. Bernard, La., 1984. Nurse aide Nursing Home, St. Bernard, La., 1984—2003; dir. Boogie's Art Gallery, St. Bernard, La., 1999—. Dir. art and craft Vacation Bible Sch., First Bapt. Ch., Verret, La. Author: (coloring book) Color with Boogie, 2002, (craft, annual project) New Yr. Craft, (picture book) Picture Perfect Book 00 , 2000. Mem.. New Orleans Art Coun. Achievements include open first Art Gallery in St. Bernard, La. with Joan Sloan, 1999. Now a non-profit Gallery/Studio.

JOHNSON, ELEANOR MAE, education educator; b. St. Paul, Mar. 22, 1925; d. Emil H. and Leona W. (Warner) Busse; m. Edward Charles Johnson, May 13, 1950; 1 child, Mary Jo Johnson Tuckwell. BS, U. Wis., Stout, 1946, MS, 1959, edn. specialist, 1981. Cert. home economist, tchr., Wis. Instr. home econs. various pub. schs., Wis., 1946-48, 56-64; home economist U. Wis. Extension, various locations, 1948-51, 52-56; tchr. educator U. Wis.-Stout, Menomonie, 1965-87; ret., 1987. Summer session guest prof. U. Man., Winnipeg, Can., 1970, 71, S.D. State U., Brookings, 1978; dir. Native Am. curriculum for home econs. Fed. Vocat. Project, U. Wis.-Stout, 1978-80; cons. vocat. evaluation team U. Wis.-Stout, 1982-90; presenter at profl. confs.; team mem. interdisciplinary consumer edn. teaching materials Joint Coun. Econ. Edn., 1980-82. Editor teaching materials for Native Ams., 1978-80. Sr. statesman Wis. Coalition on Aging, 1990-2003; adv., vol. Office of Aging, 1992-2003. Mem. Am. Home Econs. Assn. (del. nat. and internat. confs., Inner City fellow 1970), Life mem. with - Am. Vocat. Assn., Wis. Edn. Assn., U. Wis.-Stout Alumni, Assn. Tchr. Educators and Am. Assn. Ret. Persons. Avocations: national and international travel, collecting historical canning jars, stamps, antique dolls, genealogy. Home: 623 Elm Ave Barron WI 54812-1712

JOHNSON, ELIZABETH ERICSON, retired educator; b. Rockford, Ill., Oct. 5, 1927; d. Gunnar Lawrence and Victoria Amelia (Carlson) Ericson; m. Barent Olaf Johnson, June 2, 1951; children: Ann E. Arellano, Susan M. Taber. BA, U. Ill., 1949; MSEd, No. Ill. U., 1969. Tchr. Sch. Dist. 205, Rockford, Ill., 1949-53, 65-92. Mem. Ct. Appointed Spl. Advocate, Rockford, 1992—. Mem. AAUW, LWV (bd. dirs. 1994-96, local bd.), Ill. Ret. Tchrs. Assn., Winnebago Ret. Tchrs. Assn. (various bds.), Phi Delta Kappa emeritus. Avocations: music, viola, musician, violist. Home: 1902 Valencia Dr Rockford IL 61108-6818 E-mail: evebridge@aol.com.

JOHNSON, ELLEN SCHULTZ, retired music librarian, researcher; b. Beatrice, Nebr., Apr. 11, 1918; d. P. Daniel and Justina (Wiebe) Schultz; m. Dale M. Johnson, May 12, 1944; children: Richard, Dorothy, Brenda. BA, Friends U., 1939; BLS, U. Ill., 1941. Head libr. Friends U., Wichita, Kans., 1946-47; head circulation and reference libr., music lectr. Wichita State U., 1959-68; head circulation dept., catalog libr., music lectr. Western Ky. U., Bowling Green, 1968-73; head cataloging dept. U. Kans., Lawrence, 1973-77, libr. archives of recorded sound, 1977-88, emeritus, 1988—. Prin. investigator Associated Audio Archives, Washington, 1986-87. Author: Leslie Bassett, A Bio-Bibliography; contbr. articles to Flute Talk, Am. Music Tchr., Coll. Band Dirs. Nat. Assn. jour. Recipient cert. recognition Audio Engring. Soc., 1986; NEH grantee, 1986-87. Mem. AAUP (officer 1959—), Internat. Assn. Sound Archives (chmn. copyright com. 1984—, contbr. phonographic bull. 1986—), Sonneck Soc., Music Libr. Assn., Assn. for Recorded Sound Collections (assoc. audio archives com. 1984-88), Nat. Fedn. Music Clubs, Lawrence Bus. and profl. Women's Club (past pres.), Sigma Alpha Iota. Republican. Unitarian Universalist. Avocations: collecting records, outdoor activities, doll collecting. Home: 3112 Longhorn Dr Lawrence KS 66049-1958

JOHNSON, ELMER HUBERT, sociologist, researcher in criminology; b. Racine, Wis., Apr. 10, 1917; s. Elmer Dumguaard and Lucinda (Hinderholtz) J.; m. Carol Catherine Holmes, June 19, 1943; children: Joy Marjorie Boyden, Jill Catherine Lewis. BA, U. Wis., 1946, MA, 1948, PhD, 1950. Reporter Racine Jour. Times, 1935-40; from asst. prof. to prof. N.C. State U., Raleigh, 1949-66; asst. dir. N.C. State Prison Dept., Raleigh, 1958-60; prof. So. Ill. U., Carbondale, 1966-87, Disting. prof., 1984, emeritus, 1987—. Bd. dirs. Joint Commn. on Corrections, Washington, 1965-70; vis. fellow Max Planck Inst., Freiburg, Germany, 1978, Nat. Inst. Law Enforcement and Criminal Justice, Washington, 1979, UN Asia and Far East Inst., Tokyo, 1985; cons. Jao Pinheiro Found., Brazil, 2000. Author: Crime, Correction and Society, 1965; editor: International Handbook of Contemporary Development in Criminology, 2 vols., 1983; editor: Handbook on Crime and Delinquency Prevention, 1987, Japanese Corrections: Managing Convicted Offenders in an Orderly Society, 1996, Criminalization and Prisoners in Japan: Six Contrary Cohorts, 1997, Community and Corrections in Japan: Nature and Challenges, 1999. Served to capt. USAAC, 1941-46, with USAF Res. Recipient Fulbright award, UN Asia and Far East Inst., Tokyo, 1990—91. Mem. Internat. Soc. Criminology, Internat. Sociol. Assn., Am. Soc. Criminology (bd. dirs. 1975-80), Acad. Criminal Justice Scis., Am. Sociol. Assn. Avocations: scholarly reading, international contacts, music appreciation. Home: 451 E Clayton Rd Carbondale IL 62901-7104 E-mail: j1941917@siu.edu.

JOHNSON, ELMER WILLIAM, lawyer; b. Denver, May 2, 1932; s. Elmer William and Lillian Marie (Nelson) J.; m. Constance Dorothy Mahon, June 18, 1955; children: Julianne Marie, Valerie Lynn, Garrett Douglas. BA, Yale U., 1954; JD, U. Chgo., 1957. Bar: Ill. 1957. Assoc. Kirkland & Ellis, Chgo., 1956-62, ptnr., 1962—99; v.p., group exec. gen. counsel Gen. Motors Corp., Detroit, 1983-87, exec. v.p., dir., 1987-88; gen. counsel Internat. Harvester, Chgo., 1982-83; spl. counsel to chmn. of Ameritech Corp., Chgo., 1982-83; pres., CEO Aspen Inst., Washington, 1999—2002; ptnr. Jenner & Block, Chgo., 2002—. Mem. legal adv. com. N.Y. Stock Exch., 1987-91; v.p., dir. The Econ. Club of Chgo.; chmn. bd. govs. Chgo. Lighthouse for Blind. Author: Avoiding the Collision of Cities and Cars, 1993, Chicago Metropolis 2020, 2001. Trustee U. Chgo., 1977-89, Aspen Inst., Colo., 1988—. Fellow Am. Acad. Arts and Scis.; mem. ABA, Ill. Bar Assn., Chgo. Club, Old Elm. Republican. Presbyterian. Office: Jenner & Block 1 IBM Plaza Chicago IL 60611

JOHNSON, EMERY ALLEN, physician; b. Sioux Falls, S.D., Apr. 16, 1929; s. Emery Albert and Florence Emily J.; m. Nancy Mourning, June 19, 1954; children: Steven, Scott, Jennifer, Jill. BS, Hamline U., 1951; MD, U. Minn., 1954; MPH, U. Calif., Berkeley, 1964; LHD, Hamline U., 2000. Commd. med. officer USPHS, 1955-81, Indian health area dir., 1964-66, asst. and dep. dir. Indian Health Service Rockville, Md., 1966-69, dir. Indian Health Service, 1969-81, asst. surgeon gen., 1969-81; cons. in pub. health and med. care

adminstrn., 1981—. Cons. Peace Corps, WHO, AID, Nat. Med. Center, Liberia; U.S. del. UNICEF Exec. Bd., 1978 Recipient Rockefeller Public Service award, 1979; Excellence in Public Service award Am. Acad. Pediatrics; medals USPHS Mem. APHA (chmn. health adminstrn. sect.), Am. Acad. Family Practice, AMA. Office: 13826 Dowlais Dr Rockville MD 20853-2658

JOHNSON, ERIC B. state legislator; b. New Orleans, Aug. 20, 1953; m. Kathryn Johnson; children: Marcus, Righton. Degree in architecture, Tulane U. Architect Hussey, Gay, Bell and DeYoung Internat.; mem. Ga. Ho. of Reps., 1993-94; senator 1st dist. Ga. State Legislature, 1994—, pres. pro temp., 2003—. Senate minority leader; sec., appropriations vice chmn. Regulated Industries and Utilities; ex-officio Economic Devel. and Tourism, Edn., Natural Resources and the Environment; mem. Fin. Reapportionment and Redistricting Rules Com.; sponsor, mem. joint senate-house study com. on cert. of need health care facilities Ga. State Senate. Regional dir. former U.S. Senator Mack Mattingly, 1981-83; alumnus Leadership Savannah; active Inner City Night Shelter. Named Ga.'s Young Rep. of Yr., 1980. Mem. AIA, Exec. Assn. of Savannah. Mem. Savannah Christian Ch. also: 22 Marsh Point Dr Savannah GA 31406-3218 Business E-Mail: ejohnson@legis.state.ga.us.

JOHNSON, ERNEST FREDERICK, chemical engineer, educator; b. Jamestown, N.Y., Apr. 4, 1918; s. Ernest Frederick and Esther Marie (Engstrom) J.; m. Marjorie Ruth McMullin, July 15, 1944; children: David S. (dec.), Carolyn L. Walton, Arthur B., Melissa A. Bonner. BS, Lehigh U., 1940; PhD, U. Pa., 1949. Rsch. engr., tech. supr. synthetic organic chem. mfr. Barrett div. Allied Chem. Corp., Phila., 1940-46; asst. prof. dept. chem. engring. Princeton U., 1948-54, assoc. prof., 1954-59, prof., 1959-86, acting chmn. dept. chem. engring., 1959-60, chmn. dept., 1977-78, assoc. dean faculty, 1962-66, clk. of faculty, 1983-86, assoc. Plasma Physics Lab., 1955-86, prof. emeritus, 1986—, sr. advisor to pres., 1988-91. Cons. petroleum, chem., engring., environ., food processing firms, govt. agys., 1949—; bd. dirs. Autodynamics Inc. 1968-85; mem. adv. bd. Indsl. and Engring. Chemistry, 1964-67. Author: Automatic Process Control, 1967; contbr. Advances in Chemical Engineering, 1958, Ency. Chemistry, Chemistry of Fusion Power Development, 1972; contbr. articles to sci. jours. Trustee Associated Univs., Inc., 1962-68, chmn. bd., 1965-67; trustee Westminster Found., 1973-79. Recipient Nat. Engrs. Week Engring. Edn. award, 1994, Lehigh U. Alumni Assn. award, 2000, Eugene G. Grace Class of 1889 award Lehigh U., 2001; named hon. mem. Princeton Class of 1962. Fellow AAAS, AIChE (exec. com. Cen. Jersey sect. 1972—), Am. Inst. Chemists; mem. Am. Chem. Soc. (exec. com. div. indsl. and engring. chemistry 1965-67, coun. 1976-78), Princeton Engring. Assn. (sec.-treas. 1954-57, exec. com. 1954—), Adirondack Mountain Club, Appalachian Mountain Club, Tärnavrå Yacht Club, Sigma Xi, Tau Beta Pi, Phi Eta Sigma. Presbyterian (elder). Home: 47 Meadow Lakes 03U Hightstown NJ 08520 also: Indian Point Rd Stonington ME 04681-9702

JOHNSON, EUGENE CLARE, data processing company executive; b. Whitehall, Wis., Nov. 19, 1940; s. Paul Reuben and Clara Theresa (Severson) J.; m. Livia Ann Baynes, Sept. 23, 1967; children: Andrew Paul, Anthony Alexander. Student, Madison Coll., 1959, Pasadena Coll., 1961, Purdue U., 1962, Harvard U., 1974. Vol. Peace Corps, Chile, 1962-64; acct. Am. Ins. Underwriters, N.Y.C., 1964-66; advanceman to Pres. Richard M. Nixon N.Y.C., 1966-68; asst. treas. Bristol-Myers Co., N.Y.C., 1968-69; spl. asst. to Gov. Nelson Rockefeller N.Y.C., 1969-77; mgr. advanced systems div. U.S. Postal Service, Washington, 1971-80; with govt. relations dept. ITT, Washington, 1980-85; exec. v.p., chief operating officer TCom Systems, Inc., Washington, 1985-88; v.p. market devel. Diversified Data and Communications Inc., Washington, 1988-90; pres., chief exec. officer Bus. Mail Express, Inc., Washington, 1990-95, Mail 2000, Washington, 1995—. Founder Electronic Funds Transfer Assocs., Washington, 1977. Patentee performance analyzer. Sr. adviser Reagan Presdl. Transition Team, 1980; presdl. appointee U.S. Archtl. and Transp. Barriers Compliance Bd., 1988-90; adv. bd. Peace Corps., 1990-92. Mem.: Kenwood Golf and Country (Bethesda, Md.) (chmn. bd. dirs. 1987). Avocations: tennis, golf, jogging. Home: 5525 Chamberlin Ave Chevy Chase MD 20815-6643 Office: Ste 300 7316 Wisconsin Ave Bethesda MD 20814-2976

JOHNSON, EUGENE LAURENCE, lawyer; b. Wisconsin Rapids, Wis., Nov. 30, 1936; s. Elmer Hilding and Claribel May Johnson; m. Barbara Dell Braley, June 18, 1960; children: Mark, Ben, Christopher. BSCE, U. Wis., 1960, JD, 1962. Bar: Minn. 1963, Calif. 1965, U.S. Patent Office 1963. Atty. Pillsbury Co., Mpls., 1962-64; assoc. Mellin, Hanscom & Hursh, San Francisco, 1964-66; ptnr. Dorsey & Whitney, Mpls., 1966-98, Eugene L. Johnson, PA, Wayzata, Minn., 1998—. Program founder, adj. prof. intellectual property law William Mitchell Coll. of Law, 1967-75. Capt. C.E. USAR, 1960. Mem. Minn. Bar Assn. (past bd. govs.), Am. Intellectual Property Law Assn., Minn. Intellectual Property Law Assn. (past pres.), Mpls. Athletic Club, Lafayette Country Club. Republican. Office: Eugene L Johnson PA 1500 Bohns Point Rd Wayzata MN 55391-9309

JOHNSON, EVA MARIA, retired translator; b. Ludwigshafen, Rhine, Germany, Jan. 19, 1920; came to U.S., 1951; naturalized 1955; d. George and Maria Regina (Wurzel) Lenz; m. Martin L. Johnson, June 8, 1952 (dec. Jan. 1994); 1 child, Michael Andrew. Student, Ludwigshafen, 1938, Vorbeck Lang. Sch., 1940-43. Interpreter, translator German and French, Police, Lampertheim, Germany, 1945-46; reporter Deutsche Presse Dienst, Wiesbaden, Germany, 1946-48; editl. specialist U.S. Mil. Govt., Wiesbaden, Germany, 1948-51; bilingual sec. Embassy of Austria, Washington, 1951-53; translator Internat. Affairs Dept. CIO, Washington, 1953—55; translator Combat Ops. Rsch. Group, CDC, Fort Belvoir, Va., 1965-70; freelance translator top secret clearance Dept. Def., Washington, 1970-72; sr. sect., translator Holman & Stern, Patent Law Office, Washington, 1972-85; ret., 1985. Key-note spkr. Surviving POWs VA Hosp., Martinsburg, W.Va., 1996. Anti-Nazi activist, 1943-45. Mem.: The Ret. Mil. Officer Assn. (life). Avocations: photography, writing, eggeury, gardening, reading. Home: 352 Monastery Ridge Rd Stephenson VA 22656

JOHNSON, EVAN KENNETH, physical therapist, educator; b. N.Y.C., Feb. 14, 1960; m. Wendy Haberman, Aug. 21, 1993; children: Jared Ian, Ethan Francis. BA in Psychology and Biology, CUNY, 1992; MS in Phys. Therapy, Columbia U., 1994. Cert. orthopedic specialist. Phys. therapist Ball Meml. Hosp., Muncie, Ind., 1994-96; asst. chief phys. therapist Phys. Medicine and Rehab. Ctr., Englewood, N.J., 1996-98; site coord. St. Charles Hosp. Rehab. Network, Bronx/Queens, NY, 1998-2000; phys. therapy coord. Phys. Medicine and Rehab. Ctr., Bardonia, N.Y., 2000-2001; sr. therapist advanced clinician N.Y. Presbyn. Hosp.: Columbia Presbyn. Spine Ctr., 2001—. Clin. instr., lectr. Columbia U., 1996-2003, asst. prof. clin. phys. therapy, 2003—; clin. faculty assoc. N.Y. Med. Coll., 1998—; phys. therapy coord. clin. pathways com., Ball Meml. Hosp., 1994, 95. Contbr. articles to Jour. Orthopaedic and Sports Phys. Therapy. Recipient J and W Freedman award Hunter Coll., 1992, Phys. Therapy Alumni award Columbia U., 1992, 93, Mary E. Callahan award Columbia U., 1994; Paul Brachfeld grantee CUNY, 1991, 92. Mem. Am. Phys. Therapy Assn. (platform presenter, Reno, 1995, mem. performing arts spl. interest group, mem. Orthopaedic sect.), Internat. Assn. Dance Medicine and Sci., Am. Acad. Orthopaedic Manual Phys. Therapists, Phi Beta Kappa. Office: Columbia Univ Program in Physical Therapy 710 W 168th St 8th Floor New York NY 10032 E-mail: EKJ6@columbia.edu.

JOHNSON, EVELYN, minister, educator; b. Jefferson County, Ala., Jan. 18, 1945; d. Johnie Sr. and Virginia Sherrer Johnson; div.; children: Thaddeus R., Ralph D. II. BA in Philosophy and Religion, Kean U., 2000. Cert. radiol. technologist, N.J.; ordained Mount Zion AME Ch., 1997. Radiology technologist Hosp., N.J., 1968-87; sch. crossing guard Union Twp. Police Dept., N.J., 1990-99; cafeteria aide Bd. Edn., Union, N.J., 1993-99, sub. tchr. Union County, N.J., 1999—; min. St. Luke AME Ch., Newark, 1990—. Author: From The Mortar to The Glue, 1998. Dir. St. Luke Cmty. Multi-purpose OutReach Ctr., Newark; pres. Union County Women Polit. Caucus, 1984, Recreation Adv Com., Union, 1987-88; v.p. Union Twp. Betterment Com., Twp. of Union, 1987; coord. Hands Across Am., Twp. of Union, 1987. With U.S. Army, 1966-68. Named Woman of Yr., Calvary Bapt. Ch., Vauxhall, N.J., 1984; resolution Union Twp. Governing Body, 1988. Avocations: singing, walking, writing. Home: 1000 Valley St Vauxhall NJ 07088-1035 Office: St Luke AME Ch 146 Clinton Ave Newark NJ 07114-1958 Fax: 973-623-4030. E-mail: Jhnsone@Hotmail.com.

JOHNSON, EVELYN BRYAN, airport terminal executive; b. Corbin, Ky., Nov. 4, 1909; d. Edward William and Myme Estelle (Fox) Stone; m. Wyatt J. Bryan, Mar. 21, 1931 (dec. 1963); m. Morgan N. Johnson, Feb. 25, 1965 (dec. Mar. 1977). Grad., Tenn Wesleyan Jr. Coll., 1929; student, U. Tenn., 1930-32. With Morristown (Tenn.) Flying Svc., Inc., 1947-97, designated pilot examiner, 1952—, sec.-treas., 1949-62, pres., 1962-82; mgr. Moore Murrell Airport, 1962—. Gov.'s appointee Tenn. Aero. Commn., 1983—2001, vice-chmn., 1987—89, chmn., 1989, 1994—96, 1996—2001. Recipient Carnegie Hero medal, 1958, Svc. to Mankind award Morristown Sertoma Club, 1981, Kitty Hawk award, FAA, 1991, Friends of Aviation award Tenn. Aviation Assn., 1992, Stewart G. Potter Aviation Edn. award Aviation Distbrs. and Mfrs. Assn., 1992, Elder Statesman of Aviation award Nat. Aeronautics Assn., 1993, Katherine Wright Meml. award Nat. Aeronautics Assn. and the Nenety Nies, 2002; named Flight Instr. of Yr., Nashville Dist. 1973, 79, So. region 1979, Nat., 1979 (all FAA), Outstanding Alumnus Tenn. Wesleyan Coll., 1981, Inductee Women in Aviation Pioneers Hall of Fame, 1994, Hamblen Women Hall of Fame, 1997, Flight Instr. Hall of Fame, EAA Air Venture Mus., Oshkosh, 1997, Ky. Aviation Hall of Fame, 2000, Tenn. Aviation Hall of Fame, 2002, Kathryn Wright Meml. award NAA, 2002; holder of record most flying time for women pilots, 1995, Guiness Book of Records 1995—. Mem. CAP, Morristown Area C. of C., Nat. Assn. Flight Instrs. (bd. dirs., treas 1987-88, award 1992), Ninety-Nines, Whirly Girls (plaque 1992), Aircraft Owners and Pilots Assn., Silver Wings (bd. dirs. 1987—. Woman of Yr. 1981, Carl Fromhagen award 1992, Ninety Nines award of merit 1994) Republican. Baptist. Home: 775 Commanche Dr Jefferson City TN 37760-5125 Office: PO Box 1013 Morristown TN 37816-1013

JOHNSON, FERNLY ELDO, surgeon; b. Otisco, Minn., Aug. 21, 1918; BS, U. Ill., 1941, MD, 1943. Diplomate Am. Bd. Surgery. Intern U.S. Naval Hosp., Gt. Lakes, 1943-44; resident Hines VA Hosp., 1948-51; surgeon emeritus Swedish Covenant Hosp., Chgo., 1951—. Fellow AMA; mem. ACS, Alpha Omega Alpha.

JOHNSON, FRANCIS SEVERIN, physicist; b. Omak, Wash., July 20, 1918; s. Ralston Severin and Elizabeth (Gruenes) J.; m. Maurine Marie Green, Sept. 12, 1943; 1 dau., Sharan Kaye. B.Sc. with honors in Physics, U. Alta., Can., 1940; MA in Physics and Meteorology, UCLA, 1942, PhD in Meteorology, 1958. Head, high atmosphere research sect. U.S. Naval Research Lab., Washington, 1946-55; mgr. space physics research Lockheed Missiles & Space Co., 1955-62; head, atmospheric and space scis. div. S.W. Center Advanced Studies, Dallas, 1962-64, dir. earth and planetary scis. lab., 1964-69; acting pres. U. Tex. at Dallas, 1969-71; dir. Center for Advanced Studies, 1971-74, Cecil H. and Ida M. Green honors prof. natural sci., 1974-89, prof. emeritus, 1989—, exec. dean grad. studies and research, 1976-79; asst. dir. astron., atmosphere, earth and ocean scis. NSF, Washington, 1979-83. Cons. ionospheric physics subcom., space scis. steering com. NASA, 1960-62, mem. planetary atmospheres subcom., space scis. steering com., 1962-67, chmn. lunar atmospheric measurements team, Apollo sci. planning teams, 1964-67, mem. adv. bd. Mars space missions, 1964-67, mem. lunar and planetary missions bd., 1967-71; mem. adv. panel atmospheric scis. NSF, 1962-67; mem. working group IV COSPAR, 1965-80, v.p., 1975-80; mem. Nat. Acad. Scis. panel adv. to central radio propagation lab. Nat. Bur. Standards, 1962-65, mem. panel weather and climate modification Nat. Acad. Scis., 1964-70, mem. space sci. bd., 1969-81, mem. geophysics research bd., 1971-77, mem. bd. on atmospheric scis. and climate, 1984-87, mem. Nat. Acad. Scis. com. adv. to NOAA, 1966-71, mem. climate research bd., 1977-79; mem. adv. com. research to coordinating bd. Tex. Coll. and Univ. System, 1966-67; mem. sci. advisory bd. USAF, 1968-79; mem. nat. adv. com. Oceans and Atmosphere, 1971-73; pres. Spl. Com. on Solar Terrestrial Physics, 1974-77; mem. Aerocibo adv. bd. and vis. com. Nat. Astronomy and Ionsphere Ctr. Cornell U., 1985-88. Author: Satellite Environment Handbook, 1965; also numerous articles. Served with USAAF, 1942-46. Decorated Bronze Star medal; recipient Henryk Arctowski award NAS, 1972, Exceptional Sci. Achievement medal NASA, 1973, Meritorious Civilian Service award USAF, 1979, Disting. Tex. Sci. award Tex. Acad. Scis., 1984, Disting. Alumni award U. Alta., 2001. Fellow Am. Geophys. Union (vice chmn. sect. geomagnetism and aeronomy 1964-68, pres. sect. solar planetary relationships 1970-72, John Adam Fleming award 1977), AAAS (council mem. 1968-72), Am. Meteorol. Soc. (councilor 1976-78), IEEE, AIAA (chmn. tech. com. space and atmospheric physics 1961-64, Space Sci. award 1966); mem. Internat. Assn. Geomagnetism and Aeronomy (exec. com. 1967-71), Internat. Union Radio Sci. (chmn. U.S. Commn. IV 1964-67, sec. U.S. nat. com. 1967-70, vice chmn. 1970-73, chmn. 1973-76), Internat. Union Geodesy and Geophysics (U.S. nat. com. 1973-76), Sigma Xi. Office: U Tex At Dallas MS FO22 PO Box 830688 Richardson TX 75083-0688 E-mail: johnson@utdallas.edu.

JOHNSON, FRANK, educator, retired state official; b. Ogden, Utah, Mar. 12, 1928; s. Clarence Budd and Arline (Parry) J.; m. Maralyn Brewer, Aug. 15, 1950; children: Scott, Arline, Laurie, Kelly, Edward. BS, U. Utah, 1955; MS, U. Ill., 1958, PhD, 1960. Instr. U. N.D., Grand Forks, 1955-56; teaching asst. U. Ill., Urbana, 1956-59; rsch. asst. prof. U. Del., Newark, 1959-60; prof. U. Utah, Salt Lake City, 1960-93, assoc. dean, 1970-77; dir. divsn. pub. utilities State of Utah, Salt Lake City, 1989-95. Cons. Gen. Foods, Sears, Magnavox, Albertsons, Zion Bank, Nat. Food Brokers Assn., others; part-owner Old Post Office Bldg., Ogden, Utah, Seventeenth St. Storage; bd. dirs. Enterprise Mentors Internat. Legis. Utah House of Reps., Salt Lake City, 1982-88; mem. Humanitarian Svc. Mission, eastern Europe, 1998-99; trainer vols. Salt Lake City Winter Olympics, 2002. Republican. Avocations: mountains, boating, travel, reading, public service. Home: 1048 E Fairway Dr North Salt Lake UT 84054-3056

JOHNSON, FRANK, professional basketball coach; b. Weirsdale, Fla., Nov. 23, 1958; m. Amy Johnson; children: Lindsay, Natalie. Postgrad, Wake Forest U., 1981. Guard Wash. Bullets, Houston Rockets, Varese & Rimini, Italy, Phoenix Suns, asst. coach, cmty. rels. dept., head coach, 2002—. Named NBA All-Rookie honors, 1982. Office: Phoenix Suns 201 E Jefferson St Phoenix AZ 85004 also: PO Box 433 Phoenix AZ 85001

JOHNSON, FRANK WILLIAM, marketing professional; b. Sumter, S.C., Sept. 20, 1948; s. John William and Dorothy (Ferrigan) J.; m. Sally Gattshall, Nov. 25, 1970; children: Lauren Elizabeth, Mark William. BA in Polit. Sci., The Citadel, 1970; MS in Ops. Mgmt., U. Ark., 1976. Sales rep. Union Carbide Corp., Dallas, 1976-78, product mgr. N.Y.C., 1979-82; sales mgr. Steelcase Inc., Dallas, 1982-83; dir. mktg. VECTA divsn. Steelcase Inc., Dallas, 1984-86; dir. sales and mktg. Lista Internat., Dallas, 1986-87; v.p. Kewaunee Sci. Corp., Lockhart, Tex., 1987-92; v.p. sales and mktg. McCoy, Inc., Houston, 1992-95; v.p. Contract Specifix, Richmond, VA, 1995-96; pres. Saxton, Inc., Davenport, Iowa, 1996-97; dir. sales Office Furniture USA, Pelham, Ala., 1998—2003; pres., CEO Norus Office Furniture, Inc., Charlotte, NC, 2003—. Capt. USAF, 1970-76. Mem.: Sales and Mktg. Club. Republican. Mem. Ch. of God. Home: 7211 Conifer Cir Indian Trail NC 28079-9528 Office: Office Furniture USA 273 Cahaba Valley Pkwy Pelham AL 35124-1146 E-mail: fwj@quixnet.net.

JOHNSON, FRANKLYN ARTHUR, academic administrator; b. Rochester, N.Y., Nov. 6, 1921; s. Robert Barnes and Olyve Cole (Eckler) J.; m. Emily Bernetta Lingle, Aug. 15, 1945 (div. Aug. 1978); children: Franklyn Arthur Jr.(dec.), Terri A. Cochran, Sandra C. Fox; m. Elena Senese, Sept. 27, 1991. BA, Rutgers U., 1947; MA, Harvard U., 1949, PhD, 1952; LHD (hon.), Jacksonville U., 1961; DLitt (hon.), Mt. Senario Coll., Ladysmith, Wis., 1971; LLD (hon.), Flagler Coll., St. Augustine, Fla., 1976; DCL (hon.), Drury Coll., Springfield, Mo., 1976; HHD (hon.), Mo. Valley Coll., 1978. Intelligence officer CIA, Washington, 1949-51; asst., assoc. prof. govt. Rollins Coll., Winter Park, Fla., 1952-56; pres., prof. govt. Jacksonville U., Fla., 1956-63, Calif. State U., Los Angeles, 1963-65; asst. sec., dir. Job Corps OEO, Washington, 1965-67; pres., chmn., trustee Wm. H. Donner Found., N.Y.C., 1967-70; dir. Arthur Vining Davis Founds., Coral Gables, Fla., 1970-78; prof. adminstrn. Fla. Atlantic U., Boca Raton, 1970-87; pres., prof. mgmt. S.W. Fla. Coll., Naples, 1987—. Trustee Inst. for Am. Univs., Aix-en-Provence, France, 1967-97, Eckerd Coll., St. Petersburg, Fla., 1978-90; chmn. S.E. Coun. Founds., Atlanta, 1975-77. Author: Defence by Committee, 1960, Defence by Ministry, 1980, 81, One More Hill, 1949, rev. edits., 1982, 88, Santori, 1990, Castro: The Last Hurrah, 1992, The Periled Presidency, 1995, Here and There, 1995, After Thoughts, 1996, D. S. Nemenoff, Maestro, 1996, A Chance Encounter, 1996, Odds and Ends, 1996, The Gods That Failed, 1997, Pearls Are a Girl's Best Friend, 1997, The 22nd Amendment, 1998, The Reluctant Presidents, 1999, Santori Island of Evil, 1999, Key West to Cuba, 2000, The Mismated, 2001, Triangle of Terror: Trauma in Everglades City, 2003; also articles on def., civil and mil. rels., adminstrn. Mem. U.S. Com. United World Colls., N.Y.C., 1975-85, Fla. Gov.'s Coun. on Indian Affairs, Tallahassee, 1975-80, exec. adv. coun. Fla. Atlantic U., chmn.; bd. dirs. Collier Cultural and Ednl. Ctr., Naples; v.p., dir. Beachwood Assn., Inc., 1992-94; pres. Francobollo Press. Lt. U.S. Army, 1942-45, ETO. Decorated Disting. Svc. medal, Jubilee of Liberty, Croix deGuerre, Diplome de la Liberation de Normandie (France); Prisoner of War medal, Silver Star, 5 Bronze Stars, 3 Purple Hearts, Conspicuous Svc. Cross; recipient George Washington honor medal Freedoms Found., Valley Forge, 1956, Profl. Achievement award Barry U., Miami, Fla., Eric Fenby lectr., 1991; named Champion Ind. Higher Edn. in Fla., Ind. Colls. Fla., 1992 Svc. Medallion, N. Fla. Jr. Coll., Madison, Fla. Fellow Inter U. Seminar on Armed Forces and Soc.; mem. Delius Assn. Am. (life, founding pres.), Can. Inst. Strategic Studies, Phi Beta Kappa, Phi Alpha Theta, Pi Alpha Alpha (pres.), Phi Kappa Phi. Republican. Presbyterian. Avocations: classical music, writing fiction. Home: PO Box 1873 Bonita Springs FL 34133-1873 E-mail: el-francobollo@webtv.net.

JOHNSON, FREDA S. public finance consultant; b. N.Y.C., Mar. 17, 1947; m. J. Chester Johnson, May 7, 1989. BA in Polit. Sci., CUNY, 1968; grad. Advanced Mgmt. Program, Harvard U., 1986. Analyst mcpl. div. Dun & Bradstreet Corp., N.Y.C., 1968-71; sr. analyst Moody's Investor Svc., Inc. (subs. Dun & Bradstreet), N.Y.C., 1972, v.p., assoc. dir. mcpl. dept., 1973-79, sr. v.p., dir. mcpl. dept., 1979-81, exec. v.p., 1981-90; pres. Govt. Fin. Assocs., Inc. pub. fin. adv. co., 1992—. Mem. Anthony Commn. for Pub. Fin.; former sr. credit advisor Ecolink, joint Soviet-Am. pub. fin. project; Congl. testifier U.S. Senate Com. on Banking, Housing and Urban Affairs, subcom. fiscal affairs and health U.S. Ho. of Reps., U.S. Senate Com. Govtl. Affairs, Joing Econ. Com. Congress; bd. dirs. MBIA Inc., Nat. Assn. Ind. Pub. Fin. Advisors, 1993-95, Queens Coll. Corp. Adv. Bd., 1994-99; bd. govs. Coun. Mcpl. Performance, 1984-86; instr. New Sch. for Social Rsch., 1982-83; mem. adv. bd. City Almanac, 1982-84; trustee Citizens Budget Com.; spkr. numerous profl. orgns., univs.; adj. prof. Grad. Sch. Bus. Adminstrn. Columbia U., spring 1991. Avocations: theater, museums, basketball fan.

JOHNSON, G. CAROL, financial services executive; b. Hamilton, Ohio, Sept. 7, 1942; d. Carlace A. Tipton; m. Robert L. Braddock (div. 1984); children: Ryan Braddock, Lauren Braddock; m. Ed. Johnson, Feb. 17, 1985; children: Meryl, Erica. BA, U. Cin., 1965, MA, 1976. V.p. Fed. Home Loan Bank Cin., 1973-85; pres. PENN Mortgage Corp., Cin., 1985-87; dir. comms. Neighborhood Reinvestment Corp., Washington, 1989-91; dir. affordable housing investments Fed. Home Loan Mortgage Corp., Vienna, Va., 1991-94; sr. v.p. GMAC Mortgage Corp., Horsham, Pa., 1995—. Bd. dirs. MERL Holdings Inc. Active Jr. League, Cin. and Washington, 1980-92, Johnson House Historic Site; chair bd. dirs. Habitat for Humanity Internat., 1997—. Mem. Am. Homeowners (chair 1999-2000), Edn. Counseling Inst. (bd. dirs., vice chair 1997-99), Links, Inc. Office: GMAC Mortgage Corp 100 Witmer Rd Horsham PA 19044

JOHNSON, GARDINER, lawyer; b. San Jose, Calif., Aug. 10, 1905; s. George W. and Izora (Carter) J.; AB, U. Calif., 1926, JD, 1928; m. Doris Louise Miller, Sept. 28, 1935; children: Jacqueline Ann, Stephen Miller. Bar: Calif. 1928; practice San Francisco, 1928— ; ptnr. Johnson & Stanton, 1952-84. Mem. nat. drafting com. Council State Govts., 1944-47, chmn. Gov.'s Conf. Edn., 1955; chmn. Calif. delegation White House Conf. Edn., 1955; mem. Calif. Legislature from 18th Assembly Dist., 1935-47, speaker pro tem, 1940; mem. Rep. State Cen. Com., 1934-46, 50-86; mem. Alameda County Rep. Cen. Com., 1934-47, 59-86; alternate del. Rep. Nat. Conv., 1940, del., 1956, 60, 64, 68, 76; pres. Calif. Rep. Assembly, 1959; mem. Rep. Nat. Com., 1964-68; mem. Citizens Legis. Adv. Commn., 1957-61; bd. dirs. U. Calif. Hosps. Aux., 1960-70, pres., 1956-58; bd. dirs. Florence Crittenton Home, San Francisco, 1960-69, 76—, pres., 1967-69; bd. dirs. Florence Crittenton Assn. Am., 1969-75, v.p., 1973-75; pres. Calif. Hist. Soc., 1968-70; bd. dirs. Spring Opera of San Francisco, 1963-69, Child Welfare League Am., 1976-84; bd. govs. San Francisco Heart Assn., 1963-70, chmn., 1966-69; mem. council Save-the-Redwoods League, 1970—. Fellow Am. Coll. Trial Lawyers; mem. Assn. Trial Lawyers Am., Internat. Bar Assn. (alternate del. 8th Conf. Salzburg 1960), Inter-Am. Bar Assn., ABA (com. state legislation 1957-59, vice chmn. com. pub. contracts 1959), Presidio Soc. (dir. 1981—), Bar Assn. San Francisco (pres. 1958), Phi Beta Kappa, Phi Delta Phi, Kappa Delta Rho. Republican. Episcopalian. Clubs: Pacific-Union, Lawyers (San Francisco), Commonwealth Club Calif. (life, pres. 1958-59). Home: 329 Hampton Rd Piedmont CA 94611-3525 Office: 221 Sansome St San Francisco CA 94104-2307

JOHNSON, GARRETT BRUCE, lawyer; b. Akron, Ohio, Sept. 15, 1946; s. Vincent Hadar and Elizabeth Irene (Garrett) J.; m. Barbara Peters Silver, May 31, 1969; children: Emily Peters, Adam Garrett. A.B., Princeton U., 1968; J.D., U. Mich., 1971. Bar: Ill. 1973, U.S. Dist. Ct. (no. dist.) Ill. 1973, U.S. Ct. Appeals (7th cir.) 1979, U.S. Supreme Ct. 1990. Fellow Max Planck Inst. for Fgn. and Internat. Criminal Law, Freiburg, Germany, 1971-72; assoc. Kirkland & Ellis, Chgo., 1973-78, ptnr., 1978— . Article and book review editor Mich. Law Rev. 1970-71. Humboldt scholar, 1971-72. Office: Kirkland & Ellis 200 E Randolph St Fl 54 Chicago IL 60601-6636

JOHNSON, GARY EARL, former governor; b. Minot, N.D., Jan. 1, 1953; s. Earl W. and Lorraine B. (Bostow) J.; m. Dee Simms, Nov. 27, 1976; children: Seah, Erik. BA in Polit. Sch., U. N.Mex., 1975. Pres., CEO Big J Enterprises, Albuquerque, 1976—94; gov. State of N.Mex., 1995—2003. Bd. dirs. Entrepreneurship Studies at U. N.Mex., 1993-95. Named to list of Big 50 Remodelers in the USA, 1987; named Entrepreneur of Yr., 1995. Mem. LWV, C. of C. Albuquerque (bd. dirs. 1993-95). Republican. Lutheran. Achievements include Mt. Everest summit, 2003. Avocations: rock-climbing, mountain climbing, skiing, pilot, triathlete.*

JOHNSON, GARY L. publishing executive; b. Mpls., Aug. 19, 1938; s. Maurice Fred and Alta Elizabeth J.; m. Carol Ann Schlisler, Sept. 8, 1962. Diploma, Bethany Coll. of Missions, Mpls., 1959; student, Augsburg Coll., 1960-63. Mgr. Bethany Book Shop, Mpls., 1960-63, Bethany Printing Div., Mpls., 1963-76; pres. Bethany House Pubs., Mpls., 1963—. Avocation: songwriting. Office: Bethany House Pubs 11400 Hampshire Ave S Minneapolis MN 55438-2852

JOHNSON, GARY M. lawyer; b. 1947; BS, Gustavus Adolphus Coll., 1969; JD, NYU, 1973. Law clk. to justice U.S. Ct. Appeals (3d cir.), Phila., 1973-74; assoc. Dorsey & Whitney, Mpls., 1974-79, ptnr., 1980—. Fellow Am. Coll. Trust and Estate Counsel; mem. Minn. Bar Assn., Hennepin County Bar Assn., Order of Coif. Office: Dorsey & Whitney Ste 1500 50 South Sixth Street Minneapolis MN 55402-1498 E-mail: johnson.gary@dorsey.com.

JOHNSON, GARY ROBERT, political scientist; b. Shenandoah, Iowa, June 30, 1949; s. Glen Robert and Norma Jean (Otte) J.; m. Margaret Delaina Maddox, Aug. 30, 1975; children: Samuel Maddox, Katherine Elizabeth. BA, Augustana Coll., Rock Island, Ill., 1972; MA, U. Cin., 1975, PhD, 1979. Teaching asst., rsch. asst. U. Cin., 1972-78; rsch. cons. Frost & Jacobs, Attys.at Law, Cin., 1976; instr., then asst. prof. polit. sci. Lake Superior State U., Sault Ste. Marie, Mich., 1978-84, assoc. prof. polit. sci., 1984-90, head dept. social scis., 1981-89, prof. polit. sci., 1990—. Vis. lectr. Drake U., Des Moines, 1986-87; manuscript referee various jours., pubs., 1986—; mem. faculty workgroup on undergrad. instrnl. quality Gov.'s Commn. on Future of Higher Edn. in Mich., 1984. Bibliography co-editor Politics and the Life Scis. jour., 1986-91, editor, 1991-2001; contbr. articles, book revs. to profl. jours., edited books. Grantee State of Mich., 1987. Mem. Am. Polit. Sci. Assn. (panel discussant, chair 1989—, sect. program chair 1990-91), Assn. Politics and Life Sci. (exec. dir. 1996-2001, conf. chair 1998, 99, 2000), Internat. Soc. Human Ethology, Human Behavior and Evolution Soc. Avocations: genealogy, old books, racquetball. Home: 924 Johnston St Sault Sainte Marie MI 49783-3324 Office: Lake Superior State U 650 W Easterday Ave Dept Polit Sault Sainte Marie MI 49783-1643 E-mail: gjohnson@lssu.edu.

JOHNSON, GARY THOMAS, lawyer; b. Chgo., July 26, 1950; s. Thomas G. Jr. and Marcia Johnson; m. Susan Elizabeth Moore, May 28, 1978; children: Christopher Thomas, Timothy Henry, Anna Louisa. AB, Yale U., 1972; Hons. BA, Oxford U., 1974, MA, 1983; JD, Harvard U., 1977. Ba: Ill. 1977, U.S. Dist.

Ct. (no. dist.), Ill. 1977, U.S. Ct. Appeals (7th cir.) 1985, U.S. Supreme Ct. 1986, N.Y. 1993. Assoc. Mayer, Brown & Platt, Chgo., 1977-84, ptnr., 1985-94, Jones Day, Chgo., 1994—. Mem. Spl. Commn. on Adminstrn. of Justice Cook County, Chgo., 1984-88; v.p. Criminal Justice Project of Cook County, 1987-91; bd. dirs. Lawyers' Com. for Civil Rights Under Law, 1992—, trustee, 1994—, regional co-chair, 1996-2001, co-chair, 2001-2003; mem. Ill. Supreme Ct. Spl. Commn. on the Adminstrn. of Justice, 1992-94. Bd. dirs. Chgo. Lawyers' Com. for Civil Rights Under Law, 1981-90, Legal Assistance Found., Chgo., 1987-96, pres., 1994-96. Rhodes scholar Oxford U., 1972-74. Fellow Am. Bar Found. (life; state chair 2003—), Ill. Bar Found. (life); mem. ABA (Ho. of Dels. 1991-97), Am. Judicature Soc. (bd. dirs. 1987-91), Ill. State Bar Assn., Chgo. Bar Assn., Chgo. Coun. Lawyers (pres. 1981-83), Internat. Bar Assn. Office: Jones Day 77 W Wacker Dr Chicago IL 60601-1692

JOHNSON, GARY WILLIAM, environmental scientist, consultant; b. Warwick, R.I., Feb. 23, 1957; s. Donald Milton and Elaine Carin (Soderlund) J.; m. Diane Lynn Farrell, Aug. 1, 1992; children: Danielle Lynn, Kelsey Ann. BA in Biology, U. R.I., 1979; MS in Environ. Sci., U. New Haven, 1987. Cert. instr. Inst. Nuclear Power Operators; OSHA cert. safety trainer. Rschr. Nat. Marine Fisheries Svc., Narragansett, RI, 1978—79; asst. scientist N.E. Utilities, Waterford, Conn., 1979—84, assoc. scientist Berlin, Conn., 1984—86, scientist Rocky Hill, Conn., 1986—97; sr. scientist, environ. coord. N.E. Nuc. Energy Co., Waterford, Conn., 1997—2000; supr. environ. programs Millstone Nuc. Power Sta. Dominion Nuc. Conn., Waterford, 2000—. Prin. scientist Ecologic Risk Mgmt. Svcs., Monroe, Conn., 1989-94; guest lectr. U. New Haven, 1990-96; lectr. in field. Contbr. articles to profl. jours. Vol. sci. guide East Lyme (Conn.) Jr. High Sch., 1983-96; guide, lectr. Audubon Soc., Jamestown, R.I., 1983-85; chmn. Waterford Conservation Commn., 1997—; v.p. Meadow Green Homeowners Assn., 1999. Mem. Edison Electric Power Industry Biologists, Nat. Environ. Tng. Assn. Achievements include obtaining ISO 14001 environmental management systems certification for Millstone Nuclear Power Facility, Waterford, Conn.; development of state of the art computer models to perform quantitative analysis of ecologic and human health risk from exposure to toxic materials; research in condenser biofouling control efforts for the nuclear power industry; coordinated all environmental issues to support the decommissioning of a nuclear power plant. Home: 2 Melanie Dr Waterford CT 06385-1600 Office: Dominion Nuclear Conn Millstone Nuclear Power Sta PO Box 128 Waterford CT 06385-0128

JOHNSON, GEORGE H. financial services company executive; b. Boston, Aug. 30, 1941; s. Harry G. and Josephine (Grenda) J.; m. Marguerite Anne Harrington, Aug. 12, 1967; 1 child, Heather Diana. BS, Northeastern U., Boston, 1966. CLU, ChFC; cert. internal auditor; enrolled agt. IRS; cert. tax preparer; fellow life office mgmt. Sr. internal auditor U.S. Life Corp., N.Y.C., 1970-76; dir. internal audit, treas. Consumers United Group, Inc., Washington, 1976—, also bd. dirs. Former bd. dirs., chair World Hunger Edn. Svc., Washington. Participant blood bank donor program ARC, Washington, 1977—. Mem. Inst. Internal Auditors, Md. Soc. Accts., Am. Soc. CLU and ChFC, Cert. Tax Preparers, Washington Inst. Internal Auditors. Home: 11805 Bunchberry Ln Gaithersburg MD 20878-2315

JOHNSON, GEORGE LLOYD, education educator, consultant, writer; b. Dunn, NC, Aug. 13, 1955; s. George Loyd Johnson Sr. and Jean Morrison Johnson. BA in history, Campbell U., 1977, MEd, 1978; MA, East Carolina U., 1985; PhD in am. history, U. of SC, 1991. Instr. of history U. of SC, 1990—91; asst. prof. of history Campbell U., Buies Creek, NC, 1991—97, assoc. prof. of history, 1997—. Cons., advanced placement U.S. history Coll. Bd., Ednl. Testing Svc., Princeton, NJ, 1998—. Author: (history book) The Frontier in the Colonial South: South Carolina Backcountry, 1736-1800, 1997; contbr. author of book reviews, chapters to books; author of over 70 ency. articles for several academic encyclopedias including Great Athletes of the Twentieth Century, Great Events of the Twentieth Century, The African American Ency. Spl. events com. Averasboro Civil War Battlefield Commn., Dunn, NC, 1998—2001. Fellow Summer Inst. fellow, Nat. Endowment for the Humanities, Univ. of Va. and Va. Found. for the Humanities, 1998. Mem.: NC Lit. and Hist. Soc. (corr.), Bapt. History and Heritage Soc. (corr.), NC Assn. of Historians (corr.; pres. 1999—2000), Am. Hist. Assn. (corr.), So. Hist. Assn. (corr.; membership com. 2002—03), SC Hist. Soc. (assoc.), Ormohundro Inst. for the Study of Early Am. History and Culture (assoc.), Hist. Soc. NC (life), Omicron Delta Kappa (life), Phi Alpha Theta (life), Phi Kappa Phi (life). Democrat-Npl. Baptist. Achievements include research in colonial history in the South. Avocations: weightlifting, travel. Home: 203 East K St Erwin NC 28339 Office: Campbell University 211 Judge Taylor Rd D Rich Building Buies Creek NC 27506 Home Fax: 910-814-4311; Office Fax: 910-814-4311. Personal E-mail: johnson@mailcenter.campbell.edu. E-mail: johnson@mailcenter.campbell.edu.

JOHNSON, GEORGE TAYLOR, training and manufacturing executive; b. Kansas City, Mo., Jan. 12, 1930; s. George Dewey and Geneva (Van Leu) J.; m. Pamela Kay Cole, Aug. 30, 1981; children: Van L., Victoria Johnson-Beineke, Wendell O., Marcella Johnson-Stewart, Julia I. BA, Columbia U., 1977. Enlisted U.S. Army, 1947; chief instr. rotary wing sect. U.S. Army Transp. Sch., Ft. Eustis, Va., 1965-67; ret. U.S. Army, 1967; group leader aerospace publs. Beech Aircraft Corp., Wichita, Kans., 1968-79, adminstr. aerospace logistics programs, 1979-87, staff asst. program mgmt., 1987-88, staff adminstr. program mgr., 1988-92, ret., 1992; pres., CEO Diversifieed Ednl. Tng. and Mfg. Co., 1992—. Founder U.S. Army Black Pilots Reunions, U.S. Army Black Aviators Assn.; mem. Cmty. Action Agy., Wichita, 1973-75, State of Kans. Aviation Adv. Com., 1991—, Pvt. Industry Coun., Wichita, 1994—; Kans. del. White House Conf. on Small Bus., Washington, 1995. Decorated DFC, Air medal with V and four oak leaf clusters; named Welfare to Work Small Bus. Owner of Yr., SBA, 1999; recipient Black Avaition Hall of Fame, 2001. Mem.: VFW, NAACP, Wichita Ind. Bus. Assn. (bd. dirs. 1996—2001), Wichita C. of C. (bd. dirs. 1996—99), 9th and 10th Cav. Assn., Army Aviation Assn. Am., Rotary Internat. Baptist. Home: 9430 Cross Creek St Wichita KS 67206 Office: 2102 E 21st St N Wichita KS 67214-1943 E-mail: gjohn97063@aol.com.

JOHNSON, GERALD, III, cardiovascular physiologist, researcher; b. Liberty, Tex., Aug. 16, 1945; s. Gerald Jr. and Jimmie Leah (Hensley) J.; m. Delynda Juanice Wall, Sept. 20, 1985. MS, U. Okla., 1971; PhD, U. Okla., Oklahoma City, 1980. NIH stipendiary U. Okla., Oklahoma City, 1972-76, rsch. assoc., 1979-80; electrophysiologist Childrens Med. Ctr., Tulsa, Okla., 1980-82; post-doct. fellow Oral Roberts U. Sch. Medicine, Tulsa, 1982-84, asst. prof., 1984-88; sr. rsch. fellow Jefferson Med. Coll., Phila., 1988-90; assoc. prof. dept. medicine, health scis. ctr. U. Okla., 1990-98, prof. dept. medicine, 1998—2001; dir. cardiovasc. lab. W.K. Warren Med. Rsch. Inst., Tulsa, 1990—2001; cons. critical care and oncology Ely Lilly and Co., 2001—. Cons. McGee Rehab. Inst., Phila., 1990, Dept. Pediatrics City of Faith Hosp., Tulsa, 1982, Aerobics Ctr. Oral Roberts U., Tulsa, 1981; rsch. asst. to assoc. VA Hosp., Oklahoma City, 1970-72, Cen. State Hosp., Norman, Okla, 1969-70, U. Okla. Health Scis. Ctr., Oklahoma City, 1979-80; mem. numerous coms. Oral Roberts U., 1984-88; adj. assoc. prof. physiology dept. pharmacology and physiology Okla. State U. Coll. Osteo. Medicine, Tulsa; mem. faculty 3d Internat. Conf. Nuc. Cardiology, Florence, Italy, 1997. Contbr. numerous articles to profl. jours.; reviewer Jour. Nuc. Cardiology, Jour. Nuc. Medicine, Life Scis.; presenter in field. Grantee The Hearst Found., 1981-82, Am. Heart Assn., 1985-86, 97; recipient Travel award Biofeedback Soc. Am., 1981, Citation Paper awards, 1981, 82, Best Basic Rsch. Paper award Jour. Nuc. Cardiology, 1997. Fellow Coun. on Circulation; mem. AAAS, Internat. Soc. for Heart Rsch. (Am. sect.), Am. Heart Assn., Am. Physiol. Assn., Am. Soc. Nuc. Cardiology (founding), Fedn. Am. Socs. for Exptl. Biology, Soc. Nuc. Medicine, Okla. Soc. Physiologists (pres.), N.Y. Acad. Scis., Soc. of Sigma Xi, Phi Kappa Phi. Achievements include research on protective effects of exercise training in shock, adrenoceptor relationships in hypertension, morphologic differences in vasculature during hemorrhagic hypotension, protective effects of nitric oxide and sodium nitrite in ischemia/reperfusion, role of endothelium in myocardial ischemia/reperfusion. Office: Ely Lilly and Co DC 6075 Indianapolis IN 46285

JOHNSON, GERALD LEE, health facility administrator; b. May 7, 1952; MHA, Kennedy Western U., 1993, PhD, 2001. Cert. Am. Coll. Healthcare Execs. Adminstr. Heart Ctr. Manatee Meml. Hosp., Bradenton, Fla., 1983-88; dir. imaging St. Mary's Med. Ctr., Racine, Wis., 1988-90; dir. off site devel. Hardin Meml. Hosp., Etown, Ky., 1990-96; adminstr., dir. U. Louisville Hosp., 1996-2000; dir. diagnostic and therapeutic svcs. Danville (Va.) Regional Med. Ctr., 2000—. Fellow Am. Healthcare Radiol. Adminstrs., Am. Coll. Cardiology, Lions (pres.). Address: PO Box 2397 Danville VA 24541-0397 E-mail: cherhealth@gcronline.com., johnsong@drmc.drhsi.org.

JOHNSON, GERALDINE ESCH, language specialist; b. Steger, Ill., Jan. 5, 1921; d. William John Rutkowski and Estella Anna (Mannel) Pietz; m. Richard William Esch, Oct. 12, 1940 (dec. 1971); children: Janet L. Sohngen, Daryl R., Gary Michael; m. Henry Bernard Johnson, Aug. 23, 1978 (dec. 1988). BSBA, U. Denver, 1955, MA in Edn., 1958, MA in Speech Pathology, 1963; vocat. credential, U. No. Colo., 1978, postgrad., Metropolitan State Coll., U. Colo., Colo. State U., Colo. Sch. of Mines, U. Hawaii. Cert. speech therapist, Colo.; cert. tchr., class A counselor, tchr. educationally handicapped, Colo. Tchr. music Judith St. John Sch. Music, Denver, 1946-52; tchr. West High Sch., Denver, 1955-61, chmn. bus. edn. dept., 1958-61, reading specialist, 1977-78; speech therapist, founder South Denver Speech Clinic, 1965-71; tchr. Educationally Handicapped Resource Rm., Denver, 1971-74, Diagnostic Ctr., The Belmont Sch., Denver, 1974-77; speech-lang. specialist elem. and jr. high schs., Denver, 1978-86; itinerant speech-lang. specialist various elem. and jr. high schs., Denver, 1978—; ret. Denver Pub. Sch. System, 1986. Home lang tchr. Early Childhood Edn., Denver, 1975; mem. Ednl. TV Adv. com., Colo.; sec. Cen. Bus. Edn. Com., Colo; tchr. letter writing clinics, local bus., Denver, 1960—. Former judge Colo. State Speech Festivals; demonstrator, lectr. Speech-Lang. and Learning Disabilities area Colo. Edn. Assn., 1971-73; vol. communications and prereading skills tchr. YMCA (cert. recognition for 10 yrs. svc. 2001), Denver Pub. Schs. Ret. Employees Assn. (cert. of recognition for 10 yrs. cmty. svc.). Recipient Spl. Edn. award Denver Pub. Schs., 1986. Mem. Speech-Lang.-Hearing Assn. (cert.), U. Denver Sch. Bus. Alumni Bd., Beta Gamma Sigma, Kappa Delta Pi, Delta Pi Epsilon. Home: 580 S Clinton St Apt 3B Denver CO 80231-1263

JOHNSON, GLENDON E. retired insurance company executive; b. 1924; BS, U. Utah, 1948; JD, Harvard U., 1952. In charge Wash. office Am. Life Convention, Washington, 1959-68; pres. Great Southern Life Ins. Co., Houston, 1968-70; pres., chmn. bd. dirs., CEO Am. Nat. Ins. Co., Galveston, Tex., 1970-77; law ptnr. Routier & Johnson P.C., Washington, 1978-84; pres., CEO John Alden Ins. Co., Inc., 1984-87; chmn. bd., CEO John Alden Fin. Corp., Miami, Fla., 1987-98; pres., chmn. bd., CEO John Alden Life Ins. Co., 1984-98. Mem. nat. bd. Boy Scouts Am., 1971-77, 1981—, nat. exec. com., 1981—, nat. v.p., chmn. audit com., mem. nominating com., 1994—, mem. exec. bd. Fla. coun., chmn. nat. Cub Scout com., 1981-83, chmn. nat. program group, 1983-86, chmn. mktg. and relationships com., 1987-91, chmn. pers. com., 1992-93 (Silver Beaver award 1971, Silver Antelope award 1974, Silver Buffalo award 1993, Good Scout award 1993).

JOHNSON, GLENN THOMPSON, judge; b. Washington, Ark., July 19, 1917; s. Floyd and Reola (Thompson) J.; m. Elaine Bailey, May. 26, 1993; children: Evelyn A., Glenn T. BS, Wilberforce U., 1941; JD, John Marshall Law Sch., 1949, LL.M., 1950; grad., Nat. Coll. State Trial Judges, 1971, Appellate Ct. Judges Seminar, N.Y. U., 1974; LL.D. (hon.), Ark. Bapt. Coll., 1978. Bar: Ill. 1950. Pvt. practice law, 1950-57; asst. atty. gen., 1957-63; sr. asst. atty. Met. San. Dist. Chgo., 1963-66; assoc. judge Cir. Ct., Cook County, Chgo., 1966-68, judge, 1968-73; justice Ill. Appellate Ct., Chgo., 1973—. Trustee John Marshall Law Sch. Served with AUS, 1942-46. Recipient merit award John Marshall Law Sch., 1970; Merit award Beatrice Caffrey Youth Service, 1976 Mem. Nat. Bar Assn. (merit award 1970), ABA, Ill. Bar Assn., Chgo. Bar Assn., Cook County Bar Assn. (awards 1967, 73, pres. 1964-66), Am. Acad. Matrimonial Lawyers (gov.) Methodist. Home: #2203-S 5050 S Lake Shore Dr Apt 2203 Chicago IL 60615-3217

JOHNSON, GOODYEAR See O'CONNOR, KARL WILLIAM

JOHNSON, GORDON GILBERT, religion educator, minister; b. St. Paul, Nov. 19, 1919; s. Gilbert Oliver and Myrtle Isabel (Bjorklund) J.; m. Alta Fern Borden, May 21, 1945; children: Gregg A., Gayle E. Johnson Hyames. Cert., Moody Bible Inst., 1941; AA, Bethel Coll., St. Paul, 1943; student, Harvard U., 1944, 45; BA, U. Minn., 1945; BD, Bethel Theol. Sem., 1946; ThM, Princeton Theol. Sem., 1950; ThD, No. Bapt. Theol. Sem., 1960. Ordained to ministry Bapt. Gen. Conf., 1946. Pastor 1st Bapt. Ch., Milltown, Wis., 1946-48, Bethel Bapt. Ch., Montclaire, N.J., 1948-51, Central Ave. Bapt. Ch., Chgo., 1951-59; v.p., dean, prof. preaching Bethel Theol. Sem., St. Paul, 1959-84; interim sr. pastor Trinity Bapt. Ch., St. Paul, 1972-73; assoc. pastor, interim sr. pastor College Ave. Bapt. Ch., San Diego, 1984-89; interim dean Bethel Sem. West, San Diego, 1990-91; interim sr. pastor Clairemont Emmanuel Bapt. Ch., San Diego, 1990-91, First Bapt. Ch., Lakewood, Long Beach, Calif., 1991-92, New Life Ch., Woodbury, Minn., 1993, Elim Bapt. Ch., Mpls., 1995-96. Chmn. bd. publ. Bapt. Gen. Conf., Chgo., 1948-53, pres. bd. trustees, 1953-55, chmn. world mission bd., 1955-60, moderator, 1957-58, 85-86; mem. gen. coun. Bapt. World Alliance, Washington, 1965-85; lectr. in field; del. to World Congress on Evangelism, Berlin, 1965; educator for elderhostels for Bethel Coll., Minn., 1992-98; vis. prof. Regent Coll., Vancouver, 1976; pres. Minn. Sem. Consortium, 1979-81. Author: My Church; contbr. articles to profl. jours. With USN, 1944-45. Rsch. scholar Yale U. Div. Sch., 1969. Mem. Acad. Homileticians, Religious Speech Assn. E-mail: johgor@bethel.edu. *In a capricious and sometimes explosive world an underlying confidence in the gracious providence of a loving God gives peace and wholeness of life. That makes possible an optimism about life.*

JOHNSON, GORDON JAMES, artistic director, conductor; b. St. Paul, 1949; BS, Bemidji State U., 1971; MS, Northwestern U., 1977; D in Mus. Arts, U. Oreg.; studied with Leonard Bernstein, Erich Leinsdorf, Herbert Blomstedt. Music dir., condr. Great Falls (Mont.) Symphony Assn., 1981—, Glacier Orch. and Chorale, Mont., 1982-97; artistic dir., condr. Flathead Music Festival, Mont., 1987-96; music dir., condr. Mesa (Ariz.) Symphony Orch., 1997—. Grad. tchg. fellow U. Oreg, 1979—81; artist in residence Condr's Guild Inst., W.Va. U., 1984; condr. Spokane Symphony at The Festival at Sandpoint; guest condr. St. Paul Chamber Orch., 1971, Spokane Symphony, 1983, 86, Dubuque Symphony, Iowa, 1985, Charlotte Symphony, NC, 1985, Lethbridge Symphony, Alberta, Canada, 1986, Cheyenne Symphony, Wyo., 1986, West Shore Symphony, Mich., 1988, Bozeman Symphony, Mont., 1989, Kumamoto Symphony, Kyshu, Japan, 1991, Kankakee Symphony, Ill., 1993, Toulon Symphonies, France, 1994, Guam Symphony, 1995, Tokyo Lumiere Orch., 1995, Fort Collins Symphony, Colo., 1995, Wilmslow Symphony Orch., England, 1997; guest ballet condr. Alberta Ballet, 1986, Oakland Ballet, Calif., 1988, Eugene Ballet, Oreg., 1993, David Taylor Ballet, Colo., Colo., 1994, St. Petersburg Ballet, Russia, 1995, Western Ballet Theater, Oreg., 1996; spkr. regional conf. Am. Symphony Orch. League, 1987, spkr. nat. conf., 88; mem. adj. faculty U. Great Falls, 1981—, U. Mont., 1996—; lectr. U. Guam, 1995; condr. seminars L.A. Philharmonic Inst., 1983, Condr.'s Guild Inst., 1984, Festival at Sandpoint, Condr.'s Program, 1986, Am. Symphony Orch. League's Am. Condr.'s Program, N.Y. Philharmonic, 1987, Condr.'s Guild "Bruckner Seminar", Chgo. Symphony Orch., 1989, Carnegie Hall Tng. Program for Condrs., Cleve. Orch., 1993. Named to Highland Park High Sch. Hall of Fame, St. Paul, 1997; Philharmonic Condr.'s scholar St. Paul Chamber Orch., 1971, L.A. Philharmonic Inst. fellow, 1983. Mem.: ASCAP. Office: Great Falls Symphony Assn PO Box 1078 Great Falls MT 59403-1078 E-mail: gjohnson@mcn.net.

JOHNSON, GORDON SELBY, consulting electrical engineer; b. Petersburg, Ind., July 25, 1918; s. Basil Orvil and Lillian May (Selby) J.; m. Frances Marie Overstreet, June 15, 1940; children: Lowell, Anne, Judith, Martha, Carol, Gordon, Mary. BSEE, Purdue U., 1939. Registered profl. engr., Wis. Engr. Sunbeam Electric Mfg. Co., Evansville, Ind., 1939-41, Kohler (Wis.) Co., 1941-48, dept. head, 1948-55, chief engr., 1955-65, mgr. engring., 1965-76, sr. staff engr., 1976-85, cons. engr., 1985-87; pvt. practice cons. Winter Haven, Fla., 1987—. Dir. communications and tech. assistance Elec. Generating Systems Assn., Boca Raton, Fla., 1986-92, tech. dir., 1993-99, pres., 1983-84. Author: Kohler Tech. Series, 1976-85; editor: Elec. Grounding, 1992, On-Site Power Generation, 1990, 2d edit., 1993, 3rd edit., 1998; editor Powerline mag., 1986-92, tech. editor, 1993-99; contbr. numerous articles to profl. jours. Pres. Sheboygan (Wis.) County Coun. of Chs., 1965-67; lay leader N.E. Wis. Dist. United Meth. Ch., 1975-76; chmn. adv. com. Lakeshore Tech. Coll., Sheboygan, 1970-80; adv. high sch. sci. seminars. With U.S. Mcht. Marine, 1944-45, ETO, NATOUSA. Recipient L.H. Carpenter Outstanding Svc. award Elec. Generating Systems Assn., 1973. Fellow IEEE (sect. chmn. 1953-54); mem. NSPE, Soc. Automotive Engrs., Nat. Fire Protection Assn. Avocations: competitive running, bicycling, gardening. E-mial. Home and Office: 421 Flagler Rd SE Winter Haven FL 33884 E-mail: johnsonjogs@aol.com.

JOHNSON, GREG, professional hockey player; b. Thunder Bay, Ont., Can., Mar. 16, 1971; Hockey player Red Wings, 1993-96, Penguins, 1996-97; ctr. Nashville Predators, 1999—. Recipient silver medal with Team Can., Olympics, 1994. Office: Nashville Predators 501 Broadway Nashville TN 37203-3932

JOHNSON, GREGORY CARL, pilot, astronaut, career officer; b. Seattle, July 30, 1954; s. Raleigh Osmond and May Ann (Linneman) J.; m. Christine Rochelle Scott, Aug. 10, 1974; children: Scott Gregory, Kent Christopher. BS in Aeronautics and Astronautics, U. Wash., 1977; exptl. test pilot, USAF Test Pilot Sch., 1984. Cert. airline transport pilot. Head maintenance dept. USN, Oak Harbor, Wash., 1989-90; project pilot NASA Johnson Space Ctr., Houston, 1990-94, chief maintenance and engring., 1994-98, astronaut candidate pilot tng., 1998-99, astronaut support pilot, 1999—; comdg. officer Naval Sta. Rota Spain USNR, New Orleans, 1993-95, comdg. officer Naval Air Sta. New Orleans, 1995-97, comdg. officer naval rsch. lab., 1998—2000, comdg. officer Naval Coordination Protection of Shipping, 2000—02. Primary test pilot multiple projects, 84, 86, 87, 92. Capt. USNR, 1977—. Mem. AIAA, Soc. Exptl. Test Pilots, Naval Reserve Assn. Avocations: car repair, running.

JOHNSON, GUY CHARLES, music educator, musician; b. Marinette, Wis., Nov. 8, 1933; s. Everton Ellsworth and Anna Mae (Brazier) J. BFA, U. Wis., Milw., 1955; MusM, Ind. U., 1956. Asst. prof. piano Drury Coll., Springfield, Mo., 1956-57, Luther Coll., Decorah, Iowa, 1959-68; assoc. prof. music Friends U., Wichita, Kans., 1968-95. Impresario Lewis and Selma Miller Recital series, Wichita, 1976-86. Recital debut Athenaeum Hall, Milw., 1955; Chgo. debut Fullerton Hall, 1969; appearances with numerous symphonies including Rochester (Minn.) Symphony, Milw. Symphony, Santa Barbara (Calif.) Symphony; accompanist for various operas, ballet cos. Mem. Wichita-Sedgwick County Hist. Mus. Mem. Wichita Area Piano Tchrs. League (pres. 1969, 90—), Kans. Music Tchrs. Assn., Nat. Guild Piano Tchrs., Wichita Art Assn. Home: 640 N Rock Rd Wichita KS 67206-1794

JOHNSON, H. THOMAS, business educator; b. Chgo. m. Elaine B. Johnson, July 17, 1971; 1 child, Thomas C. AB, Harvard U., 1960; MBA, Rutgers U., Newark, 1961; PhD, Wis. U., 1969. Auditor Arthur Andersen & Co., Boston, 1961-64; prof. econs. U. Western Ont., London, Can., 1968-78; prof. bus. Wash., 1978-88; Retzlaff chair bus. Portland (Oreg.) State U., 1988—. Author: Relevance Lost, 1987, Relevance Regained, 1992, Profit Beyond Measure, 2000. Recipient Shingo Rsch. Prize for Excellence in Mfg., 2001. Office: Portland State U Sch Bus Portland OR 97035 E-mail: tomj@sba.pdx.edu.

JOHNSON, HANSFORD TILLMAN, civilian military employee; b. Aiken, S.C., Jan. 3, 1936; s. Wade Hansford and Julia Johnson; m. Linda Ann Whittle, June 21, 1959; children: Richard, Elizabeth, David. BS in Thermodynamics and Aerodynamics, U.S. Air Force Acad., 1959; MS in Aeros., Stanford U., 1967; MBA in Bus. Sci., U. Colo., 1970; postgrad., Nat. War Coll., 1975-76. Registered profl. engr., Colo.; lic. Nat. Assn. Securities Dealer Prin. Commd. 2d lt. USAF, 1959, advanced through grades to 4-star gen., 1989; asst. prof. U.S. Air Force Acad., Colorado Springs, Colo., 1968-71; comdr. 22d Bomb Wing USAF, March AFB, Riverside, Calif., 1979-81; plans staff officer USAF Hdqrs., Washington, 1972-75; asst. dep. for plans Strategic Air Commd., Omaha, 1981-82; dir. programs USAF Hdqrs., Washington, 1982-85, dep. ops. Offutt AFB, Neb., 1985-86; vice comdr. in chief Pacific Air Forces USAF, Hickam AFB, Hawaii, 1986-87; dep. comdr. in chief U.S. Cen. Command, MacDill AFB, Fla., 1987-88; dir., moved forces to and from Persian Gulf Joint Chiefs of Staff, Washington, 1988-89; comdr. in chief U.S. Transp. Command, Mil. Airlift Command (now Air Mobility Command), Scott AFB, Ill., 1989-92; ret. USAF, 1992; bd. dirs. USAA, San Antonio, 1987-92, chief of staff, 1993, vice chmn., 1993—95; pres., CEO USAA Capital Corp., 1993—95; v.p., CEO Credit Union Nat. Assoc., Madison, Wis., 1995—2001; asst. sec. U.S. Navy, Dept. of Def., Washington, 2001—02, 2003—, acting sec., 2003. Mem. Tex. Rsch. and Tech. Found., Decorated DFC with 2 oak leaf clusters, Legion of Merit, Silver Star, DSM, Def. DSM with 2 oak leaf clusters, Def. Meritorious Svcs. medal, Meritorious Svc. medal, Air medal with 22 oak leaf clusters, Air Force DSM with oak leaf cluster; Republic of Vietnam Armed Forces Honor medal 1st class with one svc. star, Gallantry Cross with palm. Mem. AIAA, Order of Daedalians (flight capt. 1975, 84, 85), Soc. Mil. Engrs. Office: 1000 Navy Pentagon Washington DC 20350-1000*

JOHNSON, HARDWICK SMITH, JR., school psychologist; b. Millen, Ga., Aug. 13, 1958; s. Hardwick Smith Sr. and Louise (Joiner) J. BA, Atlanta Christian Coll., 1981; MEd, Ga. So. Coll., 1984; EdS, Ga. State U., 1988; DSc (hon.), Holy Trinity Coll.; DD (hon.), St. Ephrem's Inst.; EdD, Nova Southeastern U., 2002. Cert. spl. edn. tchr., Ga.; cert. sch. psychologist. Ga. Spl. edn. resource tchr. Claxton (Ga.) High Sch., 1983-86; sch. psychologist, 1986—. Genealogist, 1980—; supervising tchr. Author: The History of the Johnson Family and Johnson Church, 1976, The Aaron Family, 1986, Some Descendants of James and Rachel Oglesby, 1785-1991, 1991. Organizing club pres. Young Reps. Coweta County. Named Tchr. of the Yr., Coun. for Exceptional Children, Claxton, 1985, Hon. Order Ky. Col., 1986, hon. admiral Tex. Navy Gov. of Tex., 1987, lt. col. a.d.c. Gov. of Ga., 1987, citizen State of Okla., citizen of L.A., col. Gov. La., lt. col. Gov. Ala., hon. mem. Coweta Tribal Town of the Creek Indian Nation (now Okla.); recipient Liberty medal with oak lead cluster SAR, Meritorious Svc. award SAR, Silver Good Citizenship medal SAR, medal of honor NSDAR, medal of honor NSDAC, Minuteman medal NSSAR, 1994. Fellow Am. Coll. Genealogists; mem. SAR (v.p. chpt. 1985-86, pres. Statesboro chpt. 1986-87, state sec. 1987—, Meritorious Service medal Ga. soc. 1987, state pres., v.p. gen. South Atlantic dist. 1991-92), SCV, Nat. Soc. Sons of Am. Colonists (nat. v.p. 1986—, gov. Ga. soc. 1987—, gov. gen. 1989-91, Mil. Order of the Stars and Bars), Coun. for Exceptional Children (pres.-elect, v.p. 1985-86), Ga. Assn. Educators (sch. rep. 1985—, pres.-elect 1986-87), NEA (sch. rep.), Ga. Assn. Sch. Psychologists, Continental Soc. Sons Indian Wars (founding gov. gen., nat. pres.), The Nat. Gavel Soc., Jamestowne Soc., Gen. Soc. Colonial Wars, Colonial Order Acorn, First Families Ga. (founding sec./treas. gen., gov. gen. 1993—), Nat. Huguenot Soc., Gen. Soc. War 1812 (former v.p. gen.), Sons Revolution in State of Ga., Hereditary Order Descendants Colonial Govs. (gov. gen. 1999—), Nat. Soc. Descs. Early Quakers, Nat. Soc. Ams. of Royal Descent (1st v.p.), Order Indian Wars of U.S., Order Ams. Armorial Ancestry, Hereditary Order Descs. Loyalists and Patriots Am. Revolution (dep. gov. gen.), Order Colonial Lords of Manors in Am., Baronial Order of Magna Charta, Order of The Three Crusades,(1096-1192), Order of The Crown of Charlemagne in the U.S.A. (1st v.p), The Colonial Soc. Pa., Descendants Washington's Army at Valley Forge (organizing cmdr. Ga. brigade), Aztec Club of 1847-Mil. Soc. of the Mex. War (former v.p.), Baronial Order of Magna Charta, St. George's Soc. (Jacksonville, Fla.), Nat. Soc. Sons and Daus. of Pilgrims (gov. gen. 1993-95), Sons and Daughters of the Colonial, Antebellum Bench and Bar, Order of Scions of Colonial Cavaliers (dep. gov. gen.), The Old Guard (Atlanta), Sons and Daus. of Antebellum Planters, DeMolay (master councilor 1977-78), Am. Priory Most Venerable Order of Hosp. of St. John of Jerusalem (comdr.), Soc. for the Preservation of Early Am. Art, City Tavern Club, Kappa Delta Pi (historian 1983—), Phi Delta Kappa. Republican. Avocations: heraldry, travel, writing, reading. Home: 1317 Winburn Drive East Point GA 30344

JOHNSON, HARMER FREDERIK, art appraiser; b. Faversham, Kent, England, Jan. 21, 1943; s. Stanley George and Lorna Mary (Clark) J.; m. Judith Rose Fischman, July 14, 1970; children: Jesse, Joanna, Eliza. Dept. asst. Sotheby & Co., London, 1961-66; dept. head, v.p. Sotheby Parke-Bernet Co., N.Y.C., 1966-73; pres. Harmer Johnson Books Ltd., N.Y.C., 1975—, Harmer Johnson Co., N.Y.C., 1973—. Author: (books) American Indian Art Magazine, Guide to the Arts of the Americas: Pre-Columbian, American Indian, 1992. Mem. Appraisers Assn. Am. (pres. 1986-88, cert.). Avocations: music, theatre. Office: Harmer Johnson 146 E 84th St New York NY 10028-2026

JOHNSON, HAROLD EARL, human resources specialist; b. Lincoln, Nebr., July 11, 1939; s. Earl W. and Evelyn Jean (Sipp) J.; m. Carol Louise Schmidt, Aug. 17, 1971 (div.); children: Andrew Brian, Daniel Earl. BS, U. Nebr., 1961. From indsl. relations trainee to mgr. profl. employment Am. Can Co., 1961-68; dir. recruitment/devel. metal mining div. Kennecott Copper Corp., 1968-73; v.p.

personnel Am. Medicorp Inc., 1973-75; v.p. employee relations. devel., then sr. v.p. employee relations and corp. adminstrn. INA Corp., 1975-79; sr. v.p. human resources Federated Dept. Stores, Inc., Cin., 1979-85; sr. v.p. corp. personnel and adminstrn. The Travelers Cos., Hartford, Conn., 1985-89; mng. ptnr. Korn/Ferry Internat., N.Y.C., 1989-92, exec. search and human resources Norman-Broadbent Internat., N.Y.C., 1992-96; sr. ptnr., bd. dirs. The Cabot Group, Washington, 1996—2002; sr. ptnr. TMP Worldwide, 1997—2001; mem. faculty Mont. Leadership Inst., Mont. State U., Bozeman, 2000—02; global practice leader Heidrick and Struggles, Internat., Denver, 2002—. Bd. dirs. Snowfly Inc., Laramie, Wyo. Mem. Sky Club (N.Y.C.), Univ. Club (N.Y.C.), Winged Foot Golf Club (Mamoroneck, N.Y.), Econ. Club (N.Y.C.), Ptarmigan Country Club, Ft. Collins/Colo., Assn. of Exec. Search Cons. Republican. Presbyterian. Office: Heidrick and Struggles Internat 1400 Sixteenth St Denver CO 80202

JOHNSON, HAROLD GENE, lawyer; b. St. Louis, July 20, 1934; s. Edward Henry Johnson and Betty (Burton) Pallister; m. Susan Ann Giesecke, Oct. 10, 1953; children: H. Mark, Deborah S. Johnson Schnitzer, Michael R., Laura A. Johnson Schwent, Mitchell D. BSBA, Washington U., St. Louis, 1961, LLB, 1962. Bar: Mo. 1962, U.S. Dist. Ct. (ea. dist.) Mo. 1964, U.S. Ct. Appeals (8th cir.) 1981. Assoc. Schomburg, Marshall & Craig, St. Louis, 1962-63, Green & Raymond, St. Louis, 1963-64; ptnr. Johnson & Hayes, St. Louis, 1978-85, Law Offices Mitchell D. Johnson, St. Louis, 1988-93, Johnson & Johnson, 1993—. Judge mcpl. ct. City of Bridgeton, Mo., 1973-85. Served with U.S. Army 1954-56. Recipient Spl. Service award City of Bridgeton, 1985; Honored with ann. presentation of The Judge Harold Johnson award Pro-Life Direct Action League, 1985. Bar: Mo. Bar Assn., Met. Bar St. Louis, St. Louis County Bar Assn. Avocation: woodworking. Office: 500 Northwest Plz Ste 715 Saint Ann MO 63074-2222

JOHNSON, HAYNES BONNER, author, journalist, television commentator; b. N.Y.C., July 9, 1931; s. Malcolm Malone and Ludie (Adams) J.; m. Julia Ann Erwin, Sept. 21, 1954 (div.); m. Kathryn A. Oberly, June 29, 2002; children—Katherine Adams, David Malone, Stephen Holmes, Sarah Brooks, Elizabeth Haynes. BJ, U. Mo., 1952; MS, U. Wis., 1956; HHD (hon.), Wheeling Jesuit U., 1997; LHD (hon.), U. Mo., 1999. Reporter Wilmington (Del.) News-Jour., 1956- 57; with Washington Star, 1957-69, reporter, copy editor, to asst. city editor, night city editor to spl. assignments corr.; nat. corr. Washington Post, 1969-73, asst. mng. editor, 1973-77, columnist, 1977-94; prof. polit. comm. and journalism George Washington U., Washington, 1994-96; Knight chair, prof. journalism U. Md., 1998—. Ferris prof. journalism and pub. affairs Princeton U., 1975-78; TV commentator PBS Washington Week in Rev., 1967-94, The News Hour with Jim Lehrer, 1994—; guest scholar Brookings Instn., 1987-91; Regents lectr. U. Calif., Berkeley, 1992; lectr. in field. Author: Dusk at the Mountain, 1963, The Bay of Pigs, 1964, (with Bernard M. Gwertzman) Fulbright: The Dissenter, 1968, (with George C. Wilson) Army in Anguish, 1972; (with Richard Harwood) Lyndon, 1973, The Working White House, 1975, In the Absence of Power, 1980; (with Howard Simons) The Landing, 1986, Sleepwalking Through History, 1991, Divided We Fall, 1994, (with David S. Broder) The System, 1996, The Best of Times, 2001; editor: The Fall of a President, 1974. Bd. dirs. Herbert Block Found. Served to 1st lt. AUS, 1952—55. Recipient Pub. Svc. prize and Grand award for reporting Washington Newspaper Guild, 1962, 68, Interpretive Reporting award, 1965, Nat. Reporting award, 1968, Pulitzer prize for nat. reporting, 1966, Headliners award for nat. reporting, 1968, Sigma Delta Chi gen. reporting award, 1969; fellow in comm. Duke U., 1973-74; prof. in residence Annenberg Sch., 1993. Mem. Nat. Acad. Pub. Adminstrn. Clubs: Gridiron (Washington); Nassau (Princeton); Fed. City (Washington). Home: 2812 Woodland Dr NW Washington DC 20008-2742 Office: Coll Journalism U Md Journalism Bldg College Park MD 20742-0001 E-mail: haynesjohnson@hotmail.com.

JOHNSON, HEIDI SMITH, science educator, educator; b. Mpls., June 1, 1946; d. Russell Ward and Eva Ninette (Holmquist) Smith; m. Alan C. Sweeney, Dec. 21, 1968 (div. 1977); m. Robert Allen Johnson, July 17, 1981. BA, U. Calif., Riverside, 1969; MA, No. Ariz. U., 1992. Park ranger U.S. Nat. Parks Svc., Pinnacles Nat. Monument, 1972-73, aide Petrified Forest Mus. Assn., Ariz., 1973-75; dispatcher police dept. U. Ariz., Tucson, 1975-76; communications operator II dept. ops. City of Tucson, 1976-78; dispatcher Tucson Police Dept., 1978-82, communications supr., 1982-85, communications coord., 1985; substitute tchr. Bisbee (Ariz.) Pub. Schs., 1985-91; instr. English Cochise Community Coll., Douglas, Ariz., 1990-92; tchr. English/creative writing Bisbee H.S., 1992-93; tchr. earth sci. and paleontology Lowell Jr. High Sch., Bisbee, 1993—. GED tchr. Cochise County Jail, 1988-89; owner Johnson's Antiques and Books, Bisbee, 1990-99. Trustee Bisbee Coun. on Arts and Humanities, 1986-88; pres. Cooper Queen Libr. Bd., Bisbee, 1988-91; book sales chmn. Shattuck Libr., Bisbee Mining Mus., 1987-92; founder Riverside (Calif.) chpt. Zero Population Growth, 1968. Mem. Mid-Am. Paleontol. Soc., Sierra Club (mem. nat. wilderness study com. 1969-72, wilderness survey leader 1969-72), S.W. Paleontol. Soc., Paleontol. Soc., Nat. Ctr. Sci. Edn., The Nature Conservancy, Paleontol. Rsch. Instn., Nat. Assn. Geosci. Tchrs., AZ Geol. Soc. Roman Catholic. Avocations: paleontology, flower gardening, book collecting.

JOHNSON, HENRY FRED, clergy; b. Colorado Springs, Aug. 23, 1948; s. Nathan Eugene Johnson Sr. and Jessie Bell (Stovall) Crowder; m. Christine Johnson, May 20, 1967; children: Diedre M., Tina D. AA in Social Work, Pikes Peak C.C., Colorado Springs, 1990; B in Biblical Studies, Nazarene Bible Coll., Colorado Springs, 1993, B in Christian Edn., 1995; M in Bibl. Studies, Andersonville Bapt. Sem., 1998, PhD in Bibl. Studies, 2000. Ordained Baptist Min. Personnel sr. sgt. U.S. Army, 1967-87; program coord. Martin Luther Home, Colorado Springs, 1988—2000; youth pastor Friendship Missionary Bapt. Ch., Colorado Springs, 1991-99; asst. pastor Chapel Pueblo (Colo.) Minimum Ctr., 1993—; writer Henry Johnson Min., Colorado Springs, 1995—; instr. Nat. Bapt. Youth Convention, New Orleans, 1995—2000; cmty. coord. Resource Exch., Colorado Springs, 2000—; interim pastor Friendship Missionary Bapt. Ch., 2001—. Bd. mem. Am. Assn. on Mental Retardation, Colo. Author: Challenge of the Teens in the 90's and Beyond, 1995, Book of James, 1998, Arise and Rebuild, 1997, Book of Revelation, 2000. Baptist. Avocations: reading the bible, writing bible studies. E-mail address. Office: Henry Johnson Ministries PO Box 17922 Colorado Springs CO 80935-7922 E-mail: reverendhenry@aol.com.

JOHNSON, HERBERT ALAN, history and law educator, lawyer, chaplain; b. Jersey City, Jan. 10, 1934; s. Harry Oliver and Magdalena Gertrude (Diemer) J.; m. Barbara Arlene (Balcerak), Sept. 24, 1955 (dec. Nov. 1980); children: Amanda Blair, Vanessa Paige.; m. Jane (McCue), June 4, 1983. AB, Columbia U., 1955, MA, 1961, PhD (Schiff fellow), 1965; LLB, N.Y. Law Sch., 1960; postgrad., Luth. Theol. So. Sem., 1981-84. Bar: N.Y. 1960; U.S. Supreme Ct. 1965; D.C. 1967; S.C. 1983; ordained vocat. deacon, 1991. Jr. clk. First Nat. City Bank of N.Y., N.Y.C., 1955; adminstrv. asst. Chase Manhattan Bank, N.Y.C., 1957—60; practiced in N.Y.C., 1960—67; rsch. asst. Papers of John Jay, Columbia U., 1961—63; lectr. Hunter Coll., N.Y.C., 1964—65, asst. prof. history, 1965—67; assoc. sem. on history of legal polit. thought Papers of John Jay, Columbia U., 1966—77; assoc. editor Papers of John Marshall, Inst. Early Am. History and Culture, Williamsburg, Va., 1967—70; assoc. sem. on early Am. history Papers of John Jay, Columbia U., 1967—77; co editor Papers of John Marshall, Inst. Early Am. History and Culture, 1970—71, editor, 1971—77; prof. law and history U. S. C., Columbia, 1977—90, Ernest F. Hollings, prof. constl. law, 1991—2002, disting. prof. law emeritus, 2002—. Lectr. Coll. William and Mary Williamsburg, 1967-77; Bostick vis. rsch. prof. So. studies program U. S. C., 1976, 77; mem. com. rsch., publ. Heritage '76 Com. Am. Revolution Bicentennial Commn., 1972-73; mem. bd. adjustments, appeals, Williamsburg, 1970-77; trustee Fund for Preservation of John Marshall House, 1972-74; Fund Coop. Editl. Rsch. Am. Antiquarian Soc., 1972-76 Author: The Law Merchant and Negotiable Instruments in Colonial New York, 1664-1730, 1963; John Jay, 1745-1829, 1970; Imported Eighteenth Century Law Treatises in Am. Libraries 1700-1799, 1978; Essays on New York Colonial Legal History, 1981; History of Criminal Justice, 1988, 3d edit., 2002; John Jay: Colonial Lawyer, 1989; The Chief Justiceship of John Marshall, 1997; Wingless Eagle: U.S. Army Aviation Through World War I, 2001; co-author: Historical Courthouses of New York State-18th and 19th Century Halls of Justice Across the Empire State, 1977; Foundations of Power, John Marshall, 1801-15, vol. 2, History of the Supreme Court of the U.S., 1981; editor: The Papers of John Marshall, Vol. 1, 1974, Vol. II, 1977, South Carolina Legal History, 1980; Am. Legal and Constitutional History: Cases and Materials, 1994, 2d edit., 2000; gen. editor Chief Justiceships of the U.S. Supreme Court Series, 1989—; contbg. articles to profl. jour. Chaplain assoc. Bapt. Med. Ctr., Columbia, 1983-2002; hospice legal svc. vol., 1986-2000; mem. ethics com. S.C. Episcopal Home, Still Hopes, 1989-99; 1st lt. USAF, 1955-57; ret. col., Res. Recipient: William P. Lyons Masters' Essay Award Loyola U., 1962; Paul S. Kerr History prize N.Y. State Hist. Assn., 1970; U. S. C. Edn. Found. Rsch. Award profl. sch., 2000; Am. Council Learned Soc. Fellow, 1974-75; Inst. Humane Studies Fellow, 1981, 85; vis. fellow Centre for Comparative Constl. Studies, U. Melbourne Law Faculty, 1992; vis. rsch. scholar U. Toronto Law Faculty, 1995; vis. prof. Univ. of Birmingham, (Eng.), 1998. Mem. Am. Hist. Assn. (Littleton-Griswold com. 1976-81, interim com. Bicentennial era 1976-77), Selden Soc. (state corr. for S.C. 1988-2002), Stair Soc., Air Force Assn., Am. Law Inst., Assn. Am. Law Sch. (chmn. legal history sect. 1979), Am. Soc. Legal History (pres. 1974-75, del. Am. Coun. Learned Soc. 1977-80, bd. dirs. 1999-2001), U. South Caroliniana Soc., Res. Officers Assn., Assn. Profl. Chaplains, Nat. Eagle Scout Assn. Episcopalian. Home: 245 Laurel Falls Rd Franklin NC 28734-9527 E-mail: janeherb@dnet.net.

JOHNSON, HERBERT FREDERICK, sales executive, former university administrator, librarian; b. St. Paul, Aug. 1, 1934; s. Herbert Oscar and Hazel Grace (Otto) J.; m. Delores Elaine Madson, Aug. 21, 1955; children: Steven F., Eric L., Kirsten M. BA, U. Minn., 1957, MA, 1959; postgrad., Kursverksamheten Vid Lunds Universitet, Betyg, 1975. Libr. U.S. Govt., Washington, 1959-61; asst. bus. libr. Columbia U., 1961-64; head libr., assoc. prof. Hamline U., 1964-71; libr., prof. Oberlin Coll., 1971-78; libr. Oberlin Pub. Library, 1971-78; dir. librs. Emory U., 1978-88, mem. faculty adv. com. Jimmy Carter Ctr. for Policy Studies, 1982-84; sales & svc. rep. Active Mobility of Ga., Marietta, 1988-91; sr. regional mgr. Williams/Howard Assocs., 1989-91; regional v.p. Primerica Fin. Svcs., Marietta, Ga., 1991—2002; registered prin. PFS Investments, Inc., 1991—; project dir. Nat. Drug Info. Ctr. Nat. Families in Action Inc., 1989-90. Lectr. U. Minn. Libr. Sch., 1967; vis. prof. Atlanta U. Sch. Libr. Svcs., 1979; charter bd. Cooperating Librs. in Consortium, St. Paul, 1969-71; libr. adv. com. Minn. Higher Edn. Coordinating Commn., 1970-71; mem. com. input standards Ohio Coll. Libr. Ctr., 1972-73, chmn. com. patron input, 1973-75; chmn. Ohio Multitype Interlibr. Cooperation Com., Ohio State Libr. Bd., 1976-78; mem. adv. and steering com. Ohio Pre-White House Conf. on Libr. and Info. Services, 1977-78; bd. dirs. Assn. Rsch. Librs., 1983-88, pres., 1987-88; chmn. librs.adv. com. Univ. Center in Ga., Atlanta, 1979-80, 85-86; del. users council OCLC Online Computer Libr. Ctr. Inc., 1981-83, 85-88; bd. dirs. Southeastern Libr. Network, 1980-83, chmn. bd., 1981-83; bd. govs. Rsch. Librs. Group, 1986-87. Contbr. articles to profl. jours. Mem. com. on internat. programs Nat. Student YMCA's, 1962-64; mem. Minn. Republican Task Force on Edn., 1966; pres., treas. Lord of Life Luth. Ch., Lorain, Ohio, 1972-75; mem. Lorain Coop. Luth. Ministry Bd., 1976-78; v.p. St. Luke Luth. Ch., Atlanta, 1979-80, 81-82; bd. dirs. Nat. Families in Action, 1979-89, 90—, pres. 1987-88, v.p., 1990-93; mem. adv. coun. DeKalb/Rockdale counties of Met. Atlanta chpt. ARC, 1981-88, Cobb/Douglas counties of Met. Atlanta chpt. ARC, 1988-92, emergency cmty. svcs. com., 1990-94; bd. dirs. Scandinavian Am. Found. Ga., 1983-, v.p. 1993-2000, chmn. bd., 2000-02; bd. dirs. Swedish Coun. Am. 1987—, chair Glenn T. Seaborg Nobel prize travel award com., 1990-2002, jr. achievement classroom cons., 1993-94. Decorated Army Commendation medal, Meritorious Service medal; George Williams fellow, 1957; Council on Library Resources fellow, 1974-75; NSF grantee, 1967-71. Mem. ALA, Nat. Family Caregivers Assn. (nat. caregivers adv. panel 2000—), Am. Scandinavian Found., Am. Swedish Inst., Ga. Libr. Assn., Southeastern Libr. Assn., Atlanta Zool. Soc., Chattahoochee Nature Ctr., Common Cause, Minn. Libr. Sch. Alumni Assn. (chmn. 1967), Wildlife Preservation Trust, Nat. Trust Hist. Preservation, Scandinavian Am. Found. Ga., Sierra Club, High Mus. Art, Rotary (dist. 6900 youth exch. com. 1994-97, treas. 1995-97, sec. North Dekalb, Ga. club 1981-82, pres. 1984-85, dir. 1998-2001, group study exch. team leader to dist. 2360 Sweden 2002—, dist. chair 2003—, Svc. Above Self award 2001, Dist. Svc. award 2002), East Cobb (Ga.) Bus. Assn. (bd. dirs. 1996-2000), Mil. Officers Assn. Am., Nordic Lodge 708 (bd. dirs. 2003—), Vasa Order of Am. (bd. dirs. 2003—), Beta Phi Mu. *Too many folks have given up realizing their dreams, yet with the Lord's help, anyone has the capacity to make their dreams a reality. The toughest part of the struggle is winning the battle between the ears- that is in believing in ones self. There is no greater thrill than having helped another win that struggle and having made a difference in that person's life!.*

JOHNSON, HERBERT MICHAEL, publisher; b. Leipzig, Germany, Mar. 19, 1936; came to U.S., 1940; s. Walter J. Johnson; m. Susan Armstrong, July 9, 1960; children: Walter J. II, Matthew G., Herbert M. Jr., Miranda S., George F. BS, Duke U., 1958. Mgr. domestic sales Acad. Press, Inc., N.Y.C., 1958-66; v.p., founder Greenwood Press, Inc., Westport, Conn., 1967-72; pres., pub., founder Johnson Assocs, Inc., Greenwich, Conn., 1972-80; founder, CEO, JAI Press, Inc., Greenwich, 1975-99; founder, pres., pub. Armstrong Pub. Co., 1993-97; pres. Ablex Pub. Co., 1997-99; dir. Nutmeg Investment Ptnrs. LLC, Greenwich, Conn., 1998—; chmn. Info. Age Pub. Inc., 2001—. Mem. council Boy Scouts Am., Greenwich, 1967-80. Home: Augustus Ln Greenwich CT 06830-7040 Office: Nutmeg Investment Ptnrs LLC 80 Wason St PO Box 4967 Greenwich CT 06831-0419 E-mail: hmjnutmeg@aol.com.

JOHNSON, HERMAN LEONALL, research nutritionist, retired; b. Whitehall, Wis., Apr. 1, 1935; s. Frederick E. And Jeanette (Severson) J.; m. Barbara Dale Matthews, July 3, 1960 (dec. May 1971); m. Barbara Ann Badger, Apr. 3, 1976. BA in Chemistry, North Cen. Coll., Naperville, Ill., 1959; MS in Biochemistry & Nutrition, Va. Poly. Inst. and State U., 1961, PhD in Biochemistry and Nutrition, 1963. Rsch. biochemist S.R. Noble Found., Ardmore, Okla., 1963-65; nutrition chemist U.S. Army Med. Rsch., Denver, 1965-74; nutrition physiologist Letterman Army Rsch., Presidio San Francisco, 1974-80, Western Human Nutrition Rsch. Ctr. USDA, Presidio San Francisco, 1980-95, ret., 1995. Contbr. numerous articles to profl. jours. Trustee 1st Meth. Ch., Ronnert Park, Calif., 1985-94, mem. fin. com., 1994—. With Med. Svc. Corps U.S. Army, 1954-56. Named one of Outstanding Young Men of Am., 1975; NIH traineeship Va. Poly. Inst. and State U., Blacksburg, 1961-63. Mem. AAAS, Am. Inst. Nutrition, Am. Soc. Clin. Nutritionists, Am. Coll. Nutritionists, Am. Coll. Sports Medicine, Sebastopol Spinners, Sigma Xi, Phi Lambda, Phi Sigma. Republican. Achievements include research on human nutrition. Home: 256 Alden Ave Rohnert Park CA 94928-3704 E-mail: barbherm@inreach.com.

JOHNSON, HOLLIS EUGENE, III, foundation executive; b. Nashville, June 24, 1935; s. Hollis Eugene Jr. and Jennie Frances (Settle) J.; m. Marie Celeste Morrison, Nov. 19, 1960; children: Hollis Eugene IV, Martha Settle. BA, Vanderbilt U., 1956. With First Am. Nat. Bank, Nashville, 1959-76, v.p., trust officer, until 1976; exec. sec.-treas. So. Bapt. Found., Nashville, from 1976, now pres. Chmn. bd. trustees Franklin Rd. Acad., 1986-88, 95—, pres. Nashville Residence for Young Women, 1973, Nashville Area Jr. C. of C., 1965; chmn. Cumberland Valley Girl Scout investment coun., 1976-79; deacon Belmont Heights Bapt. Ch., 1974—, chmn., 1984, 89. With USNR, 1956-59. Mem. Assn. Bapt. Found. Execs. (pres. 1982), Nashville Soc. Fin. Analysts, Assn. for investment mgmt and rsch. Home: 5308 Confederate Dr Nashville TN 37215-5202 Office: So Bapt Found 901 Commerce St Nashville TN 37203-3697

JOHNSON, HORTON ANTON, pathologist; b. Cheyenne, Wyo., Nov. 12, 1926; s. Horton Antonius and Katharine Mary (Tidball) J.; m. Caryl Abell Daly, Nov. 20, 1970; children by previous marriage: Katherine, Kristin, Margaret, Ann, Gregory, Marjorie. AB, Colo. Coll., 1949; MD, Columbia U., 1953. Diplomate: Am. Bd. Pathology. Intern Univ. Hosp., Ann Arbor, Mich., 1953-54, resident in pathology, 1954-57, Pondville Cancer Hosp., Walpole, Mass., 1957-58; scientist Brookhaven Nat. Lab., 1958-60, 63-70; asst. prof. pathology U. Utah, 1960-63; prof. pathology SUNY, Stony Brook, 1970-72, Ind. U., 1972-75; prof., chmn. dept. pathology Tulane U., New Orleans, 1975-84; prof. pathology Columbia U., N.Y.C., 1984-91; dir. pathology St. Luke's-Roosevelt Hosp. Ctr., N.Y.C., 1984-91. Docent Met. Mus. Art, 1993—. Served with USNR, 1944—46, USS Atlanta. Recipient Lederle Med. Faculty award, 1961 Fellow Coll. Am. Pathologists; mem. Am. Soc. Exptl. Pathology, Internat. Acad. Pathology, Biophys. Soc., Radiation Research Soc., N.Y. Acad. Scis., Assn. Clin. Scientists, Soc. Health and Human Values, Phi Beta Kappa, Alpha Omega Alpha. Achievements include rsch. on radiation injury, aging, theoretical biology. Home: 39 N Cove Rd Old Saybrook CT 06475-2538 Office: 3 Lincoln Ctr Ste 47C New York NY 10023-6566 E-mail: horton_johnson@hotmail.com.

JOHNSON, HOWARD EARL, chemist, educator; b. Denver, Jan. 18, 1921; s. Leonard Earl and Lillian Myrtle Johnson; m. Betty Mae Gilbertson, June 5, 1950; children: Karen Ann, Sheryl Lynne, Robyn Leigh. BA, U. of Denver, 1947, BA, 1948; MS, Calif. Inst. of Tech., Pasadena, 1952; post grad., U. Wash., Seattle, 1949—57. Cert. CC Instr., secondary sch. tchr. Weather officer USAAF, 1943—46; chemist Gen. Electric Co., Richland, Wash., 1948—49, 1951—53; tchr. sci Fontana HS, Calif., 1953—56; mem. tech. staff atomics internat. divsn. Rockwell Internat., Canoga Pk., Calif., 1956—73, sr. chemist, 1964—66, mem. tech. staff V, 1966—72; environ. specialist C.F. Braun & Co., Alhambra, Calif., 1973—75; tchr. Brentwood Sch., LA, 1975—82, chmn. sci. dept., 1975—82; sr. chemist Havard atomic products operation Rockwell Internat., Richland, Wash., 1982—87. Rockwell Internat. rep. Nat. Analytical Standards working com. of U.S. Atomic Energy Commn., Argonne, Ill., 1967—72; chemist Hanford Atomic Products Ops., 1948—49, 1951—53, 1982—87; instr. E. LA Ext. Divsn. U. Calif., 1977—80. Contbr. chapters to books, scientific papers;, author environmental impact reports. Bd. mem. Boise Unitarian Universalist Fellowship, 1999—2001, guest spkr., 1997—. Lt. USAAF, 1943—46, PTO. Mem.: Caltech Alumni Assn. (alumni fund coord. 1990—2000), Pi Delta Theta, Phi Delta Kappa. Unitarian Universalist. Avocations: church activities, reading, classical music, travel, camping. Home: 3504 Veranda Way Boise ID 83706

JOHNSON, HOWARD PAUL, agricultural engineering educator; b. Odebolt, Iowa, Jan. 27, 1923; s. Gustaf Johan and Ruth Helen (Hanson) J.; m. Patricia Jean Larsen, June 15, 1952; children: Cynthia, Lynette, Malcolm. BS, Iowa State U., 1949, MS in Agrl. Engring., 1950; MS in Hydraulic Engring., U. Iowa, 1954; PhD, Iowa State U., 1959. Engr., Soil Conservation Service, Sioux City, Iowa, 1949; instr. Iowa State U., Ames, 1950-53, 54-59, asst. prof., 1959-60, assoc. prof., 1960-62, prof. agrl. engring., 1962-80, head dept., 1980-88, prof. emeritus; cons., 1960-80. Contbr. numerous articles, papers to profl. lit. Co-editor Hydrologic Modeling, 1981. Patentee flow meter. Pres., Sawyer Sch. PTA, Ames, 1965; precinct rep. Republican party, Ames, 1980. Served with AUS, 1943-46, ETO. Recipient Iowa State U. Gamma Sigma Delta Merit award, 1983; EPA grantee, 1975-80; Anson Marston Disting. Prof. Engring., 1986. Fellow AAAS, Am. Soc. Agrl. Engrs. (div. chmn. 1969-70, tech. coun. 1974-76, Engr. of Yr. Iowa sect. 1981, Mid-Central sect. 1982, John Deere medal 1994). Baptist. Lodge: Rotary. Avocations: reading, photography, fishing, writing. Office: Iowa St U Dept Agrl Engring 100 Davidson Hall Ames IA 50014

JOHNSON, HOWARD WESLEY, former university president, business executive; b. Chgo., July 2, 1922; s. Albert H. and Laura (Hansen) J.; m. Elizabeth J. Weed, Feb. 18, 1950; children: Stephen Andrew, Laura Ann, Bruce Howard. BA, Central Coll., Chgo., 1943; MA, U. Chgo., 1947; cert., Glasgow (Scotland) U., 1946; LLD (hon.), Harvard U., U. Miami, 1966, U. Mass., 1969, Oklahoma City U., 1970, U. Cin., 1973, Babson Coll., 1978; ScD (hon.), Lowell Tech. Inst., Tufts U., Bryant Coll., 1967; LHD (hon.), Northea. U., 1966, Roosevelt U., 1969; LittD (hon.), Clarkson Coll. Tech., 1973. From asst. to assoc. prof., dir. mgmt. rsch. U. Chgo., 1948-51, 53-55; asst. to v.p. pers. adminstrn. Gen. Mills, Inc., 1952-53; assoc. prof., dir. exec. programs, assoc. dean Sloan Sch. Mgmt., MIT, 1955-59, prof., dean, 1959-66; pres. MIT, 1966-71; chmn. corp., 1971-83; hon. chmn. corp., 1983-90; life mem. corp., 1983-97; life mem. emeritus, 1997—. Exec. v.p. Federated Dept. Stores, 1966; chmn. Fed. Res. Bank Boston, 1968-69; trustee Putnam Funds, 1961-71; mem. Pres.'s Adv. Com. on Labor-Mgmt. Policy, 1966-68; chmn. Environ. Studies Bd. NAS-NAE, 1973-75; mem. sci. adv. com. Mass. Gen. Hosp., 1968-70; mem. Nat. Manpower Adv. Com., 1967-69, Nat. Commn. on Productivity, 1970-72; trustee Com. Econ. Devel., 1968-71, Wellesley Coll., 1968-86, trustee emeritus 1986—; trustee Radcliffe Coll., 1973-79; hon. trustee Aspen Inst. for Humanistic Studies, Inst. Deaf Analyses, 1971-79; mem. corp. Woods Hole (Mass) Oceanog. Instn. Author: Holding the Center: Memoirs of a Life in Higher Education, 1999. Trustee WGBH Ednl. Found., 1966-71, Henry Francis du Pont Winterthur Mus., 1984-87, Dibner Inst., 1992-97; mem. corp. Mus. Sci., Boston; overseer Boston Symphony Orch, 1968-72; mem.-at-large Boy Scouts Am.; pres. Boston Mus. Fine Arts, 1975-80, trustee 1971-72, chmn. bd. overseers, 1980-83, chmn. exec. com., 1983-87, hon. life trustee 1992—; trustee Alfred P. Sloan Found., 1982-95, chmn. bd. 1988-95; bd. dirs. Nat. Arts Stablzn. Found., 1983-87, Museo de Arte de Ponce, 1983-87. With AUS, 1943-46. Recipient Alumni medal U. Chgo., 1970, Gyorgy Kepes Fellowship prize MIT, 1999. Fellow AAAS, Am. Acad. Arts and Scis.; mem. Coun. Fgn. Rels., Am. Philos. Soc., Nat. Acad. Scis. (Pres.'s Circle), Nat. Acad. Engring. (Pres.'s Cir.), Inst. of Medicine (Pres.'s Cir.), Century Assn. (N.Y.C.), Comml. Club (Boston), Tavern Club (Boston), St. Botolph Club (Boston), Phi Gamma Delta. Office: MIT 77 Massachusetts Ave Cambridge MA 02139-4307

JOHNSON, IRVING STANLEY, pharmaceutical company executive, scientist; b. Grand Junction, Colo., June 30, 1925; s. Walter Glen and Frances Lucetta (Tuttle) J.; m. Alwyn Neville Ginther, Jan. 29, 1949; children: Rebecca Lyn, Bryan Glenn, Kirsten Shawn, Kevin Bruce. BS, Washburn U., Topeka, 1948; PhD, U. Kans., 1953. With Lilly Rsch. Labs., Indpls., 1953-88, v.p. rsch., 1973-88; mem. profl. edn. com. Am. Cancer Soc., 1972-82. Rschr. cancer, virus, genetic engring.; recombinant adv. com. NIH, 1985-88; mem. UCLA Symposia Bd., 1986-89; cons. biomed. rsch., 1989—; bd. dirs. Allelix Biopharms., Ligand Pharms.; sci. adv. bd. Elan Corp., 1996—; trustee La Jolla Cancer Rsch. Found., 1990-93; advisor to biomed. rsch. cos., venture capital groups. Mem. sci. adv. bd. Biotech., 1986—; mem. editorial bd. Chemico-Biol. Interactions, 1968-73; contbr. articles to profl. publs.; patentee in field. With USNR, 1943-46. Recipient 1st ann. Congl. award for sci. and tech., 1984. Fellow AAAS; mem. Am. Assn. Cancer Rsch. (Cain Meml. award for outstanding preclin. rsch. in cancer chemotherapy 1986), Am. Soc. Cell Biology (mem. pub. policy com.), Environ. Mutagen Soc., Internat. Soc. Chemotherapy, N.Y. Acad. Scis., Soc. Exptl. Biology and Medicine, Am. Soc. Immunologists (mem. sci. adv. bd. biotech), Soc. for Neurosci., Sigma Xi, Phi Sigma. Episcopalian.

JOHNSON, IVER CHRISTIAN, valuation company executive; b. N.Y.C., Oct. 21, 1928; s. Rudolph Albert and Mae Sophia (Bernhardt) J.; m. Ann E. Wells, May 15, 1954 (div. Apr. 1978); children: Christian Robert, Roberta Dawn, Brad Milton; m. Rochelle Valene Wehrheim, Dec. 6, 1986. BSME, N.Y.U., 1950; MBA, Northwestern U., 1958. Registered profl. engr. Engr. Yale & Towne Mfg. Co., Chgo., 1952-54; computer sales engr. GE, Phoenix, 1958-60; comml. broker O'Malley Investment & Realty Co., Phoenix, 1960-64; v.p. Investors Trust & Realty Co., Inc., Phoenix, 1964-66; ptnr. Shuart Bros. Constrn. Co., Phoenix, 1966-69; pres. Iver C. Johnson & Co., Ltd., Phoenix, 1970-95. Del. mem. Citizen Amb. Program Econ. Mgmt. Delegation to Soviet Union, Moscow, Kiev and Odessa, USSR, 1990; adj. instr. Ozarks Tech. Coll., S.W. Bapt. U., S.W. Baptist U. Chmn., mem. bd. appeals Ariz. State Land Dept., 1989-95, exec. com. Ariz. Appraiser Coalition, 1989-92. 1st lt. USAF, 1954-56; mem. Ash Grove (Mo.) City Coun., 1997—. Mem. Am. Soc. Appraisers (sr., pres. 1985-86, ASA award 1981, Outstanding Mem. award 1990), Inst. Indsl. Engrs., Internat. Right of Way Assn. (SRWA award 1990), Am. Mktg. Assn. (profl.). Republican. Lutheran. Avocation: freelance writing. Home and Office: 904 E Auburn Dr Ash Grove MO 65604-9100 E-mail: iverjohns@aol.com., ivercjohns@hotmail.com.

JOHNSON, J. CHESTER, financial executive, poet; b. Chattanooga, Sept. 28, 1944; m. Freda Stern; children: Juliet Christina, Guilbert Roland. Student, Harvard U., 1962-65; BSE, U. Ark., 1967. Sr. analyst Moody's Investors Svc., 1968-71; head pub. fin. rsch. and adv. group The Morgan Bank, 1972-77; dep. asst. sec. U.S. Treasury Dept., Washington, 1977-78; chmn., prin. Govt. Fin. Assocs., Inc., N.Y.C., 1979—. Bd. dirs., chair fin. com. N.Y. State Environ. Facilities Corp., 1991-95; chmn. Fed. Task Force to create Nat. Devel. Bank; chmn. Fed. Inter-agy. Task Force for Improvement Govtl. Fin. Reporting; chmn. Fund to Assure Pub. Infrastructure Fin., Nat. Infrastructure Bond Coalition, 1988-91; interviewed on pub. fin. Cable News Network, ABC Morning News Feature, PBS News Roundup, NBC Nightly News, others. Author: (poetry) OH America!, January 12th, 1967, 2d edit., 1975, Family Ties, Internecine Interregnum!, 1981, For Conduct and Innocents, 1982, Shorts: For Fun, Not for Instruction, 1985, It's a Long Way Home, An American Sequence, 1985, Shorts: On Reaching Forty, 1985, Exile/Martin, 1986, The Professional Curiosity of a Martyr, 1987, Freda's Appetite, 1991, Lazarus, Come Forth, 1993, Plain Bob

(Unbehaved), 1993; (with W.H. Auden) revised psalms in The Book of Common Prayer of The Episcopal Church, 1971-77; co-author: Original Disclosure Guidelines for Securities' Offerings by State and Local Governments, 1976, The Future of Boston's Capital Plant, 1980, Mayor's Financial Management Handbook, 1985: contbr. numerous articles to profl. jours. and poetry to anthologies. Mem. Nat. Assn. Ind. Pub. Fin. Advisors (pres. 1989-91), Nat. Soc. Mcpl. Analysts, Nat. Fedn. Mcpl. Analysts (Disting. Lifetime Contbn. award 1988). Office: Govt Fin Assocs Inc 63 Wall St Fl 16 New York NY 10005-3001

JOHNSON, JAMES A. financial organization executive; b. Benson, Minn., Dec. 24, 1943; s. Alfred I. and Adeline (Rasmussen) J.; m. Katherine Marshall, Feb. 15, 1969 (div. 1973); m. Maxine Isaacs, Jan. 12, 1985; 1 child, Alfred Isaacs. BA, U. Minn., 1965; MA, Princeton U., 1968. Spl. asst. to Sen. Walter Mondale U.S. Senate, Washington, 1972; dir. pub. affairs Dayton Hudson Corp., Mpls., 1973-76; exec. asst. to v.p. Walter Mondale The White House, Washington, 1977-81; pres. Pub. Strategies, Washington, 1981-85; mng. dir. Lehman Bros., N.Y.C., 1985-89; vice-chmn. Fannie Mae, Washington, 1990-91, chmn., CEO, 1991-98, chmn. exec. com. bd. dirs., 1999; chmn., CEO Johnson Capital Ptnrs., Washington, 2000-01; vice chmn. Perseus, 2001—. Bd. dirs. Target Corp., Goldman Sachs Inc., Temple-Inland, Gannett, Inc., KB Home. Chmn. John F. Kennedy Ctr. for Performing Arts; chmn. bd. trustees The Brookings Instn.; bd. dirs. The Enterprise Found., Nat. Housing Endowment, United HealthGroup, Nat. Assn. on Fetal Alcohol Syndrome. Democrat. Avocations: tennis, golf, travel. Office: Perseus LLC 2099 Pennsylvania Ave NW Washington DC 20006

JOHNSON, JAMES BEK, JR., library director; b. Sommerville, Mass., Oct. 1, 1943; s. James Bek and Esther Elizabeth (Cummings) J.; m. Deborah Marie Clawson, Oct. 21, 1972; children: Kirsten Eliska, Jessica Cummings. BA in History, La. State U., New Orleans, 1966; MS in LS, La. State U., Baton Rouge, 1968. Libr. La. State Penitentiary, Angola, 1968-70; cons. S.C. State Libr., Columbia, 1972-73, dir. dept. for handicapped, 1973-79, dep. dir., 1979-90, dir., 1990—. Contbr. articles to profl. jours. Mem. S.C. Gov.'s Com. on Employment of Handicapped, 1977—; vol. coach Columbia Recreation Dept., 1983-91; pres. Quail Creek Neighborhood Assn., Hopkins, S.C., 1986-90, mem. improvement coun. Lower Richland High Sch., Hopkins, 1991-93; mem., trustee First Steps to Sch. Readiness. With USMC, 1970-72. Mem. ALA (various coms.), S.C. Libr. Assn. (chmn. pub. libr. sect.), Chief Officers State Libr. Agys. (legis. com. 1990-96, sec. 1994-96), S.C. State Agy. Dirs. Orgn. (bd. dirs.), Staff Liaison, Governor's info. resource coun. Democrat. Episcopalian. Avocations: gardening, collecting opera records, baseball. Office: SC State Libr PO Box 11469 Columbia SC 29211-1469 E-mail: jim@leo.scsl.state.sc.us.

JOHNSON, JAMES DAVID, concert pianist, organist, educator; b. Greenville, S.C., Aug. 7, 1948; s. Theron David and Lucile (Pearson) J.; m. Karen Elizabeth Jacobson, Feb. 1, 1975. MusB, U. Ariz., 1970, MusM, 1972, D of Mus. Arts, 1976; MusM, Westminster Choir Coll., 1986. Concert pianist, organist Pianists Found. Am., Boston Pops Orch., Royal Philharm., Nat. Symphony Orch., Leningrad Philharmonic, Victoria Symphony, others, 1961—; organist, choirmaster St. Paul's Episcopal Ch., Tucson, 1968-74, First United Meth. Ch., Fairbanks, Alaska, 1974-89, All Saints Episc. Ch., Omaha, 1995—; prof. music U. Alaska, Fairbanks, 1974-96, chair music dept., 1991-94; Isaacson prof. of music U. Nebr., Omaha, 1994—2001, chair dept. music, 1999—2001, Robert M. Spire chair in music, 2002—. Recordings include Moszkowski Etudes, 1973, Works of Chaminade Dohnanyi, 1977, Mendelssohn Concerti, 1978, Beethoven First Concerto, 1980, Beethoven, Reinecke, Ireland Trios with Alaska Chamber Ensemble, 1988, Kabalevsky Third Concerto, Muczynski Concerto, Muczynski Suite, 1990, Beethoven Third Concerto, 1993. Recipient Record of Month award Mus. Heritage Soc., 1979, 80, Excellence in Tchg. award U. Nebr. at Omaha, 2001. Mem. Music Tchrs. Nat. Assn., Phi Kappa Phi, Pi Kappa Lambda. Episcopalian. Avocations: painting, woodworking, icon writing. Office: U Nebr Dept Music Omaha NE 68182-0001

JOHNSON, JAMES DOUGLAS (JIM JOHNSON), lawyer; b. Crossett, Ark., Aug. 20, 1924; s. Thomas William and Maudie Myrtle (Long) J.; m. Virginia Morris, Dec. 21, 1947; children: Mark Douglas, John David and Joseph Daniel (twins). LL.B., Cumberland U., 1947. Bar: Ark. 1948. Practice in, Crosset, 1948-58; assoc. justice Supreme Ct. Ark., 1958-66; practice law Little Rock, 1966—; Ark. Senate 22d Senatorial Dist., 1950-54. Served with USMCR, World War II. Mem. Ark. Jud. Council, Lamda Chi Alpha. Republican. Christian Scientist. Home: PO Box 1086 Conway AR 72033-1086

JOHNSON, JAMES ERLING, insurance executive; b. Waseca, Minn., May 19, 1942; s. Erling Olaf and Geneva Eleanor (Nyberg) J. BA cum laude, Carleton Coll., 1964; MS, U. Iowa, 1966. Sr. asst. health svcs. officer USPHS, 1966-68; with Minn. Life Ins. Co., St. Paul, 1968—, 2d v.p., actuary, 1976-79, v.p., actuary, 1979-90, sr.v.p., actuary, 1990—; pres., chief exec. officer Minn. Fire & Casualty, Minnetonka, 1984-97, also bd. dirs.; pres., chief exec. officer Adjustable Life Ins. Co., St. Paul, 1988-93, also bd. dirs. Mem. alumni bd. Carleton Coll., Northfield, Minn., 1987-90, coun., 1988-89, bd. trustees 1999—; campaign cabinet St. Paul United Way, 1988-89; bd. dirs. Minn. Landmarks, 1988—, treas., 1989-91, chmn., 1991-96; trustee ECH Found., 1989-95, asst. treas., 1990-91, treas., 1991-95; bd. dirs. Alliance of Am. Insurers, 1994-95, vice chmn., 1994-95, Saint Paul Chamber Orch., 1998—, co-chair indivdual gifts com., 1998-2000, vice chair devel., 2000—; mem. adv. bd. Minn. Ctr. for Ins. Rsch., 1995—. U. Iowa fellow, 1964-66. Fellow Soc. Actuaries; mem. Am. Acad. Actuaries, Twin Cities Actuarial Club (chmn. 1978-79), Mpls. Club, Flagship Athletic Club, Univ. Club (St. Paul), Minn. Assn. of Mutual Ins. Cos. (bd. dirs. 1984-97, pres. 1992-94), Nat. Assn. of Secondary Sch. Prins. (trustee Trust to Reach Edn. Excellence 1999—), Am. Coun. of Life Ins. (chair group ins. com., 2003—), Calhoun Beach Club, Phi Beta Kappa, Pi Mu Epsilon. Episcopalian. Avocations: travel, reading, running, swimming. Home: 2034 Lower Saint Dennis Rd Saint Paul MN 55116-2833 Office: Minn Life Ins Co 400 Robert St N Saint Paul MN 55101-2015 E-mail: james.johnson@minnesotamutual.com.

JOHNSON, JAMES HARDING, advertising executive; b. Perry, Iowa, Sept. 26, 1940; s. Richard Harding and Dorothy Margarite (Nelson) J.; m. Kathy Novak, Dec. 27, 1980; children: Ann Katherine, Alexander Simon, Elizabeth Ashely; children by previous marriage: Jennifer Lynn, James Harding. BA, U. Wash., 1963; PHD, U. Minn., 1972. Lic. psychologist, Utah, Va., Ill. Asst. prof. psychology U. Utah, Salt Lake City, 1975-77, dir. divsn. psychology Med. Sch., 1976-77; assoc. prof., vice chmn. dept. psychiatry Ea. Va. Med. Sch., Norfolk, 1977-79; chmn. Va. Consortium for Profl. Psychology, Norfolk, 1978-79; prof., dir. clin. psychology Ill. Inst. Tech., Chgo., 1979-83; pres. Human Edge Software, Inc., San Mateo, Calif., 1983-87, Text Generations Techs., San Mateo, 1987-89, Johnson Direct Advt., Palo Alto, Calif., 1988-89; CEO Connected Brands, 1989—. Author: Mental Health in the 21st Century, 1979, Technology in Mental Health Care Delivery Systems, 1980, How to Buy Almost Any Drug Legally Without a Prescription, 1990; co-author: Mind Prober, 1985; mem. editl. bd. Computers in Psychiatry and Psychology, Computers in Human Service, Behavior Rsch. Methods and Instrumentation, 1977, Computers in Psychiatry and Psychology, Computers and Behavioral Sci.; contbr. articles to profl. jours. Recipient Rush bronze medal Am. Psychiat. Assn., 1975. Mem. APA. Office: Connected Brands 400 Seaport Ct Ste 100 Redwood City CA 94063-2799

JOHNSON, JAMES J. lawyer; BA, U. Mich.; JD, Ohio State U. Bar: Ohio 1972. V.p., gen. counsel Procter & Gamble Co., Cin., 1991—, now sr. v.p., gen. counsel, 1991—, chief legal officer. Office: Procter & Gamble Co 1 Procter And Gamble Plz Cincinnati OH 45202-3393

JOHNSON, JAMES JOSEPH SCOFIELD, lawyer, judge, educator, author; b. Washington, Apr. 28, 1956; s. Richard Carl and Harriette (Benson) J.; m. Sherry Bekki Hall; children: Andrew Joel Schaeffer Johnson. AA with high honors, Montgomery Coll., Germantown, Md., 1980; BA with honors, Wake Forest U., 1982; JD, U. N.C., 1984; ThD with highest honors, Emmanuel Coll. Christian Studies, 1996, DASc with highest honors, 2000; PhD with highest honors, Cambridge Grad. Sch., Springdale, Ark., 1996, MSc, M of Liberal Arts, 1999. Bar: Tex. 1985, U.S. Dist. Ct. (no. dist.) Tex. 1986, U.S. Dist. Ct. (ea. dist.) Tex. 1987, U.S. Ct. Appeals (5th cir.) 1989, U.S. Dist. Ct. (we. and so. dists.) Tex. 1990, U.S. Supreme Ct. 2000; bd. cert. bus. bankruptcy law Tex. Bd. Legal Specialization, 1990, 95, 2000, Am. Bankruptcy Bd. Cert., 1992; cert. water quality monitor Tex. Natural Resource Conservation Commn., 1994-1997. Assoc. various orgns., Dallas, 1985—; pvt. practice law Dallas, 1993—. Adj. prof., master faculty LeTourneau U., Dallas, 1991—, Dallas Christian Coll., 1995—; lectr. History, Geography, Ecology, Culture, Norwegian Cruise Lines, 1998—; Bibl. langs. instr. Cross Timbers Inst., 2001—. Author: Introduction to Environmental Studies, 1995, 98, Doxological Zoology and Zoogeography, 1998, How Texas is Addressing Administrative Law Issues in School Law Contexts, 2003; sr. editl. staff N.C. Jour. Internat. Law and Comml. Regulation, 1983-84; conf. issue editor Harvard Jour. Law & Pub. Policy, 1984; contbr. articles to profl. jours. Protestant chaplain Boy Scouts Am., Goshen, Va., 1976; libr. vol. N.W. Bible Ch., Dallas, 1991-2000; cmty. program dir. Southwestern Legal Founds. Conf. on Internat. and Am. Law, 1991-92; scripture chmn. Gideons Internat., North Dallas, Tex., 1993-94. Recipient award for excellence in biblical studies and biblical langs. Am. Bible Soc., 1982. Mem. Near East Archaeology Soc., Sangre de Cristo Mountain Coun., Icelandic Geneal. Soc., Creation Rsch. Soc., Evangel. Theol. Soc., Norwegian Soc. Tex., Icelandic Soc. of Dallas, Sons of Norway (historian). Republican. Avocations: reading, writing, birding, traveling, hiking. Office: PO Box 2952 Dallas TX 75221-2952

JOHNSON, JAMES MCDADE, lawyer; b. Shreveport, La., Dec. 5, 1939; s. Leslie N. and Nell (McDade) J.; m. Glenda Roth, Jan. 27, 1962; children: Danielle Johnson Tuman, Kimberly Dawn. B.A., La. State U., 1962, J.D., 1964. Bar: La. 1964. First asst. dist. atty. 26th Jud. Dist. La., Minden, 1975-83; ptnr. Campbell, Campbell & Johnson, Minden, 1964—95; assoc. nat. legal counsel U.S. Jaycees, Tulsa, 1970-71, nat. legal counsel, 1971-72; mem., Ho. Rep. Dist. 10 La., 1990—. mem. State Ctrl. Democratic Com., 1990—. Chmn. Minden Democratic Exec. Com., La., 1964-74. Named Outstanding Vice Pres. La. Jaycees, 1969. Mem. Assn. Trial Lawyers Am. Episcopalian. Office: James M Johnson PLC PO Box 1015 Minden LA 71058

JOHNSON, JAMES MYRON, psychologist, educator; b. Sauk Centre, Minn., Aug. 4, 1927; s. Walfred and Sophie Catherine (Koelzer) J.; m. Constance Mary Blodgett, Apr. 15, 1950; children: Kathryn, Peter, Donna, Daniel, Amy, Linda, Eric, Christian. BA, U. Minn., 1948; MA, Clark U., 1950; PhD, Columbia, 1958; ME (hon.), Stevens Inst. Tech., 1986. Staff psychologist Lever Bros. Co., 1955-64; Adj. prof. Grad. Sch. Indsl. Engring., N.Y.U., 1963-66; dep. dir. lab. psychol. studies Stevens Inst. Tech., 1964-67, dir., 1967-73, prof. mgmt. sci. and psychology, 1966-89, prof. emeritus, 1989—, assoc. dean acad. affairs, 1972-76, dir. tech. and soc. curriculum, 1972-75; dir. Center for Mgmt. of Organizational Resources, 1976-81; sr. partner Organizational Scis. Assocs., 1980-88; v.p. G. W. Fotis Assocs., Inc., 1982-88, head, dept. of mgmt., 1988-89. Cons. to industry. Prodr.: (film) The Man Who Revolutionized Management: Frederick Winslow Taylor; co-editor: Parish Life; editor: Lyme Cath. Observer. Pres. Darien (Conn.) Mental Health Assn., 1961-64, 68-70; mem. Darien Democratic Town Com.; bd. dirs. Gateway, Inc., 1979-86. Served with USNR, 1945-46. Mem. Am. Psychol. Soc., Met. N.Y. Assn. Applied Psychology (pres. 1963-64), Sigma Xi (treas. 1984-89), Old Lyme Country Club. Democrat. Roman Catholic. Home: 4 Tantummaheag Rd Old Lyme CT 06371-1137

JOHNSON, JAMES N. corporate executive, lawyer; b. 1919; married. Ph.B., Marquette U., 1941; LL.B., Cornell U., 1943; LL.D., Coll. Racine, 1973. With Olwell & Brady, 1943-46; with Porter, Johnson, Quale & Porter, 1946-61; sec., gen. atty. A. O. Smith Corp., Milw., 1961-67, v.p., sec., gen. counsel, 1967—. Office: 3533 N 27th St Milwaukee WI 53216-2663

JOHNSON, JAMES P. religious organization executive; Pres. Christian Ch. Found., Inc., Indpls. Mem. Christian Ch. Office: Christian Ch Found Inc 130 E Washington St PO Box 1986 Indianapolis IN 46206-1986

JOHNSON, JAMES ROBERT, ceramic engineer, educator; b. Cin., Jan. 2, 1923; s. Charles William and Della Ramona (Schubert) J.; m. Virginia M. Bowen, Apr. 3, 1945; children: Cathy (Mrs. Edward Spear), Barbara Kallusky, Randy, John, Jamie (Mrs. J.R. Myers), Brian. BS, Ohio State U., 1947, MS, 1948, PhD, 1950; DSc (hon.), U. Wis., 1993. Asst. prof. U. Tex., 1950-51; tech. adviser ceramics Oak Ridge Nat. Lab., 1951-56; lab. mgr., dir., exec. scientist Minn. Mining & Mfg. Co., St. Paul, 1956-79, cons., 1979—; William L. McKnight prof. U. Minn., Duluth, 1988-89. Adj. prof. U. Wis.-Stout, U. Minn., 1979—. Contbr. articles to profl. jours.; patentee in field. Served with C.E. AUS, 1943-46. Recipient Distinguished Alumnus award Ohio State U., 1970, 3M Carlton award, 1970, Prakken award Internat. Tech. Edn. Assn., 1989, James R. Johnson award established in his honor, U. Wis. Stout, 1983, Nelva Runnalls Rsch. award, U. Wis. Stout, 1989. Fellow Am. Ceramic Soc. (pres. 1973-74, disting. life mem.), Wis. Acad. Scis., Arts and Letters (pres. 1988); mem. NAE, Nat. Inst. Ceramics Engrs. (Pace award 1959, Greaves-Walker award 1985), Am. Soc. for Metals Engring. (Materials Achievement award 1980), Research Engring. Soc. Am. Achievements include pioneering in auto catalytic converters, high temperature nuclear fuel materials, bioceramics. Home: 1829 Winding Oaks Way Naples FL 34109-1458

JOHNSON, JAMES TERENCE, lawyer, educator, minister; b. Springfield, Mo., Oct. 25, 1942; s. Clifford Lester and Margaret Jeanne (Wallace) Johnson; m. Martha Susan Mitchell, May 2, 1964; children: Jennifer Jeanne, Emily Jill. BA, Okla. Christian Coll., 1964; JD, So. Meth. U., 1967; LLD (hon.), Pepperdine U., 1980. Min., Okla., Tex., 1961—; staff counsel, asst. prof. Okla. Christian Coll., Oklahoma City, 1968-72; pvt. practice Oklahoma City, 1969—; v.p. Okla. Christian U., 1972-73, exec. v.p., 1973-74, pres., 1974-95, chancellor, 1995—2000. Co-founder Enterprise Sq., 1982, Cascade Coll., 1993. Named to Okla. Higher Edn. Hall of Fame, 2000. Mem.: Okla. Bar Assn., Phi Delta Theta.

JOHNSON, JAMES TURNER, theology studies educator; b. Crockett Mills, Tenn., Nov. 2, 1938; s. Walter Turner and Georgia Maie (Swanson) J.; m. Pamela Jane Bennett, Oct. 19, 1969; children: Christopher Edward Bennett, Ashley Elizabeth Bennett. AB, Brown U., 1960; BD, Vanderbilt U., 1963; MA, Princeton U., 1967, PhD, 1968. Instr. philosophy and religion Newberry (S.C.) Coll., 1963-65; lectr. religion Vassar Coll., Poughkeepsie, N.Y., 1968-69; asst. prof. religion Rutgers U., New Brunswick, N.J., 1969-77, assoc. prof. religion, 1977-82, prof. religion, 1982—; univ. dir. internat. programs, 1987-96. Author: Just War Tradition, 1981, Can Modern War Be Just, 1984, The Quest for Peace, 1987, The Holy War Idea in Western and Islamic Traditions, 1997, Morality and Contemporary Warfare, 1999; editl. bd. mem. Jour. Religious Ethics, 1981—; editl. adv. com. Religious Studies Rev., 1981-91; co-editor Jour. Mil. Ethics, 2001—. Fellow Rockefeller Found., N.Y.C., 1976-77, Guggenheim Found., N.Y.C., 1984, fellow for Coll. Tchrs., NEH, Washington, 1991-92. Mem.: Am. Acad. Religion. Office: Rutgers U Dept Religion New Brunswick NJ 08903 E-mail: jtj@rci.rutgers.edu.

JOHNSON, JAMES WILSON, pastor; b. Benson, N.C., Apr. 11, 1942; s. Roy Allen and Edna Mavoreen (Allen) J.; m. Charlotte Marie Smith, Aug. 15, 1964; children: Donna Marie, Johnnie Allen. BA in History and Edn., Meth. Coll., Fayetteville, N.C., 1964; postgrad., East Carolina U., 1964. Southeastern Bapt. Sem., Wake Forest, N.C., 1964—. Lic. to ministry So. Bapt. Conv., 1964, ordained, 1967. Interim pastor 15 chs., N.C., 1964-86; pastor Albertson (N.C.) Bapt. Ch., 1986-97, Concord Bapt. Ch., Rose Hill, N.C., 1997—. Driver edn. specialist N.C. Divsn. Motor Vehicles, Raleigh, 1968-2000; dir. brotherhood Ea. Bapt. Assn., Warsaw, 1987-91, chmn. nominating com., 1988-90, vice moderator, 1989-91, moderator, 1991-93, mem. numerous coms., 1968-2000. Bd. dirs. Duplin County Assn. for Retarded Citizens, 1969-79, v.p., 1975-77, pres., 1977-79. Mem. N.C. State Employees Assn. Home and Office: Concord Bapt Ch 639 E Southerland St Wallace NC 28466-2731 E-mail: jwj519@earthlink.net.

JOHNSON, JANE PENELOPE, freelance/self-employed writer; b. Danville, Ky., July 1, 1940; d. Buford Lee Carr and Emma Irene (Coldiron) Sebastian; m. William Evan Johnson, July 15, 1958; children: William Evan Jr., Robert Anthony. Grad., Famous Writer's Sch. Fiction, Westport, Conn., 1967; grad. writer's div., Newspaper Inst. Am., N.Y.C., 1969; grad., Am. Assn. Chrisitan Counselors, 2001; LittD (hon.), The London Inst. Applied Rsch., 1993. Lay counselor Caring for People God's Way. Author numerous poems; author song lyrics: Everlasting Freedom, Answered Prayer, Glory Bound, Americans Standing Tall; recs. include America, 1997-98, The Light of the World, 1998-99; contbr. Hilltop Gospel Songbook. Patron Menninger. Ennobled by Prince John, The Duke of Avram, Tasmania, Australia; semifinalist Internat. Libr. Poetry, N.Am. Poetry Open; recipient 28 Editor's Choice awards for poetry Nat. Libr. of Poetry, 1994, Editor's Choice award Internat. Libr. Poetry, 2000, Coat of Arms, Coll. of Heraldry; named to Internat. Poetry Hall of Fame, 1996, Pres. award, 2002; named World Laureate. Fellow The World Lit. Acad. Eng.; mem. NAFE, Smithsonian Assocs., Peale Ctr. for Christian Living, Sweet Adelines, Internat. Soc. Poets (life, advisor), Internat. Platform Assn., Charles Menniger Soc. (life), Internat. Order of Merit, Nat. Writer's Club, Poetry Guild N.Y., Norman Vincent Peale Fellowship (founder). Republican. Avocations: swimming, skating, dancing, piano. Office: Gardenside Br PO Box 8013 Lexington KY 40504-8013

JOHNSON, JANET GRAY ANDREWS, clinical social worker; b. Raleigh, N.C., Jan. 14, 1956; d. Junius Jackson and Alma Gray (Goff) Andrews; m. Charles Lavon Johnson, Jr., June 23, 1990. BSW, N.C. State U., 1978; MSW, U. N.C., 1980; MBA, Meredith Coll., Raleigh, 1987. Diplomate clin. social work; lic. clin. social worker, N.C.; cert. Acad. Cert. Social Workers. Social worker Johnston County Dept. Social Svc., Smithfield, N.C., 1980-81; clin. social worker Johnston County Mental Health, Smithfield, 1981-84, Holly Hill Hosp., Raleigh, 1984-87, geriatric program coord., 1987-90, adult clin. svcs. coord., 1990-91; dir. adult program Coastal Plain Hosp., Rocky Mount, N.C., 1991-93; clin. case mgr. Value Behavioral Health, Research Triangle Park, N.C., 1993-94; social work supr. III, Dorothea Dix Hosp., Raleigh, NC, 1994—; field edn. instr. UNC Sch. Social Work, 1999, 2002. Chair geriatric adv. bd. Holly Hill Hosp., 1989-91; bd. dirs. Johnston County Coun. on Aging, Smithfield, 1982-84; founder/facilitator Johnston County Alzheimers's Family Support Group, Smithfield, 1982-84. Recipient humanitarian awards. Mem. NASW (bd. dirs. N.C. chpt. 1990-94, chair eastern dist. 1991-94, co-chair Wake County chpt. 1990-91, Social Worker of Yr. award N.C. chpt. 1992). Avocations: collecting antiques, flower and vegetable gardening. Office: Dorothea Dix Hosp 820 S Boylan Ave Raleigh NC 27603-2246

JOHNSON, JANET HELEN, Egyptology educator; b. Everett, Wash., Dec. 24, 1944; d. Robert A. and Jane N. (Osborn) J.; m. Donald S. Whitcomb, Sept. 2, 1978; children: J.J., Felicia. BA, U. Chgo., 1967, PhD, 1972. Instr. Egyptology U. Chgo., 1971-72, asst. prof., 1972-79, assoc. prof., 1979-81, prof., 1981—; dir. Oriental Inst., 1983-89; research assoc. dept. anthropology Field Mus. of Natural History, 1980-84, 94-99, 2003—. Author: Demotic Verbal System, 1977, Thus Wrote Onchsheshonqy, 1986, 3d revised edit., 2000, (with Donald Whitcomb) Quseir al-Qadim, 1978, 80; editor: (with E.F. Wente) Studies in Honor of G.R. Hughes, 1977, Life in a Multi-Cultural Society, 1992. Smithsonian Instn. grantee, 1977-83; NEH grantee, 1978-81, 81-85; Nat. Geog. Soc. grantee, 1978, 80, 82 Mem. Am. Rsch. Ctr. in Egypt (bd. govs. 1979—, exec. com. 1984-87, 90-96, v.p. 1990-93, pres. 1993-96). Office: U Chgo Oriental Inst 1155 E 58th St Chicago IL 60637-1540 E-mail: j-johnson@uchicago.edu.

JOHNSON, JANET LOU, real estate company executive, writer; b. Boston, Aug. 22, 1939; d. Donald Murdoch and Helen Margaret (Slauenwhite) Campbell; m. Walter R. Johnson, Mar. 31, 1962; children: Meryl Ann, Leah Kathryn, Christa Helen. Student, Gordon Coll., Hamilton, Mass., 1962-64. Adminstr., account exec. Fuller/Smith & Ross, Boston, 1958-63; adminstr. Walter R. Johnson, P.E., Gloucester, Mass., 1970-76; broker Realty World, Gloucester, 1976-77, Hunneman & Co., Gloucester, 1977-79; pres., owner Janet L. Johnson Real Estate, Gloucester, 1979—. Author, illustrator, pub: The Ritz Carlton Cat, 1999. Mem. Nat. Assn. Realtors, Mass. Assn. Realtors (bd. dirs. 1985-87), Cape Ann C. of C., Cape Ann Bd. Realtors (pres. 1984-85, state dir. 1985-86), North Shore Assn. Bd. Realtors. Office: Janet L Johnson Real Estate 160 Main St Rockport MA 01966 Home: 160 Main St Rockport MA 01966-2017 Business E-Mail: jjrealest@aol.com.

JOHNSON, J(ANET) SUSAN, psychologist; b. Ramey AFB, P.R., Mar. 24, 1948; d. Wesley Roger and Marie Dolores (Stecher) J. BA in Psychology, San Diego State U., 1970, Ma in Psychology, 1974. Nat. exec. lab. coord. Navy Nat. Elec. Lab., San Diego, 1970-72; assoc. dir. clin. decisions Navy Health Rsch. Ctr., San Diego, 1972-78; exec. dir. The Edwards Assocs., San Diego, 1978—; clin. intern in clin. psychology TRI Cmty. Svcs. Outpatient Clinic, San Diego, 1978-80; exec. dir., v.p. Strategic Vision, San Diego, 1983—. Cons. in field; co-founder Ctr. for Value Centered Life, 1999; key spkr., program coord. for nat. presidencies, prime mins., Fortune 100 CEO's, 1978—; pvt. practice on theoretical devel. of value centered psychology, 1972—; rschr. in U.S., U.K., France, Germany, Hungry, Bulgaria, Japan, Brazil, Italy, Greece, Russia and numerous other countries.. Contbr. articles to profl. publs. Avocations: skiing, boating, scuba diving, gardening. E-mail: susan@vision-inc.com.

JOHNSON, JANICE E, education educator, writer; b. Portsmouth, Ohio, Sept. 15, 1956; d. James Elmer and Gwendolin Audrey Johnson. AD, Shawnee State U., 1986—88, B in bus. adminstrn., 1988—90; MBS, Morehead State U., 1990—92. Cert. Computer Professional Inst. for Certification of Computing Professionals, 1996, Bus. Info. Systems Inst. for Certification of Computing Professionals, 1996, Office Info. Systems Inst. for Certification of Computing Professionals, 1996; Med. Lab. Tech. Am. Soc. of Clin. Pathologists, 1977. Br. mgr. Roche Biomedical Laboratories, Livonia, Mich., 1985—86; bus. faculty Shawnee State U., Portsmouth, Ohio, 1990—. Author: (short stories) Fido, The Leading Edge, Crossroad, Planes of Reality, (novels) Heroes on Ice, Voice of Truth. Web leader Shawnee State U., Portsmouth, Ohio, 1996—2003; advisor Fantanime Club, Portsmouth, Ohio, 2001—03, Shawnee State Computer Soc., Portsmouth, Ohio, 1990—2003. Recipient Wall St. Jour. Student Achievement award, Wall St. Jour., 1989, Presdl. scholarship, 1988—89, D.P.M.A. Student award, Data Processing Mgmt. Assn., 1987. Mem.: HTML Writers Guild, Internat. Webmasters Assn., Am. Soc. of Clin. Pathologists (assoc.). Christian. Avocations: writing, web design, reading, bird watching, gardening. Office: Shawnee State University 940 2nd St Portsmouth OH 45662 E-mail: jjohnson@shawnee.edu.

JOHNSON, JAY WITHINGTON, former congressman; b. Bessemer, Mich., Sept. 30, 1943; s. Ruben W. and Catherine W. (Withington) J.; m. Jane Sholtz (div.); m. Jo Lee Works, June 26, 1982; stepchildren: Christopher, Joanna AA, Gogebic Community Coll., 1963; BA, No. Mich. U., 1965; MA, Mich. State U., 1970. Disk jockey Sta. WFMK, Lansing, Mich., 1968-69; news anchorman Sta. WILX-TV, Lansing, 1969-70; radio news reporter Sta. WOWO, Ft. Wayne, Ind., 1970-73; news anchorman Sta. WPTV-TV, West Palm Beach, Fla., 1973-76; radio news reporter Sta. WVCG/WLVE-FM, Miami, Fla., 1976; TV producer Sta. WPLG-TV, Miami, 1976; news anchorman, mng. editor Sta. WPEC-TV, West Palm Beach, 1977-80; news anchorman Sta. WOTV-TV, Grand Rapids, Mich., 1980-81, Sta. WFRV-TV, Green Bay, Wis., 1981-87, Sta. WLUK-TV, Green Bay, 1987-96; mem. 105th Congress from 8th Wis dist., 1997-98, mem. agrl., transp. and infrastructure coms.; acting dep. asst. sec. congl. rels. USDA, 1999-2000; dir. U.S. Mint, Washington, 2000-2001. Vol. Big Bros./Big Sisters, Green Bay, 1982-87 (Vol. of Yr. 1985); pres., bd. dirs. Family Violence Ctr., Green Bay, 1982-87; v.p. communications United Way, Green Bay, 1987—; adv. bd. Libertas Alcohol Treatment Ctr., 1989—. With U.S. Army, 1966-68. Recipient Gov's award Gov. Tommy Thompson, 1988; named Citizen of Yr. Masons, 1987.

JOHNSON, JEAN ELAINE, nursing educator; b. Wilsey, Kans., Mar. 11, 1925; d. William H. and Rosa L. (Welty) Irwin. BS, Kans. State U., 1948; MS in Nursing, Yale U., 1965; MS, U. Wis., 1969, PhD, 1971; DS (hon.), Univ. Wis., 1998. Instr. nursing, Iowa, 1948—58; staff nurse Swedish Hosp., Englewood, Colo., 1958—60; in-svc. edn. coord. Gen. Rose Hosp., Denver, 1960—63; rsch. asst. Yale U., New Haven, 1965—67; assoc. prof. nursing Wayne State U., Detroit, 1971—74, prof., 1974—79; dir. Ctr. for Health Rsch., 1974—79; assoc. dir. oncology nursing Cancer Ctr. U. Rochester, NY, 1979—93, prof. nursing, 1979—95, prof. emerita, 1995—. Rosenstadt prof. health rsch. Faculty Nursing, U. Toronto, 1985; vis. prof. U. Utah Coll. Nursing, 1996—97, U. Wis., Madison, 1998. Author: Self-Regulation Theory: Applying Theory to Your Practice, 1997; contbg. author Handbook of Psychology and Health, vol. 5, 1984; contbr. articles. Recipient Bd. Govs. Faculty Recognition award, Wayne State U., 1975, award for disting. contbn. to nursing sci., Am. Nurses Found. and ANA Coun. for Nurse Rschrs., 1983, Grad. Tchg. award, U. Rochester, 1991, Disting. Rschr. award, Oncology Nursing Soc., 1992, Outstanding Contbns. to Nursing and Psychology award, divsn. of health psychol-

ogy APA, 1993; grantee, NIH, 1972—95. Fellow: Am. Psychol. Soc., Acad. for Behavioral Medicine Rsch., APA (Outstanding Contbns. to Nursing and Psychology award 1993), AAAS; mem.: Inst. Medicine of NAS (com. on patient injury compensation 1976—77, membership com. 1981—86, gov. coun. 1987—89), ANA (chmn. coun. for nurse rschrs. 1976—78, commn. for rsch. 1978—82), Phi Kappa Phi, Omicron Nu, Sigma Xi. Home: 4924 Whitecomb Dr Apt 15 Madison WI 53711-2661

JOHNSON, JEFF, marketing professional; BA in Psychology, Williams Coll.; M in Psychology, PhD in Psychology, NYU. Dir. consumer behavior J. Walter Thompson, 1980; EVP, acct. dir., dir. strategic planning Scali, McCabe, Sloves; mng. ptnr., dir. new bus. devel. Wells Rich Greene BDDP, NY; mktg. dir. Structure The Limited; pres. WestWayne, 2000—, CEO, 2002—. Office: 1170 Peachtree St 15th Fl Atlanta GA 30309

JOHNSON, JEFFREY GRANT, research scientist, psychology educator; b. Ft. Hood, Tex., Jan. 9, 1956; s. Roland Franklin and Gail Ann Johnson. BA, Oakland U., 1978; MA, Temple U., 1981, PhD, 1987. Asst. prof. psychology Bloomsburg (Pa.) U., 1987-88, Gettysburg (Pa.) Coll., 1988-90; postdoctoral rsch. fellow Johns Hopkins U., Balt., 1990-92, Columbia U., N.Y.C., 1992-97, assoc. prof. clin. psychology, 1997—2003; rsch. scientist Rsch. Found. for Mental Hygiene, N.Y.C., 1997—, assoc. prof. clin. psychology, 2003—. Lectr. Psychiat. Epidemiology Tng. Program, Columbia U., 1997—; reviewer Jour. Abnormal Psychology, 1997—, Am. Jour. Pub. Health, 1999—, Archives Gen. Psychiatry, 1999—. Contbr. over 80 articles to sci. jours., including Sci., Archives Gen. Psychiatry, JAMA, Jour. Abnormal Psychology, Jour. Cons. and Clin. Psychology, Jour. Psychopathology and Behavioral Assessment, Jour. Personality Disorders, Cognitive Therapy and Rsch., Am. Jour. Psycniatry, Ednl. and Psychol. Measurement, Jour. Social and Clin. Psychology, Comprehensive Psychiatry, Psychol. Medicine, Acta Psychiatrica Scandinavica, Jour. Adolescent Health, Jour. Am. Acad. Child and Adolescent Psychiatry, Jour. of child and Family Studies; photographs exhibited in galleries, N.Y.C., Washington, Phoenix, Denver, Moscow and Berlin. Recipient nat. rsch. svc. award NIMH, 1990-93, outstanding rsch. study award Am. Profl. Soc. on Abuse of Children, 1999; postdoctoral rsch. grantee Aaron Diamond Found., 1994-97. Mem. Ridge Street Artists. Avocations: photography, travel, guitar, bicycling, hiking. Office: NY State Psychiat Inst 1051 Riverside Dr Unit 60 New York NY 10032-1013 E-mail: jjohnso@pi.cpmc.columbia.edu.

JOHNSON, JEH CHARLES, lawyer; b. N.Y.C., Sept. 11, 1957; s. Jeh Vincent and Norma (Edelin) J.; m. Susan M. DiMarco, Mar. 18, 1994. BA, Morehouse Coll., Atlanta, 1979; JD, Columbia U., 1982. Bar: N.Y. 1983, D.C. 1999. Litig. assoc. Sullivan & Cromwell, N.Y.C., 1982—84; assoc. Paul, Weiss, Rifkind, Wharton & Garrison, N.Y.C., 1984-88, 92-93; asst. U.S. atty. So. Dist. N.Y., 1989-91; ptnr. Paul, Weiss, Rifkind, Wharton & Garrison, N.Y.C., 1994-98, 2001—; gen. counsel USAF, Washington, 1998—2001. Adj. lectr. law Columbia U. Law Sch., N.Y.C., 1995—97. Trustee Adelphi U., 2001—. Mem.: Coun. Fgn. Rels. Office: Paul Weiss Rifkin Wharton & Garrison 1285 Ave of Americas New York NY 10019 Office Fax: 212-757-3990. Business E-Mail: jjohnson@paulweiss.com.

JOHNSON, JEH VINCENT, architect; b. Nashville, July 8, 1931; s. Charles Spurgeon and Marie Antoinette (Burguette) J.; m. Norma Edelin, Dec. 28, 1956; children— Jeh Charles, Marguerite Marie. AB, Columbia U., 1953, M.Arch., 1958. Architect/designer Paul R. Williams, Los Angeles, 1956; designer Adams & Woodbridge, N.Y.C., 1957-62; asso. Gindele & Johnson (P.C. Architects and predecessors), Poughkeepsie, N.Y., 1962-69, partner, 1969-71, pres., 1971-80; ptnr. LeGendre Johnson McNeil Assos., 1980-90; pvt. practice architecture Wappingers Falls, N.Y., 1990—. Sr. lectr. in art Vassar Coll., 1964—2001, lectr. in urban studies, 1995—2000, lectr. emeritus, 2001-; mem. N.Y. State Bd. for Architecture, 1974-84, chmn., 1980-82; mem. Nat. Commn. Urban Problems, 1967-69; nat. master grader Nat. Coun. Archtl. Registration Bds., 1984-91. Designer: Dutchess County (N.Y.) Mental Health Ctr., 1969, Lagrange (N.Y.) Town Hall, 1969, Newburgh (N.Y.) Houses on the Lake, 1970, Whitney Young Health Ctr., Albany, N.Y., 1973, St. Simeon Apts. for Elderly, Poughkeepsie, 1973, 93, Bedford-Stuyvesant Comml. Ctr., N.Y.C., 1978, Camp of Tomorrow, Girl Scouts U.S.A., Mt. Pleasant, N.Y., 1985, Millbrook (N.Y.) Ch. Alliance Housing, Ctrl. Bapt. Ch., Salt Point, N.Y., Hillcrest House, Poughkeepsie, 1992, The Intercultural Ctr. at Vassar Coll, 1993, St. Anna Apts., Poughkeepsie, 1996. Mem. Dutchess County Planning Bd., 1988-92; bd. dirs. Scenic Hudson, Inc., 1995—. William Kinne Fellows traveling fellow, 1958 Fellow AIA (mem. nat. task force on affordable housing, Students medal 1958); mem. Nat. Orgn. Minority Architects (charter), AAUP, NAACP, Nat. Coun. Archtl. Registration Bds., Sigma Pi Phi. Clubs: Masons. Home and Office: 14 Edgehill Rd Wappingers Falls NY 12590-1228

JOHNSON, JENNIE, chaplain, social worker; b. Houston, Sept. 18, 1952; d. James L.C. and Marilyn Mildred (Frazier) J.; children: Alan, David. BS in Social Work, Tex. Woman's U., 1976; postgrad., Bishop's Sch. of Theology, Denver, 1979-80, Samaritan Theol. Sem., L.A., 1982-84, Episcopal Theol. Sem., Austin, Tex., 1986-87. Cert. social worker, Tex.; oblate Order of St. Benedict, 1998. Comdr. 94th Ord. Det. USAR, Ft. Carson, Colo., 1978-80, evaluator 1st maneuver tng. command Denver, 1980-81; prodn. control planner Elmo Semiconductor, L.A., 1981-83; quality control planner TRW Def. and Space Guidance, L.A., 1983-84; dir. chpt. svcs. Greater Amarillo (Tex.) Red Cross, 1985-86; chaplain Austin State Hosp., 1987-88, Brackenridge Hosp., Austin, 1988-91, Hospice Austin, 1992-95; asst. dir. Centex Chpt. ARC, Austin, Tex., 1995-96; chaplain Seaton Medical Ctr., Austin, 1998—. Conveener Integrity Austin, 1989-90, 92-94, 96-97; conf. presenter Nat. Episcopal AIDS Coalition, Cin., 1990, mem., 1990—. Founding bd. dirs. Out Youth Austin/YWCA, 1990-92; mem. Tex. AIDS Network, Austin, 1992—; foster parent Casey Family Program, Austin, 1992-94; diocesan del. St. Michael's Episcopal Ch., Austin, 1988—, jr. warden, 1993-95, mem. vestry, 1993-97, mem. divsn. for spiritual devel. of diocese Mentor Edn. for Ministry; mem.-at-large Women for Social Witness Network, Nat. Episcopal Ch., 1992-96; mem. Episcopal Womens Caucus, 1993—, Nat. Hospice Orgn., 1993—, Tex. Hospice Orgn., 1992—, presenter state conf., 1995, Order of St. Luke the Physician, 1984—. 1st lt. U.S. Army, 1975-80. Democrat. Avocations: paleontology, needlework, reading, fishing, camping. E-mail: jkhaslund2@aol.com.

JOHNSON, JEROME LINNÉ, cardiologist, educator; b. Rockford, Ill., June 19, 1929; s. Thomas Arthur and Myrtle Elizabeth (Swanson) J.; m. Molly Ann Rideout, June 27, 1953; children: Susan R. Johnson, William Rideout. BA, U. Chgo., 1951; BS, Northwestern U., 1952, MD, 1955. Diplomate Nat. Bd. Med. Examiners. Intern U. Chgo. Clinics, 1955-56; resident Northwestern U., Chgo., 1958-61; chief resident Chgo. Wesley Meml. Hosp., 1960-61; mem., v.p. Hauch Med. Clinic, Pomona, Calif., 1961-88; pvt. practice cardiology and internal medicine Pomona, 1988—. Clin. assoc. prof. medicine, U. So. Calif., L.A., 1961—; mem. staff Pomona Valley Hosp. Med. Ctr., chmn. coronary care com. 1967-77; mem. staff L.A. County Hosp. Citizen ambassador, People to People; mem. Town Hall of Calif., L.A. World Affairs Coun. Lt. USNR, 1956-58; bd. dirs. Claremont chpt. ARC, 1993-2000; bd. dirs., health com. Mt. San Antonio Gardens Retirement Home, 1993-2000. Fellow Am. Coll. Cardiology, Am. Geriatrics Soc., Royal Soc. Health; mem. Galileo Soc., Am. Heart Assn. (bd. dirs. L.A. County div. 1967-84, San Gabriel div. 1963-89), Am. Soc. Internal Medicine, Inland Soc. Internal Medicine, Pomona Host Lions. Avocations: photography, swimming, bicycling, medical and surgical antiques, travel. Home: 648 Delaware Dr Claremont CA 91711-3457

JOHNSON, JERRY D. legislative staff member; b. Harlan County, Ky; From past mem. local dem. bd. elections to chmn. various campaigns State of Ky., mem. Gov. Paul Patton first gubernatorial race, mem. exec. staff with Patton adminstrn., mem. spl. asst. to the Gov.; chmn. Ky. Dem. Party. Pub. svc. dem. state ctrl. exec. com. State of Ky. Democrat. Office: 190 Democrat Dr PO Box 694 Frankfort KY 40601

JOHNSON, JERRY DOUGLAS, biology educator; b. Salina, Kans., Sept. 1, 1947; s. Maynard Eugene and Norma Maude (Moss) J.; m. Kathryn Ann Johnson, May 12, 1973; children: George Walker, Brett Arthur. BS in Zoology, Fort Hays State U., 1972; MS in Biology, U. Tex., El Paso, 1975; PhD in Wildlife Sci., Tex. A&M U., 1984. Teaching asst. biology dept. U. Tex., El Paso, 1973—75; instr. biology El Paso C.C., 1975—2000, Piper prof., 1989—90; prof. biol. scis. U. Tex., El Paso, 2000—; dir. Indio Mountains Rsch. Station, 2000—. Councilor bd. scientists Chihuahuan Desert Rsch. Inst., Alpine, Tex., 1991—. Co-author: Middle American Herpetology, 1988; editor: Meso Am. Herpetology, 2001; contbr. articles to profl. jours. Bd. dirs. Meml. Park Improvement Assn., 1987—, El Paso Coun. for Internat. Visitors, 1988—, v.p., 1996, Parks and Recreation Bd., El Paso, 1991-94. Recipient El Paso Natural Gas Faculty Achievement award, 1995—96, Nat. Inst. Staff and Orgnl. Devel. Tchg. Excellence award, 1995—96, EPCC Honors Program Outstanding Honors Faculty award, 1998—99; grantee, Sigma Xi, 1974, Theodore Roosevelt Found. Am. Mus. Natural History, 1979, Exline Corp., 1980, NSF, 1992—95, 2001—, NIH, 1992—2000, Tex. Pks. and Wildlife Dept., 1998—2000. Mem. NSF, Nat. Ctr. for Acad. Achievement, Nat. Inst. Gen. Med. Sci., Soc. for Study of Amphibians and Reptiles (elector 1980, assoc. editor Geog. Distbn. Herpetol. Rev. 1993—), Southwestern Assn. Naturalists (assoc. editor 1977-85, bd. govs. 1985-89), Tex. Herpetol. Soc. (v.p., pres. 1995-96), El Paso Herpetol. Soc. (pres. 1993-95), Herpetologists League, others. Home: 3147 Wheeling Ave El Paso TX 79930-4321 Office: U Tex Dept Biol Scis El Paso TX 79968-0001 E-mail: jjohnson@utep.edu.

JOHNSON, JIMMIE, race car driver; b. El Cajon, Calif., Sept. 17, 1975; Racecar driver Herzog Motorsports, 1999—. Commentator ESPN; spokesperson Chevrolet divsn. GM. Named champion, Mickey Thompson Stadium, 1992—94, Am. Speed Assn. Memphis Motorsports Park, 1999, Busch Series Hills Bros. Coffee 300, 2001, Rookie of the Yr., Am. Speed Assn. ACDelco Challenge Series, 1998; recipient champion, Am. Spped Assn. Orange County Speedway, 1999, 7th pl., Busch Series The Milw. Mile, 1999. Office: c/o Hendrick Motorsports 4400 Papa Joe Hendrick Blvd Charlotte NC 28262

JOHNSON, JIMMY, sports broadcaster, former professional football coach; b. Port Arthur, Tex., July 16, 1943; BA, U. Ark., 1965. Asst. coach Louisiana Tech. U., LA, 1965, Wichita State U., KS, 1967, Iowa State U., IA, 1968-68, U. Oklahoma, Norman, OK, 1970-72, U. Arkansas, AR, 1973-76, U. Pittsburg, 1977-78; head coach Oklahoma State U., OK, 1979-83, U. Miami, Miami, FL, 1983-88, Dallas Cowboys, Dallas, 1989-94; sports commentator, football analyst Fox Network, 1994-95; head coach, gen. mgr. Miami Dolphins, 1996-99; co-host NFL Sunday, Fox, 2002—. Coach NCAA Divsn. I championship team, 1987, Super Bowl (XXVII, XXVIII) championship team, 1992-93; named Coach of Yr. Walter Camp Found., 1986-87, NFL Coach of Yr. Coll. & Pro Football Newsweekly, 1990, UPI, 1990, AP, 1990, Football Digest, 1991; recipient Seattle Gold Helmet award, 1986.

JOHNSON, JOANN MARDELLE, federal agency administrator; b. Massena, Iowa, Feb. 24, 1949; BA in Edn., U. No. Iowa, 1971. Former tchr.; grain and livestock prodr.; mem. Iowa Senate from 39th dist., Des Moines, 1994—2000; mem. appropriations com., mem. commerce com.; chair ways and means com.; chair commerce com.; mem. Nat. Credit Union Admin., Alexandria, Va., 2002—, vice chair, 2003—. Mem. 4-H, Local Devel. Bd.; vol. various cmty. orgns.; campaign mgr. Rep. Dwight Dinkla, 1992, Congressman Jim Lightfoot, 1990, orgn. dir., 1986-88. Mem. Am. Legis. Exch. Coun., Farm Bur., Cattleman's Assn. Republican. Office: Nat Credit Union Admin Off of the Bd 1775 Duke St Alexandria VA 22314-3428 Office Fax: 703-518-6346. E-mail: boardmember.johnson@ncua.gov.

JOHNSON, JOEL W. food products executive; With General Foods Corp.; exec. v.p. sales and mktg. Hormel Foods Corp., 1991-92, pres., 1992-93, COO, CEO, 1993-95, bd., CEO, pres., 1995—. Bd. dirs. Overseers of The Carlson Sch. Mgmt. U. Minn.; trustee Hamilton Coll. Office: Hormel Foods Corp 1 Hormel Pl Austin MN 55912-3680

JOHNSON, JOHN, broadcast journalist; b. N.Y.C., June 20, 1938; s. John Edward and Irene Elizabeth (Tutt) J. BA, CCNY, 1961, M Art Edn., 1963; DHL (hon.), St. Thomas Aquinas Coll., 1991. Tchr., asst. prin. N.Y.C. Bd. Edn., 1960-67; assoc. prof. fine arts Lincoln U., 1967-68; prodr., dir., writer documentary unit ABC News, N.Y.C., 1968-71; corr. ABC Evening News, N.Y.C., 1971-72; reporter WABC-TV News, N.Y.C., 1972-85, sr. corr., anchor, 1985-95; anchor WCBS-TV News, N.Y.C., 1995-96; anchor, sr. corr. WNBC-TV News, N.Y.C., 1996-97; ret., 1997. Essayist: The Black Power Revolt, 1968; author Only Son, 2002; one-man show: Bridges: Recent Paintings, Walter Wickiser Gallery, Soho, N.Y., 2003. Recipient Best Enterprise Reporting award AP, 1977, Emmy award for Best Sports Programming, 1978, Best Documentary award AP, 1979, Emmy award for Best Investigative Reporting, 1983, Emmy award for Best Spot News, 1982, Emmy award for Best Svc. News, 1982, Nat. Broadcast award for Outstanding Spot News, UPI, 1982, Lifetime Achievement award in broadcast journalism N.Y. Assn. Black Journalists, 1997; named to CCNY Comm. Hall of Fame, 2000. Mem. AFTRA, Dirs. Guild Am.

JOHNSON, JOHN ANDREW, construction executive; b. Grand Rapids, Mich., Apr. 10, 1942; s. Arnold L. and Ione A. (Christenson) J.; m. Peggy J. Ruckman, June 12, 1971 (dec. Apr. 1996); children: Perry T., John C-G. (dec.); m. Luisa Moncada Ruiz, June 30, 1997; children: Andrew L., Sofia B. Assoc. in Engring., Mich. State U., E. Lansing, 1964; diploma, U.S.A. Signal Sch., Ft. Monmouth, 1966, Detroit Diesel Allison, Indpls., 1972. Tech. writer Massey-Ferguson, Inc., Indpls., 1965-66, 1969-70, svc. rep. Akron, Ohio, 1970-73, regional svc. mgr. Detroit, 1973-78, regional sales mgr. Columbus, Ohio, 1978-84; pres. Johnson and Assocs., Ind., 1984-86; svc. mgr. Hanomag Baumaschinen GmbH, Hannover, Fed. Republic Germany, 1986-90, Samsung Constrn. Equipment, Seoul, Republic of Korea, 1990-98; dir. Internat. Cons., Pierceton, Ind., 1998-99, Volvo Constrn. Equip. N.Am. Inc., Asheville, N.C., 1999—. With U.S. Army, 1966-69. Mem. Soc. Automotive Engrs., Profl. Photographers Assn., Am. Legion. Republican. Lutheran. Avocations: golf, fishing, hunting, photography. Home: 372 Kingfisher Ln Horse Shoe NC 28742 Office: Volvo Construction Equip N Amer 1 Volvo Dr Asheville NC 28803-3447 E-mail: icsjohn@acninc.net., john.johnson@volvo.com.

JOHNSON, JOHN BRAYTON, editor, publisher; b. Watertown, N.Y., Dec. 14, 1916; s. Harold Bowtell and Jessie R. (Parsons) J.; m. Catherine Amelia Common, June 21, 1941; children: John Brayton, Ann Johnson Kaiser, Deborah Johnson, Harold Bowtell II. AB, Princeton, 1939; L.H.D., St. Lawrence U., 1978, SUNY, 2000. Reporter Watertown (N.Y.) Daily Times, 1939-41, 46-49, editor and pub., 1949—. Chmn. Coun. to Health Sci. Ctr., Syracuse, 1955-98. Trustee N.Y. State Dormitory Authority, Elsmere, 1956—; trustee emeritus St. Lawrence U., Canton, N.Y. Served with M.I. AUS, 1941-46. Mem. AIA (hon.), Princeton Club N.Y., Black River Valley Club. Republican. Presbyterian. Home: Watertown, NY. Died May 2, 2001.

JOHNSON, JOHN D. grain company executive; b. Rhame, N.D. BBA, Black Hills State U. Feed cons. GTA divsn. Cenex Harvest States Cooperatives, Inver Grove Heights, Minn., 1976, regional sales mgr., dir. sales and mktg., gen. mgr. GTA Feeds, group v.p. Farm Mktg. and Supply, 1992, pres., CEO, 1995—, pres., gen. mgr., 1998—. Bd. dirs. Ventura Foods, Sparta Foods. Mem. NCRA (bd. dirs.). Office: Cenex Harvest States 5500 Cenex Dr Inver Grove Heights MN 55077

JOHNSON, JOHN EDWIN, orthodontist; b. Waverly, Ky., Aug. 9, 1931; s. Richard Spalding and Margaret (Vize) J.; m. Margaret Josephine Smith, Dec. 29, 1956; children: Catherine Margaret, Michael John. DDS, St. Louis U., 1956. Diplomate Am. Bd. Orthodontics (charter mem. coll. diplomates). Orthodontist in pvt. practice, New Albany, Ind., 1956—. Bd. dirs., sec. DePaul Sch. for Dyslexia, Louisville, 1974-78. Contbr. articles to profl. jours. Capt. U.S. Army, 1956-58. Mem. ADA, Am. Assn. Orthodontists, European Orthodontic Soc., So. Assn. Orthodontists, South Ctrl. Dental Soc., Ind. Dental Soc. (pres. south ctrl. component 1968-69), Filson Hist. Soc., Rotary (pres. New Albany, Ind. club 1992-93, founder New Albany Rotary Toast), Big Springs County Club. Roman Catholic. Avocations: golf, photography, horticulture.

JOHNSON, JOHN GRAY, retired university chancellor; b. Irwin, Pa., Aug. 8, 1924; s. John Arthur and Elizabeth (Gray) J.; m. L. Jane Wyncoop, Aug. 28, 1948; children: Scott Raymond, Lynn. BS, Carnegie Mellon U., 1949; LL.D. (hon.), U. Indpls., 1980. Alumni dir. Carnegie Mellon U., 1955-60; exec. dir. Am. Alumni Council, Washington, 1960-64; v.p. for devel. Butler U., Indpls., 1964-66, pres., 1978-88, chancellor, 1989-90; v.p. for devel. Carnegie Mellon U., Pitts., 1966-78. With AUS, 1943-46. Decorated Air medal. Named Sagamore of the Wabash. Mem. Ind. C. of C. (life), Sun City Found. (pres.), Oro Valley Country Club, Phi Kappa Phi, Omicron Delta Kappa. Home: 14326 N Green Meadow Ln Tucson AZ 85737-7120

JOHNSON, JOHN H. publisher, consumer products executive; b. Arkansas City, Ark., Jan. 19, 1918; m. Eunice Johnson; children: John Harold(dec.), Linda Johnson Rice. Student, U. Chgo., Northwestern U., Howard U.; LL.D., Central State Coll., Shaw U., N.C. Coll., Benedict Coll., Carnegie-Mellon Inst., Morehouse Coll., N.C. A. and T. State U., Syracuse U., Eastern Mich. U., Hamilton Coll., Lincoln U., Malcolm X Coll., Upper Iowa Coll., Wayne State U., Pratt Inst., Chgo. State U., Northeastern U., Am. U., Ctrl. State Coll., Clark Atlanta U., DePaul U., Harvard U., NYU, Northwestern U., Roosevelt U., U. Ark., Pine Bluff, U. D.C., U. Ill., U. So. Calif., Wilberforce U. Pub., chmn. chief exec. officer Johnson Pub. Co., Inc., Chgo. N.Y.C., L.A., Washington, 1942—; pub., editor Ebony, Jet, Ebony South Africa; pres. Sta. WLOU, Louisville, Fashion Fair Cosmetics, Chgo., Supreme Beauty Products; pub., chmn., CEO Johnson Pub. Co., Chgo. Chmn., chief. exec. officer Supreme Life Ins. Co., Chgo.; bd. dirs. Greyhound Corp., Dillard Dept. Stores, Inc., The Dial Corp.; mem. adv. bd. 1st Comml. Bank of Little Rock. Author: Succeeding Against the Odds, 1989. Trustee Art Inst., Chgo. Recipient Named Outstanding Young Man, U.S. Jaycees, 1951, Communicator of Yr., U. Chgo. Alumni Assn., 1974, Chicagoan of Yr., Chgo. Boys Club, 1983, recipient Horatio Alger award, 1966, John Russwurm award, Nat. Newspaper Pubs. Assn., 1966, Spingarn medal, NAACP, 1966, Henry Johnson Fisher award, Mag. Pubs. Assn., 1971, Columbia Journalism award, 1974, Honors Disting. Accomplishment, United Negro Coll. Fund., 1983, Robie award, Jackie Robinson Found., 1985, Disting. Contbrn. to Journalism award, Nat. Press Found, 1986, named to Acad. Disting. Entrepreneurs, Babson Coll., 1979, Chgo. Bus. Hall of Fame, 1983, named to Entrepreneur of Decade, Black Enterprise Mag., 1987, inducted into Black Press Hall of Fame, 1987, Pub. Hall of Fame Folio Ednl. Trust Inc., 1987, Ill. Bus. Hall of Fame, 1989, Nat. Sales Hall of Fame, 1989, Chgo. Journalism Hall of Fame, 1990, recipient Harold H. Hines Jr. Benefactors' award, United Negro Coll. Fund, 1988, Excel award, Internat. Assn. Bus. communicators, Founders award, NCCJ, 1989, Disting. Svc. award, Harvard U. Grad. Sch. Bus. Adminstrn., 1991, Salute to the Media award, Impact Publs., Africa's Future award, UNICEF, 1992, Booker T. Washington Speaker's award, Booker T. Washington Bus. Assn., Heritage award, Exec. Leadership Coun., 1992, Dow Jones Entrepreneurial Excellence award, Dow Jones and the Wall Street Jour., 1993, Monarch award for Comms., Alpha Kappa Alpha, 1993, Comm. award, Ctr. for Comm., Inc., 1995, Presdl. medal of Freedom, 1996, Corp. Pioneer award, Bus. Policy Rev. Coun., 1996, Lifetime Achievement award, Am. Advt. Found., 1996, Nat. Bus. Hall of Fame award, Nat. Jr. Achievement, 1997, inductee Entrepreneurship Hall of Fame, U. Ill.-Chgo., 1993. Fellow: Sigma Delta Chi; mem.: Mag. Pubs. Assn., U.S. C. of C. (dir.). Office: 1270 Avenue Of The Americas New York NY 10020-1700*

JOHNSON, JOHN HENRY, film director, producer, photographer, educator; b. Pueblo, Colo., Oct. 31, 1951; s. William Admiral "Buddy" and Matilda Marie (Trabucco) J.; m. Nadine Sue Milosavich, Aug. 24, 1974; children: Rebecca Sue, Thomas William. Student, U. So. Colo., 1970—73; Assoc. of Fine Arts, Rochester Inst. Tech., 1973, BFA summa cum laude, 1975; MFA, Cranbook Acad. Art, 1977. Photographer Colo. Hwy. Dept., Eisenhower Tunnel, 1971; cinematographer, prodn. asst., writer various prodn. co., Colo., 1979-80; prodn. asst. Metro-Goldwyn-Mayer, Canon City, Colo., 1983; studio cameraman, flr. dir. Sta. KOAA-TV, Pueblo, 1970, 1997—2001; dir., cinematographer, editor Humanities div. film series, U. So. Colo., Pueblo, 1971-72; photographer Pueblo Chieftain & Star Jour., 1975; pres., founder Tamarack Prodn., Inc., Pueblo, 1982—. Grad. tchng. asst. Cranbrook Acad. Art, Bloomfield Hills, Mich., 1977; instr. photography Arapahoe C.C., Littleton, Colo., 1978, C.C. Denver, 1979; instr. filmmaking, photography and design Colo. Inst. Art, Denver, 1978-79, U. So. Colo., 1978, 1980-81, 2001—; instr. filmmaking Learning Tree U., Chatsworth, Calif., 1992-93; instr. photography, filmmaking, art and humanities Pueblo C.C., 1994-2002. Dir., cinematographer, co-writer, co-editor (documentary film) Damon Runyon's Pueblo, 1981 (Golden Eagle award Council on Internat. Nontheatrical Events 1983); dir., writer, producer, cinematographer, editor: (documentary film) Zebulon Pike & The Blue Mountain, 1984 (Golden Eagle award Council on Internat. Nontheatrical Events 1985, Commendation cert. Am. Assn. for State and Local History 1986); dir., writer, producer, cinematographer, editor (feature film) Blue Lights, 1988 (invited feature at the Internat. Sci. Fiction and Fantasy Film Festival, Rome, 1990); photographer represented in books including Visual Concepts for Photographers, 1980 (Chinese edit. 1998), Photographic Materials & Processes, 1986 (also Italian edit. 1993), 2d edit., 2000, View Camera Technique, 5th edit., 1986, 6th edit., 1993, 8th edit., 1999, Orlin Helgoe-Shaman of the Prairie, 1986, Southwest Fine Arts Biennial Catalogue, 1976; contbg. editor: Focal Encyclopedia of Photography, 3d edit., 1993. Grantee Thatcher Found., 1973-77, Profl. Photographers Am., 1974, Cranbrook/Ford Found., 1977, NEH, 1979, Colo. Endowment for the Humanities, 1979, U. So. Colo., 1979. Avocations: skiing, music, genealogy, movies.

JOHNSON, JOHN IRWIN, JR., neuroscientist; b. Salt Lake City, Aug. 18, 1931; s. John Irwin and Ann Josephine (Freeman) J. AB, U. Notre Dame, 1952; MS, Purdue U., 1955, PhD, 1957. Instr., then asst. prof. Marquette U., Milw., 1957-60; USPHS spl. research fellow U. Wis., Madison, 1960-63; Fulbright-Hays research scholar U. Sydney, Australia, 1964-65; asso. prof. biophysics, psychology and zoology Mich. State U., East Lansing, 1965-69, prof., 1969-81, chmn. dept. biophysics, 1973-78, prof. anatomy, 1981-99, prof. radiology and neurosci., 1999—. Vis. fellow psychology dept. Yale U., New Haven, 1975-76 Recipient Career Devel. award NIH, 1965-72, research grantee, 1966-79; research grantee NSF, 1969-71, 71-73, 73-76, 78-89, 91—; 3d hon. life mem. Anat. Assn. Australia and N.Z., 1973 Mem. Soc. Neurosci., Am. Assn. Anatomists, Soc. for Comparative and Integrative Biology, Am. Soc. Mammalogists, Animal Behavior Soc., AAUP, ACLU, Sigma Xi. Home: 2494 W Grand River Ave Okemos MI 48864-1447 Office: Mich State U Dept Radiology 519A E Fee Hall East Lansing MI 48824-1316 E-mail: johnij@aol.com., johnij4@yahoo.com.

JOHNSON, JOHN PRESCOTT, philosophy educator; b. Tumalo, Oreg., Apr. 24, 1921; s. John Edward and Caroline Prescott (Eaton) J.; m. Mable Alice Dougherty, June 9, 1943; children: Grace Beth Johnson Booth), John Paul, Carol Ruth Johnson Hull. AB, Pitts. State U., 1947, MS, 1948; PhD, Northwestern U., 1959. Asst. prof. philosophy Bethany (Okla.) Nazarene Coll., 1949-57; asst. prof. U. Okla., Norman, 1957-62; assoc. prof. philosophy Monmouth (Ill.) Coll., 1962-69; prof. philosophy Monmounth (Ill.) Coll., 1969-86; chmn. dept. philosophy Monmouth (Ill.) Coll., 1967-86, emeritus prof. philosophy, 1986—. Vis. asst. prof. Northwestern U., summer 1961, Cons. research project student values U.S. Office Edn., 1967 Author: The Value Philosophy of Wilbur Marshall Urban, 1988, The Reality of Faith, 1996, The Gates of Light, 2000, The More Excellent Way, 2000, The Living Fountain: The Symbolism of Grace, 2003; contbr. articles to philos. jours. Mem. Am. Philos. Assn., Ill. Philos. Assn. (sec.-treas. 1967-69, pres. 1971-73).

JOHNSON, JOHN WARREN, retired association executive; b. Mpls., Jan. 29, 1929; s. Walter E. and Eileen L. J.; m. Marion Louise Myrland; children— Daniel Warren, Karen Louise, Nancy Marie. BA, U. Minn., 1951. CEO Am. Collectors Assn., Inc., Mpls., 1955-96; ret., 1996. Dir. Western Nat. Ins. Group, 1998—. Author: Political Christians, 1979, You Can Manage Your Money, 1981, 38 Days to Cape Town, 1981, Credit Guide for Collectors, 1984, The Pearls of Saigon, 1987, The Use of Humor in Public Speaking Is No Joke!, 1991, 53 Days to Beijing, 1991, The Strange Blood of East Africa, 1995. Mem. Mpls. City Coun., 1963-67; mem. Minn. State Ho. of Reps., 1967-74, asst. majority leader, 1972-74; Republican candidate for Gov. of Minn., 1974. With USNR, 1947-53. Mem. Am. Soc. Assn. Execs. (chmn. bd. 1986-87), U.S. C. of C. (chmn. bd. regents 1975, bd. dirs. 1990-92), Minn. Soc. Assn. Execs. (past pres.). Lutheran. Office: 4121 W 50th St Ste 1 Minneapolis MN 55424-1206

JOHNSON, JOHN WILLIAM, JR., executive recruiter; b. St. Petersburg, Fla., Dec. 10, 1932; s. John William and Elizabeth (Lowitz) J.; m. Cecelia Lynn Wescott, Feb. 6, 1960; children: William Wescott, James Robert, Gayle McCrimmon. AB, Wesleyan U., Middletown, Conn., 1954; postgrad., NYU, 1958-59. With Benton and Bowles, Inc., N.Y.C., 1958-82, v.p., account supr., 1963-70, sr. v.p., mgmt. supr., 1970-82, adminstr. profit sharing plan, 1969-82, dir., 1977-82; with Webb, Johnson Assocs., N.Y.C., 1982—2002, founder,

former pres., 1982-95, mng. dir., 1995-2000, sr. mng. dir., 2000—02; co-founder, mng. dir. Johnson & Norinsky Assocs., 2002—. Mem. Scarsdale Planning Bd., 1984-88, Scarsdale Non-Partisan Jud. Qualifications Com., 1987-92, Scarsdale Bd. Ethics, 1995-2000; pres. Rainsford House Assn., N.Y.C., 1964-66, bd. dirs., 1962-70; bd. mgrs. Jacob Riis Settlement, 1963-89; bd. dirs. St. Christopher's Inc., 1965-2000, hon. bd. dirs., 2000—; mem. parents steering com. Coll. William and Mary, 1987-91; warden Ch. St. James the Less, Scarsdale, 1993-95; trustee Healthcare Chaplaincy, 1999—. Pilot USNR, 1954-58. Decorated Air medal; co-honoree Scarsdale Hist. Soc. award, 1996. Mem. Winged Foot Golf Club, Sky Club, Mid Ocean Club, Harbour Ridge Club. Home: 43 Axtell Dr Scarsdale NY 10583-5601 Office: 1 Dag Hammarskjold Plaza 34th Fl New York NY 10017

JOHNSON, JOHNNIE DEAN, investor relations consultant; b. Wells County, Ind., Aug. 18, 1938; s. William Clayton and Anna Sarah (Woods) J.; m. Jean Johnson, June 26, 1960 (div. Aug. 1986); 1 child, Judith; m. Geraldine U. Foster, Mar. 5, 1988. BA, U. Findlay (Ohio), 1960; MBA, Bowling Green (Ohio) State U., 1976. CPA, Ohio. Spl. asst. to pres. Marathon Oil (acquired by U.S. Steel 1982), 1978-82; asst. fin. vice chmn., chief fin. officer U.S. Steel, 1982-84, asst. corp. comptr., investor, strategic planning, 1984-85, asst. corp. comptr. investor rels., 1985-86; mng. dir. Georgeson & Co. Inc., N.Y.C., 1987-91; founder, chmn., CEO Johnnie D. Johnson & Co. Inc., N.Y.C., 1991-98; chmn., CEO Strategic IR, Inc., N.Y.C., 1998—. Trustee U. Findlay (Ohio), 1989—. Mem. Nat. Investor Rels. Assn. (chmn. 1985-86), Petroleum Investor Rels. Assn. (pres. 1979-80), Investor Rels. Assn. (treas. 1988-90). Congregationalist. Home: 6 Tantummaheag Rd Old Lyme CT 06371-1137 Office: 645 5th Ave Fl 8 New York NY 10022 E-mail: jdjohnson@strategic-ir.com.

JOHNSON, JOHNNY RAY, mathematics educator; b. Chatham, La., Dec. 19, 1929; s. Dave Ernest and Bessie (Morris) J.; m. Betty Ann Moore, Oct. 21, 1960 (div. May 1982); children: Todd Michael, John Fitzgerald, Shauna Renee; m. Barbara F. Kennedy, June 1, 1990. BS, La. Tech U., 1951; MS, Auburn U., 1953, PhD, 1959. Asst. prof. math. La. Tech U., 1958-62; assoc. prof. math. Appalachian State U., 1962-63; prof. elec. engring. La. State U., Baton Rouge, 1963-83, prof. emeritus, 1983—; prof. math. U. North Ala., 1984-95, prof. emeritus, 1995—; adj. prof. elec. engring. U. Fla., Gainesville, 1976-77; mem. staff Combat Ops. Research Group, Ft. Monroe, Va., summer 1957; mathematician Boeing Co., New Orleans, summer 1965; engring. specialist Gen. Dynamics, 1983-84 Author: (with David E. Johnson) Mathematical Methods in Engineering and Physics, 1965, Graph Theory with Engineering Applications, 1972, Introductory Electric Circuit Analysis, 1981, Linear Systems Analysis, 1975; (with David E. Johnson and John L. Hilburn) Basic Electric Circuit Analysis, 1978, 3d edit., 1986, 4th edit., 1990, (with David E. Johnson, John L. Hilburn and Peter D. Scott) 5th edit., 1995, (with David E. Johnson and Harry P. Moore) A Handbook of Active Filters, 1980, (with David E. Johnson) A Funny Thing Happened on the Way to the White House, 1983, (with David E. Johnson and John L. Hilburn) Electric Circuit Analysis, 1989, 2d edit., 1991, Introduction to Digital Signal Processing, 1989, (with David E. Johnson, John L. Hilburn & Peter D. Scott) Electric Circuit Analysis, 3d edit., 1997. Pres. Wildwood PTA, 1973-74. Served with AUS, 1954-56. Mem. IEEE (sr. 1968-93), U. North Ala. Inst. for Learning in Retirement (v.p., chmn. curriculum com. 1997-98, treas. 1998-99), Sigma Xi, Tau Beta Pi, Phi Kappa Phi, Eta Kappa Nu, Pi Mu Epsilon, Kappa Mu Epsilon. Home: 209 Wesley Ct Florence AL 35630-1486 E-mail: jjohnson66@sprynet.com.

JOHNSON, JONAS TALMADGE, otolaryngologist, educator; b. Ravenna, Ohio, Jan. 3, 1947; s. J. Norman and K. Alice (Harkrader) Johnson; m. Janis Johnson, Dec. 22, 1968; children: Olin T., Rurik C., Ivar N. Postgrad., Dartmouth Coll., 1965-68; MD, SUNY, Syracuse, 1972. Diplomate Am. Bd. Otolaryngology. Asst. prof. U. Pitts., 1979-84, assoc. prof., 1984-87, prof., 1987—, vice chmn., 1982—; active staff Montefoire Hosp., Pitts., 1987—, Western Pa. Hosp., 1996—, U. Pa. Med. Ctr. Southside Hosp., 1996—. Cons. VA Med. Ctr., Pitts., 1979—80, Children's Hosp., Pitts., 1980—89. Editor: Am. Jour. Otolaryngology, 1992—2002, The Laryngoscope, 2003; co-editor: (book) Infectious Diseases and Antimicrobial Therapy of the Ears Nose and Throat, 1997, Carcinoma of the Thyroid, 1999, Tracheotomy, 1999; mem. numerous editl. bds.: ; contbr. articles to profl. jours. Maj. M.C. USAF, 1977—79. Recipient Ben Shuster award, Am. Acad. Facial Plastic and Reconstructive Surgery, 1976. Mem.: ACS, AMA, Am. Radium Soc., Am. Soc. Clin. Oncology, Am. Assn. Cancer Rsch., Am. Rhinol. Soc., Am. Head and Neck Soc. (sec. 1998—2001, v.p. 2001—02, pres.-elect 2002—03, pres. 2003—04), Triological Soc. (ea. sect. v.p. 2000), Am. Bronchoesophagologic Soc., Am. Laryngol. Assn., Am. Acad. Otolaryngology-Head and Neck Surgery (bd. dirs. 1992—94, coord. for continuing edn. 1995—2001, pres.-elect 2001—02, pres. 2002—03, Merit award in clin. rsch. 1976, Honor award 1982, Disting. Svc. award 1994). Office: Eye and Ear Inst UPMC 200 Lothrop St Ste 500 Pittsburgh PA 15213-2546

JOHNSON, JONATHAN EDWIN, II, lawyer; b. Whittier, Calif., May 1, 1936; s. Roger Edwin and Louise (Thompson) J.; m. Clare Hardy, June 23, 1963 (dec. 1995); children: Jonathan III, Hardy, Benjamin, Adam, Rufus, Bradford, Roger, Ralph; m. Garnet Kalsched, June 17, 2000. BChemE, Cornell U., 1959, MBA, 1960; JD with honors, George Washington U., 1963. Bar: Calif. 1964; cert. specialist family law, Calif. Assoc. Tuttle & Taylor, L.A., 1963-65; pvt. practice L.A., 1965-67; ptnr. Johnson & Jarvis, L.A., 1967-68, Johnson, Poulson, Coons & Slater, L.A., 1968—. Instr. paralegal probate U. West L.A. Sch. Law, 1974; mem. clergy adv. com. to supt. edn., City of L.A., 1978-81. Fellow Am. Acad. Matrimonial Lawyers (counsel So. Calif. chpt. 1998-99); mem. Calif. State Bar Assn. (legis. com. family law sect. 1978-88, chmn. 1980), Beverly Hills Bar Assn. (exec. com. family law sect. 1977-82, 86-88, 91—, chmn. 2003-2004), Inter-stake Bus. and Profl. Assn. L.A. (pres. 1974), Cornell Club of So. Calif. (pres. 1966-68), Order of Coif, Sigma Chi, Phi Delta Phi. Mem. Lds Ch. Home: 1094 Acanto Pl Los Angeles CA 90049-1604 Office: Johnson Poulson Coons & Slater 10880 Wilshire Blvd Ste 1100 Los Angeles CA 90024-4112

JOHNSON, JOSEPH CLAYTON, JR., lawyer; b. Vicksburg, Miss., Nov. 15, 1943; s. Joseph Clayton and Rose Butler (Levy) J.; m. Cherrian Frances Turpin, Oct. 24, 1970; children: Mary Clayton, Erik Cole. BS, La. State U., 1965, JD, 1969. Bar: La. 1969, U.S. Dist. Ct. (ea. and mid. dists.) La. 1969, U.S. Dist. Ct. (we. dist.) La. 1979, U.S. Ct. Appeals (5th cir.) 1982. Ptnr. Taylor, Porter, Brooks & Phillips, Baton Rouge, 1969—. Mem. civil justice reform act com. U.S. Dist. Ct. (mid. dist.) La., 1995-97, chmn. 1996-97; mem. La. Atty. Disciplinary Bd., 1997-99. Bd. editors Oil and Gas Reporter, 1988—. Pres. Baton Rouge area Am. Cancer Soc., 1987—88; adv. bd. Ctr. for Energy Law, 2000—. With U.S. Army, 1969—75. Recipient John Rogers award, 1999, Ctr. for Am. and Internat. Law. Master: Dean Henry George McMahon Am. Inn of Ct.; mem.: Ctr. for Am. and Internat. Law (bd. editors Oil and Gas Reporter), Baton Rouge Bar Assn., La. State Law Inst. (mineral code com.), La. Bar Assn. (mem. ho. of dels. 1979—92, coun. rep. mineral law sect. 1986—94, chmn. mineral law sect. 1992—93). Republican. Methodist. Office: PO Box 2471 Baton Rouge LA 70821-2471 E-mail: clay@tpbp.com.

JOHNSON, JOSEPH ERLE, mathematician; b. Memphis, Apr. 27, 1951; s. Louis Miller and Harriette Edith (Geiger) J. BS in Applied Math., Ga. Inst. Tech., 1975. Tax examiner IRS, Atlanta, 1975-77; sec., treas. Louis M. Johnson & Co., Memphis, 1977-82; grad. asst. dept. math. scis. Memphis State U., 1983-84; warehouse adminstr. The Julien Co., Memphis, 1986-89; with Venture Constrn. Co., Memphis, 1990-91, Crager Constrn. Co., Memphis, 1991-92; data processing mgr. Finishing Techs., Inc., Chattanooga, Tenn., 1993; engring. records clk. Tenn. Valley Authority, Chattanooga, 1993-99, engring. aide, 1999-2000, student intern., 2001—. Treas. Memphis Astron. Soc., 1980-81. Mem. Soc. for Indsl. and Applied Math. Home: 613 Tremont St Apt 2 Chattanooga TN 37405-4168

JOHNSON, JOY ANN, diagnostic radiologist; b. New Richmond, Wis., Aug. 16, 1952; d. Howard James and Shirley Maxine (Eidem) J.que BA in Chemistry summa cum laude, U. No. Colo., 1974; D of Medicine, U. Colo., 1978. Diplomate Am. Bd. Radiology, Nat. Bd. Med. Examiners; cert. added qualification pediatric radiology. Resident in radiology U. Colo., 1978-81, fellow in pediat. radiology, 1981-82; asst. prof. diagnostic radiology and pediatrics, chief sect. pediatric radiology Clin. Radiology Found. U. Kans. Med. Ctr., Kansas City, 1982-87; radiologist Radiology Assocs. Ltd., Kansas City, Mo., 1987-92; mem. staff Bapt. Med. Ctr., Kansas City, Mo., 1987-92; radiologist Children's Mercy Hosp., Kansas City, 1992-95, Leavenworth-Kansas City Imaging, 1996—; assoc. prof. U. Mo., Kansas City, 1992—; chief of staff Cushing Mem. Hosp., 2002—. Speaker Radiol. Soc. Republic of China, 1985, RSNA 2000 panel mem. Contbr. articles to med. jours. Nat. Cancer Inst. fellow, 1982. Mem. AMA, Am. Coll. Radiology, Radiol. Soc. N.Am., Am. Inst. Ultrasound in Medicine (mem. program com. Kansas City 1984), Soc. Pediatric Radiology (mem. com. for cmty. bsed pediat. radiologists 1998-), Am. Assn. Women in Radiology, Lambda Sigma Tau. Avocations: horseback riding, physical fitness, sports, reading. Office: Leavenworth-Kansas City Imaging 9201 Parallel Pkwy Kansas City KS 66112-1528

JOHNSON, JOYCE MARIE, psychiatrist, epidemiologist, public health officer; b. Baton Rouge, Jan. 30, 1952; d. Gene Addison and Helen Marie (Kalcik) J.; m. James Albert Calderwood, Mar. 28, 1987; 1 child, James. BA, Luther Coll., Decorah, Iowa, 1972; MA, U. Iowa, 1974; DO, Mich. State U., 1980; DFA (hon.), NY Inst. Tech., 2001. Cert. in psychiatry, pub. health and preventive medicine, and clin. pharmacology. Cooking instr. Kirkwood C.C., Iowa City, Iowa, 1974-76; health planner Iowa Regional Med. Program, Iowa City, 1974-76; commd. USPHS, advanced through grades to rear adm.; intern USPHS Hosp., Balt., 1980-81; med. epidemiologist Hepatitis Labs., Ctrs. Disease Control, Phoenix, 1981-83, AIDS, Ctrs. Disease Control, Atlanta, 1983-84; resident in psychiatry NIMH, 1984-87, staff psychiatrist, 1987-88; epidemiologist, divsn. dir. Food and Drug Adminstrn., 1988-93; asst. surgeon gen. USPHS, 1995—; dir. divsn. nat. treatment demonstrations, Substance Abuse and Mental Health Svcs. Adminstrn., 1993-97; chief med. officer USCG, 1997—. Med. Perspectives fellow, New Guinea and Thailand, 1978-79; mem. clin. faculty Mich. State U., 1983-93, Georgetown U. Med. Ctr., 1988—, Uniformed Svcs. U. of the Health Scis. Recipient Dr. Nathan Davis award for Outstanding Work in Govt. Svc., 2001. Mem. Mensa, Cosmos Club. Office: 5518 Western Ave Bethesda MD 20815-7122

JOHNSON, JULIA A. writer; b. Des Plaines, Ill., Sept. 8, 1961; d. John J. and Margaret J. Roarty; m. Quinten R. Johnson; 1 child, Raymond. BA English, Mount St. Mary's Coll., Emmitsburg, Md., 1983. Office svcs. pers. First Boston Corp., N.Y.C., 1984—86; fixed income trader Kidder Peabody, Inc., N.Y.C., 1986—88; mergers & acquisitions staff Scott Mason, Ltd., N.Y.C., 1991—92; brokerage asst. Paine Webber, Hackensack, NJ, 1997—98; pub. rels. writer In House, Inc., Vienna, Va., 2000—01; freelance writer, pub. rels. cons. Julie Johnson, Leesburg, Va., 1993—. Writer, cons. Issue Action Publs., Leesburg, Va., 1999—2000. Author: (novels) Loudoun County: Blending Tradition with Innovation, 2000; contbr. articles to profl. jours. Mem.: Loudoun C. of C. (mem. mktg. & comms. com. 1999—), Loudoun County C. of C. Democrat. Roman Catholic. Avocations: running, travel, hiking, biking, reading. Office: PO Box 285 Leesburg VA 20178-0285

JOHNSON, JULIA F. bank executive; Sr. v.p. Banc One Corp. Columbus, Ohio, 1993—; dir., office of info. and policy Bank One, 1999—; with Bank One, 1985—. Office: Banc One Corp Dept OH-0152 100 E Broad St Dept Oh-152 Columbus OH 43215-3607

JOHNSON, JULIA MAE, literature educator, poet; b. New Orleans, Nov. 4, 1971; d. Jeremie Sheehan and Eddie Howard Johnson; m. Robert John Holub Jr., Aug. 5, 2000. BA, Hollins Coll., 1993; MFA, U. Va., 1995. Instr. U. Va., Charlottesville, 1994—95; asst. dir. creative writing New Orleans Ctr. for Creative Arts, 1995—96; tchr. ESL ESS Lang. Inst., Pusan, Republic of Korea, 1996—97. Author: (book of poems) Naming The Afternoon, 2002. Recipient Fiction award, Nassau Lit. Rev., 1989, prize, Acad. Am. Poets, 1990, 1992, 1993, 2003, New Writing award for poetry, Fellowship of So. Writers, 2003. Mem.: Associated Writing Programs, Blue Ridge Writers Bd. (bd. dirs. 2002—). Home: 2445 Lofton Rd SW Roanoke VA 24015

JOHNSON, JULIE ANN, career planning administrator; b. Spalding, Lincolnshire, Eng., July 15, 1950; d. Horace Mark and Annie Stacey; m. Richard Charles Johnson, Sept. 7, 1974; children: James, Claire, Christopher. Customer svcs. rep. Blue Star Garages, London, 1969—71; acct. CV Shaw & Co., London, 1971—74, Arcade Motors, London, 1974—77, Altman Buane & Co., Edgware, England, 1978—92; advisor Citizens Advice Bur., St. Albans, England, 1992—94; mgr. Oaklands Coll., St. Albans, 1994—. Auditor Scout Group, St. Albans, 1989—; sec. NAEGA Ltd., St. Albans, 2000—02; rep. Assoc. Colls. Eastern Region, England, 1999—; network coord. Herts. Info. Advice & Guidance, England, 1998—; sec. NAEGA, 2002—. Creator Quality Care System/Guidance Coun. Stds., 1999. Fund raiser Scouts, St. Albans, 1989—; rd. agt. Residents Assn., St. Albans, 1994—. Ch. Of England.

JOHNSON, JULIE ELIZABETH SILLIN, educator; d. David Andrew and Judith Ann Sillin; m. Robert Paul Johnson, May 1996. BS, Ohio State U., 1986; MA, Miami U., Oxford, Ohio, 1995. Educator Cin. Pub. Schs., 1988—94; presenter Englefield & Arnold, Inc., Columbus, Ohio, 1997—2001; evaluator Data Recognition Inc., Mason, Ohio, 1998—2002; edn. coord., workshop developer Kids Voting, Cin., 2002—. Vol. Greyhound Adoption Greater Cin., 2002—. Grad. fellow, NEH, 1992. Mem.: LWV. Avocations: gardening, sewing, cooking.

JOHNSON, JULIE MARIE, lawyer, lobbyist, judge; b. Aberdeen, S.D., Aug. 7, 1953; d. Howard B. and Jerauldine (Dilly) J.; m. Bryan L. Hisel. BA in Govt., Comm., U. S.D., 1974, MA in Polit. Sci., JD, U. S.D., 1976. Bar: S.D. 1977, U.S. Dist. Ct. S.D. 1977. Assoc. Siegel, Barnett Law Firm, Aberdeen, 1977; law clk. Fifth Judicial Circuit Ct., Aberdeen, 1977-78; ptnr. Maloney, Kolker, Fritz, Hogan & Johnson, Aberdeen, 1978-84; dep. sec. S.D. Dept. Labor, Aberdeen, Pierre, 1983-84, sec. Gov.'s Cabinet, 1985-87; pres. Industry and Commerce Assn. of S.D., Pierre, 1987-95; sec., Gov.'s Cabinet S.D. Dept. Revenue, Pierre, 1995; exec. dir. S.D. Rural Devel. Coun., Pierre, 1995—2003; adminstrv. law judge, 2003—. Treas. S.D. Cmty. Found., Pierre, 1987-95; mem. Pvt. Industry Coun., 1985-87, S.D. Coun. on Vocat. Edn., 1985-87; bd. dirs. Mo. Shores Women's Resource Ctr., Pierre, 1988-89; chmn. S.D. Main St. Adv. Coun., 1987-91; bd. dirs. United Way, 1988-96, chmn., 1991; mem. Shortgrass Arts Coun., 1987—, South Dakotans for the Arts, 1981—, Solid Waste Mgmt. Plan Task Force, 1990, S.D. Citizens Adv. Coun. on Hazardous Waste, 1991-92, gov.'s adv. coun. on health care reform, 1992-93, gov.'s Homestate Underground Lab adv, coun., 2002—; bd. dirs. Hist. S.D. Found., 1996-99; founding mem., legal counsel Outdoor Women of S.D., Inc., 1995—; bd. trustees USD Found., 1992—; trustee, mem. bus. affairs com., 1996—, com. on trustees, Kelley Ctr. for Entrepreneurship adv. bd., presdl. search com. Dakota Wesleyan U., 1999-2000; founding mem., treas. S.D. Discovery Ctr. and Aquarium, Inc., bd. dirs., 1988-92; mem. S.D. Water Congress, 1990—97, bd. dirs., 1987-95; bd. dirs. Nyoda Girl Scout Coun., 1997-99; mem. adv. bd. W.O. Farber Ctr. for Excellence in Civic Leadership, 1998—; bd. dirs. Farber Fund, 1987—; founding mem. S.D. Chambers & Econ. Devel. Coun., 1989—; mem. Network Mgmt. Team Nat. Rural Devel. Partnership, 1998—2001; mem. Children's Care Hosp. and Sch. Found. Bd., 1997—, investment com., 1999—, bd. devel. com., 2000—; mem. Nat. Rural Devel. Partnership Presdl. Transition Team, 2000-01, Agr. and Econ. Devel. Task Force, 2001, S.D. Habitat for Humanity Bd., 2001—; bd. dir. Historic S.Dak. Found., 1995-98, Genesis of Innovation, 2000-, S.Dak. Habitat for Humanity, 2001-, ; acting exec. dir. S.Dak. Math., Sci. and Tech. Coun., 2000-03; vol. chmn. S.Dak. WWII Meml. Dedication, 2001; bd. dirs.S.D. Habitat for Humanity, 2001—; founder, treas. Friends of Discovery Ctr., S.D.; Trustee, many coms. Dakota Wesleyan U., Children's Care Hosp. Found, bd, trustees and various coms., Univ. S. D. Found.Bd. RJR Nabisco fellow Women Execs. in State Govt., Harvard, 1986; named Outstanding Young Citizen Jaycees, Aberdeen, 1982, S.D. Jaycees, 1983. Mem. S.D. Bar Assn. (chmn. adminstrv. law com. 2001-, mem. CLE com., Worker's compensation com.), Industry and Commerce Assn. S.D. (bd. dirs. 1985-87), U. S.D. Alumni Assn. (exec. com. 1987-96, pres. 1990-92), AAUW, Bus. and Profl. Women U.S.A. (nat. legis. chmn. 1987-88, 92-94, nat. chmn. issues mgmt. 1991-93, pres. S.D. 1984-85, Woman of Yr. award Aberdeen chpt. 1982), Women Execs. in State Govt. (bd. didrs. 1985-87), Coun. State Mfrs. Assn., S.D. Mining Assn. (bd. dirs. 1991-95, Gold PAC, 1995-), Nat. Indsl. Coun., Coun. State C.'s of C., Ducks Unltd., Rotary, Zonta, ABC Investment Club, Rocky Mountain Elk Found. Republican. Lutheran. Address: 1100 E Church St Apt 352 Pierre SD 57501-2354 Office: 210 E 4th St Pierre SD 57501 Home: 1414 Sharpstone Dr Mitchell SD 57301-6250 E-mail: juliem.johnson@state.sd.us.

JOHNSON, KAREN, legislation and congressional affairs secretary; BA comm., Appalachian State Univ., NC. Asst. Conv. Mgr. for Pub. Liaison Rep. Nat. Conv., 2000; instr. of Polit. comm. and Pub. Rels. Internat. Rep. Inst.; asst. sec. of edn. for legis. and congl. affairs U.S. Dept. Edn., Washington, 2003—; v.p. of Soc. Mark. and Pub. Affairs Porter Novelli. Fellow: Univ. of Pa. Annenberg Sch. for Comm. She also traveled to China and Hong Kong to serve as a delegate for the Am. Coun. of Young Polit. Leaders. Office: Dept of Ed 400 Maryland Ave SW Rm 7E307 Washington DC 20202*

JOHNSON, KAREN LEE, lawyer; b. Houston, Feb. 29, 1948; d. Bailey Edward and Frances Bette (Pfefferle) J. B.S. in Edn., Tex. Tech. U., 1970, J.D., 1973. Bar: Tex. 1973. Research asst. office legal affairs Tex. Tech. U., Lubbock, 1972-73, staff asst., 1973; univ. legal counsel W. Tex. State U., Canyon, 1973-76; asst. gen. counsel Tex. Edn. Agy., Austin, 1976-78; gen. counsel Tex. State Tchrs.' Assn., Austin, 1978— ; cons. on legal problems in edn. Tex. Jr. Coll. System, 1976-80. Council program chmn. Explorer Scouts, Amarillo, Tex., 1976; mem. Gov.'s Commn. on Juvenile Justice, San Marcus and Austin, 1983; mem. adv. council Windham Sch. Dist., Huntsville, Tex., 1984. Recipient Outstanding Service award Llano Estacado Explorer Scouts, 1976, Windham Sch. System, 1984. Mem. Tex. Bar Assn., Austin Young Lawyers, Nat. Assn. Tchr. Attys., Nat. Orgn. Legal Problems in Edn., Pi Beta Phi. Democrat. Presbyterian. Office: Texas State Tchrs Assn 7701 N Lamar Blvd Ste 518 Austin TX 78752-1025 also: State Bar of Tex PO Box 12487 1414 Colorado St Austin TX 78701-1627

JOHNSON, KARLA ANN, county official; b. Heber City, Utah, July 27, 1957; d. Henry Edward and Twila Faun (Jacobson) Kohler; m. Arthur Que Johnson, Sept. 22, 1977; children: Russell, Kohler Scott, Marc. Cattle rancher, Kanab, Utah, 1981—. Bd. dirs. S.W. Utah Dept. Health, St. George; bd. dirs., pres. Kanab C. of C.; charter mem. Nat. Coun. Women's Adv. to Congress, Washington; ambassador Mountain Am. Credit Union, St. George; sec. County Rep. Party, Kanab, Utah; pres. PTA, Kanab. Mem. Internat. Assn. Clks., Recorders, Election Ofcls., Treas., Friendship and Cultural Exch. Soc., Coalition of Resources and Economies, Utah Assn. Counties (bd. dirs.), Ariz. Strip Interpretive Assn. (adv. bd.).

JOHNSON, KATHARYN PRICE (MRS. EDWARD F. JOHNSON), civic worker; b. Smyrna, Del., Mar. 24, 1897; d. Lewis M. and Jennie Cairl (Smithers) Price; grad. Centenary Coll., 1915, LHD (hon.), 1997; student Goucher Coll., 1915-18; m. Edward F. Johnson, Nov. 16, 1920; children: Edward A., Jane Cairl Johnson Kent. With Liberty Loan Com. for Md. and Liberty Loan Assn. of Balt., 1918-20; dir. Scarsdale Woman's Club, 1933-36; dir. White Plains Thrift Shop, 1930-43, pres., 1936-43; mem. exec. com. Scarsdale Community Fund, 1934-38; active Scarsdale council Girl Scouts, 1937-53, commr., 1939-41, now hon. mem. Scarsdale-Hartsdale council, 1953-69; mem. region 2 com. Girl Scouts U.S.A., 1942-56, mem. nat. bd., exec. com., 1947-55, chmn. orgn. and mgmt. dept., 1952-55, mem. nat. field com., 1943-55, mem. equipment service com. 1956-69, mem. internat. com., 1956-60, mem. meml. gifts com., 1974-81; mem. Bd. Edn., Scarsdale, N.Y., 1943-46; disaster chmn. Scarsdale chpt. ARC, 1942-45; mem. Commn. Human Rights, 1958-69, Commn. Status of Women, 1957-69; rep. World Assn. Girl Guides and Girl Scouts to UN, 1957-71, mem. NGO com. on UNICEF, 1965-72, sec., 1968-70; participant World Confs., World Assn. Girl Guides and Girl Scouts, Greece, 1960, Denmark, 1963, Japan, 1966, Finland, 1969, Can., 1972, Eng., 1975, Iran, 1978, World Conf., U.S., 1984. Recipient Juliette Low World Friendship medal Girl Scouts USA, 1984. Mem. Nat. Coun. Women U.S., Scarsdale Hist. Soc., Olave-Baden-Powell Soc. (founder), Pi Beta Phi. Republican. Presbyterian. Clubs: Scarsdale Woman's (life), Scarsdale Golf, Nat. Women's Republican; Shenorock Shore. Home: 165 Brewster Rd Scarsdale NY 10583-2021

JOHNSON, KATHERINE ANNE, health research administrator, lawyer; b. Medford, Mass., Apr. 20, 1947; d. Lester and Eileen Anne (Henaghan) J. BS, La. State U., 1969; MSA, George Washington U., 1972; JD, Cath. U., 1985. Bar: Md. 1985. Pub. health adviser HHS, Washington, 1970-76; dir. plan implementation SE Colo. Health Sys. Agy., Colorado Springs, 1976-78; sr. mng. assoc. CDP Assocs., Inc., Atlanta, 1978-87, dir. legal affairs, 1986-87; v.p. Cancer CarePoint Inc., Atlanta, 1987; sr. mgr. Salick Health Care, Inc., Bethesda, Md., 1987-89; pvt. practice Potomac, Md., 1989-90; assoc. dir. for adminstrn. San Antonio Cancer Inst., 1990-96; assoc. dir. planning and adminstrn. CTRC Rsch. Found., San Antonio, 1996-97, v.p., 1997-98; COO Inst. Drug Devel., San Antonio, 1997-98; prin. biomed. program devel. consulting, 1998-99; dir. rsch./adminstrn. Am. Coll. Surgeons, 1999—2002; asst. prof., assoc. dir. adminstrn. Massey Cancer Ctr., Richmond, 2002—. Spkr. in field. Contbr. articles to profl. jours. Vol. Ct.-Apptd. Spl. Adv. for Abused Children. Mem. Md. Bar Assn., Am. Health Lawyers Assn., Leadership Tex. Class of 1996, Soc. Rsch. Adminstrs. Avocations: skiing, reading, antique collecting. Office: Po Box 980037 Richmond VA 23298 E-mail: kajohns@earthlink.net.

JOHNSON, KATHY VIRGINIA LOCKHART, art educator; b. Aberdeen, Miss., May 5, 1951; d. Clovis Clinton and Marium Kathleen (Bowen) Lockhart; m. Gary Wayne Johnson, Aug. 5, 1973; 1 child, Daniel Clinton. BFA, Miss. U. Women, 1973; postgrad., U. Ala., 1973—92. Cert. tchr. Ala. Inventory clk. Johnson Showroom, Columbus, Miss., 1970—73; student tchr. Amory Mid. Sch., Amory, 1973; tchr. art Huntsville Art League, Huntsville, 1974, 1983—84, Evangel Sch., 1974—75, 1st Christian Early Childhood, 1984—88, Huntsville Mus. Art, 1990, Huntsville City Schs., 1989—. One-woman shows include, 1974, Tchr. Show Youth Art Month, 1994, Ann. NASA Picnic, 1998. Mem.: Huntsville Edn. Assn., Ala. Edn. Assn., Nat. Art Edn. Assn., Alpha Delta Kappa (bd. dirs. 1999—, pres. 1996—, sec. 1999—2002). Mem. Christian Ch. (Disciples Of Christ). Avocations: painting, gardening, football. Home: 122 Regent Ctr Madison AL 35758

JOHNSON, KAY DURBAHN, real estate manager, consultant; b. Crookston, Minn., Apr. 4, 1937; d. Wilbert John and Frieda (Johnson) Durbahn; m. Ray Arvin Johnson, May 14, 1960; children: Sherry Kay Johnson Johnston, Diane Rosalind Johnson Peterson, Laura Faye Johnson. BA, U. Minn., 1959. Reference analyst Indsl. Rels. Ctr. U. Minn., Mpls., 1959-61; real estate mgr. Minnetonka, Minn., 1976—; ptnr. Broadmoor Plantation Investors, Fargo, N.D., 1976—; v.p. D&T Property, Inc., Minnetonka, 1990—, also bd. dirs.; v.p. Comreco, LLC, 2002—, bd. dirs. Tax reduction cons. R.A. Johnson & Assocs., Minnetonka, 1985—; bd. dirs. Empire Aggregate, Inc., 2001—. City of Minnetonka Planning Commn., 1972-74, vice chair, 1973-74; mem. Land Use Task Force, 1972-74; liaison Ridgedale Devel.; various coun. positions Minnetonka Luth. Ch., mem. choir; mem. GMC Motorcoach Assn. Mem. Mpls. Inst. Arts. Republican. Avocations: art, music, camping, traveling. *For greater happiness try to balance your life by making time for all aspects of living, including activities to meet social, spiritual, physical, family, work, and intellectual needs.*

JOHNSON, KEITH LIDDELL, chemical company executive; b. Darlington, England, July 22, 1939; came to U.S., 1948, naturalized, 1958; s. Arthur Henry and Beatrice (Liddell) J.; m. Margaret Elaine Meston, Aug. 29, 1959; children: Leslie Margaret, Kevin Liddell, Gregory Norman, Kathleen Elaine; 1 ward, Ann Louise Warwick. BA, U. Mich., 1960. Chem. technician Ajem Labs., Livonia, Mich., 1956-60; rsch. chemist labs. Swift & Co., Chgo., 1960-63, project mgr., 1963-67, group leader R&D ctr. Oak Brook, Ill., 1967-71, adminstrv. asst. to exec. v.p. Chgo., 1971-72, quality assurance dir., 1974-78, group mgr. plant quality assurance, 1978-82; quality assurance mgr. refinery divsn. Swift Edible Oil Co. subs. Swift & Co., Chgo., 1972-73, corp. quality assurance mgr., 1973-74; tech. dir. Norman Fox & Co., L.A., 1982-83, br. mgr., 1983-88, gen. mgr., 1988—, exec. v.p., dir., 1989—, pres., 1993—. Bd. dirs. Lexard Corp., L.A., v.p. 1990-94; bd. dirs. Chem. Distbn. Network, Des Plaines, Ill.; mem. Chgo. Manpower Area Planning Com., 1971; mem. industry adv. bd. South Coast Air Quality Mgmt. Dist., Calif., 1982-84. Contbr. articles to profl. jours. V.p., dir. St. Martha's Sr. Care Ctr., West Covina, Calif., 1993—, chmn. bd., 1995-99, vestry St. Martha's Epsicopal Ch., sr. warden 1991-96, 98-2001; bd. dirs. St. Martha's Epsicopal Sch., 1999-2001. Mem. Chgo. Chemists Club, Chem. Art Forum Chgo. (v.p. 1980, pres. 1981), Am. Chem. Soc. (chair elect so. Calif. sect. 2000-01, chair 2001—, mem. exec. com. 2000—), Soc. Cosmetic Chemists (membership chmn. Bay area chpt. 1985, chmn. 1987-88), Am. Oil Chemists Soc., Chem. Mktg. Assn. So. Calif. Episcopalian. Achievements

include 17 U.S. and 25 fgn. patents. Home: 342 Amberwood Dr Walnut CA 91789-2473 Office: Ste 150 200 Citadel Dr City Of Commerce CA 90040-1554 E-mail: keithjohnson@prodigy.net., kjohnson@norfox.ws.

JOHNSON, KENNETH LEROY, airport executive; b. Vero Beach, Fla., Oct. 30, 1965; s. Franklin Roosevelt and Helen (Perry) J. BSc, Tenn. State U., 1987. Equipment svc. employee Northwest Airlines, Orlando, Fla., 1989-91; asst. dir. ops. Hillsborough County Aviation Authority, Tampa, Fla., 1991—. Democrat. Baptist. Avocations: golf, working out. Home: 10231 Woodford Bridge St Tampa FL 33626-1819 Office: Hillsborough County Aviation Tampa Internat Airport PO Box 22287 Tampa FL 33622

JOHNSON, KENNETH F. lawyer; b. Ft. Bragg, Calif., June 10, 1938; s. Frank W. and Gertrude Johnson; m. Jane Perry Drennan, June 11, 1961; children: Erik, Mark. BSCE, U. Calif., Berkeley, 1962; JD, U. Calif., Hastings, 1969. Bar: Calif. 1970. Of counsel ReedSmith Crosby Heafey, Oakland, Calif., 2003—. Note and comment editor Hastings Law Jour., 1968-69. Officer USNR, 1962—66. Scholar U. Calif. Hastings, 1967-68, 68-69. Mem. Calif. Bar Assn., Alameda County Bar Assn., Contra Costa County Bar Assn., Bar Assn. San Francisco, Assn. Bus. Trial Lawyers Assn., Order of Coif. Office: Reed Smith Crosby Heafey 1999 Harrison St Fl 22 Oakland CA 94612-3520

JOHNSON, KENNETH HARVEY, veterinary pathologist; b. Hallock, Minn., Feb. 17, 1936; s. Clifford H. and Alma (Anderson) J.; Sept. 17, 1960; children: Jeffrey, Gregory, Sandra. BS, U. Minn., 1958, DVM, 1960, PhD, 1965. Jr. asst. health officer NIH, Bethesda, Md., 1958; practice vet. medicine Edina, Minn., 1960; USPHS-NIH non-service fellow U. Minn., St. Paul, 1960-65, asst. prof. dept. vet. pathology and parasitology, 1965-69, assoc. prof., 1969-73, prof., 1973-98, prof. emeritus dept. vet. pathobiology, 1998—, head, sect. pathology, dept. vet. biology, 1974-76, chmn. dept. vet. pathobiology Coll. Vet Medicine, 1976-83. Cons. Minn. Mining & Mfg. Co., Medtronic Inc., Natural-Y Surg. Specialties; principle and co-investigator several NIH grants, 1965-98. Mem. editl. bd. Amyloid, the Internat. Jour. of Exptl. and Clin. Investigation; contbr. chpts.: Veterinary Clinics of North America, 1971, Spontaneous Animal Models of Human Disease, 1979, Kirk's Current Veterinary Therapy; contbr. articles to sci. jours. Councilman Nativity Lutheran Ch., St. Anthony Village, Minn., 1972-75. Recipient Tchr. of Yr. award, 1968-69, Norden award for disting. tchr. in vet. medicine, 1970, Beecham award for rsch. excellence, 1989, Ralson Purina Small Animal Rsch. award, 1990, Phi Zeta faculty achievement award, 1992, Outstanding Achievement award Bd. of Regents of U. Minn., 2001. Mem.: AAUP, Am. Soc. Investigative Pathology, Am. Coll. Veterinary Pathologists (hon.), Gamma Sigma Delta, Phi Zeta, Sigma Xi. Home: 3510 Skycroft Dr Minneapolis MN 55418-1780 Office: Univ Minn Coll Vet Medicine Dept Vet Diagnostic Med Saint Paul MN 55108 E-mail: johns049@tc.umn.edu.

JOHNSON, KENNETH OSCAR, oil company executive; b. Center City, Minn., Apr. 11, 1920; s. Oscar W. and Sigrid (Hollsten) J.; m. Margery Wheeler, Apr. 18, 1945; 1 child, Eric W. BS in Chem. Engring., U. Minn., 1942. With Exxon Corp., Houston, 1942-74, heavy fuels mgr. supply dept., 1968-72, wholesale fuels sales mgr., mktg. dept., 1972-74; chmn., chief exec. officer Belcher Oil Co., Miami, Fla., 1974-88; bd. dirs. Coastal Corp., 1988—2001. Bd. dirs. Petroleum Industry Found. Patentee in field. Home: 845 Admiralty Parade Naples FL 34102 7874

JOHNSON, KENNETH OWEN, retired audiologist; b. St. Paul, Jan. 26, 1920; s. Ernest Wilbert and Anna Mae (Little) J.; m. Dorothy Schlesselman, Sept. 5, 1949 (dec. Aug. 1995). BA, Macalester Coll., St. Paul, 1946; MA, U. Minn., 1948; PhD, Stanford, 1952. Chief, audiology and speech correction program VA, Washington, 1954-56; cons. acoustical audiology, dir. San Francisco Hearing and Speech Ctr., 1956-57; asst. clin. prof. dept. surgery Stanford Med. Sch., 1957; exec. sec. Am. Speech and Hearing Assn., 1957-80. Dir. Deafness, Speech and Hearing Publs., 1959-78; sec.-treas., past pres.; chmn. Coalition Ind. Health Professions, 1970-71; cons. for speech, hearing and lang. to Head Start program, 1968-72; mem. research fellowship bd. U.S. Vocational Rehab. Adminstrn., 1964-71. Bd. dirs. Com. Handicapped, People to People Program; former trustee Am. Speech and Hearing Found. Kenneth O. Johnson Edn. Ctr. named in his honor, Rockville, Md., 1983; recipient Disting. Citizen award Macalester Coll., 1946, Svc. award Nat. Coun. on Communitive Disorders, 2000. Mem.: So. Calif. Golf Assn. (bd. dirs. 1988—92, vice chmn. rules and competition com. 1988—92, course rating com. and rules and competition com. 1988—97, v.p. Rancho Bernardo Golf Club 1994). Home: 15591 Walton Heath Row San Diego CA 92128-4477 E-mail: kojohn@san.rr.com.

JOHNSON, KERRY ANN, music therapist, music educator; d. Daniel Lee and Diane Susan Immel. Cert. in piano pedagogy, Alverno Coll., 2000, MusB, 2002. Ch. organist Trinity Luth. Ch., Campbellsport, Wis., 1994—; pvt. piano instr. Milw., 1999—; ch. musician Adoration Luth. Ch., Greenfield, Wis., 2001—; piano tchr. White House Music, West Bend, Wis., 2003—; music therapist Wis. Conservatory Music, Milw., 2003—. Mem.: Wis. Chpt. for Music Therapy, Music Tchrs. Nat. Assn., Am. Music Therapy Assn.

JOHNSON, KEVIN MAURICE, professional basketball player; b. Sacramento, Calif., Mar. 4, 1966; Student, U. Calif., 1987. Basketball player Cleve. Cavaliers, 1987—88, Phoenix Suns, 1988—. Mem. Dream Team II, 1994. Named NBA Most Improved Player, 1989; named to All-NBA 2d team, 1989—91, All-NBA 3d team, 1992, All-NBA 2d team, 1994. Office: care Phoenix Suns 201 E Jefferson St Phoenix AZ 85004-2412

JOHNSON, KEVIN BLAINE, lawyer, educator; b. Wichita, Kans., Aug. 28, 1956; s. Howard Blaine and Ruth Signe (Hornlund) Johnson; m. Candis L. Jimenez, May 30, 2003. BA, Wichita State U., 1978; JD, Washburn U., 1981. Bar: Kans. 1982, US Dist. Ct./Kans. 1982, US Ct. Appeals (10th cir.) 1991, US Supreme Ct. 1993. Sole practice Overland Pk., Kans., 1981—82; asst. dist. atty. Wyandotte, County, Kans., 1982—84; assoc. Law Office of A.B. Fletcher, Wichita, Kans., 1984—86, Law Office of Stan R. Singleton, Derby, Kans., 1986—88; pvt. practice Wichita, 1988—; prof. law Kans. Newman Coll., Wichita, 1984—96, Webster U., Wichita, 1995—99; prof. Emporia State U., 1999—. Author: (novels) The 11th Kans. Vol. Cavalry, 1986, A Summer Madness, 1988, A Short Practical Guide to Bus. Law With Forms, 1990, (rev. title) Bus. Legal Guide, 1994, At War on the Prairie, 1990, Employer's Legal Guide, 1995, Employee Law Compliance, 2001, Small Bus. Legal Guide, 2002, Office Manager's Legal Guide, 2002, Fed. Law Prohibiting Employment Discrimination, 2002, Tex. Employer's Legal Guide, 2003; contbr. articles. Mem.: Kans. Bar Assn., Wichita Bar Assn., Wichita Citizen Participation Orgn. Coun. (mem. 1985—86), High Plains Drum Corps, Inc. (bd. dir. 1987—90), Sky Ryders Drum and Bugle Corps (drum instr., Hutchinson, Kans. 1978—81, bd. dir. 1988—90). Republican. Luth. Office: PO Box 2016 Wichita KS 67201-2016

JOHNSON, KEVIN LAMONT, educator; s. Rexford and Carrie Johnson. BA in Engring., Dartmouth Coll., 1991; MBA in Fin. and Mktg., Ind. U., 1996. EIT Bur. Profl. and Occupl. Affairs, Pa., 1992. Lab. asst. James Graham Brown Cancer Ctr., Louisville, 1984—86; loan asst. Interlibrary Loan Dept., Hanover, NH, 1986—86; lab. asst. Dartmouth-Hitchcock Med. Ctr., Hanover, 1987—87; sales rep. Safety Plus, Inc., Louisville, 1987—87; cook Godfather's Pizza, Louisville, 1987—88; customer svc. mgr. Honey Baked Ham Co., Louisville, 1987—88; inventory counter Wash. Inventory Svc., Louisville, 1987—88; deli worker Price Champions Grocery Store, Hanover, 1988—88; sales rep. Carnival Shoe Store, Louisville, 1988—88; customer svc. rep. The Courier-Jour. & Louisville Times Co., 1989—89; engr. intern Louisville Gas and Electric Co., 1989—90; optical character scanner Humanities Computing, Hanover, 1990—90; pizza delivery driver Everything But Anchovies, Hanover, 1991—91; engr. and dist. coord. Betz Water Mgmt. Group, Trevose, Pa., 1991—92, dist. rep. Westlake, Ohio, 1992—94; sr. bus. devel. specialist Ashland Chem. and Distbn. Companies, Columbus, Ohio, 1996—99; network analyst Ashland Distbn. Co., Columbus, 1999—2000; assoc. instr. Ind. U., Bloomington, 2000—. Grad. Dale Carnegie Course, Columbus, Ohio, 1998—98. Contbr. chapters to books. Vol. youth worker Jr. Achievement, Phila., 1991—92. Recipient stipend, Lion's Club Louisville, 1986; fellow, Consortium Grad. Mgmt. Schs., 1994—96; scholar, Mgmt. Doctoral Student Assn., 2000—04; GE Future Faculty fellow, 2000—. Mem.: Acad. Mgmt. (strategy reviewer bus. policy and strategy divsn. 2002—, entrepreneurship reviewer entrepreneurship divsn. 2001—), Mgmt. Doctoral Student Assn., Alpha Phi Alpha (life; chpt. pres. and v.p. 1987—88). Avocations: martial arts, piano, cooking, small business management. Office: Indiana Univ 1309 East Tenth St Bloomington IN 47405 E-mail: kevljohn@indiana.edu.

JOHNSON, KEVIN ORLIN, publishing executive, writer; BA, So. Ill. U., 1974; MA, St. Louis U., 1977; PhD, U. Ill., 1988. CEO Pangaeus Cos., Dallas. Spkr. in field. Author: Rosary: Mysteries, Meditations, and the Telling of the Beads, 1997, Why Do Catholics Do That?, 1994 (best seller award Pubs. Weekly 1995), Apparitions: Mystic Phenomena and What They Mean, 1998; editor: Missal: The Order of Mass in English, 1997; contbr. articles to profl. jours. Recipient Grand award news writing, med. Coun. Advancement & Support Edn., 1985, Journalism award Cath. Press. Assn., 1988, Gold award Dallas Advt. League TOPS. 1988, 89, Excellence award Comm. Arts Mag., 1989, Best show award AR100 Award Show, 1990. Mem. AIA, Assn. for Preservation of Va. Antiquities, Ctr. for Palladian Studies in Am., Friends of Poplar Forest, Friends of Stratford Hall Plantation, Inst. of Physics (London), Internat. Soc. for Archaeoastronomy and Astronomy in Culture, Internat. Soc. for the Study of Time, Native Plant Soc. of Tex., Seed Savers, Shakespeare Oxford Soc., Tex. Classical Assn., Thomas Jefferson Meml. Found. Monticello Fund (assoc.), Canon Law Soc. Am. (assoc.). Avocations: gardening, native plant conservation. Office: Pangaeus Cos PO Box 670127 Dallas TX 75367-0127

JOHNSON, KEVIN RAYMOND, law educator; b. Culver City, Calif., June 29, 1958; s. Kenneth R. Johnson and Angela J. (Gallardo) McEachron; m. Virginia Salazar, Oct. 17, 1987; children: Teresa, Tomás, Elena. AB in Econs. with great distinction, U. Calif., 1980; JD magna cum laude, Harvard U., 1983. Bar: Calif. 1985, U.S. Dist. Ct. (no., ea. and so. dists.) Calif. 1985, U.S. Ct. Appeals (9th cir.) 1985, U.S. Supreme Ct. 1991. From rsch. asst. to Charles Haar prof. Harvard U., Cambridge, Mass., 1982-83, instr. legal writing, 1982; law clk. to Hon. Stephen Reinhardt, U.S. Ct. Appeals (9th cir.), L.A., 1983-84; atty. Heller Ehrman White & McAuliffe, San Francisco, 1984-89; acting prof. law U. Calif., Davis, 1989-92, prof., 1992—, prof. Chicano studies, 2000—, assoc. dean acad. affairs, 1998—, dir. Chicano studies program, 2000—01. Instr. civil procedure, complex litig., immigration law, refugee law, acting dir. clin. legal edn., 1992; instr. Latinos and Latines and the law, 2001; instr. critical race theory, 03; mem. legal del., El Salvador, 1987. Author: (book) How Did You Get To Be Mexican? A White/Brown Man's Search for Identity, 1999, Race, Civil Rights, and the Law: A Multiracial Approach, 2001, Mixed Race America and the Law: A Reader, 2002; editor: Harvard Law Rev., 1981—83; contbr. articles to profl. jours. Bd. dirs. Legal Svcs. No. Calif., 1996—, mem. exec. com., 1997—, v.p., 2001—03, pres., 2003—; bd. dirs. Yolo County ACLU, 1990—93, chmn. legal com., 1991—93; magistrate merit selection panel U.S. Dist. Ct. (ea. dist.) Calif.; vol. Legal Svcs. Program, San Francisco, Sacramento; mem. Lawyers Com. Civil Rights San Francisco Bay Area, 1991—; various pro bono activities. Recipient commendation, Calif. State Bar, 1985—90, Chancellor's Cmty. and Diversity award, 2001. Mem.: ABA (mem. coordinators com. immigration 1998—), Calif. Bar Assn. (mem. standing com. legal svcs. for poor 1992—94, mem. gov. com. continuing edn. bar 1993—98, mem. minority affairs com., mem. law sch. admission coun. 1999—2001), U. Calif. Alumni Assn. (class sec. Class of 1980), Phi Beta Kappa. Democrat. Roman Catholic. Office: U Calif Sch Law King Hall Davis CA 95617

JOHNSON, KEVIN ROGERS, analyst, journalist; b. Dallas, Aug. 10, 1975; s. Dan Rogers and Susan (Hearn) J.; m. Kimberly Kay Johnson, 2000. BBA, Baylor U., 1997. Electronic editor Baylor Lariat, Waco, Tex., 1994, staff writer, copy desk chief, 1995, city editor, 1996; copy editor intern Rochester (Minn.) Post-Bull., 1996; editor-in-chief Baylor Lariat, 1996, staff photographer, 1997; sr. specialist Frito-Lay, Plano, 1997—. Mem. Assn. Info. Tech. Profls., Soc. Profl. Journalists, Golden Key, Gamma Beta Phi. Avocations: camping, hiking, biking, train riding, road trips. E-mail: kevin.johnson@bigfoot.com.

JOHNSON, KEYSHAWN, professional football player; b. L.A., July 22, 1972; Student, W. L.A. Coll., U. So. Calif. Wide receiver N.Y. Jets, 1996—2000, Tampa Bay Buccaneers, 2000—. Named wide receiver coll. All-Am. first team, The Sporting News, 1995. Achievements include first round draft pick (1st pick overall) NFL, 1996; mem. AFC Ea. Conf. championship team, 1998. Office: Tampa Bay Buccaneers One Buccaneer Pl Tampa FL 33607

JOHNSON, KIRSTEN DENISE, elementary education educator; b. L.A., Sept. 21, 1968; d. Daniel Webster Johnson and Marinella Venesia (Ishem) Johnson Miller; 1 child, Khari Malik Manning-Johnson. BBA in Ins., Howard U., 1990; student, Southwestern Sch. Law, L.A., 1991-92, Calif. State U., Dominguez Hills, 1994-97. Asst. Ctr. for Ins. Edn. Howard U., Washington, 1988-89; intern Cigna Ins. Co., L.A., 1989; agt. asst. McLaughlin Co., Washington, 1989-90; legal sec. Harris & Baird, L.A., 1990-92; legal asst. Hamrick & Garrotto, L.A., 1992-94; tchr. 5th grade L.A. Unified Sch. Dist., 1993—; intern Travelers Cos., 1987—. Free-lance writer Calif. Mus. Sci., L.A., 1994—; workshop presenter in field. Participant UCLA/CSP Sci. Project; tutor Delinquent Teenage Group Home Residents, 1998—. Nat. Dean;s List, 1987, 88, All Am. scholar, 1989, John Schumacher scholar, 1991, Martin Luther King Jr. scholar, 1996. Mem. NEA (RA del.), UTLA (mem. ho. of reps.), CTA, Internat. Soc. Poets. Democrat. Avocations: reading, traveling, movies, weight lifting.

JOHNSON, KRAIG NELSON, lawyer, mediator; b. Landstuhl, Germany, July 8, 1959; came to U.S., 1966; s. Howard Arthur Sr. and Joy Anne (Nelson) J.; m. AmberJade E. Leca, Nov. 13, 1993. BA with honors, Eckerd Coll., 1981; M in Internat. Mgmt., Am. Grad. Sch. Internat. Mgmt., Glendale, Ariz., 1982; JD, Baylor U., 1992. Bar: Fla. 1993; cert. mediator and arbitrator Supreme Ct. of Fla. Mktg. mgr. Jack Eckerd Corp., Clearwater, Fla., 1982-85; mktg. systems mgr. NCS, Inc., Houston, 1985-87; dir. ops. Petro, Inc., El Paso, 1987-90; atty. and shareholder Zimmerman, Shuffield, Kiser & Sutcliffe, P.A., Orlando, Fla., 1992—2003; atty., mng. ptnr. Goodman McGuffey Lindsey & Johnson LLP, Orlando, Fla., 2003—. Editor: Florida Workers' Compensation Practice, 1994; contbr. articles to profl. jours. Mem. internat. trade and investment adv. bd. Econ. Devel. Commn. of Mid-Fla., Orlando, 1997—; mem. Task Force on Title IX, Baylor U. Bd. of Regents, Waco, 1992-93; bd. dirs. Asian-Am. C. of C., Orlando, 1994-95. Fellow Soc. of Antiquaries of Scotland; mem. Am. Immigration Lawyers Assn., St. Andrew's Soc. of Ctrl. Fla. (bd. dirs., v.p. 1996-98, pres. 1998-2000), Fla. Bar Assn. (sect. on internat. law and litig.), Order of Barristers. Avocations: sailing, flying, shooting sports, mandarin chinese and german languages. Home: 509 N Hampton Ave Orlando FL 32803-5516 Office: Goodman McGuffey Lindsey & Johnson LLP 1245 W Fairbanks Ave Winter Park FL 32789

JOHNSON, KRISTEN MARIE, art director; b. Thorton, Colo., June 17, 1969; d. William and Cheryl (Mathews) Avery; m. Christian John Johnson, May 26, 1996. Degree in visual comm., Colo. Inst. of Art, Denver, 1989; graphic design degree, Calif. Coll. Arts and Crafts, 1992. Jr. designer Steve Rank, Inc., San Francisco, 1990-92; editl. illustrator Contra Costa Times, Walnut Creek, Calif., 1992; imaging technician Miller Freeman, San Francisco, San Mateo, Calif., 1992-95; sr. designer Fawcette Tech. Publs., Palo Alto, Calif., 1995-97; pres., owner Johnson Design & Illustration, Pasadena, Calif., 1995—. Freelance graphic design Johnson Design and Illustration, Pasadena, 2000—. Graphic design adv. coun. Diablo Valley Coll., Pleasant Hill, Calif., 1994-95. Republican. Avocations: rollerblading, hiking, camping, mountain biking. Office: Johnson Design & Illustration 153 N Oak Knoll Ave # 106 Pasadena CA 91101-4102

JOHNSON, LADY BIRD (MRS. CLAUDIA ALTA TAYLOR), wife of former President of United States; b. Karnack, Tex., Dec. 22, 1912; d. Thomas Jefferson Taylor; B.A., U. Tex., 1933, B.Journalism, 1934, D.Letters, 1964; LL.D., Tex. Woman's U., 1964; D.Letters, Middlebury Coll., 1967; L.H.D., Williams Coll., 1967, U. Ala., 1975; H.H.D., Southwestern U., 1967; m. Lyndon Baines Johnson (36th Pres. U.S.), Nov. 17, 1934 (died Jan. 22, 1973); children: Lynda Bird Johnson Robb, Luci Baines. Mgr. husband's congl. office, Washington, 1941-42; owner, operator radio-TV sta. KTBC, Austin, Tex., 1942-63, cattle ranches, Tex., 1943—. Hon. chmn. Nat. Headstart Program, 1963-68, Town Lake Beautification Project; also cotton and timberlands, Ala. Mem. Advisory council Nat. Parks, Historic Sites, Bldgs. and Monuments; bd. regents U. Tex., 1971-77, mem. internat. conf. steering com., 1969; trustee Jackson Hole Preserve, Am. Conservation Assn., trustee emeritus Nat. Geog. Soc.; founder Nat. Wildflower Research Ctr., Austin, 1982. Recipient Togetherness award Marge Champion, 1958; Humanitarian award B'nai B'rith, 1961; Businesswoman's award Bus. and Profl. Women's Club, 1961; Theta Sigma Phi citation, 1962; Disting. Achievement award Washington Heart Assn., 1962; Industry citation Am. Women in Radio and Television, 1963; Humanitarian citation Vols. of Am., 1963; Peabody award for White House TV visit, 1966; Eleanor Roosevelt Golden Candlestick award Women's Nat. Press Club; Damon Woods Meml. award Indsl. Designers Soc. Am., 1972; Conservation Service award Dept. Interior, 1974; Disting. award Am. Legion, 1975; Woman of Year award Ladies Home Jour., 1975; Medal of Freedom, 1977; Nat. Achievement award Am. Hort. Soc., 1984. Life mem. U. Tex. Ex-Students Assn. Episcopalian. Author: A White House Diary, 1970. Address: LBJ Libr and Mus 2313 Red River St Austin TX 78705-5702

JOHNSON, LAEL FREDERIC, lawyer; b. Yakima, Wash., Jan. 22, 1938; s. Andrew Cabot and Gudney M. (Fredrickson) Johnson; m. Eugenie Rae Call, June 9, 1960; children: Eva Marie, Inga Margaret. AB, Wheaton Coll., 1960; JD, Northwestern U., 1963. Bar: Ill. 1963, U.S. Dist. Ct. (no. dist.) Ill. 1964, U.S. Ct. Appeals (7th cir.) 1966. V.p., gen. counsel Abbott Labs., Abbott Park, Ill., 1981-89, sr. v.p., sec., gen. counsel, 1989-94; of counsel Schiff Hardin & Waite, Chgo., 1995—. Mem., past chmn. Law Sch. bd. Northwestern U. Mem.: ABA, Assn. Gen. Counsel. Office: Schiff Hardin & Waite 6600 Sears Tower Chicago IL 60606

JOHNSON, LARRY DEMETRIC, professional basketball player; b. Tyler, Tex., Mar. 14, 1969; Student, Odessa Jr. Coll.; grad., U. Nevada, Las Vegas, 1991. Basketball player Charlotte Hornets, 1991—96, N.Y. Knicks, 1996—. Mem. NCAA Divsn. I Championship Team, 1990, Dream Team II, 1994. Named Coll. Player of Yr., Sporting News, 1991, NBA Rookie of Yr., 1992; named to All-Am. 1st team, Sporting News, 1990—91, NBA All-Rookie team, 1992, NBA All-Star team, 1993, 1994; recipient John R. Wooden award, NCAA, 1991, Naismith award, 1991. Office: NY Knicks Two Pennsylvania Plz New York NY 10121-0091

JOHNSON, LARRY CLINTON, college administrator; b. Nashville, Dec. 23, 1951; s. Mack Clinton and Christine (Davis) J.; m. Clandia Swisher, June 30, 1984; children: Mary Abigail, Elizabeth Crady, Christiana Grace. B of Engring., Vanderbilt U., 1973, MS, 1975; MDiv, Yale U., 1978. Cert. fundraising exec. Sr. planning engr. Westinghouse Elec. Corp., Pitts., 1979-86; assoc. dir. Ketchum Inc., Pitts., 1988-89, dir., 1989-94; asst. dean. sch. engring. SUNY, Buffalo, 1994-95, sr. dir. devel., 1995-97; v.p. advancement Kettering U., Flint, Mich., 1997-98, Houghton (N.Y.) Coll., 1999—2002, Niagara U., Lewiston, NY, 2002—. Mem. Coun. for Advancement and Support for Edn., Eta Kappa Nu. Republican. Episcopalian. Avocations: hiking, nordic skiing, travel, golfing. Home: 9002 Seneca Brook Rd Boston NY 14025 Office: PO Box 2008 Niagara University NY 14109

JOHNSON, LARRY ROBERT, education educator; b. Nome, N.D., Dec. 9, 1943; s. Samuel Harold and Myrtle Evelyn (Fjeld) J.; m. Mae Marie Wolf, June 12, 1965; children: Tanya Ann, Cameron Mark, Angela Marie, Sara Elizabeth. BS, Valley City State U., 1965; BD, Inter-Luth. Theol. Sem., 1969; postgrad., U. N.D., 1968-69; MA, Ind. U., 1977; ThM, Fuller Theol. Sem., 1992. Elem. tchr. Anchorage Borough Sch. Dist., Alaska, 1965-66; instr. Inter-Lutheran Theol. Sem., Plymouth, Minn., 1969-71; missionary, linguist Luth. Bible Translators, Aurora, Ill., 1971—. Instr. U. Liberia, Monrovia, 1974-75; lang. project adminstr. The Inst. for Liberian Langs., Monrovia, 1978-80, translation cons., 1985—; hon. translation advisor United Bible Soc., 1987—; teaching asst. Fuller Theol. Sem., 1990-93. Translator: St. Mark in Kisi, 1982, St. Matthew in Kisi, 1986, Luke and Acts in Kisi, 1987, Six Booklets Scripture Selections in Kisi, 1987, 88, New Testament in Kisi, 1989, (bulletin) Communication Principles Applied to Translations in Oral Societies in Current Trends in Scripture Translation, 1997. Recipient Grad. award Luth. Brotherhood Ins. Co., 1971, Nat. Def. Edn. Act Title VI award Ind. U., 1976, Bible Translation award Fuller Theol. Sem., 1992. Mem. Kappa Delta Pi. Lutheran. Avocation: amateur radio. Home: HC3 Box 3202 Theodosia MO 65761 also: Luth Bible Translators PO Box 2050 Aurora IL 60507-2050 E-mail: lrjohnson_travel@yahoo.com.

JOHNSON, LAURENCE F(LEMING), lawyer; b. Dallas, Oct. 14, 1948; s. Milton G. and Miriam Johnson; m. Mary Lou Nichols, May 10, 1980; children: Andrew, Margaret, Paul. BA, U. Md., 1970, JD, 1973. Bar: Md. 1974, D.C. 1978, U.S. Dist. Ct. Md. 1977, U.S. Dist. Ct. D.C. 1978, U.S. Ct. Appeals (4th cir.) 1977, U.S. Supreme Ct. 1977, U.S. Ct. Appeals (D.C. cir.) 1980. Staff atty. Md. Pub. Interest Rsch. Group, College Park, Md., 1974—76; pvt. practice Silver Spring, Md., 1976—77, Wheaton, Md., 1980—82; spl. asst. to commr. Pub. Svc. Commn. Md., Balt., 1977—78; asst. to U.S. Congressman Silver Spring, 1979—80; pres. Laurence F. Johnson, P.C., Wheaton, 1982—87, 1991—; mng. ptnr. Johnson & Freedman, 1987—91; ptnr. Johnson & Assocs., P.C., 1991—98, Johnson & Yang, P.C., Wheaton, 1998—. Legis. asst. Greenbelt Consumer Svcs., Inc., Savage, Md., 1976—77; rsch. asst. various state legislators, Annapolis, Md., 1976—77. Pres. Ayrlawn Citizens Assn., Bethesda, Md., 1984—87. Named one of Outstanding Young Men Am., 1977; recipient Outstanding Performance award, Montgomery County Dem. Com., Kensington, Md., 1976, Citation of Appreciation, Greenbelt Consumer Svcs., 1978. Mem.: ABA (gen. practice sect. 1984, chmn. subcom. nonimmigrant visas), Bar Assn. Montgomery County (co-chmn. immigration 1984, chmn. 1988—96), Md. State Bar Assn., Am. Immigration Lawyers Assn. (softball chmn. 1983, 1984, 1986, chmn. office tech. and econs. com. 1989, vice chair D.C. chpt. 1993—94, essential worker com. co-chair 1998—2001), Nat. Eagle Scout Assn., Alpha Phi Omega. Democrat. Roman Catholic. Office: Johnson and Yang 2730 University Blvd W Ste 500 Wheaton MD 20902-1975 E-mail: johnson@jylaw.net.

JOHNSON, LAURENCE MICHAEL, lawyer; b. N.Y.C., Feb. 8, 1940; s. Edgar and Eleanor (Kraus) Johnson; m. Margie Serrano, Mar. 15, 2003; children: Mary Serena, Lisa Arienne, Laura Elizabeth, Daniel Milton, Miguel L., Daniel B. AB cum laude, Harvard U., 1961; LL.B. cum laude, Columbia U., 1964. Bar: Mass. 1964. Research asst. Columbia U., 1962-64; law clk. Supreme Jud. Ct. Mass., 1964-65; from assoc. to ptnr. firm Nutter, McClennen & Fish, Boston, 1965-77; ptnr. firm Newman & Meserve, Boston, 1977-78, Palmer & Dodge, Boston, 1978-83; sole practice law Boston, 1983-85; ptnr. firm Johnson & Polubinski, Boston, 1985-86, Johnson & Schwartzman, Boston, 1986—91; of counsel Fordham & Starrett, Boston, 1991—96; ptnr. Mahoney, Hawkes & Goldings, Boston, 1996—2001, Davis, Malm & D'Agostine, Boston, 2001—. Arbitrator Am. Arbitration Assn., 1976—; tchg. team Harvard Trial Adv. Workshop, 1976—; mem. trial adv. faculty Mass. Contg. Legal Edn. of New Eng. Law Inst., 1979—. Author: 20 Years of Civil Rights: Epilogue and Prologue, Boston Bar Journal, 1988; contbr. articles to profl. jours. Group chmn. larger law firms United Way of Mass. Bay, 1976; mem. Sudbury Human Rights Council, 1964-68, pres., 1965-66, Patriot award, 1976 Fellow: Am. Coll. Trial Lawyers (complex litigation com. 1994—99), Boston Bar Found. (life); mem.: ABA (jud. adminstrn. divsn., litigation & anti-trust sects.), Mass. Bar Assn., Am. Law Inst., Boston Bar Assn. (steering com. lawyers com. for civil rights under law 1976—). Democrat. Home: 11 Northway Rd Randolph MA 02368-2913 *The trial lawyer's art requires a combination of knowledge, both specialized and general, experience (and the judgment that comes with it), energy, determination, uncompromising self-appraisal and receptivity to the ideas of others. Its object is effective communication and to achieve it, it draws upon not only the law, but every area of human interest. It provides boundless opportunities for creative achievement, but they are realized only in proportion to the effort actually expended.*

JOHNSON, LAVERNE ST. CLAIR, retired elementary school educator; b. Danville, Va. d. Emanuel Linwood and Lula St. Clair (Yarbrough) White; m Cornell A. Johnson, Apr. 10, 1955 (div. Apr. 1982); children: Cassandra St. Clair, LeBrahne Cornell. Student, Howard U., 1950-55, Allen U., 1955; BA, Queens Coll., 1977, MA, 1986. Cert. and lic. in reading edn., common br., N.Y. Asst. tchr. 1st Hebrew Day Nursery, Bklyn., 1967-75; tchr. United Youth Action Day Care, Bklyn., 1977-80, Charles R. Drew Day Care Ctr., Queens Village, N.Y., 1980-83, N.Y.C. Bd. Edn., Bklyn., 1983-95; ret., 1995. Composer childrens' music; author: (childrens' poems) Fall Time Fall Time, 1974. Mem.

Com. to Eliminate Media Offensive to African People, St. Albans, N.Y., 1988—, Dem. Club, St. Albans, Bklyn. Philharmonic Chorus, St. Albans Congl. Ch. choir, Howard U. Choir, Carr-Hill Singers, Cambria Heights Civic Assn., other choral groups. Mem. United Fedn. Tchrs. Howard U. Alumni Club (sec. L.I. chpt. 1970-79), Lioness (v.p. Cambria Heights, N.Y. 1980-82, cert. of appreciation 1980-89). Avocations: musical composition, poetry, aerobics, church activities, community groups.

JOHNSON, LAWRENCE ALAN, cereal technologist, educator, administrator; b. Columbus, Ohio, Apr. 30, 1947; s. William and Wyoma (Swift) J.; m. Bernice Ann Miller, June 15, 1969; children: Bradley, David. BS, Ohio State U., 1969; MS, N.C. State U., 1971; PhD, Kans. State U., 1978. Rsch. chemist Durkee Foods div. SCM Corp., Strongsville, Ohio, 1973-75; assoc. rsch. chemist Food Protein R&D Ctr. Tex. A&M U., College Station, 1978-85; dir. Ctr. for Crops Utilization Rsch. Iowa State U., Ames, 1991—. Mem. rsch. com. Am. Soybean Assn., St. Louis, 1987-91, Nat. Corn Grower's Assn., St. Louis, 1990-91. Author: (with others) Handbook of Cereals, 1991; editor: (book/procs.) Technologies for Value-Added Products from Proteins and Co-Products, 1989; contbr. more than 150 articles to profl. jours. 1st lt. U.S. Army, 1971-73, Vietnam. Recipient Rsch. award Corn Refiners Assn., 1998. Mem. Am. Assn. Cereal Chemists (assoc. editor jour. 1982-85), Am. Soc. Agrl. Engrs., Am. Oil Chemists Soc. (assoc. editor jour. 1989—, Archer Daniels Midland Rsch. award 1986, 92, 99, 2001), Royal Swedish Acad. Agr. and Forestry (fgn. mem. 1999), Inst. Food Techs. Republican. Lutheran. Achievements include 10 patents. Home: 2226 Buchanan Dr Ames IA 50010-4368 Office: Ctr Crops Utilization Rsch Iowa State U Ames IA 50011-0001

JOHNSON, LAWRENCE M. retired bank executive; b. 1940; Student, U. Hawaii. With Bank of Hawaii, Honolulu, 1963-2000, exec. v.p., 1980-84, vice chmn., 1984-89, pres., 1989-2000, now chmn. bd., CEO, until 2000, ret., 2000. Address: Ste # 230 130 Merchant St Honolulu HI 96813

JOHNSON, LAYMON, JR., management analyst; b. Jackson, Miss., Sept. 1, 1948; s. Laymon and Bertha (Yarbrough) J.; m. Charlene J. Johnson, Nov. 13, 1982. B in Tech., U. Dayton, 1970; MS in Sys. Mgmt., U. So. Calif., 1978. Mem. tech. staff Rockwell Internat., Canoga Park, Calif., 1975-77; sr. dynamics engr. Gen. Dynamics, Pomona, Calif., 1978-83; fin. sys. specialist Northrop Corp., Pico Rivera, Calif., 1983-90; utility budget analyst dept. water and power City of L.A., 1991-97; mgmt. analyst L.A. Police Dept., 1997—. Lt. comdr. USNR, 1970-92. Mem.: So. Calif. Crime and Intelligence Analysts Assn., Internat. Assn. Crime Analysts, Inst. Safety and Sys. Mgmt. Triumvirate, Calif. Crime Analysts Assn., Libr. Congress Assocs., Am. Philatelic Soc., Internat. Assn. Law Enforcement Intelligence Analysts, LA County Mus. Art, Trojan Club, Tau Alpha Pi. Democrat. Roman Catholic.

JOHNSON, LEANNE, lawyer; b. Shreveport, La., Oct. 18, 1961; BS magna cum laude, So. Ark. U., 1983; JD with high honors, U. Ark., 1986. Bar: Ark. 1986, Tex. 1987, U.S. Dist. Ct. (so. and ea. dists.) Tex. 1987; bd. cert. in personal injury trial law Tex. Bd. Legal Cert. Clk. to Hon. Nauman Scott U.S. Dist. Ct. (we. dist.) La., Alexandria, 1986-87; from assoc. to ptnr. Orgain, Bell & Tucker, LLP, Beaumont, Tex., 1987—. Former dir., sec., officer Beaumont YMCA. Mem. Jefferson County Young Lawyers Assn. (former officer, dir.), Jefferson County Bar Assn. Office: Orgain Bell & Tucker LLP 470 Orleans St Ste 400 Beaumont TX 77701-3076

JOHNSON, LELAND "LEE" HARRY, social services administrator; b. Moscow Twp., Wis., Jan. 30, 1947; s. Amos Sanford and Bethellen (Otto) J.; m. Laurel Landry; children: Najib, Zack, Jessica, Karine. B degree, Gettysburg Coll., 1969; M degree, Ind. U.-Purdue U., 1971. Supr. psychiat. social work Rock County Guidance Clinic, Beloit, Wis., 1971-73, acting adminstr. Janesville, Wis., 1974; program dir., coord. Rock County Mental Health Svcs., 1974-75; program dir. Columbia County Home & Unified Bd., Portage, Wis., 1975, svcs. program dir. Portage, Wyocena, Wis., 1975-77; dir. human svcs. Columbia County Health Svcs., Portage, 1977; exec. dir. Navajo County Guidance Clinic, Winslow, Ariz., 1977-78, Coconino Community Guidance Ctr. Inc., Flagstaff, Ariz., 1978-85; human svcs. dir Eau Claire (Wis.) County Human Svcs., 1985-89; from dep. dist. adminstr. to dist. adminstr. Fla. Dept. Children and Families, Jacksonville, 1989—2001; exec. v.p. human svcs. Sarasota (Fla.) YMCA, 2001—. Mem. NASW, Acad. Cert. Social Workers. Home: 6114 36th Ln E Bradenton FL 34203 Office: YMCA Sarasota One S School Ave Ste 301 Sarasota FL 34237 E-mail: lhJohnson@sarasota-ymca.org.

JOHNSON, LENNART INGEMAR, materials engineering consultant; b. Mpls., Dec. 23, 1924; s. Sixten Richard Wilhem and Marie Augusta Johnson; m. Muriel Grant, Oct. 7, 1961; 1 child, Sandra Lee. BS in Chem. Engring., U. Minn., 1948. Petroleum engr. Northwestern Refining Co., New Brighton, Minn., 1948-49; sr. engr. Ordnance Div. Honeywell, Hopkins, Minn., 1949-67, prin. materials engr. Def. Sys. Div., 1967-69, supr. engring. Def. Sys. Div., 1969-87; staff engr. Armament Sys. Div. Honeywell Inc., Hopkins, Minn., 1987-88; cons. Soc. Automotive Engring., Warrandale, Pa., 1989-99. Cons. Ecubed Assocs., Inc., 1993-97; forum leader and presenter, U. Wis. Engring. Inst., Madison, 1965. Contbr. articles to profl. jours. Mem. credentials com. Hennepin County Rep. Conv., Minn., 1972, alt. del., 1974. Recipient Prize Paper award, Inst. Elec. Engrs. Fellow Am. Inst. Chemists; mem. Soc. Automotive Engrs. (sec. composites com. 1986-87, chmn. 1987-88), Am. Inst. Chem. Engrs. Achievements include development of and research in injection molding technology, urethane and epoxy casting resins, and urethane foaming resins; preparation of numerous Aerospace Material Specifications published by Society of Automotive Engineers. Home and Office: 14109 Mount Ter Minnetonka MN 55345-3826

JOHNSON, LEONARD GUSTAVE, research mathematician, consultant; b. Neguanee, Mich., Mar. 12, 1918; s. Werner Leonard and Sophia (Larsson) J.; m. Taimi Marie Lappi, July 5, 1944; 1 child, Virginia. BA, No. Mich. U., 1940; MA, U. Mich., 1941. Math. tchr. Channing (Mich.) H.S., 1941-42; rsch. mathematician Gen. Motors Corp., Detroit, 1945-74; seminar leader Detroit Rsch. Inst., Grosse Pointe Farm, Mich., 1958-98. Author: The Statistical Treatment of Fatigue Experiments, 1964, Theory and Technique of Variation Research, 1964; editor Statis. Bull. Detroit Rsch. Inst., 1961-98. State Coll. scholar U. Mich., 1940-41. Fellow Am. Soc. Quality (cert. reliability engr.); mem. Soc. Automotive Engrs., Indsl. Math. Soc. (treas. 1950-51, pres. 1994-97, Gold award 1991), Kappa Delta Pi, Phi Beta Kappa. Avocations: writing poetry, computer software development. Home and Office: 31811 Bretz Dr Warren MI 48093-1670

JOHNSON, LEONARD HJALMA, lawyer; b. Thomasville, Ga., May 22, 1957; s. Hjalma Eugene and Laura Nell (McLeod) J.; m. Nancy Louise Brock, Dec. 13, 1981; children: Brock Hjalma, Paige McLeod. BSBA, U. Fla., 1978, JD, 1980. Assoc. Dayton, Sumner, Luckie and McKnight, Dade City, 1981-83, Greenfelder and Mander, Dade City, 1983-84; pres. East Coast Bank Corp., Ormond Beach, Fla., 1983-2000; pvt. practice Dade City, 1984-89; ptnr. Johnson, Auvil, Brock & Wilson, PA, Dade City, 1990—; vice chmn. Bank of Madison (Fla.) County, 1983—88, N. Fla. Bank Corp., Madison, 1983—88, Bank at Ormond By-the-Sea, 1983-2000. Vice chmn. Lake State Bank, 1989-96. Bd. dirs. Downtown Dade City Main St. Inc., 1987-96, East Pasco Habitat for Humanity, 1998-99; trustee Dade City Hosp., 1994-96, chmn., 1996; mem. Leadership Fla. Mem. ABA, Fla. Bar Assn., Pasco County Bar Assn. (sec. 1982-83), Young Pres. Orgn. (edn. chmn. Fla. chpt. 1997-98, chpt. chmn. 1998-99), Dade City C. of C., Fla. Blue Key. Republican. Methodist.

JOHNSON, LEONARD JAMES, lawyer; b. Belmond, Iowa, May 25, 1951; BA in Govt., St. Johns U., Collegeville, Minn., 1974; JD, U. Iowa, 1977. Bar: Mo. 1977, U.S. Dist. Ct. (we. dist.) Mo. 1977, Kans. 1978, U.S. Dist. Ct. Kans. 1978, U.S. Ct. Appeals (10th cir.) 1985, U.S. Ct. Appeals (8th cir.) 1986 . Assoc. Stinson Morrison Hecker LLP, Kansas City, Mo., 1977-82, ptnr., 1982—. Mem. fed. practice com. Western Dist. Mo., Kansas City, 1986-93. Mem. ABA, Mo. Bar Assn., Def. Research Inst. Home: 4330 W 207th St Bucyrus KS 66013-9647 Office: 2600 Grand Blvd Kansas City MO 64108-4606 E-mail: ljohnson@stinsonmoheck.com.

JOHNSON, LEONARD MORRIS, retired pediatric surgeon; b. Gowanda, N.Y., June 11, 1931; s. Leonard Brynolf and Helen Berdena (Morris) J.; m. Ann Marie Homer, Mar. 30, 1968; children: H. Leif B. Johnson, Nils A.C. Johnson. BA, Haverford Coll., 1954; MD, U. Pa., 1958; MS in Surgery, U. Minn., Mayo Grad. Sch., Rochester, 1966. Diplomate Am. Bd. Gen. Surgery; cert. special competence in pediatric surgery. Intern Colo. Gen. Hosp., Denver, 1958-59; fellow in gen. surgery Mayo Clinic, Rochester, 1959-63; fellow in pediatric surgery Children's Mercy Hosp., Kansas City, Mo., 1964-65; vis. pediatric surgeon Acad. Hosp., Uppsala, Sweden, 1967; registrar in pediatric urology Alder Hey Children's Hosp., Liverpool, Eng., 1967-68; gen. surgeon SS Hope (Project Hope), Guayaquil, Ecuador, 1964, gen. and pediatric surgeon Conakry, Guinea, 1965, 1965-68; pediatric surgeon Children's Hosp., Oakland, Calif., 1969-97, ret., 1997, chief of dept. of surgery, 1989-92. Bd. dirs. Children's Hosp., Oakland, Calif., 1982-91; bd. trustees Children's Hosp. Found., Oakland, 1986-95; mem. exec. bd. Mt. Diablo-Silverado Coun. Boy Scouts Am., 1996—. Recipient Order Ruben Dario, Pres. Republic of Nicaragua, Managua, 1966; recipient Bronze Bambino award Children's Hosp., Oakland, 1990. Fellow Am. Coll. of Surgeons, Surgical fellow Am. Acad. of Pediatrics; mem. AMA, Am. Trauma Soc. (founding mem.), Am. Pediat.-Surg. Assn., Pacific Assn. Pediatric Surgeons, Brit. Assn. Pediat. Surgeons, Calif. Med. Assn., Alameda-Contra Costa Med. Assn. Republican. Avocations: photography, hiking, skiing, travel, music. E-mail: lmj2544219@aol.com.

JOHNSON, LEONIDAS ALEXANDER, optometrist, minister; b. Chgo., Jan. 16, 1959; s. Leon and Dolores J.; m. Crystal Dwaun Ellington, June 23, 1990 (div. Feb. 1999). BA in Biology, Ill. Wesleyan U., 1981; BS in Visual Sci., So. Calif. Coll. of Optometry, Fullerton, 1983, OD, 1985; student, Grace Theol. Sem., Long Beach, Calif., 1986-89; MA in Practical Theology, Biola U., La Mirada, Calif., 1997. Optometrist Larry Gotlieb, O.D., Redondo Beach, Calif., 1985-86, James Moses, O.D., Inglewood, Calif., 1986-87, Eyecare U.S.A., Montclair, Calif., 1987-89, Pearle Visioncare, Brea, Calif., 1989-94, Montebello Med. Eye Ctr., Calif., 1994-95, WATTSHealth Found., Inc., L.A., 1996-2001, chief vision care svcs., 1996-2001. Mem. quality assurance com. Eyecare U.S.A., 1988—89; medicine com. UHP Healthcare, 1996—2001; vision care svcs. coord. Global Health Outreach, 2001—; mem. adv. bd. Prison Fellowship Ethiopia, 2001—; investigator Ocular Hypertension Treatment Study; founder, pres. Crystal Fountain Ministries, Inc., 1997; clin. adj. prof. So. Calif. Coll. Optometry, 1988—. Author: Go Down, Moses! Devotions Inspired by Old Negro Spirituals, 2000; co-author: What Is This Thing Called Preaching? An Authentic Collection of Sermons by Rev. Leon Johnson, Vol. One, 1996, Vol. Two, 1998; author: Bread of Heaven Songs of Praise: Daily Biblical Devotional Guide Featuring Old Meter Hymns, 1997, The Foolishness of the Message Preached-An Original Collection of Soul Food Filled Sermons, Vol.1, 1999, Vol.2, 2000, Solomon's Prayer: Heal the Land--Devotional Readings from the King, 2002; contbr. articles to profl. jours. Min., deacon Friendship Bapt. Ch., Yorba Linda, Calif., 1981—2000, The Evangelical Ch. Alliance; pastor Christian edn. New Dawn Missionary Bapt. Ch., Pasadena, Calif., 2000—, missionary, 2000—; bd. dirs. Kenya Children's Fund, 2002—. Fellow Am. Acad. Optometry; mem. Am. Acad. Religion. Home: PO Box 4434 Diamond Bar CA 91765-0434

JOHNSON, LERLEAN NEWSOME, sociologist; b. E. St. Louis, Ill., Jan. 21, 1932; d. Edward Newsome and Sarah Byndon; m. Jesse L. Johnson, Dec. 1961; children: A'Jamal Byndon, Carl Clemens, Kamau Nnamdi, Angela Jackson, Irene Harris, Verna, Kevin, Jesse, Charlotte, Sara, Rosalie, Lerlean N., Louis, Lyndon. Diploma, Attucks HS, Carbondale, Ill., 1950. Counselor, adv. Project Enable, Omaha, 1956; sec. Mothers for Adequate Welfare, Omaha, 1967—90; mem. Nat. Welfare Rights Org., Omaha, 1969—78; pres. Omaha Client Coun., Omaha, 1978—2002. Recipient Valuable Com. Ctr., United Meth. Com. Ctr., 1976, Untiring Labor and Svc., Com. Adv. of Omaha, 1979, Outstanding Svc., City of Omaha Human Rels. Dept., 1986, Client of the Yr., Region V Client Coun., 1993, Woman of the Yr., N Omaha Neighborhood Assoc., 2000. Mem.: UCAN, Charles Drew Health Ctr. Advisory Bd., Greater Omaha Com. Action, Legal Aid Bd., State of Neb. Adv. Com., Omaha Survival Coalition (assoc.). Achievements include participated in Civil Rights march in Wash. DC; marched for Decent Safe and Affordable Housing for poor people; one of the seven interveners for Integration in the Omaha Pub. Sch. Syst; an adv. people in various States. Needy people sought her help because they had heard of her love and concern for hurting people. Home: 2016 Fowler Ave Omaha NE 68111

JOHNSON, LESLIE CAROLE, editor, publisher; b. Mpls., June 16, 1942; d. Lester Carl and Lillian Irene (Barrette) Lindstrom; m. Dennis Arthur Johnson, Aug. 8, 1964 (div. Sept. 2, 1988); children: Anthony James, Renee Denise; m. Willard Bromberg Shapira, Feb. 3, 1996; stepchildren: Eve Shapira Roycraft, Joel Shapira, Stephen Shapira. BA in Journalism, U. Minn., 1964. Freelance writer, Mpls., 1964-73; editor, pub. The Mississippi Rag, Mpls., 1973—. Pres. Twin Cities Jazz Soc., Mpls., St. Paul, 1982-84, bd. dirs., 1978-84; arts adv. com. bd. dirs. Met. Coun./Regional Arts Coun., St. Paul, 1986-89; vol. driver Meals on Wheels, Mpls., 1986-89; vol. cook Loaves & Fishes, Mpls., 1988-94; vol. Midwest Cmty. Hospice, Mpls., 1991-99. Mem. NAFE, Internat. Assn. Jazz Educators, Jazz Journalists Assn. Democrat. Roman Catholic. Avocations: reading, walking, music appreciation. Home: 5644 Morgan Ave S Minneapolis MN 55419-1525 Office: The Mississippi Rag 9448 Lyndale Ave S Ste 120 Bloomington MN 55420-4245 E-mail: editor@mississippirag.com.

JOHNSON, LESTER FREDRICK, artist; b. Mpls., Jan. 27, 1919; s. Edwin August and Helma Marie (Holmes) J.; m. Josephine Valenti, Feb. 12, 1949; children: Leslie Maria, Anthony Edwin. Student, Mpls. Art Inst., 1939-41, St. Paul Art Sch., 1939-41, Art Inst. Chgo., 1943. Prof. painting Yale U., 1964—, dir. studies, 1968—. Mem. Milford (Conn.) Fine Arts Council, 1972-73; mem. art adv. com. Housatonic Community Coll., Stratford, Conn., 1969-87 One-man shows, Zabriskie Gallery, N.Y.C., Martha Jackson Gallery, N.Y.C., Donald Morris, Detroit, Walter Moos Gallery, N.Y.C., Toronto, Can., David Barnett Gallery, Milw., Mpls. Art Inst., Dayton Art Inst., Fort Worth Art Inst., Yale Univ. Mus., Gimpel Fils Gallery, London, Gimpel Hanover Gallery, Zurich, Switzerland, Westmoreland Mus. Art. Greenburg, Pa. (traveling), Augustana Coll. Centennial Hall Gallery, Pa. Acad. Fine Arts, Newport Harbor Art Mus., Edward Thorpe Gallery, N.Y.C., Gimpel-Weitzenhofer Gallery, N.Y.C., Peter Findley Gallery, N.Y.C., Denise Dade' Gallery, N.Y.C., Joseph Rickards Gallery, N.Y.C.; exhibited in numerous group shows; represented in permanent collections, Albright Knox Mus., Dayton Art Inst., Met. Mus. Art, N.Y.C., Mus. Modern Art, New Sch. for Social Research, Phoenix Art Mus., U. Nebr., Walker Art Mus. Recipient Creative Arts award Brandeis U., 1978, Jimmy Ernest award in art Am. Acad. Arts and Letters, 2003; Trumbull Coll. fellow, 1996—; Guggenheim fellow, 1973. Mem. Nat. Acad. Design (elected assoc., coun.). Home: PO Box 7582 Greenwich CT 06836-7582 Office: Yale U Sch Art York And Chapel St New Haven CT 06520

JOHNSON, LESTER LARUE, JR., artist, educator; b. Detroit, Sept. 28, 1937; s. Lester L. and Haroldine M. (Stanley) J. BFA, MFA, U. Mich. Prof. Coll. for Creative Studies, Detroit. Participant dept. art and art history 3d Ann. African Am. Lecture Series, Wayne State U., 2000, internat. conf. on African Influences in the Visual Arts of the Ams., 2001. Exhibitions include Whitney Mus. Art, Nat. Acad. Design, N.Y.C., Kalamazoo Inst. Arts, Mich., Saginaw Art Mus., Detroit Inst. Arts, Univ. Mich. Mus. Art, Ann Arbor, Centro de Memoria e Cultura dos Correios, Salvador, Bahia, Brazil, Detroit Pretty City at G.R. N'Namdi Gallery and the Univ. Cultural Assn., 2003, Represented in permanent collections Osaka U. Arts, Japan, Mus. Afro-Brasileiro at Fed. U. of Bahia, Salvador, Brazil, prin. works include Bishop Internat. Airport, Flint. Recipient John S. Newberry Purchase prize, 54th Exhibit Mich. Artists, Detroit Inst. Arts, 1964, recognition award African-Am. Music Festival; grantee Andrerw W. Mellon Found. Office: Coll for Creative Studies 201 E Kirby St Detroit MI 48202-4048 E-mail: ljohnson@ccscad.edu.

JOHNSON, LILLIAN BEATRICE, sociologist, educator, counselor; b. Wilmington, N.C., Nov. 8, 1918; d. James Archie and Mary Gaston (Atkins) J. AA, Peace Coll., 1940; BRE, Presbyn. Sch. Christian Edn., 1942; MS, N.C. State U., 1965, PhD, 1972. Dir. Christian edn. First Presbyn. Ch., Pensacola, Fla., 1945—47, Greenwood, SC, 1947—48, Durham, NC, 1948—51; club dir. Army Spl. Svcs., No. Command, Japan, 1951—53; teenage dir. YWCA, Washington, 1953—56, assoc. exec. Honolulu, 1956—59, exec. dir. Tulsa, 1959—62; instr. N.C. State U., 1962—72; asst. prof. Greensboro Coll., 1972—75; mem. faculty dept. sociology U. West Ala., 1975—89, prof. emerita, 1989—; pvt. practice family counseling Fayetteville, NC, 1989—2002; ret. Mem.: DAR. Home: 5521 Glenhope Ct Cary NC 27511-3898 Business E-Mail: pgregg@glenaire.org.

JOHNSON, LINDA ARLENE, petroleum and flatbed semi-freight transporter; b. Sparta, Wis., Mar. 6, 1946; d. Clarence Julius and Arlene Mae (Yahnke) Jessie; children: Darrick, Larissa. With Union Nat. Bank & Trust Co., Sparta, 1964-69, Hill, Christensen & Co., CPA's, Tomah, Wis., 1969-75; owner Johnson of Wis. Oil Co., Inc., Tomah, 1969-95; with Larry's Express, Inc., Tomah, 1975-78; owner Johnson Rentals, 1979—, Johnson of Wis. Transport Co., Inc., Tomah, 1982—. Mem. Forward Tomah Devel., Inc., 1999—; active St. Paul's Luth Ch., Tomah. Mem. Petroleum Marketers Assn. Am., Am. Trucking Assn., Petroleum Marketers Assn. Wis., Tomah Area C. of C., Tomah Area Credit Union (bd. dirs. 1993—, sec. 1993-94), Rotary (dir. 1997-99), Beta Sigma Phi (Laureate Phi chpt.). Home and Office: 24011 Flatter Ave Tomah WI 54660-4424

JOHNSON, LIZABETH LETTIE, small business owner, insurance agent; b. Dallas, Aug. 24, 1957; d. Winfred Herschel Johnson and Mary Francis (Flowers) Goff; children: Brandi, Elissa. Student, Georgetown (Ky.) Coll., 1975-76, U. Ky., 1976-78. Staff analyst Met. Ins. Co., Lexington, 1979-81, ins. agt., 1981-82; sr. account agt. Allstate Ins. Co., Lexington, 1982—2003; owner Fanfare Jewelry, LLC, 2002—. Vol. Big Bros./Big Sisters, 1979-84, Life Adventure Camp, 1989-92; hotline counselor Lexington Rape Crisis Ctr., 1984-92, bd. dirs., 1988-91; vol. Christians in Comty. Svc., 1986-93, Hope Ctr., 1998—; mem. Bluegrass Adoptive Parent Support Group, 1985-92. Fellow Life Underwriting Tng. Council; mem. NAACP, Nat. Assn. Life Underwriters. Democrat. Episcopalian. Avocations: aerobics, walking, racquetball, needlework, reading, breeding himalayan cats and standard poodles. Office: Fanfare Jewelry LLC PO Box 12813 Lexington KY 40583 E-mail: ljohnson82@aol.com.

JOHNSON, LOIS ANN, patient educator; b. Jersey City, Nov. 2, 1937; d. John Milton and Sadie Marie (Arbogast) Herrold; m. Lewis Clifford Johnson, Aug. 26, 1961; children: Lisa, Ann, Dosa. Diploma, Del. Hosp. Sch. Nursing, 1958; BSN, U. Del., 1960. RN, Del. Instr. Del. Hosp. Sch. Nursing, Wilmington, 1960-65, Nursing Sch. Wilmington, 1965-85; patient educator Med. Ctr. Del., Wilmington, 1986-98; diabetes edn. specialist Christiana Care Health Sys., Wilmington, 1998—. Pres. Clin. Testing Assocs., Inc., Claymont, Del., 1982-97. Contbr. to profl. publs. Mem. Am. Assn. Diabetes Educators (cert.), Am. Diabetes Assn., Tri-State Assn. Diabetes Educators, Am. Heart Assn. (instr.), Christian Bus. and Profl. Women's Assn. Avocations: travel, reading, cooking, boating, decorating. Home: 121 Hilldale Ct Claymont DE 19703-1306

JOHNSON, LOLA NORINE, retired advertising and public relations executive, educator; b. Austin, Minn., Dec. 28, 1942; d. Alton E. and Evelyn M. (Quast) Milbrath; m. Dennis D. Johnson, June 15, 1963 (div. July 1973); children: Brenda J., Erik B. Attended, Coll. of St. Thomas. Pub. rels. account rep. Kerker & Assocs. Advt. and Pub. Rels., Bloomington, Minn., 1973-78; comm. mgr. Norwest Bank Mpls., 1978-83; dir. media rels., account supr. Edwin Neuger & Assocs. Pub. Rels., Mpls., 1983-85; v.p., mng. dir. The Richards Group, Mpls., 1985-86; owner, pres. PR Plus, Edina, Minn., 1986-2000; ret., 2000. Mem. cmty. faculty, instr., counselor Met. State U., Mpls., St. Paul, 1980-93. Cons. comm. United Way, Mpls., 1982. Recipient Gold award United Way Mpls., 1982. Home: 7151 York Ave S Apt 807 Minneapolis MN 55435-4435

JOHNSON, LONNIE L., JR., information specialist; b. Bridgeton, N.J., May 16, 1964; s. Lonnie L and Ivory M. Johnson; m. B.J. F. Brown Johnson, Aug. 7, 1987; children: Nima Warfield, Nashad Warfield. BA in Bus., Kean U., 1996; MA in Libr. Sci., Rutgers U., 2000. Acct. Ortho Biotech (Johnson and Johnson), Raritan, NJ, 1996—98; CEO/pres. Calenture Pub., Plainfield, NJ, 1999—. Bd. dirs. JBW, Plainfield, NJ. Avocation: chess. Office: Calenture Publishing PO Box 2812 Plainfield NJ 07062 Fax: 908-757-1742. Personal E-mail: mbalj@hotmail.com.

JOHNSON, LOREN CHARISSE, publishing executive, writer; b. Hackensack, N.J., Sept. 6, 1960; d. Larry Lee and Peggy Garris(Stepmother), Patrick Charles (Stepfather) and Barbara Jean Lauder; m. Dennis Johnson, Jan. 24, 1992 (div. Aug. 1996); 1 child, Leah; m. Sandy Simmons, June 1982 (div. Oct. 1985); 1 child, Charisse; m. Dennis Johnson, Sept. 15, 1997. *Husband Dennis Johnson, MSU 74-78, retired NFL player running back for "Buffalo Bill" (1978-80) and "New York Giants" (1980-82). Currently Chevy auto sales consultant, NJ. Daughter Charisse Monet Johnson, 17, H.S. grad 2003, top in District in girl's H.S. basketball and track and field, currently ranked in top 19 H.S. girls long jump for state of PA, also "A Who's Who Among American High School Students" 2002 & 2003, currently attending Div. I college-NJ basketball Scholarship. Daughter Leah Iman Johnson, 11, 6th grade, scores in the 99% national standardized test, 5'8" very advanced in basketball, loves math, writing and singing. Mother Barbara Jean Bobbitt[0097]Lauder worked for coach Leatherware-NY-1963-96, first and only African American executive to work for coach during her employment, started as receptionist and worked her way up; Father Larry Lee Garris retired Teaneck, NJ fireman (1965-92), was one if the first five African American firefighters for Teaneck during time when nationally very few, currently in real-estate-NJ; stepfather Patrick Charles Lauder Sr., former Marine (1960-65) guarded President John F. Kennedy when he was in Europe (Ireland), Hoffman Las Roche Pharm, Co. retiree, Nutley, NJ, worked for 26 years.* Student, Hunter Coll., 1982; AA, U. Fla., 1981. Editl. sec. Harcourt Brace Jovanovich Pub., N.Y.C., 1982—84; adminstrv. asst. Chem. Bank, N.Y.C., 1984—88; personnel cons. Office Personnel Search, N.Y.C., 1988—91; prin., owner Licensing By Loren, Inc., NJ, 1994—; freelance mtg. loan officer Stroudsburg, Pa., 2000—. Prin., owner The Dreamers, 1996—. Author: The Dreamers, 1996, Jesus & Me, 1998, Misunderstood, 1998. Recipient 1st Runner Up, N.J. Jr. Miss Pageant, 1977. Avocations: reading, writing, movies, sports, children. Office: Licensing by Loren Inc PO Box 936 Marshalls Creek PA 18335

JOHNSON, LUAN, disaster management consultant; b. Provo, Utah, Apr. 27, 1956; d. Jack R. and Colleen (Kesler) J. BA, Brigham Young U., 1981, MA, 1984; PhD, U. Wash., 1994. Dir. Tchg. Resource Ctr., Provo, 1980-84; tchg. asst. comms. dept. Brigham Young U., Provo, 1982-83; counselor Master Acad., Salt Lake City, 1985; ednl. designer, program mgr. City of Sunnyvale, 1986-90; tchg. asst., rsch. asst., speech comm. dept. U. Wash., Seattle, 1991-93; program mgr. City of Seattle, 1993—. Recipient Best Ednl. Campaign award Internat. Assn. Emergency Mgrs., 1998, Nat. Coord. Coun. of Emergency Mgmt. Best Newsletter award, 1996, 98, 2002, 1st pl.-best ednl. campaign Internat. Assn. Emergency Mgrs., 1998, Outstanding Pub. Svc. award Seattle Police Dept., 1999, 1st pl.-best ednl. video Internat. Assn. Emergency Mgrs., 1999. Mem.: Phi Kappa Phi. Mem. Lds Ch. Avocation: collecting and flying kites. Home: 6609 224th St SW Mountlake Terrace WA 98043-2324

JOHNSON, MAGIC (EARVIN JOHNSON), professional sports team executive, former professional basketball coach; b. Lansing, Mich., Aug. 14, 1959; s. Earvin and Christine Johnson; m. Cookie Kelly; 2 children. Student, Mich. State U., 1976-79. Basketball player L.A. Lakers, 1979-91, 95-96; sportscaster NBC-TV, 1993-94; chmn. Johnson Devel. Corp., 1993—; head coach L.A. Lakers, 1994, v.p., co-owner, 1994—; chmn. Magic Johnson Entertainment, 1997—; ret., 1991. Gold medalist, U.S. Olympic Basketball Team, 1992. Author: (autobiography) Magic, 1983; (autobiography, with Roy S. Johnson) Magic's Touch, 1989; What You Can Do to Avoid AIDS, 1992; My Life, 1992. Recipient Citizenship award, 1992, All-Around Contbns. to Team Success award IBM, 1984; mem. NCAA Championship Team, 1979, NBA All-Star Team, 1980, 82-92, MVP NBA All-Star Game, 1990, 92, NBA Championship Team, 1980, 82, 85, 87, 88; named MVP NBA Playoffs, 1980, 82, 87, NBA, 1987, 89, 90, All-Star Game, 1990, 92, Player of the Year, Sporting News, 1987; recipient Schick Pivotal Player award, 1984; named to All-NBA first team, 1983-91, second team, 1982, NBA All-Rookie Team, 1980; named one of the 50 greatest players in NBA history, 1996, elected to Naismith Meml. Basketball Hall of Fame, 2002 Achievements include being a holder of NBA playoff record most assists (2320); NBA Finals single-series record highest assists-per-game avg. (14), 1985, highest assists per game, rookie (8.7), 1980, NBA Finals single game record most points by rookie (42), 1980, NBA Finals single game record

most assists one quarter (8), NBA single game record most assists (22). Office: Magic Johnson Found 1600 Corporate Pointe Ste 1080 Culver City CA 90230 also: Johnson Devel Corp 9100 Wilshire Blvd Beverly Hills CA 90212-3415 also: FX Networks Inc 1440 S Sepulveda Blvd Los Angeles CA 90025-3458

JOHNSON, MARCIA J. dental hygienist; b. Cleveland, Dec. 16, 1949; d. Bernard Exsall and Aletha Odessa (Mason) Baker; m. Gregory Carl Johnson, Apr. 24, 1987; children: Bernard, Cecelia. Grad. dental hygienist, U. Minn., Mpls., 1972. Cert. Registered Dental Hygienist Wash., Nat. Bd. Cert. Minn. Dental hygienist Children's Hosp., Mpls., 1972—74, Dr. McDonald and Dr. Kinneberg, St. Paul, 1974—77, Dr. Lorenzo Patelli, Seattle, 1978—82, Dr. Terry Thomas, Seattle, 1983—90, Dr. Charles Wallace, Seattle, 1991—98, Dr. Kathy Curtis and Dr. John Larsen, Seattle, 1999—2003, Dr. Linda FuKuda, Seattle, 2000—. Vol. Planned Parenthood, Seattle, 1984—87; pres. P.T.A., Seattle, 1996—97; Sunday sch. tchr. Grace United Meth. Ch., Seattle, 1997—99; chair Grace United Meth. Women, Seattle, 2001—. Recipient Vol. Cert., John Muir Elem. Sch., 1996—2002. Mem.: Seattle Dental Hygiene Soc. Democrat. Methodist. Avocations: flower arranging, poetry, reading, writing, walking. Home: 9212 39th Ave S Seattle WA 98118-4827

JOHNSON, MARGARET ANDERSON, writer, publishing executive, plantation owner; b. Knoxville, Tenn., Apr. 19, 1927; d. Samuel Waller and Laura Lewis (Lawhon) Anderson; m. Thomas Carlisle Johnson, Jan. 9, 1949; children: James Scott, Wendy, Laura Lynn. Student, U. Tenn. and U. Fla., 1945—49. Pub. Water Oak Pub., Tallahassee, 1990—, writer, artist. Author, illustrator: Berber, A Lamb's Tale, 1998. Past pres. Ednl. TV Coun., Tampa, Tampa Jr. Women's Club; past advisor parliamentary procedure Jr. League of Tallahassee, past bd. dirs.; past v.p. Christian Women's Club, Tampa; past pres. PTA; tchr. Sunday sch. Tallahassee Bible Ch., First Bapt. Ch., Tampa, Fla., Grace Ch., Christ Cmty. Ch., Tampa, writer, illustrator Sunday sch. materials. Named Most Outstanding Sustainer, Jr. League, Tallahassee, 1989. Mem.: Alpha Omicron Pi (coll. chpt. pres.). Republican. Avocations: painting, writing, horseback riding, providing a haven for needy animals. Home and Office: Water Oak Pub 2984 Water Oak Plantation Dr Tallahassee FL 32312 Fax: 850-668-7100.

JOHNSON, MARGARET ANN (PEGGY), library administrator; b. Atlanta, Aug. 11, 1948; d. Odell H. and Virginia (Mathiasen) J.; m. Lee J. English, Mar. 4, 1978; children: Carson J., Amelia J. BA, St. Olaf Coll., 1970; MA, U. Chgo., 1972; MBA, Met. State U., 1990. Music cataloger U. Iowa Librs., Iowa City, 1972-73; analyst Control Data Corp., Bloomington, Minn., 1973-75; br. libr. St. Paul Pub. Librs., 1975-77; head tech. svcs. St. Paul Campus Librs., U. Minn., 1977-86; collection devel. office U. Librs., U. Minn., Mpls., 1987-90; asst. dir. St. Paul Campus Librs., U. Minn., 1987-95; planning officer U. Librs. U. Minn., Mpls., 1993-97, asst. univ. libr., 1997—2003, interim univ. libr., 2002, assoc. univ. libr., 2003—. Libr. cons. Makerere U., Kampala, Uganda, 1990, U. Nat. Rwanda, 1990, Inst. Agr. and Vet. Hassan II, Rabat, Morocco, 1992—, Ecole Nat. Agr., Meknes, Morocco, 2000, China Agrl. U., Beijing, 2001. Author: Automation and Organizational Change in Libraries, 1991, The Searchable Internet, 1996; editor: New Directions in Technical Services, 1997; editor Technicalities Jour., 2000—; editor Guide to Tech. Svcs. Resources, 1994, Recruiting, Educating and Tng. Librarians for Collection Devel., 1994, Collection Mgmt. and Devel., 1994, Virtually Yours, 1998; contbr. articles to profl. jours. Recipient Samuel Lazerow Rsch. fellowship Assn. Coll. and Rsch. Librs., Inst. for Sci. Info., 1987. Mem. ALA, Minn. Libr. Assn., Internat. Assn. Agrl. Libr. and Documentatists, U.S. Agrl. Info. Network, Assn. for Libr. Collections and Tech. Svcs. (pres. 1999-2000). Office: U of Minn Librs 499 Wilson Libr 309 19th Ave S Minneapolis MN 55455-0438 E-mail: m-john@tc.umn.edu.

JOHNSON, MARGARET H. welding company executive; b. Chgo., June 3, 1933; d. Harold W. and clara J. (Pape) Glavin; m. Odean Jack Johnson, Nov. 18, 1950; children: Karen Ann, Dean Harold. Student, Moody Bible Inst., 1976-78. V.p., sec. Seamline Welding, Inc., Grayslake, Ill., 1956-96, also bd. dirs. Author: Living Faith, 1973, 80, Lord's Ladder of Love, 1976, God's Rainbow, 1982; contbr. articles to religious mags. Trustee SWCEPS, Grayslake, 1963-99; life mem. Rep. presdl. Task Force, 1982—; trustee, 1986-88; charter founder Ronald Reagan Rep. Ctr., 1987; mem. lake View Neighborhood Group, Chgo., Small Group Ch. Cmty.; active Mary, Seat of Wisdom Cath. prayer groups, 1970-90, renew facilitator, 1986-88, co-chairperson, 1986-88; Sunday sch. tchr.; mem. parish coun. St. Gilbert parish, 1995-2000, evangelization chair, 1995-99, hospitality chair, 1995-99, welcome home program, 1998-99; mem. St. Raymond Cath. Ch., Mt. Prospect, 2000—, The Moorings of Arlington Heights spiritual Life com., 2001—. Mem. AARP, ASCAP, Fedn. Ind. Small Bus., Internat. Platform Assn., Women's Aglow Fellowship, Grayslake c. of C., Exch. Club of Grayslake, Grayslake Devel. Corp. Home: 836 Crescent Dr Arlington Heights IL 60005-3263

JOHNSON, MARGARET KATHLEEN, business educator; b. Baylor County, Tex., Oct. 30, 1920; d. George W. and Julia Rivers (Turner) Higgins; m. Herman Clyde Johnson, Jr., July 27, 1949 (dec.); 1 child, Carolyn Kay. BS, Hardin-Simmons U., 1940; M in Bus. Edn., North Tex. State U., 1957, EdD, 1962. Clk. Farmers Nat. Bank, Seymour, Tex., 1940-41; adminstrv. sec. U.S. Navy, Corpus Christi, Tex., 1941-46; adminstrv. asst. Hdqrs. 8th Army, Yokohama, Japan, 1946-49; instr. Coll. Bus. Adminstrn., U. Ark., 1957-60; teaching fellow Sch. Bus. Adminstrn., North Tex. State U., 1960-62, instr., 1962-63; asst. prof. bus., tchr. edn. and secondary edn. Tchrs. Coll., U. Nebr., Lincoln, 1963-65, asso. prof., 1966-70, prof., 1970—. Guest lectr. U. N.Mex., 1967, Curriculum Devel. in Bus. Edn., N.S. Dept. Edn., 1969, North Tex. State U., 1970, East Tex. State U., 1972; in Policies Commn. for Bus. and Econ. Edn., 1979-83; mem. bd. devel. Hardin-Simmons U., 1994-97. Author: Standardized Production Typewriting Tests series, 1964-65, National Structure for Research in Vocational Education, 1966; co-author: Introduction to Word Processing, 1980, 2d edit., 1985, Introduction to Business Communication, 1981, 2d edit., 1988, Business Communication Principles and Applications, 1996; editor: Nat. Bus. Edn. Assn. Yearbook, 1980. Recipient United Bus. Edn. Assn. award as outstanding grad. student in bus. edn. North Tex. State U., 1957; award for outstanding service Nebr. Future Bus. Leaders Am., 1968; Mountain-Plains Bus. Edn. Leadership award, 1977; merit award Nebr. Bus. Assn., 1979 Mem. Nat. Bus. Edn. Assn. (exec. bd. 1975, 76-78), Mountain-Plains Bus. Edn. Assn. (exec. sec. 1970-73, pres. 1975), Nebr. Bus. Edn. Assn. (pres. 1966-67), Nebr. Council on Occupational Tchr. Edn., Delta Pi Epsilon. E-mail: margaretkhj@aol.com.

JOHNSON, MARIAN ILENE, education educator; b. Hawarden, Iowa, Oct. 3, 1929; d. Henry Richard and Wilhelmina Anna (Schmidt) Stoltenberg; m. Paul Irving Jones, June 14, 1958 (dec. Feb. 1985); m. William Andrew Johnson, Oct. 3, 1991. BA, U. La Verne, 1959; MA, Claremont Grad. Sch., 1962; PhD, Ariz. State U., 1971. Cert. tchr., Iowa, Calif. Elem. tchr. Cherokee (Iowa) Sch. Dist., 1949-52, Sioux City (Iowa) Sch. Dist., 1952-56, Ontario (Calif.) Pub. Schs., 1956-61, Reed Union Sch. Dist., Belvedere-Tiburon, Calif., 1962-65, Columbia (Calif.) Union Sch. Dist., 1965 68; prof. edn. Calif. State U., Chico, 1972-91. Avocation: travel. Home: 26437 S Lakewood Dr Sun Lakes AZ 85248-7246

JOHNSON, MARIE-LOUISE TULLY, dermatologist, educator; b. N.Y.C., July 26, 1927; d. James Henry and Mary Frances (Dobbins) Tully; m. Kenneth Gerald Johnson, June 10, 1950. AB, Manhattanville Coll., 1948; PhD, Yale U., 1954, MD, 1956. Intern, then resident Yale-New Haven Med. Ctr., 1956-59; asst. prof. medicine, dermatology Yale U., 1961-67, clin. prof. dermatology, 1980—; chief dermatologist med. svc. Atomic Bomb Casualty Commn., Hiroshima, Japan, 1964-67; assoc. prof. dermatology NYU, 1967-70, 74-76, prof. dermatology, 1976-80; assoc. prof. dermatology, coordinator continuing med. edn. Dartmouth Coll., Hanover, N.H., 1971-74; chief dermatology Bellevue Hosp., N.Y.C., 1974-80; dir. med. edn. Benedictine Hosp., Kingston, N.Y., 1980-93. Cons. Health and Nutrition Exam. Survey I, II, Health Stats., Washington, 1967-84. Contbg. author: Cecil's Textbook of Medicine, 15th edit., 1979, 16th edit., 1982, 17th edit., 1985, Dermatology in General Medicine, 2d edit., 1979. Mem. Cardinal Cooke Pro-Life Commn., Albany, N.Y., 1986-87; bd. dirs. Maternity and Early Childhood Found., Albany, 1985—, pres., 1987—. Named Disting. Alumna, Manhattanville Coll., 1977. Fellow Am. Acad. Dermatology (master, bd. dirs. 1976-80; mem. Am. Dermatol. Assn. (bd. dirs. 1986-92, v.p. 1991-92, pres. 2000-01), NAS Inst. Medicine, Internat. Physicians for Prevention of Nuclear War (del. 1982, 83, 87, 88, 89). Roman Catholic. Home: 15 Strawberry Bank Rd High Falls NY 12440-5128 Office: Kingston Hosp Med Arts Bldg Ste 202 368 Broadway Kingston NY 12401-5144

JOHNSON, MARILYN, retired obstetrician, gynecologist; b. Houston, May 7, 1925; d. William Walton and Marilyn (Henderson) J. BA, Rice Inst., 1945; MD, Baylor U., 1950. Intern New Eng. Hosp. Women and Children, Boston, 1950-51; resident Meth. Hosp., Houston, 1951-53; fellow in gynecol. pathology Harvard Med. Sch., 1952-53; resident in gynecology M.D. Anderson Tumor Inst., Houston, 1954, fellow, 1955; practice medicine specializing in ob-gyn. Houston, 1954-81, Fredericksburg, Tex., 1981-97; ret., 1997. Mem. staffs St. Joseph's, Meml., Meth., Park Plaza, Hill Country Meml. Rosewood, South Austin Cmty., Comfort (Tex.) Cmty. hosps.; clin. instr. ob-gyn Coll. Medicine, Baylor U., 1954—, Postgrad. Sch. Medicine, U. Tex., 1954—; gynecologist De Pelchin Faith Home, Houston, 1954—, also Rice U., Richmond State Sch.; med. dirs. Birthright, Inc., Houston, 1973—; chief med. staff Hill Country Meml. Hosp., Fredericksburg, Tex., 1990-92; cons. Tex. bd. Blue Cross Blue Shield; pro-life public spkr. Bd. dirs. Right to Life, Houston, Found. for Life. Grantee Sandoz Labs., 1973, 75, Delbay Pharm. Co., 1977. Fellow Am. Coll. Obstetricians and Gynecologists; mem. AMA, Am. Soc. Colposcopic Pathologists, Tex. Med. Assn., Am. Med. Women's Assn., Internat. Infertility Assn., Harris County Med. Soc., Postgrad. Med. Assembly South Tex., Houston Ob-Gyn. Soc., Tex. Folklore Soc., Zonta, Fredericksburg Rockhounds. Republican. Baptist. Home: 2301 Lakeside Ct Rockport TX 78382-3519

JOHNSON, MARK ALAN, lawyer; b. Marysville, Ohio, June 5, 1960; s. Neil Raymond and Elizabeth Johnson; m. Deborah Anne Hillis, Sept. 21, 1984. BA, Otterbein Coll., 1982; JD, Ohio State U., 1985. Bar: Ohio 1985, U.S. Dist. Ct. (so. dist.) Ohio 1985, U.S. Ct. Appeals (6th cir.) 1987, U.S. Dist. Ct. (no. dist.) Ohio 1991, U.S. Ct. Appeals (5th cir.) 1998. Assoc. Baker and Hostetler LLP, Columbus, Ohio, 1985-92, ptnr., 1993—. Mem. ABA (litigation sect., mem. bus. torts litigation com., comml. and banking litigation com.), Ohio Bar Assn., Columbus Bar Assn. Office: Baker & Hostetler LLP 65 E State St Ste 2100 Columbus OH 43215-4215 E-mail: mjohnson@bakerlaw.com.

JOHNSON, MARK ALAN, biochemist; b. El Paso, Tex., Sept. 26, 1954; s. Arthur Alan and Carole Mae (Johnson) J.; m. Susan Mae Roberson, June 23, 1979; children: Tyler, Lucas, Emma. BS in Chemistry and Biology, U. Ill., Chgo., 1976; PhD in Biochemistry, Wash. State U., 1984. Postdoctoral rsch. assoc. Wash. State U., Pullman, 1985-86; postdoctoral fellow St. Jude Children's Rsch. Hosp., Memphis, 1986-89; fellow Mead Ctr. Rsch., Chillicothe, Ohio, 1989—. Vis. scientist Mead Imaging, Miamisburg, Ohio, 1993-94. Author: Biosynthesis of Terpenoid Wood Extractives, 1985, Advances in Chemotherapy of AIDS, 1990; contbr. articles to Molecular Pharmacology, Jour. Biol. Chemistry. Mem. AAAS, Am. Chem. Soc., Soc. for Indsl. Microbiology. Achievements include research in biocatalytic uses of soybean seed hull peroxidase in the pulp and paper industry; use of protease for repulping and recycling beverage carriers; discovery that 5-Nucleotidase activates dideoxy purine nucleosides. Home: 30 Timberlane Dr Chillicothe OH 45601-1941 Office: Mead Cen Rsch PO Box 1700 232 E 8th St Chillicothe OH 45601-3478 E-mail: maj@mead.com.

JOHNSON, MARK ANDREW, lawyer; b. Plainville, Kans., Feb. 27, 1959; s. Delton Lee and Margaret Ellen (McCracken) J. BA in Chemistry, Reed Coll., 1982; JD, U. Calif., Berkeley, 1987. Bar: Oreg. 1987, U.S. Supreme Ct. 1991. Jud. clk. U.S. Dist. Ct. Oreg., Portland, 1987-88, Oreg. Ct. of Appeals, Salem, 1988-89; assoc. Gevurtz, Menashe, Larson, Kurshner & Yates, PC, Portland, 1989-93; ptnr. Findling & Johnson LLP, Portland, 1993-99; of counsel Bennett Hartman Morris & Kaplan, LLP and predecessor, Portland, 1999—. Mem. ABA, Nat. Lesbian and Gay Law Assn. (co-chmn. 1994-95), Oreg. Gay and Lesbian Law Assn. (co-chair 1990-92), Oreg. State Bar (pres. 1998-99). Office: Bennett Hartman Morris & Kaplan LLP 851 SW 6th Ave Ste 1600 Portland OR 97204-1307 E-mail: johnsonm@bennetthartman.com.

JOHNSON, MARK EUGENE, lawyer; b. Independence, Mo., Jan. 8, 1951; s. Russell Eugene and Reatha (Nixon) J.; m. Vicki Ja Lane, June 11, 1983. AB with honors, U. Mo., 1973, JD, 1976. Bar: Mo. 1976, U.S. Dist. Ct. (we. dist.) Mo. 1976, U.S. Ct. Appeals (8th cir.) 1984, U.S. Supreme Ct. 1993. Ptnr. Stinson Morrison Hecker LLP, Kansas City, Mo., 1976—. Editor Mo. Law Rev., 1974-76. Pres. Lido Villas Assn., Inc., Mission, Kans., 1979-81. Mem. ABA, Mo. Bar Assn., Kansas City Bar Assn., Lawyers Assn. Kansas City, Def. Rsch. Inst., Internat. Assn. Def. Counsel, Mo. Orgn. Def. Lawyers, Carriage Club, Order of Coif, Phi Beta Kappa, Phi Eta Sigma, Phi Kappa Phi, Omicron Delta Kappa. Republican. Presbyterian. Home: 4905 Somerset Dr Shawnee Mission KS 66207-2230 Office: Stinson Morrison Hecker LLP 2600 Grand Blvd Ste 1200 Kansas City MO 64108-4606

JOHNSON, MARK J, computer science educator; b. Dayton, Ohio, Nov. 25, 1961; s. Clifford H and Barbara M Johnson; m. Lyn R Isaacson. BA, St. Olaf Coll., 1983; PhD, U. of Wis., 1994. Assoc prof of computer sci. and math. Ctrl. Coll., Pella, Iowa, 1994—. Office: Central Coll 812 University Pella IA 50219

JOHNSON, MARK KEVIN, operating room nurse; b. Camden, N.J., Mar. 22, 1963; s. Charles James and Doris Frances (Dodd) J. Diploma, Meth. Hosp. Sch. Nursing, Phila., 1984; BS in Profl. Arts, St. Joseph's Coll., Standish, Maine, 1998, cert. in health care mgmt., 1999. Staff nurse surg. unit Meth. Hosp., Phila., 1984-85, staff nurse intravenous therapy dept., 1985-86; staff nurse surg. unit Misericordia Hosp., Phila., 1987-88, staff nurse operating rm., 1988-92; staff nurse oper. rm. West Jersey Hosp. (now Virtual Health Sys.), Voorhees, NJ, 1992-98; staff nurse operating Summit Surgical Ctr. Virtua Health Sys., 1998—. Chairperson continuous Quality Improvement Coun., West Jersey Hosp. Operating Rm., Voorhees, N.J., 1994-97; spkr. role of a nurse Jennings Elem. Sch., Oaklyn, N.J., 1991-93, St. John's Sch., Collingswood, N.J., 1998. Fellow Assn. Operating Rm. Nurses. Roman Catholic. Avocations: travel, photography, reading. Home: 111 E Beechwood Ave Apt 21 Oaklyn NJ 08107-1364

JOHNSON, MARK MATTHEW, museum administrator; b. Dec. 10, 1950; s. Charles Michael Jr. and Jean Lee (Reid) J.; m. Amy Joy Schneider, March 10, 1984; children: Rachel Amelia, Sarah Jean. BA, U. Wis., Whitewater, 1974; cert. Art Mus. Studies, MA in Art History, U. Ill., 1976. Rsch. assoc. Krannert Art Mus., Champaign, Ill., 1975, asst. dir., curator, 1981-85; lectr. dept. mus. edn. Art Inst. Chgo., 1975-77; curator dept. art history and edn. Cleve. Mus. Art, 1977-81; dir. Muscarelle Mus. Art. Coll. William and Mary, Williamsburg, Va., 1985-94; lect. dept. fine arts Coll. William and Mary, 1985-94; dir. Montgomery (Ala.) Mus. Fine Arts, 1994—. Author: Idea to Image: Preparatory Studies from the Renaissance to Impressionism, 1980, Romeyn de Hooghe, 1989, Literacy Through Art, 1990, Nissan Engel: Nouvelles Dimensions, 1994, Hans Grohs: An Ecstatic Vision, 1996, (English and French edits.) Nissan Engel, 1998; organized, curated numerous exhbns., 1980—. Rsch. and travel grantee various mus. Mem. Assn. Art Mus. Dirs., Internat. Coun. Mus., Coll. Art Assn., Am. Assn. Mus. (accreditation com.). Office: Montgomery Mus Fine Arts PO Box 230819 One Museum Dr Montgomery AL 36123-0819 E-mail: mmjmmfa@aol.com.

JOHNSON, MARK WAYNE, lawyer; b. Dallas, June 6, 1959; s. W.A. and Wanda Louise (Follis) J.; m. Helene Denise Metz, June 7, 1987; children: Benjamin Gates, Andrew Noah. BS, Belhaven Coll., Jackson, Miss., 1980; JD, U. Miss., Oxford, 1983. Bar: Miss. 1983, U.S. Dist. Ct. (no. and so. dists.) Miss. 1983, U.S. Ct. Appeals (5th cir.) 1990; cert. govt. fin. mgr. Sole practice, Jackson, Miss., 1983-86; investigative auditor Miss. Dept. Audit, Jackson, 1986-92; budget analyst Office Budget and Fund Mgmt., Jackson, 1992-2001; dir. acctg. Miss. Sec. of State, Jackson, 2001—. Owner Possum Press, 1998—; with Madison Hazard Mitigation Coun., 2000-01. Contbr. articles to profl. jours. Dir. Miss. Coun. Compulsive Gambling, 1996-98, adv. bd., 1998—; bd. dirs. Miss. Pub. Employees Credit Union, 1994—. Recipient Spl. Merit award for traffic safety and edn. Nat. Assn. Chiefs of Police, 1987; named one of Outstanding Young Men of Am., 1988. Mem. Miss. Bar. Avocations: writing, computers. Office: Sec of State 301 N President St Jackson MS 39201 E-mail: mjohnson@sos.state.ms.us.

JOHNSON, MARLENE M. nonprofit executive; b. Braham, Minn., Jan. 11, 1946; d. Beauford and Helen (Nelson) J.; m. Peter Frankel. BA, Macalester Coll., 1968. Founder, pres. Split Infinitive, Inc., St. Paul, 1970-82; pres., bd. dirs. Face to Face Health and Counseling Clinic, 1977-78; with Working Opportunities for Women, 1977-82; lt. gov. State of Minn., St. Paul, 1983-91; sr. fellow Family Support Project, Ctr. for Policy Alternative, 1991-93; assoc. adminstr. for adminstrn. GSA, Washington, 1994-95; v.p. for people and strategy Rowe Furniture Corp., McLean, Va., 1995-97; CEO NAFSE: Assn. Internat. Educators, 1998—. Founder, past chmn. Nat. Leadership Conf. Women Execs. in State Govt.; mem. exec. com., midwestern chair Nat. Conf. Lt. Govs.; bd. dirs. AFS-USA, Inc., 1992-98, Nat. Capitol Region coun. Girl Scouts U.S., 1997-, bd. trustees AFS Internat. programs, 1998-2002; mem. adv. bd. Comms. Consortium Media Ctr., 2000-, Ctr. for Children in Poverty, Columbia U.; mem. commn. on internat. edn. Am. Coun. for Edn., 1999-. Chmn. Minn. Women's Polit. Caucus, 1973-76, Dem.-Farmer-Labor Small Bus. Task Force, 1978, Child Care Task Force, 1987; dir. membership sect. Nat. Women's Polit. Caucus, 1975-77; vice chmn. Minn. Del. to White House Conf. on Small Bus., 1980; co-founder Minn. Women's Campaign Fund, 1982; bd. dirs. Nat. Child Care Action Campaign; chair Children's 2000 Commn., 1990; candidate for Mayor St. Paul, 1993. Recipient Outstanding Achievement award St. Paul YWCA, 1980, Disting. Svc. award St. Paul Jaycees, 1980, Disting. Citizen citation Macalester Coll., 1982, Disting. Contbns. to Families award Minn. Coun. on Family Rels., 1986, Minn. Sportfishing Congress award, 1986, Royal Order of Polar Star Govt. Sweden, 1988, Children's Champion award Def. Fund, 1989, Jane Preston award Minn. State Coun. on Vocat. Tech. Edn., 1989, Legis. Leadership award Am. Fedn. Tchrs., 1991; named One of Ten Outstanding Young Minnesotans, Minn. Jaycees, 1980; Swedish Bicentennial Commn. grantee, 1987. Mem. Nat. Assn. Women Bus. Owners (past pres.).

JOHNSON, MARLYS MARLENE, elementary school educator; b. Omak, Wash., Mar. 13, 1946; d. Beverly Wayne and Mary Etta (Greene) McGrath; m. Gary Vaughn Johnson, Aug. 13, 1967 (div. June 3, 2001); children: Chad, Shane, Aubrey. BS in Edn., Wash. State U., 1967, MEd, 1991. Cert. profl. educator Wash., tchr. Va. Substitute tchr. Pullman (Wash.) Sch. Dist., 1970—80, home hosp. tutor, 1973—77, tchr. 2d grade, 1980—2001; tchr. 5th grade Alexandria (Va.) City Pub. Schs., 2001—02, tchr. 1st grade, 2002—03, tchr. 3d grade, 2003—. Pres. Profl. Edn. Adv. Bd. Office Supt. Pub. Instrn. and Wash. State U., Olympia and Pullman, 2000; tchr. leader Curriculum Instrn. Leadership Coun., Pullman, 1996—2001; presenter in field. Contbr. articles to profl. jours. Host family chair Wash. State Jr. Miss, Pullman, 1998—2001; awards chairperson Pullman Swim Club; mother advisor Rainbow for Girls; mem. scholarship com. 4-H. Recipient Christa McAuliffe Excellence in Edn. award, State of Wash./OSPI, 1990; grantee Contextual Tchg. grantee, U.S. Dept. Edn., 1999—2001, Rsch. Tech. grantee, RMC Rsch. Corp., Pullman, 1999—2000. Mem.: Wash. Edn. Assn. (rep. assembly del.), Pullman Edn. Assn. (exec. sec.), Phi Kappa Phi. Methodist. Home: 1501 N Highview Ln #110 Alexandria VA 22311

JOHNSON, MARSHALL HARDY, investment company executive; b. Raleigh, N.C., Sept. 7, 1923; s. William Thompson and Evie (Barnes) J.; m. Mary Lynn Lewis, June 24, 1947 (div. 1977); children: Marshall Hardy, Lynn Lewis Johnson-Titchener, Carter Johnson Overton; m. Beverly Ray Johnson, June 2, 1984. Student, U. N.C., 1942-43, 45-46; grad. in banking, U. Pa., 1957. Reporter, analyst Dunn & Bradstreet, Raleigh, 1946-47; chmn., pres., CEO McDaniel Lewis & Co., Greensboro, N.C., 1947—; v.p. Scott & Stringfellow, Inc., Richmond, Va., 1993-96. Mem. Midwest Stock Exch., Chgo., 1960-77; dir. emeritus First Citizen Bank & Trust, Greensboro, Mcpl. Coun., Raleigh; adv. dir. Friends Home, 1985-93. Contbr. articles to profl. jours. Dir. Young Dems., Greensboro, 1962-66, Jr. C. of C., Greensboro, 1964-70; deacon First Bapt. Ch., Greensboro. With USN, 1942-46. Fellow Fin. Fedn. Am.; mem. Am. Arbitration Assn. (nat. panel bd. 1963—), Nat. Assn. Securities Dealers (nat. panel arbitration 1985—), Securities Industries Assn. (Mid-Atlantic exec. com. 1986-93), Securities Dealers of Carolinas (pres. 1976), Magna Charta Baron, Odd Fellows, Kiwanis (Hixon award 1998), Greensboro Country Club, City Club (life scout), Alpha Tau Omega. Avocations: tennis, golf, swimming. Home: 310 Kimberly Dr Greensboro NC 27408-5018 Office: McDaniel Lewis & Co PO Box 9 Greensboro NC 27402-0009 E-mail: zipjohnson@aol.com. *I've learned that our quality of life is largely determined by our own choices.*

JOHNSON, MARTIN ALLEN, publisher; b. Bklyn., Aug. 20, 1931; s. Ellis A. and Estelle (Rudnick) J.; m. Suzanne Cornbleet, Dec. 12, 1964 (div. Feb. 1979); 1 dau., Sarah.; m. Diane Schlesinger Krull, Aug. 19, 1981. AB, Bard Coll., 1954. Asso. editor Am. Printer and Lithographer mag., N.Y.C., 1956-57, mng. editor, 1957-58, editor, 1958; mng. editor Printing Impressions mag., Phila., also; Delaware Valley Printing Impressions, 1958-61; pub. PTM mag., Chgo., 1959-67; v.p. Ednl. Screen and Audio Visual Guide, Chgo., 1962-67; pres. Trade Periodical Co., Chgo., 1967—, Pub. Dynamics, Inc., Stamford, Conn., 1968—, U.S. Indsl. Publs., Inc., Stamford, 1971—, U.S. Graphics Corp., Stamford, 1974—, Landmark Comms. Corp., Stamford. Contbr. articles to profl. jours. Bd. dirs. Cornell Mus. Art Guild. Served with AUS, 1954-56. Recipient Justin P. Allman award Wallcoverings Assn., 1993. Mem. Typophiles (NYC), Ams. for Music Library in Israel, Am. Soc. Interior Designers, Am. Watercolor Soc. (sustaining), Boca Raton Mus. Art Artist Guild (profl), Fla. Watercolor Soc., Chgo. Press Club, Execs. Club (Chgo.), Landmark Club (Stamford), Wellington Club (London). Jewish. Avocations: poetry, objective biblical history, painting. Office: Pub Dynamics Inc 9506 Lantern Bay Cir West Palm Beach FL 33411 E-mail: mjtalk2me@aol.com.

JOHNSON, MARTIN CLIFTON, physician; b. Santa Fe, Nov. 16, 1933; s. Henry J. and Dorothy (Clifton) J.; m. Priscilla Bollam, June 13, 1959; children: Martin Clifton II, Kurt B., Kirsten L. Ustach, Katharine E. AB, Stanford U., 1955, MD, 1959. Diplomate Am. Bd. Neurol. Surgery, Am. Bd. Pediat. Neurosurgery, Am. Bd. Forensic Examiners, Am. Bd. Forensic Medicine. Intern in surgery Palo Alto (Calif.) Stanford U. Hosp., 1959-60; fellow in neurosurgery Mayo Found., Rochester, Minn., 1960-61; asst. resident gen. surgery Presbyn. Med. Ctr., San Francisco, 1963-64; asst. resident, sr. resident, chief resident in neurosurgery U. Cin., 1964-68; pvt. practice neurosurgery/pediat. neurosurgery Portland, Oreg., 1968-99. Col. M.C. AUS, ret.; lt. comdr. M.C. USNR, 1961-63. Fellow ACS, Am. Acad. Pediats.; mem. AMA, Portland Met. Med. Soc., Oreg. Med. Soc., Congress Neurol. Surgeons, Am. Assn. Neurol. Surgeons, Am. Assn. Pediatric Neurosurgery, Multnomah Athletic Club, Columbia Aviation Club. Office: Pacific Northwest Neurol Assocs PC 31870 SW Country View Ln Wilsonville OR 97070-7476

JOHNSON, MARVIN MERRILL, chemical engineer, chemist; b. Salt Lake City, Mar. 21, 1928; s. John Ivan and Hildur Elizabeth (Johnson) J.; m., Apr. 8, 1951; children: Mark, Jennifer, Lorelie, Maryanne. BS in Chem. Engring., U. Utah, 1950, PhD in Chem. Engring., 1958. Sr. rsch. chemist Phillips Petroleum, Bartlesville, Okla., 1956-68, rsch. chemist, 1968-74, sr. rsch. assoc., 1974-75, sr. scientist, 1978-86; prof. chem. engring. Okla. State U., Stillwater, 1986-89; sr. scientist Phillips Petroleum, 1989-91, rsch. & devel. rsch. fellow, 1991—. Contbr. articles to profl. jours.; patentee in field. Named Inventor of Yr. Okla. Bar Assn., 1981. Fellow AICE; mem. Nat. Acad. Engring., Am. Chem. Soc. (Okla. Chemist 1982, Southwest Regional award 1982, Nat. Medal Tech. 1985, IRI Achievement award 1993, hero of chemistry ACS, 1998), Sigma Xi. Home: 4413 Woodland Rd Bartlesville OK 74006-5340 Office: c/o Phillips Petroleum Co 354 Pl Phillips Rsch Ctr Bartlesville OK 74004-0001

JOHNSON, MARVIN RICHARD ALOIS, architect, consultant; b. Humphrey, Nebr., Aug. 13, 1916; s. Otto Henry and Reenste (Berends) J. AB, BA in Architecture, U. Nebr., 1943; M.Architecture, Harvard U., 1948. Designer, draftsman firm Clark & Enersen, Lincoln, Nebr., 1946-47, 48-50; cons. architect div. sch. planning N.C. Dept. Public Instrn., Raleigh, 1950-80; architect, cons. ednl. facilities, 1981—. Cons. HEW, Washington, 1960 Contbr. articles to profl. jours. Served with USNR, 1943-46. Fellow AIA (recipient Distinguished Service citation N.C. chpt. 1960, v.p. N.C. chpt. 1977-78, pres.-elect 1979, pres. 1980); mem. Council Ednl. Facility Planners, Am. Assn. School Adminstrs., Phi Beta Kappa. Democrat. Lutheran. Home: 3500 Faulkner Dr Apt D303 Lincoln NE 68516-6639 E-mail: mramrajohn@aol.com.

JOHNSON, MARY ANN, vocational school owner; b. Chgo., June 26, 1956; d. Truly and Pearlie Mae (Bell) J.; children: Pamela Ann, Russell Alan Jr. AA, Joliet (Ill.) Jr. Coll., 1990; student mgmt. info. systems, Governor State U. Student intern Argonne (Ill.) Nat. Lab., 1972-79; owner, pres. Tech. Soft Svcs., Chgo., 1991—. Lectr., condr. seminars on running small bus. Author: Running a Small Business, 1996. Avocations: self-defense, computer and software edn. Office: Tech Soft Svcs 160 E Illinois St Ste 603 Chicago IL 60611-3859

JOHNSON, MARY ELIZABETH, music educator, pianist; b. Tyler, Tex., Mar. 29, 1933; d. Robert Edward and Mamie Oberia (Walters) Spaulding; m. George Devereaux Johnson, Mar. 31, 1955; children: Bradford D., Robin Elizabeth. BFA, So. Methodist U., 1955; pvt. study with Bomar Cramer, Dallas, 1964-69. Music tchr. Dallas Country Day Sch., 1955; tchr. Dayton (Ohio) pub. schs., 1956-57; pvt. tchr. piano Dallas, 1962—; profl. accompanist, 1965—; duo-pianist, 1965—; sponsor-tchr. creative and performing arts program Dallas Ind. Sch. Dist., 1981-82, 83, 84. Sponsor Jr. Melodie and Jr. Harmonie. Mem. Northwest Bible Ch. Dallas, 3-score com. N.W. Bible Ch. Named to Hall of Fame, Am. Coll. Musicians, 1981. Mem. Nat. Guild Piano Tchrs. (cert., named to honor roll 1971), Tex. Fedn. Music Clubs (historian 1974-76, state chmn. music svc. in the community 1971-73, dist. jr. counselor 1971-78, dist. chmn. music svc. in the community 1971-78; rec. sec. 5th dist. 1975-76, 1st v.p. 1977-78, jr. festival chmn. 1977-80, dist chmn. Jr. Gold Cup awards 1980, 84, 85, 86, 87, 88, asst. chmn. North Dallas div. 5th dist. jr. festival 1981-82), Music Tchrs. Nat. Assn., Jr. Pianists Guild of Dallas (chmn. jr. recitals 1983, chmn. sr. recitals 1984, treas. 2003-2004), Tex. Music Tchrs. Assn., Dallas Music Tchrs. Assn., Music Study Club Dallas (chmn. piano program 1981-82), Music Study Club, Dallas Fedn. Music Clubs (del. 1969-78, 1st v.p. 1977), Daus. Republic Tex. (1st v.p. Bonham chpt. 1975-76), Alpha Delta Pi, Melodie Club (pres. 1969-71, 2d v.p. 1977—, choral accompanist, counselor jr. club, historian, press sec. 1981-82, 1st v.p. 2003-2004), Kalista Club (yearbook chmn. 1983-2000, v.p. 1984-85, pres. 1986-87), Park Cities Club, Tower Club, Kermis Club, Rondo-Carrousel Club, Trippers Club, 3-Score or More Com, Northwest Bible Ch., Mu Phi Epsilon (patron). Home: 3848 Cedarbrush Dr Dallas TX 75229-2701

JOHNSON, MARY ELIZABETH, retired speech educator; b. Powhatan Pt., Ohio, Mar. 10, 1905; d. John McFadden Johnson and Nancy Ramsay (Shannon) Johnson BA, Muskingum Coll., New Concord, Ohio, 1926; MA, U. Mich., 1933; postgrad., Northwestern U., 1956, 60, Ohio State U., 1946, 68. Cert. in edn., speech correction, Ohio, 1960. Tchr. Moundsville (W.Va.) High Sch., 1926-37, dean of girls, 1935-37; chmn. English dept. Martins Ferry (Ohio) High Sch., 1937-44, instr. speech, 1944-48; asst. prof. Muskingum Coll., 1948-52, assoc. prof. speech, 1952-72, emeritus assoc. prof., 1972—. Chmn. drama and poetry reading conf. Muskingum Coll., 1946-68, communications area, 1950-53, acting chmn. dept. speech, 1965-66, adviser Nat. Collegiate Players, 1957-65; author Ohio dist. state scholarship tests in English for secondary schs., 1941, 43, 46. V.p. Women's Forum, New Concord, 1966-67; mem. First Community Village Coun., Columbus, Ohio, 1984, 85; chmn. Children's Hosp. Twig #15, Columbus, 1987, 88. Mem. AAUW, Am. Assn. Retired Persons, Am. Speech and Hearing Assn., Ohio Speech and Hearing Assn., Comparative Edn. Soc. (seminar and field study in Europe 1967), Ohio Ret. Tchrs. Assn., Heritage Club, Parchment Club (pres. New Concord 1968, 78), Delta Kappa Gamma Internat. (pres. Psi chpt., Alpha Delta State 1941-43, pres. Alpha Psi chpt. 1951, state recording sec. 1965-67). Presbyterian.

JOHNSON, MARY EVANS, musicologist, musician; b. Hollywood, Calif., Oct. 30, 1924; d. Leland Hayes and Marion Reeder Evans; m. Manly Johnson, 1942 (div. 1982); children: Evan Andrew, Graham Matthew. MusB with distinction, Sch. of Music, Univ. of Mich., Ann Arbor, Mich., 1946, MusM Musical Art, 1947; Mus D, Sch. of Music, Univ. of Okla., Norman, Okla., 1979. Founding instr., lit. and materials dept. Juilliard Sch., New York, NY, 1947—52, mgr. composers forum, 1947—52, performing and lectr., 1947—. Author: (Dr. Dissertation) Characteristic Metrical Anomalies in the Instrumental Music of Robert Schumann: A Study of Rhythmic Intention, 1979 (William Poland Lectr., Ohio State Univ., "Shumann's Rhythmic Riddles", 1997). Unitarian. Achievements include discovery of Schumann's approach to Hemioles as metrically, rather than structurally, inflected. Home: 235 27th St Del Mar CA 92014

JOHNSON, MARY KATHERINE (KATIE JOHNSON), elementary education educator; b. Prescott, Wis., June 12, 1945; d. Walter Frank and Mary Jane (Larson) Johnson; m. William F. Hilton, June 23, 1968 (div. 1985); children: Bradley Eric, Karin Louise. BA, Mich. State U., 1967, MA, 1970; postgrad., U. Calif., Berkeley, 1970—. Cert. elem. tchr., Calif. Tchr. East Lansing (Mich.) Pub. Schs., 1967-68, Hall's Crossroads Sch., Aberdeen, Md., 1968-69, Oakland (Calif.) Pub. Schs., 1970-82; tchr., cons. Bay Area Writing Project, Berkeley, 1978—, Bay Area Math. Project, Berkeley, 1994—, Bay Area Calif. Arts Project, Berkeley, 1997—; cons. Child Devel. Project, San Ramon, Calif., 1985; tchr. Berkeley Unified Sch. Dist., 1986—, support provider, beginning tchr. support and assessment program, 2000—; coord. pub. programs, math. edn. program Lawrence Hall of Sci., U. Calif., Berkeley, 1996-98; curriculum developer, writer U. Calif. Bot. Gardens, 2001—. Mem. MATHTEQ U. Calif., Berkeley, 1987-90; mem. com. of credentials Commn. for Tchr. Preparation and Licensing, Sacramento, 1974-76; spkr. Asilomar Math. Conf., 1991—, mem. program com., 1995-2000; spkr. Calif. chpt. Assn. for Persons with Severe Handicaps Conf., 1992, 94, 97, 98, 2000, bd. dirs., 1997—; spkr. Assn. for Persons with Severe Handicaps Internat. Conf., 1993, 2001, Supported Life Conf., 1992; rep. No. Regional Spl. Edn. Local Plan Area Com., Region III Full Inclusion Task Force for State of Calif., 1994-98; participant Calif. Rsch. Inst., 1992; mem. adv. task force on tchr. preparation in mainstreaming Calif. Commn. on Tchr. Credentialling, 1996; adv. bd. Profl. Internship Program., U. Calif., Berkeley; tchr. leader Profl. Insvc. for New and Experienced Tchrs., 1997—; pres. AC3ME-Alameda/Contra Costa County Math Educators, 2000—; mem., tchr.-leader Profl. Instrn. for New and Established Tchrs., 1998-2002. Contbg. author: Portfolio Assessment in Mathematics, 1990, Teacher Handbook on Homework, C.M.C. Communicator, 1993. Coord. children's coun. Epworth Meth. Ch., Berkeley, 1985-88, 96-98, Youth Coun., 1993-95; cert. lay spkr. Bay View dist. Calif.-Nev. United Meth. Ch., Berkeley, 1989—, trustee, 1994-96, 98-2002; pres. bd. trustees Maya's Music Therapy Fund, 1994—; mentor tchr. Berkeley Unified Sch. Dist., 1996, 99; mem. adv. bd. Calif. Urban Partnership program U. Calif., Berkeley, 1999—. Recipient Outstanding Alumni K-12 Tchr. award Mich. State U. Coll. Edn. Alumni Assn., 2002; named Math. Tchr. of Yr. Alameda/Contra Costa Counties Math. Educators, 1996; Berkeley Pub. Edn. Found. grantee, 1988, 89, 90, 92, 94, 95, 98, 2000-03, In Dulce Jullibo Inc. grantee, 1989, 90, 92, 94, 95, 99, 2003, BAMP grantee, 1995, Calif. Math. Coun. grantee, 1995; fellow Bay Area Math. Project, 1994, Oakland-Bay Area Writing Project, 1977, Bay Area Writing Project, 1978, 98, Bay Area Calif. Arts Project, 1997. Mem. Nat. Coun. Tchrs. English, Nat. Coun. Tchrs. Math., Calif. English Coun., Calif. Math. Coun., P.E.O., Profl. Instr. for New and Established Teacher; bd. dirs. CA Chpt. Assn. Persons with Severe Handicaps, 1997—, Alameda-Contra Costa County Math. Educators (pres. 2000—). Democrat. Avocations: singing, jogging, swimming, gourmet cooking, sewing. Home: 1016 Keeler Ave Berkeley CA 94708-1404 Office: Oxford Sch 1130 Oxford St Berkeley CA 94707-2624

JOHNSON, MARY LOU, lay worker, educator; b. Moline, Ill., July 15, 1923; d. Percy and Hope (Aulgur) Sipes; m. Blaine Eugene Johnson, May 30, 1941 (dec.); children: Vivian Johnson Sweedy Maday, Michael D. (dec.), Amelia Johnson Harms Thomas, James Michael (dec.). Grad. high sch., Moline. From chmn. Christian edn. to dir. 1st Christian Ch., Moline, 1971—88, dir. Christian edn., 1988—93, ret., 1993, chmn. Christian edn., 2001—03. Sunday sch. tchr. 1st Christian Ch., Moline, 1958-84; cluster del. Christian Chs. Ill. and Wisc., Moline, 1988-89. Author: (poem) What Is A Mother?, 1965. Officer various positions PTA, Moline, 1972-75, hon. life mem. State of Ill., 1972; leader, dist. chair Girl Scouts U.S., Moline, 1955-65; chmn. skywatcher USAF Ground Observer Corps, Moline, 1955-57; vol. telethon coord. Muscular Dystrophy Assn., Moline, 1971-94; del. lt. gov.'s Commn. on Aging, Springfield, Ill., 1990; historian 1st Christian Ch., Moline, 1996—, libr., 2000—; vol. C.A.R.E. Ministry, 1999—, Ring for Care, 1999-2002, Western Ill. Area Agy. on Aging, 1998-2003. Recipient Appreciation award Muscular Dystrophy Assn., 1964-94. Republican. Home: 2014 9th St Moline IL 61265-4779 E-mail: grmalou624@aol.com. *Life hands us many challenges. I find them interesting and always have been willing to accept them. Not all my efforts have been successful; however, each attempt has helped me grow to be a better person.*

JOHNSON, MARY MURPHY, social worker, writer; b. N.Y.C., Mar. 5, 1940; d. Richard and Nora (Greene) Murphy; m. Noel James Johnson, Oct. 8, 1961 (dec.); children: Valerie Johnson Powell, Donna Homan, Noreen Marie Pettitt, Richard. BA in English/History magna cum laude, BS in Sociology magna cum laude, Jacksonville State U., 1983, MA in History, 1984, B in Social Work magna cum laude, 1988. Cert. gerontology specialist. Asst. activities dir. Jacksonville (Ala.) Nursing Home, 1985-86; social services dir. Beckwood Manor, Anniston, Ala., 1987—. Cons. in field. Editor: Vladivostak Diary, 1987. Mem. AAUW, Nat. Assn. for Family and Cmty. Edn., Ala. Archaeol. Soc., Coosa Valley Archaeol. Soc. (sec. 1982-87), Soc. Ala. Archivists, Human Svcs. Coun., Treasure Forest Assn., Vietnam Vets. Am., Soc. for Creative Anachronism (Reeve, Canton of the Peregrine), Phi Eta Sigma, Phi Alpha Theta, Sigma Tau Delta, Omicron Delta Kappa. Russian Orthodox. Avocations: collecting antiques and depression glass, hiking, reading, archaeology.

JOHNSON, MARY P. freelance writer; b. Balt., Sept. 23, 1927; d. Frederick and Marie Rosina (Walter) Manke; m. Alvin H. Walker, June 21, 1947 (div. Mar. 1955); m. Maurice P. Johnson, July 1, 1955; 1 child, Carol Joy. Student, Johns Hopkins U., 1959-63. Assoc. dir. Centennial planning and programs Johns Hopkins U., Balt., 1973-77; arts reviewer Balt. Sun-Arundel, 1997—; reviewer concerts and theater, reporter Severna Park (Md.) Voice, 1998—. Mem. Journalism and Women Symposium, 2002. Bd. dirs. Performing Arts Assn., Linthicum, Md., 1995—. Mem.: AAUW, Am. Theatre Critics Assn. Inc., Assn. for Women in Comms., Friends of Annapolis Opera, Friends of Annapolis Chorale, Friends of Annapolis Orch., Balt. Symphony, Balt. Opera, Met. Opera Guild. Democrat. Lutheran. E-mail: marybud@toad.net.

JOHNSON, MARY PAULINE (POLLY JOHNSON), nursing executive; b. Ohio, May 23, 1940; BSN summa cum laude, Ohio State U., 1962; MSN, Duke U., 1980. RN, N.C. Staff nurse psychiatry unit Univ. Hosps., Ohio, 1963-64; pediatric office nurse. Gaithersburg, Md., 1971-73; clin. nurse coord. N.C. Meml. Hosp., Chapel Hill, NC, 1973-86; grant coord. N.C. Assn. Home Care, 1988; practice cons. N.C. Bd. Nursing, Raleigh, 1988-96, assoc. dir. practice, 1996-97, exec. dir., 1997—. Adv. com. Citizens Advocacy Ctr. Mem. ANA, Nat. Coun. State Bds. Nursing (bd. dirs.), N.C. Nurses Assn., N.C. Orgn. Nurse Leaders. Office: NC Bd of Nursing 3724 National Dr Raleigh NC 27612-4070 E-mail: polly@ncbon.com.

JOHNSON, MARYL RAE, cardiologist; b. Fort Dodge, Iowa, Apr. 15, 1951; d. Marvin George and Beryl Evelyn (White) Johnson. BS, Iowa State U., 1973; MD, U. Iowa, 1977. Diplomate Am. Bd. Internal Medicine, Am. Bd. Cardiovasc. Diseases. Intern U. Iowa Hosps., Iowa City, 1977-78, resident, 1978-81, fellow, 1979-82; assoc. in cardiology U. Iowa Hosps. and Clins., Iowa City, 1982-86, asst. prof. medicine cardiovasc. divsn., 1986-88; asst. prof. medicine Med. Ctr. Loyola U., 1988-92, assoc. prof., 1992-94, Rush. U., 1994-97, Northwestern U. Med. Sch., 1998—2002; prof. medicine U. Wis. Med. Sch., Madison, 2002—. Med. dir. cardiac transplantation U. Iowa Hosp., 1986—88; assoc. med. dir. cardiac transplantation Loyola U., 1988—94, assoc. med. dir. Rush Heart Failure and Cardiac Transplant Program, 1994—97; dir. heart failure cardiac transplant program Northwestern U. Med. Sch., 1998—2001, dir. heart failure program, 2001—02; med. dir. heart failure and transplantation U. Wis. Hosp. and Clinics, 2002—. Editor (assoc. editor): Jour. Heart and Lung Transplantation, 1995—99; mem. editl. bd.:, 2000—. Mem. Nat. Heart Lung and Blood Adv. Coun., Bethesda, Md., 1979—83; mem. biomed. rsch. tech. rev. com. NIH, 1990—93, chairperson, 1992—93, chair biomed. rsch. tech. spl. emphasis panel, 1999—. Recipient Jane Leinfelder Meml. award, U. Iowa Coll. Medicine, 1977, Clin. Investigator award, NIH, 1981, New Investigator Rsch. award, 1981, 1986; scholar Barry Freeman, 1974. Mem.: ACP, AAAS, AMA, Am. Coll. Cardiology (heart failure and cardiac transplant com. 2002—), Am. Heart Assn., Ctrl. Soc. Clin. Rsch., Internat. Soc. Heart and Lung Transplantation, Order of Rose, Alpha Omega Alpha, Iota Sigma Pi, Phi Kappa Phi, Alpha Lambda Delta. Office: U Wis Madison E5/582D CSC 5710 600 Highland Ave Madison WI 53792 E-mail: mrj@medicine.wisc.edu.

JOHNSON, MATTIEDNA, nurse, retired diaconal minister; b. Amite County, Miss., Apr. 7, 1918; d. Isaac and Minnie (Ramsey) J.; m. Robert William Kelley, Oct. 19, 1943 (div. May 1980); children: Bobby Lou, Robert William Jr., Patricia Elaine, Frances Minette. RN, Terrell Meml. Hosp.; postgrad., Homer G. Phillips Hosp.; MA, Ashland Theol. Sem. RN, Tenn., Mont., Minn.; diaconal min. United Meth. Ch. Head nurse Jane Terrell Hosp., Memphis; staff nurse Homer G. Phillips Hosp., St. Louis; lab. tech. U.S. Army U. Minn., Mpls.; pvt. duty nurse Mpls. Dist. Minn. State, Mpls.; medical missionary Gbarnga (Liberia) Meth. Mission; pvt. duty night nurse Mo., Tenn., Ohio. Author: Tots Goes to Gbarnga, 1994, Johnson's Instructors Guide, 1949, Johnson's Manual-Church Nursing, 1994. Created ch. nursing Am. Red Cross., 1949—, vol. instr. Recipient Last Living Natural Scientist of 2000 Millennium award. Mem. ANA, Nat. Black Nurses Assn. (sec. 1970—). Achievements include crystallization of penicillin mold for gun shot wounds; tests of staphlococcus germs and terriable mice mold against streptococcus hymolyticus germ of scarlet fever; developed R13 Mold penicillin crystals for the injectable IV-Intra Muscular. Home: 13606 Abell Ave Cleveland OH 44120-3954

JOHNSON, M(AURICE) GLEN, political science educator; b. Pikeville, Ky., Nov. 18, 1936; s. Marvin Forrest and Norcie (Wicker) J.; m. Sipra Bose, July 13, 1963; children: Denise Bose, Robert Alexander. BA, Georgetown Coll., Ky., 1958; MA, U. N.C., Chapel Hill, 1961, PhD, 1966. Instr. polit. sci. U. Ky., Lexington, 1963-64; instr. Vassar Coll., Poughkeepsie, N.Y., 1964-66, asst. prof., 1966-72, assoc. prof., 1972-77, prof., 1977—2002, prof. emeritus, 2002—; Shirley Ecker Boskey chair in internat. rels., 1999—2002; dir. program of internat. studies Vassar Coll., Poughkeepsie, N.Y., 1985-89, acting pres., 1997-98, 2003—; dir. Am. Studies Rsch. Ctr., Hyderabad, India, 1990-93. Author: (with others) Beyond the Water's Edge, 1975, Consensus at the Crossroads, 1972, La Dèclaration Universelle des Droits de l'Homme, 1991, Ah, Columbus! The Indian Discovery of America, 1993, The Universal Declaration of Human Rights 1948-1993, 1994, The Universal Declaration of Human Rights: A History of its Creation and Implementation, 1998; editor Indian Jour. Am. Studies, 1990-93; contbr. articles to profl. jours. Trustee Poughkeepsie Day Sch., 1968-72, 85-88, 99—, pres. bd. trustees, 1986-88; trustee Eleanor Roosevelt Ctr. at Val-Kill, 1986-90, 94-2002, v.p., 1989-90, 95-97, pres., 1997-2000; bd. dirs. Friends of Fulbright in India, 1995—, chmn. bd., 2003—. Named Sr. Fulbright lectr. U. Poona, India, 1977-78, sr. Fulbright lectr. India, 1990-93. Mem. Am. Polit. Sci. Assn., Assn. for Asian Studies, Internat. Studies Assn. Home: 39 Garfield Pl Poughkeepsie NY 12601-4321 Office: Vassar Coll Box 376 124 Raymond Ave Poughkeepsie NY 12604-0376 E-mail: johnsong@vassar.edu.

JOHNSON, MAURICE VERNER, JR., agricultural research and development executive; b. Duluth, Minn., Sept. 13, 1925; s. Maurice Verner Sr. and Elvira Marie (Westberg) J.; m. Darlene Ruth Durand, June 23, 1944; children: Susan Kay, Steven Dale. BS, U. Calif., 1953. Registered profl. engr. From research engr. to dir. research and devel. Sunkist Growers, Ontario, Calif., 1953-84, v.p. research and devel., 1984-90, ret., 1990—. V.p., dir. Calif. Citrus Quality Council, Claremont. Contbr. articles to profl. pubs.; patentee in field. Sgt. U.S. Army, 1944-46, ETO. Fellow Am. Soc. Agrl. Engrs. (dir. 1969-70); mem. ASME, Am. Inst. Indsl. Engrs., Am. Assn. Advancement Sci., Nat. Soc. Profl. Engrs., Tau Beta Pi. Republican. Avocation: golf.

JOHNSON, MICAH WILLIAM, television newscaster, director; b. Pitts., July 23, 1963; s. William T. and Joann K. (Pierce) J. Student, Indiana U. Pa., 1981-84. Announcer WLEM-AM/WQKY-FM, Emporium, Pa., 1978-81; news dir., anchorman WIUP-TV, Indiana, Pa., 1981-84; anchorman, reporter WSEE-TV, Erie, Pa., 1984-85; anchorman, mng. editor WVVA-TV, Bluefield, W.Va., 1985-86; news dir., anchorman WKYN-TV, St. Mary's, Pa., 1986-87; anchorman television and radio news Cable News Network, Atlanta, 1987-89; anchorman, corr. NBC-TV News, Washington, 1989-90; sr. producer radio & TV U.S. Senate, Washington, 1990; anchorman, news dir. Sta. KTSM-TV-AM-FM, El Paso, Tex., 1990-93, Sta. WTOV-TV, Steubenville, Ohio, 1993-94; dir. news Sta. WBRE-TV, Wilkes-Barre, Pa., 1994-96; news dir. Sta. WPXI-TV, Pitts., 1996-97; dir. news and prodn. WVIT-TV Paramount Pictures, Hartford, Conn., 1997—; pres., CEO Mediastars Internat., 2001—; v.p. news ops. Meredith Corp., 2001—. Talk show host Sta. KTSM Newsradio, El Paso, 1990-93; adj. prof. Dekalb Coll., Clarkston, Ga., 1987-89; bd. dirs. Conn. Assoc. Press. Vol. fireman Morris Twp. Fire Co., Morrisdale, Pa., 1980—, Erie Emergency Med. Svcs., 1984-85; dir. choir Morrisdale United Meth. Ch., 1982-87; bd. dirs. El Paso Humane Soc., El Paso Zool. Soc.; mem. adv. bd. Salvation Army. With Pa. N.G., 1981—. Recipient Presdl. Citation for Cmty. Svc., 1992, Best of the Best award/Cmty. Svc. Nat. Assn. Broadcasters, 1992, AP award, 1985, 86, 87, 90, 91, 92, 93, 94, 95, 96, 97, 98, Nat. Pianist award Am. Coll. Musicians, 1973-79, Ind. U. Disting. Alumni award, 1990, Gold medal award Internat. Radio Festival N.Y, 1990, Gavel award State Bar of Tex., 1992, Tex. Gov.'s award/Cmty. Svc., 1992, Outstanding Contbn. to Law Enforcement award combined law enforcement assns. of Tex., 1991-92, Spl. Recognition award U.S. Marshal's Svc., 1992, Pub. Safety award Pa. Gov., 1996; nominee Emmy award for Best Newscast, 1994, 95, 96, 97; recipient Emmy award for Best Newscast, 1997. Mem. NATAS (bd. govs.), Nat. Press Club, Radio-TV News Dirs. Assn. (Overall Excellence in News award), Conn. Assoc. Press Bd. Dirs. (v.p.), Nat. Radio Broadcasters Assn., El Paso Police Officers Assn. (hon.), White House Corrs. Assn., Nat. Wildlife Fedn. (bd. dirs. Ind. U. mag.), El Paso Humane Soc. (bd. dirs.), El Paso Zool Soc. (bd. dirs.) Nat. Press Club, El Paso Downtown Lions Club, Masons. Avocations: fishing, travel, piano. E-mail: ceo@mediastars.tv.

JOHNSON, MICHAEL, former international athlete; b. Dallas, Sept. 13, 1967; m. Kerry Johnson; 1 child. Student, Baylor U., 90. Ret., 1991. BBC sports commentator. Recipient Gold medal 200 meters Goodwill Games, 1990, 94, 4 x 100 relay Barcelona Olympics, 1992, 200 meters and 400 meters Summer Olympics, Atlanta, 1996; winner 200 meters World Athletic Championships, 1991, 400 meters, 1993; U.S. Nat. champion 200 meters, 1990-92, 95; named Athlete of Yr. USA Track & Field, 1993-94; world record holder indoor 400 meters, 200 meters at 1996 Olympics; gold medal for 400 meters World Championship, 1997., gold medalist, 400m & 4 x 400m, Sydney Olympic Games, 2000; first athlete to be ranked no. 1 in the world in both the 200m and 400m; 3 time recipient of the Jesse Owens award. Office: USA Track & Field PO Box 120 Indianapolis IN 46206-0120

JOHNSON, MICHAEL A. lawyer; b. Hornell, N.Y., Mar. 5, 1955; s. Richard C. and Patricia A. J.; m. Katherine A. Sheridan, Aug. 9, 1980; children: Michael Patrick, Kaitlyn Meghan. BA, St. Vincent Coll., 1977; JD, Ohio No. U., 1980. Bar: Pa. 1980, U.S. Dist. Ct. (we. dist.) Pa. 1980, U.S. Ct. Appeals (3rd cir.) 1991, U.S. Supreme Ct. 1988. Assoc. Hammer & Pollins, Greensburg, Pa., 1981-84; pvt. practice Mt. Pleasant, Pa., 1984—. Active Boy Scouts Am., 1969. Recipient Eagle Scout Boy Scouts Am. Mem. Pa. Bar Assn. (zone 6 bd. dels. 1996-99), Pa. Trial Lawyers Assn., Mental Health Assn. (pres. 1996-97, Fred Funari award 1998), Westmoreland Bar Assn. (life, chair planning com. 1990-92, mock trial advisor Mt. Pleasant Sch. 1993-95), Lawyers Abstract Westmoreland County (bd. dirs./ officer 1997-2001, pres. 2000), Ned J. Nakles Am. Inn of Ct. (master, sec., treas. 1997—). Avocations: automotive restoration, reading, coaching soccer, football. Office: 749 N Church St Mount Pleasant PA 15666-9147 E-mail: tjktmplaw@aol.com.

JOHNSON, MICHAEL KENNETH, chemistry educator; b. Tonbridge, Kent, Eng., Mar. 8, 1953; came to U.S., 1980; s. Thomas Sydney and Eileen J.; m. Carole Ann Woodhouse, Aug. 21, 1976; children: Caroline Louise, Thomas Michael. BA, Cambridge U., 1974, MA, 1977; MSc, U. East Anglia, 1975, PhD, 1977. Postdoctoral fellow U. East Anglia, Norwich, 1977-80; postdoctoral rsch. assoc. Princeton (N.J.) U., 1980-82; asst. prof. chemistry La. State U., Baton Rouge, 1982-86; assoc. prof. chemistry U. Ga., Athens, 1987-91, prof. chemistry, 1991-98, disting. rsch. prof. chemistry, 1998—, dir., 1993—. Biophysics grant rev. panel NSF, Washington, 1990-95; biophysics study sect. NIH, Washington, 2000—. Editor: Electron Transfer in Biology and the Solid State, 1990; contbr. articles to profl. jours. Alfred P. Sloan fellow, 1986; Rsch. grantee NIH, 1984, 87, 94, 2000, NSF, 1986, 90, 94, 98. Mem.: Am. Chem. Soc., Phi Kappa Phi. Home: 1100 Double Bridges Rd Winterville GA 30683-4830 Office: U Ga Dept Chemistry Athens GA 30602 E-mail: johnson@chem.uga.edu.

JOHNSON, MICHAEL LEE, accountant, controller; b. Jamestown, N.Y., May 9, 1967; s. Eugene S. Johnson and Joanne D. (DeVoe) Flint; m. Lisa A. Tousignant, Oct. 1, 1988; children: Benjamin M., Zachary T. Degree, Jamestown C.C., 1987, U. Pitts., Bradford, Pa., 1989; MBA, Otterbein Coll., 2000. Cert. mgmt. acct., fin. mgmt. Intern Acu-Rite, Inc., Jamestown, 1987-89; acctg. mgr. Cottingham Paper Co., Columbus, Ohio, 1989-95; v.p., treas., contr., asst. sec. Ohio Bar Title Ins. Co., Cleve., 1995—; v.p., contr. Midland Title Security, Inc., 2002—; treas. Port Lawrence Title and Trust Co., 2002—. Vol. Habitat for Humanity, 1997—, Boy Scouts Am. Mem. Am. Land Title Assn. (acctg. com. 1997-99, internal audit com. 1997-99), Inst. Mgmt. Accts., Vasa Order Am., Cin., Columbus, Dayton Pitt Club, Phi Theta Kappa. Methodist. Home: 8401 Bernice Dr Strongsville OH 44149-1022 Office: First Am Title Ins Co 1111 Superior Ave Ste 700 Cleveland OH 44114 E-mail: mljohnson@firstam.com.

JOHNSON, MICHAEL LEWIS, psychiatrist; b. Louisville, May 17, 1941; s. Ralph L. and Bee (Burr) J.; children: Kirstin, Aaron, Jessica; m. Frances Bourne. AB, Earlham Coll., Richmond, Ind., 1963; MD, Ind. U., 1968. Diplomate Am. Bd. Psychiatry and Neruology. Intern Marion County Gen. Hosp., Indpls., 1968-69; resident in psychiatry Wash. U. Barnes Hosp., St. Louis, 1969-72; staff psychiatrist U.S. Naval Hosp., Portsmouth, Va., 1972-74, South Cen. Community Mental Health Ctr., Bloomington, Ind., 1974-80; psychiatrist pvt. practice, Bloomington, Ind., 1974-83; unit dir. Milford-Whitinsville (Mass.) Regional Hosp., 1983-85; staff psychiatrist Harvard Vanguard Med. Assocs., Cambridge, Mass., 1985-2000, Peabody, Mass., 1997-2000, Boston, 2000—. Instr. in psychiatry Harvard Med. Sch., Boston, 1985—, mem. comm. skills task force, 2001--; instr. in psychiatry Cambridge Hosp., 1985-92, Brigham and Women's Hosp., 1993—; mem. credentials com. Harvard Pilgrim Health Care; mem. psychopharmacology com. and ctrl. psychiat. consultation svc. Harvard Vanguard Med. Assocs., mem. com. skills task force, Harvard Med. Sch., cons. psychiatrist Pain Program Harvard Vanguard Med. Assocs.; sci. adv. bd. mem. Ott Light Sys., Santa Monica, Calif., bd. dirs. Lenair Healing Found., Inc., Newbury, Mass. Author: (book chpt.) Psychotherapists Guide to Pharmacotherapy, 1989; subject of docudrama Virtuoso, 1991. Recipient Robert H. Ebert tchg. award Harvard Vanguard Med. Assocs., 1999; Harvard Macy fellow, 2003. Mem. Soc. Of Friends. Achievements include being subject of stage play and docudrama Virtuoso, 1996. Office: Harvard Vanguard Med Assocs 147 Mil Stt Boston MA 02109

JOHNSON, MICHAEL PAUL, history educator; b. Ponca City, Okla., July 6, 1941; s. Howard W. and Maybelle P. (Fetrow) J.; m. Anne E. Thompson, June 2, 1962; children: Ian Michael, Sarah Elizabeth. AB in Chemistry cum laude, Knox Coll., 1963; MA in History, Stanford U., 1967, PhD in History, 1973. Asst. prof. LeMoyne Coll., Memphis, 1967-68; instr. San Jose (Calif.) State U., 1970-71; asst. prof. history U. Calif., Irvine, 1971-77, assoc. prof., 1977-84, prof., 1984-94, Johns Hopkins U., Balt., 1994—. Author: Toward a Patriarchal Republic, 1977, Black Masters, 1984, No Chariot Let Down, 1984, The American Promise, 1998, Reading the American Past, 2 vols., 1998, Abraham Lincoln, Slavery and the Civil War, 2000. Fellow Am. Coun. Learned Socs., 1977, NEH, 1982, Ctr. for Advanced Study in Behavioral Scis., 1999-00. Mem. Am. Hist. Assn., Orgn. Am. Historians (ABC Clip Am. History and Life award 2003), So. Hist. Assn., Phi Beta Kappa. Office: Johns Hopkins U Dept History Baltimore MD 21218

JOHNSON, MICHAEL RANDY, bank executive; b. York, Nebr., Jan. 29, 1946; s. Sheldon Albert and Mary Lynn (Barbur) J.; m. Virginia L. Allgood, Apr. 5, 1975; children: Cory Michael, Scott Alan, Adam Todd. Student, Doane Coll., 1964-66, U. Nebr., 1966-68. Farmer, Geneva, Nebr., 1968-84; field reporter Agrl. Stabilization and Constrn. Svc., Geneva, 1973-80; adjuster Fed. Crop Ins. Corp., Kansas City, Kans., 1979-81, North Ctrl. Crop Ins., Eau Claire, Wis., 1981-84, Acceptance-Redland Ins. Co./Am. Agrisurance-Agrijusters, Council Bluffs, Iowa, 1984-86, field supr., 1986-88, tng. supr., 1988-90, regional claim supr., 1990-92, v.p., asst. claims mgr., 1993-94, claims mgr., sr. v.p., 1994-98, dir. claims and compliance, sr. v.p., 1998-2001; chief field svcs. officer Am. Assurance, 2001—02; agrl. ins. adv. and cert. agrl. arbitrator/mediator, 2003—; asst. v.p. Peoples Nat. Bank, Council Bluffs, Iowa. Cons. Segura La Comml. Monterey, Mex., 1988-92, Segures Am., Mexico City, 1988-92; contbg. bd. mem. Code of Ethics Bd. Nat. Crop Ins. Svc., Overland Park, Kans., 1992—; speaker in field. Author: (reference handbook) Grop Growth Patterns and Loss Adjustment, Mexico, 1991; editor: Crop Adjusting Manual, 1990, '91, '92. Mem. Masons. Methodist. Avocations: reading, fishing, platform speaking, plant studies. Home: 21845 Hwy 183 Crescent IA 51526 Office: Peoples Nat. Bank 306 W Erie PO Box 410 Missouri Valley IA 51555

JOHNSON, MICHAEL WARREN, international relations specialist; b. Mpls., Oct. 2, 1948; s. Warren Redy and Lorraine Agnes (Capistran) Johnson; m. Jeanine Ann Tyldesley, Feb. 6, 1971 (div. 1991); children: Benjamin T., Joseph A., Katherine E.; m. Deborah V. Matthews, July 26, 1991; children: Maximilian N., Scott M. BS, U.S. Mil. Acad., 1970; MA in Internat. Rels., U. So. Calif., 1973; PhD of Polit. Sci., MIT, 1985; postgrad., Harvard U., 1987. Commd. 2d lt. U.S. Army, 1970, advanced through grades to capt., 1974; resigned, 1975; sr. Mid. East analyst U.S. Army Mil. Intelligence, 1975; stockbroker Merrill Lynch, Pierce, Fenner & Smith, Inc., Boston, 1975—81; v.p. Thomson McKinnon Securities Inc., Boston, 1981—82; 1st v.p. Jefferies & Co., Boston, 1982—84; sr. v.p. Moseley, Hallgarten, Estabrook & Weeden, Inc., Boston, 1984—88; internat. rels. cons. Geopolitical Strategist, Inc., 1984—. Fgn. policy adv. to Congl. adv., 1980. Mem.: Assn. Grads. U.S. Mil. Acad.

JOHNSON, MIKKEL BORLAUG, physicist; b. Waynesboro, Va., Jan. 2, 1943; s. Wallace A. and Anne D. (Davies) J.; m. Lynne McFadden, June 14, 1966; children: Kara Marit, Krista Lynne. BS, Va. Poly. Inst., 1966; MS, Carnegie Mellon U., 1968, PhD, 1970. Rsch. assoc. Cornell U., Ithaca, N.Y., 1970-72; staff mem., fellow Los Alamos (N.Mex.) Nat. Lab., 1972—. Vis. prof. SUNY, Stony Brook, 1981-82, Carnegie Mellon U., 1997-98. Editor: Relativistic Dynamics and Quark-Nuclear Physics, 1986, Nuclear and Particle Physics on the Light Cone, 1989, LAMPF Workshop on (Pi,K) Physics, 1991; assoc. editor Nuclear Physics, 1975-97. Lab. fellow Los Alamos Nat. Lab, 1991; recipient Humboldt award for Sr. U.S. Scientist, Humboldt Found., 1986. Fellow Am. Phys. Soc. Home: 118 Piedra Loop Los Alamos NM 87544-3828 Office: Los Alamos Nat Lab P divsn Ms H846 Los Alamos NM 87545-0001 E-mail: mbjohnson@lanl.gov.

JOHNSON, MILDRED GRACE MASH, investment company executive; b. Castle Rock, Wash., Mar. 3, 1922; d. Percival and Hilda C. (Nyberg) M.; widowed, 1988; children: John, Joy, Judy, Chris, Steven. Student, U. Wash. Pres. Johnson Investment Co., Seattle, 1988—. Deacon U. Presbyn. Ch., Seattle, 1981—. Mem. Am. Bus. Women's Assn. (v.p. 1979-89, Woman of Yr. 1981), Apt. Opt. Assn. (hon. 25 Yr. Mem.), Master Builders, Daus. Nile, Order of Ea. Star. Republican. Avocations: entertaining, skiing, writing, reading, traveling. Home: 3812 E Mcgilvra St Seattle WA 98112-2427

JOHNSON, MILLARD WALLACE, JR., mathematics and engineering educator; b. Racine, Wis., Feb. 1, 1928; s. Millard Wallace and Marian Manilla (Rittman) J.; m. Ruth Pugh Gifford, Dec. 26, 1953; children: Millard Wallace III, Jeannette Marian Brooks, Charles Gifford, Peter Allen. BS in Applied Math. and Mechanics, U. Wis., 1952, MS, 1953; PhD in Math, MIT, 1957. Rsch. asst. MIT, 1953-57, lectr., 1957-58; mem. staff Math. Rsch. Ctr. U. Wis., Madison, 1958-94, prof. mechanics, 1958-63, prof. mechanics and math., 1964-94, mem. staff Rheology Rsch. Ctr., 1970—, mem. Engine Rsch. Ctr., 1985—, prof. emeritus, 1994—. Contbr. articles to profl. jours. Adv. bd. Internat. Math. and Statis. Librs. (IMSL), 1971-92. With USN, 1946-48. Fellow ASME; mem. Soc. Rheology, Soc. Indsl. and Applied Math., Am. Acad. Mechanics, Brit. Soc. Rheology, Wis. Acad. Scis., Arts and Letters, Phi Beta Kappa. Home: 802 Blue Ridge Pkwy Madison WI 53705-1148 Office: U Wis Dept Eng Phys 1500 Engineering Dr Madison WI 53706-1609

JOHNSON, MILTON LEE, civil engineer; b. Lake Mills, Iowa, Dec. 7, 1931; s. Selmer Melvin and Dorothea Adaline (Ruby) J.; m. Myrtle J. Engelby, Mar. 22, 1953; children: Marlys, Emily, Diane, Darrell, Steven. BS in Civil Engring., Iowa State U., 1957. Registered profl. engr., Iowa. Asst. resident engr. Iowa Hwy. Commn., Britt and Decorah, 1957-62; engr. Clayton County, Elkader, Iowa, 1962-80, Wapello County, Ottumwa, Iowa, 1980-87; exec. dir. Nat. Assn. County Engrs., 1987-91; resident constrn. engr. Iowa Dept. Transp., Ottumwa, 1991—94. Mem. NSPE, ASCE (Wilber S. Smith award 1992), Nat. Assn. County Engrs. (pres. 1977-78, exec. dir. 1979-91), ARTBA (bd. dirs. 1980-92, Ralph R. Bartelsmeyer award 1992), Iowa County Engrs. Assn. (pres. 1969, Engr. of Yr. 1972, Spl. Svc. award 1985). Lutheran. Home and Office: 405 Chestnut St Box 326 Monona IA 52159

JOHNSON, MORGAN BURTON, artist, writer; b. Santa Monica, Calif., Nov. 25, 1952; s. Arnold and Roma (Burton) Johnson. BA in Psychology, U. Calif., San Diego, 1974; cert. fgn. studies, Lycee du U., Dijon, France, 1968. Mgr. Coronet Stores, Las Vegas, Nev., 1975; mgr., chef Diver's Cove Restaurant, Long Beach, Calif., 1977-80; prodn. control asst. Century Plastics, Compton, Calif., 1980; prodn. supr. Analytichem Internat., Harbor City, Calif., 1980-81; sr. planner Sci. Mfg./Am. Hosp., Emeryville, Calif., 1982-85; materials mgr. Applied Biosys. (Perkin-Elmer), Foster City, Calif., 1985-90. Owner, pres. Two Bears Restoration, 1990—. Exhibited in group shows at Medford (Oreg.) Ctr., 1993, Mills House Art Gallery, Garden Grove, Calif., 1979, San Bernardino Mus. Art, 1980-81, Calif. Poly. State U., San Luis Obispo, 1985, West Coast Biennial, Pacific Grove Art Ctr., 1985, Cunningham Meml. Art Show, Bakersfield, Calif., 1985, The Rogue Gallery, Medford, 1984-85, 90-91, C. Erickson Gallery, Half Moon Bay, Calif., 1986-90, Britt Music Festival, Jacksonville, Oreg., 1994; one-man shows include OJAC Gallery, Jacksonville, Oreg., 2002, Cache Salon, Walnut Creek, 1996, First Congl. Ch., Long Beach, 1996, Giustina Gallery, Oreg. State U., 2002, Valley View Winery, Ruch, Oreg., 2003, Coos Art Mus., 2003; represented in permanent collections; author: Trees of Other Colors, 1994, Condemned to a Life of Painting Pretty Pictures, 1994, Circle of the White Buffalo, 1996, Memories of Aunt Aura, 2000; published in Nat. Libr. Poetry Anthology, 1997-2001, Future Present, 2002. Mem. So. Oreg. Arts Coun., Medford, 1990—, San Francisco Artist's Coop, 1980-83; fin. sec. Long Beach Art Assn., 1978-79; hanging com. mem. San Diego Art Inst., 1974-76. Recipient 1st prize Recreation and Parks Dept., L.A., 1965, 66, Long Beach Art Assn., 1977, 3d pl. award Downey Mus. Art, 1977, 78, So. Oreg. Lambda Excellence award for art, 1997, 98. Avocations: hiking, gardening. Home and Office: 10370 Sterling Creek Rd Jacksonville OR 97530 E-mail: morganjart@aol.com.

JOHNSON, MURRAY H. optometrist, researcher, consultant, lecturer; b. Montreal, Que., Can., Jan. 29, 1956; arrived in U.S., 1980; s. William and Leah (Bedzowski) J.; m. Linda Fluxman, Apr. 30, 1978; children: Warren Natan, Tanya Yael, Arielle Carly. Diploma in Optometry, Witwatersrand Coll., Johannesburg, 1977; postgrad., U. Montreal, 1980; BS, OD, U. Houston, 1981, MSc in Physiol. Optics and Vision Sci., 1984; postgrad., U. Tex. Health Ctr., 1983. Lic. optometrist, Tex., 1983, therapeutic lic., Tex., 1992; cert. ocular therapeutics for treatment and mgmt. ocular disease U. Houston, 1992; cert. optometric glaucoma specialist, U. Houston, 2002. Clin. instr. U. Houston, 1981-85, postdoct. fellow, 1981-84; researcher Inst. contact Lens Rsch., Houston, 1983-88; pvt. practice optometry specializing in contact lenses Eye & Contact Lens Assocs. North Tex., Dallas, 1985—. Vis. asst. prof. U. Houston, 1984-85, adj. asst. prof., 1985-89; cons., clin. investigator Metro Optics, Inc., Dallas, 1989—; premktg. clin. evaluator, cons. and investigator to various contact lens and pharm. mfrs., 1989—; clin. investigator Paragon Optical, Mesa, Ariz., 1992; cons. Unilens Corp., Largo, Fla., 1989; clin. examiner Nat. Bd. Clin. Skills Exam., Nat. Bd. Examiners in Optometry, 1997—. Contbr. articles to profl. jours. Mem. clin. care com. Global Vision Inst., Global Vision Dallas, 1996; mem. edn. com. Akiba Acad. Dallas, 1986—88, bd. dirs., 1986—97, long range planning com., 1987—88, devel. com., 1993, v.p., treas, 1993—94, budget com., 1993—96, scholarship com, 1994—2002; bd. dirs. Congregation Share Tefilla, Dallas, 1988—92; steering com. B'nai B'rith, 1986—88, treas., 1987—88; mem.-at-large Jewish edn. com. Jewish Fedn. Dallas, 1998—99; mem. Jewish identity and values experiences com. Jewish Edn. Dept., 1999—, chair, 2000—01; local beneficiaries subcom., allocations com. Jewish Fedn. Greater Dallas, 1999—2000, mem. renaissance and renewal subcom. planning and allocations com., 2000—; chair Jewish identity and values experiences subcom. Jewish Edn. Com., 2000—01. Postdoctoral fellow U. Houston, 1981-84, grantee 1981, 82; Ezell Rsch. fellow Am. Optometric Found., 1983. Fellow Am. Acad. Optometry; mem. AAAS, Assn. Rsch. in Vision and Ophthalmology, Am. Pub. Health Assn. (vision care sect.), Am. Optometric Assn. (contact lens sect.), Tex. Optometric Assn., Dallas County Optometric Soc., Am. Optometric Found. (Ezell fellows club), Sigma Xi. Jewish. Avocations: walking, swimming, racquetball. Office: Eye & Contact Lens Assocs N Tex 18111 Preston Rd Ste 180 Dallas TX 75252-6009

JOHNSON, NANCY ANN, education educator, educator; b. Worcester, Mass., May 12, 1932; d. Arthur Eugene and Anna Evelyn (Erickson) J. BA, Clark U., 1955, MA in Edn., 1957; EdD, Boston U., 1977. Tchr. pub. schs., Auburn, Mass., 1956-63, reading supr. Groton, Mass., 1963-68; asst. prof. edn. Worcester State Coll., 1968-78, assoc. prof., 1978, prof., 1982, chair dept. edn., 1982-84, 91, coord. student teaching, 1980-83; adv. bd., local sch. Mem. pastoral com. Peoples Ch., Worcester, 1973-80, Christian edn. com., 1978-91, sec., 1990-94, ch. libr. extension, 1992-93, adult edn. coord.; mem. exec. bd. Friends of Worcester Pub. Libr., 1980—, sec., 1981-82; coord. book sale vols.; corporator Worcester YWCA; mem. state lit. coun.; bd. dirs. Brittan Sq. Neighborhood Coun.; docent Worcester Hist. Mus., 1995—; sec. Clark Alumnae Coun., 1961-66; grant writer tree project City of Worcester-Brittan Sq. Neighborhood Coun.; docent Preservation Worcester, 1999, mem. endangered prop. com.; bd. dirs., lectr. Friends of Hope Cemetery; chair scholarship com. Worcester Women's Club. Mem. AAUW, Mass. Assn. Tchr. Educators (pres. 1987-88), Delta Kappa Gamma (sec. Tay chpt. 1974-76, 1st v.p. chpt. 1976, pres. 1990-92), Pi Lambda Theta (pres Alpha Gamma chpt. 1979-81, mem. exec. bd. chpt. 1975-79), Phi Delta Kappa (Educator of Yr. 1993, advisor ctrl. chpt. chair rsch. ctrl. Mass. chpt. found. rep., scholarship chair), Kappa Delta Pi (co-counselor), Worcester Womens Club (scholarship chair), Boston U. Womens Club (pres.), Boston U. Alumni Club Worcester County (pres. 1992-94, nominating chair, scholarship chair). Friends of Hope Cemetery Program Chr. Office: 486 Chandler St Worcester MA 01602-2832

JOHNSON, NANCY ELIZABETH, bookseller; b. Des Moines, July 21, 1953; d. Walter Eugene and Frances Goodman (Eaton) J. BS, Drake U., 1975. Page Legislature State of Iowa, Des Moines, 1967-69, asst. bill clk., 1970-71; pub. rels. Conv. and Visitors Bur., Des Moines, 1975-76; antique show promoter Collector's Extravaganza, Denver, 1976—; bookseller The Library, 1977—; owner, mgr. The Libr., Des Moines, 1977—. Pres., CEO Collectors Extravaganza Corp., 1996—; dir. The Frances Goodman Johnson Found., 1998—. Mem. Internat. Booksellers Fedn., Mountains & Plains Booksellers Assn., Profl. Show Mgrs. Assn. (bd. dirs. 1999--, v.p. 2001-02, pres. 2003--), Cyclone Corvettes, Inc. (bd. dirs. 1998), Alpha Kappa Delta, Kappa Delta Pi, Psi Chi. Republican. Protestant. Avocations: languages, skiing, competition driving. Home: 2737 E Euclid Ave Des Moines IA 50317-4243 Office: PO Box 692 Des Moines IA 50303-0692

JOHNSON, NANCY LEE, congresswoman; b. Chgo., Jan. 5, 1935; d. Noble Wishard and Gertrude Reid (Smith) Lee; m. Theodore H. Johnson, June 27, 1932; children— Lindsey Lee, Althea Anne, Caroline Reid BA, Radcliffe Coll., 1957; postgrad., U. London, 1957-58. Vice chmn. Charter Commn. New Britain, Conn., 1976-77; mem. Conn. Senate from 6th dist., 1977-82, 98th-108th Congresses from 6th and 5th Conn. dist., Washington, 1983—; mem. ways and means com., chmn. health subcom. 101st-108th Congresses from 6th and 5th Conn. Dist., Washington. Pres. Friends of Libr., New Britain Pub. Libr., 1973-76, Radcliffe Club Northern Conn., 1973-75; bd. dirs., pres. Sheldon Cmty. Guidance Clinic, 1974-75; dir. religious edn. Unitarian Universalist Soc. New Britain, 1967-72; bd. dirs. United Way New Britain, 1976.79. Recipient Outstanding Vol. award United Way, 1976; English Speaking Union grantee, 1958-59 Republican. Home: 141 S Mountain St New Britain CT 06052-1511 Office: Ho of Reps 2113 Rayburn Bldg Washington DC 20515-0705

JOHNSON, NANCY PELANDER, medical/surgical nurse, writer; b. Washington, D.C., Apr. 30, 1953; d. Carl Edward and Isabelle Neff Pelander; m. Richard Paul Johnson; children: Rebecca Anne, Beverly Jean. BA in Spanish, U. Colo., 1977; nursing degree, Mesa C.C., 1999. Nurse Springdale West Healthcare, Mesa, Ariz.; freelance writer Mesa. Author: (children's book) 95 Animals of the Bible, 1997; contbr. religious articles to publs. Lutheran. Avocations: art, music, writing, fishing, camping. E-mail: nancy5356@cableaz.com.

JOHNSON, NANCY PLATTNER, secondary education educator; b. Milw., July 1, 1938; d. Paul and Mary (Kalns) Plattner; m. Orville Johnson III, July 1, 1978. BS, U. Chgo., 1960; postgrad., Ohio State U., 1965; M, U. Cen. Fla., Orlando, 1974; PhD, U. Wis., 1979. Cert. elem. tchr. Tchr. Harvard Sch. for Boys, Chgo., 1960-61; math. tchr. Boone County Schs., Columbia, Mo., 1962-64, Columbus, Ohio, 1964-66; math. instr. U. Wis., Stevens Point, 1966-72; math. educator Orange County, Orlando, Fla., 1972-76; rsch. grad. asst., instr. U. Wis., Madison, 1976-79; vis. assoc. prof. Stetson U., Orlando, 1980-81; math. educator Seminole County Sch. Bd., Sanford, Fla., 1982—. Contbr. articles to profl. jours. Bd. dirs. Crown Oaks Springs Cmty. Assn., 1974—. NSF grantee Ohio State U., 1964-65; NSF fellow U. Wis., 1976-79. Mem. NEA, Math. Assn. Am., Nat. Coun. Tchrs. Math., Fla. Teaching Profl., Fla. Math. Coun., Seminole County Math. Coun., Semimole County Edn. Assn. Avocations: art, music, writing. Home: 212 Jasmine Ln Longwood FL 32779-4908

JOHNSON, NANCY RUTH, nurse; b. Gorman, Tex., Feb. 15, 1957; d. Dale Newton and Perelene Ruth (Wright) Johnson; 1 child, Joseph Dale. BSN, Tex. Woman's U., Denton, 1980. Staff nurse Baylor U. Med. Ctr., Dallas, 1980-81; charge nurse ICU/CCU DeLeon Hosp., Tex., 1981-82; staff nurse MICU/CCU VA Med. Ctr., Phoenix, 1982-83; staff nurse Harris Hosp. Meth., Ft. Worth, 1983-84, Tex. Dept. Health, Stephenville, 1984-95; nurse Dublin Ind. Sch. Dist., 1995—. Mem. Tex. Woman's U. Alumni Assn., Epsilon Sigma Alpha. Lodges: Order Eastern Star. Home: 1124 Apache Dr De Leon TX 76444-9801 Office: 701 Thomas St Dublin TX 76446-1617

JOHNSON, NAOMI BOWERS, nurse; b. Ft. Benning, Ga., Aug. 17, 1954; d. Bob and Henrietta Violet (Hoomalu) Bowers; m. James William Johnson, Dec. 7, 1973 (div.); children: Amelia, Melissa, Charity, James-William. ADN, Troy State U., Montgomery, Ala., 1974. Office supr., lab. supr., nursing coord. physician's office, Selma, Ala.; patients care coord. West. Ala. Home Health Agy., Selma; discharge planning/social svcs., SOBRA and clin. case mgmt. coord. Vaughan Regional Med. Ctr. Hosp., Selma; DON Dunn Nursing Home, Selma, Capitol Hill Health Care Ctr.; dir. mktg. and admissions Mariner Post Acute Health Care Network, Montgomery, Ala.; DON Ball Healthcare-Lighthouse, Selma. Author (poet): Publish America/International Poet Society, 2002—03. E-mail: hoomalu@bellsouth.net.

JOHNSON, NEAL FREDERICK, psychological scientist, educator; b. Willmar, Minn., May 1, 1934; s. Malcolm Ruben and Helen Laura Johnson; m. Kathleen A. Crimmins, Sept. 9, 1960 (dec. Jan. 2000); children: Neal, Margaret (dec. Sept. 1999), Elizabeth, Michael. *Neal Johnson is an Eagle Scott, as is his son Michael. His grandson Neal III is very close to Eagle; his granddaughter Evelyn Grace Johnson is very active in Girl Scouts, and his grandsons Christopher and Alexander Taylor are active in Cubs. His paternal grandfather, N.F. Johnson, was founding member of the Green Giant Corp. BOD, later chairman. His father owned a dairy and ice cream manufacturing plant, was on BOD Boy Scouts of America, BOD of the Salvation Army, BOD Bank of Willmar, and was listed in Who's Who in Commerce and Industry (1953). His grandson Neal F. Johnson III is listed in Who's Who Among American High School Students (2001-2002).* BA, U. Minn., 1956, PhD, 1961. Prof. psychology Ohio State U., Columbus, 1961—. Vis. prof. U. Calif., Berkeley, 1965, 74, 75, 77, 78, 83. Contbr. articles to profl. jours.; assoc. editor Jour. Memory and Lang., 1984-88; consulting editor Jour. Verbal Learning and Verbal Behavior, 1965-84, Memory & Cognition, 1972-82, Jour. Exptl. Psychology: Human Perception and Performance, 1978-82, Jour. Exptl. Psychology: Learning, Memory and Cognition, 1982-89, Jour. Memory and Lang., 1988-94, Gen. Psychology Rev., 1996—. Mem. com. Troop 312 Boy Scouts Am., Columbus, 1974-81. Rsch. scholar Tozer Found., Stillwater, Minn., 1959; grantee U.S. Office Edn., NIH, NSF. Fellow APA (pres. Soc. Gen. Psychology 1995, pres. divsn. exptl. psychology 1996), AAAS (governing coun. 1998-2000, chair psychology sect. 2002—); mem. Psychonomic Soc. (pres. 1997), Coun. Sci. Soc. Presidents, Midwestern Psychol. Assn. (pres. 1987). Presbyterian. Avocations: downhill skiing, fencing. Home: 5478 Rockwood Rd Columbus OH 43229-4324 Office: Dept Psychology Ohio State U Columbus OH 43210 E-mail: johnson.64@osu.edu.

JOHNSON, NEIL ARTHUR, composer, educator; b. Minot, Nd, Sept. 16, 1945; s. Francis James and Mildred Lenore Johnson; m. Paulette Claire Olson, May 29, 1968; children: Chad Michael, Shannon Lee. BS, Minot State Univ., Minot, ND, 1967. Educator Upham Pub. Schools, Upham, ND, 1967—70, Bottineau Pub. Schools, Bottineau, 1970—83; grad. tchg. asst. Colo. State Univ., Fort Collins, 1983—84; educator Blevins Jr. H.S., Fort Collins, 1984—97, Rocky Mountain H.S., Fort Collins, 1997—. Composer Published 62 Songs. Recipient Tchr. of the Yr., Bottineau Jaycees, ND, 1980. Mem.: Music Educators Nat. Conf., Am. Choral Directors Assn. Avocation: golfing. Home: 1919 Leicester Way Fort Collins CO 80526-1204 Office: Rocky Mountain High School 1300 West Swallow Road Fort Collins CO 80526

JOHNSON, NEIL MONROE, test engineer; b. Groton, Conn., Nov. 4, 1970; s. Donald Monroe and Martha Ann (Akin) J. BS in Mech. Engring., Clemson (S.C.) U., 1992; MS in Mech. Engring., Vanderbilt U., Nashville, Tenn., 1996. Design engr. Tri-Tech Svcs., Selma, Ala., 1992-93; test engr. Oceaneering Space Sys., Houston, 1997-2000, Raytheon, Houston, 2000, U.S. Environmental Protection Agency, Ann Arbor, 2000—. Author: Small 6B Orbital Replaceable Unit Hardware to Robotic System, 1999, Plasma Contactor Unit Orbital Replaceable Unit Hardware to Robotic System Integration Standards, 1999. Named Employee of Qtr., Oceaneering Space Sys., 1997, recipient Elite Team award, 1998, Superior Svc. award, 1998, Engring. Directorate-NASA Johnson Space Ctr., 1998, Cert. of Appreciation Am. Inst. Aeronautics and Astronautics, Houston Sect., 1999. Mem. ASME, Am. Inst. of Aeronautics and Astronautics, ASM Internat., Soc. of Auto. Engrs. Avocations: auto racing, snow skiing, biking, hiking. Home: 1554 Jones Dr Ann Arbor MI 48105 Office: NVFEL 2565 Plymouth Rd Ann Arbor MI 48105 E-mail: neilmjohnson@hotmail.com., johnson.neil@epa.gov.

JOHNSON, NEWELL WALTER, oral pathologist, physician; b. Melbourne, Australia, Aug. 5, 1938; B in Dental Sci., U. Melbourne, 1961, M in Dental Sci., 1963; PhD, U. Bristol, 1967. Lectr. Univ. Coll. Hosp., London, 1963-64; scientific staff U. Bristol, UK, 1964-67; reader in exptl. oral pathology London Hosp., 1968-76; cons. dental surgeon Royal London Hosp., 1968—. Co-founder, chief exec. editor Oral Diseases; dir. WHO Collaborating Ctr. for Oral CancerPrecancer. Editor Jour. Periodontal Rsch., 1985-95; editl. bd. Jour. Clin. Periodontology, Jour. Pathology; reviewer jours. in field; contbr. numerous articles to profl. jours., chpts. to books. Fellow Royal Coll. Surgeons England, Royal Australasian Coll. Dental Surgeons, Royal Coll. Pathologists, Royal Coll. Pathologists Australasia, Acad. Med. Scis., Acad. Medicine UK; mem. Internat. Assn. Dental Rsch, Br. Soc. Dental Rsch., Br. Dental Assn., Royal Soc. Medicine (pres. sec. odontology 1989-90), Internat. Assn. Oral Pathologists, Br. Soc. Oral Medicine, Br. Soc Periodontology, Br. Assn. Head & Neck Oncologists, Royal Microscopical Soc., Zool. Soc. London, Fedn. Dentaire Internat., Pathol. Soc. Gr. Britain & Ireland, European Orgn. Caries Rsch., Br. Assn. Study of Cmty. Dentistry, Bone & Tooth Soc., Rsch. Def. Soc., European Cancer Prevention Assn., Assn. Profs. of Dentistry. Office: Guys Kings St Thomas Sch Med Dentstry Biomed Scis Kings Dentl Inst Caldecot Rd London SE5 9RW England Fax: 0171-346 3624. E-mail: newell.johnson@kcl.ac.uk.

JOHNSON, NEWKIRK LYNN, not-for-profit developer; b. Olean, N.Y., Apr. 18, 1969; s. Jeffrey Lynn and Jacquelyn Fern Johnson. BA in Philosophy, Albion Coll., Mich., 1991; M in Environ. Studies, The Evergreen State Coll., Olympia, Wash., 1999. Biol. sci. technician Rock Creek Nat. Pk., Washington, 1999; exec. dir. Friends of Allegheny Wilderness, Warren, Pa., 2001—. Author: (jour. article) Natural Areas Jour., Wild Earth Jour. County coord. Jerry Brown for Pres., Canandaigua, NY, 1992. Independent. Avocations: football, swimming, hiking, photography. Office: Friends of Allegheny Wilderness 220 Ctr St Warren PA 16365 E-mail: kjohnson@pawild.org.

JOHNSON, NICHOLAS, writer, lawyer, lecturer; b. Iowa City, Sept. 23, 1934; s. Wendell A.L. and Edna (Bockwoldt) Johnson; m. Karen Mary Chapman, 1952 (div. 1972); children: Julie, Sherman, Gregory; m. Mary Eleanor Vasey, 1991; 1 child, Alexander. BA, U. Tex., 1956, LL.B., 1958; L.H.D., Windham Coll., 1971. Bar: Tex. 1958, D.C. 1963, U.S. Supreme Ct. 1963, Iowa 1974; lic. radio amateur. Law clk. to judge John R. Brown, U.S. 5th Circuit Ct. Appeals, 1958-59; law clk. to U.S. Supreme Ct. Justice Hugo L. Black, 1959-60; acting assoc. prof. law U. Calif. at Berkeley, 1960-63; assoc. Covington & Burling, Washington, 1963-64; adminstr. Maritime Adminstrn., chmn. Maritime Subsidy Bd. U.S. Dept. Commerce, 1964-66; commr. FCC, 1966-73; adj. prof. law Georgetown U., 1971-73; Poynter fellow Yale U., 1971; vis. prof. U. Ill., Champaign-Urbana, 1976, U. Okla., Norman, 1978, Ill. State U., Normal, 1979, U. Wis., Madison, 1980, Newhouse Sch., Syracuse U., 1980, U. Iowa Coll. Law, 1981—; vis. prof. dept. communications studies U. Iowa, 1982-85; vis. prof. Western Behavioral Scis. Inst., U. Calif., San Diego, 1986-91. Vis. prof. Calif. State U., Los Angeles, 1986, New Sch. Soc. Resource ConnectEd, 1990, U. Iowa dept. theater arts, 1999; regents prof. U. Calif., San Diego, 2000; co-dir. U. Iowa Inst. for Health, Behavior and Environ. Policy, 1990-93; chmn., dir. Nat. Citizens Comm. Lobby, 1975—, Nat. Citizens Com. for Broadcasting, 1974-78; pub. access, 1975-77; commentator Nat. Pub. Radio, 1975-77, 83-86, Sta. WRC-AM, Washington, 1977, Sta. WSUI, Iowa City, 1982-87; presdl. advisor White House Conf. on Libraries and Info. Services, 1979; exec. com. World Acad. Art and Sci., 1993-97. Author: Cases and Materials on Oil and Gas Law, 1962, How to Talk Back to Your Television Set, 1970, Japanese transl., 1971, Life Before Death in the Corporate State, 1971, Test Pattern for Living, 1972, Broadcasting in America, 1973, Cases and Materials on Communications Law and Policy, 1981, 82, 83, 84, 85, 86, Readings for Law of Electronic Media, 1993-94, (with David Loundy) Law of Electronic Media in a Cyberspace Age, 1996; syndicated columnist: Gannett News Service, 1982-84, Register and Tribune Syndicate, 1984, Cowles Syndicate, 1985-86, King Features Syndicate, 1986, Iowa City Press Citizen, 1998-2001; contbr. to legal, gen., internat. publs.; contbg. editor, host PBS The New Tech Times, 1983-84. Dem. candidate for U.S. Ho. of Reps. from 3d Iowa Dist., 1974; bd. dirs. Ctr. for Study Commercialism, 1991-96, Citizens Ind. Pub. Broadcasting, 1999-2002, Common Cause, 1990-96, Internat. Soc. Gen. Semantics, 1960-2000, Iowa City Cmty. Sch. Dist., 1998-2001, Virtual Classroom Project, 1990-91, Vol. in Tech. Assistance, 1994-2000; mem. adv. bd. Ctr. Media Edn., 1993-, Cultural Environ., Movement, 1992-, Fairness and Accuracy in Reporting, 1996—, Inst. Pub. Accuracy, 1997-, Open Soc. Inst. Media Group, 1999-2000, Project Censored, 1976-, U. Iowa Info. Arcade, 1991-92, War and Peace Found., 1988-, Working Assets Long Distance, 1992-96; mem. Broadband and Telecom. Commn., Iowa City, 1981-87. Named One of 10 Outstanding Young Men in U.S., U.S. Jaycees, 1967, recipient New Republic Pub. Defender award, 1970, Civil Liberties Award Ga. ACLU, 1972, DeWitt Carter Reddick award U. Tex., 1977, George Stoney award Nat. Fedn. Local Cable Programmers, 1987; fellow World Acad. Art and Sci., 1991—. Mem. D.C., Iowa Bar Assn. (Citizenship award 1951), State Bar Tex., Golden Key, Order of Coif, Phi Beta Kappa, Phi Delta Phi, Phi Eta Sigma, Pi Sigma Alpha. Democrat. Unitarian Universalist. Home and Office: PO Box 1876 Iowa City IA 52244-1876 E-mail: njohnson@inav.net.

JOHNSON, NIEL MELVIN, archivist, historian; b. Galesburg, Ill., July 28, 1931; s. Clarence Herman and Frances Albertina (Nelson) J.; m. Verna Gail Applegate, May 1, 1952; children: Kristin, David. BA, Augustana Coll., 1953; MA, State U. Iowa, 1965, PhD, 1971. Tchr. Unit #115, Biggsville, Ill., 1954-57; asst. historian U.S. Army Weapons Command, Rock Island, Ill., 1957-60, chief historian, 1960-63; instr. Augustana Coll., Rock Island, Ill., 1967-69; asst. prof. Dana Coll., Blair, Nebr., 1969-74; vis. asst. prof. U. Nebr., Omaha, 1975-76; archivist, historian Harry S. Truman Libr., Independence, Mo., 1977-92. Pres. Portal to the Plains, Inc., Blair, Nebr., 1973-77, Am. Friends of Emigrant Inst. Sweden, East Moline, Ill., 1984-89. Author: George S. Viereck: German-American Propagandist, 1972, Portal to the Plains, 1974, Power, Money and Women: Words to the Wise from Harry S. Truman, 1999; co-author: Rockford Swedes: American Stories, 1993; contbr. articles in field to profl. jours., newspapers. Coord. New Sweden '88 com. of Greater Kansas City, Mo.; chmn. Historic Trails City Com., Independence, 1988-93. Recipient Commendation, Concordia Hist. Inst., St. Louis, 1977. Mem. Midwestern Archives Conf., Jackson County Hist. Soc., Scandinavian Assn. (pres. 1987-89). Democrat. Lutheran. Avocations: painting, writing, photography, golf, impersonator of Harry S. Truman. Home: 15804 Kiger Cir Independence MO 64055-3750

JOHNSON, NILS, JR., minister; b. Balt., Apr. 3, 1930; s. Nils and Hazel Margaret (Caulk) J.; m. Marian Baker, June 10, 1950 (div. Dec. 30, 1971); children: Nils III, Lief Todd, Marta Kristine, Peter Kurt; m. Crystal Ann Wolfe, June 22, 1979; children: Thomas Ned Wolfe, Timothy Marlowe Wolfe (dec.). BS, Ind. U., 1955; B in Divinity, Oberlin Coll., 1958; postgrad., Drew U., 1963-67. Ordained clergy Evangelical Luth. Ch. in Am. Pastor Florence (Ohio) Congregational Ch., 1958-60; assoc. pastor St. Jacobs Luth. Ch., Miamisburg, Ohio, 1960-63; pastor Epiphany Luth. Ch., Warren, N.J., 1963-72; campus pastor Kutztown (Pa.) U., 1972-92; chaplain Muhlenberg Coll., Allentown, Pa.,

1993-96. Campus ministry cons. NEPA Synod Evangelical Luth. Ch. Am., Wescosville, Pa., 1981-93, divsn. for edn., Chgo., 1993-96. Pres. bd. dirs. Reading (Pa.)-Berks Campfire Girls, 1975-76; exec. bd. dirs. Friend, Inc., Berks County, Pa., 1985-92; bd. dirs. Reading-Berks Pa. Habitat for Humanity, 1999—. With USAF, 1951—54. Monroe fellow, 1958-89. Avocations: woodworking, sailing. Home: 8 Curtis Rd Kutztown PA 19530-9205 E-mail: cryslin@msn.com.

JOHNSON, NOBLE MARSHALL, research scientist; b. San Francisco, Feb. 23, 1945; BSEE cum laude, U. Calif., Davis, 1967, MSEE, 1970; PhD, Princeton U., 1974. Rsch. staff SRI Internat., Menlo Park, Calif., 1974—76; from rsch. staff to sr. rsch. staff Xerox Palo Alto Rsch. Ctr., Palo Alto, 1976—87, prin. scientist Electronic Materials lab., 1987—; mgr. Optoelectronic Materials and Devices, 1999—. Vis. lectr. Princeton (NJ) U., 1986, U. Erlangen-Nürnberg, Germany, 1988; presenter in field. Co-editor: 5 books; contbr. over 325 articles to profl. jours.; patentee in field. Recipient Disting. Sr. U.S. Scientist award Alexander von Humboldt Found., Germany, 1987; Nat. Def. Grad. fellow, Princeton U., 1969-72. Fellow Am. Phys. Soc.; mem. IEEE (sr.), Materials Rsch. Soc. (coun. 1986-88), Sigma Xi. Office: Palo Alto Rsch Ctr Electronic Materials Lab 3333 Coyote Hill Rd Palo Alto CA 94304-1314

JOHNSON, NOEL LARS, biomedical engineer; b. Palo Alto, Calif., Nov. 11, 1957; s. LeRoy Franklin and Margaret Louise (Lindsley) J.; m. Elise Lynnette Moore, May 17, 1986; children: Margaret Elizabeth, Kent Daniel. BSEE, U. Calif., Berkeley, 1979; ME, U. Va., 1982, PhD, 1990. Mgr. R&D Hosp. Products divsn. Abbott Labs., Mountain View, Calif., 1986-99; founder, chief tech. officer HealtheTech., Inc., 1999—. Contbr. articles to profl. jours. Fellowship NIH 1980-85; rsch. grantee Abbott Labs. 1989. Mem. IEEE, Biomed. Engrng. Soc., Delta Chi (founder, 1st pres. chpt. U. Calif. at Berkeley). Achievements include invention of metabolic monitor, patented automated drug delivery system, pharmacokinetic drug infusion, and critical care disposables. Home: 14586 Aloha Ave Saratoga CA 95070-6004 E-mail: njohnson@healthetech.com.

JOHNSON, NORMA HOLLOWAY, federal judge; b. Lake Charles, La. d. H. Lee and Beatrice (Williams) Holloway; m. Julius A. Johnson, June 18, 1964. BS, D.C. Tchrs. Coll., 1955; JD, Georgetown U., 1962. Bar: D.C. 1962, U.S. Supreme Ct. 1967. Pvt. practice law, Washington, 1963; atty. civil divsn. Dept. Justice, Washington, 1963-67; asst. corp. counsel Office of Corp. Counsel, Washington, 1967-70; judge D.C. Superior Ct., 1970-80, U.S. Dist. Ct. (D.C. dist.), Washington, 1980-97, chief judge, 1997-2001; senior judge U.S. Dist. Ct. (D.C. dist), Washington, 2001. Bd. dirs. Judiciary Leadership Devel. Coun. Fellow Am. Bar Found.; mem. Nat. Bar Assn., Fed. Judges Assn., Am. Judicature Soc., Supreme Ct. Hist. Soc., Am. Inns of Ct. (William Bryant inn). Office: US Dist Ct US Courthouse 333 Constitution Ave NW Washington DC 20001-2802

JOHNSON, NORMA LOUISE, accountant; b. Cin., June 21, 1951; d. Raymond and Geneva (Cheesbrough) Banks; m. Raymond D. Johnson, Aug. 31, 1973; children: Raymond, Rhea, Amos, Dorian. AD summa cum laude, Southwestern Coll. Bus., 1992; cert., H&R Block; BA, Union Inst., 1998; postgrad. in taxation, Golden Gate U., 2002—. Confidential sec. NCR, Dayton, Ohio, 1969-70; receiving clk. Delco Products, Dayton, 1972-73; sr. clk. GM Assembly, Cin., 1973-74; primary order clk. AC Delco, Cin., 1974-76; with customer svc. dept. Nacom, Cin., 1982; acctg. clk. CCSI, Cin., 1993; pres. Johnson's Fin., Cin., 1994-2000; ptnr. RG Group, 2000—. Tax analyst Provident Bank, 2001; pres. Johnson's Fin. Extensions, 2003. Avocation: writing poetry. Home: 460 Vista Glen Ct Cincinnati OH 45246

JOHNSON, NORMAN JAMES, physician, lawyer, medicological consultant; b. Bklyn., Apr. 15, 1921; s. James Henry and Florence Gertrude (Crilley) J.; m. Bernadette Frances Lowe, Jan. 17, 1948; children: Michael Lowe, Christopher Day, Mark Hughes, Matthew Day (dec.), David Hughes. AB magna cum laude, Fordham U., 1942; MD, SUNY, 1945; JD, U. Ga., 1979. Bar: Ga. 1981; cert. Am. Bd. Pediat. Intern Kings County Hosp., Bklyn., 1945-46; intern pediatrics The L.I. Coll. Hosp., Bklyn., 1948-49; resident cardiology Irvington House, Irvington-on-Hudson, N.Y., 1949-50; resident pediatrics Cin. Children's Hosp., 1950-51, chief resident pediatrics, 1951-52; assoc. prof. pediatrics U. Ark., Little Rock, 1952-56; chief pediats. Miners Meml. Hosp., Williamson, W.Va., 1956-59; asst. prof. pediatric medicine U. Tenn. Med. Sch., Memphis, 1959-61; from asst. chief to chief pediatrics Met. Hosp., Detroit, 1961-71; practice medicine specializing in pediats. Athens, Ga., 1972-77; clin. dir emergency medicine St. Mary's Hosp., Athens, 1976-86; with emergency medicine Hilton Head Hosp., Hilton Head Island, S.C., 1986-87; with Newton Gen. Hosp., Covington, Ga., 1987-95. Instr. pediatrics U. Cin., 1951-52, assoc. prof. pediatrics U. Ark., Little Rock, 1952-56, asst. prof. pediatrics U. Tenn., Memphis, 1959-61; expert civilian cons. pediatrics, Army & Navy Gen. Hosp., Hot Springs, Ark., 1953-56. Contbr. articles to profl. jours. Pres. PTA, Athens, 1975-76, Friends of Ga. Mus. of Art, Athens, U. Ga., 1985-86, 95-96. Capt. U.S. Army, 1946-48, PTO. Mem. Am. Acad. Pediat., Am. Coll. Emergency Physicians, Irish and Am. Pediat. Soc. Democrat. Roman Catholic. Avocations: singing, running. Home and Office: PO Box 305 Watkinsville GA 30677-0008

JOHNSON, OLIN CHESTER, education educator; b. Phila., Sept. 19, 1941; s. Benjamin F. and Eva M. Johnson; m. Vernetta Dudley, Nov. 22, 1964; children: Quanda, Olin Jr. BS, Cheyney State Coll., 1965; MEd, Temple U., 1969; MS, U. Pa., 1972. Cert. elem. edn., social studies, elem. prin., secondary prin., supt., Pa. Tchr. Phila. Sch. Dist., 1965-68, supr., 1968-72, dir., coord. urban career ednl. ctr., 1973-75, prin., 1976—, William Bryant Sch., 1977-80, Charles R. Drew Sch., 1981—. Mem. secondary sch. com. U. Pa., Phila.; adj. asst. prof. Drexel U., Phila., 1989—, mem. ednl. adv. com. Chmn. Cmty. Concern 13, Inc., 1970—, B.F. Johnson Scholarship Fund, 1971—; vice-chmn. Phila. M.H. Multi-Purpose Learning Ctr., 1975-85; bd. dirs. Open Door Bapt. Ch.; exec. adminstr. B.F. Johnson Found., 1989—. Recipient award Nat. Tchr. Corp., 1970, Four Chaplains Cmty. Svc. award, 1971, 73, Phila. Prin. Merit award Phila. Sch. Dist. #1, 1978, OIC commendation, 1973, Pa. Dept. Edn. Planning and Testing citation, 1987, Prin. Outstanding Leadership C.R. Drew award, 1987, Strawbridge Civic award, 2001; Ford Found. fellow U. Pa., 1971-74. Mem. Am. Assn. Sch. Adminstrs., Pa. Congress Sch. Adminstrs., Phi Delta Kappa, Kappa Alpha Psi.

JOHNSON, OLIN GLYNN, computer science educator; b. Waxahachie, Tex., Dec. 21, 1935; s. Olin Tivis and Ruth (Sutton) J.; m. Ferol Marie Gibson, Jan. 20, 1961; children: Olin Wesley, Glynna Marie. BS, So. Meth. U., 1957, MS, 1960; MA, U. Calif., Berkeley, 1966, PhD, 1968. Rsch. scientist IBM, Houston, 1968-70; exec. v.p. Internat. Math. and Statis. Librs., Houston, 1970-73; assoc. prof. U. Houston, 1973-83, prof., 1983—, acting, assoc. or chair computer sci. dept., 1975—. Author: Computer Organization and Programming, 1984. Mem. Assn. Computing Machinery (coun. mem. 1972-75, nominating com. 1976-78, chmn. nominating com. 1977). Office: Computer Sci Dept Univ Houston Houston TX 77204-0001 E-mail: johnson@cs.uh.edu.

JOHNSON, OLIVER THOMAS, JR., lawyer; b. San Antonio, July 3, 1946; s. Oliver Thomas and Joan Elizabeth (Edwards) J.; m. Susan Caroline Nelson, Nov. 6, 1976; children: Caroline Elizabeth, Thomas Christian. Student, U. Redlands, 1964-65; BA, Stanford U., 1968, JD, 1971. Bar: Calif. 1972, D.C. 1975, U.S. Ct. Internat. Trade 1983, U.S. Supreme Ct. 1991. Atty. office of legal adviser U.S. Dept. State, Washington, 1971-73, spl. asst. to legal adviser, 1973-75; assoc. Covington & Burling, Washington, 1975-80, ptnr., 1980—. Co-author: The Registration of Foreign Agents in the United States, 1981, Private Investors Abroad: Problems and Solutions, 1987, The North American Free Trade Agreement: Issues, Options, Implications, 1992, The International Lawyer's Deskbook, 1996; contbr. articles to profl. jours. Bd. dir. U.S.-Azerbaijan Coun., Washington, 1995. Mem.: ABA, Inst. Transnat. Arbitration (adv. bd.), Washington Inst. Fgn. Affairs (bd. dirs.), Am. Soc. Internat. Law, Met. Club, Order of Coif. Office: Covington & Burling 1201 Pennsylvania Ave NW Washington DC 20004-2401 E-mail: tjohnson@cov.com.

JOHNSON, OMOTUNDE EVAN GEORGE, economist; b. Freetown, Sierra Leone, Mar. 27, 1941; came to U.S., 1961; s. Evan George and Elizabeth O. (Allen) J.; m. Octavia Olayemi John, Oct. 30 1965; children: Olatunde Cheryl, Omoyemi Evan, Olubayo Darryl. BA, UCLA, 1965, MA, 1967, PhD, 1970. Lectr. in econs. Calif. State U., Long Beach, 1967-69; lectr. U. Sierra Leone, Freetown, 1969-73; vis. asst. prof. U. Mich., Ann Arbor, 1973-74; economist IMF, Washington, 1974-79, sr. economist, dep. divsn. chief, 1979-82, advisor, 1992-94, divsn. chief, 1994-98, asst. dir., 1998-2000; econ. rschr. and cons. McLean, Va., 2000—. Vis. rsch. fellow U. Oxford, Eng., 1996-97; resident rep. IMF, Ghana, 1987-90. Contbr. numerous articles to profl. jours. Mem. Am. Econ. Assn., U.S. Chess Fedn., Royal Econ. Soc. U.K., Nat. Symphony Orch. Assn., Met. Opera Guild. Episcopalian. Avocations: chess, piano, classical music, reading. Home and Office: 6401 Oak Meadow Way Mc Lean VA 22101-5342 E-mail: oegjohnson@aol.com.

JOHNSON, ORRIN WENDELL, lawyer; b. Mpls., Nov. 7, 1920; s. Elmer Godfrey and Lydia (Carlson) J.; m. Patsy Elizabeth Coons, Apr. 2, 1951; children: Forrest, Wendell, Carol, Laura. BA cum laude, U. Tex., 1942, JD cum laude, 1947. Bar: Tex. 1947, U.S. Ct. Appeals 1948, U.S. Supreme Ct. 1964. Assoc. Karl Gibbon, Harlingen, Tex, 1947-49; ptnr. Gibbon, Coneway, Johnson, Harlingen, 1949-51, Gibbon & Johnson, Harlingen, 1951-53; pvt. practice law Harlingen, 1953-67; ptnr. Johnson & Davis, Harlingen, 1967-95; of counsel Rodriguez, Colvin and Chaney, Brownsville, Tex., 1995—. Assoc. editor Tex. Law Rev., 1946-47; contbr. articles to profl. jours. Pres. Cameron County Good Govt. League, 1979-82, bd. dirs., 1980-86; trustee Marine Mil. Acad., 1964-91, v.p., 1982-86, pres., 1986-89; adv. dir. Valley Baptist Hosp., 1964-72. Maj. USMCR, 1942-57. Recipient Pub. Service Achievement award Common Cause, 1981. Fellow Am. Coll. Trial Lawyers, Am. Coll. Trust and Estate Attys., Tex. Acad. Trust and Probate Lawyers, Am. Bar Found., Tex. Bar Found. (trustee 1977, chmn. fellows 1980-81, sustaining life mem., Lola Wright Found. award 1989, Five Outstanding Fifty Yr. Lawyers in Tex. 1999); mem. ABA (del. Tex. chpt. 1989-90), State Bar Tex. (bd. dirs. 12th dist. 1972-75, pres. 1982-83, chmn. rules ethics com. 1986-88, Pres.' award 1986, Frank J. Scurlock award 1983, trustee Tex. Ctr. for Legal Ethics and Professionalism 1990-94), Immigration Law Reform Inst. (bd. dirs., exec. com. 1987-90), Order of Coif, Masons, Phi Delta Phi. Methodist. Office: Law Offices of Orrin Johnson 402 E Van Buren Ave Harlingen TX 78550-6834

JOHNSON, OWEN VERNE, historian, educator; b. Madison, Wis., Feb. 22, 1946; s. Verner Lalander Johnson and Marianne Virginia (Halvorson) Muse; m. Marta Kucerova, July 17, 1969 (div. Jan. 26, 2001); children: Eva, Hana; m. Ann Coonradt Tyron, May 12, 2001. BA in History with distinction, Wash. State U., 1968; MA in History, U. Mich., 1970, cert. in Russian Ea. European studies, PhD in History, U. Mich., 1978. Reporter Pullman (Wash.) Herald, 1961-67; reporter, announcer Sta. KWSU Radio-TV, Pullman, 1965-68; reporter, editor, producer Sta. WUOM, Ann Arbor, Mich., 1969-77; adminstrv. asst. Ctr. Russian and Ea. European Studies U. Mich., Ann Arbor, 1978-79; asst. prof. Sch. Journalism So. Ill. U., Carbondale, Ill., 1979-80; asst. prof. Ind. U., Bloomington, 1980-87, assoc. prof., 1987—, acting dir. Polish studies, 1989-90, dir. grad. studies, 1990-91, dir. Russian and Ea. European Inst., 1991-95. Mem. Modern Sweden Seminar, Uppsala, 1967; mem. Studia Academica Slovaca Comenius U., Bratislava, Czech Republic, 1973; field advisor journalism Am. Coun. Tchrs. Russian, 1993—96; adj. prof. Ind. U., Bloomington, 1996—. Author: (book) Slovakia 1918-38: Education and the Making of a Nation, 1985; co-author: Eastern European Journalism Before, During and After Communism, 1999; contbr. articles to profl. jours.; mem. editl. bd., Slovakia, 1978—89, Journalism Monographs, 1986—88, Kosmas, 1996—, Mediyska istrazivanja, 2002—; corr. editor: Journalism History, 1985—2000, cons. editor: Slavic Rev., 1985—91. Capt. USAR, 1971—79. Recipient Excellence in Journalism award, Sigma Delta Chi, 1966; grantee, Nat. Coun. Soviet and E. European Rsch., 1988—90, Am. Coun. Learned Socs./Social Sci. Rsch. Coun. Joint Com. Ea. Europe, 1983, Internat. Rsch. and Exchs. Bd., 1973—89, 2003—. Mem.: Slovak Studies Assn. (pres. 1988—91), Orgn. Am. Historians, Internat. Assn. Media Comm. Rsch., Czechoslovak History Conf. (editor newsletter 1980—84, mem. exec. com. 1988—92, Stanley Pech award 1987—88), Assn. Edn. Journalism and Mass. Comm. (head history divsn. 1985—86), Am. Assn. Advancement Slavic Studies (mem. edn. com. 1988—90), Am. Hist. Assn. Democrat. Presbyterian. Office: Ind U Sch Journalism 222C Ernie Pyle Hall Bloomington IN 47405 Fax: 812-855-0901. E-mail: johnsono@indiana.edu.

JOHNSON, P. H. federal agency administrator; b. May 12, 1948; Grad., U. Miss. Elected Miss. State Auditor, 1988; apptd. Miss. State Gen. Dir. Farmer's Home Adminstrn.; atty. Johnson Bobo, Clarksdale, Miss.; fed. co-chmn. Delta Regional Authority, 2001—. Office: Delta Regional Authority 236 Sharkey Ave Ste 400 Clarksdale MS 38614

JOHNSON, PAM, former newspaper editor, communications educator; Mng. editor Phoenix Gazette, 1989—93, Ariz. Republic, Phoenix, 1993-96, sr. v.p. news, exec. editor, 1996—2001; educator, Poynter Inst., St. Petersburg, Fla., 2001—. Office: The Poynter Institute 801 3rd St S Saint Petersburg FL 33701 E-mail: pjohnson@poynter.org.*

JOHNSON, PATRICIA ELLEN, humanities educator; b. Richmond, Ind., July 22, 1951; d. Everett Orville and Mary Finch Johnson; m. Dennis Charles Dougherty; 1 child, Thomas Dougherty. BA, Earlham Coll., 1973; PhD, U. of Minn., 1985. Asst. prof. of english The U. of Ala. in Huntsville, Huntsville, Ala., 1985—89; assoc. prof. of humanities and lit. Pa. State Harrisburg, Middletown, Pa., 1989—. Coord. lit. maj. Pa. State Harrisburg, 1991—95, coord. humanities masters degree program, 1996—99. Author: Hidden Hands: Working-Class Women and Victorian Social-Problem Fiction, 2001; contbr. chapters to books, articles to profl. jours. Fellow, 83U. of Minn., 1983—84; grantee, Nat. Endowment for the Humanities, 1992, Inst. for the Arts and Humanistic Study, 1992. Mem.: MLA, Phi Beta Kappa. Office: Penn State Harrisburg 777 West Harrisburg Pike Middletown PA 17057

JOHNSON, PATRICK, JR., lawyer; b. New Orleans, June 6, 1955; s. Patrick and Louise J.; m. Gayle Marie Daniel, Feb. 24, 1979; children: Patrick III, Daniel Hartman, Michael Joseph. BS, U. New Orleans, 1977; JD magna cum laude, Tulane U., 1979; diploma with distinction, U. Stockholm, 1980. Bar: La. 1980, U.S. Dist. Ct. (ea. and mid. dists.) La. 1980, U.S. Ct. Appeals (5th and 11th cirs.) 1981, U.S. Supreme Ct. 1985, U.S. Dist. Ct. (we. dist.) La. 1986. Assoc. Lemle & Kelleher, L.L.P., New Orleans, 1980-85, ptnr., 1985—. Lectr. in field. Articles editor Tulane U. Law Rev., 1978-79, mem. bd. student editors, 1977-78. Mem. ABA (bus. bankruptcy com., chpt. 11 and secured creditors subcom.), Am. Bankruptcy Inst., La. Bar Assn. Home: 403 Atherton Dr Metairie LA 70005-3809 Office: Lemle & Kelleher LLP Pan-Am Life Ctr 21st Fl 601 Poydras St New Orleans LA 70130-6029 E-mail: pjohnson@lemle.com.

JOHNSON, PAUL BRETT, writer, illustrator; b. Mousie, Ky., May 19, 1947; s. Paul and Harriet Johnson. MA in Edn., U. Ky., 1970. Author, illustrator: children's picture books The Cow Who Wouldn't Come Down, 1993, Lost, 1995, Farmers' Market, 1997, Old Dry Frye, 1999, Bearhide and Crow, 2000, Fearless Jack, 2001, Jack Outwits the Giants, 2002, others. Named to N.Y. Pub. Libr. "100" list, 1993, 1999, 2001, 2002; recipient Best Book award, Sch. Libr. Jour., 1993, 1996, Notable Book award, Smithsonian Instn., 1997, Calif. Young Readers medal, 2000. Mem. Soc. Children's Book Writers and Illustrators. Avocation: travel. Home: 444 Fayette Park Lexington KY 40508-1331 E-mail: pbj@paulbrettjohnson.com.

JOHNSON, PAUL OREN, lawyer; b. Mpls., Feb. 2, 1937; s. Andrew Richard and LaVerne Delores (Slater) J.; children: Scott, Paula, Amy. BA, Carleton Coll., 1958; JD cum laude, U. Minn., 1961. Bar: Minn. 1961. Atty. Briggs & Morgan, St. Paul, 1961-62, Green Giant Co., Le Sueur, Minn., 1961-66, asst. sec., 1967-74, sec., 1975-79, v.p., gen. counsel, 1971-79, v.p. corporate rels., 1973-79, mem. mgmt. com., 1976-79; gen. counsel H.B. Fuller Co., St. Paul, 1979-84, sr. v.p., sec., 1980-90, mem. mgmt. com., 1981-90. Bd. dirs. The Fulcrum Group, chmn. bd. dirs. Coun. v.p., exec. com. Boy Scouts Am.; bd. dirs. Rep. County Com., 1965; bd. dirs. Minn. State U., 1979-82, v.p., 1980-82; chmn. bd. dirs. Minn. Com. Serving Deaf and Hard of Hearing; bd. dirs. vice chair Minn. Acads. Office: Lexington-Riverside 403-1077 Sibley Meml Hwy Saint Paul MN 55118-3680

JOHNSON, PAULINE BENGE, nurse, anesthetist; b. London, Ky., May 10, 1932; d. Chester G. and Bertha M. (Hale) Benge; m. Scottie W. Johnson, Apr. 29, 1950 (dec. 1976); children: Rita Johnson, Nita Johnson Yaw, Gina Johnson Carlson. AA, U. Ky., 1968; diploma, U. Cin. Sch. Nurse Anesthesia, 1971; BS summa cum laude, U. Cin., 1974, M., 1977, D., 1981. RN, Ohio, Ky., Tenn., Ind., W.Va., Fla., Tex. Staff anesthetist Jewish Hosp., Cin., 1971-72, Mercy North Hosp., Hamilton, Ohio, 1972-86, Ft. Hamilton Hosp., Hamilton, 1972-86, McCullough-Hyde Hosp., Oxford, Ohio, 1986-88; freelance anesthetist multiple hosps. Ohio, Ky., 1982-88; staff anesthetist, ind. contractor Shriner Burn Inst., Cin., 1989; staff anesthetist, ind. contractor multiple hosps. Pauline B. Johnson Co., Inc., Ohio, Ky., Tenn., Ind., W. Va., Fla., Tex., 1989—. Provider hosp. anesthesia relief svcs. to under-serviced rural hosp. oper. rms., 1990—. Ch. clk. Lindenwald Bapt. Ch., Hamilton, 1955-72, mem. 1955-85, instr., 1955-76; mem. 1st Bapt. Ch., Hamilton, 1985—, NOW, 1978—, nominating com. major polit. party, Hamilton, 1986-89; mem., med. com. Planned Parenthood, Hamilton, 1987—. Scholar U. Cin., 1969-71, 77-81; recipient Spl. Recognition Higher Edn., Laurel County Homecoming, London, Ky., 1988. Mem. Am. Assn. Nurse Anesthetists (speaker nat. conv. 1982, speaker rsch. forum nat. meeting 1989, mem. nominating com. 1978), Ohio State Assn. Nurse Anesthetists (state bd. dirs. 1989-92, 88-90, 79-80, chair bylaws com. 1991-92, 92-93, nominating com. 1993-94, chair edn. com. 1990-91, pres. 1982-84, state editor Highlights 1974-82, co-chair state meeting 1982, pres. dist. 5 Cin. 1978, govt. rels. chpt. Greater Cin. chpt. 1976-87, speaker meetings), Kappa Delta Pi. Avocations: politics, reading, music, travel, swimming. Home: 76 Picadilly Dr Hamilton OH 45013-3621

JOHNSON, PETER FORBES, transportation executive, business owner; b. Salem, Mass., May 7, 1934; s. William Bennett and Sarah Loraine (Nee) J.; m. Mikell Kraus, Oct. 11, 1958; children: Krista, Todd, Karyn, Jennifer. BS, U.S. Mcht. Marine Acad., 1957. Deck officer Texaco, Port Arthur, Tex., 1958-63; from deck officer to master Reynolds Metals Co., Corpus Christi, Tex., 1963-65, port capt., 1965-68, operating mgr., 1968-71; internat. marine mgr. Gulf Miss. Marine Corp., New Orleans, 1971-72; cons. Peter F. Johnson & Assocs., New Orleans, 1972-73; exec. v.p. Pyramid Marine, Inc., New Orleans, 1973-76; pres., owner, chmn. bd. Pacific-Gulf Marine, Inc., New Orleans, 1976—. Trustee U.S. Mcht. Marine Acad., Kings Point, NY. Lt. (j.g.) USNR, 1959-63. Mem. Coun. Am. Master Mariners, Soc. Naval Architects and Marine Engrs., Propeller Club U.S. (Maritime Man of Yr, 1986), U.S. Navy League, Southern Yacht Club, English Turn Country Club. Republican. Roman Catholic. Avocations: fly fishing, golf, hunting, sailing. Home: 3 Lakeway Ct New Orleans LA 70131-3322 Office: Pacific Gulf Marine Inc PO Box 6479 New Orleans LA 70174-6479 E-mail: pfj@pac-gulf.biz.

JOHNSON, PHILIP EDWARD, lawyer; b. Denver, Oct. 17, 1947; s. William Edward Johnson and Margarete Eileen (Brandon) Schmaltz; m. Mary Lou Raders, Jan. 1, 1996; children: Brooke, Brandon, Dara, Bryce. BA, U. Colo., 1969; JD, U. Denver, 1974. Bar: Colo. 1975, U.S. Dist. Ct. Colo. 1975, U.S. Ct. Appeals (10th cir.) 1981. Corp. counsel Tosco Corp., Denver and Los Angeles, 1975-76; assoc., ptnr. Mosley, Wells, Johnson & Ruttum P.C., Denver, 1976-93; ptnr. Bennington, Johnson & Reeve, P.C., Denver, 1993—2002, Bennington Johnson Biermann & Craigmile, LLC, Denver, 2002—. Vol. U.S. Peace Corps, Panama, 1969, 1970; pres. bd. trustees Denver Acad. Avocations: athletics, fishing, travel. Home: 444 Clayton St Denver CO 80206-4231 Office: Bennington Johnson Biermann & Craigmile LLC 370 17th St Ste 3500 Denver CO 80202-1371 E-mail: pej@benningtonjohnson.com.

JOHNSON, PHILIP LESLIE, lawyer; b. Beloit, Wis., Jan. 24, 1939; s. James Philip and Christabel (Williams) J.; m. Kathleen Rose Westover, May 12, 1979; children: Celeste Marie, Nicole Michelle. AB, Princeton U., 1961; JD, U. South Calif., 1973. Bar: Calif. 1973, U.S. Ct. Appeals (9th cir.) 1975, U.S. Ct. of Military Appeals, 1978, U.S. Supreme Ct. 1980. Pilot U.S. Marine Corps., 1961-70; assoc. Law Office Wm. G. Tucker, L.A., 1973-78; ptnr. Engstrom, Lipscomb & Lack, L.A., 1978-92; judge pro tem Calif. State Bar Ct., 1990-95; ptnr. Lillick & Charles, Long Beach, Calif., 1993-99, Shaw, Terhar & LaMontagne, L.A., 2000—. Chmn. aerospace law com. Def. Rsch. Inst. Contbr. articles to profl. jours. Pres., bd. dirs. U. So. Calif. Legion Lex, 1992-93; chmn. com. to nom. alumni trustees Princeton U., 1996-97, mem. exec. com. of alumni coun., 1996-97; chmn. Marine Corps Scholarship Found. L.A. Ball, 1997-99. Mem. ABA, (aviation & space law com., torts & ins. practice section), Princeton Club (So. Calif., bd. dirs.). Avocations: flying, snow skiing, jazz. Home: 5340 Valley View Rd Palos Verdes Peninsula CA 90275-5089 Office: Shaw Terhar & LaMontagne 707 Wilshire Blvd Ste 3060 Los Angeles CA 90017 E-mail: avnlawyer@aol.com.

JOHNSON, PHILIP MCBRIDE, lawyer; b. Springfield, Ohio, June 18, 1938; AB with honors, Ind. U., 1959; LLB, Yale U., 1962. Bar: Ill. 1962, D.C. 1983, N.Y. 1984. Ptnr. Kirkland & Ellis, Chgo., 1962-81; chmn. Commodity Futures Trading Comm., Washington, 1981-83; ptnr. Wiley, Johnson & Rein, Washington, 1983-84, Skadden, Arps, Slate, Meagher & Flom, Washington, 1984—; lectr. on commodities regulation U. Va. Law Sch., 1993—. Spkr. panelist on Commodity Exch. Act Fed. Bar Assn., others; mem. adv. com. definition and regulation Commodity Futures Trading Commn., adv. com. state jurisdiction and responsibility; adv. com. regulatory coordination, adv. com. fin. products, adv. com. tech., adv. com. global markets Commodity Futures Trading Commn. Author: Commodities Regulation, 2 vols., 1997, Derivatives: A Manager's Guide to the World's Most Powerful Financial Instruments, 1999; mng. editor Yale U. Law Jour, 1962, Agrl. Law Jour; contbr. articles to legal jours. Mem. ABA (founder, chmn. com. on futures regulation 1975-81, mem. governing coun. sect. on bus. law 1981-83), Futures Industry Assn. (bd. dirs. 1980-81, 86-87), Internat. Bar Assn. (founder, chmn. subcom. on commodities, futures and options law 1986-90), N.Y. Stock Exch. (mem. regulatory adv. com. 1988—). Office: Skadden Arps Slate Meagher & Flom 1440 New York Ave NW Ste 700 Washington DC 20005-2111 E-mail: pjohnson@skadden.com.

JOHNSON, PHILIP WAYNE, judge; b. Greenwood, Ark., Oct. 24, 1944; s. John Luther and Flora (Joyce) J.; m. Carla Jean Newsom, Nov. 6, 1970; children: Betsy, Carl, Jeff, Laura, Philip. BA, Tex. Tech. U., 1965, JD, 1975. Bar: Tex. 1975, U.S. Dist. Ct. (no. and we. dists.) Tex. 1976, U.S. Ct. Appeals (5th cir.) 1984, U.S. Supreme Ct. 1984; cert. in civil trial and personal injury trial law, Tex. Bd. Legal Specialization. Assoc. Crenshaw Dupree & Milam, Lubbock, Tex., 1975-80, ptnr., 1980-98; justice Tex. State Ct. of Appeals (7th dist), Amarillo, 1999—2002, chief justice, 2003—. Bd. dirs., pres. Lubbock County Legal Aid Soc., Tex., 1977-79; bd. dirs., chmn. Trinity Christian Schs., Lubbock, 1978-83, 85-89; bd. dirs., pres. S.W. Lighthouse for Blind, Lubbock, 1978-85. Served to capt. USAF, 1965-72. Decorated Silver Star, D.F.C.; Cross of Gallantry (Vietnam). Fellow: Tex. Bar Found. (life), Am. Bar Found. (life); mem.: Lubbock County Bar Assn. (pres. 1984—85), Amarillo Bar Assn., Tex. Bar Assn., Phi Delta Phi. Home: 7818 Covington Pkwy Amarillo TX 79121-1940 Office: Seventh Ct of Appeals 501 S Fillmore St Rm 2A Amarillo TX 79101-2449

JOHNSON, PHYLLIS ELAINE, chemist, researcher; b. Grafton, N.D., Feb. 19, 1949; d. Donald Gordon and Evelyn Lorraine (Svaren) Lanes; m. Robert S.T. Johnson (dec. Mar. 2001), Sept. 12, 1969; children: Erik, Sara. BS, U. N.D., 1971; PhD, 1976. Instr. chemistry Mary Coll., Bismarck, N.D., 1971-72; postdoctoral rsch. fellow U. N.D., Grand Forks, 1975-79, chemist, 1977-79; rsch. chemist USDA Human Nutrition Rsch. Ctr., 1979-87, rsch. leader for nutrition, biochemistry and metabolism, 1987-91; assoc. dir. Pacific West Area USDA-ARS, 1996-97; dir. Beltsville Area USDA, ARS, 1997—; Disting. Chemistry Alumni lectr. U. N.D., 1998. Editor: Stable Isotopes in Nutrition, 1984; mem. editl. bd. Jour. Micronutrient Analysis, 1988-91, Jour. Nutrition, 1998—; contbr. articles to profl. jours. Chmn. Parents of Gifted and Talented, 1984—86. Recipient Arthur S. Flemming award Outstanding Sci. Achievement, 1989, Women in Sci. and Engrng. award, 1993, Sioux award N.D. Alumni Found., 1998, Fed. Energy and Water Mgmt. award, 1998, Presdl. Rank award of Meritorious Exec., Pres. of U.S., 1999, White House Closing the Circle award for Environ. Mgmt. from Pres. Bush, 2002, for Biobased Products Program, 2003. Mem. Am. Soc. Clin. Nutrition, Am. Chem. Soc., Am. Inst. Nutrition, Internat. Soc. Trace Element Rsch. in Humans (sec. 1992-98), Exec. Women in Govt., Sr. Exec. Assn., Soc. Exptl. Biology Medicine, Rotary, Sons of Norway (dist. v.p. 1984-86, dist. pres. 1986-88, internat. bd. dirs. 1988-92), Phi Beta Kappa, Sigma Xi, Gamma Sigma Delta. Lutheran. Avocations: cooking, skiing, needlework, camping. Home: 7868 Manet Way Severn MD 21144-1649 Office: USDA Bldg 003 Rm 223 10300 Baltimore Ave Beltsville MD 20705-2350 E-mail: johnsonp@ba.ars.usda.gov.

JOHNSON, RALPH THEODORE, JR., physicist; b. Salina, Kans., Apr. 29, 1935; s. Ralph Theodore and Mary Alice (Wallerius) J.; m. Ruth Elaine Rohrer, Jan. 25, 1958; children: Barbara A., Thomas T., Gregory E., Janet E. MS in Physics, Kans. State U., 1959, PhD, 1964. Staff mem. GE, Cin., 1957-58; rsch. and teaching asst. Kans. State U., 1958-63; from rsch. scientist to mgr. Sandia Nat. Lab., Albuquerque, 1965-97. Mem. N.Mex. Govs. Energy Task Force, 1974; mem. assessment panel Nat. Rsch. Panel, 1978-90; mem. Am. Nat. Std. Writing Com., 1990-97 Contbr. articles to profl. jours. Pres., bd. dirs. Marriage Enrichment Nonprofit Corp. 1st lt. USAF, 1963-65. Achievements include patent for neutron radiation detector; memory phenomenon in amorphous semiconductors; ionic conduction in solid electrolytes; radiation effects in semiconductors and electronics; metrology program development; marriage program development. Home: 6601 Arroyo Del Oso Ave NE Albuquerque NM 87109-2733

JOHNSON, RANDALL CLYDE, mortgage banker; b. Tulsa, Okla., Feb. 12, 1949; s. Clyde O. and Barbara Grace Johnson; m. Mary Dan Peck, June 25, 1971 (div. Aug. 1981); 1 child, Paul C.; m. Frances Evelen Wigelious, Oct. 1, 1982; 1 child, Tyler B. BA, U. Miami, Coral Gables, Fla., 1971. V.p. Baker Mortgage Co., Miami, Fla., 1971-75; S.E. U.S. regional mgr. Gen. Electric Credit Corp., Coral Gables, Fla., 1975-77; pres., CEO Equitable Mortgage Resources, Inc., Clearwater, Fla., 1977-89; chmn., CEO Market St. Mortgage Co., Clearwater, 1989-2000. Mem. adv. bd. Avondale Funding Corp., Chgo., 1998—, Residential Funding Corp./GM Acceptance, Bloomington, Minn., 1999, Fannie Mae Corp., Washington, 2000—. Contbr.: Real Estate Financing Desk Book, 1977. Pres. Mental Health Assn. Pinellas County, Clearwater, 1986-89; participant Leadership Pinellas, Clearwater, 1988-98; dir. Clearwater Marine Sci. Ctr., 1990-91; vice chmn. Mortgage Bankers Polit. Action Com., Washington, 1996-98; hon. chmn. Pinellas County March of Dimes, 2000; mem. pres.'s coun. U. Miami, 1998—. Recipient Schumacher-Bolduc award, 1999; named Outstanding Young Men in Am., JCs Internat., 1979, Floridans to Watch in the Next Ten Years, Fla. Trend Mag., Miami, 1980, Significant Sig, Sigma Chi Nat. Fraternity, Evanston, Ill., 1998; faculty fellow Sch. Mortgage Banking, Washington, 1988. Mem. Mortgage Bankers Assn. Am. (cert. mortgage banker, profl. mem., bd. govs. 1995—, Legion of Honor 1999), Mortgage Bankers Assn. Fla. (profl. mem., pres. 1987-88), Belleair Country Club (mem.-guest tournament champion 1994), Carlouel Yacht Club. Republican. Episcopalian. Avocations: spending time with my family, golfing, fishing. Address: 2130 Summit way Palm Harbor FL 34684-1772 Fax: 727-791-4136. E-mail: JohnsonMSM@aol.com., rjohnson@msmc.net.

JOHNSON, RANDY (RANDALL DAVID JOHNSON), professional baseball player; b. Walnut Creek, Calif., Sept. 10, 1963; Student, U. So. Calif. With Montreal Expos, 1985—89; pitcher Seattle Mariners, 1989—98, Houston Astros, 1998—99, Ariz. Diamondbacks, 1999—. Named Pitcher of Yr., Sporting News, 1995, Am. League Strikeout Leader, 1995; named to All-Star Team, 1990, 1993—95; recipient Cy Young award, 1995. Achievements include leading Am. League Strikeouts, 1992. Office: c/o Ariz Diamondbacks BankOne Ballpark 401 E Jefferson St Phoenix AZ 85004-2438

JOHNSON, REBECCA GROOMS, music educator; b. Columbus, Ohio, Dec. 9, 1952; d. Fred Paul and Hazel (Burr) Grooms; m. Stephen Allen Johnson, Feb. 1, 1975. MusB, Capital U., 1975; MA in Piano Pedagogy, Ohio State U., 1977, PhD in Piano Pedagogy, 1982. Asst. prof. Circleville (Ohio) Bible Coll., 1978-81; adj. asst. prof. Mercy Coll., Detroit, 1982-84; mem. faculty Cmty. Music Sch./Capital U., Columbus, 1988-95; lectr. Ohio State U., Columbus, 1995-98; dir. Cmty. Music Sch., adj. assoc. prof. Capital U., 1998—, dir. keyboard pedogogy program. Founder, dir. piano pedagogy conf. presented by Capital U. Conservatory of Music, 1988-95; dir. seminars and presenter papers in field nat. confs.; mem. learning theories com. Nat. Conf. on Piano Pedagogy, 1988-94. Composer: (piano arrangement) O Come, O Come Emmanuel, 1993; contbr. articles to mus. jours. Mem. MTNA (nat. chair pedagogy com. 2000-03), Ohio Music Tchrs. Assn. (state pres. 1996-98, 4th v.p. state bd. 1992-96, chmn. cen.-ea. dist. 1990-92, active adjudicator dist. and state competitions, lectr. workshop clinician state conv. 1986, 90, 96, nat. conv. 1994, 98, dist. confs.), Phi Kappa Phi, Pi Kappa Lambda. Mem. Church of God. Avocations: hiking, skiing, reading. Office: Cmty Music Sch Capital Univ Columbus OH 43209

JOHNSON, REVERDY, lawyer; b. NYC, Aug. 24, 1937; s. Reverdy and Reva (Payne) J.; m. Pamela Forbes, Mar. 10, 1961 (div.); m. Marta Schneebeli, Apr. 4, 1970 (div.); children: Deborah Ghiselin, Reverdy Payne; m. Robbie M. Williams, Feb. 20, 1994. AB cum laude, Harvard U., 1960, LLB, 1963. Bar: Fla. 1963, Calif. 1964, N.Mex. 1997. Assoc. Brobeck, Phleger & Harrison, San Francisco, 1963-66; from assoc. to ptnr. Pettit & Martin, San Francisco, 1966-95; of counsel Steinhart & Falconer LLP, San Francisco, 1995-97, Scheuer Yost & Patterson, Sante Fe, NMex., 1996—, Fenwick and West, LLP, Mountain View, Calif., 1999—2003. Co-owner Johnson Turnbull Vineyards, Napa Valley, Calif., 1977-93; tech. adv. com., com. open space lands Calif. Joint Legislature, 1968-69, chmn., 1969-70. Bd. dir. Planning and Conservation League, 1966-72, League to Save Lake Tahoe, 1972-77, Found. for San Francisco's Archtl. Heritage, 1975-84, San Francisco Devel. Fund, 1986-96; bd. dir. Santa Fe Shakespeare Co.2001—, pres., 2002—. Mem. Urban Land Inst. (vice chmn. recreational devel. council 1975-78, comml. and retail devel. council 1980-99), Napa Valley Vintners Assn. (bd. dir. 1985-88, v.p. 1987, pres. 1988), Am. Coll. Real Estate Lawyers, Lambda Alpha. also: Scheuer Yost & Patterson 125 Lincoln Ave Ste 223 Santa Fe NM 87501-2053 E-mail: reverdyj@santafelawyers.com.

JOHNSON, RICHARD JAMES VAUGHAN, newspaper executive, retired; b. San Luis, Potosi, Mex., Sept. 22, 1930; s. Clifton Whatford and Myrtle Louise (Hinman) Johnson; m. Belle Beraud Griggs, Aug. 6, 1955; children: Shelley Beraud, Mark Hinman. BBA, U. Tex., Austin, 1954. Asst. to exec. dir. Tex. Daily Newspaper Assn., 1955—56; from with to chmn. Houston Chronicle Pub. Co., 1956—2000; chmn. Houston Chron., 2000—02, ret., 2002. Chmn., CEO, dir. Robert A. Welch Found.; bd. visitors M.D. Anderson Cancer Ctr.; bd. dir. Tex. Med. Ctr. With U.S. Army, 1952—54. Mem.: Am. Newspaper Pubs. Assn. (past pres. and chmn.), Tex. Daily Newspaper Assn. (pres. 1978), Coronado Club, Houston Club, River Oaks Club. Unitarian Universalist. Office: Houston Chronicle 801 Texas St Houston TX 77002-2996

JOHNSON, RICHARD ARLO, lawyer; b. Vermillion, S.D., July 8, 1952; s. Arlo Goodwin and Edna Marie (Styles) J.; m. Diane Marie Zephier, Aug. 18, 1972 (div. Jan. 1979); m. Sheryl Lavonne Mader, June 5, 1981; 1 stepchild, Chadwick O. Wagner; 1 child, Sarah N. BA, U. S.D., 1974, JD, 1976. Bar: S.D. 1977, U.S. Dist. Ct. S.D. 1977. Ptnr. Pruitt, Matthews, Muilenberg & Strange, Sioux Falls, S.D., 1977-92, Strange, Farrell & Johnson, P.C., Sioux Falls, 1992—. Mem. Pub. Defender Adv. Bd., Sioux Falls, 1983-98; mem. S.D. Dental Peer Rev. Com. S.E. Dist. Fellow Am. Acad. Matrimonial Lawyers; mem. ATLA, ABA, S.D. Trial Lawyers Assn., State Bar S.D. (chmn. family law com. 1989-92), Sioux Falls (S.D.) Jazz and Blues Soc. (bd. dirs., 1998—, pres. 2003), Phi Delta Phi (pres. 1976-77), Masons, Shriners (past potentate). Democrat. Lutheran. Home: 409 E Lotta St Sioux Falls SD 57105-7109 Office: Strange Farrell & Johnson PC 141 N Main Ave Ste 200 Sioux Falls SD 57104-6429

JOHNSON, RICHARD ARNOLD, statistics educator, consultant; b. St. Paul, July 10, 1937; s. Arnold Verner and Florence Dorothy J.; m. Roberta Anne Weinard, Mar. 21, 1964; children— Erik Richard, Thomas Robert B.E.E., U. Minn., Mpls., 1960, MS in Math., 1963, PhD in Stats., 1966. Asst. prof. stats. U. Wis., Madison, 1966-70, assoc. prof., 1970-74, prof. stats, 1974—, chmn. dept. stats., 1981-84; head Greentree Statis. Consulting, Madison, Wis., 1978—. Cons. industry, Dept. Energy; cooperating scientist Dept. Agr. Co-author: Statistical Concepts and Methods, 1977, Applied Multivariate Statistical Analysis, 1982, 5th edit., 2002, Probability and Statistics for Engineers (4th edit. 1990, 5th edit. 1994, 6th edit. 00), Statistics-Principles and Methods, 1985, 4th edit., 2001, Business Statistics-Decision Making with Data, 1997, Statistical Reasoning and Methods, 1998. Recipient Frank Wilcoxon prize, 1991; NATO sr. postdoctoral fellow, 1972; numerous grants NSA, NSF, ONR, Air Force, NASA. Fellow Inst. Math. Stats. (program sec. 1980-86, mem. of council 1980-86), Am. Statis. Assn. (sect. rep. to council 1980-82), Royal Statis. Soc.; mem. Internat. Statis. Inst. Lutheran. Avocations: fishing, cross-country skiing. Office: Greentree Statis Cons 7122 Valhalla Trl Madison WI 53719-3039

JOHNSON, RICHARD AUGUST, English language educator; b. Washington, Apr. 18, 1937; s. Cecil August and Esther Marie (Nelson) J.; m. Michaela Ann Memelsdorff, Aug. 20, 1960; children— Nicholas, Patrick, Hong, Loeun. BA, Swarthmore Coll., 1959; PhD, Cornell U., 1965. Instr. English U. Va., Charlottesville, 1963-65; asst. prof. Mt. Holyoke Coll., South Hadley, Mass., 1965-71, assoc. prof., 1971-74, prof., chmn. dept., 1974-80, 1988-91, prof. Alumnae Found., 1980-86, Lucia, Ruth and Elizabeth MacGregor prof. English, 1986—. Vis. prof. Amherst Coll., 1979, 84-88. Author: Man's Place: An Essay on Auden, 1973; co-author: Common Ground: Personal Writing and Public Discourse, 1992, Finding Common Ground, 1996; contbr. articles to profl. jours. Mem. MLA, AAUP, Phi Beta Kappa Democrat. Episcopalian. Office: Mount Holyoke Coll Dept English 50 College St South Hadley MA 01075-1423 E-mail: rjohnson@mtholyoke.edu.

JOHNSON, RICHARD CLARK, lawyer; b. Knoxville, Tenn., Feb. 5, 1937; s. Paul R. and Bernice (Whittaker) J.; m. Suzanne M. O'Meara, Apr. 13, 1969. AB magna cum laude, Harvard U., 1958, JD magna cum laude, 1962. Bar: Mass., D.C., Va. Asst. and acting exec. dir. FPC, Washington, 1966-68; assoc., then ptnr. Vom Baur, Coburn, Simmons & Turtle, Washington, 1968-79; ptnr. Seyfarth, Shaw, Fairweather & Geraldson, Washington, 1979-94, mng. ptnr., 1983-94; ptnr. Jenner & Block, Washington, 1995—2002, Smith, Pachter, McWhorten and Allen, Vienna, Va., 2002—. Served to capt. USAF, 1962-65. Fulbright scholar U. Bonn, Fed. Republic Germany, 1958-59. Mem. ABA, Mass. Bar Assn., D.C. Bar Assn., Va. Bar Assn., Harvard Club (Boston), University Club, Met. Club (Washington). Avocations: civil war studies, gardening, distance running, watercolor painting, languages. Office: Smith Pachter McWhorter & Allen PLC 8000 Towers Crescent Dr Ste 900 Vienna VA 22182 E-mail: rjohnson@smithpachter.com.

JOHNSON, RICHARD DARRELL, management consultant; b. Columbus, Ohio, Aug. 1, 1935; s. Darrell Dean and Gretchen Price (Motz) Johnson; m. Ann Elizabeth Sektnan, Apr. 9, 1960; children: Julie Ann, Jennifer Lynn, Douglas Richard. B in Indsl. Engring., Ohio State U., 1958, MBA, 1962. CPA Ohio, Ill.; cert. in computer processing Inst. Cert. Computer Profls.; registered profl. engr., Ohio. Consulting staff Arthur Andersen & Co., Cleve., 1962-65, consulting mgr., 1965-70, consulting ptnr., 1970, consulting mng. ptnr., 1971-75, cons. retail industry head, 1969-75, chmn. adv. coun., 1976-78, country mng. ptnr., 1975-77, mng. ptnr. profl. edn. Chgo., 1977-79, mng. ptnr. edn. consulting, 1979-86; mng. ptnr. change mgmt. Andersen Consulting, Chgo., 1986-91, ret. ptnr., 1991; pres. VIA Internat. Ltd., Chgo., 1992-99; chmn. VIA Internat. LLC, Chgo., 1998-99; pres. RDJ Ltd. Mgmt. Conss., 1999—. Mem. Ill. Dist. 67 Bd. Edn., Lake Forest, 1984—90, sec., 1984—85, chmn. edn. com., 1987—90, chmn. strategic planning com., 1989—90; trustee Ravinia Festival Assn., Highland Pk., Ill., 1988—95, Highland Park, Ill., 1996—, vice chmn. Highland Pk., Ill., 1998—2002, chmn. devel. com., 1998—2002, long range planning com. Highland Park, Ill., 1996—, fin. com., ann. fund com., 1979—; treas. Lake Forest (Ill.) Symphony Assn., 1979—81, v.p., 1981—83, exec. v.p., 1983—89, adv. bd., 1989—; gen. coord. Chgo. campaign Am. Cancer Soc., 1983; dir. United Way Lake Forest, Lake Bluff, Ill., 1981—, treas., 1984—86, pres., 1986—88; mem. Chgo. adv. bd. Coll. Engring., Ohio State U., 1988—91, alumni adv. coun., 1996—99; chmn. Alumni Assn. Bd., 1999—, vice chmn., 2001—02; mem. Coll. Bus. Adv. Coun., 1976—83, 1st v.p., 1978—79; mem. Ruth Weimer Mt. Leadership Initiatives Fund, 1997—. 1st lt. USAF, 1958—61. Recipient Internat. Disting. Svc. award, Assn. Sys. Mgmt., 1976, Gerlach award, 1998, Alumni Citizenship Award, OSU Alumni Assoc., 1998, Disting. Alumni Award, Fishe Coll. of Bus., 2002. Mem.: Chgo. Coun. Fgn. Rels., Vail (Colo.) Racquet Club, Sloane Gardens Club (London) (treas. 1993—94), Pelican Isle Yacht Club (Naples, Fla.), Exec. Club Chgo., Pelican Marsh Golf Club (Naples), Sigma Chi (Significant Sig award 2002). Avocations: skiing, boating, classical music, tennis, golf, internat. Home: 351 Sussex Ln Lake Forest IL 60045-2057 Office: RDJ Ltd 351 Sussex Lane Lake Forest IL 60045-2057 E-mail: rdjltd@earthlink.net.

JOHNSON, RICHARD DAVID, retired librarian; b. Cleve., June 10, 1927; s. Robert Emanuel and Emma (Lindhorst) J.; m. Harriett Herzog, Sept. 8, 1956; children: Ruth Ellen, Royce Emanuel. BA, Yale U., 1949; MA in Internat. Rels., U. Chgo., 1950, MALS, 1957. Libr. Nat. Opinion Rsch. Ctr. U. Chgo., 1956-57; reference libr. Stanford, 1957-59; cataloger Stanford U., 1959-60, 61-62, adminstrv. asst. to dir., 1960-61, head acquisitions, 1962-64, chief undergrad. libr. project, 1964-67, chief libr. tech. svcs., 1967-68; dir. librs. Claremont (Calif.) Colls., 1968-73, SUNY, Oneonta, 1973-94; ret., 1994. Editor: Calif. Libr., 1966-68, Coll. and Rsch. Librs., 1974-80, Choice, 1982, Lexington Books series on librs., 1981-87, N.Y. Libr. Assn. Bull., 1986-91, Assn. Libr. Collections and Tech. Svcs. Newsletter, 1989-91, Glimmerglass Opera Guild Newsletter, 1995—; mng. editor: Jour. Libr. Automation, 1980. Trustee Four County Libr. System, Binghamton, N.Y., 1978-88, South Cen. Rsch.Libr. Coun., Ithaca, 1986-90. With inf. AUS, 1952-54. Decorated Bronze Star; recipient Acad./Rsch. Libr. of Yr. award Assn. Coll. and Rsch. Librs., 1984, Trustees award for outstanding svc. South Ctrl. Rsch. Libr. Coun., 1994, Ptnr. in Excellence award Opera Vols. Internat., 2000. Mem. ALA, Calif. Libr. Assn. (pres. 1972), N.Y. Libr. Assn. (pres. acad. and spl. librs. sect. 1981-82, 2d v.p. 1982, Spirit of Librarianship award 1992). Beta Phi Mu. Presbyterian. Home: 2 Walling Blvd Oneonta NY 13820-1918

JOHNSON, RICHARD DEAN, pharmaceutical consultant, educator; b. DeKalb, Ill., July 8, 1936; s. Arthur Dean Johnson and Evelyn Alice (Telford) Williams; m. Paula Marcellus Jennings, Nov. 3, 1942; children: Janet Telford Bijur, Julie Tess, Richard Dean Jr., Jennings Brodie. BS, U. Calif., Berkeley, 1960; PharmD, U. Calif., San Francisco, 1961, MS, 1962, PhD, 1965; MBA, Rockhurst Coll., Kansas City, Mo., 1984. Cert. tchr. Calif., lic. pharmacist Calif. Sect. head R&D Allergan Inc., Irvine, Calif., 1965-67; dir. regulatory affairs Syntex Labs., Inc., Palo Alto, Calif., 1967-73; mng. dir. licensing Marion Labs., Inc., Kansas City, Mo., 1973-79, v.p. licensing, 1980-82, v.p. corp. devel., 1983-87, v.p. bus. alliances, 1987-89; corp. v.p. Marion Merrell Dow, Inc., Kansas City, 1989-91; ret., chmn., CEO KC Pharma, LLC, Mo., 1991—. Adj. prof. Sch. Pharmacy, U. Mo., Kansas City, 1991-95, R&D coun., 1993—, adj. grad. prof., 1995—; bd. dirs. Dey Labs., Inc., Concord, Calif., Tanabe-Marion Labs., Kansas City, U.S. Biosci., Inc., Blue Bell, Pa., ImmunoPharmaceutics, Inc., San Diego, Lovelace Respiratory Rsch. Inst., Albuquerque, Micrologix Biotech Inc., Vancouver, B.C., mem. comp. and audit coms., Tima Tech., Inc., Kansas City, AusAm Biotech., Inc., Santa Monica, Calif., mem. comp. and intellectual property coms.; guest lectr. U. S.C. Sch. Bus. Adminstrn., Columbia, 1975-79; pharm. analyst, SunTrust Robinson Humphrey, 2002, Cottonwood Capital Mgmt., LLC, 2002—. Contbr. articles to pharm. jours. Presdl. exch. exec. White House, Washington, 1970-71, U.S. Pharmacopeia Com. of Rev., 1990-94, 95-2001; trustee U. Mo., Kansas City Pharmacy Found., 1993—, v.p., 1994-96, pres., 1996-98, fin. com., 1996 , pres. emeritus, 1998—, chmn. devel. com., 1994-96, chmn. exec. and fin. coms., 1996-98, dean's adv. bd., 1995—; trustee Kansas City Cmty. Found., 1993—, U. Kansas City Bd., Mo., 1996-2001, U. Mo., Kansas City, 2001—; fin. and real estate coms., 1998—; mem. Kansas City Life Sci. Initiative and Undergrad. Rsch. coms., 2001—; dean's adv. bd. Sch. Pharmacy U. Calif., San Francisco, 1994-97, bd. counsellors, 1997-2001; dean's adv. bd. Sch. Pharmacy U. Mo., Kansas City, 1995-2001, 2003—; trustee Conservatory of Music, U. Mo., Kansas City, 1998-2002; Henry W. Bloch Sch. Bus. and Pub. Adminstrn. exec. roundtable U. Mo., Kansas City, 1998-2003; active Internat. Rels. Coun., Kansas City, 1998—; active De La Salle Sch. Devel. Com., 1993-2001, St. Lukes Hosp. Stroke Com., 1993—, U.S. Pharmacopeia Drug Nomenclature Com., 1990-94, 95-2001, vet. drug com., 1998-2001, ARC, Kirkwood Soc. Recipient Grad. award Borden Co., 1962; NIH Pub. Health Svc. Tng. grantee, 1962-65; Am. Found. for Pharm. Edn. fellow, 1962-65, Sir Henry S. Wellcome Meml. fellow, 1962-63, Am. Inst. Chemists fellow, 1965-70. Mem.: ACS, AAAS, Licensing Exec. Soc., Fedn. Internat. Pharmacy, Pharm. Mfrs. Assn., N.Y. Acad. Sci., Acad. Pharm. Sci., Am. Pharm. Assn., Am. Assn. Pharm. Scis., Am. Found. for Pharm. Edn. Centurion, ARC Kirkwood Soc., La Jolla Country Club, La Jolla (Calif.) Beach and Tennis Club, Carriage Club (Kansas City, Mo.), Hallbrook Country Club (Kansas City, Mo.), Balboa Bay Club (Newport Beach, Calif.), Phi Lambda Sigma, Rho Chi, Sigma Xi. Home: 5330 Ward Pky Kansas City MO 64112-2369 Office: KC Pharma LLC 222 W Gregory Blvd Kansas City MO 64114-1110 also: 8486 El Paseo Grande La Jolla CA 92037-3013

JOHNSON, RICHARD FRED, lawyer; b. July 12, 1944; s. Sylvester Hiram and Naomi Ruth (Jackson) Johnson; m. Sheila Conley, June 26, 1970; children: Brendon, Bridget, Timothy, Laura. BS, Miami U., Oxford, Ohio, 1966; JD cum laude, Northwestern U., 1969. Bar: Ill. 1969, U.S. Dist. Ct. (no. dist.) Ill. 1969), U.S. Dist. Ct. (ctrl. dist.) Ill. 2000, U.S. Ct. Appeals (7th cir.) 1977, U.S. Ct. Appeals (2d cir.) 1980, U.S. Ct. Appeals (9th cir.) 1991, U.S. Ct. Appeals (5th cir.) 1993, U.S. Supreme Ct. 1978. Law clk. U.S. Dist. Ct. (no. dist.) Ill., Chgo., 1969-70; assoc. firm Lord, Bissell & Brook, Chgo., 1970-77, ptnr., 1977—. Lectr. legal edn. Contbr. articles to profl. jours. Recipient Am. Jurisprudence award 1968. Mem. Chgo. Bar Assn., Union League. Home: 521 W Roscoe St Chicago IL 60657-3518 Office: Lord Bissell & Brook 115 S La Salle St Ste 3200 Chicago IL 60603-3902

JOHNSON, RICHARD FREDERICK, psychologist, researcher, educator; b. Boston, July 11, 1943; s. Frederick and Alice Hilda (Kullen) J.; m. Sharyn Lois Doyle, Sept. 11, 1965; children: Wendy Kullen, Adam Bruns. BA with honors, Northeastern U., 1966; MA in Psychology, Brandeis U., 1968, PhD, 1970. Lic. psychologist, Mass. Rsch. psychologist Medfield (Mass.) Found., 1972-76; rsch. psychologist Human Factors and Physiology Group U.S. Army Natick R&D Labs., 1976-83; rsch. psychologist Mil. Performance div. U.S. Army Rsch. Inst. Environ. Medicine, Natick, 1983—. Mem. faculty Medfield State Hosp., 1974-76; sr. lectr. psychology Northeastern U., 1971-76, 84—; U.S. nat. leader panel HUM-TP6 Tech. Coop. Program, 2001—; cons. in field. Editl. cons. Jour. Cons. and Clin. Psychology, 1973-83, Exercise and Sport Scis. Revs., 1985-87, Psychosomatic Medicine, 1987-92, Jour. Aging and Health, 1991-96, Human Factors, 1992—, Armed Forces and Society, 1993—, Aviation, Space and Environ. Medicine, 1997—, Psychol. Reports, 1999—, Perceptual and Motor Skills, 1999—, The Gerontologist, 2000—, Medicine and Sci. in Sports and Exercise, 2000—, Ergomomics, 2002—; corr. assoc. commentator Behavioral and Brain Scis., 1978—; contbr. over 100 articles to profl. jours., book chpts., tech. reports. Capt. Med. Svc. Corps U.S. Army, 1970-72, with Res., 1966-74. Recipient Milton H. Erickson Sci. Excellence award Am. Soc. Clin. Hypnosis, 1977; grantee Nat. Inst. Mental Health, 1972-76; fellow Brandeis U. 1967-70. Fellow Am. Psychol. Assn. (chmn. conv. program div. gen. psychology 1974-75), Am. Psychol. Soc.; mem. AAAS, Aerospace Med. Assn., Human Factors and Ergonomics Soc., Soc. Applied Exptl. Engring. Psychologists, Sigma Xi (local chmn. program com., 1989-90, pres.-elect 1990, pres. 1991). Office: US Army Rsch Inst Environ Medicine Mil Performance Divsn Natick MA 01760 E-mail: richard.johnson@na.amedd.army.mil.

JOHNSON, RICHARD KARL, hospitality company executive; b. Gaylord, Minn., May 27, 1947; s. Karl S. and Mildred (Tollefson) J.; m. Eva Margaret Wick, Oct. 12, 1973; children: Michelle, Richard, Ryan. BA, Gustavus Adolphus U., St. Peter, Minn., 1969. Gen. mgr. Green Giant Restaurants, Inc., Mpls., 1969-71, Mpls. Elks Club, Mpls., 1971-73; dir. concept devel. Internat. Multifoods, Mpls., 1972-75; v.p. concept devel. A&WFood Svcs. Can., North Vancouver, B.C., 1975-81; dir. food and beverages Ramada, Reno, 1981-82; pres., owner R.K. Johnson & Assoc., Reno, 1981—; owner D.J. Mgmt., 1990—; pres., owner Metzker Johnson Group, 2002—. Asst. gen. mgr. Gold Dust West Casino, Reno, 1983-85; gen. mgr. P&M Corp., Reno, 1985-86; v.p. ops. C.P.S.W. Inc., Reno and Tempe, Ariz., 1986-87, Lincoln Fairview, Reno, 1987-89; v.p. corp. affairs Prudential Realty, Nev., 1991-2002. Mem. Aircraft Owners and Pilots Assn., Nat. Restaurant Assn., Nev. Realtor, Elks Club. Lutheran. Avocations: flying, scuba diving. Home and Office: RK Johnson & Assoc 825 Meadow Springs Dr Reno NV 89509-5913

JOHNSON, RICHARD KENT, publishing executive; b. Moberly, Mo., Mar. 22, 1952; s. Edward and Elizabeth Johnson; m. Susan Dale Fersh, Sept. 4, 1976; children: Alexis, Claire. BA, Am. U., 1974. TV prodn. specialist Smithsonian Inst., Washington, 1974-77; dir. pub. rels. Congl. Info. Svc., Bethesda, Md., 1977-80, dir. advt. and promotion, 1980-83, dir. communications, 1983-89, dir. mktg., 1989-90, v.p. mktg., 1990-96, Univ. Publs. Am., Bethesda, 1990-96; sr. v.p. Congl. Info. Svc. and Univ. Pubs. Am., 1997-98; enterprise dir. Scholarly Pub. and Acad. Resources Coalition, Washington, 1998—. Bd. dirs. BioOne; mem. steering com. SPARC Europe, 2001—; mem. governing bd. Cornell U. Project Euclid, 2002—; mem. NIH PubMed Ctr. Nat. Adv. Com., 2003—. Recipient Echo Leader award Direct Mktg. Assn., 1986, Mktg. Achievement award Info. Industry Assn., 1985, 89, 90. Home: 5622 Lamar Rd Bethesda MD 20816-1350 Office: 21 Dupont Cir NW Ste 800 Washington DC 20036-1543 E-mail: rick@arl.org.

JOHNSON, RICHARD TENNEY, lawyer; b. Evanston, Ill., Mar. 24, 1930; s. Ernest Levin and Margaret Abbott (Higgins) J.; m. Marilyn Bliss Meuth, May 1, 1954; children: Ross Tenney, Lenore, Jocelyn. AB with high honors, U. Rochester, 1951; postgrad., Trinity Coll., Dublin, Ireland, 1954-55; LLB, Harvard, 1958. Bar: D.C. 1959. Trainee Office Sec. Def., 1957-59; atty. Office Gen. Counsel. Dept. Def., 1959-63; dep. gen. counsel Dept. Army, 1963-67, Dept. Transp., 1967-70; gen. counsel CAB, 1970-73, mem., 1976-77; gen. counsel NASA, 1973-75, ERDA, 1975-76; chmn. organizational integration Dept. Energy Activation, Exec. Office of Pres., 1977; ptnr. firm Sullivan & Beauregard, 1978-81; gen. counsel Dept. Energy, 1981-83; ptnr. Zuckert, Scott, Rasenberger & Johnson, 1983-87; prin. Law Offices of R. Tenney Johnson, Esq., Washington, 1987-2001; gen. counsel Assn. of Univs. for Rsch. in Astronomy, 1987—. Lt. USNR, 1951-54. Mem. ABA, Fed. Bar Assn., Cosmos Club, Phi Beta Kappa, Theta Delta Chi. E-mail: marandten@starpower.net.

JOHNSON, RICHARD TIDBALL, neurology, microbiology and neuroscience educator, research virologist; b. Grosse Pointe, Mich, July 16, 1931; s. Horton and Katharine (Tidball) J.; m. Frances W. Johnson, Sept. 18, 1954; children: Carlton, Erica, Matthew, Nathan. AB cum laude, U. Colo., Boulder, 1953; MD, U. Colo., Denver, 1956. Diplomate Am. Bd. of Psychiatry and Neurology. Intern Stanford U. Hosp., San Francisco, 1956-57; clin. pathologist dept. virus diseases Walter Reed Army Inst. of Research, Washington, 1957-58, asst. chief dept. of virus diseases, 1959; asst. resident in neurology Mass. Gen. Hosp., 1959-60, clin. fellow neuropathology, 1959-61, sr. resident neurology, 1961-62; teaching fellow in neurology Harvard Med. Sch., Boston, 1959-60, teaching fellow neuropathology, 1959-61, teaching fellow neurology, 1961-62; exchange teaching fellow, 1st asst. in neurology Med. Sch. of King's Coll., U. Durham, Newcastle-Upon-Tyne, 1962; hon. fellow dept. microbiology Australian Nat. U., Canberra, 1962-64; assoc. neurologist Cleve. Met. Gen. Hosp., 1964-69; asst. prof. neurology Case Western Res. U., Cleve., 1964-68, assoc. prof. neurology, 1968-69; assoc. prof. microbiology Johns Hopkins U. Sch. of Medicine, Balt., 1969-74, Dwight D. Eisenhower prof. neurology, 1969-88, prof. microbiology, 1974—, prof. neurosci., 1983—; joint appointment dept. molecular microbiology & immunology Johns Hopkins U. Bloomberg Sch. Pub. Health, 1984—. Neurologist Johns Hopkins Hosp., Balt., 1969—, neurologist-in-chief, 1988-97, prof., dir. dept. neurology, 1988-97; cons. neurology Balt. City Hosp., 1974; vis. prof. U. Peruana Cayetano Heredia, Lima, Peru, 1971, Imperial Coll. of Health Sci., Teheran, Iran, 1974, Inst. fur Virologie und Immunobiologie, U. Wurzburg, 1976; vis. prof. neurology and neuropathology Mahidol U., Bangkok, 1984; vis. sci. Armed Forces Research Inst. of Med. Sci., Bangkok, Thailand, 1984; founding dir. Nat. Neurosci. Inst., Singapore, 1997-2000. Author (with others): Amotrophic Lateral Sclerosis: Recent Research Trends, 1976; author: Infections of the Nervous System, 1987, Viral Infections and the Developing Nervous System, 1988, Viral Infections of the Nervous System, 1982, 1998, Current Therapy in Neurologic Diseases, Vol. 2, 1987, Current Therapy in Neurologic Diseases, Vol. 3, 1990, Current Therapy in Neurologic Diseases, Vol. 4, 1993, Current Therapy in Neurologic Diseases, Vol. 5, 1997, Current Therapy in Neurologic Diseases, Vol. 6, 2001; mem. editl. bd. 10 profl. jours.; editor: Annal. Neurol., 1988—. Mem. adv. bd. Nat. Multiple Sclerosis Soc., 1971—, exec. com., 1981—, chmn., 1985—89; spl. cons. to NIH on transmissible spongiform encephalopathis, 2001—; mem. adv. coun. James A. Baker Inst. for Animal Health, Cornell U., 1977—89; program dir. Pew Neurosci. Program, Pew Charitable Trusts, 1985—91. Decorated comendador Order of Hipolito Unanue; recipient Jean Martin Charcot aard Internat. Fedn. of Multiple Sclerosis Soc. 1985, Smadel medal Infectious Disease Soc. of Am., 1986, Multiple Sclerosis Soc. medal Assn.of Brit. Neurologists, 1986,; Pioneer award Int. Soc. Neuroviro, 1999, fellow Royal College of Physicians of London (hon), 2003, numerous others. Fellow Am. Acad. of Neurology (2d v.p. 1975-77); mem. Assn. of Am. Physicians, Am. Soc. for Virology, Australian Assn. of Neurologists (hon.), Interurban Clin. Club, Acad. Brasileira de Neurologia, Assn. for Rsch. in Nervous and Mental

Diseases, Internat. Brain Rsch. Orgn., Peripatetic Club, Soc. for Neurosci., Soc. Peruana de Psiquiatria, Johns Hopkins Med. Soc. (pres. 1970-71), Balt. Neurol. Soc. (pres. 1973-74), Am. Soc. for Clin. Investigation, Am. Neurol. Assn. (councillor 1977-81, v.p. 1984-85, pres. 1986-87), Am. Assn. of Neuropathologists (assoc.), World Fedn. of Neurology (chmn. research group on neuroimmunology and virology 1979—), Am. Soc. for Microbiology, AAAS, Philippine Neurol. Assn. (hon. fellow), Internat. Soc. for Antiviral Rsch., Inst. of Medicine of the Nat. Acad. of Sci., Am. Fedn. of Clin. Rsch., Alpha Omega Alpha, Phi Beta Kappa. Avocations: photography, travel. Office: Johns Hopkins U Sch Medicine Dept of Neurology 600 N Wolfe St Meyer 6-181 Baltimore MD 21205 E-mail: rtj@jhmi.edu.

JOHNSON, RICK, state official; m. Cindy Johnson. Former commr., bd. chmn. Osceola County; Spkr. of Ho. Mich. Ho. Reps., Dist. 102, 2001—. Mem. Pine River Sch. Bd. Edn.; dist. dir. Mich. Farm Bur. Mem.: Osceola County Republican Party (chmn.). Republican. Office: 166 Capitol Bldg PO Box 30014 Lansing MI 48909-7514 Office Fax: 517-373-9371. Business E-Mail: rijohnson@house.mi.gov.

JOHNSON, ROBERT ALAN, lawyer; b. Harrisburg, Pa., June 18, 1944; s. Harry Andrew and Minna Melissa (Ebert) J.; m. Selina Braham Pedersen, Aug. 25, 1979; children: Isabella P., Robert A. Jr. BA, Washington and Jefferson Coll., 1966; JD, Harvard U., 1969. Bar: Pa. 1969. Assoc. Buchanan Ingersoll, Pitts., 1969-76, ptnr., 1977—. Contbr. legal articles to profl. jours. Pres. Bach Choir Pitts., 1979-81; bd. dirs. Pitts. Opera, 1985-94, River City Brass Band, Pitts., 1986-95, Renaissance and Baroque Soc., Pitts., 1994—, Friends of the Music Libr., Carnegie Libr. of Pitts., 1995—, CTC Found., 1999—, River City Brass Band Charitable Endowment, Pitts., 2000—, Early Music Am., 2002-. Fellow Am. Coll. Tax Counsel, Am. Coll. Employee Benefits Counsel; mem. ABA, Allegheny County Bar Assn., Allegheny Tax Soc. (chmn. 1982-83), Pitts. Tax Club, Duquesne Club. Republican. Presbyterian. Avocation: avid collector classical music recs. Home: 601 St James St Pittsburgh PA 15232-1434 Office: Buchanan Ingersoll 301 Grant St Ste 20 Pittsburgh PA 15219-1410 E-mail: johnsonra@bipc.com.

JOHNSON, ROBERT ALLISON, life insurance company executive; b. Canandaigua, N.Y., Sept. 8, 1928; s. Allison Fisher and Thelma Marie (Beers) J.; m. Suzanne Amundsen Stone, Dec. 18, 1951; children— Pamela Suzanne, Carol Alison, Elizabeth Stone, Cynthia Marie. BA in History, Harvard U., 1950; MBA, Western New Eng. Coll., 1963. With Mass. Mut. Life Ins. Co., Springfield, 1951—, employment mgr., 1958-72, dir. personnel, 1972-76, sr. v.p., 1976—. Active ARC. Served with U.S. Army, 1951-53. Mem. Life Office Mgmt. Assn., Am. Soc. C.L.U.'s. Home: 181 Windjammer Dr Leesville SC 29070 Office: 1295 State St Springfield MA 01111-0001

JOHNSON, ROBERT BRUCE, historic preservationist; b. Salina, Kans., Dec. 14, 1941; s. Robert Alexander and Virginia Belle (Keen) J.; m. Dora Koundakjian, May 14, 1966 (div. May 1986); children: Martin, Alicia; m. Genevieve Whittemore, Oct. 18, 1986; 1 child, James Trevor Johnson. BA, Wheaton Coll., 1964; JD, Cath. U. Sch. of Law, Washington, 1976. Orgnl. sales leader The Southwestern Co., Nashville, 1963-65; asst. housing mgr. Nat. Capitol Housing Authority Housing Urban Devel., Washington, 1966-67; project dir. Archdiocese of Washington Office of Edn., Washington, 1967-70; dep. dir. Dept. Labor Youth Svcs., Washington, 1970-75; pres. Intown Properties Inc., Washington, 1977-81, Mt. Vernon Realty Inc., Washington, 1981-86, Premier Realty Svcs. Inc., Washington, 1986-90; sr. v.p. AmeriFund Inc., Washington, 1990-95; devel. dir. Patrick Henry Inst., Lynchburg, Va., 1995-98; pres. Monument Real Estate Historic Properties, 1994—; 576992. Cons. Nat. Trust for Hist. Preservation, Washington, 1982-83, New Covenant Schs., Lynchburg, Va.; ptnr. Towne Ctr. Assocs., Staunton, Va., 1979-92, Capitol Link Devel. Assocs., Washington, 1986-89, Coolidge House Assocs., Washington, 1987-94. Contbr. articles to profl. jours. Treas., co-founder New City Montessori Sch., Washington, 1969—73; mem. Cmty. Advisors on Equal Employment, Washington, 1967—70; patron Nat. Children's Choir, 1979—89; treas., initiator Bottle Bill Initiative Campaign, Washington, 1985—86; hon. chmn. Bus. Adv. Coun., 2002; commr. Presdl. Bus. Commn., 2002. Recipient Silver Palm Eagle Scout Boy Scouts Am., 1957. Mem. Nat. Trust for Hist. Preservation, Hist. Staunton Found. (ann. preservation award 1982, 83), Victorian Soc. Am., Lynchburg Acad. Music Theatre (co-chmn. bus. adv. coun.). Home: Villa Mozart 517 Washington St Lynchburg VA 24504

JOHNSON, ROBERT BRUCE, company director; b. 1944; MS, U. Ariz., 1980, BS, 1968. Hydrologist W.S. Gookin & Assocs., Scottsdale, Ariz., 1972-75; hydrologist II City of Tucson, 1975-78, chief hydrologist, 1978-97, lead adminstr., 1997-98, asst. dir., 1998—. Office: City Tucson PO Box 27210 Tucson AZ 85726-7210

JOHNSON, ROBERT EUGENE, historian, academic administrator; b. NYC, Aug. 7, 1943; s. Robert E. and Eileen Mary (Holden) J.; m. Laura Zoe Climenko; children: Byron, Alexander. BA, Antioch Coll., 1965; PhD, Cornell U., 1975. History lectr. Erindale Coll. U. Toronto, 1971-74, asst. prof. history, 1975-79, assoc. prof. history, 1979-95; prof., 1995—; dir. Ctr. for Russian and East European Studies U. Toronto, 1989-2000. Author: Peasant and Proletarian, 1979, The Seam Allowance, 1982, Contadini e Proletari, 1993; editor: The 1937 Census of USSR, 1992. Rsch. grantee Social Sci. and Humanities Rsch. Coun. Can., Toronto and Moscow, 1994-99. Mem. Am. Hist. Assn., Am. Assn. for Advancement of Slavic Studies, Can. Assn. Slavists (v.p. 1985-86). Avocations: mycology, cross-country skiing, canoeing. Office: U Toronto CREES Munk Ctr 1 Devonshire Pl Toronto ON Canada M5S 3K7 E-mail: johnson@chass.utoronto.ca.

JOHNSON, ROBERT GLENN, geology and geophysics educator; b. Iowa, Dec. 12, 1922; m. Elizabeth Louise Gulliver, July 17, 1949. BS, Case Western Res. U., 1947; PhD, Iowa State U., 1952. Project engr. Bendix Aviation Inc., Red Bank, N.J., 1952-55; scientist Honeywell Inc., Mpls., 1955-74, staff scientist, 1974-90; adj. prof. dept. geology and geophysics U. Minn., Mpls., 1990—. Contbr. articles to profl. publs. Achievements include 23 patents on control technology sensors; pioneering research in silicon microstructure sensor technology; contributions to understanding of glacial climate change. Office: U Minn Dept Geology-Geophys 310 Pillsbury Dr SE Minneapolis MN 55455-0219 E-mail: johns088@johns088.email.umn.edu.

JOHNSON, ROBERT HENRY, political science educator; b. Hannaford, N.D., Jan. 23, 1921; s. Albert Idan and Alma (Peterson) J.; divorced; children: Mark Olin, Eric Lowell, Hilary Jean. BA, Concordia Coll., Moorhead, Minn., 1942; MS, Syracuse U., 1943; PhD, Harvard U., 1949. Tchg. fellow Harvard U., 1948-49, instr. govt., 1949-51; asst. to exec. sec. NSC, 1951-54, mem., sec. spl. staff, 1954-59, dir. planning bd. secretariat, 1959-61, mem. sr. staff, 1961-62; mem. policy planning coun. State Dept., 1962-67; sr. fellow Brookings Instn., 1966-68, guest scholar, 1970, 71, 73, 80; Harvey Picker prof. internat. rels. Colgate U., 1968-71, 80-84, Charles Evans Hughes prof. govt., 1971-80, chmn. dept. polit. sci., 1979-82, 83-84. Vis. fellow Overseas Devel. Coun., 1974-75, 76-77, 84-86, 87-88; sr. fellow Nat. Policy Assn., 1988—; cons. to dir. internat. divsn. GAO, 1978-82; resident assoc. Carnegie Endowment for Internat. Peace, 1982-83, 86-87. Author: Improbable Dangers, U.S. Conceptions of Threat in the Cold War and After, 1994; contbr. articles to profl. jours. and newspapers. With USNR, 1943-46. Recipient Rockefeller Pub. Svc. award, 1958; Alumni Achievement award Concordia Coll., 1975; fellow Social Sci. Rsch. Coun., 1948-49; Ford Found. grantee, 1966 Mem. Am. Polit. Sci. Assn., Coun. on Fgn. Rels. Congregationalist. Home: 3120 Wellington Rd Alexandria VA 22302-2228 Office: Nat Policy Assn 1424 16th St NW Washington DC 20036-2211

JOHNSON, ROBERT LEE, JR., physician, educator, researcher; b. Dallas, Apr. 28, 1926; s. Robert L. and Doris (Miller) J.; m. Aileen Johnson, 1952; children: Stephen Lee, Robert Edward. BS, So. Meth. U., 1947; MD, Northwestern U., 1951. Intern Cook County Hosp., Chgo., 1951-52; resident in internal medicine Parkland Meml. Hosp., Phila., 1952-55; fellow nat. foun. infantile paralysis and clin. instr. U. Tex. Southwestern Med. Ctr., Dallas, 1955-56; fellow dept. physiol. and pharmacology Grad. Sch. Medicine U. Pa., Phila., 1956-57; asst. prof. U. Tex. Southwestern Med. Ctr., Dallas, 1959-65, assoc. prof., 1965-69, prof. medicine, 1969—; John Butler Meml. lectr. U. Wash., Seattle, 2001. Vis. staff Parkland Meml. Hosp., Dallas, 1957—, Zale Lipshy U. Hosp., Dallas, 1989—, St. Paul Hosp., Dallas, 2000-; cons. chest diseases VA Hosp., Dallas, 1966—; dir. sarcoidosis clinic Parkland Meml. Hosp., 1983—; mem. parent rev. com. Nat. Heart, Lung, and Blood Inst. for Spl. Ctrs. of Rsch. proposals, 1983-85; mem. Nat. Heart, Lung, and Blood Rsch. Rev. Com., 1985-89; mem. respiratory and applied physiology study sect. NIH, 1991-94. Mem. editl. bd.: Jour. Clin. Investigation, 1972—77, Jour. Applied Physiology, 1980—82, Circulation, 1996—, guest referee editor: Jour. Applied Physiology, —, Am. Jour. Physiology, —, Chest, —, Circulation, —, Circulation Rsch., —, Am. Jour. Med. Sci., —, Am. Jour. Respiration and Circulation Medicine, —, Jour. Clin. Investigation, —, Early Human Devel., —, Kidney Internat., —. With Naval ROTC, 1945-46; with USNR, 1944-46; maj. USAR, 1962. Mem. Am. Heart Assn. (cardiopulmonary coun. exec. com. mem. 1990-92, nominating com. cardiopulmonary coun. 1989-93, chmn. 1990-92), Am. Thoracic Soc. (planning com. mem. 1987-90, com. proficiency standards 1985-94, Scientific Accomplishment award 1996), Am. Coll. Chest Physicians, Am. Fedn. Clin. Rsch., Am. Physiol. Soc., Am. Soc. Clin. Investigation, Assn. Am. Physicians, Cen. Soc. Clin. Rsch., So. Soc. Clin. Rsch., Soc. Sigma Xi. Office: UT Southwestern Med Ctr 5323 Harry Hines Blvd Stop 9034 Dallas TX 75390-9034

JOHNSON, ROBERT LOUIS, cable television company executive; b. Hickory, Miss., Apr. 8, 1946; m. Sheila Crump, Jan. 19, 1969. BA in History, U. Ill., 1968; M in Pub. Affairs, Princeton U., 1972. Press. sec. Hon. Walter E. Fauntroy, Congl. del. from Washington, 1973—76; v.p. govt. rels. Nat. Cable TV Assn., 1976—79; founder, pres. Black Entertainment TV, Washington, 1979—, Dist. Cablevision, Inc., 1980—; chmn., pres., CEO BET Holdings, Inc. (formerly Black Entertainment TV), Washington, 1993—. Recipient Image award, NAACP, 1982, Bus. of Yr. award, D.C. C. of C., 1985, Exec. Leadership Coun. award, Turner Broadcasting, 1993, 20/20 Vision award, Cablevision Mag., 1995, Hall of Fame award, Broadcasting and Cable Mag., 1997, Good Guys award, Nat. Women's Polit. Caucus, 1998, Disting. Alumni award, Princeton U., 1998. Office: BET Holdings Inc 1900 W Pl NE Washington DC 20018-1211

JOHNSON, ROBERT WOOD, IV, sports team executive; Owner N.Y. Jets, Hempstead, 2000—; chmn., CEO The Johnson Co. Inc. Office: NY Jets 1000 Fulton Ave Hempstead NY 11550-1030

JOHNSON, ROGER, science educator; b. Dayton, Ohio, Apr. 22, 1939; m. Lori Johnson; m. Lori Johnson, Aug. 16, 1968; children: Allison, Erika Story. PhD, U. Conn., Storrs, 1966. Asst. prof. Amherst (Mass.) Prof., 1968, Tufts U., Medford, Mass., 1968—71; prof. Ramapo Coll., Mahwah, NJ, 1971—. Author: Aggression in Man and Animals; contbr. articles. Sr. Fulbright fellow, 1979, rsch. grant, H.F. Guggenheim Found., 1991, 1995. Office: Ramapo Coll Sch Theoretical/Applied Scis Mahwah NJ 07430

JOHNSON, ROGER CHRISTIE, environmental engineer; b. Belmond, Iowa, Aug. 12, 1925; s. Elmer Adolph and Goldie Evelyn (Christie) Johnson; m. Constance Jean Benson, July 26, 1953; children: Christie Clark, Gregory, Jamie, Bradley, Wade, Eric. BS in Chemistry, Calif. Inst. Tech., Pasadena, 1949. Qualified environ. profl, Iowa, cert. waste water operator. Lab technician Gen. Mills, Belmond, 1956-61, asst. quality assurance mgr. West Chgo., Ill., 1961-63; plant chemist Ctrl. Soya, Belmond, 1963-66, quality assurance mgr., 1966-83; environ. engr. Eaton Corp., Belmond, 1983—. Cubmaster, Webelos leader Boys Scouts Am., Belmond, 1964—69; chair, vice-chair Belmond-Klemme Bd. Edn., 2001—, Wright County (Iowa) Dems., 1972—2003; bd. dirs. Belmond Cmty. Retirement Apts., 1970—89. With U.S. Army, 1943—45. Named mem. honor roll, NIACC, 1994; recipient cert. of recognition for protection of Iowa natural resources, State of Iowa, 2000. Mem.: LEPC (Region V), AAAS, Internat. Union Pure and Applied Chemistry, Nat. Resources Def. Coun., Union Concerned Scientists, Inst. Profl. Environ. Practice, Iowa Water Pollution Control Assn., Iowa Environ. Coun., Water Environ. Fedn., Air and Waste Mgmt. Assn., Am. Indsl. Hygiene Assn., Am. Chem. Soc., Sierra Club, Wildlife Fedn. Congregational. Home: 312 4th Ave NE Belmond IA 50421-1314 Office: Eaton Corp 700 Luick Ln S Belmond IA 50421-0303

JOHNSON, ROGER WARREN, chemical engineer; b. Huntsville, Ala., Oct. 25, 1960; s. Frederic Allen and Joan (Bickum) J.; m. Margaret Jane Major, June 16, 1984. BChemE, Auburn U., 1984. Process engr. fibers divsn. E.I. DuPont de Nemours & Co., Waynesboro, Va., 1984-86, devel. engr. imaging systems Brevard, N.C., 1986-87; R & D engr. Hercules Inc.-A&TP, Oxford, Ga., 1987-92; account mgr. Hercules Inc.-Absorbents and Textile Products, Oxford, Ga., 1992-95; product mgr. Hercules Inc.-A&TP, Oxford, Ga., 1995-96; staple II plant mgr. FiberVisions LLC, Oxford, Ga., 1997-98; fiber and film tech. svc. mgr. BP Amoco Polymers, Alpharetta, Ga., 1998—. Mem. Auburn Alumni Assn., Phi Kappa Phi. Home: 1410 Mclendon Ave NE Atlanta GA 30307-2129 Office: BP Amoco Polymers 1410 McLendon Ave NE Atlanta GA 30307

JOHNSON, ROGERS BRUCE, retired chemical company executive; b. Boston, Apr. 8, 1928; s. Rogers Bruce and Dorothy Squires (Aiken) J.; m. Margery Ruth Howe, June 25, 1951 (dec. July 1997); children: Wynn, Carol, Stephen, Herrick; m. Alexandra Caroline Luckes Peacock Lee, Nov. 28, 1998. BA, Harvard U., 1949, MBA, 1955. Field salesman Dow U.S.A., Pitts., 1956-61; mgr. molding materials Dow Europe, Zurich, Switzerland, 1961-65; bus. mgr. styrene polymers Dow U.S.A., Midland, Mich., 1965-70; corp. products dir. Dow Chem. Co., Midland, Mich., 1970-76; v.p. supply, distbn. and planning Dow Chem. U.S.A., Midland, Mich., 1976-81, group v.p. adminstrv. services, 1981-89. Dir. Dow Can., Sarnia, Ont., Can., 1973-77, Dow Pacific, Hong Kong, 1973-77; bd. dirs. Strategic Planning Inst., 1987-88. Bd. dirs. Midland Community Tennis Ctr., (Mich.), 1974-89, Mich. Citizens' Research Council, 1985-89; pres. Midland Community Tennis Ctr. (Mich.), 1975-78, treas., 1972-76, 79-80; pres. Midland County Growth Council, 1985-89. Served to 1st lt. USAF, 1951-53. Decorated Bronze Star Republican. E-mail: bruce1928@aol.com.

JOHNSON, ROLAND ERIC, internist; b. Hackensack, N.J., Jan. 15, 1949; m. Virginia Mary Peterson, June 6, 1970; children: Jennifer Michelle, Ian Eric, Keri Lynn. BA in chemistry, Columbia Coll., 1970, MD, 1974. Diplomate Am. Bd. Internal Medicine. Attending physician Newton Meml. Hosp., Newton, N.J., 1977—. Mem. ACP, Am. Med. Soc., Sussex County Med. Soc., Med. Soc. N.J., Masons. Episcopal. Avocations: cattle farming, skiing, scuba diving, hunting. Home: 555 Stanhope Rd Sparta NJ 07871-2819 Office: Newton Med Ctr 183 High St Newton NJ 07860-9699

JOHNSON, RONALD CARL, chemistry educator; b. Milw., Sept. 5, 1935; s. Carl Walter and Valeska Ella (Schulz) J.; m. Susan Nancy Anderson, Aug. 27, 1960; children: Erica Susan, Laura Karen. BS, Lawrence Coll., 1957; PhD, Northwestern U., 1961. From asst. prof. to prof. Emory U., Atlanta, 1961-75, prof., 1975-2001, prof. emeritus, 2001—. Author: Coordination Chemistry, 1964, 2d edit. 1987; Descriptive Chemistry, 1965, General Chemistry, 1974. Mem. AAAS, AAUP, Am. Chem. Soc. (chair Ga. sect. 1974-75, counselor 1977-80), Ga. Acad. Sci. (pres. 1977-78), Phi Beta Kappa, Sigma Xi. Presbyterian. Avocations: jogging, racquetball, bridge. Office: Emory U Dept Chemistry Atlanta GA 30322-0001 E-mail: rjohn04@emory.edu.

JOHNSON, RONALD E. grocery company executive; With Harris-Teeter; mgmt. positions at Food Loin, Bi-Lo, Food Giant and Richfood; chmn., pres., CEO Kash n'Karry Food Stores Inc., Fla., 1995—97, Farm Fresh, Norfolk, Va., 1997—98; pres., COO Jitney-Jungle Stores of Am. Inc., Jackson, Miss., 1998—99, CEO, 1999—. Office: Jitney Jungle Stores Am Ste D20 1855 Lakeland Dr Jackson MS 39216-4947

JOHNSON, RONALD KAY, retail company executive; b. Abilene, Tex., Feb. 26, 1939; s. Vernon Floyd and Mattye Sue (Milburn) J.; m. Sally Ann Fleet, Nov. 22, 1962 (div.); 1 child, Sheri May. AA, Spokane Falls Coll., 1970; BA in Theatre Arts with honors, Eastern Wash. State U., 1971; AS with honors, Portland C.C., 1992. Divsn. mgr. Nutrition Ctrs. Fred Meyer, Inc., Portland, Oreg., 1971—. V.p. Nutrition Ctrs. Divsn., 1979-87; owner, mgr. Valley Mist Farm, San Diego, 1957-65; med. massage therapist, 2003. Actor Lake Oswego Cmty. Theatre, 1979—, Portland Civic Theatre. Recipient Best Supporting Actor award Spokane Civic Theatre, 1967-68, Best Actor award Oreg. Theatre Soc., 1980-81. Avocation: raising race horses. Home: 2319 Old Maypearl Rd Waxahachie TX 75167 E-mail: RKJohnson@ectisp.net.

JOHNSON, RONDA JANICE, professional not-for-profit fundraiser; b. Muleshoe, Tex., Sept. 28, 1943; d. Randolph Revere and Betty Jo (Pool) J. BS in Edn., U. Tex., Austin, 1966; MBA, Houston Bapt. U., 1980. Cert. fund raising exec. Tchr. Galena Park Ind. Sch. Dist./Houston Ind. Sch. Dist., 1966-68; adminstrv. asst. Houston-Galveston Area Coun., 1968-69, Johns Hopkins U. Applied Physics Lab., Columbia, Md., 1969-73; dir. adminstrn. Edmondson Coll. Bus., Chattanooga, 1973-76; dir. Branell Women's Coll., Atlanta, 1976-78; dir. devel. U. Tex. Health Sci. Ctr., Houston, 1978-84, Houston Symphony Orch., 1984-85, Houston Child Guidance Ctr., 1985-87; pres. ctrl. divsn. Douglas M. Lawson Assocs., Inc., Houston, 1987-96; sr. cons. Cargill Assocs., Ft. Worth, 1996-97; vice chancellor instnl. advancement Tex. Tech. U., Health Scis. Ctr., Lubbock, 1997-2000; exec. dir. U. Cin. Found., 2000—02; dir. devel. Columbia U. Health Scis. Ctr., N.Y.C., 2003—. Instr. Vol. Support Ctr., Houston, 1992, continuing edn. div. Rice U., Houston, 1992-95. Adv. bd. Houston Achievement Pl., 1992; bd. dirs. Escape Ctr., Houston, 1992-94. Named Woman of the Yr. by S.W. Houston News, 1994. Mem. Nat. Soc. Fundraising Execs. (bd. dirs. 1989—, pres. 1994-95; mem. found. bd. 1997—), Planned Giving Coun., Houstonian Network. Republican. Avocations: reading, photography, travel, cooking, gardening. Office: Univ Cincinnati Found Exec Dir PO Box 19970 Cincinnati OH 45219 Address: 3778 Brighton Manor Cincinnati OH 45208 Fax: (513) 556-4340. E-mail: ronda.johnson@uc.edu.

JOHNSON, ROSEMARY WRUCKE, personnel management specialist; b. Leith, N.D., Sept. 21, 1924; d. Rudolph Aaron and Metta Tomina (Andersen) Wrucke; m. Robert Johnson Jr., Sept. 28, 1945 (div. 1964). Student, George Washington U., 1944-45, 47, Nat. Art Sch., Washington, 1943-45. Supr. Displaced Persons Commn., Frankfurt, Germany, 1950-52, FBI, Washington, 1952-81; cons. position mgmt. orgn. design Arlington, Va., 1981—. Mem. NAFE, Classification and Compensation Soc., Soc. FBI Alumni (membership chmn. 1985-91), Internat. Platform Assn. Lutheran. Avocations: painting, sketching. Home and Office: 3710 Lee Hwy Arlington VA 22207-3721

JOHNSON, ROSS, state legislator; b. Sept. 28, 1939; m. Diane Morris; 2 children. BA in History, Calif. State U., Fullerton; JD, Western State U. Mem. Calif. Assembly, 1978-95, Republican leader, 1988-91; mem. Calif. State Senate, 1995—, mem. appropriations com., edn. com., ins. com., mem. fin., investment and internat. trade com. Mem. Republican State Ctrl. Com.; former chair Orange County Citizens for Law and Order. Served with USN. Republican. Office: State Capitol Rm 305 Sacramento CA 95814 also: 18552 Macarthur Blvd Ste 395 Irvine CA 92612-1226*

JOHNSON, ROY RAGNAR, electrical engineer, researcher; b. Chgo., Jan. 23, 1932; s. Ragnar Anders and Ann Viktoria (Lundquist) J.; m. Martha Ann Mattson, June 21, 1963; children: Linnea Marit, Kaisa Ann. BSEE, U. Minn., 1954, MS, 1956, PhD, 1959. Rsch. fellow U. Minn., 1957-59; from rsch. engr. to sr. basic rsch. scientist Boeing Sci. Research Labs., Seattle, 1959-72; prin. scientist KMS Fusion, Inc., Ann Arbor, Mich., 1972-74, dir. fusion expts., 1974-78, tech. dir., 1978-91, dept. head for fusion and plasmas, 1985-88; tech. dir. Innovation Assocs., Inc., Ann Arbor, 1992; inertial confinement fusion classification/records mgr. Lawrence Livermore Nat. Lab., 1992—. Vis. lectr. U. Wash., Seattle, 1959-60; vis. scientist Royal Inst. Tech., Stockholm, 1963-64; cons. Dept. Edn., Washington, 1995, 98, 2000, 03. Author: Nonlinear Effects in Plasmas, 1969, Plasma Physics, 1977, Research Trends in Physics, 1992; contbr. articles to profl. publs.; patentee in field. Bd. advisors Rose-Hulman Inst. Tech., 1982— . Decorated chevalier Order of St. George; comdr. Order of Holy Cross of Jerusalem. Fellow: Am. Phys. Soc.; mem.: AIAA, IEEE (life), AAAS, N.Y. Acad. Scis., Am. Def. Preparedness Assn., Nuc. Plasma Scis. Soc. of IEEE (exec. com. 1972—75), Swedish Club Detroit, Swedish Coun. Am., Am. Swedish Inst., Swedish Am. Hist. Soc., Commonwealth Club Calif., Assn. Old Crows, Torpar Riddar Orden, Vasa Order Am. (past chmn. Svea lodge), Gamma Alpha, Eta Kappa Nu. Lutheran. Home: PO Box 166 Livermore CA 94551-0166 Office: Livermore Nat Lab PO Box 808 Livermore CA 94551-0808 E-mail: johnson3@llnl.gov.

JOHNSON, RUFUS WINFIELD, lawyer; b. Montgomery County, Md., May 1, 1911; s. Charles L. and Margaret (Smith) J.; m. Rosena L. Allen, June 21, 1939 (div. May 1971); m. Vaunda Louise Griffith, May 29, 1971; step-children: Yvonne, Jackie, Karen, Rodney, Michelle. AB, Howard U., 1934, postgrad., 1934-36, LLB, 1939. Bar: Calif., Ark., Supreme Ct. Ark., Supreme Ct. Calif., D.C. Dist. Ct., U.S. Ct. Appeals, D.C., U.S. Supreme Ct., Supreme Ct. of South Korea; cert. counsel Judge Advocate Gen. Sch., Washington. Pvt. practice, D.C., Calif., Ark., 1945—. Originator Lawyer's Pro Bono Svc. Ret. Lt. Col. USAR. Decorated Combat Inf. badge, Purple Heart, Bronze Star with 2 oak leaf clusters, Spl. Citation for Bravery. Mem. VFW (life), Am. Judicature Soc., Am. Acad. Polit. and Social Sci., Mil. Order Purple Heart, Internat. Soc. Poets, Am. Kempo Karate Assn., Sr. Citizens Coalition, Ret. Officers Assn., Am. Legion, Masons, Am. Karate Assn. (5th degree Shorin-Ryu Black Belt), Lions. Baptist. Home: PO Box 776 Mason TX 76856-0776

JOHNSON, RUPERT HARRIS, JR., finance company executive; BA, Washington and Lee U., 1962. With Franklin Resources, Inc., San Mateo, Calif., 1965—, exec. v.p., chief investment officer, dir.; sr. v.p., asst. sec. Franklin Templeton Distbrs., Inc.; pres. Franklin Advisers, Inc.; now v.p. Traiting Portfolio. Mem. exec. com., bd. govs. Investment Co. Inst.; trustee Santa Clara U., Washington and Lee U.; chmn. bd. dirs. Franklin Mgmt., Inc.; exec. v.p., sr. investment officer Franklin Trust Co.; dir. various Franklin Templeton funds; portfolio mgr. Franklin DynaTech Fund. With USMC, 1962-65. Mem. Nat. Assn. Securities Dealers (dist. conduct com.). Office: Franklin Resources Inc Templeton Group 777 Mariners Island Blvd San Mateo CA 94404-1585*

JOHNSON, SALLY A. nurse, educator; b. Rockford, Ill., Apr. 24, 1923; d. Herbert A. and Aileen (Peyton) Johnson; children: Ann Elizabeth Scannell, Stacey Aileen Lerager. RN Good Samaritan Hosp., 1945; nurse obstetrics delivery Women's Hosp., N.Y.C., 1947-49, St. Francis Hosp., Evanston, Ill., 1953; charge, head nurse Broward Gen. Hosp., Ft. Lauderdale, Fla., 1968; night supr. Ashbrook Convalescent and Nursing Hosp., Scotch Plains, N.J., 1968—. Owner Thomas A. Edison Brick Co., Sally Johnson Enterprises. Coun. chmn. Betty Merit Tchrs. Scholarship, 1962; area nat. organizer Girl Scouts U.S.A., 1962-65; Westfield (N.J.) Round-Up and Health chmn., 1962-63; pres. Tamaques Sch., 1965, adviser Parent Tchr. Orgn., 1966, fgn. relationship chmn., 1967-68; exec. bd. chmn. Westfield HS PTA Newsletter, 1968-70; chmn. Nat. Space Edn., Westfield, 1964; Westfield chmn. fgn. nurses Overlook Hosp., Summit, N.J., 1964-69. Recipient scholarship to Harvard U. Coll. Bus. Mem. Nat. Assn. Investors Corp., Nat. Dist. Nurses Assn., NOW (N.J. coord. 1967-68), Am. Contract Bridge League, Bridge Tchrs. Assn., Naples Investment Club (sec. 1995-96). Republican. Achievements include patent for marking devices. Office: 50 Quiche Ct Fort Myers FL 33912 Home: 8415 Excalibur Cr B-3 Naples FL 34108 E-mail: sallyjohnson@comcast.net.

JOHNSON, SAMIRA EL-CHEHABI, marketing professional; b. Niagara Falls, N.Y., Mar. 2, 1958; d. Munzir and Ismat (Zakaria) El-Chehabi; m. Kenneth M. Johnson, Sept. 21, 1991; 1 child, Davis B. BS in Med. Tech. magna cum laude, SUNY, Buffalo, 1980. Component lab. supr. ARC, Detroit, 1982-85; sr. med. technologist Rush Presbyn. St Lukes Med. Ctr., Chgo., 1985-86; tech. cons. Baxter Internat., Deerfield, Ill., 1986-88, ednl. svcs. mgr., 1988-89, market mgr., 1989-93, sr. market mgr., 1993-99; dir. mktg. Cerus Corp., Concord, Calif., 1999—2003; freelance cons., 2003—. Assoc. editor Continuous Flow, 1988-90, Component Therapy Digest, 1988-90; patentee in field. Mem. Nat. Blood Data Resource Ctr., 1996—. Mem. ANA (program adminstr. 1988-98), Am. Soc. Clin. Pathologists, Am. Soc. Med. Technologists (program adminstr. 1988-98), Am. Assn. Blood Banks, Internat. Soc. Blood Transfusion. Avocations: sailing, scuba diving, theater, horseback riding, rollerblading. Home and Office: 25023 N Abbey Glenn Dr Hawthorn Woods IL 60047-9759 E-mail: samira_johnson@direcway.com.

JOHNSON, SAMUEL (SAM JOHNSON), congressman; b. San Antonio, Tex., Oct. 11, 1930; m. Shirley L. Melton; children: James R., Gini Mulligan, Beverly Briney. BBA, So. Meth. U., 1951; M in Internat. Affairs, George Washington U.; grad., Armed Forces Staff Coll., Nat. War Coll. Joined USAF, 1950, fighter pilot, prisoner of war, 1966-73, former dir. Air Force Fighter Weapons Sch., former mem. Thunderbirds, wing commdr., air div. commdr., ret., 1979; founder home bldg. co., 1979; mem. Tex. Ho. of Reps., 1984-91, U.S. Congress from 3d Tex. dist., Washington, 1991—; mem. ways and means com.; mem. edn. and the workforce com., chmn. employer-employeerels. subcom. Edn. and the workforce com., early childhood, youth and families subcom. Chmn. Conservative Action Team. Decorated 2 Silver Stars, Disting. Flying Cross, 4 Air medals, 2 Purple Hearts. Republican. Office: 1211 Longworth Ho Office Bldg Washington DC 20515-0001 also: 801 E Campbell Rd Ste 425 Richardson TX 75081-1867*

JOHNSON, SAMUEL CURTIS, chemical company executive; b. Racine, Wis., Mar. 2, 1928; s. Herbert Fisk and Gertrude (Brauner) J.; m. Imogene Powers, May 8, 1954; children: Samuel Curtis III, Helen Johnson-Leipold, Herbert Fisk III, Winifred Johnson Marquart. BA, Cornell U., 1950; MBA, Harvard U., 1952; LLD (hon.), Carthage Coll., 1974, Northland Coll., 1974, Ripon Coll., 1980, Carroll Coll., 1981, U. Surrey, 1985, Marquette U., 1986, Nijenrode U., 1992. With S.C. Johnson & Son, Inc., Racine, 1954—, internat. v.p., 1962-63, exec. v.p., 1963-66, pres., 1966-67, chmn., pres., chief exec. officer, 1967-72, chmn., chief exec. officer, 1972-88, chmn., 1988—; CEO S.C. Johnson Commercial Markets, 1996—. Bd. dirs. Deere & Co., Moline, Ill., H.J. Heinz Co., Phila., Mobil Corp., N.Y.C.; chmn. bd. dirs. Johnson Worldwide Assocs., Inc., Johnson Internat. Inc. Trustee Am. Mus. Natural History, N.Y.C.; trustee emeritus The Mayo Found., Cornell U., presdl. councillor; chm Johnson's Wax Fund, Inc., Johnson Found., Inc.; founding chmn. emeritus Prairie Sch., Racine; chmn. adv. coun. Cornell U. Grad. Sch. Mgmt.; regent emeritus Smithsonian Instn.; hon. mem. Bus. Coun.; mem. nat. bd. govs. The Nature Conservancy. Mem. Chi Psi. Clubs: Cornell (N.Y.C., Milw.); Univ. (Milw.); Racine Country. Home: 4815 Lighthouse Dr Racine WI 53402-2666 Office: S C Johnson Commercial Markets 8310 16TH St Sturtevant WI 53177

JOHNSON, SANDRA ANN, educator, counselor; b. Houston, Apr. 27, 1958; d. Johnnie and Area (Bradford) Johnson. AA, Houston C.C., 1991; BBA, Tex. So. U., 1994; MA, Prairie View A&M U., 1998; PhD, Tex. So. U., 2000; PhD in Psychology, Berne U. Lic. profl. counselor. Tchr. computers Houston Sch. Dist., 1981—. Instr. North Harris Coll., Houston, 1996—, Houston C.C.; counselor Houston C.C. Sys.; rsch. resident, Saint Kitts and Nevis. Vol. Herman Hosp., Houston, 1987—88, U. Tex. Health Sci. Ctr.; intern, vol. DePelchin Children Ctr., 1997—98; counselor Vision of Hope Women, Houston, 1996—97, Cmty. Devel. Corp.; contact person Houston Mayor's Camp, 1997; pres., bd. dirs. Vision of Hope; pres. CAP Cmty. Devel.; pro bono counselor Black Ams. in low income areas; summer resident St. Kitts, West Indies. Named Disting. Role Model of Houston, North Main Ch. of God in Christ, 1998; recipient Outstanding Counselor, Houston C.C. Sys. Mem. Chi Sigma Iota. Democrat. Baptist. Avocations: tennis, golf, jogging, reading, racquetball. Office: Houston Cmty Coll System Southeast Campus Houston TX 77088-7102 E-mail: sondra_johnson@yahoo.co.uk.

JOHNSON, SANDRA LYNN TERRY, education consultant; b. Mesa, Ariz., Apr. 14, 1942; d. Kenneth Cade and Merlyn Grace (Mattes) Terry; m. Olin Neal Johnson, June 2, 1961; children: Diane Lynn Johnson McLean, Keith Terry Johnson. BS, Tex. Tech U., 1967; MA, U. Tex., 1983, PhD, 1994. Cert. secondary, elem., kindergarten, and gifted edn. tchr., Tex. Tchr. various pvt. schs., Austin, Tex., 1969-84, Austin Ind. Sch. Dist., 1974-76; dir. University Avenue Early Learning Ctr., Austin, 1976-84; cons. Johnson Cons., Austin, 1984-91, ednl. cons., 1998—; cons. region XIII, Edn. Svc. Ctr., Austin, 1991-98; adj. faculty U. Tex., Austin, 1998. Trainer AP Environ. Sci. for Coll. Bds., 1996-98. Editor: Hands Across Texas, 1991, Fulfilling a Dream, 1997, And There Was Light, 1998, Foundation for the Future, 2000; contbg. author mongraph: Perspectives in Gifted Education: Young Gifted Children, Rickes Center for Gifted Children, U. Denver; contbr. articles to profl. jours., mags., newspapers and profl. newsletters; featured in PBS video The Equitable Classroom. Sunday sch. tchr. University Avenue Ch. of Christ, Austin, 1975-83; master tchr. Nat. Tchr. Tng. Inst. for PBS, 1993-96. Scholar Nat. Honor Soc., 1960, Hardin Simmons U., 1960; Advanced Micro Devices grantee, 1997, Eisenhower grantee, 1997. Mem. Nat. Sci. Tchrs. Assn., Nat. Assn. for Rsch. in Sci. Tchg., Nat. Assn. for Gifted Children, Austin Assn. for Edn. Young Children (v.p. 1971-73, pres. 1973-74, chmn. Week of Young Child 1974-75, newsletter editor 1975-76, historian 1983-86, conf. chmn. 1971-72), Tex. State Tchrs. Assn., Phi Kappa Phi, Kappa Delta Pi. Democrat. Avocations: swimming, reading, painting, hiking, camping, yoga. Office: Johnson Cons Svcs 604 E Covington Dr Austin TX 78753-2712 E-mail: dr_s_johnson@hotmail.com.

JOHNSON, SANKEY ANTON, manufacturing company executive; b. Bremerton, Wash., May 14, 1940; s. Sankey Broyd and Alice Mildred (Norum) J.; m. Carolyn Lee Rogers, Nov. 30, 1968; children: Marni Lee, Ronald Anton. BS in M.E., U. Wash.; MBA, Stanford U. V.p., gen. mgr. Cummins Asia Pacific, Manila, Philippines, 1974-78; v.p. automotive Cummins Engine Co., Columbus, Ind., 1978-79; v.p. North Am. Bus., 1979-81; pres., chief exec. officer Onan Corp., Mpls., 1981-85; exec. v.p. Pentair Inc., St. Paul, from 1985, chief operating officer, 1985—, pres., 1986-89; chmn. Hidden Creek Industries, Mpls., 1989—. Trustee Mfr.'s Alliance. Bd. advisors Stanford Grad. Sch. Bus. Mem. Lafayette Club. Home: 2310 Huntington Point Rd W Wayzata MN 55391-9743 Office: Hidden Creek Industries 294 Grove Ln E Wayzata MN 55391

JOHNSON, SARAH LYNN (LEWIS), librarian, editor; b. New Britain, Conn., Oct. 21, 1969; d. Stephen Harry and Judith Ann (Orman) Lewis. BA in French, Drew U., 1991; MA in Linguistics, Ohio State U., 1992; M Info. and Libr. Studies, U. Mich., 1994. Reference and sys. libr. Bridgewater (Mass.) State Coll., 1995—2002; asst. prof. libr. svcs. Ea. Ill. U., Charleston, 2002—. N.Am. regional editor jour. Reference Revs., 2001—; coord. editor Hist. Novels Rev., 2000—; hist. fiction editor NoveList Readers Adv. Svc., 2001—, Electronic Resources Rev., 2000. Co-author: The Information Professional's Guide to Career Development Online, 2002. Mem. ALA, Assn. Coll. and Rsch. Librs. Office: Eastern Illinois Univ Booth Library Charleston IL 61920 Fax: 217-581-7534. E-mail: cfsln@eiu.edu.

JOHNSON, SCOTT LOREN, sales executive; b. Detroit, July 13, 1963; s. Ronald Fred Johnson and Barbara Ruth (Everett) Dahm. A in Bus. Adminstrn., Oakland C.C., Auburn Hills, Mich., 1989; BBA cum laude, Walsh Coll., 1997. Sales engr. Wilson Agy., Inc., Troy, Mich., 1983-87; pres. Metalex, Inc., Troy, 1987-88; regional sales mgr. Mascotech, Inc., Fraser, Mich., 1988-92, sales dir., 1992-95, sales mgr., 1995-99; dir. sales New Venture Gear, Metaldyne, Inc., Royal Oak, Mich., 1999—. Avocations: alpine skiing, golf, boating.

JOHNSON, SHANNON, professional basketball player; b. Aug. 18, 1974; Attended, U. S.C. Mem. 2 ABL Champion Columbus Quest; profl. basketball player Spain, Orlando Miracle, 1999—. Named All-WNBA 2nd Team, 1999, 2000, East team, Inaugural WNBA All-Star Game, 1999, Ea. Conf. Ers., WNBA All-Star Game, 2000. Office: RDV Sports Complex Orlando Miracle 8701 Maitland Summit Rd Orlando FL 32810

JOHNSON, SHAUN DARRIN, music educator; b. Patchogue, N.Y., May 10, 1968; s. Kenneth Howard and Grace Marie Johnson. MusB, SUNY, 1993, MusM, 1994. Cert. music tchr. N.Y. Music tchr. Glen Cove (N.Y.) Elem. Sch., 1994—95, Westhampton Beach (N.Y.) Mid. Sch., 1995—; dir. music and art Westhampton Beach (N.Y.) Sch. Dist., 2000—. Music dir. Suffolk C.C., Selden, NY, 1997—, stage dir., 2000—. Vol. firefighter Ctr. Moriches (N.Y.) Fire Dept., 1985—2001. Mem.: Hamptons Music Educators Assn. (sec. 1998—), Suffolk County Music Educators Assn. (chmn. 1997—99). Avocations: racquetball, golf, cooking, sailing, reading.

JOHNSON, SHIRLEY ELAINE, management consultant; b. Terre Haute, Ind., Sept. 15, 1946; d. Mervil Ray and Sarah Kathryn (Tucker) W.; children: Richard Alan, Gary Michael. BA, DePaul U., 1991. Sec. to v.p. fin. Cenco Inc., Oak Brook, Ill., 1972-74, exec. asst. to group pres., 1974-75, asst. to chmn., 1975-77, corp. personnel/office mgr., 1977-80; corp. sec. Acadia Petroleum Corp., Denver, 1980-82; mgr. office Chapman, Klein & Weinberg, PC, Denver, 1982-84; asst. to chmn. The Heidrick Ptnrs., Inc., Chgo., 1984-92, v.p., 1992-98; assoc. Heidrick & Struggles Inc., Chgo., 1998-99; cons. Ray & Berndtson, Chgo., 1999—2003, Davis-Burns Group, Roswell, Ga., 2003—. Mem. NAFE, Am. Mgmt. Assn., Exec. Women Internat., Rsch. Roundtable. Home: 6363 Brandywine Trl Norcross GA 30092 Office: 700 Old Roswell Lakes Pkwy Ste 310 Roswell GA 30076

JOHNSON, SHIRLEY Z. lawyer; b. Burlington, Iowa, Mar. 6, 1940; d. Arthur Frank and Helen Martha (Nelson) Zaiss; m. Charles Rumph, Jan. 19, 1979. BA summa cum laude, U. Iowa, 1962; JD with honors, U. Mich., 1965. Bar: Calif. 1966, D.C. 1976, U.S. Supreme Ct. 1979. Trial atty. antitrust divsn. U.S. Dept. Justice, San Francisco, 1965-72; counsel antitrust subcom. U.S. Senate Jud. Com., Washington, 1973-75; ptnr. Baker & Hostetler, Washington, 1976-85; pvt. practice Washington, 1985-98; ptnr., chair antitrust and trade regulations dept. Greenberg Traurig, Washington, 1998—. Adv. bd. BNA Antitrust & Trade Regulations Reporter, 2000—; mediator U.S. Dist. Ct., Washington, 1990—. Contbr. articles to profl. jours. Trustee The Textile Mus., Washington, 1991—, v.p. bd. trustees, 1991—. Mem. ABA, Women's Bar Assn. (bd. dirs. 1989-91), Am. Law Inst., Order of Coif, Phi Beta Kappa. Democrat. Avocation: collecting asian art. Office: Greenburg Traurig 800 Connecticut Ave NW Washington DC 20006-2709 E-mail: Johnson@gtlaw.com.

JOHNSON, SIDNEY MALCOLM, foreign language educator; b. New Haven, Aug. 17, 1924; s. Everett Caswell and Eleanor (Eckman) J.; m. Lora Louise Dunbar, Sept. 29, 1945; children: Thomas Malcolm, Frederick William, Karl Everett. BA, Yale U., 1944, MA, 1948, PhD, 1953. Asst. instr. Yale U., 1946-51; instr. U. Kans., 1951-53, asst. prof., 1953-58, asso. prof., 1958-62, prof., 1962-65; prof. German, chmn. dept. Emory U., Atlanta, 1965-72; prof. German, Ind. U., Bloomington, 1972-93, chmn. dept., 1972-78, 91-92, prof. emeritus, 1993—. Dir. Ind.-Purdue U. Study Program, U. Hamburg, W.Ger., 1978-79 Translator: (with M.E. Gibbs) Willehalm (Wolfram von Eschenbach), 1984, Titurel and the Songs (Wolfram von Eschenbach), 1988, Kudrun, 1992; author: (with M.E. Gibbs) Medieval German Literature. A Companion, 1997, paperback edit., 2000; contbr. articles on medieval German lit. to profl. jours. Served to lt. (j.g.) USNR, 1943-46. Research grantee Am. Philos. Soc., 1963 Mem. MLA, Am. Assn. Tchrs. German, AAUP, Wolfram von Eschenbach Gesellschaft, Internat. Assn. Germanic Studies, Medieval Acad. Home: 2320 E Covenanter Dr Bloomington IN 47401-5402 E-mail: johnsons@indiana.edu.

JOHNSON, SILAS R., JR., consultant, retired air force officer; b. Ft. Worth, Jan. 29, 1945; s. Silas Robert and Lucille (Burns) J.; m. Paulette Kamykowski, Apr. 12, 1968; children: Jennifer, Tyler. BBA, U. Miami, Coral Gables, Fla., 1967; MPA, Pepperdine U., 1979; postgrad., Air U., Montgomery, Ala., 1975, 83, 89. Commd. 2d lt. USAF, 1968, advanced through grades to major gen., 1998; co-pilot, aircraft comdr. 416 Bombardment Wing, Griffiss AFB, N.Y., 1969-74; spotlight officer, chief of tanker assigments Strategic Air Command, Offutt AFB, 1974-77; RF-4C pilot 363d Tactical Reconnaissance Wing, Shaw AFB, S.C., 1977-80; co-pilot, aircraft comdr., flight comdr. 60th Bombardment Squadron, Anderson AFB, Guam, 1981-83; air staff action officer to asst. dir. air force issues team USAF Hdqrs./The Pentagon, Washington, 1983-86; comdr. 46th Bombardment Squadron/319th Bombardment Wing, Grand Forks AFB, N.D., 1986-88; dir. Joint Flag Officer Warfighting Course, Maxwell AFB, Ala., 1989-90; asst. dep. comdr. maint., later vice comdr. 319th Bombardment Wing, Grand Forks AFB, 1990-91; vice comdr. 4th Wing, Seymour Johnson AFB, N.C., 1991-92; comdr. 93d Bomb Wing, Castle AFB, Calif., 1992-94, 552d Air Control Wing, Tinker AFB, Okla., 1994-96; dep. dir. ops. joint chiefs of staff The Pentagon, Washington, 1996-98; vice comdr. 21st Air Force, McGuire AFB, N.J., 1998-99; comdr. Air Mobility Warfare Ctr. USAF, Ft. Dix, N.J., 1999-2000; chief U.S. Mil. Tng. Mission, Riyadh, Saudi Arabia, 2000—02; ret. USAF, 2002; pres. SRJ Cons. Inc., 2002—; v.p. Burdeshaw Assocs., Bethesda, Md., 2002—. Decorated Def. Disting. Svc. medal, Def. Superior Svc. medal, Legion of Merit with 2 oak leaf clusters, Air medal with 2 oak leaf clusters, Air Force Commendation medal, Vietnam Svc. medal; recipient Moeller Trophy for outstanding wing comdr. in air combat command, 1996. Mem. Daedalians (chpt. pres.), Sigma Chi. Avocations: golf, reading.

JOHNSON, SONDRA LEA, accountant; b. Kansas City, Mo., May 11, 1952; d. Albert John Oscar and Dorothy Mae (Hudgens) Johnson. AA, Longview Coll., 1972; BSBA in Acctg. cum laude, Ctrl. Mo. State U., 1974, MBA, 1980. CPA Mo. Acct. Farmland Industries, Kansas City, 1974-76; acct., auditor Ernst & Whinney, Kansas City, 1976-79, Laventhol & Horwath, Kansas City, 1980-81; corp. acct., mgr. Butler Mfg. Co., Kansas City, 1981-84; audit supr. Grant Thornton Internat., Kansas City, 1984-89; sr. fin. analyst Hoechst Marion Roussel, Kansas City, 1989-95; with fin. reporting dept. UtiliCorp United, Inc., Kansas City, 1996-99; sr. fin. analyst ERC/GE, Overland Park, Kans., 1999—2000; internal auditor Met. CC, Kansas City, 2000—. Specialized instr. nat. continuing edn. tng. program Grant Thornton Internat., various locations; acctg. instr. Ctrl. Mo. State U., Warrensburg, 1979—80, Rockhurst Coll., Kansas City, 1981—82, Avila Coll., Kansas City, 1989—90. Mem.: AICPA, Mo. Soc. CPAs, Inst. Mgmt. Accts., Women's C. of C. Kansas City, Phi Kappa Phi. Democrat. Lutheran. Avocations: travel, collecting limited edition figurines, sports, music. Office: Met CC 3200 Broadway Kansas City MO 64111

JOHNSON, STANFORD LELAND, marketing, international business educator; b. Mapleton, Utah, July 31, 1924; s. Leland Stanford and Mary Alice (Thompson) J.; m. Lucy E. Watts, Sept. 14, 1945 (div. 1976); children: Janet, Debbie, Stanford Leland, Robert, Gregory, Kent; m. Heidi G. Ivanoff, Jan. 1977 (div. 1996); m. Linda M. Sartain, Oct., 1998 (dec. Dec. 13, 2001). BS in Bus. and Social Sci., Utah State U., 1949; MS in Mktg. and Retailing, NYU, 1950; PhD in Bus, N.Y. U., 1965. Cert. comml. pilot. Field research Dept. Commerce, 1949-51; asst. mgr. Wickel's Men's Wear Store, Logan, Utah, 1951-52; asst. prof. Sch. Bus., Utah State U., 1951-54; asst. dean, instr. N.Y. U., 1954-64; mem. faculty San Francisco State U., 1964-89, prof. mktg., transp. and world bus., 1968-89, chmn. dept., 1972-76. Cons. to industry, 1960—; lectr. U. Calif. Med. Sch., Pharm. Adminstrn., 1969-85. Editorial cons., McGraw-Hill Book Co., Houghton Mifflin Co., Wadsworth Pub. Co., Sci. Research Assos. Bd. dirs., acad. adviser Schiller Internat. U., Heidelberg, Germany, 1969— . Served as pilot USAAF, 1943-45. Ins. fellow Am. Assn. U. Tchrs., 1953; Forum and Finance fellow, 1954; Found. for Econ. Edn. fellow, 1955; recipient Founder's Day award NYU, 1965. Mem. Sales and Mktg. Execs. Assn. Republican. Mem. Ch. of Jesus Christ of Latter Day Saints. Home: 4609 Park Woods Dr Pollock Pines CA 95726-9508 E-mail: drslj@jps.net.

JOHNSON, STEPHEN L. federal agency administrator; b. Washington, Mar. 21, 1951; s. William Arrett and Nell (Easler) J.; m. Deborah Lynn Jones, Aug. 5, 1972; children: Carrie, Matthew, Allison. BA, Taylor U., 1972; MS, George Washington U., 1976. Dir. tech. ops. Litton Bionetics, Kensington, Md., 1976-80; sr. sci. advisor EPA, Washington, 1980-84, 86-88, dir. field ops. disvn., 1984-86, dep. dir. hazard evaluation divsn., 1988-90, dir. registration divsn., 1990—, dep. dir., pesticide programs, 1997—99, asst. adminr. prevention pesticides and toxic substances, 2000—, acting dep. adminstr., 2003—. Dir. tech. ops. Hazleton Labs. Corp., Falls Church, Va., 1984-86; chmn. FIFRA sci. adv. panel EPA, Washington, 1988-90; exput cons. WHO, Geneva, Switzerland, 1988-90. Contbr. articles to profl. jours. Bd. dirs. Frederick (Md.) County Crisis Pregnancy Ctr., 1987; deacon Fredricktown Bapt. Ch., Walkerville, Md., 1991; commr. USTA Jr. League, Frederick County, Md., 1993; bd. dirs. Frederick Tennis Patrons. Mem. USTA (bd. dirs., v.p. Md. dist.). Avocation: tennis. Office: EPA Prevention Pesticides and Toxic Substanc 1200 Pennsylvania Ave NW MC 7101 Washington DC 20460 Office Fax: 202-260-1847.*

JOHNSON, STEVEN BOYD, lawyer; b. Springfield, Tenn., July 19, 1953; s. Ammon and Dorothy Jean (Anderson) J.; m. Martha Jane Yoakum, 1981 (div. Mar. 1987); 1 child, Eleanor Danielle; m. Betsy Lou Brown, Jan. 4, 1989. BA, Vanderbilt U., 1975; MA, Webster Coll., 1977; JD, U. Memphis, 1979. Bar: Tenn. 1979, U.S. Dist. Ct. (we., mid. and ea. dists.) Tenn., U.S. Ct. Appeals (6th cir.). Law clk. to Judge Robert M. McRae U.S. Dist. Ct. (we. dist.) Tenn., Memphis, 1980-81; assoc. Apperson, Crump, Duzane & Maxwell, Memphis, 1981-83; ptnr. Horne & Peppel, Memphis, 1983-84; mem., ptnr. Butler Vines & Babb, P.L.L.C., Knoxville, 1985—. Assoc. prof. entertainment law U. Memphis, 1980. Co-author: Tennessee Workers Compensation Practice, 1995. Served with USN, 1975-77. Mem. Tenn. Bar Assn., Knoxville Bar Assn., Def. Rsch. Inst., Delta Theta Phi, Omicron Delta Kappa. Republican. Avocations: skiing, water skiing, boating, reading. Home: 3434 Harbour Front Way Knoxville TN 37922-9422 Office: Butler Vines & Babb PLLC First Am Bank Ctr Ste 810 Knoxville TN 37902

JOHNSON, STEVEN CARL, educational consultant; b. Detroit, Nov. 18, 1959; s. Lloyd Thoralf and Anna Mae (Gluesing) Johnson. BSME, U. Detroit Mercy, 1985; student, U. Mich.-Flint, 1992, Wayne State U., 1994. Census clerk U.S. Bur. of Census, Detroit, 1980; student mech. engr. Southeastern Mich. Transp. Authority, Detroit, 1981; detail drafter Irving M. Moskovitz & Son Inc., Detroit, 1981; plant engr. asst. Beaumont Hosp.-Royal Oak, Mich., 1982; applications engr. Time Engring., Troy, Mich., 1985; engring. support analyst Creative Indus., Auburn Hills, Mich., 1986—88; CAD detailer Troy Design, Flint, Mich., 1989—90; substitute tchr. Flint Cmty. Sch., 1991—92; gatekeeper Entech Personnel, Livonia, Mich., 2001—02; substitute tchr. Dearborn Cmty. Sch., Mich., 2002; clerical worker Spherion, Southfield, Mich., 1997—; owner, lead cons. On-Site Tutoring, Detroit, 1989—. Author: Teach Me, Lord Jesus: A Work-in-Progress Concerning Gayness Under Christ, 1999. Sec. Mich. Citizens Against Casino Gambling, Detroit, 1998—2000. Mem.: Soc. of Mfg. Engrs. Achievements include development of method of tutoring that uses socratic dialogue to help students move on towards ind. study. Avocations: reading, walking, finding pictures in clouds. Home: 15894 Evergreen Rd Detroit MI 48223-1239 E-mail: ihsscj@juno.com.

JOHNSON, STEWART WILLARD, civil engineer; b. Mitchell, S.D., Aug. 17, 1933; s. James Elmer Johnson and Grace Mahala (Erwin) Johnson Parsons; m. Mary Anis Giddings, June 24, 1956; children: Janelle Chiemi, Gregory Stewart, Eric Willard. BSCE, S.D. State U., 1956; BA in Bus. Adminstrn. and Polit. Sci., U. Md., 1960; MSCE, PhD, U. Ill., 1964. Registered profl. engr., Ohio. Commd. 2d lt. USAF, 1956, advanced through grades to lt. col., prof. mechs. and civil engring. Air Force Inst. Tech., 1964-75, dir. civil engring. Seoul, Republic of Korea, 1976-77, chief civil engring. research div. Kirtland AFB, N.Mex., 1977-80, ret., 1980; prin. engr. BDM Corp., Albuquerque, 1980-94, Johnson and Assocs., Albuquerque, 1994—; engr. Northrop Grumman, Albuquerque, 2003—. Cons. in site surveys, found. design, constrn. of ground stas. for satellite comm. sys., 1992-2001; engr. NorthropGrumman, Albuquerque, 2003—; cons. space sci. and lunar basing NASA, U. N.Mex., N.Mex. State U. and Los Alamos Nat. Lab., 1987-92; adj. prof. civil engring. U. N.Mex., 1987-92; prin. investigator devel. concepts for lunar astron. obs. U. N.Mex., N.Mex. State U., NASA, 1987-94; tech. chmn. Space '88, Space '90, Space '94, Space '96, Space '98, Space 2000, Space 2002, Internat. Confs., Albuquerque; vis. lectr. Internat. Space U., Japan, 1992, Huntsville, Ala., 1993, Barcelona, Spain, 1994, Stockholm, 1995; mem. panel on siting lunar base European Space Agy., 1994; gen. chair Space 96 and RCEII Conf., Albuquerque, 1996; gen. chmn. Space Conf., Albuquerque, 1998, 2000, Robotics Conf., Albuquerque, 1998, 2000. Editor Engineering, Construction, and Operations in Space, I, 1988. II, 90, V, 96, Space 2000 Procs., Space 2002 Procs.; contbr. articles to profl. jours. Pres. ch. coun. Ch. of Good Shepherd United Ch. of Christ, Albuquerque, 1983-85, chmn. bd. deacons, 1991-93, 2000, moderator, 1996-97, clk., 2002; S.W. Conf. (United Ch. Christ) del. to Gen. Synod XIX, St. Louis, 1993, Gen. Synod XX, Oakland, Calif., 1995, Gen. Synod XXI, Columbus, Ohio, 1997; trustee Lunar Geotech. Inst., 1990—; mem. adv. bd. Lab. for Extraterrestrial Structures Rsch., Rutgers U., 1990—. Fellow Nat. Acad. Scis. NRC, 1970-71; recipient World Bar Assn. Space Humanitarian award, 1996. Fellow: ASCE (chmn. exec. com. aerospace divsn. 1979, tech. activities com. 1984, chmn. com. space engring. and constrn. 1987—, mem. nat. space policy com. 1988—96, chmn. 1990—96, Outstanding News Corr. award 1981, Aerospace Scis. and Tech. Applications award 1990, Edmund Friedman Profl. Recognition award 1989); mem.: AAAS, AIAA (space logistics com., Engr. of Yr. Region IV 1990), Nat. Space Soc., Am. Geophys. Union, Soc. Am. Mil. Engrs., Sigma Xi, Pi Sigma Alpha. Republican. Mem. United Ch. of Christ. Avocations: photography, swimming, walking, gardening, hiking.

JOHNSON, SYLVIA SUE, university administrator, educator; b. Abiline, Tex., Aug. 10, 1940; d. SE Boyd and Margaret MacGillivray (Withington) Smith; m. William Ruel Johnson; children: Margaret Ruth, Laura Jane, Catherine Withington. BA, U. Calif., Riverside, 1962; postgrad., U. Hawaii, 1963. Elem. edn. credential, 1962. Chmn. bd. regents U. Calif., 2000—. Mem. bd. regents U. Calif.; mem. steering com. Citizens Univ. Com., chmn., 1978-79; bd. dirs., charter mem. U. Calif.-Riverside Found., chmn. nominating com., 1983—; pres., bd. dirs. Friends of the Mission Inn, 1969-72, 73-76, Mission Inn Found., 1977—, Calif. Bapt. Coll. Citizens Com., 1980—; bd. dirs. Riverside Cmty. Hosp., 1980—, Riverside Jr. League, 1976-77, Nat. Charity League, 1984-85; mem. chancellors blue ribbon com., devel. com. Calif. Mus. Photography; state bd. dirs. C. of C., 2003. Named Woman of Yr., State of Calif. Legislature, 1989, 91, Citizen of Yr., C. of C., 1989; recipient Golden Key award Soroptimist Internat., 2000, Chancellor's medal U. Calif. Riverside, 2002; recipient Silver Raincross medal, Jr. League Riverside, 1993. Mem. U. Calif.-Riverside Alumni Assn. (bd. dirs. 1966-68, v.p. 1968-70), Calif. C. of C. (bd. dirs. 2003—).

JOHNSON, TESLA FRANCIS, data processing executive, educator; b. Altoona, Fla., Sept. 2, 1934; s. Tesla Farris and Ruby Mae (Shockley) J.; m. Eleanor Mary Riggs, Oct. 17, 1975. BSEE, U. S.C., 1958; MS in Ops. Rsch., Fla. Inst. Tech., 1968; PhD in Adminstrv. Mgmt., Walden U., Mpls., 1989. Machinist apprentice Seaboard Airline Ry., 1952-54; asst. computer engr. So. Ry. System, Washington, 1958-61; sr. sci. programmer NCR, Dayton, Ohio, 1961-66; staff programmer IBM, East Fishkill, N.Y., 1966-72; mgr. Jay Turner Co., Grace, Idaho, 1973-74; programmer, analyst Ccybernetics & Systems, Inc., Jacksonville, Fla., 1974-77; systems analyst lst Nat. Bank Md., Balt., 1977-78; sr. systems analyst GM, Detroit, 1978-80; tech. analyst Sunbank Data Corp., Orlando, Fla., 1980-81; mgr. data adminstrn. dept. Martin Marietta Corp., Orlando, 1981-92; dir. technology Computer Bus. Assocs., 1993-96; program mgr. GTE Through Computer Horizons, 1997-2000; ret., 2000—. Adj. prof. bus. adminstrn. Valencia C.C., Orlando, 1989-94, Orlando Coll., 1990-92, Fla. Inst. Tech., Melbourne; mentor grad. sch. of computer resource mgmt. Webster U., 1993-94. Recipient cert. of appreciation NASA, 1969, Excalibur award. Mem. Tau Beta Pi, Sigma Phi Epsilon. Republican. Baptist. Avocations: stamp and coin collecting, playing the organ. Home: 36649 Sundance Dr Grand Island FL 32735 E-mail: teslafjohnson@hotmail.com.

JOHNSON, THEODORE MEBANE, investment executive; b. Denver, Jan. 25, 1934; s. Harold Theodore and Flora Luella (Cunningham) J.; m. Sandra Hall, May 23, 1970 (dec.). BS, U. Denver, 1956; postgrad. Advanced Mgmt. Program, Harvard U. Partner, Hornblower Weeks-Hemphill, Noyes, 1961-78, sr. v.p., dir., exec. com., until 1978; exec. v.p., divsn. dir. PaineWebber, Inc., N.Y.C., 1978—2003. Chmn. bd. dirs., CEO Cross Match Techs., 1997—. Co-founder, past dir. N.Am. Housing Corp. Served to lt. (j.g.) USNR, 1956-57. Mem. Securities Industry Assn. (govt. rels. com., past chmn. Mid-Atlantic chpt.). Clubs: Bond (Washington), Congressional Country (Washington), Univ. Club (Washington), City Tavern (Washington), N.Y. Athletic, Robert Trent Jones Country (Manasas, Va.), Pine Tree Country Club (Boynton Beach, Fla.). Presbyterian. Home: 140 Atlantic Ave Palm Beach FL 33480-3707

JOHNSON, THOMAS DALE, management consultant; b. DeKalb, Ill., Aug. 9, 1942; s. Orville J. and Dorace G. (Gonterman) Johnson; m. Patricia T. Riley, Sept. 6, 1969; children: Christopher, Todd, Shawn, John Scott. BS in Chem. Engring., Purdue U., 1965, MS in Indsl. Adminstrn., 1966. Cons. Price Waterhouse & Co., Washington, 1969-71; adminstrv. mgr. Nat. Coun. Equal Bus. Opportunity, Washington, 1971-73; owner Riley & Johnson, Washington, 1971—. V.p. Washington Mgmt. Group, 1978—83, Wayne Mid-Atlantic, 1980—90; v.p. fed. regulatory products Info. Handling Svcs., 1983—87; pres. Bus. Rsch. Svcs., Inc., 1991—; v.p. mktg., sales and sys. gen. mgr. Asia UPI, 1996—97; pub. Bradford's Directory Mktg. Rsch. Agys., 1999—; founder, pres., dir. Biosupplies, 1999—; dir. Tangerine Techs. Inc., 2000—02; exec. v.p. Carroll Pub. Co., 2002—. Contbr. articles to profl. jours. Pres. Nat. Dir. Pub. Assn., 1993—; pub. mktg. rsch. directories, govt. adv. newsletter; co-founder Capital Content Network, D.C. Tech. Coun.; treas. St. Columba's Ch., 1980—82. Served with Chem. Corps U.S. Army, 1967—68. Episcopalian. Office: 4201 Connecticut Ave NW Washington DC 20008-1158

JOHNSON, THOMAS EDWARD, plastic and reconstructive surgeon; b. Ft. Dodge, Iowa, Oct. 27, 1953; s. Arthur Harold and Ann Marie Johnson. BA in Gen. Sci., U. Iowa, 1976, MD, 1980. Diplomate Am. Bd. Ophthalmology.

Intern Maricopa County Gen. Hosp., Phoenix, 1980—81; resident U. Colo. Health Sci. Ctr., Denver, 1981; fellow, ophthalmic pathology Pacific Presbyn. Med. Ctr., San Francisco, 1985; fellow, oculoplastic surgery King Khaled Eye Specialist Hosp., Riyadh, Saudi Arabia, 1986—87; fellow, oculoplastic and reconstructive surgery Bascom Palmer Eye Inst., U. Miami, Fla., 1992—93; clin. asst. prof. King Saud U., Riyadh, 1987—92, U. Miami, clin. assoc. prof., 1997—. Contbr. articles to profl. jours. Fellow: Am. Acad. Ophthalmology; mem.: Am. Soc. Oculoplastic and Reconstructive Surgery (edn. com. 1993—). Lutheran. Office: Bascom Palmer Eye Inst U Miami 900 NW 17th St Miami FL 33136

JOHNSON, THOMAS FLOYD, former academic administrator, educator; b. Detroit, June 1, 1943; s. Edward Eugene and Adella Madeline (Norton) J.; m. Michele Elizabeth Myers, Mar. 26, 1965; children: Jason, Amy, Sarah. BPh, Wayne State U., 1965; BD, Fuller Theol. Sem., 1968; ThM, Princeton Sem., 1969; PhD, Duke U., 1979. Pastor Presbyn. Ch. U.S.A., Pa., Mich., 1969-76; asst. prof. U. Sioux Falls, S.D., 1978-83; acad. dean Sioux Falls (S.D.) Coll., 1981-83, pres., 1988-97; prof. N.Am. Baptist Sem., Sioux Falls, 1983-88; dean George Fox Evang. Sem., Portland, Oreg., 1997—2001; interim pres. George Fox U., Newberg, 1997-98, prof. bibl. theol., 1997—. Contbr. 9 articles to Internat. Standard Bible Ency., 1988; author: 1, 2, and 3 John New International Biblical Commentary, 1993. Bd. dirs. Children's Home Soc. S.D., Sioux Falls, 1980-86, S.D. Symphony Orch., 1988-92, Carroll Inst., 1989-93, Coalition Christian Colls. and Univs., 1992-97. Mem. Am. Bapt. Assn. Colls. and Univs. (pres. 1992-94), Soc. Bibl. Lit., Sioux Falls C. of C. (bd. dirs. 1992-95), Rotary (bd. dirs. Downtown Club 1991-95, pres. 1993-94). Office: George Fox Univ 414 N Meridian St Newberg OR 97132 E-mail: tjohnson@georgefox.edu. *Every day, with all its tasks and relationships, is a gift from God. Our response is to live thankfully, in service to God and God's world.*

JOHNSON, THOMAS G., JR., lawyer; b. Norfolk, Va., Apr. 4, 1942; BA, U. Va., 1964, LLB, 1969. Bar: Va. 1969. Atty. Willcox & Savage P.C., Norfolk, Va.; chmn. Willcox & Savage P.C., Norfolk, Va. Bd. editors: Va. Law Rev., 1967-69. Mem. Raven Soc., Order of Coif, Phi Beta Kappa, Norfolk Sch. Bd., 1976-90, chmn., 1981-90. Office: Willcox & Savage PC One Commercial Plz Ste 1800 Norfolk VA 23510

JOHNSON, THOMAS HAROLD, radiologist; b. El Dorado, Ark., Dec. 11, 1933; MD, U. Ark., 1957. Diplomate Am. Bd. Radiology. Intern Washington U./City Hosp., St. Louis, 1957-58; resident in internal medicine Washington U./VA Hosp., St. Louis, 1958-59; resident Baylor Hosp., Houston, 1959-60; resident in radiology Cin. Gen. Hosp., 1960-63; radiologist Okla. Meml. Hosp., Oklahoma City; prof. radiol. scis. U. Okla. Health Sci. Ctr., Oklahoma City. Mem. AMA, Am. Coll. Radiology, Radiol. Soc. N.Am. Office: Univ of Okla Health Sci Ctr Dept Radiol Scis PO Box 26307 Oklahoma City OK 73126-0307

JOHNSON, THOMAS JERALD, lawyer; b. Huron, S.D., Aug. 22, 1953; s. Jerald L. and Kathleen A. J.; m. Susan L. Willroth, Aug. 5, 1978. BA, U. Mont., 1975; JD, U. S.D., 1978. Bar: S.D. 1978, U.S. Dist. Ct. S.D. 1978, U.S. Ct. Appeals (8th cir.) 1979, U.S. Supreme Ct. 1981. Sole practice, Sioux Falls, S.D., 1977-80; ptnr. Quaintance, Swanson & Johnson, Sioux Falls, 1980-85; ptnr. Quaintance & Johnson, 1986-90, Quaintance, Johnson, Nadolski & Starnes, 1991-92; atty. pvt. practice, 1993—; instr. Am. Bankers Assn.; bd. dirs. E. River Legal Services, Sioux Falls, 1979-83. Bd. dirs. Parent to Parent Inc.; chmn. S.D. Bd. Pardons and Paroles. Mem. ABA, Am. Trial Lawyers Assn., S.D. Trial Lawyers Assn., S.D. Bar Assn., Minnehaha County Bar Assn., Alpha Tau Omega. Republican. Lodge: Elks. Home: 3060 S Coral Ct Sioux Falls SD 57103-4830 Office: PO Box 899 Sioux Falls SD 57101-0899

JOHNSON, THOMAS STEPHEN, banker; b. Racine, Wis., Nov. 19, 1940; s. H. Norman and Jane Agnes (McAvoy) Johnson; m. Margaret Ann Werner, Apr. 18, 1970; children: Thomas Philip, Scott Michael(dec.), Margaret Ann. AB in Econs., Trinity Coll., 1962; MBA, Harvard U., 1964. Instr. Grad. Bus. Sch. Ateneo de Manila U., Philippines, 1964-66; spl. asst. to contr. U.S. Dept. Def., Washington, 1966-69; with Chem. Bank, N.Y.C., 1969-89, pres., 1983-89, Mfrs. Hanover Trust Co., N.Y.C., 1989-91; chmn., CEO GreenPoint Fin. Corp., GreenPoint Bank, N.Y.C., 1993—. Bd. dirs. Alleghany Corp., R.R. Donnelley & Sons, Inc., The Phoenix Cos., Inc., Lower Manhattan Devel. Corp. Trustee, past chmn. Trinity Coll.; chmn., bd. trustees U.S. Japan Found.; chmn. bd. dirs. Inst. Internat. Edn.; bd. dirs. Cancer Rsch. Inst., Channel 13-WNET, United Way N.Y.C. Mem.: Coun. Fgn. Rels., Harvard Club N.Y.C., Links N.Y.C., River Club N.Y.C., Palm Beach Polo and Country Club, Montclair Golf Club. Roman Catholic. Office: GreenPoint Fin Corp 90 Park Ave Fl 4 New York NY 10016-1301

JOHNSON, THOMAS STUART, lawyer; b. Rockford, Ill., May 21, 1942; s. Frederick C. and Pauline (Ross) J. BA, Rockford Coll., 1964, LLD, 1989; JD, Harvard U., 1967. Bar: Ill. 1967. Ptnr., past pres. Williams & McCarthy, Rockford, 1967—. Lectr. in field. Contbr. numerous articles to profl. jours. Chmn. bd. trustees Rockford Coll., 1986—89; trustee Eastern Ill. U., 1996—2000, Emanuel Med. Ctr., Turlock, Calif., 1984—86, Swedish Covenant Hosp., Chgo., 1984—86, Lincoln Acad. of Ill., 1999—; chmn. bd. dirs. Ill. Inst. Continuing Legal Edn., Chgo., 1984—86; treas. Lawyers Trust Fund of Ill., Chgo., 1984—86; bd. govs. Regent's Coll., London, 1985—89; bd. dirs., mem. benevolence bd. Covenant Ch. Am., Chgo., 1984—86; chmn. Regent's Found. for Internat. Edn., London; chancellor Ill. Acad. Lawyers, 1999. With U.S. Army, 1968—70. Fellow Am. Bar Found., Am. Coll. Trust and Estate Counsel; mem. ABA (ho. of dels. 1982-89, chmn. commn. on advt. 1984-88), Ill. Bar Assn. (bd. govs. 1976-82, sec. 1981-82, medal of honor 1997), Winnebago County Bar Assn. (pres. 1990), Am. Judicature Soc. (bd. dirs. 1986-90), Rockford Country Club, Rotary (pres. Rockford 1992-93), Univ. Club Rockford. Republican. Home: 913 N Main St Rockford IL 61103-7068

JOHNSON, THOMAS WEBBER, JR., lawyer; b. Indpls., Oct. 18, 1941; s. Thomas W. and Mary Lucinda (Webber) J.; m. Sandra Kay McMahon, Aug. 15, 1964 (div. 1986); m. Deborah Joan Collins, May 17, 1987 (div. 1990); m. Barbara Joyce Walter, Mar. 13, 1992. BS in Edn., Ind. U., 1963, JD summa cum laude, 1969. Bar: Ind. 1969, Calif. 1970. Law clk. Ind. Supreme Ct., Indpls., 1968-69; assoc. Irell & Manella, L.A., 1969-76, ptnr., 1976-84, Irell & Manella, Newport Beach, Calif., 1984—99; atty. Irell & Manella, of counsel, 2000—. Chair Com. on Group Ins. Programs for State Bar of Calif., San Francisco, 1978-79; adj. prof. law UCLA, 1996-2001; lectr. for Practicing Law Inst., Calif. Continuing Edn. of the Bar, Calif. Judges Assn., seminars on ins. and bus. litigation. Editor-in-chief: Ind. Law Review, 1968-69; contbr. articles to profl. jours. With USNR, 1959-65. Named Outstanding Grad. Province XII, Phi Delta Phi legal fraternity, 1969. Mem. ABA (lectr. chair ins. coverage litigation com., tort and ins. practice sec. 1995-96), Calif. Bar Assn., Orange County Bar Assn., Masons, Newport Beach Country Club. Republican. Mem. Christian Ch. Office: Irell & Manella 840 Newport Center Dr Ste 400 Newport Beach CA 92660-6323

JOHNSON, TIGE CHRISTOPHER, lawyer; b. Morris, Ill., Oct. 20, 1970; s. H. Craig and Sandra K. J.; m. Yvonne C. Rubio, May 22, 1993. BA with distinction, U. N.Mex., 1992; JD, Vanderbilt U., 1996; LLM with merit, London Sch. Econ. and Polit. Sci., 1997. Bar: Mich. 1998, D.C. 1999, Ill. 2000. Assoc. Varnum, Riddering, Schmidt & Howlett LLP, Grand Rapids, Mich., 1997-99, Altheimer & Gray, Chgo., 1999—2001; asst. v.p., asst. gen. counsel CNA Fin. Corp., Chicago, 2001—. Adj. prof. depts. legal studies and criminal justice Grand Valley State U., 1999; cons. Jr. Achievement, Grand Rapids, 1998; pres., bd. dirs. Montreux Condominium Assn.; v.p., bd. dirs. City Ctr. Condominium Assn.; prof. dept. liberal edn. Columbia Coll., Chgo., 2001—. Mem. Mich. Bar Assn., Grand Rapids Bar Assn., Ill. Bar Assn., Mich. Bar Assn., D.C. Bar Assn., Phi Alpha Delta (pres. 1995-96, law-related instr. 1995-96), Alpha Tau Omega (various coms. 1988-92). Republican. Lutheran. Avocations: snowboarding, traveling, reading, in-line skating. Home: 208 W Washington St #1704 Chicago IL 60606 Office: CNA Plz 333 S Wabash Chicago IL 60685-7482 Fax: 312-817-3145. E-mail: Tige.Johnson@cna.com.

JOHNSON, TIMOTHY D. music educator, composer, poet; b. Salina, Kans., June 8, 1943; s. Dwight Howard and Lucy Polly Johnson; m. Vickie Ellen Ohmer, Aug. 19, 1972; children: Michael Anthony, Brandon Curtis, Rae Ann Rachelle. BME, Kans. State Teachers Coll., 1966; MME, Emporia State U., 1997. Cert. music tchr. Ariz., 1997. Mem., formerly brass contractor/rd. mgr. Jerry Presley Band, Lenexa, Kans., 1985—; dir. bands Wickenburg H.S., Ariz., 2002—. Performer (arranger, composer): A Prairie Lullaby, The TreeTop, author of poems. Freelance musician, spkr., entertainer various religious, youth, prisons, 1970—2002. Mem.: Music Educators Nat. Conf., Ariz. Music Educators Assn. R-Conservative. Protestant. Avocations: travel, reading. Home: 625 Aircleta Dr #2 Wickenburg AZ 85390 Personal E-mail: victims@localnet.com.

JOHNSON, TIMOTHY PETER, senator; b. Canton, S.D., Dec. 28, 1946; s. Vandal Charles and Ruth Jorinda (Ljostveit) J.; m. Barbara Brooks, June 6, 1969; children: Brooks Dwight, Brendan Vandal, Kelsey Marie. BA, U. S.D., 1969, MA, 1970, JD, 1975; postgrad., Mich. State U., 1970-71. Bar: S.D. 1975, U.S. Dist. Ct. S.D. 1976. Fiscal analyst Legis. Fiscal Agy., Lansing, Mich., 1971-72; pvt. practice Vermillion, S.D., 1975-86; mem. S.D. Ho. of Reps., 1978-82, S.D. Senate, 1982-86, U.S. Ho. of Reps., 1987-97; U.S. senator from S.D., 1997—. Adj. inst. U. S.D., Vermillion, 1974-83; mem. S.D. Code Commn., Pierre, 1982-86. Mem. Vermillion City Planning Commn., 1977-78; treas. Clay County Dem. Com., Vermillion, 1978; del. Dem. Nat. Conv., 1988, 92, 96. NSF grantee, 1969-70. Mem. S.D. Bar Assn., Clay County Bar Assn., Phi Beta Kappa, Omicron Delta Kappa. Democrat. Lutheran. Office: 324 Hart Senate Ofc Bldg Washington DC 20510-0001 also: 320 S First St Ste 103 Aberdeen SD 57401-1554*

JOHNSON, TIMOTHY R. B. obstetrician-gynecologist, educator; b. Duluth, Jan. 13, 1950; s. Timothy and Myra Johnson; m. Jo Wiese, June 17, 1972; children: Bradley, Clark, Anna. AB, AM, U. Mich., 1971; MD, U. Va., 1975. Diplomate Am. Bd. Ob-gyn., Am. Bd. Maternal-Fetal Medicine. Asst. prof. Uniformed Svcs. U., Bethesda, Md., 1983-85; assoc. prof. gynecol. obstetrics, pediats., dir. pediats. Johns Hopkins U. Hosp., Balt., 1985-93; prof., chair dept. ob-gyn. U. Mich., Ann Arbor, 1993—, prof. women's studies, 1995—. Mem. faculty group practice bd. U. Mich., 1995-97, chair clin. redesign program, 1998, chair med. sch. rev., 1997. Bd. dirs. Ann Arbor Art Ctr., 1994—; bd. dirs. S.E. Mich. March of Dimes, 1998—. Fellow Am. Coll. Ob-Gyn. (chair internat. com. 1991-95), West African Coll. Surgeons (hon.); mem. Soc. for Maternal and Fetal Medicine (bd. dirs. 1993-97), Am. Assn. Med. Colls. (com. on advancing women in the acad.), Alpha Omega Alpha. Office: 1500 East Med Ctr Dr Ann Arbor MI 48109 E-mail: trbj@umich.edu.

JOHNSON, TIMOTHY VINCENT, congressman; b. Champaign, Ill., July 23, 1946; Mem. from 104th Dist. Ill. Ho. of Reps, 1976-2000; mem. U.S. Congress from 15th Ill. dist., Washington, 2001—; mem. agr. com., sci. com., transp. and infrastructure com. Republican. Home: 129 W Main St Urbana IL 61801-2714 Office: 1541 Longworth HOB Washington DC 20515*

JOHNSON, TOD STUART, market research company executive; b. Mpls., June 6, 1944; s. David Z. and Helen R. (Connor) J.; m. Cindy Schwartz, Aug. 28, 1966; children: Scott, Stacey BS, Carnegie Mellon U., 1966, MSI.A., 1967. Vice pres. Market Sci. Assocs., Inc., Des Plaines, Ill., 1967-71; pres., chief exec. officer NPD Research, Inc., Port Washington, N.Y., 1971-89, Home Testing Inst., Inc., Port Washington, N.Y., 1980-89, OPOC Computing, Inc., Port Washington, N.Y., 1980-89, NPD Group, Port Washington, N.Y., 1982—, The NPD Group Inc. (merger of NPD Rsch. Inc., Home Testing Inst. Inc., and OPOC Computing), Port Washington, N.Y., 1989—; chmn., dir. NPD/Nielsen, Inc., 1987-91; chmn. ISL Internat. Surveys Ltd., Toronto, 1990-98; mng. dir. GFK Mktg. Svcs. Europe GmbH, 1995-99; chmn., CEO Jupiter Media Metrix, N.Y.C., 1998—2001. Bd. dirs. Advt. Rsch. Found., N.Y.C., sec., 1988, vice chmn., 1989, chmn., 1990; founding co-chmn. Coun. Mktg. and Opinion Rsch., 1992-94. Contbr. articles to profl. jours.; patentee in field Trustee Carnegie-Mellon U., Pitts., 1980—, chmn., trustee student affairs com., 1982-85, co-chmn. devel. com., 1993-2000. Mem. Young Pres. Orgn. Republican. Jewish. Home: 10 Heathcote Rd Scarsdale NY 10583-4414 Office: NPD Group 900 W Shore Rd Port Washington NY 11050-4624

JOHNSON, TOM MILROY, academic dean, medical educator, physician; b. Northville, Mich., Jan. 16, 1935; s. Waldo Theodore and Ruth Jeanette (Christensen) J.; m. Emily Chapin Rhoads, June 13, 1959 (div. Aug. 1983); children— Glenn C., Heidi R.; m. Jane Susan Robb, June 10, 1987; 1 stepchild, Elizabeth K. BA in Psychology with honors, Coll. of Wooster, 1956; MD, Northwestern U., 1961; postgrad. in health systems mgmt., Harvard U., 1974. Rotating intern Detroit Receiving Hosp., 1961-62; resident in internal medicine U. Mich. Med. Ctr., Ann Arbor, 1962-65, fellow in pulmonary disease, 1967-68; asst. prof. internal medicine Mich. State U., East Lansing, 1968-71, assoc. prof., asst. dean Coll. of Medicine Grand Rapids, 1971-77; prof. medicine, dean Sch. of Medicine U. N.D., Grand Forks, 1977-88; prof., assoc. dean Coll. Human Medicine, Mich. State U., 1988-94; campus dean, CEO Kalamazoo Ctr. for Med. Studies Mich. State U., 1994-98, prof. emeritus medicine, 1999—; cons. in med. edn. Fla. State U., 1999—2001. Bd. dirs. No. Mich. Regional Health Svcs., Petosky, 1991—2001. Contbr. articles to profl. jours. Capt. M.C., USAF, 1965-67. A. Blaine Brower Traveling scholar ACP, 1977; Tom M. Johnson lecture hall named in his honor Grand Rapids Med. Ctr., 1982; recipient Physician Leadership award Mich. Hosp. Assn., 1999, Disting. Alumni award Coll. of Wooster, 2003. Fellow ACP (Laureate award Mich. chpt.); mem. AMA, Mich. State Med. Soc., Studebaker Drivers Club, Antique Automobile Club of Am., Alpha Omega Alpha. Avocation: restoration of antique automobiles and older farm houses. Home and Office: 4815 Barton Rd Williamston MI 48895-9305

JOHNSON, VAHE DUNCAN, lawyer; b. Providence, Dec. 18, 1938; s. Vahe D. and Katharine (Simpson) J.; m. Diana E. Lepow, Apr. 13, 1964; children: Alexandra, Mark Adam. AB, Harvard U., 1960, LLB, 1963. Bar: R.I. 1964. From assoc. to ptnr. Edwards & Angell, Providence, 1963—. Bd. dirs. Fleet Nat. Bank, Fleet Bank of Mass., N.A., Fleet Bank, N.A. Trustee Providence Found., 1985, Providence Pub. Libr, 1988, Miriam Hosp., Providence, 1990, Lifespan Corp., Capitol Ctr. Commn., Tufts Vet. Sch., 1999. Office: Edwards & Angell 2800 Fin Plz Providence RI 02903 E-mail: djohnson@ealaw.com.

JOHNSON, VAN R. health facility administrator; b. Idaho; BS, Brigham Young U.; MS, U. Minn. Past sr. mgr. Intermountain Healthcare Corp., Salt Lake City; past sr. v.p., COO Sutter Health, Sacramento, now pres., CEO. Bd. dirs. Boy Scouts Am. Golden Empire Coun. Recipient award of distinction Hosp. Coun. No. and Ctrl. Calif., 1996. Office: Sutter Health 2200 River Plaza Dr Sacramento CA 95833-4134

JOHNSON, VERNON EUGENE, history educator; b. Norfolk, Va., Oct. 25, 1930; s. Ellis Moses and Maude Louvenia (Wilkins) J.; m. Barbara Lucy Wynder, June 6, 1959; children: Troy Eugene, Stacy Yvette. AB with distinction, Va. State Coll., 1951; MA, U. Pa., 1964; diploma with honors, Army Command-Gen. Staff Coll., 1968; postgrad., Old Dominion U., 1977-78; advanced cert. in edn., Coll. William and Mary, 1979, EdD, 1982. Commd. 2d lt. U.S. Army, 1951, advanced through grades to lt. col., 1966; ret., 1979; adminstr. Hampton (Va.) U., 1980—96; sr. prof. history Tidewater Va. Ctr., St. Leo U. Fla., 1980—. Collection mgr., adj. instr. Hampton U., Va., 1980—. Active Boys Clubs. Decorated Legion of Merit with oak leaf cluster; recipient Brotherhood award, 1981, Jefferson Cup, 1982; named Man of Yr., 1981. Mem. Am. Assn. Higher Edn., Am. Hist. Assn., Assn. for Study Higher Edn., Nat. Hist. Assn., Assn. U.S. Army, Beau Brummell Civic and Social Club, Alpha Kappa Mu, Phi Alpha Theta, Omega Psi Phi (3d dist. rep.). Methodist.

JOHNSON, VERONICA ANN WILKERSON, information and government services director; b. Detroit, Aug. 5, 1952; d. James Henry and Alberta (Dixon) Wilkerson; B.A., Wayne State U., 1975; M.A., U. Mich., 1977; m. Melvin Lee Johnson, Nov. 3, 1973; children— Dichondra Rosalyn, Christopher Lee, Jonell Henry. Lab. technician Wayne County Health Dept., Project Prescad, 1978-79; children's librarian Inkster (Mich.) br. Wayne Oakland Library Fedn., 1979, head community librarian, 1979-85; government relations specialist State Library of Mich., 1985-87, dir. info. and govt. services, 1987—; owner Verondee Cons. Co., East Lansing, Mich.; adminstrv. aide State Rep. Hansen Clarke, Mich.; legis. liaison Gov. James J. Blanchard; speaker, presenter workshops in field; bd. dirs. U. Mich. Lansing Svc. Ctr., 1993—. Newspaper columnist Library Lines; author manuals on mktg. govt. publs., cost effective methods and community needs/pub. library; v.p. Info. Movers, Inc., Mich. City of Inkster adviser Vol. Tng. for Youth Leadership Devel., Sister Cities Internat. Mem. City of Inkster Cable TV Task Force, 1981—, East Lansing (Mich.) Planning Commn., 1995—; chmn. workshop com. Inkster Internat. Friendship Force Exchange, 1981— ; sec. Inkster Community Project Pride, 1979-80; apptd. Selective Svc. Bd., State of Mich., 2002—. U. Mich. Sch. Library Sci. fellow, 1976-77. Recipient State of Mich. Young Librarian of Yr. award, 1982. Mem. NAACP, ALA (chmn. ASCLA/SLAS com. 1986-87, mem. ASCLA planning com. 1986-87), Med. Library Assn., Mich. Library Assn., Council of State Agy. Librarians (sec./treas), Gamma Phi Delta. Mem. Ch. of Christ. Home: 915 Darlington Ave East Lansing MI 48823-1882 Office: Dir Univ Mich Lansing Svc Ctr 101 S Washington Sq Lansing MI 48933 E-mail: veronicj@umich.edu.

JOHNSON, VICKI VALEEN, paramedic, technical advisor movie studios; b. Houston, May 26, 1958; d. Louis Reginald and Nobie Jeanine (Johnson) Vanderburg; 1 child, Jacqueline Monique. Cert EMT, U. Tex., San Antonio, 1991; cert. paramedic, Ctrl. Tex. Coll., 1993; cert. advanced life support, Metroplex Hosp., Killeen, Tex., 1983; cert. CPR instr., ARC, Burnet, Tex.; AAS in Emergency Medicine, U. Ctrl. Tex. Lic. paramedic, EMT, Tex.; cert. CPR, ARC. Free lance film, spl. events and commls. paramedic, tech. advisor various studios including Warner Bros., CBS, 20th CenturyFox, L.A., 1994—; paramedic Internat. Olympics Diving Competition, Atlanta, 1996. Event dir. Sea World of Tex., San Antonio, 1995; health supr. Girl Scouts Am. of Tex., 1998; sr. publicist, writer feature films, music industry and spl. events, pub. rels., on-tour promotions groups like SOS Band, The Whispers, Ramone Carter, others; profl. songwriter, speechwriter Atty. Gen. Jim Mattox, Tex., 1983—; talent coord. various local, state and nat. beauty pageant prodns.; pub. rels. coordr. Fat Trax Band tour to Japan; promotional coord. LA Raiders Monday Night Football, 1985; stunt paramedic maj. feature film industry; feature editor U. Ctrl. Tex., 1999—2002. Named Princess of Kingsland, Kingsland, Tex. C. of C., 1978, Imperial Miss Houston, 1981-82; Miss Imperial Houston Exhibit, San Antonio Livestock Show and Rodeo, 1996, Outstanding Young Women of Am., Atty. Gen.'s Office, Tex.; elected to San Antonio chpt Women's Hall of Fame, 1994. Mem. Internat. Profls. Assn. (hon. mem.), Internat. Alliance Stage and Theatrical Employees Union 484 (med. com. 1995-97), Internat. Cinematographers Guild LA Local 600 (publicists divsn.), Tex. Assn. Film and Tape Profls., Order of Ea. Stars. Democrat. Methodist. Avocations: writing, travel, movies, spending time with daughter. Home: 307 Presidio Dr Leander TX 78641

JOHNSON, VICTOR CHARLES, association executive; b. Pitts., July 24, 1941; s. Anne M. Byers; children: Christine Johnson Payne, Timothy Mark. BA, Whitworth Coll., 1963; MA, San Francisco State U., 1971; PhD, U. Wis., 1975. Tng. assoc. Ford Found., Bogota, Colombia, 1967-69; subcom. staff assoc. U.S. Ho. of Reps., Washington, 1975-81, subcom. staff dir., 1981-93; assoc. dean internat. edn. Jacksonville U., 1997-98; assoc. exec. dir. pub. policy NAFSA: Assn. of Internat. Educators, Washington, 1998—. Vol. U.S. Peace Corps, Liberia, West Africa, 1963-65, regional dir. internat.-Am. ops., 1993-97. Office: NAFSA Assn of Internat Educators 1307 New York Ave NW Washington DC 20005-4704

JOHNSON, VICTOR LAWRENCE, banker; b. Phila., Feb. 8, 1928; s. Paul J. and Eleanor (Moskowitz) J.; m. Joan Markovitz, Dec. 4, 1955; children: Linda E., Sally A. Grad., Phillips Exeter Acad., 1945; BA, Haverford Coll., 1949; MBA, Wharton Sch. of U. Pa., 1951. Vice pres. Ocean City Mfg. Co., Phila., 1953-58; pres. Johnson Computing Co., Phila., 1958-68, chmn. bd., dir., 1968—; with Provident Nat. Bank, Phila., 1969—, sr. v.p., 1971—; pres., dir. Allen Data Systems, Inc., Phila., 1970; pres. JCI Data Processing Inc., 1976—. Bd. dirs. Sircom Knitting Co., Spring City, Pa., pres., 1980-81; chmn. Wordco Data Systems Inc., 1992. Bd. dirs., mem. budget com. Phila. United Fund, 1954-67; bd. dirs. Nicetown Club Boys and Girls, Phila., 1954-57, Huntingdon Valley (Pa.) Civic Assn., 1956-64; bd. dirs., exec. com. Rydal/Meadowbrook (Pa.) Civic Assn., 1969—; mem. planning and devel. com. Germantown Friends Sch., 1970-73; vol. trustee Not-For-Profit Hosps. Bd., v.p., 1984-87, chmn. planning com., 1987-89; vice chmn., 1989-96, trustee, exec. com. Albert Einstein Med. Ctr., 1973—, vice chmn., 1980, chmn. bd. govs. No. divsn., 1981-84, chmn. bd. dirs., 1987-90; chmn. bd. trustees Health Care Found., 1987-90; dir. Jefferson Health System, 1998; sec., treas. Delaware Valley Hosp. Couns., 1982-95; chmn. bd. Delaware Valley Health, Edn. and Rsch. Found., 1982-85; bd. dirs. Phila. Festival Theatre for New Plays, 1989-94. With U.S. Army, 1951-52. Fellow Coll. Physicians Phila. (trustee 2002—); mem. Pa. Bankers Assn., Bank Automation Assn. Delaware Valley, Am. Hosp. Assn. (coun. governing bds. 1989), Hosp. Trustees Assn. Pa. (vice chmn. bd. 1991-92, chmn. bd. 1992). Clubs: Locust (Phila.); Philmont Country (Huntingdon Valley) (bd. dirs., exec. v.p.). Home: Hidden Glen Jenkintown PA 19046 Office: 200 Route 130 S Cinnaminson NJ 08077-2892

JOHNSON, VICTORIA HOUSTON, elementary school educator, poet; b. Cleve., Dec. 6, 1961; s. Daniel Arron and Margaret Mildred Houston; m. Clyde Bowman Johnson, Nov. 15, 1980; children: Lamont Anthony, Ronald Clyde. AA, Social Svc. Tech. Sch., 1997. Cert. day care Cuyaga County Child Care, 80. Day care adminstr., youth leader Greater Love Bapt. Ch., Cleve., 1996—; tchr. extended learning program Cleve. City Schs., 2000—01; co-owner C.J. Famous Angus, Cleve. Noon-time supr. Cleve. City Schs., 1995—2000. Contbr. poetry to lit. publs. (Hon. Mention, Nat. Libr. Poetry, 99, Editor's Choice award, 98). Named Poet of Merit, Nat. Libr. Poetry, 1997; recipient Pres.' Recognition of Lib. Excellence award, Nat. Authors Registry. Avocations: reading, writing, dog shows. Office: Greater Love Missionary Bapt Ch 3630 E 116th St Cleveland OH 44105

JOHNSON, VINCENT ROBERT, law educator, educator; b. Latrobe, Pa., Oct. 10, 1953; s. Harry Paul and Anna Ruth (Gozlick) J. BA, St. Vincent Coll., 1975; JD, U. Notre Dame, 1978; LLM, Yale U., 1979; LLD, St. Vincent Coll., 1991. Bar: Pa. 1978, U.S. Ct. Appeals (7th cir.) 1981, Tex. 1985, U.S. Supreme Ct. 1986. Law clk. Hon. Bernard S. Meyer, N.Y.C., Albany, N.Y., 1979-80, Hon. Thomas E. Fairchild, Chgo., 1980-82; asst. prof. St. Mary's U., San Antonio, 1982-85, assoc. prof., 1985-88, prof., 1988—, assoc. dean for adminstrn., 2001—02, assoc. dean acad. and student affairs, 2002—. Jud. fellow U.S. Supreme Ct., 1988-89; dir. St. Mary's Inst. on World Legal Problems, Innsbruck, Austria, 1989-2001; vis. prof. Vt. Law Sch., 1991, St. Petersburg State U., Russia, 1999, Shandong U., China, 2001. Author: Mastering Torts, 1995, 2d edit., 1999; co-author: Studies in American Tort Law, 1994, 2d edit., 1999, Teaching Torts, 1995, 2d edit., 1999; mem. editl. adv. bd. Carolina Acad. Press. Chair Mayor of San Antonio's Task Force on Ethics in Govt., 1997-98; mem. adv. bd. Chinese Rev. Common Law, 2002—. Fulbright sr. scholar, Beijing, China, 1998. Mem. ABA, Am. Law Inst., State Bar Tex. (lawyer advt. com. 1985-88, rules of profl. conduct com. 1996-99), Assn. Am. Law Schs. (chmn. teaching methods sect. 1987-88), Order of Art and Culture (Innsbruck, Austria), Phi Delta Phi (Teaching Excellence award 1986), Phi Alpha Delta (Disting. Svc. award 1984). Democrat. Roman Catholic. Home: 124 W Gramercy Pl San Antonio TX 78212 Office: St Marys U Sch Law One Camino Santa Maria San Antonio TX 78228-8602 E-mail: vjohnson@stmarytx.edu.

JOHNSON, VIRGIL EVANS, JR., research scientist; b. Tampa, Fla., Feb. 26, 1927; s. Virgil Evans Sr. and Opal Florence (Harper) J.; m. Emma Frances Kinard, Nov. 20, 1948; children: Cynthia Latimer, Lynn Langer, Shirley Brott. BEE, Ga. Inst. Tech., 1949; SM, MIT, 1955; PhD, Johns Hopkins U., 1988. Hydraulics engr. U.S. Waterways Exptl. Sta., Vicksburg, Miss., 1949-50, 52-53; rsch. asst. Hydrodynamics Lab., MIT, Cambridge, 1953-55; aero. rsch. scientist Nat. Adv. Com. for Aeronautics-NASA Langley, Hampton, Va., 1955-60; from chief engr. to pres. Hydronautics Inc., Laurel, Md., 1960-83; chief engr. Tracor Hydronautics Inc., Laurel, 1983-91; v.p., chief scientist, co-founder Hydronautics Rsch. Inc., Fulton, Md., 1991—. Contbr. articles to profl. jours.; inventor and patentee in field. With USN, 1945-46, PTO; capt. U.S. Army, 1950-52, Korea. Republican. Methodist. Avocations: fishing, sailing. Home: 24011 Woodfield Rd Gaithersburg MD 20882-2827 Office: 7605 Airpark Rd Ste D Gaithersburg MD 20879-4183 E-mail: francesk@erols.com.

JOHNSON, W. TAYLOR, physician; b. Suffolk, Va., Jan. 17, 1936; s. Walter Taylor and Ethel (Storey) J.; m. Bettie Ann Orenduff; children: Elizabeth Ann, Patricia Ellen. Grad., Duke U., 1957, MD, 1961. Diplomate Am. Bd. Dermatology, Am. Bd. Dermatopathology. Commd. ensign USN, 1954; advanced through grades to capt. Nat. Naval Med. Ctr., 1975, intern, 1961-62; resident in dermatology U.S. Naval Hosp., San Diego, 1964-66; fellow in dermatopathology Armed Forces Inst. Pathology, Washington, 1967-68; staff physician U.S.

Naval Tng. Ctr., San Diego, 1962-64; staff dermatologist Nat. Naval Med. Ctr., Bethesda, 1967-72, asst. chief of dermatology, 1972-78, chief of dermatology, 1978-81, ret., 1981; asst. prof. medicine Georgetown U., Washington, 1969-88; pvt. practice Gaithersburg, Md., 1981—. Contbr. articles to profl. jours. Mem. AMA, Assn. Mil. Dermatologists (pres. 1979), Washington, D.C. Soc. Dermatology (pres. 1983), Am. Acad. Dermatology, Am. Soc. Dermatopathology, Montgomery County, Md. Med. Soc., Med. and Chirurgical Faculty of Md., Internat. Soc. for Dermatol. Surgery. Republican. Presbyterian. Avocations: tennis, computers. Home: 12301 Rivers Edge Dr Potomac MD 20854-1072

JOHNSON, W. THOMAS, JR., media executive; b. 1941; BJ, U. Ga., 1963; MBA, Harvard U., 1965. With Tex. Broadcasting Corp., Austin, 1971—73, exec. v.p., 1971—73; pub. Dallas-Herald Times, 1975; with L.A. Times, 1975—, pres., 1977, pub., 1980, sr. v.p., 1986, vice chmn., chmn. bd. dirs.; pres., bd. dirs., chmn., CEO Cable News Network, 1990—. Dep. press sec., spl. asst. Pres. Lyndon B. Johnson, 1969; chmn. bd. dirs. Times Mirror Newspaper mgmt. com.; v.p. Turner Broadcasting Sys., Atlanta. Chmn. Lyndon B. Johnson Found., Stanford Profl. Journalism Program; bd. trustees Mayo Found., Knight Found. Named Pub. of Yr., Adweek Mag., 1984, Cable Exec. of Yr., 1991; recipient Horatio Alger Disting. Am. award, 1987; White House fellow, 1965. Office: Cable News Network 1CNN Ctr NW PO Box 105366 Atlanta GA 30348-5366

JOHNSON, WAINE CECIL, dermatologist; b. Mt. Vernon, Tex., Sept. 30, 1928; s. Tulley Bell and Lizzie J.; m. Deanna Glutz, Dec. 1973; children: Susan Lynn, Carol Ann, Sandra Kay. BS, E. Tex. State U., 1949; MD, U. Tex., 1953. Intern Brooke Army Hosp., 1953-54; resident in dermatology Walter Reed Army Hosp., 1955-58; fellow in dermal pathology Armed Forces Inst. Pathology, 1960-61; mem. staff Skin and Cancer Hosp., Phila., 1962-78, asst. dir. lab., 1962, dir., 1970-78; mem. faculty Temple U. Med. Sch., Phila., 1962-78, prof. dermatology, 1970-78; clin. prof. U. Pa. Med. Sch., 1978—; chmn. dept. dermatology Grad. Hosp. U. Pa., 1978-98; mng. ptnr. Delaware Valley Dermatopathology LLP, 1998—2000; co-mng. dir. Delaware Valley Dermatopathology divsn. Inst. for Dermatopathology, Conshohocken, Pa., 2001—. Author numerous papers in field.; Co-editor: Dermal Pathology, 1974. Served to maj. M.C. USAR, 1953-62. Recipient Gold medal sci. exhibit Am. Soc. Clin. Pathologists-Coll. Am. Pathologists, 1962 Mem. AMA, ACP, Am. Acad. Dermatology (chmn. pathology com. 1976-80), Am. Dermatol. Assn., Internat. Acad. Pathology, Am. Registry Pathology (pres. 2003—), Am. Soc. Dermatopathology (pres. 1988) Soc. Investigative Dermatology, Histochem. Soc., Phila. Dermatol. Soc. (pres. 1979-80), Atlantic Dermatol. Conf. (pres. 1979-80), Coll. Physicians of Phila. (chmn. dermatology sect. 1994-97). Home: 744 Crosswicks Rd Rydal PA 19046-3004 Office: Ste 310 20 Ash St Millenium 1 Conshohocken PA 19428 E-mail: wjohnson@ameripath.com.

JOHNSON, WALLACE, retired army officer; b. Oklahoma City, Aug. 8, 1939; s. Carroll Wallace and Pauletta (Bibbs) J.; m. Lela Mae Johnson, Dec. 25, 1959; children: Wallace, Steven, Valerie Lynne, Sharon Denise. BS, U. Okla., 1961; MBA, Ala. A&M U., 1973. Commd. 2d lt. U.S. Army, 1961, advanced through grades to lt. col., 1978; lt. inf. platoon leader, exec officer 1/58th Inf. (Mech), Ft. Benning, Ga., 1962-64; detachment comdr. Co. A-29 C 10th spl. forces Bad Tolz, West Germany, 1964-66, detachment comdr. A333, 5th spl. forces group, Republic Vietnam, 1966-67; br. chief instr. USAMMCS Redstone Arsenal, Ala., 1969-71; security plans, ops. officer 23d support group, Republic Korea, 1971-72; chief orgn. br. USAMMCS, Redstone Arsenal, 1973-75; exec. officer 101st Ordnance Bn., Heilbronn, W. Ger., 1976-78; surety insp. Office of Insp. Gen., Heidelberg, W. Ger., 1978-79; sr. logistics instr. Command and Gen. Staff Coll., Ft. Leavenworth, Kans., 1979-84; chief materiel and logistics systems div. Army Ordnance Missile and Munition Ctr. and Sch., 1984-85; sr. program analyst CAS, Inc., 1985-86; mgr. logistics integration Acustar, Inc. Mil.-Pub. Electronic Systems, 1986-88, mgr. bus. devel. dept., automatic test equipment (ATE)/test program sets (TPS) and electroluminescent display products Chrysler Corp., 1986-91; dir. mktg. Automation Rsch. Systems Ltd., 1991-93, program mgr., 1993-94 GMU, 1994—; dir., mentor-protege program; instr. U.S. Army service schs.; sr. parachutist, jump master. Decorated Combat Inf. Badge, Bronze Star. Mem. Assn. U.S. Army, Am. Def. Preparedness Assn., Internat. Platform Assn., Soc. Logistics Engrs., Unmanned Vehicle Assn., Spl. Forces Assn., Nat. Def. Industry Assn. Republican. Baptist. Club: Jaywalkers of Ft. Leavenworth (v.p. 1980-81), Kiwanis, Nat. Space Club (vice chmn.). Lodge: Sertoma (Leavenworth chpt. pres. 1981-84). Home: 9513 Retriever Rd Burke VA 22015-4515 Office: George Mason U Fairfax VA 22030-3409

JOHNSON, WALLACE HAROLD, lawyer; b. Cleve., Oct. 7, 1939; s. Wallace H. and Esther Johnson; m. Donna Simpson, June 9, 1962; children: Kimberly, W. Todd, Vicki, Eric. BA in Polit. Sci., Ohio U., 1961; postgrad., Rutgers U., 1961; JD, U. Toledo, 1965. Bar: Ohio 1965, U.S Dist. Ct. D.C., 1969, U.S. Ct. Claims 1974, U.S. Supreme Ct. 1968, Nebr. 1975, Colo. 1993, Wyo. 1993. Trial atty. organized crime and racketeering sect. U.S. Dept. Justice criminal divsn., Washington, 1965-69; minority counsel subcom. criminal laws and procedures U.S. Dept. Justice, Washington, 1969-70, assoc. dep. atty. gen., 1970-72; spl. asst. to Pres. White House, Washington, 1972-73; asst. atty. gen. land and resources divsn. U.S. Dept. Justice, Washington, 1973-75; ptnr. Kutok Rock, Washington, 1975-90. Gen. counsel, NCBA, 1995-98. Recipient Scholastic Achievement award Bur. Nat. Affairs. Mem. Order of Coif, Phi Beta Delta, Omicron Delta Kappa. Home: 3129 Southfork Rd Cody WY 82414-8009 Office: Old Post Office Cody WY 82414

JOHNSON, WALLACE STEPHEN, JR., Asian languages educator; b. Hampton, Va., Nov. 6, 1932; s. Wallace Stephen and Ellen Virginia (Weston) J.; m. Diantha Sibley Haviland, June 3, 1970; 1 child, Wallace Stephen III BA, Johns Hopkins U., 1957; PhD, U. Pa., 1968; postgrad., Harvard U. Law Sch., 1970-71. Prof. Asian langs. U. Kans., Lawrence, 1965—. Translator: The T'ang Code: General Principles, 1979; editor: A Concordance to the T'ang Code, 1965, An Index to the Pien-tzu lei-pien, 1967, A Concordance to the Kuan-tzu, 1970, A Concordance to the Han-fei tzu, 1975, A Reader in Chinese Literature, 1976, A Reader in Chinese Anthropology-Sociology, 1976, A Reader in Chinese International Relations, 1976, A Reader in Chinese Art History, 1976, (with Grace Wan) A Reader in Chinese History, 1972; editor Jour. Asian Legal History. Fellow Am. Council Leared Soc., 1970, Harvard U. Law Sch., 1970, Howard Found., 1972, Humboldt Found., 1972 Mem. Assn. for Asian Studies Home: 1633 Stratford Rd Lawrence KS 66044-2529 Office: U Kans Dept East Asian Langs Lawrence KS 66045-0001

JOHNSON, WALTER CURTIS, electrical engineering educator; b. Weikert, Pa., Jan. 6, 1913; s. David C. and Mary (Ely) J.; m. Carolyn Shirk, Sept. 1, 1934; children: Walter Curtis, William Stanford, David Edward. BS, Pa. State Coll., 1934; student in advanced engring., Gen. Electric Co., 1934-37; E.E., Pa. State Coll., 1942. Instr., dept. elec. engring. Princeton, 1937, prof. elec. engring., 1948—, Arthur LeGrand Doty prof. engring., 1963-81, Arthur LeGrand Doty prof. emeritus, 1981—, chmn. dept., 1950-65. Engring. cons. various cos.; resident visitor Bell Telephone Labs., 1968 Author: Mathematical and Physical Principles of Engineering Analysis, 1944, Transmission Lines and Networks, 1950, (with P.R. Clement) Electrical Engineering Science, 1960; articles tech. and sci. publs. Recipient Western Elec. award for excellence in engring. edn.; Am. Soc. Engring. Edn., 1967; Nat. award for Best Initial Paper Am. Inst. Elec. Engrs., 1939 Fellow IEEE, AIEE, IRE; mem. Am. Soc. Engring. Edn. (chmn. elec. engring. div. 1955-56), Am. Phys. Soc., Sigma Xi. Presbyterian. Home: 31 Meadow Lks # O7 Hightstown NJ 08520-3372

JOHNSON, WALTER EARL, geophysicist; b. Denver, Dec. 16, 1942; s. Earl S. and Helen F. (Llewellyn) J.; m. Ramey Kandice Kayes, Aug. 6, 1967; children: Gretchen, Roger, Aniela. Grad. in Geophys. Engring., Colo. Sch. of Mines, 1966. Registered profl. engr., Colo.; cert. geologist, Colo. Geophysicist Pan Am. Petroleum Corp., 1966-73; seismic processing supr. Amoco Prodn. Co., Denver, 1973-74, marine tech. supr., 1974-76, divsn. processing cons., 1976-79; geophys. supr. No. Thrust Belt, Denver, 1979-80; chief geophysicist Husky Oil Co., Denver, 1981-82; exploration mgr. Rocky Mountain and Gulf Coast divsn., Denver, 1982-84; geophys. mgr. ANR Prodn. Co., Denver, 1985-99; pres. Exploration GeoCons., Inc., Denver, 2000—. Pres. Sch. Lateral Ditch Co.; cons. engr. Bd. dirs. Rocky Mountain Residence. Mem. Denver Geophys. Soc., Soc. Exploration Geophysicists. Republican. Baptist. Office: 645 Court Pl Ste 309 Denver CO 80202-4507

JOHNSON, WALTER FRANK, JR., lawyer; b. Georgiana, Ala., 1945; s. Walter F. and Marjorie Ellen (Carnathan) J.; m. Emily Waldrep, Nov. 23, 1969; children: Brian W., Stacey E. BS, Auburn U., 1968; JD, Samford U., 1973. Bar: Ala. 1973, Ga. 1974. Acct. Union Camp Corp., 1968-70; assoc. Hatcher, Meyerson, Oxford and Irvin, Atlanta, 1973-74, Thompson and Redmond, Columbus, Ga., 1974-78, pvt. practice, 1978—. Asst. pub. defender, Columbus, 1978. Mem. ABA, Ala. State Bar, State Bar Ga., Columbus Lawyers Club. Methodist. Home: 3235 Flint Dr Columbus GA 31907-2029 Office: PO Box 6507 3006 University Ave Columbus GA 31907-2106 E-mail: wfjattorney@earthlink.net.

JOHNSON, WALTER KLINE, civil engineer; b. Mpls., Aug. 28, 1923; s. Horace Edward and Ida Axelina (Kline) J.; m. Geneva Lorraine Olson, Sept. 2, 1950; children: Kristine Idelle, Karen Margaret, Konstance Louise. BCE, U. Minn., 1948, MS, 1951, PhD, 1963. Registered profl. engr., Minn. With Greeley and Hansen, Chgo., 1948-49, Infilco, Inc., Tucson, 1951-52, Toltz, King, Duvall, Anderson & Assocs., St. Paul, 1952-55; faculty U. Minn., Mpls., 1955—, assoc. prof. civil engring., 1965-74, prof., 1974-75; dir. planning Met. Waste Control Commn., St. Paul, 1975-89; mgmt. cons. in environ. engring. St. Paul, 1989—. Patentee wastewater sampler. Capt. USAAF, 1943-46. EPA rsch. fellow Brit. Water Pollution Rsch. Lab., 1971. Fellow ASCE (pres. N.W. sect. 1972-73), Am. Water Works Assn., Cen. State Water Environment Assn.; mem. Am. Acad. Environ. Engrs. (diplomate). Lutheran. Achievements include rsch. on biol. waste water treatment, sludge bulking, nitrogen removal by denitrification. Home: 5321 29th Ave S Minneapolis MN 55417-2010 E-mail: WKJ1@JUNO.COM.

JOHNSON, WALTER L. transportation company executive; b. Flint, Mich., Aug. 31, 1927; s. Fred T. and Nellie L. (Niswonger) J.; m. Ida E. Laukonen (div.); children: Eric, Mary, David; m. Rozann Randazo. BA in Math., U. Mich., 1950. Indsl. engr. Kaiser Motors, Willow Run, Mich., 1951-53; various positions including N.Am. coordinator Brazil Kaiser-Willys, Toledo, 1953-68; gen. mgr. plant AM Gen., South Bend, Ind., 1968-74; v.p. mfg. automotive group Midland Ross, Southfield, Mich., 1974-76; exec. v.p. ops. Midland Steel Products, Cleve., 1976-79; pres. Midsco div. Lamson & Sessions, Cleve., 1979-85, exec. v.p. transp. equipment products, 1985-88, also bd. dirs. Served with USN, 1945-46. Home: 590 Wedgewood Way Naples FL 34119-1811

JOHNSON, WARREN, foreign language educator; b. Geneva, Ill., Apr. 16, 1958; s. Martin A. and Eleanor J. Johnson. BA with honors, U. Iowa, 1978; AM, U. Mich., 1984, PhD, 1989. Lectr. U. Paul Valéry, Montpellier, France, 1989-90; asst. prof. French Moorhead (Minn.) State U., 1990-91, U. Ala., Tuscaloosa, 1991-95; asst. prof. French and Spanish, Ark. State U., 1998—2003, assoc. prof. French, 2003—. Contbr. articles to profl. jours. Mem. MLA, Am. Assn. Tchrs. French, Soc. des Etudes Romantiques et Dix-neuviémistes. Avocations: classical music, art. Office: Ark State U Dept Langs PO Box 2400 State University AR 72467 E-mail: wjohnson@astate.edu.

JOHNSON, WARREN CHARLES, retired lawyer; b. Wahoo, Nebr., Mar. 22, 1920; s. Wilmer G. and Florence E. (Slama) J.; children: Warren, Lucinda, Lauri, Genevieve. BSBA with high distinction; JD cum laude, U. Nebr. Bar: Nebr. 1948, U.S. Dist. Ct. Nebr. 1948. Assoc. Cline Williams Wright Johnson & Oldfather, Lincoln, Nebr., 1948-50, ptnr., 1951-2000; ret., 2000. Bd. dirs. First Nat. Bank, Lincoln, First Nat. Bank, Fairbury, Nebr., Farmers & Traders Bank, Waco, Nebr., First Nat. Bank, Bradshaw, Nebr., Blue River Bank, McCool Junction, Nebr. Vice-chmn. U. Nebr. Found., 1984-85; pres. S.W. Cmty. Ctr., Lincoln, 1963-67, Nebr. Conf. United Ch. of Christ, 1962-68. Maj. USAAF, 1942-46; PTO. Mem. ABA, Nebr. Bar Assn., Lincoln Bar Assn. (pres. 1966), Masons, Shriners. Republican. Congregationalist. Home: 6801 Hickory Crest Rd Lincoln NE 68516-2458

JOHNSON, WARREN DONALD, retired pharmaceutical executive, former air force officer; b. Blackwell, Okla., Sept. 2, 1922; s. Charles Leon and Vera Ruth (Tucker) J.; children: Richard Johnson, Patricia Suzanne Johnson Peak, Lindabeth Johnson Brown, Ross Anthony. Student, Oklahoma City U., 1940-41. Served to 1st lt. U.S. Army, 1942-45; commd. 1st lt. USAAF, 1945; advanced through grades to lt. gen. USAF; chief of staff SAC Offutt AFB, Nebr., 1971-73; dir. Def. Nuclear Agy., Washington, 1973-77; ret., 1977; corp. v.p. Baxter Internat. Inc., Deerfield, Ill., 1977-91. Cons., tchr. Lake Forest Grad. Sch. Mgmt., 1991-99; ptnr. Cort & Assoc. Aircraft Sales and Charter. Decorated D.S.M., Legion of Merit with 2 oak leaf clusters, Joint Commendation medal. E-mail: generaldon@aol.com.

JOHNSON, WAYNE D. gas industry executive; b. Winterset, Iowa, Sept. 20, 1932; s. Leslie E. and Ruth N. J.; m. Lynne Alice Brouwer, June 15, 1963; children: Christopher W., Kevin B. BA, U. Nebr., 1954; LLB, Harvard U., 1959. Bar: Ill. bar 1959. Assoc., then ptnr. Ross, Hardies, O'Keefe, Babcock & Parsons, Chgo., 1959-72; asst. gen. counsel Peoples Gas Co., Chgo., 1972-75; sr. v.p., gen. counsel Entex, Inc., Houston, 1975-78, pres., 1978-86, utility cons., 1986-87; pres. United Tex. Transmission Co., 1987-93, Am. Natural Gas Power, Inc., Houston, 1993-97; utility cons., 1997—. Dir. Simmons & Co., Internat., 1980—. Past chmn. Galveston Bay Found.; vice chmn. Sam Houston Area Coun., Boy Scouts Am.; mem. data integration team and demand task force Nat. Petroleum Coun., Com. on Natural Gas, 1998-2000. With U.S. Army, 1954-56. Woodrow Wilson fellow, 1954 Mem. Am. Gas Assn., So. Gas Assn. (past chmn.), Lawyer's Club (Chgo.). Home: 5517 Cedar Creek Houston TX 77056

JOHNSON, WAYNE EATON, writer, editor, former drama critic; b. Phoenix, May 9, 1930; s. Roscoe and Marion (Eaton) J.; children: Katherine, Jeffrey. BA, U. Colo., 1952; postgrad., Duke U., 1952-53; postgrad. (KLM polit. reporting fellow 1957), U. Vienna, Austria, 1955-56; MA, UCLA, 1957. Reporter Internat. News Service, Des Moines, 1958, Wheat Ridge (Colo.) Advocate, 1957, Pueblo (Colo.) Chieftain, 1959, Denver Post, 1960, editl. writer, music critic, 1961-65; arts and entertainment editor Seattle Times, 1965-82, drama critic, 1980-92. Instr. journalism Colo. Woman's Coll., 1962 Author: Show: A Concert Program for Actor and Orchestra, 1971, America! A Concert of American Images, Words and Music, 1973, From Where the Sun Now Stands: The Indian Experience, 1973, Let's Go On: Pacific Northwest Ballet at 25, 1997; editor, co-pub.: Secrets of Warmth, 1992, Footprints on the Peaks, 1995, The Burgess Book of Lies, 1995. With CIC AUS, 1953-55, Korea. Home: 11303 Durland Pl NE Seattle WA 98125-5926 E-mail: waynojay@comcast.net.

JOHNSON, WAYNE HAROLD, librarian; b El Paso, Tex., May 2, 1942; s. Earl Harold and Cathryn Louise (Greeno) J.; m. Patricia Ann Froedge, June 15, 1973; children: Meredith Jessica (dec.), Alexandra Noëlle Victoria. BS, Utah State U., 1968; MPA, U. Colo., 1970; MLS, U. Okla., 1972. Circulation libr. Utah State U., Logan, 1968, adminstrv. asst. libr., 1969; with rsch. dept. Okla. Mgmt. and Engring. Cons., Norman, 1972; chief adminstrv. svcs. Wyo. State Libr., Cheyenne, 1973-76, chief bus. officer libr. archives and hist. dept., 1976-78, state libr., 1978-89; county grants mgr. Laramie County, Wyo., 1989-2001; cons. in field. Trustee Bibliog. Ctr. for Rsch., Denver, pres., 1983, 84; mem. Cheyenne dist. Longs Park coun. Boy Scouts Am., 1982-86; active Cheyenne Frontier Days, 1975—; mem. admissions and allocation com. United Way, 1991-94; mem. Ho. of Reps., Wyo. Legislature, 1993—; chmn. Transp. Hwys. Com., 1999—. Served with USCG, 1960-64. Mem. Aircraft Owners and Pilots Assn., Cheyenne C. of C. (chmn. transp. com. 1982, 83, mil. affairs com. 1994—), Am. Legion, Masons (Grand Lodge libr. 2001--), Kiwanis (bd. dirs. 1986-87), No. Colo. Yacht. Club. Republican. Presbyterian.

JOHNSON, WILLARD CHAPIN, surgeon, researcher; b. Waterbury, Conn., Nov. 4, 1937; s. Edward Oscar and Dorothy (Graves) J.; m. Elsie Ernest, Dec. 16, 1964 (dec. Nov. 1994); children: Karen, Thomas, David; m. Regina Ruth Kobett, Jan. 5, 1996. BS, MIT, 1959, MS, 1960; MD, Tufts U., 1964. Diplomate Am. Bd. Surgery. Intern Phila. Gen. Hosp., 1964-65; resident Boston City Hosp., 1965-70; chief vascular surgery Boston VA Med. Ctr., 1982-99, chief surgery, 1988-99; prof. surgery Tufts U. Sch. Medicine, Boston, 1982-92, Boston U. Sch. Medicine, 1992—, vice chmn. dept. surgery, 1998-99. Comdr. USN, 1970-72. Mem. ACS, Soc. Vascular Surgery, Internat. Soc. Cardiovascular Surgery, New Eng. Surg. Soc., New Eng. Soc. Vascular Surgery, Boston Surg. Soc.

JOHNSON, WILLARD RAYMOND, political science educator, consultant; b. St. Louis, Nov. 22, 1935; s. Willard and Dorothy (Stovall) J.; m. Vivian Robinson, Dec. 15, 1957; children: Caryn L., Kimberly E. BA, UCLA, 1957; MA, Johns Hopkins U., 1961; PhD, Harvard U., 1965. Asst. prof. polit. sci. MIT, Cambridge, Mass., 1964-69, assoc. prof., 1969-73, prof. polit. sci., 1973-96, prof. emeritus, 1996—. Vis. assoc. prof. Harvard U. Sch. Bus., Cambridge, 1969; exec. dir. Circle Inc., Roxbury, Mass., 1968-70; adj. prof. Fletcher Sch., Medford, Mass., 1971-82; cons. U.S. Nat. Commn. for Minority Enterprise, Washington, 1969; bd. dirs. Interfaith Housing Corp., Boston, 1970; chmn. bd. Circle Inc. subs. Greater Roxbury Devel. Corp., 1970; mem. U.S. Commn. for UNESCO, Washington, 1960-66 Author: The Cameroon Federation, 1970, (with Vivian R. Johnson) West African Governments and Volunteer Development Organizations, 1990; contbr. articles to Daedalus, 1973-82; New Eng. dir. Jour. African Civilizations, 1979-82, Jour. Modern African Studies, 1983, Negro History Bull., 2001; mem. editl. bd. Africa Today, 1975-2001. Bd. dirs. TransAfrica and TransAfrica Forum, Washington, 1978-95, chmn., 1984-86, pres. Boston chpt., 1980-84, 89-90; chmn. Africa Policy Task Force, McGovern for Pres. campaign, 1972, sr. adv. bd. Boston Pan-African Forum, Inc., 1997—; pres. Kans. Inst. African Am. and Native Am. Family History, 1997—. Recipient M.L. King Jr. award MIT Pres.'s Office, 1982—, YMCA Black Achiever's award, 1988; fellow and grantee Ford Found.; grantee Social Sci. Research Council, 1975, Rockefeller Found., 1977; Fulbright grantee, 1987; resident fellow Rockefeller Study Ctr., Bellagio, Italy, Sept. 1987; Fulbright scholar Indonesia, summer 1991. Mem. Coun. Fgn. Rels., Assn. Concerned African Scholars (bd. dirs. 1977—, nat. co-chmn. 1984-89), African Studies Assn., Nat. Conf. of Black Polit. Scientists. Democrat. Baptist. Office: MIT Dept Polit Sci 30 Wadsworth St Cambridge MA 02142-1320 *I believe that personal and social health is based on responsible engagememt, creative action, reflective credulity, disciplined energy, and mutual respect.*

JOHNSON, WILLIAM ALEXANDER, clergyman, philosophy educator; b. Bklyn., Aug. 20, 1934; s. Charles Raphael and Ruth Augusta (Anderson) J.; m. Carol Genevieve Lundquist, June 11, 1955; children— Karin Ruth, Karl William, Krister Frederick. BA, Queens Coll., City U. N.Y., 1953; B.D. (Univ. fellow, Morrow Meml. fellow, Daniel Delaplaine fellow), Union Theol. Sem., 1956; Teol. Kand., Lund U., 1957, Teol. Lic., 1958, Teologie Doktor, 1962; MA, Columbia U., 1958, PhD (Univ. fellow, Rockefeller Bros. fellow), 1959. Ordained deacon Meth. Ch., 1955, priest Episcopal Ch., 1968. Profl. baseball player N.Y. Giants, 1949-51; dir. Boys Club, Salvation Army, Jamaica, N.Y., 1952-54; minister Mt. Hope and Teabo Meth. chs., Wharton, N.J., 1954-56; elder Meth. Ch., 1956; minister Immanuel and Union Meth. chs., Bklyn., 1957-59; asst. in instrn. Columbia U., N.Y.C., 1957, Union Theol. Sem., N.Y.C., 1958; instr., asst. prof. religion Trinity Coll., Hartford, Conn., 1959-63; lectr. philosophy and theology Hartford Sem. Found., 1961-62; assoc. prof. religion, chmn. dept. religion Drew U., Madison, N.J., 1963-66; research prof. religion NYU, N.Y.C., 1966; vis. lectr. Union Theol. Sem., N.Y.C., 1966; vis. prof. religion Princeton (N.J.) U., 1966-68; prof., chmn. dept. religion Manhattanville Coll., Purchase, N.Y., 1967-71; vis. prof. Christian ethics Gen. Theol. Sem., N.Y.C., 1970; Albert V. Danielsen prof. Christian thought, prof. philosophy and history of ideas Brandeis U., Waltham, Mass., 1971—, prof. Near Ea. and Jewish studies, 1988—; canon residentiary Cathedral Ch. of St. John The Divine, N.Y.C., 1973—. Vis. Prof. Protestant theology N.Am. Coll., Vatican City, 1969-75; vis. prof., Tokyo, Stockholm, 1979, U. Gothenburg, Sweden, 1979, U. Copenhagen, 1994-95, Univ. Perth, Australia, 1997, 99, 2001; examining chaplain Diocese of Arctic, 1982; lectr., Europe, Asia, Africa, S.Am., Australia, Caribbean, Arctic. Author: The Philosophy of Religion of Anders Nygren, 1958, Christopher Polhem: The Father of Swedish Technology, 1963, Nature and the Supernatural in the Theology of Horace Bushnell, 1963, On Religion: A Study of Theological Method in Schleiermacher and Nygren, 1964, Problems in Christian Ethics, 1965 (with Nels F.S. Ferré) Swedish Contributions to Modern Theology, 1966, The Search for Transcendence, 1974, The Christian Way of Death, 1974, Invitation to Theology, 1979, Philosophy and the Gospel, 1979, (with Moorhead Kennedy) Christianity and Terrorism, 1986, O Boundless Salvation, 1987; also articles; debut as Popolo in Aida, Met. Opera, 1989, Tosca, 1990, La Boheme, 1992. Democratic committeeman Hartford, 1960-63; mem. exec. com. Am. Friends Service Com., Coll. Div., 1966-70; bd. dirs. Queens Coll. CUNY; priest-in-charge Korean Episc. Ch., N.Y.C., 1992—. Recipient David F. Swenson-Kierkegaard Meml. award, 1964, Harbison award for Tchr. of Yr. Danforth Found., 1965; named Outstanding Young Man in Am. Jr. C. of C., 1964; Disting. Alumnus Queens Coll., 1980; Scandinavian-Am. Found. fellow, 1956, 85; Fulbright scholar U. Copenhagen, 1957-58; Dempster Grad. fellow Meth. Ch., 1958; Am. Philos. Soc. fellow, 1971, 85. vis. rsch. fellow Princeton, 1972; Guggenheim fellow for study in Rome, Italy, 1972; NSF grantee, 1978; Rockefeller fellow Aspen Inst., 1978, fellow Aspen Inst., Jerusalem, 1982; Nat. Endowment Humanities grantee, 1978, 86; grantee Arthur Vining Davis Found., 1981; grantee Trinity Ch. of N.Y.C., 1982, 84; grantee Tauber Inst. Study of European Jewry; named All-Am. Baseball Player, Amateur Athletic Assn., 1952, 53, All-Am. Soccer Player, Amateur Athletic Assn., 1953. Mem. Am. Acad. Religion, Asia Soc., Japan Soc., Scandinavian-Am. Heritage Soc., Am. Philos. Assn., Danforth Assos., Soc. for Sci. Study Religion, Soc. for Religion in Higher Edn. (Kent fellow 1959), Soc. Anglican Theologians, Vasa Order Am., Am. Soc. Christian Ethics, Swedish Pioneer Hist. Soc., Soc. for Scandinavian Study, Danish-Am. Soc., Australian Am. Soc., Willa Cather Pioneer Meml. Found., Authors Guild, Episcopal Churchmen for S.Africa, New Haven Theol. Group, Westchester Inst. Psychiatry and Psychoanalysis (dir.), Ecumenical Found. for Christian Ministry, English Speaking Union, Ch. Soc. for Coll. Work, Paris Am. Club, Columbia University Club, Met. Opera Club, The Pilgrims, The Coffee House, Lotos Club, Century Club, Explorer's Club, Phi Beta Kappa, Pi Gamma Mu, Phi Sigma Tau. Democrat. Episcopalian. Office: 27 Fox Meadow Rd Scarsdale NY 10583-2903 also: 44 Pascal Ave Rockport ME 04856-5918 *I have attempted in my life to fulfill the simple prayer of St. Francis: Lord, make me an instrument of your peace/Where there is hatred . . . let me sow love/Where there is injury . . . pardon/Where there is doubt . . . faith/Where there is despair . . . hope/Where there is darkness . . light/Where there is sadness . . . joy. For it is giving that we receive; it is pardoning that we are pardoned; and it is dying that we are born to eternal life.*

JOHNSON, WILLIAM ASHTON, retired lawyer; b. St. Louis, June 26, 1933; s. William Stuart and Adele (Balmer) J.; m. Anne Chartrand, Nov. 11, 1961; children: Mark, Anthony, Jocelyn, Jennifer. BA, St. Louis U., 1955, JD, 1957; postdoctoral, Northwestern U., 1969. Bar: Mo. 1957. Asst. sec. Mercantile Bank NA, St. Louis, 1969-73, asst. trust officer, 1973-76, trust officer, 1976-78, asst. v.p., 1978-83, v.p., 1983-86; sr. atty. trust Mercantile Bancorporation Inc., St. Louis, 1996—99; ret., 1999. Author St. Louis U. Law Rev., 1971. Served with U.S. Army, 1957-59. Mem. Alpha Sigma Nu. Democrat. Roman Catholic. Home: 4732 Prague Ave Saint Louis MO 63109-2708

JOHNSON, WILLIAM DAVID, retired university administrator; b. Bloomington, Ind., Aug. 9, 1924; s, Ben and Ida Grace (Garlock) J.; m. Audrey Aelise Thurston; 1 child, Sheryn Aelise Johnson Peters BS, Ind. U., 1946. Asst. bursar U. Va., Charlottesville, 1947-54, comptroller George Washington U., 1954-69, dir. planning and budgeting, 1969-82, assoc. provost, 1982-84, provost, 1984-89. Served to 1st lt. U.S. Army, 1943-46; ETO Mem. Fin. Exec. Inst. (chpt. pres. 1969-70), Eastern Assn. Coll. and Univ. Bus. Officers, Nat. Assn. Coll. and Univ. Bus. Officers, Omicron Delta Kappa, Delta Chi Republican. Presbyterian. Avocations: woodworking; golf; skeet shooting. Home: 3440 S Jefferson St Apt 705 Falls Church VA 22041-3125

JOHNSON, WILLIAM DEAN, power company executive; b. Pa., Jan. 9, 1954; BA, Duke U., 1978; JD, U. N.C., 1982. Law clk. Hon. J.D. Philips Jr., U.S. Ct. Appeals, 4th Cir., 1982-83; assoc. Hunton & Williams, 1983-90, ptnr., 1990-92; assoc. gen. counsel Carolina Power & Light, Raleigh, 1992-95, v.p., corp. sec., 1995-1999, sr. v.p., corp. sec., 1999-2001; exec. v.p., gen. counsel, sec. Progress Energy, Inc., Raleigh, 2001—02; pres., CEO, Progress Energy Svc. Co., Raleigh, 2002—. Mem. ABA, N.C. Bar Assn. Office: Progress Energy Inc 411 Fayetteville Street Mall Raleigh NC 27601-1748

JOHNSON, WILLIAM HOWARD, agricultural engineer, educator; b. Sidney, Ohio, Sept. 3, 1922; s. Russell Earl and Dollie (Gamble) J.; m. Wyoma Jean Swift, Oct. 2, 1943; children: Lawrence Alan, Cheri Ellen, Dana Sue. BS, Ohio State U., 1948, MS, 1953; PhD, Mich. State U., 1960. Registered profl. engr. Mem. faculty Ohio Agrl. Expt. Sta., Wooster, 1948-64; mem. faculty Ohio Agrl. Research and Devel. Center, Wooster, 1964-70, prof., asso. chmn. dept. agrl.

engring., 1959-70; part-time prof. Ohio State U., 1964-70; prof., head dept. agrl. engring. Kans. State U., Manhattan, 1970-81, dir. Engring. Experiment Sta., 1981-87. Cons. farm equipment cos. Author: (with B.J. Lamp) Principles, Equipment and Systems for Corn Harvesting, 1966; also articles. Recipient Distinguished Alumnus award Coll. Engring., Ohio State U., 1974; named to Coll. Engring. Kans. State U. Hall of Fame, 1992; recipient Cyrus Hall McCormick-Jerome Increase Case medal Am. Society of Agricultural Engineers, 1994 Fellow Am. Soc. Agrl. Engrs. (pres. 1986-87, McCormick-Case Gold Medal award 1994), Kans. Engring. Soc. (pres. 1985-86), Sigma Xi, Tau Beta Pi. Achievements include research on soil-plant-machine relationships, harvesting, design for soiltillers, planters, harvesters. Home: 2121 Meadowlark Rd #131 Manhattan KS 66502 Office: Kans State Univ Dept Agrl Engring Seaton Hall Manhattan KS 66506 E-mail: wjohnson@ksu.edu.

JOHNSON, WILLIAM JENNINGS, marketing consultant, entrepreneur; b. Sioux Falls, S.D., Sept. 16, 1955; s. Jennings Pearson and Donna E. (Kelley) J.; m. Suzanne Reando, Mar. 8, 1980; children: Krista Marie, Daniel William. BSBA, Black Hills State U., 1978. Salesman Met. Life, Rapid City, S.D., 1978-79, EMSCO Industries, Rapid City, 1979-80; salesman, pres., founder, chmn. Diversified Fin. Svcs., Inc., Rapid City, 1981—; co-owner Sibco Inc., Rapid City, 1984—; pres., co-founder Success Inc., Rapid City, 1991—. Guest authority spkr. Paul Strassels Radio Talk Show Annuities, 1990; mktg. cons. Control Tech. Internat., Rapid City, 1994; group conf. mktg. facilitator S.D. Bus. 20, 1994. Co-author: (sales tng. guide) Moneytalks, 1991. Active Rimrock Evang. Free Ch. Recipient cert. merit S.D. SBA, 1978, Key Club Disting. Sales award Keystone Mass Distbrs., Inc., Boston, 1983, Million Dollar Premium Prodr. award Am. Investors Life Ins., Topeka, 1988, Chmn.'s Club award Life USA Ins. Co., Mpls., 1989, 90, 91, 92, 93, Nat. Sales Achievement award Nat. Assn. Life Underwriters, 1992; named Million Dollar Round Table Ct. of the Table, 1992, 97, 98. Mem. Million Dollar Round Table. Republican. Avocations: golf, fishing, reading. Office: Diversified Fin Svcs Inc 1508 Mt View Rd Ste 101 Rapid City SD 57702-4349

JOHNSON, WILLIAM JOSEPH, investment manager; b. Cleve., Apr. 10, 1941; s. Robert David and Ann (Sercely) J.; m. Joan Donna Anshutz, June 18, 1966; children: Donna, Jennifer. BA, Ohio State U., 1966; postgrad., NYU, 1971-75. Account exec. Merrill Lynch, N.Y.C., 1966-73, Cyrus J. Lawrence, N.Y.C., 1973-77; v.p. Kuhn Loeb, N.Y.C., 1977-78; sr. v.p. Donaldson Lufkin and Jenrette, N.Y.C., 1978-2000; founder, mng. gen. ptnr. Xantos Ptnrs., 2001—; mng. dir. Second Curve Capital, 2001. Served with USNR, 1961-63. Named Outstanding Broker, Reg. Rep mag., Newport Beach, Calif., 1986. Roman Catholic. Avocations: windsurfing, hiking, sailing, history, folk music. Home: 14 Green Hill Rd Madison NJ 07940-2526

JOHNSON, WILLIAM POTTER, newspaper publisher; b. Peoria, Ill., May 4, 1935; s. William Zweigle and Helen Marr (Potter) J.; m. Pauline Ruth Rowe, May 18, 1968; children: Darragh Elizabeth, William Potter. AB, U. Mich., 1957. Gen. mgr. Bureau County Rep., Inc., Princeton, Ill., 1961-72; pres. Johnson Newspapers, Inc., Sebastopol, Calif., 1972-75, Evergreen, Colo., 1974-86, Canyon Commons Investment, Evergreen, 1974—, Johnson Media, Inc., Granby, Colo., 1987—. Author: How the Michigan Betas Built a $1,000,000 Chapter House in the '80s. Alt. del. Rep. Nat. Conv., 1968. Lt. USNR, 1958-61. Mem. Colo. Press Assn., Nat. Newspaper Assn., Maple Bluff Country Club, Madison Club, Beta Theta Pi. Home: 8820 S Sea Oaks Way 204 Vero Beach FL 32963 Office: PO Box 409 Granby CO 80446-0409

JOHNSON, WILLIAM R. food products company executive; Grad., UCLA; MBA, U. Tex. With H.J. Heinz Co., Pitts., 1982—, pres., COO, 1996-98, chmn., pres., CEO, 1998—. Office: PO Box 57 600 Grant St Pittsburgh PA 15219-2702

JOHNSON, WILLIAM RAY, insurance company executive; b. West Union, Ohio, Feb. 12, 1930; s. A. Earl and Helen (Walker) J.; m. Anne Abrams, Mar. 27, 1954; children: Elizabeth Anne, William Randall. BS in Edn., Wilmington Coll., 1951. Tchr., theatre dept. Miami U., Oxford, Ohio, 1951; divsn. mgr. Prudential Ins. Co. of Am., Waco, Tex., 1956-60; nat. tng. cons., gen. agt. Paul Revere Life Ins. Co., Dallas, 1960—65; health and accident ins. cons. Dallas, 1965—68; ptnr. Wiedemann & Johnson, Cos., Dallas, 1965—93. Mem. exec. com. Cullen Frost Bank, Dallas, 1986-94, mem. trust com., 1986-94, chmn. 1991-94, also bd. dirs. Bd. dirs. Suicide Prevention of Dallas, 1973-81, pres. 1975-76; bd. dirs. Routh St. Ctr., 1975-78, Turtle Creek Manor, 1977-79, Sr. Citizens of Greater Dallas, Inc., 1977-81, Dallas Child Guidance Clinic, 1977-83; mem. Bishops Adv. Com. on Planning and Devel., Episcopal Diocese of Dallas, 1976-81; sr. warden St. Michael's Episcopal Ch., 1979-81; trustee Episcopal Theol. Sem. of SW, Austin, Tex., 1981-87, mem. exec. com., 1984-86; mem. bd. theol. edn. Episcopal Ch., N.Y.C., 1982-88; mem. exec. coun. Episcopal Diocese of Dallas, 1983-86, standing com., 1987-90; trustee St. Michael Sch., 1989-91, Greater Dallas Community of Chs., 1986-89, mem. exec. com. 1987-88; bd. trustees Jubilee Park and Cmty. Ctr. Corp., 1997—. Served to 1st lt. USAF, 1951-55. Mem. Multiple Sclerosis Soc. (bd. dirs. N. Texas Divsn. 1987-89), Anglican Sch. Theology (bd. trustees 1986-89, 98—, chmn. 1988-89), Dallas Country Club.

JOHNSON, WILLIAM W. dental educator; b. Monroe, Wis., Jan. 31, 1952; s. Herbert T. and Edna J.; m. Veronica A. Hartman, Aug. 4, 1973. DDS, Marquette U., 1977, MS, 1989. Pvt. dental practice, Lancaster, Wis., 1977-79, Monroe, Wis., 1979-90; assoc. prof. U. Tenn., Memphis, 1990-97; chmn., assoc. prof. Minn. State U., Mankato, 1997—2000; assoc. prof. adult restorative dentistry U. Nebr., Lincoln, 2000—. Adj. asst. prof. Marquette U., Milw., 1989—95. Contbr. articles to profl. jours. Pres. faculty orgn. U. Tenn. Coll. of Dentistry, Memphis, 1994—95. Mem. Wis. Dental Assn. (rep. to mem. svcs. divsn. 1985-90), Green CountyDental Soc. (pres. 1985-88), Am. Assn. Dental Schs., Am. Dental Assn., Acad. Gen. Dentistry, Acad. Operative Dentistry, Chgo. Dental Soc., Internat. Assn. Dental Rsch., Omicron Kappa Upsilon, Alpha Sigma Nu. Office: Coll of Dentistry U Nebr 40th and Holdrege Sts Lincoln NE 68583

JOHNSON, YVONNE AMALIA, elementary education educator, science consultant; b. DeKalb, Ill., July 1, 1930; d. Albert O. and Virginia O. (Nelson) J. BS in Edn., No. Ill. State Tchrs. Coll., 1951; MS in Edn., No. Ill. U., 1960. Tchr. Love Rural Sch., DeKalb, 1951-53, West Elem. Sch., Sycamore, Ill., 1953—2002; coord. Media Ctr. West Sch. Ill. honors sci. tchr., ISU, 1985-87. Contbr. articles to profl. publs. Bd. dirs. Sycamore Pub. Libr., 1974-98, pres. bd. dirs., 1984-98, chmn. maj. fund drive for addition to libr., 1994-98; founder Dekalb County Excellence in Edn. award, 1999. Named DeKalb County Conservation Tchr., 1971, Gov.'s Master Tchr., State of Ill., 1984, Outstanding Agrl. Tchr. in the Classroom Dekalb County Farm Bur., 1993; grantee NSF, 1961, 62, 85, 86, 87, NASA, 1988; Sci. Lit. grantee State of Ill., 1992-94. Mem. NEA, NSTA (cert. in elem. sci.), Ill. Sci. Tchrs. Assn., Ill. Edn. Assn., Sycamore Edn. Assn., Coun. for Elem. Sci. Internat. Office: West Elem Sch 240 Fair St Sycamore IL 60178-1641

JOHNSON, ZANE QUENTIN, retired petroleum company executive; b. Bristow, Okla., Mar. 5, 1924; s. Sylvester B. and Meta B. (Biggs) J.; m. Nila Jean Caylor, June 4, 1949; children: Zane Quentin, Mark Caylor, Janis Lyn. BS in Chem. Engring, U. Okla., 1947. With Gulf Oil Corp. (and subs. cos.), from 1947; pres., chief operating officer Gen. Atomic, Inc., San Diego, 1969-70; exec. v.p. Gulf Oil Corp., Pitts., 1970-75; pres. Gulf Sci. & Tech. Co., Pitts., from 1975, now ret. Faculty Sch. Chem. Engring., U. Okla. Mayor, Port Arthur, Tex., 1957-58; bd. dirs. United Community Services of San Diego County, 1969-70, Boy Scouts Am., Duquesne U.; trustee Shadyside Hosp. Served to 1st lt. USAAF, PTO. Decorated Air medal with three oak leaf clusters; recipient U. Okla. Coll. Engring. Hall of Fame award. Mem. AIChE, Am. Petroleum Inst., Port Royal Club, Royal Poinciana Golf Club, Hound Ears Golf Club (Blowing Rock, N.C.). Republican. Presbyterian. Home: 8410 Abbington Cir # A-34 Naples FL 34108-7733

JOHNSON-CHAMP, DEBRA SUE, lawyer, educator, writer, artist; b. Emporia, Kans., Nov. 8, 1955; d. Bert John and S. Christine (Brigman) Johnson; m. Michael W. Champ, Nov. 23, 1979; children: Natalie, John. BA, U. Denver, 1977; JD, Pepperdine U., 1980; postgrad., U. So. Calif., 1983-84. Bar: Calif. 1981. Pvt. practice, Long Beach, Calif., 1981-82, L.A., 1981-87, Woodland Hills, Calif., 1993-99; of counsel Greenbaum & Champ, 1999—. Legal reference librarian, instr. Southwestern U. Sch. Law, L.A., 1982-88; adj. prof. law, 1987-88; atty. Contos & Bunch, Woodland Hills, 1988-93; free lance writer/artist; owner The Purple Iguana, 1997—; of counsel Greenbaum & Champ LLP, 1999—. Editor-in chief: Southern Calif. Assn. Law Libraries Newsletter, 1984-85; mem. law rev. Pepperdine U., 1978-80; contbr. articles to profl. jours. Trustee United Meth. Ch., Tujunga, Calif., 1986-88. West Pub. Co. scholar, 1983; recipient H. Wayne Gillis Moot Ct. award, 1980, Vincent S. Dalsimer Best Brief award 1979. Mem. ABA, So. Calif. Assn. Law Libr., Am. Assn. Law Libr., Calif. Bar Assn., Southwestern Affiliates, Friends of the Libr. L.A. Democrat. Home and Office: 5740 Valerie Ave Woodland Hills CA 91367-3967 E-mail: legaldebi2@prodigy.net.

JOHNSON-COUSIN, DANIELLE, French literature and cultural studies educator; b. Geneva; d. Edouard Henri and Suzanne Louise Cousin; m. Harry Morton Johnson, Jan. 25, 1970; 1 child, Eliza Suzanne Johnson. Cert. de Maturité cum laude, Coll. of Geneva, 1962; BA, U. Alaska, 1966; MA, Purdue U., 1968; PhD, U. Ill., 1977; postgrad., Oxford U., 1968, Northwestern U., Evanston, Ill., 1968-69, Maximilian U., Munich, 1970, Mellon Regional Seminar Lit. Crit., Vanderbilt U., 1987. Vis. lectr. U. Ill., Urbana-Champaign, 1976-77; asst. prof. French Amherst Coll., 1979-82; asst. prof. French, Andrew W. Mellon fellow Vanderbilt U., Nashville, 1982-88, dir. Vanderbilt-in-France program Aix-en-Pce, 1984-85; assoc. prof. French Fla. Internat. U., 1988—2002. Cons. Social Scis. and Humanities Rsch. Coun. of Can., Ottawa, 1994—. Contbr. articles to profl. jours. Named U. Mass. Oxford scholar, 1968; fellow, U. Ill., 1971—73, Inst. Advanced Studies in Humanities, U. Edinburgh, Scotland, 1979, numerous others. Mem. Nat. Assn. Scholars, Am. Assn. Tchrs. French (emeritus), Am. Soc. 18th-Century Studies, Assn. Lit. Scholars and Critics, Soc. des Professeurs Francais et Francophones en Am., Assn. J.J. Rousseau (Neuchatel), Soc. Vaudoise d'Histoire & d'Archéologie (Lausanne), Internat. Soc. for Study of European Ideas, Internat. Parliament of Writers (Strasbourg), Internat. Dir. of 18th Century Studies, Oxford, Oglala Lakota Coll. Alumni (hon.), Pi Delta Phi (hon.). Home: 9805 SW 115th Ct Miami FL 33176-2582

JOHNSON-D'ALESSIO, ANNA MARIA, writer; b. Villa Lottorio, Italy, June 19, 1959; arrived in Canada, 1964; d. Frank and Rosa D'Alessio; m. Robert Johnson, June 29, 1985. Student, St. Clair Coll., 1980—81, Internat. Corr. Sch., 1984, Lifetime Career Schs., 1986, Nat. Edn. Corp., 1990—91. Waitress, hostess, cashier La Cuising Restaurant, Windsor, 1979—82; hostess Viscount Hotel, Windsor, Canada, 1982—83; sales agt. Jacobson's, Grosse Pointe, Mich., 1989—99. Author: (poetry) A Place Within, 2001; contbr. poems to lit. publs.; rec. artists: CD You Don't Really Know. Mem.: Detroit Inst. Arts, Famous Poet Soc. (award 1990—, trophy of excellence 2002), Internat. Soc. Poetry (award 1989—, Poet of Merit award 2003, Bronze Commemorative award medallion 2002). Roman Catholic. Avocations: photography, art, floral arrangement, writing, reading. Home: 665 W Warren Ave Apt 312 Detroit MI 48201 Office: 1st Books Libr 2595 Vernal Pike Bloomington IN 47404 E-mail: Anjohns313@aol.com.

JOHNSON-GRAUER, LOIS EILEEN, artist; b. Shafter, Calif., July 20, 1942; d. Pete S. and Martha (Sawatzky) Unruh; m. William Howard Johnson, Aug. 13, 1960 (div. 1987); 1 child, Cindy Eileen; m. Ronald G. Grauer, Feb. 2, 2001. Student, Fresno City Coll., 1959-60, North Tex. State U., 1962-63, No. Ariz. U., 1970-75, Scottsdale Artists' Sch., 1984-87. Art cons. grades 7 and 8 Auberry (Calif.) Elem. Sch., 1987-92, pvt. portrait com., 1979-82. Exhibited in group shows at Husberg Fine Art and El Prado Galleries, Sedona, Ariz., 1970-79, O'Brien's Art Emporium, Scottsdale, 1982-93, Congl. Reception, U.S. Congress, Washington, 1992, Georgetown U. Art Gallery, Washington, 1992, SUNY Butler Gallery, 1992, Port History Mus., Phila., 1992, Ellis Island, N.Y., 1992, JFK Mus. and Libr., Boston, 1992, Nat. Hist. Mus., L.A., 1993, Transamerica Twr., San Francisco, 1993, GWS Big Horn Gallery Carmel, Calif., 1993-94; others represented in permanent collections Valley Nat. Bank, U.S. Dept. Justice, Wickenburg Art Mus., Johnson's Wax, Firestone Tire, General Motors, Max Factor, Vertex Mgmt., Inc., others; representations Joanne Chappell Gallery, San Francisco, Californiaview Fine Art Gallery, Los Gatos.; paintings included in Contemporary Western Artists, Prentice Hall Lit., Images of Am. Immigration. Host Internat. Coll. Students, Dallas, Tex. and Flagstaff, Ariz., 1962-78; co-founder Campus Ambs., 1965-78; fundraiser in community, 1966—. Recipient scholarship Nat. Portrait Seminar, Washington, 1983, 1st Pl. Best and Brightest Competition, Scottsdale (Ariz.) Art Sch., 1986, 2d Pl. Immigration and Naturalization Svc. Internat. Competition, U.S. Dept. Justice, Washington, 1992. Avocations: photography, hiking. Home: PO Box 153 Ben Lomond CA 95005-0153 E-mail: graurog@yahoo.com.

JOHNSON-LAIRD, PHILIP NICHOLAS, psychologist; b. Rothwell, Eng., Oct. 12, 1936; s. Frederick Ryberg and Dorothy (Blackett) J.-L.; m. Maureen Mary Sullivan, Aug. 1, 1959; children: Ben, Dorothy. BA with honors, Univ. Coll., London, 1964; PhD, Univ. Coll., 1967; Doctorate (hon.), U. Gothenburg, Sweden, 1983, Padua (Italy) U., 1997, Trinity Coll., Dublin, Ireland, 2000, Nat. U. Distance Edn., Madrid, Spain, 2000, U. Ghent, Belgium, 2002. Asst. lectr., then lectr. psychology Univ. Coll., London, 1966-73; vis. mem. Inst. for Advanced Study, Princeton, N.J., 1971-72; reader, prof., chair exptl. psychology Sussex U., Brighton, Eng., 1973-82; spl. appointment, asst. dir. Med. Rsch. Coun. Applied Psychology Unit, Cambridge, Eng., 1982-89; prof., Stuart prof. psychology Princeton U., 1989—. Vis. prof. cognitive sci. Stanford (Calif.) U., 1980, vis. prof. psychology, 1985; vis. prof. Trieste (Italy) U., 1990, Univ. Coll., 1992, NYU, 1996, Padua, 2000. Author: Mental Models, 1983, The Computer and the Mind, 1988, (with Ruth Byrne) Deduction, 1991, 7 others; contbr. over 200 articles to profl. jours. Mem. Campaign for Disarmament, London, 1959-82. Recipient Medaglia D'Onore, U. Florence, Italy, 1989, Fyssen prize, 2002. Fellow: Royal Soc. U.K., Brit. Acad.; mem.: Soc. Exptl. Psychologists, Brit. Psychol. Soc. (Spearman medal 1974, Pres.'s award 1985), Am. Psychol. Soc. Avocations: modern jazz piano, arguing. Office: Princeton U Dept Psychology Princeton NJ 08544-0001 E-mail: phil@princeton.edu.

JOHNSON-LANS, SHIRLEY B. economist, educator; b. Wichita, Kans. d. Howard A. and Kathryn Augusta Johnson; m. Asher B. Lans, June 28, 1967 (dec. Feb. 2002); 1 child, Andrea Elisabeth Lans Donahue. BA magna cum laude, Harvard U., 1956; MA with 1st class honors, Edinburgh (Scotland) U., 1958; PhD, Columbia U., 1966. Lectr. Mt. Holyoke Coll., South Hadley, Mass., 1959, CCNY, 1959—62; instr. Barnard Coll., N.Y.C., 1962—65; asst. prof. NYU, 1965—67; prof. Vassar Coll., Poughkeepsie, NY, 1967—. Vis. prof. St. Andrews (Scotland) U., 1972; rsch. assoc. Nat. Bur. Econ. Rsch., Inc., N.Y.C., NY, 1961—63, Survey Rsch. Ctr., U. Mich., Ann Arbor, 1964. Contbr. articles to profl. jours. Bd. dirs. N.Y. State Energy Rsch. Devel. Authority, 1987—2000, State of N.Y. Mortgage Agy., N.Y.C., 1978—86; mem. vestry, warden The Episcopal Parish of Calvary/St. Georges, N.Y.C., 1978—. Fellow Ford, 1964; grantee Woodrow Wilson Found., 1956—57; scholar Marshall, 1956—58. Mem.: Am. Econ. Assn., Poughkeepsie Tennis Club, Nat. Arts Club, Harvard Club of N.Y. Episcopalian. Avocations: keyboard playing, tennis, swimming, choral singing. Office: Vassar Coll Box 378 Poughkeepsie NY 12604 E-mail: sjlans@vassar.edu.

JOHNSON-LEESON, CHARLEEN ANN, former elementary school educator, insurance agent, insurance consultant, regional executive assistant; b. Battle Creek, Mich., June 10, 1949; d. Kenneth Andrews Leeson and Ila Mae (Weed/Lesson) McCutcheon; m. Lynn Boyd Johnson, Aug. 8, 1970; children: Eric Andrew, Andrea Johnson McGrath. BA, Spring Arbor Coll., 1971; MS, Reading Specialist, Western Ill. U., 1990. Cert. elem. and secondary tchr., Mich., elem. tchr., Ill., reading K-9, Ill. Tchr. Hanover (Mich.) Horton Schs., 1972-73, Virden (Ill.) Elem. Sch., 1984-90; ins. agt. State Farm Ins., Virden, Ill., 1991-95, cons. Springfield, Ill., 1995-97, regional exec. asst. Bloomington, Ill., 1997-99, agt. Myrtle Beach, S.C., 1999—. Cofounder girl and jr. high sch. cheerleading advisor in field; course leader Agt. Schs. 1, 2, and 3. Music dir., pianist Zion Luth. Ch., Farmersville, Ill., 1979-88, organist, pianist Olive St. Friends, Battle Creek, 1961-67. Recipient Honor the Educator award World Book, 1988, 89, Soaring Eagle award Millionair/Amb. Club, 1991-98, Amb. Club, 2001-02; Wilson Stone scholar, 1990, Mich. State scholar, 1967. Mem. AUA, Internat. Reading Assn., S.C. Assn. Life Underwriters, Nat. Assn. Ins. and FIn. Advisors, Alpha Upsilon Alpha. Avocations: music (piano and organ), writing. Home: 9621 Chestnut RIdge Dr Myrtle Beach SC 29572 Office: 119 Waccamaw Med Park Conway SC 29526-8902 Office Fax: 843-347-9326. E-mail: charleen.johnson.cyxd@statefarm.com.

JOHNSON-LIBKIND, JEAN SUE See LIBKIND, JEAN SUE JOHNSON

JOHNSON-MILLER, CHARLEEN V. teacher coordinator; b. Cleve., Ohio, Jan. 17, 1948; d. Leroy and Alice Vivian Carter; m. Sammy Richard Miller, Dec. 24, 1980; 1 child, Patrice. BS in Edn., Ctrl. State U., 1970; MS in Edn., Cleve. State U., 1979; postgrad., Clevel. State U., 1985, John Carrol U., 1983. Permanent tchg. cert. Ohio, 1985. Cleve. Tchrs. Union rep. Cleve. Pub. Schs., 1982—86, cons. tchr., mentor, 1988—93, guidance/drug liaison, 1992—95; lead tchr. Cleve. Mcpl. Schs., 1995—99, grade level chairperson, 1996—2000, safety patrol dir., 1998—, Helping One Student to Succeed/tutor vol. coord., 1999—. Cons. tchr., facilitator human devel. Kent (Ohio) State U., 1983—90; program developer, curriculum planner guidance program Cleve. Pub. Schs., 1985—91, dist. prof. developer, 1993—99. Mem. Present Day Bapt. Ch. Scholar Martha Holden Jenning scholar, Martha Holden Jennings Found., Cleve., 1990. Mem.: Cabinettes, Scrabblers (past pres., v.p., sec.), Alpha Kappa Alpha, Phi Delta Kappa, Inc. (life). Avocations: tennis, bowling, aerobics, kickboxing, line dancing.

JOHNSON-PAYTON, LORI RENEE, systems engineer; b. Jacksonville, N.C., Dec. 27, 1967; d. Robert Russa and Louise Margaret Johnson; m. Daryl Spencer Payton, June 8, 1996; 1 child, Joshua Payton. BS in Sys. Engring., U. Va., 1991; MS in Indsl. Engring., Ga. Inst. Tech., 1992; M Cert. in Project Mgmt., George Washington U., 1998; PhD, U. of Va., 1997. Solutions/product planner desktop sys. pers. computing divsn. IBM Corp., Research Triangle Park, NC, 1997—99, program mgr. desktop sys., 2000; spl. bids and ops. program mgr. desktop sys. IBM Corp., Research Triangle Park, NC, 2000—01; engring. cons. bid re-engring. group IBM Corp., Research Triangle Park, 2001—. Contbr. articles to profl. jours. Fellow, GEM Found., 1991—92; scholar, NSF, 1993—95. Mem.: PMI Inst., Inst. For Ops. Rsch. and the Mgmt. Sci., Soc. of Risk Analysis, Nat. Soc. of Black Engineers, Tau Beta Pi, Delta Sigma Theta, Alpha Kappa Psi. Avocations: running, travel, swimming, aerobics, piano. Home: 101 Covewood Court Durham NC 27713 Office: IBM Corporation 3039 Cornwallis Rd Bldg 002/JJ326 Research Triangle Park NC 27709 Home Fax: 919-544-7524, Office Fax: 919-543-4253. Personal E-mail: ljohnson_payton@hotmail.com. E-mail: ljp@us.ibm.com.

JOHNSTON, ALAN COPE, lawyer; b. Evanston, Ill., Mar. 4, 1946; S. Alan Rogers and Eleanor Cope (Smith) J.; m. Kathryn Elizabeth Edwards, June 21, 1969; 1 child, Eliza. BA, Yale U., 1968; JD, Harvard U., 1975. BAR: Calif. 1975, D.C. 1979, u.S. Dist. Ct. (no., ea., ctrl. and so. dists.) Calif., U.S. Dist. Ct. D.C., U.S. Ct. Appeals (9th fed. and D.C. cirs.)., U.S. Supreme Ct., Gaikoku Jimu Bengoshi, Japan. Assoc. Morrison & Foerster, San Francisco, 1975-79, Washington, 1979-81, ptnr. San Francisco, 1981-85, Palo Alto, Calif., 1986—2002, Tokyo, 2002—. Lt. USNR, 1969-72. Avocations: sailing, reading. Office: Morrison & Foerster 755 Page Mill Rd Palo Alto CA 94304-1018 E-mail: acjohnston@mofo.com.

JOHNSTON, ALASTAIR J. sports association executive; b. Glasgow, Scotland; Degree, U. Strathclyde. From intern to pres. Internat. Mgmt. Group, Cleve., 1969—2001, pres., COO, 2001—03; pres. Internat. Mgmt. Group Internat., 2003—, co-CEO, 2003—; COO Arnold Palmer Enterprises. Mem. adv. bd. World Golf Village and Hall of Fame. Author: The Chronicles of Golf: 1457-1857, Vardon to Woods: A Pictorial History of Golfers in Advertising. Office: International Management Group 1360 East 9th St Ste 1000 Cleveland OH 44114*

JOHNSTON, BARRY ALGENE, housing loan administrator; b. Evansville, Ind., May 12, 1960; s. Benjamin Algene and Marie Cunningham Johnston; m. Jamie Lee Leach, June 6, 1992. BS in Bus. Mgmt., Western Ky. U., 1994. Owner, head coach River City Gymnastics, Owensboro, Ky., 1984—89; drafter Michael Wells Arch., Owensboro, 1989—93; account analyst Am. Gen. Fin., Evansville, Ind., 1995—96; real estate owned mgr. Firstar Home Mortgage, Owensboro, 1995—2000; housing program mgr. Green River Area Devel. Dist., Owensboro, 2001—. Pres. Ohio Valley Homeless Coun., Owensboro, 2002—; coun. mem. AmeriCorp/Vista, Owensboro, 2002—. Mem.: YMCA. Baptist. Home: 4111 Foxtail Pl Owensboro KY 42303 Office: Green River Area Devel Dist 3860 US Hwy 60 West Owensboro KY 42303

JOHNSTON, BERNARD FOX, foundation executive, writer; b. Taft, Calif., Nov. 19, 1934; s. Bernard Lowe and Georgia Victoria (Fox) J.; m. Audrey Rhoades, June 9, 1956 (div. Sept. 1963); 1 child, Sheldon Bernard. BA in Creative Arts, San Francisco State U., 1957, MA in World Lit., 1958. Lectr. philosophy Coll. of Marin, Kentfield, Calif., 1957-58; lectr. humanities San Francisco State U., 1957-58, 67-68; instr. English Contra Costa Coll., San Pablo, Calif., 1958-63; Knowles Found. philosophy fellow, 1962; fellow Syracuse U., 1964-66; freelance writer Piedmont, Calif., 1968-77; pres. Cinema Repertory, Inc., Point Richmond, Calif., 1978-89; pres., exec. dir. Athena Found., Tiburon, Calif., 1990—, Incline Village, Nev., 1990—. Exec. prodr. (TV series) The Heroes of Time, (TV documentary) The Shudder of Awe; CEO The Athena Found., Inc., 1997, Mahler Festival, U. Colo., Boulder, 1998. Author: (screenplay) Point Exeter, 1979, Ascent Allowed, 1988 (award); author, editor: Issues in Education: An Anthology of Controversy, 1964, The Literature of Learning, 1971; festival pianist Lake Tahoe Internat. Film Festival, 1998; resident pianist Tahoe-Chrysler Corp., 1998; pianist (CD) Time Remembered; musical dir., featured pianist Lake Tahoe Summer Music Series, 2000, piano soloist Sierra Nevada Coll. Presdl. Dinner, 2000; featured pianist Lake Tahoe Hebrew Assn. Concert, 2001, Tahoe Forest Hosp. benefit, Lake Tahoe; pianist San Francisco State U. Athletic Awards Ceremony, 2001, Squaw Creek Resort Lake Tahoe Forest Benefit, concert, featured pianist, 2001, 03; essay Bound for Glory. Arts grantee Silicon Valley Cmty. Found., 1998; recipient TV Arts award Krisch Found., 2001; Bell-Brook Talent TV Award, 1950. Mem. Dirs. Guild Am., Writers Guild Am., Coun. for Basic Edn., Wilson Ctr. Assocs., Assn. Lit. Scholars and Critics, Smithsonian Instn., Donner Land Trust, Nat. Assn. Scholars, Calif. Assn. Scholars, San Francisco State Alumni Assn., Commonwealth Club of Calif. Avocations: classical and jazz piano, backpacking, softball. Office: 845 Southwood Blvd Ste 50 Incline Village NV 89451-946 E-mail: athenaprods@powernet.net.

JOHNSTON, BRUCE FOSTER, economics educator; b. Lincoln, Nebr., Sept. 24, 1919; s. Homer Klotz and Ethel Matilda (Hockett) J.; m. Harriet L. Pollins, Mar. 31, 1944; children— Bruce C., Patricia C. BA, Cornell U., 1941; MA, Stanford U., 1950, PhD, 1953. Agrl. mktg. adminstr. Dept. Agr., 1941-42; chief food br. econ. and sci. sect. SCAP, Tokyo, 1945-48; agrl. economist Food and Agr. div. U.S. Mission to NATO and European Regional Orgn., Paris, 1952-54; assoc. prof. econs., assoc. economist Food Research Inst., Stanford U., Calif., 1954-59, prof. econs., economist, 1959—. Cons. World Bank, FAO, other. Author: (with Tomich and Kilby) Transforming Agrarian Economies: Opportunities Seized, Opportunities Missed, 1995, (with Clark) Redesigning Rural Development: A Strategic Perspective, 1982, (with Anthony, Jones and Uchendu) Agricultural Change in Tropical Africa, 1979, (with Kilby) Agriculture and Structural Transformation: Economic Strategies in Late-Developing Countries, 1975; co-editor:, contbr.: (with Ohkawa and Kaneda) Agriculture and Economic Growth: Japan's Experience, 1969. Guggenheim fellow, 1962; Internat. Inst. Applied Systems Analysis fellow, 1978-79, Adminstr.'s fellow AID, 1991. Fellow Am. Agrl. Econs. Assn.; mem. Am. Econ. Assn., African Studies Assn., Phi Beta Kappa, Phi Kappa Phi Home: 613 Walnut St Pacific Grove CA 93950-3932 Office: Stanford U Food Rsch Inst Stanford CA 9430 E-mail: bfjohn@stanford.edu.

JOHNSTON, COYT RANDAL, lawyer, poet; b. Wheeler, Tex., Nov. 17, 1946; s. Coyt Edward Johnston and Valrea Joyce (Hirons) Chase; m. Sandra Susan Ramos, Sept. 4, 1970 (div. Aug. 1993). BA, Brigham Young U., 1971; JD with honors, U. Tex., 1974. Bar: Tex. 1974. Assoc. Baker & Botts, Houston, 1974-78, Hewett, Johnson, Swanson & Barbee, Dallas, 1979-81; owner Coyt Randal Johnston, Dallas, 1981-82; atty. Davenport & Brown, Dallas, 1982-84; shareholder Johnston & Budner, Dallas, 1984-97; founder, shareholder Johnston & Tobey, Dallas, 1997—. Mem. Tex. Bd. Legal Specialization, Austin, 1980-83; mem. personal injury adv. commn., 1990—. Author poems. Avocations: water skiing, poetry and song writing, guitar playing. Office: Johnston & Tobey PC 900 Jackson St Ste 710 Dallas TX 75202-4437

JOHNSTON, CYRUS CONRAD, JR., medical educator; b. Statesville, N.C., July 16, 1929; m. Marjorie Tarkington, Feb. 20, 1960; 2 children. BA, Duke U., 1951, MD, 1955. Diplomate Am. Bd. Internal Medicine. Intern Duke Hosp., Durham, N.C., 1955-56; resident in medicine Barnes Hosp., St. Louis, 1956-57; rsch. fellow in endocrinology and metabolism Ind. U., Indpls., 1959-61, instr. medicine, 1961-63, asst. prof., 1963-67, assoc. prof., 1967-69, prof. medicine, 1969-97, disting. prof. medicine, 1997—; assoc. dir. Gen. Clin. Rsch. Ctr. Ind. U. Med. Ctr., Indpls., 1962-67, program dir., 1967-72, prin. investigator, 1968-88, dir. divsn. endocrinology and metabolism, 1968-94. Mem. aging rev. com. Nat. Inst. Aging, 1982-85, chmn. geriatrics rev. com., 1985-86; mem. nursing sci. rev. com. NIH, 1988-89; mem. com. for protection of human subjects Ind. U.-Purdue U., Indpls., 1966—, chmn., 1978—; chmn. Nat. Osteoporosis Found. Sci. Adv. Bd., 1986—; med. adv. panel Paget's Disease Found., 1989—; v.p. Nat. Osteoporosis Found., 1992—; mem. Nat. Adv. Coun. on Aging, 1992-95. Assoc. editor Bone and Mineral, 1985-94, Bone, 1995—; editl. bd. Jour. Bone and Mineral Rsch., Jour. Clin. Endocrinology and Metabolism, 1988-91. Capt. USAF, 1957-59. Recipient Career Rsch. Devel. award USPHS, 1963-68, Sandoz prize Internat. Assn. Gerontology, 1993. Mem. ACP, AAAS, AMA, Am. Assn. Clin. Endocrinologists (Yank D. Coble, Jr. M.D. Disting. Svc. award 1998), Am. Fedn. Clin. Rsch., Am. Soc. for Bone and Mineral Rsch. (Frederic C. Bartter award 1996), Am. Clin. and Climatological Soc., Ctrl. Soc. for Clin. Rsch., Endocrine Soc., Sigma Xi. Office: Indiana U Dept Medicine 541 N Clinical Dr CL 459 Indianapolis IN 46202-5112 E-mail: cjohnsto@iupui.edu.

JOHNSTON, DAVID FREDERICK, lawyer; b. Tiffin, Ohio, Sept. 9, 1943; s. Frederick Walter and Aleta Marguerite (Ruehle) J.; m. Ona Lee Graham, June 18, 1966; children: Matthew, Rebecca, Elisabeth, Benjamin. BA in Chemistry, Oreg. State U., 1965; JD, Golden Gate U., 1971. Bar: Calif. 1972, Oreg. 1973, U.S. Ct. Mil. Appeals 1974, U.S. Supreme Ct. 1983. Commd. officer U.S. Coast Guard, 1965; sea duty U.S. Coast Guard Cutter Magnolia, 1966-67; staff atty. U.S. Coast Guard, 1971-79; dept. chief U.S. Coast Guard Marine Safety Office, Norfolk, Va., 1979-82; appeal decision supr. U.S. Coast Guard Hdqrs., Washington, 1982-85; sole practice Portland, Oreg., 1985-86; workers compensation ins. EBI Ins., Portland, Oreg., 1986-95. Author: Suspension and Revocation of Mariner's Licenses, Certificates and Documents, 1984. Elder, Presbyn. Ch., Green Acres Ch., Portsmouth, Va., 1979, Multnomah Ch., Portland, 1986; com. chmn. Clermont Sch., Fairfax County, Va., 1983, bd. co-chair, 1996-99, land use co-chair, Collins View Neighborhood Assn., Portland, 1999— Mem. Oreg. State Bar, Phi Kappa Phi, Phi Lambda Upsilon. Home and Office: 0550 SW Palatine Hill Rd Portland OR 97219-7830

JOHNSTON, DENNIS ROY, computer systems integrator; b. Wahoo, Nebr., June 29, 1937; s. Roy Alfred and Wilma Jean (Weidensall) J.; m. Dorothy McLay Carr, June 19, 1965; children: Kristin Anne, Ami Carr. Student, U. Nebr., 1955-56, 57-58, U. Colo., 1961-64. City planner Denver Urban Renewal Authority, 1965-69; dir. graphics Haines, Lundberg & Waehler, N.Y.C., 1969-72; sr. v.p., sr. project mgr. LCP Assocs., Inc., N.Y.C., 1972-90; prin., computer cons. Chatham Cons. Group, 1990—. Mem. Am. Mgmt. Assn., Adminstrv. Mgmt. Soc.)cert. of merit), Nat. Computer Assn., Southport Hist. Soc., Southport Lions, Southport Presbyn., St. James Members Club. Republican. Presbyterian. Home and Office: 3212 Wexford Way Southport NC 28461-8410

JOHNSTON, DIANE MILLER, librarian; b. Attleboro, Mass., Nov. 30, 1947; d. Gordon William and Rena Mae (Miller) J. BA, Wheaton Coll., 1969; MA in Classics, NYU, 1970; MLS, Columbia U., 1981. Libr. N.Y. Pub. Libr., N.Y.C., 1970—2002; libr. Robert F. Wagner Archives Tamiment Inst. Libr. NYU, N.Y.C., 2003—. Selection officer for classics, women's studies, Romanian and Albanian, N.Y. Pub. Libr., N.Y.C., 1981—. Office: Tamiment Wagner Archives New York U 70 Washington Square South New York NY 10012-1091 E-mail: dmj5@nyu.edu.

JOHNSTON, E. RUSSELL, JR., civil engineer, educator; b. Phila. s. E. Russell and Ethel (Doherty) J.;m. Ruth Alice Phillips, Dec. 29, 1951; children: E. Russell III, Bruce P. BSCE, U. Del., 1946; ScD, MIT, 1949. Asst. prof., then assoc. prof. civil engring. Lehigh U., Bethlehem, Pa., 1949-57; prof. civil engring. Worcester (Mass.) Poly. Inst., 1957-63, U. Conn., Storrs, 1963—89, head dept. civil engring., 1972-77. Author: Mechanics for Engineering, 1956, 4th edit., 1987, Vector Mechanics for Engineers, 1962, 7th edit., 2003, Mechanics of Materials, 1981, 3d edit., 2002. Recipient Benjamin Wright award Conn. Soc. Civil Engrs. Home: PO Box 525 Storrs Mansfield CT 06268-0525 Office: Univ Conn Dept Civil Engring Storrs Mansfield CT 06269

JOHNSTON, EDWARD ALLAN, lawyer; b. Balt., Sept. 25, 1921; s. William Henry and Hattie Frisby (Sanner) J.; m. Dorothy Janet Swart, June 23, 1951 (dec. Jan. 1994); children: Elizabeth Janet, Jean Taylor; m. Mary Ellen Kinnaird, Apr. 15, 1995. BBA, U. Balt., 1942, BS, 1947, LLB, 1949, LLM, 1957. Bar: Md. 1949; CPA, Md. Assoc. Whiteford, Taylor & Preston, Balt., 1954-62, ptnr., 1962—. Lectr. taxes U. Balt., 1948-65; bd. dirs. Dunbar Armored Express Inc. Pres. Dickeyville Assn., 1960; bd. dirs. Contact-Balt., 1974-80, chmn. bd., 1976-80; trustee Asbury Found., 1970—; trustee The Wesley Home, Inc., 1985-92; v.p., gen. counsel Soc. of Srs., 1983—; gen. counsel Ea. Srs. Golf Assn., Inc., 1988—; chmn. of adminstrv. bd. Meth. Ch., 1965-69, 88-90, trustee, chmn. bd., 1977-87. Recipient Alumnus of Yr. award U. Balt., 1980 Mem. U. Balt. Alumni Assn. (pres. 1975-76), Md. Golf Assn. (v.p. 1960-67, pres. 1968), Mid. Atlantic Golf Assn. (v.p. 1978-81, pres. 1982, gen. counsel 1983—), Balt. Country Club (golf com., house commn., bd. govs. 1989-95, exec. com., treas. fin. com. 1991-95, v.p. 1992-93, pres. 1993-95). Home: 4104 Ravenhurst Cir Glen Arm MD 21057-9767 Office: Whiteford Taylor & Preston 210 W Pennsylvania Ave Ste 400 Baltimore MD 21204-5332 Fax: 410-832-2015. E-mail: ejohnston@wtplaw.com.

JOHNSTON, ELAINE CURRY, librarian; b. Hot Springs, Ark., Oct. 1, 1944; d. Aaron B. and Leta M. (Tisdale) C.; m. James Robert Johnston, Aug. 12, 1967; children: Gregory Joseph, James Scott. BA, U. Ark., 1966; MLS, U. Ky., 1981. Tchr. English Harrisburg (Ark.) High Sch., 1966-67, Raytown (Mo.) High Sch., 1967-70; ins. corr. Bus. Men's Assurance Co., Kansas City, Mo., 1970-71; reference libr. La. State Libr., Baton Rouge, 1982-87; assoc. dir. Med. Libr. of Mecklenburg County, Learning Resource Ctr. Charlotte AHEC, 1987—. Mem. N.C. Libr. Assn., Med. Libr. Assn., Phi Beta Kappa, Beta Phi Mu, Alpha Delta Pi. Home: 7420 S Norwood Ave Tulsa OK 74136-6907 Office: Med Lib/AHEC PO Box 32861 Charlotte NC 28232-2861

JOHNSTON, FRANK C. psychologist; b. West Hartford, Conn., June 21, 1955; s. Frank C. and Chris (Butler) J.; m. Susan H. Leffert, July 26, 1981; 1 child, Daniel Frank. BA, Fairfield U., 1977; MEd, MA, Columbia U., 1979; PhD, SUNY, Albany, 1984. Sch. psychologist bd. coop. ednl. svcs. Herkimer, N.Y., 1979-80; intern Counseling Ctr., SUNY, Buffalo, 1983-84; psychologist Family Svc. Rochester, N.Y., 1985-87, Child and Youth div. Rochester Mental Health Ctr., 1988; pvt. practice Rochester, 1988—. Cons. Brockport (N.Y.) Day Care Ctr., 1989-90, Learning Devel. Ctr., Rochester Inst. Tech., 1989-90; co-founder Behavioral Health Consortium Rochester, 1993—. Mem. APA, N.Y. State Psychol. Assn. (managed care task force), Genesee Valley Psychol. Assn. (mem. legal legis com. 1988-90, mem. ins. com. 1990-92, chmn. ins. com. 1990-93, pres. 1994, past pres. 1995), Rochester Cmty. Individual Practice Assn. (mem. psychology subcom. 1988-98, mem. health subcom. 1988-2000, mem. mental health task force Preferred Care 1999-2000), Rochester Area Assn. Clin. Psychologists, Nat. Register Health Svc. Providers in Psychology. Office: 480 White Spruce Blvd Rochester NY 14623-1608

JOHNSTON, GEORGE W. lawyer; b. Syracuse, N.Y., Aug. 8, 1950; s. Norman Fero and Mary Jane (Innes) J. BA, Johns Hopkins U., 1972; JD, Georgetown U., 1975. Bar: Md. 1975. Law clerk U.S. Dist. Ct., Balt., 1975-76; atty. Venable, Baetjer & Howard, Balt., 1976—; chief oper. officer Venable, Baetjer & Howard, LLP, 1999—2001. Lectr. in field. Author: BNA Aids Guide, 1990, Affirmative Action Workbook, 1992, Maryland Employer's Guide, 1991; contbr. articles to profl. jours. Vice chmn. Md. Citizens for the Arts. Mem. ABA, FBA, Md. Bar Assn., Balt. City Bar Assn. Office: Venable Baetjer & Howard 1800 Mercantile Bank 2 Hopkins Plz Ste 1800 Baltimore MD 21201-2982

JOHNSTON, GERALD E. manufacturing company executive; b. Whittier, Calif. BS, Cal. St. Fullerton. V.p. corp. devel. and planning Procter and Gamble; with Clorox Co., Oakland, Calif., 1981—, v.p., corp. devel and planning, 1992—93, v.p., gen mgr., Kingford Products Div., 1993—96, group v.p., 1996—99, pres., COO, 1999—2003, pres., CEO, 2003—. Office: Clorox Co 1221 Broadway Oakland CA 94612-1888*

JOHNSTON, GERALD SAMUEL, physician, educator; b. Johnstown, Pa., Aug. 4, 1930; s. Fleurence Gerald and Lorna Freda (Lawhead) J.; m. Dorothy Anna Jones, June 18, 1956; children: Joy Johnston Biciocchi, Jill A. Verna, Jana S. Moritzkat, Gerald S. Jr., Amy L. Tapparo, Douglas S. BS, U. Pitts., 1952, MD, 1956. Diplomate Am. Bd. Internal Medicine, Am. Bd. Nuclear Medicine. Intern Walter Reed Gen. Hosp., Washington, 1956-57; resident in internal medicine Brooke Gen. Hosp., San Antonio, 1958-61; commd. med. officer U.S. Army, 1955-71, advanced through grades to col., 1971; capt. USPHS, 1971-82; surgeon 358 Gen. dispensary, Seoul, Korea, 1961-62; chief nuclear medicine Walter Reed Gen. Hosp., Washington, Md., 1963-69, Letterman Gen. Hosp., San Francisco, 1969-71, NIH, Bethesda, Md., 1971-82, U. Md., Balt., 1982-93, acting chmn. dept. radiology, 1989-92, prof. medicine, radiology and oncology, 1982-93; chmn. dept. nuclear medicine Washington Hosp. Ctr., 1993-99, staff nuclear med. physician, 1999—; established nuclear medicine svc. Royal Hobart Hosp., Tasmania, Australia, 1999. Author two books; contbr. over 250 articles to profl. jours. Decorated Legion of Merit, 1970. Fellow ACP, Am. Coll. Radiology; mem. AMA, AAUP, Am. Coll. Nuclear Medicine (pres. 2002-03), Soc. Nuclear Medicine. Republican. Avocations: carpentry (home crafts), history, philosophy, running. Office: Washington Hosp Ctr 110 Irving St NW Washington DC 20010-2975 E-mail: docgsj@starpower.net.

JOHNSTON, GLADYS STYLES, university official; b. St. Petersburg, Fla., Dec. 23, 1942; d. John Edward and Rosa (Moses) Styles; m. Hubert Seward Johnston, July 30, 1966. BS in Social Sci., Cheney U., 1963; MEd in Ednl. Adminstrn., Temple U., 1969; PhD in Ednl. Adminstrn.-Orgnl. Theory, Cornell U., 1974. Tchr. Chester (Pa.) Sch. Dist., 1963-66, West Chester (Pa.) Sch. Dist., 1966-67, asst. prin., elem. prin., dir. Summer Sch., 1968-71; dir. Head Start Chester County Bd. Edn., West Chester, 1967-69; teaching asst., rsch. asst. Cornell U., Ithaca, N.Y., 1971 74; asst. prof. ednl. adminstr. and supervision Rutgers U., New Brunswick, N.J., 1974-79, assoc. prof., chmn. dept. Grad. Sch. Edn., 1979-83, chmn. dept. mgmt. Sch. Bus., 1983-85; dean, prof. Coll. Edn., Ariz. State U., Tempe, 1985-91; provost, v.p. for acad. affairs DePaul U., Chgo., 1991-93, chancellor, 1993—. Disting. Commonwealth vis. prof. Coll. William and Mary Sch. Edn., Williamsburg, Va., 1982-83; manuscript reviewer Jour. Higher Edn., Jour. Ednl. Leadership, Prentice Hall Pub. Co., Englewood Cliffs, N.J.; speaker and conf. presenter in field; cons. AT&T, Ednl. Testing Svc., Prentice-Hall Pub. Co.; cons. to coordinating bd. Tex. Coll. and Univ. System. Author: Research and Thought in Administration Theory, 1986; mem. editorial bd. Ednl. Evaluation and Policy Analysis, Ednl. Adminstrn. Quar., Ednl. and Psychol. Rsch. Jour.; contbr. articles and book revs. to profl. jours., chpts. to books. Bd. dirs. Edn. Law Ctr., 1979-86, Sta. KAET-TV, Phoenix, 1987—, Found. for Sr. Living, 1990-91; mem. adv. coun. to bd. trustees Cornell U., 1981-86; trustee Middlesex Gen. Univ. Hosp., 1983-86. Recipient Outstanding Alumni award Temple U.; Andrew D. White fellow Cornell U. Mem. ASCD, Am. Assn. Colls. for Tchr. Edn., Nat. Conf. Profs. Ednl. Adminstrn., Am. Ednl. Rsch. Assn. (proposal reviewer 1979 , chmn. task force for participation and membership 1981—, chmn. E.F. Linquist award com. 1985, mem. govt. rels. com. 1986—, publ. com. 1986—), Phi Kappa Phi, Phi Delta Kappa, Alpha Phi Sigma. Office: U of Nebraska at Kearney Office of Chancellor 905 W 25th St Kearney NE 68845-4238

JOHNSTON, HAROLD S(LEDGE), chemistry educator; b. Woodstock, Ga., Oct. 11, 1920; s. Smith L. and Florine (Dial) Johnston; m. Mary Ella Stay, Dec. 29, 1948; children: Shirley Louise, Linda Marie, David Finley, Barbara Dial. AB, Emory U., 1941, ScD (hon.), 1965; PhD, Calif. Inst. Tech., 1049. Instr. to assoc. prof. chemistry Stanford (Calif.) U., 1947—56; assoc. prof. Calif. Inst. Tech., Pasadena, 1956—57; prof. U. Calif., Berkeley, 1957—91, dean, coll. chemistry, 1966—70, prof. emeritus, 1991—. Vis. prof. U. Rome, 1964; adv. com. Calif. Statewide Air Pollution Rsch. Ctr., 1969—73, Nat. Ctr. Atmospheric Rsch., 1975—78, FAA High Altitude Pollution Program; vis. adv. com. Brookhaven Nat. Lab., 1970—73; faculty rsch. lectr. U. Calif., Berkeley, 1989. Author: Gas Phase Reaction Rate Theory, 1966, Gas Phase Reaction Kinetics of Neutral Oxygen Species, 1968, Reduction of Stratospheric Ozone by Nitrogen Oxide Catalysts from Supersonic Transport Exhaust, 1971; contbr. articles. Recipient Tyler prize, Environ. Achievement, 1983, Disting. Alumni award, Calif. Inst. Tech., 1985, Award for Chemistry in Svc. to Soc., NAS, 1993, Nat. Medal of Scis., 1997; grantee, Materials and Molecular Rsch. divsn. Lawrence Berkeley Lab., 1966—. Fellow: Am. Assn. Arts and Scis., NAS (adv. panel to Nat. Bur. Standard 1965—67, com. motor vehicle emissions 1971—75, Svc. to Soc. award in chemistry 1993), Am. Geophys. Union (Roger Revelle medal 1998), Am. Phys. Soc., Am. Chem. Soc. (Gold medal award Calif. sect. 1956, Pollution Control award 1974, award in chemistry of contemporary technol. problems 1985), AAAS; mem.: Sigma Xi (nat. lectr. 1973). Home: 132 Highland Blvd Berkeley CA 94708-1023 Office: U Calif Dept Chemistry Berkeley CA 94720-0001*

JOHNSTON, JAMES C. neurologist, lawyer; b. Wash., Nov. 20, 1959; s. Rufus L. and Dorothy M. Johnston. MD, U. Tex., San Antonio, 1984; JD, U. Oreg., 1997. Diplomate Am. Bd. Psychiatry and Neurology. Intern in surgery U. Tex. Health Sci. Ctr., San Antonio, 1984-85; resident in neurology Tex. Med. Ctr., Houston, 1985-88; dir. vocat. rehab. State of Idano, Idaho Falls, 1988-89; cons. neurologist, dir. rehab. Eastern Idaho Neurology Clinic, Idaho Falls, 1988-90; cons. neurologist, med. dir. Objective Med. Evaluations, P.A., Houston, 1990—95; dir. Neurology Svcs., Eugene, Oreg.; pres., CEO Legal Medicine Consultants, Ltd., Eugene, 1995—. Fellow: Coll. Legal Medicine; mem.: ABA, Royal Soc. Medicine (London), State Bar Tex., Am. Coll. Med. Examiners, Am. Acad. Neurology, Am. Soc. Neurorehab. (cert.). Office: Ste 171 2852 Willamette St Eugene OR 97405-8200

JOHNSTON, JAMES ROBERT, library director; b. Wheaton, Ill., June 3, 1947; s. Robert W. and Elizabeth S. (Townsend) J.; m. Carol Ann Trezza, June 14, 1969; children: Steven J., Julie M. BA, U. Notre Dame, 1969; MLS, Fla. State U., 1973. Head librarian Grande Prairie Library Dist., Hazel Crest, Ill., 1973-76; chief librarian Joliet (Ill.) Pub. Library, 1976—; pres. bd. dirs. Ill. Library Employees Benefit Plan. Mem. automation com. Heritage Trail Libr. Sys., Shorewood, Ill.; pres. Ill. Libr. Employees Benefit Plan, Joliet; bldg. cons. Co-author: Illinois Library Trustees Association Booklet "Selecting Consultants", 1986; contbr. speeches and articles in field. V.p. Joliet/Will County Project Pride; mem. events com. C. of C. Mem. Ill. Libr. Assn. (pub. libr. sect. 1977-78, legis. devel. com. 1977-82, jr. mems. roundtable 1976-77, regional planning com. 1996, Title III rev. com. 1996—, interlibr. coop. subcom.,), Kiwanis, Beta Phi Mu. Avocations: ho guage model railroading, softball, bowling, golf. Home: 2208 Graystone Dr Joliet IL 60431-8785 Office: Joliet Pub Library 150 N Ottawa St Joliet IL 60432 4192

JOHNSTON, JAMES WESLEY, retired tobacco company executive; b. Chgo., Apr. 11, 1946; s. Ted and Irma (Hacker) J.; children: Amanda E., Emily S. BS in Accountancy, U. Ill., 1967; MBA, Northwestern U., 1971. C.P.A., Ill. Fin. analyst Ford Motor Co., 1967-69; with N.W. Industries, 1969-79, dir. corp. devel., 1973-75, v.p. mktg., 1975-79; exec. v.p. Asia/Pacific R.J. Reynolds Tobacco Internat. Inc., 1979, pres., chief exec. officer Asia/Pacific, 1979-81; exec. v.p. R.J. Reynolds Tobacco Co., U.S., 1981-84; divsn. exec. consumer banking N.E. U.S. Citicorp, N.Y.C., 1984-89; chmn. CEO R.J. Reynolds Tobacco Co., Winston-Salem, N.C., 1989-95; chmn. R.J. Reynolds Tobacco Worldwide, Winston-Salem, N.C., 1993-96; vice chmn. RJR Nabisco, Inc., 1995-96, ret., 1996. Bd. dirs. Sealy Corp., Trinity, N.C., Pilot Therapeutics, Charleston, S.C., RemoteLight.com, Inc., Research Triangle Park, N.C. Treas., trustee, pres. Village of Bolingbrook, Ill., 1973-75; bd. dirs. Winston-Salem Bus. Inc., 1989—; active N.C. Bus. Coun. Mgmt. and Devel., Raleigh, 1989—; trustee Wake Forest U., Winston-Salem, 1991—; mem. bd. visitors Wake Forest U. Bapt. Med. Ctr., Winston-Salem, 1991—. Mem.: Piedmont Club, Old Town Club. Office: 380 Knollwood St Ste 570 Winston Salem NC 27103-1849

JOHNSTON, JOANNE SPITZNAGEL, lawyer, writing consultant; b. Peoria, Ill., Mar. 11, 1930; d. Elmer Florian and Anna E. (Kolb) Spitznagel; m. Charles Helm Bennett, June 12, 1951 (div. 1978); children: Mary Jaquelin Bennett Graub, Ariana Holliday Bennett, Caroline Helm Bennett Ammerman, Joanne Mary Bennett Jeffers; m. Donald Robert Johnston, Nov. 25, 1981. A.B., Vassar Coll., 1951; MA, Ind. U., 1970, PhD, 1974; JD, Ind. U.-Indpls., 1980. Bar: Ind. 1980, Minn. 1985. Lectr. Ind. U., Indpls., 1968-81, U.-Indpls., 1970-76; writing cons. U. Minn., Mpls., 1982-91; sole practice Indpls., 1980-86, Mpls., 1986-91. Mem.: Garden Club Am. (Indpls. chpt.), Indpls. Womans, Dramatic. Methodist. Home: 1066 Winterthur Indianapolis IN 46260-2232 also: 1469 Landings Circle Sarasota FL 34231

JOHNSTON, JOCELYN STANWELL, paralegal; b. Evanston, Ill., Feb. 16, 1954; d. Gerald and Dorothy Jeanne (Schoenfield) Stanwell; m. Thomas Patrick Johnston, Nov. 28, 1986. BA, U. Minn., 1981; cert., Phila. Inst. Paralegal Tng., Phila., 1986. Paralegal Fredrikson & Byron PA, Mpls., 1981-84, Reed, Smith, Shaw and McClay, Phila., 1984-85, McCausland, Keen & Buckman, PC, Radnor, Pa., 1985-86, Harris, Guenzel, Meier & Nichols, PC, Ann Arbor, Mich., 1986 87, Conner & Bentley, PC, Ann Arbor, 1987-88, Cichocki & Armstrong, Ltd., Oak Park, Ill., 1988-90, Bishop and Bishop, Oak Brook, Ill., 1994-95, Martin, Breen & Merrick, Oak Park, 1994-95, Saitlin, Patzik, Frank & Samotny, Ltd., Chgo., 1995, Bryson R. Cloon, Esquire, Leawood, Kans., 1996—. Democrat. Home: 14501 Marty St Overland Park KS 66223-2300 Office: Bryson R Cloon Esquire 11350 Tomahawk Creek Pkwy Leawood KS 66211-2670 E-mail: johnstont@umkc.edu.

JOHNSTON, JOHN BENNETT, JR., former senator, consultant; b. Shreveport, La., June 10, 1932; m. Mary Gunn, 1956; children: Bennett, Hunter, Mary, Sally. Student, Washington and Lee U., U.S. Mil. Acad.; LL.B., La. State U., 1956. Bar: La. 1956. Mem. firm Johnston, Johnston & Thornton, 1959; mem. La. House Reps., 1964-68, La. Senate, 1968-72; U.S senator from La., 1972-96; chmn. Dem. senatorial campaign com., 1975-76; ptnr., CEO Johnston & Assocs., Washington, 1996—. Former mem. appropriations com., ranking minority subcom. on energy and water devel., ranking minority com. on energy and natural resources, former mem. budget com., former mem. spl. com. on aging, former mem. select com. on intelligence; bd. dirs. Chevron Corp.. Served to 1st lt. U.S. Army, 1956-59. Democrat. Office: Johnston & Assocs Ste 200 1455 Pennsylvania Ave NW Washington DC 20004-1024

JOHNSTON, JOHN CLIFFORD, JR., lawyer; b. Wooster, Ohio, July 30, 1916; s. J. Clifford and Estella Marie (Smith) J.; m. Marie Wolf, Sept. 6, 1947; children— J.C., Gordon W. B.A., Coll. of Wooster, 1938, J.D., U. Mich., 1941. Bar: Ohio 1941. Counsel Critchfield, Critchfield & Johnston, Wooster, Ohio, 1945— . Served to capt. AUS, 1941-45. Decorated Bronze Star. Fellow Am. Bar Found.; mem. ABA, Ohio State Bar Assn. (pres. 1961-62, exec. com. 1957-63), Ohio State Bar Found. (trustee 1973-76), Am. Judicature Soc. (bd. dirs. 1973-76), Ohio Legal Ctr. Inst. (trustee 1961-63). Home: 275 W Henrietta St Wooster OH 44691-2878 Office: 225 N Market St Wooster OH 44691-3511

JOHNSTON, JOHN DEVEREAUX, JR., law educator, retired; b. Asheville, N.C., Oct. 1, 1932; s. John D. and Marion R. (Green) J.; m. Beryl R. Watson, Dec. 21, 1952; m. Diana Armatage, June 10, 1972; children: Catherine, Patricia, Sharon, Laura, Jackie, John. AB, Duke U., 1954, LL.B., 1956. Bar: N.C. 1956, U.S. Ct. Appeals (4th cir.) 1969, U.S. Supreme Ct. 1969. Mgmt. trainee J.P. Morgan & Co., 1956-58; pvt. practice Asheville, 1959-62; asst. prof. Duke U. Law Sch., Durham, N.C., 1963-64, asst. dean, 1963-65, assoc. prof., 1965-67, prof., 1968-69; prof. law NYU Law Sch., N.Y.C., 1969-89, prof. law emeritus, 1990—. Vis. prof. Vanderbilt U., 1972, UCLA, 1975, Washington U., St. Louis, 1981, Hastings Coll. Law U. Calif., San Francisco, 1984. Author: (with G. Johnson) Land Use Control, 1977; contbr. articles to profl. jours. Home: 21 Stuyvesant Rd Asheville NC 28803-3022 E-mail: JDJJR@worldnet.att.net. *As a young law teacher, I was mentored by two wise elders. One emphasized preparation: Don't ever go into class without knowing where you intend to take it. The other counselled flexibility: Be prepared for anything, and let student input determine how the class will unfold. A third elder provided a synthesis: Never overestimate what your students already know, nor underestimate what they are capable of learning.Applying that maxim, I determined to introduce new subjects slowly and carefully, even spoon-feeding the students for a while. Thereafter, development of the topic proceeded at their speed. After they reached a level of sophistication well beyond my expectations, I concluded that the third elder was the wisest.*

JOHNSTON, JOHN ERIC, chemist; b. Detroit, Feb. 5, 1948; s. John Edmondson and Lorraine Therese (Rivard) J.; m. Cathleen Adele Higgins, Aug. 31, 1985. BS in Chemistry, U. Notre Dame, 1970; PhD in Polymer Sci., U. Akron, 1975. Chemist Union Carbide Corp., Charleston, W.Va., 1976-79, project scientist, 1979-80; staff chemist Exxon Chem. Co., Linden, N.J., 1980-81, leader, 1981-90, section head rsch. & engring. dept., 1990—2001; sr. scientific adv. strategic planning, 2001—. Capt. U.S. Army, 1970-80. Inductee N.J. Inventors Hall of Fame, ACS Hero of Chemistry, 1998. Mem. AAAS, Soc. Automotive Engrs., Am. Chem. Soc. Achievements include over 30 U.S. and foreign patents for polymers and lubricant additives. Office: Exxon Mobil Rsch & Engring Rt 22E Clinton Twp Annandale NJ 08801 E-mail: john.e.johnston@exxonmobil.com.

JOHNSTON, JOHN STEVEN, lawyer; b. Kansas City, Mo., Dec. 5, 1948; s. Herschel Wayne and Dixie June J.; m. Deb Neal, Feb. 19, 1977; children: Benjamin, Will. BA in Math., William Jewell Coll., 1970; MA in Psychology, U. Mo., 1975, JD, 1980; postgrad. in clin. psychology, U. Minn., 1975—77. Bar: Mo., 1980, U.S. Dist. Ct. Kans., 1999. Assoc. Linde, Thomson, Fairchild, Langworthy & Kohn, Kansas City, 1980-81, Shook, Hardy & Bacon LLP, Kansas City, 1981-85, ptnr., 1986—, chmn. tort law sect., 1998—2002. Bd. dirs. Lawyers Encouraging Acad. Performance. Author (contbg.): Missouri Methods of Practice-Litigation Guide, 1991; contbr. articles articles to profl. jours. Bd. dirs. Big Bros. and Big Sisters, Kansas City, 1989—, Ozanam Home for Boys, Kansas City, 1990-2002, Lawyers Encouraging Acad. Progress, 2002—. Recipient Outstanding Contbn. to Cmty Health award S. Kansas City Mental Health Resource Network, 1975, Michael Coburn award for cmty. svc. Legal Aid of We. Mo., 1999; named to William Jewell Coll. Hall of Fame, 1999. Mem.: Kansas City Met. Bar Assn. (chmn. civil law and procedure com. 1991—92, bd. dirs. 1993—, pres. 1998, 7th Ann. Pres. award for bar svc. 1993), Mo. Bar Assn. (bd. govs. 1999—), Kansas City Met. Bar Found. (bd. dirs./exec. com. 1995—, chair lawyers for children com. 1998—2002, v.p. 2000—, 1st Ann. Pres.'s award for bar svc. 2001), Ross T. Roberts Inn of Ct. (master 1995—). Home: 25004 Timberlake Trl Greenwood MO 64034 Office: Shook Hardy & Bacon LLP 1200 Main St Kansas City MO 64105 Fax: 816-421-4066. E-mail: jjohnston@shb.com.

JOHNSTON, KENNETH JOHN, astronomer, scientific director naval observatory; b. N.Y.C., Oct. 9, 1941; s. Marion Nugent Johnston; m. Therese M. Clasen, June 25, 1966. BEE, Manhattan Coll., 1964; PhD, Georgetown U., 1969. NAS, NRC postdoctoral assoc. Naval Rsch. Lab., Washington, 1969-71, radio astronomer, 1971 80, supr. physicist, 1980-90, chief scientist ctr. for advanced space sensing, 1990-92, supt. remote sensing divsn., 1992-93; sci. dir. U.S. Naval Observatory, Washington, 1993—. Contbr. over 400 articles to Astron. and Astrophys. Lit. Recipient NRL Sigma Xi Pure Sci. award, 1985, Alexander von Humboldt Sr. Scientist award, 1985, Max Planck Soc. Rsch. award, 1990. Mem. Internat. Astron. Union, Union of Radio Sci., Royal Astron. Soc., Am. Astron. Soc. Achievements include development of a program that applied interferometric techniques for high resolution imaging at optical and radio wavelengths; directed a pioneering effort to develop the first imaging optical interferometer to be located at Flagstaff, Ariz.; established a global inertial reference frame at optical/ radio wavelengths; developed radio techniques to probe the surface of asteroids, and the first images of interstellar masers. Office: US Naval Observatory 3450 Massachusetts Ave NW Washington DC 20392-0001

JOHNSTON, LAURANCE SCOTT, foundation director; b. St. Paul, Aug. 4, 1950; s. Scott D. and Laura L. (Wallace) J. BS, Hamline U., 1972; MS, Northwestern U., 1973, PhD, 1976; MBA, George Mason U., 1985. Postdoctoral fellow Chgo. Med. Sch., 1977-78; regulatory scientist Bur. Foods, FDA, Washington, 1978-81; exec. sec. NIH, Bethesda, Md., 1981-86; dir. div. sci. rev. Nat. Inst. Child Health and Human Devel., NIH, Bethesda, 1986-92; dir. spinal cord rsch. and edn. founds. Paralyzed Vets. of Am., 1992-97, with Dept.

Biomed. and Disability Rsch., 1997—. Contbr. articles to profl. jours. Damon Runyon/Walter Winchell Cancer Found. fellow, 1978. Home: 637B S Broadway St PMB 241 Boulder CO 80305 E-mail: laurancejohnsto@aol.com.

JOHNSTON, LAWRENCE D. career officer; b. Okla., Apr. 28, 1947; BS in Econ., Okla. State U., 1970; grad., Squadron Officer Sch., 1975; MS in Mgmt., Troy State U., 1979; grad., Air Command and Staff Coll., 1982; student, Nat. Def. U., 1982; MS in Nat. Security and Strategic Studies, Naval War Coll., 1990; Sr. Officials in Nat. Security, Harvard U., 1992, Sr. Execs. in Nat./Internat. Security, 1997. Commd. 2d lt. USAF, 1970, advanced through grades to brig. gen., 1996; F-4 flight leader, fast forward air controller 388th Tactical Fighter Wing, Korat Royal Thailand AFB, 1971-72; F-4 instr. 35th Tactical Fighter Wing 35th Tactical Fighter Wing, George AFB, Calif., 1972-75; F-4 fighter weapons instr., flight comdr. and chief wing weapons and tactics 347th Tactical Fighter Wing, Moody AFB, Ga., 1975-78; fighter weapons instr., chief weapons tng. 406th Tactical Fighter Tng. Wing, Zaragoza AFB, Spain, 1978-79; staff action officer Hdqs. USAF in Europe, Ramstein AFB, W. Germany, 1980-81; chief wing weapons and tactics, asst. ops. officer 474th Tactical Fighter Wing, Nellis AFB, Nev., 1982-87, chief wing maintenance tng. div., ops. officer, F-16 squadron comdr., 1982-87; dir. assignments Hdqs. Tactical Air Command, Langley AFB, Va., 1987-89; comdt. USAF Fighter Weapons Sch., Nellis AFB, Nev., 1990-91; vice-comdr. 363rd Fighter Wing, Shaw AFB, S.C., 1991-93; comdr. various AFB's, 1993-98; dir. plans and programs Hdqs. Air Combat Command, Langley AFB, 1998-2000; comdr. Air Warfare Ctr., Nellis AFB, Nev., 2000—. Decorated Legion of Merit with oak leaf cluster, D.F.C. with three oak leaf clusters, Purple Heart, Air medal with 17 oak leaf clusters. Office: Nellis AFB AWFC / CC 4370 N Washington Blvd Ste 117 Nellis AFB NV 89191-7076

JOHNSTON, LAWRENCE R. food products executive; BS, Stetson U., Deland, FL. Merchandising mgr. GE Appliances; region mgr. GE; gen. mgr. Eastern Sales & Distbn. Opers., GE Appliances; pres. Internat. GE Puerto Rico; gen. mgr. Domestic Sales Opers., GE; v.p. sales & distbn. GE Appliances; pres. & CEO GE Med. Sys., Europe; sr. v.p. GE; pres. & CEO GE Appliances, 1999—2001, Albertson's, Inc., 2001—. Chmn. GE's European Exec. Coun.; bd. mem. Food Mktg. Inst., Washington, CIES World Food Forum, Paris. Office: 250 Park Ctr Blvd Boise ID 83706

JOHNSTON, LELAND MANN, JR., physician; b. Jackson, Tenn., July 2, 1947; s. Leland Mann and Helen (Presley) J. BA, Vanderbilt U., 1969; MD, Emory U., 1978; grad. in adult, Seattle Inst. Psychoanalysis, 1990, grad. in child, 1996. Diplomate Am. Bd. Psychiatry and Neurology; cert. in adult psychoanalysis and child psychoanalysis. Intern U. Wash., Seattle, 1978-79, resident in adult psychiatry, 1978-81, fellow in child psychiatry, 1982-83, U. Colo., Denver, 1981-82; pvt. practice Seattle, 1983-2001; mem. faculty Seattle Inst. Psychoanalysis, 1990—; clin. instr. dept. psychiatry & behavioral scis. U. Wash., Seattle, 1993-2001; pvt. practice, Boulder, Colo., 2001—; mem. faculty Denver Inst. for Psychoanalysis, Denver, 2002—. Mem. faculty Denver Inst. for Psychoanalysis, 2001—; clin. instr. dept. psychiatry U. Colo. Sch. Medicine, 2002—. Mem. AMA, Am. Psychoanalytic Assn. (cert. psychoanalyst 1992, cert. child psychoanalyst 1997, assoc. child tng. analyst 1998—), Am. Psychiat. Assn, Assn. for Child Psychoanalysis, Edith Buxbaum Found. (pres. 1998-2000). Avocations: skiing, backpacking, scuba diving, music. Office: 1740 Sumac Ave Boulder CO 80304-0814 E-mail: lmjohnstonmd@attbi.com.

JOHNSTON, LINDA TIDWELL, municipal official; BA in Psychology, U. Fla., 1969. Tchr. English, speech and drama Cocoa H.S., Rockledge, Fla., 1969-70; exec. trainee Burdines Dept. Store, West Palm Beach, Fla., 1970-72; adminstrv. asst., counselor Fortune Personnel, Cocoa Beach, 1972-73; social worker State of Fla., Cocoa, 1973-74; dir. ret. sr. vol. program City of Raleigh, 1974-79, dir. citizen involvement divsn., 1979-91, dir. neighborhood svc. divsn. cmty. svcs. dept., 1996—, divsn. dir. cmty. svcs. dept, 1991—96. Mem. N.C. Assn. Vol. Adminstrs., Woman's Club Raleigh. Office: Cmty Svcs Dept 310 W Martin St # 201 Raleigh NC 27601-1326

JOHNSTON, LLOYD DOUGLAS, social scientist; b. Boston, Apr. 18, 1940; s. Leslie D. and Madeline B. (Irvin) J.; 1 child, Douglas Leslie. BA in Econs., Williams Coll., 1962; MBA, Harvard U., 1965, postgrad., 1965-66; MA in Social Psychology, U. Mich., 1971, PhD, 1973. Research asst. Grad. Sch. Bus. Adminstr., Harvard U., Boston, 1965-66; asst. study dir. Inst. Social Research, U. Mich., Ann Arbor, 1966-73, asst. research scientist, 1973-75, assoc. rsch. scientist, 1975-78, sr. rsch. scientist and program dir., 1978-98; disting. sr. rsch. scientist Inst. Social Rsch., U. Mich., Ann Arbor, 1998—; chmn. exec. com. U. Mich. Substance Abuse Rsch. Ctr. Excellence, 1990-95, acting dir., 1994-95. Prin. investigator Monitoring the Future: A Continuing Study of Lifestyles and Values of Am. Youth, 1975—, Youth, Education and Society, 1996—, also other nat. and internat. survey studies; cons. to WHO, UN, EEC, Coun. of Europe, Pan Am. Health Orgn., White House, U.S. Congress, various founds., numerous fgn. govts., fed. agys., univs., rsch. insts., TV networks, Nat. Partnership for Drug Free Am., 1975—; chmn. tech. planning group; mem. Resource Group for Goal Seven, Nat. Ednl. Goals Panel, 1991-2002; mem. extramural sci. adv. bd. Nat. Inst. on Drug Abuse, 1990-94; mem., also chmn. prevention subcom., Nat. Adv. Coun. on Drug Abuse, 1982-86, Presdl. appointee White House Conf. for a Drug-Free Am., 1987-88, Presdl. appointee Nat. Commn. for Drug Free Schs., 1989-90; chmn. drug epidemiology sect. Internat. Coun. on Alcohol and Addictions, 1982—; mem. Com. on Problems of Drug Dependence, 1982-86; mem. or chmn. various adv. coms. various univs., founds.; mem. various working groups NAS; mem. various coms. and adv. groups Nat. Inst. Drug Abuse, 1975—; mem. or chmn. 7 working groups WHO, 1975—; invited lectr. nat. and internat. confs. and convs.; testimony before Congress and fed. regulatory agys. Author: Drugs and American Youth, 1973, Student Drug Use in America, 1975-81, 82, Monitoring the Future Nat. Survey Results on Drug Use 1975-2002, vol. 1 and 2, 2003, 40 other books and monographs on drug use and lifestyles of Am. secondary sch. students and young adults, 1972—, 26 reference vols.; editor: Conducting Follow Up Research on Drug Treatment Programs, 1977; contbr. 100 chpts. to books, articles to profl. jours. Recipient Nat. Pacesetter award in rsch. Nat. Inst. on Drug Abuse, 1982, 1st Sr. Rsch. Scientist award and lectureship U. Mich., 1987, Regents award for disting. pub. svc., 1998, Disting. Rsch. Scientist award, 2002. Fellow Coll. on Problems of Drug Dependence; mem. APA, Soc. for Psychol. Study Social Issues (sec.-treas. 1976-79), Am. Sociol. Assn., Am. Pub. Health Assn. Home: 5538 Lawrence Ct Pinckney MI 48169-9257 Office: U Mich Inst Social Rsch Ann Arbor MI 48109

JOHNSTON, LOGAN TRUAX, III, lawyer; b. New Haven, Dec. 9, 1947; s. Logan Truax Jr. and Elizabeth (Josey) J.; m. Celeste Linguere; children: Charlotte Hathaway, Logan Truax IV, Owen Conrad, Oritse J., Gboyega P. BA, Yale U., 1969; JD, Harvard U., 1973. Bar: Ill. 1973, Ariz. 1984, U.S. Ct. Appeals (2d cir.) 1982, U.S. Ct. Appeals (7th cir.) 1973, U.S. Ct. Appeals (9th cir.) 1986, U.S. Ct. Appeals (fed. cir.) 1990, U.S. Supreme Ct. 1991. Assoc. Winston & Strawn, Chgo., 1973-79, ptnr., 1979-83, Phoenix, 1983-89; mng. ptnr. Johnston Maynard Grant & Parker, Phoenix, 1989-97, Johnston & Kelly, Phoenix, 1997—2003. Spl. asst. state's atty. Du Page County, Ill., Wheaton, 1976-77; cons. Community Legal Svcs., Phoenix, 1984—. Contbg author: Arizona Appellate Handbook, Vol. III. Served with U.S. Army N.G., 1970-76. Mem. ABA, Maricopa County Bar Found., Maricopa County Bar Assn., Ariz. Bar Found., Ariz. State Bar Assn., Phoenix Heroes Endowment Fund. Presbyterian. Avocations: books, movies, golf, hiking, travel. Office: Johnston Law Offices PLC 1 N 1st St Phoenix AZ 85004-2357

JOHNSTON, MALCOLM (CALUM), bank executive; b. Glasgow, Scotland, July 10, 1934; s. Malcolm and Margaret Brown (MacPherson) J.; m. Anna Maria Bindels, Sept. 7, 1963; children: Margareta J.M., Malcolm H.A. Grad., Kelvinside Acad., Glasgow. With Standard Bank of Ghana Ltd, 1955-62, Standard Bank of Nigeria Ltd., 1962-69, The Bank of Nova Scotia, 1969-97, asst. agt., 1969-72, spl. rep. Hong Kong, 1972-74, mgr. Kuala Lumpur, Malaysia, 1974-76, Kingston, Jamaica, 1976-78, from asst. gen. mgr. to gen. mgr., 1979-83, sr. v.p. comml. credit, 1983-86, exec. v.p. internat. banking, 1986-97; also bd. dirs.; pres., CEO Bank NT Butterfield, 1997—. Mil. Svc. The Royal Highland Regiment, The Black Watch. Fellow Inst. Can. Bankers (gold medal 1983); mem. Nat. Club (Toronto), Hong Kong Club, Kelvinside Academicals, Glasgow, Coral Beach and Tennis Club (Bermuda). Office: Bank of Butterfield PO Box HM 195 Hamilton HM AX Bermuda E-mail: calumjohnston@bntb.bm.

JOHNSTON, MANLEY RODERICK, research and development company executive, chemist; b. Edmonton, Canada, Oct. 2, 1942; s. Roderick Oliver and Leona Inez Johnston; m. Marian Fern Kragness, Oct. 7, 1967; children: Christine Michelle, Cindy Katherine. BSc, U. of Alta., 1960—64; MS, U. of Ill., 1964—66, PhD, 1964—68. Sr. chemist/ supr./mgr 3M, St. Paul, 1968—89, tech. dir. Europe, 1989—92, v.p. internat. tech. ops., 2000—. Mem.: IRI. Avocations: curling, golf, music, travel. Office: 3M 3M Center Saint Paul MN 55144 E-mail: mrjohnston@mmm.com.

JOHNSTON, MARGUERITE, journalist, author; b. Birmingham, Ala., Aug. 7, 1917; d. Robert C. and Marguerite (Spradling) J.; m. Charles Wynn Barnes, Aug. 31, 1946; children: Susan, Patricia, Steven, Polly. AB, Birmingham-So. Coll., 1938. Reporter Birmingham News, 1939-44; Washington corr. Birmingham News, Birmingham Age-Herald, London Daily Mirror, 1945-46; columnist Houston Post, 1947-69, fgn. news editor, mem. editorial bd., 1969-85, assoc. editor editorial page, 1972-77, asst. editor editorial page, 1977-85. Lectr. in field, 1947— ; instr. creative writing U. Houston, 1946-47, lectr. feature writing, 1965-66; lectr. Baker Coll., Rice U., 1977-78; del. Asian Am. Women Journalists Conf., Honolulu, 1965, 1st World Conf. Women Journalists, Mexico City, 1969 Author: Public Manners, 1957, A Happy Worldly Abode, 1964, Houston: The Unknown City, 1836-1946, (Winedale Historical Ctr. Ima Hogg award, Otis Lock award East Tex. Historical Assn.), 1991. Bd. dirs. Tex. Bill of Rights Found., 1962-64; bd. dirs. Planned Parenthood, 1953-55, Population Inst., 1985-91; mem. Mcpl. Art Commn., 1971-76, Houston Com. Fgn. Relations. Recipient Theta Sigma Phi Headliner award, 1954, 1st ann. award of merit Houston Com. Alcoholism, 1956, cert. of merit Gulf Coast chpt. Am. Soc. Safety Engrs., 1960, Agnese Carter Nelms award Planned Parenthood, 1968, Sch. Bell award Tex. State Tchrs. Assn., 1974, 75, Gold Key award Nat. Council Alcoholism, 1975, Global award Population Inst., 1981. Mem. Tex. Soc. Architects (hon.), Philos. Soc. Tex., Phi Beta Kappa, Pi Beta Phi Home: 2929 Buffalo Speedway Houston TX 77098

JOHNSTON, MARILYN FRANCES-MEYERS, physician, medical educator; b. Buffalo, Mar. 30, 1937; BS, Dameon Coll., 1966; PhD, St. Louis U., 1970, MD, 1975. Diplomate Am. Bd. Pathology, Diplomate Nat. Bd. Med. Examiners. Fellow in immunology Washington U., St. Louis, 1970-72; resident in pathology Washington U. Hosp., St. Louis, 1975-77, St. John's Mercy Med. Ctr., St. Louis, 1977-79; research fellow hematology St. Louis U. Sch. Medicine, 1979-80; instr. biochemistry St. Louis U., 1972-75, asst. prof. pathology, 1980-87, assoc. prof., 1987-92, prof., 1992-99, prof. emeritus, 1999—, dir. transfusion svcs., 1980-99; staff pathologist Christian Hosp. Barnes Jewish Christian Hosps., St. Louis, 1999—. Med. dir. Mo./Ill. Regional Red Cross, 1983-88; area chmn. for inspection and accreditation Am. Assn. Blood Banks, Arlington, Va., 1984; med. dir. transfusion svc. Christian Hosps., Barnes-Jewish-Christian Hosp. Sys., St. Louis, 1999—. Author: Transfusion Therapy, 1985. Named Goldberger fellow, AMA, 1979; recipient Transfusion Medicine Acad. award, Nat. Heart, Blood and Lung Inst., 1984—. Mem. Am. Assn. Blood Banks, Am. Assn. Immunologists, Internat. Soc. Blood Transfusion, Am. Soc. Clin. Pathologists, Sigma Xi. Office: Christian Hosp NE 11133 Dunn Rd Saint Louis MO 63136

JOHNSTON, MARK DAVID, language educator; b. Puyallup, Wash., Nov. 23, 1952; s. Arthur David and Carol Mae Johnston; m. Anne Clark Bartlett, Nov. 19, 1960; children: Matthew Augustine Johnston-Urey, Benjamin Gregory Johnston-Urey. BA, U. Oreg., 1974; PhD, The Johns Hopkins U., 1978. Asst. prof. Spanish Wash. U., St. Louis; asst. prof. English Ill. State U., Normal, 1982—83, from assoc. prof. to prof. Spanish, 1983—97; corp. desktop support supr. US Cellular Corp., Chgo., 1998—99; info. tech. dir. The Newberry Libr., 1999—2003; prof. Spanish DePaul U., Chgo., 2003—. Vis. prof. history and Spanish St. Xavier U., Chgo., 2000; vis. prof. comparative lit. U. Iowa, Iowa City, 1990. Author: The New Rhetoric of Ramon Llull (Hermagoras Press), The Book of the Lover and the Beloved of Ramon Llull (Aris & Phillips), (scholarly monograph) The Spiritual Logic of Ramon Llull (Oxford, Clarendon Press), The Evangelical Rhetoric of Ramon Llull (Oxford University Press). Pres. Independence Pk. Adv. Coun., Chgo., 2000—03. Recipient John Nicholas Brown prize Outstanding First Book, Medieval Acad. Am., 1991; fellow, Am. Coun. Learned Societies, 1979, 1982, NEH, 1980, 1998, 1994—95. Mem.: Ill. Medieval Assn. (pres. 2001—02), Midwest MLA, MLA Am. D-Liberal. Lutheran. Avocations: old house renovation, greyhound rescue, bagpiping. Office: Dept Modern Langs DePaul U 802 W Belden Chicago IL 60614 E-mail: mjohnst4@depaul.edu.

JOHNSTON, MARY ELLEN, retired nursing educator; b. Roswell, N.Mex., June 4, 1951; d. E. Bernard and Jane (Shugart) J. BSN, Baylor U., 1973; MSN, Oral Roberts U., 1982. Staff nurse crit. care dept. Tucson Med. Ctr., 1973-74; charge nurse med. unit St. Mary's Hosp., Roswell, 1975; instr. nursing Ea. N.Mex. U., Roswell, 1975-2000; ret., 2000. Mem. ANA (cert. med.-surg. nurse), N.Mex. Nurses Assn. (past pres. dist. V), Baylor U. Nurses Alumni Assn., Philanthropic and Ednl. Orgn. (N.Mex. state officer), Daus. of Am. Colonists, Altrusa Club Roswell, DAR, Sigma Theta Tau. Republican. Methodist. Home: 2715 N Kentucky Ave Apt 16 Roswell NM 88201-5868

JOHNSTON, MICHAEL (WILLIAM JOHNSTON), political science educator, university administrator; b. Omaha, Nebr., Nov. 1, 1949; s. William M. and Margaret Mary (Ryan) J.; m. Bette Bennett, 1976; children: Michael Joseph, Patrick Brendan Ryan. BA in Polit. Sci summa cum laude, Macalester Coll., St. Paul, 1971; MPhil in Polit. Sci., Yale U., 1974, PhD in Polit. Sci., 1977. Teaching fellow, acting instr. Yale U., 1972-76; instr. U. Pitts., 1976-77, asst. prof., 1977-82, assoc. prof., 1982-86; from assoc. prof. to prof. Colgate U., Hamilton, NY, 1986—2003, Charles A. Dana prof. polit. sci., 2003—. Chmn. Colgate U. Rsch. Coun.; vis. lectr. politics, vis. fellow Ctr. Urban and Regional Rsch. U. Glasgow, Scotland, 1983—84; vis. fellow dept. politics and Inst. Rsch. in Social Scis. U. York, England, 1991; vis. fellow St. Aidan's Coll., 1997; vis. fellow dept. politics U. Durham, England, 1997; rsch. assoc. Cogen, Holt and Assocs., New Haven, 1974—75; Pitts. on-site coord. cmty. devel. block grants evaluation ABT Assocs., Cambridge, Mass., 1979—80; leader US Info. Agy. Seminar on corruption and democracy, Mongolia, 1999; participant anti-corruption confs.; participant, working group chair Ditchley (Eng.) Conf., 1998; coord. rsch. on case studies Internat. Political Bribery, Italy, 2000; bd. dirs., coun. governance Transparency Internat. USA; co-organizer program on governance and democratization 2nd Conv. European Assn. Advancement Social Scis., Cyprus, 1997, U.S. AID Ptnrs.' Conf., Washington, 2000; spkr. in field; cons. in field; presenter in field. Author: Political Corruption and Public Policy in America, 1982, Fraud, Waste and Abuse in Government, 1986, Political Corruption: A Handbook, 1989; co-editor: Political Corruption, 2002; contbr. articles to profl. jours. NSF fellow, 1972-76; grantee U. Pitts., 1983, Nuffield Found., 1984, Fulbright/British Coun. Higher Edn., 1984, Colgate U. Rsch. Coun. Maj. Grants com., 1987, New Liberal Arts program Colgate U./Sloan Found., 1988, 90, Leverhulme Trust/Social and Cmty. Planning Rsch., 1998, NEH fellow 2002-03. Mem. Internat. Polit. Sci. Assn., Internat. Studies Assn., Am. Polit. Sci. Assn., Beta Kappa, Pi Sigma Alpha. Democrat. Roman Catholic. Avocations: computing, baseball, trains. Home: 41 W Main St Earlville NY 13332-1900 Office: Colgate U Dept Polit Sci 13 Oak Dr Hamilton NY 13346-1383 Fax: 315-228-7883. E-mail: mjohnston@mail.colgate.edu.

JOHNSTON, NEIL CHUNN, lawyer; b. Mobile, Ala., Feb. 23, 1953; s. Vivian Gaines and Sara Niel (Chunn) J.; m. Ashley Monroe Hocklander, Dec. 20, 1980; children: Katie, Neil Jr. BA, Southwestern at Memphis (name changed to Rhodes Coll.), 1975; JD, U. Ala., 1978. Atty. Hand, Arendall L.L.C., Mobile, Ala., 1978—. Practice group leader, land use and environment Contbr. articles to profl. jours. Pres. Project CATE Found, Inc., Mobile, 1987—; trustee Nature Conservancy, Ala., 1990-96; bd. dirs. Am. Jr. Miss Program, 1996-2003; bd. dirs., (pres. 2003—),Ala. Coastal Found. Recipient Ala. Gov.'s award-Water Conservationist, Ala. Wildlife Fedn., 1987, EPA Region IV Wetlands Recognition award, 2000, Nat. Wetlands award Environ. Law Inst., 2003. Mem. ABA (vice-chair forestry com. sect. environment, energy, resc.), Ala. State Bar Assn. (chmn. environ. law sect. 1984-91, corp. banking, bus. law sect. 1993), Mobile Bar Assn., Ala. Forestry Assn., Ala. Law Inst., Rotary (pres. Mobile 1996-97). Office: Hand Arendall LLC 3000 FNB Bldg 107 St Francis St Mobile AL 36602

JOHNSTON, NORMAN JOHN, retired architecture educator; b. Seattle, Dec. 3, 1918; s. Jay and Helen May (Shultis) J.; m. Lois Jane Hastings, Nov. 22, 1969. BA, U. Wash.-Seattle, 1942; B.Arch., U. Oreg., 1949; M. in Urban Planning, U. Pa.-Phila., 1959, PhD, 1964. Registered architect, Wash. City planner Seattle City Planning Commn., 1951-55; asst. prof. arch. U. Oreg.-Eugene, 1956-58; assoc. prof. architecture and urban planning U. Wash.-Seattle, 1960-64, prof., 1964-85, prof. emeritus, 1985—, assoc. dean, 1964-76, 79-84, chmn. dept. architecture, 1984-85. Mem. nat. exams. com. Nat. Coun. Archtl. Registration Bds., Washington, 1970-81, 88-99; vis. prof. Tokyo Inst. Tech., 1991, 98; Fulbright prof. Istanbul Tech. U., 1968-69; mem. Wash. State Archtl. Registration Bd., 1989-2000, chmn., 1988-89. Author: Cities in the Round, 1983, Washington's Audacious State Capitol and its Builders, 1988 (Gov.'s Book award 1984, 89), The College of Architecture and Urban Planning, 75 Years at the University of Washington: A Personal View, 1991, The Fountain and the Mountain - The University of Washington Campus, 1895-1995, 1995-2003, National Guide Series: The University of Washington, 2001; editor: NCARB Architectural Registration Handbook, 1980; contbr. articles to profl. jours. Mem. King County Policy Devel. Commn., Seattle, 1970-76; mem. Capitol campus design adv. com. State of Wash., Olympia, 1982-2000, chmn., 1980-88, 96; trustee Mus. History and Industry, 1997-2000. Recipient Wash. Disting. Citizen award, 1987, Barney award AIA Coll. of Fellows, 2003. Fellow AIA (pres. Seattle chpt. 1981, AIA medal Seattle chpt. 1991, Wash. Coun. medal 1997); mem. Phi Beta Kappa, Sigma Chi, Tau Sigma Delta. Presbyterian. Home: 900 University St Apt Au Seattle WA 98101-1778 Office: U Wash C Architecture & Urban Planning PO Box 355726 Seattle WA 98195-5726 E-mail: njjo@u.washington.edu.

JOHNSTON, OLIVER MARTIN, JR., animator; b. Palo Alto, Calif, Oct. 31, 1912; s. Oliver Martin and Arclissa Florence (Boggs) J.; m. Marie Estelle Worthey, Jan. 23, 1943; children: Richard Oliver, Kenneth Andrew. Student, Stanford U., 1931-34, U. Calif., Berkeley, 1932, Chouinard Art Inst., 1934-35. Directing animator Walt Disney Co., Burbank, Calif., 1935-78. Lectr., spkr. in field. Asst. animator Snow White and the Seven Dwarfs, 1937; animation supr. Fantasia, 1940, Bambi, 1942; animator Pinnochio, 1940, The Fox and the Hound, 1981, Victory Through Air Power, 1943, The Three Caballeros, 1945, Make Mine Music, 1946; directing animator Song of the South, 1946, Melody Time, 1948, The Adventures of Ichabod and Mr. Toad, 1949, Cinderella, 1950, Alice in Wonderland, 1951, Peter Pan, 1953, Lady and the Tramp, 1955, Sleeping Beauty, 1959, 101 Dalmatians, 1961, Sword in the Stone, 1963, Mary Poppins, 1964, The Jungle Book, 1967, The Aristocats, 1970, Robin Hood, 1973, Rescuers, 1977, also shorts and TV cartoons; author: Disney Animation -- The Illusion of Life, 1981, Too Funny For Words, 1987, Bambi-the Story and the Film, 1990, Jungle Book Portfolio, 1992, The Disney Villain, English edit., 1993, French edit., 1995; contbg. editor sketch book series; subject of documentary Frank and Ollie; drawings exhibited in Whitney Mus., NYC, 1981. Guest spkr. Russian Govt. and Soyuzmultifilm, 1976, other East European Countries, US Info. Agy. Cultural Exch. Program, 1986. Recipient Pioneer in Film award Delta Kappa Allpha, 1978, honor award Mus. Modern Art, 1978, Annie award Internat. Animated Film Soc., 1980, Disney Legend award, 1989, Grand Prix of the Am., 1995; Academy Tribute to Ollie Johnston & Frank Thomas, The 8th Marc Davis Lecture on Animation presented by the Acad. of Motion Picture Arts and Sci. and the Academy Found., 2003. Avocations: trains, reading, studying, sports. Address: 748 Flintridge Ave Flintridge CA 91011-4027

JOHNSTON, OSCAR BLACK, III, lawyer; b. Tulsa, Oct. 1, 1941; s. Oscar Black Jr. and Carol (VanDerwiele) J.; m. Ruth Archdeacon Darrough; children: Eric Oscar, David Darrough. BBA, Baylor U., 1963; JD, U. Tulsa, 1966. Bar: Okla. 1966, U.S. Dist. Ct. (no., ea., we. dists.) Okla., U.S. Ct. Claims, U.S. Ct. Appeals (10th cir.), U.S. Supreme Ct. Asst. U.S. attorney U.S. Dist. Ct. (we. dist.) Okla., 1970-76; ptnr. Logan & Lowry, L.L.P., Vinita, Okla., 1979—. Assoc. editor Tulsa Law Review, 1964-66. Presiding judge divsn. 54 Okla. Temp. Ct. Appeals, 1980-81, judge divsn. XIV, 1991-93; presiding judge panel VI Lawyer-Staffed Ct. Appeals, 1992. Capt. JAGC, U.S. Army, 1966-70. Fellow Am. Bar Found. (state chair 2001—), Okla. Bar Found. (trustee 1988-96, pres. 1995); mem. ABA (sects. litigation, family law and criminal), Fed. Bar Assn. (pres. Oklahoma City chpt. 1975), Craig County Bar Assn. (pres. 1986-88), Okla. Bar Assn. (adminstrn. of justice, bench and bar coms., assoc. editor, mem. bd. editors Okla. Bar Jour. 2000—), Okla. Trial Lawyers Assn., Rotary (pres. Vinita 1983-84), Phi Alpha Delta. Republican. Methodist. Office: Logan & Lowry PO Box 558 Vinita OK 74301-0558 Home: 116 Westwood Ave Vinita OK 74301-2703

JOHNSTON, PAULINE KAY, chemist; b. Elgin, Ill., Mar. 17, 1951; d. Joseph Kenneth and Beryl Frances (Ferguson) Gogola; m. Laurance Scott Johnston, Aug. 30, 1975 (div. Dec. 1998). BS with highest honors, U. Ill., 1973; MS, Northwestern U., 1974, PhD, 1979. Environ. scientist Sci. Applications Internat. Corp., McLean, Va., 1979-85; sr. chemist U.S. Consumer Product Safety Commn., Bethesda, Md., 1985-87, U.S. EPA, Washington, 1987—94, 1996—. Contbr. articles to profl. jours. Mem. Alpha Lambda Delta. Avocations: pottery, gardening, hiking.

JOHNSTON, PHILIP CONNELLY, lawyer; b. N.Y.C, June 6, 1968; s. John Martin and Suzanne (Shephardson) J. AB, U. Mich., 1990; MA in Internat. Studies, Johns Hopkins U., 1994; JD, Columbia U., 2000. Corr. UPI, Moscow, 1995-97; law clk. to Hon. Joan A. Lenard, U.S. Dist. Ct. for So. Dist. Fla., Miami, Fla., 2000—02; assoc. Skadden, Arps, Slate, Meagher & Flom, NYC, 2002—. Avocations: Russian, German, Spanish langs., travel. Office: US Dist Ct for So Dist Fla 301 N Miami Ave 7th Fl Miami FL 33121

JOHNSTON, RICHARD ALAN, lawyer; b. Buffalo, Mar. 18, 1950; s. Richard W. and Virginia (Holmes) J.; m. Patricia Downing, Aug. 28, 1971; children: Matthew, Sarah, Elizabeth, Michael. BA, Cornell U., 1972; JD, Harvard U., 1976. Bar: Mass. 1977, U.S. Dist. Ct. Mass. 1977, U.S. Ct. Appeals (1st cir.) 1977. Law clk. to presiding justice Mass. Ct. Appeals, Boston, 1976-77; assoc. Hale and Dorr LLP, Boston, 1977-82, sr. ptnr., 1982—. Co-chmn. North Area Task Force, Charlestown, Mass., 1981—; trustee Dennis (Mass.) Conservation Trust, 1988—, pres., 1995—; mem. transition team Mass. Gov. William Weld, 1990-91; internat. election observer Internat. Human Rights Law Group, Nepal, 1991; dir. Friends of City Square Park, 1993—; trustee Hockey Humanitarian Award Found., 1997—; pres. Friends of Tanzanias Schs., Inc., 1997—, Compact of Cape Cod Conservation Trusts, 2001—. Mem. ABA, Internat. Bar Assn., Boston Bar Assn., Nat. Health Lawyers Assn., Mass. Bar Assn. Home: 43 Monument Ave Charlestown MA 02129-3323 Office: Hale & Dorr LLP 60 State St Boston MA 02109-1816

JOHNSTON, RICHARD BOLES, JR., pediatrician, educator, biomedical researcher; b. Atlanta, Aug. 23, 1935; s. Richard Boles and Jane (Dillon) Johnston; m. Mary Anne Claiborne, Aug. 13, 1960; children: Richard B. III, S. Claiborne, Kristin M. BA, Vanderbilt U., 1957, MD, 1961; MS (hon.), U. Pa., 1986. Diplomate Am. Bd. Pediat., Am. Bd. Pediat. Infectious Disease. Resident in pediat. Vanderbilt U., 1961-63, Harvard U., 1963-64, fellow pediat. immunology, 1967-70; asst. prof., assoc. prof. depts. pediat. and microbiology U. Ala. Med. Ctr., Birmingham, 1970-76; vis. assoc. prof. Rockefeller U., N.Y.C., 1976-77, vis. prof., 1983-84; prof. pediat. U. Colo. Sch. Medicine, Denver, 1977-86; chmn. dept. pediat. Nat. Jewish Ctr. Immunology and Respiratory Medicine, Denver, 1977-86, U. Pa. Sch. Medicine, Phila., 1986-90, Wm. H. Bennett prof. pediat., 1986-92; med. dir. March of Dimes Birth Defects Found., White Plains, N.Y., 1992-98. Adj. prof. pediat, chief sec. pediat. immunology Yale U. Sch. Medicine, 1992-98; prof. pediat. Sch. Medicine U. Colo., Denver, 1999—, assoc. dean rsch. devel., 2001-; trustee Internat. Pediat. Rsch. Found., 1983-87, 95-98, chmn. 1984-87, 97-98; chmn. adv. bd. for vaccines and related biols. FDA, Bethesda, Md., 1990-93; chmn. com. vaccine safety, Inst. Medicine, 1992-93, chmn. com new rsch. in vaccines, 1993-94, chmn. forum vaccine safety, 1995-98, chmn. com. asthma and indoor air, 1998-99, bd. health promotion disease prevention, 1994-2001, chmn. com. rsch. in multiple sclerosis, 1999-2001. Mem. editl. bd. 7 profl. jours., 1978—; contbr. 260 articles to profl. jours.; editor Current Opinion in Pediatrics, 1997—. Capt. M.C., U.S. Army, 1964-66. Faculty scholar Josiah Macy Jr. Found., 1976-77; recipient Commr. citation and Wiley medal FDA, 1994. Fellow AAAS; mem. Inst. Medicine NAS, Am. Soc. Clin. Investigation, Am. Pediat. Soc. (pres. 1996-97), Assn. Am. Physicians, Soc. Pediat. Rsch. (pres. 1980-81). Office: Office of Dean C-290 U Colo Sch Medicine 4200 E 9th Ave Denver CO 80262 E-mail: richard.johnston@uchsc.edu.

JOHNSTON, RICHARD FOURNESS, biologist, educator; b. Oakland, Calif., July 27, 1925; s. Arthur Nathaniel and Marie (Johnson) J.; m. Lora Lee Bliler, Feb. 7, 1948; children: Regan, Janet, Cassandra. BA, U. Calif., Berkeley, 1950, MA, 1953, PhD, 1955. Asst. prof. dept. biology N.Mex. State U., 1956-58; mem. faculty depts. zoology and ecology U. Kans., Lawrence, 1958—, prof., 1968-92, prof. emeritus, 1992—, chmn., 1979-82, editor mus. publs., 1974-76, 86-91; program dir. systematic biology NSF, Washington, 1968-69; editor Ann. Rev. Ecology and Systematics, 1968-92, Current Ornithology, 1981-87. Mem. adv. panel biol. scis. Smithsonian Fgn. Currency Program, 1969-71 Served with AUS, 1943-46. Am. Acad. Arts and Scis. grantee, 1957; nat. Acad. Sci. grantee, 1959; NSF grantee, 1959-83. Fellow Am. Ornithol. Union (Coues award 1975), AAAS, mem. Ecol. Soc. Am., Soc. Systematic Zoology (editor jour. 1967-70, pres. 1977), Soc. Study Evolution. Home: 615 Louisiana St Lawrence KS 66044-2337 Office: U Kans Mus Natural History Lawrence KS 66045-0001 E-mail: rjon@ku.edu. *Variability or heterogeneity or pluralism is present in nearly everything humans do or to which they are exposed.*

JOHNSTON, ROBERT EVERETT, information management executive; b. New Haven, Oct. 28, 1939; s. Robert Frederick Jr. and Viola Gladious (Hartling) J.; m. Carol Ann Rayner; children: Nikki Ann, Michael, Pamela, Alan, James. Grad. high sch., East Hartford, Conn. Cert. info. sys. security profl. From pvt. to CWO U.S. Army, 1958-69; ret. USAR, 1984; mgr. data processing The Travelers, Hartford, Conn., 1969-79, The Hartford, Hartford, 1979-81; dir. data processing Phoenix Mut. Life, Hartford, 1981-89; sr. cons. Andersen Cons., Hartford, 1989-90; asst. v.p. Shawmut Nat. Corp., Hartford, 1990-91; gen. mgr. Arbitration Svcs. Corp., Hampton, NH, 1991-95; computer security practice dir. M. Corby & Assocs., inc., Worcester, Mass., 1996-99; sr. security architect Hewlett-Packard Co., Burlington, Mass., 1999-2000; chief security officer, chief privacy officer, security adv. to bd. dirs. Cogentric, Inc., Portsmouth, NH, 2000—02; security adviser ASC, Kingston, NH, 2001—02, chief tech. officer Enfield, Conn., 2003—, ISC2, Framingham, Mass., 2002—03. Dir. ops. Commonly Accepted Security Practices & Recommendations, 2001—03 lectr. info. security. Author: Should BS 7799 Become an ISO Standard?, 1999. Dist. coord. United We Stand Am., 1994-96, state coord., 1996-98; chmn. Kingston Hist. Dist. Commn., 1997-98, 2000-2003. Mem. Am. Philatelic Soc., Am. Soc. for Indsl. Security, Info. Sys. Security Assn., Computer Security Inst., N.Y. Acad. Sci., Internat. Computer Security Assn., Internat. Info. Sys. Security Cert. Consortium, Info. Sys. Audit and Control Assn., Am. Legion, Toastmasters (pres. 1974-82). Republican. Methodist. Avocations: philately, motorcycling. Home: 92 Carriage House Enfield CT 06082 Office: ASC PO Box 564 Broad Brook NH 06014 E-mail: bjohnston@e-computer-security.com. *When entrusted to process you are obligated to safeguard.*

JOHNSTON, ROBERT FOWLER, venture capitalist; b. Phila., Aug. 15, 1936; s. William S. and Elinor (Fowler) J.; m. Lynn Dixon, Feb. 5, 1972; children: William McCord, Bradford Dixon, Alexandra Fowler. BA, Princeton U., 1958; MBA, NYU, 1964. With F.S. Smithers & Co., N.Y.C., 1960-61, Smith Barney & Co., N.Y.C., 1963-67; pres. Johnston Assocs. Inc., Princeton, N.J., 1967—. Bd. dirs. Vela Pharm., Inc., Lawrenceville, N.J., Target Inc., Princeton, N.J., ExSAR Corp., Princeton, N.J. Co-author: Entrepreneural Science: New Links Between Corporations, Universities and Government. Mem. adv. coun. Princeton U. Dept. Molecular biology, 1983—; mem. exec. com. Friends of Inst. Advanced Study, Princeton, 1992—, chmn., 1998—2002; founder Edn. Ventures Found. With USAF, 1961-62. Mem. Nat. Venture Capital Assn., Univ. Club of N.Y.C. Avocations: archaeology, art. Home: Sycamore Creek 48 Elm Ridge Rd Pennington NJ 08534 Office: Johnston Assoc Inc 181 Cherry Valley Rd Princeton NJ 08540-7911 E-mail: rjohnston@jaivc.com.

JOHNSTON, ROBERT JAKE, federal magistrate judge; b. Denver, Sept. 30, 1947; m. Julie Ann Black; children: Jennifer, Robert, Jr., Michelle. BS, Brigham Young U., 1973; JD, U. Pacific, 1977. Bar: Nev. 1977, U.S. Dist. Ct. Nev. 1978, U.S. Ct. Appeals (9th cir.) 1984. Law clk. to Hon. Merlyn Hoyt Nev. 7th Judicial Dist., Ely, 1977-78; dist. atty. White Pine County, Ely, 1979-82; pvt. practice Johnston & Fairman, Ely, 1979-82; deputy dist. atty. Office Clark County Dist. Atty., Las Vegas, Nev., 1983-84; asst. U.S. atty. Office U.S. Atty., Las Vegas, 1984-87, chief civil div., 1986-87; U.S. magistrate judge U.S. Dist. Ct., Las Vegas, 1987—. Dir. Boy Scouts Am. Boulder Dam Area Coun., Las Vegas. With U.S. Army, 1967-70. Mem. Nev. Bar Assn., Fed. Magistrate Judicial Assn. (dir. 1990-92), Las Vegas Track Club, 9th Jud. Cir. Hist. Soc., Southwest Oral History Soc. Office: US Dist Ct Ste 3005 333 Las Vegas Blvd S Las Vegas NV 89101

JOHNSTON, ROY G. consulting structural engineer; b. Chgo., Jan. 7, 1914; s. Karl Gunnar and Esther M. (Youngberg) J.; m. Naomi Harmon, July 30, 1936 (dec.); children: Judith R., Robert K.; m. Lucille Peterson, Dec. 28, 1991. BSC.E., U. So. Calif., 1935. Cert. civil and structural engr., Calif. Plan checker County of Los Angeles, 1935; structural designer C. Devel., Los Angeles, 1936-44; structural engr. Lummis Co., Los Angeles, 1944-45, Brandow & Johnston, Los Angeles, 1945-64; v.p., structural engr. Brandow & Johnston Assocs., Los Angeles, 1964—. Mem. structural safety com. VA, 1973-91; mem. Calif. Bd. Registration Engrs., 1971-78, pres., 1975-76; past chmn. Bldg. Seismic Safety Coun., Washington, 1982-85; mem. State Bldg. Stds. Commn., Calif., 1985-94; mem. steering com. 8th World Conf. Earthquake Engring., 1984; cons. U.S.-Japan Seismic Rsch. Program, 1980-87; lectr. earthquake engring. seminars. Contbr. articles to profl. jours. Trustee Westmont Coll., 1964—, chmn., 1972-88. Recipient Disting. Alumni award U. So. Calif., 1972, 2 George Washington award Inst. Advancement Engring., L.A., 1985; named Constrn. Man Yr., Constrn. Industry so. Calif., 1981, Engr. of Yr. SEOSC, 1990, Pres. award Tall Bldg. Coun., 1994, SEAOSC S.B. Barnes Lifetime Achievement award, 2000. Fellow ASCE, Am. Concrete Inst.; mem. NAE, Earthquake Engring. Rsch. Inst. (bd. dirs., v.p.), Structurals Engr. Assn. (Calif. pres.), Structurals Engrs. So. Calif. (pres., engr. of Yr. 1990), Nat. Acad. Engrs. Republican. Avocations: travel, golf. Office: Brandow & Johnston Assocs 1660 W 3rd St Los Angeles CA 90017-1138

JOHNSTON, RUTH D. film studies, English literature, and women's studies educator; b. La Paz, Bolivia, Nov. 8, 1944; came to U.S., 1948; d. Wolf and Anna Sara Goldstein; m. Harry M. Johnston III, Nov. 22, 1970. BA in English, Barnard Coll., 1965; MA in English, U. Chgo., 1966; PhD in English, NYU, 1980, MA in Cinema Studies, 1982. Adj. lectr. Bklyn. Coll., 1970-72, John Jay Coll. of Criminal Justice, N.Y.C., 1972-77, Rutgers U., Newark, 1980-81, St. Peter's Coll., Jersey City, 1981-82; adj. instr. Pace U., N.Y.C., 1980-82, asst. prof., 1982-88, assoc. prof., 1988-94, prof., 1994—. Mem. adv. bd. Pace N.Y. Women's Studies, 1990—; reader NYU Press, 1990, 92, U. Pa. Press, 1995. Contbr. articles to profl. jours., including Camera Obscura, Cinema Jour., others. Mem. MLA, Soc. Cinema Studies, Northeast MLA, U. Film and Video Assn., Northeast Victorian Studies Assn., Soc. for the Study of Narrative Lit. Office: Pace U Pace Plz New York NY 10038

JOHNSTON, STANLEY HOWARD, JR., rare books curator, bibliographer; b. Cleve., Apr. 28, 1946; m. Carol Ann Lewis, June 19, 1976. BA, Columbia Coll., 1968; MA, U. Western Ontario, London, Ontario, Can., 1970, PhD, 1977; MS in Libr. Sci., Case Western Reserve U., 1979. Tchg. asst. U. Western Ontario, London, Can., 1971-72; asst. to editors Spenser Newsletter, London, Ontario, Can., 1972-73; bibliographer Cleve. Herbals Project, Cleve, 1984-90; curator of rare books Holden Arboretum, Kirtland, Ohio, 1990—. Internet columnist Coun. on Botanical and Horticultural Librs., 1995—; libr. adv. com. The Herb Soc. Am., Kirtland, Ohio, 1997-99. Author: The Cleveland Herbal, Botanical and Horticultural Collections, 1992, Cleveland's Treasures from the World of Botanical Literature, 1998; contbr. articles to profl. jours.; internet columnist. Mem. MLA, Bibliographical Soc. Am., Soc. for History of Natural History, Am. Libr. Assn. (rare books and manuscripts sect.), The Bibliographical Soc., Coun. on Botanical and Horticultural Librs. (mem. publs. com., electronic comm. com., 1996—, documentation strategy com. 1996-2001, long term planning com., 1997-2001, preservation and access com. 2001—), Medieval Acad. Am., Am. Philatelic Soc., No. Ohio Bibliophilic Soc. Republican. Presbyterian. Avocations: philately, collecting mysteries, fantasy, sci.-fiction. Home: 7226 Grant St Mentor OH 44060-4704 Office: The Holden Arboretum 9500 Sperry Rd Kirtland OH 44094-5149 E-mail: stanley177@aol.com.

JOHNSTON, SUMMERFIELD K., JR., food products executive; b. 1954; V.p. Johnston Food Group, Inc., 1983-85; officer Cleveland (Tenn.) Coca-Cola, 1986-87; v.p., gen. mgr. Midwest Coca-Cola (subsid. Johnston Coca-Cola Bottling Co.), Mpls., 1987-2000, pres., regional ops., from 1987; chmn., CEO Coca-Cola Enterprises, Inc., Atlanta, 1997—2002. Office: Coca-Cola Enterprises 2500 Windy Ridge Pkwy Atlanta GA 30339

JOHNSTON, THOMAS MCELREE, JR., retired church administrator; b. Coral Gables, Fla., June 10, 1934; s. Thomas McElree and Lorine (Davis) J.; m. Anna Youel Armstrong, July 2, 1960; children: Kathryn Armstrong, Timothy Armstrong, Sara Helen. BA, Amherst Coll., 1956; MDiv, Yale U., 1959; ThM, Princeton Theol. Sem., 1963; D of Ministry, San Francisco Theol. Sem., 1978. Ordained to ministry Presbyn. Ch., 1959. Assoc. coord. religious affairs NC State U., Raleigh, NC, 1959-62; min. community svc. Tabernacle Presbyn. Ch., Phila., 1963-66; organizer, head of staff Ch. of the Reconciler, Clearwater, Fla., 1966-78; assoc. Presbytery devel. Synod of the Covenant, Columbus, Ohio, 1978-83, assoc. exec., 1985-88; exec. Synod of the Trinity, Camp Hill, Pa., 1988-2000; ret. Pres. Pa. Coun. Chs., Harrisburg, 1995-98; chair Synod Exec. Forum, 1997; chmn. gen. assembly Synod Staff Forum, 1997; corr. mem. Gen. Assembly Coun., Louisville, 1993-94. Publisher: (newspaper) Trinitarian. Pres., organizer Religious Cmty. Svcs., Inc. Clearwater, 1968-70; pres. Pinellas County Head Start, Inc., Clearwater, 1968-72; mem. Pinellas County Sch. Bd., Pinellas County Coun., Clearwater, 1972-76; bd. dirs. Cmty. Svc. Found., Largo, Fla., 1969-78, Drug Free Pa., Inc., 1999-2002. Named Vol. of Yr., Civic Coun., Pinellas County, Fla., 1972; recipient Humanitarian award Lions Club, 1975. Mem. Rotary Internat. (club. pres. 2003—). Presbyterian. Home: 1041 Country Club Rd Camp Hill PA 17011-1049

JOHNSTON, VIRGINIA EVELYN, retired editor; b. Spokane, Wash., Apr. 26, 1933; d. Edwin and Emma Lucile (Munroe) Rowe; m. Alan Paul Beckley, Dec. 26, 1974; children: Chris, Denise, Rex. Student, Portland C.C., 1964, Portland State U., 1966, 78-79. Proofreader the Oregonian, Portland, 1960—62, teletypsetter operator, 1962—66, operator Photon 200, 1966—68, copy editor, asst. women's editor, 1968—80, spl. sects. editor, 1981—83, editor FOOD day, 1982—2001; ret., 2002. Pres. Matrix Assocs., Inc., Portland, 1975—, chmn. bd., 1979—; past pres. Bones & Brew, Inc. Editor Principles of Computer Systems for Newspaper Mgmt., 1975-76. Cons. Dem. Party Oreg., 1969, Portland Sch. Dist. No. 1, 1978. Democrat. Home: 4140 NE 137th Ave Portland OR 97230-2624

JOHNSTON, WILLIAM DAVID, biotechnology executive; b. Chgo., Nov. 5, 1944; s. Samuel David and Jeanne (Williams) J.; m. Susan Diane Ward, Aug. 19, 1966; children: Kimberly Dawn Sites, Kirk David, Tiffany Dee Hansen, Kyle Donald, Ryan Daryl. BS in Chemistry, Brigham Young U., 1969, PhD in Organic Chemistry, 1974. V.p. Parish Chem. Co., 1973-75; mgr. materials control Baxter Healthcare Corp., 1975-80; group mgr., polymer rsch. and material control Travenol Labs., Inc., 1980-84, v.p. Material and Membrane Tech. Ctr., 1984-86, v.p. applied scis., 1987-93; v.p., gen. mgr. gene therapy div. Baxter Healthcare Corp., Round Lake, Ill., 1993-97; pres., CEO Inhibitex, Inc., Atlanta, 1997—. Mem. adv. bd. Ill. Jr. Acad. Sci., Springfield, 1984-86, GDITT, 2003; bd. dirs. Ga. Biomed. Ptnrs., 1999—, Biotechnology Industry Orgn., emerging co. sect. governing bd., 2002—; co-chair BioSci. Coun. for Metro Atlanta; mem. adv. bd. Coll. Engring., U. Ill., Chgo., 1988-92, dept. chem. engring. Northwestern U., Evanston, Ill., 1989-98; bd. dirs. Neocrin Co., 1992-96, Ga. Biomedical Ptnrs., 1999—. Contbr. articles to profl. jours.; patentee in field. Stake pres. LDS Ch., Buffalo Grove, Ill., 1988-97; exec. coun. N.E. Ill. coun. Boy Scouts Am., 1989-97; chmn. bd. LDS Social Svcs., Naperville, Ill., 1990-97. Brigham Young U. scholarship. Mem. AAAS, Am. Chem. Soc., Internat. Soc. for Artificial Organs, Internat. Soc. Blood Purification (exec. bd. 1991-96), Soc. for Biomaterials, Internat. Soc. of Cell Transplantation, Sigma Xi. Home: 1422 Spyglass Hill Dr Duluth GA 30097-5948 E-mail: bjohnston@inhibitex.com.

JOHNSTON, WILLIAM FREDERICK, emergency services administrator; b. Oakridge, Tenn., Mar. 4, 1945; s. Leonard E. and Helene C. (Spicker) J.; m. Kathleen Jo Hotaling, Nov. 17, 1988; 1 child, Lindsey Anne. BS, U. Wash., 1969, MS, 1971, MD, 1974, MBA, 1998. Diplomate Am. Bd. Emergency Medicine. Med. intern U. Wash. Affiliated Hosps., Seattle, 1974-75; emergency medicine resident Valley Med. Ctr. Fresno/U. Calif. San Francisco, Fresno, 1975-77; pres., CEO N.W. Emergency Physicians, Seattle, 1977-81; med. dir. emergency svcs. N.W. Hosp., Seattle, 1977—. Bd. dirs. First Choice Health Plan, Inc., First Choice Health Network, Inc., Washington Casualty Co., N.W. Healthcare Ins. Svcs. Contbr. articles to med. jours. Fellow Am. Coll. Emergency Physicians. Avocations: skiing, hiking, kayaking. Home: 4731 Beach Dr SW Seattle WA 98116-4340 Office: N W Hosp 1550 N 115th St Seattle WA 98133-8498 E-mail: billj@nwlink.com.

JOHNSTON, WILLIAM WEBB, pathologist, educator; b. Statesville, N.C., Aug. 26, 1933; s. Jesse Clyde and Pauline Elizabeth (Massey) J. BS, Davidson Coll., 1954; MD, Duke U., 1959. Diplomate Am. Bd. Pathology, Am. Bd. Cytopathology, Internat. Bd. Cytopathology. Intern Duke U., 1959-60, resident in pathology, 1960-63, mem. faculty, 1963—, prof. pathology, 1972-97, dir. div. cytopathology and cytotechnology tng. program, 1966—; ret., 1996. Bd. dirs. Anatomical Pathology Svc.; cons. pathologist Durham VA Hosp., Duncan County Hosp.; chmn. Internat. Bd. Cytopathology, 1992-98. Author: (with W.J. Frable) Respiratory Cytopathology, 1974; Diagnostic Respiratory Cytopathology, 1979; (with S.H. Bigner) The Cytopathology of the Central Nervous System, 1981, 2d edit., 1994, Pulmonary Cytology (with James Linder), 1992; assoc. editor Acta Cytologica, 1978—, sr. mem. editorial bd., 1992; editor: Masson Monographs in Cytopathology; mem. editorial bd. Am. Jour. Clin. Pathology, 1986; editorial cons. Masson Publs., N.Y.C.; mem. editorial adv. bd. Jour. Nat. Cancer Inst. Fellow Internat. Acad. Cytology (Maurice Goldblatt award 1995), Am. Soc. Clin. Pathologists, Coll. Am. Pathologists, Royal Soc. Medicine; mem. AMA (del. 1982-96), Am. Soc. Cytology (rev. bd., pres. 1981-82, Papanicolaou award 1986), Am. Assn. Pathologists, Arthur Purdy Stout Soc. Surg. Pathology, Internat. Acad. Pathology, Am. Assn. for Cancer Rsch. Republican. Presbyterian (organist). Home: 8200 Bromley Rd Hillsborough NC 27278-9709

JOHNSTON, YNEZ, artist, educator; b. Berkeley, Calif., May 12, 1920; BFA, U. Calif., Berkeley, 1941, MFA, 1946. Lectr. art U. Calif., Berkeley, 1950-51, Colorado Springs Fine Arts Center, 1954, 55, Chouinard Art Inst., 1956, Calif. State U., Los Angeles, 1966, 67, U. Judaism Sch. Fine Arts, Los Angeles, 1967, Otis Art Inst., Los Angeles, 1978-81; artist-in-residence Fullerton Coll. (Calif.), 1982 One-man exhbns. include: San Francisco Mus. Art, 1943, Redlands U., 1947, Santa Barbara (Calif.) Mus. Art, 1952, 57, Pasadena (Calif.) Mus. Art, 1955, 62, Colorado Springs (Colo.) Fine Arts Center, 1955, Calif. Palace Legion of Honor, 1956, The O'Hana Gallery, London, 1958, Paul Kantor Gallery, Los Angeles, 1952, 53, 55, 57, 58, 61-62, 63, Beloit (Wis.) Coll., 1961, Barbara Cecil Gallery, New Orleans, 1963, Mex., 1959, Occidental Coll., L.A., 1955, Esther Bear Gallery, 1967, Ball State U., 1967, Stewart-Verde Galleries, San Francisco, 1966, San Francisco Mus. Art, 1967, Mekler Gallery, L.A., 1970-82, 84, 89, Tokyo Shoten Gallery, N.Y.C., 1976, Mitsukoshi Gallery, Tokyo, 1977, Wiener Gallery, N.Y.C., 1977, Worthington Gallery, Chgo., 1982, 85, 88, Mekler Gallery, 1987, 89, Tomlyn Gallery, Fla., 1990-99, 2003, Fresno Mus. Art, 1992, Tortue Gallery, Santa Monica, 1994-96, Tobey Moss Gallery, L.A., 1994, 2003, Kennedy Museum, Athens, Ohio, 1997, Lyman Allyn Mus, New London, Conn., 1998, Schmidt-Bingham Gallery, N.Y.C., 1998, 99, 2001, Santa Cruz Mus., Calif. 1998, Norton-Simon Mus., Pasadena, Calif., 2004; also exhibited numerous group shows including: Whitney Mus. Am. Art, 1953-56, Mus. Modern Art, 1952, 54, Carnegie Inst., 1951, 55, I.F.A. Gallery, Washington, 1963, 100 Prints of the Year, N.Y.C., 1963, Bklyn. Mus., 1966, Vancouver (B.C., Can.) Print Internat., World Print Competition, San Francisco, 1977, Met. Mus., 1978, L.A. County Mus., 1980-81, Drawings from Their Collection, Nat. Gallery Smithsonian, Washington, Wight Gallery UCLA, 1988, Nat. Gallery Modern Art, New Delhi, 1988, Memory Gallery, Nagoya, Japan, 1990, Gallery IV, L.A., 1990, Worcester Art Mus., 1991, Amon Carter Mus., 1991, Women's Art Mus., Washington, 1994, Met. Mus. Fresno, Calif., 1994, Brigitie Haasner Gallery, Wiesbaden, Germany, Norton-Simon Mus., 1999, Traveling Show in China, Macao, Municipal Gallery, Rio Honda Coll., L.A., Taiwan, 2001, others; represented in permanent collections numerous museums including, Santa Barbara Mus. Art, Mus. Modern Art, Philbrook Art Center, Los Angeles County Mus., City Art Mus. St. Louis, Whitney Mus. Am. Art, Phila. Mus. Art, San Diego Mus. Art, U. Ill., Met. Mus. Art, Hirshhorn Collection, Herbert F. Johnson Collection (Cornell U.), San Francisco Mus. Art, Otis Art Inst., Milw. Art Center, Worcester Art Mus. (travelling print exhbn. to Terra Mus., Chgo., Amon Carter Mus., Ft. Worth, 1990), Santa Fe Mus. of Fine Art, The Nat. Mus. Israel, Jerusalem, Gift Gardens Bot./Sculpture Pk., Fla., Norton-Simon Mus., numerous schs. and colls., other museums, also pvt. collections. Recipient San Francisco Mus. Art award oil painting, 1946; awards Calif. State Fair, 1951, 61, 62; award etching Los Angeles County Mus., 1950; exhbn. first award Met. Mus. Art, 1952; purchase award Exhbn. Fgn. Artists, Rome, Italy, 1952; purchase award Otis Art Inst., 1963; purchase award Los Angeles Municipal Art Dept., 1967; also commns.; John Simon Guggenheim Found. grantee, 1952; Louis Comfort Tiffany grantee, 1955, 56; Huntington Hartford grantee, 1957; James Phelan grantee, 1958; MacDowell Colony grantee, 1959; Tamarind workshop fellow, 1966; Nat. Endowment Arts painting grantee, 1976, 85 Home and Studio: 579 Crane Blvd Los Angeles CA 90065-5019

JOHNSTONE, BRIAN, medical educator; b. Bilbrook, Staffordshire, U.K., Nov. 1, 1960; m. Veronique Sarie Hazan, Nov. 8, 1986; children: Timothy George, Emma Victoria. BS, Brunel U., Uxbridge, U.K., 1983; PhD, U. London, 1987. Assoc. prof. Case Western Res. U., Cleve., 1995—. Section editor (textbook) Orthopaedics. Mem. med. and sci. com. Arthritis Found., Cleve. Recipient Volvo award for low back pain rsch., 1988, 1994, Arthritis Foundation's 50 Shining Stars for svcs. to charity, Arthritis Found., 2000. Mem.: Am. Soc. Matrix Biology, Orthop. Rsch. Soc. Achievements include patents for; patents pending for probes for chondrogenesis. Avocations: pottery, soccer. Office: Case Western Reserve University 10900 Euclid Ave Cleveland OH 44106 Office Fax: 216-368-1332. E-mail: bxj9@po.cwru.edu.

JOHNSTONE, C. BRUCE, investment company executive; b. N.Y.C., Nov. 7, 1940; s. R. Adam and Muriel S. (Smith) J.; m. Helen Louise Lott, Aug. 27, 1963; children: Brent Paul, Reed Evan. AB cum laude, Harvard U., 1962, MBA, 1966. CFA. V.p. portfolio mgr. Fidelity Equity Income Fund, Boston, 1972-90; portfolio group leader income and growth funds Fidelity Mgmt. & Rsch. Co., Boston, 1981-90, sr. v.p., 1984-89, bd. dirs., 1989-90, exec. v.p. chmn. investment com., 1990; sr. v.p. Fidelity Mgmt. Trust Co., Boston, 1982-90, also bd. dirs.; mng. dir. Fidelity Investments, Boston, 1983—; chief investment officer, mng. dir. Fidelity Internat. Ltd., 1990—92; sr. mktg. investment strategist Fidelity Investments, 1992—; chmn. HBS Fund, 1998—2003. Founding mem., dir. Needham Edn. Found. Class chair Harvard U. Bus. Sch., 1966—, class sec., 1986—; Mem. com. on univ. resources Harvard U., 1987—. Lt. USNR, 1962-68. Mem. Chartered Fin. Analysts, Boston Security Analysts Soc., Premiere Club, Wellesley Country Club, Harvard Varsity Club, Harvard Club Boston. Home: 827 Charles River St Needham MA 02492-1007 Office: Fidelity Investments 82 Devonshire St Boston MA 02109-3605

JOHNSTONE, CAROL JOANNE, physicist; b. Dallas, Tex., Dec. 19, 1953; d. Jerry Lynn Harvey and Isla Beatrice Creighton; m. John Allistair Johnstone; children: Kira, David, Ian. BA, BS, U. of Tex., 1977, PhD in nuc. physics, 1985. Post-doctoral rsch. fellow U. of N.Mex, 1984—85; rsch. scientist Fermi Nat. Accelerator Lab, Batavia, Ill., 1985—89, assoc. scientist, 1989—95, applications physicist, 1995—2000, applied scientist, 2000—; rsch. prof. Ill. Inst. of Tech., Chgo., 2001—. Contbr. articles to profl. jours. Recipient Fermilab Tech. award, Dept. of Energy, 1984.

JOHNSTONE, IRVINE BLAKELEY, III, lawyer; b. Newark, Dec. 21, 1948; s. Irvine Blakeley Jr. and Ruth (Morton) J.; m. Phyllis Nevins, Oct. 16, 1983. BA with honors, Lehigh U., 1972; JD, Duke U., 1975. Bar: N.J. 1975, U.S. Dist. Ct. N.J. 1975, U.S. Ct. Appeals (3d cir.) 1979, N.Y. 1981; cert. civil trial adv. Nat. Bd. Trial Advocacy. Assoc. Riker, Danzig, Scherer & DeBevoise, Newark, 1975-76, Shanley & Fisher, Newark, 1976-80; ptnr. Johnstone, Skok, Loughlin & Lane, Westfield, N.J., 1980—. Mem. bd. of govs. Blair Acad., 1978-84; atty. Rahway Lifers Group (N.J.) State Prison, 1980-85, Planning Bd., Clark, N.J., 1981-82, Bd. of Adjustment, Clark, 1982-84. Mem. ABA, ATLA, Nat. Bd. Trial Advocacy (civil trial advocate), N.J. Bar Assn., Union County Bar Assn., Def. Rsch. Inst., Union County Arbitration Bd. (cert. civil trial atty. N.J. Supreme Ct.), N.J. Trial Lawyers Assn., R.J. Hughes Am. Inns of Ct. (master 1995—). Clubs: Baltusrol (Springfield, N.J.). Republican. Presbyterian. Avocations: flying, golf, sports. Home: 5 Bartles Rd Lebanon NJ 08833-4606 E-mail: ibj@jsll-lawfirm.com., attys@jsll-lawfirm.com.

JOHNSTONE, JOHN WILLIAM, JR., retired chemical company executive; b. Bklyn., Nov. 19, 1932; s. John William and Sarah J. (Singleton) J.; m. Claire Lundberg, Apr. 14, 1956; children: Thomas Edward, James Robert, Robert Andrew. BA, Hartwick Coll., Oneonta, N.Y., 1954; DSc (hon.), Hartwick Coll., 1990; grad. advanced mgmt. program, Harvard U., 1970. With Hooker Chem. Corp., 1954-75, group v.p., 1973-75; pres. Airco Alloys divsn. Airco, Inc., 1976-79; v.p., gen. mgr. indsl. products, then sr. v.p. chems. group Olin Corp., 1979-80, corp. v.p., pres. chems. group, 1980-85, pres., 1985-87, chief operating officer, 1986-87, chmn., pres., CEO, 1988-96, chmn. of bd., 1996, bd. dirs., ret., 1996. Bd. dirs., Rsch. Corp. Techs. Inc., McDermott Internat., Inc., Arch Chem. Inc. Trustee Hartwick Coll., 1983-91, 92—. Mem. Soc. Chem. Industry, Soap and Detergent Assn. (former chmn. bd. dirs.), Chem. Mfrs. Assn. (chmn. bd. dirs. 1991), Woodway Country Club, Blind Brook Club. Episcopalian.

JOHNSTONE, MARTIN E. state supreme court justice; BA, Western Ky. U.; JD, U. Louisville. Bar: Ky. Judge 3d Magisterial Dist., Ky., 1976-78; dist. judge Jefferson County, Ky., 1978-83; chief judge, 1987-93; circuit judge, 1985-87; justice Ky. Ct. Appeals, 1993-96, chief judge pro tem, 1996; justice Ky. Supreme Ct., 1996—, dep. chief justice, 1998—. Recipient Outstanding Trial Judge award Ky. Acad. Trial Attys., 1991. Mem. Louisville Bar Assn. (Judge of Yr. 1981). Office: State Capitol Capitol Bldg 700 Capitol Ave, Suite 1000 Frankfort KY 40202-2761*

JOHNSTONE, PHILIP MACLAREN, lawyer; b. Sharon, Conn., Mar. 24, 1961; s. Rodney Stuart and Frances Louise (Davis) J.; m. Elizabeth Laird McGovern, Sept. 10, 1988. BA in Econs. magna cum laude, Duke U., 1983; JD, U. Pa., 1986. Bar: Mass. 1986, Conn. 1987, U.S. Dist. Ct. Conn. 1988, R.I. 1998. Ptnr. Waller, Smith & Palmer, P.C., New London, Conn., 1997—. Bd. dirs. J Boats, Inc., Newport, R.I., 1987—. Trustee Denison Pequotsepos Nature Ctr., Mystic, Conn., 1998-2002, Pine Point Sch., Stonington, Conn., 2000—. Mem. ABA, Mass. Bar Assn., Conn. Bar Assn., R.I. Bar Assn. Republican. Episcopalian. Avocations: tennis, golf. Home: 17 Cliff St Stonington CT 06378-1249 Office: Waller Smith and Palmer PC 52 Eugene Oneill Dr New London CT 06320-6324 E-mail: pmjohnstone@wallersmithpalmer.com.

JOHNSTONE, QUINTIN, law educator, writer; b. Chgo., Mar. 29, 1915; s. Quintin and Wegia (Metsker) J.; m. Nancy McMullen; children: Robert Dale, Katherine Mary. AB, U. Chgo., 1936, JD, 1938; LL.M., Cornell U., 1941; J.S.D., Yale U., 1951; DHL, Quinnipiac Coll., 1993. Bar: Ill. 1939, Oreg. 1948. Pvt. practice, Chgo., 1939-41; atty. OPA, 1941-47; mem. law faculty Willamette U., 1947-50, U. Kans., 1950-55, Yale U., 1955—, Justus S. Hotchkiss prof., 1969-85, prof. emeritus, 1985—; dean law, prof. Haile Selassie I U., Ethiopia, 1967-69. Prof. N.Y. Law Sch., 1985-2000. Author: (with D. Hopson) Lawyers and Their Work, 1967; (with C. Berger) Land Transfer and Finance, 4th edit., 1993; (with M. Wenglinsky) Paralegals, 1985; contbr. articles to profl. jours. Mem. ABA, Conn. Bar Assn., Oreg. Bar Assn. Home: 22 Morris St Hamden CT 06517-3423 Office: Yale Law Sch PO Box 208215 New Haven CT 06520-8215

JOHNSTONE, ROBERT PHILIP, lawyer; b. Bellefonte, Pa., Dec. 1, 1943; s. B. Kenneth and Helene (Hetzel) J.; m. Susan Alice Hardy, June 22, 1968; children: Natalie, Nancy. BS with honors, Denison U., 1966; JD magna cum laude, U. Mich., 1969. Bar: Ind. 1969. Assoc. Barnes, Hickam, Pantzer & Boyd, Indpls., 1969-75, ptnr., 1976-82, Barnes & Thornburg, Indpls., 1982—. Chmn. litigation dept. Barnes & Thornburg, 1988-89, mem. mgmt. com., 1988-89; lectr., panelist legal seminars and trial advocacy programs. Sec.-treas. Contemporary Art Soc. of Indpls. Mus. Art, 1983—84; v.p., bd. dirs. Friends of Herron Gallery, Herron Sch. Art, 1981—85; bd. dirs. Eagle Creek Park Found., 2001—. Fellow Am. Coll. Trial Lawyers (state com. 1992-97, state chair 1995-96); mem. U.S. 7th Fed. Cir. Bar Assn., Ind. Bar Assn., Fed. Bar Assn., Indpls. Bar Assn., Order of the Coif, Woodstock Club (Indpls., bd. dirs. 1988-90, v.p. 1989, pres. 1990), Indpls. Art Ctr. (bd. dirs. 1991-97), Dramatic Club (Indpls.), Phi

Beta Kappa, Omicron Delta Kappa. Home: 1065 W 52nd St Indianapolis IN 46228-2463 Office: Barnes & Thornburg 11 S Meridian St Indianapolis IN 46204-3535 E-mail: bob.johnstone@btlaw.com.

JOHNSTONE, ROSE MAMELAK (MRS. DOUGLAS JOHNSTONE), biochemistry educator; b. Lodz, Poland, May 14, 1928; d. Jacob Shea and Esther (Rotholz) Mamelak; m. Douglas Johnstone, Aug. 9, 1953; children: Michael, Eric. BSc, McGill U., 1950, PhD, 1953. Nat. Cancer Inst. of Can. fellow Nat. Inst. for Med. Rsch., London, Strangeway Rsch. Lab., Cambridge, Eng., 1954-56; rsch. assoc. McGill-Montreal Gen. Hosp. Rsch. Inst., 1956-60; faculty McGill U., Montreal, Que., Can., 1961-97, assoc. prof. biochemistry, 1967-76, prof., 1977-97, prof. emeritus, 1997—, chmn. dept., 1980-90. Gilman Cheney chair biochemistry McGill U., Montreal, 1985-96, emeritus chair, 1997-98. Contbr. articles to profl. jours. Grantee Nat. Cancer Inst. Can., 1965-67, Med. Rsch. Coun. of Can., 1965-2001, NIH, 1987-90, 92-96. Fellow Royal Soc. Can. (treas. 1991-94); mem. McGill Assn. U. Tchrs. (membership sec. 1967-70, treas. 1995-96), Biol. Chemists Am., Can. Biochem. Soc. (pres. 1985-86), Internat. Assn. Women Bioscientists (sec. 1985-88). Home: 4064 Oxford Montreal QC Canada H4A 2Y4 Office: McGill U McIntyre Med Sci 3655 Sir Wm Osler Promenade #804 Montreal QC Canada H3G 1Y6 E-mail: rose.johnstone@mcgill.ca.

JOHNS-TREAT, CORINNE V. management consultant; b. San Francisco, Nov. 9, 1953; d. Joseph Sal and Mildred (Balisha) Johns; m. Harold Kenneth Treat, June 3, 1982; children: Nicolas, Rachel. BS in Bus., San Jose State U., 1976; MA in Mgmt., U. Phoenix, San Jose, Calif., 1986. Dept. mdse. mgr. Capwells, Fremont, Calif., 1976-77; records auditor Ford Motor Corp., Milpitas, Calif., 1977-80; sr. analyst Xerox Corp, Hayward, Calif., 1980-81; advanced products project mgr. Amdahl Corp., Sunnyvale, Calif., 1981-87, mgr. engring. change control, 1983-85, mgr. advanced products planning, 1985-87; mng. prin. CINTAM Cons., San Jose, 1987—. Author: Project Management, 1986; contbr. articles to profl. jours., including San Jose Bus. Jour. Room parent D.M. Bagby Sch., San Jose, 1994—; team mgr. Cal. Valley Youth Soccer Assn., San Jose, 1997—; active 1st Congl. Ch., San Jose, 1998-99. Avocations: singing, guitar, soccer, golf. Fax: 408-264-7900. E-mail: cintam@attglobal.net.

JOHNTING, WENDELL, law librarian; b. Winchester, Ind., Aug. 30, 1952; s. Ernest K. and Jewell G. (Browning) J. AB, Taylor U., 1974; MLS, Ind. U., 1975. Asst. dir. tech. svcs. Ind. U. Sch. Law Libr., Indpls., 1975—. Project dir. Indpls. Law Cataloging Consortium, 1980-92; vis. libr. Cambridge U., Squire Law Libr., Cambridge, Eng., 1985; founding mem. Info. Online Project Leaders, 1987-90; spkr. in field; mem., sec. Ind. U. Librs. Faculty Coun., 2001-02. Libr. vol. Beech Grove (Ind.) Pub. Libr., 1993-95; reader, vol. Marion County Health Care Home, Indpls., 1989. Mem.: Ind. U. Libr. Faculty Coun. (sec. 2001—02), Indpls. Law Librs. Assn. (sec.-treas. 1999—2001), Ind. Libr. Fedn. (pers. com. 2000—), Christian Legal Soc. (faculty adv. 2001—), Ind. U. Librs. Assn. (exec. bd. 1982—85, v.p. 1986—87, treas. 1999—2001), Ohio Region Assn. Law Librs. (sec. 1982, exec. bd. 1982—85), Knights of Pythias, Dramatic Order Knights of Khorassen, Alpha Phi Gamma, Chi Alpha Omega, Beta Phi Mu. Republican. Baptist. Avocations: gardening, astronomy, cooking. Home: 420 N 23rd Ave Beech Grove IN 46107-1032 Office: Ind U Sch Law Libr 530 W New York St Indianapolis IN 46202 E-mail: wjohntin@iupui.edu.

JOHNTZ, JOHN HOFFMAN, JR., lawyer; b. Alva, Okla., Apr. 26, 1937; s. John H. and Veenetia E. (Burchfiel) J.; m. Linda B. Dover, June 9, 1962; children: John H., Jason Dover. BA, Harvard U., 1959; JD, U. Kans., 1965. Bar: Kans. 1965, U.S. Supreme Ct. 1971. Ptnr. Payne & Jones, P.C., Overland Park, Kans., 1965—. Mem. family adv. com. Kans. Jud. Coun.; mem. Kans. Bd. Law Examiners; head draftsman Kans. Domestic Rels. Law; bd. dirs. Brookside Bank, Olathe Fin. Svcs. Corp.; spkr. domestic rels. law. Co-author: Tax Aspects of Litigation; contbr. articles to profl. jours.; bd. editors Kans. Bar Jour. Bd. dirs. mem. coun. Soc. Fellows Nelson-Atkins Mus. Art; bd. dirs. Kansas City-Xion, China Sisters City Com., Kans. Citizens for the Arts, Mid-Am. Arts Alliance, Kansas City Artists Coalition, Arts Coun. Johnson County, Mo. Repertory Theatre, Kemper Mus. Contemporary Art. Lt. (j.g.) USN, 1959—61. Named Shawnee Mission North Disting. Alumnus. Fellow: Am. Acad. Matrimonial Lawyers; mem.: ABA, Kans. State Hist. Soc. (bd. dirs.), Phi Beta Kappa, Phi Delta Phi (grad. of yr. 1965). Home: 4424 W 84th St Shawnee Mission KS 66207-1811 Office: Payne & Jones Chartered PO Box 25625 Shawnee Mission KS 66225-5625 E-mail: jjohntz@paynejones.com.

JOICE, NORA LEE, clinical dietitian; b. Kearney, Nebr., Mar. 5, 1948; d. Frank Rogers and Clarrisa Blanche (Drinnan) Jackson; m. David Wayne Joice, Dec. 21, 1973. BS, U. Ariz., 1971. Registered dietitian; lic. dietitian. Clin. dietitian St. Francis Hosp., Tulsa, 1972-76; pub. health nutritionist Tulsa City County Health Dept., 1976-81; clin. dietitian City of Faith Hosp., Marriott Corp., Tulsa, 1982-84, asst. chief dietitian, 1984-86, chief clin. dietitian, 1986-87, clin. nutrition specialist, 1987-89; cons. dietitian in long-term health facilities Marriott Corp., Tulsa, 1990-92; pvt. practice cons. dietitian Tulsa, 1992—; clin. dietitian Broken Arrow (Okla.) Med. Ctr., 1993-94; outpatient clin. dietitian St. John's Med. Ctr., Tulsa, Okla., 1995-2000. Cons., dietitian Health Care Facilities, a practice group with Am. Dietetic Assn. Mem. Okla. Dietetic Assn., Am. Dietetic Assn., Okla. Cons. Dietitians in Health Care Facilities. Democrat. Pentecostal. Avocations: crafts, painting, piano. Home and Office: 2320 S Urbana Ave Tulsa OK 74114-3627

JOINER, CHARLES WYCLIFFE, judge; b. Maquoketa, Iowa, Feb. 14, 1916; s. Melvin William and Mary (von Schrader) J.; m. Ann Martin, Sept. 29, 1939; children: Charles Wycliffe, Nancy Caroline, Richard Martin. BA, U. Iowa, 1937, JD, 1939. Bar: Iowa 1939, Mich. 1947. With firm Miller, Huebner & Miller, Des Moines, 1939-47; part-time lectr. Des Moines Coll. Law, 1940-41; faculty U. Mich. Law, 1947-68, assoc. dean, 1960-65, acting dean, 1964-65; dean Wayne State U. Law Sch., Detroit, 1968-72; U.S. dist. judge, sr. judge, 1972—. Assoc. dir. Preparatory Commn. Mich. Constl. Conv., 1961, co-dir. research and drafting com., 1961-62; civil rules adv. com. U.S. Jud. Conf. Com. Rules Practice and Procedure, 1959-70, evidence rules adv. com., 1965-70; rep. Mich. Atty. Gens. Com. Ct. Congestion, 1959-60 Author: Trials and Appeals, 1957, Civil Justice and the Jury, 1962, Trial and Appellate Practice, 1968; Co-author: Introduction to Civil Procedures, 1949, Jurisdiction and Judgments, 1953, (with Delmar Karten) Trials and Appeals, 1971. Mem. charter rev. com. Ann Arbor Citizens Coun.cil, 1959-61; mem. Mich. Commn. Uniform State Laws, 1963-97; Mem. Ann Arbor City Coun.cil, 1955-59. Served tot lt. USAAF, 1942-45. Fellow Am. Bar Found. (chmn. 1977-78); mem. ABA (chmn. com. specialization 1952-56, spl. com. uniform evidence rules fed. cts. 1959-64, adv. bd. jour. 1961-67, spl. com. on specialization 1966-69, ethics com. 1961-70, council mem. sect. individual rights and responsibilities 1967-77, chairperson 1976-77), State Bar Mich. (pres. 1970-71, chmn. joint com. Mich. procedural revision 1956-62, commr. 1964—), Am. Judicature Soc. (chmn. publs. com. 1959-62), Am. Law Student Assn. (bd. govs.), Am. Law Inst., Scribes (pres. 1963-64)

JOINER, GARY DILLARD, cartographer, history educator, author; b. El Dorado, Ark., Aug. 30, 1951; s. Frank Dillard and Rudy Rachel Joiner; m. Marilyn Murrell Segura, Aug. 7, 1982. BA, La. Tech. U., 1973; postgrad., Lancaster (Eng.) U., 1999—, La. Tech. U., 2000—02. Pres. Precision Cartographics, Shreveport, La., 1982—; instr. history La. State U., Shreveport, 1996—, dir. Red River Regional Studies Ctr., 1999—. Author: (journal) Civil War Regiments, 1994, Red River Steamboats, 1999, Historic Shreveport-Bossier, 2000, One Damn Blunder from Beginning to End: The Red River Campaign - 1864; editor: Historians of the Western Theater of Civil War, 2000—. Pres. North La. Civil War Roundtable, Shreveport, 1994-98; bd. dirs. North La. Stroke Assn., Shreveport, 1998—; treas., bd. dirs. Oakland Cemetery Preservation Soc., Shreveport, 1999—; bd. dirs. McNeill Street Pumping Sta. Preservation Soc., Shreveport, 1998—. Mem. Mem. Am. Hist. Assn., Soc. Hist. Assn., Soc. for Mil. History, The Hist. Soc., North La. Hist. Soc. (bd. dirs. 1996—, jour. editor 2000—), DeSoto Parish Hist. Soc. (pres. Mansfield 2000—), Tarshar Soc. Methodist. Avocations: reading, travel, writing, archaeology. Home: 1039 Blanchard Pl Shreveport LA 71104 Office: La State U One University Pl Shreveport LA 71115 also: Precision Cartographics 1029 Blanchard Pl Shreveport LA 71104 Fax: 318-222-0662. E-mail: gjoiner@pilot.lsus.edu., gdjoiner@bellsouth.net.

JOINER, MICHAEL CHARLES, radiation biologist, researcher; b. London, July 3, 1954; s. Eric Charles and Doreen Elsie Joiner; m. Barbara Dixon, Sept. 13, 1985; children: Gregory Ian, Beth Imogen. MA, Cambridge U., England, 1976; PhD, London U., 1980. MRCR (Hon) Royal Coll. of Radiologists, 1999. Head, exptl. oncology Gray Cancer Inst., London, England, 1980—2001; leader, radiation biology program Wayne State U. and Karmanos Cancer Inst., Detroit, Mich., 2001—. Office: Wayne State Univ 4100 John R Detroit MI 48201-2013 Office Fax: 313-966-2659.

JOKL, ALOIS LOUIS, electrical engineer; b. Vienna, Mar. 16, 1924; came to the U.S., 1939; s. Samuel and Ernestine (Fischer) J.; m. Agnes Antoinette Wozniak, Dec. 29, 1951; children: Justine Ann, Martin Louis, James Anthony. B in Engring., U. So. Calif., 1944; PhD, U. Colo., 1973. Registered profl. engr., Va., N.Y. Elec. engr. Westinghouse Electric Corp., Buffalo, 1946-51; chief elec. engr. R&D div. Continental Motors Corp., Detroit, 1955-64; br. chief power tech. div. USA Belvoir RDE Ctr., Ft. Belvoir, Va., 1964-72, chief power generation div., 1972-88, sr. scientist logistics equipment, 1988-89; cons. Alexandria, Va., 1989—. Lectr. Cath. U. Am., Washington, 1981—; mem., chief U.S. delegation Quadripartite Working Group Elec. Power Sources, London, Auckland, New Zealand, 1983-89; judge Sch. Sci. Fairs, Alexandria, 1980-91. Contbr. articles to profl. jours. With U.S. Army, 1944-46, ETO. Mem. IEEE (sr. life), Sigma Xi (v.p. Belvoir chpt. 1983-85). Roman Catholic. Achievements include four patents; research in magnetic field calculations, electrical machinery design methods, waveform predictions. Home and Office: 2607 N Stevens St Alexandria VA 22311-1512 E-mail: ajokl@att.net.

JOKLIK, WOLFGANG KARL, biochemist, virologist, educator; b. Vienna, Nov. 16, 1926; s. Karl F. and Helene (Giessl) J.; m. Judith Vivien Nicholas, Apr. 9, 1955 (dec. Apr. 1975); children: Richard G., Vivien H.; m. Patricia Hunter Downey, Apr. 23, 1977. B.Sc. with 1st class honors, U. Sydney, Australia, 1948, M.Sc., 1949; D.Phil. (Australian Nat. U. scholar), U. Oxford, Eng., 1952. Australian Nat. U. research fellow, Copenhagen, Denmark, 1953, Canberra, Australia, 1954-56; fellow, 1957-62; assoc. prof. cell biology Albert Einstein Coll. Medicine, Bronx, N.Y., 1962-65, prof. cell biology, 1965-68, Siegfried Ullmann prof. biochem. virology, 1966-68; prof., chmn. dept. microbiology and immunology Duke U. Med. Ctr., Durham, N.C., 1968-92, James B. Duke Disting. prof. microbiology and immunology, 1972-92, James B. Duke prof. microbiology, 1992-96, James B. Duke prof. emeritus, 1996—. Sr. author: Zinsser Microbiology, 15th, 16th, 17th, 18th, 19th, 20th edits.; editor-in-chief Virology, 1975-93, Microbiological Rev., 1991-95; contbr. articles to profl. jours. Recipient Sr. U.S. award Alexander Humboldt Found., 1985, ICN Internat. prize for virology, 1991. Mem. NAS, Inst. Medicine of NAS, Am. Soc. Virology (pres. 1982-83), Am. Soc. Microbiology, Am. Soc. Biol. Chemists. Address: Duke U Med Ctr Dept Molecular Genetics and Microbiology PO Box 3020 Durham NC 27710-0001 E-mail: joklikb@aol.com.

JOLAS, BETSY, composer, educator; b. Paris, Aug. 5, 1926; d. Eugene and Maria (MacDonald) J.; m. Gabriel Illouz, Aug. 27, 1949; children: Frederic, Claire, Antoine. BA, Bennington Coll., 1946; student, Conservatoire Nat. Paris, 1946. Replaced Olivier Messiaen Paris Conservatory, 1971-74, prof. advanced analysis and composition, 1975—. Prof. composition Tanglewood, 1976-77, SUNY, Buffalo, 1976, Yale U., 1979, 82, Boston U., 1985, Darius Milhaud prof. Mills Colls., Fromm prof. Harvard, 1994; resident Am. Acad., Rome, 1999; Berlin Prize fellow Am. Acad. Berlin, 2000. Compositions include Points d'or for one saxophonist playing four saxophones and ensemble, 1982, Episode Sixiéme pour alto, 1983; Trois Duos Pour Tuba et Piano, 1983; O Wall, for wind quintet, 1976; Well Met, for ensemble, 1973; Tales of a Summer Sea, for orch., 1977, Stances, for piano and orch., 1978, Points D'Aube, for ensemble and viola solo; Preludes Fanfares Interludes Sonneries, for wind orch. and percussion, 1983; Trois Rencontres, for orch., 1973, Sonate á 12, for 12 voice soloists a capella, 1970; Motet II, for choir and orch., 1965; Caprice á deux voix, for soloists without accompaniment, 1978; Quatuor II for solo voice and string trio, 1964; Le pavillon au bord de la riviére, chamber opera in 4 acts, 1975; Le Cyclope, chamber opera in one act, 1986; Schliemann opera in 3 acts, 1989; Frauenleben 9 Lieder for viola and orch., 1992, Sigrancia Ballade for baritone and orch., 1995, Lumor 7 sacred lieder for saxophone and orch., 1996, Petite Symphonie Concertante for violin and orch., 1997, Quatvor VI avec clarinette, 1997, Sonate ā 8, for cello octet, 1998, Motet III, for 5 soloists, chorus and baroque orch., 1999, Trio Sopra, for clarinet, violin and piano, 2000, Concerto-Fantaisic, for piano and mixed chorus, 2001, Motet IV for soprano, flute, clarinet, violin, chello and harp, 2002; many recs.; contbr. articles to profl. jours. Performer French Radio, Paris, 1955-65. Decorated Officier de l'Ordre Nat. du Mérite, Commandeur des Arts et Lettres, chevalier de la Legion d'Honneur; recipient Internat. Conducting Competition prize, Besançon, 1953, Copley Found. Chgo. award, 1954, ORTF award, 1961, Am. Acad. Arts award, 1973, Grand Prix de la Music, 1974, Grand Prix de la Ville de Paris, 1981, Grand Prix de la SACEM, 1982, Koussevitsky Found. award, 1974, Prix Internat. Maurice Ravel, 1992, Personnalité de l'année, 1993, Prix SACEM de la Meilleure Création, 1994. Mem. Am. Acad. Arts and Letters, Am. Acad. Arts and Scis. Office: Conservatoire Nat Supérieur de Musique 209 Ave Jean Jaurés 75019 Paris France E-mail: betsyjolas@noos.fr.

JOLICOEUR, PAUL, molecular biologist; b. Beauceville, Que., Can., Jan. 4, 1945; s. Philippe Jolicoeur and Eva Rodrigue; m. Claudine Tremblay, Apr. 10, 1976. BA, Laval U., Que., 1964, MD, 1968, PhD, 1973. Intern Royal Victoria Hosp., Montreal, Que., Can., 1968-69; med. dir Lama-Kara Hosp. (SUCO), Togo, Africa, 1968-79; pvt. practice Gaspésie, P.Q., 1970; postdoctoral fellow MIT, Cambridge, 1973-76; dir. lab. molecular biology Clin. Rsch. Inst. Montreal, Que., 1976—. Contbr. articles to profl. jours. Recipient medal Lt. Gov. of Que., 1964. Mem. Med. Rsch. Coun. (study sect. 1978-81, Centennial fellow 1975-76), Nat. Cancer Inst. (study sect. 1982-84, 96-98, adv. com. on rsch. 1984-88), Royal Soc. Can. Home: 5296 Durocher Outremont QC Canada H2V 3Y1 Office: Montreal Inst Clin Rsch 110 W Ave des Pins Montreal QC Canada H2W 1R7 Fax: 514-987-5794.

JOLIE, ANGELINA, actress; b. L.A., June 4, 1975; d. Jon Voight and Marcheline Bertrand; m. Jonny Lee Miller, 1995, (div. Feb. 1999), Billy Bob Thonton, 2000, (div. 2003). 1 child: Maddox (adopted). Student, Strasberg Theatre Inst.; Grad. in Film, NYU. Actress. Former profl. model, London, N.Y., L.A. Actress: (films) Lara Croft Tomb Raider: The Cradle of Life, 2003, Life or Something Like It, 2002, Original Sin, 2001, Lara Croft: Tomb Raider, 2001, Gone in Sixty Seconds, 2000, Dancing in the Dark, 2000, Girl, Interrupted, 1999, The Bone Collector, 1999, Pushing Tin, 1999, Playing by Heart, 1998, Hell's Kitchen, 1998, Gia, 1998, Playing God, 1997, George Wallace, 1997, True Women, 1997, Love Is All There Is, 1996, Mojave Moon, 1996, Foxfire, 1996, Without Evidence, 1995, Hackers, 1995, Angela & Viril, 1993, Cyborg 2, 1993, Lookin' to Get Out, 1982; (music videos) Loaf, Meat, Lenny Kravitz, Antonello Venditti, The Lemonheads; actress five student films for U. So. Calif. Sch. of Cinema. Recipient BFCA award Best Supporting Actress: Girl, Interrupted, 2000; Oscar award for Girl, Interrupted, 1999, nominated Emmy award Outstanding Supporting Actress: George Wallace, 1998; recipient Golden Globe awards Best Performance Actress in a Supporting Role: Girl, Interrupted, 2000, Best Peformance Actress in a Mini-Series: Gia, 1999, George Wallace, 1998, L.A. Outfest award for Outstanding Actress: Gia, 1998, Nat. Bd. of Rev. award for Playing by Heart, 1998, Screen Actors Guild award, Gia, 1999. Avocations: collecting knives, mortuary sci. Office: William Morris Agency 151 El Camino Dr Beverly Hills CA 90212-3635*

JOLISSAINT, STEPHEN LACY, pathologist; b. Honolulu, Oct. 7, 1951; s. John Mire and Joyce Marie (Lacy)) J.; m. Belle Kamille Bowen, Dec. 29, 1988; children: Taylor Elise, Stephen Lacy Jr., Barrett Claire. BS, La. State U., Baton Rouge, 1973; MD, La. State U., New Orleans, 1976. Intern, then resident U.S. Army, Fitzsimons Army Med. Ctr., Aurora, Colo., 1976-80; staff pathologist U.S. Army, 1980-82; pathologist Pecot, Padgett & Jolissaint, APMC, Opelousas, La., 1982-97, Pathology Group of La., Baton Rouge, 1997—; staff pathologist Woman's Hosp. La., 1997—, Summit Hosp., 1997—; med. dir. SW Med. Ctr., 2000—. Fellow Am. Coll. Pathologists (keyperson 1986-88), Am. Soc. Clin. Pathology; mem. AMA (del. young physicians sect. 1986-91), La. Med. Soc. (del. 1985-88, 90-91, chmn. young physicians com. 1988-91), La. Pathology Soc., St. Landry Parish Med. Soc. (pres. 1985-86), Lafayette Parish Med. Soc., La. Thoroughbred Owners and Breeders Assn., Alpha Omega Alpha. Roman Catholic. Avocations: thoroughbred racing and breeding, saltwater fishing. Home: 134 N Emily Cir Lafayette LA 70508-5044 E-mail: sjolissaint@pathgroupla.com.

JOLLES, BERNARD, lawyer; b. N.Y.C., Oct. 5, 1928; s. Harry and Dora (Hirschorn) J.; m. Lenore Madison Jolles, Oct. 11, 1953 (div. Jan. 1984); children: Abbe, Jacqueline, Caroline. BA, N.Y.U., 1951; LLB, Lewis & Clark Coll., 1961. Bar: Oreg. 1963, U.S. Dist. Ct. Oreg. 1964, U.S. Dist. Ct. (no. dist.) Miss. 1968, U.S. Ct. Appeals (9th cir.) 1965, U.S. Supreme Ct. 1979. Assoc. Anderson Franklin Jones & Olsen, Portland, Oreg., 1963-68; ptnr. Franklin Olsen Bennett & Desbarsay, Portland, Oreg., 1968-79, Jolles Bernstein & Garone and predecessor firms Jolles Sokol & Bernstein, Portland, Oreg., 1979—. Editor: Damages, 1974. Bd. dirs. ACLU, Portland, Oreg., 1975—. Fellow Am. Coll. Trial Lawyers; mem. Oreg. State Bar Assn. (pres. 1986-87), Am. Inns of Ct. (sr. barrister 1985—). Avocations: cooking, reading. Office: Jolles & Bernstein 721 SW Oak St Fl 2 Portland OR 97205-3712

JOLLES, JANET K. PILLING, lawyer; b. Akron, Ohio, Sept. 5, 1951; d. Paul and Marjorie (Logue) Kavanaugh; m. Martin Jolles, Mar. 6, 1987; children: Madeleine Sloan Langdon Jolles, Jameson Samuel Rhys Jolles. BA, Ohio Wesleyan U., 1973; JD, U. Mo., 1976; LLM, Villanova U., 1985. Bar: Pa. 1976, U.S. Tax Ct. 1976, U.S. Dist. Ct. (ea. dist.) Pa. 1976, Ohio 1996. Atty. Schnader, Harrison, Segal & Lewis, Phila., 1976-83; gen. counsel Kistler-Tiffany Cos., Wayne, Pa., 1983-95; lawyer Janet Kavanaugh Pilling Jolles & Assocs., Berea, Ohio, 1996-99; v.p. First Union Trust Co., Wilmington, Del., 1999—2002, Wachovia Trust Co., Wilmington, 2002—. Mem. Estate Planning Coun. Del., Wilmington Tax Group, Phila. Estate Planning Coun., Estate Planning Coun. Cleve., Estate Planning Coun. Del. Mem.: ABA, Wilmington Women in Bus., Pa. Bar Assn., Phila. Bar Assn. (probate sect., tax sect.), Cuyahoga County Bar Assn., Cleve. Bar Assn., Ohio State Bar Assn., Berea Women's League, Phi Beta Kappa, Phi Delta Phi. Office: 3 Beaver Valley 4th Fl Wilmington DE 19803 E-mail: janet.jolles@wachovia.com., jjolleslaw@aol.com.

JOLLY, BRUCE DWIGHT, manufacturing company executive; b. Wheeling, W.Va., Aug. 27, 1943; s. Edward and Martha Elizabeth (Glass) J.; m. Alice Marie O'Beirne, May 25, 1974 (div. Sept. 1997); children— Mara O'Beirne, Brock Thomas; m. Anne Caroline Rist, Dec. 22, 2001. AB, Dartmouth Coll., 1965; MBA, U. Va., 1967. Systems engr. IBM Corp., Richmond, Va., 1967-68; fin. analyst Keystone Consol. Industries, Peoria, Ill., 1970-73; contr. HON Industries, Inc., Muscatine, Iowa, 1973-76, sec., treas., 1976-79; v.p. fin. Hawkeye Steel Products, Inc., Waterloo, Iowa, 1979-83, Cosco, Inc., Columbus, Ind., 1983-90; chief fin. officer Kiel Bros. Oil Co. Inc., Columbus, Ind., 1990-96; v.p. fin. Riverton Investment Corp., Winchester, Va., 1996—. With AUS, 1968-70, Vietnam. Decorated Bronze Star. Mem. Rotary, Phi Kappa Psi. Republican. Presbyterian. Home: 1420 Ramseur Ln Winchester VA 22601-6738 Office: Riverton Investment Corp 158 Front Royal Pike Ste 305 Winchester VA 22602-4324 E-mail: bdjolly@direcway.com.

JOLLY, BRUCE OVERSTREET, retired newspaper executive; b. Bay City, Tex., July 2, 1912; s. Irvin and Alice Gretchen (Overstreet) J.; m. Sarah Clark Tate Jeffress, Jan. 22, 1946; children: Bruce Overstreet, Jr., Edwin Jeffress. AB in English and Journalism, Franklin Coll., 1938. Reporter Indpls. News 1938-40, Post Tribune, Gary, Ind., 1940-42, 47-48; Washington corr. Daily News, Greensboro, N.C., 1949-65; with pub. rels. dept. So. Ry., Washington, 1965-72. Author: The First Hundred Years, 1977, Keeping Up With Yesterday, 1985, A Century of Progress, 1990, Travels With Barbara, 1992, Midst the Shifting Winds (The South and Civil Rights--Truman to Johnson, 1998, Billy Goat and The Twins, 2000; editor: The Brightness of His Presence, 1980. Pres. EBJ, Ltd., 2000; mem. planning commn. N.C. Tercentenary Celebration, 1962. With USAF, 1942-46, CBI. Recipient Cert. of Merit, State of N.C., 1963, alumni citation Franklin Coll., 1977. Mem. Nat. Press Club, Soc. of the South Pole (corr. Antartic 1963), Soc. Profl. Journalists, Arlington Knights of the Round Table (pres. 1982-83). Episcopalian. Avocations: golf, swimming, travel. Home: 4800 Fillmore Ave Apt 458 Alexandria VA 22311-5055

JOLLY, CHARLES NELSON, lawyer, pharmaceutical company executive; b. New Brunswick, N.J., Aug. 14, 1942; s. Nelson Frederick and Marie Mercedes (Montemayor) J.; m. Laurie Cherie Puryear, Feb. 5, 1992; children: T Christopher, Susan Noel. BS, Holy Cross Coll., 1964; LLB, George Washington U., 1967. Bar: D.C. 1968, Tenn. 1984. Atty. Swift & Co., 1966-70, Miles Labs. 1970-71, dir. legis. affairs, 1971-75, assoc. gen. counsel Elkhart, Ind., 1975-77, v.p., sec., gen. counsel, bd. dirs. Chattem Inc., Chattanooga, 1977-94; of counsel Baker, Donelson, Bearman, Caldwell & Spencer, Chattanooga, Tenn., 1999—. Cand. for U.S. Congress, 1994, 96; past bd. dirs. Sr. Neighbors of Chattanooga Inc., Tenn. Conservation League. Mem.: ABA, Van Buren County C. of C. (past bd. dirs.), BBB Chattanooga (past chmn., past bd. dirs.), Coun. Better Bus. Burs. U.S. (past bd. dirs.), Non-Prescription Drug Mfrs. Assn. (past bd. dirs. vice chmn. exec. com.), DC Bar Assn., Chattanooga Bar Assn., Tenn. Bar Assn. Chattanooga Retriever Club (past bd. dirs., past sec.), Mid. Tenn. Amateur Retriever Club (past sec.).

JOLLY, DANIEL EHS, dental educator; b. St. Louis, Aug. 25, 1952; s. Melvin Joseph and Betty Ehs (Koehler) Jolly; m. Paula Kay Haas, 1972 (div.); 1 child Farrell. BA in Biology and Chemistry, U. Mo., Kansas City, 1974, DDS, 1977. Resident in hosp. dentistry VA Med. Ctr., Leavenworth, Kans., 1977-78; pvt. practice Newcastle, Wyo., 1978-79; asst. prof. U. Mo., Kansas City, 1979-87; chief restorative dentistry Truman Med. Ctr., Kansas City, 1979-87; dir. dental oncology Trinity Luth. Hosp., 1982-87; assoc. prof., dir. gen. practice residency program Ohio State U., Columbus, 1987—, prof., dir. gen. practice residency program, 1993—. Dir. Honduras Clinic Project, 1992—; bd. dirs. Rinehart Found. U. Mo. Dental Sch., Kansas City, 1985—87; cons. Lee's Summit (Mo.) Care Ctr., 1984—87, Longview Nursing Ctr., Grandview, 1986—87; sec. Combined Hosp. Dental Staff, Columbus, 1989—90, v.p., 1990—91, pres. 1991—92. Author: (manual) Hospital Dental Hygiene, 1984, Hospital Dentistry, 1985, OSU Manual Hospital Dentistry, 1989—, (booklet) Nursing Home Dentistry, 1986, Dental Oncology, 1986. Mem. profl. adv. coun. Easter Seal Soc., 1986—92, sec. bd. dirs. Easter Seal Rehab. Ctr., 1990—93, mem. regional coun. Kansas City, 1985—87; pres. Health Profls. Serving Humanity. With U.S. Naval Sea Cadet Corps, 1998—99. Recipient Alumni Achievement award in dentistry, U. Mo., Kansas City, 1995. Fellow: Pierre Fauchard Acad., Am. Coll. Dentistry, Acad. Dentistry Handicapped (pres. 1992), Am. Assn. Hosp. Dentists (regional v.p. 1993—, sec., pres.-elect 2002—03, pres. 2003—), Am. Soc. Dentistry Children, Acad. Gen. Dentistry, Am. Soc. Geriatric Dentistry, Acad. Dentistry Internat.; mem.: ADA, Ohio Dental Assn. (Humanitarian award 1998), Internat. Soc. Oral Oncology, S.W. Oncology Group, Fedn. Spl Care Orgns. Dentistry (chmn. 1992—93), Greater Kansas City Dental Soc., Internat. Assn. Dentistry handicapped (pres. 1994—96, past pres. 1996—98, editor 1998—), Magna Charta Barons Club. Avocations: photography, skiing, scuba diving, swimming, horses. Home: 1601 W Fifth Ave # 118 Columbus OH 43212-2310 Office: Ohio State U Coll Dentistry PO Box 182357 305 W 12th Ave Columbus OH 43218-2357 E-mail: jolly.4@osu.edu.

JOLLY, E. GRADY, federal judge; b. Oct. 3, 1937; BA, U. Miss., 1959, LLB, 1962. Trial atty. NLRB, Winston-Salem, NC, 1962—64; asst. U.S. atty. No. Dist. Miss., 1964—67; trial atty. Dept. Justice Tax Div., Washington, 1967—69; pvt. practice Jolly, Miller & Milam, Jackson, Miss., 1969—82; judge U.S. Ct. Appeals (5th cir.), Jackson, 1982—. Office: James O Eastland US Courthouse 245 E Capitol St Rm 202 Jackson MS 39201*

JOLLY, WILLIAM THOMAS, foreign language educator; b. Helena, Ark., Apr. 8, 1929; s. Sidney Eugene and Eva (Jones) J. BA, Southwestern at Memphis, 1952; MA, U. Miss., 1958; PhD, Tulane U., 1968. Assoc. ancient langs., chmn. dept. Millsaps Coll., Jackson, Miss., 1959-65; assoc. prof. Greek and Latin Rhodes Coll., Memphis, 1965-75, prof., 1975-94, chmn. dept. fgn. langs., 1975-79, prof. emeritus, 1994—. With USN, 1953-55. Recipient Clarence Day award Day Found., 1991. Mem. Am. Philol. Assn/, Linquistic Soc. Am., Archaeol. Inst. Am., Classical Assn. Mid. West & South, Tenn. Classical Assn., Tenn. Philol. Assn., Am. Classical Legue. Democrat. Methodist. Home: 697 University St Memphis TN 38107-5138 Office: Rhodes Coll. 2000 N Parkway Memphis TN 38112-1690

JONARIS, GEORGE G. electrical engineer, computer engineer; b. Cairo, Feb. 2, 1962; s. Jonaris G Kreiz, Nawal L Morcos; m. Lily M. Iskander, June 10, 1995; children: Claire children: Christine. PhD, N.C. State U., 1992. Sr. software engineer Cadence Design Systems, San Jose, 1992—99, project leader, 1999—. Recipient Student Achievement award, Syndicate of Engineers, Cairo, Egypt, 1984. Mem.: IEEE, Toastmasters Internat., Phi Kappa Phi. Achievements include patents for circuit layout technique with template-driven placement using Fuzzy logic. Office: Cadence Design Systems 555 River Oaks Pkwy San Jose CA 95134

JONAS, GARY FRED, philanthropy executive; b. N.Y.C., Apr. 26, 1945; s. Otto and Hilde (Levy) Jonas; m. Rosalyn Ethel Levy; children: Lauren, Rachel. BS in Ops. Rsch., Columbia U., 1966; MBA, Harvard U., 1968. Mgmt. cons. Fry Cons., Washington, 1968-69; div. dir. Univ. Rsch. Corp. Ctr. Human Svcs., Chevy Chase, Md., 1970-73, exec. v.p., 1973-75, pres., chief exec. officer, 1975-85, chmn., chief exec. officer, 1985-88, also bd. dirs.; pres., chief operating officer The Earle Palmer Brown Cos., Bethesda, Md., 1988-93, also bd. dirs.; pres., CEO 20/20 Laser Ctrs., Inc., Bethesda, 1993-97, also bd. dirs.; exec. v.p., dir. TLC Laser Eye Ctrs., Inc., Bethesda, 1997-2000; mng. ptnr. Venture Philanthropy Ptnrs., Inc., Reston, Va., 2000—02; CEO Strategic Philanthropic Advisors, LLC, 2002—; pres. Alase Laser Hair Removal Ctrs., 2002—. Pres. Alase Laser Hair Removal Ctrs., Vienna, 2002—; faculty assoc. Johns Hopkins U., 1999—. Contbr. articles to profl. jours. Mem.: Young Pres.'s Orgn. (exec. com., chmn. Washington metro chpt. 1987—88), Washington Bd. Trade, Am. Soc. Tng. and Devel., Conf. Bd., Nat. Contract Mgmt. Assn., Profl. Svcs. Coun. (past bd. dirs., v.p.), Inst. Mgmt. Cons. (cert.), Woodmont Country Club, Harvard Club. Home: 6716 Melody Ln Bethesda MD 20817-3115 E-mail: gary@jonas.com.

JONAS, GILBERT, public relations and fund raising executive; b. July 22, 1930; s. Harry and Mitzi (Rosenstein) J.; m. Barbara L. Selby, Sept. 1953 (div. Nov. 1961); 1 child, Susan; m. P. Joyce Theise, Dec. 27, 1964; children: Jillian, Stephanie. BA, Stanford U., 1951; grad. cert. Chinese studies, Columbia U., 1953, MA in Internat. Affairs, 1955. Pub. rels. counsel African Independence movements and East Asian govts., 1955-67; exec. sec. Am. Friends of Vietnam, N.Y.C., 1956-57; v.p. Harold L. Oram, Inc., N.Y.C., 1958-61; exec. sec. Am. Med. Ctr. for Burma, N.Y.C., 1959-61; cons., acting dir. Far East, Peace Corps, Washington, 1961; pres., owner Gilbert Jonas Co., Inc., N.Y.C., 1962—2003. Author: One Shining Moment--A History of the Student World Federalist Movement, 1942-1953, 2000. Dir. pub. info. N.Y. Youth for Stevenson, 1956; mem. exec. com. N.Y. Com. for Dem. Voters, 1959-62; pres. Reform Ind. Dem. of N.Y., 1958-59; mem. civil rights staff Nat. Citizens for Kennedy-Johnson, 1960; devel. and pub. rels. counsel NAACP, 1965-95, mem. exec. com. Mid-Manhattan br., 1997-2000, life mem.; mem. steering c om. N.Y. Citizens for Humphrey-Muskie, 1968; nat. coord. Charles Evers for Gov. Miss., 1971; co-founder N.Y.C. Reform Movement, Dem. party, 1958-63; bd. dirs. Am. Com. on Africa, 1955-59, League Indsl. Democracy, 1972-91, Harlem Youth Devel. Found., 1998—; nat. coord. Holy Land Conservation Fund, 1977-82; cons. Internat. Civil Rights Ctr. and Mus., Greensboro, N.C., 1996-97, Chinese Dissidents; founding bd. mem., treas. The Wei Jingsheng Found., 1998-2002; chmn. World Federalist Assn. Greater Metro N.Y., 2001-2002; mem. nat. bd. World Federalist Assn., 2002-; mem. coun. World Federalist Movement, 2001-. With U.S. Army, 1953-55. Recipient Ann. Freedom award Miss. NAACP, 1970, Ann. Humanitarian award Manhattan NAACP, 1989. Mem. Phi Beta Kappa, Sigma Delta Chi. Home: 215 E 80th St Apt 5L New York NY 10021-0545 E-mail: partisanme@aol.com.

JONAS, HARRY S. medical education consultant; b. Kirksville, Mo., Dec. 3, 1926; s. Harry S. and Sarah (Laird) J.; m. Connie Kirby, Aug. 6, 1949; children— Harry S., III, William Reed, Sarah Elizabeth. BA, Washington U., St. Louis, 1949, MD, 1952. Intern St. Luke's Hosp., St. Louis, 1952-53; resident Barnes Hosp., St. Louis, 1952-56; practiced medicine specializing in ob-gyn., Independence, Mo., 1956-74; prof. ob-gyn, chmn. dept. ob-gyn Truman Med. Center; asst. dean U. Mo-Kansas City Sch. Medicine, 1975-78, dean, 1978-87, med. edn. cons., 2000—, spl. cons. to the dean; asst. v.p. med. edn. AMA, Chgo., 1987-2000. Mem. Independence City Council, 1964-68; mem. Jackson County (Mo.) Legislature, 1973-74. Mem. ACOG (pres. 1986-87), Ctrl. Assn. Obstetricians and Gynecologists, Assn. Profs. Gynecology and Obstetrics, Assn. Am. Med. Colls., A.C.S., AMA, Mo. Med. Assn., Jackson County Med. Soc., Kansas City Gynecol. Soc., Chgo. Gynecol. Soc. Home: 207 NW Spruce St Lees Summit MO 64064-1430 Office: U Mo-Kansas City Sch Medicine 2411 Holmes St Kansas City MO 64108-2741

JONAS, JIRI, chemist, educator; b. Prague, Czechoslovakia, Apr. 1, 1932; s. Frantisek and Jirlna (Vondrak) Jonas; m. Ana M. Masiulis, June 1, 1968. BSc, Tech. U. Prague, 1956; PhD, Czechoslovak Acad Sci., 1960; D (honoris causa) (hon.), U. Rio de Janeiro. Research assoc. Inst. Organic Chemistry, Czechoslovak Acad. Sci., Prague, 1960-63; vis. scientist, dept. chemistry U. Ill., Urbana, 1963-65, from asst. to assoc. prof., 1966-72, prof., 1972—2001, prof. Ctr. for Advanced Study, 1996-2001, prof. emeritus, 2001—, sr. staff mem. Materials Research Lab., 1970-93, dir. sch. chem. scis., 1983-93, dir. Beckman Inst. Advanced Sci. and Tech., 1993—2001, dir. emeritus, 2001—. Mem. editl. bd. Jour. Magnetic Resonance, 1975—2000, Jour. Chem., 1980—83, Jour. Chem. Physics, 1986—89, Accts. Chem. Rsch., 1990—93, Ann. Rev. Phys. Chemistry, 1991—95; contbr. articles to profl. jours. Recipient U.S. Sr. Scientist award, Alexander von Humboldt Found., 1988; Alfred P. Sloan fellow, 1967—69, J. S. Guggenheim fellow, 1972—73, Sr. scholar, U. Ill., 1985—88. Fellow: AAAS, Am. Phys. Soc., Am. Acad. Arts and Scis.; mem.: NAS, Materials Rsch. Soc., Am. Chem. Soc. (assoc. editor. Jour. Am. Chem. Soc., Joel Henry Hildebrand award 1983), Am. Philos. Soc., NBTC Club (Naples, Fla.), U. Ill. Tennis Club. Roman Catholic. Office: Univ of Ill 166 Roger Adams Lab 600 S Mathews Urbana IL 61801 E-mail: j-jonas@uiuc.edu.

JONAS, MANFRED, historian, educator; b. Mannheim, Germany, Apr. 9, 1927; came to U.S., 1937, naturalized, 1944; s. Walter and Antonie (Dannheiser) J.; m. Nancy Jane Greene, July 19, 1952; children: Andrew Miles, Kathryn Leslie, Emily Susan, Matthew Greene. BS, CCNY, 1949; A.M., Harvard U., 1950; PhD (Teaching fellow), Harvard, 1959. Mil. intelligence analyst U.S. Dept. Def., 1951-54; teaching fellow Harvard, 1954-59; vis. prof. Am. history Free U., Berlin, 1959-62; asso. prof. PMC Colls., 1962-63; faculty Union Coll., Schenectady, 1963-96, dir. grad. program Am. studies, 1964-74, prof. history, 1967-81, chmn. dept. history, 1970-81, chmn. div. social sci., 1971-74, Washington Irving prof. modern lit. and hist. studies, 1981-86, John Bigelow prof. history, 1986-96, prof. emeritus, 1996—, chmn. div. social sci., 1971-74. Lectr. CCNY, 1950, U. Md. Extension, 1954, Northeastern U., 1958; dir. NDEA Insts. for Advanced Study in History, 1966-68; cons. U.S. Office Edn., 1966, NEH, 1985; sr. Fulbright-Hays lectr. U. Saarland, Germany, 1973; Charles Warren fellow Harvard U., 1977-78; Salgo vis. prof. Eötvös Lorand U., Budapest, 1983-84. Author: Die Unabhängigkeitserklärung der Vereinigten Staaten, 1964, Isolationism in America, 1935-41, 1966, 90, American Foreign Relations in the Twentieth Century, 1967, The United States and Germany, 1984; co-editor: Roosevelt and Churchill: Their Secret Wartime Correspondence, 1975, 90, New Opportunities in a New Nation, 1982; editorial bd. Diplomatic History, 1980-83; contbr. articles profl. jours. Mem. N.Y. State Regents Exam. Com. in Am. History, 1970-87; moderator Forum 17 WMHT-TV, 1965; bd. dirs. Freedom Forum, Inc., 1965-76, chmn., 1969-70, 75-76. Served with USNR, 1945-46. Mem. Am. Hist. Assn., Orgn. Am. Historians, Soc. for Historians Am. Fgn. Relations, AAUP (pres. chpt. 1969-71, chair conf. com. 1988-93), Phi Beta Kappa (pres. Alpha chpt. N.Y. 1990-92, 93-95), Phi Alpha Theta. Home: 33 Front St Schenectady NY 12305-1301 E-mail: jonasm@union.edu.

JONAS, RICHARD ANDREW, medical educator; b. Adelaide, South Australia, Nov. 28, 1951; came to US, 1982; s. Lyall Richard Jonas; m. Dianne E. Wearne, Apr. 12, 1980 (div. May 1996); children: Andrew William, Michael Richard; m. Katherine Vernot, Nov. 6, 1999; 1 child, Nicole Sofia. MBBS with honors, U. Adelaide, 1974; MA, Harvard U., 1994. Gen. surgery resident Royal Melbourne Hosp., Australia, 1975-79; cardiac surgery resident Green Ln. Hosp., Auckland, New Zealand, 1980-82; resident in cardiac surgery Brigham & Women's Hosp., Boston; surg. fellow Brighmam and Women's Hosp., Boston, 1982-83; chief resident in cardiac surgery Children's Hosp., Boston, 1983-84; prof. surgery Harvard Med. Sch., Boston, 1994—; chief of cardiac surgery Children's Hosp., Boston, 1994—. Author: Cardiopulmonary Bypass in Neonates and Infants, 1994, Brain Injury and Cardiac Surgery, 1995. Fellow ACS, Soc. of Neurosci.; mem. Am. Assn. of Thoracic Surgery v.p., Soc. of Thoracic Surgery, Am. Surg. Assn. Episcopalian. Avocations: snow skiing, mountain trekking. Office: Dept Cardiac Surgery Children's Hosp 300 Longwood Ave Boston MA 02115-5724 E-mail: richard.jonas@tch.harvard.edu.

JONAS, RUTH HABER, psychologist; b. Tel Aviv, Aug. 24, 1935; d. Fred S. and Dorothy Judith (Bernstein) Haber; m. Saran Jonas, Sept. 16, 1956; children: Elizabeth, Frederick. AB, Barnard Coll., 1957; MA, New Sch. for Social Rsch., 1977, PhD, 1987; grad. psychotherapy and psychoanalysis, NYU, 1996. Lic. psychologist, N.Y. 1st and 2d yr. intern clin. psychology NYU Med. Ctr.-Bellevue Hosp., N.Y.C., 1985-87; postdoctoral rsch. fellow NYU Med. Ctr., N.Y.C., 1987-88; clin. instr. psychiatry NYU Sch. Medicine, N.Y.C., 1987, clin. asst. prof. psychiatry, 1991; sr. psychologist forensic svc. Bellevue Hosp., N.Y.C., 1988—; pvt. practice psychology N.Y.C., 1988—. Fellow Am. Orthopsychiat. Assn.; mem. APA, N.Y. State Psychol. Soc., Manhattan Psychol. Assn., Am. Heart Assn. (fellow stroke coun.). Office: 200 E 33d St Ste 10B New York NY 10016-4827

JONAS, SARAN, neurologist, educator; b. N.Y.C., June 24, 1931; s. Myron and Margaret (Wurmfeld) J.; m. Ruth Haber, Sept. 16, 1956; children: Elizabeth Ann, Frederick Jonathan. BS, Yale U., 1952; MD, Columbia U., 1956. Diplomate Am. Bd. Psychiatry and Neurology, Am. Bd. Internal Medicine. Intern Bellevue Hosp., N.Y.C., 1956-57, resident and fellow in medicine and neurology, 1957-62; practice medicine specializing in neurology N.Y.C., 1964—; from clin. instr. to assoc. prof. clin. neurology NYU Sch. Medicine, 1964-77, prof. clin. neurology, 1977—, acting chmn. dept. neurology, 1987-91. Assoc. dir. neurology NYU Hosp., 1970-87, dir., 1987-91, dir. electroencephalography, 1969-94; acting dir. neurology Bellevue Hosp., N.Y.C., 1987-91, assoc. dir., 1991—, dir. electroencephalography, 1994—. Served with USN, 1962-64. N.Y. State fellow in rheumatic diseases, 1962-64 Mem. Am. Acad. Neurology, Assn. for Rsch. in Nervous and Mental Diseases, Am. Heart Assn. (Stroke Coun., Epidemiology Coun.), Am. Epilepsy Soc. Office: 530 1st Ave New York NY 10016-6402

JONAS, STEPHEN P. investment company executive; b. 1953; BA in Math. magna cum laude, Boston U., 1974, MBA with highest honors, 1975. CFO, Graphic Sys., Inc., Hudson, N.H., 1975-78; from head of fin. to divsn. CFO, Wang Labs., Lowell, Mass., 1978-87; v.p. fin. investor info. svcs. Fidelity Investments, Boston, 1987, various fin. mgmt. positions, sr. v.p., CFO Personal Investments and Brokerage Group, sr. v.p., CFO, 1998—. Office: Fidelity Investments 82 Devonshire St Boston MA 02109

JONAS, STEVEN, public health physician, health policy analyst, writer; b. N.Y.C., Nov. 22, 1936; s. Harold Jacob and Florence Jane (Kyzor) J.; m. Josephine Gear, June 19, 1964 (div.); m. Linda Sue Friedman, Nov. 23, 1971 (div.); children: Jacob Henry, Lillian Sara. BA cum laude, Columbia Coll., 1958; MD, Harvard U., 1962; MPH, Yale U., 1967; MS, NYU, 1997. Diplomate Am. Bd. Preventive Medicine-Pub. Health. Intern Lenox Hill Hosp., N.Y.C., 1962-63; postdoctoral rschr. Univ. Coll. London and London Sch. Econs., 1963-65, resident in preventive medicine and pub. health, 1965—67; dist. health officer, 1967-68; dir. ambulatory care planning and devel., 1969; dir. dept. social medicine Morrisania City Hosp., Bronx, NY, 1969-71; asst. prof. Albert Einstein Coll. Medicine, Bronx, 1969—71; lectr. Mt. Sinai Sch. Medicine, N.Y.C., 1969-89, asst. prof. dept. cmty. medicine, 1971—74; coord. ambulatory svcs. Univ. Hosp., 1971-74, assoc. prof. dept. cmty. and preventive medicine, 1974-83; prof. dept. preventive medicine SUNY Stony Brook Sch. Medicine, 1983—; attending physician Nassau County Med. Ctr., East Meadow, NY, 1973-86. Cons. dept. medicine Winthrop-U. Hosp., Mineola, N.Y., 1979-93; adj. assoc. prof. Columbia U. Sch. Architecture, 1977-79; adj. assoc. prof. med. edn. Tex. Coll. Osteo. Medicine, Ft. Worth, 1980-85; adj. prof. legal edn. Touro Coll. Sch. of Law, Huntington, N.Y., 1998—; mem. N.Y. State Bd. Medicine, 1979-88. Author: Quality Control of Ambulatory Care: A Task for Health Departments, 1977, Medical Mystery: The Training of Doctors in the United States, 1978, Triathloning for Ordinary Mortals, 1986, revised, 1999, An Introduction to the U.S. Health Care System, 5th edit., 2003, The New Americanism, 1992, Take Control of Your Weight, 1993, Regular Exercise: A Handbook for Clinical Practice, 1995, The Essential Triathlete, 1996, Talking About Health and Wellness with Patients, 2000; editor, co-author: Health Care Delivery in the United State (Book of Yr. award Am. Jour. Nursing 1982), 1977, 81, 86, co-editor, 1999, 2002, Health Promotion and Disease Prevention in Clinical Practice, 1996; co-author: Pacewalking: The Balanced Way to Aerobic Health, 1988, The "I Don't Eat (But I Can't Lose)" Weight-Loss Program, 1989, Just the Weigh You Are, 1997, Help Your Man Get Healthy, 1999, 30 Secrets of the World's Healthiest Cuisines, 2000; chief editor: (Springer series) Health Care and Society, 1976-79, Medical Education, 1978-2000; mem. editl. bd. Preventive Medicine, 1983—, ACSM's Health & Fitness Jour., 1999—, Am. Jour. of Preventive Medicine, 1987-99; book rev. editor Am. Jour. Preventive Medicine, 1991-92; mem. editl. bd. Am. Med. Athletic Assn. Quarterly, 1988—, columnist, 1999—, editor-in-chief (J), 2002-; staff writer, Am. TRI, 2002-; contbr. articles to profl. jours.; reviewer in field. Sr. advisor U.S. Preventive Svcs. Task Force, 1984-89. Fellow Am. Pub. Health Assn., Am. Coll. Preventive Medicine (con. chmn. 1979-82), N.Y. Acad. Medicine (med. edn. com. 1983-92); mem. AMA, Am. Hosp. Assn. (life), Assn. Am. Med. Colls., Profl. Ski Instrs. Am. (cert. level I 1995), Assn. Tchrs. Preventive Medicine (pres. 1977-78), NYS Bd. Med. (1977-87), Phi Beta Kappa. Democrat. Jewish. Avocations: cycling, pacewalking and running, weight lifting, triathlon competition, skiing. Home: 105 Washington Ave Port Jefferson Station NY 11777-2003 Office: SUNY Sch Med Stony Brook NY 11794 E-mail: sjonas@notes.cc.sunysb.edu.

JONAS, TONY, television executive; Dir. dramatic series Aaron Spelling Prodns.; v.p. dramatic series and long form programming MGM/UA TV Group; sr. exec. in charge of devel. Winkler/Rich Prodns., Paramount; v.p. devel. Disney TV; sr. v.p. drama devel. Warner Bros. TV (previously Lorimar TV), 1989-91, exec. v.p. creative affairs, 1991-95, pres., 1995-98, Tony Jonas Prodns., Burbank, Calif., 1999—. Office: Tony Jonas Prodns Bldg 34 Rm 100 4000 Warner Blvd Burbank CA 91522-0001

JONASSAINT, JEAN, French and Francophone literatures educator; MA in Lit. Studies, U. Que., Montreal, 1981; PhD in French Studies, U. Montreal, 1990. Sr. lectr. U. Que., Montreal, 1979-96; cultural adviser City of Montreal, 1988-95; asst. prof. French and francophone lit. Duke U., Durham, N.C. Literary commentator News Paper, Le Devoir, Montreal, 1991-92. Author: La Déchirure du texte et autres brèches, 1984, Le Pouvoir des mots, les maux du pouvoir. Des romanciers haïtiens de l'exil, 1986, Des romans de tradition haïtienne. Sur un récit tragique, 2002; editor, guest editor De l'autre littérature québécoise Autoportraits, supplement Lettres Québécoises, 1992; editor, pub. Dérives, 1975-87; mem. assoc. editors bd. Nepantla: Views from South; mem. reading and evaluation com. Jour. Études Francophones; contbr. articles to profl. jours. Rsch. grantee Can. Coun. for the Arts Explorations, 1981, Can. Coun. for the Arts, 1986, Sec. State Can./Multiculturalism, 1994-95, Trent Found., Duke U., 2000; PhD fellow Fonds Formation Chercheur et Action Concertée, 1983-85. Mem. MLA, Conseil Internat. d'etudes Francophones, Am. Comparative Lit. Assn., Assn. des éditeurs de périodiques culturels québécois (pres. 1979-80). Office: Duke Univ Romance Studies Box 90257 Durham NC 27708-0257 Office Fax: 919-684-4029. E-mail: /jonj1996/@duke.edu.

JONASSEN, GAYLORD D. computer company executive, new products and market development; b. East Orange, N.J., Oct. 13, 1932; s. Jonas M. and Alma M. (Stelter) Jonassen; m. Shirley Ann Christophel, June 15, 1956; children: Glenn, Brenda. BSME, Ariz. State U., 1960. Cert. profl. cons. Devel. engr. Motorola Semiconductor, Phoenix, 1956—60; plant and facilities rsch. and devel. engr. Western Electric, N.Y.C., 1960—65; new products mgr. Deutsch Relays, L.I., NY, 1965—67; new product mktg., sales mgr. Kinemotive Corp., Farmingdale, NY, 1967—69; divsn. mgr. Atlantic Sci. Corp., Plainview, NY, 1969—70; exec. v.p., tech. dir. Telecomm. Industries, Inc., Copaigue, NY, 1970—73; founder, pres. Internat. Protein Industries, Inc., Hauppauge, NY, 1973—84, chmn. bd., 1973—84; mgmt. cons. Gaylor Jonassen Assocs., 1984—85; computer sys. engring. project engring. program mgmt. Norden Sys. UTC, 1985—91, Gaylord D. Jonassen/Group, 1991—; founder, pres. Scan-trol Sys., Inc., 1997—. Contbr. articles to various publs. Served with USN, 1950—54. Recipient Disting. Achievement award, Coll. Engring. and Applied Sci., Ariz. State U., 1982; fellow, ASTM, 1958. Mem.: L.I. Assn. Commerce and Industry. Achievements include patents in field. Home: 1293 Poplar St East Earl PA 17519-0271

JONASSEN, JAMES O. architect; b. Aberdeen, Wash., July 23, 1940; s. James E. and Marjorie E. (Smith) J.; m. Patricia E. Glen, June 9, 1958 (div. Oct. 1975); m. Marilyn Joan Kampa, June 11, 1977; children: Christian A., Steven E. BArch, U. Wash., 1964; MS in Architecture, Columbia U., 1965. Registered architect Ala., Alaska, Ariz., Calif., Colo., Fla., Ga., Idaho, Ill., Kans., La., Minn., Mo., Mont., Nebr., Nev., N.Mex., N.C., Ohio, Okla., Oreg., S.D., Tex. Wash., Utah., Wis., D.C., Del. Mass. Miss., N.H., N.Y., R.I., Vt., P.R., British Columbia, Can. Designer NBBJ Group, Seattle, 1965-70, ptnr., 1970—; CEO NBBJ West, 1983-96, mng. ptnr., 1997—. Bd. dirs. Health Insights Found. Prin works include Bettelle Meml. Lab., Richland, Wash., 1965 (lab of yr. award 1968), Heath Profl. Bldg., 1970, Children's Orthopedic Hosp., Seattle, 1972 (AIA Honor award 1976), St. Mary's Hosp., Surg. Pavilion, Rochester, Minn., 1982, St. Vincent Med. Office Bldg., Portland, Oreg., 1983, Scottsdale Meml. Hosp. N., Ariz., 1984, Seattle VA Hosp., 1985, Stanford U. Hosp., 1986, St. Joseph Host. Med. Ctr., 1988, Providence Med./ Ctr., Seattle, 1990 (AIA Merit award), David Grant Med. Ctr., Fairfield, Calif., 1986 (USAF Honor award 1989, Spl. citation DOD 1988, Type i Honor award USAF 1989, Excellence in Design award DOD 1991), Alaska Native Med. Ctr., 1997, Kangbuk Med. Ctr., Seoul, Korea, 1998, Capital Coast Health Med. Ctr., Wellington, New Zealand, 2000. Bd. dirs. Health Facilities Rsch. and Edn. Project, 1991—98, Swedish Med. Ctr. Found., 1993—, Sch. Zone Inst., 1990—; pres.bd. Architecture and Children project, 1990; mem. vis. com. U. Washington Sch. Medicine, 2001—. Recipient Seattle Newsmaker Tomorrow award, Time Mag., 1978, Modern Health Care award, Swedish Med. Ctr., 1997—2000, Seattle Archtl. Found. Bd., 2000—; fellow fellow, Naramore Found., 1969; scholar Columbia U. shcolar, 1964. Fellow AIA (chmn. steering com. 1983-85, nat. com. architecture for health, mem. Nat. Life Cycle Task Force 1977, bd. dirs. Seattle chpt. 1985-87, Modern Healthcare award 1998); mem. Sr. Coun. Archs. (pres. 1999, 2000), Wash. Athletic Club, Columbia Tower Club, Rotary. Office: NBBJ 111 S Jackson St Seattle WA 98104-2881

JONASSON, RALPH GEORGE, research chemist; b. Hamilton, Ont., Can., July 8, 1957; s. Werner and Cecilia (Liedtke) Jonasson. BSc, McMaster U., Hamilton, 1980; PhD, U. Western Ont., London, Can., 1986. Postdoctoral fellow McMaster U., Hamilton, 1986-87, rsch. assoc., 1987-88; rsch. officer Alta. Rsch. Coun., Edmonton, Can., 1989-98; rsch. chemist Vulcan Performance Chems., Columbus, Ga., 1998—2002. Author: (book chpt.) Advances in Lignocellulosics Characterization, 1999; inventor in field; contbr. articles to profl. jours. Mem. AAAS, Internat. Assn. Water Quality (reviewer 1998-2001), Chem. Inst. Can. (chair Edmonton local sect. 1996, past chair Edmonton local sect. 1997), Am. Chem. Soc., Royal Soc. Chemistry, Geochem. Soc. Avocations: history, philosophy, silviculture, wine appreciation. Home: 62 Juanita Dr Hamilton ON Canada L9C 2G3

JONCKHEERE, ALAN MATHEW, physicist; b. Howell, Mich., Feb. 12, 1947; s. August Peter and Elizabeth Gertrude (Nash) Jonckheere; m. Barbara Jean Minter, Aug. 16, 1969; children: Jessica, Susan, Laura Jean and Amanda Jean (twins). BS, Mich. State U., 1969; MS, U. Wash., 1970, PhD, 1976. Instr. physics dept. Fermi Nat. Accelerator Lab., Batavia, Ill., 1976-78, staff physicist, 1978—, assoc. dept. head meson dept., 1981-83, assoc. dept. head exptl. areas, 1983-84, Beams group coordinator, 1984-85, accelerator div. exptl. support dept., 1985-89, researcher div. D0 dept., 1989—. Researcher elem. particle physics Stanford Linear Accelerator Ctr., Lawrence Berkeley Lab., Calif. Contbr. papers to physics publs. Office: Fermi Natl Accelerator Lab PO Box 500 Batavia IL 60510-0500 E-mail: Jonckheere@fnal.gov.

JONDAHL, TERRI ELISE, importing and distribution company executive; b. Ukiah, Calif., May 6, 1959; d. Thomas William and Rebecca (Stewart) J. AA in Bus. Adminstrn., Mendocino Coll., 1981; BA in Adminstrn. and Mgmt., Columbia Pacific U., 1993. Office systems analyst County of Mendocino, Ukiah, 1980-83; micro systems analyst Computerland of Annapolis, Md., 1983-84; controller Continental Mfg. Inc., Nacogdoches, Tex., 1984-87, mktg. mgr., 1987-89, dir. sales and mktg., 1989-95; exec. v.p., chief oper. officer CAB Inc., Oakwood, Ga., 1995—2002; CEO Cab Inc., 2002—. Co-author: National Federation of Business & Professional Women Local Organization Revitalization Plan, 1989. Mem. Hall Co. C. of C. Mem.: NAFE, Am. Bus. Women's Assn., Ukiah Bus. and Profl. Women (pres. 1981—82), Nacogdoches Bus. and Profl. Women (pres. 1987—88), Tex. Fedn. Bus. and Profl. Women (state pres. 1994—95), Gwinnett County C. of C. (CEO exec. roundtable), Nacogdoches County C. of C. (small bus. adv. com. 1990). Home: 6344 Green Oak Rdg Flowery Branch GA 30542-6630 Office: CAB Inc 4161 Chamblee Rd Oakwood GA 30566-3518 E-mail: tjondahl@cabinc.com.

JONES, A. ELIZABETH, federal agency administrator; married; 2 children. BA in history, Swarthmore Coll., 1970; studied Arabic, in Beirut, Tunis and Cairo, 1975—77; in Internat. Rels., Boston U., 1986. Joined Fgn. Svc., 1970; fgn. svc. post Kabul, Afghanistan, 1971—72; pub. affairs officer Near East and South Asia Bur., 1972—73; polit. officer, 1973—75, Amman, Jordan, 1977—79; dep. prin. officer U.S. Interests Sect., Baghdad, Iraq, 1979—80; dep. chief mission Islamabad, Pakistan, 1988—92; Lebanon desk officer, 1981—83; dep. dir. for Lebanon, Jordan, Syria, and Iraq, 1983—84; head econ./comml. sect. U.S. Mission, West Berlin, 1985—88; dep. chief mission Bonn, Germany, 1992—93; exec. asst. Sec. of State, 1993—94; amb. Rep. of Kazakhstan, 1995—98; prin. dep. asst. sec. bus. Near Eastern Affairs U.S. State Dept., 1998—2000; sr. advisor Caspian Basin Energy Diplomacy, 2000—01; asst. sec. for European and Eurasian affairs U.S. Dept. of State, Washington, 2001—. Office: US Dept of State European and Eurasian Affairs 2201 C St NW Washington DC 20520 Office Fax: 202-647-5575.

JONES, ABBOTT C. investment banking executive; b. Lexington, Ky., Aug. 14, 1934; s. John Catron and Lois (Sauters) J.; m. Carol Donahue, June 29, 1957; children: Cynthia, Alison, Hilary. BA, Principia Coll., 1956; MBA, Harvard U., 1958. Salesman Carnation Co., 1959-60; account exec. Benton & Bowles, N.Y.C., 1960-63; with Ogilvy & Mather, N.Y.C., 1963-77, sr. v.p., dir., 1973-77; sr. v.p., gen. mgr. Foote, Cone & Belding, N.Y.C., 1977-82; pres. Foote, Cone & Belding, Associated Communications Cos., N.Y.C., 1982-86; pres., chief operating officer Foote, Cone, Belding Communications, Inc., N.Y.C., 1986-89; pvt. cons. practice Greenwich, Conn., 1989-90; mng. dir. AdMedia Ptnrs. Inc., N.Y.C., 1990—. Served with U.S. Army, 1958-59. Mem.: Belle Haven (Greenwich, Conn.). Office: 19th Flr 444 Madison Ave New York NY 10022-6903 E-mail: ajones@admediapartners.com.

JONES, AIDAN DREXEL, lawyer; b. Wilmington, Del., Dec. 17, 1945; s. Richard Leonard and Dorothy Drexel (Walsh) J.; m. Kathleen Dellert, Aug. 19, 1972; 4 children. BA, Wesleyan U., 1967; JD, Georgetown U., 1974. Bar: D.C. 1975, U.S. Supreme Ct. 1984, Md. 1996. Law clk. U.S. Dist. Ct., Washington, 1974—75; assoc. Edward Greensfelder Jr. P.C., Washington, 1975—77, Haight, Gardner, Poor & Havens, Washington, 1977—83; ptnr. Finley, Kumble, Wagner, Heine, Underberg, Manley, Myerson & Casey, Washington, 1983—87, Laxalt, Washington, Perito & Dubuc, Washington, 1988—90, Washington, Perito & Dubuc, Washington, 1990—91, Graham & James, Washington, 1991—95; pvt. practice, 1995—. Contbr. articles to profl. jours. Mem. nat. alumni com. Wesleyan U., Middletown, Conn., 1987-89, 1967 class agt., 1985-92; trustee River Road Unitarian Ch., 1992-94; co-treas. Sidwell Friends Sch. Parents Assn., 1995-97, v.p., 1997-98, pres. 1998-99. Lt. USN, 1968-71. Mem. ABA (vice chmn. aviation and space law com. 1985 91). Office: 1818 N St NW Ste 700 Washington DC 20036-2477

JONES, ALAN D. music educator; b. Columbus, Ohio, July 6, 1955; s. Gene Alden and Mary Elizabeth Jones; m. Joanne Marie Pawlukewicz, Aug. 5, 1989. BA, Capital U., Columbus, Ohio, 1973—77; Masters of Music, Eastman Sch. of Music, Rochester, NY, 1977—80. Dir. choral music Spencerport Ctrl. Schools, Spencerport, NY, 1980—. Sectional festival vocal jazz chair NY State Sch. Music Assn., NY, 1992—, manual com. vocal jazz chair, NY, 1992—. Recipient Rochester Philharm. Orch. outstanding music educator, Rochester Philharm. Orch., 2002. Mem.: Music Educators Nat. Conf. (com. chair 1980), NY State Music Assn. (committe chair 1980). Avocations: golf, landscaping. Home: 74 Queensland Dr Spencerport NY 14559

JONES, ALAN PORTER, JR., food manufacturing executive; b. Milw, Minn, Feb. 27, 1925; s. Alan Porter and Eleanor Pratt (Bright) J.; m. Jean Drummond, Sept. 12, 1953; children: Richard, Susan, Cynthia, Alexandra. BA cum laude, Harvard U., 1948, MBA, 1950. With Jones Dairy Farm, Ft. Atkinson, Wis., 1950—, asst. treas., 1953-61, treas., 1961-74, v.p., treas., 1974-93, also bd. dir. Pres. Uncle Josh Bait Co., 1978-1992. Dir. Dwight Foster Pub. Libr., 1952-87, Wis. Livestock and Meat Coun., 1981-97, Ft. Atkinson C. of C., 1985-88; mem. Ft. Atkinson Sch. Bd., 1968-69, Wis. Gov.'s Adv. Com. on Internat. Trade, 1981-97, Wis. Internat. Trade Coun., 1997—, Wis. Citizens Environ. Coun., 1980-84, Wis. Radioactive Waste Policy Coun., 1984-87; trustee Ripon Coll., Wis., 1974-77; bd. dir. Wis. Nature Conservancy, 1992-95. With Inf. US Army, 1943-45. Decorated Bronze Star, Combat Inf. Badge, Presdl. Unit citation. Mem. Nat. Audubon Soc., Sierra Club, Nature Conservancy, Wilderness Soc., Am. Legion, Internat. Crane Found. Republican. Home: 433 Adams St Fort Atkinson WI 53538-1401 Office: Jones Dairy Farm PO Box 808 Fort Atkinson WI 53538-0808

JONES, ALBERT CECIL, consulting engineer; b. Montevallo, Ala., July 29, 1938; s. Albert Cecil and Thelma Evelyn (Hearn) J.; children: Trey, Scott, Shannon. BCE, Auburn U., 1959. Sr. design engr. Rust Engr., Birmingham, Ala., 1969-73; assoc. ptnr. Harland Batholomew & Assoc., Memphis, 1973-83; pres., CEO Cecil Jones and Assoc. Inc., Birmingham, 1983-97; v.p. mktg. Neel-Schaffer Inc., Birmingham, 1997—. 1st lt. USAR, 1960-62. Fellow ASCE, Inst. of Transp. Engrs.; mem. Am. Pub. Works Assn. (past pres.). Office: Neel-Schaffer Inc 1 Chase Corp Ctr Ste 200 Birmingham AL 35244

JONES, ALEX S. journalist, writer, broadcaster; b. Greeneville, Tenn., Nov. 19, 1946; m. Susan E. Tifft, Sept. 21, 1985. BA, Washington and Lee U., 1968. Editor Greeneville (Tenn.) Sun, 1978-83; press reporter N.Y. Times, 1983-92; host On the Media Nat. Pub. Radio, 1993-97; host, exec. editor Media Matters PBS, 1995—; Eugene C. Patterson prof. Practice Journalism Duke U., 1998—2000. Sr. fellow Media Studies Ctr., 1996-97; dir. Joan Shorenstein Ctr. on the Press, Politics, and Pub. Policy, Harvard U., 2000—. Author: (with Susan E. Tifft) The Patriarch: The Rise and Fall of the Bingham Dynasty, 1991, The Trust: The Private and Powerful Family Behind The New York Times, 1999. Recipient Pulitzer prize for specialized reporting, 1987; Nieman fellow, 1981-82. Home: Apt 61 1 Waterhouse St Cambridge MA 02138-3612

JONES, ALLEN, JR., lawyer; b. Washington, May 24, 1930; s. Allen Sr. and Gladys May (Bunch) J.; m. Gloria Jean Clyma, Nov. 29, 1952 (div. June 1989); children: Victoria, Jennifer, Matthew; m. Cheryl B. Crook, Aug. 11, 1991. BA, Mich. State U., 1952; JD, Georgetown U., 1957. Bar: D.C. 1957, U.S. Supreme Ct. 1961, Md. 1962. Sales rep. Ethyl Corp., Salt Lake City, 1952; sr. atty. Wilkes Artis Chartered, Washington, 1957-2000; of counsel Hamilton and Hamilton, LLP, Washington, 2001—. Mem. exec. com., treas. Coun. for Ct. Excellence, Washington, 1988-98; mem. D.C. study devel. coun. Mich. State U., 1999—. Mem. Civil Delay Reduction Task Force, Washington, 1988-92; co-founder Washington Lawyers Against Drugs, 1986-87; mediator Superior Ct. of D.C., 1986—; vice chmn. Children's Hosp. Found., Washington, 1988-92; chmn. Children's Hosp. Telethon, Washington, 1988-89; v.p. Rotary Found. Washington, 2001, pres., 2002. Mem. ABA (Ho. of Dels. D.C. chpt. 1986-87), D.C. Bar Assn. (pres. 1986-87, pres. rsch. found. 1984-85), The Barristers (pres. 1982-83), Lawyers Club, The Counsellors, Jud. Conf. of D.C., Rotary Club Washington (pres.-elect 1997, pres. 1998-99). Republican. Lutheran. Avocations: golf, biking, hiking. Home: 703 Penny Dr Stevensville MD 21666-3731 Office: Hamilton and Hamilton LLP Ste 1100 1775 Pennsylvania Ave NW Washington DC 20006-4605 E-mail: aj@hamiltonlaw.com.

JONES, AMOS NATHANAEL, journalist, violist; b. Lexington, Ky., Oct. 6, 1977; s. LaMont and Kay Grimes Jones. BA cum laude, Emory U., 2000. News copy editor The Atlanta Journ.-Consitution, 1999; violist The Charlotte Philharmonic, NC, 2000—; news copy editor The Charlotte Observer, NC, 2000—. Del. Am. Acad. Achievement, Washington, 2000. Author: Major Houses, 2001, Drama Behind the Gates, 2001; creator (web page) Historic African Am. Chs. of Lexington, 1999. Mem. Friendship Bapt. Ch., Charlotte, NC, 2000—. Mem.: Soc. Profl. Journalists, Nat. Assn. Black Journalists, Am. Copy Editors Soc. American Baptist. Office: The Charlotte Observer 600 S Tryon St Charlotte NC 28206

JONES, ANCIL ARTHUR, cardiologist; b. Bethesda, Md., June 5, 1948; s. James R. and Betty C. Jones; m. Pamela H. Hensel, May 15, 1950; children: Christopher P, Katherine A. BA, Dartmouth Coll., 1970; MD, Yale U., 1974. Diplomate Am. Bd. Internal Medicine, 1981, cardiovascular medicine Am. Bd. Internal Medicine, 1982, interventional cardiology Am. Bd. Internal Medicine, 2000, critical care medicine Am. Bd. Internal Medicine, 2002. Cardiologist Hartford Hosp., Conn., 1980—81, Crozer Chester Med. Ctr., Upland, Pa., 1981—, dir. cardiac catheterization lab. Chester, Pa. Lt. cmdr. U.S. Pub. Health Svc., 1976—78, Bethesda, MD. Fellow: Soc. Cardiac Angiography and Inverventions, Am. Coll. Cardiology (dist. counselor, pa, 1999). Office: Cardiology Cons Phila Prof Office Bldg No 2 #224 1Med Ctr Blvd Upland PA 19013

JONES, ANDREW WILLIAM, pharmaceutical executive; b. Midland, Mich., Feb. 15, 1970; s. William Clarence Jones, Mary Constance Jones; m. Christine Marie Cullen. BS, U. Del., 1992. Assoc. dir. quality assurance Cardinal Health, Somerset, NJ, 2001—; tech. mgr. RTP Region KMI / PAREXEL, Durham, NC, 1998—2001; sr. assoc. Biogen, INC, Cambridge, Mass., 1997—98; scientist /engr. Nanosystems (Kodak), Collegeville, Pa., 1993—97. Presenter in field. Author: My Sophomore Year, 2001, Signed Books and spoke on work at a variety of stores in the Raleigh, NC area., 2001, Signed books in the Princeton, NJ., 2002; contbr. Mem.: Internat. Pharm. Acad., Am. Assn. Pharm. Scientists, Inst. of Validation Tech., Parenteral Drug Assn., Internat. . of Pharm. Engrs. Office: Cardinal Health 14 School House Rd Somerset NJ 08873 Office Fax: 732-537-6466. Business E-Mail: andrew.jones@cardinal.com.

JONES, ANDRUW RUDOLF, professional baseball player; b. Willemstad, Curacao, The Netherlands, Apr. 23, 1977; Outfielder Atlanta Braves, 1996—. Office: Atlanta Braves PO Box 4064 Atlanta GA 30302 Fax: 404-614-1391.

JONES, ANITA KATHERINE, computer scientist, educator; b. Ft. Worth, Mar. 10, 1942; d. Park Joel and Helene Louise (Voigt) J.; m. William A. Wulf, July 1, 1977; children: Karin, Ellen. AB in Math., Rice U., 1964; MA in English, U. Tex., 1966; PhD in Computer Sci., Carnegie Mellon U., 1973, PhD in Sci. and Tech. (hon.), 2000. Programmer IBM, Boston, Washington, 1966-69; assoc. prof. computer sci. Carnegie-Mellon U., Pitts., 1973-81; founder, v.p. Tartan Labs. Inc., Pitts., 1981-87; free-lance cons. Pitts., 1987-88; prof., head computer sci. dept. U. Va., Charlottesville, 1988-93, prof., 1997—, univ. prof., 1998—, Lawrence A. Quarles prof. engring. and applied sci., 1999; dir. def. rsch. and engring. Dept. Def., Washington, 1993-97. Mem. Def. Sci. Bd., Dept. Def., 1985-93, 98—; mem. sci. adv. bd. USAF, 1980-85; governing bd. Nat. Sci. Found.; vice-chair governing bd. NSF, 1998-2000; bd. dirs. Sci. Applications Internat. Corp., InQTel; trustee Mitre Corp., 1989-93, chair Va. Rsch. and Technology Adv. Commn., 1999-2002, Commonwealth of Va. Advs. Commn.; mem. corp. Charles Stark Draper Labs., 1999—. Editor: Perspectives on Computer Science, 1977, Foundations of Secure Computation, 1971. Recipient Air Force Meritorious Civilian Svc. award, 1985, Medal for Disting. Pub. Svc. Dept. of Def., 1996, Disting. Svc. award Computing Rsch. Assn., 1997. Fellow IEEE, AAAS, Assn. Computing Machinery (editor-in-chief Transactions on Computer Sys. 1983-91), Am. Acad. Arts and Scis.; mem. Nat. Acad. Engring., Sci. Found. of Ireland (bd. dirs. 2000—), Sigma Xi. Avocation: gardening. E-mail: jones@virginia.edu.

JONES, ANTHONY RAY, military career officer; m. Nancy Erwin; children: Regan, Erin, Holly. BS in Bus., Ind. U., 1970; M in Sys. Mgmt., U. So. Calif., L.A., 1982; grad., Army Command/Gen. Staff Coll., U.S. Army War Coll. Commd. 2nd lt. U.S. Army Infantry, 1970, advanced through grades to maj. gen., 1998, inf. platoon leader, co. exec. officer 1st bn. 30th Inf., aviation platoon leader, HHC co. comdr. 9th inf. divsn. Ft. Lewis, Wash., exec. officer 213th Aviation Co. Camp Humphreys, Korea, co. comdr. E Co., task force 160, exec. officer 160th Spl. Ops. Aviation Group, comdr. 3d bn., 227th Aviation Regiment, 3d Armored Divsn. Ft. Hood, Tex., Germany, Saudi Arabia, comdr. Combat Aviation Brigade, 24th Inf. Divsn. Ft. Stewart, Ga., chief ops. and contingency plans, dep. chief staff ops. Washington, dep. dir. ops. J3 Joint Staff, asst. divsn. comdr.-forward 1st Armored divsn. Tuzla, Bosnia-Herzegovina; asst. ops. officer, test concepts and project officer U.S. Army Aviation Bd., Ft. Rucker; ops. rsch., sys. analysis for force modernization office U.S. Army Mil. Pers. Ctr., Alexandria, Va.; aviation ops. officer Spl. Ops. Office, dep. chief of staff U.S. Army, Washington. Decorated Def. Superior Svc. medal, Legion of Merit with oak leaf cluster, Bronze Star, Meritorious Svc. medal with seven oak leaf clusters, Air medal, Army Commendation medal with oak leaf cluster, Nat. Def. Svc. medal with oak leaf cluster, Armed Forces Expeditionary medal, S.W. Asia Svc. medal, Kuwait Liberation medal, Joint Meritorious Unit award with oak leaf cluster. Office: US Army Aviation Ctr Fort Rucker AL 36362

JONES, ARTHUR EDWIN, JR., library administrator, English and American literature educator; b. Orange, N.J., Mar. 20, 1918; s. Arthur Edwin and Lucy Mabel (Alpaugh) J.; m. Rachel Evelyn Mumbulo, Apr. 24, 1943; 1 child, Carol Rae Jones Jacobus BA, U. Rochester, 1939; MA, Syracuse U., 1941, PhD in English, 1950; MLS, Rutgers U., 1964. Instr. English Syracuse U., N.Y., 1946-49, Drew U., Madison, N.J., 1949-52, asst. prof., 1952-55, assoc. prof., 1955-60, prof. English and Am. lit., 1960-86, dir. libraries, 1956-85, prof., libr. emeritus, 1986—. Evaluator Middle States Assn. Colls., Phila., 1955-85. Author: Darwinism and American Realism, 1951; contbr. articles to profl. jours.; book reviewer Library Jour., 1956-75, Choice, 1969— Trustee Madison Pub. Library, N.J., 1958-79, pres., 1976-79. Served to 1st lt. U.S. Army, 1941-46 Named to U. Rochester Athletic Hall of Fame, 1997; Lilly Endowment scholar Am. Theol. Libr. Assn., 1963-64 Mem. MLA, Nat. Coun. Tchr. of Eng., ALA (councillor 1970-71), Am. Theol. Libr. Assn. (pres. 1967-68), AAUP, Lions Club, Habitat for Humanity. Democrat. Home: 400 Avinger Ln Apt 409 Davidson NC 28036-9718

JONES, AUDREY BEYER, dietitian; b. Madison, Wis., Feb. 1, 1921; d. Adelbert John and Hazel Mae (Crocker) Beyer; m. Frank C. Jones, July 11, 1954 (dec. Jan. 23, 2003); children: Philip Lynn(dec.), Paul Douglas, David Scott. BS, Milw.-Downer Coll., 1941; BA, U. Wis., 1947; Tchg. Cert., U. Corpus Christi, Tex., 1962. Lic. dietitian, Tex. Dietitian Charity Hosp., New Orleans, 1942-43, 12th Evac Hosp./U.S. Army, 1943-44, VA Hosp., Wood, Wis., 1948-51; clinic dietitian VA Reg. Office, Milw., 1951-53; chief dietitian Kuakini Hosp., Honolulu, 1954-55; nutrition cons. various hosps. Corpus Christi, 1964—. Docent Art Mus. So. Tex., Corpus Christi, 1990-93. 1st lt. U.S. Army, 1943-44; ETO. Recipient Cmty. Bldr. award Masonic Grand Lodge of Tex., 2000. Mem. AAUW (pres. Corpus Christi br. 1994-96), Am. Dietetic Assn. (registered dietitian), Tex. Dietetic Assn., Corpus Christi Dietetic Assn. (pres. 1972). Republican. Lutheran. Avocations: travel, birding, reading, crossword puzzles, bridge. Home: 4621 Monette Dr Corpus Christi TX 78412-2344

JONES, B. TODD, lawyer, former prosecutor; s. Paul and Sylvia Jones. Grad., Macalester Coll., 1979; JD, U. Minn., 1983. Mng. ptnr. Greene Espel, Mpls., 1996—97; asst. U.S. atty. for Minn., 1997—98; U.S. atty. Minn. dist. U.S. Dept. Justice, 1998—2001; ptnr. Robins, Kaplan, Miller & Ciresi, Mpls., 2001—. With USMC. Office: Robins Kaplan Miller & Ciresi 2800 LaSalle Plaza 800 LaSalle Ave Minneapolis MN 55402

JONES, BARBARA ANN, elementary education educator; b. Rockville Centre, N.Y., Nov. 2, 1946; d. Robert C. and Doris M. (Felten) J. BS in Edn., St. John's U., 1968; MA, Hofstra U., 1971; MS, Coll. New Rochelle, 1996. Tchr. Our Lady of Peace Sch., Lynbrook, N.Y., 1968-86, Uniondale (N.Y.) Pub. Schs., 1986—; pers. trainer A & S, Hempstead, 1985-87. Leader 4-H Club, Franklin Square, N.Y., 1973-84, corr. sec. leaders coun.; active PTA. Roman Catholic. Avocations: crafts, needlework, stamp collecting. Office: Uniondale Pub Schs Smith St Sch 780 Smith St Uniondale NY 11553-3399

JONES, BARBARA CHRISTINE, educator, linguist, creative arts designer; came to U.S., 1964, naturalized, 1971; d. Martin and Margarete (Roth-Rommel) Schulz von Hammer-Parstein; m. Robert Dickey, 1967 (div. 1980); m. Raymond Lee Jones, 1981. Student, U. Munich, 1961, Philomatique de Bordeaux, France, 1962; BA in German, French, and Speech, Calif. State U., Chico, 1969, MA in Comparative Internat. Edn., 1974. Cert. secondary tchr., C.C. instr., Calif. Fgn. lang. tchr. Gridley Union H.S., Calif., 1970-80, home econs., decorative arts instr., cons., 1970-80, English study skills instr., 1974-80, ESL coord., instr. Punjabi, Mex. Ams., 1970-72, curriculum com. chmn., 1970-80; program devel. adv. Program Devel. Ctr. Supt. Schs., Butte County, Oroville, Calif., 1975-77; opportunity tchr. Esperanza H.S., Gridley, Calif., 1980-81, Liberty H.S., Lodi, Calif., 1981-82, resource specialist coord., 1981-82; Title I coord. Bear Creek Ranch Sch., Lodi, Calif., 1981-82, instr., counselor, 1982-83; sub. tchr. Elk Grove (Calif.) Unified, 1982-84. Freelance decorative arts and textiles designer, 1982-95; internat. heritage and foods adv. AAUW, Chico, Calif, 1973-75; lectr. German, Schreiner Coll., Kerrville, Tex., 1993; workshop dir. Creative Arts Ctr., Chico, 1972-73; workshop dir., adv. Bus. Profl. Women's Club of Gridley, 1972-74; mem. Cowboy Artists Mus., Kerrville, 1996-99; v.p. Golden State Mobile Home League, Sacramento, 1980-82; mem. publicity Habitat for Humanity, Kerrville br., 1992-94. Weavings-wall hangings (1st pl. 10 categories, Silver Dollar Fair, Chico, Calif., 1970). Vol. Ariz. Superior Ct., Foster Care Review Bd., 2003. Mem.: AAUW (publicity dir. cultural activities Kerrville br. 1991—92), Am. Assn. German Tchrs., German Texan Heritage Soc., Turtle Creek Social Cir. (pioneer 1992—99), USAR Non-Commd. Officer's Assn. (ednl. adv. 1984—86), Am. Cancer Soc. (publicity 1992—95), Kerrville Garden Club (publicity 1993—97), United European Am. Club, Kappa Delta Pi. Avocations: textile design, swimming, travel, real estate, mosaics. Home: 3350 Pasadena Ave Kingman AZ 86401-5046

JONES, BARBARA ELLEN, neuroscientist, educator; b. Phila., Dec. 19, 1944; d. Charles and Ella (Yeager) J.; m. John Gordon Galaty, Aug. 12, 1972; 1 child, James Gordon. BA, U. Del., 1966, MA, 1969, PhD, 1971. Rsch. assoc., asst. prof. U. Chgo., 1972-77; asst. prof. dept. neurology and neurosurgery McGill U., Montreal, 1977-82, assoc. prof., 1982-88, prof., 1989—. Vis. lectr. U. Nairobi, Kenya, 1974-75; vis. scientist Oxford U., Eng., 1984-85; vis. prof. U. Geneva, 1991-92, 98-99. Contbr. articles to profl. jours. Postdoctoral fellow Coll. de France, Paris, 1970-72. Mem. Am. Neurosci. Soc., Sleep Rsch. Soc. Avocations: horseback riding, skiing. Home: 97 Arlington Ave Westmount QC Canada H3Y 2W5 Office: McGill Univ 3801 Univ St Montreal QC Canada H3A 2B4

JONES, BENJAMIN ANGUS, JR., retired agricultural engineering educator, administrator; b. Mahomet, Ill., Apr. 16, 1926; s. Benjamin Angus and Grace Lucile (Morr) J.; m. Georgeann Hall, Sept. 11, 1949; children: Nancy Kay Jones-Kepple, Ruth Ann Jones-Sommers. BS, U. Ill., 1949, MS, 1950, PhD, 1958. Registered profl. engr., Ill. Asst. prof., asst. ext. engr. U. Vt., Burlington, 1950-52; instr., agrl. engr. U. Ill., Urbana, 1952-54, asst. prof., agrl. engr., 1954-58, assoc. prof., agrl. engr., 1958-64, prof., agrl. engr., 1964-92, prof. emeritus, 1992—, assoc. dir., agrl. exptl. sta., 1973-92; assoc. dir. emeritus, 1992—, U. Ill., Urbana, 1992. Cons. various Ill. Drainage Dists., 1958—. Co-author: (textbook) Engineering Application in Agriculture, 1973; contbr. articles to Jour. Soil & Water Conservation, Encyclopedia Britannica, Agrl. Engring., Transactions of ASAE, Proceedings of ASCE, Soil Sci. Soc. Am. Proceedings, Crops and Soils, Jour. Hydrology, Water Resources Bulletin. Merit badge examiner Boy Scouts Am., Burlington, 1950-52; lay mem. Cen. Ill. Con. United Meth. Ch., 1978-81. With USN, 1944-46. NSF fellow. Fellow Am. Soc. Agrl. Engrs. (bd. dirs., trustee); mem. Soil and Water Conservation Soc., Am. Soc. for Engring. Edn., Sigma Xi, Gamma Sigma Delta, Alpha Epsilon. Home: 2012B Eagle Ridge Ct Urbana IL 61802-8617

JONES, BEVERLY ANN MILLER, nursing administrator, retired patient services administrator; b. Bklyn, July 14, 1927; d. Hayman Edward and Eleanor Virginia (Doyle) Miller; m. Kenneth Lonzo Jones, Sept. 5, 1953 (dec.); children: Steven Kenneth, Lonnie Cord. BSN, Adelphi U., 1949. Chief nurse regional blood program ARC, NYC, 1951-54; asst. dir., acting DON M.D. Anderson Hosp. and Tumor Inst., Houston, 1954-55; DON Sibley Meml. Hosp., Washington, 1959-61; assoc. dir. nursing svc. Anne Arundel Gen. Hosp., Annapolis, Md., 1966-70; asst. adminstr. nursing Alexandria Hosp., Va., 1972-73; v.p. patient care svc. Longmont United Hosp., Colo., 1977-93; pvt. cons., 1993-99; ret. Instr. ARC, 1953-57, chmn. nurse enrollment com. D.C. chpt., 1959-61; mem. adv. bd. Boulder Valley Vo.-Tech. Health Occupations Program, 1977-80; del. nursing adminstrs. good will trip to Poland, Hungary, Sweden and Eng., 1980. Contbr. articles to profl. jours. Mem.-at-large exec. com. nursing svc. adminstrs. sect. Md. Nurses' Assn., 1966-69; bd. dir. Meals on Wheels, Longmont, 1978-80, Longmont Coalition for Women in Crisis, Applewood Living Ctr., Longmont; mem. utilization com. Boulder (Colo.) Hospice, 1979-83; mem. task force on nat. commn. on nursing Colo. Hosp. Assn., 1982, mem. coun. labor rels., 1982-87; mem. U. Colo. Task Force on Nursing, 1990; vol. Champs program St. Vrain Valley Sch. Dist., Prestige Plus program Longmont United Hosp., 1999—. Named Outstanding Vol. of Yr., St. Vrain Valley Sch. Dist., 2002. Mem. Am. Orgn. Nurse Exec. (chmn. com. membership svc. and promotions, nominee recognition of excellence in nursing adminstrn.), Colo. Soc. Nurse Exec. (dir. 1978-80, 84-86, pres. 1980-81, mem. com. on nominations 1985-86, Outstanding Vol. of Yr. 2002). Home: 853 Wade Rd Longmont CO 80503-7017

JONES, BILL, former state official, rancher; b. Coalinga, Calif., Dec. 20, 1949; s. C.W. and Cora Jones; m. Maurine Abramson, Aug. 29, 1971; children: Wendy, Andrea. BS in Agribus. and Plant Sci., Calif. State U., Fresno, 1971. Ptnr. ranch, nr. Firebaugh, Calif.; mem. Calif. Assembly, Sacramento, 1983—, Rep. leader, 1991—; Sec. of State State of California, 1994—2003. Former chmn. Fresno County Rep. Cen. Com. Named Outstanding Young Farmer, Fresno C. of C. Mem. Fresno County and City C. of C. (past bd. dirs.). Republican. Methodist. Avocations: horseback riding, golf, flying, travel.*

JONES, BILLY ERNEST, dermatology educator; b. Daytona Beach, Fla., Jan. 29, 1933; s. Bibb Ernest and Marjorie (Eyre) J.; m. Hannah Warren, June 12, 1958; children: Alan W., Lawrence W., Marjorie E. BS, The Citadel, 1954; MD, Duke U., 1958. Diplomate Am. Bd. Dermatology. Commd. 2d lt. U.S. Army, 1958, advanced through grades to maj., 1964, intern William Beaumont Hosp., 1958-59, gen. med. officer Henry Barracks Cayey, P.R., 1959-61, resident in dermatology The Presidio San Francisco, 1961-64, chief dermatology Ft. Gordon, Ga., 1964-67, resigned, 1967; practice medicine specializing in dermatology Greenville, N.C., 1967-80; prof. medicine East Carolina U., Greenville, 1991-97, ret., 1997. Recipient Clin. Tchr. award Sr. Class, 1983, 84, 88, Teaching Recognition award 1st yr. residents, 1982, 3d yr. residents, 1985 Med. Sch. East Carolina U. Fellow Am. Acad. Dermatology; mem. AMA, N.C. Med. Soc. Republican. Episcopalian. Avocations: tennis, horticulture.

JONES, BOB, III, academic administrator; b. 1939; m. Beneth Jones; 3 children. BA, MA, Bob Jones U.; D (hon.), Pillsbury Bapt. Bible Coll., San Francisco Bapt. Theological Seminary, Maranatha Bapt. Bible Coll. Various positions with Bob Jones U., pres., 1971—. Mem. exec. com., bd. trustees Bob Jones U.; v.p. bd. dirs. Gospel Fellowship Assn. Office: Bob Jones U Office Of Pres Greenville SC 29614-0001*

JONES, BOISFEUILLET, JR., publishing executive; b. Atlanta, Ga., Nov. 14, 1946; s. Boisfeuillet and Laura (Coit) J.; m. Barbara Frost Pendleton, Sept. 13, 1969; children: Lindsay Pendleton, Theodore Boisfeuillet. AB, Harvard U., 1968, JD, 1974; D.Phil., Oxford U., 1981. Bar: Mass. 1974, D.C. 1979. Law clk. Judge Levin H. Campbell, US Ct. Appeals (1st cir.), Boston, 1974-75; atty Hill and Barlow, Boston, 1975-80; v.p., counsel Washington Post, DC, 1980-95 pres., gen. mgr., 1995-2000, pub., CEO, 2000—. Dir. Bowater Mersey Paper Co., Ltd., N.S., Assoc Press, NY, Robinson Terminal Warehouse Corp. Alexandria, Va., Fed. City Coun., Washington, Eugene & Agnes Meyer Found. Washington, Newspaper Assn. Am. Rhodes scholar Rhodes Trust, 1968. Episcopalian. Home: 4331 Forest Ln NW Washington DC 20007-1137 Office Washington Post 1150 15th St NW Washington DC 20071-0002

JONES, BONNIE DAMSCHRODER, government agency administrator; b. Cocoa, Fla., Dec. 20, 1945; d. Eugene Edward and Lu Jeanette (Hufford) Damschroder; m. Robert Kirk Jones, June 8, 1968; children: Kelly Anne Jennifer Graham. BS in Edn., Capital U., Columbus, Ohio, 1967; MS in Edn. George Mason U., 1976; transition specialist cert., U. Hawaii, 1988; EdD Columbia U., 2000. Tchr. mental retardation Waterford (Conn.) Pub. Schs. 1967-68; tchr. mentally retarded Escambia County Schs., Pensacola, Fla. 1968-70; tchr. learning disabilities Fairfax County Schs., Fairfax, Va., 1975-78 curriculum specialist Newport News (Va.) Pub. Schs., 1978-80; program coord Peninsula Area Coop. Ednl. Svcs. Day Treatment Regional Sch., Newport News, 1980-81; dist. transition coord. Hawaii Dept. Edn., Honolulu, 1984-88 program specialist Kans. Dept. Edn., Topeka, 1988-90; rsch. asst. Columbia U Tchrs. Coll., N.Y.C., 1991-92; tchr. learning disabilities Fairfax County Pub Schs., Fairfax, Va., 1992-94, tchr., dept. chairperson, 1994-96; program specialist U.S. Dept. Edn. Office of Spl. Edn. Programs, 1997—2002, edn. rsch analyst, 2002—. Adj. faculty Grad. Sch. Edn., George Mason U., Fairfax, 1976 Fairfax, 1997—, Baruch Coll., 1992, Grad. Sch. Edn., Johns Hopkins U. Columbia, Md., 2002—; supervising tchr. Hampton (Va.) Inst., 1981, U Hawaii, Honolulu, 1998, George Mason U., 1996; mem. exceptional needs standards com. Nat. Bd. for Profl. Tchg. Standards, 1994—98; nat. adv. com. on assessment of exceptional needs standards, 1998—. Co-author: Identifying Handicapping Conditions, 1978, Career Awareness for Students with Handicaps, 1986, Implementing Transition Goals, 1992, 2d edit., 1999, Student Led IEPs, 2000; mem. editl. bd. Career Devel. for Exceptional Individuals, 2000—. Mem. Jr. League, Portland, Maine, Honolulu, Topeka, and No. Va., 1983— pres. USCG Officers' Wives Club, Portland, 1983, bd. dirs. Newport News 1978-79, Honolulu, 1984-88, N.Y.C., 1991; co-chmn. carnival booth Punahou Sch., Honolulu, 1987, 88; treas. Red Hill Sch. PTA, Honolulu, 1985-87; bd dirs. Internat. Divsn. Career Devel., 1989-94, treas., 1992-94; pres. Kans Divsn. Career Devel., 1989-90. Recipient cert. of appreciation USCG, Boston 1983, community svc. award, N.Y.C., 1991; Vocat. Educator of Yr. award Hawaii Vocat. Edn. Assn., 1987, Outstanding Contbn. to Transition award Kans Div. on Career Devel., 1990, Outstanding Alumni award George Mason U Grad. Sch. Edn., 1998. Mem. ASCD, Am. Ednl. Rsch. Assn., Coun. fo Exceptional Children (subcom. on knowledge and skills profl. standards com 1990-94, rsch. com. tchr. edn. divsn. 2000—), Phi Delta Kappa. Home: 772 Silver Sage Ct Springfield VA 22153-2126 E-mail: bonnie.jones@ed.gov.

JONES, BRENDA GAIL, school district administrator; b. Winnipeg, Man. Can., Nov. 5, 1949; d. Glen Allen and Joyce Catherine (Peckham) McGregor BA, San Francisco State U., 1972; MA, U. San Francisco, 1983. Cert. tchr., sch adminstr., Calif. Tchr. Lakeport (Calif.) Unified Sch. Dist., 1973-82, asst. prin. 1982-88, dir. ednl. svcs. and spl. projects, 1988-2000; dir. pupil personnel svcs Redwood City (Calif.) Sch. Dist., 2000—. Instr. English Mendocino Coll. Ukiah, Calif., 1977-82. Mem. Assn. Calif. Sch. Adminstrs. (past pres. 1987 Lake County charter), Order Ea. Star (past matron Clear Lake chpt. 1995, dep grand matron 1999). Democrat. Episcopalian. Avocations: health, fitness walking, reading, gardening. Home: 1315 20th St Lakeport CA 95453-305 Office: Redwood City sch Dist 750 Bradford St Redwood City CA 94063

JONES, BRIAN W. federal agency administrator; BSBA in Fin., Georgetown U.; JD, UCLA. Atty. Sheppard, Mullin, Richter & Hampton, San Francisco pres. Ctr. New Black Leadership, Washington; counsel U.S. Sen. Jud. Com. Washington, 1999; dep. legal affairs sec. to Calif. Gov. Pete Wilson, 1999; atty Curiale Dellaverson Hirschfield Kelly & Kraemer, LLP, San Francisco; gen counsel Dept. Edn., Washington, 2001—. Contbr. (on air polit. and new analysis) MSNBC-TV. Office: Dept Edn Gen Counsel 400 Maryland Ave SW Washington DC 20202-2110

JONES, BRUCE ALLEN, pathologist; b. Indpls., Feb. 23, 1953; BS, U. Mich 1975; MD, Wayne State U., 1979. Diplomate in anat. and clin. pathology an cytopathology Am. Bd. Pathology. Resident in internal medicine Harper Hosp Detroit, 1979-80; fellow in diagnostic electron microscopy William Beaumont Hosp., Royal Oak, Mich., 1984-85; resident in pathology St. John Hosp Detroit, 1980-84, assoc. pathologist, 1985-94, dir. pathology residency pro gram, 1992—, dir. clin. pathology, 1994—; dir. St. John Clin. Pathology Labs Romeo Plank br. St. John Health Sys., Clinton Twp., Mich., 1997—. Bd. dir Joint Venture Hosp. Labs., Detroit. Contbr. articles to profl. jours. Mem. Col Am. Pathologists (chmn. quality practices com.), Detroit Acad. Medicine, Am Soc. Clin. Pathologists, Am. Coll. Physician Execs. Office: St John Hosp 2210 Moross Rd Detroit MI 48236-2172 E-mail: bruce.jones@stjohn.org.

JONES, C. PAUL, lawyer, educator; b. Grand Forks, N.D., Jan. 7, 1927; s Walter M. and Sophie J. (Thorton) J.; m. Helen M. Fredel, Sept. 7, 1957 children— Katherine, Sara H. BBA, JD, U. Minn., 1950; LLM, William Mitchell Coll. of Law, 1955. Assoc. Lewis, Hammer, Heaney, Weyl & Halverson, Duluth, Minn., 1950-51; asst., chief dep. Hennepin County Atty

Mpls., 1952-58; asst. U.S. atty. U.S. Atty's. Office, St. Paul, 1959-60; assoc. Maun & Hazel, St. Paul, 1960-61; ptnr. Dorfman, Rudquist, Jones, & Ramstead, Mpls., 1961-65; state pub. defender Minn. State Pub. Defender's Office, Mpls., 1966-90. Adj. prof. law William Mitchell Coll. of Law, St. Paul, 1953-70, prof. law, 1970—2001, prof. emeritus, 2001-. assoc. dean for acad. affairs, 1991-95; adj. prof. U. Minn., Mpls., 1970-90; mem. adv. com. on rules of criminal procedure Minn. Supreme Ct., 1970—. Author: Criminal Procedure from Police Detention to Final Disposition, 1981; Jones on Minnesota Criminal Procedure, 1955, 64, 70, 75; Minnesota Police Law Manual, 1955, 67, 70, 76 Mem. Minn. Gov.'s Crime Commn., St. Paul, 1970s, Minn. Fair Trial-Free Press Assn., Mpls., 1970s, Citizens League, Mpls., 1955—, Mpls. Aquatennial Assn., Mpls., 1955-60, Minn. Coun. on Crime and Justice, 1991—. Recipient Reginald Heber Smith award Nat. Legal Aid and Defender Assn., 1969 Fellow Am. Coll. Trial Lawyers; mem. Am. Bd. Trial Advs., ABA, Minn. State Bar Assn., Hennepin County Bar Assn., Ramsey County Bar Assn., Nat. Legal Aid & Defender Assn. Clubs: Suburban Gyro of Mpls., Mpls. Athletic. Lodges: Rotary. Democrat. Lutheran. Avocations: fishing; hunting; golfing; desert watching. Home: 5501 Dewey Hill Rd Edina MN 55439-1906 Office: William Mitchell Coll Law 875 Summit Ave Saint Paul MN 55105-3030

JONES, CARL E., JR., bank executive; Pres. First Ala. Bancshores, Inc., Montgomery; chmn., chief exec. officer First Ala. Bank/Mobile, 1981-96; pres., COO Regions Fin. & Regions Bank, Birmingham, Ala., 1997-98, pres., CEO, 1998—, chmn., 2001—. Office: Regions Fin Corp 417 N 20th St PO Box 10247 Birmingham AL 35202-0247

JONES, CARLETON SHAW, information systems company executive, lawyer; b. N.Y.C., Sept. 8, 1942; s. Carlyle Herman and Virginia Ann (Sloat) J.; m. Dona Baker VanArsdale, July 15, 1972; children: Emily Baker, Timothy Dustin. BA, Denison U., 1964; LLB, Yale U., 1967. Bar: Ohio 1967, Fla. 1971, D.C. 1973. Law clk. to chief judge U.S. Ct Appeals (6th cir.), Akron, Ohio, 1967; dep. gen. counsel Price Commn., Exec. Office of Pres., Washington, 1971-73; assoc. Shaw, Pittman Potts & Trowbridge, Washington, 1973-77, ptnr., 1978-91; sr. v.p., counsel Sysorex Info. Sys., Fairfax, Va., 1992, pres., 1992-97, also bd. dirs.; pres. Vanstar Govt. Sys. (formerly Sysorex Info. Sys.), Fairfax, 1997-99; advisor, bd. mem. high tech. cos., 1999—; pres. Info Ops Govt. Solutions, Arnold, Md., 2000—01; pres., COO Multimax, Inc., Landover, Md., 2001—. Spkr. on fed. high-tech. procurement issues. Lt. (j.g.) USNR, 1967-71. Mem. ABA, FBA, Chevy Chase Club, Met. Club.

JONES, CAROLYN ELLIS, publisher, retired employment agency and business service company owner; b. Marigold, Miss., Feb. 21, 1928; d. Joseph Lawrence and Willie Decelle (Forrest) Peeples; m. David Wright Ellis, May 30, 1945 (div. 1966); children: David, Lyn, Debbie, Dawn; m. Frank Willis Jones, Jan. 1, 1980. Student, La. State U., 1949. Owner, mgr. Personnel and Bus. Svc., Inc., Greenwood, Miss., 1962-88, now v.p.; owner Honor Pub. Co., Greenwood, 1988—. ESL tchr. at a Spanish Mission, nr. Sunflower, Miss. Author: The Lottie Moon Storybook, 1985; editor: An Old Soldier's Career, 1974; contbr. articles to religious and gen. interest publs. Mem. adv. bd. career edn. Greenwood Pub. Schs., 1975-76, mem. adv. bd. vocat.-tech. dept., 1975-88; conf. leader Miss. Bapt. Convention Singles Retreat, 1980; Mission Svc. Corps del. Home Mission Bd., So. Bapt. Conv., Hawaii, 1979. Mem. Greenwood C. of C. (edn. com. 1980—, guest spkr. career day program local high sch.), Mothers Against Drunk Drivers, Altrusa Internat., Nat. Fedn. Ind. Bus., Miss Delta Rose Soc., Miss. Native Plant Soc., Gideon Aux. (pres. 1986-88). Avocations: writing, rose exhibitions, wildflowers. Office: 802 W President Ave Greenwood MS 38930-326

JONES, CAROLYN EVANS, writer, speaker; b. Middleboro, Mass., Sept. 5, 1931; d. King Israel and Kleo Estelle (Hodges) Evans; m. John Homer Jones, Sept. 9, 1966 (dec. July 1986); 1 child, David Everett. BA in English, Tift Coll., 1952; M Religious Edn., Carver Sch. Missions and Social Work, 1958; BA in Art, Mercer U., 1982. Cert. secondary tchr., Ga. Tchr. McDuffie County Bd. Edn., Thomson, Ga., 1952-53, Colquitt County Bd. Edn., Norman Park, Ga., 1953-55; missionary Home Mission Bd. SBC, New Orleans and Macon, 1958-66; spl. edn. tchr. Bibb County Bd. Edn., Macon, 1968-70, 75-79; owner, operator Laney Co. Imprinted Specialties, Macon, 1986-97; writer, 1998—. Contbr. numerous articles and poems to profl. jours. Bible tchr. YWCA, Macon, 1980-85; deacon 1st Bapt. Ch., Macon. Mem.: Bapt. Women in Ministry, Southeastern Writers Assn., Ga. Writers Inc. Democrat. Avocations: reading, travel, attending conferences.

JONES, CATESBY BROOKE, retired banker; b. Lexington, Va., Mar. 7, 1925; s. Catesby and Elizabeth (Cox) J.; m. Margaret Gordon Gaffney, June 13, 1953 (dec. Apr. 1995); children: Catesby II, Margaret Brooke, Elizabeth Gordon; m. Barbara Jeffreys Webb, Mar. 16, 1996. Grad., St. Paul's Sch., 1943; BA in Econs, Yale, 1949; grad., Stonier Grad. Sch. Banking, Rutgers U., 1956, U. Va. Grad. Sch. Bus., 1961. With United Va. Bank, Richmond, 1949-85, sr. v.p., head nat. div., 1965-85; fin. cons. Marsh & McLennan Inc., 1985-88; former pres., dir. Buffalo Creek & Gauley R.R. Co.; former dir. Spindale Mills, Inc. Bd. dirs. Regency Bank, former dir., vice chmn. Richmond Ind. Bicentennial Commn., 1975-1983 Chmn. fin. com., bd. dirs. Richmond Area Community Coun., 1959-63; div. chmn. United Givers Fund, 1965, 72; treas., bd. dirs. MCV Hosp. Hospitality House, 1985-92. 1st Lt. AUS, 1944-46. Mem. Va. C. of C. (treas., dir. 1964-67), Richmond C. of C. (chmn. membership relations com. 1957-59), Soc. Colonial Wars in Va. (gov. 1976), Soc. Cincinnati (pres. Va. chpt. 1979-82, gen. pres. 1983-86), Jamestown Soc., Beta Theta Pi. Clubs: Yale of Va. (past pres.); Country of Va. (Richmond); Edgartown Golf. Episcopalian. Home: 1 Chatham Sq 6161 River Rd Richmond VA 23226-3318

JONES, CHARLES CALHOUN, estate and business planning consultant; b. Bedford, Pa., Jan. 12, 1940; s. Charles Stauffer and Marjorie Vesta (Calhoun) J.; m. Patricia Jean Diehl, Aug. 12, 1960; children: Kathryn Lynn, Suzanne Elizabeth, Christopher Andrew. BS in Econs., Widener U., 1961. CLU; chartered fin. cons.; registered investment advisor. Field dir. Bus. Men's Assurance, Kansas City, Mo., 1970-76; pres. Agrl. Bus. Adminstrn., Kansas City, 1976-78; br. mgr. E.F. Hutton, Raytown, Mo., 1978-79; pres. C.C.J. Inc., Kansas City, 1979-90; chmn. coun. John Hancock Mut. Life Ins. Co., 1992-98, gen. agts. adv. com., mktg. chmn., 1992-99. Chmn. bd. dirs. Pentrust Advisors; advisor Nat. Cattleman's Assn., Denver, 1976-79. Author: Financial Management Pentrust, 1987; contbr. articles to profl. jours. Gov. Am. Royal, Kansas City, 1981; mem. adminstrv. bd. and coun. Luth. Ch., Kans.; bd. dirs. Providence/ St. John Hosp. Found., 1999—. Mem. Lees Summit C. of C. (econ. devel. com. 1982-85), Soc. Fin. Svc. Profls. (bd. dirs. 1998—), Assn. Internat Fin. Planners (bd. dirs. 1976-80), Planned Giving Coun. (charter), Rotary Internat., Soc. of Fin. Svc. Profls., Loch Lomond Club (Luss, Scotland), Blue Hills C.C. Avocation: golf. Office: Pentrust Advisors PO Box 481993 Kansas City MO 64148-1993

JONES, CHARLES E. chief justice supreme court; b. June 12, 1935; BA, Brigham Young U., 1959; JD, Stanford U., 1962. Bar: Calif. 1963, U.S. Dist. Ct. Ariz. 1964, U.S. Ct. Appeals (9th cir.) 1963, Ariz. 1964, U.S. Ct. Appeals (10th cir.) 1974, U.S. Supreme Ct. 1979. Law clk. to Hon. Richard H. Chambers U.S. Ct. Appeals (9th cir.), 1962-63; assoc., ptnr. Jennings, Strouss & Salmon, Phoenix, 1963-96; appd. justice Ariz. Supreme Ct., Phoenix, 1996, vice chief justice, 1997—2002, chief justice, 2002—. Bd. visitors Brigham Young U. Law Sch., 1973-81, chmn., 1978-81, Univ. Arizona Coll. Law, 2003—. Named Advocat du Consulat-Gen. de France, 1981—; Alumni Dist. Svc. award Brigham Young U., 1982; recipient Aaron Feuerstein award U. Ariz., 1998. Fellow Am. Bar Found., Ariz. Bar Found.; mem. ABA, State Bar Ariz., Fed. Bar Assn. (pres. Ariz. chpt. 1971-73), J. Reuben Clark Law Soc. (nat. chmn. 1994-97), Maricopa County Bar Assn., Am. Coll. Labor & Employment Lawyers, Conf. Chief Justices of Fifty States, Nat. Com. Pub. Trust and Confidence in the Cts. (chmn.), Pi Sigma Alpha. Office: Ariz Supreme Court 1501 W Washington St Phoenix AZ 85007-3222

JONES, CHARLES EDWIN, historian, bibliographer, chaplain; b. Kansas City, Mo., June 1, 1932; s. Dess Dain and Dove (Barnwell) J.; m. Beverly Anne Lundy, May 30, 1956; 1 child, Karl Laurence. BA, Bethany-Peniel Coll., 1954; MALS, U. Mich., 1955; MS, U. Wis., 1960, PhD, 1968; postgrad., Episcopal Div. Sch., Cambridge, Mass., 1975-76. Ordained to ministry Reformed Episcopal Ch. as deacon, 1990. Libr. Park Coll., 1961-63; manuscript curator Mich. Hist. Coll. U. Mich., Ann Arbor, 1965-69; assoc. prof. history Houghton Coll., 1969-71; hist. cataloguer Rockefeller Libr. Brown U., 1971-76; chaplain-in-residence Quail Creek Nursing Ctr., Oklahoma City, 1989-98, 2001—. Author: Perfectionist Persuasion, 1974, Guide to the Study of the Holiness Movement, 1974, Guide to the Study of the Pentecostal Movement, 1983, Black Holiness, 1987, The Charismatic Movement, 1995; contbr. articles to scholarly jours. With U.S. Army, 1956-58. Mem. Am. Theol. Libr. Assn., Can. Ch. Hist. Soc. Democrat. Mem. Reformed Episcopal Ch. Home: 12300 Springwood Dr Oklahoma City OK 73120-1724

JONES, CHARLES HILL, JR., banker; b. July 14, 1933; s. Charles Hill and Susan Roy (Johnston) J.; m. Hope Haskell, Jan. 28, 1961; children: Hope H., Charles Hill III, Henry M.T. Grad., Groton (Mass.) Sch., 1952; BA in Econs., U. Va., 1956. With Wood, Struthers & Winthrop, Inc., N.Y.C., 1956-73, gen. ptnr., 1968-69, v.p., dir., dir. rsch., 1969-73; sr. v.p., chief investment officer Midlantic Nat. Bank, Edison, 1974-87; gen. ptnr. Edge Ptnrs., 1987—. Bd. dirs. N.J. Title Ins. Co., chmn., 2000-01; bd. dirs. NJT Holdings, chmn., 2000-. Author: (with Joseph D. Davis) Toll Road Bonds, 1959, The Growth Rate Appraiser, 1968. Treas. N.Y. chpt. R.E. Lee Meml. Found., 1964-69; trustee, chmn. fin. com. Monmouth Med. Ctr., 1975-81, pres. bd. trustees Rumson (N.J.) Country Day Sch., 1982-85; trustee Hampden-Sydney Coll., 1995-99, 2002-. Mem. Inst. Chartered Fin. Analysts, Bond Club, City Midday Club (trustee, treas. 1965-71, v.p. 1972-74). Home: 218 Via Linda Palm Beach FL 33480-3405 Office: Edge Ptnrs 1129 Broad St Shrewsbury NJ 07702-4333

JONES, CHARLES IRVING, bishop; b. El Paso, Tex., Sept. 13, 1943; s. Charles I. Jr. and Helen A. (Heyward) J.; m. Ashby MacArthur, June 18, 1966; children: Charles I. IV, Courtney M., Frederic M., Keith A. BS, The Citadel, 1965; MBA, U. N.C., 1966; MDiv, U. of the South, 1977, DD, 1989. CPA. Pub. acctg. D.E. Gatewood and Co., Winston-Salem, N.C., 1966-72; dir. devel. Chatham (Va.) Hall, 1972-74; instr. acctg. U. of the South, Sewanee, Tenn., 1974-77; coll. chaplain Western Ky. U., Bowling Green, 1977-81; vicar Trinity Episcopal Ch., Russelville, Ky., 1977-85; archdeacon Diocese of Ky., Louisville, 1981-86; bishop Episcopal Diocese of Mont., Helena, 1986-2001. Bd. dirs. New Directions Ministries, Inc., N.Y.C.; mem. standing com. Joint Commn. on Chs. in Small Communities, 1988-91, Program, Budget and Fin., 1991-94; v.p. province VI Episcopal Ch., 1991-94, mem. Presiding Bishop's Coun. Advice, 1991-94. Author: Mission Strategy in the 21st Century, 1989, Total Ministry: A Practical Approach, 1993; bd. editors Grass Roots, Luling, Tex., 1985-90; contbr. articles to profl. jours. Founder Concerned Citizens for Children, Russelville, 1981; bd. dirs. St. Peter's Hosp., Helena, 1986-2001; bd. dirs. Christian Ministry in Nat. Parks, 1992—. With USMCR, 1961-65. Mem. Aircraft Owners and Pilots Assn. Episcopalian. Avocations: running, flying, writing, skiing. Office: Diocese Mont 515 N Park Ave Helena MT 59601-2703 E-mail: bpci@aol.com.

JONES, CHARLES J. wood products manufacturing executive; b. Marshfield, Oreg., Jan. 29, 1940; s. Charles J. Cotter and Lois C. (Smith) Meltebeke; m. Sharon S. Madsen, Mar. 29, 1969; children: Mary E., Judith A., Kari C., April M., Autumn C. AS in Fire Sci. Tech., Portland Community Coll., 1974; BS in Fire Adminstrn., Eastern Oreg. State Coll., 1983; diploma, Nat. Fire Acad., 1983, 85; MPA, Lewis and Clark Coll., 1989. Cert. class VI fire officer, Oreg., hazardous materials instr., fire instr. I; lic. real estate agt. From firefighter to capt. Washington County Fire Dist., Aloha, Oreg., 1964-74, battalion chief, 1974-81, dir. comms., dir. research and devel., 1981-85, dir. strategic planning, 1986-88; cons. Tualatin Valley Fire & Rescue, Aloha, 1989-90; pres., CEO Palletoys, 1989—. Basic and advanced 1st aid instr. ARC, 1965-80; cons. Washington County Consol. Communications Agy., 1983-86, chmn. 9-1-1 mgmt. bd., 1982-83; mem. adv. bd. Washington County Emergency Med. Svcs., 1981-83; owner/instr. Internat. Vocat. Inst. and Family Tree Learning Ctrs. Jones Internat., Ltd., 1990-95. Editor local newsletter Internat. Assn. Firefighters, 1970; contbr. articles on fire dept. mgmt. to jours. Active Community Planning Orgn., Washington County, 1979-90, chmn. 1988-89. With USAF, 1957-59. Mem. Oreg. Fire Chiefs Assn. (chmn. seminar com. 1982-83, 89, co-chmn. 1981, 84, 86, 87, 88). Republican. Mem. Congl.Ch. Avocations: photography, genealogy, antique auto restoration, traveling, writing. Office: Palletoys PO Box 86 Forest Grove OR 97116-0086

JONES, CHARLIE, television sports announcer; b. Ft. Smith, Ark. m. Ann; children: Chuck, Julie. JD, U. Ark., 1953. Play-by-play broadcaster Am. Football League, ABC-TV, 1960-64, NFL, NBC, 1965-98, Cin. Reds TV Network, 1973-74, USC Basketball, 1974-75, Seattle Seahawks preseason football, Sta. KING-TV, 1985-89; commentator for Wide World of Sports ABC, 1961-64; sports dir. Sta. WFAA-TV, Dallas, 1962-65, Sta. WMAQ-TV, Chgo., 1974; sports commentator NBC-TV, 1965-98; play-by-play broadcaster Colo. Rockies TV Network, 1993-95. Author: What Makes Winners Win (N.Y. Times Bestseller), 1997; co-author: You Go Girl, 2000, Be the Ball, 2000, That's Outside My Boat, 2001, Game, Set Match, 2002; TV broadcasting firsts include Super Bowl I, first Am. Football League Championship game, first Am. Football League nationally televised game, first NBC SportsWorld, first World Cup Gymnastics, first World Cup Marathon, first World Championships of Track and Field, Helsinki, 1983, first World Indoor Championships of Track and Field, Indpls., 1987, first Sr. Skins Game, Hawaii, 1988; broadcaster 50 coll. bowl football games; host TV shows: Seahawks Insider, Almost Anything Goes, Pro-Fan; appeared in TV series: Ironside, McMillan and Wife, Columbo, The Dick Van Dyke Show, Rich Man, Poor Man; appeared in several Movies of the Week and motion pictures Personal Best, Without Limits, Return of the Killer Tomatoes, and Killer Tomatoes Strike Back. Recipient Emmy award for documentary Is Winning the Name of the Game, 1982, Outstanding Achievement award Freedoms Found. of Valley Forge, 1982, Bronze medal for co-producing, co-hosting, co-writing The American Frontier, PBS-TV, Internat. TV Festival of N.Y., 1982, Headliner of Yr. award for outstanding contbns. in field of TV San Diego Press Club, 1986, Disting. Alumnus award U. Ark., 1989; inductee Pro Football Hall of Fame, 1997, Aks. Sports Hall of Fame, 2000. Mem. Confrerie des Chevaliers du Tastevin. Office: 8080 El Paseo Grande La Jolla CA 92037-3284 E-mail: jonesvoice@aol.com.

JONES, CHARLOTTE, principal; b. Elk City, Okla., Dec. 21, 1949; d. S.G. and Mary Kathryn (Hartman) McLaury; m. Ray Loyd Jones, Apr. 3, 1969; children: Kathryn Denise, Ryan MacRay, Joshua Kyle. BS in Edn., U. Okla., 1976; MEd, Southwestern Okla. State U., 1991. Cert. tchr. math., counseling, social studies, lang. arts. Prin. Madison Elem. Sch., Norman, Okla. Mem.: ASCD, Nat. Assn. Elem. Sch. Prins., Okla. Assn. Elem. Sch. Prins., Rotary, Phi Delta Kappa. Home: 4409 Oxford Way Norman OK 73072-3160 E-mail: cjones@norman.K12.OK.us.

JONES, CHRISTINE MASSEY, retired furniture company executive; b. Columbus, Ga., Nov. 7, 1929; d. Louis Everett and Donia (Spivey) Massey; divorced; children— James Raymond, Jr., James David. Student, Ga. Southwestern Coll., 1947-48. With Muscogee Mfg. Co., Columbus, Ga., 1948-56, sec. to pres., 1956; sec. to pres. and treas., corp. sec. Haverty Furniture Cos., Inc., Atlanta, 1956-59, sec. to pres. and treas., 1959-63, sec. to pres., 1963-72, sec. to pres., adminstrv. asst., 1972-74, sec. to pres., adminstrv. asst., corp. sec., 1974-78, corp. sec., 1978-86, corp. sec., asst. v.p., 1986 93; v.p. stockholder rels., sec. Haverty Furniture Cos., Atlanta, 1993-97, ret., 1997. Mem. Am. Soc. Corp. Secs. (securities industry com.)

JONES, CHRISTOPHER, advertising company executive; m. Sara Jones; children: Laura, Gus. Former co-pres., exec. v.p. Worldwide Agy. Ops. J. Walter Thompson Co., N.Y.C., former mng. dir. multinational accounts; chief exec. J. Walter Thompson, London, 1989-92; CEO J. Walter Thompson Co., N.Y.C., 1997—. Office: J Walter Thompson Co 466 Lexington Ave New York NY 10017-3140

JONES, CHRISTOPHER PRESTIGE, classicist, historian; b. Kent, U.K., 1940; s. William Prestige and Irene May (McCreddie) J. BA, Oxford U., 1962; PhD Classical Philology, Harvard U., 1965. From lectr. to prof. U. Toronto, Can., 1965-92, chair dept. classics, 1986-90; prof. classics and history Harvard U., Cambridge, 1992-97, George Martin Lane prof. classics and history, 1997—. Vis. lectr. Harvard U., 1968; assoc. prof. Ecole Normale Supérieure de Jeunes Filles, Paris, 1979, Ecole Normale Supérieure, Paris, 1992; acting vice dean Faculty Arts and Scis., U. Toronto, 1985-86. Author: Philostratus: Life of Apollonius of Tyana, 1971, Plutarch and Rome, 1971, The Roman World of Dio Chrysostom, 1978, Culture and Society in Lucian, 1986, Kinship Diplomacy in the Ancient World, 1999; co-editor: Le Martyre de Pionios, prêtre de Smyrne, 1994; contbr. numerous articles to profl. jours. Fellow Royal Soc. Can., Am. Numismatic Soc.; mem. Am. Philol. Assn. (chair subcom. epigraphical bibliog. 1981-89, subcom. cartography 1986-90), Am. Acad. Arts and Scis., German Archeol. Inst. (corr. mem. 1992—), Am. Philos. Soc. Home: 130 Mount Auburn St Apt 107 Cambridge MA 02138-5757 Office: Harvard U Boylston Hall Cambridge MA 02138 E-mail: cjones@fas.harvard.edu.

JONES, CLARIS EUGENE, JR., botanist, educator; b. Columbus, Ohio, Dec. 15, 1942; s. Claris Eugene and Clara Elizabeth (Elliott) J.; m. Teresa Diane Wagner, June 26, 1966; children: Douglas Eugene, Philip Charles, Elizabeth Lynne. BS, Ohio U., 1964; PhD, Ind. U., 1969. Asst. prof. botany Calif. State U., Fullerton, 1969-73, assoc. prof., 1973-77, prof. botany, 1977—, chmn. dept. biol. sci., 1989—, dir. Fullerton Arboretum, 1970-80, dir. Faye MacFadden Herbarium, 1969—; disting. faculty mem. Sch. Natural Sci. and Math., 1999—. Adj. instr. Marshall Coll. Natural Sci. and Math., 2000. Author: A Dictionary of Botany, 1980; editor: Handbook of Experimental Pollination Biology, 1983; contbr. articles to profl. jours. Mem. Am. Inst. Biol. Sci., AAAS, Bot. Soc. Am., Internat. Assn. Plant Taxonomy, Am. Soc. Plant Taxonomists, Soc. Study Evolution, Systematics Assn., Ecol. Soc. Am., Calif. Bot. Soc., Sigma Xi Methodist. Office: 800 N State College Blvd Fullerton CA 92834-6850

JONES, CLARK POWELL, JR., financial services executive; b. Gainesville, Fla., Nov. 1, 1964; s. Clark Powell and Mary Evelyn (Eddins) J.; m. Patricia Ann Pagli, Sept. 26, 1993; children: Kylie Elizabeth, Erin Nicole. BA in Econs. and Polit. Sci., Emory U., 1986; MBA in Fin., NYU, 1994. Cert. cash mgr. Corp. svcs. officer First Am. Corp., Nashville, 1986-89; v.p. Berkshire Capital Corp., NYC, 1989-95; v.p., sr. mgr.-bus. svc. group Barnett Banks, Inc., Jacksonville, Fla., 1995-98; sr. v.p., dir. bus. planning and analysis Fleet Boston Fin., 1998—. Bd. dir. Eddins Broadcasting Co., Inc. Mentor INROADS, 1998, 99, Jr. Achievement volunteer, 1998, 99, 2000. Mem. Emory Univ. Alumni Assn. Republican. Methodist. Avocations: reading, golf. Office: Fleet Boston Fin/Small Bus Svcs 1075 Main St 2nd Fl Waltham MA 02451 Fax: (781) 788-1037.

JONES, CLEON BOYD, research engineer; b. Norwalk, Calif., Nov. 9, 1961; s. Cleon Earl and Marjorie Helen (McDade) J. BS in Math., Biola U., 1983. Rsch. libr. Christian Rsch. Inst., San Juan Capistrano, Calif., 1981-84; flight control engr. Leading Systems, Inc., Irvine, Calif., 1984-90; sr. staff engr. Dynamic Rsch., Inc., Torrance, Calif., 1990-98; sr. flight dynamics engr. Frontier Systems, Inc., Irvine, Calif., 1998—. Recipient NASA Group Achievement award Pilot Project Team, 1994. Republican. Avocations: reading, soccer, music, theology, aviation. Home: 720 N Markwood St Orange CA 92867-7214

JONES, CLIFFORD ALAN, lawyer; b. Auston, Tex., Aug. 14, 1953; s. Paul Dale and Marylu (Farnum) J.; m. Lynda Lee Kaid, Jan. 31, 1972. BA in Govt., So. Ill. U., 1974; JD, U. Okla., 1977; MPhil, U. Cambridge, 1995, PhD, 1997. Bar: Okla. 1977, U.S. Dist. Ct. (we. dist.) Okla. 1978, U.S. Ct. Appeals (10th cir.) 1978, U.S. Supreme Ct. 1980, U.S. Ct. Appeals (fed. cir.) 1984, Tex. 1994. Assoc. Fagin, Hewett, Mathews & Fagin, Oklahoma City, 1977-79, 80-81; mem. firm. Bradford, Haswell, Jones, Oklahoma City, 1981-86, Clifford A. Jones & Assocs., 1986-96. Vis. asst. prof. law Oklahoma City U., 1979-80, adj. prof. law, 1980; spl. lectr. law U. Okla., Norman, 1979, 81; temporary judge Okla. Ct. Appeals, 1982-83; vis. prof. law and bus. U. Okla., 1996-2001; lectr. Coll. Law U. Fla., 2001—. Author: Private Enforcement of Antitrust Law in the EC, UK and USA, 1999; contbr. articles to profl. jours. Mem. ABA (antitrust and litigation sect.), Assn. Trial Lawyers Am., Okla. Bar Assn. (co-editor Desk Man., antittrust sect., patent trademark adn copyright sect.), Oklahoma County Bar Assn., Internat. Bar Assn. (bus., gen. practice, energy and natural resource law sects.). Home: 2230 NW 26th Ave Gainesville FL 32605 E-mail: jonesca@law.ufl.edu.

JONES, CLIVE GARETH, ecologist, researcher; b. Circencester, Eng., Mar. 3, 1951; came to U.S., 1978; s. Maldwyn Henry and Marianne (Weisz) J. BSc in Biology with honors, U. Salford, Eng., 1975; PhD in Biology, U. York, Eng., 1978. Fellow U. Ga., Athens, 1978-80; asst. scientist Inst. of Ecosystem Studies, Millbrook, N.Y., 1980-87, assoc. scientist, 1987-92; scientist Inst. Ecosystem Studies, Millbrook, 1993—. Author: Ecological Understanding, 1994; editor: Microbial Mediation of Plant Herbivore Interactions, 1991, Linking Species and Ecosystems, 1995; contbr. over 130 articles to profl. jours. Recipient Travelling fellowship Brit. Ecol. Soc., 1987, Winston Churchill fellowship English Speaking Union, Australia, New Zealand, 1990; named John Simon Guggenheim Meml. fellow, 1994. Fellow AAAS; mem. Internat. Soc. Chem. Ecol. (coun. 1986-89, bylaws com. 1990), Ecol. Soc. Am. (fellowship com. 2002—), Entomol. Soc. Am., British Ecol. Soc., Sigma Xi (editl. bd. Functional Ecology 2001—). Office: Inst Ecosystem Studies Millbrook NY 12545-0129 E-mail: jonesc@ecostudies.org.

JONES, CLYDE WILLIAM, anesthesiologist; b. Barbados, West Indies, Sept. 29, 1929; came to U.S., 1947; s. Lewis F. and Albertha B. (Lewis) J.; m. Norma Anita, Sept. 14, 1963; children: Michael W., Ronald C., Stephen T. BS, City Coll., N.Y.C., 1954; MD, Howard U., 1958. Diplomate Am. Bd. Anesthesiology. Capt. U.S. Navy, 1959-79, med. officer, 1959-63; resident in anesthesiology U.S. Naval Hosp., San Diego, 1963-66, staff anesthesiologist Camp Pendleton, Calif., 1966-67, chief of anesthesiology, 1967-69, 1st Hosp. Co., Danang, Vietman, 1968, U.S. Naval Hosp., Marianas Island, Guam, 1969-71; staff anesthesiologist Naval Regional Med. Ctr., San Diego, 1971-73, chief of anesthesiology, 1973-79; staff anesthesiologist Kaiser Permanente Med. Ctr., San Diego, 1979-81, 87—, chief of anesthesiology, 1981-87. Contbr. articles to profl. jours. Acolyte lay reader, sub Deacon All Sts. Episc. Ch., San Diego, 1971—; acolyte, chalice bearer, lay eucharistic min. St. Dunstan's Episco. Ch., San Diego; bd. dirs. Bishop's Sch., San Diego, 1980—81, San Diego Civic Light Opera, Inc., 1980—83. Recipient Meritorious Svc. medal, certificate of merit Surgeon Gen. U.S. Navy, 1979. Fellow Am. Coll. Anesthesiologists; mem.Am. Soc. Anesthesiologists (delegate), Assn. Mil. Surgeons of U.S., Am. Soc. Clin. Hypnosis, Internat. Anesthesia Rsch. Soc., Naval Inst., Sigma Pi Phi. Democrat. Avocations: hypnosis, coin collecting, medical volunteer. Home: 5201 Countryside Dr San Diego CA 92115-2136 Office: Kaiser Permanente Med Ctr 4647 Zion Ave San Diego CA 92120-2507 E-mail: cwjretired@yahoo.com.

JONES, COBI, professional soccer player; b. Detroit, June 16, 1970; Student, UCLA. Midfielder Coventry City, 1994—95, Vasco da Gama, 1995—96, L.A. Galaxy, 1996—, U.S. Nat. Team, 1996—. With gold medal U.S. Team Pan Am. Games, 1991; with U.S. Olympic Team, 1992, U.S. Nat. Team, 1992—95, including victory over Ivory Coast, 1992. Host (TV series) Megadose (MTV), guest appearance Beverly Hills 90210, 1994. Achievements include tied for all-time assist lead, with 11. Office: c/o US Soccer Fedn 1801-1811 S Prairie Ave Chicago IL 60616 and: LA Galaxy 1640 S Sepulveda Blvd Los Angeles CA 90025-7510

JONES, CRAIG WARD, lawyer; b. Pitts., June 14, 1947; s. Curtis Edison and Margaret (McFarland) J.; m. Sarah Dowding; children: Laura McFarland, Rebecca Long, Nancy Harper. BA, Carleton Coll., 1969; JD, U. Pitts., 1976. Bar: Pa. 1976, U.S. Dist. Ct. (we. dist.) Pa. 1976, U.S. Ct. Appeals (3d cir.) 1981. Ptnr. Reed Smith LLP, Pitts., 1976—. Served to lt. USNR, 1969-73. Mem. Allegheny County Bar Assn. Presbyterian. Home: 208 Cornwall Dr Pittsburgh PA 15238-2639 Office: Reed Smith LLP Mellon Sq 435 6th Ave Pittsburgh PA 15219-1886

JONES, CYNTHIA TERESA CLARKE, artist; b. Bklyn., Aug. 12, 1938; d. Arthur Ottio and Emma (Gibbs) Clarke; m. Robert H. Jones. Apr. 21, 1968 (div. Sept. 1977); 1 child, Kim Marie. Student, Bklyn. Mus., 1954-57, Art Career Sch., 1958, Hunter Coll., N.Y.C., 1963-65. One woman shows include Queens Borough Pub. Libr., Jamaica, N.Y., 1986, Baruch Coll., 1972; exhibited in group shows Queens Coun. on Arts Exhibit at Gertz Dept. Store, 1972, Queens Coll. Arts Festival, 1972, Dist. Coun. 37, First Art Exhbn., 1972, Artist Equity Group Shows Union Carbide, 1975, 77, Queensborough Community Coll. Invitational Show at Holocaust Resource Ctr., 1985, Pen and Brush, 1990, AQA Gallery, 1990, AQA at Chung Cheng Gallery at St. Johns U., 1987-90, Lowenstein Libr. Gallery Fordham U., 1989, Arlington Arts Ctr., 1991, Pursuit of Peace Ceres Gallery, 1991; designer cover Rsch. Papers Stats. Dept. Bernard

M. Baruch Coll., 1973; works reprinted in Locally Speaking Local 384 newsletter. Donator work to MUSE Gallery, 1990, to Hale House Ctr., Inc.; active Women's Caucus for Art. Recipient Joseph Grumbacher Co. award, 1958, Scholastic Art award and key, 1957, Fine Arts award Queensboro Soc., 1973, Outstanding Painting award, 1973, France Lieber Meml. award Nat. Assn. Women Artists, Inc., 1992, two certs. of merit Latham Found., 1956-58; scholar Latham Found., 1958. Mem. Artists Equity Assn., Inc. N.Y., Alliance of Queens Artists, Coll. Art Assn., Queens Coun. on Arts, Ind. Arts Assn., Arlington Arts Ctr. Va., Queensboro Coll. Art Gallery (assoc.), Nat. Assn. Women Artists (The Kreindler Meml. award 1995), Print Club, Guild Am. Papercutters. Office: 11332 Mayville St Jamaica NY 11412-2410

JONES, D. PAUL, JR., banker, lawyer; b. Birmingham, Ala., Sept. 26, 1942; s. D. Paul and Virginia Lee (Mount) J.; m. Charlene Dale Angelich, Aug. 1964; children: Holly, Allison, Paul, III. BS, U. Ala., 1964, JD, 1967; LL.M., N.Y. U., 1968. Bar: Ala. Mem. firm Balch, Bingham, Baker, Hawthorne, Williams & Ward, Birmingham, 1970-78, of counsel, 1978-86; exec. v.p., gen. counsel, dir. Compass Bancshares, Inc., Birmingham, 1978-84, vice chmn., 1984-89, pres., COO, 1989-91, chmn., CEO, 1991—. Bd. dirs. Compass Bank, Golden Enterprises, Inc., Russell Lands Co., Bus. Coun. Ala., Compass Bancshares, Inc.; exec. com. Pub. Affairs Rsch. Coun. Ala.; mem. Internat. Fin. Conf. Chmn. Ala. Bus. Charitable Trust Fund; mem. adv. bd. Better Bus. Bur. Birmingham; adv. bd. Salvation Army, Birmingham; bd. visitors Sch. Commerce and Bus. Adminstrn., U. Ala.; mem. pres.'s coun. U. Ala., Birmingham, Ala. Inst. Deaf and Blind; ptnr. Econ. Devel. Partnership Ala.; grad. bd. trustees Leadership Birmingham; grad. Leadership Ala.; mem. adv. bd. Juvenile Diabetes Found., Ala., corp. chmn. Walk to Cure Diabetes, 1999; co-chmn. Advantage 21 Leadership Coun.; mem. adv. coun. Nat. Multiple Sclerosis Soc.; bd. dirs. Region 2020, Inc., Fed. Res. Bank Atlanta; dinner chmn. 32d ann. awards dinner Nat. Conf. for Cmty. and Justice, 2000; adv. bd. Svc. Corp. Ret. Execs. Mem. ABA, Ala. Bar Assn. (chmn. sect. corp., banking and bus. law 1973-75, bd. bar examiners 1975-78), Birmingham Bar Assn., Am. Bankers Assn. (mem. govt. rels. coun. 1985-88), Ala. Bankers Assn. (pres. 1989-90, chmn. fin. com. 1990-91, exec. coun.), Fin. Svcs. Roundtable (bd. dirs., banking and fin. markets com.), Soc. Internat. Bus. Fellows, Newcomen, Birmingham C. of C., Birmingham C. of C. Found., Birmingham Bus. Leadership Group, Svc. Corps Ret. Execs. (adv. bd.), The Club, Old Overton, Country Club Birmingham, Willow Point Golf and Country Club (Alexander City), Rotary. Home: 2010 Garden Pl Birmingham AL 35223-1156 Office: Compass Bancshares Inc PO Box 10566 Birmingham AL 35296-0001 also: Compass Bancshares Inc 15 20th St S Birmingham AL 35233-2000

JONES, DALE EDWIN, public defender; b. Rahway, N.J., Oct. 22, 1948; s. Horatio Gates and Audrey Irma (Morgan) J.; m. Karen Anne Woodhall, June 19, 1971; children: Sharon, Michael, Stephan; m. Maria D. Noto, Aug. 2, 1987 (div. 1989); m. Joan E. DiTullio, Oct. 18, 1991; 1 child, Trevor. BA, Rutgers U., 1970, JD, 1973. Bar: N.J. 1973, U.S. Dist. Ct. N.J. 1973, U.S. Supreme Ct. 1977, N.Y. 1983. 1st asst. pub. defender Office Pub. Defender, Newark, 1974-84, dep. pub. defender in charge of capital litigation, 1984-87; asst. pub. defender, dir. of policy Office of Pub. Defender, Trenton, NJ, 1987—, dir. policy, dir. of policy, 1987—. Mem. model jury charge com., N.J. Supreme Ct., 1983-88, criminal practice com., Trenton, 1983—, com. media rels., 1987-89, strategic planning com., 1996-98, rules of evidence com., 1998-2002. Mem. editorial bd. N.J. Lawyer. Mem. ACDL-N.J., Nat. Assn. Criminal Def. Lawyers (cert. criminal atty.), Amnesty Internat. Democrat. Office: Pub Defender Office PO Box 850 Trenton NJ 08625-0850 Personal E-mail: djones2411@yahoo.com. Business E-Mail: Dale.Jones@opd.state.nj.us.

JONES, DAN BRIGMAN, ophthalmologist, educator; b. Raleigh, N.C., June 12, 1936; m. Marilyn Woodall; children: Danny Brigman Jr., Allen Walker. BA, Duke U., 1958, MD, 1962. Diplomate Am. Bd. Ophthalmology. Intern Duke Hosp., Durham, 1962-63; resident in ophthalmology Bascom Palmer Eye Inst., U. Miami (Fla.) Sch. Medicine, 1965-69; fellow in cornea and external disease Moorfields Eye Hosp., Inst. Ophthalmology, London, 1967-68; asst. prof. then assoc. prof. ophthalmology dept. surgery Vanderbilt U. Sch. Medicine, Nashville, 1969-71; assoc. prof. then prof. ophthalmology Cullen Eye Inst., Baylor Coll. Medicine, Houston, 1972-78, Sid W. Richardson prof., chmn. dept. ophthalmology, 1981—, Margarett Root Brown chair ophthalmology, 1991—; mem. staff, then chief ophthalmology svc. Ben Taub Gen. Hosp., 1972—, Meth. Hosp., Houston, 1972—; mem. staff St. Luke's Episcopal Hosp., Houston, 1973—. Chief ophthalmology sect. VA Hosp., Houston, 1973-78; mem. sci. adv. com. Knights Templar Eye Found., Inc., 1984-2002; mem. various coms. and couns. Nat. Eye Inst., 1975-76; mem. adv. panel on ophthalmology U.S. Pharmacopeial Conv., 1980-84; mem. ophthalmic drugs adv. com. FDA, 1975-78; cons. in field; vis. prof. to numerous schs., including Johns Hopkins U., Balt., 1975, 79, Washington U., St. Louis, 1975, Tipler Army Hosp., Honolulu, 1974, Yale U., New Haven, 1988, others; lectr. in field. Contbr. numerous articles to profl. jours. Bd. dirs. William C. Connor Found., Tex. Christian U., 1981—, Tex. Soc. to Prevent Blindness, 1981—; bd. dirs. The Lighthouse of Houston, 1981-89, mem. adv. coun., 1989—; mem. exec. med. com. Lions Eye Bank of Tex., 1981—, bd. dirs., 1989—. Epidemic intelligence officer USPHS, 1963-65. Recipient Honor award in Edn. Am. Acad. Ophthalmology and Otolaryngology, 1976; grantee NIH, 1978—, Sid W. Richardson Found., 1977-82. Mem. AMA (mem. program com. sect. ophthalmology 1970-73), Am. Acad. Ophthalmology (mem. faculty of basic and clin. sci. course 1970-76, mem. ophthalmology knowledge assessment com. 1972-80, mem. adv. com. 1973-77, mem. long range planning com. 1976-80, mem. program adv. com. 1986-89, sec. instrn. 1989—, trustee 1989—, Sr. Honor award 1986), Am. Ophthalmol. Soc., Am. Soc. for Microbiology, Assn. for Rsch. in Vision and Ophthalmology, Assn. Univ. Profs. Ophthalmology (chmn. resident and fellowship edn. com. 1986-88, chmn. edn. com. 1988-93, trustee 1988-93, pres. bd. trustees 1993-94), Harris County Med. Soc., Houston Ophthal. Soc. (pres. 1979-80), Ocular Microbiology and Immunology Group, Inc. (exec. sec. 1973-89, bd. dirs. 1989-93), Pan Am. Assn. Ophthalmology, Tex. Ophthal. Assn. (mem. bd. councillors 1982-85), Tex. Soc. Infectious Diseases, Baylor Ophthalmology Alumni Assn., Inc., Bascom Palmer Alumni Assn., Phi Beta Kappa, Phi Eta Sigma, Alpha Omega Alpha. Office: Cullen Eye Inst 6565 Fannin NC 205 Houston TX 77030

JONES, DAN L. academic administrator; m. Daisy Jones; 2 children. BA, doctorate, Univ. Utah. Pres. Towson Univ., 2002—, asst. prof. english, 1966, chair english dept., dean coll. liberal arts. Office: Towson U Adminstrn Rm 331 8000 York Rd Baltimore MD 21252-0001

JONES, DAN LEWIS, psychologist; b. Halifax, Va., Oct. 8, 1951; s. Ernest Lewis and Mary Elizabeth (Francis) J.; m. Temple Kiger Jones, Aug. 17, 1974; children: Natalie Temple, Layla Michelle. BA, Appalachian State U., 1974; MA, West Ga. Coll., 1976; PhD, U. Kans., 1986. Lic. psychologist, N.C., Calif., Va.; diplomate in counseling psychology Am. Bd. Profl. Psychology; cert. treatment of alcohol and other psychoactive substance use disorders, APA Coll. of Profl. Psychology. Instr. psychology N.C. Ctrl. U., Durham, 1976-79; counselor Adult Life Resource Ctr., U. Kans., Lawrence, 1979-84; psychology intern Counseling Ctr. U. Calif., Irvine, 1984-85; acting dir. adult life resource ctr. U. Kans., 1985-86; staff psychologist Counseling Ctr. Utah State U., Logan, 1986-88; psychologist Counseling Ctr. East Tenn. State U., Johnson City, 1988-89; sr. psychologist, dir. tng., asst. dir. Counseling and Psychol. Svcs., Appalachian State U., Boone, N.C., 1989-97, dir., 1996—; part-time pvt. practice. Cons. IRS, 1985, Bristol (Tenn.) Mental Health Ctr., 1989, N.C. Ct. Counseling Svcs., 1979. Author: (with others) Counseling Adults, 1985, editor; author (manual) The Stress management Workshop, 1985, (with others) AACD Stress Workshop Manual, 1985; ad hoc reviewer Jour. Psychotherapy Integration, Jour. Coll. Student Devel., Jour. of Am. Coll. Health, others. Fellow Acad. of Counseling Psychology; mem. APA (chmn. spl. interest group on coll. counseling ctrs. divsn. 17, mem. program com. divsn. 29), Am. Coll. Health Assn., Am. Counseling Assn., Am. Coll. Counseling Assn., NC Psychol. Assn., Am. Coll. Pers. Assn. (directorate commn. VII), Soc. of Psychotherapy Integration, Internat. Assn. Counseling Svcs. (bd. dirs., pres. elect). Democrat. Avocation: racquetball. Home: 357 Fawn Dr Boone NC 28607-8461 E-mail: jonesdl@appstate.edu.

JONES, DANIEL EDWIN, JR., bishop; b. Westcliffe, Colo., Jan. 31, 1942; s. Daniel Edwin and Vivian Mary (Falkenberg) Jones. BA, Carroll Coll., Helena, Mont., 1964; MA, Am. Coll., Louvain, Belgium, 1968. Ordained priest Roman Cath. Ch., 1968, ordained to ministry Ch. of Jesus Christ, 1994, consecrated to bishop Ch. of Jesus Christ. Parish priest Diocese of Pueblo, Colo., 1968-72; itinerant mission priest Traditional Cath. Movement, Westcliffe, 1972-93; itinerant bishop Ch. of Jesus Christ, St. Jovite, Canada, 1994—. Editor, pub.: Sangre de Cristo Newsnotes, 1973—. 3d order mem. Order Magnificat Mother of God. Avocations: rockhounding, golf, hunting, fishing, gardening. Office: Sangre de Cristo Newsnotes PO Box 89 Westcliffe CO 81252-0089

JONES, DANIEL HARE, librarian, consultant; b. Charleston, S.C., Jan. 18, 1949; s. Daniel Hare and Maria Clare (Duffy) J.; m. Rajia Christina Tobia, Dec. 15, 1979; children: Andrew Duffy, Patrick Joseph. BS, Clemson U., 1971; MLS, Emory U., 1977. Tchr. pub. schs., Blackville, S.C., 1971-73; tchr. Peace Corps., Malaysia, 1973-74; libr. Biomed. Libr. U. So. Ala., Mobile, 1977-79; libr. Briscoe Library U. Tex. Health Sci. Ctr., San Antonio, 1979-98; pres. Libr. Cons. NA, Inc., Mobile, Ala., 1998—2003; dir. R&D for N.Am. representing Otto Harrassowitz, Wiesbaden, German, 1998—2003; libr. P.G. Northrup Meml. Lib. S.W. Found. Biomedical Rsch., San Antonio, 2003—. Indexer publs. Nat. Inst. Arthritis, Metabolism and Digestive Diseases, 1978; cons. Georgetown U. Med. Ctr. Libr., Washington, 1985-87, S.W. Found. for Biomed. Rsch., 1994-95; mem. libr. adv. coun. Springer-Verlag Pub. Co., 1992-96. Mem. editl. bd. Serials Rev., 1991-97, Newsletter on Serial Pricing Issues, 1990-98, Library Collections, Acquisitions, and Tech. Svcs., 1999-2002. Mem. ALA, Acad. Health Info. Profls. (disting.), Med. Libr. Assn., Tex. Libr. Assn. Roman Catholic. Avocations: swimming, gardening. Home: 223 Clearview Dr San Antonio TX 78228-1940 Office: PG Northrup Meml SW Found Biomedical Rsch PO Box 760549 San Antonio TX 78245-0549 E-mail: djones@sfbr.org.

JONES, DARYNDA DEAN, interpreter, educator; b. Friona, Tex., Aug. 21, 1965; d. Garold Eugene Eakins and Wanda Faye Metcalf; m. Daniel Lynn Jones, Oct. 19, 1986; children: Jerrdan Rhyder, Casey Dakota. BS in Sign Lang. Interpreting, U. N.Mex., 2001. Sign program asst. U. N.Mex., Albuquerque, 1999—2000; instr. sign program Clovis (N.Mex.) C.C., 2001—, staff interpreter, 2001—. Adv. bd. Clovis C.C., 2001—. Mem.: Golden Key, Phi Kappa Phi. Avocations: writing, reading. Home: 1412 S Abilene Portales NM 88130 E-mail: darynda_jones@yahoo.com.

JONES, DAVID ALWYN, geneticist, botany educator; b. Colliers Wood, Surrey, Eng., June 23, 1934; came to U.S., 1989; s. Trefor and Marion Edna Jones; m. Hazel Cordelia Lewis, Aug. 29, 1959; children: Catherine Susan, Edmund Meredith, Hugh Francis. BA, MA in Natural Scis., U. Cambridge, Eng., 1957; DPhil in Genetics, U. Oxford, Eng., 1963. Chartered biologist, UK. Lectr. genetics U. Birmingham, Eng., 1961-73; prof. genetics U. Hull, Eng., 1973-89, head dept. plant biology and genetics, 1983-88; prof. botany U. Fla., Gainesville, 1989—2003, chmn. dept. botany, 1989—98. Chmn. membership com. Inst. of Biology, London, 1982-87. Co-author: Variation and Adaptation in Plant Species, 1971, Analysis of Populations, 1976, What is Genetics?, 1976, Zmiennosc i przystosowanie roslin, 1977; contbr. over 100 articles to profl. jours. Fellow Linnean Soc., Inst. Biology; mem. AAAS, Am. Soc. Naturalists, Bot. Soc. Am., Internat. Soc. Chem. Ecology (coun. 1983-84, 89-91, keynote spkr. ann. meeting 1984, pres. elect 1986-87, pres. 1987-88, past pres. 1988-89, co-editor Jour. Chem. Ecology 1994-2000, Outstanding Svc. award 2001), Brit. Assn. Advancement of Sci. (chmn. coord. com. for cytology and genetics 1974-87), Genetical Soc. Gt. Britain (convenor ann. meetings profs. of genetics 1983-88), Ecol. Genetics Group, Population Genetics Group, Soc. for Study of Evolution, Gamma Sigma Delta, Sigma Xi (pres. U. Fla. chpt. 2000-01). Achievements include research in practical population biology especially in ecological genetics and chemical ecology of cyanogenic plants. Home: 7201 SW 97th Ln Gainesville FL 32608-6378 Office: U Fla Dept Botany 220 Bartram Hall Gainesville FL 32611-8526

JONES, DAVID ALLEN, health facility executive; b. Louisville, Aug. 7, 1931; s. Evan L. and Elsie F. (Thurman) Jones; m. Betty L. Ashbury, July 24, 1954. BS, U. Louisville, 1954; JD, Yale U., 1960. Bar: Ky. 1960. Founder Humana Inc. (formerly Extendicare Inc.), Louisville, 1961—97, also chmn., dir., 1997—; ptnr. Greenebaum, Doll and McDonald and predecessor, Louisville, 1965—69, of counsel, 1969—74. Dir. Abbott Labs. Lt. (j.g.) USN, 1954—57. Mem.: Louisville Area C. of C. Office: Humana Inc 500 W Main St Ste 300 Louisville KY 40202-4268

JONES, DAVID CHARLES, retired air force officer, former chairman Joint Chiefs of Staff; b. Aberdeen, S.D., July 9, 1921; s. Maurice and Helen Alice (Meade) J.; m. Lois M. Tarbell, Jan. 23, 1942; children: Susan Jones Coffin, Kathy Jones Franklin, David Curtis. Student, U. N.D., Minot State Coll.; grad., Flying Sch., Roswell, N.Mex., 1943, Nat. War Coll., Washington, 1960; H.L.D., U. Nebr., 1974, La. Tech. U., 1975, Minot State Coll., 1979, Boston U., 1980, Troy State U. Commd. 2d lt. U.S. Air Force, 1943, advanced through grades to gen., 1971; dep. comdr. ops. Vietnam; vice comdr. 7th Air Force; comdr.-in-chief U.S. Air Force Europe; comdr. 4th Allied Tactical Air Force; chief of staff U.S. Air Force, Washington, 1974-78; chmn. Joint Chiefs of Staff, Dept. Def., Washington, 1978-82, ret., 1982. Decorated Def. D.S.M., Air Force D.S.M., Navy D.S.M., Army D.S.M., Legion of Merit, D.F.C., Bronze star, Air medal, numerous others. Mem. Air Force Assn., Falcon Found., Mgmt. Execs. Soc., Coun. on Fgn. Rels., Alfalfa Club, Army-Navy Country Club, Bohemian Club. E-mail: dcji@aol.com.

JONES, DAVID JOHN, III, preventive medicine physician, medical executive; b. Ellwood City, Pa., Jan. 1, 1933; s. David John Jr. and Margaret Sarah (Liebendorfer) J.; m. Marie Anne Butler, Aug. 13, 1955; children: Sharon Jones Olszewski, David John IV, Marcie Jones Walsh. BS in Chemistry cum laude, Grove City Coll., 1954; MD, Jefferson Med. Coll., Phila., 1958; MPH in Med. Care Adminstrn., U. Pitts., 1965. Diplomate Am. Bd. Preventive Medicine. Intern Western Pa. Hosp., Pitts., 1958-59; resident in preventive medicine U. Pitts., Pa. Dept. of Health, 1963-65; pvt. practice Sharon, Pa., 1961-63; asst. prof. cmty. health U. Mo., Columbia, 1965-69; assoc. prof. medicine, dir. cmty. medicine U. Md. Sch. Med., Balt., 1969-76; dir. cmty. medicine York (Pa.) Hosp., 1969-76; v.p. Pa. Blue Shield, Camp Hill, 1976-83, Silver Spring Health Plan, Mechanicsburg, Pa., 1984-87; med. dir. All Health, Harrisburg, Pa., 1987—. Bd. dirs. Vision Benefits of Am., Pitts.; trustee Presbyn. Homes, Inc.; chmn. Am. Bd. Med. Quality, 1998—. Editor Am. Jour. Med. Quality, 1986—. Lt. cmdr. (sr. surgeon), USPHS, 1959-61. Milbank Faculty fellow, N.Y.C., 1967. Fellow Am. Coll. Med. Quality (disting.; v.p., pres.-elect, pres., 1992-96, Disting. Svc. award), Masons. Republican. Presbyterian. Avocations: music, art, gardening, bridge. Home: 1455 Virginia Ave York PA 17403-3629 Office: All Health 4750 Lindle Rd Harrisburg PA 17111-2428

JONES, DAVID M. zoological park administrator; b. Cheshire, Eng., Aug. 14, 1944; arrived in U.S., 1994; m. Janet Jones; 3 children. BSc in Zoology, Royal Vet. Coll., London, 1966; B in Vet. Medicine, Royal Veterinary Coll., London, 1969. 1st resident vet. surgeon Whipsnade pk. Zool. Soc. London, 1969-75, sr. vet. officer, 1975, responsible for animal collection London and Whipsnade, 1981, dir. zoos London and Whipsnade, 1984, CEO, 1991; dir. conservation and consultancy London and Whipsnade, 1993; dir. N.C. Zool. Pk., Asheboro, 1994—, Dept. Environ. Health, Natural Resources State of N.C., 1994—. Chmn. Fauna and Flora Internat., London, 1987—94; chmn. conservation com. World Wide Fund Nature, England, 1988—94, trustee, England; chmn. Brooke Hosp. Animals, London, Pakistan, 1990—98, India, 2000—02, Yadkin Pee-Dee Lakes Project, 1998—; mem. coun. World Wildlife Fund U.S., 1996—2002. Contbr. articles to profl. jours. Mem.: Royal Coll. Vet. Surgeons. Home: 1688 Sylvan Way Asheboro NC 27205-2546 Office: 4401 Zoo Pkwy Asheboro NC 27205-1425

JONES, DAVID MILTON, economist, educator; b. Newton, Iowa, June 22, 1938; s. Charles Raymond and Mary Evelyn (Corrough) J.; m. Becky Ann Jones Strait, Aug. 4, 1962; children: David, Jennifer, Stephen. BA with honors, Coe Coll., 1960; MA, U. Pa., 1961, PhD, 1969. Economist Fed. Res. Bank N.Y., N.Y.C., 1963-68; v.p., fin. economist Irving Trust Co., N.Y.C., 1968-72; vice-chmn., chief economist, bd. dirs. Aubrey G. Lanston & Co., Inc., N.Y.C., 1972-2000; owner DMJ Advisors LLC, N.Y.C., 2000—, Crystal Lake Resort, Pine, Colo. Advisor panel Fed. Res. Bank N.Y., 1982-93, cons. bd. govs., 1996—; mem. bd. vis. U. Pa.; former dir. pub. interest Suffolk County Savs. and Loan, Centerreach, N.Y.; bd. dirs. Aubrey G. Lanston & Co., Inc., Coe Coll., Union Theol. Sem.; lectr. AIMR security analysts seminar, Northwestern U. Author: Fed Watching and Interest Rate Projections: A Practical Guide, 1986, The Politics of Money: The Fed under Alan Greenspan, 1991, The Buck Starts Here: How the Federal Reserve Can Make or Break Your Financial Future, 1995, Unlocking the Secrets of the Fed: How Monetary Policy Affects the Economy and Your Wealth Creation Potential, 2002. Chmn. fin. and investment com. United Ch. Bd. for World Ministries, N.Y.C., 1975-86; mem. bond com. Twp. of Montclair, 1982-83. Woodrow Wilson Found. fellow, 1960; NDEA fellow, 1960 Mem. Nat. Assn. Bus. Economists, Econ. Club of N.Y., Nat. Econ. Club (bd. dirs.). Home: 483 E Gulf Dr Sanibel FL 33957-7219 Office: PO Box 529 Pine CO 80470

JONES, DAVID PROCTOR, academic administrator; b. Eugene, Oreg., Apr. 16, 1970; s. John Edwin Jones and Mary Elizabeth (Proctor) Brown; m. Jen B. Jones. BA in Secondary Edn., SUNY, Oswego, 1992; MS in Counseling, U. Nebr., Kearney, 1995; PhD in Ednl. Policy, Planning and Leadership, Coll. William and Mary, 2002. Tchr. Carlisle (Iowa) H.S., 1993; resident hall dir. U. Nebr., Kearney, 1993-95; area dir. office of residence life Coll. of William and Mary, Williamsburg, Va., 1995-2000; asst. dir. housing and residential edn. U. N.C., Chapel Hill, 2000—. Mem. program com. Upper Midwest Region-Assn. of Coll. and Univ. Housing Officers. Author computer program R.A. Train, 1995; contbr. articles to profl. jours. Dance-A-Thon organizer Habitat for Humanity, Kearney, 1993-94. Pres. scholar Upper Midwest Region-Assn. of Coll. and Univ. Housing Officers, 1994; recipient Outstanding New Profl. award, 1994. Mem. Southeastern Assn. Housing Officers (newcomers workshop chmn. 1996-98, membership svcs. com. chmn. 1998-2002, rsch. and info. com. chmn. 2002-, case study winner 1996, Svc. award 1999), So. Assn. Coll. Student Affairs, Order of Omega, Sigma Tau Chi. Avocations: reading, sports, juggling, writing. Office: U NC Housing & Residential Edn CB # 5500 101 Car Bldg Chapel Hill NC 27599-5500 E-mail: david_jones@unc.edu. davidpjones@usa.com.

JONES, DAVID RHODES, consulting editor; b. Connellsville, Pa., Sept. 13, 1932; s. David Rhodes and Ruth Elizabeth (Dillon) J.; m. Mary Lee Lauffer, Oct. 8, 1955; 1 dau., Elizabeth Lee. BA, Pa. State U., 1954; MA, N.Y. U., 1961. Reporter Wall Street Jour., N.Y.C., 1957-61, bur. chief Pitts., 1961-63; with N.Y. Times, 1963—97, corr., Detroit, 1963-65, nat. labor reporter, Washington, 1965-68, asst. nat. editor, N.Y.C., 1969-72, nat. editor, 1972-87, editor nat. editions, 1987-97, asst. mng. editor, 1989-97. Trustee Pa. State U. Served to 1st lt. USAF, 1955-57. Mem.Tau Kappa Epsilon.

JONES, DAVID ROBERT, zoology educator; came to Can., 1969; s. William Arnold and Gladys Margery Jones; m. Valerie Iris Gibson, Sept. 15, 1962; children: Melanie Ann, Vivienne Samantha B.Sc., Southampton U., 1962; PhD, U. East Anglia, Norwich, Eng., 1965. Rsch. fellow U. East Anglia, Eng., 1965-66; lectr. zoology U. Bristol, Eng., 1966-69; prof. zoology U. B.C., Vancouver, B.C., Can., 1969—. Contbr. numerous articles to profl. jours. Recipient Killam rsch. prize, 1993; fellow Killam Found., Can., 1973, 89; scholar Disting. scholar, Peter Wall Inst. Advanced Studies, Vancouver, 2002. Fellow Royal Soc. Can. (Flavelle medal 2000); mem. Soc. Exptl. Biology, Am. Physiol. Soc., Can. Zool. Soc. (Fry medal 1992), Order of Canada. Office: Zoology Animal Care U BC 6199 S Campus Rd Vancouver BC Canada V6T 1W5 E-mail: jones@zoology.ubc.ca.

JONES, DAVID STANLEY, lawyer; b. Columbus, Ohio, July 16, 1948; s. Herbert Morton and Gertrude Olivia (McKeon) J.; m. Mary Elizabeth Lyman, July 8, 1972; children— Colin David, Brian Christopher, Scott Lyman, Megan Elizabeth. B.B.A., U. Notre Dame, 1970; J.D., U. Houston, 1976. Bar: Tex. 1976, U.S. Dist. Ct. (no. dist.) Tex. 1979, (ea. and we. dists.) Tex. 1980, U.S. Ct. Appeals (5th and 11th cirs.) 1981, U.S. Supreme Ct. 1983. trial atty. U.S. Dept. Labor, Office Solicitor, Dallas, 1978-80 ; ptnr. Baldwin, Gilliland & Jones, Dallas, 1984-88; pvt. practice, Dallas, 1988—. Editor U. Houston Law Rev., 1975-76. Mem. State Bar Assn. Tex. (labor law specialist Tex. Bd. Legal Specialization, 1981, author and editor Tex. Practice Guide 1983), ABA (contbr. labor law sect. ann. report 1981-82, 84-88), Fed. Bar Assn. Dallas (pres. elect 1987-88, pres. 1988-89), Dallas Bar Assn., Phi Delta Phi. Roman Catholic. Home: 3072 Ponder Dr Dallas TX 75229-5860 Office: PO Box 31 Dallas TX 75221-0031

JONES, DIANA WYNNE, writer; b. London, Aug. 16, 1934; d. Richard Aneurin Jones and Marjorie (Jackson) Hughes; m. John Anthony Burrow, Dec. 22, 1956; children: Richard, Michael, Colin. BA, St. Anne's Coll. U. Oxford, Eng., 1956. Free-lance writer part-time, Essex, Oxford, Eng., 1944-70; full-time writer Oxford, Bristol, Eng., 1970—. Panel judge Guardian Award for Children's Books, London, 1979-83, Whitbread Prize for Lit., Children's Sect. London, 1988; judge World Fantasy Awards, 2001. Author: (children's and young adults' books) Wilkins' Tooth (in U.S. Witch's Business), 1973, The Ogre Downstairs, 1974, Eight Days of Luke, 1975, Cart and Cwidder, 1975, Dogsbody, 1975, Power the Three, 1976, Drowned Ammet, 1977, Charmed Life, 1977 (Guardian award 1978), Who Got Rid of Angus Flint, 1978, The Spellcoats, 1979, The Magicians of Caprona, 1980, The Homeward Bounders, 1981, The Time of the Ghost, 1981, Witch Week, 1982, Warlock at the Wheel, 1984, Archer's Goon, 1984 (Boston Globe/Horn Book award), Fire and Hemlock, 1985, Howl's Moving Castle, 1986 (Boston Globe/Horn Book award), A Tale of Time City, 1987, The Lives of Christopher Chant, 1988, Chaos Person, 1989, Wild Robert, 1989, Hidden Turnings, 1989, Castle in the Air, 1990, Black Maria, 1991, A Sudden Wild Magic, 1992, The Crown of Dalemark, 1993, Stopping for a Spell, 1993, Hexwood, 1993, Fantasy Stories, 1994, Everard's Ride, 1995, The Tough Guide to Fantasyland, 1996, Minor Arcana, 1996, Deep Secret, 1997, Dark Lord of Derkholm, 1998, (retelling of) Puss n' Boots, 1999, Mixed Magics, Year of the Griffin, 2000, The Merlin Conspiracy, 2003. Recipient, Mythopoeic Soc. award, 1995, 99, Joseph Wagner award Brit. Fantasy Soc., 1999. Mem. Soc. of Authors, Brit. Fantasy Soc. Avocations: cooking, hiking, owning a cat. Home: 9 The Polygon Bristol BS8 4PW England Office: care Greenwillow Books 105 Madison Ave New York NY 10016-7418

JONES, DONALD LEE, religious studies educator; b. Xenia, Ohio, Aug. 1938; s. Dana Dalphon and Alice Lenore (Lewis) J.; m. Susan Alicia Haas, Aug. 19, 1961; children: Douglas Haas, Kevin Scott Jones, Darin Andrew. BA, Ohio Wesleyan U., 1960; MDiv, Meth. Theol. Sch. in Ohio, 1963; PhD, Duke U., 1966. Asst. prof. religion Earlham Coll. and Sch. Religion, Richmond, Ind., 1966-67, U. S.C., Columbia, 1967-70, assoc. prof. religion, 1970-75, prof. religious studies, 1975—, chmn. religious studies, 1980-89, grad. dir. religious studies, 1986-92, 95—. Contbr. articles to profl. jours. Bd. dirs. Richland County Guardian Ad Litem Project, Columbia, 1990-97, chair 1994-95; bd. dirs. Family Svc. Ctr., Columbia, 1990-96, chair 1994-95; chair pastoral counseling svc. com. Trenholm Road United Meth. Ch., Columbia, 1979—; trustee Ministry Resources Found., 1990—; pres. Columbia Kiwanis Club, 1991-92; chmn. Atlas Road Elem. Sch. adv. coun., Columbia, 1983; founding mem. Christian-Jewish Congress of S.C., 1976; mem. S.C. Coun. for Human Rights, 1968-70. Mem. Soc. of Biblical Lit. (S.E. chair regional secs. 1984; Columbia Torch Club Internat. (pres. 1996-97), Soc. of Biblical Lit. (nat. coun. 1981-84, S.E. pres. 1972-73, regional sec. 1981-87), S.C. Acad. of Religion (pres. 1975-76). Democrat. United Methodist. Avocations: golf, reading, music. Home: 848 Malibu Dr Columbia SC 29209-2446 Office: Dept Religious Studies U Sc Columbia SC 29208-0001

JONES, DONALD PAUL, communications educator, consultant; b. St. Paul, Minn., July 27, 1947; s. Kenneth Paul and Vivian Savino Jones; m. Cheryl Lyn Skiba, June 30, 1979. BA Speech Comm., U. Minn., Mpls., 1969; AM Speech U. Ill., Champaign, Ill., 1970; PhD Speech Comm., So. Ill. U., Carbondale, Ill., 1989. Dir. of forensics U. ND, Grand Forks, ND, 1974—77, U. Dayton, Dayton, Ohio, 1979—83; dir. of on-campus debate Ball State U., Muncie, Ind., 1983—86; asst. prof. SW Mo. State U., Springfield, Mo., 1989—95; adj. prof. Drury Coll. and Cox Coll. of Nursing, Springfield, Mo., 1995—96; chair and assoc. prof., english and communication Tri-State U., Angola, Ind., 1996—. Cons. Continental Cablevision, Dayton, Ohio, 1981—83. Faculty pres. Tri-State U., Angola, Ind., 2001—03; speech writer and cons. various Dem. candidates, Minneapolis and other cities, Minn., 1970—79. Recipient Nichols Ehninger Award for top paper in rhetoric and comm., Nat. Comm. Assn., 198[illegible] Barrenbrugge Award for Faculty Excellence, Tri-State U., 2002, Helen Smi[illegible] McKetta Excellence in Tchg. Award, 2000, Top Argumentation Paper, Ct[illegible]

States Comm. Assn., 1994; NSF Fellowship, NSF, 1980-1981. Democrat-Npl. Unitarian Universalist. Avocation: chess. Home: 802 Village Green Dr Angola IN 46703-9308 Office: Tri-State Univ 1 Univ Ave Angola IN 46703-1764 E-mail: jonesd@tristate.edu.

JONES, DONNA MARILYN, state agency administrator, former legislator; b. Brush, Colo., Jan. 14, 1939; d. Virgil Dale and Margaret Elizabeth (McDaniel) Wolfe; m. Donald Eugene Jones, June 9, 1956; children: Dawn Richter, Lisa Shira, Stuart. Student, Treasure Valley Community Coll., 1981-82; grad., Realtors Inst. Cert. residential specialist. Co-owner Parts, Inc., Payette, Idaho, 1967-79; dept. mgr., buyer Lloyd's Dept. Store, Payette, Idaho, 1979-80; sales assoc. Idaho-Oreg. Realty, Payette, Idaho, 1981-82; mem. dist. 13 Idaho Ho. of Reps., Boise, 1987-90, mem. dist. 10, 1990-94, mem. dist. 9, 1995-98; assoc. broker Classic Properties Inc., Payette, 1983-91; owner, broker ERA Preferred Properities Inc., 1991-98; mem. dist. 9 Idaho Ho. of Reps., 1992-98. Co-chmn. Apple Blossom Parade, 1982; mem. Payette Civic League, 1968-84, pres. 1972; mem. Payette County Planning and Zoning Commn., 1985-88, vice-chmn. 1987; field coordinator Idaho Rep. Party Second Congl. Dist., 1986; mem. Payette County Rep. Cen. Com. 1978—; precinct II com. person, 1978-79, state committeewoman, 1980-84, chmn. 1984-87; outstanding county chmn. region III Idaho Rep. Party Regional Hall of Fame, 1985-86; mem. Payette County Rep. Women's Fedn., 1988—, bd. dirs., 1990-92; mem. Idaho Hispanic Commn., 1989-92, Idaho State Permanent Bldg. Adv. Coun., 1990-98; bd. dirs. Payette Edn. Found., 1993-96, Western Treasure Valley Cultural Ctr., 1993-96; nat. bd. dirs. Am. Legis. Exchange Coun., 1993-98; mem. legis. adv. coun. Idaho Housing Agy., 1992-97; committeeperson Payette County Cen.; chmn. Ways and Means Idaho House of Reps., 1993-97, House Revenue & Taxation Com., 1997-98; mem. Multi-State Tax Compact, 1997-98; Idaho chmn. Am. Legis. Exchange Coun., 1991-95; exec. dir. Idaho Real Estate Commn., 1998—. Recipient White Rose award Idaho March of Dimes, 1988; named Payette/Washington County Realtor of Yr., 1987. Mem. Idaho Assn. Realtors (legis. com. 1984-87, chmn. 1986, realtors active in politics com. 1982-98, polit. action com. 1986, polit. affairs com. 1986-88, chmn. 1987, bd. dirs. 1984-88), Payette/Washington County Bd. Realtors (v.p. 1981, state dir. 1984-88, bd. dirs 1983-88, sec. 1983), Bus. and Profl. Women (Woman of Progress award 1988, 90, treas. 1988), Payette C. of C., Fruitland C. of C., Wiesr C. of C.. Republican. Avocations: reading, interior decoration. Home: 1911 1st Ave S Payette ID 83661-3003 Office: Idaho Real Estate Commn 633 N 4th St Boise ID 83720-0001

JONES, DOROTHY JOANNE, social services professional; b. L.A. d. Joseph Anthony and Florence (Chaffin) Ghiotto; divorced; children: Teri McKane, Carole Shroll, Christopher Jones. BA, La Verne U., 1980; MS, Calif. State U., Fullerton, 1983. Lic. marriage, family/child counselor. Dep. sheriff L.A. County Sheriff Office, 1972-76; dir. A.I.C., L.A., 1976-80; mgr. McDonnell Douglas, Long Beach, Calif., 1980-93; pvt. practice Los Alamitos, Calif., 1980—, Long Beach, Calif., 1980—. Program specialist CAO Dept., Los Angeles County, 2000-. Author: When to SayNo, 1983; contbr. poems to lit. publs. Mem. Ctr. for Performing Arts, L.A., 1976&, Transpacific Mgmt., Long Beach, 1982-83. Recipient Spl. Svc. award Assn. Labor and Mgmt., Orange County, Calif., 1983. Mem. Employee Assistance Profls. Assn. (pres. 1980-82), Alcoholism Info. Ctr. (v.p. 1980-91), Counseling Assocs. (v.p. 1976-83), Calif. Assn. Marriage and Family Therapists (cons. Los Angeles County 1993—). Democrat. Episcopalian. Avocations: dancing, swimming, sailing.

JONES, DOROTHY VINCENT, diplomatic historian; b. Washington, Dec. 14, 1927; d. Guy Morgan and Margaret Hildora (Magnusen) Vincent; m. Robert R. Jones, Sept. 3, 1947; children: Daniel R., Mark A. BA, Washburn Mcpl. U., 1949; MA, U. Mo.-Columbia, 1971; PhD, U. Chgo., 1979. Past mem. staff Belleville (Kas.) Telescope, stringer, 1950-51; past co-publisher Lebanon (Kas.) Times, stringer, 1952-55, Shorewood (Wis.) Herald, 1963—67; ind. scholar, 1979—; curator 2 exhibits U. Chgo. Libr., 1982-85; vis. scholar U. Chgo., 1986-91; scholar-in-residence The Newberry Libr., Chgo., 1986—; assoc. history dept. Northwestern U., Evanston, Ill., 1991—. Cons. to editors of Peace/Mir, Syracuse U. Press, 1992; cons. Peace Task Force, Evang. Luth. Ch. in Am., 1992; mem. editl. adv. bd. for Ethics & Internat. Affairs, N.Y., 1993-2001; bd. trustees Carnegie Coun. on Ethics & Internat. Affairs, 1996-2001. Author: Code of Peace, 1991 (Gelber award 1991), Splendid Encounters, 1984, License for Empire, 1982, Toward a Just World, 2002; co-author: Traditions of International Ethics, 1992, On Cultural Ground, 1994, Ethics and Statecraft, 1995, The Dumbarton Oaks Conversations and the United Nations, 1998, Power and Responsibility in World Affairs, 1999; contbr. The Oxford Companion to United States History, 2001, Dictionary of American History, 2002; contbr. articles to profl. jours. Recipient Saxton fellowship Harper Pub., 1961-62, Excellence in Writing award Western History Assn., 1970, Grad. fellowship U. Chgo., 1972-73, MacArthur fellowship MacArthur Found., 1986-88. Democrat. Baptist. Avocation: gardening. Home and Office: 1213 Main St Evanston IL 60202-1650 E-mail: jonesd@newberry.org.

JONES, DOUGLAS GORDON, retired literature educator; b. Bancroft, Ont., Can., Jan. 1, 1929; s. Gordon Wilfred and Arlene (Ford) Jones; m. Betty Jane Kimbark, Sept. 23, 1950 (div.); children: Stephen, Skyler, Tory Joanne, North; m. Monique Baril, Dec. 1, 1976; 1 stepchild, Nicolas Grandmangin. BA in English, McGill U., 1952; MA in English, Queen's U., 1954; DLitt (hon.), Guelph U., 1982. Instr. Royal Milit. Coll., Kingston, Ont., 1954-55, Ont. Agrl. Coll., Guelph, 1955-61, Bishop's U., Lennoxville, 1961-63; prof. dept. letters and comm. U. Sherbrooke, Que., Can., 1963-94. Vis prof Univ Victoria, BC, Canada, 1978, Univ Canadienne en France, Villefranche-sur-Mer, 1987; mem arts adv panel, juries Can Coun. Author: (poetry) Frost on the Sun, 1957, The Sun is Axeman, 1961, Phrases from Orpheus, 1967, Under the Thunder the Flowers Light Up the Earth, 1977 (Gov Gen Award for Poetry, 1977, A J M Smith Award for Poetry, 1977), A Throw Particles: New and Selected Poems, 1983, Balthazar and Other Poems, 1988 (QSPELL Prize for Poetry, 1989), A Thousand Hooded Eyes, 1991, The Floating Garden, 1995 (QSPELL Prize for Poetry, 1995), Wild Asterisks in Cloud, 1997, Grounding Sight, 1999; translator: The Terror of the Snows: Selected Poems of Paul-Marie Lapointe, 1976, The Fifth Season: Poems by Paul Marie Lapointe, 1995, Normand de Bellefeuille Categories, One, Two & Three, 1993 (Gov Gen Award for Translation, 1993), Emile Martel, For Orchestra and Solo Poet, 1996; ed, contbg translator: poetry The March to Love: Selected Poems of Gaston Miron, 1986, Esprit de Corps: Quebec Poetry of the Late Twentieth Century in Translation, 1997; contbr. articles to profl jours. Mem.: League Canadian Poets, Royal Soc Can, Asn for Can and Que Literatures. Home and Office: 120 Houghton St North Hatley QC Canada J0B 2C0 E-mail: dgjones@abacom.com.

JONES, DOUGLAS WILEY, lawyer; b. Fort Lauderdale, Fla., 1948; AB, Princeton U., 1970; JD, Harvard U., 1973. Bar: N.Y. 1974. Mem. Milbank, Tweed, Hadley & McCloy LLP, N.Y.C. Mem. ABA, Assn. of the Bar of the City of N.Y. Office: Milbank Tweed Hadley & McCloy LLP 1 Chase Manhattan Plz Fl 47 New York NY 10005-1413

JONES, E. MICHAEL, editor, writer; b. Phila., Pa., May 4, 1948; s. Eugene J. Jones and Florence M. Jones; m. Ruth Price Jones; children: Adam, Peter, Rebecca, Sarah, Samuel. PhD, Temple U., Phila., 1979, MA, 1975; BA, St. Joseph's U., Phila., 1971. Editor Culture Wars, 1981—; asst. prof. St. Mary's Coll., 1979—81; lectr. Gymnasium Haus Aspel, Germany, 1973—76. Author: (book) Libido Dominandi: Sexual Liberation and Political Control, 2000, Monsters From the ID: Horror in Fiction and Film, 2000, The Slaughter of Cities: Urban Renewal as Ethnic Cleansing. Avocations: music, rowing. Home: 206 Marquette Ave South Bend IN 46617 Office: Culture Wars 135 Marquette Ave South Bend IN 46617 Office Fax: 574-289-1491. E-mail: jones@culturewars.com.

JONES, E. STEWART, JR., lawyer; b. Troy, N.Y., Dec. 4, 1941; s. E. Stewart and Louise (Farley) J.; m. Constance M., Dec. 28, 1968; children: Christopher, Brady, Erin. BA, Williams Coll., 1963; JD, Albany Law Sch., 1966. Bar: N.Y. 1966, U.S. Dist. Ct. (no. dist.) N.Y. 1966, U.S. Dist. Ct. (so. and ea. dist.) N.Y. 1994, U.S. Dist. Ct. (we. dist.) N.Y. 1987, U.S. Claims Ct. 1991, U.S. Ct. Appeals (2d cir.) 1976, U.S. Supreme Ct. 1976. Asst. dist. atty. Rensselaer County (N.Y.), 1968 70, spl. prosecutor, 1974; ptnr. E. Stewart Jones, Troy, 1974—. Lectr. in field; mem. com. on profl. standards of 3d jud. dept. State of N.Y., 1977-80, mem. 3d jud. screening com., Albany County; mem. merit selection panel for selection and appointment of U.S. magistrate for No. Dist. N.Y., 1981, 91; bd. dirs. Univ. Found. at Albany, trustee Troy Savs. Bank. Contbr. numerous articles to profl. jours. Trustee The Albany Acad., Albany Law Sch.; active Nat. Alumni Coun. Albany Law Sch. With USNG. Fellow: Am. Bar Found., N.Y. Bar Found., Inner Circle Advs., Internat. Soc. Barristers (chmn. Upstate N.Y. 1988—), Am. Bd. Trial Lawyers, Am. Inns. of Ct., Internat. Acad. Trial Lawyers, Am. Coll. Trial Lawyers, Am. Bd. Profl. Liability Attys. (diplomate), Internat. Soc. Barristers; mem.: Coll. Master Advs. and Barristers (sr. counsel), Saratoga County Bar Assn., Am. Coll. Barristers (sr. counsel), Internat. Acad. Litigators (diplomate), Civil Justice Found. (founding sponsor), Trial Lawyers for Pub. Justice (founder), Inst. Injury Reduction (founder), Am. Bd. Trial Advs. (adv.), N.Y. State Assn. Criminal Def. Lawyers, Nat. Assn. Criminal Def. Lawyers, Nat. Bd. Trial Advocacy (diplomate), Fed. Bar Coun., Dispute Resolutions, Inc. (nat. panel of arbitrators), Am. Arbitration Assn. (nat. panel of arbitrators), N.Y. State Defenders Assn., Albany County Bar Assn., Am. Soc. Law and Medicine, Rensselaer County Bar Assn., Am. Judicature Soc. (sustaining), Practising Law Inst., ABA (numerous coms.), Capital Dist. Trial Lawyers Assn. (bd. dirs. 1973—76), N.Y. State Trial Lawyers Assn. (bd. dirs. 1982—91, dir. emeritus 1991), N.Y. State Bar Assn. (mem. exec. com. trial lawyers sect. 1977—90, 1981—94, mem. spl. com. med. malpractice, other coms., Outstanding Practitioner award 1980), Williams Club (N.Y.C.), Stone Horse Yacht Club (Harwich Port, Mass.), Ft. Orange Club, Schuyler Meadows Club. Home: 46 Schuyler Rd Loudonville NY 12211-1447 Office: 28 2nd St Troy NY 12180-3986 E-mail: info@esjlaw.com.

JONES, E. THOMAS, lawyer; b. Buffalo, July 19, 1950; s. Thomas Kenneth and Marian Arlene (Turk) J.; m. Jennifer Dee Lowery, Oct. 19, 1974; children: Evan Thomas III, Courtney Bree. BA, SUNY, Buffalo, 1972; JD, Cleve. State U., 1981. Bar: N.Y. 1982, U.S. Dist. Ct. (we. dist.) N.Y. 1982, U.S. Ct. Appeals (2d cir.) 1987. Mem. mgmt. staff Marine Midland Bank, Buffalo, 1971-76, M&T Bank, Buffalo, 1976-78, 81-82, Nat. City Bank, Cleve., 1978-81; sole practice Buffalo, 1982—. Hearing officer Buffalo City Ct., 1997—. Committeeman Amherst Rep. Party, N.Y., 1984—; fire fighter Getzville Fire Co., Inc., Amherst, 1988-91; town councilman, Amherst, 1990-91; coach, bd. dirs. Amherst Youth Hockey Assn.; dep. town atty. Town Amherst, N.Y., 1996-2001, town atty., 2002—. Mem. ABA, N.Y. State Bar Assn., Erie County Bar Assn. Home: 1375 N French Rd Amherst NY 14228-1908

JONES, EDGAR ALLAN, JR., law educator, arbitrator, lawyer; b. Bklyn., Jan. 8, 1921; s. Edgar Allan and Isabel (Morris) J.; m. Helen Callaghan, Sept. 15, 1945; children: Linda Marie, Anne Marie, Carol Marie, Edgar Allan III, Denis James, Robert Morris, David Llewellyn, Therese Marie, Catherine Marie, Nancy Marie, Daniel Anthony. BA, Wesleyan U., 1942; LLB, U. Va., 1950. Bar: Va. 1948. Faculty UCLA, 1951—, prof. law, 1958-91, emeritus, 1991—, asst. dean, 1957-58; dir. Law-Sci. Rsch. Ctr., 1963-66; labor dispute arbitrator, mediator, fact finder for pvt. and pub. employers and unions, 1953—. Appeared as judge ABC-TV network programs Accused, 1958-59, Traffic Ct., 1958-61, Day in Court, 1958-64; moderator ednl. TV program Forum West, 1966; author: (novel) Mr. Arbitrator, 2000; editor: Law and Electronics: The Challenge of a New Era, 1960; founding editor Va. Law Weekly, 1948-50, NAA Chronicle, 1977-78; contbr. numerous labor law, arbitration and polygraph articles to law revs. Pres. Creddalt Rsch., Inc., 1959-90; dir. Deauville Restaurant, Inc. (Jimmy's 1978 94); pub. mem. Calif. Commn. Manpower Automation and Tech., 1963-67, Calif. Manpower Adv. Com., 1964-67; nat. enforcement commr. WSB, 1951; sec. Californians for Kennedy, 1960. Mem. ABA, Nat. Acad. Arbitrators (pres. 1981). Home: PO Box 1347 Pacific Palisades CA 90272-1347

JONES, EDITH HOLLAN, federal judge; b. Phila., Apr. 7, 1949; BA Cornell U., 1971; JD with honors, U. Tex., 1974. Bar: Tex. 1974, U.S. Supreme Ct. 1979, U.S. Ct. Appeals (5th and 11th cirs.), U.S. Dist. . (so. and no. dists.) Tex. Assoc. Andrews & Kurth, Houston, 1974—82, ptnr., 1982—85; judge U.S. Ct. Appeals (5th cir.), Houston, 1985—. Gen. counsel Rep. Party of Tex., 1981—83. Master: ABA; mem.: State Bar Tex. Presbyterian. Office: 515 Rusk Ave Ste 12505 Houston TX 77002-2655

JONES, EDITH IRBY, physician; b. Conway, Ark., Dec. 23, 1927; d. Robert and Mattie (Buice) Irby; m. James Beauregard Jones, Apr. 16, 1960 (dec. Oct. 1989); children: Gary Ivan, Myra Vonceil Jones Romain, Keith Irby. BS, Knoxville Coll., 1948; MD, U. Ark., 1952. Intern Univ. Hosp., Little Rock, Ark., 1952-53; gen. practice medicine Hot Springs, Ark., 1953-59; resident in internal medicine Baylor Coll. Medicine, Houston, 1959-62; practice medicine specializing in internal medicine Houston, 1962—; mem. staff Meth. Hosp., Houston, Hermann Hosp., Houston, Riverside Gen. Hosp., Houston, St. Elizabeth Hosp., Houston, St. Anthony Ctr., Houston, St. Joseph Hosp., Houston, Thomas Care Ctr., Houston, Town Park, Houston, chief of staff. Clin. asst. prof. medicine Baylor Coll. Medicine, U. Tex. Sch. Medicine, Houston; dir. Prospect Med. Lab.; bd. dirs., sec. Mercy Hosp. Comprehensive Health Care Group; ptnr. Jones, Coleman and Whitfield; grand med. examiner Ct. Calanthe Jurisdiction, Tex.; cons. Social Security Agy., Tex. Pub. Welfare Dept., Vocat. Rehab. Assn., Tex. Rehab. Commn.; bd. dirs. Standard Savs. Assn., Houston; others. Contbr. articles to profl. jours. Bd. dirs. Houston Internat. U., Drug Addiction Rehab. Enterprise, March of Dimes, Houston, Odessey House, Houston; adv. bd. Houston Coun. on Alcoholism; com. for revising justice code, Harris County, Tex.; chmn. bd. trustees Knoxville Coll.; impartial hearing officer Houston Ind. Sch. Dist.; trustee Mut. Assn. for Profl. Service; mem. Cmty. Welfare Planning Assn., Friends of Youth, Human Svcs. Adv. Council, Houston; bd. visitors U. Houston; others. Dr. Edith Irby Jones Day proclaimed by State of Ark., 1985, City of Little Rock, 1985, City of N.Y.C., 1986; named one of 30 Most Influential Black Women Houston, 1984; named to Tex. Black Women's Hall of Fame, 1986; commended by Calif. Senate, 1969; proclamation by city council, Houston, 1985, Mayor of Houston, 1986; recipient cert. of citation Ho. of Reps. State of Tex., 1986, Volunteerism and Cmty. Svc. award Tex. Acad. Internal Medicine, 2000, Scroll of Merit award Nat. Med. Assn., 2001; portrait placed in entrance hall U. Ark. for Med. Scis., 1985; others; named one of 100 Leading Black Physicians Black Enterprise mag., 2001. Fellow Am. Coll. Medicine, Am. Soc. Internal Medicine (Oscar E. Edward award 2001); mem. AMA, Am. Med. Women's Assn. (v.p. Houston chpt.), Nat. Med. Assn. (past pres., Scroll of Merit 2001), Lone Star Med. Assn., Harris County Med. Assn., Houston Med. Forum, Tex. Assn. Disability Examiners, Bus. and Profl. Women, Nat. Coun. Negro Women, Inc. (v.p. Dorothy Height chpt.), NAACP, PTA, YMCA, Alpha Kappa Mu, Delta Sigma Theta, Eta Phi Beta. Clubs: Links, Inc., Top Ladies of Distinction, Girl Friends, Inc., Women of Achievement, Inc. (Hall of Fame 1985). Lodges: Order Eastern Star. Democrat. Avocations: travel, walking, swimming. Home: 3402 S Parkwood Houston TX 77021 Office: 2601 Prospect St Houston TX 77004-7737 E-mail: eijones@advmed.com.

JONES, EDWARD, pathologist; b. Wellington, Kans., Mar. 21, 1935; s. Thomas S. and Grace W. (Sydebotham) Imel; m. Barbara A. Blount, Aug. 30, 1956; children: Kimberly Riegel, Sheila, Matt, Tom. AB in Chemistry, U. Kans., 1957, MD, 1961. Diplomate Am. Bd. Pathology in Anat. and Clin. Pathology; cert. med. rev. officer. Intern St. Francis Hosp., Wichita, Kans., 1961-62; sr. asst. USPHS, Yuma, Ariz., 1962-64; gen. practice medicine Lawrence (Kans.) Meml. Hosp., 1964-65; resident in pathology St. Luke's Hosp., Kansas City, Mo., 1965-69; pathologist Ctrl. Kans. Med. Ctr., Gt. Bend, 1969-2001, dir., 1974-76, pres., 1976-78; ret., 2001. Physician cons. Hoisington Luth. Hosp., Kans., 1969—, St. Joseph's Meml. Hosp., Larned, Kans., 1969—, Edwards County Hosp., Kinsley, Kans., 1969—. Bd. dirs. Cedar Park Place, Gt. Bend, 1980-88; bd. dirs. Ctrl. Kans. Med. Ctr., 1999—, chmn., 2002. Fellow Coll. Am. Pathologists (del., foreman 1978-87), Am. Soc. Clin. Pathologists; mem. Kans. Soc. Pathologists (pres. 1980-81), Gt. Bend Cmty. Theater Club. Avocations: theater, musical theater. Home: 3208 Broadway Ave Great Bend KS 67530-3716

JONES, EDWARD ALLEN, engineer; b. Piqua, Ohio, Nov. 28, 1946; s. Thomas Loya and Bessie Faith (Coffman) J.; m. Angeliki Athanasiou, Oct. 4, 1969; children: Faith H., Thomas A. BSME, Union Coll., 1978, postgrad., 1985—. Toolmaker GE, Schenectady, N.Y., 1970-74, foreman, 1974-75, instr., 1976-78, project engr., 1978-84, mfg. engr., 1984-92; sr. project engr. Westinghouse Electric, Schenectady, 1992-95; engring. tech. writer, 1995-99, tech. manual support engr., 1999—. Exec. officer Advance Base Functional Component, Albany, 1988-92; cons. to GE. Author: Reactor Support Cost Estimating Manual, 1989, Steam Generator and Reactor Servicing Equipment Technical Manual, 1996. Co-provider Family Care Home for Adults, Schenectady, 1972—. With USN, 1966-70, ret Res., 1992. Mem. Soc. Mfg. Engrs., Naval Enlisted Res. Assn. (v.p. 1984-85), GE Apprentice Alumni Assn. Eastern Orthodox Ch. Avocations: wood working, reading, computer software and hardware. Office: Bechtel Plant Machinery Inc 600 Liberty St Schenectady NY 12305-2105 E-mail: toolmaker@global2000.net.

JONES, EDWARD DOUGLASS, III, economist; b. L.A., May 15, 1945; s. Edward Douglass Jones and Alice (Stanton) Serrao; m. Holly Cabrini Smith, June 15, 1968 (div. Aug. 1987); children: Darragh Wesley Cheleden, Devon Koster Smith Coleman. AB, U. Chgo., 1966; MA, Washington U., St Louis, 1968, postgrad., 1968-70. Sr. rsch. economist CIA, Washington, 1970-74; sr. econ. adviser U.S. Dept. Justice, Washington, 1974-81; rsch. dir. INCOG, Tulsa, Okla., 1981-84; pvt. practice cons. Tulsa, 1984-85; sr. analyst Nat. Econ. Rsch. Assocs., L.A., 1985-86; pvt. practice cons. N.Y.C., L.A., 1986-88; cons. U.S. Sentencing Commn., Washington, 1988-89; pvt. practice cons. Atlanta, 1989-90, Nat. Acad. of Scis., Washington, 1989-90; co-founder, sec.-treas., exec. v.p. Med. Rev. Sys., Inc., Atlanta, 1990 93; sr. v.p. Centris Group, 1993 99; pvt. practice cons. Charleston, SC, 2000—; co-founder, pres. and CEO HIPAA Corp., Johns Island, SC, 2000 ; chmn. Workgroup for Electronic Data Interchange, Reston, Va., 2003—. Commr. Electronic Healthcare Network Accreditation Commn. Contbr. articles to profl. jours., books.

JONES, EDWARD GEORGE, neuroscience professor; b. Upper Hutt, Wellington, N.Z., Mar. 26, 1939; came to U.S., 1972; s. Frank Ian and Theresa Agnes (Riordan) J.; m. Elizabeth Suzanne Oldham, Apr. 27, 1963; children: Philippa Emilie, Christopher Edward. MD, U. Otago, Dunedin, N.Z., 1962; PhD, U. of Oxford, Eng., 1968. Med. and surg. intern Tauranga Hosp., New Zealand, 1963; demonstrator to assoc. prof. dept. anatomy U. Otago Med. Sch., Dunedin, New Zealand, 1964-72; Nuffield Dominions demonstrator and lectr. Balliol Coll., U. of Oxford, Eng., 1964-72; assoc. prof. to prof., dept. anatomy and neurobiology Washington U. Sch. Medicine, St. Louis, 1972-84, George H. and Ethel Ronzini Bishop scholar, 1981-84, dir. div. exptl. neurology, 1981-84; prof. and chmn. dept. anatomy and neurobiology U. Calif., Irvine, 1984-98; dir. Ctr. Neurosci. U. Calif. Davis, 1998—; prof. psychiatry U. Calif., 1998—. Cons. NIH, 1972—; dir. Neural Systems Lab., Frontier Rsch. Program in Neural Mechanisms of Mind and Behavior, Riken, Japan, 1988-96; vis. sr. rsch. fellow St. John's Coll. at U. Oxford, Eng., 1989-90. Author: The Thalamus, 1984; co-author: Thalamus, 1997, The Thalamus and Basal Telencephalon, 1982; co-editor: (book series) Cerebral Cortex, 1984-2001; author, reviewer numerous sci. and hist. articles, chpts. in books, 1964—. Mem. Pres.'s Adv. Bd. Calif. State U., Long Beach, 1986-90. Named one of 100 most cited biol. scientists, Sci. Citation Index, 1982, 151 Thompson scientific highly cited scientist database, 2001; recipient Rolleston Meml. prize, U. Oxford, 1970, Lashley award, Am. Philos. Soc., 2001; grantee rsch. grantee, NIH, 1971—. Fellow: AAAS; mem.: Anat. Soc. Gt. Brit. and Ireland (Sumington Meml. prize 1968), Am. Assn. Anatomists (Cajal medal 1999, Henry Gray award 2001), Soc. Neurosci. (com. chair 1978—81, 1988—89, pres.-elect 1997—98, pres. 1998—99). Democrat. Avocations: reading, writing, carpentry. Office: U Calif Ctr Neurosci 1544 Newton Ct Davis CA 95616-4859

JONES, EDWARD LOUIS, historian, educator; b. Georgetown, Tex., Jan. 15, 1922; s. Henry Horace and Elizabeth (Steen) J.; m. Dorothy M. Showers, Mar. 1, 1952 (div. Sept. 1963); children: Cynthia, Frances, Edward Lawrence, Lynne Ann McGreevy, Oct. 7, 1963; children Christopher Louis, Teresa Lynne. BA in Philosophy, BA in Far East, U. Wash., 1952, BA in Speech, 1955, postgrad., 1952-54; JD, Gonzaga U., 1967. Social worker Los Angeles Pub. Assistance, 1956-57; producer, dir. Little Theatre, Hollywood, Calif. and Seattle, 1956-60; research analyst, cons. to Office of Atty. Gen., Olympia and Seattle, Wash., 1963-66; coordinator of counseling SOIC, Seattle, 1966-68; lectr., advisor, asst. to dean U. Wash., Seattle, 1968—. Instr. Gonzaga U., Spokane, Wash., 1961-62, Seattle Community Coll., 1967-68; dir. drama workshop, Driftwood Players, Edmonds, Wash., 1975-76. Author: The Black Diaspora: Colonization of Colored People, 1988, Tutankhamon: Son of the Sun, King of Upper and Lower Egypt, 1978, Black Orators' Workbook, 1982, Black Zeus, 1972, Profiles in African Heritage, 1972, From Rulers of the World to Slavery, 1990, President Zachary Taylor and Senator Hamlin: Union or Death, 1991, Why Colored Americans Need an Abraham Lincoln in 1992, Forty Acres and a Mule: The Rape of Colored Americans, 1994, Mister Moon Goes to Japan, A children's story, 2001; editor pub. NACADA Jour. Nat. Acad. Advising Assn., more. V.p. Wash. Com. on Consumer Interests, Seattle, 1966-68. Served to 2d lt. Fr. Army, 1940-45. Recipient Outstanding Teaching award U. Wash., 1986, Tyee Inst. Yr. U. Wash., 1987, appreciation award Office Minority Affairs, 1987, acad. excellence award Nat. Soc. Black Engrs., 1987, Appreciation award Fla. chpt. Nat. Bar Assn., 1990; Frederick Douglass scholar Nat. Coun. Black Studies, 1985, 86. Mem. Nat. Assn. Student Personnel Adminstrs., Smithsonian Inst. (assoc.), Am. Acad. Polit. and Social Sci., Nat. Acad. Advising Assn. (bd. dirs. 1979-82, Cert. of Appreciation 1982, editor Jour. 1981—, award for Excellence 1985), Western Polit. Sci. Assn. Democrat. Baptist. Avocations: travel, research, chess. Office: U Wash Ethnic Cultural Ctr Seattle WA 98195-0001

JONES, EDWIN CHANNING, JR., electrical and computer engineering educator; b. Parkersburg, W.Va., June 27, 1934; s. Edwin Channing and Helen M. J.; m. Ruth Carol Miller, Aug. 14, 1960; children: Charles, Cathleen, Helene. BSEE, W.Va. U., 1955; Diploma, U. London, 1956; PhD, U. Ill., 1962. Lic. profl. engr., W.Va. Engr. GE, Syracuse, N.Y. and Bloomington, Ill., 1955, 62, Westinghouse Electric Co., Balt., 1959; asst. prof. elec. engring. U. Ill., Urbana, 1962-66; asst. prof. Iowa State U., Ames, 1966-67, assoc. prof., 1967-72, prof., 1972—2001, univ. prof., 1995—2001, assoc. chair dept., 1997—2001, univ. prof. emeritus, 2001—. Mem. Accreditation Bd. Engring. Tech., N.Y.C., 1984-87. Author handbook chpts. on electronic engring. Lt. U.S. Army, 1956—58. Recipient Linton F. Grinter Disting. Svc. award, Accreditation Bd. Engring. Tech., 2001. Fellow AAAS, IEEE (pres. edn. soc. 1975-76, mem. ednl. activities bd. 1975-76, 78-81, 84-87, accreditation activity award), Am. Soc. Engring. Edn.; mem. Soc. History of Tech., Sigma Xi, Tau Beta Pi, Eta Kappa Nu, Phi Kappa Phi, Phi Beta Delta. Avocations: photography, slide rule collecting. Office: Iowa State U 2216 Coover Hl Ames IA 50011-0001

JONES, EFFIE L. social sciences educator; b. Sarepta, Miss., Feb. 16, 1945; d. Joe N. and Oleta P. Erby; children from previous marriage: Robin, Chandra, Robert. BA in Christian Edn., Mid South Bible Coll., Memphis, 1979; MS in Edn., Memphis State U., 1990. Assoc. prof. social scis. Crichton Coll., Memphis, 1986—, exec. dir. Am. Humanics, 1999—. Cons., ind. Christian edn. various chs., Memphis, 1980—. Campus dir. Mid South Am. Humanics Collaborative, Memphis, 1999—, Am. Humanics, Inc., Kansas City, Mo., 1999—; dir. Christian edn. Tabernacle Bapt. Ch., Memphis, 1994—2003. Mem.: NASW, Nat. Coun. Social Scis., Orgn. Am. Historians. Baptist. Avocations: reading, witnessing. Office: Crichton Coll 255 N Highland Memphis TN 38111

JONES, ELAINE HANCOCK, humanities educator; b. Niagara Falls, N.Y., Feb. 17, 1946; d. Roy Elmer and June Edna (Clark) Hancock; m. Ralph Jones III, Oct. 9, 1971 (div. June 1981). AAS in Comml. Design, U. Buffalo, 1962; BFA, SUNY, Buffalo, 1971, MFA in Painting, 1975; postgrad., Fla. State U., 1993—. Med. illustrator Roswell Park Meml. Inst., Buffalo, 1967-70; designer, animator Acad. McLarty Film Prodns., Buffalo, 1970-73; publs. designer Buffalo/Erie County Hist. Soc., 1974-78; dir. publs. Daemen Coll., Amherst, N.Y., 1978-80; owner, art dir. Plop Art Prodns., Melbourne, Fla., 1981-86; instr. humanities Brevard C.C., Melbourne, 1986—; prof. humanities Brevard campus Rollins Coll., Melbourne, 1995—. One-woman shows include SUNY, Buffalo, 1974, Upton Gallery, N.Y., 1975, Gallery Wilde, Buffalo, 1978; exhibited in group shows at Fredonia Coll., N.Y., 1975, Upton Gallery, 1975, Brevard Art Mus., Melbourne, Fla., 1987. Mem. docent program Art Mus./Sci. Ctr., Melbourne, 1983-84, mem. edn. com., 1995—; officer Platinum Coast chpt. Sweet Adelines Internat., 1984-90. Nat. Merit scholar, 1971-75; recipient cert. of merit Curtis Paper Co., 1977; N.Y. State Coun. on Arts grantee, 1975. Republican. Home: 2240 Sea Ave Indialantic FL 32903-2524 Office: Brevard CC Liberal Arts Dept 3865 N Wickham Rd Melbourne FL 32935-2310

JONES, ELI, III, marketing/sales educator; b. Houston, Nov. 24, 1961; s. Eli Jones, II and Elvira Jones; m. Fern Cecilia Walker; children: Necia, Tracia, Christopher, Elicia. BS in Journalism, Tex. A & M U., 1979—82, MBA, 1985—86, PhD in Mktg., 1993—97. Key acct. mgr. Quaker Oats, Houston,

1986—88, zone sales planning mgr. Jacksonville, Fla., 1988—89, key accts. exec. Charlotte, NC, 1989—90; sales mgr. Nabisco, Houston, 1990—92; zone mgr. Frito Lay, Houston, 1992—93; instr. Tex. A & M U., College Station, 1993—97; assoc. prof. mktg. U. Houston, 1997—. Dir. Program for Excellence in Selling, Houston, 1997—; faculty advisor Program for Excellence in Selling Alumni Assn., Houston, 1998—; chair doctoral dissertation U. Houston, 1997—; pres., CEO Eli Jones & Assoc., Inc., Houston, 2001—; mentor, charter mem. KPMG's PhD Project mktg. chap., 1997—; adv. bd. The Fischer Inst., Akron, 1999—; sales coach Baylor U. Nat. Collegiate Sales Competition, Waco, 1999—2002; exec. sales instr., rschr., cons. various nat. and local firms and orgns., 1997—; keynote spkr. Cougar Preview, Houston, 1997—; adv. bd. Charter Sch., Victoria, 2000—; guest spkr. Sales & Mktg. Execs. Assn., Houston, 1999—2000. Dir.: (Sales Certification Program) Program for Excellence in Selling, —; co-editor: Sales Professional Network, 2001—; editl. rev. bd.: Indsl. Mktg. Mgmt., 2001—, Jour. Personal Selling and Sales Management, 2000—. Judge H.S. DECA competition, Humble, 2001; instr. Seeds of Life Ministry Workshop, Houston, 1999. Mem.: Nat. Conf. in Sales Mgmt., Southwestern Mktg. Assn., Acad. Mktg. Sci. (Outstanding Mktg. Tchr. 2001), Am. Mgmt. Assn., Alpha Mu Alpha. Avocations: Contemporary Christian Music Ministry, A/V technology, travel, basketball. Home: 19030 Cloyanna Ln Humble TX 77346 Office: University of Houston 4800 Calhoun Rd Houston TX 77204-6028 Home Fax: 281-852-5822. Personal E-mail: eli-fern-jones@msn.com. Business E-Mail: eli-jones@uh.edu.

JONES, ELIZABETH NORDWALL, county government official; b. Glendale, Calif., Sept. 1, 1934; d. Darrell Robert and Rosita (Hopps) Nordwall; m. William Maurice Jones, Jan. 28, 1956; children: Kevin Scott, Sigrid Elizabeth, Kimberly Anne. Student, DePauw U., 1952-54; BA, U. So. Calif., 1956; EdS, MA, U. Fla., 1975. Outreach librarian Santa Fe Regional Library, Gainesville, Fla., 1966-72; testing coordinator CETA Program, Gainesville, 1974-75; supr. Alachua County Crisis Ctr., Gainesville, 1975-79, dir., 1979-84, Dept. Vol. Services, Gainesville, 1983-89, Dept. Human Svcs., Gainesville, 1989-91; Dept. Community Svcs., 1991-97; retired, 1997. Trustee Santa Fe Community Coll., Gainesville, 1974-85; mem. Fla. Adv. Council on Libraries, Talahassee, 1977-87; mem. State community Coll. Coordinating Bd., Tallahassee, 1983-84. Bd. dirs., past pres. Friends of Five Pub. TV; bd. dirs. Child Adv. Ctr.; county ct. mediator. Mem. Am. Assn. Suicidology (nat. treas. 1983-85, nat. bd. dirs. 1985-87, nat. pres. 1987-88, nat. cert. examiner 1991-94), Fla. Assn. C.C. (past state bd. dirs.), Altrusa Internat. (pres. Gainesville chpt. 1983-84), LWV (past pres. Gainesville chpt.), Women's Forum Gainesville, Rotary (chpt. sec. 1994, bd. dirs. 1995, pres.-elect 1999, pres. 2000), Fla. Free Speech Forum (pres. 2002—), Leadership Fla. Class XIV, Alpha Chi Omega. Avocations: reading mysteries, camping, fishing. Home: 5915 NW 27th Ave Gainesville FL 32606-6440 E-mail: jones@chem.ufl.edu.

JONES, EMIL, JR., state legislator; b. Chgo., Oct. 18, 1935; s. Emil Sr. and Marilla (Mims) J.; m. Patricia Sterling, Dec. 14, 1974 (dec.); children: Debra, Renee, John, Emil III. A in Bus. Adminstrn., City Coll. Chgo., 1970. Mem. Ill. Ho. Reps., Springfield, 1972-82, Ill. Senate, Springfield, 1982—, Senate Dem. leader, mem. exec. com., mem. joint com. adminstrv. rules, pres., 2002—. Active Task Force on Long Term Care, Morgan Pk. Civic League, Chgo. Recipient Beautiful People award Chgo. Urban League, 1981, Friend of Edn. award Ill. State Bd. Edn., 1983, Legis. Leadership award Ill. Dept. Human Rights, 1984, Leadership award Nat. Bar Assn., 1985, Mem. Nat. Black Caucus State Legislators, Nat. Conf. State Legislators, Knights of St. Peter Claver, Shriners. Democrat. Roman Catholic. Home: 11357 S Lowe Ave Chicago IL 60628-4714 Office: 507 W 111th St Ste 16-600 Chicago IL 60628-4019 also: James R Thompson Ctr 100 W Randolph St Ste 16 600 Chicago IL 60601-3220*

JONES, ERIC E. lawyer; b. Wheatland, Wyo., Feb. 25, 1969; s. Frank J. and Berneta Marie Jones. BSBA in Acctg., U. Ariz., 1991; JD, U. Wyo., 1997. Bar: Wyo. 1997, Colo. 1997. Sr. acct. Ernst & Young, Denver, 1991-94; pvt. practice, Wheatland, 1997—. Mem. Wyo. Jaycces (state legal counsel 1998-99, local treas. 1999-2003, pres. 2003—). Republican. Episcopalian. Avocations: outdoor activities and sports, theatre. Office: PO Box 9 Wheatland WY 82201-0009

JONES, ERIKA ZIEBARTH, lawyer; b. Washington, June 10, 1955; d. Thomas Arthur and Ruth (Helm) Ziebarth; m. Gregory Monroe Jones, June 2, 1978; 1 child, Katherine Anne. AB, Georgetown U., 1976, JD, 1980. Bar: D.C. 1980, U.S. Ct. Appeals (D.C. cir.) 1987, U.S. Supreme Ct. 1987. Atty., regulatory analyst U.S. Office Mgmt. and Budget, Washington, 1980-81; spl. counsel Nat. Hwy. Traffic Safety Adminstrn., Washington, 1981-85, chief counsel, 1985-89; of counsel Mayer, Brown Rowe & Maw, Washington, 1989-90; ptnr. Mayer, Brown and Platt, Washington, 1991—. Bd. dirs. Immaculata Coll. High Sch., 1985-88. Mem. ABA, D.C. Bar Assn., Phi Beta Kappa. Republican. Roman Catholic. Home: 6612 31st Pl NW Washington DC 20015-2302 Office: 1909 K St NW Washington DC 20006 E-mail: ejones@mayerbrown.com.

JONES, EUGENE GORDON, pharmaceutical company executive; b. Lookout, W.Va., June 26, 1929; s. Alphus Raymond and Mona Blanche (Bobbitt) J.; m. Nancy Lee Hall, Aug. 19, 1951; children: Gene Douglas, Michael Gordon, Rebecca Lee, Jody Lynn. BS, Va. Tech. U., 1951. Med. rep. The Upjohn Co., Charlottesville, Va., 1956-60, profl. svcs. mgr. Washington, 1960-63, sr. med. rep. Roanoke, Va., 1963-68, hosp. med. rep. Richmond, Va., 1968-70, dist. sales mgr., 1970-73, tng. specialist, 1973-76, tng. mgr., 1976-87, nat. tng. dir., 1987-90; pres., owner Global Meeting Planners, 1991—. Author: (self instrn. course) Managed Health Care, 1985, Arthritis Primer, 1976. Pres. Am. Diabetes Assn., Roanoke chpt., 1967, Richmond chpt., 1971, state del., 1970; bd. dirs. United Way, Kalamazoo, 1990, 91, Mich. Diabetes Assn., Detroit, 1979; deacon River Rd. Presbyn. Ch.; mem. Rep. Presdl. Task Force. Lt. U.S. Army, 1951-53, Korea, capt. USAR, 1953-60. Mem. VFW (founder of the Kalamazoo Mi Korea War chpt., life), Nat. Soc. Pharm. Sales Trainers (hon., pres. Western chpt. 1980-81, pres. nat. orgn. 1987-88, dir. 1985-90, founder newsletter 1987), Meeting Planners Internat., Internat. Meeting Planners, Mil. Order World Wars (treas. 1964-68), Kalamazoo Aviation History Mus., Charles Garfield Group (hon.), Korean War Vets. Assn, Res. Officers Assn. of U.S. (life), PGA Assocs. (life), Am. Legion. Avocations: volunteering, golf, reading, walking, travel. Home: 2828 Kalarama Rd Kalamazoo MI 49024-2321

JONES, EUINE FAY, architect, educator; b. Pine Bluff, Ark., Jan. 31, 1921; s. Euine Fay and Candie Louise (Alston) J.; m. Mary Elizabeth Knox, Jan. 6, 1943; children: Janis Fay, Jean Cameron. BArch, U. Ark., 1950; MArch, Rice U., 1951; DFA (hon.), Kans. State U., 1984; LHD (hon.), Drury Coll., 1985, Hendrix Coll., 1991; DHL (hon.), U. Ark., 1990, Lindsey Wilson Coll., 1997. Asst. prof. architecture U. Okla., 1951-53; Frank Lloyd Wright Taliesin fellow, 1953; prof. architecture U. Ark., 1953-88, chmn. dept., 1966-74, dean Sch. Architecture, 1974-76; pvt. practice architecture, 1953-97. Rome Prize fellow in architecture and design, 1981; dean, u. prof. emeritus U. Ark., 1988. Served as lt., naval aviator USNR, 1942-45. Recipient nat. awards for archtl. design, Gold medal for distinction in archtl. design Tau Sigma Delta, 1984, Disting. Alumnus award U. Ark., 1982, Rice U., 1989; subject of book by Robert Ivy, Jr., AIA Press, 1992. Fellow AIA (Gold medal for Lifetime Achievement 1990); mem. Assn. Collegiate Schs. Architecture (Disting. Prof. award 1985), Soc. Archtl. Historians Home: 1330 N Hillcrest Ave Fayetteville AR 72703-1924

JONES, EVAN WIER, lawyer; b. Warwick, R.I., Sept. 25, 1966; s. Richard Morris and Suzanne Wier J.; m. Andrea Squire, Aug. 15, 1992; children: Connor Evan, Sarah Kathryn, Jacob Squire. BA with honors, U. Ga., 1988, JD, 1991. Bar: Ga. 1991, U.S. Army Ct. Appeals 1996, Ga. Supreme Ct. 1996. Legal assistance atty. 7th inf. div. U.S. Army, Monterey, Calif., 1991-92, spl. asst. U.S. atty. 7th inf. div., 1992-93, trial counsel U.S. SETAF Vicenza, Italy, 1994-95; assoc. Sistrunk & Assocs., Atlanta, 1995-99; ptnr. Insley & Race, LLP, 1999-2000, Allen & Weathington PC, Atlanta, 2000—03; mem. Evan W. Jones, LLC, Atlanta, 2003—. Lectr. basic med. malpractice ICLE, 1999; faculty Ga. Trial Skills Clinic, 1999; lectr. med. malpractice issues Nat. Bus. Inst., 1998-2000; lectr. in field. Mem. Aspiring Youth Program, 1998-99, Ga. Pro Bono Honor Roll, 1997-99. Capt. U.S. Army, 1991-95. Mem. ATLA, Ga. State Bar Assn. (Pro Bono Honor Roll), Gridiron Secret Soc., Christian Bus. Men's Coun., Ga. Trial Lawyers Assn. Avocations: running, weightlifting, reading, fishing, history. Office: Evan W Jones LLC Ste 1700 3490 Piedmont Rd Ste 650 Atlanta GA 30305 E-mail: evan.jones@ewslaw.us.

JONES, EVELYN GLORIA, medical technologist, educator; b. Roanoke, Va., Aug. 13, 1940; d. William Darnell and Elizabeth (Harris) Powell; m. Theodore Joseph Jones, Aug. 21, 1965. BS in Biology, Tenn. State U., 1973; cert. in med. tech., Vanderbilt U., 1974; MEd in Adminstrn. and Supervision, Tenn. State U., 1993. Cert. clin. lab. scientist Nat. Cert. Agy. Med. Lab Pers. Med. technologist Metro Gen. Hosp., Nashville, 1974-78, Vanderbilt Med. Ctr., Nashville, 1978-97; microbiologist Tenn. Dept. Health Lab. Svcs., Nashville, 1997—. Tech. cons. Vanderbilt Point of Care Program, 1993-96; lectr. St. Thomas Program Med. Tech., Nashville, 1991-94, Tenn. State U./Meharry Med. Tech. Program, Nashville, 1991—; instr. tchg. faculty Pub. Health Lab. Svcs., State Tenn., Nashville. Nashville bd. dirs. Tenn. Valley Region ARC Blood Svcs., 1996-2002; asst. sec. Henderville area chpt. The Links, Inc., 1997-2002; docent Frist Mus.; info. guide Fisk U.; mem. adv. com. Tenn. State U. Mem.: AAAS, So. Assn. Clin. Microbiology, Am. Soc. Clin. Pathologist (assoc.; cert. med. technologist), Alpha Kappa Alpha, Phi Delta Kappa. Roman Catholic. Home: 1003 Cross Bow Dr Hendersonville TN 37075-9403 Office: Tenn Dept Health Lab Svcs Dept Microbiology Nashville TN 37202 E-mail: EvelynJones@mail.state.tn.us.

JONES, EVERETT BRUCE, retired civil engineer, hydrologist; b. Ft. Collins, Colo., Sept. 23, 1933; s. Donald Lee and Muriel Virginia (Gwynn) J.; m. Margie Raben, May 27, 1956; children: Elizabeth Gwynn, Janet Lee. BS, U. Wyo., 1955; MS, Pa. State U., 1957; PhD, Colo. State U., 1964. Registered profl. engr., Wyo., Colo., Mont., Alaska. Chief of water devel. State of Wyo., Cheyenne, 1959-61; engr., hydrologist D.W. Barr Assocs., Mpls., 1964-65; asst. dir. inst. land/water rsch. Pa. State U., University Park, 1965-68; coord. water resources EG&G, Inc., Boulder, Colo., 1968-70; v.p. M.W. Bittinger and Assocs., Ft. Collins, 1970-77; pres. Resource Cons., Inc., Ft. Collins, 1977-87; regional mgr. spl. projects ESE, Inc., Englewood, Colo., 1987-88; outside dir. N.Am. Weather Cons., Salt Lake City, 1987-88; assoc. Bisop-Brogden Assocs., Lakewood, Colo., 1988-90; dist. mgr., dir. midwest regional govt. svcs. Groundwater Tech., Inc., Englewood, 1990-91; with Jacobs Engring. Group, Inc., Denver, 1991—94. V.p., bd. dirs. Wyo. Well Svc., Inc., Cody, 1965-71; v.p. rsch. Land and Water Cons., Inc., Ft. Collins, 1972-75; pres. Aetech West, Inc., Ft. Collins, 1982-83; v.p. Altair, Inc., Lakewood, 1989-90. Contbr. numerous articles to tech. jours.; editor tech. procs. Vol., Wyo. Presbytery Coms., Habitat for Humanity, Cody C. of C.; mem. adv. coun. for geoscis. dept. Colo. State U. 1st lt. U.S. Army, 1955-57. NDEA fellow, 1961-64. Mem. ASCE, Am. Soc. Agrl. Engrs., Am. Geophys. Union, Am. Meteorol. Soc., Wyo. Engring. Soc., Rotary Internat., Sigma Xi, Phi Kappa Phi, Xi Sigma Pi, Sigma Gamma Epsilon. Republican. Presbyterian. Avocations: fishing, ham radio, western history.

JONES, EVERETT RILEY, JR., oil company executive; b. Leitchfield, Ky., July 28, 1918; s. Everett Riley and Margie (Hatfield) J.; m. Lois Gibbins, July 15, 1950; children: Stacey Rae, Rande Leigh. Student, Spencerian C.C., 1936-37, U. Louisville, 1946-47. Lic. pub. acct., Ky. Sec. treas., dir. Lafitte Oil Corp., Louisville, 1947-49; ptnr. Fryer & Hanson Drilling Co., Dallas, 1950-58; pres., dir. Bengal Producing Co., Dallas, 1959—. Dir. Dallas County Small Bus. Devel. Ctr., Inc. Contbr. articles/stories to newspapers, publs. Trustee S.W. Engring. Found. Served to capt. USAAF, 1942-45. Decorated D.F.C., Air medal with 4 oak leaf clusters. Mem. Engrs. Club Dallas (past pres.) Dallas Petroleum Club (past pres.), Royal Air Force Club in London, Northwood Country Club Dallas. Episcopalian. Office: 8080 N Central Expy Dallas TX 75206-1838

JONES, FARRELL, retired judge; b. May 6, 1926; BA, Lincoln U., 1950; JD, NYU, 1957. Social investigator N.Y.C. Dept. Social Svcs., 1957-58; asst. counsel Gov. Harriman's Com. to Rev. N.Y. State Parole Sys., 1958; field rep. N.Y. State Commn. for Human Rights, 1958-60, sr. field rep., 1960-61, regional dir. L.I. region, 1961-63; exec. dir. Nassau County (N.Y.) Commn. on Human Rights, 1963-70; dep. county exec. Nassau County, 1970-71; assoc. dir., clin. asst. prof. divsn. alcohol./drug depend. SUNY Downstate Med. Ctr., 1971; 1st dep. adminstr. N.Y.C. Human Resources Adminstrn., 1971-74; asst. v.p. Blue Cross and Blue Shield Greater N.Y., 1974-88; pvt. practice Port Washington, N.Y., 1988-90; judge adminstrv. law N.Y. State Workers Compensation Bd., 1990-95; ret., 1996. Bd. dirs. Mental Health Assn. Nassau County, Health Watch Info. & Promotion Svcs., Bklyn., N.Y. (nat.), Am. Com. on Africa; cons. N.Y. State Dept. Edn. on Intergroup Rels.; cons. L.I. Sch. Dists.; pres. Sci. Mus. L.I., Plandome, N.Y., 1984-90. Bd. dirs. Family Svc. Assn. Nassau County, N.Y.C. Comprehensive Health Planning Agy., 1971-74, Cow Bay Housing, Port Washington, 1975-85; chmn. Nassau County Econ. Opportunity Commn., 1971-72; pres. Nassau County Law Svcs. Com., 1969-71; bd. dirs. Health and Welfare Coun. of Nassau County, Nassau County Cmty. Econ. Devel. Corp., Nassau Cmty. Health Svcs. Found., 1966-69, Cmty. Health Plan of Suffolk County, N.Y., 1981-86, chmn. labor com., 1981-86; mem. Nassau County Crime Coun., 1966-71; trustee Adelphi U., mem. adv. bd. Sch. Social Work, 1964-70, chmn., 1970—; assoc. trustee North Shore Hosp., 1991—; trustee Port Washington Pub. Libr., 1976-91, Urban League, L.I., 1976-91; mem. Nassau County Youth Bd., 1964-71; life mem., pres. North Shore Br. NAACP, 1983-87; mem. adv. coun. Hofstra U., 1967-72, v.p., 1971-72; pres. Levitt Found., 1994—; village justice, Manorhaven, N.Y., 1996—. With AUS, 1951-53. Address: 9 The Quarter Deck Port Washington NY 11050-1431

JONES, FERDINAND TAYLOR, JR., psychologist, educator; b. N.Y.C., May 15, 1932; s. Ferdinand Taylor and Esther (Haggie) J.; m. Antonina Laub, Sept. 26, 1953 (div. Mar. 1967); children: Joanne Esther, Terrie Lynn; m. Myra Jean Rogers, Nov. 25, 1967. AB, Drew U., 1953; PhD, U. Vienna, Austria, 1959. Staff psychologist Riverside Hosp., Bronx, N.Y., 1959-62; chief psychologist Westchester County Community Mental Hosp. Bd., White Plains, N.Y., 1962-67; tng. cons. Lincoln Hosp. Mental Health Services, Bronx, 1967-69; tchr. psychology Sarah Lawrence Coll., Bronxville, N.Y., 1968-72; prof. psychology Brown U., Providence, 1972-97, prof. emeritus, 1997, dir. psychol. svcs., 1972-1992; clin. lectr. Emeritus in Psychiatry and Human Behavior, 2002. Scholar-in-residence The Schomburg Ctr. for Rsch. in Black Culture, 1987; cons. St. Peter's Head Start, Yonkers, N.Y., 1967-71, Bronx State Hosp., 1969-72; vis. prof. U. Dar es Salaam, Tanzania, 1993, Oberlin Coll., 1997, 98, U. Cape Town, 1999, Sarah Lawrence Coll., 2001. Co-editor: The Triumph of the Soul: Cultural and Psychological Aspects of African American Music. Bd. dirs. Am. Orthopsychiat. Assn., 1984-87. Served with AUS, 1953-56. Mem. APA, Am. Orthopsychiat. Assn. (pres. 1989-90), Ea. Psychol. Assn., Westchester County Psychol. Assn. (past pres.), Assn. Black Psychologists, Soc. Psychol. Study Social Issues, Internat. Assn. for Jazz Edn. Achievements include developing (with Myron W. Harris) small group method for reduction of distance and dissonance in interracial communication. Home: 182 Sessions St Providence RI 02906 Office: Brown U 79 Waterman St Providence RI 02912-9079 E-mail: ferdinand_jones@brown.edu. *Dedicated to channeling a lifelong fascination with people into skilled understanding of human behavior and the alleviation of problems in human functioning.*

JONES, FLETCHER, JR., automotive company executive; CEO Fletcher Jones Mgmt., Las Vegas, Nev., pres. Office: Fletcher Jones Mgmt 175 E Reno Ave Ste C-6 Las Vegas NV 89119-1102*

JONES, FLORENCE M. music educator; b. West Columbia, Tex., Apr. 11, 1939; d. Isaiah and Lu Ethel (Baldridge) McNeil; m. Waldo D. Jones, May 29, 1965; children: Ricky, Wanda, Erna. BS, Prairie View A&M U., 1961, MEd, 1968; postgrad., Rice U., 1988, U. Houston, 1980. Cert. tchr. elem. edn., math. Tchr. English and typing Lincoln High Sch., Port Arthur, Tex., 1961-62; tchr. grades three and four Houston Ind. Sch. Dist., 1963-90, tchr. gifted and talented, 1990-94; tchr. piano Windsor Village Liberal Arts Acad., Houston, 1994—. Dist. tchr. trainer Houston Ind. Sch. Dist., 1985-90; shared decision mem. Sch. decision Making Team, 1993-94; coord. gifted/talented program, Petersen Elem. Sch., Houston, 1990-94; participant piano Recital Hartzog Studio, 1985-88; film previewer Houston Media Ctr. Curriculum writer Modules to Improve Science Teaching, 1985; author sci. pop-up book, 1980, gifted/talented program, 1994; contbr. poems to lit. jours. Youth camp counselor numerous non-denominational ch. camps, U.S., 1961-89; active restoration of Statue of Liberty, Ellis Island Found., N.Y.C., 1983-85; lay minister Ch. of God, 1961-94; charter founder The Am. Family History Immigration Ctr., Ellis Island, N.Y.C. Recipient Letter of Recognition for Outstanding Progress in Edn., Pres. Bill Clinton, 1994, Congresswoman Sheilia Jackson Lee, Tex. Gov. George Bush, State Rep. Harold V. Sutton Jr., Houston Mayor Bob Lanier, Tex. Gov. Ann Richards; Gold Cup/Highest Music award Hartzog Music Studio, 1987, Diamond Key award Nat. Women of Achievement, 1995, Editors Choice awarc Nat. Library Poetry, 1995, cert. recognition Quaker Oats Co. and NCNW Inc. 1999, Youth Advisors trophy and New Millennium Leader plaque Nat. Womer Achievement, 2001, others; inductee The Internat. Poetry Hall of Fame. Mem NEA, Houston Assn. Childhood Edn. (v.p. 1985-88), Assn. for Childhood Edn (bd. dirs. 1979-91), Houston Zool. Soc., World Wildllife Fund, Nat. Storytelling Assn., Tejas Storytelling Assn. (life), Soc. Children's Book Writers anc Illustrators, Nat. Audubon Soc., Am. Mus. Natural History, Tex. Ret. Tchrs Assn. (life), Internat. Soc. Poets (disting. life mem.), others. Democrat Avocations: writing, reading, storytelling, collecting sea shells, arts and crafts Home: 3310 Dalmatian Dr Houston TX 77045-6520

JONES, FRANK A., JR., psychiatrist, educator; MD, Case Western U., Cleve. 1972. Diplomate Am. Bd, Psychiatry and Neurology, 1977. Psychiatry interr Boston State Hosp., Dorchester, Mass., 1972—73; resident in psychiatry Worcester State Hosp., Dorchester, Mass., 1973—75; physician dept. psychiatry Univ. Behavioral Health Ctr., Piscataway, NJ, 1977—2002. Prof. psychiatry Robert Wood Johnson Med. Sch., 1977—. Office: 3055 Rte 27 Franklin Park N. 08823

JONES, FRANK CATER, retired lawyer; b. Macon, Ga., June 19, 1925; s Charles Baxter and Carolyn (Cater) J.; m. Annie Gantt Anderson, Mar. 31 1951; children: Eugenia Anderson Henderson, Annie Gantt Blattner, Carolyı Corley, Frank Cater. BBA, Emory U., 1947; LLB, Mercer U., 1950, LLD (hon.) 1996. Bar: Ga. 1950. Pvt. practice, Macon, 1950—77; mem. firm Jones, Cork & Miller (and predecessor), 1950—77, King & Spalding, Atlanta, 1977—2001 Bd. dirs. So. Trust Corp. Trustee Wesleyan Coll., Macon, 1966—, chmn. bd dirs., 1981-86; pres. Atlanta Symphony Orch. League, 1982-84; chmn. Ga. Gt Park Authority, 1980-83, Ga. Pub. Telecom. Commn., 1983-98, Met. Atlanta chpt. ARC, 1987-88; bd. dirs. Carter Ctr., Emory U., 1987—; chmn. Michael C Carlos Mus., 1991-96; trustee Emory U., Atlanta, 1991-95, trustee emeritus 1995—. Fellow: ACTL (bd. regents 1986—, sec. 1990—92, pres. 1993—94) mem.: ABA (ho. of dels. 1972—94), U.S. Supreme Ct. Hist. Soc. (pres 2002—), State Bar of Ga. (pres. 1968—69), Ga. Bar Assn. (pres. young lawyer sect. 1956—57), Macon Bar Assn. (pres. 1954), Greater Macon C. of C. (pres 1965), Rotary. Home: 4957 Wellington Dr Macon GA 31210-4427 Office: King & Spalding 191 Peachtree St Atlanta GA 30303-1763 E-mail fjones@kslaw.com

JONES, FRANK GRIFFITH, lawyer; b. Houston, Sept. 11, 1941; s. A Gordon and Grace (Griffith) Jones; m. Deborah Ann Young, July 5, 1969 children: Russell G., Sarah G., Christopher Y. BS, Rice U., 1963; JD, U. Tex. 1966. Bar: Tex. 1966, U.S. Dist. Ct. (so., no. and ea. dists.) Tex., U.S. Ct Appeals (5th and 8th cirs.), cert.: (civil trial specialist). Ptnr. Fulbright & Jaworski, L.L.P., Houston, 1966, co-ptnr. in charge, 2001—. Chmn. Fulbright & Jaworski Employment Commn., 1988—92, mem. lit. mgmt. com. and policy com., head practice devel. com. Chmn. troop com. Boy Scouts Am., Houston 1986—88; mem. Greater Houston. Partnership; bd. dirs. Houston Symphony Holly Hall Retirement Cmty., Friends Fondren LIbr.; mem. Rice U. Fun Coun., Houston, 1987—93; pres. Baker Coll. Rice U., 1962—63. Lt. (j.g. USNR, 1967—72. Fellow Keeton, U. Tex. Law Sch., 1993—. Fellow: Internat Acad. Trial Lawyers, Am. Coll. Trial Lawyers (ADR com. 1986—96, chmn 1992—94, ethics com. 1996—2001); mem.: ABA, Chartered Inst. Arbitrators Tex. Gen. Counsel Forum, Products Liability Adv. Coun., Def. Rsch. Inst., Am Counsel Assn., Tex. Assn. Def. Counsel, Houston Assn. Cert. Civil Trial an Appellate Specialists, Am. Bar Found., Houston Bar Found., Tex. Bar Found. Tex. Bar Assn., Houston Young Lawyers Assn. (pres. 1972—73), Houston Ba Assn. (chmn. 2003), Internat. Assn. Def. Counsel, Am. Bd. Trial Advs., Greate Houston Partnership, Houston City Club, Rotary, Phi Delta Phi (past pres.) Avocations: tennis, travel. Office: Fulbright & Jaworski LLP 1301 Mckinney S Ste 5100 Houston TX 77010-3095

JONES, FRANK WYMAN, management consultant, mechanical engineer; b Ironton, Ohio, Jan. 20, 1940; s. Kylius and Kathleen (McDonald) J.; m Margaret Kwitek, Sept. 1, 1962; children: Kelly, Connie, Katie, Colleen Carolyn. BSME, U. Cin., 1963; MBA, Ind. U., 1965. V.p., gen. mgr. G & Machine Tool Divsn., Fond du Lac, Wis., 1976-80; exec. v.p. Giddings & Lewi Inc., Fond du Lac, Wis., 1980-81, pres., CEO, 1982-86; mgmt. cons. Tucson 1987—. Bd. dirs. Modine, Racine, Wis., Star Cutter Co., Farmington Hills Mich., Gardner Publs., Inc., Cin. Gen. Tool Co., Cin. Mem. Am. Mgmt. Assn Nat. Assn. Corp. Dirs. Republican. Roman Catholic. Home: 6740 N Sair Andrews Dr Tucson AZ 85718-2619

JONES, FRANKLIN CHARLES, judge; b. Hanover, N.H., July 2, 1948; s Laurence Harry and Dorothy Selma (Covey) J.; m. Jan Lynn Griggs, June 18 1966; children— Gregory Allen, Matthew Scott, Benjamin Albert, Kathry Covey. B.A., U. N.H., 1970; J.D., Boston U., 1973. Bar: N.H. 1973, U.S. Dis Ct. N.H. 1978, U.S. Ct. Appeals (1st cir.) 1978, U.S. Supreme Ct. 1979. Atty Michael & Wallace, Rochester, N.H., 1973-76; ptnr. Michael & Jones, Rochester, 1976-78, Michael Jones & Wensley, 1979-1992, Jones, Wensley, Wirth & Azcrian, 2001—.; presiding justice Rochester Dist. Ct., 2001-. Office: Rochester Dist Ct 76 N Main St Rochester NH 03867

JONES, FRANKLIN ROSS, education educator; b. Charlotte, N.C., Jan. 3 1920; s. William Morton and Olive Ruth (Moser) J.; divorced; childrer Franklin Ross, C. Morton, Susan Noel. AB, Lenoir Rhyne Coll., 1941; MA, U N.C., 1951; DEd, Duke U., 1960. Tchr. schs., N.C., 1944-48; prin. Jr. High Sch Henderson, N.C., 1948-54; dist. sch. prin. Wake County, N.C., 1954-56; dis supt. Roxboro (N.C.) schs., 1956-58; chmn. dept. edn. Randolph-Macon Coll Ashland, Va., 1959-64; interim dean U. Richmond (Va.), 1962; dean Sch. Edı Old Dominion U., 1964-69; Eminent prof. Old Dominion U., 1974-94; founde Child Study Center, 1965, disting. prof., 1969—, social founds. program leade 1973-77, doctoral program liaison rep., 1974-77, faculty chmn., 1981—. Di Forest Ridge Corp., 1985; vis. rsch. scholar Duke U., 1967; cons. HEW, Stat Sch. Sys. and Colls.; lectr. in field; mem. com. White house Conf. Children an Youth, 1968-71, Ea. regional chmn., 1968-71; mem. Va. Gov.'s Com. Implementation, 1971-73; spkr. 25th Internat. Congress of Psychology, Brussels 1992; symposium chmn. European Congress of Psychology, Athens, Greece 1995; cons. to dean on test score stats., Old Dominion U., 1995—; adj. prof. U Va., 1959-64. Author: Psychology of Human Devel., 1969, 2d edit. 1985, 3 edit. 1992, Handbook on Testing, 1972, Understanding the Middlescent Year. 1978, Theory of Adult Development, 1980; Radio series Sta. WTAR, Norfolk 1973-75; test item writer for N.Y. Regency exams, 1987, Ednl. Testing Svc 1989; guest editor of Education, 1990—. Mem. Norfolk Urban Coalition 1969-73; chmn. March of Dimes, Person County, N.C., 1956-57; mem. adv. bo Tidewater Rehab. Ctr., 1967-69; chmn. Hull Scholarship Fund, 1983-85; coor U. Joy Fund Drive, 1974-95; univ. chmn. United Fund, 1982, 84; chmn assessment com. Va. Reading to Learn Program, 1990-91; cons. to sch. system ETS, HEW, Coll. 1966—; dir. Praxis Ctr., 1993—; adminstr. Nat. Bd. for Cer Counselors Ctr., Nat. Lang. and Music Bd. of Certification; chmn. scholarshi fund Brewton Parker Coll., Mt. Vernon, Ga., 1999-2003; chmn. drive fo low-paid faculty Old Dominion U., 2002-. Recipient Dean's Svc. award Ol Dominion U., 1984, Univ. award for Fund RAising, 1994, Heritage Foun award, 1996, Football recognition and scholar Brewton Parker Coll., Ga., 199 Va. Golden Olymnpics tennis doubles champion, 1982-84, 880 meter run Gol medal, 1983, 100 meter dash Silver medal, 1984. Mem. Am. Psychol. So (charter), S.E. Psychol. Assn., Va. Assn. U. Profs. (dir. 1962-64), South Atlant Philosophy Edn. Soc. (pres. 1966-69, dir. 1969—), Va. Assn. Rsch. in Ed (Disting. Rsch. awards 1972, 73, 78),N.C. Edn. Assn. (pres. North Cen. chp 1951, pres. North Cen. Prins. 1956), Ea. Ednl. Rsch. Assn., Nat. Urban Ed Assn., Bicycle Relay Jr. Marathon World's Record Team, 1933, Alpha Ta Kappa, Kappa Delta Pi, Phi Delta Kappa, Phi Kappa Phi, Pi Gamma Mu (se 1962-64) Clubs: Harbor (Norfolk). Lodges: Lions, Rotary. Home: 102 Manchester Ave Norfolk VA 23508-1243

JONES, GALEN RAY, physician assistant; b. Salt Lake City, Feb. 1, 1948; Leonard Ray and Veda (Whitehead) J.; m. Patricia Ann Poulson, Jan. 21, 197 children: Brian, Marci, Natalie. Grad. with honors, Med. Field Svc. Sch. F Sam Houston, San Antonio, 1971; BS, U. Utah, 1982. Missionary Ch. of Jesu Christ of Latter Day Saints, Alta., Sask., Can., 1967-69; asst. mgr. Cowan Frostop Hamburger Stand, Salt Lake City, 1969-70; with Safeway Stores, Inc Salt Lake City, 1970; o.r. tech. Latter Day Saint Hosp., Salt Lake City, 1973-7 physician asst. Lovell Clinic Inc., Lovell, Wyo., 1975-77, Family Health Car

Inc., Tooele, Utah, 1977-86, West Dermatology and Surgery Med. Grp., Redlands, Calif., 1986-95; with blood and marrow transplant program Univ. Hosp. and Primary Childrens Med. Ctr. U. Utah, Salt Lake City, 1996-98; physician asst. D. Edgar Allen Dermatology, Ogden, 1998—. Maturation lectr. Tooele Sch. Dist., 1978-86; course dir., instr. EMT, North Big Horn County Search and Rescue, 1976; instr. EMT, Grantsville Ambulance Inc., 1979-85; lectr. on skin care and changes to sr. citizen groups, hosp. auxs., health fairs, 1986—; Boy Scouts Am. scoutmaster 1987-89, scout com. chair, 2001—; high sch. sophomore sem. tchr. religion, 1991-96; owner Adventureland and TopHat Video, Magna, Utah, 1982-96. Author: (with others) The P.A. Clinical Practice, 1995. Chmn. County Health Teen Pregnancy Prevention Project, Tooele, 1980-81; adv. bd. State Dept. Health-Rural Health Network, Salt Lake City, 1985-86; health lectr. County Health & Edn. Dept. Progs., Tooele, 1977-86; mormon bishop/pastor Lakeview Ward, Latter Day Saints Ch., Tooele, 1982-86; mem. Utah Acad. Physician Assts. (pres. 1980-81, editor newsletter 1979-80); mem. People to People Ambs. P.A. del. to China, Beijing, Xian, Guillin, Yangshou, Hong Kong, 2000-01. With U.S. Army, 1971-73. U. Utah grantee, 1966, 67, 69. Fellow Am. Acad. Physician Assts., Utah Acad. Physicians Assts. Republican. Mem. Lds Ch. Avocations: gardening, hiking, camping, skiing, photography, travel. Home: 2670 Willow Wick Dr Sandy UT 84093-1929 Office: D Edgar Allen Dermatology 3860 Jackson Ave Ogden UT 84403-1956

JONES, GENIA KAY, emergency supervising nurse, consultant; b. Dallas, Dec. 21, 1954; d. Joe and Juanita Sue (White) Self; m. Paul L. Jones, June 1, 1986. ADN, Tarrant County Jr. Coll., 1976; mgmt. cert., Cedar Valley Coll., 1980; sci. update, Mountain View Coll., Dallas, 1984; BSN, Regent's U., 2001. RN; cert. emergency nurse; cert. BLS, ACLS, ACLS instr. Instr. Steven's Pk. Hosp., Dallas, 1972-77; asst. dir. nursing svcs. Four Season's Conv. Ctr., Dallas, 1977-78; with surgery dept. Dallas/Ft. Worth Med. Ctr., 1978-80; dir. nursing Med. Staffing Svcs., Dallas, 1980, Reproductive Svcs., Inc., Dallas, 1981; adminstrv. supr. Dallas Family Hosp., 1982-85; patient care coord., emergency dept. Dallas S.W. Med. Ctr., 1985-90, staff nurse, emergency dept., 1990-99; medical consultant Needham, Johnson, Lovelace, and Johnson, 1992—; emergency nurse dir. Rockwall Minor Emergency Ctr., 1999—2001; emergency nurse Virtual Healthcare Svcs. Meth. Med. Ctrs. Dallas, 2001—03, Med. Ctr. of Arlington, 2002—. Internat. flight nurse Air Ambulance Network, Inc., Dallas, 1987—; instr. intravenous therapy, 1980—; cons., adv., 1980—; medico-legal cons., 1990—; clin. instr. Edn. Am., 1999—2001. Recipient Citizens award, Certs. Appreciation, HOSA Nat. Leadership Conf., Silver medal of Honor; Internat. Biog. Assn. fellow, 1990. Mem. NAFE, Am. Heart Assnb., Nurses' Svc. Orgn., Tex. Nurses' Assn., Emergency Nurses' Assn. Home: 108 Burkett Ln Red Oak TX 75154-7602

JONES, GEOFFREY KYLE, telecommunications industry executive; b. New Orleans, Dec. 21, 1972; s. Stephen Randall and Julie Anne Jones. B in Sociology, Tex. Tech. U. Account rep. AT&T, Marietta, Ga., 1997—2000, comm. technician Tulsa, Okla., 2000—. Mem.: Telecom Pioneers Am. (treas. 2003—). Home: Unit 133 4870 E 68th St Tulsa OK 74136 Office: AT&T 424 S Detroit Ave Tulsa OK 74120

JONES, GEOFFREY MELVILL, physiology research educator; b. Cambridge, Eng., Jan. 14, 1923; s. Benett and Dorothy Laxton (Jotham) J.; m. Jenny Marigold Burnaby, June 21, 1953; children: Katharine, Francis, Andrew, Dorothy. BA, Cambridge U., 1944, MA, 1947, MB, BCh, 1949. House surgeon Middlesex Hosp., London, Eng., 1949-50; sr. house surgeon Addenbrookes Hosp., Cambridge, Eng., 1950-51; sci. med. officer Royal Air Force Inst. Aviation Medicine, Farnborough, Eng., 1951-55; sci. officer Med. Rsch. Coun., Eng., 1955-61; assoc. prof. physiology, dir. aviation med. rsch. unit McGill U., Montreal, Que., Can., 1961-68, prof., dir., 1968-88, Hosmer rsch. prof., 1978-91, emeritus prof. physiology, 1991—. Rsch. prof. clin. neuroscis. U. Calgary, Alta., Can., 1991—, Coll. France, 1979, 95; vis. prof. Stanford U., 1971-72. Author: (with another) mammalian Vestibular Physiology, 1979; editor: (with another) Adaptive Mechanisms in Gaze Control, 1985; contbr. numerous articles to profl. jours. Served to squadron leader Royal Air Force, 1951-55 Sr. rsch. assoc. Nat. Acad. Sci., 1971-72; recipient Skylab Achievement award NASA, 1974, 1st recipient Dohlman medal Dohlman Soc. Toronto U., 1987, Quinquennial Gold medal Barany Soc. Internat., 1988, Ashton Graybiel award U.S. Naval Aerospace Labs., 1989, Wilbur Franks Annual award Can. Soc. Aerospace Medicine, Buchanan-Barbour award Royal Aeronautical Soc., 1991, Mc Laughlin Medal, 1991, Royal Soc. Can. Fellow Can. Aeronautics and Space Inst., Aerospace Med. Assn. (Harry Armstrong award 1968, Arnold D. Tuttle award 1971), Royal Soc. Can. (McLaughlin medal 1991), Royal Soc. London, Royal Aeronautical Soc. London (Stewart Meml. award 1989, Buchanan Barbour award 1990); mem. U.K. Physiol. Soc., Can. Physiol. Soc., Can. Soc. Aerospace Med. Soc., Internat. Collegium Otolaryngology, Soc. Neurosci. Avocations: tennis, sailing, outdoor activities, reading, piano playing/composition. Office: U Calgary Dept Clin Neuroscis 3330 Hospital Dr NW Calgary AB Canada T2N 4N1

JONES, GEORGE FLEMING, international consultant; b. San Angelo, Tex., June 27, 1935; s. George Fleming and Cora (Brewer) J.; m. Maria Rosario Correa, Apr. 23, 1960; children: George III, Robert, Michael, Mary Louise. AB magna cum laude, Wabash Coll., 1955; AM, Tufts U., 1956; MA, Stanford U., 1967; LLD, Wabash Coll., 2000. Joined Fgn. Svc., Dept. State, 1956; with Econ. Bur., Dept. State, Washington, 1956-58; with Am. Embassy Ecuador, 1958-60, Ghana, 1961-63, Venezuala, 1963-66; officer in charge Venezuelan affairs Dept. State, Washington, 1967-69, officer in charge Colombian affairs, 1969-71; polit. advisor U.S. Mission to IAEA, Vienna, 1971-74; counselor for polit. affairs Am. Embassy, Guatemala, 1974-77; student Nat. War Coll., Washington, 1977-78; Latin Am. adviser U.S. del. U.S.-Soviet Conventional Arms Talks, 1978; dep. dir. office Latin Am. regional polit. affairs Dept. State, 1978-80, dir., 1980-82; dep. chief of mission Am. Embassy Costa Rica, 1982-85, Chile, 1985-89; sr. adviser for Latin Am. and Caribbean affairs U.S. del. UN Gen. Assembly, N.Y.C., 1990, 95; amb. to Republic of Guyana, 1991-95; dir. programs for the Ams., Internat. Found. for Election Sys., Washington, 1996-99. Dir. Democracy and Governance Ctr. Devel. Assocs., Inc., 2000—. Recipient Superior Honor award Dept. State, 1987. Mem. Am. Fgn. Svc. Assn. (v.p. 1989-90, 2003—, bd. dirs. 1999-2001), Sr. Fgn. Svc. Assn. (bd. dirs. 1990-92). Home: 3804 Acosta Rd Fairfax VA 22031-3804 E-mail: geojones@erols.com., gjones@devassoc1.com.

JONES, GEORGE HILTON, retired history educator, writer; b. Baton Rouge, Jan. 11, 1924; s. William Carruth and Elizabeth Fly (Kirkpatrick) J. BA, La. State U., 1947; DPhil, Oxford (Eng.) U., 1950. Instr. Hofstra Coll., Hempstead, N.Y., 1950-51; asst. prof. Ind. U., Bloomington, 1951-52; asst. editor Am. Book Co., N.Y.C., 1953-54; asst. prof. Washington Coll., Chestertown, Md., 1954-56, Tex. Technol. Coll., Lubbock, 1958-61, Kans. State U., Manhattan, 1961-64; assoc. prof. Olivet (Mich.) Coll., 1964-66; from assoc. to full prof. Ea. Ill. U., Charleston, 1966-89, prof. emeritus, 1989—. Ednl. advisor R.J. Best, Inc., San Francisco, 2001—. Author: The Main Stream of Jacobitism, 1955, Charles Middleton, The Life and Times of a Restoration Politician, 1968, Convergent Forces, Immediate Causes of the Revolution of 1688 in England, 1991, Great Britain and the Tuscan Succession Question, 1999; co-author: Southern Regional Education Board, 1960; maj. contbr. Huguenot Soldiering Project, 2002—. Cpl. U.S. Army, 1943-45. Rhodes scholar, Oxford, 1947-50; fellow Newberry Libr., Chgo., summer 1959, Guggenheim Found., London, 1960-61. Fellow Royal Hist. Soc.; mem. AAUP, N.Am. Conf. on Brit. Studies, United Oxford and Cambridge Univ. Club. Democrat. Avocation: writing light verse. Home: 1530 3rd St Charleston IL 61920-3312

JONES, GEORGE HUMPHREY, retired healthcare executive, hospital facilities and communications consultant; b. Kansas City, Mo., July 10, 1923; s. George Humphrey and Mary R. (Marrs) J.; m. Peggy Jean Thompson, Nov. 23, 1943; children: Kenneth L., Daniel D., Kathleen Jones Smith, Carol R. Jones Johnson, Janet S. Jones Fitts. Student, U. Mo., Kansas City, 1940-43, Wis. State U., Oshkosh, 1943. Police officer Kansas City (Mo.) Police Dept., 1947-51; elec. contr. Paramount Elec. Svc., Kansas City, 1947-50; electrician Automatic Temp. Control Co., Kansas City, 1951-57; pres., chief ops. George H. Jones Co., Kansas City, 1957-65; sales mgr. Nycon Inc., Lee's Summit, Mo., 1965; design engr. Midland Wright Corp., Kansas City, 1966; dist. sales mgr. Comm. Electronics, Kansas City, 1967; plant ops. supr. Rsch. Med. Ctr., Coll. of Nursing and hdqrs. Health Midwest, Kansas City, 1968-77, dir. plant ops. and comm., 1977-90; hosp. facilities and comm. cons. Overland Park, Kans., 1990-99; ret. Guest lectr. Nat. U., San Diego, 1987. Vol. Salvation Army Emergency Svcs.; bd. dirs. Camellot Fine Arts Acad., 1974—76, v.p., bd. dirs., 1975—76; adv. dir. Rsch. Med. Ctr., 1990—; mem. Heart of Am. Wing Commemorative Air Force. With USAF, 1942—46, with U.S. Army, 1950—51. Fellow Am. Soc. Hosp. Engring., Healthcare Info. and Mgmt. Systems Soc.; mem. Kansas City Area Hosp. Engrs. (pres. 1985, bd. dirs. 1985-89), Am. Legion, Alpha Phi Omega. Presbyterian. Avocations: fishing, photography. Home and Office: 6022 W 86th St Shawnee Mission KS 66207-1521 E-mail: gjones@everestkc.net.

JONES, GEORGE STEVEN, civil engineer; b. Belgrade, Yugoslavia, June 2, 1927; m. Sofia Jones, 1960; 1 child, Appta. BSCE, Northwestern U., 1951, MSCE, 1956, PhD in Bus. Adminstrn., 1958; PhD, Hamilton State U., U. Fla., 1972. Civil engr. Hollabird & Root, Chgo., 1956—57; profl. engr., gen. mgr. Arcadia Engring. Internat., Inc., 1956—70, chmn. bd., 1970—. Civil engr. US C.E., 1951—54; prof. structural engring. Northwestern U., Evanston, Ill.; chmn. dept. econs. U. Ill., Chgo.; legis. asst. Gen. Assembly, Ill.; pres. Tetrakear & Assocs., Inc.; bd. dirs. 1st Nat. Bank of Chgo., Skokie Cmty. Hosp. Author: The Pneumatic Tube Goes Modern, 1958, Opportunities in Construction, 1960, Management and Labor, 1962; contbr. Bd. chmn. Oakton Coll.; pres. Hamilton State U. Mem.: NSPE, ASCE. Avocation: swimming. Address: 6804 Avenida Marbella Sarasota FL 34238-2738

JONES, GEORGE WASHINGTON, JR., lawyer; b. Balt., July 27, 1953; s. George W. and Mattie Alice (Reed) Jones; m. Loretta Phylis Pleasant, Aug. 5, 1978; children: Melissa Grace, George Charles, Jessica Michelle. BA, U. Chgo., 1975; JD, Yale U., 1980. Bar: D.C. 1980, U.S. Dist. Ct. D.C. 1980, U.S. Ct. Appeals (D.C. cir.) 1983, U.S. Supreme Ct. 1986. Law clk. to judge U.S. Ct. Appeals (7th Cir.), Chgo., 1978-79; assoc. O'Melveny & Myers, Washington, 1979-80; asst. to solicitor gen. U.S. Dept. Justice, Washington, 1980-83; assoc. Sidley & Austin, Washington, 1983-87, ptnr., 1988—. Mem.: NBA, ABA, DC Bar (pres. 2002—03). Office: Sidley Austin Brown & Wood LLP 1501 K St NW Washington DC 20005

JONES, GEORGIA ANN, publisher; b. Ogden, Utah, July 6, 1946; d. Sam Oliveto and Edythe June Murphy; m. Lowell David Jones; children: Lowell Scott, Curtis Todd. Sculptor, 1964-78; journalist, 1968-80; appraiser real property Profl. Real Estate Appraisal, San Carlos, Calif., 1980-95; online columnist, 1995-97; owner, pub. Ladybug Press, Sonora, 1996—. Leader workshops for writers, 1994—; founder, prodr. internat radio stas. Ladybughive, 1998—, Teen Talk Network, 1999—, Moose Meals, 2001—; owner IA Connections Network, 2001—. Author: A Garden of Weedin', 1997, Write What You Know: A Writer's Adventure, 1998, In Line at the Lost and Found, 2000, The Real Dirt on the American Dream: Home Ownership and Democracy, 2000; patentee Scruples-tag, 1980; editor, pub. Women on a Wire, 1996, vol. 2, 2001; author, playwright, A Stitch in Time, 1995, The Usual Suspects, 1995. Spkr. Jubillenium Interfaith Conf. for World Peace, 1999. Mem. Internat. Forum of Lit. and Culture (bd. dirs., U.S. chpt., Pave Peace keynote spkr. internat. congress 1999). Avocations: drawing, designing and building homes, landscape gardening. Office: 16964 Columbia River Dr Sonora CA 95370

JONES, GERALD EDWARD, religion educator; b. Gettysburg, S.D., June 20, 1933; s. Otis Clinton and Alma May (Gorman) J.; m. Joyce Nadine Lindstrom; children: Eric Otis, JanEtta, Angela, Nadine, Sylvia, Gerald L. BS, Brigham Young U., 1957, MA, 1960, PhD, 1972; postgrad., U. Minn., U. Iowa. Seminary prin. LDS Ch. Ednl. System, St. Johns, Ariz., 1957-59, Grantsville, Utah, 1960-63, Rexburg, Idaho, 1964-66, Pocatello, Idaho, 1966-67; dir. Inst. Religion U. Wyo., Laramie, 1967—70, pres. Sch. Religion, 1969—70; dir. Inst. Religion U. Calif., Berkeley, 1971-85, Stanford U., Palo Alto, Calif., 1985-92, Yale U., New Haven, 1992-95. Tour dir. Brigham Young U., Provo, Utah, 1978-80; lectr., cons. various orgns. Utah, Calif., Idaho, 1970-90; bd. dirs. Internat. Network for Religion and Animals, No. Wales, Pa. Author: Animals and the Gospel, 1980; contbg. editor: Between the Species Jour., Berkeley, 1984—; contbr. articles to profl. jours. Bd. govs. Nat. Coun. of Christians and Jews, San Franciscio, 1986-92, nat. trustee, N.Y.C., 1988-92; pub. policy expert Heritage Found., Washington, 1982-94. Recipient commendation Merritt Hosp., Oakland, Calif., 1984. Mem. S.D. Hist. Soc. (life), Utah Hist. Soc. (life), Soc. Christian Philosophers. Mem. Lds Ch. Avocations: world travel, book collector, church activities. Home: 1311 Edinburgh Ct Concord CA 94518-3918 E mail: gejphd@juno.com.

JONES, GERALD PAUL, software educator; b. South Gate, Calif., July 11, 1946; AB, U. So. Calif., L.A., 1968, MSEd, 1978, PhD, 1985. Mem. staff U. So. Calif., L.A. Contbr. articles to profl. jours. Mem. Phi Beta Kappa. Home: PO Box 18425 Los Angeles CA 90018-0425 Office: U So Calif JEF 214 1020 W Jefferson Blvd Los Angeles CA 90089-0251 E-mail: gpjones@usc.edu.

JONES, GERRE LYLE, marketing and public relations consultant; b. Kansas City, Mo., June 22, 1926; s. Eugene Riley and Carolyn (Newell) J.; m. Charlotte Mae Reinhold, Oct. 30, 1948; children: Beverly Anne Jones Putnam, Wendy S. Jones Stout. BJ, U. Mo., 1948, postgrad., 1953-54. Exec. sec. Effingham (Ill.) C. of C., 1948-50; field rep. Nat. Found. Infantile Paralysis, N.Y.C., 1950-57; dir. pub. rels. Inst. Logopedics, Wichita, Kans., 1957-58; owner Gerre Jones & Assocs., Pub. Rels., Kansas City, Mo., 1958-63; info. officer Radio Free Europe Fund, Munich, Fed. Republic of Germany, 1963-65, spl. asst. to dir. pub. rels., 1965-66; exec. asst. pub. affairs Edward Durell Stone, 1967-68; dir. mktg. and comms. Vincent G. Kling & Ptnrs., Phila., 1969-71; mktg. cons. Ellerbe Architects, Washington, 1972; v.p. Gaio Assocs., Ltd., Washington, 1972-73, exec. v.p., 1973-76; exec. v.p. Bldg. Industry Devel. Svcs., Washington, 1973-76; pres. Gerre Jones Assocs. Inc., Albuquerque, 1976-89, ret., 1989; sr. v.p. Barlow Assocs., Inc., Washington, 1977-78; lectr. numerous colls. and univs. Author: How to Market Professional Design Services, 1973, 2d edit., 1983, How to Prepare Professional Design Brochures, 1976, (with Stuart H. Rose) How to Find and Win New Business, 1976, Public Relations for the Design Professional, 1980; contbr. articles to profl. jours. Served with USAAF, 1944-45, maj. USAF (ret.). Mem. Nat. Assn. Sci. Writers, AIA (hon.), Assn. Former Intelligence Officers, Sigma Delta Chi, Alpha Delta Sigma, Phi Delta Phi, Masons. Republican.

JONES, GLENN EARLE, property management executive; b. Greensboro, N.C., May 11, 1946; s. Harold Clifford and AnnaBelle (Goodwin) J. B.S., Cornell U. Sch. Hotel and Restaurant Mgmt., 1968. Asst. to gen. mgr. Warwick Hotel, Houston, 1968-69; Northeastern Ohio sales rep. L.G. Balfour Co., Attleboro, Mass., 1969-72; resident mgr. Chase Park Plaza Hotel, St. Louis, 1972-74; gen. mgr. Holiday Inn, Steamboat Springs, Colo., 1974, Santa Fe Hilton Inn, 1975, Sheraton Inn, New Orleans, 1976-79; pres. Landmark Systems, Inc., New Orleans, 1979— ; chmn. Sheraton, So. Regional Owners and Mgrs. Council, 1981— . mem. com. membership Greater New Orleans Tourist and Conv. Commn.; mem. dist. com. United Fund. Mem. New Orleans Hotel and Motel Assn. (treas.), Cornell Soc. Hotelmen, Am. Hotel Mgmt. Assn. (cert., mem. fund devel. com. Ednl. Inst.). Episcopalian. Home: 3101 Rue Parc Fontaine # 1408 New Orleans LA 70131-

JONES, GLOWER WHITEHEAD, lawyer; b. Atlanta, May 4, 1936; s. Samuel L. and Alma (Powell) J.; m. Joanna Dayvault, Apr. 5, 1980; children: Mark, Jeff, Tom, Frank, Michael. Grad. Dartmouth Coll. 1958; JD, Emory U., 1963. Bar: Ga. 1962, U.S. Dist. Ct. Ga. 1963, U.S. Ct. Appeals (5th and 11th cirs.), U.S. Ct. Claims, U.S. Supreme Ct. Assoc. Smith, Swift, Currie, McGhee & Hancock, Atlanta, 1963-65; ptnr. Smith Currie & Hancock, Atlanta, 1967-99, of counsel, 2000—. Author: Legal Aspects of Doing Business in North America and Canada, 1987, Alternative Clauses to Standard Construction Contracts, 1990, editor 2d edit., Construction Subcontracting: A Legal Guide for Industry Professionals, 1991, Wiley Construction Law Update, 1992, 93, 94, Construction Contractors: The Right To Stop Work, 1992, Remedies for International Sellers of Goods, 1993; mem. editl. bd. Ga. State Bar Jour.; contbr. articles to profl. jours. Mem. exec. bd. Met. Atlanta Boys' & Girls' Clubs, Inc., asst. sec., 1973-80, sec., 1980-83; bd. dirs. Samuel L. Jones Boys' & Girls' Club, Inc., So. Region Boys Clubs Am.; trustee, past pres. Atlanta Florence Crittendon Svcs., Inc.; bd. dirs. Carrie Steele Pitts Home, Gate City Day Nursery Assn.; treas. IBA Found. Recipient Golden Boy award Met. Atlanta Boys' Club, 1971. Fellow Chartered Inst. Arbitrators; mem. ABA, Fed. Bar Assn., Internat. Bar Assn. (chmn. internat. sales com., chmn. UNCITRAL subcom., chmn. membership com., mem. governing coun. sect. bus. law), Ga. Bar Assn., State Bar Ga., Atlanta Bar Assn. (former chmn. prepaid legal svcs. com., engr. lawyers rels. com.), Lawyers Club Atlanta, Am. Judicature Soc., Assn. Trial Attys. Am., Ga. Assn. Trial Lawyers, Dartmouth Coll. Alumni Club, Baylor Alumni Club, Emory U. Alumni Club, Atlanta Athletic Club, Ansley Park Golf Club, Dartmouth Club, World Trade Club, Phi Delta Theta. Home: 78 Peachtree Cir NE Atlanta GA 30309-3519 Office: Smith Currie & Hancock Harris Tower 233 Peachtree St NE Ste 2600 Atlanta GA 30303-1530

JONES, GORDON KEMPTON, dentist; b. Rochester, NY, July 22, 1946; s. Joseph Kempton and Eunice (Patten)J.; m. Kathleen Anne FitzSimmons, July 24, 1971; children: Bryan Kempton, Brendan Austin, Graeme Meghan, Michael Cameron, Meredith Hunter, Mallory Sterling. BA in Chemistry, U. N.C., 1968, DDS, 1976; MS in Restorative Dentistry, U. Mich., 1984. Lic. dentist, Ill., N.C. Commd. lt. USN, 1976, advanced through ranks to capt., 1993; resident Naval Regional Med. Ctr., Camp Pendleton, Calif., 1977; dentist U.S.S. Holland USN, Holy Loch, Scotland, 1977-80; head dept. operative dentistry Naval Dental Clinic, Great Lakes, Ill., 1984—90, 1993—97, cons. operative dentistry, 2000—; dentist regional med. ctr. USN, Great Lakes, Ill., 1980-82; head dept. operative dentistry Naval Dental Ctr., Norfolk, Va., 1990-93, dir. managed care Great Lakes, Ill., 1993-97, clinic dir., 1996-97; comdg. officer Naval Dental Rsch. Inst., 1997-99; splty. leader for dental rsch. USN, 1997-2000, program mgr. mercury abatement, 2001—. Cons. Naval Hosp. Great Lakes, 1984—86, 1993—2002, asst. dir. advanced edn. in gen. dentistry, 2002—; asst. clin. prof. Northwestern U. Dental Sch., Chgo., 1985—90, Chgo., 1995—98; quality assurance coord., head advanced clin. program in gen. dentistry, Norfolk, 1990—93; com. chmn. Am. Bd. Operative Dentistry, 1987—, pres., 1996—2000, exec. coun., 1996—2002, chair examination com., 2000—; VISN-12 rsch. com. U.S. VA, 1998—. Contbr. articles to profl. jours.; speaker in field. Course dir. ARC, Great Lakes, 1984-90. Fellow Internat. Coll. Dentists; mem. ADA, Acad. Operative Dentistry (mem. jour. editl. bd. 1993-95, 96—), Am. Assn. Dental Rsch. (pres. Chgo. sect. 2000-01, chair local organizing com. 2000-01), Am. Dental Edn. Assn., Internat. Assn. Dental Rsch., Acad. Gen. Dentistry, Am. Assn. Dental Schs., Am. Legion, Omicron Kappa Upsilon, Alpha Phi Omega, Delta Sigma Delta. Avocations: computer science, reading, walking. Home: 1541 N Mckinley Rd Lake Forest IL 60045-1377 E-mail: gkjones@gl.med.navy.mil.

JONES, GRANT, retired state legislator, lawyer, insurance agent; b. Abilene, Tex., Nov. 11, 1922; s. Morgan and Jessie (Wilder) Jones; m. Anne Smith, Aug. 21, 1948; children: Morgan Andrew, Janet Jones Pliego. BBA, So. Meth. U., 1947; MBA, U. Pa., 1948; D (hon.), Abilene Christian U., 1981, McMurry U., 1983, Hardin Simmons U., 1985. CPCU; bar: Tex. 1974. Casualty underwriter Trezevant and Cochran, Dallas, 1950-54; ins. agt. Abilene, 1948-73; pvt. practice law, mediator, ind. ins. agt., 1954—. Mem. Tex. Ho. of Reps. from 62d Dist., 1965—72, Tex. Senate from 24th Dist., 1973—89. Pilot USAF, WWII. Mem.: Tex. Assn. Ins. Agts. (past pres.), Nat. Assn. Ins. Agts. (dir. 1963). Methodist. Home: 3818 S Lake Dr Belton TX 76513 Office: PO Box 2143 Temple TX 76503-2143

JONES, GRANT RICHARD, landscape architect, planner; b. Seattle, Aug. 29, 1938; s. Victor Noble and Iona Belle (Thomas) J.; m. Ilze Grinbergs, 1965 (div. 1983); 1 child, Kaija. Student in liberal arts, Colo. Coll., 1956-58; BArch, U. Wash., 1962; M in Landscape Arch., Harvard U., 1966, postgrad. (Frederick Sheldon fellow), 1967-68. Draftsman Jones Lovegren Helms & Archs., Seattle, 1958-59; designer Landscape Archs., Seattle, 1961-65, state conservation planner Honolulu, 1968-69; rsch. assoc. landscape architecture rsch. office Harvard U., 1966-67; prin. Archs. and Landscape Archs., Ltd., Seattle, 1969—. Instr., vis. critic U. Oregon, U. Washington, U. Calif. at Berkeley, CSN Calpoly, U. Va., Harvard U.; lectr. and spkr. in field 30 univs., U.S.; chmn. landscape archtl. registration bd., State of Wash., 1974-79; mem. coun. Harvard U. Grad. Sch. Design, 1978-82, 91-96; vis. com. Harvard U. Grad. Sch., 1993—; bd. visitors U. Oregon Sch. Arch. and Allied Artists; bd. dirs. Scenic Am., Stewardship Ptnrs., Landscape Arch. Found. Author: The Nooksack Plan: An Approach to the Investigation and Evaluation of a River System, 1973; (with B. Gray and J. Burnham) A Method for the Quantification of Aesthetic Values for Environmental Decision Making, 1975, Design as Ecogram, 1975; (with J. Coe and D. Paulson) Woodland Park Zoo: Long Range Plan, Development Guidelines and Exhibit Scenarios, 1976, Landscape Assessment. . .Where Logic and Feelings Meet, 1978, Design Principles for Presentation of Animals and Nature, 1982, What Are Zoos?, 1984, An Arboretum on a Landfill, 1984, Beyond Landscape Immersion to Cultural Resonance, 1989, Some Thoughts on Power and Influence, 1993; prin. works include Nooksack River Plan, Bellingham, Wash.; Yakima (Wash.) River Regional Greenway, Union Bay Teaching and Research Arboretum, U. Wash., Seattle, Newhalem Campground, North Cascades Nat. Park, Woodland Park Zool. Gardens, Seattle, Washington Park Arboretum, U. Wash., Seattle, zoo master plans for Kansas City, Roanoke, Va., Detroit and Honolulu, Dallas Arboretum and Bot. Garden, Toledo Zoo African Savannah Complex, Thai Elephant Forest at Woodland Park Zoo, Singapore Bot. Gardens, Paris Pike Hist. Hwy, Denver Commons Park, others. Recipient Nat. award Am. Zoo Assn., 1981-84. Fellow Am. Soc. Landscape Architects (chmn. Wash. chpt. 1972-73, trustee 1979—, v.p., 1988-90, Merit award in community design 1972, Honor award in regional planning 1974, Merit award in regional planning 1977, Merit award in park planning 1977, Merit award in instnl. planning 1977, Pres.'s award of excellence 1980, merit awards in landscape planning), Nature Conservancy, Am. Hort. Soc., Am. Assn. Bot. Gardens and Arboreta, Audobon, Sierra Club, Phi Gamma Delta, Diet, Rainier Club. Office: Jones & Jones Archs and Landscape Archs Ltd 105 S Main St Ste 300 Seattle WA 98104-2578

JONES, GRIER PATTERSON, lawyer; b. Ft. Worth, June 26, 1942; s. Kenneth Hugh and Nancy (Culver) J.; m. Mary Ransford, Mar. 17, 1979; children: Allison Culver, Megan Elizabeth. BA, U. of South, 1964; JD, U. Tex., 1967. Bar: Tex. 1967, Ill. 1978. Asst. sec. and counsel Southland Fin. Corp., Dallas, 1969-74; atty. Mobil Oil Corp., Dallas, 1974-77, litigation mgr. Chgo., 1977-79; corp. counsel Hunt Energy Corp., Dallas, 1979-83; pvt. practice Dallas, 1983-95; asst. dist. atty. Dallas County, 1995-2001, asst. atty. gen., 2001—. Mem. Tex. Unauthorized Practice of Law Com., 1987-95; asst. Atty. Gen. Speaker to various groups. Lay reader, vestryman Good Shepherd Episcopal Ch. Fellow Coll. State Bar Tex., Dallas Bar Found.; mem. Dallas Bar Assn. (bd. dirs. 1998-99, chmn. house com. 1996-98), Tex. Steeplechase Club, Phi Gamma Delta. Republican. Home: 9048 Stone Creek Pl Dallas TX 75243-6213 Office: Office Atty Gen Ste 700 1600 Pacific Ave Dallas TX 75202 Fax: 214-965-7132. E-mail: grier.jones@cs.oag.state.tx.us.

JONES, GWENYTH ELLEN, publishing information systems/technology executive; b. Omaha, Sept. 21, 1952; d. Robert Lester and Mary Ellen (Ouren) J.; m. William F. Knoff Jr.. BA, U. Va., 1974, MA in English, 1982. Mktg. dir. John Wiley & Sons, N.Y.C., 1986-89, pub., 1989-90, dir. info. systems and tech., 1990-97, exec. dir. pub. info. systems and techs., 1997—2001; v.p. Pub. INfo. Sys. and Techs., 2001—. Mem. Am. Mgmt. Assn. Avocations: dancing, tennis. Office: John Wiley and Sons 605 3rd Ave Fl 6 New York NY 10158-0012

JONES, HAROLD ANTONY, banker; b. Bklyn., Nov. 5, 1943; s. Harold Edward and Marie Albertine (Schwietering) J.; m. Jo Ann T. Titone, Oct. 8, 1966; children: Christopher, Gregory. BA, Pace Coll., 1968; postgrad., Am. Inst. Banking, 1970; AAS., Grad. Sch. Savs. Banking, Brown U., 1975; grad., Exec. Mgmt. Program, U. Mass., 1977. With Mfrs. Trust Co., N.Y.C., 1961-64; with Lincoln Savs. Bank, N.Y.C., 1964-90, dir. mktg., 1978-79, sr. v.p., corp. sec., 1979-81, dir. retail banking div., 1980-90; sr. v.p. bank adminstrn. Ridgewood Savs. Bank, N.Y.C., 1990—. Guest lectr. money and banking NYU; guest lectr. corp. social responsibility Columbia U.; pres. N.Y. Savs. Banks Life Ins. Council, 1985 Decorated knight Holy Sepulchre of Jerusalem; named Outstanding Banker in Cmty. Revitalization Brighton Beach Neighborhood Assn., 1978, Banker of Yr. Manhattan C. of C., 1990. Mem. Fin. Advt. and Mktg. Assn. N.Y. (dir.), Bank Mktg. Assn., Cmty. Bankers Assn. NY State (com. on pub. info.), Thrift Inst. Mktg. (chmn. exec. com.), Harbour Green Assn. (pres. 1992). Office: Ridgewood Savings Bank 71-02 Forest Ave Ridgewood NY 11385

JONES, H(AROLD) GILBERT, JR., lawyer; b. Fargo, N.D., Nov. 2, 1927; s. Harold Gilbert and Charlotte Viola (Chambers) J.; m. Julie Squier, Feb. 15, 1964; children: Lenna Lettice Mills Jones Carroll, Thomas Squier, Christopher Lee. B of Engring., Yale U., 1947; postgrad., Mich. U., 1948-49; JD, UCLA,

1956. Bar: Calif. 1957. Mem., ptnr. Overton, Lyman & Prince, L.A., 1956—61; founding ptnr. Bonne, Jones, Bridges, Mueller & O'Keefe, L.A., 1961—89, of counsel, 1990—92, Lewis, Brisbois, Bisgaard & Smith, 1992—. Bd. dirs. Wilshire YMCA, 1969-75. With U.S. Army, 1950-52. Fellow Am. Coll. Trial Lawyers, Am. Bd. Trial Advs. (nat. pres. 1988-89, nat. exec. com. 1990, 92, 96, nat. bd. dirs. 1977—, pres. L.A. chpt. 1980, Calif. Trial Lawyer of Yr. 1999), Internat. Acad. Trial Lawyers: mem. ABA, Calif. Bar Assn., Los Angeles County Bar Assn. (past. chmn. legal-med. rels. com.), Orange County Bar Assn., So. Calif. Assn. Def. Counsel, Jonathan Club, Transpacific Yacht Club (commodore 1996-98), Newport Harbor Yac ht Club (commodore 1998), Cruising Club Am., L.A. Yacht Club, Univ. Athletic Club, Ctr. Club. Home: 818 Harbor Island Dr Newport Beach CA 92660-7228 Office: 650 Town Center Dr Ste 1400 Costa Mesa CA 92626-7020 E-mail: hg5150@aol.com., gjones@lbbslaw.com.

JONES, HARTWELL KELLEY, JR., lawyer; b. Columbia, S.C., Mar. 4, 1941; s. Hartwell Kelley and Lora (Bussey) J. BA in Journalism, U. S.C., 1963, MA in Internat. Studies, 1966, JD, 1970. Bar: S.C. 1970, U.S. Ct. Appeals (4th cir.) 1974, U.S. Dist. Ct. 1975, U.S. Supreme 1976. Reporter Columbia Record, 1961-64; press sec. to U.S. Rep. A. W. Watson, 1964-67; reporter govt. affairs The State newspaper, Columbia, 1967-68, night city editor, 1968-70; legal asst., press sec. to Gov. of S.C., 1970-74; gen. counsel S.C. Ins. Dept., Columbia, 1974-78; sole practice Cayce, S.C., 1978-83, West Columbia, S.C., 1983-92, Columbia, S.C., 1992—. Exec. v.p., legis. counsel Profl. Ins. Agents S.C.; gen. counsel S.C. Optometric Assn.; exec. dir. and legis. counsel S.C. Assn. Veterinarians; legis. counsel S.C. Child Care Assn., legis. counsel S.C. Soc. of Accountants. Bd. dirs. Riverland Park Neighborhood Assn.; Cayce planning commn. WOLO-TV Citizens Adv. Com., S.C. With U.S. Army, 1964-70. Decorated Order of Palmetto, State of S.C. Highest Civilian award. Mem. S.C. Bar, S.C. Law Enforcement Officers Assn., S.C. Sheriffs Assn., S.C. Soc. Accts. (legis. counsel). Baptist. Office: 1226 Pickens St Ste 203 Columbia SC 29201-3462 E-mail: kelley@sc.rr.com.

JONES, HELENE RASBERRY, nursing educator; b. Weleetka, Okla., Apr. 16, 1940; d. John Milburn and Florence Loretta (King) Rasberry; m. Thomas Graves Jones, June 29, 1974; children: Kimberly Anne, Kendall Lee. BSN, Okla. Bapt. U., 1962; MN, Emory U., 1970. RN, Okla., Miss. Instr. Bapt. Sch. Nursing, Oklahoma City, 1963-66; staff nurse Presbyn. Hosp., Oklahoma City, 1966-67; instr. William Rufus King State Tech. Inst., Selma, Ala., 1967-69; prof. Sch. Nursing U. Miss., Jackson, 1970-80, coord., asst. prof., 1986-90; asst. DON div. staff devel. Univ. Hosp., Jackson, 1990-95; dir. dept. of staff devel. Univ. Hosps. and Clinics, Jackson, 1995-99, ret., 1999; assoc. prof. U. Tulsa, 1981; asst. dir., coord. divsn. staff devel. Hillcrest Med. Ctr., 1983-86; staff nurse St. Dominics Hosp., Jackson, 1991—99; mem. Jackson Right To Life, 2002—; counselor Jackson Ctr. for Pregnancy Choices, 2002—. Cons. Miss. Regional Med. Program, Jackson, 1972; chair accreditation rev. com. Schs. Nursing and bd. trustees instns. higher learning, Jackson, 1979-80. Mem. coms. health check and awards, Jackson, 1986-90, Am. Heart Assn., 1986—, PTA, Jenks, Okla. and Jackson, 1970-84; Citizens Better Edn., Jackson, 1978-80. Lt. U.S. Army, 1961-63. Mem. ANA, Miss. Nurses Assn. (dist. #13 nurse educator II award 1993), Sigma Theta Tau. Republican. Baptist. Avocations: walking, tennis, canoeing, reading, needlepoint. Home: 65 Glenway Pl Brandon MS 39042-2530

JONES, HERMAN OTTO, JR., corporate professional; b. Jacksonville, Fla., Dec. 1, 1933; s. Herman Otto Sr. and Esther (Powell) J.; m. Marjorie Seaver, June 4, 1955 (dec. June 1996); two children (dec.); m. M. Beth Seaver, May 10, 1997. BSA, U. Fla., 1956. V.p. Oak Crest Hatcheries, Inc., Jacksonville, 1956-71; exec. v.p. Oak Crest Enterprises, Inc., Jacksonville, 1958-71; dir. sales Diversified Imports, Inc., Lakewood, N.J., 1971-73, BEC Ltd., Winchester, Eng., 1973-78; sales rep. Paul Revere Ins. Co., Jacksonville, 1978-81; v.p. Anitox Corp., Buford, Ga., 1981-85; pres. Gateway Suppliers, Inc., Jacksonville, 1986-98; v.p. Sales Agritek Bio Ingredients Corp., Montreal, Quebec, Can., 1993-97; pres. Gateway Bio-Nutrients, Inc., 1998—. Contbr. articles to profl. jours. Vice chmn. bd. deacons Riverside Bapt. Ch., 1988-89, deacon, 1991-94, sec. of deacons, 1991-92, dir. Sunday Sch., 1992-93; bd. dirs. South Shore Condos, 1998-2001, treas., 1998-2001, 2003, pres., 2001—03; past pres. Duval Co. Farm Bur., 1964, Fla. Poultry Assn., 1964, Fla. Hatchery, 1964, Fla. Breeders Assn., 1965, Fla. Poultry Fedn., 1965. Named Outstanding Mem., Fla. Poultry Fedn., 1965, Southeastern Poultry and Egg Assn., 1963, State Outstanding Young Farmer, Fla. Jaycees, 1968; recipient Disting. Service award, Jacksonville Jaycees, 1970. Mem.: Fla. Feed Assn., U.S. Poultry and Egg Assn., Greater Jacksonville Fair Assn. (bd. dirs. 2002—), South Shore Condo Assn. (treas. 1998—2001, pres. 2001—03, treas. 2003—), Mandarin Mus. and Hist. Soc., Beaches Sea Turtle Patrol, Order of DeMolay (Chevalier degree state master councilor state of Fla. 1953), Order Ea. Star (past patron), Jesters, Shriners, Masons (master), Rotary (bd. dirs. South Jacksonville 1989—91). Republican. Avocations: golf, travel. Home: CND #703 1551 1st St S Jacksonville FL 32250-6360 E-mail: hjones@gatewaybio-nutrients.com.

JONES, HOBERT W. health physics and radiochemistry consultant; b. Lexington, Ky., Aug. 12, 1957; s. John E., Jr. and Peggy Ann (Pickle) J. BS in physics, U. Ky., 1980; MS in Health Physics, Ga. Inst. Tech., 1985. Cert. health physicist; registered radiation protection technologist. Radiochemical lab. analyst Tenn. Valley Authority, Soddy-Daisy, 1981-84; health physicist Am. Electric Power Svc. Corp., Columbus, Ohio, 1985-91; sr. health physicist EG&G Mound Applied Techs., Miamisburg, Ohio, 1991-92, tech. specialist health physics, 1992-93; health physicist, radiochemist Labyrinth Group, Dayton, Ohio, 1993-95; health physicist Internat. Cons., Inc., 1997-98; health physics and radiochemistry cons. Enercon Svcs., Inc., 1998—2002, Horizon Environ. Group, Inc., 2002—. Mem. Am. Nuclear Soc. (assoc.), Health Physics Soc. (plenary), Cin. Radiation Soc. (bd. dirs. 1993-94, pres.-elect 1993-95, pres. 1994-95), Ky. Cols.. Home: 550 E Whipp Rd Centerville OH 45459-2256 Office: Fluor Fernald Uno Bldg 11003 Hamilton-Cleves Hwy Harrison OH 45030 E-mail: hobertjones@hotmail.com.

JONES, HOUSTON GWYNNE, history educator; b. Yanceyville, N.C., Jan. 7, 1924; s. Paul Hosier and Lemma Sue (Fowlkes) J. BS, Appalachian State Coll., 1949; MA, George Peabody Coll., 1950; postgrad., NYU, 1951-52; cert. archival adminstrn., Am. U., 1957; PhD, Duke U., 1965. Prof. history Oak Ridge (N.C.) Mil. Inst., 1950-53; chmn. div. soc. scis. West Ga. Coll., Carrollton, 1955-56; state archivist of N.C. State Dept. Archives & Hist., Raleigh, N.C., 1956-68; dir. State Dept. Archives & History, Raleigh, N.C., 1968-74; adj. prof. history U. N.C., Chapel Hill, 1974-94, dir. N.C. Coll., 1974-94, Thomas W. Davis rsch. historian, 1994—. Mem. Nat. Hist. Publs. and Records Commn., Washington, 1978-86, N.C. Hist. Commn., Raleigh, 1977—. Author: Books For History's Sake, 1966, The Records of a Nation, 1969, Local Government Records, 1980, North Carolina Illustrated, 1983, North Carolina History: An Annotated Bibliography, 1995, Historical Consciousness in the Early Republic, 1995; editor-in-chief N.C. Hist. Rev., 1968-74; gen. editor: North Caroliniana Society Imprints, 1978—. Chmn. Am's. 400th Anniversary Com., Raleigh, 1978-80; sec.-treas. North Caroliniana Soc., Chapel Hill, 1975—; sec. Joint Commn. on Status of Nat. Archives, Washington, 1967-68. Served with USN, 1942—46. Recipient Disting. Alumnus award Appalachian State U., 1971, Cannon Cup hist. preservation N.C. Soc. for Preservation of Antiquities, 1971, Univ. Svc. award U. N.C. Gen. Alumni Assn., 1990, Disting. Svc. award in documentary publ. and preservation Nat. Hist. Publs. and Records Commn., Washington, 1990, John Tyler Caldwell award in humanities N.C. Humanities Coun., 2001, N.C. awrd State of N.C., 2002. Fellow Soc. Am. Archivists (pres. 1968-69, Waldo G. Leland prize 1967, 81), Soc. North Caroliniana (Soc. award 1994); mem. N.C. Literary and Hist. Assn. (sec. 1969-75, pres. 1975-76, Crittenden Meml. award 1977), N.C. Writers Conf. (chmn. 1982, Conf. award 1994), Am. Assn. for State and Local History (sec. 1978-82, award of merit 1968, award of distinction 1989), Nat. Assn. State Hist. Preservation Officers (com. chmn. 1972-74), Hist. Soc. N.C. (pres. 1979-80, R.D.W. Connor award 1956), Soc. History Discoveries (coun. 2003—), Carolina Club. Democrat. Home: 302 Country Club Rd Chapel Hill NC 27514-3906 Office: U NC Libr NC Collection Chapel Hill NC 27599-3930

JONES, HOWARD LANGWORTHY, retired educational administrator, consultant; b. Pelham, N.Y., Nov. 16, 1917; s. Dyer Tillinghast and Margaret (Langworthy) J.; m. Margaret Irene Lloyd, Apr. 27, 1940; 1 son, D. Lloyd. AB, Colgate U., 1939; MA, Syracuse U., 1948, Ed.D., 1951; LL.D., Colgate, 1969. Tchr., coach secondary sch., East Hampton, N.Y., 1939-42; mem. faculty Colgate U., 1947-61, prof., 1947-55, v.p., 1956-61; pres. Northfield (Mass.) Mt. Hermon Sch., 1961-79; spl. asst. to pres. Colgate U., Hamilton, N.Y., 1979—; ptnr. Joerger, Jones, & Krehel, 1990-1998; ret., 1998. Dir. Imagetics Corp., Greenfield.; Bd. dirs. A Better Chance, Inc., Boston, 1962—, Elderhostel Inc.; trustee Good Hope Sch., St. Croix, V.I., 1966-73, Cushing Acad., Asburnham, Mass., 1967-73, Colgate U., 1969—, Coll. V.I., 1962— Served as pilot USAAF, 1943-47. Mem. Am. Mgmt. Assn. (dir. 1965-71), Nat. Assn. Ind. Schs. (dir. 1971—), Phi Delta Kappa, Phi Kappa Tau. Clubs: Univ. (N.Y.C.). Home: 22 E Pleasant St Hamilton NY 13346-1330

JONES, HOWARD ST. CLAIRE, JR., electronics engineering executive; b. Richmond, Va., Aug. 18, 1921; s. Howard St. Claire and Martha Lillian (Mason) J.; m. Evelyn Mercer Saunders, Nov. 27, 1946. BS, Va. Union U., 1943, DSc (hon.), 1971; cert. engring., Howard U., 1944; MSEE, Bucknell U., 1973; DHL (hon.), Trinity Coll., Hartford, Conn., 1997. Registered profl. engr., D.C., Va., Md. Indsl. engring. aid Bur. Ships USN, Washington, 1943; electro mech. engring. aide U.S. Bur. Standards, Washington, 1944, electronic physicist, 1946-53; electronic scientist, engr., supervisory phys. scientist Harry Diamond Labs., AUS, Washington, 1953-80; tech. cons. microwave electronics, 1980—. Tchr. radio physics Hilltop Radio-Electronics Inst., Washington, 1946-52; assoc. prof. elec. engring. Howard U., 1958-63, adj. prof., 1982; cons. microwave engring., 1965-69; cons. univ. relations, 1983—. Contbr. tech. reports and publs. Served as instr. mech. engring. AUS, 1944-46. Recipient four Sustained Superior Performance or Spl. Act awards Harry Diamond Labs AUS, 1956, 68, 70, 75, Inventor of Year award, 1972; Sec. Army Fellowship award, 1972; Army Research and Devel. award, 1975; Meritorious Civilian Service award, 1976, 80 Fellow IEEE (Harry Diamond Field award 1985), AAAS, Washington Acad. Sci.; mem. ASEE, NAE (elect mem.). Achievements include holding 31 U.S. patents microwave field. Home: 3001 Veazey Ter NW Apt 1310 Washington DC 20008-5407

JONES, J. GILBERT, private investigator; b. San Francisco, June 1, 1922; s. Enoch Roscoe (L.) Jones, Sr. and Remedios (Ponce de Leon) Jones. Student, U.S. Mcht. Marine Acad., 1942—44, San Francisco City Coll., 1941—42, student, 1946—47; AB, U. Calif., Berkeley, 1949, MA, 1952. Pvt. investigator. Ins. insp. Ins. Cos. Insp. Bur., San Francisco, 1959—62; pub. rels. cons. San Francisco, 1962—67; ins. insp. Am. Svc. Bur., San Francisco, 1967—72; propr., mgr. Dawn Universal Internat., San Francisco, 1972—, Dawn Universal Security Svc., San Francisco, 1983—. Mem.: SAR, Libr. Congress Assocs., U. Calif. Alumni Assn., World Affairs Coun. N. Calif., Commonwealth Club of Calif., Sons Spanish-Am. War Vets. Soc. Republican. Office: PO Box 424057 San Francisco CA 94142-4057

JONES, J. KENLEY, journalist; b. Greenville, S.C., Feb. 24, 1935; s. J. Clyde and Mildred Idel (Smith) J.; m. Margaret Jean McPherson, Dec. 11, 1965; children— Stephanie, Jason, Eleanor. Student, Furman U., 1953-55; BS in Speech, Northwestern U., 1957, MS in Journalism, 1963; postgrad., Columbia U., 1964-65. Reporter City News Bur. of Chgo., 1962; reporter, cameraman KRNT-TV, Des Moines, 1963-64, WSB-TV, Atlanta, 1965-69; fgn. corr. NBC News, Asia, 1969-72; corr. NBC News (Southeast Bur.), Atlanta, 1972-98. Served with USNR, 1958-61. Recipient Overseas Press Club award for best television reporting from abroad, 1970 Mem. AFTRA, Nat. Acad. Television Arts and Scis. Presbyterian. Office: 1175 W Peachtree St NW Atlanta GA 30309-3432

JONES, JAMES ALLEN, secondary education educator; b. Detroit, May 2, 1925; s. David and Cornelia (Lula) J. BS, Wayne State U., 1946; MA, Oakland U., 1949; PhD in Bibl. Studies, Am. Coll. Metaphysical Theology, Mpls., 1998. Tchr. Detroit Pub. Schs., 1949-87; prin., tchr. Roman Catholic Archdiocese, Detroit, 1987-93; supervisor student tchrs. Wayne State U., Detroit, 1993-97; tchr. Loyola Jesuit H.s., Detroit, 1997-2000; lectr., supr. student tchrs. Ea. Mich. U., Ypsilanti, 2000—. Instr. U. Mich., Dearborn, 1981—; ind. distributor seminar workshop in wellness Nikken, 1999. Author: A Guide to Teens Who Take Their Own Lives, 1987. Mem. English Speaking Union, Mich. Assn. Mid. Sch. Educators. Office: PO Box 2097 Detroit MI 48202-0097 Fax: 313-873-2299.

JONES, JAMES CLYDE, management consultant, researcher; b. Harlan, Ky., Sept. 14, 1944; s. Clyde Jones and Tina Wilson; m. Carolina Zumaran Sanjines, Oct. 29, 1993. BS, U. of Ky., Lexington, 1966; PhD, U. of Fla., Gainesville, 1980, MS, 1981. Latin Am. regional advisor UN Office on Drugs and Crime, Vienna, 1997—99; ind. cons., 1987—97; assoc. project dir. U. of Fla., Gainesville. Recipient Global Security grant for rsch. on conflict and drug control in Colombia and the Andes, John D. and Catherine T. MacArthur Found., 2002—03, PhD Rsch. in Bolivia fellowship, Fulbright Commn., 1977—79, NSF, 1978, Inter-American Found., 1969—77. Avocations: jogging, reading. Personal E-mail: jonesjcz@prodigy.net. E-mail: jonesjcz@hotmail.com.

JONES, JAMES EARL, actor; b. Arkabutla, Miss., Jan. 17, 1931; s. Robert Earl and Ruth (Williams) J.; m. Cecilia Hart, Mar. 15, 1982; 1 child, Flynn Earl. BA, U. Mich., 1953, LHD (hon.), 1970; diploma, Am. Theatre Wing, 1957; studied with Lee Strasburg, Ted Danielewsky; DFA (hon.), Princeton U., 1980, Yale U., 1982; LHD (hon.), Columbia Coll., 1982; ArtsD (hon.), NYU, 1994. Appeared in plays: Much Ado About Nothing, 1955-59, 1961, Stalag 17, 1955-59, The Caine Mutiny, 1955-59, Arsenic and Old Lace, 1955-59, The Desperate Hours, 1955-59, Othello numerous appearances (Drama Desk award for best performance, 1964, Vernon Rice award, 1965), Egghead (Broadway debut), Sunrise at Campobello, 1958, The Big Knife, 1959, King Henry V, 1960, Measure for Measure, 1960, Richard II, 1961, A Midsummer Night's Dream, 1961, The Apple (Obie award best actor) 1961, Clandestine on the Morning Line (Obie award best actor) 1961, Richard III, 1961, Taming of the Shrew, 1961, Moon on a Rainbow Shawl (Obie award best actor) 1961, The Merchant of Venice, 1962, The Tempest, 1962, Toys in the Attic, 1962, Macbeth, 1962, The Winter's Tale, 1963, The Emperor Jones, 1964, 1967, Baal (Obie award best performance) 1965, Coriolanus, 1965, Troilus & Cressida, 1965, The Great White Hope, 1969 (Drama Desk award outstanding performance 1969, Golden Globe award new male star of yr. 1971, Tony award for best actor, Antoinette Perry award best actor in a dramatic play, 1969), Les Blancs (Drama Desk award outstanding performance) 1970, Hamlet (Drama Desk award outstanding performance) 1973, King Lear, 1973, The Cherry Orchard (Drama Desk award outstanding performance) 1973, The Iceman Cometh, 1973, Of Mice and Men, 1974, Paul Robeson, 1977, Hedda Gabler, 1980, Master Harold and The Boys, 1982-83, Fences, 1985-87 (Drama Desk award, Antoinette Perry award, Outer Critics Circle award for Best Actor, 1987, Tony award for Best Actor, Drama Critics award); appeared in movies: Dr. Strangelove, 1963, The Great White Hope, 1970 (Acad. Award nom. best actor 1970, Golden Globe award new male star of 1971), King: A Filmed Record Montgomery to Memphis, 1970, The Man, 1972, Malcolm X, 1972, Claudine, 1973 (Image award best actor NAACP, 1974, Golden Glove award non. best actor in a musical or comedy, 1974) The River Niger, 1975, The Bingo Long Traveling All-Stars and Motor Kings, 1976, Star Wars, 1977 (voice of Darth Vader), The Greatest, 1977, A Piece of the Action, 1978, The Empire Strikes Back, 1980 (voice of Darth Vader), Conan the Barbarian, 1982, Return of the Jedi, 1983 (voice of Darth Vader), Soul Man, 1986, Allan Quartermain & the Lost City of Gold, 1987, Matewan, 1987, Gardens of Stone, 1987, Coming to America, 1988, Field of Dreams, 1989, The Hunt For Red October, 1990, Sneakers, 1991, Patriot Games, 1992, Meteor Man, 1993, Sommersby, 1993, The Sandlot, 1993, (voice) The Lion King, 1994, Clear and Present Danger, 1994, Cry The Beloved Country, 1995, A Family Thing, 1996, Looking for Richard, 1996, Gang Related, 1997, Summer's End, 1998, (voice) The Lion King II: Simba's Pride, 1998, Undercover Angel, 1999, On the Q.T., 1999, Finder's Fee, 2001, (voice) Recess Christmas: Miracle on Third Street, 2001; TV movies include: The Cay, 1974 (Golden Gate award, Golden Hugo award, Gabriel award, 1975), King Lear, 1974, Jesus of Nazareth, 1977, Roots: The Next Generation, 1979, Guyana Tragedy: The Story of Jim Jones, 1980, The Atlanta Child Murders, 1985, The Last Elephant (Ace nomination) 1990, Heatwave, 1990 (Ace award, best actor in a supporting role, Emmy award best supporting actor in a spl. or mini-series 1991), By Dawn's Early Light, 1990 (Emmy award nomination outstanding supporting actor 1991), The Vernon Johns Story, 1993, What the Deaf Man Heard, 1997; TV series: (narrator) Malcolm X, 1972, (host) Black Omnibus, 1973, (host) Vegetable Soup, 1975, Sojourner, 1975, Third and Oak (Ace award); star TV series Paris, 1979-80, Gabriel's Fire, 1990 (Outstanding Lead Actor in Dramatic Series Emmy award 1991), Pros & Cons, 1991 (Emmy award best actor in a drama series, Best Actor NAACP), Under One Roof, 1995; appeared on TV shows Guiding Light, As The World Turns, The Defenders, East Side, West Side, Dr. Kildare, Tarzan, Highway to Heaven, L.A. Law, Homicide: Life on the Street, Lois & Clark: The New Adventures of Superman, Frasier, Law & Order, Touched by an Angel, Picket Fences, (voice) The Simpsons, Garfield and Friends; appeared, narrated TV specials including Black Omnibus: Negro in the Arts, 1973, (narrator) Beauty & The Beast CBS Library Misunderstood Monsters, 1981, Aladdin & His Wonderful Lamp Fairie Tale Theatre, 1986, Wonderworks, 1986, Soldier Boys CBS Schoolbreak Special, 1987, The 41st Annual Tony Awards, 1987, Square One Television, 1987, America Picks The All-Time Favorite Movies, 1988, Teach 109 American Playhouse, 1988, (narrator) A Hard Road to Glory: The Black Athlete, 1988, (narrator) Michael Jackson: Motown on Showtime, 1988, (host, narrator) The Way We Hear Smithsonian World, 1988, (host narrator) Who Lives Who Dies, 1988, Saturday Night with Connie Chung, 1989, Third and Oak: The Pool Hall American Playwrights Theatre, 1989, The 43rd Annual Tony Awards, 1989, Reflections on the Silver Screen with Prof. Richard Brown, 1990, America's All Star Tribute to Oprah Winfrey, 1990, World Series, 1990, 44th Annual Tony Awards, 1990, Golden Glove awards, 1990, Nat. Meml. Day Concert, 1990, 42d Annual Primetime Emmy Awards, 1991, A Party for Richard Pryor, 1991, 17th Annual People's Choice Awards, 1991, 12th Annual Ace Awards, 1991, (narrator) Visitors from the Unknown, 1991, Muhammad Ali, Biography, 1991, Portrait of Castro's Cuba, 1991, Twenty-Third Annual NAACP Image Awards, 1991, When It Was A Game, 1991, (narrator) The Creative Spirit, 1992, AFI Salute to Sidney Poitier, 1992, Shelly Duvall's Bedtime Stories, 1992, (narrator) Ivory Wars: Lincoln Memorial Day Concert, 1993, 47th Annual Tony Awards, 1993, The Second Civil War, 1996, Alone, 1997, Lincoln Memorial Day Concert, 1997; recordings include: Great American Documents (with Orsen Welles, Henry Fonda, Helen Hayes), 1976, The People Could Fly, Oedipus Rex, To be Young, Gifted and Black, Poems from Black Africa, The Emperor Jones, Native Son, The Great White Hope, John Henry, The New Testament, Portraits of Freedom; appeared in Bell Atlantic Commercials; the voice behind CNN Lincoln Portrait, 1993; vocal introduction 3rd Rock from the Sun; co-author: (with Penelope Niven) James Earl Jones: Voices and Silences, 1993. Recipient The Village Voice Off-Broadway award, 1962, Theatre World award, 1962, Hon. Doctoral Degree Black Am. Culture Festival, 1969, Grammy award, 1976, medal for spoken lang. Am. Acad. Arts and Letters, 1981, Office of Black Ministries Toussaint medallion, 1982, Theater Hall of Fame award, 1985, Emmy award for performance in children's programming, Soldier Boys, CBS Schoolbreak Spl., 1987-88, L.A. Film Tchrs. Assn. Jean Renoir award, 1990, Commonwealth award Disting. Svc. in the Dramatic Arts, Bank of Del., 1991, Nat. Medal of Arts for outstanding contbn. to cultural life of country, 1992, Hall of Fame Image award for great contbn. to arts, NAACP, 1992, UCLA medal, 1993; named Disting. Artist, L.A. Music Ctr. Club, 1994, John Houseman award The Acting Co., 1995; numerous other acting awards, nominations-Obie, Drama Desk, Tony, Golden Globe, Outer Critics Cir., ACE, others. Mem. Nat. Council of Arts (Presdl. appt. to adv. bd. 1962, presdl. appointee 1970-76), Actors' Equity Assn., SAG, Am. Fedn. TV and Radio Artists, Theatre Comm. Group (bd. dirs. 1962) Address: Horatio Prodns PO Box 610 Pawling NY 12564-0610*

JONES, JAMES EDWARD, JR., retired law educator; b. Little Rock, June 4, 1924; BA, Lincoln U., Mo., 1950; MA, U. Ill. Inst. Labor and Indsl. Relations, 1951; JD, U. Wis., 1956. Bar: Wis., U.S. Supreme Ct. Indsl. relations analyst U.S. Wage Stabilization Bd., Region 7, 1951-53; legis. atty. Dept. Labor, Washington, 1956-63, counsel for labor relations, 1963-66, dir. office labor mgmt., policy devel., 1966-67, assoc. solicitor labor div. labor relations and civil rights, 1967-69; vis. prof. law and indsl. relations U. Wis.-Madison, 1969-70, prof., 1970-93, Bascom prof. law, 1983-91, Nathan P. Feinsinger prof. labor law, 1991-93, prof. emeritus, 1993—. Dir. Inst. Relations, Research Inst., 1971-73, assoc. Inst. for Research on Poverty, 1970, dir. Ctr. for Equal Employment and Affirmative Action, Indsl. Relations Research Inst., 1974-93; mem. research and edn. staff Pulp, Sulphite and Paper Mill Workers, AFL-CIO, 1958; mem. Fed. Service Impasses Panel, 1978-82; mem. pub. rev. bd. Internat. Union UAW, 1970—; mem. adv. com. NRC Nat. Acad. Scis., 1971-73; mem. Wis. Manpower Planning Council, 1971-76; mem. spl. com. on criminal justice, standards and goals Wis. Council Criminal Justice, 1975-76; bd. dirs. labor law sect. Wis. State Bar, 1976; mem. Fed. Mediation and Conciliation Arbitration Panel, 1975—; spl. arbitrator U.S. Steel and United Steel Workers, 1976-86; mem. expert com. on family budget revision Dept. Labor Series, 1978-79; cons. in field. Mem. Madison Police and Fire Commn., 1973-77, 94-95, pres., 1976-77. Recipient Sec. Labor Career Svc. award Dept. Labor, 1963, Hilldale award (Social Sci. Divsn.), 1990-91, Wis. Law Alumni Disting. Svc. award, 1995, tchr. of yr. award Soc. Am. Law Tchrs., 1998, disting. alumni award U. Ill., 1996; John Hay Whitney fellow, 1953, 54. Mem. Labor Law Group Trust (chmn. editorial policy com. 1978-82), Indsl. Relations Research Assn. (treas. Washington chpt. 1968-69, exec. bd. 1977-80), Fed. Bar Assn. (chmn. labor law com. 1967-69, dep. chmn. council on labor law and labor relations 1979-80), State Bar Wis., Nat. Bar Assn. (nat. adv. com. of equal employment clin. project 1970-79, Hall of Fame 1999), Nat. Acad. Arbitrators, Order of Coif, Phi Kappa Phi. Office: Univ Wisconsin Sch of Law Madison WI 53706

JONES, JAMES EDWARDS, SR., religion educator; b. Balt., Apr. 9, 1946; s. Temple and Rosemary (King) Jones; m. Emma Pettway, Oct. 1976 (div. May 1994); children: James Jr., John, Tracy, Malik; m. Matiniah Yahya, Sept. 11, 1995; children: Shakur, Abdul-Nur, Mustaffah, Khabirah, Muhammad, Abdul Hakim, Haneefah, Ibraheem. BS in Secondary Edn., Hampton U., 1968; MA in Religion, Yale U., 1983; DMin, Hartford Seminary, 1989. Exec. dir. Black Coalition of Greater New haven, 1974-79; assoc. dir. NARCO Inc., New Haven, 1968-73; dir., assoc. prof. N.H. Coll., New Haven, 1979-89; ednl. coord. APT Found., Yale U., New Haven, 1989-90; assoc. prof. world religions/African studies Manhattanville Coll., Purchase, N.Y., 1990—. Cons. New Haven Housing Auth., 1999—; Al Bashaer Schs., Cairo, 1998—. Mem. new haven Bd. Edn., 1975-79; Islamic chaplain New Haven Jail, 1980—. Mem. Nat. Tng. Labs. Inst., Assn. Muslim Social Scientists. Moslem. Home: 153 Greenwood St New Haven CT 06511-5310 Office: Manhattanville Coll 2900 Purchase St Purchase NY 10577-2131

JONES, JAMES FLEMING, JR., academic administrator, Roman language and literature educator; b. Atlanta, Apr. 9, 1947; s. James F. and Sarah Kate (Smith) J.; m. Jan Sheets, Nov. 15, 1969; children:Jennifer, Justin, Jason BA, U. Va., 1969; MA, Emory U., 1972; cert., U. Paris-Sorbonne, 1972; MPhil, Columbia U., 1974, PhD, 1975. Tchr., chmn. dept. fgn. langs. Woodward Acad., College Park, Ga., 1969-72; preceptor Columbia U., 1973-75; prof. Romance langs. and lit. Washington U., St. Louis, 1975-91, chmn. dept. Romance langs., 1982-91; vice provost, dean Dedman Coll., So. Meth. U., Dallas, 1991-96; pres. Kalamazoo Coll., 1996—. Sr. visitor for Hilary term, Oxford, 1987. Precentor, Ch. of St. Michael and St. George, Clayton, Mo., 1978-91. Decorated chevalier Ordre des Palmes Académiques; recipient Avis Blewett award Am. Guild Organists, 1989, Faculty award Washington U., 1990, Disting. Alumnus award Ga. Mil. Acad.-Woodward Acad. Alumni Assn., 1990; NEH fellow, 1976, Folger Inst. fellow, 1982. Mem. MLA, Am. Assn. Tchrs. of French, Am. Soc. 18th Century Studies, Soc. Rousseau Studies, Soc. Prévost d'Exiles Office: Kalamazoo Coll Office of Pres 1200 Academy St Kalamazoo MI 49006-3295

JONES, JAMES L., JR., military officer; b. Kansas City, Mo., Dec. 19, 1943; BS Sch. Fgn. Svc., Georgetown U., 1966; student, Amphibious Warfare Sch., Quantico, Va., 1973-74; grad., Nat. War Coll., 1985. Commd. 2d lt. USMC, 1967, advanced through grades to gen., 1999; platoon and co. comdr. Vietnam, 1967-68; co. comdr., 1968-70, Marine Barracks, Washington, 1970-73, 3d Marine Divsn., Okinawa, Japan, 1974-75; served in officer assignments sect. Marine Hdqrs., Washington, 1976-79; liasion officer to U.S. Senate Washington, 1979-84; comdr. 3d bn. 9th Marines 1st Marine Divsn., Camp Pendleton, 1985-87; from sr. aide to comdt. to mil. sec. to comdt. Hdqrs. Marine Corps., Washington, 1987-89; comdg. officer 24th Marine Expeditionary Unit, Camp Lejeune, N.C., 1990-92; dep. dir. U.S. European Command, Stuttgart, Germany, 1992-94; comdg. gen., 2d Marine Divsn., Camp Lejeune, 1994-96; dep. chief of staff plans, policies, and ops. Hdqrs. Marine Corps, Washington, 1996-99, sr.

mil. aide to Sec. of Def., 1997-99; 32d commdt. USMC, Washington, 1999—2003; comdr. U.S. European Command, 2003—; supreme allied comdr. Europe, 2003—. Decorated D.S.M., Silver Star, Legion of Merit with 3 gold stars, Bronze Star with Combat V.*

JONES, JAMES LEONARD, lawyer; b. Helena, Mont., Sept. 25, 1945; s. Vernon Leonard and Mary Elizabeth (Conn) J.; m. Madilyn Charmaine Bell, June 17, 1967; children— Mathew James, Aaron Christopher, Steven Ryan. B.A., U. Mont., 1967, J.D., 1970. Bar: Mont. 1970, U.S. Dist. Ct. Mont. 1970, U.S. Ct. Appeals (9th cir.) 1973. Law clk. to chief judge U.S. Dist Ct. Mont., Missoula, 1970-71; asst. U.S. atty. U.S. Dept. Justice, Billings, Mont., 1971-74; prin. Anderson, Brown, Gerbase, Cebull & Jones, P.C., Billings, 1974-86, ptnr. Dorsey & Whitney, 1986—. Mem. Yellowstone County Republican Central Com. Served to capt. USAR, 1970. Mem. Mont. Bar Assn. (pres. young lawyers sect. 1974-75), ABA, Yellowstone County Bar Assn., Mont. Assn. Def. Counsel (pres. 1981-82), Def. Research Inst. (state dir. 1983-84), Internat. Assn. Ins. Counsel. Methodist. Office: Anderson Brown Gerbase Cebull 315 N 24th St Billings MT 59101-1395 Home: Dorsey & Whitney 1200 First Inerstate Ctr 401 N 31st St Billings MT 59101-1200

JONES, JAMES PARKER, federal judge; b. Tampa, Fla., July 3, 1940; s. Edmund Leroy and Nellie (Parker) J.; m. Mary Duke Trent, June 24, 1964; children: J. Trent, Benjamin P., Jonathan E. AB, Duke U., 1962; LLB, U. Va., 1965. Bar: Va. 1965. Asst. atty. gen. Va. Atty. Gen., Richmond, 1965-66; law clk. U.S. Ct. Appeals, Richmond, 1966-68; atty. Penn, Stuart, Eskridge & Jones, Abingdon and Bristol, Va., 1968-96; judge U.S. Dist. Ct., Abingdon, Va., 1996—. Bd. dirs. Va. Ctr. for Innovative Tech., Reston, Va., 1987-90. State senator Commonwealth of Va., 1983-88; mem. Dem. Nat. Com., 1982-92; mem. State Bd. Edn., 1990-96, pres., 1992-96. Fellow Am. Coll. Trial Lawyers (mem. Va. state com. 1995-96); mem. The Nature Conservancy (trustee Va. chpt. 1988-96). Democrat. Espicopalian. Office: US Dist Ct 180 W Main St Abingdon VA 24210-2844

JONES, JAMES RICHARD, business administration educator; b. Saginaw, Mich., May 25, 1940; s. George B. and Rena Jones; m. Sheila I. Jones; children: Kimme Ann, Kriste Gay, Kelly Lyn, Karme Jill. BA, Mich. State U., 1962, MBA, 1964; PhD, Ariz. State U., 1969. Research analyst Mich. Public Service Commn., Lansing, 1962; systems analyst Allis-Chalmers Mfg. Co., West Allis, Wis., 1964-65; asst. prof. transp. U. Houston, 1967-70; asso. prof. mktg. U. Ga., Athens, 197— 72; spl. asst. Dept. Transp., Washington, 1972-74, transp. economist, 1974-76; Disting. prof. transp. Memphis State U., 1976-81; George R. Brown Disting. prof. bus. Trinity U., San Antonio, 1981—. Cons. in field. Author books in field; contbr. articles to profl. jours.; bd. editors: Jour. Mktg. Theory and Practice, 1992—. Keeshin fellow, 1963 Mem. Am. Soc. Traffic and Transp., Am. Mktg. Assn., Council Logistics Mgmt., Transp. Research Forum, Transp. Research Bd., So. Mktg. Assn., Assn. Mktg. Theory and Practice, Am. Inst. Decision Scis. Home: 1711 Brush Creek Dr San Antonio TX 78248-2003 Office: Trinity U 715 Stadium Dr San Antonio TX 78212-3104 E-mail: jjones@trinity.edu.

JONES, JAMES RICHARD, mechanical engineer; b. Danville, Ky., Jan. 9, 1947; s. James Elkin and Ophelia (Faulkner) J.; m. Patricia Ann Harlen, May 20, 1967 (div. 1979); children: Jerri Ann (dec.), James Patrick; m. Betty Lou Polk, May 26, 1985. AAS in Mfg. Tech., Lexington Tech. Inst., Ky., 1974. With IBM, Lexington, Ky., 1967-81, Charlotte, N.C., 1981-86, procurement mfg. engr., 1986-87, assoc. engr., 1987-1992, sr. assoc. engr., 1992-93; document control adminstr. Accuride Inc., Charlotte, 1994-95; prodn. support Philip Morris USA, 1995-96, prodn. tech. II, 1996 ; instr. technology U. Ky., Lexington. Internal auditor, Internat. Standards Orgn. 9000; quality assurance auditor. Mem. Masons. Democrat. Mem. African Methodist Episcopal Zion Ch. Avocations: hunting, fishing, photography. Home: 7117 Ludwig Dr Charlotte NC 28215-1822 E-mail: kyjrj@worldnet.att.net.

JONES, JAMES ROBERT, ambassador, former congressman, lawyer; b. Muskogee, Okla., May 5, 1939; m. Olivia Barclay, 1968; children: Geoffrey Gardner, Adam Winston. AB in Journalism and Govt., U. Okla., 1961; LLB, Georgetown U., 1964. Bar: Okla. 1964, D.C. 1964. Legis. asst. Congressman Ed Edmondson, 1961-64; spl. asst. Pres. Lyndon Johnson, 1965-69; mem. 93d-99th congresses from 1st Dist. Okla., Washington, 1973-87; chmn. budget com 97th and 98th Congress, Washington; chmn. social security subcom. 99th Congress, Washington; ptnr. Dickstein, Shapiro & Morin, Washington, 1987-89; chmn. bd., chief exec. officer Am. Stock Exch., N.Y.C., 1989-93; U.S. amb. to Mexico, 1993-97; pres. Warnaco Internat., 1997-98; CEO Manatt, Jones Global Strategies, Washington. Bd. dirs. Kaiser Family Found., Grupo Modelo, Kansas City So. Ind., Anheuser Busch, Keyspan, Inc.; co-chmn. U.S.-Mex. Bus. Com.; chmn. Meridian Internat. Ctr., World Affairs Couns. of Am. Served to capt. CIC AUS, 1964—65. Mem.: D.C. Bar Assn., Okla. Bar Assn. Office: 1501 M St NW Ste 700 Washington DC 20005-1737 E-mail: jjones@manatt.com. *In essence, I try to follow the admonition of Thomas Aquinas, "To work as if everything depends upon you, and pray as if everything depends on God.*

JONES, JANE, artist; b. Denver, Apr. 3, 1953; d. Leslie Richard and Dorothy Mae (Hays) J.; m. John Q. Gaddis, Apr. 2, 1983. BS, Met. State Coll., 1976. Tchr. Red Rocks Cmty. Coll., Lakewood, Colo., 1990—. One person shows include: Le KAE Gallery, Scottsdale, Az., 1996, 98, 99, 2003, Turner Art Gallery, Denver, 1998, Akontempo Gallery, Delray Beach, Fla., 1996-97, Horizon Fine Art, Jackson, Wyo., 2001; invitational exhbns.: Am. Art in Miniature, Gilcrease Mus., 2001, 02, Western Visions, Nat. Mus. of Wildlife Art, 2001, 02, Annual Realism Invitational, van de Griff/Marr Gallery, Santa Fe, N.Mex., 2001, 02, West Valley Art Mus., Phoenix, 2003; group exhbns. include: Women Artists of the West Show, San Juan Capistrano, Calif., 1998, Denver Art Mus., 1994, Nabisco Art Gallery, E. Hanover, N.J., 1993, Nat. Mus. of Wildlife Art, Jackson, Wyo., 2001, 02, van de Griff/Marr Gallery Realism Invitational, Santa Fe, N.Mex., 2001, 02, Gilerease Mus., Tulsa, Okla., 2002; juried shows include: Am. Artists Profl. League, N.Y., 1997, Port Royal Mus. Galleries, Naples, Fla., 1994, Oil Painters of Am. Prince Gallery, Chgo., 1992, Aspen Art Mus., 1989.; contbr. articles to profl. jours. Recipient Juror's Choice award, Colo. History Mus., Denver, 1997, Floral award, Am. Artists Profl. League, N.Y., 1992, 94, 99, First Place Purchase award, 30th Annual Fall Art Festival, Glenwood Springs, Colo., 1992, Juror's award, Arvada Ctr. for Arts/Humanities, Colo., 1991, Florence & Ernst Thorne Thompson Meml. award Allied Artists of Am. Mem.: Allied Artists of Am. (Florence and Ernst Thorne Thompson Meml. award 2002), Am. Artists Profl. League, Oil Painters Am. Meth.

JONES, JANET DULIN, writer, film producer; b. Hollywood, Calif., Sept. 6, 1957; d. John Dulin and Helen Mae (Weaver) J. BA, Calif. State U., Long Beach, 1980. Developer mini-series and TV series Embassy Comm., L.A., 1981-84; assoc. to producer Hotel Aaron Spelling Prodns., L.A., 1984-85; writing intern Sundance Film Inst., L.A., 1985; feature film story analyst Carson Prodns., L.A., 1985-86; freelance screenplay and play writer, L.A. and N.Y.C., 1986—. Author: (screenplays) Fad Away, 1986, Alone in the Crowd, 1987, Story of the Century, 1988, The Long Way Home, 1989, (plays) Cousin Judy, 1989, The Set-up, 1990, Roommates, 1991, Local Girl, 1991, Dickens and Crime, 1992, Little Bear Books, Vols. 1-5,[;] actor: A Weighty, Waity Matter-My Adventures with India, 1992; author: (screenplays) Coming and Going, 1993, Watching the Detectives, 1994, The Ambassadors, 1994, Words of Love, 1995, Map of the World, 1995, Katherine, 1996, Vanity Fair, 1996, Sarah's Mark, 1998; dir.: Words of Love, 1998, Custom of the Country (Edith Wharton, 1999, Nevermore, 2002; author: (non-fiction) Cook & Tell, 2002. Bd. dirs. Sterling Cir. of Aviva Ctr. for Girls, 1990; bd. dirs., rec. sec., steering com. The Creative Coalition, 1991-92; mem. Canine Hosp. Vols., Santa Monica Hosp. Mem. ACLU, Women in Film, Earth Communication Office (TV and film coms.), Writers Guild Am., Ind. Feature Project, Am. Film Inst., Sundance Film Inst. (pre-selection com. 1985-87), People for Am. Way, Habitat for Humanity, Amnesty Internat., Delta Gamma. Address: 1518 Franklin St # 4 Santa Monica CA 90404

JONES, JANICE COX, elementary education educator, writer; b. Jackson, Miss., Nov. 4, 1937; d. Eugene Debs and Thelma Corelli (Beard) Cox; m. June 20, 1959 (div. June 1985); children: Allison Jones Griffiths, Tamara Jones McKee. BS with highest distinction, Miss. Coll., 1959; MEd magna cum laude, U. Miami, 1968. Cert. elem. edn. Tchr. Jackson Pub. Sch., 1959-60, Arlington (Tex.) Pub. Schs., 1960-63, Houston Pub. Schs., 1963-64, Miami-Dade County Pub. Schs., 1967-1980, 1988—97; pres. Palm Tree Prodns., Ltd., 1980-88. Tchr. English ESOL Say Sch., Tokyo, 1985; tutor, child welfare worker CBS, Twentieth Century Fox, N.Y.C., Miami, 1981-; pvt. tutor, owner Think, Ink!, Miami, 1983-; piano tchr. MDCPS Cmty. Sch., Miami, 1991-; participant Miss. Gov.'s Edn./Econ. Task Force, 1990-91; workshop presenter Children's Cultural Coalition & Arts for Learning; speaker/poet in field; usher Coconut Grove Playhouse, Actor's Playhouse, Gablestage, Biltmore. Author several books of poetry, Geography Fun Facts: A Trip Across the U.S.A. in Poetry, Numbered & Name: A Preventive for Math Anxiety in Children and Adults. Dist. exec. adv. com. to sch. bd. for gifted edn. Miami-Dade County Pub. Schs., 1987-91; adv. bd. Metro-Dade Rapid Transit, 1974-77; parent sponsor Olympics of the Mind Team, 1984; parent sponsor Queen's Ct., Jr. Orange Bowl, Coral Gables, Fla., 1983; vol. pianist, organist, music dir. Village Green Baptist Mission, Miami, 1973; vol. Habitat for Humanity, 1991-. Recipient nat. poetry award, Byline Mag., 2002, ann. conf. scholarship, World Future Soc.; grantee, NEA, 1973. Mem. Am. Fedn. Tchrs., Dade Heritage Trust (edn. com., writer), Miami Writer's Club, Fla. Freelance Writers Assn., Nat. Writers Assn. South Fla. chapt. (bd., exec. sec. 1997 , nat. writing contest chair, 1998-2001), United Tchrs. Dade (bldg. steward 1976-78), Tropical Audubon Soc., Coun. for Internat. Visitors, Internat. Platform Assn. (red carpet com.), Soc. Children's Book Writers and Illustrators, Miami Arts Exch., Nature Conservancy, Sierra Club. Avocations: Broadway plays and musicals, museums, fishing, photography, travel, accordion, accordion. Home: 6301 SW 93rd Ct Miami FL 33173-2317

JONES, JANIS SUE, women's health nurse; b. Frederick, Okla., May 29, 1947; d. O. Frank and Dorothy Jean (Grayson) Gouchie; married; children: Christopher Elmore, Randle Elmore, Stanley Elmore, Garron Elmore. Diploma, Greenville Vocat. Nursing Sch., 1978; AAS, Assoc. Nursing, Grayson County Coll., 1989; student, U. Houston, East Tex. State U. RN, cert. inpatient obstetrics nurse. Office nurse Sherman Ob/Gyn Assoc., Tex., 1984-87; staff nurse Wilson N. Jones Hosp., Sherman, 1981-84; charge nurse Med. Plaza Hosp., Sherman, 1989-91; nurse, women's care unit Poudre Valley Hosp., Ft. Collins, Colo., 1991-93; with Apothecare, Inc. Wound Care Liasion, Ft. Collins, 1993-95; dir. Maxim Home Care, Ft. Collins, 1996-98; nurse educator Rocky Mt. Surg. Specialists, Ft. Collins, 1998—; instr. Inst. Bus. and Med. Careers, 2000—03; nurse ed. Ft. Collins Women's Clinic. Instr. maternal nutrition Med. Plaza Hosp., preceptor orientation ob-gyn.; asst. in devel. 1st ann. perinatal conf., North Tex., So. Okla. Mem. com. March of Dimes. Mem. Pottsboro Bus. and Profl. Women (past pres.), Phi Eta Sigma. Home: 289 Pin Oak Dr Loveland CO 80538 E-mail: cowgirls53@yahoo.com.

JONES, JAY H. biology and biochemistry educator; b. Springfield, Ill., Nov. 29, 1951; s. Joseph Henry and Sadie Marie (Penman) J.; m. Melinda Bell, May 24, 1971; children: Jennifer Helen, Karl Geoffrey. BA, So. Ill. U., 1973, BS, 1975, MS, 1976; MA, Ind. U., 1979, PhD, 1984. Undergrad. rsch. asst. So. Ill. U., Carbondale, 1970-73, NASA rsch. asst., 1973-75, grad. tchg. asst., 1975-76; assoc. instr. Ind. U., 1977-79, 81-83; instr. biology Ripon (Wis.) Coll., 1979-81; sr. rsch. geobotanist ARCO Exploration Tech., 1984-85; asst. prof. U. La Verne, Calif., 1986-89, assoc. prof., 1989-96, prof. biology and biochemistry, 1996—, acting chair biology, 1990, chair dept. acad. computing svcs., 1991-2000, dir. instrnl. tech. and rsch. support, 2000—. Rsch. group dir. NSF H.S. Sci. Student Inst., 1979, 81; vis. asst. prof. Ind. U./Purdue U., Indpls., summer 1986; naturalist Gulf Island Nat. Seashore, summer 1982; cons. NASA/Lockheed, spring 1990, 91; manuscript reviewer for various profl. publs. Contbr. articles to profl. jours. Senator scholar in biol. scis., 1969; fellow Ind. U., 1976-77, Floyd fellow, 1978, 79, 80, 81, 83; grantee Sigma Xi, 1976, U. Ind., 1978, Ind. Acad. Sci., 1979, 83, Ky. Acad. Sci., 1981, Fletcher Jones Found., 1987, 90, 96, 2002, Parsons Found., 1988, 98, NSF, 1988, 97, 98, Ahmanson Found., 1998, Weingart Found., 2003. Mem. Am. Chem. Soc., Internat. Orgn. Paleobotany, Internat. Assn. Wood Anatomists, Bot. Soc. Am., Ind. State Acad. Scis., So. Calif. Botanists, Sigma Xi, Phi Kappa Phi. Avocations: amateur radio, aviation. Office: U LaVerne Dept Biology La Verne CA 91750 E-mail: jonesj@ulv.edu.

JONES, JAY PAUL, environmental engineer; b. Wilmington, Del., Sept. 17, 1953; s. H. Walton and Eleanor Jane (Slaybaugh) Jones; m. Cecilla A. Betts, Mar. 9, 1970; children: Jay Paul Jr., Stephanie Camille Koons, Shaun M. BS in Agr. Engring. Tech., U. Del., 1976. Registered profl. engr. Del. Lectr. agr. engring. U. Del., Newark, 1976-79; water resources engr. Water Resources Del. DNREC, Dover, 1979-87; program mgr. Hazardous Waste Mgmt. br. Del. DNREC, Dover, 1987-89; regional dir. James C. Anderson Assocs., Inc., Dover, 1989-95; mktg. dir. CABE Assocs., Inc., Dover, 1995—. Mem. Del. Citizen and Tech. Adv. Com., Source Water Assessment and Protection Program, 2002—; mem. Del. Chronic Violators Regulation Devel. Com., 2002. Author: Hazardous Wastes in Delaware, 1991, 93. Pres. Dover H.S. Basketball Boosters, 1992; campaign mem. Com. to Elect Pat Lynn, Dover, 1992; mem. Holy Cross Home Prayer Ctrs., Dover, 1990—2000, core group leader, 1996—99, Alpha course coord., 1999—2001, 2003—, Men of Malvern, 1993—; leader Holy Cross Visitation Ministry, Dover, 1993—94, confirmation instr., 1991—97, RCIA sponsor, 1996—97; mem. Holy Cross Devel. Campaign, Dover, 1995, Holy Cross Competion Campaign, Dover, 1998; instr. Jr. Achievement, 1996—97. Mem.: NSPE (Kent Sussex chpt. v.p. 1994—95, pres. 1995—96, v.p. 1999—2000, pres. 2000—02), Air and Waste Mgmt. Assn., Ctrl. Del. Econ. Devel. Coun., Del. Consulting Engrs. Coun. (sec. 2001—), Del. Assn. Profl. Engrs. (bd. dirs. 2001—, chair govt. affairs and by-laws com. 2002—), Del. Engring. Soc., Rehoboth Beach Patrol Alumni Assn., Sci. Math. and Tech. Alliance, Capitol City Rotary. Republican. Roman Catholic. Avocations: hunting, golf. Home: 180 Merion Rd Dover DE 19904-2323 Office: CABE Assocs Inc PO Box 877 Dover DE 19903-0877 E-mail: ud7man1@comcast.net.

JONES, JEAN CORREY, organization administrator; b. Denver, Jan. 12, 1942; d. Robert Magnie and Elizabeth Marie (Harpel) Evans; m. Stewart Hoyt Jones, Aug. 3, 1963; children: Andrew and Correy. BS in History, Social Studies and Secondary Edn., Northwestern U., 1963. Cert. non-profit mgr. History tchr. Glenbrook South H.S., Glenview, Ill., 1963-65; advocacy rsch. dir. Episc. Diocese of Denver, 1977-80; pub. affairs adminstr. United Bank of Denver, 1980-82; pres., CEO Mile Hi coun. Girl Scouts U.S., Denver, 1982—. Substitute tchr. Denver Pub. Schs., 1965-80. Active Minoru Yasui Cmty. Vol. Award com., 1979-201, Women's Forum of Colo., 1989-2002, Leadership Denver (Member of Yr., 1988), 1988—; pres. Jr. League, Denver, 1979-80, Rotary, Denver, 1995—, pres., 1995-96, commr., chair Colo. Civil Rights commn., Denver, 1987-96, vice chair Health One, Denver, 1996; bd. dirs. Hist. Denver, Inc., 1994—, Samaritan Inst., Denver, 1999; chair, trustee Colo. Trust, 2002; pres. Women's Forum of Colo. Inc., 1999—; trustee Rotary Found., Am. Humane Assoc., 2002—, Colo. Health Inst., 2003—; v.p. Univ. Club, 2002—. Named Profl. Woman of Achievement Colo. Women's Leadership Coalition and Colo. Easter Seal Soc., 1995, Martin Luther King Social Responsibility award. Mem. Denver Metro C. of C., Univ. Club. Republican. Episcopalian. Avocations: swimming, tennis, reading. Office: Girl Scouts Mile High Coun PO Box 9407 Denver CO 80209-0407

JONES, JEAN GRACE, speech educator; b. Paterson, N.J., Aug. 16, 1954; d. Robert L. and Diane E. (Patri) J.; m. Bradley Evans Wilson, Oct. 10, 1997; children: Cheryl Schoonmaker-Shafer, Adam Schoonmaker. BS, Wright State U., Dayton, Ohio, 1988, MA, 1989; PhD, U. Pitts., 1995. Cert. secondary English and speech tchr., Ohio; cert. secondary English and comm. tchr., Pa. Tchg. asst. Wright State U., 1987-89; tchg. fellow U. Pitts., 1990-95; asst. prof. dept. speech and comm. studies Edinboro U. Pa., 1995-99, assoc. prof. dept. speech & comm., 1999—. Recipient grad. rsch. writing award Ohio U. Comm. Rsch. Conf., 1993, Excellence in Tchg. award Internat. Comm. Assn., 1994, Educator of Yr. award Meadville (Pa.) YWCA, 2000. Fellow Western Pa. Writing Project; mem. Nat. Comm. Assn. (conf. top paper award 1992), Ea. Comm. Assn., Internat. Comm. Assn. Democrat. Avocations: piano, aerobics, camping. Office: Edinboro U Pa Dept Speech Comm Studies Edinboro PA 16444-0001

JONES, JEANNE PITTS, pre-school administrator; b. Richmond, Va., Oct. 19, 1938; d. Howard Taliaferro and Anne Elizabeth (Warburton) Pitts; m. Jack Hunter Jones, Nov. 17, 1962; children: Jack Hunter, Jr., Judith Anne, James Howard, Jon Martain. BA, Marshall U., 1961, postgrad., 1962, Presbyn. Sch. Christian Edn., Richmond, 1974, 94, Va. Commonwealth U., 1987-88, MEd in Early Childhood Edn., 2000. Cert. tchr. Va. Tchr. Richmond Pub. Schs., 1961-65; founder Bon View Sch. Early Childhood Edn., Richmond, 1971, tchr., 1971-91, dir., 1971—. Validator Nat. Assn. for Edn. of Young Children, 1993—, mentor, 1994-98; acad. affairs chmn. Good Shepherd Episcopal Sch. Bd., Richmond, 1985-88; mentor Ecumenical Child Care Network Nat. Coun. Chs., Washington, 1990-92. Chmn. room parents Crestwood Sch. PTA Bd., Richmond, 1974-80; publicity chmn. Va. Swimming, Richmond, 1978-88, children's coord. Bon Air United Meth. Ch., Richmond, 1985-93, v.p. Bon Air United Meth. Women, 1991-94; dir. Camp Friendship, Bon Air UMC, Richmond, 1992—; Va. Children's Action Network, Va. Conf. of United Meth. Ch., rep., 1993-95; Va. Conf. United Meth. Ch., weekday com. 1992-94. Recipient Spl. Mission recognition Bon Air United Meth. Women, Richmond, 1987. Mem.: Success by Six Mentor, Va. Assn. for Early Childhood Edn. (bd. dirs. 2002—, mentor "Success by Six" 2002), Chesterfield Coalition Early Childhood Educators (bd. dirs. 1993—97), Presch. Assn. Ch. Ednl. Dirs. (pres. 1993—95), Richmond Early Childhood Assn. (mem.-at-large 1994—96, rec. sec. 1996—98, 1998—2000, v.p. membership 2000—02, pres.-elect 2001—02, pres. 2002—, Early Childhood Adv. of the Yr. 2002). Republican. Avocations: aerobics, reading. Home: 9103 Whitaker Cir Richmond VA 23235-4053 Office: Bon View Sch Early Childhood Edn 1645 Buford Rd Richmond VA 23235-4271

JONES, JEFFERY LYNN, software engineer; b. Aug. 5, 1960; s. Robert Meryl and Ione Dell (Eaves) J. Ptnr., co-owner Megabyn Assocs (previously JJ Enterprises), Oklahoma City, 1982—; v.p., co-owner Oklahoma Digital Techs., Inc., Oklahoma City, 1987—; ptnr. Nighthawk Bus. Ideas, Jones, Okla. Contract cons. Bank Tech Inc., Oklahoma City, 1985-86, Phillips Petroleum Corp., Bartlesville, Okla., 1986-87; cons. Union Oil Co. of Calif., Oklahoma City, 1989—. Co-author: (software) PetroTrak 2000 Lease/Production Petroleum Tracking System, 1991. Pres. Atari Computer Club, Oklahoma City, 1983-84. With USAF, 1978-80. Recipient Paul Harris award Rotary Internat., 1991. Achievements include co-design of PXI 512 Medical Image Processing System and CompuLanx Computerized Forklift Data System; software engineer for international manufacturer of high speed video webb inspection systems. Home and Office: Nighthawk Bus Ideas 7833 NE 95th St Jones OK 73049-5801

JONES, JENK, JR., editor, educator; b. Tulsa, June 24, 1936; s. Jenkin Lloyd and Juanita Rose (Carlson) J.; m. Carol Beatrice Jaros, June 27, 1959; children: Janette Lloyd Jones Strickland, Landon Lloyd. BA in Polit. Sci., U. Colo., 1958. Sports writer Mpls. Tribune, 1959; reporter, news editor Anchorage Times, 1959-61; state capital corr. Tulsa Tribune, Oklahoma City, 1961-62, Washington corr., 1962-63, copy editor Tulsa, 1963-64, chief copy desk, 1964-65, asst. city editor, 1965-66, asst. mng. editor, 1966-67, mng. editor, 1968-74, exec. editor, 1974-88, editor, 1988-91, editor, pub., 1991-92; chief copy editor, writer, photographer South Ctrl. Golf Mag., Tulsa, 1993—, Hurricane Tracker Mag., 1995—. Prof. journalism Okla. State U., 1993-95, prof. polit. sci. Rogers U., Tulsa, 1995-96; cons. editor The Tulsa Sentinel, 1992-93; juror Pulitzer Prize, 1982-83. With USAFR, 1958-64. Unitarian Universalist. Home: 6447 S Louisville Ave Tulsa OK 74136-1532 Office: South Ctrl Publs 2723 S Memorial Dr Tulsa OK 74129 E-mail: jenknjerri@webzone.net.

JONES, JENKIN LLOYD, retired newspaper publisher; b. Madison, Wis., Nov. 1, 1911; s. Richard Lloyd and Georgia (Hayden) J.; m. Ana Maria de Andrada Rocha, July 30, 1976; children: Jenkin Lloyd, David, Georgia; step-children: Maria Alice Glaser, Paulo Rocha. PhB, U. Wis., 1933; various hon. degrees. Reporter Tulsa Tribune, 1933, mng. editor, 1938, editor, 1941-88, pub., 1963-1991; ret., 1992. Author: The Changing World, 1966. Served to lt. comdr. USNR, 1944-46, PTO. Recipient William Allen White award Okla. Hall of Fame, 1957; Fourth Estate award Am. Legion, 1970; Freedom Leadership award Freedoms Found., 1969; Disting. Service award U. Wis., 1970; Disting. Service award U. Okla., 1971; Disting. Service award Okla. State U., 1972. Mem. Am. Soc. Newspaper Editors (pres. 1957), Inter Am. Press Assn., U.S. C. of C. (pres. 1969), Internat. Press Inst. Clubs: So. Hills Country (Tulsa). Republican. Unitarian Universalist. Home: 6683 S Jamestown Pl Tulsa OK 74136-2616

JONES, JERRY (JERRAL WAYNE JONES), professional football team executive; b. L.A., Oct. 13, 1942; m. Gene Jones; children: Stephen, Charlotte, Jerry Jr. Grad., U. Ark., 1965, MBA, 1970. Exec. v.p. Modern Security Life, Springfield, Mo., 1965-69; prin. oil and gas bus., 1970—; pres., gen. mgr. Dallas Cowboys, 1989—. Nat Paralysis Assn.; Boys Clubs Am. Avocations: hunting, fishing, tennis, water-skiing, skiing. Office: Dallas Cowboys 1 Cowboys Pkwy Irving TX 75063-4999

JONES, JEWEL, social services administrator; b. Oklahoma City, Okla., Dec. 7, 1941; d. Joseph Samuel and Jewell (Hathyel) Fisher; m. Maurice Jones, July 17, 1976; children: Anthony, Carmen. BA in Sociology, Langston (Okla.) U., 1962; MA in Pub. Adminstrn., U. Alaska, Anchorage, 1974. Tchr. Seidman Sch., L.A., 1962; correctional offfcer State of Calif. Dept. Corrections, Corona, 1963-65; probation officer County of San Bernardino, Calif., 1965-67; dep. exec. dir. Cmty. Action Agy., Anchorage, 1967-70; social svcs. dir. City of Anchorage, 1970-87; social svcs. mgr. Municipality of Anchorage, 1987-2000, dir. health & human svcs., 2000—. Chmn. bd. Alaska Housing Fin. Corp., Anchorage, 1995—; pres. Anchorage KidsPlace Project, 1994-95; chair Alaskan of the Yr. Scholarship Com., 1985—; chmn. bd. Janet Helen Tolan Gamble and Toby Gamble Ednl. Trust, 1998—. Mem. adv. bd. Salvation Army, Anchorage, 1982-87, Alaska R.R., Anchorage, 1990—;m trustee United Way of Anchorage, 1990-97; bd. dirs Alaska Ctr. for Performing Arts, 1987-97. Recipient Pres.'s award Alaska Black Caucus, 1984, Employment of Handicapped award Mayor of Anchorage, 1979, Execs. in Profile award Region X Blacks in Govt. award, 1998. Mem. NAACP (Harambe award 1973), Alaska Black Leadership Conf. (Cmty. Svc. award 1979-80), Links Inc., Quota Club Intenrat., Valli Vue Homeowners Assn. (v.p.), Zeta Phi Beta. Democrat. Avocations: cooking, reading, gardening. Office: Municipality Anchorage PO Box 196650 Anchorage AK 99519-6650

JONES, JIMMY WAYNE, JR., historian, educator; b. Wynne, Ark, Jan. 25, 1968; s. Jimmy Wayne Jones and Bonnie Jean Speer; m. Kimberly Marie Babcock Chenault, Mar. 10, 1999; children: Haley Brooke, Hannah Blake, Donovan Avery, Truman Alexander. BA, Ark. State U., 1991, MA, 1993; PhD, U. Ark., 2002. Master lectr. U. Ark., Fayetteville, 1996—2001, asst. editor, 1999—2001; vis. asst. prof. history Southeast Mo. State U., Cape Girardeau, 2001—02; Franklin fellow, vis. asst. prof. history U. Ga., Athens, 2002—. Contbr. articles to profl. jours. and encys. Mem.: Orgn. Am. Historians, So. Hist. Assn., Am. Hist. Assn. Democrat. Avocation: hiking. Office: U Ga Dept History 220 Le Conte Athens GA 30602 E-mail: jwjones@uga.edu.

JONES, JOAN MEGAN, anthropologist; b. Laramie, Wyo., Sept. 7, 1933; d. Thomas Owen and Lucille Lenoir (Magill) J. BA, U. Wash., 1956, MA, 1968, PhD, 1976. Mus. educator Burke Mus. U. Wash., Seattle, 1969-72; anthropologist Quinault Indian Nation, Taholah, Wash., 1976-77; researcher, corp. officer Profl. Anthropology Consulting Team/Social Analysts, Seattle, 1977-79; research assoc. dept. anthropology U. Wash., Seattle, 1982-91. Research investigator Dept. Social and Health Services State of Wash., Seattle, 1977; vis. lectr. Dept. Anthropology U. B.C., Vancouver, 1978; research specialist Artsplan Arts Alliance Wash. State, Seattle, 1978; vis. instr. Dept. Anthropology Western Wash. U., Bellingham, 1981; rsch. and archives dir. Samish Indian Nation, Anacortes, Wash., 2001—; cons. in field. Author: Northwest Coast Basketry and Culture Change, 1968, Basketry of Quinault, 1977, Native Basketry of Western North America, 1978, Art and Style of Western Indian Basketry, 1982, Northwest Coast Indian Basketry Styles. Wenner-Gren Found. Anthrop. Research fellow, 1967-68; Ford Found. fellow, 1972-73; Nat. Mus.'s. Can. grantee, 1973-74. Fellow Am. Anthrop. Assn., Soc. Applied Anthropology; mem. Nat. Assn. Practicing Anthropologists, Assn. Women in Sci., Skagit Valley Weavers Guild (v.p. Skagit County chpt. 1985-86, 89-90, corr. sec. 1988-89), Whidbey Weavers. Avocations: handweaving, hand spinning, knitting.

JONES, JOHN ARTHUR, lawyer; b. San Antonio, Fla., Oct. 9, 1921; s. Charles Garfield and Catherine Magdalene (Smith) J.; m. Margarette Lorraine (Sally) Johnson, Sept. 17, 1949; children: Matthew, Lisa, Malcolm, Darby. AA, U. Fla., 1947, JD with honors, 1949. Bar: Fla. 1949, U.S. Dist. Ct. (so. dist.) Fla. 1952, U.S. Ct. Appeals (5th cir.) ( ) 1959, U.S. Ct. Appeals (11th cir.) 1982, U.S. Supreme Ct. ( ) 1978. Assoc. Holland & Knight and predecessors, Tampa, Fla., 1949-54, ptnr., 1954—. Faculty Fla. Sch. of Banking, 1969-81. Editor, contbr.:

How to Live and Die with Florida Probate, 1972, Practice Under Florida Probate Code, 1976-2002. Served in U.S. Army, 1940-46; lt. col. USAR. Decorated Bronze Star. Fellow Am. Coll. Trust and Estate Counsel; mem. ABA, Fla Bar Assn. (cert. wills, trusts and estates, chmn. real property probate and trust law sect. 1980-81), Hillsborough County (Fla.) Bar Assn., Internat. Acad. Estate and Trust Lawyers, Am. Coll. Real Estate Lawyers, Am. Bar Found., Masons, Shriners, Tampa Club, Univ. Club. Home: 5027 W San Miguel St Tampa FL 33629-5428 Office: Holland & Knight LLP PO Box 1288 100 N Takpa St Ste 4100 Tampa FL 33602 E-mail: jajones@hklaw.com.

JONES, JOHN ELLIS, real estate broker; b. Odum, Ga., Oct. 28, 1941; s. Roland Warnell and Agnes Carridean (Brown) J.; m. Nellie Ann Dougherty, June 21, 1963; children: John Richard, Katherine Ann. BSBA, U. Fla., 1967. Cert. residential broker. With FBI, Washington, D.C., 1959-64; mgr. Fed. Res. Bank, Jacksonville, Fla., 1967-69; asst. mgr. Blue Cross/Blue Shield of Fla., Jacksonville, 1969-72; mgr. Heavener Realty Co., Jacksonville, 1972-75; pres., owner John Jones Realty Inc., Jacksonville, 1975-77, ERA Mid. Ga., Macon, 1977-79, ERA-Jones Realty Co., Macon, 1979-81; assoc. broker McNair Realty Co., Macon, 1981-89, Sheridan Solomon Kernaghan Realtors, Macon, 1989-91; with Fickling and Co., Macon, Ga., 1991—. Instr. real estate Macon Coll., 1980—, instr. real estate sales seminar, 1988—. Deacon San Jose Bapt. Ch., Jacksonville, 1975; Bible tchr. Vineville Bapt. Ch., Macon, 1979. Mem. Nat. Assn. Realtors (nominee Educator of Yr. 1996), Ga. Assn. Realtors (bd. dirs.), Mid. Ga. Assn. Realtors (bd. dirs., sec. 1995, v.p. 1996, pres. elect 1997, pres. 1998, past pres. 1999, Realtor of Yr. 1996), Ga. Realtors Inst., Realtors Nat. Mktg. Inst., Real Estate Educators Assn., Ga. Real Estate Educators Assn., Macon C. of C. (hon. life, bd. dirs. 1996-98, amb. 1989, Ambs. award 1995), River North Country Club (bd. dirs. 1992-94), Cert. Residential Specialists (Ga. chpt. sec. 1995, pres.-elect 1996, pres. 1997. Realtor of Yr. 1997). Republican. Avocations: bible study, self development. Home: 193 Rivoli Lndg Macon GA 31210-8633 Office: Fickling & Co 2960 Riverside Dr Macon GA 31204-1275 E-mail: johnejones@aol.com.

JONES, JOHN FRANK, retired lawyer; b. Carrington, N.D., Feb. 24, 1922; s. Dwight Frank and Veronica Esther (Sheehy) J.; m. Sally Oppegard; children: Janna Jones Bellwin, John M., Jeramy Ridder, Jill Jones Nester, Julie, Jeffrey, J. David. BS, U. N.D., 1946; MS in Organic Chemistry, U. Wis., 1953; JD, U. Akron, 1956 Bar: Ohio 1956 U.S. Patent Office, U.S. Ct. Appeals. Patent atty. B. F. Goodrich Co., Akron, Ohio, 1956-62; sr. patent atty. Standard Oil Co., Cleve., 1962-70, patent counsel, 1970-81, food and drug atty. Vistron Corp. subs. Standard Oil Co., Cleve., 1968-81, ret., 1981; cons. to Standard Oil Co., Cleve. and Ashland Chem. Co. (div. Ashland Oil Co.), Columbus, Ohio, 1981-95, B.F. Goodrich Co. Served with USAAF, 1943-46. Decorated D.F.C., Air medal. Mem. Am. Chem. Soc., Ohio Bar Assn., ABA, Cleve. Intellectual Property Law Assn., CBI Hump Pilots Assn. Republican. Patentee in chem. and polymer fields; contbr. articles on polymer sci. to profl. jours. Home and Office: 2724 Cedar Hill Rd Cuyahoga Falls OH 44223-1226

JONES, JOHN HARDING, photographer; b. Pitts., Apr. 28, 1923; s. John F. and Emma Eleanor (West) J.; 1 child, Blair Harding; m. Teresa Watras, June 23, 1999. BFA, Rochester Inst. Tech., 1949; MBA, Pepperdine U., 1978; PhD, U. London, 1983; M in Photography (hon.), Brantridge Forest, Eng.; DLitt (hon.), Ky. Christian U.; EdD, St. John's U. Seaman U.S. Naval Air, 1940, advanced through grades to comdr., 1948; ret., 1963; chief photographer U.S. Steel Corp., Pitts.; mgr. art & photo dept. Magnavox Corp., Urbana, Ill.; chief photographer rehab. medicine sect. U.S. Vet. Adminstrn., L.A.; coord. rehab. medicine domiciliary sect. Wadsworth VA Hosp., L.A. Tchr. Carnegie Mellon Inst., Pitts., Earl Wheeler Schs., Pitts., Seattle U., Art Inst. Pitts.; dir., owner The Little Studio, Panorama City, Calif., 1989—, The Little Studio West, Panorama City, 1994—; owner The Little Studio, Pitts., The Little Studio West, The Howling Publ. Author: Photography, 1972, The Correspondence Educational Directory, 1976, 79, 84, 94, Correspondence Courses for High School Credit & GED Preparation, 1994. Comdr. USNR, ret. Recipient award Writers Guild, 1977, Merit award Cooking, 1986; elected to Am. Police Hall of Fame, 1996 Mem. Profl. Photographers Am., Masons, Shriners, Order of the Eastern Star (worthy patron 1986). Presbyterian. Avocations: bowling, writing, travel, civic activities, stamp collecting, publishing. E-mail: jjones2823@sti.net., jonesusn@yahoo.com.

JONES, JOHN HARRIS, lawyer; b. New Blaine, Ark., Apr. 9, 1922; s. Ira Burton and Byrd (Harris); m. Marjorie Crosby Hart, 1983. AB, U. Central Ark., 1941; postgrad., George Washington U. Law Sch., 1941-42; LL.B., Yale, 1947. Bar: Ark. 1946, U.S. Supreme Ct. 1963. Comms. clk. FBI, 1941-42; practice in Pine Bluff, 1947—; spl. judge Circuit Ct., 1950; spl. chief justice Ark. Supreme Ct., 1997. Chmn. bd. Pine Bluff Nat. Bank, 1964-77, pres., 1966-76; Mem. Ark. Bd. Law Examiners, 1953-59; Republican nominee for U.S. Senate, 1974; Rep. presdl. elector, 1980; v.p., dir. John Rust Found., 1953-60. Served to 1st lt. USAAF, 1943-45. Decorated Purple Heart, Air medal. Mem. Ark. Bar Assn., Jefferson County Bar Assn. (pres. 1959-60). Mem. Christian Ch. (elder 1963-65, trustee 1965-71, 78-84). Clubs: Eden Park (Pine bluff), Little Rock Club. Home: 4001 S Cherry St Pine Bluff AR 71603-7156 Office: 104 S Main St Pine Bluff AR 71601-4320

JONES, JOHN LOU, arbitrator, retired railroad executive; b. July 22, 1929; s. Ira S. and Myrtle C. (Flagel) J.; m. Nancy H. Sikes, Feb. 2, 1953; children: Nanette, Robert, Eleanor, Stefani, Amanda, Jennifer, Eric. BA, Luther Coll., 1950; MS, MIT, 1954; AMP, Harvard U., 1974. Staff engr. Chrysler Corp., Detroit, 1957-59; br. chief USAF, 1959-63; dir. computer activities So. Ry. Co., Washington, 1963-64, asst. v.p.-data processing Atlanta, 1964-69, v.p.-mgmt. info. svcs., 1969-82; exec. v.p.-adminstrn. Norfolk So. Corp., Va., 1982-87. Bd. dirs. Norfolk & Western Ry., Roanoke, Va., So. Ry. Co., Atlanta; also bd. dirs. various ry. subs.; arbitrator in massive dispute on intellectual property rights between IBM and Fujitsu Co., 1985-97. Bd. dirs. Va. Symphony, 1986-92, Urban League of Hampton Rds., 1985-87. Capt. USAF, 1951-57; bd. dirs. Cultural Alliance of Greater Hampton Rds., 1984-87. Recipient Disting. Svc. award Luther Coll., 1976. Mem. Conf. on Data Sys. Langs. (chmn. 1967-85), COBOL Devel. Com. (chmn. 1960-67), Am. Assn. R.R.s (data sys. divsn., chmn. 1969-70), Am. Mgmt. Assn. (v.p. planning coun. 1970-72, Disting. Svc. award 1972), BBB Norfolk (bd. dirs. 1983-87), Coun. BBB (bd. dirs. 1984-90). Lutheran. Office: 909 Unicorn Trl Chesapeake VA 23322-7365 E-mail: bigmean@hiddenwood.com.

JONES, JOHN MARTIN, JR., lawyer; b. Balt., Dec. 31, 1928; s. John Martin and Nannalee (Rogers) J.; m. Dayle Fort Nesbitt, July 27, 1969; children—David Mallory, Kelly Anne, Jeffrey Wallace Arthur, Kathleen Celeste; stepchildren— Martha Nesbitt Dewey, William Fort Nesbitt, Howard Scott Nesbitt. AB, U. Md., 1951, LLB, 1953. Bar: Md. 1953, U.S. Dist. Ct. Md. 1953, U.S. Ct. Appeals (4th cir.) 1954, U.S. Supreme Ct. 1959. Assoc. Piper & Marbury, Balt., 1954-59, ptnr., 1960-86; pvt. practice, 1986-99; asst. atty. gen. State of Md., 1959-60; counsel Wilmer, Cutler & Pickering, Balt., 2000-01; legal cons. to law firms, 2001—. Mem. Md. Gov.'s Commn. to Study Tax Laws. Mem. Balt. Area council Boy Scouts Am.; publ. adv. Regional Planning Council, Greater Balt., 1977. Mem. ABA, Md. Bar Assn., Bar Assn. Balt. City, Am. Judicature Soc. (life), Am. Law Inst. (life), Center Club, Yale Club of N.Y.C., Order of Coif, Delta Theta Phi, Delta Kappa Epsilon. Clubs: Center, Yale of N.Y.C, DKE of N.Y.C. Achievements include being a mem. adv. com. in drafting and preparation of Am. Law Inst.'s Model Land Development Code, 1970-77. Home: 8025 Strauff Rd Baltimore MD 21204-1834 Office: 200 Saint Paul Pl Ste 2121 Baltimore MD 21202-2004 E-mail: johnmartinj01967@aol.com. *Palma Non Sine Pulvere.*

JONES, JOHN O. state legislator; Ill. state rep. Dist. 107, 1995—. Office: PO Drawer 1787 1116 Main St Mount Vernon IL 62864-3819*

JONES, JOHN PAUL, probation officer, psychologist; b. Blanchard, Mich., July 23, 1944; s. Lawrence John and Thelma Blanche (Eldred) J.; m. Joan Margaret Bruder, Aug. 18, 1972; children: Jason John, Justin John, Jessica Joan-Margaret. BS, Cen. Mich. U., 1970, MA, 1974; PhD, Wayne State U., Detroit, 1980. Diplomate Am. Bd. Forensic Medicine, Am. Bd. Cert. Forensic Examiners, Am. Bd. Psychol. Specialties, Am. Acad. of Experts in Traumatic Stress; diplomate in psychotherapy; cert. addictions counselor. Mgr. F. W. Woolworth Co., Bay City, Mich., 1970; probation officer Oakland County Cir. Ct., Pontiac, Mich., 1970-74, probation officer supr., 1974-78, dir. spl. probation program, 1978-80; chief probation officer County of Oakland, Pontiac, 1980-93; outpatient clin. dir. Auro Med. Ctr., Bloomfield Hills, 1993—. Lectr. Oakland U., Rochester, Mich., 1978-82; lic. psychologist Psychol. Svcs. of Bloomfield Hills, Mich., 1980-82, Family Treatment Ctr., Pontiac, Mich., 1983-84, Associated Profls., Bloomfield Hills, 1984-85, Auro Med. Ctr., Bloomfield Hills, 1985—. Pres. Pontiac Lions Club, 1986-87; study subcom. Oakland County Jail, 1982-84; mem. Oakland County Child Sexual Abuse Task Force, 1982-83. With U.S. Army, 1966-68. Mem. APA (bd. govs.), Internat. Neuropsychol. Assn., Am. Correctional Psychologist Assn., Am. Acad. Experts in Traumatic Stress, Am. Coll. Forensic Examiners (BCFE, BCFM), Am. Psychotherapy Assn., Mich. Corrections Assn., Mich. Assn. Probation Officers Svcs., Mich. Psychol. Assn., Fraternal Order of Police, Cen. Mich. U. Alumni Assn. (bd. dirs. Mt. Pleasant chpt. 1989-93), Mich. Neuropsychol. Soc., Am. Psychol. Assn. Republican. Avocations: travel, horseback riding, reading, fencing. Home: 2915 Masefield Dr Bloomfield Hills MI 48304-1951 Office: Auro Med Ctr Ste 102 1711 S Woodwood Ave Bloomfield Hills MI 48302

JONES, JOHN STANLEY, urban development executive; b. Scranton, Pa., Mar. 25, 1947; BA, SUNY, Stony Brook, 1968; MS, U. Ariz., 1977. Prin. planner Pima County, Tucson, 1979-84; planning cons. pvt. practice, Tucson, 1984-89; dir. devel. svcs. ctr. City of Tucson, 1989-90, dir. devel. svcs. dept., 1990-93, acting water dir., 1993-94, dir. spl. projects, 1995-99; dir. Rio Nuevo Devel. Project, Tucson, 1999—. Recipient Local Official award, Nat. Assn. Homebuilders, 1995. Mem. Am. Planning Assn., Am. Inst. Cert. Planners. Office: City Tucson PO Box 27210 Tucson AZ 85726-7210 E-mail: jjones1@ci.tucson.az.us.

JONES, JOHN WESLEY, entrepreneur; b. Wenatchee, Wash., Nov. 15, 1942; s. Richard F. and Hazel F. (Hendrix) J.; m. Melissa L. Meyer, June 22, 1968 (div. 1982); children: John E., Jennifer L.; m. Deborah G. Matthews, Apr. 24, 1993. BA in Bus./Econs., Western Wash. U., Bellingham, 1966. Trainee Jones Bldg., Seattle, 1967-69, mgr., 1969-78; owner/mgr. N.W. Inboards, Bellevue, Wash., 1974-78, Jones Bldg., Seattle, 1978-86; pvt. investor Bellevue, 1987—; owner/mgr. J. Jones Enterprises, 1994—. Trustee BOMA Health & Welfare Trust, 1982-86, chmn. 1986; mem. Seattle Fire Code Adv. Bd., 1979-86. With USMCR, 1966-72. Mem. Seattle Bldg. Owners and Mgrs. Assn. (trustee 1979-86), Bldg. Owners and Mgrs. Internat., N.W. Marine Trade Assn., Am. Assn. Individual Investors, Composite Fabricators Assn., Soc. Naval Architects and Marine Engrs., Boat U.S., Seattle Yacht Club, NRA, Internat. Show Car Assn., Nat. Street Rod Assn., Specialty Equipment Mktg. Assn. Republican. Avocations: boating, water skiing, snow skiing, automobiles, photography. Home and Office: PO Box 2088 Port Townsend WA 98368

JONES, JOIE PIERCE, entrepreneur, acoustician, educator, writer, scientist; b. Brownwood, Tex., Mar. 4, 1941; s. Aubrey M. and Mildred K. (Pierce) J.; m. Kay Becknell, June 12, 1965. BA (Jr. fellow 1961-63), U. Tex., Austin, 1963, MA, 1965; PhD, Brown U., 1970. Sr. scientist Bolt Beranek & Newman, Inc., Cambridge, Mass., 1970-75; assoc. prof., dir. ultrasonics research lab. Case Western Res. U. Sch. Medicine, Cleve., 1975-77; prof., chief med. imaging, dir. grad. studies, dept. radiol. scis. U. Calif., Irvine, 1977—. Cons. acoustics; pres. Computer Sci. Systems, 1978—; founding gen. ptnr. Of Food and Wine, 1982—, Meditherm Assocs., Ltd., 1983-85, Spar Techs., 1987-90, Surgisonics Inc., 1991—, Dermasonics, Inc., 2002—; proposal reviewer NSF/NIH, 1974—; appointee sci. and tech. adv. com. Pres. Carter, 1977-81. Author: Acoustical Imaging, 1995, Acoustics and Society: Applications of Ultrasound in Medicine, 1972; co-author (with Z.H. Cho, M. Singh): Foundations of Medical Imaging, 1993; mem. editl. bd. Ultrasound in Medicine and Biology, 1976—; contbr. more than 300 articles to profl. jours. Active vol. local govt. Fellow Am. Inst. Ultrasound in Medicine, IEEE, Acoustical Soc. Am., Am. Phys. Soc.; mem. AAAS, Am. Assn. Physicists in Medicine, Calif. Wine and Food Soc., Phi Beta Kappa. Democrat. Achievements include more than 50 patents in field. Home: 2094 San Remo Dr Laguna Beach CA 92651-2628 Office: U Calif Dept Radiol Sci Irvine CA 92697-5000 E-mail: jpjones@ucl.edu.

JONES, JOSEPH SEYMOUR, small business owner, poet; b. Gadsden, Ala., July 4, 1962; s. Jimmie and Sallie Carstarphen Jones. AS in Bus., Bishop State Jr. Coll., Mobile, Ala., 1983; BS in Bus., U. Mobile, 1986; MA in Tchg., Spring Hill Coll., 1994. Cert. elem. tchr. Ala. Dept. Edn. Acctg./engring. support staff U.S. Army Corps Engrs., Mobile, 1979—87; parts clk. Mobile County Pub. Schs., 1988—90, fuel specialist, 1990—94, cert. elem. tchr., 1994—98; owner, mng. founder Believe Enterprises, LLC, Mobile, 2001—. Author: A Poet's Poetic Expressions: Mustard Seeds, 2001, poetry, Lady! The World Forever Thands You!, 1998, Lady! Le Monde a Jamais Vous Remercie!, 1999. Recipient Poet of Merit awards, Internat. Soc. Poets, Washington, 1998—2000. Avocations: restoring classic cars and antique homes, fishing, photography. Office: Believe Enterprises LLC PO Box 40216 Mobile AL 36640-0216

JONES, JOSEPH WAYNE, business executive, entrepreneur; b. Wilmington, Del., Dec. 17, 1936; s. Joseph West Jones and Harriet (Bryan) Flink; m. Shirley Claire Sawyer, Sept. 5, 1959 (div. Sept. 1969); children: Summer, Jackson West, Jay Wayne; m. Patricia Lee Cossin, Dec. 26, 1970; 1 child, Jordan W. BS in Advt., U. Fla., 1958; M, Rollins Coll., 2000. Mgmt. trainee W.T. Grant & Co., Miami, Fla., 1958; with sales and mktg. The Coca-Cola Co., Atlanta, 1959-72; gen. mgr., v.p. The Coca-Cola (Japan) Co., Tokyo, 1972-77; sr. v.p., gen. mgr. Coca-Cola Europe & Africa, London, 1977-83; corp. v.p. The Coca-Cola Co., Atlanta, 1983-84; exec. v.p. The Stroh Brewery Co., Detroit, 1984-88; chmn. Mom's Best Cookies, Orlando, Fla., 1988-94; chmn., pres. Orlando Internat. Inst. for Advanced Edn., 1996-97; pres. Asia-Pacific region, corp. exec. v.p. S.C. Johnson Profl., Singapore, 1997-2001; mng. dir. Graybeard Capital LLC, 2002—. Chmn. code enforcement bd. City of Winter Park, 1991-97. Contbg. author newspaper articles to Japan News, 1973-74. Coord. day care ctr. United Appeal, Atlanta, 1961; founding mem. Internat. Triangle, London, 1981-83; contbr. Nat. Playing Fields Assn., London, 1982; bd. dirs. YMCA, Winter Park, 1988-94, also past chmn.; trustee, sec.-treas. Winter Park Meml. Hosp., 1991—; sec.-treas. Winter Park Health Found., 1994-97; mem. mgmt. com., coun. ministries, stewardship chmn. 1st United Meth. Ch., Winter Park, 1991-92; mem. external adv. bd. Univ. Fla. Ctr. Internat. Studies, 2001; mem. adv. bd. Hamilton Holt Sch., Rollins Coll.; chmn. alumni bd. Rollins Coll., 2002—. With U.S. Army, 1958-59. Named Outstanding Trainee Cadet, U.S. Army Signal Corps, Ft. Gordon, S.C., 1958; recipient Aid to Children Worldwide award Variety Club Internat., London, 1981. Mem. Assn. Nat. Advertisers (bd. dirs. 1987), Winter Park C. of C. (bd. dirs. 1994-96), Grosse Pointe Club (Mich.), Renaissance Club (Detroit), Interlachen Country Club (membership devel. com. 1994), Singapore Island Country Club, Univ. Club, Sigma Nu. Avocations: shooting, fishing, boating, golfing, reading. Home: 455 Beloit Ave Winter Park FL 32789 Fax: (407) 622-6670.

JONES, KACY DOUGLAS, accountant; b. Lancaster, Ohio, Feb. 6, 1955; s. Jack Victor and Barbara Jean (Unkle) J.; m. Lisa Marie Elliott Bells, 1981 (div. 1987); 1 child, Paul Andrew. BS, Franklin U., 1986. CPA, Ohio. Acct. Capital Tax Planning, Columbus, Ohio, 1986-87; tax assoc. Coopers & Lybrand, Columbus, 1988-91; acctg. supr. Ameriflora '92, Columbus, 1992-93; acctg. mgr. Rite Rug, Columbus, 1993-97, TS Trim Industries, Inc., Canal Winchester, Ohio, 1997—. Chamber scholar Columbus Area C. of C., 1986. Mem. Ohio Soc. CPAs, Inst. Mgmt. Accts. Democrat. Methodist.

JONES, KAREN ANNETTE, civic volunteer; b. Breckenridge, Tex., Feb. 16, 1941; d. Ballard Dorsie and Iris Alvern (Hampton) Hutchison; m. Jerry Raymond Jones, Mar. 16, 1963; children: Lisa Rene Jones Story, Karen DeAnn Jones. BS, McMurry U., Abilene, Tex., 1963. Sec. McMurry Coll., Abilene, 1959-63, Continental Oil Co., Abilene, 1963; substitute tchr. Abilene Pub. Schs., 1967-68; tchr. continuing edn. Mountainview Community Coll., Dallas, 1974; floral designer/sec. Christopher Design, Dallas, 1978-80. Bd. dirs., sec. Wesley Rankin Community Ctr., Dallas, 1989-97; adminstrv. bd. Inglewood United Meth. Ch., Grand Prairie, Tex., 1986—, Breckenridge (Tex.) United Meth. Ch., 2001—; bd. dirs., Brighter Tomorrows Abused Women's Shelter, Grand Prairie, 1994-97; mentor, Breckenridge Jr. H.S., 2001—; regional dir., liaison Guillain-Barre Syndrome Found. Internat., 1999-. Mem. AAUW (sec. 1988—), Grand Prairie Women's Club (bd. dirs. 1986-88). Democrat. Methodist. Address: 10101 County Road 197 Breckenridge TX 76424-7005

JONES, KEITH ALDEN, lawyer; b. Tulsa, July 11, 1941; s. Leonard Virgil and Bernadine (Hutchison) J.; m. Renata Skuta, June 15, 1974; children: Emily Isobel, Alden Rivendale. BA, Harvard U., 1963, LLB, 1966. Bar: Mass. 1966, D.C. 1978, U.S. Supreme Ct. 1972. Asst. prof. Boston U. Law Sch., 1966-67; lectr. Harvard U. Law Sch., 1967-68; assoc. Ropes & Gray, Boston, 1968-70; minority counsel U.S. Senate Select Com. on Small Bus., 1970-72; asst. to Solicitor Gen. of U.S., 1972-75; dep. solicitor gen., 1975-78; ptnr. Fulbright & Jaworski, Washington, 1978-94; of counsel Beck, Redden & Secrest, Houston, 1995—. Mem. ABA, Am. Law Inst.

JONES, KELLEY RAYLIN, labor relations specialist; b. Woodbridge, Va., June 30, 1973; d. Wilfred Ray and Mary Linda Jones. BA in Anthrop., George Mason U., 1995; MA in Anthrop., Cath. U. of Am., 2000. Cert.: Va. (paralegal) 2002; mediator Justice Ctr. of Atlanta, Ga., 2000, labor rels. practioner Fpmi, Ala., 2001. Office automation clk. Army Mgmt. Staff Coll., Fort Belvoir, 1995—97; libr. technician Smithsonian Instn., Washington, 1997—98; adminstrv. asst. USDA, Washington, 1999—2000, labor rels. specialist, 2000—. Tchr. Cath. U. of Am., Washington, 1998—2000. Mem.: Am. Anthrop. Assn. Office: United States Department of Agriculture 1400 Independence Ave SW Room 0756-SB Washington DC 20250 Office Fax: 202-720-4837.

JONES, KEN PAUL, lawyer; b. DeRidder, La., Jan. 5, 1959; s. Benjamin Paul and Frances (Causey) J.; m. Kari Stuart, 1990. BS in Fin., U. Utah, Salt Lake City, 1980; BS in Mgmt., U. Utah, 1980, JD, 1983. Bar: Tex. 1983, Utah 1984, U.S. Dist. Ct. Utah 1984. Assoc. McGinnis, Lochridge & Kilgore, Austin, Tex., 1983-84; mem. firm Watkiss & Saperstein, Salt Lake City, 1984-92, Parsons, Davies, Kinghorn & Peters, Salt Lake City, 1992—2002. Mem. Order of the Coif. Avocations: running, reading, biking. Office: Jones Waldo Holbrook & McDonough 170 South Main Ste 1500 Salt Lake City UT 84101 E-mail: Kjones@joneswaldo.com.

JONES, KENNETH B., JR., surgeon; b. Shreveport, La., 1940; MD, Tulane U., 1966. Diplomate Am. Bd. Surgery. Intern Confederate Meml. Med. Ctr., Shreveport, La., 1966-67; resident in gen. surgery La. State U. and affiliated hosp., Shreveport, 1969-73; fellow in pediat. surgery Ala. Children's Hosp., 1973; chief of staff Christus Schumpert Med. Ctr., Shreveport, 1999-2001; asst. prof. surgery La. State U. Med. Ctr. Fellow: ACS; mem.: AMA, Surg. Assn. La., Am. Soc. Gen. Surgeons, Am. Soc. Bariatric Surgery (chmn. surg. access com. 1997—98, sec. treas. 1998—2000, pres. 2001—02), Southeastern Surg. Congress. Office: 1801 Fairfield Ave Ste 408 Shreveport LA 71101-4468 Home: 950 McCormick St Shreveport LA 71104 E-mail: pbsurgkj@aol.com.

JONES, KENNETH BRUCE, surgeon; b. Scottsville, Ky., Apr. 17, 1953; s. Kenneth C. and Betty (Miller) J.; m. Carol Jean Munger, June 28, 1980; children: Daniel, Christopher, Elizabeth. BS, U. Ky., 1974; MD, Vanderbilt U., Nashville, 1978. Diplomate Am. Bd. Surgery; cert. advanced trauma life saving. Surg. intern and resident U. Louisville Med. Sch., 1978-80; resident in surgery East Tenn. U. Med. Sch., Johnson City, 1980-82, chief resident, 1983; surgeon Claiborne Surg. Group, Tazewell, Tenn., 1983-84, N.E. Ark. Surg. Clinic, Jonesboro, Ark., 1984—; sec. med. staff Meth. Hosp., 1986-87, chief of surgery, 1988-90, vice chief of staff, 1989-91, chief of staff, 1992-94; chief of surgery St. Bernard's Regional Med. Ctr., 1996-97; mem. hosp. bd. Regional Med. Ctr. N.E., 1997. Asst. clin. prof. surgery U. Ark. Area Health Edn. Ctr., Jonesboro, 1985—; cancer liaison of ACS Commn. on Cancer to St. Bernard's, 1996—. Contbr. articles on surgery to profl. jours. Active sch. bd., 1993-98; deacon So. Bapt. Ch. Justin Potter med. scholar, 1974-78. Fellow: ACS; mem.: NRA, Am. Soc. Bariatric Surgery, Soc. Am. Gastrointestinal Endoscopic Surgeons, Am. Soc. Gen. Surgery, Am. Cancer Soc. (pres. Craighead County unit 2000—01), Nat. Wild Turkey Fedn., Dove Sportsman Soc., Ducks Unltd., Phi Beta Kappa. Baptist. Avocations: hunting, sporting clays shooting, jogging, toy trains. Home: 2600 Nix Lake Dr Jonesboro AR 72404-0917 Office: NE Ark Surg Clinic 800 S Church St Ste 104 Jonesboro AR 72401-4154 E-mail: jonesfamily@cox-internet.com.

JONES, KENSINGER, advertising executive; b. St. Louis, Oct. 18, 1919; s. Walter C. and Anna (Kensinger) J.; m. Alice May Guseman, Oct. 7, 1944; children: Jeffrey, Janice A. Jones Geary. Student, Washington U., St. Louis, 1938-39. TV writer, advt. agy. supr. Leo Burnett Co., 1952-57; exec. v.p., creative dir. Campbell-Ewald Co., Detroit, 1957-68; sr. v.p., creative dir. D.P. Brother & Co., Detroit, 1968-70; sr. v.p., exec. creative dir. Leo Burnett Co., Inc., Chgo., 1970-73; regional creative dir. Leo Burnett Pty. Ltd., Sydney, Australia, 1973-75, Leo Burnett, SE Asia, 1975-77; creative supr. Biggs/Gilmore, 1981-83; lectr. Mich. State U., 1982-95; emeritus, 1996. Vis. lectr. People's Republic China, 1988, Taipei, Taiwan, Jakarta, Indonesia, 1990, Dalhousie U., N.S., 1992. Author: Enter Singapore, 1974, Looking For the Best, 1994; co-author: Cable Advertising-New Ways to New Business, 1986, A Call From the Country, 1989, Love Poems of a Business Man, 1997, Case Histories in Co-operation, 1999, (as R.N. Lake) Not Guilty, Just Dead, 1999; writer; radio series Land We Live IN, 1945-52; contbr. poems and articles to mags. Chmn. Barry County Planning and Zoning Commn., Parks and Recreation Commn.; county grants coord. Barry County, 1977-78, mem. futuring steering com., 1988—; mem. Econ. Devel. Action Group, 1988-96, Mich. State U. Dean's Cmty. Coun. on the Arts, 1993-96, Mich. State U. Co-op. Ext. Adv. Coun., 1993-95; mem. comms. com. Nat. Coun. Boy Scouts Am., 1966-92; bd. dirs. World Med. Relief, Inc., 1961-92, dir. emeritus, 1993. With U.S. Army, 1940—44. Recipient Silver Beaver award Boy Scouts Am., Silver Salute Mich. State U., 1982, award Freedoms Found., 1984, Positive Action for Tomorrow award Barry County, 1995; named Barry County Sr. Citizen of Yr., 1999; body of his work added to John W. Hartman Collection, Duke U., 2001. Mem. The Players Club, Circumnavigators Club, Adcraft Club of Detroit. Home: 425 Pritchardville Rd Hastings MI 49058-9328 *The opportunity to absorb, examine, synthesize and then utilize facts and experience is what makes creative endeavor fascinating. Somehow the individual mind finds new and meaningful relationships between previously unrelated data. An idea is born. It becomes an advertising campaign, a book or movie, a new product. Trying to find those new relationships makes life rewarding in so many ways. Dissatisfaction with the status quo is the prod toward all progress. Use your talents broadly. Not just to make a living, but to improve your life, your environment, your society. By doing so you'll improve your talents.*

JONES, KENT ALBERT, economist, educator; b. Wilmington, Del., May 5, 1953; s. Albert Hyatt and Sylvia Esther (Phelps) J.; m. Tonya Diantha Price, May 21, 1977; children: Ana-Lisa, Diantha. Student, U. Bonn, Fed. Republic Germany, 1974-75; AB, Oberlin Coll., 1976; MA in Law and Diplomacy, Tufts U., 1979; D of Polit. Sci., U. Geneva, 1981. Economist U.S. Internat. Trade Commn., Washington, 1981; asst. prof. Babson Coll., Wellesley, Mass., 1982-88, assoc. prof., 1988-93, Edward Madden term chair, 1992-97, prof., 1993—, chair econs. dept., 1998—; sr. economist U.S. Dept. State, Washington, 1988-89. Cons. Internat. Labour Office, Geneva, Switzerland, 1987, NSF, Washington, 1984. Author: Impasse and Crisis in Steel Trade Policy, 1983, Politics vs. Economics in World Steel Trade, 1986, Export Restraint and the New Protectionism, 1994, Who's Afraid of the WTO?, 2003; contbr. articles to profl. jours. Elder Needham Presbyn. Ch., Mass., 1986—. Recipient scholarship, Rotary Internat., 1974, McJannet fellowship, Grad. Inst. U. Geneva, 1979, Cabot Corp. fellowship, Tufts U., Fletcher Sch. of Law and Diplomacy, 1976. Mem. Am. Economic Assn., So. Economic Assn., Western Economic Assn., Atlantic Econ. Soc., Phi Beta Kappa. Presbyterian. Office: Babson Coll Econs Dept Babson Park MA 02457 E-mail: kjones@babson.edu.

JONES, KRISTIN ANDREA, artist; b. Washington, Aug. 1, 1956; d. Frank W. and Arlene (Swift) Jones; m. Andrew Ginzel, June 14, 1986. Student, St. Martins Sch. Art, London, 1978-79; BFA, R.I. Sch. Design, 1979; MFA, Yale U., 1983. Artistic cons. Hudson River Park Conservancy, N.Y.C., 1997. Executed art works for Oreg. Conv. Ctr., Portland, 1990, Pa. Conv. Ctr., 1994, Battery Park City, N.Y.C., 1992, Olympic Arts Festival, Atlanta, 1996, MTA, N.Y.C., 1997. Executed art works for Oreg. Conv. Ctr., Portland, 1990, Battery Park City, N.Y.C., 1992, Pa. Conv. Ctr., 1994, Olympic Arts Festival, Atlanta, 1996, MTA, N.Y.C., 1999, Metronome Union Sq. S., N.Y.C., 1999, Tevereterno, 2002—. Recipient Pollack-Krasner Found. award, 1994, Louis Comfort Tiffany Found. award, 1991; Visual Arts fellow Nat. Endowment for the Arts, 1986, 94; Fulbright fellow, 1983-84, 2001-02; Am. Acad. in Rome fellow, 1994-95. Home: 289 Bleecker St New York NY 10014-4106 E-mail: kristin@honesginzel.com.

JONES, L. Q. See MCQUEEN, JUSTICE ELLIS

JONES, LARRY DARNELL, tax specialist; b. Birmingham, Ala., Feb. 21, 1959; s. Londene Jones. Student, Rutgers U., 1980-84, Camden County Coll., 1982. Tax specialist LDJ, Inc., Camden, N.J., 1983-95, AMA, 1993—, GAU, 1995—. Home and Office: 3199 Westfield Ave Apt 202 Camden NJ 08105 Office: 655 Line St Camden NJ 08103

JONES, LARRY WAYNE "CHIPPER", JR., baseball player; b. De Land, Fla., Apr. 24, 1972; m. Sharon Jones. Shortstop Jacksonville Jaguars, 1990—95; 3rd baseman Atlanta Braves, 1995—2001, leftfield, 2002—. Office: Turner Field PO Box 4064 Atlanta GA 30302-4064*

JONES, LAUREN EVANS, lawyer; b. Lawrence, Kans., Jan. 10, 1952; s. Kevin Rice and Marcia Jo Ann (Peterson) J.; m. Vivien Craig Long, Mar. 26, 1978; children: Dylan Tyler, Hayden Blake, Carson Reed. BA in History, U. Mich., 1973; JD, Duke U., 1977. Bar: R.I. 1978, U.S. Dist. Ct. R.I. 1978, U.S. Ct. Appeals (1st cir.) 1985, U.S. Ct. Appeals (9th cir.) 1994, U.S. Supreme Ct. 1991. Assoc. Lovett, Morgera, Schefrin & Gallogly, Providence, R.I., 1979-83; ptnr. Jones & Aisenberg, Providence, 1983-89; owner Jones Assocs., Providence, 1990—. Mem. Jud. Performance Eval. Commn., 1993—; mem. R.I. Supreme Ct. Com. on Profl. and Civility, 1995-96. Editor R.I. Bar Jour., 1989-95, 2002-; contbr. articles to profl. jours. Nominee R.I. Supreme Ct., 1993, 95, 96, 97. Mem. R.I. Bar Assn. (exec. com. 1989-2000, 2002—, sec. 1995, v.p. 1996, pres. elect 1997, pres. 1998-99). Office: Jones Assocs 72 S Main St Providence RI 02903-2907 E-mail: ljones@appeallaw.com.

JONES, LAURETTA MARIE, artist, designer, computer science researcher; b. Cleve., Mar. 13, 1953; d. Richard Llewellyn and Loretta (Jares) J. BFA, Cleve. Inst. Art, 1975; postgrad., N.Y. Inst. Tech., 1981, 87. Instr. Sch. Visual Arts, N.Y.C., 1984-94, dir. undergrad. computer studies, 1988-90. Adj. prof. art Manhattanville Coll., Purchase, NY, 1985—86; instr. N.Y. Bot. Gardens, 2000—, Western Conn. State U., 2001—; cons. Trintex/Prodigy, White Plains, NY, 1986—87, IBM Gallery Sci. and Art, N.Y.C., 1987—88; cons. graphic design IBM T.J. Watson Rsch Ctr., Yorktown Heights, NY, 1988—90, adv. graphic designer, 1990—95, devel. engr., 1995—; rsch. staff mem. Network Transaction Systems, 1997—99, mgr., 1997—99; mgr. Cognitive Human Computer Interaction, 1999—2000, Next Web HCI Components, 2001—. Exhibited paintings, drawings in shows worldwide, 1983—; represented in permanent collection Franklin Inst., Phila., Mus. Sci. and Industry, Chgo. Mem. ACLU, Assn. for Computing Machinery-Spl. Interest Group on Computer Human Interactions, Nat. Computer Graphics Assn. (speaker 1987), Guild of Nat. Sci. Illustrators (rec. sec. N.Y. chpt.), Am. Soc. of Bot. Artists (edn. adv. com.), Small Computers Arts Network (speaker 1984-89), Computer Arts Discipline Graphic Artists Guild (founding, steering com. 1984-88), ACM-SIGGRAPH (N.Y.C. chpt. editor newsletter, bd. dirs. 1986-92, speaker 1991, nat. courses com. 1991-92, design show jury 1993), Am. Inst. Graphic Arts, Amnesty Internat., NOW, Nature Conservancy, Nat. Resources Def. Coun. Avocations: tandem biking, hiking, ballroom dancing, gardening, botanical art. Office: IBM TJ Watson Rsch Ctr PO Box 704 Yorktown Heights NY 10598-0704

JONES, LAURIE GANONG, sales and marketing executive; b. Owatonna, Minn., Feb. 22, 1954; d. Harvey Mathias and Elaine Ione (Mauren) Ganong; m. Daniel Lee Jones, Sept. 6, 1975; 1 child, Jonathon Alexander. AB in Econs., U. Calif., Davis, 1979; MBA, Pepperdine U., Malibu, Calif., 1987. Cert. internal auditor, cert. info. systems auditor. EDP auditor Nat. Blvd. Bank, Chgo., 1980-82; sr. EDP auditor Carnation Co., L.A., 1982-85, Wickes Cos., Santa Monica, Calif., 1985-87; sr. audit mgr. Watt Industries, Santa Monica, 1987-89; dir. audit svcs. Canaudit, Inc., Simi Valley, Calif., 1988-93; prin. Jones & Jones, Sterling, Colo., 1989—; pres. Jones Techs, Inc., Sterling, Colo., 1991-92; dir. support svcs. Sykes Enterprises, Tampa, Fla., 1992-97, dir. product planning, 1998-2000; pres. DLJones, Inc., 1993—. Guest lectr. Calif. Poly. Inst., Pomona, 1985-87, Calif. State U., Long Beach and Domingez Hills, Calif., 1985-87; conf. spkr. Inst. Internal Auditors, Orlando, Fla., L.A., 1988—; spkr. Software Support Profl. Assn., 1993—; chair Sterling Regional Med. Ctr. Found., 1995-01; chmn. adv. bd. Northeastern Jr. Coll., 1994-97. Author: (monograph) Internal Audit Involvement in the Joint Venture Process, 1990, The Successfull In Charge Auditor, 1990, Introduction to Internal Auditing, 1990, 11A Cash Operations Practice Set, 1991, 11A Risk Assessment Tool Kit, 1990, Self Healing Technology, 1999. Disaster preparedness coord. Watt Industries, Santa Monica, 1988-89; mem. Colo. Econ. Devel. Commn., 2000—. Named Bus. Person of the Year Logan County C. of C., 1992. Mem. EDP Auditors Assn. (3d pl. rsch. award 1988), Inst. Internal Auditors (bd. govs. L.A. 1987-89, bd. govs. Denver 1990, internat. bd. regents 1988-91, outstanding rsch. paper 1988, Outstanding Mem. 1988, Outstanding Colo. Citizen 1994), Assn. Support Profls. Republican. Methodist. Sterling Country Club. Avocations: farming, cycling, reading, travel, skiing. Office: DLJones PO Box 1882 Sterling CO 80751-0882 E-mail: laurie@dljones.com.

JONES, LAURIE LYNN, magazine editor; b. Kerrville, Tex., Sept. 2, 1947; d. Charles Clinton and Jean Laurie (Davidson) J.; m. C. Frederick Childs, June 26, 1976; children: Charles Newell (Clancy), Cyrus Trevor; 1 stepchild, Ariel Childs. BA, U. Tex., 1969. Asst. to dir. coll. admissions Columbia U., N.Y.C., 1969-70; asst. to dir. Office Alumni-Columbia U., N.Y.C., 1970-71; asst. advt. mgr. Book World, 1971-72, Washington Post-Chgo. Tribune, 1971-72; editorial asst. N.Y. Mag., N.Y.C., 1972-74, asst. editor, 1974, sr. editor, 1974-76, mng. editor, 1976-92, Vogue Mag., N.Y.C., 1992—. Mem. Am. Soc. Mag. Editors, Women in Coummunication, Advt. Women N.Y. Republican. Methodist. Home: 40 Great Jones St New York NY 10012-1109 Also: 62 Giles Hill Rd Redding Ridge CT 06876 Office: Vogue Magazine 4 Times Sq New York NY 10036-6561 E-mail: laurie_jones@vogue.com.

JONES, LAWRENCE DONALD, economics educator; b. Columbus, Ohio, Apr. 24, 1931; s. Lawrence Donald and Alice Bradford (Colton) J.; m. Sheila Ann Conlin, June 30, 1962; children: Thomas Conlin, David Lawrence. BA in Math., Ohio State U., 1953, MA in Econs., 1954; PhD in Econs., Harvard U., 1959. Instr. econs. Harvard U., Cambridge, Mass., 1959-62; asst. prof. Wesleyan U., Middletown, Conn., 1962-66; assoc. prof. Ind. U., Bloomington, 1966-69; assoc. dir. SEC, Washington, 1969-70; assoc. prof. U. Pa., Phila., 1969-76; prof. U. B.C., Vancouver, Canada, 1976—96, prof. emeritus, 1996—. Vis. prof. U. Calif. Berkeley, 1986-87. Author: Investment Policies of Life Insurance Companies, 1968 (Clarence Arthur Kulp award). Contbr. articles to profl. jours. Mem. Am. Econ. Assn., Am. Fin. Assn., Am. Real Estate and Urban Econs. Assn. Home: 4263 W 14th Ave Vancouver BC Canada V6R 2X7 Office: U BC Faculty Commerce & Bus Adminstrn 2053 Main Mall Vancouver BC Canada V6T 1Z2 E-mail: Lawrence.Jones@commerce.ubc.ca.

JONES, LAWRENCE NEALE, university dean, minister; b. Moundsville, W.Va., Apr. 24, 1921; s. Eugene Wayman and Rosa (Bruce) J.; m. Mary Ellen Cooley, Mar. 29, 1945; children: Mary Lynn, Rodney Bruce. B.Ed., W. Va. State Coll., 1942, LL.D., 1965; MA, U. Chgo., 1948, B.D., Oberlin Grad. Sch., 1956; PhD, Yale U., 1961; LL.D., Jewish Theol. Sem., 1971. Ordained to ministry United Ch. Christ, 1956; student Christian Movement Middle Atlantic Region, 1957-60; dean chapel Fisk U., 1960-65; dean students Union Theol. Sem., N.Y.C., 1965-71; prof. Union Theol. Sem. (Afro-Am. ch. history), 1970; dean Union Theol. Sem., 1971-74, acting pres., 1970; dean Sch. Div. Howard U., Washington, 1975-91, ret., 1991. Pres. Civil Rights Coordinating Council, Nashville, 1963-64 Bd. dirs. Sheltering Arms and Children's Svc., 1970-75, Inst. Social and Religious Studies Jewish Sem., United Ch. Bd. for World Ministries, 1969-75; bd. dirs., sec. exec. com. Assn. Theol. Schs., U.S. and Can.; chmn. exec. com. Fund for Theol. Edn., 1978—. With AUS, 1943-46, 47-53. Rockefeller Doctoral grantee; Lucy Monroe scholar; Rosenwald scholar; Am. Assn. Theol. Schs. Study grantee. Mem. Am. Ch. History Soc., Am. Acad. Religion, Soc. Study Black Religion (pres. 1973-75), Nat. Com. Black Churchmen.

JONES, LAWRENCE TUNNICLIFFE, lawyer; b. Mineola, N.Y., Jan. 20, 1950; s. Carroll Hudson Tunnicliffe and Florence Virginia (Greene) J. BA, U. Va., 1972; JD, U. Richmond, 1975. Bar: Va. 1975, D.C. 1976, N.Y. 1976, U.S. Dist. Ct. (ea. and so. dist.) N.Y. 1976, U.S. Supreme Ct. 1986. Bus. mgr. law review U. Richmond, Va., 1974-75; ptnr. Carroll Hudson Tunnicliffe Jones and Lawrence Tunnicliffe Jones Attys. at law, Mineola, 1976-91; owner, 1992—. Trustee Nassau County Hist. Soc., 1976—, pres., 1983-89; bd. dirs. Friends of Hist. St. George's Ch., Hempstead, N.Y., 1982—, v.p., 1990-92, pres., 1992-94; bd. dirs. St. Mary's Devel. Fund, Garden City, N.Y., 1983-89, pres., 1987-89; pres. coun. Cathedral Sch. St. Paul Alumni Fund, Inc., Garden City, 1984—; bd. govs. Cathedral Sch. St. Mary, Garden City, 1983-86. Recipient Mineola Bus. Person of Yr. award, 2000. Mem. ABA, Nat. Acad. Elder Law Attys., Va. State Bar Assn., N.Y. State Bar Assn., Nassau County Bar Assn., Nassau County Tax and Estate Planning Coun., Univ. Club (N.Y.C.), Univ. Club (L.I., pres. 1986-87, 93-94, bd. dirs. 1983-86, 89—), Mineola C. of C. (dir. 1993—), Garden City Golf Club, Mineola-Garden City Rotary (dir. 1991-94), Garden City Fellowship (pres. 1993-94, dir. 1994—), Cathedral Club (Garden City) (pres. 1993-95), Garden City C. of C. Episcopalian. Avocation: historic building preservation. Home: 158 Cathedral Ave Hempstead NY 11550-1140 Office: Jones & Jones 1000 Franklin Ave Ste 302 Garden City NY 11530-2910

JONES, LAWRENCE WILLIAM, retired educator, physicist; b. Evanston, Ill., Nov. 16, 1925; s. Charles Herbert and Fern (Storm) J.; m. Ruth Reavley Drummond, June 24, 1950; children: Douglas Warren, Carol Anne, Ellen Louise. BS, Northwestern U., 1948, MS, 1949; PhD, U. Calif. at Berkeley, 1952. Research asst. U. Calif. Radiation Lab., Berkeley, 1950-52; mem. faculty U. Mich., Ann Arbor, 1952—, prof. physics, 1963-98, chmn. dept. physics, 1982-87, prof. emeritus, 1998—. Physicist Midwestern U. Rsch. Assn., 1956-57; vis. physicist Lawrence Radiation Lab., Berkeley, 1959—, cons., 1964-66; vis. scientist CERN, Geneva, Switzerland, 1961-62, 65, 85—, assoc., 1988—; vis. physicist Brookhaven Nat. Lab., Upton, N.Y., 1963—, Fermi Nat. Accelerator Lab., Batavia, Ill., 1971—; vis. prof. Tata Inst. Fundamental Rsch., Bombay, India, 1979, U. Sydney Australia, 1991; elem. particle physics panel of physics survey com. NRC, 1984; cons. ctrl. design group Superconducting Super Collider Nat. Lab., 1985-87, vis. physicist, 1991-94; cons. NASA, 1974-81, 2002; trustee Univs. Rsch. Assn., 1982-87; disting. vis. scholar U. Adelaide, 1991; vis. scientist U. Auckland, 1991; co-chmn. sci. adv. com. Mich. Environ. Coun., 2000—; mem. internat. adv. com. Bilivian Obs. of Mt. Chacaltaya, 2001—. Mem. adv. panel for Cosmic Rays Jour. of Physics G., 1991-95. Guggenheim fellow, 1965; Sci. Rsch. Coun. fellow, 1977. Fellow Am. Phys. Soc. Home: 2666 Parkridge Dr Ann Arbor MI 48103-1731 Office: U Mich Dept Physics Ann Arbor MI 48109-1120 E-mail: lwjones@umich.edu.

JONES, LAWRENCE WORTH, poet, editor, performance art producer, songwriter; b. Norman, Okla., Jan. 5, 1950; s. Walter Neil and Jane Elizabeth (McCauley) J. BA in English magna cum laude, CUNY, 1991, postgrad., alumni scholar, CUNY, 2002, tchg. fellow, 2003. Supr. Fidelity Svc. Co., Boston, 1978-83; compliance dir. Alliance Fund Svcs., N.Y.C., 1985-88; dir. Cafe Nico, artists, writers, photographers collective, N.Y.C., 1991-2000. Advisor ABC No Rio, N.Y.C., 1991—. Author: We Become a Picnic, 1994; contbr. poetry to Downtown Poets, 1999. Coord. Gay Liberation Front, N.Y.C., 1970; plaintiff Gay Cmty. Alliance, Norman, Okla., 1972; campaign coord. Nader NYC '96, 1996. Fellow Tchg. fellow, CUNY, 2003; scholar Alumni scholar, 2002. Mem. Poets and Writers, Poetry Project. Avocations: art history, watercolors, collage. Home: 994 Bushwick Ave Apt 4R Brooklyn NY 11221-3749 E-mail: ljones11221@yahoo.com.

JONES, LEANDER CORBIN, educator, media specialist; b. Vincent, Ark., July 16, 1934; s. Lander Corbin and Una Bell (Lewis) J.; A.B., U. Ark., Pine Bluff, 1956; M.S., U. Ill., 1968; Ph.D., Union Grad. Inst., 1973; m. Lethonee Angela Hendricks, June 30, 1962; children: Angela Lynne, Leander Corbin. Tchr. English pub. high schs., Chgo. Bd. Edn., 1956-68, vol. English-as-fgn. lang. tchr. Peace Corps, Mogadiscio, Somalia, 1964-66; TV producer City Colls. of Chgo., 1968-73; communications media specialist Meharry Med. Coll., 1973-75; assoc. prof. Black Americana studies Western Mich., U., 1975-89, prof., 1989—, chmn. African studies program, 1980-81, co-chmn. Black caucus, 1983-84; pres. Corbin 22 Ltd., 1986—; dir. 7 art workshop Am. Negro Emancipation Centennial Authority, Chgo., 1960-63. Mem. Mich. Commn. on Crime and Delinquency, 1981-83; mem. exec. com. DuSable Mus. African Am. History, 1970—; mem. Prisoners Progress Assn., 1977-82, South African Solidarity Orgn., 1978—, Dennis Brutus Def. Com., 1980-83; chmn. Kalamazoo Community Relations Bd., 1977-79; bd. dirs. Kalamazoo Civic Players, 1981-83; pres. Black Theater of Kalamazoo, 1978-85; dir., dramaturg Mich. Black Repertory Theatre, 1987 90; exec. prodr. Ransom Street Playhouse, Kalamazoo, 1993—. Served with U.S. Army, 1956-58. Faculty Enrichment grantee Govt. Can., 1992. Mem. Assn. Study African-Am. History, NAACP (exec. com. Kalamazoo br. 1978-82), Theatre Arts and Broadcasting Skills Ctr. (pres. 1972—), AAUP, Mich. Orgn. African Studies, Nat. Council Black Studies, Popular Culture Assn., 100 Men's Club, Kappa Alpha Psi. Dir. South Side Ctr. of Performing Arts, Chgo., 1968-69, Progressive Theatre Unltd., Nashville, 1974-75, Mich. Black Repertory Theatre, 1987-90; chmn. Tenn. Region N.AM. Zone of 2d World Festival Black and Artican Arts and Culture, 1975, Nat. Black Media Consortium, 1985; writer, producer, dir. TV drama: Roof Over my Head, Nashville 1975; designer program in theatre and TV for hard-to-educate; developer edn. programs in Ill. State Penitentiary, Pontiac, and Cook County Jail, Chgo., 1971-73. Writer, dir. 10 Score!, 1976, Super Summer, 1978; dir. Trouble in Mind, 1979, Day of Absence, 1981, 85, Happy Ending, 1981, Who's Got His Own, 1983, Take A Giant Step, 1985; producer For Colored Girls Who Have Considered Suicide When the Rainbow is Enuf, 1984; featured at Civic Theater, Kalamazoo, in Great White Hope, 1979, Dutchman, 1980, Moon On a Rainbow Shawl, 1980, Five on the Black Hand Side, 1982, Who's Got His Own, Guys and Dolls, Black Girl, Tambourines to Glory, 1983, Day of Absence, Take a Giant Step, 1985, Soldier's Play, 1986, Beef, No Chicken, 1989, Black Eagles, 1994; author: Roof Over My Head, 1975, Africa is for Reel, 1983, Journal of Black Studies, 1985; exec. producer and host TV series Fade to Black, 1986—. Home: PO Box 2404 Portage MI 49081-2404 Office: Western Mich U 3721 S Westnedge Ave Ste 222 Kalamazoo MI 49008-2979

JONES, LEE BENNETT, chemist, educator, university official; b. Memphis, Mar. 14, 1938; s. Harold S. and Martha B. J.; m. Vera Kramar, Feb. 8, 1964; children: David B., Michael B. BA magna cum laude, Wabash Coll, 1960; PhD, M.I.T., 1964; DSC (hon.), Wabash Coll., 1992. Faculty U. Ariz., Tucson, 1964-85, prof. chemistry, 1972-85, asst. head dept. chemistry, 1971-73, head dept., 1973-77, dean Grad. Coll., 1977-79, provost Grad. Studies and Health Scis., 1979-82, v.p. rsch., 1982-85; prof. chemistry, exec. v.p., provost U. Nebr., Lincoln, 1985—2002, exec. v.p., provost emeritus, 2002—. Chmn. bd. dirs. Coun. Grad. Schs., 1986; mem. Grad. Records Exam. Bd., 1986-91; mem. Midwest Higher Edn. Commn., 1995—. Mem. editl. bd. Jour. Chem. Edn, 1975-79; contbr. numreous articles to sci. jours. Mem. Nebr. R&D Authority, 1985—, Midwest Higher Edn. Commn.; vice chmn. Nebr. Ednl. Telecomm. Commn., 1987-88, 91-92. NSF fellow, 1961-63, 64— Mem. AAAS, AAUP, Am. Chem. Soc., Chem. Soc. (London), N.Y. Acad. Scis., Phi Beta Kappa. Home: 1611 Kingston Rd Lincoln NE 68506-1526 Office: U Nebr 106 Varner Hall 3835 Holdrege St Lincoln NE 68503-1435

JONES, LEONADE DIANE, media publishing company executive; b. Bethesda, Md., Nov. 27, 1947; d. Leon Adger and Landonia Randolph Jones. BA with distinction, Simmons Coll., 1969; JD, MBA, Stanford U., 1973. Bar: Calif. 1973, D.C. 1979. Summer assoc. Davis Polk & Wardwell, N.Y.C., summer 1972; securities analyst Capital Rsch. Co., L.A., 1973-75; asst. treas. Washington Post Co., 1975-79, 86-87, treas., 1987-96; dir. fin. services Post-Newsweek Stas., Inc., Washington, 1979-84, v.p. bus. affairs, 1984-86; ind. mgmt. cons., pvt. equity investor, 1997-99, 2001—; CFO, sec. VentureThink, LLC, 1999-2001; exec. v.p., CFO Versura, Inc., 2000-01. Bd. dirs. Am. Balanced Fund, Inc., Income Fund Am., Inc., Fundamental Investors, Growth Fund Am., Inc., The New Economy Fund, Smallcap World Fund, Inc.; mem. investment mgmt. subcom. of benefit plans com. Am. Stores Co., 1992—99; mem. investment adv. com. N.Y. State Tchrs. Retirement Sys., 1999—; mem. investment mgmt. subcom. Albertson's Inc., 1999—. Bd. dirs. The Women's Found. Named D.C. Women's Hall of Fame, 1992; recipient Candace award for bus., 1992, Serwa award, 1993. Mem.: D.C. Bar Assn., Calif. Bar Assn., Nat. Bar Assn., Stanford U. Bus. Sch. Alumni Assn. (bd. dirs. 1986—88, pres. Washington-Balt. chpts. 1984—85).

JONES, LEROY WELWOOD (WRY WELWOOD), mental health services professional; b. Troy, N.Y., Apr. 28, 1952; s. Alfred Welwood Jones and Barbara Adams Froelich; m. Martha Gammons, June 14, 1980; children: Cally Gammons, Ian Reid. BS in Drama and Theatre Edn., Emerson Coll., 1975; MA in Expressive Therapy, Lesley Coll., 1981. Lic. mental health counselor Mass., 1993. Expressive therapist ATLANTICARE, Lynn, Mass., 1991—93, psychiat. crisis clinician, 1993—94, Health And Edn. Svcs., Beverly, 1994—96; clin. case mgr. Mass. Behavioral Health Partnership, Boston, 1996—; owner Welwood Works, North Hampton, NH, 2001—. Author of poems, The Wonderful Powers Of Being. Founder Nine Step Pagans (recovery support group)., North Hampton. Recipient cert. Appreciation, Cmty. Health and Alternative Opportunity Svcs., 1987, Best Short Story, Wakefield Item, 1988, 1St prize Poem, Mass. State Poetry Soc., 1992, 1St prize Poetry, Eagle Tribune, Lawrence Mass., 1994. Achievements include originated Jones Visual Model of the Psyche; development of wood finishing innovations using flame; nine steps toward health and freedom from chemical or behavioral slavery. Avocations: hiking, bicycling, canoeing, reading, flute. Office: Welwood Works 109 Shel-Al Estates North North Hampton NH 03862 Personal E-mail: wrywj@yahoo.com. E-mail: wry@welwoodworks.com.

JONES, LEWIS ARNOLD, JR., physician, radiologist, consultant; b. Detroit, Sept. 16, 1950; s. Lewis Arnold, Sr. and Berlene (Irish) J.; m. Pamela Denise Jennings, Nov. 14, 1992; children: Jennifer Tiffany, Alicia Dawn, Lewis Alexander. Student, Highland Park Coll., 1968-69, Wayne State U., 1969-72; MD, U. Mich., 1978. Diplomate Am. Bd. Radiology. Radiology residency Providence Hosp., Southfield, Mich., 1978-82; diagnostic radiologist Tri-County Radiology, P.C., West Bloomfield, Mich., 1983-84; clin. instr. of radiology Wayne State U. Sch. of Medicine, Detroit, 1984-91, clin. asst. prof. radiology, 1991-97; physician cons. Mich. Dept. Cmty. Health, Lansing, 1997-2000; radiologist Henry Ford Hosp., Detroit, 2000—02, Genesys Physicians Integrated Diagnostics, Burton, Mich., 2002—. Mem. cmty. adv. com. Karmanos Cancer Inst., Detroit, 1994-97; adv. bd. African Am. anti-platelet stroke prevention Wayne State U., 1996-97; co-investigator Women's Health Initiative, Detroit, 1996-97; co-chmn. 1997 Mich.'s Year of Women's Health, Mich. Dept. Cmty. Health, Lansing, 1997-98. Vol. spkr. Am. Cancer Soc., 1986—. Co-creator, co-presenter seminars Ptnrs. for Life, A women's health empowerment program, Mich., 1996—; bd. dirs. Oakland County Am. Cancer Soc., 1988—. Recipient Life Saver award Am. Cancer Soc., Southfield, Mich., 1990, Frederick Douglass award Nat. Assn. Negro Bus. and Profl. Women's Clubs, New Met. Detroit Club, 1996, winner "What a Man" contest, Essence Mag./ Preferred Stock Cologne, N.Y.C., 1995. Mem. AMA, Mich. State Med. Soc., Wayne County Med. Soc., Am. Coll. Radiology, Assn. Univ. Radiologists, Soc. Breast Imaging. Avocation: jazz and classical music collector. Home: 4951 Champlain Cir West Bloomfield MI 48323-3529

JONES, LINCOLN, III, army officer; b. Ft. Benning, Ga., Jan. 23, 1933; s. Lincoln and Doris G. (Baltz) J.; m. Alexandra Ann Archbald, June 21, 1958; children: Peter L., Patricia A. BS, U.S. Mil. Acad., 1958; MS, Auburn U., 1969. Commd. 2d lt. U.S. Army, 1958; advanced through grades to maj. gen.; brigade comdr. 9th Inf. Div., 1978-79, chief staff div. and, 1980, asst. div. comdr., 1980-82; dep. chief of staff LANDSOUTH, Verona, Italy, 1982-85; dep. comdg. gen. V Corps, Frankfurt, Germany, 1985-87; comdg. gen. USASETAF, Vicenza, Italy, 1987-90; pres., CEO ENRON Power Corp., Houston, 1991-93; pres. ENRON Engring. and Constrn. Co., Houston, 1994-96; vice chmn. ENRON Europe Ltd., London, 1996-98; pres. Lincoln Assocs. Inc., Houston, 1999—, Internat. Bus. and Energy Devel. Corp. for Pakistan; chmn. World Wide Strategic Ptnrs. Corp., Houston, 2003—. Exec. prof. U. Houston. Mem. Com. on Fgn. Rels., Houston; bd. dirs. World Coun. Fgn. Affairs, Nat. Def. U. Decorated D.S.M. with oak leaf cluster, Def. Superior Svc. Medal, Legion of Merit with oak leaf cluster, D.F.C., Bronze Star for valor with oak leaf cluster, others. Mem. Assn. U.S. Army (vice-chmn.), Assn. Grads. U.S. Mil. Acad. Episcopalian. Home: 9 Fernglen Dr The Woodlands TX 77380-3957

JONES, LINDA, communications educator; BA in English, U. Mich., 1972; MS in Journalism with distinction, Northwestern U., 1985. Reporter The Chelsea (Mich.) Standard, 1973-75; county govt., police reporter The Marshall (Mich.) Evening Chronicle, 1975-77; edn. reporter The Bay City (Mich.) Times, 1977--79, asst. met. editor, 1979-81, met. editor, 1981-86; vis. asst. prof. dept. journalism Roosevelt (Mich.) U., 1986-88, assoc. prof. journalism, 1992—, interim head, faculty of journalism and comm. studies, 1995-96, dir. sch. comm., 1996; asst. prof. Medill Sch. Journalism Northwestern U., 1988-92. Acting dir. Multicultural Journalism Ctr., Urban Journalism Ctr.; pub. com. StreetWise, 1995—; cons. The Times, 1993; adviser advising ctr., 1994-95; tchr. workshop sessions Journalism Edn. Assn./Nat. Scholastic Press Assn. conventions, 1992-96, chair Multicultural Scholarship com., 1996, spkr. com. Ill. host orgn., 1996. Contbr. articles to profl. jours.; judge and lectr. in field. Recipient Parent-Tchr. Assn. Mich. spl. award for edn. coverage, 1977, Mich. AP second place, breaking news, team coverage of major fire, 1980; Regents-Alumni scholarship U. Mich., 1968. Office: Roosevelt Univ 1751-T Robin Hall 600F 430 S Michigan Ave Chicago IL 60605-1394

JONES, LINDA MAY, tour guide; b. El Dorado, Kans., Nov. 9, 1937; d. Forrest Edward and Edith May Carlson; m. William Stanley Conard, Sept. 1, 1957 (div. Nov. 1970); children: Chris Dale Conard, Carin Dene Conard, Curtis Dean Conard; m. Verl Ray Jones, Nov. 6, 1982. Student, U. Kans., 1955-57, U. Colo., 1970-71. Tour guide Queen City Tours, Denver, 1976-84, tour guide coord., 1977-84, Am. Travel Brokers, Denver, 1977-84; owner Columbine Tours, Denver, 1984-92; tour dir. Backyard Tours, Englewood, Colo., 1993—2002, Mountains and More Tour Co., Golden, Colo., 1993—, JPS Enterprises, 1998—, Great Times Tours, 2002—. Mem. tourism adv. com. Metro Denver Conv. and Visitors Bur., 1990; seminar presenter; staff writer Colo. Gambler, 1994—. Co-author: Mile High Denver, A Guide to the Queen City, 1981; contbr. hist. articles to mags. V.p. Rep. Ctrl. Com., Gilpin County, Colo., 1983-93; v.p. Gilpin County Hist. Soc., Central City, Colo., v.p. 1988-90, pres., 1990—. Mem. Mt. Lookout DAR, Rotary, Alphi Phi. Methodist. Avocations: hiking, horseback riding. Home: PO Box 615 Black Hawk CO 80422 E-mail: linda@fairburnmountain.com.

JONES, LINDA R. WOLF, company executive; b. Jersey City, Sept. 4, 1943; d. Eugene Leon and Lottie (Pinkowitz) Rubin; m. Frank Paul Jones, Oct. 21, 1973 (div. Nov. 1987); 1 child, Elisabeth Noel. AB, Bryn Mawr Coll., 1964; MA, Yale U., 1968; DSW, Yeshiva U., N.Y.C., 1985. Dir. planning and tng. N.Y.C. Dept. Employment, 1971-77; dir. legislation N.Y.C. Community Devel. Agy., 1977-78; supervisory legis. analyst N.Y.C. Human Resources Adminstrn., 1978; sr. policy analyst Community Svc. Soc. N.Y., 1978-85; dir. pub. policy YMCA Greater N.Y., 1985-89; dir. spl. projects Phoenix House, N.Y.C., 1990-92; dir. income security policy Community Svc. Soc., N.Y.C., 1992-94; exec. dir. Therapeutic Communities Am., Washington, 1994—2002; dir. internat. ops. Conwal divsn. Axiom Resource Mgmt., Falls Church, Va., 2002—. Mem. adj. extension faculty Cornell U./N.Y. State Sch. Indsl. and Labor Rels., N.Y.C., 1975-80; dir. Nonprofit Coordinating Com. N.Y., N.Y.C., 1986-94, Govt. Affairs Profls., N.Y.C., 1989-94. Author (book) Eveline M. Burns and the American Social Security System 1935-60, 1991; mem. editorial bd. New Eng. Jour. Human Svcs., 1981—; contbr. articles to profl. jours. Mem. Civic Affairs Forum, N.Y.C., 1985-94; mem. legis. task force N.Y. State Gov.'s Office Vol. Svc., N.Y.C., 1987 90. Mem. Women in Govt. Rels., Am. Pub. Welfare Assn. (dir. 1982), Bryn Mawr Club Westchester (bd. dirs., past pres. 1974-94), Bryn Mawr Club Washington. Home: 6621 7th Pl NW Washington DC 20012 Office: Conwal Divsn Axiom Resource Mgmt Inc Ste 300 5203 Leesburg Pike Falls Church VA 22041

JONES, LINDY DON, lawyer; b. Vernon, Tex., Aug. 20, 1949; s. Earl Irven Jones and Avis June (Koontz) McDowell; m. M. Kathryn Sanders, June 6, 1969; children: Brandi Kim, Megan Dawn, Ty Jeffrey. BBA in Mgmt. with honors, U. Tex., Arlington, 1971; JD, So. Meth. U., 1974. Bar: Tex. 1974, U.S. Ct. Appeals (5th cir.) 1974, U.S. Dist. Ct. (we. dest.) Tex. 1977, U.S. Dist. Ct. (ea. dist.) Tex. 1978, U.S. Dist. Ct. (so. dist.) Tex. 1979. Ptnr. Moseley, Jones, Enoch & Martin and predecessors, Dallas, 1974-81, Moseley, Jones, Allen & Fuquay, Dallas, 1981-86, Jones, Allen & Fuquay, Dallas, 1986—. Pres. Highland Park United Meth. Ch. Mens Club, Dallas, 1979; chmn. bd. dirs. Dickinson Pl. Charitable Corp., Dallas, 1984-86. Recipient hon. life membership Highland Park United Meth. Ch. Mens Club, 1980. Mem. ABA, Dallas Bar Assn. (com. mem. 1974—), State Bar Tex., Delta Theta Phi. Republican. Home: 8068 Moss Meadows Dr Dallas TX 75231-3915 Office: Jones Allen & Fuquay LLP 8828 Greenville Ave Dallas TX 75243-7160 E-mail: ljones@jonesallen.com.

JONES, LOUIS, JR., (BUCKY JONES), academic administrator; Dir. Fayetteville (Ark.) regional campus Webster U. Mem. Ark. Bar Assn. (pres. 1999—). Office: Webster U 3448 N College Ave Fayetteville AR 72703-5105

JONES, LOUIS WORTH, retired management analyst, journalist; b. St. Louis, Jan. 8, 1908; s. Ed C. and Vida Pearl (Wrather) J.; m. Pauline Marie Ernest, May 24, 1947; children: David Worth, Roger Louis, Ethan Ernest, Faye Frances, Arthur Carlyle. Student, Washington U., St. Louis, 1925-27. Trainee, adminstrv. officer Farm Security Adminstrv., USDA, Washington, 1934-46; mgmt. analyst War Assets Adminstrn., San Francisco, 1946-48, US AEC, Los Alamos, N.Mex., 1948-50, USN Radiol. Def. Lab., San Francisco, 1950-68; ret., 1968. Co-founder, trustee emeritus The World U., Benson, Ariz.; founder, exec. dir. Intergroup Rels. of No. Calif., 1966-73. Editor, pub. Lou Jones Newsletter, 1959-70; author: (scripts) Meet Mary Wollstonecraft, 1977, Servetus: Why Did He Die?, 1977, Meet Alexander Meiklejohn, 1978, So You Think We Have Democracy?, 1988. Vol. alt. coord. Civil Def., San Mateo County, 1957-58; pres. Mid-Peninsula Coun. Civic Unity, 1959-60; co-founder Bi-County Commn. Human Rels.; trustee Unitarian Ch., San Mateo, Calif., 1958. Hon. Soc. scholar Washington U., 1925-27; recipient Mem. of Yr. award Unitarian-Universalist, 1977. Mem.: Internat. Platform Assn., Intergroup Rels. Assn. No. Calif. (founder), Nat. Assn. Ret. Fed. Employees. Avocations: piano, photography. Home: 511 Verano Ct San Mateo CA 94402-3261 Fax: 650-344-0334. E-mail: louiswj@aol.com.

JONES, LOVANA S. state legislator; b. Mansfield, Ohio, Mar. 28, 1935; 2 chilren. BA, Ohio State U. Mem. from 5th dist. Ill. Ho. of Reps., formerly asst. majority leader. Mem. children and family law com., edn. fin. elections com., pub. safety and infrastructure appropriationcoms., chmn. reapportionment com., mem. state govt. com. Supr. anti-gang program Chgo. Intervention Network. Office: Ill State Senate State Capitol 109 State House Springfield IL 62706-0001*

JONES, LUCIAN COX, lawyer; b. Kew Gardens, N.Y., Dec. 22, 1942; m. Ann Waters, Aug. 22, 1964; children— L. Rustin, Norman W., Warren R. AB, Davidson Coll., 1964; JD, Columbia U., 1967. Bar: N.Y. 1967. Assoc. Shearman & Sterling, N.Y.C., 1967-68, 70-76, ptnr., 1976-98; lectr.Cameron Sch. Bus. U. N.C., Wilmington, 1998—. Served to capt. U.S. Army, 1968-70 Mem. ABA, N.C. State Bar Assn., Assn. Bar City N.Y. Office: U NC Cameron Sch Bus 601 S College Rd Wilmington NC 28403-3297

JONES, LUPE SIRENA, insurance agent; b. Pasadena, Calif., Jan. 12, 1970; d. Luis Prado and Antonia Diaz Ixta; m. Anthony Laschint Jones-Carroll, June 13, 1992 (div. Aug. 1999).

JONES, LYLE VINCENT, psychologist, educator; b. Grandview, Wash., Mar. 11, 1924; s. Vincent F. and Matilda M. (Abraham) Jones; m. Patricia Edison Powers, Dec. 17, 1949 (div. 1979); children: Christopher V., Susan E., Tad W. Student, Reed Coll., 1942—43; BS, U. Wash., 1947, MS, 1948; PhD, Stanford U., 1950. Nat. Research fellow, 1950—51; asst. prof. psychology U. Chgo., 1951—57; vis. assoc. prof. U. Tex., 1956—57; assoc. prof. U. N.C., 1957—60, prof., 1960—69, Alumni disting. prof., 1969—92, rsch. prof., 1992—, dir. L.L. Thurstone Psychometric Lab., 1957—74, 1979—92, vice chancellor, dean Grad. Sch., 1969—79. Pres. Assn. Grad. Schs., 1976—77; cons. in field. Author: Studies in Aphasia: An Approach to Testing, 1961, The Measurement and Prediction of Judgment and Choice, 1968, An Assessment of Research-Doctorate Programs in the United States, 5 vols., 1982, Indicators of Precollege Education in Science and Methematics, 1985; Psychometrika, 1956—61, mem. editl. com. for psychology Mc-Graw-Hill, 1965—77; contbr. articles to profl. jours. Mng. trustee J. McKeen Cattell Fund, 1974—. With Air Corps U.S. Army, 1943—46. Recipient Thomas Jefferson award, U. N.C., 1979; fellow, Ctr. Advanced Study in Behavioral Scis., 1964—64; grantee, NIH, 1957—63, NSF, 1960—63, 1971—74, 1982—84, 1993—97, NIMH, 1963—74, 1979—87. Fellow: AAAS, APA (pres. divsn. 1963—64), Am. Statis. Assn., Am. Psychol. Soc., Am. Acad. Arts and Scis.; mem.: Psychometric Soc. (pres. 1962—63), Inst. Medicine, Nat. Coun. Measurement Edn., Am. Ednl. Rsch. Assn. Home: 6578 US Highway 15 501 N Pittsboro NC 27312-7793 Office: U NC CB 3270 Davie Hl Chapel Hill NC 27599-0001 E-mail: lvjones@email.unc.edu.

JONES, LYNNE CHRISTINE HEILENMAN, orthopaedic surgery educator; b. Phila., Dec. 26, 1956; d. Benjamin Franklin and Phyllis Marie (Lindholm) Heilenman; m. Paul Alan Jones, Feb. 18, 1978; children: Amy, Christine. BS, Ursinus Coll., 1977; MS, Towson (Md.) State U., 1987; PhD, Johns Hopkins U., 1997. Rsch. technician Johns Hopkins U., Balt., 1977-78, lab. coord., 1979-84, coord. rsch., 1984-85, rsch. assoc., 1985-97, asst. prof. orthopaedic surgery, 1997-2000, assoc. prof. orthopaedic surgery, 2000—. Mem. faculty Johns Hopkins Sch. Medicine; tech. dir. Arthritis Surgery Bone Bank, 1987—; adj. faculty Harford C.C., 1990; dir. Ctr. for Osteonecrosis Rsch. and Edn., 1995—; treas. ARCO Internat., 1998—; rsch. cons. Contbr. articles to profl. jours., chpts. to books. Leader Girl Scouts U.S., 1993—. Named one of Outstanding Young Women Am., 1984. Mem. ASTM, Orthopaedic Rsch. Soc., Soc. Biomaterials, Nat. Osteonecrosis Found. (sec., treas. 1999—). Republican. Presbyterian. Avocations: golf, hiking, reading. Home: 3510 Glen Oak Dr Jarrettsville MD 21084-1836 Office: Johns Hopkins U Dept Orthopaedics Ste 201 Good Samaritan Profl Bldg Baltimore MD 21239-2905 E-mail: lcjones@jhmi.edu.

JONES, M. DOUGLAS, JR., pediatrics educator; b. San Antonio, Apr. 22, 1943; BA, Rice U., 1964; MD, U. Tex., 1968. Diplomate Am. Bd. Pediat. Intern U. Colo. Sch. Medicine, Denver, 1968-69, resident, 1969-71, fellow neonatal-perinatal medicine, 1973-75; pediatrician-in-chief Children's Hosp., U. Hosp., Denver; prof., chmn. pediatrics U. Colo. Sch. Medicine. Mem. Am. Bd. Pediat., Am. Acad. Pediat., Am. Pediat. Soc., Soc. for Pediat. Rsch. Office: Childrens Hosp 1056 E 19th Ave Denver CO 80218-1088

JONES, MALINDA THIESSEN, telecommunications company executive; b. Perryton, Tex., Jan. 23, 1947; d. Chester Francis Thiessen and Bobbye Pearson (Wallis) Schwalm; m. Hollis Bass Jones, Mar. 21, 1969 (div. 1972); 1 child, Reshad. BA in Psychology, U. Mo.-Kansas City, 1975. Rsch. asst. U. Kans. Med. Ctr., Kansas City, 1975-77; owner, mgr., regional mgr. U.S. Telecom, Dallas, 1981-82, staff asst. to pres., 1983-84, sr. planner, 1984-85; dir. mktg. Telinq Systems Inc., Richardson, Tex., 1985-86, dir. bus. devel. and corp. communications, 1986—. V.p. mktg. Dakota Group, Inc., 1989—; cons. in field. Editor conf. presentations, bus. plans. Vol. tchr. Sch. for Learning Disability, Operation Discovery, Kansas City, 1973-75; corp. liaison exec. assistance program Dallas C. of C./Dallas Ind. Sch. Dist., 1984; chmn. com. Therapeutic Riding Tex., Dallas, 1985. Recipient Outstanding Contbr. award Dallas Ind. Sch. Dist., 1984. Mem. NAFE, Nat. Mus. Assn. for Women in Arts, Assn. Women Enterpreneurs Dallas, Nat. Soc. Washington Family Descendants. Home: 1122 Overlake Dr Richardson TX 75080-6937 Office: Dakota Group Inc 1217 Digital Dr Richardson TX 75081-1970 E-mail: mthiesse@swbell.net.

JONES, MALLORY See DANAHER, MALLORY

JONES, MARIE C. language educator; b. La Charité-sur-Loire, France, July 27, 1968; arrived in U.S., 1993; d. Jean-Claude and Paulette B. Conin. BA, U. F. Rabelais, 1991, MA, 1992; PhD, U. North Tex., 1999. Tchg. fellow, adj. lectr. English U. North Tex., Denton, 1994—2001, lectr. English, 2001—. Pub. Basilisk Press. Author (poetry chapbook): Lovg Song, with Mass Extinction, 2003; translator: La ville où je t'aime, 2003; translator: (endnote) At Fault, 2001; translator: Lacan et la pensée chinoise, 2000; translator: (scholarly articles) Kate Chopin: An Annotated Bibliography, 1999; contbr. Mem.: Associated Writing Programs, Am. Lit. Translators Assn., Modern Lang. Assn.

JONES, MARION, track and field athlete; b. L.A., Oct. 12, 1975; m. C.J. Hunter, 1998 (div. 2001); 1 child, Timothy Montgomery. Named Women's Athlete of the Yr., Track and Field News, 1997, 1998, Track & Field News, 2000; recipient 11th place long jump, U.S.A., 1995, 5th place, Olympic Trials, 1992, 4th place 100m, NCAA, 1994, 6th place 200m, 1994, 2nd place, 1994, 4th place long jump, 1995, 3 gold medals for 100, 200, 4x100, Sydney Games, 2000, 5 time world champion 100m (1997-99), 200m (2001), 4x100m (1997,01), Jesse Owens award winner, 1999, AP and USOC Female Athlete of the Yr., 2000. Office: c/o USA Track & Field 1 Rca Dome Ste 140 Indianapolis IN 46225-1023

JONES, MARK ALAN, broadcast technician; b. San Francisco, 1957; m. Stephanie Phillips, 1983. BA in Communication Studies, Calif. State U., 1979. Chief operator Sta. KXPR, Sacramento, 1979-80, with ops./prodn.dept., 1980—. Recipient pub. radio program award for Excellence, Corp. Pub. Broadcasting, 1981. Office: Capital Pub Radio Inc 3416 American River Dr Ste B Sacramento CA 95864-5715 E-mail: jones@csus.edu.

JONES, MARK LOGAN, educational association executive, educator; b. Provo, Utah, Dec. 16, 1950; s. Edward Evans and Doris (Logan) J.; m. Catherine A. Bailey. BS, Ea. Mont. Coll., 1975; postgrad. in labor rels., Cornell U.; postgrad., SUNY, Buffalo. Narcotics detective Yellowstone County Sheriff's Dept., Billings, Mont., 1972-74; math tchr. Billings (Mont.) Pub. Schs., 1975-87; rep. Nat. Edn. Assn. of N.Y., Buffalo, Jamestown, 1987-91, Nat. Edn. Assn. Alaska, Anchorage, 1991—. Mem. Alaska Tchr. Licensure Task Force, Tchr. Edn. Adv. Coun., Adv. Com. on Tchr. Stds., Alaska Partnership Tchr. Enhancement; bd. mem. Alaska staff Devel. Network; mem. various coms. Alaska Dept. Edn. Photographs featured in 1991 N.Y. Art Rev. and Am. Artist. Committeeman Yellowstone Dem. Party, Billings, 1984-87; exec. com. Dem. Cen. Com., Billings, 1985-87; bd. dirs. Billings Community Ctr., 1975-87; concert chmn. Billings Community Concert Assn., 1980-87; bd. dirs. Chautauqua County Arts Coun.; bd. dirs. Big Brothers and Big Sisters Anchorage. With U.S. Army, 1970-72. Recipient Distinguished Svc. award, Billings Edn. Assn., 1985, Mont. Edn. Assn., 1987. Mem. ACLU, Billings Edn. Assn. (bd. dirs. 1980-82, negotiator 1981-87, pres. 1982-87), Mont. Edn. Assn. (bd. dirs. 1982-87), Ea. Mont. Coll. Tchr. Edn. Project, Accreditation Reviewer Team Mont. Office Pub. Edn., Big Sky Orchard, Masonic, Scottish Rite. Avocations: bonsai, photography, reading, classical and jazz music, hunting, fishing. Home: PO Box 102904 Anchorage AK 99510-2904 Office: Nat Edn Assn Alaska 1840 S Bragaw St Ste 103 Anchorage AK 99508-3463

JONES, MARSHALL BUSH, education educator, researcher; b. Portchester, NY, Jan. 25, 1928; s. Donald and Muriel Marshall Jones; m. Beverly Ratner, Mar. 7, 1952; children: Donald Ratner, Susan Story Marshall. BA, Yale U., 1946—49; PhD, Univ. of Calif. at LA, 1950—53. Lt. j.g. (med. svc. corps) U.S. Naval Sch. of Aviation Medicine, Pensacola, Fla., 1953—55, rsch. psychologist, 1956—62; asst. prof. of psychiatry U. of Fla., 1962—68; assoc. prof. of behavioral sci. Penn State Coll. of Medicine, Hershey, Pa., 1968—72, prof. of behavioral sci., 1973—2003, prof. and chair of behavioral sci., 1979—. Chair, bd. of directors Keystone Human Services, Harrisburg, Pa., 1996—. Contbr. articles to profl. jours. Pres. ACLU of Fla., Gainesville, Fla., 1966—68; chair, bd. of directors Keystone Human Services, Harrisburg, Pa., 1996—2003. Lt. j.g. Navy Med. Svc. Corps, 1956—62, Pensacola, Fla. Recipient McLaughlin Vis. Prof., McMaster U., 1985. Mem.: AAAS (assoc.). D-Liberal. Achievements include development of isoperformance technology; the theory of behavioral contagion; the risk-factor model of complex genetic diseases. Home: 41 West Caracas Ave Hershey PA 17033 Office: Penn State Coll of Medicine 500 University Dr Hershey PA 17033 Office Fax: 717-531-6916. E-mail: mbj1@psu.edu.

JONES, MARTHA LEE, social worker, consultant; b. Bklyn., Dec. 6, 1945; d. Harold L. and Janet R. (Holcomb) Utts; m. Steve R. Jones; 1 child, Erin R. BS, Juniata Coll., 1967; postgrad., Columbia U., 1967-68; MSW, U. Md., 1972; PhD, Fielding Inst., 1990. Lic. social worker, Pa. Dir. Child Welfare Svcs., Huntingdon, Pa., 1968-70, supr. Carlisle, Pa., 1970-75; dir. child care Meth. Children's Home, Mechanicsburg, Pa., 1975-76; pvt. practice Camp Hill, Pa., 1976-78; pres. Common Sense Assoc., Mechanicsburg, 1979-96, Common Sense Adoption Svcs., Mechanicsburg, 1993—; adminstr. Pa. Statewide Adoption Network, Mechanicsburg, 1995—2000. Contbr. articles to profl. jours. E-mail: mluj@aol.com.

JONES, MARY ANN, geriatrics nurse; b. Suffern, N.Y., July 15, 1943; d. Ralph and Hilva (Kelly) Osborne; m. Richard D. Jones, Aug. 31, 1985. AAS, Rockland C.C., Suffern, 1963; BS, St. Thomas Aquinas Coll., Sparkill, N.Y., 1983. Cert. dir. nursing adminstrn./long term care. Supr. to asst. DON Ramapo Manor Nursing Ctr., Suffern, 1964-87; dir. staff devel. Carnegie Gardens Coor to DON Nursing Ctr., Melbourne, Fla., 1987—2003; staff devel. coord. Carnegie Gardens Nursing Ctr., Melbourne, Fla., 2003—. Inducted into Nadona Acad. Fellows, 1997. Mem. Nat. Assn. Dirs. Nursing Adminstrn. in Long Term Care, Fla. Assn. Dirs. Nursing Adminstrn. in Long Term Care (cert. Dir. Nursing Adminstrn. in Long Term Care 1995), Gericulture Soc. Home: 426 Lackland St SW Palm Bay FL 32908-7111

JONES, MARY ELIZABETH, school counselor; b. Lake Charles, La.; d. Annie Walter and Thelma (Griffin) J. BS in Recreation, So. U., 1969; MA, 1977; Licensed profl. counselor. Program dir. YWCA, Baton Rouge, 1969-72; instr. So. U., Baton Rouge, 1972-74, career counselor, 1974-84; student personnel officer Baton Rouge Vocat. Tech. Inst., 1984-86; resource person Women's Skill Tng. Program, Baton Rouge, 1984-86; placement officer Jumonville Sr. Vocat. Tech. Sch., Baton Rouge, 1987-88; counselor, job developer, 1988—; cons. ind. contractor, 1988-90; substance abuse coord., La. State Penitentiary; advisor So. U. Tchrs. Job Fair, Baton Rouge, 1980—; resource person Women's Skill Tng. program, ednl. specialist Foster Care Pre-Vocat. project, 1988—. Bd. dirs. Battered Women's Program, Baton Rouge, 1985, also mem. exec. com., chmn. nominating com.; chmn. scholarship com. Scotlandville Area Adv., 1982. Recipient Community Services award Scotlandville Area Adv. Council, 1982. Mem. Nat. Family Opinion, Smithsonian Assn., Am. Assn. for Counseling and Devel., La. Sch. Counselors Assn., La. Vocation Assn., Am. Soc. For Tng. and Devel., 100 Black Women, Democrat. Roman Catholic. Avocations: traveling, reading, monogramming, hook rug weaving, interior design. Home: 1631 79th Ave Baton Rouge LA 70807-5431

JONES, MARY JEANNE A. investment adviser; b. Hartford, Conn., May 30, 1934; d. Buist Murfee and Dorothy (Crawford) Anderson; m. Richard F. Jones III, June 23, 1956 (div. Feb. 23, 1998); children: Laura O. Jones Shafer, Heidi A. Jones Hunter, Richard F. IV. AB cum laude, Smith Coll., 1956; MA in History, U. Va., 1962. Analyst, registered rep. Conning & Co., 1970-74; analyst, bond investment dept. Aetna Life & Casualty, 1974-76; pres. Mary Jeanne Jones, Inc., Farmington, Conn., 1976—, trustee, 1987—, conservator, 1999—2002. Registered rep. Nat. Assn. Securities Dealers, 1971-74, N.Y. Stock Exch., 1971-74. Author: The Fundamental Orders of Connecticut, 1988, Congregational Commonwealth, Connecticut, 1636-1662, 1968; co-author: Pharmacology at the University of Virginia School of Medicine, 1966; contbr. articles to profl. jours.; patentee diaper dunker. Notary pub. State of Conn., 1976—2001; trustee Conn. Hist. Soc., 1986—92, 1998—, treas., 1987—91, 1998—, mem. fin. com., 1986—92, 1996—; trustee Kingswood-Oxford Sch., 1976—80; treas. Nick Schaus for Congress 6th Dist., Conn., 1980, 1982; mem. investment com. Asylum Hill Congl. Ch., 1997—2001, chmn., 1999—2001, chmn. bd. adminstrn. fin., 2003—, deacon, mem. exec. com.; mem. planned giving adv. com. U. Hartford, 1997—99; mem. investment com. Conn. Valley Girl Scouts USA Coun., 1999; pres. Smith Coll. Class of 1956, 1976—81. Mem.: Hartford Soc. Fin. Analysts (bd. dirs. 1983—89, treas. 1983—84, v.p. 1984—86, pres. 1986—87), Inst. CFAs (coun. examiners 1979—81), Assn. Investment Mgmt. and Rsch., Town & Country Club, 1892 Club. Republican. Avocations: skiing, travel, gardening. Home and Office: 37 Prattling Pond Rd Farmington CT 06032-1803

JONES, MARY M. landscape architect; Student, U. Tex., Austin, 1974—75; Bachelor of Landscape Arch. magna cum laude, Tex. A&M, 1979. Registered landscape arch., Mass., Calif., Tex., Ohio, Ariz., Mich., Minn. Arch. Johnson Johnson & Roy, Inc., Ann Arbor, Mich.; prin. Hargreave Assocs., 1983—. Mem. Mayor's Inst. on City Design, 2002, 03; mem. Sch. Arch. found. adv. coun. U. Tex., Austin, 2002; mem. dean's external adv. coun. Sch. Arch. Tex. A&M, 2001—02; co-chair Landscape Arch. CEO Roundtable, 2000—01; mem. landscape adv. coun. dept. landscape arch. and environ. planning U. Calif., Berkeley; mem. adv. bd. and publ. com. Designed Landscape Forum; mem. design rev. bd. Bay Conservation Devel. Commn.; lectr. in field; vis. critic landscape arch. Harvard Design Sch. Contbr. articles to profl. jours. and mags.; prin. works include Sydney Olympics Master Concept Design, U. Cin. Master Plan, Guadalupe River Pk., Byxbee Pk., Crissy Field, San Francisco. Mem.: Am. Soc. Landscape Artists (Honor award for excellence in the study of landscape arch. 1979), San Francisco Planning and Urban Rsch. Assn., Am. Acad. Rome (Prince Charitable Trusts fellow 1997—98). Office: Hargreaves Assocs 118 Magazine St Cambridge MA 02139 also: Hargreaves Assocs 2020 17th St San Francisco CA 94103*

JONES, MARY TRENT, endowment fund trustee; b. Durham, N.C., July 15, 1940; d. Josiah Charles Trent and Mary Duke (Biddle) Semans; m. James Parker Jones, June 27, 1964; children: James Trent, Benjamin Parker, Jonathan Edmund. AB, Duke U., 1963. Trustee The Duke Endowment, Charlotte, N.C., 1988—. Chmn. Josiah Charles Trent Found., Durham, 1978-83; bd. dirs. Mary Duke Biddle Found., Durham, 1983—, Concert Artists Guild, N.Y.C., 1996-00. Mem. Va. Perinatal Svcs. Adv. Bd., Richmond, 1986-91; sec. Va. Arts Commn., Richmond, 1989-92, bd. dirs., 1984-92; trustee Va. Intermont Coll., Bristol, Va., 1986-91, 98-2001; mem. State Coun. Higher Edn. Va., Richmond, 1991-95; trustee Va. Mu. of Fine Arts, Richmond, 1992-97; mem. bd. Washington County Pub. Libr. Found., 1997—; trustee William King Regional Arts Ctr., 1998—, Emory and Henry Coll., 1999—. Recipient outstanding alumni award Durham Acad., 1991. Mem. Va. Highlands Festival Bd. Episcopalian. Avocations: reading, walking, hiking. Home: 107 Hillside Dr NE Abingdon VA 24210-2013

JONES, MATTHEW O. engineering educator; b. Anchorage, Dec. 4, 1974; s. Everett O. and Susan S. Jones; m. Patricia B. Jones, May 19, 2001. B in Math. and Physics, Mid. Tenn. State U., 1999. Guitarist various rock bands, Birmingham, Ala., 1994—99; loan closer Irwin Mortgage Corp., Brentwood, Tenn., 1999—2000; tchg. asst. indsl. and sys. engrng. Ga. Tech., Atlanta, 2001—, instr. dept. indsl. and sys. engrng., 2002. Musician: (lead guitarist) Bands: East of Eden, Fishtank Jonah, Sylvia's Crib, Onion Spyders. Scholar, Mid. Tenn. State U., Dept. Physics, 1997—98. Mem.: Inst. for Ops. Rsch. and Mgmt. Scis. Avocations: guitar, gardening, cooking, building guitars, making wine.

JONES, MICHAEL LYNN, financial consultant, branch operations manager; b. Tulsa, Okla., Aug. 24, 1967; s. Leonard A. and Loretta F. (Howard) J.; m. Renee D. Carter, Aug. 2, 1986; 1 child, Jonah Jacob. Student, U. Okla., 1985-88, Am. Coll., 1997-98. CFP, Internat. Bd. Cert. Fin. Planners. Retail mgr. The Finish Line, Broken Arrow, Okla., 1985-88; stockbroker Stuart James Co., Tulsa, 1988-89; rep. Am. Bank and Trust, Tulsa, 1989-91; fin. advisor Am. Express Fin. Advisors, Tulsa, 1991-97; fin. cons. PrimeVest Fin. Svcs., Tulsa, 1997-98, s/b Wachovia Securities, Tulsa, 1998—. Mem. Young Dems., Tulsa, Promise Keepers, Tulsa; vol. Soc. for Prevention of Cruelty to Animals, Salvation Army, Boys Club, Broken Arrow, 1987-92; mem. Jr. C. of C., Tulsa. Mem. Internat. Assn. for Fin. Planning (regional chpt. v.p. 1995-99), Inst. of CFP, Okla. U. Alumni Assn., Tulsa Running Club, Green Country Classic Mustangs, Tulsa Optimist Club, Toastmasters Internat. Tulsa, Mensa, Forest Ridge Country Club, Jr. C. of C. Democrat. Avocations: reading, music, physical fitness, family activities. Home: 9226 S Maplewood Ave Tulsa OK 74137-4123 Office: s/b Wachovia Securities 6120 S Yale Ave Ste 1650 Tulsa OK 74136-4218

JONES, MICHAEL STUART, music educator; b. East Point, Ga., Aug. 9, 1964; s. Charles Kenneth and Sue Hinton Jones. B in Music Edn., U. S.C., 1986. Cert. tchr. S.C., 1987. Band dir. Johnsonville (S.C.) HS, 1987—91, West Florence HS, Florence, SC, 1991—. Mem.: Am. Sch. Band Dir.'s Assn., Internat. Assn. Jazz Educators, S.C. Music Educator's Assn., S.C. Band Dir.'s Assn. (region chmn. 1995—), Music Educator's Nat. Conf., Phi Beta Mu, Phi Mu Alpha Sinfonia (life), Kappa Kappa Psi (life). Office: West Florence High Sch 221 N Beltline Dr Florence SC 29501 Office Fax: 843-664-8475. E-mail: bdjock@aol.com.

JONES, MILES JAMES A. pathologist, consultant; b. Abington, Pa., Nov. 22, 1952; s. James. A. and Jessie L. (Brisbane); m. Linda Darlene Ableitner, Oct. 14, 1979; children: Dominick, Jessica. Student, Princeton U., 1973; MD, Howard U., 1977. Am. Bd. Pathology. Research fellow, Washington, 1975; intern in gen. surgery Cleve.Clinic, 1977-78; resident in anatomic & clin. pathology Mayo Clinic, Rochester, Minn., 1978-82; emergency room physician Mt. Sinai Hosp., Mpls., 1979-81; jr. staff pathologist Armed Forces Inst. of Pathology, Washington, 1982-84; pathologist, dir. Profl. Arts Lab., West Frankfort, Ill., 1985-91; pathologist, lab. dir. LaPorte (Ind.) Hosp. and Found., 1991—93. Lectr. various colls. and univs.; mem. step 1 pathology test com. Nat. Bd. Med. Examiners. Recipient Stowell-Orbison award, 1982. Fellow Am. Soc. Clin. Pathologists, Coll. Am. Pathologists; mem. AMA, Coll. Am. Pathologists, Internat. Soc. Gynecologic Pathologists, Herrin C. of C., Rotary. Avocations: tropical fish hobbyist, horticulture, microcomputer hobbyist. Home: 1704 SE 11th St Lees Summit MO 64081-3157

JONES, MILTON BENNION, retired agronomist, educator; b. Cedar City, Utah, Jan. 15, 1926; s. William Lunt and Claire (Bennion) J.; m. Grace Elaine Guymon, Sept. 8, 1951; children: Milton B. Jr., Richard W., Jo Layne, Tamera, Sherilee, Karolyn. BS, Utah State U., 1951; PhD, Ohio State U., 1955. Successively jr. agronomist, asst. agronomist, assoc. agronomist, agronomist, lectr. emeritus U. Calif., Hopland, Davis, 1955—. Cons. IRI Rsch. Inst., Campinas, Brazil, 1963-65, CSIRO, Australia, 1974, BLM, Ukiah, Calif., 1970-77, Sulphur Inst., Washington, 1967-88, AID U. Evora, Portugal, 1984, Basque Govt., Bilbao, Spain, 1987, MAF, Invermay, New Zealand, 1990. Contbr. articles to profl. jours. Mem. Sch. bd. Ukiah Elem. Sch. Dist., 1962-63; scout leader local chpt. Boy Scouts Am., Ukiah, 1962-70. With USN, 1944-47. Fellow Agronomy Soc., Soil Sci. Soc. Home: 3501 Leland Ln Ukiah CA 95482-6911 Office: U Calif 4070 University Rd Hopland CA 95449-9717 E-mail: mbjggj@juno.com.

JONES, MILTON WAKEFIELD, publisher; b. Burbank, Calif., Apr. 18, 1930; s. Franklin M. and Lydia (Sinclair) J.; m. Rita Strong, May 4, 1959; 1 son, Franklin Wayne. Student, Santa Monica City Coll., 1948-50; AA, U. So. Calif., 1950-52. V.p. mktg. Sav-Ink Co., Newport Beach, Calif., 1956-58; account exec. KDES-Radio, Palm Springs, Calif., 1958-60; pres. Milton W. Jones Advt. & Pub. Rels. Agy., Palm Springs, 1960—, Desert Publs., Inc., Palm Springs, 1965—, Riverside Color Press, Inc., Palm Springs, Olman Travel Svc., Palm Springs, 1979-84. Pres. Franklin Comms. (Sta. KPSL-Radio), 1987-98, Airport Displays Ltd., 1972—; vice chmn. Palm Springs Savings Bank, 1981-96; bd. dirs., treas. Canyon Nat. Bank. Pub. Palm Springs Life Mag., 1965—, Wheeler Bus. Letter, Palm Springs, 1969-77, San Francisco mag., 1973-79, Guest Life, Orange County, N.Mex., Carmel/Monterey, St. Petersburg/Clearwater, Vancouver, Can., El Paso, Houston, 1978—, Orange County mag., 1987-89, McCallum Theatre Program, 1989—, Ofcl. Guide to Houston, 1993, El Paso Guest Life, 1993, Pebble Beach, The Magazine, 2002, Pub. Record newspaper, 1996, Official Guide to Ontario, 2001, Official Guide to Galveston Island, 2003. Mem. Desert Press Club (pres. 1965). Home: 422 N Farrell Dr Palm Springs CA 92262-6559 also: 206 Abalone Ave Newport Beach CA 92662-1304 Office: 303 N Indian Canyon Dr Palm Springs CA 92262-6015 E-mail: milt@palmspringslife.com.

JONES, MONIAREE PARKER, legal nurse consultant; b. Montgomery, Ala., Oct. 20, 1953; d. Jeffie Knod and Amanda Gertrude (Grier) Parker; m. C. Emile Jones, May 24, 1980; 1 child, William Andrew. Assoc. Nursing, Troy State U., 1974; BSN, U. Ala., 1980. Cert. occupational health nurse; cert. case mgr. Nurse emergency rm. Elmore County Hosp., Wetumpka, Ala.; med. auditor State of Ala. Med. Svcs. Adminstrn., Montgomery; instr. women's tng. program State of La., Baton Rouge; occupational health nurse Georgia Gulf Corp., Plaquemine, La., 1984-91; dir. occupational health svcs. River West Med. Ctr., Plaquemine; occupational rehab. cons. Am. Internat. Health and Rehab. Svcs., Birmingham, Ala.; internal coord. CompSolution, Birmingham, Ala., 1992—; client svcs. mgr. Lake Shore Rehab. Ctr.; occupational health nurse State Farm Ins. Co., Birmingham; health and disabilities coord. Jefferson County Com. Econ. Opportunity, 2000—; legal nurse cons. Haskel, Slaughter, Young and Rediker, LLC. Mem. La. Assn. Occupational Health Nurses (pres. Baton Rouge chpt.), Ctrl. Ala. Occupational Nurses Assn. (pres.), Am. Assn. Occupational Health Nurses (pres. ctrl. Ala. chpt.). Home: 505 Highgate Hill Rd Indian Springs AL 35124-3835 Office: 1400 Park Place Tower Park Place N Birmingham AL 35203 E-mail: Nightingalempj@aol.com.

JONES, NANCY LANGDON, financial planning practitioner; b. Chgo., Mar. 24, 1939; d. Lewis Valentine and Margaret (Seese) Russell; m. Lawrence Elmer Langdon, June 30, 1962 (div. 1970); children: Laura Kimberley, Elizabeth Ann;

m. Claude Earl Jones, Jan. 1, 1973. BA, U. Redlands, Calif., 1962; MS, Coll. for Fin. Planning, 1991. CFP; registered investment advisor; accredited tax advisor; cert. sr. advisor. Bookkeeper Russell Sales Co., Santa Fe Springs, Calif., 1962-70; office mgr. Reardon, McCallum & Co., Upland, Calif., 1970-77; broker, assoc. ERA Property Ctr., Upland, 1977-84; registered rep. Fin. Network Investment Corp., Pasadena, Calif., 1984-92; pvt. practice fin. planning Upland, 1984—; ptnr. Jones, Graham & Assocs., Registered Investment Advisors, Upland, Calif., 1994; pres. NLJones, Inc., 2000—. Mem. adj. faculty Coll. Fin. Planning, Denver, 1986-94; mem. nat. comprehensive exam. question writing com. CFP Bd. Stds., 1994-98; del. U.S. fin. and investment leaders study mission to China and Hong Kong, 1993; industry spkr. N.Am. Securities Adminstrs. Assn. Investment Advisor Workshop, 1999; panelist L.A. Times Annual Investment Strategies Conf., 1999, 2000; featured planner L.A. Times Money Makeover, 1999, 2001, 02. Author: (textbook for UCLA Course) So You Want to Be a Financial Planner: Your Guide to a New Career, 2001. Leader Spanish Trails coun. Girl Scouts U.S., 1974-81; mem. exec. com. Corp. 2000 Coun., San Antonio Cmty. Hosp.; mem. planned giving adv. bd. Goodwill Industries of the Inland Counties, 1997-98; mem. planned giving roundtable Inland Empire. Recipient Hon. Svc. award Valencia Elem. Sch., 1978, Top Ten, Am. Bus. Womens Assn., 2003; selected 1 of Top 100 Women Owned Businesses in Inland Empire, Bus. Press, 1996; named One of the Most Influential People in the Fin. Planning Profession, readers of Fin. Planning Mag., 2002. Mem. SAG, N. Am. Securities Adminstrs. Assn., Inc. (investment adv. coun. 2000—), Inland Soc. Tax Cons., Internat. Assn. Fin. Planners (pres. San Gabriel Valley chpt. 1987-88, mem. exec. bd. So. Calif. conf. 1992-98, chmn. So. Calif. Conf., 1996-97), Am. Bus. Women's Assn. (pres. Upland chpt. 1989-90, gen. chmn. 1995, Pacific Spring Conf. Woman of Yr. award 1988), Fin. Planning Assn., Inst. CFP San Gabriel Valley Soc. (pres. 1992-93, chmn. 1993-94, bd. dirs. 1990-97), Inst. CFPs (nat. practice mgmt. and tech. com. 1996), Nat. Coun. Exchangers (sec. 1986-87), Fin. Planning Assn., Estate Planning Coun. Pomona Valley (bd. dirs. 1995—, pres. 1998-99), Women's Bus. Network (pres. 1987-88), Registry Fin. Planning Practitioners, Inland Valley Profl. Aux. (charter, bd. dirs. 1991-92), Assistance League Upland, Upland C. of C. Avocations: traveling, acting. Home and Office: 2485 Mesa Ter Upland CA 91784-1078 E-mail: nancy@nljones.com.

JONES, NANCY STEED, small business owner; b. Brunswick, Ga., Sept. 19, 1944; d. Robert Leonard Steed and Sylvania Elizabeth (Ford) Steed McLeroy; m. James Lee Messer, Sept. 16, 1960 (div. July 1962, deceased); 1 child, Sharlene Elizabeth Messer Garner; m. Jeremiah Timothy Ford, Sept. 12, 1969 (div. Sept. 1990); 1 child, Rebecca Lynne Ford; m. Alvin L. Jones Sr., Oct. 21, 1992. BS in Mktg./Mgmt., LaSalle U., 1995, MS/PhD in Mktg./Mgmt., PhD (hon.), LaSalle U. Sec., bookkeeper Steed Bros. Heating & Air Conditioning, Augusta, Ga., 1963-65; sec. Dixie Bearings, Inc. subs. Bearings, Inc., Augusta, Ga., 1967-72, dist. sec., 1972-81, exec. sec. to regional mgr., pers. coord. regional office, 1981-90, Atlanta, 1990-94; owner Funtime Enterprises dba Columbia County Net, Appling, Ga., 1992—; spl. edn. para-profl. Columbia County (Ba.) Bd. Edn., 2002—. Substitute tchr. Columbia County schs., 2001—02; adj. prof. La Salle U., 1995—. Mem. Order Eastern Star, Page (profession assn. of GA Educators); NASE (Nat. Assn. of self-employed). Republican. Baptist. Avocations: music, reading, aerobics, cooking, computers. Home and Office: 2960 Old Thomson Rd Appling GA 30802-1901 E-mail: nasone@comcast.net.

JONES, NATHANIEL RAPHAEL, retired federal judge; b. Youngstown, Ohio, May 13, 1926; s. Nathaniel B. and Lillian (Rafe) J.; m. Lillian Graham, Mar. 22, 1974; children: Stephanie Joyce, Pamela Haleystepchildren: William Hawthorne, Rickey Hawthorne, Marc Hawthorne. AB, Youngstown State U., 1951, LL.B., 1955, LL.D. (hon.) (hon.), 1969, Syracuse U., 1972. Editor Buckeye Rev. newspaper, 1956; exec. dir. FEPC, Youngstown, 1956—59; practiced law, 1959—61; mem. firm Goldberg & Jones, 1968—69; asst. U.S. atty., 1961—67; asst. gen. counsel Nat. Adv. Commn. on Civil Disorders, 1967—68; gen. counsel NAACP, 1969—79; judge U.S. Ct. of Appeals, 6th Circuit, 1979—2002, sr. judge, 1995—2002; sr. ptnr. Blank Rome Comisky & McCauley LLP, Cin., 2002—. Adj. prof. U. Cin. Coll. Law, 1983—; trial observer, South Africa, 1985; dir. Buckeye Rev. Pub. Co.; chmn. Con. on Adequate Def. and Incentives in Mil.; mem. Task Force-Vets. Benefits; lectr. South African Judges seminar, Johannesburg, Co-chmn. Cin. Roundtable, Underground R.R. Freedom Ctr.; observer Soviet Union Behalf com. on Soviet Jewry. With USAF, 1945—47. Mem.: FBA, ABA (co-chmn. com. constl. rights criminal sect. 1971—73, chmn. Africa coun., chmn. jud. clerkship initiative 1999—2000, chmn. spl. advisor coun. on racial and ethnic justice 1994—97), Cin. Bar Assn., Nat. Conf. Black Lawyers, Urban League, Am. Arbitration Assn., Nat. Bar Assn., Mahoning County Bar Assn., Ohio State Bar Assn., Houston Law Club (Youngstown), Elks, Kappa Alpha Psi. Baptist. Office: Blank Rome LLP 201 E 5th St Ste 1700 Cincinnati OH 45202 E-mail: Jones-n@blankrome.com.*

JONES, NEIL FORD, surgeon, educator; b. Merthyr Tydvil, Wales, Nov. 30, 1947; s. John Robert and Kathleen Mary (Ford) J.; m. Barbara Rose Unterman, Feb. 18, 1978; 1 child, Nicholas Huw. MBBS, MA, Oxford (Eng.) U., 1975. Registrar N.E. Thames Regional Plastic Surgery Centre, Billericay, Eng., 1982; fellow in hand surgery and microsurgery Mass. Gen. Hosp. Harvard U., Boston, 1983; asst. prof. surgery U. Pitts., 1984-89, assoc. prof. surgery, 1989-93, dir. hand and microsurgery, 1987-93; prof., chief hand surgery UCLA Sch. Medicine, 1993—, prof. orthop. surgery, prof. plastic and reconstructive surgery. Contbr. articles to profl. jours. Fellow ACS, Royal Coll. Surgeons Eng.; mem. Am. Assn. Plastic Surgeons, Am. Soc. Surgery of Hand (mem. coun. 2000—), Am. Soc. Reconstructive Microsurgery (sec. 1999-2001), Internat. Soc. Reconstructive Microsurgery. Avocation: travel. Home: 524 N Bonhill Rd Los Angeles CA 90049-2326 Office: 200 UCLA Medical Plz # 140 Los Angeles CA 90095-8344 E-mail: njones@mednet.ucla.edu.

JONES, OLIVER HASTINGS, consulting economist; b. Altoona, Pa., Dec. 9, 1922; s. Oliver Hastings and Mary (Herman) J.; m. Margaret Ann Vogel, July 4, 1942; children: Thomas, William, David, Robert, Richard. BA, St. Francis Coll., Loretto, Pa., 1948; MA, Pa. State U., 1949, PhD, 1961. Analyst, divsn. bank ops., bd. govs. Fed. Res. System, 1951-55; sr. economist, rsch. dept. Fed. Res. Bank, Cleve., 1955-59; assoc. rsch. economist, real estate rsch. program Grad. Sch. Bus. Adminstrn., U. Calif., L.A., 1959-61; economist Stanford Rsch. Inst., 1961-62; dir. rsch. Mortgage Bankers Assn. Am., 1962—68, exec. v.p., 1968—77; cons. economist Oliver Jones & Assocs., 1977—. Professorial lectr. Am. U., 1967— Author: (with Leo Grebler) The Secondary Mortgage Market, 1961, Financial Futures Market, 1983. Served with AUS, 1942-45. Mem. Am. Statis. Assn., Am. Econ. Assn., Am. Finance Assn., Nat. Assn. Bus. Economists, Conf. Bus. Economists, Lambda Alpha. (internat. pres. 1976-77) Clubs: Cosmos (Washington), Metropolitan (Washington). Home: 67 Greenfield Dr Carlisle PA 17013-7682

JONES, OSCAR CALVIN, minister, dean; b. San Antonio, Sept. 1, 1932; s. Oscar Sr. and Nonnie Lee (Cunningham) Jones Simpson; m. Peggy Ann Helm, June 12, 1977; children: Dennis Ray, Shawntelle Janora. BTh, Am. Sch. Divinity, 1968, ThM, 1971; PhD, Trinity Theol. Sem., 1981, DMin, 1982, postgrad., 1982—. Ordained to ministry Am. Bapt. Chs., 1957. Pastor, counselor St. John Bapt. Ch., Long Beach, Calif., 1965-69; exec. dir. M.A.T.E., Inc., L.A., 1969-71; area rep. ABC, N.Y.C., 1971-83; pastor, counselor Shiloh Bapt. Ch., Sacramento, 1983-85; pres. Guardalupe Coll., San Antonio, 1995-97; dean Am. Internat. Theol. Inst. & Sem., San Antonio, 1996—, acad. dean, 1998—; pastor Corinthian Bapt. Ch., Fairbanks, Ak., 1998; interim pastor New Union Missionary Bapt. ch., San Antonio, 1999, Martin Luther King Jr. Meml. Bapt. Ch., Renton, Wash., 2000—01; ret., 1995. Prof. Calif. State U., Sacramento, 1985; instr. golden age srs. Greater Corinth Bapt. Ch., San Antonio; we. rep. M&M benefit bd. Am. Bapt. Chs. U.S.A., N.Y.C., 1985-95; mem. supr. com. Am. Bapt. Credit Union, 1986-95; mem. We. Commn. on Ministry, Oakland, 1986-94. Author: The Preacher's Dilemma, 1978, The 10 Crowns of the Bible, 1974, The Psychological View-Point on Counseling The Black American, 1982, Motifs for Ministry, The Call to the Ministry. Mem. exec. com. Am. Bapt. Black Chs., Valley Forge, Pa., 1969-84; mem. exec. bd. Inter-Faith Svc. Bur., Sacramento, 1983-84; trustee Am. Bapt. Sem. West, Oakland, Calif., 1985—, Am. Bapt. Homes of West, pastoral clin. edn., fellow, 1982-84. Mem. Alpha Phi Alpha. Democrat. Office: New Union Missionary Bapt Ch 818 N Mittman San Antonio TX 78202-1507

JONES, OWEN DONALD, law educator; b. Glen Ridge, N.J., May 29, 1963; s. Donald Irvine and Margaret Rosalind Jones; m. Lydia Alyce Clougherty, Dec. 8, 1996. BA, Amherst Coll., 1985; JD, Yale U., 1991. Bar: Pa. 1991, D.C. 1992. Jud. clerk to. Judge Thomas Penfield Jackson U.S. Dist. Ct. D.C., 1991—92; assoc. Covington & Burling, Washington, 1992—94; assoc. prof. law Ariz. State U., Tempe, 1994—98, prof. law, 1998—, prof. biology, 2002—. Editor-in-chief Jurimetrics: The Jour. of Law, Sci. and Tech., 1997-98. Mem. Soc. Evolutionary Analysis in Law (pres. 1998—). Avocations: skiing, scuba, whitewater kayaking. Office: Ariz State U Coll Law Tempe AZ 85287

JONES, PATRICIA BENGTSON, sculptor; b. Janesville, Wis., Aug. 5, 1932; d. Clarence Edward and Phyllis Ann (Eau Clair) Bengtson; m. Robert S. Jones, July 3, 1953 (div. Aug. 1986); children: Pamela Ann Eau Clair, Diane Marie. AA, DeAnza Jr. Coll., Cupertino, Calif., 1974; BA in Painting, San Jose State U., 1977, MA in Sculpture, 1983. Cmty. colls. instr. credential, Calif. Exhibit curator Yucca Gallery, Albuquerque, 1964-67. Curator N.Mex. Art League, Albuquerque, 1966-67, Peninsula Art Assn., San Mateo, Calif., 1969; co-chmn. fine arts San Mateo Fair, 1969; chmn. fine arts San Mateo County Fair, 1970; asst. installor De Young Mus., San Francisco, 1976; restorer Santa Clara Artist's Foundry, 1981-84; marble cons. Leitch & Co., San Francisco,, 1984-86; instr. Studio Carlos Nicoli, Carrara, Italy, 1995; cutlery cons. R.H. Macy's, San Leandro, Calif., 1986-97; restoration cons., subcontractor, workshops, 1985—; sculpture, 1985-2003; mentor John F. Kennedy U., Berkeley, Calif., 1989—. Group exhbns. at New Leaf Garden Gallery, Calif., 1992-2003, The Art Foundry Gallery, 1999, Heritage Mus., Seattle, 1998, Claudia Chapline Gallery, Stinton Beach, Calif., 1998-2003, Contract Design Ctr., San Francisco, 1996-2003, Triton Mus. of Art, Santa Clara, Calif., 1967-94; group exhbns. include N.Mex. Art Mus., Santa Fe, 1965-66, Frye Art Mus., Seattle, 1987, Bedford Gall., Walnut Creek, CA, 1991, Spectrum Gallery, San Francisco, 1991, Downey (Calif.) Mus. Art, 1990-92, Sho-en Sculpture and Gallery, Ramona, 1992-94, Contract Design Ctr. for San Francisco, 1993, N.Am., The Foothill Art Ctr., Colden, Colo., 1985-91-94, One Bush Gallery, San Francisco, 1994, Oakland (Calif.) Mus., 1994. Bd. dirs. YWCA, Beloit, Wis., 1956-60; various positions Gen. Fedn. Women's Clubs, Wis., 1956-60; vol. fund drives Mental Health Drive Wis., Beloit, 1956-60; room mother Campfire Girls, Albuquerque, 1961-62. Recipient John Cavanaugh Meml. award N.Am. Sculpture Exhbn., Golden, Colo., 1985. Mem. Internat. Sculptors Assn., Pacific Rim Sculptors Group (founder), Nordic Fine Arts Group (chmn. & curator, 2003), Fine Arts Mus. San Francisco, Sculptors Guild San Jose, World Affairs Coun., San Francisco Mus. Modern Art, Sierra Club, Commonwealth Club Calif. Democrat. Studio: 2019 2d St Berkeley CA 94710

JONES, PATRICIA LOUISE, elementary counselor; b. Moorhead, Minn., Aug. 20, 1942; d. Harry Wilfred and Myrtle Louise Rosenfeldt; m. Edward L. Marks (div.); m. Curtis C. Jones, July 16, 1973; children: Michon, Andrea, Nathan, Kirsten, Leah. BS, Moorhead State U., 1965; MS, Mankato State U., 1990. Cert. K-12 sch. counselor, Minn. Tchr. Anoka (Minn.) Hennepin Schs., 1966-68; pvt. practice Youth Ctr., Truman, Minn., 1969-72; bookkeeper Fairmont (Minn.) Glass & Sign, 1973, Truman Farmers Elevator, 1973-87; libr. Martin County Libr., Truman, 1988-89; sch. counselor St. James (Minn.) Schs., 1989—. Coord. Internat. Fun Fest, St. James, 1992, 96; originator, advisor Armstrong After Sch. Hispanic Club, St. James, 1991-2001. Coord. Truman Days Parade, 1991, 92, 94-2000; mem. adv. bd. Watonwan County Big Buddy Program, 1993—; mem. Watonwan County Corrections Adv. Bd., 1998-2002; foster parent, 1999. Mem. ACA, Am. Sch. Counselors Assn., Minn. Sch. Counselors Assn. (bd. dirs. 1997-99), S.W. Minn. Counselors Assn. (Elem. Counselor of Yr. 1993, pres. 1997-99). Avocations: genealogy, walking, photography. Office: Saint James Sch Dist 500 8th Ave S Saint James MN 56081 E-mail: pjones@stjames.k12.mn.us.

JONES, PAUL LAWRENCE, lawyer; b. Snow Hill, N.C., Mar. 15, 1948; s. LeRoy and Esther Belle (Harper) J.; m. Asonia Lynette Battle, June 14, 1980; 1 child, Krystle Paulette. B.S., N.C. Agrl. and Tech. State U., 1971; J.D., N.C. Central U., 1974. Bar: N.C. 1975, D.C. 1976, U.S. Tax Ct. 1976, U.S. Ct. Mil. Appeals 1976, U.S. Ct. Claims 1976, U.S. Dist. Ct. (ea. dist.) N.C. 1979, U.S. Supreme Ct. 1982. Atty., asst. clk. U.S. Supreme Ct., Washington, 1974-76; assoc. firm Beech & Pollock, Kinston, N.C., 1979-80, mng. atty. Eastern Carolina Legal Services, Wilson, N.C., 1980-82; ptnr. firm Beech & Jones, Kinston, 1982-88. Mem. N.C. State Banking Commn., Raleigh, 1983; treas. Lenoir County Dem. Com., Kinston, 1983-86; bd. dirs. Lenoir Meml. Hosp.; mem. Lenoir Ind. Devel. Commn. Maj. USAR. Paul Harris fellow. Mem. ABA, N.C. Bar Assn., Assn. Trial Lawyers Am., N.C. Acad. Trial Lawyers, Lenoir County Bar Assn. (pres. 1983), Lenoir County C. of C. (bd. dirs. 1983), Phi Alpha Delta, Kappa Alpha Psi. Mem. Methodist Episcopal Zion Ch. Lodges: Rotary, Masons, Shriners. Home: 1102 N Queen St Kinston NC 28501-3948 Office: 1102 N Queen St Kinston NC 28501-3948

JONES, PETER ANTHONY, medical research administrator; b. Cape Town, South Africa, Jan. 21, 1947; naturalized citizen U.S. married; 3 children. BSc with 1st class honors, U. Coll. Rhodesia, 1969; PhD, U. London, 1973. NIH tng. fellow divsn. hematology-oncology Children's Hosp. of L.A., 1973-75; dir. basic rsch. and dir. Urol. Cancer Lab. U. So. Calif., L.A., 1984-93, assoc. dean for acad. and sci. affairs Sch. Medicine, 1991-94, interim chmn. dept. molecular microbiology and immunology, dir. Comprehensive Cancer Ctr., 1993—. Mem. integration panel breast cancer program U.S. Army Med. Rsch. and Devel. Command to date; mem. cancer5 ctr. support rev. com. Nat. Cancer Inst., 1988-92; mem. Bladder Cancer Working Group of the Organ Sys. Program, 1986-89; mem. cellular biology and physiology study sect. NIH, 1984-87, mem. chem. pathology, spl. study sect., 1985, ad hoc mem. cellular physiology rev. group, 1983, ad hoc mem. pathology B study sect., 1981, mem. spl. study sect. tumor promoters, 1982. Assoc. editor Cancer Rsch., 1983—, Molecular Carcinogenesis, 1987—, Carcinogenesis, 1990-93, Invasion and Metastasis, 1982—. Cancer Assn. Rhodesia Jr. Rsch. fellow, 1969-70, U. Rhodesia Postgrad. fellow, 1971; rsch. grantee Am. Cancer Soc., 1977-78, 78-79, 79-82, Nat. Cancer Assn. South Africa, Nat. Inst. Gen. Med. Scis., 1982-85, Nat. Cancer Inst., 1978-89, 82-89, 89—. Mem. AAAS, Am. Soc. Biochemistry and Molecular Biology, Am. Assn. for Cancer Rsch. (pubs. com., bd. dirs. 1989-92, program com. 1988, chmn. biology sect. 1989, chmn. local arrangements com. ann. meeting 1986), Am. Urol. Assn. (affiliate), DNA Methylation Soc., Soc. for Basic Urol. Rsch. Achievements include research in DNA methylation and cell differentiation; molecular biology of cancer. Office: Norris Comprehen Cancer Ctr 1441 Eastlake Ave Los Angeles CA 90089-9181

JONES, PETER D'ALROY, historian, writer, retired educator; b. Hull, Eng., June 9, 1931; arrived in U.S., 1959, naturalized, 1968; s. Alfred and Madge (Rutter) d'Alroy; m. Johanna Maria Hartinger, Feb. 20, 1987; 1 child, Heather Marie; children from previous marriage: Kathryn Beauchamp Fly Ebert, Barbara Collier Rosenberg. BA, Manchester (Eng.) U., 1952, MA, 1953; PhD, London U. Sch. Econ., 1963; postgrad., U. Brussels, Belguim, 1954. Freelance editor, London, 1953-56; lectr. U.S. history dept. Am. studies Manchester U., 1957-58; vis. asst. prof. econs. Tulane U., 1959-60; from asst. to full prof. Smith Coll., 1960-68; Kennan prof. Am. instns. and values Trinity Coll., Hartford, 1980-81; prof. history U. Ill., Chgo., 1968-98, prof. emeritus, 1998—. Vis. prof. Columbia U., U. Mass., U. Hawaii, U. Warsaw, Poland, U. Düsseldorf, Fed. Republic Germany, U. Salzburg, Austria; mem. com. examiners Grad. Record Exams. Ednl. Testing Svc., Princeton, N.J., 1966-70; mem. Am. studies com. Am. Coun. Learned Socs., 1973-75; lectr. U.S. Dept. State, 1973-87; adv. to publs. Author: Economic History of U.S.A. Since 1783, 1956, 2nd edit., 1965, The Story of the Saw, 1961, America's Wealth, 1963, The Consumer Society, 2d edit., 1967, The Christian Socialist Revival, 1968, The Robber Barons Revisited, 1968, Robert Hunter's Poverty: Social Conscience in the Progressive Era, 1965, La Sociedad Consumidora, 1968, Since Columbus: Poverty and Pluralism in the History of the Americas, 1975, The U.S.A.: A History of Its People and Society, 2 vols., 1976, Henry George and British Socialism, 1991; co-editor: Biographical Dictionary of American Mayors, 1820-1980, 1981, Ethnic Chicago, 1981, rev. and enlarged edit., 1984, 4th edit., 1995; contbr. several entries to Ency. World Biography, 1988, 94; contbr. numerous articles and book revs to profl. jours., popular newspapers. R.W. Emerson prize com Phi Beta Kappa, 1991—94. With RAF, 1956—57. Mem. London Sch. Econs. Soc. (life). E-mail: verdi1901@aol.com.

JONES, PHILIP HOWARD, broadcast journalist; b. Marion, Ind., Apr. 27, 1937; s. Thomas Howard and Charline (Shugart) J.; m. Paricia Ann Powell, June 4, 1961; children: Pamela Lynn, Paul Howard. BS in Arts and Scis., Ind. U., 1959. Dir. news Sta. WTHI-TV, Terre Haute, Ind., 1960-61; polit. corr. Sta. WCCO-TV, Mpls., 1961-69; White House corr. CBS News, Washington, 1974-76, Capitol Hill corr., 1977-89, nat. corr., 1989-90; corr. 48Hrs. Broadcast, 1990-95; Washington corr. CBS News, 1995—2001, Washington polit. corr., 1996—2001; ret., 2001. With USAF, 1961-62. Recipient Internat. News award Radio-TV News Dirs. Assn., 1965, award for Vietnam war reporting, 1966, Emmy award for CBS Indochina air war coverage NATAS, 1971, (6) Emmy awards CBS News 48 Hours Broadcast Coverage, 1992. Mem. Masons. Home: 5105 Westport Rd Chevy Chase MD 20815-3713 E-mail: phil.jones@verizion.net.

JONES, PHILIP KIRKPATRICK, JR., lawyer; b. Baton Rouge, June 26, 1949; s. Philip Kirkpatrick and Mary Jane (Kincade) J.; m. Serena Catherine Cockayne, Apr. 5, 1980; children: Veronica Cockayne, Nicola Kincade, Clare Kirkpatrick, Philip Carruth Elliot. BA in Govt., Dartmouth Coll., 1971; JD, La. State U., 1974; LLB, diploma in legal studies, Cambridge (U.K.) U., 1976. Bar: La. 1974, U.S. Dist. Ct. (ea. and we. dist.) La. 1980, U.S. Ct. Appeals (5th and 11th cirs.) 1981, U.S. Dist. Ct. (mid. dist.) La. 1987, U.S. Supreme Ct. 1992. Law clk. to John A. Dixon Jr. Supreme Ct. La., New Orleans, 1974-75; staff atty. Presdl. Clemency Bd., Washington, 1975; lectr. U. Singapore, 1977-79; from assoc. to ptnr. Liskow & Lewis, New Orleans, 1980—. 1st lt. USAF, 1975. Republican. Presbyterian. Office: Liskow & Lewis PC 50th Fl One Shell Square New Orleans LA 70139 E-mail: pkjones@liskow.com.

JONES, PHILIP NEWTON, physician, medical educator; b. Billings, Mont., May 27, 1924; s. Robert Newton and Edith (Woodbury) J.; m. Rebecca Ann Means, June 13, 1948; children: Robert Newton II, Rebecca Ann, Margaret Jane. Student, Stanford, 1942-43, U. Wis., 1944; MD, Washington U., St. Louis, 1948. Diplomate Am. Bd. Internal Medicine. Intern St. Luke's Hosp., Chgo., 1948-49, resident in internal medicine, 1949-51; rssch. fellow internal medicine Northwestern U., Chgo., 1953, clin. asst. medicine, 1954-57; practice medicine, specializing in internal medicine and hepatology Chgo., 1954-94; clin. asst. medicine U. Ill., Chgo., 1957-58, from clin. instr. to clin. assoc. prof. medicine, 1958-71; assoc. prof. medicine Rush Coll. Medicine Chgo., 1971-75, prof. medicine, 1975-94, prof. emeritus, 1994—. Sr. attending physician Presbyn.-St. Luke's Hosp., Chgo., 1954-94, treas. med. staff, 1960-62, mem. exec. com., med. staff, 1960-62, 72-77, sec. med. staff, 1972-73, pres. med. staff, 1973-75; mem. exec. bd. Rush-Presbyn.-St. Luke's Med. Ctr., Chgo., 1973-75, trustee, 1973-77. Contbr. articles to books and profl. jours. Mem. bd. edn., Kenilworth, Ill., 1962-68, pres., 1965; mem. Welfare Council Met., Chgo., 1965-66; bd. dirs. Presbyn. Home, Evanston, Ill., 1978-88, 93—. Served with AUS, 1943-46, to capt. USAF, 1951-53. Fellow Am. Coll. Physicians, Inst. Medicine Chgo.; mem. Am. Assn. Study Liver Disease, Chgo. Soc. Internal Medicine, Am. Fedn. Clin. Research, AMA, Ill. Med. Assn., Chgo. Med. Soc., Nu Sigma Nu. Republican. Congregationalist (pres. bd. trustees). Clubs: Comml. (Chgo.); Indian Hill. Home: 868 Pembridge Dr Lake Forest IL 60045-4200

JONES, PHYLLIS EDITH, nursing educator; b. Barrie, Ont., Can., Sept. 16, 1924; d. Colston Graham and Edith Luella (Shand) J. BScN, U. Toronto, 1950, MSc, 1969; DNSc (hon.), U. Turku, Finland, 1993. With Victorian Order Nurses, Toronto, 1950-53, asst. dir., 1959-63; supr. Vancouver Dept. Health, 1953-58; prof. nursing U. Toronto, 1963-89, dean Faculty Nursing, 1979-88, prof. emeritus, 1989—. Cons. WHO, 1985, 86 Contbr. articles to profl. jours. Can. Nurses Found. fellow, 1967-69; recipient grants Nat. Health Research and Devel.; recipient grants Ont. Ministry Health. Fellow Am. Public Health Assn.; mem. Coll. Nurses Ont., Registered Nurses Assn. Ont., Can. Public Health Assn., Can. Soc. Study Higher Edn., N.Am. Nursing Diagnosis Assn. (charter), ProNursing Finland (hon.). Home: RR 2 Owen Sound ON Canada N4K 5N4

JONES, PHYLLIS GENE, judge; b. Fargo, N.D., May 29, 1923; d. Joseph C. and Rosina Belle (Pinkham) Bambusch; m. Dwight Bangs Jones, May 29, 1945 (dec.); children: Stephanie Martineau, Jacqueline Ridge, Kent Carroll; m. David D. Norman, Oct. 9, 1970 (dec.). BA, Macalester Coll., 1944; JD, William Mitchell Coll. Law, 1960. Bar: Minn. 1960. Wirephoto operator AP, St. Paul, 1943-45; reporter St. Paul Pioneer Press, 1945-46; asst. county atty. Ramsey County, St. Paul, 1960-71; gen. counsel Minn. Urban County Attys. Bd./Minn. County Attys. Coun., St. Paul, 1971-75; pvt. practice St. Paul, Cottage Grove, Minn., 1975-84; judge Minn. Dist Ct. 10th Jud. Dist., Anoka, 1984-93. Mem. Minn. Adv. Coun. to State Investment Bd., 1983-84; mem. Washington County Pers. Com., Stillwater, Minn., 1982-84. Supr., Grey Cloud Town Bd., Minn., 1971-75. Mem. ABA, Minn. State Bar Assn. (chmn. victimless crimes com. 1974-75, co-chair sr. lawyers com. 1997-99), Ramsey County Bar Assn. (exec. com. 1982-83), Washington County Hist. Soc. (dir. 2000—). Achievements include distinction of being the first full-time female prosecutor in Minnesota.

JONES, PIRKLE, photographer, educator; b. Shreveport, La., Jan. 2, 1914; s. Alfred Charles and Wilie (Tilton) J.; m. Ruth-Marion Baruch, Jan. 15, 1949 (dec. Oct. 1997). Grad., Calif. Sch. Fine Arts, 1949; PhD in Fine Arts (hon.), San Francisco Art Inst, 2003. Profl. free-lance photographer, 1949—; asst. to Ansel Adams, 1949—53; faculty Calif. Sch. Fine Arts, 1953-58, San Francisco Art Inst., 1971-97. Tchr. Ansel Adams Workshops, Yosemite.; Mem. Archtl. Adv. Com., Mill Valley, Calif., 1963-67 Exhibited in leading art mus.; photographic archive established Spl. Collections Libr., U. Calif., Santa Cruz; author: Portfolio One, 1955, (with Dorothea Lange) Death of a Valley, 1960, Portfolio Two, 1968; (with Ruth-Marion Baruch) Black Panthers, 1968, 2d edit., 2002, The Vanguard, A Photographic Essay on the Black Panthers, 1970; author: Berryessa Valley, The Last Year, 1995, Pirkle Jones California Photographs, 2001. Nat. Endowment for Arts photography fellow, 1977; recipient award of honor for exceptional achievement in field of photography Arts Commn. of City and County of San Francisco, 1983 Home: 663 Lovell Ave Mill Valley CA 94941-1086 E-mail: pirkle@earthlink.net.

JONES, PRISCILLA LEE, community health nurse, counselor; b. Ft. Ord, Calif., Jan. 7, 1950; d. Mary Elizabeth (Clark) Jones; children: Jacob D. Sipple, Edward F. Strickler III. AA in Psychology, U. Del., 1985; ADN, Del. Tech. and Community Coll., 1985; BS in Behavioral Sci., Wilmington Coll., 1987. RN, Del. Nurse emergency dept. St. Francis Hosp., Wilmington, 1986; psychiat. charge nurse Meadowwood Adolescent Hosp., New Castle, Del., 1990-91; nurse emergency dept. Beebe Med. Ctr., Lewes, Del., 1991-92; pvt. practice Millsboro, Del., 1992-96; family practice nurse Beebe Med. Ctr., Lewes, Del., 1992-96, infectious disease nurse, 1996—97; clin. nurse mgr. cmty./migrant health Delmana Rural Ministries, Dover, Del., 1998-99, health planning specialist, 1999-2000, dir. nursing, 2000; provider rels. coord. Compassionate Care Hospice, Wilmington, Del., 2001—. Mem. legis. com. Del. Bd. Nursing. Author: A Christmas Poem, 1990. Campaign scheduler M. Jane Brady Del. Atty. Gen., 1994. Mem. ANA, Clin. Regional Adv. Network, Del. Nurses Assn., Mayflower Soc., Clin. Regional Adv. Network, DAR. Republican. Avocations: writing poetry, photography, listening to music, reading, politics. Office: Compassionate Care Hospice 5610 Kirkwood Hwy Wilmington DE 19808 E-mail: priscilla.jones@mchsi.com.

JONES, QUINCY, producer, composer, arranger, conductor, trumpeter; b. Chgo., Mar. 14, 1933; s. Quincy Delight and Sarah J.; children: Kidada, Rashida, Jolie, Martina-Lisa, Quincy III, Rachelle, Kenya. Student, Seattle U., Berklee Coll. Music; pvt. study with, Nadia Boulanger; student, Boston Conservatory; hon. degree, Berklee Coll. Music, 1983, Howard U., 1985, Seattle U., 1990, Wesleyan U., 1991, Loyola U., 1992, Brandeis U., 1992, Clark U., 1993. Trumpeter, arranger Lionel Hampton Orch., 1950-53; arranger for orchs., singers including Frank Sinatra, Dinah Washington, Count Basie, Sarah Vaughan, Peggy Lee, USA For Africa; organizer, trumpeter Dizzy Gillespie Orch. for Dept. of State tour of Near East, Mid. East, S.Am., 1956; music dir. Barchlay Disques, Paris; leader own orch. European tour, concerts, TV, radio, 1960; music dir., Mercury Records, 1961, v.p., 1964; composer: background scores The Boy in the Tree, 1964; condr. (film music) The Pawnbroker, Mirage, The Slender Thread, 1965, Walk Don't Run, Made in Paris, 1966, Banning (Acad. awd. nom. best song 1967), The Deadly Affair, Enter Laughing, In Cold Blood (Acad. awd. nom. best score 1967), In the Heat of the Night, 1967, For the Love of Ivy (Acad. awd. nom. best song 1968), The Split, Mirage, A Dandy in Aspic, The Hell with Heroes, Jigsaw, 1968, Bob and Carol and Ted and Alice, Cactus Flower, John and Mary, The Italian Job, The Lost Man, MacKenna's

Gold, 1969, Eggs, Of Men and Demons, The Out-Of-Towners, Up Your Teddy Bear, The Last of the Mobile Hotshots, They Call Me Mr. Tibbs, 1970, The Anderson Tapes, Brother John, Honky, $, 1971, Come Back Charleston Blue, The Hot Rock, 1972, The New Centurions, 1972, The Getaway, 1972, Mother, Jugs, and Speed, 1976, The Wiz, 1978, (also co-producer) The Color Purple (Acad. awd. noms., best picture, best song 1985), Fever Pitch, (exec. music producer) The Slugger's Wife, 1985, Listen Up: The Lives of Quincy Jones, 1990; composer, actor (film) Blues for Trumpet and Koto, Life Goes On; rec. artist numerous platinum albums including Body Heat, 1974, Mellow Madness, 1975, I Heard That, 1976, The Dude, 1981, Back on the Block, 1989, Snackwater Jack, 1991; producer videotape Portrait of An Album: Frank Sinatra with Quincy Jones and Orchestra, 1986 (platinum); producer recordings Michael Jackson's Off the Wall, 1980, Thriller, 1982 (world's best selling record), Bad; producer (with Steven Spielberg) The E.T. Storybook, (TV series) Fresh Prince of Bel Air, 1990—; composer (television) Hey Landlord, 1966-67, Ironside, 1967-75, The Bill Cosby Show, 1969-71, The New Bill Cosby Show, 1972-73, Sanford and Son, 1972-77, Sanford Arms, 1977, The Cosby Show, 1984-92, The Oprah Winfrey Show, 1989—; mini-series Roots (Emmy awd., best music composition, 1977), 1977; founder Vibe Magazine, 1992, exec. prodr. A Call for Reunion concert Lincoln Meml. for Clinton Inauguration, 1993. Recipient 76 Grammy nominations, 26 Grammy awards, numerous Readers Poll awards Downbeat Mag., Trendsetters awards Billboard Mag., Golden Note award ASCAP, 1982, Image award NAACP, 1974, 80, 81, 83, 90, 91, Hollywood Walk of Fame, 1980, Man of the Yr. award City of Hope, 1982, Whitney Young Jr. award Urban League, 1986, Humanitarian of Yr. award T.J. Martell Found., 1986, Lifetime Achievement award Nat. Acad. Songwriters, 1989, Grammy Living Legend award, 1990, Grammy award for Best Jazz instrumental, individual or group 1994 for "Miles and Quincy Live ath Montreux", Scopus award Hebrew U., 1991, Spirit of Liberty award People for the Am. Way, 1992; named Entrepreneur of the Yr. USA Today/Fin. News Network, 1991; film biography: Listen Up: The Lives of Quincy Jones, 1990. Office: Eliot Sekuler Publicist Rogers & Cowan 3800 Barham Blvd Ste 503 Los Angeles CA 90068-1042

JONES, RANDALL MARVIN, chemist; b. Beaver Falls, Pa., May 13, 1959; s. Edward Henry and Geraldine Barbara (Woodson) J. BS in Chemistry, Carnegie Mellon U., 1980. Cert. profl. chemist, 1998. Technician, student Johns Hopkins Sch. Medicine, Balt., 1980—82; chemist The Upjohn Co., Kalamazoo, 1982-88; teaching asst. Mich. State U., East Lansing, 1988-90; adj. chemistry instr. Duquesne U., Pitts., 1991-92; analytical chemist Carlisle (Pa.) SynTec Inc., 1992-94, sr. analytical chemist, 1994-2000; rsch. chemist Pharmacia Corp., Kalamazoo, 2000—. Recipient National Merit scholarship Armstrong Cork Co., 1976. Mem. Am. Inst. Chemists, Am. Chem. Soc. Office: Pharmacia Corp 7000 Portage Rd Kalamazoo MI 49001

JONES, RAYFORD SCOTT, surgeon, medical educator; b. Dallas, Aug. 24, 1936; MD, U. Tex., Galveston, 1961. Diplomate Am. Bd. Surgery. Intern U. Tex., 1961-62; resident U. Pa. Hosp., Phila., 1962-67; mem. staff Duke U. and VA Hosp., Durham, N.C.; then prof. surgery Duke U.; now prof. surgery U. Va., Charlottesville. Mem. Am. Surg. Assn., Am. Coll. Surgeons, Soc. Clin. Surgery, So. Surg. Assn., Soc. Univ. Surgeons. Office: U Va Hosps Dept Surgery Box 800709 Jefferson Park Ave Charlottesville VA 22908-0709

JONES, RAYMOND EDWARD, JR., brewing executive; b. New Bern, N.C., Jan. 27, 1927; s. Raymond Edward and Ellen LaVerne (Mallard) J.; children: Leslie Anne, Raymond Edward III. BS, U. Md., 1953; LL.B., U. Balt., 1962. Bar: Md. 1962. Office mgr. Hopkins Furniture Co., Annapolis, Md., 1953-55; sr. v.p. legal, sec. Nat. Brewing Co., Balt., 1956-75; (merged with Carling Brewing Co. 1975); sr. v.p. legal and indsl. relations, dir. Carling Nat. Breweries, Inc., 1975-78; sec., assoc. gen. counsel Miller Brewing Co., 1978-84, v.p., gen. counsel, sec., 1984-89. House counsel and/or officer Divex, Inc., Laco Products, Inc., Laco Corp., C.W. Abbott, Inc., Pompeian, Inc., Interhost Corp., Solarine Co., Balt. Baseball Club, Inc., 1967-75 Bd. dirs. Soc. Preservation Md. Antiquities, 1969-71. Served with USNR, 1942-45. Mem. ABA, Md. Bar Assn., Balt. Bar Assn., Sigma Chi, Sigma Delta Chi. Presbyterian. Home: 24848 Deepwater Point Dr Saint Michaels MD 21663-2324

JONES, RAYMOND MOYLAN, strategy and public policy educator; b. Phila., Dec. 28, 1942; s. Raymond and Elizabeth (Shaw) J.; m. Barbara Ann Donaghue, May 22, 1965; children: Andrea Marie, Audra Marie. BS, U.S. Mil. Acad., 1964; MBA, Harvard U., 1971; JD, U. Tex., 1973; PhD, U. Md., 1993. Bar: Tex. 1973, U.S. Supreme Ct. 1993. Commd. 2d lt. U.S. Army, 1964, advanced through grades to capt., 1966, ret., 1969; legal asst. to chmn. Occidental Petroleum Corp., L.A., 1973-75; pres. Oxy Metal Industries Internat., Geneva, 1975-77, Occidental Resource Recovery Corp., Irvine, Calif., 1978-81; v.p. Hooker Chem. Corp., Houston, 1977-78; pvt. practice cons. Austin and Irvine, 1981-86; lectr. Calif. State U., Long Beach, 1986, U. Md., College Park, 1986-90, Loyola Coll., Balt., 1990—. Cons. to multinational and domestic orgns. Author: Strategic Management in a Hostile Environment: Lessons from the Tobacco Industry, 1998; contbr. articles, book rev. to profl. publs. Mem. Friends of Austin Symphony Orch.; mem. Ludwig Von Mises Inst., Burlingame, Calif., 1987—, Intercoll. Studies Inst., Bryn Mawr, Pa., 1987—; mgmt. con. ARC, Balt., 1988—. Grantee U. Md. 1987, Loyola Coll. 1993. Mem. Am. Econ. Assn., Acad. Internat. Bus., Strategic Mgmt. Soc., Acad. Mgmt., State Bar Tex., Harvard Club. Roman Catholic. Home: 305 Kerneway Baltimore MD 21212-4714 Office: Loyola Coll Sellinger Sch Bus Mgmt Baltimore MD 21210-2699 E-mail: rjones@loyola.edu.

JONES, REBA (BECKI) PESTUN, elementary school educator, music educator; b. Logan, W.Va., Apr. 30, 1949; d. John Rohac and Carolyn Kelly Pestun; m. Edgar Roger Jones, Aug. 22, 1968; 1 child, Karaleah Sabina Reichart. MusB in Edn., W.Va. U., 1970; EdM in Music Edn., U. Md., 1986; DMA, Shenandoah U., 2003. Cert. postgrad. prof. in music edn. grades K-12 Va., 1986, tchr. Am. Orff Schulwerk Assn., 1986. Choir dir. Asbury United Meth. Ch., Charles Town, W.Va., 1976—86; music tchr. grades K-5 Columbia Elem. Sch. - Fairfax County Pub. Schs., Annandale, Va., 1986—2002; music tchr. grades K-6 Herndon (Va.) Elem. - Fairfax County Pub. Schs., 2002—. Musician (composer/educator): (creative musical unit) A Musical Physical Fitness Workout (Semi-Finalist for the Nat. Music Found., 2000), (creative music units for grades k-3) Rabbit on My Mind (Winner of Impact II Nat. Grant and Va. Commn. for the Arts Grant for Outstanding Achievement, 1999), (original musical for grades k-6) Coal Mining Musical (Impact II Nat. Award Winner, 2001), (original musical unit for grades k-3) Sea Turtle Rhapsody (Impact II Nat. Award Winner, 2002), (original music unit for grades k-6) A True Whale Story (Winner Outstanding Achievement from the Va. Commn. for the Arts, 1998), (original musical with appalachian songs) Journey From the Mountain to the Sky (Hon. Mention from Nat. Music Found., 1999), (original music teaching unit) Musical Manatees (Impact II Nat. Grant Award Winner, 2003), (musical teaching unit and performance) Forever Free (Wash. Post Grant in Edn. Winner, 1998). Mem.: Music Educator's Nat. Conf., Appalachian Studies Assn., Am. Orff Schulwerk Assn., Fairfax Gen. Music Educators Assn., Fairfax Edn. Assn. Office: Herndon Elem Sch 630 Dranesville Rd Herndon VA 20170 E-mail: becki.jones@fcps.edu.

JONES, REBECCA ALVINA PATRONIS, nurse; b. Quincy, Fla., Sept. 14, 1952; d. Eugene T. Patronis and Ada Lee (Allen) Poole; m. Robert Gerald Jones, Dec. 29, 1979; 1 child, Aislan Hlynn. BS in Nursing, U. Fla., 1974; MS in Nursing, U. S.C., 1988; D in Nursing Sci., Ind. U., Indpls., 1991. RN, Ill.; cert. in nursing adminstrn. advanced. Team leader, teaching staff nurse Shands Teaching Hosp., Gainesville, Fla., 1974—76; commd. 1st Lt. U.S. Army, 1976, advanced through grades to lt. col., 1985, various nursing positions, 1976—83, ret., 2001; cmty. health nurse Gorgas Army Hosp., Panama City, Panama, 1984—86; nursing rsch. asst. U. S.C., Columbia, 1986—87; asst. dir. nursing Kershaw County Meml. Hosp., Camden, SC, 1988—89; assoc. instr. Ind. U., Indpls., 1989—91; asst. prof., assoc. dir. nursing La Salle U., Albert Einstein Med. Ctr., Phila., 1991—94; dir., prof. Sch. Nursing and Health Scis., Tex. A&M U., Corpus Christi, 1994—2001; pres. West Surburban Coll. Nursing, Oak Park, Ill., 2001—. Clin. faculty assoc. U. Tex. Health Sci. Ctr. Sch. Nursing and Grad Sch. Biomed. Scis., 1996—2002; dep. dir. Coastal Bend Health Edn. Ctr. Tex A&M U. Sys. Health Sci. Ctr., 1999—2001. Contbr. articles to profl. jours. Mem.: Fedn. Ill. Ind. Colls. and Univs., Ill. Nurses Assn., Nat. Assn. Ind. Colls. and Univs., Am. Assn. Pres. of Ind. Colls. and Univs., Internat. Assn. Human Caring, Coun. on Grad. Edn. for Adminstrn. Nursing, Am. Assn. Colls. Nursing, Coun. Nurse Execs., Nat. League Nursing, Sigma Theta Tau Internat. Republican. Avocations: computers, reading, swimming. Office: West Suburban Coll Nursing 3 Erie Ct Oak Park IL 60302 Office Fax: 708-763-1531. E-mail: wsjonesra@wscn.edu., rebeccajo@palm.net.

JONES, RENEE KAUERAUF, health care administrator; b. Duncan, Okla., Nov. 3, 1949; d. Delbert Owen and Betty Jean (Marsh) Kauerauf; m. Dan Elkins Jones, Aug. 3, 1972. BS, Okla. State U., 1972, MS, 1975; PhD, Okla. U., 1989. Diplomate Am. Bd. Sleep Medicine. Statis. analyst Okla. State Dept. Mental Health, Okla. City, 1978-80, divisional chief, 1980-83, adminstr., 1983-84; assoc. dir. HCA Presbyn. Hosp., Oklahoma City, 1984-2000; mng. ptnr. Sleep Assocs., LLC, Oklahoma City, 2000—, Sleep REMedies, LLC, Okalhoma City, 2003—. Adj. instr. Okla. U. Health Sci. Ctr., 1979—; assoc. staff scientist Okla. Ctr. for Alcohol and Drug-Related Studies, Okla. City, 1979—; cons. in field. Assoc. editor Alcohol Tech. Reports jour., 1979-84; contbr. articles to profl. jours. Mem. assoc. bd. Hist. Preservation, Inc., treas. 1994. Mem. APHA, NAFE, Assn. Health Svcs. Rsch., Alcohol and Drug Problems Assn. N.Am., Am. Sleep Disorders Assn., N.Y. Acad. Scis., So. Sleep Soc. (sec.-treas. 1989-91), Phi Kappa Phi. Democrat. Methodist. Avocations: skiing, scuba diving, racewalking, bicycling, painting. Home: 401 NW 19th St Oklahoma City OK 73103-1911 Office: The Sleep Clinic 5530 N Francis Ave Oklahoma City OK 73118

JONES, RICHARD JEFFERY, internist, educator; b. Cleve., Apr. 6, 1918; s. Edward Safford and Frances Christine (Jeffery) J.; m. Helen Hart, Oct. 5, 1946; children: Christopher, Ruth, Jeffery, Catherine. AB, Oberlin Coll., 1938; MA, SUNY, Buffalo, 1942, MD, 1943. Diplomate Am. Bd. Internal Medicine. Intern U. Chgo. Hosps., 1944, resident in internal medicine, 1947-49; assoc. prof. medicine U. Chgo., 1958-76; assoc. prof. clin. medicine Northwestern U., Chgo., 1976-92, pvt. practice specializing in cardiology, 1976—92. Vis. assoc. prof. Rockefeller U., 1965. Author: Chemistry and Therapy of Chronic Cardiovascular Disease, 1961; mem. editl. bd. Nutrition Revs., 1964-72. Lt. USNR, 1944-46, PTO. Recipient Presdl. letter of commendation Pres. of U.S., 1946. Fellow Am. Heart Assn.; mem. AMA (dir. sci. activities 1976-83, coun. sec. 1976-83), Ctrl. Soc. Clin. Rsch., Soc. Exptl. Biol. and Medicine (editl. bd. 1964-74). Unitarian Universalist. Home: 5550 South Shore Drive Ste 1014 Chicago IL 60637-5058 E-mail: rjones@ais.net

JONES, RICHARD LAMAR, entomology educator; b. Charleston, Miss., May 31, 1939; s. Raymond Lee and Tyna Louise (Holland) J.; m. Anne Marchman, June 6, 1964; children: Katherine Mathis, Margaret Holland; m. Joan Marie Wood, Nov. 29, 1997. BS, Miss. State U., 1963, MS, 1965; PhD, U. Calif., Riverside, 1968. Rsch. entomologist Agrl. Rsch. Svc., USDA, Tifton, Ga., 1968-77; assoc. prof. entomology U. Minn., St. Paul, 1977-84, prof., head dept., 1984-91, dean Coll. Agr., 1991-95; dean of rsch., dir. Fla. Agrl. Expt. Sta. U. Fla., Gainesville, Fla., 1995—. Editor, author: Semiochemicals, 1974; also over 70 articles. With USN, 1958-60. Scholar NIH, 1965-68, Fulbright scholar, Leiden, The Netherlands, 1980. Mem. AAAS, Entomol. Soc. Am. (fin. com. 1989-96), Am. Chem. Soc. Avocations: golf, fishing. Office: U Fla PO Box 110200 Gainesville FL 32611-0200

JONES, RICHARD MELVIN, bank executive, former retail executive; b. Eldon, Mo., Nov. 26, 1926; m. Sylvia A. Richardson, 1950; 3 children. BSBA, Olivet Nazarene Coll., 1950, LLD (hon.), 1983; grad. advanced mgmt. program, Harvard U., 1973. With Sears, Roebuck & Co., 1950-89, store mgr., 1963-68, gen. mgr., 1974, exec. v.p.-East, 1974-80, corp. v.p., 1980, vice-chmn., CFO, 1980-85, pres., CFO, 1986-88; chmn., CEO Guaranty Fed. Savs. Bank, Dallas, 1989-91. Trustee Field Mus. Natural History, Northwestern Univ. Assocs., Chgo.; adv. coun. J.L. Kellogg Grad. Sch. Mgmt. Northwestern U.

JONES, RICHARD MICHAEL, lawyer; b. Chgo., Jan. 16, 1952; s. Richard Anthony and Shirley Mae (Wilhelm) J.; m. Catherine Leona Ford, May 25, 1974. BS, U. Ill., 1974; JD, Harvard U., 1977. Bar: Colo. 1977, U.S. Dist. Ct. Colo. 1977. Assoc. Davis, Graham & Stubbs, Denver, 1977-81; corp. counsel Tosco Corp., Denver, 1981-82; asst. gen. counsel Anschutz Corp., Denver, 1982-88, gen. counsel, v.p., 1989—. Mem. ABA, Colo. Bar Assn., Denver Bar Assn. Office: Anschutz Corp 555 17th St Ste 2400 Denver CO 80202-3987

JONES, RICHARD WALLACE, interior designer; b. Canandaigua, N.Y., Dec. 6, 1929; s. William Wallace and Maybelle Louise (Smith) J.; m. Patricia Hardwick, June 24, 1957 (div. 1973). Student, Hobart Coll., 1946-47; tchr.'s cert., Longy Sch., Cambridge, Mass., 1952; postgrad., Yale U. Sch. Music, 1952-53. Owner, operator Richard W. Jones studios, Boston, Hartford, Conn., 1954-63; designer, mgr. House of Good Taste Pavilion, N.Y. World's Fair, 1963-66; design editor Redbook Mag., N.Y.C., 1967-72; sr. design editor Better Homes & Gardens mag., Des Moines, 1972-76; pres., dir. Circanow Interior Design Firm, Des Moines, N.Y.C., 1974-90; designer, mgr. D.H. Hershel Inc., Nantucket, Mass., 1978-81; ptnr., designer, buyer Portobello, Nantucket, 1981-83; dir. design Laura Ashley Inc., Ridgewood, N.J., 1989-90; interior designer Godfrey & Assocs., Naples, Fla., 1994-97; prin. Richard W. Jones Designs, Naples, Fla., 1997—. Curator Hammond Mus., Gloucester, Mass., 1950-60, Hill-Stead Mus., Farmington, Conn., 1962; del. Internat. Fedn. Interior Designers, Amsterdam, The Netherlands, 1975-76. Editor in chief Interiors mag., Residential Interiors, 1976-78. Mem. Pres.' Com. on Barrier Free Design, Washington, 1972-74. Recipient Dorothy Dawe award Sr. Design Editor, 1974. Fellow Am. Soc. Interior Designers (nat. pres. 1976. Disting. Svc. medal 1977); mem. Nat. Soc. Interior Designers (nat. pres. 1972-74), Nantucket C. of C. (bd. dirs. 1980-82, sign approval com. 1982-84). Presbyterian. Avocations: collecting contemporary and african art, travel.

JONES, RICK H. arts administrator; b. Dayton, Ohio, Jan. 23, 1948; s. Huston Benjamin and Mildred Garnet J.; m. Christine Renee Elliott, Dec. 18, 1971; children: LeAnna, Brandt. BFA, Wright State U., 1970; MFA, Md. Inst. Coll. of Art, 1972. Exec. dir. Wayne Ctr. for the Arts, Wooster, Ohio, 1979-91, Fitton Ctr. for Creative Arts, Hamilton, Ohio, 1991—. Author: An Arts Center In Our Community: How Do We Begin, 1990, The Arts Center Handbook, 1997. Chmn. Vision 2020 Focus Gp., Hamilton, Ohio, 1999-2000, Hamilton Vision Commn., 2001—, Main Street Wooster, Wooster, Ohio, 1988-90, Design Commn., Wooster, Ohio, 1989-91; bd. mem. Regional Cultural Planning Com., Cin., 1997-99, Fairfield (Ohio) C. of C., Regional Cultural Alliance, Cin., 2000-01, Ohio Citizens for the Arts, 2000—; pres. Leadership Hamilton Alumni; co-chair S.E. Butler County Chamber Leadership. Recipient Ohio Governor's award for Arts Adminstrn., Ohio Arts Council, 1991. Mem. ASCD, Nat. Art Edn. Assn., Music Educators Nat. Conf., Ohio Art Edn. Assn. (Disting. Citizen award 1987), Ohio Mus. Assn., Ams. for the Arts, Ohio Cizitens for the Arts, Ohio Arts Presenters Network, Ohio Alliance Arts Edn., Rotary. Avocations: golf, reading, gardening, 5-string banjo, african art. Home: 405 Oakwood Dr Hamilton OH 45013-3466 E-mail: rick@fittoncenter.org.

JONES, RITA ANN, retired speech, theater educator; b. Tupelo, Miss., Sept. 9, 1947; d. Sammie Lee and Helen Juanita (Stone) J. AA, Itawamba Jr. Coll., 1967; BS, Miss. State U., 1969; MA, Miss. U. for Women, 1972. Tchr. Tremont (Miss.) High Sch., 1969-71, Winona (Miss.) Separate Sch. Dist., 1972-80, Holmes C.C., Goodman, Miss., 1980—2000; ret., 2000. Dir. Little Theatre, Fulton, Miss., 1977-80, 84; pres. Bus. and Profl. Women, Winona, 1977-78; active local Meth. Ch. Mem. Tchr.'s Assn. Republican. Avocations: reading, crafts, needlepoint. Home: PO Box 236 Fulton MS 38843-0236 Office: Holmes CC Hill St Goodman MS 39079

JONES, ROBERT ALFRED, retired clergyman; b. Buffalo, July 19, 1930; s. Ralph A. and Edna Mae (Carver) J.; m. Helen T. Webster, July 20, 1957; children: Marc E., Paul R., Nancy L. BA, Houghton Coll., 1953; MA, Alfred U., 1959. Ordained to ministry United Meth. Ch., 1959. Assoc. pastor University United Meth. Ch., Buffalo, 1959-63; campus min. SUNY, Buffalo, 1963-67; pastor Woodside United Meth. Ch., Buffalo, 1967-74; sr. pastor Baker Meml. United Meth. Ch., East Aurora, N.Y., 1974-80; supr. Rochester dist United Meth. Ch., 1980-86; sr. pastor Ctrl. Park United Meth. Ch., 1986-89; asst. to bishop N.Y. west area United Meth. Ch., Syracuse, 1989-91; sr. pastor Williamsville (N.Y.) United Meth. Ch., 1991—99. Home: 146 Farber Ln Williamsville NY 14221-5754

JONES, ROBERT ALONZO, economist; b. Evanston, Ill., Mar. 15, 1937; s. Robert Vernon and Elsie Pierce (Brown) J.; m. Ina Turner Jones; children: Lindsay Rae, Robert Pierce, Gregory Alan, William Kenneth. AB, Middlebury Coll., 1959, LLD, 1992; MBA, Northwestern U., 1961. Economist Hahn, Wise & Assocs., San Carlos, Calif., 1966-69; sr. rsch. officer Bank of Am., San Francisco, 1969-74; v.p., dir. fin. forecasting Chase Econometrics, San Francisco, 1974-76; chmn. bd. Money Market Svcs., Inc., Belmont, Calif., 1974-86, MMS Internat., Redwood City, Calif., 1986-89, chmn. emeritus, 1989-2000; chmn. bd. dirs. Market News Internat., N.Y.C.; chmn. emeritus Geonomics Inst., Middlebury, Vt., 1995—, chmn. bd., 1986-95, Jones Interant., 1990—, Digital Integrator, Inc., Incline Village, Nev., 1993—. Chmn. bd. Jones Fin. Network, Inc., Incline VIllage; dean coun. Harvard U. Div. Sch., Cambridge, Mass., 1991—; mem. Kellogg Alumni Adv. Bd., Northwestern U., 1993—; trustee Middlebury Coll., 1998—; instr. money and banking Am. Inst. Banking, San Francisco, 1971, 72. Author: U.S. Financial System and the Federal Reserve, 2974, Power of Coinage, 1987. Councilman, City of Belmont, Calif., 1970-77, mayor, 1971, 72, 75, 76; dir. San Mateo County Transit Dist., 1975-77; chmn. San Mateo County Coun. Mayors, 1975-76; trustee Incline Village Gen. Improvement Dist., 1984-85, Carlmont United Meth. Ch., 1978-81. 1st lt. USAR, 1961-68. Recipient Ernst & Young Entrepreneur of the Yr. award, 1986, Stanton Recognition award North Shore Country Day Sch., 1996; named Hon. life mem. Calif. PTA, ordo honorum Kappa Delta Rho Nat. Frat.; John Harvard fellow Harvard U., 1996. Mem. Nat. Assn. Bu. Economists, San Francisco Bond Club. Republican. Methodist. Office: Jones Internat Inc PO Box 7498 Incline Village NV 89452-7498 *The entrepreneurial spirit is distinguished by passion, creativity, and the fulfillment of mission through other people.*

JONES, ROBERT BRENT, electrical engineer; b. Provo, Utah, 1969; s. Brent M and Marybeth Reynolds Jones; m. Dina Newell Berke; m. Debra Lee Shelton (dec.); children: Mikayla Newell, Jack Newell, Adam Robert, Austin Brent. BS summa cum laude, in elec. engring., Brigham Young U., 1993; MS in elect. engring., PhD in elect. engring., Stanford U., 1999. Summer intern Lawrence Livermore Nat. Lab., Livermore, Calif., 1987—88, Intel Corp., Various, Oreg., 1991—95; rsch. staff Strategic CAD Labs, Intel Corp., Hillsboro, Oreg., 1995—2003, prin. engr., 2003—. Author: Symbolic Simulation Methods for Industrial Formal Verification; contbr. articles various profl. jours. Recipient Eagle Scout, Boy Scouts of Am., 1986; fellow Nat. Def. Sci., Engring. Grad. fellowship, Elec. Engring., US Gov., 1993-1997, NSF Grad. fellowship, Computer Engring. (funding declined), NSF, 1993. Mem.: IEEE, Assn. for Computing Machinery, Tau Beta Pi. Mem. Lds Ch. Achievements include patents for Applications of symbolic simulation in formal verification; patents pending for. Avocations: piano, photography. Office: Strategic CAD Labs Intel Corp 2111 NE 25th Ave JF4-211 Hillsboro OR 97123

JONES, ROBERT CLAIR, middle school educator; b. Norfolk, Va., Apr. 9, 1949; s. Leon Herbert and Barbara Dean (Jones) J.; m. Geri Lee Siebels, Feb. 13, 1977; children: Adam, Matthew, Aaron, Lee. BS, Old Dominion U., 1971, MS, 1981. Tchr. Virginia Beach (Va.) Jr. High Sch., 1971-73, Kempsville Jr. High Sch., Virginia Beach, 1973—. Adj. faculty Old Dominion U., Norfolk, Va., 1990—; co-chmn. faculty coun. Kempsville Mid. Sch., 1992-93, curriculum coord., grade level chair, 1993—; program devel. com. for mid. schs., Virginia Beach City Schs., 1990-91, chmn. social studies curriculum adv. com., 1990-91, instr. staff devel., 1989-91; speaker in field. Contbr. articles to profl. jours.; featured in Oasis mag. Baseball coach Pony Colt League, Virginia Beach, 1991-92; vol. Make A Wish Found., Virginia Beach, 1990-92. Named Tchr. of Yr., Va. Coun. Social Studies, 1987—. Mem. ASCD, NEA, Nat. Coun. Social Studies, Va. Edn. Assn., Va. Coun. Social Studies, Virginia Beach Edn. Assn. Avocations: profl. musician, collecting records, Beatles memorobilia. Home: 812 Yearling Ct Virginia Beach VA 23464-3214 Office: Kenpsville Mid Sch 260 Churchill Dr Virginia Beach VA 23456

JONES, ROBERT CLAUDE, editor; b. Troup, Tex., July 20, 1931; s. Paul David and Frances Marie (Hixon) Jones; m. Nancy Dale Torrance, June 6, 1953; children: Susan Louise, Christopher Michael, Amy Robin Weber Jones, Elizabeth Ann Hanley. JB, U. Tex., 1952, MJ, 1953, PhD in English, 1958. Instr. English U. Colo., Boulder, 1957—58; asst. prof. English William Jewell Coll., Liberty, Mo., 1958—61; prof. English Ctrl. Mo. State U., Warrensburg, Mo., 1961—91; ret., 1991; editor The Mid-Am. Press, Inc., Warrensburg, 1976—. Sr. Am. lectr. in Am. Lit. U. Timisoara, Romania, 1982—83, Aristotle U., Thessaloniki, Greece, 1986—87; pres. Mo. Assn. Tchrs. English, 1983—84. Editor: Living Off the Land, 1999, The Long Journey, 2001, The Mid-Am. Poetry Rev., 2000—. Avocations: reading, music, chess, writing, poetry. Home: 222 W Gay St Warrensburg MO 64093 Office: The Mid-Am Press Inc PO Box 575 222 W Gay Warrensburg MO 64093-0575

JONES, ROBERT EDWARD, federal judge; b. Portland, Oreg., July 5, 1927; s. Howard C. and Leita (Hendricks) J.; m. Pearl F. Jensen, May 29, 1948; children— Jeffrey Scott, Julie Lynn BA, U. Hawaii, 1949; JD, Lewis and Clark Coll., 1953, LHD (hon.), 1995; LLD (hon.), City U., Seattle, 1984. Bar: Oreg. Trial atty., Portland, Oreg., 1953-63; judge Oreg. Circuit Ct., Portland, 1963-83; justice Oreg. Supreme Ct., Salem, 1983-90; judge U.S. Dist. Ct. Oreg., Portland, 1990—. Mem. faculty Nat. Jud. Coll., Am. Acad. Jud. Edn., ABA Appellate Judges Seminars; former mem. Oreg. Evidence Revision Commn., Oreg. Ho. of Reps.; former chmn. Oreg. Commn. Prison Terms and Parole Stds.; adj. prof. Northwestern Sch. Law, Lewis and Clark Coll., 1963—, Willamette Law Sch., 1988-90. Author: Rutter Group Practice Guide Federal Civil Trials and Evidence, 1999—. Mem. bd. overseers Lewis and Clark Coll., mem. bd. visitors to Northwestern Sch. Law. Served to capt. JAGC, USNR. Recipient merit award Multnomah Bar Assn., 1979; Citizen award NCCJ, Legal Citizen of the Yr. award Law Related Edn. Project, 1988; Service to Mankind award Sertoma Club Oreg.; James Madison award Sigma Delta Chi; named Disting. Grad., Northwestern Sch. Law; Outstanding Profl. Achievement Alumnus award, U.S. Merchant Marine Acad., 1998; Judge Robert E. Jones Oreg. Justice award, Am. Judicature Soc., 1999. Mem. Am. Judicature Soc. (bd. dirs. 1997-2001), State Bar Oreg. (past chmn. Continuing Legal Edn.), Oregon Circuit Judges Assn. (pres. 1967-1968), Oreg. Trial Lawyers Assn. (pres. 1959, chair 9th cir. edn. com. 1996-97). Office: US Dist Ct House 1000 SW 3rd Ave Ste 1407 Portland OR 97204-2944 E-mail: robert_jones@ord.uscourts.gov.

JONES, ROBERT EMMET, French language educator, novelist; b. N.Y.C., Sept. 16, 1928; s. Robert Emmet and Lois Kathryn (UpdeGrove) J. AB, Columbia U., 1948, PhD, 1954; certificat de phonetique Sorbonne, Paris, 1949. Vis. instr. French Columbia U., 1953-54; asst. prof. French U. Ga., Athens, 1954-61, U. Pa., 1961-67; asso. prof. French and humanities M.I.T., 1967-71, prof. French and humanities, 1971-92, prof emeritus, 1992—; tchr. French cooking, 1976—. Author: The Alienated Hero in Modern French Drama, 1961, Panorama de la nouvelle critique en France, 1968, Gerard de Nerval, 1974, H.R. Lenormand, 1984, Botticelli's Face, 2002; contbr. articles to profl. jours. Mem. MLA, Am. Assn. Tchrs. French, French Library Boston. Clubs: St. Anthony, St. Botolph. Episcopalian. Home: 452 Beacon St Boston MA 02115-1001 E-mail: r.e.jones@comcast.net.

JONES, ROBERT GEAN, religion educator; b. Magnolia, Ark., Feb. 17, 1925; s. Emless Bunyan and Eunice (Gean) J.; m. Marian Laverne Alexander, July 23, 1946; 1 dau., Carolyn Ann. BA cum laude, Baylor U., 1947; B.D. cum laude, Yale, 1950, MA, 1957, PhD, 1959. Ordained to ministry Bapt. Ch., 1946; minister Deep River (Conn.) Bapt. Ch. and; First Bapt. Ch. of, Saybrook, 1950-59; asst. prof. religion George Washington U., Washington, 1959-61, asso. prof., 1961-64, prof., 1964-91, prof. emeritus, 1991—, chmn. dept. religion, 1963-79, univ. marshal, 1969-89. Adj. prof. U. Tenn., Chattanooga, 1991-93, Maryville Coll., 1993-95. Author: The Rules for the War of the Sons of Light With the Sons of Darkness, 1957, The Manual of Discipline (1QS), The Old Testament and Persian Religion, 1964. Mem. Soc. Bibl. Lit. and Exegesis, Am. Acad. Religion, Alpha Chi, Omicron Delta Kappa. Home: 307 Amohi Ln Loudon TN 37774-3013 E-mail: robgjones@aol.com.

JONES, ROBERT HENRY, automotive distribution executive; b. Willow Springs, N.C., Dec. 31, 1935; s. Kenneth Tomas and China Christiana (Blalock) J.; m. Margaret Ann Page; children: Julie Beth, Jeffrey Bert, Jay Brent. AA in Acctg., Kings Coll., 1960. Acct. Jones & Guerrero Co., Inc., Agana, Guam, 1961-63, gen. mgr., 1963-67, v.p., 1967-73, exec. v.p., 1973-84; pres., chief exec. officer Triple J Enterprises, Tamuning, Guam, 1984—. Chmn. bd. Guam Visitors Bur., 1974-76, bd. dirs., 1968-89; chmn. Pacific Asia Travel Assn.,

Micronesia chpt., 1988-89; v.p. Boy Scouts Am., Hawaii, 1968—. Served with U.S. Army, 1957-59. Recipient Silver Beaver award Boy Scouts Am., 1975, Silver Antelope award, 1991; Mr. Tourism award Guam Visitors Bur., 1976. Mem. Guam C. of C. (chmn. 1980, Bus. Man of Yr. award 1983); Guam Hotel and Restaurant Assn. (pres., founder 1969-71). Lodges: Rotary (bd. dirs. Guam). Republican. Presbyterian. Avocations: snow skiing, dirt bike riding, traveling.

JONES, ROBERT JEFFRIES, lawyer; b. Atlantic City, N.J., Sept. 7, 1939; s. Robert Lewis and Mildred Laura (Jeffries) J.; m. Joan Mary Feichtner, Aug. 17, 1963; children: Christopher, Kendall, Stephen. BA, Colgate U., 1961; LLB with honors, U. Pa., 1964. Bar: Pa. 1965, U.S. Dist. Ct. (ea. dist.) Pa. 1965, U.S. Ct. Appeals (3d cir.) 1965. Assoc. Saul, Ewing LLP, Phila., 1964-71, ptnr., 1971—. Mem. steering com. Bond Atty.'s Workshop, Chgo., 1980. Mem. Montgomery County Rep. Com., Norristown, Pa., 1967-71; chmn. Whitpain Twp. Park and Recreation Bd., Blue Bell, Pa., 1980-84; bd. dirs. Phila. YMCA Camps, 1970-76; trustee Colgate U., 1999—; mem. gen. counsel alumni corp., 1993-99, pres. Phila. chpt., 1980-84. Fellow Am. Coll. Bond Counsel (founder); mem. ABA, Phila. Bar Assn. (chmn. tax exempt fin. com. 1985-86), Pa. Bond Lawyers Assn. (founder Harrisburg, Pa. 1987), Pa. Economy League (bd. dirs. 1994—). Avocations: skiing, golf, history. Office: Saul Ewing LLP 3800 Centre Sq W Philadelphia PA 19102 E-mail: rjjboilerplate@aol.com., rjones@saul.com.

JONES, ROBERT LAWTON, architect, planner, educator; b. McAlester, Okla., May 12, 1925; s. Lawton Henry and Josephine (Troy) J.; m. Lynn Scott, Dec. 2, 1950; children: Jayme, Mark, Paul, Gregory, Laure, Christi, Matthew. BArch cum laude, U. Notre Dame, 1949; MS, Ill. Inst. Tech., 1953; postgrad., Tech. U., Karlsruhe, Fed. Republic Germany, 1954. With Perkins & Will, Chgo., 1949-52; mgr. civic ctr. project Tulsa, 1954-55; arch. David G. Murray & Assocs., Tulsa, 1955-56; dir. planning and design Murray Jones Murray Inc., Tulsa, 1957-88; prof., dir. architecture U. Okla., 1986-88, prof., dir. urban design, 1988-95; campus planner U. Tulsa, 1993-98. Prin. works include Chapman Hall Tulsa U., Tulsa Internat. Airport, Okla. U. Coll. Nursing, St. Patrick's Ch., First Nat. Bank, Ctr. Pla., Okla. Coll. Osteol. Medicine and Surgery, Hilti Western Hemisphere Hdqrs., Cities Svc. Tech. Ctr. Chmn. Community Rels. Commn., Tulsa, 1968, Arts Commn., Tulsa, 1970-71, chmn. Tulsa Pollution Control Task Force, 1970; v.p. Arts and Humanities Coun., Tulsa, 1971-74, pres. 1975-76 (Pres.'s award 1986); bd. dirs. Nat. Rsch. Found. on Aging, 1974-78, Tulsa Met. Ministry, 1977-82 (interfaith award 1986). With USNR, 1943-46. Fulbright grantee 1953-54; recipient Tchng. Excellence award Coll. of Arch., U. Okla., 1992-93. Fellow AIA (chmn. nat. jury 1989); mem. NCCJ (chmn. Tulsa chpt., v.p. 1970-73, 90-94, chmn. long-range planning task force 1984, nat. bd. trustees 1984-90, Brotherhood award 1972), Am. Planning Assn., Am. Inst. Cert. Planners, Met. Tulsa C. of C. (dir. 1974-76). Democrat. Roman Catholic. Home and Office: 1916 E 47th St Tulsa OK 74105-4917

JONES, ROBERT LYLE, emergency medical services leader, financial planner, educator; b. Washington, Feb. 14, 1959; s. Herman Aven and Dorothy Edith J.; m. Cynthia Celia Bogdanowicz, May 15, 1996. B in Gen. Sci., U. Kans., 1982; MA in Adult and Continuing Edn., U. Mo., 1990. Registered paramedic, Kans.; cert. emergency med. svcs. instr./coord.; chartered mut. funds counselor; accredited investor SEC. Paramedic team leader Johnson County (Kans.) Med. Action, 1983-89, dist. supr., 1989-92, edn. supr., 1992—2002, bn. chief, 2002—; chmn., CEO Bercalso Investments, 2001—; pres., chief investment officer NorthTail Real Estate Co., 2002—. BCLS instr., 1979-87, affiliate faculty, 1987—, ACLS instr., 1985-88, prehosp. trauma life support instr., 1986—, affiliate faculty, 1988—, PALS instr., 1993—; PEPP instr./coord., 2003—. Served to Capt. USAR, 1979-94. Mem.: Fin. Planning Assn., Assn. Profls. in Infection Control and Epidemiology. Avocations: bicycling, backpacking, running. Office: Johnson County Med Action 111 S Cherry St Ste 300 Olathe KS 66061-3421

JONES, ROBERT RUSSELL, magazine editor; b. Topeka, Oct. 19, 1927; s. Russell Alonzo and Marie (Carter) J.; m. Dorothy Jean Vincent, Sept. 3, 1947; children— Daniel Robert, Mark Alan. AB in Polit. Sci. and History, Washburn U., Topeka, 1949; MS in Tech. Journalism, Kans. State U., Manhattan, 1959. Expt. sta. editor, asst. prof. agrl. econs. Kans. State U., 1957-60; asst. editor Agrl. Pubs. Inc., Milw., 1960-67; sci. editor, asst. prof. expt. sta. U. Mo., Columbia, 1967-72; assoc. editor Indsl. Research mag., Chgo., 1972-74, editor, 1974-78; editorial dir. Indsl. Research & Devel. mag., Barrington, Ill., 1978-83; editor, editorial dir. Research & Devel. Mag., Barrington, 1984-89, exec. editor Des Plaines, Ill., 1989-91; editorial dir. Chromatography Forum Mag., Barrington, 1986, Chromatography Mag., Barrington, 1987. Chmn. R & D Scientist of Yr. award ann. program, 1974-91, I-R 100 new products awards ann. program, 1974-87, R & D 100 new product awards ann. program, 1988-91; pres., CEO, editl. dir. Applied Sci. Communications, 1991—. Editor: The Unsettled Earth, 1975, Foresight mag., 1991-93, First Notes mag., 1991-95, The Spire mag., 1995—. Served with USNR, 1945-46. Mem. AAAS, Am. Bus. Press (Jesse H. Neal Editorial Achievement award 1976), Am. Soc. Bus. Press Editors, Nat. Assn. Sci. Writers. Democrat. Baptist. Home: 1213 Main St Evanston IL 60202-1650

JONES, ROGER ALAN, chemistry educator, researcher, consultant; b. York, Pa., Mar. 25, 1947; s. Galen Victor and Frieda (Shaull) J. BS, U. Del., 1969; PhD, U. Alberta, 1974. Postdoctoral fellow MIT, Cambridge, Mass., 1974-77; asst. prof. chemistry Rutgers U., New Brunswick, N.J., 1977-82, assoc. prof., 1982-88, prof., 1988—, chmn. dept. chemistry and chem. biology, 1996—. Contbr. articles to profl. jours. NIH rsch. grantee, 1982—; faculty rsch. awardee Am. Cancer Soc., 1986-91. Fellow AAAS, Am. Chem. Soc. E-mail: jones@rutchem.rutgers.edu.

JONES, R(OGER) KENT, civil engineer, educator; b. Streator, Ill., Sept. 5, 1926; s. Thales Winsor and Dorothy Lucille (Smith) J.; m. Pauline Rose Bartkoski, Sept. 13, 1947 (div. Jan. 1972); children: Michael, Dorothy, Raymond, Margaret, Virginia, Charles, Teresa, Stanley; m. Agnes Chaesun Baek, Feb. 6, 1972 (div. Apr. 1995); children: Edgar Kim, Sara Su. BCE, Marquette U., 1952. Registered profl. engr., Ill., Tex., Mo. Product engr. Southwestern Petroleum, Ft. Worth, 1963-66; constrn. engr. Ambursen Engring. Co., Houston, 1966-67; facilities engr. VA Hosp., Houston, 1967-68; prin. civil engr. Metro. Water Reclam Dist., Chgo., 1968-94; commr. edn. Esperanto League N.Am., Chgo., 1994—2002, also bd. dirs.; dir. Aviation Lang. Devel. Project, 1998—. Instr. civil tech. U. Houston, 1967-68; tech. advisor Harold W. Coll., Chgo., 1992. Adminstr. translation: General Chemistry, 1990 (prize 1994); editor: The Esperanto Language in Elementary Schools, 1997. Candidate Ft. Worth City Coun., 1959; mem. Cath. Interracial Coun., Ft. Worth, 1961-66; coord. Am. Disabled Accessible Pub. Transit, Chgo., 1983-84. Electronic technician USN, 1944-49. Recipient Appreciation award Am. Assn. Tchrs Esperanto, 1996. Avocation: piano. Home and Office: 5048 N Marine Dr Apt D6 Chicago IL 60640-3200 Fax: 773-5616582. E-mail: KentJones9@aol.com.

JONES, ROGER L. mathematician, educator; b. Holland Patent, N.Y., June 2, 1949; m. Kathleen Jones, June 22, 1974. PhD, Rutgers U., 1974. Prof. math. DePaul U., Chgo., 1974—. Achievements include research in harmonic analysis, probability and ergodic theory. Office: DePaul Univ 2320 N Kenmore Chicago IL 60614

JONES, ROGER WALTON, English language educator, writer; b. Morristown, N.J., Nov. 22, 1953; s. Chastine Walton and Gloria (Gamble) J.; m. Sue Chang, Aug. 3, 2003. BA in eng., Kenyon Coll., 1976; MA in eng., Southern Ill. U., 1979; PhD in eng., Tex. A&M U., 1989. Teaching asst. Southern Ill. U., Carbondale, 1978-79; adj. prof. Kean Coll., Newark, N.J., 1980; instr. Lamar U., Beaumont, Tex., 1981-83; teaching asst. Tex A&M U., College Station, 1984-89, lecturer, 1990; asst. prof. Howard Payne U., Brownwood, Tex., 1990-91; dir. acad. honors Ranger (Tex.) Coll., 1991—, head dept. humanities and social & behavioral scis., 1998—. Author: Larry McMurtry and the Victorian Novel, 1994; contbr. articles to profl. jours. Contbr., mem. Dem. Nat. Com., Washington. Recipient Merit Incentive award Lamar U., 1983. Mem. Modern Lang. Assn., S. Cen. Modern. Lang. Assn. Democrat. Episcopalian. Avocations: reading, writing, oil painting, swimming. Office: Ranger Coll College Cir Ranger TX 76470 E-mail: rjones@ranger.cc.tx.us.

JONES, ROGER WAYNE, electronics executive; b. Riverside, Calif., Nov. 21, 1939; s. Virgil Elsworth and Beulah (Mills) J.; m. Sherill Lee Bottjer, Dec. 28, 1975; children: Jerrod Wayne, Jordan Anthony. BS in Engring., San Diego State U., 1962. Br. sales mgr. Bourns, Inc., Riverside, 1962-68; sales and mktg. mgr. Spectrol Electronics, Industry, Calif., 1968-77, v.p. mktg., 1979-81; mng. dir. Spectrol Reliance, Ltd., Swindon, England, 1977-79; sr. v.p. S.W. group Kierulff Electronics Corp., L.A., 1981-83; v.p. sales and mktg. worldwide electronic techs. div. Beckman Instruments, Fullerton, Calif., 1983-86; pres., ptnr. Jones & McGeoy Sales, Inc., Newport Beach, Calif., 1986—. Author: The History of Villa Rockledge, A National Treasure in Laguna Beach, 1991, California From the Conquistadores to the Legends of Laguna, 1997, Laguna Beach, California, An Illustrated Narrative History, 2003. Republican. Office: 5100 Campus Dr Newport Beach CA 92660-2101

JONES, RONALD DAVID, lawyer; b. Oneida, N.Y., Jan. 2, 1930; s. Keith Walton and Winnie (Thomas) J.; children: Susan D., Stephen T.; m. Hildegard Vetter, June 9, 1984. BS, Yale U., 1951; JD cum laude, Harvard U., 1958. Bar: N.Y. 1958, U.S. Ct. Appeals (1st, 2nd, 4th, 5th, 6th and D.C. cirs.), U.S. Supreme Ct. 1980. Assoc. LeBoeuf, Lamb, Leiby & MacRae, N.Y.C., 1958-64, ptnr., 1965-89, of counsel, 1990—. Pres. Coun. Econ. Regulation, 1988-92; chmn. United Distbn. Cos., 1990-97; chmn. Upper Housatonic Valley Nat. Heritage Area, Inc., 2000—. Served to lt. USNR, 1951-55 Mem. ABA (chmn. sect. on pub. utilities law 1986-87), Internat. Bar Assn. (chmn. SBL com. on utility law 1988-90), Univ. Club (N.Y.C.). Avocations: running, writing, history. Office: 27 Woodcrest Ln PO Box 1942 Lakeville CT 06039 E-mail: rdjones@discovernet.net.

JONES, RONALD H. computer information systems executive; b. San Diego, Feb. 11, 1938; s. Henry G. and Geneva H. (Hodges) J.; m. Carol Sue Carmichael, Dec. 9, 1967. BS, San Diego State Coll., 1959, MS, 1961. Project mgr. UNIVAC, San Diego, 1961-67, Computer Scis. Corp., San Diego, 1967-75; v.p. Interactive, Inc., San Diego, 1975-92; owner Consulting Co., San Diego, 1992—; ind. cons., programmer various mfg. & distbg. cos., San Diego, 1992—. Contbr. articles to profl. jours; tech. advisor to Internat. Spectrum Mag. Advisor San Diego State Univ.; Rep. nat. committeeman, 1979—. Mem. AARP, Am. Prodn. and Inventory Control Soc., Assn. for Computing Machinery, Calpirg and Ucan. Presbyterian. Avocations: golf, tennis, fishing, collecting. Home and Office: 2484 Pine St San Diego CA 92103-1042 also: Ron Jones Cons PO Box 370083 San Diego CA 92137-0083

JONES, RONALD LEE, lawyer, writer; b. Ames, Iowa, Apr. 11, 1942; s. L. Meyer and Mary Elizabeth (Homer) J.; m. Cynthia Jane Spitzer, Oct. 1, 1994. BA, Ill. Wesleyan U., 1965; cert., Naval Justice Sch., Camp Pendleton, Calif., 1968; JD, Calif. Western Sch. Law, 1972. Bar: Nebr. 1973, U.S. Ct. Appeals (8th cir.) 1973, U.S. Supreme Ct. 1979. Corp. counsel Gene Fuller, Inc., San Diego, 1972-73; asst. gen. counsel Daniel Internat. Corp., Greenville, S.C., 1974-79; v.p., gen. counsel, sec. Royster Co., Norfolk, Va., 1979-83; writer Virginia Beach, Va., 1983—; counsel Peter Kiewit Sons, Inc., Omaha, 1984-87, Occidental Chem. Corp., Dallas, 1988—, The Williams Cos., 1997, Hall Estill Law Firm, Tulsa, Okla., 2002—. Chmn. lawyers coordinating com. Fla. Phosphate Council, Tampa, 1980. Author: Practice Preventive Corporat Law, 1985, How to Counsel Corporate Clients: Ten Reasons Business People Don't Take Legal Advice (And What You Can Do About It), ALI-ABA, 2000; editor (newsletter) Corp. Counsel Reporter, 1985—; contbr. articles to profl. jours. Capt. USMC, 1965-69. Mem. ABA (corp., banking and bus. law sect., constrn. law forum com.), Fertilizer Inst., Am. Mfrs. Assn. Home: 1 Royal Dublin Ln Broken Arrow OK 74011-1127

JONES, RONALD WINTHROP, economics educator; b. Louisville, July 5, 1931; s. August F. and Bess (White) J.; m. Sarah Jay-Smith, July 20, 1956 (div. 1964); 1 child, Deane; m. Catherine L. Maitland, June 14, 1969; children: Laura, Dylan, Brenn, Polly. AB, Swarthmore Coll., 1952; PhD, MIT, 1956. Instr. MIT, 1955-56, Swarthmore Coll., 1956-57; prof. econs. U. Rochester (N.Y.), 1958—. Co-author: World Trade and Payments; author: International Trade-Essays in Theory, 1979, Globalization and the Theory of Input Trade, 2000. Fellow NAS, Econometric Soc., Am. Acad. Arts and Scis. Office: U Rochester Dept Econs Rochester NY 14627 E-mail: jonr@troi.cc.rochester.edu.

JONES, RONDALL EUGENE, lab administrator; b. San Angelo, Tex., Nov. 15, 1942; s. Willie France Jones and Zona Irene Baker; m. Mary Esther Smith, Dec. 20, 1975; children: Caleb, Drew. BS, Tex. Tech, 1961—65; MS, U. of Wis., 1965—67; PhD, U. of N.Mex, 1969—85. Prin. mem. of tech. staff Sandia Nat. Labs, Albuquerque, N.Mex., 1967—. Ch. leader Hope Evang. Free Ch., Albuquerque, N.Mex., 1967—2003. Achievements include patents for method and apparatus for automated assembly. Office: Sandia National Laboratories Dept 6523 PO Box 5800 Albuquerque NM 87185-0974 Personal E-mail: rejones7@msn.com. E-mail: rejones@sandia.gov.

JONES, RUSSEL CAMERON, civil engineer, educator; b. Tarentum, Pa., Oct. 18, 1935; s. Frederick Russel and Helena Doris (Elliot) J.; m. Sharon Ann Keillor; children: Amy Sue, Kimberly Nicole, Tamara Melissa. BS, Carnegie Inst. Tech., 1957, MS, 1960, PhD, 1963; MALS, U. Del., 1994. Structural engr. Hunting, Larsen & Dunnels, Pitts., 1957-59; asst. prof. civil engring. M.I.T., 1963-66, assoc. prof., 1966-71; prof., chmn. dept. civil engring. Ohio State U., Columbus, 1971-76; dean Sch. Engring., U. Mass., Amherst, 1977-81; v.p. acad. affairs Boston U., 1981-87, v.p. acad. devel., 1985-87; pres. U. Del., Newark, 1987-88, univ. rsch. prof., 1988-95; exec. dir. NSPE, Alexandria, Va., 1995-98; mng. ptnr. World Expertise LLC, Falls Church, Va., 1998—. Named Del. Engr. of Yr., 1994; recipient Collingwood prize, ASCE, 1966, Edmund Friedman profl. recognition award, 1981, Internat. medal for disting. contbns. to engring. edn., Australasian Assn. Engring. Edn., 1993; fellow, NDEA, 1959—62, ASCE, 1962—63. Fellow AAAS, ASCE (bd. dirs. 1969-71, 72-75, v.p. 1976-77), NSPE, Am. Soc. Engring. Edn., Accreditation Bd. Engring. and Tech. (bd. dirs. 1983-86, pres. 1987-88), Royal Soc. for Encouragement of Arts, Mfrs. and Commerce, Instn. of Engrs. of Ireland; mem. IEEE, Am. Assn. Higher Edn., Nat. Assn. for Sci., Tech. and Soc. (bd. dirs. 1992-95), Sigma Xi, Tau Beta Pi, Phi Kappa Ph, Chi Epsilon, Sigma Nu. Office: 2001 Mayfair Mclean Ct Falls Church VA 22043-1761 E-mail: rcjonespe@aol.com.

JONES, SALLY DAVIESS PICKRELL, writer; b. St. Louis, June 4, 1923; d. Claude Dildine and Marie Daviess (Pittman) Pickrell; m. Charles William Jones, Sept. 2, 1943 (dec.); 1 child, Matthew Charles (dec.). Student, Mills Coll., Oakland, Calif., 1941-43, U. Calif.-Berkeley, 1944, Columbia U., 1955-58. Author: (novel) The Lights Burn Blue, 1947. Mem. Met. Mus. Art, Nat. Coun. Women, Asia Soc., Fgn. Policy Assn., UN Assn. Episcopalian. Address: 1603 Bayhouse Point Dr Apt 107 Sarasota FL 34231-6774

JONES, SAMUEL LEANDER, conductor; b. Inverness, Miss., June 2, 1935; s. Samuel Leander and Ella Mae (Spencer) J.; m. Nancy Ruth Peacock, Jan. 29, 1957 (div.); children: Rachel Ann, Alison Frances; m. Kristin Barbara Schutte, Dec. 22, 1975. BA, Millsaps Coll., 1957; MA, U. Rochester, 1958, PhD, 1960; D (hon.), Millsaps Coll., 2000. Dir. instrumental music Alma (Mich.) Coll., 1960-62, instr., 1960-61, asst. prof., 1961-62; music dir. Saginaw Symphony Orch., 1962-65; asst. condr. Rochester Philharm. Orch., N.Y., 1965-67, assoc. condr., 1967-69, resident condr., 1969-70, condr., 1970-72; dean Shepherd Sch. of Music Rice U., Houston, 1973-79, prof. of conducting and composition, Shepherd Sch. Music, 1973-97, prof. emeritus, 1997—; prof. of conducting and composition, dir. orchestral studies Carnegie-Mellon U., Pitts., 1988-89. Assoc. dir. Am. Symphony Orch. League Inst. of Orchestral Studies, Orkney Springs, Va., 1966-76; mus. advisor Flint Symphony Orch., 1974-76; guest condr. Pitts. Symphony, Detroit Symphony, Houston Symphony, Buffalo Philharm., Prague Symphony; composer-in-residence Seattle Symphony Orch., 1997—. Founder Alma Symphony, 1961; condr., Saginaw (Mich.) Symphony, 1962-65, also, dir., Saginaw Choral Soc., composer-in-residence, Delta Coll., Univ. Ctr., Mich., 1964-65; founder, conductor: Festival Orch, Univ. Ctr., 1964-65; guest condr., Pitts. Symphony, Buffalo Philharmonic, Shenandoah Valley Music Festival, Naumberg, Iceland symphonies, others.; Composer: Symphony 1, 1960, In Retrospect, 1959, Overture for a City, 1964, Festival Fanfare (commd. Am. Symphony Orch. League), 1964, Elegy in Memory of John Fitzgerald Kennedy, 1917-63, 1963, Let Us Now Praise Famous Men (commd. Shenandoah County Bicentennial Commn.), 1972, Spaces, 1974, Contours of Time, 1975, Fanfare and Celebration (commd. Houston Symphony), 1980, A Symphonic Requiem (commd. Sioux City Symphony), 1983, The Trumpet of the Swan (commd. Millsaps Coll.), 1985, Listen Now, My Children (commd. Midland-Odessa Symphony), 1985, (opera) A Christmas Memory, 1982, Canticles of Time, Symphony No. 2 (commd. Millsaps Coll.), 1990, Symphony No. 3 (commd. Amarillo Symphony), 1991, The Seas of God (commd. Greensboro Choral Soc.), 1992, (oratorio) The Temptation of Jesus (commd. 2d Presbyn. Ch. Richmond), 1995, Cello Sonata, 1997, Janus (commd. Seattle Symphony), 1998, (commd. Amarillo Symphony) Roundings, 1999-2000, Aurum Aurorae (commd. ASCAP Found. and Meet The composer), 2001, Eudora's Fable: The Shoe Bird (commd. Miss. Boychoir), 2002, Chorale - Overture for Organ and Orchestra (commd. Seattle Symphony), 2003; orchestral works, 1958—, solos, songs, chamber works, 1958—; writer/narrator: ednl. TV series for N.Y. State Dept. Edn. The World of Music. Recipient Founders medal Millsaps Coll., 1957, rec. publ. award Ford Found., 1976; Woodrow Wilson fellow, 1958; Martha Baird Rockefeller Found. grantee, 1973; music award Miss. Inst. Arts and Letters, 1986, 91, 2003; Internat. Angel award, 1997; named to Miss. Musicians Hall of Fame, 2000. Mem. ASCAP, Am. Music Ctr., Condrs. Guild (pres. 1987-89), Meet the Composer, Am. Symphony Orch. League, Omicron Delta Kappa, Lambda Chi Alpha. Methodist. Avocations: birding, reading. Home: 35247 34th Ave S Auburn WA 98001-9034 Office: Seattle Symphony Orch Benaraya Hall PO Box 21906 200 University St Seattle WA 98111-3906 E-mail: campanile@earthlink.net.

JONES, SARA SUE FISHER, librarian; b. Rupert, Idaho, May 2, 1962; d. Richard Sherman and Dana Louise Fisher; m. Martin R. Jones, Jan. 7, 1984; children: Russel, Elaine. BA in Comms., Boise State U., 1983; MLS, Syracuse U., 1999. Libr. dir. Stanley (Idaho) Cmty. Libr., 1984-86; English tchr. Minidoka County Schs., Rupert, Idaho, 1986-88; children's librarian Elko (Nev.) County Libr., 1988-95, libr. dir., 1995-2000; state libr., divsn. adminstr. Nev. State Libr. and Archives, 2000—. Commr. State Nev. Commn. on Ednl. Tech. Elko County Libr. Bd. scholar, 1997-99. Mem. Nev. Libr. Assn. (pres. 2000—, pub. trustee, chair, Dorothy McAlindin award 1995, scholar 1997-98), Nev. Libr. Orgn. (chair N.E. dist.), Philanthropic Edn. Orgn., Soroptimist Internat. (pres. 1995-96). Avocations: reading, camping, golf. Office: 100 N Stewart St Carson City NV 89701

JONES, SEABORN GUSTAVUS, poet; b. Macon, Ga., Oct. 10, 1942; s. Seaborn Gustavus and Anne (Reynolds) J.; 1 child from previous marriage, Bronwyn Price Jones; m. Loyce Kirkland, Oct. 10, 1989. Student, Mercer U., 1961-63, San Francisco City Coll., 1972-73. Faculty (summer) Wesleyan Coll., Macon, 1985-95; mem. adv. bd. Ga. Poetry Cir., 1986-90, artist in edn. and lit. orgns. Ga. Arts Coun., 1992-93. Author: Drowning from the Inside Out, 1981, Lost Keys, 1996 (Violet Reed Haas prize for poetry 1996); contbr. numerous poems to mags. With USMCr, 1961-67. Named Ga. Author of Yr. Ga. Coun. of Authors and Journalists, 1988; Alan Collins scholar ini poetry Bread Loaf Writers Conf., 1991. Home: PO Box 469 Lizella GA 31052-0469

JONES, SHANNON SHAWNA MARIE, elementary guidance counselor; b. Colorado Springs, Colo., July 6, 1974; d. James Spencer and Virginia Marie (Parkes) Weaver; m. Michael Andrew Jones, July 18, 1998. BA in Psychology, Pa. State U., 1996, MEd in Counseling Edn., 1997. Cert. ednl. specialist II Pa. Child and adolescent counselor intern The Meadows Psychiat. Hosp., Boalsburg, Pa., 1996; elem. guidance counselor Manheim (Pa.) Ctrl. Sch. Dist., 1997—. Tchg. asst. health and human devel. and family studies Pa. State U., University Park, 1995, rsch. infant rsch. lab., 95; counselor Families and Schs. Together, State College, Pa., 1995—98; counselor intern Corl St. Elem. Sch.-State College Sch. Dist., 1997; tutor Manheim Ctrl. Sch. Dist., 2001—; article cons. The Lancaster (Pa.) New Era Newspaper, 2001. Mem. Congl. Bible Ch., Marietta, Pa., 1998—. Grantee Parent Resource Libr. grant, Manheim Ctrl. Sch. Dist. Stiegel Elem., 1997, Drug and Alcohol Coun., 2002; scholar Liberal Arts Endowment Fund, Pa. State U., 1992—96, George Doughman Meml. scholar, 1992—96. Mem.: Lancaster County Counseling Assn. Avocations: antiquing, gardening, playing board games. Home: 210 Wild Cherry Ln Marietta PA 17547

JONES, SHELDON ATWELL, lawyer; b. Melrose, Mass., Apr. 20, 1938; s. Sheldon Atwell and Hannah Margaret (Andrews) J.; m. Priscilla Ann Hatch, Sept. 10, 1966; children: Sarah Percy, Abigail Atwell. BA, Yale U., 1959; LLB, Harvard U., 1965. Bar: Mass. 1965, U.S. Dist. Ct. Mass. 1967, Calif. 2001. Assoc. Gaston, Snow, Motley & Holt, Boston, 1965-72; ptnr. Gaston Snow & Ely Bartlett, Boston, 1972-87, Dechert LLP, Boston, Newport Beach, 1987—. Past sec. H&Q Healthcare Investors, Boston. Contbr. articles to profl. jours. Lt. (j.g.) USN, 1959-62. Mem. ABA (past chmn. subcom. on investment cos., state regulation of securities com.), Mass. Bar Assn., Boston Bar Assn. (past co-chmn. subcom. on investment cos. and investment advisers), Calif. State Bar Assn., Orange County Bar Assn., Yale Club, Harvard Club. Congregationalist. Avocations: skiing, sailing. Home: 701 Garrett Dr Corona Del Mar CA 92625 Office: Dechert LLP 14th Fl 4675 MacArthur Ct Newport Beach CA 92660 E-mail: sheldon.jones@dechert.com.

JONES, SHERMAN J. academic administrator, management educator, investment executive; b. Newport News, Va., Jan. 12, 1946; s. Sherman Edward and Leola Mae (Pryor) J.; children: Kimberly, Sherman Edward. BA in Am. Studies with honors, Williams Coll., 1968; MBA, Harvard U., 1970, EdD, 1978. Woodrow Wilson adminstrv. intern, asst. to pres. Cen. State U., Ohio, 1970-71; asst. dir. Office Coop. Acad. Planning Inst. for Svc. to Edn., Washington, 1971-72; mgmt. cons. Cresap, McCormick & Paget, Inc., Washington, 1972-75; mgmt. cons. mgmt. div. Acad. for Ednl. Devel., Inc., Washington, 1975-77; v.p. for adminstrn. Fisk U., Nashville, 1977-80, v.p., acting dean, 1980-82; exec. v.p., prof. mgmt. Tuskegee (Ala.) U., 1982-84, prof. mgmt., exec. v.p., provost, 1984-91; prof. mgmt., provost, v.p. for acad. affairs Clark Atlanta U., 1991-93; pres., headmaster So. Normal Sch., Brewton, Ala., 1993-96; investment rep. Edward D. Jones & Co., 1996-99; fin. advisor Prudential Securities, Inc., Atlanta, 1999—2002; v.p. devel. Knoxville (Tenn.) Coll., 2000—; fin. advisor Raymond James, Atlanta, 2002—. Bd. dirs. Better Bus. Bur. Nashville/Middle Tenn., 1978-82; mgmt. bd. John A. Andrew Community Hosp., 1982-85; adv. bd. St. Andrews Sewanee Sch., Tenn., 1986-92, bd. trustees, 1993-97; mem. Nashville Coun. on Fgn. Rels.; bd. trustees YMCA, Brewton, Ala., 1995—. Harvard Grad. Sch. Edn. teaching fellow in edn., 1976-77. Mem. Alumni Coun. Harvard Grad. Sch. Edn., Williams Coll. Exec. Coun. Alumni Soc, Kiwanis (Atlanta). Republican. Episcopalian. Avocations: sports, reading, tennis, weight lifting, cooking. Home: PO Box 11222 Knoxville TN 37939 Office: Raymond James 3500 Piedmont Rd Ste 215 Atlanta GA 30305

JONES, SHIRLEY, actress, singer; b. Smithton, Pa., July 31, 1934; d. Paul and Marjorie (Williams) J.; m. Jack Cassidy, Aug. 5, 1956 (div. 1975); children: Shaun, Patrick, Ryan; m. Marty Ingels, 1977. Grad. high sch., 1952; student, Pitts. Playhouse. Appeared with chorus South Pacific, 1953, in Broadway prodn. Me and Juliet, 1954; other state appearences include The Beggar's Opera, 1957, The Red Mill, 1958, Maggie Flynn, 1968, On a Clear Day, 1975, Show Boat, 1976, Bitter Suite, 1983; films include role of Laurey in Oklahoma, 1954, later stage tour Paris and Rome, sponsorship U.S. Dept. State, Carousel, 1956, April Love, 1957, Never Steal Anything Small, 1959, Bobbikins, 1959, Elmer Gantry, 1960 (Acad. Best Supporting Actress award 1961), Pepe, 1960, The Two Rode Together, 1961, The Music Man, 1962, The Courtship of Eddie's Father, 1963, A Ticklish Affair, 1963, Bedtime Story, 1964, The Secret of My Success, 1965, Fluffy, 1965, The Happy Ending, 1969, The Cheyenne Social Club, 1970, Beyond the Poseidon Adventure, 1979, Tank, 1984, There Were Times, Dear, 1985; night club tour with husband, 1958, later TV and summer stock; star TV series The Partridge Family, 1970-74, Shirley, 1979; guest star: TV series McMillan, 1976; TV films include: Silent Night, Lonely Night, 1969, But I Don't Want To Get Married!, 1970, The Girls of Huntington House, 1973, The Family Nobody Wanted, 1975, The Lives of Jenny Dolan, 1975, Winner Take All, 1975, Yesterday's Child, 1977, Evening in Byzantium, 1978, Who'll Save Our Children, 1978, A Last Cry for Help, 1979, The Children Of An Lac, 1980, Inmates: A Love Story, 1981, There Were Times Dear, 1987; one-woman concert: TV series Shirley Jones' America 1981; author: Shirley and Marty: An Unlikely Love Story, 1990. Nat. chairwoman Leukemia Found. Named Mother of Yr. by Women's Found., 1978.

JONES, SHIRLEY GREEN, librarian; b. St. Matthews, S.C., Jan. 25, 1954; d. Ezekiel and Annie B. (Anderson) Green; m. Charles Elvin Jones, Oct. 25, 1975; children: Candace, Charlton, Carmen. BS in Libr. Sci., S.C. State U., 1976, MS in Counseling Edn., 1991. Cert. media specialist, S.C. Circulation libr. Benedict

Coll., Columbia, S.C., 1977-80; caseworker, periodicals libr. Calhoun DSS, St. Matthews, 1980-81; elem. libr. North (S.C.) Elem. Sch., 1981-83; social worker Orangeburg (S.C.) WSS, 1984-90; libr. St. John Elem., 1984-86, Bethlehem Elem., 1984-86; elem./mid. sch. libr. Webber Sch., Eastover, S.C., 1990—. Exec. bd. PTA, Webber Sch., 1992—. Mem. S.C. Assn. Sch. Librs. Avocations: reading, travel, meeting interesting people, painting ceramics, bicycle. Office: Webber Sch 140 Webber School Rd Eastover SC 29044-9032 Home: 537 Tea Ticket Orangeburg SC 29118-3219

JONES, SHIRLEY JOYCE, small business owner, fashion designer; b. Chgo., Aug. 13; d. Roman C. Carpen and Mary A. Mleczko; m. William T. Jones, May 2, 1959; children: Debra Ann, Lisa Courtney. Student, Wright Coll., 1955-56, Triton Coll., 1963-64; grad., Ippolito Beauty Sch., 1973. Lic. cosmetologist, Ill. Pres. St. Vincent Ferrer, River Forest, Ill., 1973-74; owner Shirley Jones Beauty Studio, Chgo., 1979-93, Flare Schaumburg, 1983-87, Surprise Boutique, Oakbrook, Ill., 1988-96, Shirley Jones Boutique, Chgo., 1993-96; founder, chmn. gala cancer charity September Surprise, Oak Brook, Burr Ridge, Ill., 1990—. V.p. Oak Brook Republican Womens Club, 1999; active Dupage Fedn. Republican Women, Nat. Fedn. Republican Women, Ill. Fed. Repub. Women (chief of protocol, vice chmn., chaplain). Grantee Ippolito Beauty Sch., 1973. Mem. Fashion Group Internat., Chgo. Fashion Group, Nat. Arts and Letters Soc., Oakbrook, Ill. Roman Catholic. Avocations: golf, dancing, travel, antiques, gourmet cooking. Home and Office: 6812 Fieldstone Dr Burr Ridge IL 60527-6967

JONES, SIDNEY LEWIS, economist, researcher, educator; b. Ogden, Utah, Sept. 23, 1933; s. Lewis W. and Anna Vernal (Evans) J.; m. Marlene Stewart, Nov. 24, 1953; children— Randall Sidney, Stanna, Bryan Lewis, Blake Stewart, Allyson. BS with honors in Econs, Utah State U., 1954; MBA, Stanford, 1958, PhD, 1960. Asst. prof. finance Northwestern U., Evanston, Ill., 1960-64, assoc. prof., 1964-65; prof. finance U. Mich., Ann Arbor, 1965-69, 71-72; sr. staff economist Pres.'s Council Econ Advisers, 1969-71, spl. asst. to chmn., 1970-71; minister-counselor for econ. affairs to NATO, Brussels, Belgium, 1972-73; asst. sec. for econ. affairs Dept. Commerce, Washington, 1973-74; dep. asst. to Pres., also; dep. counsellor for econ. policy White House, 1974-75; counselor to sec. Treasury, Washington, 1975; asst. sec. for econ. policy Dept. Treasury, 1975-77; fellow Woodrow Wilson Internat. Center for Scholars, Washington, 1977-78; asst. to bd. govs. FRS, 1978; research scholar Am. Enterprise Inst., Public Policy Research and lectr. Georgetown U., 1979-84; under sec. for econ. affairs Commerce Dept., Washington, 1984-86; prof. Georgetown U., Washington, 1986-89; assoc. faculty Brookings Inst., Washington, 1986-89; asst. sec. for econ. policy U.S. Dept. of the Treasury, Washington, 1989-93; vis. prof., rsch. assoc. Carleton Coll., 1993—. Vis. prof. Cornell U., 1994-95, Dartmouth Coll., 1993, Ariz. State U., 1996, U. North Carolina, 1999. Co-author: The Generalist-Specialist Dichotomy in the Management of Creative Personnel, 1960, Managerial Problems in Finance, 1964, Financial Institutions, 4th edit, 1966, The Development of Economic Policy, 1980, Public and Private Economic Adviser: Paul W. McCracken, 2000. Served to 1st lt. Q.M.C. AUS, 1954-56. Recipient Distinguished Alumni award Utah State U., 1971; Newell scholar; McKinsey fellow; Ford Found. fellow, 1957-60 Home: 8505 Parliament Dr Potomac MD 20854-4001

JONES, STANLEY BOYD, health policy analyst, priest; b. Balt., July 27, 1938; s. Arthur Boyd and Lillian Ailene (Powell) J.; m. Judith K. Miller, Mar. 9, 1981; children— Andrew, Jeffrey, Lisa, Julia. BA, Dartmouth Coll., 1960; postgrad., Yale U., 1960-63. Ordained Episc. priest., 1992. Mem. profl. staff, staff dir. Subcom. on Health, U.S. Senate, Washington, 1970-76; program devel. officer Inst. of Medicine, Nat. Acad. Scis., Washington, 1976-78; v.p. Fullerton, Jones & Wollkstein (Health Policy Alternatives), Washington, 1978-80; v.p. for Washington representation Nat. Assns. Blue Cross and Blue Shield Plans, 1980-83; prin. Health Policy Alternatives, 1983-86; pres. Consol. Healthcare, 1986-89; ind. cons. on health policy Washington, 1989—; clergyman Diocese of W.Va., 1992—; dir. Health Ins. Reform Project George Washington U., 1994-99. Commr. D.C. Gen. Hosp. Mem. Inst. of Medicine of Nat. Acad. Scis. Office: 2021 K St NW Washington DC 20006-1003 E-mail: stan@stanleyjones.com.

JONES, STANTON WILLIAM, management consultant; b. New Orleans, May 24, 1939; s. Albert DeWitt and Clara Arimenta (Stanton) J.; m. Gladys Marina Caceres, Aug. 22, 1990; children: Hazel Nathalye, Albert Stanton, 1 child from a previous marriage, Ellen Marie. BS, Embry-Riddle Aero. U., Daytona Beach, Fla., 1973; MBA, Syracuse (N.Y.) U., 1977. Cert. internal auditor. Commd. 2d lt. U.S. Army, 1963, advanced through grades to lt. col., 1979, fixed wing pilot, 1965-72, rotary wing pilot, 1972; mgmt. cons. Stanton W. Jones & Assocs., San Francisco, 1987—. Joint venture ptnr. Budget Analyst to Bd. Suprs., San Francisco, 1988—. Bd. dirs. Hunter's Point Boys & Girls Club, San Francisco, 1987—. Decorated Meritorious Svc. medal. Mem. Alpha Phi Alpha (pres. 1988-90). Roman Catholic. Avocations: chess, reading, jogging. Home: 1948 Cortereal Ave Oakland CA 94611-2632 Office: Stanton W Jones & Assocs 57 Post St Ste 713 San Francisco CA 94104-5025 E-mail: stantonj@aol.com.

JONES, STEPHANIE J. photojournalist, artist; b. Waukesha, Wis., July 24, 1973; d. Richard A. and Gretchen J. (Koegel) J. Student, U. Wis., 1991-92, Mpls. Coll. Art and Design, 1992-94, Milw. Inst. Art and Design, 1994-95. Printer Moto Photo and Portrait Studio, Brookfield, Wis., 1991-99; photojournalist Oconomowoc (Wis.) Enterprise Waukesha Freeman, 1999—2001. Recipient 1st place Overall Newspaper Photography award Wisc. Newspaper Assn., 2000. Avocations: travel, volleyball. E-mail: ebb@execpc.com.

JONES, STEPHANIE TUBBS, congresswoman, lawyer; b. Cleve., Sept. 10, 1949; BA, Case Western Res. U., 1971, JD, 1974. Bar: Ohio 1974, U.S. Dist. Ct. (no. dist.) Ohio 1975, U.S. Ct. Appeals (6th cir.) 1981, U.S. Supreme Ct. 1981. Asst. gen. counsel, EEO adminstr. N.E. Ohio Regional Sewer Dist., 1974-76; asst. prosecutor Cuyahoga County Prosecutor's Office, 1976-79; trial atty. Cleve. dist. office EEO, 1979-81; judge Cleve. Mcpl. Ct., 1982-83, Cuyahoga County Ct. of Common Pleas, 1983-91; prosecutor Cuyahoga County, Cleve., 1991-98; mem. U.S. Congress from 11th Ohio dist., 1999—; mem. banking and fin. svcs. com., 1999—; mem. com. on small bus., 1999—. Mem. Stds. Ofcl. Conduct, 1999-; vis. com. bd. overseers Franklin Thomas Backus Sch. Law, Case Western Res. U. Bd. trustees Comty. Re-entry Program; bd. trustees class of 1984 Leadership Cleve. Alumnae; mem. Task Force on Violent Crime, Substance Abuse Initiative; trustee Cleve. Police Hist. Soc.; bd. trustees Bethany Bapt. Ch. Recipient Outstanding Vol. Svcs. in Law and Justice award Urban League Greater Cleve., 1986, Women of Yr. award Cleve. chpt. Nat. Assn. Negro Bus. and Profl. Women's Clubs, Inc., 1987, award in recognition of outstanding svc. to judiciary and black comty. Midwest region Nat. Black Am. Law Student Assn., 1988, Career Women of Achievement award YWCA, 1991, Disting. Svc. award Cleve. chpt. NAACP, 1997; named Black Profl. of Yr., Black Profl. Assn. Cleve., 1995, 1994 Ohio Dem. of Yr., Ohio Dem. Party, 1995; inductee Collinwood H.S. Hall of Fame, 1994, Soc. Benchers of Case Western Res. U. Sch. of Law, 1996. Mem. ABA, Nat. Black Prosecutor's Assn., Nat. Dist. Atty.'s Assn. (met. prosecutor's com.), Nat. Coun. Negro Women, Nat. Coll. Dist. Attys. (bd. regents), Ohio State Bar Assn. (Nettie Cronise Lutes award 1997), Ohio Prosecuting Attys. Assn. (exec. com.), Cleve. Bar Assn. (trustee), Norman S. Miner Bar Assn. (past treas.), Cuyahoga Women's Polit. Caucus, Delta Sigma Theta (Greater Cleve. Alumnae chpt., Althea Simmons award 1993). Democrat. Office: Ho of Reps 1009 Longworth Hob Washington DC 20515-3511 also: Dist Office 3645 Warrensville Ctr Rd Ste 204 Shaker Heights OH 44122*

JONES, STEPHEN, lawyer; b. Lafayette, La., July 1, 1940; s. Leslie William and Gladys A. (Williams) J.; m. Virginia Hadden (dec.); 1 child, John Chapman; m. Sherrel Alice Stephens, Dec. 27, 1973; children: Stephen Mark, Leslie Rachael, Edward St. Andrew. Student, U. Tex., 1960-63; LLB, U. Okla., 1966. Sec. Rep. Minority Conf., Tex. Ho. of Reps., 1963; personal asst. to Richard M. Nixon N.Y.C., 1964; adminstrv. asst. to Congressman Paul Findley, 1966-69; legal counsel to gov. of Okla., 1967; spl. asst. U.S. Senator Charles H. Percy and U.S. Rep. Donald Rumsfeld, 1968; mem. U.S. del. to North Atlantic Assembly NATO, 1968; staff counsel censure task force Ho. of Reps. Impeachment Inquiry, 1974; spl. U.S. atty. No. Dist. Okla., 1979; spl. prosecutor, spl. asst. dist. atty. State of Okla., 1977; judge Okla. Ct. Appeals, 1982; civil jury instrn. com. Okla. Supreme Ct., 1979-81; adv. com. ct. rules Okla. Ct. Criminal Appeals, 1980; now mng. ptnr. Stephen Jones & Assoc., Enid, Okla. Adj. prof. U. Okla., 1973-76; instr. Phillips U., 1982-90; bd. dirs. Coun. on the Nat. Interest Found. Author: Oklahoma and Politics in State and Nation, 1907-62, 1974, Others Unknown: The Oklahoma City Bombing Case and Conspiracy, 1998; co-author: France and China, The First Ten Years, 1964-74, 1991, Vernon's Oklahoma Forms 2d Criminal Practice & Procedure Vols. I, II, 1999; contbr. articles to various jours. Bd. dirs., coun. mem. Nat. Interest Found.; acting chmn. Rep. State Com., Okla., 1982; Rep. nominee Okla. atty. gen., 1974, U.S. Senate, 1990; spl. counsel to Gov. Okla., 1995; apptd. chief def. counsel by U.S. Dist. Ct., Oklahoma City, U.S. vs. Tim McVeigh, Oklahoma City Bombing Case, 1995-97; mem. vestry St. Matthews Episc. Ch., 1974, sr. warden, 1983-84, 89-90. Mem. ABA, Okla. Bar Assn., Garfield County Bar Assn., Beacon Club. Office: PO Box 472 Enid OK 73702-0472

JONES, STEPHEN WITSELL, lawyer; b. Honolulu, Aug. 12, 1947; s. Allen Newton Jr. and Maude Estelle (Witsell) J.; m. Judy Kaye Mason, Aug. 13, 1977; children: MaryAnn, Adam, Kathleen. Student, Hendrix Coll., 1965—66; AB with high honors, U. Ill., 1969; JD with highest honors, U. Ark., Little Rock, 1978. Bar: Ark. 1978, U.S. Dist. Ct. (ea. and we. dists.) Ark. 1978, U.S. Ct. Appeals (7th and 8th cirs.) 1978, U.S. Supreme Ct. 1984. Rsch. statistician Ark. Dept. Parks and Tourism, Little Rock, 1971—72, dir. tourist info. ctr., 1972—74; affirmative action specialist Office of the Gov., Little Rock, 1974—75; dir. pers. Ark. Social Svcs. Div., Little Rock, 1975—77; mgmt. info. specialist Ark. Health Dept., Little Rock, 1977—78; assoc. House, Holmes & Jewell, Little Rock, 1978—84; ptnr. House, Wallace, Nelson & Jewell, Little Rock, 1984—86; ptnr., founding mem. Jack, Lyon & Jones, P.A., Little Rock, 1986—2002. Adj. instr. div. lifelong edn. U. Ark., Little Rock, 1992-95. Co-author: Employment Law Deskbook for Arkansas Employers, 1997; editor-in-chief U. Ark. Little Rock Law Rev., 1977; editor Ark. Employment Law Letter, 1996—; contbr. chpt.: Employment Discrimination Law, 2d edit., 1983. Bd. dirs. United Cerebral Palsy of Ctrl. Ark., Little Rock, 1978—; bd. dirs. Ark. Ice Hockey Assn., 1992-2000; pres. Ctrl. Ark. Youth Hockey Assn., 2000. With U.S. Army, 1969-71. Recipient Svc. Recognition award United Cerebral Palsy of Ctrl. Ark., 1986, 95. Fellow Coll. Labor and Employment Lawyers, Greater Little Rock C. of C.; mem. ABA (labor/litigation law practice mgmt. sect.), Ark. Bar Assn., Def. Rsch. Inst., Ark. State C. of C. (bd. dirs., chair health com.). Episcopalian. Avocations: photography, golf. Home: 1724 S Arch St Little Rock AR 72206-1215 Office: Jack Lyon & Jones PA 3400 TCBY Tower 425 W Capitol Ave Little Rock AR 72201-3405

JONES, SUSAN CHAFIN, management consultant; b. Bryan, Tex., July 14, 1951; d. Othel Viron and Norma Beatrice (Bartley) Chafin; m. Robert Lewis Jones, Apr. 9, 1973 (dec.); 1 child, Kelli Sanness. BS in Edn., Stephen F. Austin State U., 1973; MA, U. Tex., Austin, 1976. Cert. rehab. counselor; lic. marriage and family therapist. Tng. coord. Behavioral Systems Scis. Assocs., Austin, 1973-76; pres., CEO Jones Counseling & Cons., Inc. (formerly Jones, Bright Internat.), The Woodlands, Tex., 1976—; CEO Jones, Ragain Internat., Inc., The Woodlands, 1997-99; team leader Guatemala Med. Mission, 1999-2000; interim exec. dir. Interfaith of the Woodlands, Tex., 1999—2001. Author: Feelings Beneath Words and Messages in Action, 1974, Supervisor's Notes: Guidelines on Employee Counseling, 1977, Youth Ministry: A Manual for Youth Counselors, Leaders and Workers, 1991, 360o Intermetrics, Assessment for Individuals and Organizations, 1993, Therapeutic Approaches to Women's Health: A Program of Exercise and Education, 1995. Active McCullough High Sch. PTA, The Woodlands, 1992-95; v.p. McCullough Highsteppers Parent Club, 1993-95; dir. Stephen Ministry The Woodlands United Meth. Ch., 1992-96, mem. adminstrv. bd., 1993-96; bd. mem. Montgomery County Young Life, 1991-92. Mem. Montgomery County C. of C., Am. Assn. Marriage and Family Therapy (clin.), Am. Assn. Christian Counselors (profl., charter), Christian Counselors Tex., Rotary Internat., Women's Energy Network. Republican. Avocations: playing piano, skiing, writing. Office: Jones Counseling & Cons Inc 10655 Six Pines Dr #160 The Woodlands TX 77380-0655

JONES, SUSAN EMILY, fashion educator, administrator, educator emeritus; b. N.Y.C., Sept. 9, 1948; d. David and Emily Helen (Welke) J.; m. Henry J. Titone, Jr., Oct. 21, 1974 (div. 1980); m. Douglas S. Robbins, Aug. 21, 1985 B.F.A., Pratt Inst., Bklyn., 1970. Designer Sue Brett, N.Y.C., 1970-74, St. Tropez, 1975; prof. fashion Pratt Inst., Bklyn., 1972-2000, chairperson fashion dept., 1981-2000, chairperson merchandising and design programs fashion dept., 1983-2000; computer software cons., 1988-89; owner, designer Sej Wearable Artworks, 1992—. Internat. observer Jeunes Createurs de Mode, Paris, 1987, judge, 1988; U.S. rep. SAGA Internat. Design Ctr., Copenhagen, 1992, serdesigns, Hawaii, 2001—. Tech. book reviewer, 1994—. Recipient Young Am. Designer award Internat. Ladies Garment Workers Union, 1970, Ptnr. in Edn. award N.Y.C. Pub. Sch. System Chancellor, 1992-93. Mem. Fashion Group (regional com. 1983-87, mem. com. 1990-93, ednl. com. 1995-96, co-chair ednl. com. 1996-98), Nat. Retail Fedn., Under Fashion Assn. Home: 79-7199 Mamalahoa Hwy 351 F Holualoa HI 96725 Office: Pratt Inst Dept of Fashion Design 200 Willoughby Ave Brooklyn NY 11205-3899 E-mail: sejpratt@aol.com., sjones@pratt.edu.

JONES, SUSIE MATHIS, social worker; b. Montgomery, La., May 4, 1933; d. John Frank and Maud Mathis; m. Michael Moore, Mar. 15, 1998; children: Leonard, Gary, Gregory, Regina. BS, Northwestern St. U., Natchitoches, La., 1955; MSW, La. State U., 1982. Lic. social worker, La. Program specialist, geriatric psychiat. unit Briarwood Psychiatrist Hosp., Alexandria, La.; social work supr. Regional Program Spl. Health and Human Resources, Winnfield, La.; pvt. practice Winnfield. Chmn. region IV La. Conf. Social Welfare; mem. governing bd. Rapides Health Care Sys.; La. state trainer AARP; cons. in field. Active in St. Pauls Episcopal Ch. Recipient Chareles E. Dunbar Jr. Career Svc. award, Hilda Simon award Internat. Leaders in Achievement, Internat. Book of Honor award; recognized Community Leaders of Am., LA NASW Dorothy Schenthal Leadership Award. Mem. NASW, Kiwanis, Winnfield C. of C. Home: PO Box 127 Winnfield LA 71483-0127

JONES, SUZANNE LOUISE, physical therapist; b. Scranton, Pa., Dec. 13, 1962; d. Clayton Fuller and Louise Decker Northup; m. Bruce Michael Jones, May 21, 1988; 1 child, Lindsay Louise. BS magna cum laude, U. Del., 1984. Lic. phys. therapist. Phys. therapist Allied Svcs. Rehab. Hosp., Scranton, Pa., 1994—, 1985-86, 91-95, stroke program mgr., 1991—; phys. therapist Pa. Home Health Svcs., Dunmore, Pa., 1985-91; asst. phys. therapy lab. instr. U. Scranton, 1990, 92. Guest lectr. Coll. Misericordia, Dallas, 1995. Com. mem. Jewish Cmty. Ctr. Daycare com., Scranton, 1999—. Mem. Pa. Phys. Therapy Assn., Am. Phys. Therapy Assn., Nat. Stroke Assn. Avocations: reading, swimming.

JONES, SYBLE THORNHILL, dietitian; b. Summit, Miss., July 10, 1932; d. Hurby Lee and Iva Mae (Brown) Thornhill; children: Bruce Clifford, Janice Jones Duvall, Kent Christopher. BS, U. So. Miss., Hattiesburg, 1954; MS, La. Tech. U., Ruston, 1972. Lic. dietitian, La.; registered dietitian. Supr. food svc. U. So. Miss., Hattiesburg, 1954-55; sec. U.S.F. & G. Claims Office, Natchez, Miss., 1955-56; exec. sec. Gen. Agt. Aetna Life, New Orleans, 1956-57; unit mgr. Progressive Cafeterias, Houston, 1959-66; chief dietitian Ctrl. La. State Hosp., Pineville, 1966-68; dir. food and nutrition svc. Rapides Parish Sch. Bd., Alexandria, La., 1968—. Trustee Tchrs. Ret. Sys. La., Baton Rouge, 1990-. Mem. adv. bd. Rapides Coun. on Aging, Alexandria, 1973-75. Mem. Am. Dietetic Assn., Am. Food Svc. Assn. (Pres. Gold award 1987, Silver Spirit award 1990), La. Dietetic Assn. (pres. 1971-72, Outstanding Dietitian 1972), La. Sch. Food Svc. Assn. (pres. 1986-87), La. Assn. Sch. Execs. (exec. com. 1980-81), La. Assn. Sch. Bus. Ofcls. (regional dir. 1976-77). Democrat. Methodist. Avocations: motor home travel, reading, dining out, old movies. Home: 138 Ron Mar Ln Pineville LA 71360-4547 Office: Rapides Parish Sch Bd 619 6th St PO Box 1230 Alexandria LA 71309-1230 E-mail: jonessy@rapides.k12.la.us.

JONES, SYLVANUS BENSON, adjudicator, consultant, lawyer; b. Southport, N.C., Nov. 21, 1928; s. Thomas Henry and Katie Mable J.; m. Karen Ann Charbonneau, Aug. 10, 1970 (div. May 1975); 1 child, Donovan; m. Brenda Castleyoung-Jones, Sept. 9, 1999. Student, Howard U., 1945-48; AD in Fin., Peter's Bus. Coll., Washington, 1955; postgrad., Fgn. Svc. Inst., Arlington, Va., 1956, George Washington U., 1959-60, Bibliothèque de la Sorbonne U. de Paris, Paris, 1962, Georgetown U., Washington, 1962, Am. U., 1966-68. Lic. real estate agt.; lic. gen. contractor, Md.; lic. ins. agt., Md., D.C. Enumerator, IBM computer operator U.S. Census Bur., Suitland, Md., 1950-51; clk. typist, claims div. VA, Washington, 1951-52; rsch. clk. Bur. Security and Consular Affairs, U.S. Dept. State, Washington, 1952-53, supr. passport processing sect., 1953-56, from jr. to sr. adjudicator domestic adjudication div., 1956-61, consular affairs officer adv. opinions div., 1961-63, chief pvt. bill staff, office of dep. dir. for ops., 1963-68, chief fraud and investigation unit, 1968-72; adjudicator, gen. cons., 1972—. Editor-in-chief The Washington Press, 1957-63; founder, dir. Mut. Fund Investment Program for Govt. Employees, Washington, 1969-73; instr. Tennis U. Puebla (Mex.), 1973-75; editor-in-chief The Annapolis (Md.) Press, 1989—; chmn. ad hoc com. to repeal the utilities tax, Annapolis, 1992—. Contbr. articles to profl. jours; grantee hub cap locking device. Treas. Annapolis City Dem. Ctrl. Com., 1992, 97; Dem. candidate for mayor, Annapolis, 1993, 97, 2001; chmn. trans. adv. bd., Annapolis, 1992-98. Recipient Cert. of Disting. Citizenship, City of Annapolis, 1987, 97, 99, Gov.'s Citation for Outstanding Svc. to Citizens, State of Md., 1997, 99, Red Cross Citizenship award, Trailblazer award U.S. Dept. State, 1998; numerous meritorious svc. awards; Howard U. scholar. Home: 16 Bausum Dr Annapolis MD 21401-4309 E-mail: syl_jones@juno.com.

JONES, TERRELL B. travel company executive; Grad., Denison U. Travel agt. Vega Travel, Chgo.; v.p. Travel Advisors, Sabre Applications and Devel.; v.p. product devel. Sabre Travel Info. Network; pres. Sabre Decision Techs.; dir. product devel. Am. Airlines, 1978, pres. Sabre Computer Svcs., 1993-96; pres. Sabre Computer Svcs., 1996-99, Sabre Interactive, 1996-99; sr. v.p. Sabre Inc.; pres. Travelocity.com. Mem. customer adv. bd. Intel, Lotus; mem. The Rsch. Bd. Office: care Sabre Group 4255 Amon Carter Blvd Fort Worth TX 76155-2603

JONES, THOMAS BROOKS, lawyer, educator; b. Atmore, Ala. s. John Maxwell and Marjorie Lee (Brooks) J. BA, U. Ala., 1949, JD, 1951; LLM, Columbia U., 1958; postgrad. legal studies, U. Stockholm, 1973. Bar: Ala. 1951. Sole practice, Escambia County, Ala., 1951-52; judge, 1953-57; interim asst. prof. U. Fla. Law Sch., Gainesville, 1958-60; atty. Dept. of the Army, various cities, 1961-83; instr. Anchorage Community Coll., Chapman Coll., Anchorage, 1982—. Author: Munich, 1977; contbr. articles to profl. jours. With AUS, 1946-47. Mem. ABA, Fla. Bar Assn. Democrat. Baptist. Avocations: foreign travel, sports. Home and Office: 836 M St Apt 208 Anchorage AK 99501-3355

JONES, THOMAS E. bank executive; b. 1939; Joined Citibank, N.Y.C., 1980; sr. v.p., chief acctg. officer Citicorp and Citibank, N.Y.C., 1980-88, fin. contr., 1980-88, sr. corporate officer, 1988-90; exec. v.p., prin. fin. officer Citigroup, N.Y.C., 1990—, chmn & CEO, Global Investment Management & Private Banking Group, and chmn & CEO, Citigroup Asset Management N.Y.C. Office: Citigroup 399 Park Ave New York NY 10022-4614

JONES, THOMAS EDWARD, medical technologist; b. Los Angeles, Dec. 1, 1948; s. Leonard Martin and Ada Frances (Sprague) J. BS in Microbiology, San Diego State U., 1974; MBA, U. Calif., Riverside, 1991. Supr. microbiology Plasma Inc., Long Beach, Calif., 1977-80, supr. microbiology and hematology, 1981-84; med. technologist San Bernardino (Calif.) County Med. Ctr., 1984-85, supervising med. technologist, 1985—99, expert surveyor U.S. Health Care Fin. Adminstrn., 1994-95; supervising med. technologist Arrowhead Regional Med. Ctr., Colton, Calif., 1999—. Served with U.S. Army, 1969-71. Mem. AAAS, Am. Soc. Microbiology, Am. Soc. Clin. Pathology (assoc., bd. cert. med. technologist, diplomate in lab mgmt.), Am. Assn. Clin. Chemistry, Clin. Lab. Mgmt. Assn., Exptl. Aircraft Assn., Internat. Aerobatic Club. Democrat. Avocations: flying, photography. Home: PO Box 441 Crestline CA 92325-0441 Office: Arrowhead Regional Med Ctr Clin Lab 400 N Pepper Ave Colton CA 92324-1801 E-mail: tomjones@pe.net.

JONES, THOMAS OWEN, computer industry executive; b. Phila., Apr. 6, 1932; s. Paul John and Katharine (McCahey) J.; m. Mary Louise Russell, Sept. 19, 1959 (div. Aug. 1979); children: SusanR., Thomas H., Andrew S. BS in Engring., U. Pa., 1954, MBA, 1958. Account mgr. IBM Corp., Phila., 1958-66; asst. to sec. HEW, Washington, 1966-67; v.p. Donaldson, Lufkin & Jenrette, Inc., N.Y.C., 1967-72; pres. Jones/Hosplex Sys., N.Y.C., 1973-84, Carnegie-Madison Inc., N.Y.C., 1984-87, Fifth Generation Computer Corp., N.Y.C., 1987—, Golden Enterprises, Inc., Melbourne, Fla., 1999. Cons. to sec. HEW, Washington, 1967-68; mem. Edn. Commr.'s Adv. Coun. on Copyright Policy, Washington, 1967-70. Mem. N.Y. State Adv. Coun. on Edn., Albany, 1970-75; mem. N.Y.C. #4 Cmty. Planning Bd., 1973-75. With U.S. Army, 1954-56. White House fellow U.S. Commn. on White House Fellows, Washington, 1966-67; named Outstanding Young Man of the Main Line, Jr. C. of C., Bryn Mawr, Pa., 1966. Mem.: IEEE, NY Acad. Scis., Wharton Alumni Assocs. (exec. bd. 1993—2000), Am. Legion, Union League Club Phila., NY Athletic Club. Avocations: tennis, travel. Office: Fifth Generation Computer Corp 876 Kinderkamack Rd # 202 River Edge NJ 07661 E-mail: tojones@aol.com.

JONES, THOMAS OWEN, JR., business educator, military officer; b. Washington, June 24, 1935; s. Thomas Owen Jones and Annie May Bell; m. Jasie Barringer, Nov., 1982 (div. Nov. 1989); m. Phyllis Stepp Cage, Oct. 10, 1990; stepchildren: Rebecca Lynn, Julie Gayle Cage. BSME, U. Pa., 1957; BSBA, U. Southwestern La., 1966; MBA, George Washington U., 1968, D of Bus. Adminstrn., 1972. Lic. comml. pilot, bldg. contractor, N.C.; cert. flight instr. Officer (ret.), naval aviator USN, 1958-2000; asst. and acting dean Coll. Bus. Loyola U., New Orleans, 1971-74; dean Sch. Bus. Eastern Ill. U., 1974-78; pres., CEO Galleries One, N.Y.C., 1978-85; founder, chmn. TJA Consulting, Washington, 1976-85; founder, CEO, chmn. BillPayers, Inc., Greensboro, N.C., 1985-99; chmn. divsn. bus. Greensboro Coll., 1986—. Fred L. Proctor Sr. prof. bus. Founding ptnr. Boston Consulting Group, Cambridge, Mass., 1966. Bd. dirs. Prison Ministry of N.C., 1998-2000. Rear admiral USNR, 1958-2000, ret.. Recipient Gold medal Pan Am. Games, Mexico City, 1955, Gold medal Am. Canoeing Assn., 1957, Silver medal Olympic Games, Melbourne, Australia, 1956; 12 rowing championships Am. Rowing Assn., 1952-61., Fellow Acad. Mgmt.; mem. Assn. Exptl. Test Pilots, Greensboro City Club, Kiwanis, Beta Gamma Sigma. Republican. Presbyterian. Avocations: home building, teaching sunday school, demonstration piloting, coaching rowing. Home: 3614 Pinetop Rd Greensboro NC 27410 Office: Greensboro Coll 815 W Market St Greensboro NC 27401 E-mail: billpayers@aol.com.

JONES, THOMAS PETER, priest; b. N.Y.C., Nov. 21, 1932; s. John Edwin Jones and Katherine Veronica Stoll Jones. BA in Philosophy, St. Bonaventure U., 1956; MA in Theology, Washington Theol. Union, 1976. Missionary to Brazil Franciscan Order, Gioas, Brazil, 1960—80, 1985—88, pastor; vicar gen. Prelacy of Cristalandia, Gioas, Brazil; parochial vicar Hispanic Apostolate Holy Cross Parish-Archdiocese N.Y., Bronx, 1988—90; parachial vicar Brazilian Apostolate East Boston Archdiocese of Boston, 1990—96; pastor St. Francis Xavier Parish, Narrowsburg, NY, 1996—. Roman Catholic. Avocations: music, guitar, piano, reading. Home and Office: 135 Bridge Narrowsburg NY 12764

JONES, THOMAS ROBERT, social worker; b. Escanaba, Mich., Jan. 3, 1950; s. Gene Milton and Alica Una (Mattson) J.; m. Joy Sedlock. BA, U. Laverne, 1977; MSW, U. Hawaii, 1979. Social work assoc. Continuing Care Svcs., Camarillo, Calif., 1973-78; psychiat. social worker Camarillo State Hosp., 1980-84; psychotherapist Terkensha Child Treatment Ctr., Sacramento, Calif., 1984-86; psychiat. social worker Napa (Calif.) State Hosp., 1986-87, Vets. Home Calif., Yountville, 1987-98, chief of social work svc., 1998—. Mem. Nat. Assn. Social Workers, Soc. Clin. Social Work, Acad. Cert. Social Workers. Avocations: creative writing, reading, meditation, classical music. Home: PO Box 1095 Yountville CA 94599-1095 Office: Vets Home Calif Yountville CA 94599 E-mail: Thomas.Junes@cdva.ca.gov.

JONES, THORNTON KEITH, research chemist; b. Brawley, Calif., Dec. 17, 1923; s. Alfred George and Madge Jones; m. Evalee Vestal, July 4, 1965; children: Brian Keith, Donna Eileen. BS, U. Calif., Berkeley, 1949, postgrad., 1951-52. Research chemist Griffin Chem. Co., Richmond, Calif., 1949-55; western product devel. and improvement mgr. Nopco Chem. Co., Richmond, Calif., 1955; research chemist Chevron Research Co., Richmond, 1956-65, research chemist in spl. products research and devel., 1965-1982; product quality mgr. Chevron USA, Inc., San Francisco, 1982-87, ret. Patentee in field. Vol. fireman and officer, Terra Linda, Calif., 1957-64; mem. adv. com. Terra

Linda Dixie Elem. Sch. Dist., 1960-64. Served with Signal Corps, U.S. Army, 1943-46. Mem. Am. Chem. Soc., Forest Products Research Soc., Am. Wood Preservers Assn., Alpha Chi Sigma. Republican. Presbyterian. Avocations: music, gardening, wine and food.

JONES, TIMOTHY MARK, graphic designer, painter; b. Washington, May 20, 1969; s. William Harry and Susan (Dorfman) J. Student, Brandeis U., 1987-89; BFA, Tufts U./Sch. Mus. Fine Arts, Boston, 1993. Art dir. Inner Tradition Press, Rochester, Vt., 1993-97; prodn. mgr., designer Steerforth Press, South Royalton, Vt., 1997-99; sr. designer Harvard U. Press, Cambridge, Mass., 1999—. Office: 79 Garden St Cambridge MA 02138-1423 Home: 759 East Seventh St Boston MA 02127 E-mail: tim_jones@harvard.edu.

JONES, TOM, publishing executive; Publisher Computer Shopper, N.Y.C. Office: Computer Shopper 28 E 28th St Fl 10 New York NY 10016-7930

JONES, TOMMY LEE, actor; b. San Saba, Tex., Sept. 15, 1946; s. Clyde L. and Lucille Marie (Scott) J.; m. Kimberlea Gayle Cloughley, May 30, 1981. BA cum laude in English, Harvard U., 1969. Broadway debut in A Patriot for Me, 1969; other stage appearances include Fortune and Men's Eye's, 1969, Four on a Garden, 1971, Blue Boys, 1972, Ulysses in Nighttown, 1974, True West, 1981; film debut in Love Story, 1970; other film appearances include Eliza's Horoscope, 1972, Life Study, 1972, Jackson County Jail, 1976, Rolling Thunder, 1977, The Betsy, 1978, Eyes of Laura Mars, 1978, Coal Miner's Daughter, 1980, Back Roads, 1981, Nate and Hayes, 1983, River Rat, 1984, Black Moon Rising, 1986, The Big Town, 1987, Stormy Monday, 1988, The Package, 1989, Fire Birds, 1990, JFK, 1991 (Acad. award nominee), Under Siege, 1992, The Fugitive, 1993 (Golden Globe award for best supporting actor 1994, Acad. award for best supporting actor 1993), House of Cards, 1993, Heaven and Earth, 1993, Blown Away, 1994, The Client, 1994, Natural Born Killers, 1994, Blue Sky, 1994, Cobb, 1994, Batman Forever, 1995, Men in Black, 1997, Volcano, 1997, U.S. Marshals, 1997, (voice) Small Soldiers, 1998, Rules of Engagement, 2000, Double Jeopardy, 1999, Space Cowboys, 2000, Men in Black II, 2002, The Hunted, 2003; TV movies include Smash-Up on Interstate 5, 1976, Charlie's Angels, 1976, The Amazing Howard Hughes, 1977, The Rainmaker, 1982, The Executioner's Song (Emmy award), 1982, The Park is Mine, 1985, Yuri Nosenko, KGB, 1986, Broken Vows, 1987, Stranger on My Land, 1988, April Morning, 1988, Gotham, 1988, The Good Old Boys, 1995; appeared in TV miniseries, Lonesome Dove, 1989.

JONES, TRACEY KIRK, JR., minister, educator; b. Boston, Mar. 16, 1917; s. Tracey Kirk and Marion (Flowers) J.; m. Martha Clayton, Sept. 12, 1942 (dec. June 1975); children: Judith Grace Watson, Tracey Kirk Jones, III, Deborah Anita Jones Breitenbach; m. Junia K. Moss, July 1, 1978. BA, D.D., Ohio Wesleyan U.; B.D., Yale Div. Sch., 1942. Ordained to ministry Meth. Church, 1945; missionary Meth. Ch., China, 1946-50, 1952-55, exec. bd. mission, 1955; exec. sec. S.E. Asia, 1955-62; assoc. gen. sec. div. world missions, 1962-64; assoc. gen. sec. world div., 1964-68; gen. sec. bd. missions, 1968-72; gen. sec. bd. global ministries, 1972-80. Adj. prof. Drew Theol. Sch., Madison, N.J., 1980-89; mem. governing bd. Nat. Coun. Chs., 1st v.p., 1978-80. Author: Our Mission Today, 1963. Home: 700 John Ringling Blvd Apt W308 Sarasota FL 34236-1588

JONES, TREVOR OWEN, biomedical industry executive, management consultant; b. Maidstone, Kent, Eng., Nov. 3, 1930; came to U.S., 1957, naturalized, 1971; s. Richard Owen and Ruby Edith (Martin) J.; m. Jennie Lou Singleton, Sept. 12, 1959; children: Pembroke Robinson (dec.), Bronwyn Elizabeth. Higher Nat. Cert. in Elec. Engring., Aston Tech. Coll., Birmingham, Eng., 1952; Ordinary Nat. Cert. in Mech. Engring., Liverpool (Eng.) Tech. Coll., 1957. Registered profl. engr., Wis.; chartered engr., U.K. Student engr., elec. machine design engr. Brit. Gen. Electric Co., 1950-57; project engr., project mgr. Nuc. Ship Savannah, Allis-Chalmers Mfg. Co., 1957-59; with GM, 1959-78, staff engr. in charge Apollo computers, 1967, dir. electronic control sys., 1970-72, dir. advanced product engring., 1972-74; dir. GM Proving Grounds, 1974-78; v.p. engring., automotive worldwide TRW Inc., Cleve., 1978-80, v.p. transp. electronics group, 1980-87; chmn. bd. dirs. Libbey-Owens-Ford Inc., 1987-94; chmn., CEO Internat. Devel. Corp., 1987—; from vice chmn. to chmn. Echlin Inc., 1995-98, chmn. bd. dirs., interim pres. and CEO, 1997; chmn., founder, CEO Biomec Inc., 1998—; chmn. Ohio Fuel Cell Coalition. Vice chmn. Motor Vehicle Safety Adv. Coun., 1971; chmn. Nat. Hwy. Safety Adv. Com., 1976. Author, patentee automotive safety and electronics. Trustee Lawrence Inst. Tech., 1973-76; mem. exec. bd. Clinton Valley coun. Boy Scouts Am., 1975; mem. bd. govs. Cranbrook Inst. Sci., 1977; mem. Sec. of Def. Def. Sci. Bd. Task Force on Internat. Arms Devel. Cooperation, 1995-98; chmn. Nat. Rsch. Coun. Com. Partnership for a New Generation Vehicle, 1994-2001; vice chair bd. trustees Cleve. State U., 2001. Officer Brit. Army, 1955-57. Recipient Safety award for engring. excellence U.S. Dept. Transp., 1978. Hon. Fellow, Brit. Instn. Mechanical Engrs., Fellow Brit. Instn. Elec. Engrs. (Hooper Mem. prize 1950), IEEE (life, exec. com. vehicle tech. soc. 1977-81), Royal Soc. of the Arts, Mfg. and Commerce, Soc. Automotive Engrs. (Arch T. Colwell paper award 1974, 75, Vincent Bendix Automotive Electronics award 1976, Edward N. Cole award 1988), Engring. Soc. Detroit, Engring. Soc. Cleve., Instn. Mech. Engrs. (hon.); mem. NAE, Union Club, Royal Poinciana Country Club (Naples, Fla.). Republican. Episcopalian. Home: Two Bratenahl Pl Bratenahl OH 44108 also: Ste 2001 4151 Gulf Shore Blvd N Naples FL 34103 E-mail: tojones@biomec.com. *Innovation and the acceptance of change are fundamental seeds of progress, and only hard work and an open mind will permit you to harvest its fruits.*

JONES, TRINA WOOD, special education educator; b. Murfreesboro, N.C. d. James Elton I and Sarah Virginia (Bishop) Wood; 1 child, Ashleigh Erin. BA in Early Childhood Edn., N.C. Cen. U., 1977, MEd in Mental Retardation, 1978. Educator Granville County Pub. Schs., Stovall, N.C., 1978-81, Norfolk (Va.) Pub. Schs., 1981-84, Chgo. Pub. Schs., 1984—. Mem. Coun. for Exceptional Children. Avocations: coin and stamp collecting, writing, reading, travel. Home: 5230 S Cornell Ave Chicago IL 60615-4200 Office: Jackie Robinson Elem Sch 4225 S Lake Park Ave Chicago IL 60653 3064 E-mail: twj195@aol.com.

JONES, VAUGHN PAUL, healthcare marketing executive; b. Johnstown, Pa., Apr. 25, 1947; s. Gordon Kenneth and Luella Jane (Seesholtz) Jones; m. Karen Tolbert, Nov. 22, 1985; children: Stewart Conway, Shelly Marie. BS in Acctg., Ferris State U., 1971; MBA, Capital U., 1985; grad., Columbus (Ohio) Area Leadership Program, 1985-86. Lic. health care risk mgr. Fla. Auditor John W. Galbreath, Columbus, 1972-74; mgmt. analyst State of Ohio, Columbus, 1974-76; contrr. Functional Planning, Inc., Columbus, 1976-82; pres. N. Area Mental Health Svcs., Inc., Columbus, 1982-87; assoc. exec. dir. Lakeside Alternatives, Inc., Orlando, Fla., 1987-90; adminstrv. svcs. mgr. Prog. Cos. Fla. Divsn., Tampa, 1991-92; v.p. corp. svcs. Harbor Behavioral Health Care Inst., Inc., New Port Richey, Fla., 1992-98; dep. devel. officer Fla. Housing Fin. Corp., Tallahassee, 1998; project mgr. Itasca Constrn. Assocs., Tampa, 1998—2001, dir. bus. devel. healthcare divsn., 2001—. Vol. United Way Campaign; chmn. polit. letterwriting com. gubernatorial campaign Columbus, 1985. Recipient Senatorial citation, State of Ohio, 1985, Ho. of Reps. citation, 1986. Mem.: Fla. Soc. Healthcare Risk Mgrs., MBA Execs., Rotary (v.p. Capital City West Club 1981). Avocations: collecting antique tools, collecting bamboo fly rods. Home: 1648 Parker Point Blvd Odessa FL 33556 Office: Itasca Constrn Assocs 7884 Woodland Center Blvd Tampa FL 33614-2409

JONES, VERNON QUENTIN, surveyor; b. Sioux City, Iowa, May 6, 1930; s. Vernon Boyd and Winnifred Rhoda J.; m. Rebeca Buckovecz, Oct. 1981; children: Steve Vernon, Gregory Richard, Stanley Alan, Lynn Sue. Student, UCLA, 1948-50. Draftsman III, city engr. City of Pasadena, Calif., 1950-53; sr. civil engring. asst. L.A. County Engrs., L.A., 1953-55; v.p. Treadwell Engring. Corp., Arcadia, Calif., 1955-61, pres., 1961-64, Hillcrest Engring. Corp., Arcadia, 1961-64; dep. county surveyor Ventura County, Calif., 1964-78; propr. Vernon Jones Land Surveyor, Bullhead City, Ariz., 1978—; city engr. City of Needles, Calif., 1980-87. Instr. Mohave Community Coll., 1987-90. Chmn. graphic tech. com. Ventura Unified Sch. Dist., 1972-78, mem. career adv. com., 1972-74; mem. engring. adv. com. Pierce Coll., 1973; pres. Mgmt. Employees of Ventura County, 1974; v.p. Young Reps. of Ventura County, 1965; pres. Marina Pacifica Homeowners Assn., 1973. Mem. League Calif. Surveying Orgns. (pres. 1975), Am. Congress on Surveying and Mapping (chair so. Calif. sect. 1976), Am. Soc. Photogrammetry, Am. Pub. Works Assn., County Engrs. Assn. Calif. Home: PO Box 20761 Bullhead City AZ 86439-0761

JONES, VIRGINIA MCCLURKIN, retired social worker; b. Anniston, Ala., Mar. 13, 1935; d. Louie Walter and Virginia Keith (Beaver) McClurkin; m. Charles Miller Jones, Jr., Mar. 16, 1957; children: Charles Miller III, V. Grace. BA, Agnes Scott Coll., 1957; MA, U. Tenn., 1965, MSSW, 1979. English instr. U. Tenn., Knoxville, 1967-71; religious edn. dir. Oak Ridge Unitarian Ch., 1972-73, 76-78; co-owner, mgr. The Bookstore, 1973-76; English instr. Roane State C.C., 1975-80; pvt. practice clin. social work Oak Ridge, 1980-98. Cons. Mountain Cmty. Health Ctr., Coalfield, Tenn., 1980-83, Valley Ridge Hospice, 1987-89. Contbr. articles to local newspapers. Mem.: NASW, Oak Ridge Ministerial Assn., Knoxville Area Agnes Scott Alumnae (pres.), Concord Yacht Club, Rotary. Democrat. Episcopalian. Office: 1345 Oak Ridge Turnpike Oak Ridge TN 37830-6554

JONES, WALTER BEAMAN, congressman; b. Pitt County, N.C., Feb. 10, 1943; m. Joe Anne Jones; 1 child. BA in History, Atlantic Christian Coll., 1967. Mgr. Walter B. Jones Office Supply Co., 1967-73; salesman Dunn Assoc., 1973-82; pres. Benefit Reserves, Inc., 1989-94, Judson Co., 1990-94; rep. N.C. Ho. of Reps., 1983-92; mem. 104th-108th Congress from 3d N.C. dist., 1995—; mem. armed srvc. com., resources com., banking & financial com. Republican. Office: US House Reps 422 Cannon Bldg Ofcbldg Washington DC 20515-0001*

JONES, WALTER HARRISON, chemist, educator; b. Griffin, Sask., Can., Sept. 21, 1922; s. Arthur Frederick and Mildred Tracy (Walter) J.; m. Marion Claire Twomey, Oct. 25, 1959 (dec. Jan. 1976); m. Dorothy-Lynne Byrne, 1979 (div. 1981, remarried 1994, div. 1997). BS with honors, UCLA, 1944, PhD in Chemistry, 1948. Rsch. chemist Dept. Agr., 1948-51, Los Alamos Sci. Lab., 1951-54; sr. rsch. engr. N.Am. Aviation, 1954-56; mgr. chemistry dept. Ford Motor Co., 1956-60; sr. staff and program mgr., chmn. JANAF-ARPA-NASA Thermochem. panel Inst. Def. Analyses, 1960-63; head propulsion dept. Aerospace Corp., 1963-64; sr. scientist, head advanced tech. Hughes Aircraft Co., 1964-68; prof. aero. systems, dir. Corpus Christi Ctr. U. West Fla., Pensacola, 1969-75, prof. chemistry, 1975-95; vis. rsch. chemist UCLA, 1994—. Vis. prof. U. Toronto, 1979, 92, U. Queensland 1998; cons. pvt., fed. and state agys. Author: (fiction) Prisms in the Pentagon, 1971; contbr. numerous articles to tech. jours., chpts. to books; patentee in field. Mem. Gov.'s Task Force on Energy, Regional Energy Action Com., Fla. State Energy Office, adv. com. Tampa Bay Regional Planning Coun.; judge regional and state sci. fairs. Grantee fed. and state, rsch. corp., NSF, 2000—. Fellow ASEE/ONR, NATO, Am. Inst. Chemists; mem. AIAA, AAUP, AAAS, Am. Astron. Soc. (propulsion com.), Am. Chem. Soc. (chmn. Pensacola sect.), N.Y. Acad. Scis., Am. Phys. Soc., Internat. Solar Energy Soc., Combustion Inst. World Assn. Theoretical Organic Chemists, Am. Ordnance Assn., Air Force Assn., Philos. Soc. Washington, Pensacola C. of C., Phi Beta Kappa, Sigma Xi (pres. local chpt.), Pi Mu Epsilon, Phi Lambda Upsilon (sec. local chpt.), Alpha Mu Gamma, Alpha Chi Sigma (pres. local chpt.). Home and Office: 355 Calle Loma Norte Santa Fe NM 87501-1256

JONES, WALTON LINTON, internist, former government official; b. McCaysville, Ga., Dec. 4, 1918; s. Walton Linton and Pearl Josephine (Gilliam) J.; m. Caroline Wells Schachte, June 5, 1943; children— Walton Linton III, Francis Stephen, Kathleen Caroline BS, Emory U., 1939, MD, 1942. Diplomate Am. Bd. Preventive Medicine. Commd. lt. (j.g.) U.S. Navy, 1942, advanced through grades to capt., 1956; rotating intern U.S. Naval Hosp., Charleston, S.C., 1942-43, aerospace medicine, 1944; flight surgeon USMC Aircraft Squadrons, 1944-47; head aero. med. safety Navy Dept., 1947-53; sr. med. officer U.S.S. Randolph, 1953-55; dir. aero. med. ops. and equipment Bur. Medicine and Surgery, Navy Dept., 1955-64; dir. biotech. and human research div. NASA, 1964-66; ret. U.S. Navy, 1966; civilian dir. biotech and human research div. NASA, Washington, 1966-70, dep., dir. life scis., 1970-75, dir. occupational medicine, 1975-82, dir. occupational health, 1982-85; cons. aerospace medicine, 1985—. Mem. exec. com. hearing and bioacoustics Nat. Acad. Scis., 1964-85, chmn., 1970, mem. exec. com. on vision, 1964-85; Kober lectr. Georgetown U., 1968 Leader, mem. com. Nat. Capital Area council Boy Scouts Am., Falls Church, Va., 1956-64 Decorated Legion of Merit; recipient Exceptional Service medal NASA, 1979, Outstanding Leadership medal NASA, 1985. Fellow Aerospace Medicine Assn. (Bauer award 1970, pres. 1980), AIAA (assoc., recipient John Jeffries award 1970), Royal Soc. Health; mem. Internat. Astronatics Acad., Assn. Mil. Surgeons (Founders award 1956), Internat. Acad. Aerospace Medicine.

JONES, WARREN THOMAS, computer science educator; b. Gainesville, Ga., Nov. 5, 1942; s. Hammond C. and Thelma (Brewer) J.; m. Bobbie Jean Collins, June 12, 1964; children: Warren Thomas. B.E.E., Ga. Inst. Tech., 1965, MS, 1971, PhD, 1973. Registered profl. engr., Ky. Asst. prof. engring. U. Louisville, 1973-77, assoc. prof., 1977-79; prof., chmn. computer sci. U. Ala., Birmingham, 1979—2003, prof. emeritus, 2003—. Author: Computer Literacy, 1983. Mem. Assn. for Computing Machinery, Internat. Soc. for Computational Biology, IEEE Computer Soc. Home: 1525 Wingfield Ct Birmingham AL 35242-5851 Office: Univ Ala Dept Computer And Info Sci Birmingham AL 35294-1170

JONES, WAYNE ALLEN, publisher; b. Bisbee, Ariz., Feb. 10, 1945; s. Earl Wayne and Mary Elizabeth Brown Jones; m. Susheel Dheer, Dec. 30, 1967; children: Sangita (Bete) Adrienne Pfister, Alexander Subhash. A.B. in Biology, Harvard Coll., 1967; A.M. in English, Harvard U., 1970, Ph.D. in English and Am. Lit. and Lang., 1974; M.A. in English, U. Mich., 1969. Lectr., asst. prof. U. Ill., Chgo., 1972—76; asst. prof. U. Miami, Coral Gables, Fla., 1976—80, adj. asst. prof., 1980—89; documentation specialist and other positions Digital Equipment Corp., Maynard, Mass., 1980—98; alliance mgr. Compaq Computer Corp., Marlborough, Mass., 1998—2002; global alliance mgr. Hewlett-Packard Co., Littleton, Mass., 2002—03. Adv. bd. Nathaniel Hawthorne Soc., Bloomfield Hill, Mich., 1974—77; founder, co-dir. The Snarks - A Miami Writer Workshop, 1978—80; pub. Fractal Edge Press, Stow, Mass., 2002—. Contbr. The Nathaniel Hawthorne Calendar, editor, collaborator (three-act play) The Shift by Bernard McCabe, assoc. editor Nathaniel Hawthorne Jour., 1977—80; contbg. editor: Nathaniel Hawthorne Soc. Newsletter, 1975—76; mem. adv. bd., contbr. First Printings of Am. Authors, 1974—80; author: Stone Works, 2002, Decades of Rehearsal, 2003; author: (with Barnard McCabe) The A Poems, 2003. Juried poet Houston Poetry Fest, 2000, 2002, 2003, Chgo. Poetry Fest, 2003; pres. bd. dirs. Studio Potter, Dunbarton, NH, 2000—03. Named to Greybeard - DTR-SIG Hall of Fame, Datatrieve Spl. Interest Group, 1982; recipient award of merit, Soc. Tech. Comm., 1981, 1991, Recognition for Outstanding Partnering and Customer Presentations, Platinum Technologies Corp., 1998; fellow, U. Ill., Chgo., 1975, Huntington Libr., San Marino, CA, 1976, Am. Coun. Learned Socs., 1977; grantee, U. Ill., Chgo., 1974; Max Orovitz Summer fellow in arts and humanities, U. of Miami, 1979. Mem.: Phi Kappa Phi (chpt. sec.-tras. 1979—80). Independent. Taoist. Achievements include discovery of Nathaniel Hawthorne's first review of another author; Hawthorne's means of funding Fanshawe, his first novel; Hawthorne's income from The Token and Twice-Told Tales; a previously unknown Hawthorne love letter; 2 volumes of Manning Estate records in Nathaniel Hawthorne's hand. Avocation: photography. Home: 2234 W Leland Ave FL 2 Chicago IL 60625-2006 Office Fax: 773-561-5939. Personal E-mail: wayne.jones@att.net.

JONES, WELLINGTON DOWNING, III, banker; b. Topeka, Feb. 16, 1945; s. Wellington Downing Jr. and Nancy (Neiswanger) J.; m. Andrea Loftus, May 2, 1970; children: Wellington Downing IV, Heather, Lindsey. BSBA, Northwestern U., 1967; postgrad., Grad. Sch. Banking, Madison, Wis., 1980, Harvard U., 1987. Mktg. rep. IBM, Chgo., 1969-76; v.p. data processing 1st Bank & Trust (name 1st Source Bank 1981), South Bend, Ind., 1976-79, v.p. retail banking, 1979-81; sr. v.p. 1st Source Bank, South Bend, 1981-88; pres. 1st Nat. Bank Mishawaka (acquired by 1st Source Bank 1983), Ind., 1983; exec. v.p. 1st Source Corp., South Bend, 1988—98, pres., 1998—. Bd. dirs. Trustcorp Mortgage, South Bend. Bd. dirs. Neighborhood Housing Svcs., South Bend, 1986—, Entertainment Dist. Bd., South Bend, 1991—, United Way St. Joseph County, South Bend, 1991—; chmn. South Bend Mayor's Housing Forum, 1991—; pres. No. Ind. Hist. Soc., South Bend, 1991—. Sgt. USMCR, 1967-73. Mem. Signal Point Club (Niles, Mich.), Morris Park Country Club. Presbyterian. Avocations: golf, platform tennis, reading, investments. Office: 1st Source Bank 100 N Michigan St South Bend IN 46601-1630

JONES, WENDELL E. state legislator; b. Nov. 4, 1937; m. Jane; 3 children. BS in Speech & Hearing Therapy, Ball State U. Speech therapist, dir. spl. edn. Dist. 15, Palatine, Ill.; mem. Ill. Senate, Springfield, 1998—. Rep. precinct capt.; pres. Village Palatine, 1973-77, trustee, 1967-73. Republican. Office: State Capitol 611 C Capitol Bldg Springfield IL 62706-0001 also: 110 W Northwest Hwy Palatine IL 60067-3558*

JONES, WILL(IAM) (WILLIAM ARNOLD JONES), writer, former newspaper columnist; b. Dover, Ohio, Jan. 29, 1924; s. Vinton W. and Eva M. (Ringheimer) J.; m. Ruth Hines Johnson, May 4, 1968; children by previous marriage— Judson D., Jeffrey B., Brinley W., Megan A., Snake C. Student, Ohio State U., 1942-45, U. Minn. Law Sch., 1945-46. Movie reviewer Tuscarawas County Republican News, Ohio, 1938-39; reporter Dover Daily Reporter, 1939-42, Columbus Citizen, Ohio, 1942-45, Mpls. Tribune, 1945-47, entertainment and food columnist, 1947-84. Creative cons., freelance writer advt. agencies 1962— . Author: cook book Wild in the Kitchen, 1961; also numerous articles. Founder S.H.A.M.E. Smokers, anti-smoking group, 1964. Served with USAAF, 1943. Home and Office: 2102 Cedar Lake Pkwy Minneapolis MN 55416-3616

JONES, WILLIAM ALLEN, lawyer, entertainment company executive; b. Phila., Dec. 13, 1941; s. Roland Emmett and Gloria (Miller) J.; m. Margaret Smith, Sept. 24, 1965 (div. 1972); m. Dorothea S. Whitson, June 15, 1973; children— Darlene, Rebecca, Gloria, David. BA, Temple U., 1967; MBA, JD, Harvard U., 1972. Bar: Calif. 1974. Atty. Walt Disney Prodns., Burbank, Calif., 1973-77, treas., 1977-81; atty. Wyman Bautzer et al, L.A., 1981-83, MGM/UA Entertainment Co., Culver City, 1983, v.p., gen. counsel, 1983-86; sr. v.p., corp. gen. counsel, sec. MGM/UA Communications Co., Culver City, Calif., 1986-91; exec. v.p., gen. counsel, sec. Metro-Goldwyn-Mayer Inc., Santa Monica, Calif., 1991-95, exec. v.p. corp. affairs, 1995-97, sr. exec. v.p., 1997—. Bus. mgr. L.A. Bar Jour., 1974-75; bd. dirs. The Nostalgia Network Inc.; mem. bd. of govs. Inst. for Corp. Counsel, 1990-93. Charter mem. L.A. Philharm. Men's Com., 1974-80; trustee Marlborough Sch., 1988-93, Flintridge Preparatory Sch., 1993-96. With USAF, 1960-64. President's scholar Temple U., 1972 Mem. Harvard Bus. Sch. Assn. So. Calif. (bd. dirs. 1985-88). Home: 1557 Colina Dr Glendale CA 91208-2412 Office: Metro Goldwyn Mayer Inc 2500 Broadway Santa Monica CA 90404-3065

JONES, WILLIAM AUGUSTUS, JR., retired bishop; b. Memphis, Jan. 24, 1927; s. William Augustus and Martha (Jones) J.; m. Margaret Loaring-Clark, Aug. 26, 1949; 4 children. BA, Southwestern at Memphis, 1948; B.D., Yale U., 1951. Ordained priest Episcopal Ch., 1952; priest in charge Messiah Ch., Pulaski, Tenn., 1952-57; curate Christ Ch., Nashville, 1957-58; rector St. Mark Ch., LaGrange, Ga., 1958-65; asso. rector St. Luke Ch., Mountainbrook, Ala., 1965-66; dir. research So. region Assn. Christian Tng. and Service, Memphis, 1966-67; exec. dir. Assn. Christian Tng. and Service, 1968-72; rector St. John's, Johnson City, Tenn., 1972-75; bishop of Mo. St. Louis, 1975-93. Adj. staff Christ Ch., Wilmington, Del., 2001. Episcopalian.

JONES, WILLIAM BENJAMIN, JR., electrical engineering educator; b. Fairburn, Ga., Sept. 17, 1924; s. William Benjamin and Katherine (Davenport) J.; m. Mary Pierce Hammond, Sept. 8, 1948; children: William Benjamin III, Katherine P., Joseph L. BS, Ga. Inst. Tech., 1945, MS, 1948, PhD, 1953. Mem. tech. staff Hughes Aircraft Co., Culver City, Calif., 1954-58; prof. elec. engring. Ga. Inst. Tech., 1958-67; prof. Tex. A&M U., 1967-90, head dept. elec. engring., 1967-84. Vis. prof. U. Fla., 1984-85 Author: Introduction to Optical Fiber Communication Systems, 1987. Served with USNR, 1943-46. Mem. IEEE (sr. mem., editor transactions on communication systems 1960-61, chmn. communication tech. group 1966-67, mem. tech. activities bd. 1966-69, v.p. communications soc. 1972-73, chmn. elec. engring. dept. heads assn. 1983-84), Sigma Xi, Tau Beta Pi, Eta Kappa Nu. Home: Apt 1125 3801 Village View Dr Gainesville GA 30506 E-mail: wjones1125@charter.net.

JONES, WILLIAM BOWDOIN, political scientist, retired diplomat, lawyer; b. L.A., May 2, 1928; s. William T. and LaValle (Bowdoin) J.; m. Joanne Fairchild Garland, June 27, 1953; children: Lisa, Stephanie, Walter. AB in Polit. Sci., UCLA, 1949; JD, U. So. Calif., 1952; postgrad., U. Southampton, Eng., 1949, Sch. Internat. Rels., U. So. Calif., 1955-60. Bar: Calif. 1953, U.S. Supreme Ct. 1964, D.C. 1968, U.S. Ct. Internat. Trade 1988. Pvt. practice law, L.A., 1953-62; joined Fgn. Svc., Dept. State, Res., 1962-68, active svc., 1968-84; dep. dir. Office African Programs, 1964-67; dir. program analysis staff, 1967-68; dir. Office Program Devel. and Evaluation, 1968; dep. asst. sec. state for edn. and cultural affairs, 1969-73; chmn. U.S. del. to 17th Gen. Conf. UNESCO, Paris, 1972; permanent rep. minister Dept. State, 1973-77; mem. U.S. del. to European Ministers Edn. Conf., Bucharest, Rumania, 1973, Internat. Oceanographic Commn. Gen. Conf., Paris, 1973, 18th Gen. Conf. UNESCO, 1974; head U.S. del. Conf. on Cultural Policies, Africa, Accra, Ghana, 1975; mem. U.S. del., chmn. legal com. 19th Gen. Conf. UNESCO, Nairobi, Kenya, 1976; chmn. performance standards bds. U.S. Fgn. Svc., 1976; amb. to Haiti Port-au-Prince, 1977-80; diplomat-in-residence Hampton (Va.) Inst., 1980-81; with law of sea mgmt. ops. Dept. State, Washington, 1981-84, ret., 1984; Amb.-in-residence prof. U. Va., 1984-85; fellow Woodrow Wilson Found., Princeton (N.J.) U., 1986—; ptnr. law firm, 1989—. Bd. dirs. Nat. Cap. Assn. UN, U.S. Coun. UN U.; disting. vis. prof. Pepperdine U., 1993-95, vis. prof., 1995; adj. prof. Hamden Sydney Coll., 1991-94, 97, amb.-in-residence, 1996-98, William A. Johns prof. polit. sci., amb.-in-residence, 2001, trustee, 2000; staff dir. subcom. on Western hemisphere affairs, fgn. affairs com. Ho. of Reps., 1987; White House del. to observe elections in Suriname, 1987; cons. internat. affairs, Washington, 1989; exec. com. Legion Lex, U. So. Calif. Law Ctr., 2002. Chmn. exec. com. Am. Soc. African Culture, 1961-62; mem. L.A. World Affairs Coun., 1945-62; mem. pres.'s adv. coun. St. Mary's Coll., Md., 1988-94, mem. pres.' coun., 1989-92, trustee Hampden-Sydney Coll., Va., 1992-95, 2000—; bd. dirs. Ctr. for Excellence in Pub. Affairs, Hampden-Sydney Coll., 1998—; mem. U.S. Coun. UN U., 1998—. Recipient Alumni Profl. Achievement award UCLA, 1978, Alumni Merit award U. So. Calif., 1980. Mem. ABA, Am. Acad. Polit. and Social Sci., Academia de Derecho Internacional, Am. Fgn. Svc. Assn., Assn. Black Am. Ambs. (bd. dirs. 1995), Univ. Club, Kappa Alpha Psi, Pi Sigma Alpha, Sigma Pi Phi Boule. Home and Office: 4807 17th St NW Washington DC 20011-3705 *As a Black American, I have always strongly resisted being stereotyped. My family for generations was well educated, with a tradition of excellence, pride and achievement. I have always felt I could compete with anyone and that I had a right to expect to achieve positions of highest authority. My advice is to stand on your own two feet. Work with determination to suceed.*

JONES, WILLIAM ERNEST, chemistry educator; b. Sackville, N.B., Can. s. Frederick W. and Jennie E. (Tuttle) J.; m. Norma Florence McKinney Reid, Aug. 9, 1958; children: Mary Ellen E., Jennifer A.J., Sarah A.L., K. Martha M. B.Sc., Mt. Allison U., 1958, M.Sc., 1959; PhD, McGill U., 1963. Asst. prof. Dalhousie U., Halifax, 1962—68, assoc. prof., 1968—73, prof. chemistry, 1973—91, chmn. dept. chemistry, 1974—83, chmn. univ. senate, 1983—89, Saint Mary's U., Halifax, 1989—91, prof. chemistry, dean faculty sci., 2001—; prof. chemistry, v.p. acad. affairs U. Windsor, 1991—98, prof. chemistry, 1991—2001; adj. prof. chemistry St. Mary's U., 2001—, acting dean faculty grad. studies and rsch. Contbr. articles to profl. jours. Fellow Chem. Inst. Can. Home: 17 Shaw Crescent Halifax NS Canada B3P 1V2 Office: St Mary's U Office Faculty Grad Studies & Rsch Halifax NS Canada B3H 3C3 E-mail: wjones@stmarys.ca.

JONES, WILLIAM HENRY, retired military officer; b. Black Diamond, Wash., Apr. 1, 1924; s. Stanley Ernest Jones and Lena Ellenor Nott; m. Barbara Ann Liestman, May 17, 1960; 1 child, Denise; m. Shirley Ann Williams, Jan. 27, 1946 (div. May 12, 1960); 1 child, Robert. Grad. summa cum laude, Naval Sch. Hosp. Adminstrn., 1950; AA, San Diego City Coll., 1963; BA, San Diego State Coll., 1964; grad., Fed. Health Care Execs. Inst., Chgo., 1972. Apprentice seaman USN, 1942, advanced through grades to capt., combat hosp. corpsman various WWII battles, 1942—45, various enlisted assignments, 1945—50, commissioned ensign med. svc. corps, 1950, asst. fin. officer Naval Hosp. Mare Island, 1950—54, adminstrv. officer med. dept. USS Hancock, 1954—56, asst.

adminstrv. officer Naval Hosp. Bethesda, Md., 1956—58, adminstrv. officer Naval Hosp. Corps Sch. San Diego, 1958—60, dir. Amphibious Med. Indoctrination Coronado, Calif., 1960—64, chief patient affairs Naval Hosp. Oakland, Calif., 1964—66, med. adminstrn. officer Hosp. Ship USS Repose - Vietnam War, 1966—67, adminstrv. officer Naval Hosp. St. Albans, NY, 1967—69, with Naval Hosp. Yokosuka, Japan, 1969—71, dir. Health Care Adminstrn. Naval Regional Med. Ctr. Long Beach, Calif., 1971—73, exec. officer Nat. Naval Med. Ctr. Bethesda, Md., 1973—74, commissioned officer Field Med. Svc. Sch. Camp Pendleton, Calif., 1974—79, mem. officers selection bd., 1974—79, ret., 1979. Decorated Meritorious Svc. medal (2), Navy Commendation medal, Legion of Merit; recipient Poet of the Year, Famous Poet Soc., 2003. Mem.: Fleet Res. Assn., Fed. Health Care Execs., Am. Coll. Hosp. Adminstrs., Internat. Poetry Hall of Fame (mem. 1996), Internat. Poets Soc. (disting. mem. 1995). Avocations: reading, walking, writing. Home: 947 San Pablo Way San Marcos CA 92069

JONES, WILLIAM JOHNSON, lawyer; b. Orange, N.J., Aug. 14, 1935; s. William Johnson and Amelia (Opdyke) J.; children— Elizabeth, Jane. A.B., Princeton U., 1957; J.D., Harvard U., 1960. Bar: N.Y. 1961. Asst. dist. atty. N.Y. County, N.Y.C., 1960-66; atty. Western Electric, N.Y.C., 1966-72; gen. atty. N.Y. Telephone, N.Y.C., 1972-75, 78-79; atty. AT&T, N.Y.C., 1975-78, 79-83; gen. solicitor AT&T Techs., Berkeley Heights, N.J., 1983-86, AT&T, Berkeley Heights, 1986-89, AT&T, Basking Ridge, N.J., 1990—. Author: Fifty Years on Fifth, 1957. Mem. ABA, Ctr. Pub. Resources, Ctr. for Litigation Risk Analysis (bd. advs.), Lewis Carroll Soc. Clubs: Princeton (N.Y.), Nassau (Princeton). Home: 67 Park Ave # 10-d New York NY 10016-2557 Office: AT&T 295 N Maple Ave Basking Ridge NJ 07920-1002

JONES, WILLIAM KINZY, materials engineering educator; b. Miami, Fla., July 23, 1946; s. Harold Grover and Josephine (Kinzy) Jones; m. Sharon Mattingly, June 6, 1981; children: Kelli, Kinzy, Brent. BS, Fla. State U., 1967, MS, 1968; PhD, MIT, 1972. Mgr. engring. Cordis Corp., Miami, 1977-87; group head C.S. Draper Lab., Cambridge, Mass., 1972-77; assoc. prof. engring. Fla. Internat. U., Miami, 1987-91, prof., assoc. dean for rsch., 1991—. Dir. Fla. Mfg. Extension Partnership, Advanced Material Rsch. and Engring. Inst.; chmn. advanced rsch. workshop NATO, 1994-95; gen. chair Internat. Microelectronics Conf., 1992, Multi-Chip Module Conf., 1995; tech. co-chair Electronic Packaging Conf., China, 1996, 98; trustee Ednl. Found.; cons. in field. Contbr. articles to profl. jours.; patentee in field. Recipient Rsch. award Fla. Internat. U., 1991, 2001. Fellow Internat. Microelectronic and Packaging Soc.(pres. 1992-93, v.p. membership 1998, trustee Ednl. Found., Tech. Achievement Wagnon award 1991, Hughes award 1996); mem. IEEE (sr.). Republican. Home: 75550 Overseas Hwy # 534 Islamorada FL 33036-4005 Office: Fla Internat U University Park Campus Coll Of Engring Eas 3442 Miami FL 33199-0001 E-mail: jones@fiu.edu.

JONES, WILLIAM OSBORNE, II, physician assistant; b. Corbin, Ky., May 30, 1951; s. William Osborne and Rebecca Marie (Grover) J.; div.; children: Anastasia Marie Rising, William Osborne III, Thomas Adam. BS, George Washington U., 1985; MA, Webster U., 1988. Enlisted USN, 1970, hosp. corpsman, technician, physician asst., 1970-94, advanced through grades to lt., ret., 1994; pvt. practice physicia asst. Gaffney, S.C., 1994; with Spartanburg (S.C.) Nephrology Assocs., 1994—. Med. lectr. nephrology. Contbr. articles to profl. jours. Named to Hon. Order Ky. Cols. Fellow Am. Acad. Physician Assts.; mem. Am. Acad. Nephrology Physician Assts. (v.p. 1997-98, sec. 1998-99), S.C. Acad. Physician Assts. (pres., v.p. 1996-99), Naval Assn. Physician Assts., Mensa. Avocations: mountain and road cycling, weight lifting, motorcycling. Home: 268 Wilford Rd Blacksburg SC 29702-9651 Office: Spartanburg Nephrology Assocs 128 Dillon Dr Spartanburg SC 29307-1018 E-mail: wojones@aol.com.

JONES, WILLIAM RANDOLPH, history educator; b. Little Rock, Apr. 6, 1930; s. John Riley Jones and Jewell Esther Spears; m. Anne Steed, Nov. 13, 1960; children: Anne, Brantley, Mark, Adam. AB in History and Lit., Harvard Coll., 1951; MA in History, Harvard U., 1952, PhD in History, 1958. Prof. Ga. State U., Atlanta, 1956-58, Coll. Charleston, S.C., 1958-59, Ohio Wesleyan U., Delaware, 1959-62, U. N.H., Durham, 1962-95, Armstrong Atlantic State U., Savannah, Ga., 1997—2000. Cons. Testing Svc., Princeton, N.J., 1975-82; cons. in world history and silk road projects UNESCO, Paris, 1978-95; mem. seminar on legal history Columbia Law Sch., 1975-82; founder, co-dir. Internat. Conf. Group on China and Europe in the Middle Ages, 1988-95. Author: Relations of the Two Jurisdictions: Studies in Medieval and Renaissance History, 1970; contbr. articles to profl. jours. With U.S. Army, 1955-58. French Govt. fellow U. Paris, 1951, Fulbright fellow King's Coll., London U., 1958. Democrat. Home: PO Box 13264 Jekyll Island GA 31527-0264 E-mail: billannejone@aol.com.

JONES, WILLIAM REX, law educator; b. Murphysboro, Ill., Oct. 20, 1922; s. Claude E. and Ivy P. (McCormick) J.; m. Miriam R. Lamy, Mar. 27, 1944; m. Gerri L. Haun, June 30, 1972; children: Michael Kimber, Jeanne Keats, Patricia Combs, Sally Horowitz, Kevin. BS, U. Louisville, 1950; JD, U. Ky., 1968; LLM, U. Mich., 1970. Bar: Ky. 1969, Ind. 1971, U.S. Supreme Ct. 1976. Exec. v.p. Paul Miller Ford, Inc., Lexington, Ky., 1951-64; pres. Bill's Seat Cover Ctr., Inc., Lexington, Ky., 1952-65, Bill Jones Real Estate, Inc., Lexington, Ky., 1965-70; asst. prof. law Ind. U., Indpls., 1970-73, assoc. prof., 1973-75, prof., 1975-80; dean Salmon P. Chase Coll. Law. No. Ky. U., Highland Heights, 1980-85, prof., 1980-93, prof. emeritus, 1993—. Vis. prof. Shepard Broad Law Ctr., Nova Southeastern U., Ft. Lauderdale, Fla., 1994-95; mem. Ky. Pub. Advocacy Commn., 1982-93, 97-2000, chmn., 1986-93; chmn. existing structures appeal bd., City of Newport, Ky., 2002—. Author: Kentucky Criminal Trial Practice, 3d edit., 2001, Kentucky Criminal Trial Practice Forms, 3d edit., 2000. 1st sgt. U.S. Army, 1940-44. Cook fellow U. Mich., 1969-70, W.G. Hart fellow Queen Mary Coll. U. London, 1985. Mem. Order of Coif. E-mail: jonesw@nku.edu, wrexjones@zoomtown.com.

JONES, WILLIAM RICHARD, database administrator; b. Morgantown, Ky., Sept. 27, 1952; s. James Edward Jones and Mahalia Jane (Kuykendall) Bratton; m. Marina del Pilar Lagario, Nov. 20, 1981. AA, Excelsior Coll., 1982, BS, 1984; student, U. Tenn., 1987—90; MS in Info. Sci., Capella U., 2002. Cert. computer profl. Supr. radar work ctr. USS Midway (CV-41), Yokosuka, Japan, 1980-81; calibration technician Naval Oceanographic Facility, Ford Island, Hawaii, 1981-84; leading petty officer oe divsn. USS Cimarron (AO-177), Pearl Harbor, Hawaii, 1984-85; engring. assoc. Tenn. Valley Authority, Chattanooga, 1986-90, programmer analyst, 1990-92, database administr., 1992-95; open systems product support rep. BMC Software, Inc., Austin, Tex., 1995-98; database adminstr. Acxiom Corp., Little Rock, 1998-2000, Alistia Inc., Austin, 2000—01; cons. Volt Tech. Resources, 2001—. Tchg. asst. ZD Net U. on Compuserve, 1996. Cert. database adminstr. Team leader web page regional judging team Info. Superhighway Competition sponsored by Blacks in Govt. and The Alliance of Black Tech. Orgns. Recipient Ednl. & Rsch. Found. Essay Scholar Mensa, 1988, Grosswirth-Salny Essay Scholar, Magellan Web Page design award. Mem. Internet Soc., HyperText Markup Lang. Writer's Guild, Assn. for Computing Machinery, Black Data Processing Assocs., Am. Numis. Assn., Intertel, Tenn. State Numis. Soc., Am. Mensa Ltd., Am. Legion, Colloquy. Republican. Avocations: authoring web pages, numismatics, reading. Home: 11500 Jollyville Rd Apt 2414 Austin TX 78759 Office: Volt Tech Svc 4210 Sprewood Spr Ste 100 Austin TX 78744 E-mail: webmaster@aawc.com.

JONES-ATKINS, DEBORAH KAYE, state official; b. Bradenton, Fla. July 2, 1958; d. Ralph and Jewelle Vanessa (Gayle) Jones; m. Larry Bobby Atkins, July 30, 1983; 1 child, Omari Gayle Jones-Atkins. AS with distinction, cert. in human svcs., Monroe C.C., Rochester, N.Y., 1986; BIS, Va. State U., Petersburg, 1995; postgrad., SUNY, Brockport, 1998. Credit investigator Sears Roebuck & Co., Rochester, NY, 1980; customer svc. rep. B. Forman Co., Rochester, NY, 1980-81; youth counselor Brighton Youth Agy., Rochester, NY, 1976-81; staff asst. Makro Inc., Capitol Heights, Md., 1981-82; customer svc. rep. MetroVision Inc., Capitol Hts., 1983-84; teen parent counselor Urban League of Rochester, 1985, program coord., 1988; job developer YWCA of Rochester, 1985-87; prog. support technician, sr. Dept. Med. Assistance Svc., Commonwealth of Va., Richmond, 1989-96; alt. health care supr. Commonwealth of Va. Med. Assist. Svc., 1989-96; subs. tchr. Rochester City Sch. Dist., 1996-2000; SOL tudor, subs. tchr. Henrico County Pub. Sch., 2000; social worker County of Henrico Dept. Social Svc. Mem. Women's Resource Ctr., Richmond, 1989—; heir link The Links Inc., Rochester, 1982—; vol. United Negro Coll. Fund Telethon, Rochester, 1988, N.Y. State Dept. Labor Career Edn. Expo, 1989, WXXI Auction 21, Rochester, 1989, YMCA Greater Rochester, 1989, Arts Coun., Richmond, Richmond Children's Festival, 1989, Sci. Mus. Va., Richmond, 1989, Arts Coun. Richmond 15th Ann. June Jubilee, 1990, Children's Book Festival, 1990, Maymont Found. Flower Garden Show, 1990, 91, Va. Spl. Olympics, 1990—, Jr. League Richmond 45th Book and Author Dinner, 1990, dinner asst. ticket chairperson 46th Book and Author Dinner, 1991, hostee 45th Dinner, Children's Book Festival Arts Coun. Richmond; mem. agy. svc. com. Friends Assn. for Children, 1990—; mem. student adv. com. Va. Commonwealth U. Health Svcs., 1991, Friends of Art Richmond Mus. Fine Arts, 1991; mem. membership com., audience devel. com. Richmond Profl. Women's Network; placement counselor placement com. Jr. League Richmond, 1991, mem. tng. com., 1991; mem. adv. com. Children's Mus. Richmond; mem. exec. bd. YWCA of Richmond, 1992-95, mem. fin. com., 1996—; mem. policy bd. Jr. League Richmond, 1992-93; bd. dirs. Urban League of Richmond, 1996-2001; 3rd v.p. vols. PTA Echo Lake Elem. Sch.; mem. Echo Lake Elem. PTA County Coun, 2001; mem. architect com. 2001 Springcreek Assn. Named one of Outstanding Young Women of Am., 1988. Mem. NAFE, Nat. Coun. Negro Women, Jr. League of Rochester, Nat. Trust Hist. Preservation, Richmond Profl. Women's Network (rec. sec., exec. bd. 1992—), Richmond Jaycees. Democrat. Avocations: jogging, aerobics, tennis, racquetball, the arts, reading, travel. Home: PO Box 6582 Glen Allen VA 23058 Office: 8600 Dixon Powers Rd Richmond VA 23228

JONES-GLAZE, BARBARA ANN, library media specialist; b. Dalton, Ga., Dec. 20, 1946; d. Jack and Beatrice (Walls) Jones; m. Steven Glaze, June 21, 1980; 1 child, Kipp-Cailean. BA in English, West Ga. Coll., 1968; BA in Music, U. Tenn., 1971; MEd, EdS, U. Ga., 1973; EdD, Vanderbilt U., 1991. Libr. media specialist Whitfield County Bd. Edn., Dalton, Ga., 1975, Westside Mid. Sch., Rocky Face, Ga., 1975—. Pres. Phoebus Apollo, Inc., Dalton, Ga., 1985—. Author: Dewey Song, 1973. Mem.: Whitfield Fedn. Tchrs. (pres.), Ga. Fedn. Tchrs. (state exec., sec., exec. coun., career ladder task force, legis. com., constl. com., health edn. com., minority report com., legal affairs com. chair), Am. Fedn. Tchrs., Kappa Delta Pi, Delta Theta Pi. Home: 912 W Lakeshore Dr Dalton GA 30720-5501

JONES GREGORY, PATRICIA, secondary art educator; b. La Grange, Ga., Apr. 15, 1944; d. Eddie Burrel Jones (dec.), Samuel Lee (stepfather) and Mildred Jones (Johnson) Turrentine; m. Bernard Gregory, Oct. 12, 1985. BFA in Art Edn., Pratt Inst., 1966; MS in Photography, Ill. Inst. Tech., 1970; postgrad. in African Studies and Rsch., Howard U., 1970-74; EdD in Ednl. Adminstrn. and Supervision, Seton Hall U., 1994. Cert. prin./supr., supr., ednl. adminstrn. and supervision, art tchr. grades K-12. Art tchr. Westfield (N.J.) Sch. Dist., 1966-68; art instr. Howard U., Washington, 1970-71; art tchr. Newark (N.J.) Sch. Dist., 1974-79, Irvington (N.J.) Sch. Dist., 1979-80, South Orange (N.J.)-Maplewood (N.J.) Sch. Dist., 1980-81, Montclair (N.J.) Sch. Dist., 1981-82; art instr., docent Newark (N.J.) Mus., 1982-84; art tchr. Weequahic H.S., Newark, 1983-98. Mem. com. textbook evaluation curriculum svcs. Bd. Edn., Newark, 1983—; art dir. Ergo-Weequahic H.S., Newark, 1984-93, founder, advisor Kuumba Art Club, 1989-94, PB Graphics Design, liasion, City Without Walls Art Reach mentor program, 1997-98. Author: Many Moods of the Afro-American Woman, 1971, Multicultural Arts Exhibition Catalog, 1992, Pathways to Empowerment, 1997; editor, pub. The Harvester, 1979-83, The Beauty of Holiness, 1997, The Clarion: The Voices That Lead to Righteousness, 1999-2000, Friendship With the World, 2000, Metamorphosis of the Christian, 2001, Intermezzo in l'Italia. Rschr. Goldman and Kennedy The New York Urban Athlete, Simon and Schuster, N.Y., 1983; vol. tchr., counselor local ch. Grace B. Monroe grantee Pratt Inst., Bklyn., 1964; Grad. scholar Ill. Inst. Tech., Chgo., 1968-70; Rsch. fellow Howard U., Washington, 1972-73; recipient Cert. of Recognition, Gov.'s Tchr. Recognition Program, N.J., 1993. Mem. ASCD, Nat. Assn. for Multicultural Edn., Nat. Assn. Art Educators, Newark Mus., Newark Art Coun., Studio Mus. in Harlem, Kappa Delta Pi. Avocations: art, travel, discussion, reading, writing. Home: 78 Woodland Ave East Orange NJ 07017-2006

JONES-GROMACKI, LISA DAWN, health facility administrator; b. Crystal, Minn., Sept. 3, 1970; d. Edward Harry Jones and Jean Marie (Pulkkinen) Fiorini; m. Michael Paul Gromacki, May 24, 1997. AA in Journalism, Mesabi C.C., Virginia, Minn., 1992; BA in Bus. and Pub. Adminstrn., St. Cloud State U., 1994. Lic. nursing home adminstr., Minn. Environ. svcs. supr., asst. mgr. vol. svcs., adminstrv. intern St. Benedict's Ctr., St. Cloud, Minn., 1993-94; mgr. clin. Planned Parenthood, Little Falls, Minn., 1994-96; mgr. ops. Digestive Healthcare, Mpls., 1996-97; adminstr. Dentistry Children, Edina, Minn., 1997—99. Mem. adv. bd. HIV/STD, Duluth, Minn., 1994-96. Mem. NAFE, Am. Health Care Adminstrn. Assn., Med. Group Mgmt., Pub. Adminstrn. Assn. Avocations: down hill skiing, kick boxing. Office: Dentistry Children and Adolescents 7373 France Ave S Edina MN 55435-4534

JONES-JOHNSON, GLORIA, sociologist, educator, consultant; b. Donaldsonville, Ga., Feb. 4, 1956; d. Willie James Jones and Annie Lois (Backey) Facen; m. Willie Roy Johnson, Aug. 14, 1982; children: Kyle Jamary Johnson, Nia Kiara Johnson. BA, Talladega Coll., 1978; MA, Bowling Green State U., 1980; PhD, U. Mich., 1986. Teaching asst. Bowling Green (Ohio) State U., 1978-80; rsch. asst. U. Mich., Ann Arbor, 1980-84, teaching asst., 1984-85; lectr. Wayne State U., Detroit, 1986; asst. prof. Iowa State U., Ames, 1986-92, assoc. prof., 1992-2000, prof., 2000—, administrv. intern, 1997-98. Cons. United Rubber Workers, Des Moines, 1988—, TVA, Nashville, 1987—; vis. scholar U. Ga., Athens, 1996—. Grant reviewer NSF, 1988—, U.S. Dept. Edn., 1991—; editl. bd. The Sociol. Quar. and the Nat. Jour. of Sociology; contbr. articles to Jour. Social Psychology, Jour. Applied Social Psychology, Am. Sociologist, and others. Mem. Am. Sociological Assn., Midwest Sociological Soc. (state dir. Iowa 1991—), Assn. Black Sociologists, Rural Sociological Soc. (assoc. editor 1990—), Indsl. Rels. Rsch. Assn., Alpha Chi, Sigma Xi. Democrat. Roman Catholic. E-mail: GJJ@iastate.edu.

JONES-KOCH, FRANCENA, school counselor, educator; b. Bunnell, Fla., Dec. 3, 1948; d. Roosevelt Jones and Naomi Stafford; m. William H. Koch, July 1976 (div. Aug. 1980); 1 child, Ahmad Yussef Shaw. BS, Fla. Meml. Coll., 1972; M in Elem. Edn., Nova Southeastern U., 1984, specialist degree, 1994. Intermediate tchr. Miami (Fla.) Dade County Pub. Schs., 1973—88, guidance counselor, 1988—. Adj. prof. Fla. Meml. Coll., Miami, 1984—87; juvenile GED instr. Women's Detention Ctr., Miami, 1994—96; planner summer 2000 Inmate to Inmate Tutoring Program Dept. Corrections, Miami, 2000; mem. region 5 steering com. Dade County Pub. Schs., Miami, mem. dist.'s student svcs. adv. coun., 2002—; amb. United Way-Dade County Pub. Schs., Miami; pres. Dade Counseling Assn., Miami, 2002—; dir. comms. Herstory Inc., 1975—2000. Vol. United Way Dade County, Miami, 1999—. Mem.: Am. Sch. Counselor Assn., AAUW (Miami br. chair Gwen Cherry awards 2000—, designer 21st Century Women's Wisdom Project 2001, prodr. 21st Century Women's Wisdom Project 2001), Fla. Counseling Assn., United Tchrs. Dade County, United Way of Dade County, Zeta Phi Beta Sorority, Inc. (pres. Beta Zeta chpt. 1997—99). Avocations: reading, community service, creative writing, travel, visiting book stores. Home: 10850 SW 164th St Miami FL 33157

JONES-MORTON, PAMELA, human resources specialist; b. Balt., Aug. 21, 1947; d. Robert Alfred and Lois Enola (Skilliter) Jones; m. Wayne Daniel Morton, Sept. 7, 1968 (div. Aug. 1990). BS, Frostburg State U., 1970; MA, Mich. State U., 1976; PhD, Ohio State U., 1989. Tchr. Alleghaney High Sch., Cumberland, Md., 1970-72, Am. Sch. in Japan, Tokyo, 1972-74, dept. head, 1974-77; tchr. The Tatnall Sch., Wilmington, Del., 1977-78; dept. head, athletic dir. Internat. Sch. Dusseldorf, West Germany, 1979-82; athletic dir. Escola Americana De Rio de Janeiro, 1982-85, Am. Cmty. Sch., London, 1985-86; grad. asst. Ohio State U., Columbus, 1986-89; univ. prof. W.Va. U., Morgantown, 1989-91; mgr. human and bus. devel. Honda of Am. Mfg., Inc., Columbus, 1991-95, mgr. expatriate adminstrn. dept., 1995-98, mgr. orgnl. devel. expatriate adminstrn., 1998-99, mgr. strategic sect., orgnl. devel., 1999—2002, mgr. expatriate adminstrn. dept., 2002—. Pres. Kanto Plains Athletic Assn., Tokyo, 1973-77; mem accreditation team European Coun., London, 1982; spkr., trustee I Know I Can, Columbus, Ohio; mem. TARGET, The Ohio State U. and Columbus Japanese/Am. Bus. Cmty. Author: (chpt.) Transferring Learning to the Work Place, 1997; contbr. articles to profl. jours. Active Dolphin Rsch. Ctr., Marathon Shores, Fla., 1992—, Marine Conservation, 1994—. Mem. AAUW, Am. Soc. Tng. and Devel. (benchmarking forum 1991-95, spkr. 1993, 94, 95), Soc. Human Resource Mgmt., Inst. Internat. Human Resources, Phi Delta Kappa. Democrat. Avocations: gardening, scuba diving, traveling, photography, puzzles. Office: Honda of Am Mfg Inc 24000 Honda Pkwy Marysville OH 43040-9251

JONES-RAFFERTY, BRENDA ANNE, personal growth and development company executive; b. Mobile, Ala., Nov. 7, 1943; d. Carl Hubert and Willie (Cathey) Jones; m. Virgil Dean King, Dec. 11, 1963 (div. 1967); children: Jenny Louise, Diana Maria; m. James Matthew Rafferty, May 15, 1993. AA, Stephens Coll., 1963; BS, U. West Fla., 1970, MBA, 1972. Cert. info. sys. auditor, data processor. Instr. Pensacola (Fla.) Jr. Coll., 1970-73; sys. analyst Dept. Social Svc., Columbia, S.C., 1973-74; asst. EDP auditor Bankers Trust, Columbia, S.C., 1974-76; vis. asst. prof. Lander Coll., Greenwood, S.C., 1976-78; internal auditor South New Eng. Telephone Co., New Haven, 1978; asst. v.p. Citytrust, Bridgeport, Conn., 1978-91; pres. Paar Enterprises, Asheville, N.C., 1985—; owner Rafferty Constrn. Corp., Asheville, 1999—. Seminar teaching staff Inst. Internal Auditors, Altamonte Springs, Fla., 1979-91, internat. com. info. systems, 1983-84; seminar leader Ctrs. Network, N.Y., Boston, New Haven, 1981-85; coord. coach Herment, San Francisco, 1984-86; regional rep. courses divsn. Werner Erhard and Assocs., New Haven, 1986-87; assoc. Al Williams, New Haven, 1989-92; ind. distbr., Nuskin, New Haven, 1990-92; lic. Avatar master and wizard Star's Edge Internat, 1992—; signature sound practitioner, New Haven, 1994-96, Hypnotherapist, New Haven, 1995-97; owner, officer Rafferty Constrn. Corp., Asheville, 1999—. Mem. Electronic Data Processing Auditors Assn. (bd. dirs. 1981-82), Inst. Internal Auditors. Democrat. Unitarian Universalist. Home: PO Box 8282 Asheville NC 28814-8282 Office: Paar Enterprises PO Box 8282 Asheville NC 28814-8282 E-mail: parexcel@paarenterprises.com.

JONES-WILLS, EUNICE STEPHANIE, mental health nurse, researcher; b. Guyana, Nov. 14, 1955; came to the U.S., 1967; d. Esther (Fredericks) Elder; m. Bernard Jones, June 3, 1974 (div. Sept. 1989); m. Aloysius Ignatius Wills, May 25, 1991; children: Dwayne, Anton, Denise, Brandon, Andrew. AAS, N.Y.C. Tech. Coll., Bklyn., 1987; BS, U. Md., 1994, MS, 1996. RNC; RN, Md., D.C., Va; clin. specialist of psychiat. and mental health. Med.-surg. nurse Providence Hosp., Washington, 1987-88; charge nurse Crownsville (Md.) Hosp. Ctr., 1988-92; team leader Dept. Mental Health Svcs., Washington, 1992-96, psychiat. rsch. nurse NIH, Bethesda, Md., 1996-98; clin. nurse Bureau of Prisons Fed. Dentention Ctr., Miami, Fla., 1998—. CPR instr. Dept. Health and Human Svcs., Washington, 1993-96; head judge sci. fair regionals Pub. Health Svc., Rockville, Md., 1997, 98, presenter pub. schs. health week, 1997, 98. Lt. comdr. USPHS, 1996—. Mem. ANA (psychiat. and mental health cert.), Res. Officer Assn., Commd. Officer Assn., Sigma Theta Tau, Phi Theta Kappa. Democrat. Roman Catholic. Avocations: reading, traveling, shopping, biking. Home: 4010 NW 73rd Ave Coral Springs FL 33065-2142 Office: Federal Dentention Ctr 33 NE 4th St Miami FL 33132-2111

JONES-WILSON, FAUSTINE CLARISSE, education educator emeritus; b. Little Rock, Ark., Dec. 3, 1927; d. James Edward and Perrine Marie (Childress) Thomas; m. James T. Jones, June 20, 1948 (div. 1977); children: Yvonne Dianne, Brian Vincent; m. Edwin L. Wilson, July 10, 1981. AB, Ark. A.M.&N. Coll., 1948; AM, U. Ill., 1951, EdD, 1967; LLD, U. Ark., Pine Bluff, 2003. Tchr., sch. librarian Gary pub. schs. (Ind.), 1955-62, 1964-67; asst. prof. Coll. Edn., U. Ill., Chgo., 1967-69; assoc. prof. adult edn. Fed. City Coll., Washington, 1970-71; prof. edn., grad. prof. Howard U., Washington, 1969-70, 71-93, acting dean Sch. Edn., 1991-92, prof. emeritus, 1993—. Author: The Changing Mood in America; Eroding Commitment, 1977, A Traditional Model of Educational Excellence: Dunbar High School of Little Rock, Arkansas, 1981; co-author: Paul Laurence Dunbar High School of Little Rock, Arkansas, 2003; editor Jour. Negro Edn., 1978-91, 92-93; co-editor: Encyclopedia of African-American Education, 1996; assoc. editor Jour. of Edn. for Students Placed at Risk, 1996-2000; co-author: Take from Our Lips A Song, Dunbar to Thee. Chmn. East Coast steering com. Nat. Coun. on Educating Black Children, 1986—88, 1990—92, 3d v.p., 1992—94, bd. dirs., 1994—98. Recipient Frederick Douglass award Nat. Assn. Black Journalists, 1979, Disting. Scholar-Tchr. award Howard U., 1985, Exemplary Leadership award Am. Assn. Higher Edn. Black Caucus, 1988, Gertrude E. Rush award Nat. Bar Assn., 1990, Disting. Career award V.P. for Acad. Affairs, Howard U., 1993, Disting. Alumni award Coll. Edn. U. Ill., 1997; Phelps Stokes Fund sr. fellow, 1993-2000. Mem. Am. Ednl. Studies Assn. (pres. 1984-85), John Dewey Soc., Soc. Profs. of Edn. (Mary Anne Raywid award 2002), Phi Delta Kappa (pres. Howard U. chpt. 1986-87, Svc. key 1990). Democrat. Methodist. Home: 6605 Allview Dr Columbia MD 21046-1005

JONG, ERICA MANN, writer, poet; b. N.Y.C., Mar. 26, 1942; d. Seymour and Eda (Mirsky) Mann; m. Michael Werthman, 1963 (div. 1965); m. Allan Jong (div. Sept. 1975); m. Jonathan Fast, Dec. 1977 (div. Jan. 1983); 1 child, Molly; m. Kenneth David Burrows, Aug. 5, 1989. BA, Barnard Coll., 1963; MA, Columbia U., 1965. Faculty, English dept. CUNY, 1964-65, 69-70, overseas div. U. Md., 1967-69; mem. lit. panel N.Y. State Council on Arts, 1972-74; faculty Breadloaf Writers Conf. Middlebury, Vt., 1982; mem. faculty Saltzburg Seminar, Saltzburg, Austria, 1993, 98. Author: (poems) Fruits and Vegetables, 1971, reissued edit., 1997, Half Lives, 1973, Loveroot, 1975, At the Edge of the Body, 1979, Ordinary Miracles, 1983, Becoming Light: Poems New and Selected, 1992; (novels) Fear of Flying, 1973, How to Save Your Own Life, 1977, Fanny: Being the True History of the Adventures of Fanny Hackabout-Jones, 1980, Parachutes and Kisses, 1984, Serenissima, 1987 (reissued as Shylock's Daughter, 1995), Any Woman's Blues, 1990, Inventing Memory, 1998, Sappho's Leap, 2003, (poetry and non-fiction) Witches, 1981, reissued edit., 1997, (juvenile) Megan's Book of Divorce, 1984 (reissued as Megan's Two Houses, 1995), (memoir) The Devil at Large, 1993, What Do Women Want?, 1998, (autobiography) Fear of Fifty, 1994, (non-fiction) What Do Women Want?, 2001; composer lyrics: Zipless: Songs of Abandon from the Erotic Poetry of Erica Jong, 1995, (fiction) Inventing Memory, 1997. Recipient Bess Hokin prize Poetry mag., 1971, Prix Literaire, Deauville Film Festival, 1997; named Mother of Yr., 1982; Woodrow Wilson fellow; Nat. Endowment Arts grantee, 1973. Mem. PEN, Authors Guild U.S.A. (coun. 1975—, pres. 1991-93), Poets and Writers Bd., Writers Guild Am.-West, Poetry Soc. Am. (Alice Faye di Castagnola award 1972), Phi Beta Kappa. Office: Erica Jong Prodns care Kenneth David Burrows 425 Park Ave New York NY 10022-3506

JONG, NANCY, financial consultant; b. San Francisco, Mar. 18, 1967; d. David Jong and June Moriguchi. BS, San Francisco State U., 1990, MBA, 1996. Fin. analyst Am. Appraisal Assocs., San Francisco, 1991—93; sr. acct. Bunje, Buss & Lloyd, San Francisco, 1994—96; freelance cons. San Francisco, 1997—98; v.p. banking group GateCapital, San Francisco, 1998—2000; fin. cons. San Francisco, 2000—02; pvt. practice fin. cons., 2003. Mem.: Inst. Mgmt. Cons., Nat. Assn. Women Owned Bus., Assn. Fin. Planners. Democrat-Npl. Avocations: piano, cooking.

JONGEWARD, GEORGE RONALD, retired systems analyst; b. Yakima, Wash., Aug. 9, 1934; s. George Ira and Dorothy Marjorie (Cronk) J.; m. Janet Jeanne Williams, July 15, 1955; children: Mary Jeanne, Dona Lee, Karen Anne. BA, Whitworth Coll., 1957; postgrad., Utah State U., 1961. Sr. systems analyst Computer Scis. Corp., Honolulu, 1969-71; cons. in field Honolulu, 1972-76; prin. The Hobby Co., Honolulu, 1977-81; sr. systems analyst Computer Systems Internat., Honolulu, 1981-96, asst. v.p., 1994-96; instr. EDP Hawaii Pacific U., Honolulu, 1982-90. Mem. car show com. Easter Seal Soc., Honolulu. 1977-82; active Variety Club, Honolulu, 1978-81. Mem. Mensa (Hawaii pres. 1967-69), Triple-9. Presbyterian. Avocations: travel, professional pianist, theater, classic cars. Home: 4108 Avalanche Ave Yakima WA 98908-2915

JONGEWARD, GREGG DUANE, biology educator, researcher; b. Denver, Oct. 16, 1964; s. Darrell Duane and Sarah Cleone Jongeward; m. Lisa Anne Wrischnik, Sept. 9, 1994. BS, U. Minn., 1986; PhD, Calif. Inst. Tech., 1993. Postdoctoral Am. Cancer Soc. fellow U. Calif., San Francisco, 1993-96, instr. Berkeley, 1996; asst. prof. biology U. of the Pacific, Stockton, Calif., 1996—. Cons. Neuromark, 2000. Contbr. articles to profl. jours. Mem. bd., Micke Grove Zool. Soc., 1999-2001. Holmok Cancer Rsch. fellow, U. Pacific, 1999-2000. Mem. Genetics Soc. Am. Avocation: ice hockey. Office: U of the Pacific 3601 Pacific Ave Stockton CA 95211 E-mail: gjongewa@uop.edu.

JONOVIC, DONALD J. management consultant, writer; b. Milw., Sept. 1, 1943; s. Joseph E. and Ann J.; m. Pamela J. McNeil, Dec. 4, 1970. BS, Marquette U., 1965; MA, U. Wis., 1976, PhD, 1982. Pub., editor Electrical Info. Pubs., Madison, Wisc., 1972-77; ptnr. Ctr. for Family Bus., Cleve., 1977-82; pres. Family Bus. Mgmt. Svcs., Cleve., 1982—. Author: Outside Directors in the Family-Owned Business, 1981, The Second Generation Boss, 1982, Someday It'll All Be Yours...or Will It?, 1984, Iron, Industry, and Independence, 1985, Passing Down the Farm, 1986, The Ultimate Legacy, 1997; editor: Encyclopedia of Telemarketing, 1989. Lt. USN, 1965-70, Vietnam. Mem. Family Firm Inst. Office: Family Bus Mgmt Svcs PO Box 201400 Cleveland OH 44120 E-mail: djonovic@familybusinessmgt.com.

JONSEN, ALBERT R(UPERT), retired medical ethics educator; b. San Francisco, Apr. 4, 1931; s. Albert R. and Helen (Sweigert) Jonsen; m. Mary Elizabeth Carolan. BA, Gonzaga U., 1955, MA, 1956; STM, U. Santa Clara, 1963; PhD, Yale U., 1967. Mem. S.J., 1949—76; ordained priest Roman Cath. Ch.; instr. philosophy Loyola U., L.A., 1956—59; asst. in instrn. Yale Div. Sch., 1966—67; asst. prof. theology and philosophy U. San Francisco, 1967—72, pres., 1969—72; prof. med. ethics Sch. Medicine, U. Calif.-San Francisco, 1972—87; adj. assoc. prof. dept. community medicine and internat. health Sch. Medicine, Georgetown U., 1977; prof. med. ethics, chmn. dept. med. history and ethics Sch. Medicine U. Wash., Seattle, 1987—99; prof. emeritus. Vis. prof. Yale U., 1999—2000; mem. artificial heart assessment panel Nat. Heart and Lung Inst., 1972—73, 1984—86; mem. Am. Bd. Med. Spltys., 1978—81; cons. Am. Bd. Internal Medicine, 1978—82, ACOG, 1983—88; mem. Pres.'s Commn. for Study of Ethical Problems in Medicine, 1979—82, Nat. Commn. for Protection Human Subjects of Biomed. and Behavioral Rsch., HEW, 1974—78, Nat. Bd. Med. Examiners, 1985—87, Commn. on AIDS Rsch., NRC, 1986—92, Panel on Social Impact of AIDS (chmn.), 1989—91; chmn. nat. adv. bd. Ethics and Reprodn., 1991—96; mem. ethics adv. bd. GERON Corp., 2000—; vis. prof. Stanford U. Sch. Medicine, 2002, U. Va. Law Sch., 2002. Author: Responsibility in Modern Religious Ethics, 1968, Patterns of Moral Responsibility, 1969, Christian Decision and Action, 1970, Ethics of Newborn Intensive Care, 1976, Clin. Ethics, 1982, The Abuse of Casuistry: A History of Moral Reasoning, 1987, The New Medicine and the Old Ethics, 1990, The Social Impact of AIDS in the United States, 1993, Bioethics, 1997, The Birth of Bioethics, 1998, A Short History of Medical Ethics, 2000. Bd. trustees Inst. Ednl. Mgmt., Harvard U., 1971—74, Ploughshares Found., 1980—84; mem. San Francisco Crime Com., 1969—71; bd. dirs. Found. Critical Care Medicine, 1983—86, Sierra Health Found., 1987—. Fellow, Guggenheim, 1995—96. Fellow: The Hastings Ctr.; mem.: Am. Osler Soc. (McGovern award 1986), Am. Coll. Cardiology (Convocation Medal 1996), Am. Soc. for Bioethics and Humanities (Lifetime Achievement award 1999), Blue Cross and Blue Shield Assn. (med. adv. panel, tech. assessment program 1985—), Instituto de Bioetica (Madrid), Inst. Medicine (com. human values 1973, coun. 1983—85, 1990—92), Soc. Christian Ethics, Am. Soc. Law and Medicine (bd. dirs. 1986—88), Soc. Health and Human Values (pres. 1986—87). Home: 1333 Jones St # 502 San Francisco CA 94109 E-mail: arjonsen@aol.com.

JONSEN, ERIC RICHARD, lawyer; b. San Francisco, June 5, 1958; s. Richard William and Ann Margaret (Parsons) J.; m. Ida-Marie, May 8, 1982; children: Kaitlyn, Jeremy, Michelle. BA, Hartwick Coll., 1980; JD, U. Colo., 1985. Bar: Colo., N.Y., U.S. Dist. Ct. Colo., U.S. Ct. Appeals (10th cir., Fed. cir.), U.S. Ct. Appeals (fed. cir.). Assoc. William P. DeMoulin, Denver, 1986-88, Fairfield & Woods, Denver, 1988—91; ptnr. Ciancio & Jonsen PC, Denver, 1994—2001, Jonsen & Assoc. LLC, Broomfield, Colo., 2001—. Bd. dirs. Broomfield Blast Soccer Club, 2000—. Mem. ABA, Colo. Bar Assn., Rotary (pres. Broomfield Crossings 2000--). Office: Jonsen & Assocs LLC 10901 W 120th Ave # 240 Broomfield CO 80021 E-mail: erjonsen@jonsen.net.

JONSEN, RICHARD WILIAM, retired educational administrator; b. San Francisco, Mar. 29, 1934; s. Albert Rupert and Helen Catherine (Sweigert) J.; m. Ann Margaret Parsons, Nov. 20, 1955; children: Marie Wood, Eric, Gregory, Stephen, Matthew. BA, U. Santa Clara, 1955; MA, San Jose (Calif.) State U., 1970; PhD, Stanford U., 1973. Pub.'s rep. Hearst Advt. Service, San Francisco, 1955-58; alumni dir. U. Santa Clara, Calif., 1958-70; dir. admissions, asst. dean. Sch. Edn., asst. prof. Syracuse (N.Y.) U., 1972-76; project dir. Edn. Commn. States, Denver, 1976-77, Western Interstate Commn. Higher Edn., Boulder, Colo., 1977-79, dep. dir., 1979-90, exec. dir., 1990-99; ret., 1999; instr. ESL Front Range Cmty. Coll., Colo., 1999—. Vis. prof. U. Tamaulipas, Mex., 1996-97; cons. Consortium for N.Am. Higher Edn. Collaboration; bd. regents U. Santa Clara, 2002—. Author: State Policy and Independent Higher Education, 1975, Small Liberal Arts Colleges, 1978, Lifelong Learning: State Policies, 1978, The Environmental context for Postsecondary Education, 1986; editor: Higher Education Policies in the Information Age, 1987. Roman Catholic. Home: 363 Troon Ct Louisville CO 80027-9592 E-mail: dickjonsen@att.net.

JONSSON, BJARNI, mathematician, educator; b. Draghals, Iceland, Feb. 15, 1920; came to U.S., 1941, naturalized, 1963; s. Jon and Steinunn (Bjarnadottir) Petursson; m. Amy Sprague, Dec. 16, 1950 (div. 1967); children: Eric M., Meryl S.; m. Harriet Parkes, Jan. 17, 1970; child, M. Kristin. BA, U. Calif. at Berkeley, 1943, PhD, 1946. Faculty Brown U., 1946-56, asst. prof., 1948-56; vis. prof. U. Iceland, 1954-55; vis. asso. prof. U. Calif. at, Berkeley, 1955-56; vis. prof., research mathematician U. Calif., Berkeley, 1962-63; faculty U. Minn., 1956-66, assoc. prof., 1956-59, prof., 1959-66; disting. prof. Vanderbilt U., Nashville, 1966-93, disting. prof. emeritus, 1993—. Mem. AAUP, Am. Math. Soc. Achievements include research, publs. in lattice theory, universal algebra, founds. of algebra, group theory. Office: Vanderbilt U Dept Math 2305 W End Ave Nashville TN 37203-1700 Address: 5810 Vine Ridge Dr Nashville TN 37205-1326 E-mail: jonsson@vanderbilt.edu.

JONTZ, JEFFRY ROBERT, lawyer; b. Stuart, Iowa, May 28, 1944; s. John Leo Jontz and Leora Burnette (Pittman) Myers; m. Sharyn Sue Kopriva, June 8, 1968; 1 son, Eric Barrett. BA, Drake U., 1966; JD with distinction, U. Iowa, 1969. Bar: Iowa 1969, Fla. 1971, Ohio 1972, U.S. Dist. Ct. (mid. dist.) Fla. 1971, U.S. Ct. Appeals (5th cir.) 1971, fla. 1972, U.S. Ct. Appeals (11th cir.) 1981, U.S. Tax Ct. 1983. Law clk. to Hon. Charles R. Scott U.S. Dist. Ct. (mid. dist.) Fla., Jacksonville, 1969-70; to Hon. Bryan Simpson U.S. Ct. Appeals (5th cir.), Jacksonville, 1970-71; assoc. Jones, Day, Cockley & Reavis, Cleve., 1971-72; asst. U.S. atty. U.S. Dist. Ct. (mid. dist.) Fla., Orlando, 1972-74; pvt. practice Orlando, 1974—; ptnr. Young, Turnbull & Linscott, Orlando, 1974-79, Baker & Hostetler, Orlando, 1979, DeWolf, ward & Morris, Orlando, 1979-84, Jontz, russell & Hull, Orlando, 1985-86, Holland & Knight, 1986-96, Carlton Fields, Orlando, 1996—. Contbr. articles to profl. jours.; mem. editl. bd. Iowa Law Rev., 1968. Chmn. Fed. Judicial Rels. Com., 2001—; Past bd. dirs. The Door Drug Rehab. Ctr. of Ctrl. Fla.; bd. dirs. Fla. Symphony Orch., 1985—93, Jr. Achievement Ctrl. Fla., 1997—; mem. Rollins Coll. Tar Boosters; mem. code enforcement bd. City of Maitland, Fla., 1990—92; chmn bd. adjustment City of Winter Park, Fla., 1995—; mem. parents com. Dartmouth Coll., 1995—99; mem. long range planning com., former county commiteeman Orange County (Fla.) Reps., past chmn. bd. trustees First Congregational Ch., Winter Park, Fla. Recipient Outstanding Individual Cmty. Leadership award Vol. Ctr. Ctrl. Fla., 1991. Mem. Am. Bankruptcy Inst., Ctrl. Fla. Bankruptcy Lawyers Assn., Fla. Bar (9th cir. grievance com. 1979-82, chmn. comml. litigation com. 1981-82, bankruptcy and creditor's rights com. corp. bus. and banking law sect., com. on jud. adminstrn., selection and tenure 1985-86, mem. jud. nominating procedures com. 1995-96, lectr. seminars), Orange County Bar Assn. (chmn. jud. rels. com. 1995—, bankruptcy com.), ABA (mem. comml. transactions litigation com., others), Drake U. Nat. Alumni Assn. (past chmn. ctrl. Fla. chpt., sec., bd. dirs. 1981-93, pres.'s circle coun.), Iowa State Bar Assn., Order of Coif, Winter Park Racquet Club (mem. bd. govs., sec., v.p., pres. 1989-94, 96-98), Tiger Bay Club Orlando, Citrus Club, U. Iowa Alumni Assn. (bd. dirs. 2003—), Omicron Delta Kappa, Tau Kappa Epsilon, Phi Delta Phi. Office: 450 S Orange Ave Ste 500 Orlando FL 32801-3370 E-mail: jjontz@carltonfields.com., jontz@worldnet.att.net.

JONZE, SPIKE, film director; b. Rockville, Md., 1969; s. Arthur Spiegel III and Sandy Granzow; m. Sofia Coppola, June 26, 1999. Prodr.: (films) Human Nature, 2001; exec. prodr., prodr., writer, actor : (TV series) Jackass, 2000; writer, dir. : (video) Beastie Boys: Sabotage, 1994; writer, prodr. : (films) Jackass: The Movie, 2000; actor: Mi vida loca, 1993, The Game, 1997; actor, dir. : Being John Malkovich, 1999 (N.Y. Film Critics Cir. Award for Best First Film, 1999, Broadcast Film Critics Assn. Award for Breakthrough Performer, 1999, Online Film Critics Soc. Award for Best Debut, 1999); dir.: (video) R.E.M. Parallel, 1995; (films) How They Get There, 1997, (video) Bjork: Volumen, 1998; (films) Clip Cult Vol. 1: Exploding Cinema, 1999, Adaptation, 2002; actor: (video) Beastie Boys: A Video Anthology, 2000; (films) Three Kings, 1999 (Broadcast Film Critics Assn. Award for Breakthrough Performer, 1999). Recipient MTV Video Music Award for Best Direction for Buddy Holly, 1995. Office: Creative Artists Agy Attn Tony Metzger 9830 Wilshire Blvd Beverly Hills CA 90212-1825*

JOO, DOUGLAS D.M. newspaper and video production executive; b. Hamheung, Korea, July 14, 1945; came to U.S., 1985; s. Soo Jang and Syn Duk (Choi) J.; m. Myung Mi, Oct. 21, 1970; children: Hoon Hwi, Hoon Pal, Hoon Chul. BS, Seoul Nat. U., 1967; MA, Kyung Hee U., Seoul, 1979; MPhil, George Washington U., 1993. Pres. News World Comms., Washington, 1992—, Washington Times Corp., 1992—, Noticias PanAm Corp., 1996—; chmn., CEO Atlantic Video, Inc., 1991—; pres. U.S. Property Devel. Corp., 1991—, Nat. Hospitality Corp., 2000—; chmn., CEO UPI, 2000—. Pres. Concept Comms., Washington, 1992—, chmn., CEO GoodLife TV Network; pres. Washington Times Aviation, 1997—. Trustee U. Bridgeport, Conn.; chmn. bd. dirs. Internat. Coalition for Religious Freedom, Washington, 1998—. Mem. World Media Assn. (pres. 1992—), Washington Times Found. (pres. 1992—). Office: Washington Times Corp 3600 New York Ave NE Washington DC 20002-1996

JOO, MICHAEL, artist, educator; b. Ithaca, N.Y., 1966; BFA, Washington U., 1989; MFA, Yale U., 1991. Adj. instr. The Cooper Union Sch. Art, N.Y.C., 1996, guest artist, 2000—. Adj. instr. The Cooper Union Sch. Art, N.Y.C., 1996, guest artist, 2000—. One-man shows include Nordanstad-Skarstedt, N.Y., 1992, Thomas Nordanstad Gallery, 1994—96, Stedelijk Mus., Amsterdam, 1995, Galerie Anne de Villepoix, Paris, 1995, Anthony D'Offay Gallery, London, 1995, Anton Kern Gallery, N.Y., 1997, exhibited in group shows at Ctr. Arts at Yerba Buena, San Francisco, 1993, Queens (N.Y.) Mus. Art, 1993, New Mus. Contemporary Art, N.Y., 1993, The Interart Ctr., 1994, Kumho Mus., Seoul, 1994, Cohen Gallery, N.Y., 1994, Serpentine Gallery, London, 1994, Inst. Contemporary Art, 1995, Randolph St. Gallery, Chgo., 1995, Mus. Contemporary Art, 1995, Kwangju Contemporary Mus., Sydkorea, 1995, Bloom Gallery, Amsterdam, 1996, The Post Office, London, 1996, Mus. Africa, Johannesburg, 1997, Anton Kern Gallery, N.Y., 1997, P.S. 1, 1998, others. Office: care Cooper Union Sch Art 30 Cooper Sq New York NY 10003-7120

JOO, SEUNG-HO, political scientist, educator; b. Incheon City, Republic of Korea, Dec. 6, 1959; s. Hong-Rin Joo and Soon-Hee Kim; m. Soon-Mi Hwahng, May 21, 1963; children: Esther Y.M., Danielle Y.H., Andrew Y.S. BA, Yonsei U., Seoul, 1982; PhD, Pa. State U., 1993. Asst. prof. polit. sci. U. of Minn.-Duluth, Duluth, Minn., 1994—95; assoc. prof. polit. sci. U. of Minn.-Morris, Morris, Minn., 1995—. Author: Gorbachev's Foreign Policy Toward the Korean Peninsula, 2000, Korea in the 21st Century, 2002. Fellow Humphrey Inst. Policy Fellow, Hubert H. Humphrey Inst. of Pub. Affairs, 1997—98; grantee IREX Travel Grant, Internat. Rsch. and Exch. Bd., 2001; Disting. Rsch. fellow, Korea Inst. Nat. Unification, 1999—2000. Mem.: Internat. Studies Assn., Assn. of Korean Polit. Studies in N.Am. (exec. sec., treas. 1999—2003), Am. Polit. Sci. Assn. Home: 4 Riverside Rd Morris MN 56267 Office: U Minn-Morris 109 Camden 601 E 4th St Morris MN 56267 Office Fax: 320-589-6117. E-mail: joos@mrs.umn.edu.

JOOS, FELIPE MIGUEL, mechanical engineer, researcher; b. Montevideo, Uruguay, Sept. 4, 1952; arrived in U.S., 1973, naturalized, 2003; s. Carlos Jose and Alma Elena Joos; children: Carolina Lucia, Catrina Aneliese, Celina Maria. BS in Applied Sci. and Engring., Calif. Inst. Tech., 1976; MSME, MIT, 1978, PhDME, 1983. Cert. engr., Uruguay. Engr. Ingenieros Consultores Latinoamericanos Limitada, Montevideo, Uruguay, 1978-79; mech. engr. research and devel. div. Gen. Electric Corp., Schenectady, N.Y., 1982-85; project engr. Creare, Inc., Hanover, N.H., 1985-87; tech. assoc. Eastman Kodak Co., Rochester, N.Y., 1987—. Indsl. fellow Ctr. for Interfacial Engring., U. Minn., Mpls., 1991-92. Contbr. articles to profl. jours.; presenter at internat. symposium and conf. in field; patentee in field. Mem. ASME, Internat. Soc. Coating Sci. and Tech. (tech. session chair 1994, 98, 2000), Soc. Hispanic Profl. Engrs. (award 1993, v.p. 1989-90, treas. 1990-92, treas. Ea. Tech. and Career conf. 1991), Tau Beta Pi. Avocations: scuba diving, community affairs. Home: 75 Wood Creek Dr Pittsford NY 14534-4415 Office: Eastman Kodak Co Kodak Park Rochester NY 14652-3703

JOOS, STEVEN LEE, sports editor; b. Peoria, Ill., Feb. 4, 1955; s. Charles Edward and Shirley Ann (Clary) J. AA in English, Ill. Ctrl. Coll., East Peoria, Ill., 1976; BSJ, Bradley U., 1978. Asst. editor Metamora (Ill.) Herald, 1978; corr. Tazewell Pub., Morton, Ill., 1978-79; editor Mason County Dem., Havana, Ill., 1979; staff announcer WDUK-FM Radio, Havana, 1979-88; corr. Pekin (Ill.) Daily Times, 1982-83; reporter Times-Advocate, West Salem, Ill., 1988-89; sports editor Posey County News, Poseyville, Ind., 1989—. Recipient awards for writing. Avocations: writing poetry, historical study. Home: PO Box 372 Poseyville IN 47633-0372 Office: Posey County News 604 Lockwood St Poseyville IN 47633 E-mail: sjoos_44@yahoo.com.

JOOS, WINNIE J. home and community educator; b. Humbird, Wis., Mar. 21, 1926; d. Samuel Robert and Maude Mary Newton; m. Thane William Joos, July 14, 1945; children: Charles, Susan, David, Karen. Grad. pub. schs., Alma Center, Wis. Pres. Jackson County, Ext. Homemakers, Black River Falls, Wis., 1973-75, pres. Eau Claire County Eau Claire, Wis., 1991-93, dir. N.W. dist., 1994-96; pres.-elect Wis. Assn. Home and Cmty. Edn., Eau Claire, 1997, pres., 1998-2000, past pres., 2002—. Mem. Order Ea. Star (sec. 1985-2000, worthy matron 2000-03). Democrat. Methodist. Avocations: camping, crafts, tatting, crochet, knitting. Home: 2883 Green View Dr Eau Claire WI 54703

JOOSTEN, MICHAEL JOHN, music educator; b. Stevens Point, Wis., Dec. 17, 1959; s. Anthony and Viola Joosten; m. Elizabeth Joan Anderson, July 8, 1989; children: Heidi, Daniel, Sarah. BSc, U. Wis., 1983; student in Music, U. So. Oreg., 2002—03. Music tchr. Cameron (Wis.) Sch. Dist., 1984—. Instr. U. Wis., Rice Lake, Wis.; adjudicator WSMA, 1985—, hons. band coach, 1999—2001; cmty. band dir. Rice Lake (Wis.) Mcpl. Band, 1992—; dir. State of Wis. FFA Band, 1990—97; music clinician Son Solo Ensemble and Band Festival. Govt. rels. officer Coalition for Music Edn., Madison, Wis., 1994—97. Mem.: Wis. Music Educators Assn. (govt. rels. officer 1994—97), Cameron (Wis.) Civic Club. Avocations: woodworking, gardening, golf. Office: Cameron School Dist 600 Wisconsin Cameron WI 54822

JOPLIN, JULIAN MIKE, lawyer; b. Littlefield, Tex., Aug. 30, 1936; s. Charles Arbie and Gladys (Douglass) J.; m. Barbara Maye McKinney, Sept. 1, 1957; children: Erin Colleen, Jeffrey Miles. BBA in Fin., Tex. Tech U., 1958; JD, U. Tex., 1963. Bar: Tex. 1963. Ptnr. Strasburger & Price, Dallas, 1963—. Bd. dirs. Notre Dame Spl. Sch., 1986-91, Presbyn. Hosp., Dallas, 1988-93, Ctrl. Dallas Assn., 1989-98, Children's Hosp., Dallas, 1998-2001, ruling elder Highland Pk. Presbyn. Ch., Dallas, 1982-2000; elder First Presbyn. Ch., Kerrville, 2003—. Capt. U.S. Army and Tex. N.G., 1958-63. Mem.: U. Tex. Law Sch. Alumni Assn. (bd. dirs. 1987—90, mem. exec. com. 1998—2001), Dallas Bar Found. (bd. dirs., chmn. 1997—98), Dallas Bar Assn. (bd. dirs., pres. 1988), State Bar Tex. (bd. dirs. 1989—92), Rotary, Riverhill Country Club, Salesmanship Club. Republican. Avocation: racquet sports. Home: 1542 Saddle Club Dr Kerrville TX 78028 Office: Strasburger & Price 901 Main St 4300 Bank of Am Plz Dallas TX 75202 E-mail: mjoplin@ktc.com.

JOPPEN-HELLWIG, SANDRA, linguist, researcher; b. Krefeld, Germany, Jan. 22, 1965; d. Werner Wilhelm and Ingeborg Maria (Fercho) Joppen; m. Joerg Olaf Hellwig, June 4, 1994; children: Naomi, Lennart. MA, Heinrich-Heine-U., Duesseldorf, Germany, 1991, PhD, 2000. Rsch. asst. Heinrich-Heine-U., Duesseldorf, 1991—. Author: Causatives in Basque, 1993, Case Alternation and Its Conceptual Basis, 1995, Structural Arguments with Semantic Case: The Case of Causees and Recipients in 4-Place Verbs, 1999, Verbclasses and Argument Linking. Non-Canonical Arguments, Expletives, and 4-Place Causatives in Ergative Versus Accusative Languages, 2001; co-author: Argument Linking in Basque, 1994, The Representation of Argument Linking in a Unification Based Formalism, 1996, First Steps in the Acquistion of German Phonology, 1998. German Acad. Exch. Svc. scholar, 1990. Mem. German Assn. for Sprachwissenschaft. Office: HH-Uni Sprachwiss Universitaetsstr 1 40225 Düsseldorf Germany

JORDAN, ALEXANDER JOSEPH, JR., lawyer; b. New London, Conn., Oct. 11, 1938; s. Alexander Joseph and Alice Elizabeth (Mugovero) J.; m. Mary Carolyn Miller, Aug. 8, 1964; children: Jennifer, Michael, Stephanie. BS, U.S. Naval Acad., 1960; LLB, Harvard U., 1968. Ptnr. Gaston & Snow, Boston, 1968-91, Bingham, Dana & Gould, Boston, 1991-93, Nixon Peabody LLP, Boston, 1994—. Mem., past chmn. adv. com. Town of Hingham, Mass., 1989-95, mem. govt. study com., 2000-2001. With USN, 1960-65, capt. USNR, 1965-94, ret. Mem. ABA, Mass. Bar Assn., Boston Bar Assn., U.S. Naval Inst., Naval Res. Assn., Harvard Alumni Assn. (regional dir. 1998-2001), U.S. Naval Acad. Alumni Assn., Harvard Club Hingham (trustee, chmn. com. schs. and scholarships, past pres.), Harvard Club of Boston. Office: Nixon Peabody LLP 101 Federal St Fl 13 Boston MA 02110-1832

JORDAN, AMOS AZARIAH, JR., foreign affairs educator, retired army officer; b. Twin Falls, Idaho, Feb. 11, 1922; s. Amos Azariah and Olive (Fisher) J.; m. MarDeane Carver, June 5, 1946; children: Peggy Jordan Hughes, Diana Jordan Paxton, Keith, David, Linda Jordan Mabey, Kent. BS, U.S. Mil. Acad., 1946; BA, Oxford U., Eng., 1950, MA, 1955; PhD, Columbia U., 1961. Commd. 2d lt. U.S. Army, 1946, advanced through grades to brig. gen., 1972; instr. U.S. Mil. Acad., 1950-53, prof. social scis., 1955-72; arty. battery comdr. U.S. Army, Korea, 1954-55; asst. S-3 7th Divsn. Arty. Korea, 1955; adviser econ. and fiscal policy U.S. Econ. Mission to Korea, 1955; ret. U.S. Army, 1972; dir. Aspen Inst., 1972-74; prin. dep. asst. sec. for internat. security affairs Dept. Def., Washington, 1974-76; dep. undersec. and acting undersec. for security assistance Dept. State, Washington, 1976-77; with Ctr. for Strategic and Internat. Studies, Washington, 1977-94, pres., chief exec. officer, 1983-88, vice chmn., 1988-94, pres. Pacific Forum Honolulu, 1990-94; sr. adviser CSIS, 1994—; counselor Pacific Forum, 1994—. Mem. staff Pres.'s Com. to Study Fgn. Assistance Program, 1959; staff dir. Adv. Com. to Sec. Def. on Non-Mil. Instrn., 1962; spl. polit. advisor to U.S. amb. to India, 1963-64; cons. NSC, 1979; mem. Nat. Com. on Security and Econ. Assistance, 1983; Henry Kissinger rsch. chair in nat. security policy CSIS, 1988-92; mem. Pres.'s Intelligence Oversight Bd., 1989-93; internat. co-chmn. Coun. on Sec. Coop. in the Asia Pacific, 1993-96, chmn. U.S. com., 1993-98; co-chmn. Korean-Am. Wisemen Coun., 1991-98; Asia area adminstr. Latter Day Saint Charities, 1998-99; spl. asst. to pres. Brigham Young U., Hawaii, 2001-02; bd. dirs. Pacific Forum, Ctr. for Strategic and Internat. Studies. Author: Foreign Aid and the Defense of Southeast Asia, 1962, Issues of National Security in the 1970's, 1967; co-author: American National Security Policy and Process, 1981, 5th edit., 1999; contbr. chpts. to books and articles to profl. jours. Decorated D.S.M., Legion of Merit with oak leaf cluster, Disting. Civilian Svc. medal Dept. Def. Mem. Coun. Fgn. Rels., Assn. Am. Rhodes Scholars, Pacific Coun. Internat. Policy, Bretton Woods Com. Office: Pacific Forum CSIS Pauahi Tower 1001 Bishop St Ste 1150 Honolulu HI 96813-3407

JORDAN, ANGEL GONI, electrical and computer engineering educator; b. Pamplona, Spain, Sept. 19, 1930; came to U.S., 1956, naturalized, 1966; s. Hilario and Perpetua (Goni) J.; m. Nieves Alfonso Cuartero, July 8, 1956; children: Xavier, Edward, Arthur. MS, PhD, Carnegie Inst. Tech., 1959; Dr. h.c., Poly. U. Madrid, Spain, 1985, U. Publica de Navarra, 2001. With Naval Ordnance Lab., Madrid, 1952-56; instr. elec. engring. Carnegie-Mellon U., 1956-58, asst. prof. elec. engring., 1959-62, assoc. prof., 1962-65, prof., 1965-90, univ. prof., 1990-97, U.A. and Helen Whitaker prof., 1972-80, head dept., 1969-79; dean engineering Carnegie-Mellon U. (Carnegie Inst. Tech.), 1979-83; provost Carnegie-Mellon U., 1983-91, J.F and N.P. Keithley univ. prof. elec., computer engring., 1997-99, univ. prof. emeritus, 1999—. Rsch. fellow Mellon Inst. Indsl. Rsch., 1958—59; cons. to industry; bd. dirs. Magnascreen Corp., Mirror Sys., Inc., SOCINTEC. Contbr. articles to profl. jours. Dir. Pitts. High Tech. Council, 1983— ; bd. dirs. Pa. Sci. and Engring. Found, 1981-83. Recipient Enterprise award Pitts. Bus. Times, 1985; NATO sr. scientist fellow, 1976; Fulbright Disting. scholar, 1988; named Edn. Man of the Yr, Pitts, 1987. Fellow IEEE, AAAS; mem. Am. Phys. Soc., Nat. Acad. Engring., Acad. Engring. Spain, Sigma Xi, Eta Kappa Nu, Phi Kappa Phi, Tau Beta Pi. Home: 5874 Aylesboro Ave Pittsburgh PA 15217-1446 Office: Carnegie-Mellon U Wean Hall # 4618 Pittsburgh PA 15213 E-mail: ajordan@cs.cmu.edu.

JORDAN, ANNE DEVEREAUX, writer, educator; b. Franklin, Pa., Dec. 11, 1943; d. Frederic William and Helen Anne Wilson; m. Robert Crouse (div. May 20, 1994); 1 child, David Frederic Crouse. MA, U. of Mich., Ann Arbor, Michigan, 1969, BA, 1968. English educator Ea. Conn. State U., Willimantic, Conn., 1991—; lectr. Wesleyan U., Middletown, Conn., 1990—; sr. editor TALL, Brandon, Vt., 1994—98; mng. editor The Mag. of Fantasy and Sci. Fiction, Cornwall, Conn., 1979—89; english educator Ctrl. Conn. State U., New Britain, Conn., 1991—93, U. of Hartford, Hartford, Conn., 1979—83; lectr. U. of Conn., Storrs, Conn., 1973—75; english educator Western Mich. U., Kalamazoo, Mich., 1970—73. Cons. Fross Zelnick Lehrman and Zissu, New York, NY, 1990—; founder The Children's Lit. Assn., 1972. Contbr. articles to profl. jours. Chair, bd. of commissioners Mansfield Housing Authority, Storrs, Conn., 1992—2003. Recipient Lifetime Membership to the Children's Lit. Assn., The Children's Lit. Associaiton, 1976, Avery and Jule Hopwood Award for short story and poetry, U. of Mich., 1968, Anne Devereaux Jordan award, Children's Lit. Assn., 1992; scholar Oakland's Writer's Conf., Detroit Women's Writers, 1969. Avocations: reading, travel.

JORDAN, ANNE E. DOLLERSCHELL, journalist; b. Mpls., Mar. 30, 1964; d. Allen L. and Marcia G. (Landeen) Dollerschell; m. James Lawrence Jordan, Aug. 16, 1986; children: Davyd, Scott. BA, U. Wis., 1986. From editl. asst. to mng. editor Governing Mag., Washington, 1987—. Mem. Phi Beta Kappa, Phi Kappa Phi, Phi Theta Kappa. Office: Governing Mag Ste 1300 1100 Connecticut Ave NW Washington DC 20036-4109

JORDAN, BERNICE BELL, retired elementary school educator; b. Calvert, Tex. d. Ocie Wade and Nannie B. (Westbrook) Bell; m. William B. Jordan, Sept. 28, 1956; children: Beverly, Terrence, Keith. Student, Prairie View A&M, Tex. Western Coll.; BA, San Jose State Coll., 1959, MA, 1985. Cert. elem. edn., fine arts, multi-cultural tchr., specially designed acad. instrn. English. Writer curriculum guide, fine arts Alum Rock Union Elem. Sch. Dist., San Jose, Calif., elem. tchr., 1959—99; writer sch. plan Goss Elem.; ret., 1999. Mem. adv. com., tchr.-cons. writing project San Jose U., 1992—. Mem.: NEA, ASCD, Calif. Ret. Tchrs. Assn., Santa Clara County Reading Coun., Calif. Elem. Edn. Assn., Calif. Reading Assn., Calif. Tchrs. Assn., Alum Rock Edn. Assn., Nat. Coun. Negro Women, Delta Kappa Gamma, Alpha Delta Kappa. Home: 3282 Fronda Dr San Jose CA 95148-2015

JORDAN, BETH MCANINCH, artist, educator; b. Corn, Okla., Nov. 23, 1918; d. Abraham Willems Siemens and Marie (Richert) Siemens; m. Roy David McAninch, Mar. 5, 1946 (dec. Apr. 1982); children: David McAninch, Susan McAninch Munkres; m. H. Dale Jordan, Nov. 29, 1985. Student, Tabor Coll., 1937; BFA, S. Western State U., Weatherford, Okla., 1940. One-woman shows include Philbrook Art Ctr., Tulsa, Oklahoma City Art Ctr., Linda Howell & Assocs., Oklahoma City. Home and Office: 1606 Drakestone Ave Oklahoma City OK 73120-1207

JORDAN, BRENDA MOORE, artist; b. Roanoke Rapids, NC, Feb. 4, 1946; d. John Leroy and Sarah (Williams) Moore; m. John Richard Jordan, Jr., June 26, 1982; m. James Edwin Harlow, Nov. 27, 1966 (div.); 1 child, Edwin Scott Harlow. BS cum laude in Art Edn. and Painting, U. N.C., Greensboro, 1980. One-woman shows include Chowan College, Murfreesboro, N.C., 2001, Wake County Mcpl. Bldg., Raleigh, N.C., 2001, Wilson (N.C.) Art Coun. Bldg., 2001, Barton Coll., Wilson, N.C. Bd. dirs. (3 gubernatorial appointments) Murfreesboro Hist. Commn.; bd. dirs. U. N.C. Thurston Arthritis Rsch. Ctr., Chapel Hill, NC, 1966—99, N.C. divsn. Am. Cancer Soc., Raleigh, NC, 1982—92, N.C. Tri-Agy. Health Bd., Raleigh, NC, 1990—92; bd. dir. Sch. Pub. Health, Chapel Hill, NC, N.C. Lit. and Hist. Assn., Raleigh. Democrat. Baptist. Home: 809 Westwood Dr Raleigh NC 27607

JORDAN, BRUCE LESLIE, music educator, musician; b. Dayton, Ohio, Oct. 6, 1944; s. Robert Leslie and Lois Evelyn Jordan; m. Brenda Sue Jordan, July 28, 1979; children: Amanda Lynn, Robert Eugene. MusB, Miami U., 1966; MusM, Ind. U., 1969. Prof. Sinclair C.C., Dayton, 1973—. Performer (Saxophone): S.C.C. Jazz Ensemble; performer: (CD) Water Music.

JORDAN, BRYCE, retired university president; b. Clovis, N.Mex., Sept. 22, 1924; s. W. Joseph and Kittie (Cole) J.; children: Julia Cole, Christopher Joseph; m. Barbara E. Brueggebors, Oct. 28, 2000. Student, Hardin-Simmons U., 1941-42; MusB, U. Tex., 1948, MusM, 1949; PhD, U. N.C., 1956; LLD, Juniata Coll., 1985, Milliken U., 1990. Asst. prof. music Hardin-Simmons U., 1949-51; from asst. prof. to prof. music U. Md., 1954-63; prof. music, chmn. dept. U. Ky., 1963-65, U. Tex., 1965-68, v.p. student affairs, 1968-70, pres. ad interim, 1970-71, pres. Dallas, 1971-81; exec. vice chancellor for acad. affairs U. Tex. System, 1981-83; pres. Pa. State U., 1983-90. Mem. faculty Salzburg (Austria) Seminar Am. Studies, 1960, 62, 98; occasional lectr. Fgn. Svc. Inst., Dept. State, 1962-63; mem. Yale Coun. on Music, 1971-73, Nat. Commn. on Higher Edn. Issues, 1982-83. Author: (with Homer Ulrich) Student Manual for Music: A Design for Listening, 1957, Designed for Listening, 1962, also articles, revs.; assoc. editor: Coll. Music Symposium, 1961-66. Bd. dirs. Dallas Grand Opera Assn., 1973-75, Pa. Econ. Devel. Ptnrship, 1987-90; trustee St. Marks Sch. Tex., 1973-81, Dallas Symphony Assn., 1972-81, Presbyn. Hosp., Dallas, 1976-83; v.p. Dallas Civic Music Assn., 1978-79, pres., 1979-80, exec. com. 1980-81; bd. dirs. Dallas County chpt. ARC, 1976-79; divsn. chmn. United Way Met. Dallas, 1979; Pa. state chmn. Am. Heart Assn., 1983-84; trustee Com. on Econ. Devel. 1988-90; adv. bd. comml. programs NASA, 1988-90; nat. chmn. higher edn. U.S. Treasury Savs. Bond Programs, 1988-89, 89-90; presiding elder Presbyn. Ch.; chmn. Austin Lyric Opera, 1991-94; vis. com. Eastman Sch. Music U. Rochester, 1991-94; chmn. fine arts adv. coun. U. Tex., Austin, 1994-96; chmn. adv. bd. U. Tex. Press, 1997-99; mem. Knight Found. Commn. on Intercollegiate Athletics, 1991-93, 2000-01. Recipient Hon. Alumni award Pa. State U., 1987, medal, 1990, Doty medal U. Tex., 1996, Presdl. citation U. Tex., 2002; named Disting. Alumnus, U. N.C., 1985, Hardin-Simmons U., 1987, U. Tex., Austin, 1991. Mem. Coll. Music Soc. (v.p. 1963-65, coun. mem. 1968-70), Am. Musicol. Soc. (chmn. greater Washington chpt. 1958-60), Music Educators Nat. Conf. (pres. Md. br. 1963), Music Tchrs. Nat. Assn., Philos. Soc. Tex., Dallas C. of C. (dir. 1970-82), So. Assn. Colls. and Schs. (commn. on colls. 1981-83), Pa. Assn. Colls. and Univs. (chmn. 1988-89), Phi Kappa Phi, Pi Kappa Lambda, Phi Mu Alpha, Golden Key. Home: 7801 Comfort Cove Austin TX 78731-1471 E-mail: bigbendboy@austin.rr.com.

JORDAN, CAROLE JEAN, political organization administrator; married; 1 child. Sec. exec. com. Nat. Fedn. Rep. Women, 1995-97, mem. at large, dir. region 3, 1997—. Pres. Fla. Rep. Women, 1992-97, bd. dirs.; regent, co-chair Orlando 87 conv. Nat. Fedn. Rep. Women; pres. Rep. Women Indian River; mem. exec. com. Fla. Rep. Com.; nat. committeewoman, Fla., 1996-, rep. rules com. Rep. Nat. Com.; del.-at-large Rep. Nat. Conv., San Diego; del., at-large alternative Rep. Nat. Conv., Houston, 1992, del. to pres. I, II, II; co-chmn. RPOF Election 1996 com.; joint owner Jordan Irrigation and Well Drilling, Inc. Active George bus. for Pres.; active statewide steering com. Jeb Bush for Gov.; candidate for U.S. Congress, 1994; sec., vice chmn. Rep. Exec. Com. Indian river County; vol. Indian River County Mental Health Soc., Indian River Meml. Hosp. Woman's Bur., Indian River Hist. Soc., Environ. Learning Ctr., Jr. League, Vera Beach Ctr. for Arts; past pres. St. Edward's Sports Assn. Mem. Nat. Small Bus. Assn., Nat. Fedn. Ind. Businesses, Vero Beach/Indian River C. of C., Coast Builders Assn. (treas.). Office: Nat Fedn Rep Women 124 N Alfred St Alexandria VA 22314-3011 Fax: 703-548-9836.*

JORDAN, CATHELEEN, social worker, educator; b. Kansas City, Mo., June 1, 1947; d. J. Lon and Mary Joyce (Perdue) Jordan; m. Richard Hoefer, May 29, 1999; children: Mary Catheleen, Christopher Jordan, Sharon Elizabeth. BA, U. Houston, 1973; MSW, U. Tex., Arlington, 1979; PhD, U. Calif., Berkeley, 1986. Social worker Tex. Dept. Human Svcs., Belton, 1974-77; prog. evaluation specialist City of Ft. Worth, Tex., 1978; statis. analyst Inst. for Sci. Analysis, San Francisco, 1979-80; teaching/rsch. assoc. U. Calif., Berkeley, 1981-83; instr. Dana Coll., Blair, Nebr., 1983-84; clin. social worker Parenting Guidance Ctr., Ft. Worth, 1984-85; project coord. Tex. Rsch. Inst., Ft. Worth, 1984-85; vis. asst. prof. U. Tex., Arlington, 1985-86, asst. prof. social work, 1986-91, assoc. prof., 1991-95, dir. cmty. svc. clinic, 1991-96, prof., 1995—, dir. PhD program, 2000—02, co-dir. work & life project, 1999—. Vol., Arlington Night Shelter, 1989-93; adv. bd. Foster Child Advocates, Ft. Worth, 1985-88; bd. dirs. Am. Cancer Soc., 1999—, Dallas LifeWalk, 1992-97. Recipient Torgeson Teaching award, U. Tex., 1988. Mem. Nat. Assn. Social Workers (chair Tarrant County 1999—), Coun. on Social Work Edn., Soc. for Social Work Rsch., Southwestrn Social Sci. Assn. Democrat. Methodist. Avocations: tennis, dancing, reading, writing, skiing. Office: U Tex PO Box 19129 Arlington TX 76019-0001 Business E-Mail: jordan@uta.edu.

JORDAN, CHARLES MILTON, lawyer; b. Houston, Apr. 3, 1949; m. Jeanette Jordan; children: Nicole, John, Rebecca. BBA, U. Tex., 1971, JD, 1975, BBA, 1971, JD, 1975. Bar: Tex. 75, U.S. Dist. Ct. (so. dist.) Tex. 76, U.S. Supreme Ct. 78, U.S. Ct. Appeals (5th cir.) 79, U.S. Dist. Ct. (no. dist.) Tex. 82, U.S. Dist. Ct. (we. and ea. dists.) Tex. 83. Assoc. Troutman, Earle & Hill, Austin, 1975-76, Simpson & Burwell, Texas City, 1976-78, Smith & Herz, Galveston, Tex., 1978-80; ptnr. Dibrell & Greer, Galveston, 1980-85, Barlow, Todd, Crews & Jordan PC, Houston, 1986-88, Barlow, Todd, Jordan & Oliver, LLP, Houston, 1988-99, Barlow, Todd, Jordan & Jones, LLP, Houston, 1999—2002, Daughtry, Scott & Jordan, P.C., Houston, 2003—. Commr. Commn. Texas City/Galveston Ports, 1984. 1st lt. USAF, 1971-77. Recipient Outstanding Young Man Am. award, U.S. Jaycees, 1980. Mem. Tex. Bar Assn., Galveston County Bar Assn. (pres. 1981-82, bd. dirs. 1985-88), Tex. Young Lawyers Assn (bd. dirs. 1982-85, Outstanding Dir. award 1983-84), Galveston County Young Lawyers Assn. (pres. 1979-80, Outstanding Young Lawyer award 1981). Office: Daughtry Scott & Jordan PC 17044 El Camino Real Ste 400 Houston TX 77058-2630 E-mail: cmjordan@daughtryscott.com.

JORDAN, CHARLES MORRELL, retired automotive designer; b. Whittier, Calif., Oct. 21, 1927; s. Charles L. and Bernice May (Letts) J.; m. Sally Irene Mericle, Mar. 8, 1951; children: Debra, Mark, Melissa. BS, MIT, 1949; grad. advanced mgmt. program, Harvard U., 1979; Doctorate (hon.), Art Ctr. Coll. Design, 1992, Ctr. for Creative Studies, 2001. With GM, Warren, Mich., 1949—, chief designer Cadillac Studio, 1957-61, group chief designer, 1961-62, exec. in charge automotive design, 1962-67, dir. styling Adam Opel A.G., 1967-70, exec. in charge Cadillac, Oldsmobile, Buick Studios, 1970-73, exec. in charge Chevrolet, Pontiac and Comml. Vehicle Studios, 1973-77, dir. design, 1977-86, v.p. design staff, 1986-92; retired, 1992. 1st lt. USAF, 1952-53. Recipient First Nat. award Fisher Body Craftsman's Guild, 1947, disting. svc. citation Automotive Hall of Fame, 1990, Wally B. Ford award Ctr. for Creative Studies, 1992; named Hon. Judge, Pebble Beach Concours d'Elegance, 1970—. Mem. Calif. Scholastic Fedn. (life), Ferrari Club Am. Address: PO Box 8330 Rancho Santa Fe CA 92067-8330 E-mail: cmjdesign@aol.com.

JORDAN, CHARLES WESLEY, retired bishop; b. Dayton, Ohio, May 28, 1933; s. David Morris and Naomi Azelia (Harper) J.; m. Margaret May Crawford, Aug. 2, 1959; children: Diana, Susan. BA, Roosevelt U., 1956; MDiv, Garrett Evangel. Theol. Sem., Evanston, Ill., 1960; LHD (hon.), Morningside Coll., 1994; DD (hon.), Rust Coll., 1995, Simpson Coll., 2000. Ordained to ministry United Meth. Ch., 1960. Pastor Woodlawn United Meth. Ch., Chgo., 1960-66; dir. of urban ministries Rockford, Ill., 1966-71; prog. staff No. Ill. Con./United Meth. Ch., Chgo., 1971-82; dist. supt. Chgo./So. Dist. United Meth. Ch., 1982-87; sr. pastor St. Mark United Meth. Ch., Chgo., 1987-92; bishop Iowa Area United Meth. Ch., Des Moines, 1992-2000; ret., 2000. Del. United Meth. Gen. Conf., 1976, 80, 84, 88, 92, Gen. Bd. Global Ministries, 1972-80, Gen. Coun. on Ministries, 1980-88; trustee Garrett Evangel. Theol. Sem., 1982-97. Commnr. Rockford Housing Authority, 1969-71; bd. dirs. Cmty. Mental Health Coun., Chgo., 1989-91, Project Image, Inc., Chgo., 1987-92, Cen. Iowa Health System, 1993-2000, Mid-Iowa coun. Boy Scouts Am., 1995-2000; pres. United Meth. Gen. Bd. Ch. amnd Society, 1996-2000, Ecumenical Ministries Iowa, 1999. Named to Hall of Fame Wendell Phillips High Sch., Chgo., 1989. Mem. NAACP (life, chmn. religious affairs 1990-92), Kappa Alpha Psi, Sigma Pi Phi. Home: 1014 Deborah St Upland CA 91784-1206

JORDAN, CHESTER I. communication educator, theater educator; b. Floral Park, N.Y. s. Chester H. and Emma S. J.; m. Marla J. Johnson, Aug. 3, 1961; children: Jennifer Beckman, Suzanne. BA, Emory & Henry Coll., 1961; MA, U. Wyo., 1968; PhD, Bowling Green State U., 1975. Asst. prof. James Madison U., Harrisonburg, Va., 1970-75, Sul Ross State U., Alpine, Tex., 1975-79; prof. U. N.C., Pembroke, 1979—. Faculty senate UNCP, 1981—2002. Dir. over 90 theatre prodns., 1963—. Bd. dirs. Caroline Civic Ctr., Lumberton, N.C., 1994-2000, Robeson County Arts Coun., 1984-94. Mem. AAUP (chpt. pres., v.p. 1984—), N.C. Reading Assn. (parliamentarian 1989—). Avocation: travel. Office: U NC at Pembroke 1 University Dr Pembroke NC 28372-1510 Fax: 910-521-6552. E-mail: chet.jordan@uncp.edu.

JORDAN, CLIFFORD HENRY, management consultant; b. New Orleans, Dec. 27, 1921; s. Clifford Henry and May Rosalie (Duke) J.; m. Clara H. Nordberg, June 1, 1955. Grad. RN, Pa. Hosp. Sch. Nursing, 1949; BS in Nursing Edn., Temple U., 1954, EdD, 1975; MS in Edn., U. Pa., 1957. R.N., Pa. Assoc. dir. Episc. Hosp. Sch. Nursing, Phila., 1958-63, DON, 1963-66; prof. nursing U. Pa., Phila., 1966-82, prof. emeritus, 2002—; exec. dir. Assn. Oper. Rm. Nurses, Denver, 1982-90; mgmt. cons. Phila., 1990—. Cons. in nursing adminstrn. Pa., N.J., Calif. hosps.; edn. cons. in organizational devel. Pa., Kans., N.J. univs. Mem. Pa. Gov.'s Commn. on Health, 1975-77; bd. govs. Health Systems Agy. So. Pa., 1975-79. Recipient U. Pa. Lindbach award, 1980; named Outstanding alumni U. Pa., 1982 Fellow Am. Acad. Nursing (designated as Living Legend 1996); mem. Am. Nurses Assn. (bd. dirs.), Pa. Nurses Assn. (pres. 1962-66, 72-76), Am. Nurses Found. (v.p. 1980-82). Republican. Roman Catholic. Home and Office: The Wellington # 1610 135 S 19th St Philadelphia PA 19103-4912

JORDAN, DANIEL PATRICK, JR., law librarian; b. Bklyn., July 15, 1951; s. Daniel Patrick and Nan (Sinnott) J. BA, Bklyn. Coll., 1975; JD, U. Pacific, 1980; MLS, Pratt Inst., 1982. Ref. librarian Touro Coll., Huntington, N.Y., 1982-83, head pub. services, 1983-86, head law libr., 1986—. Mem. ABA, Calif. Bar Assn., Am. Assn. Law Libraries. Office: Touro Coll Jacob D Fuchsberg Law Ctr 300 Nassau Rd Huntington NY 11743-4346 E-mail: DanJ@tourolaw.edu.

JORDAN, DANIEL PORTER, JR., foundation administrator, history educator; b. Philadelphia, Miss., July 22, 1938, s. Daniel Porter and Mildred M. (Dobbs) J.; m. Lewellyn Lee Schmelzer, Dec. 18, 1961; children: Daniel P., Grace Dobbs, Katherine Lewellyn. BA, U. Miss., 1960, MA, 1962; PhD, U. Va., 1970. Various tchg. positions overseas divsn. U. Md., 1962-65, Richmond, Va., 1968-69, U. Va., summers 1970-72; prof. history Va. Commonwealth U., Richmond, 1969-84, Ariz. State, 1995; dir. Stratford Hall Summer Sem., 1981-91; exec. dir. Thomas Jefferson Found. (Monticello), 1985—, pres., 1994—. Scholar in residence U. Va., 1985—. Author: Political Leadership in Jefferson's Virginia, 1983, A Richmond Reader, 1733-1983, 1983, Tobacco Merchant: The Story of Universal Leaf Tobacco Company, 1995. Mem. adv. com. Papers of Thomas Jefferson, Princeton U.; mem. Sec. of Interior's adv. bd. Nat. Pk. Sys., 1984-88, chmn., 1987-88; mem. Jeffersonian Restoration Adv. Bd., U. Va., 1985—; mem. rev. bd. Va. Hist. Landmarks Commn., 1981-92, chmn., 1989-92; mem. Nat. Pks. and Conservation Bd., 1989-92, Ea. Nat. Bd., 1991-2001; pres. Richmond Civil War Roundtable, 1983; trustee Nat. Trust for Hist. Preservation, 1999—; bd. dirs. Fund for the U.S. Capitol Visitor Ctr., 2000—; mem. adv. bd. Freedom Forum Mus., 2002—, Eudona Welty Found., 2002—. Served with inf. U.S. Army, 1962-65. Thomas Jefferson Found. fellow, 1965-68; recipient award of merit Am. Assn. for State and Local History, 1977, 88, Pub. Svc. award U.S. Dept. of Interior, 1990, Medal for Va. Svc., AIA, 1993. Mem. Am. Antiquarian Soc., Va. Hist. Soc. (bd. dirs. 1986-91), Mass. Hist. Soc., So. Hist. Assn. (life), Orgn. Am. Historians (life), Walpole Soc., Phi Beta Kappa (pres. Alpha of Va. 1995-98), Omicron Delta Kappa, Sigma Chi. Methodist. Home and Office: Monticello Home of Thomas Jefferson PO Box 316 Charlottesville VA 22902-0316 E-mail: djordan@monticello.org.

JORDAN, DEOVINA NASIS, administrative nurse; b. Bangued, Abra, Philippines, May 7, 1960; d. Demetrio Villamor Nacis and Francisca Bicarme Baptista; m. James Lowell Jordan, July 25, 1992. BS in nursing, Perpetual Help U., Philippines, 1980; D in medicine, U. Santo Tomas, Philippines, 1985; M in pub. health, Loma Linda U., 2001; MS in nursing, UCLA, 2004. Cert. Edni. Comm. for Foreign Med. Grads. Phila., Pa.; Ped. Nursing, Am. Nursing Credentialing Ctr., Wash. DC. Clin. nurse Hosp. for Joint Dis. Ortho. Inst., NYC, 1987—88; clin. nurse III Mattel Children's Hosp, UCLA, Los Angeles, 1988—; admin. nurse IV UCLA Med. Ctr., 2002—; v.p., founder Jordan Rsch. Inst., Murietta, Ga., 1994—; pres Fil-Am Assoc., Murietta, 1994—. Rsch. adv. bd. Am. Biographical Inst., 2002—. Contbr. articles various prof. jours. Recipient Outstanding Profl. Woman award, Am. Biographical Inst., 2001. Mem.: Calif. Nurses Asn., Am. Coll. of Healthcare Execs.

JORDAN, DUPREE, JR., management consultant, educator, journalist, publisher, business executive; b. May 14, 1929; s. DuPree and Roslyn (Moncrief) J.; m. Margaret Virginia Malone, Dec. 28, 1948; children: Peggy Jordan DeSear, DuPree III, Lyn Jordan Whitworth, Terri Lee. AB, Mercer U., 1947; MEd, Emory U., 1954; LLB, Atlanta Law Sch., 1951, LLD, 1963, DLitt, 1971; postgrad., Crozer Theol. Sem., 1948-49, Nat. Inst. Pub. Affairs, summer 1967, Inst. Life-Long Learning-Harvard U., 1979, Inst. Edn. Mgmt.-Harvard U., 1981. Ordained to ministry So. Bapt. Conv., 1945. Pastor Eden Bapt. Ch., Savannah, Ga., 1946-47, Duluth (Ga.) 1st Bapt. Ch., 1953-55; reporter Chester (Pa.) Times, 1948-49; assoc. dir. Radio and TV Commn. So. Bapt. Conv., Atlanta, 1949-52, acting dir., 1952-53; tchr. history, speech Ga. State U., Atlanta, 1952-55; tchr. Bible, English Westminster Schs., Atlanta, 1954-55; editor, pub., owner West End Star, Atlanta, 1955-66, N. DeKalb Record, Chamblee, Ga., 1956-64, TriCounty Graphic, Atlanta, 1962-64, Piedmont Satellite, 1967-68; pres. Jordan Enterprises, Inc., 1957—, Jordan Internat. Enterprises Inc., 1991—, Jordan & Jordan Advt. and Pub. Rels., 1954—, Fun Products, Inc., 1968-69. Pres. Success Publs., Inc., 1969—; pub. Success Orientation, 1969—; ptnr. WE Inc., convenience food stores, 1968-69; dir. pub. affairs and congl. rels. exec. office Pres. U.S., So. region Office Econ. Opportunity, Atlanta, 1965-69; nat. coord. Religious Orgs., OEO, Washington, 1968-69; news reporter, panelist TV stas., Atlanta, 1955-76; exec. dir. Assn. Pvt. Colls. and Univs. in Ga., 1970-81; dir. Successful Selling Seminars; pres. Ga. Coll. for Leadership Devel., 1969—; profl. spkr. and trainer. Mem. Gov.'s Rapid Transit Com., 1963-64, Gov.'s Com. for World's Fair in Atlanta, 1962-64; pres. Christian Coun. Met. Atlanta, 1973; chmn., CEO Jordan Family Found. Svcs., Inc., 1997—; bd. dirs. Atlanta Girls Club, YMCA, Boy Scouts Am. Named Man of Yr. radio stas., Atlanta, 1962, 63, West End Jaycees, 1962; recipient Quill award Sigma Delta Chi, 1962, 63; named Ky. Col., 1967; mem. hon. staff Gov. Ga., 1962-66, 70-74, 74-78; honored with Rev. Dr. DuPree Jordan, Jr. Day by Gov. Jimmy Carter, 1973. Mem. AIM, ASTD, Nat. Press Club, West End Bus. Men's Assn. (pres. 1962-63), Chamblee-Doraville Bus. Men's Assn. (pres. 1963-64), Fulton County Grand Jurors Assn. (dir. 1961), Ga. State Chamber/Bus. and Industry Assn., Atlanta, DeKalb County Chambers (dir. 1961), World Future Soc., Pub. Rels. Soc. Am., Adminstrv. Mgmt. Soc., Am. Soc. Pub. Adminstrn., Sales and Mktg. Execs. Internat., Soc. Advancement Mgmt., Am. Mgmt. Assn., Am. Mktg. Assn., Am. Soc. Assn. Execs., Soc. Assn. Mgrs., Am. Assn. Coll. and Univ. Execs., So. Assn. Colls. (State Execs. Coun. coordinating chmn. 1980), State Assn. Execs. Coun., Ga., Internat. assn. bus. communicators, Internat. Soc. Ednl. Planners, Am. Acad. Polit. and Social Sci., Meeting Planners Internat., Nat. Spkrs. Assn. (founding mem. 1974, profl. awards com. 1980-81, dir. exec. com. 1982-84, sec. bd. 1983-84), Assn. Mgmt. Cons., Internat. Mgmt. Coun., Inst. Mgmt. Cons., Internat. Group Agys. and Burs. (gen. program chmn. 1994, co-founder), Sigma Delta Chi (dir. 1963), Blue Key, Phi Delta, Alpha Chi Omega, Alpha Psi Omega, Kappa Sigma. Home and Office: 965 Oakhaven Dr Roswell GA 30075-1231 Business E-Mail: info@jie.com., info@slss.com.

JORDAN, ELKE, molecular biologist, government medical research institute executive; b. Gottingen, Germany, Apr. 8, 1937; came to U.S., 1953, naturalized, 1961; d. Peter Friederich and Elisabeth A.K. (Lehmann) J.; m. Thomas H. Edelson, Aug. 21, 1972 (div. 1991). BA, Goucher Coll., 1957; Ph.D, Johns Hopkins U., 1962. In various rsch. positions Harvard U., 1962-64, U. Cologne, Fed. Republic Germany, 1964-68, U. Wis., Madison, 1968-69, U. Calif., Berkeley, 1969-72; grants assoc. NIH, Bethesda, Md., 1972-73; coord. for collaborative rsch. Nat. Cancer Inst., NIH, Bethesda, Md., 1973-76; health scientist adminstr. Nat. Inst. Gen. Med. Scis., NIH, Bethesda, 1976-82, assoc. dir., 1982-88; dir. Office of Human Genome Rsch., NIH, Bethesda, 1988-89; dep. dir. Nat. Human Genome Rsch. Inst., NIH, Bethesda, 1989—2002; with Found. for NIH, Bethesda, 2002—. Contbr. articles on molecular biology of E. coli and bacteriophage lambda to profl. jours. NIH fellow, 1959-65; Helen Hay Whitney Found. fellow, 1965-68. Fellow AAAS; mem. Am. Soc. for Human Genetics. Office: Found for NIH 1 Cloister Ct Ste 152 Bethesda MD 20814-1460

JORDAN, FRANK J. lawyer; b. New Canaan, Conn., June 13, 1929; s. Michael and Anna (Markva) J.; m. Sheila Filene, June 19, 1960. BS, U.S. Mcht. Marine Acad., 1953; JD, N.Y. Law Sch., 1961. Bar: N.Y. 1961, U.S. Patent and Trademark Office 1961, U.S. Dist. Ct. (so. and ea. dists.) N.Y. 1963, U.S. Supreme Ct. 1967, U.S. Ct. Appeals (fed. cir.) 1968. Atty., Am. Standard, N.Y.C., 1963-65; assoc. Brown and Seward, N.Y.C., 1965-66; atty. Am. Can Co., Greenwich Conn., 1966-68; sole practice, N.Y.C., 1969-79; ptnr. Jordan & Hamburg, N.Y.C., 1979— . Contbr. regular column on patent law to bi-monthly publ. Lt. USN, 1953-55, Korea. Mem. Assn. Bar City N.Y., Internat. Patent and Trademark Assn., N.Y. Patent Law Assn., N.Y. Law Sch. Alumni Assn., U.S. Mcht. Marine Acad. Alumni Assn. Home: 205 3rd Ave New York NY 10003-2506 Office: Jordan & Hamburg 122 E 42nd St Rm 4000 New York NY 10168-0069

JORDAN, GLENN, director; b. San Antonio, Apr. 5, 1936; BA, Harvard U., 1957; postgrad., Yale U. Drama Sch., 1957-58. Dir. regional and stock theatre, including Cafe La Mama, late 1950s; N.Y. directorial debut with Another Evening With Harry Stoones, 1961; other plays include A Taste of Honey, 1968; Rosencrantz and Guildenstern Are Dead, 1969, A Streetcar Named Desire at Cin. Playhouse in the Park, 1973, All My Sons at Huntington Hartford Theatre, 1975; founder, N.Y. TV Theater, 1965, dir. various plays, including Paradise Lost and Hogan's Goat; dir. mini-series Benjamin Franklin, CBS, 1974 (Emmy award 1975, Peabody award); Family, ABC-TV series, 1976-77, including segment Rights of Friendship (Dirs. Guild Am. award); numerous TV plays for public TV, including Eccentricities of a Nightingale, 1976; The Displaced Person, 1976; TV movies including Shell Game, 1975, One Of My Wives Is Missing, 1975, Delta County U.S.A, 1977, In The Matter of Karen Ann Quinlan, 1977, Sunshine Christmas, 1977, Les Miserables, 1978, Son-Rise, A Miracle of Love, 1979, The Family Man, 1979, The Women's Room, 1980, Lois Gibbs and the Love Canal, 1982, Heartsounds, 1984 (Peabody award), Toughlove, 1985, Dress Gray, 1986, Something In Common, 1986, Promise, 1986 (2 Emmy awards for producing, directing, Peabody award, Golden Globe award), Echoes in the Darkness, 1987, Jesse, 1988, Home Fires Burning, 1988, Challenger, 1989, The Boys, 1990, Sarah Plain and Tall, 1990, Aftermath, 1990, O Pioneers!, 1991, Barbarians at the Gate, 1992 (Emmy award Outstanding Made for TV Movie, 1993, Golden Globe award, Best Mini-series or movie made for TV, 1994), To Dance with the White Dog, 1994, Jane's House, 1994, My Brother's Keeper, 1994, A Streetcar Named Desire, 1995, Jake's Women (Neil Simon), 1996, After Jimmy, 1996, Mary and Tim, 1996, A Christmas Memory, 1997, The Long Way Home, 1998, Legalese, 1998, Night Ride Home, 1999, Winter's End: Sarah Plain & Tall III, 1999, Midwives, 2000; dir: feature film Only When I Laugh (Neil Simon), 1981, The Buddy System, 1983, Mass Appeal, 1984. Recipient Emmy awards for N.Y. TV Theater Plays, 1970, Actors Choice, 1970. Office: Creative Artists Agy 9830 Wilshire Blvd Beverly Hills CA 90212-1825 also: 9401 Wilshire Blvd Ste 700 Beverly Hills CA 90212-2920

JORDAN, HOWARD EMERSON, retired engineering executive, consultant; b. State College, N.Mex., May 14, 1926; s. Howard E. and Elizabeth (Bruden) J.; children: Blair, Julie. BSEE, U. Wis., 1946; MS, Case Western Res. U., 1958, PhD, 1962. With Rayovac Co., Madison, Wis., 1946-52, Reliance Elec., Cleve., 1954-93, dir. corp. R & D, 1993—; pvt. cons.; rsch. scientist U. Tex. Author: Energy Efficient Electric Motors and Their Application, 1983, 2d edit., 1994; contbg. author: Handbook of Electric Machines, 1987. Served to 1st lt. USAF, 1952-54. Recipient Disting. Svc. citation U. Wis., 1989. Fellow IEEE (sr.); mem. Nat. Electrical Mfrs. Assn. (chmn. motor and generator sect. 1979). Methodist.

JORDAN, IRVING KING, university president; Pres. Gallaudet U., Washington, 1988—. Office: Gallaudet U Office of President 800 Florida Ave NE Washington DC 20002-3660 E-mail: president@gallaudet.edu.

JORDAN, JACK D. art educator; b. St. Louis, Oct. 17, 1928; s. Rupert James Jordan and Audrey Fayette Morris; m. Roberta Kay Hughes, Nov. 1, 1969 (div. Dec. 1986). Grad. H.S., DesMoines. Staff artist Register and Tribune, Des-Moines, 1948—52; art dir. Union and Evening Tribune, San Diego, 1952—71, art supr., picture editor, 1952—71; fine artist, 1971—2002; gallery owner Jordan Gallery, Inc., El Cajon, Calif., 1986—90; art instr. Grossmont Cuyamaca Coll., San Diego, 1989—. Illustrator: Pathways to Freedom, 1966, Brand Book Seven, 1983, How To Paint the Old West, 1999; one-man shows include Borrego Desert Art Ctr., Borrego Springs, Calif., 1971, A. Huney Gallery, San Diego, 1982, Project Wildlife, Alpine, Calif., 1985, La Vae Gallery, La Mesa, Calif., 1985, Desert Princess Hotel, Cathedral City, Calif., 1986, Jordan Gallery, El Cajon, 1992, Perspective Gallery, Scripps Oceanog. Soc., La Jolla, Calif., 2001. Mem.: East County Art Assn., Mus. Contemporary Art Calif., San Diego Mus. Art Artists Guild, San Diego Mus. Art, Scripps Oceanog. Soc. (fundraiser for Birch Aquarium 2000). Home: Apt 4 421 Shady Ln El Cajon CA 92021-6430

JORDAN, JAMES JACKSON, architect; b. Oklahoma City, Jan. 7, 1926; s. George Smith Jordan, Esther Lee Jordan; m. Louella Shaw Shaw; children: James J. Junior, Lyndon K., Jonathan D. BS Engring., Okla. State U., 1950, BArch, 1951. Lic. architect, Okla., Calif.; registered profl. engr., Okla. Designer Oklahoma City Planning Commn., Oklahoma City, 1951—52; master planning, architect, supv. engr. Base Civil Engring. Office, Tinker Air Force Base, Okla., 1952—65, chief engring. sect. then deputy base engr. McClellan Air Force Base, Calif., 1965—81; owner J.J.Jordan Architect/Engineer, Sacramento, 1981—94, J.J.Jordan, Architect and Author, 1994—. Assoc. architect & engr. Associated Architects & Engrs., Bethany, 1957—65; master commr. & expert cons. Calif. Architects Licensing Bd., Sacramento, 1982—. State Exposition Park, 1949 (2d medal Nat. Archtl. Competition 1949), Nationally Copyrighted Buildese Modules, 1993; contbr. articles to profl. jours.; author: Christ! I want your body, 2003. Pres. bd. trustees St Mk's Meth. Ch., Sacramento, 1982—83, NM Presbyn. Ch., 1998—99. Recipient Civilian Engr. of Yr. Profl. Excellence award, Headquarters USAF, Washington, 1964. Mem.: Westar Inst. (assoc.). Methodist. Avocation: Teaching Religious Studies and Writing Religious books..

JORDAN, JAMES LOWELL, educator, writer; b. Mpls. s. Lowell Stephen Jordan and Rose Mary Servatius; m. Deovina Bicarme Nasis, July 25, 1992. BA, U. Calif., Riverside, 1976; grad. cert. in adminstrn., U. Calif., 1982; M in Adminstrn., U. Calif., Riverside, 1983; cert. mfg. engring., U. Calif., L.A., 1990; PhD, Iowa State U., 1981, U. Iowa, 1987. Asst. prof. Ctrl. Wash. U., 1986-94, dir. ungergrad. bus. program, 1986-87; lectr. U. Calif., Riverside, 1988-92; prof. So. Calif. U., 1994—, U. Lethbridge, Can., 1994—, pres. Jordan Rsch. Inst., 1994—. Reviewer, contbr. articles to profl. publs.; author: sci. and rel. books.

JORDAN, JOE J. architect; b. Phila., May 5, 1923; s. Edmund F. and Elizabeth N. (Jungkurth) Jordan; m. Sarah Jeanne Connolly, Nov. 1, 1974. BS in Architecture, U. Ill., 1949. Prin. Joe J. Jordan, FAIA, Phila., 1961-81; ptnr. Delta Group, Phila., 1972-74; prin., pres. Jordan, Mitchell Inc., Phila., 1981-93. UN tech. assistance expert Mid. E. Tech. U., Ankara, Turkey, 1958—60, acting head dept. architecture, 1959, archtl. advisor to univ. pres., 60; mem. faculty dept. architecture Drexel U., Phila., 1962, adj. prof., 64, head dept., 1965—77. Author: (book) Senior Center Facilities, 1975, Senior Center Design, 1978, Cape May Point - The Illustrated History, 2003; contbr. articles to profl. jours. Mem. citizens coun. city planning, Phila., 1956—70; bd. dirs. Phila. Sr. Ctr., 1964—70, Reed St. Neighborhood Ho., 1968—69; mem. mayor's com. housing Phila., 1973—76; mem. Gov. Task Force Multi-Svc. Sr. Ctrs. Pa., 1975—77, N.J. Assisted Living Facilities Task Force, 1995—96; v.p. Greater Cape May Hist. Soc., 1998—. Recipient numerous archtl. awards, award of excellence, Urban Design Mag.; Fulbright fellow, 1954—55. Fellow: AIA (emeritus, Citation for Excellence, Phila. chpt. Honor award, others). Home: PO Box 22 Cape May Point NJ 08212-0022 Personal E-mail: joejordan@comcast.net.

JORDAN, JOHN RICHARD, JR., lawyer; b. Winton, N.C., Jan. 16, 1921; s. John Richard Jordan and Ina Love (Mitchell) J.; m. Patricia Exum Weaver, June 19, 1949 (div.); children: Ellen Meares Jordan McCarren, John Richard, III.; m. Brenda Moore Harlow, June 27, 1982. BA, U. N.C., 1942, JD, 1948. Founding sr. partner law firm Jordan, Price, Wall, Gray Jones and Carlton, Raleigh, NC. Mem. staff Atty. Gen. N.C., 1948-51; mem. N.C. Senate (3 regular sessions, 1 spl. session), 1959, 61, 63 Contbr. articles and revs. to newspapers and mags.; editor: Why the Democratic Party, 1955. Candidate for lt. gov. N.C., 1964; mem. N.C. Bd. Higher Edn., 1964; mem. N.C. Commn. Higher Edn. Facilities, 1964—; chmn. N.C. Bd. Social Svcs., 1969-73; trustee U. N.C., 1969-73, bd. govs. U. N.C., 1973-97, chmn. bd. govs., 1980-84; trustee Chowan Coll., 1979, 1981, 97-98, chmn., 1998; trustee Ravenscroft Found., 1971-87, N.C. Supreme Ct. Hist. Soc., 1993—; mem. dirs. coun. Nat. Humanities Ctr, 1991; permanent chmn. N.C. Dem. Conv., 1974; chmn. bd. dirs. N.C. div. Am. Cancer soc., 1959, pres., 1960; mem. Gov.'s Cancer Commn., 1962-64; N.C. chmn. ARC, 1966, Nat. Soc. Crippled Children and Adults, 1963; pres. N.C. Arthritis Found., 1966-70; bd. dirs. N.C. Med. Found., pres. co-founders club of Found.; bd. dirs. Myesthenia Gravis Found. (Carolinas chpt, 1991—); bd. dirs. State Capitol Found.; pres. Friends of N.C. Archives, 1984-86; chmn. N.C. Council Econ. Edn., 1984-87; bd.dirs. N.C. Mus. History Assocs., 1983-86; pres. Henry Lee Soc., 1991-93; mem. Jud. Conf. U.S. Ct. Appeals; bd. dirs. N.C. Cmty. Found.; treas. N.C. Supreme Ct. Hist. Soc. Recipient award for scholarship and leadership Phi Delta Phi, 1948; Disting. Service award as Raleigh's Young Man of Yr., 1955; Disting. Service award N.C. Public Health Assn., 1964; Gold Medal award Am. Cancer Soc.; Disting. Alumnus award Chowan Coll., 1983, U. N.C. Sch. Law, 1995; inducted into N.C. Bar Hall of Fame, 1995. Mem. Wake County Bar Assn. (chmn. exec. com. 1955), N.C. Bar Assn., Am. Bar Assn., Am. Judicature Soc., N.C. Acad. Trial Lawyers, Internat. Bar Assn., English Speaking Union (dir.), Coral Bay Club, Pi Kappa Alpha, Phi Delta Phi. Clubs: Carolina Country, Carolina, Sphinx, Capital City of Raleigh, Torch, Lions, Assembly of Raleigh. Baptist. Home: 809 Westwood Dr Raleigh NC 27607-6644 Office: Jordan Price Wall Gray ones and Carlton 1951 Clark Ave Raleigh NC 27605

JORDAN, JOHN W., II, holding company executive; b. 1948; Grad., U. Notre Dame, 1969. With Carl Marks & Co., 1972—82, The Jordan Co., N.Y.C., 1982—; CEO Jordan Industries, Inc., Deerfield, Ill., 1982—. Office: Jordan Industries 1751 Lake Cook Rd Ste 550 Deerfield IL 60015-5624 also: Jordan Industries Inc 875 N Michigan Ave Chicago IL 60611-1803*

JORDAN, JON BYRON, lawyer; b. Jefferson City, Mo., June 18, 1968; s. Jan Byron and Ivonne Marie Jordan; m. Elizabeth Ann Cintron, June 21, 1997; 1 chld, Taylor Elizabeth. BS in Bus. Mgmt., Fla. State U., 1990; JD cum laude, Loyola U., New Orleans, 1994. Bar: Fla. 1994, D.C. 1997, U.S. Dist. Ct. (so. dist.), Fla., 1995, U.S. Dist. Ct. (middle dist.), Fla., 1996. Assoc. Wicker, Smith, Tutan, O'Hara, McCoy, Graham and Ford, P.A., Miami, Fla., 1995-97; sr. counsel S.E. Regional Office, U.S. SEC, Miami, 1997-99; assoc. Baker Botts L.L.P., Washington, 1999—2002; sr. counsel divsn. enforcement U.S. SEC, Washington, 2001—. Contbr. articles to law jours., including Columbia Bus. Law Rev., Northwestern Jour. Internat. Law and Bus., U. Miami Entertainment and Sports Law Rev., Mich. State U. Jour. Internat. Law. Mem. ABA, D.C. Bar (mem. steering com. Corp., Fin. and Securities Law sect., 2000—), Assn. SEC Alumni, Rep. Nat. Lawyers Assn., Phi Delta Phi, Alpha Sigma Nu, Sigma Phi Epsilon. Roman Catholic. Avocations: writing, fishing, golf. Home: 504 H North Thomas St Arlington VA 22203 Office: US SEC Enforcement Div 450 Fifth St NW Mail Stop 8-6 Washington DC 20549-0806 Fax: 202-942-9630.

JORDAN, JOSEPH LOUIS, education educator, government official; Degree in bus. adminstrn. and mktg., St. Lawrence Coll.; MBA, Clarkson U. Prof. bus. St. Lawrence Coll., Brockville, Can., 1984-87, St. Lawrence Coll, Brockville, Can., 1988-93; coord. operational rev. Ministry Colls. and Univs., 1987-88; coord., prof. internat. edn. dept. St. Lawrence Coll, Brockville, Can., 1993—; owner summer retail bus. Brockville, 1990-93. Designer, implementor computer tng. courses, Africa; fulltime provincial campaign exec., 1987, 88, 92, 93, 96. Fed. mem. parliament Leeds-Grenville, 2000—02, parliamentary sec. to prime min., 2000—02. Office: 422 Confederation Bldg House of Commons Ottawa ON Canada K1A 0A6

JORDAN, JUDITH VICTORIA, clinical psychologist, educator; b. Milw., July 28, 1943; d. Claus and Charlotte (Backus) J.; m. William M. Redpath, Aug. 11, 1973. AB, Brown U., 1965; MA, Harvard U., 1968, PhD, 1973; DHL (hon.) (hon.), New Eng. Coll., 2001. Diplomate Am. Bd. Profl. Psychology. Psychologist Human Relations Service, Wellesley, Mass., 1971-73; assoc. psychologist McLean Hosp., Belmont, Mass., 1978-93, psychologist, 1993—, dir. women's studies program, 1988—, dir. tng. in psychology, 1991, dir. Women's Treatment Network, 1992—. Vis. scholar Stone Ctr. Wellesley Coll., 1985—; asst. prof. psychiatry Harvard Med. Sch., 1988—; co-dir. Jean Baker Miller Tng. Inst., Wellesley Coll. 1998; adv. bd Fox TV Network, Women First healthcare., 1998; disting. prof. Menninger Clinic, 1999. Author: Empathy and Self Boundries, 1984, Women's Growth in Connection, 1991, (with others) The Self in Relation, 1986; editor, author: Relational Self in Women; editor: Women's Growth in Diversity, 1997. Recipient Outstanding Contbn. award, Feminist Therapy Inst., 2002. Fellow Am. Psychol. Assn.; mem. Mass. Psychol. Assn. (bd. dirs. 1983-85, Career Achievement award for outstanding contbns. to advancement of psychology as a sci. and a profession), Phi Beta Kappa. Office: McLean Hosp 114 Waltham St Lexington MA 02421-5415

JORDAN, KARIN BALTEN-BABKOWSKI, health facility administrator; b. Hannover, Germany, July 26, 1958; came to U.S., 1979; d. Ekkehard and Liselotte (Pache) Babkowski; m. Wayne Donald Jordan, June 13, 1981. BA in Biology cum laude, Colo. Christian Coll., Denver, 1987; MA in Counseling, Rollins Coll., Winter Park, Fla., 1989; PhD in Child and Family Devel., U. Ga., 1992. RN; lic. marriage and family therapist, Colo.; cert. kindergarten tchr., Germany; diplomate/bd. cert. expert in traumatic stress. Intern in counseling Hope and Help Ctr., Orlando, Fla., 1989; intern in marriage and family therapy McPhaul Ctr., Athens, 1990-91; asst. clin. dir. Cross Keys Counseling Ctr., Atlanta, 1991-93; practicum supr. U. Colo., Denver, 1993, clin. dir., 1994-99, mem. faculty, 1994-97, asst. prof., 1997-2000, U. Nev., Las Vegas, 2000-01; assoc. prof., dept. chair George Fox U., Newburg, Oreg., 2001—. Bd. dirs. Maria Drost Svcs.; rsch. asst. dept. child and family devel. U. Ga., Athens, 1989-91; bd. dirs., counselor Sun Valley Family Hope Counseling Ctr., Denver, 1996—98; rsch. cons. Jefferson Couty Pub. Sch. Mental Health Group, Jefferson County Substance Abuse Counseling Dept.; guest lectr. in Russia, Moscow, 2003. Author: Public Assessment Handbook, 2003; mem. editl. bd. Jour. Counseling Devel., 2003—, Jour. Brief Therapy and Crisis Intervention, 2003—; contbr. articles to profl. jours. Mem. mental health com. 9News Health Fair, Denver, 1995—98; mem. com. Colo. Okla. Resource Coun., Denver, 1996-97; apptd. to augmenting panel Colo. State Grievance Bd., 1997-98; mental health vol. N.Y.C. World Trade Ctr. Attack, 2001. Mem. APA (divsn. 16 com. children, youth, families 1996—), ACA (founter Trauma Networking Group 2003—), Am. Assn. Marriage Family Therapy (cert. therapist, supr.), Colo. Assn. Marriage Family Therapy (pub. rels. com. 1996—, v.p.), Colo. Counseling Assn., Internat. Assn. Marriage Family Counselors, Nat. Acad. Cert. Family Therapists. Avocations: reading, drawing, traveling. Office: George Fox U Dept Grad Counseling 414 N Meridian St Newberg OR 97132-2697 E-mail: DrKBJordan@cs.com.

JORDAN, KARLA SALGE, early childhood education educator; b. Berlin, July 4, 1943; came to U.S. 1965; d. Hubert Ernst Richard and Irmgard Klara Salge; m. William Jackson Jordan, May 28, 1963 (div. 1980); 1 child, Michael Bond. BA, Berlin Tchrs. Coll., 1964, Meth. Coll., Fayetteville, N.C., 1974; MA, Fayetteville State U., 1986. Cert. tchr., N.C., ednl. supr., 1995, cert. early childhood generalist Nat. Bd. Edn., 2000. Tchr. Eastover Elem. Sch., Fayetteville, 1974-75, Montclair Elem. Sch., Fayetteville, 1975—. Workshop presenter Cumberland County Sch., Fayetteville, spring 1983, 92-95; mem. bldg. leadership team Montclair Elem. Sch., 1992-93, chair, 1994-95, grade chair, 1980-90, 99-2001, 2002-03, sch. improvement team chair, 1995-98, 2001-03. Treas. Montclair PTA, 1987-88, sec., 1988-90, pres. 1985, 86; youth choir dir. Eureka Bapt. Ch., Fayetteville, 1990—, min. of music, 1995—; mem., bible study leader for German fellowship Walstone Bapt. Ch., Fayetteville, German fellowship coord., 1999 . Fayetteville Jr. League mini grantee, 1991; named Tchr. of the Yr. Montclair Elem. Sch., 1987-88; recipient Fayetteville Tchr. of the Week Jr. League and the Huntington Learning Ctr., 1997. Mem. ASCD, Cross Creek Reading Coun. (rec. sec. 1990), Fayetteville Assn. for Edn. of Young Children, N.C. Assn. of Edn. (bldg. rep. 1981-83), Pi Lambda Theta. Republican. Baptist. Avocations: sewing, crafts, gardening, travel, reading. Home: 845 Mary Jordan Ln Fayetteville NC 28311-7075 Office: Montclair Elem Sch 555 Glensford Dr Fayetteville NC 28314-2326 E-mail: karla-sjs@msn.com., karlajordan@ccs.k12.nc.us.

JORDAN, KEITH M, band director, musician; b. Alamogordo, N.Mex., 1956; s. Melvin Vernon and Billie Helen Birdwell Jordan; m. Mary Helen Birdwell Jordan; children: Mariah Bird, Ashley Bird. MusB Edn., N.Mex State U., Las Cruces N.M., 1974—78, U. of Utah, Salt Lake City, Utah, 1978—80. Asst. band of dir. U. of Utah, Salt Lake, Utah, 1978—80; h.s. band dir. Murray H.S., Murray, Utah, 1980—86, La Cueva H.S., Albuquerque, 1986. V.p. of bands N.Mex Music Educ Assn., New Mexico, N.Mex., 1991—93, pres. of nmmea, 1993—, post pres. of nmmea, 1995—97. Founder hoffmentown acad. of mu Hoffmantown Ch., Albuquerque, 1994; organist Hoffmantown Ch. Orch., Albuquerque, 1992—96, condr., 1993—96. Recipient Sweepstakes Award, heritage music festivals, New Orleans, LA, 2000, Sweepstakes Awards in Band, Heritage Music Festivals, San Diego,CA, 2001, Sweepstakes Award in Band, Heritage Music Festivals-Los Vegas, Nev., 1999. Mem.: New Mex. Teachers Fedn. (assoc.), New Mex.Music Edn. Assc. (assoc.; v.p. pres, p.prs. 1986), Inter. Assoc Of Jazz Edn. (assoc.). Office: La Cueva High School 7801 Wilkshire Blvd NE Albuquerque NM 87122 Office Fax: 505-857-0177. E-mail: jordan-k@aps.edu..

JORDAN, KEVIN DAVID, director, educator, minister; A.B., Princeton U., 1979; M.Div., Union Theol. Sem., 1983; Ed.D., Dowling Coll., 2003. Ordained min. AME Ch., Phila., 1983. Asst. dir. Higher Edn. Opportunity Program Dowling Coll., Oakdale, NY, 1985—, adj. asst. prof., 1990—. Home: 87 Central Blvd Oakdale NY 11769 Office: Dowling Coll Idle Hour Blvd Oakdale NY 11769-1999 Fax: 631-244-1098. E-mail: kdjministry@yahoo.com.

JORDAN, LEO JOHN, lawyer; b. Pittston, Pa., Nov. 24, 1931; s. Joseph Thomas and Agnes (Granahan) J.; children: Leo John, Michael, Paul, Mary Terese; m. Carla Temple. AB in Econ., King's Coll., 1953; JD, U. Md., 1960. Bar: Md. 1960, Tex. 1965, Ill. 1990, N.Y. 1997. Claim supr. Ins. Co. N.AM., Phila., 1956-62; atty. State Farm Ins. Cos., Bloomington, Ill., 1962-96; ret., 1996—. Contbr. articles to profl. jours. Commr. Richardson City Planning Commn., Tex., 1964-68. With USN, 1954-56. Mem. ABA (ho. of dels., chair tort and ins. practice sect. 1992-93), Chgo. Bar Assn., Nat. Com. Property Ins. (chmn. bd. dirs. 1978-79), N.Y. State Bar Assn., Assn. Bar City N.Y., Fedn. Def. and Corp. Counsel, Def. Rsch. Inst., Md. State Bar Assn., Tex. State Bar Assn., Ill. State Bar Assn. Democrat. Roman Catholic. Avocations: tennis, reading, marathon running. Home: 50 Whalen Ct West Orange NJ 07052

JORDAN, LOIS WENGER, foundation official; b. Madison, Wis., Dec. 28, 1943; d. Alfred and Phyllis Mae (Shaffer) Wenger; m. William Malcolm Jordan, Dec. 28, 1963; children: William Andre, Christopher Allan Wenger. BS, Millersville (Pa.) U., 1969. Tchr. Hempfield Sch. Dist., Lancaster, Pa., 1969-70, Lancaster Sch. Dist., 1975-80; dir. Upward Bound, Millersville U., 1980-82; dir. devel. St. Joseph Hosp., Lancaster, 1982-87; assoc. dir. devel. Pa. State U. Coll. Medicine, Hershey, 1987-97; dir. devel. Pa. State U., Capital Coll., 1997-2000; nat. dir. revenue devel. Am. Coll. Physicians/Am. Soc. Internal Medicine, 2000—02; pres. Jordan Assocs., 2002—. Author: (children's book) What's a Hospital Like?, 1972. Mem. Lancaster Jr. League, 1975—; trustee St. Joseph Hosp., 1979—82, James Buchanan Found., Lancaster, 1982—94; bd. trustees Penn Manor Found., 1998—2000; trustee Highland Presbyn. Ch., Lancaster, 1982—85. Recipient Cheston M. Berlin Svc. award Pa. State U. Alumni Assn., 1995, Outstanding Cmty. Svc. award Jr. League Assn., 1995. Mem. Assn. Healthcare Philanthropy (bd. dirs. 1990-92). Republican. Avocations: travel, hiking, international cooking. Home: 1734 Colonial Manor Dr Lancaster PA 17603-6034 E-mail: jordanl@blazenet.net.

JORDAN, LYNDON KIRKMAN, family practice physician; b. Mount Olive, N.C., Jan. 6, 1935; s. Lyndon Kirkman and Rachael Loucille (Hazelton) J.; m. Beverly Hayes Brooks, Aug. 19, 1961; children: Lyndon III, Christopher, Patrick. BA, Duke U., 1957, MD, 1961. Diplomate Am. Bd. Family Practice. Intern Watts Hosp., Durham, N.C., 1961-62; flight surgeon Beale AFB, Marysville, Calif., 1962-64; pvt. practice Smithfield, NC, 1964—2001; dir. family medicine residency program Duke U. Sch. Medicine, Durham, 1972-74. Cons. Roche Biomed. Labs., Burlington, N.C., 1987-92, Pfizer Pharms. Co., Mahwah, N.J., 1994-92; chmn. Johnston County Bd. of Health, Smithfield, N.C., 1998-2000 dirs. Centura Bank of Smithfield, 1996-2002n. bd. dirs. Millennium Healthcare Network of N.C. and S.C., 1996-99; nat. lectr. in field of allergy. Capt. USAF, 1962-64. Named family physician of yr. N.C. Acad. Family Physicians, 1982, N.C. Tarheel of the Week, News & Observer Newspaper, Raleigh, 1983; Paul Harris fellow Rotary Internat., 1989. Fellow Am. Acad. Family Physicians. Episcopalian. Avocations: flying, hunting, fishing, painting. Home: 105 Mariah Dr Four Oaks NC 27524-8433

JORDAN, MARK HENRY, retired consulting civil engineer; b. Lawrence, Mass., Apr. 10, 1915; s. Joseph Augustine and Gertrude (O'Connell) J.; m. Louise Sullivan, June 23, 1939; children: Mary Elizabeth (Mrs. Delio Giant-urco), Margaret Michaela. BS, U.S. Naval Acad., 1937; M. Civil Engring., Rensselaer Poly. Inst., 1942, MS, 1965, PhD, 1968. Registered profl. engr., N.J., N.Y. Commd. ensign U.S. Navy, 1937, advanced through grades to capt., 1955; comdr. 6th Seabee Battalion South Pacific, 1943-44; comdr. 103d Seabee Battalion, 1951-52; comdr. Civil Engr. Corps. Sch., 1960-63; ret., 1963; assoc. prof. civil engring. U. Mo., Columbia, 1966-67; prof. civil engring. Rensselaer Poly. Inst., 1968-77, prof. emeritus, 1977—, dean continuing studies, 1967-72, chmn. civil engring., 1972-73. Cons. engr. Smith & Mahoney, Albany, N.Y., 1975-78; individual practice as cons. engr., 1978— Author: (with others) Saga of the Sixth, 1950, Iron Brigade General, 1993. Mem. Rensselaer County Charter Commn., 1969-71; Bd. dirs. United Community Services, Troy, N.Y., 1969-75. Decorated Bronze Star with V, Presdl. Unit citation. Fellow ASCE (life); mem. NSPE, Am. Arbitration Assn., Am. Soc. Engring. Edn., Soc. Am. Mil. Engrs. (local post pres.), Am. Pub. Works Assn., Sigma Xi, Chi Epsilon. Clubs: Fort Orange (Albany, N.Y.). Roman Catholic. Home and Office: 46 East Rd Troy NY 12180 6861

JORDAN, MARVIN EVANS, JR., record company executive; b. Muskogee, Okla., Aug. 13, 1944; s. Marvin Evans and May Elizabeth (Williams) J.; m. Suonja Summirs, Aug. 23, 1969 (div. 1983); m. Kristine Lynn Johnson, Nov. 8, 1984; children: Marvin Edwin, Mary Elizabeth, Michael Evans-Lyman; stepchildren: Daniel Noah Winger, David Paul Winger, Karen LaVohn Winger Van Hofer, Cory Brent Winger, Jay Martin Winger, Aaron Thomas Jones, Benjamin Arthur Jones Jordan, Seth Ailean Jones, Sara Jean Jones Jordan. BS, City U., Bellevue, Wash., 1981, MBA, 1983. Producer, promoter Natures Green Oratory Presents, Seattle, 1966—67; v.p. North Hollywood Releasing, Seattle, 1967-68; prin. Jordan Assocs., Seattle, 1969-89; chmn. bd. Western-Internat. Artists, Inc., 1976-78; pres. Standard Record Co., Spokane, Wash., 1989—; mem. agy. mktg. network Star Power, 1991 93; pres. Millenial Entertainment Network, 2000—; sr. ptnr., CEO Aztec Mgmt. Sys., Spokane, Wash., 2000—. Artistic dir. Concerts Nimbus, Seattle, 1981-84; co-dir. Kids Khorus Klub, Olympia, Wash., 1985-87. Composer, lyricist, collaborator (song) Heart Songs, 1994; vocalist (album) After All, 1994; numerous unpub. songs. Asst. dist. commr. Whatcom dist. Mount Baker coun. Boy Scouts Am., 1987-91, 94-98, chmn. coun. exploring svc. team, 1993-94, membership chair Thunderbird dist. Inland N.W. Coun., 2001—2003, unit commr., 2003—; steering com. Adult Attention Deficit Disorder Assn., 1993-94. With U.S. Army, 1963-66. Named Disting. Commr. Boy Scouts Am., 1992, recipient Wood Badge, 1990. Mem. Northwest Area Music Assn. Mem. Lds Ch. Avocations: residential design, computer programming, reading. Fax: 419-730-0308.

JORDAN, MARY, editor-in-chief, reporter; m. Kevin Sullivan; 2 children. Grad., Georgetown U., 1983; student, Trinity Coll., Dublin; M in Journalism, Columbia U., 1984; postgrad., Georgetown U., 1994—95, Stanford U., 1999—2000. Nat. edn. reporter Washington Post, mem. met. and nat. staffs, 1984, co-bur. chief N.E. Asia bur., 1995—99, co-bur. chief Mexico City bur., 2000—. Recipient Nieman fellowship, Harvard U., 1989—90, Pulitzer prize for internat. reporting, 2003. Office: Washington Post 1150 15th St NW Washington DC 20071

JORDAN, MICHAEL HUGH, information technology executive; b. Kansas City, Mo., June 15, 1936; m. Kathryn Hiett, Apr. 8, 1961 (div.); children: Kathryn, Stephen; m. Hilary Cecil, Mar. 4, 2000. BSChemE, Yale U., 1957; MSChemE, Princeton U., 1959. Cons., prin. McKinsey & Co., Toronto, London and Cleve., 1964—74; dir. fin. planning PepsiCo, Purchase, NY, 1974—76, sr. v.p. planning and devel., 1976—77; sr. v.p. mfg. ops. Frito-Lay divsn. PepsiCo Internat., Dallas, 1977—82, pres., CEO Frito-Lay divsn., 1983—85; pres. PepsiCo Foods Internat., 1982—83; exec. v.p., CFO PepsiCo Inc., Purchase, 1985—86, pres., 1986; pres., CEO PepsiCo Worldwide, Dallas, 1987—92; ptnr. Clayton, Dubilier and Rice, N.Y.C., NY, 1992—93; chmn., CEO Westinghouse Electric Corp./CBS, Pitts., 1993—98; ptnr. Beta Capital Group LLC; chmn., CEO Electronic Data Systems Corp., Plano, Tex., 2003—. Bd. dirs. Aetna, eOriginal Inc., WPP Group plc, i2 Techs. Inc.; chmn. Nat. Fgn. Trade Coun.; mem. Brookings Instn. Bd. dirs. United Negro Coll. Fund, 1986—, Ctr. for Excellence in Edn., Washington, 1988—92. Recipient cert. nuclear engring., Bettis Labs. Atomic Power Labs., Pitts.

JORDAN, MICHAEL JEFFREY, retired professional basketball player, former professional sports team executive, retired baseball player; b. Bklyn., Feb. 17, 1963; s. James and Deloris Jordan; m. Juanita Vanoy, Sept. 1989; children: Jeffrey Michael, Marcus James, Jasmine. Student, U. N.C., 1981—84. Basketball player Chgo. Bulls, 1984—93; baseball player Chicago White Sox AA Team, 1994-95; basketball player Chgo. Bulls, 1995—98; pres. basketball ops. Washington Wizards, 1999—2000, player, 2001—03. Mem. NCAA Championship Team, 1982, U.S. Olympic Team (received Gold Medal), 1984, 92. Author: RareAir: Michael on Michael, 1993. Named Rookie of Yr., NBA, 1985, Slam-Dunk Championship winner, 1987, 1988, NBA All-Star Game Most Valuable Player, 1988, 1996, 1998, NBA Def. Player of Yr., 1988, NBA Most Valuable Player, 1988, 1991—92; named to Sporting News All-Am. first team, 1983—84, NBA All-Star team, 1985—93, 1996—98, 2002—03, All NBA First Team, 1987—93, 1996—98, NBA All-Def. Team, 1988—93, NBA championship team, 1991—93, 1996—98; recipient Naismith award, 1984, Wooden award, 1984, IBM award, 1985, 1989, Schick Pivotal Player award, 1985, 1989, Seagram's NBA Player of Yr., 1987, NBA All-Def. Team, 1996—98, NBA Most Valuable Player, 1996—98, NBA Finals MVP, 1991—93, 1996—98. Achievements include holder record for most points in an NBA playoff game with 63; mem. NCAA divsn. 1 championship team, 1982.*

JORDAN, NAPOLEON BONAPARTE, educational consultant; b. Ft. Valley, Ga., May 22, 1929; s. James Lee J. and Lillie Mae Jordan; m. Bernice Miriam Evans, Jan. 27, 1957; children: Harold, Kenneth, Cheryl, Constance. BS, Ft. Valley State Coll., 1950; MA, Northwestern U., 1956. Tchr. social studies, dept. head Detroit Pub. Schs., 1957-67; instr. history Wayne C.C. & Marygrove Coll., Detroit, 1969-71, Wayne State U., Detroit, 1971-84; asst. prin. Knudsen Jr. High Sch., Detroit, 1967-69; prin. Butzel Mid. Sch., Detroit, 1969-96; coord. New Global Learning Pathway 21st Century Schs., Detroit, 1999—. Author: (tchrs. guide) Negro in American Life 1865-1965, 1965. Mem. edn. com. NAACP, Detroit, 1965. Pres. Virginia Park Citizens Svc. Corp., 1980. Edn. Specialist U.S. Army, 1951-53. Recipient Merit award Mayor of Detroit, 1989, Spirit of Detroit City Coun., 1986. Mem. Ft. Valley State U. Alumni Assn. (pres. Detroit chpt., bd. dirs.). Avocations: classical music, chess. Home: 18025 Oak Dr Detroit MI 48221-2774

JORDAN, NICOLE T.N. historian, educator; d. Frederick Loring Seely and Lucille Fisher Jordan; m. David A. Herrup, June 28, 1992; 1 child, Rachel Ming Tal Herrup. BA, Wellesley Coll., Mass., 1972; B.A. Honours (M.A. Oxon), Oxford U., 1975; Ph.D., London Sch. of Econs., 1984. Lectr. Trinity Coll., Oxford U., Oxford, England, 1980—81; lectr., asst., assoc. prof. of history U. of Ill., Chgo., 1984—. Com. mem. and chair, midwest regional Mellon fellowships in humanistic studies competition Andrew W. Mellon Found., Princeton, Ill., 1995—. Author: (historical monograph) The Popular Front and Central Europe: the Dilemmas of French Impotence, 1919-1940 (George Louis Beer Prize of the Am. Hist. Assn., Selection of the Am. Coun. of Learned Societies History E-book Project, 1992); contbr. Fellow Guggenheim fellow, John Simon Guggenheim Found., 1998—99, Univ. Tchrs. fellow, NEH, 1997—98; Inst. for the Humanities, U. Ill.-Chgo. fellow, 1988—89. Mem.: Am. Hist. Assn. Jewish. Avocations: listening to music, reading, walking. Office: Univ of Illinois Dept History 913 University Hall m/c 198 Chicago IL 60607-7109 Personal E-mail: njordan@uic.edu. E-mail: njordan@uic.edu.

JORDAN, PAUL, music director; b. N.Y.C., Mar. 12, 1939; s. Henry Paul and Irene B (Brandt) J.; m. Xilin Feng, Dec. 20, 1993; 1 child, Libai Henry Feng Jordan. State degree in Sacred Music, Staatliche Hochschule für Musik, Frankfurt, Germany, 1963; MusM, Yale U., 1967; D of Mus. Arts in Conducting, Am. Conservatory Music, Chgo., 1998. Music dir. United Ch. on the Green, New Haven, 1964-74; prof. music SUNY, Binghamton, 1973-95; music dir. Stratford (Conn.) United Meth. Ch., 1996—2001; dir. music First Congl. Ch., Guilford, Conn., 2001—; instr. Neighborhood Music Sch., New Haven, 1997—. Solo concerts in more than 100 venues on 4 continents including Leipzig Gewandhaus, Berlin State Playhouse, Freiburg and Vienna cathedrals; comml. recs.; composer of 40 works for orchestral, choral and chamber ensembles and for keyboard; contbr. articles to profl. jours. Recipient Deutscher Schallplatten-preis nomination German Phon Acad., 1976, European prize for Bach Interpretation, Fondation Europeenne de la Culture, Lucerne, 2003; Solo Recitalist's fellow Nat. Endowment for Arts, Washington, 1983. Mem. Conductors Guild, Am. Guild Organists. Home: 16 Hughes Pl New Haven CT 06511-4904 E-mail: pxjordan@yahoo.com.

JORDAN, PAUL RICHARD, journalist, writer; b. Wayland, Ky., Apr. 1, 1926; s. Pual Jackson Jordan and Versa Hall Jordan-Moore; m. Dorothy Ruth Wright, Apr. 20, 1954; 1 child, Paul R. II. AB in Journalism, U. Ky., 1950. News editor Paintsville (Ky.) Herald, 1950—51; news reporter Huntington (W.Va.) Herald-Dispatch, 1951—52; newsman AP, Louisville and Frankfurt, Ky., 1952—62; PIO Office of Saline Water, Dept. of Interior, Washington; chief info. office Office of Coal Rsch., 1973—75; ret., 1981. Editor: (book) Coal Camp Kids--Coming Up Hard and Making It, 1990; author: So Little Time for Dying, 2001; editor: Our Heritage Mag., 1963—67; contbr. articles, reports, and brochures to various publs.; author: Journey from Beaver Creek, 2003. Adviser to two Ky. govs. Frankfurt, Ky., 1962—67. Cpl. U.S. Army, 1944—46, ETO. Mem.: VFW (dist. comdr. 1988—89, 1992—93), Moose, Am. Legion. Avocation: photography. Home: 115 Hollyfield Ln Vaughan NC 27586

JORDAN, RANDALL WARREN, optometrist; b. Camilla, Ga., May 19, 1952; s. Billie Howard and Sara Ann (Richards) Jordan; m. Angela Marie Farmer, May 15, 1982; 1 child, Samantha Marie. BS in Biology, So. Coll. Optometry, 1987, OD, 1989. Diplomate So. Coun. Optometrists. Supply and distbn. mgr. Phoebe Putney Meml. Hosp., Albany, Ga., 1981-85; ophthalmic technician Omni Eye Svcs., Memphis, 1987; optometrist Albany Retinal-Eye Ctr., Albany, 1989-90, Eyecare Assocs. Ga., Brunswick, 1990-91; Eye Med, Chamblee, 1992-95, Drs. Shelton, Spooner, and Jordan, 1995-2000, Jordan Eye Care, 2000—. Optometrist Dougherty County Health Dept., Albany, 1989-90, Dept. Children's Med. Svcs., Albany, 1989-90, Lion's Club Vision Screening, Montezuma, Ga., 1989; mem. Emory Vision Correction Ctr. With U.S. Army, 1972-74. Mem. Am. Optometric Assn., Ga. Optometric Assn., Kiwanis, Beta Sigma Kappa, Omega Delta, Phi Theta Upsilon. Avocations: water skiing, scuba diving, photography, reading, music. Home: PO Box 5103 Cordele GA 31010-5103 Office: PO Box 5103 Cordele GA 31010-5103

JORDAN, ROBERT ANDREW, accountant; b. Chillicothe, Ohio, Jan. 10, 1955; s. Robert Dulaney and Juanita (Clark) J.; m. Darlynne Marie Shrader, Oct. 8, 1977; children: Justin Andrew, Lindsey Dara, Jarrett Cole. AA in Bus. Adminstrn. with honors, Cerritos Coll., Norwalk, Calif., 1974; BA in Acctg. cum laude, David Lipscomb U., Nashville, 1976. CPA, Fla., Tenn. Supervising sr. acct. Peat, Marwick, Mitchell & Co., CPAs, Miami, Fla., 1976-81; audit supr. Blankenship, Summar & Assocs., CPAs, Nashville, 1981-82; audit mgr. Bishop, Bussell & Assocs., CPAs, Brentwood, Tenn., 1982-86; controller Cone Oil Co., Inc. & Cone Solvents, Inc., Nashville, 1986-89; acct., cons. R. Andrew Jordan, CPA, 1986—. Sec., treas., bd. dirs. B& C Aviation Co., Inc., 1987—89; v.p. fin. Fetorgon Corp., Nashville, 1986—89; sec., treas. Rustoff Products, Inc., 1990—94; treas., contr. FL Co., Inc, 1991—94; rep. Waller Equity Mgmt., Nashville, 1994—97; mgr. ops. and compliance officer LBMC Investment Advisors, LLC, Brentwood, Tenn., 1998—. Mem. bus. adv. coun. David Lipscomb U., 1986—89; pres. Ogelsby Cmty. Club, 1989—91; asst. coach

Brentwood (Tenn.) Civitan Baseball, 1991—93, 1999—2001; coach Brentwood Civitan Baseball, Tenn., 2001—02; deacon fin. ministry Antioch Ch. of Christ, 1984—91. Mem. AICPA, Tenn. Soc. CPAs, Tenn. Hist. Soc. Avocations: golf, running, bicycling, fishing, travel. Home: 701 Edmondson Pike Brentwood TN 37027-8205

JORDAN, ROBERT ELIJAH, III, lawyer; b. South Boston, Va., June 20, 1936; s. Robert Elijah and Lucy (Webb) J.; children: Janet Elizabeth, Jennifer Anne, Robert Elijah IV. SB, MIT, 1958; JD magna cum laude, Harvard U., 1961. Bar: D.C. 1962, Va. 1964. Spl. asst. civil rights Office Sec. Def., Washington, 1963-64; asst. U.S. atty. for D.C., 1964-65; exec. asst. for enforcement Office Sec. Treasury, 1965-67; dep. gen. counsel Dept. Army, 1967, acting gen. counsel, 1967-68; gen. counsel of Army, spl. asst. for civil functions to Sec. Army, 1968-71; ptnr. Steptoe & Johnson, Washington, 1971—2003, mng. ptnr., 1988-90. Mem. bd. cert. U.S. Cir. Cts. of Appeals Cir. Execs., 1987-88; pres. Langley Sch., 1981-82; mem. civil pro bono com. U.S. Dist. Ct., 1991-92. Contbr. articles to profl. jours. Mem. bd. dirs. Washington Humane Soc., 2000-03. Served to 1st lt. AUS, 1961-63. Recipient Karl Taylor Compton award, 1958, Arthur S. Flemming award, 1970, award for exceptional civilian svc. Dept. Army, 1971; Sloan Found. scholar; Edward J. Noble Found. fellow. Mem. Va. State Bar, D.C. Bar (chmn. ethics com. 1978-83, spl. com. on model rules profl conduct 1983-89, pres. 1987-88), Calif. State Bar, D.C. Bar Found. (pres. 1993-94, 97-98), Atlantic Coun. (bd. dirs. 1993—, exec. com. 1994—2001, chmn. nominating com. 1997-2001), Tau Beta Pi, Tau Kappa Alpha. Democrat. Home: 5239 Siesta Cove Dr Sarasota FL 34242 Office: 1330 Connecticut Ave NW Washington DC 20036-1795 E-mail: rjordan@steptoe.com.

JORDAN, ROBERT LEON, lawyer, educator; b. Reading, Pa., Feb. 27, 1928; s. Anthony and Carmela (Votto) J.; m. Evelyn Allen Willard, Feb. 15, 1958 (dec. Nov. 1996); children: John Willard, David Anthony BA, Pa. State U., 1948; LLB, Harvard U., 1951. Bar: N.Y. 1952. Assoc. White & Case, N.Y.C., 1953-59; prof. law UCLA, 1959-70, 75-91, prof. law emeritus, 1991—, assoc. dean Sch. Law, 1968-69. Vis. prof. law Cornell U., Ithaca, N.Y., 1962-63; co-reporter Uniform Consumer Credit Code, 1964-70, Uniform Comml. Code Articles 3, 4, 4A, 1985-90; Fulbright lectr. U. Pisa, Italy, 1967-68 Co-author: (with W.D. Warren) Commercial Law, 1983, 5th edit., 2000, Bankruptcy, 1985, 5th edit., 1999. Lt. USAF, 1951-53. Office: UCLA Sch Law 405 Hilgard Ave Los Angeles CA 90095-9000

JORDAN, ROBERT LEON, judge; b. Woodlawn, Tenn., June 28, 1934; s. James Richard and Josephine (Broadbent) J.; m. Dorothy Rueter, Sept. 8, 1956; children: Robert, Margaret, Daniel. BS in Fin., U. Tenn., 1958, JD, 1960. Atty. Goodpasture, Carpenter, Dale & Woods, Nashville, 1960-61; mgr. Frontier Refining Co., Denver, 1961-64; atty. Green and Green, Johnson City, Tenn., 1964-66; trust officer 1st Peoples Bank, Johnson City, 1966-69; v.p., trust officer Comml. Nat. Bank, Pensacola, Fla., 1969-71; atty. Bryant, Price, Brandt & Jordan, Johnson City, 1971-80; chancellor 1st Jud. Dist., Johnson City, 1980-88; dist. judge U.S. Dist. Ct. (ea. dist.) Tenn., Knoxville, 1988—2001, sr. dist. judge, 2001—. Mem. adv. com. U. Tenn. Law Alumni, 1978-80; sec. Tenn. Jud. Conf., 1987-88, mem. exec. com., 1988; del. Tenn. State-Fed. Judicial Coun., 1993—. Bd. dirs., v.p. Tri-Cities estate Planning Coun., Johnson City, 1969; bd. dirs. Washington County Tb Assn., Rocky Mount Hist. Assn., High Rock Camp, Johnson City, Jr. Achievement of Pensacola Inc.; bd. dirs., treas. N.W. Fla. Crippled Children's Assn., Pensacola; chancellor's assoc. U. Tenn. With U.S. Army, 1954-56. Named Boss of Yr. Legal Secs. Assn., Washington, Carter County, Tenn., 1982. Mem. Tenn. Bar Assn., Tenn. Bar Found., Knoxville Bar Assn. (bd. govs. 1999), Washington County Bar Assn. (pres.-elect 1980), Johnson City C. of C., Hamilton Burnett Am. Inn of Ct. (pres. 1993-94), Kiwanis (pres. Met. Johnson City Club 1969, Kiwanian of Yr. award 1986-87). Republican. Mem. Ch. of Christ. Office: Howard H Baker US Courthouse 800 Market St Ste 141 Knoxville TN 37902-2303

JORDAN, ROBERT REED, geologist, educator; b. N.Y.C., June 5, 1937; s. Herbert and Irene (Reed) J.; m. Jane H. Jordan, June 28, 1958; children: Richard P., Judith H. AB, Hunter Coll., 1958; MA, Bryn Mawr Coll., 1962, PhD, 1964. Cert. profl. geologist, Del.; lic. geologist, N.C. Geologist Del. Geol. Survey, Newark, 1958-64, asst. state geologist, 1964-69, state geologist, dir., 1969—2003; instr. U. Del., Newark, 1962-64, asst. prof., 1964-68, assoc. prof., 1968-88, prof., 1988—. Mem. Del. Air and Water Commn., Dover, 1966-73; chmn. Del. State Boundary Commn., Newark, 1971-2003; mem. Del. State Bd. Registration of Geologists, 1972-2003; mem. Outer Continental Shelf policy com. U.S. Dept. Interior, 1974-77, 85-2003, chmn., 1993-94; mem. N.Am. Commn. on Stratigraphic Nomenclature, 1978—, chmn., 1984, 92; mem. U.S. Nat. Com. on Geology, 1990-96. Contbr. numerous articles to profl. jours. Recipient tributes Del. Gen. Assembly, 2003; named Hon. Mountaineer, State of W.Va., 1997, Ky. col., 1997. Fellow Geol. Soc. Am.; mem. Del. Acad. Sci. (pres. 1990, 2002), Am. Inst. Profl. Geologists (hon. mem. award 1996, editor 1989-90, Galey Mem. Pub. Svc. award 1992), Am. Geol. Inst. (fin. com. 1992—, treas., exec. com. 1992-93, Outstanding Svc. award 1992, 93, Ian Campbell award 1996,), Assn. Am. State Geologists (hon.; pres. 1983-84, Achievement award), Am. Assn. Petroleum Geologists (hon. mem. award 1993, Disting. Svc. award 1988, Cohee Pub. Svc. Ea. award 1990, Galey award Ea. 1995, John T. Galey Sr. meml. medal 1998, Pres.'s award divsn. environ. geology 2001).

JORDAN, ROBERT SMITH, political science educator; b. Los Angeles, Calif, June 11, 1929; s. Ralph Burdette and Mary Wright (Smith) J.; m. Sara Jane Hatch, Sept. 19, 1961; children: Sara Jane, Mary Rebecca Leming, Robert Hatch, David Thomas. AB, UCLA, 1951; MS, U. Utah, 1955; MA (DuBois fellow), Princeton U., 1957, PhD, 1960; PhD (Fulbright scholar), St. Antony's Coll., Oxford U., Eng., 1960; Henry P. DuBois, 1953—54. Instr. dept. politics Princeton U., 1956-57; asst. prof. pub. and internat. affairs, exec. asst. to dean Grad. Sch. Pub. and Internat. Affairs, U. Pitts., 1959-60; assoc. professorial lectr. George Washington U., 1960-62; asst. dir. Army War Coll. Center, 1960-61; dir. Air U. Center, 1961-62, assoc. prof. polit. sci. and internat. affairs, 1962-70, asst. to pres., 1962-64; dir. Fgn. Affairs Intern Program, Sch. Pub. and Internat. Affairs, 1968-70; dean faculty econ. and social studies, head dept. polit. sci. Fourah Bay Coll., U. Sierra Leone, 1965-67; prof. polit. sci. State U. NY at Binghamton, 1970-76, chmn. dept., 1970-74; dir. rsch. UN Inst. for Tng. and Rsch., NYC, 1975-79; Dag Hammarskold vis. prof. internat. rels. U. SC, Columbia, 1979-80; prof. polit. sci., rsch. prof. U. New Orleans, 1980—2002, dean Grad. Sch., 1980-82. Disting. vis. prof. Naval War Coll., 1984-86; Fulbright prof. Cen. Study of Arms Control and Internat. Security, U. Lancaster, Eng., Jan.-June, 1988; vis. prof. internat. rels. US Air War Coll., 1992-94. Author/co-author, editor/co-editor: The NATO International Staff/Secretariat, 1967, Government and Power in West Africa, 1970, rev. edit., 1977, Europe and the Superpowers, 1971, rev. edit., 1990, International Administration, 1971, Multinational Cooperation, 1972, The World Food Conference and Global Problem Solving, 1976, Political Leadership in NATO, 1979, Changing Role and Concepts in the International Civil Service, 1980, Dag Hammarskjold Revisited: The UN Secretary-General as a Force in World Politics, 1983, Europe in the Balance: The Changing Context of European International Politics, 1986, Generals in International Politics: NATO's Supreme Allied Commander, Europe, 1987, Maritime Strategy and the Balance of Power: Britain and America in the Twentieth Century, 1989, Norstad: Cold War NATO Supreme Commander, 2000, International Organizations: A Comparative Approach of the Management of Cooperation, 2001. Served with USAF, 1951—53. Decorated Bronze Star; named Disting. Alumnus, Hinckley Inst., U. Utah, 1964; NATO rsch. fellow, 1969—70, Hooper postdoctoral fellow, U.S. Naval Hist. Ctr., 1987, 1997. Mem. ASPA (chmn. sect. on internat. and comp. adminstrn.), Assn. Princeton Grad. Alumni (pres.), Internat. Studies Assn. (v.p., chmn. sect. internat. orgn.), Acad. Coun. UN, Internat. Inst. Strategic Studies (London), Royal Inst. Internat. Affairs (London), Cosmos Club (Washington), Plimsoll Club (New Orleans), Sigma Chi (UCLA and Utah). Mem. Lds Ch. E-mail: smitty1929@charter.net.

JORDAN, RONALD P. pharmacist, pharmaceutical executive, consultant; b. Hartford, Conn., Dec. 25, 1952; s. James P. Jordan Jr. and V. Antionette Jordan; m. Karen W. Jordan, Oct. 11, 1986. BS in Pharmacy, U. R.I., 1976. Registered pharmacist. Dir. drug benefits Blue Cross & Blue Shield of R.I., Providence, 1983-87, asst. v.p., 1987-89; pres. Drug Benefit Mgmt. Systems, Inc., West Greenwich, R.I., 1989-95, HCaliber Consulting Corp., West Greenwich, 1995—; sr. v.p., chief info. officer Hospice Pharmacia, LLC, Phila., 1996—99; also bd. dirs.; sr. v.p., chief info. officer ExcelleRx Inc., Phila., 1999—2000; also bd. dirs. Mem. adv. bd. Allscrips Inc., Chgo., 1999—; spl. govt. employee HHS-HCFA, MCAC, Balt., 1999—; sr. v.p. global strategies PharmasMarket-.com, 2000; pres. HealthNation, Inc., Wheaton, Ill., 2002—. Mem. Gov.'s Adv. Coun. on Health, Providence, 1998—. Named one of 50 Most Influential Pharmacists of Yr., Am. Druggist Mag., N.Y.C., 1997, 98, Pharmacist of Yr., R.I. Pharm. Assn., 1998; recipient Founder award N.E. Pharm. Coun., 1999, Bowl of Hygeia award A.H. Robins, R.I. Pharm. Assn., 1983. Fellow: Am. Pharm. Assn. (pres. 1998—99), Am. Soc. Cons. Pharmacists; mem.: Nat. Coun. Prescription Drug Programs (Time award 1992), Pharm. Soc. Israel (hon.), Wickford Yacht Club. Office: HCaliber Consulting Corp 10 Taggart Ct East Greenwich RI 02818-1085

JORDAN, RUTH ANN, physician; b. Oct. 12, 1928; d. Willard and Esther (Fouts) J.; children: Diane J., Linda J. AB, Ind. U., 1950; MD, Columbia U., 1957. Intern St. Luke's Hosp., N.Y.C., 1957—58, asst. resident, 1958—59; physician Met. Life Ins. Co., N.Y.C., 1960—62, Standard Oil Co. of N.J., N.Y.C., 1962, MIT, Cambridge, Mass., 1963—71, New Eng. Mut. Life Ins. Co., Boston, 1963—66, asst. med. dir., 1971—74; fellow internal medicine Mass. Gen. Hosp., Boston, 1974—75; physician Simmons Coll., Boston, 1975—78, Northeastern U., Boston, 1976—78; assoc. med. dir. New Eng. Telephone Co., Boston, 1978, med. dir. clin. svcs., 1978—86; dir. occupl. medicine Gen. Med. Assn., Boston, 1986—91; assoc. med. dir. Allmerica, Worcester, Mass., 1991—97; plant med. dir. GM, Westwood, Mass., 1995—; physician Health Resource, Woburn, Mass., 1996—. Therapeutic dietitian Meth. Hosp., Indpls., 1951-53, Presbyn. Hosp., N.Y.C., part-time 1954-57; nat. coord. com. on cholesterol, 1986—, Mass. Adv. Coun. for Workers Compensation, 1986-89. Fellow: Am. Coll. Occupl. and Environ. Medicine (health edn. com. 1984—, membership com. 1985—88, bd. dirs. 1986—92); mem.: PEO, DAR, AMA, Mass. Med. Soc. (mem. Ho. of Dels. 1984—, chmn. environ. and occupl. health com. 1985—88, mem. interspecialty com. 1985—88, mem. nutrition com. 2001—, mem. bylaws com. 2001—), Norfolk Dist. Med. Soc. (v.p. 1998—99, mem. edn. com. 1998—, mem. exec. com. 1998—, pres. 1999—2001, alt. to Mass. Med. Soc. nominating com. 2000—, alt. to Mass. Med. Soc. bd. trustees 2000—03, bd. trustees 2003—), New Eng. Occupl. Med. Assn. (bd. dirs. 1980—89, pres. 1981—84), The Country Club, Columbia U. Club of New Eng. (v.p. 1981—84, pres. 1989—91), Alpha Chi Omega. Home: 105 Rockwood St Brookline MA 02445-7100

JORDAN, SANDRA, public relations professional; b. Pasadena, Tex., Oct. 10, 1952; d. Royal Wilson and Kathryn Ann (Speck) J.; m. William Anderson Mintz, Aug. 10, 1974 (div. 1980). B of Journalism, U. Tex., 1974. Reporter Austin (Tex.) American Statesman, 1974-76; news dir. KTAE Radio, Taylor, Tex., 1974-76; dir. of news and info. Inst. of Texan Cultures, San Antonio, 1976-82; pub. rels. dir. San Antonio Mus. Assn., 1982-83; dir. news/info. Univ. Tex., San Antonio, 1983-86; sr. publicist Rogers & Cowan, Inc., Washington, 1986-87; communications dir. NARAL, Washington, 1987-88; assoc. Parker, Vogelsingers & Assocs., Washington, 1988-90; pub. rels. and mktg. dir. Girl Scout Coun., Washington, 1990-99; mgr. media rels. Planned Parenthood Fedn. Am., Washington, 1999-2000; fellow Population Leadership Program, Washington, 2000—; dir. comms. and outreach USAID, Washington, 2000—. Pub. rels. cons. YWCA, Washington; judge, ad contest, Women in Comm., Iowa, 1993; workshop organizer Washington Ind. Writers, 1990; publicity com. CASE Conf., San Antonio, 1986, Smithsonian Nat. Assoc. Prog., San Antonio, 1980; panelist Women in Comms. Roundtable, 1996, Global Health Coun., Washington, 2003; presenter in field. Contbg. author: Folk Art in Texas, 1985. Prog. cons. KLRN-TV (pub.) San Antonio, 1981, 82; del. Dem. Nat. Conv., Taylor, 1976; docent Kennedy Ctr., Washington, 1989. Recipient Apex award, 1991-93, 95, 97-98, Comm. Concepts, 1991, Design honors, Tex. Assn. of Mus., 1993, IABC Silver Inkwell award, 1995, Silver Anvil award, 1996. Mem. Women in Comm. (D.C. chpt., literacy project 1992, mentoring program com., v.p. for programs 1998—), Women in Advt. and Mktg., Am. Soc. Assn. Execs., The Writers Ctr., Pub. Rels. Soc. Am. Avocations: fiction writing, quilt making. Home: 6305 E Halbert Rd Bethesda MD 20817-5409 Office: USAID G/PHN/POP The Ronald Reagan Bldg 1300 Pennsylvania Ave Washington DC 20523 E-mail: sjordan@usaid.gov.

JORDAN, STEPHEN M. university president; m. Ruth Kinnie; 3 children. BA in Polit. Sci., U. No. Colo., 1971; MPA in Fin. Adminstrn., U. Colo., Denver, 1979, PhD in Pub. Adminstrn./Policy Analysis, 1990. Vice chancellor for budgets and facilities U. Colo. Health Scis. Ctr., 1985—, asst. sec. bd. regents, 1985—; dep. exec. dir. fin. and planning, Bd. Regents Ariz. State U., 1989—; exec. dir. Kans. Bd. Regents, 1994—; pres. Eastern Wash. U., Cheney, 1998—. Mem. Spokane Valley High Tech. Coun.; bd. dirs. Spokane Symphony, 2000, Wash. Tech. Ctr., 2000, Wash. State Inst. for Pub. Policy, 2002. Mem. Spokane Area C. of C. (bd. dirs. 2000), Providence Svcs. Ea. Wash., Wash. Campus Compact. Office: Eastern Wash U Showalter Hall Rm 214 Cheney WA 99004-2444

JORDAN, THOMAS E. retired academic researcher; b. Leeds, Eng., July 23, 1929; s. Edward Thomas Jordan and Nora Mullarkey; m. Catherine J. Jordan, Sept. 5, 1953; children: Julia, Joseph, Daniel. EdD, Ind. U., 1955. Curators' prof., dean Grad. Sch., assoc. vice chancellor U. Mo., St. Louis, 1968-98. Author: 30 scholarly books and monographs; researcher: 30 scholarly books and monographs; contbr. over 150 articles to prof. jours. Recipient Rsch. prize Royal Soc. Health. Avocation: reading. Home: 2361 Broadmont Ct Chesterfield MO 63017-7830

JORDAN, THOMAS FREDRICK, physics educator; b. Duluth, Minn., June 4, 1936; s. Thomas Vincent and Mildred (Nystrom) J. BA, U. Minn., 1958; PhD, U. Rochester, 1962. Rsch. assoc. U. Rochester, 1961-62, instr., 1962-63; NSF postdoctoral fellow U. Bern, Switzerland, 1963-64; asst. prof. U. Pitts., 1964-67, assoc. prof., 1967-70; prof. U. Minn., Duluth, 1970—. Vis. prof., workshop participant U. Wis., 1965, Aspen (Colo.) Inst. for Humanistic Studies, 1966, Summer Inst. for Theoretical Physics, U. Colo., 1967, Internat. Ctr. for Theoretical Physics, Trieste, Italy, 1968, U. Rochester, 1976-77, Syracuse U., Nat. Inst. for Nuclear Rsch., Firenze, Italy, U. Geneva., U. Paris 1982, Internat. Ctr. for Theoretical Physics, Trieste, workshop on early universe, Erice, Italy, Geneva, U. Bern, 1986, U. Calif. at Santa Barbara, 1988, U. Tex., 1990, 94, 2003. Author: Linear Operators for Quantum Mechanics, 1969, Quantum Mechanics in Simple Matrix Form, 1985; contbr. numerous article to profl. jours. Rsch. fellow Alfred P. Sloan Found., 1965-67, Temple U., 1984, Bush Found. fellow U. Tex., 1994; Fulbright Rsch. grantee U. Göttingen, Fed. Republic of Germany, 1991-92, 2003.

JORDAN, THOMAS HILLMAN, geophysicist, educator; b. Coco Solo, C.Z., Republic of Panama, Oct. 8, 1948; s. Clarence Eugene and Beulah J.; m. Margaret Jordan; 1 child, Alexandra Elyse. BS, Calif. Inst. Tech., 1969, MS in Geophysics, 1970, PhD in Geophysics and Applied Math., 1972. Asst. prof. Princeton (N.J.) U., 1972-75, Scripps Instn. of Oceanography, U. Calif. San Diego, La Jolla, 1975-77, assoc. prof., 1977-82, prof., 1982-84, MIT, Cambridge, 1984-85, U. So. Calif., L.A., 2000—. Contbr. over 140 articles to profl. jours. Fellow AAAS, Am. Geophys. Union (James B. Macelwane award 1983, George P. Woolard award 1998); mem. NAS, Am. Philosophical Soc. Office: Dept Earth Scis U So Calif Los Angeles CA 90089-0740 E-mail: tjordan@usc.edu.

JORDAN, TRACEY ALYS, librarian; b. Clearwater, Fla., Dec. 16, 1965; d. Albert Abraham Jordan and Sarah Frances Hamn; 1 child, Alexzander Albert Abraham Walker. BS in Polit. Sci., Fla. State U., 1996, MS in Info. Studies, 1997, EdS in Libr. Sci., 1999, PhD in Religion, 2001. Cert. sch. libr. media specialist Fla. State U., 1999. Info. specialist Ednl. Services Program, Tallahassee, 1998—2000; reference libr. Fla. Agr. and Mech. U., 2000—01. Dir. Media Ministry, Midway, 1998—99, Single Parent Support Group, Tallahassee, 2000—01. Named Outstanding Student of Yr., St. Petersburg Jr. Coll., 1986; recipient Outstanding Svc. award, Fla. Black Student Assn. Inc., 1988; fellow Delores Auzenne fellow, Fla. State U., 2002; scholar, Bus. and Profl. Women, 1985, Am. Theol. Libr. Assn., 2001, J. Chungam Yau scholar, Fla. State U., 2002. Mem.: Orgn. Am. Historians, Southeastern ALA, Am. Religion Assn., Black Alliance Edn. Options. Office: Fla State U M05 Dodd Hall Tallahassee FL 32306-1520 Home Fax: 850-644-7225; Office Fax: 850-644-7225. E-mail: tdb1116@fsu.edu.

JORDAN, VERNON EULION, JR., lawyer, former association official; b. Atlanta, Aug. 15, 1935; s. Vernon Eulion and Mary (Griggs) J.; m. Shirley M. Yarbrough, Dec. 13, 1958 (dec. Dec. 29, 1985); 1 child, Vickee; m. Ann Dibble Cook, Nov. 22, 1986. BA, DePauw U., 1957; JD, Howard U., 1960; hon. degrees, DePauw U., Howard U., Boston Coll., Brandeis U., CUNY, U. Ill. Chgo. Duke U., U. Mass., NYU, Princeton U., Tulane U., Rutgers U., Tuskegee Inst., Yale U., Notre Dame U., Harvard U., plus 50 other instns. higher edn. Bar: Ga. 1960, Ark. 1964. Practice law, Atlanta, 1960-61, Pine Bluff, Ark., 1964-65; Ga. field dir. NAACP, 1961-63; dir. Voter Edn. Project So. Regional Council, 1964-68; atty. OEO, Atlanta, 1969; exec. dir. United Negro Coll. Fund, N.Y.C., 1970-71; pres. Nat. Urban League, 1972-81; sr. ptnr. firm Akin, Gump, Strauss, Hauer & Feld, LLP, Washington, of counsel, 2000—; sr. mng. dir. Lazard Freres & Co., LLC, N.Y.C., 2000—. Bd. dirs. Am. Express Co., Am. Online Latin Am., Asbury Automotive Group, Dow Jones & Co., J.C. Penney Co., Inc., Xerox Corp., Revlon, Inc., Sara Lee Corp; frequent guest on maj. nat. TV programs including Meet The Press, Face the Nation; chmn. Clinton Presdl. Transition Bd.; apptd. to Pres.'s adv. com. Points of Light Initiative Found., 1989. Mem. Nat. Adv. Commn. on Selective Svcs., 1966-67, Am. Revolution Bi-Centennial Commn., 1972—, Presdl. Clemency Bd., 1974; adv. coun. Social Security, 1974; trustee Ford Found., LBJ Found., Urban Inst. (life), Howard U.; mem. steering com. Bilderberg Meetings; mem. Coun. on Fgn. Rels.; adv. trustee DePauw U., bd. dirs. NAACP Legal Def. and Ednl. Fund; hon. mem. Ralph Bunche Inst. on the UN. Fellow 2Met. Applied Research Center, 1968; Fellow Harvard Inst. Politics, 1969; recipient Alexis de Tocqueville award United Way Am., 1977. Mem. ABA, D.C. Bar Assn., Nat. Bar Assn., Nat. Conf. Black Lawyers, Am. Law Inst., University Club, Board Room, Council on Fgn. Relations, Century Assn.. Mem. A.M.E. Ch. Office: Lazard Freres & Co LLC 30 Rockefeller Plz New York NY 10112-0002

JORDAN, WILLIAM CHESTER, history educator; b. Chgo., Apr. 7, 1948; s. Johnnie Parker and Marguerite Jane (Mays) J.; m. Christine Kenyon Hershey, May 30, 1970; children: Victoria Marie, John Mark, Clare Kenyon, Lorna Janice. AB, Ripon Coll., 1969; PhD, Princeton U., 1973. Instr. Princeton U., 1973-74, lectr., 1974-75, asst. to assoc. prof. history, 1975-86, prof. history, 1986—, Behrman sr. fellow in humanities, 1990—94; dir. Shelby Cullom Davis Ctr. for Hist. Studies, 1994-99. Vis. lectr. U. Pa., Phila., 1981-82; vis. assoc. prof. history Swarthmore (Pa.) Coll., 1985; mem. adv. com. history Grad. Records Exam, 1976-86, chmn., 1980-86; Morgan lectr. Dickinson Coll., Carlisle, Pa., 1985. Co-editor: Order and Innovation in the Middle Ages, 1976; author: Louis IX and the Challenge of the Crusade, 1979, From Servitude to Freedom, 1986, The French Monarchy and the Jews, 1989, Women and Credit, 1993, The Great Famine, 1996, The Middle Ages: An Encyclopedia for Students, 1996, The Middle Ages: A Watts Guide for Children, 2000, Europe in the High Middle Ages, 2001, Ideology and Royal Power in Medieval France, 2001; contbr. articles on medieval history and medieval law to profl. jours. Fellow Woodrow Wilson Found., Ford Found., Danforth Found, Mellon Found., Rockefeller Found., Annenberg Rsch. Inst. Fellow Medieval Acad. Am. (Haskins medal 2000); mem. Am. Hist. Assn. (co-chair program com. 1985), Am. Coun. Learned Socs. (sec. 1986-95, bd. dirs. 1982-95), Am. Philos. Soc. (elected), Soc. French Hist. Studies, Soc. Study of the Crusades and Latin East, Haskins Soc. Office: Dept of History Princeton U Princeton NJ 08544-0001 E-mail: wchester@princeton.edu.

JORDAN, WILLIAM DAVIS, lawyer; b. Palestine, Tex., Aug. 5, 1940; s. Henry Latimer and Evelyn (Davis) J.; m. Toby Stall Feb. 8, 1964; children: Russell Stall Jordan, Stephen Monnig Jordan. BBA with honors, U. Tex., 1963, LLB with honors, 1964. Bar: Tex. 1964; cert. estate planning and probate law Tex. Bd. Legal Specialization. Assoc., then ptnr. Jackson and Walker, Dallas, 1964—97; shareholder Johnson, Jordan, Nipper & Monk, P.C., Dallas, 1997—. Chmn. U. Tex. Tax Conf., 1977, also planning com.; spkr. in field. Contbr. articles to profl. jours. Active Dallas Estate Planning Coun.; chmn. Southwestern Legal Found. Oil and Gas Tax Inst., 1981-86, planning com.; dir., past chmn. Dallas Met. YMCA; past dir. Baylor U. Med. Ctr. Found., YMCA Rockies, Colo., King Found.; vice chmn. YMCA Found.; adv. dir. Cmtys. Found. Tex., Dallas Found. Mem. Tex. Bar Assn. (co-chmn. peer com. 1967-68), Dallas Bar Assn. (chmn. tax sect. 1977), Dallas Estate Planning Coun. (past bd. dirs.), Rotary (found. trustee Dallas 1985-91), Dallas Country Club, Beta Theta Pi. Presbyterian. Office: Johnson Jordan Nipper & Monk PC 13155 Noel Rd Ste 1050 LB3 Dallas TX 75240-1531

JORDAN, WINTHROP DONALDSON, historian, educator; b. Worcester, Mass., Nov. 11, 1931; s. Henry Donaldson and Lucretia Mott (Churchill) J.; m. Phyllis Henry, Aug. 30, 1952 (div. 1979); children: Joshua H., J. Mott, W. Eliot; m. Cora Miner Reilly, Feb. 27, 1982. AB, Harvard U., 1953; MA, Clark U., 1957; PhD, Brown U., 1960. Instr. history Phillips Exeter (N.H.) Acad., 1955-56; lectr. in history Brown U., Providence, 1959-61; fellow Inst. Early Am. History and Culture, Williamsburg, Va., 1961-63; from asst. prof. to prof. history U. Calif., Berkeley, 1963-82, assoc. dean for minority group affairs Grad. div., 1968-70; vis. prof. history and black studies U. Miss., Oxford, 1981, prof. history and Afro-Am. studies, 1982—. Vis. asst. prof. history U. Mich., Ann Arbor, 1966; vis. prof. history U. Calif., Berkeley, 1989; William F. Winter prof. history and prof. Afro-Am. studies, U. Miss., 1993—, F.A.P. Barnard Disting. prof., 1998—; vis. prof. history U. Zimbabwe, 1994. Author: White Over Black, 1968, Tumult and Silence at Second Creek, 1993; co-author: The United States, 1979, The Americans, 1982, The American People, 1986; mem. editorial bd. various scholarly jours. Council mem. Inst. Early Am. History and Culture, 1977-79. Recipient Ralph Waldo Emerson award Phi Beta Kappa, 1968, Parkman prize Soc. Am. Historians, 1969, Nat. Book award for History and Biography Am. Book Pubs., 1969, Bancroft prize Columbia U., 1969, 94, Landry award LSU Press, 1992, Eugene M. Kayden award, 1994, Disting. Alumnus citation Brown U. Grad. Sch., 1993; fellow Charles Warren Ctr. for Study Am. History Harvard U., 1965, Social Sci. Rsch. Coun., 1966, Guggenheim Found., 1967, Ctr. for Advanced Study Behavioral Scis., Palo Alto, 1975-76; grantee NIMH, 1970-73. Mem. Am. Antiquarian Soc. (elected), Am. Hist. Assn., Orgn. Am. Historians, So. Hist. Assn., Mass. Hist. Soc. (elected), Miss. Hist. Soc., Krokodiloes Club. Home: 400 Murray St Oxford MS 38655-2914 Office: Dept History U Miss University MS 38677 E-mail: hsjordan@olemiss.edu.

JORDAN-BYCHKOV, TERRY GILBERT, geography educator; b. Dallas, Aug. 9, 1938; s. Gilbert John and Vera Belle (Tiller) J.; m. Bella Bychkova; children: Tina, Sonya, Eric. BA, So. Meth. U., 1960; MA, U. Tex., 1961; PhD, U. Wis., 1965. Asst. prof. geography Ariz. State U., Tempe, 1965-69; prof., dept. chmn. U. North Tex., Denton, 1969-82; Walter Prescott Webb prof. geography. U. Tex., Austin, 1982—. Author: German Seed in Texas Soil, 1966, Texas Log Buildings, 1978, Trails to Texas, 1981, Texas Graveyards, 1982, American Log Buildings, 1985, American Backwoods Frontier, 1989, North American Cattle Ranching Frontiers, 1993, The European Culture Area, 4th edit 2002, The Mountain West: Interpreting the Folk Landscape, 1997, The Human Mosaic, 9th edit., 2003, North America, Particularly Texas, in the Year 1849, 1999, Siberian Village: Land and Life in the Sakha Republic, 2001, Anglo-Celtic Australia, 2002.The Upland South, 2003; contbr. articles to profl. jours. Fellow Am. Geog. Soc., Tex. State Hist. Assn., Tex. Inst. of Letters, Assn. Am. Geographers (v.p. 1986-87, pres. 1987-88, Honors award 1982). Avocations: travel, genealogy. Office: The U of Tex at Austin Dept Geography Austin TX 78712 Fax: 512-471-5049. E-mail: tgjordan@mail.utexas.edu.

JORDANIA, VAKHTANG, conductor, educator; b. Tbilisi, Republic of Georgia, Dec. 9, 1942; came to U.S., 1983; s. Givi and Varvara J.; children: Giorgi, Nina, Maria, Dimitri. Student, Tbilisi Conservatory, 1966, Leningrad Conservatory, 1969; MusD, Moscow Conservatory, 1971, People's Artist, 1983. Asst. condr. Leningrad Philharm., 1970-71, assoc. condr., 1971-73; condr. Tchaikovsky Competition, 1972, 78; condr., artistic dir. Leningrad Radio Orch., 1973-74; prof. music Saratov (USSR) Conservatory, 1974-77; condr., music dir. Saratov Philharm., 1974-77; condr., artistic dir. Kharkov (USSR) Philharm., 1976-83, Chattanooga Symphony and Opera Assn., 1985-92; condr., music dir. Spokane Symphony, 1991-94. Prin. guest condr. K.B.S. Symphony, Seoul, Republic of Korea, 1984-96; music dir. St. Petersburg Festival Orch., 1993—, Russian Fed. Orch., 1994—, Kharkov Philharm. and Kharkov Opera, 1993—, music dir., Daegu City Symphony, Korea, 2002; founder Vakhtang Jordania Internat. Conducting Competition, 2001. Over 75 recs., TV broadcasts, radio broadcasts, film, and numerous others. Recipient 1st place USSR Nat. Audition for Internat. Competition, 1971, Herbert Von Karajan prize, 1971, Grammy

award nominee, 1993; Jordania prize named in his honor IBLA Internat. Competition, 1999—. Mem. Internat. Acad. Scis., Edn., industry and Arts (elected). Avocations: horseback riding, dogs, fishing.

JORDEN, DOUGLAS ALLEN, lawyer, zoning hearing officer; b. Ft. Smith, Ark., July 17, 1950; s. James Roy and Gordon P. J.; m. Mary Zoe Arendt, Apr. 23, 1983; children: Michael, Willie, Julia. BA, U. Ark., 1972, JD, 1976. Bar: Ark. 1976, Ariz. 1976, U.S. Dist. Ct. Ariz. 1976, U.S. Ct. Appeals (9th cir.) 1977, Calif. 1992, Colo. 1992, U.S. Supreme Ct. 1996. Assoc. Harold Mott Esq., Phoenix, 1976-78; town atty. Town of Paradise Valley, Ariz., 1978-82; assoc. Fennemore Craig, Phoenix, 1982-84; ptnr. Slavin, Kane & Paterson, Phoenix, 1984-88, Lancy, Scult, McVey, Phoenix, 1988-90, Jorden Law Firm, Phoenix, 1990-92, Kane, Jorden, von Oppenfeld, Phoenix, 1992-98, Jorden, Bischoff, McGuire & Rose, PLC, Phoenix, 1998—. Co-author: Arizona Land Use Law, 1988, 3d rev. edit. 1998. Mem. Paradise Valley Village Planning Com. 1988-90; chmn. Phoenix Environ. Quality Commn., 1988-95. Mem. State Bar Ariz. (continuing legal edn. com. 1990-94), Rocky Mt. Land Use Inst. (regional adv. bd. 1992—). Democrat. Methodist. Avocation: hiking. Office: Jorden Bischoff McGuire & Rose PLC Ste 205 7272 E Indian Sch Rd Scottsdale AZ 85251-6268 E-mail: djorden@jordenbischoff.com.

JORDEN, ELEANOR HARZ, linguist, educator; b. N.Y.C. d. William George and Eleanor (Funk) Harz; m. William J. Jorden, Mar. 3, 1944 (div.); children: William Temple, Eleanor Harz, Marion Telva. AB, Bryn Mawr Coll., 1942; MA, Yale U., 1943, PhD, 1950; D.Litt. (hon.), Williams Coll., 1982; D.H.L. (hon.), Knox Coll., 1985; D. Langs. (hon.), Middlebury Coll., 1991; D. Univ. (hon.), U. Stirling, Scotland, 1993. Instr. Japanese Yale U., 1943-46, 47-48; dir. Japanese lang. program and Fgn. Service Inst. Lang. Sch., Am. Embassy, Tokyo, 1950-55; sci. linguist Fgn. Service Inst., Dept. State, Washington, 1959-69; acting head Far East langs., 1961-64; chmn., 1964-67, 69; chmn. Vietnamese lang. div., 1967-69; vis. prof. linguistics Cornell U., 1969-70, prof., 1970-87, Mary Donlon Alger prof. linguistics, 1974-87, prof. emeritus, 1987—. Bernhard disting. vis. prof. Williams Coll., 1985—86, vis. prof., 1986—87, adj. prof., 1987—92; dir. Japanese FALCON program, 1972—87; Univ. prof., Disting. fellow Nat. Fgn. Lang. Ctr. Sch. Advanced Internat. Studies Johns Hopkins U., 1987—91; acad. dir. Exchange: Japan's Tchr. Tng. Inst., 1988—; sr. cons. prep. framework Japanese lang. curriculum and Japanese coll. bd. exam, 1991—93; sr. cons. Japanese multi-media project U. Md., 1995—97, cons. Part 2, Ohio State U., 2002—03; dir. SPENG Program, 1980—; co-dir. Survey on Japanese Lang. Study, 1988—92; guest scholar Wilson Ctr. Smithsonian Instn., 1982; cons., permanent disting. dir. Nat. Assn. Self-Instrnl. Lang. Programs, pres., 1977—78, 1984—85; mem. Fulbright-Hays Com. on Internat. Exch. Scholars, 1972—75; mem. area adv. com. for East Asia, 1972—76; chmn. Social Sci. Rsch. Coun. Task Force on Japanese Lang. Tng., 1976—78; mem. adv. com. Japan Found., 1979—81; mem. Lang. Attrition Project, 1981—87; advisor Ctr. for Japanese Studies, Stirling U., Scotland, 1988—92; mem. Yale U. Coun. Com. Langs. and Lit., 1990—98. Author: (with Bernard Bloch) Spoken Japanese, 1945, Syntax of Modern Colloquial Japanese, 1955, Gateway to Russian, 1961, Beginning Japanese, Part 1, 1962, Part 2, 1963, (with Sheehan, Quang and others) Basic Vietnamese, vols. I, II, 1965, (with Quang) Vietnamese Familiarization Course, 1969, (with Hamako Chaplin) Reading Japanese, 1976, (with Mari Noda) Japanese: The Spoken Language, part 1, 1987, part 2, 1988, part 3, 1990, (with Richard Lambert) Japanese Language Instruction in the U.S.: Resources, Practice and Investment Strategic, 1992. Decorated Order of Precious Crown Emperor of Japan, 1985; recipient Superior Svc. award Dept. State, 1965, Japan Found. and Social Sci. Rsch. Coun. sr. fellow, 1976, Toyota award Twentieth Anniversary Fund grantee, 1978, Japan Found. award, 1985, Papalia award for Excellence Tchr. Tng., 1993, N.E. Conf. award Disting. Svc. and Leadership in Profession, 1994; honoree Eleanor Harz Jorden Festival, Portland State U., 1995. Mem. Assn. Asian Studies (v.p. 1979-80, pres. 1980-81), Linguistic Soc. Am., Am. Coun. Tchrs. Fgn. Langs., Nat. Assn. Self-Instrnl. Lang. Programs (pres. 1978, 85, permanent disting. dir. 1991—), Assn. Tchrs. Japanese (exec. com., pres. 1978-84), Japan Soc. N.Y. (bd. dirs. 1982-88), Exchange: Japan (bd. dirs., v.p., sec. 1998—). Office: 3300 Darby Rd Apt 1302 Haverford PA 19041-1067 Fax: 610-658-2563. E-mail: ejorden@brynmawr.edu.

JORDEN, JAMES ROY, oil company engineering executive, consultant; b. Oklahoma City, Apr. 16, 1934; s. James Roy and Gordon (Peeler) J.; m. Shirley Ann Swan, Nov. 17, 1956; children: Philip Taylor, David Emerson. BS in Petroleum Engring., U. Tulsa, 1957. Engr. Shell Oil Co., various locations, 1957, 1960-81, petrophys. engr. advisor Houston, 1981-85; mgr. petroleum engring. rsch. Shell Devel. Co., Houston, 1985-88, mgr. head office prodn., tech. tng., 1988-93; mgr. CPI tng. Shell Oil Co., Houston, 1993-95; retired, 1995; cons. Quicksilver Resources, Inc., 1998—. Mem. industry adv. bd. petroleum engring. U. Tulsa, 1987-92, chmn., 1988; vis. com. petroleum engring. Colo. Sch. Mines, Golden, 1988-95. Co-author: Well Logging I, 1984, Well Logging II, 1986; co-inventor in field. 1st lt. USAF, 1957—60. Named to Hall of Fame, Petroleum Engring. Dept. U. Tulsa, 1985. Mem. Am. Inst. Mining, Metall. and Petroleum Engrs. (trustee 2000-02), Soc. Petroleum Engrs. (hon., pres. 1984, Disting. Svc. award 1988, DeGolyer Disting. Svc. medal 1991, bd. dirs. 1975-79, dir. svc. corps. 1984-90, life trustee found., treas. found. 1991-92, sr. v.p. found. 1993-95, pres. found. 1995-97), Kappa Alpha. Republican. Presbyterian. Avocations: golf, reading, wine. Home: PO Box 8111 Horseshoe Bay TX 78657-8111

JORDEN, WILLIAM JOHN, writer, retired diplomat; b. Bridger, Mont., May 3, 1923; s. Hugh G. and Jane Ann (Temple) J.; m. Eleanor Harz, 1944 (div.); children: William Temple, Eleanor Harz, Marion Telva; m. V. Mildred Xiarhos, 1972. BA with honors, Yale, 1947; MS, Columbia, 1948. Instr. Japanese Yale, 1945—46; reporter Vineyard Gazette, Edgartown, Mass., 1947; radio news writer N.Y. Herald Tribune, 1948; fgn. corr. A.P., Japan and Korea, 1948—52, N.Y. Times, Japan and Korea, 1952—55, chief of bur. Moscow, 1956—58; diplomatic corr. N.Y. Times (Washington bur.), 1958-61; mem. Policy Planning Coun., State Dept., 1961-62, spl. asst. to under sec. polit. affairs, 1962-65, dep. asst. sec. state pub. affairs, 1965-66; sr. mem. staff NSC, 1966-68, 72-74; mem., spokesman Am. del. Vietnam Peace Talks, Paris, 1968-69; asst. to former Pres. Lyndon B. Johnson, 1969-72; U.S. ambassador to Panama, 1974-78. Scholar-in-residence LBJ Libr.; adj. prof. LBJ Sch. Pub. Affairs, U. Tex., 1978-80; U.S. chmn. U.S.-Panama Consultative com., 1992-95. Author: Panama Odyssey; co-author: Japan Between East and West. Served with AUS, 1943-45. Shared Pulitzer prize for internat. corr., 1958; Recipient Disting. Honor award Dept. State, 1978; Pulitzer traveling fellow, 1948-49; Council Fgn. Relations fellow, 1955-56; Decorated order of Vasco Nunez de Balboa (Republic of Panama) Mem. Coun. Fgn. Rels., Acad. Polit. Sci., Author's Guild. Clubs: Yale of Washington, Washington Golf and Country, Fgn. Corrs. Japan (pres. 1952-53).

JORDON, ROBERT EARL, physician; b. Buffalo, May 7, 1938; s. James Wallace and Helen Viola (Sampson) J.; m. Mary Ann Michels, July 12, 1969; children: James H., Kathryn L., Marie H. BA, Hamilton Coll., 1960; MD, SUNY-Buffalo, 1965; MS, U. Minn., 1970. Diplomate: Am. Bd. Dermatology, Am. Bd. Dermatological Immunology, Am. Bd. Diagnostic and Laboratory Immunology. Intern straight medicine Buffalo Gen. Hosp., 1965 66; resident, fellow in dermatology Mayo Clinic and Mayo Found., Rochester, Minn., 1966-69, asso. cons., 1971-73, cons. dermatology, 1973-77; instr. pathology U. Minn. Hosps., Mpls., 1971-73; Nat. Inst. Arthritis and Metabolic Diseases spl. research fellow U. Minn., Mpls., 1972-73; asst. prof. dermatology Mayo Grad. Sch. Medicine, Rochester, 1971-73, Mayo Sch. Medicine, Rochester, 1973-76, asst. prof. immunology, 1974-77, asso. prof. dermatology, 1976-77; prof. medicine, chmn. dermatology Med. Coll. Wis., Milw., 1977-82; med. career investigator VA, 1978-82; chief dermatology Froedtert Meml. Luth. Hosp., Milw., 1980-82; chmn. dept. dermatology U. Tex. Health Sci. Ctr., Houston, prof., 1983—; chief dermatology Hermann Hosp., Houston, 1983—2003; mem. study sect. NIH, 1983-86. Mem. nat. arthritis adv. bd. Nat. Inst. aRthritis and Metabolic Diseases, NIH; mem. nat. adv. bd. Arthritis, Musculoskeletal and Skin Diseases, 1989-91, chmn. 1992-93. Mem. editl. bd. Jour. Investigative Dermatology, 1977-82, Jour. Clin. and Lab. Immunology, 1977—, Archives of Dermatology, 1978-87, sect. editor Am. Jour. Dermatopathology, 1981-83, Clin. Aspects Autoimmunity, 1989-92. Elder Grace Presbyn. Ch., Houston, 1987—; bd. dirs. CAnCare of Houston, 1991-2001, pres. bd. dirs., 1997-99, chmn. bd., 1999-2001. Lt. comdr. M.C., USN, 1965 71. Recipient Bacelli Research award SUNY, Buffalo, 1965, Med. Spltys. Outstanding Achievement award Mayo Found., 1969, Marion B. Sulzberger award Am. Soc. Dermatologic Allergy and Immunology, 1983, award Am. Skin Assn., 1999, JB & Blanche Earthman award 2002. Mem. Soc. Investigative Dermatology (com. nominations 1986—, dir. 1977-82), Am. Acad. Dermatology (co-chmn. com. lab. proficiency and quality control in immunodermatology 1980-83, dir. Immunopathology Symposium 1981-86, bd. dirs. 1993-98), AAAS, Am. Assn. Immunologists, Am. Dermatol. Assn., Am. Fedn. Clin. Research, AMA, Am. Soc. Clin. Investigation, Assn. Profs. Dermatology (bd. dirs. 1987-89), Central Soc. Clin. Research, Dermatology Found. (chmn. med. and sci. com. 1980-81, trustee 1993-98, discovery award 2000), Soc. Exptl. Biology and Medicine, Lupus Erythematosus Soc. Wis. (mem. med. adv. bd. 1977-83), Wis. Dermatol. Soc. (pres. 1979-80), Wis. State Med. Soc., Chgo. Dermatol. Soc., Tex. Med. Assn., Houston Dermatol. Soc., Lupus Soc. Houston (adv. bd. 1986—90), Sigma Xi. Home: 376 Green Cove Dr Montgomery TX 77356-8267 Office: U Tex Health Sci Ctr Houston TX 77030

JØRGEN, ULM, retired computer scientist; b. Odense, Denmark, Mar. 23, 1934; s. Laurits and Rigmor (Andersen) Nielsen; m. Solveig Pedersen, Mar. 23, 1957; children: Hans-Henrik, Frank, Helle. Commd. officer Danish Army, 1954, advanced through grades to capt.; database adminstr. Danish Forces, 1972-80; ret., 1980; database adminstr. Danish Securities Ctr., Tåstrup, Denmark, 1980-84, ops. mgr., 1984-94, v.p., 1986-94; dir. Danish Backup Ctr., 1994-97; ret., 1997. Avocation: yachting. Home: Lyovej 24 DK-2000 Frederiksberg Denmark E-mail: ulm@ddf.dk.

JORGENSEN, ALFRED H. retired data processing executive; b. South Gate, Calif., May 1, 1934; s. Peter Hansen and Anna Christine (Nielsen) J.; m. Carole Jean Scott, Sept. 3, 1959; children: Mark Alan, Lora Jean. AA, El Camino Coll., 1958; student, UCLA, 1958-60. Assoc. engr. Litton Industries, Beverly Hills, Calif., 1957-60; engr. Daystrom, Inc., 1960-64; with control sys. divsn. Foxboro Co., Pitts., 1964-67, dist. and regional mgr., 1967-69; with Interactive Scis., Pitts., 1969-72, v.p., 1970-71, Computeria Inc., 1971, pres., 1971-72; v.p. Interactive Scis. Corp., Braintree, Mass., 1972-77, pres., CEO, 1977-80; exec. v.p. Nat. Data Corp., Atlanta, 1980-83; v.p. nat. sales Cullinet Software Inc., 1983-85; v.p., gen. mgr. Sys. and Computer Tech., 1985-87; pres., COO Infosafe Corp., Atlanta, 1987-88; pres. Corp. Playmakers, 1988-90; dir. bus. alliances Sprint Comm., Atlanta, 1990-95; gen. mgr. Applied Tech. Ctr., 1995—2000; ret., 2000. Bd. dirs. Process Corp., Pitts., Chestatee State Bank; adj. prof. Emory U., 1998—2000. Chmn., Relay for Life Am. Cancer Soc., 2001; bd. dirs. Mass. Assn. Mental Health, 1977—79, v.p., 1978—79; bd. dirs. Satisfy (Drug Rehab. Program), Dawson Humane Soc., 2003. Mem. IEEE, Data Processing Mgmt. Assn., Assn. Iron and Steel Engrs., Instrument Soc. Am., Cash Mgmt. Assn., Am. Mgmt. Assn., Nat. Platform Assn., Pearson Yacht Club (commodore 1984). Home: 927 Liberty Church Rd Dawsonville GA 30534-7354 E-mail: aljorgy@aol.com.

JORGENSEN, ANN, farmer; b. Cedar Rapids, Iowa, Sept. 16, 1940; d. Kenneth Edward and Velma Ann (Baumhoefener) Fry; m. Marlyn L. Jorgensen, Feb. 27, 1961; children: Christopher, Peter, Timothy, Jennifer. BA, U. Iowa, 1962. Lic. commodity broker. Tax acct. Bill Burrell Tax Svc., Urbana, Iowa, 1968-70, Hansen Acctg., Vinton, Iowa, 1970-75; commodity broker First Mid. Am., Cedar Rapids, 1975-85; owner Lakeview Enterprises, Osage Beach, Mo., 1975-85; v.p., treas. Timberlane Hogs, Ltd., Garrison, Iowa, 1970-97; ptnr., owner Jorg-Anna Farms, Garrison, 1963—; pres., founder Farm Home Offices, Vinton, 1980-97; mem., farm credit adminstr. Bd. Farm Credit Adminstr., 1997—2002, chair Farm Credit Sys. Ins. Corp., 2000—02; dir. state and fin. rels. risk mgmt. agy. USDA, 2002—. Mem. Bennett Agrl. Round Table, 2000; bd. dirs. Farm Bur. Mut. Funds, Des Moines, commr. Interstate Agrl. Grain Commn. Midwest Compact, 1988-97; mem. Agriculture Products Adv. Bd., Des Moines, 1990—, bd. dirs.; spkr. in field; mem. environ. com. Nat. Pork Producers Coun., 1996-2000; chair info. tech. com. Am. Farm Bur. Fedn., 1996—. Author: Put PaperWork in its Place, 1982; contbr. articles to profl. jours. Mem., chair Iowa Arts Coun., 1973-79; regent Iowa Bd. Regents, 1979-85; dir., pres. Iowa Alcoholic Beverages Commr., Des Moines, 1985-88; nat. chair Tauke for U.S. Senate, Iowa, 1987-88; bd. dirs. Iowa Dept. Econ. Devel., 1988—; chair bd. Iowa Rural Devel. Coun., 1991-95; mem. Iowa Supreme Ct. Study Com., 1995-96. Named to Iowa Vol. Hall of Fame, 1989. Mem. AACC (bd. dirs. 1995—), Vinton Am. Assn. U. Women (various offices 1980—), Iowa Pub. TV Found. (sec. 1987-95), Alpha Zeta. Avocations: golf, bridge, photography. Home: 2703 Woodley Rd NW Washington DC 20008 Office: Dir State Fin Rels Ris Mgmt Agy USDA 1500 Independence Ave W Washington DC 20250-0801 E-mail: jorgensena@fca.gov.

JÖRGENSEN, BETH ELLEN, Spanish language educator; b. S.I., N.Y., Oct. 11, 1953; d. Charles William and Dorothy (Gralow) J.; m. Thomas Scott Covell; children: Megan J., Benjamin J. BA in Spanish with high honors, Oberlin Coll., 1975; MA in Spanish, U. Wis., 1978, PhD in Spanish-Am. Lit., 1986. Tchg. asst. U. Wis., Madison, 1976-82, lectr. dept. Spanish and Portuguese, 1982-83; asst. prof. Spanish U. Rochester, N.Y., 1986-93, assoc. prof. Spanish, 1993—, chair dept. modern langs. and cultures, 1994-98. Assoc. chair undergrad. programs modern langs. and cultures U. Rochester, 1993-94, undergrad. advisor Spanish, mem. steering com. Multimedia Ctr., mem. study abroad com. Coll. Arts and Scis., 1993-94, dean's fellow, 1987-88; assoc. Susan B. Anthony Ctr. for Women's Studies, mem. seminar and speakers com., 1992-94; manuscript appraiser U. Tex. Press, U. Ariz. Press; book reviewer Hispanic Review, Letras Femeninas; presenter in field. Author: The Writing of Elena Poniatowska: Engaging Dialogues, 1994; co-editor: The Contemporary Mexican Chronicle, 2002; contbr. articles to profl. jours. Vilas fellow U. Wis., 1978-79, Dipman Grad. fellow Oberlin Coll., 1984-85. Mem. MLA, Am. Assn. Tchrs. Spanish and Portuguese, L.Am. Studies Assn., Midwest MLA, N.E. MLA, New Eng. Coun. L.Am. Studies, Assn. de Literatura Femenina Hispánica, Feministas Unidas (v.p. 2001, pres. 2002—), Phi Beta Kappa (chpt. pres. 1992-94). Office: U Rochester Modern Langs and Cultures Rochester NY 14627 E-mail: bjgn@mail.rochester.edu.

JORGENSEN, DANIEL FRED, academic executive; b. May 3, 1947; m. Susan Jorgensen, June 20, 1969; children: Kari, Becky. BA in Journalism, S.D. State U., 1969, MS in Journalism, 1974; postgrad., Colo. State U.; grad. with honors, U.S. Army's Def. Info. Sch., 1970. Writer news and sports Sioux Falls (S.D.) Argus-Leader, 1969-70; asst. editor news and sports, part-time instr. S.D. State U. Comm. Office, 1972-74; from publ. editor to asst. dir. Colo. State U., 1974-78; editor news and sports Hot Springs (S.D.) Star, 1978-81; exec. dir. Black Hills (S.D.) Girl Scout Coun., 1981-83; dir. devel. and pub. rels. St. Martin's Acad., Rapid City, S.D., 1983-84; dir. news svc. St. Olaf Coll., Northfield, Minn., 1984-88, dir. pub. rels., 1988-97; v.p. comm. Scholarship Am., 1997-2000; dir. pub. rels. Augsburg Coll., 2000—. Author and co-author six books; contbr. numerous articles to mags. and jours. Chair bd. Northfield Hosp., 1990-2001, United Way, 1989-91, chair 1990-91; chair bd. Northfield Rotary, 1987-92, v.p., 1990-91, pres. 1991-92; officer various other cmty. orgns.; mem. coms. Northfield Sch.; governing bd. Minn. Hosp. Assoc., 1998—2003. 1st lt. U.S. Army, 1970-72. Named to first class Leadership Rapid City, 1982-83; honored for community svc. City of Northfield, 1992; recipient Rice County Vol. award, 1992. Mem. Coun. for the Advancement and Support of Edn. (nat. coms. mem. 1991—), Nat. Assn. Sci. Writers, Nat. Edn. Writers Assn., Kappa Tau Alpha, Sigma Delta Chi. Avocations: sports, youth activities, writing, community theatre. Home: 505 Wilson Ct Northfield MN 55057-1374 Office: Augsburg Coll 2211 Riverside Ave Minneapolis MN 55454 E-mail: jorgensd@augsburg.edu.

JORGENSEN, ERIK, forest pathologist, educator, consultant; b. Haderslev, Denmark, Oct. 28, 1921; emigrated to Can., 1955, naturalized, 1960; s. Johannes and Eva Bromberg (Hansen) J.; m. Grete Moller, June 13, 1946; children: Marianne, Birthe. M. Forestry, Royal Vet. and Agrl. Coll., Copenhagen, 1946. Forest pathologist Royal Vet. and Agrl. Coll., Copenhagen, 1948-55; forest pathologist sci. service Agr. Can., 1955-59; asst. prof. U. Toronto, 1959-63, assoc. prof., 1963-67, prof. forest pathology and urban forestry, 1967-73; chief urban forestry program Can. Forestry Service, Environ. Can., 1973-78; arboretum dir., prof. environ. biology U. Guelph, Ont., 1978-87; cons. in field, 1987-89. Author: The Development of an Urban Forestry Concept, 1967; contbr. articles to sci. jours. Served to 2d lt. Danish Army, 1946-48. Recipient Authors citation Internat. Shade Tree Conf., 1970; recipient Maple Leaf award Internat. Shade Tree Conf., 1975, Can. Patents and Devel. Ltd. Inventors cert., 1975, Trees for Tomorrow award Can. Forestry Assn., 1993. Fellow Can. Inst. Forestry; mem. Ont. Profl. Foresters Assn., Internat. Soc. Arboriculture, Ont. Shade Tree Council (life, Jaap Salm Meml. award 1975), Sigma Xi. Lutheran. Home: 172 Metcalfe St Apt 507 Guelph ON Canada N1E 6T6 *A dedication to the application of forest science to the service of mankind.*

JORGENSEN, GERALD THOMAS, psychologist, educator, lawyer; b. Mason City, Iowa, Jan. 15, 1947; s. Harry Grover and Mary Jo (Kollasch) J.; m. Mary Ann Reiter, Aug. 30, 1969; children: Amy Lynn, Sarah Kay, Jill Kathryn. BA, Loras Coll., Dubuque, 1969; MS, Colo. State U., Ft. Collins, 1970, PhD, 1973; Juris Canonici Licentiae, Cath. U. Am., 1998. Lic. psychologist, Iowa, canonist Cath. Ch.; cert. health svc. provider Nat. Register, Iowa; ordained to ministry Roman Cath. Ch. as deacon, 1979. Psychology intern Counseling Ctr., Colo. State U., Ft. Collins, 1971-72, VA Hosp., Palo Alto, Calif., 1972-73; psychologist Loras Coll., Clarke Coll., Dubuque, 1973-76; asst. prof. psychology Loras Coll., 1976-80, assoc. prof., 1981-93, dir. Ctr. for Counseling and Student Devel., 1977-86, assoc. dean of students, 1985-86, dean of students, v.p. for student devel., 1986-93; cons. and supervising psychologist Gannon Ctr. for Cmty. Mental Health, 1977—. Assoc. med. staff Mercy Med. Ctr., 1989—. mem. credentials com., 1992—; asst. dir. for formation Office of Permanent Diaconate, Archdiocese of Dubuque, 1979-93, dir., 1993-96, auditor, 1993-98; cons. psychologist Met. Tribunal, 1993—, judge, 1998—; mem. Iowa Bd. Psychology Examiners, Des Moines, chairperson, 1984-90, coord. continuing edn., 1983; sec.-gen. First Internat. Congress on Licensure, Certification and Credentialing of Psychologists, New Orleans, 1995. Contbr. articles to profl. jours. Treas. Dubuque County Assn. Mental Health Inc., 1975-82, v.p., 2002—. NDEA fellow, 1969-72. Fellow Assn. State and Provincial Psychology Bds. (exec. com. 1986-89, pres. 1989-92, Morton Berger award 1996); mem. Am. Coll. Pers. Assn. (chmn. com. VII 1980-82), Am. Assn. Counseling Devel., Am. Psychol. Assn., Iowa Psychol. Assn. (treas. 1976-80, mem. exec. coun. 1980-83, highest honors 1990), Nat. Assn. Diaconate Dirs. (sec. 1983-85, treas. 1985-90, award 1991), Canon Law Soc. Am. (sec. 2002—), Iowa Student Pers. Assn., Fedn. Assns. Reg. Bds. (v.p. 1993-94, 96-97, pres. 1994-96), Delta Epsilon Sigma, Phi Kappa Phi, Sigma Tau Phi. Democrat. Roman Catholic. Office: Archdiocesan Ctr 1229 Mount Loretta Ave Dubuque IA 52003-7826 Home: 480 Woodland Ridge Dubuque IA 52003-6723 E-mail: dbqcmtaud@arch.pvt.k12.ia.us.

JORGENSEN, GORDON DAVID, retired engineering company executive; b. Chgo., Apr. 29, 1921; s. Jacob and Marie (Jensen) J.; m. Nadina Anita Peters, Dec. 17, 1948 (div. Aug. 1971); children: Karen Ann, David William, Susan Marie; m. Barbara Noel, Feb. 10, 1972 (div. July 1976); m. Ruth Barnes Chalmers, June 15, 1990. BSEE, U. Wash., 1948, postgrad. in bus. and mgmt., 1956-59. Registered profl. engr., Alaska, Ariz., Calif., Colo., Nev., N.Mex., N.D., Utah, Wash., Wyo. With R.W. Beck & Assocs., Cons. Engrs., Phoenix, 1948—, ptnr., 1954-86; pres. Beck Internat., Phoenix, 1971—; ret. Project mgr. for mgmt., operation studies and reorgn. study Honduras power sys., 1969-70. Served to lt. (j.g.) U.S. Maritime Svc., 1942-45. Recipient Outstanding Svc. award Phoenix Tennis Assn., 1967, Commendation, Govt. Honduras, 1970. Mem. IEEE (chmn. Wash.-Alaska sect. 1959-60), NSPE, Am. Soc. Appraisers (sr. mem.), Ariz. Cons. Engrs. Assn., Ariz. Soc. Profl. Engrs., Internat. Assn. Assessing Officers, Southwestern Tennis Assn. (past pres.), U.S. Tennis Assn. (pres. 1987-88, chmn. U.S. Open com.), chmn. U.S. Davis Cup com., chmn. Internat. Tennis Fed., Davis Cup com.). Presbyterian (elder). Home: 74-574 Palo Verde Dr Indian Wells CA 92210-7314

JORGENSEN, JAMES H. pathologist, educator, microbiologist; b. Dallas, July 11, 1946; m. Jane Drummond, Feb. 18, 1978. BA, North Tex. State U., 1969, MS, 1970, PhD, 1973. cert. microbiologist. Rsch. assoc. Shriners Hosp. for Crippled Children, 1970-73; assoc. dir. Bexar County Hosp., 1973-75; instr. dept. pathology and dept. microbiology, Health Sci. Ctr. U. Tex., San Antonio, 1973-75, asst. prof., 1975-78, assoc. prof., 1978-84; dir. clin. microbiology labs. Univ. Hosp., 1975—; prof. dept. pathology, dept. medicine, dept. microbiology, dept. clin. lab. scis., Health Sci. Ctr. Univ. Ctr. Hosp., 1984—. Mem. editl. bd. Antimicrobial Agts. and Chemotherapy, 1982—, Jour. Clin. Microbiology, 1986-99, Clin. Infectious Diseases, 1995, Diagnostic Microbiology and Infectious Diseases, 1983-87, reviewer, 1992-93; reviewer of numerous sci. jours.; chairholder Nat. Com. for Clin. Lab. Stds., subcom. on antimicrobial susceptibility testing, 1990-97; chair Nat. Com. for Clin. Lab Stds., Microbiol. Area Com., 1998-2002. Author: In Vitro Detection of Methicillin Resistant Staphylococci, 1985, A Clinician's Dictionary of Bacteria and Fungi, 1986, Progress and Pitfalls in Staphylococcus Susceptibility Testing, 1987; editor Automation in Clinical Microbiology, 1987, Manual of Clinical Microbiology, 1995, 2d edit., 1999. Recipient Becton-Dickenson and Co. award in Clin. Microbiology, 1992; James W. McLaughlin Pre-Doctoral fellow in Infection and Immunity, Med. Br., U. Tex., 1971-73; Pre-Doctoral scholarship, North Tex. State U., 1969-70. Fellow Infectious Diseases Soc. of Am., Am. Acad. Microbiology; mem. Am. Soc. for Microbiology (Tex. branch chmn. clin. divsn. 1987-88), Southwestern Assn. of Clin. Microbiology, Tex. Infectious Diseases Soc. (pres. 1985-86), South Tex. Assn. of Microbiology Profls. (program dir. 1981-86, pres. 1989-90). Office: Univ of Texas Health Sciences Dept of Pathology 7703 Floyd Curl Dr San Antonio TX 78284-6200

JORGENSEN, LELAND HOWARD, aerospace research engineer; b. Rexburg, Idaho, Nov. 1, 1924; s. Leland Maeser and Anne Molyneaux (Howard) J.; m. Lynone Watkins, Mar. 24, 1949; children: Leland Ronald Jorgensen, Paul Victor Jorgensen, Jonathan Arthur Jorgensen, Sara Anne Jorgensen. BS in Mech. Engring. with honors, U. Utah, 1948; MS in Mech. Engring. with honors, Stanford U., 1949; PhD in Mech. Engring. with high honors, Calif. We. U., 1977. Rsch. engr. NACA-Ames Aero. Lab., Moffett Field, Calif., 1949-59; rsch. scientist NASA-Ames Rsch. Ctr., Moffett Field, Calif., 1959-66, tech. asst. chief thermo and gas dynamics div., 1966-68, tech. asst. chief aeronautics div., 1968-71, aerospace rsch. scientist, 1971-80; aerospace cons. Sandy, Utah, 1980—. Mem. aerodyn. panel for space shuttle NASA, 1978-80; cons. on Agile missile USN, 1972; cons. on air-slew missile USAF, 1973. Contbr. over 50 articles on aerodyns. of missiles and aircraft at subsonic, transonic, supersonic and hypersonic speeds to profl. jours. Trustee Saratoga (Calif.) Sch. Dist., 1977-81; v.p., pres. Eagle Scout Assn. Santa Clara (Calif.) coun. Boy Scouts Am., 1962-72; pres. Neighborhood 5 Granite Cmty., Sandy, 1990-93; high priest LDS Ch. Lt. USNR, 1944-46, PTO. Recipient Apollo Achievement award, NASA, 1969, Merit of Honor award, U. Utah Emeritus Alumni Assn., 2003. Fellow AIAA (assoc.); mem. SAR (pres. Salt Lake City chpt. 1989-90, pres. Utah Soc. 1992-93, chaplain 1994-97, Meritorious Svc. medal 1993, Patriot medal 1997, Silver Good Citizenship medal 2001, trustee 1999-2001), Sons of the Utah Pioneers (life), Tau Beta Pi, Pi Tau Sigma, Sigma Nu, Theta Tau. Achievements include basic wind-tunnel tests of models of the command module for the Apollo program that sent men to the moon in 1969; development of analytical method for computing aerodynamics of missile and airplane-life configurations to very high angles of attack; service on committee that approved aerodynamics of the space-shuttle orbiter for the first flight. Office: Aerospace Cons 3 La Montagne Ln Sandy UT 84092-6024

JORGENSEN, LOU ANN BIRKBECK, social worker; b. Park City, Utah, May 14, 1931; d. Robert John and Lillian Pearl (Langford) Birkbeck; m. Howard Arnold Jorgenson, June 9, 1954; children: Gregory Arnold, Blake John, Paul Clayton. Student, Westminster Coll., 1949-51; BS, U. Utah, 1953, MSW, 1972, PhD, 1979; grad., Harvard Inst. Ednl. Mgmt., 1983. Social work adminstr. nursing home demonstration project, dept. family and cmty. medicine U. Utah Med. Ctr., Salt Lake City, 1972-74; mental health ednl. specialist Grad. Sch. Social Work U. Utah, Salt Lake City, 1974-77, 77-80, asst. prof., 1974-80, assoc. prof., 1980-94, prof., 1994-97, prof. emeritus, 1997—, dir. doctoral program, 1984-89, 94-97, assoc. dean, 1986-94. Regional mental health cons. Author: Explorations in Living, 1978, Social Work in Business and Industry, 1979, Handbook of the Social Services, 1981, (with others) Women as They Are, 2d edit., 2001; edit. bd. Jour. of Women and Aging; contbr. articles to profl. jours. Bd. dirs. Info. and Referral Ctr., 1975-82, United Way of Utah, 1976-82, Pioneer Trail Parks, 1977-83, Rowland Hall-St. Mark's Sch., 1980-86, Salt Lake County Housing commr., 1980-86, Utah State Health Facilities Bd., 1991-2001, chmn., 1994-95, 97-98; pres. Human Svcs. Conf. for Utah, 1979-80; bd. dirs. Alzheimer's Assn., Utah chpt., 1990-97, Salt Lake County Coalition Bus. and Human Svcs., 1990-94; mem. Valley Mental Health Bd., 1990-2000; bd. dirs. Ballet West, 2000-02; bd. dirs., Norman S. Anderson MD Mental Health Award, 1988-2000, chair, 1999-2000. Mem. NASW (pres. Utah chpt. 1978-79), Coun. on Social Work Edn., Commn. Women in Higher Edn. Adminstrs. Pub. Agys. Assn., Human Svcs. Assn. Utah, Jr. League Salt Lake

City (pres. 1969-70), Town Club (pres. bd. dirs. 2000-2002), Phi Kappa Phi. Episcopalian. Home and Office: 1458 Kristianna Cir Salt Lake City UT 84103-4221 E-mail: ljorgensen@uofu.com.

JORGENSEN, NORMAN ERIC, lawyer; b. Oakland, Calif., July 13, 1938; s. Peter Wesley and Janet Marie Jorgensen; m. Concetta Finocchio, Aug. 3, 1963 (div.); children: Eric Vincent, Joseph Peter, Catherine Ann Jorgensen Martinsen, Lara Lynn; m. Connie Engelking, Feb. 4, 1979. BS in Physics, MIT, 1960; postgrad., Princeton U., 1960-61, U. Calif., Berkeley, 1961-65, JD, 1968. Bar: Calif. 1969, U.S. Dist. Ct. (no. dist.) Calif. 1969, U.S. Ct. Appeals (9th cir.) 1969, Oreg. 1973, U.S. Ct. Claims 1973, U.S.Dist. Ct. (ctrl. dist.) Calif. 1974, U.S. Dist. Ct. Oreg. 1976, U.S. Supreme Ct. 1976, U.S. Ct. Appeals (fed. cir.) 1982, U.S. Patent and Trademark Office 1993. Pvt. practice, Oakland, 1969-71; ptnr. Grose Rose & Jorgensen, Oakland, 1971-73; assoc. gen. counsel Tektronix Inc., Beaverton, Oreg., 1973-90; group counsel Intel Corp., Santa Clara, Calif., 1990-91; pvt. practice, San Jose, Calif., 1991—; chmn. bd., gen. counsel Mindego, Inc., San Jose, 2003—. Mem. Calif. State Bar, Oreg. State Bar, Santa Clara County Bar Assn. Office: 3465 Sierra Rd Ste 1000 San Jose CA 95132-3000 E-mail: ericjorgensen@alum.mit.edu.

JORGENSEN, PALLE ERIK TIKOB E T, mathematician, educator; b. Copenhagen, Oct. 8, 1947; came to U.S., 1973, naturalized, 1979; s. Soren A.W. and Gyrit D. (Baden) J.; m. Soon-Min Park, Jan. 4, 1975; children: Anton Y., Greta S., Tina S. AB, U. Aarhus, Denmark, 1968, MS, 1970, PhD, 1973. Asst. prof. math. Stanford (Calif.) U., 1977-79; assoc. prof. U. Aarhus, 1979-83; prof. U. Iowa, Iowa City, 1983—. Vis. assoc. prof. U. Pa., Phila., 1982-84; mem. internat. faculty Danish Govt. Rsch. Acad. Author: Operator Commutation Relations, 1984, other books on advanced math.; editor Acta Applicandae Mathematicae, 1983—, Proceedings of the Am. Math. Soc.; contbr. articles to profl. jours. Grantee Danish Rsch. Coun., 1976-77, NSF, 1977-79, 82—; U. Iowa faculty scholar, 1992—. Mem. Am. Math. Soc., Danish Math. Soc., Math. Assn. Am., Danish Acad. Sci. (internat. faculty), Soc. Indsl. and Applied Math. Office: U Iowa Dept Math Mlh Iowa City IA 52242 E-mail: jorgen@math.uiowa.edu.

JORGENSEN, PAUL J. research company executive; b. Midway, Utah, Sept. 1, 1930; s. Joseph and Alice P. Jorgensen; m. Ardelle M. Bloom, Sept. 11, 1959; children: Paula, Mark, Janet, LaDell, Brett, Scott. Student, U. Utah, 1948-50, PhD, 1960; BS, Brigham Young U., 1954. Scientist Gen. Electric Co., Schenectady, N.Y., 1960-68; mgr. ceramics group Stanford Research Inst., Menlo Park, Calif., 1968-74, dir. materials research ctr., 1974-76; exec. dir. phys. sci. div. SRI Internat., Menlo Park, 1976-77, v.p. phys. and life sci. div., 1977-80, sr. v.p. scis. group, 1980-88, exec. v.p., COO, 1988-94, also bd. dirs., exec. v.p., 1994—. Cons. GTE, 1971-82; mem. com. high temperature chemistry NRC, 1972-75, nat. materials adv. bd., 1982-85; mem. Internat. Panel of Advisors on Tech., Singapore Inst. Stds. & Indsl. Rsch. Contbr. articles to profl. jours.; patentee in field. Served with U.S. Army, 1954-56. Recipient IR-100, Indsl. Research Mag., 1967. Fellow Am. Ceramic Soc. (chmn. basic sci. div. 1975). Republican. Mem. Lds Ch. Office: SRI Internat 333 Ravenswood Ave Menlo Park CA 94025-3453 E-mail: paul.jorgensen@sri.com.

JORGENSEN, RALPH GUBLER, lawyer, accountant; b. N.Y.C., Mar. 12, 1937; s. Thorvald W. and Florence (Gubler) J.; m. Patricia June Spivey, June 21, 1971 (dec. Oct. 1997); 1 child, Misty. AB, George Washington U., 1960, LLB, 1962. Bar: D.C. 1963, Md. 1963, N.C. 1972, U.S. Dist. Ct. D.C. 1963, U.S. Ct. Appeals (D.C. cir.) 1963, U.S. Dist. Ct. Md. 1964, U.S. Dist. Ct. (ea. dist.) N.C. 1972, U.S. Dist. Ct. (mid. dist.) N.C. 1977, U.S. Ct. Appeals (4th cir.) 1974, U.S. Tax Ct. 1976, U.S. Ct. Claims 1979, U.S. Supreme Ct. 1971; CPA, Md., Nev., N.C. Sole practice, Washington, Silver Spring, Md., 1963-71, Tabor City, NC, 1971—. Bd. dirs. Columbus County ARC, N.C., 1974. Mem. ABA, ATLA, Am. Assn. Atty.-CPAs, N.C. Bar Assn., N.C. Acad. Trial Lawyers, Alpha Kappa Psi. Democrat. Baptist. Home: 101 Pireway Rd Tabor City NC 28463-2021 Office: 116 W 4th St PO Box 248 Tabor City NC 28463-0248 E-mail: R.G.Jorgensen@weblink.net.

JORGENSON, DALE WELDEAU, economist, educator; b. Bozeman, Mont., May 7, 1933; s. Emmett B. and Jewell (Torkelson) J.; m. Linda Ann Mabus, July 24, 1971; children: Eric Mabus, Kari Ann. BA, Reed Coll., 1955; AM, Harvard U., 1957, PhD, 1959; PhD (hon.), Uppsala U., 1991, Oslo U., 1991, Keio U., 2003. Mem. faculty U. Calif., Berkeley, 1959-69, prof. econs., 1963-69, Harvard U., 1969-80, Frederic Eaton Abbe prof. econs., 1980—2002, Frank William Taussig rsch. prof. econs., 1992-94, Samuel W. Morris. prof., 2002—. Ford research prof. econs. U. Chgo., 1962-63 Author: (with J.J. McCall and R. Radner) Optimal Replacement Policy, 1967, Econometric Studies of U.S. Energy Policy, 1975, (with R. Landau) Technology and Economic Policy, 1986 (with F.M. Gollop and B.M. Fraumeni) Productivity and U.S. Economic Growth, 1987, (with R. Landau), Technology and Capital Formation, 1989, (with Lars Bergman, Erno Zalai) General Equilibrium Modeling and Economic Policy Analysis, 1990, (with Kun-Young Yun) Tax Reform and the Cost of Capital, 1991, (with Li Jingwen, Zheng Youjing and Masahiro Kuroda) Productivity and Economic Growth in China, USA and Japan, 1993, (with R. Landau) Tax Reform and the Cost of Capital: An International Comparison, 1993, Postwar U.S. Economic Growth, 1995, International Comparisons of Economic Growth, 1995, Capital Theory and Investment Behavior, 1996, Tax Policy and the Cost of Capital, 1996, (with E. Hanushek) Improving America's Schools, 1996, Aggregate Consumer Behavior, 1997, Measuring Social Welfare, 1997, Econometric General Equilibrium Modeling, 1998, Energy, The Environment and Economic Growth, 1998, Econometric Modeling of Producer Behavior, 2000, (with Kun-Young Yun) Lifting the Burden: Tax Reform, the Cost of Capital, and U.S. Economic Growth, 2001,(with Charles Wessner) Measuring and Sustaining The New Economy, 2002, Economic Growth int the Information Age, 2002. Fellow AAAS, NAS (chair sect. 54 Econ. Scis. 2000-03), Am. Philos. Soc., Econometric Soc. (pres. 1987), Am. Statis. Assn., Am. Acad. Arts and Scis.; mem. Am. Econ. Assn. (John Bates Clark medal 1971, pres. 2000), Royal Swedish Acad. Scis. Home: 1010 Memorial Dr Cambridge MA 02138-4859 Office: Harvard U Littauer 122 Cambridge MA 02138-3001 E-mail: djorgenson@harvard.edu.

JORGENSON, MARY ANN, lawyer; b. Gallipolis, Ohio, 1941; BA, Agnes Scott Coll., 1963; MA, Harvard U., 1964; JD, Case Western Res. U., 1975. Bar: Ohio 1975, N.Y. 1982. Ptnr., chair firm's corp. practice Squire, Sanders & Dempsey, 1990—. Office: Squire Sanders & Dempsey LLP 127 Public Sq Ste 4900 Cleveland OH 44114-1284 E-mail: mjorgenson@ssd.com.

JORIS-QUINTON, LIESBET, internal medicine physician; b. Antwerpen, Belgium, Oct. 2, 1958; MD, U. Instelling, 1984. Diplomate Am. Bd. Internal Medicine. Resident internal medicine U. Antwerp, 1984-87, 91-92; fellow physiology Stanford U., Calif., 1987—88, resident internal medicine, 1993—95; fellow physiology U. Calif. Riverside, 1988-91, 92-93; internist Scripps Clinic, San Diego, 1997—. Mem. ACP. Office: Green Hosp of Scripps Clinic 10666 N Torrey Pines Rd La Jolla CA 92037-7387 E-mail: lquinton@scrippsclinic.com.

JORIZZO, JOSEPH L. dermatology educator; b. Rochester, N.Y., Oct. 6, 1951; s. Joseph Lucius and Margaret R. (Volpe) J.; m. Susan MacLeod, Aug. 23, 1975 (div.); children: John Joseph, Michael Wesley; m. Irene Carros, Dec. 30, 1995; 1 child, Melina Margaret. AB, Boston U., 1972, MD magna cum laude, 1975. Diplomate Am. Bd. Dermatology. Intern in internal medicine N.C. Meml. Hosp., Chapel Hill, 1975-76, resident in dermatology, 1976-78, chief resident, 1978-79; overseas registrar Dermatology Inst. St. John's Hosp. for Diseases of the Skin, London, 1979-80; clin. asst. prof. dept. dermatology U. Tex. Med. Br., Galveston, 1979-80, from asst. prof. dept. dermatology to assoc. prof. dept. dermatology, 1980-86; prof. Sch. Medicine of Wake Forest U., Winston-Salem, NC, 1986—, prof. and founding chair dept. dermatology, 1986—2002. Cons. VA Clinic, Winston-Salem, 1986—, Forsyth Meml. Hosp., Winston-Salem, 1989—, VA Hosp., Salisbury, N.C., 1991—; mem. med. adv. bd. Am. Behcet's Disease Assn., 1988—, Winston-Salem/Forsyth County Lupus Found., 1989—; co-chmn. Southeastern Consortium for Dermatology, 1990, steering com., 1987—; mem. internat. steering com. Bechet's Disease, 1989—; mem. adv. com. Nat. Student Rsch. Forum, 1981-86; speaker more than 100 meetings, symposia, U.S. and Europe; vis. prof. Cath. U. Rome Med. Sch., 1981, U. Ark. Med. Scis., Little Rock, 1982, Brooke Army Med. Ctr., San Antonio, 1982, U. Louisville, 1982, U. N.Mex., Albuquerque, 1985, U. Mich., Ann Arbor, 1985, Duke U. Med. Ctr., 1986, U.Va., Charlottesville, 1986, Emory U., Atlanta, 1986, 92, U. South Fla., Tampa, 1987, Brown U. Med. Ctr., Providence, R.I., 1990, U. Ind., Indpls., 1991, NYU Med. Ctr., 1991, Columbia U., N.Y.C., 1993, U. Pitts., 1993, many others; invited speaker numerous meetings including Chapel Hill Alumni Dermatology Conf., 1981, Immunology Club Meeting, Galveston, 1984, Fla. Dermatol. Soc. Ann. Meeting, Ft. Lauderdale, 1984, Stetson lectr. N.Mex. Dermatol. Soc., Albuquerque, 1985, Mich. Dermatological Soc., Shanty Creek, 1985, Charlotte Dermatol. Soc., 1986, Greensboro Dermatopathology/Dermatology Semiann. Meeting, 1987, N.C. Med. Soc., 1987, Richmond-Tidewater Dermatologic Soc., Williamsburg, Va., 1988, AARP, Winston-Salem, 1988, No. Calif. Dermatologic Assn., North Lake Tahoe, Calif., 1989, Stiefel Can. Symposium, Key Biscayne, Fla., 1990, Dermatologic Soc. Greater N.Y., 1990, Westwood Conf. Clin. Dermatology, Hilton Head, S.C., 1990, Westwood Conf., Charleston, S.C., 1991, Charlotte Dermatol. Soc. Meeting, 1992, N.C. Med. Soc. Dermatology Sect., 1992, Charlotte Family Practice Soc., 1993. Co-author: Dermatological Signs of Internal Disease, 1988; contbr. chpts. to books, more than 90 articles to profl. jours.; author abstracts in field; reviewer Archives of Dermatology, 1981—, Jour. Am. Acad. Dermatology, 1981—, Pediatric Dermatology, 1986—, Jour. Investigative Dermatology, 1986—, Internat. Jour. Dermatology, 1984—, JAMA, 1988—, others; mem. editorial bd. Clin. and Exptl. Dermatology, 1988—, Jour. Am. Acad. Dermatology, 1988-93, Archives of Dermatology, 1990—, Jour. European Acad. of Dermatology and Venereology, 1992—, Current Problems in Dermatology, 1992—, Practical Cases in Dermatology, 1993—, others. Trustee Forsyth County Day Sch., Winston-Salem, 1990-94, chmn. devel. com., 1991-92, coord. new parent's bldg. fund, 1987-88; participant med bowl fund raiser for Crisis Control, Winston-Salem, 1990. William Reed traveling fellow, 1979, Am. Acad. Dermatology fellow, 1982, 84, Dermatology Found. fellow, 1983, Upjohn Pharm. Co. Spl. grantee, 1982, Ital. Dermatology Soc. grantee, 1981, Italian Found. Rsch. Dermatology grantee, 1981, Wellcome Trust/Royal Soc. Medicine grantee, 1993, Dermatology Found. grantee, 1984, 86, 87, Noah Worcester Dermatologic Soc. grantee, 1986, Nat. Inst. Dental Rsch. grantee, 1985-86, Neutrogena grantee, 1986, Am. Cyanamid Co. grantee, 1987, Hoechst-Roussel grantee, 1988, numerous other grants including Herbert Labs., Genderm, Dermik Labs., R.W. Johnson Pharms., Stiefel Labs., Pfizer Labs., Curatek Pharms., Allergan Herbert, Bristol-Myers Squibb, Hoffman LaRoche Dermatologics, Glaxo Pharm. Co., RJR Nabisco, Ortho-McNeil Pharms. Fellow ACP; mem. AMA, Soc. Investigative Dermatology (sec.-treas. So. sect. 1984-85, v.p. So. sect. 1985-86, pres. So. sect. 1986-87, membership com. 1987-90, chmn. membership com. 1989-90), Am. Acad. Dermatology (mem. numerous coms. including internat. affairs 1981-84, summer session com. 1989—, chmn. clin. studies session 1990, nominating com. 1993—, v.p.-elect 2002--, chmn. various awards coms., media tng. recipient 1984), Am. Coll. Cyrosurgery, Dermatology Found. (dir. membership subcom. 1983-85, devel. com. 1983-86), So. Med. Assn., Forsyth County Med. Soc. (Membership Task Force 1989-90), N.C. Med. Soc., N.C. Dermatology Soc., Am. Fedn. Clin. Rsch., Psoriasis Found., Noah Worcester Dermatologic Soc., N.Am. Clin. Dermatological Soc., Pacific Dermatologic Assn. (hon.), Am. Dermatologic Assn., Am. Bd. Dermatology (Part I test com.), Societe Francaise de Dermatologie et de Venereologie, Am. Skin Assn., Internat. Soc. Tropical Dermatology, St. John's Dermatological Soc. (U.K.), Sir James Saunders Soc., Academia Medicorum Litteratorum (Italy), South Ctrl. Dermatological Soc. (organizing com. 1981-84, program com. 1984-86),Italian Soc. Dermatology and Venereology (corr.), Brit. Assn. Dermatologists (overseas mem.), Assn. Profs. Dermatology (internal medicine com. 1984-86), Dowling Club (U.K.), Phi Beta Kappa, Sigma Chi Rsch. Soc., Alpha Omega Alpha. Home: 4424 Bent Tree Farm Rd Winston Salem NC 27106-4252 Office: Wake Forest U Sch Med Dept Dermatology Med Ctr Blvd Winston Salem NC 27157-0001

JORJANI, MARYAM, psychotherapist; b. Paris, May 26, 1953; Degree, Sorbonne U., Paris, 1982, Tropagen Sch., N.Y.C., 1974, Queens Coll., 1972; DMS methaphysical, psychology, Univ. of Methaphucie, L.A. Skills tng. for mind/bodychange Harvard Med. Sch. Various positions to designer merchandise Faslo, N.Y.C., 1982—92; sales broker Garrick Aug., N.Y.C., 1992—2000; psychotherapist N.Y.C., 2000—01. Home: 201 E 35th St New York NY 10016

JORNDT, LOUIS DANIEL, former retail drug store chain executive; b. Chgo., Aug. 24, 1941; s. Louis Carl and Margaret Estelle (Teel) J.; m. Patricia McDonnell, Aug. 1, 1964; children— Kristine, Michael, Kara BS in Pharmacy, Drake U., 1963; MBA, U. N.Mex., 1974. Various mgmt. positions Walgreen Co., Chgo., 1963-68, dist. mgr., 1968-75, regional dir. Deerfield, Ill., 1975-79, regional v.p., 1979-82, v.p., treas., 1982-85, sr. v.p., treas., 1985-89, pres., chief oper. officer, 1989-97, CEO, chmn., 1997—2003; ret., 2003. Bd. dirs. Better Bus. Bur. Chgo., 1982—, Chgo. Assn. Commerce and Industry; nat. chmn. Drake U. Pharmacy Alumni Fund. Mem. Nat. Assn. Corp. Treas., Fin. Execs. Inst. Clubs: Economic (Chgo.); Glen View (Ill.) Golf. Avocations: golf; swimming; reading.*

JORRES, DANIEL, literature educator; b. Caguas, P.R., Mar. 9, 1961; arrived in U.S., 1984; s. Vicente Jorres and Antonia Rodriguez. BA in Comparative Lit., U. P.R., Rio Piedras, 1984; MA in L.Am. Poetry, SUNY, Stony Brook, 1986; PhD in L.Am. Baroque, U. Cin., 1990. Tchg. asst. SUNY, Stony Brook, 1984—86, U. Cin., 1986—88; instr. Ohio State U., Columbus, 1988—90; assoc. prof. Ohio U., Athens, 1990—. Author Thoriras si da ura prithavera novels; contbg. editor: Cin. Roman Langs. Rev., 1990—, Chasqui: L.Am. Rev., 2000—, author poetry and criticism. Activitst, bd. mem. United Campus Ministry, Athens, Ohio, 1993—2003. Named Book of Yr., Pen Club, P.R., 1990. Mem.: MLA, Internat. Inst. Iberoamerican Lit., L.Am. Studies Assn. Avocations: reading, dancing, travel, music, driving.

JORTNER, JOSHUA, physical chemistry scientist, educator; b. Poland, Mar. 14, 1933; s. Arthur and Regina Jortner; m. Ruth Sanger, Jan. 1, 1960; 2 children. PhD, Hebrew U. Jerusalem; D (hon.), Ben Gurions U. of Negev, Israel, 1985, Pierre and Marie Curie U., Paris, 1986, Tech. U. Munich, 1996. Instr. dept. phys. chemistry Hebrew U. Jerusalem, 1961-62, sr. lectr., 1963-65; assoc. prof. Tel Aviv U., 1965-66, prof., 1966—, head Sch. Chemistry, 1966—72, dep. rector, 1966-69, v.p., 1970-72. Rsch. assoc. U. Chgo., 1962—64, vis. prof., 1965—71, H.C. Orsted Inst., U. Copenhagen, 1974, 78, U. Calif., Berkeley, 1975, Calif. Inst. Tech., 1977, Oxford U., 1995; Blaise Pascal prof. Ecole Normale Supérieure, Paris, 1999—2000. Contbr. over 680 articles to profl. jours. Recipient award, Internat. Acad. Quantum Sci., 1972, Weizmann prize, 1973, Rothschild prize, 1976, Kolthof prize, 1976, Israel prize in Chemistry, 1982, Wolf prize, 1988, Hon. J. Heyrovsky Gold medal, 1993, August-Wilhelm-von-Hofmann medal, 1995, R.S. Mulliken medal, 1998, J.O. Hirschfelder prize, 1999. Mem.: Am. Acad. Arts and Scis., Internat. Union Pure and Applied Chemistry (v.p. 1996—97, pres. 1998—99, past-pres. 2000—01), Royal Netherlands Acad. Arts and Scis. (fgn.), Learned Soc. of Czech Repub., U.S. Nat. Acad. Scis. (fgn. assoc.), Indian Acad. Sci., German Acad. Scis. Leopoldina, Romanian Acad. Scis., European Acad. Scis. and Arts, Russian Acad. Scis. (fgn.), Polish Acad. Scis., Danish Acad. Scis. and Letters (fgn. mem.), Am. Philos. Soc., Internat. Acad. Quantum Molecular Scis, Israel Acad. Scis. and Humanities (v.p. 1980—86, pres. 1986—95). Avocation: science policy. Office: Tel Aviv U Sch Chemistry Ramat-Aviv 69978 Tel Aviv Israel also: Israel Acad Scis-Humanities Einstein Sq PO Box 4040 91040 Jerusalem Israel

JOSBENO, LARRY JOSEPH, physics educator; b. Elmira, N.Y., Oct. 21, 1938; s. Samuel Joseph and Katherine Lorena (Jessup) J.; m. Cecile Ann Quatrano, Sept. 15, 1962; children: Deborah Ann, John Lawrence. BS in Math., St. Bonaventure U., 1962; MS in Chemistry, U. N.H., 1970. Cert. tchr., N.Y. Tchr. Horseheads (N.Y.) High Sch., 1965-89; prof. Corning (N.Y.) C.C., 1989—; faculty assn. chair, 1995. Vis. scientist Cornell U., Ithaca, N.Y., 1986-87; adj. prof. Elmira Coll.; cons. State Edn. Dept., Albany, N.Y., 1987, Math Matrix, Ithaca, 1987—. Author: ARCO Physics Review Book, 1983; contbr. articles to profl. jours. Mem. bd. govs. Notre Dame H.S., Elmira, 1977-82; trustee Steele Meml. Lab., Elmira, 1985-94, pres., 1993; obs. presenter Elmira Corning Astron. Soc., Corning, 1968—; trustee So. Tier Libr. Sys., 1995-2000. Capt. arty. U.S. Army, 1963-65. Recipient N.Y. State Chancellor's award, 1995, Excellence in Tchg. award Bd. Trustees, 1998. Fellow Sci. Tchrs. Assn. N.Y. (pres. 1989-90); mem. Math. Assn. Am., Am. Phys. Soc. (N.Y. state sec./treas. 2001—), Am. Chem. Soc., Am. Physics Tchr. Assn. (N.Y. state sect., bd. dirs. 1996-2000, pres. 2002—, N.Y. State svc. award 2000), So. Tier Libr. Assn. (trustee 1995), Alpha Sigma Lambda (Tchr. of Yr. 1985). Democrat. Roman Catholic. Home: 539 W Franklin St Horseheads NY 14845-2356 E-mail: josbenlj@corning-cc.edu.

JOSCELYN, KENT B(UCKLEY), lawyer; b. Binghamton, N.Y., Dec. 18, 1936; s. Raymond Miles and Gwen Buckley (Smith) J.; children: Kathryn Anne, Jennifer Sheldon. BS, Union Coll., 1957; JD, Albany (N.Y.) Law Sch., 1960. Bar: N.Y. 1961, U.S. Ct. Mil. Appeals 1962, D.C., 1967, Mich. 1979. Atty. adviser hdqts. USAF, Washington, 1965-67; assoc. prof. forensic studies U. Ind., Bloomington, 1967-76; dir. Inst. Rsch. in Pub. Safety, 1970-75; head policy analysis divsn. Highway Safety Rsch. Inst. U. Mich., Ann Arbor, 1976-81; dir. transp. planning and policy Urban Tech. Environ. Planning Program, Ann Arbor, 1981-84; prin. Joscelyn and Treat P.C., Ann Arbor, 1981—93, Joscelyn, McNair & Jeffrey P.C., Ann Arbor, 1993-2001. Cons. Law Enforcement Assistance Adminstrn., U.S. Dept. Justice, 1969-72; Gov.'s appointee as regional dir. Ind. Criminal Justice Planning Agy., 1969-72; vice chmn. Ind. Organized Crime Prevention Coun., 1969-72; commr. pub. safety City of Bloomington, Ind., 1974-76. Editor Internat. Jour. Criminal Justice. Capt. USAF, 1961-64. Mem. NAS, ABA, NRC, D.C. Bar Assn., N.Y. State Bar Assn., Internat. Bar Assn., Transp. Rsch. Bd. (chmn. motor vehicle and traffic law com. 1979-82), Am. Soc. Criminology (life), Assn. for Advancement Automotive Medicine (life), Soc. Automotive Engrs., Acad. Criminal Justice Scis. (life), Assn. Chiefs Police (assoc.), Nat. Safety Coun., Assn. Former Intelligence Officers (life), Product Liability Adv. Coun., Sigma Xi, Theta Delta Chi. Office: Kent B Joscelyn PC PO Box 130589 Ann Arbor MI 48113-0589 E-mail: kbjpc@earthlink.com.

JOSE, SHIBU, agriculture educator, researcher; b. Cochin, Kerala, India, May 8, 1970; s. P.J. and Mariamma Jose; m. Sheena Jose, Oct. 21, 1996. BS, Kerala Agrl. U., 1991; MS, Purdue U., 1994, PhD, 1997. Rsch. fellow Kerala Agrl. U., 1991-92; grad. instr. Purdue U., West Lafayette, Ind., 1992-97; rsch. assoc. U. Minn., St. Paul, 1997-98; asst. prof. U Fla., Milton, 1998—. Cons. editor Agroforestry Systems; assoc. editor Forest Sci. Recipient Jawaharlal Nehru Meml. award Jawaharlal Nehru Trust, 1992; Aga Khan Found. internat. fellow, Switzerland, 1996-97. Mem. AAAS, Soc. Am. Foresters (Best Poster award 1996), Ecol. Soc. Am., Phi Kappa Phi. Avocations: painting, cooking, stamp collecting. Office: U Fla 5988 Highway 90 Milton FL 32583-1713

JOSEFF, JOAN CASTLE, manufacturing executive; b. Alta., Can., Aug. 12, 1922; naturalized U.S. citizen, 1945; d. Edgar W. and Lottie (Coates) Castle; BA in Psychology, UCLA; widowed; 1 son, Jeffrey Rene. With Joseff-Hollywood, jewelry manufacture and rental and aircraft components and missiles, Burbank, Calif., 1939—, chmn. bd., pres., sec.-treas. Numerous TV appearances including CBS This Morning, Australia This Morning, Am. Movie Channel. Mem. Burbank Salary Task Force, 1979—, L.A. County Earthquake Fact-Finding Commn., 1981— ; bd. dirs. San Fernando Valley area chpt. Am. Cancer Soc., treas., Genesis Energy Systems, Inc., 1993—; mem. Rep. Cen. Com.; del. Rep. Nat. Conv., 1980, 84, 88, 92, 96, 2000; voting mem. Calif. Rep. Party; chmn. Women Legis.; active Beautiful People Award Com. Honoring John Wayne Carcer Clinic; appointed by Gov. Wilson to Barber and Cosmotology Bd; appointed br Pres. Clinton to Selective Svc. System. Recipient Women in Achievement award Soroptimist Internat., 1988. Mem. Women of Motion Picture Industry (hon. life), Nat. Fedn. Rep. Women (bd. dir., Caring for Am. award 1986), Calif. Rep. Women (bd. dir., treas. 1986-90), North Hollywood Rep. Women (pres. 1981-82, parliamentarian), Nat. Fedn. of Rep (voting mem., program chair, 1994—, bylaws chair 1998—), Calif. Fedn. of Rep. Women (chaplain, Americanism chmn. so. div., regent chmn. Women of Achievement award 1988), L.A. County Fedn. of Rep. Women (scholarship chmn.). Home: 10060 Toluca Lake Ave Toluca Lake CA 91602-2924 Office: 129 E Providencia Ave Burbank CA 91502-1922

JOSEFOWICZ, GREGORY P. retail executive; Grad., Mich. State U.; MBA, Northwestern U. Kellogg Sch. Mgmt., 1979. With Jewel-Osco (Albertson's Inc.), 1968—99; pres. Jewel-Osco, 1997—99; pres., CEO Borders Group Inc., Ann Arbor, Mich., 1999—, mem. bd. dirs., 1999—, chmn., 2002—. Mem. bd. advisors C.S. Mott Children's Hosp., Ann Arbor, Key Bank (Mich. dist.), Ann Arbor; mem. bd. dirs. Spartan Stores, Inc., Grand Rapids, Mich., Ryerson Tull, Chgo.; mem. advisory bd. Northwestern U. Kellogg Sch. Mgmt. Recipient Retailer Yr., Ill. Retail Merchants Assn., 1999. Office: Borders Group 100 Phoenix Dr Ann Arbor MI 48108*

JOSELL, JESSICA (JESSICA WECHSLER), public relations executive; b. Balt., June 17, 1943; d. Maury J. and Rose E. (Lodin) Snyder; m. Neil B. Josell, Apr. 30, 1965 (dec. Nov. 1967); m. Steven James Wechsler, Jan. 12, 1980. BA, U. Fla., 1965. V.p., gen. mgr. Morton Dennis Wax & Assocs., N.Y.C., 1976-81; v.p. The Raleigh Group, Ltd., N.Y.C., 1981-87; pres. Josell Communications, Inc., N.Y.C., 1981—. Exec. officer, bd. dirs. The Bridge, Inc., N.Y.C. Mem.: N.Y. Women in Film and TV. Home and Office: Josell Communications Inc 185 W End Ave Ste 22C New York NY 10023-5549

JOSELYN, JO ANN, space scientist; b. St. Francis, Kans., Oct. 5, 1943; d. James Jacob and Josephine Felzien (Firkins) Cram. BS in Applied Math., U. Colo., 1965, MS in Astro Geophysics, 1967, PhD in Astro Geophysics, 1978. Research asst. NASA-Manned Space Ctr., Houston, 1966; physicist NOAA-Space Environ. Lab., Boulder, Colo., 1967-78; space scientist NOAA-Space Environ. Ctr., Boulder, 1978-99; chief Geospace Branch, 1992-95; sec.-gen. Internat. Union Geodesy and Geophysics, 1999—. U.S. del. study group 6 Consultive Com. for Ionospheric Radio, 1981, 83; mem. com. on data mgmt. and computation NASA Space Sci. Bd., 1988. Mem. U. Colo. Grad. Sch. Alumni Coun., 1986-90, U. Colo. Engring. Devel. Coun., 1991-99, U. Colo. Adv. Coun. for the Women in Engring. Program, 1992-98, Grad. Sch. Adv. Coun.; bd. trustees U. Colo. Found., 2002-. Recipient unit citation NOAA, 1971, 80, 85, 86, sustained superior performance award 1985, 87-90, 92, 94; group achievement award NASA, 1983, Disting. Engring. Alumnus award U. Colo., 1987, Dir.'s award Space Environ. Lab., 1991, 95, Pacesetter award Boulder County, 1994, Sec. Commerce award for Customer Svc. Excellence, 1994, George Norlin award U. Colo. Alumni Assn., 2000; elected to U. Colo. Disting. Alumni Gallery, 1995; named Woman of Achievement, Zonta Club, Boulder, 1996; named to Colo. Women's Hall of Fame, 2002; fellow Sci. and Tech. Agy. Japan, 1990-91. Mem. AAAS, AAUW, PEO, Am. Women in Sci., Am. Geophys. Union, Union Radio Sci. Internat. (commns. G and H, membership chair of commn. H 1993-96), Internat. Assn. Geomagnetism and Aeronomy (co-chair Divsn. V on observatories, instruments, indices and data 1991-95, sec.-gen. 1995-99), Internat. Astron. Union (commns. 10 and 49), Rotary Internat., Ikebana Internat., Sigma Xi, Tau Beta Pi, Sigma Tau. Republican. Methodist. Office: Univ Colo CIRES Campus Box 216 Boulder CO 80309-0216 E-mail: jjoselyn@cires.colorado.edu.

JOSEPH, BURTON M. retired grain merchant; b. Mpls., Apr. 2, 1921; s. I.S. and Anna J.; m. Geri Mack, Apr. 2, 1953; children: Shelley, Scott, Jonathan. BA, U. Minn., 1942. Vice pres. I.S. Joseph Co., Inc., Mpls., 1945-53, pres., 1953-80, chmn. bd., 1980-85, vice chmn. bd., 1985-97, ret., 1997. Vice chmn. Martrade Ltd., 1985; mem. agrl. policy adv. com. for trade U.S. Dept. Agr., 1980—; pres. Joseph Co. Inc. Mpls. (JCI), 1990, pres. Am. Energy Mktg., 1999—. Commr. Duluth Port Authority, Mpls. Human Relations Commn.; treas. Nat. Commn. Anti-Defamation League, 1969-76; nat. chmn. Anti-Defamation League of B'nai B'rith, 1976-78, hon. nat. chmn., 1978; trustee Am. Freedom from Hunger Found.; trustee, bd. govs. Hebrew Union Coll.-Jewish Inst. Religion, 1970-75, vice chmn., 1976; commr. Met. Airports Commn., 1985. Mem. Am. Energy Mktg. (pres. 2000—). Home: 1201 Yale Pl Apt 502 Minneapolis MN 55403-1956

JOSEPH, DANIEL DONALD, aeronautical engineer, educator; b. Chgo., Mar. 26, 1929; s. Samuel and Mary (Simon) J.; m. Ellen Broida, Dec. 18, 1949 (div. 1979); children: Karen, Michael, Charles; m. Kay Jaglo, Feb. 9, 1990. MA in Sociology, U. Chgo., 1950; BS in Mech. Engring, Ill. Inst. Tech., 1959, MS, 1960, PhD, 1963. Asst. prof. mech. engring. Ill. Inst. Tech., 1962-63; mem. faculty U. Minn., 1963—, assoc. prof. fluid mechanics, 1965-69, prof. aerospace engring. and mechanics, 1969-90, Russell J. Penrose prof., 1990—. Author 4 books on stability and bifurcation theory and fluid dynamics; editor 3 books; editorial bd. SIAM Jour. Applied Math, Jour. Applied Mechanics, Jour. Non-Newtonian Fluid Mechanics, others; contbr. articles to sci. jours. Guggenheim fellow, 1969-70, Timoshenko medal Am. Soc. of Mechanical Engineers,

1995. Mem. NAS, ASME, NAE, Am. Phys. Soc., Am. Acad. Arts and Scis., Soc. Engring. Sci. (G.I. Taylor medal 1990, Bingham medal Soc. of Rheology). Achievements include contbns. to math. theory of hydrodynamic stability; rheology of viscoelastic fluids. Home: 1920 S 1st St Apt 2302 Minneapolis MN 55454-1279 Office: U Minn Dept Aerospace Engring 110 Union St SE Minneapolis MN 55455-0153

JOSEPH, DANIEL MORDECAI, lawyer; b. Paterson, N.J., Aug. 20, 1941; m. Susan Fields, July 30, 1972; 1 child, Nicholas. AB, Columbia U., 1963; LLB, Harvard U., 1966. Bar: N.J. 1967, U.S. Supreme Ct. 1970, D.C. 1974. Law clk. to judge U.S. Ct. Appeals (5th cir.), Dallas, 1966-67; atty. civil div. U.S. Dept. Justice, Washington, 1967-71; asst. gen. counsel EPA, Washington, 1971-72; spl. asst. environ. affairs gen. counsel U.S. Dept. Transp., Washington, 1972-74; ptnr. Akin, Gump, Strauss, Hauer & Feld, Washington, 1974—. Mem. D.C. Bar (rules of conduct rev. com. 1991-2000, chmn. 1996-99, spl. com. on multidisciplinary practice 1999—, legal ethics com. 2000—). Office: Akin Gump Strauss Hauer & Feld Ste 400 1333 New Hampshire Ave NW Washington DC 20036-1564

JOSEPH, EDITH HOFFMAN, retired editor; b. Syracuse, N.Y., Jan. 4, 1928; d. Max and Ida (Hodis) Finkelstein; m. Irving Hoffman, Sept. 4, 1949 (dec. Dec. 1965); children: Kenneth R., Maxine E. Neuhauser; m. William Jacob Joseph, May 19, 1968; stepchildren: David E., Harlan L., Saul J., Gail C. (dec. Nov. 1999). BS in Journalism/Bus. Adminstrn., Rider Coll., 1949. Copywriter advt. Swern's-Lit Bros., Trenton, N.J., 1949-51; pub. info. asst. N.J. Div. Pensions, Trenton, 1967-69; pub. rels. asst. N.J. Dept. Labor & Industry, Trenton, 1969-70; mng. editor newsletter N.J. Dept. Environ. Protection, Trenton, 1971-74; environ. news editor N.J. Dept. Environ. Protection-N.J. Outdoors Mag., 1974-84; editor newsletter N.J. Dept. Environ. Protection-Environ. News, 1985-90; editor environ. news sect. N.J. Dept. Environ. Protection-N.J. Outdoors Mag., 1991. Contbr. articles to profl. jours. Avocations: travel, reading, walking, theatre, volunteer work. Home: 1 Highgate Dr Apt 113 Trenton NJ 08618-2001

JOSEPH, ELEANOR ANN, health science association administrator, consultant; b. Cleve., Mar. 6, 1944; d. Emil and Eleanor (Leelais) Dienes; m. Abraham Albert Joseph, Oct. 28, 1984. BS in Math. cum laude, Cleve. State U., 1978, MPA in Health Care Adminstrn., 1991. Cert. profl. healthcare quality, coding specialist, accredited records technician, registered record adminstr., health info. adminstr. Asst. dir. med. records Suburban Hosp., Warrensville Heights, Ohio, 1963-77; coder Shaker Med. Ctr., Shaker Heights, Ohio, 1965, Huron Rd. Hosp., Cleve., 1965; instr. Cuyahoga C.C., Cleve., 1970-72; dir. med. records Hillcrest Hosp., Mayfield Heights, Ohio, 1977-84; med. records technician Vis. Nurse Assn., Cleve., 1985; coord. med. record svcs. Ctr. for Health Affairs Greater Cleve. Hosp. Assn., 1985-88, dir. coding svcs. Ctr. Health Affairs, 1988-89, dir. health record svcs. Ctr. Health Affairs, 1989-98; v.p. health info. mgmt. svcs. Greater Cleve. Healthcare Assn., 1999—, privacy officer Ctr. Health Affairs, 2001—. Coding instr. cmty. edn. dept. Cleve. State U., 1998—; instr. cmty. edn. Lakeland CC, coding tchr., 1999; spkrs. bur. Hillcrest Hosp., Mayfield Heights, 1978—84; adv. com. Cuyahoga C.C., 1973—80, 1994—, faculty, 1999—2003; coord. seminars in field; cons. in field. Co-author: (manual) Quality Assurance Program for Medical Records Deparment, 1981, Dollars and Sense: A Reference Guide to Coding and Prospective Payment System Reimbursement Issues, 1988; co-editor: Care and Management of Health Care Records, 1988, 1992. Active Holden Arboretum, Kirtland, Ohio, 1975—, Ohio Hist. Soc., Columbus, 1975—; mem. adv. task force cert. program med. office mgmt. Lakeland CC, 1997—96. Recipient Outstanding Svc. award, Ctr. Health Affairs/Greater Cleve. Healthcare Assn., 1997. Mem.: N.E. Ohio Health Info. Mgmt. Assn. (chmn. coding roundtable 1993—), Ohio Health Info. Mgmt. Assn. (project leader alliances 1992—94, data quality reimbursement coun. 1992—, liaison to ambulatory sect. 1994—96, project leader developing coding seminars 1996—97, co-chmn. data quality and reimbursement coun. 1996—98, pres.-elect 1998—99, pres. 1999—2000, dir. and del. coord. 2000—01, del. to Am. Health Info. Mgmt. Assn. 2002—03, Disting. Mem. award 1997, Profl. Achievement award 2003), Ohio Assn. Healthcare Quality, Ohio Med. Record Assn. (alt. del. 1982, med. record coun. 1985—92, del. for state assn. mem. at nat. ann. mtg. 1989, legis. com. 1989—90, del. for state assn. mem. at nat. ann. mtg. 1990), N.E. Ohio Med. Record Assn. (treas. 1979, v.p. 1980, pres. 1982—83, counselor 1983, ednl. com. 1984, chmn. nominating com. 1986, ednl. com. 1987, cons. com. 1987—91, audit com., membership com., bylaws com., pub. rels. com.), East Ohio Med. Record Assn., Nat. Assn. Healthcare Quality, Am. Guild Patient Accts. Mgrs., Am. Health Info. Mgmt. Assn. (quality assurance and long term care sects., ambulatory records sec. 1992—2001, del. 1997—2000, item writing panel for cert. coding exams 1997—2003, accredited record tech. practitioner 2000—02, co-chmn. coun. cert. 2001, chair coun. on cert. 2002, nominating com. 2002—03), Am. Med. Record Assn. (cons. roster 1976, charter mem. assembly on edn. 1989), Am. Acad. Profl. Coders (treas. local chpt. 1994, endorsed as tchr. for profl. med. coder curriculum, cert.), Holden Arboretum, Northeastern Ohio Assn. for Healthcare Quality, Cleve. City Club. Lutheran. Avocations: cultural events, nature walks, golf, music. Office: Greater Cleve Healthcare Assn Ctr for Health Affairs 1226 Huron Rd E Cleveland OH 44115-1702 E-mail: eleanor.joseph@chanet.org.

JOSEPH, GERI MACK (GERALDINE JOSEPH), former ambassador, educator, journalist; b. St. Paul, June 19, 1923; BS, U. Minn., 1946; LLD, Bates Coll., 1982; DHL (hon.), Macalester Coll., 1997; LLD, Carleton Coll., 1998; DHL (hon.). Staff writer Mpls. Tribune, 1946-53, contbg. editor, 1972-78; amb. to The Netherlands, Am. Embassy, The Hague, 1978-81; sr. fellow internat. programs U. Minn. Hubert H. Humphrey Inst. Pub. Affairs, Mpls., 1984-94, chmn. adv. bd., 1997—; dir. Mondale Policy Forum, 1990-94. Bd. dirs. Nat. Dem. Inst. for Internat. Affairs, George A. Hormel Co.; mem. U.S. President's Commn. on Mental Health, Minn. Supreme Ct. Commn. on Mentally Disabled and the Cts., mem. Coun. on Fgn. Rels., 1985—; mem. com. on Mid. East, Brookings Instn., 1987. Vice chmn. Gov.'s Commn. on Taxation, 1983-84; trustee Carleton Coll., 1975-94; mem. Democratic Nat. Com., 1960-72, vice chmn., 1968-72; pres. Nat. Mental Health Assn., 1970-72, co-chairperson Minn. Women's Campaign Fund, 1982-84; co-chmn. Atty. Gen.'s Com. on Child Abuse within the Family, 1986. Democrat. E-mail: gerimj@cs.com.

JOSEPH, GREGORY NELSON, media critic, writer, actor; b. Kansas City, Mo., Aug. 25, 1946; s. Theodore Leopold and Marcella Kathryn (Nelson) J.; m. Mary Martha Stahler, July 21, 1973; children: John, Jacqueline, Caroline. AA, Met. C.C., Kansas City, 1967; BA with honors, U. Mo., Kansas City, 1969. Intern, cub reporter Kansas City Star-Times, 1965-67; feature writer, asst. city editor The Pasadena (Calif.) Union, 1971-73; investigative reporter The Pasadena Star-News, 1973-75; bus. writer The Riverside (Calif.) Press Enterprise, 1975-76; reporter, consumer writer, feature writer, TV critic The San Diego Tribune, 1976-90; TV columnist The Ariz. Republic, Phoenix, 1990-94; media critic, writer, 1994—. Recipient various writing awards Copley Newspapers, Pasadena and San Diego, 1971-73, 83, Pub. Awareness award San Diego Psychiat. Physicians, cert. of appreciation Epilepsy Soc. San Diego County, 1989. Mem.: Internat. Platform Assn., TV Critics Assn., NATAS (bd. govs. 1990—92), SAG, SAG Nat Com. for Performers with Disabilities, Phi Kappa Phi. Roman Catholic. Avocations: scriptwriting, reading, writing about hollywood, appearing at schools and on radio and tv to discuss tv and film. Home: 4864 W Alice Ave Glendale AZ 85302-5107 Address: Victoria Allen Literary Agy 1489 E Thousand Oaks Blvd Ste 2 Thousand Oaks CA 91362-6207 also: Dani's Talent Agency One E Camelback Rd Ste 550 Phoenix AZ 85012

JOSEPH, GREGORY PAUL, lawyer; b. Mpls., Jan. 18, 1951; s. George Phillip and Josephine Sheha (Nofel) J.; m. Barbara, Jan. 19, 1979. BA summa cum laude, U. Minn., 1972, JD cum laude, 1975. Bar: Minn. 1975, N.Y. 1979, U.S. Dist. Ct. Minn. 1975, U.S. Dist. Ct. (so. and ea. dist.) N.Y. 1979, U.S. Ct. Appeals (8th cir.) 1976, U.S. Ct. Appeals (2d cir.) 1979, U.S. Ct. Appeals (D.C. cir.) 1980, U.S. Supreme Ct. 1983, U.S. Tax Ct. 1987, U.S. Ct. Appeals (7th cir.) 1989, (5th cir.) 1992, (6th cir.) 1999, (11th cir.) 2002. Pvt. practice, Mpls., 1975-79; assoc. Fried, Frank, Harris, Shriver & Jacobson, N.Y.C., 1979-82, ptnr., 1982-01, chair litigation dept., 2000-01; chmn. Gregory P. Joseph Law Offices, LLC, N.Y.C., 2001—. Asst. U.S. spl. prosecutor N.Y.C., 1981—82, Washington, 1981—82; mem. adv. com. on fed. rules of evidence U.S. Judicial Conf, 1993—99; co-chair 3d Circuit Task Force on Selection of Class Counsel, 2001; chair com. of lawyers to enhance the jury process N.Y. State Cts., 1998—99, mem. adv. com. on civil practice, 1999—2002. Author: Modern Visual Evidence, 1984, Sanctions: The Federal Law of Litigation Abuse, 1989, 3rd edit., 2000, Civil RICO: A Definitive Guide, 1992, 2nd edit., 2000; co-author: Evidence in America, 1987; editor: Emerging Problems Under the Federal Rules of Evidence, 1983, reporter 2d edit., 1991; co-editor: Sanctions: Rule 11 and Other Powers, 1986, 2d rev. edit., 1988; editorial bd. Moore's Fed. Practice, 1995—, contbr. articles to profl. jours. Fellow Am. Bar Found., Am. Coll. Trial Lawyers (chmn. fed. rules of civil procedure com. 2000-02, regent 2002—); mem. ABA (chmn. litig. sect. 1997-98), Am. Law Inst., N.Y. Bar Assn. (chair trial evidence com. 1988-94), Minn. Bar Assn., N.Y. County Lawyers Assn., Assn. of Bar of City of N.Y. (chmn. profl. responsibility com. 1993-96, mem. exec. com. 1999—). Home: 390 West End Ave Apt 10G New York NY 10024 Office: Gregory P Joseph Law Offices LLC 805 Third Ave Fl 31 New York NY 10022 E-mail: gjoseph@josephnyc.com.

JOSEPH, J. JONATHAN, interior designer; b. Gloucester, Mass., Jan. 14, 1932; s. George Stephen and Maryann (Lattof) J. Cert., Vesper George Sch. Art, Boston, 1952; student theater design, Boston Conservatory Music, 1951. Assoc. designer Reva Lewitt, Boston, 1952-67, Peter Schifando & Co., L.A., 1993—; owner interior design bus. Boston, 1967—; pres. Seraphim Galleries, Inc., L.A., 1998—. Cons. in fine arts; spl. research 19th century glass in Am., also Tiffany glass; exhibited Tiffany glass collection Mus. Fine Art, Boston, 1965, Worcester (Mass.) Art Mus., 1968. Important decorating works include: assoc. designer on the restoration of Plaza Hotel, N.Y.C., assoc. designer Ronald Reagan Presdl. Libr., Simi Valley, Calif., 1991. Author: Jane Peterson, An American Artist, 1981; co-curator: (exhbn.) Jane Peterson: An Impression, Hickory (N.C.) Mus. of Art, 1987; contbr. revs. and articles to profl. publs. Recipient award Internat. V'Soske Rug Design. Mem. Am. Soc. Interior Designers (chmn. bd. New Eng. chpt. 1965-66, chpt. v.p. 1969-71, pres. 1971-72, bd. dirs. 1986-87), Nat. Early Am. Glass Club (1st v.p. 1967-69), Mus. Fine Arts Boston. Address: PO Box 1220 Back Bay Annex Boston MA 02117

JOSEPH, JAMES ALFRED, ambassador; b. Opelousas, La., Mar. 12, 1935; s. Adam and Julia Lee (Jones) J.; m. Mary Braxton; children: Jeffrey, Denise. BA, So. U., 1956; MDiv, Yale U., 1963; hon. degree, Loyola U. of Chgo., U. Md., Winthrop Coll., Southeastern U., Fla. Meml. U., Shaw U., Ind. U., Pomona Coll. Ordained to ministry United Ch. Christ, 1963. Asso. dir. Assn. of Founds., Columbus, Ind., 1967-69; chaplain Claremont (Calif.) Colls., 1969-70; exec. dir. Irwin-Sweeney-Miller Found., Columbus, 1970-72; v.p. Cummins Engine Co., 1972-77, 81-82; also pres. Cummins Found., Columbus, 1972-77, 81-82; ambassador to So. Africa, U.S. Dept. State, 1996-99; prof. Duke U., Durham, N.C., 2000—. Under sec. U.S. Dept. Interior, Washington, 1977-81; chmn. Commn. on No. Mariana Islands, 1980-86; pres., CEO, Coun. on Founds., 1982-95; mem. faculty Stillman Coll., Tuscaloosa, Ala., 1963-64, Pitzer Coll., Claremont, 1966, Claremont Sch. Theology, 1970, Yale U., 1981-82; mem. adv. com. nat. Sci. Acad., Agy. Internat. Devel. Author: The Charitable Impulse, 1990, Remaking America, 1995; co-editor: Three Perspectives on Ethnicity, 1976; contbr. articles to profl. publs. Chmn. Spl. Commn. on Racism and Devel., World Council Chs., Geneva, chmn., U.S. del. to UN Conf. in Kenya, Bilateral Consultation with Mex. Pres. Claremont Intercultural Coun., 1965-67; chmn. nat. bd. NCCJ; mem. City Park and Recreation Commn., Claremont, 1965-67, apptd. by Pres. Clinton chmn. bd. dirs. Corp. for Nat. Svc., chmn. ofcl. U.S. govt. dels. to Mex., Micronesia, Canada; pres. Nat. Black United Fund; bd. dirs. Pitzer Coll., Brookings Inst., Nat. Endowment for Democracy, Points of Light Found., Colonial Williamsburg Found., Africare, Opportunity Funding Corp., Union Theol. Sem., N.Y.C., African-Am. Inst. N.Y., Children's Def. Fund, New Transcentury Found.; bd. visitors Inst. Policy Scis., Duke U. Served to 1st lt., Med. Service Corps U.S. Army, 1956-58. Fellow Met. Applied Research Center, N.Y.C., 1958; vis. fellow Nuffield Coll., Oxford U. Mem. Assn. Black Found. Execs. (chmn. 1970-76), Council Fgn. Relations, Hague Club, Alpha Phi Alpha. Office: Am Embassy/Pretoria Dept State Washington DC 20521-0001

JOSEPH, JAMES MICHAEL, music educator; b. Springfield, Pa., July 21, 1970; s. James Lewis and Anita Louise (Iacono) Joseph. BS, Westchester U of Pa, Westchester, Pa, 1988—92. Tchr. T/E Sch. Dist., Berwyn, Pa., 1992—. Band dir. Conestoga HS, Berwyn, Pa. Democrat. Catholic. Avocation: travel. Home: 213 N Maryland Ave Wilmington DE 19804-1337 Office: Conestoga HS 200 Irish Rd Berwyn PA 19312

JOSEPH, JAMES WILLIAM, political analyst; b. Gilroy, Calif., Jan. 1, 1960; s. William A. and Carmina M. J.; m. Mildred P. Maxwell, July 9, 2000. BA in Polit. Sci., Calif. State U., Fresno, 1982; D. U. Calif., Riverside, 1990; MA in Internat. Rels., Calif. State U., Fresno, 1984. Calif. lifetime tchg. credential. Asst. prof. polit. sci. U. Tex., Tyler, 1993—99; prof. polit. sci., dir. model UN programs Fresno (Calif.) City Coll., 1999—. Author: Between Realism and Reality: The Reagan Administration and International Debt, 1994; polit. commentator Sta. KFSN-TV, Fresno; contbr. articles to profl. jours. Mem. Am. Polit. Sci. Assn., Internat. Studies Assn. Republican. Avocations: cycling, reading. Office: Fresno City Coll 1101 E University Ave Fresno CA 93741 Home: 5623 W Fallon Ave Fresno CA 93722-2813 E-mail: jjospolsci@aol.com., james.joseph@scccd.com.

JOSEPH, JERRY, b. N.Y.C., Oct. 12, 1919; s. Ralph Joseph, Clara Schwartzman; m. Floria Ruff; children: Denice Fox, Robert. Pres. Toujay Designs, N.Y.C., 1962—70; pres., dir. Internat. Hi-F- Expo., N.Y.C., 1970—78; pres., founder (SAC) Soc. Audio Cons., N.Y.C., 1970—88; pub. Audio & Electronics Digest, N.Y.C., 1976—84; exec. recruiter DBA Jerry Joseph, Beverly Hills, Calif., 1985—2000. Author: Pilot 1940-45, 2001, The Doctor and the Prostitute, Forever Tomorrow, Incident at Cactus Ridge, 2001. Dir. Music Against Drugs, N.Y.C., 1972—73; Director M.A.D. Music Against Drugs, New York City, NY, 1972—73. Lt. USAF, 1940—45. Recipient Award for Outstanding Promotion of the High Fidelity Industry, Inst. of High Fidelity, 1971. Fellow: Inst. of Profl. Designers. Avocations: flying, golf, softball, skiing. Home: 78656 Golden Reed Drive Palm Desert CA 92211 Personal E-mail: JJoseph@dc.rr.com.

JOSEPH, JOHN, history educator; b. Baghdad, Iraq, Sept. 1, 1923; came to U.S., 1946, naturalized, 1961; s. Joseph Shukur and Rebecca (Alkhas) J.; m. Beatrice Paul Malick, July 20, 1956; children: Paul Faris, Lawrence John, Deena Joseph Kinsky. BA, Franklin and Marshall Coll., 1950; MA, Princeton U., 1953, PhD, 1957. Instr. Princeton U., 1956-58, lectr., 1958-59; assoc. prof. history Thiel Coll., Greenville, Pa., 1960-61; assoc. prof. Franklin and Marshall Coll., Lancaster, Pa., 1964-69, prof. history, 1969—, Lewis Audenreid prof. history, 1972, prof. emeritus, 1988—. Author: The Nestorians and Their Muslim Neighbors, 1961, Muslim-Christian Relations and Inter-Christian Rivalries in the Middle East, 1983 (named an outstanding acad. book Choice mag. 1983-84), The Modern Assyrians of the Middle East, Encounters with Western Christian missions, Archaeologists, and Colonial Powers, 2000. Recipient Excellence in Teaching award Christian R. and Mary F. Lindback Found., 1978; fellow Ford Found., 1954-56, NEH, 1979; grantee Am. Council Learned Socs.-Social Sci. Research Council Joint Com., 1966 67 Fellow Middle East Studies Assn.; mem. Phi Beta Kappa. Democrat. Home: 88 Orchard Rd Lancaster PA 17601-3228 Office: Franklin and Marshall Coll College Ave Lancaster PA 17604 Address: 88 Orchard Rd Lancaster PA 17601-3228 E-mail: j_joseph@fandm.edu.

JOSEPH, JULES K. retired public relations executive; b. Cin., Jan. 18, 1927; s. Leslie Bloch and Ellen (Kaufman) J.; m. Elizabeth Levy, Sept. 9, 1948; children— Ellen Beth, Barbara Ann, John Charles. BA in Journalism, U. Wis., 1948. Mem. press relations staff Gimbels, Milw., 1948-52; bur. chief Fairchild Publs., Milw., 1952-60; co-founder, chmn. emeritus Zigman-Joseph-Stephenson Assocs. in Pub. Rels., Milw., 1960-94; ret., 1994. Pres. Friends of Art of Milw. Art Ctr., 1961-62; v.p. Milw. County Mental Health, 1967; bd. dirs. Milw. Repertory Theatre, Camp Webb, Milw. Pks. Bd., St. John's Home for the Aged, Milw., DePaul Hosp., Charles Allis Art Libr., Wis. Olympics Com.; bd. dirs. Frank Lloyd Wright Heritage Tourism Program; adv. bd. Salvation Army. Recipient Chancellor's award for outstanding contbn. to mass communication U. Wis., 1988. Mem. Pub. Rels. Soc. Am. (accredited, treas. Wis. 1970-71, bd. dirs. counselors sect. 1991-92), Soc. for Profl. Journalists, Phi Kappa Phi. Episcopalian. Home: 10610 N Magnolia Dr Mequon WI 53092-5054 Office: 735 W Wisconsin Ave Milwaukee WI 53233-2413 *During my first job (summer '47) as a reporter on the Cincinnati Enquirer I was told to leave if I did not get the story. I have translated this to mean there's no excuse for not getting the job done— or reaching your goal.*

JOSEPH, LEONARD, lawyer; b. Phila., June 8, 1919; s. Harry L. and Mary (Pollock) J.; m. Norma Hamberg, 1947; children: Gilbert M., Stuart A., Janet H. Fitzgerald. BA, U. Pa., 1941; LLB, Harvard U., 1947. Bar: N.Y. 1949. Law clk. to chief judge U.S. Ct. Appeals, Boston, 1947-48; since practiced in N.Y.C.; ptnr. and of counsel Dewey Ballantine, 1957—. Bd. dirs., exec. com. Legal Aid Soc. N.Y., 1986-89; mem. panel of disting. neutrals CPR Inst. for Dispute Resolution. Bd. editors Harvard Law Rev., 1946-47. Served with AUS, 1943-46. Fellow Am. Bar Found., Am. Coll. Trial Lawyers Office: Dewey Ballantine 1301 Avenue Of The Americas New York NY 10019-6022

JOSEPH, LURA ELLEN, librarian, geologist; b. Tulsa, Jan. 24, 1947; d. Don Roscoe and Ruth Elizabeth (Taplin) J. Student, St. Paul Bible Coll., 1965-67, Pan Am. Coll., 1967-68; BA in Anthropology, U. Okla., 1971, MS in Geology, 1981; MA in Psychology with honors, U. Cen. Okla., 1992; M of Libr. and Info. Studies, U. Okla., 1994. Cert. petroleum geologist. Exploration geologist Getty Oil Co., Oklahoma City, 1977-84; geologist Harper Oil Co., Oklahoma City, 1984-86, consulting geologist, 1986-88; sr. geologist Grace Petroleum, Oklahoma City, 1988-93, cons. geologist, 1993-95; phys. scis. libr. N.D. State Univ. Libr., Fargo, 1995—2001; asst. prof. libr. adminstrn. U. Ill., Urbana-Champaign, 2001—. Author: (with others) Hugo Reservoir I, 1971; contbr. articles to profl. jours. Mem. Am. Assn. Petroleum Geologists, Geol. Soc. of Am., Spl. Libr. Assn., Geosci. Info. Soc. (v.p.), Sigma Gamma Epislon, Psi Chi, Beta Phi Mu. Avocations: travel, photography, reading, art. Office: U Ill Geology Libr 223 Natural History Bldg 1301 W Green St Urbana IL 61801

JOSEPH, MARIO ALEXIS, lawyer; b. Cordoba, Argentina, Jan. 16, 1971; m. Naomi Joseph, June 24, 1992. Student, Yeshiva U., 1989-90; BA, CUNY, Queens, 1992; JD, Benjamin N. Cordozo Sch. Law, 1995. Bar: N.Y., N.J. Asst. ombudsman Dept. of State, Office of Gov., N.Y.C., 1991-92; clk., liaison Franklin H. Williams, Jud. Commn. on Minorities, N.Y.C., 1993-94; pin. law clk. N.Y. State Supreme Ct., N.Y.C., 1993-94; cons. Interpublic Group, N.Y.C., 1995-96; prin. Law Offices of Mario A. Joseph, N.Y.C., 1997—. Clk., liaison Jud. Commn. on Minorities, N.Y.C., 1993-94; asst. ombudsman Office of the Gov., Dept. State, N.Y.C., 1991-92. Mem. young leadership com. mem. Am. Israel Pub. Affairs, 1999. Recipient Cert. of Achievement Nat. Multiple Sclerosis Soc., 1997, Cert. of Merit N.Y. Acad. Scis., 1994. Mem. AMA, Chinese Am. Bar Assn. (dir., founder 1998-99), N.Y. State Bar Assn. Avocations: skiing, horseback riding, painting. Office: Law Office of Mario A Joseph 401 Broadway New York NY 10013-3005

JOSEPH, MICHAEL SARKIES, accountant; b. Peoria, Ill., Dec. 10, 1950; s. Sarkas M. and Theresa I. (Kelch) J.; m. Christine L., June 28, 1975; children: Brian, Christopher, Patrick. BS, No. Ill. U., 1972. CPA. Ptnr. Ernst & Young, Cleve. and Chgo., 1972-89, ptnr. N.Y.C., 1989—; profl. acct. fellow Fed. Home Loan Bank Bd., Washington, 1981-83. Roman Catholic. Avocations: golf, swimming, youth athletic programs. Home: 38 Kellogg Hill Rd Weston CT 06883-2620 Office: Ernst & Young LLP 5 Times Sq New York NY 10036

JOSEPH, MICHAEL THOMAS, broadcast consultant; b. Youngstown, Ohio, Nov. 23, 1927; s. Thomas A. and Martha (McCarius) J.; m. Eva Ursula Boerger, June 21, 1952. BA, Case Western Res. U., 1949. Program dir. Fetzer Broadcasting, Grand Rapids, Mich., 1952-55; nat. program dir. Founders Corp., N.Y.C., 1955-57; program cons. to ABC, CBS, NBC, Capital Cities, Infinity, Cox, Entercom, Gannett, Greater Media, Tribune, N.Y. Times, 1958—; v.p. radio Capital Cities, N.Y.C., 1959-60; v.p. owned radio stas. NBC, N.Y.C., 1963-65. Mem. Internat. Radio and TV Soc., Nat. Assn. Broadcasters

JOSEPH, RAMON RAFAEL, physician, educator; b. N.Y.C., May 17, 1930; s. Felix R. and Helen Joseph; m. Mary Ann Kowalchik, June 16, 1956; children: Ricardo George, Maria Ann Thompson, Lisa Marie Benson. BS, Manhattan Coll., 1952; MD, Cornell U., 1956. Diplomate Nat. Bd. Med. Examiners, Am. Bd. Internal Medicine. Intern Meadowbrook Hosp., Hempstead, N.Y., 1956-57, resident, 1957, Wayne County Gen. Hosp., Westland, Mich., 1959-62, dir. gastroenterology, 1962-84, asst. dir. internal medicine, 1964-73, dir., chmn., 1973-84, pres. med. staff, 1971-72; cons. internal medicine and gastroenterology Annapolis Hosp., 1962-87; from instr. internal medicine to prof. U. Mich., 1962-85, prof. emeritus, 1998—; asst. dean U. Mich. Med. Sch., 1973-84; 1st v.p., dir. Univ. Med. Affiliates PC, 1981-84; pres., CEO Univ. Med. Affiliates (P.C.), 1985-87; med. dir. Henry Ford Hosp. Westland (Mich.) Ctr., 1987-94; sr. attending physician Henry Ford Hosp., Detroit, 1987-95. Cons. gastroenterology St. Mary Hosp., Livonia, Mich., 1966—, chmn. divsn. of gastroenterology, 1987-93. Contbr. articles to profl. jours. Mem. Community Commn. on Drug Abuse, Livonia and Westland, Mich., 1970-73; mem. Mich. Dept. Edn. Council on Drug Abuse, cons. on drug abuse public schs., Livonia, 1968-74; pres. Livonia Sch. Bd. Adv. Council, 1970-71. Capt. U.S. Army, 1957-59. Fellow ACP; mem. Am. Fedn. Clin. Research, Am. Gastroent., Assn., AAAS, Assn. Am. Med. Colls., AMA, N.Y. Acad. Sci., Detroit Gastroent. Soc. (pres. 1969-70), Mich., Wayne County Med. Socs., Am. Assn. Lab. Animal Sci., Am. Soc. Gastrointestinal Endoscopy, Am. Soc. Internal Medicine, Mich. Soc. Gastrointestinal Endoscopy (pres. 1982-86), Mich. Soc. Internal Medicine, Assn. Program Dirs. in Internal Medicine. Roman Catholic. Home: 5593 Stratford Dr West Bloomfield MI 48322-1540 also: 13755 W Via Montoya Sun City West AZ 85375-2054 E-mail: rjoseph514@aol.com.

JOSEPH, RAYMOND, lawyer; b. Lansing, Mich., Jan. 21, 1924; s. John Gamel and Lena (Tobia) J.; divorced; children: Gina Marie, Mark Raymond. Student, Mich. State U., 1948; JD, Wayne State U., 1951. Law clk. to Leland Carr, presiding chief justice Mich. Supreme Ct., 1953—54; with Raymond Joseph & Assocs., Lansing, Mich. Former pres. Lansing Symphony Assn.; officer, dir. Opera Co. Mid-Mich., Kresge Art Mus., Lansing Art Gallery, Lansing Ballet Assn., Mich. Orchestral Assn. Lt. USAAF, 1943-45, ETO. Decorated 7 Air medals; recipient presdl. citations. Mem. ABA, Mich. Bar Assn., Ingham County Bar Assn. (former sec.), Assn. Trial Lawyers Am., Mich. Trial Lawyers Assn., Am. Judicature Soc. (fed. ct. mediator), Def. Rsch. Inst. Democrat. Mem. Christian Ch. Avocations: art and art history, classical music, reading, tennis. Home and Office: 2710 Applegate Ln East Lansing MI 48823-2109 E-mail: raymond.joseph@eudoramail.com.

JOSEPH, RICHARD SAUL, cardiologist, educator; b. N.Y.C., Mar. 27, 1937; s. Charles Irving and Lillian (Horowitz) J.; m. Frances B. Rappaport, Jan. 27, 1963; children: Lauryl, James, Alisa, Jennifer. BA magna cum laude, Hofstra Coll., 1958; MD, Albert Einstein U., 1962. Intern U. Utah Affiliated Hosp., Salt Lake City, 1962-63; resident in chest medicine Bronx (N.Y.) Mcpl. Hosp., 1963-64; resident in internal medicine Mt. Sinai Hosp., N.Y.C., 1966-68; fellow in cardiology Nassau County Med. Ctr., East Meadow, N.Y., 1968-69; pvt. practice cardiology Huntington (N.Y.) Hosp., 1969—, chief cardiology, 1981-90, attending cardiology, 1973—; asst. prof. clin. medicine (cardiology) SUNY, Stony Brook, 1973—. Cons. in cardiology Kings Park (H.Y.) Hosp., 1971—; electro cardiographer Huntington Hosp., 1971—, co-dir. cardiac stress lab., 1975—; dir. Huntington Cardiac Rehab., 1977-94; adj. attending cardiologist St. Francis Hosp., Roslyn, N.Y., 1993-2000. Contbr. articles to profl. jours. Speaker med. adv. bd. Suffolk County Heart Assn., Blue Point, N.Y., 1971-73; speaker med. dir. Huntington (N.Y.) YMCA, 1973-77. Lt. USN, 1964-66. Recipient Pres. prize Hofstra Coll., Uniondale, N.Y., 1954; named Valedictorian Hofstra Coll., Uniondale, N.Y., 1958. Fellow Am. Coll. Cardiology; mem. Alpha Omega Alpha. Jewish. Avocations: jogging, classical and popular piano. Office: 205 E Main St Huntington NY 11743-2923

JOSEPH, ROBERT THOMAS, lawyer; b. June 12, 1946; s. Joseph Alexander and Clara Barbara (Francis) J.; m. Sarah Granger, May 22, 1971; children: Paul, Timothy. AB, Xavier U., 1968; JD, U. Mich., 1971. Bar: Mich. 1971, Ill. 1976, U.S. Dist. Ct. (no. dist.) Ill. 1976, U.S. Ct. Appeals (7th cir.) 1983. Staff atty. FTC Bur. Competition, Washington, 1971-76, asst. to dir., 1972-74; atty. Sonnenschein Nath & Rosenthal, Chgo., 1976—, ptnr., 1978—. Trustee Northbrook (Ill.) Libr. Bd., 1979-89, pres., 1983-85. Recipient Disting. Svc. award FTC, 1976. Mem. ABA (chair franchising com. of antitrust law sect. 1984-87, chair videotapes com. 1987-90, chair publs. com. 1991-94, coun.

1994-97, program officer 1997-99, com. officer 1999-2000, vice-chair 2000-2001, chair 2001-02, mem. governing bd. forum on franchising), Met. Club. Roman Catholic. Office: Sonnenschein Nath Rosenthal 233 S Wacker Dr Ste 8000 Chicago IL 60606-6491

JOSEPH, RODNEY RANDY, artist, arts society executive; b. Providence, July 13, 1945; s. Sidney Wilson and Philomena Joseph; m. Rumiko Antoinette Joseph, Jan. 29, 1971; children: Randy P., Reiner Scott. Student, Sch. Practical Art, Boston, 1964-67, Boston Conservatory Music, 1972-73; BFA, Art Inst. Boston, 1994. With Joseph Art Studio, Plymouth, Mass., 1973-76; arbitrator Better Bus. Bur., Fair Haven, Mass., 1977-79; prodr. Cape 11-Cable, Yarmouth, Mass., 1980-81; pres. Creative Life for Humanitary Arts Soc., Plymouth, 1992—. Pres. Creative Life Inc., Plymouth, 1976-92; cons. Creative Life Rsch., 1979—; program designer Office for Children of Boston, Plymouth, 1978-79; legal rsch. pres., 1976; cons. to govtl. policy on social welfare programs without the cost of taxation, 1994—; cons. svcs. to Pres. Clinton's Program, 1994—. Prodr. children's video: Captain Randy and Scott Terrific Adventures; author: (video) Saga of Old Plimoth Indians Cat the First Thanksgiving, 1999. Designed programs and campaigned for revitalization policies, talent laws; authored Act Naturally Talented Children, Mass., Nat. Campaign "Joseph Universal Welfare Act," Proposal for Resolution Article to cover local real estate tax cost and protection of hist. lands, Old Plymouth/Plymouth, Ma., Program of the Joseph Univ. Welfare Act proposal for constnl. programs for U.S. Sec. of Interior and Pres. Clinton Joint Social Pilot Project, recognized by Mass. State Senate for dedication and commitment in establishing Nov. 13 as Massasoit Compact Day, 1997; campaign for World Peace by C-Life Inc.; mem. Sandwich Hist. Soc. Recognized by Pres. Reagan Pvt. Sector Initiatives, 1982, Internat. Bio Ctr. Eng. Man of Yr. award, 1992-93, 93-94; recognized by House of Commons, London, Prime Min. John Major, Social Security divsn., leader of the opposition Tony Blair for the Joseph Universal Welfare Act, 1995. Mem. Internat. Platform Assn. (arts presentation 1993, nat. conv., presenter of poetry, theatre, works of art, speech), Boston Social Libr. (life), Sandwich Hist. Soc. Republican. Avocations: painting, antique collecting, art exhibitions. Home: 558 Wareham Rd Plymouth MA 02360-3239

JOSEPH, STEVEN JAY, lawyer; b. Baker, Oreg., Sept. 7, 1950; s. Jay Hyrum and Patricia Jean (Cahill) J.; m. Melissa Davis Joseph, Jan. 1, 1978; children: Lindsey Joseph, Logan Joseph. BS, Ea. Oreg. State Coll., 1972; JD, U. Oreg., 1975. Bar: Oreg. 1975, U.S. Dist. Ct. Oreg. 1975. Assoc. Willard K. Carey P.C., LaGrande, Oreg., 1975-76; ptnr. Carey & Joseph P.C., LaGrande, Oreg., 1976-88, Carey, Joseph & Mendiguren, LaGrande, Oreg., 1988-95, Joseph & Mendiguren P.C., LaGrande, 1995-96; atty. pvt. practice, LaGrande, 1997—. Pres. La Grande Indsl. Devel. Corp., 1999—. Councilor City of LaGrande, Oreg. 1990-94, 97-98; adv. bd. Salvation Army, 1995-2001; trustee E.O.S.C. Found., 1980-95, pres. 1988-90, East Oreg. U.-East Oreg. U. Found., 2000—, La Grande Sch. Dist. Bd., 2001— Mem.: LaGrande-Union County C. of C. (bd. dirs. 1982—84, chmn. 2003), Rotary, Elks. Republican. Avocations: polo, racquetball, skiing, hunting, golf. Home: 806 Highland Pl La Grande OR 97850-3216 Office: PO Box 3230 La Grande OR 97850-7230 E-mail: sjoseph@uwtc.net.

JOSEPH, TIMOTHY WACHT, writer; b. Hartford, Conn., May 10, 1944; s. William Gordon and Lillian Teresa Joseph; m. Marsha A. Raggi; children: Timothy I., Kimberly K. BS, BS in Edn., MA, Truman State U.; PhD, U. N.D. Cert. tchr. Mo. Sr. scientist U.S. Dept. Energy, Oak Ridge, Tenn., 1980—; divsn. dir. Resource Scis. Corp., Tulsa, 1978—80; sect. mgr. Environ. Rsch. and Tech., Ft. Collins, Colo., 1976—78; prof. Chapman Coll., Cheyenne, Wyo.; tchr., head dept. sci. Northwestern H.S., Mendon, Mo.; prof. Joliet Jr. Coll., Ill.; assoc. limnologist Midwest Rsch. Inst., Kansas City, Mo., 1974—76. Writer Cetacean Freelance, Knoxville, Tenn. Author: (novels) Four-Fifths, 2000, (poetry) Reflections On Love, 2002. Recipient Tech. Comm. award for excellence in writing tech. doc. for pub., Soc. Tech. Comm., 1999, Word Wesver award for Excellence, Novel Writing, 2000. Mem.: Nat. Environ. Health Assn., Knoxville Writers' Guild. Avocations: woodworking, sailing, rowing, crafts. Home: 11458 N Couch Mill Rd Knoxville TN 37931 Personal E-mail: joseph@esper.com.

JOSEPH, WENDY EVANS, architect; B in Design of Environ. (summa cum laude), U. Pa., 1977; MArch (with hons.), Harvard U., 1981. With Archl. Resources Cambridge, Inc., Boston, 1978, Pei Cobb Freed, 1985—93; pvt. practice NYC, 1994—. Mem. archl. team US Holocaust Meml. Mus., Washington. Chair alumni coun. Harvard U. Recipient Rome prize, 1983. Mem.: Archl. League (v.p. architecture), AIA (chair nat. com. design). Office: 500 Park Ave New York NY 10022*

JOSEPHBERG, ROBERT GARY, ophthalmologist, consultant, retina and vitreous surgeon; b. N.Y.C., Oct. 22, 1950; s. Sol and Sally (Lampert) J.; m. Lisa Monique Harth, Sept. 18, 1958; children: Sari, Daniel. BS, U. Wis., 1972; MD, Albany (N.Y.) Med. Coll., 1976. Diplomate Am. Bd. Ophthalmology. Intern in medicine Meml. Hosp., Worcester, Mass., 1976-77; resident in ophthalmology UMD, N.J., 1977-80; fellow in retina and vitreous surgery U. Baylor, Houston, Tex., 1980-82. Asst. clin. prof. N.Y. Med. Coll., Valhalla, 1985—, N.J. Coll. Medicine, Newark, 1985—, N.J. Coll. Medicine, New Brunswick, 1982—; chief of retina Westchester Med. Ctr.-N.Y. Med. Coll. Vol. surgeon Project Orbis, 1982, 85, 87. Mem. AMA, Fla. Med. Assn., Assn. Rsch. and Vision in Ophthalmology, Am. Acad. Ophthalmology, N.Y. State Med. Soc, N.Y. State Ophthal. Soc., N.J. Retina Soc., Atlantic Coast Retina Group, N.J. Ophthal. Soc., Vitreous Soc. (nominating com. 1996-98), Aspen Retinal Detachment Soc., Westchester County Med. Soc., Phi Kappa Phi. Achievements include patents for portable vitrectomy machine for endophthalmitis (Visitrec). Avocation: skiing. Office: 984 N Broadway Ste 511 Yonkers NY 10701-1308 E-mail: lisarirob@earthlink.net.

JOSEPHIAN, JENNY ADELE, acupuncturist, artist; b. Berkeley, Calif., Mar. 5, 1959; d. Roger Eslie Josephian and Carolyn Marie Wrasse. BA, Antioch U. West, San Francisco, 1986; diploma of competence, Traditional Acupuncture Inst., Columbia, Md., 1988, M Acupuncture, 1990. Lic. acupuncturist, Calif. Mem. office staff, acupressure practitioner Acupressure Inst., Berkeley, 1981-85; pvt. practice acupressure, Berkeley, 1981-88; pvt. practice acupuncture, 1988—. Exhibited works in show at Nexus Gallery, Berkeley, Calif., 2000. Avocations: travel, gardening, dancing. Office: 1502 Walnut St Ste A Berkeley CA 94709-1563

JOSEPH-KORDELL, SHELLEY M. geriatric care administrator; b. Jan. 18, 1947; BA, U. Minn., 1970. Fin. v.p. Kordell & Co. Inc., Mpls., 1979-81; pres. Estates in Transition Inc./Rent A Dau., Mpls., 1982—; v.p. The Joseph Co. Inc., Mpls., 1990—; income tax preparer H&R Block, Mpls., 1996-97. Mediator West Suburban Mediation Ctr., Hopkins, Minn., 1987—; bd. dirs. Temple Israel, Mpls., 1987—91, 1998—2000, Joseph Found., Mpls., 1990—. Office: Estates In Transition Inc 5427 Pompano Dr Minnetonka MN 55343-9405 E-mail: info@rentadaughter.com.

JOSEPHS, BABETTE, legislator; b. N.Y.C., Aug. 4, 1940; d. Eugene and Myra A. Josephs; children: Lee Aaron Newberg, Elizabeth Master. BA, Queens Coll., 1962; JD, Rutgers U., 1976. Sole practice, Phila., 1976-78; exec. dir. Nat. Abortion Rights Action League of Pa., Phila., 1978-80, Citizens Coalition for Energy Efficiency, Phila., 1980-81; pvt. practice cons., fundraiser Phila., 1981-84; mem. Pa. Ho. of Reps., Phila., 1984—. Bd. dirs. ACLU. Mem. Phila. Bar Assn. Democrat. Jewish. Office: 1528 Walnut St Philadelphia PA 19102-3604

JOSEPHS, RAY, public relations and advertising executive, writer, international relations consultant; b. Phila., Jan. 1, 1912; s. Isaac and Eva (Borsky) J.; m. Juanita Wegner, Feb. 22, 1941. Student, U. Pa., 1927-29. Staff writer Phila. Evening Bull., 1929-40; columnist Buenos Aires Herald, 1940-44, Latin-Am. corr., 1940-55; representing at various times Wash. Post, Christian Sci. Monitor, Pitts. Post-Gazette, Newark Star Ledger, Chgo. Sun, P.M., Variety, Nat. Monthly, others; co-founder, chmn. Internat. Pub. Relations Co., Ltd., N.Y.; chmn. bd. Ray Josephs-David E Levy, Inc.; pub. rels. counsel maj. industries, comml. concerns including Hitachi, Toshiba, Hong Kong Shanghai Bank, Bass Charrington, Fuji Bank, Seiko Time, Nikko Securities, Kubota Ltd., New Otani Hotels, Newhouse Newspapers, House & Garden, Mitsui & Co., Toray Industries, Am. Inst. Imported Steel.; dir. Concorde News Bur., N.Y.C. Lectr. Columbia Inst. Arts and Scis., Ind. U., Cornell Coll., Sweet Briar, Union Coll., Town Hall of West, San Francisco, Detroit, Indpls., Atlanta, Louisville, Spokane, Los Angeles Town Halls, numerous forums, town meetings from coast to coast; broadcaster NBC, CBS, MBS; cons. on Latin Am. affairs to coordinater Inter-Am. Affairs Brit. Ministry Information, RKO Radio Pictures, Asso. Export Adv. Agys.; cons. Bus. Coun. for Internat. Understanding, others pub. svc. orgns. Author: Argentine Diary, 1944, Spies and Saboteurs in Argentina, 1943, Latin America: Continent in Crisis, 1984, (with James Bruce) Those Perplexing Argentines, 1952, How to Make Money From Your Ideas, 1954, How to Gain an Extra Hour Every Day, 1955, 92; (with David Kemp) Memoirs of a Live Wire, 1956, Streamlining Your Executive Workload, 1958; (with Oscar Steiner) Our Housing Jungle and Your Pocketbook, 1960; (with Stanley Arnold) The Magic Power of Putting Yourself Over With People, 1962 (books pub. in Brit., French, Japanese, Spanish, Italian, German, Korean, Norwegian, Russian, Hungarian, Chinese, other edits.); contbr. to mags. and profl. jours. Mem. Brandeis U. Devel. Council. Recipient Achievement is Ageless award, N.Y. State, 2002. Mem. Writers Guild Am., Public Relations Soc. Am. (charter, accredited), Soc. Mag. Writers. Clubs: American (Buenos Aires); Overseas Press (N.Y.C.). Home: 860 United Nations Plz New York NY 10017-1810

JOSEPHSON, DIANA HAYWARD, not-for-profit company executive; b. London, Oct. 17, 1936; came to U.S., 1959; d. Robert Hayward and Barbara Bailey. BA with honors, Oxford U., Eng., 1958, MA, 1962; M in Comparative Law, George Washington U., 1962. Bar: Eng. and Wales 1959, D.C. 1963. Assoc. Covington & Burling, Washington, 1959-68; asst. dir. Office of the Mayor, Washington, 1968-74; exec. dir. Nat. Capital Area ACLU, Washington, 1975-78; dep. asst. adminstr. policy and planning, satellites NOAA, U.S. Dept. Commerce, Washington, 1978-82; pres. Am. Sci. and Tech. Corp., Bethesda, Md., 1982-83, Space Am., Bethesda, 1983-85; v.p. mktg. Arianespace, Inc., Washington, 1985-87; v.p. Martin Marietta Comml. Titan Inc., Washington, 1987-89; dir. bus. devel. Martin Marietta Advanced Launch Systems, Denver, 1989-90, Martin Marietta Civil Space and Communications Co., Denver, 1990-93; dep. under sec. commerce oceans and atmosphere, NOAA U.S. Dept. Commerce, Washington, 1993-97; prin. dep. asst. sec. for installations and environ. Dept. Navy, Washington, 1997-2000; sr. v.p. Environ. Def., N.Y.C., 2000—. Mem. Space Applications Bd., NRC, 1988-89, Comml. Space Transp. Adv. Commn., U.S. Dept. Transp., Washington, 1984-85; adv. bd. Washington Space Bus. Roundtable, 1985-87. Mem. D.C. Law Revision Commn., Washington, 1975-78, D.C. Internat. Women's Yr. State Coordinating Com., 1977. Mem. Am. Astronautical Soc. (bd. dirs. 1985-88), Nat. Space Club (bd. govs.), Women in Aerospace, Washington Space Bus. Roundtable (adv. bd. 1985-87). Avocations: sailing, reading. Office: Environ Def 257 Park Ave S 17th Fl New York NY 10010

JOSEPHSON, KENNETH BRADLEY, artist, retired educator; b. Detroit, July 1, 1932; s. Ernest Gustav and Hilda Christine (Wick) J.; m. Carol A. Compeau, Feb. 1954 (dec. Apr. 1958); m. Sherill A. Petro, Oct. 28, 1960 (div. 1973); children: Matthew W. (dec.), Bradley J., Anissa C.; m. Sally D. Garen, Jan. 30, 1973 (div. 1978); m. Katherine R. Bateman, June 7, 1991 (div. 1998). BFA, Rochester Inst. Tech., 1957; MS, Inst. Design Ill. Inst. Tech., 1960. Photographer Chrysler Corp., Detroit, 1957-58; exch. tchr. Konstfackskolan, Stockholm, 1966-67; assoc. prof. U. Hawaii, Honolulu, 1967-68; vis. prof. Tyler Sch. Art, Temple U., Phila., 1975, UCLA, 1981-82; prof. Sch. Art Inst. Chgo., 1960-97. Fellowship panelist Nat. Endowment Arts, Washington, 1975; vis. artist Ecole Régionale des Beaux Arts De Saint-Etienne, France, fall 1995. One-person shows include Visual Studies Workshop, Rochester, N.Y., 1971, U. Iowa Mus. Art, Iowa City, 1974, 291 Gallery, Milan, 1974, Cameraworks Gallery, L.A., 1976, Reicher Gallery Barat Coll., Lake Forest, Ill., 1977, Fotoforum, Kassel, Germany, 1978, Photographer's Gallery, London, 1979, Delpire Galerie, Paris, 1981, Young Hoffman Gallery, Chgo., 1981, Swen Parson Gallery No. Ill. U., 1983, Vision Gallery, Boston, 1983, Retrospective Exhbn. Mus. Contemporary Art, Chgo., 1983, Friends of Photography, Carmel, Calif, 1984, Rhona Hoffman Gallery, Chgo., 1991, 99, La Serre Gallery, Beaux-Arts de Saint Etienne, France, 1996, Retrospective Exhbn. Art Inst. Chicago, 1999, Retrospective Exhbn. Whitney Mus. Art, N.Y., 2001, Yancey Richardson Gallery, N.Y., 2001, 02, Priebe Art Gallery, U. Wis., Oshkosh, 2001, Kenneth Josephson Ctr. Photography, Lectoure, France, 2003; group shows include Fla. State Mus., Gainesville, 1965, Sheldon Meml. Art Gallery, Lincoln, 1968, Fogg Art Mus., Harvard U., 1967, Eastman House, Rochester and Nat. Gallery of Can., Ottawa, 1967, Mus. Contemporary Crafts, N.Y.C., 1971, Corcoran Gallery, 1972, Art Inst. Chgo., 1973, 93, Walker Art Ctr., Mpls., 1973, Madison Art Ctr., 1973, Mus. Art, Indpls., 1973, Incontri Internazionali d'Arte Precheggio di Villa Borghese, Rome, 1973-74, Atkins Art Gallery, 1974, Kunsthaus, Zurich, 1977, Mus. Contemporary Art, Chgo., 1977, 96, Leslie Tonkonow Art Works and Projects, N.Y.C., 1998, Carol Ehlers Gallery, Chgo., 1999; Mus. Art. R.I. Sch. Design, 1978, Mus. Modern Art, N.Y.C., 1978, Light Gallery, N.Y.C., 1980, Photokina, Koln, Germany, 1980, Seibu Mus. Art, Tokyo, 1982, Barbican Art Gallery, London, 1985, L.A. County Mus. Art, Nat. Mus. Modern Art, 1989, State of Ill. Art Gallery, 1989, U. Hawaii Art Gallery, 1990, Art Inst. Chgo., 1990, Rockford Coll. Art Gallery, 1990, Catherine Edelman Gallery, Chgo., 1991, Davenport Mus. Art, 1992, Seagram Bldg. Gallery, 1992, Renaissance Soc., Chgo., Montreal Mus. of Fine Arts, 1993, Art Inst. Chgo., 1993, Chgo. Cultural Ctr., 1994, U. Ariz., 1994, Mus. Modern Art, 1995, Laurence Miller Gallery, 1995, Ehlers Caudill Gallery, Chgo., 1996, Gallery 312, Chgo., 1996, Mus. Contemporary Photography, Columbia Coll., Chgo., 1996, VIII Fotobienal Vigo (Spain), 1998, Whitney Mus. Am. Art, N.Y., 2002, Art Inst. Chgo., 2002, San Francisco Mus. Modern Art, 2002, Phila. Mus. Art, 2002, Stephen Daiter Gallery, Chgo., 2002, Mus. Contemporary Art, Chgo., 2002, Carl Solway Gallery, Cin., 2002; permanent collections include Mus. Modern Art., N.Y.C., Contemporary Arts Mus., Houston, Addison Gallery Am. Art, Art Inst. Chgo., Bibliothéque Nationale, Paris, Ctr. for Creative Photography, U. Ariz., Fotografiska Museet, Stockholm, Hallmark Collections, Kansas City, Mo., Mpls. Inst. Arts, Mus. Fine Arts, Boston, Grunwald Ctr. Graphic Arts, UCLA, Nat. Mus. Art Smithsonian Instn., Washington, Nat. Mus. Modern Art, Kyoto, L.A. County Mus. Art, San Francisco Mus. Modern Art, Cartier Internat. Found., Paris, U.S. Trust Co., Art. Inst. of Chgo., Hunter Mus., Chattanooga, Tenn., Deloitte and Louche, Chgo., John D. and Catherine T. MacArthur Found., Seagram Collection, High Mus. Art., Libr. Congress, Internat. Ctr. Photography, N.Y., Cleve. Mus. Art, Tokyo Met. Mus. Photography, Whitney Mus. Am. Art., N.Y.. Served with U.S. Army, 1953-55. Guggenheim fellow, 1972, Nat. Endowment for Arts fellow, 1975, 79, Ruttenberg Arts Found. grantee, 1983, Ill. Acad. of Fine Arts Photographer award, 1993. Mem. Soc. for Photog. Edn. (founding mem.)

JOSEPHSON, MARVIN, talent and literary agency executive; b. Atlantic City, Mar. 6, 1927; s. Joseph and Eva (Rounick) J.; m. Tina Tann Chen, Apr. 12, 1973; children: Celia M., Claire A., Nancy A., Joseph T. Josephson; YiLing L.T. and YiPei R.T. Chen-Josephson. BA, Cornell U., 1949; LL.B., N.Y. U., 1952. Atty. CBS, N.Y.C., 1952-55; pres., then chmn. ICM Holdings Inc. (and predecessors), N.Y.C., 1955—. Pres., then chmn. exec. com. Internat. Creative Mgmt., Inc. subs. ICM Holdings Inc., N.Y.C., 1975. Served with USN, 1945-46. Office: ICM Holdings Inc 40 W 57th St 16th Fl New York NY 10019-4098 Fax: 212-556-6886. E-mail: mjosephson@icmtalent.com.

JOSEPHSON, NANCY, talent agent; d. Marvin J.; m. David Stern; 3 children. Grad., Brown U., 1980, Harvard Law Sch., 1982. Atty., 1982-86, Internat. Creative Mgmt., Beverly Hills, 1986, head N.Y. TV dept.; various positions as an agent, 1979-87; head TV lit. dept. Internat. Creative Mgmt., Beverly Hills, 1987-95, exec. v.p. of TV, 1995—, co-pres., 1998—. Developer (TV shows) Friends, Nash Bridges, Caroline in the City, The Simpsons. Named one of top twenty-five most important women in entertainment Hollywood's Reporter. Office: Internat Creative Mgmt 8942 Wilshire Blvd Ste 219 Beverly Hills CA 90211-1934

JOSEPHSON, RICHARD CARL, lawyer; b. Washington, Nov. 20, 1947; s. Horace Richard and Margaret Louise (Loeffler) J.; m. Jean Carol Attridge, Aug. 1, 1970; children: Lee Margaret, Amy Dorothy. AB, Case Western Res. U., 1969; JD, Coll. of William and Mary, 1972. Bar: Oreg. 1973. Law clk. Hon. John D. Butzner, Jr., U.S. Ct. Appeals, 4th Cir., Richmond, Va., 1972-73; mem. Stoel Rives LLP, Portland, Oreg., 1973—. Bd. dirs. Tucker-Maxon Oral Sch., Portland, 1987—, Vis. Nurse Assn., Portland, 1978-89, Healthlink, Portland, 1984-89, St. Mary's Acad., Portland, 1998-2001. 1st lt. U.S. Army, 1973-79. Fellow Am. Coll. Bankruptcy, Am. Coll. Comml. Fin. Lawyers; mem. ABA, Am. Bankruptcy Inst., Oreg. Bar Assn. (chmn. debtor-creditor sect. 1980-81). Avocations: skiing, white water rafting, running, cycling, theatre. Office: Stoel Rives LLP 900 SW 5th Ave Ste 2300 Portland OR 97204-1229 E-mail: rcjosephson@stoel.com.

JOSEPHSON, WILLIAM HOWARD, lawyer; b. Newark, Mar. 22, 1934; s. Maurice and Gertrude (Brooks) J.; m. Barbara Beth Haws, June 18, 1995. AB, U. Chgo., 1952; JD, Columbia, 1955; commoner, St. Antony's Coll., Oxford (Eng.) U., 1958-59. Bar: N.Y. 1956, D.C. 1966, U.S. Supreme Ct. 1959. Assoc. Paul, Weiss, Rifkind, Wharton & Garrison, N.Y.C., 1955-58, Joseph L. Rauh, Jr., Washington, 1959; Far East regional counsel ICA, 1959-61; spl. asst. to dir. Peace Corps, 1961-62, dep. gen. counsel, 1961-63, gen. counsel, 1963-66; asso. Fried, Frank, Harris, Shriver & Jacobson, N.Y.C., 1966-67, ptnr., 1968-94, counsel, 1994-99; asst. atty. gen. in charge charities bur. N.Y. State Law Dept., 1999—. Spl. counsel N.Y.C. Human Resources Adminstrn., 1966-67, City Univ. Constrn. Fund, 1967-96, N.Y.C. Bd. Edn., 1968-71, N.Y.C. Employees' Retirement Sys., 1975-86; Nat. Dem. vice presdl. campaign coord., 1972; pres. Peace Corps Inst., 1980—; mem. N.Y. State Gov. Task Force Pension and Investment, 1987-89, N.Y. State His. Records Adv. Bd., 1990-96, N.Y. State Archives Preservation Trust, 1994-96. Bd. editors: Columbia Law Rev, 1953-55. Trustee and treas. St. Antony's Coll. trust, 1994-99. Recipient William A. Jump award exemplary achievement pub. adminstrn., 1965, Disting. Svc. award, Valerie Kantor award, Corp. Social Responsibility award Mex. Am. Legal Def. and Edn. Fund, 1980, 81, 93. Mem. Assn. Bar City N.Y. (spl. com. on Congl. ethics 1968-70), Council on Fgn. Relations. Jewish. Home: 58 S Oxford St Brooklyn NY 11217-1305 Office: Charities Bur NY State Law Dept 120 Broadway Fl 3 New York NY 10271

JOSEY, E(LONNIE) J(UNIUS), librarian, educator, former state administrator; b. Norfolk, Va., Jan. 20, 1924; s. Willie and Frances (Bailey) J.; m. Dorothy Johnson, Sept. 11, 1954 (div. Dec. 1961); 1 dau., Elaine Jacqueline. AB, Howard U., 1949; MA, Columbia U., 1950; MLS, SUNY, Albany, 1953; LHD, Shaw U., 1973; DPS, U. Wis., Milw., 1987; HHD, N.C. Cen. U., 1989; LittD, Clark Atlanta U., 1995; LHD (hon.), Clarion Univ. of Pa., 2001. Desk asst. Columbia U. Libraries, 1950-52; libr. tech. asst. central br. N.Y. Pub. Libr., N.Y.C., 1952; libr. I Free Libr., Phila., 1953-54; instr. social scis. Savannah State Coll., 1954-55, libr., assoc. prof., 1959-66; libr., asst. prof. Del. State Coll., 1955-59; assoc. divsn. libr. devel. N.Y. State Edn. Dept., Albany, 1966-68; chief Bur. Acad. and Rsch. Libraries, 1968-76, Bur. Specialist Libr. Svcs., 1976-86; prof. U. Pitts. Sch. Libr. and Info. Scis., 1986-95, prof. emeritus, 1995—. Mem. bd. advisors Children's Book Rev. Service, Bklyn., 1972— Editor, contbg. author: The Black Librarian in America, 1970, What Black Librarians Are Saying, 1972, New Dimensions for Academic Library Service, 1975; co-compiler, co-editor: Handbook of Black Librarianship, 1977; co-editor: A Century of Service: Librarianship in the United States and Canada, 1976, Opportunities for Minorities in Librarianship, 1977, The Information Society: Issues and Answers, 1978, Libraries in the Political Process, 1980, Ethnic Collections in Libraries, 1983, Libraries, Coalitions, And the Public Good, 1987, Politics and the Support of Libraries, 1990, Festchaift E.J. Josey: an Activist Librarian, 1992, The Black Librarian in America Revisited, 1994, Handbook of Black Librarianship, 2001; mem. editl. bd. Dictionary of Am. Library History, 1974— ; mem. editl. adv. bd. ALA Yearbook, 1975-83; spl. advisor: World Ency. Black People, 1974-80; contbr. numerous articles to profl. jours. Mem. Albany Interracial Coun., 1972—86; state youth advisor Ga. Conf., 1962—66, 1st v.p., 1981—82, pres., 1982—86, life mem., 1971—, chmn. program, 1972—76, trustee; mem. tech. task force Econ. Opportunity Authority of Savannah, 1964—66; mem. adv. coun. Sch. Libr. Sci. N.C. Ctrl. U.; mem. adv. coun. Sch. Libr. and Info. Sci. SUNY, Albany, Sch. Libr. and Info. Sci. Queen's Coll. CUNY; mem. exec. bd. Savannah (Ga.) br. NAACP, 1960—66; mem. exec. bd. Albany br. Ga. Conf., 1970—72; mem. exec. bd. Albany Opportunity Authority; bd. dirs. Freedom to Read Found., 1987—91. With AUS, 1943—46. Recipient cert. of Appreciation Savannah br. NAACP, 1963, NAACP award Savannah State Coll. chpt., 1964, Merit award for work on econ. opportunity task force Savannah Chatham County, 1966, award for disting. service to librarianship Savannah State Coll. Library, 1967, Jour. Library History award, 1970, N.Y. Black Librarians Inc. award, 1979, N.J. Black Librarians Network award, 1984, Joseph W. Lippincott award, 1980, Disting. Alumnus of Yr. award SUNY Albany Sch. Library and Info. Sci. and Policy, 1981, 89, Disting. Service award Library Assn. of CUNY, 1982, Martin Luther King Jr. award for disting. community leadership SUNY, Albany, 1984, award for contbns. to librarianship D.C. Assn. Sch. Librarians, 1984, award Kenyan Library Assn., 1984, Disting. Service award Afro-Caribbean Library Assn., Eng., 1984; ALA Hon. Mem. Award, 2002. Mem.: ACLU, AAUP, ALA (hon.; founder, chmn. Black Caucus 1970—71, mem. coun. 1970—, mem. exec. bd. 1979—86, v.p./pres.-elect 1983—84, pres. 1984—85, John Cotton Dana award 1962, 1964, Black Caucus award 1979, ALA Equality award 1991, Black Caucus Demco award for disting. svc. to librarianship 1994, Wash. office award 1996—, Humphrey/OCLC/Forest Press award for contbns. to internat. librarianship 1998), Am. Soc. Info. Scis., Internat. Platform Assn., N.Y. Libr. Assn. (Disting. Svc. award 1985), Am. Acad. Polit. and Social Sci., Assn. Study Afro-Am. Life and History, Pa. Libr. Assn. (Disting. Svc. award 1996), N.Y. Libr. Club, Kappa Phi Kappa, Alpha Phi Omega. Democrat. Home: 5 Bayard Rd Unit 505 Pittsburgh PA 15213-1905 Office: U Pitts Sch Info Scis Bldg Pittsburgh PA 15260 E-mail: ejjosey@mail.sis.pitt.edu.

JOSHI, ATUL B. physician; s. Balwantrai B. and Gunvventiben B. Joshi; m. Seema A. Nimbker, Nov. 24, 1982; children: Pooja A., Shweta A. MB, BChir, Topiwala Nat. Med. Sch., Bombay, 1979; MChir in Orthopedics, U. Liverpool, 1990. Faculty at JPS Health Network, Ft. Worth & Univ. Med. Ctr., Tex. Tech. Univ., Lubbock; pvt. practice Lubbock, Tex., 2002—. Fellow: Royal Coll. Edinbrugh; mem.: TMA, AMA (assoc.), Am. Acad. Orthop. Surgeon (assoc.). Office: 3601 22nd Pl Lubbock TX 79410

JOSHI, GIRISH PREMJI, anesthesiologist, researcher; b. Pune, India, Mar. 7, 1959; came to U.S., 1992; s. Premji Punja and Shanta Premji J. MB, BS, U. Pune, 1981, MD in Anesthesiology, 1985; MD, U. Coll. Dublin, Ireland, 1994. Diplomate Am. Bd. Anesthesiology. Lectr. King Edward Meml. Hosp., Pune, 1986-87; registrar Regional Gen. Hosp., Limerick, Ireland, 1988-89, Beaumont Hosp., Dublin, 1990; cons. anesthetist Cappagh Hosp. and Mater Misericordia Hosp., Dublin, 1991; asst. prof. Oreg. Health Scis. U., Portland, 1992, U. Tex. S.W. Med. Ctr., Dallas, 1993-97, assoc. prof., 1997—2001, prof., 2001—. Dir. perioperative medicine and ambulatory anesthesia Parkland Health and Hosp. Sys., Dallas, 1999—, chmn. pain com., 1998-2002; vice-chmn. clin. rsch. com. U. Tex. S.W. Med. Ctr., Dallas, 1997-2002. Editor: Anesthesia for Laparoscopy Thoracoscopy, Hysteroscopy, 2001; mem. editl. bd. Jour. Evaluation in Clin. Practice, 1998-2001. Nat. Merit scholar Govt. India, Pune, 1980-81; named Man of Yr., B.J. Med. Coll. Students Assn., 1980; recipient Cost-Effectiveness award Anesthesiology News & Stuart Pharm., 1993, 96. Fellow Royal Coll. Surgeons; mem. Am. Soc. Anesthesiologists (subcom. mem. 1999—), Internat. Anesthesia Rsch. Soc., Soc. for Ambulatory Anesthesia (chair publs. 2000—), Tex. Soc. Anesthesiologists, Dallas County Anesthesiology Soc. (pres. 1998). Hindu. Avocation: travel. Office: Univ Tex SW Med Ctr 5323 Harry Hines Blvd Dallas TX 75390-9068

JOSHI, HARIHAR S. medical laboratory executive; b. Manjarkhed, India, Aug. 20, 1931; came to U.S., 1962; s. Sopandeo Waman and Manakarnika Narayan J.; m. Vaijayanti Pushpa Laxman Kukade, June 6, 1957; children: Chandrashekhar, Wandana, Sharad. B in Vet. Sci., M.P. Vet. Coll., 1954; MS, U. Hawaii, 1964; PhD, U. Guelph, 1971. Vet. officer Dept. Vet. & Animal Husbandry, India, 1954-58; rsch. assoc., lectr. Bombay Vet. Coll., India, 1958-62; asst. prof. U. Guelph, Ont., Canada, 1964-69; rsch. fellow Worcester Found. Exptl. Biology, Shrewsbury, Mass., 1971-75; tech. supervisor, dir. Ind. Med. Labs., Worcester and Cambridge, Mass., 1975-80; pres. Omega Med. Labs, Oxford, Mass., 1980-95. Head religious matters India Soc. Worcester, Shrewsbury, 1972-95; Hindu priest, 1972—. Mem. Am. Assn. Clin. Chemists. Home: 65 Locust Ave Worcester MA 01604-1129

JOSHI, HEM RAJ, educator; b. Shera, Baitadi, Nepal, May 18, 1963; arrived in U.S., 1997; s. Khem Raj and Haripriya Joshi; m. Rashika Bhattarai, Jan. 16, 1996; children: Umang Raj, Imani. MSc, Garhwal U., Dehradun, India, 1989; MS in Indsl. Math., U. Kaiserslautern, Germany, 1995; PhD, U. Tenn., 2002. Asst. prof. Tribhuwan U., Kathmandu, Nepal, 1995—; post doctoral rsch. assoc.

U. Tenn., Knoxville, 2002—. Program officer German Tech. Cooperation, Kathmandu, 1996—97. Pres. SIAM U. Chpt., Knoxville, 1999—2002. Recipient Mahendra Vidya Bhusan, His Majesty Nepal, 1990; DAAD fellow, German Acad. Exch. Program, 1993—95, Yates Dissertation fellow, U. Tenn., 2001—02. Mem.: Soc. for Indsl. and Applied Math. Achievements include research in optimal control of an HIV immunology model. Home: 1611 Laurel Ave 1315 Knoxville TN 37916 Office: Univ Tenn 121 Ayres Hall Knoxville TN 37996-1300 E-mail: joshi@math.utk.edu.

JOSHI, JAGMOHAN, agronomist, consultant; b. Dhanoa, Panjab, India, Mar. 20, 1933; came to U.S., 1966; s. Gian Chand and Savitri Devi J.; m. Santosh Sharma, Feb. 19, 1961; children: Shallin, Shushen, Shailesh. MS, Panjab U., Chandigarh, India, 1961; PhD, Ohio State U., 1972. Cert. profl. crop scientist. Lectr. Extension Tng. Ctr., Mashobra, India, 1956-61; asst. agrl. officer Ministry Agr., Nairobi, Kenya, 1961-66; rsch. assoc. Ohio State U., Columbus, 1966-73, U. Md. Ea. Shore, Princess Anne, 1973-77, rsch. asst. prof., 1977-85, rsch. assoc. prof., 1985-96, prof., 1997—, dir. Soybean Rsch. Inst., 1976—. Cons. N.C. Agrl. & Tech. U., Greensboro, 1988, Transkel Washington Bur., 1990; internat. cons. in Zambia, Zimbabwe, Kenya, Nigeria, India, Republic of China, Sri Lanka, the Caribbean Islands, Egypt, Macedonia, and Russia, 1976—; co-team leader China Tech. and Sci. Exch., USDA, Washington, 1990. Co-author: Soybeans for the Tropics, 1987; contbg. editor: Technologies for Sustainable Agriculture in the Tropics, 1993; contbr. articles to profl. jours. Pres. India Assn. Ea. Shore, Salisbury, 1979. Grantee USDA, NASA, 1973—. Mem. Am. Soc. Agronomy, Crop Sci. Soc. Am., Am. Soybean Assn., Assn. Agrl. Scientists of Indian Origin. Achievements include research on host plant resistance, on cultural control of soybean pests, on winged bean, on agronomy of hydrocarbon producing plants and development of high yielding and promiscuous soybean varieties for Zambia; patentee in development of foliar spray for soybeans, and method of treating plants. Office: Univ Md Ea Shore Trigg Hall Princess Anne MD 21853

JOSHI, JAMES BIKRAM DHOJ, information scientist, educator; s. Hem Bikram Dhoj and Prava Joshi; m. Tripti Onta, Apr. 15, 2002. B in Engring., Motilal Nehru Regional Engring. Coll., India, 1993; MS in computer Sci., Purdue U., Ind., 1998, PhD in Computer Engring., 2003. Cert. Applied Mgmt. Principles Purdue U., 2000. Lectr. Kathmandu U., Nepal, 1993—96; rsch. asst. Purdue U., West Lafayette, Ind., 1996; asst. prof. dept. info. sci. and telecomm. U. Pitts. Computer cons. Goodwill Fin. and Ins. Co. Pvt. Ltd., Kathmandu, Nepal, 1993—94. Author: (book chpt.) Advances in Digital Governement: Technology, Human Factors, and Policy.; song writer, composer, singer (songs in nepali, newari and english) Music Album produced in Nepal; contbr. articles to profl. jours. Recipient Children Rep., Govt. of Bulgaria, 1984, Gold medal, Vanasthali Inst., 1986, Youth Exch. Participation, Govt. of Japan, 1995; grantee Student Travel Grant, IEEE Computer Soc., 2000; scholar Colombo Plan Scholarship, Govt. of India, 1989—93. Mem.: Assn. of Computing Machinery, IEEE. Achievements include research in A model for secure multimedia documents in distributed environments; A generalized temporal role based access control model. Office: U Pitts 721 IS Bldg 135 N Bellefield Ave Pittsburgh PA 15260

JOSHI, JANARDAN SHANTILAL, surgeon; b. Ahmedabad, Gujarat, India, Oct. 19, 1931; came to U.S., 1977; s. Shantilal Jatashanker and Ramlaxmi S. Joshi; m. Hansa Janardan, May 14, 1954; children: Mukesh J., Chetana K. MB BChir, Med. Coll., Baroda, India, 1955; Diploma in Laryngology and Otology, M.S. U., Baroda, 1957. Bd. cert. Am. Bd. Otolaryngology. Prof., head ear, nose and throat dept. NHL Mcpl. Med. Coll. and KM Sch. Postgrad. Medicine/Rsch., Ahmedabad, 1964-76; pvt. practice Ahmedabad, 1966-76, San Jose, Calif., 1983—. Fellow: Am. Acad. Otolaryngology-Head and Neck Surgery Inc., Royal Coll. Surgeons Edinburgh. Avocations: foreign travel, photography, wind surfing. Office: 244 N Jackson Ave Ste 201 San Jose CA 95116-1604

JOSHI, PRABHAKAR G. educator; b. Thane, Bombay, India, June 28, 1931; came to U.S., 1963; s. Ganesh Laxman and Saraswatibai G. J.; m. Savita P. Joshi; 1 child, Chandrashekhar P. BA, U. Bombay, 1954, LLB, 1960; MA, Tex. State U., 1966; ABD, Cath. U., 1976; PhD, Southea. U., 1978; MA in Sci. of Creative Intelligence, Maharishi U. Mgmt., 2003. Mem. vol. Indo-Am. liaison faculty, admissions office staff Maharishi U. Mgmt., Fairfield, Iowa, 1997—. Rsch. assoc. Kans. State U., Manhattan, 1980, U.S. Army Depot, Oakland, Calif., Alexandria, Va., Phila.; vis. prof., rsch. assoc. The Pentagon, Washington, Morris Coll., S.C., 1972-97. Author: India-U.S. Satellite Educational Program, 1978, Problems of Modernization in India, 1978, Problems and Prospects of Economic Development in India, 1977, Boondoggle of Conferences, 1997, An Example for All, 2d edit., 1995, India-U.S. Staellite Educational Program, rev. edit., 2000, others. Canditate for U.S. Ho. of Reps., 1996. Recipient Hind Rattan (Jewel of India), Non-Resident Indians Welfare Soc., 1995, Trophies, Sr. Citizens Sports Sumter County, Sumter, S.C., 1994, 95, 96. Mem. ASPA (life mem., mem. planning com. 1978 annual conf.) Avocations: table tennis, travel, learning to transcend, writing, lecturing. Home: MUM DB1130 Fairfield IA 52557-0001 E-mail: Joshipps@hotmail.com.

JOSHI, PRATIBHA C. immunologist, researcher; b. Bombay, Dec. 30, 1955; came to U.S., 1980; d. Shankar R. and Mrunalini S. Gokhale; m. Chandrashekhar V. Joshi, Mar. 23, 1980; children: Neil, Nina. BSc, Bombay U., 1976, MSc, 1978; PhD, Miss. State U., 1988. Postdoctoral fellow NIH, Jackson, 1989-90, 92-93; from rsch. assoc. to sr. rsch. assoc. U. Miss. Med. Ctr., Jackson, 1993-96, assoc. prof. surgery, rschr., 1996—. Contbr. articles to profl. jours. Mem. AAAS, Am. Assn. Immunologists, N.Y. Acad. Scis. Avocations: travel, reading, painting.

JOSHI, SATISH DEVDAS, organic chemist; b. Bombay, Maharashtr, India, Sept. 29, 1950; came to U.S., 1982; s. Devdas Ganesh and Premlata (Prabhu) J.; m. Shima Janakimohan Bhadra, May 2, 1974; children: Shruti, Shilpa. BS, Bombay U., 1970, MS, 1972; PhD in Chemistry, Bombay U., Bombay, 1977. Rsch. fellow State U. Gent, Belgium, 1979-81, Louvain Med. Sch., Brussels, 1981-82; rsch. assoc. Mt. Sinai Sch. Medicine, N.Y.C., 1982-85; group leader Bachem, Inc., Torrance, Calif., 1985-87; dir. Bachem Biosci. Inc., Phila., 1987-89; pres., chief exec. officer Star Biochems., Torrance, 1989-91; tech. dir. Mallinckrodt Inc., St. Louis, 1991-2001; exec. v.p. Peptisyntha, Inc. (Solvay GR), 2001—. Mem. AAAS, ACS, Am. Peptide Soc., Torrance C. of C., Protein Soc. Home: 1928 Via Estudillo Palos Verdes Estates CA 90274-1910

JOSHI, SURESH MEGHASHYAM, research engineer; b. Poona, India; came to U.S., 1969, naturalized 1982. B.S., Banaras U., India, 1967; M.S., Indian Inst. Tech., Kanpur, 1969; Ph.D., Rensselaer Poly. Inst., 1973. Engr., Stone & Webster Corp., Boston, 1972-73; rsch. assoc. NASA, Hampton, Va., 1973-75, sr. scientist, 1983—; rsch. prof. Old Dominion U. Research Found., Norfolk, Va., 1975-83; vis. prof. U. Va., Charlottesville, 1992-93. Author: Control of Large Flexible Space Structures, 1989; co-author: Control of Nonlinear Multibody Flexible Space Structures, 1996; contbr. articles to profl. jours. Recipient Allen B. DuMont prize Rensselaer Poly. Inst., 1973; Group Achievement award NASA, 1977, Cert. of Recognition, 1981, Quality award, 1984, 1988, 90, 91; Spl. Achievement award, 1987, 89, 94, 95; Outstanding Tech. Contributions award, 1989, 90, 92, Floyd Thompson award, 1992, Dual Career Ladder award, 1992. Fellow AIAA, IEEE (control sys. tech. award 1995, Judith A. Resnick award 2003), ASME. Avocation: amateur cartoonist. Office: NASA Langley Rsch Ctr Mail Stop 132 Hampton VA 23681

JOSHI, VIJAY V. pathologist, educator; b. Poona, India, Mar. 10, 1936; came to U.S., 1965; m. Jayashree Nene. MBBS, Byramjee Jeejibhoy Med. Coll., India, 1959; MD, Grant Med. Coll., India, 1962; resident, Med. Coll. Va., 1965-68; PhD, U. Western Ontario, Canada, 1970. Diplomate Am. Bd. Pathology, Am. Bd. Anatomic Pathology, Am. Bd. Pediatric Pathology. Resident in pathology Grant Med. Coll., Bombay, Med. Coll. Va., Richmond, 1965-68; lectr. in pathology Grant Med. Coll., 1962-65; rsch. fellow U. Western Ont., Can., 1968-70; asst. prof. pathology Mont. (Can.) Children's Hosp., 1970-72; asst. prof. pathology and pediatrics Med. Coll. Va., 1972-74, assoc. prof., 1974-75; pediatric pathologist Postgrad. Inst. Med. Edn. and Rsch., Chandigarh, India, 1975-78; prof. pathology Govardhandas Sunderdas Med. Coll., Bombay, 1978-80; assoc. prof. pathology and pediatrics coterminus U. Medicine and Dentistry N.J., N.J. Med. Sch., Newark, 1981-86, prof. coterminus, 1986-88; prof. dept. pathology and lab. medicine, clin. prof. pediatrics E. Carolina U. Sch. Medicine, Greenville, 1988-96. Dir. pediatric pathology Children's Hosp. N.J., 1980-88, Pitt County Meml. Hosp., Greenville, 1988-96; dir. pediatric pathology Ct. Children's Med. Ctr., Hartford, 1996—; collaborator with pathology ctr., nat. Wilm-tumor study Chi ldren's Hosp. Denver, 1986; cons. to collaborative ctr. investigation of AIDS, Armed Forces, Instn. Pathology, Washington, 1986-87; cons. in pediatric pathology Beth Israel Med. Ctr., N.Y.C., 1992; U.S. coord. and participant joint CME programs Med. Coun. India, 1988—; mem. numerous nat. coms. Author: Common Problems in Pediatric Pathology, 1994, Handbook of Placental Pathology, 1994; editor: Pathology of AIDS and Other Manifestations of HIV Infection, 1990; contbr. numerous chpts. to books and articles to refereed jours., periodic reviewer prof. jours.; mem. editl. bd. Pediatric Pathology and Pediatric AIDS and HIV Infection: Fetus to Adolescent, 1990. Grantee AIDS Found., 1985, Pediatric Oncology Group, 1989, NIH, 1991. Mem. Am. Soc. Clin. Pathologists, Indian Assn. Pathologists and Microbiologists, Internat. Acad. Pathology (study group complications of perinatal care 1984—), Internat. Paediatric Pathology Assn. (coun.), Soc. Pediatric Pathology Assn. (coun.), Soc. Pediatric Pathology (chmn. mem. com. 1985-88, rsch. com. 1988-89, editl. bd. jour. 1987). Office: Hartford Hosp Dept Pathology Dept Pathology and Lab Medicine 80 Seymour St Hartford CT 06102-8000

JOSHUA, PERCY, English educator; b. Jonesville, Tex., May 5, 1952; s. Clint and Mildred (Lewis) J. BA, U. Dallas, 1974; MEd, Centenary Coll. of La., 1992, postgrad., 1996. Cert. tchr., Tex., La. Tchr. Irving (Tex.) Ind. Sch. Dist., 1975-78, Caddo Parish Schs., Shreveport, La., 1986—; chair English dept. Caddo Parish Magnet H.S., Shreveport, 1993-96. Mgr. Mr. B's Beauty Supply, Dallas, 1978-85. Bd. dirs. Shreveport Met. Ballet; mem. Shreveport Opera. Fellow La. Endowment for Humanities, 1990, 92, 93, 94, 96. NEH, 1993, 2001, Japanese Studies Inst., 1998. Mem. NEA, Nat. Coun. Tchrs. English (scholarship to Adelaide, Australia conf. 1993), La. Assn. Educators, La. Coun. Tchrs. English, Caddo Assn. Educators (assn. rep. 1987—), Caddo Coun. Tchrs. English (SLATE rep. 1995-2000), Shreveport C. of C. (leadership coun. 1996—). Baptist. Avocations: travel, reading, arts, chess, writing. Home: 259 Merrick St Shreveport LA 71104-2433 Office: Caddo Parish Magnet HS 1601 Viking Dr Shreveport LA 71101-5245 E-mail: percy836@bellsouth.net.

JOSKOW, JULES, economic research company executive; b. N.Y.C. s. Abraham and Mollie (Neuberg) J.; m. Charlotte Epstein, June 24, 1945; childern: Paul, Margaret, Andrew. BS, CCNY, 1941; MA, Columbia U., 1942, PhD, 1953. Mem. faculty dept. econs. CCNY, 1941=60; dir. rsch. Boni, Watkins, Jason & Co., N.Y.C., 1952-61; v.p. Nat. Econ. Rsch. Assocs., N.Y.C., 1961-70, sr. v.p., 1970-76, exec. v.p., 1976 85, pres., 1985-91, spl. cons., 1991—. Contbr. articles to profl. jours. Mem. nat. governing coun. Am. Jewish Congress, N.Y.C., 1968-71; v.p. Temple Emanuel, Great Neck, N.Y., 1974-77. Mem. Glen Head Country Club L.I. (pres. 1988-91). Home: 127 Station Rd Great Neck NY 11023-1721

JOSKOW, PAUL LEWIS, economist, educator; b. Bklyn., June 30, 1947; s. Jules and Charlotte Joan (Epstein) J.; m. Barbara Zita Chasen, Sept. 10, 1978; 1 child, Suzanne Zoe. BA, Cornell U., 1968; M.Phil., Yale U., 1971, PhD, 1972. Asst. prof. econs. MIT, Cambridge, 1972-75, assoc. prof. econs., 1975-78, prof. econs., 1978—, Mitsui prof., 1989-96, Elizabeth and James Killian chair, 1996—, head dept. econs., 1994-98, dir. Ctr. for Energy and Environ. Policy Rsch., 1999—. Vis. prof. J.F.K. Sch. Govt., Harvard U., Cambridge, Mass., 1979-80; rsch. assoc. Nat. Bur. Econ. Rsch., 1988—; Joel Dean meml. lectr. Oberlin Coll., Ohio, 1983; cons. NERA, White Plains, N.Y., 1972-97, The World Bank, 1991-92, Rand Corp., Santa Monica, Calif., 1972-87; pub. mem. Adminstrv. Conf. U.S., Washington, 1980-82; mem. adv. coun. EPRI, Palo Alto, Calif., 1980-84; mem. acid rain adv. com. EPA, 1990-93, mem. sci. adv. bd., 1998-2002; chmn. rsch. adv. bd. Com. for Econ. Devel., 1991-94, sci. adv. bd. Inst. d'Organization Industrielle, Toulouse, France, 1991—; bd. dirs. New Eng. Electric Sys., Westborough, Mass., 1987-2000, State Farm Indemnity Co., Bloomington, Ill., 1993-2002, Nat. Grid Group, London, 2000-02, Nat. Grid Transco, London, 2002—, Whitehead Inst. for Biomed. Rsch., Cambridge, Mass.; trustee Putnam Mutual Funds, Boston, 1997—. Co-author: Electric Power in the U.S., 1979, Markets For Power, 1983, Markets For Clean Air, 2000; author: Controlling Hospital Costs, 1981, Economic Regulation, 2000; also numerous articles, chpts.; co-editor, then assoc. editor Bell Jour. Econs., 1976-85; co-editor Jour. of Law, Econs. and Orgn., 1992-95; bd. editors Am. Econ. Review, 1993-98. Pres. Yale U. Coun., 1993—. Fellow Am. Acad. Arts and Scis., Econometric Soc.; mem. ABA (assoc.), Am. Econ. Assn., Econometric Soc., Internat. Assn. for Energy Econs.(Best Paper award, 1994), Internat. Soc. for New Instnl. Econs. (v.p. 2000-2001, pres.2002-03). Home: 7 Chilton St Brookline MA 02446-3902 Office: MIT Dept Econs 50 Memorial Dr Cambridge MA 02142-1347 E-mail: pjoskow@mit.edu.

JOSLIN, DAVID BRUCE, bishop; b. Collingswood, N.J., Jan. 8, 1936; s. Elizabeth (Andrews) J.; m. Kathrine E. Brockett, June 15, 1958; children: Paul Gregory, Suzanne Marie. BA, Drew U., Madison, 1958; M of Divinity (cum laude), Drew U., 1961; Assoc. in Anglican Studies, Episcopal Div. Sch., 1965. Assoc. rector St. Paul's Ch., Montvale, N.J., 1965-67; rector St. David's Ch., Wilmington, Del., 1967-74, Christ Ch., Westerly, R.I., 1974-87, Ch. of St. Stephen the Martyr, Edina, Minn., 1987-91; Episcopal Bishop Diocese of Ctrl. N.Y., 1991—2000; assisting Bishop Diocese of N.J., Trenton, 2000—. Keynote spkr. for retreats and confs., cons. liturgies and ch. design, chmn. bd. various state and nat. ch. bds.; mem. Standing Commn. on Ecumenism, 1995—, Coun. for the Devel. of Ministry, 1993—; leader Relationship of Anglican and Old Caths., 1994—. Author: Apostle in Our Midst-the Office of Bishop, 1982. Mem. Downtown Revelopment Task Force, Westerly, 1983-87; Citizen's Adv. Bd. Westerly, 1982-87; deputy gen. conv. Episcopal Ch., 1985. Mem. Fellowship of Sts. Alban and Sergius, Anglican Soc. of the U.S.A. (v.p. 1980-87), Rotary. Episcopalian. Avocations: traveling, collector of antique autos.

JOSLIN, JANINE ELIZABETH, preservation consultant; b. Kansas City, Mo., Mar. 16, 1948; d. James Bryce and Isabel Quezon (Carr) Traner; m. Jack Leslie Joslin, Dec. 4, 1971; children: Jaclyn, Aaron, Amanda. BA in History, U. Mo., Kansas City, 1971; MA in Heritage Preservation, Ga. State U., 1992. Pvt. practice cons., Rome, Ga., 1989—92; dir. Chieftains Mus., Rome, 1992—94; pres. Gaia Walkers Inc., Leawood, Kans., 1996—99; pvt. practice cons. Leawood, 1999—. Bd. mem. Women Vision Internat., Overland Park, Kans., 1996—; pres. bd. Donnelly Internat., Kansas City, Kans., 1997—98; team leader Sci. City Mus., Kansas City, Mo., 1998—99. Contbr. articles to mags. Commr. Leawood Hist. Commn., 1998—; bd. mem. Kans. Preservation Alliance, Topeka, 2001—. Grantee, IMS, 1994, Ga. Heritage 2000, 1995, Kans. Why 150, 1999. Avocations: rowing, hiking, rafting. Home: 12508 Catalina Leawood KS 66209

JOSLIN, JOE EDWARD, JR., secondary school educator; b. Cleveland, Miss., Jan. 23, 1971; s. Joe E. Joslin Sr. and Sharon Perkins Joslin; m. Stacey Welborn Joslin, Nov. 18, 1995; children: Emma Suzanne, Aubrey Anne. B in Music Edn., Northwestern State U., 1994; EdM, McNeese State U., 2002. Tchr. Hughes Spring (Tex.) H.S., 1994—95, DeRidder (La.) Jr. High, 1995—2001, Merryville (La.) H.S., 2001—. Prin. trumpet First Bapt. Ch. Orch., 1988—. Recipient Key to the City, DeRidder Police Jury, 1989. Mem.: Tex. Music Educators Assn., La. Music Educators Assn., La. Bandmasters Assn., Music Educators Nat. Conf., Kappa Alpha (sec. 1993—94), Kappa Delta Pi. Democrat. Baptist. Avocations: golf, music, fishing. Home: 1009 S Texas St Deridder LA 70634 Office: Merryville HS 7061 Hwy 110 W Merryville LA 70653

JOSLIN, LESLIE ALLEN, writer; b. Chelsea, Mass., Apr. 15, 1943; s. Leslie Hugh and Lorieta (Mogford) J.; m. Patricia King, Dec. 5, 1970; children: Amy, Wendy. BA, San Jose State Coll., 1966; MA, U. Colo., Boulder, 1974; MPhil, U. London, 1984. Intelligence officer USN, 1967-88; instr. Cen. Oreg. Cmty. Coll., Bend, 1989—; adj. Oreg. State U., Bend, 1999—; owner, pub., cons. Wilderness Assocs., Bend, Oreg., 1992—. Author: (books) Uncle Sam's Cabins, 1995, Toiyabe Patrol, 1993, Wilderness Concept and the Three Sisters Wilderness, 2000; editor: (book) Walt Perry, 1999. Wilderness educator/ ranger, Deschutes Nat. Forest, Bend, Oreg., 1990—. Recipient Cmty. Achievement award, Deschutes Nat. Forest, 1997, Nat. Wilderness Edn. Leadership award, USDA Forest Svc., 2000, Meritorious Svc. medal, Dept. Defense, Washington, 1978, 87, U.S. Navy, 1988, Joint Svc. Commendation medal, Dept. Defense, 1984. Mem. Ret. Officers Assn. (cen. oreg. chap.), Forest History Soc., Archaeol. Soc. Cen. Oreg., Deschutes Co Historical Soc. Avocations: writing, reading, walking, restoring historic ranger stations. Office: Wilderness Assocs PO Box 5822 Bend OR 97708-5822 E-mail: lesjoslin@aol.com.

JOSLIN, ROBERT SCOTT, pharmaceutical company executive; b. Indpls., May 28, 1929; s. Fred A. and Mildred A. Joslin; m. Mary C. Flannagan (div. Aug. 1978); children: Jeffrey S., Mark W., Jennifer A.; m. Nancy J. Korbar, Aug. 11, 1984. BS in Pharmacy, Purdue U., 1951, MS in Pharm. Chemistry, 1955, PhD in Ind./Phy. Pharm., 1959. Registered pharmacist, Ind. Sr. pharm. chemist Eli Lilly & Co., Indpls., 1958-65; dir. pharm. rsch. William H. Rorer, Inc., Ft. Washington, Pa., 1965-74; assoc. dir. pharm. R & D G. D. Searle & Co., Skokie, Ill., 1974-78; corp. dir. pharm. R & D Baxter Labs., Deerfield, Ill., 1978; cons., recruiter Joslin & Assoc., Ltd., Barrington, Ill., 1978—. Contbr. articles to profl. publs. Capt. USNR, 1947—. Recipient Nat. Lunsford-Richardson award, 1957. Fellow Am. Inst. Chemists, Am. Assn. Pharm. Sci., Acad. Pharm. Sci.; mem. AAAS, Am. Chem. Sci., Parenteral Drug Assn., N.Y. Acad. Scis., Midwest Pharm. Discussion Group, Internat. Pharm. Fedn., Chicagoland Pharm. Discussion Group (founder, past chmn.), Sigma Xi, Phi Lambda Upsilon, Kappa Psi, Rho Chi. Achievements include patents for drug delivery and processing. Home and Office: 291 Deer Trail Ct Ste C Lake Barrington IL 60010-1773

JOSLIN, ROGER SCOTT, insurance company executive; b. Bloomington, Ill., June 21, 1936; s. James Clifford Joslin and Doris Virginia (McLaflin) Joslin Browning; m. Stephany Moore, June 14, 1958; children: Scott, Jill, James BS in Bus., Miami U., 1958; JD, U. Ill., 1961. Bar: Ill. 1961. Assoc. Davis, Morgan & Witherell, Peoria, Ill., 1961-63; controller Union Ins. Group, Bloomington, Ill., 1963-64; asst. v.p. State Farm Mut., Bloomington, 1964-69, v.p., controller, 1969-77, v.p., treas., 1977-87, sr. v.p., treas., 1989-98, vice chmn., CFO, 1998—2003; ret. Chmn. bd. State Farm Fire and Casualty Co.; v.p., bd. dirs. State Farm Gen. Ins. Co.; bd. dirs. State Farm Mutual; treas. State Farm County Mut. Co. Tex.; v.p., treas., bd. dirs. State Farm Lloyds, Inc., State Farm Internat. Services, Inc., State Farm Investment Mgmt. Corp., State Farm Growth Fund, Inc., State Farm Balanced Fund, Inc., State Farm Interim Fund, Inc., State Farm Mcpl Bond Fund, Inc.; bd. dirs. State Farm Life Ins. Co., State Farm Life and Accident Assurance Co., State Farm Annuity and Life Ins. Co. Mem. Bloomington Bd. Edn., 1980-91, pres., 1983-84, 85-86; trustee 2d. Presbyn. Ch., 1971-74, pres. bd. trustees, 1973-74; bd. dirs. Brokaw Hosp., 1981-84; pres. BroMenn Healthcare, 1984-86, bd. dirs., 1984-89; bd. dirs. Western Ave. Cmty. Ctr., 1979-85, pres., 1981-83; bd. overseers RAND's Inst. for Civil Justice, 1989-98; chmn. Ins. Info. Inst., 1998—; chmn. bd. trustees Neighborhood Housing Svcs. Am., 1994—, The Social Compact, 1995-98, Natural Disaster Coalition, 1997-98—. Mem. ABA, Ill. State Bar Assn., McLean County Bar Assn., Ill. Soc. C.P.A.s, Miami U. Alumni Assn. (exec. council 1971-74) Presbyterian. Home: 2001 E Cloud St Bloomington IL 61701-5733

JOSLYN, WALLACE DANFORTH, retired psychologist; b. Cape Girardeau, Mo., Apr. 13, 1939; s. Lewis Danforth and Margaret Bernice (Gallup) J.; m. Annette Andre, Aug. 27, 1966 (div. Feb. 1969); m. Moreen V. Drescher, May 26, 1979; children: Jonathan David, Sarah Analisa Malathi. BA, U. Va., 1961; MS, U. Wis., 1965, PhD, 1967. Diplomate V. Frankl Inst. Logotherapy, 1993. Rsch. assoc. Oreg. Regional Primate Rsch. Ctr., Beaverton, 1967-71; clin. psychologist Knoxville divsn. VA Ctrl. Iowa Health Care Sys., Iowa, 1972-97; ret. Asst. prof. U. Oreg. Health Scis. U., 1970. Contbr. articles to profl. jours. NIMH fellow. Avocations: photography, track and field, travel, investing, history. Home: 802 E Competine Knoxville IA 50138-1955 E-mail: wdjoslyn@lisco.com.

JOSS, PAUL CHRISTOPHER, astrophysicist, atmospheric physicist, educator; b. Bklyn., May 7, 1945; s. Everett Henry and Magda Anna (Hohorst) J.; m. Marjorie Jean Axton, Jan. 24, 1970 (div.); 1 child, Susan Elizabeth; m. Karen Elizabeth Murray, July 3, 1992 (div.); 1 child, Matthew Albert Henry. BA, Cornell U., 1966, PhD, 1971. Mem. Inst. for Advanced Study, Princeton, N.J., 1971-73; asst. prof. MIT, Cambridge, 1973-78, assoc. prof., 1978-83, prof., 1983—, mem. Ctr. for Theoretical Physics, 1973—, mem. Ctr. for Space Rsch., 1973—, assoc. head astrophysics divsn., 1983-88. Vis. scientist Weizmann Inst. Sci., Rehovot, Israel, 1974—75, 1978, Inst. Astronomy, Cambridge, England, 1977, 93; vis. staff mem. Los Alamos (N.Mex.) Sci. Lab., 1979—80, cons., 1980—92, Visidyne Inc., Burlington, Mass., 1979—82, 1992—93, spl. asst. to pres., 1993—2000, sr. scientist, 2000—; mem. adv. com. Inst. Geophysics and Planetary Physics Los Alamos Nat. Lab., 1987—92; mem. High Energy Astrophysics Mgmt. Ops. Working Group NASA, 1988—91; mem. Astronomy and Space Physics Sci. Coun. Univs. Space Rsch. Assn., 1988—92; mem. Inst. for Theoretical Physics U. Calif., Santa Barbara, 1991; pres. Joss Consulting Assocs., 1992—. Contbr. 140 articles to profl. jours.; editor 140 articles to profl. jours. Woodrow Wilson Found. fellow, 1966; NSF fellow, 1970; Alfred P. Sloan Found. fellow, 1976. Mem. Am. Astron. Soc. (Helen B. Warner Prize 1980, exec. com. High Energy Astrophysics div. 1983-85), Am. Phys. Soc., Internat. Astron. Union, Phi Beta Kappa. Avocations: classical music, chess. Office: MIT Dept Of Physics Rm 37-607 Cambridge MA 02139 E-mail: joss@space.mit.edu.

JOST, LAWRENCE JOHN, lawyer; b. Alma, Wis., Oct. 9, 1944; s. Lester J. and Hazel L. (Johnson) J.; m. Anne E. Fisher, June 10, 1967; children— Peter, Katherine, Susan. BSCE, U. Wis., 1968, JD, 1969. Bar: Wis. 1969, U.S. Dist. Ct. (ea. dist.) Wis. 1969, U.S. Ct. Appeals (7th cir.) 1969, U.S. Supreme Ct. 1980. Law clk. to judge U.S. Dist. Ct., Milw., 1969-70; assoc. firm Brady, Tyrrell, Cotter & Cutler, 1970-74; assoc. Quarles & Brady, 1974-76, ptnr., 1976—, chair real property sect., 2002—, coord. real estate group, 1985—. Vis. tchr. gen. practice Wis. Law Sch. Bd. dirs. Milw. Chamber Theatre, 1998-2001, Marcus Ctr. for the Performing Arts, 2003—; pres. Vis. Nurse Assn. Milw., 1982-85, VNA, Corp., 1982-86; bd. dirs. Wis. Heritage Inc., 1980-82, Vis. Nurse Found., 1986-95, pres., 1993-94; bd. dirs. Milw. Repertory Theater, 1995-2001—, pres., 1990-92; bd. dirs. United Performing Arts Fund, 1989-93. Mem. ABA, Wis. Bar Assn. (lectr. seminars), Milw. Bar Assn., Am. Coll. Real Estate Lawyers, Am. Coll. Mortgage Attys. Mem. Plymouth United Ch. of Christ Office: Quarles & Brady LLP 411 E Wisconsin Ave Ste 2550 Milwaukee WI 53202-4497

JOST, TIMOTHY STOLTZFUS, law educator; b. Reedley, Calif., Nov. 25, 1948; s. Arthur P. and Esther Ruth (Goosen) J.; m. Ruth Stoltzfus, Jan. 2, 1982; children: Jacob, Micah, David. BA, U. Calif., Santa Cruz, 1970; JD, U. Chgo., 1975. Bar: Ill. 1975, Ohio 1982. Atty. Legal Assistance Found. of Chgo., 1975-81; from asst. to assoc. prof. law Ohio State U., Columbus, 1981-87, prof. law, 1987-92, acting dir. Health Policy Ctr., 1994-96, Newton, Baker, Baker & Hostetler prof., 1992-2001; Robert L. Willett Family prof. Washington and Lee U., Lexington, Va., 2001—. Cons. Inst. of Medicine, 1984-85, 2000-01; guest prof. U. Gottingen (Germany), 1996-97. Author: Readings in Comparative Health Law and Bioethics, 2001, Disentitlement, 2003, (casebook) Health Law, 1987, 4th edit., 2001, Property Law, 1989, Regulation of the Health Care Professions, 1997, The Law of Medicare and Medicaid Fraud and Abuse, 1998, 2d edit., 2000. Supervising mem. State Mental Bd. of Ohio, Columbus, 1967-92. Deutsche Acad. Austausch Dienst grant, 1995, Fulbright grant, 1989, 1996-97. Mem. Am. Soc. Law and Med. Ethics, Nat. Health Laywers Assn., AALS (aging and law sect. chair 1990), Nat. Acad. Social Ins. Democrat. Mennonite. Home: 1370 Lincolnshire Harrisonburg VA 22802 Office: Washington & Lee U Sch Law Lexington VA 24450 E-mail: jostt@wlu.edu.

JOTCHAM, THOMAS DENIS, marketing communications consultant; b. Llandudno, Wales, Feb. 21, 1918; s. George James and Marion (Brand) J.; m. Margaret Jean Thirlwell, Aug. 10, 1940 (dec.); children: Patricia, Douglas, Joy, Candace (dec.), m. Thelma M. Archer, April 29, 2002. Student, Lower Can. Coll., 1929-36, McGill U., 1937-39. Sales rep. Montreal Lithographing Co., Ltd., Montreal, 1945—47; sales mgr. Wesco Waterpaints Can., Ltd., Montreal, 1947—48; advt. mgr. Pepsi-Cola Co. Can., Ltd., Montreal, 1948—52, mgr., 1952—54; asst. advt. mgr. Reader's Digest Assn., Ltd., Montreal, 1954—56; mgr., v.p. Foster Advt. Ltd., Montreal, 1956—73, exec. v.p., 1973—75, pres., 1977—81, vice chmn., 1981—83; pres. Sherwood Communications Group Ltd., Toronto, 1977—81, vice chmn., 1981—83. Mem. coun. Montreal Bd. Trade, 1973-75, v.p., 1977-78, pres., 1979, hon. chmn., 1980-81. Bd. dirs. Grace Dart Hosp., 1973-83, pres., 1979-83; bd. dirs. Can.Coun. Christians and Jews, 1978-81, Les Grands Ballets Canadien, 1976-77; mem. Venetion Condominium, Inc., pres. 1984, 88-92; treas. Freedom Found.-Broward, 1999-2000.

Maj. Can. Army, 1940-45. Recipient ACA Gold medal, 1978; charter recipient McGill Mgmt. Achievement award, 1981. Fellow: Inst. Can. Advt. (pres. 1976—77); mem.: Advt. Agy. Coun. Que. (pres. 1975—76), Advt. and Sales Assocs. Montreal (pres. 1948—49), Advt. and Sales Execs. Club (pres. 1956—58), Can. Advt. and Sales Assn. (pres. 1960—61), Can.- South African Soc. (bd. dirs. 1980—89, chmn. 1983—86), Internat. Swimming Hall of Fame (chmn. 1998—99), Coral Ridge Yacht Club (gov. 1993—97, commodore 1997), St. James Club (com. chmn. 1979—81), Mt. Stephen Club (pres. 1967—68), Royal Montreal Golf Club, Ft. Lauderdale Golf and Country Club (bd. dirs. 1990—92), Thistle Curling Club (pres. 1977—78), Ont. Club, Psi Upsilon. Home and Office: 2000 S Ocean Dr #1510 Fort Lauderdale FL 33316-3813 Office Fax: 954-524-1653.

JOTHI, RISHYUR K. surgeon; b. Calcutta, India, July 19, 1939; s. Rishyur Subrahmaniam and Uma (Krishnamurthi) Krishnam; m. Chandrika Jothi, Feb. 5, 1971; children: Shambhavi, Sumana. MBBS, Madras Med. Coll., Madras, India, 1963. Diplomate Am. Bd. Surgery. Chief thoracic and vascular surgery Naval Hosp., Oakland, Calif., 1989-91; pvt. practice in gen. and vascular surgery Mt. Diablo Med. Ctr., Concord, Calif., 1991—, John Muir Med. Ctr., Walnut Creek, Calif., 1991—. Served to capt. M.C., USN, 1970-91. Decorated Navy Commendation medal. Fellow ACS. Avocations: tennis, photography. Office: 2485 High School Ave Concord CA 94520-1819

JOU, JERWEN, psychology educator; b. Chechiang, China, Sept. 22, 1945; came to U.S., 1978; s. Sushiao and Yinfang Jou; m. Chian-hua Tsai, Apr. 21, 1974; children: Henry, Chin. BA in Edn., Nat. Chengchi U., Taipei, Taiwan, 1969; MA in Linguistics, Fujen U., Taipei, 1975; MS in Psychology, East Tex. State U., 1980; PhD in Psychology, Kans. State U., 1990. H.s. tchr., Taiwan, 1970-72; asst. editor Far East Book Co., Taipei, 1972-75; instr. linguistics Providence U., Taichung, Taiwan, 1975-78; instr. psychology Kans. State U., Manhattan, 1989-90; asst. prof. psychology Ga. So. U., Statesboro, 1990-93; lectr. psychology U. Tex.-Pan Am., Edinburg, 1993-94, from asst. prof. to assoc. prof. psychology, 1994-2000, prof., 2000—. Contbr. articles, papers, and abstracts to profl. jours. Mem. Am. Psychol. Soc., Psychonomic Soc. Avocations: reading, exercise, watching discovery channel. Home: 410 N Depot Rd Edinburg TX 78541 Office: U Tex-Pan Am Edinburg TX 78541-2999 E-mail: jjou@panam.edu.

JOUKOWSKY, ARTEMIS A. W. private investor; b. Shanghai, Dec. 26, 1930; s. Artemis M.W. and Helen (Skvorzov) J.; m. Martha Content Sharp, June 9, 1956; children: Nina Lydia Koprulu, Artemis W. III, Michael A. AB, Brown U., 1955, LLD (hon.), 1985. Dep. to dir. Am. Internat. Underwriters, Milan, 1960-66, dep. to regional dir. for Europe, 1963-66, regional v.p. for Middle East, North Africa Beirut, 1966-72, pres., regional dir. S.E. Asia Hong Kong, 1972-74, v.p. N.Y.C., 1974-77; mng. dir. Middle East Assurance and Reinsurance Co., Beirut, 1966-72; dir. Tam Sigorta, Istanbul, Turkey, 1967-72, Union Atlantique de Reassurance SA, Brussels, 1979-88, European Am. Underwriters, Vienna, 1979-87; dir., shareholder's rep. AIG Joint Ventures with Govt. Agencies, N.Y.C., 1979-87, pres. socialist countries div. and spl. world markets div., 1977-87. Founder, chmn. Brown U. Sports Found., 1983—; trustee Brown U., Providence, 1985—, vice chancellor 1988-97, chancellor, 1997-98, chancellor emeritus, 1998--, mem. bd. fellows, 1998—; chmn. campaign for rising generation for Brown U., 1991-96, chmn. campaign for Brown Med. Sch., 1997-2002; mem. bd. overseers Thomas J. Watson Inst. for Internat. Studies, 1981—; mem. vis. com. Ctr. for Old World Archaeology and Art, 1981-92; vice chmn. bd. govs. John Carter Brown Libr., 1988—; trustee Lawrenceville Sch., N.J., 1984—, pres. bd. trustees, 1997-2001; chmn. Archaeol Inst. Am., 1992—; pres. bd. trustees Am. Ctr. Oriental Rsch., Amman, Jordan, 1992—; mem. vis. com. Boston Mus. Fine Arts, 1985-92; dir. Clear Pool Camp, 1976-85; co-founder Am. Sch. Milan, 1962, bd. govs., 1961-65, pres. 1963-64, fin. com. 1962-65; trustee St. Croix Landmark Soc., Fredericksted, U.S. V.I., 1995—; trustee Internat. Rsch. and Exchs. Bd., 1998—. Decorated Order of the Cedars Govt. Lebanon, Order of Independence medal Jordan. Mem. U.S. C. of C. (gov. Hong Kong chpt.), U.S.-USSR Trade and Econ. Coun. (tourist and travel com. 1974-77), Hungarian-Am. Trade and Econ. Coun. (vce chmn. 1984-87), Exploreer's Club (N.Y.C.), India House (N.Y.C.), Hong Kong Club (life), Brown Club (N.Y.C.), Larchmont (N.Y.) Yacht Club, St. Croix Yacht Club (U.S. V.I.) Univ. Club (Providence), Hope Club (Providence), Knickerbocker Club (N.Y.C.). Office: Brown U 5 Benevolent St Providence RI 02912-9018

JOUNG, JOHN J. chemical engineer, researcher; b. Chungsong, Kyung sang buk-Do, Republic of Korea, June 29, 1941; arrived in U.S., 1968; s. Kee B. Joung and Chae N. Kim; m. Catherine K. Joung, Jan. 20, 1968; children: Thomas K., Sandra K. BSChemE, Seoul Nat. U., 1963, MSChemE, 1967; PhD in Chem. Engring., U. N.Mex., 1970. Rsch. assoc. U. Chgo., 1971—76; sr. rsch. scientist Colgate-Palmolive, Barrington, Ill., 1976—78; sci. advisor Am. Hosp. Supply Corp., Glendale, Calif., 1978—81; rsch. dir. Amoco Corp., Naperville, Ill., 1981—96; v.p. Xytel Corp., Elk Grove Village, Ill., 1996—98; prin. proposal engr. ADV Solutions and Svcs., Schiller Park, Ill., 1998—. Contbr. articles to profl. jours. Lt. Korean Mil., 1963—65. Postdoctoral Rsch. fellow, USAEC, 1970. Mem.: AIChE. Achievements include patents for polymer, biotechnology and medical device. Avocations: reading, gardening, hiking. Home: 6095 Mill Bridge Ln Lisle IL 60532

JOURDREN, MARC HENRI, investment banking company executive; b. Paris, Dec. 28, 1960; s. Pierre Auguste Jourdren and Berthe Augustine Dubois. Diploma in econs. and fin., Essec, Paris, 1983; MBA, Harvard U., 1987. Pres., founder Essec Enterprises Internat., Paris, 1982-83; attache French Ministry of Economy and Fin., N.Y.C., 1983-85; assoc. Goldman Sachs & Co., N.Y.C. and Tokyo, 1987-88, Goldman Sachs Internat., London, 1988—2003, v.p., exec. dir., 1991—2000, head Japanese equities, 1996-99, head global products group, 1999—2003, mng. dir., 2000—03, Lehman Bros., 2003—. Fgn. advisor Harvard U., Cambridge, Mass., 1989—. Mem. Wigmore Hall London, Soc. Couserans Pyrenees, Brit. Mensa Ltd. Avocations: piano, russian art, gastronomy, nature, skiing. Home: 48 Macready House Crawford St London W1H 5LP England Office: Lehman Bros 25 Bank St London E14 England Business E-Mail: marc.jourdren@lehman.com.

JOURNEY, DREXEL DAHLKE, lawyer; b. Westfield, Wis., Feb. 23, 1926; s. Clarence Earl and Verna L. Gilmore (Dahlke) Journey Gilmore; m. Vergene Harriet Sandsmark, Oct. 24, 1952; 1 child, Ann Marie. *Wife Vergene Journey, Registered Nurse St Mary's School of Nursing, 1947 and a member of the National Capitol Harp Ensemble, Holds various concert harp performance credits, including ensemble appearances at the White House and the John F. Kennedy Center for the Performing Arts.* BBA, U. Wis., 1950, LLB, 1952; LLM, George Washington U., 1957. Bar: Wis. 1952, U.S. Dist. Ct. (we. dist.) Wis. 1953, U.S. Supreme Ct. 1955, U.S. Ct. Appeals (4th cir.) 1960, U.S. Ct. Appeals (5th cir.) 1961, U.S. Ct. Appeals (D.C. cir.) 1965, U.S. Ct. Appeals (7th and 9th cirs.) 1967, U.S. Ct. Appeals (1st cir.) 1969, D.C. 1970, U.S. Dist. Ct. D.C. 1970, U.S. Ct. Appeals (2d, 3d, 6th, 8th and 10th cirs.) 1976, U.S. Ct. Appeals (11th cir.) 1981. Counsel FPC, Washington, 1952-66, asst. gen. counsel, 1966-70, dep. gen. counsel, 1970-74, gen. counsel, 1974-77; ptnr. Schiff, Hardin & Waite, Washington, 1977—. Mem. mediation program U.S. Dist. Ct. (D.C. cir.), 1989—, early neutral evaluation program, 1989-95; mem. case evaluation program D.C. Superior Ct., 1991—. Author: Corporate Law and Practice, 1975; contbr. articles to profl. jours. Pres. Am. U. Park Citizens Assn., Washington, 1970-72; trustee Lincoln-Wesmoreland Housing Project, Washington, 1978-79. With Mcht. Marine Res., USNR, 1944-46, USNG, 1948-50. Knapp scholar U. Wis., 1952. Mem. ABA, FBA, Energy Bar Assn., Masons, Army and Navy Club, Phi Kappa Phi, Phi Eta Sigma, Theta Delta Chi. Republican. Congregationalist. Home: 4540 Windom Pl NW Washington DC 20016-2452 Office: Schiff Hardin & Waite 1101 Connecticut Ave NW Ste 600 Washington DC 20036-4390 E-mail: djourney@schiffhardin.com.

JOVANOVIC, MIROSLAV N. economics educator; b. Novi Sad, Yugoslavia, Jan. 19, 1957; s. Nikola and Elena (Mocko) J.; m. Ljiljana Vilhar, Apr. 23, 1983; children: Jovan, Nikola. BA, U. Belgrade, Yugoslavia, 1979; postgrad., U. Armsterdam, 1980-81; MA, U. Belgrade, Yugoslavia, 1985; postgrad., Queen's U., Kingston, Ont., Can., 1986-87; PhD, U. Belgrade, Yugoslavia, 1988. Teaching asst. dept. econs. Queen's U., Kingston, Can., 1986-87; econ. NAFTA-GAS, Novi Sad, 1982-89; assoc. econ. officer Ctr. on Transnat. Corps. UN, N.Y.C., 1989-92; assoc. econ. affairs officer ECE, UN, Geneva, 1992—. Vis. lectr. European Summer Acad., Spetsae, Greece, U. Geneva. Author: Economics of the European Economic Community, 1985, International Economic Integration, 1992, 2d edit., 1998, European Economic Integration: Limits and Prospects, 1997, Geography of Production and Economic Integration, 2001; co-author: EEC and the Developing Countries, 1990; editor: International Economic Integration: Critical Perspectives on the World Economy, 4 vols., 1998; co-editor: The Challenge of Free Economic Zones in Central and Eastern Europe, 1991. Recipient award Vojvodina Coun. for Sci. Rsch., 1988, award Govt. Can., 1986, award Dutch Govt., 1980. Mem. Am. Econ. Assn., Royal Econ. Soc., European Community Studies Assn. Serbian Orthodox. Avocations: bicycling, skiing. Home: Rue de St Jean 32A CH-1203 Geneva Switzerland Office: UN ECE-Transport Divsn Palais des Nations CH-1211 Geneva Switzerland E-mail: miroslavjovanovic@hotmail.com., miroslav.jovanovic@unece.org.

JOVE, RICHARD, molecular biologist; b. Barcelona, Catalunya, Spain, Feb. 5, 1955; came to U.S., 1960; s. Ricardo and Maria Rosa (Calmet) J.; m. Hua Yu, June 21, 1984. BA, SUNY, Buffalo, 1977, MS, 1978; M in Philosophy, Columbia U., 1981, PhD, 1984. Postdoctoral fellow Rockefeller U., N.Y.C., 1984-88; asst. prof. U. Mich., Ann Arbor, 1988-94, assoc. prof., 1994-95, dir. molecular oncology program Cancer Ctr., 1992-95; prof. oncology, biochemistry and pathology U. So. Fla. Sch. Medicine, Tampa, 1995—; Frank and Carol Morsani prof. molecular oncology U. South Fla. Sch. Medicine, Tampa, 2003—; dir. molecular oncology program Moffitt Cancer Ctr. and Rsch. Inst., Tampa, 1995—; assoc. dir. basic rsch. Moffitt Rsch. Inst., Tampa, 2003—. Recipient John S. Newberry prize Columbia U., 1984, Jr. Faculty Rsch. award Am. Cancer Soc., 1988-91; Damon Runyon-Walter Winchell Cancer Fund fellow, 1984-87; named Scientist of the Yr., Moffitt Cancer Ctr., 2002, named Frank and Carol Morsani prof. molecular oncology, 2003—. Mem. The Harvey Soc., Sigma Xi. Office: U So Fla Moffitt Cancer Ctr 12902 Magnolia Dr Tampa FL 33612-9416 E-mail: richjove@moffitt.usf.edu.

JOVICK, ROBERT L. lawyer; b. Butte, Mont., Oct. 2, 1950; m. Stacy Towle, June 23, 1976; children: Janelle, Torey, Jay. BS in Indsl. Engring., Mont. State U., 1972; JD, U. Mont., 1975. Bar: Mont. 1975, U.S. Dist. Ct. Mont. 1975, U.S. Supreme Ct. Pvt. practice, Livingston, Mont., 1975—. City atty. City of Livingston, 1975-95. Sec. Livingston Community Trust, 1987—. Mem. Livingston Golf Club (pres. 1990). Methodist. Avocations: fly fishing, hiking, history of montana. Office: PO 1245 227 S 2nd St Livingston MT 59047-3001

JOWDY, JEFFREY WILLIAM, development executive; b. New Bern, N.C., Oct. 1, 1959; s. Albert Willoughby and Millicent (McKendry) J. BA in Journalism, U. Ga., 1983, postgrad. in speech communication, 1983-85; MA in Pers. Mgmt., Troy (Ala.) State U., 1987. Cert. fund raising exec. Employee relations mgr. Phoebe Putney Meml. Hosp., Albany, Ga., 1985-87; dir. South Ga. chpt. March of Dimes Birth Defects Found., Macon, Ga., 1987-90; devel. dir. Mount de Sales Acad., Macon, 1990-94; sr. mng. dir. Jerold Panas, Linzy & Ptnrs., 1994—97; sr. v.p. YMCA of Mid. Tenn., Franklin, 1997—2003; pres. Lighthouse Counsel, 1999—. Bd. dirs. Hamilton Holt Ednl. Loan Fund, mem. Nat. Ctr. for non-profit Bds. Alumni bd. dirs. Henry Grady Coll. Journalism, U. Ga.; bd. dirs. Joe C. Davis YMCA Outdoor Ctr.; mem. Ga. Coun. on Planned Giving; mem. Christian Stewardship Assn. Mem. Assn. Fundraising Profls. (pres. Nashville chpt.), SAR (founder, pres. Ocmulgee chpt.), Macon C. of C., Macon Heritage Found., Assn. Fundraising Profls. (pres.-elect Nashville chpt.), Mid. Ga. Cedars Club (v.p., chmn. pub. rels., bd. dirs.), Kiwanis (v.p., pres. Macon chpt., Kiwanian of Yr. award 1989), Rotary Club of Nashville, Commerce Club, Phi Kappa Theta (sec. Delta Rho Found., founder, pres. Gamma Sigma Alumi chpt.). Home: PO Box 681325 Franklin TN 37068-1325 Office: 228 Circle View Dr Franklin TN 37067

JOWERS, RONNIE LEE, university health sciences center executive; b. Columbia, S.C., July 4, 1951; s. Talbert Joseph and Mary Helen (Reed) J.; m. Kay Byars, July 6, 1974; children: C. Ryan, Ivey Amanda. BA, Furman U., 1973; MBA, Clemson U., 1984. Acct., mortgage banker First Piedmont Mortgage Co., Greenville, S.C., 1972-76; fin. mgr. Greenville Hosp. System, 1976-80; bus. mgr. Greenville Gen. Hosp., 1980-81; adminstr., med. edn. Greenville Hosp. System, 1981-87; adminstv. dept. medicine Emory U., Atlanta, 1987-91, assoc. v.p. for health affairs, 1991-2000, v.p. for health affairs, 2000—; CFO Emory Healthcare, 1995—. Bd. dirs. Clifton Casualty Ins. Co.; co-mgr. Emory Med. Care Found., Atlanta, 1989—90; chmn. adv. coun. S.C. Consortium of Cmty. Tchg. Hosps., Charleston, SC, 1982—86; adj. asst. prof. Med. U. S.C.; bd. dirs. Emory Adventist Hosp., 2002—, vice chmn. bd. dirs., 2003—. Transp. chmn. Beat Leukemia Celebrity Classic, 1988—97; Sunday sch. tchr. Smoke Rise Bapt. Ch., Stone Mountain, Ga., 1989—94, 2000—, deacon, 1991, fin. com., 1989—94, 1998—2000, 2002—, chmn., 1996, 1998; mem. nat. planning com. Sr. Adminstrn. of Acad. Health Ctr. meetings, program chmn., 1997; treas. Greenville Hosp. Sys. Credit Union, 1980—84, pres., 1985. Mem. Am. Coll. Healthcare Execs. (assoc.), Acad. Health Ctrs. Assn., mem. of Ways and Means Com., Emory Univ., Beta Gamma Sigma. Baptist. Avocations: baseball card and autograph collecting, magic. Home: 1980 Grace Arbor Ct Atlanta GA 30329

JOY, BILL See JOY, WILLIAM

JOY, CARLA MARIE, history educator; b. Denver, Sept. 5, 1945; d. Carl P. and Theresa M. (Lotito) J. AB cum laude, Loretto Heights Coll., 1967; MA, U. Denver, 1969, postgrad., 1984-87. Instr. history Cmty. Coll., Denver; prof. history Red Rocks C.C., Lakewood, Colo., 1970—. Cons. for innovative ednl. programs; reviewer fed. grants, 1983-89; mem. adv. panel Colo. Endowment for Humanities, 1985-89. Contbr. articles to profl. publs. Instr. vocat. edn. Mile High United Way, Jefferson County, 1975; participant Jefferson County Sch. Sys. R-1 Dist., 1983-88; active Red Rocks C.C. Spkrs. Bur., 1972-89, strategic planning com., 1992-97; chair history discipline Colo. Gen. Edn. Core Transfer Consortium, 1986-96, faculty transfer curriculum coun., 1997—; mem. Colo. C.C. curriculum com., 1999—; mem. history, geography, civics stds. and geography frameworks adv. com. Colo. Dept. Edn., 1995-96; steering com. Ctr. Tchg. Excellence, 1991-92, 96-97; with North Ctrl. Self-Study Process, 1972-73, 80-81, 86-88, 96-98; with K-16 Linkages Colo. Commn. for Higher Edn., 1997-98; mem. evaluation team for Colo. Awards, edn. and civic achievement for Widefield Sch. Dist. #3, 1989; mem. Red Rocks C.C.-Clear Creek Sch. Sys. Articulation Team, 1990-91; mem. Statue of Liberty-Ellis Island Found. Inc., 1987—. Ford Found. fellow, 1969; recipient Cert. of Appreciation Kiwanis Club, 1981, Telecomm. Coop. for Colo.'s Cmty. Colls., 1990-92, Master Tchr. award U. Tex.-Austin, 1982. Mem. NEA, Am. Hist. Assn., Am. Assn. Higher Edn., Nat. Coun. Social Studies, Nat. Geog. Soc., Omohundro Inst. Early Am. History and Culture, Colo. Edn. Assn., Colo. Coun. Social Studies, World Hist. Assn., Orgn. Am. Historians, The Colo. Hist. Soc., Colo. Geog. Alliance, Soc. Hist. Edn., Phi Alpha Theta. Home: 1849 S Lee St Apt D Lakewood CO 80232-6252 Office: Red Rocks C C 13300 W 6th Ave Lakewood CO 80228-1213

JOY, EDWARD BENNETT, electrical engineer, educator; b. Troy, N.Y., Nov. 15, 1941; s. Herman Johnson and Elizbeth (Bennett) J.; m. Patricia Marie Huddleston, Aug. 27, 1966; children: Frederick Huddleston, Rebecca Elizabeth. BEE, Ga. Inst. Tech., 1963, MSEE, 1967, PhDEE, 1970. Asst. prof. elec. engring. Ga. Inst. Tech., Atlanta, 1970-75, assoc. prof., 1975-80, prof., 1980-98, prof. emeritus, 1998—; pres. Joy Engring. Co., Boulder, Colo., 1981—. Cons. to cos., govtl. agys., orgns. Patentee in field; contbr. to profl. publs. Lt. USN, 1963-65, Vietnam. Fellow IEEE; mem. Antenna Measurements Techniques Assn. (past vice-chmn., tech. coord., disting. achievement award). Republican. Presbyterian. Avocations: amateur radio, electronics, hiking. Home and Office: 1450 Rembrandt Rd Boulder CO 80302-9478

JOY, ROBERT JOHN THOMAS, medical history educator; b. South Kingstown, R.I., Apr. 5, 1929; s. Angelo Francois and Mary Frances (Egan) Joy; m. Beverly June Boxer, July 5, 1952 (div. May 1984); children: Robert L.F., Lisa; m. Janet Lucille Brady, July 12, 1985. BS, U. R.I., 1950; MD, Yale U., 1954; MA, Harvard Coll., 1965; cert., Armed Forces Staff Coll., 1968. Commd. 1st lt. U.S. Army, 1954, advanced through grades to col., 1970; intern, then resident Walter Reed Army Med. Ctr., Washington, 1954-58; asst. dir. environ. medicine U.S.A. Med. Rsch. Lab., Fort Knox, Ky., 1959-61; comdr. U.S.A. Rsch. Inst. for Environ. Medicine, Natick, Mass., 1961-62; chief comdr. U.S.A. Med. Rsch. Team, Saigon, Vietnam, 1965-66; chief med. rsch. div. Office of Surgeon Gen., U.S. Army, Washington, 1968-69; dep. med. and life scis. Office of Dir. Def. Rsch. and Engring., Washington, 1969-71; dep. dir., then dir. Walter Reed Inst. Rsch., Washington, 1971-76; prof., chmn. mil. medicine Uniformed Svcs. U. Health Scis., Washington, 1976-81, prof., chmn. med. history, 1981-96, prof. emeritus, 1996—; ret. U.S. Army, 1981. Hon. mem. faculty Indsl. Coll. Armed Forces, Washington, 1990; faculty mem. USAF Sch. Aerospace Medicine, 1992—. Editor: Jour. History Medicine and Allied Scis., 1983—87; contbr. :, editor (monographs on mil. medicine). Decorated Disting. Svc. medal, Legion of Merit (4); recipient John Shaw Billings award, Am. Mil. Surgeons of U.S., 1986, William P. Clements award Uniformed Svcs., U. Health Scis., 1980. Fellow: Coll. Physicians Phila., AAAS, ACP (Davies award Med. Humanism 2002); mem.: Am. Physiol. Soc., Am. Assn. History Medicine (coun. 1979-81) (William Osler medal 1954), Osler Soc. (bd. govs. 1986-89). Home: 5821 Highland Dr Bethesda MD 20815-5531 Office: Uniformed Svcs U Dept Med History 4301 Jones Bridge Rd Bethesda MD 20814-4712

JOY, WILLIAM N. (BILL JOY), former computer company executive; BSEE, U. Mich., 1975, MSEE and Computer Sci., 1982. Co-founder Sun Microsystems Inc., Mountain View, Calif., 1982, v.p. rsch., 1996—98, chief scientist, 1998—2003. Prin. designer U. Calif. (Berkeley) version of UNIX operating sys.; co-designer Java tech., SPARC microprocessor architecture. Recipient Lifetime Achievement Award, USENIX Assoc., 1993. Mem. NAE; co-chmn., Presidential Info. Tech. Adv. Com., 1997.*

JOYAUX, ALAIN GEORGES, art museum director; b. East Lansing, Mich, Oct. 28, 1950; s. Georges Jules and Jane (Peckham) J.; 1 child, Daniel Edgar BFA in Studio Art, Mich. State U., 1973, MFA in Studio Art, 1976, MA in Art History, 1978. Acting dir. Kresge Art Mus., Mich. State U., East Lansing, 1978; asst. dir. Flint Inst. Arts, Mich., 1978-83; dir. Ball State U. Art Gallery (name changed to Mus. of Art), Muncie, Ind., 1983—. Author exhbn. catalogues, 1981—. Mem. Am. Assn. Mus., Intermus, Conservation Assn. (bd. dir. 1985-93). Office: Ball State U Museum of Art 2000 W University Ave Muncie IN 47306-1022 E-mail: ajoyaux@bsu.edu.

JOYCE, ANNE RAINE, editor, director of publications; b. South Bend, Ind., Oct. 2, 1942; d. James Agee and Marjorie Elizabeth (Gilstrap) Raine; m. Glenn Russell Joyce, Aug. 19, 1962; 1 child, Adam Russell. AB, Cen. Meth. Coll., 1962; MA in French, U. Mo., 1966; MA in Linguistics, U. Iowa, 1979. Cert. tchr., Mo. Tchr. Centralia (Mo.) High Sch., 1962-64; instr. Coe Coll., Cedar Rapids, Iowa, 1978-79, Georgetown U., Washington, 1980-83; asst. editor Am.-Arab Affairs, Washington, 1983-84; editor, dir. publs. Mid. East Policy, Washington, 1984—; gen. sec. Mid. East Policy Coun., Washington, 1991—, v.p., 1993—. Mem. edn. com. Fairfax County (Va.) PTA Bd., 1986-88. U.S. Dept. Def. fellow, 1964-66; recipient Recognition award Am.-Arab Affairs Coun., 1988, Disting. Alumni award. Cen. Meth. Coll., 1990. Mem. Middle East Studies Assn., LWV (fin. chair Fairfax county chpt. 1981—). Home: 6916 Tulsa Ct Alexandria VA 22307-1730 Office: Middle East Policy Coun 1730 M St NW Ste 512 Washington DC 20036-4516

JOYCE, BERNITA ANNE, former federal government agency administrator; d. Albert A. and Margaret C. Joyce; m. Kenneth B. Lucas, Aug. 2, 1975. BA, Duchesne Coll.; MBA, U. Santa Clara, PhD, 1974. With Wolfe & Co. CPAs, Washington, 1971-72; fin. dir. Nat. Forest Products Assn., Washington, 1972-74; budget and fiscal officer ICC, Washington, 1974-77, Office Mgmt. and Budget, 1977-80; asst. dir. mgmt. svcs. Bur. Mines, Dept. Interior, 1980-85; asst. dir. Office Policy Analysis, Dept. Interior, 1985-96, asst. spl. trustee Am. Indians, 1996—99; asst. treas. S.J. Cmty. Georgetown U., 2000—. Author: Financial Viability of Private Elementary Schools. Mem. AICPAs, Sr. Execs. Assn., Assn. Govt. Accts., Cosmos Club, Beta Gamma Sigma, Cosmos Club. Home: 6001 Bradley Blvd Bethesda MD 20817-3807

JOYCE, EDWARD ROWEN, retired chemical engineer, educator; b. St. Augustine, Fla., Oct. 20, 1927; s. Edward Rowen and Annie Margaret (Cobb) J.; m. Leland Livingston White, Sept. 11, 1954; children: Leland Ann, Julia, Edward Rowen III, Theo, Adele. BS in Chem. Engring., U. Miss., 1950; M of Engring., U. Fla., 1969; MBA, U. North Fla., 1975. Registered profl. engr., Fla. Petroleum engr. Texaco, Harvey, La., 1953-55; project engr. Freeport Sulphur Co., New Orleans, 1955-59; chem. engr. SCM Corp., Jacksonville, Fla., 1959-81; profl. engr. Jacksonville Electric Authority, 1981-93, ret., 1993. Adj. prof. U. North Fla., Jacksonville, 1977—, Jacksonville U., 1989—; newspaper columnist Fla. Times Union, Jacksonville, 1970-87. Co-author: Sulfate Turpentine Recovery, 1971; author booklet; patentee in field. Sci. fair judge Duval County Sch. System, Jacksonville, 1960-92; co-chmn. adv. com. U. North Fla., 1981-85; merit badge advisor Boy Scouts Am., Jacksonville, 1960—; advisor Jr. Achievement, Jacksonville, 1963; vestryman, lay Eucharistic minister, sr. warden local Episcopal ch. Comdr. USN, 1950-53, Korea. Fellow Fla. Engring. Soc. (pres. Jacksonville chpt. 1983); mem. AICE (pres. Peninsular Fla. chpt. 1963-64), Phi Kappa Phi, Alpha Pi Mu, Gamma Sigma Epsilon. Democrat. Avocations: stamp collecting, coin collecting, water sports, camping. Home: 5552 Riverton Rd Jacksonville FL 32277-1361

JOYCE, JAMES DANIEL, clergyman; b. Spencer, Va., Jan. 12, 1921; s. James Garfield and Mary (Taylor) J.; m. Dorothy Beatrice Campbell, Aug. 2, 1946; 1 son, Kevin Campbell. AB in Religion, Johnson Bible Coll., 1945, Lynchburg Coll., 1946; BD, Butler U., 1949; MA in Biblical Theology, Yale U., 1952, PhD, 1958. Ordained to ministry Disciples of Christ Ch., 1943. Pastor Hanover Ave. Christian Ch., Richmond, Va., 1954-59; sr. student leader ecumenical inst. World Council Chs., Geneva, 1960; prof. New Testament and Bible theology Christian Theol. Sem., Indpls., 1961-62; dean grad. sem. Phillips U., Enid, Okla., 1962-74; pastor Bethany Christian Ch., Houston, 1974-80, Covenant Christian Ch., Houston, 1980—. W.E. Garrison lectr. Disciple students Yale U., 1963; Jesse M. Bader lectr. evangelism Drake U., 1968; columnist Christian Jour., 1962-80; bass soloist rec. Joy-ce Sounds, 1977; pres. World Conv. Chrs. of Christ, 1970-74, mem. exec. com., 1974—; lectr. for armed forces in Far East, 1968; adj. prof. speech and creative writing U. Houston and Houston Community Coll., 1981-82; prof. speech and writing Houston Community Coll., 1982—, also head dept. speech; mem. bd. mgrs. Pension Fund Disciples of Christ. Author: The Living Christ in Our Changing World, 1962, The Place of the Sacraments in Worship, 1967. Recipient cert. of merit Methodist Bishop of Korea, 1972. Mem. Am. Assn. Theol. Schs. (exec. com. 1966-72), Theta Phi. Home: 5211 Carew St Houston TX 77096-1319

JOYCE, KENNETH THOMAS, electronics company executive; BS in Acctg., St. Joseph's U., 1971; MBA in Fin., Drexel U., 1989. CPA. Acctg. KPMG Peat Marwick, 1971; v.p. fin., CFO Selas Corp. Am.; CFO Selas fluid Processing Corp. (subs. Linde AG); v.p., ops. controller Amkor Tech., Inc., West Chester, Pa., 1997; exec. v.p.; CFO, 1999—. Office: Amkor Tech Inc 1900 S Price Rd Chandler AZ 85248 Office Fax: 480-821-2616. Business E-Mail: kjoyce@amkor.com.

JOYCE, LARRY WAYNE, physician; b. Richlands, Va., June 7, 1962; s. Estil Larry and Charlotte Pearline (Dye) J. AS summa cum laude, Southwest Va. C.C., 1982; BS in Biology & Chemistry cum laude, East Tenn. State U., 1984; DO, U. Health Scis., 1989. Med. lab. tech. Mattie Williams Hosp., Richlands, Va., 1978-86; instr. biology lab. Southwest Va. C.C., Richlands, 1984-85, instr. microbiology lab., 1987, instr. chemistry, 1986; resident East Tenn. U., Quillen Coll. Medicine, Johnson City, 1989-94; asst. prof. dept. pathology East Tenn. State U., Johnson City, Tenn., 1994-98, asst. clin. prof. pathology, 1998—. Staff pathologist VA Med. Ctr., Mountain Home, 1994-98, Clinch Valley Med. Ctr., Richlands, Va., 1998-2003. Author: HIV Disease 1993, 94, 95, 96, 97, 98, 99, 2000, 01. HIV ednl. outreach Tri-Cities AIDS Project, Johnson City, 1990-92 (svc. awards 1990, 91); HIV educator Lambda Soc., Johnson City, 1990. Mem. Am. Assn. Med. Pers., Am. Soc. Clin. Pathologists, Coll. Am. Pathologists, Am. Osteopathic Assn., Am. Osteopathic Coll. Pathologists. Avocations: computer, tennis, hiking, movies, music. Home: 128 Birch St Raven VA 24639 E-mail: riverwayne@hotmail.com.

JOYCE, MARY ANN, principal; b. Bklyn., May 29, 1935; d. Alfred and Antoinette (Polito) Lo Sasso; m. Michael J. Joyce, Jr., Mar. 2, 1957 (dec. 1982); children: Michael, Debra Grammer, Patricia Sommers. BA in Elem. Edn., Social Scis., Mount St. Mary Coll., 1972; MS in Elem. Edn., Reading, SUNY, New Paltz, 1975, CAS in Ednl. Adminstrn., 1983. Cert. tchr. N-6, N.Y., reading tchr., K-12, N.Y., sch. dist. administr., N.Y., sch. administr./supr., N.Y. Tchr.

grades 3 and 4 Temple Hill Sch., Newburgh, N.Y., 1972-74, tchr. reading, 1974-83, tchr. gifted and talented, 1976-83, asst. prin., 1983-85; prin. Horizons-on-the-Hudson Magnet Sch., Newburgh, 1985-98; exec. dir. curriculum and instrn. Newburgh Enlarged City Schs., 1998—. Tchr. summer sch. Newburgh (N.Y.) Free Acad., 1976-81; adj. prof. SUNY, New Paltz, 1989-91; nat. review panelist Blue Ribbon Sch. Competition, 1991, 92, FIRST family-sch. partnership program, 1992; speaker numerous confs., seminars. Recipient Elem. Sch. Recognition award U.S. Dept. Edn., 1989-90, 93-94, Excellence in Adminstrn. award Mid-Hudson Sch. Study Coun., 1993, award for Outstanding Leadership, Achievements and Contributions Toward Making the Edn. of our Nation's Youth a Safe and Productive Experience, 1991. Mem. ASCD, Am. Assn. Female Execs., Nat. Assn. Elem. Sch. Prins. (Excellence in Edn. award 1990, 94), State Adminstrs. Assn. N.Y. State (Elem. Schs. Excellence award 1990, 94), Newburgh Suprs. and Adminstrs. Assn., United Univ. Profs., Delta Kappa Gamma. Avocations: reading, sewing, needlework. Office: Newburgh Enlarged City Schs 124 Grand St Newburgh NY 12550-4615

JOYCE, MARY HOLT, retired social worker; b. Denver, July 10, 1915; d. Robert Vail and Mary Sayre (Stearns) Barkalow; m. Marmaduka Burrell Holt, Jr., Oct. 3, 1942 (wid. Oct. 1976); children: John S., Peter B., Katherine B.; stepchildren: Marmaduke B. III, Robert W., Alan M.; m. Robert Henry Joyce, May 1, 1981 (wid. Jan. 1985); 1 stepchild, Nancy J. Woodward. BA, Colo. Coll., 1938; Grad., U. Denver, 1941. Social worker Big Sister Agy., Denver, 1939-40; probation officer Denver Juv. Ct., 1940-42. Bd. dirs. Florence Crittendom Home, Denver, 1945-48; bd. trustees Graland Country Day Sch. 1940; pres. Women Vestry, St. John's Cathedral/Episcopal, 1960-61, founder Referral Svc. for Srs., 1987, co-chair search com. for dean, 1990-91. Mem. Colonial Dames, Monday Literary Club, Denver Art Mus., Colo. Symphony, Univ. Club. Episcopalian. Avocations: reading, music, travel, family. Home: Emerson St Apt 325 111 Park Ave W Denver CO 80205-3209

JOYCE, MICHAEL DANIEL, personal resource management therapist and consultant, neurolearning therapist; b. St. Cloud, Minn., June 8, 1948; s. Francis Daniel and Bernadette (Ferkinhoff) J.; m. Patricia Mary Boom, July 7, 1969. BA in Psychology and Sociology, St. Cloud State U., 1973, postgrad., 1977, Moorhead State U., 1993, Atwood Inst., 1993, Biofeedback Tng. and Treatment Ctr., 1994. Cert. behavior analyst, rsch. analyst, Minn., master practitioner of neuro-linguistic programming, Colo.; cert. hypnotherapist, neurolearning therapist; cert. in hemisphere specific auditory stimulation; cert. to practice hemisphere specific auditory stimulation; cert. in biofeedback; cert in EEG neurofeedback. Resident mgr. Dan J. Brutger, Inc., St. Cloud, 1969-71; rsch. analyst Faribault (Minn.) State Hosp., 1974-75, behavior analyst, 1975-76; therapist/behavior analyst Ctrl. Minn. Mental Health Ctr., St. Cloud, 1977-78; emotional/behavior disabled facilitator, chpt. 1 tutor Perham (Minn.) Dent Schs., 1978-92, dir. neurofeedback svcs. Tech. cons. Inclusive Edn. Tech. Assistance Team, Region IV, State of Minn., Perham, 1991-93, Personal Resource Strategies, Vergas, Minn., 1994-99; dir. neurotechnology svcs. A Chance To Grow, Mpls., 1999—; trainer and mentor Minn. Learning Resource Ctr., Mpls., 1999—. Co-author: Life-Threatening Behavior: Analysis and Intervention, 1982, Audio-Visual Entrainment Program as a Treatment for Behavior Disorders in a School Setting—Journal of Neurotherapy, 2001. Coord. Youth Assn. for Retarded Citizens, St. Cloud, 1977-78; respite care provider Ctrl. Minn. Mental Health Ctr., St. Cloud and Perham, 1977-78, 79 86; vol. Perham Schs., 1978—, Spl. Olympics - Winter Games, Duluth, Minn., 1980, 81. Named Mem. of Yr. Minn. Sch. Employees Assn., 1989. Mem. Neuro-Linguistic Programming (cert. master level), Internat. Med. and Dental Hypnotherapy Assn. (cert. neurolearning therapist). Avocations: organic gardening and orcharding, tree farming, basketball, computers, psycho-technology hardware and software. Home: 1749 Roselawn Ave W Saint Paul MN 55113-5757 E-mail: mdmjoyce@hotmail.com., mjoyce@mail.actg.org.

JOYCE, MICHAEL PATRICK, lawyer; b. Omaha, Oct. 3, 1960; s. Thomas Hunt and Joan Clare (Berigan) J. Student, Miami U., Oxford, Ohio, 1978-79; BSBA, Creighton U., 1982; JD, U. Houston, 1988. Bar: Mo., Kans., U.S. Dist. Ct. (we. dist.) Mo. 1988, U.S. Dist. Ct. Kans. 1989, U.S. Ct. Appeals (8th and 10th cirs.) 1988, U.S. Supreme Ct. 1994. Assoc. mgr. Avco Fin. Svcs. Internat., Inc., Omaha, 1983-85; assoc. Wyrsch, Atwell, Mirakian, Lee & Hobbs, P.C. (formerly Koenigsdorf & Wyrsch, P.C.), Kansas City, Mo., 1988-94; shareholder Wyrsch, Hobbs, Mirakian, & Lee, PC, Kansas City, Mo., 1995-97; pvt. practice, 1997-98; pres. The Joyce Law Firm, LLC, Kansas City, Mo., 1998-2000; shareholder Van Osdol, Magruder Erickson & Redmond, PC, Kansas City, 2000—. Adj. prof. U. Mo. Kansas City Sch. Law, 1997-2001. Asst. editor (newsletter State Bar Tex.) Caveat Vendor, 1987-88. Grad. NITA, 1992; bd. dirs. Creighton U., 1997-99. Mem. ABA, Nat. Assn. Criminal Def. Lawyers, Am. Health Lawyers Assn., Mo. Bar Assn., Mo. Assn. Criminal Def. Lawyers, Kans. Bar Assn., Kansas City Metro Bar Assn., Johnson County Bar Assn., Creighton U. Alumni Assn. (dir. region IV nat. alumni bd. dirs. 1994-96, pres. 1997-99), Creighton U. Alumni Club (pres. Kansas City area 1992-94). Roman Catholic. Avocations: golf, basketball, community service. Office: 2400 Commerce Tower 911 Main St Kansas City MO 64105-2009 E-mail: mpjoyce@vomer.com.

JOYCE, ROBERT E. philosopher, educator; b. Chgo., May 13, 1934; s. Peter J. and Mildred Wurtz J.; m. Mary Rosera, Aug. 12, 1961. BA, U. St. Mary of the Lake, 1957; MA, DePaul U., 1959; PhD, Internat. Coll., 1978. Instr. philosophy U. Notre Dame, South Bend, Ind., 1961-62; prof. philosophy St. John's U., Collegeville, Minn., 1962-94, prof. emeritus, 1994—. Author: New Dynamics in Sexual Love, 1970, Let Us Be Born, 1970, Human Sexual Ecology, 1980, Affirming Our Freedom in God, 2001; contbr. articles to profl. jours. Recipient Lumen Gentium award Thomas More Inst., 1972. Mem. Metaphys. Soc. Am., Am. Cath. Philos. Assn., Minn. Philos. Soc. Inst. Theol. Encounter Sci. Tech., Fellowship Cath. Scholars. Office: St Johns U Dept Philosophy Collegeville MN 56321 E-mail: rjoyce@csbsju.edu.

JOYCE, STEPHEN MICHAEL, lawyer; b. Los Angeles, Mar. 19, 1945; s. John Rowland and Elizabeth Rose (Rahe) J.; m. Bernadette Anne Novey, Aug. 18, 1973; children: Natalie Elizabeth, Vanessa Anne. BS, Calif. State U., Los Angeles, 1970; JD, U. LaVerne, 1976. Bar: Calif. 1976, U.S. Dist. Ct. (cen. dist.) Calif. 1977, U.S. Ct. Claims 1981. Pvt. practice, Beverly Hills, Calif., 1976-93; ptnr. Gold & Joyce, Beverly Hills, 1982-84. Personal atty. to Stevie Wonder and various other celebrities, 1977—. Contbr. articles to profl. jours. Served to pvt. USAR, 1963-69. Mem.: ABA, San Fernando Valley Bar Assn., Consumer Atty. of So. Calif. Assn., Beverly Hills Bar Assn., L.A. County Bar Assn., Calif. Bar Assn., Calabasas Tennis & Swim Club. Democrat. Roman Catholic. Avocation: long distance running. Home: 4724 Barcelona Ct Calabasas CA 91302-1403 Office: 15260 Ventura Blvd Ste 640 Sherman Oaks CA 91403-5340 E-mail: enjoyce2@aol.com.

JOYCE, VERONICA DELORES, writer, educator; b. N.Y.C., N.Y., Feb. 4, 1939; d. Otto Paul Mueller, Julia Madeline (Fraites) Mueller; m. Alfred Robert Joyce, Feb. 12, 1982; 1 child, Jennifer Venus Mackenzie. BS in Edn., Fordham U., 1973, MA in English, 1975; PhD of English Edn., NYU, 1978. Tchr. Leonia Jr. and Sr. H.S., Leonia, NJ, Bloomingdale H.S., Valrico, Fla. Cons. writing U. So. Fla., Tampa, Hillsborough County Bd. Edn., Tampa. Contbr. ; author (poem): Sunscripts. Mem.: Classroom Tchrs. Assn., Hillsborough Coun. Tchrs. English, Fla. Coun. Tchrs. English, Am. Fedn. Tchrs., Nat. Coun. Tchrs. English. Avocations: gardening, swimming, writing, travel, stamp collecting. Home: PO Box 5634 Sun City Center FL 33571 Office: Bloomingdale HS 1700 Bloomingdale Ave E Valrico FL 33594

JOYCE, WILLIAM GEORGE, JR., transportation executive; b. Oswego, N.Y., Nov. 24, 1949; s. William George and Nannette Davies J.; m. Patricia L., July 1, 1983; children: Tara, Kendra, Andrew. Student, SUNY, Oswego, 1967-71. Ops. mgr. Lake Shore Transp. Lines, Oswego, 1971-96; pres., CEO N.Y. State Motor Truck Assn., Inc., Albany, 1997—. Gen. chmn., treas. Maintenance Coun., Alexandria, Va., 1994-95; chmn. bd. dirs. N.Y. Motor Truck, Albany, 1994-96; first v.p. N.Y. Motor Carrier Conf., Buffalo, 1993-95. Mem. Am. Trucking Assn. (v.p. 1994-97), Am. Soc. Assn. Execs., Trucking Assns. (exec. coun., regional vice chair), N.Y. State Soc. Assn. Execs. Republican. Roman Catholic. Office: NYS MTA 828 Washington Ave Albany NY 12203 E-mail: bjoyce@nytrucks.org.

JOYCE, WILLIAM H. chemist; b. 1935; BS, Pa. State U., 1957; MBA, NYU, 1971, PhD, 1984. With Union Carbide Corp., Danbury, Conn., 1957—2001, past exec. v.p. ops., pres., COO, 1993—95, pres., CEO, 1995—96, chmn., pres., CEO, 1996—2001; vice chmn. The Dow Chem. Co., Danbury, 2000—. Bd. dirs. CVS Corp., Reynolds Metals Co. Recipient Nat. medal of Tech., NSF, 1993, Industry Achievement award, Plastics Acad., 1994, Lifetime Achievement award, 1997. Mem.: NAE, Am. Plastics Coun. (bd. dirs.), Soc. Chem. Industry (treas., bd. dirs.). Office: The Dow Chem Co 39 Old Ridgebury Rd Danbury CT 06810-5103

JOYCE, WILLIAM LEONARD, librarian; b. Rockville Centre, N.Y., Mar. 29, 1942; s. John Francis and Mabel Clare (Leonard) J.; m. Carol Gail Bertani, Aug. 13, 1967; children: Susan, Michael. BA, Providence Coll., 1964; MA, St. John's U., 1966; PhD, U. Mich., 1974. Manuscripts libr. William L. Clements Libr. U. Mich., Ann Arbor, 1968-72; curator manuscripts Am. Antiquarian Soc., Worcester, Mass., 1972-81, edn. officer, 1977-81; asst. dir. for rare books and manuscripts N.Y. Pub. Libr., N.Y.C., 1981-86; assoc. univ. libr. for rare books and spl. collections Princeton U., 1986-2000, Dorothy Foehr Huck chair for spl. collections Pa. State U., 2000—. Numerous cons. assignments including assessment and reporting project Nat. Hist. Publs. and Records Commn., Washington, 1982; lectr. Clark U., 1975-77; adj. faculty Sch. Library Service, Columbia U., N.Y.C., 1984-92; vis. prof. Grad. Sch. Libr. & Info. Sci. UCLA, 1994. Author: Editors and Ethnicity: A History of the Irish-American Press, 1848-1883, 1976; co-author: Documenting America: Assessing the Condition of Historical Records in the States, 1984; booklet Evaluation of Archival Institutions, 1982; co-editor: Printing and Society in Early America, 1983; editor: Catalog of Manuscripts Collections of the American Antiquarian Society, 4 vols., 1979; contbr. articles, revs. to profl. jours. Bd. dirs. Conservation Ctr. for Art and Hist. Artifacts, 1992-2000, chmn., 1995-98; mem. J.F.K. Assassination Records Rev. Bd., 1994-98; mem. adv. bd. Cannery Row Mus. Found., 1998-2000; mem. adv. com. Ctr. for Jewish History, 2000—, chmn., 2001—. Fellow Soc. Am. Archivists (coun. mem. 1981-85, pres. 1986-87); mem. Am. Hist. Assn. (mem. profl. div. com. 1979-81), Bibliog. Soc. Am. (chmn. fellowship com. 1982-85), Orgn. Am. Historians, Am. Antiquarian Soc., ALA (rare books and manuscripts sect., publs. com. 1985-88, chmn. 1987-88, mem. ARL spl. collections task force 2000-), Grolier Club (coun. 1990-93), Internat. Coun. on Archives (com. on lit. and art, 1993-97), Princeton Club (N.Y.C.). Office: Pa State Librs 110 Paterno Library University Park PA 16802-1808 E-mail: wlj2@psulias.psu.edu.

JOYCE, WILLIAM ROBERT, textile machinery company executive; b. Springfield, Ohio, Mar. 18, 1936, s. Robert Emmet and Christel Beatrice (Beekman) J.; m. Betty Arlene Provonsha, Aug. 29, 1959; children: Jennifer Lynn, Janet Cathleen. BA in Bus., Calif. We. U., 1982. Cert. mfg. engring. tech., Soc. Mfg. Engrs.; registered investment securities rep. Mfg. engring. Heinicke Instruments, Hollywood, Fla., 1964—68; div. mgr. Jensen Corp., Pompano Beach, Fla., 1969—72; pres. Textiles Supply, Inc., Gerton, NC, 1972—82; v.p., gen. mgr. Tex-Fab, Inc., Gerton, 1980—82; pres. Tex-nology Sys., Inc., Gerton, 1982—90, Corrib Enterprises Ltd., Automation Cons., Dana, NC, 1981—; owner The Silver Hammer Jewelry Store Chain, NC. Co-founder Assoc. Woodland Owners N.C.; mem. Hickory Nut Gorge Vol. Fire Dept., Gerton. Served with USAF, 1958 64. Recipient Innovative Devel. award, 1985, award, Optimist Club, 1953—54. Mem.: NSPE, Handmade in Am. Craft Orgn., We. Carolina Entrepreneurial Coun., Mountain Comml. Lending Consortium, Am. Inst. Design and Drafting, Soc. Mfg. Engrs., Guild Master Craftsmen (internat. mem.), Profl. Engrs. N.C., NRA. Republican. Baptist. Achievements include patents in field.

JOYCE-BRADY, MARTIN FRANCIS, medical educator, physician, researcher; b. Wilmington, Del., Sept. 25, 1953; s. Robert Lawrence and Marjorie Theresa (Martin) Brady; m. Jean Marie Joyce, Sept. 17, 1977; children: Jessica, Erin, Emily. BA in Arts & Scis., U. Del., 1975; MD, U. Md., Balt., 1979. Medicine intern Boston City Hosp., 1979-80, medicine resident, 1980-82, chief med. resident, 1982-83; pulmonary fellow Pulmonary Ctr., Boston U. Sch. Medicine, 1982-87, asst. prof. medicine, 1987-96, assoc. prof. medicine, 1997—; dir. pulmonary function lab. Boston City Hosp., 1987-96; dir. ventilator care unit Jewish Meml. Hosp., Boston, 1988—, dir. pulmonary and respiratory therapy, 1996—. Contbr. articles to profl. jours.; peer reveiwer articles to profl. jours. H. Fletcher Brown scholar Bank of Del., Wilmington, 1975, E.L. Trudeau scholar Am. Lung Assn., 1990-92; program project grantee on lung devel. NIH, 1991-96, 97-2002, 2002—. Mem. AAAS, Am. Soc. for Cell Biology, Mass. Med. Soc., Am. Thoracic Soc., Mass. Thoracic Soc. (chmn. rsch. grant com., 2003—) Achievements include proposition of alternative pathway hypothesis for type 1 alveolar epithelial cell differentiation during lung development; described novel role for lung surfactant in distributing amphipathic signal anchor proteins throughout the gas exchange surface of the lung; described novel role for gamma-glutamyl-transferase and its protein isoform in an endoplasmic reticulum stress response; described role of gamma glutamyl transferase-mediated glutatione metabolism in lung alveolar epithelial cell biology and lung redox homeostasis at the gas exchange surface of the lung. Office: Pulmonary Ctr 80 E Concord St Boston MA 02118-2307 E-mail: mjbrady@lung.bumc.bu.edu.

JOYNER, CHRISTOPHER CLAYTON, international relations educator; b. Aberdeen, Md., May 16, 1948; s. Houston Clay Joyner and Besse Hyde Sowers; m. Nancy Douglas, Dec. 27, 1972; children: Kristin Elizabeth, Clayton Douglas. BA magna cum laude, Fla. State U., 1970, MA, 1972, 73; PhD, U. Va., 1977. Co-dir. Ctr. for Peace and Environ. Studies Fla. State U., 1971-73, instr. dept. govt., 1972-73; asst. prof. polit. sci. Muhlenberg Coll., 1977-80; vis. prof. dept. govt. and fgn. affairs U. Va., 1980-81; asst. prof. polit. sci. George Washington U., Washington, 1981-85, assoc. prof., 1985-90, prof. dept. polit. sci. and Elliott Sch. Internat. Affairs, 1991-94; prof. dept. govt. sch. fgn. svc. Georgetown U., Washington, 1995—. Editl. advisor Internat. Legal Materials, 1988-90; vis. prof. government, Dartmouth Coll., 1989, 91, 93, 95, 97; profl. lectr. Sch. Advanced Internat. Studies Johns Hopkins U., 1991, 92; mem. editl. adv. bd. Rowman & Littlefield Pub., Prentice Hall Internat. Relations series, Transnat. Pubs.; mem. editl. adv. coun. U. Tasmania Antarctic and So. Oceans Law and Policy Paper Series. Author: Antarctica and the Law of Sea, 1992, Eagle Over the Ice: The U.S. in the Antarctic, 1997, Teaching International Law, 1997, Governing the Frozen Commons: The Antarctic Regime and Environmental Protection, 1998; editor: International Law of the Sea and the Future of Deep Seabed Mining, 1975, The Antarctic Legal Regime, 1988, The Persian Gulf War: Lessons for Strategy, Law and Diplomacy, 1990, United Nations Legal Order, 1995, The United Nations and International Law, 1997, Reining in Impunity for International Crimes and Serious Violations of Fundamental Human Rights, 1998, Governing the Frozen Commons: The Antarctic Regime and Environmental Protection, 1998; sr. editor Va. Jour. Internat. Law, 1973-77; mem. editl. bd. Polar Record, Va. Jour. Internat. Law, Internat. Studies Notes, Internat. Studies Quarterly, Global Governance, Case Western Res. Jour. Internat. Law, Ocean Devel. and Internat. Law, Terrorism: An Internat. Jour., 1988-92, Internat. Jour. Marine and Coastal Law, Polar Record contbr. numerous articles to profl. jours. Mem. governing bd., bd. dirs. Acad. Coun. on the UN Sys., 1999-2002, vice chair governing bd., 2001. With USAR, 1970-76. Grantee Inst. World Order, Inc., 1971-73, Ford Found., 1989-94, Nansen Inst./Tinker Found., 1992-94, Fridtjof Nansen Inst., 1995—; rsch. fellow Antarctic Ctr. for Rsch. and Cooperation, U. Tasmania, 1994, U. Canterbury, 2001, sr. rsch. fellow Woods Hole Oceanographic Instn., 1986-87. Mem. Am. Polit. Sci. Assn., Am. Soc. Internat. Law (life, exec. com. 1984-87, 1997-2000), Antarctican Soc. (bd. dirs. 1984-87), Internat. Studies Assn. (pres. internat. law sect. 1985-86, 1997-98, mem. governing coun. 1985-86, 96-97), Internat. Law Assn., Law of Sea Inst., Nat. Eagle Scout Assn., UN Assn., Golden Key Hon. Soc., Raven Soc. Hon., Phi Beta Kappa, Omicron Delta Kappa, Phi Kappa Phi, Pi Sigma Alpha, Phi Theta Kappa, Phi Alpha Theta. Democrat. Methodist. Avocations: jogging, autograph seeking, writing. Home: 3151 Borge St Oakton VA 22124 Office: Georgetown U Dept Govt Washington DC 20057-0001 E-mail: joynerc@georgetown.edu.

JOYNER, CLAUDE REUBEN, JR., physician, medical educator; b. Winston-Salem, N.C., Dec. 4, 1925; s. Claude R. and Lytle (Mackie) J.; m. Nina Glenn Michael, Sept. 21, 1950; children: Emily Glenn, Claude Courtney. BS, U. N.C., 1947; MD, U. Pa., 1949. Intern Hosp. U. Pa., 1949-50; resident Bowman Grey Med. Sch., 1950, U. Pa., 1954-55, fellow in cardiology; Nat. Heart Inst. trainee, 1952-53; asst. instr. medicine Hosp. U. Pa., Phila., 1951-53, instr., 1953-56, assoc. medicine, 1956-59, asst. prof., 1959-64, assoc. prof., 1964-72; prof. medicine U. Pitts., 1972-87, Med. Coll. Pa., 1987-96, vice dean, 1989-96; chief medicine Allegheny Gen. Hosp., Pitts., 1972-96. Contbr. articles to profl. jours. Served to lt. M.C. USNR, 1950-52. Fellow Am. Coll. Cardiology, ACP, Councils on Circulation, Arteriosclerosis and Cardiovascular Radiology of Am. Heart Assn.; mem. AAAS, Am. Heart Assn., Am. Clin. and Climatol. Soc. Home: Pulpit Rock 45 Little Sewickley Creek Rd Sewickley PA 15143 8393 Office: Allegheny Gen Hosp Pittsburgh PA 15212

JOYNER, DEE ANN, bank official; b. Alton, Ill., Feb. 26, 1947; d. T. Claxton and Dorothy M. (Troeckler) Burroughs; m. Orville Joyner, Mar. 15, 1973; 1 child, Dawn L. Kotva. BA in Govt., So. Ill. U., 1971, MS in Govt., 1973; MBA, St. Louis U., 1985. Adminstrv. asst. So. Ill. U., Edwardsville, 1970-72; staff assoc. Marshall Kaplan, Gans and Kahn, Washington, 1972-73; dir. community affairs East-West Gateway Coordinating Council, St. Louis, 1973-78; exec. dir. Coro Found., St. Louis, 1978-80, St. Louis County Econ. Council, Clayton, Mo., 1985-89; planning dir. St. Louis County, 1980-84, chief of staff to county exec., 1989-90; sr. v.p. Commerce Bank St. Louis, 1990—. Mem. Civil Svc. Bd., University City, Mo., 1984—93, Better Bus. Bur., 1991—93, Tax Increment Financing Commn./Indsl. Devel. Authority, University City, Mo., 1993—97, Alzheimers Assn., 1992—99, Girl Scout Coun. of Greater St. Louis, 1993—96, St. Louis Boundary Commn., 1999—2002; bd. dirs. Boys and Girls Town, 1994—, St. John's Mercy Med. Ctr., 1997—2000, Deaconness Found., 2002—; Bd. dirs. Confluence, St. Louis, 1983—89, Focus St. Louis, 1996—2002, bd. chmn., 1996—98; bd. dirs. Forest Park Forever, 2003—; mem. Automobile Club of Mo., 1995—, Delta Dental Mo., 1998—. Recipient Joseph E. Boland Meml. Outstanding Alumnus award St. Louis U., 1992, Spl. Leadership award YWCA, St. Louis, 1987, Janet Roede Ashcroft award for Cmty. Svc., Alzheimers Assn., 1999, Above and Beyond award for cmty. svc. St. Louis Bus. Jour., 2002. Mem. Leadership St. Louis, So. Ill. U. Alumni Assn. (Alumnus of Yr. 1994), Mo Women's Forum (bd. dirs. 1989-90, 2000-02), Univ. Club (bd. dirs. 1994-97). Office: 8000 Forsyth Blvd Saint Louis MO 63105-1707

JOYNER, J(AMES) CURTIS, judge; b. Newberry, S.C., Apr. 18, 1948; s. George C. and Joan C. (Glenn) J.; m. Mildred Ann Carter, Apr. 5, 1975; children: Jennifer Christine, Nicole Marie, Jacqlyn Ann. Student, Peirce Jr. Coll., Phila., 1967; BS in Acctg., Ctrl. State U., Wilberforce, Ohio, 1971; JD, Howard U., 1974. Bar: Pa. 1975, U.S. Dist. Ct. (ea. dist.) Pa. 1981. Contr. D.C. Project, Washington, 1972-73; legal publ. specialist Fed. Register, Washington, 1974-75; asst. dist. atty. Dist. Atty. Office Chester County, West Chester, Pa., 1975-80, chief dep. dist. atty., 1980-84, 1st asst. dist. atty., 1984-87; judge Ct. of Common Pleas, 15th Jud. Dist., West Chester, 1987-92, U.S. Dist. Ct. (ea. dist.) Pa., Phila., 1992—. Mem. coun. trustees West Chester U., 1983-2000, trustee emeritus, 2001. Named Trailblazer in Law Enforcement Gov. Thornburgh, 1986; recipient Outstanding Svc. award to law enforcement Pa. Criminal Investigators, 1987, Disting. Law and Justice award County and State Detectives Assn., 1988, Donald K. Anthony Alumni Achievement Hall of Fame Ctrl. State U., 1994, Pres.' Medallion for Svc. West Chester U., 2001. Mem. Fed. Bar Assn. (hon.), Chester County Bar Assn. Avocations: sports, jazz, golf. Office: US Dist Ct Rm 8613 601 Market St Philadelphia PA 19106-1714

JOYNER, JOHN WESLEY, psychologist, educator; b. Memphis, Dec. 2, 1928; s. Eli Green and Ritter Mae Joyner. Student, Mich. State U., 1954-58, Ferris State U., 1958; BS, Tenn. State U., 1960, MS, 1962; PhD, Ohio State U., 1972. Lic. tchr., Tenn., counselor, Ill., Ky., Psychologist, Ohio. Mgr. Pinnacle Lanes, Nashville, 1961-63; counselor Armstrong H.S., Washington, 1963-64, Sumner H.S., Cairo, Ill., 1964-67, Cairo H.S., 1967-69, West Ky. Area Vocat. Sch., Paducah, 1969-71; rschr. assoc. Ctr. for Vocat. Edn./Ohio State U., Columbus, 1971-72; staff counselor, instr. Psychol. Ctr. Coll. Edn./Ohio State U., Columbus, 1973; assoc. prof. psychology, dir. student devel. svcs. Counseling and Testing Ctr./Tenn. State U., Nashville, 1973-84; prof. psychology Tenn. State U., Nashville, 1984—. Adv. bd. multi cultural edn. enrichment program Tenn. State U., Nashville, 1998-2000; adminstrv. asst. Psychol. Cons. Ctr., Columbus, 1971-73; owner Test Preparation, Nashville, 1984—; cons. in field. Author: Student Self Directed Manual for the ACT, 2000. Active CORE, 1963-65, So. Poverty Law Ctr., 2000—. Staff sgt. U.S. Army, 1948-52, Germany. Recipient Rogers award for best counselor Fla. State U., 1965. Mem. NAACP, ACLU, AAUP, Am. Sch. Counseling Assn., Tenn. Counseling Assn., Phi Delta Kappa. Methodist. Avocations: politics, wildlife, sports, tv. Home: 3512 Geneva Cir Nashville TN 37209-1525 E-mail: jjoyner@tnstate.edu.

JOYNER, WALTON KITCHIN, lawyer; b. Raleigh, N.C., Apr. 1, 1933; s. William Thomas and Sue (Kitchin) J.; m. Lucy Holmes Graves, Sept. 23, 1955; children: Sue Carson Clark, Walton K. Jr., James Y. II. AB in Polit. Sci., U. N.C., 1955, JD with honors, 1960. Bar: N.C., cert. mediator; lic. comml. pilot. Ptnr. Joyner & Howison, Raleigh, 1960-80, Hunton & Williams, Raleigh, 1980—. Sec., treas. N.C. R.R. Co., Raleigh, 1966; bd. dirs. United Title Ins. Co., Raleigh; bd. mgrs. Wachovia Bank, N.C., 1969-98; bd. govs. U.S. Power Squadrons, 1974-81. Assoc. editor U. N.C. Law Rev. Pres. Rehab. and Cerebral Palsy Ctr. Wake County, Raleigh, 1974; trustee St. Mary's Coll., 1990-91; bd. dirs. Peace Coll. Found., 2001—. Mem.: Law Alumni Assn. U. N.C. (bd. dirs.), Wake County Bar Assn. (chmn., bd. dirs. 1977), N.C. Bar Assn. (treas. probate sect. 1983), Carolina Country Club (pres. 1983—84, 2000—01), Order of Coif, Phi Beta Kappa. Presbyterian. Avocation: flying. Home: 815 Marlowe Rd Raleigh NC 27609-7022 Office: Hunton & Williams 1 Hannover Sq PO Box 109 Fl 14 Raleigh NC 27602-0109

JOYNER, WEYLAND THOMAS, physicist, educator, business consultant; b. Suffolk, Va., Aug. 9, 1929; s. Weyland T. and Thelma (Neal) J.; m. Marianne Steele, Dec. 3, 1955; children: Anne, Weyland, Leigh. BS, Hampden-Sydney Coll., 1951; MA, Duke U., 1952, PhD, 1955. Teaching fellow Duke U., Durham, N.C., 1954, rsch. assoc., 1958; physicist Dept. Def., Washington, 1954-57; rsch. physicist U. Md., 1955-57; asst. prof. physics Hampden-Sydney Coll., 1957-59, assoc. prof., 1959-63, prof., 1963—, physics chmn., 1968-82, 85-87, Elliott prof., 1995-98; rsch. assoc. Ames Lab. AEC, 1964-65; vis. prof. Pomona Coll., 1965; staff Commn. on Coll. Physics, Ann Arbor, Mich., 1966-67; vis. fellow Dartmouth Coll., 1981. Mem. Panel on Preparation Physics Tchrs., 1967-68; nuclear physics cons. Oak Ridge Inst. Nuclear Studies, 1960-67; NASA-Lewis faculty fellow, 1982-84; pres. Piedmont Farms, Inc., 1958-75, Windsor Supply Corp., 1966-82, Three Rivers Farms, Inc., 1971-74, Windsor Seed & Livestock Co., 1969-83; ednl. cons. numerous colls. and univs., 1965-75; mgmt. cons., 1966—. Contbr. articles profl. jours. Bd. dirs. Prince Edward Acad., 1971-92, exec. com., 1975-92; trustee Prince Edward Sch. Electoral Bd., 1979-80. NASA prin. investigator, 1985-87. Fellow AAAS; mem. Am. Phys. Soc., Am. Assn. Physics Tchrs., IEEE, Va. Acad. Sci. (past mem. council, sect. pres.), Am. Inst. Physics (regional counselor, past dir. Coll. Program), Phi Beta Kappa, Sigma Xi, Lambda Chi Alpha. Presbyn. (trustee). Home: Venable Pl Hampden Sydney VA 23943 Office: Hampden Sydney Coll Gilmer Sci Ctr Hampden Sydney VA 23943

JOYNER KERSEE, JACQUELINE, former track and field athlete; b. East St. Louis, Ill., Mar. 3, 1962; d. Alfred and Mary Joyner; m. Bob Kersee, Jan. 11, 1986. BA in History, UCLA, 1985; LLD (hon.), Washington U., St. Louis, 1992, Iona Coll., 1994; DHL (hon.), Harris-Stowe State Coll., 1993, Fontbonne Coll., St. Louis, 1998, Spelman Coll., 1998, Howard U., 1999, George Washington U., St. Louis, 1999. Winner 4 consecutive Nat. Jr. Pentathlon Championships; winner heptathlon Goodwill Games, Moscow, 1986, U.S. Olympic Festival, 1986; winner USA/Mobil Outdoor Track and Field Championship, 1987; winner, long jump and heptathlon World Track and Field Championships, 1987; winner Grand Prix Indoor Championships, winner indoor world record 55m hurdles 7:37 seconds, 1989; winner heptathlon Goodwill Games, St. Petersburg, Russia, 1994; ret., 2001. Pres., founder JJK & Assocs., Inc. Author: (autobiography) A Kind of Grace: the Autobiography of the World's Greatest Female Athlete, 1997; co-author: A Woman's Place Is Everywhere, 1994. Founder JJK Cmty. Found. (name now JJK Found.); chmn. St. Louis Sports Commn., 1996-2000, chmn. emeritus, 2001—; Barbie Amb. of Dreams. Recipient Silver medal for heptathlon L.A. Summer Olympic Games, 1984, Sullivan award, 1986, Jesse Owens award, 1986, 87, Am. Black Achievement award Ebony mag., 1987, Gold medal for long jump at 24 ft. 3 1/2 in. and heptathlon Seoul Summer Olympic Games, 1988, 1st Female Athlete of Yr. award Sporting News, 1988, Gold medal for heptathlon Barcelona Summer Olympic Games, 1992, Bronze medal for long jump Barcelona Summer

Olympic Games, 1992, Gold medal for heptathlon World Track and Field Championships, 1993, Bronze medal in long jump in Atlanta, 1996, Jim Thorpe award, 1993, Jackie Robinson "Robie" award, 1994, Grand Prix Outdoor Champion, 1994, Parenting Leader award Parenting mag., Jesse Owens Humanitarian award, 1999, Humanitarian award Women Sports and Fitness, Pres.'s award Nat. Conf. Black Mayors; named Athlete of Yr., Track & Field News, 1986, Female Athlete of Yr., AP, 1987, Female of Yr. IAAF, 1994, St. Louis Ambassadors Sportswoman of Yr., Hon. Harlem Globetrotter, Goodwill Game heptathlon champion, 1986, 90, 94, 98, Woman Athlete of Century, Sports Illustrated, 1999; inductee Nat. Boys and Girls Club Hall of Fame Achievements include setting world record of 7161 points at U.S. Olympic Festival, 1986; set world record of 7291 points at Seoul Summer Olympic Games for heptathlon, 1988; holder Am. record in long jump, 1994, 50 meter hurdles, 60 meter hurdles. Office: Elite Internat Sports Mktg and Mgmt 1034 S Brentwood Blvd Ste 1530 Saint Louis MO 63117-1215

JOYNT, ROBERT JAMES, academic administrator, physician; b. Le Mars, Iowa, Dec. 22, 1925; MD, 1952, PhD, 1963. Diplomate Am. Bd. Psychiatry and Neurology (past pres.). Intern Royal Victoria Hosp., Montreal, Canada, 1952—53; chief neurology Strong Meml. Hosp., Rochester, NY, 1966—84; assoc. U. Iowa, Iowa City, 1957—58, asst. prof. neurology, 1958—61, assoc. prof., 1961-66; prof. neurology U. Rochester, 1966—, chmn. dept., 1966—84; dean U. Rochester Sch. Medicine and Dentistry, 1984—89; v.p. and vice provost for health affairs U. Rochester Sch. Medicine & Dentistry, 1989—94. Named Disting. Univ. Prof., 1997; fellow Neurology, USPHS, 1954—57; scholar Fulbright scholar, Cambridge U., 1953—54. Fellow: AAAS; mem.: AMA (chief editor Arch Neurology 1982—97), Am. Acad. Neurology (past pres.), Am. Neurol. Assn. (past pres.), Inst. Medicine, Royal Soc. Medicine, Am. Electroencephalographic Soc. Office: U Rochester Sch Medicine and Dentistry PO Box 673 Rochester NY 14642-0001 E-mail: robert_joynt@urmc.rochester.edu.

JOZEFOWICZ, RALPH FRANCIS, neurologist; b. Queens, N.Y., July 12, 1953; s. Henry Francis and Gabrielle T. Jozefowicz. BA, Johns Hopkins U., 1975; MD, Columbia U., 1979. Diplomate Am. Bd. Internal Medicine, Am. Bd. Psychiatry and Neurology. Resident U. Rochester, N.Y., 1979-85, fellow, 1985-87, asst. prof., 1987-92, asosc. prof., 1992-98, prof. neurology and medicine, assoc. chair edn., 1998—. Author: Case Studies in Neurology, 1998. Fellow ACP, Am. Acad. Neurology; mem. Am. Neurol. Assn. (Disting. Tchr. award 1998). Democrat. Roman Catholic. Avocation: choral music. Office: U Rochester Dept Neurology 601 Elmwood Ave Rochester NY 14642-0001 E-mail: ralph_jozefowicz@urmc.rochester.edu.

JOZWIAK, STEVEN JAY, lawyer; b. N.Y.C., Apr. 19, 1957; s. Leon and Selma Fern (Chaikin) J.; m. Erin Jo Chilbert, Dec. 27, 1994; 1 child, Theodore Samuel. BA, Rutgers Coll., 1979; Diplomate, San Diego U., 1981, Inst. Comparative & Internat. Law Oxford U., 1981; JD, Widener U., 1982; LLM, NYU, 1987. Bar: N.J. 1982, Pa. 1983, N.Y. 1984, U.S. Dist. Ct. N.J. 1983, U.S. Ct. Appeals (3rd cir.) 1986, U.S. Dist. Ct. (ea. dist.) Pa., 1992, U.S. Tax Ct., U.S. Supreme Ct., 2000; CPA N.J. Atty., owner Law Offices of Steven J. Jozwiak, Cherry Hill, N.J., 1986—. Adj. faculty Glassboro State Coll., 1983-84. Contbr. article to profl. jour. Bd. dirs. non-profit health orgs. Recipient Am. Jurisprudence award. Fellow N.J. Soc. CPA's; mem. ABA (mem. com. on tax acctg. problems taxation sect. 1980), Am. Asn. Atty. CPA's (pres. Phila. and greater Del. Valley chpt. 1998-2000), Nat. Assn. Accts., Camden County Bar Assn., Epsilon Delta Epsilon Hon. Fraternity, Phi Delta Phi Law Hon. Fraternity, Sigma Pi. Office: 2201 Route 38 Ste 200 Cherry Hill NJ 08002-4370 E-mail: jozco@aol.com.

JU, SEMMY, educational administrator; b. Peking, People's Republic of China, Sept. 11, 1945; came to U.S., 1970; B of Archtl. Engring., Chung-Yuan Christian Coll. Sci. and Engring., Chung-Li, Republic of China, 1969; M of Regional Planning, U. Mass., 1972. Planner, office phys. planning and constrn. U. Chgo., 1972-79; assoc. dir. office budget and planning No. Ill. U., DeKalb, 1979-88, project dir. remodeling Coll. of Law, 1979-82, project dir. planning and constrn. Student recreations Ctr., 1979-85; dir. for facilities planning and space mgmt. U. Ill., Chgo., 1988—94; dir. campus planning and constrn. mgmt. U. Fla., Gainesville, 1994—2000; assoc. v.p. facilities mgmt. Montclair (NJ) State U., 2000—. Mem. Nat. Assn. Coll. and Univ. Bus. Officers, Soc. Coll. and Univ. Planning. Avocation: tennis. Home: 100 Hepburn Rd Apt 12B Clifton NJ 07012-2232 Office: Montclair State U Office Facilities Mgmt Montclair NJ 07043

JU, WILLIAM DAVID, pharmaceutical executive; b. N.Y.C. s. David M.C. and Lily Ju. AB, Princeton U.; MD, U. Pa. Diplomate Am. Bd. Dermatology. Sr. staff fellow Nat. Cancer Inst., Bethesda, Md., 1991—92; asst. med. dir. Hoffmann-LaRoche, Nutley, NJ, 1992—94; assoc. dir. regulatory affairs Merck Rsch. Labs., Rahway, NJ, 1994—95, assoc. dir. clin. pharmacology, 1995—97, dir. clin. pharmacology, 1997—99, dir. project planning & mgmt., resource & rsch. planning, 2000—01; v.p. product devel. Pharmacia Corp., Peapack, NJ, 2001—03; COO, PTC Therapeutics, South Plainfield, NJ, 2003—. Contbr. articles to Jour. Investigative Dermatology. Bd. dirs. Chinese Am. Med. Soc., N.Y.C., 1997-2000; trustee The Peck Sch., Morristown, N.J., 1999—, Caldwell (N.J.) Coll., 1998—. Fellow Am. Acad. Dermatology (Stellwagon award 1990); mem. Phi Beta Kappa, Alpha Omega Alpha. Office: PTC Therapeutics 100 Corporate Ct South Plainfield NJ 07080

JU, YIGUANG, engineering educator; b. Tong Cheng, Anhui, China, July 21, 1964; BS, Tsinghua U., Beijing, 1986; MS, Tsinghua U., 1988; PhD, Tohoku U., Sendai, Japan, 1994. Rsch. assoc. Tohoku U., Sendai, 1994—95, asst. prof., 1995—98, assoc. prof., 1998—2000; prof. Tsinghua U., Beijing, 2000—01; asst. prof. dept. mech. and aerospace engring. Princeton U., NJ, 2001—. Dir. Inst. of Thermo Physics, Beijing, 2000—01. Recipient Young Rschr. award, Asia Pacific Combustion Com., Taiwan, 1999, Outstanding Young Rschr. award, Chinese Nat. Sci. Found., 2001; grantee Fluid Sci. grantee, Fluid Sci. Found., Japan, 1995. Mem.: ASME. Office: Princeton University Dept Mech/Aerospace Engring Olden St Princeton NJ 08544

JUANG, CHARNG HSEIN, adult education educator; m. Anne Yang; children: Kevin Anderson, Michael Andrew. PhD, Purdue U., 1978—81. EIT S.C. State, 1987. Prof., civil engring. Clemson U., 1992—. Contbr. more than 75 articles in refereed journals (T K Hsieh Award for best paper pub. by the Instn. of Civil Engineers, 2001). Grantee Research Grants, NSF, Multiple research grants since 1991. Mem.: Am. Soc. of Civil Engineers. Office: Clemson U 214 Lowry Hall Clemson SC 29634-0911 E-mail: hsein@clemson.edu.

JUAN-RAMON, V. HUGO, economist; b. Tucuman, Argentina, Oct. 21, 1951; s. Eulogio and Rosa (Presti) J. MA, U. Tucuman, Argentina, 1976, Ctr. Macroeconomic Studies Argentina, 1980; PhD in Econs., U. Chgo., 1988. Adj. prof. The Am. U., Washington, 1989-90; economist IMF, Washington, 1992-93, sr. economist, 1994-97, dep. divsn. chief, 1998—. Cons. The World Bank, Washington, 1989-90, Inter-Am. Devel. Bank, Washington, 1991-92. Office: IMF 700 19th St NW Washington DC 20431 E-mail: vjuanramon@imf.org.

JUARBE, FREDERICO, JR., federal agency administrator; b. P.R. Student, U. N.Mex., 1971—73. Mgmt. trainee Dale Carnetig Leadership Tng., Inst., 1965—71; asst. dir. VFW, 1971—78, dir., 1978—2001; asst. sec. vets. employment and tng. svcs. U.S. Dept. Labor, Washington, 2001—. With U.S. Army, 1962—65. Office: US Dept Labor 200 Constitution Ave NW Washington DC 20210

JUAREZ, ANTONIO, psychotherapist, consultant, counselor, educator; b. El Paso, Tex., Nov. 6, 1952; s. Juan Antonio and Amelia (Rivas) J. BS in Psychology, U. Tex.-El Paso, 1976, MA in Clin. Psychology, 1982; postgrad., N.Mex. State U., 1987—, Calif. Coast U., 1990—. Cert. counselor; cert. diplomate, Am. Psychotherapy Assn., lic. profl. counselor, Tex., PhD of Martial Arts, Ea. USA Internat. Coll. Martial Arts, Pittsburgh, 2000. Caseworker asst. El Paso Mental Health Ctr., 1978-79, caseworker III, 1982-83; clin. specialist S.W. Mental Health Ctr., Las Cruces, N.Mex., 1979-80; therapist, trainer S.W. Cmty. House, El Paso, 1980-81; psychol. cons. El Paso Guidance Ctr., 1981-82, psychotherapist, 1983—, dir. N.E. svcs.; pvt. practice El Paso, 1987—. Mem. Nat. Bd. for Cert. Counselors; dir. Cross-Cultural Counseling Ctr., 1988—; instr. psychology El Paso C.C., 1988-90, counselor, cons.; cons. Citizens and Students Together, El Paso, 1983—, group facilitator Tai Chi Chuan Instr., Sun Valley Regional Hosp., El Paso, Tex., 1988; psychotherapist, treatment team coord. El Paso State Ctr., 1997—; adj. prof. counseling Webster U., Ft. Bliss, Tex., 1995—. Mem. Latin Am. com. N.Mex. State U., 1985. Served with USAF, 1972-76. Fellow Am. Assn. Integrative Medicine, U.S.-N.Mex. Border Health Assn., El Paso Psychol. Assn., Tex. Assn. for Counseling and Devel., Tex. Assn. for Children of Alcoholics, Golden Key, Nat. Acad. for Clin. Mental Health Counselors, Ea. U.S.A. Martial Arts Assn. (Black Belt Hall of Fame 1996, Master of Wushu 2000), Ea. U.S.A. Internat. Martial Arts Assn. (named Man of Yr. 2003, Black Belt Hall of Fame 2003). Democrat. Roman Catholic. Avocations: martial arts, playing stringed instruments. Home: PO Box 1493 Santa Teresa NM 88008-1493 Office: Cross-Cultural Counseling Ctr 2112 Trawood Dr # 3B El Paso TX 79935-3318

JUAREZ, JOSÉ ROBERTO, JR., law educator; b. Laredo, Tex., May 25, 1955; s. José Roberto Sr. and María Antonia (Martínez) J.; m. Lorene Martínez Juárez, Aug. 8, 1981; children: Marisa Celia, José Roberto III, Marco Andrés. AB, Stanford U., 1977; JD, U. Tex., Austin, 1981. Bar: Tex. 1981, U.S. Ct. Appeals (5th cir.) 1983, U.S. Ct. Appeals (9th cir.) 1989, U.S. Dist. Ct. (so. and we. dists.) Tex. 1984. Staff atty. Gulf Coast Legal Found., Galveston, Tex., 1982, Mex. Am. Legal Def. & Ednl. Fund (MALDEF), San Antonio, 1983-87; regional counsel, dir. employment program MALDEF, L.A., 1987-90; assoc. prof. law St. Mary's U. Sch. Law, San Antonio, 1990-95, prof. law, 1995—, assoc. dean, 1997-99. Cons. Ford Found., N.Y.C., 1990-99, Intercultural R & D Assn., San Antonio, 1991. Contbr. articles to profl. jours., including Jour. Law & Inequality, St. Mary's Law Jour. Mem. ABA, Assn. Am. Law Schs. (chair sect. on employment discrimination 1994), State Bar Tex. Roman Catholic. Home: 108 Cas Hills Dr Castle Hills TX 78213-3322 Office: St Mary's U Sch Law One Camino Santa María San Antonio TX 78228 E-mail: bjuarez@stmarytx.edu.

JUAREZ, MARTIN, priest; b. Kansas City, Kans., Mar. 23, 1946; s. Martin Huerta and Hermelinda (Rocha) J. AS, Colby Community Coll., 1971; BA in sociology, U. Mo., Kansas City, 1974; MDiv, St. Thomas Sem., Denver, 1985; cert. in Hispanic ministry, Oblate Sch. of Theology, San Antonio, 1991, Mexican-Am. Cultural Ctr., 1991. Priest Archdiocese of Kansas City, Kans., 1981—. Bd. dirs. Pioneer Village, Topeka, 1983-88; co-dir. El Centro, Topeka, 1989. Mem. N.Am. Veterinary Tech. Assn. Office: PO Box 410695 Kansas City MO 64141-0695

JUBELIRER, ROBERT C. lieutenant governor; b. Altoona, Pa., Feb. 9, 1937; s. Samuel H. and Darothy (Brett) J.; 4 children. Grad., Pa. State U., Dickinson Sch. Law. Bar: Pa. Mem. Pa. Senate, Dist. 30, Harrisburg, 1974—; majority leader Pa. Senate, 1981-84, pres. pro tem, 1984—92, 1994—; lt. gov. Commonwealth of Pa., 2001—02. Chmn. Blair County Multiple Sclerosis Soc.; bd. dirs. Allegheny chpt. Nat. Multiple Sclerosis Soc.; mem. adv. coun. Hollidaysburg Vets. Home; past hon. chmn. Tuckahoe dist. Penns Woods coun. Boy Scouts Am.; hon. chmn. Jr. Achievement. Recipient 1st Freedom of Info. Day award Am. Sch. Counselors Assn., Miracle Mile Disting. Svc. award Pa. Rural Electric Assn., 1988, State Guardian of Sml. Bus. award Pa. chpt. Nat. Fedn. Ind. Bus., Disting. Svc. award Nat. Constable Assn., 1990, Fulton County Human Svcs. Coun. award for Leadership on Rural Health Issues, 1991; named Legislator of Yr., one of ten Outstanding Legislators of Yr. Nat. Rep. Legislators, Assn., 1985. Mem. Pa. Bar Assn., Blair County Bar Assn., Rotary, Masons. Republican. Office: 292 Capital Building Harrisburg PA 17120*

JUBERG, RICHARD KENT, b. Cooperstown, N.D., May 14, 1929; s. Palmer and Hattie Noreen (Nelson) J.; m. Janet Elisabeth Witchell, Mar. 17, 1956 (div.); children: Alison K., Kevin A., Hilary N., Ian C.T.; m. Sandra Jean Vakericks, July 8, 1989. BS, U. Minn., 1952, PhD, 1958. Asst. prof. U. Minn., Mpls., 1958-65; sci. faculty fellow Univerista di Pisa, Italy, 1965-66; assoc. prof. U. Calif., Irvine, 1966-72, U. Sussex, Eng., 1972-73; prof. U. Calif., Irvine, 1974-91, prof. emeritus, 1991—. Vis. prof. U. Goteborg, Sweden, 1981; mem. Courant Inst. Math. Scis., NYU, 1957-58. Contbr. articles to profl. jours. With USN, 1946-48, Guam. NSF Faculty fellow, Univ. Pisa, Italy, 1965-66. Mem. Am. Math. Soc., Tau Beta Pi. Democrat. Avocation: bird watching.

JUBINSKA, PATRICIA ANN, ballet instructor, choreographer, artist, artist; b. Norfolk, Va. d. Joseph John and Lucy (Babey) Topping; children: Vanessa Meredith, Courtney Hilary. Student, Md. State Ballet Sch., Sch. Am. Ballet, N.Y.C.; BA, R.I. Coll.; MA, Wesleyan U.; PhD, Union Inst., 1999. Mem. N.Y.C. Ballet; freelance artist Chamber Ballet of L.A., San Antonio Ballet, Md. State Ballet; artistic dir. Blackstone Valley Ballet, Harrisville, R.I., 1983-84, Am. Ballet, Pascoag, R.I., 1984-92; asst. artistic dir. Odessa Ukrainian Dancers, Woonsocket, R.I., 1991-92; freelance guest artist, 1992—; mem. Mandrivka Dancers of Boston, 1993—; mem. faculty Fine Arts West Warwick Sch., 1995—; mem. faculty Roger Williams U., 2000—. Avocation: equestrian. Home: 110 Gold Mine Rd Chepachet RI 02814

JUCEAM, ROBERT E. lawyer; b. NYC, June 16, 1940; s. Benjamin T. and Amelia B. (Spatz) J.; m. Eleanor Pam, May 24, 1970; children: Daniel, Jacquelyn, Gregory. AB cum laude, Columbia U., 1961, LLB, 1964, JD, 1972; LLM, NYU, 1966. Bar: NY 1965, US Dist. Ct. (so. and ea. dists.) NY 1966, US Tax Ct. 1968, US Ct. Appeals (2d cir.) 1967, US Supreme Ct. 1971, US Ct. Appeals (5th cir.) 1978, US Ct. Appeals (DC cir.) 1980, US Ct. Appeals (11th cir.) 1987, US Ct. Appeals (7th cir.) 1989, US Ct. Appeals (9th cir.) 1999. Law clk. US Dist. Ct., NY, 1964-66; assoc. Fried, Frank, Harris, Shriver & Jacobson, NY, 1966-73, ptnr., 1974—. Bd. dir. Nat. Network Def. of the Right to Counsel, Inc., 1985-89, Lawyers Com. for Human Rights, 1986-94, Bar Assurance and Reins. Ltd., 1991—, Am. Immigration Law Found., 1987—, pres., 1991-2000, treas., 2000—; gen. counsel US Supreme Ct. Hist. Soc., 1995—, trustee, mem. exec. com., 1999—; mem. arbitration panel US Dist. Ct. (ea. dist.) NY, 1986—; mem. comml. and constrn. panels Am. Arbitration Assn., 1972-94; dir. civil rights Washington Lawyers Com., 1996-99; mem. bd. advisors DC Bar Found., 1996-2001; treas., bd. dir. Pro Bono Inst., 1997—. Contbr. articles to legal jours. Trustee Mex.-Am. Legal Def. and Edn. Fund, 1986-90, chmn. program and planning com., 1988-90; adv. com. to task force on racial, gender and minority discrimination US Ct. Appeals for 2d Circuit, 1994-96; bd. dir. Appleseed Found., Inc., 1997-99; mem. bd. advisors Atlantic Legal Found., 2001—. Recipient Lester Zazuly medal, 1958, Columbia Coll. Alumni Achievement award, 1961, Edward Foxx prize Columbia Coll., 1961, Maldef Corp. Responsibility award, 1993, Valerie J. Kantor award for extraordinary achievement, 1997, Am. Immigration Law Found. hon. fellow and Founder's award, 1989, Lifetime Achievement award Ctr. for Human Rights and Constl. Law, 1993. Fellow Am. Bar Found. (life), NY State Bar Found.; ABA (ho. of dels. 1983—, chmn. com. on immigration sect. litigation 1985-90, immigration pro bono adv. task force, 1992-98, vice chmn., 1995-96, mem. coordinating com. on immigration law 1984-87, chmn. 1989-92, mem. com. environ. controls sect. banking, 1983-86, vice chmn. com. on constrn., sec. gen. practice 1989-90, mem. standing com. lawyers pub. svc. responsibility 1993-96, mem. coun. fund justice and edn. 1994-2000, 03—, adv. mem., 2000-02, chmn. major gifts com. 1997-98, Pro Bono award 1992); mem. Internat. Bar Assn. (chmn. Sect. Gen. Practice com. bus. migration 1987-88), NY State Bar Assn., Assn. Bar City of NY (com. on trademarks and unfair competition 1983-86, com. immigration 1986-89, com. on profl. and jud. ethics 1989-92, com. Human Rights Law 1994-96), Nat. Assn. Criminal Def. Lawyers (co-chmn. com. on immigration 1988-90), Am. Judicature Soc. (life), Am. Bar Endowment, Nat. Conf. Bar Presidents (assoc.), Am. Immigration Lawyers Assn. (pres. 1982-83, bd. gov. 1971—, chmn. NY chpt. 1971-72, gen. counsel 1986-91, liaison to ABA commn. on nonlawyer practice 1993-94, editor Ann. Symposium Handbook 1985-88, assoc. editor 1989-90, Edith Lowenstein Meml. award 1981, Pro Bono award 1992), Soc. Sachems, Fed. Bar Assn., NY County Lawyers Assn. (reporter NY Equitable Distbn. Law Proposals 1968, bd. dir. 1996-98), Def. Rsch. Inst., NY Criminal Bar Assn., NY State Trial Lawyers Assn., Assn. Profl. Responsibility Lawyers, Assn. Fed. Def. Lawyers, Cow Neck Peninsula Hist. Soc. (life), Italy and Colonies Philat. Soc. of Gt. Brit. (life), Jack Knight Soc. (life), LI Postal History Soc. (life), Am. Helvetia Philatelic Soc. (life), Am. Philat. Soc. (life), Internat. Fedn. Postcard Dealers, India House Club, Alpha Epsilon Pi. Home: 106 Hemlock Rd Manhasset NY 11030-1214 Office: Fried Frank Harris Shriver & Jacobson 1 New York Plz Ste 2500 New York NY 10004-1901

JUCHEM, ELMAR, musicologist, music educator, consultant; b. Frankfurt am Main, Hesse, Germany, Aug. 30, 1966; arrived in U.S., 1998; s. Gerhard Juchem and Irene Müller. PhD, Georg-August-Universität, Göttingen, Germany, 1998. Mgr. spl. projects Kurt Weill Found. for Music, N.Y.C., 1998—2000, dir. publs. and rsch., 2001—. Vis. prof. Folkwang Hochschule, Essen, North Rhine-Westphalia, Germany, 2002—. Author: (book) Kurt Weill und Maxwell Anderson: Neue Wege zu einem amerikanischen Musiktheater, 2000; co-author: (biography) Kurt Weill: A Life in Pictures and Documents, 1999; editor: (journal) Kurt Weill Newsletter, 2001—, (music edition) Unsung Weill: Songs Cut from Broadway Shows and Hollywood Films, 2002; co-editor: (corr. edit.) Kurt Weill: Briefe an die Familie, 2000—; translator: (biography) Kurt Weill: Ein Leben in Bildern und Dokumenten, 2000 (Süddeutsche Zeitung Non-fiction book of the month, 2000); curator (exhibitions) Kurt Weill: Making Music Theater, 2002; contbr. articles to profl. jours. Grantee, German Academic Exch. Svc., 1994, Kurt Weill Found. for Music, 1994, 1995, 1997; scholar, German Academic Exch. Svc., 1990—91, ERASMUS (European Union), 1993; vis. fellow, Yale U., 1995. Avocations: clarinet, volleyball, travel. Home: 140 Sixth Ave Brooklyn NY 11217 Office: Kurt Weill Found for Music 7 East 20th St New York NY 10003 Office Fax: 212-353-9663.

JUCKEM, WILFRED PHILIP, manufacturing company executive; b. Sheboygan, Wis., Apr. 27, 1915; s. Arvin M. and Martha (Henning) J.; m. Dorothy Iris Dean, Dec. 8, 1941; children— Jean Audrey, Philip Dean. Grad., Sheboygan Bus. Coll., 1934. With Jenkins Machine Co., Sheboygan Falls, Wis., 1933-34, Kohler of Kohler, Wis., 1934-42, Rock Island (Ill.) Arsenal, 1942-45; with Eagle Signal Corp., Moline, Ill., 1947-63, v.p. mfg., 1958-63; asst. to pres. E.W. Bliss Co., Canton, Ohio, 1963-64, adminstrv. v.p., 1964-66, v.p. press div., 1966-67, v.p. corporate devel., 1967-68; v.p., div. mgr. E.W. Bliss Co. (Eagle Signal div.), 1968-77; chmn. bd. Sears Mfg. Co., Davenport, Iowa, 1977-86. Dir. Long Mfg. N.C. Chmn. bd. dirs. Davenport Osteo. Hosp., 1969-80, chmn., 1980-82; bd. dirs. Ridgecrest Retiremenet Village, 1969-87. Chmn. bd. dirs. Davenport Osteo. Hosp., 1979-80, chmn., 1980-82; bd. dirs. Ridgecrest Retirement Village. Recipient Honorary Alumnus award St. Ambrose Coll., Davenport. Mem. Nat. Elec. Mfrs. Assn. (chmn. emeritus traffic control systems sect. 1972-77), Am. Ordnance Assn. (pres. Iowa-Ill. chpt. 1975-76), Asso. Employers Quad Cities (dir., past pres.) Lutheran. Home: Ridgecrest Village C-1 4130 Northwest Blvd Davenport IA 52806-4243

JUDA, RICHARD JOHN, anesthesiologist, critical care specialist; b. Glastonbury, Conn., Aug. 12, 1967; s. Richard Joseph and Frances Ann (Urbansky) J.; m. Mary deGroot. Student, Stonehill Coll., North Easton, Mass., 1985-86; BS in Biology/Health Sci., U. Hartford, 1989; cert. paramedic, Mohegan Cmty. Coll., Norwich, Conn., 1990; postgrad., Ctrl. Conn. State U., 1990-91; MD, St. George's U., Grenada, 1996. Cert. ACLS instr., Advanced Trauma Life Support, Pediatric Advanced Trauma Life Support. Intern U. Conn., 1996-97, resident in surgery, 1997-99, resident in anesthesia, 1999-2002, chief resident in anesthesia, 2001-2002; fellow in critical care anesthesia Yale U., 2002—; attending physician Manchester (Conn.) Meml. Hosp., 2003—. Asst. faculty dept. EMS edn. Hartford Hosp., 1990—, rsch. asst., 1986-91, 93-94; physician asst. Kingstown Med. Coll.-Kingstown Gen. Hosp., St. Vincent, W.I., 1993, Simon Bolivar Clin.-St. George's U. Sch. Med., 1992-93; presenter in field; med. cons. Glastonbury Fire Dept. Contbr. articles to profl. jours. Polish Nat. Alliance scholar, 1986-89, Geoffrey H. Bourne Meml. scholar, 1991-96. Mem. AMA, Am. Soc. Anesthesiologists, Am. Med. Student Assn., Nat. Assn. Grad. and Profl. Students, Internat. Trauma Anesthesia and Critical Care Soc., Conn. State Soc. Anesthesiologists, Soc. Critical Care Medicine. Roman Catholic. Home: 54 Partridge Landing Glastonbury CT 06033-2850

JUDAH, FRANK MARVIN, retired school system administrator; b. Guymon, Okla., Sept. 13, 1941; s. Frank Morris and Margaret (Vaughan) J.; m. Rita Kay Paschal, Oct. 28, 1966; children: Frances Margaret (dec.), Frank Martin. BA, Tex. Tech. U., 1965; MA, Tex. A&M U., 1975, PhD, 1980. Cert. tchr., ednl. adminstr., Tex. Tchr. Reagan County Ind. Sch. Dist., Big Lake, Tex., 1967-73; adminstrv. asst. City of Sweetwater, Tex., 1974-76; dir. purchasing Killeen (Tex.) Ind. Sch. Dist., 1977-81; asst. supt. for adminstrn. Seguin (Tex.) Ind. Sch. Dist., 1981-85; asst. supt. for bus. DeSoto (Tex.) Ind. Sch. Dist., 1985-97; ret., 1997. Civil svc. commr. City of DeSoto, 1988-93; trustee DeSoto Ind. Sch. Dist., 2000-2003, bd. sec., 2003. Mem. Tex. Assn. Sch. Bus. Ofcls. (vice-chmn. cert. com. 1984-97), Assn. Sch. Bus. Ofcls. Internat., Rotary (pres., sec. DeSoto club 1986-89), Masons (treas. DeSoto lodge 1409 1987-90, 98-99). Avocations: numismatics, gardening, physical fitness, recreational reading. Home: PO Box 90 Moody TX 76557-0090 E-mail: texpony@ev1.net.

JUDAH, NORMAN, information technology executive; married; 2 children. BSc in Engring., U. Witwatersrand; MSc in Applied Sci., U. Toronto. With Imperial Oil Ltd.; from mem. staff to v.p. Microsoft Corp., Redmond, Wash., 1990, v.p. bus. devel. Office: One Microsoft Way Redmond WA 98052-6399

JUDD, ASHLEY, actress; b. Granada Hills, Calif., Apr. 19, 1968; d. Michael Ciminella and Naomi Judd; m. Dario Franchitti, Dec. 12, 2001. Movies include Ruby in Paradise, 1993, Smoke, 1995, Heat, 1995, A Time to Kill, 1996, Kiss the Girls, 1997, Simon Birch, 1998, Eye of the Beholder, 1999, Double Jeopardy, 1999, Dexterity, 2000, Where the Heart Is, 2000, Someone Like You, 2001, High Crimes, 2002, Divine Secrets of the Ya-Ya Sisterhood, 2002, Frida, 2002(TV) Norma Jean and Marilyn, 1996, The Ryan Interview, 2000. Office: William Morris Agy 1 William Morris Pl Beverly Hills CA 90212-2775

JUDD, BRIAN RAYMOND, physicist, educator; b. Chelmsford, Eng., Feb. 13, 1931; s. Harry and Edith (Saltmarsh) J. BA, Brasenose Coll., Oxford U., 1952, MA, D.Phil., Brasenose Coll., Oxford U., 1955. Fellow Magdalen Coll., Oxford U., 1955-62; instr. U. Chgo., 1957-58; assoc. prof. U. Paris, 1962-64; staff mem. Lawrence Radiation Lab., Berkeley, Calif., 1964-66; prof. physics Johns Hopkins U., Balt., 1966-96, chmn. dept., 1979-84, Gerhard H. Dieke prof., 1992-96, prof. emeritus, 1997-98, Gerhard H. Dieke prof. emeritus, 1998—. Vis. Erskine fellow U. Canterbury, Christchurch, New Zealand, 1968; vis. fellow Australian Nat. U., Canberra, 1975; hon. fellow Brasenose Coll., Oxford U., 1983—. Author: Operator Techniques in Atomic Spectroscopy, 1963, reprinted, 1998, Second Quantization and Atomic Spectroscopy, 1967, (with J.P. Elliott) Topics in Atomic and Nuclear Theory, 1970, Angular Momentum Theory For Diatomic Molecules, 1975. Recipient Spedding award for rare-earth rsch. Rhone-Poulenc, Inc., 1988. Fellow Am. Phys. Soc. Office: Johns Hopkins U Dept Physics and Astronomy Baltimore MD 21218

JUDD, BURKE HAYCOCK, geneticist; b. Kanab, Utah, Sept. 5, 1927; s. Zadok Ray and Elva (Haycock) J.; m. Barbara Ann Gaddy, Mar. 21, 1953; children: Sean Michael, Evan Patrick, Timothy Burke. BS, U. Utah, 1950, MS, 1951; PhD, Calif. Inst. Tech., 1954. Postdoctoral fellow Am. Cancer Soc. U. Tex., Austin, 1954-56, from instr. to prof., 1956-79, dir. Genetics Inst., 1977-79; geneticist Atomic Energy Commn., Germantown, Md., 1968-69; chief lab. genetics Nat. Inst. Environ. Health Sci., Research Triangle Park, N.C., 1979-95. Vis. asst. prof. Stanford U., Palo Alto, Calif., 1960; Gosney vis. prof. Calif. Inst. Tech., Pasadena, 1975-76; adj. prof. U. N.C., Chapel Hill, 1979-99, Duke U., Durham, 1980-2002; mem. panel genetic biology NSF, Washington, 1969-73, genetics study sect. NIH, Washington, 1974, 77, 79, 88, com. on germplasm resources NAS, Washington, 1976-77; chmn. human genome initiative rev. panel Dept. of Energy, Washington, 1988. Author: Introduction to Modern Genetics, 1980; editor: Molecular and Gen. Genetics, 1986-95; assoc. editor Genetics, 1973-78; contbr. articles to profl. jours. With U.S. Army, 1946-47. Fellow AAAS; mem. Am. Soc. Naturalists (sec. 1968-70), Genetics Soc. Am. (sec. 1974-76, v.p., pres. 1979-80). Avocations: travel, poetry, fiction. Home: 411 Clayton Rd Chapel Hill NC 27514-7613 E-mail: bhjudd@bellsouth.net.

JUDD, DENNIS L. lawyer; b. Provo, Utah, June 27, 1954; s. Derrel Wesley and Leila (Lundquist) J.; m. Carol Lynne Chilberg, May 6, 1977; children: Lynne Marie, Amy Jo, Tiffany Ann, Andrew, Jacquelyn Nicole. BA in Polit. Sci. summa cum laude, Brigham Young U., 1978, JD, 1981. Bar: Utah 1981, U.S. Dist. Ct. Utah 1981. Assoc. Nielson & Senior, Salt Lake City and Vernal, Utah, 1981-83; dep. county atty. Uintah County, Vernal, 1982-84; ptnr. Bennett & Judd, Vernal, 1983-88; county atty. Daggett County, Utah, 1985-89, 91-99; pvt. practice Vernal, 1988—; county atty. Daggett County, 2000—; prosecutor City of Naples, Naples, 1996-99; legal counsel Uintah County Sch. Dist., 1996—; city atty. Naples City, Utah, 1999—, Vernal City, Utah, 2000—; atty. City of Vernal, 2000—. Mem. governing bd. Uintah Basin applied Tech. Ctr., 1991-95,

v.p., 1993-94, pres., 1994-95. Chmn. bd. adjustment Zoning and Planning Bd., Naples, 1982-91, 94—; mem. Naples City Coun., 1982-91; mayor pro tem City of Naples, 1983-91; legis. v.p. Naples PTA, 1988-90; sec. Friends of Utah Field House of Natural History, 2000—; v.p. Uintah Dist. PTA Coun., 1990-92; mem. resolution com. Utah League Cities and Towns, 1985-86, small cities com., 1985-86; trustee Uintah Sch. Dist. Found., 1988-97, vice chmn., 1991-93; mem. Uintah County Sch. Dist. Bd. Edn., 1991-95, v.p., 1991-92, pres., 1992-95; chmn. Uintah County Rep. Conv., 1998. Hinkley scholar Brigham Young U., 1977. Mem. Utah Bar Assn., Uintah Basin Bar Assn., Statewide Assn. Prosecutors, Vernal C. of C. Republican. Mem. Lds Ch. Avocations: hunting, photography, lapidary. Home: 460 E 1555 S Naples UT 84078 Office: 461 W 200 S Vernal UT 84078-3049

JUDD, JAMES, conductor, music director; b. Eng. Grad., Trinity Coll. Music, London. Asst. conductor Cleve. Orch.; assoc. music dir. European Cmty. Youth Orch., artistic dir.; conductor Berlin Philharmonic, Israel Philharmonic; music dir. Fla. Philharmonic, 1987—2001, New Zealand Symphony Orch., 2002—. Guest condr. Vienna Symphony, Gewandhaus Orch., Leipzig, Germany, Prague Symphony Orch., Orch. Nat. France, Orch. Suisse Romande, Nat. Arts Ctr. Orch., Ottawa, Cin. Symphony, NHK Symphony, Tokyo, Mozarteum Orch.; co-founder Chamber Orch. Europe. Office: PO Box 6640 Wellington 6038 New Zealand

JUDD, O'DEAN P. physicist; b. Austin, Minn., May 26, 1937; MS in Physics, UCLA, 1961, PhD in Physics, 1968. Staff physicist and project dir. Hughes Rsch. Lab., Malibu, Calif., 1959-67; postdoctoral fellow UCLA Dept. Physics, 1968-69; researcher Hughes Rsch. Lab., Malibu, Calif., 1969-72; researcher, group leader Los Alamos Nat. Lab., 1972-82, chief scientist for def. rsch. and applications, 1981-87; chief scientist Strategic Def. Initiative Orgn., Washington, 1987-90; energy and environ. chief scientist, lab. fellow Los Alamos (N.Mex.) Nat. Lab., 1990-93; nat. intelligence officer for sci. and tech. Nat. Intelligence Coun., Washington, 1993-94; ind. tech. advisor and cons. Los Alamos, 1995—. Mem. numerous govt. coms. related to sci. and tech., def. and nat. security policy; adj. prof. physics U. N.Mex., Albuquerque. Patentee in sci. and tech.; contbr. numerous articles to sci. and def.-related jours. Fellow IEEE, AAAS, Los Alamos Nat. Lab. Inst. Advanced Engring.; mem. Am. Phys. Soc. Office: Los Alamos Nat Lab MS F650 Los Alamos NM 87544-2648

JUDD, RICHARD LOUIS, academic administrator; b. Bridgeport, Conn., Mar. 22, 1937; s. Wilbur Franklin and Priscilla (Nagy) J.; m. Nancy Ruth Fox, Nov. 30, 1963; children: Sarah, Jonathan. BS with honors, Cen. Conn. State U., 1959; MA, Ohio State U., 1961; PhD, U. Conn., 1971; LLD (hon.), Briarwood Coll., 2000; MD (hon.), Kyung Hee U., Seoul, Korea, 2000. Prof. emergency med. scis. Ctrl. Conn. State U., New Britain, 1992—, v.p., 1992-96, pres., 1996—. Vis. exec. Am. Coun. Edn., USDA, 1981; mem. adv. com. United Tech. Corp., 1994—97, New Eng. Coun. Spl. Commn. Hightech Workforce, 2000; chmn. devel. adv. com. Pratt and Whitney, 1994. Sr. author: First Responder 3rd edit., 1994, Geriatric Emergencies, 1986. Commr. New Britain Police Dept., 1981—89, 1993—95; chmn. Conn. Adv. Bd. EMS, 1992—97; campaign chmn. United Cmty. Svcs., New Britain, 1987—88, pres., 1990—92, Verdienstkreuz, Germany, 1990; chmn. New Britain Mus. Am. Art, 1993—98; bd. dirs. New Britain Gen. Hosp., 1996—. Named Citizen of Yr., 1990, Outstanding Alumni Educator, U. Conn. Sch. Edn., 1999, Disting. Advocate for the Arts, Conn. Commn. on the Arts, 2003; recipient Lifetime Achievement award, Nat. Assn. Emergency Med. Technicians, 1996; Demi fellow, 1970. Home: 119 Ten Acre Rd New Britain CT 06052-1531 Office: Cen Conn State U 1615 Stanley St New Britain CT 06053-2439 E-mail: judd@ccsu.edu.

JUDD, STEPHEN ALAN, biomedical researcher, educator, marketing professional; b. Concord, Calif., Mar. 30, 1965; s. David Stuart Judd and Sybil Marie White, Myke Elise Judd (Stepmother) and Brian Lee White(Stepfather); m. Jill Denise Adler, July 30, 1988; children: Caitlyn Morgan, Alexander Michael, Connor Matthew, Cameron Bradley. BS, Humboldt State U., 1983—88; MS, U. of Calif., Davis, 1991—93. Cert. in Mktg. Am. Mgmt. Assn., 2000. Biomedical rsch. scientist Lawrence Livermore Nat. Lab., Calif., 1988—91; grad. tchg./rsch. asst. U. of Calif., Davis, 1991—93; biology instr. Los Rios C.C. Dist., Sacramento, Calif., 1993—95; sr. product mgr., worldwide genotyping services Applera Corp., Norwalk, Conn., 1994—2000; dir. of mktg. and bus. devel., indsl. and agrl. markets Motorola, Schaumburg, Ill., 2000—02. Mem., working group on ethical, legal & social issues in toxicogenomics NIH-Nat. Inst. of Environ. Health Sciences' Nat. Ctr. for Toxicogenomics, Washington, 2000—02. Asst. cub master Boy Scouts of Am., Davis, Calif., 1997—2000; cert. area referee Am. Youth Soccer Orgn., Calif., 1996—2003. Recipient Vanguard Emerging Tech. Award for Achievement, Vision and Innovation, Comstock Mag./Coopers and Lybrand, 1996, VIP Vision Award, Zoogen Inc., 1996. Achievements include patents for 8 US and Internat. patents issued on the use of emu oil and fractions thereof as an insect repellent; first to Conceived, developed and launched DNA PawPrint genetic pedigree analysis service for purebred dogs. Avocations: family, soccer, travel, guitar, reading. Office: Motorola Life Sciences 126 West Del Mar Boulevard Pasadena CA Personal E-mail: mktrodin@hotmail.com.

JUDD, THOMAS ELI, electrical engineer; b. Salt Lake City, Apr. 12, 1927; s. Henry Eli Judd and Jennie Meibos; m. Mary Lu Edman, June 21, 1948; children: Shauna, Kirk E., Blake E., Lisa. BSEE, U. Utah, 1950. Registered profl. engr., Utah. Mech. engr. Utah Power & Light Co., Salt Lake City, 1950-55; chief engr. Electronic Motor Car Corp., Salt Lake City, 1955-56, Equi-Tech Corp., Salt Lake City, 1978-79; hydraulic devel. engr. Galigher Co., Salt Lake City, 1956-58; pres. Toran Corp., Salt Lake City, 1958-71, T M Industries, Salt Lake City, 1971-78; chief exec. officer, mgr. Ramos Corp., Salt Lake City, 1979—. Project cons. Eimco Corp., Salt Lake City, 1966; design cons. to tech. cos. Patentee in field in U.S. and fgn. countries; contbr. editor U.S. Rail News, 1982—. Cons. Nat. Fedn. Ind. Bus., 1983—. With USNR, 1945-46, PTO. Mem. Tau Beta Pi. Republican. Mem. Lds Ch. Avocation: flying. Office: Ramos Corp 956 Elm Ave Salt Lake City UT 84106-2330

JUDD, WILLIAM ROBERT, engineering geologist, educator; b. Denver, Aug. 16, 1917; s. Samuel and Lillian (Israelske) J.; m. Rachel Elizabeth Douglas, Apr. 18, 1942; children: Stephanie (Mrs. Chris Wadley), Judith (Mrs. John Soden), Dayna (Mrs. Erick Grandmason), Pamela, Connie. AB, U. Colo., 1941, postgrad., 1941-50. Registered profl. engr., Colo., engring. geologist, Oreg. Engring. geologist Colo. Water Conservation Bd., 1941-42; supervisory engring. geologist Denver & Rio Grande Western R.R., Colo. and Utah, 1942-44; head geology sect. No. 1, acting dist. geologist-Alaska U.S. Bur. Reclamation, Office of Chief Engr., Denver, 1945-60; head basing tech. group RAND Corp., Santa Monica, Calif., 1960—66; prof. rock mechanics Purdue U., Lafayette, Ind., 1966-87, head geotech. engring., 1976-86; tech. dir. Purdue U. Underground Excavation and Rock Properties Info. Center, 1972-79, prof. emeritus civil engring., 1988—. Geotech. cons., U.S., Mexico, Cuba, Honduras, Greece, 1950— ; geoscience editor Am. Elsevier Pub. Co., 1967-71; chmn. panel on ocean scis. Com. on Instl. Cooperation, 1971-85; founder and chmn. Nat. Acad. Sci. U.S. Nat. Com. on Rock Mechanics, 1963-69, co-chmn. panel on rsch. requirements, 1977-81, chmn. panel on awards, 1972-82; mem. U.S. Army Adv. Bd. on Mountain and Arctic Warfare, 1956-62, USAF Sci. Adv. Bd. Geophysics Panel Study Group, 1964-67; com. on safety dams NRC, 1977-78, 82-83; Nat. dir. Nat. Ski Patrol System, Inc., 1956-62; Alex du Toit Meml. lectr., S.Africa and Rhodesia, 1967; owner Rayanbill Galleries, 1986—. Author: (with E.F. Taylor) Ski Patrol Manual, 1956, (with D. Krynine) Principles of Engineering Geology and Geotechnics, 1957, Sitzmarks or Safety, 1960; editor: Rock Mechanics research, 1966, State of Stress in the Earth's crust, 1964; co-editor: Physical Properties of Rocks and Minerals, 1981; editor-in-chief: Engring. Geology, 1972-92, hon. editor, 1996—. Recipient Spl. Rsch. award NRC, 1982; named to Colo. Ski Hall of Fame, 1983; named hon. life mem. Nat. Ski Patrol System, Inc., 1988. Fellow ASCE, Geol. Soc. Am. (Disting. Practice award engring. geology divsn. 1989), South African Inst. Mining and Metallurgy; mem. Assn. Engring. Geologists (hon.), Internat. Assn. Engring. Geologists (Hans Cloos medal 1994), Ind. Soc. Engring. Geology (life), Ind. Acad. Scis., U.S. Com. on Large Dams (exec. com. 1977-83, com. on earthquakes 1976-90), U.S. Ski Assn. (hon. life), U.S. Recreational Ski Assn. (hon. life). Home and Office: 1051 Cumberland Ave West Lafayette IN 47906 *Are you important? Take your thumb out of a bowl of water, then measure the hole it left.*

JUDELL, HAROLD BENN, lawyer; b. Milw., Mar. 9, 1915; s. Philip Fox and Lena Florence (Krause) J.; m. Maria Violeta van Ronzelen, May 5, 1951 (div.); m. Celeste Seymour Grulich, June 24, 1986. BA, U. Wis., 1936, JD, 1938; LLB, Tulane U., 1950. Bar: Wis. 1938, La. 1950. Mem. Scheinfeld Collins Durant & Winter, Milw., 1938; spl. agt., adminstrv. asst. to dir. FBI, 1939-44; legal attache U.S. Embassy Peru, 1942-44; ptnr. Foley & Judell, LLP, New Orleans, 1950—; v.p., dir. Dauphine Orleans Hotel Corp., 1970—, chmn. bd., 1999—. Mem. Tulane U. Bus. Sch. Coun.; trustee Greater New Orleans YMCA, 1981—; dir. Sizeler Property Investors, Inc., 1986—. Fellow Am. Coll. Bond Counsel (founding); mem. ABA, La. Bar Assn., Nat. Assn. Bond Lawyers (bd. dirs., pres. 1984-85), New Orleans Country Club, Lawn Tennis Club, Met. Club (N.Y.C.). Office: Foley & Judell LLP 365 Canal St New Orleans LA 70130-1112 E-mail: hjudell@foleyjudell.com.

JUDEX, STEFAN, psychologist, educator; b. Starnberg, Germany, Nov. 25, 1968; s. Erhard and Gudrun Judex; m. Angeline Yeo, Aug. 22, 1998. PhD, U. Calgary, 1994—99. Asst. prof. SUNY, Stony Brook, 2001—. Home: 222 Glenwood Ln Port Jefferson NY 11777 Office: SUNY Stony Brook Psychology A Bldg Stony Brook NY 11794 Office Fax: 631-632-8577. E-mail: stefan.judex@stonybrook.edu.

JUDGE, BERNARD MARTIN, editor, publisher; b. Chgo., Jan. 6, 1940; s. Bernard A. and Catherine Elizabeth (Halloran) J.; m. Kimbeth A. Wehrli, July 9, 1966; children: Kelly, Bernard R., Jessica. Reporter City News Bur., Chgo., 1965-66; reporter Chgo. Tribune, 1966-70, city editor, 1974-79, asst. mng. editor met. news, 1979-83; editor, gen. mgr. City News Bur. Chgo., 1983-84; assoc. editor Chgo. Sun-Times, 1984-88; from editor to pub. Chgo. Daily Law Bull., 1988—; pub. Chgo. Lawyer, 1989—; v.p. Law Bull. Pub. Co., Chgo., 1988—. Bd. dirs. Constnl. Rights Found., Chgo., 1992—, chmn. bd. dirs., 1995-97; trustee Fenwick Cath. Prep. H.S., Oak Park, Ill., 1989—. Named to Chgo. Journalism Hall of Fame, 2000. Mem. Sigma Delta Chi. Home: 360 E Randolph St Apt 1905 Chicago IL 60601-7335 Office: Law Bull Pub Co 415 N State St Chicago IL 60610-4631

JUDGE, CHARLES A. physician, statistician; b. Phila., Aug. 4, 1950; s. Charles A. Judge and Ella M. Snyder; m. Ruby C. Alonzo, Oct. 9, 1982; children: Stephanie, Christine. BA, Holy Cross, 1972; postgrad., MIT, 1973-74; MD, Georgetown U., 1978. Bd. cert. Am. Bd. Internal Medicine. Intern in medicine Boston VA Hosp., 1978-79, resident, 1979-81; physician Mountain Comprehensive Health Corp., Whitesburg, Ky., 1981-83; dir. Calvert Internal Medicine Group, Prince Frederick, Md., 1983—. CIO Calvert Internal Medicine, Prince Frederick, 1984—; pres. Caj Software, Inc., Huntingtown, Md., 1996—. Author (software) Track Judge, 1998. Avocations: thoroughbred breeding, aviation. Office: CIMG Ste 310 110 Hospital Rd Prince Frederick MD 20678

JUDGE, DOLORES BARBARA, real estate broker; b. Plymouth, Pa. m. Richard James Judge; children: Susan, Nancy, Richard Jr. Student, North Harris County Coll., 1984-85, U. Tex., 1985, Houston Community Coll., 1988-89. Real estate agt. comml. real estate cos. in area, 1981-84; owner D-J Investment Properties, Conroe, Tex., 1984—; pres., ptnr. J&M Mgmt. Co., 1996-97; pres. Judge Mgmt. Co., 1997—. Mem. first adv. bd. First Nat. Title Co., Conroe, 1989-90. Chmn. North Houston Econ. Devel. Showcase, 1990; bd. dirs. Montgomery County Crime Stoppers, Inc., 1993—. Mem. Conroe C. of C., Comml. Real Estate Assn. Montgomery County (pres. 1986-87, bd. dirs. 1988), Conroe Art League (exec. bd.) Avocations: golf, travel, computers, reading. Office: D-J Investment Properties 306 Tara Park Conroe TX 77302-3756

JUDGE, GEORGE GARRETT, economics educator; b. Carlisle, Ky., May 2, 1925; s. William Everett and Etna (Perkins) J.; m. Sue Dunkle, Mar. 17, 1950; children: Lisa C., Laura S.; m. Margaret C. Copeland, Oct. 8, 1976. BS, U. Ky., 1948; MS, Iowa State U., 1949, PhD, 1952. Asst. prof. U. Conn., Storrs, 1951-55; prof. U. Okla., Stillwater, 1955-58; vis. prof. Yale U., New Haven, 1958-59; prof. econs. U. Ill., Urbna, 1959-86, U. Calif., Berkeley, 1986—. Vis. disting. prof. U. Ga., 1977-79; cons. Internat. Wool Secretariat, London, 1976-77. Author: Markov Processes, 1970, Spatial Equilibrium, 1972, Allocation Over Space and Time, 1975, Pre-Test and Stein Rule Estimators, 1978, Theory and Practice of Econometrics, 1980, 85, Introduction to the Theory and Practice of Econometrics, 1982, 88, Improved Methods of Inference, 1986, Learning and Practicing Econometrics, 1993, Maximum Entropy Econometrics, 1996, Undergraduate Econometrics, 2000, Econometric Foundations, 2000. With USSAF, 1943-45, PTO. Social Sci. Rsch. Coun. fellow, 1958-59, NSF fellow, 1965-66, Jour. Econometrics fellow; grantee NSF, 1976-87. Fellow Econometric Soc.; mem. Am. Statis. Assn., Am. Econ. Assn., Dial Club. Avocations: golf, sailing. Office: U Calif 207 Giannini Hall Berkeley CA 94720-3310

JUDGE, JAMES CARL, quality assurance officer, information systems specialist; b. Casper, Wyo., Aug. 26, 1945; s. Herbert B. and E. Francis (Sheehan) J.; m. Judith Karen Stillwell, May 15, 1971; children: Tracy Michelle, Eric James Michael, Casey McKay. BA in Mgmt. with honors, St. Mary's Coll., 1996; MS in Quality Assurance, Calif. State U., Dominguez, 2000. Micrographics technician Chevron Oil Co., Denver, 1969-77; mgr. micro-image processing EG&G Idaho Inc., Idaho Falls, 1977-81; engring. assoc. U. Calif. Lawrence Livermore (Calif.) Nat. Lab., 1981-93; ops. mgr. Hazardous Waste Mgmt., 1996—; quality assurance officer Environ. Protection Dept., 1996—. Editor newsletter Hard Copy, 1977. Mem. adv. com. Community Coll. Denver, 1976. With U.S. Army, 1965-69. Mem. Nat. Micrographics Assn. (chmn. edn. com. Rocky Mountain chpt. 1974-75, Mem. of Yr. award 1977), Dept. Energy-Contractors Image and Info. Assn. (conf. host 1986, exec. com. 1984-90, vice chmn. 1985-86, chmn. 1986-87), Assn. Info. and Image Mgmt. (mem. adv. bd. 2002-), Phi Kappa Phi Republican. Roman Catholic. Avocations: computer programming, optics, baseball, bowling. Home: 961 Hazel St Livermore CA 94550-2334 Office: Lawrence Livermore Nat Lab PO Box 808 Livermore CA 94551-0808

JUDGE, JEAN FRANCES, management consultant; b. N.J., Aug. 25, 1922; d. Frank Theodore and Frances Marie (O'Brien) J. BS, Coll. St. Elizabeth, 1944. Asst. dietitian Hoffman LaRoche, Inc., 1944-45; dir. sch. lunch program for handicapped children Jersey City Sch. System, 1945-51; dir. field home econs. United Fruit Co., 1951-55; extension prof. consumer food mktg. Rutgers U., New Brunswick, N.J., 1955-70; dir. consumer affairs Grand Union Co., Elmwood Park, N.J., 1970-74; owner, pres. Jean Judge Assocs., Inc., Hackensack, N.J., 1974-93. Trustee Coll. St. Elizabeth, 1987-96, mem. mktg. com., capital fund campaign, mem. planned giving com. Recipient Mother Xavier award Coll. St. Elizabeth, 1973. Mem. Soc. Consumer Affairs Profls. in Bus. (charter bd. dirs. 1974-75, Outstanding Svc. award 1975, Individual Achievement award 1985), SOCAP Found. (bd. trustees 1986-96).

JUDGE, JERRY, business executive; b. Eng. Pres. Lowe Lintas & Ptnrs. Interpublic Group of Cos., Inc., NYC, 1997—2001; CEO Lowe & Ptnrs. Worldwide, 2001—. Office: Lowe Lintas & Ptnrs Interpublic Group Cos Inc 1114 Avenue Of The Americas New York NY 10036-7703

JUDGE, RAJINDER, psychiatrist; b. Jullundur, India, Mar. 22, 1961; arrived in Eng., 1964,arrived in U.S., 1996; d. Sadhu and Parkash Judge. MD, U. Birmingham, Eng., 1984. Intern Wordsley Hosp. and Russells Hall Hosp., Dudley, England, 1984—85; sr. house officer psychiatry Midland Nerve Hosp., Birmingham, 1985—86; physician Riyadh, Saudi Arabia, 1986—87; psychiatry registrar North Worcester, England, 1987—89; assoc. med. dir. Smith Kline Beecham, England, 1991—96; dir., global physician for Prozac, Lilly & Co., Indpls., 1997—2000; psychiatrist Nat. Health Svc., 1991—94; registrar, sr. registrar London Charing Cross Rotation, 1989—91; v.p. neuroscience Novartis, East Hanover, NJ, 2000—. Forensic med. examiner London Met. Police Force, 1991—. Contbr. articles to profl. jours. Mem.: ENCP, Royal Coll. Psychiatrists. Avocations: automobiles, movies, travel. Office: Novartis One Health Plz East Hanover NJ 07936-1080

JUDGE, ROSEMARY ANN, oil company executive; b. Jersey City; d. Frank T. and Frances M. (O'Brien) J. AB, Seton Hall U. Exec. sec. Socony Vacuum, N.Y.C., 1944-56; sec., confidential asst. to v.p. and dir. Socony Mobil, N.Y.C., 1956-59; sec., confidential asst. to pres. Mobil Oil Co. Div., N.Y.C., 1959-61; sec., adminstrv. asst. to pres. Mobil Oil Corp., N.Y.C., 1961-69, adminstrv. asst. to chmn., 1969-71, asst. to chmn., sec. exec com., 1971-84, corp. sec., 1975-76; asst. to chmn., sec. bd. and exec. com. Mobil Corp., 1976-84; pres. Mobil Found., N.Y.C., 1973-85. Mem. bd. regents Seton Hall U., 1982-88. Mem. Women's Econ. Round Table, Spring Lake (N.J.) Golf Club, Pelican Yacht Club (Fla.).

JUDICE, MARC WAYNE, lawyer; b. Lafayette, La., Oct. 22, 1946; s. Marc and Gladys B. Judice; 1 child, Renee. BS, U. La., 1969; MBA, U. Utah, 1974; JD, La. State U., 1977. Bar: La. 1977; bd. cert. civil trial law, civil trial advocacy Nat. Bd. Trial Advocacy. Ptnr. Voorhies & Labbe, Lafayette, 1977-85, Juneau, Judice, Hill & Adley, Lafayette, 1985-93, Judice & Adley, Lafayette, 1993—. Bd. dirs. Univ. Med. Ctr., Lafayette, 1991, chmn.; bd. dirs. Home Savs. Bank, Lafayette, 1996—, Women's & Childrens Hosp., Lafayette, 1992-94; bd. trustees Med. Ctr. Southwest La., 1998-2001, chmn. bd. dirs., 1999-2003. Republican. Roman Catholic. Office: Judice & Adley 926 Coolidge Blvd Lafayette LA 70503-2434 E-mail: mwj@judice-adley.com.

JUDIE, JOYCE FOX, tax specialist, educator; b. St Louis, May 27, 1959; d. Billy Martin and Lavada Fox; m. Thomas Melvin Toye, June 17, 1978 (div. Aug. 24, 1994); children: Ebonie M. Toye, Corey M. Toye; m. Edward Judie, July 10, 1998; stepchildren: Milika Ward, Kareem, Khalil. AAS in Paralegal, Ctrl. Tex. Coll., 1996; BS in Pub. Adminstrn., Upper Iowa U., 1996; MPA, Troy State U., 2001. Enlisted US Army, 1978, advanced through grades to sgt. 1st class, 1992; personnel/records clk. 759th Mil. Police Bn., Ft. Dix, NJ, 1978—79; personnel/mgmt. asst. HHC CENTAG, Heidelberg, Germany, 1979—82; personnel adminstrv. ctr. sgt. Fgn. Support Command, Ft. Meade, Md., 1982—88; personnel staff sgt. 11th Aviation Brigade (including Desert Storm), Illesheim, Germany, 1988—91; sr. pers. staff supr. Divsn. Support Command, Ft. Ord, Calif., 1991—93; sr. enlisted advisor Readiness Group, Ft. Riley, Kans., 1993—96; sr. personnel adminstrv. supr. Divsn. Artillery Command, Ft. Drum, NY, 1996—98; tax rep. IRS, Seattle, 1998—. Voting asst. El Paso Sch. Dist., Tex., 1999; parliamentarian Seoul Am. HS, 2000—01; mentor Lincoln HS, Tacoma, 2002—. Mem.: ASPA, Phi Delta Kappa (sec. 2002—). Avocations: aerobics, reading, research, volunteering. Home: 8929 Milbanke Ct SE Olympia WA 98513 Office: IRS M/S W&I 915 Second Ave Seattle WA 98174

JUDOVITZ, DALIA, language educator; b. Romania, Sept. 23, 1951; BA, Brandeis U, 1973; MA, Johns Hopkins U, 1976, PhD, 1979. Asst. prof. U Pa., State College, Pa., 1979—82, U. Calif., Berkeley, 1982—88; assoc. prof. Emory U., Atlanta, 1988—94, prof., 1994—2002, NEH prof. French and Italian, 2002—. Vis. fellow Inst. Humanities U. Mich., 1994. Author: Subjectivity and Representation in Descartes: The Origins of Modernity, 1988; co-editor: Dialectic and Narrative, 1993; author: Unpacking Duchamp: Art in Transit, 1998, Déplier Duchamp: Passages de l'art (French edit.), 2000, The Culture of the Body: Genealogies of Modernity, 2001. Fellow Mellon Fellowship, Columbia U Soc. of Fellows in the Humanities, 1981—82, Am. Coun. of Learned Soc., 2002. Mem.: MLA, N. Am. Assn. 17th Century French Lit., Internat. Assn. for Philos. and Lit. Home: 676 North Parkwood Rd Decatur GA 30030 Office: French and Italian Dept Emory U Atlanta GA 30322

JUDSON, ARNOLD SIDNEY, management consultant; b. Brockton, Mass., Mar. 29, 1927; s. Moses Joel and Fanny (Becker) J.; m. June Brenner, June 19, 1949; children: Pamela F., Jill E. BS in Chem. Engring., MIT, 1947, MS in Orgnl. Behavior, 1948. Prodn. foreman U.S. Rubber Co., Providence, 1948-50; pers. mgr., mfg. mgr., then dir. tng. and devel. Polaroid Corp., Cambridge, Mass., 1950-62; mgmt. cons. The Emerson Cons., Ltd., London, 1962-66; sr. mgmt. cons. Arthur D.Little, Inc., Cambridge, 1966-76; dir., mgmt. cons. The Berwick Group, Inc., Boston, 1976-81; pres., CEO Gray-Judson-Howard, Inc., Cambridge, 1981-90, chmn., 1990-94; pres. The Judson Co., Inc., 1994-2001. Cons. Exec. Svc. Corps. Author: A Manager's Guide to Making Changes, 1966, Making Strategy Happen, 1990, 2nd edit., 1996, Changing Behavior in Organizations, 1991; contbr. articles to bus. publs.; composer orchestral and chamber music. Chmn. bd. dirs. Greater Boston Rehab. Svcs., Cambridge, 1984-2001. With USN, 1945-46. Mem. Univ. Club Boston. Office: The Judson Co Inc 2 Hawthorne Pl Ste 3E Boston MA 02114

JUDSON, C(HARLES) JAMES (JIM JUDSON), lawyer; b. Oregon City, Oreg., Oct. 24, 1944; s. Charles James and Barbara (Busch) J.; m. Diana L. Gerlach, Sept.11, 1965; children: Kevin, Nicole. BA cum laude, Stanford U., 1966, LLB with honors, 1969. Bar: Wash. 1969, U.S. Tax Ct. 1970, D.C. 1981. Ptnr. Davis Wright Tremaine, Seattle, 1969—. Bd. dirs. Port Blakely Tree Farms, Garrett and Ring, Joshua Green Corp., China Unicom; spkr. in field. Author: State Taxation of Fin. Instns., 1981; contbr. articles to profl. jours. Chmn. Bus. Tax Coalition, Seattle, 1987; chmn. lawyers div. United Way, Seattle, 1986, 87, commerce and industry div., 1989-91; trustee Wash. State Internat. Trade Fair, Seattle, 1981-86; bd. dirs. Seattle Prep. Sch., 1986-88; bd. dirs. Olympic Park Inst., 1988—, Yosemite Nat. Insts., 1993—; mem. Assn. Wash. Bus. Tax Com., 1978—; tax advisor Wash. State House Reps. Dem. Caucus; advisor Wash. State Dept. Revenue on Tax and Legis. Matters; mem. Seattle Tax Group, 1983—. Fellow Am. Coll Tax Counsel; mem. ABA (chmn. com. on fin. orgns. tax sect. 1978-82, subcom chmn. state and local tax com. tax sect. 1979—, chmn. excise tax com. 1983-90, interorgn. coordination com. 1985—, chmn. environ. tax com. 1991—), Wash. State Bar Assn. (chmn. tax sect. 1984-86, chmn. western region IRS/bar liaison com. 1987-88, mem. rules com. 1991—), Seattle-King County Bar Assn. (mem. tax sect. 1973-86), Seattle C. of C. (tax com. 1982—), Wash. Athletic Club (Seattle), Broadmoor Golf Club (Seattle), Bear Creek Golf Club (Redmond). Avocations: skiing, golf, basketball, wood working, hiking. Office: Davis Wright Tremaine 2600 Century Sq 1501 4th Ave Seattle WA 98101-1688

JUDSON, FRANKLYN NEVIN, physician, educator; b. Cleve., Apr. 14, 1942; s. Franklyn S. and Nancy Elizabeth (Nevin) J.; m. Kathleen A. Thompson, June 24, 1972 (div. 1977); m. Marti J. Sachse, Dec. 12, 1981; children: Jennifer, Rachel. BA, Wesleyan U., 1964; MD, U. Pa., 1968. Intern U. Wis. Hosps., Madison, 1968-69, resident, 1969-70; epidemic intelligence svc. officer Ctrs. Disease Control, Atlanta, 1970-72; fellow in infectious diseases U. Colo., Denver, 1972-74, from asst. prof. to assoc. prof. depts. medicine and preventive medicine, 1976-87, prof., 1987—; dir. Denver Disease Control Service, 1976-86; chief infectious disease service Denver Gen. Hosp., 1982—; dir. Dept. Pub. Health City of Denver, 1986—; pres. med. staff Denver Health, 1996-98. Chmn. anti-infective agts. adv. com. FDA, 1993-95; mem. Colo. State Bd. Health. Editor: Diagnosis of Sexually Transmitted Diseases, 1985; assoc. editor Sexually Transmitted Diseases, 1988-99; mem. editorial bd. Genitourinary Medicine, 1984-94; contbr. articles to profl. jours. Pres. met. council Colo. chpt. Am. Lung Assn., Denver, 1988-90, bd. dirs.; pres. Coalition for A Tobacco Free Colo., 1995-96. Mem. Am. Veneral Disease Assn. (bd. dirs. 1981-88, pres. 1983-85, Outstanding Investigator 1980), Am. Social Health Assn. (bd. dirs. 1983-90, 97—, v.p. 1987, chmn. 2002), Group Against Smokers' Pollution (bd. dirs., v.p. Colo. chpt. 1982—), Internat. Soc. Sexually Transmitted Diseases Rsch. (pres. 1997-99), Internat. Union Against the Secually Transmitted Infections (pres.-elec 2001-). Mem. Soc. Of Friends. Avocations: running, skiing, farming. Home: 662 Josephine St Denver CO 80206-3723 E-mail: fjudson@dhha.org.

JUDSON, J. RICHARD, retired art educator, historian; b. L.I., N.Y., July 5, 1925; s. Bernard Judson and Sylvia Siegl; m. Carolyn French Judson, June 21, 1953; children: Pieter Moulton, Matthew Bowditch, Sarah Mercer, Nicolaas French. AB, Oberlin Coll., 1948; MA, NYU, 1953; PhD, Utrecht (The Netherlands) U., 1956. Asst. prof. Smith Coll., Northampton, Mass., 1956—62, assoc. prof., 1962—67, prof., 1967—74; W.R. Kenan Jr. prof. U. N.C., Chapel Hill, 1974—93. Chmn. art dept. Smith Coll., 1967—69, U. N.C., 1974—80; vis. assoc. prof. Columbia U., N.Y.C., 1966—67. Author: (books) Dirck Barendsz, 1534-1592, 1970, The Drawings of Jacob de Gheyn, 1973, Passion of Christ, VI, Corpus Rubenianum Ludwig Burchard, 2000, (exhbn. catalogs) Rembrandt after Three Hundred Years, Catalogue of Paintings, 1969—70, P.P. Rubens als Boekillustrator, 1977; co-author: (books) Book Illustrations and Title Pages, XXI, Corpus Rubenianum Ludwig Burchard, 1978, The Age of Bruegel: Netherlandish Drawings in the Sixteenth Century, 1986, Gerrit van Hothorst, 1999, (exhbn. catalog) The Age of Bruegel, 1986—87. With USNR, 1943—44. Recipient Rubens medal, City of Antwerp, Belgium, 1977; fellow C.R.B., Belgian-Am. Ednl. Found., Brussels, 1953, sr., Southea. Inst. Medieval and

Renaissance Studies, 1976, Netherlands Inst. Advanced Studies, Wassenaar, 1986; grantee, Am. Coun. Learned Socs., 1974; scholar Fulbright, 1954—55, 1955—56, 1964—65, Am. Acad., Rome, 1981—82; Fellow John Simon, Guggenheim Found., 1960—61. Mem.: Catboat Assoc., Nantucket Yacht Club. Avocation: sailing. Home: PO Box 118 Etna NH 03750 E-mail: jud.judson@valley.net.

JUDSON, JOHN IRVING, retired English educator, poet, writer, editor; b. Stratford, Conn, Sept. 9, 1930; s. Irving John and Edna May (Hewitt) J.; m. Joanne Carol Aker, Oct. 30, 1959; children: William, Lisa, Gary, Sara. AB, Colby Coll., 1958; postgrad., U. Maine, 1962; MFA, U. Iowa, 1965. Electronics technician Norden-Ketay Co., Milford, Conn., 1957, Lab. for Electronics, Boston, 1958-59; tchr. English, Grinell (Iowa) Jr. H.S., 1963-64, Coburn Classical Inst., Waterville, Maine, 1964-65; instr. U. Iowa, Iowa City, 1965; prof. English, U. Wis., La Crosse, 1965-92, prof. emeritus, 1992—. Editor, pub. Juniper Press, Maine, Iowa, Wis., 1962—; bd. dirs. Wis. Poets In Schs. Program, Madison. Author 6 books and 8 chapbooks of poetry, 1965— (5 awards); editor: Voyages to the Inland Sea, 1971-79. Mem. Wis. Arts Bd., Madison, 1967-70. With USAF, 1951-55, Korea. Recipient award Coun. for Wis. Writers, 1971, 74, 96, Midwestern Book award U. Ky., 1974, Earplay award Corp. for Pub. Broadcasting, 1974, award Authors League Am., 1970. Avocations: letter press printing, golf. Home: 1310 Shorewood Dr La Crosse WI 54601

JUDSON, PHILIP LIVINGSTON, lawyer; b. Palo Alto, Calif., Oct. 25, 1941; s. Philip MacGregor and Elizabeth Stuart (Peck) J.; m. Dorothy Louisa Lebohner, Sept. 6, 1963 (div. Jan., 1996); children: Wendy Patricia, Philip Lebohner, Michael Lee; m. Danielle DuPuis Kane, May 18, 1996. BA, Stanford U., 1963; JD, U. Calif., Hastings, 1969. Bar: Calif. 1970, Tex. 1999, U.S. Dist. Ct. (no. dist.) Calif. 1970, U.S. Ct. Appeals (9th cir.) 1970, U.S. Dist. Ct. (ctrl. dist.) Calif. 1984, U.S. Dist. Ct. (ea. dist.) Calif. 1985, U.S. Supreme Ct. 1987, D.C. 1988, U.S. Dist. Ct. (so. dist.) Calif. 1989, Tex. 1999, U.S. Dist. Ct. (no. and we. dists.) Tex. 2000, U.S. Dist. Ct. (ea. dist.) Tex. 2002. Assoc. Pillsbury, Madison & Sutro, San Francisco, 1969-76, ptnr., 1977-99, Skjerven Morrill MacPherson, LLP, San Jose, Calif., 1999, Austin, Tex., 1999—2002; shareholder Winstead Sechrest & Minick, P.C., Austin, Tex., 2002—. Lectr. Practising Law Inst., U. Tex. Advanced Intellectual Property Law Inst., Inst. for Am. and Internat. Law Intellectual Property Law Program. Pres. St. Mark's Sch., San Rafael, 1983-85, founding mem. trustee 1980-86; trustee Marin Acad., San Rafael, 1985-91. 1st lt. U.S. Army, 1963-65. Mem. ABA (antitrust and litigation sects.), San Francisco Bar Assn., Am. Judicature Soc., Austin Intellectual Property Law Assn., Travis County Bar Assn., Order of Coif, Phi Delta Theta. Republican. Episcopalian. Home: 8004 High Hollow Dr Austin TX 78750-7872 Office: 100 Congress Ave Ste 800 Austin TX 78701 E-mail: pjudson@austin.rr.com., pjudson@winstead.com.

JUE, SUSAN LYNNE, interior designer; b. Berkeley, Calif., July 7, 1956; d. Howard Lynn and Rosie (Fong) J. AA with honors, Cabrillo Coll., 1977; BA, Calif. Coll. Arts and Crafts, 1979. Interior designer Lucasfilm Ltd., San Anselmo, Calif., 1980-81, Whisler-Patri Architects and Planners, San Francisco, 1982, Barry Reischmann Design Studio, San Francisco, 1983, Kaplan, McLaughlin, Diaz Architects and Planners, San Francisco, 1984-85; Gensler & Assocs., Architects San Francisco, 1985, Hirano Assocs., San Francisco, 1987-88, Clocktower Design, San Ramon, Calif., 1988-89, Reel/Grobman & Assocs., San Francisco, 1989-90; interior designer Primo Angeli Inc., San Francisco, 1990-92, Guillermo Rossello, Architect, Berkeley, Calif., 1992-94, Jean Coblentz & Assocs., San Francisco, 1995, Safeway, Pleasanton, 1996—. Chmn. Children's Discovery Mus. of San Jose, 1996. Recipient No. Calif. Home & Garden Design Achievement award 1992. Mem. Internat. Interior Design Assn. (newsletter editor No. Calif. chpt. 1987-88, resource index com. 1987-88, chmn. graphic com. 1987-88, Ronald McDonald House com. 1988-89, chmn. Salvation Army project com. 1990-91, chmn. Bread and Roses project com. 1991, chmn. Ctr. for AIDS, 1991-92, chmn. Maitri AIDS Hospice, 1995-97, chmn. ARIS, 1995-96, guide dogs for blind 1997-98, bd. dirs. 1991—, Cert. of Appreciation 1989, 91, 92, 97, 98, 99, Cmty. Svc. Program award 1993, 97, 98, pres. No. Calif. chpt. 1999—). Avocations: travel, graphic design. Home: 3339 Montevideo Dr San Ramon CA 94583-2606

JUEL, TWILA EILEEN EILEEN, elementary education educator; b. Audubon, Iowa, Feb. 8, 1948; d. Niels Christian and Norma Eileen (Wahlert) J. BE, Dana Coll., Blair, Nebr., 1970; MEd, U. Nebr. Omaha, 1975. Cert. tchr., Nebr. Tchr. Millard Pub. Schs., Omaha, 1970—2003; ret., 2003. Mem. NEA, Nebr. Edn. Assn., Millard Edn. Assn., Phi Delta Kappa. Democrat. Lutheran. Home: 16146 Arbor Ct Omaha NE 68130-1736

JUERGENS, BONNIE KAY, not-for-profit company executive; b. Denver, Sept. 11, 1947; d. Robert and Patricia Elaine (Carnahan) Beckman; adopted d. Donald Frederick Ruschmyer; m. Theodore Louis Juergens, Feb. 2, 1968 (div. 1976); m. Hugh Avery Standifer, Apr. 14, 1979. BA, MacMurray Coll., 1969; MLS, U. Ariz., 1972. Libr. liaison officer SUNY Ctrl. Adminstrn., Albany, 1973-75; spl. project dir. AMIGOS Bibliog. Coun., Inc., Dallas, 1975-77, assoc. dir., 1988-89; exec. dir. Amigos Libr. Svcs. Inc. (formerly AMIGOS Bibliog. Coun. Inc), Dallas, 1989—; customer rep. C.L. Systems, Inc., Newtonville, Mass., 1977-78; mgr. automation Austin (Tex.) Pub. Libr., 1978-83; ptnr. Justan Enterprises Mgmt. Cons., Austin, 1978-88. Vis. assoc. prof. Tex. A&M U., College Station, 1984; mem. users coun. OCLC Inc., Dublin, Ohio, 1979-83, 89-98. Author: Self-Instructional Intro to OCLC Mod 100 Terminal, 1976, revised edit., 1981; contbr. articles to profl. jours. Mem. Ctr. for Nonprofit Mgmt., Dallas, 1990—; bd. advisors U. North Tex. Grad. Libr. Sch., Denton, 1990—. Mem. ALA (mem. coun. 1981-89), Libr. and Info. Tech. Assn. (bd. dirs. 1980-89), Tex. Libr. Assn. Avocations: reading, sewing, travel, literacy-program support activities. Office: Amigos Libr Svcs Inc 14400 Midway Rd Dallas TX 75244-3509 E-mail: juergens@amigos.org.

JUERGENS, GEORGE IVAR, history educator; b. Bklyn., Mar. 20, 1932; s. George Odegaard and Magnhild (Julin) J.; m. Bonnie Jeanne Brownlee; children: Steven Erik, Paul Magnus. BA, Columbia Coll., 1953; BA, MA, Oxford U., 1956; PhD, Columbia U., 1965. Instr. Dartmouth Coll., Hanover, N.H., 1962-65; asst. prof. Amherst (Mass.) Coll., 1965-67; assoc. prof. Ind. U., Bloomington, 1967-80, prof. history, 1980—. Cons. Nat. Endowment Humanities, Washington, 1971— Author: Joseph Pulitzer and the New York World, 1966, News From The White House, 1981; assoc. editor: Jour. Am. History, 1968-69. With U.S. Army, 1956-58. Recipient Disting. Teaching award Amoco Found., 1982; Kellett fellow Columbia U., 1954-56; sr. faculty fellow Nat. Endowment Humanities, 1971-72; fellow Rockefeller Found., 1981-82 Mem. AAUP, Orgn. Am. Historians, Phi Beta Kappa Home: 2111 E Meadow Bluff Ct Bloomington IN 47401-6885 Office: Ind U Dept History Bloomington IN 47405 E-mail: juergens@indiana.edu.

JUERGENSMEYER, JOHN ELI, lawyer; b. May 14, 1934; s. Irvin Karl and Clara Augusta (johannaber) J.; m. Elizabeth Ann Bogart, Sept. 10, 1963; children: Margaret Ann, Frances Elizabeth. BA, U. Ill., 1955; JD, 1963; MA, Princeton U., 1957; PhD, 1960. Bar: Ill. 1963, U.S. Supreme Ct. 1968. Mem. faculty extension div. U. Ill., 1961-63; 73-74, U. Hawaii, 1958-60; mem. firm Kirkland, Brady, McQueen, Martin & Schnell, Elgin, Ill., 1963-64; founder, sr. ptnr. Juergensmeyer, Zimmerman, Smith & Leahy, Elgin, Ill., 1964-81, Juergensmeyer-Strain & Assocs., Elgin, Ill., 1981-95, Juergensmeyer & Assocs., 1995—. Mgr., owner Tollview Office Complex, 1976-95; asst. pub. defender Kane County, 1964-67, asst. states atty., 1976-78; spl. asst. atty. gen. State of Ill., 1978-85; hearing officer Ill. Pollution Control Bd., 1971-74; commr. U.S. Nat. Commn. on Libraries and Info. Scis., 1982-88; lectr. Inst. for Continuing Legal Edn.; trustee ALA Endowment Fund, 1970-84; assoc. prof. Judson Coll., Elgin, 1963—; bd. dirs. Elgin Nat. Bank. Author: President, Foundations, and the People-to-People Program, 1965; dontbr. articles to profl. jours.; contbr. publs. in field. Chmn. Hiawatha Dist. Boy Scouts Am.; v.p. Elgin Family Svc. Assn., 1967-71, Elgin Sister City Comm., 1990—; sec. Lloyd Morey Scholarship Fund, 1967-73; commr. Elgin Econ.Devel. Commn., 1971-75; chmn. Kane County Rep. Ctrl. Com., 1978-80; adv. bd. Ill. Youth Commn., 1964-68; bd. dirs Wesley Found of U. Ill., 1971-75; pres. adv. bd. Elgin Salvation Army, 1973-75. Served to capt. Intelligence Svc., USAF, 1958-60. Recipient Anti-Pollution Echo award Defenders of the Fox River, Inc., 1971, Cert. Merit, Heart Fund, 1971, Outstanding Young Man award Jr. C. of C., Elgin, 1967; Princeton U. fellow, 1955-56, Merrill Found. fellow, 1956-58. Mem. Assn. Trial Lawyers Am., ABA (local govt. law sect. spl. taxing dists. com. 1978—), Ill. State Bar Assn. (chmn. local govt. com. 1974-75, editor local govt. law newsletter 1973-74, mem. seminar in USSR 1979), Chgo. Bar Assn. (chmn. local govt. com. 1975-76), Kane County Bar Assn. (chmn. legis. com. 1974, chmn. local govt. com. 1992-93), 7th Cir. Bar Assn. (membership com.), Am. Arbitration Assn. (arbitrator), Am. Polit. Sci. Assn. (panel spkr. 1960 convention, mem. Sfrican Politics seminar 1966), Fed. Bar Assn., Midwest Polit.Sci. Assn., Ill. Polit. Sci. Assn. Northwest Suburban Bar Assn. Elgin Bar Assn. (chmn. legal aid 1964-67), Rotary (pres. 1977-78, Paul Harris fellow), Jaycees (legal counsel, bd. dirs. 1965-71), Phi Beta Kappa, Phi Alpha Delta, Alpha Kappa Lambda. Methodist. Club: Union League (Chgo.). Lodges: Masons, Shriners, Rotary (pres. 1977-78). Office: Assoc Prof Govt Judson College Elgin IL 60123

JUETT, SAMUEL JOSEPH, administrative officer, consultant; b. Seymour, Ind., June 24, 1960; s. Melvin Royce Juett and Marilyn Joan Motsinger; Stepfather Roy Motsinger; m. JoAnne Crum Juett, June 11, 1983; children: Jarred, Jacqueline. BS, U. Indpls., 1982; MA, U. Louisville, 1986; DOA, U. Ga., Athens, 1991; diploma, US Army Command & Gen. Staff, Ft. Leavenworth, Kans., 1989-92. Prof. mgmt. Mercer U., Atlanta, 1989-96; city mgr. City of Monroe, Ga., 1997-99, exec. adminstrv. officer, 2000—. Cons. Work-Ethics.com, Washington, 1998-01. Author: The Efficacy of Performance Appraisal Systems in the Public Sector, 1996, An Analysis of Job Characteristics in State Mental Hospitals, 1986. Capt., US Army, CONUS, 1981-93. Mem. Internat. City County Mgmt. Assn., Internat Fire Chiefs Assn., Rotary Internat., Masonic Lodge. Mem. Alliance of Baptists. Avocations: internat. travel, WWI studies, antique fire trucks. Office: 410 4th Ave Eau Claire WI 54703-5542 E-mail: sjjuett@earthlink.net.

JUETTNER, DIANA D'AMICO, lawyer, educator; b. N.Y.C., Jan. 21, 1940; d. Paris T.R. and Dina Adele (Antonucci) D'Amico; m. Paul J. Juettner, June 29, 1963; children: John, Laura. BA, Hunter Coll., 1961; postgrad., Am. U., 1963; JD cum laude, Touro Coll., 1983. Bar: N.Y. 1984, U.S. Dist. Ct. (so. dist.) N.Y. 1984, U.S. Supreme Ct. 1987. Office mgr. Westchester County Dem. Com., White Plains, NY, 1976-79; dist. mgr. for Westchester County U.S. Bur. Census, N.Y.C., 1979-80; pvt. practice Ardsley, NY, 1984—; prof. law, program dir. for legal studies Mercy Coll., Dobbs Ferry, NY, 1986—, co-chair social and behavioral scis. divsn., 2002—, asst. chair dept. law, criminal justice-safety adminstrn., 1994-98, pres. faculty senate, 1996—98, 2000—02. Arbitrator small claims matters White Plains City Ct., 1985-89. Co-author: (booklet) Your Day in Court, How to File a Small Claims Suit in Westchester County, 1976; assoc. editor N.Y. State Probation Officers Assn. Jour., 1990-92; editor-in-chief Jour. Northeast Acad. Legal Studies in Bus., 1996-98; contbr. articles to profl. jours. Councilwoman Town of Greenburgh, N.Y., 1992—; vice chair law com. Westchester County Dem. Com., White Plains, 1987-91; corr. sec. Greenburgh Dem. Town Com., Hartsdale, N.Y., 1986-91; mem. Westchester County Citizens Consumer Adv. Coun., White Plains, 1975-91, chair, 1991; chair Ardsley (N.Y.) Consumer Adv. Commn., 1974-79. Mem. Am. Assn. for Paralegal Edn. (model syllabus task force 1992-95, chair legis. com. 1995-97), N.Y. State Bar Assn. (elder law sect. com. on pub. agy. liaison and legis. 1992-95), Westchester County Bar Assn. (chair paralegal subcom. 1990—, chair bicentennial U.S. Constitution com. 1987-91), Westchester Women's Bar Assn. (v.p. 1989-91, dir. 1994-96, co-chair tech. com. 1996-2000), Women's Bar Assn. State N.Y. (chair profl. ethics com. 1997-98). Avocations: sailing, walking. Office: Mercy Coll 555 Broadway Dobbs Ferry NY 10522-1134 Business E-Mail: djuettner@mercy.edu.

JÜGELT, KARL-HEINZ BURKHARD, librarian, researcher; b. Auma, Thüringen, Germany, Sept. 11, 1934; s. Helmut and Gertrud (Blauert) J.; m. Margot Fischer Pohlenz, Nov. 22, 1958 (div. 1970); children: Burkhard, Henriette; m. Ingelore Henk, Jan. 28, 1972; children Konstantin, Karoline. Diploma in Linguistics, Humboldt U., Berlin, 1957, diploma in Libr. Sci., 1962; PhD, U. Rostock, 1976, Extraord.prof., 1988. Rschr. U. Bibliothek, Jena, Germany, 1958; head various depts. Deutche Staats-Bibliothek, Berlin, 1959-71; univ. libr. U. Rostock, 1972-92; custodian U. Rostok, 1993-99, retired, 1999. Mem. editl. bd. Zentralblatt Für Bibliothekswesen, 1987-90; contbr. articles to profl. jours. Mem. Libr. Assn. (last GDR pres. 1987-90) Mem. Verband Deutscher Bibiothekare, Vereinigung Österreichischer Bibliothekarinnen und Bibiothekare (mem. 1990—), Nemzetközi Magyarsagtudomanyi Társaság, Lions Club Rostock (sec. 1994—). Avocation: collecting type specimen books. E-mail: karl-heinz.juegelt@web.de.

JUGENHEIMER, DONALD WAYNE, advertising and communications educator, university administrator; b. Manhattan, Kans., Sept. 22, 1943; s. Robert William and Mabel Clara (Hobert) J.; m. Bonnie Jeanne Scamehorn, Aug. 30, 1970 (dec. 1983); 1 child, Beth Carrie; m. Kaleen B. Brown, July 25, 1987. BS in Advt., U. Ill.-Urbana, 1965, MS in Advt., 1968, PhD in Communications, 1972. Advt. copywriter Fillman & Assocs, Champaign, Ill., 1963-64, 66; media buyer Leo Burnett Co., Chgo., 1965-66; asst., assoc. prof. U. Kans., Lawrence, 1971-80, prof. jounralism, dir. grad. studies and rsch., 1980-85; Manship prof. journalism La. State U., Baton Rouge, 1985-87; prof., chmn. dept. communications and speech Fairleigh Dickinson U., Teaneck, N.J., 1987-89, 92-95, dean coll. liberal arts, 1989-92; chair dept. English, lang. and philosphy, 1995; prof. Sch. Journalism So. Ill. U., Carbondale, 1995—. Dir. Sch. Journalism So. Ill. U., Carbondale, 1995-2002; adj. faculty Turku (Finland) Sch. Econs., 1999—; adv. cons. U.S. Army, Fort Sheridan, Ill., Pentagon, Washington, 1981-90, Am. Airlines, 1989-91, IBM Corp., 1989—, U.S. Dept. Def.; cons. editor Grid Publ., Columbus, Ohio, 1974-84; grad. and rsch. dir. U. Kans., 1978-84, adv. chmn., 1974-78; adj. prof. Turku (Finland) Sch. Econs. and Bus. Adminstrn., 1998—. Author: Advertising Media Sourcebook and Workbook, 1975, 3d edit., 1989, 4th edit. 1996, Strategic Advertising Decisions, 1976, Basic Advertising, 1979, 2d edit., 1991, Advertising Media, 1980, Problems and Practices in Advertising Research, 1982, Advertising Media: Strategy and Tactics, 1992, Advertising Media Planning: A Brand Management Approach, 2003; bd. editors Jour. Advt., 1985-89, Jour. Interactive Advt., 2000—, Jour. Current Issues and Rsch. in Advt., 1990—. Advvertising Needs Planning: A Broad Management Approach, 2003. Subscription mgr. Jour. of Advt., 1971-74, bus. mgr., 1974-79; chmn. U. Div. United Fund, Lawrence, 1971-72; pres. Sch.-Cmty. Rels. Coun., Lawrence, 1974-75. Recipient Hope Tchg. award U. Kans, 1977, 78, Kellogg Nat. fellow W.K. Kellogg Found., 1984-88; named Outstanding Young Men in Am. Nat. Jaycees, 1978. Mem. AAUP, Am. Acad. Advt. (pres. 1984-86), Assn. For Edn. in Journalism (head advt. divsn. 1977-78), Kappa Tau Alpha, Alpha Delta Sigma. Presbyterian. Avocations: skiing; sailing; writing; travel; reading. Home: 110 Tecumseh Dr Carbondale IL 62901-7113 Office: So Ill U Sch Journalism Carbondale IL 62901-6601

JUHANI, ERMA, lawyer, former stock exchange executive; b. Tampere, Finland, Nov. 29, 1946; LLM, U. Helsinki, Finland, 1969, Lic. Laws, 1977. Asst. Heikki Haapaniemi Law Office, 1969; lawyer legal affairs dept. Enso-Gutzeit Oy, 1972; legal ops. mgr. Union Bank of Finland, Ltd., 1979, asst. gen. mgr. sect. for investment banking and legal ops., 1981, branch mgr. Helsinki-Eteläsatama branch, 1982; mng. dir. Unitas Ltd., 1983, Indsl. Bank Finland, Ltd., 1988; pres., CEO The Helsinki Stock Exch., 1989-97; CEO HEX Helsinki Exchs., 1997—2000; sr. advisor Borenius & Kemppinen Ltd., Helsinki, Finland, 2002—. Mem. bd. dirs. The Helsinki Stock Exchg., 1986, 88, The Finnish Found. for Share Promotion, 1989. Office: Borenius & Kemppinen Ltd Yrjönkatu 13A FIN-00120 Helsinki Finland

JUHL, DANIEL LEO, manufacturing and marketing firm executive; b. Sioux City, Iowa, Aug. 18, 1935; s. Burnett Andrew and Margret Anne (Osinger) J.; m. Colleen Ann Eagan, Dec. 20, 1958; children: Gregory, Michael, Jennifer. Student, U. S.D., 1956; BSME, UCLA, 1959; postgrad., Harvard U., 1976. Design engr. Edler Industries, Newport Beach, Calif., 1959-61; v.p. mfg. Raybestos-Manhattan Corp. (now Rayteck Corp.), Trumbull, Conn., Can. and Europe, 1961-80; v.p. ops. Easco/KD Tools, Lancaster, Pa., 1980-83; mgr. ops. S.K. Wellman Corp., Bedford Heights, Ohio, 1983-86; gen. mgr. N.Am. Systems, Bedford Heights, 1986; indsl. mgmt. cons., 1987; pres., chief exec. officer Stanhope Products Co., Brookville, Ohio, 1987-2000, Nat. Extrusions Co., Bellefontaine, Ohio, 1987—, Nathan Hale Furniture Co., 1987-2000; pres., CEO DJ Ventures Inc., Centerville, Ohio, 2000—. Contbr. numerous articles to trade jours.; patentee high temperature lightweight plastic insulation, molecular sieve used in auto air conditioning. Fund raiser United Way, 1980-2000. Recipient Disting. Alumni award UCLA, 1991. Mem. Soc. Automotive Engrs. (chmn. com. 1987), Soc. Plastics Industry, Elks. Avocations: travel, sports, woodworking.

JUHL, HAROLD ALEXANDER, retired career officer, construction executive; b. Kearney, Nebr., June 24, 1950; s. Harold Ferdinand and Vivian Lea Louise (Simshauser) J.; m. Becky Sue Adams, July 30, 1971; children: Aaron A., Shane B. Student, Kearney State Coll., 1968-71, Pensacola (Fla.) Jr. Coll., 1977-79; BA, Colo. State U., 1985. Electronic technician GTE Corp., Chgo., 1971-73; enlisted USMC, 1973, advanced through grades to lt. col., 1990; helicopter pilot HML-267, Camp Pendleton, Calif., 1974-76; flight instr. USN VT-3, Milton, Fla., 1976-79; air officer 2d Bn. 4th Marines, Okinawa, Japan, 1979-80; KC-130 pilot, weapons-tactics instr. VMGR 252, Cherry Point, N.C., 1980-83, aviation safety officer, 1986-88; dir. of safety and standardization VMGR-252, 1988-89, Marine Aircraft Group 36, Okinawa, Japan, 1989-90; C-130 class desk officer Navair-Syscom, Washington, N.C., 1990-94; spl. ops. officer Marine Forces Atlantic, Camp LeJuene, N.C., 1994-97; ret., 1997; owner Juhl Designs, Swansboro, N.C., 1997—. Cons. Colo. State U. ROTC, Ft. Collins, 1984-85, Aerial Refueling Systems Adv. BGroup, Oxford, Eng., 1987—, KC-130 Aircraft Symposium, El Toro, Calif., 1987-94; presenter to NATO's Partnership for Peace Coordination Cell, Mons, Belgium, 1996; guest lectr. USN Acad., Annapolis, Md., 1983-84; mem. joint US-Japan Battle Studies Program, 1989-90; participant Warfighting Symposium, Okinawa, Japan, 1989, 90; exercise planner for Norway/NATO Exercises, 1994, 95, 96. Cubmaster Boy Scouts Am., Quantico, Va., 1985-86; coach, referee Quantico Youth Soccer League, 1985; commr. Quantico Little League, 1986; coach Pop Warner Football, Newport, N.C., 1987, 88, 90; coach Ea. Carolina Soccer Assn., 1990-91. Recipient Shield of Service Boy Scouts Am., 1986. Mem. Marine Corps Assn., Marine Corps Aviation Assn., Golden Key, Experimental Aircraft Assn. (charter, bd. dirs. Beafort, N.C. chpt.) Clubs: Kearney Aero (pres. 1970-71). Avocations: art collecting, metalcrafts, home improvements, travel, airplane constrn. Home: 223 Star Hill Dr Swansboro NC 28584-8935

JUHOLA, MICHAEL DUANE, lawyer; b. Ashtabula, Ohio, May 11, 1955; s. Kenneth Duane and Lois Rosemary (England) J.; m. Denise H. Juhola, May 2, 1987. BA, Hiram Coll., 1977; JD, Ohio State U., 1980. Bar: Ohio 1980, U.S. Dist. Ct. (so. dist.) Ohio 1987, U.S. Ct. Appeals (6th cir.) 1992. Asst. dir. Ohio Legal Ctr. Inst., Columbus, 1980-88; staff atty. Smith, Clark & Holzapfel, Columbus, 1988-89; exec. dir. Ohio div. Profl. Edn. System, Inc., Columbus, 1989-91; pvt. practice law Columbus, 1991—. Coun. mem. North Community Luth. Ch., Columbus, 1989-93. Mem. Ohio Bar Assn., Columbus Bar Assn., Worthington Estate Planning Coun., Phi Beta Kappa. Office: 867-B High St Worthington OH 43085

JULANDER, PAULA FOIL, health care and political consultant, state senator; b. Charlotte, N.C., Jan. 21, 1939; d. Paul Baxter and Esther Irene (Earnhardt) Foil; m. Roydon Odell Julander, Dec. 21, 1985; 1 child, Julie McMahan Shipman. Diploma, Presbyn. Sch. Nursing, Charlotte, N.C., 1960; BS magna cum laude, U. Utah, 1984; MS in Nursing Adminstrn., Brigham Young U., 1990. RN, Utah. Nurse various positions, Fla. and S.C., 1960-66; co-founder Am. Laser Corp., 1970-79; tchg. asst. U. Utah, Salt Lake City; mem. Utah Ho. of Reps., Salt Lake City, 1989-92; Dem. nominee lt. gov. State of Utah, 1992; minority whip Utah State Senate, Dist. 1, Salt Lake City, 1998—2000; health care/polit. cons. Salt Lake City, 1998—2000. Mem. adj. faculty Brigham Young U. Coll. Nursing, 1987—95; bd. dirs. Block Fin. Svcs.; mem. Utah state exec. bd U.S. West Comm., 1993—96; bd. regents Calif. Luth. U., 1994—97; trustee KUED TV, 2000—, Intermountain Health Care Hosps., 2000—. Med. cons. ("Health Tracks, A Practical Guide to Mng. Your Health"), 2000; co-author (cookbook): Utah State Fare, 1995. Pres. Utah Nurses Found., 1986—88; mem. Nat. Conf. of State Legis. Com. on Families and Children, 1999—, The Coun. of State Govt. Com. on Health and Aging, 1999—, Women's Polit.Caucus, Statewide Abortion Task Force, 1990; bd. dirs. Cmty. Nursing Svc. Home Health Plus, 1992—94; mem. Planned Parenthood Assn. Utah, 1994—, Utahns for Choice, 1995—; trustee Westminster Coll., 1994—, HCA-St. Mark's Hosp., 1994—95; elected sen. State of Utah, 1998—. Recipient Utah pub. health hero award, 2000. Mem.: Nat Orgn. Women Legislators, Utah Nurses Assn. (legis. rep. 1987—88, Lifetime Achievement award), ANA, Phi Kappa Phi (Susan Young Gates award 1991), Sigma Theta Tau.

JULANDER, ROYDON O. political science educator, lobyist; b. Washington, Feb. 07; s. Odell and Ora (Hansen) J.; m. Sandra Prows; children: Dirk, Jori, Tracy, Treg; m. Paula Foil, Oct. 21, 1985. MS in Philosophy, U. Utah, 1962, PhD in Polit. Sci., 1985. Instr. dept. polit. sci. Weber State U, Ogden, Utah, 1960, asst. prof., 1960—65, assoc. prof., 1965-86, prof., 1986—. Mem. Utah Senate, Salt Lake City, 1972-74; chmn. Utah Family Svcs. Bd., Salt Lake City, 1986-92; vice chmn. Utah Dem. Com., Salt Lake City, 1997—; mem. Utah Radiation Control Bd., Salt Lake City, 1999—. With U.S. Army, 1954-56. Rsch. grantee U.S. Aging Coun., 1981. Mem. ASPA, Sierra Club. Avocation: woodcarving. Home: 476 B St Salt Lake City UT 84103 Office: Weber State U 1203 University Cir Ogden UT 84408 E-mail: rjulander@weber.edu.

JULESZ, BELA, experimental psychologist, educator, electrical engineer; b. Budapest, Hungary, Feb. 19, 1928; came to U.S., 1956; s. Jeno and Klementin (Fleiner) J.; m. Margit Fasy, Aug. 7, 1953 Dipl. Elec. Engring., Tech. U., Budapest, 1950; Dr. Ing., Hungarian Acad. Sci., Budapest, 1956. Asst. prof. dept. communication Tech U. Budapest, Hungary, 1950-51; mem. tech. staff Telecommunication Research Inst., Budapest, 1951-56, Bell Labs., Murray Hill, N.J., 1956-64, head sensory and perceptual processes, 1964-83; rsch. head visual perception rsch. AT&T Bell Labs., Murray Hill, N.J., 1984-89; State of N.J. prof. psychology, dir. lab. of vision rsch. Rutgers U., Piscataway, N.J., 1989-99, ret., 1999—. Continuing vis. prof. biology dept. Calif. Inst. Tech., Pasadena, 1985-94. Author: Foundations of Cyclopean Perception, 1971, Dialogues on Perception, 1995; author over 200 sci. papers on visual perception; discover computer generated random-dot stereogram technique. Fairchild disting. scholar Calif. Inst. Tech., 1977-79, 87, assoc. Neurosci. Research Progam, 1982; MacArthur Found. fellow, 1983-87; Dr. H.P. Heineken prize Royal Netherlands Acad. Arts and Scis., 1985; Karl Spencer Lashley award Am. Philos. Soc., 1989. Fellow AAAS, Am. Acad. Arts and Scis., Optical Soc. Am.; mem. NAS, Goettingen Acad. Scis. (corr.), Hungarian Acad. Scis. (hon.), Am. Philos. Soc. Home: 30 Valleyview Rd Warren NJ 07059-5229 Office: Rutgers U Lab Vision Rsch Psychology 152 Frelinghuysen Rd Piscataway NJ 08854-8020

JULIAN, J. R. lawyer; b. Wilmington, Del., Apr. 6, 1943; BA, Am U., 1966; JD, Cath. U. Am., 1970. Bar: Del. 1971, U.S. Dist. Ct. Del., U.S. Ct. Appeals (3d cir.), U.S. Supreme Ct. Pvt. practice, Wilmington, Del. Mem. bd. bar examiners Supreme Ct. State Del., 1985-89; mem. rules com. Del. Indsl. Accident Bd. Bd. dirs. Hist. Soc. Ct. Chancery. Mem. ABA (litig. sect., bus. law sect.), ATLA, Del. Bar Assn. (v.p. New Castle County chpt., former vice chair jud. appointments com., exec. com., litig. com., alt. dispute resolution com., ins. com., workers' compensation com., pres.), Am. Bd. Trial Advocates, Def. Rsch. Inst., Am. Judicature Soc., Del. Trial Lawyers Assn., Federalist Soc. for Law and Pub. Policy Studies (bd. adv. Del. chpt. lawyers divsn.), St. Thomas More Soc. Del. (pres.), Pi Sigma Alpha, Delta Theta Pi. Office: Ste 1001 Market St Mall PO Box 2171 Wilmington DE 19899-2171*

JULIAN, MICHAEL, grocery company executive; b. 1950; With Human Sys. Inc., Florham Pk., NJ, 1975-85, Richfood Inc., Mechanicsville, Va., 1985-87; COO, exec. v.p. Farm Fresh Inc., 1987—, chmn., CEO, 1988—; pres., CEO Jitney Jungle, Jackson, Miss., 1997-1999. Office: Jitney Jungle 1855 Lakeland Dr STE D20 Jackson MS 39216-4947

JULIAN, RAYMOND CHARLES, financial planner, investment company executive; b. Beverly, Mass., Oct. 23, 1952; s. Raymond W. and Marjorie (Vendettouli) J.; m. Michele D. Simpson, May 28, 1979. BS in Mgmt., Boston Coll., 1975. Cert. fin. planner, registered investment advisor. Exec. producer Beacon Sport Network, Boston, 1975-79; field underwriter N.Y. Life Ins. Co., Boston, 1978-80; account exec. Am. Mut. Ins. Cos., Chestnut Hill, Mass., 1980-81; asst. v.p. First Svc. Ins. Agy., Watertown, Mass., 1981-91; exec. v.p., prin. Compass Securities Corp., Newton, Mass., 1991—; investment advisor Compass Capital Corp., Newton, 1991-96. Cert. fin. planner NE Savs. FA,

Watertown, 1987-91. Mem. Fin. Planning Assn. (pres. Greater Boston Soc. 1992-93), Rotary, Newton Club. Office: Compass Capital Corp One Gateway Ctr Newton MA 02458 E-mail: ray@CompassSecurities.com.

JULIAN, ROSE RICH, music educator, director; b. Asheboro, N.C., Sept. 9, 1937; d. Herbert C. and Esther Dennis Rich; m. Cecil Perry Julian, May 30, 1959 (div. Apr. 1977); children: Alan Perry, Keri Dawn Julian Sorensen, Derrick Kyle. AA in Voice, Mars Hill Coll., 1957; BS in Music, East Carolina U., 1959; postgrad., U N.C., 1971—79, Western Carolina U., 1995. Cert. music tchr. N.C. Dir. music USAF Chapel Choir, 1960—71; tchr. Rowan/Salisbury (N.C.) Schs., 1972—79, 1988—; dir. music Thyatira Pres Ch., Salisbury, 1982—88, Coburn U. N.C., Salisbury, 1991—97. Conductor Salisbury Choral Soc., 1993; pianist 1st Bapt. Ch., Salisbury, 1999—; judge Protestant Chapels of Europe, Frankfurt, Germany, 1970. Mem.: AOSA, NAE, Nat. Assn. Tchrs. Singing, Music Educators Assn., Piano Guild. Baptist. Home: 36 Old Farm Rd Salisbury NC 28147

JULIANA, JAMES NICHOLAS, ordnance company executive; b. Camden, N.J., Apr. 1, 1922; s. Nicholas and Rosa (de Noti) J.; m. Elizabeth D. Sutton, Nov. 8, 1947, children— James S., Patrick C., Mary E., Thomas E., David J., Richard S., Robert Francis, Ronald Joseph (dec.). BS, Washington Coll., Md., 1944. Spl. agt. FBI, 1947-53; asst. exec. dir., exec. dir., chief counsel to minority Senate Permanent Sub-com. on Investigations, 1953-58; exec. dir. CAB, 1958-61; pres., dir. Internat. Fact Finding Inst., 1961-62; pres. James N. Juliana Assocs., Washington, 1962-81, 84—; sec., dir. Alaska N.Am. Corp., Washington, 1970-77; v.p. fed. affairs Braniff Internat., 1977-81; prin. dep. asst. sec. for manpower, res. affairs and logistics Dept. Def., Washington, 1981-84; dir. Tround Internat., 1984-97; chmn., CEO, pres., 1993-97; dir. IX Sys., 1985-98. Mem. Pres.'s Com. on Mental Retardation, 1971-77; exec. v.p. Armed Forces Mktg. Council, Washington, 1974-81; bd. visitors, bd. govs. Washington Coll., Chestertown, Md., 1978-84. Served with USNR, 1944-46. Mem. Soc. Former Spl. Agts., FBI, Coalition of Mil. Distributors (exec. dir. 1990—), Capital Hill Club, Kappa Alpha, Omicron Delta Kappa. Home: 11013 Rosemont Dr Rockville MD 20852-3650 also: 66 W 17th St Ocean City NJ 08226-2924 Office: 11013 Rosemont Dr Rockville MD 20852-2606

JULIANO, JOHN LOUIS, lawyer; b. Oct. 21, 1944; s. John Carmine and Jeannette Helen (Ciotti) J.; m. Maryjane Theresa Groccia, July 4, 1966 (dec.); children: Jennifer, Jonathan. BBA, St. John's U., 1966; JD, Bklyn. Law Sch., 1969. Bar: N.Y. 1970, U.S. Dist. Ct. (ea. and so. dists.) N.Y., U.S. Ct. Appeals (2d cir.), U.S. Supreme Ct. Ptnr. Juliano, Karlson, Weisberg, 1970-72; pvt. practice East Northport, N.Y., 1972—. Pres., dir. Hillside United Van Lines, Inc.; mem. N.Y. State 10th Jud. Grievance Com., 1998—; lectr. Suffolk Acad. Law. Mem. ATLA, N.Y. State Bar Assn., Suffolk County Bar Assn. (pres. 1996-97, v.p. 1995-96, treas. 1994-95, sec. 1993-94, bd. dirs. 1998-2001), N.Y. State Trial Lawyers Assn., ICC Practitioners, Criminal Bar Assn., Columbian Lawyers Assn. (sec. 1972, treas. 1973, pres. 1974-75), Am. Inns of Ct. Address: 39 Doyle Ct East Northport NY 11731-6404

JULIBER, LOIS, manufacturing executive; b. 1949; m. John Adams. BA, Wellesley Coll.; MBA, Harvard U. Former v.p. Gen. Foods Corp.; from gen. mgr. to pres. Far East/Can. divsn. Colgate-Palmolive Co., N.Y.C., 1988-92, chief tech. officer, 1992-94, pres. Colgate—N.Am. divsn., 1994—. Bd. dirs. DuPont Corp. Trustee Brookdale Found., Wellesley Coll. Mem. Harvard Bus. Sch. Club N.Y. (bd. dirs.) Avocations: tennis, gardening, cooking. Office: Colgate Palmolive Co 300 Park Ave Fl 8 New York NY 10022-7499

JULIEN, ROBERT MICHAEL, anesthesiologist, writer; b. Port Townsend, Wash., Mar. 24, 1942; s. Frank Felton and Mary Grace (Powers) J.; m. Judith Dianne DeChenne, Feb. 26, 1963; children: Robert Michael, Scott M. BS in Pharmacy, U. Wash., 1965, MS in Pharmacology, 1968, PhD, 1970; MD, U. Calif.-Irvine, 1977. Intern Good Samaritan Hosp., Portland, Oreg., 1977-78; resident Oreg. Health Scis. U., 1978-80; asst. prof. pharmacology U. Calif.-Irvine, 1970-74, asst. clin. prof., 1974-77; assoc. prof. anesthesiology and pharmacology U. Oreg., Portland, 1980-83; staff anesthesiologist St. Vincent Hosp., Portland, 1983—. Author: Primer of Drug Action, 1975, 9th edit., 2001, Understanding Anesthesiology, 1984, Drugs and the Body, 1987. Recipient Svc. award Am. Epilepsy Soc., 1975. Mem. Am. Soc. Anesthesiologists, Am. Assn. Pharmacology and Exptl. Therapeutics, Soc. Neurosci., Oreg. Med. Assn., Western Pharmacology Soc. Roman Catholic. Home: 1212 SW Hessler Dr Portland OR 97239-2807 Office: St Vincent Hosp Dept Anesthesia 9205 SW Barnes Rd Portland OR 97225-6603 E-mail: drsjulien@comcast.net.

JULIEN, TERRENCE DARRYL, neurosurgeon, researcher; b. Washington, Oct. 12, 1966; s. Selwyn McGregor and Thelma Sally J.; m. Thuy-An H., June 23, 1990. BA, U. Del., 1988; MD, Howard U., 1993. Intern Med. Ctr. Del., Newark, 1993-94; fellow in neurosurgery NYU Med. Ctr., N.Y.C., 1994-95, resident in neurosurgery, 1995-96, SUNY, Syracuse, 1996-2001, asst. chief resident neurosurgery, 1999-2000, chief resident in neurosurgery, 2000-01; fellow in neurosurg. oncology Meml. Sloan-Kettering Cancer Ctr., N.Y.C., 2001—02; instr. neurosurgery H. Lee Moffitt Cancer Ctr., Tampa, Fla., 2002—03. Recipient cancer rsch. scholarship, AACR, 2001; fellow, Mitchel Found., Howard U., 1991. Mem.: AMA, Congress Neurol. Surgeons, Am. Assn. Cancer Rsch. (Minority Scholar in Cancer Rsch. 2001), Am. Asn. Neurolog. Surgeons (joint sect. tumors 1988, joint sect. spine guidelines com. 1998—2001, Preuss award 1999). Office: H Lee Moffitt Cancer Ctr Dept Neurosurgery 12902 Magnolia Dr Ste 3136 Tampa FL 33612 E-mail: Julient@mac.com.

JULIEN, THOMAS THEODORE, religious denomination administrator; b. Arcanum, Ohio, June 27, 1931; s. Russel Ray and Clara (Cassel) J.; m. Doris Mardella Briner, Aug. 21, 1953; children: Becky Jean, Terry Lee, Jacqueline Sue. BA, Bob Jones U., 1953; MDiv, Grace Theol. Sem., Winona Lake, Ind., 1957, DD (hon.), 1996; cert. French lang., U. Grenoble, France, 1960. Ordained to ministry Fellowship of Grace Brethren Chs., 1956. Pastor Grace Brethren Ch., Ft. Wayne, Ind., 1955-58; missionary Grace Brethren Fgn. Missions, Grenoble, 1959-64, field supt. Macon, France, 1964-78, dir. for Europe, 1964-86; exec. dir. Grace Brethren Internat. Missions, Winona Lake, 1986-2000. Author: Handbook for Young Christians, 1959, Inherited Wealth, 1976, Spiritual Greatness, 1979, Seize the Moment, 2000. Decorated chevalier de Republique (Ctrl. African Republic). Home: 545 S Circle Dr Warsaw IN 46580 Office: Grace Brethren Internat Missions PO Box 588 Winona Lake IN 46590-0588 E-mail: tomjulien@compuserve.com.

JULIFS, SANDRA JEAN, community action agency executive; b. Jersey City, July 12, 1939; d. Roy Howard and Irma Margrete (Barkhausen) Walters; m. Harold William Julifs, July 22, 1961; children: David Howard, Steven William. BA, U. Va., 1961; postgrad., U. Minn., 1962-63, Mankato State Coll., 1963. Cert. comty. action profl. Tchr. St. James (Minn.) Pub. Schs., 1961-62; substitute tchr. Sleepy Eye (Minn.) Pub. Schs., 1963-67, home bound tutor, 1967; lay reader, rater U. Wis., Stevens Point, 1968; co-founder Family Planning Service Portage County, Stevens Point, 1970-72; family planning dir. Tri-County Opportunities Coun., Rock Falls, Ill., 1971-77, energy programs coord., 1977-78, planner, EEO officer, 1978-83, pres., chief exec. officer, 1983—. Sec. Ill. Ventures for Comty. Action Springfield, 1983-91, bd. dirs. 1991-94, 96—. Mem. Nat. Cmty. Action Found., Washington, 1987—; bd. dirs. Twin Cities Homeless Coalition, 1989-96; mem. adv. coun. Sauk Valley Coll. Human Svcs., 1990-99; mem. Sauk Valley Coll. Workforce Devel. Coun., 1999—; mem. Whiteside County Overall Econ. Devel. Coun., 1990-99; mem. adv. coun. Inst. for Social and Econ. Devel., 1992-95; cons. com. No. Ill. Synod, Evang. Luth. Ch. Am., 1993-99, churchwide assembly del., 1995; mem. Statewide Rural Poverty Conf. Com., 1996-97; mem. Ill. State Microenterprise Initiative; mem. cmty. svcs. adv. com. Ill. Dept. Commerce and Cmty., 1998—. Recipient Appreciation award Western Ill. Agy. on Aging, 1980, 81, Spl. Recognition award Ill. Head Start and Day Care Assn., Recognition award Ill. Community Action Fund, 1984, Recognition award Ill. Ventures for Cmty. Action, 1996. Mem. AAUW, NAFE, Whiteside County Welfare Assn., Lee County Welfare Assn. (sec.-treas. 1983-84), Nat. Cmty. Action Assn., Cmty. Action Partnership, Ill. Cmty. Action Assn. (com. chair 1985-88, dir. exec. com. 1986-95, treas. 1988, 89, sec. 1989, 90, v.p. 1991-93, pres. 1993-95, dir. 2000-03, Recognition award 1985-95, 2000-03). Lutheran. Avocations: travel, reading. E-mails. Office: Tri-County Opportunities Coun PO Box 610 Rock Falls IL 61071-0610 E-mail: sjulifs@wmccinc.com., hwjulifs@essex1.com.

JULSTROM, ROSA DRAKE, music educator; b. Harrisburg, Ill., Apr. 12, 1925; d. Charles Bryant Drake and Rosa Bauer Streng; m. Clifford Arthur Julstrom, Aug. 21, 1948 (dec. Mar. 1991); childre: Bryant Arthur, Stephen Drake. BA, U. Rochester, 1946; MA, Eastman Sch. Music, 1947. Tchr. piano Middlebury (Vt.) Coll., 1947-48; ind. music tchr. Macomb, Ill., 1948—. Pub. music by Clifford Arthur Julstrom, Julstrom Enterprises. Mem. Music Tchrs. Nat. Assn., Ill. State Music Tchrs. Assn., Phi Beta Kappa. Democrat. Home and Office: 226 E Grant St Macomb IL 61455-3230

JUMA, CALESTOUS, international development educator; b. Busia, Kenya, June 9, 1953; s. John Juma Kwada and Clementina Okhubedo Juma; m. Alison Thornycroft Field, Sept. 9, 1987; 1 child, Eric Kwada Field. MSc, U. Sussex, Falmer, Brighton, U.K., 1983, DPhil, 1986. Sch. tchr., Mombasa, 1974-78; rschr., editor Environment Liaison Ctr., Nairobi, 1979-82; exec. dir., founder African Ctr. for Tech. Studies, Nairobi, 1988-95; exec. sec. UN Conv. on Biol. Diversity, Geneva and Montreal, 1995-98; rsch. fellow Kennedy Sch. Govt. Harvard U., Cambridge, Mass., 1999-2000, sr. rsch. fellow, program dir. Kennedy Sch. Govt., 2000 01; prof. Kennedy Sch. Govt., 2002 ; chancellor U. Guyana, 2002—. Author: Long Run Economics, 1987, The Gene Hunters, 1989, The Adaptive Economy, 1993, Open the Social Sciences, 1996. Recipient Pew Scholars award Pew Charitable Trusts, 1991, UN Global 500 Roll of Honor, UN Environ. Program, 1993, Henry Shaw medal Mo. Bot. Garden, 2001. Fellow Kenyan Nat. Acad. Scis., N.Y. Acad. Scis., World Acad. Art and Sci.; mem. AAAS, NAS (bd. agr. and natural resources), Internat. Soc. for Study of Time. Avocations: hiking, bicycling. Home: 363 Concord Ave Cambridge MA 02138 Office: Kennedy Sch of Govt 79 JFK St Cambridge MA 02138 E-mail: calestous_juma@harvard.edu.

JUMONVILLE, FELIX JOSEPH, JR., physical education educator, realtor; b. Crowley, La., Nov. 20, 1920; s. Felix Joseph and Mabel (Rogers) J.; m. Mary Louise Hoke, Jan. 11, 1952; children: Carol, Susan. BS, La. State U., 1942; MS, U. So. Calif., 1948, EdD, 1952. Assoc. prof. phys. edn. Los Angeles State Coll., 1948-60; prof. phys. edn. Calif. State U., Northridge, 1960-87, emeritus prof. phys. edn., 1987—. Owner Felix Jumonville Realty, Northridge, 1974-82, Big Valley Realty, Inc., 1982-83, Century 21 Lamb Realtors, 1983-86, Cardinal Realtors, 1986-87; varsity track and cross-country head coach L.A. State Coll., 1952-60, Calif. State U., Northridge, 1960-71. Served with USCGR, 1942-46. Named to, Baton Rouge H.S. Hall of Fame; recipient U.S. Commendation medal. Mem. Assn. Calif. State Univ. Profs., AAHPER, Pi Tau Pi, Phi Epsilon Kappa, Kappa Sigma. Home: Unit N98 2001 E Camino Parocela Palm Springs CA 92264-8283

JUMONVILLE, FLORENCE M. librarian, historian; b. New Orleans; d. Warren P. and Florence E. (Seither) J. BA, U. New Orleans, 1971, MEd, 1976, MA, 1988, PhD, 1997; MS, La. State U., 1972. Libr. Hist. New Orleans Collection, 1972-74, 78-82, head libr., 1982-96; libr. Belle Chasse (La.) State Sch., 1974-78; head La. and spl. collections Earl K. Long Libr., U. New Orleans, 1997—. Adj. instr. libr. sci. La. State U., Baton Rouge, 1994, 96. Author: Bibliography of New Orleans Imprints, 1764-1864, 1989, Louisiana History: An Annotated Bibliography, 2002; editor: LLA Bull., 1990—95; co-editor: A History of the Louisiana Library Association, 1925-2000, 2003; contbr. articles to profl. jours. Adv. bd. Ethel and Herman L. Midlo Ctr. for N.O. Studies, La. Hist. Records; bd. dirs. Theatre Libr. Assn. Recipient Lucy B. Foote award La. Libr. Assn., 1985, Fannie Simon award Spl. Librs. Assn. Mus., Arts and Humanities Divsn., 1997. Mem. ALA, Am. Antiquarian Soc., Am. Hist. Assn., Am. Printing History Assn., Assn. Moving Image Archivists, Bibliog. Soc. Am., Soc. for the History of Authorship, Reading and Pub., La. Hist. Assn., La. Libr. Assn., Beta Phi Mu, Phi Delta Kappa, Kappa Delta Pi. Avocations: needlework, classic movies, reading. Office: Earl K Long Libr Univ New Orleans Lakefront New Orleans LA 70148-0001 E-mail: fjumonvi@uno.edu.

JUMP, CHESTER JACKSON, JR., clergyman, church official; b. Covington, Ky., Mar. 31, 1918; s. Chester Jackson and Inez (Moore) J.; m. Margaret Elizabeth Savidge, Sept. 5, 1942; children— Karen Jane, Richard Alan, Catherine Louise, Robert Jon. AB, Albright Coll., 1938; MA, Columbia U., 1940; BD, Union Theol. Sem. N.Y.C., 1943; postgrad., Ecole Coloniale, Brussels, Belgium, 1950-51; DD, Eastern Bapt. Theol. Sem., 1965. Ordained to ministry Bapt. Ch., 1943. Pastor N.E. Larger Parish, Lyndon Center, Vt., 1943-44; missionary Belgian Congo, Republic of Congo, 1945-62; regional rep. Am. Bapt. Fgn. Mission Socs., Valley Forge, Pa., 1961-64, exec. dir., 1965-83; assoc. gen. sec. Am. Bapt. Chs., 1965-83, dir. world relief, 1983-88, interim gen. sec., 1987-88; mem. gen. bd. Nat. Council Chs., 1965-75, mem. program bd., exec. com. div. overseas ministries, 1965-83, mem. gov. bd., 1965-75, 87-88; mem. exec. com. Bapt. World Alliance, 1965-85, 87-88, v.p., 1980-85; bd. dirs., exec. com. Am. Bapt. Chs., Pa., Del., 1989-97; chmn., budget commn. Commn. on New Ch. Planting and Adminstrv. Svcs., 1989-99. Trustee Eastern Bapt. Theol. Sem.; mem. Ch. World Service Commn., 1983-88, fin. com., 1983-88; mem. Bapt. World Aid, 1970-85; mem. bd. personnel com. IMPACT. Author: (with wife) Congo Diary, 1950, Coming, Ready or Not, 1959. Mem. Pi Gamma Mu. Home and Office: 240 Applewood Dr Apt 2 Lewisburg PA 17837 E-mail: cjmsjump@ptd.net.

JUMP, SHARYL A. special events coordinator; b. Tecumseh, Nebr., June 23, 1953; d. Evelyn Annabelle and Edgar Franklin Knox; m. Donald H. Jump, May 10, 1975; children: Thomas James, Lisabeth Ann. Devel. spl. events coord. Naval War Coll. Found., Newport, RI, 1989—. Various duties St. Peter's Luth. Ch., Newport, RI, 1989—2003. Mem.: Naval War Coll. Found. (life). Lutheran. Avocations: golf, skiing, travel.

JUMPER, DOUGLAS CAMERON, publication coordinator, media consultant; b. Dallas, Mar. 4, 1958; s. Millard Bishop Jr. and Elizabeth McCulloch Jumper; m. Kirsten Rae Evenson, May 2, 1993. BS, Tex. Christian U., 1980. Mng. editor Ft. Worth News-Tribune, 1978-90; mktg. dir. LeWay-AURA Inc., Ft. Worth, 1990-97; editor, pub. North Lake Travis Log, Lago Vista, Tex., 1997-99; publ. specialist Tex. Dept. Health, Austin, 2000—. Pub. info. officer City of Jonestown, Tex., 2001—. Alderman City of Jonestown, 2001—. Recipient Outstanding Continuous Coverage, Tex. State Tchrs. Assn., 1988. Mem. Soc. Profl. Journalists (pres. Ft. Worth chpt. 1997-2001), Jonestown C. of C. (pres. 1993-94), Sigma Chi (Ft. Worth and Austin alumni chpt.). Presbyterian. Avocations: cooking, gardening, reading. Home: 10904 First St Jonestown TX 78645 Office: Tex Dept Health 1100 W 49th St Austin TX 78756 E-mail: doug.jumper@tdh.state.tx.us.

JUMPER, JOHN PHILLIP, chief of staff US Air Force; b. Paris, Tex., Feb. 4, 1945; s. Jimmy Jefferson and Maree Loretta (Nowell) J.; m. Ellen Elizabeth McGhee, Mar. 29, 1969; children: Catherine, Janet, Melissa. BSEE, Va. Mil. Inst., 1966; MBA, Golden Gate U., 1978; postgrad., Air Command and Staff Coll., Maxwell AFB, Ala., 1977-78, Nat. War Coll., Washington, 1981-82. Commd. 2d lt. USAF, 1966, advanced through grades to gen., 1997; instr. pilot 414th Fighter Weapons Squadron, Nellis AFB, Nev., 1974-77; action officer Directorate for Ops. and Tng., Washington, 1978-81; comdr. 430th Tactical Fighter Squadron, Nellis AFB, Nev., 1983; exec. officer to comdr. Hdqrs. Tactical Air Command, Langley AFB, Va., 1983-86; comdr. 33d Tactical Fighter Wing, Eglin AFB, Fla., 1986-87, Egling AFB, Fla., 1987-88, 57th Fighter Weapons Wing, Nellis AFB, 1988-90; dep. dir. politico-mil. affairs Joint Staff, Washington, 1990-92; sr. mil. asst. for sec. def. Office Sec. Def., Washington, 1992-94; comdr. 9th AF, Shaw AFB, 1994-96; Deputy Chief of Staff, Air and Space HAF, Washington, 1996-97; commdr. Allied Air Forces Ctrl. Europe, Ramstein AB, Germany, 1997-2000, HQ Air Combat Command, Langley AFB, 2000—01; chief of staff US Air Force, Washington, 2001—. Contbr. articles to mil. pub. Decorated Def. DSM with oak leaf cluster, Legion of Merit DSM with oak leaf cluster, DFC with 2 oak leaf clusters, Air medal with 17 oak leaf clusters. Mem. Air Force Assn. Roman Catholic. Avocations: racquet ball, jogging, piano, guitar, golf, sports cars. Office: 1670 AF Pentagon Washington DC 20330

JUMPER, ROY DAVIS LINVILLE, writer, educator; b. Boston, Mass., Aug. 30, 1959; s. Roy Eulliss Jumper and Mary Ruth Linville. BA, Ind. U., Bloomington, IN, 1982; MPA, U. Maine, Orono, ME, 1985; PhD, U. Tenn., Tn, 1996. Librarian's asst. Ind. U., Ind., 1979—80; intern Cummins Engine Found., Columbus, Ind., 1980—81; asst. mng. dir. Internat. Bus. Associates, Cairo, 1983; assoc. instr. Ariz. State U., Tempe, Ariz., 1985—86; adj. prof. Middlesex Rsch. Ctr., U.S. Navy, 1997—. Cons. The Linville Family L.L.C., South Padre Island, Tex., 1999—. Author: (book) Power and Politics: The Story of Malaysia's Orang Asli, Orang Asli Now: The Orang Asli in the Malaysian Political World, Death Waits in the Dark: The Senoi Praak, Malaysia's Killer Elite; contbr. articles to profl. jours. Recipient Scholar, French History and French Civil Law, U. Dijon, France, 1977-1979. Mem.: Assn. Asian Studies, Am. Polit. Sci. Assn., Pi Sigma Alpha, U. Maine. Address: PO Box 2824 South Padre Island TX 78597 Fax: 812 339 5877.

JUN, INSOO, nuclear scientist, researcher; b. Inchon, Republic of Korea, Oct. 3, 1963; arrived in U.S., 1983; s. Si-Won and Chan-Bok Jun; m. Seung-Ah Lee. BS, U. Mass., 1986; PhD, UCLA, 1991. Post-doctoal fellow UCLA, LA, 1992—95; scientist Hughes Space and Comm. Co., El Segundo, Calif., 1996—2000; sr. tech. staff Jet Propulsion Lab., Pasadena, Calif., 2001—. Contbr. articles to profl. jours. Mem.: Am. Geophys. Union, Americal Nuc. Soc. Office: Jet Propulsion Laboratory 4800 Oak Grove Drive Pasadena CA 91109

JUN, JONG SUP, public administration educator; b. Sunsan, Korea, July 26, 1936; s. Myung D. and Jeum S. (Pai) J.; m. Soon Y. Jun, Sept. 16, 1964; children: Eugene, Amy. LLB, Yeungnam U., Taegu, Korea, 1960; MA, U. Oreg., 1964; PhD, U. So. Calif., 1969. Prof. Calif. State U., Hayward, 1968—. Vis. prof. Hosei U., Tokyo, 1992-93, Korea U., 2000-2001; coord. Pub. Adminstrn.Theory Network, 1993—; coord. The Pub. Adminstrn. Theory Network Internat. Author: Public Administration: Design and Problem Solving, 1986, Philosophy of Administration, 1994; editor: Rethinking Administrative Theory, 2002; co-editor Globalization and Decentralization, 1996; editor: Development in the Asia Pacific, 1994, Jour. Adminstrn. Theory and Praxis, 1993—; chief editor Jour. Adminstrv. Theory and Praxis, 1994-99; editl. mem. Internat. Rev. Adminstrv. Sci., 1991. Recipient Rsch. Grant award Social Rsch.Coun., N.Y., 1979, Outstanding Acad. Achievement award Am. Soc. Pub. Adminstrn., San Francisco, 1982; Fulbright scholar Yonsei U., Korea. Fellow Nat. Acad. Public Adminstrn. Avocation: japanese gardening. Home: 18698 Mount Lassen Ct Castro Valley CA 94552-1955 Office: Calif State U Hayward CA 94552

JUNDI, BILAL, principal; b. Beirut, Jan. 1, 1964; s. Mohamad Amin Al Jundi and Hanife Al Bahloul; m. Rawaa Merhi, May 20, 1995. BA in edn., BA in Islamic studies, MA in edn., Aldawaa U. Lic.: Ministry of Justice, Québec, Can. (Commr. Oaths) 1998. Prin. Ecole Ali Ibn Abi Talib, St. Laurent, Canada, 1991—; orator Nation Musulmane du Québec, Montréal, Canada, 1998—. Chief exec. Muslim Cmty. of St. Laurent, St. Laurent, Canada, 1995—. Prodr.: (theatre) Shaqaek AL Noman The Coquelicot; contbr. (television documentary) Peace and Religion. Recipient Migration Award, Ministry of Migration, 1995. Liberal. Moslem. Avocations: writing, reading, swimming, travel, arts. Office: Ecole Ali Ibn Abi Talib 275 Houde Saint-Laurent QC Canada H4N 2J3 Office Fax: 514-748-5407. Personal E-mail: bilaljundi@ecoleali.com.

JUNE, DAVID HAROLD, information technology specialist; b. Alameda, Calif., Mar. 26, 1948; s. Harold Burton and Lois (Baugh) J.; m. Leise Palm Purtle; 1 child, Sean Christopher Purtle. BS in Materials Engring., San Jose State U., 1979. Process engr. Fairchild Semiconductor, Mt. View, Calif., 1979-84; process engring. mgr. Intel, Rio Rancho, N.Mex., 1984-85; tech. team mgr. No. Telecom Elec., San Diego, 1985-89; dir. engring. Thesis Group, Dallas, 1989-91; CIM mgr. Read Rite, Milpilas, Calif., 1992-94; dir. engring. and data mgmt. Cell Net Data Sys., San Carlos, Calif., 1994-99; dir. program mgmt. BCN Data Sys., San Francisco, 1999-2000; v.p. engring. Telephia, San Francisco, 2000—01, pres. NextGen Metrics, Pleasanton, Calif., 2001—. Inventor in field; contbr. articles to profl. jours. Office: NextGen Metrics 4847 Hopyard Rd #4 Pleasanton CA 94588 E-mail: david@nextgenmetrics.com.

JUNE, ROY ETHIEL, lawyer; b. Forsyth, Mont., Aug. 12, 1922; s. Charles E. and Elizabeth F. (Newnes) J.; m. Laura Brautigam, June 20, 1949; children: Patricia June, Richard Tyler. BA, U. Mont., 1948, BA in Law, 1951, LLB, 1952. Bar: Mont. 1952, Calif. 1961. Sole practice, Billings, Mont., 1952-57; atty. Sanders and June, 1953-57; real estate developer Orange County, Calif., 1957-61; ptnr. Dugan, Tobias, Tornay & June, Costa Mesa, Calif., 1961-62; city prosecutor Costa Mesa, 1962-63; asst. city atty., 1963-67; city atty., 1967-78; sole practice, 1962—. Atty., founder, dir. Citizens Bank of Costa Mesa, 1972-92; atty. Costa Mesa Hist. Soc., Costa Mesa Playhouse Patron's Assn., Red Barons Orange County, Costa Mesa Meml. Hosp. Aux., Harbor Key, Child Guidance Ctr. Orange County, Fairview State Hosp. Therapeutic Pool Vols., Inc. Active Eagle Scout evaluation team Harbor Area Boy Scouts Am., YMCA; atty. United Fund/Cmty. Chest Costa Mesa and Newport Beach; bd. dirs. Boys' Club Harbor Area, Mardan Ctr. Ednl. Therapy, United Cerebral Palsy Found., Orange County; docent Palm Springs Mus., 1996—. With USAF, WWII. Decorated Air medal with oak leaf cluster, DFC. Mem. Calif. Bar Assn., Costa Mesa C. of C. (bd. dirs.), Masons, Scottish Rite, Shriners, Santa Ana Country, Amigos Viejos, Los Fiestadores, Palm Springs Calif. Air Mus. (docent). E-mail: RoyJune655@cs.com.

JUNEJA, HARINDER SINGH, hematologist; b. India, Nov. 25, 1947; MD, All India Inst. Med. Scis., 1984. Cert. internal medicine, oncology, hematology. Fellow in hematology-oncology U. Fla., Gainesville, 1975-77; resident in internal medicine St. Mary's Hosp., Rochester, 1977-79; fellow in hematology-oncology U. Tex. Med. Br., Galveston, 1979-80; active staff U. Tex. Med. Br. Hosps., 1979-91. Active teaching staff Herman Hosp., Houston, 1991—; active staff LBJ Hosp. Harris County Med. Dist., 1991—; instr. internal medicine U. Tex. Med. Br., 1980-81, asst. prof., 1981-89, assoc. prof., 1989-91; assoc. prof. U. Tex., Houston, 1991-2002, prof., 2002—; adj. assoc. prof. and cons. M.D. Anderson Cancer Ctr., Houston, 1997—. Fellow ACP; mem. Am. Fedn. for Clin. Rsch., Am. Soc. Hematology, Internat. Soc. Exptl. Hematology. Office: U Tex Med Sch/Hematology Divsn Rm 5-284 M5B 6431 Fannin St Houston TX 77030-1501

JUNEK, HEATHER DIANE, medical/surgical nurse; d. James Milton and Kellye Diane Forster; m. Carl David Junek, Oct. 9, 1973. Diploma, Bapt. Sch. Profl. Nursing, 1999. RN Tex., 1999. Staff nurse Bapt. Health Sys., San Antonio, 1999—. Democrat. Baptist. Avocations: watercolor painting, embroidery. Home: 6807 Linkway St San Antonio TX 78240-3048

JUNEWICZ, JAMES J. lawyer; b. Oct. 1, 1950; s. John and Genevieve J.; m. Virginia Bornyas. BS, Georgetown U., 1972; JD, Duquesne U., 1976; LLM, NYU, 1978. Bar: Pa. 1977, D.C. 1978, Ill. 1984. Asst. gen. counsel SEC, Washington, 1982—84; ptnr. Mayer, Brown, Rowe & Maw LLP, Chgo., 1987—. Office: Mayer Brown Rowe & Maw 190 S La Salle St Ste 3900 Chicago IL 60603-3410

JUNG, ANDREA, cosmetics executive; Grad. magna cum laude, Princeton U. Sr. v.p. gen. mdse. I. Magnin; exec. v.p. Neman Marcus; sr. v.p. Avon Products, Inc., N.Y.C., 1994-97, pres., 1998-2000; CEO, 2001—. Bd. dirs. Fragrance Found., Cosmetic Exec. Women. Sale Corp., Donna Karan Internat. Office: Avon Products Inc 1345 Avenue Of The Americas New York NY 10105-0302

JUNG, BETTY CHIN, epidemiologist, research analyst, educator, medical/surgical nurse; b. Bklyn., Nov. 28, 1948; d. Han You and Bo Ngan (Moy) C.; m. Lee Jung, Oct. 1, 1972; children: Daniel, Stephanie. AA, King's Coll., 1968; BS, Columbia U., 1971; MPH, So. Conn. State U., 1993. RN, Conn., Miss., N.Y.; cert. health edn. specialist. Adminstrv. asst. Columbia U., N.Y.C., 1968-69; practical nurse Babies Hosp., N.Y.C., 1969-70, charge nurse, 1974-76; staff nurse Columbia-Presbyn. Hosp., N.Y.C., 1971-73; sch. nurse Nassau County Sch. System, Long Island, N.Y., 1984-85; grad. asst. So. Conn. State U., New Haven, 1991-92; coop. edn. intern Conn. Dept. Health Svcs., Hartford, 1991-92; intern North Ctrl. Dist. Health Dept., Enfield, Conn., 1992; epidemiologist Conn. Dept. Pub. Health, Hartford, Conn., 1992-98, health program assoc., 1998-2001, epidemiologist 3, 2003—; staff nurse Quinnipiac Coll. Student Health Svcs., 1998; mem. multicultural adv. coun. Conn. Dept. Children and Families, assoc. rsch. analyst, 2001—03. Health promotion cons. dept. pub. health So. Conn. State U., New Haven, 1991, mem. adv. coun. dept. pub. health, 1999—, lectr., adj. faculty, 1998—, tchg. asst., 1992, curriculum developer, 92, vol. rsch. analyst, 93, founder grad. alumni mentor program, 1993—94, mem. adv. coun., 1997—; webmaster E-comm. web site, 2000—, univ. asst. webmaster, 2001—; instr. Albertus Magnus Coll., 1995—96; computer cons., course dir. contg. edn. program dept. pub. health So. Conn.

State U., 1998—; health columnist Baldwin Newcomers Club, NY, 1977—78; coord. Dept. Pub. Health and Svcs./Conn. EPI Info. Network, Hartford, 1994—2001; mem. Nat. Lead Info. Ctr. Spkrs. Bur., 1997—98; vol. scientist Sci.-By-Mail, 1997—98; mem. Nat. Safety Coun. Environ. Health Ctr. Spkrs. Referral Bur., 1998—2001; apptd. mem. Conn. Dept. Pub. Health's Affirmative Action Employee Adv. Com., 1998—2001; mem. permanent commn. Status of Women, 1996—, chair news subcom., editor affirmative action newsletter, 2001; apptd. mem. multicultural adv. coun. Conn. Dept. Children and Families, 2002—03. Mem. editl. bd.: Data Quality, 1994—98, mem. manuscript rev. bd.: Jour. Clin. Outcomes Mgmt., 1995—, Pub. Health Reports, 1997—98, Women's Health in Primary Care, 1998—; contbg. editor: Episource, A Guide to Resources in Epidemiology, 1998—99; editor/web pub.: SCSU Pub. Health E-News Bull., 2000—01, Public Health E-news, 2001—, Public Health Jobs Electronic Newsletter, 2000—, pilot reviewer: Ctr. for Disease Control, 2003—; contbr. articles to profl. jours. Vol. nurse health educator, coord. Chinatown's First Ann. Health Fair, 1971-72; treas. Tenant Assn., Bronx, N.Y., 1976-77; pre-confirmation tchr. Bethlehem Luth. Ch., Baldwin, N.Y., 1981-85. Grantee, USPHS, 1992—98, Fed. HUD, 1995—98, U.S. Preventive Health and Health Svcs., 1998, block grant, Maternal Child Health, 1998—2001, Cardiona Secular Health, CDC, 2003—; scholar Merit, Kings Coll., 1968, Columbia U., 1968—69, Women's Florist Assn., 1968, Bessie Lee Gambrill scholar, So. Alumni Assn., 1992. Fellow: Soc. for Pub. Health Edn.; mem.: Pub. Health Expertise Network of Mentors (program dir. 2002—), Internat. Assn. Webmasters and Designers, Boston Mus. Sci., Nat. Acad. Sci. (mentor career planning ctr. beginning scientists & engrs. 1997—98), Columbia U. Sch. Nursing Alumni Assn. (survey cons. 1994—95), Conn. Women in Healthcare Mgmt., Inc., So. Conn. State U. Alumni Assn. (founder pub. health chpt. 1994, interim pres, then pres. 1994—98, founder, coord. pub. health alumni mentor program 1994—2002, chair coms. 1994—, numerous other positions 1994—, editor MPH Alumni Record 1995—, founder, dir., coord. pub. health alumni spkrs. bur. 1997—, founder, program dir. pub. health expertise network of mentors 2002—, Alumni Appreciation award 1998), Internat. Assn. IT Trainers (assoc.), Conn. Pub. Health Assn., Nat. Lead Info. Ctr. Spkrs. Bur., Conn. State and Territorial Epidemiologists (alternate cons. 1996—, co-leader Healthy People 2010 1999—2001, lead diabetes 2002—, lead cardiovasc. disease 2002—), Am. Statis. Assn. (OSPA media experts list 1997—), Am. Med. Writers Assn., APHA (health care reform activist network, peer assistance the model stds. project). Avocations: reading, writing, research, web development and design, bicycling. Home: 25 Driftwood Ln Guilford CT 06437-1929 Office: Conn Dept Pub Health 410 Capitol Ave Hartford CT 06106

JUNG, BEVERLEY C. accountant, advocate; b. N.Y.C., May 11, 1927; d. Yock Low Joe and Katherine Woo Chu; m. Gokmun Jung, May 2, 1945. Student, CCNY, 1967. Owner G&G Sales, Inc., N.Y.C., 1968—75, 1982—95; chief fiscal officer CPC/Chinatown Planning Coun., N.Y.C., 1975—80; cmty. field rep. Cmty. Svc. Adminstrn., N.Y.C., 1980—82; cmty. coord. N.Y.C. Dept. Housing, 1995—98, N.Y.C. Dept. Aging/Foster Grandparent Program, 1998—. Dist. leader Rep. Party, N.Y.C., 1977; v.p. N.Y. Rep. County Com., N.Y.C., 1985—. Recipient Ethnic Cmty. award, Mayor Koch, N.Y.C., 1985; scholar, The New Sch., N.Y.C., 1982. Mem.: Orgn. Chinese Ams. (founder, pres., award 1981). Lutheran. Avocations: crocheting, knitting, tatting, sewing, jewelry making. Home: Apt 3M 10 Confucius Plaza New York NY 10002-6731 Office: NYC Dept for the Aging Rm 1419 2 Lafayette St New York NY 10007-1392

JUNG, DORANNE, public relations, marketing and advertising consultant; b. Los Angeles, June 11, 1948; d. Harry Gordon and Frances (Wong) J. BA, Mills Coll., 1970; postgrad., U. Calif., Berkeley, 1969, Fla. Presbyn. Coll., London, 1970; MS, Boston U., 1972. Media asst. Young & Rubicam Internat., N.Y.C., 1970; comms. coordinator New Eng. Spl. Edn. Instrnl. Materials Center, Boston, 1972-73; media dir./account exec. Harcomm Assocs., Cambridge, Mass., 1973-76; promotion, advt. and pub. rels. mgr. Westinghouse Broadcasting, WBZ Radio, Boston, 1976-79; pres. Corcoran & Doranne, Inc., Cambridge, 1979-84; asst. prof. Boston U. Sch. Pub. Comm., 1980-89; prodr./dir. video TV and radio shows; cons. mem. pub. affairs com. Boston chpt. ARC, 1979-88, CHIAT/DAY, San Francisco, 1988, FCB/IMPACT, L.A., 1989; dir. mktg. original programming MCA Home Video/MCA, Inc., 1989-94; v.p. Vineyard Prodns., 1994-95; owner Jung & Assocs., 1995-98, 99—; v.p. creative svcs. DIVX Entertainment, 1998-99; prof. Calif. State U., 2002—, Santa Monica C.C., 2002—; adj. prof. Santa Monica Coll., 2001—. Contbg. author: Teaching About Funerals, 1980; author/dir. radio series Fishing and Our Law, 1979-80. Mem. pub. rels. com. Am. Heart Assn., 1978; mem. Hale House/Back Bay Aging Concerns Benefit Com., 1981-83; mem. pub. rels. com. Family Service Assn. Greater Boston, 1983—. Recipient award Ohio State Inst. Edn. by Radio/TV award, 1978, Broadcast Promotion Assn., 1978; Clarion award Women in Communications, 1978. Mem. Press Club Boston, Broadcast Promotion Assn., New Eng. Broadcasters Assn., Nat. Assn. TV Program Execs., Women in Direct Mktg. Assn. So. Calif., Coalition Pacific Asians Entertainment, Direct Mktg. Club of So. Calif., Venice Interactive.

JUNG, DORIS, dramatic soprano; b. Centralia, Ill., Jan. 5, 1924; d. John Jay and May (Middleton) Crittenden; m. Felix Popper, Nov. 3, 1951; 1 son, Richard Dorian. Ed., U. Ill., Mannes Coll. Music, Vienna Acad. Performing Arts; student of, Julius Cohen, Emma Zador, Luise Helletsgruber, Winifred Cecil. Debut as Vitellia in: Clemenza di Tito, Zurich (Switzerland) Opera, 1955, other appearances with, Hamburg State Opera, Munich State Opera, Vienna State Opera, Royal Opera Copenhagen, Royal Opera Stockholm, Marseille and Strasbourg, France, Naples (Italy) Opera Co., Catania (Italy) Opera Co., N.Y.C. Opera, Met. Opera, also in Mpls., Portland, Oreg., Washington and Aspen, Colo.; soloist: Wagner concert conducted by Leopold Stokowski, 1971; with, Syracuse (N.Y.) Symphony, 1981, voice tchr., N.Y.C., 1970— . Home: 40 W 84th St New York NY 10024-4749 *Whether performing as a singer or teaching, attempting to understand the voice is tremendously daunting. As with life itself, the human voice defies understanding with its day to day differences and one's everchanging points of view. The secret of unflagging devotion to this life's work lies in accepting its elusiveness.*

JUNG, GLENN HAROLD, retired oceanographer educator, researcher; b. Lyons, KS, Oct. 11, 1924; s. Walter Benjamin and Elsie Esther Jung; m. Jean McLean Clements, Aug. 28, 1948; children: Lynn Stockton Parsons, Lawrence Ervin, Margaret Leslie Blankenship, Richard Brooks, Kenneth Dale. BS, MIT, 1949, MS, 1952; PhD, Tex. A & M U., 1955. Fulbright fellow U. of Oslo, 1954—55; oceanography rschr. Gulf Consultants, Tex., 1955—58; asst. prof. Tex. A&M U., 1955—57; assoc. prof. of meteorology and oceanography Naval Postgraduate Sch., 1958—65, prof. of oceanography, 1965—84, emeritus prof. of oceanography, 1984—. Ruling elder Carmel Presbyn. Ch., Calif. First lt. USAAF, 1943—47. Mem.: Sigma Xi. Protestant-Presbyterian. Avocation: travel. Home: 24651 Cabrillo St Carmel CA 93923

JUNG, HENRY HUNG, mechanical engineer; b. Hong Kong, Aug. 3, 1957; s. Cheuk-Sun and Siu-Kuen (Ma) J.; m. Mi-Ying Miranda, Mar. 28, 1986. BS MechE, Ariz. State U., 1980; MS MechE, U. Ill., 1983; MBA, Santa Clara U., 1994. Engr. Lockheed Aircraft, Burbank, Calif., 1981-82; researcher U. Ill., Champaign-Urbana, 1982-83; engr. Pratt & Whitney Aircraft, West Palm Beach, Fla., 1983-84; sr. scientist Lockheed Missiles & Space Co., Palo Alto, Calif., 1984-94; sr. mfg. engr. Sun Microsystems Co., Mountain View, Calif., 1994-96; sr. supplies engr. Apple Computer, Cupertino, Calif., 1996-97; sr. mech. project mgr. Intel, Santa Clara, Calif., 1997-2000; staff engr. in packaging Sun Microsys. Co., Palo Alto, Calif., 2000—. Contbr. numerous articles on electronic cooling to profl. jours. Mem. ASME, AIAA, N.Y. Acad. Scis., Sigma Xi, Tau Beta Pi, Pi Tau Sigma. Avocations: tennis, swimming. Home: 21486 Holly Oak Dr Cupertino CA 95014-4928 Office: Sun Microsys 901 San Antonio Rd USUN 12342 Palo Alto CA 94303-4900 E-mail: henry.jung@sun.com.

JUNG, HILDA ZIIFLE, retired physicist; b. Gretna, La. d. William Christian and Leonora Margaret (Giboney) Ziifle; m. Julius Robert Jung Jr., Nov. 2, 1968. BS, Tulane U., 1943. Engring. release clk. Higgins Aircraft Co., Michoud, La., 1943-44; rsch. physicist So. Regional Rsch. Ctr., USDA, New Orleans, 1944-79; retired, 1979. Contbr. articles to profl. jours.; patentee chem. process. Named Woman of Yr. New Orleans Fed. Exec. Bd., 1978. Mem. AAAS, AARP (program dir. Terrytown chpt. 1991-95, chmn. social com. 1989), Am. Chem. Soc. (sec. La. sect. 1977), Orgn. Profl. Employees Dept. Agrl. (life, pres. 1978, Profl. of Yr. 1979), Am. Legion Aux. (post 64 chaplain, 1995, 96, 97, 98, 2002, color bearer 1999, 2000), Nat. Assn. Ret. Fed. Employees (life, 1st v.p., legis. chmn. 1980, pres. 1981, 92, pub. rels. officer 1984, 89-91, 2000, 01, pub. rels. officer 2002, 2003, newsletter editor 1993, program chair 1995, 96, 97, 98, 99, 2000, 2001, 2002, 2003), Gretna Hist. Soc., German Heritage Cultural & Geneal. Soc. La., Sigma Xi. Lutheran. Avocations: stamps, reading, fishing, antique cars.

JUNG, PATRICK JOSEPH, humanities educator; b. Milw., Dec. 6, 1963; s. Robert Joseph and Georgia Lee (Winter) Jung; m. Rochelle Marie Weidensee, Sept. 6, 1987; children: Katherine Mary, Aloysius John, Francis Andrew. BA, U. Wis. Whitewater, 1986; MA, Marquette U., 1992, PhD, 1997. Rsch. asst. Milw. Pub. Mus., 1996—97; adj. prof. Marquette U., 1997—; adminstr. devel. Legal Aid Soc. Milw., 2002—03; asst. prof. history political sci. Milw. Sch. Engring., 2003—. Rsch. analyst Marquette U., Milw., 1997—2000; dir. devel. Novus Group, Milw., 2000—02; instr. donor rsch. Archdiocese Milw., 2003—; hist. cons. Indian Treaties Lord Cultural resources, Ottawa, Ont., Canada, 2003—. Contbr. Capt. U.S. Army, 1986—90, res. officer Nat. Guard, 1990—94. Decorated Commendation Medal with 3 Oak Leaf Clusters; fellow, Arthur J. Schmitt Found., 1994; Rev. John Raynor fellow, 1991. Mem.: Assn. Fundraising Profls., Wis. Hist. Soc., Am. Hist. Assn. Roman Catholic. Office: Milw Sch Engring 1025 N Broadway Milwaukee WI 53202

JUNG, SEONG-OOK, engineer; s. Hakwon Jung and Kuyrae Kang; m. Aeran Cho; 1 child, Dayeon. PhD, U. Ill., 2002. Rsch. asst. Yonsei U., Seoul, Republic of Korea, 1987—89; sr. staff rschr. Samaung Electronics, Yong-In, Republic of Korea, 1989—98; rsch. asst. U. Ill., Urbana, 1998—2001, tchg. asst., 2000—02; prin. circuit design engr. T-RAM, San Jose, Calif., 2001—. Rsch. staff U. Santa Cruz, 2001. Contbr. articles to profl. jours. Fellow, Samsung Electronics, 1986—89, 1998—2000; scholar, Yonsei U., 1983—85. Mem.: IEEE (sr.). Achievements include patents for memory device with address transition for skipping failed memory blocks; merged memory and logic (MML) integrated circuits including independent memory bank signals and methods; graphic RAM having a dual port and serial data access method thereof; mode setting circuit and method of a semiconductor memory device; semiconductor memory device and method for gating the columns thereof; video ram method for outputting serial data; flash write for a semiconductor memory device; dual port video random access memory with block write capability; data output buffer circuit with precharged bootstrap circuit.

JUNG, TIMOTHY TAE KUN, otolaryngologist; b. Seoul, Korea, Dec. 1, 1943; came to U.S., 1969; s. Yoon Yong and Helen Chung-Hyuk (Im) J.; m. Lucy Moon Young, Sept. 10, 1972; children: David, Michael, Karen. BS, Seoul Nat. U., 1966, Loma Linda U., 1971, MD, 1974; PhD, U. Minn., 1980. Diplomate Am. Bd. Otolaryngology. Med. intern Loma Linda (Calif.) U. Med. Ctr., 1974-75; resident in surgery U. Minn. Med. Sch., Mpls., 1975-76, resident in otolaryngology, 1976-80, asst. prof. otolaryngology, 1980-84, clin. asst. prof., dir. prostaglandin lab., 1984-85; assoc. prof., dir. otolaryngology rsch. Loma Linda U., 1985-90, prof., dir. otolaryngology rsch., 1990-92, clin. prof., dir. otolaryngology rsch., 1992—. Mem. deafness and communications disroders rev. com. Nat. Inst. Deafness and Communications, NIH, 1989-92. Mem. bd. editors Annals of Otology, Rhinology & Laryngology, 1994—; mem. internat. bd. editors Acta Otolaryngologica, 1999—; contbr. numerous chpts. to med. books, over 100 articles and abstracts to med. jours. Sec. gen. Korean-Am. Otolaryngcology Soc., 1992—. Sgt. Korean Army, 1966—69. Recipient Edmund Price Fowler award. Fellow ACS, Triological Soc., Am. Acad. Otolaryngology (honor award 1990), Am. Acad. Surgeons; mem. AMA, Am. Otol. Soc., Am. Neurotol. Soc., Soc. Univ. Otolaryngologists, Assn. Rsch. in Otolaryngology, Centurions, Collegium Otorhinolaryngogicum Amicetiae Sacrum, Korean-Am. Otolaryngology Soc. (sec. gen. 1990--), Alpha Omega Alpha. Seventh-day Adventist. Avocations: horticulture, photography, hiking. Home: 11790 Pecan Way Loma Linda CA 92354-3452 Office: 3975 Jackson St Ste 202 Riverside CA 92503-3947 E-mail: tjung1790@aol.com.

JUNGBLUTH, CONNIE CARLSON, wealth strategist; b. Cheyenne, Wyo., June 20, 1955; d. Charles Marion and Janice Yvonne (Keldsen) Carlson; m. Kirk E. Jungbluth, Feb. 5, 1977; children: Tyler, Ryan. BS, Colo. State U., 1976. CPA, Colo., Ariz. Sr. acct. Rhode Scripter & Assoc., Boulder, Colo., 1977-81; mng. acct. Arthur Young, Denver, 1981-85; asst. v.p. Dain Bosworth, Denver, 1985-87; v.p. George K. Baum & Co., Denver, 1987-91; acct. Ariz. Luth. Acad., 1994-95; sr. tax acct. Ernst & Young, LLP, Phoenix, 1995-96; nat. tax mgr. personal wealth mgmt. RSM McGladrey, Inc., Phoenix, 1996-2000; mgr. pvt. client svcs. Arthur Andersen, Phoenix, 2000—01; sr. v.p., wealth strategist Bank of Am. Pvt. Bank, Phoenix, 2002—. Mem. adv. bd. Ariz. Cmty. Found., 2002—, Jewish Cmty. Found., 2002. Active Denver Estate Planning Coun., 1981-85, Ctrl. Ariz. Estate Planning Coun., 1997-98; organizer Little People Am., Rocky Mountain Med. Clinic and Symposium, Denver, 1986; adv. bd. Children's Home Health, Denver, 1986-89; fin. adv. bd. Gail Shoettler for State Treas., Denver, 1986; campaign chmn. Kathi Williams for Colo. State Legislature, 1986; mem. Sch. dist. 12 Colo. Edn. Found. Bd., 1991, Napa Sch. Dist. Elem. Site com., 1992-94; apptd. Ariz. Gov.'s Coun. Developmental Disabilities, 1998-99, chmn. planning com., 1998-99; mem. profl. adv. bd., editor Charitable Giving Guide, Ariz. Cmty. Found., 2002—. Named one of 50 to watch, Denver mag., 1988. Mem. AICPA, Fin. Planning Assn., Colo. Soc. CPAs (strategic planning com. 1987-89, instr. bank 1983, trustee 1984-87, pres. bd. trustees 1986-87, bd. dirs. 1987-89, chmn. career edn. com. 1982-83, pub. svc. award 1985-87), Little People of Am., Colo. Mcpl. Bond Dealers, Ariz. Herb Assn., Metro North C. of C. (bd. dirs. 1987-90), Denver City Club (bd. dirs. 1987-88), Phi Beta Phi. Avocations: faith, family, horticulture, philanthropy, gourmet cooking. Office: Bank of America Pvt Bank 201 E Washington Ste 2300 Phoenix AZ 85004

JUNGBLUTH, KIRK E. b. Lima, Ohio, Apr. 5, 1949; s. Harold A. and Marjorie J. (Brown) J.; m. Connie Carlson, Feb. 5, 1977; children: Tyler, Ryan. Student, Mesa Coll., Grand Junction, Colo., Regis Coll., Denver. Cert. Gen. real estate appraiser, Ariz. Loan officer, real estate appraiser Home Fed. Savs. & Loan, Ft. Collins, Colo., 1973-76; real estate appraiser Jungbluth & Assocs., Ft. Collins, 1976-83; pres., bd. dirs. Security Diamond Corp., Denver, 1982-90; nat. sales dir. InfoAm. Computers, Denver, 1982-90; chmn. bd. dirs., CEO U.S. Capital Lending Corp., Denver, 1987-91; ct.-appointed receiver Dist. Ct. State of Colo., 1990; mgr. real estate appraisal World Savs. & Loan Assn., Walnut Creek, 1992-93, Pleasanton, Calif., 1993—94, Phoenix, 1994—2000; pres., CEO Real Estate Rsch. Corp., Phoenix, 2000—. Sgt. USMC, 1969-71. Republican. Avocations: golf, skiing, scuba diving. Home: 958 E Dava Dr Tempe AZ 85283-4761 Office: PO Box 28382 Tempe AZ 85285

JUNGEBERG, THOMAS DONALD, lawyer; b. Berea, Ohio, June 12, 1950; s. Wilbert Donald and Carolyn Francis (Gaube) J.; m. Kathleen Ann Killmer, Oct. 5, 1973; children: Kimberlee Ann, Allison Lynn, Zebulun Thomas, Nathan Aaron. BA, Kent State U., 1972; JD, Cleve. State U., 1976. Bar: Ohio 1976, Mass. 2001, U.S. Dist. Ct. (no. dist.) Ohio 1977, U.S. Tax Ct. 1980, U.S. Supreme Ct. 1980. Tchr. Berea City Schs., Ohio, 1972-75; staff atty. Palmquist & Palmquist, Medina, Ohio, 1977-80, Gibbs & Craze, Parma Heights, Ohio, 1980-81; sole practice Medina, 1981-87; v.p., gen. counsel, corp. sec. Shelby (Ohio) Ins. Co., 1987-95; prin. Lexington (Ohio) Ins. Cons., 1995-96; sole practice Lexington, 1995-96; v.p. legal Reliance Nat., Cleve., 1996-98; asst. v.p., asst. gen. counsel Commerce Ins. Group, Webster, Mass., 1999—. Tchr. First Bapt. Christian Sch., Medina, 1981-84; elder, sec. First Bapt. Ch. of Medina, 1979-86, chmn. First Bapt. Christian Sch., Medina, 1984; bd. govs. Ohio Med. Profl. Liability Underwriting Assn., 1993-95; dir. Inst. Inst. Ind., 1994-95. Mem. Ohio State Bar Assn.Mass. Bar Assn., Am. Corp. Counsel Assn., Gideons Internat. Republican. Avocations: piano, archery, gospel music composition, flying. Home: 66 Westview Dr Danielson CT 06239 E-mail: tdjungeberg@aol.com., tjungeb@commerceinsurance.com.

JUNGER, MIGUEL CHAPERO, acoustics researcher; b. Dresden, Germany, Jan. 29, 1923; came to U.S., 1941, naturalized, 1946; s. José and Adrienne (Junger) Chapiro; m. Ellen Sinclair, 1960; children: M. Sebastian, A. Carlotta. BS, MIT, 1944, SM, 1946; ScD (Gordon McKay scholar), Harvard U., 1951. Postdoctoral rsch. fellow in acoustics Harvard U., 1951-55; partner Cambridge Acoustical Assocs., Inc., 1955-59, pres., 1959-89, chmn. bd. dirs., 1989-97. Sr. vis. lectr. ocean engring. dept. MIT, Cambridge, 1968-78; vis. prof. U. Technologie de Compiègne, 1975, 77-82 Author: Sound, Structures and Their Interaction, 1972, 2d edit., 1986, rev. edit., 1993, Eléments d'Acoustique Physique, 1978, Handbook of Acoustic Characteristics of Turbomachinery Cavities, 1997; guest editor, author: Structural Acoustics, 1997; contbr. articles to profl. jours. Fellow ASME (Rayleigh lectr., Per Bruel Noise Control and Acoustics Gold medal 1992), Acoustical Soc. Am. (Trent-Crede medal 1987). Achievements include patents in field. Home: 90 Fletcher Rd Belmont MA 02478-2017 E-mail: ellenandmiguel@earthlink.net.

JUNGERMAN, JOHN ALBERT, physics educator; b. Modesto, Calif., Dec. 28, 1921; s. Albert Augustus and Freda (Durst) J.; m. Nancy Lee Kidwell, Oct. 23, 1948; children: Mark, Eric, Roger, Anne. AB, U. Calif., Berkeley, 1943, PhD, 1949. Research physicist Manhattan Project, Oak Ridge, Tenn. and Berkeley, 1944-45, Los Alamos, N.Mex., 1945-46, Lawrence Berkeley Lab., Berkeley, 1946-49, 50-51; asst. prof. physics U. Calif., Davis, 1951, prof. physics, 1960-91, prof. emeritus, 1991, founding dir. Crocker Nuclear Lab., 1965-80, chmn. physics dept., 1981-82, 83-87; assoc. mem. faculty Starr King Sch. for Ministry, Berkeley, Calif., 1992-93. Vis. prof. U. Grenoble, France, 1972; prin. investigator nuclear physics Atomic Energy Commn., U. Calif., Davis, 1956-71; cons. OAS U. Chile, Santiago, 1982, OAS, 1971, Internat. Atomic Energy Agy., 1982. Author: Nuclear Arms Race: Technology and Society, 1986, 2d edit., 1990, World in Process, 2000. Organizer, instr. Davis Summer Insts. on Nuclear Age Edn. for Secondary Sch. Instrs., 1986-93. NSF Nuclear Physics grantee, 1971-73, NSF Sci. Edn. grantee, 1990-93. Fellow Am. Physical Soc.; mem. Am. Solar Soc., Sigma Xi. Democrat. Avocations: piano, sailing, bicycling, painting. Office: U Calif Dept Physics Davis CA 95616 E-mail: jajungerman@ucdavis.edu.

JUNGMAN, JONATHAN WAYNE, accountant; b. Yonkers, N.Y., Feb. 12, 1948; s. John L. and Frances E. (Ashmall) J.; m. Lois W. Friedlander, Aug. 26, 1973; children: Susan, Rebecca. BS, NYU, 1970; MBA, St John's U., N.Y.C., 1977. Acctg. supr. ops. The Singer Co., N.Y.C., 1971-74; sr. fin. analyst Am. Airlines, Lake Success, N.Y., 1974-76; asst. contr. Werner Mgmt. Cons., N.Y.C., 1976-84; contr. Compensation Resources, Elmsford, N.Y., 1984-88, Andrews & Clark, Inc., N.Y.C., 1988-90; mgr. budget and fin. reporting Paul, Weiss, Rifkind, Wharton & Garrison, N.Y.C., 1990—. Served as 1st lt. U.S. Army, 1970-71. Mem. Nat. Assn. Accts. Home: PO Box 128 Croton On Hudson NY 10520-0128 Office: Paul Wiess Rifkind Wharton & Garrison 1285 Ave Of The Americas New York NY 10019-6028

JUNIKER, ANTHONY MICHAEL, economic developer, consultant; b. Jackson, Miss., Aug. 30, 1948; s. John and Aleen J.; m. Kathleen Akright, Oct. 9, 1982; 1 child, Margaret Aleen. BS in Acctg., Miss. State U., 1971. Comptroller Capital Security Svcs., Jackson, Miss., 1982-84; small bus. cons. Miss. R&D Ctr., Jackson, 1984-87, mgr. comml. bus. assistance, 1987-88; mgr. entrepreneurial devel. Miss. Dept. Econ. & Cmty. Devel., Jackson, 1988-90, mgr. cmty. ops. br., 1990-96; sr. bus. devel. officer Enterprise Corp. Delta, Jackson, 1996-2000; exec. dir. Magnolia (Ark.) Econ. Devel. Corp., 2000—. Lt.col. U.S. Army. Mem.: Ark. Econ. Developers. Republican. Methodist. Avocations: reading, electric trains. Office: Magnolia Econ Devel Corp PO Box 2262 Magnolia AR 71754-2262

JUNKER, BOBBY RAY, research and development executive, physicist; b. San Antonio, Tex., Aug. 29, 1943; s. Richard Eugene and Alice Emma (Gruetzmacher) J.; m. Judith Lynne Combs, Sept. 12, 1968 (div. Aug. 1974); 1 child, Bryce Allyn; m. Sheryl Ann Watson, Oct. 8, 1976 (div. July 1995); children: Melissa Sheryl, Evan Ryan; m. Virginia C. Katt, July 13, 1996. BS, U. Southwestern La., 1965; MA, U. Tex., 1967, PhD in Chemistry, 1969. Instr. chemistry U. Tex., Austin, 1969-70; rsch. assoc. physics U. Pitts., 1970-72; asst. prof. physics U. Ga., Athens, 1972-76; sci. officer Office Naval Rsch., Arlington, Va., 1977-84, dir. physic. divsn., 1983-86, dir. math. and phys. scis. dept., 1986-93, head electronics, info. and surveillance dept., 1993—. Contbr. chpts. to books. Treas. PTA, Fairfax, Va., 1988-89, county rep., 1990-92; treas. Fairfax Christian Ch., 1982-87, 92-95. Recipient Presdl. Meritorious Rank award U.S. Govt., 1989, 99. Mem. AAAS, Am. Phys. Soc., Sigma Xi. Achievements include rsch. theoretical atomic physics, including electron-atom and ion-atom collisions. Office: Office Naval Rsch Info Electronics and Surveillance Dept 800 N Quincy St Arlington VA 22203-1906

JUNKER, JAMES A. radiologist; b. St. Louis, Apr. 27, 1954; s. Anthony F. and Joan C. Junker; m. Mary Kay Junker, Apr. 11, 1981; children: Thomas P., Margaret A. AB, St. Louis U., 1975, MD, 1979. Diplomate Am. Bd. Radiology, Am. Bd. Vascular and Interventional Radiology, Am. Bd. Neuroradiology. Intern in pediatrics St. Louis U. Hosp., 1979-80; resident Mallincknodt Inst. Radiology, 1980-83; radiologist Scott Radiol. Group, St. Louis, 1983—. Mem. governing bd. Southpointe Hosp.-Tenet, St. Louis, 1993-2001. Fellow Am. Coll. Radiology; mem. AMA, Radiol. Soc. N.Am., Soc. Cardiovascular and Interventional Radiology, Mo. State Med. Assn., Mo. Radiol. Soc. (pres. 2000), Greater St. Louis Soc. Radiologists (pres. 1995), Jefferson County Med. Soc. Avocations: golf, travel. Home: 16 Fox Mdws Saint Louis MO 63127-1401 Office: Scott Radiol Group 2344 Hampton Ave Saint Louis MO 63139-2909

JUNKERMAN, WILLIAM JOSEPH, retired lawyer; b. N.Y.C., May 5, 1904; s. Otto J. and Margaret Anne (McCarthy) J.; m. Helen Veronica Barrett, June 28, 1930. AB, NYU, 1925; LLB, Fordham U., 1928. Bar: N.Y. 1929, U.S. Dist. Ct. (so. and ea. dists.) N.Y. 1929, U.S. Ct. Appeals (1st, 2d and 3d cirs.), U.S. Supreme Ct. 1946. Ensign naval aviation USNR, 1925-41; with USN, 1941-46; comdr. ret. ; asst. counsel L.I. State Park Commn., 1929-32; sole practice, N.Y.C., 1932-41; regional atty. CAA, 7th Region, Seattle, 1947-48; mem. Haight, Gardner, Poor & Havens, N.Y.C., 1948-50, gen. ptnr., 1950-80. Spl. master N.Y. Supreme Ct., N.Y. County; abitrator U.S. Dist. Ct. Edn., N.Y. Fellow Am. Coll. Trial Lawyers; mem. Nat. Pilots Assn., Naval Order of U.S., Am. Legion (past comdr.). Clubs: Quiet Birdmen, Wings. Address: 271 Madison Ave Ste 1107 New York NY 10016-1001

JUNOD, DANIEL AUGUST, podiatrist; b. Vandalia, Ill., Sept. 12, 1928; s. Louis August and Nettie Louise (Martin) J.; m. Joanne Alice Denton, Mar. 29, 1952; children: Paul, John, Timothy, David, Stephen. Student, Greenville (Ill.) Coll., 1946-48; DPM, Scholl Coll. Podiatric Med., Chgo., 1952. Lic. podiatric physician, Ill. Pvt. practice podiatrist, Greenville, 1952—; staff podiatrist Fair Oaks Nursing Home, Greenville, 1970—, Brauns Terrace, Greenville, 1989—, Faith Countryside Homes Nursing Ctr., Highland, Ill., 1992—2003, Highland (Ill.) Health Care Ctr., 1993-2000. Staff podiatrist 25 different nursing homes in several south ctrl. Ill. cities, many yrs. Contbr. articles to profl. jours. Avocations: photography, volksmarching, video photography, photography and artwork. Home: 511 S 2nd St Greenville IL 62246-1742 Office: 309 W College Ave PO Box 697 Greenville IL 62246-0697

JUNOD, SUZANNE WHITE, historian, consultant; b. Decatur, Ga., Aug. 10, 1959; d. James Roy and Jane (Langley) White; m. Louis John Junod, Nov. 7, 1993; children: Christine Rebecca, Carter Louis. BA hist., Valdosta State Univ., Valdosta, Ga., 1981; MA hist., PhD hist., Emory Univ., Atlanta, 1994. Historian U.S. Food and Drug Adminstrn., Rockville, Md., 1985—. Cons. Adv. Com. on Human Radiation Experiments (apptd. by William Clinton), Washington, 1994—95. Contbr. articles to profl. jour. Editl. bd. Journal of the History of Medicine, 1999—. Recipient Award of Merit, FDA, 1989. Mem.: Am. Inst. for the Hist. of Pharmacy, Am. Assn. for the Hist. of Medicine, Soc. for Hist. in Fed. Govt. (Thomson Prize 2000, 2002). Achievements include established the first prof. hist. office within the FDA. Office: FDA Hist Office HFC-24 Rm 12-69 Rockville MD 20857

JUNZ, HELEN B. economist; d. Samson and Dobra Bachner. BA, PhD, U. Amsterdam; MA, New Sch. Social Rsch. Acting chief consumer price sect. Nat. Indsl. Conf. Bd., N.Y.C., 1953-58; research officer Nat. Inst. Econ. and Social Research, London, 1958-60; economist Bur. Econ. Analysis, Dept. Commerce, Washington, 1960-62; adviser div. internat. fin. bd. govs. Fed. Res. System, Washington, 1962-77; dep. asst. sec. Office of Asst. Sec. for Internat. Affairs, Dept. Treasury, Washington, 1977-79; v.p., sr. advisor 1st Nat. Bank Chgo., 1979-80; v.p. Townsend Greenspan & Co., Inc., N.Y.C., 1980-82; sr. advisor European dept. IMF, 1982-87, dep. dir. exch. and trade rels. dept., 1987-89, spl. trade rep., dir. Geneva office, 1989-94; dir. gold econs. svc. World Gold Coun., Geneva, Switzerland, 1994-96; pres. HBJ Internat., London, 1996—. Adviser OECD, Paris, 1967-69; sr. internat. economist Council of Econ. Advisers, The White House, Washington, 1975-77. Author: Where did all the money go?,

2002; contbr. articles to profl. jours. Mem. Am. Econ. Assn., Coun. Fgn. Rels., Cosmos Club, Reform Club. Office: HBJ Intnat 39 Chalcot Sq London NW1 8YP England E-mail: hbjunz@planet.nl.

JUODVALKE, EGLE See JUODVALKÉ, EGLIS

JUODVALKÉ, EGLIS (EGLE JUODVALKE, JUODVALKE), writer; b. East Chicago, Ind., Jan. 28, 1950; d. Antanas and Ona (Norkutė) J.; m. Henryk Skwarczynski, Sept. 2, 1989. BA, U. Chgo., 1973. Sr. editor Radio Free Europe/Radio Liberty, Inc., Munich, 1976-95. Author: (poetry) If You Touch Me, 1972, Who Has the Ring?, 1983, The Necklace of Mnemosine, 1996, (prose) Sugar Mountain or The Adventures of a Lithuanian Diabetic in America and Other Exotic Places, 2000, (bilingual poetry and CD of author's reading) Veidrodis ir tuštuma/The Mirror and the Void, 2002. Mem. Santara-Šviesa, Korp! Neo-Lithuania. Avocation: touring Greece. Home: 8608 Sayre Ave Burbank IL 60459-2260

JUODVALKIS, JUDITH L, human resources specialist; b. Cleveland, Ohio, May 24, 1973; d. Kathleen E and James H Hoffmann; m. Vincent V Juodvalkis, Aug. 12, 2000. BA, Allegheny Coll., Meadville, Pa., 1991—95; MA, U. of Akron, Akron, Ohio, 1995—97. Certificate in Salary Administration World at Work, 2003. Adminstrv. asst. Stephens Assoc, Ltd., Columbus, Ohio, 1997—99; human resources adminstr. Human Resources Solutions, Columbus, Ohio, 1999—99; compensation analyst Big Lots, Inc., Columbus, Ohio, 1999—2001; compensation cons. The Longaberger Co., Newark, Ohio, 2001—. Mem.: Human Resource Assn of Ctrl. Ohio, Columbus Compensation Assn., Soc. for Human Resource Mgmt., World at Work, Phi Beta Kappa, Alpha Gamma Delta (activities coord. 1994—95). United Methodist. Office: The Longaberger Company 1500 East Main Street Newark OH 43055 E-mail: jjuodval@longaberger.com.

JUPINA, ANDREA ANN, executive search consultant; b. Pottsville, Pa., May 23, 1950; d. Andrew Jupina and Anna (Kavalecs) J. Student, Douglass Coll., 1969-70; BA in Biology/Psychology, Antioch Coll., 1973. Rsch. assoc. Booz, Allen & Hamilton, Inc., N.Y.C., 1977-81; founder, mng. dir. A. Jupina Co., N.Y.C., 1983-93; sr. v.p. Boyden Consulting Corp., N.Y.C., 1993-94. Founder Stuyvesant Group Internat., Amsterdam, 1987—. Author: The Handbook of Executive Search Research-A How-To Guide for Researchers, Search Consultants, Corporate Recruiters and Line Executives, 1992; contbr. articles to profl. jours. Dir. Antioch Coll. Alumni Assn., 1986-89, mem. devel. com., 1989; founding mem. The City Ch., N.Y., 1993; adv. coun. Women's Internat. Leadership Program, Kellogg Found., 1993—; founding mem. Rsch. Roundtable, 1979. Mem. Princeton Club of N.Y. (squash and athletics com. 1992), Netherlands C. of C.

JUPITER, JESSE BERNARD, orthopedic surgeon; b. N.Y.C., Sept. 23, 1946; s. Samuel Jacob and Miriam (Kabakoff) J.; m. Beryl Stephanie Abrams, June 19, 1971; children: Stacy Deborah, Benjamin Scott. AB, Brown U., 1968; MD, Yale U., 1972. Diplomate Am. Bd. Orthopedic Surgery. Resident in surgery Mass. Gen. Hosp., Boston, 1975-76, resident in orthop., 1976-79, orthopedic trauma chief, 1989-94, chief orthopedic hand, 1995—; trauma fellow Swiss Assn. for Study of Internal Medicine, Basel, Switzerland, 1980; hand/microsurgery fellow Louisville Ky. Hand, 1980-81, orthop. hand/trauma surgeon dept. orthop. surgery Mass. Gen. Hosp./Harvard Med. Sch., Boston, 1981-89; prof. orthopaedic surgery Harvard Med. Sch., Boston, 1997—, Hansjörg Wyss/AO chair prof., 2003—. Trustee Assn. for Study of Internal Medicine Found., Zurich, Switzerland, 1992—, chmn. edn., 1994—. Editor: Flynn Hand Surgery, 1991, Skeletal Trauma, 1991 (award 1992), Fractures of the Distal Radius, 1995 (with Dr. Diego Fernandez). With USPHS, 1973-75. Avocation: adult soccer league. Home: 15 None Such Way Weston MA 02493-1021 Office: Mass Gen Hosp 15 Parkman St Boston MA 02114-3117 E-mail: jjupiter1@partners.org.

JURA, JAMES J. electric utility executive; b. Creston, Nebr., Dec. 9, 1942; s. Joseph James and Edna Helena (Mackenstadt) J.; m. Sylvia; children: Joseph, James, John, Fredericka. BA, U. Wash., Seattle, 1967; MBA, Seattle U., 1971; postgrad., Harvard U., 1985. With indsl. rels. staff Boeing Co., Seattle, 1968-71; with policy devel. staff OSHA, Washington, 1971-73; legis. and budget analyst Office Mgmt. and Budget, Washington, 1973-78; asst. adminstr. Bonneville Power Adminstrn., U.S. Dept. Energy, Washington, 1978-80, from exec. asst. adminstr. to adminstr. Portland, Oreg., 1980-91; CEO, gen. mgr. Assoc. Electric Coop. Inc., Springfield, Mo., 1991—. Bd. dirs. Assn. Mo. Elec. Coops., Mo. Employers Mut. Ins. Co. With U.S. Army, 1963-65. Republican. Office: Associated Electric Coop PO Box 754 Springfield MO 65801-0754 E-mail: jjura@aeci.org.

JURAFSKY, DANIEL, linguist; b. Yonkers, NY, 1962; BA in Linguistics, U. Calif., Berkeley, 1983, PhD in Computer Sci., 1992. Software engr.; postdoc. rsch. Internat. Computer Sci. Inst., 1992—96; assoc. prof. U. Colo., 1996—. Drummer Too Many Notes. Mem. editl. bd.: Computer Speech Lang.; coauthor: Speech and Language Processing. Recipient CAREER award, NSF; fellow MacArthur Found. fellow, 2002. Office: U Colo Dept Linguistics 295 UCB Boulder CO 80309-0295*

JURAN, JOSEPH MOSES, engineer, consultant; b. Braila, Rumania, Dec. 24, 1904; arrived in U.S., 1912, naturalized, 1917; s. Jakob and Gitel (Goldenberg) Juran; m. Sadie Shapiro, June 5, 1926; children: Robert, Sylvia, Charles, Donald. BS in Elec. Engring., U. Minn., 1924; JD, Loyola U., 1935; DEng (hon.), Stevens Inst. Tech., 1988; DSc (hon.), U. Minn., 1992, Rochester Inst. Tech., 1992; LLD (hon.), U. New Haven, 1992. With Western Electric Co., Inc., 1924—41; asst. adminstr. Office Lend-Lease Adminstrn., 1941—43, Fgn. Econ. Adminstrn., 1943—45; prof., chmn. dept. adminstrv. engring. NYU, 1945—51, prof. ind. engr., 1951; pvt. cons. N.Y.C., 1951—79; chmn. Juran Inst., Inc., Wilton, Conn., 1979—87, chmn. emeritus, 1987—. Cons. numerous indsl. cos. and govt. agys., 1945—; vis. lectr. numerous Am. and Fgn. univs.; founder, chmn. Juran Found., Inc., 1986—. Author (video cassette series): Juran on Quality Improvement, 1981; author: Juran on Planning for Quality, 1988, Juran on Leadership for Quality, 1989, Juran on Quality by Design, 1992; lectr., author (numerous papers on mgmt.). Decorated Order of Sacred Treasure (Japan); recipient alumni medal, U. Minn., 1954, Scroll of Appreciation, Japanese Union Scientists and Engrs., 1961, 250th Anniversary medal, Czech Higher Inst. Tech., 1965, Wallace Clark medal, 1967, ann. medal, Technikhaza Esztergom, Hungary, 1968, medal, Fedn. Tech. and Sci. Industries, Hungary, 1968, medal of honor camera, Official de la Industria, Madrid, 1970, Plaque Appreciation, Republic Korea, 1978, Stevens medal, Stevens Inst. Tech., 1984, Chairman's award, Am. Assn. Engring. Socs., 1988, Nat. medal Tech. U.S., 1992, Mng. Automation award, Automation Hall of Fame, 1995. Fellow: AAAS, ASME (hon. Warner medal 1945, Eli Whitney award 1995, Soichior Honda medal 1995), Am. Mgmt. Assn., Am. Inst. Indsl. Engrs. (Gilbreth medal 1981), Internat. Acad. Mgmt., Am. Soc. for Quality Control (hon. Brumbaugh award 1958, Edwards medal 1962, Eugene L. Grant medal 1967); mem.: NAE, Spanish Soc. for Quality Control, Brit. Inst. Quality Assurance, Spanish Assn. for Quality Control, European Orgn. Quality Control (hon. medal 1993), Philippine Soc. for Quality Control, Argentine Orgn. for Quality Control, Australian Orgn. for Quality Control (Juran medal named in his honor 1975), Romanian Acad. (academician 1992, established Juran award 1992), mem., sometime officer many profl. assns., Alpha Pi Mu, Tau Beta Pi, Sigma Xi. Office: Juran Inst Inc PO Box 811 Wilton CT 06897-0811*

JURAN, SYLVIA LOUISE, editor; b. Chgo. d. Joseph Moses and Sadie (Shapiro) J. BA, U. Minn.; MA, Columbia U., 1960; PhD, Harvard U., 1975. Project editor Macmillan Pub. Co., N.Y.C., 1981-91; editor Ralph Appelbaum Assocs. Inc., N.Y.C., 1991—. Faculty The New Sch., N.Y.C., 1980-82. Project editor: Ency. of the Holocaust, 1990 (Dartmouth medal ALA, 1990), Ency. of the Third Reich, 1991; editor scripts for mus. exhbns.; contbr. articles to profl. jours. Nat. Def. fgn. lang. fellow, 1960-61, 62-63. Mem. Harvard Club of N.Y.C., Harvard Grad. Sch. Alumni Assn. (N.Y. exec. com. 1984—), James Beard Found. Office: Ralph Appelbaum Assocs Inc 88 Pine St New York NY 10005-1801

JURAND, JERRY GEORGE, periodontology educator, researcher; b. Gostyn, Piaski, Poland, Apr. 23, 1923; came to US, 1956; s. Piotr and Maria (Mizerska) J.; m. Ruth Edith I. Kujus, 1950; children: Lydia U., Robert B., Darlene S. Diploma, Polish Humanistic Lyceum, Ingolstadt, Germany, 1947; Dr.Med-.Dent., Friedrich Alexander U., Erlangen, Germany, 1956; DDS, U. Tenn., Memphis, 1965. Cancer rsch. scientist in biochemistry Roswell Park Meml. Inst., Buffalo, 1957-62; rsch. assoc. in immunology St. Jude Children's Rsch. Hosp., Memphis, 1962-65; assoc. prof. periodontology U. Tenn., Memphis, 1965-70, prof. periodontology, 1970—, rsch. dir. in periodontology, 1965-75, clinic dir. in periodontology, 1975-80; prof. emeritus U Tenn, Coll. Dentistry, Memphis, 2002—. Cons. in periodontics St. Jude Children's Rsch. Hosp., 1965—. Contbr. to book: Surface Chemistry and Dental Integuments, 1973; contbr. articles to profl. jour. Advisor Boy Scouts Am., Memphis, 1965-75; discussion panelist Amnesty Internat., Memphis, 1982. Capt. Dental Corps US Army, 1953-56. NIH rsch. grantee, 1965-75. Mem. ADA (life), AAAS, Am. Assn. Dental Rsch. (life), Internat. Assn. Dental Rsch. (life), N.Y. Acad. Scis. Avocations: camping, scouting, nature preservation, canoeing, painting. Office: U Tenn Coll Dentistry 875 Union Ave Memphis TN 38103-3513 E-mail: jjurand@utmem.edu.

JURASEK, JOHN PAUL, mathematics educator, counselor; b. Flushing, NY, June 23, 1959; s. John Steven and Eleanor Rita Jurasek; m. Gale Marie Abrahamsen, May 22, 1993; 1 child, John IV. BS, Fairleigh Dickinson U., 1982; BA, SUNY, New Paltz, 1991; MS, Iona Coll., 1995. Cert. pub. sch. math. tchr., N.Y., N.J. Acct. Sony Corp., Park Ridge, N.J., 1982-85; learning ctr. coord. Rockland C.C., Suffern, NY, 1985-91; math. instr. Collegiate Sch., Passaic, N.J., 1991-92, Ridgefield Park (N.J.) Schs., 1992—99, Cresskill (NJ) Schs., 2000—. Map chair NY/NJ Trail Conf. Contbr. articles to profl. jours. Mem. Town Dem. Com., Piermont, N.Y., 1980. Recipient Above and Beyond award RAMAQUOIS, Pomona, 1990, Counselor of Yr. award 1990. Mem. Internat. Soc. Technology in Edn., Math. Assn. Am., Nat. Coun. Tchrs. Math., N.J. Edn. Assn., Northvale Rifle and Pistol Club, Am. Mensa, Brit. Mensa, Appalachian Mountain Club. Democrat. Roman Catholic. Avocations: model rocketry, target shooting, computer programming, hiking. Home: 193 Howard Ave Orangeburg NY 10962-2314 Office: Cresskill Schs 1 Lincoln Dr Cresskill NJ 07626 E-mail: jurasek@optonline.net.

JURASEK, RANDALL JOHN, educational consultant; b. Rockford, Ill, Nov. 19, 1954; s. Walter John and Florence (Misuraca) J.; m. Elizabeth Leigh Lichter, Sept. 22, 1979; children: Nicholas John, Alex Joseph. BS in Edn., Western Ill. U., 1977; MEd, Nat. Coll. Edn., 1986; Cert. Advanced Studies, Nat. Louis U., 1997. Tchr. spl. edn. Kankakee Area Spl. Edn. Coop., 1977-78, Harlem Consol. Dist. 122, Loves Pk., Ill., 1978-79, Rockford Sch. Dist. 205, Ill., 1980-88; systems engr. IBM, Rockford, 1988-91, edn. specialist, 1991-93; networking specialist, trainer, 1993-95; staff developer Byron Comm. Unit Sch. Dist. 226, Ill., 1995-97; project mgr. IBM K-12 Cons. Svc., Indpls., 1997-99; edn. transformation specialist IBM Bus. Consulting Svc., Chgo., 1999—. Cons., presenter in field. Mem. regional adv. bd. Discovery Ctr. Rockford, 1992—98, Coun. Exceptional Children, Rockford, 1984—88, pres., 1987—88; mem. bus. adv. coun. Goodwill Industries, 1991—93; mem. No. Ill. Ctr. Adaptive Techs., 1987—93; mem. sch. bd. Byron Cmty. Unit Sch. Dist., 2001—; mem. parish coun. St. Mary's Ch., Byron, 1995—. Mem. ASCD, Phi Delta Kappa (newsletter editor 1986-88). Roman Catholic. Avocations: model railroading, o-guage, gardening, technology.

JURCH, GEORGE R., JR., retired science educator; b. New Britain, Conn., Feb. 1, 1934; s. George and Alice Jurch; m. Molly Irene Brown; children: George III, Steven, Carol. BS in Chemistry, U. Fla., 1957; MS in Chemistry, U. Ky., 1961; PhD, U. Calif., San Diego, 1965. Technician Thorton Chem. Lab., Tampa, Fla., 1952—56; rsch. chemist IBM, Lexington, Ky., 1961; rsch. assoc. Yale U., New Haven, 1965—66; prof. U. South Fla., Tampa, 1966—99; ret., 1999. Cons. USDA, Fla., 1975—99. Author: (book) Lab Manual General Chemistry, 1969, Lab Manual Organic, 5 edits., 1975—99. Sgt. U.S. Army, 1957—59. Democrat. Roman Catholic. Achievements include patents in field. Avocation: wine consultant. Home: 1215 E Brandon Blvd Brandon FL 33511

JURGENSEN, KAREN, newspaper editor; BA in Eng., U. N.C., 1971. Editorial and feature writer, columnist, editorial page layout editor Charlotte (N.C.) News, 1972-75; writer, editor Sea Grant Coll. Program U. N.C., Raleigh, 1976-79; from asst. lifestyle editor to lifestyle editor Miami News, 1979-82, asst. city editor, 1982; topics editor, life dept. USA Today, McLean, Va., 1982, spl. projects editor, life dept., 1983-85, dep. mng. editor, life dept., 1985-86, mng. editor, cover stories dept., 1986-87, sr. editor, days/spl. projects, 1987-91, editor of editorial page, 1991-99, editor of newspaper, 1999—. Participant Penney-Mo. Workshop, Columbia, Mo., 1981, Am. Press Inst. Workshops, 1981, 84, newspaper execs. mktg. sem. Am. Newspaper Pubs. Assn., 1986. Bd. vis. Chapel Hill Sch. Journalism and Mass Comm., U. N.C., chair, 1996-99. Recipient Matrix award Women in Comm. D.C. chpt., 2000, Women's Leadership Nat. Lifetime Legacy award D.C. Chamber of Commerce, 2002; named to U. N.C. Sch. Journalism Hall of Fame, 2001; Exchange scholar U. P.R., 1969-70. Mem. Am. Soc. Newspaper Editors (chair/vice chair press bar com. 1993-95, convention com. 1991-94, vice chair convention com. 1995-96, vice chair, chair literacy com. 1989-91, future of newspapers com. 1988-90, 91, writing awards bd. 1989-91). Office: USA Today 7950 Jones Branch Dr Mc Lean VA 22108

JURGENSEN, MONSERRATE, clinical nurse, consultant; b. Guyanailla, P.R., Oct. 25, 1945; d. Francisco and Felicita (Feliciano) Muniz; m. Timothy J. Jurgensen, Dec. 1, 1978; children: Timothy J. Jr., Jeremy J. Diploma, Presbyn. Hosp. Sch. Nursing, San Juan, P.R., 1967; BSN, Barry U., 1990; postgrad., Webster U., 1992—. RN, Fla. Surg. unit and surg. ICU staff nurse U. Hosp., P.R., 1967-69; commd. 2d lt. USAF, 1969, advanced through grades to maj., 1986; pediat. unit staff nurse USAF Hosp., Sheppard AFB, Tex., 1969-70, orthopedic and psychiat. unit staff nurse Cam Ranh Bay, Vietnam, 1970-71, staff nurse obstetrics unit Torrejon AFB, Spain, 1971-74, obstetrics head nurse K.I. Sawyer AFB, Mich., 1974-78, staff nurse obstetrics unit, head nurse pediatric clinic Langley AFB, Va., 1978-81; med.-surg. nurse USAFR, Langley AFB, Va., 1984-86, staff nurse Primary Care Clinics Norfolk, Va., 1985-86; staff nurse Cigna HMO, Miami, Fla., 1986-87; staff nurse long-term care unit VA Hosp., Miami, 1988-90, med.-surg. nurse psychiat. unit, 1990-91; quality control nurse, infection control Immunization Clinic, Duke Field, Fla., 1989-91; evening-night supr., mgr. med.-surg. unit same day surgery Army Hosp., Ft. Jackson, S.C., 1991-94; mgr. same day surgery med.-surg. unit Reynolds Army Cmty. Hosp., Ft. Sill, Okla., 1994—. Mem. Soc. Presbyn. Hosp. Sch. Nursing. Republican. Avocations: tennis, cooking, sewing. Office: US Army Fort Sill Lawton OK 73503

JURGENSEN, W.G. insurance company executive; BSBA, MBA, Creighton U. Corp. banking officer thru exec. v.p. corp. banking Northwest Investment Svcs.; mgmt. First Chicago NBD Corp.; exec. v.p. Bank One Corp.; CEO Nationwide Ins. Office: Nationwide Ins 1 Nationwide Plz Columbus OH 43215

JURICIC, DAVOR, mechanical engineering educator; b. Split, Croatia, Aug. 2, 1928; came to U.S., 1968; s. Mate and Slavka (Franceschi) J.; m. Milesa L. Harris, Mar. 10, 1984; 1 child, Ivanna Albertin. Dipl.Ing., U. Belgrade, Yugoslavia, 1952, DSc, 1964. Stress analyst Icarus Aircraft Industries, Zemun, Yugoslavia, 1953-58; rsch. engr. Inst. Aeronautics, Belgrade, 1958-63; asst. prof. U. Belgrade, 1963-65, assoc. prof., 1965-68, S.D. State U., Brookings, 1968-73, prof., 1973-75; vis. prof. Stanford (Calif.) U., 1975-78; prof. mech. engring. U. Tex., Austin, 1978-98, prof. emeritus, 1998—. Contbr. numerous articles to profl. jours. Rsch. grantee various agencies, 1962—. Mem. ASME, Am. Soc. Engring. Edn. (Chester F. Carlson award 1993), Sigma Xi. Achievements include research in suspension system for railway vehicles (patent). E-mail: juricic@mail.utexas.edu.

JURIGA, RAYMOND MICHAEL, dentist; b. Uniontown, Pa., May 29, 1949; s. John Martin and Elizabeth Ann (Vanek) S.; m. Barbara Diane Menni, Aug. 13, 1972; children: Vanessa Rae, Max Nicholas. BS, Calif. State Coll., 1971; DMD, U. Pitts., 1975. Diplomate Am. Bd. Forensic Dentistry. Dentist Office of Patrick Piovesan, White Oak, Pa., 1975-76, Westmore Dental Arts Group, Mt. Pleasant, Pa., 1976-78, dentist, ptnr., 1980—; dentist Office of Robert Sepp DDS, Connellsville, Pa., 1978-80. Staff dentist Health South Outpatient Surg. Ctr., Mt. Pleasant, 1990—; cons. staff Harmon House, Mt. Pleasant, 1990—; part-time clin. instr. dental hygiene Westmoreland C.C., Youngwood, Pa., 1994—. Fellow Acad. Gen. Dentistry, Am. Endodonic Soc., Acad. Dentistry Internat., Internat. Coll. Dentists, Am. Coll. Dentists, Am. Acad. Forensic Scis.; mem. Pa. Dental Assn. (10th dist. rep. 1997—, forensic odontology com., dental identification team PADIT), Am. Soc. Forensic Odontology (mem. region III DMORT). Democrat. Roman Catholic. Avocations: photography, model railroading, stamp collecting, racquetball, bicycling. Office: Chestnut Hills Dental 220 Bessemer Rd Ste 301 Mount Pleasant PA 15666-9141

JURIGA, ROSEMARIE, social services administrator; b. Akron, Ohio, Sept. 4, 1949; d. Emil Paul and Wanda Theresa (Pelka) Juriga. AAS in Community Svcs., U. Akron, 1977, BA in Social Work, 1981; MS in Social Adminstrn., Case Western Res. U., 1992. Lic. social worker Ohio. Office supr. Vocat. Devel. Ctr., Akron, 1978-80; assoc. exec. dir. Goodwill Industries Akron, 1980-82; coord. Akron Cmty. Svc. Ctr. and Urban League, 1982-84; dir. Akron 70001, 1984-90; exec. dir. Tri-County Ind. Living Ctr., Akron, 1990—. Commn. grantee rev. U.S. Dept. Edn., Washington, 1993—95; dean appointment Summit County Adv. Mandel Sch. Applied Social Sci., Cleve., 1992—. Candidate Akron Sch. Bd., 1993; mem. Mayor's Commn. Children, Akron, 1994; mem allocations panel United Way Summit County, 1986—92; v.p., pres. Cmty. Welfare Forum, 1998—2000, Housing Network, 2000; chair Cath. Commn., 2001—03, bd. dirs., 1986—; bd. dirs., treas. Women's Entrepreneurial Growth Orgn., Akron, 1991—93; bd. dirs. United Way Women, Akron, 1993; Christmas in April, 2000, 2001; bd. dirs. Multi-County Housing Devel. Corp. Named Employer of Yr., Summit County Com. Employment and Advocacy Persons with Disability, 1994, Woman of the Yr., Women's History Project Summit County, 1994; recipient Bishop Anthony Pilla Leadership award, 1999, Michael Powell award for humanitarianism, 2002. Mem.: NASW, Women's Network Akron. Avocations: walking, hiking, fishing, travel. Office: Tri-County Ind Living Ctr 680 E Market St Ste 205 Akron OH 44304-1640 E-mail: rose@tcilc.org.

JURKA, EDITH MILA, psychiatrist, researcher; b. N.Y.C., Dec. 4, 1915; d. Charles Anton and Edith Dorothy (Schevcik) J. *Grandfather 1863 graduate, Bellevue Hospital Medical School. Private practice in Manhattan: Owned four pharmacies. Both parents were doctors.* BA, Smith Coll., 1936; postgrad., Charles U., Prague, Czechoslovakia, 1936-38; MD, Yale U., 1944. Diplomate Am. Bd. Psychiatry and Neurology. Intern in children's med. svc. Bellevue Hosp., N.Y.C., 1944-45, asst. alienist, 1947-49; rotating intern Gallinger Hosp., Washington, 1945-46; intern N.Y. State Psychiat. Inst., N.Y.C., 1946-47; asst. psychiatrist Mt. Sinai Hosp., N.Y.C., 1949-51; pvt. practice N.Y.C., 1949—; asst. psychiatrist Roosevelt Hosp., N.Y.C., 1954-57; chief psychiatrist Pleasantville (N.Y.) Cottage Sch., 1961-74. Bd. dirs. intuition network Inst. Noetic Scis.; dir. Wind Song Inst. Sec. Jane Coffin Childs Fund, 1938-41. Fellow Am. Orthopsychiat. Assn.; mem. Am. Psychiat. Assn., N.Y. Coun. Child and Adolescent Psychiatry, N.Y. County Med. Soc., N.Y. State Med. Soc. (psychiat. medicine com.), Westchester Psychiat. Soc. Avocations: architecture, parapsychology, travel, gardening, theater. Home: 16 Apple Bee Farm Ln Croton On Hudson NY 10520-3612 Office: 116 E 66th St New York NY 10021-6547

JURKAT, MARTIN PETER, mathematician, statistician, management educator; b. Berlin, July 23, 1935; came to U.S., 1946, naturalized, 1951; s. Ernest Herman and Dorothy (Bergas) J.; m. Mayme Porter, May 31, 1958; children; Martin Alexander, Susanna, Maria. BA in Math. and Stats. with honors, Swarthmore (Pa.) Coll., 1957; MA, U. N.C., 1961; PhD, Stevens Inst. Tech., Hoboken, N.J., 1972. Programmer Burroughs Corp. Research Lab., Paoli, Pa., 1960-61; sr. program analyst ITT Corp., Paramus, N.J., 1961-64; dir. Center Mcpl. Studies and Services Stevens Inst. Tech., 1975-77, chief transp. analysis div. Davidson Lab., 1964-75, Alexander Crombie Humphreys prof. mgmt. sci., 1979—2001. Cons. Tank-Automotive Devel. Command, U.S. Army, 1975-88, AT&T, 1995-2001, Lucent, 1996-2001; dir. Cause project NSF, 1978-81. Co-author: The NATO Reference Mobility Model, 1980; author studies, reports on mobility, transp., human factors, math. edn. Mem. Assn. Computing Machinery. Democrat. Mem. Soc. Of Friends. Home and Office: 2822 Don Quixote Santa Fe NM 87505 E-mail: mpeterj@comcast.net.

JURKIEWICZ, MARGARET JOY GOMMEL, secondary education educator; b. Indpls., Sept. 5, 1920; d. Dewey Ezra and Joy Agnes (Edie) Gommel; m. Walter Stephen Jurkiewicz, Jan. 1, 1942; children: Mary Margaret, Dewey John, Walter Stephen Jr., Hugh Louis. BS, Ind. U., 1941; postgrad., U. Minn., 1942-43, Butler U., 1950-51, U. Cin., 1958-60, Ind. U., 1971-72, Ball State U., 1974-75. Cert. secondary tchr., Ind., Ohio. Tchr. home econ. Plymouth HS, Ind., 1941-42, Indpls. Pub. Sch., Ind., 1949-57, Mt. Confort-Hancock Co. Sch., Mt. Comfort, Ind., 1957-58, Cin. Pub. sch., 1958-61; tchr. 6th grade Plymouth Sch. corp., Ind., 1961-63; tchr. home econ. and art Argos Cmty. Sch., Ind., 1963-67; tchr. home econ. Penn-Harris-Madison Sch., Mishawaka, Ind., 1967-83; tchr. chpt. I South Bend Sch. Corp., Ind., 1983-85; vol. tchr. art various sch., Ind., 1985—, various sch., Mich., 1985—96, various sch., Ill., 1985-96. Author newsletter and booklet Polish Cultural Soc., 1979—. Bd. dir. Area Agy. on Aging Coun., Plymouth, Ind., 1987-94, Garden Cts. Sr. Housing, Plymouth, 1989—; mem. legis. com. Five County Area Agy. on Aging, 1994--; vol. tchr. sch., libr., children's mus. and sr. ctr., 1985—. Mem.: AARP (editor newsletter Marshall County chpt. 1993—), AAUW (pres., chair various coms.), Plymouth Pub. Libr. Friends (pres., chair various coms.), Marshall County Ret. Tchr. (pres. 1993—95), Ind. Assn. Family and Consumer Sci., Am. Assn. Family and Consumer Sci., PEO, Tippecanoe Audubon Soc., Ind. Polish Cultural Soc. (v.p., chair various coms.). Methodist. Avocations: gardening, camping, travel, football games, sewing. Home: 11570 9th A Rd Plymouth IN 46563-9581 E-mail: mjjurkiewicz@yahoo.com.

JURKIEWICZ, MAURICE JOHN, surgeon, educator; b. Claremont, N.H., Sept. 24, 1923; s. Charles B. and Mary (Ostrowska) J.; m. Mary de Forest Freeman, July 7, 1951; children— Elizabeth de Forest, John Christopher. D.D.S. magna cum laude, U. Md., 1946; MD, Harvard U., 1952. Diplomate: Am. Bd. Surgery, Am. Bd. Plastic Surgery (mem. bd. 1971-77, chmn. 1977-78). Intern Barnes Hosp., Washington U., St. Louis, 1952-53, resident, 1953-58, clin. fellow, 1958-59, instr. surgery, 1957-59; mem. staff U. Fla. Hosp., Gainesville; asst. prof. surgery U. Fla., 1959-64, assoc. prof., 1964-67, prof., 1967-71, chief div. plastic and reconstructive surgery, 1959-71; chief of surgery VA Hosp., Gainesville, 1968-71; prof. surgery, chief of plastic and reconstructive surgery Emory Affiliated Hosps., Atlanta, 1971-92; chief surg. services Grady Meml. Hosp., Atlanta, 1972-77; chief of surgery VAMC, Atlanta, 1989-93. Cons. in plastic surgery Walter Reed Gen. Hosp., Washington, 1971-91; sci. counselor Nat. Inst. Dental Rsch., 1966-71; chmn. com. on study of evaluation procedures Am. Bd. Med. Spltys., 1979-81; mem. at large Nat. Bd. Med. Exams., 1985-93; commr. Joint Commn. on Accreditation of Health Care Orgns., 1985-94 (sec. 1989-90, treas. 1990-91, vice chmn. 1991-92), Nat. Cons. in Plastic Surgery to the Shriners Hosp., 1995—. Editor: Operative Techniques in Plastic Surgery, 1994-99; assoc. editor: Plastic and Reconstructive Surgery, 1972-78, 79-83, co-editor, 1985-89; assoc. editor Am. Surgeon, 1977-87. Served to lt. (j.g.) USNR, 1946-48. Fellow Royal Australasian Coll. Surgeons (hon.); mem. AMA, Am. Cancer Soc., Am. Cleft Palate Assn., ACS (bd. regents 1979-88, vice chmn. 1985-88, pres.-elect 1988, pres. 1989 90), Am. Soc. Plastic and Reconstructive Surgeons, Southeastern Soc. Plastic and Reconstructive Surgeons, Ga. Soc. Plastic and Reconstructive Surgeons, Southeastern Surg. Congress, Am. Soc. Head and NEck Surgeons (pres. 1989), Edn. Founds. Plastic Surgery Coun., Am. Assn. Plastic Surgeons (pres. 1989-81), Am. So, surg assns. (1st v.p. 1993-94), Med. Assn. Ga. Home: 715 Old Post Rd NW Atlanta GA 30328-4758 Office: Emory U Clinic 550 Peachtree St 8th Fl Ste 4300 Atlanta GA 30308

JURKOWITZ, DANIEL S. lawyer, prosecutor, judge; b. Tucson; s. Harvey and Chaya Jurkowitz; m. Lisa A. Klein. BA, U. Ariz., 1994, JD, 1997. Bar: Ariz. 1997, U.S. Dist. Ct. Ariz. 1998, U.S. Ct. Appeals (9th cir.) 1998, U.S. Supreme Ct. 2000. Intern Ariz. Atty. Gens. Office, Dept. Econ. Security, Tucson, 1994; appeals clk. criminal divsn. Pima County Attys. Office, Tucson, 1995—96, student prosecutor criminal divsn., 1996; Westlaw student rep. West Pub. Corp., Tucson, 1996—97; law clk. civil divsn. Pima County Attys. Office, Tucson, 1997, dep. county atty. criminal divsn., 1997—98, dep. county atty. civil divsn., law clk. supr., 1998—2001; adminstrv. law judge Ariz. Dept. Transp., Tucson, 2001—; judge pro tempore Ariz. Superior Ct., 2003—; arbitrator State Bar of Ariz. Fee Arbitration Pgm, 2003—; hearing officer Sunnyside Unified Sch. Dist., 2002—. Legal columnist: Daily Jour. Corp., 2000. Teen ct. judge Pima

County Teen Ct., 2001—02; treas. Fountain Park Homeowners Assn., 2002—03; mem. City of Tucson Citizens' Transp. Adv. Com., 2001—03; state and precinct committeeman Ariz. Rep. Party, Tucson, 1994—2001; vice chmn., sec. exec. com. Pima County Rep. Party, 1999—2001; v.p, pres. Sienna Homeowners Assn., Tucson, 1998—2000. Nat. merit scholar. Mem.: ABA, Pima County Bar Assn. (co-chair, sch. coord., tutor Lawyers for Literacy, Young Lawyers div. 1997—2002, bd. dirs. Young Lawyers divsn. 1999—2003, bd. dirs. 2002—), Mensa, Phi Beta Kappa. Jewish. Avocations: guitar, tennis, reading. Office: Arizona Dept Trans Motor Vehicle Exec Hearing Office 3565 S Broadmont Dr Second Fl Tucson AZ 85713-5240 Fax: 520-838-2779. E-mail: daniel.jurkowitz@azbar.org.

JURKOWSKI, ODIN LECH, medical librarian, educator; s. Donald Eugene and Bonnie Jean Jurkowski; m. Deanna Lynn Jurkowski, Oct. 21, 1995; children: Kalina Mai, Byron Tyr, Acacia Jade, Amelia Blythe. BS in Sci. and Tech. in Context, Ill. Inst. of Tech., 1992; MS in Libr. and Info. Sci., Dominican U., 1994; MS in Tech. Comm. and Info. Design, Ill. Inst. of Tech., 1997; EdD in Instrnl. Tech., No. Ill. U., 2003. Access services libr. Ill. Inst. of Tech., Chgo., 1994—97; head libr. Ill. Inst. of Tech. Rice Campus Br., Wheaton, Ill., 1997—98; libr. dir. St. Anthony Coll. of Nursing, Rockford, Ill., 1998—2002; asst. prof. Ctrl. Mo. State U., Warrensburg, Mo., 2002—. Mem.: ALA, AAUP, Mo. Libr. Assn., Mo. Assn. of Sch. Librarians, Assn. for Libr. and Info. Sci. Edn., Kappa Delta Pi, Alpha Sigma Phi. Atheist. Avocations: swimming, martial arts, reading. Office: Central Missouri State University Lovinger 3132 Warrensburg MO 64093 Office Fax: 660-543-4164. E-mail: jurkowski@cmsu1.cmsu.edu.

JURMAIN, SUZANNE TRIPP, freelance writer and editor; b. N.Y.C., Aug. 13, 1945; d. Paul and Ruth (Enders) Tripp; m. Richard B. Jurmain, Aug. 14, 1966; children: Sara, David. BA with honors, UCLA, 1966. TV actress, 1949-65; asst. editor TV Guide, L.A., 1966; editor Legal Directories Pub. Co., L.A., 1967; editor, pub. rels. coord. UCLA Mus. Cultural History (now UCLA Fowler Mus.), 1968-77; freelance writer and editor, 1978—. Author: From Trunk to Tail: Elephants Legendary and Real, 1978, Once Upon a Horse: A History of Horses and How They Shaped Our History, 1989 (ALA Notable Book 1989, award for nonfiction So. Calif. Coun. on Lit. for Children and Young People 1990), Freedom's Sons: The True Story of the Amistad Mutiny, 1998 (VOYA nonfiction honor book 1999). Mem. Phi Beta Kappa. Office: McIntosh & Otis 353 Lexington Ave New York NY 10016

JUROE, SUSAN E. lawyer; b. Detroit, Jan. 9, 1961; d. James Blickson and Ellen (Emmy) Juroe. BA in Lit., Am. U., 1983; JD, Cath. U., Washington, 1986. Bar: D.C. Atty. Sanders & Assocs., Washington, 1987-89, Paddock & Stone, Washington, 1989-96, Holland & Knight Miller Canfield, Washington, 1996—. Bd. dirs. Nat. Leased Housing, Washington, Housing and Devel. Reporter, Affordable Housing Fin. Mag., Housing Bond Report. Bd. dirs. Cmty. Residences Found., Arlington, VA. Republican. Avocation: breeding and exhibiting paint horses. Home: 1530 33d St Washington DC 20007 Office: Holland & Knight LLP 2100 Pennsylvania Ave NW Washington DC 20037-3295

JURTSHUK, PETER, JR., microbiologist, educator; b. N.Y.C., July 28, 1929; s. Peter and Mary (Ferens) J.; m. Rebecca Jones, Jan. 2, 1971; children: Peter, Larissa. AB, NYU, 1951; MS, Creighton U., 1953; PhD, U. Md., 1957. Asst. prof. pharmacology Bklyn. Coll. Pharmacy, L.I. U., 1957-59; asst. prof. enzyme chemistry U. Wis.-Madison, 1962-63; asst. prof. microbiology U. Tex., Austin, 1963-69; assoc. prof. biology and biochemistry U. Houston, 1970-76, prof., 1976—, undergrad. chmn., 1976—80, dir. program in microbiology, 1990—. Mem. vis. biol. program Am. Inst. Biol. Scis., 1969-72 Contbr. chpts. to books. Recipient Disting. Service award Tex. br. Am. Soc. Microbiology, 1982; NIH grantee, 1964-75; NSF grantee, 1986-89. Fellow Am. Acad. Microbiology; mem. Am. Soc. Microbiology (pres. Tex. br. 1972-74), N.Y. Acad. Scis., Am. Soc. Biochemistry and Molecular Biology, Am. Chem. Soc., Sigma Xi (pres. U. Houston chpt. 1979-80). Russian Orthodox. Home: 879 Ramada Dr Houston TX 77062-5607 Office: U Houston Biology and Biochemistry Dept Houston TX 77204-5001 E-mail: jurtshuk@uh.edu.

JUSKENAS, NELLIE K. retired anesthesiologist; b. Rochester, N.Y., 1919; MD, Vytauto Didziojo U., Kaunas, 1943. Diplomate Am. Bd. Anesthesiology. Intern City Hosp., Kaunas, 1942-43; resident in ob-gyn Marymount Hosp., Garfield Heights, Ohio, 1953-54, resident in anesthesiology, 1954-56, staff. Fellow Am. Coll. Anesthesiology; mem. AMA, Am. Soc. Anesthesiology.

JUSKO, WILLIAM JOSEPH, pharmaceutical scientist, educator; b. Salamanca, N.Y., Oct. 26, 1942; s. Joseph Chester and Pauline Helen (Wrona) J.; m. Malgorzata J. Sidor, Oct. 26, 1996; children: Suzanne, Marjorie, Katherine, Natalie, Nicole. BS in Pharmacy, SUNY, Buffalo, 1965, PhD, 1970; Doctor Honoris Causa, Med. Acad. of Cracow, Poland, 1987. Rsch. pharmacologist VA Hosp., Boston, 1969-72; asst. prof. Boston U. Sch. Medicine, 1970-72, SUNY, Buffalo, 1972-74, assoc. prof., 1974-77, prof., 1977—, chair dept. pharm. scis., 2001—. Dir. Clin. Pharmacokinetics Lab., Buffalo, 1972-81; vis. scientist Mario Negri Inst. for Pharmacology, Milan, 1978-79; cons. Wyeth Labs., Radnor, Pa., 1976—, various other cos. Editor: (book) Applied Pharmacokinetics, 1980, 2d rev. edit., 1992; contbr. numerous rsch. articles to profl. jours. Recipient Rorer award Am. Coll. Gastroenterology, Toronto, Can., 1980. Fellow AAAS, Am. Assn. Pharm. Sci. (Rsch. Achievement award 1998), Am. Coll. Clin. Pharmacology (Russell Miller award 1988), Am. Coll. Clin. Pharmacy (Disting. Svc. award 1989); mem. Am. Soc. Clin. Pharm. Therapy (Rawls-Palmer award 1987). Office: SUNY Sch Pharmacy Buffalo NY 14226

JUSKOWIAK, TERRY EUGENE, career military officer; b. Danville, Pa., May 29, 1951; s. Joseph Leon and Betty Lorraine (Dilliplane) J.; m. Susan Kay Renn, Sept. 15, 1974; children: John, Christopher, Jennifer. BA, The Citadel, Charleston, S.C., 1973; MS, Fla. Inst. Technology, Melbourne, 1981. Commd. 2d lt. U.S. Army, 1973, advanced through ranks to major gen., 1999, contract cost mgmt. analyst Army Mat. Ctr., 1980-84, aide-de-camp Sec. Army Washington, 1984-85, dep. V Corps logistics officer Frankfurt, Germany, 1986-88, exec. officer 122 Main 3d Armored Divsn. Hanau, Germany, 1988-89, from divsn. staff to battalion cmdr. 82d Airborne Divsn. Ft. Bragg, NC, 1989-92, spl. asst. to chief of Staff Washington, 1992-94, brigade cmdr. 10th Mtn. Divsn. Ft. Drum, NY, 1994-96, asst. divsn. cmdr. support 10th Mtn. Divsn., 1996—; dep. comdg. gen. NATO SFOR Spt Cmd, 1996-98; dir. logistics I4 U.S. Atlantic comd. Norfolk, Va., 1997-98; comdr. 1st Corps Support Command (Airborne), Ft. Bragg, NC, 1998-2000; dir. logistics U.S. Forces Command, Ft. McPherson, Ga., 2000-01; quartermaster gen., comdt. Quartermaster Sch., 2001—02; comdr. Combined Arms Support Command, 2002—. Decorated Def. Superior Svc. medal, Legion of Merit, Bronze Star, Def. Meritorious Svc. medal. Mem. Assn. Citadel Men, Assn. U.S. Army, Quartermaster Assn., 82d Airborne Assn., 10th Mtn. Divsn. Assn. Presbyterian. Avocations: reading, running, skiing.

JUST, FAYE JORDAN, antique restoration company executive; b. Carthage, Miss., June 6, 1925; d. Neadham Guice and Ethel (Doude) Jordan; m. Virgil Louis Just, May 2, 1970; children: Babetta, Sandra, Audrey. Student, UCLA, 1943-62, U. So. Calif., 1950-52; AA in ME, Pierce Coll., 1965; BSBA in Math. and Ops. Rsch., U. Calif., Northridge, 1969. Loftswoman/flying wing Northrope Aircraft, Hawthorne, Calif., 1943-45; with Rockwell Internat., L.A. and Canoga Park, Calif., 1947-70, sr. rsch. engr. rocket engines, to 1970. Co-owner Just Marine Engring., 1972-77, Just Enterprises, Ventura, Calif., 1977—. Office: Just Enterprises 679 Santa Ysabel Ave Los Osos CA 93402-1143 E-mail: just@antique-restoration.com.

JUST, GEMMA RIVOLI, retired advertising executive; b. N.Y.C., Nov. 29, 1921; d. Philip and Brigida (Consolo) Rivoli; m. Victor Just, Jan. 29, 1955. BA, Hunter Coll., N.Y.C., 1943. Copy group head McCann Erickson, N.Y.C., 1958-62; copy supr. Morse Internat., N.Y.C., 1962-67; v.p., dir. creative svcs. Deltakos divsn. J. Walter Thompson, N.Y.C., 1967-75; v.p., copy dir. Sudler & Hennessey divsn. Young & Rubicam, N.Y.C., 1980-87, sr. v.p., assoc. creative dir. copy, 1987-88, ret., 1989. Mem. Episcopal Ch. Women of Ch. of Incarnation, N.Y.C., also ch. altar guild pres. and acolyte. Recipient Aesculapius awards Modern Medicine mag., 1980-88; named Best Writer, Art Dirs. Club N.Y., 1979, Best Writer Young & Rubicam, 1981. Mem. Coun. Comms. Soc., Pharm. Advt. Coun., Am. Med. Writers Assn. (exec. com. 1973). Home: 155 E 38th St Apt 5D New York NY 10016-2663

JUST, JENNIFER RAMSAY, television and video producer, writer; b. Lake Forest, Ill., Dec. 30, 1958; d. Ward Swift Just and Jean Claudia (Ramsay) Bower; m. F. Corey Darling, Sept. 10, 1988; children: Cameron, Evan. BA in Psycholinguistics, Brown U., 1981. Editorial asst. The Writer, Inc. and Plays, Inc., Boston, 1981-82, asst. editor, 1982-83, assoc. editor, 1983-84; prodn. asst. Sta. WGBY-TV, pub. TV, Springfield, Mass., 1984-86, assoc. producer, 1986-88, producer, 1988-90; freelance writer, video producer Easthampton, Mass., 1990-95; freelance writer Southington, Woodbridge, Conn., 1990—; columnist On the Homefront. Mem. Easthampton Conservation Commn., 1990—94, Southington Parent-Tchr. Coun., 1998—2000, Southington Arts Coun., 1999—2000, Beecher Road Sch. PTO, 2000—, Woodbridge Cable Adv. Coun., 2001—; bd. mem. C.B. Ramsay Found., F. Ward Just Scholarship Fund, 2001—. Recipient 1st place award Advt. Club. Western Mass., 1987, ACE award, 1990, Excellence in Cable Programming awards, 1991-96, Emmy award nomination, 1996, ACE award nomination, 1996. Mem.: Internat. Women Writers Guild, Sisters in Crime, Mystery Writers Am. Inc. Democrat. Avocations: gardening, geneology, reading, travel. Home: 157 Center Rd Woodbridge CT 06525-1840 E-mail: jenniferjust@yahoo.com.

JUST, PHILIP RAY, auditor; b. Kingsport, Tenn., Jan. 12, 1955; s. Avolt Bernard and Margaret Rebecca (Luttrell) J.; m. Ruth Rangel, June 30, 1980; children: Jonathan Philip, Bree Anne Celeste. BBA, Southwestern Adventist Coll., Keene, Tex., 1977. CPA, Tex. Dir. purchasing Marion County Hosp., Jefferson, Tex., 1977-79; staff auditor S.W. Adventist Health Svcs., Inc., Keene, 1979-80; treas. Valley Grande Manor Assn., Inc., Ft. Worth, 1980-81; staff auditor Gen. Conf. Auditing Svc., Burleson, Tex., 1981-84, dist. dir., 1984-87, area dir., 1987—. Mem. Am. Inst. CPAs, Tex. Soc. CPAs, Lions. Adventist. Office: Gen Conf Auditing Svc 777 S Burleson Blvd PO Box 1177 Burleson TX 76097-1177

JUST, RICHARD EUGENE, agricultural and resource economics educator consultant; b. Tulsa, Feb. 18, 1948; s. William and Leah (Flaming) J.; m. Janet Lee Humphries, Aug. 26, 1989; children: Angela K. Eisinger, David R., Ronald L. Mawer. BS, Okla. State U., 1969; MA, U. Calif., Berkeley, 1971, PhD, 1972. Prof. agrl. econs. and stats. Okla. State U., Stillwater, 1972-75; prof. agrl. and resource econs. U. Calif., Berkeley, 1975-85, U. Md., College Park, 1985-92, chmn. dept., 1992-95, disting. univ. prof., 1995—. Cons. The World Bank, Washington, 1976—, Oak Ridge Nat. Lab., 1976-81, Winrock Internat., 1979-81, Electric Power Rsch. Inst., 1981-83, Stanford Rsch. Inst., 1981, Safeway Stores, Inc., Oakland, Calif., 1983-86, Price Waterhouse, 1987-91, The Pillsbury Co., Mpls., 1988-89, U.S. Gen. Acctg. Office, Washington, 1978-79, 90-95, U.S. Dept. Justice, 1999, others; prin. Law and Econs. Consulting Group, 1993—; vis. prof. Ben Gurion U. Negev, 1977, Brigham Young U., 1977, 79-80, 94; sr. rsch. fellow The Inst. for Policy Reform, 1991—; sr. cons. Charles River Assocs., 2001—. Author: A Comprehensive Assessment of the Role of Risk in U.S. Agriculture, 2002, Applied Welfare Economics and Public Policy, 1982, Commodity and Resource Policies in Agricultural Systems, 1991, Conflict and Cooperation on Trans-Boundary Water Resources, 1998, (monographs) Econometric Analysis of Production Decisions, 1975, Econometric Analysis of Processing Tomatoes, 1978; editor Am. Jour. Agrl. Econs., 1984-86, editl. com., 1978-80; mem. editl. bd. Jour. Devel. Planning Lit., 1985—, Springer-Verlag, 1989—; mem. editl. coun. Western Jour. Agrl. Econs., 1982-84; also articles to jours. Mem. task force on economy Calif. Dem. Com., 1981-83; mem. agrl. policy task force for speaker Calif. Assembly, 1983-84; bishop LDS Ch., 1993-97, stake pres., 1997—. Internat. Inst. Ecol. Econs. fellow, 1991—. Fellow Am. Agrl. Econs. Assn. (dissertation awards com. 1976-78, selected papers com. 1981-93, com. on jour. pub. 1986, fellows election com. 1991-96, mem. pub. enduring quality com. 1998—02, Quality of Rsch. Discovery award 1977, 80, 83, 89, 90, 96, 2002, Outstanding Jour. Article award 1981, 93, Enduring Quality award 1992, 94, 98, 2003); mem. Western Agrl. Econs. Assn. (editl. coun. 1982-84, Outstanding Pub. Rsch. award 1974, 83, 96, 2003), Am. Econ. Assn., Royal Econ. Soc., Econometric Soc., Atlantic Econ. Soc., Alpha Zeta. Office: Agrl/Resource Econs U Md College Park MD 20742-0001

JUST, WARD SWIFT, author; b. Michigan City, Ind., Sept. 5, 1935; s. F. Ward and Elizabeth (Swift) J. Student, Lake Forest (Ill.) Acad., 1949-51, Cranbrook (Mich.) Sch., 1951-53, Trinity Coll., Hartford, Conn., 1953-57. Reporter Waukegan (Ill.) News-Sun, 1957-59, Newsweek, 1959-61, Reporter mag., 1962-63; corr. Newsweek, 1963-65, Washington Post, 1965-70; writer Vineyard Haven, Mass., 1970—. Author: To What End, 1968, A Soldier of the Revolution, 1970, Military Men, 1970, The Congressman Who Loved Flaubert and Other Washington Stories, 1973, Stringer, 1974, Nicholson at Large, 1975, A Family Trust, 1978, Honor, Power, Riches, Fame, and the Love of Women, 1979, In the City of Fear, 1982, The American Blues, 1984, The American Ambassador, 1987, Jack Gance, 1989, Twenty-One Selected Stories, 1990, The Translator, 1991, Ambition & Love, 1994, Echo House, 1997, A Dangerous Friend, 1999; (play) Lowell Limpett, 2000, The Weather in Berlin, 2002; contbr. Best Am. Short Stories, 1972-73, 76. Recipient O. Henry award, 1985, 86, 93.

JUSTER, KENNETH IAN, federal agency administrator; b. N.Y.C., Nov. 24, 1954; s. Howard H. and Muriel (Uchitelle) J. AB, Harvard U., 1976, MS in Pub. Policy, JD, Harvard U., 1980. Bar: D.C. 1981, U.S. Dist. Ct. D.C. 1981, U.S. Ct. Appeals (D.C. cir.) 1982, U.S. Ct. Internat. Trade 1984, U.S. Ct. Appeals (Fed cir.) 1985, U.S. Supreme Ct. 1985. Staff Nat. Security Coun., 1978; law clk. to judge U.S. Ct. Appeals (2nd cir.), Brattleboro, Vt., 1980-81; assoc. Arnold & Porter, Washington, 1981-87, ptnr., 1988-89, 93-97, sr. ptnr., 1998—2001; dep., sr. adviser to the dep. Sec. of State, Washington, 1989-92; acting counselor U.S. Dept. State, Washington, 1992-93; under sec. export admin. U.S. Dept. Commerce, Washington, 2001—02, under sec. industry and security, 2002—. Mem. faculty Internat. Law Inst., 1987-89, 93-95; vis. fellow Coun. Fgn. Rels., W ashington, 1993. Editor Harvard U. Internat. Law Jour., 1979-80; contbr. articles to profl. jours. Mem. ABA (internat. law sect., chair internat. investment and devel. com. 1994-96, coun. mem. 1996-99, chair tech. legal assistance bd. 2000-01) coun., 2003-., D.C. Bar Assn. (internat. law sect., mem. faculty continuing legal edn. program 1987-89), Am. Coun. on Germany, Coun. on Fgn. Rels., U.S.-Panama Bus. Coun. (bd. mem.), Phi Beta Kappa. Office: US Dept Commerce Bur Idustry and Security 14th & Constitution Ave NW Washington DC 20230 Office Fax: 202-482-2387.

JUSTESEN, BENJAMIN RAY, II, writer; b. Dunn, N.C., June 13, 1949; s. Wayne Quay and Elizabeth (Massengill) J.; m. Helen Thomas Pridgen, June 30, 1973 (div. 1982); 1 child, Fredrika Elizabeth; m. Margaret Rose Cadien, Jan. 5, 1985. BA in English Lit. and Am. History, U. N.C., Chapel Hill, 1974, postgrad., 1981-83, N.C. State U., 1976-80. Editor Brunswick Beacon, Shallotte, N.C., 1971-72; reporter News Reporter, Whiteville, N.C., 1972-73, Sanford (N.C.) Herald, 1973-74, Fayetteville (N.C.) Observer, 1974-75; v.p., gen. mgr. Bragg Office Supply Inc., Fayetteville, 1975-81; grad. instr. sch. journalism U. N.C., Chapel Hill, 1981-83; commd. fgn. svc. officer U.S. Dept. State, Washington, 1983-97; consular officer Am. Embassy, Kingston, Jamaica, 1983-85, gen. svcs. officer Copenhagen, 1985-87, adminstrv. officer Paramaribo, Surinam, 1989-90; press. officer pub. affairs bur. U.S. Dept. State, Washington, 1987-89; regional pers. officer Am. Embassy, Singapore, 1991-92, adminstrv. officer, 1992-93; Russian ops. officer nuclear risk reduction ctr. U.S. Dept. State, Washington, 1994-96, internat. rels. officer, 1996-97. Freelance writer, editor, 1997—; with GED Testing Svc., Am. Coun. on Edn. Author: George Henry White: An Even Chance in the Race of Life, 2001; editor Cross Current, 1980-82; spl. projects dir. GED Testing Svc., Am. Coun. on Edn., 2001—. Active Alexandria-Gyumri Sister City Com., 1994-97, chmn., 1995-96. Whitaker scholar U. N.C., 1967-69, Vt. Royster fellow U. N.C., 1981-83. Mem. U. N.C. Gen. Alumni Assn. (life), So. Hist. Assn., NC Lit. and Hist. Assn., Phoenix Hist. Soc. Episcopalian. Avocations: writing, book collecting, travel. Home: 206 Aspen St Alexandria VA 22305-1812 E-mail: justesen2@hotmail.com.

JUSTESEN, DON ROBERT, psychologist; b. Salt Lake City, Mar. 8, 1930; s. Richard Carvel and Elizabeth Agnes (Gustafson) J.; m. Patricia Ann Larson, Feb. 14, 1957; children: Lyle Richard, Jonille Jacelyn, Tracy Ann, Anthony Ray. BA in Psychology and Philosophy, U. Utah, 1955, MA, 1957, PhD, 1960. Asst. prof., chmn. dept. psychology Westminster Coll., Salt Lake City, 1959-62; lectr. to prof. dept. psychology U. Mo.-Kansas City, 1963-75; vis. prof. U. Colo., Boulder, 1965; asst. prof. to prof. dept. psychiatry U. Kans. Sch. Medicine, Kansas City, 1963-96; dir. behavioral radiology labs. VA Med. Ctr., Kansas City, 1962-95. Cons. Nat. Coun. on Radiation Protection and Measurements, Washington, 1977-98, EPA, NAS, NIH, NSF, USN, 1972-95, to assocs. programs NRC/NAS, 1988-94. Contbr. articles to profl. jours.; assoc. editor Jour. Microwave Power and Electromagnetic Energy, 1975-88; editor Spl. Supplements to Radio Sci., Washington, 1977-79; editor in chief Bioelectromagnetics, 1988-93; mem. editorial bd. Bioelectromagnetics Soc., 1979-83, 88-93. Pres. Fountains Homes Assn., Grandview, Mo., 1974-75. Served with USN, 1948-52, ATO; served to lt. USNR, 1962-65. Recipient First Cash prize in psychopharmacology Am. Psychol. Assn., 1968; VA Research Career Scientist, 1980; USPHS grantee, 1971-86. Fellow AAAS, APA, Am. Psychol. Soc.; mem. IEEE (sr.), Soc. for Neurosci., Bioelectromagnetics Soc. (pres. 1984-85), Brit. Soc. Philosophy of Sci., Nat. Acad. Sci., Internat. Union Radio Sci. (U.S. nat. com., commn. on metrology) Home: 12416 Ewing Ct Grandview MO 64030-1834 *My father, the late Richard Carvel Justesen, was an inventor who never sought a patent or a penny for his inventions. When I asked why he invented, he said his reward was a complex ecstacy that bloomed at the moment of creation, a rapture of elation tinged with sadness. I failed to understand this paradox of affect until experiencing it myself. The elation derives from making or thinking something significant that's never been made or thought before. The sadness inheres in the utter inability to share the emotional joy. One is confined, to paraphrase Hume, to the solipsism of the creative moment.*

JUSTICE, BLAIR (DAVID BLAIR JUSTICE), psychology educator, author; b. Dallas, July 2, 1927; s. Sam Hugh and Lou-Reine (Hunter) J.; m. Rita Norwood, July 26, 1972; children: Cynthia, David, Elizabeth (dec.). BA, U. Tex., Austin, 1948; MS, Columbia U., 1949; MA, Tex. Christian U., 1963; PhD, Rice U., 1966. Diplomate Am. Bd. Med. Psychotherapists; cert. expert in traumatic stress. Reporter Ft. Worth Star-Telegram, 1952-55; sci. writer N.Y. Daily News, 1955-56, Ft. Worth Star-Telegram, 1956-64; sci. editor, columnist Houston Post, 1964-73; exec. asst. to Mayor Houston, 1966-72; prof. psychology Sch. Pub. Health, U. Tex., Houston, 1968—2001, prof. emeritus, 2001—; assoc. dean for acad. affairs U. Tex., Sch. Pub. Health, Houston, 1994-2000; dir. Project Support, Imagery & Immune Function in Breast Cancer, 1993-99; co-investigator Alt. Medicine Ctr. for Cancer Rsch. U. Tex. Sch. Pub. Health, Houston, 1995-98, patient advocate M.D. Anderson Cancer Ctr., Houston, 2000—. Co-investigator U. Tex. Ctr. for Alternative Med. Cancer Rsch.; sr. psychologist, group therapist, psychiat. residency faculty Tex. Rsch. Inst. Mental Scis., 1973-85; cmty. assoc. Rice U., Lovett Coll.; cons. child abuse Tex. Dept. Human Resources; faculty assoc. Ctr. for Health Promotion, R & D, U. Tex. Health Sci. Ctr., mem. inter-faculty coun., 1991-92; dir. Ctr. for Prevention of Violence and Injury, 1987-89, chmn. faculty Sch. of Pub. Health, 1990-91, chmn. faculty policy com., 1989-90, faculty marshal, 1990, mem. exec. com., 1991-93, vice chair interfaculty coun., 1992-93; vis. scholar U. Colo., 1990—; founding assoc. Blaffer Gallery U. Houston. Author: Violence in the City, 1969, Detection of Potential Community Violence, 1967, (with Rita Justice) The Abusing Family, 1976, The Broken Taboo: Sex in the Family, 1979, Perspectives in Public Mental Health, 1982, Who Gets Sick: Thinking and Health, 1987, Who Gets Sick: How Beliefs, Moods and Thoughts Affect Your Health, 1988, revised edit., 2000, The Abusing Family, rev. edit., 1990, A Different Kind of Health: Finding Well-Being Despite Illness, 1998; Visits with Violet: Lessons on How to Be Happy 100 Years, 1999; editor: Your Child's Behavior, 1972; editorial bd.: Internat. Jour Mental Health, 1980—. Gen. chmn. Houston Job Fair, 1967-73; chmn. Houston Manpower Area Planning Council, 1972-74; mem. Tex. Urban Devel. Commn., 1970-72; bd. dirs. Houston Housing Devel. Corp., Tex. Citizens Human Devel., 1979-84, Greater Houston Com. Prevention of Child Abuse, 1982-88; sec. bd. mgrs. Tarrant County Hosp., Dist., 1961-64; pres. Greater Houston Youth Council, 1978-79, Houston Area Council on Sudden Infant Death Syndrome, 1977-78; mem. nat. adv. com. Marine Biomed. Inst., U. Tex. Med. Br., 1971-84; mem. Office of Minority Affairs, Resource Persons Network, HHS, 1988—; mem. community bd. Tex. Youth Council; vestry, chmn. adult edn. St. John The Divine Episc. Ch., 1984-88. Served with USNR, 1945-46. Recipient most outstanding book award Tex. Writers Roundup, 1970, award of recognition City of Houston, 1973, Benjamin Franklin Book award Pubs. Mktg. Assn. Am., 1988, Excellence in Media award APA, 1988, Friends of Fondren Libr. book award Rice U., 1989, 91, Heritage award for child abuse rsch. Child Abuse Prevention Coun., 1989, award for outstanding contbn. to sci. Tex. Psychol. Assn., 2001, Living Principles award Internat. Assn. Transactional Analysis, 1999; named One of Five Outstanding Young Men of Tex., 1962; recipient numerous awards for sci. writing; grantee NIH. Fellow Am. Coll. Psychology, Am. Inst. Stress, Phi Beta Kappa (dir. Houston chpt. 1979-89, pres. Houston chpt. 1982-83); mem. APHA (chmn. mental health sect. 1980-81, governing coun. 1983-85, action bd. 1985-87, mental health sect. award 1989), Nat. Assn. Sci. Writers (life; exec. com. 1965-67), Houston Psychol. Assn. (pres. 1975, Lifetime Achievement award for contbn. to psychology 2002)), Knights of the Vine. Home: 6416 Sewanee St Houston TX 77005-3760 Office: 1200 Hermann Pressler Dr Houston TX 77030-3900 E-mail: bjustice@sph.uth.tmc.edu.

JUSTICE, BOB JOE, corporate development executive; b. Ardmore, Okla., Dec. 14, 1946; s. Jesse William and Nora Estell (Boston) J.; m. Patricia Ann Thorpe, Dec. 26, 1970; children: Chad Andrew, Melanie Katherine, Kimberly Ann. MBA, Coll. William and Mary, 1973. Landman Mobil Oil Co., Oklahoma City, 1970-71; planning analyst DuPont Corp., Wilmington, Del., 1973-75; planning specialist Houston Oil & Minerals Corp., Houston, 1976-79; mgr. planning and econs. Dome Petroleum Corp., Denver, 1979-82; mgr. investment and bus. analysis Union Pacific Resources, Ft. Worth, 1982-89; mgr. fin. Lasmo Energy, Tulsa, 1989-90; mgr. corp. devel. Aquila Energy Corp., Omaha, 1990-94; cons., 1994—. Served with U.S. Army, 1971-73. Am. Assn. Petroleum Landmen scholar, 1968-70. Mem. Planning Forum, Assn. Corp. Growth, Am. Petroleum Inst. Republican. Mem. Reformed Ch. Am. Home and Office: 15818 Howard St Omaha NE 68118-2108 E-mail: bjustice47@aol.com.

JUSTICE, BRADY RICHMOND, JR., medical services executive; b. Albertville, Ala., Dec. 26, 1930; s. Brady R. and Kate (McEachern) J.; m. Sandra Gearner, Dec. 29, 1956; children: David, Michael, Lori Blankenship, Kathryn Justice. BBA, Baylor U., 1953. CPA, Ind. Ptnr. Arthur Andersen & Co., Dallas, 1953-64, Indpls., 1964-72; exec. v.p. Basic Am. Industries, Inc., Indpls., 1972-83; pres. Basic Am. Med., Inc., Indpls., 1983-92; sr. v.p. Columbia Hosp. Corp., 1992-93; chmn. Heritage Capital Corp., Indpls., 1993—. Mem. Columbia Club, Lions (pres. Indpls. chpt.). Republican. Baptist. Home: 8037 Clymer Ln Indianapolis IN 46250-4236 Office: Heritage Capital Corp 6900 Gray Rd Indianapolis IN 46237-3209

JUSTICE, DONALD RODNEY, poet, educator; b. Miami, Fla., Aug. 12, 1925; s. Vascoe J. and Mary Ethel (Cook) J.; m. Jean Catherine Ross, Aug. 22, 1947; 1 son, Nathaniel Ross. BA, U. Miami, 1945; MA, U. N.C., 1947; postgrad., Stanford U., 1948-49; PhD, U. Iowa, 1954. Instr. English U. Miami, 1947-51; asst. prof. Hamline U., St. Paul, Minn., 1956-57; lectr. U. Iowa, 1957-60, asst. prof., 1960-63, assoc. prof., 1963-66, prof., 1971-82, Syracuse U., 1966-70, U. Fla., Gainesville, 1982-92. Author: The Summer Anniversaries, 1960, Night Light, 1967, Departures, 1973, Selected Poems, 1979, Platonic Scripts, 1984, The Sunset Maker, 1987, A Donald Justice Reader, 1992, New and Selected Poems, 1995, Oblivion: On Writers and Writing, 1998, Orpheus Hesitated beside the Black River, 1998, Donald Justice in Conversation with Philip Hoy, 2002; editor: The Collected Poems of Weldon Kees, 1962. Rockefeller Found. fellow in poetry, 1954, Ford Found. fellow, 1964, Guggenheim Found. fellow in poetry, 1976, Acad. Am. Poets fellow, 1988; Nat. Endowment for the Arts grantee, 1967, 73, 80, 89; recipient Pulitzer Prize in poetry for Selected Poems, 1980, Bollingen prize for poems, 1991, Lannan Literary award, 1996. Mem. Am. Acad. Arts and Letters, Acad. Am. Poets (chancellor 1997). Home: 338 Rocky Shore Dr Iowa City IA 52246-3836

JUSTICE, FRANKLIN PIERCE, JR., oil company executive; b. Wanego, W.Va., May 5, 1938; s. Franklin Pierce and Jeneta Ruth (Cooley) J.; m. Eva Mae Hartley, June 8, 1960; children: Kerry, Kelly, Kevin. BSBA, W.Va. State Coll., 1967; MBA in Fin., Marshall U., 1977; postgrad., U. Louisville, 1971-72. Reporter Dun & Bradstreet, Inc., Charleston, W.Va., 1960-63, reporting mgr., 1963-65, office mgr., Huntington, W.Va., 1966-68; domestic trade specialist U.S. Dept. Commerce, Charleston, 1968-70; pres., investment mgr. Equal

Opportunity Fin., Inc., Ashland, Ky., 1970-93; adminstrv. asst. to v.p. personnel Ashland Oil, Inc., 1973-74, adminstrv. asst. to v.p. external affairs, 1974-75, mgr. spl. projects, 1975-76, dir. pub. affairs, 1976-78, v.p. pub. rels., 1978-82, v.p., 1985-93; v.p. ops. support Ashland Services Co., 1982-85; ret., 1993; exec. dir. Rsch. and Econ. Devel. Ctr. Marshall U., Huntington, W.Va., 1993-95, v.p. devel., 1995-99; pres. Marshall U. Rsch. Corp., 1993-98; assoc. dean Southeastern Community Coll., 1999-2000; dir. major gifts Marshall U., 2002—03. Pres. Roundtable Venture Fund; cons. in field. Vice chmn. Ky. Ctr. for Arts, Louisville, 1982-92; bd. dirs. Ky. Coun. Econ. Edn., 1978-90, chmn. bd., 1980-83; dir. Marshall U. Bus. Adv. Bd., 1982—; exec. com. bd. dirs. W.Va. State Coll. Found., Inc., 1988-95; bd. dirs. Delta Dental of Ky. Mem. W.Va. C. of C. (life; chmn. bd. dirs. 1992-94, exec. com.), Ashland Area C. of C. (1st v.p. 1978-79, pres. 1980, bd. dirs. 1978-98), Ky. C. of C. (chmn. bd. dirs. 1983, life). Republican. Home: 2010 Turnberry Ln Murrells Inlet SC 29576-6804 Fax: (843) 357-8483. E-mail: fpjemj@aol.com.

JUSTICE, GEORGE LEWIS, language educator; b. Phila., Nov. 16, 1964; s. Jack Burton and Martha Monser Justice, Judith Justice (Stepmother); m. Devoney Kay Looser. BA, Wesleyan U., 1986; MA, U. Pa., 1990, PhD, 1994. Editl. sec. Harper & Row, Pubs., N.Y.C., 1987—88; asst. prof. English Marquette U., Milw., 1995—2002; asst. prof. U. Mo., Colubmia, 2002—. Vis. asst. prof. La. State U., Baton Rouge, 2001—02. Author: The Manufacturers of Literature, 2002; editor: Women's Writing and the Circulation of Ideas, 2002. Recipient Mellon Dissertation award, Mellon Found., 1993-1994; fellow Winchester, Wesleyan U., 1989-1994, Van Pelt Libr., U. Pa., 1994-1995, Noel Library, 2002. Mem.: MLA, Soc. History Authorship, Reading, and Pub., Johnson Soc. Ctrl. Region (pres. 2000—01), Am. Soc. Eighteenth-Century Studies, Jane Austen Soc. N.Am. (life; book rev. editor 2001). Office: U Mo Dept English Columbia MO 65211 Office Fax: 573-882-5785. Personal E-mail: g.justice@mchsi.com. Business E-Mail: justiceg@missouri.edu.

JUSTICE, JACK BURTON, retired lawyer, writer; b. Hardy, Ky., Aug. 2, 1931; s. George Edward and Goldia (Alley) J.; m. Martha Monser, Dec. 28, 1957 (dec. Feb. 1974); m. Judith Farquhar Lang, Apr. 26, 1975; children—Jonathan Burton, George Lewis, Paul Williamson. AB in Polit. Sci, W.Va. U., 1952, postgrad. in law, 1954-55; BA in Jurisprudence, Oxford (Eng.) U., 1954, MA, 1960. Bar: Pa. 1956. Assoc. firm Drinker Biddle & Reath, Phila., 1956-62, ptnr., 1962-82, White & Williams, Phila., 1982-96. Bus. mgr. Am. Oxonian, 1967-86; lectr. in field. Contbr. articles to profl. and lit. jours. Pres. Youth Svc., Phila., 1962-65; chmn. Phila. Com. on City Policy, 1966-67, Southeastern Pa. chpt. Ams. for Democratic Action, 1968-70; bd. overseers William Penn Charter Sch., Phila., 1978-91, clk., 1986-89. Rhodes scholar, 1952-54. Mem. Assn. Am. Rhodes Scholars (sec. 1967-86, pres. 1986-94). Democrat. Home: 10 Coyote Pass Rd Santa Fe NM 87508

JUSTICE, PHILLIP HOWARD, marketing professional; b. Pikeville, Ky., Aug. 29, 1948; s. Howard and Opal Fanny (Hatfield) J.; children: Phillip Wayne, Benjamin Howard. Student, Pikeville Coll., 1966, 67, Free Will Bapt. Coll., 1972; DD (hon.), Welcome Bapt. Inst., 1987; AS, Vincennes U., 2001. Sales rep. Reynolds and Reynolds, Evansville, Ind., 1978-81; account exec. Merrill Lynch, Evansville, 1981-83, E.F. Hutton, Evansville, 1983-88; assoc. v.p. investments Dean Witter Reynolds, Inc., Evansville, 1988-91, Prudential Securities, Evansville, 1991-95, Citizen's Nat. Bank, Evansville, 1995, Advantage Payroll Svcs., 1996—2003; mgr. Justice Funeral Home, Pikeville, Ky., 2003—. Bd. dirs. Evansville unit Am. Heart Assn., 1990, 91. Mem. Rockport Area C. of C. (v.p. 1990, pres. 1991), Lions, Optimists, Rotary Club (bd. dirs. 1995—). Republican. Avocation: gospel singing. Home: PO Box 1517 Pikeville KY 41502 Office: Justice Funeral Home 1118 S Mayo Trail Pikeville KY 41501 E-mail: philjustice@yahoo.com.

JUSTMAN, DICK JOSEPH, public works administrator; b. Mitchell, SD, Nov. 25, 1943; s. LeRoy Joseph and Lorraine Rita Justman; children: Teresa, Laura, Joe. BSBA, Dakota State U., 1970. Controller City of Sioux Falls, S.D., 1973-97, pub. works adminstr. Chmn. Diabetes Assn. Sioux Falls; pres. Sioux Falls Libr. Bd., 1979-85; active Good Shepherd Ctr., Sioux Falls, 1999—; religious edn. tchr., St. Michael's Parish, 1992—; Sunday Sch. tchr. Children's Home Soc., 1999—; vol. Children's Miracle Network, 1996—. With USN, 1961-64, master sgt., USAR. Named Civil Servant of Yr., 1982, Sioux Falls. Mem. Am. Legion, SD Mcpl. League, SD Mcpl. Fin. Officers (pres. 1998-99), Kiwanis (pres. Sioux Falls chpt. 1999-2000, Kiwanian of Yr. 2002). Republican. Roman Catholic. Avocation: volunteering. Home: 5401 W 26th St Apt 110 Sioux Falls SD 57106 Office: City of Sioux Falls 224 W 9th St Sioux Falls SD 57104 Fax: (605) 367-4605. E-mail: djustman@siouxfalls.org., dickjustman@hotmail.com..

JUSTMAN, MOSHE, economics educator; b. N.Y.C., Sept. 22, 1948; arrived in Israel, 1961; s. Joshua and Nina (Dunevitch) J.; m. Valerie Brand, Oct. 10, 1977; children: Ariella, Lillie, Yonatan. BSc, Hebrew U., Jerusalem, Israel, 1972, MSc, 1974; PhD, Harvard U., 1982. Systems analyst Israel Aircraft Industries, 1974-79; lectr. Ben Gurion U., Beer Sheva, Israel, 1982-87, from sr. lectr. to prof., 1987-2001, chair dept. econs., 1995-97. Vis. prof. Carnegie-Mellon U., Pitts., 1988-89, People's U. Beijing, 1989, 91; dir. Monaster Ctr. for Econ. Rsch., 2000-02. Editor series of 4 books on technology policy in Israel, 1990-96; contbr. articles to profl. jours. Allon fellow Coun. Higher Edn. in Jerusalem, 1982-85; Ameritech fellow, 1990; Gass fellow Jerusalem Inst. Office: Ben Gurion U Dept Econs 84105 Beer Sheva Israel E-mail: justman@bgumail.bgu.ac.il.

JUSTMAN, RICHARD ALLEN, pediatrician; b. N.Y.C., Oct. 4, 1945; AB, Cornell U., 1966; MD, SUNY, Buffalo, 1970. Diplomate Am. Bd. Pediatrics. Intern U. Chgo. Hosps. and Clinics, 1970-71, resident, 1971-72, U Wis. Hosps., 1975-76; fellow Johns Hopkins Hosp., 1972-73; nat. med. dir. United Healthcare, Mpls., 1992—. Maj. USAF, 1973-75. Office: United Healthcare 5901 Lincoln Dr Edina MN 55436-1611 E-mail: richard_a_justman@uhc.com.

JUSTUS, ADALU, writer, designer; b. Lawrenceville, Ill., Aug. 5, 1928; d. Edward G. and Zerma E. (Ike) Johnston; m. Gary Hunt; children: Brett Justus, Richard Lee, Sheryl Marlene, Ira James, Jeffrey Lynn, Melinda Sue. Diploma in child psychology, San Fernando (Calif.) U., 1957. Freelance writer (first novel pub.), Calif., 1960—; owner child care ctr., 1968-73; mastecomy advisor Orange County Physicians, Victor Valley, Calif., 1976-87; owner The Elegant Lady Boutique, Calif., 1974-89. Lectr. Ariz., Ill., Calif., Tex., Nev., 1975-90; instr. tng. seminars Custom Undergarment Com., Calif., Ariz., Nev., Tex., 1974-89; instr. breast clinic, breats exam. classes Victor Valley Hosp., 1973-87; owner Calif. Silo Pub., Calif., 1985-92; designer doll clothes, wardrobes, Calif., Ariz., Tenn., 1987-94; designer custom undergarments Bjene, Calif., 1976-82, Bejene, Calif., 1985; designer, instr., cons. Command Performance, Waco, Tex., 1985-89. Author: In The Shadow of Death, 1960; co-author: Dorit's Soft Sculpture Doll Techniques, 1988, Justus Ike Family Cookbook, 1989, Please Don't Say Good-Bye, 1998, So You're Married to One of Those, 1998, Wanta See My Attic, 1998, (screenplay) Body & Soul, 1963, Mommy Please Don't Kill Me, 1983, (with Ira S. Marlin) My Son, My Mother, 1985, Please Don't Say Good-Bye, 1998, So You're Married to One of Those, 1998, The Gift of Peace, 1999 (children's book) Bipity-Bop, 1999, The StoryTeller House, 1999, Wanta See My Attic, 1999. Pres., founder Friends for Life, Victor Valley. Mem. Friends of Libr. (sponsor), Christian Found. Children & Aging (sponsor), Women St. Anne Parish. Republican. Roman Catholic. Avocations: reading, embroidery, quilting. Home: 32 Bland Ave Sumter SC 29150-3816

JUSZCZAK, NICHOLAS MAURO, psychology educator; b. Chorely, Lancashire, Eng., May 19, 1955; came to U.S. 1956; s. Adam and Augusta (Lugnan); 1 child, Amanda; m. Margie Nina Malkin, Oct. 9, 1988; children: Kimberly, Melissa, Nina, Nicole. BA cum laude, Baruch Coll., N.Y.C., 1980; MS, Hunter Coll., N.Y.C., 1984. Rschr. psychophysiology lab Baruch Coll., N.Y.C., 1980-88, instr. psychology, 1984—. Cons. statistics BOE/CUNY Student Mentor Program, 1987-91; creator, pres. world wide web Homeroom Dot Net, 1997—. Contbr. articles to profl. jours. Cons. Office of Instructional Tech., N.Y. State Bd. Edn., 1999—. Mem. N.Y. Acad. Sci. Home: 26 Spiral Ln Levittown NY 11756 E-mail: nmj@homeroom.net.

JUSZCZYK, JAMES JOSEPH, artist; b. Chgo., Jan. 30, 1943; s. Joseph Peter and Pauline (Polak) J.; m. Phyllis Ann Pozar, May 30, 1965 (dec. Jan. 1992). BFA, Cleve. Inst. of Art, 1966; MFA, U. Pa., 1969. Artist pvt. practice, Zurich, 1986-92; lectr., cons. Binney & Smith Liquitex Paints, Easton, Pa., 1992-94, Lascaux Colours & Restauro, Alois Diethelm AG, Zürich, Switzerland, 1995-98; lectr. Daler-Rowney USA, Cranbury, N.J., 1998—. Adj. prof. art CCNY, 1996—; presented master class workshops in acrylic techniques in the Benelux countries (Amsterdam, DeHaag, Antwerp, Brussels), 1996-97, 98, 99. Artist: solo exhibitions include Phila. Coll. of Textiles and Sci., 1970, Rosa Esman Gallery, N.Y.C., 1974, 76, 1978-79, Gimpel-Hanover Galerie, Zurich, 1975, 82, Galerie Christel, Stockholm, 1980, Jan Cicero Gallery, Chgo., 1980, 83, 92, Galerij S65, Aalst, Belgium, 1981, Andre Emmerich Galerie, Zurich, 1982, Galerie Konstructiv Tendens, Stockholm, 1982, Galerie Storrer, Zurich, 1987, Galerie Meissner Edition, Hamburg, 1987, Merril Lynch Internat., Zurich, 1987, ACP Viviane Ehrli Galerie, Zurich, 1988, 93, 94, 97, 2000, Galerie Bruno Bucher, Poitiers, France, 1992, Galerie Vromans, Amsterdam, 1995, Fine Arts Gallery L.I. U., Southampton, 1997, Found. for Concrete and Constructivist Art, Zurich, 1991, Galerie Albergo Giardino, Ascona, Switzerland, Ann Reid Art Gallery, Princeton, N.J., 1998, Pearl Conard Gallery, Ohio State U., Mansfield, Ohio, 1999, Bohem Press Galerie Moderne Kunst, Zurich, 2001; group exhbns. include Mondrian House Gallery, Amersfoort, Netherlands, 1999, 16 Young Artists, Inst. Contemporary Art, Phila., 1969, Eight Abstract Painters, 1978, Andre Zarre Gallery, N.Y., The Geometry of Color, 1977, Cleve. Mus. Art, Centenary Exhibition, 1982, Bronx Mus. of the Arts, 50th Anniversary Exhibition of The American Abstract Artists, Editions Fanal, Basel, Paris, Saga '93, '96, 97, 98, 99, 2000, 01, 02, 03, ACP Viviane Ehrli Gallerie Art-Frankfurt, 1994-96, The Noyes Mus., Oceanville, N.J. Am. Abstract Artists Persistence of Abstraction, 1994, Mus. Coopmanhus, Franeker, Netherlands, 1995, DePaul U. Art Gallery, Chgo., 1997; Forum Konkrete Kunst, Erfurt, Germany, 1998, Mus. fuer Moderne Kunst, Hiebuell, Germany, 1999, Hunter Coll. Times Sq. Gallery, N.Y.C., 2001, Nat. Mus. Szezecin, Poland, 2002, Hunter Coll-Times Sq. Gallery, N.Y.C., 2003; represented in corp. and pub. collections, AT&T, N.Y.C., Arco. Internat.-Anaconda Aluminum, Chgo., Art Inst. Chgo., Chase Manhattan Bank, N.Y.C., Citicorp, N.Y.C., Lehman Bros, N.Y.C., Madison (Wis.) Art Ctr., Merrill Lynch Internat., Zurich, Prudential Life Ins., Newark, Shearson Am. Express, N.Y.C., Svenska Handelsbanken, Stockholm, Swiss Bank Corp., N.Y.C., N.J. State Mus., Whitney Mus. of Am. Art., Mondrian House Found., Amersfoort, Netherlands, Nat. Mus. Szezecin, Poland. Recipient Student Work scholarship Cleve. Inst. Art, Angel Fund award U. Pa.; Ford Found. Undergrad. grantee Cleve. Inst. Art, 1965, Pollock-Krasne Found., 1995; 50th Anniversary Print Portfolio, Am. Abstract Artists, 1987, 60th, 1997. Mem. Am. Abstract Artists. Home: 6601 Broadway #6-L Bronx NY 10471-2075

JUUSELA, KARI HENRIK, dean; b. Helsinki, Finland, Sept. 15, 1954; s. Oiva Henrik Juusela and Kaija Inkeri Naakka; m. Deborah Juusela, June 11, 1979; children: Alexander, Katherine. BM, Berklee Coll. Music, Boston, 1977; MM, Ga. State U., 1988; DMA, U. Md., 1992. Instr. music Montgomery Coll., Rockville, Md., 1989—93; coord. music theory/composition Stetson U. Sch. Music, Deland, Fla., 1993—98, assoc. dean, 1998—. Composer: opera Meet Me Tonight in Dreamland, 1995, choral work Kyrie, 1996 (1st prize Composer's Guild, 1998), cello quartet Bliss, 1997 (Grand prize, 1998). Recipient Composition award, ASCAP, 1996—; Fla. Arts fellow, State of Fla., 1997. Mem.: Soc. of Composers, Asian Cultural Assn., Phi Kappa Phi. Avocations: kayaking, surfing, tennis. Home: 615 Forest Ln Deland FL 32724 Office: Stetson U Sch Music Presser Hall Deland FL 32720

JUVAN, DENNIS PAUL, securities trader; b. Ravenna, Ohio, Nov. 2, 1950, s. Henry William and Geraldine Ann J.; m. Vicki Ann Kline, June 10, 1995; children: Andrew, Jayne, John, Lori, David, Lisa, Danny. BS, Ashland (Ohio) U., 1973. Registered securities rep.; lic. health and life ins. V.p. Juvan Mfg., Ravenna, 1974-89, Butler Wick & Co., Kent, Ohio, 1989—. Mem. Sales and Mktg. Execs., Akron, 1998—. Bd. dirs. Leadership Portage County, Kent, Ohio, 1999—; mem. Saint Joseph's Ch., Suffield, Ohio, 1988—; 1st Dan Black belt World Black Belt Bur., 2000—, Mus. of Am. Fin. History, N.Y., 1999—. With Army N.G., 1971-77. Mem. Mfrs. Circle of Distinction, Am. Funds All Am. Team, Akron Toastmasters (treas. 1996—, sponsor Hudson chpt. 1996-2000. Roman Catholic. Avocations: tae kwon doe, running, public speaking, golf, reading. Home: 1282 Congress Lake Rd Mogadore OH 44260 Office: Butler Wick & Co PO Box 990 149 N Water St Kent OH 44240 Fax: 330 678 6515.

JUVET, RICHARD SPALDING, JR., chemistry educator; b. L.A., Aug. 8, 1930; s. Richard Spalding and Marion Elizabeth (Dalton) J.; m. Martha Joy Myers, Jan. 29, 1955 (div. Nov. 1978); children: Victoria, David, Stephen, Richard P.; m. Evelyn Raeburn Elthon, July 1, 1984. BS, UCLA, 1952, PhD, 1955. Research chemist Dupont, 1955; instr. U. Ill., 1955-57, asst. prof., 1957-61, assoc. prof., 1961-70; prof. analytical chemistry Ariz. State U., Tempe, 1970-95, prof. emeritus, 1995—. Vis. prof. UCLA, 1960, U. Cambridge, Eng., 1964-65, Nat. Taiwan U., 1968, Ecole Polytechnique, France, 1976-77, U. Vienna, Austria, 1989-90; air pollution chemistry and physics adv. com. EPA, HEW, 1969-72; adv. panel on advanced chem. alarm tech., devel. and enging. directorate, def. sys. divsn. Edgewood Arsenal, 1975; adv. panel on postdoctoral associateships NAS-NRC, 1991-94; mem. George C. Marshall Inst., 1998—. Author: Gas-Liquid Chromatography, Theory and Practice, 1962, Russian edit., 1966; editl. advisor Jour. Chromatographic Sci., 1969-85, Jour. Gas Chromatography, 1963-68, Analytica Chimica Acta, 1972-74, Analytical Chemistry, 1974-77; biennial reviewer for gas chromatography lit. Analytical Chemistry, 1962-76. Deacon Presbyn. Ch., 1960—, ruling elder, 1972—, commr. Grand Canyon Presbytery, 1974-76; moderator, communion com. Valley Presbyn. Ch., Scottsdale, Ariz., 1999-2001. NSF sr. postdoctoral fellow, 1964-65; recipient Sci. Exch. Agreement award to Czechoslovakia, Hungary, Romania and Yugoslavia, 1977. Fellow Am. Inst. Chemists; mem. AAAS, Am. Chem. Soc. (nat. chmn. divsn. analytical chemistry 1972-73, nat. sec.-treas. 1969-71, divsn. com. on chem. edn., subcom. on grad. edn. 1988—, councilor 1978-89, coun. com. analytical reagents 1985-95, co-author Reagent Chemicals, 7th edit. 1986, 8th edit. 1993, 9th edit. 2000, chmn. U. Ill. sect. 1968-69, sec. 1962-63, directorate divsn. officers' caucus 1987-90), Internat. Union Pure and Applied Chemistry, Internat. Platform Assn., Am. Radio Relay League (Amateur-Extra lic.), Sigma Xi, Phi Lambda Upsilon, Alpha Chi Sigma (faculty adv. U. Ill. 1958-64, Ariz. State U. 1975-95, profl. rep.-at-large 1989-94, chmn. expansion com. 1990-92, nat. v.p. grand collegiate alchemist 1994-96, trustee ednl. found. 1994—). Achievements include rsch. on gas and liquid chromatography, instrumental analysis, computer interfacing, plasma desorption mass spectroscopy. Home: 4821 E Calle Tuberia Phoenix AZ 85018-2932 Office: Ariz State U Dept Chem and Biochem Tempe AZ 85287-1604 E-mail: rsjuvet@juno.com.

JUVILER, PETER HENRY, political scientist, educator; b. London, Mar. 26, 1926; s. Adolphe Adam and Katie (Henry) J.; m. Anne C. Stephens, June 20, 1982; children: Gregory, Geoffry. BE, Yale U., 1948, ME, 1949; PhD, Columbia U., 1960. Project engr. Sperry Gyroscope Co., 1949-52; taught polit. sci. Princeton U., 1957-58, Columbia U., 1959-60, Hunter Coll., CUNY, 1960-64; prof. Barnard Coll., 1974—, prof. emeritus and dir. human rights studies, 2001—. Co-dir. Columbia U. Ctr. for Study Human Rights, 1986—. Author: Revolutionary Law and Order, 1976, Freedom's Ordeal: The Struggle for Human Rights and Democracy in Post-Soviet States, 1998; co-editor, contbr. Gorbachev's Reforms: U.S. and Japanese Assessments, 1988, Human Rights for the 21st Century, 1993, Religion and Human Rights: Competing Claims?, 1999; contbr. numerous articles. With USN, 1944-46. E-mail: phj1@columbia.edu.

JYRINGI, DARLENE M. gerontologist; b. Worcester, Mass., Apr. 23, 1950; d. Waino I. and Dorothy M. Jyringi; children: Lindsey Malbon, Hailey Malbon. BA, SUNY, Stony Brook, 1994; MPS, L.I. Univ., Southampton, 1999. Cons. Suffolk County Archeol. Assn., Stony Brook, 1991-96; gerontologist Alzheimer's Disease Ctr. L.I., Stony Brook, 1996—. Mem. Aging L.I. Network Consortium (bd. dirs. 1998), Gerontology Profls. L.I. Home: 25 William Penn Dr Stony Brook NY 11790 Office: Stony Brook U Hosp Alzheimers Disease Asst Ctr Stony Brook NY 11794-8101 Office Fax: (631)444-6358. E-mail: djyringi@notes.cc.sunysb.edu.

KAAG, CYNTHIA STEWART, library and information scientist, educator, librarian; b. LaCrosse, Wis., Mar. 29, 1948; d. Harold Gillingham and Janice Smith Stewart; m. Donald Bricker Kaag, June 28, 1979; 1 child, Sierra Elizabeth. BA in History, U. of Wis., 1969, MS in Libr. and Info. Sci., 1975. Head of collection devel. Owen Sci. and Engring. Libr., Pullman, Wash., 1986—96; head, Brain Edn. Libr. Wash. State U., Pullman, 1997—99, head Owen Sci. and Engring. Libr., 2000—. Chair Nat. Inst. on Collection Devel. in an Electronic Age, Chgo., 1995—97. Editor (compiler, author): (internet database on yellowstone science) Science and Scientific Research in Yellowstone National Park; author: (book) Collection Evaluation Techniques; contbr. Bd. mem. and leader Girl Scouts of the Inland Empire, Moscow, Idaho, 1989—2000. Fellow Torger Thompson fellow, U. of Wis., 1970—71, NDEA, 1969—70. Mem.: Ref. and User Svcs. Assn. (pres. 2002—), ALA (chair collection devel. and evaluation sect. program com. 1988—90, chair collection evaluation com. 1988—93, chair collection devel. and evaluation sect. 1996—97, chair orgn. and edn. com. 1999—2001), Beta Phi Mu, Phi Alpha Theta. Avocations: conservation work, quilting. Home: 1316 N Mountain View Rd Moscow ID 83843 Office: Washington State University Owen Science and Engineering Library Pullman WA 99164-3200 Office Fax: 509-335-2534. E-mail: kaag@wsu.edu.

KAAKE, NORMAN BRADFORD, quality assurance professional; b. Upper Darby, Pa., July 5, 1954; s. Norman Howard and Dorothy (Harris) K.; m. Kathy May Alexander, Dec. 27, 1983; 1 child, Mikeala Alexandra. BA in Polit. Sci., U. Maine, 1976. Restaurant mgr. That Seafood Place, Virginia Beach, Va., 1981; import/boarding mgr. Containership Agy., Inc., Norfolk, Va., 1982-84, equipment mgr., 1984-86; ops. cost. control mgr. Tricom Shipping Agys., Inc., Norfolk, 1986-87; examiner asset based comml. lending Casco No. Bank, Portland, Maine, 1987-88, sr. examiner, 1988-90, comml. lender, 1991-95; mgr. distbn and quality sys. Merrill Industries, Inc., 1995-98; quality assurance engr. DOCdata New Eng., 1998-99; credit officer, lender Pepperell Bank and Trust, Biddeford, Maine, 2000—, 2000—. Mem. 20th Maine Honor Brigade, 1975—; com. mem. Hampton Roads Steamship Trade Com., Norfolk, 1982-87; asst. scoutmaster troop 323 Boy Scouts Am., Hollis, Maine, 1987-95, merit badge counselor, York County, 1987—; mem. Hollis Planning Bd. and Comprehensive Planning Com., 1990-98, 2002—, Hollis Budget Com., 1991-94; Pheresis donor ARC, 1988—; active United Way Campaigns, 1987—; vice chmn. Hollis Planning Bd., 1992-93, chmn., 1993-98. Served to capt. U.S. Army, 1976-80, USAR, 1980-87. Mem. Am. Inst. Banking, Internat. Register Cert. Auditors (cert. auditor quality sys.), Internat. Platform Assn., Hampton Roads Traffic Club, York County Riders, Inc. (v.p. 1990-91, bd. dirs. 1991-92), York County Vets. Alliance, Nat. Eagle Scout Assn., So. Maine Vets. Assn. (bd. dirs.), No. York County Family YMCA Steering Com. Republican. Avocations: antique collecting, boating, camping, downhill skiing, photography. Home and Office: 15 History Ln Hollis Center ME 04042-3236

KABACINSKI, STANLEY JOSEPH, health and physical education educator, consultant, speaker; b. Duryea, Pa., May 23, 1949; s. Bernard Merlyn and Anna (Polaski) K.; m. Mary Claire Finnerty, June 26, 1971; children: Ryan Michael, Michael Joseph. BS in Health, Phys. Edn. and Dance, East Stroudsburg State Coll., 1971, MEd in Health, Phys. Edn. and Dance, 1975; postgrad., Millersville U., 1981. Tchr., coach basketball, softball, soccer, volleyball Washington (N.J.) Boro Elem., 1971-78; asst. football coach, head coach offense, scouting coord. East Stroudsburg (Pa.) State Coll., 1971-78, cooperating tchr. for student tchrs., 1974-78; asst. prof. Millersville (Pa.) U., 1978—, offensive coord., adminstrv. asst., recruiting coord., strength coach, 1978-88, coord., minor in athletic coaching, 1989—, grad. program coord. MEd in sport mgmt., 1999—, chair health and phys. edn. dept., 1999—. Chair dept. health and phys. edn.; cons. Sch. Dist. of Lancaster, 1991—, Clarion (Pa.) U., 1991—, Gov's. Coun. on Phys. Fitness and Sports, Harrisburg, Pa., 1991—, East Stroudsburg U., 1994—, Mansfield U., 1998—; rschr. U.S. Mil. Acad. Performance Enhancement Ctr., West Point, N.Y., 1989, Am. Coaching Effectiveness Program and Coaching Minor Nat. Survey, Millersville, 1989; motivational cons., 1991—; ASEP instr. coaching principles, sport 1st aid, sport psychology; clinician various tng. programs and spkr. in field; also TV appearances. Dir., instr. activities in field Warren County Elem., Washington, N.J., Willow St. (Pa.) Elem., Ch. of Apostles Pre-Sch., Rohrerstown, Pa., Hans Herr Elem., Lampeter, Pa., Willow St. Family Festival, Fulton Elem. Sch., Lancaster, Pa.; head coach, cons. Willow St. Youth Baseball, 1987-91; cons. Willow St. PTO, 1983-87; coord. Elks Hoop Shoot, Washington, N.J., 1971-78. Mem. AAHPERD, Am. Football Coaches Assn., Pa. State Assn. Health, Phys. Edn., Recreation and Dance, Assn. Pa. State Coll. and Univ. Profs., Pa. Scholastic Football Coaches Assn., N.J. State Football Coaches Assn., Lancaster County Quarterback Club, Phi Epsilon Kappa. Avocations: coaching, baseball and football card collecting, model railroading, landscaping. Office: Millersville U Pucillo Gymnasium Millersville PA 17551

KABACK, ELAINE, career counselor, family therapist, consultant; b. Phila., Feb. 22, 1939; d. Sol and Evelyn Zitman; children: Douglas, Stephen, Michelle. Student, Pa. State U., 1956-58; BA, Temple U., 1960; MS, Calif. State U., 1977; PhD, Calif. Grad. Inst., 1998. Nat. cert. career counselor; cmty. coll. counselor credential; lic. marriage and family therapist. Tchr. English Sayre Jr. H.S., Phila. Pub. Schs., 1960-62; tchr. English and history Beth Tfiloh Pvt. Day Sch., Balt., 1968-72; mgmt. cons., trainer SWA, Palos Verdes, Calif., 1975-85; counselor Career Planning Ctr. and Mid-Life Ctr. Long Beach City Coll., 1977-78; dir. program devel. Univance Career Ctrs., Inc., L.A., 1978-80; pvt. practice career counseling, 1980—; pvt. practice, marriage and family therapy, 1998—. Outplacement cons. Exec. Horizons, Inc., Newport Beach, Calif., 1985-96; coord. career transition program, trainer, instr. UCLA Extension, 1980—; cons. in career systems, outplacement and orgnl. devel. Pres. Palos Verdes chpt. NOW, 1974-76; treas. S.W. chpt. Nat. Women's Polit. Caucus, 1973, 78; bd. dirs. STEP Adult Edn. Programs, Palos Verdes, 1974—. Mem. Calif. Counseling and Devel., Am. Counseling Assn., Calif.. Assn. Marriage and Family Therapy, Orgn. Devel. Network, Phi Kappa Phi. Office: 11530 W Olympic Blvd Ste 255 Los Angeles CA 90064-1697 E-mail: ekaback1@aol.com.

KABACK, MICHAEL, medical educator; b. Phila., Sept. 1, 1938; MD, U. Pa., 1963. Diplomate Am. Bd. Med. Genetics, Am. Bd. Pediatrics. Intern Johns Hopkins Hosp., Balt., 1963—64, resident pediatrics, 1966—68; fellow molecular biology and genetics NIH, Bethesda, Md., 1964—66; mem. staff Children's Hosp., San Diego; prof. pediatrics and reproductive medicine U. Calif., San Diego. Recipient William Allan Meml. award, Am. Soc. Human Genetics, 1993, Harland Sanders award, March of Dimes, 2000. Fellow: AAAS; mem.: NAS, AMA, Soc. for Pediatric Rsch., Am. Soc. Human Genetics, Am. Coll. Med. Genetics, Am. Pediatric Soc., Am. Acad. Pediatrics, Inst. Medicine. Office: Childrens Hosp San Diego 8110 Birmingham Way San Diego CA 92123-2758 E-mail: mkaback@ucsd.edu.

KABAK, BERNARD JOSHUA, lawyer; b. Bronx, N.Y., Dec. 22, 1941; s. Samuel Louis and Jeanne (Sirotin) K.; m. Ilana Etta Stern, June 15, 1982. AB, Columbia U., 1963; LLB, Harvard U., 1966; M Urban Planning, Hunter Coll., 1968. Bar: N.Y. 1967, Israel 1975. Sr. atty. N.Y.C. Dept. City Planning, N.Y.C., 1968-73; spl. advisor Ministry of Justice, Jerusalem, Israel, 1974-75; counsel Office of Dep. State Comptroller for N.Y.C., 1976—; counsel Nat. Civic League, Council Mcpl. Performance, 1985—. Contbr. in field. Trustee Lincoln Square Synagogue, N.Y.C., 1986—; divisional chmn. United Jewish Appeal-Fedn. Jewish Philanthropies, N.Y.C., 1973; mem. exec. com. Coalition to Free Soviet Jews, N.Y.C., 1978—. Avocation: silversmith. Home: 393 W End Ave New York NY 10024-6138 Office: Office Dep Comptroller NYC 270 Broadway New York NY 10007-2306

KABAK, DOUGLAS THOMAS, lawyer; b. Elizabeth, N.J., Nov. 19, 1957; s. Aaron and Marilyn Virginia (Johnson) K.; m. Elisabeth Wiggin McDuffie, Oct. 21, 1989; 1 child, Matthew Thomas McDuffie Kabak. BA, Rutgers U., 1979, MBA, MBA, Rutgers U., 1990; postgrad., U. Exeter, Eng., 1980; JD, Seton Hall U., 1982. Bar. N.J. 1982, U.S. Dist. Ct. N.J. 1982. Law clk. Superior Ct. N.J., Elizabeth, 1982-83; assoc. Z. Lance Samay, Morristown, N.J., 1983-86; asst. dep. pub. defender Office Pub. Defender, Elizabeth, 1986—. Legal rep. St. Joseph's the Carpenter Bd. Edn., Roselle, N.J., 1985-87. Dir. St. Joseph the Carpenter Cath. Youth Orgn., Roselle, 1986-88, coach, 1981-88. Mem. KC. Roman Catholic. Home: 16 Indian Spring Rd Cranford NJ 07016-1616 Office: Pub Defender Office 65 Jefferson Ave Ste 3 Elizabeth NJ 07201-2441 E-mail: mckabak@juno.com.

KABALIN, JOHN NICHOLAS, urologist; b. L.A., Dec. 23, 1958; s. Nicholas Augustin and Mary Jane (Engleman) Kabalin; m. Pamela Grace White, July 11, 1981. BS, Stanford U., 1980; MD, Johns Hopkins U., 1984. Diplomate Am. Bd. Urology. Intern in surgery Stanford U. Med. Ctr., 1984-85, resident in surgery,

1985-86, resident in urology, 1986-90, chief resident in urology, 1989-90; chief urology sect. Va Med. Ctr., Palo Alto, Calif., 1990-97; asst. prof. urology Stanford (Calif.) U., 1990-97; asst. prof. surgery U. Nebr. Coll. Medicine, 1999—. Contbr. . Fellow: ACS, Am. Soc. for Laser Medicine and Surgery, Internat. Coll. Surgeons; mem.: AAAS, AMA, Am. Bd. Forensic Medicine, N.Y. Acad. Scis., Internat. Soc. Urology, Biomed. Optics Soc., Am. Lithotripsy Soc., Endourol. Soc., Soc. Univ. Urologists, Soc. Urol. Oncology, Am. Soc. Clin. Oncology, Am. Urol. Assn., Am. Assn. Clin. Urologists, Alpha Omega Alpha, Phi Beta Kappa. Roman Catholic. Achievements include adaptation and clinical development of Holmium laser sources for soft tissue and prostatic surgery. Office: Ste 2200 3911 Ave B Scottsbluff NE 69361-4669

KABAT, LINDA GEORGETTE, civic leader; b. Cleve., Nov. 26, 1951; d. Michael G. and Georgette (deVos) Paul; m. John Edward Kabat Jr., Apr. 23, 1977; 1 child, Susan Marie. Student, Cleve. Inst. Music, 1969-72. With sales dept. Higbee Co., Fairview Park, Ohio, 1972; customer svc. rep. Ashland Chem. Co., Cleve., 1972-74, Celanese Corp., Lakewood, Ohio, 1974-76; with sales dept. May Co., North Olmsted, Ohio, 1979; customer svc. rep. Diamond Shamrock Corp., Cleve., 1979-82; in sales May Co., North Olmsted, 1989-97; with Concepts Direct, Longmont, Colo., 1999—. Chpt. pres. Cath. War Vets. Aux., Cleve., 1973-75, pres. Ohio, 1975-77, nat. sec., 1977-79, state sec., 1991-92. Mem. Mu Phi Epsilon (pres. 1971-72, historian 1970-71). Republican. Avocations: camping, traveling, needlework, music.

KABBES, DOUGLAS JOHN, physician; b. Effingham, Ill., Oct. 27, 1959; s. John Robert and Jane Claire K.; m. Cheryl Ann Gennaro, Oct. 27, 1990; children: Courtney, Connor, Christa. BA with honors, So. Ill. U., 1981, MD, 1985. Diplomate Am. Bd. Family Practice. Dir., chmn. dept. emer. medicine St. Anthony's Hosp., Effingham, Ill., 1997—. Founder, CEO Emergency Cons., Effingham, 1999—; founding ptnr. Effingham Ptnrs. progress, 1999—; founder KKG Devel. Corp., 1995—, pres., 1995-97; founding ptnr. Kabbes Properties, Inc., Effingham, 1994—; founder, pres. Effingham State Bank Land Trust 1951, 1997—; ptnr. Nat. Trail LLC, Effingham. Chmn. ch. picnic St. Anthony's Ch., Effingham, 1994; mem. adv. bd. St. Anthony's Hosp., Effingham, 1996-2001; tech. planning com. St. Anthony's Sch., Effingham, 1996; v.p. Effingham chpt. Am. Cancer Soc. So. Ill. U. Pres. scholar, 1977-81. Mem. Am. Coll. Emergency Physicians, Am. Acad. Family Physicians, Am. Coll. Physicians [illegible], KC, Phi Eta Sigma. Republican. Roman Catholic. Avocations: golf, travel, real estate development. Home: 903 Park Hills Dr Effingham IL 62401 Office: St Anthony's Meml Hosp 503 N Maple Effingham IL 62401 E-mail: DougKabbes@hotmail.com.

KABDEBO, THOMAS GEORGE, library director; b. Budapest, Hungary, Feb. 5, 1934; arrived in U.K., 1956; s. Bela and Klara (Kelen) K.; m. Agnes Wohl, June 29, 1959 (div. 1984); children: Lilian, Andrea; m. Anna Kane, Dec. 22, 1986; 1 child, Istvan. BA, U. Wales, 1959; diploma in Libr., U. London, 1960, MPhil, 1968; PhD in History, U. Manchester, 1983. Asst. libr. U. Wales, 1959, U. London, 1960-69; libr. U. Guyana, 1969-72, U. Westminster, 1973-74; sublibr. U. Manchester, 1975-82; libr. Nat. U. Ireland, Maynooth, 1983—. Author 43 books in English, Hungarian and Welsh including Amonnan, 1993 (quality prize 1994), The Danube Trilogy, 1992-97 (award 1995), Dictionary of Dictionaries, 1992, Attila Jozsef (Fust Prize award), 1997. Decorated Order of Merit (Hungary); recipient Rakoczi essay prize, Hungarians of N.Am., Ottawa, Pro Patria Hungarica, Hungarian Republic, Budapest, 1992, Arany Janos prize for Lit., 1998, Nagy Imre plaque for 1956 Activities, 1999, Arany Janos prize for Lit., 2000, Attila Jozef prize for Lit., 2001. Fellow Libr. Assn.; mem. P.E.N. Roman Catholic. Avocations: fishing, swimming, chess. Home: 92 Aylmer Rd Newcastle Co Dublin Ireland Office: Nat U Ireland Maynooth County Kildare Ireland Fax: 00353-1-4589691. E-mail: tkabdebo@gofree.indigo.ie.

KABEL, ROBERT JAMES, lawyer; b. Burbank, Calif., Nov. 30, 1946; s. Herman James and Margaret Elizabeth (Doyle) K. BA, Denison U., 1969; JD, Vanderbilt U., 1972; LL.M. in Taxation, Georgetown U., 1979. Bar: D.C., Tenn., Ohio, U.S. Supreme Ct. Adminstrv. asst. to Gov. Winfield Dunn of Tenn., Nashville, 1972-75; legis. asst. to Senator Paul Fannin, Washington, 1975-77; legis. dir. Senator Richard G. Lugar of Ind., Washington, 1977-82; spl. asst. to pres. White House, Washington, 1982-84; ptnr. Manatt, Phelps & Phillips and precedessor firm, Washington, 1985—2002, Baker & Daniels, Washington, 2002—; sr. v.p. Sagamore Assoc., Washington, 2002—. Part-time mem. Fgn. Claims Settlement Commn., 1987-91; chair Greater Washington Bd. Trade Task Force Internat. Trade & Intellectual Property, 1996-97. Mem. Bretton Woods Commn.; Vanderbilt Law Sch. Alumni Bd., 1997-2000; bd. trustees Denison U., 1999—; chmn. bd. dirs. Log Cabin Reps., 1994-99; chmn. Liberty Edn. Fund, 1999—; mem. D.C. Rep. Com., vice chmn. Recipient citation Denison U. Alumni. Mem. ABA, Rep. Lawyers Assn., Denison U. Alumni Soc. (pres. 1994-96), Met. Club Washington, The Federalist Soc. Republican. Presbyterian. Office: Baker & Daniels 805 15th St NW Ste 700 Washington DC 20005 E-mail: RKabel@bakerd.com.

KABEL, ROBERT LYNN, chemical engineering educator; b. Champaign, Ill., Apr. 3, 1932; s. Myron Charles and Marietta Lovina (Lynn) K.; m. Barbara Jean Robb, June 8, 1958; children: Joseph Robb, Douglas Alan. BS, U. Ill., 1955; PhD, U. Wash., 1961: Registered profl. engr., Pa. Engr. Conoco, Ponca City, Okla., 1954, Sun Oil Co., Marcus Hook, Pa., 1955, Chevron Rsch. Co., LaHabra and Richmond, Calif., 1967, 68; rsch. scientist NASA Ames Rsch. Ctr., Palo Alto, Calif., 1969; engr. Exxon, Linden, N.J., 1976-78; prof. chem. engring. Pa. State U., University Park, 1963—. Invitational prof. chem. and bioengring. Ariz. State U., Tempe, 1984-85; vis. prof. Tech. U. Norway, Trondheim, 1971-72, Pahlavi U., Shiraz, Iran, 1978, U. N.S.W., Sydney, Australia, 1988, 89, U. Canterbury, Christchurch, New Zealand, 1989, Chulalongkorn U., Bangkok, 1989; co-editor/author: Scaleup of Chemical Processes, 1985; cons. in field. Co-author: Sources and Control of Air Pollution, 1998. Bd. dirs. Oreg.-Calif. Trails Assn., 1999-2002. With USAF, 1961-63. Decorated Air Force Commendation medal; recipient Outstanding Tchg. award Amoco Found., 1983, award for Excellence in Instrn., Western Electric, 1983, Nat. Catalyst award for Excellence in Chem. Tchg., Chem. Mfrs. Assn., 1984, Disting. Achievement award Ariz. State U., 1985, ASEE Corcoran award, 1989; ASEE faculty fellow, 1969, Royal Norwegian Coun. for Sci. and Indsl. Rsch. fellow, 1971-72, NATO fellow, 1974, Erskine fellow, 1989. Fellow AIChE (editl. bd. 1980-85); mem. Am. Chem. Soc., Sigma Xi, Phi Lambda Upsilon, Alpha Chi Sigma, Tau Beta Pi, Phi Eta Sigma. Republican. Presbyterian. Office: 130 Fenske Lab University Park PA 16802-4400 E-mail: r8k@psu.edu.

KABINGUE, KEN, biochemist; b. Tacloban, Leyte, The Philippines, Jan. 17, 1976; came to U.S., 1992; s. Ben and Virginia Kabingue. BS in Biochemistry, La Sierra U., 1997. Rsch. assoc. Baxter Healthcare Corp., Duarte, Calif., 1997—. Mem. AAAS, Assn. Biomolecular Resource Facilities, Am. Assn. Pharm. Scientists, Am. Chem. Soc., Internat. Union Pure and Applied Chemistry. Avocations: music, sports. Office: Baxter Healthcare Corp 1710 Flower Ave Duarte CA 91010-2923 E-mail: ken_kabingue@baxter.com.

KABIR, FIROZ, wood technologist, researcher; b. Chapai Nawabgonj, Rajshahi, Bangladesh, Feb. 1, 1961; s. Azhar Ali Biswas and Serina Begum; m. Flora Parveen, Jan. 1, 1966; children: Fariha B, Wasiq A. PhD, U. Putra Malaysia, Selangor, 1998. Rsch. scientist Bangldesh Forest Rsch. Scientist, Chittagong, Bangladesh, 1987—98; postdoctoral scientist Va. U. Tech, Blacksburg, Va., 1999—. Contbr. articles and revs. to profl. jours. Fellow: Inst. Wood Sci. Home: 700 Appalachian Dr Apt 7 Blacksburg VA 24060 Office: Virginia Tech Brooks Forest Products Ctr Blacksburg VA 24061-0503 Office Fax: 540-231-1383. E-mail: firozk@vt.edu.

KABIR, MOHAMMED ANOWARUL, pharmacologist; s. Sekender Ali and Asia Khatun; m. Noorun Nahar, June 26, 1992; 1 child, Navid. PhD, L.I. U., 2003. Tchg. fellow L.I. U., 1997—; summer intern Novartis Pharm., East Hanover, NJ, 2002. Rsch. fellow Forest Pharm., Inwood, NY, 2001. Fellow Forest Lab Rsch., 2001. Mem.: AAPS (assoc.), Rho Chi (hon.). Achievements include patents for Cell coated microdialysis. Home: 88-09 148th St # 1C Jamaica NY 11435 Home Fax: 718-780-4586. Personal E-mail: kabirliu@aol.com.

KABRIEL, MARCIA GAIL, psychotherapist; b. El Reno, Okla., Jan. 8, 1938; d. Gail Frederick and Katherine (Marsh) Slaughter; m. J. Ronald Kabriel, May 25, 1957; children: Joseph Charles, Jeffrey Gail, Jae B. BA, U. Okla., 1965, MSW, 1968; postgrad., Am. U. Psychiat. social worker Dept. Mental Hygiene, N.Y.C., 1968-69, Washington Hosp. Ctr., 1970—82, assoc. mem. dept. psychiatry, 1972-75, sr. psychotherapist Counseling Ctr., 1972-75, chief dept. social svcs., 1976-82, cons. spl. projects, 1974-82; psychotherapist Md. Inst. Pastoral Counseling, Annapolis, Md., 1972-97; supr. continuing protective svcs. State Md., 1983-91; supr. rsch. project on child sexual abuse AACO, 1991-93; forensic social worker Anne Arundel Cir. Ct., 1991-97; exec. v.p. Kent Island Transport, Inc., 1985-97; pvt. practice Woodstock, Va., 1998—. Program dir. Shenandoah Meml. Hosp., Life Ctr. of Galax, Woodstock, 1996-97; field instr. Cath. U., Washington, 1973-75, U. Md., 1976-91; adjunct prof. U. Md. 1992-97. Mem. NASW, Acad. Cert. Social Workers (bd. cert. diplomate). Democrat. Presbyterian. Home: 547 Zepp Rd Star Tannery VA 22654 Office: 238 N Main St Woodstock VA 22664-1417

KAC, VICTOR G. mathematician, educator; b. Buguruslan, USSR, Dec. 19, 1943; came to U.S., 1977; s. Gersh and Clara (Landman) K.; m. Elena Bourdenko; children: Luba, Marianne. Diploma, Moscow State U., 1965, cand. of sci., 1968. Asst. Moscow Inst. Electronic Machine Bldg., 1968-71; sr. tchr. MIEM, Moscow, 1971-76; assoc. prof. MIT, Cambridge, Mass., 1977-81, prof., 1981—. Author two books on infinite-dimensional Lie algebras, a book on vertex algebra and a book on quantum calculus; contbr. numerous articles to profl. jours. Recipient Medal Coll. de France, 1981, Wigner medal Group Theory Found., 1994; Guggenheim fellow, 1985, Sloan fellow, 1981. Mem. Am. Math. Soc., Moscow Math. Soc. (hon.). Achievements include structure and representation theory of infinite-dimensional groups and algebras that arise in mathematics and physics. Home: 273 Mason Ter Brookline MA 02446 Office: MIT Math Dept 77 Massachusetts Ave Cambridge MA 02139-4307

KACHERGIS, JOYCE W. designer; b. Omaha, Feb. 9, 1925; d. Lawrence Benjamin Webster and Olga Agnes Olsen; m. George J. Kachergis, July 6, 1946 (dec. Aug. 1974); children: Peter W., Karl George, Anne Olga; m. Jess G. Bell, 1986 (dec. Apr. 2001). AA, Stephens Coll., 1945; BFA, Sch. of the Art Inst., Chgo., 1947. Prodn. design mgr. U. N.C. Press, Chapel Hill, 1963-77; prodn. and design mgr. Stanford U. Press, Palo Alto, Calif., 1977-80; founder, pres., designer Kachergis Book Design, Pittsboro, N.C., 1980—. Vis. prof. Radcliffe Sch. Pub., Cambridge, Mass., 1979-82. Mem. Am. Assn. Univ. Presses (bd. dirs. 1978-80). Office: Kachergis Book Design 14 Small St N Pittsboro NC 27312-5453 E-mail: jwkb@mindspring.com.

KACHUR, ALEXANDER VICTOR, chemist; b. Tal'ne, Cherkasy, Ukraine, Oct. 30, 1959; came to U.S., 1992; s. Victor Z. and Nonna S. (Cherepenko) K.; m. Elena A. Kachur, May 18, 1985; 1 child, Dan. MS in Chemistry, Kiev (Ukraine) U., 1981, PhD in Chemistry, 1987. Cert. in chemistry edn. From asst. prof. to assoc. prof. Kiev U., 1982-92; postdoctoral rschr. U. Pa., Phila., 1992-96, rsch. assoc., 1996-99, sr. rsch. investigator, 1999—. Adj. prof. St. Joseph U., Phila., 1999-2000; adj. prof. Univ. of Scis., Phila., 2000—. Contbr. articles to profl. jours.; patentee in field. Mem. Am. Chem. Soc., Radiation Rsch. Soc. Office: U of Pa 195 J Morgan Bldg Philadelphia PA 19104 E-mail: kachur@mail.med.upenn.edu.

KACHUR, BETTY RAE, elementary education educator; b. Lorain, Ohio, June 12, 1930; d. John and Elizabeth (Stanko) Kachur. BS in Edn., Kent State U., 1963; MEd, U. Ariz., 1971. Cert. tchr., in reading. Tchr. Lorain City Schs., 1961-94. Bd. dirs. Habitat for Humanity Lorain County, 1997—2001, Lorain Pub. Libr., Ohio Friends LIbrs.; treas. Lorain Downtown Ministerial Assn.; profl. storyteller Northeastern Ohio Western Res. Assn. for Preservation and Perpetuation of Storytellers. Mem.: AAUW (social com., scholarship com. 1999), Daniel T. Gardner Reading Assn. (pres. 1978—79, treas. 1988—94), Internat. Reading Assn. (by-laws com. Ohio Coun.). Mem. United Ch. Of Christ. Avocations: reading, writing, quilting, travel.

KACKLEY, JAMES R. former financial services executive; b. Hammond, Ind. m. Barbe Kackley; children: Shannon, John. Grad., Northwestern U., 1964. Ptnr. Arthur Andersen & Co., Chgo., mng. ptnr.; mng. ptnr. fin. adminstrn. Andersen Worldwide, Chgo., 1998-99. Bd. dirs. Chgo. Urban League, Cities in Schs., Adler Planetarium, Pres.'s Coun. for Mus. of Sci. and Industry; co-chmn. exec. coun. Inst. for Ill.; prin. Chgo. United; chmn. west div. campaign United Way, 1990; mem. adv. coun. Chgo. area coun. Boy Scouts Am.; chmn. fin. com. Winnetka Bible Ch. Mem. Mid-Am. Com., Nat. Strategy Forum, Attic Club, Chgo. Club, Econ. Club,, Indian Hill Club, Kenilworth Club, Univ. Club. Office: Andersen Worldwide 225 N Michigan Ave Fl 16 Chicago IL 60601-7600

KACPROWICZ, DONNA MARIE (DONNA LEONETTI), staff nurse; b. Lower Merion, Pa., Feb. 1, 1965; d. Robert G. Leonetti and Rosemary G. (Noone) Anastasia; m. Kenneth Kacprowicz, Mar. 20, 1999; 1 child, John Francis. AAS, C.C. of Phila., 1988. RN. Staff nurse Kindred Hosp. Del. County, Darby, Pa., 2000—.

KACUBA, ALICE MARIE, nurse; b. Montrose, Pa., July 7, 1960; d. Leonard and Dolores (Monahan) K. Diploma, Robert Packer Hosp., 1981; BSN, U. Md., 1993; MSN, Marymount U., 1997. RN, Pa., Md.; cert. CCRN, RAC. Staff nurse, ICU Robert Packer Hosp., Sayre, Pa., 1981-83, The Traveling Nurse Corps., Malden, Mass., 1983-86; clin. nurse IV The Nat. Insts. Health, Bethesda, Md., 1986-98; regulatory project mgr. FDA, Rockville, Md., 1998—. Mem. AACN, ANA, Regulatory Affairs Profl. Soc., Drug Info. Soc., Sigma Theta Tau. Office: 5600 Fishers Ln Rockville MD 20857-0001

KACULI, XHEMAL T. oil industry executive, researcher; B in Mech. Engring., Poly. U. Albania, Tirana, 1995; M in Engring. Sci., Lamar U., 1999, D in Engring., 2002. Rschr. Lamar U., Beaumont, Tex., 1997—2003; engring. analysis and design, product devel. dept. Dril-Quip, Inc., Houston, 2001. Contbr. articles to profl. jours. Pres. Albanian Am. Assn., Houston, 2001—03. Fellow, Lamar U., 2001—02; scholar, 1998, 1999, 2000. Mem.: ASME, Nanotechnology Inst., Am. Soc. Metals, Am. Soc. Petroleum Engrs. Achievements include research in effect of mechanical alloying and bulk shear processing on the quality of Tungsten Carbide Tool products; microstructure and properties of mechanical alloyed and equal channel angular extruded Tungsten Carbide; integration of mechanical alloying and equal channel angular extrusion for production of nanostructured materials; application of mechanical alloying and bulk shear processing to produce superior quality oil field tool products; use of mechanical alloying and ECAE for production of nanostructured titanium silicide. Personal E-mail: kaculi@hotmail.com.

KACUR, LOIS MARIE, obstetric and pediatric nurse; b. Perry, Ohio, Nov. 19, 1915; d. Mark Benjamin and Floy Vivian (Penhollow) Johnson; m. Michael Kacur, Aug. 31, 1947; children: Michael Brian, Barton Winslow, David Lyle, Ellen Marie. Diploma, Cleve. City Hosp., 1939. RN. Ret. Mem. Cleve. Met. Gen. Hosp. Nurses' Alumni Assn. (life).

KACZKA, DAVID WALTER, physician, biomedical engineer; b. Boston, Sept. 8, 1967; s. Walter Stanley and Shirley Ann K.; m. Monica Lynn Hawley, Aug. 10, 1996. BS summa cum laude, Boston U., 1990, MS, 1993, MD, PhD, 2000. Rsch. assoc. Boston U., 2000-2001; resident physician St. Vincent Hosp., Worcester, Mass., 2000-2001; resident in anesthesiology Johns Hopkins Hosp., Balt., 2001—. Contbr. articles to profl. jours. Mem. IEEE (assoc.), Biomed. Engring. Soc., Tau Beta Pi, Alpha Eta Mu Beta, Sigma Xi (assoc.), Golden Key Nat. Honor Soc. Home: 105 S Ann St Baltimore MD 21231 Office: Dept Anesthesiology and Critical Care Medicine Blalock 1412 600 N Wolfe St Baltimore MD 21287 Fax: 410-955-5607. E-mail: dkaczka1@jhmi.edu.

KACZMARCZYK, JEFFREY ALLEN, journalist, classical music critic; b. Patuxent River Naval Air Base, Md., Jan. 7, 1963; s. Frank Joseph and Diane Catherine Kaczmarczyk; m. Cynthia L. Shimmel, Aug. 13, 1988; children: Jessica, Michael, David. BA, Western Mich. U., 1986; postgrad., Calif. State U. Editor-in-chief Western Herald, Kalamazoo, Mich., 1986-87; staff writer, acting editor Albion (Mich.) Recorder, 1987; staff writer, columnist Hastings (Mich.) Banner, 1987-92; arts writer, classical music critic The Grand Rapids (Mich.) Press., 1992—. Freelance arts writer, critic Kalamazoo (Mich.) Gazette, 1990-93; editor The Weekender, Hastings, 1991-93. Dir., sec. Thornapple Arts Coun., Hastings, 1992-97; dir. Grand Rapids Area Coun. for Humanities, 1995-2001; vestryman Emmanuel Episcopal Ch., Hastings, 1997-99, sr. warden, 1999. Episcopalian. Home: 314 S Park St Hastings MI 49058-1635 Office: The Grand Rapids Press 155 Michigan St NW Grand Rapids MI 49503-2353

KACZMAREK, CARLA, lawyer; b. Detroit, Sept. 6, 1953; d. Leo Joseph and Charlotte (Schwanke) K.; m. Andrzej Poplawski, Apr. 29, 2000. BS, Eastern Mich. U., 1975; JD, U. Detroit, 1978. Bar: Mich. 1978, Ill. 1979. Law clk. State of Mich. Dept. Mental Health, Detroit, 1977; staff atty. Sr. Citizens Legal Aid Project, Legal Aid and Defenders Assn., State of Mich., Detroit, 1977-82; ptnr. Kaczmarek P.C., Hamtramck, Mich., 1982—. Bd. dirs. Regina H.S., Harper Woods, Mich., 1997—. Mem. AAUW, Advocates (prs. 1982-83). Avocations: powerboating, waterskiing, fishing. Office: Kaczmarek PC 2930 Holbrook St Hamtramck MI 48212-3512

KACZOROWSKI, GREGORY JOHN, biochemist, researcher, science administrator; b. South Bend, Ind., Nov. 20, 1949; s. John Walter and Jean (Bankowski) K.; m. Maria L. Garcia, June 21, 1982. BS in Chemistry summa cum laude, U. Notre Dame, 1972; PhD in Biochemistry, MIT, 1977. Helen Hay Whitney postdoctoral rsch. fellow Roche Inst. Molecular Biology, 1977-80; sr. rsch. biochemist Merck Inst. for Therapeutic Rsch., Rahway, N.J., 1980-84, assoc. dir. dept. membrane biochemistry and biophysics, 1986-88, dir., 1988-96, sr. dir., 1996—; rsch. fellow Biochemistry, Fundamental and Exploratory Rsch., Rahway, 1984-86. Reviewer NIH, NSF, U.S.-Israel Binational Sci. Found.; invited speaker, presenter papers at various profl. meetings; adj. prof. dept. pharmacology and physiology UMDNJ, 1995—. Contbr. numerous articles, revs. to profl. jours.; patentee in field. Hoosier scholar, 1968-72, Notre Dame scholar, 1968-72. Mem. AAAS, Am. Chem. Soc., Am. Soc. Biol. Chemists, Am. Physiol. Soc., Biophys. Soc., N.Y. Acad. Sci., Phi Beta Kappa. Home: 5 Ashbrook Dr Edison NJ 08820-4318 Office: Merck Sharp & Dohme Rsch Labs PO Box 2000 Rahway NJ 07065-0900 E-mail: gregory_kaczorowski@merck.com.

KADAMUS, JAMES ALEXANDER, educational administrator; b. Syracuse, N.Y., Oct. 26, 1949; s. Alexander J. and Alice M. Kadamus; m. Carol Ann Wierzchowski, June 26, 1971; children: Christopher James, Benjamin Andrew. BA in Polit. Sci., Union Coll., Schenectady, 1971; M Regional Planning, U. N.C., 1973. Planner, rsch. Syracuse-Onondaga County Planning Agy., 1968-71; asst., then assoc. planner Office Long Range Planning N.Y. State Edn. Dept., Albany, 1974-78; exec. asst. to dep. commr. elem., secondary-continuing edn. N.Y. State Edn. Dept., Albany, 1978-79, chief Bur. Proprietary Sch. Supervision, 1979-82, asst. commr. Office Elem., Secondary and Continuing Edn., 1982-88, asst. commr. Office Higher and Continuing Edn., 1988-93, assoc. commr. Office Fin., Mgmt. and Info. Svcs., 1992-95, dep. commr. elem., mid., secondary-continuing edn., 1995—. Mem. Nat. Skill Standards Group, Washington, 1992-94; mem. Congl. Commn. on Tech. and Literacy, Washington, 1991-92; mem. Nat. Commn. to Assess Vocat. Edn., Washington, 1989-90; mem. Nat. Rsch. Coun. Com. on Ednl. Excellence and Testing Equity, 1999—. Author: New Directions for Vocational Edn. at the Secondary Level, 1987; also articles; appearances on Today Show, NBC Nightly News, CNN News, others. Bd. dirs. Jr. Achievement, Albany, 1993-96; trustee Capital Dist. YMCA, Albany, 1995—; v.p. Guilderland (N.Y.) Cmty. Ctr. YMCA, 1993-98; coach Guilderland Soccer Club, 1983-93; chief Guilderland YMCA Indian Guides. Mem. Am. Edn. Fin. Assn., Nat. Assn. State Dirs. Vocat. Edn. (pres. 1990-91). Avocations: soccer, golf, boating. Office: NY State Edn Dept Washington Ave Albany NY 12234-0001 E-mail: jkadamus@mail.mysed.gov.

KADANE, JOSEPH B. statistics educator; b. Washington, Jan. 10, 1941; s. David Kurzman and Helene Margret (Born) K.; m. Kathleen Coleman, 1969 (div. 1975); m. Caroline Mitchell, 1992. BA cum laude in Math., Harvard Coll., 1962; PhD in Stats., Stanford U., 1966. Asst. prof. Yale U., New Haven, 1966-68; staff analyst Ctr. for Naval Analysis, Arlington, VA., 1968-71; prof. stats. Carnegie-Mellon U., Pitts., 1971-86, L.J. Savage prof., 1996—, univ. prof., 2000—. Mem. Commn. on Behavioral and Social Scis. and Edn., NRC, 1986-92; mem. Bd. on Math Scis., 1988-91. Assoc. editor Jour. Am. Statis. Assn., 1968-73, dep. editor, 1976-78, editor, 1983-85; assoc. editor Annals of Stats., 1974-76; contbr. articles to profl. jours. NSF grantee; Office Naval Research grantee; Japan Soc. for Promotion of Sci. fellow, 1978 Fellow Am. Statis. Assn. (Pitts. statistician of yr. 1980), Inst. Math. Stats., AAAS; mem. Internat. Statis. Inst. Democrat. Jewish. Home: 2 Darlington Ct Pittsburgh PA 15217-1502 Office: Carnegie-Mellon U Dept Stats Pittsburgh PA 15213

KADANOFF, LEO PHILIP, physicist, educator; b. N.Y.C., Jan. 14, 1937; s. Abraham and Celia (Kibrick) Kadanoff; children: Marcia, Felice, Betsy. AB, Harvard U., 1957, MA, 1958, PhD, 1960. Fellow Neils Bohr Inst., Copenhagen, 1960—61; from asst. prof. to prof. physics U. Ill., Urbana, 1961—69; prof. physics and engring., univ. prof. Brown U., Providence, 1969—78; prof. physics U. Chgo., 1978—82, John D. MacArthur Disting. Service prof., 1982—. Mem. tech. com. R.I. Planning Program, 1972—78, mem. human svcs. rev. com., 1977—78; pres. Urban Obs. R.I., 1972—78. Author: Electricity Magnetism and Heat, 1967; co-author: Quantum Statistical Mechanics, 1963; adv. bd. Sci. Year, 1975—79, editl. bd. Statis. Physics, 1972—79, Nuc. Physics, 1980—. Recipient Wolf Found. prize, 1980, Boltzmann medal, Internat. Union Pure and Applied Physics, 1990, Grande Medaille d'Or, Acad. Scis. Inst. France, 1998, Nat. med. Sci., 1999; fellow NSF, 1957—61, Sloan Found., 1963—67. Fellow: Am. Acad. Arts and Scis., Am. Phys. Soc. (Buckley prize 1977, Onsager prize 1998); mem.: NAS. Home: 5421 S Cornell Ave Apt 15 Chicago IL 60615-5678 Office: U Chgo James Franck Inst 5640 S Ellis Ave Chicago IL 60637-1433

KADAR, KARIN PATRICIA, librarian; b. Oil City, Pa., May 30, 1951; d. Michael Joseph and Bette Lee (Painter) Kadar; divorced; 1 child, Michael L. BS, Clarion U., 1973; MLS, U. Pitts., 1975; postgrad., U. S.C. Lic. instrnl. II in libr. sci. and elem. edn., pub. libr. lic. Substitute tchr. McKeesport (Pa.) Area Schs., 1973, elem. sch. libr., 1973-75, 3d grade tchr., 1975-78, elem. sch. libr., 1978-81; adj. prof. Pa. State U., McKeesport, 1988; periodicals libr. Seton Hill Coll., Greensburg, Pa., 1986-89; dir. Penn Twp. Pub. Libr., Level Green, Pa., 1989-90; grade sch. libr. substitute St. Agnes Sch., North Huntington, Pa., 1992; mid. sch. libr. substitute Belle Vernon (Pa.) Area Sch. Dist., 1993-95; dir. West Newton (Pa.) Pub. Libr., 1993-95, Highland Cmty. Libr., Richland, Pa., 1996; libr. Ridgeland (S.C.) Elem. Sch., 1996-98; spl. orders coord. Barnes and Noble, Hilton Head Island, SC, 1998-99; mgr. Bluffton (S.C.) Cmty. Libr., 1998-99; media specialist Jasper (S.C.) County H.S., 1999—, dist. libr./ media specialist coord., 1999—2001; sch. tech. coord. West Hardeeville Sch., 2002—. Mem. consumer appeals bd. Ford Motor Co., 1989-92, coord. Sch. Dist. Libr. Media Svcs., 2000—; staff writer Current Diversions. Author: (booklet) Sammy the Smokeless Dragon, 1976. Panelist Scan Trak Shoppers, 1984—. Nat. Family Opinion, 1984—; vol. Am. Cancer Soc., 1969-94, pub. edn. chmn., 1974-80, cancer prevention study II chmn., 1982-88, pub. affairs chmn., 1984-86, residential area crusade chmn., 1984-85. Named Vol. of Yr. Am. Cancer Soc. Mon Youch Unit, 1983-84; recipient Crusade award Am. Cancer Soc., Mon Yough unit, 1985-86. Mem. ALA, Pa. Libr. Assn., Parent-Tchr. Guild, Pa. State Edn. Assn., Low Country Reading Assn. (pres-elect), S.C. Assn. Sch. Librs. (regional rep. Jasper County, writer and mem. editl. bd. Messenger), Westmoreland County Hist. Soc., McKeesport Coll. Club, Heritage Hist. Assn. (Hilton Head, S.C.). Avocations: freelance writing, collecting books, genealogical research. Office: West Hardeeville Sch Hwy 46 Hardeeville SC 29927

KADEL, LEE A. computer engineer; s. Lee A. and Billie R. Kadel; m. Patricia M. Pond, Feb. 19, 1947; children: Elizabeth Cruver, Melody Bowman. Cert. sys. engr. Microsoft Corp., 1998, security adminstr. Checkpoint Software, 2001, NT cert. ind. profl. Lanop, 2001. Pres., CEO B.I.R.T. Systems Inc., Lake Geneva, Wis., 1986—95; v.p. Custom Indsl. Sales, Inc., Elkhorn, Wis., 1995—98; tech. cons. Teksystems, Inc., Brookfield, Wis., 1998—2002; sr. network analyst Covenant Healthcare / WFSI, Milw., 2002—. Mem.: Assn. Info. Tech. Profls. (bd. dirs. 2003—), Info. Systems Security Assn. (assoc.). Republican. Achievements include development of computer application testing methodology; computer application deployment methodology; Project Lead - Total Network Rebuild (servers, mail, Internet). Office: Covenant Healthcare / WFSI 5000 W Chambers St Milwaukee WI 53210

KADEN, BRUCE RICHARD, hematologist, oncologist; b. Chgo., Mar. 16, 1947; BS, U. Ill., 1968, MD, 1972. Diplomate Am. Bd. Internal Medicine, Am. Bd. Hematology, Am. Bd. Oncology. Intern Duke Med. Ctr., Durham, N.C., 1972-73, resident in internal medicine, 1973-75, fellow in hematol. oncology, 1975-78; pvt. practice North Suburban Med. Cons., 1978. Mem. staff Luth. Gen. Hosp., Park Ridge, Ill., Holy Family Med. Ctr., Des Plaines, Ill.; clin. asst. prof. medicine U. Chgo. Mem. AMA, Am. Soc. Clin. Oncology, Am. Soc. Hematology, Alpha Omega Alpha. Office: North Suburban Med Consultants 8915 W Golf Rd Niles IL 60714-5825

KADEN, LEWIS B. law educator, lawyer; b. 1942; AB, Harvard U., 1963, LLB, 1967. Bar: N.Y. 1970, N.J. 1974. Harvard scholar Emmanuel Coll., Cambridge U., 1963-64; law clk. U.S. Ct. Appeals, 1967; legis. asst. Senator Robert F. Kennedy, 1968; ptnr. Battle, Fowler, Stokes & Kheel, 1969-73; chief counsel to gov. State of N.J., 1974-76; assoc. prof. Columbia U., 1976-79, prof., 1979-84, adj. prof., 1984—, dir. Ctr. for Law and Econ. Studies, 1979-83; ptnr. Davis, Polk & Wardwell, N.Y.C., 1984—. Bd. dirs. Bethlehem Steel Corp.; chmn. U.S. Govt. Overseas Presence Adv. Panel, 1999. Chmn. N.Y. State Indsl. Coop. Coun., 1986-92. Office: Davis Polk & Wardwell 450 Lexington Ave Fl 31 New York NY 10017-3982 E-mail: kaden@dpw.com.

KADER, FRED J. pediatric neurologist; b. Antwerp, Belgium, 1938; s. Jacob and Rivka (Krystal) Jeruzalski; m. Sarah Brona Kader, May 31, 1964; children: Howard, Eileen, Darrin. MD, McGill Univ., Canada, 1964. Int. Jewish Gen. Hosp., Montreal, Canada, 1964—65; res. int. med. Montreal Gen.. Hosp., Montreal, 1965—66; res. neurologist Balt. City Hosp., 1966—67, Johns Hopkins Hosp., 1967—69; fellow pediat. neurology Montefiore Hosp., Einstein, NY, 1969—71; courtesy staff Childrens Meml. Hosp., Omaha, 1974—78, staff, 1978—, U. Nebr. Med. Ctr., Omaha, 1974—78; cons. neurologist Hastings Regional Ctr., Omaha, 1975—79; courtesy staff Bergan Mercy Med. Ctr., Omaha, 1978—99; assoc. staff Bishop Clarkson Meml. Hosp., Omaha, 1978—83; cons. ped. neur. Ehrling Bergquist Hosp., Bellevue, Nebr., 1978—85; cons. pediat. neurologist Boys Town Inst. Communication Disorders, Omaha, 1978—81; courtesy staff Immanuel Med. Ctr., Omaha, 1978—92, 1995—97, Lutheran Med. Ctr., Omaha, 1978—80; vis. staff St. Josephs Hosp., Omaha, 1978—81; cons. Midlands Cmty. Hosp., Papillion, Nebr., 1979—99, Nebr. Meth. Hosp., Omaha, 1978—80, Meth. Richard Young Hosp., Omaha, 1978—; courtesy staff Nebr. Meth. Hosp., Omaha, 1980—; cons. neurologist Albany Regional Med. Ctr., Albany, NY, 1980—83; cons. Mercy Hosp., Council Bluffs, Iowa, 1981—86, St. Josephs Ctr. for Mental Health, Omaha, 1989—99; asst. clin. prof. in pediat. and neurology U. Nebr. Coll., Omaha, 1978—; asst. prof. Creighton U. Sch. Med., Omaha, 1974—78, asst. clin. prof. neurology, 1978—, asst. clin. prof. ped., 1981—; courtesy staff Boys Town Inst. Comm. Disorders, Omaha, 1981—, St. Luke's Regional Med. Ctr., Sioux City, Iowa, 1994—96, consulting staff, 1996—2000; courtesy staff Marian Health Ctr., Sioux City, Iowa, 1994—2000; consulting staff Bishop Clarkson Meml. Hosp., Omaha, 1998—. Profl. adv. bd. mem. Epilepsy Assn. of Nebraska and Western Iowa, 1989—, Nebraska Epilepsy League & Assn., 1975-89; cons. ped. neurologist, Area Edn. Agency, Council Bluffs, IA, 1986—. Presenter in field. Mem., coach Omaha Met. Amateur Hockey Assn., 1975—90; bd. trustees Beth El Synagogue, Omaha, 1995—, com. chmn., 1995—. Mem. Am. Acad. Neurology, Am. Acad. Pediats. Nebr. chpt. (comm. mem. handicapped and chronically ill children 1980-81), Child Neurol. Soc., Muscular Dystrophy Assn., Nat. Tuberous Assn. (life mem.), Tourette Syndrome Assn. (founding mem. Nebr. chpt.), Tuberous Sclerosis Assn. Am., Epilepsy Assn. Nebr. and Western Iowa (profl. adv. bd. mem. 1989), Greater Omaha Assn. Retarded Citizens, Nebr. Acad. Neurologists and Neurosurgeons, Spina Bifida Assn. Nebr., Omaha Jewish Fedn. Dept. Jewish Edn. (com. on learning disabilities 1979—), 1976-B'nai Brith Henry Monsky Lodge, Nebr. Republican. Jewish.

KADER, NANCY STOWE, nurse, consultant, bioethicist; b. Ogden, Utah, May 29, 1945; d. William Hessel and Mildred (Madsen) Stowe; m. Omar Kader, Jan. 25, 1967; children: Tarik, Gabriel, Aron, Jacob. BSN, Brigham Young U., 1967; postgrad., U. Md. RN ICU Glendale (Calif.) Adventist Hosp., 1970-75, Utah Valley Hosp., Provo, 1975-83; campaign coord. Matheson for Gov., Salt Lake City, 1976-85, Wilson for Senate, Salt Lake City, 1980; RN cons. MESA Corp., Reston, Va., 1984-85; mgr. cost containment Health Mgmt. Strategies, Washington, 1985-88; nurse cons. Birch & Davis, Washington, 1988-90; cons. Inst. Medicine NAS, Washington, 1990-92; cons. Pal-Tech Inc., Arlington, Va., 1992—. Vice chmn. Utah State Bd. Nursing, Salt Lake City, 1977—83; adj. prof. Hood Coll., Md., 2000; ethics cons. to Healthcare Systems, Washington; cons. in field. Dem. county chmn., Utah, 1977-79; del. Dem. Nat. Conv., 1980; del. Va. State Dem. Conv., 1984-95; vice chmn. Gov.'s Commn. on Status of Women, Salt Lake City, 1975-78; bd. dirs. Health Systems Agy. of No. Va., 2000—. Democrat. Home: 11401 Tanbark Dr Reston VA 20191-4121

KADIM, SATYANARAYANA VENKATA, cardiologist; b. Lingapuram, Andhra Pradesh, India, Apr. 10, 1945; arrived in US, 1976, naturalized; s. Subbarao Kadim and Anjamma Pasupuleti; m. Samarla Premilarani, May 14, 1983; children: Rajeshkumar, Subhashkumar. MBBS, Osmania U., Warangal, India, 1972. Diplomate Am. Bd. Internal Medicine, cert. nuclear physician lic. Rotating intern MGM Hosp., Warangal, 1972—73; jr. then sr. house officer in internal medicine Ards Hosp., New Townards, Northern Ireland, 1973—75; sr. house officer in internal medicine No. Ireland Fever Hosp., Belfast, 1975—76; house physician St. John's Riverside Hosp., Yonkers, NY, 1976—77; PG-Y I, II, III in internal mediicne Mt. Vernon (N.Y.) Hosp., 1977—80; cardiology fellow Waterbury (Conn.) Hosp., 1980—81, V.A. Hosp., Dayton, Ohio, 1981—82; pvt. practice in cardiology and internal medicine River Valley Health Sys., Ironton, Ohio, 1982—2001, Our Lady Bellefonte Hosp., Ashland, Ky., 2001—. Physician sports physical exams for children of Ironton, 1982—2001; physician River Valley Health Sys. (Lawrence County Med. Ctr.). Fellow: Royal Soc. Medicine, ACP, Am. Coll. Internat. Physicians, Am. Biograph. Inst., Internat. Biograph. Assn. (life); mem.: Soc. Nuclear Medicine, Lawrence County Med. Soc. (pres. 1986), Ohio State Med. Assn., Am. Soc. Nuclear Cardiology, Am. Coll. Medicine, AMA, Am. Coll. Cardiology. Avocations: basketball, volleyball, badminton, chess. Home: 903 McGovney Ave Ironton OH 45638 Office: 411 Center St Ironton OH 45638

KADIR, DJELAL, literature educator, writer, translator, editor; b. St. Theodoros, Larnaca, Cyprus, Jan. 21, 1946; m. Juana Celia Cohen, May 24, 1969; 1 child, Aixé. BA, Yale U., 1969; PhD, U. N.M., 1972. Prof., chair comparative lit. Purdue U., West Lafayette, Ind., 1973-91; Disting. prof. lit. U. Okla., Norman, 1991-95, Neustadt prof. comparative lit., 1995-97; E.E. Sparks prof. of comparative lit. Pa. State U., 1998—; dir. Internat. Sch. Theory in humanities, 1999—; founding pres. Internat. Am. Studies Assn., 2000. Editor World Literature Today, U. Okla., Norman, 1991-96; cons. Libr. Congress, Washington, 1975—; vis. scholar Russian Acad. Scis., Moscow, 1992; lectr. in field; sr. rsch. assoc. U. Leipzig, 1994—, Borges Ctr., Aarhus U. Denmark; bd. dirs. Coun. on Nat. Lits., Internat. Writers Ctr.; sr. rsch. fellow, mem. exec. bd. Internat. Sch. of Theory in the Humanities, Santiago, Spain, 1997-99. Author: Juan Carlos Onetti, 1977, Questing Fictions, 1986, Columbus and the Ends of the Earth, 1992, The Other Writing, 1993; editor, translator selected poetry of Joao Cabral de Melo Neto, 1994; editor: Oxford History of Latin American Literature, 2003, Longman Anthology of World Literature, 2003; mem. editl. bd. PMLA 1998-2002. Mem. State Arts Coun. Okla., Oklahoma City, 1991-96; cons. Indpls. Mus. Art. Resident fellow Rockefeller Found., Bellagio, Italy, 1993. Mem. MLA (chmn. Del. Assembly 1999-2000), Internat. Comparative Lit. Assn. (exec. bd. com. Lit. Histories, 1992—, chmn. com. on theory 1998—), Am. Comparative Lit. Assn., Internat. Found. Global Studies (sec. 1998-2000), Internat. Coll. Global Studies (v.p. 1998-2000). Avocations: music (cello), hiking, horseback riding, polo. Office: Dept Comparative Lit Pa State U 311 Burrowes Bldg University Park PA 16802-6203 E-mail: dxk50@psu.edu.

KADIS, JONATHAN BRYNN, information technology executive; b. Patuxent River, Md., Sept. 14, 1956; s. Alvin Paul Jr. and Beverly (Jones) K.; m. Tami Louise Stoneking, May 25, 1979; children: Jared Brynn, Justin Brett, Tarissa Lynn, Tasha Lee. AA, AS, Bellevue Community Coll., 1983; Bachelors, Brigham Young U., 1985, Masters, 1986. Service technician Sta. KIRO-TV, Seattle, 1982-83; asst. prodn. mgr., videographer, editor Sta. KBYU-TV, Provo, Utah, 1983-87; producer, dir. Sta. KUID-TV, Moscow, Idaho, 1987-93; mgr. multimedia and distance learning svcs. Utah State U., Logan, 1993-97, supr. Faculty Assistance Ctr. for Tchg., 1993-97, dir. multimedia and distance learning svcs., 1997—2000, dir. tech. support svcs., 2000—, adj. prof. comms. Freelance producer, dir., editor, videographer N.W. Region, 1987—; lectr. U. Idaho, Moscow. Author: Corporate Media Management, 1986. Asst. scoutmaster Boy Scouts Am., Stanwood, 1975-76, chartered orgn. rep., 1990-91, River Heights, Utah, 1996-97, cubmaster, Moscow, 1991-92, scoutmaster and chartered orgn. rep., 1993-97. With Air N.G., 1983—. Recipient Nat. Variety Spl. Emmy award nomination NATAS, IRIS nomination for Outdoor Idaho, Phys. Fitness award. Nat. U. for Continuing Edn. Assn., Emmy nomination for Best of Outdoor Idaho, UPI Documentary Excellence award, Corp. for Pub. Broadcasting-Pub. TV Program award for Bears, Idaho Press Club award, N.Am. film/Video award, 1st pl. All-Media Editorial award Idaho Press Club, award of merit Elkhorn dist. Boy Scouts Am., 1996. Avocations: travel, golf, landscaping, antique video equipment collecting. Office: Utah State U Tech Support Svcs 3740 Old Main Hill Logan UT 84322-3740 Home: 215 S Sherwood Dr Providence UT 84332-9688

KADISH, RICHARD L. lawyer; b. Newark, Dec. 1, 1943; s. Irving Jerome and Henrietta (Appleblatt) K.; m. Bethany Tortis, Aug. 6, 1972; children: Jennifer, Andrew, Jill. BA, U. Pa., 1965; MA, Rutgers U., 1968, JD, 1970. Deputy atty. gen. N.J. Atty Gen., Trenton, N.J., 1971-74; deputy exec. dir. N.J. Housing Fin. Agy., Trenton, N.J., 1974-77; sr. v.p. CRI Inc., Rockville, Md., 1978-87, exec. v.p., 1987-94; pres. Capital Apt. Properties, Inc., Rockville, Md., 1994-97, CAPREIT, Inc., Rockville, Md., 1998—. Dir. Nat. Multifamily Housing Coun. Mem. ABA, N.J. Bar Assn. Office: CAPREIT Ste 100 11200 Rockville Pike Rockville MD 20852-3154

KADISH, SANFORD HAROLD, law educator; b. N.Y.C., Sept. 7, 1921; s. Samuel J. and Frances R. (Klein) K.; m. June Kurtin, Sept. 29, 1942; children: Joshua, Peter. B Social Scis, CCNY, 1942; LLB, Columbia U., 1948; JD (hon.), U. Cologne, 1983; LLD (hon.), CUNY, 1985, Southwestern U., 1993. Bar: N.Y. 1948, Utah 1954. Pvt. practice law, N.Y.C., 1948-51; prof. law U. Utah, 1951-60, U. Mich., 1961-64, U. Calif., Berkeley, 1964-91, dean Law Sch., 1975-82, Morrison prof., 1973-91, prof. emeritus, 1991—. Fulbright lectr. Melbourne (Australia) U., 1956; vis. prof. Harvard U., 1960-61, Freiburg U., 1967; lectr. Salzburg Seminar Am. Studies, 1965; Fulbright vis. lectr. Kyoto (Japan) U., 1975; vis. fellow Inst. Criminology, Cambridge (Eng.) U., 1968. Author: (with M.R. Kadish) Discretion to Disobey— A Study of Lawful Departures from Legal Rules, 1973, (with Schulhofer) Criminal Law and Its Processes, 6th edit., 1995, Blame and Punishment—Essays in the Criminal Law, 1987; editor-in-chief Ency. Crime and Justice, 1983; contbr. articles to profl. jours. Reporter Calif. Legis. Penal Code Project, 1964-68; pub. mem. Wage Stblzn. Bd., region XII, 1951-53; cons. Pres.'s Commn. Adminstrn. of Justice, 1966; mem. Calif. Coun. Criminal Justice, 1968-69. Lt. USNR, 1943-46. Fellow, Ctr. Advanced Study Behavioral Scis., 1967—68, Guggenheim fellow, Oxford U., 1974—75, vis. fellow, All Souls Coll. Oxford U., 1983. Fellow AAAS (v.p. 1984-86), Brit. Acad. (corr.); mem. AAUP (nat. pres. 1970-72), Am. Assn. Law Schs. (exec. com. 1960, pres. 1982), Order of Coif (exec. com. 1966-67, 74-75), Phi Beta Kappa. Home: 774 Hilldale Ave Berkeley CA 94708-1318 E-mail: shk@law.berkeley.edu.

KADISON, RICHARD VINCENT, mathematician, educator; b. N.Y.C., July 25, 1925; married, 1956; 1 child. MS, U. Chgo., 1947, PhD, 1950; hon. doctorate, U. d'Aix-Marseille, 1986, U. Copenhagen, 1987. NRC fellow math. Inst. Advanced Study, 1950-52; from asst. prof. to prof. Columbia U., 1952-64; Kuemmerle prof. math. U. Pa., 1964—. Fulbright rsch. grantee, Denmark, 1954-55; Sloan fellow, 1958-62; Guggenheim fellow, 1969-70. Mem. NAS (chmn. math. sect. 2003—), Am. Math. Soc. (Steele prize for lifetime achievement 1999), Royal Danish Acad. Sci. and Letters (fgn. mem.), Norwegian Acad. Sci. and Letters (fgn. mem.), Sigma Xi. Office: U Pa Dept Math Philadelphia PA 19104-6395

KADISON, STUART, lawyer, educator, writer; b. Richmond, Va., Nov. 17, 1923; s. Elliot Theodore and Rebecca (Lesser) K.; m. Carita Silverman, June 23, 1946; children: Dana, Brian, Warne. Student, NYU, 1938-40; AB, U. Md., 1942; LL.B., Stanford U., 1948. Bar: Calif. 1948. Practiced law, Los Angeles; now ret. ptnr. Sidley & Austin, Los Angeles. Lectr. Southwestern U. Sch. Law, L.A., 1948-52, Stanford U. Sch. Law, 1977-82; Herman Phleger vis. prof. Stanford Law Sch., 1994; vis. prof. Brigham Young U. Law Sch., 1995-99, U. Chgo. Law Sch., 2000; co-chmn. ABA-Am. Newspaper Pubs. Assn. Task Force, 1977-83. Bd. visitors Stanford Law Sch., 1964-72, chmn., 1969-70; bd. dirs. Friends of Huntington Libr., v.p. and treas., 1977-82, pres., 1983-85, bd. overseers, 1978-91; chmn. lawyers adv. com. Constl. Rights Found., 1978-81; trustee Santa Barbara Mus. Art, 1991-97, 2001-. Lt. USNR, 1942-46. Elected to Townsend Harris Hall of Fame, 1994. Fellow Am. Coll. Trial Lawyers, Am. Bar Found.; mem. ABA (chmn. spl. com. on delivery of legal svcs. 1973-75, chmn. resource devel. coun. 1983-84), Am. Law Inst. (life), L.A. County Bar Assn. (pres. 1971-72, chmn. com. on judiciary 1976-77, Shattuck-Price Meml. award 1986), State Bar Calif. (gov. 1973-76), Destroyer Escort Commanding Officers WWII. Home: 4853 Glencairn Rd Los Angeles CA 90027-1135

KADIYALA, KOTESWARA RAO, econometrics educator; b. Mustabada, India, Apr. 20, 1933; came to U.S. 1962, naturalized 1981; s. Venkayya and Anna Poorna (Korivi) K.; m. June 15, 1957; children— Ravindra Kumar, Rajendra Kumar, Rajeswarrao, Suseela Anna. B.Sc. with honors, Andhra U., 1957; M.S. in Stats., Indian Statis. Inst., 1959; Ph.D., Minn. U., 1966. Asst. prof. Wayne State U., Detroit, 1966-67; asst. prof. U. Western Ont., London, Can., 1967-69, assoc. prof., 1969-70, prof., 1970-71; prof. Purdue U., West Lafayette, Ind., 1971— . Mem. Am. Statis. Assn. Home: 1341 King Arthur Dr Lafayette IN 47905 Office: Purdue U 4033 Rahls Hall 100 S Grant St West Lafayette IN 47907 E-mail: Kadiyala@mgmt.Purdue.edu.

KADLOWEC, JENNIFER, engineering educator; b. Ohio; BS in Physics, Baldwin-Wallace Coll., 1993; MS in Mech. Engring., U. Mich., 1995, PhD in Mech. Engring., 1999. Grad. rsch./tchg. asst. U. Mich., Ann Arbor, 1993—99; mfg. engr. BFGoodrich Landing Gear Divsn., Cleve., 1996; mech. engr. Erico, Inc, Solon, Ohio, 1999; asst. prof. Rowan U., Glassboro, NJ, 1999—. Faculty fellow NASA Glenn Rsch. Ctr., Cleve., 2000—01. Recipient Gen. Electric Faculty of the Future award, Gen. Electric/U. Mich.; Rsch. scholar, Gt. Lakes Ctr. for Truck and Transit Rsch., NASA-ASEE Faculty fellow, NASA Glenn Rsch. Ctr., 2000, 2001. Mem.: ASME (assoc.), Soc. Engring. Scis. (assoc.), Am. Chem. Soc. (assoc.; Rubber divsn.), Am. Soc. for Engring. Edn. (assoc.). Office: Rowan Univ 232 Rowan Hall 201 Mullica Hill Rd Glassboro NJ 08028 E-mail: kadlowec@rowan.edu.

KADNER, CARL GEORGE, biology educator emeritus; b. Oakland, Calif., May 23, 1911; s. Adolph L. and Otilia (Pecht) K.; m. Mary Elizabeth Moran, June 24, 1939; children: Robert, Grace Wickersham, Carl L. BS, U. San Francisco, 1933; MS, U. Calif., Berkeley, 1936, PhD, 1941. Prof. biology Loyola Marymount U., Los Angeles, 1936-78, prof. emeritus, 1978—. Trustee Loyola U., Los Angeles, 1970-73. Served to maj. U.S. Army, 1943-46. Mem. Entomol. Soc. Am. (emeritus), Sigma Xi, Alpha Sigma Nu. Republican. Roman Catholic. Avocation: insect photography. Home: 8100 Loyola Blvd Los Angeles CA 90045-2639

KADO, CLARENCE ISAO, molecular biologist; b. Santa Rosa, Calif., June 10, 1936; s. James Y. and Chiyoko K.; m. Barbara M. Kawahara, June 30, 1963; children: Deborah, Diana M. B.Sc., U. Calif., Berkeley, 1959, PhD, 1964. Rsch. asst. Virus Lab., U. Calif., Berkeley, 1960-64, NIH postdoctoral fellow, 1964-67, asst. rsch. biochemist, 1967-68; asst. prof. plant pathology U. Calif., Davis, 1968-72, assoc. prof., 1972-76, prof., 1976—. Dir. Fallen Leaf Lake Confs., 1985—. Author: (textbook) Principles and Techniques in Plant Virology, 1972; editor: (novels) Molecular Mechanisms of Bacterial Virulence, 1994, Horizontal Gene Transfer, 1998, 2d edit., 2002; editor: (assoc. editor) Virology, 1970—73, (Jours.) Jour. Bacteriology, 1987—93, Molecular Microbiology, 1989—. Recipient Bronze medal for virus rsch., WHO, 1968; fellow Sr. fellow, NATO, 1974—75; grantee, NIH, 1968—2001, Am. Cancer Soc., 1969—73, 1980—82, SEA, 1979—85, CRGO, 1985—99. Fellow: Am. Acad. Microbiology (U.S. Presdl. Sci. award), Am. Phytopath. Soc.; mem.: Internat. Soc. Molecular Plant-Microbe Interactions, Am. Soc. Biochemistry and Molecular Biology, Am. Soc. Microbiology, N.Y. Acad. Scis., AAAS, Fly Fishers Davis (dir, past pres.), Fly Fishers, Sigma Xi. Office: U Calif Davis Crown Gall Group One Shields Ave Davis CA 95616

KADOHIRO, JANE K. educator, nurse, diabetes consultant; b. Lima, Ohio, July 20, 1947; d. Howard M. and Betty J. (Johoske) Keller; m. Howard M. Kadohiro, Dec. 27, 1969; children: Christopher, Jennifer. BA in Sociology and Edn., U. Hawaii, Manoa, 1969; BS in Nursing, U. Hawaii, Honolulu, 1977, MPH, 1990; MS, U. Hawaii, 1994, DrPH, 1999; postgrad., Yale U., 2001—. Staff nurse Children's Hosp., Honolulu, 1977-78; staff pub. health nurse Hawaii State Dept. Health, Honolulu, 1978-80, coord. hypertension and diabetes, 1980-85, projects adminstr., 1985-89, chief chronic diseases, 1989-91; office mgr. Hanalei Trends, Honolulu, 1985-89; clin. nurse specialist Queen's Med. Ctr., Honolulu, 1991-94; cons. Aiea, Hawaii, 1991—; nurse investigator Honolulu Heart Program, 1991-95; asst. prof. U. Hawaii at Manoa, Honolulu, 1991—; dep. dir. health State of Hawaii, 2003—. Leader, advisor, life mem. Girl Scouts U.S., Honolulu, 1978—; mem. diabetes project Office of Hawaiian Affairs, 1993-95. Named Disting. Alumni U. Hawaii Sch. Nursing, 1987; one of Hawaii's Unsung Heroes, Honolulu Star Bull., 1993. Mem. ANA (polit. action com. 1994—), APHA, Hawaii Nurses Assn. (Excellence in Clin. Practice award 1995), Am. Diabetes Assn. (nat. del. yearly, nat. programs com. nat. youth congress 1993-95, nat. youth task force and design team 1996-97, nat. profl. edn. com. 1997-98, Pacific N.W. regional pres.-elect 1998-99, pres. health care and edn. 1999-2000, Reaching People award 2002, outstanding contbns. to diabetes and camping nat. award 1994, Hawaii affiliate founding bd. dirs. 1978—, camp nurse and camp dir. 1982, past pres. 1986, chair mem. coms. 1978—, Reaching People award Pacific NW Region 2002), Hawaii Pub. Health Assn., Am. Assn. Diabetes Educators (bd. dirs. 1997—, chair 1999-2001, rsch. com. 2001-03, awards com. 2001-02, pub. affairs com. 2002-03, 1st v.p. 2000-01, pres.-elect 2001-02, nat. pres. 2002-03), Hawaii Assn. Diabetes Educators (founding mem., bd. dirs. 1989—, pres. 1996—, state legis. coord. 1996-2001, treas. 1994-95, pub. affairs chair 1996-2001, diabetes camp edn. nat. award 1995), Diabetes Advocacy Alliance Hawaii (convener and chair 1997—), Assn. Asian and Pacific Health Orgns. (adv. bd. 2002—), Internat. Diabetes Fedn., Internat. Soc. Pediat. and Adolescent Diabetes (steering com. Internat. Diabetes camping program 1989—), Am. Heart Assn. (cardiovasc. nursing coun. 1985-97), Sigma Theta Tau (founding mem., chair nominating com. 1995-97 Gamma Psi chpt. and chpt.-at-large, chmn. recognition com. 1986-89). Avocations: travel, people, community and organization work, lifelong learning. Home: 1629 Wilder Ave Apt 504 Honolulu HI 96822-4652 E-mail: kadohiro@hawaii.edu.

KADONAGA, JAMES TAKURO, biochemist; b. Ft. Bragg, N.C., Aug. 24, 1958; s. Tadashi and Alice Ayako K.; m. Anne Kadonaga, Sept. 15, 1984; children: William, Natalie. SB, MIT, 1980; AM, Harvard U., 1982, PhD, 1984. Fellow U. Calif., Berkeley, 1984-88, asst. prof. molecular biology San Diego, 1988-92, assoc. prof., 1992-94, prof., 1994—, vice chmn., 2000—03, chmn-.,Molecular Biology, 2003—. Mem. editl. bd. Molecular Cell Jour., 1997—, Genes and Devel. Jour., 1994—, Molecular and Cellular Biology, 1993-2001, Protein Expression and Purification, 1990—; contbr. articles to profl. jours. Recipient Biochemistry grant award Eli Lilly, 1989-91, Am. Inst. of Chemists/MIT award, 1980, prize Alpha Chi Sigma/MIT, 1980; named to Hall of Fame, East Side Union H.S. Dist., San Jose, Calif., 1991; DuPont fellow Harvard U., 1983-84, Miller fellow, 1984-86, sr. fellow Am. Cancer Soc. (Calif. div.), 1986-87, Presdl. Faculty fellow Pres. George Bush, 1992-97; Lucille P. Markey scholar, 1987-93. Fellow AAAS, Am. Acad. Microbiology; mem. Am. Chem. Soc., Am. Soc. Microbiology, Am. Soc. Biochemistry and Molecular Biology. Office: U Calif San Diego 9500 Gilman Dr La Jolla CA 92093-0347

KADOTA, TAKASHI THEODORE, mathematician, electrical engineer; b. Omogo, Ehime-Ken, Japan, Nov. 14, 1930; s. Shigeru and Kikuko (Tominaga) K.; m. Helena Littau, Dec. 21, 1956 (div.); children: Mari, Amy, Kimberley; m. Charlie Frances Hampton. BSEE, Yokohama (Japan) Nat. U., 1953; MSEE, U. Calif., Berkeley, 1956, PhDEE, 1960. Mem. tech. staff AT&T Bell Labs., Whippany, N.J., 1960-66, Murray Hill, N.J., 1966-94; ret., 1994. Vis. prof. U. Hawaii, Honolulu, 1978, U. Calif., Berkeley, 1975, Stanford U., 1974. Fellow IEEE (assoc. editor 1977-80).

KADOUS, TAMER ADEL, research scientist; b. Al-Mahal Al-Koubra, Gharbia, Egypt, Sept. 19, 1970; arrived in U.S., 1998; s. Adel Abd El-Ghany Kadous and Rawia Abd El-Hamid El-Ghanam; m. Nermeen Ahmed Bassiouny; children: Sarah children: Mariam. MSc, Alexandria (Egypt) U., 1997, U. Wis., 1999, PhD, 2001. Registered engr. Sys. engr. Thorn Security, Alexandria, 1994—97; rsch. asst. U. Wis., Madison, 1998—2001; rsch. intern NOKIA INC., Dallas, 1999—2000; rsch. engr. QUALCOMM INC., San Diego, 2001—. Tchg. asst. Alexandria U., 1994—97, U. Wis., Madison, 1998—2000. Contbr. articles to profl. jours. Mem., pres. Muslim Student Assn., Madison, 1998—2001. Soldier Egyptian Air Force, 1995—96. Mem.: IEEE. Office: QUALCOMM INC 5775 Morehouse Dr San Diego CA 92121 Office Fax: 858-658-1560.

KADOW, CATHI, academic counselor; b. Chgo. AA, South Suburban Coll., South Holland, Ill., 1987, AS, 1988; BA in Writing, Purdue U. Calumet, Hammond, Ind., 1990, MA in English Lit., 1992; postgrad., Loyola U., Chgo., 1998—. Sec. South Suburban Coll., 1984-90; adj. instr. prep. writing Prairie State Coll., Chicago Heights, Ill., 1991, Lewis U., Romeoville, Ill., 1994; grad. asst. Purdue U. Calumet, 1990-92, vis. instr. English, 1992-94, acad. counselor, 1995—, editor univ. catalog, 1991-93. Contbr. poetry to lit. jours., including Skylark, Crossroads Poetry Jour., World of Poetry (hon. mention 1988, Silver Poet awrd 1989), Chasing Rainbows, Midwest Poetry Anthology, Interior Lighting, Impressions, Writer II, Am. Poetry Anthology; pub. in online jours. Recipient 3d place award writing contest Woman's Day, 1985; scholar South Suburban Coll., 1986, President's scholar, 1988-89. Mem. Nat. Acad. Advising Assn., Ind. Acad. Advising Network, Phi Theta Kappa, Alpha Chi. Avocations: travel, photography. Office: Purdue U Calumet 2200 169th St Hammond IN 46323-2068

KADOW, CLEMENS MARTIN JOACHIM, engineer, researcher; s. Hermann and Hildegard Kadow. MS in Mech. Engring., U. Pitts., 1998; Diplom Ingenieur in civil engring., Universitaet Hannover, 2000; MS in Math. Sci., PhD, Carnegie Mellon U., 2003. Mgmt. cons. McKinsey & Co., Hamburg, Germany, 2000; rsch. asst. Carnegie Mellon U., Pitts., 2000—. Fulbright scholar, 1997—98. Mem.: Soc. Indsl. and Applied Math., Sigma Xi. Office: Carnegie Mellon U 5615 Hobart St Pittsburgh PA 15217 E-mail: kadow@cmu.edu.

KADUK, JAMES ALBERT, crystallographer; b. Cleve., June 21, 1952; s. Edward Eugene and Patricia Ann (Getts) K.; m. Catherine Ann Goodnetter, Aug. 27, 1978; children: Anne Elizabeth, Benjamin James. BS, U. Notre Dame, 1973; MS, Northwestern U., 1975, PhD, 1977. Rsch. chemist Amoco Chem. Co., Naperville, Ill., 1977-81, staff rsch. chemist, 1981-85, BP Chems., Naperville, 1985-88, sr. rsch. scientist, 1988-91, assoc. rsch. scientist, 1997—. Vis. lectr. North Ctrl. Coll., Naperville, Ill. Patentee synthesis of the zeolite ferrierite using chelating templates, process for the preparation of an alkali metal/silica gel catalyst having a uniform metal dispersion; contbr. articles to profl. jours. Pres. Naperville Cmty. Chorus, 1989-91; bd. dirs. DuPage Symphony, 1991-94, v.p., 1992-93. 1st. lt. USAF, 1979. Mem. Internat. Ctr. for Diffraction Data (chmn. sales and mktg. subcom. 1992-96, new product R&D 1992-94, PDF database 1990-92, 94-96, rep. to U.S. Nat. Com. for Crystallography 1992-94, rep. to Internat. Union Crystallography Commn. on crystallographic data 1994-96, mem.-at-large bd. dirs. 1990-94, 96-2000, chmn. tech. com. 2000—), Am. Crystallographic Assn. (chmn. svc. crystallographic spl. interest group 1990-92, chmn. materials sci. spl. interest group 1996-98, apparatus and stds. com. 1994-96, U.S. nat. com. for crystallography 1996-2000, 2002—, sec-treas. 1998-2000, vice chair 2000—), Internat. Union Crystallography (calendar com. 1994-2002). Achievements include 2 patents, others pending. Office: BP Naperville Complex Box 3011 150 W Warrenville Rd Naperville IL 60566 E-mail: kadukja@bp.com.

KADYK, FOLKERT HERPEL, music educator; b. Tulsa, Okla., June 25, 1932; s. Jacob Merion and Elizabeth (Herpel) K.; m. Jean Erickson, Sept. 1, 1956; children: Charles C., Winona Kadyk Smith. BA, Coll. of Wooster, Ohio, 1955; MEd, Temple U., 1961; MA, Villanova U., 1978; D.Mus. Art, Temple U., 1987. Music therapist Phila. State Hosp., 1956-58; tchr. music grades 8 10 Pennsbury Schs., Yardley, Pa., 1958-60; tchr. music K-12 Bridgeport (Pa.) Schs., 1960-62, Great Valley Schs., Malvern, Pa., 1962-86; adj. faculty Delaware County C.C., Media, Pa., 1987-2000, Pa. State U., Media, 1989—2002. Adj. faculty Immaculata (Pa.) Coll., 1976—; hymnal coord.

Friends Gen. Conf., Phila., 1996-97. Editor: (hymnal) Worship in Song, 1997. Bd. dirs. Main Line Symphony Orch., Wayne, Pa., 1974—. Mem. Am. Fedn. Musicians. Mem. Soc. Of Friends. Avocations: woodworking, carpentry, walking, computers. Home: 945 Conestoga Rd Berwyn PA 19312-1305

KAEGEL, RAY MARTIN, real estate and insurance broker; b. St. Louis, Dec. 7, 1925; s. Ray E. and Loyola (Mooney) K.; BS in Secondary Edn., Washington U., St. Louis, 1948, MBA, 1955; m. Daniel Marilyn Dugger, July 2, 1943. Mgr., St. Louis Amusement Co., Inc., 1941-43, 46-52; gen. mgr. Md. Real Estate & Ins. Agy., Inc., Granite City, Ill., 1953-60; pres., gen. mgr., dir. Kaegel Real Estate & Ins. Agy., Inc., Granite City, 1961-2003. Sec., Granite City Bd. Realtors, 1959-63, 66-77, pres, 1964-65, 79-81, 86-87. Vice chmn. Tri-Cities Area Red Cross, 1972; bd. dirs., v.p. Lighthouse for Blind, St. Louis, 1985-87, vice-chmn. 1987-91. Served to lt. (j.g.) USNR, 1943-46. Named Realtor of Yr. Granite City Bd. Realtor, 1990. Mem. Tri-Cities Ind. Ins. Agts. Assn. (pres. 1971-73), Granite City Multiple Listing Service, Inc. (sec.-treas. 1971-82, 88-92, 96-97, pres. 1982-88, 92-95). Home: 660 Pine Creek Dr Chesterfield MO 63017-5922 Office: Kaegel Real Estate & Ins Agy 660 Pine Creek Dr Town And Country MO 63017-5922

KAEHELE, BETTIE LOUISE, accountant; b. Sherwood, Tenn., Oct. 29, 1950; d. James Henry and Ruby Katherin (Clark) Shetters; divorced; children: Josiah Dean, Dana Marie. AAS, Albuquerque Tech. Vocat. Inst., 1980; BSBA, Nat. Coll., Albuquerque, 1991. Acctg. clk. Am. Auto Assn., Albuquerque, 1980-81, Ryder Truck Rental, Inc., Albuquerque, 1981-82; bookkeeper, sec. Grants Steel Sash & Hardware, Albuquerque, 1986-87; owner Sherwood Svcs., 1982-86; acctg. specialist Burton & Co., Albuquerque, 1987, Neff & Co., Albuquerque, 1987-91; acctg. tech. U. N.Mex. Found., Albuquerque, 1991-92, acct., 1992—2002, sr. acct., 2002—; acct. biology dept., acct. II U. N.Mex., Albuquerque, 1997—2002, sr. acct., 2002—. Bible study Bernalillo County Detention Ctr. Republican. Avocations: reading, dance, theatre, poetry, writing. Home: 7408 Desert Canyon Pl SW Albuquerque NM 87121-6424

KAEMPEN, CHARLES EDWARD, manufacturing company executive; b. Quincy, Ill., Mar. 10, 1927; s. Charles Herman and Margo (Gochicoa) K.; m. Inger Margareta Nystrom, Aug. 5, 1951; children: Charles Robert, Donald Michael, Annette Darlina, Laura Inger. BS in Aeron. Engring., U. Ill., Urbana, 1950; DSc in Astronautics, Internat. Acad. Astronautics, Paris, 1964. Registered profl. engr., Calif., Conn. Sr. designer Saab Aircraft Co., Linkôping, Sweden, 1950-52; design analyst Sikorsky Helicopter United Aircraft, Stratford, Conn., 1952-56; space mission analyst Missle div. N.Am. Rockwell, Downey, Calif., 1957-60; staff scientist Hughes Aircraft, Fullerton, Calif., 1961-63; lunar systems analyst Northrop Space Lab., Hawthorne, Calif., 1963-64; pres. Am. Space Transport Co., Tustin, Calif., 1964-66; transport systems analyst Dashaveyor Co., Venice, Calif., 1966-67; pres. Kaempen & Assocs., Orange, Calif., 1967-68; sr. rsch. engr. Baker Oil Tools Inc., L.A., 1968-69; pres. Kaempen Industries, Inc., Santa Ana, Calif., 1969-82, Kaempen & Assocs., 1982—; pres., CEO Kaempen Composite Products, Inc., 1996-2000; pres. Kaempen Corp., Inc., 2000-. Author papers on fiberglass composites and filament winding; patentee in field. With U.S. Army, 1944-47. Reciepient Cert. of Merit Pictionary of Internat. Biography, London, 1965, Fellow AIAA; mem. ASME, ASTM, Soc. Aerospace Materials and Process Engring., Soc. of Plastics Industry, Nat. Soc. Profl. Engrs., Mason. Republican. Lutheran. Home: 3202 E Larkstone Dr Orange CA 92869-5546 Office: Kaempen Composite Products Inc 681 S Tustin St Ste 110 Orange CA 92866-3345

KAESBERG, PAUL JOSEPH, virology researcher; b. Engers, Germany, Sept. 26, 1923; came to U.S., 1926, naturalized, 1933; s. Peter Ernst and Gertrude (Mueller) K.; m. Marian Lavon Hanneman, June 13, 1953; children— Paul Richard, James Kevin, Peter Roy. BS in Engring, U. Wis., Madison, 1945, PhD in Physics, 1949; D. Natural Scis. (hon.), U. Leiden, The Netherlands, 1975. Instr. biometry and physics U. Wis., 1949-51, asst. prof. biochemistry, 1956-58, assoc. prof., 1958-60, prof., 1960-63, prof. biophysics and biochemistry, 1963—, Beeman prof. biophysics and biochemistry, 1983-87, chmn. Biophysics Lab., 1970-88, Wis. Alumni Research Found. prof., 1981—, Beeman prof. molecular virology and biochemistry, 1987-90, prof. emeritus, 1990. Cons. in field. Contbr. chapts. to books and articles to profl. jours. Mem. NAS, Am. Soc. Virology (pres. 1987-88). Home: 5002 Bayfield Ter Madison WI 53705-4811 Office: U Wis Inst Molecular Virology 1525 Linden Dr Madison WI 53706-1534 E-mail: pjkaes@aol.com.

KAESS, JOHN PHILIP, music educator, choir director; b. St. Paul, Jan. 9, 1942; s. Romen Albert and Lucy Belle (Houle) Kaess. MusB, U of St. Thomas, St. Paul, MN, 1960—65; MusM, U of MN, Mpls., MN, 1965—67, MusM further studies, 1968—73; PhD music performance, Pacific Western U, Los Angeles, CA and Honolulu, HI, 1997—99. Cert. tchr. K-12 State of MN. Music coord. and tchr. Guardian Angels Ch. & Sch., Chaska, Minn., 1971—73; tchr., choir dir., organist,and diocesan ch. and sch. Curriculum comm. Archdiocese St. Paul& Mpls., St. Paul, 1968—72; music dir. Regina Coeli Youth Choir, St. Paul, 1973—79; organist, accompanist Twin Cities Schola Cantorum, St. Paul & Mpls., Minn., 1973—99; curriculum comm. Archdiocese St. Paul& Mpls., St. Paul, 1978—88. Author 10 articles (Catholic publ.). Organist music dir. St. Ambrose Ch., St. Paul, 1979—89. Mem.: Ch. Music Assoc. of Am. (assoc.), Minn. Music Tchr. Assoc. (assoc.), The Evergreen Club (assoc.). Republican. Roman Catholic. Achievements include known in Catholic cir. around the country and locally as a ch. musician (choir dir. and organist)and music tchr., organist, music tchr., St. Mary's Academy and Coll., St. Mary's, Kans. 2000-present. Avocations: collecting cars, travel. Home: 3622 Cleveland St NE Minneapolis MN 55418

KAESS, KEN, advertising executive; Grad., Vassar Coll., 1976. Acct. exec. Doyle Dane Bernbach, 1976; pres. DDB Worldwide, N.Y.C., 1999—, CEO, 2000—. Mem.: Am. Assn. Advt. Agys. (chmn.). Office: DDB Worldwide Omnicom Group Inc 437 Madison Ave New York NY 10022*

KAESTNER, JOHN THOMAS, beverage company executive; b. St. Louis, Nov. 25, 1950; s. Albert Theodore and Dolores Marion Kaestner Jr.; m. Linda Sue Kincaid, Feb. 16, 1973 (div. Sept. 1991); children: Jennifer, John Jr.; m. JoAnn M. Rhodus Breheny, Dec. 19, 1992; stepchildren: Patrick Breheny, Julie Breheny Morris, Kathleen Breheny. BA in Elem. Edn., Harris Tchrs. Coll., 1973; MA in Edn., St. Louis U., 1977. Cert. tchr., prin., Mo. Tchr. Parkway Sch. Dist., Chesterfield, Mo., 1973-78; sales tng. instr. Anheuser-Busch Cos., Inc., St. Louis, 1978-80, mgr. beer mktg. mgmt. devel., 1980-86, mgr. mktg. planning and analysis, 1986-89, sr. mgr. consumer awareness and edn., 1989-94, sr. group, dir. consumer awareness and edn., 1994—2002, v.p. consumer affairs, 2002—. Planning and adv. com. Characters Plus, St. Louis, 1995—; com. mem. 2004, St. Louis, 1997—; bd. dirs. BACCHUS/Gamma Peer Edn. Network, 1999—, Family and Relationship Ctr., La Jolla, 1997—, Nat. Bus. Alliance of the Am. Sch. Counselor Assn., Alexandria, 1995—, Nat. Acad. League, Salt Lake City, 1997—; bd. dirs., Ea. Mo. Better Bus. Bur., 2001—. Recipient Disting. Alumni award Harris Tchrs. Coll., 1997 Roman Catholic. Avocations: golf, snow skiing, softball. Home: 777 Carman Meadows Dr Manchester MO 63021-7174 Office: Anheuser-Busch Cos Inc One Busch Place Saint Louis MO 63118

KAFARSKI, MITCHELL I. chemical processing company executive; b. Detroit, Dec. 15, 1917; s. Ignacy A. and Anastasia (Drzazgowski) K.; m. Zofia Drozdowska, July 11, 1967; children: Erik Michael, Konrad Christian. Student, U. Detroit, 1939-41, Shrivenham (Eng.) Am. U., 1946. Process engr. Packard Motor Car Co., Detroit, 1941-44; organizer, dir. Artist and Craftsman Sch., Esslingen, Germany, 1945-46; with Nat. Bank of Detroit, 1946-50; founder, pres. Chem. Processing Inc., Detroit, 1950-65, also bd. dirs.; chmn. bd., pres., treas. Aactron Inc., Madison Heights, Mich., 1965—; chmn. bd., pres. Imtech of Mich., Inc., 1988-92. Treas. Detroit Magnetic Insp. Co., 1960-65; also dir.; v.p. KMH Inc., Detroit, 1960-64; also dir.; treas. Packard Plating Inc., Detroit, 1962-67, also dir. Commr. Mich. State Fair, 1965-72; mem. com. devel. and planning to build Municipal Stadium State of Mich., 1965-88; benefactor, mem. Founders Soc., Detroit Inst. Arts, 1965— ; trustee Founders' Soc., Detroit Inst. Arts, 1982-90; sponsor, host world celebrity for World Preview Mich., 1965-66; mem. dist. adv. council SBA, 1971-73; del. White House Conf. on Aging, 1971; organizer, treas. Mich. Reagan for Pres. Com., 1980; treas. Straith Meml. Hosp., Southfield, Mich., 1972—, chmn. bd., 1976; trustee Mich. Opera Theater, 1982— ; bd. dirs. Gilbert and Sullivan Light Opera Soc., Palm Beach, Fla., 1985— ; White House rep. to opening of first U.S. Trade Center, Warsaw, Poland, 1972; chmn. fund-raising Bloomfield Arts Assn., Birmingham, Mich., 1973-74; mem. Space Theatre Consortium, Inc., Seattle, 1981-83; bd. regents Orchard Lake (Mich.) Schs., 1981-83; Vice chmn. Republican State Nationalities Council Mich., 1969-73; bd. dirs. Bloomfield Arts Assn., 1973-84, Friends of Kresge Library, Oakland U., 1973-86; presdl. appointee bd. dirs. U.S.A. Pennsylvania Ave. Devel. Corp., Washington, 1973-81; chmn. bd. Straith Meml. Hosp., Detroit, 1971—, Detroit Sci. Center, 1972—, corp. dir.; mem. Internat. Soc. Palm Beach; trustee Greater Palm Beach Symphony, 1986; mem. Citizen's Commn. to Improve Mich. Cts., 1986-88; contbr. Kravis Ctr. for Performing Arts, West Palm Beach, 1989; mem. Bus. Com. for the Arts, Palm Beacvh, 1991—. Served with AUS, 1944-46, ETO. Recipient Nat. award for war prodn. invention War Prodn. Bd., 1943; decorated knight's Cross Order of Poland's Rebirth Restituta, 1975, chevalier Chaine des Rotisseurs, 1982, Knight of Malta Order of St. John. Mem. Nat. Assn. Metal Finishers, Mich. Assn. Metal Finishers (dir., chmn. bd. 1976), N.A.M., Am. Electroplaters Soc., Cranbrook Acad. Arts, Am.-Polish Action Coun. (chmn. 1971-76), Am. Assn. Mus. (treas. Detroit), Poinciana Club, Village Club. Clubs: Capitol Hill (Washington); Detroit Athletic. Home: 21 Kingsley Manor Ct Bloomfield Hills MI 48304-3520 Office: Aactron Inc 29306 Stephenson Hwy Madison Heights MI 48071-2394 *A basic ingredient to success usually is determined by special events in one's life. In the course of my experiences, a sprinkling of tribulations were a must. From these were gleaned the principles, goals and conduct in attaining success. During the course of my life's pursuit, the ability to help others ensured a complete fulfillment of my goals.*

KAFENTZIS, JOHN CHARLES, journalist, educator; b. Butte, Mont., Aug. 18, 1953; s. Christian and Betty Ann (Gaston) K.; m. Teresa Marie Nokleby, June 5, 1976; children: Kathryn Anne, Christian John. BA in Journalism, U. Mont., 1975. Reporter The Missoulian, Missoula, Mont., 1974-76, The Hardin (Mont.) Herald, 1976, The Spokesman-Rev., Spokane, Wash., 1976-80, copy editor, 1980-83, chief copy desk, 1983-89, news editor, 1989-94, news designer, 1994—. Adj. faculty Ea. Wash. U., Cheney, 1982—, Whitworth Coll., 1998. Greek Orthodox. Avocation: competitive swimming. Office: The Spokesman Rev 999 W Riverside Ave Spokane WA 99201-1098

KAFF, ALBERT ERNEST, journalist, author; b. Atchison, Kans., June 14, 1920; s. John and Ethel Mae (Worley) K.; m. Lee Chuan Diana Fong, Oct. 15, 1960; children: Arthur Fong, Alban Fong. BA in Econs., U. Colo., 1942. Reporter Atchison Globe, summers 1939-41, Ponca City (Okla.) News, 1946-48, Daily Oklahoman, Oklahoma City, 1948-50; fgn. corr. U.P.I., Korea and Japan, 1952-56, bur. mgr., 1956—58, Taipei, Taiwan, 1958—61, Manila, Philippines, 1961—63, news editor, 1963-72, dir. Asian svcs., 1972-75, asst. dir., dir. pers. rels., 1975-78, v.p., gen. mgr. Asia-Pacific Hong Kong, 1978-84, v.p., mgr. N.Y., 1984-85; media cons., 1985; bus. internat. editor Cornell U. News Svc., 1986-93. Freelance journalist Stamford, Conn., Alexandria, Va., Fairfield, Conn., 1993—; columnist Overseas Press Club Bull. Contbg. author: How I Got That Story, 1967, Eyewitness on Asia, 1997, Foreign Correspondents in Japan: Covering a Half Century of Upheavals from 1945 to the Present, 1998; author: (with Avner Arbel) Crash: Ten Days in October. . . Will It Strike Again?, 1989. Served with AUS, 1943-46, 50-52. Decorated Bronze Star Mem. Fgn. Corrs. Club Japan (pres. 1967-68), Fgn. Corrs. Club Hong Kong (pres. 1974-75), Overseas Press Club Am. (v.p. 1984-86, bd. dirs. 1988-92, trustee Found. 1992—), Ithaca Press Club (vice chmn. 1987-88) Sigma Chi. Episcopalian. Home and Office: 393 Unquowa Rd Fairfield CT 06824-5028 *During 52 years of reporting, writing and editing the news, I missed several opportunities because I ignored a basic rule: If you can accomplish the assignment today or tomorrow, do it today. Tomorrow will bring new demands.*

KAFFENBERGER, ERNST WILHELM, engineer; b. Worms, RhineHesse, Germany, Dec. 13, 1931; s. Ernst Wilhelm and Friedericke (Roth) K.; m. Erna Cicillie Hansen, Mar. 9, 1957; children: Rüdiger, Sievert. Grad. automotive electrician, Worms Rhine, Germany, Worms Rhine, Fed. Republic of Germany, 1951; BSEE, Hochschule für Technik, Mannheim Rhine, Germany, 1957. Automotive electrician Rhine Engr. Depot U.S. Army, Kaiserslautern, Palatina, Germany, 1951-52; devel. engr. ANT Nachrichtentechnik, Backnang, Baden Wtbg, Germany, 1957-69, dept. head Devel. Dept. for Microwave guides and components, 1969-93, specialist embedded software in contrs., 1993-95. Vice chmn. subcom. 412.4 German Electrotech. Commn., 1980-95 Contbr. articles to tech. jours. Coach Judo-sport Gymnastics and Sports Community, Backnang, Fed. Republic of Germany, 1982—. Mem. Jagdspaniel Club. Evangelic Christian. Achievements include invention of microwave antenna component, microwave waveguides. Home: Tannenweg 6 Ostalb-Kreis D-73565 Spraitbach Germany E-mail: ernst.kaffenberger@t-online.de.

KAFFER, ROGER LOUIS, bishop; b. Joliet, Ill., Aug. 14, 1927; s. Earl Louis and Helen Ruth (McManus) K.. BA, St. Mary of the Lake, Mundelein, Ill., 1950, STB, 1952, MA, 1953, licentiate in sacred theology, 1954; licentiate of canon law, Pontifical Gregorian U., Rome, 1958; D of Pastoral Ministry, St. Mary of the Lake, Mundelein, Ill., 1983; MEd, DePaul U., 1965; LHD (hon.), Felician Coll., 1986; DHL (hon.), Coll. St. Francis, 1990; doctorate (hon.), Lewis U., 1990. Ordained priest Roman Cath. Ch., 1954; cert. K-14 supr. Ill. Eccles. notary Roman Cath. Diocese of Joliet, 1954—56; asst. chancellor Roman Cath. Diocese Joliet, 1958—65; aux. bishop Roman Cath. Diocese of Joliet, 1985—, vicar gen., vicar for clergy, 1985—; rector St. Charles Borromeo Sem., Lockport, Ill., 1965—70; prin. Providence High Sch., New Lenox, Ill., 1970—85; rector Cathedral of St. Raymond, Joliet, 1985; consecrated bishop, 1985; ret., 2002. Past. mem. Marriage Tribunal, Diocesan Sem. Bd., Diocesan Bd. Religious Edn. Named Cleric of Yr., KC, 1973, Citizen of Yr., New Lenox Assn. Commerce, 1976, Man of Yr., Joliet Cath. High Alumni Assn., 1978, Citizen of Yr., UNICO, Joliet, 1996; recipient DeLa Salle medallion, Lewis U., 1984, Lifetime Achievement award, Joliet C. of C., 1999, award, Paluch Family Found., 2002. Mem.: Nat. Conf. Cath. Bishops Conf. Ill., KC (Ill. state chaplain 1993—). Roman Catholic. Avocations: youth work, retreat work. Address: 425 Summit St Joliet IL 60435-7155

KAFIN, ROBERT JOSEPH, lawyer; b. Phila., Jan. 1, 1942; s. Jacob A. and Anna C. (Cohen) K.; m. Carol A. Friedman, June 20, 1965; children: Tammy Ellen, Peter Douglas. AB, Franklin & Marshall Coll., 1963; JD, Harvard U., 1966. Bar: N.Y. 1967, U.S. Dist. Ct. (so. dist.) N.Y. 1968, U.S. Dist. Ct. (no. dist.) N.Y. 1971, U.S. Dist. Ct. (we. dist.) N.Y. 1974, U.S. Ct. Appeals (2d cir.) 1971, U.S. Supreme Ct. 1972, D.C. 1997. Ptnr. Kafin and Needleman, Glens Falls, N.Y., 1971-78; prin. Miller, Mannix, Lemery & Kafin, Glens Falls, N.Y., 1978-87; assoc. Proskauer Rose LLP, N.Y.C., 1967-71, ptnr., 1987-91, chief operating officer, ptnr., 1991—. Trustee Adirondack Conservancy Com., Elizabethtown, N.Y., 1980-87; judge Glens Falls City Ct., 1976; counsel N.Y. State Senate, Albany, N.Y., 1973-87. Editor: N.Y. Environmental Law Handbook, 1988, 92. Bd. dirs. Environ. Planning Lobby, Albany, 1977-88; active Manhattan Solid Waste Adv. Bd., N.Y.C., 1987—; dir. N.Y. Parks and Conservation Assn., 1995—, chmn., 1999; trustee Preservation League N.Y. State, 1997—. Mem. N.Y. Bar Assn. (sec. environ. law sect. 1988, treas. 1989, 1st vice chmn. 1991, chair 1992-93), Assn. Bar City N.Y. (environ. law com. 1987-89). Democrat. Jewish. Home: 340 E 72d St Apt 3-SE New York NY 10021 Office: Proskauer Rose LLP 1585 Broadway Fl 27 New York NY 10036-8299

KAFKA, GERALD ANDREW, lawyer; b. Martins Ferry, Ohio, Sept. 9, 1951; s. Andrew and Mary (Spustek) K.; m. Rita A. Cavanagh; children: Andrea, Sarah, Justin. BA, Wheeling Jesuit Coll., 1972; JD, U. Cin., 1975; LLM in Taxation, Georgetown U., 1979. Bar: Ohio 1975, D.C. 1982, Md. 1984, U.S. Tax Ct. 1977, U.S. Claims Ct. 1978, U.S. Supreme Ct. 1979, D.C. 1982, U.S. Dist. Ct. (D.C. dist.) 1983, U.S. Ct. Appeals (D.C., fed., 3d, 4th, 5th, 6th, 7th 8th and 9th cirs.). Trial atty. honors program tax div. U.S. Dept. Justice, Washington, 1975-79; ptnr. Scribner, Hall & Thompson, Washington, 1979-84, Sutherland, Asbill & Brennan, Washington, 1984-92, Dewey Ballantine, Washington, 1992-2000, Mokee Nelson, LLP, Washington, 2000—03, Latham & Watkins, 2003—. Mem. adj. faculty Georgetown U. Law Ctr., Washington, 1979—; master J. Edgar Murdoch Am. Inn of Ct., U.S. Tax Ct., 1989—. Author: Litigation of Federal Tax Civil Controversies, 1996; editor procedure dept. Jour. Taxation; contbr. articles to profl. jours. Named Outstanding Atty., Tax Divsn. U.S. Dept. Justice, Washington, 1977. Fellow Am. Coll. Tax Counsel; mem. ABA (chair ct. procedure com. tax sect. 1993-95, chmn. task force civil tax litigation process 1989-90, task force on large case audits and litigation 1990-91, ad hoc joint com. tax ct. jurisdiction 1987, task force on taxpayer bill of rights legis 1987-88), D.C. Bar Assn. (steering com. tax sect. 1986-91, chmn. com. audits and litigation tax sect. 1987). Office: 555 Eleventh St NW Washington DC 20004 E-mail: gkafka@mckeenelson.com.

KAFKA, JOHN ABRAHAM, pediatrician; b. Petach-Tikva, Israel, Sept. 21, 1950; s. Heinz Leopold and Miriam K.; m. Betsy R. Frank; children: Benjamin E., Abigail E., Simon M. BA, U. Calif., San Diego, 1972, MD, 1977. Diplomate Am. Bd. Pediats. Attending pediatrician, asst. clin. prof. U. Calif. Med. Ctr., San Diego, 1981—; chair dept. pediats. Sharp Rees Stealy Med. Group, San Diego, 1992-98, regional med. dir., 1998—. Fellow Am. Acad. Pediats. Office: 5525 Grossmont Ctr Dr PO Box 9012 La Mesa CA 91944-9012

KAFKA, MARIAN STERN, neuroscientist; b. Richmond, Va., Mar. 30, 1927; d. Henry Sycle and Adele (Lewit) Stern; m. John S. Kafka, Oct. 3, 1952; children: David Egon, Paul Henry, Alexander Charles. AB in Zoology, Conn. Coll., 1948; PhD in Physiology, U. Chgo., 1952. Rsch. asst. dept. physiol. chemistry Emory U. Sch. Medicine, Atlanta, 1952-53; rsch. assoc. Ill. Neuropsychiat. Inst., U. Ill. Sch. Medicine, Chgo., 1953-54; rsch. asst. dept. internal medicine Yale U. Sch. Medicine, New Haven, 1954-57; USPHS postdoctoral fellow endocrinology br. Nat. Heart, Lung and Blood Inst. NIH, Bethesda, Md., 1965-68, physiologist hypertention-endocrine br., 1968-74, physiologist sect. biochemistry and pharmacology Biol. Psychiatry Br., 1974-82; physiologist Clin. Neurosci. Br. NIMH, Bethesda, 1982-86, exec. sec. neurobehavioral rsch. rev. subcom., neuroscis. rsch. rev. com. Rockville, Md., 1986, exec. sec. cellular neurobiology & psychopharmacology com., 1986-90, chief clin. rev. br. divsn. extramural activities, 1990. Contbr. articles, revs. to sci. publs. Recipient Adminstr.'s award for Meritorious Achievement, ADAMHA, 1989; Marie J. Mergler fellow in physiology, 1950. Mem. AAAS, Am. Physiol. Soc. (mem. pub. affairs and pub. info. com. 1974-79, chair pub. info. com. 1980-84, centennial com. 1979-85), Soc. for Neurosci., Endocrine Soc., Biophys. Soc., Internat. Soc. Chronobiology, Fedn. Am. Soc. for Exptl. Biology (pub. info. com. 1977-82), Phi Beta Kappa, Sigma Xi. Achievements include research in neurotransmitter receptors in animals and humans, molecular interactions between neurotransmitters, receptors and cell membranes, central nervous system control of circadian rhythms. Home: 7834 Aberdeen Rd Bethesda MD 20814-1102 Office: NIMH Parklawn Bldg 5600 Fishers Ln Rm 902C Rockville MD 20852-1750

KAFKER, FRANK A. historian, educator; b. N.Y.C., Dec. 18, 1931; s. Robert and Ida (Schear) K.; m. Serena Lipton, Dec. 20, 1953; children: Scott, Roger. BA, Columbia Coll., 1953, MA, 1954, PhD, 1961. From instr. to assoc. prof. Corning (N.Y.) C.C., 1958-62; from asst. prof. to prof. U. Cin., 1962-98, emeritus prof., 1998—. Author: The Encyclopedists as a Group, 1996; co-author: The Encyclopedists as Individuals, 1988; editor: Notable Encyclopedias of the 17th & 18th Centuries, 1981, Notable Encyclopedias of Late 18th Century, 1994; co-editor: The French Revolution, 1968, 5th edit., 2002, Napoleon and His Times, 1989. Fulbright fellow, 1954-55, Camargo Found fellow, 1993, Am. Philosophical Soc. fellow, 1978. Mem. Soc. French Hist. Studies (co-editor 1985-92), Soc. 18th Century French Studies (pres. 1995-97), Am. Soc. 18th Century Studies, Soc. Diderot, Br. Soc. 18th Century Studies, 18th Century Scottish Studies Soc. Home: 31 Brimmer St Apt 4 Boston MA 02108-1014 E-mail: fkafker@msn.com.

KAFOURE, MICHAEL D. food products executive; BS in Mgmt. and Adminstrn., Ind. U. Pres., COO U.S. baking ops. Interstate Bakeries Corp., Kansas City, Mo.; pres. Merico, Inc., St. Louis. Office: Interstate Bakeries Corp 12 E Armour Blvd Kansas City MO 64111

KAGAN, ANDREW BESDIN, lawyer, educator; b. Pittsfield, Mass., Apr. 26, 1949; s. David Bernard and Irene Sylvia (Besdin) K. BA in Psychology, Syracuse U., 1971; MA in Psychiat. Social Work, U. Chgo., 1975; JD with honors, Rutgers U., 1980. Bar: Ill. 1980, U.S. Dist. Ct. (no. dist.) Ill. 1980, U.S. Ct. Appeals (7th cir.) 1980, U.S. Tax Ct. 1994. Psychiat. social worker Austen Riggs Ctr., Stockbridge, Mass., 1971-73, Michael Reese Hosp., Chgo., 1975-77; assoc. Mandel, Lipton & Stevenson, Ltd., Chgo., 1980-82; sole practice Chgo., 1982-85; of counsel Lawrence Y. Schwartz, Ltd., Lincolnwood, Ill., 1985—. Arbitrator, comml. panel Am. Arbitration Assn., Chgo., 1984, Better Bus. Bur., Chgo., 1984; instr. Northeastern Ill. U., Chgo., 1984. Mem. Cmty. Devel. Citizens' Adv. Coun., Village of Oak Park, Ill., 1986. Recipient Am. Jurisprudence award Lawyer's Coop. Pub. Co., Rochester, N.Y., 1980. Mem. Ill. Bar Assn., Chgo. Bar Assn. (lawyer referral svc. 1984). Office: 7366 N Lincoln Ave Ste 404 Lincolnwood IL 60712-1741

KAGAN, BRUCE LAURENCE, psychiatrist, scientist; b. N.Y.C., Aug. 1, 1953; s. Marshall Joseph Kagan and Eileen Barbara (Karsh) Hammond; m. Fay Ellen Read, Sept. 24, 1989. BA, Yale U., 1975; MD, PhD, Albert Einstein Coll. Medicine, 1982. Diplomate Am. Bd. Psychiatry and Neurology. Prof. psychiatry UCLA Sch. Medicine, 1998—; dir. Post Traumatic Stress Disorder Program West L.A. VA Med. Ctr., 1990-94. Contbr. articles to profl. jours. Recipient Pfizer Postdoctoral award, 1986, VA Career Devel. award, 1986, Am. Psychiat. Assn.-Burroughs-Wellcome fellowship, 1984, First award Nat. Inst. Mental Health, 1988, VA Merit Rev. award, 1987, Nat. Inst. Mental Health Rsch. Scientist Devel. award, 1994. Fellow Am. Psychiat. Assn. Achievements include discovery of channel forming properties of toxins such as colicins, diphtheria toxin, yeast killer toxin, tumor necrosis factor, defensins, protegrins, amylin, prions. Office: UCLA Med Sch 760 Westwood Plz Los Angeles CA 90095-8353

KAGAN, DONALD, historian, educator; b. Kurshan, Lithuania, May 1, 1932; arrived in US, 1934, naturalized, 1940; s. Max and Leah (Benjamin) K.; m. Myrna Dabrusky, Jan. 13, 1955; children: Robert William, Frederick Walter. AB, Bklyn. Coll., 1954; MA, Brown U., 1955; PhD, Ohio State U., 1958. Instr. history Pa. State U., University Park, 1959-60; asst. prof. ancient history Cornell U., 1960-64, asso. prof., 1964-67, prof., 1967; sterling prof. classics & history Yale U., 1969—2002, master Timothy Dwight Coll., 1976-78, acting dir. athletics, 1987-88, dean Yale Coll., 1989-92. Author: The Great Dialogue, 1965, The Outbreak of the Peloponnesian War, 1969, The Archidamian War, 1974, The Western Heritage, 1979, (with Frank Turner and Steven Ozment) The Peace of Nicias and the Sicilian Expedition, 1981, The Fall of the Athenian Empire, 1987, Pericles of Athens and the Birth of Democracy, 1991, On the Origins of War and the Preservation of Peace, 1995, (with Frederick W. Kagan) While America Sleeps, 2000; The Peloponnesian War, 2003. Recipient Nat. Humanity Medal, 2002. Home: 37 Woodstock Rd Hamden CT 06517-2949 Office: Yale Univ Hall of Grad Studies 215 New Haven CT 06502 E-mail: donald.kagan@snct.net.

KAGAN, ELENA, law educator; b. 1960; BA summa cum laude, Princeton, 1981; MPhil, Worchester Coll., Oxford, 1983; JD magna cum laude, Harvard Law School, 1986. Law clk. US Ct. of Appeals for Judge Abner Mikva of the US Supreme Ct. for the DC Circuit, 1986—87, US Ct. of Appeals for Justice Thurgood Marshall of the US Supreme Ct., 1987—88; assoc. Williams & Connolly, Wash., DC, 1989—91; faculty mem. Univ. of Chgo. Law Sch., Chgo. 1991—99; nominated to serve as judge US Supreme Ct. of Appeals, Wash., DC 1999—99; asst. prof. Univ. of Chgo. Law Sch., 1991, prof. of law tenure, 1995 assoc. counsel to the Pres. White House, Wash., DC, 1995—96, dep. asst. to the Pres. for Domestic Policy, 1997—99, dep. dir. of the Domestic Policy Coun. 1997—99; vis. prof. Harvard Law Sch., Cambridge, Mass., 1999, prof., 2001—, dean, 2003—, Charles Hamilton Houston prof. of law, 2003—. Author: (article) Harvard Law Rev. Article, "Pres. Admin.", 2001 (honored as the year's top scholarly article by the Am. Bar Assoc. Section on Admin. Law and Reg. Pract. 2001). Kagan has also written on a range of First Amendment issues, including the role of governmental motive in different facets of First Amendment doctrine, and the interplay of libel law and the First Amendment. Mem. Harvard Law Sch. faculty appt. comm., Harvard Law Sch. Locational options comm. (chair 2001—02). Kagan is a prof. of law at Harvard fLaw Sch. where she teaches admin. law, constitutional law, and civil procedure. Her recent sholarship focuses primarily on the role of the Pres. of the US in formulating and influencing fed. admin. and regulatory law. Office: Harvard Law Sch Griswold 200 1563 Mass Ave Cambridge MA 02138*

KAGAN, ILSE ECHT, research librarian, village historian; b. Free City of Danzig, Sept. 23, 1927; d. Samuel and Hella Echt; m. Robert A. Kagan, Aug. 26, 1951 (dec. Oct. 1994); children: Jonathan, Miki. BA (hon.), Oxford (Eng.) U., MA, 1954; MLS, Columbia U., 1960. With Pira Energy, N.Y.C., 1987—; village historian Village of Gt. Neck (N.Y.) Estates, 1996—. Past pres. Gt. Neck Estates Civic Assn., sec., 2000—; past pres. Gt. Neck chpt. Hadassah; bd. dirs. Am. Jewish Com. Mem.: Oxford U. Club, Brit. Schs. Univ. Club, Harvard Club. Avocations: tennis, theater, music. Home: 25 Elm St Great Neck NY 11021 Office: Pira Energy 3 Park Ave New York NY 10016 E-mail: piraiek@concentric.net.

KAGAN, JEROME, psychologist, educator; b. Newark, Feb. 25, 1929; s. Joseph and Myrtle (Liebermann) K. BS, Rutgers U., 1950; PhD, Yale, 1954. Instr. psychology Ohio State U., 1954-55; research assoc. Fels Research Inst., Yellow Springs, Ohio, 1957-59, chmn. dept. psychology, 1959-64; assoc. prof. psychology Antioch Coll., 1959-64; rsch. prof. psychology Harvard U., 1964-2000, dir. Mind Brain Behavior Initiative, 1996-2000, rsch. prof., 2000—. Adv. com. Nat. Inst. Child Health and Devel. Author (with G.S. Lesser): Contemporary Issues in Thematic Apperceptive Methods, 1961; author: (with Moss) Birth to Maturity, 1962; author: (with Mussen, Conger and Huston) Child Development and Personality, 7th edit., 1990; author: (with Segal) Psychology, 7th edit., 1991; author: (with Janis, Mahl and Holt) Personality, 1969, Understanding Children, 1971, Change and Continuity in Infancy, 1971; author: (with Kearsley and Zelazo) Infancy, 1978; author: (with Brim) Constancy and Change, 1980, The Second Year, 1981, The Nature of the Child, 1984; author: Unstable Ideas, 1989, Galen's Prophecy, 1994, Three Seductive Ideas, 1998, Surprise, Uncertainty and Mental Structures, 2002. Served with AUS, 1955-57. Recipient Lucius Cross medal Yale U., 1981; Phi Beta Kappa scholar, 1988-89. Fellow AAAS, APA (Disting. Sci. Contbn. award 1987, G. Stanley Hall award 1995), Am. Acad. Arts and Scis., Soc. Rsch. Child Devel. (Disting. Sci. Contbn. award 1989); mem. NAS, Inst. Medicine, Ea. Psychol. Assn. Home: 210 Clifton St Belmont MA 02478-2605 Office: Harvard U Dept Psychology William James Hall 33 Kirkland Hl Cambridge MA 02138 E-mail: jk@wjh.harvard.edu. *My success has been aided by a combination of hard work, openess to new ideas, a readiness to discard beliefs that are proven invalid; a desire to nurture the growth of others; and belief in the beauty of ideas and the perfectibility of man.*

KAGAN, JULIA LEE, magazine editor; b. Nurnberg, Fed. Republic Germany, Nov. 25, 1948; d. Saul and Elizabeth J. Kagan. AB, Bryn Mawr Coll., 1970. Rschr. Look Mag., N.Y.C., 1970-71; editl. asst., asst. editor McCall's mag., N.Y.C., 1971-74, assoc. editor, 1974-78, sr. editor, 1978-79; articles editor Working Woman mag., N.Y.C., 1979-85, exec. editor, 1985-88; editor Psychology Today, 1988-90; sr. editor McCalls, 1990-91; contbg. editor Working Woman, 1991-93; editor-in-chief Lamaze Parents' Mag., 1992-93, Lamaze Baby Mag., 1993; spl. projects dir. Child Mag., 1993-94; sr. v.p. EDK Assocs., N.Y.C., 1994; psychology/health dir. Fitness Mag., N.Y.C., 1995-96; dep. editor Consumer Reports Mag., Yonkers, NY, 1996, editor, 1996-2000; v.p. and editl. dir. Consumers Union, 2000—. Vis. J. Stewart Riley prof. journalism Ind. U., 1991-93. Co-author: Manworks: A Guide to Style, 1980; contbg. author: The Working Woman Success Book, 1981, The Working Woman Report, 1984. Pres. Appleby Found., N.Y.C., 1982-84; trustee Bryn Mawr Coll., 2000—. Recipient 2d Ann. Advt. Journalism award Compton Advt., 1983 Mem. Am. Soc. Mag. Editors, Womens Media Group (bd. dirs.), Journalism and Women Symposium (treas. 1993-94, pres. 1995-96). Clubs: Princeton (N.Y.C.). Office: Consumer Reports 101 Truman Ave Yonkers NY 10703-1044*

KAGAN, MARILYN D. retired architect; b. Providence, Nov. 13, 1930; d. Jacob L. and Emma Kenner Kagan. BS in Arch., Drexel U., 1972. Cartographer U.S. Army Map Svc., Providence, 1952-53, Redevel. Authority, Phila., 1958-58; architect George Ewing Inc., Phila., 1969-70, City of Phila. Water Dept., 1971-91; ret., 1991. Designer jewelry. Bd. dirs. Philly Walks-Pedestrian Safety Coalition, 1996-98; chair Soviet Jewry Com. of Society Hill Synagogue, Phila., 1980-90. Recipient Cert. of Appreciation, Jewish Family Svc., 1993-96. Mem.: Na'Amat/Pioneer Women (pres. R.I. chpt. 2002—). Democrat. Jewish. Avocations: jewelry design, painting, photography, gardening, travel. Home: 311 Rochambeau Ave Providence RI 02906-3507

KAGAN, RON, zoological park administrator; Gen. curator Dallas Zoo and Dallas Aquarium; curator Jerusalem Zool. Gardens; dir. Detroit Zool. Inst., 1992—. Bd. dirs. Mich. Natur Conservancy. Mem.: Am. Zool. Assn. (accreditation commn., nominations com.), Assn. of Wildlife Sanctuaries (bd. dirs.), Mich. Museums Assn. (bd. dirs.). Office: Detroit Zool Inst PO Box 39 8450 W Ten Mile Rd Royal Oak MI 48068-0039

KAGAN, STEPHEN BRUCE (SANDY KAGAN), chief financial officer; b. Elizabeth, NJ, Apr. 27, 1944; s. Herman and Ida (Nadel) K.; m. Susan D. Kaltman, July 3, 1966; children: Sheryl, Rachel BS in Econs., U. Pa., 1966; MBA in Fin., Bernard Baruch Coll., 1969. Chartered fin. analyst. Security analyst Merrill Lynch Pierce Fenner & Smith, N.Y.C., 1966-68; dir. rsch. Deutschmann & Co., N.Y.C., 1968-70; v.p. Equity Sponsors, Inc., N.Y.C., 1970-72; v.p., investment counselor Daniel H. Renberg & Assocs., Inc., LA, 1972—78; CFO, COO Carlson Travel Network, Van Nuys, Calif., 1978—95; ep. Excel Telecomms., Van Nuys, Calif., 1995—; CFO, ptnr. Tatum CFO Ptnrs., LLP, 2000—. Vice pres. bd. Temple Beth Hillel, North Hollywood, Calif., 1976-83 Mem. Inst. Cert. Fin. Analysts, Beta Gamma Sigma Avocations: golf, skiing, poker, travel. Home and Office: 13952 Weddington St Van Nuys CA 91401-5751

KAGAN, VAL ALEXANDER, engineer, researcher, educator; b. Odessa, Ukraine, Aug. 24, 1940; arrived in U.S., 1991, naturalized, 1998; m. Rina V. Kaplan, July 5, 1969; children: Atalia, Anna. BS, MS in Mech. Engring., Tech. U. Kaunas, Lithuania, 1964, PhD in Engring., 1970; DSc, Acad. Scis., Moscow, 1985. Design engr. R&D Co. Priekalas, Kaunas, 1965-66; postgrad. course scientist Tech. U. Kaunas, 1967-69, postdoctoral fellow, 1970-71, asst. prof., 1971-72; assoc. prof. Tech. U., Vilnius, Lithuania, 1972-84, prof., rsch. fellow, lead ctr., 1984-91; engr., sr. engr. Honeywell Internat. (formerly Allied Signal, Inc.), Morristown, NJ, 1992-95, sr. prin. scientist, 1996-98, applied technology leader, 1998—2002, BASF Corp., Mount Olive, NJ, 2003—. Mem. adv. bd. Vilnius U., 1983—91; sr. cons. Acad. Sci., Vilnius, 1984—91; mem. sci. coun. Russian Acad. Sci., Moscow, 1986—91. Editor: (magazine) Applied Mechanics, 1986—91; contbr. over than 300 articles to profl. jours. Mem.: ASME, AIAA, ASTM, Soc. Plastics Engrs. Achievements include 24 U.S. and European patents. Home: 122 Edgefield Dr Morris Plains NJ 07950-1960 Office: Honeywell Internat 101 Columbia Rd Morristown NJ 07960-4658 E-mail: val.kagan@honeywell.com.

KAGAWA, FRANK TAKESHI, critical care physician; b. San Francisco, May 1, 1957; s. Francis Takeshi and Lori Fusa (Shinsato) K.; m. Marjorie Harue Higashi, Oct. 11, 1987; children: Alan, Kirsten, Kelly. BA, U. Calif., Santa Cruz, 1979; MD, U. Calif., San Diego, 1983. Diplomate Am. Bd. Internal Medicine, Am. Bd. Critical Care, Am. Bd. Pulmonary Diseases. Resident in internal medicine Santa Clara Valley Med. Ctr., San Jose, Calif., 1983-86, chief resident in internal medicine, 1986-87; fellow pulmonary and critical care medicine Stanford (Calif.) U., 1987-89, clin. asst. prof., 1989-90; asst. chief respiratory and critical care medicine Santa Clara Valley Med. Ctr., San Jose, 1990-92, assoc. chief respiratory and critical care medicine, 1992—. Clin. assoc. prof. Stanford U., 1992-99, clin. prof., 1999—; dir. med. intensive care Santa Clara Valley Med. Ctr., San Jose, 1992—. Contbr. articles to profl. jours. Named one of Best Drs. in the Bay Area, San Francisco Focus mag., 1997, Best Drs. in Am., 1996, 1997, 2000, 2001, 2002, Top Drs. in Silicon Valley, San Jose mag., 1999—2002; recipient Best Drs. in the Bay Area, San Francisco Focus mag., 2003. Fellow Am. Coll. of Chest Physicians; mem. AMA, ACP, Am. Thoracic Soc., Soc. of Crtl. Care Medicine. Avocation: family. Office: Santa Clara Valley Med Ctr 751 S Bascom Ave San Jose CA 95128-2604

KÅGE, JONAS, ballet company artistic director; b. Stockholm; m. Deborah Dobson; 1 child, Isabelle. Student, Royal Swedish Ballet Sch. Mem. Royal Swedish Ballet, Am. Ballet Theatre, 1971-75, soloist, 1972-75, prin. dancer, 1973-75, Stuttgart (Germany) Ballet, 1975-76, Geneva (Switzerland) Ballet, 1976-78, Zürich (Switzerland) Ballet, 1978-88; artistic dir. Malmo (Sweden) Opera Ballet, 1988-95; freelance guest artist, master tchr., 1995-97; artistic dir. Ballet West, Salt Lake City, 1997—. Guest artist Am. Ballet Theatre, 1977—, Frankfort Ballet, Germany, Basel Ballet, Switzerland, Royal Swedish Ballet, 1980—81, Deutsche Opera Berlin, 1982, Pitts. Ballet, 1984—85, Nat. Ballet of Can., 1984—86, Milw. Ballet, 1984—85, NAPAC Dance Co., 1985—86, Munich Opera Ballet, 1985—86, Nat. Ballet of Portugal, 1986—87, Ariz. Ballet, 1987—88. Dancer prin. (ballets) Swan Lake, Coppélia, La Bayadere, Tales of Hoffmann, Lander's Etudes, Shadowplay, Leaves are Fading, Balanchine's Theme and Variations, Am. Ballet Theatre, 1971—75, Gemini, Some Times, Intermezzo, Les Noces, 1971—75, Swan Lake, Don Quixote, Sphinx, Voluntaries, 1977, The Taming of the Shrew, Romeo & Juliet, Onegin, Gemini, La Sacre de Printemps, Greening, Stuttgart Ballet, 1975—76, Apollo, The Four Temperaments, Agon Symphony in C, Who Cares?, Geneva Ballet, 1976—77, Romeo & Juliet, The Sleeping Beauty, Sphinx. Rosalinda, London Festival Ballet (now English Nat. Ballet), 1977, Cinderella, Swan Lake, Giselle, Romeo & Juliet, 1982—83, Swan Lake, Frankfort Ballet, 1980—81, Giselle, Basel Ballet, 1980—81, Don Quixote, Vienna Ballet, 1980—81, The Taming of the Shrew, Manon, Royal Swedish Ballet, 1980—81, La Sylphide, Deutsche Opera Berlin, 1982, Coppélia, Giselle, Greening, Apollo, Spoleto and Naples, 1982, Swan Lake, Pitts. Ballet Theatre, 1984—85, Romeo & Juliet, Nat. Ballet of Can., 1984—85, Swan Lake, 1985—86, The Merry Widow, Milw. Ballet, 1984—85, Apollo, NAPAC Dance Co., 1985—86, Romeo & Juliet, Munich Opera Ballet, 1985—86, Apollo, Nat. Ballet of Portugal, 1986—87, The Nutcracker, Ariz. Ballet, 1987—88; creator prin. role (ballets) Chopin Pas de Deux, Malmo Opera Ballet, 1993—94; choreographer (ballets) Swedish TV, 1983, Simple Symphony, Zurich Ballet, 1984, Baroque Variations, Malmo Opera Ballet, 1988, Swan Lake, 1992—93 (Thalia prize, 1993); master of ceremonies dance competition, Swedish TV, 1997. Bd. dirs. Swedish Dance U., Stockholm, Dalhalla amphitheater, Rattvik, Sweden. Recipient Dance medal, Carina Ari Found., 1994. Avocations: photography, skiing, mountain climbing, horseback riding, wilderness guide training.*

KAGGEN, LOIS SHEILA, non-profit organization executive; b. N.Y.C., Jan. 2, 1944; d. Elias and Sylvia (Muntner) K.; m. Harold Jay Burns, June 29, 1969 (dec. June 1975); 1 child, David Henry (dec.); m. Michael Francis McCann, Sept. 26, 1984. BS in Fine Arts, Skidmore Coll., 1964; postgrad., Cooper Union, 1967-70; MA in Art Edn., CCNY, 1973; PhD in Art Edn., NYU, 1997. Tchr. fine arts grades 7-9 Jr. H.S. 149, Bronx, N.Y., 1967-74; founder, pres. Resources for Artists With Disabilities, N.Y.C., 1987—. Traumatic Brain Injury Consumer Adv., 1977—; mem. adv. bd. com. Art in Edn. Project, N.Y. State Coun. on the Arts, Ctr. for Safety in the Arts, N.Y.C., 1987; cons. Ea. Paralyzed Vets. Assn., Guggenheim Mus. Art, N.Y.C., 1990; mem. bd. advisors Ind. Arts Gallery, Queens Ind. Living Ctr., Jamaica, N.Y., 1987-97, 98; mem. steering com. Ann. Disability Independence Day March, 1992-93, mem. Media Outreach, 1992; provider written and oral testimony in field to orgns. including N.Y. City Coun., 1992, 93, Severely Injured TBI Survivors Cognitive Dysfunctions and Needs, Coun. of City of N.Y. (com. on mental health, mental retardation, alcoholism, drug abuse and disability svcs., 2002), Nat. Coun. on Disability, N.Y.C., 1994, Washington, 1995, N.Y. State Assembly mems. and N.Y. State senators, 1994, 99, N.Y. State Standing Com., 1996, mem. citizens adv. coun. Andrew Heiskell Libr. for the Blind and Physically Handicapped, N.Y.C., 1997—; bd. dirs. Ctr. for Independence of the Disabled of N.Y., Inc., N.Y.C., 1996—, Gov.'s appt. to Traumatic Brain Injury Svcs. Coordinating Coun., Albany, 1997-2001, others; presenter NIH Consensus Devel. Conf. on Rehab. of Persons with Traumatic Brain Injury, Bethesda, Md., 1998, 5th Ann. Conf., Traumatic Brain Injury Program, N.Y. State Dept. Health, Albany, 1998, Info. and Comm. Com. TDISEC (TBI Coun.) NYS-DOH, Delmar, N.Y., 2001, N.Y. State Assembly task force on people with disabilites: pub. hearing City U. N.Y. Grad. Ctr., N.Y., 2001; originator, conf. com. co-organizer, consumer panelist NYU Moses Ctr. for Students with Disabilities and Ctr. for Independence of Disabled of N.Y., Loeb Student Ctr., NYU, N.Y.C., 1998; panel organizer, moderator, presenter Inst. for Rsch. on Women's 16th Ann. Celebration of Our Work Conf., Douglass Coll., Rutgers U., New Brunswick, N.J., 1998; art presenter in field. Photography exhbns. include 80 Washington Sq. East Galleries, N.Y.C., 1977, Soho Photo Gallery, N.Y.C., 1978, 4th St. Photo Gallery, N.Y.C., 1979, Womanart Gallery, N.Y.C., 1979, Leslie-Lohman Gallery, N.Y.C., 1980, 81, Window Gallery, Met. Savs. Bank, N.Y.C., 1980, Cathedral St. John-the-Devine Gallery, N.Y.C., 1980, Donnell Libr. Gallery, 1981; originator, organizer various exhbns. African-Am. Artists with Disabilities, Artists with Phys. Disabilities; contbr. articles, photographs to profl. jours. Mem. Nat. Inst. Disability and Rehab. Rsch.; mem. Office Spl. Edn. and Rehab. Svcs. U.S. Dept. Edn., Washington, mem. per rev. registry, 1995—; active Disabled in Action of Greater N.Y., 1989—, Manhattan Borough Pres. Disability Adv. Coun., 1988—98, 1999—; access subcom. 504 Dem. Club for Persons with Disabilities, 2000—; mem. Mayor's Adv. Com. on People with Disabilities, N.Y.C., 1991—93, Citywide Coalition on Disability, N.Y.C., 1994—95; active in assistive signage needs Planning Meeting NYC Coun./Dept. Disabled, 2000; mem. info. subcom. NYC Coun. Planning Com. Dept. Disabled, 2000—; mem. Disabilities Network of NYC, 2000—; mem. disability rights steering com. 504 Dem. Club for Persons with Disabilities, 1987—88, mem. exec. com., 1990—2002; mem. N.Y. County Dem. Com. 102ED, 1995—; mem. at-large exec. bd. Village Ind. Dems., 2003. Grantee Whitney Mus. Am. Art and the Smithsonian Instn., summer 1967, summer film inst. Stanford U., 1968; Cooper Union scholar, 1967-70; recipient Appreciation cert. Manhattan Borough Pres., 1991, Dean's Disting. Alumni Achievement award NYU, N.Y.C., 1998. Mem. Coll. Art Assn. (com. mems. with disabilities for accessible programs and places 1990—), N.Y.C. Coun. dept. for disabled. Office: Resources for Artists with Disabilities 77 7th Ave Ste PH-H New York NY 10011-6645

KAGIWADA, REYNOLD SHIGERU, electronics executive; b. LA, July 8, 1938; s. Harry Yoshifusa and Helen Kinue (Imura) K.; children: Julia, Conan. BS in Physics, UCLA, 1960, MS in Physics, 1962, PhD in Physics, 1966. Asst. prof. in residence physics UCLA, 1966-69; asst. prof. physics U. So. Calif., 1969-72; mem. tech. staff TRW (now NGST), Redondo Beach, Calif., 1972-75; scientist, sect. head TRW (now NGST), 1975-77, sr. scientist, dept. mgr., 1977-83, lab. mgr., 1984-87, project mgr., 1987-88, MIMIC chief scientist, 1988-89, asst. program mgr., 1989-90, advanced technology mgr., 1990—2001, dir. advanced electronics, 2002—. Presenter in field. Contbr. over 40 articles to profl. jours.; patentee 9 solid state devices. Recipient Gold Medal award TRW, 1985, Ramo Tech. award, 1985, Transfer award, IEEE MTT-S N. Walter Cox award, 1997. Fellow IEEE (v.p. IEEE MTT-S adminstrn. com. 1991, pres. 1992, Disting. Svc. award 2001); mem. Assn. Old Crows, Sigma Xi, Sigma Pi Sigma. Home: 3117 Malcolm Ave Los Angeles CA 90034-3406 Office: NGST Bldg M5 Rm 1492 One Space Park Bldg Redondo Beach CA 90278 E-mail: reynold.kagiwada@ngc.com.

KAGLE, JOSEPH LOUIS, JR., artist, arts administrator, art educator; b. Pitts., May 2, 1932; s. Joseph Louis and Edith (Marcellus) K.; m. Anne Cornelia Schiller, Jan. 19, 1957; children: Samantha Anne, Christopher Yung Wook. Student, Carnegie Mus. Sch. Art, 1938-51; BA in English, Dartmouth Coll., 1955; MFA in Art and Art History, U. Colo., 1958; MEd in Gifted and Talented Edn., U. Ark., Little Rock, 1984. Instr. Wis. State U., Whitewater, 1958-60; head dept. art, asst. prof. Washington and Jefferson Coll., Pa., 1960-64; head dept. art, assoc. prof. Keuka Coll., 1964-68; artist in residence Chapman Coll., World Campus Afloat, 1968-69; prof., head dept. fine arts, visual arts, dance, music and theatre U. Guam, 1970-76; prof. art Community Coll. Finger Lakes, 1976-78; exec. dir. S.E. Ark. Arts and Sci. Center, Pine Bluff, 1978-84; dir. Brockton (Mass.) Art Mus., 1984-86, The Art Ctr., Waco, Tex., 1987—2000, Bridgewater State Coll., 1986-87. Artist in residence Wash. State U., Spokane, 1965—66, Naples Mill Sch., 1976—2001, Internat. Plentary of Artists, Kutaisi, Georgia, 2001; bd. contbrs. Waco Tribune-Herald Opinion Edits.; lectr. USIS, Taiwan, 1970—76; critic Pine Bluff (Ark.) News. Work exhibited in over 400 nat. and internat. exhbns. including Nat. Gallery, Washington, Nat. Mus., Tiblisi, Georgia; dir. 50 TV shows on art; muralist, Hafa Adai Theatre, Bank of Guam, Fine Arts Bldg. U. Guam; author: Death Is All the Time, 1976. Mem. planning bd. Pine Bluff Com. Gifted and Talented, 1979-80; mem. adv. bd. Sta. KCTF, 1989-92; bd. dirs. Greater Waco Coun. on the Arts, 1989—; bd. dirs. Assn. for Retarded Citizens., chmn., 1990-92, 93-94. Named Fulbright scholar, Taiwan, 1965, Georgia, 2001—02, Smithsonian Instn. Kellog Found. Project scholar, 1983, artist of yr., Pacific chpt. AIA, 1976—77. Mem. Am. Mus. Assn., Coll. Art Assn., Tex. Assn. Mus., Coll. Art Assn., Am. Mus. Assn., Waco Assn. Mus. (chmn. bd. dirs. 1995-97), Waco C. of C. (bd. dirs. 1994-97). Home: 2924 Savannah Ct Waco TX 76710-1739 E-mail: joe_kagle@hotmail.com.

KAHALAS, HARVEY, business educator; b. Boston, Dec. 3, 1941; s. James and Betty (Bonfeld) K.; m. Dianne Barbara Levine, Sept. 2, 1963; children: Wendy Elizabeth, Stacy Michele. BS, Boston U., 1965; MBA, U. Mich., 1966; PhD, U. Mass., 1971. Data processing coord. Ford Motor Co., Wayne, Mich., 1963-66; lectr. Salem (Mass.) State Coll., 1966-68; asst. prof. bus. Worcester (Mass.) Poly. Inst., 1970-72; asst. prof. Va. Poly. Inst. and State U., Blacksburg, 1972-75, assoc. prof., 1975-77; SUNY, Albany, 1977-79, assoc. dean, 1979-81, prof., 1979-89, dean, 1981-87; pres. HKE Inc., 1987-97; prof. U. Mass., Lowell, 1989-94, dean, 1989-94, exec. dir. Ctr. Indsl. Competitiveness, 1990-94, Commonwealth disting. prof., 1994-97; dir. Ctr. for Bus. Rsch. and Competitiveness, U. Mass., Dartmouth, 1994-97; prof., dean Wayne State U., 1997—, exec. dir. Inst. for Orgn. and Indsl. Competitiveness, 2001—. Program dir. Aspen Inst., 1994—97; exec. dir. Inst. Orgnl. and Indsl. Competitiveness Wayne State U., 2001—; bd. dirs. Lumigen Inc., Southfield, Mich.; cons. Aspen Inst./Fund for Corp. Initiatives, N.Y.C., 1980—94, GE, Schenectady, NY, 1981—85, GM, Tarrytown, NY, 1987—89. Contbr. articles to profl. jours. Bd. dirs. Nat. Found. Ileitis and Colitis, Albany, NY, 1982—89, Fund for Corp. Initiatives, N.Y.C., 1980—, Blue Cross Northeastern N.Y., Albany, 1983—89, Capital Dist. Bus. Rev., Albany, 1984—, Greater Detroit Area Health Coun., 1998—2001, Greater Detroit Conv. and Visitors Bur., 2001—. Named Disting. Alumni, U. Mass., 1982, Disting. Lectr. USIA, 1985, Am. Participant USIA, 1989; Fulbright scholar, 1987, 88, Aspen Inst. scholar, 1997. Mem. Fulbright Assn. (life), Acad. Mgmt. (treas. 1971-73, mem. exec. com.), Human Resource Planning Soc. (hon.), Human Resource Systems Profls. (hon.), Pers. Accreditation Inst. (life), Beta Gamma Sigma, Sigma Iota Epsilon, Delta Tau Kappa. Office: Wayne State Univ Sch Bus Adm 226 Prentis Bld 5201 Cass Ave Detroit MI 48202-3930

KAHAN, BARRY DONALD, surgeon, educator; b. Cleve., July 25, 1939; s. Jacob Marvin and Pearl (Schultz) K.; m. Rochelle Liebling, Sept. 22, 1963, 1 child, Kara. BS, U. Chgo., 1960, PhD, 1964, MD, 1965. Intern Mass. Gen. Hosp., Boston, 1965-66, resident in surgery, 1968-72; staff asso. in immunology NIH, 1966-68; asst. prof. surgery and physiology Northwestern U. Sch. Medicine, Chgo., 1972-74, asso. prof., 1975-76; prof. surgery U. Tex. Med. Sch., Houston, 1977—, also dir. divs. organ transplantation dept. surgery, dir. program immunology, grad. sch. Bd. dirs. Ill. Kidney Found., 1974-76. Mem. ACS, AAAS, Soc. Univ. Surgeons, Am. Soc. Clin. Investigation, Am. Soc. Transplant Surgeons (pres. 1989—), Am. Surg. Assn., Internat. Transplantation Soc. (charter, treas. 1990—), Am. Surg. Assn., Am. Assn. Immunologists, Am. Assn. Cancer Rsch., Am. Physiol. Soc. Office: U Tex Houston MSB 6-240 6431 Fannin St Houston TX 77030

KAHAN, DAVID MICHAEL, education educator; b. Los Angeles, Sept. 21, 1967; s. Osher and Bernice Golden Kahan; m. Amy Laura Waldman, Sept. 5, 1993; children: Jeremy Aaron, Rachel Lyn. BS, UCLA, 1990, MEd in Tchr. Edn., 1991; PhD in Phys. Edn., Ohio State U., 1995. Asst. prof. U. Texas, Odessa, 1995—98, U. N. Mex., Albuquerque, 1998—2000; asst. prof. in phys. edn. San Diego State U., 2000. Author: (articles) various profl. jours., 1995—. Soccer coach Am. Youth Soccer Orgn., San Diego, 2002. Recipient Friend of Edn., Ector County Ind. Sch. Dist., 1998, Outstanding Tchrs. of Am., Ector Canty Ind. Sch. Dist., 2000. Mem.: Am. Alliance for Health Phys. Edn., Recreation & Dance, Nat. Assn. for Phys. Edn. in Higher Edn., Calif. Assn. for Health Phys. Edn., Recreation & Dance, Phi Kappa Phi (hon.). Democrat. Office: San Diego State U 5500 Campanile Dr San Diego CA 92182-7251

KAHAN, MARLENE, professional association executive; b. Bronx, N.Y., June 10, 1952; d. Meyer and Ruth (Baroth) Schmulewitz. BA in Psychology, CUNY, 1973. Tchr. elem. sch., Bronx, 1974-75; asst. to pres. Mag. Pubs. Am., N.Y.C., 1976-83; asst. dir. Am. Soc. Mag. Editors, N.Y.C., 1983-90, exec. dir., 1990—. Recipient Gold Key award PR News, 1991. Mem. Am. Soc. Assn. Execs., N.Y. Soc. Assn. Execs. (bd. dirs. 2000—), Women in Comms. (program com. N.Y.C. 1991-93, bd. dirs. 1993-95, v.p. programs 1993-95). Avocations: ballet, jazz dance and music. Office: Am Soc Mag Editors 919 3rd Ave New York NY 10022-3902 E-mail: mkahan@magazine.org.

KAHAN, MITCHELL DOUGLAS, art museum director; BA, U. Va., 1973; MA, Columbia U., 1975; M of Philosophy, CUNY, 1978, PhD, 1983. Mus. aide Nat. Mus. Am. Art, Washington, 1978; curator Montgomery (Ala.) Mus. Fine Art, 1978-82, N.C. Mus. Art, Raleigh, 1982-86; dir. Akron (Ohio) Art Mus., 1986—. Cons. La. World's Exposition, New Orleans, 1983-84. Author: Art Inc.: American Paintings in Corporate Collections, 1979, Roger Brown, 1981, Minnie Evans, 1986, Art Since 1850-Akron Art Museum, 2001. Columbia U. fellow, 1973, Smithsonian Inst. fellow, 1976-78, CUNY grad. research fellow, 1978, Nat. Endowment for Arts fellow, 1987. Mem. Coll. Art Assn., Intermus Conservation Assn. (trustee 1986-95, pres. 1990-92, 95), Assn. Art Mus. Dirs., Akron Area Arts Alliance (pres. 2003—), Akron Roundtable (pres. 2001). Office: Akron Art Mus 70 E Market St Akron OH 44308-2084

KAHAN, ROCHELLE LIEBLING, lawyer, concert pianist; b. Chgo., Sept. 5, 1939; d. Arnold Leo and Helly (Ichilson) Liebling; m. Barry D. Kahan, Sept. 22, 1962; 1 child, Kara. BA, Northwestern U., 1959, JD, 1963. Bar: Ill. 1963, Tex. 1977. Atty. Treasury Dept., Chgo., 1964-65, Boston, 1965-66, 68-72, Washington, 1966-67, pvt. practice, Chgo. and Houston, 1972—. Mem. ABA, Tex. Bar Assn., Houston Bar Assn., Houston Tuesday Musical Club (pres.), Treble Clef Club (past pres.), Kappa Beta Pi (past pres.), Mu Phi Epsilon. Avocation: early music.

KAHAN, SHELDON JEREMIAH (CHRISTOPHER REED), musician, singer; b. Honolulu, Mar. 5, 1948; s. Aaron Kahan and Marianne (Royjiczek) Sann. Student, Tel Aviv U., 1967-69, Merritt Coll., 1972-74. Guitarist The Grim Reapers, Miami Beach, Fla., 1965-66; bassist The Electric Stage, Jerusalem, 1969-71; music dir., musician Fanfare, L.A., 1974-75, Jean Paul Vignon & 1st Love, L.A., 1975-76; musician Jenny Jones & Co., L.A., 1976; musician, vocalist Fantasy, L.A., 1977-79; leader, musician, vocalist Fortune, L.A., 1980-83; bassist Johnny Tillotson Show, Nev., 1983; ptnr., musician, vocalist Heartlight, L.A., 1983-84; leader, musician, vocalist The Boogie Bros., L.A., 1984—; arranger, conductor L.A. Rock Chorus, 1988; musician, vocalist Jeremiah Kahan, L.A., 1988; bass player LIX, L.A., 1990—; solo act Sheldon Kahan, L.A., 1990—. Spokesman Moore Oldsmobile & Cadillac, Valencia, Calif., 1987. Compiled musical work Sheldon Jeremiah Kahan The Early Years - Vol. I, rec. artist Bandana Records; musician (albums): City Lights, Out of the Shadows; prodr.(and disk jockey): Kaleidoscope Radio Mag., Am. Radio Network; one-man shows include El Capitan, Irvine, Calif., 1990, Sagebrush Cantina, Calabassas, Calif., 1990, Don Jose, Artesia, Calif., Pineapple Hill, Tustin, Calif., 1991, The Fling, Tustin, 1992, Beverly Garland, North Hollywood, Calif., Brian Patch, Garden Grove, Calif., Sugar Suite, Granada Hills, Calif., 1993, The Blarney Stone, Fountain Valley, Calif., 1994, Sunset Lounge, Fullerton, Calif., Rembrandts, Placentia, Calif., 1995, Chez Lynn, Orange, Calif., 1996, Maxwells, Anaheim Hills, Royal Crown, Fullerton, Calif., 1997, The Oasis, Garden Grove, 1997, Azar's Red Robin, Newbury Park, Calif., The Stovepiper, Northridge, Calif., Volare, Northridge, 1998, On Grady's, Granada Hills, 1998, Sportspage, Placentia, 1998, Mary White & Christopher Reed (duo) The Odyssey, Granada Hills, 1999, Aussie Bobs, Van Nuys, Calif., 1999, Galios, Woodland Hills, Calif., 2000, The Sugar Mill, Tarzana, Calif., 2000, Paolis, Woodland Hills, The Pete Oden Show, 2001, The Sutler, Nashville, Hall of Fame Lounge, Just Pams, Clarksville. Mem. AFTRA, Am. Fedn. Musicians. Democrat. Jewish. Achievements include research in comparative religions. Avocations: chess, aerobics, weight training, comparative religions. Home: 7930 Hwy 70 S Nashville TN 37221 E-mail: boogiebro@aol.com.

KAHANA, EVA FROST, sociology educator; b. Budapest, Hungary, Mar. 21, 1941; came to U.S., 1957; d. Jacob and Sari Frost; m. Boaz Kahana, Apr. 15, 1962; children: Jeffrey, Michael. BA, Stern Coll., Yeshiva U., 1962; MA, CCNY, CUNY, 1965; PhD, U. Chgo., 1968; HLD (hon.), Yeshiva U., 1991. Nat. Inst. on Aging predoctoral fellow U. Chgo. Com. on Human Devel., 1963-66; postdoctoral fellow Midwest Council Social Research, 1968; with dept. sociology Washington U., St. Louis, 1967-71, successively research asst., research assoc., asst. prof.; with dept. sociology Wayne State U., Detroit, 1971-84, from assoc. prof. to prof., dir. Elderly Care Research Ctr., 1971-84; prof. Case Western Res. U., Cleve., 1984—, Armington Prof., 1989-90, chmn. dept. sociology, 1985—, dir. Elderly Care Research Ctr., 1984—, Pierce and Elizabeth Robson prof. humanities, 1990—. Cons. Nat. Inst. on Aging, Washington, 1976-80, NIMH, Washington, 1971-75. Author: (with E. Midlar-

sky) Altruism in Later Life, 1994; editor: (with others) Family Caregiving Across the Lifespan, 1994; mem. editl. bd. Gerontologist, 1975-79, Psychology of Aging, 1984-90, Jour. Gerontology, 1990-94, Applied Behavioral Sci. Rev., 1992—; contbr. articles to profl. jours., chpts. to books (recipient Pub.'s prize 1969). Bd. dirs. com. on aging Jewish Community Fedn., Cleve.; vol. cons. Alzheimer's Disease and Related Disorders Assn., Cleve. NIMH Career Devel. grantee, 1974-79, Nat. Inst. Aging Merit award grantee, 1989—; Mary E. Switzer Disting. fellow Nat. Inst. Rehab., 1992-93; recipient Arnold Heller award excellence in geriatrics and gerontology Menorah Park Ctr. for Aged, 1992, Diekhoff awrd for disting. grad. tchg., 2002; named Disting. Geontological Rschr. in Ohio, 1993. Fellow Gerontol. Soc. Am. (chair behavioral social sci. com. 1984-85, chair 2000—, Disting. Mentorship award 1987, Polisher award 1997); mem. Am. Sociol. Assn. (coun. sect. on aging 1985-87, Disting. Scholar award sect. on aging and life course 1997, chair sect. on aging and life course, 2000-2001), Am. Psychol. Assn., Soc. for Traumatic Stress, Wayne State U. Acad. Scholars (life), Sigma Xi. Avocations: reading, antiques, travel.

KAHANE, JEFFREY, conductor, pianist; b. L.A., Sept. 12, 1956; BMus, San Francisco Conservatory, 1977. Prof. piano Eastman Sch. Music, 1988-95; music dir. Santa Rosa (Calif.) Symphony, 1995—, L.A. Chamber Orch., 1996—, Green Music Festival, 2001—. Office: IMG Artists 825 7th Ave New York NY 10019-6014 E-mail: artistsny@imgworld.com.

KAHARICK, JEROME JOHN, lawyer; b. Johnstown, Pa., Apr. 15, 1955; s. Stanley Joseph and Emily (Solic) K.; m. Carolyn Marie Safko, Aug. 7, 1977; children: Natalie, Allison. BA summa cum laude, U. Pitts., 1977; JD, Duquesne U., 1991. Bar: Pa. 1991, N.Y. 2000, U.S. Dist. Ct. (we. dist.) Pa. 1991, U.S. Dist. Ct. (we. dist.) Mich. 1998, U.S. Dist. Ct. (no. dist.) N.Y. 1998, U.S. Ct. Appeals (3d cir.) 1992, U.S. Supreme Ct., 1997. Sales rep. Met. Life, Johnstown, Pa., 1977-84; owner, stockholder Planned Fin. Svcs., Johnstown, Pa., 1984-88; law clk. Wayman, Irvin & McAuley, Pitts., 1988-89; legal analyst Elliott Co., Jeannette, Pa., 1989-92; pvt. practice Johnstown, 1992-95, 97—; asst. pub. defender Cambria County, Pa., 1993-99; ptnr. Weaver and Kaharick, 1995-97; atty. in pvt. practice Johnstown, Pa., 1997—. Exec. production editor Duquesne Law Rev., 1990-91. Mem. ABA, ATLA, N.Y. Bar Assn., Nat. Assn. Criminal Def. Lawyers, Pa. Bar Assn., N.Y. State Bar Assn., Order of Barristers. Republican. Roman Catholic. Office: Wallace Bldg 406 Main St Ste 301-302 Johnstown PA 15901-1906

KAHIKINA, MICHAEL PUAMAMO, social services administrator, state legislator; b. Honolulu, Jan. 16, 1950; m. Naomi Abigail Barros; children: Puamamo, Kealoha, Kaua'i, Kanoe. AA, Leeward C.C., Pearl City, Hawaii, 1988; BS in Pub. Adminstrn., U. Hawaii-West Oahu, 1990. Utility electrician U.S. Navy Exch., Pearl Harbor, Hawaii, 1972-74; electrician City & County of Honolulu, 1974-75; outreach counselor Waianae Rap Ctr., 1975-79; social worker II Queen Liliuokalani Ctr., Nanakuli, Hawaii, 1979-85; agrl. specialist Honolulu Cmty. Action Program, Waianae, 1985-87; cmty. outreach . Hale Ola Ho'opakolea, Nanakuli, 1987-90; unit dir. Boys & Girls Club-Waianae, 1990—. Mem. State Ho. Reps. (Dist. 43), 1994—; bd. dirs. Neighborhood Bd.-Waianae, 1988-92; mem. Tchr. Retention Task Force, Waianae, 1987, Sch. Cmty. Based Mgmt. Task Force, Honolulu, 1988. Sgt. USAF, 1968-72. Democrat. Avocations: songwriting, music. Home: 89-416 Nanakuli Ave Waianae HI 96792-4037 Office: Ho Reps State Capitol 435 S Beretania St Honolulu HI 96813-2410*

KAHL, WILLIAM FREDERICK, retired college president; b. May 23, 1922; s. William Frederick and Bessie (Glading) K.; m. Mary Carson, Jan. 25, 1964; children: Frederick Glading, Sarah Hartwell. BA, Brown U., 1945; MA, Harvard U., 1947, PhD, 1955, LHD, 1993. Lectr. history Boston U., 1947-48, 50; from instr. to prof. Simmons Coll., Boston, 1948-76, provost, 1965-76; pres. Russell Sage Coll., Troy, N.Y., 1976-88. Bd. dir. Norstar. Author: The London Livery Companies: An essay and bibliography, 1960; contbr. articles to profl. jours. Vice-chmn. Hudson River Valley Assn.; bd. dirs. Albany Symphony Orch., Lower East Side Conservancy; chmn. bd. Tenement Mus., N.Y. State Nature Conservancy, Albany Inst. History and Art, Friends of the Hudson River Valley, Hudson River Valley Coordinating Coun., Russell Sage Pres. Adv. Coun.; pres., trustee, Albany Acad. for Girls, Wildwood Sch., Albany C. of C. Found. Social Sci. Coun. rsch. grantee, 1957-58. Mem. Am. Hist. Assn., Anglo-Am. Hist. Conf. Episcopalian. Home: 29 Old Niskayuna Rd Albany NY 12211-1349 Office: Russell Sage Coll Troy NY 12180

KAHLE, ANNE B. geophysicist; b. Auburn, Wash., Mar. 30, 1934; d. Charles O. Lewis and Elfrida Jenkins; m. James E. Kahle, Oct. 7, 1928; children: Richard D., Sheree L., Vicki I., Jeffrey P. BS, U. Alaska, 1955, MS, 1962; PhD, UCLA, 1974. Sr. scientist The RAND Corp., Santa Monica, Calif., 1962—74; sr. rsch. scientist Jet Propulsion Lab., Pasadena, Calif., 1974—; leader, U.S. ASTER Sci. Team NASA, 1989—. Contbr. articles to sci. publs. Mem.: Am. Geophys. Union. Office: Jet Propulsion Lab 4800 Oak Grove Dr Pasadena CA 91109 Office Fax: 818-354-0966. E-mail: anne@aster.jpl.nasa.gov.

KAHLE, BREWSTER, communications executive; m. Mary Austin; 1 child, Caslon. Grad., MIT. Founder Wide Area Info. Servers Inc., 1996—; pres. Internet Achives, San Francisco, Calif., 1996—; CEO Alexa Internet, San Francisco, 1996—.

KAHLENBECK, HOWARD, JR., lawyer; b. Ft. Wayne, Ind., Dec. 7, 1929; s. Howard and Clara Elizabeth (Wegman) K.; m. Sally A. Horrell, Aug. 14, 1954; children: Kathryn Sue, Douglas H. BS with distinction, Ind. U., 1952; LLB, U. Mich., 1957. Bar: Ind. 1957. Ptnr. Krieg DeVault, LLP, Indpls., 1957—. Sec., bd. dirs. Maul Tech. Corp. (formerly Buehler Corp.), Indpls., 1971-81, Am. Monitor Corp., Indpls., 1971-86, Am. Interstate Ins. Corp. Wis., Milw., 1973-84, Am. Interstate Ins. Co. Ga., Am. Underwriters Group, Inc., Indpls., 1973-86, Pafco Gen. Ins. Co., 1987-88. With USAF, 1952-54. Mem. ABA, Ind. Bar Assn., Indpls. Bar Assn., Alpha Kappa Psi, Delta Theta Phi, Beta Gamma Sigma, Delta Upsilon Internat. (sec., bd. dirs. 1971-83, chmn. 1983-86, trustee found. 1983-98). Lutheran. Home: 6320 Old Orchard Rd Indianapolis IN 46226-1041 Office: Krieg DeVault LLP One Indiana Sq Ste 2800 Indianapolis IN 46204 Business E-Mail: hk@kdlegal.com.

KAHLENBERG, JEANNETTE DAWSON, retired civic organization executive; b. Chgo., May 22, 1931; d. Horace and Frances Jeannette (Ledlie) Dawson; m. Richard Walter Kahlenberg, Sept. 3, 1955; children: Joy Kahlenberg Fallon, Trudi Kahlenberg Picciano, Richard Dawson. BA, Wellesley Coll., Wellesley, Mass., 1953; MA, Union Theol. Sem.-Columbia U., 1956. Dir. Christian edn. The Presbyterian Ch., Madison, N.J., 1955-56; dir. fin. devel. LWV of Minn., St. Paul, 1978-80; cons. fin. devel. Nat. Bd. YWCA of U.S.A., N.Y.C., 1981-84; v.p. adminstrn. China Inst. in Am., N.Y.C., 1984-86; exec. dir. Citizens Union of City of N.Y., 1986-98. Author: A History of Citizens Union, 1897-1997; co-author: What's the Score in Minnesota, Equal Opportunity for Girls in Athletics, 1979; editor (newsletter) Citizens Union Reports, 1986-98. Mem. sch. bd. White Bear Lake (Minn.) Area Schs., 1975-80, Spl. Vocat. Tech. Sch. Dist., NE Suburban St. Paul, 1978-80; trustee United Theol. Sem. of the Twin Cities, New Brighton, Minn., 1975-80; local pres. state bd. dirs. LWV, Minn., 1973-79; pres. Ridgewood LWV, 2001—; pres. Ch. Women United of Ridgewood and Vicinity, 1999—2003. Presbyterian. Home: 480 Fairway Rd Ridgewood NJ 07450-3412 also: 10 Scott Ave Chautauqua NY 14722 E-mail: kahlenb@attglobal.net.

KAHLER, HERBERT FREDERICK, diversified business executive; b. St. Augustine, Fla., Sept. 20, 1936; s. Herbert E. and Marie (Strieter) K.; m. Erika Rozsypal, May 16, 1964; children: Erik, Stephen, Christopher, Michael, Craig. AB, Johns Hopkins, 1958; LLB, Harvard U., 1961. Bar: N.Y. bar 1962. With Simpson, Thacher & Bartlett, N.Y.C., 1961-65; sec., gen. counsel Insilco Corp., Meriden, Conn., 1965-70; pres., CEO W.H. Hutchinson & Son, Inc., Chgo., 1970-73, Miles Homes Co., Mpls., 1973-86; v.p., dir. Insilco Corp., 1979-88; pres. Kahler & Assocs., 1988—; pres., CEO Crown Fixtures, Inc., Plymouth, Minn., 1990—, Power Generation Svc., Inc., 1990—97, chmn., 1997—; pres., CEO Crown Tonka Calif., Inc., 2000—. Hon. consul Republic of Austria, 1998—. Bd. corporators Meriden Hosp., 1965-70, Harvard, 1970; bd. govs. Meriden/Wallingford Hosp., 1987; bd. dirs. St. Paul Chamber Orch., 1974-87, St. Paul Opera Assn., 1975-77, Minn. Opera Co., 1977-87. Lt., arty. AUS, 1962-64. Mem. ABA, Mpls. Club, Phi Beta Kappa. Office: Crown Fixtures Inc 10700 Highway 55 Ste 160 Plymouth MN 55441-6134

KAHLER, NANCY J. music educator, director; d. Frederick Charles and Grace Miriam (Moyer) Knerr; children: Denise Marie, Timothy Charles, Debra Joan Bucklin, Allan Curtis, Donald James. B in Music Edn., Esther Boyer Coll. Music, Phila., 1983. Music tchr. Camden Bd. Edn., NJ, 1984—. Organist, choir dir. Karmel UCC, Phila., 1982—2000; organist St. Hedwig's, Phila., 1983; dir. music Temple Lutheran, Pennsauken, NJ, 2000—; elections' chair Camden Edn. Assn., NJ, 2000. Contbr. articles to profl. jours. Mem.: Music Tchrs. Nat. Assn., Music Educators Nat. Convention, Am. Guild Organists, Delta Mu. Avocations: baking, gardening, composing. Home: 7703 West Chester Pike Upper Darby PA 19082-1418 E-mail: studiok@snip.net.

KAHLER, RAY WILLIAM, lawyer; b. Longview, Wash., Oct. 29, 1970; s. Ray E. and Karen G. Kahler. BA in English, U. Puget Sound, 1993; JD, Harvard U., 1996. Bar: Wash. 1996, U.S. Dist. Ct. (we. dist.) Wash. 1997. Lawyer Stritmatter Kessler Whelan Withey Coluccio, Hoquiam, Wash., 1996—. Office: Stritmatter Kessler Whelan Withey Coluccio 413 8th St Hoquiam WA 98550-3607 E-mail: ray@skwwc.com.

KAHLFUSS, HANS JÜRGEN WILHELM, retired librarian; b. Königsberg/Ostpreussen, Germany, Aug. 27, 1936; s. Bruno Richard and Elsa (Ulrich) K.; m. Gisela Hanßen, Sept. 24, 1965; children: Torsten, Melanie. Abitur, Realgymnasium Geesthacht, Germany, 1956; Staatsexamen Lehramt höhere Schule Math. Geogra., U. Kiel, Germany, 1962, D in Natural Scis., 1964; Bibliotheksassessor, Bibliothekarlehrinstitut, Köln, 1966. Jr. libr. U. Libr., Kiel, Schleswig-Holstein, Germany, 1966-70; sr. libr. Senckenbergische Biblio., Frankfurt/M., Hessen, Germany, 1970-75; head of libr. Gesamthochschulbibliothek, Kassel, Hessen, Germany, 1975-99; ret., 1999. Beiratsmitglied, Arbeitsgemeinschaft d. Spezialbibliotheken Cologne, 1973-80; pres. Verein fuer hessische Geschichte und Landeskunde, 1985—. Author: Zentrale Kartensammlungen an westdeutschen Hochschulen, 1968, Landesaufnahmen u. Flurvermessungen in den Herzogtümern Schleswig, Holstein und Lauenburg vor 1864, 1969, Geschichte der amtlichen Kartographie der Herrschaft Schmalkalden, 2001; author, editor: Ex bibliotheca Casselana, 400 Jahre Landesbibliothek 1580-1980, 1980, 125 Jahre Murhardsche Stiftung der Stadt Kassel und ihrer Bibliothek 1863-1988, 1988. Recipient Wissenschaftspreis Stadt Kiel, 1966. Fellow Historische Kommission für Hessen; mem. Verein Deutscher Bibliothekare, Gesellschaft für Schleswig-Holsteinische Geschichte, Verein für Hessische Geschichte und Landeskunde. Avocations: german local and regional historical geography, genealogy. Home: Am Fuchsberg 9 34225 Baunatal Germany Fax: 0561 4 915911. E-mail: kahlfuss@vhghessen.de.

KAHLOW, BARBARA FENVESSY, statistician; b. Chgo., June 26, 1946; d. Stanley John and Doris (Goodman) Fenvessy; m. Lloyd Fitch Reese, Dec. 6, 1969 (div. 1977); m. Allan Howard Young, Mar. 31, 1979 (div. 1982); m. Ronald Arthur Kahlow, Sept. 28, 1985 (div. 1990). BA, Vassar Coll., 1968. Statistician U.S. Govt./Dept. HEW, Nat. Ctr. Health Statistics, 1968-70, Nat. Ctr. for Ednl. Statistics, 1970-72, Exec. Office of Pres. Office Mgmt. and Budget, Washington, 1972-98. Dep. staff dir. subcom. on energy policy, natural resources and regulatory affairs House Govt. Reform Com., 1998—. Author: Motor Vehicle Accident Deaths in the U.S.: 1950-69, 1970; contbr. articles to profl. jours. N.Y. State Regents scholar, 1964-68. Mem. Am. Statis. Assn., Foggy Bottom Assn., League of Rep. Women of D.C., Friends of the Kennedy Ctr., Friends of the Corcoran, Smithsonian Assocs., Washington Vassar Club. Republican. Episcopalian. Home: Apt #404 2555 Pennsylvania Ave NW Washington DC 20037-1640 Office: House Govt Reform Com Bldg # B-377 Rayburn House Office Bldg Washington DC 20515-0001

KAHMANN, SARAH STUBER, retired foundation administrator; b. Clay, Pa., Jan. 18, 1928; d. Harry Miles and Mamie (Stauffer) Stuber; div. 1993; children: Lynne Einhaus, Ed III, Susan Hasty, Barbara Amato; m. Paul J. Kahmann, Aug. 31, 2002. V.p. Nat. Coalition for Protection Children and Families, Cin., 1989-93; ret., 1993. Active Federated Women's Club and St. Luke Found. Bd.; founder Enough is Enough Bd., 1996-2002; apptd. by gov. Ky. Commn. Women, 1998—; grad. Leadership Ky., 2000; bd. dirs. Women's Crisis Ctr., 2003—. Named Woman of Yr. Cin. Enquirer, 1997. Protestant. Avocations: community service, politics, art, travel. *My experience has been a willingness to risk, along with the belief that set-backs are not failures but an opportunity to learn and grow--these principles have led me to risk much, and thus accomplish much and enriched my life tremendously.*

KAHN, ALAN EDWIN, lawyer; b. N.Y.C., Aug. 9, 1929; s. Joseph and Harriet Rose (Rubel) K.; m. Regina Wolf, Aug. 7, 1960 (div. Jan. 1978); 1 child, Jolie Galen; m. Patricia Ann Dugan, June 4, 1978. BBA, CCNY, 1950; JD, Bklyn. Law Sch., 1956. Bar: N.Y. 1956, U.S. Dist. Ct. (so. and ea. dists.) N.Y. 1978, U.S. Tax Ct. 1978; CPA, N.Y. Staff asst.-acct. Feinberg, Jacobs & Furman, N.Y.C., 1956-57; pvt. practice N.Y.C., 1957-96, 98—; prin. Law Office of Alan E. Kahn, N.Y.C., 1957-99; sr. ptnr. Kahn, Boyd, Levychin CPAs, N.Y.C., 1993; pvt. practice, 1998—. Tax cons. to various nonprofit orgns., N.Y.C., 1977—. Cons. Vol. Lawyers for the Arts, N.Y.C., 1978—. Sgt. U.S. Army, 1951-52. Mem. ATLA (mem. com. 1990—), N.Y. State Bar Assn. (elder law com.), N.Y. State Trial Lawyers Assn. (chmn. subcom. on legis. estate and trusts 1979, spkr. bd. 1990—, mem. com. 1991—, chair 2000—), N.Y. County Lawyers Assn. (taxation com. 1988—, sec. com. on taxation 1996-2000, chair com. on taxation 2000—), Spkr.'s Bur., Assn. Trial Lawyers City N.Y., Jewish Lawyers Guild, N.Y. State Soc. CPAs, Nat. Sculpture Soc. (patron mem.), Odd Fellows (grand adv. bd. N.Y. chpt. 1979-80, gen. counsel grand lodge 1989—), Mchts. Club (bd. govs., asst. treas., treas. and gov. 1992—, award chmn. legal com. 1995—). Democrat. Avocations: collecting prints, paintings and oriental ceramics. Home: 370 1st Ave New York NY 10010-4923 Office: 99 Wall St New York NY 10005-3101 E-mail: aekwacs@aol.com.

KAHN, ALFRED EDWARD, economist, educator, government official; b. Paterson, N.J., Oct. 17, 1917; s. Jacob and Bertha (Orlean) K.; m. Mary Simmons, Oct. 10, 1943; children: Joel, Rachel, Hannah. AB, NYU, 1936, MA, 1937; postgrad., U. Mo., 1937-38; PhD, Yale U., 1942; LLD (hon.), Colby Coll., 1978, U. Mass., 1979, Ripon Coll., 1980, Northwestern U., 1982, Colgate U., 1983; DHL (hon.), SUNY, Albany, 1985. Mem. staff Brookings Inst., 1940, 51-52; with anti-trust div. Dept. Justice, 1941-42, Dept. Commerce, 1942, WPB, 1943; economist on Palestine surveys, 1943-44, Twentieth Century Fund, 1944-45; asst. prof., chmn. dept. econs. Ripon Coll., 1945-47; asst. prof. Cornell U., 1947-50, asso. prof., 1950-55, prof., 1955-89, chmn. dept. econs., 1958-63, Robert Julius Thorne prof. econs., 1967-89, emeritus, 1989—, dean Coll. Arts and Scis., 1969-74; chmn. N.Y. State Pub. Service Commn., 1974-77, CAB, 1977-78, Council on Wage and Price Stability (adviser to Pres. on inflation), 1978-80. Mem. atty. gen's nat. com. to study anti-trust laws, 1953-55; sr. staff U.S. Coun. Econ. Advisers, 1955-57; spl. cons. Boni, Watkins, Jason & Co., N.Y.C., 1957-61, Nat. Econ. Rsch. Assocs., 1961-74, 80—, U.S. Fgn. Agrl. Svc., Israel, 1960-61, Dept. Justice, 1963-64, FTC, 1965, Ford Found., 1967; econ. adv. coun. AT&T, 1968-74; econ. adv. com. U.S. C. of C., 1964-66; mem. environ. adv. com. Fed. Energy Adminstrn., 1974-77; mem. rev. com. sulfur emissions from power plants Nat. Acad. Scis., 1974-75; adv. bd. Electric Power Rsch. Inst., 1974-77; mem. Nat. Antitrust Law Rev. Com., 1978-79; adv. to N.Y. gov. on comm. regulation, 1980-81; mem. usage panel Am. Heritage Dictionary, 1982—; mem. N.Y. Gov.'s Adv. Com. on Pub. Power for L.I., 1986, N.Y. Gov.'s Fact-Finding Panel on Shoreham Nuclear Plant, 1983, N.Y. State Coun. on Fiscal and Econ. Priorities, 1983-89; chmn. adv. com. on price reform and competition in the USSR Internat. Inst. for Applied Systems Analysis, 1990-92; econ. commentator Nightly Bus. Report (pub. TV), 1981-97; mem. Ohio Blue Ribbon Panel Telecomm. Regulation, 1992-93; mem. N.Y. State Telecomm. Exch., 1992-94; Ct.-apptd. expert U.S. Dist. Ct., 1993-94; com. study of competition U.S. airline industry Nat. Rsch. Coun., 1999—. Author: Great Britain in the World Economy, 1946; co-author (with J.B. Diriam): Fair Competition, The Law and Economics of Anti-Trust Policy, 1954; co-author: (with M.G. de Chazeau) Integration and Competition in the Petroleum Industry, 1959; author: The Economics of Regulation, 2 vols., 1970, 71, reprinted/new intro., 1988, Letting Go: Deregulating The Process of Deregulation, 1998, Whom the Gods Would Destroy, Or How Not to Deregulate, 2001. Trustee Cornell U., 1964-69; mem. nat. governing bd. Common Cause, 1982-85; chmn. Blue Ribbon Panel to Investigate Pricing of Electricity in Calif., 2000. Fulbright Rsch. fellow Italy, 1954-55; recipient Wilbur Cross medal for outstanding achievement Yale U., 1995, L. Welch Pogue award for Lifetime Contbn. to Aviation, 1997, Soverign Fund award 1997, J. Rhoads Foster award, 1999. Mem. Am. Econ. Assn. (v.p. 1981-82), Nat. Assn. Regulatory Utility Commrs. (exec. com., chmn. com. on electricity 1975-77), Am. Acad. Arts and Scis., Phi Beta Kappa. Home: 221 Savage Farm Dr Ithaca NY 14850-6501 Office: 308 N Cayuga St Ithaca NY 14850-4209

KAHN, ALFRED JOSEPH, social worker and policy scholar, educator; b. N.Y.C., Feb. 8, 1919; s. Meyer and Sophie (Levine) K.; m. Miriam Kadin, Sept. 3, 1949 (div. 1984); 1 child, Nancy Valerie. B in Social Sci., CCNY, 1939; B in Hebrew Lit., Sem. Coll. Jewish Studies, N.Y.C., 1940; MS, Columbia U., 1946, D in Social Welfare, 1952; DHL (hon.), Adelphi U., 1984; DSc (hon.), U Md., 1989; Dr. (hon.), York U., Eng., 1998. Psychiat. social worker Jewish Bd. Guardians, N.Y.C., 1946-47; mem. faculty Sch. Social Work Columbia U., 1947-89, prof. Sch. Social Work, 1954-89, prof. emeritus, 1989; co-dir. Cross Nat. Studies Rsch. Program, 1973—; Disting. vis. prof. Grad. Sch. Social Svc., Fordham U., 1990-2001. Staff cons. Citizens Com. for Children, N.Y.C., 1948-72; mem. summer faculty Smith Coll. Sch. Social Work, 1949-54; cons. govts., founds., vol. agys., 1949—; mem. numerous adv. coms.; mem. adv. com. child devel. NRC-Nat. Acad. Scis., 1971-76, mem. com. child devel. rsch. and pub. policy, Acad. Scis., 1977-83, chmn., 1980-83; mem. adv. bd. Inst. Rsch. Poverty, U. Wis., 1967-2002. Author: A Court for Children, 1953, Planning Community Services for Children in Trouble, 1963, Neighborhood Information Centers, 1966, (with Anna Mayer) Day Care as a Social Instrument, 1966, Theory and Practice of Social Planning, 1969, Studies in Social Policy and Planning, 1969, Social Policy and Social Services, 1973; co-author: Not for the Poor Alone, 1975, Social Service in the U.S., 1976, Social Services in International Perspective, 1977, Child Care, Family Benefits and Working Parents, 1981, Helping America's Families, 1982, Maternity Policies and Working Women, 1983, Income Transfers for Families With Children, 1983, Child Care: Facing the Hard Choices, 1987, The Responsive Workplace, 1987, Mothers Alone, 1988, Social Services for Children, Youth and Families in the United States, 1989, Social Services for Children, Youth and Families: The New York City Study, 1990, A Welcome for Every Child, 1994, Social Policy and the Under 3s, 1994, Starting Right, 1995, Big Cities in the Welfare Transition, 1998, Contracting for Child and Family Services, 2000; contbr. monographs, articles to profl. jours., chpts. to books; editor: Issues in American Social Work, 1959, Shaping The New Social Work, 1973; co-editor: Family Policy: Government and Families in Fourteen Countries, 1978, Child Support, From Debt Collection to Social Policy, 1988, Privatization and the Welfare State, 1989, Child Care, Parental Leaves and The Under 3s: Policy Innovation in Europe, 1991, Children and Their Families in Big Cities, 1996, Family Change and Family Policies in Great Britain, Canada, New Zealand, and the United States, 1997, Beyond Child Poverty: The Social Exclusion of Children, 2002. With USAAF, 1942-46. Mem. AAUP, Nat. Assn. Social Workers (chmn. div. practice and knowledge 1963-66, bd. dirs. 1967-70), Council Social Work Edn., Assn. for Policy Analysis and Mgmt. Home: 250 Gorge Rd Apt 17B Cliffside Park NJ 07010-1309 Office: Columbia U Sch Social Work New York NY 10025 E-mail: ajk7@columbia.edu.

KAHN, ALFRED ROBERT, toy manufacturing company executive; b. Bklyn., Jan. 18, 1947; s. Murray and Lilyane K. (Kaplan) Kahn. BA in Bus., C.W. Post Coll., N.Y., 1964—68. Exec. v.p. mktg. Coleco Industries, Inc., West Hartford, Conn. Office: 4 KIDS ENTERTAINMENT 1414 Ave of the Americas New York NY 10019

KAHN, ANNETTE LEE, clinical social worker, psychotherapist; b. Grantsboro, N.C., June 22, 1935; d. Robert Earl and Mildred (McCotter) Lee; m. Charles Howard Kahn, May 12, 1956; children: Kathryn Lauren, Sarah Elizabeth, Benjamin Arthur. BA in Piano and Pub. Sch. Music, Meredith Coll., Raleigh, N.C., 1957; MSW, U. Kans., 1973. Bd. cert. diplomate in clin. social work Am. Bd. Examiners in Clin Social Work; lic. clin. social worker, N.C. Dir., family therapy trainer Family Focus Bert Nash CMHC, Inc., Lawrence, 1981-84, dir. screening and emergency svcs., 1981-84, dir. children's svcs., 1979-81, 84-86, chief social worker, 1979-85, clin. social worker, 1973—2000; pvt. practice psychotherapy. Adminstrv. dir. N.C. State Cert. Program for Piano Tchrs., 1963-65. Bd. dirs. Hdqtrs. (drug and crisis counseling), Lawrence, 1976-79, The Shelter, Inc., Lawrence, 1979-84; bd. dirs., sec., chmn. Trinity Episcopalian. Foster Home, 1974-80; bd. dirs., treas., sec. Mental Health Assn. Lawrence, 1980-85; docent N.C. Mus. Art, 1965-68, U. Kans. Spencer Art Mus., 1969-71. Fellow: Kans. Soc. Clin. Social Work (chmn. ethics 1977, chmn. by-laws 1976); mem.: NASW, Mediation Network (N.C.), N.C. Soc. Clin. Social Workers (pres. 1995—97, bd. dirs. 1993—2000, co-chair local programs & continuing edn. 1998—2000). Avocations: tennis, sailing, chamber music, piano, travel. Home and Office: 25B Mt Bolus Rd Chapel Hill NC 27514-2638 E-mail: kahnac@aol.com.

KAHN, ANTHONY F. lawyer; b. Washington, Apr. 29, 1954; s. Henry and Claudia F.; m. Cynthia Marie Farhart, Aug. 11, 1979; children: Brian, Andrew, Stephen. BA, Wake Forest U., 1976; MBA summa cum laude, JD magna cum laude, U. Notre Dame, 1980. Bar: N.Y. 1981. Ptnr. White & Case LLP, N.Y.C., 1980—. Office: White & Case LLP 1155 Avenue of the Americas New York NY 10036-2711 E-mail: AKAHN@WHITECASE.com.

KAHN, BENJAMIN ALEXANDER, lawyer; b. Boston, July 8, 1970; s. Michael David and Ruth Jacobson Kahn. BA cum laude, Tufts U., 1992; visiting law student, U. Colo., 1994; JD, U. Mich., 1995. Bar: Colo. 1997, U.S. Dist. Ct. Colo. 1998, U.S. Ct. Appeals (10th cir.) 1999. Clk. to Hon. Justice George E. Lohr, Denver, 1995-96; assoc. Kennedy & Christopher, P.C., Denver, 1998-2001, Brownstein, Hyatt & Farber, P.C., Denver, 2001—. Contbr. articles to profl. jours. including Stanford Jour. of Internat. Law, ABA Tort and Ins. Law Jour., William Mitchell Law Rev. Clara Belfield-Henry Bates Law Travel fellow, 1997. Mem. Colo. Bar Assn. (environ., natural resources, water, litigation, and other coms.), Adminstrn. Law Forum Com., Denver Bar, Colo. Def. Lawyers Assn., Colo. Indian Bar Assn. Avocations: art, music, outdoor activities, antiques, travel. Home: 2590 Cherry St Denver CO 80207-3145 Office: 410 17th St Ste 2200 Denver CO 80202-4437 E-mail: bkahn@bhf-law.com.

KAHN, BERND, radiochemist, educator; b. Pforzheim, Baden, Germany, Aug. 16, 1928; came to U.S., 1938; s. Eric Herman and Alice Dora (Meyer) K.; m. Gail Pressman, Aug. 6, 1961; children: Jennifer, Elizabeth. BSChemE, N.J. Inst. Tech., 1950; MS in Physics, Vanderbilt U., 1952; PhD in Chemistry, MIT, 1960. Commd. officer USPHS, 1954, advanced through grades to capt., 1970, health physicist, radiochemist, Oak Ridge (Tenn.) Nat. Lab., 1951-54, engr. various facilities, 1954-74, ret., 1974; prof. nuc. engring. and health physics Ga. Inst. Tech., Atlanta, 1974-96, prof. emeritus, 1996—, dir. Environ. Resources Ctr., 1974—. Co-editor: Management of Low-Level Radioactive Waste, 1979; co-inventor recovery of magnesium salts from sea water. Mem. Nat. Coun. Radiation Protection and Measurments (hon.), Am. Chem. Soc., Am. Phys. Soc., Health Physics Soc. Achievements include research specialization: radiochemistry and environmental radioactivity. Office: Ga Inst Tech Nuclear Engring Health Physics Atlanta GA 30332-0335 E-mail: bernd.kahn@me.gatech.edu.

KAHN, BERT L. lawyer; b. Milw., July 5, 1938; s. David and Rose (Glusman) K.; m. Erika Apt, Sept. 1, 1963; children: Rita, Mitchell, Abigail. BBA, U. Wis., 1960, JD, 1963. Bar: Wis. 1964, Ill. 1971, U.S. Tax Ct. 1966. Atty. Estate & Gift Tax div., IRS, Chgo., 1963-65; trial aty. Reg. Counsels Office-U.S. Treasury Office, St. Paul and Chgo., 1965-72; ptnr. Hirschtritt, Hirschtritt, Gold, P.C., Chgo., 1972-77, Mardell & Kahn, Ltd., Chgo., 1977-81; pvt. practice Bert L. Kahn, Ltd., Skokie, Ill., 1981—. Lectr. in field. Pres. Religious Zionists of Chgo., 1979-80, co-nat. pres. 1996-98; bd. dirs. Airie Crown Hebrew Day Sch., Chgo., 1981; chmn. subcom. lawyers div. Jewish United Fund, 1989-90; v.p., past co-pres. Religious Zionists of Am. Mem. ABA (tax com.), Chgo. Bar Assn. (tax com.). Office: 8707 Skokie Blvd Ste 107 Skokie IL 60077-2200

KAHN, BRUCE MEYER, lawyer; b. Memphis, Feb. 28, 1952; s. Sidney Louis, Jr. and Maxine March (Meyer) K. B.A., Trinity Coll., 1974; J.D., Tulane U., 1977. Bar: Tenn. 1977. Assoc., Buchignani & Greener, Memphis, 1977-80; ptnr. Goodman, Glazer, Greener, Schneider & McQuiston, Memphis, 1981—; sec.-treas., dir. Paper Products Co., 1984— . Mem. legal com. B'Nai B'Rith

Home and Hosp. for Aged, Memphis, 1981-84, Temple Israel Synagogue, 1984— ; vol. Memphis in May Internat. Festival, 1984— ; chmn. Trinity Coll. Alumni Support Program, 1981-84; v.p. Temple Israel Brotherhood, 1984— . Mem. Memphis and Shelby County Bar Assn., Tenn. Bar Assn., ABA, Tax Watch Group, Greater Memphis Employee Benefits Council. Jewish. Club: Racquet of Memphis. Home: 4995 Normandy Ln Memphis TN 38117-2701 Office: Goodman Glazer Greener Schneider & McQuiston 1500 Commerce Bldg Memphis TN 38103

KAHN, CARL RONALD, research laboratory administrator; b. Louisville, Jan. 14, 1944; s. David L. and Reva W. (Waldman) K.; m. Susan Becker; children: Stacy, Jeffrey. BA, U. Louisville, 1964, MD, 1968, MS, 1984; MA (hon.), Harvard U., 1984; DSc (honoris causa), U. Louisville, 1984, U. Paris-Pierre and Marie Curie, 1990, U. Geneva, 2000. Diplomate Am. Bd. Internal Medicine, Am. Bd. Endocrinology and Metabolism. Intern and resident in ward medicine Barnes Hosp., St. Louis, 1968-70; clin. assoc., sr. clin. assoc., clin. endocrinology br. Nat. Inst. Arthritis, Metabolism and Digestive Diseases, NIH, Bethesda, Md., 1970-73; sr. investigator Diabetes Br. NIH, Bethesda, Md., 1973-78, chief diabetes br., 1979-81; rsch. dir Joslin Diabetes Ctr., Boston, 1981-2000, dir., 1997-99, exec. v.p., dir., 1997-99; assoc. prof. Harvard Med. Sch., Boston, 1981-84, prof. medicine, 1984—, Mary K. Iacocca prof. medicine, 1986—; pres. Joslin Diabetes Ctr., 2000—. Lectr. symposia, meetings, thesis supr., course dir. and devel. numerous med. instns.; admitting and attending physician NIH Clin. Ctr., 1972-81; physician Brigham and Women's Hosp., Boston, 1981, chief div. Diabetes and Metabolism, 1981-92; assoc. staff Endocrinology/Internal Medicine, New Eng. Deaconess Hospital, Boston, 1982, active staff, 1986; clin. assoc. prof. medicine, Uniformed Svcs. U. Health Scis, Bethesda, Md., 1979-81; vis. scientist Centre de Moleculaire, Centre National de la Recherche Scientifique, Gif-sur-Yvette, France, 1979-80; adj. prof. genetics George Washington U., 1980-81; overseas vis. prof. Royal Melbourne Hosp., Australia, 1985; vis. prof. Royal Postgrad. Hosp., London, 1985; Rosemary Sarver vis. prof. in endocrinology and metabolism, The Hosp. of the Good Samaritan, L.A., 1985. Author or co-author over 430 publs. in field; mem. editl. bds. Jour. Clin. Endocrinology and Metabolism, 1977-80, Diabetes, 1977-84, Am. Jour. Medicine, 1979-84, Jour. Clin. Investigation, 1979-84, Jour. Receptor Rsch., 1980-83, Hormone and Metabolic Rsch., 1980-83, Endocrinology, 1981-85, Jour. Biol. Chemistry, 1983-88, Diabetes and Metabolism Revs., 1984, Receptor, 1989—; exec. editor Trends in Endocrinology and Metabolism, 1989-90; cons. editor Jour. Clin. Investigation; assoc. editor Diabetes, 1996-2001. Mem. Nat. Diabetes Adv. Bd., 1981-85, co-chmn. rsch. com., 1982-85. Recipient David Rumbough Meml award for Sci. Achievement Juvenile Diabetes Found., 1977, CIBA-Geigy Drew award for biochem. rsch., 1981, Mary Jane Kugel award Juvenile Diabetes Found., 1982, AFCR award for Outstanding Clin. Rsch. under Age 40, 1983, Sol Berson Meml. lectureship NIH, 1983, Hehnemann Lectr. in Pharmacology U. Calif.,1984, Pfizer Biomed. Rsch. award, Pfizer inc., 1986, Cristobal Diaz award Internat. Diabetes Fedn., 1988, Banting award Am. Diabetes Assn., 1993, Nat. Acad. Scis. award, 1999, Inst. Medicine, 1999, Hamden award U.A.E., 2000, Lawson-Wilkins Lectr. Pediatric Endocrine Soc., 2001, others. Fellow AAAS; mem. Nat. Acad. Scis., Am. Acad. Arts & Scis., Am. Fedn. Clin. Rsch., The Endocrine Soc. (Edwin B. Astwood lectr. 1987, Kocl award 2000), Am. Diabetes Assn. (Eli Lilly award for rsch. 1980, Otto Brandman award N.J. affiliate 1989, Elliott P. Joslin medal Mass. affiliate, Albert Renold award 1998), Am. Soc. Clin. Investigation (nat. coun. 1986—, pres. elect 1987-88, pres. 1988-89), Am. Soc. Biol. Chemistry, Assn. Am. Physicians, Sigma Xi, Alpha Epsilon Delta, Phi Kappa Phi, Alpha Omega Alpha. Achievements include rsch. in insulin receptors and insulin action, insulin-like growth factors, diabetes mellitus, hypoglycemia, immunity, autoimmunity and viruses in endocrine disorders. Office: Joslin Diabetes Ctr One Joslin Pl Boston MA 02215 E-mail: c.ronald.kahn@joshn.harvard.edu.

KAHN, CHARLES HOWARD, architect, educator; b. Birmingham, Ala., Feb. 10, 1926; s. Benjamin Arthur and Dorothy (Goldman) K.; m. Annette Lee, May 12, 1956; children: Kathryn Lauren, Sarah Elizabeth, Benjamin Arthur. AB, U. N.C., 1946; BCE, N.C. State U., 1948, BArch, 1956; MS, MIT, 1949; Fulbright grantee, Inst. di Urbanistico, Rome, 1957-58; postgrad., U. N.C., 1991. With Robert & Co. (architects and engr.), Atlanta, 1949-51, Frederick Snare Corp., N.Y.C., 1951-52, F. Carter Williams (AIA), Raleigh, N.C., 1952-54; propr. Charles Howard Kahn & Assocs. Architects and Engrs., Raleigh, N.C., 1954-68, Lawrence, Kans., 1968-91; dean Sch. Architecture and Urban Design, U. Kans., Lawrence, 1968-81; prof. Sch. Architecture and Urban Design U. Kans., 1968-91; prof. emeritus Sch. Architecture and Urban Design, U. Kans., Lawrence, 1991—; pvt. practice Charles H. Kahn, FAIA & Assoc., Chapel Hill, N.C., 1991—. Vis. prof. Sch of Design, N.C. State U., 1992—; arch. revue and selection com. U. N.C., 2000—. Prin. works include Carter Stadium, N.C. State U., 1966, Minges Auditorium, E. Carolina Coll., 1967, Poliedro, Caracus, Venezuela, 1973; mem. editorial bd.: Jour. Archtl. and Planning Rsch. Bd. dirs. Cmty. Devel. Ctr., 1968-75; bd. dirs. Environ. R&D Found., 1968-91, v.p., 1975-87, pres. 1987-91; mem. Kans. Bldg. Commn., 1978-80. Recipient Hon. Alumnus and Disting. Alumnus awards U. Kans., 1989; Fulbright vis. rsch. scholar Gt. Brit., 1977-78 Fellow AIA; mem. Assn. Collegiate Schs. of Architecture, Kans. Soc. Architects (pres. elect 1986, pres. 1987), Phi Beta Kappa, Phi Kappa Phi, Sigma Xi, Tau Beta Pi. Democrat. Jewish.

KAHN, DAVID, editor, author; b. N.Y.C., Feb. 7, 1930; s. Jesse and Florence (Abraham) K.; m. Susanne Monika Fiedler, Oct. 22, 1969 (div. Jan. 1995); children: Oliver, Michael. AB, Bucknell U., 1951; DPhil, Oxford (Eng.) U., 1974. Reporter Jersey Jour., Jersey City, 1952-53; copyboy N.Y. Daily News, 1953-55; reporter Newsday, Garden City, N.Y., 1955-63; freelance writer, 1963-65, 67-74; news desk editor Internat. Herald Tribune, Paris, 1965-67; prof. journalism NYU, 1974-79; asst. viewpoints editor Newsday, Melville, N.Y., 1979-94, mem. editorial bd., 1988-94; scholar in residence Nat. Security Agy., 1995; asst. editor features Newsday, Melville, N.Y., 1996-98; ret., 1999; freelance author, 1999—. Adj. prof. modern polit. and mil. intelligence Yale U., New Haven, 1985, Columbia U., N.Y.C., 1986-88; founding co-editor Cryptologia mag., 1977—; mem. editorial bd. Intelligence and Nat. Security, 1986—, Internat. Jour. Intelligence and Counterintelligence, 1986—, Jour. Cryptology, 1991-2001; witness Congl. coms.; adj. prof. journalism, State U. of New York, Stony Brook, 1991-94. Author: Two Soviet Spy Ciphers, 1960, Plaintext in the New Unabridged, 1963; The Codebreakers, 1967, Hitler's Spies, 1978, Seizing the Enigma, 1991 (named Notable Naval Book of 1991 U.S. Naval Inst.); editor: Kahn on Codes, 1983; editor, translator: Clandestine Operations, 1983; cons. on cryptology to Oxford English Dictionary; contbr. articles to profl. jours. and encys. Bd. trustees St. Antony's Coll. Trust, ret., 2000; bd. dirs. Nat. Cryptologic Mus. Found.; sr. assoc. mem. St. Antony's Coll., Oxford U., 1972-74; bd. dirs. Great Neck Libr., 2002-. Recipient spl. award Nat. Security Agy., 1991, Nat. Intelligence Study Ctr., 1992. Mem. Am. Cryptogram Assn. (pres. 1965-67), World War II Studies Assn. (bd. dirs. 1987—), Internat. Intelligence Study Group, Internat. Spy Mus. (mem. adv. bd. dirs.), Internat. Assn. for Cryptologic Rsch. (bd. dirs. 1980-90), Century Assn., Phi Beta Kappa. Democrat. Jewish. Avocation: tennis. Home and Office: 120 Wooleys Ln Great Neck NY 11023-2301 E-mail: davidkahn1@aol.com.

KAHN, DOUGLAS ALLEN, legal educator; b. Spartanburg, S.C., Nov. 7, 1934; s. Max Leonard and Julia (Rich) K.; m. Judith Bleich, Sept. 24, 1959; m. Mary Briscoe, June 12, 1970; children— Margery Ellen, Jeffrey Hodges. BA, U. N.C., 1955; JD with honors, George Washington U., 1958. Bar: D.C. 1958, Mich. 1965, U.S. Ct. Appeals (D.C. cir.) 1958, U.S. Ct. Appeals (5th and 9th cirs.) 1959, U.S. Ct. Appeals (3d, 4th and 6th cirs.) 1960, U.S. Supreme Ct. 1963. Atty. Civil and Tax div. U.S. Dept. Justice, 1958-62; assoc. Sachs and Jacobs, Washington, 1962-64; prof. law U. Mich., Ann Arbor, 1964—, Paul G. Kauper Disting. prof., 1984—. Vis. prof. Stanford Law Sch., 1973, Duke Law Sch., 1977, Fordham Law Sch., 1980-81, U. Cambridge, 1996. Author: (with Gann) Corporate Taxation, 1989, (with Lehman) Corporate Income Taxation, 2001, (with Waggoner and Pennell) Federal Taxation of Gifts, Trusts and Estates, 1997, Federal Income Tax, 1999; comment editor George Washington U. Law Rev., 1956-58; contbr. articles to profl. jours. Recipient Emil Brown Found. prize, 1969 Mem. ABA, Order of Coif. Republican. Jewish. Office: U Mich Law Sch 625 S State St Ann Arbor MI 48109-1215 E-mail: dougkahn@umich.edu.

KAHN, EDWIN LEONARD, lawyer; b. N.Y.C., Aug. 1, 1918; s. Max L. and Julia (Rich) K.; m. Myra J. Green, Oct. 20, 1946 (dec. 1994); children: Martha L., Deborah K. Spiliotopoulos. AB, U. N.C., 1937; LLB cum laude, Harvard U., 1940. Bar: N.C. 1940, D.C. 1949. Atty., asst. head legislation and regulations div. Office Chief Counsel IRS, 1940-52, dir. tech. planning div., 1952-55; ptnr. Arent, Fox, Kintner, Plotkin & Kahn, Washington, 1955-86, of counsel, ret., 1986—. Lectr. NYU Tax Inst., mem. adv. bd., 1959-70; lectr. tax insts. Coll. William and Mary, U. Chgo., U. Tex. Editor: Harvard Law Rev, 1939-40; editorial adv. bd. Tax Advisor of Am. Inst. CPA's, 1974-86. Bd. dirs. Jewish Community Ctr. Greater Washington, 1972-78; trustee Cosmos Club Found., 1989-93, chmn., 1989-91, With U.S. Army, 1943-46, ETO. Decorated Bronze Star. Fellow Am. Bar Found. (life); mem. ABA (coun. 1963-66, vice chmn. sect. taxation 1965-66), Fed. Bar Assn. (chmn. taxation com. 1967-68), D.C. Bar Assn., Nat. Tax Assn.-Tax Inst. Am. (adv. coun. 1967-69, bd. dirs. 1969-73), Am. Law Inst. (life), Am. Coll. Tax Counsel, J. Edgar Murdock Am. Inn Ct. (master bencher 1988-91), Phi Beta Kappa (life mem. fellows). Jewish. Home: 4104 40th St N Arlington VA 22207-4805 Office: 1050 Connecticut Ave NW Washington DC 20036-5303

KAHN, EDWIN SAM, lawyer; b. N.Y.C., Jan. 22, 1938; m. Cynthia Chutter, May 30, 1966; children: David, Jonathan, Jennifer. BA, U. Colo., 1958; JD, Harvard U., 1965. Bar: Colo. 1965, U.S. Dist. Ct. (Colo.) 1965, U.S. Ct. Appeals (10th cir.) 1965, U.S. Supreme Ct. 1968. Assoc. Holland & Hart, Denver, 1965-70, ptnr., 1970-77; ptnr., shareholder Kelly, Haglund, Garnsey & Kahn, LLC, Denver, 1978—. 1st lt. USAF, 1959-62. Fellow Am. Coll. Trial Lawyers; mem. Denver Bar Assn. (pres. 1984-85). Home: 2345 Leyden St Denver CO 80207-3441 Office: Kelly Haglund Garnsey & Kahn LLC 1441 18th St Ste 300 Denver CO 80202-1255 E-mail: edkahn@4dv.net.

KAHN, ELLIS IRVIN, lawyer; b. Charleston, S.C., Jan. 18, 1936; s. Robert and Estelle Harriet (Kaminski) Kahn; m. Janice Weinstein, Aug. 11, 1963; children: Justin Simon, David Israel, Cynthia Kahn Nirenblatt. AB in Polit. Sci., Citadel, 1958; JD, U. S.C., 1961. Bar: S.C. 1961, U.S. Ct. Appeals (5th cir.) 1963, U.S. Ct. Appeals (4th cir.) 1964, U.S. Supreme Ct. 1970, DC 1978, U.S. Claims Ct. 1988, diplomate: Nat. Bd. Trial Advocacy, Am. Bd. Profl. Liability Attys. (trustee 1989-), cert.: (civil ct. mediator). Law clk. U.S. Dist. Ct. S.C., 1964—66; prin. Kahn Law Firm, Charleston. Adj. prof. med.-legal jurisprudence Med. U. S.C., 1978—87; mem. rules com. U.S. Dist. Ct., 1984—96. Mem. nat. coun. Am. Israel Pub. Affairs Com., 1982—88, Hebrew Benevolent Soc., pres., 1994—96; mem. Hebrew Orphan Soc., S.C. Organ Procurement Agy., 1989—94; chmn. campaign Charleston Jewish Fedn., 1986 –87, pres., 1988—90. Capt. USAF, 1961—64. Fellow: Internat. Soc. Barristers; mem.: ATLA (state committeeman 1970—74), ABA, S.C. Trial Lawyers Assn. (pres. 1976—77), 4th Cir. Jud. Conf. (life), S.C. Bar. Home: 316 Confederate Cir Charleston SC 29407-7431 Office: PO Box 31397 Charleston SC 29417-1397

KAHN, EUGENE S. department store chain executive; BA, CCNY, 1971. Asst. buyer Gimbels East, 1971-73, buyer, 1973-76; various merchandising positions Bamberger's, from 1976, sr. v.p., gen. mdse. mgr., 1984-88; group sr. v.p. Macy's Northeast, 1988-89, Macy's South/Bullock's, 1989-90; pres., CEO G. Fox divsn. May Dept. Stores, 1990-92, pres., CEO Filene's divsn., 1992-98, vice chmn. parent co., 1996-97, exec. vice chmn., 1997-98, pres., CEO, 1998-2001, chmn., CEO, 2001—. Trustee Washington U., St. Louis; trustee, treas. Mary Inst./Country Day Sch., St. Louis. Office: May Dept Stores 611 Olive St Saint Louis MO 63101-1721

KAHN, FREDRICK HENRY, internist; b. L.A., Aug. 26, 1925; s. Julius and Josephine Leone (Langdon) K.; m. Barbara Ruth Visscher, Feb. 14, 1952; children: Susan, Kathryn, William. AB, Stanford U., 1947, MD, 1951. Diplomate Am. Bd. Internal Medicine. Rotating intern San Francisco Gen. Hosp., 1950-51, fellow pathology, 1951-52; resident medicine Los Angeles VA Hosp., 1954-57, sr. resident, 1956-57; asst. clin. prof. medicine UCLA Sch. Medicine, 1957—; attending physician Cedars Sinai Med. Ctr., L.A., 1957-96, attending physician emeritus, 1996—; attending physician UCLA, 1957-95. Med. advisor Vis. Nurse Assn., Los Angeles, 1957-87. Contbr. articles to med. jours.; inventor blow-through high altitude chamber; promoter iodine method of personal water disinfection for travelers and hikers. Served with USNR, 1943-46; lt. (M.C.), USNR, 1952-54. Fellow ACP; mem. AMA, Microscope Soc. So. Calif. Am. Handel Soc., Sierra Club. Home: 3309 Corinth Ave Los Angeles CA 90066-1312 E-mail: fredandbarbara@attbi.com.

KAHN, HERTA HESS (MRS. HOWARD KAHN), retired securities trader; b. Wuerzburg, Germany;, naturalized, U.S. d. Ferdinand and Lilly (Suesser) Hess; m. Herbert Levy (dec.); 1 child, Linda Levy; m. Howard Kahn (dec.). Student, Northwestern U. Sch. Commerce. Joined Paine, Webber, Jackson & Curtis, Inc., Chgo., 1941; registered rep. Paine, Webber Inc., acct. v.p., v.p. investments; ret., 1994; mktg. cons., 1995—. Author: (book) What Every Woman Should Know About Investing Her Money, 1968. Hon. life mem. nat. commn., hon. life. mem. Chgo. exec. com. Anti-Defamation League B;nai B'rith; bd. dirs. Found. Hearing and Speech Rehab., Chgo. Mem.: Chgo. Crime Commn., Chgo. Fin. Exch., Assn. Investment Mgmt. and Rsch., Investment Analysts Soc. Chgo., N.Y. Soc. Security Analysts, Tamarisk Country Club (Rancho Mirage, Calif.), Execs. Club (Chgo.), Econ. Club, Std. Club, Northmoor Country Club (Highland Park, Ill.).

KAHN, IRWIN WILLIAM, industrial engineer; b. N.Y.C., Feb. 3, 1923; s. Milton and Clara (Clark) K.; BS, U. Calif.-Berkeley, 1949; student Cath. U., 1943-44; m. Mildred Cross, May 14, 1946 (dec. May 1966); children: Steven Edward, Michael William, Evelyn Ruth, Joanne Susan; m. 2d, Marajayne Smith, Oct. 9, 1979. Chief indsl. engr. Malsbary Mfg. Co., Oakland, Calif., 1953-57, Yale & Towne Mfg. Co., San Leandro, Calif., 1957-60; sr. indsl. engr. Eitel McCulloch, San Carlos, Calif., 1961-62, Lockheed, Sunnyvale, Calif., 1962-69; v.p. Performance Investors, Inc., Palo Alto, 1969-74; with Kaiser-Permanente Svcs., Oakland, 1974-76; nat. mgr. material handling Cutter Labs., Berkeley, Calif., 1976-83; sr. mgmt. engr. Children's Hosp. Med. Ctr., Oakland, 1983; sr. indsl. engr. Naval Air Rework Facility, Alameda, Calif., 1983-85, Naval Supply Ctr., Oakland, 1985-88; vis. lectr. U. Calif., Berkeley, 1986; tchr. indsl. engring. Laney Coll., Oakland, 1967—, Chabot Coll., Hayward, Calif.; pres. East Bay Table Pad Co., 1990. Chmn. Alameda County Libr. Adv. Commn., 1965—. Served with AUS, 1943-46. Registered profl. engr., Calif. Mem. Am. Inst. Indsl. Engrs. (chpt. pres. 1963-64, chmn. conf. 1967 nat. publ. dir. aerospace div. 1968-69), Calif. Soc. Profl. Engrs. (pres. chpt.). Club: Toastmasters (dist. gov. 1960-61).

KAHN, JAMES ROBERT, lawyer; b. Indpls., Apr. 11, 1953; s. Robert D. and Rose Doris (Hyman) K.; m. Debra Amper, Oct. 21, 1984; children: Adam Joshua, Aliza Toby. BA, U. Pa., 1974; JD, Harvard U., 1978. Bar: Pa. 1978, U.S. Dist. Ct. (ea. dist.) Pa. 1978, U.S. Ct. Appeals (3d cir.) 1982, N.J. 1985, U.S. Dist. Ct. N.J. 1985, U.S. Dist. Ct. (ea. and so. dists.) N.Y. 1988. Jud. clk. U.S. Dist. Ct. Dist. N.J., Camden, 1978-79; assoc. Blank, Rome, Comisky & McCauley, Phila., 1979-88, ptnr., 1988-95, Margolis Edelstein, 1995—. Chair Phila. Bar state civil cts. com., 1994; mem. Gov.'s Task Force on Med. Malpractice, 2002-2003. Bd. dirs., v.p., sec. Jewish Family and Children's Svcs., Phila., 1988—; bd. dirs. Phila. Pride, Inc., 1994-97; bd. dirs., sec. Schylkill River Devel. Coun., Inc., 1993-2002; trustee Jewish Fedn. Greater Phila., 1993—; mem. United Jewish Appeal Young Leadership Cabinet, 1992-96. Recipient Young Leadership award Jewish Fedn. of Greater Phila., 1993, Stella Moore award for contbns. to dance in Phila., 1994. Mem. Pa. Bar Assn., Phila. Bar Assn., Assn. Trial Lawyers Am., Pa. Trial Lawyers Assn., Phila. Trial Lawyers Assn., Phila. Bicycle Club. Avocation: biking. Home: 2420 Fitlers Walk Philadelphia PA 19103-5562 Office: Margolis Edelstein Curtis Ctr 4th Fl Independence Sq W Philadelphia PA 19106-3304 E-mail: jkahn@mangolisedelstein.com.

KAHN, JAMES STEVEN, retired museum director; b. N.Y.C., Oct. 14, 1931; 3 children. BS in Geology, CCNY, 1952; MS in Minerology, Pa. State U., 1954; PhD in Geol. Sci., U. Chgo., 1956. Instr. U. R.I., Kingston, 1957, asst. prof., 1958-60, research assoc. Narragansett Marine Lab., 1957-60; group leader U. Calif., Livermore, 1960-70; dept. head Physics Internat. Co., San Leandro, Calif., 1970-71; div. head geophysics U. Calif., Livermore, 1972—74, dep. assoc. dir. human resources, 1975-78, assoc. dir. nuclear testing, 1978-80, dep. dir. lab., 1980-87; pres., chief exec. officer, dir. Mus. Sci. and Industry, Chgo., 1987-97; retired, emeritus. Trustee Mus. Sci. and Industry; mem. math. scis. cdn. bd. NAS, 1991-94; chmn. sci. adv. com. Gov. Ill., 1994-98; IMAX Corp. Co-author: Statistical Analysis in Geological Sciences, 1962; cntbr.: Microstructure, 1968; contbr. articles to scientific jours. Trustee Geol. Soc. Am. Found., 1997—, fellow Geol. Soc. Am.; bd. dirs. Franklin and Eleanor Roosevelt Inst., 1994-2001, Dubuque (Iowa) Art Inst., 1999-02, emeritus trustee Dubuque Mus. Art; rector sci. and medicine Lincoln Acad. Ill., 1994-2002; mem., vice-chmn. Bd. Natural Resources and Conservation, State of Ill. Centennial fellow Pa. State U. Coll. Earth and Mineral Scis., 1996. Mem. Missions Hills (Calif.) Country Club, Sigma Xi. Unitarian Universalist. E-mail: j.bk@verizon.net

KAHN, JAN EDWARD, manufacturing company executive; b. Dayton, Ohio, Aug. 29, 1948; s. Sigmond Lawrence and Betty Jane K.; m. Deborah Ann Deckinga, Nov. 28, 1975; children: Jason Edward, Justin Allen, Julie Ann. BS in Metall. Engring., U. Cin., 1971. Mgmt. trainee U.S. Steel Corp., Gary, Ind., 1971-72; plant metallurgist Regal Tube Co., Chgo., 1972-74, gen. foreman, 1974-76, supt., 1976-77, mgr. tech. svc., 1978-80, materials mgr., 1980-81; mgr. quality contrl Std. Tube Co., Detroit, 1977-78; dir. ops. Boye Needle Co., Chgo., 1981-82, v.p. ops., 1982-83, v.p., gen. mgr., 1984-85, pres., 1985-88; v.p. sales and mktg. Caron Internat., Washington, N.C., 1988 . Bd. dirs. Warm Up Am., Craft Yarn Coun. Mem. Am. Soc. Metals, AIME, ASTM, Ravenswood Indsl. Coun. (bd. dirs. 1983-84, pres. 1985), hand Knitting Assn. (chmn. 1986-88). Republican. Mem. Christian Reformed Ch. Home: 13909 Teakwood Dr Lockport IL 60441-8697 Office: Caron Internat PO Box 3000 Orland Park IL 60462-1099 E-mail: wa8lis@accesschicago.net.

KAHN, JASON S. investment banker, consultant; b. Huntington, N.Y., Dec. 5, 1979; s. Donald and Ann Kahn. Bachelor's Degree, U. Vt., 2002. Real estate investment banker Credit Suisse First Boston, N.Y.C., 2002—. Avocations: snowboarding, rock climbing. Office: Credit Suisse First Boston 11 Madison Ave New York NY 10010

KAHN, JESSICA ANNETTE, pediatrics educator, researcher; b. Birmingham, Ala., Dec. 2, 1964; d. Henry and Iris Rubin Spira; m. Robert Steven Kahn, Apr. 14, 1991; children: Rebecca Natalie, Ethan Henry. BArch summa cum laude, Princeton U., 1986; MD, Harvard U., 1992, MPH, 1999. Diplomate Am. Bd. of Pediats. Instr. in pediats. Harvard Med. Sch., Boston, 1998—99; asst. prof. of pediats. U. of Cin., 1999—. Recipient Young Investigator award, N.Am. Soc. for Pediat. and Adolescent Gynecology. Mem.: Assn. of Reproductive Health Profls., Soc. for Adolescent Medicine (New Investigator award), Am. Acad. of Pediat., Phi Beta Kappa. Office: Cin Children's Hosp Med Ctr 3333 Burnet Ave Cincinnati OH 45229 Office Fax: 513-636-8844.

KAHN, JIM, magazine publisher; m. Cyd Kahn; 1 child, Miranda. BS in Bus. Mgmt., SUNY, Binghamton, 1980. Account exec. Golf Mag. Properties, N.Y.C., 1986, west coast mgr. L.A., assoc. pub. N.Y.C., 1990-96, pub., sr. v.p., 1996—. Office: Golf Mag Times Mirror Mags Inc 2 Park Ave Rm 1101 New York NY 10016-5604*

KAHN, LAURENCE MICHAEL, lawyer, business consultant; b. Chgo., May 15, 1947; s. Ernest Newman and Louise (Schoenberg) K.; m. Geraldine Marie Hirsch, July 31, 1971 (div. Oct. 1985); children: Eric M., Melissa M.; m. Candace L. Ross, Sept. 7, 1991. BA magna cum laude, U. Pa., 1969, MS in Edn., 1971; JD cum laude, U. Mich., 1977. Bar: Mich. 1977, D.C. 1980, Md. 1981, U.S. Dist. Ct. Md. 1981, U.S. Dist. Ct. D.C. 1981, U.S. Ct. Claims 1989, U.S. Ct. Appeals (D.C. cir) 1992, Calif. 1994. Tchr. Northbrook (Ill.) Sch. Dist. 27, 1969-70, Abington (Pa.) Sch. Dist., 1971-73, Phila. Sch. Dist., 1973-74; staff atty. FTC, Washington, 1977-81; from assoc. to ptnr. Sherman Meehan & Curtin, PC, Washington, 1981-91; pres. Negotiated Solutions, San Diego, 1991—, Washington, 1991—; dep. city atty. San Diego City Atty.'s Office, 1994-95; bus. cons. The Thomas Group, Medford, Oreg., 2001—. Adj. prof. U. Md., College Park, 1981, Nat. U., San Diego, 1997, San Diego State U., 1999-2001. Bd. dirs. San Diego Urban League, San Diego Civic Light Opera Assn. Mem. ATLA, Phi Beta Kappa. Avocations: jogging, participating in team sports, canoeing, hiking, ornithology.

KAHN, LINDA MCCLURE, actuary, consultant; b. Jacksonville, Fla. d. George Calvin and Myrtice Louise (Boggs) McClure; m. Paul Markham Kahn, May 20, 1968. BS with highest honors, U. Fla.; MS, U. Mich., 1964. Actuarial trainee N.Y. Life Ins. Co., N.Y.C., 1964-66, actuarial asst., 1966-69, asst. actuary, 1969-71; v.p., actuary U.S. Life Ins., Pasadena, Calif., 1972-74; mgr. Coopers & Lybrand, L.A., 1974-76; sr. cons. San Francisco, 1976-82; dir. program mgmt. Pacific Maritime Assn., San Francisco, 1982-97; pres., CEO P.M. Kahn & Assocs., 1997—; chmn., CEO Paul and Linda Kahn Found., 1998—. Bd. dirs. San Francisco Nat. Maritime Mus. Libr., 1998—; trustee ILWU-PMA Welfare Plan, 1982—97, SIU-PD-PMA Pension and Supplemental Benefits Plans, 1982—90, Seafarers Med. Ctr., 1982—90; bd. dirs. Pacific Heights Residents Assn., 1978—93, sec.-treas. bd. dirs., 1981; bd. dirs. Friends of St. Frances Childcare Ctr., 2002—, CFO, 2003. Fellow Soc. Actuaries (chmn. com. on minority recruiting 1988-91, chmn. actuary of future sect. 1993-95), Conf. Cons. Actuaries; mem. Internat. Actuarial Assn., Internat. Assn. Con. Actuaries, Actuarial Studies Non-Life Ins., Am. Acad. Actuaries (enrolled actuary), Western Pension and Benefits Conf. (newsletter editor 1983-85, sec. 1985-88, treas. 1989-90), Actuarial Club Pacific States, San Francisco Actuarial Club (pres. 1981), Met. Club, Commonwealth Club, Soroptimists (v.p. 1973-74), Concordia-Argonaut Club, Pacific Club (Honolulu), Book Club Calif., Colophon Club. Home and Office: 2430 Pacific Ave San Francisco CA 94115-1238

KAHN, MARC JEFFREY, science educator; b. Phila., June 7, 1961; S. Neal Stanley and Marlene Joyce (Tanenbaum) K.; m. Chris M. Matteo, April 25, 1987; children: Benjamin Aaron, Abigail Sarah. BA, U. Pa., 1979-83, MD, 1983-87. Resident Hosp. U. Pa., Phila., 1987-90, chief med. res., 1990-91, fellow hematology, 1991-94; internal med. program dir. Tulane U. Sch. of Medicine, New Orleans, 1994—, student programs assoc. dir., 1996—2002, assoc. dean for student affairs, 2002—. Contbr. articles to Biochemistry, Am. Jour. Hematology, Acad. Medicine, Focus and Opinion in Internal Medicine, Am. Jour. Medicine, Jour. Clin. Oncology, Jour. Cancer Edn. Recipient Nat. Rsch. Svc. award Nat. Inst. Health, 1993. Fellow: ACP; mem.: Assn. Program Dirs. in Internal Medicine, Am. Soc. Hematology, Alpha Omega Alpha (treas., councilor). Office: Tulane Sch of Med 1430 Tulane Ave New Orleans LA 70112-2699 E-mail: mkahn@tulane.edu.

KAHN, MARC LESLIE, orthopedic surgeon; b. Phila., Mar. 12, 1956; s. Sigmund and Joanne (Pokras) K.; m. Cynthia Petrowsky; 4 children. AB, Lafayette Coll., 1978; MD, Hahnemann Med. Coll., 1982. Resident in orthopedics Monmouth Med. Ctr., Long Branch, N.J., 1987; surgeon, maj. U.S. Army, Ft. Dix, N.J., 1987-91; orthopedic surgeon Garden State Orthopedics, Pennsauken, N.J., 1991—. Clin. instr. N.J. Sch. Osteo. Medicine. Contbr. articles. Decorated Army Achievement medal with 2 oak leaf clusters, Meritorious Svc. medal. Fellow: Arthroscopy Assn. N.Am., Am. Acad. Orthop. Surgeons; mem.: AMA, N.J. Acad. Medicine, Camden County Med. Soc, Orthop. Surgeons of N.J. (bd. dirs., sec.), N.J. Orthop. Soc. (sec., bd. dirs.), N.J. Med. Soc. Home: 6 Regan Ct Kirkwood Voorhees NJ 08043

KAHN, MARILYN ZELDIN, artist, art educator; b. N.Y.C., Nov. 21, 1928; d. Jacob and Sarah Zeldin; m. Ernest Joseph Kahn, June 4, 1950; children: David Lawton, Richard Barry. Cert., Traphagen Sch., N.Y.C., 1948, Art Students League, 1950; student, Bklyn. Mus. Sch., 1949. Art tchr. studio classes, Sharon, Mass., 1960—. Juror Mansfield Art Festival, 1985, Easton Art Festival, 1987, Stoughton Art Assn. Show, 1988, 94, Franklin Art Assn., 2000. One-woman show Audubon Gallery at Moosehill Sanctuary, Sharon, Mass., 1992, Stonehill Coll., Easton, Mass., 1987; group shows include Perkins Gallery, Stoughton, Mass., 1998, 2000, Moosehill Gallery, Sharon, Mass., 1998, 2000, Caccivio & Sons Gallery, 1990-92, Cambridge Art Assn. Gallery, 1968—, Wenninger's Gallery, Rockport, Mass., 1970-89, Attleboro (Mass.) Mus., 1972, Easton Art Festival, 1989, Fuller Art Mus., Brockton, Mass., 1994, 95, Ogunquit Art Ctr., 1995, 96, Perkins Gallery, Stoughton, Mass., 1998, Audubon Gallery, Sharon, 1998, Artistic Appetites Gallery, Hyannis, Mass., 1998, 99, 2000, 01, 02, Lilac Moon, Sharon, Mass., 1999, 2000, 2001, Book and Cup, Inc., Sharon, 1999-00. Pres. Sharon (Mass.) League of Women Voters, 1975-76; chairperson Sharon (Mass.) Planning Bd., 1980, 85, active, 1976-86. Recipient numerous 1st Prizes, and other honorable mentions. Mem. Nat. Mus. Women in Arts, New Eng. Watercolor Soc. (assoc.), Cambridge Art Assn., Sharon Creative Arts Assn.

(program co-chair 1993-95, past pres. 1972, 73), Fuller Art Mus. Avocations: square dancing, ballroom dancing, weight training, gardening. Home: 114 Ames St Sharon MA 02067-2118 E-mail: mzkahn@comcast.net.

KAHN, MARIO SANTAMARIA, international marketing executive; b. Manila, Jan. 16, 1956; came to U.S., 1980; s. Rene L. and Dolores (Santamaria) K.; m. Maria Victoria Legaspi, Dec. 28, 1987; 1 child, Marc Daniel. AB in Mktg. & Comm., De La Salle U., Manila, 1977; MA in Comm. Mgmt. cum laude, U. So. Calif., 1982; postgrad., Stanford U., 1989. Account mgr. McCann-Erickson, Manila, 1977—80; teaching asst. U. So. Calif., L.A., 1980—82; ops. mgr. Dayton-Hudson Corp., Mpls., 1982—85; dir. trademark licensing Sunkist Growers, Sherman Oaks, Calif., 1986—. Bd. dirs. Sunkist Soft Drink Internat., Travelers Century. Mem. Am. Mktg. Assn., Am. Mgmt. Assn., Stanford Alumni Assn., Annenberg Alumni Assn., De La Salle Alumni Assn., USC Gen. Alumni Assn. Office: Sunkist Growers Inc 14130 Riverside Dr Sherman Oaks CA 91423-2313

KAHN, MARK LEO, arbitrator, educator; b. N.Y.C., Dec. 16, 1921; s. Augustus and Manya (Fertig) K.; m. Ruth Elizabeth Wecker, Dec. 21, 1947 (div. Jan. 1972); children: Ann Mariam, Peter David, James Allan, Jean Sarah; m. Elaine Johnson Morris, Feb. 12, 1988. BA, Columbia U., 1942; MA, Harvard U., 1948, PhD in Econs., 1950. Asst. economist U.S. OSS, Washington, 1942-43; tchg. fellow Harvard U., 1947-49; dir. case analysis U.S. WSB, Region 6-B Mich., 1952-53; mem. faculty Wayne State U., Detroit, 1949-85, prof. econs., 1960-85, prof. emeritus, 1985—, dept. chmn., 1961-68, dir. indsl. rels. M.A. program, 1978-85. Arbitrator union-mgmt. disputes. Co-author: Collective Bargaining and Technological Change in American Transportation, 1971; mem. editl. bd. Employee Responsibilities and Rights Jour., 1988-96; contbr. articles to profl. jours. Bd. govs. Jewish Welfare Fedn. Detroit, 1976-82; bd. dirs. Jewish Home for Aged, Detroit, 1978-93, Lyric Chamber Ensemble, Southfield, Mich., 1995-97, Detroit Empowerment Zone Devel. Corp., 1996-99. Pvt. to Capt. AUS, 1943-46. Decorated Bronze Star; recipient Disting. Svc. award U.S. Nat. Mediation Bd., 1987, Am. Arbitration Assn., 1992. Mem. AAUP (past chpt. pres.), Nat. Acad. Arbitrators (bd. govs. 1960-62, v.p. 1976-78, chmn. membership com. 1979-82, pres. 1983-84, chmn. nominating com. 1993-96), Indsl. Rels. Rsch Assn. (pres. Detroit chpt. 1956, exec. sec. 1979-89, nat. exec. bd. 1985-88), Soc. Profls. in Dispute Resolution (v.p. 1982-83, pres. 1986-87). Home and Office: 15151 Ford Rd Apt 321 Dearborn MI 48126-5027 E-mail: mleokahn@aol.com.

KAHN, MARTIN L. physician, educator; b. N.Y.C., Apr. 29, 1939; s. Harry and Bess Kahn; m. CArol LynnAnn Kahn, Aug. 12, 1962; children: Matthew E., Michael A. BS, Queens Coll., 1959; MD, NYU, 1963. Diplomate in internal medicine and cardiovascular disease Am. Bd. Internal Medicine. Asst. prof. medicine NYU Sch. Medicine, N.Y.C., 1972-77, assoc. prof. clin. medicine, 1977-82, prof. clin. medicine, 1982—, Joel E. and Joan L. Smilow prof. cardiology, 2002—. Contbr. chpt. to book, articles to profl. jours. Capt. U.S. Army, 1967. Jonas Salk scholar City of N.Y., 1963. Fellow Am. Coll. Cardiology; mem. Am. Heart Assn., Harvey Soc., NYU Sch. Medicine Alumni Assn. (pres. 1986-87, bd. dirs. 1981—, Gt. Tchr. award 1998), Phi Beta Kappa. Office: NYU Sch Medicine 530 1st Ave New York NY 10016-6402 E-mail: Martin.Kahn@med.nyu.edu.

KAHN, MELVIN A. political science educator; b. N.Y.C., Nov. 17, 1930; s. Meyer Miles Shomer and Hannah Abrams Shomer Kahn; m. Adrienne Phyllis Iseberg, Aug. 17, 1958 (div. Apr. 1974); children: David Kahn, Sharonah Greenberg, Miriam Sichel; m. Helen Joan Gleeson, May 24, 1986. BA, U. Fla., 1952; MA, U. Chgo., 1958; PhD, Ind. U., 1964. Lectr. Ind. U. Labor Inst., Bloomington, 1959-61; asst. prof. Ind. State U., Terre Haute, 1961-65; assoc. prof. So. Ill. U., Carbondale, 1965-70; prof. polit. sci. Wichita State U., 1970—, chair polit. sci., 1970-76. Co-dir. Kans. Seminar, Taft Inst., N.Y.C., 1976-88; Alexander Hamilton portrayer and lectr., 1986—. Author: The Politics of American Labor, 1970; co-author: The Winning Ticket, 1983; contbr. articles to profl. jours. Bd. dirs. Mid-Kans. Jewish Fedn., 1999—; downstate campaign mgr. Gov. Shapiro Com., Ill., 1968; exec. dir. Dem. County Com., Wichita, 1982; mem. state com. Kans. Dem. Party, 1995-96, 2000—; del. Dem. Nat. Conv., 2000. Recipient Excellence in Tchg. award Wichita State Bd. Regents, 1983, John M. Barrier Disting. Tchg. award, 1997, Mortar Bd. Educator Appreciation award, 1999-2000; named Kans. Prof. of Yr., Coun. for Advancement and Support of Edn., 1989; Nat. Endowment fellow Princeton U., 1986, Andrus Found.-AARP grantee, 1980. Mem. AAUP, Am. Polit. Sci. Assn., Wichita Downtown Lions (bd. dirs. 1982-86). Democrat. Jewish. Home: 7700 E 13th St N Unit 4 Wichita KS 67206-1289 Office: Wichita State U Campus Box 17 Polit Sci Dept Wichita KS 67260-0017

KAHN, MICHAEL, stage director; b. N.Y.C. s. Frederick J. and Adele (Gaberman) K. BA, Columbia U.; DHL (hon.), U. S.C., 1994, Kean Coll., 1974. Artistic dir. Am. Shakespeare Theatre, Stratford, Conn., 1969-77, The Acting Co., 1978-88, Chautauqua Conservatory Theatre Co., 1985-88, Shakespeare Theatre, Washington, 1986—; dir. Chautauqua Inst. Theatre Sch., 1983-88; dir. drama divsn. Juilliard Sch., N.Y.C., 1992—; acad. chmn. Brit. Am. Drama Acad., Oxford, Eng., 1992-96; artistic dir. The Shakespeare Theatre Acad. for Classical Acting George Washington U., Washington, 2000—. Mem. faculty Circle in the Square, N.Y.C., Princeton U.; mem. faculty grad. program Sch. Arts, NYU; mem. panel League of Profl. Theatre Tng. Programs; bd. dirs. Theatre Comm. Group, Theatre Panel, N.Y. State Coun. of Arts; mem. theatre panel Nat. Endowment for Arts; panel mem. D.C. Commn. on Humanities and the Arts; artistic dir. Shakespeare Theater Acad. for Classical Acting, George Washington U., 2000—. Dir. Romeo and Juliet (Helen Hayes nomination), The Winter's Tale, Macbeth (Helen Hayes nomination), All's Well that Ends Well (Helen Hayes nomination), Anthony and Cleopatra, As You Like It, Twelfth Night (Helen Hayes award 1989), Merry Wives of Windsor (Helen Hayes nomination), Richard III, 1990 (Helen Hayes nomination), King Lear, 1991, Much Ado About Nothing, 1992, Measure for Measure, 1992, Hamlet, 1993 (Helen Hayes award 1993), Mother Courage (Helen Hayes award), 1993, Richard II, 1993, The Doctor's Dilemma, 1994, Henry IV, 1994 (Helen Hayes award), Henry V (Helen Hayes nomination), Volpone, 1996, Henry VI (Helen Hayes award), 1996, Mourning Becomes Electra, (Helen Hayes Award) 1997; Peer Gynt (1997); Sweet Bird of Youth, 1998, A Woman of No Importance, 1998, King John, 1999, The Merchant of Venice, 1999, King Lear, 1999, Coriolanus, 1999, Camino Real, 2000, Timon of Athena, 2000, Don Carlos, 2001 (Helen Hayes nomination), The Oedipus Playe, 2001, The Duchess of Malfi, 2002, Hedda Gabler, 2001, The Winters' Tale, 2002, The Silent Woman, 2003; producing dir. McCarter Theater, Princeton, N.J.; plays including Beyond The Horizon, Mother Courage, Grave Undertaking, The Heiress, Angel City, The Torchbearers, A Month in the Country, Put Them All Together, 1974—; dir. Broadway prodns. The Death of Bessie Smith, 1967, Here's Where I Belong, 1968, Cat On A Hot Tin Roof, 1974, Night of the Tribades, 1977, Whodunnit, 1983, Showboat, 1983 (Tony nomination); off-Broadway prodns. Funnyhouse of A Negro, 1966, Rimers of Eldritch, 1967, Thorton Wilder plays, 1967, N.Y. Shakespeare Festival's Measure for Measure, 1966, Grand Magic, Manhattan Theatre Club, 1978, A Month in the Country, Roundabout, 1980, Hedda Gabler, Roundabout, 1981, Flux, 1982, Something Different, 1983, Ten By Tennessee, 1986, Sleep Deprivation Chamber, 1996, Goodman Theatre, Chgo., Old Times, 1972, Tooth of Crime, 1973, Tis Pity She's a Whore, 1974, Showboat, Cairo, Egypt, 1987, Five By Tennessee, 1989, Moscow, Leningrad, Vilmius Warsaw, Belgrade, 1990, Signature Theatre Otabenga, Va., 1994, The Oedipus Plays, Athens Festival, 2003; TV prodn. Beyond the Horizon, WNET, 1975; San Francisco Opera Julio Cesare, 1978, The Acting Co., 1978—, A New Way to Pay Old Debts, 1984, The White Devil, 1979, Carmen, Houston Grand Opera, 1981, Carmen, Washington Opera, 1982, The Glass Menagerie, Chautauqua Conservatory Theatre, 1985, Tis Pity She's a Whore (Am. Repertory Theatre), 1988, Much Ado About Nothing, McCarter Theatre, 1993, Vanessa, Dallas Opera, 1994, Washington Opera, 1995. Recipient Best Dir. Revival award Saturday Rev., 1966; Charles MacArthur award for best dir. Old Times, 1973, Joseph Jefferson award, 1974, Washington Post award, 1989; named Best Dir. N.J. Drama Critics, 1974, 76, Washingtonian of Yr. Washingtonian mag., 1989; nominated for 4 Vernon Rice awards, 1967, John Houseman award, Globe Theater award, Bravo award Opera Music Theatre Internat., 1997, D.C. Mayor's Art award, 1997, Champs Cmty. award, 2000, William Shakespeare award for Classical Theatre, 2002, Univ. Club Cultural award of the Yr., 2002, GLAAD Capitol Area award, 2002, Lifetime Achievement award SETC, 2003. Home: 1 W 72nd St New York NY 10023-3486 Office: The Shakespeare Theatre 301 E Capitol St SE Washington DC 20003-3808 E-mail: mkahn@shakespeardc.org.

KAHN, NANCY VALERIE, publishing and entertainment executive, consultant; b. N.Y.C., Dec. 15, 1952; d. Alfred Joseph and Miriam (Kadin) K. BA magna cum laude, Princeton U., 1974. Dir. prodn. and devel. Bus. Rsch. Publs., Inc.-MacRAE's Directories, N.Y.C., 1984-86; assoc. pub., exec. editor Leadership Directories Inc., N.Y.C., 1987-88; dir. new product devel. Gale Rsch. Inc., N.Y.C., 1988-89; pub., editorial dir. directories and info. devel. Adweek, N.Y.C., 1989—93; v.p. Everlink Corp., N.Y.C., 1993—94; prin. NVK Comm., N.Y.C., 1994—. Univ. scholar Princeton U., 1974. Mem. Directory and Database Pubs. Forum & Network, Manhattan Assn. Cabarets. Avocations: arts, musical theatre, cabaret, foreign travel, walking. Office: NVK Comm PO Box 826 New York NY 10021

KAHN, NORMAN, pharmacology and dentistry educator; b. N.Y.C., Dec. 28, 1932; s. Louis Meyer and Dorothy (Simon) Kohn; m. Dale Krasnow, Mar. 30, 1958 AB, Columbia U., 1954, D.D.S., 1958, PhD, 1964. Lic. dentist, N.Y. State. Dental intern Montefiore Hosp., Bronx, N.Y., 1958-59; instr. Coll. Physicians and Surgeons, Columbia U., N.Y.C., 1962-65, asst. prof., 1965-72, assoc. prof., 1972-80, prof. pharmacology, 1980-99, prof. dentistry, 1980-92, Edwin S. Robinson prof. dentistry, 1992-99; assoc. dean acad. affairs Sch. Dental and Oral Surgery, Columbia U., 1989-94, acting dean, 1994-95; attending dentist Presbyn. Hosp., N.Y.C., 1985-99, Robinson prof. dentistry & pharm. emeritus, spl. lectr., 1999—, cons. dentist, 1999—. Vis. assoc. prof. UCLA, 1978; chair instl. rev. bd. Columbia-Presbyn. Med. Ctr., N.Y.C., 1981-91; cons. pharmcologist Harlem Hosp., N.Y.C., 1966-80; vis. scientist U. Pisa, Italy, 1965-66. Contbr. chpts. to books, articles to profl. jours. NIH grantee, 1969-75, Nat. Fund Med. Edn. grantee, 1973; recipient Outstanding Contbn. to Teaching award Columbia U. Coll. Physicians and Surgeons, 1980, Physicians & surgeons Disting. Svc. award in Pre-Clinical Yrs., 2001; hon. research fellow Univ. Coll., London, 1986. Mem. Am. Physiol. Soc., ADA, Am. Assn. Dental Schs., Confrerie des Chevaliers du Tastevin, Alpha Omega Alpha, Omicron Kappa Upsilon Jewish. Avocation: oenology. Office: Columbia U 630 W 168th St New York NY 10032-3795

KAHN, PAUL FREDERICK, executive search company executive; b. Indpls., Oct. 10, 1935; s. Paul L. and Florence (Copeland) K.; m. Helen Gail Bass, Dec. 27, 1961; children— Hartley, Meredith. BS, Purdue U., 1957; MBA, Harvard U., 1963. Brand mgr. Procter and Gamble, Cin., 1963-69; v.p. Foote, Cone & Belding, N.Y.C., 1969-70; sr. v.p. Wilson Sporting Goods, Chgo., 1970-78, Sara Lee Corp., Chgo., 1978-87; pres., chief exec. officer Kayser-Roth Hosiery Co., 1988; mng. ptnr. Heidrick & Struggles, Chgo., 1989—. With USMC, 1957—60. Mem.: Sharon Country Club, Hillsboro Club, Harvard Club (N.Y. chpt.), Univ. Club, Indian Hill Country Club. Presbyterian. Home: 177 Scott Ave Winnetka IL 60093-1529 also: 100 Low Rd Sharon CT 06069-2015

KAHN, PETER B. physics educator; b. N.Y.C., Mar. 18, 1935; s. Morton E. and Lillian E. (Miller) K.; m. Lois Gibbs, Sept. 16, 1956 (div. 1986); children: Miriam, David, Jeffrey; m. Victoria McLane, Jan. 8, 1989. BS, Union Coll., 1956; PhD, Northwestern U., 1960. Research assoc. U. Iowa, Iowa City, 1960-61; from asst. to assoc. prof. physics SUNY, Stony Brook, 1961-71, prof. physics, 1971—2003, emeritus prof., 2003—, chmn. dept. physics, 1974-85. Fellow Am. Physics Soc. Office: SUNY Dept Physics Stony Brook NY 11794-3800

KAHN, RICHARD DREYFUS, lawyer; b. N.Y.C., Apr. 25, 1931; s. David Effrian and Lucille (Kahn) K.; m. Judith Raff, Sept. 10, 1961 (div. 1977); children— Jason, Adam, Alexander; m. Elaine H. Peterson, July 21, 1983 AB, Harvard U., 1952, JD, 1955. Bar: N.Y. 1955. Assoc. Debevoise & Plimpton, N.Y.C., 1955-62, ptnr., 1963-90, of counsel, 1991-93. Editor Harvard Law Rev., 1953-55 Trustee Am. Soc. Psychical Rsch., N.Y.C., 1966-73; bd. dirs. The Emerson Sch., N.Y.C., 1968-71, J. M.R. Barker Found., N.Y.C., 1968—, C. G. Jung Found. Analytical Psychology, 1984-90, Concerned Citizens of Montauk, 1991—, Group for the South Fork, 1993—; bd. dirs. Found. Child Devel, N.Y.C., 1970-88, coun. vice chmn., 1996-2000; mem. Montauk Citizens Adv. Com., 1992—. Mem. Assn. of Bar of City N.Y. (chmn. com. atomic energy 1965-68), Harvard Club N.Y.C. (bd. mgrs. 1991-93), Phi Beta Kappa. Home: 224 W Lake Dr Montauk NY 11954-5235 E-mail: arcon@optonline.net.

KAHN, ROBERT E. electrical engineer; b. Dec. 23, 1938; BEE, CCNY; MEE, PhD Elec. Engring., Princeton U. Mem. tech. staff Bell Telephone Labs.; asst. prof. elec. engring. MIT, Cambridge; sr. scientist Bolt, Beranek & Newman; dir. info. processing techniques DARPA; founder, pres. Corp. Nat. Research Initiatives, Reston, Va., 1986—. Recipient Nat. medal of Tech., U.S. Dept. of Commerce, 1997. Fellow: IEEE; mem.: NAE. Office: Corp for Nat Rsch Initiaves 1895 Preston White Dr Ste 100 Reston VA 20191-5434

KAHN, ROBERT L(OUIS), psychologist, educator; b. Detroit, Mich., Mar. 28, 1918; s. George Arthur and Mabel Jeanette Kahn; m. Beatrice Hilary Goldstein, Aug. 25, 1940; children: Judith, Marcia, Janet. BA, Univ. Mich., 1939, MA, 1940, PhD, 1952, Univ. Amsterdam, Amsterdam, Netherlands, 1985. Tchr. H.S., Detroit, 1940—41; survey dir. Work Projects Adminstrn., Detroit, 1941—42; survey analyst U.S. Bur. of the Census, Washington, 1942—48; prof., rsch. scientist Univ. Mich., Ann Arbor, 1948—88, prof., rsch. scientist, emeritus, 1988—. Bd. mem. Westport Adv. LTD, Palm Beach Gardens, 1990—, Buck Inst. on Aging, Novato, Calif., 1991; bd. mem., v.p. SPRY Found., Washington, 1992. Co-author: Dynamics of Interviewing, 1957, Organizational Stress, 1964, Social Psychology of Organization, 1978, Work and Health, 1981, ORganizations and Nation-States, 1990, Successful Aging, 1998. Fellow: Inst. of Medicine Nat. Acad. Sci., Am. Acad. of Arts and Sci.; mem.: Phi Beta Kappa. Democrat. Jewish. Home: 2115 Nature Cove 301A Ann Arbor MI 48104 Office: Inst for Soc Rsch 426 Thompson St Ann Arbor MI 48106-1248

KAHN, RONALD N. investment researcher; b. Schenectady, N.Y., Aug. 6, 1956; s. Ernest H. and Gloria K. Kahn. AB in Physics, Princeton U., 1978; PhD in Physics, Harvard U., 1985. Dir. rsch. Barra, Inc., Berkeley, Calif., 1991-98; global head equity rsch. Barclay Global Investors, San Francisco, 1998—. Editorial adv. bd. Jour. Portfolio Mgmt., N.Y.C., 1998—, Jour. Investment Cons., Denver, 1998—; author: Active Portfolio Management, 1995, 2d edit., 2000; contbr. articles to profl. jours. Recipient Journalism award Investment Mgmt. Cons. Assoc., Denver, 1995; Mass Media Sci. fellow AAAS, Washington, 1983. Avocations: travel, reading. Office: Barclays Global Investors 45 Fremont St San Francisco CA 94105-2204 E-mail: ron.kahn@barclaysglobal.com.

KAHN, SANDRA J. anesthesiologist; b. N.Y.C., Nov. 27, 1957; MD, Cornell U. Med. Coll., 1984. Diplomate Am. Bd. Anesthesiology. cert. pain mgmt. Intern Pa. Hosp., Phila., 1984-85; resident in anesthesiology U. Pa. Hosp., 1985-87, fellow in pain mgmt./cardiac anesthesia, 1987-88; staff Grad. Hosp., 1988—2002, Pa. Hosp., 2002—. Clin. asst. prof. anesthesiology U. Pa, 1989-97, Hahnemann Sch. Medicine, Phila., 1998-2001. Mem. Am. Soc. Anesthesiology. Office: Penn Hosp Dept Anesthesiology 800 Spruce St Philadelphia PA 19107-6192

KAHN, SANDRA S. psychotherapist; b. Chgo., June 24, 1942; d. Chester and Ruth Sutker; m. Jack Murry Kahn, June 1, 1965; children: Erick, Jennifer. BA, U. Miami, 1964; MA, Roosevelt U., 1976. Tchr. Chgo. Pub. Schs., 1965-67; pvt. practice psychotherapy, Northbrook, Ill., 1976—. Host Shared Feelings, Sta. WEEF-AM, Highland Park, Ill., 1983—; author: The Kahn Report on Sexual Preferences, 1981, The Ex Wife Syndrome Cutting The Cord and Breaking Free After The Marriage Is Over, 1990; columnist Single Again mag. Mem. Ill. Psychol. Assn., Chgo. Psychol. Assn. (past pres. 1990). Jewish. Office: 801 Skokie Blvd Northbrook IL 60062-4039

KAHN, SIGMUND BENHAM, retired internist and dean; b. Phila., May 18, 1933; s. Maxwell Louis and Clara (Parris) K.; m. Joanne Pokras, June 11, 1955; children: Marc L., Elissa Kahn Petrosky, Hillary Kahn Roth, Lauren B. Westlake. BA, U. Pa., 1954, MD, 1958. Diplomate Am. Bd. Internal Medicine; cert. hematology and med. oncology. Rotating intern Albert Einstein Med. Ctr., Phila., 1958-59; resident in internal medicine Hosp. of U. Pa., Phila., 1959-61, fellow in hematology, 1961-62, USPHS rsch. fellow dept. hematology, 1962-63; assoc. in hematology medicine Hahnemann U. Hosp., Phila., 1963-66, asst., assoc., then prof. medicine, 1966-99; prof. dept. neoplastic disease Hahnemann Univ. Hosp., Phila., 1978-99, dir. edn., vice chmn. dept., 1978-94; assoc. dean Hahnemann U., Phila., 1986-94; prof. emeritus, 1999—2002; prof. dept. medicine divsn. hematology/ med. oncology Med. Coll. Pa./Hahnemann U., Phila., 1992-94, assoc. dean edn., 1992-94, prof. emeritus, 1999—2002, Drexel U. Coll. of Med., 2002—. Cons., chmn. dean's com. Wilkes-Barre (Pa.) VA Hosp., 1987-92. Mem. editl. bd. Jour. Cancer Edn., 1985-95, Am. Jour. Clin. Oncology; contbr. articles to profl. jours. Instl. rep. Boy Scouts Am., 1970-75; pres. Temple Beth Sholom, Cherry Hill, N.J., 1977-80; mem. med. bd. Lupus Found., Delaware Valley, 1977-79. Mem. AMA, ACP, Phila. County Med. Soc., Phila. Hematology Soc., Pa. Med. Soc., Am. Fedn. Clin. Rsch., Am. Hematology Soc., Am. Assn. Cancer Rsch., Am. Soc. Clin. Oncology, Am. Assn. Cancer Edn., Am. Cancer Soc. (chmn. patient svc. com. Phila. divsn. 1981-83, chmn. med. subcom. profl. edn. com. 1979-81, fin. com. 1981), Phi beta Kappa, Alpha Omega Alpha. Jewish. Home: 2307 Sagemore Dr Marlton NJ 08053-4315

KAHN, STEVEN EMANUEL, medical educator; b. Durban, South Africa, July 28, 1955; m. Stephanie Berk Kahn; 2 children. MB, ChB, U. Cape Town, South Africa, 1978. Diplomate Am. Bd. Internal Medicine. Intern depts. ob./gyn. and medicine Somerset Hosp., Cape Town, South Africa, 1979; resident dept. ob./gyn. 2 Mil. Hosp., Wynberg, South Africa, 1980, resident and coord. dept. ob./gyn., 1981; resident dept. medicine divsn. endocrinology Groote Schuur Hosp., Cape Town, 1982; rsch. fellow diabetes and endocrine rsch. group U. Cape Town, 1983; resident dept. medicine Albert Einstein Med. Ctr., Phila., 1983—86; sr. rsch. fellow divsn. metabolism, endocrinology and nutrition Dept. Medicine U. Wash. Sch. of Medicine, VA Med. Ctr., Seattle, 1986—88; assoc. investigator, staff physician divsn. endocrinology and metabolism Dept. Medicine VA Med. Ctr., Seattle, 1988—91, rsch. assoc., staff physician divsn. endocrinology and metabolism Dept. Medicine, 1991—95; acting instr. divsn. metabolism, endocrinology and nutrition Dept. Medicine U. Wash. Sch. of Medicine, Seattle, 1988—92, asst. prof. divsn. metabolism, endocrinology and nutrition Dept. Medicine, 1992—95, assoc. prof. divsn. metabolism, endocrinology and nutrition Dept. Medicine, 1995—2001, prof. divsn. metabolism, endocrinology and nutrition, 2001—; dir. R&D VA Puget Sound Health Care Sys., 2001—. Prizer vis. prof. Case Western Res. U., 1999. Mem. editl. bd. Jour. Clin. Endocrinology and Metabolism, 1995—98, Diabetes Care, 1997—99; contbr. articles to profl. jours. Named Assoc. Investigator, Dept. VA, 1988, Rsch. Assoc., 1991; recipient Career Devel. award, Juvenile Diabetes Found., 1988, NIH, 1999, Feasibility award, Dana Found., 1989, Clin. Investigator award, NIH, 1991, New Investigator award, Diabetes Rsch. Coun., 1992—94, rsch. award, NIH, 1997, Novartis Young Investigator award in diabetes rsch., 2001; scholar Amelia Schenkman, 1973—75. Mem.: ACP, Gen. Med. Coun. (U.K.), Western Soc. Clin. Investigation (councillor 1998—), Endocrine Soc., Am. Soc. for Clin. Investigation, Am. Fedn. Clin. Rsch. (chair program com. for metabolism 1994, 1996, councillor western sect. 1994—96, pres.-elect western sect. 1996, pres. western sect. 1997, nat. councillor 1996), Am. Diabetes Assn. (bd. dirs. Wash. affiliate 1993—94, exec. bd. dirs. 1994—98, rsch. grant rev. panel 1994—97, rsch. award 1996, mentor award 1999). Office: VA Puget Sound Health Cr Dept Medicine 151 1660 S Columbian Way Seattle WA 98108-1532

KAHN, SUSAN, artist; b. N.Y.C., Aug. 26, 1924; d. Jesse B. and Jenny Carol (Peshkin) Cohen; m. Joseph Kahn, Sept. 15, 1946 (dec.); m. Richard Rosenkranz, Feb. 1, 1981. Grad., Parsons Sch. Design, 1945; student, Moses Soyer, 1950-57. Subject of: book Susan Kahn, with an essay by Lincoln Rothschild, 1980; One-woman shows include Sagittarius Gallery, 1960, A.C.A., Galleries, 1964, 68, 71, 76, 80, Charles B. Goddard Art Center, Ardmore, Okla., 1973, Albrecht Gallery Mus. Art, St. Joseph, Mo., 1974, N.Y. Cultural Center, N.Y.C., 1974, St. Peter's Coll., Jersey City, 1978, Heidi Neuhoff Gallery, N.Y.C., 1989, Sindin Galleries, 1996; exhibited in group shows Audubon Artists, N.Y.C., Nat. Acad., N.Y.C., Springfield (Mass.) Mus., City Center, N.Y.C., A.C.A., Galleries, N.Y.C., Nat. Arts Club, N.Y.C., Butler Inst., Youngstown, Ohio, Islip Art Mus., East Islip. N.Y., 1989, Fine Arts Mus. of S., Mobile, Ala., 1989, Chatanooga Regional History Mus, 1989, Longview (Tex.) Mus. Art, 1990; represented in permanent collections, Tyler (Tex.) Mus., St. Lawrence U. Mus., Canton, N.Y., Fairleigh Dickinson U. Mus., Rutherford, N.J., Syracuse U. Mus., Sheldon Swope Gallery, Terre Haute, Ind., Montclair (N.J.) Mus. Fine Arts, Butler Inst. Am. Art, Youngstown, Ohio, Reading (Pa.) Mus., Albrecht Gallery Mus. Art, St. Joseph(Mo.), Cedar Rapids (Iowa) Art Center, N.Y. Cultural Center, N.Y.C., Edwin A. Ulrich Mus., Wichita, Kans., Wichita State U., Johns Hopkins Sch. Advanced Internat. Studies, Washington, Joslyn Mus., Omaha, U. Wyo., Laramie. Recipient Knickerbocker prize for best religious painting, 1956; Edith Lehman award Nat. Assn. Women Artists, 1958; Simmons award, 1961; Knickerbocker Artists award, 1961; Nat. Arts Club award, 1967; Knickerbocker Medal of Honor, 1964; Famous Artists Sch. award, 1967 Mem. Nat. Assn. Women Artists (Anne Barnett Meml. prize 1981, Solveig Stromsoe Palmer Meml. award 1987, Dorothy Schweitzer award 1990), Artists Equity, Met. Mus., Mus. Modern Art, Nat. Assn. Women Artists (meml. award 1987). *I choose to be a realist and humanist in my work. The most important objects of my concern are people, their lives and times. I believe that art is a way of communicating, subject matter translated into color, form and line, so that the work will express the idea convincingly.*

KAHN, SY MYRON, humanities educator, poet; b. N.Y.C., Sept. 15, 1924; s. Max Kahn, Sophie (Wagner) Kahn; m. Marion Belefant, June 15, 1947 (div. Oct. 1, 1962); 1 child, David Matthew; m. Nancy Dennis, Apr. 20, 1963 (div. Apr. 20, 1979); m. Janet Aline Baker, Nov. 25, 2000. BA, U. Pa., 1948; MA, U. Conn., 1951; PhD, U. Wis., 1957. Prof. English and drama U. of Pacific, Stockton, Calif., 1963—86. Exec. dir. Fallon House Theatre, Columbia, Calif., 1970—84; vis. prof. Am. Studies U. Wales, Swansea, 1987, Swansea, 97; vis prof. theatre Justus Liebig U., Giessen, Germany, 1987; prof. Am. Lit. Fulbright Commn., Salonika, Greece, 1957—58, Warsaw, 1966—67, Vienna, 1970—71, Porto, Portugal, 1985—86. Author: Between Tedium and Terror, 1993; author (poetry) Our Separate Darkness, 1963, Triptych, 1964, A Later Sun, 1966, Fight is With Phantoms, 1966, Another Time, 1968, Facing Mirrors, 1980; editor Interculture, 1975, Devour the Fire, 1984. Cpl. U.S. Army, 1943—45, PTO. Recipient Gardner Writing award, 1955, 1956, Borestone Poetry award, 1964, Promethean Lamp prize, 1966, Grand Prize Poetry, 1985, Angel of the Arts award, Port Townsend, 2003. Mem.: Modern Lang. Assn., Key City Players (v.p. 2000—, pres. 2002—03). Home: 1212 Holcomb St Port Townsend WA 98368

KAHN, THOMAS, medical educator; b. Offenburg, Germany, June 23, 1938; s. Ludwig and Ellen (Kaufman) K.; m. Si Mi Pak, Nov. 7, 1968; children: Diana, David, Philip. BA, NYU, 1958, MD, 1962. Intern medicine Balt. City Hosps., 1962-63, U. Pitts. Hosps., 1963-64, Mt. Sinai, N.Y.C., 1964-65, resident in nephrology, 1965-67; chief renal sect. Bronx VA Med. Ctr., 1979-96; prof. medicine Mt. Sinai Sch. Medicine, N.Y.C., 1988—. Maj. U.S. Army, 1967-69. Office: VA Med Ctr 130 W Kingsbridge Rd Bronx NY 10468-3904

KAHN, WOLF, artist; b. Stuttgart, Germany, Oct. 4, 1927; came to U.S., 1940, naturalized, 1946; s. Emil and Nellie (Budge) K.; m. Emily Mason, Mar. 2, 1957; children: Cecily, Melany. Student, Hans Hofmann Sch., 1948-49; BA, U. Chgo., 1951. Vis. prof. painting U. Calif., Berkeley, 1960; adj. assoc. prof. Cooper Union Art Sch., 1961-77; jury mem. numerous regional art shows artist-in-residenceDartmouth Coll., 1984. One-man shows include Borgenicht Gallery, N.Y.C., 1957-95, Beadleston Gallery, N.Y.C., 1998, 2000, Thoma Segal Gallery, Balt., 2000, Jerald Melberg Gallery, Charlotte, N.C., 1993-2000, Ft. Lauderdale Mus. Art, 1991, Boca Raton Mus. of Art, 1997; group shows include Whitney Mus., N.Y.C., 1960, 77, Met. Mus., N.Y.C., 1975-76; represented in permanent collections Mus. Modern Art, N.Y.C., Whitney Mus. Houston Mus. Fine Arts, Chase Manhattan Coll., Va. Mus., Met. Mus., N.Y.C., L.A. County Mus., Hirschhorn Mus., Washington; author: Pastel Light, 1983, Wolf Kahn pastels, 2000; contbr. articles to profl. jours. Trustee Brattleboro Mus. Vt., 1979—, Vt. Studio Sch.,1988—; apptd. N.Y.C. Art Commn., 1993-95. With USNR, 1945-46. Recipient award for art Am. Acad. Arts and Letters, 1979; Fulbright fellow Italy, 1964-65; Guggenheim fellow, 1967-68; Ford Found. grantee, 1969 Mem. Nat. Acad. Design (coun. mem. 1982-96), Nat. Art Club, Am. Acad. Arts and Letters. Democrat. Jewish. Office: care Beadleston Gallery 724 5th Ave New York NY 10019-4106

KAHNE, STEPHEN JAMES, systems engineer, educator, academic administrator, engineering executive; b. N.Y.C., Apr. 5, 1937; s. Arnold W. and Janet (Weatherlow) Kahne; m. Irena Nowacka, Dec. 11, 1970; children: Christopher, Kasia. BEE, Cornell U., 1960; MS, U. Ill., 1961, PhD, 1963. Asst. prof. elec. engring. U. Minn., Mpls., 1966-69, assoc. prof., 1969-76; dir. Hybrid Computer Lab., 1968-76; founder, dir., cons. InterDesign Inc., Mpls., 1968-76; prof. dept. sys. engring. Case Western Res. U., Cleve., 1976-83, chmn. dept., 1976-80; dir. divsn. elec., computer and sys. engring. NSF, Washington, 1980-82; prof. Poly Inst. N.Y., 1983-85, dean engring., 1983-84; pres. Oreg. Grad. Ctr., Beaverton, 1985-86, prof. dept. applied physics and elec. engring., 1985-89; chief engr. civil systems divsn. MITRE Corp., McLean, Va., 1989-90, chief scientist Washington Group, 1990-91, cons. engr. Ctr. for Advanced Aviation Sys. Devel., 1991-94; exec. dir., CEO Triangle Coalition for Sci. and Tech. Edn., 1994; chancellor, v.p. Embry-Riddle Aeronautical U., Prescott, Ariz., 1995-97, prof. engring., 1995—. Cons. in field; exchange scientist NAS, 1968, 75. Editor: IEEE Transactions on Automatic Control, 1975-79; hon. editor: Internat. Fedn. of Automatic Control, 1975-81, dep. chmn. mng. bd. publs., 1976-87, chmn., 1999—, v.p., 1987-90, pres.-elect, 1990-93, pres., 1993-96, advisor, 1999—; assoc. editor: Automatica, dep. chmn. editl. bd., 1976-82; mem. editl. bd. IEEE Spectrum, 1979-82; contbr. articles to sci. jours. Active Mpls. Citizens League, 1968-75; regent L.I. Coll. Hosp., Bklyn., 1984-85; trustee Yavapi Regional Med. Ctr., 1999—; chmn. Beaverton Sister Cities Found., 1986-89. Served with USAF, 1963-66. Recipient Amicus Poloniae award POLAND Mag., 1975, John A. Curtis award Am. Soc. Engring. Edn., Outstanding Svc. award Internat. Fedn. Automatic Control, 1990; Case Centennial scholar, 1980 Fellow: AAAS, IEEE (life; pres. Control Sys. Soc. 1981, bd. dirs. 1982—86, v.p. tech. activities 1984—85, Centennial medal 1984, Disting Mem. award 1983, Richard Emberson award 1991, Disting. Lectr. 1998—2000); mem.: Air Traffic Control Assn., Am. Soc. Engring. Edn., Eta Kappa Nu. Office: Embry Riddle Aero U 3700 Willow Creek Rd Prescott AZ 86301-3721 E-mail: s.kahne@ieee.org.

KAHNEMAN, DANIEL, psychology educator; b. Tel Aviv, 1934; BA in Psychology and Mathematics, The Hebrew U., Jerusalem, Israel, 1954; PhD in Psychology, U. Calif., 1961; DSc (hon.), U. Pa., 2001. Lectr. in psychology The Hebrew U., Jerusalem, 1961—66, sr. lectr. in psychology, 1966—70, assoc. prof., 1970—73, prof., 1973—78, fellow Ctr. for Rationality, 2000—; prof. psychology U. B.C., Canada, 1978—86, U. Calif., Berkeley, 1986—94; Eugene Higgins prof. psychology, prof. pub. affairs in the Woodrow Wilson Sch. Princeton U., NJ, 1993—. Vis. scientist dept. psychology U. Mich., 1965—66; fellow, Ctr. for Cognitive Studies, lectr. in psychology Harvard U., 1966—67; vis. scientist Applied Psychol. Rsch. Unit, Cambridge, England, 1968—69; fellow Ctr. for Advanced Studies in the Behavioral Scis., 1977—78; assoc. fellow Canadian Inst. Advanced Rsch., 1984—86; vis. scholar Russell Sage Found., 1991—92. Mem. editl. bd. Jour. Behavioral Decision Making, Jour. Risk and Uncertainty, Thinking and Reasoning, Econs. and Philosophy. Named Katz-Newcomb lectr. in social psychology, 1979; recipient Fitts Lectures, U. Mich., 1987, Disting. Scientific Contbn. award, Soc. Consumer Psychology, 1992, Tanner Lecture on Human Values, U. Mich., 1994, Bartlett Lecture, Exptl. Psychology Soc., Eng., 1995, Hilgard award lifetime contbn. to gen. psychology, 1995, Nobel prize in econs., Royal Swedish Acad. Scis., 2002. Fellow: Econometric Soc., Canadian Psychol. Assn., Am. Psychol. Assn., Am. Psychol. Soc. (Disting. Scientific Contbn. award 1982), Am. Acad. Arts and Scis.; mem.: NAS, Soc. Judgment and Decision Making, Soc. Econ. Sci., Psychonomic Soc., Soc. Exptl. Psychologists (pres. 1992—93, Warren medal 1995). Office: Princeton U Dept Psychology Princeton NJ 08544-1010

KAHRMANN, LINDA IRENE, child care supervisor; b. Newark, Feb. 25, 1949; d. Mitchell Augustus and Irene Constance (Banta) Bradshaw; m. Robert George Kahmann, Aug. 22, 1993; children: Jeannette Regan Longo, Kellie Ann Bradshaw, Jeffrey Robert. Student, Mansfield State Coll., 1967, Middlesex County Coll., 1968-70. Tchr. K-2d grade Holy Spirit Sch., Perth Amboy, N.J., 1970-75; child care supr. North Brunswick (N.J.) Bd. Edn., 1985—. Mathworks aide Parsons Sch., North Brunswick, 1991-93; ESL child care coord., megaskills child care coord. North Brunswick Bd. Edn., 1990—. Tchr. summer elem. enrichment program North Brunswick Bd. Edn., 1988—; v.p. North Brunswick Band Parents, 1989-92. Named to Band Parent Hall of Fame, Band Parents Assn. North Brunswick, 1992. Episcopalian. Avocations: needlework, reading, travel, gourmet cooking. Home: 21 Allison Ct Monmouth Junction NJ 08852-2624 Office: John Adams Sch Old Georges Rd North Brunswick NJ 08902

KAHRMANN, ROBERT GEORGE, educational administrator; b. New Brunswick, N.J., Dec. 12, 1940; s. Robert George and Susan Rose (Budish) K.; m. Linda Irene Bradshaw, Aug. 22, 1993; children: Kellie, Jeffrey, Jeannette. BS, Monmouth U., West Long Branch, N.J., 1963; MA in Edn., Seton Hall U., 1964; EdD, NYU, 1970. Tchr. social studies Middletown Twp. (N.J.) H.S., 1964—66; asst. dir. Jersey City State Coll., 1968—71; dir. continuing edn. Somerset County Coll., Somerville, NJ, 1971—77, Seton Hall U., South Orange, NJ, 1977—78, 1978—84; mgr. continuing engring. edn. IEEE, Piscataway, NJ, 1984—95; dean Pa. Inst. of Tech., Media, 1995—98; v.p. acad. affairs Berkeley Coll., West Paterson, NJ, 1998—99; assoc. dean enrollment svcs. Hudson County C.C., Jersey City, 1999—2001; dir. enrollment svcs. Middlesex C.C., Edison, NJ, 2001—02; ret., 2002. Adj. prof. Seton Hall U., 1977-83; cons. N.J. Funeral Dirs. Assn., 1978-84, Westmoreland County (Pa.) C.C., 1975, N.Y.C. Fire Lts. Assn., 1974-75. Editor: Fire Problems in Modern Building, 1971; contbr. articles to profl. jours. Pres., treas. H.S. Band Parents, North Brunswick, N.J., 1985-93; chmn. Charter Study Commn., North Brunswick, 1981-82; chmn. and mem. Parks and Recreation Com., North Brunswick, 1984-92, Devel. Com., 1977-83. Recipient TAB Pioneer award IEEE Computer Soc., 1988, Edn. award N.J. Ind. Ins. Agts., 1982, Founder's Day award NYU, 1971. Mem.: Am. Philat. Soc., Internat. TV Assn., Phi Delta Kappa. Avocations: travel, stamp collecting, model trains. Personal E-mail: robkahrmann@aol.com.

KAIBORIBOON, KITTI, neurologist; b. Lampang, Thailand, Dec. 24, 1971; s. Suwat and Jurairat Kaiboriboon. MD, Mahidol U., Bangkok, Thailand, 1995. Physician No. Regional Hosp., Ministry of Pub. Health, Lampang, Thailand, 1995—97; neurology fellow Chulalongkorn U., Thailand, 1997—98; neurology resident St. Louis U. Sch. of Medicine, St. Louis, 1999—. Contbr. Scholar Am. Acad. Ann. Meeting Scholarship for Residents, 2002. Mem.: Am. Epilepsy Soc., Am. Acad. of Neurology. Office: Dept of Neurology 3635 Vista Ave at Grand Blvd Saint Louis MO 63110

KAID, LYNDA LEE, communications educator; b. Harrisburg, Ill., Aug. 22, 1948; d. Billy Cameron and Leona Elizabeth (Oglesby) K.; m. Clifford Alan Jones. BA, So. Ill. U., 1970, MS, 1972, PhD, 1974. Prof. dept. comm. U. Okla., Norman, 1974—2001, dir. Polit. Comm. Ctr., 1984—2001; sr. assoc. dean Coll. Journalism. and Comm. U. Fla., Gainesville, 2001—. Mem. adv. bd. Mus. of Broadcast Comm., Chgo., 1990—. Co-author: Political Campaign Communication: A Bibliography and Guide to the Literature, 1974 (Outstanding Reference Book of 1974, Choice mag.); co-editor Political Communication Yearbook 1984, 1985, Political Campaign Communication: A Bibliography and Guide to the Literature, Vol. 2, 1973-1982, 1985, New Perspectives on Political Advertising, 1986, The Political Commercial Archive: A Catalog and Guide to the Collection, 1991, Mediated Politics in Two Cultures: Presidential Campaigning in the United States and France, 1991, Die Massenmedien im Wahlkampf, 1993, The Lynching of Language: Gender, Politics and Power in the Hill-Thomas Hearings, 1996, Political Advertising in Western Democracies: Parties and Candidates on Television, 1995, The Electronic Election, 1999; contbr. numerous articles to profl. jours. Recipient Rsch. award on Polit. Advt., NSF & Nat. Endowment for Humanities, 1992—; Fulbright scholar USIA-Fulbright Commn., Western Europe, 1987-88, 1997. Mem. Am. Film Inst., League of Women Voters, Internat. Comm. Assn. (pres. polit. comm. divsn. 1979-81). Avocation: travel. Office: U Fla Weimer Hall Gainesville FL 32611

KAIDY, MITCHELL, journalist, writer, legislative staff member; b. Bklyn., Mar. 23, 1925; s. Murad Abdallah and Asma Araman Kaldy; m. Jean Harris Kaldy; children: Kristen, Mark. Student, U. Miss., 1943—44, Clemson (S.C.) A&M Coll., 1944; BS in Journalism, NYU, 1948. Reporter, editor Monticello (N.Y.) Evening News, 1948—49, Middletown (N.Y.) Times Herald, 1949—50, Rochester (N.Y.) Dem. Chronicle, 1950—65; legis. aide and speech writer N.Y. State Legis., Albany, 1966—83; freelance TV comml. prodr. Rochester, 1983—90; freelance writer, 1983—. Dir. rsch. N.Y. State Joint Legis. Com. on Conservation, 1967; legis. aide N.Y. State Assembly Com. on Labor, Albany, 1972; pres., sec. Rochester (N.Y.) Newspaper Guild, 1953—60, N.Y. State Newspaper Guild. Contbr. columns in newspapers, articles to profl. jours.; manuscript editor Becoming American: The Early Arab Immigrant Experience, by Alixa Naff, 1985. Founder Peace and Justice Edn. Ctr., Rochester, 1962; candidate Congress, 1982—84. Cpl. U.S. Army, 1943—46, Europe. Decorated Bronze Star medal 87th Infantry Divsn., U.S. Army, 3 Battle Stars, Combat Infantry Badge, named Journalist of Yr., Utica, N.Y., 1966; fellow, Am. Newspaper Guild, 1963. Democrat. Achievements include conceiving U.S. Supreme Ct. suit by ACLU granting registration and voting rights to pre-trial detainees held on misdemeanor charges, 1974; research in initiated, wrote, and presided over four plaque placements in Belgium, commemorating 87th Infantry Divsn. engagements during Battle of the Bulge, 1996. Avocations: travel, journalism. Home: 921 Crittenden Rd Rochester NY 14623-1157 Fax: 585-424-4746.

KAIER, EDWARD JOHN, lawyer; b. Sewickley, Pa, Sept. 23, 1945; s. Edward Anthony and Mary Patricia (Crimmins) K.; m. Annette Thomas, July 31, 1976; children: Elizabeth Anne, Charles Crimmins, Thomas Edward, AB, Harvard U., 1967; JD, U. Pa., 1970. Bar: DC 1970, Pa. 1970, US Dist. Ct. (ea. dist.) Pa. 1971, US Ct. Appeals (3rd and DC cir.) 1971, US Dist. Ct. DC, 1971. Law clk. to presiding justice US Dist. Ct. for DC, Washington, 1970-71; assoc. Dechert Price & Rhoads, Phila., 1971-74; ptnr. Kaier and Kaier, Phila., 1974-77, Hepburn Willcox Hamilton & Putnam, Phila., 1977—. Pres. Savoy Co., Phila., 1978-80; bd. dir. Mgr. Funds, Norwalk, Conn., Mgr. AMG Funds, Boston, Third Avenue Funds, NY Vice chmn. Rosemont (Pa.) Sch. of Holy Child, 1981-90. Mem. ABA, Phila. Bar Assn. (chmn. office practice com. probate sect. 1987-90, exec. com. 1990-92, 2002-2003), Merion Cricket Club, Phila. Club, Phila. Country Club, Avalon Yacht Club (trustee 1987-90, 92-93, treas. 1990-92), Harvard-Radcliffe Club (Phila., sec. 1989—). Republican. Roman Catholic. Avocations: sailing, golf. Home: 111 N Lowrys Ln Bryn Mawr PA 19010-1408 Office: Hepburn Willcox Hamilton & Putnam 1100 One Penn Ctr Philadelphia PA 19103 E-mail: ejkaier@hepburnlaw.com., macoejk@aol.com.

KAIL, KENNETH STONER, lawyer; b. N.Y.C., Oct. 14, 1955; s. Morton and Adrienne (Stoner) K.; m. Ivy Hwang, Apr. 18, 1986. BS, SUNY, Albany, 1977; JD, U. Pa., 1980. Bar: N.Y. 1981. Law clk. to presiding justice U.S. Ct. Appeals (fed. cir.), Washington, 1980-81; assoc. Simpson Thacher & Bartlett, N.Y.C., 1981-90; of counsel Morrison & Forster, N.Y.C., 1990-92, ptnr., 1992-95; ptnr., head tax practice group Morgan, Lewis & Bockius, LLP, N.Y.C., 1995—. Mem. ABA, N.Y. State Bar Assn. Office: Morgan Lewis Bockius LLP 101 Park Ave Fl 33 New York NY 10178-0060 E-mail: kkail@morganlewis.com.

KAILAS, LEO GEORGE, lawyer; b. N.Y.C., May 28, 1949; s. George and Evanthia (Skoulikas) K.; m. Merle S. Duskin; children: Arianne, George, Shirley. AB, Columbia U., 1970, JD, 1973. Bar: N.Y. 1974. Assoc. Olwine, Connelly, Chase, O'Donnell and Weyher, N.Y.C., 1973-77; ptnr. specializing in internat., comml.-admiralty litigation Milgrim Thomajan Jacobs & Lee, PC (now Piper & Marbury LLP), N.Y.C., 1977-2000, mem. internat. trade and litigation group, until 2000; ptnr. Reitler Brown LLC, N.Y.C., 2000—. Mem. ABA, Assn. Bar City N.Y. (chmn. admiralty com. 1985-88). Office: Reitler Brown LLC 800 3d Ave 21st Fl New York NY 10022 E-mail: lkailas@reitlerbrown.com.

KAILASAM, MALA TRICHUR, physician; b. Madras, India, Feb. 5, 1965; d. Trichur Krishnaiyer and Radha (Ramaswamy) K.; m. Raman Murli Krishna, June 14, 1989; 1 child, Aparna Krishnan. MBBS, Bangalore (India) Med. Coll., 1988; MPH, San Diego State U., 1997. Jr. resident Mysore (India) Med. Coll., 1989, LNJP Hosp., New Delhi, 1990; postdoctoral rsch. fellow U. Calif., San Diego and UCLA, 1991-99; resident in internal medicine Griffin Hosp., Derby, Conn., 1999—2002; physician Internal Medicine Assocs., Wallingford, Conn., 2002—. Contbr. articles to Am. Jour. Hypertension, Ethnicity and Health, Hypertension, others. Recipient Pres.'s Silver medal Govt. of India, 1987, Victoria Hosp. Gold medal Bangalore U., 1988, Outstanding Intern of Yr. award, 2000, Outstanding House Officer, Hushpuppy award, 2001; Phi Beta Delta scholar, 1997. Mem. ACP, APHA, Phi Kappa Phi. Home: 8 Park Ln Woodbridge CT 06525 Office: Internal Med Assocs 97 Barnes Rd Wallingford CT 06492 E-mail: mkailasam@hotmail.com.

KAILATH, THOMAS, electrical engineer, educator; b. Poona, India, June 7, 1935; arrived in U.S., 1957, naturalized, 1976; s. Mamman and Kunjamma (George) K.; m. Sarah Jacob, June 11, 1962; children: Ann, Paul, Priya, Ryan. BE, U. Poona, 1956; SM, MIT, 1959, ScD, 1961; Dr. Tek (hon.), Linkoping U., Sweden, 1990; Doctorate (hon.), U. Carlos III, Madrid, 1999; D honoris causa, Strathclyde U., Scotland, 1992, U. Bordeaux, France, 2003. Comm. rschr. Jet Propulsion Labs., Pasadena, Calif., 1961-62; faculty Stanford (Calif.) U., 1963—, prof. elec. engring., 1968—, Hitachi Am. prof. engring., 1988—2001, Hitachi Am. prof. emeritus, 2001—; dir. Info. Systems Lab., 1971-81, assoc. chmn. dept., 1981-87. Vis. prof., cons. univs., industry, govt. Author: Linear Systems, 1980, Least-Squares Estimation, 2d edit, 1981, Linear Estimation, 2000; mem. editl. bd. various jours.; contbr. articles to profl. jours. Recipient Edn. award Am. Control Coun., 1986, Tech. Achievement and Soc. awards Signal Processing Soc. IEEE, 1989, 91, Donald G. Fink Prize award, 1996, Shannon award, 2000; Sr. Vinton Hayes fellow MIT, 1992, Guggenheim fellow, 1970, Churchill fellow, 1977, Michael fellow Weizmann Inst., Israel, 1984, Royal Soc. guest rsch. fellow, 1989; Alexander Humboldt fellow, 2003. Fellow: IEEE (Edn. medal 1995), Am. Acad. Arts and Scis., Inst. Math. Stats.; mem.: NAS, Royal Spanish Acad. Engring., Third World Acad. Scis., Soc. Indsl. and Applied Math., Am. Math. Soc., Nat. Acad. Engring., Indian Nat. Acad. Engring., Sigma Xi. Home: 1024 Cathcart Way Palo Alto CA 94305-1047 Office: Stanford U Dept Elec Engring Stanford CA 94305-9510 E-mail: kailath@stanford.edu.

KAILIAN, ARAM HARRY, architect, consultant; b. Phila., Oct. 23, 1949; s. Harry G. and Louise (Haledjian) Caily; m. Kathryn I. Zakian, May 27, 1973; children: Arsine K., Aram E. BS, Temple U., 1973; student, Tyler Sch. Fine Art, Phila., 1967-69, Drexel U., 1970-71. Project architect Kuljian Corp., Phila., 1970-73, Urban Engrs. Inc., Phila., 1973-76; project designer Wm. F. Lotz Designers, Horsham, Pa., 1976-78; prin./architect Clyde H. Goff & Assocs./A.H. Kailian, Architects, Interior Design, Constrn. Mgmt., Bala Cynwyd, Pa., 1982-94, Kailian Assocs., Bryn Mawr, Pa., 1978-94; spl. asst. to the commr. Pub. Bldgs. Svc./Gen. Svcs. Adminstrn., Washington, 1994-96, sr. adviser to commr., 1997-2001; interagency coord./office v.p. Pres. Cmty. Empowerment Bd., 1997-2001; prin. Aram H. Kailian Architect/Constrn. Cons., 2002—. Bd.dirs. NIBS CADD Coun., 1994-2001, Aram H. Kailian, AIA Architect/Constrn. Cons., 2001-. Contbr. articles to profl. jours. Mem. Dem. Nationalities Coun., Washington, 1976—, Nat. Rep. Heritage Groups Coun., 1976—; bd. dirs. Armenian Nat. Com. Am., 1983-89. Mem. AIA, D.C. Soc. Architects, Am. Arbitration Assn., Nat. Acad. Conciliators, Nat. Trust for Historic Preservation, Acad. Polit. Sci. Democrat. Armenian Orthodox. E-mail: akailian@hotmail.com.

KAIMOWITZ, GABE HILLEL, lawyer; b. N.Y.C., May 5, 1935; s. Abraham and Esther (Bialogursky) K.; children: David, Beth. BS, U. Wis., 1955; MA, U. Cen. Fla., 1988; LLB, NYU, 1967. Bar: N.Y. 1969, Mich. 1971, Fla., 1987, U.S. Dist. Ct. (mid. dist.) Fla., 1987, U.S. Ct. Appeals (6th cir.) 1971, U.S. Ct. Appeals (3d cir.) 1982, U.S. Ct. Appeals (2d cir.) 1983, U.S. Ct. Appeals (11th cir.), 1989 U.S. Ct. Appeals (7th cir.) 1990, U.S. Ct. Appeals (D.C. cir.) 1998. Atty. Ctr. Social Welfare, Politics and Law, N.Y.C., 1967-70; sr. atty. Mich. Legal Services, Detroit, 1971-79; assoc. P.R. Legal Def., N.Y.C., 1980-84; exec. dir. Greater Orlando (Fla.) A. Legal Services, 1985-86; equal opportunity investigator Alachua County, Fla., 1999—2002; pvt. practice. Atty. Attys. Against Am. Apartheid, Fla. and various other civil rights orgns., 1969—; lectr., adj. prof. numerous univs. Contbr. articles to profl. jours.; author poems. Served with U.S. Army, 1956-57, with Res. 1958-60. Smith fellow, 1970-71, Legal Services Corp. fellow, 1979-80. Mem. N.Y. State Bar Assn., Fla. Bar Assn. Jewish. Avocation: writing and editing. Home: 4411 SW 34th St Gainesville FL 32608-2562 Office: PO Box 140119 Gainesville FL 32614-0119 E-mail: gabehk@aol.com.

KAIMOWITZ, JEFFREY HUGH, librarian; b. N.Y.C., Nov. 3, 1942; AB, Johns Hopkins U., 1964; PhD in Classics, U. Cin., 1970; MS in Libr. Svc., Columbia U., 1976. Asst. prof. Miami U. Ohio, Oxford, 1969—73; libr. trainee N.Y. Pub. Libr., N.Y.C., 1973—77; curator Watkinson Libr. Trinity Coll., Hartford, Conn., 1977—2001, curator Enders Ornithology Collection, 1994—, head libr., 2001—. Home: 27 Stoneham Dr West Hartford CT 06117 Office: Trinity College Watkinson Library 300 Summit St Hartford CT 06106-3186

KAIMSTHORN, LORD RENFREW OF See RENFREW, ANDREW

KAINE, PAUL, performing company executive; Exec. dir. Nashville Ballet, 2002—. Office: Nashville Ballet 3630 Redmon St Nashville TN 37209

KAINE, TIMOTHY M. lieutenant governor; m. Anne Holton; children: Annella, Woody, Nat. AB summa cum laude, U. Mo., 1979; JD cum laude, Harvard U., 1983. Law clk. to judge R. Lanier Anderson III U.S. Ct. Appeals (11th cir.), mem. law firm; mem. City Council, Richmond; mayor City of Richmond, 1998—2001; lt. gov. State of Virginia, 2002—. Mem. local and state govt. adv. com. FCC. Contbr. articles to profl. jours. Bd. dirs. Historic Jackson Ward Found. Mem. ABA, Va. Bar Assn., Richmond Bar Assn. Democrat. Office: Office Lt Gov 900 E Main St Ste 1400 Richmond VA 23219*

KAINEN, ANNA, writer; b. Cluz, Romania, Feb. 17, 1913; came to U.S., 1929; d. Carl and Sally Newman; divorced; 1 child, Carol Lippman. BA in Creative Writing, CUNY, 1980. Garment worker, 1929-75. Author: Another Place, 1988 (awards Barbara Deming Meml. Fund, Nat. Coun. Sr. Citizens, Internat. Libr. Poetry), (poetry) The Archives of Memories, 2000; contbg. author: What We Know So Far, 1995, The Quarterly, 1981, 91; playwright: Mama's World, Am. Jewish Theater, 1985, Taking My Turn, 1980, others. Woolrich writing fellow Columbia U., 1988-89. Democrat. Jewish. Home: 689 Columbus Ave New York NY 10025

KAINTHLA, RAMESH CHAND, manufacturing company executive; b. Shimla, India, Feb. 18, 1954; came to U.S., 1983; s. Hira Nand and Belku (Devi) K.; m. Neetu Dua, Aug. 9, 1981; children: Priyanka, Radhika. BS, HP Univ., Shimla, 1973, MS in Physics, 1975; PhD in Physics, IIT Delhi, India, 1980. Rsch. assoc. IIT Delhi, 1980-81, U. NSW, Sydney, Australia, 1981-83, Tex. A&M U., College Station, 1984-86, sr. rsch. assoc., 1986-88, rsch. scientist, 1988-89; v.p. Rechargeable Battery Corp., College Station, 1989 . Dir. Rechargeable Battery Corp., 1990—. Contbr. articles to profl. jours.; patentee in field. Mem. Electrochem. Soc. Avocations: music, movies, gardening, web creation. Office: Rechargeable Battery Corp 809 University Dr # 100E College Station TX 77840-1431 E-mail: kainthla@tca.net.

KAIPA, PRASAD LAKSHMI NARASIMHA, educational researcher and consultant; b. Anantapur, India, Sept. 25, 1955; came to U.S. 1981; s. Lakshmi Narayana and Kamala Kumari (Sadali) K.; m. Vinoda Kumari, Dec. 31, 1982; children: Pravin, Vidya. BSc, Sri Venkateswara U., India, 1974; MSc, Sri Venkateswara U., 1976; PhD, Indian Inst. Tech., 1981. Geophysicist Oil & Natural Gas Commn., Nazira, Assam, India, 1981; rsch. assoc. U. Utah, Salt Lake City, 1981-82, rsch. asst. prof., 1983-87; mgr. tech. mkts. Apple Computer Inc., Cupertino, Calif., 1987-88; mgr., tech. advisor Apple Univ., Cupertino, Calif., 1988-89; fellow Apple Computer Inc., Cupertino, Calif., 1989-90; founder Mithya Inst. for Learning, Campbell, Calif., 1990—. Pres. Macwiz Cons., Campbell, 1985-87; CEO, Selfcorp., 1999; founding dir., Inst. for Entrepreneurs, 2002—; part-time prof. Saybrook Grad. Sch., San Francisco, 1994—. Author: Review of Computer Software and Hardware, 1986-88; cons. editor MacToday, MacWorld, 1987-88; publisher "An ongoing dialogue on learning" newsletter, 1990-93. U. Utah rsch. grantee, 1985-87. Mem.: Soc. for Organized Learning (trustee 2002—). Avocations: tennis, reading, chess, table tennis. Office: Selfcorp 268 E Hamilton Ave Ste D Campbell CA 95008-0239

KAIPER, DONALD DIXON, historian, educator; b. Ft. Smith, Ark., Mar. 23, 1941; s. Daniel Bottenus Kaiper and Nan Dixon Kaiper Slygh; 1 child from previous marriage, Lief Eric. BA, Colgate U., 1962; MDiv, Andover Newton (Mass.) Theol. Sch., 1967; MA, U. Hawaii, 1968; PhD, U. Calif., Santa Cruz, 1980. Tchg. assoc. U. Calif.-Santa Cruz, U. Calif.-Berkeley, San Francisco State U., Holy Names Coll., Oakland, Calif., 1978—81; instr. history and polit. sci. Tex. A&I U., Chabo Coll., Reedley Coll., 1982—85; instr. history, program coord. Los Medanos Coll., Pittsburg, Calif., 1985—. Author, narrator pub. svc. TV series on citizen competence and democracy, 2001—02; editor: 3 vols. of Am. Indian readers for social sci. instrs. Recipient Mabeek McLeod Lewis award, 1980, award, Sagan Found., 1980, Affirmative Action award, Contra Costa C.C. Dist.; fellow, NEH, 2001. Mem.: Nat. Social Sci. Assn., Conf. Polit. and Social Thought, Orgn. Am. Historians, Pittsburg Hist. Soc. Avocations: reading, research, travel, gardening. Home: 3501 Dameron Pl Antioch CA 94509 Office: Los Medanos Coll 2700 E Leland Rd Pittsburg CA 94565 E-mail: kaiperd@aol.com.

KAISCH, KENNETH BURTON, psychologist, priest; b. Detroit, Aug. 29, 1948; s. Kenneth R. Kaisch and Marjorie F. (Howe) Bourke; m. Suzanne Carol LePrevost, Aug. 31, 1969; 1 child, Samuel. BA, San Francisco State U., 1972; MDiv, Ch. Divinity Sch. Pacific, 1976; MS, Utah State U., 1983, PhD in Clin. Psychology, 1986. Ordained deacon Episcopal Ch., 1976, priest, 1977; lic. clin. psychologist, Calif.; diplomate Nat. Inst. Sports Psychologists. Intern local parish, 1973-76; ordinand tng. program Ch. of the Good Shepherd, Ogden, Utah, 1976-77; pastor St. Francis' Episc. Ch., Moab, Utah, 1977-80, St. John's Episc. Ch., Logan, Utah, 1980-84; psychol. asst. Peter Ebersole, Ph.D., Fullerton, Calif., 1984-86; intern in clin. psychology Patton State Hosp., Calif., 1985-86; psychol. asst. Ronald Wong Jue, Ph.D., Fullerton and Newport Beach, Calif., 1986-88; pvt. practice clin. psychologist Calif., 1988—; clin. dir. Anxiety Clinic, Fullerton, 1993—. Exec. dir. Contemplative Congress, Fullerton, 1988-91, Inner Peace Conf., 1995-97; founder, pres. OneHeart, 1986-98, Contemplative Visions, Fullerton, 1990-2000; supply priest Episc. Diocese of L.A.; invited lectr. Acad. Sch. Profl. Psychology, Moscow, 1992, 93, Moscow Med. Acad., 1998. Co-author: Fundamentals of Psychotherapy, 1984, Developing Your Feel for Golf, 1998; author: Finding God: A Handbook of Christian Mediation, 1994, The Mental Golf Inventory, 1998, Hit it With Your Best Shot: How to Play Golf in the Zone, 2000; co-editor: God in Russia: The Challenge of Freedom, 1999, Turning the Heart to God, 2001; contbr. numerous articles to profl. jours. Mem. St. Andrew's Episc. Ch., Fullerton. Mem. APA, Calif. Psychol. Assn., Anxiety Disorders Assn. Am., Nat. Register of Health Svc. Providers in Psychology, Phi Kappa Phi, Rotary (past bd. dirs., past officer). Episcopalian. Office: 2555 E Chapman Ave Ste 617 Fullerton CA 92831-3621 E-mail: ken_kaisch@yahoo.com.

KAISER, ALBERT FARR, diversified corporation executive; b. N.Y.C., May 14, 1933; s. Albert Louis and Lucille (Daggett) K.; m. Joy E. White, Sept. 16, 1961; children— Elizabeth Ann, Albert Farr. BA, Hamilton Coll., Clinton, N.Y., 1955; MBA, Harvard U., 1960. With acquisitions dept. AMF Inc., 1960-61; with data processing div. IBM Corp., 1961-84; with Sperry and Hutchinson Co., 1974-82; pres. The Gunlocke Co., Inc., 1977-79, pres. promotional services div., also chmn. motivation and travel div., 1979-80; corp. exec. v.p. Sperry and Hutchinson, Inc., N.Y.C., 1980-82; investment banker J.J. Lowrey & Co., N.Y.C., 1983-84; pres. ABB Power Distbn. Inc., 1984-92; ret., 1992—. Served to lt. (j.g.) USNR, 1955-58. Mem. Hamilton Coll. Aumni Assn. (former pres. Westchester County chpt.), Fox Meadow Tennis Club (Scarsdale), Bradenton Country Club. Republican. Mem. Reformed Ch. Am. Home: PO Box 2205 105 Sunset Ln Anna Maria FL 34216 Home (Summer): 25 Camp Rich Rd Milton VT 05468 E-mail: alkaiser@sprintmail.com.

KAISER, ANN CHRISTINE, magazine editor; b. Milw., Apr. 7, 1947; d. Herbert Walter and Annette G. (Werych) Gohlke; m. Louis Dan Kaiser; children: Richard L., Michael D. BS in Journalism, Northwestern U., 1969. Reporter Waco (Tex.) Tribune-Herald, 1969-71; editor Country Woman, Greendale, Wis., 1971—; mng. editor Taste of Home, Greendale, 1993—. Named among People of the Yr., Milw. Mag., 1998. Lutheran. Avocations: sailing, tennis, golf, travel. Office: Reiman Publs 5400 S 60th St Greendale WI 53129-1404

KAISER, DANIEL HUGH, historian, educator; b. Phila., July 20, 1945; s. Walter Christian and Estelle Evelyn (Jaworsky) K.; m. Jonelle Marie Marwin, Aug. 10, 1968; children: Nina Marie, Andrew Eliot. AB, Wheaton Coll., 1967; AM, U. Chgo., 1970, PhD, 1977. Asst. prof. history U. Chgo., 1977-78, Grinnell (Iowa) Coll., 1979-84, assoc. prof., 1984-86, prof. history, 1986—, Joseph F. Rosenfield prof. social studies, 1984—, chair dept. history, 1988-90, 96-98. Mem. adv. bd. Soviet Studies in History, 1979-85; rsch. assoc. dept. Slavonic studies, vis. mem. Darwin Coll., Cambridge (Eng.) U., 1992-93; vis. prof. dept. Slavic langs. and lits. Ctr. for Medieval and Renaissance Studies, UCLA, 1996. Author: The Growth of the Law in Medieval Russia, 1980; editor: The Workers' Revolution in Russia, 1917, 1987; translator, editor: The Laws of Rus' Tenth to Fifteenth Centuries, 1992; co-editor: (with Gary Marker) Reinterpreting Russian History 860-1860s, 1994; editl. bd. Slavic Rev., 1996-2001. Elder 1st Presbyn. Ch., Grinnell, 1985, 87-89. Fellow Nat. Endowment Humanities, 1979, 92-93, 2000, John Simon Guggenheim Meml. Found., 1986, Fulbright-Hays Faculty Rsch. Abroad Found., 1986, Woodrow Wilson Internat. Ctr. Scholars, 1986, Internat. Rsch. Exchs. Bd. fellow to USSR/Russia, 1974-75, 78-79, 86, 93. Mem. Am. Assn. for Advancement Slavic Studies, Am. Hist. Assn., Early Slavic Studies Assn. (v.p. 1995-97, pres. 1997-99), Slavonic and East European Medieval Studies Group (U.K.), Study Group on 18th Century Russia (U.K.), 18th Century Russian Studies Assn. Office: Grinnell Coll Dept History Grinnell IA 50112-1670 E-mail: kaiser@grinnell.edu.

KAISER, DANIEL ROBERT, research scientist; b. Cudahy, Wis., Dec. 16, 1969; s. Harold and Elaine Kaiser. BEE, U. of Wis., 1988—93; MS, U. of Minn., 1995—99, PhD, 1997—2001. Scientist St. Paul Heart Clinic, St. Paul, 1999—2003, Medtronic Inc, Mpls., 2003—; engr. Electronic Theatre Controls, Middelton, Wis., 1992—95. Home: 1418 Hartford Ave St. Paul MN 55116 Office: Medtronic Inc 7000 Central AveNE msB181 Minneapolis MN 55432 Personal E-mail: dankaiser@attbi.com. E-mail: daniel.r.kaiser@medtronic.com.

KAISER, FRAN ELIZABETH, endocrinologist, gerontologist; b. N.Y.C., Dec. 6, 1949; d. Philip Francis and Bronia (Weiss) K. BS, CCNY, 1970; MD, N.Y. Med. Coll., N.Y.C., 1974. Diplomate Am. Bd. Internal Medicine, Am. Bd. Geriatrics. Intern Beth Israel Med. Ctr., N.Y.C., 1974-75, resident to chief resident, 1975-78, fellow in endocrinology and metabolism U. Minn., Mpls., 1978-81, instr. dept. medicine, 1980-81, asst. prof., 1981-86; asst. prof. in residence UCLA Sch. medicine, 1986-89; assoc. prof. medicine St. Louis U., 1989-94, prof., 1994-97, assoc. dir. divsn. geriatric medicine, 1989-97, prof., 1994-97; sr. regional med. dir. Merck & Co., Inc., Irving, Tex., 1997—. Adj. prof. medicine St. Louis U, 1997—; chief sect. endocrinology and metabolism Dept. Internal Medicine, St. Paul Ramsey Med. Ctr./U. Minn. Hosps., St. Paul, 1981-86; John A. Hartford Geriatric Faculty Devel. award scholar Hartford Found., N.Y.C./UCLA Sch. Medicine, 1986-87; chief geriatric medicine Olive View Med. Ctr./UCLA San Fernando Valley Program, Sylmar, Calif., 1987-89; med. dir. Hosp. Based Home Care, VA Med. Ctr., Sepulveda, 1987-89. Mem. editl. bd.: Jour. Clin. Endocrinology and Metabolism, ad hoc reviewer: Endocrinology, Jour. AMA, Jour. Am. Geriatrics Soc., past mem. editl. bd.: Am. Geriatric Soc., Internat. Medicine Bull., cons. editor: Am. Health Mag.; contbr. articles. Grantee NIH, 1980-81, 97, Genetech, 1987-89, Syntex Corp. 1990-92, Hoechst-Roussel, 1992-94, Bur. Health Professions, 1991-97, VIVUS, 1993-97, Merck, 1994-97, Upjohn, 1995-97. Fellow: Am. Geriat. Soc.; mem.: Am. Assn. Home Care Physicians, Am. Geriatrics Soc. (past mem. editl. bd. Internal Medicine Bull., Jour. Geriatric Nephrology & Urology), Gerontol. Soc. Am., N.Y. Acad. Sci., Am. Fedn.Clin. Rsch., Endocrine Soc. (mem. women in endocrinology group), Am. Diabetes Assn., AAAS. Achievements include research on hormonal changes with aging, studies of therapy of erectile dysfunction, testosterone, estrogen and frailty and women's health and sexuality. Office: Merck & Co Inc 222 Las Colinas Blvd W Ste 1465 Irving TX 75039-5451 E-mail: fran_kaiser@merck.com.

KAISER, GEORGE B. corporate financial executive; married; 3 children. BS, MS, Harvard U. Chmn. Bok Fin., Tulsa; prin. owner Kaiser-Francis Oil Co. Founder Tulsa Cmty. Found., 1998. Office: Bok Fin Bank of Okla Tower PO Box 2300 Tulsa OK 74192

KAISER, GERARD A. senior vice president; Postgrad, Columbia U. Sr. v.p. med. affairs Jackson Meml. Hosp., prof. of cardiothoracic surgery; deputy dean clinical affairs U. Miami Sch. of Medicine; residency U. Hosp. Thoracic Surgery. Mem.: Am. Bd. Thoracic Surgery, Am. Bd. Surgery, Am. Assn. Thoracic Surgery. Office: Jackson Meml Hosp 118 W Wing Miami FL 33136

KAISER, GREG CHRISTOPHER, pediatric gastroenterologist; b. Tampa, Fla., Mar. 24, 1966; s. Alexander and Elinor (Blackwell) K. BS, Furman U., 1988; MD, U. Fla., 1992. Diplomate Am. Bd. Pediatrics, Am. Bd. Pediatric Gastroenterology. Intern Orlando (Fla.) Regional Healthcare Sys., 1992-93, resident in pediats., 1993-95; chief resident in pediats. Orlando Regional Hosp., 1994-95; fellow in pediat. gastroenterology Vanderbilt U. Med. Ctr., Nashville, 1995-98; pediat. gastroenterologist All Children's Hosp., St. Petersburg, Fla., 1998—. Contbr. articles to profl. jours. Football referee Fla. H.S. Athletic Assn., Tampa, 1996—. Recipient Elliot V. Newman Rsch. award Vanderbilt U., 1998. Mem. AMA (polit. action com. 1992—), Am. Acad. Pediats., Am. Gastroenterology Assn., N.Am. Soc. for Pediat. Gastroenterology and Nutrition (Rsch. award 1997, 98), Phi Beta Kappa. Republican. Office: All Childrens Hosp Dept Pediat Gastroent 480 7th Ave S Saint Petersburg FL 33701-4839

KAISER, HANS ELMAR, pathology educator, researcher; b. Prague, Czech Republic, Feb. 16, 1928; arrived in U.S., 1961. s. Rudolf and Charlotte (Thiel) K.; m. Charlotte (Moehring), Oct. 12, 1960. ScD, U. Tuebingen, Fed. Republic of Germany, 1958. Rsch. prof. U. Md., Balt., 1988; hon., sci. dir. Internat. Inst. Anticancer Rsch., Attiki, Greece. Hon. cons. Bulgarian Med. Acad., Sofia; vis. prof. Martin Luther U., Halle-Wittenberg, Fed. Republic of Germany, U. Vienna, Austria; pres. Internat. Soc. for Study of Comparative Oncology, German Soc. Comparative Oncology, Inc. Author: Das Abnorme in der Evolution, 1970; Morphology of Sirenia, 1972; Species Specific Potential of Invertebrates, 1980; editor, author: Nepolasms, Comparative, Pathology of Growth. . ., 1981; Cancer Growth and Progression, 10 vols., 1989; others; mem. editorial bd. Anticancer Rsch., in Vivo. Mem.: Physikalisch Medizinische Societaet Erlangen (corr.), Turkish Kanseroloji ve Ekoloji Dernegi (hon.). Home: 433 Southwest Dr Silver Spring MD 20901-4420

KAISER, KEITH ALLEN, music educator, researcher, conductor; b. Cheyenne, Wyo., June 30, 1966; s. Alfred Joseph and Shirley Ann Kaiser; m. Jennifer Ellen Ehrhorn, Nov. 10, 2001. MusB in Music Edn., U. Wyo., Laramie, 1988; MusM in Music Performance, U. Redlands, Calif., 1995; PhD in Music Edn., Fla. State U., Tallahasee, 1995—98. Cert. Tchr.(Music K-12) Wyoming, 1988. Dir. of bands and dept. chair (grades 6-12, instrumental music) Goshen County Sch. Dist., Torrington, Wyo., 1988—93; founder and condr. U. of Redlands (Calif.) Wind Ensemble for Young Musicians, 1994—95; instrumental music tchr. (grades 4-12) Beaumont (Calif.) Sch. Dist., 1993—94; asst. prof. music edn. Ithaca Coll., NY, 1998—, chair music edn., 2003—. Presenter seminars and workshops. to a variety of Musical Socs. and Orgns. nationally.; condr. Ithaca (N.Y.) Concert Band (comty. band), 1999—. Contbr. articles to profl. jours. Condr. Syracuse (N.Y.) Signature Youth Band (inner city youth), 2000—; mem. Lion's Club, Torrington, Wyo., 1989—93. Named Outstanding Grad. Student, U. Redlands, 1995; scholar Presser Scholar, The U. of Wyo. Music Dept., 1988. Mem.: Pi Kappa Lambda, Phi Kappa Phi, Tau Beta Sigma (hon.), Phi Mu Alpha Sinfonia (hon.), Kappa Kappa Psi (life; chpt. pres., chpt. vice-president, dist. rep. 1985—88), NY State Sch. Music Assn. (state certification chairperson and liason 2002), Music Educators Nat. Conf.

KAISER, LARRY ROBERT, thoracic surgeon; b. St. Louis, Aug. 31, 1952; s. Patricia Glaser; children: Jonathan, Jeffrey. BS, MD, Tulane University, News Orleans, 1970—77. Diplomate Am. Bd. Thoracic Surgery. Resident in surgery UCLA, 1977—83, fellow in surg. oncology, 1979—81; resident in thoracic and cardiovasc. surgery U. Toronto, Canada, 1983—85; asst. attending surgeon Meml. Sloan-Kettering Cancer Ctr., 1985—88; asst. and assoc. prof. surgery Washington U. Sch. Medicine, 1988—91; prof. and chief thoracic surgery U. of Pa. Sch. of Medicine, Phila., 1991—2001, John Rhea Barton prof. and chmn. dept. surgery, 2001—. Home: 408 Barbara Lane Bryn Mawr PA 19010 Office: Hosp of the Univ of Pa 3400 Spruce St 4 Silverstein Philadelphia PA 19104 Office Fax: 215-614-0363. Business E-Mail: larry.kaiser@uphs.upenn.edu.

KAISER, LINDA SUSAN, lawyer; b. Alexandria, Va., Apr. 7, 1956; d. Thomas Raymond Kaiser and Joanne May (Wilber) Raynolds. BA, Pa. State U., 1978; JD, U. Pitts., 1981. Asst. counsel Pa. Ins. Dept., Harrisburg, 1981-85; sr. counsel Cigna Corp., Phila., 1985-92; asst. gen. counsel Reliance Ins. Co., Phila., 1992-95; ins. commr. Commonwealth of Pa., Harrisburg, 1995-97; sr. v.p., gen. counsel and sec. Reliance Ins. Co., Phila., 1997-2000; ptnr. Saul Ewing, LLP, 2000—. Property casualty steering com. Ins. Fedn. Pa., Phila., 1992-95; alternate Pa. Workers Compensation Gov. Bd., 1993-95; bd. dirs. Nat. Assn. Ind. Insurers, 1997-2000, vice-chair membership com., 1999-2000; bd. dirs. Ins. Fedn. Pa., 1998-2000; vice chair Issues Com., 2003—. Pres. Huntington's Disease Soc. Am., Delaware Valley, Phila., 1993-96, v.p., 1996-2002; bd. dirs. Phila. Theatre Co., 2002— Mem. ABA, Soc. CPCU, Soc. Nat. Assn. Ins. Commrs. (vice chair N.E. zone 1997), Order of Coif, Barristers, Com. of Seventy Office: Centre Square West 3d Fl Philadelphia PA 19102-2186 E-mail: lkaiser@saul.com.

KAISER, MARK JOHN, research scientist, science educator; b. Ft. Thomas, Ky, June 22, 1965; Degree in agr. engring., Purdue U., 1985, degree in indsl. engring., 1988, degree in indsl. engring., 1991. Rsch. asst. Purdue U., West Lafayette, Ind., 1985-91, instr., 1988-91, rsch. fellow, 1990-91; instr. Ind. Vocat. Tech. Coll., Lafayette, Ind., 1990-91; asst. prof. indsl. engring. Auburn U., Ala., 1991-94; vis. asst. prof. Am. U. Armenia, Yerevan, 1995, vis. assoc. prof. earthquake and indsl. engring., 1996; asst. prof. indsl. and mfg. engring. Wichita State U., Kans., 1996—, grad. coord. dept. indsl. and mfg. engring., 1997—2001; assoc. prof. La. State U., 2001—. Assoc. prof., Ctr. Energy Studies, La. State U., 2001-. Contbr. articles to profl. jour. Achievements include the initiation of the fields of geometric metrology and constructive convex geometry, developed meta-modeling analysis of fiscal regimes; national expert on LIHEAP and WAP allocation mechanisms. Office: Center for Energy Studies, LSU Energy Coast & Environ Bldg Nicholson Extension Dr Baton Rouge LA 70803-0301

KAISER, MARTIN, newspaper editor; b. Milw., Oct. 11, 1950; Sports editor Chicago Sun-Times; assoc. mng. editor Baltimore Sun; mng. editor Milw. Jour.-Sentinel, 1994—97, editor, 1997—. Mem.: Am. Soc. Newspaper Editors (bd. dir., chmn. readership issues com. 2003—). Office: Milwaukee Journal PO Box 661 333 W State St Milwaukee WI 53203-1309*

KAISER, MICHAEL M. performing company executive; B magna cum laude, Brandeis U.; M in Mgmt., MIT. Rsch. economist for Wassily Leontief; past. owner Kaiser Assoc.; past exec. dir. Royal Opera House, Am. Ballet Theatre; past. exec. dir. Ailvin Ailey Dance Theater Found.; past assoc. dir. Pierpont Morgan Libr.; past gen. mgr. Kansas City Ballet; pres. John F. Kennedy Ctr. for Performing Arts, Washington, 2001—. Cons. arts orgn.; adj. prof. arts adminstrn. N.Y. U.; lectr. U. Witwatersrand, Johannesburg. Author: Understanding the Competition: A Practical Guide of Competitive Analysis, 1981, Developing Industry Strategies: A Practical Guide of Industry Analysis, 1983, Strategic Planning in the Arts: A Practical Guide, 1995. Office: John F Kennedy Ctr Performing Arts 2700 F St NW Washington DC 20566

KAISER, NINA IRENE, health care consultant; b. San Diego, Nov. 29, 1953; d. Louis Frederick and Mary Elizabeth (Wright) K.; children: Kellen Anne Kaiser, Ethan Andrew Kaiser-Klimist. BSN, BA in Women Studies, San Francisco State U., 1980; MBA, U. Phoenix, 2001. RN, Calif. RN Calif. Pacific Med. Ctr., San Francisco, 1980-81, Ralph K. Davies Med. Ctr., San Francisco, 1982-85, Planned Parenthood, San Francisco, 1985-86, Visiting Nurses and Hospice, San Francisco, 1986-88; RN supr. St. Mary's Home Care, San Francisco, 1991-93; RN dir. St. Vincent's Homecare and Hospice, Fremont, Calif., 1993-94, Home Health Link, San Leandro, Calif., 1994-99; acting site mgr. Kaiser Home Health, Oakland, Calif., 2003—. Mgmt. cons., 1999-2002; regional coun. chair San Francisco Bay Area, 1999—. Pres. Daus. of Bilitis, San Francisco, 1977-78; founding mem. Buena Vista Lesbian and Gay Parents Assn., San Francisco, 1985; treas., bd. dirs. Holladay Ave. Homeowners Assn., San Francisco, 1984-96; bd. dirs. Midrasha High Sch., Berkeley, Calif., 1996. With USN, 1971-74. E-mail: missnynak@aol.com.

KAISER, PHILIP MAYER, retired diplomat; b. Bklyn., July 12, 1913; s. Morris and Temma (Sloven) K.; m. Hannah Greeley, June 16, 1939; children: Robert Greeley, David Elmore, Charles Roger. AB, U. Wis., 1935; BA, MA (Rhodes scholar), Balliol Coll., Oxford (Eng.) U., 1939. Economist, bd. govs. Fed. Res. System, 1939-42; chief project ops. staff, also chief planning staff enemy br. Bd. Econ. Warfare and Fgn. Econ. Adminstrn., 1942-46; expert on internat. orgn. affairs State Dept., 1946; exec. asst. to asst. sec. labor in charge internat. labor affairs, 1946-47; dir. Office Internat. Affairs, Dept. Labor, 1947-49, asst. sec. labor for internat. affairs, 1949-53; labor adviser to Com. for Free Europe, 1954; spl. asst. to Gov. W. Averell Harriman of N.Y., 1955-58; prof. internat. rels. Sch. Internat. Svc. Am. U., 1958-61; U.S. ambassador to Republic Senegal, Islamic Republic Mauritania, 1961-64; minister Am. Embassy, London, Eng., 1964-69; chmn. Ency. Brit. Internat. Ltd., London, 1969-75; dir. Guinness Mahon Holdings, Ltd., 1975-77; amb. to People's Republic of Hungary, 1977-80, Austria, 1980-81; professorial lectr. Johns Hopkins Sch. Advanced Internat. Studies, 1981—83, Woodrow Wilson vis. fellow, 1984; sr. cons. SRI Internat., 1981-97. Mem. interdept. com. to develop programs under Marshall Plan, 1947—48, interdept. com. to develop programs for Greek-Turkish aid and Point 4 Tech. Assistance, 1947—49, Internat. del. to Hungary's Parliamentary elections, 1990; spl. amb. for Pres. Kennedy to Rwanda for its ind. day, 62. Author: Journeying Far and Wide: A Political and Diplomatic Memoir, 1993. Bd. dirs. Am. Ditchley Found., Ptnrs. for Dem. Change, Coun. Am. Ambs., Assn. Diplomatic Studies, Am. Acad. Diplomacy. Decorated knight comdr. Austrian Govt., Cross of Order of Merit of Republic of Hungary. Mem. Am. Assn. Rhodes Scholars, Coun. Fgn. Rels., Washington Inst. for Fgn. Affairs, Phi Beta Kappa. Home: 2101 Connecticut Ave NW Washington DC 20008-1728 Fax: 202-332-6124.

KAISER, RICHARD ALAN, surgeon; b. Newburgh, N.Y., Dec. 15, 1944; AB cum laude, Dartmouth Coll., 1966; MD, Harvard U., 1969. Diplomate Am. Bd. Surgery. Intern Beth Israel Hosp., Boston, 1969-70, resident in surgery, 1970-71, 74-77, Children's Hosp. Med. Ctr., Boston, 1975-76. Attending surgeon Mountainside Hosp., Montclair, N.J., 1977—. Lt. comdr. USNR Med. Corps, 1971-73. Fellow ACS; mem. AMA. Office: 73 Park St Montclair NJ 07042-2903 E-mail: rkaiser@worldnet.att.net.

KAISER, ROBERT GREELEY, newspaper editor; b. Washington, Apr. 7, 1943; s. Philip Mayer and Hannah (Greeley) K.; m. Hannah Jopling, July 14, 1965; children: Charlotte Jerome, Emily Eli. BA, Yale U., 1964; M.Sc., London Sch. Econs., 1967; postgrad., Columbia U., 1970-71. Reporter met. staff Washington Post, 1967-69, corr. Saigon Bur., 1969-70, bur. chief Moscow Bur., 1971-74, nat. corr., 1975-82, assoc. editor, columnist, 1982-85, asst. mng. editor for nat. news, 1985-90, dep. mng. editor, 1990-91, mng. editor, 1991-98, assoc. editor, sr. corr., 1998—. Vis. prof. Duke U., 1974-75, adj. prof., 1980-90. Author: Cold Winter, Cold War, 1974, Russia, The People and The Power, 1976, (with Jon Lowell) Great American Dreams, 1979, (with Hannah Jopling Kaiser) Russia From the Inside, 1980, Why Gorbachev Happened, 1991, The News About the News, (with Leonard Downie Jr.), 2002. Recipient Overseas Press Club award for best reporting from abroad, 1975. Mem. Coun. Fgn. Rels., Elihu Club. Office: Washington Post Co 1150 15th St NW Washington DC 20071-0002

KAISER, ROBERT LEE, engineering executive, retired; b. Louisville, June 28, 1935; s. Harlan K. and LaVerne (Peterson) K.; m. Margaret Siler; children: Robin Lee, Robert Lee. Student, U. Louisville, 1953-54, U. Ky., 1958-61. Registered profl. engr., Fla., Ky. Draftsman, designer E.R. Ronald & Assocs., Louisville, 1953-54, Thompson-Kissell Co., 1954-56; estimator, engr. George Pridemore & Son, Lexington, Ky., 1956-58; designer, engr., supr. Frankel & Curtis, Lexington, 1958-61; engr. Hugh Dillehay & Assocs., 1961-65; owenr, engr., operator K-Svc., Inc., 1965-74; project engr. Mason & Hanger, Silas Mason Co., Inc., 1974-77; v.p. Webb-Dillehay Design Group, 1977-81; pres. Kaiser-Taulbee Assocs., Inc., Lexington, Louisville, Orlando, Fla., ret., 2000. Past chmn., pres. and bd. dirs. Opportunity Workshop Lexington; vis. lectr. mech. engring. and Coll. Architecture, U. Ky.; mem., past chmn. Ky. State Bd. of Registration for Engrs, and Land Surveyors, Ky. Task Force to Develop New Engring. and Surveying Laws; charter commn. merger Lexington-Fayette County govts.; mem. Ky. Airport Zoning Comsn., mem. Gov.'s Task Force on Ednl. Constrn. Criteria; past trustee, chmn. Humana Hosp., Lexington, Aviatior Mus. Ky. Chmn. storm water task force Lake County Water Authority, Fla engring. advisor to Harris chair of Lake's Restoration Coun.. Mem. ASME NSPE, ASHRAE (past pres. local chpt.), Ky. Soc. Profl. Engrs. (life), Fla Engring. Soc., Mt. Dora C. of C. (bd. dirs.), Rotary. Episcopalian. Home: 138(Skyline Dr Tavares FL 32778-2533 Business E-Mail Bob.Kaiser@ampam.com. E-mail: rmk22578@earthlink.net.

KAISER, ROY, artistic director; b. Perth Amboy, N.J. Studied ballet with Karen Irvin; student, San Francisco Ballet Sch., Sch. Pa. Ballet. With Pa. Ballet 1979, prin. dancer, 1980-92, asst. ballet master, 1987-92, ballet master, 1992 assoc. artistic dir., 1993, interim artistic dir., 1994-95, artistic dir., 1995— Featured artists (with brothers) N.Y. World's Fair and throughout the U.S. performer on TV with Wayne Newton Music Carnival, Cleve.; performer on TV NBC-TV's Kraft Music Hall. Leading classical roles include Siegfried in Swan Lake, Franz in Coppelia, the Cavalier in The Nutcracker, Bolero, Symphonic Etudes, A Musical Offering, other prin. roles include George Balanchine's Symphony in C, Western Symphony, Symphony in Three Movements, Iago in The Moor's Pavane, Franklin Ct. Office: Pennsylvania Ballet 1101 S Broad S Philadelphia PA 19147-4410*

KAISER, SUZANNE BILLO, investment banker; b. Bronxville, N.Y., Apr. 9 1948; d. Otto Emile and Barbara (Leggett) Billo; divorced; 1 child, Kate Student, U. Lausanne, Switzerland, 1968, U. Paris, 1969; BA in Politics with honors, Hollins Coll., 1971; MBA, Georgetown U., 1997; MS, Columbia U Sch Journalism, 1999. Staff mem. U.S. Congresswoman Margaret Heckler Washington, 1971-72; adminstrv. officer internat. divsn. Kidder, Peabody & Co., Inc., N.Y.C., 1980-86; v.p., corp. sec. Concord Internat. Investments N.Y.C., 1986—. Bd. dirs. Coun. Jr. Leagues Westchester, 1976-77, Bronxville (N.Y.) Mid. Sch. Coun., 1989-90, Bronxville Pub. Libr., 1990-95; mem. H.S Coun., Bronxville Sch., 1992-93; mem. coun. women N.Y. Bot. Garden 2003—. Mem. Soc. Profl. Journalists, Pen and Brush, Hollins Club of N.Y. Georgetown U. Club (N.Y.C.). Office: Concord Internat Investment 66 Madison Ave New York NY 10021-8029

KAISER, WALTER, English language educator; b. Bellevue, Ohio, May 31 1931; AB magna cum laude, Harvard Coll., 1954; PhD, Harvard U., 1960 Allston Burr sr. tutor Eliot House Harvard U., 1957-58, from instr. to assoc prof. English, comparative lit., 1960-62, prof. English, comparative lit., 1969 chmn. dept., 1969-75, 82-85. Mem. coms. degrees in history and lit. Harvard U. 1960—, Faculty coun., 1971-74, libr. com., 1971-74; dep. dir. Villa I Tatti Florence, 1971-86, dir. 1988-2002. Author: Praisers of Folly: Erasmus, Rabelais, Shakespeare, 1964, Essays of Montaigne, 1964; co-author Program in Literature and the Arts for the Core Curriculum, 1977; transl.: (with intro.) Three Secret Poems, (George Seferis), 1969, Alexis (Marguerite Yourcenar) 1984, Two Lives and a Dream (Marguerite Yourcenar), That Mighty Sculptor Time (Marguerite Yourcenar), 1992; edit. bd. Studies in English Lit., 1977-88 editor-in-chief I Tatti Studies: Essays in the Renaissance, 1988-2002; editor (with M. Mallon) On Artists and Art Historians: Selected Book Reviews of John Pope Hennessy, 1994; contbr. numerous articles, reviews, poems to profl. jours Chair ad hoc vis. com. to Addison Gallery Am. Art, 1978; trustee Michael Rockefeller Meml. Fellowship, 1965-68, 69-70, Rockefeller Family Fund 1973-79, Mus. Fine Arts, Boston, 1978-88, Bogliasco Found., 2001—; bd. dirs Philip H. Rosenbach Found., 1974-78. Fulbright fellow U. Paris, 1954-55 Tower fellow Ecole Normale Supérieure Paris, 1955-56; fellow to Rome Am Coun. Learned Socs., 1964-65; Walter Channing Cabot fellow Fac. Arts. and Scis., 1977-78. Mem. PEN, Boston Athenaeum, Am. Comparative Lit. Assn. Renaissance Soc. Am., Signet Soc. (assoc.), Modern Greek Studies Assn. Shakespeare Assn. Am., Coun. Fgn. Rels., Knickerbocker Club, Somerset Club Harvard Club, Old Salopian, Boston Libr. Soc., Century Assn., Phi Beta Kappa Home and Office: 25 Sutton Pl S Apt 20M New York NY 10022 E-mail walter_kaiser@harvard.edu.

KAISER-BOTSAI, SHARON KAY, early childhood educator; b. Waterloo Iowa, Aug. 9, 1941; d. Peter A. Ley and Lorraine (Worthington) Burton; m Hugh W. Kaiser, Aug. 28, 1968 (div. 1981); 1 child, Kiana; m. Elmer E. Botsai Dec. 5, 1981; children: Kiana, Don, Kurt. BSBA, U. Ariz., 1963; MEd, U Hawaii, Honolulu, 1970; postgrad., U. Hawaii, 1972-88. Cert. elem. edn. tchr Hawaii. Sec. Donald M. Drake, San Francisco, 1964-66; tchr. St. Mark' Kindergarten, Honolulu, 1966-73; head tchr. Cen. Union Preschool, Honolulu 1967-77; tchr. Waiokeola Preschool, Honolulu, 1974-76, 77-88; tchr. staf instruction Honolulu Dist. Dept. of Edn., 1989-90; tchr. students of ltd. English proficiency Kaahumanu Sch., Honolulu, 1990-94; tchr. kindergarten Palolo Sch., Honolulu, 1991-97, Waialae Chartered Sch., 1997—2003. Pvt. instr. in Hawaiian dance, 1977-79; workshop leader marine sea crafts Sea Grant Inst. for Marine Educators, 1977, HAEYC Conf., 1979, 82, 84, 85, 86, chair workshop in music and creative drama, 1977, drama workshop, 1994, Drama Nat. Conf workshop leader, 1982, multiple intelligences workshop leader, 1998; speaker Celebration of Life Sta. KHON-TV, 1979; workshop leader MECAP Conf 1985; mem. com. Improvement Symphony Performance for Preschoolers 1977; art advisor, coord. Sunday sch. program Waiokeola Ch., 1973, speaker creative communication, 1984; validator accreditation program Nat. Acad. for Edn. of Young Children, 1986—; asst. to co-chair conf. Hawaii Assn. for Edn Young Children, 1987-88; Hawaii State Tchrs. Assn. rep. Palolo Sch., 1993 lectr. in field. Author: Creative Dramatics, 1990; co-author: Preschool Activities, 1990. Actress Presido Playhouse, San Francisco, 1962, Little Theatre Honolulu Zoo, 1976; instr. spl. edn. students Kaneohe YWCA, 1967; troo co-leader Girl Scouts U.S.A., 1981-84; bd. dirs. Zoo Hui, 1984-86; trustee stewardship chmn. Waiokeola Ch., 1986-88. Mem. Hawaii Assn. for Edn. c Young Children (First recipient Phyllis Loveless Excellence in Teaching awar 1979), Delta Delta Delta. Lutheran. Avocations: tennis, water and snow skiing creative drama, traveling, scuba diving. Home: 321 Wailupe Cir Honolulu H 96821-1524

KAISERLIAN, PENELOPE JANE, publishing company executive; b. Paisley, Scotland, Oct. 19, 1943; came to U.S., 1956; d. W. Norman and Magdalen Jeanette (Houlder) Hewson; m. Arthur Kaiserlian, June 29, 1968; 1 child Christian BA, U. Exeter, Eng., 1965. Copywriter, sales rep. Pergamon Press Elmsford, N.Y., 1965-68; exhibits mgr. Plenum Pub., N.Y.C., 1968-69; ass mktg. mgr. U. Chgo. Press, 1969-76, mktg. mgr., 1976-83, assoc. dir 1983-2001; dir. U. Va. Press, 2001—. Mem. Soc. for Scholarly Pub., Am. Geog Assn., Colonnade Club. Office: Univ Va Press PO Box 400318 Charlottesville VA 22904-4318

KAISERMAN, DAVID NORMAN, music educator; b. Cleve., July 15, 193 m. Sonia Uvezian, Jan. 12, 1962. BS, The Juilliard Sch., N.Y.C., 1959, MS 1960; DMA, U. Iowa, 1977. Asst. prof. Iowa State U., Ames, 1963-68; assoc prof. U. Puget Sound, Tacoma, 1968-75, prof., 1975-77, U. Okla., Norman 1977-80, U. Louisville, 1980-85, chmn. piano dept., 1983-85; prof. Northwestern U., Evanston, Ill., 1985—2002, chmn. piano dept., 1985-91, prof. emeritu 2002—; founder, pres., pub. Siamanto Press, 2001—. Performer concert recitals, adjudications, master classes and radio/TV programs worldwide 1958—; contbr. articles to profl. jours. Finalist various piano competition N.Y.C., Chgo., 1958—65; recipient various awards and scholarships, Th Juilliard Sch., 1954—60, Josephine Fry Bi-Annual award, Piano Tchrs. Congress of N.Y., 1963, Soc. Town Hall award, 1963, Grand prize tchr. divsn., Na Guild Piano Tchrs., 1973, 1983, winner auditions, Hour of Music, N.Y.C., 196 others. Mem.: Pubs. Mktg. Assn., Am. Liszt Soc., Coll. Music Soc., Mus Tchrs. Nat. Assn. (master tchr. cert. 1983), Pi Kappa Lambda. Office: PO Bo 458 Northbrook IL 60065-0458

KAISH, LUISE CLAYBORN, sculptor, former educator; b. Atlanta, Sept. 1925; d. Harry and Elsa (Brown) Meyers; m. Morton Kaish, Aug. 15, 1948; child, Melissa. BFA magna cum laude, Syracuse U., 1946, MFA, 1951; studen Escuela de Pintura y Escultura, Escuela de las Artes del Libro, Taller Grafic Mexico, 1946-47. Artist-in-residence Dartmouth Coll., 1974; prof. sculptur and painting, 1980-93, chmn. div. painting and sculpture Columbia U., 1980-8 prof. emerita, 1993; vis. artist U. Wash., Seattle, Battelle seminars and stud program, Seattle, 1979; artist-in-residence U. Haifa, Israel, 1985. One-ma shows Meml. Art Gallery, Rochester, N.Y., 1954, Sculpture Ctr., N.Y.C., 195 58, Staempfli Gallery, N.Y.C., 1968, 81, 84, 87, 88, Minn. Mus. Art, St. Pau 1969, Jewish Mus., N.Y.C., 1973, U. Ark., 1990, The Century Assn., 199 exhibited (with Morton Kaish), Rochester Meml. Art Gallery, 1958, USI

Rome, 1973, Dartmouth Coll., 1974, Oxford Gallery, Rochester, 1988; represented in permanent collections Whitney Mus. Am. Art, N.Y.C., Met. Mus. Art, N.Y.C., Jewish Mus., N.Y.C., Export Khleb, Moscow, Minn. Mus. Art, Gen. Mills Corp., Minn., Rochester Meml. Art Gallery, Smithsonian Instn., Nat. Mus. Am. Art, Washington, also numerous pvt. collections, commns., Syracuse U., Temple B'rith Kodesh, Rochester, Temple Israel, Westport, Conn., Holy Trinity Mission Sem., Silver Springs, Md., Temple Beth Shalom, Wilmington, Del., Beth-El Synagogue Ctr., New Rochelle, N.Y., Temple B'nai Abraham, Essex City, N.J., Continental Grain Co., N.Y. Trustee Am. Acad. in Rome, 1973-81, mem. exec. com., 1975-81, trustee emerita, 1994; trustee St. Gaudens Found., 1978-90, mem. exec. com., 1980-90. Recipient awards Everson Mus., Syracuse, 1947, awards Rochester Meml. Art Gallery, 1951, awards Ball State U., 1963, awards Ch. World Service, 1960, awards Council for Arts in Westchester, 1974, Emily Lowe award, 1956, Audubon Artists gold medal, 1963, Honor award AIA, 1975, Arents Pioneer medal, Syracuse U., 1989; Louis Comfort Tiffany grantee, 1951; Guggenheim fellow, 1959; Rome prize fellow Am. Acad. in Rome, 1970-72 Mem. Nat. Acad. Design, The Century Assn., Eta Pi Upsilon. Home and Office: 610 W End Ave # 9-a New York NY 10024-1605

KAISH, MORTON, artist, educator; b. Newark, Jan. 8, 1927; s. Morris and Sophie (Furman) K.; m. Luise H. Meyers, Aug. 15, 1948; 1 dau., Melissa. BFA, Syracuse U., 1949; postgrad., Academie de la Grande Chaumiere, Paris, 1951, Istituto d' Arte, Florence, Italy, 1952, Accademia delle Belle Arti, Rome, 1957. Vis. critic Parsons Sch. Design, N.Y.C., 1966-70, Phila. Coll. Art, 1983; mem. faculty Art Students League, N.Y.C., 1974—; guest critic Sch. Visual Arts, N.Y.C., 1967; vis. prof. Queens Coll., Flushing, N.Y., 1979; vis. artist U. Wash., Seattle, 1979; fellow MacDowell Colony, 1976; artist-in-residence Dartmouth Coll., 1974, U. Haifa, Israel, 1985; prof. Fashion Inst. Tech., SUNY, N.Y.C., 1973—; vis. artist Susquehanna U., 1985; dir. Carl Fischer Mus. Instrument Co., 1964-70. Vis. artist Columbia U., N.Y.C., 1986, Boston U., 1987. One-man shows include Manhattanville Coll., Purchase, N.Y., 1955, Rochester (N.Y.) Meml. Art Gallery, 1955, Guild Hall, Easthampton, L.I., 1969, U.S. Info. Service, Rome, 1973, Dartmouth,Coll., Hanover, N.H., 1974, Staempfli Gallery, N.Y.C., 1964, 67, 71, 73, 79, 83, 86, 89, Oxford Gallery, Rochester, N.Y., 1989, Century Assn., N.Y., 1989, Hollis Taggart Galleries, Washington, 1993, N.Y.C., 1996; group shows Mus. Galleria 11 Torcoliere, Rome, 1957, Barone Gallery, N.Y.C., 1959, Art Inst. Chgo., 1964, Sheldon Meml. Art Gallery, Lincoln, Nebr., 1964, U. Nebr., Lincoln, 1964, Krannert Art Mus., U. Ill., Urbana, 1965, 68, Herron Mus. Art, Indpls., 1965, Mary Washington Coll., Fredericksburg, Va., 1965, Am. Acad. Arts and Letters, N.Y.C., 1966, Pa. Acad. Fine Arts, Phila., 1966, Ark. Art Ctr., Little Rock, 1966, Whitney Mus. Am. Art, N.Y.C., 1966, Finch Coll. Mus. Art, N.Y.C., 1966, N.J. State Mus., Trenton, 1966, Krannert Art Mus., 1968, Kent (Ohio) State U., 1970, U.S. Info. Service, Rome, 1972, New Sch. Social Research, N.Y.C., 1973, Child Hassam Purchase Fund Exhbn., N.Y.C., 1973; invitational exhbns. Child Hassam Purchase Fund, 1975, Am. Acad. Arts and Letters, 1975, Drawings U.S.A., 1975, Minn. Mus. Art, St. Paul, 1975, Springfield Art Mus., 1975, Springfield Mus. Art, Mo., 1975, Galerie Brusberg, Berlin, W.Ger., 1980, Taft Mus., Cin., 1981, NAD, N.Y.C., 1983, 85, 89, 91; represented in permanent collections Met. Mus. Art, N.Y.C., Whitney Mus. Am. Art, N.Y.C., Bklyn. Mus., Nat. Mus. Art, Smithsonian Instn., Washington, Brit. Mus., London, The Fitzwilliam Mus., Cambridge, Guild Hall, Easthampton, N.Y., Williams Coll., Williamstown. Mass., Syracuse U., N.Y., Swarthmore Coll., Indpls. Mus. Art, U. Mich. Mus. Art., Guilford Coll., Greensboro, N.C., Rochester (N.Y.) Meml. Art Gallery, Bates Coll., Lewiston, Maine, New Britain (Conn.) Mus. Am. Art, Newark Mus., N.J. Recipient SUNY Rsch. Found. award, 1983, Gervasi award, 1985, William Ward Ranger Fund purchase award, 1983, 85, Benjamin Altman prize, 1989, Andrew Carnegie prize, 1992, Adolph and Clara Obrig prize, 2003, Disting. Alumni award for Achievement in the Visual Arts Syracuse U., 1989; faculty exch. scholar SUNY, 1987. Mem. NAD (corr. sec., William A. Paton prize 1983), Century Assn., Artists' Choice Mus. (bd. artists), Artists' Fellowship (trustee, v.p.). Address: 610 W End Ave New York NY 10024-1605

KAJI, AKIRA, microbiology scientist, educator; b. Tokyo, Jan. 13, 1930; came to U.S., 1954; s. Kiichi and Chiyo (Hanai) K.; m. Hideko Katayama, Aug. 22, 1958; children: Kenneth, Eugene, Naomi, Amy. BS, Tokyo U., 1953; PhD, Johns Hopkins U., 1958; MS (hon.), U. Pa., 1973. Rsch. fellow Johns Hopkins Hosp., Balt., 1958-59; guest investigator Rockefeller U., N.Y.C., 1959; rsch. assoc. microbiology Vanderbilt Med. Sch., Nashville, 1959-62; vis. scientist Oak Ridge (Tenn.) Nat. Lab., 1962-63, assoc. U. Pa. Med. Sch., Phila., 1963-64, asst. prof. microbiology, 1964-67, assoc. prof., 1967-72, prof., 1972—. Permanent mem. bd. sci. councilors Nat. Eye Inst., Bethesda, Md., 1987-92; prof., chair Tokyo U. Faculty Pharm. Scis., 1972-73; vis. prof. Kyoto U. Virus Rsch. Inst., 1985. Contbr. over 200 articles to profl. jours. Recipient Fulbright-Smith-Mundt award, 1954, Helen Hay Whitney award, 1964-69, John Simmon Guggenheim award, 1972-73, Fogarty Internat. Sr. award, 1985-86 Mem. Am. Soc. Biol. Chemistry and Molecular Biology, Am. Soc. Cell Biology, Am. Soc. Microbiology, Am. Soc. Chemistry. Avocations: ice dancing, swimming. Office: U Pa Sch Medicine Dept Microbiology Johnson Pavilion Philadelphia PA 19104

KAJI, HIDEKO, pharmacology educator; b. Tokyo, Jan. 1, 1932; came to U.S., 1954; d. Sakae and Tsuneko (Matsuda) Katayama; m. Akira Kaji, Aug. 23, 1958; children: Kenneth, Eugene, Naomi, Amy. BS, Tokyo U. Pharm. Scis., 1954; MS, U. Nebr., 1956; PhD, Purdue U., 1958. Vis. scientist Oak Ridge (Tenn.) Nat. Lab., 1962-63; assoc. U. Pa., Phila., 1963-64; rsch. assoc. The Inst. Cancer Rsch., Phila., 1965-66, asst. mem., 1966-76; vis. mem. Max Planck Inst. Molek. Gen., Berlin, 1972-73, Nat. Inst. Med. Rsch., London, 1973; assoc. prof. Jefferson Med. Coll., Phila., 1976-82; vis. prof. Wistar Inst., Phila., 1984-85; prof. biochemistry and molecular pharmacology Jefferson Med. Coll., Phila., 1983—. Cons. Nippon Paint Co., Ltd., Tokyo, 1990—, Coatesville (Pa.) VA Hosp., 1982-84. Contbr. articles to profl. jours. Fellow NIH (bd. dirs. 1986-89); mem. Am. Soc. Biochemistry and Molecular Biology, Am. Soc. Pharmacol. and Exptl. Therapeutics, Am. Soc. Microbiology, Sigma Xi. Home: 334 Fillmore St Jenkintown PA 19046-4328 Office: Jefferson Med Coll 1020 Locust St Philadelphia PA 19107-6731 Business E-Mail: hideko.kaji@jefferson.edu.

KAJITANI, MOTOHISA, sociology educator; b. Kamioka, Gifu, Japan, May 8, 1937; s. Miyokichi and Nui (Taguchi) K.; m. Yoko Shimizu, Nov. 1969; 1 child, Kuri BA, Tokyo U. Fgn. Studies, 1961; Diploma in Social Sci., U. Tokyo, 1961; MA, Kyoto (Japan) U., 1964. Lectr. Meijo U., Nagoya, Japan, 1964-69, prof., 1976—, chmn. libr., 1991-2001, univ. prof. grad. sch., 2002—; joint lectr. Tokyo U. Fgn. Studies, 1965—72, 1975—82. Vis. prof. dept. sociology UCLA, 1990; non-resident mem. Queen Elizabeth House, Oxford, 1972-74; guest prof. U. Klagenfurt, Austria, 1996; guest lectr. Nagoya City U., 1997—. Assoc. editor History of Sociology, 1981-87; author: Shakaigaku to Nippon, New Steps to Internatl. Sociology, 2002; Press and Empire, 1981; author, editor: Shakaigaku no Rekishi: A History of Sociology, 1982, 89; editor: (with Hisao Naka) Sociologie Globale, 1987; editor: (with J. Langer) Shakaigatu to Europa, 1994; contbr. articles to Global, 1984-87. Recipient prize of social thought Akegarasu Fund, Tokyo and Kanazawa Univs., 1964, Outstanding Achievement award in edn., Cambridge, Eng., 1999; over 10 grants in Japan. Mem.: others, Japanese Sociol. Assn., Internat. Sociol. Assn. (life). Avocations: opera, concerts. Office: Meijo U 1-501 Shiogamaguchi Nagoya 468 Japan Fax: (52) 853-3936. E-mail: kajitani@meijo-u.ac.jp.

KAKADIARIS, IOANNIS, computer science educator; b. Athens, Greece, May 16, 1966; m. Maria Gasi, Jan. 13, 1996; children: Eugenia, Alexandra. PhD in Computer Sci., U. Pa., 1997. Tchg. asst. Northeastern U., Boston, 1990—90, rsch. asst., 1990—91; rsch. fellow U. Pa., Phila., 1991—96, post-doctoral fellow, 1996—97; asst. prof. U. Houston, 1997—, dir. visual computing lab, 1997—2002, coord. external rels. Virtual Environments Rsch. Inst., 1998—2000, mem. Tex. Learning and Computation Ctr., 1999—, thrust leader bioimaging and biocomputation Virtual Environments Rsch. Inst, 2000—02, interim dir. Virtual Environments Rsch. Inst, 2000—02, co-dir. Visual Computing Lab., 2002—, dir. divsn. bioimaging and biocomputation Inst. for Digital Informatics and Analysis, 2002—. Adj. asst. prof. dept. health informatics Health Info. Scis. U. Tex., Houston, 1999—; adj. asst. prof. dept. plastic surgery U. Tex. M.D. Anderson Cancer Ctr., Houston, 2000—; mem. The W.M. Keck Ctr. for Computational and Structural Biology, 2002—. Editor: Proceedings of the IEEE Human motion analysis and synthesis workshop; contbr. chapters to books, articles to profl. jours. Recipient award, Schlumberger Tech. Found., 1998—99, SHELL Interdisciplinary award, 1999; fellow, Bodosakis Found., 1989—91, Gerondelis Found., 1991—92; grantee, SGI Inc., 1998, NSF, 1998, U. Houston Internat. Space Systems Ops., 2000—02, NSF, 2000—, Tex. Higher Edn. Coordinating Bd., 2000—03, Am. Honda R&D, Inc., 2000—01, MD Anderson Cancer Ctr., 2000—, NSF, 2001—02, Sun Microsystems, 2001—, Tex. Higher Edn. Coordinating Bd., 2001, Keck Ctr. for Computational Biology, 2002—03, Juvenile Diabetes Rsch. Found., 2002—, U. of Houston Faculty Devel. Initiative Program, 2002—03, U. Houston, 2002, Real Time Innovations Inc., 2002. Mem.: IEEE (Disting. Visitor 2002—), Brit. Machine Vision Assn., Internat. Soc. for Computer Aided Surgery, Hellenic Soc. Scientists in Computer and Info. Sci., Assn. for Computing Machinery, Am. Heart Assn., Sigma Xi (pres. 2002—03). Achievements include research in understanding diagrams in technical documents; data interrogation in visual computing; adaptive fuzzy connectedness-based medical image segementation; automatic hybrid segmentation of dual contrast cardiac MR data; g-HDAF multiresolution deformable models for shape modeling and reconstruction; teleoperating robonaut; m-HDAF multiresolution deformable models; automatic computation of the ejection fraction using dual contrast short-axis cardia MR images; estimating the motion of the LAD; tracking methods for medical augemented reality; multi-sensory investigation of geoscientific data; application of virtual reality in surgery; improvement of anthropometry and pose estimation from a single uncalibrated image; numerous others. Office: Univ Houston 4800 Calhoun MS CSC 3010 Houston TX 77204-3010 Office Fax: 713-743-1250. E-mail: ioannisk@uh.edu.

KAKAR, SANJAY, gastrointestinal and liver pathologist; b. Chandigarh, India, June 17, 1968; s. Ramesh Kumar and Savita Kakar; m. Shalini Sahai, June 22, 1971. MB, Christian Medical Coll., 1986—91; BChir, Christian Med. Coll., 1986—91; MD, Postgraduate Inst., 1992—94. Registered med. practioner Haryana Med. Coun., India, 1992, anatomic and clinical pathology Am. Bd. of Pathology, 2000, MD Minn., 2000, Calif., 2002, bd. cert. Am. Bd. of Pathology, U. of Ill., 2000. Sr. ho. officer Postgraduate Inst., Chandigarh, India, 1995—96; clin. ho. officer U. of Ill. Med. Ctr., Mayo Clinic, Rochester, Minn., 2000—02; asst. prof. U. of Calif. Med. Ctr., 2002—, Vet. Affairs Med. Ctr., 2002—; staff pathologist and cons., GI-Liver pathologist U. Calif. San Francisco and VA Med. Ctr., 2002—. Contbr. articles to profl. jours. Rsch. grant, Mayo Clinic, Rochester MN, 2001, 2002. Fellow: Am. Coll. of Pathology (life); mem.: Am. Gastroent. Assn., Am. Soc. of Clin. Pathologists, US and Can. Acad. of Pathology. Avocations: astronomy, badminton, cricket, art. Home: 233 Rock Harbor Lane Foster City CA 94404 Office: UCSF and VA Med Ctr 4150 Clement St San Francisco CA 94121 Office Fax: 415-750-6947. E-mail: skakar@itsa.ucsf.edu.

KAKU, MICHIO, theoretical nuclear physicist, educator; b. San Jose, Calif., Jan. 24, 1947; s. Toshio and Hideko (Maruyama) K. BA, Harvard U., 1968; PhD, U. Calif., Berkeley, 1972; PhD (hon.) Hofstra U., 1997, SUNY, Old Westbury, 1997. Rsch. assoc. Princeton U., N.J., 1972-73; assoc. prof. CCNY and Grad. Ctr., 1973-83, prof., 1983—; vis. prof. NYU, 1988, Inst. for Advanced Studies at Princeton U., 1990. Author: Nuclear Power: Both Sides, 1983; Beyond Einstein, the Cosmic Quest for the Theory of the Universe, 1986, Introduction to Superstrings, 1988, Strings, Conformal Fields, and Topology, 1991, Quarks, Symmetries, and Strings, 1991, Quantum Field Theory: A Modern Introduction, 1993, Hyperspace: A Scientific Odyssey Through Parallel Universes, Time Warps, and the 10th Dimension, 1994, Frontiers in Quantum Field Theory, 1996, Visions: How Science Will Revolutionize the 21st Century, 1997, Einstein's Cosmos, 2004, Parallel Worlds, 2004; contbr. 70 articles to profl. jours. Fellow Am. Phys. Soc. Avocations: nuclear arms control, nuclear power. Office: CCNY Physics Dept 138th St at Convent Ave New York NY 10031

KALABA, ROBERT EDWIN, applied mathematician; b. Mt. Vernon, N.Y., Sept. 21, 1926; s. Edwin Albert and Leona Margaret (Winkler) K.; m. Wilma Joy Becker, Dec. 23, 1950; children: Robert John, Darlene Day, Kathy Lynn, Richard William. BA, NYU, 1948, PhD, 1958. Mathematician Rand Corp., Santa Monica, Calif., 1951-70; prof. econs., elec. and biomed. engring U. So. Calif., Los Angeles, Calif., 1969—. Author: Invariant Imbedding and Radiative Transfer in Slabs of Finite Thickness, 1963, Quasilinearization and Nonlinear Boundary-Value Problems, 1965, Dynamic Programming and Modern Control Theory, 1965, Imbedding Methods in Applied Mathematics, 1973, Integral Equations via Embedding Methods, 1974, Control, Identification and Input Optimization, 1982, Numerical Derivatives and Nonlinear Analysis, 1986, A New Analytical Dynamics, 1995; founding editor Jour. Applied Math. and Computation, 1975; contbr. articles to profl. jours. Served with USN, 1945-46. Mem. IEEE (life), Assn. Computing Machinery, Math. Assn. Am., Riviera Country Club, Am. Econ. Assn., Phi Beta Kappa. Home: 370 Aderno Way Pacific Palisades CA 90272-3344 Office: U So Calif Los Angeles CA 90089-0251

KALAFUT, MICHAEL FRANCIS, civil engineer; b. Trenton, N.J., Feb. 28, 1954; s. Michael R. and Margaret A. (Simonelli) K.; m. Claire E. Cullen, May 23, 1981; children: Alison K., Scott M. B Engring., Stevens Inst. Tech., 1976; MSCE, Rutgers U., 1985. Registered profl. engr., N.J., Pa. Sr. engr. Mercer County, Trenton, 1977; asst. engr. N.J. Dept. Transp., Trenton, 1977-79; contract adminstr. Foster Wheeler Energy Corp., Livingston, N.J., 1979-83; project engr. Gilbane Bldg. Co., Princeton, N.J., 1983-85, West Windsor-Plainsboro Regional Sch. Dist., Plainsboro, N.J., 1985-88; v.p. Lehrer McGovern Bovis, Inc., Princeton, 1988—97; project exec. Skanska USA, Parsippany, NJ, 1997—. Mem. NSPE, Am. Mensa, Ltd. Republican. Office: Lehrer-McGovern Bovis Inc 100 Nassau Park Blvd Princeton NJ 08540-5932

KALAHASTI, VIDYASAGAR, cardiologist; s. Lakshminarayana and Adilakshmi Kalahasti; m. Priya Kalahasti, Sept. 7, 1997; 1 child, Ananya. MBBS, Sri Venkateswara Med. Coll., 1987—94; MD, Cleve. Clinic Found., 1998—2002. Cert. foreign med. grad. Ednl. Commn. Fgn. Med. Graduates(ECFMG), 1994, perm. lic. to practice State Med. Bd. Ohio, 2002, cert. bd. cert. Am. Bd. Internal Medicine(ABIM), 2002, basic life support (BLS) Am. Heart Assn. (AHA), 2002, advanced cardiac life support(ACLS) Am. Heart Assn. (AHA), 2002. Ho. officer, dept. internal medicine Swarna Nursing Home, Tirupati, India, 1994, Medwin Hospitals, Hyderabad, 1995; ho. officer anesthesiology Mt. Hope Maternity Hospitals, Mount Hope, 1996—98; internship in anesthesiology Cleve. Clinic Found., Ohio, 1998—99, internship in internal medicine, 1999—2000, residency in internal medicine, 2000—02, cons., 2002—02, fellowship in cardiovascular diseases, 2002—. Recipient Gold Medal in Pharmacology, Sri Venkateswara Med. Coll., Tirupati, A.P. India, 1989, Gold Medal in Forensic Medicine, 1990, Gold Medal in Ophthalmology, 1991, Gold Medal in Social and Preventive Medicine, 1991. Mem.: AHA, AMA, ACP (assoc.), Am. Coll. Cardiology (assoc.). Achievements include research in QRS duration as a predictor of Mortality. Home: 35 Severance Cir Dr Apt 205 Cleveland Heights OH 44118 Office: Cleveland Clinic Found 9500 Euclid Ave Cleveland OH 44195

KALAI, EHUD, decision sciences educator, researcher in economics and decision sciences; b. Tel Aviv, Dec. 7, 1942; came to U.S., 1963; s. Meir and Elisheva (Rabinovitch) K., m. Marilyn Lott, Aug. 24, 1967; children: Kerren, Adam. AB with distinction, U. Calif. at Berkeley, 1967; MS, Cornell U., 1971, PhD in Applied Math., 1972. Asst. prof. dept. statistics Tel Aviv U., 1972-75; vis. asst. prof. decision scis. J.L. Kellogg Grad. Sch. Mgmt. Northwestern U., Evanston, Ill., 1975-76, assoc. prof. decision scis., 1976-78, prof. managerial econs. and decision scis., 1978-82, The Charles E. Morrison Chair prof. decision scis., 1982-2001, prof. math., 1990—, IBM rsch. chair managerial econs., 1980-81, J.L. Kellogg rsch. chair in decision theory, 1981-82, chmn. meds. dept., 1983-85; dir. Ctr. for Strategic Decision-Making Kellogg Sch. Mgmt., Northwestern U., 1995—. Oskar Morgenstern rsch. prof. game theory NYU, 1991; expert testimony in ct. cases, 1982—; cons. Israeli Def. Forces, 1974-75, 1st Nat. Bank Chgo., 1987, Arthur Anderson, 1990, Kaiser Permanente, 1995, Nath Sonnenschein and Rosenthal, 1999, Baxter Healthcare Corp., 1999—; James J. O'Conner Distinguished Prof. of Decision and Game Scis., 2001—. Founder, editor Games and Econ. Behavior Jour., 1988—; editl. bd. Math. Social Scis., 1980-90, Jour. Econ. Theory, 1980-88, Internat. Jour. Game Theory, 1984—; contbr. numerous articles on game theory and econs. to profl. jours. Sgt. Israeli Def. Forces, 1960-63. NSF grantee, 1979—; Sherman Fairchild Disting. scholar, Calif. Inst. Tech., 1994-95. Fellow Econometrics Soc.; mem. Am. Math. Soc., Pub. Choice Soc., Game Theory Soc. (founder, exec. v.p. 1998—), Beta Gamma Sigma. Home: 1110 N Lake Shore Dr Apt 23S Chicago IL 60611-1023 Office: Kellogg Grad Sch of Mgmt Northwestern Univ Evanston IL 60208-0001 E-mail: kalai@kellogg.northwestern.edu.

KALAINOV, SAM CHARLES, insurance company executive; b. Steele, N.D., May 11, 1930; s. George and Celia Mae (Makedonsky) K.; m. Delores L. Holm, Aug. 10, 1957; children: John Charles, David Mark. BS, N.D. State U., 1956. CLU. Life ins. agt. Am. Mut. Life Ins. Co., Fargo, N.D., 1956-60, supt. agys. Des Moines, 1960-70, sr. v.p. mktg., 1972-80, pres., chmn., CEO, 1980-95; v.p. agy. Western States Life Ins. Co., Fargo, 1970-72; chmn. bd. dirs. Am. Mut. Holding Corp., Amerus Life, 1995-2000. Bd. dirs. Am. Coun. Life Ins., Washington, Bankers Trust, Des Moines; past chmn. Des Moines Devel. Corp. Bd. dirs. Luth. Health Sys., Fargo, 1974-91, City Corp., Des Moines, 1981-95, Civic Ctr. Ct., 1981-95, Iowa Luth. Hosp., 1982-91; trustee Drake U.; past chmn. Des Moines Conv. and Visitors Bur.; civilian aide to Sec. Army at Large, 1991; past state dir. Selective Svc. Sys.; bd. mem. N.D. State U. Devel. Found. With inf. AUS, 1947-49, lt., 1952-55. Decorated Bronze Star; recipient Alumni Achievement award N.D. State U., 1983, Patrick Henry award Army Nat. Guard, 1998. Mem. Nat. Assn. Life Underwriters, Greater Des Moines C. of C. (past chmn., Nat. Leadership award 1978), Corp. for Internat. Trade (chmn.), Alexis de Tocqueville Soc., Am. Legion, Rotary (past pres. Des Moines chpt.), Grand Lodge Iowa, Royal Order of Jesters, Za-Ga-Zig Temple. Home: 681 50th St Des Moines IA 50312-1807 Office: AmerUs Group 699 Walnut St Des Moines IA 50309-3929

KALAJIAN-LAGANI, DONNA, publishing executive; b. Mountainside, N.J., Feb. 8, 1955; d. Jack and Analid Kalajian; m. Ron Galotti, Oct. 14, 1981. BS, Penn State U., 1975. Internat. credit analyst Irving Trust Co., N.Y.C., 1976—77; ad sales rep. BMT Pub., N.Y.C., 1977—79, Woman's Day Mag., N.Y.C., 1979—81, cosmetics mgr., 1981—83, ea. mgr., 1984—87; v.p., advt. dir. Ladies' Home Jour., N.Y.C., 1987—89, v.p., pub., 1989—95; pub./sr. v.p. Cosmopolitan Mag., 1996—99; publ. dir. Cosmopolitan Group, N.Y.C., 1999—, sr. v.p., 1999—. Home: 100 Park Ave New York NY 10017-5516 Office: Cosmopolitan Hearst Magazines 224 W 57th St New York NY 10019-3299*

KALAMAROS, PHILIP E. lawyer; b. South Bend, Ind., Apr. 21, 1962; s. Edward N. and Marilyn J. Kalamaros; m. Lynn E. K., July 10, 1999. BBA, U. Notre Dame, 1984, JD, 1987. Bar: Ind. 1987, Mich. 2001, U.S. Dist. Ct. (no. and so. dists.) Ind. 1987, U.S. Ct. Appeals (7th cir.) 1987, U.S. Supreme Ct. 1995. Shareholder atty. Edward N. Kalamaros & Assocs., P.C., South Bend, 1987-2000, mng. shareholder, pres., 1996-2000; ptnr. Hunt Suedhoff Kalamaros LLP, South Bend, 2000—. Panelist def. seminar, Ins. Inst. Ind., 1998. Contbr. articles to profl. jours. Dir. Redbud Trail Retreat, Buchanna, Mich., 1989-91; dir. Southold Restorations, South Bend, 1993-97, New Carlisle (Ind.) Hist. Soc., 1994-98. Fellow Ind. Bar Found.; mem. ATLA, Def. Rsch. Inst., Nat. Coun. Self Insurers, Nat. Health Lawyers Assn., 7th Cir. Bar Assn., Ind. State Bar Assn., Ind. Trial Lawyers Assn., Def. Trial Counsel of Ind. (amicus chair 1992-97, dir. 1997-2000, participant seminars 1995, 97, 99, 2000, 02, 03), Ind. Self Insurers Assn., St. Joseph County Bar Assn. (chair young lawyers 1987-89, bd. govs. 1989-90, sec. 1990-2003), Notre Dame Law Assn., Porsche Club of Am. (past pres. Michiana region). Avocations: motor sports, auto and marine. Office: Hunt Suedhoff Kalamaros LLP 120 W LaSalle PO Box 4156 South Bend IN 46634-4156 E-mail: phil@HSK-Law.com.

KALAMOTOUSAKIS, GEORGE JOHN, economist, merchant banker, educator; b. Chios, Greece, July 26, 1936; came to U.S., 1953; s. John S. and Marika (Nikolaides) K.; 1 child, Yannis. BA, CUNY, 1956, MA, 1958; PhD, NYU, 1966. Instr. Fairleigh Dickinson, U., Teaneck, N.J., 1958-59; asst. prof. Ithaca (N.Y.) Coll., 1959-62; chief economist Brown Engr., N.Y.C., 1963-64; instr. Washington Sq. Coll., NYU, 1963-65; econ. cons. N.Y. State Office Regional Devel., Albany, 1964-66; adv. economist IBM, Armonk, N.Y., 1969-73; internat. economist Am. Standard, Inc., N.Y.C., 1973-76; prof. finance Grad. Sch. Bus., NYU, 1971-77. External dir. Rank-Xerox, Hellas, Greece, Atlantic Union Ins. Co., Athens, Greece; vis. prof. U. Md. European divsn. USAF, 1960, 67-68; head dept. pub. fin. Ctr. of Planning and Econ. Rsch., Athens, Greece; dir. econ. rsch. Bank of Greece, 1977-79; chief exec. officer, vice-chmn. bd. Bank of Crete, Athens, 1979-84; exec. dir., country head, gen. mgr. Greece, head Middle Ea. region Am. Express Bank Ltd., N.Y.C., 1985-94, fin. svcs. cons., 1995—; mem. William J. Fulbright Scholarship com., Athens; bd. dirs. Egyptian Am. Bank, Cairo, 1989-94. Contbr. articles to profl. jours.; Author books on internat. fin., Cyprus and self determination, common market and econ. devel. Greece. Bd. dirs., trustee Hellenic Theatre Found., bd. dirs. Aegian U., Greece. Am. Ford Found. Faculty Research fellow, 1962 Mem. Am. Econ. Assn., AAUP (v.p. chpt. 1961), Omicron Delta Epsilon. Home: 124 Lakeview Ave Lynbrook NY 11563-1755 Office: 43 Diamantidou Ave Paleo Psychico 15452 Athens Greece

KALAN, GARY EDWARD, anesthesiologist; b. White Plains, N.Y., Dec. 19, 1953; MD, U. Vt., 1982. Diplomate Am. Bd. Anesthesiology. From intern to resident in internal medicine R.I. Hosp., Providence, 1982-84; resident in anesthesiology U. Conn., Farmington, 1984-87; dir. dept. anesthesiology Greenwich (Conn.) Hosp., 1994—, co-dir. dept. integrative medicine, 2002; v.p. Greenwich Anesthesiology Assocs. PC, 1998—; pvt. practice, 1987—. Mem. AMA, Am. Soc. Anesthesiologists, Conn. State Soc. Anesthesiologists. Office: Greenwich Anes Assoc PC PO Box 772 Greenwich CT 06836-0772

KALANA, DAVID STERLING, director of information systems; b. Houston, Aug. 1, 1964; s. Frank and Sylvia Anne (Nicol) Kalana; m. Dawn Marie Strate, Sept. 28, 1996; children: Shaelynn, Ashley. Diploma, Computer Learning Ctr., Houston, 1990. Computer operator Western Atlas Internat., Houston, 1990-91; sr. computer sys. operator Exxon Co. USA, Houston, 1991-93; network sys. adminstr. Univ. Hosp., Salt Lake City, 1993-95; sys. cons. Bus. Enterprise Sys. Technology, Salt Lake City, 1995-96; nat. sys. engring. instr. Astron/Advanced Tech. Ctr., Salt Lake City, 1996-98; global sys. engr. Iomega Corp., Roy, Utah, 1998-2000; dir. info. sys. Net Voyage Corp. dba Net Documents, Inc., Orem, Utah, 2000—. Republican. Mem. Ch. Latter Day Saints. Avocations: golf, aviation, reading, family. Home: 7381 S Union Creek Way 11 D Salt Lake City UT 84047 E-mail: dkalana@netdocuments.com., dkalana@hotmail.com.

KALANTZIS, GEORGE, historian, educator; s. Apostolos and Polyxeni Kalantzis; m. Irene Kalantzis, Oct. 31, 1987. BS, U. of Ill., 1990; MABS, Moody Grad. Sch., 1993; MS, Northeastern Ill. U., 1993; MTS, Garrett-Evangelical Theol. Sem., 1994; PhD, Northwestern U., 1997. Asst. prof. of the history of christianity Garrett-Evangelical Theol. Sem., Evanston, Ill., 1997—. Dir. of ednl. technologies Garrett-Evangelical Theol. Sem., 1997—. Editor: The Greek New Testament; author, Theodore of Mopsuestia: Commentary on John, 2003, (albums) Digital Resources for the History of Christianity, I-Duo filii and the homo assumptus in the Christology of theodore of Mopsuestia, 2002, Ephesus as Roman, Christian and Jewish Metropolis in the First and Second Centuries C.E., 1997. Fellow Hartman fellowship, Garrett-Evangelical Theol. Sem., 1994, Ernest W. Saunders Endowed Doctoral fellowship, 1996—97; grantee, Wabash Ctr. for Tchg. and Learning in Theology and Religion, 2000; scholar, Northwestern U., 1994—97, Ester Y. Armstrong scholarship, Garrett-Evangelical Theol. Sem., 1994—95. Mem.: L'Association Internationale des Études Patristiques (AIEP), Am. Soc. of Ch. History, Soc. of Bibl. Rsch., Am. Schs. of Oriental Rsch., N.Am. Patristics Soc., Am. Philol Assn. Office: Academic 2121 Sheridan Road Evanston IL 60201 Office Fax: 847-866-3957. E-mail: george-kalantzis@northwestern.edu.

KALAPATHY, URUTHIRA PASUPATHY, food scientist, researcher; b. Jaffna, Sri Lanka, Nov. 8, 1953; s. Nagalingam and Kamaladevi Uruthirapasupathy; m. Bhavani Thevasigamany; children: Mathanki, Branavan. BS, U. Jaffna, 1979; PhD, N.D. State U., 1992. Hydrogeochemist Water Resources Bd., Jaffna, 1982—86; rsch. scientist U. Ark., Fayetteville, 1993—2001; prof. Claflin U., Orangeburg, SC, 2002—. Contbr. articles to profl. jours., chpts. to books. Grantee, U.S. Dept. Agr., 2000—. Mem.: Inst. Food Technologists. Home: 3200 Fernandina Rd Columbia SC 29210 Office: Claflin Univ Orangeburg SC 29115 Office Fax: 803-535-5776. Personal E-mail: ukalapat@hotmail.com. E-mail: ukalapat@claflin.edu.

KALAPOS, FELICIA ZERA, elementary school educator, writer; b. Bridgeport, Conn., July 5, 1953; d. Aloyzy John and Florence (Dobieski) Zera; m. George Julius Kalapos, Jr., May 26, 1974; children: Jennifer, Jessica, Jaclyn, Jeffrey. BS Elem. Edn. cum laude, So. Conn. State U., 1974; MS Elem. Edn., U. Bridgeport, 1976. Cert. profl. educator Conn. State Bd. Edn. Grade 6 tchr. Fairfield (Conn.) Bd. Edn., 1974—77, gifted tchr., 1979—81, grade 5 tchr., 1988—90, chpt. I math tutor, tchr., 1991—92, math resource tchr., 1993—, gifted math tchr., 2000—; homebound pvt. corp. tutor Fairfield and Stratford (Conn.) Bd. Edn., 1981—88. Ednl. cons. Environ. Mgmt. Con., Shelton, Conn., 1990; guest lectr. ESOL class Fairfield (Conn.) U., 2000; guest lectr. U. R.I., Kingston, 2000; spkr. in field. Author: (novels) Love on a Shoestring, 2000. Active PTA, 1974—. Mem.: Nat. Edn. Assn., Conn. Edn. Assn., Fairfield Edn. Assn., Nat. Coun. Tchrs. Math. Republican. Roman Catholic. Avocations: collecting old books, cooking, writing. Home: 502 Allyndale Dr Stratford CT 06614-4308 Office: Fairfield Bd Edn Stratfield Sch 1407 Melville Ave Fairfield CT 06825

KALAS, FRANK JOSEPH, JR., financial, information systems consultant; b. Stafford Springs, Conn., Dec. 31, 1943; s. Frank Joseph and Margaret Mary (LaPanne) K.; m. Minh Tran, June 24, 1972; children: Jennifer Ann, Joanne Catherine. BBA, U. N.Mex., 1966; MS, U. Ark., London, Eng., 1974. Sr. auditor Knox & Scott, CPAs, Albuquerque, 1963-66; commd. officer USN, 1967, advanced through grades to capt., 1987; dir. fin. mgmt. office Naval Sea Systems Command, Washington, 1988-93; ret., 1993; mgr. material and prodn. svcs. Intermarine USA, Savannah, Ga., 1993-95; sr. prin. Am. Mgmt. Systems, Inc., Fairfax, Va. Adj. prof. acctg. R.I. Coll., 1978-80, Far East divsn. U. Md., 1980-82. Author: Food Service Operations and Contracting, 1987. Decorated Meritorious Svc. medal, Legion of Merit. Mem. Am. Soc. Naval Engrs., Soc. Logistics Engrs. (pres. 1979-80), Profl. Picture Framer's Assn. (cert.), Am. Soc. Mil. Comptrs. (Outstanding Mem. award 1985), Nat. Amateur Press Assn., Inst. of Mgmt. Accts., Am. Prodn. and Inventory Control Soc. Roman Catholic. Achievements include invention of automated data capture system for engineering inspections. Avocations: amateur journalism, clocks, russian history, competition dancing, WW II history. Office: Am Mgmt Systems Inc 4114 Legato Rd Fairfax VA 22033-4002

KALATA, MARY ANN CATHERINE, architect; b. Passaic, N.J., Sept. 7, 1962; d. John Joseph Kalata and Filomena Katherine Kurnat. BS Archl. Technology, N.Y. Inst. Technology, 1984. Model builder, field coord. Perkins & Will, Russo & Sonder Architects, N.Y.C., 1984—94; archl. designer Andrew G. Antoniades Architects, N.Y.C., 1994—97; archl. coord. MIchael J. Romanik Architects, Paterson, NJ, 1997—. Mem. Rep. Nat. Com., Washington. Recipient gold medal in archl. technology, N.Y. Inst. Technology, 1984. Mem.: ASC/AIA, U.S. Navy League. Republican. Roman Catholic. Avocations: photography, travel, model building, audio technology. Home: 8 Baker Ct Clifton NJ 07011

KALAVAR, JYOTSNA MIRLE, education educator; b. Bangalore, India, May 17, 1963; d. Mirle Subbarao and Sharadamba Krishnaswamy; m. Gopinath Shankar Kalavar, May 29, 1988; children: Abhinav Rao, Samir Rao. PhD, U. of Md., College Park, 1990; postgrad., U. of Mich., Ann Arbor, 1993. Lic. psychologist Mich. Asst. prof. Fayette campus Pa. State U., Uniontown, 1997—2000, assoc. prof. New Kensington campus Upper Burrell, 2000—. Grantee, Ctr. for Rural Pa., 2000, Nat. Inst. on Aging, 2000—02. Mem.: AASTHA Found. (life) (hon.), Assn. Gerontology (v.p. psychosocial 2002—), Gerontol. Soc. of Am. Achievements include research on homebound elderly; institutionalized elderly; immigrant elderly. Office: Pa State U New Kensington campus 3550 7th Street Rd New Kensington PA 15068 Office Fax: 724-334-6039. E-mail: jmk18@psu.edu.

KALAYCIOGLU, SERDAR, space robotics engineer, manager; b. Luleburgaz, Kirklareli, Turkey, Aug. 8, 1963; arrived in Can., 1984; s. Vedat and Aynur (Vural) K.; m. Banu Ayse Kunas, June 28, 1985; children: Dennis Serkan, Isabel Selin. BSc with honors, Mid. East Tech. U., Ankara, Turkey, 1984; PhD, McGill U., Montreal, Que., Can., 1988. Registered profl. engr. Teaching asst., dept. mech. engring. McGill U., Montreal, 1984-88, rsch. asst., dept. mech. engring., 1984-88, rsch. assoc., dept. mech. engring., 1985-86, aux. prof., dept. mech. engring., 1987-88; systems engr. Thomson-CSF Systems Can. Inc., Ottawa, Ont., 1988-89, project mgr., 1989-90, mgr. space robotics and automation, 1990-92; mgr. REACH, Can. Space Agency, St. Hubert, Canada, 1992-96, mgr. dynamics group, mgr. space technologies, 1996—2001. Cons. Comm. Rsch. Ctr., Ottawa, 1985—86; referee Natural Scis. and Engring. Rsch. Coun. Can., Ottawa, 1989—90; invited spkr. Rensselaer Poly. inst., Troy, NY, 1990, Mfg. Rsch. Corp. Ont., Toronto, 1991, U. Waterloo, 1991; organized and chaired sessions Internat. Conf. on Intelligent Teleopration, 1991—; adj. prof. U. Ottawa, 1989—92, McGill U., Montreal, 1994—; adj. assoc. prof. elec. and computer engring. Concordia U., Montreal, 1994—; gen. mgr. Glengo, Istanbul, Turkey, 1998—99; pres. Bensa Sys. Can. Inc., 1999—. Reviewer IEEE, AAIA, AAS, Jour. Can. Aeros. and Space Inst., 1989; contbr. more than 85 articles to profl. jours. Recipient Math. award, Turkish Sci. and Rsch. Coun., 1980, Chemistry award, 1980, Achievement awards ASME, 1994, 96. Mem. IEEE, ASME, AIAA, Am. Astronautical Soc. (sr.), Am. Inst. Aeros. and Space Instrn., Can. Soc. Elec. and Computer Engrs., Can. Astronautics and Space Inst., Assn. Profl. Engrs. Ont., Can. Soc. Mech. Engrs. Achievements include development of a supervised autonomous robots system for Space Station; optimal deployment schemes for space appendages; found analytical solution for deployment of flexible space appendages, dynamics and control techniques for spacecraft and its appendages; special expertise in international financing and bank instruments including letter of credits and bank guarantees; coordinated over $300M USD international loans and bank instruments; introduced international banking and financing in Canada for project funding. Home: 1775 Socrate Brossard QC Canada J4X 1L6 Office: 1 Wood Ave Ste 602 Westmount QC Canada H3Z 3C5

KALAYJIAN, ANIE, psychotherapist, nurse, educator, consultant; b. Aleppa, Syria; came to U.S., 1971; d. Kevork and Zabelle (Mardikian) Kalayjian; m. Shahé Navasart Sanentz, Dec. 16, 1984 (div. 1999). BS, L.I. U., 1979; MEd, Columbia U., 1981, EdD, 1985, profl. nursing tng. course, 1984; cert. photography, Pratt Inst., 1979; DSc (hon.), L.I. U., 2001. RN, N.Y., N.J., Conn.; cert. psychiat. mental health specialist; Dutch diplomate in logotherapy; advanced cert. in Eye Movement Desensitization and Reprocessing, advanced cert. in disaster mgmt. ARC; bd. cert. expert in traumatic stress; cert. expert in crisis mgmt. Psychiat. nurse Met. Hosp., N.Y.C., 1979-84; staff psychiat. mental health nurse Project Renewal, N.Y.C., 1978-2000; instr. Hunter Coll., N.Y.C., 1980-82; prof. Bloomfield Coll., N.J., 1984-85; lectr. Jersey City Coll., N.J., 1985; prof. Seton Hall U., South Orange, N.J., 1985-87; assoc. prof. grad. program St. Joseph Coll., 1987-91; prof. criminal justice John Jay Coll. Fairleigh Dickinson U., 1991-92; vis. prof. John Jay Coll. Criminal Justice Fairleigh Dickinson U., 1991-92, Pace U., N.Y.C., 1994-95. Adj. prof. Coll. Mt. St. Vincent, Riverdale, NY, 1995—97, Fordham U., 1998—, Coll. New Rochelle, 1998—99; disting. lectr. Columbia U., N.Y.C., 1995; spkr. in field; keynote spkr. Mid Am. Logotherapy Inst., 1995, Coll. Mt. St. Vincent, 1995, Hollins Coll., Va., 1995, UN; NGO exec. com. vice-chair, 2000—; chair DPI/NGO annual conf. Author: Disaster and Mass Trauma: Global Perspectives on Post Disaster Mental Health Management, 1995; contbr. articles to profl. jours., chapters to books; reviewer: Readings: A Journal of Reviews and Commentary in Mental Health, 1990—; TV appearances ABC, CNN, NY1, Tokyo TV, —, radio appearances WSOU, WFUV, —. Active com. for presdl. task force on nursing curriculum Soc. for Traumatic Stress Studies; co-founder, East coast coord. Mental Health Outreach to Earthquake Survivors in Armenia; program dir. Mental Health Outreach to Earthquake Survivors in Turkey, 1999; dir. Julia Richman-Pace U.-N.Y. State Bd. Edn.-Visiting Nurse Svc.-Partnership program, 1991-92; UN rep. World Fedn. for Mental Health, mem. mental health/human rights com., 1996—. Recipient Clark Found. scholarship award, 1985, Outstanding Rsch. award Columbia U., 1993, ABSA Outstanding Achievement award APA, 1995; rsch. grantee Pace U., 1992; Endowed Nursing Edn. Columbia U., scholar, 1984; Armenian Relief Soc. scholar, 1976-77, Armenian Students Assn. Am. scholar, 1976-78, Columbia U. Tchrs. Coll. Outstanding Rsch. award, 1993. Fellow Am. Orthopsychiat. Assn., N.Y. State Nursing Assn. (planning com. nursing edn.), APA (outstanding achievement award 1995); mem. Coun. on Continuing Edn., Psychiat. and Mental Health Nursing, Am. Psychol. Soc., Am. Psychiat. Nurses Assn., Am. Acad. Experts in Traumatic Stress, Internat. Coun. Psychologists, Internat. Trauma Counselors, Inst. for Psychodynamics and Origins of Mind, Armenian Students Assn. (treas. 1980-81, pres. 1981-83, scholarship chairperson 1983-85, v.p. ctrl. exec. com. 1987-88, pres. 1988-89, nat. pres. 1988-90), Armenian Info. Profls. (corr. sec. 1992—), Armenian-Am. Soc. for Studies on Stress and Genocide (founder, pres. 1988—), N.Y. RN's Assn. (chair edn. com. 1989-99), World Fedn. for Mental Health (UN rep. 1994—, treas., sec., UN com. on human rights 1994—, chair human rights com. 1996—), Univ. for Peace (cor. sec. UN com.), Internat. Soc. Traumatic Stress Studies (v.p. N.Y. chpt. 1993-95, pres. 1995—), Global Soc. for Nursing and Health (pres., co-founder), N.Y. Counties RN Assn. (Jane Delano Disting. Svc. award 1994), Kappa Delta Pi (advisor 1989-90), Sigma Theta Tau. Avocations: aerobics, photography, acting, hiking. Office: 130 W 79th St New York NY 10024-6477 E-mail: kalayjiana@aol.com.

KALB, BENJAMIN STUART, television producer, director; b. L.A., Mar. 17, 1948; s. Marcus and Charlotte K. BS in Journalism, U. Oreg., 1969. Sportswriter Honolulu Advertiser, 1971-76. Traveled with tennis profl. Ilie Nastase; contbr. articles N.Y. Times, Sport Mag. and Tennis U.S.A., 1976; editor Racquetball Illustrated, 1978-82; segment producer PM Mag. and Hollywood Close-Up, 1983-86; exec. producer Ben Kalb Prodns., 1986—; instr. sports in soc. U. Hawaii, 1974-75. Prodr. (video) The Natural Way to Meet the Right Person, 1987; prodr., dir. (video) Casting Call: Director's Choice, 1987, The Natural Way to Meet the Right Person (Best Home Videos of Yr. L.A. Times), (TV pilot and home video) Bizarro, 1988, (infomercial) How To Start Your Own Million Dollar Business, 1990, The Nucelle Promise, 1993-94, Koolatron Companion, 1997, Radiant Health, 1999, Facial Toner, 1999, AbTronic Fitness Sys., 2000; prodr.-dir. (infomercials) Banamex USA Credit Card, 1995, Slimaster Exerciser, 1996, Koolatron Companion, 1997, Yonex Golf, 1998, Toski's Touch, 2001, Beon Computer, 2001, Buffalo Milke, 2001, Restform Airbed, 2002, Abs & More, 2002, Chef O'Matic, 2003; segment dir. (home video) Movie Magic, 1990, (TV show) Totally Hidden Video; writer-segment dir. (home video) Making of The American Dream Calendar Girl, 1991; prodr., host (cable TV show) Delicious Sports, 1987-88; segment dir. Totally Hidden Video (Fox TV Network), 1991-92; prodr., dir. short feature film Love Match, 1995; contbr. articles to mags. and newspapers. Served with Hawaii Army N.G., 1970-75. Named Outstanding Male Grad. in Journalism, U. Oreg., 1969. Mem. Sigma Delta Chi (chpt. pres. 1968). Democrat. Jewish. Home: 4008 Thunder Hawk St Las Vegas NV 89129 Office: 5045 Rogers Ste 7 Las Vegas NV 89118 E-mail: bkalbprod@aol.com.

KALB, MARVIN, public policy and government educator; Diploma, CCNY; MA, postgrad. in Russian History, Harvard U. Prof. press and pub. policy John F. Kennedy Sch. Govt. Harvard U., dir. Joan Shorenstein Ctr. on Press, Politics, and Pub. Policy, 1987—99; Edward R. Murrow prof. press and pub. policy JFK Sch. Govt., 1987-99; sr. fellow/lectr. in pub. policy Shorenstein Ctr., Washington, 1999—; faculty chair Washington Programs KSG., Wahington, 1999—. Host PBS series: Candidates '88; chief diplomatic corrs. CBS News, NBC News; moderator Meet The Press; sr. rsch. assoc. Ctr. for Sci. and Internat. Affairs; exec. com. Harvard's Russian Rsch. Ctr. Co-author: (with Hendrik Hertzberg) Candidates '88, (with Stephen Hess) The Media and the War on Terrorism; author or co-author 7 non-fiction books, including: One Scandalous Story, The Nixon Memo, Kissinger, Roots of Involvement: The U.S. and Asia, and 2 best-selling novels. Recipient numerous awards for excellence in diplomatic reporting including two Peabody prizes, U. Ga., DuPont prize, Columbia U., and numerous Overseas Press Club awards. Mem. Coun. on Fgn. Rels., Am. Acad. Arts and Scis. Avocations: rsch. of ethical/polit. legacy of the Ten Commandments; Washington Redskins football. Office: Harvard U Joan Shorenstein Ctr Kennedy Sch Govt 1779 Massachusetts Ave WW Ste 810 Washington DC 20036

KALB, PAUL EDWARD, lawyer, internist; b. New York, NY, Oct. 18, 1958; s. Seymour Kalb and Carol Cohen; m. Susan Michelle Ascher, May 4, 1986. JD, Yale Law Sch., New Haven, CT, 1987—90; MD, Boston U Sch. of Medicine, Boston, Mass., 1979—83. Bar: NY State Bar Assn. (Bar of New York) 1990; cert. Diplomate Am. Bd. of Internal Medicine, 1986. Ptnr. and head, health care group Sidley Austin Brown & Wood LLP, Washington, 1997—; assoc. Sidley & Austin, Washington, 1990—97; attending physician Meml. Sloan-Kettering Cancer Ctr., New York, NY, 1986—87; intern and resident NY Hosp., New York, NY, 1983—86. Author: (textbook) Health Care Fraud: Enforcement and Compliance, (article (JAMA) Legal Issues in Sci. Rsch., Health Care Fraud and Abuse. Founding bd. mem. Spinal Bifida Found., Washington, 1996—2002. Avocation: travel. Office: Sidley Austin Brown & Wood LLP 1501 K Street NW Washington DC 20005 E-mail: pkalb@sidley.com.

KALB, VIRGINIA GROVER, retired school library administrator, educator; b. Trenton, N.J., Apr. 19, 1936; d. Charles Rue and Mary Beatrice (App) Grover; m. John Garrison Kalb, Dec. 21, 1957; children: John Charles, Thomas Rue. BA, William Smith Coll., Geneva, N.Y., 1958; MA, Calif. State U., Long Beach, 1976. Cert. in elem. edn., libr. svcs., adminstrv. svcs., Calif. Libr. media specialist Montebello (Calif.) Unified Sch. Dist., 1976-84, coord. media svcs., 1984-95; cons. learning resources Fountain Valley, Calif., 1995—. Asst. prof. Calif. State U., L.A., 1987-93; asst. prof. Calif. State U., Long Beach, 1990—. Author column in Sch. Libr. Media Quar., 1988-91. Mem. ALA, Am. Assn. Sch. Librs., Calif. Media and Libr. Educators Assn. (pres. 1987-88), So. Calif. Coun. on Lit. for Children and Young People, Phi Kappa Phi. Office: 8782 La Zana Ct Fountain Valley CA 92708-3329

KALBA, KAS, international telecommunications consultant; b. Wangen, Germany, Apr. 13, 1945; came to U.S., 1950; s. Simon J. and Sophia Kalba; m. Patricia A. Carvalho, June 18, 1966; children: Simon Michael, Sontine. BA, Yale U., 1966; MA in Communications, U. Pa., 1967, PhD, 1974. Staff asst. Sloan Commn. on Cable Communications, N.Y.C., 1970-71; lectr., instr. communications planning Harvard U., Cambridge, Mass., 1971-76; vis. lectr. mass media MIT, Cambridge, 1976-77; pres. Kalba Internat. Inc., Lincoln, Mass., 1973—. Mem. adv. com. Cable World (China). Trustee Cambridge Ctr. for Adult Edn., 1984-85, Pacific Telecomms. Coun., trustee, 1997-2001; mem. satellite comms. adv. com. U.S. Info. Agy., 1989-93; mem. cable TV adv. com., Town of Lincoln, 2002—. Mem. Internat. Inst. Comms., Internat. House of Japan.

KALBFLEISCH, JOHN MCDOWELL, cardiologist, educator; b. Lawton, Okla., Nov. 15, 1930; s. George and Etta Lillian (McDowell) K.; m. Jolie Harper, Dec. 30, 1961. AS, Cameron A&M U., Lawton, 1950; BS, U. Okla., 1952, MD, 1957. Diplomate Am. Bd. Internal Medicine, Am. Bd. Cardiovascular Disease. Intern U. Va. Hosp., 1957-58; resident and fellow U. Okla. Med. Ctr., 1958-62, instr. medicine, 1964-66, asst. prof., 1966-69, assoc. clin. prof., 1970-78, clin. prof. Tulsa br., 1978—; pvt. practice Tulsa, 1969—; founder, chmn. bd., CEO Cardiology of Tulsa, Inc., 1969—; dir. cardiovascular svcs. St. Francis Hosp., Tulsa, 1975—. Physician adv. bd. City of Tulsa, 1978-81; bd. dirs. St. Francis Hosp., exec. com., 1987-97, 2001—; exec. v.p., chief med. officer St. Francis Health Sys., 1998-99; treas. Tulsa Med. Edn. Found., 1988-89, v.p., 1990-92, pres., 1992-94; med. dir., chmn. bd. Warren Clinics, 1990-97; mem. Okla. Ctr. for Advancement of Sci. and Tech., 1989-95; mem. adv. com. Ctr. for Lasser Devel. and Applications, Okla. State U. Contbr. articles to profl. jours. With USPHS, 1962-64. Recipient Lifelong Svc. award, Tulsa Med. Edn. Found./U. Okla. Coll. Medicine, 2002. Fellow ACP (gov.-elect Okla. 1990-91, gov. 1991-95, Okla. Laureate award 1995), Am. Coll. Cardiology (gov. Okla. 1978-81); mem. AMA, AAAS, Tulsa County Med. Soc., Okla. State Med. Assn., Am. Heart Assn. (Fellow coun. on clin. cardiology), tchg. scholar 1967-69), Okla. Soc. Internal Medicine v.p., pres.-elect 1983-84, pres. 1985-86), Am. Soc. Internal Medicine, Am. Fedn. Clin. Rsch., Am. Inst. Nutrition, U. Okla. Med. Alumni Assn. (Physician of Yr. in Pvt. Practice 1999), Delta Upsilon. Republican. Presbyterian. Office: 6151 S Yale Ave Ste 400 Tulsa OK 74136-1933

KALBOUSS, GEORGE, retired language educator; b. N.Y.C., June 21, 1939; s. Leonid (Lonya) Igor and Irene Kalbouss; children: Christina McGarvey, Katherine Mielke. AB, Columbia U., 1960, MA, 1961; PhD, NYU, 1968. Adminstr. Port N.Y. Authority, N.Y.C., 1961—66; asst. prof. Dartmouth Coll., Hanover, NH, 1967—73; assoc. prof. slavic langs and lits. Ohio State U., Columbus, 1973—2001; ret., 2001. Cons. various orgns., Columbus, 1985—; spkr. Ohio Humanities Coun., Columbus, 1999—. Author: (book) Plays of the Russian Symbolists, 1982, Russian Culture, 1998; prodr.: (documentaries) Road Show, 2002. Bd. dirs. Ukrainian Mus. Archives, Cleve., 1998—; heritage program prodr. Ohio Bicentennial Commn., Columbus, 2002—. Officer USAR, 1962—92. Mem.: Am. Assn. Tchrs. Slavic and E. European Langs., Am. Assn. Advancement Slavic Studies (exec. sec. 1973—75, bd. dirs. 2000—). Avocation: model trains. Home: 1370 Wyandotte Rd Columbus OH 43212 Office: Ohio State U 1841 Millikin Rd Columbus OH 43212 Home Fax: 614-688-3107. Personal E-mail: kalbouss@mac.com.

KALCEVIC, TIMOTHY FRANCIS, airline pilot, educator; b. Glenwood Springs, Colo., May 11, 1950; s. Victor and Marjorie Ann (Golden) K. BA in Acctg., Mich. State U., 1972; MBA cum laude, Roosevelt U., 1982; MA in Econs., U. Ill., Chgo., 1986; postgrad, U. Ill. CPA, Ill.; lic. airline transport pilot. Officer, pilot USN, various, 1972-79; pilot Am. Airlines, Chgo., 1979-81, 1984—; acct. Morton Mfg., Libertyville, Ill., 1981-82; acctg. mgr. Dexter Corp., Midland div., Waukegan, Ill., 1982-84. Instr. McHenry County (Ill.) Coll., 1983; ind. cons. acctg. Waukegan, 1984-85. Lt. USN, 1972-79. Mem. Am. Econ. Assn., Allied Pilots Assn. (chmn. scheduling com. Chgo. chpt. 1989-91, chmn. chgo. chpt. 1991-93), Am. Ind. Cockpit Alliance (chmn. fin. 1994). Avocation: fishing. Office: Pilot-Am Airlines O'Hare Internat Airport PO Box 66065 AMF Ohare IL 60666-0065 E-mail: timkalc@dellepro.com.

KALDOBSKY, PHOEBUS REEVEMAN, retired transportation engineer, retired management consultant; b. Vilnius, Lithuania, Mar. 13, 1919; s. Zalman and Fania (Reeveman) Kaldobsky; married; 2 children. Cert., U. London, 1947; B in Aero. Engring. with honors, Rensselaer Poly. Inst., 1953; postgrad., U. Mich., 1953-55, Wayne State U., 1953-55. Devel. engr. engring. divsn. Chrysler Corp., Highland Park, Mich., 1953-55; sr. porject engr. Ford Motor Divsn., Dearborn, Mich., 1955-59; group leader large jet engine dept. GE Co., Evendale, Ohio, 1959-60, sr. devel. engr. Worthington, Ohio, 1961-65, product mgr. specialty materials dept., 1965-69; with mgmt. devel. br./assignments Far East and Ea. Europe, UN/ILO, Geneva, 1970-74; mgr. automotive tech. devel. project Indonesian Petroleum Inst., Jakarta, 1975—76; project mgr. indsl. sys. testing equipment devel. Sun Elec. Corp., Madison Heights, Mich., 1977-78; sr. staff mem. transp. sys. ctr. U.S. Dept. Transp., Cambridge, Mass., 1978-82; ret. Lectr. mech. engring. Lawrence Tech. U., Southfield, Mich., 1954—69. Contbr. articles to profl. jours. Troop treas. Boy Scouts Am., 1964; v.p. local sch. PTA, 1965, pres., 1966. With Brit. Army, 1948—50, WWII, with Isreali Air Force. Rensselaer Poly. Inst. scholar, 1950—53. Mem.: AIAA, ASME, Nat. Hon. Aero. Soc., Soc. Automotive Engrs., Rensselaer Poly. Inst. Alumni Assn. (Mich. chpt. v.p. 1963, pres. 1964, chmn. scholarship com. 1955, 1958, 1961, 1964, area dist. sci. ctr. fund 1966—67). Home: 4143 Emerald Pines Dr Walled Lake MI 48390-1312

KALEBA, RICHARD JOSEPH, healthcare consultant; b. Chgo., Mar. 29, 1949; s. Joseph John and Josephine (Rogoszewski) K.; m. Kathleen Ann McCormick, June 13, 1970; children: Matthew, John, Daniel, Nicholas, David. BS in Biology, DePaul U., 1971, MBA in Systems Mgmt., 1974. Diplomate Am. Coll. Healthcare Execs.; cert. healthcare cons. Am. Assn. Healthcare Cons. Support svcs. supr. Augustana Hosp., Chgo., 1973; dir. materials mgmt. Westlake Cmty. Hosp., Melrose Park, Ill., 1974-76, adminstrv. asst. planning, 1977-86; v.p. planning and ancillary svcs. Mercy Hosp., Davenport, Iowa, 1977-86; COO Manatee Meml. Hosp., Bradenton, Fla., 1986-89; CEO Rome (N.Y.) Hosp., 1989-94; sr. mgr. bus. devel. Gilbane Bldg. Co., Chgo., 1994-95; prin. PRISM Healthcare Consulting, Glen Ellyn, Ill., 1995—. Cons. in field, Rome, 1992-94. Co-author: Returning the ER to Financial Viability, 1991. Bd. dirs. Leadership Manatee County, Bradenton, 1987-89, Diocese of Venice (Fla.) Sch. Bd., 1987-90. Mem. Chgo. Health Exec. Forum, Am. Soc. Healthcare Engrs. (mem. com.). Avocations: flyfishing, gardening, cooking. Office: PRISM Healthcare Consulting 799 Roosevelt Rd Ste 317 Glen Ellyn IL 60137-5908 E-mail: rkaleba@consultprism.com.

KALECH, MARC, newspaper editor; Mng. editor New York Post, N.Y.C., 1993—. Office: NY Post 10th Fl 1211 Avenue Of The Americas New York NY 10036 E-mail: mkalech@nypost.com.

KALER, ROBERT JOSEPH, lawyer; b. Boston, July 20, 1956; s. Robert Joseph and Joanne (Bowen) K. BA, Dartmouth Coll., 1978; JD, Am. U., 1981. Bar: D.C. 1981, Mass. 1983, U.S. Dist. Ct. D.C. 1982, U.S. Dist. Ct. Mass. 1984, U.S. Ct. Appeals (D.C. cir.) 1983, U.S. Ct. Appeals (1st cir.) 1984, U.S. Supreme Ct. 1986. Law clk. Sullivan & Cromwell, Washington, 1979-80, U.S. Dept. Justice, Washington, 1980-81; assoc. McKenna, Connor & Cuneo, Washington, 1981-83; ptnr. Gadsby & Hannah, Boston, 1983—. Contbr. articles to profl. jours. Mem. ABA, Internat. Bar Assn., Mass Bar Assn. Office: Gadsby & Hannah 225 Franklin St Boston MA 02110-2804

KALES, PAUL ALBERT, engineering educator, cartoonist; b. Boston, Dec. 8, 1937; s. Maurice H. and Eleanor (Kopp) K.; m. Judith Freund, Feb. 27, 1977. BS, Northeastern U., Boston, 1960, MS, 1965. Registered profl. engr., Mass. Engr. GE Co., Lynn, Mass., 1960-64; sr. engr. Avco Corp., Wilmington, Mass., 1964-68, Raytheon Co., Wayland, Mass., 1968-82, C.S. Draper Lab., Cambridge, Mass., 1982-85; assoc. prof. engring. tech. U. Mass., Lowell, 1985-99. Cons., trainer Statis. Process Control and Reliability/Maintainability Engring.; lectr. engring. Northeastern U. Boston, 1979-84. Author: Reliability for Technology, Engineering and Management, 1998, Betty and Jenn, 2002; cartoons published in Moment, Union Communications Services, Boston Globe, Eat and Run, others; contbr. articles to profl. jours. Originator, awards com. Mass. Coun. for Quality, Lowell, 1990-91. Mem. NSPE, Profl. Engrs. in Edn., Mass. Soc. Profl. Engrs., Nat. Asst. Indsl. Tech., Am. Soc. Quality Control (founding mem., sec. edn. divsn. 1994). Democrat. Jewish. Office: PO Box 179 Nantucket MA 02554

KALFATOVIC, MARTIN ROBERT, librarian, writer; b. San Jose, Calif., Apr. 20, 1961; s. Martin John Kalfatovic and Theresa Ressler; m. Mary Clare Corkery, Nov. 6, 1987; 1 child, Grace. BA in English, Catholic U. Am., 1983, MLS, 1990. Interlibr. loan libr. Nat. Mus. Am. Art/Nat. Portrait Gallery Libr., Washington, 1986-93; info. access coord. Smithsonian Instn. Librs., Washington, 1993-99, digital projects libr., 1999—2001, head new media office, 2001—. Adj. prof. Catholic U., 1996—. Author: Nile Notes of a Howadji, 1992, New Deal Fine Arts Projects, 1994, Creating a Winning Online Exhibition, 2002; editor Libr. Info. Tech. Assn. Newsletter, 1997-2000; contbr. articles to profl. jours. including Am. Nat. Biography, Jour. Popular Culture; reviewer Libr. Jour., RQ, Art Documentation, others. 5em. ALA, Assn. for the Study of Travel in Egypt and the Near East, Catholic U. Am. Sch. Libr. and Info. Sci. Alumni Bd. (bd. dirs.s 1994-95, v.p. 1995-96, pres. 1996-98). Roman Catholic. Office: Smithsonian Instn Librs 10th & Constitution Ave NW Washington DC 20560-0001 Business E-Mail: kalfatovicm@si.edu.

KALICH, RICHARD BARRY, writer; b. N.Y.C., Mar. 18, 1947; s. Kalmen and Beatrice Kalich. BA, CCNY, 1969. Prin., owner Kalich Org., N.Y.C., 1970—. Author: The Nihilesthete, 1987 (selected as one of twenty four most noteworthy novels Phila. Enquirer, 1987), The Zoo, 2003. Home and Office: 65 Central Park West New York NY 10023

KALICKI, JAN H. economist, political scientist; b. London, Aug. 5, 1948; s. Jan and Mireya (Jaimes-Freyre) Kalicki; m. Jean Ellen Engelmayer, Oct. 22, 1989; children: Jan Harlan, Alexander Van, Peter Daniel. AB with honors, Columbia Coll., 1968; PhD, London Sch. Econ., 1971. Rsch. assoc., lectr. Princeton U., 1971-72, Harvard U., Cambridge, Mass., 1972; Fgn. Svc. officer U.S. Dept. State, Washington, 1972-75, mem. policy planning staff, 1974-77; chief fgn. policy advisor to Senator Edward Kennedy, U.S. Senate, Washington, 1977-84; adj. prof. Georgetown U., Washington, 1983-85; adj. prof., asst. to pres. Brown U., Providence, 1985-88, exec. dir. Ctr. Fgn. Policy Devel., 1985-88, sr. advisor, 1988-94; v.p. Lehman Bros., N.Y.C., 1984—88, sr. v.p., 1988—93; sr. fellow Watson Inst. Internat. Studies, N.Y.C., 1994—99; U.S. ombudsman for energy and comml. cooperation with NIS Washington, 1994—2001; counselor U.S. Dept. Commerce, Washington, 1994—2001; pub. policy scholar Woodrow Wilson Internat. Ctr., Smithsonian Instn., Washington, 2001—; internat. policy scholar EastWest Inst., 2002—. Counselor internat. strategy ChevronTexaco Corp., San Francisco, 2001—; mem. Coun. Fgn. Rels. Internat. Inst. Strategic Studies, Royal Inst. Internat. Affairs, London; trustee World Affairs Coun. No. Calif. Author: The Pattern of Sino-American Crises, 1975; editor: Russian-Eurasian Renaissance?, 2003; contbr. numerous chpts. to books and articles to profl. jours. Office: ChevronTexaco Corp 575 Market St San Francisco CA 94105

KALIDINDI, SURYA RAJU, science educator; b. Hyderabad, India, June 21, 1964; came to U.S., 1985; s. Ramaraju and Aravinda (Rudraraju) K.; m. Manjula Penmetsa, June 7, 1987; children: Arvind, Bharath. B Tech, Indian Inst. Tech., Madras, 1985; MS, Case Western U., 1987; PhD, MIT, 1992. Assoc. prof., dir. mech. testing lab. and biomaterials lab. Drexel U., Phila., 1992—2000, prof., head dept. materials engring., 2000—. Vis. scientist Johnson Matthey Electronics Inc., Spokane, Wash., 1997, Katholieke U., Belgium, 1999, Fla. State U., 2000, Fla. A&M U., Tallahassee, 2000, Army Rsch. Lab., 2001; presenter in field. Contbr. numerous articles to profl. jours. Recipient Whitaker Found. Young Investigator award, 1995—99, Drexel Rsch. Achievement award, 2003; NSF grantee, 1992—. Achievements include patents for biomedical implants and advanced materials processing; development of novel algorithms for crystal plasticity simulations of deformation processing of metallic alloys; an improved understanding of the role of deformation twinning on mechanical properties of materials; a new concept for fixation of implants in bone in the human body; a novel design for stents that can treat aneurysms in the human vascular system. E-mail: skalidin@coe.drexel.edu.

KALIHER, MICHAEL DENNIS, historian, librarian; b. Santa Monica, Calif., Nov. 7, 1947; s. Eugene Charles and Phyllis Joan (McCrary) K. Student, Calif. State Coll., Hayward, 1969—70; BA, U. Ariz., 1990. Bookseller B. Dalton Bookseller, Newport Beach, Calif., 1991—94; correctional officer Ariz. Dept. Corrections, Winslow, 1994—97, libr., 1997—2001; eligibility specialist Ariz. Long-Term Care Sys., Flagstaff, Ariz., 2001—02; libr. II State of Ariz., 2002—. Pres. Klamath County (Oreg.) Hist. Soc., 1985; founder Native Am. History Week, Klamath County Mus., 1985-86. Contbr. articles to profl. jours. Mem. Ariz. Libr. Assn., Flagstaff Friends of Traditional Music, Pi Lambda Theta, Phi Alpha Theta. Avocations: backpacking, trout fishing. Home: 600 N Pantano Rd #1527 Tucson AZ 85710-2382

KALIKOW, PETER STEPHEN, real estate developer, former newspaper owner, publisher; b. N.Y.C., Dec. 1, 1942; s. Harold J. and Juliet K.; m. Mary T. Jacobatos; children: Nicholas, Kathryn. BSBA, Hofstra U., 1965, LLD (hon.), 1986. With H.J. Kalikow & Co., N.Y.C., 1966—, pres., 1973—; owner N.Y. Post, 1988-93. Bd. dirs. N.Y. State Mortgage Agy., 1981-86, chmn. ins. com. Gov. N.Y. Hosp. and Presbyn. Hosp.; trustee Hofstra U., Mus. Jewish Heritage; gen. chmn. real estate and constrn. divsn. Israel Bonds; apptd. to Met. Transp. Authority, 1994, chmn., 2001--; mem. Port Authority of N.Y. and N.J., 1995. Recipient Israel Peace medal, Israeli Govt. 1982; named Alumnus of Yr., Hofstra U., 1988. Mem. N.Y. Athletic Club, Palm Beach Country Club, Fenway Club (Scarsdale, N.Y.), Royal Automobile Club (London). Office: H J Kalikow & Co LLC 101 Park Ave Fl 25 New York NY 10178-0002

KALIKOW, RICHARD R. lawyer; b. N.Y.C., 1949; BS, Cornell U., 1971; JD, Fordham U., 1974; LLM, NYU, 1979. Bar: N.Y. 1975, Fla. 1979. Mem. Skadden, Arps, Slate, Meagher & Flom, N.Y.C. Office: Skadden Arps Slate Meagher & Flom 4 Times Sq Fl 24 New York NY 10036-6595

KALIKOW, THEODORA JUNE, university president; b. Lynn, Mass., June 6, 1941; d. Irving and Rose Kalikow AB, Wellesley Coll., 1962; ScM, MIT, 1970; PhD, Boston U., 1974. From instr. to prof. Southeastern Mass. U., North Dartmouth, 1968-84; dean Coll. Arts and Scis., U. No. Colo., Greeley, 1984-87; dean of the coll. Plymouth (N.H.) State Coll., 1987-94, interim pres., 1992-93; pres. U. Maine, Farmington, 1994—. Contbr. articles to profl. jours., 1975—Chair steering com. Maine ACE/NIP, 1995—; chair Coun. Pub. Liberal Arts Colls., 1997-99. Named to, Maine Women's Hall of Fame, 2002; recipient Am. Coun. on Edn. fellow, Brown U., Providence, 1983—84, Mary Ann Hartman award, 2000; grantee, NSF, 1978. Mem.: Assn. Am. Colls. and Univs. (bd. dirs. 2000—), Western Mountains Alliance (chmn. 2000—03), Am. Coun. on Edn. (commn. on women 1994—97, 2000—03), Soc. Values in Higher Edn. (bd. dirs. 1991—94). Office: U Maine at Farmington Office of the Pres 224 Main St Farmington ME 04938-1911

KALIL, JAMES, SR., investment executive; b. Buffalo, Oct. 22, 1919; s. Harry and Nazira (Owens) Rossi; m. Claire Homsey, May 5, 1947; children: Donald, Janice, Laura, James Jr. BSChemE, CCNY, 1941; M in ChemE, Poly. U., Bklyn., 1947, PhDChemE, 1951. Rsch. engr. DuPont Co., Wilmington, Del., 1951-80; investment mgr., chmn. bd. dirs. Affinity Wealth Mgmt., Inc., Wilmington, 1974—. Contbr. articles to newspapers; patentee chem products and processes. Fellow Poly. U., 1989. Avocations: reading, travelling, writing. Office: Affinity Wealth Mgmt Inc 1702 Lovering Ave Wilmington DE 19806-2120

KALIL, NELSON, oncologist, researcher; b. Bage, RS, Brazil, July 30, 1959; s. Felipe and Gloria K.; m. Maria I.C. Marques, July 12, 1980; children: Artur, Patricia. MD, Pontificia U. Cath. Do Rio Grande Do Sul, Porto Alegre, Brazil, 1982. Diplomate Am. Bd. Internal Medicine. Resident Hosp. São Lucas-Pontificia U. Cath., Porto Alegre, Brazil, 1983-85, resident in oncology, 1985-87, asst. prof. medicine, 1987-93; med. resident Jackson Meml. Hosp., Miami, Fla., 1993-96; clin. fellow Nat. Heart-Lung-Blood Inst., Bethesda, Md., 1998-99; clin. assoc. Nat. Cancer Inst., Bethesda, 1996—. Author: (with others) Quick Reference in Oncology, 1999, Chemotherapy for Advanced Epithelial Ovarian Carcinoma: Best Practice and Research, 2002; contbr. articles to profl. jours., chpts. to books and textbooks. Mem. ACP, Am. Soc. Med. Oncology, Am. Soc. Hematology, Brazilian Soc. Med. Oncology. Office Fax: 443-777-8405. E-mail: ngkalil@hotmail.com.

KALIN, D(OROTHY) JEAN, artist, educator; b. Kansas City, Mo., Feb. 11, 1932; d. William Warner and Esther Dorothy (Peterson) Johnson; m. John Baptist Kalin, Jr., Jan. 5, 1952; children: Jean Loraine, Debra Ann, Diana Yvonne. AA, St. Joseph (Mo.) Jr. Coll., 1951. Artist Hallmark Cards, Inc., Kansas City, Mo., 1952-53, 73-93; freelance artist Kansas City, 1953-72; owner Portraits of Life, Kansas City, 1986—, art tchr., 1988—. Illustrator article for Directory of Am. Portrait Artists, 1985; featured in Rockport Pubs. Best of Watercolor 2 and Painting Light and Shadow, 1997, Am. Artist Mag., 1998, 2000, Splash 5, 1998, Best of Collected Watercolor, 2002, Midwest Art, 2003, The Artists' Mag., 2003. Kansas City Art Inst. scholar, 1951-52. Mem. Nat. Oil and Acrylic Painters Soc. (signature mem.), Nat. Acrylic Painters Assn. (signature mem.), Kans. Watercolor Soc. (signature mem.), Women Artists of the West (signature mem.), Am. Watercolor Soc. (assoc.), Nat. Watercolor Soc. (assoc.), Midwest Watercolor Soc. (assoc.), Nat. Mus. Women in the Arts (charter mem.), Mo. Watercolor Soc. (signature mem., bd. dirs. 1999—), Western Colo. Watercolor Soc. (signature mem.), Internat. Platform Assn. Avocations: gardening, traveling. Address: 20650 State Rt 371 Platte City MO 64079-9344

KALIN, GEORGE BRUNO, pathologist, educator; b. Chgo., Feb. 22, 1948; s. Paul Peter and Rosemary (Nelson) K. B.S., U. Ill.-Chgo., 1970. Research asst. Rush-Presbyn.-St. Luke's Med. Ctr., Chgo., 1971-75; research asst. Northwestern Meml. Hosp., Chgo., 1975-78; instr. pathology, chief technologist E. Tenn. State U., Johnson City, 1978— ; lectr. Tenn. Soc. Histotech. Mem. Nat. Soc. Histotech., S. Central Flow Cytometry Assn., Sigma Xi. Roman Catholic. Contbr. articles to profl. jours. Home: 3314 Wildflower Ln Johnson City TN 37604-3337 Office: E Tenn State U James H Quillen Coll Med PO Box 70568 Johnson City TN 37614-1707

KALIN, KARIN BEA, retired secondary school educator, consultant; b. N.Y.C., June 22, 1943; d. Lawrence Leon and Celia (Siskind) Elkind; children: Laura, Howard. BS, SUNY, Oswego, 1965; MS, CUNY, 1967. Cert. social studies tchr., N.Y. Tchr. Benjamin Franklin H.S., N.Y.C., 1965-66, Grover Cleveland H.S., Ridgewood, N.Y., 1967-73, Aviation H.S., L.I. City, N.Y., 1979-99, sex equity coord., 1982-90, local equal opportunity coord., 1983-91, sch. recruiter, 1985-91; ret., 1999. Curriculum developer OEO N.Y.C. Bd. Edn., fall, 1985; global studies curriculum writing, 1997—98; panelist Aerospace Edn. Workshop for Elem. Tchrs., Career Exploration Seminar, Aerospace Edn. Conf., 1990; placement counselor East Meadow (N.Y.) Sch. Dist., 1989—; cons. Coll. Aerospace, NY, 1986, Profl. and Clerical Employees of Internat. Ladies Garment Workers Union, N.Y.C., 1989; with L.I. Coun. for Equal Edn. and Employment, 1990; placement counselor N.Y.C. H.S., 2000—; with N.Y.C. H.S. Transfer Ctr., 2000. Mem. Women on the Job, Port Washington, NY, 1986—91, L.I. Coun. Equal Edn. and Employment, 1990—, Coalition to Advocate for Women of Color in Edn.; vol. Goodwill Games, 1998, Empire State Games, 1999, Hamlet Cup, 1999—, Friends of the Arts, 1999—, L.I. Fair at Old Bethpage Restoration, 1999, L.I. Studies Inst., 2000, Divsn. 1 NCAA Women's Swimming & Diving Championship, 2001, Big East NCAA Women's Swimming & Diving Championship, 2001, 2002; mem. com. Nassau Dem. Com., Westbury, NY, 1988—. William Robertson Coe fellow, 1992; grantee Columbia U., 1967, 69, N.Y.C. Bd. Edn., 1983, Nat. Coun. for Humanities, 1985, Project Voice/Move, 1984-85; named to Nat. Women's Hall of Fame. Mem.: AFL-CIO, LWV, NAFE, AAUW (roundtable on gender equity in classroom 1992, co-chair social justice 2000—, Nassau County chair Sister to Sister 2001), NOW (chair conciousness raising com. 1982, chair women and employment com. 1987—90, chair social justice), Nat. Women's Hall of Fame, Nat. Women's History Mus., Assn. Tchrs. of Social Studies, United Fedn. Tchrs., Nat. Women's Hall of Fame, Nat. Women's Polit. Caucus (chair polit. action com. 1990—96, bd. dirs.), N.Y. State Alliance for Women and Girls in Tech., Bachelor and Bachelorettes for Square Dancing (pres. L.I. chpt. 1994—96, founder). Jewish. Avocations: swimming, reading, visiting museums, square dancing, round dancing, bridge. Home: 700 Barkley Ave East Meadow NY 11554-4501 E-mail: karin622@att.net.

KALIN, NANCY JAGGER, interior designer; b. Akron, Ohio, July 7, 1935; d. Paul Warren and Evelyn Marie (Conrad) Jagger; 1 child, Mark. BS in Edn., U. Akron, 1957. Interior designer, owner Nancy Kalin Antique Interiors, Middlebranch, Ohio, 1972—. Designs featured in over 85 internat. publs. Home and Office: PO Box One Middlebranch OH 44652-0001

KALIN, ROBERT, retired mathematics educator; b. Everett, Mass., Dec. 11, 1921; s. Benjamin and Celia (Kraff) K.; m. Shirley Sharney, Oct. 22, 1944; children: Susan Leslie, John Benjamin; m. 2d Madelyn Pildish, Aug. 17, 1962; 1 child, Richard Dean. Student, Northeastern U., 1940-43; BS, U. Chgo., 1947; MAT, Harvard U., 1948; PhD, Fla. State U., 1961. Tchr. math. Holten H.S., Danvers, Mass., 1948-49, Beaumont H.S., Hadley Tech. Sch., Soldan-Blewitt H.S., St. Louis, 1949-52; ednl. statistician Naval Air Tech. Tng. Ctr., Norman, Okla., 1952-53; test specialist, assoc. in research Ednl. Testing Svc., Princeton, N.J., 1953-55; exec. asst. Commn. on Math. of Coll. Entrance Exam. Bd., 1955-56; instr. dept. math. edn. Fla. State U., Tallahassee, 1956-61, asst. prof., 1961-63, assoc. prof., 1963-65, prof., 1965-90, prof. emeritus, 1990, assoc. dept. head, 1968-73, program chmn., 1975-78. Co-author: Elementary Mathematics, Patterns and Structure, 11 vols., 1966, (with George Green) Modern Mathematics for the Elementary School Teacher, 1966, (with E.D. Nichols) Analytic Geometry, 1973, Holt School Mathematics, 9 vols., 1974, rev. 1978, Holt Mathematics, 9 vols., 1981, rev., 1985, (with M.K. Corbitt) Prentice Hall Geometry, 1990, rev. edit., 1993. Mem., treas. Brownsville-Haywood County Libr. Bd., 1991-95, chmn., 1995-97; bd. dirs. Friends of Tenn. Librs., 1995-2002, sec., 1996-97, pres.-elect, 1997-99, pres., 1999-2000, past pres., 2000-02; pres. Temple Adas Israel, 1992-94, treas., 1994-2000; bd. dirs. Jewish Hist. Soc. of Memphis and the Mid-South, 1998-2001, sec., 2000-01. Mem. Math. Assn. Am. (sec.-treas. Fla. sect. 1985-91, Svc. award Fla. sect. 1991), Fla. Coun. Tchrs. Math. (pres. 1960-61), Fla. Assn. Math. Educators (pres. 1984-86), Nat. Coun. Tchrs. Math. (chmn. external affairs com. 1972-73), Nat. High Sch. and Jr. Coll. Math. Clubs (gov. 1972-75, pres. 1978-80). Home: 7 Stoneleigh Pl Brownsville TN 38012-2463 E-mail: r_kalin@bellsouth.net.

KALINA, ROBERT EDWARD, opthalmologist, educator; b. New Prague, Minn., Nov. 13, 1936; s. Edward Robert and Grace Susan (Hess) K.; m. Janet Jessie Larsen, July 18, 1959; children: Paul Edward, Lynne Janet. BA magna cum laude, U. Minn., 1957, BS, MD, U. Minn., 1960. Diplomate Am. Bd. Ophthalmology (dir. 1981-89). Intern U. Oreg. Med. Sch. Hosp., Portland, 1960-61, resident in ophthalmology, 1961-62, 63-66; asst. in retina surgery Children's Hosp., San Francisco, 1966-67; Nat. Inst. Neurol. Diseases and Blindness Spl. fellow Mass. Eye and Ear Infirmary, Boston, 1967; instr. ophthalmology U. Wash., 1967-69, asst. prof., 1969-71, acting chmn. dept. ophthalmology, 1970-71, asso. prof., 1971-72, chmn. dept. ophthalmology, 1971-96, prof., 1972—. Mem. staffs Univ. Hosp., Harborview Hosp., Children's Hosp., Seattle; cons. VA Hosp., Seattle, Madigan Hosp., Tacoma; assoc. head divsn. ophthalmology dept. surgery Children's Hosp., Seattle, 1975-86; pres. U. Wash. Physicians, 1990-93. Contbr. author: Introduction to Clinical Pediatrics, 1972, Ophthalmology Study Guide for Medical Students, 1975; contbr. numerous articles to profl. publs. Served to capt., M.C. USAF, 1962-63. Fellow ACS, Am. Acad. Ophthalmology (Sr. Honor award 1989); mem., Assn. Univ. P rofs. Ophthalmology (pres. 1983-84, exec. v.p. 1989-94), Assn. Rsch. in Vision and Ophthalmology, Pacific Coast Oto-Ophthalmol. Soc. (councilor 1972-74), King County Med. Soc., Wash. State Acad. Ophthalmology, Phi Beta Kappa. Office: U Wash Dept Ophthalmology Box 356485 1959 NE Pacific St Seattle WA 98195-0001

KALINER, MICHAEL ARON, physician, researcher; b. Balt., Apr. 27, 1941; m. Jean A. Andrews, June 17, 1972; children: Aaron F., Matthew E., Leslie S. BS, U. Md., 1963, MD, 1967. Diplomate Am. Bd. Internal Medicine, Am. Bd. Allergy and Immunology (chmn. 1994). Intern Hosp. U. of Md., 1967-68; resident U. Calif., San Francisco, 1968-70; fellow Harvard U., Boston, 1970-73; scientist NIH, Bethesda, Md., 1975-93; physician Inst. for Asthma and Allergy, Washington, 1993—. Bd. dirs. Allergy and Asthma Network, Fairfax, Va.; cons. numerous pharm. cos. Editor: Allergy and Immunology Internat., 1992—2002; contbr. over 450 articles to profl. jours.; holder 3 patents in field. Recipient Outstanding Med. Alumni award, U. Md. Med. Sch., 1994, numerous other profl. awards. Mem.: Internat. Assn. Allergy and Immunology (exec. com. 1986—, treas. 1994—, v.p. 2001—), Am. Acad. Allergy, Asthma and Immunology (pres. 1995—). Home: 6515 Hillmead Rd Bethesda MD 20817-3021 Office: 11160 Veirs Mill Rd #414 Wheaton MD 20902 also: 5454 Wisconsin Ave #1700 Chevy Chase MD 20815 Office Fax: 301-962-9585.

KALININA, OLGA, economist; b. Moscow, June 21, 1974; d. Julia Melnikova and Igor Kalinin; m. Victor Podvalny, Aug. 16, 1997; 1 child, Victor Thomas Podvalny. MBA in Fin., Pace U., 1998; BA in Economics (hon.), Moscow State U., 1995; MA in Cinematography (hon.), Inst. Cinematography, Moscow, 1995. Portfolio mgmt. asst. Novos Planning Assoc., Inc., N.Y.C., NY, 1996—98; assoc. Std. & Poor's, N.Y.C., 1998—.

KALINOWSKI, JOE, humanities educator, researcher; b. Concord, Mass., Nov. 7, 1958; s. Anthony Stanley and Mary Frances Kalinowski; m. Barbara Oxman, June 12, 1988; children: Alissa Sadie, Amy Ilana. PhD, U. of Conn., 1994. Asst. prof. Dalhousie U., Halifax, Canada, 1991—95, East Carolina U., Greenville, NC, 1995—2000, assoc. prof., 2000—. Contbr. articles to profl. jours. Recipient New Faculty Mem. grant, Dalhousie U., 1992. Liberal. Roman Catholic. Achievements include invention of all-in the ear device that generates auditory alterations in how stutterers hear their own speech that allows them to produce speech fluently; numerous patents to ameliorate stuttering; research in new paradigm how stuttering is inhibited that will hopefully better help those who suffer from this disorder; construction of new theoretical or the underpinnings observed in the natural and free-flowing speech induced by altered auditory feedback, i.e., mirror neurons. Avocations: recovery, working out, reading, hanging out with my kids. Home: 1610 Paramore Dr Greenville NC 27858 Office: East Carolina U Belk Annex #5 Ogelsby Dr Greenville NC 27858 Personal E-mail: kalinowskij@mail.ecu.edu.

KALINSKE, THOMAS J. education, video game and toy company executive; b. 1944; married. BS, U. Wisconsin, 1966; MBA, U. Arizona, 1968. Acct. rep. Strauss Broadcasting Co., 1966-68, J. Walter Thompson, 1968, sr. acct. rep., 1969; sr. acct. rep., acct. supr. Case & Krone Inc., 1970-72; product mgr. Mattel Toys Mattel Inc., 1972-73, dir. product planning, 1973-77, dir. mktg., 1977-78, v.p. mktg., 1978-79, sr. v.p. mktg., 1979-82, sr. v.p. domestic, worldwide mktg., 1982-83, sr. v.p., gen. mgr. mktg., 1983-84, pres. Mattel USA, 1984-85, pres., CEO, 1985-87; pres., chief oper. officer Universal Matchbox Group, N.Y.C., 1987-90; pres., CEO Sega of Am., Redwood City, Calif., 1990-96; ceo Knowledge Universe, Menlo Park, Calif, 1996—. Office: Knowledge Universe 3351 El Camino Ste 200 Menlo Park CA 94027

KALISCH, BEATRICE JEAN, nursing educator, consultant; b. Tellahoma, Tenn., Oct. 15, 1943; d. Peter and Margaret Ruth Petersen; children— Philip P., Melanie J. BS, U. Nebr., 1965; MS, U. Md., 1967, PhD, 1970. Pediatric staff nurse Centre County Hosp., Bellefonte, Pa., 1965-66; instr. nursing Philipsburg (Pa.) Gen. Hosp. Sch. Nursing, 1966; pediatric staff nurse Greater Balt. Med. Center, Towson, Md., 1967; asst. prof. maternal-child nursing Am. U., 1967-68; clin. nurse specialist N.W. Tex. Hosp., Amarillo, 1970; assoc. prof. maternal-child nursing, curriculum coordinator nursing Amarillo Coll., 1970-71; chmn. baccalaureate nursing program, asso. prof. nursing U. So. Miss., 1971-74; prof. nursing, chmn. dept. parent-child nursing U. Mich. Sch. Nursing, Ann Arbor, 1974-86, Shirley C. Titus Disting. prof., 1977—, Titus Disting. prof. nursing mgmt., 1989—, dir. nursing bus. and health sys. program, 2000—; prin., dir. nursing consultation svcs. Ernst & Young, Detroit, 1986-89. Prin. investigator USPH grant to study image of nurses in mass media and the informational quality nursing news, U. Mich., 1977-86, prin. investigator to study intrahosp. transport of critically ill patients, 1991—; prin. investigator to study use of HIA nurse in N.Y.C. labor market, U. Mich.; prin. investigator to study the impact of managed care on critical care, U. Mich.; vis. Disting. prof. U. Ala., 1979, U. Tex., 1981, Tex. Christian U., 1983. Author: Child Abuse and Neglect: An Annotated Bibliography, 1978; co-author: Nursing Involvement in Health Planning, 1978, Politics of Nursing, 1982, Images of Nurses on Television, 1983, The Advance of American Nursing, 1986, revised, 1994, The Changing Image of the Nurse, 1987; co-editor: Studies in Nursing Mgmt.; contbr. articles to profl. jours. Recipient Joseph L. Andrews Bibliog. award Am. Assn. Law Libraries, 1979; Book of Yr. award Am. Jour. Nursing, 1978, 83, 86, 87, Outstanding Achievement award U. Md., 1987, Distinguished Alumni award U. Nebr., 1985, Shaw medal Boston Coll., 1986; USPHS fellow. Fellow Am. Acad. Nursing; mem. Am. Coll. Healthcare Execs., ANA, APHA, Am. Orgn. Nurse Execs., Sigma Theta Tau, Phi Kappa Phi. Presbyterian. Home: 27675 Chatsworth St Farmington MI 48334-1821 Office: U Mich Sch Nursing 400 N Ingalls St Ann Arbor MI 48109-0482 E-mail: bkalisch@umich.edu.

KALISCHER, ALAN LESTER, cardiologist; b. N.Y.C., Mar. 14, 1950; BA, NYU, 1973; MD, N.Y. Med. Coll., 1977; spl. competency exam., Nat. Bd. Echocardiography, 2000. Diplomate in internal medicine, cardiology and nuc. cardiology Am. Bd. Internal Medicine. Intern Kings County-Downstate Med. Ctr., Bklyn., 1977-78, resident in internal medicine, 1978-80; fellow in cardiology Columbia-Presbyn. Med. Ctr., N.Y.C., 1980-84; cardiologist Muhlenberg Hosp., Plainfield, N.J., 1984—, Overlook Hosp., Summit, N.J., 1984—, Morristown (N.J.) Meml. Hosp., 1987—, John F. Kennedy Med. Ctr., Edison, N.J., 1998—; asst. prof. clin. medicine R.W. Johnson Med. Sch., 1984—. Fellow: AMA; mem.: Med. Soc. N.J. Union County, Am. Soc. Nuc. Cardiology, Am. Coll. Cardiology. Office: Semer-Kalischer Cardiol Assocs Pa 2253 South Ave Scotch Plains NJ 07076

KALISH, ARTHUR, lawyer; b. Bklyn., Mar. 6, 1930; s. Jack and Rebecca (Biniamofsky) K.; m. Janet J. Wiener, Mar. 7, 1953; children: Philip, Pamela. BA, Cornell U., 1951; JD, Columbia U., 1956. Bar: N.Y. 1956, D.C. 1970. Assoc. Paul, Weiss, Rifkind, Wharton & Garrison, N.Y.C., 1956-64, ptnr., 1965-95, of counsel, 1996—. Lectr. NYU Inst. Fed. Taxation, Hawaii Tax Inst., Law Jour. Seminars Contbr. articles to legal jours. Assoc. trustee L.I. Jewish Med. Ctr., New Hyde Park, N.Y., 1978-82, trustee, 1982-95, hon. trustee, 1995-97; trustee emeritus North Shore - L.I. Jewish Health Sys., 1997-98, life trustee, 1998-2003, trustee, 2003—; bd. dirs. Cmty. Health Program of Queens Nassau Inc., New Hyde Park, 1978-94, pres., 1981-89, chmn. emeritus, 1994-97; bd. dirs. Managed Health, Inc., New Hyde Park, 1990-98, chmn., 1994-95. Fellow Am. Coll. Tax Counsel; mem. ABA, N.Y. State Bar Assn., Assn. Bar City N.Y., Columbia Law Sch. Assn. (bd. dirs. 1990-94). Home: 2 Bass Pond Dr Old Westbury NY 11568-1307 Office: Paul Weiss Rifkind Wharton & Garrison 1285 Avenue Of The Americas New York NY 10019-6064 E-mail: akalish@paulweiss.com.

KALISH, MYRON, lawyer; b. N.Y.C., Dec. 3, 1919; s. Louis and Bertha (Nacht) K.; m. Evelyn J. Zobler, Apr. 1, 1944; children— Nita Jane, Pamela Sue. BS in Social Sci., CCNY, 1940; LLB cum laude, Harvard U., 1943. Bar: N.Y. bar 1944. Since practiced in, N.Y.C.; sr. ptnr. Arthur, Dry & Kalish and predecessor firms, 1961-84; gen. counsel UNIROYAL, Inc., 1961-84; spl. ptnr. Shea & Gould, N.Y.C., 1985-91, of counsel, 1992-94, Parker Duryee Rosoff & Haft, N.Y.C., 1994—2002; sole practice, 2002—. Editor: Harvard Law Rev, 1942-43. Adv. bd. Southwestern Legal Found. Lt. USNR, 1943-46. Mem. ABA, N.Y. State Bar Assn., Assn. Bar City N.Y., NAM (mem. lawyers adv. com. to gen. counsel), Harvard Club, Bellport Country Club, Rockefeller Ctr. Luncheon Club, Westhampton Yacht Squadron. Home and Office: 50 E 79th St New York NY 10021-0232 E-mail: mkalish@earthlink.net.

KALISKI, MARY, psychologist; b. Bratislava, Czechoslovakia, Dec. 9, 1938; came to U.S., 1950; d. Frank and Margaret (Fleischman) Reichenthal; m. Thomas Kaliski, Sept. 21, 1957; children: Karen, Kenneth. BS summa cum laude, C.W. Post Coll., 1978; MS, profl. diploma, St. John's U., 1980, PhD, 1987. Psychologist North Shore Schs., L.I., 1977-79, Herricks Schs., L.I., 1979—. Speaker in field. Chief psychologist Stepfamily Found. L.I., 1987-92; bd. dirs. Nassau Psychol. Svcs. Inst., 1989—. Mem. Am. Psychol. Assn., Nassau County Psychol. Assn.

KALISKI, STEPHAN FELIX, economics educator; b. Warsaw, Nov. 4, 1928; emigrated to Can., 1941, naturalized, 1947; s. Jacob and Ludwika (Romanus) K.; m. Marian Ieleen Nelson, Oct. 6, 1960; 1 dau., Susan Maria. BA, U. B.C., 1951; MA, U. Toronto, 1953, postgrad., 1953-54; PhD, U. Cambridge, Eng., 1959. Statistician I Dominion Bur. Statistics, 1951-52; Alexander Mackenzie Research fellow U. Toronto, 1953-54; lectr. Queen's U., Kingston, Ont., 1954-56, prof. econs., 1969-94; chmn. div II Queen's U. (Grad. Sch.), 1971-73; prof. emeritus, 1994—; research fellow in econ. statistics Manchester (Eng.) U., 1958-59; asst. prof. Carleton U., Ottawa, Ont., 1959-62, asso. prof., 1962-65, prof., 1965-69, cmn. dept. econs., 1962-63, 64-66; research supr. Royal Commn. Taxation, 1963-64; Can. Council Sr. fellow, Dept. Labour-Univs. Research Com. research grantee, research asso. U. Calif., Berkeley, 1966-67; Can. Council leave fellow, 1973-74; hon. research asso. in econs. Harvard U., 1973-74. Social Sci. and Humanities Research Council Can. leave fellow, 1980-81, research grantee, 1978, 81; bd. dirs. Nat. Bur. Econ. Research, 1978-84; cons. Royal Commn. on Econ. Union, 1984-85, Commn. of Inquiry on Unemployment Ins., 1985-86. Author: Adjustment Assistance under the U.S. Trade Expansion Act, 1963, The Tradeoff Between Inflation and Unemployment, Some Explorations of Recent Evidence for Canada, 1972; editor, author: Canadian Economic Policy since the War, a Series of Six Public Lectures in Commemoration of the Twentieth Anniversary of the White Paper on Employment and Income of 1945, 1966; mng. editor: Can. Jour. Econs, 1976-79; contbr. articles to profl. publs. Can. Council research grantee, 1969, 77-81; Social Sci. Research Council research fellow, 1956-57 Fellow Royal Soc. Can.; mem. Can. Econs. Assn. (v.p. 1984-85, pres.-elect 1985-86, pres. 1986-87, past pres. 1987-88), Queen's Univ. Club. Home: 649 Fernmoor Dr Kingston ON Canada K7M 8K5 Office: Queen's U Dept Econs Kingston ON Canada K7L 3N6 E-mail: kaliskis@qed.econ.queensu.ca.

KALKHOFF, WILLIAM WEBSTER, sociologist, educator; b. Milw., May 26, 1971; s. Rhea Lynn Kalkhoff. BA summa cum laude, Marquette U., 1994; MA, U. Iowa, 1997. Contbr. articles to profl. jours. Rsch. grantee NSF, 2000-2001; Disting. honor scholar Ripon Coll., 1989-92, acad. scholar Marquette U., 1991-94. Mem. Am. Sociol. Assn. (nominations com. 1999-2000, Rsch. Paper award social psychology sect. 1998), Phi Beta Kappa. Avocations: blues and jazz saxophone, long-distance running, camping.

KALKSTEIN, JOSHUA ADAM, lawyer; b. Phila., Oct. 1, 1943; s. Abraham and Helen (Ponemone) K.; children: Alexa L., Trevor W., Maxim J. AB, Brown U., 1965; JD, U. Pa., 1968. Bar: N.Y. 1968, N.J. 1971, Mass. 1978, U.S. Dist. Ct. N.Y. 1968, U.S. Dist. Ct., N.J. 1971, U.S. Dist. Ct., Mass. 1978, U.S. Ct. of Appeals (3d cir.) 1973, U.S. Ct. Mil. Appeals 1969. Asst. gen. counsel Pfizer Inc., Groton, Conn., 1978—; assoc. Hellring, Lindeman & Landau, Newark, 1972-75; corp. counsel Hooper Holmes Inc., Basking Ridge, N.J., 1975-78. Vis. counsel Harvard U., MIT Ctr. for Exptl. Pharmacology and Therapeutics, Cambridge, 1995—. Bd. dirs. Howland Art Ctr., Beacon, N.Y., 1987-91, Congregation Beth El, New London, Conn., 1995-96, Main Street New London, 2000—; commr. Waterfront Redevel. Commn., Beacon, 1990-91. Lt. USNR, 1969-72. Mem. N.Y. State Bar Assn., N.J. Bar Assn., Mass. Bar Assn. Jewish. Avocations: art collecting, book collecting, golf. Home: 76 Library St Mystic CT 06355-2420 Office: Pfizer Inc 50 Pequot Ave New London CT 06320 E-mail: joshua_a_kalkstein@groton.pfizer.com.

KALKUS, STANLEY, librarian, administrator, consultant; b. Prague, Czechoslovakia, Apr. 27, 1931; came to U.S., 1952; s. Frank and Zdenka (Hynkova) K.; m. Marta J. Pokorna, Jan. 12, 1952; children: Michaela Z., Olen A., Hynek P. Abitur, Classical Gymnasium, Prague, 1950; Cert. in Germanistics, Charles U., Prague, 1951; MA, U. Chgo., 1959. Librarian, audio-visual coordinator Chgo. Bd. Edn., 1960-62; base librarian U.S. Air Force, Sidi Slimane, Morocco, 1962-63, Hahn AFB, Fed. Republic Germany, 1963-68; slavic bibliographer U. N.C., Chapel Hill, 1968-69; head library dept. Naval Underwater Systems Ctr., Newport, R.I., 1969-77; dir. U.S. Dept. Navy Library, Washington, 1977-86, coord., 1986-89, libr. of Navy, 1990-92; asst. prof. Charles U., Prague, Czech Republic, 1992—. Lectr. U. N.C., Chapel Hill, 1968-69; participant tech. info. panel AGARD (NATO), Brussels, 1974, Copenhagen, 1975, Washington, 1976, Oslo, 1977; adv. com. Intergovtl. Libr. Cooperation, 1981-82; exec. adv. com. Fedlink, 1986-88; rep. Dept. of Navy on Fed. Libr. and Info. Ctrs. com., 1991-92; chmn. libr. com. Ctrl. European Rsch. and Grad. Edn., 1998--, Econ. Inst., Acad. Scis., Prague, 1994—; mem. libr. com. Parliament of Czech Republic, 1997—; adv. bd. U. Koblenz (Germany) Exernal LS Studies, 1998-2000. Editor Navy Libraries in 1980s, 1976; contbr. articles to profl. jours. Mem. core com. R.I. Gov.'s Conf. on Libraries, 1976-77. Served with U.S. Army, 1953-55 Fellow U. Chgo., 1957-58 Mem. ALA (pres. Armed Forces sect. 1974), Spl. Libr. Assn. (chmn. mil. librs. div. 1978-79), Internat. Fedn. Libr. Assns. (mem. standing com. on social librs. 1986-96, mem. standing com. edn. and tng. 1996-2000), Am. Translators Assn., Czech Libr. and Info. Profl. Assn. (mem. exec. bd. 1999—), Assn. Americans Residing Overseas. Clubs: Newport Ski, Friends of Newport Pub. Library. Roman Catholic. Avocations: skiing, tennis. Office: Charles U Prague FF UISL U Krize 8 150 00 Prague Czech Republic also: 7009 Dreams Way Ct Alexandria VA 22315-4245 Fax: +420 2 510 80 413. E-mail: skalkus@yahoo.com., kalkus@cuni.cz.

KALKWARF, LEONARD V. minister; b. Parkersburg, Iowa, Mar. 17, 1928; s. John Jr. and Helen Kalkwarf; m. Beverly Jane Hardy, May 22, 1954; children— Deborah Joy, Cynthia Sue, Scott Craig. BA, Central Coll., Pella, Iowa, 1950; BD, New Brunswick Sem., 1953; MA, NYU, 1957; STM, Luth. Sem., Phila., 1973; DMin, Princeton Sem., 1980; DD (hon.), Central Coll., 1983. Ordained to ministry Ref. Ch. in Am., 1953. Assoc. pastor Bellevue Ref. Ch., Schenectady, N.Y., 1953-55; assoc. pastor Levittown (N.Y.) Community Ch., 1955-57; pastor Ref. Ch., Willow Grove, Pa., 1957-64, 65-91, Nat. Evang. Ch., Kuwait, Kuwait, 1964-65. Pres. Particular Synod of N.J., 1969-70, 70-71, Gen. Synod of Ref. Ch. in Am., 1983-84 Author: History, 1st Reformed Church of Philadelphia, 1960, God Loves His World, Book I, 1963, Book II, 1964; contbr. articles to religious jours. Pastoral asst. Abington, Pa. Presbyn. Ch., 1998—. Served as Chaplain CAP, 1960-62. Mem. Canterbury Cleric Club. Lodges: Rotary. Republican. Home: 812 Roslyn Ave Glenside PA 19038-3807 E-mail: kalkway@cs.com.

KALLA, ALEC KARL, writer, rancher; b. Pitts., Feb. 7, 1950; s. Milton Miklos and Marion Dorothy Kalla. Attended, Boston U., 1968-72. Rancher, Conifer, Colo., 1977—2001; v.p. Health Care Assocs., Evergreen, Colo., 1989; freelance writer, 1990—. Guest author, panelist Rocky Mountain Book Fesitval, Denver, 1993-95. Author: Velvet, 1993, Standing in the Zone, 1998, The Creature Vampyre, 1999, 57 Good Things About Chemotherapy, 2001; patentee in field, 1984. Honoree Colo. Authors Program, 1998. Mem. Mystery Writers Am. Avocations: folk guitar and banjo, archery, shooting sports. Home and Office: 8733 W Summit Circle Dr French Lick IN 47432

KALLAHER, MICHAEL JOSEPH, mathematics educator; b. Cin., Sept. 4, 1940; s. Martin Henry and Lou Will (Huff) K.; m. Donalyn May Laraway, Aug. 17, 1963; children: Jay, Michael, Christopher, Daniel, Raymond. BS, Xavier U., 1961; MS, Syracuse U., 1963, PhD, 1967. Postdoctoral fellow U. Man., Winnipeg, Can., 1967-69; from asst. prof. prof. math. Wash. State U., Pullman, 1969—, assoc. dean scis., 1979-84, acting dean scis., 1982, chmn. math dept., 1984-92; vis. prof. Auckland U., New Zealand, 1988. Author: Affine Planes with Transitive Collineation Groups; contbg. editor Finite Geometries, 1982; contbr. articles to profl. jours. Grantee NSF; Fulbright Research scholar, Kaiserslautern, Fed. Republic Germany, 1975-76. Fellow Inst. Combinatories and Its Application (founding); mem. Am. Math. Soc., Math. Assn. Am., N.Y. Acad. of Scis., Assn. of Research Profs. (pres. 1986-87), Sigma Xi. Home: 235 NW Joe St Pullman WA 99163-3410 Office: Wash State U Dept Of Math Pullman WA 99163

KALLAKIS, ACHILLEAS MICHALIS S. shipping company executive; b. London, Sept. 3, 1968; s. Michalis and Erinoula (Angelinakis) K.; m. Pamela Anne Stachowsky, Sept. 1995; children: Erinoula, Michalis and Aristotelis (twins), Dionysios. BSc in Econs. with honors, 1989. Dir. Global Transport, Del., N.Y., 1989-91; chmn., CEO The Pacific Group of Cos., London, N.Y.C., 1991—, 1991—, Pacific Risk Corp., 2000—. Dir. U.S. C of C, London, 1997—, Ocean Group USA, 1989—, Pacific Maritime, N.Y., 1991—, Bernouli Trust Corp., NY, 1994—, South Pacific Adv. Bd., Sydney, Australia, 1994—2000, Brit. Am. Bus., Inc.; chmn., CEO Pacific Coffee Corp., Hellenic Capital Mgmt., Pacific Real Estate Corp., 2000—, Atlas Alliance Group, 2000—, Atlas E-Risk, 2000—01; chmn. Pacific Vending Group; mem. devel. bd. Nat. Portrait Gallery, London, 2000—. Author: Maritime Registers of the World, 1994, Transport Economics, 1996; co-editor: The Wonders of Italy, 1996. Pres. Youth Anglo-Hellenic Soc. U.K., London, 1986-88; dir. Friends of Florence, Italy, 1997—; mem. com. Youth Enterprise Initiative, London, 1989-92; mem. Royal Opera, London, Met. Opera Guild, N.Y., Navy League. Recipient Churchill award for Excellence Churchill Enterprise Found., 1993, Pres.'s Golden Honor award South Pacific Action, Foru, 1995, Prime Min.'s award South Pacific Action Forum, 1996, Outstanding Emerging Leader award Office of Maritime Affairs, 1997; fellow Duke of Edinburgh Internat., 2003--. Fellow Inst. Dirs., Inst. Transport and Tourism; mem. Friends of Conservation,, Queen's Club, Met. Opera Guild (N.Y.C.), Met. Club (N.Y.C.), Nat. Trust (London), Soc. for the Protection of Ancient Bldgs. (London), The Landmark Tust (Eng.). Greek Orthodox. Avocations: travel, italian studies, back-gammon, fencing, tennis, antiques, poker. Office: Pacific Group Cos 8 Carlos Pl Mayfair London W1K 3AS England

KALLAKURY, BHASKAR VENKATA SATYA, pathologist, educator; b. Narsapur, India, May 9, 1960; came to U.S., 1990; s. Subrahmanyam and Laxmi (Munamarti) K.; m. Ramani L. Kharidehal, Aug. 16, 1989; children: Adarsh, Anish. B Medicine B Surgery, Osmania (India) Med. Coll., 1982. Diplomate Am. Bd. Pathology in anatomic and clin. pathology and hematology. Resident in pathology Albany (N.Y.) Med. Ctr., 1991-96, chief resident, 1993-94, fellow in molecular pathology, 1996-97; fellow in hematopathology Georgetown U., Washington, 1997-98, clin. instr., 1997-98, instr. in pathology, 1998-99; asst. prof. Pathology Albany Med. Coll., 1999-01, dir. electron microscopy, 2000-01; prof. Pathology Georgetown U. Hosp., DC, 2001—. Contbr. numerous articles to profl. jours. Recipient Ann. Resident Scholarly award Albany Med. Coll., 1994. Fellow Am. Coll. Pathologists; mem. U.S. and Can. Acad. Pathologists, Am. Assn. Cancer Rsch. Achievements include research in field of prostate cancer. Office: Georgetown U Hosp Dept Pathology 3900 Reservoir Rd NW Washington DC 20007 E-mail: kallakub@gunet.georgetown.edu.

KALLAY, MICHAEL FRANK, II, medical devices company official; b. Painesville, Ohio, Aug. 24, 1944; s. Michael Frank and Marie Francis (Sage) K.; m. Irma Yolanda Corona, Aug. 30, 1975; 1 son, William Albert. BBA, Ohio U., 1967. Salesman Howmedica, Inc., Rutherford, N.J., 1972-75, Biochem Procedures/Metpath, North Hollywood, Calif., 1975-76; surg. specialist USCI divsn. C.R. Bard, Inc., Billerica, Mass., 1976-78; western and ctrl. regional mgr. ARCO Med. Products Co., Phila., 1978-80; midwest reigonal mgr. Intermedics, Inc., Freeport, Tex., 1980-82; western U.S. rep. Minntech Renal Systems, Mpls., 1982—. Pres. Kall-Med, Inc., Anaheim Hills, Calif., 1982—. Mem. Am. Mgmt. Assn., Phi Kappa Sigma. Home and Office: 7539 E Bridgewood Dr Anaheim CA 92808-1407

KALLBERG, JEFFREY, musicologist; b. Glencoe, Minn., Oct. 17, 1954; s. Delmer Clarence Kallberg and Elaine Adeline Patchett; m. Charlotta Thunander, Oct. 26, 1991; 1 child, Erik Hans. AB magna cum laude, UCLA, 1975; PhD, U. Chgo., 1982. Prof. music history U. Pa., Phila., 1982—. Author: (non-fiction book) Chopin at the Boundaries: Sex, History, and Musical Genre. Dir. at large Am. Musicological Soc., Phila., 1997—99. Named Guest of Honor, Internat. Frydyeryk Chopin Competition, Warsaw, Poland, 1990, 2000; fellow, NEH, 1985—86, John Simon Guggenheim Meml. Found., 1992. Achievements include discovery of unknown Chopin prelude in E-flat minor (Devil's Trill). Office: Univ Pa 201 S 34th St Philadelphia PA 19104-6313 Office Fax: 215-573-2106. E-mail: kallberg@sas.upenn.edu.

KALLENBERG, JOHN KENNETH, retired librarian; b. Anderson, Ind., June 10, 1942; s. Herbert A. and Helen S. K.; m. Ruth Barrett, Aug. 19, 1965; children: Jennifer Anne, Gregory John. AB, Ind. U., 1964, M.L.S., 1969. With Fresno County Library, Fresno, Calif., 1965-70, dir., 1976; librarian Fig Garden Pub. Library br., 1968-70; asst. dir. Santa Barbara (Calif.) Pub. Library, 1970-76. Mem. Calif. Libr. Svcs. bd., 1990—99, v.p., 1992—95, pres., 1996—98; mem. Libr. of Calif. Bd., 1999—, pres., 2003; Beth Ann Harnish lectr. com., 1988—91; mem. adv. bd. Pacific S.W. Regional Med. Libr., 1999—; mem. Heartland Regional Libr. Network Bd., 2000—02. Mem.: ALA, Am. Soc. Pub. Adminstrn., Libr. Adminstrn. and Mgmt. Assn., Calif. Libr. Authority for Sys. and Svcs. (chmn. authority adv. coun. 1978—80), Calif. County Librs. Assn. (pres. 1977), Calif. Libr. Assn. (councilor 1976—77, v.p., pres. 1987), Pub. Libr. Assn., Kiwanis (pres. Fresno 1981—82, lt. gov. divsn. 5 1991—92, co-editor Cal-Nev-Ha News 1993—94, 1995—96, bd. dirs. 1999—2001, 2002—). Presbyterian. E-mail: john.kallenberg@fresnolibrary.org.

KALLENDORF, CRAIG WILLIAM, English, speech and classical languages educator; b. Cin., June 23, 1954; s. Earl Roy and Hazel Greene (Griffith) K.; m. Hilaire Richey, Oct. 16, 1993. BA, Valparaiso U., 1975; MA, U. N.C., 1977, PhD, 1982. Asst. prof. dept. English Tex. A&M U., College Station, 1982-88, assoc. prof. English and classics, 1988-93, prof. English, classics and speech, 1993—, interim head modern and classical langs., 2001—. Cons. NEH, Washington, 1987—. Author: Bibliography of Latin Influences..., 1982, Petrarch: Selected Letters, 1987, In Praise of Aeneas, 1989, Epistle of St. Paul to the Romans, 1991, A Bibliography of Venetian Editions of Virgil, 1470-1599, 1991, Vergil: The Classical Heritage, 1993, A Bibliography of Renaissance Italian Translations of Virgil, 1994, Aldine Press Books, 1998, Virgil and The Myth of Venice, 1999, Landmark Essays on Rhetoric and Literature, 1999, Humanist Educational Treatises, 2002; editor Jour. Allegorica, 1989-2000, Rhetorica, 1993-96, Neo-Latin News, 1992—; contbr. articles to prof. jours. Grantee Tex. A&M U., 1983—, South Ctrl. MLA, 1984, NEH, 1985, 90-92, Delmas Found., 1987, 92, ACLS, 1992, Humanities Rsch. Ctr., U. Tex., 1994., U. Utah Humanities Ctr., 2000-01. Lutheran. Office: Tex A&M U Dept English College Station TX 77843-4227 E-mail: kalendrf@tamu.edu.

KALLET, HARRIET FELDMAN, real estate broker; b. Jersey City, Aug. 4, 1941; d. Emanuel and Clara (Holstein) Feldman; m. Stephen M. Kallet, Aug. 15, 1965; children: Jill, Beth. BA, Elmira Coll., 1962; postgrad., Bank St. Coll. Edn., 1963-64. Cert. elem. sch. tchr., N.J., N.Y. Tchr. grade 4 Teaneck (N.J.) Bd. Edn., 1962-68; tchr. jr. high sch. Barnstable Acad., Glen Rock, N.J., 1979-84, 1984-87; real estate salesperson Murphy Realty, Montvale, N.J., 1986-93; real estate broker, sales assoc. ReMax Real Estate Assocs., Woodcliff Lake, N.J., 1994—. Mem. Sisterhood Temple Emanuel. Mem.: Pascack Valley Bd. Realtors-N.W. Bergen Bd. Realtors (com. chmn. 1992—95, chmn. realtors polit. action com. 1992—98, bd. dirs. 1993—95), N.J. Assn. Realtors Disting. Sales Club, N.J. Assn. Realtors (Million Dollar Sales Club 1988—99), Real Source Assn. Realtors (com. chmn. 1995—, bd. dirs. 1998—), Nat. Assn. Realtors, Park Ridge Rotary (bd. dirs. 1994—, v.p. 2003—, Walter Head award 2002). Avocations: golf, cooking, travel, walking. Home: 326 Spring St Upper Saddle River NJ 07458-2216 Office: ReMax Real Estate Assocs 188 Broadway Woodcliff Lake NJ 07677-8067 E-mail: shkallet@optonline.net.

KALLET, RICHARD HUBBARD, medical researcher; b. Syracuse, N.Y., July 16, 1956; s. Richard Hubbard and Jean Lee K. MS, San Francisco State U., 1996. Registered respiratory therapist. Clin. rsch. coord. critical care divsn. Dept. Anesthesia San Francisco Gen. Hosp., 1998—; clin. rsch. coord. Cardio Rsch. Inst., U. Calif., San Francisco, 1996—. Editl. bd. Respiratory Care Jour., 2001—; contbr. articles to profl. jours. Fellow Am. Assn. for Respiratory Care; mem. Soc. of Critical Care Medicine, Am. Coll. of Chest Physicians, Am. Thoracic Soc. Mem. Agnostic. Avocations: musician, percussionist. Office: San Frncisco Gen Hosp NH:GA-2 Potrero Ave San Francisco CA 94110 Fax: 415-206-5735. E-mail: rkallet@sfghsom.ucsf.edu.

KALLFELZ, FRANCIS A. veterinary medicine educator; b. Syracuse, NY, July 17, 1938; s. Alois Joseph and Josephine Marie (Honold) K.; m. Leonie Heidi Gantner, June 26, 1965; children: Andrew F., Susan E., Douglas P. Student, Lemoyne Coll., 1956-58; DVM, Cornell U., 1962, PhD, 1966. Diplomate Am. Coll. Vet. Nutrition (charter). Asst. prof. vet. medicine Cornell U., Ithaca, N.Y., 1966-73, assoc. prof., 1973-80, prof., 1980—; dir. Vet. Med. Tchg. Hosp., 1990-98, James Law prof. medicine (nutrition), 1997—. Sr. Fulbright lectr., Zagreb, Yugoslavia, 1978; cons. FAO/IAEA, Vienna, 1977-78, Indonesia, 1980-83; vis. prof. Johns Hopkins U. Sch. Medicine, 1999; mem. NRC-CAN subcom. Nutrient Requirements of Dogs and Cats, 2000-03. Contbr. articles to profl. jours. Mem. Am. Soc. Nutrition Sci., Soc. Nuclear Medicine, AVMA (coun. on rsch. 1983-89, Am. Bd. Vet. Specialties 1988-2000, chmn. 1999-2000), Soc. Exptl. Biology and Medicine, NY State Vet. Med. Soc. (pres. 2001), NY State Comm. on Animal Health Issues, NY State Bd. for Vet. Medicine. Republican. Roman Catholic. Avocations: handball, philately, camping. Home: 11 Bean Hill Ln Ithaca NY 14850-9775 Office: Cornell Univ Coll Vet Medicine Dept Clin Sci Ithaca NY 14853 E-mail: fak1@cornell.edu.

KALLGREN, EDWARD EUGENE, retired lawyer; b. San Francisco, May 22, 1928; s. Edward H. and Florence E. (Campbell) K.; m. Joyce Elaine Kislitzin, Feb. 8, 1953; children: Virginia K. Pegley, Charles Edward. AB, U. Calif., Berkeley, 1951, JD, 1954. Bar: Calif. Assoc., ptnr. Brobeck, Phleger & Harrison LLP, San Francisco, 1954-93, of counsel, 1993—2003; ret., 2003. Bd. dirs. Olivet Meml. Park, Colma, Calif., 1970-98, pres., 1991-98; chair, pres. Five Bridges Found., 1998—; mem. Berkeley City Council, 1971-75; bd. dirs., v.p./treas. Planned Parenthood Alameda/San Francisco, 1984-89. Served to sgt. USMC, 1945-48. Mem. ABA (ho. of dels. 1985-2000, state del. 1997-98, coun. sr. law divsn. 1996-2001, chair 1999-2000), State Bar of Calif. (bd. govs. 1989-92, v.p. 1991-92), Found. of State Bar Calif. (bd. dirs. 1993-98, v.p., 1994-96, chair fellows soc. 1996-98), Bar Assn. San Francisco (pres. 1988, bd. dirs.), San Francisco Lawyers Com. Urban Affairs (co-chair 1983-85), Lawyers Com. Civil Rights Under Law (trustee 1985—), The TenBroek Soc. (chair bd. dirs. 1992-95). Democrat. E-mail: ekallgren@brobeck.com.

KALLICK, DAVID A. lawyer; b. Chgo., Nov. 7, 1945; s. Joseph N. and Elizabeth A. (Just) K.; m. Arline E. Chizewer, Nov. 26, 1972; children: Michelle, Robert. AB in History, Princeton U., 1967; JD, Northwestern U., 1971. Bar: Ill. 1971, Calif. 1972. Law clk. to presiding justice Ill. Appellate Ct., Chgo., 1971-72; assoc. McCutchen, Doyle, Brown & Enersen, San Francisco, 1972-74; asst. dean U. So. Calif. Law Ctr., L.A., 1974-76, Ill. Inst. Tech.-Kent Coll. Law, Chgo., 1976-79; ptnr. Hurley Kallick & Schiller, Ltd., Deerfield, Ill., 1979-92, Tishler & Wald, Ltd., Chgo., 1992—. Past bd. dirs. Congregation Solel, Highland Park, Ill., Birchwood Club, Highland Park; past bd. mem., pres. Sch. Dist. 107, Highland Park; former trustee Legacy 107 Edn. Found., Highland Park. With USAR, 1968-74. Mem. ABA, Calif. Bar Assn., Ill. Bar Assn., Chgo. Bar Assn., Princeton Univ. Club. Home: 1887 Spruce Ave Highland Park IL 60035-2150 Office: 200 S Wacker Dr Ste 3000 Chicago IL 60606-5807 E-mail: dkallick@tishlerandwald.com.

KALLIN, BRITTA, language educator; b. Badsegeberg, Germany, Feb. 13, 1969; d. Klaus and Edelgard Kallin; m. Protip Biswas, May 10, 2002. MA, U. Cin., 1994, U. Hamburg, 1995; PhD, U. Cin., 2000. Asst. prof. German Ga. Inst. Tech., Atlanta, 2000—. Mem.: Internat. Brecht Soc. (assoc. editor 2001—). Office: Ga Tech Sch Modern Lang 613 Cherry St Atlanta GA 30332-0375

KALLIONIEMI, OLLI PEKKA, geneticist, researcher; MD, U. Tampere, 1985, PhD, 1988. Resident and rschr. Tampere (Finland) U. Hosp., 1985-90; vis. scientist U. Calif., San Francisco, 1990-93; prof. cancer biology U. Tampere, 1994-95; investigator, sect. head Nat. Human Genome Rsch. Inst., NIH, Bethesda, Md., 1996-99, sr. investigator, sect. head, 2000—. Office: NHGRI/NIH Bldg 50, Rm 5318 50 South Dr Bethesda MD 20892-8000 E-mail: okalli@nhgri.nih.gov.

KALLIR, JANE KATHERINE, art gallery director, author; b. NYC; d. John Otto and Joyce (Ruben) Kallir. BA, Brown U., 1976. Asst. to dir. Lefebre Gallery, NYC, 1977, Galerie St. Etienne, NYC, 1977-78, co-dir., 1979—. Guest lectr. NYU, 1982—85, Mus. Am. Folk Art, NYC, 1982—85; guest curator NY State Mus., Albany, 1983, Internat. Exhbn. Found., Washington, 1984—85, Mus. of City of Vienna, 1986, Austrian Nat. Gallery, 1990, Nat. Gallery Art, Washington, 1994, Indpls. Mus. Art, 1994, San Diego Mus. Art, 1994; guest lectr. Nat. Gallery Art, 1994, Ft. Lauderdale Mus. Art, 1996, guest curator, Fla., 96; guest lectr. Mus. Modern Art, 1997, Internat. Found. for Art Rsch., 1998, Wexner Ctr., Columbus, Ohio, 1999, NYU, 1999, San Diego Mus., 2001; guest curator Nat. Mus. of Women in the Arts, 2001, Orlando Mus. of Art, Fla., 2001, Museo del Vittoriano, Rome, 2001, San Diego Mus. Art, 2001; guest lectr. Columbus Mus. of Art, 2002, Clark Art Inst., 2002. Author: Gustav Klimt-Egon Schiele, 1980, Austria's Expressionism, 1981, The Folk Art Tradition, 1981, Grandma Moses, The Artist Behind the Myth, 1982, Arnold Schoenberg's Vienna, 1984, Viennese Design and the Wiener Werkstaette, 1986, Gustav Klimt: 25 Masterworks, 1989, Egon Schiele: The Complete Works, 1990, rev., 1998, Richard Gerstl/Oskar Kokoschka, 1992, Egon Schiele, 1994, Egon Schiele: 27 Masterworks, 1996, Grandma Moses, 25 Masterworks, 1997, Grandma Moses in the 21st Century, 2001, The Essential Grandma Moses, 2001, Egon Schiele, Watercolors and Drawings, 2003. Mem.: Egon Schiele: Drawings and Watercolors, Art Dealers Assn. Am. (bd. dir. 1994—97, chmn. pub. rels. com. 2001—, v.p. 2003—). Democrat. Office: Galerie St Etienne 24 W 57th St New York NY 10019-3918 E-mail: gallery@gse.art.com.

KALLMAN, BURTON JAY, foods association director; b. N.Y.C., Nov. 1, 1927; s. Leo Melville and Muriel Kallman; m. Ellis Katherine Hachikian, Dec. 12, 1958; children: Lisa, David. BS, Bethany Coll., 1947; MS, U. So. Calif., 1951, PhD, 1958. Research biochemist U.S. Govt., Denver, Los Angeles, 1959-67; mem. profl. staff TRW Systems, Redondo Beach, Calif., 1967-76; sr. scientist Sci. Applications Inc., La Jolla, Calif., 1976-80; prin. Interdisciplinary Sci. Assocs., Torrance, Calif., 1980-82; lab. dir. Applied Biol. Scis., Glendale, Calif., 1982-85; dir. sci. and tech. Nat. Nutritional Foods Assn., Newport Beach, Calif., 1985-96, cons. Cons. Children's Asthma Research Inst., Denver, 1961-63, Behavioral Health Services, Redondo Beach, 1973-77, Centinela Child Guidance, Inglewood, Calif., 1984-86, Nat. Nutritional Foods Assn., Newport Beach, 1997-. Mem. editl. bd. Jour. Applied Nutrition, 1991-99, Jour. Optimal Nutrition, 1992-96; reviewer sci. books and films, 1978—; contbr. articles to profl. jours. Bd. dirs. Drum Barracks Civil War Mus., Wilmington, Calif., 2000—. Recipient Merit award NASA, 1976, Burton Kallman Scientific Achievement award, Nat. Nutritional Foods Assn., 1997. Mem. Am. Chem. Soc., Sigma Xi. Democrat. Jewish. Home: 23214 Robert Rd Torrance CA 90505-3244 E-mail: Kallman2@aol.com.

KALLMAN, KATHLEEN BARBARA, marketing and business development professional; b. Aurora, Ill., Mar. 23, 1952; d. Kenneth Wesley and Germaine Barbara (May) Eby. Legal sec. Sidley & Austin, Chgo., 1973-76, Winston & Strawn, Chgo., 1976-78; exec. sec. Beatrice Cos., Inc., Chgo., 1978-81, adminstrv. asst., 1981-83, asst. v.p., chmn. bd. dirs., 1983—84, v.p., 1984-85; pres., mng. dir. Stratxx Ltd., Charlotte, N.C., 1985—. Mem. Chgo. Coun. on Fgn. Rels., 1986—. Mem. Am. Soc. Profl. and Exec. Women, Nat. Assn. Women Bus. Owners, Charlotte Women Bus. Owners Assn., Charlotte Assn. Profl. Saleswomen, Chgo. Assn. Profl. Saleswomen, Internat. Assn. Bus. Communicators. Avocation: photography. Office: Stratxx Ltd PO Box 470008 Charlotte NC 28247-0008

KALLMANN, HELMUT MAX, music historian, retired music librarian; b. Berlin, Aug. 7, 1922; emigrated to Can., 1940, naturalized, 1946; s. Arthur and Fanny (Paradies) K.; m. Ruth Singer, Dec. 31, 1955 (dec. July 1993); 1 stepdaughter, Lynn Salter. MusB, U. Toronto, Ont., Can., 1949, LLD, 1971. With CBC Music Libr., Toronto, 1950-70, supr., 1962-70; chief music divsn. Nat. Libr. Can., Ottawa, Ont., 1970-87, ret., 1987. Can. del. Internat. Assn. Music Librs., 1959-71 Author: A History of Music in Canada, 1534-1914, 1960; editor; Catalogue of Canadian Composers, 1952, Music for Orchestra I, Vol. 8, 1990, (with Gilles Potvin and Kenneth Winters) Ency. of Music in Canada, 1981, French edit., 1983, (with Potvin) 2nd edit., 1992, French 2nd edit., 1993, Music for Piano III, vol. 22, 1998; contbr. articles to profl. publs. Decorated Order of Can., 1986; dedicatee Musical Canada, Words and Music Honouring Helmut Kallmann, 1988; recipient Award of Merit Assn. for Can. Studies, 1998. Mem. Can. Music Coun. (v.p. 1971-76, medal 1977), Can. Assn. Music Librs. (co-founder 1956, past chmn.), Can. Mus. Heritage Soc. (chmn. 1982-2000), Faculty Music Alumni Assn. U. Toronto (pres. 1963-64), Order of Can. Home: 38 Foothills Dr Nepean ON Canada K2H 6K3 E-mail: hkallmann@comnet.ca.

KALLMANN, STANLEY WALTER, lawyer; b. Bklyn., June 6, 1943; s. Silve and Erna Kallmann; m. Carolee A. McDonald, Aug. 23, 1969; 1 child, Alexander;1 child, Andrew. BA, Rutgers U., New Brunswick, 1964; LLB, Rutgers U., Newark, 1967. Bar: N.J. 1967, U.S. Dist. Ct. N.J. 1967, N.Y. 1984. Law clk. to judge U.S. Dist. Ct. N.J., Newark, 1967-69; assoc. Stryker, Tams & Dill, Newark, 1969-71; asst. U.S. atty. U.S. Atty.'s Office, Newark, 1971-75; ptnr. Gennet, Kallmann, Antin & Robinson, Parsippany, N.J., 1975—. Mem. ABA, N.J. Bar Assn. Office: Gennet Kallmann Antin & Robinson 6 Campus Dr Parsippany NJ 07054-4406

KALLSHIAN, JAN, electronics manufacturing company executive; b. 1954; CPA. With Coopers & Lybrand; cons., CFO Datamarine Internat., Inc., Mountlake, Wash., 1995, CFO, 1997—. Office: 7030 220th SW Mountlake Terrace WA 98043

KALLSTROM, CHARLES CLARK, dentist; b. Chgo., Jan. 15, 1943; s. Charles Edward and Margaret Jane (Clark) K.; m. Roberta Lou Easterday, June 19, 1965; children: Cynthia Ann, Heidi Lynn, Karen Kristine. BS in Chem. Engring., Purdue U., 1965; DDS, Northwestern U., Chgo., 1971. Project engr. Chgo. Bridge & Iron Co., Oakbrook, Ill., 1965-67; pvt. practice dentistry Geneva, Ill., 1973—. Mem. dental staff Cmty. Hosp., Geneva, 1974—, chmn., 1980-81; chmn. Elgin C.C. Dental Assisting Adv. Bd., 1994—, chmn., 1995-99. Author, editor: Dental Assisting for the Red Cross Aide, 1971. Bd. dirs. Tri City Family Svcs., Geneva, 1983-90, v.p., 1985-87, pres., 1988-90, chmn. capitol gifts campaign, 1992-93; bd. dirs. Men's Found. Delnor Cmty. Hosp., Geneva, 1979—; pres. Geneva chpt. Am. Cancer Soc., 1986-88. Lt. USN, 1971-73. Fellow Am. Coll. Dentists, Internat. Coll. Dentists, Acad. Gen. Dentistry (master); mem. ADA, Ill. State Dental Soc. (dental edn. com.1989-92, bd. trustees 1992-95, access to care com. 1992-93, fin. and planning com. 1992-95, chmn. annual planning com. 1993-94, dental benefits com. 1994-95, ins. com. 1995-2002, chmn. 1999-2002), Fox River Valley Dental Soc. (sec. 1986, treas. 1987, v.p. 1988, bd. dirs. 1988-91, pres. 1989), Ill. Acad. Dental Practice Adminstrn., Geneva Golf Club (sec. 1988, bd. dirs. 1986-88, 92-96, 2001—, v.p. 1995, pres. 1996, treas. 2002—). Republican. Presbyterian. Avocations: traveling, golf, paddle tennis. Home: 615 Carriage Dr Batavia IL 60510-1159 Office: 302 Randall Rd Ste 105 Geneva IL 60134-4209

KALLSTROM, JAMES DAVID, lawyer; b. Akron, Ohio, Sept. 20, 1950; s. David H. and Mary (Joshua) K.; m. Phebe Gay Zimmerman, Jan. 2, 1982; 1 child, Adam J. AB, Kenyon Coll., 1973; JD, Case Western Res. U., 1976. Bar: Ohio 1976, Okla. 1982. Gen. counsel Kallstrom Real Estate, Akron, Ohio 1976-81; ptnr. Kallstrom & Ming, Edmond, Okla., 1982-84, Reed, Kallstrom, Shadid & Pipes, Oklahoma City, 1984-86; of counsel Speck, Philbin, Fleig, Trudgeon & Lutz, Oklahoma City, 1987-99, Lynn & Neville, Oklahoma City 1999-2000, Hartzog,Conger, Cason & Neville, Oklahoma City, 2000—. Instr. real estate law Akron U., 1979-81, Cen. State U., Edmond, 1982-84; instr. bus law Okla. Christian Coll., Edmond, 1984. Mem. Okla. Bar Assn., Oklahoma City Real Property Lawywers Assn., Federalist Soc. Office: Hartzog Conger et al 1600 Bank of Okla Plz 201 Robert S Kerr Ave Oklahoma City OK 73102 E-mail: jkallstrom@hartzoglaw.com.

KALM, ARNE, investment banker; b. Tallinn, Estonia, Apr. 4, 1936; arrived in U.S., 1945; s. Juri and Aino (Kalm) Sammul; m. Celia Riddle, June 14, 1975; children: Michael, Linda, Peter. BS, Calif. Inst. Tech., 1956, MS, 1957; MBA Harvard, 1961. V.p. Shareholders Mgmt. Co., L.A., 1970-72, Hollywood Turf Club, Inglewood, Calif., 1972-73; pres. Berry Enterprises, Long Beach, Calif. 1973-82, Berry Industries Corp., Santa Fe Springs, Calif., 1975-84, First Arcadia (Calif.) Corp., 1984—. Bd. dirs. Cresco Ltd., Estonia, Scanforest Ltd. Estonia; mem. employment tng. panel State of Calif., 1990-92. Bd. dirs. Meth

Hosp. So. Calif., 1995-2001, chmn. 1999-2001; v.p. Estonian League West Coast, 1961-63, pres. 1997-99; v.p. Americans for Congl. Action to Free the Baltic States, 1961-71; West Coast dir. Estonian/Am. Nat. Coun., 1966-74; pres. Calif. Rep. Heritage Groups Coun., 1971-73; nat. chmn. Calif. Inst. Tech. Alumni Fund, 1979-80. Mem. Calif. Inst. Tech. Alumni Assn. (pres. 1982-83). Lutheran. Office: First Arcadia Corp 444 E Huntington Dr Arcadia CA 91006-6203

KALMAN, ANDREW, manufacturing company executive; b. Hungary, Aug. 14, 1919; came to U.S., 1922, naturalized, 1935; s. Louis and Julia (Bognar) K.; m. Violet Margaret Kish, June 11, 1949; children: Andrew Joseph, Richard Louis, Laurie Ann. With Detroit Engring. & Machine Co., 1947-66, exec. v.p., gen. mgr., 1952-66; exec. v.p. and dir. Indian Head, Inc., 1966-75, also dir. Dir. Acme Precision Products, 1959-80, Reef Energy Corp., 1980-84. Trustee emeritus Alma (Mich.) Coll.; bd. dirs. Am. Hungarian Found., New Brunswick, N.J.; mem. adv. coun., mem. exec. com., U. Mich. Ctr. for Communication Disorders. Home: 708 S Military St Dearborn MI 48124-2108 Office: The Buhl Bldg 535 Griswold Ste 1900 Detroit MI 48226 Office Fax: 313-496-1300.

KALMAN, BERNADETTE, neurologist, researcher; d. Ilona Nemeth and Janos E. Kalman. MD summa cum laude, Med. U. Pecs, 1982; PhD, Thomas Jefferson U., 1995, Hungarian Acad. Scis. Med. diploma Med. Licensing, 1982. Resident in neurology County Hosp., Hungary, 1982—86; neuroimmunology fellow Neurology, Huddinge Hosp., Karolinska Inst., Stockholm, 1987—88. Immunogenetics fellow Nat. Inst. Hematology and Immunology, Budapest, 1988—89; jr. faculty Nat. Inst. Neurology, Budapest, 1990, visting neurology fellow, London, 1998—99; neuroimmunology fellow Neurology, Thomas Jefferson U., Philadelphia, 1990—93, rsch. asst. prof., 1993—96; asst. prof., dir. of neuroimmunology Neurology, Hahnemann U., Philadelphia, 1996—2002; dir. of MS rsch., assoc. prof. Neurology, SLRHC, Columbia U., New York, 2002—; vis. scientist Wellcome Trust Ctr. for Human Genetics, Oxford, 2000—01. Contbr. articles to profl. jours. Mem. internal rev. bd. Hahnemann U., Phila., 1997—2001. Recipient Recognition outstanding accomplishments Med. U., Hungarian Republic, 1978, 1980, 1981; grant, Nat. MS Soc., 1992, 1994—95, 1996—97, 1996—2000, Celgene, 1996, Nat. MS Soc., 2000—02, 2002—, Traveling grant, Buuroughs Wellcome Fund, 2000—01, grant, Wadsworth Found., 2002—. Mem.: Am. Acad. of Neurology. Achievements include research in immunological, immunogenetic and genetic characterization of multiple sclerosis; screening for mutations in genes of Complex I; screening for pathogenic mutations in mitochondrial DNA. Avocations: art, running, hiking, literature, classical music. Office: Neurology SLRHC Columbia University 432W 58th Street New York NY 10019 Office Fax: 212-523-8859.

KALMAN, MARC, radio station executive; b. Appleton, Wis. m. Gail Thoen; children: Robert, Todd, Stacie. Student, Am. U. Disc jockey Sta. WJPD, Ishpeming, Mich., 1967, Sta. WMBD, Peoria, Ill., 1967; account exec. Sta. WMIN, 1968, Sta. KRSI, 1968-69, Sta. WDGY, 1969-74, gen. sales mgr., 1974-81; v.p./gen. mgr. Blair Radio, 1981-88; gen. sales mgr. Sta. WCCO, 1988-92; v.p./gen. mgr. Sta. WLOL, Mpls. Bd. dirs. Variety Children's Hosp. Mem. Minn. Broadcasters Assn. (bd. dirs.). Avocation: spectator sports. Office: WLOL 60 S 6th St Ste 930 Minneapolis MN 55402 4409

KALMAN, RUDOLF EMIL, research mathematician, system scientist; b. Budapest, Hungary, May 19, 1930; s. Otto and Ursula (Grundmann) Kalman; m. Constantina Stavrou, Sept. 12, 1959; children: Andrew E.F.C., Ellisabeth K. SB, MIT, 1953, SM, 1954; DSc, Columbia U., 1957; DEng (hon.), U. Bologna, 1988; DSc (hon.), U. Kyoto, Japan, 1990; PhD (hon.), Heriot Watt U., Edinburgh, Scotland, 1990, Tech. U. Crete, 1993, Budapest Tech. U., 1999. Staff engr. IBM Research Lab., Poughkeepsie, NY, 1957—58; research mathematician Research Inst. Advanced Studies, Balt., 1958—64; prof. engring. mech. and elec. engring. Stanford U., 1964—67, prof. math. system theory, 1967—71; grad. rsch. prof. Ctr. for Math. System Theory U. Fla., 1971—92; dir. Center for Math. System Theory, U. Fla., 1971—92, prof. emeritus, 1992—; prof. math. sys. theory Swiss Fed. Inst. Tech., Zurich, 1973—97. Sci. adviser Ecole Nationale Superieure des Mines de Paris, 1968—; mem. sci. adv. bd. Laboratorio di Cibernetica, Naples, 1970—73. Author: Topics in Mathematical System Theory, 1969, over 150 sci. and tech. papers; editl. bd. Internat. Jour. Math. Modelling, Jour. Computer and Systems Scis., Jour. Nonlinear Analysis, Jour. Optimization Theory and Applications, Applied Math. Letters, Math. of Control, Signals and Systems, Jour. Forecasting, Revue Internationale du Systemique. Named Outstanding Young Scientist, Md. Acad. Sci., 1962; recipient IEEE medal of honor, 1974, Rufus Oldenburger medal, ASME, 1976, Centennial medal, IEEE, 1984, 1st Kyoto prize, Inamori Found., 1985, Steele prize, Am. Math. Soc., 1987, Bellman prize, Automatic Control Coun., 1997; fellow Guggenheim, IHES Bures-sur-Yvette, 1971. Fellow: Am. Acad. Arts and Scis.; mem.: NAS (U.S.), NAE (U.S.), Russian Acad. Scis. (fgn.), Inst. de France (fgn.), Academie des Scis., Hungarian Acad. Scis. (fgn.). Office: ETH Zentrum CH-8092 Zurich Switzerland

KALMANSON, JENNIFER DAWN, systems engineer, physicist; BA in Physics, BA in French, Hiram Coll., 1996; MS, Fla. Inst. Technology, 1998. Software engr. Software Technology, Inc., Alexandria, Va., 1998-2000; sys. engr. Lockheed Martin Info. Tech., Lanham, Md., 2000—02, High Tech. Solutions, Crystal City, Va., 2003—. Mem. AIAA, Am. Phys. Soc., Am. Geophys. Union, Zonta Internat. Avocations: scuba diving, singing opera.

KALMAR, CARLOS, music director; m. Britta Kalmar; children: Svenja, Katja. Condr. Vienna Volksoper, Vienna, 1987; music dir. Hamburg Symphony, 1987—91, Stuttgart Philharmonic, 1991—95, Anhaltisches Theater Dessau and Philharmonie Dessau, 1996—2000, Vienna Niederosterreichisches Tonkunstlevorchester, Vienna, 2000—. Prin. condr. Grant Park Music Festival, Chgo.; guest condr. numerous symphonies and orch. Avocations: hiking, cooking. Office: Ste 200 921 SW Washington Portland OR 97205Austria*

KALNICKI, SHALOM, radiologist, educator; b. Tel Aviv, July 18, 1951; s. Samuel and Dina K.; m. Rachel Leia Cukier, May 20, 1975; children: Miriam, Michael, Dina Eva. MD, U. Sao Paulo, 1974. Resident Montefiore Hosp. Med. Ctr., Bronx, 1975-78, chief resident, 1978-79; med. instr. U. Sao Paulo Med. Sch., Brazil, 1979-83; asst. prof., dir. radiotherapy dept. Hosp. of Albert Einstein Coll. Medicine, Bronx, 1983-84; asst. prof. clin. radiotherapy Mt. Sinai Med. Ctr., N.Y.C., 1984-88; assoc. prof. Magee Women's Hosp., oncologist dept. radiation oncology, U. Pitts., 1988—; chmn. dept. radiation oncology Allegheny Gen. Hosp., Pitts., 1993-2000; vice chmn. for clin. affairs, dept. radiation oncology U. Pitts. Med. Ctr., 2000—; vice chmn. clin. affairs U. Pitts. Cancer Inst., 2000—; prof. radiation oncology U. Pitts., 2000—. Contbr. articles to profl. jours. Named Outstanding House Officer, Montefiore Hosp. Med. Ctr. Alumni Assn., 1979; Sao Paulo Rsch. Found. grantee, 1972. Mem. Am. Soc. Therapeutic Radiologists, Am. Soc. Clin. Oncology, N.Y. Acad. Sci., N.Y. Cancer Soc., N.Y. Roentgen Ray Soc. Home: 5520 Northumberland St Pittsburgh PA 15217-1131 Office: UPMC Cancer Ctr 5th Fl 544 5150 Center Ave Pittsburgh PA 15232

KALNINS, ANDIS IMANTS, civil engineer; b. Teaneck, N.J., June 7, 1969; s. Imants and Dorothy Ann (Klauser) K. BS in Civil Engring., N.J. Inst. Tech., 1992; MBA in Mgmt. Info. Sys., Montclair State U., 2001. Lic. profl. engr., N.J. Project mgr. Siciliano Consulting Engrs., Wood Ridge, N.J., 1987-92; constrn. engr. Port Authority of NY/NJ, N.Y.C., 1993-97; engring. mgr. Verizon, Farmingdale, NJ, 1997—. Mem. ASCE, Nat. Soc. Profl. Engrs. Republican. Episcopalian. Avocations: skiing, golf, Judo. Office: Verizon 5100 Belmar Blvd Farmingdale NJ 07727 Home: 3 Omaha Dr Cranford NJ 07016-3317

KALNITZ, PAUL RICHARD, software developer; b. Rochester, N.Y., Mar. 31, 1958; MSCS, U. Buffalo, 1986. Software engr. Strippit, Akron, N.Y., 1986-90, Azatar, AIC, Rochester, N.Y., 1990-95; owner, software engr. Soft Landing Computer, Inc., Rochester, N.Y., 1995—. Cons. Asher Computing Svcs., Inc., Rochester, 1996-97. Author: (booklet) Tutorial on Fuzzy Logic, 1996. Mem. Assn. for Computing Machinery. Home: 1 Crescent Hill Rd Pittsford NY 14534-2404

KALOF, LINDA HENRY, sociologist, educator; b. Norfolk, Va., Dec. 17, 1946; d. William Douglas Henry and Mary Elizabeth Bailey; m. Thomas Michael Dietz; children: Alexandra Kalof, Adam Henry. BA, U. Fla., 1975; PhD, Am. U., 1989. Asst. prof. SUNY, Plattsburgh, 1989—95, assoc. prof., 1995-96, George Mason U., Fairfax, Va., 1996—2002, prof., 2002—03, Mich. State U., East Lansing, 2003—. Co-author: (book) Evaluating Social Science Research, 1996; author: Race, Gender and Sexual Harassment, 2001; contbr. articles to profl. jours. Office: Mich State U Dept Sociology East Lansing MI 48824 E-mail: lkalof@msu.edu.

KALOOSDIAN, ROBERT ARAM, lawyer; b. Watertown, Mass., Oct. 29, 1930; s. Paul and Grace (Mugrditchian) K.; m. Marianne Kaloosdian, June 30, 1957; children: Paul, Lori, Sonia. AB, Clark U., 1952; JD, Boston U., 1957, LLM, 1962. Bar: Mass. 1957, U.S. Supreme Ct. 1962. Assoc. Miles, Curran & Malkasian, Boston, 1958-60; pvt. practice Watertown, 1960—; assoc. Kaloosdian, Ciccarelli & Lerman, Watertown, 1982-99; law offices Robert A. Kaloosdian, 1999—. Corporator Watertown Savs. Bank, 1972—2003, trustee, 1976—2002, mem. cmty. reinvestment com. Corporator Mt. Auburn Hosp., Cambridge, Mass., 1978—2002; pres. Armenian Nat. Inst., Washington, 1996—. Kaloosdian/Mugar Chair of Genocide and History Clark U., 2002. Bd. dirs. Armenian Assembly of Am., 1972-2000, co-chmn., 1974-83, chmn., 1990-92; assoc. dir. State Dept. AID Grant to Lebanon, 1978—; mem. Gov.'s Task Force on Ethinic Heritage, Boston, 1976. With U.S. Army, 1952-54. Recipient Prince of Cilicia award, Catholosate of Antelias, Beirut, 1980, Dist. Svc. award Armenian Assembly, 2000. Mem. ATLA, Middlesex Bar Assn., Mass. Bar Assn. (spl. asst. to pres. 2000), Rotary (pres. 1975-76), Delta Theta Phi. Democrat. Mem. Armenian Apostolic Ch. Home: 25 Fletcher Rd Belmont MA 02478-2014 Office: 43 Mount Auburn St Watertown MA 02472-3924 E-mail: kaloosdian@aol.com.

KALOW, DAVID ARTHUR, lawyer; b. Queens, N.Y., May 6, 1953; s. Samuel Jay and Joan Elaine (Peirce) K.; m. Janet Lee Samuels, June 18, 1978; children: Margaret Emily, Jacob Richard, Benjamin Charles. BA, U. Chgo., 1974, JD, 1976. Bar: N.Y. 1977, U.S. Dist. Ct. (so. and ea. dists.) N.Y. 1977, U.S. Ct. Appeals (5th cir.) 1983, U.S. Ct. Appeals (2d cir.) 1984, U.S. Ct. Appeals (fed. cir.) 1984, U.S. Supreme Ct. 1987. Assoc. Chadbourne, Parke, N.Y.C., 1976-79, Amster, Rothstein, N.Y.C., 1980-81, Lieberman, Rudolph & Nowak, N.Y.C., 1981-85, ptnr., 1986-96, Kalow, Springut & Bressler, N.Y.C., 1996—. Mem. ABA (com. on sci. and tech., patent, trademark and copyright, computer law). Office: Kalow Springut & Bressler 380 Lexington Ave # 4300 New York NY 10168 0002 Address: 122 E 42nd St Fl 43 New York NY 10168-4399

KALOW, WERNER, pharmacologist, toxicologist; b. Cottbus, Germany, Feb. 15, 1917; emigrated to Can., 1951, naturalized, 1957; s. Johannes Bernhard and Maria Elisabeth (Heyde) K; m. Patricia M. Arnold, May 3, 1991; children from earlier marriage: Peter Bernard, Barbara Irene. Student in medicine, U. Greifswald, Ger., 1935-36, U. Graz, Austria, 1936-37, U. Gottingen, Ger., 1939-40; MD, U. Konigsberg, Ger., 1941. Research asst. Berlin U., 1947-49; research fellow, instr. U. Pa., 1949-51; lectr. U. Toronto, Ont., Can., 1951-53, asst. prof. pharmacology, 1953-55, assoc. prof., 1955-62, prof., 1962—, chmn. dept. pharmacology, 1966-77. Dir. biol. research C.H. Boehringer Sohn, Ingelheim, Ger., 1965-66 Author: Pharmacogenetics, Heredity and the Response to Drugs, 1962; editor: (with B.N. La Du) Pharmacogenetics, 1968, (with R.A. Gordon and B.A. Britt) International Symposium on Malignant Hyperthermia, 1973, (with H.W. Goedde and D.P. Agarwal) Ethnic Differences in Reactions to Drugs and Xenobiotics, 1986, Pharmacogenetics of Drug Metabolism, 1992, (with U.A. Meyer and R. Tyndale) Pharmacogenomics, 2001. Recipient Drug Info. Assn. Disting. Career award, 1997. Fellow Royal Soc. Can.; mem. Pharm. Soc. Can. (pres. 1963-64, Upjohn award 1982), Can. Physiol. Soc., Am. Soc. Pharmacology and Exptl. Therapeutics (Oscar B. Hunter Meml. award 1993), Can. Anaesthetist Soc. (hon., Rsch. Recognition award 1993, Killam award 2001), Deutsche Pharmakologische Gesellschaft. Achievements include discovering pharmacogenetic variants of cholinesterase, 1956, thereby initiating the science of pharmacogenetics, 1962; devel. pharmaco-diagnosis of malignant hyperthermia, 1970; promoted studies of pharmacoanthropology (interethnic drug comparisons), 1983-84; used caffein metabolism as a tool of biochemical epidemiology, 1986. Home: 130 McGill St Toronto ON Canada M5B 1H6 Office: U Toronto Med Scis Bldg Toronto ON Canada M5S 1A8 Business E-Mail: w.kalow@utoronto.ca. *It is good to be curious. It is better if being curious is one's work.*

KALSNER, STANLEY, pharmacologist, physiologist, educator; b. N.Y.C., Aug. 21, 1936; s. William Louis and Sadie (Feldman) K.; m. Jenny Book, Aug. 4, 1963; children— Lydia, Pamela, Louisa. AB, NYU, 1958; postgrad., SUNY Downstate Med. Ctr., 1959-62; PhD, U. Man., Can., 1966; postgrad., Cambridge (Eng.) U., 1966-67. Asst. prof. pharmacology U. Ottawa, Ont., Can., 1967-72, assoc. prof., 1972-77, prof., 1977-85; prof. joint dept. physiology and pharmacology CUNY, 1985—. Med. rsch. scientist on heart disease and blood vessel function; sci. referee Med. Rsch. Coun. Can., Can. Heart Found. Editor, contbr. chpts. to books, articles to jours.; asso. editor Can. Jour. Physiology and Pharmacology, until 1985; mem. editorial bd.: Jour. Autonomic Pharmacology, Blood Vessels. USPHS fellow, 1960-67; Med. Rsch. Coun.-NRC and Ont. Heart Found. grantee; Am. Heart Assn. grantee, 1987—. Mem. AAAS, AAUP, Can. Pharmacology Soc., Am. Soc. Pharmacology and Therapeutics. Home: 21 Hillcrest Rd Suffern NY 10901-6834 Office: CUNY Med Sch 138th St and Convent Ave New York NY 10031 *I believe that the greatest mystery of all is life and that it is worth devoting oneself to its solution.*

KALTCHEV, IVO, musician, educator; b. Vladimirovo, Bulgaria, Jan. 12, 1961; arrived in U.S., 1990; s. Lyubomir Kaltchev and Vera Kaltcheva. MusB in Piano Performance, Sofia (Bulgaria) State Acad. Music, 1987; MusM in Piano Performance, Yale U., 1992; Mus D, Rutgers U., 1996. Asst. prof. piano Sofia State Acad. of Music, Sofia, 1988—90; asst. prof. Sofia State U., 1987—90; artist piano faculty Westminster Choir Coll./Conservatory, Princeton, NJ, 1996—2000; asst. prof. Cath. U. Am., Washington, 2000—. Faculty World Piano Pedagogy Conf., 1996—; competition adjudicator U. Md., College Park, 2001; competiton adjudicator Wash. Music Teachers Assn., Washington, 2001—; competition adjudicator 15th Concurso Juvenil de Piano, Toledo, 2002, Broad Creek Music Festival, Washington, 2001—02. Musician: (CD recordings) Piano Works by Soler, Chopin, Debussy, Rachmaninov and B'Racz, 1995, Concertos for Marimba and Piano by Creston and Kurka (with G. Giannascoli), 1997, Piano Works of Charles T. Griffes, 1998, Concerto for Marimba and Piano by J. Basta (with G. Giannascoli), 1999, World Premiere Recording of Piano Works of Florent Schmitt, 2002; musician: (solo pianist) Complete Solo Piano Music of Claude Debussy, 1994; musician: (pianist) Complete Songs for Voice and Piano by Henry Duparc, 2002; musician: (concerts) World, Europe and US Premieres of works by Schmitt, Antheil, Copland, Samonov, Griffes, Spassov, Miki, B'Racz, Basta, Creston, Kurka, Zorman, D.Chavez., solo, concerto, chamber music performances, 2002. Recipient 2nd prize, Obretenov Nat. Competition, Bulgaria, 1979, 1978, 6th Citta di Salerno Internat. Piano Competition, Italy, 1979, 4th prize and prize Musicians' Assn. Bulgaria, 1st P. Vladigerov Internat. Piano Competition, 1986, Disting. Performer prize, 7th Palm Beach Invitational Internat. Piano Competition, 1993, Genia Robinor Pedagogy award, Piano Tchrs. Soc. Am., 2000, 1999, award for Tchg. Excellence, Princeton Steinway Soc., 2000. Mem.: Musicians Assn. Bulgaria, Coll. Music Soc., Music Teachers Nat. Assn. Office: Cath U Am Benjamin T Rome Sch Music Washington DC 20064 Office Fax: 202-319-6280. Personal E-mail: kaltchev@cua.edu. Business E-Mail: kaltchev@cua.edu.

KALTENBACH, C(ARL) COLIN, dean, educator; b. Buffalo, Wyo., Mar. 22, 1939; s. Carl H. and Mary Colleen (McKeag) K.; m. Ruth Helene Johnson, Aug. 22, 1964; children: James Earl, John Edward. BSc, U. Wyo., 1961; MSc, U. Nebr., 1963; PhD, U. Ill., 1967. Postdoctoral fellow U. Melbourne, Australia, 1967-69; from asst. prof. to prof. U. Wyo., Laramie, 1969-89, assoc. dean, dir. Agrl. Expt. Sta., 1980-89; vice dean, dir. Agrl. Expt. Sta. U. Ariz., Tucson, 1989—. Contbr. 200 articles to profl. publs. Named Outstanding Alumnus Coll. Agriculture U. Wyo., 1991. Mem. Nat. Assn. State Univs. and Land Grant Colls. (mem. policy bd. dirs. 2003--), Soc. for Study Reprodn. (treas. 1979-82), Am. Soc. Animal Sci., Civitan (officer 1972-85), Agrl. Experiment State Dirs. (chair 1996-97). Office: U Ariz Coll Agriculture Tucson AZ 85721-0001 E-mail: kltnbch@ag.arizona.edu.

KALTENBACH, JANE COUFFER, zoology educator; b. Chgo., Dec. 21, 1922; d. Robert William and Frances Jane (Rayner) C.; m. John Paul Kaltenbach, 1946; m. Robert Leslie Townsend, Aug. 26, 1966. BS, Beloit Coll., 1944; MA, U. Wis., 1946; PhD, U. Iowa, 1950. Tchr. asst. in zoology U. Wis., Madison, 1944-47, rsch. assoc., 1950-53; asst. zoology U. Iowa, Iowa City, 1947-50; Am. Cancer Soc. fellow Wenner-Grens Inst., Stockholm, 1953-56; asst. prof. zoology Northwestern U., Evanston, Ill., 1956-58; asst. prof., then assoc. prof. zoology Mt. Holyoke Coll., South Hadley, Mass., 1958-70, prof. biology, 1970-93, chair biology, 1980-86, prof. emeritus, 1993—. Contbr. articles to profl. publs. Grantee Northwestern U. Grad. Sch., 1957, 58, NSF, 1960 63, Mt. Holyoke Coll., 1966-91, Rsch. Corp., 1987-90. Fellow AAAS; mem. Soc. for Integrative and Comparative Biology, Am. Soc. Anatomists, Soc. Devel. Biology, Corp. Marine Biol. Lab., Soc. Biology and Medicine, Phi Beta Kappa, Sigma Xi. Home: 139 Cold Hill Granby MA 01033-9705 Office: Mt Holyoke Coll Dept Biol Scis South Hadley MA 01075 E-mail: jtownsen@mtholyoke.edu.

KALTER, ALAN, advertising agency executive; m. Chris Lezotte. With W.B. Doner & Co., Southfield, Mich., 1967—, exec. v.p., dir. retail divsn., 1990, vice chmn. account mgmt., 1990-92, pres., COO, 1992-95; CEO, chmn. W. B. Doner & Co., Southfield, Mich., 1995—. Office: W B Doner & Co 25900 Northwest ern Hwy Southfield MI 48075-1067*

KALTON, GRAHAM, survey statistician; b. Bromley, Kent, Eng., Mar. 5, 1936; came to U.S., 1979; s. Gordon and Stella (Vickery) K.; m. Francis Helen Johnson, Mar. 31, 1962; children: Alan Gordon, Alison Frances. BS in Econs., London Sch. Econs., 1958, MS, 1960; PhD, U. Southampton (Eng.), 1979. Grade B tchr. The Polytechnic, Regent St, London, 1959-60; asst. lectr. London Sch. Econs., 1961-64, lectr., 1964-68, sr. lectr., 1968-70, reader, 1970-71; prof. U. Southampton, 1971-79; prof. dept biostats., rsch. scientist U. Mich., Ann Arbor, 1979-91, prof. dept. stats., 1989-91; sr. statistician, sr. v.p. Westat Inc., 1992—; rsch. prof. joint program in survey methodology U. Md., 1995—2001, 2003—. Nat. assoc. Nat. Acads. Author: The Public Schools: A Factual Survey, 1966, (with C.A. Moser) Survey Methods in Social Investigation, 1971, Introduction to Survey Sampling, 1983, Compensating for Missing Survey Data, 1983. Fellow AAAS, Royal Stats. Soc. U.K. (chmn. social stats. sect. com. 1976-78), Internat. Statis. Inst. (chmn. nominations com. 1987), Am. Statis. Assn. (chmn. survey rsch. methods sect. 1986), Internat. Assn. Survey Statisticians (pres. 1991-93), Am. Assn. for Pub. Opinion Rsch., Wash. Stats. Soc. (pres. 1997-98), Nat. Acads. (nat. assoc.). Office: Westat 1650 Rsch Blvd Rockville MD 20850

KALTSOS, ANGELO JOHN, electronics executive, educator, photographer; b. Boston, Aug. 19, 1930; s. John Angelo and Rita Thomas (Goudas) K.; m. Verna Kay Wilson, June 30, 1952 (dec. Jan. 1973); children: Pamela, Elaine, Gregory, Stephanie, Lenora, Demetra, Dana. Student, Mass. Radio and TV Sch., Boston, 1955-57, Harvard Coll. Extension, 1964, Boston State Coll., 1965-67, U. N.M., 1976, Fitchburg State Coll., 1977. Clk. U.S. Postal Svc., Boston, 1954-57; electronic rsch. technician Crosley div. Avco, Cin., 1957; electronic rsch. production technician Raytheon Mfg. Co., Waltham, Mass., 1957-63; educator Cambridge (Mass.) Sch. Dept., 1961-81; ind. ethnology rsch. N.Mex., 1969—; mgr. Pampas, Inc., Boston, 1987-90. Bd. dirs. Expansion Dance Co., Boston; cons. 5 P.I.E., Albuquerque, 1976—, Indian Tribal Group, N.Mex.; lectr. S.W. Indian Culture in Boston, Cambridge area, 1990—; pres., treas. Spartan Enterprises, Inc., 1965-69. Author: Southwest Indian, 1986; one man shows include Christmas Tree Gallery, Manteo, N.C., 1977, 4th St. Photo Gallery, N.Y.C., 1980, Cambride Rindge and Latin Sch., Mass., 1981, Jay's, Cambridge, Mass., 1983, Here Today Gallery, Boston, 1984, Andover (Maine) Town Hall, 1984, 86, Piedmont Art Assn., Martinsville, Va., 1985-86, Cambalache Gallery, Boston, 1986-87, The 4th St. Gallery, N.Y.C., 1990, Andover (Maine) Pub. Libr., 1997-98; contbg. journalist in field. Chmn. No Thank Q Hydro Quebec, Andover, Maine, 1988-91, coord., Dryden, Maine, 1991-2001; regional and media coord. N.E. Alliance to Protect James Bay, 1990-91, exec. bd., adv. bd., treas., 1991-2001, project dir., 1995-2001; project dir., treas. Hydro Electric Watch, 2001—; senate faculty Cambridge Sch. Dept., 1980-81; sec. New Eng. Model Car Assn. of Raceways, 1966-69; educator Cambridge Adult Ctr., 1990-97, Paulist Ctr., Boston, 1991-92; judge Andover amateur photo contest, 1996-99, coord., judge, 2001—. Recipient Robert Sweeney award Rindge Alumni Assn., 1996. Mem. Appalachian Mountain Club (life). Greek Orthodox. Avocations: ethnography, entomology, cooking, gardening, hiking. Home: PO Box 33 Andover ME 04216-0033

KALTVEDT, LARRY DEAN, elementary school educator; b. Estherville, Iowa, June 22, 1944; s. Lester Salmer and Marion Lorraine (Myhre) Kaltvedt; 1 child, Otis Antares. AA, Coll. Marin, 1972; BA in Edn., Ctrl. Wash. U., 1980; EdM, Harvard U., 1986; postgrad., U. Tex., U. Calif., Santa Cruz, U. Saskatchewan, Mankato State U., Rio Salado Coll., Iowa Lakes C.C. Cert. profl. educator Wash., Iowa, Mass., Tex., Calif., Ariz. Author: SJNA's Saga, 1995, (screenplays) Girl From Botany Bay, 1997. With USCG, 1965—69. Mem.: Harvard Alumni Assn. Avocations: wilderness trekking, travel.

KALU, KALU NDUKWE, public administration educator, researcher, consultant; s. Ndukwe Kalu Ndukwe and Ogbenyalu Ndukwe Kalu; children: Rose Chinyere, Renee Aluba N. BSc, Rutgers State U., 1977—79; MBA, Atlanta U., 1980—82; PhD, Tex. Tech U., 1988—94; Post-Doctoral Fellow, Yale U., Sch. of Medicine, 1996—2000. Lectr. polit. sci., pub. adminstrn., health polit. and policy Lamar U., Beaumont, Tex., 1994—96, U. of Conn., 1997—2001; asst. prof., dir. pub. affairs program Emporia State U., Kans., 2000—; rsch. fellow Yale Ctr. for Internat. and Area Studies (Yale U.), 2001—. Mem., bd. of directors ASPA (Am. Soc. for Pub. Adminstrn.) Kans. Chpt., Topeka, 2002—. Schedule programs, policy input to nat. office ASPA , 2002. Mem.: ASPA, Pi Sigma Alpha (hon.), Pi Alpha Alpha (hon.). E-mail: kalukalu@emporia.edu.

KALUDIS, GEORGE, management consultant, book company executive, educator; b. Balt., Oct. 7, 1938; s. Steven George and Theresa (Topal) K.; m. Eugenia Leone Mihalakis, July 21, 1962; children: Stephen George, Michele Maria, William Michael, Kirk Jamie. BA, U. Md., 1960, MEd, 1965; PhD, Fla. State U., 1968. Asst. dean student life U. Md., 1960-65; resident instr. U. S. Fla., 1965-66; dir. div. planning and evaluation State Univ. Sys. Fla., 1966-70; vice chancellor ops. and fin. planning, assoc. prof. mgmt. Vanderbilt U., 1970-76, adj. assoc. prof. mgmt., 1976-78; exec. v.p. Ingram Book Co., 1976-78; chmn., pres. Kaludis Consulting, Washington, 1978—. Mem. tech. coun. Nat. Ctr. Higher Edn. Mgmt. Sys., 1970—72, bd. dirs., 1972—76, chmn. bd., 1975—76; pres., bd. dirs. Frat. Advisors Group, Inc., Tallahassee, 1968—70; mem. com. chmn. Nat. Com. on Financing Postsecondary Edn., 1972—74. Editor: Strategies for Budgeting, new Directions in Higher Education, 1973; mem. editl. bd.: On the Horizon, 1996—2001, contbg. author: Mission Management a New Synthesis, vol. 1, Dollars, Distance and Online Education. Bd. dirs. NCCJ, Nashville, St. Photios Nat. Shrine, 1986-87; 1st v.p. Family and Children's Svcs., Inc., 1978-80; chmn. Spl. Com. on Cable TV, Nashville, 1982-95; mem. parish coun. Holy Trinity Greek Orthodox Ch., 1971-94, pres., 1972-78, 81-83, 92-94, Stewardship Commn., Greek Orthodox Archdiocese, 1993-95, archdiocesan coun., 1994-98, 2000—, co-chmn. com. on strategic and long range planning, 1994-97, diocese coun., N.J., 1999—, v.p.; parish coun. St. George Greek Orthodox Ch., Bethesda, 1998, sec., chair stewardship com., 2000, pres.; del. World Clergy-Laity Congress, Greek Orthodox Ch., Istanbul, 2000, mem. Leadership 100, 2001; mem. Order of St. Andrew; mem. Nat. Capital campaign com. Fla. State U., 2001; bd. trustees Internat. Orthodox Christian Charities, 2003—. With U.S. Army, 1962-64. Recipient Medal of St. Paul award Greek Orthodox Archdiocese, 1992, Disting. Alumnus award U. Md. Coll. Edn., 1995, Order of St. Andrew of Ecumenical Patriarch, 2003—. Mem. Am. Assn. Higher Edn., Assn. Instnl. Rsch., Nat. Assn. Coll. and Univ. Bus. Officers, Fin. Execs. Inst. (pres. Nashville chpt. 1975), Nashville Area C. of C. (gov.), Am. Hellenic Ednl. Progressive Assn., U. Md. alumni ctr. cabinet, U. Md. arena seating planning com., Omicron Delta Kappa, Pi Sigma Alpha, Sigma Phi Epsilon (chmn. commn. on univ. rels. 1992-93). Office: Ste 440 1919 M St NW Washington DC 20036

KALUGER, GEORGE, clinical psychologist, educator; b. Tataria, Alba Iulia, Romania, Sept. 20, 1921; s. Niculae and Valeria (Suteu) K.; m. O. Meriem Fair, June 11, 1947. BS in Edn., Slippery Rock (Pa.) U., 1946; MEd, U. Pitts., 1948, PhD, 1950; postdoctoral, Pa. State U., Univ. Park, 1955. Lic psychologist, Pa., tchr., Pa. Tchr. science and math. Butler (Pa.) City Schs., 1946 49, guidance counselor, 1949-53; prof. edn. and psychology Shippensburg (Pa.) U., 1953-72, prof. psychology, 1972-89, chair dept. psychology, 1972-76; part time pvt. practice in clin. psychology, 1954-93. Cons. rsch. learning disabilities Capital Area Inter. Unit, Camp Hill, Pa., 1960-74, Lincoln Intermediate Unit, Cross

Keys, Pa., 1970-76; psychol. cons. Bur. Vocat. Rehab., Harrisburg, Pa., 1954-64; cons. perceptual devel. ctr. Shippensburg Area Schs., 1970-74. Co-author: Clinical Aspects of Remedial Reading, 1963, 5th printing; Psychology and Sociology, 1969, Profiles in Human Development, 1976, Reading and Learning Disabilities, 1969, 78 (2 edits.), Human Development: Span of Life, 1974, 79, 84 (3 edits.), Walk on the Sunny Side of Life, 2002. Pres. Tuesday Club, Shippensburg, 1958, Shippensburg Hist. Soc., 1961, Rotary Club, Shippensburg, 1963; nat. co-chmn. Shippensburg Univ. Found., 1987. 1st Lt. USAAF, 1942-45. Recipient Commonwealth Disting. Chair award Commonwealth of Pa., 1978-79, Commonwealth Disting. Tchg. Fellow award, 1978-79, Citation for Humanitarian Svc. Pa. Cerebral Palsy, 1964, Shippensburg U. Alumni Exceptional Svc. award, 1982. Fellow Pa. Psychol. Assn. (pres. acad. divsn. 1972); mem. Am. Psychol. Assn., Phi Delta Kappa (Educator of the Yr. award 1990). Avocations: adventure travelling, cultural photography, workshops in neuropsychology, writing. Home: 625 Brenton St Shippensburg PA 17257-2113

KALUGER, MERIEM FAIR, psychologist, educator; b. Butler, Pa., Oct. 27, 1921; d. Julian Harvey and Frances Ada (Reynders) Fair; m. George Kaluger, June 11, 1947. BS in Edn., Slippery Rock U., 1943; M of Letters, U. Pitts., 1946; ABD, Shippensburg U., 1976. Cert. tchr., Pa.; lic. psychologist, Pa. Elem. tchr. Butler City Schs., 1943-47; asst. prof. Shippensburg (Pa.) U., 1955; tchr., supr. student tchrs. Rowland Lab. Sch., Shippensburg, 1956; psychologist Bur. Vocat. Rehab., Harrisburg, Pa., 1967-69; program coord. learning disabilities Capital Area Inter. Unit, Camp Hill, Pa., 1970-72, psycho-edn. cons., 1972-74, Lincoln Inter. Unit, Cross Keys, Pa., 1974-76; pvt. practice as psychologist Shippensburg, 1976-93. Adj. prof. Shippensburg U., 1975-76, learning assistance ctr. diagnostic evaluator, 1985-93; cons. perceptual devel. Shippensburg Area Schs., 1970-74. Co-author: Profiles in Human Development, 1976, Reading and Learning Disabilities, 1969, 2d edit., 1978, Human Development: Span of Life, 1974, 3d edit., 1984. Pres. Civic Club, Shippensburg, 1966-67, Coll. Club, Shippensburg, 1986, Shippensburg U. Faculty Wives, 1957-59, 74-75, 96-98; nat. co-chairperson Shippensburg U. Found., 1987; 1st v.p. Shippensburg Hist. Soc., 1997-98, pres., 1999-2000. Recipient Paul Harris award Rotary Club, 1995, Shippensburg U. Alumni Exceptional Svc. award, 1996. Mem. Pa. Psychol. Assn., Order of Ea. Star, Order of White Shrine, Civic Club, Phi Delta Kappa. Avocations: traveling, cultural photography, writing, illustrating. Home: 625 Brenton St Shippensburg PA 17257-2113

KALVER, GAIL ELLEN, dance company executive, musician; b. Chgo., Nov. 25, 1948; d. Nathan Eli and Alice Martha (Jaffe) K. BS in Music Edn., U. Ill., 1970; MA in Clarinet Chgo. Musical Coll., Roosevelt U., 1974. Profl. musician, Chgo., 1970-77; assoc. mgr. Ravinia Festival, Highland Park, Ill., 1977-83; exec. dir. Hubbard Street Dance Chgo., 1984—. Bd. dirs. Chicago Dancers United, Ill. Arts Alliance; mem. dance panel Ill. Arts Council, Chgo., 1983-85; mem. grants panels Chgo. Office Fine Arts, 1985. Editor: Music Explorer (for music edn.), 1983-86. Mem. grants panels NEA, 1992-94; cons. music Nat. Radio Theatre, Chgo., 1983—; mem. adv. coun. Dance Initiative Chgo. Cmty. Trust, Dancers Responding to AIDS; mem. exec. com. Dance for Life, 2003. Office: Hubbard St Dance Chgo 1147 W Jackson Blvd Chicago IL 60607-2905

KALWARA, JOSEPH JOHN, engineer; b. Syracuse, N.Y., June 4, 1953; s. Stanley W. and M. Bonita (Caraglin) K; m. Edith Ann Doust, 1980; children: John C., Joseph S., James V. BS in Forestry, Syracuse U., 1977; BS in Wood Products Engring., SUNY, Syracuse, 1977; AAAS in Archtl. Tech., Onondaga County C.C., 1980. Asst. engr. Firestone Bldg. Products, Carmel, Ind., 1983-84, regional tech. coord., 1984-86, product assurance engr., 1986-88, sr. engr., 1988—. Contbr. articles to profl. jours. Mem. Single-Ply Roofing Inst., Riviera Club (Indpls.). Achievements include research in the development and engineering of building products, insulations and adhesives, sealants, and tapes relative to single-ply roofing membranes and systems; patentee in field. Home: 6050 Broadway St Indianapolis IN 46220-1808 Office: Firestone Bldg Products 525 Congressional Blvd Carmel IN 46032-5644

KALYANARAMAN, RAMKI, education educator, researcher; b. Bareilly, UP, India, Apr. 23, 1968; arrived in U.S., 1995; s. Sivaramakrishnan and Uma Kalyanaraman; m. Veena Gopal, Dec. 24, 1998. BA, IIT, Kharagpur, India, 1991; MA, IIT, Kanpur, India, 1994; PhD, N.C. State Univ., Raleigh, N.C., 1998. Postdoctoral rsch. fellow Oak Ridge Nat. Lab and Lucent Tech., Murray Hill, NJ, 1999—2001; asst. prof. Wash. Univ., St. Louis, 2001—. Contbr. chapters to books, articles to profl. jour. Mem.: IEEE, Materials Rsch. Soc., Sierra, Phi Kappa Phi. Achievements include patents for A processs to fabricate a semiconductor device; discovery of Sci. findings publ. in leading internat. sci. jour. Avocations: squash, music, travel. Home: 7315 Lindell Ave Saint Louis MO 63130 Office: Wash Univ St Louis One Brookings Dr Saint Louis MO 63130

KALYON, DILHAN M(EHMET), chemical engineering educator; b. Bursa, Turkey, June 9, 1954; s. Ahmet Zeki and Meliha Altun K.; m. Safiye Beysel, Aug. 18, 1976; children: Bilgé D., Deniz E. M in Engring., McGill U., Montreal, Can., 1977, D of Engring., 1980; M of Engring. (hon.), Stevens Inst. Tech., 1994. Asst. prof. Stevens Inst. Tech., Hoboken, N.J., 1984-88, assoc. prof., 1988-90, prof. chem. engring., 1990—, Inst. Prof. chair, 1999—; dir. Highly Filled Materials Inst., Hoboken, 1989—. Bd. dirs. Materials Processing and Rsch. Inc., 1989—; cons. for 20 cos., 1987—. Contbr. over 200 articles to profl. jours. and book chpts. Recipient numerous grants from federal and state govts. Mem. N.Y. Acad. Scis., Soc. Plastic Engrs., Soc. of Rheology, British Soc. Rheology, Polymer Processing Soc. Achievements include development of mathematical models of various polymer processing operations including blow molding, injection molding, single and twin screw extrusion; inventions with patents include new on-line rheometer, materials and processes in electromagnetic field shielding, method for particle size determination, and disposal of very toxic liquids. Office: Castle Point St Hoboken NJ 07030-5907

KAM, FREDERICK ANTHONY, internist, physician; b. Port-of-Spain, Trinidad, Feb. 9, 1961; came to U.S., 1979; s. Frederick and Joan Yvonne K.; m. Charlene; children: Brendan, Allison, Charlton. BS, U. Miami, 1983, MD, 1986. Diplomate Am. Bd. Internal Medicine. Intern Jackson Meml. Hosp., 1986-87, resident in internal medicine, 1988-89; co-dir. Gen. Medicine Clinics, Jackson Meml. Hosp. dir. U. Miami Sch. Medicine, 1989-92; med. dir., CEO UM Care, Miami, 1992-95; v.p. med. affairs Collegiate Health Care, Norwalk, Conn., 1995-97; exec. dir. Auburn (Ala.) U. Med. Clinic, 1997—. Mem.: ACP, AMA, Med. Assn. State Ala., Lee County Med. Soc. Roman Catholic. Avocations: tennis, travel, football, fishing. Office: Auburn U Med Clinic 307 W Magnolia Ave Auburn AL 36830-4801

KAM, MITCHELL M.T. business professional; b. Honolulu; BA in Psychology, UCLA, 1986; JD, U. San Diego, 1991; MBA, U. Tex., 1993. Bar: Tex. 1993, D.C. 1996; cert. sr. profl. in Human Resources, 2002. Project coord. Hawaii Transfer Co., Ltd., Honolulu, 1987-88; legal rsch. specialist U. San Diego Sch. Law, 1989-91; cons./group mgr. Novotel Hotel, Venlo, The Netherlands, 1992; dir. bus. devel. and mktg. Pia Piasecki Hurt i Detal, Kielce, Poland, 1994-95; asst. program coord., program liaison Ctr. Internat. Bus. Edn. and Rsch., Austin, Tex., 1997, 2002—03; cons. MBA Enterprise Corps, San Francisco, 1996-97; internat. career specialist U. Tex. Ford Career Ctr., McCombs Sch. Bus., Austin, 1998-2000; sr. mgr. Charles Schwab & Co., Inc., San Francisco, 2000—01; assoc. dir., Career Svcs. Office U. Tex. Sch. Law, Austin, 2003—. Bd. dirs. MBA Enterprise Corps, 1999, 2000. Sr. editor Jour. Contemporary Legal Issues, U. San Diego Sch. Law, 1989-91; assoc. editor: Motions Newspaper, U. San Diego Sch. Law, 1989-91. Mem. ABA, Am. Mktg. Assn., Soc. Competitive Intelligence Profls., Soc. Human Resources Mgmt. Global Forum, State Bar of Tex., D.C. Bar, Phi Kappa Tau. Republican. Roman Catholic.

KAM, THOMAS KWOCK YUNG, accountant educator; b. Honolulu, Nov. 12, 1955; s. William Kwock Yung and Mae S. M. (Yee) K.; m. Sally Ben Huai, July 9, 1983; children: Tiffany L. M., Stephen C. M. BBA, U. Hawaii, 1975, MBA, 1978, postgrad., 1993—. CPA, Hawaii; CMA. Intern Coopers & Lybrand, Honolulu, 1975-76; instr. Beckers CPA Rev. Course, Honolulu, 1982-83; statis. asst. Hawaiian Elec. Co., Inc., Honolulu, 1976-78, assoc. budget analyst, 1978-86; adult edn. tchr. Farrington Cmty. Sch., Honolulu, 1978-84, McKinley Cmty. Sch., Honolulu, 1978-86; lectr. West Oahu Coll., Honolulu, 1986; asst. prof. acctg. and fin. Hawaii Pacific U., Honolulu, 1984—. Mem. Neighborhood Bd. (Liliha-Kapalama), 1980-83; treas., fin. com. chmn. Neighborhood Bd. (Pearl City), 1985-88, vice chair health, edn. and welfare com. 1985, chmn., 1988-93, chmn. devel., planning and zoning com. 93-97; auditor Kams' Soc., 1984-89, 3d v.p., 1990-91, 2d v.p., 1992-93, 1st v.p., 1994-95, pres., 1996-97, bd. dirs. 1998—; mem. loan com. Native Hawaiian Revolving Loan Fund, 1989-91; co-facilitator Pearl City Highlands Elem. Sch. SCBM Coun., 1992-93, 95-96; dir. Pearl City Highlands Elem. Sch., Kokua Hui, 1992-93, treas., 1993-97, pres. 1998-2001; chmn. Leeward Dist. Sch. Adv. Coun., 1995-97. Named Co-Adult Edn. Tchr. of Yr., Hawaii Adult Edn. Assn., 1988. Mem. AICPA, Hawaii Adult Edn. Assn. (dir. 1978-79, treas. 1979-81, pres. 1981-83), Hawaii Bus. Educators Assn., Inst. Mgmt. Accts., Hui Luna Club (dir. 1978, 85, auditor 1979, treas. 1980, 81), Friends of the Libr. of Hawaii, Toastmasters (Kam 720 Club treas. 1981-82, Disting. Toastmaster 1985, Dist. 49 audit com. chmn. 1981-82, treas. 1982-84, speechcraft chmn. 1984-85). Office: Hawaii Pacific Univ 1188 Fort Street Mall Ste 252 Honolulu HI 96813-2713 E-mail: tkam@hpu.edu.

KAMACK, HARRY JOSEPH, retired chemical engineer; b. Waterbury, Conn., Dec. 5, 1918; s. Henry William and Elfrida (Withey) K. BS in Chem. Engring., Ga. Inst. Tech., 1941; MS in Nuclear Engring., Oak Ridge Sch. Reactor Tech., 1954; MS in Math., U. Delaware, 1956. Chem. engr. Gen. Chem. Co., Claymont, Del., 1941-42, E.I. Du Pont Ala. Ordnance Works, Birmingham, 1942-43; rsch. asst. E.I. du Pont Manhattan Project, Chgo., Oak Ridge, Tenn., Richland, Wash., 1943-45; rsch. engr. E.I. du Pont de Nemours, Wilmington, Del., Oak Ridge, 1946-54, process design engr. Wilmington, Augusta, Ga., 1954-69, sr. design cons., 1969-73, prin. design cons. Wilmington, 1973-78; ret., 1978. Cons. engr., Wilmington, 1979-92. Contbr. articles to profl. jours. Mem. AIChE. Home: # 301 490 Stamford Dr Newark DE 19711-2774

KAMAL, ABU HENA M. electrical engineer, researcher; s. Abdul Hannan and Golenoor Begum; m. Shamima M. Shimu, Sept. 14, 1989; 1 child, Ishmam A. Nawar. BS in Elec. and Electronic Engring., Bangladesh U. of Engring. and Tech., Dhaka, Bangladesh, 1988; MS in Elec. and Electronic Engring., Muroran Inst. of Tech., Japan, 1993; PhD in Elec. Engring., Ariz. State U., 1997. Lectr. Bangladesh U. of Engring. and Tech., Dhaka, 1988—90; sr. process engr. Nat. Semiconductor Corp., Santa Clara, Calif., 1997—99, sr. circuit design rschr., 1999—2001, staff circuit design engr., 2001—. Team leader of cobalt silicide group Nat. Semiconductor Corp., Santa Clara, Calif., 1997—99. Author: (jour. paper) IEEE Trans. of Semiconductor Mfg.; author: (and speaker) (conf.) Silicon Nanoelectronics Workshops; reviewer IEEE, 2000—; dir.(and wrote): (4 bengali dramas), 1995—2003; bur. chief: Exec. Times; contbr. articles to profl. publs. Dir., founder drama group BiNa, Santa Clara; founding mem. U.S. nonprofit orgn. SpaandanB, Sunnyvale, Calif., 1998—2003. Recipient Silver award, Nat. Semiconductor Corp., 1997; scholar Monboshu Scholarship, Ministry of Edn., Japan, 1990—93. Mem.: Inst. of Electrochem. Soc. (assoc.), Inst. of Elec. and Electronic Engring. (assoc.). Achievements include patents for Low power analog equalizer with current mode digital to analog converter; Method for the formation of a boron-doped silicon gate layer underlying a cobalt silicide layer; Process for the formation of cobalt salicide layers employing a sputter etch surface preparation step; Method for the formation of a poly silicon layer with a controlled, small silicon grain size during semiconductor device fabrication; patents pending for Apparatus and method for employing gain dependent biasing to reduce offset and Noise in a current conveyer type amplifier; Low power analog equalizer with current mode digital to analog converter; Operational amplifier circuit with improved feedback factor. Avocations: writing mag. articles, novels, travel, reading history, music. Home: 3351 Tracy Dr Santa Clara CA 95051 Office: Nat Semiconductor Corp 2900 Semiconductor Dr M/S-E-170 Santa Clara CA 95052 Office Fax: 408-721-1415. Personal E-mail: ishmam@attbi.com. E-mail: abu.kamal@nsc.com.

KAMALAKAR, PERI, pediatrician; b. Proddutur, Andhra, India, Dec. 9, 1944; came to U.S., 1969; s. Prasadarao L. and Veerabhadramma (Tata) Peri; m. Lakshmi Mantravadi, Aug. 18, 1973; children: Guatam, Sarada. MB, BS, Guntur (India) Med. Coll., 1967. Diplomate Am. Bd. Pediatrics. Fellow in pediatric hematology and oncology Buffalo Children's Hosp., 1974-76, attending, 1976-77; resident in pediatrics Newark-Beth Israel Med. Ctr., 1970-73, dir. pediatric hematology and oncology Children's Hosp. N.J., 1978—. Recipient community svc. award Orange Sickle Cell Orgn., 1982. Fellow Am. Acad. Pediatrics; mem. Am. Soc. Clin. Oncology, Am. Soc. Hematology, Am. Soc. Pediatric Hematology and Oncology. Democrat. Hindu. Home: 7 Nicholas Ct Edison NJ 08820-2244 Office: Children's Hosp of NJ Newark-Beth Israel Med Ctr 400 Osborne Ter Newark NJ 07112-2046

KAMALI, NORMA, fashion designer; b. N.Y.C., June 27, 1945; d. Sam and Estelle (Mariategui) Arraez. Grad., Fashion Inst. of Tech., 1965. Established Kamali Ltd., N.Y.C., 1967-78; owner, designer On My Own Norma Kamali, N.Y.C., 1978—. Designer costumes for Emerald City in The Wiz, 1978; for Twyla Tharp dance In the Upper Room, 1986; Parachute Designs displayed Met. Mus. of Art, N.Y.C., 1977; prodr., dir. (video) Fall Fantasy; dir. (video) Fashion Aid, 1985. Recipient CFDA award, 1982, 1985, Coty award, 1981, 82, 83, Ernie awards Earnshaw Rev., 1983, Fashion Inst. Design and Merchandising award, 1983, Annual Interiors award Interiors Mag., 1985, Salute to Women award N.Y. Fashion Group, 1986, Disting. Arch. award N.Y. chpt. AIA, 1986, Outstanding Grad. award Pub. Edn. Assn. N.Y., 1988, Award of Merit, Internat. Video Culture Competition, 1988, Am. Success award Fashion Inst. Tech., 1989, Youth Friends award Sch. Art League, 1997, Pencil award, 1999, Willow award Lower East Side Girls Club, 1999, Fashion Outreach Style award, 1999, Bus. Outreach award Manhattan C. of C., 2002-, Entrepreneur award Fashion Group, 2002-, Women's History Month award N.Y.C. Controllers Office, 2002-; featured exhibit Met. Mus. Exhibit, 2001-; inducted into Fashion Walk of Fame Fashion Ctr. Bus. Improvement Dist. Office: 11 W 56th St New York NY 10019-3902

KAMATOY, LOURDES AGUAS, artist; b. San Fernando, Pampanga, Philippines, June 29, 1945; came to U.S., 1966; d. Juan Gutierrez and Segunda Mercado (De La Cruz) Aguas; m. Ernesto Gabriel Kamatoy, Apr. 28, 1973; 1 child, Lisette Marie. BA in English, U. Santo Tomas, Manila, Philippines, 1964; MA in Ednl. Theatre, NYU, 1972; overseas cert. theatre, Rose Bruford Coll. Speech, Kent, Eng., 1966. Supr. Arthur Andersen & Co., N.Y.C., 1966-73; instr. theatre U. So. Ind., Evansville, 1973-75; pres. Bodega, Evansville, 1975-79; artist rep. Lulu Represents, Chgo., 1986-92; ptnr. MK Videostar, Chgo., 1989-92; account exec. Kamatoy Creative, Encino, Calif., 1992—2001; exec. dir. Valley Women's Ctr., Tarzana, Calif., 2001—. Pres. Evansville Arts and Edn. Coun., 1983; v.p. U. Evansville Theatre Soc., 1984; panelist Ind. Arts Commn., Indpls., 1985; bd. dirs. Arts Insight, Indpls., 1985, USI Soc. Arts and Humanities, Evansville, 1988, Valley Cultural Ctr., Woodland Hills, Calif., 1996, v.p., 1997—2000. Mem. Rotary Club (officer Warner Ctr. chpt.). Roman Catholic. Avocations: going to theatre, eating at fine restaurants. Office: 5530 Corbin Ave Ste 325 Tarzana CA 91356

KAMBER, VICTOR SAMUEL, political consultant; b. Chgo., May 7, 1944; s. Samuel J. and Cordelia A. Kamber. BA, U. Ill., 1965; MA, U. N.Mex., 1966; JD, Am. U., 1969; LLM, George Washington U., 1971. Adminstrv. asst. Congressman Seymour Halpern, Washington, 1969-72; asst. to pres. Bldg. & Constrn. Trades Dept., Washington, 1974-78; dir. AFL-CIO Labor Law Reform Task Force, Washington, 1978-80; pres., chief exec. officer The Kamber Group, Washington, 1980—. Nat. v.p. Ams. for Dem. Action, Washington; bd. dirs. BB&T Bank, Washington; sr. adv. bd. Am. League Lobbyists, Washington; bd. trustees The Nat. Theatre. Mem. Nat. Dem. Club. With U.S. Army, 1972-74. Mem. ACLU, NOW, Internat. Assn. Polit. Cons., Am. Assn. Polit. Cons. (bd. dirs. 1987-92, treas. 1991-92), Coalition Labor Union Women, Indsl. Rels. Rsch. Assn., Nat. Press Club, Local 35 Newspaper Guild, Phi Gamma Delta. Democrat. Presbyterian. Home: 4730 Massachusetts Ave NW Washington DC 20016 Office: Kamber Group 1920 L St NW Ste 700 Washington DC 20036-5018 E-mail: vkamber@kamber.com.

KAMBERG, MARY-LANE, writer, journalist; b. Kansas City, Mo., Jan. 3, 1948; d. Frederick Kenneth and Jessie Marie (Lorenz) Ladewig; m. Kenneth Dee Kamberg, June 22, 1968; children: Rebekka Dyan, Johanna Lynne. BS in Journalism, U. Kans., 1981. Freelance writer, Olathe, Kans., 1985—; creative writing tchr. Johnson County C.C., Overland Park, Kans., 1987—, Avila Coll., Kansas City, 1987-90; corr. Kansas City Star, 1990—. Presenter workshops in field; pres. bd. dirs. Whispering Prairie Press, Prairie Village, Kans., 1996-98, adv. bd. 1998—; mem. adv. bd. fiction editor Potpourri Publs. (hon. mention Nat. Poetry Month award, Potpourri, 1999), Prairie Village, 1994-97; contbg. editor Hydro Rev. Mag., Kansas City, 1991—. Author: From Patient to Payment, 1993, Tips from Tina, 1995, Cabin Fever Relievers, 1997, Little Star: A Christmas Story, 2001; editor (project leader, author): (anthology) Handprint in the Woods, 1997; editor: Alzheimer's Legal Survival Guide, 2000; contbr. . Recipient Hon. Mention award Writers Digest Mag., 1987, 88, 89, 4th pl. award Writers Digest Mag., 1990, 3d pl. award Kans. State Poetry Soc., 1992, James P. Immroth Meml. award ALA, 1996, 1st pl. humor award Springfield Writers Guild, 2002, also Ozark Creative Writers Contest, 2002. Mem. Kansas City Writers Group (co-leader 1991-97, 2000—), Writers Place, Sisters in Crime, Kansas City Press Club, Soc. Profl. Journalists, Okla. Writers Fedn., Mo. Poetry Soc., Nat. League Am. Pen Women (First Place Poetry and Fiction 2003), Mo. Writers Guild. Republican. Avocation: coaching swimming. Home and Office: 2128 E 144th St Olathe KS 66062-2355 E-mail: kamberg202@comcast.net.

KAMBOH, M. ILYAS, geneticist; b. Mian Channu, Pakistan, Nov. 1, 1956; came to U.S., 1985; s. M. Saeed and Shamim A. (Haq) K.; m. Shaheen A. Kamboh, Oct. 27, 1984; children: Hafsa I., Sundas I., Ali M. BS, Punjab U., 1976, MS, 1979; PhD, Australian Nat. U., 1984. Rsch. assoc. U. Pitts., 1985-86, asst. prof., 1987-91, assoc. prof., 1991-96, prof., 1997—. Mem. Pitts. Cancer Inst., 1993-96; mem. nutrition rsch. sci. adv. com. for Nat. Dairy Promotion Bd., Nat. Dairy Coun., Rosemont, Ill., 1993-96. Mem. editl. bd. Ethnicity and Disease, 1991—93, Human Biology, 1994—, assoc. editor Annals of Human Genetics, 2003. NIH grantee, 1988—, Samuel and Emma Winters Found. grantee, 1989-90, Nat. Dairy Bd. grantee, 1990-95, Lupus Found. Am. grantee, 1993-94, 2001-03. Fellow: Am. Heart Assn.; mem.: Am. Soc. Human Genetics, AAAS, Delta Omega Nat. Honor Soc. Home: 1265 Cardinal Dr Pittsburgh PA 15243-1207 Office: U Pitts 130 Desoto St Pittsburgh PA 15213-2535 E-mail: ikamboh@mail.hgen.pitt.edu.

KAMBOUR, ROGER PEABODY, retired polymer physical chemist, researcher; b. Wilmington, Mass., Apr. 1, 1932; s. George Constantine and Ada Grace (Mattraw) K.; m. Virginia L. Dyer, Oct. 4, 1958 (div. Dec. 1982); children— Annaliese S., Christian R.; m. Barbara Jean Vivier, June 23, 1984; 1 child, Joshua V. BA cum laude, Amherst Coll., 1954; PhD in Chemistry, U. N.H., 1960. Rschr. GE R & D Co., Schenectady, N.Y., 1960-91; U. Mass. rsch. prof., 1994-99. Vis. prof. MIT, 1991; vis. scientist Nat. Inst. Standards & Tech., Washington, 1993. Mem. editl. bd. Polymer Engring. and Sci., 1968-87, Ann. Revs. of Materials Sci., 1985-89; contbr. articles on polymer physics and phys. chemistry to profl. publs.; patentee in field Supr. 1st ward Schenectady County Bd. Suprs., N.Y., 1964-65; mem. Schenectady County Charter Commn., 1964-65; mem. Schenectady City Hist. Dist. Commn., 1975-81; mem. art com. Schenectady Mus., 1975-82; mem. Nat. Ski Patrol, 1988-93; chmn. Freedom Forum, 1975-76. Fellow Am. Phys. Soc. (Ford High Polymer Physics prize 1985); mem. NAE, Am. Chem. Soc. (Union Carbide Chems. award 1968) Democrat. Unitarian Universalist. Avocations: choral singing, skiing, sailing. Home: 2572 Rosendale Rd Niskayuna NY 12309-1312 E-mail: kamviv@worldnet.att.net.

KAMEEN, JOHN PAUL, newspaper publisher; b. Carbondale, Pa., June 2, 1941; s. Joseph Charles and Mary Veronica (O'Neill) K.; m. Carole Helen McCusker, Nov. 8, 1969; 1 child, Patricia. BS in Electronics, U. Scranton, 1963, postgrad., 1964-65. Publisher The Forest City (Pa.) News, Inc., 1967—. Sec. Greater Forest City (Pa.) Industry, Inc., 1968-98, bd. dirs., 1998—; bd. dirs. Cmty. Bancorp, Inc., Clarks Summit, Pa., 1978—; mem. Pa. Ind. Devel. Authority, 2001—. Contbr. numerous articles on hunting to mags. and pubs. Mem. Forest City Rep. Com., 1968-78; councilman Forest City Borough, 1974-78; vice chmn. Susquehanna County Rep. Party, 1994-96, chmn. 1996-2000; pres. Susquehanna County Rep. Club, 1991-92; mem. Susquehanna County Econ. Devel. Bd., 1998—. Recipient Cmty. Betterment award, Pa. C. of C., Harrisburg, 1970, Cert. of Nat. Merit, U.S. Dept. HUD, Washington, 1982; Paul Harris fellow, 1996. Mem. Pa. Newspaper Assn. (bd. dirs. 1980-84), Nat. Newspaper Assn., Susquehanna County C. of C. (dir. 1994-2000), Lions Club. Roman Catholic. Avocations: big game hunting, fishing, golf. Office: The Forest City News 636 Main St Forest City PA 18421-1430 E-mail: fcnews@nep.net.

KAMEMOTO, FRED ISAMU, retired zoologist; b. Honolulu, Mar. 8, 1928; s. Shuichi and Matsu (Murase) K.; m. Alice Takeyo Asayama, July 20, 1963; children: Kenneth, Garett, Janice. Student, U. Hawaii, 1946-48; AB, George Washington U., 1950, MS, 1951; PhD, Purdue U., 1954. Research assoc., acting instr. Wash. State U., 1957-59; asst. prof. zoology U. Mo., 1959-62; asst. prof. U. Hawaii, Honolulu, 1962-64, assoc. prof., 1964-69, prof. zoology, 1969-94, prof. emeritus, 1995—, chmn. dept., 1964-65, 71-80, 81-90, dir. biology program, 1992-94. Vis. rsch. scholar Ocean Rsch. Inst., U. Tokyo, Biol. Lab., Fukuoka U., 1968-69; vis. prof. Coll. Agr. and Vet. Medicine, Nihon U., Tokyo, summer 1973, 1979; vis. scholar dept. biology Conn. Wesleyan U., 1975-76; sr. scientist dept. fisheries Nihon U., Tokyo, 1986; vis. fgn. rschr. Tropical Biosphere Rsch. Ctr. U. of Ryukyus Okinawa, Japan, 1994. Contbr. articles to profl. jours. Chmn. Hawaii State Natural Areas Reserve System Commn., 1985-88. Served with AUS, 1954-57. NSF grantee, 1960-79; National Oceanic and Atmospheric Administration grantee, 1985-89. Fellow AAAS; mem. Sigma Xi. Buddhist. Home: 3664 Waaloa Way Honolulu HI 96822-1151 Office: U Hawaii Dept Zoology Honolulu HI 96822

KAMEN, CHERYL L. HEIBERG, social worker; b. Bklyn., Sept. 29, 1959; d. Carl Harold and Sylvia (Thorhild) Heiberg; m. Kevin Brian Kamen, June 18, 1995. BA in Sociology/Religion, Gettysburg Coll., 1982; MSW, Fordham U., 1984; postgrad., Hunter Coll., 1992. Cert. social worker, N.Y.; cert. in aging. Social worker Bay Ridge Nutrition and Home Care, Bklyn., 1984; dir. S.W. Bklyn. Sr. Svcs., Bklyn., 1984-88; exec. dir. Bay Ridge Ctr. for Older Adults/Ctr. for Cmty. Svcs., Bklyn., 1988—. Bd. dirs. Coun. Sr. Ctrs. and Svcs., N.Y.C., 1995-97; congl. del. White House Conf. on Aging, Washington, 1995; del. N.Y. State Gov.'s Conf. on Aging, Sarasota Springs, 1995. Pres. Bay Ridge Cmty. Coun., Bklyn., 1997—98, bd. dirs., 1998—2001. Recipient citation for outstanding cmty. svc., N.Y. State Assembly, 1998, 2001, Resolution for outstanding cmty. svc., N.Y. State Senate, 1998, 2001, others; fellow Melvin Jones fellow, Lions Club Internat., 1997. Mem.: NASW, Bay Ridge Coun. on Aging (pres. 1990—94, 2001—03), Lions Club Internat. (pres. 1999—2001), Bay Ridge Bus. and Profl. Women's Club (pres. 1998—99, 2002—03). Republican. Lutheran. Avocations: travel, gardening, reading. Home: 3009 Grand Blvd Baldwin NY 11510-4719 Office: Bay Ridge Ctr for Older Adults 411 Ovington Ave Brooklyn NY 11209-1504

KAMEN, DEAN, biomedical engineer; BS, Worcester Poly. Inst. Founder AutoSyringe, Inc., 1976; biomed. engr. DEKA R&D Corp., Manchester, NH, 1988—92, pres., 1992—. Founder Sci. Enrichment Encounters, 1985, FIRST (For Inspiration & Recognition of Sci. & Tech.), 1989. Named N.H. Bus. Leader of the Year, 1996; recipient Engineer of the Year award, Design News Magazine, 1994, Hoover Medal, 1995, Edwin Church medal, ASME, 1997, Heinz Award, 1998. Mem.: NAE. Achievements include developer of the first portable insulin pump, 1978; developer portable dialysis machine (awarded 'medical product of the year' by Design News Magazine), 1993; holder of more than 100 US patents. Office: DEKA R&D 340 Commercial St Manchester NH 03101-1121*

KAMEN, HARRY PAUL, retired life insurance company executive, lawyer; b. Montreal, Que., Can., June 17, 1933; came to U.S., 1936, naturalized, 1945; s. Benjamin and Manya (Manishin) K.; m. Susan J. Klein, Feb. 1, 1958 (dec. Feb. 1996); children: Katherine, Abigail; m. Barbara J. Levine, March 9, 1997. AB, U. Pa., 1954; LLB, Harvard U., 1957; postgrad., MIT. Bar: Ohio 1957, N.Y. 1958. With Met. Life Ins. Co., N.Y.C., 1959-98, v.p., sec., assoc. gen. counsel, 1979-83, sr. v.p., sec., 1983-85, sr. v.p., dep. gen. counsel, 1985-86, sr. v.p., gen. counsel, 1987-89, exec. v.p., gen. counsel, 1989-91, exec. v.p., 1991, sr. exec. v.p., 1991-93, chmn., chief exec. officer, 1993-98. Bd. dirs. BDC Fin. Inc., Bethlehem (Pa.) Steel Corp., NASD, MetLife, Inc.; mem. internat. adv. group of Santander Ctrl. Hispano, Madrid. Co-author: Commentaries on Debenture Indentures, 1971, New York Life Insurance Law, 1990. International Adv. Group Santander Ctrl. Hispano, Madrid; mem. bd. overseers Sch. Arts and Scis., U. Pa., 1994—; global adv. coun. of conf. bd., trustee Cultural Instns.

Retirement Sys., Chamber Music Soc. of Lincoln Ctr., Jewish Mus., N.Y. Bot. Garden; hon. trustee Am. Mus. Natural History; bd. advisors Mailman Sch. Pub. Health, Columbia U. Mem. Harvard Club (bd. mgrs.), East Hampton Tennis Club, Phi Beta Kappa.

KAMEN, ROBERT IRWIN, research company executive; b. N.Y.C., Aug. 6, 1944; s. Abraham and Lillian (Kovacs) K.; m. Ruth Hope Kamen, June 14, 1964 (div. 1985); m. Geertruida M. Veldman, Jan. 18, 1986; children: Daniel Martin, Annelies Eva. AB summa cum laude, Amherst Coll., 1965; PhD in Molecular Biology/Biochemistry, Harvard U., 1970. Postdoctoral fellow Inst. Molecular Biology U. Zürich, 1970-73, Imperial Cancer Rsch. Fund Labs., London, 1974-76, sr. staff scientist, 1976-82; dir. rsch. Genetics Inst., Inc., Cambridge, Mass., 1982-84, v.p. rsch., 1984-86, sr. v.p. scientific affairs, 1986-89; ind. cons. Sudbury, Mass., 1989-91; pres. BASF Biorsch. Corp., Worcester, Mass., 1991—2000, Abbott Biorsch. Ctr., Worcester, Mass., 2001—02; divsn. v.p. Abbott Labs., Worcester, Mass., 2001—02; ret., 0202. Contbr. articles to profl. jours. Mem. Am. Soc. Microbiology, European Molecular Biology Orgn., Am. Assn. Cancer Rsch. Home: 60 Woodmere Dr Sudbury MA 01776-1776

KAMENETSKY, LEONID G. physician, cardiologist; b. Lwiw, Ukraine, Apr. 7, 1934; came to U.S., 1949; s. Julian and Angela Kamenetsky; m. Ulana Nimylovych, June 20, 1959; children: mark, Myron. BS in Chemistry, U. Ill., 1957; MD, St. Louis U., 1961. Diplomate Am. Bd. Internal Medicine. Resident in internal medicine San Joaquin Gen. Hosp., Stockton, Calif., 1962-64, chief resident, 1964-65; fellow in cardiology USPHS Hosp., San Francisco, 1965-67; dir. cardiology San Joaquin Gen. Hosp., 1967-72, St. Joseph's Hosp., Stockton, 1972-80; pres. Stockton Cardiology, 1980-90, mem., 1990—. Maj. USPHS, 1965-67. Mem. AMA, ACP, Am. Soc. Internal Medicine, Aerospace Med. Assn., Ukrainian Med. Assn. Office: Stockton Cardiology Med Grp 415 E Harding Way Stockton CA 95204-6118

KAMENKOVICH, VLADIMIR MOISEEVICH, oceanographer, educator; b. Moscow, Dec. 22, 1931; came to the U.S., 1990; s. Moisey Solomonovich and Antonina Vladimirovna Kamenkovich; m. Inna Petrovna Kamenkovich, Dec. 2, 1964; children: Igor Vladimirovich, Asya Vladimirovna. Diploma in highest edn., Moscow State U., 1954, Candidate Sci., 1961; DSc, Inst. Oceanology, Moscow, 1969. Jr. scientist, sr. scientist, head lab. P.P. Shirshov Inst. Oceanology, Moscow, 1957-90, 92-94; assoc. prof., prof. dept. marine sci. U. So. Miss., Stennis Space Center, 1996—. Part-time prof. Moscow Inst. Physics and Tech., 1966-90, 92-94; vis. prof. MIT, Cambridge, Mass., 1990-91; vis. sr. rsch. scientist Lamont-Doherty Earth Obs., Columbia U., N.Y.C., 1991-92, 94-96. Fellow Am. Meteorol. Soc. (H.U. Sverdrup Gold medal 1972); mem. Am. Geophys. Union. Avocation: tennis. Office: DMS U South Miss Bldg 1020 Rm 182 Stennis Space Center MS 39529 E-mail: vladimir.kamenkovich@usm.edu.

KAMENSKY, JOHN MICHAEL, management consultant; b. Washington, Jan. 13, 1953; s. John Thomas and Margaret Kamensky; m. Jeanne Marie Berrang, Oct. 8, 1983; children: John Andrei, David Michael. BA, Angelo State U., 1975; MPA, U. Tex., 1977. Asst. dir. U.S. Gen. Acctg. Office, Washington, 1977-93; deputy dir. Nat. Partnership for Reinventing Govt., Washington, 1993-2001; asst. to deputy dir. for mgmt. U.S. Office Mgmt. & Budget, Washington, 1996-2001; dir. PricewaterhouseCoopers Global, 2001—02; assoc. ptnr. IBM Bus. Consulting Svcs., Arlington, Va., 2002—. Contbr. articles to profl. jours. Capt. USAFR, 1975-81. Recipient Pub. Innovator Leadership award Alliance Redesigning Govt., Washington, 1997. Mem. Am. Soc. Pub. Adminstrn. (sect. chair 1988). Democrat. Roman Catholic. Office: IBM Bus Consulting Svcs 1616 N Fort Myer Dr Arlington VA 22209 E-mail: john.kamensky@us.ibm.com.

KAMENTSKY, LOUIS AARON, biophysicist; b. Newark, July 28, 1930; s. Harry and Etta (Brodsky) K.; m. Marcia Alpern, Aug. 28, 1955; children: Lee, Howard, Ellen. BSEE, N.J. Inst. Tech., 1952; PhD, Cornell U., 1956. Mem. staff Columbia U. ERL, N.Y.C., 1954-55, Bell Telephone Labs., Murray Hill, N.J., 1956-60, IBM Research, N.Y.C., 1960-68; pres. Biophysics Systems, Mahopac, N.Y., 1968-76; v.p. rsch. Ortho Diagnostics Systems, Cambridge, Mass., 1976-88; chmn. CompuCyte Corp., Cambridge, Mass., 1988—. Vis. scientist Karolinska Inst., Stockholm, 1966; sr. rsch. scientist MIT, Cambridge, 1981-88. Patentee in field; contbr. articles to profl. jours. Home: 180 Beacon St Boston MA 02116-1408 Office: Compucyte Corp 12 Emily St Cambridge MA 02139-4507

KAMERICK, EILEEN ANN, corporate financial executive, lawyer; b. Ravenna, Ohio, July 22, 1958; d. John Joseph and Elaine Elizabeth (Lenney) K.; m. Victor J. Heckler, Sept. 1, 1990; 1 child, Connor Joseph Heckler. AB in English summa cum laude, Boston Coll., 1980; postgrad., Exeter Coll., Oxford, Eng., 1981; JD, U. Chgo., 1984, MBA in Finance and Internat. Bus. with honors, 1993. Bar: Ill. 1984, U.S. Dist. Ct. (no. dist.) Ill. 1985, Mass. 1986, U.S. Ct. Appeals (7th cir.) 1988, U.S. Supreme Ct. 1993. Assoc. Reuben & Proctor, Chgo., 1984-86, Skadden, Arps et al, Chgo., 1986-89; atty. internat. Amoco Corp., Chgo., 1989-93, sr. fin. mgr. corp. fin., 1993—96, dir. banking and fin. svcs., 1996-97, v.p., treas., 1998-99, Whirlpool Corp., Benton Harbor, Mich., 1997; v.p., gen. counsel GE Capital Auto Fin. Svcs., Barrington, Ill., 1997-98; v.p., CFO BP Am., 1998—2000; exec. v.p. & CFO United Stationers Inc., Des Plaines, Ill., 2000—01; exec. v.p., CFO Bcom3, Chgo., 2001—. Advisor fin. com. Am. Petroleum Inst., 1992; bd. dirs. Heartland Alliance, Info. Resources, Inc., Stelmar Shipping, Ltd. Vol. adv. 7th Cir. Bar Assn., Chgo., 1987—; bd. dirs. Boys & Girls Clubs of Chicago. Mem. Phi Beta Kappa. Roman Catholic. Home: 2627 N Greenview Ave Chicago IL 60614 Office: Bcom3 Ste 2200 35 W Wacker Dr Chicago IL 60601 Personal E-mail: eakes1@aol.com.

KAMERMAN, SHEILA BRODY, educator, social worker; b. Jan. 7, 1928; d. S. Lawrence and Helen (Golding) Brody; m. Morton Kamerman, Sept. 11, 1947; children: Nathan Brody, Elliot Herbert, Laura Kamerman-Katz. BA, NYU, 1946; MSW, Hunter Coll., 1966; D in Social Welfare, Columbia U., 1973; PhD (hon.), York U., Eng., 1998. Social worker N.Y.C. Dept. Social Svcs., 1966-68; social work supr. Bellevue Psychiat. Hosp., 1968-69; assoc. prof. social work Hunter Coll., 1977-79; from rsch. assoc. to sr. rsch. assoc. Columbia U. Sch. Social Work, 1971-79, assoc. prof. social policy and planning, 1979-81; prof. Sch. Social Work Columbia U., 1981—, Compton Found. Centennial prof., 1996—, interim dean Sch. Social Work, 2001—02. Dir. Columbia U. Inst. for Child and Family Policy, 1998—; chair NAS-NRC panel on work, family and community, 1980-82; mem. Com. Child Devel. Rsch. and Pub. Policy, 1983-88; mem. com. on prenatal care Inst. Medicine, 1986-88; cons. in field; mem. numerous social welfare coms. and adv. bds.; mem. Gov. Cuomo's Task Force on Poverty and Welfare Reform, 1986-87, adv. com. on Work and Family, 1987-88, UN Expert groups on social welfare and family policies; mem. Inst. Medicine/Nat. Rsch. Coun. bd. on children and families, 1998—. Author: (with Alfred J. Kahn) Not for the Poor Alone, 1975, Social Services in the United States, 1976, Social Services in International Perspective, 1977, Family Policy: Government and Families in Fourteen Countries, 1978, Child Care, Family Benefits and Working Parents, 1981, Parenting in an Unresponsive Society, 1980, Maternity and Parental Benefits and Leaves, 1980, Helping America's Families, 1982, Maternity Policies and Working Women, 1983, Income Transfers for Families with Children, 1983, Child Care: Facing the Hard Choices, 1987, The Responsive Work Place, 1987, Child Support: From Debt Collection to Social Policy, 1988, Mothers Alone: Strategies for a Time of Change, 1988, Privatization and the Welfare State, 1989, Social Services for Children, Youth and Families in the United States, 1990, Child Care, Parental Leave, and the Under 3's, 1991, A Welcome for Every Child, 1994, Starting Right: How America Neglects Its Youngest Children and What We Can Do About It, 1995, Children in big Cities, 1996, Confronting the New Politics of Child and Family Policies, (series of 6 reports), 1997, Family Change and Family Policies in Britain, Canada, New Zealand and the United States, 1998, Big Cities in the Welfare Transition, 1998, Contracting for Child and Family Services, 2000; editor: Early Childhood Education and Care, 2001; co-editor: (with Ronald A. Feldman) The Columbia University School of Social Work, 2001, (with Alfred J. Kahn) Beyond Child Poverty, the Social Exclusion of Children, 2002; contbr. over 200 articles to profl. jours. Recipient Hexter award Hunter Coll. Sch. Social Work, 1977, Nat. Leadership award in Social Policy, Heller Sch. Brandeis U., 1989, Social Welfare Policy & Practice Lifetime Achievement award, 2002; named to Hunt Coll. Hall of Fame, 1981; fellow Ctr. Advanced Study in Behavioral Scis., 1983-84, named to Columbia U Sch. of Social Work Hall of Fame, 2003. Mem. NASW, Am. Pub. Human Svcs. Assn., Assn. Policy Analysis and Mgmt., Phi Beta Kappa. Home: 1125 Park Ave New York NY 10128-1243 Office: Columbia U Sch Social Work 622 W 113th St New York NY 10025-7982 E-mail: sbk2@columbia.edu.

KAMEROW, DOUGLAS BIRON, epidemiologist, physician; b. Washington, Mar. 26, 1950; s. Allan Lee and Betty Jean (Clayman) Kamerow; m. Celia Dean Shapiro, May 25, 1986; children: Anna Malka, Eli Joseph, Simon David. AB, Harvard Coll., 1972; MD, U. Rochester, 1978; MPH, Johns Hopkins U., 1984. Diplomate Am. Bd. Family Practice, Am. Bd. Preventive Medicine. Intern Harbor-UCLA Med. Ctr., Torrance, 1978-79; gen. practitioner USPHS, Rochester, N.Y., 1979-81; resident Highland Hosp., Rochester, N.Y., 1981-83; chief primary care rsch. program NIMH, Rockville, Md., 1986-88; dir. clin. preventive svcs. staff Office of Disease Prevention & Health Promotion USPHS, Washington, 1988-94, asst. surgeon gen., 1997—2001; dir. Ctr. for Practice and Tech. Assessment Healthcare Rsch. and Quality, 1994—2001; chief scientist Research Triangle Inst. Internat., 2001—. Clin. prof. dept. family medicine Georgetown U., Washington, 1997—. Editor: Guide to Clinical Preventive Services, 1989, Guide to Clinical Preventive Services, 2d edit., 1995, BMJ USA, 2003—; assoc. editor: Am. Family Physician, 1989—94. Fellow Epidemiology, NIMH, 1983—85. Fellow: Am. Coll. Preventive Medicine, Am. Acad. Family Physicians; mem.: APHA, AMA, Assn. Tchrs. Preventive Medicine, Soc. Tchr. Family Medicine. Jewish. Home: 5403 Center St Chevy Chase MD 20815-7123 Office: RTI Internat 1615 M St NW Ste 740 Washington DC 20036

KAMEROW, MARTIN LAURENCE, accountant; b. Washington, Aug. 25, 1931; s. Jacob and Anne (Adler) K.; m. Corinne Perlmeter, Mar. 24, 1951; children: Deborah, Jacqueline, Haskell. BCS, Benjamin Franklin U., 1951, MCS, 1952. CPA D.C., Md. Staff acct. various CPA firms, Washington, 1949-52; pvt. practice acctg., 1952-59; ptnr. Kamerow & Serber, Washington, 1959-63; sr. ptnr. Harab, Kamerow & Serber, Washington, 1963-74; pres. Harab, Kamerow & Assocs., P.C., Washington, 1974-94, Snyder, Kamerow & Assocs., P.C., Rockville, Md., 1994—96; ptnr. Kamerow, Weintrabu & Swain, 1996—. Con. to editor U.S. News and World Report, 1972-84; expert witness on legal and tax matters, D.C., Md., 1975—; lectr. Am. U., 1956-65, tax seminars N.Y. U. Law Inst. and others; mem. faculty 39th NYU Inst. on Fed. Taxation, 1980; comml. arbitrator Am. Arbitration Assn.; mem. Ginat Food Adv. Bd., 1997-98. Author: (with S.A. Kaufman) Consolidated Financial Statements, 1958), (with U.S. News and World Reports Book on Income Taxes, 1971, 4th edit., 1974, (with Margaret Daly) Teach Your Wife to Be a Widow, How to Save on Taxes and Stay Out of Trouble, (with others) Statements on Responsibility in Tax Practice, 1988, (with others) Matthew Bender's Tax Service, 1988; contbr. articles to profl. jours. Bd. dirs. World Coun. Synagogues, Suburban Hosp. Inc., Suburban Hosp. Health Care Sys. Inc., Suburban Hosp. Found.; chmn. Jewish Chaplaincy Svcs.; pres. Brandeis Dist. Zionist Orgn. Am., Shma V'Ezer Sch., Hebrew Free Burial Soc. Wolfson Cardiac Surgery Found., 1993-95, Save A Child's Heart Found., 1996—; mem. fin. com., bd. dirs. Suburban Hosp., Bethesda, Md.; active United Jewish Appeal Fedn. Greater Washington, advance gifts chmn., treas., trustee endowment fund. Recipient Nat. Svc. award Kidney Found., 1972, Disting. Alumni award Benjamin Franklin U. Alumni Assn., 1977, Louis D. Brandeis award, 1982, Pub. Svc. award D.C. Inst. CPAs, 1990, Joseph Ottenstein award for Pub. Svc., Jewish Social Svc. Agy., 1993. Mem. AICPA (fed. tax civ. subcom. on responsibilities, Pub. Svc. award 1990), Assn. Practicing CPAs (pres. 1972-73), Greater Washington Soc. CPA's (Profl. Achievement award 2002), Cosmos Club. Home: 7420 Westlake Ter Bethesda MD 20817 Office: Kamerow Weintraub & Swain LLP 11400 Rockville Pike Ste 800 Rockville MD 20852-3004 E-mail: MKamerow@KWSCPA.com.

KAMEROW, NORMAN WARREN, business owner, financial services executive; b. Balt., Aug. 27, 1927; s. Jacob A. and Anna M. (Adler) K.; m. Helen Adele Rosenthal, Dec. 5, 1948; children: Susan K. Meyers, Brenda K. Cohen, Julie K. Skalkos. Cert. CLU, Am. Coll., 1965, cert. in chartered fin. cons., 1982, MS in Fin. Svcs., 1984. Pres. J.A. Kamerow & Co., Washington, 1956-61; prin. Norman W. Kamerow & Assoc., Washington, 1961-79; co-owner Kamerow & Meyers, Bethesda, Md., 1979—; chmn. bd. KHHM Chartered, Silver Spring, Md., 1980-84, Capital Fin. Group, Bethesda, 1986—. Chmn. bd. Capital Fin. Group, Bethesda, 1986—; bd. dirs. H. Beck, Inc., Bethesda. With U.S. Army, 1946-47. Fellow Life Underwriter Tng. Coun. (trustee 1987-90); mem. Assn. for Advanced Life Underwriting, Am. Soc. CLUs/Chartered Fin. Cons., Internat. Assn. Fin. Planners, D.C. Estate Planning Coun., Million Dollar Round Table. Avocations: tennis, travel, family. Office: Capital Fin Group 11140 Rockville Pike Fl 4 Rockville MD 20852-3144 E-mail: nkamerow@cfginc.com.

KAMERSCHEN, DAVID ROY, economist, educator; b. Chgo., Dec. 8, 1937; s. Robert R. and Elsie D. Kamerschen Barkell; m. Gena Faye Hampton, Apr. 27, 1985; children: Christine, Steven, Laura, Robert, David, Caroline. Student, Ind. U., 1959-60; BS in Econs., Miami U., Oxford, Ohio, 1959, MA, 1960; PhD in Econs., Mich. State U., 1964. Instr. dept. econs. Miami U., Oxford, Ohio, 1960-61; asst. instr. Mich. State U., summer 1962, 64; asst. prof. econs. U. Washington, St. Louis, 1964-65 65-66; assoc. prof. econs. U. Mo.-Columbia, 1966-68, prof., 1968-74; prof., head dept. econs. U. Ga., Athens, 1974-80, Disting. prof., Jasper N. Dorsey chair, 1980—. Cons. numerous cases or hearings in antitrust, pub. utilities and personal injury fields; guest appearance Mac Neil-Lehrer Report; host TV show Kamerschen Report Author: Readings in Microeconomics, 1969, (with Walter L. Johnson) Macroeconomics: Selected Readings, 1970, Readings in Economic Development, 1972, (with George M. Vredeveld) Economics, 1975, (with Lloyd Valentine) Intermediate Microeconomic Theory, 1981, (with Albert L. Danielsen) Current Issues in Public-Utility Economics, 1983, (with Albert L. Danielsen) Telecommunications in the Post-Divestiture Era, 1986, (with James C. Bonbright and Albert L. Danielsen) Principles of Public Utility Rates, 2nd edit., 1988, (with Richard McKenzie and Clark Nardinelli) Economics, 1989, Money and Banking, 10th edit., 1992; editor Rev. Social Theory, 1973-74; mem. editorial bds.: Bus. and Govt. Rev., 1968-72, Internat. Behavioral Scientist, 1970—, Indsl. Orgn. Rev., 1974-80, Rev. Indsl. Orgn., 1982-91, Rev. Fin. Econ., So. Econ. Jour., 1978-82, Mgmt. and Decision Econs., 1980-94; contbr. approximately 200 articles to profl. jours. Recipient Outstanding Grad. Tchr. award U. Ga., 1978; Swift Outstanding Tchr. of Yr. award, 1985; Amy Hayden scholar, 1959; Mich. State U. fellow, 1964; Disting. Research award U. Ga. Coll. Bus. Adminstrn., 1984; Swift Outstanding Teaching award, 1985. Mem. Am. Econ. Assn., So. Econ. Assn., Nat. Assn. Forensic Economists, ABA, (assoc), Phi Kappa Phi, Delta Sigma Pi, Beta Gamma Sigma, Omicron Delta Kappa, Sigma Alpha Epsilon Home: 3818 Sweet Bottom Dr Duluth GA 30096-1416 Office: Department of Economics Terry Coll Bus 536 Brooks Hall Athens GA 30602-6254 Office Fax: 706-542-8774. Personal E-mail: davidrkamerschen@aol.com. Business E-Mail: davidk@terry.uga.edu.

KAMERSCHEN, ROBERT JEROME, consumer products executive, investor; b. Laurium, Mich., Feb. 16, 1936; s. Robert Raymond and Elsie D (Barsanti) Kamerschen; m. Judith A Campbell, July 26, 1958; children: Kathryn, Carol, Jean. BS, Miami U., Oxford, Ohio, 1957, MBA, 1958. Exec. sales trainee Nat. Cash Register, Gary, Ind., 1958—59; mgmt. trainee Foote Cone & Belding, Chgo., 1959—60; dir. consumer mktg. Scott Paper Co., Phila., 1960—71; v.p. mktg. Revlon Inc., N.Y.C., 1971—73; sr. v.p. mktg. ops. Dunkin Donuts Inc., Randolph, Mass., 1973—77; pres., COO Chanel Inc. and Christian Dior Parfums Inc., N.Y.C., 1977—79; pres., CEO Max Factor & Co., Hollywood, Calif., 1979—83; sr. v.p. Norton Simon Inc., N.Y.C., 1980—83; pres., CEO Max Factor & Co., Hollywood, Calif., 1979—83; exec. v.p., office of chmn. sector exec. Norton Simon Inc., 1981—83; pres., COO Mktg. Corp. of Am., 1984-87; pres., CEO RKO Six Flags Entertainment, Inc. div. Wesray Capital Corp., N.Y.C., 1987—88; chmn., CEO ADVO Inc., Windsor, Conn., 1988—99; CEO Dimac Mktg. Corp, Windsor, 1999—2002. Disting. practitioner, lectr. U. Ga. Coll. Bus. Adminstrn., 1979—81; guest lectr. various univs. and trade assns.; bd. dirs. Radio Shack Corp., IMS Health Inc., R.H. Donnelley Corp., Memberworks Inc., Linens 'n Things, Inc., MDC Corp., Memberworks, Inc.; mem. bus. adv. coun., exec.-in-residence Miami U., 1979—82; pvt. investigator, strategic adv., 2002. Trustee, 1st vice chmn. Emerson Coll., 1984—89; trustee Columbia Coll., 1993—96, trustee Bushnell Hall, 1995—2002; trustee Wadsworth Atheneum, 1990—; regent U. Hartford, 1998—. Mem.: Metropolitan Club, NY Athletic Club, Sigma Alpha Epsilon, Delta Sigma Pi, Beta Gamma Sigma. Home: 204 Parade Hill Rd New Canaan CT 06840-4132 E-mail: RKamerschen@msn.com.

KAMERY, ROB HERLONG, economics educator, management consultant; b. Plainfield, N.J., Apr. 16, 1955; s. Lester Weidmann and Mary Ann (Padgett) K. DBA, U. Miss., 1976; MS, Winthrop U., Rockhill, S.C., 1978, U. Ark., 1981, MS, 1982, MS, 1998, MS, 1999; MBA, Christian Bros. U., 2000, BS, 2001; MA, Webster U., 2003. Fin. analyst Control Data Corp., Charlotte, NC, 1978; tchr. Charlotte (N.C.)-Mecklenburg Schs., 1977-78; lectr. Memphis State U., 1978-79; instr. econs. Christian Bros. U., Memphis, 1979-83, asst. prof., 1987-94, assoc. prof., 1994—2001, prof., 2001—. Vis. asst. prof. U. Ark., Fayetteville, 1982-83; cons. U.S. Army C.E., Memphis, 1988—. Contbr. articles to profl. jours., also monographs. Lt. USN, 1983-87, mem. Res. Mem. Soc. for Advancement Mgmt., Am. Econ. Assn., Missouri Valley Econ. Assn., Delta Sigma Pi (life), Pi Sigma Epsilon, Tau Kappa Epsilon (nat. advisor 1979). Republican. Avocation: british classic car restoration. Office: Christian Bros U 650 E Parkway S Memphis TN 38104-5519 E-mail: rkamery@cbo.edu.

KAMIENSKA-CARTER, EVA HANNA, designer, artist; b. Warsaw, Feb. 19, 1960; came to U.S., 1987; d. Witold and Kamilla (Karwowska) K.; m. Bernard Owen Carter, July 25, 1992; children: Lisa Camille, Maya Lee, Olav Bernard. MArch, Warsaw Tech. U., 1983; grad. with honors, Art Inst. Pitts., 1991. Certificate to practice art Ministry of Culture. Freelance artist, design cons., Warsaw, 1983-87, N.Y.C., Detroit, Boston, Pitts., 1987-92; design cons., ptnr. Carter-Kamienska Design, Pitts., 1992—. Freelance set designer in motion picture prodn., Pitts., 1994—; art tchr. Carnegie Mus. Art, Pitts., 1991-92, Pitts. Ctr. Arts, 1991-92. Storyboard illustrator: (software) The Ripper, 1995; one woman shows include Zdzisiaj Gallery, Warsaw, Poland, 1981, Na Brechta Gallery, Warsaw, 1984. At 700 PArker, Detroit, 1988; group exbhns. include Manfred Schuller Gallery, Zurich, 1985, Zdzisiaj Gallery, 1985, Tripoli Gallery, Phila., 1987, Pitts. Ctr. Arts, 1989. Birmingham Loft, Pitts., 1989, Mendelson Gallery, Pitts., 1989, Monroeville (Pa.) Libr. Gallery, 1989, IUP Gallery, Indiana, Pa., 1998, Carnegie (Pa.) Libr., 1992, Associated Artists Pitts. Gallery, 1993, ZPAP Gallery, Warsaw, 1998. Mem. Assoc. Artists Pitts., Pitts. Soc. Artists, Pitts. Ctr. Arts. Avocations: attending cultural and social events, hiking, canoeing, computers. Home and Office: Carter-Kamienska Design 1 Simplon St Pittsburgh PA 15202

KAMIL, ELAINE SCHEINER, pediatric nephrologist, educator; b. Cleve., Jan. 26, 1947; d. James Frank and Maud Lily (Severn) Scheiner; m. Ivan Jeffery Kamil, Aug. 29, 1970; children: Jeremy, Adam, Megan. BS magna cum laude, U. Pitts., 1969, MD, 1973. Diplomate Am. Bd. Pediats., Am. Bd. Pediat. Nephrology. Intern in pediats. Children's Hosp. Pitts., 1973-74, resident in pediats., 1974-76; clin. fellow in pediat. nephrology Sch. Medicine, UCLA, 1976-79, acting asst. prof. pediats., 1979-80; rsch. fellow in nephrology Harbor-UCLA Med. Ctr., Torrance, Calif., 1980-82; med. dir. The Children's Clinic of Long Beach, Calif., 1984-87; med. dir. pediat. nurse practitioner program Calif. State U., Long Beach, 1984-87; asst. clin. prof. pediats. Sch. Medicine, UCLA, 1988-91, assoc. clin. prof. pediats., 1991-97, clin. prof. pediats., 1997—; assoc. dir. pediat. nephrology and transplant immunology Cedars-Sinai Med. Ctr., L.A., 1990—2001, clin. dir. pediatric nephrology, 2001—. Adj. asst. prof. pediats. Harbor-UCLA, Torrance, Calif., 1983-87, UCLA, 1987-88, cons. in pediat. nephrology Hawthorne (Calif.) Cmty. Med. Group, 1981-2000. Author chpts. to books; contbr. articles to profl. jours. Pres.-elect med. adv. bd. Nat. Kidney Found. So. Calif., 2000-2002, pres. exec. com., 2002—. Recipient Vol. Svc. award Nat. Kidney Found., 1998. Mem. AAUW, Am. Soc. Nephrology, Am. Soc. Pediat. Nephrology, Am. Fedn. Clin. Rsch., Internat. Soc. Nephrology, Internat. Soc. Pediat. Nephrology, Internat. Soc. Peritoneal Dialysis, Renal Pathology Soc., So. Calif. Pediat. Nephrology Assn. (chair steering com. 1998—), Nat. Kidney Found. So. Calif. (med. adv. bd. 1987-96, rsch. com. 1987-90, chmn. pub. info. med. adv. bd. 1988-92, handbook com. 1988, co-chair med. adv. bd. cmty. svcs. com. 1992-93, chair-elect patient svcs. and cmty. edn. com. 1993-94, chair patients svcs. and cmty. edn. com. 1994-95, kidney camp summer vol. physician 1988-91, 93, 94, 97, 99-2003, Arthur Gordon award 1991, Exceptional Svc. award 1992, Exceptional Leadership and Support award 1995, bd. dirs. 1995-96, 2002—), Alpha Omega Alpha, Phi Beta Kappa. Office: Cedars Sinai Med Ctr 1165 WT 8700 Beverly Blvd Los Angeles CA 90048-1865

KAMILLI, ROBERT JOSEPH, geologist; b. Phila., June 14, 1947; s. Joseph George and Marie Emma (Clauss) K.; m. Diana Ferguson Chapman, June 28, 1969; children: Ann Chapman, Robert Chapman. BA summa cum laude, Rutgers U., 1969; AM, Harvard U., 1971, PhD, 1976. Geologist Climax Molybdenum Co., Empire, Colo., 1976-79, asst. resident geologist, 1979-80, project geologist Golden, Colo., 1980-83; geologist U.S. Geol. Survey, Saudi Arabian Mission, Jeddah, 1983-87, mission chief geologist, 1987-89; rsch. geologist, project chief U.S. Geol. Survey, Tucson, Ariz., 1989-96, scientist-in-charge, 1996-2001, project chief, scientist-in-charge, 2001—. Adj. prof. U. Colo., Boulder, 1981-83, U. Ariz., Tucson, 1997—. Editor: Geologic Highway Map of Arizona; contbr. articles to profl. jours. Henry Rutgers scholar Rutgers U., 1968-69. Fellow Geol. Soc. Am., Soc. Econ. Geologists; mem. Ariz. Geol. Soc. (v.p. 1995-98, 2004—, pres. 1999, past pres. 2000, counselor 2001-03), Phi Beta Kappa, Sigma Xi. Avocations: travel, swimming, bicycle riding, music, photography. Home: 5050 N Siesta Dr Tucson AZ 85750-9652 Office: US Geol Survey SW Field Office 520 N Park Ave Ste 355 Tucson AZ 85719-5035 E-mail: bkamilli@usgs.gov.

KAMIN, BLAIR DOUGLASS, newspaper critic; b. Red Bank, N.J., Aug. 6, 1957; s. Arthur Z. and Virginia P. Kamin. BA, Amherst Coll., 1979; M in Environ. Design, Yale U., 1984. Reporter Des Moines Register, 1984-87; suburban reporter Chgo. Tribune, 1987—91; culture news reporter, 1992; architecture critic, 1992—. Nominating juror Pulitzer Prize, 2000, 02. Author Why Architecture Matters: Lessons from Chicago, 2001, contbr. articles to profl. jours. Recipient Nat. Edn. Reporting award Edn. Writers Assn., 1985, Edward Scott Beck award Chgo. Tribune, 1990, George Polk award for Criticism, 1996, Pulitzer Prize for Criticism, 1999, Inst. Honor for Collaborative Achievement, AIA, 1999, Peter Lisagor award for Exemplary Journalism, 1993, 94, 95, 96, 97, 98, 2001. Jewish.

KAMIN, CHESTER THOMAS, lawyer; b. Chgo., July 30, 1940; s. Alfred and Sara (Liebenson) K.; m. Nancy Schaefer, Sept. 8, 1962; children— Stacey Allison, Scott Thomas AB magna cum laude, Harvard Coll., 1962; JD, U. Chgo., 1965. Bar: Ill. 1965, U.S. Dist. Ct. (no. dist.) Ill. 1965, U.S. Dist. Ct. D.C. 1994, U.S. Ct. Appeals (fed. cir.) 1967, U.S. Ct. Appeals (7th cir.) 1970, U.S. Ct. Appeals (5th cir.) 1975, U.S. Ct. Appeals (2d cir.) 1987, U.S. Ct. Appeals (6th cir.) 1996, U.S. Supreme Ct. 1971. Law clk. Ill. Appellate Ct., 1965-66; assoc. Jenner & Block, Chgo., 1966-72, ptnr., 1975—; spl. counsel to Gov. Ill., Springfield, 1973-74. Mem. steering com. Com. on Cts. and Justice, 1971— ; mem. Ill. Law Enforcement Commn., 1975-77; adj. prof. U. Chgo. Law Sch. Contbr. articles to profl. jours. Fellow Am. Bar Found., Am. Coll. Trial Lawyers; mem. ABA, Ill. State Bar Assn., Chgo. Bar Assn., Chgo. Coun. Lawyers, Lawyers Club, Quadrangle Club. Office: Jenner & Block 1 E Ibm Plz Fl 4700 Chicago IL 60611-3599 E-mail: ckamin@jenner.com.

KAMIN, KAY HODES, financial planner, journalist, lawyer, entrepreneur, educator, financial columnist; b. Chgo., July 3, 1940; d. Barnet and Eleanor (Cramer) H.; m. Malcolm S. Kamin, June 12, 1963; children: Kim Alison, Kyle Barret. BA, Vassar Coll., 1961; MA, U. Chgo., 1962, PhD, 1970; JD cum laude, Northwestern U., 1981. Registered investment advisor, Ill., cert. CFP; bar: Ill. 1981, (U.S. Dist. Ct. (no. dist.) Ill.) 1981. History tchr. Lincoln Park H.S., Chgo., 1963—67; social studies coord. U. Chgo., 1968—69; assoc. prof. edn. Dominican U., River Forest, Ill., 1970—76; jud. law clk. Ill. Appellate Ct., Chgo., 1981—83; assoc. Mayer, Brown & Platt, Chgo., 1983—85; v.p., gen. counsel Glencorp, Inc. dba Benetton, Chgo., 1985—93; also bd. dirs. Glencorp, Inc., Chgo., 1985—93; pres. Sutton Pl. Fin., Inc., Chgo., 1992—. Co-author Contract Law, 1983; fin. editor, columnist Today's Chgo. Woman, 1996—; frequent guest on Making Money, CLTV, Crain's Chgo. Bus.; contbr. articles to profl. jours. Pres. Chgo. Coun. for Social Studies, 1967—69, bd. govs., life mem. Chgo. Art Inst., 1974—; pres. Soc. for Contemporary Art, 1974—76, Sedoh Found., 1986—; v.p., bd. dirs. Women's Bd. of Northwestern U., 1998—99; mem. exec. com., v.p., treas. collectors forum and guide Chgo. Mus. Contemporary Art, 1997—; mem. U. Chgo. Women's Bd. Fellow U. Chgo.

Grad. Sch., 1967-70. Mem.: Chgo. Bar Assn. (vice chair fin. svcs. com. 1995—96), Chgo. Capital Club (founder 1995, pres. 1995—2001), John Evans Club (Northwestern U.), Arts Club. Avocations: golf, jogging, art collecting. Office: Sutton Place Financial Inc 1305 N Sutton Pl Chicago IL 60610-2007 E-mail: khkamin@aol.com.

KAMIN, SHERWIN, lawyer; b. N.Y.C., Feb. 5, 1927; s. Theodore and Esther K.; children: Lawrence O., Samuel N., Janet C., David W., Julia E.; m. S. Jeanne Hall, Oct. 1, 1993. BBA, CCNY, 1948; LLB, Harvard U., 1951. Bar: N.Y. 1953. Asst. to reporter Fed. Income Tax Project, Am. Law Inst., Cambridge, Mass., 1951—52; assoc. Botein, Hays, Sklar & Herzberg, N.Y.C., 1952—62, ptnr., 1962—68, Kramer, Levin, Naftalis & Frankel, N.Y.C., 1968—93, of counsel, 1993—2001, Fulton, Rowe & Hart and predecessors, N.Y.C., 2002—. Served with USN, 1945-46. Mem. ABA, Assn. of Bar of City of N.Y., N.Y. State Bar Assn., Am. Law Inst., Am. Coll. Tax Counsel. Home: 163 W 76th St New York NY 10023-8325 Office: Fulton Rowe & Hart One Rockefeller Plz New York NY 10020-2002 E-mail: sherwink@aol.com.

KAMIN, WILLIAM STEPHEN, food company executive, photographer; b. Chgo., Feb. 3, 1930; s. Emil Zola and Berta Magid; m. Adrienne Bloomberg, Aug. 28, 1955 (dec. June 15, 2001); children: Steven B., Andrew G. PhB, U. Chgo., 1947; BS, U. Ill., 1952. CPA, Ill. Staff acct. D. Himmelblau & Co., Chgo., 1955-57; budget analyst Westinghouse Electric Co., West Mifflin, Pa., 1957-63; contr. Std. Fruit Co., La Ceiba, Honduras, 1963-68, gen. mgr. Guayaquil, Ecuador, 1968-70; v.p. fin. Dole Fruit Co., Honolulu, 1970-72; v.p. ops. Castle & Cooke, Inc., San Francisco, 1972-78, v.p. strategic planning, 1978-82; pvt. practice photography Menlo Park, Calif., 1985—. Cons. William S. Kamin Cons., Atherton, Calif., 1982-85; adj. prof. Coll. Notre Dame, Belmont, Calif., 1984-85, U. Santa Clara, Calif., 1986, Golden Gate U., San Francisco, 1987. Author, photographer: Tenderloin, 1989. Bd. dirs., fin. cons. Valley Inst. of Theatre Arts, Saratoga, Calif., 1986-87; docent Coyote Point Mus., San Mateo, 1992-95, Fitzgerald Marine Res., Pacifica, Calif., 1995-97. Mem. Sons in Retirement. Avocations: tennis, travel. Home and Office: 169 Stone Pine Ln Menlo Park CA 94025-3050

KAMINER, MICHAEL SETH, dermatologist; b. Bklyn., Sept. 1, 1961; BS, Haverford Coll., 1983; MD, Tufts U., 1987. Physician SkinCare Physicians, Chestnut Hill, Mass. Office: SkinCare Physicians 1244 Boylston St Ste 302 Chestnut Hill MA 02467

KAMINOW, IVAN PAUL, physicist; b. Union City, N.J., Mar. 3, 1930; s. Benjamin and Belle (Glazer) K.; m. Florence Fischer, Nov. 26, 1952; children: Paula, Leonard, Ellen. BSEE, Union Coll., Schenectady, N.Y., 1952; MS, UCLA, 1954; AM, Harvard U., 1957, PhD, 1960. Diplomate Am. Bd. Laser Surgery. Physicist Hughes Aircraft Co., Culver City, Calif., 1952—54, AT&T Bell Labs., Holmdel, NJ, 1954—96, Lucent Bell Labs., Holmdel, 1996—97. Vis. lectr. Princeton U., 1968, U. Calif., Berkeley, 1977, Columbia U., 1986; vis. prof. Tokyo U., 1990-91; IEEE Congrl. fellow, 1996; cons. Kaminow Lightwave Tech., 1997—. Author: Introduction to Electrooptic Devices, 1974; co-editor: Optical Fiber Telecommunications, 1988, 1997, 2002; contbr. Mem. Tinton Falls Bd. Edn., 1966-74; mem. sci. com. U.S. House of Reps. Hughes fellow UCLA, 1954, Bell Labs. fellow Harvard U., 1957-60. Fellow IEEE (life, Quantum Electronics award 1983, Congl. fellow 1996, Millennium medal 2000), Am. Phys. Soc., Optical Soc. Am. (Charles Hard Townes award 1995, Tyndall award 1997); mem. NAE. Achievements include patents in field. Office: Kaminow Lightwave Tech 12 Stonehenge Rd Holmdel NJ 07733-1929 E-mail: kaminow@post.harvard.edu.

KAMINS, BARRY MICHAEL, lawyer; b. Oct. 3, 1943; s. Abe and Evelyn Bertha (Goffen) K.; m. Fern Louise Kamins, Mar. 30, 1968; 1 child, Allyson. BA, Columbia U., 1965; JD, Rutgers U., 1968. Bar: N.Y. 1969, U.S. Dist. Ct. (ea. and so. dists.) N.Y. 1973, U.S. Supreme Ct. 1974. Asst. dist. atty., 1969-73; dep. chief Criminal Ct. Bur., 1971-73; ptnr. Flamhaft, Levy, Kamins & Hirsch, 1973—. Chmn. grievance com. 2d and 11th Jud. Dist., 1994-98; adj. prof. Fordham Law Sch., Bklyn. Law Sch., Bklyn. Law Sch.; adj. prof. in criminal law N.Y. Tech. Coll.; apptd. spl. prosecutor, Kings County, 1990-92; chmn. oversight com. Criminal Def. ORgn. 2d Appellate Divsn., 1997—. Author: The Social Studies Student Investigates the Criminal Justice System, 1978, New York Search and Seizure, 1991; contbr. numerous articles on criminal law to profl. jours. Mem. ABA, N.Y. State Bar Assn. (mem. ho. dels., chair com. prof. discipline 1999—), Bklyn. Bar Assn. (past pres., chair jud. com. 1994-98), Kings County Criminal Bar Assn. (past pres.), Assn. Bar City of N.Y. (chair jud. com. 1998-2001, exec. com. 2001—). Office: 16 Court St Brooklyn NY 11241-0102

KAMINS, THEODORE I. electrical engineer; b. San Francisco, Nov. 11, 1941; s. Mandle and Myra Kamins. BS, U. Calif., Berkeley, 1963, MS, 1964, PhD, 1968. Acting asst. prof. U. Calif., Berkeley, 1968-69; rsch. staff Fairchild Semiconductor, Palo Alto, Calif., 1969-74; prin. scientist Hewlett-Packard Co., Palo Alto, 1974—; cons. prof. Stanford U., 1999—. Short course instr. Semiconductor Equipment and Materials Internat., U. Calif., Oxford U., Am. Vacuum Soc. Co-author: Device Electronics for ICs, 1978, 1986, 2003; author: Polycrystalline Silicon, 1988, 1998. Fellow IEEE, Electrochem. Soc. (Electronics divsn. award 1989).

KAMINSKI, DONALD LEON, medical educator, surgeon, gastrointestinal physiologist; b. Elba, Nebr., Nov. 9, 1940; s. Edwin and Irene (Syntek) K.; m. Maureen M. Cudmore, Nov. 28, 1964; children: Christian, Julie, Jane, Kathryn. BS, Creighton U., 1962, MD, 1966. Diplomate: Am. Bd. Surgery. Intern. St. Louis U., 1966-67, resident in surgery, 1967-71; attending surgeon St. Louis U. Hosp., 1972—, dir. gen. surgery, 1982—. Mem. Soc. Univ. Surgeons, Am. Physiol. Soc., Am. Gastroent. Assn., Am. Surg. Assn., Central Surg. Soc., Alpha Omega Alpha Republican. Roman Catholic. Home: 1025 Joanna Ave Saint Louis MO 63122-1821 Office: St Louis U 3635 Vista at Grand PO Box 15250 Saint Louis MO 63110-0250

KAMINSKI, JANUSZ, cinematographer; b. Ziembice, Poland, June 27, 1959; arrived in U.S., 1981; s. Marian Kaminski and Jadwiga Celner; m. Holly Hunter, May 20, 1995. BA in Film, Columbia Coll., 1987. Dir. photography (films) Lisa, 1988 (Line Eagel award Ill. Film Festival), Absence, 1988, Selling Short, 1988, Grim Prairie Tales, 1989, All the Love in the World, 1989, Rain Killer, 1990, The Terror Within II, 1991, The Adventures of Huck Finn, 1992, Cool as Ice, 1992, Mad Dog Coll, 1992, Trouble Bound, 1993, Schindler's List, 1993 (Acad. award best cinematography), How to Make an American Quilt, 1995, Jerry Maguire, 1996, Lost World, 1997, Amistad, 1997, Saving Private Ryan, 1998 (Acad. award best cinematography), A.I.-2001, Minority Report, 2001; dir.: Lost Souls, 2000. Office: 1223 Wilshire Blvd # 645 Santa Monica CA 90403-5400

KAMINSKI, PAUL GARRETT, federal agency administrator, investment banker; b. Cleve., Sept. 16, 1942; s. Theodore Albert and Eleanor Marie (Dobranski) K.; m. Julia Kent Crafts, Oct. 8, 1966; children: Laura Denise, Garrett Kent. BS, USAF Acad., 1964; MS in Aerospace and Astronautics, MSEE, MIT, 1966; PhD in Aeronautics and Astronautics, Stanford U., 1971. Commd. 2d lt. USAF, 1964, advanced through grades to col., 1979, spl. asst. to under sec. of def., 1977-81; dir. low observables tech. Office Dep. Chief Staff for R&D, Dept. Air Force, 1981-84; ret., 1984; pres., COO, Tech. Strategies & Alliances, Burke, Va., 1985-93, chmn., CEO, 1993-94; under sec. of def. for acquisition and tech. Dept. Def., Washington, 1994-97; chmn., CEO Technovation, Inc., 1997—; sr. ptnr. Global Tech. Ptnrs. LLC, 1998—. Chmn. Def. Sci. Bd., Washington, 1993-94. Contbr. articles to sci. jours. Dir. Spl. Olympics, Palos Verdes (Calif.) H.S., 1971-73. Decorated Legion of Merit, D.S.M. Office Sec. Def., Disting. Pub. Svc. medal, Medal of Merit in gold Netherlands Ministry Def. Fellow: IEEE, AIAA; mem.: NAE, AAAS, Sigma Gamma Tau, Tau Beta Pi, Sigma Xi. Avocations: golf, tennis, jogging, cross-country skiing. Office: Technovation Inc 6691 Rutledge Dr Fairfax Station VA 22039-1733

KAMINSKY, ALICE RICHKIN, English language educator; b. N.Y.C. d. Morris and Ida (Spivak) Richkin; m. Jack Kaminsky (dec.); 1 son, Eric (dec.). BA, NYU, 1946, MA, 1947, PhD, 1952. Mem. faculty dept. English NYU, 1947-49, Hunter Coll., 1952-53, Cornell U., 1954-57, Broome Community Coll., 1958-59, Cornell U., 1959-63, SUNY, Cortland, 1963—, prof., 1968-91, prof. emerita, 1991—, faculty exchange scholar. Author: George Henry Lewes as Critic, 1968, Logic: A Philosophical Introduction, 1974; editor: Literary Criticism of George Henry Lewes, 1964, Chaucer's Troilus and Criseyde and the Critics, 1980, The Victim's Song, 1985; contbr. more than 75 articles and revs. to numerous jours. Mem. MLA, Chaucer Soc. *At a very early age I learned that life is fragile, that many loved and lovely things die or disappear. My way of coping with that knowledge was to latch on to the work ethic. This meant working to achieve some end.*

KAMINSKY, ANATOL, educator, writer; b. Ukraine, May 17, 1925; came to U.S., 1960; s. Gregory and Eudokia Kaminsky; m. Tatjana Kripacky; 1 son, Taras. PhD, Ukrainian Free U., Munich, 1990; cert. in internat. rels., London Sch. Econs./Polit. Sci., 1958. Editor Ukrainian Ind., Munich, 1953-58; v.p. rsch. Prolog Assocs., N.Y.C., 1960-81; sr. editor Suchasnist, N.Y.C., 1962-83; dir., chief editor Ukrainian svc. Radio Free Europe/Radio Liberty, Munich, 1983-89; prof. internat. rels. Ukrainian Free U., 1993—, dean faculty of law and socio-econ. scis., 1996-98. Guest prof. Lviv (Ukraine) State U., 1993— Author: 13 books in Ukrainian. Chmn. polit. coun. Rep. of Ukrainian Supreme Liberation Coun., N.Y.C. and Munich, 1996—; assoc. mem. nat. coun. Dem. Party of Ukraine, 1996—. Recipient Internat. Orlyk prize Dem. Party of Ukraine, 1994. Mem. Orgn. Ukrainian Nationalists (chmn. 1991—). Home: 68 The Rise Warwick NY 10990-4234

KAMINSKY, GLENN FRANCIS, retired protective services official, business owner, teacher; b. Passaic, N.J., Apr. 29, 1934; s. Francis Gustave and Leona Regina (Tubach) K.; m. Janet Lindesay Strachan (div. June 1985); childrenn: Lindesay Anne, Jon Francis; m. Melanie Sue Rhamey, Mar. 11, 1989. BS in Police Sci., San Jose (Calif.) State Coll., 1958; MS in Adminstrn., San Jose State U., 1975. Cert. tchr., Alaska, N.Y., Calif., Colo., Fla., N.Mex., Oreg., Wyo., Va., Oreg., also others. Police officer San Jose Police Dept., 1957-65, sgt., 1965-75, lt., 1975-81; dep. chief Boulder (Colo.) Police Dept., 1981-92; ret. Pres. Kaminsky & Assocs., Inc., Longmont, Colo. 1981—. Author, editor: (textbook) The Field Training Concept in Criminal Justice Agencies, 2000; contbr. articles to profl. jours. Exec. dir. Nat. Assn. Field Tng. Officers Assn., 1993-2000. Sgt. U.S. Army, 1957-61, Korea. Recipinet Lifetime Achievement award Am. Soc. L.E. Trainers, 2000. Mem. Police Mgmt. Assn. (sec. 1983-88), Calif. Assn. Police Tng. Officers, Internat. Assn. Women Police, Calif. Assn. Adminstrn. of Justice Educators, Internat. Assn. Chiefs of Police (use of deadly force com.). Republican. Episcopalian. Avocations: bowling, softball, art collecting. Home and Office: 8965 Sage Valley Rd Longmont CO 80503-8885 E-mail: kaminskygf@msn.com.

KAMINSKY, IRA SAMUEL, lawyer; b. Feb. 3, 1936; s. Louis J. and Gertrude (Leff) K.; m. Barbara Handmaker, Feb. 11, 1954; children: Sherry, Louis, Jay, Phillip; m. 2d, Phyllis Levitt, June 24, 1971; 1 child, Glenn. BA, U. Mich., 1957, JD, 1960. Bar: Pa. 1960, U.S. Dist. Ct. (we. dist.) Pa. 1961. Assoc. Kaminsky & Kelly, Johnstown, Pa., 1960-67; ptnr. Kaminsky, Thomas, Wharton and Lovette, Johnstown, 1967—2001, of counsel, 2002—. Hearing examiner Pa. Liquor Control Bd., 1970-92; mem. regulatory task force U.S. SBA, 1980-85; mem. com. on fed. assistance for alternative fuels U.S. Dept. Energy, 1982-86. Mem. ABA, Pa. Bar Assn. (ho. of dels. 1969-2001, bd. govs. 1989-92). Office: 360 Stonycreek Street Johnstown PA 15901-1925 E-mail: isk@ktwllaw.com.

KAMINSKY, MANFRED STEPHAN, physicist; b. Koenigsberg, Germany, June 4, 1929; came to U.S., 1958; s. Stephan and Kaethe (Gieger) K.; m. Elisabeth Moellering, May 1, 1957; children: Cornelial K.B., Mark-Peter. First diploma in physics, U. Rostock, Germany, 1951; PhD in Physics magna cum laude, U. Marburg, Germany, 1957. German Research Soc. fellow and grad. asst. in physics U. Rostock, 1950-52; lectr. Rostock Med. Tech. Sch., 1952; German Research Soc. fellow and research asst. Phys. Inst., U. Marburg, 1953-57, sr. asst., 1957-58; research asso. Argonne (Ill.) Nat. Lab., 1958-59, asst. physicist, 1959-62, assoc., 1962-70, sr. physicist, 1970-86, dir. Surface Sci. Center-CTR Program, 1974-80, dir. Tribology Program, 1984-86; sole propr. Surface Treatment Sci. Internat., Hinsdale, Ill., 1986—. Cons. Office Tech. Assessment U.S. Congress, 1986, NRC com. on tribology, 1986-88; guest prof. Inst. Energy, U. Que., Montreal-Varennes, 1976-82; E.W. Mueller lectr. U. Wis., Milw., 1978; symposium chmn. Internat. Conf. Metall. Coatings, 1985-93. Author: Atomic and Ionic Impact Phenomena on Metal Surfaces, 1965; contbr. articles to profl. jours.; editor: Radiation Effects on Solid Surfaces, 1976; co-editor: Surface Effects on Controlled Fusion, 1974, Surface Effects in Controlled Fusion Devices, 1976, Dictionary of Terms for Vacuum Science and Technology, 1980; patentee in field. Bd. dirs. Com. 100, Hinsdale, 1970-75, 90-92, pres., 1973-74; pres. St. Vincent de Paul Soc., Hinsdale, 1972-73. Named Outstanding New Citizen of Year Citizenship Council Chgo., 1968; Japanese Soc. Promotion of Sci. fellow, 1982. Fellow Am. Phys. Soc.; mem. Am. Chem. Soc., Scientific Research Soc., Research Soc. Am., AAAS, Union German Phys. Socs., Am. Vacuum Soc. (sr., trustee 1982-84, chmn. Midwest sect. 1967-68, co-founder Gt. Lakes chpt., dir. 1968-70, chmn. fusion tech. div. 1980-81, editorial bd. jour. 1978-83, hon. 1986), Internat. Union Vacuum Sci., Techs. and Applications (chmn. fusion div. 1984-86), Sigma Xi. Home: 906 S Park Ave Hinsdale IL 60521-4519 also: 300 Galen Dr Apt 506 Key Biscayne FL 33149-2177 Office: Surface Treatment Sci Internat PO Box 175 Hinsdale IL 60522-0175

KAMINSKY, RICHARD ALAN, lawyer; b. Toledo, Nov. 15, 1951; s. Jack and Sally (Kale) K. BA, Johns Hopkins U., 1973; JD, U. Mich., 1975. Bar: Ill. 1976, U.S. Dist. Ct. (no. dist.) Ill. 1976. Assoc. Vedder, Price, Kaufman & Kammholz, Chgo., 1976-83; atty. Borg-Warner Corp., Chgo., 1983-89; v.p., assoc. gen. counsel CNA Ins. Cos., Chgo., 1989—. Bd. dirs. DePaul U. Inst. Bus. & Profl. Ethics. Contbr. chpt. to book. Mem. ABA, Chgo. Bar Assn., Ill. State C. of C. Home: 47 Williamsburg Rd Evanston IL 60203-1813 Office: CNA Ins Cos Cna Pla Chicago IL 60685-0001 E-mail: richard.kaminsky@cna.com.

KAMISAR, YALE, lawyer, educator; b. N.Y.C., Aug. 29, 1929; s. Samuel and Mollie (Levine) K.; m. Esther Englander, Sept. 7, 1953 (div. Oct. 1973); children: David Graham, Gordon, Jonathan; m. Christine Keller, May 10, 1974 (dec. 1997); m. Joan Russell, Feb. 28, 1999. AB, NYU, 1950; LLB, Columbia U., 1954; LLD, CUNY, 1978. Bar: D.C. 1955. Rsch. assoc. Am. Law Inst., N.Y.C., 1953; assoc. Covington & Burling, Washington, 1955-57; assoc. prof., then prof. law U. Minn., Mpls., 1957-64; prof. law U. Mich., Ann Arbor, 1965-92, Clarence Darrow disting. univ. prof., 1992—. Vis. prof. law Harvard U., 1964-65, San Diego U., 2000-02; disting. vis. prof. law Coll. William and Mary, 1988; cons. Nat. Adv. Commn. Civil Disorders, 1967-68, Nat. Commn. Causes and Prevention Violence, 1968-69; mem. adv. com. model code pre-arraignment procedure Am. Law Inst., 1965-75. Reporter-draftsman: Uniform Rules of Criminal Procedure, 1971-73; author: (with J.H. Choper, S. Shiffrin and R.H. Fallon), Constitutional Law: Cases, Comments and Questions, 9th edit., 2001; (with W. LaFave, J. Israel and N. King) Modern Criminal Procedure: Cases and Commentaries, 10th edit., 2002, Criminal Procedure and the Constitution: Leading Cases and Introductory Text, 2002; (with F. Inbau and T. Arnold) Criminal Justice in Our Time, 1965; (with J. Grano and J. Haddad) Sum and Substance of Criminal Procedure, 1977, Police Interrogation and Confessions: Essays in Law and Policy, 1980; contbr. articles to profl. jours. Served to 1st lt. AUS, 1951-52. Recipient Am. Bar Found. Rsch. award, 1996. Home: 2910 Daleview Dr Ann Arbor MI 48105-9684 Office: U Mich Law Sch 625 S State St Ann Arbor MI 48109-1215

KAMLER, KENNETH MARK, microsurgeon; b. NYC, Oct. 4, 1947; s. William and Ethel Kamler; children: Jonathan, Jennifer. BA in Biology, CUNY, N.Y.C., 1968; MD, U. Marseille, France, 1975. Resident orthoped. surgery L.I. Jewish Med. Ctr., N.Y.C., 1980; fellow hand and microsurgery Columbia-Presbyn. Med. Ctr., N.Y.C., 1981; microsurgeon specializing in hand surgery New Hyde Park, N.Y., 1981—. Mt. Everest (Nepal) expdn. doctor Nat. Geog., 1992-93, 95-96; chief high altitude physician NASA/Yale Comml. Space Ctr., Mt. Everest, 1998, 99; expdn. doctor Andes, Amazon, Arctic, Galapagos, Antarctica, Peru, Ecuador, 1981, 87-89; tech. advisor IMAX Movie Everest, 1997; lectr. in field. Author: Doctor on Everest, 2000; contbg. author: Everest: Mountain Without Mercy, 1997. Fellow Explorers Club (dir. 1995-2001, 2003—, sci. adv. bd. 1996—, v.p. membership 1996-99, v.p. rsch. and edn. 1999-2003, heroism and altruism on Everest award 1999, Sci. Achievement award 2002); mem. Sigma XI. Jewish. Avocations: sailing, scuba diving, mountain climbing, drawing. Home: 15041 Village Rd Jamaica NY 11432-1024 Office: 410 Lakeville Rd New Hyde Park NY 11042-1101 E-mail: kkamler@aol.com.

KAMLET, MARK, provost; B in Math., Stanford U.; M in Econs. and Stats., PhD in Econs., U. Calif., Berkeley. Former assoc. dean Coll. Humanities and Social Scis. Carnegie Mellon U., Pitts., former head dept. social and decision scis., former dean H. John Heinz III Sch. Pub. Policy and Mgmt., provost, H. John Heinz III prof. econs. and pub. policy. Past mem. U.s. Panel on Cost Effectiveness in Health and Medicine; past mem. NIH panels; courtesy faculty appointment dept. psychiatry U. Pitts. Sch. Medicine. Contbr. articles to profl. jours. Mem. exec. com. Ford Found. Pub. Policy and Internat. Affairs Fellowship Program; 1st vice chair Pitts. Partnership for Neighborhood Devel.; sec. Pitts. Parks Conservancy; chair Allegheny County Coun. Econ. Devel. Advisors, Pitts. Recipient Vernon prize for outstanding article of yr., Jour. Policy Analysis and Mgmt., 1992. Mem.: Nat. Assn. Schs. Pub. Affairs and Adminstrn. (exec. com.), Assn. Pub. Policy Analysis and Mgmt. (exec. com.). Office: Carnegie Mellon U Office of Provost 5000 Forbes Ave Pittsburgh PA 15213

KAMLOT, ROBERT, performing arts executive; b. Vienna, Nov. 28, 1926; came to U.S., 1938, naturalized, 1943; s. Paul and Elsa (Wilhelm) K.; m. Jayne Bullard, Sept. 18, 1948. Student, CCNY, Syracuse U., Hunter Coll., N.Y.C. Freelance mgr. Broadway prodns., 1964-71; prodn. exec. Zev Bufman Prodns., N.Y.C., 1969-71; co.-mgr. Much Ado About Nothing, N.Y.C., 1972, Two Gentlemen From Verona (nat. co.), Los Angeles, 1973. Gen. mgr. N.Y. Shakespeare Festival, 1973-83; gen. mgr. The Real Thing, Sunday in the Park With George, Biloxi Blues, The Odd Couple, Moon for the Misbegotten, Whoopi Goldberg, Social Security, Long Day's Journey Into Night, 1983-86, (nat. tour) Catskills on Broadway, Fool Moon, Wrong Turn at Lungfish; prodr. Hayfever, 1986; gen. mgr. Carole Shorenstein Hays Enterprises; prodr. Fences, 1987; gen. mgr. Martin Starger/The Really Useful Co. Lend Me a Tenor, 1988, Cates Films-Elmer Gantry, 1991-92, Martin Starger The Red Shoes, 1992, Fool Moon (European prodn.), 1994, BIG The Musical, 1995. Served with AUS, 1944. Mem. Assn. Theatrical Press Agts. and Mgrs., Tony Nominating Commn. Home: 175 W 93rd St New York NY 10025-9313 E-mail: jaybob175@aol.com.

KAMM, LAURENCE RICHARD, television producer, director; b. Long Branch, NJ, Oct. 10, 1939; s. Herbert and Phyllis Irene (Silberblatt) K.; m. Claire Louise Cadieux, Oct. 5, 1977; children: Lauren Michelle, Kristin Marie. BS in Speech, Northwestern U., 1961. Prodn. asst. ABC-TV, NYC, 1962-64; assoc. dir. ABC Sports, NYC, 1964-70, dir., prodr., 1970-95; coord. dir. Turner Sports, Atlanta, 1995—2000, YES Network, 2000—; Coll. Football Dir. ABC Sports, 2000—. Dir. numerous major sports events including: Super Bowl XXII, Super Bowl XXV Pre-Game, Half-Time and Post Game Shows, Super Bowl XXXVII Pre-game Show, Super Bowl TV spls., Coll. Football Scoreboard Show, Monday Night Football Half-Time Show, Summer Olympic Games, 1972, 76, 84 (Emmy award 1984), world dir. gymnastics Summer Olympic Games4s, 1996, Winter Olympic Games, 1976-88 (Emmy award 1976), Nagano Olympic Winter Games, 1998, Goodwill Games, 1998, Great Am. Bike Race, 1983 (2 Emmy awards), Indianapolis 500, 1980-87 (Emmy award 1982), Western States 100 Mile Endurance Race, 1985, 86, 20th anniversary spl. for Wide World of Sports (Emmy award 1981), New York Marathon, 1985, 86, Monday Night Football, 1987 (Emmy award), CFA Big 10 and Pac 10 Coll. Football, Major League Baseball, Tour de France Bicycle Race, Profl. Bowler Tours, Grand Prix of Monaco, Indy and NASCAR Racing, Coll. and NBA Basketball, Amateur and Profl. Figure Skating Championships; mem. directing team 25th Anniversary Spl. for Wide World of Sports (Emmy award 1986); scenic design Yes Network Studio (N.Y. local Emmy award); directing team ABC News Coverage Election Night, 1972, 76, 80, 84, 88, 92, 2000, Reagan, Bush and Clinton Inaugurations, numerous ABC News Specials including Millennium 2000; dir. team 1994 World Cup Soccer Championships; coord. dir. Goodwill Games, 1994. Recipient Emmy award for Wide World of Sports, 1986, 88, 90, Individual Achievement Emmy award for Winter Olympics spl. camera mount project, 1988, NY Emmy Award-Scenic Design, YES Network, Lifetime Achievement award in sports Dirs. Guild Am., 1997, Emmy award for tech. achievement TNT Virtual Studio, 1997. Mem.: NATAS, Dir.'s Guild Am. (Lifetime Achievement in Sports award 1996). Home Fax: 212-829-0820. E-mail: KammL@aol.com.

KAMM, LINDA HELLER, lawyer; b. N.Y.C., Aug. 25, 1939; d. Seymour A. and Mary Heller; children: Lisa, Oliver. BA in History, Brandeis U., 1961; LLB, Boston Coll., 1967. Bar: Mass. 1967, D.C. 1978, U.S. Supreme Ct. 1985. Counsel Dem. Study Group, Washington, 1968-71; counsel select com. on coms. U.S. Ho. of Reps., Washington, 1973-75, gen. counsel budget com., 1975-77; gen. counsel U.S. Dept. Transp., Washington, 1977-80; ptnr. Foley and Lardner, Washington, 1980-84, of counsel, 1984-95; pvt. practice, 1995—; of counsel Boies, Schiller & Flexner, 2001—.

KAMM, ROGER DALE, biomedical engineer, educator; b. Ashland, Wis., Oct. 10, 1950; s. Rudolph Wilhelm and Betty Jane (White) K.; m. Judith Mary Brown, Sept. 1, 1974; 1 child, Peter Martin. BS, Northwestern U., 1972; SM, MIT, 1973, PhD, 1977. Lectr. MIT, Cambridge, 1977-78, asst. prof., 1978-81, assoc. prof., 1981-87, prof. mech. engring. and bioengring., 1987—, assoc. dir. Ctr. for Biomed. Engring., 1995—. Vice chmn. U.S. Nat. Com. on Biomech., 2003—. Contbr. more than 130 articles to profl. jours. Fellow Am. Inst. Med. and Biol. Engring. (founding); mem. ASME (chmn. summer bioengring. conf.), Am. Physiol. Soc., Biomed. Engring. Soc. (sr., chmn. awards com. 1989-91, bd. dirs. 1994-97), World Coun. on Biomechanics (sec./treas., vice-chmn. 2002—). Home: 31 Nonesuch Rd Weston MA 02493-1021 Office: MIT 77 Massachusetts Ave Rm NE47-321 Cambridge MA 02139-4307

KAMMAN, ALAN BERTRAM, communications consulting company executive; b. Phila., Jan. 25, 1931; s. Daniel Lawrence and Sara Belle K.; m. Madeleine Marguerite Pin, Feb. 15, 1960; children: Alan Daniel, Neil Charles. BCE, Swarthmore Coll., 1952. With Bell Tel. Co. Pa., Phila., 1952-69, Arthur D. Little, Inc., Cambridge, Mass., 1969-85, v.p. telecommunications scis., 1977-81, v.p. corp. staff, 1981-86; nat. dir. telecommunications markets KPMG Peat Marwick, Lexington, Mass., 1987-91; mng. dir. Global Consulting Group, St. Helena, Calif., 1991—; dir. Cambridge (Mass.) Strategic Mgmt. Group, 1992—; v.p. Symmetrix, Lexington, Mass., 1994-96; exec. dir. Vt. Telecomm. Application Ctr., 1998—. Chmn. adv. bd. grad. program telecommunications U. San Francisco, Intelevent, Europe, Telecom 75, Telecom 79, Telecom 83, Telecom 91, Telecommunications Mag.; world rep. KPMG Peat Marwick to Internat. Telecommunications Union, UN. Contbr. articles to jours. in field. Bd. dirs. U.S. Coun. World Communications Yr. Mem. Appalachian Club (v.p. ops., bd. dirs.).

KAMMAN, CURTIS WARREN, retired ambassador; b. Chgo., Jan. 15, 1939; s. Glenn Forrest and Mildred Isabel (Merry) Kamman; m. Mary Glasgow Curtis, Feb. 10, 1962; children: Edward, John, W Stephen. BA, Yale U., 1959; postgrad., U. Washington, 1964-65. Joined Fgn. Service, U.S. Dept. State, 1960-2000; various diplomatic positions Am. embassies, Washington, Mexico City, Hong Kong, Moscow, Nairobi, 1960-80; dir. East African Affairs, Washington, 1980-82; polit. counselor Am. embassy, Moscow, 1982-84, minister, counselor, 1984-85; prin. officer U.S. Interests sect. Swiss embassy, Havana, Cuba, 1985-87; dep. asst. sec. U.S. Dept. State, Washington, 1987-91; amb. to Chile Santiago, 1991-94; amb. to Bolivia, 1994-97; amb. to Colombia, 1997-2000; ret., 2000. Vis. instr. Univ. Notre Dame, 2001—. Mem. vestry All Saints Ch., Saugatuck, Mich., 2002—; bd. dirs. Fgn. Students Sch., Havana, 1985—87. Mem.: Am. Acad. Diplomacy, Phi Beta Kappa. Episcopalian. Avocation: choral singing. Address: 2236 Lakeshore Dr Fennville MI 49408-9715

KAMMAN, WILLIAM, historian, educator; b. Geneva, Ind., Mar. 23, 1930; s. Harry August and Ruth Lois (Shoemaker) K.; m. Nancy Ellen Prichard, Apr. 19, 1957; children: Frederick William, Elizabeth Ellen, David Paul. AB, Ind. U., 1952, PhD, 1962; MA, Yale U., 1958. Tchr. pub. schs., Bloomington, Ind., 1955-57, 58-59; asst. prof. history U. North Tex. (formerly North Tex. State U.), Denton, 1962-66, assoc. prof., 1966-69, prof., 1969—, chmn. dept. history, 1977-89, 93-94, assoc. dean arts and scis., 1996—2002, interim dean arts and scis., 1997-98. Author: A Search for Stability: United States Diplomacy Toward

Nicaragua, 1968; contbg. author: Makers of American Diplomacy, 1974, Ency. World Biography, 1973, 87—, Ency. Am. Fgn. Policy, 1978, 2002, The War of 1898 and U.S. Interventions, 1898-34: An Ency., 1994. Mem. Denton Planning and Zoning Commn., 1976-79, 86-92. Served with U.S. Army, 1952-54. Mem. Am. Hist. Assn., Orgn. Am. Historians, Soc. Historians Am. Fgn. Relations (exec. sec.-treas. 1985-89), Phi Alpha Theta Methodist. Home: 2225 Scripture St Denton TX 76201-3707 Office: U North Tex History Dept Denton TX 76203

KAMMEN, CAROL KOYEN, historian, educator; b. Plainfield, N.J., Nov. 14, 1937; d. Elmer Albert and Helen Edith (Kingberry) Koyen; m. Michael Kammen, Feb. 26, 1961; children: Daniel Merson, Douglas Anton. BA, George Washington U., Washington, 1959. Tchr. Am. history Ithaca (N.Y.) H.S., 1971-73; lectr. history Tompkins Cortland C.C., Dryden, N.Y., 1973-84, Cornell U., Ithaca, 1983-85, lectr., 1986-92, sr. lectr., 1992—. Cons. Nat. Humanities Faculty, Atlanta, 1981—; project dir. Nat. Youth Grant Ithaca H.S., 1972—74; dir. Tompkins County Arts Coun., Ithaca, 1984; cons., historian Empire State Partnership on Arts in Edn. Program, Hangar Theater, 1991—2001; appt. historian Tompkins County, Ithaca, 2000—; lectr. and cons. various hist. socs.; local history adv. bd. N.Y. Commr. Edn., 2002—. Author: Simeon DeWitt Proprietor of Ithaca, 1969, author: What They Wrote, 1978, Lives Passed, 1984, Peopling of Tompkins County, 1986 (RCHA award of Merit 1987), On Doing Local History, 1986, repub., 1996 (Merit award 1987), rev. edit., 2003, Plain as a Pipestem, 1989; editor: One Day in Ithaca, 1989 (Spl. award 1989), The Finger Lakes of New York, 1996, Pursuit of Local History, 1997, Cornell University: Glorious to View, 2003; author plays, including: Central New York (video script) 1978, Between the Lines, 1985, Testimony for Black Voices, 1986, Counting Wheat Street, 1986, Jazz a la Mode, 1987, A Chamber Entertainment with Clowns, 1988, Flight to Ithaca, 1995, Womens' Proper Place, 1997, Peaches and Bird, 1998, Ain't I a Man, Too?, 1998, Escape to the North, 1999, Juneteenth: The Ithaca Connection, 2000, The Day the Women Met, 2000; columnist The Ithaca Jour., 1978—; ednl. writer History News, 1995—; contbg. editor Ency. of New York; editor: The Local History Ency., 2000; contbr. articles to profl. jours. Local history adv. coun. NY State Commr., 2002—. Recipient award of excellence Tompkins County Trust Co., Ithaca, 1995. Mem. Am. Assn. State and Local History (editl. writer History News 1995—), Assn. Pub. Historians N.Y. State. Democrat. Home: 16 Sun Path Ithaca NY 14850-9781 Office: Cornell U Dept History 433 McGraw Hall Ithaca NY 14853 E-mail: ckk6@cornell.edu.

KAMMEN, MICHAEL, historian, educator; b. Rochester, N.Y., Oct. 25, 1936; s. Jacob M. and Blanche (Lazerow) K.; m. Carol Koyen, Feb. 26, 1961; children: Daniel Merson, Douglas Anton. AB, George Washington U., 1958, LHD (hon.), 1991; MA, Harvard U., 1959, PhD (Bowdoin prize), 1964. Mem. faculty Cornell U., 1965—, Newton C. Farr prof. Am. history and culture, 1973—, chmn. dept. history, 1974-76, dir. ctr. for humanities, 1977-80. 1st holder chair in Am. history Ecole des Hautes Etudes en Sciences Sociales, Paris, France, 1980-81; Commonwealth Fund lectr. in Am. history U. London, 1976. Author: A Rope of Sand: The Colonial Agents, British Politics and the American Revolution, 1968, Deputyes and Libertyes: The Origins of Representative Government in Colonial America, 1969, People of Paradox: An Inquiry Concerning the Origins of American Civilization, 1972 (Pulitzer Prize for history, 73), Colonial New York: A History, 1975, A Season of Youth: The American Revolution and the Historical Imagination, 1978, Spheres of Liberty: Changing Perceptions of Liberty in American Culture, 1986, A Machine That Would Go of Itself: The Constitution in American Culture, 1986 (Francis Parkman and Henry Adams prizes, 87), Selvages & Biases: The Fabric of History in American Culture, 1987, Sovereignty and Liberty: Constitutional Discourse in American Culture, 1988, Mystic Chords of Memory: The Transformation of Tradition in American Culture, 1991, Meadows of Memory: Images of Time and Tradition in American Art and Culture, 1992, The Lively Arts: Gilbert Seldes and the Transformation of Cultural Criticism in the United States, 1996, In the Past Lane: Historical Perspectives on American Culture, 1997, American Culture, American Tastes: Social Change and the 20th Century, 1999, Robert Gwalthmey: The Life and Art of a Passionate Observer, 1999; editor: What is the Good of History?: Selected Letters of Carl L. Becker, 1900-1945, 1973, The Origins of the American Constitution: A Documentary History, 1986; editor-in-chief: The Past Before Us: Contemporary Historical Writing in the United States, 1980. Bd. dirs. Social Sci. Research Council, 1980-83. Fellow NEH, 1967, 72-73, 84-85, 97-98, Humanities Ctr. Johns Hopkins U., 1968-69, Ctr. for Advanced Study in Behavioral Scis., Stanford, 1976-77; Guggenheim fellow 1980-81, Regents fellow Smithsonian Instn. 1990, Times-Mirror Found. Rsch. Prof. Am. Studies, The Huntington Libr., San Marino, Calif., 1993-94; guest scholar Woodrow Wilson Ctr., Washington, 1997-98. Mem.: AAAS, Soc. Am. Historians, Mass. Hist. Soc., Am. Antiquarian Soc., N.Y. State Hist. Assn., Orgn. Am. Historians (exec. bd. 1989—92, pres. 1995—96), Am. Hist. Assn. (coun. 1976—79), Phi Beta Kappa. Home: 16 Sun Path Ithaca NY 14850-9781 Office: Cornell U Dept History McGraw Hall Ithaca NY 14853

KAMMER, RAYMOND GERARD, JR., government official; b. Arlington, Va., Jan. 5, 1947; s. Raymond Gerard and Kathleen Elizabeth (Nahow) K.; m. Mauna Kathleen Vogan, Mar. 23, 1967 (div. Aug. 1981); 1 child, Kathleen J.; m. Wilma Norma McMasters, May 15, 1985 BA, U. Md., 1969. Budget analyst Nat. Bur. Standards, Gaithersburg, Md., 1974-75, program analyst, 1975-76, sr. program analyst, 1976-78, assoc. dir. programs, budget and finance, 1978-80, dep. dir., 1980-91; dep. under sec. for oceans and atmosphere NOAA, 1991-93; dep. dir. Nat. Inst. Standards and Tech., 1993-96, dir., 1997—2000; acting chief fin. officer, acting asst. sec. for adminstrn. Dept. of Commerce, 1996-97; cons., 2000—. Recipient Silver medal Dept. Commerce, 1977, Gold medal Dept. Commerce, 1983, William J. Jump Meml. award William A. Jump Found., 1984, Meritorious Exec. award Dept. Commerce, 1980, 86, Roger W. Jones Exec. Leadership award, Am. U., 1988. Home: 14301 Bubbling Spring Rd Boyds MD 20841-4303

KAMMER, ROBERT ARTHUR, JR., lawyer; b. Boston, July 31, 1945; s. Robert Arthur and Lorraine B. (Edgar) K.; m. Elizabeth Britton Helmes, Aug. [illegible], 1968; children: Scott, Betsy. BA, Northwestern U., 1967; JD cum laude, Syracuse U., 1975. Bar: Ill. 1975, U.S. Supreme Ct. 1980, U.S. Dist. Ct. (no. dist.) Ill. 1975, Wis. 1983, U.S. Dist. Ct. (ea. and we. dists.) Wis. 1983. Atty. Lord Bissell & Brook, Chgo., 1975-83, Mulcahy & Wherry, Milw., 1983-86; assoc. gen. counsel, dir. litigation Sentry Ins., Stevens Point, Wis., 1986-99; sr. claims counsel Wausau (Wis.) Ins., 1999; regional litigation mgr. Liberty Mut. Group, Wausau, 1999—. Mem. Lake Bluff (Ill.) Sch. Bd., 1980-83; chmn. bd. dirs. Achievement Ctr. Early Intervention Program, Inc., 1993—; bd. dirs. Portage County Legal Aid Soc., 1994-98. Mem. ABA (vice chmn. TIPS corp. counsel com. 1992-95, co-chmn. litigation mgmt. subcom.), Wis. Bar Assn. chmn. corp. counsel com. 1988-92), Stevens Point Country Club (bd. dirs. 1998—). Avocations: golf, tennis. Home: 600 7th St Plover WI 54467-2234 Office: Liberty Mut Group 2100 Stewart Ave Ste 200 Wausau WI 54401

KAMMERER, ANN MARIE, geotechnical engineer; b. Sacramento, Calif., May 24, 1968; d. Rodney Dean and Karen Christine (Hvolboll) K.; m. Brian Louis Faudoa. AS, City Coll. of San Francisco, 1994; BS, U. Calif Berkeley, 1996, MS, 1998, PhD, 2002. Cert. engr. Engr. Olivia Chen Cons., San Francisco, 1995-96, GEI Cons., San Francisco, 1996-97; grad. rschr. U. Calif. Berkeley, 1997—2002, lectr., 2002, postdoc. rschr., 2003—; sr. geotech. engr. Arup USA, San Francisco, 2002—; lectr. Santa Clara U., 2003. Contbr. articles to profl. jour. Chair City Coll. San Francisco Women's Resource Ctr., 1993—94; chair student leadership coun. Pacific Earthquake Engring. Ctr., 1999—2000; student trustee San Francisco C.C. Dist., 1994. Recipient Calif. Alumni Assn. Leadership scholarship, 1994, Howard D. Eberhart Meml. scholarship, 1996, Nat. Sci. Found. grad. fellowship, 1997-2000; Earthquake Engring. Rsch. Inst./Fed. Emergency Mgmt. Agy. Nat. Earthquake Hazards Reduction Program grad. fellow, 2001. Mem. ASCE, Earthquake Engring. Rsch. Inst., Pacific Earthquake Engring. Rsch. Ctr., Golden Key Nat. Honor Soc., Tau Beta Pi (pres. 1995). Democrat. Avocations: scuba diving, skiing, rock hunting. Office: Arup 901 Market St Ste 260 San Francisco CA 94103-0001 E-mail: annie.brian@mindspring.com., Annie.Kammerer@Arup.com.

KAMMERER, KELLY CHRISTIAN, lawyer; b. N.Y.C., Nov. 29, 1941; s. William Henry and Edith (Langley) K.; m. Nancy Davis Frame, Oct. 2, 1999. BA, U. Notre Dame, 1963; LLB, U. Va., 1968. Bar: Va. 1968, N.Y. 1969, D.C. 1969, Fla. 1969. Peace Corps vol., Colombia, 1963-65; Reginald Heber Smith atty./fellow U. Pa., Washington, 1968-70; atty.-advisor, dep. gen. counsel Peace Corps, Washington, 1970-74; atty.-advisor AID, Dept. State, Washington, 1975-76, asst. gen. counsel, 1976-78, sr. dep. gen. counsel, 1978-82, legal counselor, 1981-82, dir. congl. rels., 1983-89; mission dir. Kathmandu, Nepal, 1989-93, counselor to the agy., 1994-99; vice chmn., U.S. rep. OECD/DAC, Paris, 1999—. Recipient Disting. Honor award AID, 1979, 83, Equal Opportunity award, 1982; presdl. rank of Disting. Sr. Exec., 1984, 89, Meritorious Sr. Exec., 1997. Mem. Inter-Am. Bar Assn., Soc. Internat. Law. Address: Psc 116 Box Oecd/aid Apo AE 09777-5000 also: 11 bis Blvd Jules Sandeau 75016 Paris France

KAMMERZELL, SUSAN JANE, elementary school educator, music educator; b. Greeley, Colo., Mar. 4, 1953; d. Carl Warren and Charlotte Josephine Strandberg; m. Arnold Henry Kammerzell, Sept. 11, 1976; 1 child, Jeffrey Scott. BA in Elem. Edn., U. No. Colo., 1975. Elem. tchr. grade 1 Ft. Morgan (Colo.) Sch. Dist., 1975—76; presch. dir., tchr. Wiggins (Colo.) Presch., 1987—89; elem. tchr. grade 1 Wiggins Sch. Dist., 1989—91, elem. tchr. kindergarten, 1991—96, elem. tchr. gen. music, 1996—. Sunday sch. tchr. grades 4 and 5 Wiggins Cmty. Ch., 1996—. Mem.: Nat. Assn. for Music Edn. Republican. Mem. United Church Of Christ. Avocations: travel, reading, music. Home: 5446 Road O Wiggins CO 80654 Office: Wiggins Sch Dist RE-50J Wiggins Elem 320 Chapman Wiggins CO 80654

KAMMEYER, SONIA MARGARETHA, real estate agent; b. Stockholm, June 21, 1942; came to U.S., 1964; d. Bengt Henrik and Margot Elsa M. (Hodin) Sjoberg; m. Whitman Ridgway, June 13, 1964 (div. 1978); children: Sean, Siobhan; m. Kenneth C.W. Kammeyer, Dec. 28, 1982. Student, Fleisher's Art Meml. Sch., Phila., 1966-69. With Ben Bell Real Estate, Lanham, Md., 1972-73, Robert L. Gruen Real Estate, Silver Spring, Md., 1973-81, Panarama Real Estate, Silver Spring, 1981-82, Long & Foster Real Estate, Inc., Silver Spring, 1982—. Named to Montgomery County Bd. Realtors Hall of Fame, 1994; recipient Nat. Sales Award, Realty Alliance, 1997. Mem. Montgomery County Bd. Realtors (life), Howard County Bd. Realtors, Swedish Profl. Women. Avocations: sculpture, painting, jewelry making, gardening, guitar playing. Home: 14600 Triadelphia Mill Rd Dayton MD 21036-1217 Office: Long & Foster Real Estate 3901 National Dr Burtonsville MD 20866-1141

KAMP, ARTHUR JOSEPH, JR., lawyer; b. July 22, 1945; s. Arthur Joseph and Irene Catherine (Ehrstein) K.; m. Barbara Hays, Aug. 24, 1968; children: Sara, Nathaniel. BA, SUNY, 1968, JD, 1970. Bar: N.Y. 1971, U.S. Dist. Ct. (we. dist.) N.Y. 1971, Va. 1973, U.S. Dist. Ct. (ea. dist.) Va. 1973. Atty. Neighborhood Legal Svcs., Buffalo, 1971; assoc. Diamonstein & Drucker, Newport News, 1972-77; ptnr. Diamonstein, Drucker & Kamp, Newport News, 1977-84, Kamp & Kamp, Newport News, 1984-87, Kaufman & Canoles, 1987-96, David, Kamp & Frank, L.L.C., 1996—; v.p. Peninsula Legal Aid Ctr., Inc., 1978-92. Chmn. Newport News Planning Commn., 1994-95, commr., 1990-97; mem. bd. visitors Ea. Va. Med. Sch., 1997—, vice rector, 2001, rector, 2002. Lt. USAF, 1971-72. Mem. Va. State Bar Assn., Newport News Bar Assn. (past bd. dirs., chmn. legal aid com.), Va. Bar Assn., Va. Peninsula C. of C. (bd. dirs., exec. com., chmn. 1997, gen. counsel 1999-2001). Democrat. Office: David Kamp & Frank LLC 301 Hiden Blvd Ste 200 Newport News VA 23606-2939 E-mail: ajkamp@davidkampfrank.com.

KAMP, CYNTHIA LEA, elementary education educator; b. Johnstown, Pa., June 29, 1956; d. Charles Jr. and Helen Lois (Paff) Lane; m. Robert Thomas Kamp, June 9, 1979; children: Jason, Meghan, Jordan. BFA, Miami U., Oxford, Ohio, 1978, MA, 1984. Cert. fine arts tchr., Ohio. Tchr. art Mt. Healthy City Schs., Cin. Mem. ASCD, Ohio Arts Edn. Assn., Ohio Edn. Assn. Home: 25 Brompton Ln Cincinnati OH 45218-1314 Office: Greener Elem Sch 2400 Adams Rd Cincinnati OH 45231

KAMP, PHILIP, food products executive; b. Orrville, Ohio, Oct. 31, 1963; s. Kenneth and Norma Jean K.; m. Brenda, July 3, 1993; 1 child, Nicholas. Grad., U. Akron, 1990. Assoc. Smith Dairy Products Co., Orrville, Ohio, 1990—. Inventor in field. Mem. planning commn. City or Orrville, 1999—. With USMC, 1986-90. Mem. Internat. Soc. Itellectually Gifted, Mensa. Republican. Avocations: theatre, opera, writer. Office: Smith Dairy Products Co 234 N Vine St Orrville OH 44667-1644 Home: Apt 301 1825 Paradise Rd Orrville OH 44667-9402

KAMPEL, DONNE, academic administrator, educator; b. New York, Ny, Apr. 8, 1947; d. Hyman and Kate Spielberg Kampel; m. Michael Braff. BA, NYU, New York, NY, 1977, MPA, 1982. Sr budget analyst City U., New York, NY, 1985—91, assoc. dir. student affairs, 1991—98; spl. asst. NYU, New York, NY, 1998—2000; sr adminstr. academic affairs Yeshiva U., New York, NY, 2000—. V.p. Muffin Country Farms, Brooklyn, NY, 1987—89. Vol. Dem. Committees, New York, NY, 1986—92. Mem.: AAUP. Avocations: antique glass collecting, music, needlework, fishing. Office: Yeshiva University 500 W 185th St New York NY 10033 E-mail: kampel@ymail.yu.edu.

KAMPELMAN, MAX M. former ambassador, lawyer; b. N.Y.C., Nov. 7, 1920; s. Joseph and Eva (Gottlieb) Kampelmacher; m. Marjorie Buetow, Aug. 21, 1948; children: Anne, Jeffrey, Julie, David, Sarah. AB, NYU, 1940, JD, 1945; MA, U. Minn., 1946, PhD, 1951; PhD (hon.), Hebrew U. of Jerusalem, 1982; PhD (hon.), Ben Guiron U. of Negev, 1992; LHD (hon.), Hebrew Union Coll., 1984, Georgetown U., 1984; LLD (hon.), Bates Coll., 1986, Bar Ilan U., 1987, Jewish Theol. Sem. of Am., 1988, NYU, 1988, Adelphi U., 1992, Brandeis U., 1993; LHD (hon.), U. Minn., 1987, Yeshiva U., 1990, Fla. Internat. U., 1993. Bar: N.Y. 1947, D.C. 1950, Md. 1956, U.S. Supreme Ct. 1951. Mem. research staff Internat. Ladies Garment Workers Union, N.Y.C., 1940-41; instr. polit. sci. U. Minn., 1946-48; legis. counsel to U.S. Senator Hubert H. Humphrey, Washington, 1949-55; ptnr. Fried, Frank, Harris, Shriver & Kampelman, Washington, 1956-85, 89, Fried, Frank, Harris, Shriver & Jacobson, 1989-91, of counsel, 1991—; sr. advisor U.S. Delegation to UN, 1966-67; amb., chmn. U.S. Delegation to Conf. on Security and Cooperation in Europe, Madrid, 1980-83; amb., head U.S. Delegation to Negotiations on Nuclear and Space Arms, 1985-89; counselor of the U.S. Dept. of State, 1987-89. Amb., head U.S. del. Copenhagen meeting of Conf. Human Dimension of the CSCE, 1990, Geneva meeting of Conf. on Nat. Minorities of CSCE, 1991, Moscow Meeting on Human Dimension of CSCE, 1991; vice chmn. Mayor's Com. on Charter Reform, Mpls., 1947-48; faculty Sch. for Workers U. Wis., summers, 1947-48; faculty polit. economy Bennington Coll., Vt., 1948-50; vis. professorial lectr. dept. govt. Howard U., 1954-56; vis. prof. polit. sci. Claremont Coll., Calif., 1963 Author: Entering New Worlds: The Memoirs of a Private Man in Public Life, 1991, The Communist Party vs The C.I.O.: A Study in Power Politics, 1957, (with Kirkpatrick) The Strategy of deception, 1963, Three Years at the East-West Divide, 1983, Entering New Worlds: The Memoirs of a Private Man in Public Life, 1991; co-author: (with Kirkpatrick) Congress Against the President, 1976; contbr. articles to profl. publs.; moderator Washington Week in Rev. program Eastern Ednl. Network, 1967-70. Pres. Friends of Nat. Zoo, 1958-60, now hon. pres.; hon. vice chmn. Anti-Defamation League B'nai Brith, 1981—, vice chmn., 1977-81; pres. Am. Friends of Hebrew U., 1975-77, chmn. bd., 1977-80, now chmn. emeritus; co-chmn. U.S. Delegation to observe elections in El Salvador, 1984; chmn. Freedom House, N.Y.C., 1983-85, 89-93, now hon. chmn., Jerusalem Found., 1989-93; chmn. adv. com. JINSA; mem. bd. Ethics & Pub. Policy Ctr.; chmn. bd. govs. UN Assn. U.S., 1989-1992; chmn. emeritus Greater Washington Telecomm. Assn. (WETA-TV); v.p. Helen Dwight Reid Ednl. Found., 1959-85, Jewish Publ. Soc., 1978-85; hon. gov. The Hebrew U. Jerusalem, gov., 1973-85, chmn. Truman Research Inst. for Advancement of Peace, 1983-85; mem. exec. com. Com. on Present Danger, 1976-85; vice chmn. Coalition for a Dem. Majority, 1977-85; overseer Coll. V.I., 1963-80; bd. govs. U. Haifa, 1984-85, Tel Aviv U., 1984-85; bd. advisors Kennedy Inst. Ethics, 1984-85; chmn. Woodrow Wilson Internat. Ctr. for Scholars, 1979-81, trustee, 1979-90, chmn., 2002, Georgetown U. Inst. for Study of Diplomacy, 1994-2002; trustee Law Cen. Found. NYU, 1978-85; bd. dirs. Georgetown U., 1978-84, Mt. Vernon Coll., 1972-80, Hebrew Immigrant Aid Soc., 1981-85, Am. Peace Soc., 1973-85, Builders for Peace, 1993—; vice chmn. Internat. Media Fund, 1990-92; bd. dirs. U.S. Inst. Peace, 1985-86, vice chmn., bd. dirs. 1992-2000; mem. steering com. Action Coun. Peace in Balklans, 1993-1999; chmn. nat. adv. coun. Am. Jewish Com., 1993-1998. Mem. ABA (mem. standing com. on law and nat. security 1979-85, 90—, mem. exec. bd. East and Ctrl. European Law Inst. 1990), Coun. on Fgn. Rels., Fed. Bar Assn., Bar Assn. D.C., Am. Polit. Sci. Assn. (treas. 1956-58), D.C. Polit. Sci. Assn. (pres. 1955), Cosmos Club. Home: 3154 Highland Pl NW Washington DC 20008-3241 Office: Fried Frank Harris 1001 Pennsylvania Ave NW Washington DC 20004-2505 *The fatherhood of God presupposes the brotherhood of Man. However defined, this is a good guide for life's conduct.*

KAMPF, MARILYN JEANNE, medical analyst; b. Kenton, Ohio, Apr. 6, 1940; d. Earl Eugene and Vivian Ruth (Linke) Brown; m. Robert C. Kampf, June 27, 1964 (dec. 1999); 1 child, Robert W. (dec. 1998). Diploma, Lima (Ohio) Meml. Sch. Nursing, 1962, Ohio No. U., 1960. Head nurse pediatrics Lima Meml. Hosp., 1962-77; supr. med. fl. Van Wert (Ohio) County Hosp., 1977-82; sr. med. analyst Cen. Ins. Co., Van Wert, Ohio, 1982—2002. Utilization rev. agt. Workers Compensation Claims, Mass., N.J., Conn. Mem. Am. Bus. Women's Assn., Nat. Assn. Ins. Women (pres.), County RN Assn., Twigs, Nat. Managed Care Cert. (cert. managed care 1998—, hearth and home RN).

KAMPFE, DORIS ELAINE, storyteller, folk artist, poet; b. Monona, Iowa, Feb. 2, 1926; d. Frederick Conrad and Alvina Ulrika (Hass) Daugs; m. LaVern Arthur Kampfe, June 1, 1945; children: Lanny, Elisa Kay. Student, U. No. Iowa, 1965-68. Sec. Singer Sewing Machine Co., Denver, 1943, Interstate Power Co., Dubuque, Iowa, 1944, Ill. Supreme Ct., Chgo., 1979; tchr., mem. adv. bd. Headstart, Waterloo, Iowa, 1965-68; sec., tutor Japan Trade Ctr., Chgo., 1979—; feature writer Shopping News, Cedar Falls, Iowa, 1981-85, writer column Personalities and Wandering Around Waverly, 1981; folk artist Iowa Arts Coun., Des Moines, 1986—; storyteller Very Spl. Arts Iowa, Des Moines, 1992—. Cruise storyteller Delta Steamboat Line, New Orleans, 1990—; storyteller at folk and art festivals, mus., librs., chs., schs., colls., retirement ctrs., Spl. Olympics, theatre, Old Opera House, Chgo. (Ill.) Hist. Lincoln Soc., Brucemore Mansion Ragtime, restaurants, nature ctrs. and parks, banquets and confs., reunions, parties, county homes and country clubs, civic ctrs., Brucemore Mansion, Hawkeye Coll., Chgo. Hist. Soc., Rockford, Ill. Author: (play) Caramella, The Curious Camel, 1982; contbr. poetry to various publs., anthologies. Advisor N.W. opportunity bd. Headstart, Hoffman Estates, Ill., 1979; mem. social concerns bd. St. Paul's Luth. Ch., Waverly, Iowa, 1981, mem. cable TV cmty. bd., 1990; dinner vol. Waverly Dem. Com., 1995. Recipient award for poetry Pen Women, Inc., 1995, 96, 98; grantee Iowa Arts Coun., 1992, 95, 97, 98, 2000. Mem. AAUW, Nat. League Am. Pen Women, Nat. Assn. Storytellers, Iowa Poetry Assn., Northlands Storytellers, Haiku Club, Women in Arts, Friends of Ctr., Print Club. Avocations: watercolor, gourmet cooking, reading, gardening. Home: 1508 Circle Dr Waverly IA 50677-1001 E-mail: doriskampfe@aol.com.

KAMPFE, NANCY LEE, communications educator; b. Lemmon, S.D., May 6, 1946; d. Kenneth and Joyce Rose (Bartell) Preszler; m. Gregory Stephen Kampfe, Aug. 15, 1970; children: Leanne, Janice, Carole, Amy. BA in English, U. S.D., 1968; MA in English, S.D. State U., 1970. Cert. secondary tchr., S.D. Halftime freshman composition S.D. State U., Brookings, 1968-70; tchr. speech and English Sioux Valley Sch., Volga, S.D., 1970-72; tchr. White River (S.D.) Sch. Dist., 1977-78; tchr. English Crazy Horse Sch., Wanblee, S.D., 1985-90; tchr. English, speech and journalism Bennett County Schs., Martin, S.D., 1990—. Yearbook adv., photographer Bennett County H.S., 1990-2002; com. co-chair lang. arts. curriculum revision com., 1991-93; com. chair reading curriculum revision com., 1992-94. Organist St. Paul's Evang. Luth. Ch., White River, S.D.; mem. SD Lang. Arts Stds. Revision Com., 2002-03. Mem. Nat. Coun. Tchr. of Eng., NEA, S.D. Edn. Assn., Bennett County Edn. Assn., S.D. Coun. Tchrs. of Eng. (v.p. 1999-01, pres. 2001-03), Nat. Writing Project (pub. chair Y2K Regional NCTE-NWP Conf. 2000), Dakota Writing Project (presenter regional workshops 2000, 02, 03). Avocations: piano, reading, cooking, writing poetry. Home: PO Box 536 Martin SD 57551-0536 Office: Bennett County H S PO Box 580 Martin SD 57551-0580

KAMPINE, JOHN P. anesthesiology and physiology educator; MD, PhD, U. Wis. Prof., chair dept. anesthesiology Med. U. Wis., Milw., prof. physiology. Mem.: Inst. Medicine-NAS. Office: Froedtert Meml Hosp PO Box 26099 9200 W Wisconsin Ave Milwaukee WI 53226-3596

KAMPITS, EVA, accrediting association administrator, educator; b. Budapest, Hungary, Feb. 22, 1946; came to U.S., 1951; d. Ernest Michael and Ilona (Gondi) K.; m. Dan Catalin Stefanescu, Aug. 4, 1979; children: Andreea N., Cristina F. Cert., U. Innsbruck, Austria, 1963; BA, Harvard U., 1968; MA, Boston Coll., 1971, PhD, 1977. Instr. freshman seminars MIT, Cambridge, 1973—80, freshman advisor, 1975-80, sophomore advisor, 1976-80, adminstrv. officer Artificial Intelligence Lab., 1967-78, asst. to dir. Lab. for Computer Sci., 1987-88, rsch. affiliate Media Lab., 1987-88; acad. dean Pine Manor Coll., Chestnut Hill, Mass., 1980-94, dir. sponsored programs, grad. sch. dean, 1994; dir. sch. and coll. rels. New Eng. Assn. Schs. and Colls., Inc., Bedford, Mass., 1994—2003, Ctr. Ednl. Improvement, 2003. Mem. NEARnet, 1989-94, Gov.'s Ednl. Tech. Adv. Coun., 1990-93; mem. steering com. Mass. Telecomputing Coalition, 1991-95, New Eng. Network Acad. Alliances in Fgn. Langs. and Lits., 1995-98, Eisenhower Regional Alliance for Math. and Sci. Reform, 1996-98; trustee Boston Archtl. Ctr., 1996-2000, overseer, 2000—; cons. Regional Ednl. Lab. of Northeast and Islands, Brown U., 1997—; mem. editl. adv. bd. Dominion Press, Eng., 1998—; rsch. assoc. Nat. Ctr. for Cmty. Innovation, Montpelier, Vt., 1999—; adv. bd. Dorcas Place, 2000; bd. dirs. Nat. Staff Devel. Coun., 2000; cons. Ministry of Edn., China, 2001—; advisor PBS Access to Coll. documentary, 2003—. Founding mem. bd. editors NERComp Jour. Founding mem. bd. visitors Brimmer and May Sch., Chestnut Hill, Mass., 1992-97. Republican. Roman Catholic. Avocations: natural history, marine studies, arts, travel, tennis. Office: New Eng Assn Schs & Colls Inc 209 Burlington Rd Bedford MA 01730-1422

KAMPMEIER, CURT, management consultant; b. Evanston, Ill., Aug. 15, 1941; s. Carlos Otto and Neva Lou (Brown) K.; m. Susan Brooks, Dec. 30, 1961; children: Rand, Elizabeth, Paul, John. BA with honors, Coll. of Wooster (Ohio), 1964; cert. bus. program, Alexander Hamilton Inst., N.Y.C., 1967. Cert. mgmt. cons. Sales rep. Westminster Press, Phila., 1964-67, Random House, Inc., N.Y.C., 1967-73; founder, chmn. The Kampmeier Group, LLC, Columbus, Ohio, 1973—. Author numerous articles and The Bus. Skills Inventory; assoc. editor, book rev. editor: Consulting to Management; former assoc. editor, book rev editor Jour. Mgmt. Consulting. Trustee Ohio Presbyn. Retirement Svcs., Columbus, 1984-87, Westminster Thurber Community, Columbus, 1984-87; commencement speaker Shawnee State Coll., Portsmouth, Ohio. Mem. Inst. Mgmt. Cons., Columbus C. of C. E-mail: curtkampmeier@aol.com.

KAMPMEIER, JACK AUGUST CARLOS, chemist, educator; b. Cedar Rapids, Iowa, June 11, 1935; s. Carlos and Nevalou (Brown) K.; m. Anne Margaret Derk, June 14, 1958; children— Scott, Margaret, Stephen. AB, Amherst Coll., 1957; PhD (NSF fellow), U. Ill., 1960. From instr. to prof. chemistry U. Rochester, N.Y., 1960-71, prof., 1971—, chmn. dept. chemistry, 1975-79, assoc. dean grad. studies Coll. Arts and Sci., 1982-88, dean Coll. Arts and Sci., 1988-91. Co-author: Peer-Led Team Learning, A Guidebook, 2001, Peer-Led Team Learning, Organic Chemistry, 2001; contbr. sci. and pedagogical articles to profl. jours. Recipient Nat. Catalyst award Chem. Mfrs. Assn., 1999; NSF sci. faculty fellow U. Calif., Berkeley, 1971-72; Fulbright Hays sr. rsch. scholar U. Freiburg, Germany, 1979-80; NATO sr. scientist, 1979-80. Mem. Am. Chem. Soc., Sigma Xi. Home: 86 Reservoir Ave Rochester NY 14620-2754 Office: U Rochester Dept Chemistry Rochester NY 14627 E-mail: kamp@chem.rochester.edu.

KAMRATH, ALAN DALE, lawyer; b. Canby, Minn., May 16, 1952; s. Paul Elmer and Verna Marie (Haugen) K.; m. Maria Teresa Victoria Ruiz de Somocurcio, Jan. 20, 1984. B.M.E., Inst. Tech., U. Minn., 1973; J.D., Hamline U., 1977. Bar: Minn. 1977, U.S. Dist. Ct. Minn. 1977, U.S. Patent Office 1976, Can. Patent Office 1977, U.S. Ct. Appeals (8th cir.) 1977. Assoc. Peterson, Wicks, Nemer & Kamrath, P.A., Mpls., 1972—. Mem. Am. Intellectual Property Law Assn., Minn. Intellectual Property Law Assn., Hennepin County Bar Assn., Minn. State Bar Assn., Silver Gavel Honor Soc. Republican. Lutheran. Home: 316 Burntside Dr Golden Valley MN 55422-5229 Office: Peterson Wicks Nemer & Kamrath 1407 Soo Line Bldg 105 S 5th St Minneapolis MN 55402-1201

KAMRIN, MICHAEL ARNOLD, toxicology educator; b. Bklyn., Aug. 5, 1940; s. Benjamin Barnett and Bessie (Bloom) K.; m. Ritva Anneli Nieminen, July 19, 1964; children: Kari and Edward (twins). BA in Chemistry, Cornell U., 1960; MS in Biophys. Chemistry, Yale, 1962, PhD in Biophys. Chemistry, 1965. Teaching asst. then rsch. asst. dept. chemistry Yale U., New Haven, 1960-63; rsch. assoc. biology div. Oak Ridge (Tenn.) Nat. Lab., 1963-66; NIH postdoctoral trainee Hopkins Marine Sta. Stanford (Calif.) U., 1966-67; asst. prof. natural sci. Mich. State U., East Lansing, 1967-72, assoc. prof., 1972-79, prof., 1979-89, prof. Inst. for Environ. Toxicology, 1982-2000, prof. resource devel., 1990-2000, prof. emeritus, 2000—. Vis. lectr. dept. zoology U. Turku, Finland, 1973-74, docent, 1996—; vis. scientist Legis. Office Sci. Advisor, State of Mich., 1980-81; participant numerous confs. and workshops, 1965—; mem. internat. evaluation team on environ. toxicology Acad. Finland, Helsinki, 1988; expert Media Resource Ctr., Scientists' Inst. for Pub. Info.; mem. risk comm. project planning group, grant reviewer USDA; peer reviewer for agy.-sponsored rsch. projects Agy. for Toxic Substances and Disease Registry, HHS; numerous others. Author: Toxicology: A Primer on Toxicology Principles and Applications, 1988, (with D.J. Katz and M.L. Walter) Reporting on Risk: A Journalist's Handbook, 1995; also other; editor: (with F.M. D'Itri) PCBs: Human and Environmental Hazards, 1983, (with P. Rodgers) Dioxins inthe Environment, 1985; editor: Pesticide Profiles, 1997, Environmental Risk Harmonization, 1997; contbr. numerous articles and abstracts to sci. jours. Numerous presentations to Rotary, Consumers Coun., LWV, county commrs., Ch. Women United, sch. dists., Mich. Med. Soc.; participant in news broadcasts, radio call-in shows and interview programs. Recipient Meml. medal U. Turku, 1974; grantee USDA, 1983-84, 86-87, 88-89, 91-98, All-Univ. Rsch. Initation grantee, 1989, All-Univ. Outreach grantee, 1995-96, EPA, 1992-95, Agy. for Toxic Substances and Disease Registry, 1992-2000, Nat. Food Safety and Toxicology Ctr., 1993-94, grantee Nat. Inst. Environ. Health Scis., 1995-2000. Fellow AAAS; mem. Am. Chem. Soc., Soc. Toxicology (editor newsletter Mich. chpt. 1984-87, chmn. nominating com. 1986, pres.-elect 1992-93, pres. 1993-94; nat. pub. comm. com. 1987-90, Nat. Pub. Comm. award 1994), Soc. Environ. Toxicology and Chemistry (bd. dirs. Ctrl. Gt. Lakes chpt. 1985-87, v.p. 1988, pres. 1989-90, Disting. Svc. award 1993; nat. govt. affairs com. 1986-2000), Soc. for Risk Analysis. E-mail: kamrin@msu.edu.

KAMROWSKI, GEROME, artist, educator; b. Warren, Minn., Jan. 29, 1914; s. Felix and Mary (Rizke) K.; m. Mary Jane Dodman, Sept. 12, 1965; children: Felix, Kirby Jay. Student, St. Paul Sch. Art, 1933-36, Art Students League, N.Y.C., 1933-34, New Bau Haus, Chgo., 1937, Hans Hofmann Sch., N.Y.C., 1938—. One-man shows Washburn Gallery, 1987; group shows Mus. Modern Art, N.Y.C., 1978, Hayward Gallery, London, 1981, Met. Mus. Art, N.Y.C., 1993. Solomon R. Guggenheim fellow, 1938; Horace H. Rachkam fellow, 1982 Home: 1501 Beechwood Dr Ann Arbor MI 48103-2941

KAMYS, WALTER, artist, educator; b. Chgo., June 8, 1917; s. Ludwik and Honorata (Krawczyk) K.; m. Eleanor Severine Hanson, Aug. 31, 1944 (div. Feb. 1971); children: Kristofer Jan, Timothy Marc. Diploma, Art Inst. of Chgo., 1943. Tchr. Putney (Vt.) Sch., 1945-46; art instr. George Walter Vincent Smith Art Mus., Springfield, Mass., 1947-60; prof. U. Mass., Amherst, 1962-87, dir. art acquisition program, 1962-74. Cons. Greenfield (Mass.) Regional Augmented Ctr. Innovative Edn., 1966; juror Springfield Art League, 1969, Student Art Festival, Westfield (Mass.) State Coll., 1980; mem. adv. com. Thorne-Sagendorph Art Gallery, Keene State Coll., 1985-89. One-man exhbns. include Carpenter Gallery, Dartmouth Coll., 1944, Margeret Brown Gallery, Boston, 1949, Mortimer Levitt Gallery, N.Y.C., 1954, Muriel Latow Gallery, Springfield, 1954, Bertha Schaefer Gallery, N.Y.C., 1955, 57, 60-61, New Vision Centre Gallery, London, 1960, Stanhope Gallery, Boston, 1963, Easthampton Gallery, N.Y.C., 1970, Castleton (Vt.) Coll., 1981, Herter Art Gallery, U. Mass., 1986, Nada/Mason Gallery, Northfield, Mass., 1990, Amherst Gallery Fine Art, 1991; also collections Recipient Prix de Rome, Am. Acad., N.Y.C., 1942, James Nelson Raymond travelling fellowship Art Inst. Chgo., 1943-44, 2nd prize Boston Arts Festival, 1955, Purchase prize Westfield State Coll., 1968. Avocations: reading and collecting books on art, travel, history, poetry, building stacked-stone sculptures. Office: PO Box 104 Sunderland MA 01375-0104

KAMYSZEW, CHRISTOPHER D. museum curator, executive educator, art consultant; b. Warsaw, May 7, 1958; came to U.S., 1982; s. Mieczyslaw and Zofia (Kubik) K.; children: Oliver G., Samuel. BA, U. Warsaw, 1982, MA in Polish Lit. and Lang., 1984. Freelance writer and translator, Poland, 1977-81; freelance theatre dir. Dearborn Theatre Co., Chgo., 1982-83, Ossetynski Actors Lab., L.A., 1982-83; head lit. sect. Krag-Underground Publishers, Warsaw, 1980-83; head archives dept. Polish Mus. Am., Chgo., 1985-88, dir., curator, 1988-93; pres. Soc. for the Arts, Chgo., 1993—. Bd. dirs. Gallery 58, Chgo.; pres. Inst. Symbological Rsch., Chgo., 1986-95, Internat. Ind. Theatre Found., Washington, 1985-86; exec. dir. Polish TV-USA, 1994-97. Co-author, editor: Collective Works of L.-F Celine, 1983, Literary Essays by L. Tyrmand, 1983; curated more than 120 exhbns. in U.S. Dir., chmn., CEO Polish Film Festival, 1988—, Europe Film Festival, 1996—; founder, pres. Chgo. Internat. Documentary Festival, 2003—. Recipient Zycie Warszawy award, 1977, Audience award Edinburgh Theatre Festival, 1980, award for disting. translation Assn. Polish Translators, 1990, award Found. of Friends of Polish Mus., 1991, award of the Ministry of Fgn. Affairs of Poland, 1993, Laterna Magica award for disting. achievements in film, 1994; Wiehmann Found. scholar, 1982, Golden Cross of Merit, 2001, Copernican award, 2002. Avocations: reading, classical music, map collecting, cross-country skiing. Office: Society for Arts 1112 N Milwaukee Ave Chicago IL 60622-4017 E-mail: christopherkamyszew@msn.com.

KAN, DIANA ARTEMIS MANN SHU, painter, art educator, writer; b. Hong Kong, Mar. 3, 1926; came to U.S., 1949, naturalized, 1964; d. Kam Shek and Sing-Ying (Hong) K.; m. Paul Schwartz, May 24, 1952; 1 son, Kan Martin Meyer Sing-Si. Student, Art Students League, 1949-51, Beaux Arts, Paris, 1951-52, Grande Chaumiere, 1951-52, Ecole Beau Arts, 1952—54. Instr. watercolor Phila. Mus. Art, 1972, Sumi-e Soc., 1974—2003, Art Students League of NY, 1985, The Nat. Acad. Design, 2001, The Smithsonian Inst., Wash., DC. Fgn. corr., city editor Cosmorama Pictorial Mag., Hong Kong, 1968; art reviewer Villager, N.Y.C., 1960-69; lectr. Birmingham So. U., N.Y. U., Mills Coll., St. Joseph's Coll., Phila. Mus., Smithsonian Instn; keynote spkr. Wellsley's Coll. Asia Week, MA, 1993. Author: White Cloud, 1938, The How and Why of Chinese Painting, 1974, Am. Artist Magazine, 1974, 86; One-man shows, London, 1949, 63, 64, Paris, 1949, Hong Kong, 1937, 39, 41, 47, 48, 52, Shanghai, 1935, 37, 39, Nanking, 1936, 38, Macao, 1947, 48, Bankok, 1947, Casablanca, 1951, 52, San Francisco, 1950, 67, N.Y.C., 1950, 54, 59, 67, 71, 72, 74, 78, Naples, 1971, Elliot Mus., Stuart, Fla., 1967, 73, Bruce Mus., Greenwich, Conn., 1969, Nat. Hist. Mus., Taipei, Taiwan, 1971, N.Y. Cultural Center Mus., 1972, Galerie Barbarella, Palm Beach, Fla., 1972, Hobe Sound (Fla.) Galleries, 1976, 81, Nat. Arts Club, 1979, Dyansen Galleries, 1987-Shenchen Mus., China, 1996, Hong Kong Art Ctr., 1996, 90 others; exhibited in group shows Allied Artists of Am., 1957-90, Royal Acad. Fine Arts, London, 1963-64, Royal Soc. Painters, London, 1964, Nat. Arts Club, N.Y.C., 1964-90, Am. Water Color Soc., N.Y.C., 1966-90, Nat. Acad. Design, N.Y.C., 1967-2003, Charles and Emma Frye Mus., Seattle, 1968, Willamette U., Salem, Oreg., 1968, Columbia (S.C.) Mus. Art, 1969, Audubon Artist, 1974-90, Evansville (Ind.) Mus., 1991, Dyansen Gallery, Boston, 1991; represented permanent collections, Met. Mus. Art, Phila. Mus. Art, Nelson Gallery, Elliot Mus., Fla., Bruce Mus., Dalhousie U., Atkin Mus., Kansas City, Nat. Hist. Mus., Taipei, The Government House, Vancouver, BC, Can.; subject of film Eastern Spirit, Western World—A Profile of Diana Kan; paintings were published by UNICEF (christmas cards): Four Children Going Fishing, 1996, Lantern Festival, 1999, Flower Drum Song, 2002, Snow Mountain, 2002. Recipient Summer Festival award N.Y.C., 1959, 1st Prize Nat. Art Club, 1982; named most Outstanding Profl. Woman of the Yr., Washington Sq. chpt. N.Y. League Bus. and Profl. Women's Club, 1971, 79, Gold medal of honor Knickerbocker Artists, 1990, Gold medal of honor Audubon Artists, 1991, 2000, Salmagundi Club, Pres. Gold medal of honor, 1998; Diana Kan Appreciation Day proclaimed by Mayor of Boston, 1991, Diana Kan Appreciation Day proclaimed by Mayor of NY, 2000; offl. citation proclaimed by Pres. Senate of Mass., 1991. Fellow Royal Soc. Arts; mem. Pen and Brush Club (dir. 1968, Brush Fund award 1968, Alice S. Buell Meml. award 1969, Margaret Sussman award 1991), Nat. Acad. Design (assoc., John Pike Meml. award 1987, cert. of merit 1991), Am. Watercolor Soc. (traveling award 1968, Marthe T. McKinnon award 1978, dir. 1975-77), Art Students League, Nat. League Pen Women, Audubon Artists (v.p. 1983), Allied Artists Am. (Barbara Vassilieff Meml. award 1969, Ralph Fabri Meml. award 1975, corr. sec. 1975-78), Catharine Lorillard Wolf Art Club (Anna Hyatt Huntington bronze medal 1970, 74, Gold medal of honor 1982), NYC Cultural Affairs Adv. Commn., 1999. Clubs: Overseas Press Am., Lotos, The Nat. Arts (NYC), The Salamagundi. Mailing: The Nat Arts Club 15 Gramercy Park S New York NY 10003-1705 E-mail: dianakan@dianakan.com. *Failure is the mother of success.*

KAN, YUET WAI, hematologist, educator; b. Hong Kong, China, June 11, 1936; arrived in U.S., 1960; s. Tong-Po and Lai-Wan (Li) Kan; m. Alvera Lorraine Limauro, May 10, 1964; children: Susan Jennifer, Deborah Ann. BS, MB, U. Hong Kong, China, 1958, DSc, 1980, DSc (hon.), 1987, Chinese U., Hong Kong, China, 1981; MD (hon.), U. Cagliari, Sardinia, Italy, 1981. Investigator Howard Hughes Med. Inst., San Francisco, 1976—; prof. lab. medicine U. Calif., San Francisco, 1977—, Louis K. Diamond prof. hematology, 1991—. Mem. NIDDK adv. coun. NIH, 1991—95; trustee Croucher Found., Hong Kong, 1992—, chmn., 1997—. Contbr. chapters to books, over 250 articles to med. jours. Recipient Dameshek award, Am. Soc. Hematology, 1980, George Thorn award, Howard Hughes Med. Inst., 1980, Gairdner Found. Internat. award, 1984, Allan award, Am. Soc. Human Genetics, 1984, Lita Annenberg Hazen award for Excellence in Clin. Rsch., 1984, Waterford award, 1987, ACP's award, 1988, Genetic Rsch. award, Sanremo Internat., 1989, Warren Alpert Found. prize, 1989, Albert Lasker Clin. Med. Rsch. award, 1991, Christopher Columbus Discovery award, 1992, City of Medicine award, 1992, Excellence 200 award, 1993, Helmut Horten Rsch. award, 1995. Fellow: AAAS, Am. Acad. Arts and Scis., Third World Acad. Scis., Royal Soc. (London), Royal Coll. Physicians (London); mem.: Nat. Acad. Sci., Soc. Chinese Bioscientists in Am. (pres. 1998—99), Am. Soc. Hematology (pres. 1990), Assn. Am. Physicians, Chinese Acad. Scis. (fgn. mem.), Acad. Sinica (Taiwan). Avocations: tennis, skiing. Office: U Calif 533 Parnassus Ave # U432 San Francisco CA 94143-0793 E-mail: kanyuet@labmed2.ucsf.edu.

KANADA, GARY N. KAHAHO'OMALU, adult education educator; s. Richard N. and Carole A. Kanada. BA in Japanese Lang., U. Hawaii, 1988, MA in East Asian Langs. & Lit., 1992, cert. in East Asian Langs. & Lit., 1993. Lifeguard City & County of Honolulu, DPR, Manoa Pool, 1991—; instr. Japanese lang. DOE, Kaimuki Cmty. Sch. Adults, 1991—93; lectr. Hawaiian lang. U. Hawaii, 1993—97; instr. Japanese & Hawaiian langs. Hawaii Pacific U., 1993—; instr. Hawaiian lang. DOE, Windward Sch. Adults, Kailua, 1996—; instr. swim classes Samuel M. Kamakau Sch., 'Aha Punana Leo, 2000—01; program chmn. Dept. Modern Langs. Hawaii Pacific U., Honolulu, 2002—. Advisor Halau Na Wainohia, Honolulu, 1997—, Hui Aloha 'Aina Ua Kukalahale-HPU, 1995—, Japanese Conversation Club-HPU, 1993—2000; mem. HPU Arts & Sciences Curriculum Com., 1999—2001. Vol. Manoa Valley Dist. Pk., Honolulu, 1994—; head coach DOE McKinley H.S. Boys' Swim Team, 1994—97. Scholar, Monbusho, Japanese Govt. Ministry Edn., 1988—89. Mem.: Hawaii Assn. Lang. Teachers (Excellence Tchg. Fgn. Languages 2002), 'Ahahui 'Olelo Hawai'i. Avocations: swimming, reading, music, travel, movies.

KANAGA, LAWRENCE WESLEY, lawyer; b. Chgo., Dec. 25, 1940; s. Lawrence W. and Virginia (Honold) K.; m. Kareen DiBlanda, Sept. 1, 1962 (div. June 1984); children: Kerry Ann, Matthew Lawrence. BA, Williams Coll., 1962; LLB, Harvard U., 1965. Bar: Conn. 1965, U.S. Dist. Ct. Conn. 1965, U.S. Ct. Appeals (2d cir.) 1968. Assoc. Goldstein & Peck, Bridgeport, Conn., 1965-71; mem. firm Zeldes Needle & Cooper, Bridgeport, 1971-87, Senie, Stock & LaChance, Westport, 1988—; mem. grievance com. U.S. Dist. Ct. Conn., 1984— . Mem. Assn. Trial Lawyers Am., ABA, Conn. Bar Assn. (mem. judiciary com. 1980-83), Conn. Trial Lawyers Assn. Democrat. Home: 131 Hillside Ave Milford CT 06460-7811 Office: Senie Stock & LaChance 125 Main St PO Box 336 Westport CT 06881-0336

KANAGY, STEVEN ALBERT, foundation administrator; b. Chgo., Sept. 26, 1956; s. John West and Hazel Elizibeth (Montgomery) K. Student, Kendall Coll., Evanston, Ill., 1974—76, W. Carey Coll., Hattiesburg, Miss., 1980, U. Southern Miss. Staff worker Longbeach Pub. Libr., Miss., 1978; mgr. Kanagy Art Found., Inc., Longbeach, Miss., 1982—, lead dir., 1997—; distbr. Amway Corp., Ada, Mich., 1984—2000, IBO Quixtar, 2001—; cmty. devel. explorer Harbour Dist., Gulfport, Miss., 1985-89, mng. ptnr., 1989—. Mng. ptnr. Archival Restorations, 1992—; lead dir. Kanagy Art Found., Inc., 1997. Contbr. article to mag. Kendall Coll. scholar. Mem. Am. Mgmt. Assn., Nat. Trust for Hist. Preservation, Internat. Platform Assn., N.Am. Hunting Club (life). Republican. Roman Catholic. Avocations: building restoration, archery, photography. Home: PO Box 1014 Long Beach MS 39560-1014 E-mail: sueme@mindspring.com.

KANAN, GREGORY BRIAN, lawyer; b. El Paso, Tex., Sept. 19, 1949; s. John Emil and Adeline (Bexell) K.; m. Linda M. Lilly, Aug. 22, 1970; children— Jeffery J., Lisa M., Stephanie A. B.A., U. Colo., 1972, J.D., 1975. Bar: Colo. 1975, U.S. Dist. Ct. Colo. 1975, U.S. Ct. Appeals (l0th cir.) 1975. Jud. clk. to chief justice Colo. Supreme Ct., Denver, 1975-76; assoc. Rothgerber, Appel, Powers & Johnson, Denver, 1976-80, ptnr., 1981— ; adj. prof. health law U. Denver; vis. lectr. U. Colo. Sch. Law, Boulder, 1975, 77-78. Chmn. U. Colo. Sch. Law Alumni Reunion, Class of 1975; participant Denver Thursday Night Bar, 1980— . Mem. Denver Bar Assn., Colo. Bar Assn., ABA, Order of Coif. Democrat. Lutheran. Office: Rothgerber Appel Powers 1200 17th St Ste 3000 Denver CO 80202-5855 Home: 2604 Cherry Creek South Dr Denver CO 80209-3235

KANARKOWSKI, EDWARD JOSEPH, data processing company executive; b. Jersey City, May 5, 1947; s. Joseph Anthony and Lillian Dorothy (Pietrowicz) K.; m. Carol Ann Miller, Sept. 14, 1969; children: Edward, Kelly, Paul, Karen, Kevin, Casey Michael. BA, St. Peter Coll., 1969; grad., U.S. Army Command and Gen. Staff Coll., Ft. Leavenworth, Kans., 1985. Corp. communications cons., N.J., 1973-75; staff writer Daily and Sunday Register, Shrewsbury, N.J., 1975-77; corp. staff writer ADP, Roseland, N.J., 1977, dir. corp. communications, 1983-88, v.p. corp. communication, 1988-93; comm. cons., 1993—. Adj. vis. prof. communications St. Peter's Coll., 1985—; corp. career adv. grad. sch. bus. Rutgers U., N.J. Author: The ADP Story, 1999. Capt. U.S. Army, 1971-73, maj. N.G. Decorated Army Commendation medal (3); named Hon. Ky. Col. Commonwealth of Ky., 1988. Mem. Internat. Assn. Bus. Communicators, Meeting Planners Internat., 3d U.S. Inf. Div. Assn., N.J. Mil. Acad. (assoc.), VFW (life), U.S. Golf Assn., U.S.O. Orgn. (contbg. mem.). Roman Catholic. Home: 132 Yellowbank Rd Toms River NJ 08753-3167

KANAROWSKI, STANLEY MARTIN, chemist, chemical engineer, government official; b. Beausejour, Man., Can., Dec. 12, 1912; came to U.S., 1923, naturalized, 1928; s. Joseph and Caroline Kanarowski; m. Pearl Lewus, Aug. 8, 1936 (dec.); children: Stanley Martin Jr., Janice Ellen, Nancy Carol Kanarowski Cioffari. BS, U. Toledo, 1934; postgrad., Ohio State U., 1938-42, U. Akron, 1943-47, NYU, 1954, Xavier U., 1969, U. Wis., U. Mich., U. Ill., U. Mo. Chemist, chief chemist Ohio Dept. Liquor Control, Columbus, 1936-42; sr. cons. chemist Nebr. Ordnance Plant Firestone Tire and Rubber Co., Fremont, 1942-43; asst. dir. corp. gen. lab., chief factory product chem. engr., R & D compounding engr. Firestone Tire and Rubber Co., Akron, Ohio, 1943-49; lab. dir., asst. rsch. and devel. mgr. Fremont (Ohio) Rubber Co., 1949-52; rsch. and devel. chem. engr. Glass Fibers, Inc., Waterville, Ohio, 1952-53; chief rsch. and devel. chemist-engr., mgr. quality control Dairypak Butler, Inc., Toledo, 1953-60; chief chemist No. Ohio Region Lab. Liquor Control Enforcement Div. State of Ohio, Cleve., 1960-62; rsch. and devel. chemist-engr. Consol Paper Co., Monroe, Mich., 1962-63; chemist City of Toledo, 1963-64; project engr., head chemist investigations sect. Ohio River Div. U.S. Army Engr. Div. C.E., 1964-69; project leader, prin. investigator U.S. Army Constrn. Engring. Rsch. Lab., Champaign, Ill., 1969-86, ret., 1986. Mem. U. Ill. Symphony Orch., 1970-86, Montgomery Coll. Symphony Orch., 1987—. Recipient Army-Navy E award, 1943, Corps of Engrs. awards and certs., 1974, 80, 84. Mem. AIChE, Am. Chem. Soc., N.Y. Acad. Scis., Nat. Def. Indsl. Assn., Chem. Soc. Washington, A.C.S. Rubber Divsn. Achievements include development of paint test kit and test procedures for evaluating quality of paints and coatings before use; evaluation and introduction of new construction materials and techniques including design of testing equipment, e.g., for sealing and waterproofing concrete and corrugated galvanized steel structures and foundations, joint sealants for concrete pavements, reflective solar control films for windows, protective coatings for concrete and maple floors, bentonite clay and membrane waterproofing, prevention of windblown rain penetration, repair techniques for leaky shower rooms, evaluation of fiber reinforced plastic tanks for underground storage of flammable liquids, dining facilities as collective protection centers against chemical-biological warfare; research on state highways for reflection cracking in asphaltic concrete overlay pavements versus new materials, introduction and management of system for identification and classification of chemical hazardous materials in all laboratories at U.S. Army CERL and disposal of hazardous substances and waste products. Materials problems consultant to Corps of Engineers installations, districts, divisions, other government agencies and civilian organizations. Address: 1329 Excaliber Ln Sandy Spring MD 20860-1117

KANDAL, TERRY R. sociology educator, consultant; b. Chgo., Sept. 17, 1940; s. Terry Olaf and Gertrude Linda Kandal; m. Nancy Jean Fried, 1965 (div. 1973); 1 child, Joshua Terry; m. Anita Aurora Acosta, Feb. 13, 1998 (div. 2003). AA, City Coll. San Francisco, 1963; BA, U. Calif., Berkeley, 1965, MA, 1967, PhD, 1974. Rsch. asst. U. Calif., Berkeley, 1965, tchg. asst., 1966-67, Davis, 1965-66; from asst. prof. to assoc. prof. Calif. State U., L.A., 1968-83, prof. dept. sociology, 1983—. Cons. Mex.-Am. Edn. Commn., L.A., 1969-70, others. Author: The Woman Question in Classical Sociological Theory, 1988, Introduction to Reissue of Robert Michels, Sexual Ethics, 2002; editor: Studies of Development and Change in the Modern world, 1989; editor spl. issue Calif. Sociologist, 1992, editor, 1984-93; reviewer for numerous publs. V.p. cmty. adv. coun. Glassell Park elem. sch., L.A., 1981-82. Mem. Am. Sociol. Assn., Pacific Sociol. Assn., Calif. Sociol. Assn., S.W. Labor Studies Assn., Internat. Soc. for Comparative Study of Civilizations, Golden Key (hon.), Phi Beta Kappa. Achievements include writing of first history of the ways founding fathers of sociology in the 19th and early 20th centuries responded to the feminist movements of their times. Home: 440 W Ave 46 Los Angeles CA 90065-5006 Office: Calif State U Dept Sociology Los Angeles CA 90032

KANDEL, ABRAHAM, computer scientist; b. Tel-Aviv, Israel, Oct. 6, 1941; s. Jacob and Dina K.; m. Nurit Kandel, Aug. 23, 1966; children: Sharon, Gill, Adi. BS, Technion, Haifa, Israel; MS, U. Calif., Santa Barbara; PhD, U. N.Mex. Assoc. prof. Computer Sci. Dept., NMIMT, Socorro, N.Mex., 1970-78; founding chmn., prof. Computer Sci. dept. Fla. State U., Tallahassee, 1978-91; chmn., prof. endowed chair Computer Sci. and Engring. dept. U. South Fla., Tampa, 1991—. Head tech. adv. bd. Expert Systems Industries, Ltd., Israel, 1984—. Editor: Fuzzy Control Systems, 1994; author: Fuzzy Mathematical Techniques and Their Applications, 1986, Fuzzy Techniques in Pattern Recognition, 1982, 28 books; contbr. over 400 articles to tech. publs. Israeli Air Force, 1959-62. Fellow IEEE, N.Y. Acad. Scis., AAAS, Assn. Computing Machinery; mem. IFSA, Am. Soc. Engring. Edn., N.Am. Fuzzy Info. Processing Soc., Nat. Inst. for Systems Test and Productivity (exec. dir. 2000—). Office: U South Fla Computer Sci & Engring Dept Tampa FL 33620

KANDEL, DENISE BYSTRYN, sociologist; b. Paris, Feb. 27, 1933; came to U.S. 1949; d. Iser and Sara (Wolsky) Bystryn; m. Eric R. Kandel, June 10, 1956; children: Paul, Minouche. BA in French, Acad. Paris, 1950; BA, Bryn Mawr (Pa.) Coll., 1952; MA, Columbia U., 1953, PhD, 1960. Social scientist NIMH, Bethesda, Md., 1959-60; postdoctoral rsch. fellow Harvard Med. Sch., Boston, 1960-62; rsch. assoc. Harvard Sch. Edn., Cambridge, Mass., 1964-69; rsch. scientist VII N.Y. State Psychiatric Inst., N.Y.C., 1969—; from asst. prof. to prof. dept. psychiatry, dept. sociomed. scis. Columbia U. Sch. of Pub. Health, NYC, 1973—. Cons. Nat. Inst. on Drug Abuse, Rockville, 1973—; editl. bd. Jour. Rsch. on Adolescence, 1990—, extramural sci. adv. bd., 1990—93; etiology sci. adv. panel Am. Legacy Found., 2000—; H. David Archibald lectr. Addiction Rsch. Found. Ctr. for Addiction and Mental Health, Ont., Canada, 2002. Author (with G. Lesser): (Book) Youth in Two Worlds., 1972; contbg. author: Parental Influences on Adolescent Marijuana Use and the Baby Boom Generation: Findings from the 1979-1996 National Household Surveys on Drug Abuse, 2001; editor: Longitudinal Research on Drug Use, 1978, Stages and Pathways of Drug Involvement: Examining the Gateway Hypothesis, 2002; assoc. editor: Jour. Health and Social Behavior, 1975—78, consulting editor Am. Jour. Sociology, 1981—83; contbr. articles to profl. jours. Active Nat. Adv. Coun. on Drug Abuse, 1986—90. Recipient Pacesetter award, Nat. Inst. on Drug Abuse, 1979, Rsch. Scientist award, 1981—, Ann. Norman E. Zinberg Meml. Lectr. award, Cambridge Hosp./ Harvard Med. Sch., 1993, R. Brinkley Smithers Disting. Scientist award, Am. Soc. Addiction Medicine, 2002, Prevention Sci. award, Soc. for Prevention Rsch., 2003. Mem.: Soc. for Life History Rsch., Internat. Sociol. Assn., Am. Sociol. Assn., Sociol. Rsch. Assn., Soc. for Rsch. on Adolescence (chmn. pubs. 1990—92). Democrat. Jewish. Avocation: collecting art nouveau furniture and glass. Office: Columbia Univ Dept of Psychiatry 1051 Riverside Dr Unit 20 New York NY 10032

KANDEL, ERIC RICHARD, neuroscience educator; b. Vienna, Nov. 7, 1929; arrived in U.S., 1939; married, 1956; 2 children. BA, Harvard Coll., 1952; MD, NYU, 1956. Intern Montefiore Hosp., N.Y.C., 1956—57; rsch. assoc. neurophysiology lab. NIH, Washington, 1957—60; psychiatrist Mass Mental Health Ctr. Harvard Med. Sch., 1960—62, 1963—64; dir. Mass. Mental Health Ctr., Boston, 1960—65; from assoc. to prof. physiology and psychiatry NYU Sch. Medicine, 1965—74; prof. physiology, biochemistry and psychiatry, dir. ctr. neurology and behavior Columbia U. Coll. Physicians and Surgeons, N.Y.C., 1974—83, Univ. prof., sr. investigator Howard Hughes Med. Inst., 1983—. Recipient Lasker award, 1983, Harvey prize, Technion, 1993, Wolf prize, Israel, 1999, Nobel prize, 2000, Heineken prize, 2000. Fellow: AAAS; mem.: NAS, N.Y. Acad. of Scis. (Mayor award excellence in sci. and tech. 1994), Internat. Brain Rsch. Orgn., Soc. Neuroscis. (pres. 1980—81), Am. Acad. Arts and Scis. Office: Columbia U Coll Physicians & Surgeons Howard Hughes Med Inst 1051 Riverside Dr New York NY 10032-2603*

KANDEL, NELSON ROBERT, lawyer; b. Balt., Sept. 15, 1929; m. Brigitte Kleemaier, Feb. 28, 1957; children: Katrin, Christopher, Peter. BA, U. Md., 1951, LLB, 1954. Bar: Md. 1954, U.S. Supreme Ct. 1964, D.C. 1980. Pres. Kandel & Assocs. P.A., Balt., 1957—. With U.S. Army. Mem. Md. Bar Assn., Balt. Bar Assn. Democrat. Lutheran. Office: The World Trade Ctr Ste 1252 40 E Pratt St Baltimore MD 21202

KANDEL, WILLIAM LLOYD, lawyer, mediator, arbitrator, educator, writer; b. NYC, Apr. 25, 1939; s. Morton H. and Lottie S. (Smith) K.; m. Joyce Roland, Jan. 27, 1974; 1 child, Aron Daniel (Ari). AB cum laude, Dartmouth Coll., 1961; JD, Yale U., 1964; LLM in Labor Law, NYU, 1967. Bar: N.Y. 1965, U.S. Dist. Ct. (ea. dist.) N.Y. 1978, U.S. Dist. Ct. (so. dist) N.Y. 1980, U.S. Dist. Ct. (no. dist.) N.Y. 1988, U.S. Ct. Appeals (2d cir.) 1982, U.S. Ct. Appeals (3d cir.) 1997, U.S. Ct. Appeals (5th cir.) 2000. Assoc. Lorenz, Finn & Giardino, N.Y.C., 1964-66; labor atty. NAM, N.Y.C., 1966-68; with Singer Co., N.Y.C., 1968-79, asst. v.p. pers. dept., 1973-76, mng. counsel pers. office of gen. counsel, 1976-79; assoc. Skadden, Arps, Slate, Meagher & Flom, N.Y.C., 1979-85; ptnr. Finley, Kumble, Wagner, Heine, Underberg, Manley, Myerson & Casey, N.Y.C., 1985-87, Myerson & Kuhn, N.Y.C., 1987-89, McDermott Will & Emery, 1989-97, Orrick, Herrington & Sutcliffe, 1997-2000; full-time mediator and arbitrator, 2000—; mediator U.S. Dist. Ct. (so. and ea. dists.), Supreme Ct. N.Y., 2001—; pvt. mediator and arbitrator, 2000—. Adj. prof. employment law Fordham U., 1983-86; lectr. Practising Law Inst.'s Ann. Inst. on Employment Law, 1980—, co-chair, 1995, chair, 1996-2002; vol. mediator U.S. EEO Commn., 2000—; spl. master Appellate Divsn. of Supreme Ct., N.Y., 2002—; panelist comml. and employment, Am. Arbitration Assn., 2002—; arbitrator Nat. Assn. Securities Dealers, 2002—. Contbg. editor: Employee Rels. Law Jour., 1975—; contbr. over 100 articles to profl. jours. V.p., bd. dirs. Assn. for Integration Mgmt., 1979-85; bd. dirs. N.Y. chpt. Am. Jewish Com., 1980-82; mem. human resources com. N.Y. YMCA, 1994—. Recipient award of Merit Nat. Urban Coalition, 1979. Mem.: Am. Arbitration Assn. (comml. and employment panels 2001—), Bar Assn. of City of N.Y., University Club. Democrat. Jewish. Home and Office: Mediator/Arbitrator 880 Fifth Ave New York NY 10021 E-mail: wlkandel@hotmail.com.

KANDELL, HOWARD NOEL, pediatrician; BS, U. Miami, 1956; MD, Tulane U., 1959. Diplomate Am. Bd. Pediatrics. Intern Phila. Gen. Hosp., 1959-60; resident N.Y. Hosp. Cornell Med. Ctr., N.Y.C., 1960-62; pediatrician Phoenix, 1965-2001; retired, 2001. Chief pediatrics Health Maintenance Assocs., Ltd., Phoenix, 1977-82; assoc. chmn. dept. pediatrics, Maricopa County Hosp., Phoenix, 1965-71, svc. chief dept. pediatrics, 1972-77; assoc. prof. pediatrics U. Ariz. Coll. Medicine, 1970-82, clin. instr. 1982-83; asst. prof. 1983-87; chmn. pediatric dept. CIGNA Healthplan of Ariz., Phoenix, 1984-87

dj. faculty mem. Ariz. State U. Coll. Nursing, 1986-95; med. dir. INA Iealthplan (CIGNA) South Fla., 1982-83. Capt. MC USAF, 1962-64. Recipient Tchr. of Yr. award dept. pediatrics Maricopa County Gen. Hosp., 1972. Fellow Am. Acad. Pediatrics (Ariz. chpt. treas., exec. com. 1970-76, Phoenix chpt. v.p. 970-72). Home: 7257 E Echo Ln Scottsdale AZ 85258-2768

KANDHAL, PRITHVI SINGH, civil engineer, manager; b. Bikaner, Rajastan, India, May 6, 1935; came to U.S., 1968; parents Dal and Sugan (Kunwar) Singh; m. Ummed Kumari, May 28, 1958; children: Ravindra S., Mitra K. BSCE, U. Rajasthan, 1957; MSCE, Iowa State U., 1969. Profl. engr., Pa. Asst dist. engr. Rajasthan State Hwy Dept., Jaipur, India, 1957-65, dist. engr., 965-68; hwy. engr. Berger Assocs., Camp Hill, Pa., 1969-70; chief asphalt engr. Pa. Dept. Transp., Harrisburg, Pa., 1970-88; assoc. dir. emeritus Nat. Ctr. Asphalt Tech. Auburn (Ala.) U., Auburn, Ala., 1988—. Author book on asphalt technology; contbr. numerous articles to profl. jours. Recipient Best Speaker award Toastmasters Internat., Camp Hill, 1972, Boss of Yr. award U.S. Jaycees, Harrisburg, 1973, Outstanding Mgmt. award Pa. Dept. Transp., Harrisburg, 981, Gov.'s Mgmt. Performance award Commonwealth of Pa., Harrisburg, 986, Walter J. Emmons award for Best Paper, Assn. Asphalt Paving Tech., 990. Fellow ASCE, ASTM (chmn. 1998-99), Assn. Asphalt Paving Tech. (pres. 999-2000, Transp. Rsch. Bd. (chmn. com. 1982-88). Hindu. Avocations: reading, photography. Home: 635 Woody Dr Auburn AL 36832-3413 Office: Auburn U Nat Ctr for Asphalt Tech 277 Technology Pkwy Auburn AL 36830 E-mail: pkandhal@eng.auburn.edu.

KANDIL, MAGDA ELSAYED, economist; b. Suez, Egypt, May 5, 1958; arrived in US, 1981; d. ElSayed Kandil and Wafaa Farag; m. Mohammed Sarhan, Feb. 15, 1979; 1 child, Hanaan Sarhan. BS in econ., Cairo U., Egypt, 978; MA in econ., U. Notre Dame, 1982; MBA, Ind. U., South Bend, 1984; PhD in econ., Wash. State U., 1988. Prod. planner Miles Lab. Inc., Mishawaka, Ind., 1982—84; tchg. asst. Wash. State U., Pullman, 1984—86; rsch. asst. Nat. Sci. Found., Wash. State U., 1986—88; asst. prof. So. Ill. U., Dept. Econ., Carbondale, 1988—92; asst. prof. to assoc. prof. U. Wis., Wilw., 1992—97; vis. assoc. prof. Justus-Liebig U., Giessen, Germany, 1994; prof. U. Wis., Dept. Econ., 1997—2001; adv. to exec. dir. Internat. Monetary Fund, Wash., DC, 999—2000; vis. scholar Internat. Monetary Fund, Inst. Rsch. Dept., 2000—01; r. economist Internat. Monetary Fund, Gen. Resources SDR Pol. Divsn. Treas. Dept., 2001—, Internat. Monetary Fund, Mid. Ea. Divsn., 2001—. Chair U. Wis., 1998—99. Author: (articles) various profl. jours.; contbr. chapters to books. Grantee, Econ. Rsch. Forum for Arab Countries, 1998, Egyptian govt., 992—96, Georges Lurcy Rsch. fellowship in Econ., Brookings Inst., Wash. D.C., 1988, Peace fellowship, Am.-Mideast Edn. Tng. Svcs., 1981—82, Acad. fellowship, Arabic Strategic Studies, 1978—78. Mem.: Arab Soc. for Econ. Rsch., Can. Econ. Assn., Am. Econ. Assn. Achievements include presentations of various topics at economic conferences. Home: 7631 Huntmaster Ln Mc Lean VA 22102 Office: Internat Monetary Fund 1825 Eye St Washington DC 0431 Office Fax: 202-589-4696. E-mail: mkandil@imf.org.

KANDIMALLA, EKAMBARESWARA RAO, molecular medicinal chemist; . Machilipatnam, India, Aug. 19, 1957; came to U.S., 1992; s. Venkateswara Rao China and Baby Tulasi (Ambati) K.; m. Seetha Baile, June 20, 1986; children: Kranthi, Bhavya. BS, MS, Andhra, Waltair, India, 1980, PhD, 1984. Rsch. assoc. Indian Inst. Sci., Bangalore, 1985-87, U. Alberta, Can., 1987-92; r. rsch. scientist Hybridon, Inc., Milford, Mass., 1992-99, dir. functional genomics Cambridge, Mass., 1999—2003, sr. dir. antisensor and functional genomics, 2003—. Contbr. articles to profl. jours. Jr. Rsch. fellow Coun. for Sci. Indsl. Rsch., 1981, Sr. Rsch. fellow, 1983. Mem. AAAS. Office: Hybridon Inc 45 Vassar St Cambridge MA 02139

KANDLER, JOSEPH RUDOLPH, financial executive; b. Vienna, Dec. 13, 921; arrived in Can., 1952; s. Franz and Maria Franziska (Stanzel) K.; m. Lubomyra-Melitta Melnechuk, June 15, 1963. D.Rerum Commercialium, Sch. Econs., Vienna, 1949. Sales exec. Philips, Vienna, 1951; acct. Brown & Root, Ltd., Edmonton, Canada, 1952-54, 56, chief acct., 1957-64; v.p. fin. Healy Ford Ctr. and Assoc. Cos., Edmonton, 1964-89; pres. Sentha Investments, Ltd., Edmonton, 1978—. Bd. dirs. Edmonton Symphony, 1969-72, Alta. Cultural Heritage Coun., 1973-81, Edmonton Opera, 1982-84, Tri-Bach Festival, 1982-4; founder Johann Strauss Found., Alta., bd. dirs., 1975-84, pres., 1975-78; founder, pres. Johann Strauss Found., B.C., 1985—; bd. govs. U. Alta., 982-86, mem. senate, 1973-79, 82-86; mem. adv. com. on cultural and conv. r. City of Edmonton, 1974-78, vice-chmn., 1976-78. Recipient Achievement award for svc. to cmty. Govt. Alta., 1975, Johann Strauss medal in gold Vienna Tourist Bd., 1989, Knight's Cross of Honor 1st Class, Republic of Austria, 990, Golden Emblem of Honor City of Vienna, 1991, Golden Emblem of Honor Sch. Econs., Vienna, 1995, Disting. Svc. award Inst. Chartered Accts. Alta., 2001. Mem. Inst. Chartered Accts. Alta. (chartered acct.). Address: Sentha Investments Ltd 392 Langs Rd Salt Spring Island BC Canada V8K 1N3

KANDRAVY, JOHN, lawyer; b. Passaic, N.J., May 9, 1935; s. Frank and Anna (Chan) K.; m. Alice E. Sullivan, Feb. 17, 1962; children: Elizabeth Ann (Mrs. Joseph P. Cassidy), Katherine Ann. BA, Wesleyan U., Middletown, Conn., 957; JD, Columbia U., 1960. Bar: N.J. 1960, D.C. 1969, U.S. Supreme Ct. 973, N.Y. 1982. From assoc. to ptnr. Shanley & Fisher, Newark, 1961-80, ptnr. Morristown, N.J., 1980-99, mng. ptnr., 1983-85, 89-99; ptnr. Drinker Biddle & Reath LLP, Florham Park, NJ, 1999—. Bd. dirs. Tingue, Brown & Co., GAR Internat. Corp.; mem. adv. bd. Ridgewood Savs. Bank of N.J. (divsn. Boiling Springs Savings Bank). Mem. Gov.'s Mgmt. Commn., State of N.J., 1970; chmn. Planning Bd., Ridgewood, N.J., 1981-85, Zoning Bd. Adjustment, 979-81; mem. bd. advisors Coll. Bus. Adminstrn., Fairleigh Dickinson U., 983-87, chmn. bd. advisors, 1985-86; mem. Soc. of Valley Hosp., Ridgewood, 971—, chmn. bd. trustees Cen. Bergen Comty. Mental Health Ctr., N.J., 970-73; trustee Palisades Counseling Ctr., Rutherford, 1968-81, The Forum Sch., Waldwick, N.J., 1987—, The Forum Sch. Found., Waldwick, 1978—; trustee The Valley Hosp., Ridgewood, 1992—, chmn. 2001—; trustee Peer Found. for Plastic Surgery and Rehab., Florham Park, 1996—, Valley Health Sys., Inc., Paramus, 1997—, Children's Aid and Family Svcs., Inc., Paramus, N.J., 1998—; lawyers' adv. coun. Rutgers Law Sch., Newark, 1994-98, vis. com., 1994-98. Edward John Noble Found. grant, 1957-60. Mem. ABA, N.J. Bar Assn., Essex County Bar Assn., D.C. Bar Assn., Morris County Bar Assn., Essex Club (gov. 1976-85), Wesleyan U. Alumni Assn. (chmn. 1981-83), Ridgewood Country Club, Park Ave. Club (gov. 1992-97). Republican. Presbyterian. Home: 56 Monte Vista Ave Ridgewood NJ 07450-2428 Office: Drinker Biddle & Reath LLP 500 Campus Dr Fl 4 Florham Park NJ 07932-1047 E-mail: john.kandravy@dbr.com.

KANDT, RAYMOND S. neurologist; b. Rochester, N.Y., July 8, 1950; m. Ilene Kandt; children: Melanie, Lauren. AB cum laude, U. Va., 1972; MD, U. Va. Sch. Medicine, 1976. Diplomate Am. Bd. Med. Examiners, Am. Bd. Pediatrics, Am. Bd. Psychiatry & Neurology with spl. competence in child neurology and with added qualifications in clin. neurophysiology; cert. neurovascular & pediat. neurosonologist; cert. MRI/CT. Intern, resident in pediatrics Johns Hopkins Hosp., Balt., 1976-78, resident in pediatric neurology, fellow in devel. pediatrics, 1978-81; instr. depts. neurology, pediatrics U. Mich., Ann Arbor, 1981-82, asst. prof. depts. neurology & pediatrics, 1982-84; asst. prof. pediatrics div. pediatric neurology Duke U. Med. Ctr., Durham, N.C., 1984-89, assoc. prof. pediatrics div. pediatric neurology, 1989-92, asst. prof. medicine div. neurology, 1990-92; assoc. prof. neurology, pediatrics Bowman Gray Sch. Medicine, Winston-Salem, N.C., 1992-97; clin. assoc. prof. pediatrics Wake Forest U./Bapt. Med. Ctr., Winston-Salem, 1997—. Chief sect. child neurology Bowman Gray Sch. Medicine, 1992-97, grad. med. edn. com. 1993-97, clin. faculty adv. coun., 1993-97; faculty advisor pediatric house staff U. Mich., 1981-84, faculty advisor med. students, 1983-84, com. on edn., 1982-84; pediatric rep. continuing med. edn. com. Duke U. Med. Ctr., 1985-92; mem. gen. clin. rsch. ctrs. com. nat. ctr. for rsch. resources NIH, 1991-95; cons. in field. Reviewer: Am. Jour. Human Genetics, 1995, Jour. Neurol. Scis., 1993—97, Nature Genetics, 1993, Annals of Neurology, 1998—2002; Annals of Neurology, 2001; contbg. editor: Annals of Behavioral Medicine, 1991—93. Adv. bd. My Father's House Group Homes, 1993; med. adv. com. Children's Ctr. for the Physically Handicapped, Winston-Salem, N.C., 1993—. Grantee NIH, 1986-91, 89-92, Nat. Tuberous Sclerosis Assn., 1992-93, grantee Glaxo, 1995-96; recipient Merck award, 1976. Mem.: Profs. Child Neurology, Tuberous Sclerosis Alliance (mem. profl. adv. bd. 1990—, scientific adv. bd. 1995—, chmn. clin. care adv. bd. 1995—97, scientific grant rev. com. 1995—, chmn. med. adv. com. N.C. chpt. 1988—), Child Neurology Soc., N.C. Med. Soc., Am. Neurol. Assn., Phi Sigma, Alpha Omega Alpha. Home: 3428 Jameson Ln Winston Salem NC 27106-4771 Office: Johnson Neurologic Clinic 606 N Elm St High Point NC 27262-4336

KANE, AGNES BREZAK, pathologist, educator; b. Danbury, Conn., Nov. 3, 1946; d. John Edward and Mary Elizabeth (Hatfield) Brezak; m. David E. Kane, June 22, 1970. BA, Swarthmore Coll., 1968; MD, Temple U., 1974, PhD, 1976. Diplomate Am. Bd. Pathology. Resident Temple U. Hosp., Phila., 1975-76, 77-78; postdoctoral fellow Karolinska Inst., Stockholm, 1976-77; asst. prof. Temple U. Sch. Medicine, Phila., 1977-82, Brown U., Providence, 1982-87, assoc. prof. pathology, 1987-95, prof. pathology, 1995-96, chair dept. pathology and lab. medicine, 1996—. Mem. merit rev. bd. for basic scis. VA, Washington, 1984-86; cons. R.I. Commn. for Safety and Occupational Health, Providence, 1986—; commr. Commn. to Identify Occupational Diseases, Providence, 1987-88; mem. rev. com. Nat. Inst. Environ. Health Scis., Research Triangle Park, N.C., 1988—. Assoc. editor Am. Jour. of Pathology, 1992—; contbr. articles on exptl. pathology to sci. publs. Lucretia Mott fellow Swarthmore Coll., 1969-71, recipient Rsch. Career Devel. award NIH, 1981-86. Mem. Am. Assn. Pathologists (women's com. 1987—, program com. 1990—), Assn. Women Med. Faculty Brown U. (founder, coord.), Women in Medicine (faculty advisor Brown U. chpt.; Mary Putnam Jacobi award 1986), Phi Kappa, Sigma Xi. Avocation: gardening. Office: Brown Univ Box G Providence RI 02912

KANE, ALAN HENRY, lawyer; b. Seattle, Nov. 7, 1940; s. Henry and Alice (Harbak) K.; m. Martha Dressler, June 25, 1966; children: Karen, Graham, Amy. BA in Law, U. Wash., 1963, JD, 1965. Bar: Wash. 1965. Ptnr. Sax & Maciver, Seattle, 1966-84, Preston Gales & Ellis, LLP, Seattle, 1985—. Fellow Am. Coll. Trusts and Estates Counsel (Wash. State chair 1985-88). Avocations: boating, water and snow skiing, fishing. Office: Preston Gates & Ellis LLP 701 5th Ave Ste 5000 Seattle WA 98104-7078 E-mail: alank@prestongates.com.

KANE, ALICE THERESA, lawyer; b. N.Y.C., Jan. 16, 1948; AB, Manhattanville Coll., 1969; JD, NYU, 1972; grad., Harvard U. Sch. Bus. Program Mgmt. Devel., 1986. Bar: N.Y. 1973, U.S. Dist. Ct. (so. dist.) N.Y. 1974. Atty. N.Y. Life Ins. Co., N.Y.C., 1972-83, v.p., assoc. gen. counsel, 1983-85, v.p. dept. pers., 1986, sr. v.p., gen. counsel, 1986-89, corp. sec., 1989-94, exec. v.p., gen. counsel, sec., 1992-95, exec. v.p. asset mgmt., 1995-98; exec. v.p. Am. Gen. Investment Mgmt. Corp., N.Y.C., 1998—. Mem. ABA (chmn. employee benefits com., tort and ins. practice sect. 1984-85, mem. corp., banking and bus. law sects., tort and ins. practice sects.), NASD, Assn. Life Ins. Counsel (deps. solvency com.). Office: Am Gen Investment Mgmt Corp 390 Park Ave 6th Fl New York NY 10022 E-mail: alice_kane@agfg.com.*

KANE, ANNETTE PIESLAK, religious organization executive; b. Trenton, N.J., May 2, 1933; d. Theodore P. and Stella (Mackiewicz) Pieslak; m. Joseph P. Kane, Sept. 6, 1958; children: Paula M., Stephen J., Brian P., Christine A. BA, Trinity Coll., Washington, 1954; MA, U. Pa., 1956. Asst. prof. Rosemont (Pa.) Coll., 1955-58, Trinity Coll., Washington, 1958-61, editor alumni jour., 1973-79; program dir. Nat. Coun. Cath. Women, Washington, 1979-86, exec. dir., 1986—. Bd. dirs. Nat. Coun. Aging, Washington, 1985-87, CARA-Ctr. for Applied Rsch. in Apostolate, Washington, 1989—, Nat. Relig. Partnership for Environ., 1993—. Roman Catholic. Office: Nat Coun Cath Women 1275 K St NW Ste 975 Washington DC 20005-4006 E-mail: akane1@winstar.mail.com.

KANE, CHERYL MARIE, education program developer; b. Great Barrington, Mass., Dec. 26, 1947; d. Alexander and Mildred (Tatsapaugh) Shmulsky. BA, U. Mass., 1969; MA, U. Colo., 1979; PhD, Fla. State U., 1988. Project dir. Colo. State Dept. Edn., Denver, 1977-79; rsch. assoc. Nat. Inst. Edn., Washington, 1979-81; pvt. practice cons. Washington, 1981-88; assoc. exec. dir. Nat. Found. for the Improvement of Edn., Washington, 1988-92; dir. rsch. Nat. Edn. Commn. on Time and Learning, Washington, 1992-94; dir. strategy New Am. Schs. Devel. Corp., Arlington, Va., 1994-99; sr. assoc. office ednl. rsch./improvement U.S. Dept. Edn., 1999-2000, exec. dir. nat. commn. on H.S. sr. yr., 2000—01, sr. rsch. assoc., 2001—. Cons. U.S. Dept. Edn., Washington, World Bank, Washington, Acad. for Edn. Devel., Washington, 1981—88. Author: Prisoners of Time: What We Know and What We Need to Know, 1994; contbr. Sec. Logan Circle Cmty. Assn., Washington, 1993. Mem.: Am. Edn. Rsch. Assn., Phi Delta Kappa. Avocations: sailing, gardening, photography, travel. Home: 1325 13th St NW Apt 6 Washington DC 20005-4453 Office: Rm 4W307 400 Maryland Ave SW Washington DC 20202

KANE, DIANE GRINKEVICH, architectural historian, educator, planner; b. Cleve., Mar. 9, 1947; d. Alex Grinkevich and Helen Magdalene Miko; m. John Jasper Kane, Sept. 3, 1972. BA, UCLA, 1969; MA, U. Calif., Berkeley, 1973; PhD, U. Calif., Santa Barbara, 1996. Tchr. Carondelet H.S., Concord, Calif., 1973-76; archtl. historian Louisville Landmarks Commn., 1978-79; exec. dir. Downtown Fullerton (Calif.) Assn., 1983; program rep. UCLA Ext., L.A., 1984-85, instr., 1986-89; archtl. historian Caltrans, L.A., 1989—; prof. New Sch. Architecture, San Diego, 1999—. Chair 1st Nat. Historic Rds. Conf., 1998. Contbg. author: Saving Historic Roads, 1998. Trustee Calif. Preservation Found., Oakland, 1996-2002, program chair conf., 2001; planning commr. City of La Habra Heights, Calif., 1983-90, mem. coun., 1990-92, mayor, mayor pro-tem, 1993-94. Scenic Byways Corridor Mgmt. Plan grantee Fed. Hwy. Adminstrn., 2000, Transp. Enhancement Activity grantee, 2000, Critical Issues Tng. grantee Nat. Pks. Svc., 1998; recipient Tranny award Calif. Trans. Found., 1997, 2002, 03, Strive for Excellence Team award Fed. Hwy. Adminstrn., 1999, Caltrans Excellence Transp. award, 1999, 2000, 2002, 2003, Calif. Preservation Found. Design award, 2002, 2003, L.A. Conservancy Preservation award, 2002. Mem. Am. Inst. Cert. Planners, Am. Planning Assn., Soc. Archtl. Historians (treas., v.p., pres. 1989-93), Soc. Comml. Archaeology (bd. dirs. 1996-98, conf. chmn. 1996). Democrat. Avocations: swimming, scuba, hiking, bicycling, travel.

KANE, EDWARD JOSEPH, educator; b. Somers Point, N.J., Sept. 26, 1951; s. Joseph James and Ruth Marina (Ramirez) K.; m. Joan L. Davis, Feb. 11, 1978; children: Jonathan E., Daniel J., Rebecca A. BA, LaSalle Coll., Phila., 1978; MEd, Widener U., Chester, Pa., 1988. Cert. tchr. Rsch. technician Franklin Inst. Rsch., Phila., 1971-74; auditor Holiday Inn Midtown, Phila., 1975-76; corr. officer Pa. Dept. Justice, Graterford, Pa., 1976-78; tchr. St. Gabriel's Hall, Phoenixville, Pa., 1978-79, Harriton High Sch., Rosemont, Pa., 1979, William Penn Sch. Dist., Yeadon, Pa., 1979-89; tchr. English and Spanish Faith Mennonite High Sch., Kinzers, Pa., 1989-97; tchr. math. Manheim Twp. Middle Sch., Lancaster, Pa., 1997—2001; tchr. project Landis Valley, 2001—. Mem. Nat. Sci. Tchrs. Assn., Internat. Reading Assn., Nat. Coun. Tchrs. Math., Nat. Middle Sch. Assn., Hist. Soc. Pa., Phila. Libr. Co., Lancaster Mennonite Hist. Soc., Appalachian Trail Conf., Nat. Council Tchrs. English. Amish-Mennonite. Avocations: astronomy, walking, bicycling, writing. Home: 167 Maple St Gordonville PA 17529-9546 Office: Manheim Twp Mid Sch School Rd Lancaster PA 17601-5134 E-mail: ejkane@redrose.net., ed_kane@mail.mtwp.K12.pa.us.

KANE, GEORGE FRANCIS, systems analyst; b. Palo Alto, Calif., Aug. 11, 1948; s. John Francis and Dorothy Desdemona (De Leito) K.; m. Tandy Jo Warnow, July 20, 1974 (div. Feb. 1981); 1 child, Kristin Aviva. BA in Philosopy, U. Calif., Berkeley, 1970. With Unisys Corp., 1979, engring. documentation specialist, 1985-90, product info. specialist Rancho Bernardo, Calif., 1990-94, product info. analyst Roseville, Minn., 1994—. Author: (chess instructions books) Chess and Children, 1974, What's My Next Move, 1974; contbr. New Unionist Monthly Newsletter, 1984—. Active New Union Party, Mpls., 1984—; sec. Minn. Atheists, 1998—. Mem. Unisys Toastmasters Club (various offices, Dist. 6 Divsn. Gov. of Yr. 2001-02) Home: Apt 210 1280 Larpenteur Ave W Saint Paul MN 55113-6340 Office: Unisys Corp 2276 Highcrest Rd Roseville MN 55113-2529 E-mail: george.kane@unisys.com.

KANE, GRACE MCNELLY, maternal, women's health and pediatrics nurse; b. Auburn, Ill., Mar. 31, 1939; d. Irving Benjamin and Ruby Louise (Stinnett) McNelly; m. Robert John Kane, July 23, 1960 (dec. 1994); children: Scott Robert, Timothy Phillip, Pamela Collette, Glenn Randall, Andrew Keith, Bruce Ryan. Diploma, Mem. Hosp. Sch. Nursing, Springfield, Ill., 1960; BS in Profl. Arts, St. Joseph's Coll., North Windham, Maine, 1985. RN Ill., cert. in occpl. hearing conservation, fetal monitoring I and II, ALCS. Staff nurse nursery-newborn units Walther Meml. Hosp., Chgo., 1962-67; staff nurse rooming-in nursery Luth. Gen. Hosp., Park Ridge, Ill., 1977-85; staff nurse med.-surg. unit Swedish Covenant Hosp., Chgo., 1989; staff nurse occupational clinic Rush-Presbyn-St. Luke's, Elk Grove Village, Ill., 1988; nurse various hosps., Arlington Heights, Ill., 1989-93; staff nurse couplet care St. Joseph's Hosp., Phoenix, 1997—. Address: 5821 E Acoma Dr Scottsdale AZ 85254-2413

KANE, JAMES PATRICK, superintendent of schools; b. Staten Island, N.Y., Apr. 4, 1933; s. Frank J. and Della A. (Harte) K.; m. Maureen D. Kane, Aug. 13, 1955; children: Deirdre, Donna. BS in edn., Fordham U., 1954; MA, Columbia U., 1962, profl. diploma, 1964; PhD in Edn., Fairleigh Dickinson U., 1974. Diplomate in sch. adminstrn. Eng. tchr. Peekskill (N.Y.) MA, 1958-66, dean of students, 1958-66; headmaster Nyack Prep. Sch., Southampton, N.Y., 1966-75; supr. of schs. Hamburg (N.J.) Pub. Schs., 1975—; lectr. William Paterson U. Adj. faculty post Ramapo Coll., Mahwah, N.J., 1983—; adj. prof. William Paterson U., Wayne, N.J., 1998—; spkr. Americana Lectrs., Newton, N.J., 1999; author school plays, Hamburg Drama Soc., 1981—. Contbr. articles to profl. jours. Trustee Franklin Mineral Mus., Franklin, N.J., 1985—; trustee Green Chimneys Sch., Brewster, N.Y., 1962-66; active Hamburg Drug Alliance Coun., 1985—. Capt. USMC, 1954-58. Recipient Reinhardt Excellence in Edn. award SCSAA, 1989, Cummings Disting. Svc. award SCEA, 1993, Fordham U. Alumni Achievement award, 1995, Excellence in Arts award SC Arts Coun., 1991, Disting. Svc. award NJASA; named Man of Yr. Hamburg, N.J., 1985, N.J. Gov.'s Award in Arts, 1997. Mem. N.J. Assn. Sch. Adminstrs. Disting. Svc. award), Am. Legion, N.J. Congress of Parents & Tchrs. (life), Roundtable Assn., Phi Delta Kappa. Avocation: summer cruising. Home: 38 Elmwood Ter Wayne NJ 07470-4334 Office: Hamburg Pub Sch Dist Linwood Ave Hamburg NJ 07419

KANE, JAMES ROBERT, financial executive; b. Pitts., Mar. 22, 1959; s. John William Sr. and Helen Mary (Neimeier) K. AS, Allegheny County Community Coll., 1979; BBA, Robert Morris Coll., 1981; MBA, So. Meth. U., 1993. CPA, Tex.; cert. mgmt. acct.; cert. fin. mgmt. Staff acct. UCCEL Corp., Dallas, 1982-83, fin. reports analyst, 1983-85, fin. systems analyst, 1985-86, fin. reporting, analysis supr., 1986; acct. Zoecon Corp., Dallas, 1986, sr. acct., 1987-90, mgr. acctg., 1990-93; mgr. corp. acctg. Kimball Internat., Inc., Jasper, Ind., 1994-96, dir. acctg., 1996-98, dir. treasury, 1998-2000; contr. URS Corp., Austin, Tex., 2000—02; v.p. acctg. Centerpulse USA Inc., Austin, 2002—. Cons. in field. Recipient Achievement award UCCEL Corp., 1985. Mem. AICPAs. Republican. Methodist. Home: 16618 Malaga Hills Dr Round Rock TX 78681 Office: 9900 Spectrum Dr Austin TX 78717

KANE, JAY BRASSLER, banker; b. Bklyn., June 4, 1931; s. Arthur Ferris and Margaret (Brassler) K.; m. Marian Albertson, Oct. 15, 1960 (dec. 1993); children: Lisa Kane Brown, James Brassler. Grad., Poly. Prep. Sch., 1949; AB, Columbia, 1953; MBA, NYU, 1961. With Met. Life Ins. Co., N.Y.C., 1954-55, Bankers Trust Co., N.Y.C., 1955—, asst. v.p., 1965-68, v.p., 1968-88, BT Brokerage Corp., 1988-90; regional dir. Frank Russell Trust. Co., N.Y.C., 1990-97; assoc. P.P.I. Internat., 1997—. Co-pres. Cotton Club, 1999—2000, mgr. corp. pension funds, mktg. dir. trust svcs.; spkr. Am. Bankers Assn.; lectr New Sch. Social Rsch.; Attach bd. dirs.; bd. dirs. Pickwick Soc. Contbr. articles to profl. jours. Mem. N.Y. Soc. Security Analysts, Fin. Analysts Fedn., Am. Pension Conf., Riverside (Conn.) Yacht Club, N.Y. Yacht Club. Home and Office: Hilton Heath Cos Cob CT 06807 E mail: jbkane1@aol.com.

KANE, JOELLE K.K.S. lawyer; b. Kealakekua, Hawaii, Nov. 16, 1969; d. Howard Kenji and Mary Jo Segawa; m. Micah Alika Kane, Jan. 14, 1996; children: Ka'ilihiwa Mary Kiyomi, Sunny Hi'ilei Akiko, Ka'ohu Jean Hiroko. BA, U. Wash., 1991; JD, U. Hawaii, 1995. Bar: Hawaii 1995. Law clk. Corp. Counsel Honolulu, 1993; legis. aide Office of Hawaiian Affairs, Honolulu, 1994-95; law clk. First Cir. State Hawaii, Honolulu, 1995-96; sr. assoc. Gallagher & Assocs., Honolulu, 1996-2000; ptnr. Henderson Gallagher & Kane, Honolulu, 2000—. Bd. dirs. WSRSLAA, Honolulu, 1996-98, v.p., 1998-99. Active Office Hawaiian Affairs, Honolulu, 1990—; grass roots organizer Hawaii Rep. Party, Honolulu, 1998—. Mem. ABA, Hawaii State Bar Assn., Hawaii Women Lawyers, Delta Theta Phi, Elks Club. Roman Catholic. Avocations: longboarding, running, gardening. Home: 45-135 Moamahi Way Kaneohe HI 96744-5329 Office: Henderson Gallagher & Kane 220 S King St Ste 2100 Honolulu HI 96813-4510

KANE, JOHN, political organization administrator; b. Md., 1961; Chmn. Md. Rep. Party, 2002—; chief exec., owner Kane Co., Elkridge. Fundraiser, advocate Intercounty Connector. Office: Md Rep Party 15 West St Annapolis MD 21401

KANE, JOHN LAWRENCE, JR., judge; b. Tucumcari, N.Mex., Feb. 14, 1937; s. John Lawrence and Dorothy Helen (Bottler) K.; m. Stephanie Jane Shafer, Oct. 5, 1993; children: Molly Francis, Meghan, Sally, John Pattison. BA, U. Colo., 1958; JD, U. Denver, 1961, LL.D. (hon), 1997. Bar: Colo. 1961. Dep. dist. atty., Adams County, Colo., 1961-62; assoc. firm Gaunt, Byrne & Dirrim, 1961-63; ptnr. firm Andrews and Kane, Denver, 1964; pub. defender Adams County, 1965-67; dep. dir. eastern region of India Peace Corps, 1967-69; with firm Holme Roberts & Owen, 1970-77, ptnr., 1972-77; judge U.S. Dist. Ct. Colo., Denver, 1978-88, U.S. sr. dist. judge, 1988—. Adj. prof. law U. Denver, U. Colo., 1996—; vis. lectr. Trinity Coll., Dublin, Ireland, winter 1989; adj. prof. U. Colo., 1996, philosophy, 2003. Contbr. articles to profl. jours. Recipient St. Thomas More award Cath. Lawyers Guild, 1983, U.S. Info. Agy. Outstanding Svc. award, 1985, Outstanding Alumnus award U. Denver, 1987, Lifetime Jud. Achievement award Nat. Assn. Criminal Def. Lawyers, 1987, Civil Rights award B'nai B'rith, 1988, Justice Gerald Le Dain award Drug Policy Found., 2000. Fellow Internat. Acad. Trial Lawyers, Am. Bd. Trial Advs. (hon.). Roman Catholic. Office: US Dist Ct US Courthouse 901 19th St Denver CO 80294-1929 E-mail: john_L_Kane@cod.uscourts.gov. *There is a tendency to gild the past with uncritical generosity but an even more pronounced one to forget Santayana's dictum that one who forgets history is bound to repeat it. Law is that indispensable mechanism by which we may survive as a free people if we use it to apply a critical understanding of history to a confusing and dynamic present.*

KANE, KAREN MARIE, public affairs consultant; b. Colorado Springs, Colo., Mar. 7, 1947; d. Bernard Francis and Adeline Marie (Logan) K. Student, Mills Coll., Oakland, Calif., 1965-66; BA, U. Wash., 1970, MA, 1973, PhC, 1977, postgrad. Pub. affairs cons., housing subcom. Seattle Ret. Tchrs. Assn., 1981-84; pub. affairs cons. 1st U.S. Women's Olympic Marathon Trials, 1982-83, Seattle, 1985—. Contbr. articles to newsletters and mags. Chmn. hist. preservation LWV, Seattle, 1989—, co-chmn. land use com., 2000—; trustee Allied Arts of Seattle, 1987—96, past chmn. hist. preservation com., sec. bd. trustees, mem. exec. com., 1987—96; trustee Allied Arts Found., 1999—, mem. sponsorship application approval com., 2002—; mem. Mayor's Landmark Theatre Adv. Group, 1991—93, Pike Place Market Hist. Commn., Seattle, 1992—98, chmn., 1997—98; mem. Pike Place Market Com. to Rev. the Hildt Agreement, 1998—99, The Market Constituency, 1999—, Friends of the Market, 1999—; vol. various polit. campaigns, Seattle; bd. dirs. Showboat Theatre Found./Bravo (formerly Showboat Theatre Found.), 1984—2002. Recipient Award of Honor Wash. Trust for Hist. Preservation, 1990, Recognition award Found. for Hist. Preservation and Adaptive Reuse, Seattle, 1991; Am. Found. grantee, 1989, 91. Mem. AAUW, Internat. Platform Assn., Mills Coll. Alumnae Assn., U. Wash. Alumni Assn., Nat. Trust for Hist. Preservation, Hist. Hawai'i Found., Found. for San Francisco's Archtl. Heritage, Wash. Trust for Hist. Preservation, Hist. Seattle Preservation and Devel. Authority.

KANE, LUCILE M. retired archivist, historian; b. Maiden Rock, Wis., Mar. 17, 1920; d. Emery John and Ruth (Coty) Kane BS, River Falls State Tchrs. Coll., 1942; MA, U. Minn., 1946. Tchr. Osceola (Wis.) High Sch., 1942-44; asst. publicity dept. U. Minn. Press, Mpls., 1945-46; rsch. fellow, editor Forest Products History Found., St. Paul, 1946-48; curator manuscripts Minn. Hist. Soc., St. Paul, 1948-75, sr. rsch. fellow, 1979-85, sr. rsch. assoc., 1985—, mem. hon. coun., 1988—. State archivist, 1975—79. Author, compiler: A Guide to the Care and Administration of Manuscripts, 2d edit., 1966, (with Kathryn A. Johnson) Manuscripts Collections of the Minnesota Historical Society, Guide No.2, 1955, The Waterfall That Built a City, 1966 (updated edit. pub. as The Falls of St. Anthony, 1987), (with Alan Ominsky) Twin Cities: A Pictorial History of Saint Paul and Minneapolis, 1983; transl., editor, Military Life in

Dakota, The Jour. of Philippe Regis de Trobriand, 1951; editor: (with others) The Northern Expeditions of Major Stephen H. Long, 1978; contbr. articles to profl. jours. Recipient award of Merit Western History Assn., 1982, Disting. Svc. award Minn. Humanities Commn., 1983, award of Distinction Am. Assn. State and Local History, 1987; co-recipient Theodore C. Blegen award Minn. Hist. Soc., 1996. Fellow: Soc. Am. Archivists. Home: 1298 Fairmount Ave Saint Paul MN 55105-2703

KANE, MARGARET BRASSLER, sculptor; b. East Orange, N.J., May 25, 1909; d. Hans and Mathilde (Trumpler) Brassler; m. Arthur Ferris Kane, June 11, 1930; children: Jay Brassler, Gregory Ferris. Student, Packer Collegiate Inst., 1920-26, Syracuse U., 1927, Art Students League, 1927-29, N.Y. Coll. Music, 1928-29, John Hovannes Studio, 1932-34; PhD (hon.), Colo. State Christian Coll., 1973. Head craftsman sculpture, arts and skills unit ARC, Halloran Gen. Hosp., NY, 1942—43; jury mem. Bklyn. Mus., 1948, Am. Machine & Foundry Co., 1957; com. mem. An Am. Group, Inc. Exhibitions include, Phila. Mus., Chgo. Art Inst., Am. Fedn. Arts, N.Y. Bot. Garden, 1981, 60th Anniversary Exhbn. Lever House, 1987—98, Sculptors Guild 50th Anniversary Exhbn., Lever House, 1987—96, 1st Bi-Coastal exhibits San Francisco, Collection Donald Trump, 1988, Collection Rene Anselmo, 1991, Shidoni Galleries, Santa Fe, N.Mex., 1989, Am. Sculpture, Hofstra Mus., 1990, exhibitions include nat. tour Am. sculpture by EducArt Projects Inc., 1992, exhibitions include, Stamford Mus. and Nature Ctr., 1996, Zimmerli Art Mus. Historical Exhibit, 1999—2000, Smithsonian Mus. Tour, 2000—02, numerous others, Represented in permanent collections, Zimmerli Art Mus., Rutgers U., N.J., 1992, Nat. Mus. Am. Art, Smithsonian Instn., Washington, 1993, 2000, Bruce Mus., Greenwich, Conn., 1996, Packer Collegiate Inst., Bklyn., 2003, one-woman shows include sculpture, Friends Greenwich (Conn.) Library, 1962, prin. works include 18 foot carving in limewood, 2002, prin. works include six oot carving Reaching the Galaxies, 2002—, prin. works include sculpture Packer Collegiate Inst., Bklyn., 2003, prin. works include plaque Burro Monument, Fair Play, Colo.; reprodns. Contemporary Stone Sculpture, 1970, Contemporary Am. Sculptures, Am. References, Chgo.; CD-ROM, Smithsonian Nat. Mus. Am. Art, Washington, 1995; contbr. articles to mags. Recipient Hyatt Huntington award, 1942, Am. Artist Profl. League and Monclair Art Assn. awards, 1943, 1st Henry O. Avery prize, 1944, Sculpture prize, Bklyn. Soc. Artists, Bklyn. Mus., 1946, John Rogers award, 1951, Lawrence Hyder prize, 1952, 1954, David H. Zell Meml. award, 1954, 1963, Hon. Mention, U.S. Maritime Commn., 1941, A.C.A. Gallery Competition, 1944, medal of Honor for Sculpture, Nat. Acad. Galleries, N.Y., prize for carved sculpture, 1955, prize for animal sculpture, 1956, 1st award for sculpture, Ann. New Eng. Exhbns., Silvermine, Conn. Fellow: Internat. Inst. Arts and Letters (life); mem.: Nat. Trust Hist. Preservation, silvermine Guild Artists, Internat. Soc. Artists (charter), Internat. Sculpture Ctr., Greenwich Soc. Artists (mem. coun.), Bklyn. Soc. Artists, Artists Coun. U.S.A., Pen and Brush (emeritus 1992), Nat. League Am. Pen Women, Inc. (OWL award for the Arts 1991), Nat. Assn. Women Artists (2d v.p. 1943—44), Sculptors Guild, Inc. (life; sec. to exec. bd. 1942—45, chmn. exhbn. com. 1942, 1944). Home and Studio: 30 Strickland Rd Cos Cob CT 06807-2729 *It is not possible to overestimate the deep satisfaction experienced in having created countless direct carvings in marble, stone, wood and models for bronze. I strongly believe mankind needs to express itself in some meaningful way. My recent mahogany woodcarvings are dedicated to Peace, Love and an end to Violence. If these goals should inspire the many thousands of viewers of my art form, then I am content that my sculpture is a worthwhile contribution to American culture.*

KANE, MARGARET MCDONALD, lawyer; b. Long Beach, Calif. d. James LaSalle and Nora Margaret (Foley) McDonald; m. Donald D. Hoytt, Oct. 28, 1967 (div. 1974); children: Lawrence Andrew, Elyse Caron ; m. John J. Kane, May 18, 1985. BA, U. So. Calif., 1967; JD, Southwestern U., 1980. Bar: Calif. 1980, U.S. Dist. Ct. (cen. dist.) Calif. 1981, U.S. Ct. Appeals (9th cir.) 1981. Prin. Silver & Freedman P.C., Los Angeles, 1981—. Mem. Los Angeles County Bar Assn., Century City Bar Assn. Office: Silver & Freedman PC 1925 Century Park East Suite 2100 Los Angeles CA 90067-2722 E-mail: mkane@silfre.com.

KANE, MARILYN, real estate company executive; Co-pres. Butler Kane, Inc., N.Y.C. Founder N.Y. chpt. Nat. Coalition for Family Justice. Office: Butler Kane Inc 171 Madison Ave #1000 New York NY 10016

KANE, MARY KAY, dean, law educator; b. Detroit, Nov. 14, 1946; d. John Francis and Frances (Roberts) K.; m. Ronan Eugene Degnan, Feb. 3, 1987 (dec. Oct. 1987). BA cum laude, U. Mich., 1968, JD cum laude, 1971. Bar: Mich. 1971, N.Y., Calif. Rsch. assoc., co-dir. NSF project on privacy, confidentiality and social sci. rsch. data sch. law U. Mich., 1971-72, Harvard U., 1972-74; asst. prof. law SUNY, Buffalo, 1974-77; mem. faculty Hastings Coll. Law U. Calif., San Francisco, 1977—, prof. law, 1979—, assoc. acad. dean, 1981-83, acting acad. dean, 1987-88, acad. dean., 1990-93, dean, 1993—; chancellor U. Calif., San Francisco, 2001—. Vis. prof. law U. Mich., 1981, U. Utah, 1983, U. Calif., Berkeley, 1983-84, sch. law U. Tex., 1989; cons. Mead Data Control, Inc., 1971, 74, Inst. on Consumer Justice, U. Mich. Sch. Law, 1972, U.S. Privacy Protection Study Commn., 1975-76; lectr. pretrial mgmt. devices U.S. magistrates for 6th and 11th cirs. Fed. Jud. Ctr., 1983; Siebenthaler lectr. Samuel P. Chase Coll. Law, U. North Ky., 1987; reporter ad hoc com. on asbestos litigation U.S. Jud. Conf., 1990-91, mem. standing com. on practice and procedure, 2001—; mem. 9th Cir. Adv. Com. on Rules Practice and Internal Oper. Procedures, 1993-96; spkr. in field. Author: Civil Procedure in a Nutshell, 1979, 5th edit., 2003, Sum and Substance on Remedies, 1981; co-author: (with C. Wright and A. Miller) Pocket Supplements to Federal Practice and Procedure, 1975—, Federal Practice and Procedure, vols. vol. 7, 3d edit., 2001, 10, 10A and 10B, 3d edit., 1998, vols. 7-7C, 2d edit., 1986, vols. 6-6A, 2d edit., 1990, vols. 11-11A, 2d edit., 1995, (with J. Friedenthal and A. Miller) Hornbook on Civil Procedure, 3d edit., 1999, (with C. Wright) Hornbook on the Law of Federal Courts, 2002, Federal Practice Deskbook, 2002; mem. law sch. divsn. West. Adv. Editl. Bd., 1986—; contbr. articles to profl. jours. Mem. standing com. on rules of practice and procedure U.S. Jud. Conf., 2000—. Mem. ABA (mem. bar admissions com. 1995-2000), Assn. Am. Law Schs. (com. on prelegal edn. statement 1982, chair sect. remedies 1982, panelist sect. on prelegal edn. 1983, exec. com. sect. on civil procedure 1983, 86, panelist sect. on tchg. methods 1984, spkr. new tchrs. conf. 1986, 89, 90, chair sect. on civil procedure 1987, spkr. sects. civil procedure and conflicts 1987, 91, chair planning com. for 1988 Tchg. Conf. in Civil Procedure 1987-88, nominating com. 1988, profl. devel. com. 1988-91, planning com. for workshop in conflicts 1988, planning com. for 1990 Conf. on Clin. Legal Edn. 1989, chair profl. devel. com. 1989-91, exec. com. 1991-93, 2000-02, pres.-elect 2000, pres. 2001), Am. Law Inst. (co-reporter complex litigation project 1988-93, coun. 1998—), ABA/Assn. Am. Law Schs. Commn. on Financing Legal Edn., State Bar Mich. Home: 8 Admiral Dr Ste 421 Emeryville CA 94608-1567 Office: U Calif Hastings Coll Law 200 Mcallister St San Francisco CA 94102-4707

KANE, MELISSA L. fundraiser; b. Holyoke, Mass., Nov. 29, 1972; d. Robert A. and Mary M. Silva; m. James G. Kane, Oct. 4, 1997. BA in History, Providence Coll., 1994; mus. studies grad. cert., Tufts U., 1996. Devel. asst. DeCordova Mus. and Sculpture Park, Lincoln, Mass., 1995-96, asst. dir. devel., 1996-98, dir. devel., 1998—. Guest lectr. Boston U., 1998. Pres. Northborough Cultural Coun., 1999—. Mem. Am. Assn. Mus., Assn. Fundraising Profls., Planned Giving Group New England, New England Mus. Assn. (lectr. 1997, 98), Women in Devel. Democrat. Roman Catholic. Avocations: art, american history, reading, theater, music. Office: DeCordova Museum & Sculpture Park 51 Sandy Pond Rd Lincoln MA 01773-2600

KANE, MICAH, political party official; B in Bus. Adminstrn., Menlo Coll., Calif.; M in Bus. Adminstrn., U. Hawaii. Govt. affairs liaison Bldg. Ind. Assn. Hawaii; exec. dir. Hawaii Rep. Party, 1999—. Office: Rep Party Hawaii 725 Kapi'olani Blvd Honolulu HI 96813 Office Fax: 808-593-7742.

KANE, MICHAEL BARRY, social science research executive; b. Taunton, Mass., July 2, 1944; s. Julius J. and Dorothy M. (Moscoff) K.; children: Jared E., Stacey E., Matthew D. BA in Polit. Sci., NYU, 1966; MA in Ednl. Adminstrn., Columbia U., 1968, MEd in Ednl. Adminstrn., 1970, EdD in Ednl. Adminstrn., 1974. Tchr. Roosevelt Sch., Stamford, Conn., 1966-67; asst. to dir. New Lincoln Sch., N.Y.C., 1969; spl. asst. to dep. commr. for devel. U.S. Office of Edn., Washington, 1970-71; headmaster Downtown Community sch., N.Y.C., 1971-73; coord. program for situational analysis and program for ednl. leadership Columbia U. Tchrs. Coll., N.Y.C., 1970-73; group mgr., project dir. Abt Assocs., Inc., Cambridge, Mass., 1973-79; asst. dir., assoc. dir. Nat. Inst. Edn., U.S. Dept. Edn., Washington, 1979-82; pres. MCK Assocs., Inc., Tallahassee, Fla., and Annapolis, Md., 1982-87; prin. Pelavin Assocs., Inc., Washington, 1988-94; v.p. Am. Inst. for Rsch., Washington, 1995—, sr. v.p., dir. program on individual and orgnl. performance, 1998—. Chmn. Profl. Tchr. Career Devel. Coun., Fla.; vis. scholar Fla. State U.'s Ctr. for Needs Assessmtn and Planning; pres. Citizen's Coun. Edn., Fla.; chmn. Fla. Bus. and Edn. Coalition; lectr. numerous workshops. Author, co-author or editor: Minorities in Textbooks: A Study of Their Treatment in Social Studies Texts, Improving Schools: Using What We Know, Changing the Odds: Factors Increasing Access to College, Implementing Performance Assessments: Promises, Problems, and Challenges, Principles and Practices of Performance Assessment; contbr. articles to profl. jours. Avocations: boating, photography, scuba diving. Home: 1307 35th St NW Washington DC 20007

KANE, MICHAEL JOEL, physician; b. Erie, Pa., July 2, 1951; BS, U.S. Naval Acad., 1973; MD, N.J. Med. Sch., 1983. Diplomate Am. Bd. Internal Medicine. Med. intern Thomas Jefferson U. Hosp., Phila., 1983-84, resident in medicine, 1984-86; fellow in neoplastic diseases Mt. Sinai Med. Ctr., N.Y.C., 1986-88; attending physician Jefferson Med. Coll., Phila., 1988-91, Med. Ctr. at Princeton, N.J., 1991-96, Cancer Inst. N.J., Hamilton, 1996—. Served to lt. U.S. Navy, 1969-79. Decorated Navy Achievement medal. Fellow ACP, Acad. Medicine of N.J., Am. Soc. Clin. Oncology, Am. Assn. Cancer Rsch., Am. Soc. Hematology, Oncology Soc. N.J. Office: Cancer Inst NJ at Hamilton 5 Hamilton Health Pl Ste 120 Hamilton NJ 08690-3542 E-mail: mkane@rwjuhh.net.

KANE, MICHAEL JOSEPH, director; b. N.Y.C., July 9, 1922; s. Max and Sophie (Kuznets) Cohen; m. Winifred June Fay, Oct. 1, 1947 (div. 1972); children: Amy Lynn, Jennifer Ann. Student, King-Smith Playhouse and Sch. of Theatre Arts, 1939-41. Actor, stage mgr. in Mister Roberts Leland Hayward Prodns., N.Y.C., 1947-51; stage mgr., assoc. dir. CBS-TV, Hollywood, Calif., 1951-53; freelance dir. Art Linkletter's House Party, Hollywood, 1953-70; dir., producer various commls., Hollywood, 1957-85; producer, dir. Can You Top This?, Hollywood, 1969-70; lectr. TV/film writing, cable TV prodn., directing for the camera Calif. State U., Fullerton, 1987-92. Mem. Radio and TV Dirs. Guild, 1952-58; co-founder The Fullerton Acting Lab., 1992. Dir.: (stage prodn.) Happy Birthday, Wanda June, 1970, (TV prodns.) Gilligan's Island, Hawaiian Eye, The Brady Bunch, Quincy, Hardcastle and McCormick. Served as staff sgt. USAAF, 1942-46. King-Smith Playhouse and Sch. Theatre Arts scholar, 1939-41. Mem. AFTRA, SAG, Soc. Stage Dirs. and Choreographers, Actors Equity Assn., Dirs. Guild Am. (trustee DGA producers pension and health plans). E-mail: maishkane@aol.com.

KANE, PATRICIA LANEGRAN, language professional, educator; b. St. Paul, June 23, 1926; d. Walter B. and Lita E. (Wilson) Lanegran; m. Donald Patrick Kane, Apr. 1, 1947; children: Laura Kane Gustafson, Maura L. Kane Hackenmueller. BA cum laude, Macalester Coll., St. Paul, 1947; MA, U. Minn., 1950, PhD, 1961. Mem. faculty Macalester Coll., 1950-91, prof. English, 1971-91, DeWitt Wallace prof., 1978-91, prof. emeritus, 1992—, chmn. dept., 1977-86, faculty assoc., office of v.p. acad. affairs, 1979-83; mem. Minn. planning com. nat. identification project advancement women in acad. adminstrn. Nat. Council Edn., 1979-81. Co-author: A St. Paul Omnibus, 1979; Contbr. articles to profl. jours. Recipient Jefferson prize for teaching excellence, 1980, Disting. Alumni citation Macalester Coll., 1992; Danforth grantee, 1957-58. Mem. MLA, Soc. Study So. Lit.

KANE, PATRICK J. high school principal; b. Cleve., June 14, 1955; s. Eugene F. and Elizabeth A. Kane; m. Heidi C. Kane, Oct. 9, 1982; children: Erin E., Jacqueline A. BS in Edn., Kent State U., 1977; MS in Athletic Adminstrn., Seattle Pacific U., 1989, cert. adminstrn., 2000. Cert. elem. tchr., Wash. Spl. edn. instr. Mentor (Ohio) Sch. Dist., 1977-78, Browning (Mont.) Sch. Dist., 1978-79; elem. tchr. Cut Bank (Mont.) Sch. Dist., 1979-81; mem. collections staff Ford Motor Credit, Portland, Oreg., 1981-84; tchr. Port Angeles (Wash.) Schs., 1984—; track coach Port Angeles H.S., 1984-93, soccer coach, 1993—2000. Intern Sport for Understanding, Washington, summer 1989, West Seattle YMCA, summer 1988. Pres. Port Angeles Jr. Soccer, 1986-91, North Olympic Soccer Referees, 1986-92; tournament dir. Jr./Sr. Babe Ruth, Port Angeles, 1990-92. Mem. Nat. Soccer Coaches Assn. Am. Avocations: hiking, weight lifting, reading. Home: 350 Viewcrest St Port Angeles WA 98362-6979 Office: Port Angeles HS 304 E Park Ave Port Angeles WA 98362-6934

KANE, PETER BAYARD, physician; b. Bryn Mawr, Pa., Apr. 3, 1938; MD, U. Pa., 1964. Diplomate Am. Bd. Anesthesiology. Intern Wis. Hosps., Madison, 1964-65; resident Hosp. U. Pa., Phila., 1965-67, fellow in rsch., 1967-69; mem. staff SUNY Hosp., Syracuse; prof. SUNY Upstate Med. U., Syracuse. Mem. AMA, Am. Soc. Anesthesiology, Internat. Anesthesia Rsch. Soc., N.Y. State Soc. Anesthesia. Office: SUNY- Upstate Med Univ 750 E Adams St Syracuse NY 13210-2306

KANE, ROBERT ALAN, radiologist, researcher; b. Boston, Jan. 18, 1946; BS in Biology, Boston Coll., 1967; MD, Tufts U., 1971. Diplomate Am. Bd. Radiology (examiner 1982—). Internship Mt. Auburn Hosp., Cambridge, Mass., 1971-72; radiology resident Mass. Gen. Hosp., Boston, 1972-75; fellow New England Deaconess, Boston, 1975, staff radiologist, 1975-95; vice chmn. radiology Deaconess Hosp., Boston, 1994-96; assoc. chief radiology Beth Israel Deaconess Med. Ctr., Boston, 1996—. Prof. radiology Harvard Med. Sch., Boston, 1999. Editor: Intraoperative Laparascopic and Endoluminal Ultrasound, 1998. Capt. USAR, 1975-81. Recipient Roscoe Miller award Soc. Gastrointestinal Radiology, 1986. Fellow Am. Coll. Radiology, Soc. Radiologists in Ultrasound; mem. Radiol. Soc. N.Am. (counselor 1986-90), Mass. Radiology Soc. (pres. 1992-93), New England Roentgen Ray Soc. (pres. 1990-91), Alpha Omega Alpha. Office: Beth Israel Deaconess Med Ctr 1 Deaconess Rd Boston MA 02215-5321

KANE, ROBERT BARRY, career officer; b. Astoria, N.Y., Aug. 13, 1951; s. Murray K. and Virginia Bolin; m. Anita Louise Van Deursen, Aug. 25, 1984; children: Virginia Marie, David Matthew. BA with high honors, Clemson U., 1973; MA, U. S.C., 1975; Edn. Splst., George Washington U., 1979; PhD, UCLA, 1997. Commd. 2d lt. USAF, 1973, advanced through grades to lt. col., 1991; sq. sect. comdr. 1st component repair Sq. USAF, Langley AFB, Va., 1976-79; chief base adminstr. 5072nd Air Base Sq. USAF, Galena Airport, Alaska, 1979-80, sq. sect. comdr. 401st Supply Sq. Torrejon AFB, Spain, 1980-83, exec. officer Navstar Global Positioning Sys. Program Office L.A. AFB, 1983-85, exec. officer/hqrs. sq. sect. comdr. 340th Air Refuel Wing Altus AFB, Okla., 1985-87, DET 9 comdr., chief aerial mail term 7025th Air Post Sq. Frankfurt, Germany, 1987-90, dir. resource mgmt. Directorate of Prog. Mgmt. L.A. AFB, 1990-94, chief edn./tng. flight 61st Mission Spt. Sq., 1994-96, nonresident studies faculty Air War Coll. Maxwell AFB, 1996—2001; chief instrn. divsn. Internat. Officer Sch., Maxwell AFB, Ala., 2001—03; ret. USAF, 2003. Ajd. faculty St. Leo's Coll., Langley AFB, Va., 1977-79, U. Alaska, Galena, 1979-80, Troy State U., Torrejon Air Base, Spain, 1980-83, We. Okla. State Coll., Altus, 1987, City Coll. Chgo., Wiesbaden, Germany, 1990, Chapman U., Manhattan Beach, Calif., 1990, Troy State U., Montgomery, Ala., 1998—. Author: Disobedience and Conspiracy in the German Army 1918-1945, 2002. Deacon, tchr. Hawthorne (Calif.) Seventh Day Adventist Ch., 1994-96, Montgomery (Ala.) First Seventh Day Adventist Ch., 1996—; usher, tchr. base chapel, various locations, 1976-94. Strom Thurmond scholar Clemson U., 1969. Avocations: military history, sightseeing, amateur photography. E-mail: rbkane@mindspring.com.

KANE, ROBERT FRANCIS, lawyer, former ambassador, consultant; b. Denver, Mar. 15, 1926; s. James Hanley and Helen Mary (Gray) K.; m. Mary Catherine Galligan, Sept. 1, 1951; children: Stephen, Anne Kane Coogan, Thomas, Mary. Student, Menlo Coll., 1946—47, U. So. Calif., 1948; AA, Coll. San Mateo, Calif., 1948; JD, U. San Francisco, 1952. Bar: Calif. 1952, U.S. Dist. Ct. (no. dist.) Calif. 1952, U.S. Dist. Ct. (ctrl. dist.) Calif. 1992, U.S. Ct. Appeals (9th cir.) 1952, U.S. Supreme Ct. 1983. Assoc. Bronson, Bronson & McKinnon, San Francisco, 1952-54; ptnr. Roos & Jennings, San Francisco, 1954-55, Ropers, Majeski & Kane, Redwood City, Calif., 1955-61, Kane, Owen & Melbye, Redwood City, 1961-68; judge Superior Ct., Redwood City, 1969-71; justice Calif. Ct. Appeals, San Francisco, 1971-79; dir. Ropers, Majeski, Kohn, Bentley, Wagner & Kane, San Francisco, 1979-94; U.S. Amb. to Ireland, Dublin, 1984-85. Arbitration mediation, spl. master, trial anc appellate cons.; lectr. in field; law educator; U.S. arbitrator in treaty dispute witl Poland, 1982. Contbr. articles to profl. jours. Bd. dirs. various schs. Served witl USN, 1944-66. Recipient Freedoms Found. award, 1980. Fellow Am. Coll Trial Lawyers; mem. ABA (life fellow found.), Calif. Bar Assn., Internat. Soc Barristers, Am. Bd. Trial Advs., Internat. Assn. Ins. Counsel, Internat. Acad Trial Judges, Calif. Acad. Appellate Lawyers. Republican. Roman Catholic Office: Profl Jud Svcs PO Box 6729 630 N San Mateo Dr San Mateo C 94401-2328 E-mail: jdgkane@jarsinc.com.

KANE, ROBERT LEWIS, public health educator; b. N.Y.C., Jan. 18, 1940; m Rosalie Smolkin, June 17, 1962; children: Miranda, Ingrid, Kate AB, Columbi Coll., N.Y.C., 1961; MD, Harvard U., 1965. Acting coordinator sr. clerkshi program dept. community medicine U. Ky., Lexington, 1968-69; svc. unit di USPHS Indian Hosp., Shiprock, N.Mex., 1969-70; spl. asst. to regional healt dir. USPHS HEW Region VIII, Denver, 1970-71; from asst. to assoc. pro family and community medicine U. Utah Sch. Medicine, Salt Lake City 1970-77; sr. researcher The Rand Corp., Santa Monica, Calif., 1977-85; fror assoc. prof. to prof. medicine UCLA Sch. Medicine, 1978-85; prof. Sch. Pub Health UCLA, 1980-85, U. Minn., 1985—, dean, 1985-90; intern U. Ky. Med Ctr., Lexington, 1965-66, resident in community medicine, 1966-69. Adj. pro Leonard Davis Sch. Gerontology, U. So. Calif., 1982-85; mem. expert com. o aging WHO, 1986—; Minn. endowed chair in long-term care and aging 1989—; mem. adv. com. on Alzheimer's Disease, Washington, 1988-96; mem com. on quality Inst. Medicine, 1988-90. Co-author: A Will and A Way, 1985 Long-term Care: Principles, Programs, and Policies, 1987, Essentials of Clinica Geriatrics, 5th edit., 2003, Understanding Health Care Outcomes Research 1997, The Heart of Long Term Care, 1998, Assessing Older Persons, 2000. Wit USPHS, 1969-70. Home: 2715 E Lake Of The Isles Pky Minneapolis M 55408-1053

KANE, SAM, meat company executive; b. Spisske Pohrdie, Czechoslovaki June 23, 1919; came to U.S., 1948, naturalized, 1953. s. Leopold and Berth (Narcisenfeld) Kannengiesser; m. Aranka Feldbrand, Jan. 15, 1946; childrer Jerry, Harold Ira, Esther Barbara. Grad., Rabbinical Coll. Galanta, 1939. Pre Sam Kane Wholesale Meat, Inc., Corpus Christi, 1956—, Sam Kane Meat, Inc Corpus Christi, 1956—, Sam Kane Packing co., Corpus Christi, 1962—, Kan Enterprises, Inc., Corpus Christi, 1956—; pres., chmn. bd., CEO Sam Kan Beef Processors, Inc., 1956—. Pres., Jewish Welfare Appeal, 1962—; pre Combined Jewish Appeal, 1962—, chmn. bd., 1962-65; mem. nat. cabin United Jewish Appeal; bd. dirs. Tex. Coun. on Econ. Edn.; mem. Gov. Tex. 200 Commn. Recipient award chmn. bd edn. B'nai Israel Synagogue, 1965, Isra Service award, 1966, Koach award State of Israel, 2976, Prime Minister c Israel Peace medal, 1980, Brotherhood award Corpus Christi chpt. NCCJ, 198 Torch of Liberty award Anti Defamation League, 1984; named Outstandin Jewish Citizen of Corpus Christi, 1969. Mem. Tex. Coun. on Econ. Edn. (b dirs.), Tex. Taxpayers Assn., B'nai B'rith. Jewish (pres. synagogue 1964-65 Home: 27 Hewitt Dr Corpus Christi TX 78404-1662 Office: San Kane Be Processors 9001 Leopard St Corpus Christi TX 78409-2502

KANE, SIEGRUN DINKLAGE, lawyer; b. N.Y.C., Sept. 21, 1938; d. Ralp Dieter and Lisbeth (Adam) Dinklage; m. David H.T. Kane, Jan. 24, 196 children: David D., Brendon T. BA cum laude, Mt. Holyoke Coll., 1960; LL Harvard U., 1963. Bar: N.Y. 1963, U.S. Ct. Appeals (2d cir.) 1964, U. Supreme Ct. 1967, U.S. Ct. Appeals (7th cir.) 1984, U.S. Ct Appeals (5th cir 1997. Ptnr. Kane, Dalsimer, Sullivan, Kurucz, Levy, Eisele & Richard, N.Y.C 1970—99, Morgan & Finnegan, N.Y.C., 1999—. Bd. mem. Bur. Nat. Affai Adv. Com., Washington, 1988—; mem. U.S. Patent and Trademark Office Pu Adv. Com., Washington, 1989-95, 2000-; lectr. trademarks Practicing Law Ins N.Y.C., 1980—; designated mem. INTA Panel Neutrals, 2000-; mem. adv. b McCarthy Ctr. Intellectual Property and Tech. Law, U. San Francisco, 2001 Author: Trademark Law: A Practitioner's Guide, 1987, 4th edit., 2002, annu supplements, 1998—; contbr. articles on trademark law to profl. jours. Me Briarcliff Zoning Bd. Appeals, Briarcliff Manor, N.Y., 1978-90, Briarcliff His Soc. Bd., Briarcliff Manor, 1986-90. Mem. ABA, Internat. Trademark Ass N.Y. Patent Law Assn. Avocations: aerobics, tennis, travel. Office: Morgan Finnegan LLP 345 Park Ave Fl 22 New York NY 10154-0053

KANE, STANLEY BRUCE, food products executive; b. N.Y.C., June 5, 192 s. Jacob and Anna (Epstein) K.; m. Janet Marilyn Haas, May 23, 1948; childre Katherine, Betsy, Priscilla. Student, NYU, 1938-39. With Kane-Miller Cor N.Y.C., 1938—, chmn. bd., 1959-77, pres., chief exec. officer, 1977—, also b dirs. Served with USAAF, 1942-45. Home: 539 Norsota Way Sarasota F 34242-1029 Office: Kane-Miller Corp 220 White Plains Rd Tarrytown N 10591-5837

KANE, STANLEY PHILLIP, insurance company executive; b. St. Paul, Oc 3, 1930; s. Bernard J. and Bertha (Pusin) K.; m. Judith Zaikaner, July 1, 195 children: Brian, Debra, Elizabeth, David. Student, Beck Radio Sch., Mpl 1948-49. V.p. Arlan Agys., Inc., Mpls., 1950-57; pres. BOMA Inc., Mpl 1957-68, North Central Life, St. Paul, 1972-76; exec. v.p. North Central Co St. Paul, 1968-76; chmn. bd., pres., chief exec. officer Early Am. Life Ins. C St. Paul, 1976-90; cons., 1990—; cons. ins. asset mgmt. Radio announce writer, WJMC, Rice Lake, Wis., 1949-50. Scoutmaster Boy Scouts Am 1967-69, dist. chmn., 1971-74; Bd. dirs., v.p. Jewish Family Service, 1975-8 chmn. bd. Alfred Adler Inst. of Minn., 1980-84; pres.-elect Mt. Zion Temple, S Paul, 1987-89, pres., 1989-91. With M.C. AUS, 1952-54. Mem. Life Unde writers Assn., Presidents Assn. Jewish (bd. dir. temple 1960-64, 75-79, pre men's club 1960-64), Am. Council Life Ins. (chmn. exec. roundtable 1985-8 bd. dirs. 1989-91) Home: 3486 Trails End Rd Saint Paul MN 55123

KANE, STEVEN EDWARD, human resources executive; b. Milw., Sept. 1949; s. Edward Thomas and Marion Jean (Regan) K.; m. Jacqueline Peacoc children: Clifford, Stacy. BS in Indsl. Relations, Cornell U., 1972, MBA, 197 JD, U. Akron, 1977. Bar: Ohio 1977, Tex. 1977. Labor relations staff B Goodrich, Akron, Ohio, 1973-77; cons. Modern Mgmt., Bannockburn, Il 1978; dir. employee relations Am. Hosp. Supply, Evanston, Ill., 1979-85; v human resources adminstrn. Baxter Internat. (formerly Baxter Travenol Labs Deerfield, Ill., 1986-87, v.p. human resources, corp. groups, 1987-89, v human resources hosp. and alternate site group, 1989-90, v.p. human resourc alternate site group, chief labor counsel, 1990-91, v.p. employee rels., asso gen. counsel, 1992-94, v.p. compensation, 1995-96, v.p. govt. affairs, 1996-9 cons. StevenKane.com, Hillsborough, Calif., 1999; sr. v.p. human resource legal, comm. Neoforma, Inc., 2000—02; prin. Kane Ptnrs., 2003—. Mem ABA, Tex. Bar Assn., Ohio Bar Assn. Home: 1425 San Raymundo Hillsborough CA 94010-6658

KANE, STEVEN MICHAEL, psychotherapist, educator; b. Boston, July 2 1947; s. Harry and Annette (Oranburg) K. AB, Boston U., 1971; MA, U. N. 1973; PhD, Princeton U., 1979. Staff psychotherapist Mass. Treatment C Bridgewater, Mass., 1985-86; staff psychologist Bridgewater State Hos 1986-89; pvt. practice psychotherapy Providence, R.I., 1990—; psycholog R.I. Sex Offender Treatment Program, 1995-2000. Dir. sr. empowerme program Westminster Sr. Ctr., Providence, 1998-2003; vis. asst. prof. U. N. 1978-79, Conn. Coll., New London, 1982-83; asst. prof. Gen. Motors Ins Flint, Mich., 1981-82; rsch. scientist Brown U. Child Study Ctr., 1984-85; ins Brown U. Learning Cmty., 1998—; dir. clin. edn. Interfaith Counseling C Providence, 1988-2002; part-time faculty RISD, Providence, 1989-99, U. R Providence, 1992—; spl. lectr. Providence Coll., 1990-94; cons. and spkr. field. Reviewer Internat. Assn. of Jazz Record Collectors Jour.; contbr. articl to profl. jours. Bd. dir. The Music Sch., Providence, 1993-95; founder, d Life-Enrichment Ctr. New Eng., Providence, 2002-. Recipient Outstandi Faculty award U. R.I./Providence Ctr., 1997; Nat. Def. Edn. Act Title IV fell Fed. Govt.-U. N.C., 1971-73, Postdoctoral Social Sci. Rsch. fellow NIM 1979-81; Rsch. grantee NSF, 1975-76; RI Dept. Elderly Affairs minority hea promotion grantee, 1998-2003. Fellow Am. Anthropol. Assn.; mem. Soc. Psychol. Anthropology, Soc. for the Anthropology of Consciousness, Am. As of Pastoral Counselors, Broadway Renaissance (pres. 2001--), Psi Chi. Avo tions: jazz pianist, writer on jazz, jazz educator. Home and Office: 4 Broadway Providence RI 02909-1625

KANE, SYDELL, elementary school principal; b. N.Y.C., Jan. 13; d. Harry and Ruth Friedman; m. Howard E. Kane; children: Bradford, Marcia Kane Hittner. BA, NYU, 1951; MA, Queen's Coll., 1968. Cert. guidance counselor, adminstr., supr., prin., N.Y. Tchr. N.Y.C. Pub. Schs., 1972; asst. prin. P.S. 220, N.Y.C., 1973-88; prin. P.S. 144, N.Y.C., 1988-99; ednl. cons., 1999—. Adj. prof. St. John's U., Hunter Coll. Author skills books. Named Supr. of Yr., Dist. 28, 1995, Outstanding Sch. Supr., St. John's U. Sch. Edn. and Human Svcs., 1997. Mem. ASCD, Queensboro Coun. on Reading, Phi Delta Kappa (pres. 1989).

KANE, THOMAS JAY, III, orthopaedic surgeon, educator; b. Merced, Calif., Sept. 2, 1951; s. Thomas J. Jr. and Kathryn (Hassler) K.; m. Marie Rose Van Emmerik, Oct. 10, 1987; children: Thomas Keola, Travis Reid, Samantha Marie. BA in History, U. Santa Clara, 1973; MD, U. Calif., Davis, 1977. Diplomate Am. Bd. Orthopaedic Surgery. Intern U. Calif. Davis Sacramento Med. Ctr., 1977-78, resident in surgery, 1978-81; resident in orthopaedic surgery U. Hawaii, 1987-91; fellowship adult joint reconstruction Rancho Los Amigos Med. Ctr., 1991-92; ptnr. Orthop. Assocs. of Hawaii, Inc., Honolulu, 1992—; asst. prof. surgery U. Hawaii, Honolulu, 1993—, chief divsn. implant surgery, 1993—. Contbr. articles to profl. jours. Mem. AMA, Am. Assn. Hip and Knee Surgeons, Hawaii Med. Assn., Hawaii Orthop. Assn. (v.p. 2003—), Am. Acad. Orthop. Surgery, Western Orthopedic Assn., Alpha Omega Alpha, Phi Kappa Phi. Avocations: tennis, golf, skiing, music, surfing. Office: Orthopaedic Svcs Co LLP 1380 Lusitana St Ste 608 Honolulu HI 96813-2442

KANE, THOMAS REIF, engineering educator; b. Vienna, Mar. 23, 1924; came to U.S., 1938, naturalized, 1943; Ernest Kanitz and Gertrude (Reif) K.; m. Ann Elizabeth Andrews, June 4, 1951; children: Linda Ann, Jeffrey Thomas. BS, Columbia U., 1950, MS, 1952, PhD, 1953; D Tech. Scis. (hon.), Tech. U. Vienna, Austria, 1990. Asst. prof., assoc. prof. U. Pa., Phila., 1953-61; prof. Sch. Engring. Stanford U., Calif., 1961-93, prof. emeritus, 1993—. Cons. NASA, Harley-Davidson Motor Co., AMF, Lockheed Missiles and Space Co., Vertol Aircraft Corp., Martin Marietta Co., Kellet Aircraft Co. Author: (vol. 1) Analytical Elements of Mechanics, 1959, (vol. 2), 1961, Dynamics, 1972, Spacecraft Dynamics, 1983; Dynamics: Theory and Applications, 1985; contbr. over 150 articles to profl. jours. Served with U.S. Army, 1943-45, PTO. Recipient Alexander von Humboldt prize, 1988. Fellow Am. Astron. Soc. (Dirk Brouwer award 1983); mem. ASME (hon.), Sigma Xi, Tau Beta Pi. Office: Stanford University Dept Mechanical Engring Stanford CA 94305

KANE, YVETTE, lawyer, federal judge; b. Donaldsonville, La., Oct. 11, 1953; d. Thomas R. Pregeant and Julia Tucker; children: Kathleen, Madeline. BA, Nicholls State U., Thibodeaux, La., 1973; JD, Tulane U., 1976. Bar: Pa. Trial atty. U.S. Equal Employment Opportunity Commn., 1977-78; asst. atty. gen. Colo. Atty. Gen.'s Office, 1978-80; dep. dist. atty. Denver Dist. Atty.'s Office, 1980-86; dep. atty. gen. rev. and advice sect. Pa. Office Atty. Gen., 1986-91; chief counsel Pa. Ind. Regulatory Rev. Commn., 1991-92; sr. assoc. Wolf, Block, Schorr & Solis-Cohen, Harrisburg, Pa., 1993-95; sec. state Commonwealth of Pa., 1995-98; U.S. dist. judge U.S. Dist. Ct. (mid. dist.) Pa., Harrisburg, 1998—. Office: US Dist Ct Box 11817 228 Walnut St 8th Fl Harrisburg PA 17108

KANEB, GARY R. oil industry executive; b. 1961; Grad., U. Notre Dame, 1983. Chase Manhattan Bank, N.Y.C., 1984-86; pres. Catamount Mgmt. Corp., Chelsea, Mass., 1988—; gen. ptnr., pres. Gulf Oil LP, Chelsea, Mass., 1986—, CEO, 1997—. Office: Gulf Oil LP 90 Everett Ave Chelsea MA 02150-2337*

KANEB, JOHN A. corporate executive; CEO, pres., chmn. HP Hood, Chelsea, Mass., 1995—. Office: HP Hood 90 Everett Ave Chelsea MA 02150-2301*

KANEDA, DAVID KEN, electrical engineering company executive; b. Norristown, Pa. s. Ben and Sumako Kaneda; m. Stephania Kaneda, Nov. 16, 1993; children: Giselle, Aaron. B Archtl. Engring., Pa. State U., 1981; MBA, U. London Bus. Sch., 1993. Registered profl. engr., Ill., Calif., Wash.; registered architect, Wis.; chartered engr., U.K., European Engr. Tech. instr. Internat. Edn. Svcs., Tokyo, 1981-82; assoc. Skidmore, Owings & Merrill, Chgo., 1982-87, London, 1987-91, L.A., 1991; regional mgr. Elliptipar Inc., New Haven, 1993-95; prin. Am. Cons. Engrs. Inc., Santa Clara, Calif., 1995-99; pres., ceo Integrated Design Assoc., Inc., Santa Clara, Calif., 1999—. Cons. Pinniger & Lum./Franz Sill, Gmbh, London and Berlin, 1992, ECS Lighting Controls Ltd., London, 1993. Recipient Edison award GE, 1987, achievement award Pa. Electric Assn., 1981, award of merit Chgo. Lighting Inst., 1987, E.F. Guth award of merit Illuminating Engring. Soc., 1987, Design award IES, 1987, design award Santa Clara Valley AIA, 1996, 98. Mem.: AIA (bd. dirs. 1998—2003, v.p. 2000, pres. Santa Clara Valley chpt., bd. dirs. Calif. coun. 2000), Nat. Assn. Asian Am. Profls., Nat. Coun. Examiners for Engring. and Surveying, Illuminating Engring. Soc. N.Am., European Fedn. Nat. Engring. Assns., Engring. Coun. U.K., Chartered Inst. Bldg. Svcs. Engrs. U.K., Asian Am. Archs. and Engrs., Alpha Phi Omega (pres. Alpha Beta chpt. 1979—80). Avocations: Karate, skiing, international travel. Office: Integrated Des Assoc Inc 3140 De La Cruz Blvd Ste 110 Santa Clara CA 95054-2435

KANEDA, MASAYOSHI, mathematics educator, researcher; b. Kashiwazaki-shi, Niigata, Japan, Nov. 7, 1971; s. Ichiro and Mutsuko Kaneda. BS in Physics, Kyoto U., Japan, 1995; MS in Physics, U. Tokyo, 1997, MS in Math. Scis., 2001; MS in Math., U. Houston, 2002, PhD in Math., 2003. Tchg. asst. U. Tokyo, Meguro-ku, 1998—98; tchg. fellow, rsch. asst. dept. math. U. Houston, 1998—2003; lectr. U. Calif., Irvine, 2003—. Contbr. articles to profl. jours. Mem.: Math. Soc. Japan, Math. Assn. Am., Am. Math. Soc., Gakushikai U. Alumni Assn. Home: 989 Victoria St Apt C4 Costa Mesa CA 92627-4055 Office: U Calif Irvine 103 Multipurpose Sci and Tech Bldg Irvine CA 92697-3875 Office Fax: 949-824-7993. E-mail: kaneda@math.uh.edu.

KANEHIRO, KENNETH KENJI, insurance educator, risk analyst, consultant; b. Honolulu, May 10, 1934; s. Charles Yutaka and Betty Misako (Hoshino) K.; m. Eiko Asari, June 23, 1962; 1 child, Everett Peter. BA in Counseling Psychology, U. Hawaii, 1956, grad. cert. in Counseling Psychology, 1957; grad. cert. in ins., The Am. Inst., 1971. CPCU; cert. continuing profl. devel. Claims adjustor Cooke Trust Co., Honolulu, 1959-62, underwriter, 1962-66; account supr. Alexander & Baldwin, Honolulu, 1966-68; spl. risk exec. Hawaiian Ins. & Guaranty, Honolulu, 1968-71, br. mgr. Hilo, Hawaii, 1971-72; chief of office Marsh & McLennan, Inc., Hilo, 1972-78; sr. mktg. rep. Occidental Underwriters, Honolulu, 1978-87; pvt. practice Honolulu, 1987—. Coord. Ins. Sch. of Pacific, Honolulu, 1978—; lectr. ins. Hawaii State Cts., 1986—; adv. bd. Ins. Commn., 2000—; mem. adv. bd. Real Estate Commn., 2003—; cons. Dai Tokyo Royal State Ins. Co., 1992—; mem. arbitration panel, ct. observer panel Hawaii State Cts., 1993-96, Hawaii Criminal Ct., 1994—; proctor Hawaii State Bar Exam., 1994—; ins. expert witness, 1995—; instr. ins. agt.'s lic. course, 1995—; dir. edn. Profl. Ins. Agts. Hawaii, 2001—; bd. dirs. Royal Ins. Agy.; mem. bd. ethical inquiry Am. Inst. for Chartered Property Casualty Underwriters, 2002—. Adult leader Boy Scouts Am., Hilo and Honolulu, 1956—, risk mgr. Aloha coun., Honolulu, 1980—; edn. chmn. Gen. Ins. Assn., Hawaii, Hilo, 1971-77; ins. cons. Arcadia Retirement Residence, Honolulu, 1987—; cons. Waikole Cmty. Assn.; bd. govs. U. Hawaii Founders Alumni Assn., Honolulu, 1993—, scholarship chmn., 1993—. With U.S. Army, 1957-59. Recipient First Lady's Outstanding Vol. award, First Lady/State of Hawaii, 1990, Pres.'s award, Boy Scouts Aloha Coun., 1997. Mem.: Profl. Ins. Agts. of Hawaii (dir. edn. 2001—), Soc. Ins. Trainers and Educators, Soc. Chartered Property and Casualty Underwriters (pres. 1986—87, nat. publs. com. 1996—, contbr. to jour., Excellence award 2000). Avocations: art, photography, music. Home: 1128 Ala Napunani St Apt 705 Honolulu HI 96818-1606

KANE HITTNER, MARCIA SUSAN, bank executive; b. N.Y.C. d. Howard Eugene and Sydell (Friedman) Kane; m. Ellis Hittner. cert. fin. planning, BA in Comm., NYU. Cert. Nat. Ret. Plans Tng. Ctr., software capability maturity model cert. interim profile adminstr. Carnegie Mellon U. Pension specialist Union Dime Savs. Bank, N.Y.C., 1978-81; money market specialist Goldome (formerly Union Dime Savs. Bank), N.Y.C., 1981-82; customer svc. mgr. Citibank, N.A., N.Y.C., 1982-85, mktg. product mgr., 1986-87, shareholder comms. mgr., 1988-89, asst. v.p., tax shelter conversions, 1990-93, asst. v.p. tech. client interface, 1993-95, asst. v.p. U.S., Europe consumer bank, 1995-99; with product design and devel. Software Engring. Process Group, 1995-99; v.p. mktg. strategy EAB subs. ABN-AMRO, 1999—2001, bus. and mktg. strategy cons., 2001—. Author: (with others) Critical Reading-Level G, 1980. Bd. dirs. Forest Hills Owners Corp., N.Y.C., 1991-92, 99—.

KANEKO, SYLVIA YELTON, clinical social worker, educator; b. Marion, N.C., Mar. 31, 1935; d. Harvey Rayburn and Annie Laurie (Phillips) Yelton; m. Shozo Kaneko, 1960 (div. 1963). BA, U. N.C., 1959; MSW, U. Hawaii, 1964; PhD, Smith Coll., 1971. Lic. clin. social worker, Mass.; bd. cert. diplomate Am. Bd. Examiners Clin. Social Work. Editl. asst. TV Guide mag., Hollywood, Calif., 1957-59; psychiat. social worker Ceders-Sinai Med. Ctr., L.A., 1965-69; pvt. practice Brookline and Newton, Mass., 1971—; asst. prof. treatment methods Smith Coll., Northampton, Mass., 1971-72; dir. social work Valley-head Psychiat. Hosp., Carlisle, Mass., 1972-75; assoc. prof., chair casework Boston U., 1978-86; assoc. prof. dept. social work U. N.H., Durham, 1995-96; faculty mem. human svcs. doctoral program Walden U., 1999—; Schwartz rounds facilitator New Eng. Sinai Hosp., 2001—. Adj. asst. prof. treatment methods and rsch. Smith Coll., Northampton, 1973-88; participant Brit.-Am. Conf. on Psychodynamic Social Work, 1979, faculty mentor doctoral program Human Svcs., Walden U., 1998—. Contbr. articles to profl. jours. Internat. Women's Yr. grantee Internat. Mktg. Inst., 1979. Fellow Am. Orthopsychiat. Assn.; mem. NASW (chair inst. com. 1978-82, bd. dirs. 1988-90), Mass. Acad. Clin. Social Workers (legis. and ednl. com. 1972-83, 86-89). Unitarian Universalist. Avocations: theatre, dance, art, music, writing, traveling. Office: Acorn Psychotherapy Assocs 1400 Center St Ste 105 Newton Centre MA 02459-1754 E-mail: sykjp@aol.com., skaneko@waldenu.edu.

KANEKO, YOSHIHIRO, cardiologist, researcher; b. Shizuoka, Japan, Jan. 22, 1922; s. Rokurohei and Yoshino (Momochi) K.; m. Toyo Nozaki, Apr. 8, 1962; children: Kyoko, Eriko, Hiroko. MD, Tokyo U. Med. Sch., Japan, 1945, DMS, 1951. Clin. assoc. dept. internal medicine Tokyo U. Hosp., Japan, 1945-53, instr., 1953-70; rsch. fellow Cleve. Clinic Found., 1958-61, 1962-63; asst. prof. 2d dept. internal medicine Tokyo U. Med. Sch., 1971-73; prof. medicine, chmn. dept internal medicine Yokohama City (Japan) U. Med. Sch., Japan, 1973-87, emeritus prof., 1987—; dir. Yokohama Hypertension Rsch. Ctr., 1987—; prof. emeritus Yokohama City U., 1987—; hon. dir. Nishi-Yokohama Internat. Hosp., 1987-93. Contbr. articles to profl. jours. Com. mem. Pharm. Bur. Japan Ministry Health & Welfare, Tokyo, 1974-87, Med. Affairs Bur., Tokyo, 1976-79. Grantee NIH, 1965-67; recipient award Japanese Kidney Found., 1986, Internat. Soc. Hypertension, 1988. Fellow High Blood Pressure Coun.; mem. Japanese Soc. Hypertension (1st pres. 1978-79, dir. 1978-89), Japanese Soc. Internal Medicine (councilor), Japan Circulation Soc., Japan Soc. Nephrology (dir. 1974-87), Am. Heart Assn. (coun. mem.), Internat. Soc. Hypertension, (coun. 1982-90, chmn. 1988). Avocations: reading, gardening. Home: 2-27-14 Nishishiba Kanazawa-ku Yokohama 236-0017 Japan Office: Yokohama Hypertension Rsch Ctr Deiki 2-8-19-402 Kanazawa-k Yokohama 236-0021 Japan

KANELLOS, NICOLAS, foreign language and liberal studies educator, publisher; b. N.Y.C., Jan. 31, 1945; s. Constantino and Inés (de Choudens) K.; m. Cristelia Pérez, May 12, 1984; 1 child, Miguel José. BA, Fairleigh Dickinson U., 1966; MA, U. Tex., 1968, PhD, 1974; postgrad., U. Mex., Mexico City, 1964-65, U. Portugal, Lisbon, 1969-70. From asst. to assoc. prof. Ind. U. N.W., Gary, 1970-79; assoc. prof. U. Houston, 1979-85, prof., 1985—, Brown Found. prof., endowed chair, 1996—. Founder, dir. Teatro Desengano del Pueblo, Gary, 1972-79; founder, pub. Arte Publico Press/U. Houston, 1979—; pub. The Americas Rev.; apptd. to Literature Policy Panel, Nat. Endowment for Arts, 1987; apptd. to Arts Adv. Com., Edul. Testing Svc./The Coll. Bd., 1987; apptd. Pres. Clinton Nat. Coun. on the Humanities, 1994; presenter papers in field assns., confs., univs., symposia U.S., Europe, Mex. Author: Mexican American Theatre: Legacy and Reality, Hispanic Bibliography, 1988, Biographical Dictionary of Hispanic Literature in the United States, 1989, The History of Hispanic Theatre in the United States up to World War II, 1990 (SW Con. Latin Am. Studies Book award 1991, Tex. Inst. Letters award 1991, San Antonio Conservation Soc. Book award, 1990), The Hispanic American Almanac: A Reference Work on Hispanics in the United States, 1993 (ALA award best reference work 1993), Thirty Million Strong: Reclaiming the Hispanic Image in American Society, 1998, Hispanic Firsts, 1997; editor: Mexican American Theater, 1983, Las aventures de Don Chipote, Hispanic Theater in the United States, 1985 Short Fiction by U.S. Hispanic Authors, 1993; co-editor: Ginn Literature Series textbooks for h.s. English, Nuevos Pasos: Chicano and Puerto Rican Drama, 1979, 2d edit., 1989, Latino Short Fiction, 1980, Handbook of Hispanic Cultures in the United States 4 vols., 1993-94; mem. editorial bd. Latin Am. Theatre Rev., 1982—, Critica, 1983—, Confluencia, 1984—, Southwest Rev., 1990—, Latino Studies Jour., 1990—; contbr. numerous articles to profl. jours.; contbr. chpts to books; prodr. videos. Member Ind. Civil Rights Commn., Gary, 1974-75; mem. arts adv. com. N.Y. Coll. Bd., 1989—; lit. cons. NEA, Washington, 1985-90; pres. Bishop's Com. for the Spanish Speaking, Gary, 1974-76. Recipient Hispanic Heritage award Pres. Reagan, 1988, award Tex. Assn. Chicanos in Higher Edn., 1989, Commendation from Gov. Tex. for high standards of acad. excellence, 1989, Am. Book award pub., editor category, 1989; named 100 most Influential Hispanic in U.S. by Hispanic Bus. mag., 1989, 93, 97; inducted Tex. Inst. Letters, 1984; NEH fellow, 1979, Eli Lilly Faculty Open fellow, 1976-77, Ford Found./Nat. Rsch. Coun. fellow, 1986-87, other awards, fellowships. Mem. Inst. Hispanic Culture of Houston, Hispanic Forum of Houston, Modern Lang. Assn. (N.Y.C. chpt.), Nat. Assn. Chicano Studies, Nat. Assn. Puerto Rican Studies. Avocations: jogging, tennis, guitar, singing. Office: U Houston Arte Publico Press Houston TX 77204-0001

KANENAKA, REBECCA YAE, microbiologist; b. Wailuku, Hawaii, Jan. 9, 1958; d. Masakazu Robert and Takako (Oka) Fujimoto; m. Brian Ken Kanenaka, Nov. 10, 1989; children: Kent Masakazu, Kym Sachiko. Student, U. Hawaii, Manoa, 1976-77, MS in Microbiology, 2000; BS, Colo. State U., 1980. Lab. asst. Colo. State U., Ft. Collins, 1979-80; microbiologist Foster Farms, Livingston, Calif., 1980-81, Hawaii Dept. Health, Lihue, 1981-86, Honolulu, 1986—, with disease outbreak control divsn., disease investigation br., 2003—. Mem. Am. Soc. Microbiology (Hawaii chpt.), Nat. Registry of Microbiologists, Am. Soc. Microbiology, Brown Bag Club (Lihue, pres. 1985-86), Golden Ripples (4-H leader), Clover Kids (4-H leader). Avocations: tennis, fishing, golf, jogging. Home: 485 Luakini St Honolulu HI 96817-1449 Office: Hawaii Dept Health Disease Investigation Br Disease Outbreak Control Divsn 1132 Bishop St Ste 1900 Honolulu HI 96813

KANER, CEM, lawyer, computer software consultant, educator; b. Detroit, July 8, 1953; s. Harry and Wilma Kaner; 1 child, Virginia Rose. Student, U. Windsor (Ont., Can.), 1971-72; BA, Brock U., St. Catharines, Ont., 1974; postgrad., York U., Toronto, Ont., 1975-76; PhD, McMaster U., Hamilton, Ont., 1984; JD, Golden Gate U., 1993. Bar: Calif., 1993. Cert. quality engr. Asst. mgr. Gallenkamp Shoes, Toronto, 1975; systems analyst Kaners and 1 plus 1, Windsor, 1981-83; lectr. McMaster U., 1981-83; software testing supr. Micro-Pro (WordStar), San Rafael, Calif., 1983-84; human factors analyst, software engr. Telenova, Los Gatos, Calif., 1984-88; software testing mgr. creativity div. Electronic Arts, San Mateo, Calif., 1988; software devel. mgr., documentation group mgr., dir. of documentation and software testing Power Up Software, San Mateo, 1989-94; pvt. practice, Santa Clara, Calif., 1994-2000; prof. computer sci. Fla. Inst. Tech., 2000—. Sr. assoc. Psylomar Orgn. Devel., San Francisco, 1983-85; lectr. U. Calif., Berkeley Ext., 1995-2000, U. Calif., Santa Cruz Ext., 1998-2000; spkr. in field. Author: Testing Computer Software, 1988, (with Jack Falk and Hung Q Nguyen) Testing Computer Software, 2d edit., 1993 (award for excellence No. Calif. Tech. Publ. Competition 1993), (with David Pels) Bad Software: What to do when Software Fails, 1998; (video course) Testing Computer Software, 1995, (with James Bach and Bret Pettichord) Lessons Learned in Software Testing: A Context-Driven Approach, 2001; columnist Software QA; contbr. articles to profl. publs. Cons. Dundas (Ont.) Pub. Library, 1982-83; vol. Santa Clara County Dept. Consumer Affairs, San Jose, 1987-88; alt. mem. San Mateo County Dem. Central Com., 1988-89; chmn. Foster City Dem Club, 1989; vol. dep. dist. atty. County of Santa Clara, Calif., 1994; grievance handler, intellectual property, book contract advisor Nat. Writers Union, San Francisco, Calif., 1994—; bd. dir. No. Calif. Hemophilia Found., Oakland, Calif., 1995-97; participating observer NCCUSL drafting com. for UCC article 2B, NCCUSL com. for uniform electronic transaction act. Scholar, Can. Nat. Rsch. Coun., 1977-78, Can. Natural Scis. and Engring. Rsch. Coun., 1979, Golden Gate U. Tuition scholar, 1989-93. Mem. IEEE (Computer Soc.), ABA, ATLA, APA, Assn. for Computing Machinery, Assn. Support Profls., Am. Soc. Quality (sr.), Am. Law Inst. (elected), Human Factors and Ergonomics Soc., Soc. for Tech. Comm. (sr.), Software Support Profls. Assn. Jewish. Avocation: development of the law of software products liability. Office: Fla Inst Tech Dept Computer Sci 150 W University Blvd Melbourne FL 32901-6988 E-mail: kaner@kaner.com.

KANESTA, NELLIE ROSE, chemical dependency counselor; b. Zuni, N.Mex., Aug. 8, 1939; d. Paxton E. and Bessie (Thompson) Boone; m. Patrick Tsethlikia, Apr. 10, 1959 (div. Mar. 1973); children: Nina, Frederick William, Pamela, Judson, Marie Christine, Paxton, Clifford. AA in Human Svcs., U. N.Mex., Gallup, 1996, B Univ. Studies, 2000. Lic. alcohol and drug abuse counselor, N.Mex. Alcoholism counselor Zuni (N.Mex.) Indian Hosp., 1985-86; counselor Friendship Svcs., Inc., Gallup, N.Mex., 1986-87; trainer Hazelden Found., Center City, Minn., 1987-88; intense residential guidance counselor Ramah (N.Mex.) Navajo Dormitory, 1988-89; Title V counselor, dir. Pine Hills (N.Mex.) Schs., 1989-91, phys. ednl. aide, 1992-93, group home life skills counselor, 1993—; substance abuse counselor Cibola County Correctional Ctr., Milan, N.Mex., 1995-96, Western Correctional Facility, Grants, N.Mex., 1997-99; adult counselor Zuni Recovery Ctr., N.Mex., 1996-97; social worker Zuni Indian Health Hosp. Counselor Zuni Pub. Health Svc. Indian Hosp., 1985, Regional Conf. on Children of Alcoholics, Albuquerque, 1985; insvc. tng. confs. Western N.Mex. U., 1986, Native Am. Cultural Issues in Substance Abuse, Coll. of Santa Fe, 1986, Chem. Dependency and Intervention, The N.Mex. Alcoholism and Drug Abuse Counselors, 1986, In-Svc. Tng. on Battered Families and Its Relation to Alcohol/Drug Abuse, 1987, N.Mex. Alcoholism and Drug Abuse Counselors Assn., 1986-88, Hazelden Chem. Dependency Counselor Tng. Program, 1988; family advocate for mentally ill Zuni Pub. Health Svc., 1993-95; court offender case worker Teen Health Ctr., 1997-99, mental health specialist, 2000-02. Avocations: reading, fishing, pottery making, basketball, listening to music. Home: PO Box 1479 Zuni NM 87327-1479 Office: Cibola County Correctional Ctr Milan NM 87021

KANET, JOHN JOSEPH, management educator; b. Chgo., Mar. 13, 1946; s. Johann Jakob and Irene Redmond Kanet; m. Christa Ursula Tuffentsammer, Oct. 20, 1994; children: Caroline I. Peani, John A., Colleen E. BS, Lehigh U., 1967; MBA, Loyola Coll., 1971; PhD, Penn State U., 1979. Materials mgr. Black & Decker Mfg. Co., Hampstead, Md., 1967—84; assoc. prof. mgmt. U. Ga., Athens, 1978—84; asociate prof. bus. analysis and rsch. Tex. A&M U., College Station, 1983—86; Burlington prof. mgmt. Clemson U., SC, 1986—2002; Niehaus chair ops. mgmt. U. Dayton, Ohio, 2002—. Konrad Zuse guest prof. U. Erlangen/Nuernberg, U. GH Essen, 1993—94; guest prof. Inst. Advanced Studies, Vienna, 1988. Contbr. articles to profl. jours. Fellow, Fulbright Commn., 1984, 1993, 2002. Mem.: Sigma Iota Epsilon, Beta Gamma Sigma. Avocations: jogging, swimming. Office: U Dayton 300 College Park Dayton OH 45469-2130 E-mail: kanet@udayton.edu.

KANET, ROGER EDWARD, political science educator; b. Cin., Sept. 1, 1936; s. Robert George and Edith Mary (Weaver) K.; m. Joan Alice Edwards, Feb. 16, 1963; children: Suzanne Elise Zelle, Laurie Alice Burhart. PhB, Berchmanskolleg, Pullach-bei-Muenchen, Ger., 1960; AB, Xavier U., Cin., 1961; MA, Lehigh U., 1963; AM, Princeton U., 1965, PhD, 1966. Asst. prof. polit. sci. U. Kans., Lawrence, 1966-69, assoc. prof., 1969-74; joint sr. fellow Russian Inst. and Rsch. Inst. Communist Affairs, Columbia U., N.Y.C., 1972-73; from vis. assoc. prof. U. Ill., Champaign, Ill., 1973—97, prof. Urbana, 1997—2002; from dean sch. internat. studies to prof. dept. internat. studies U. Miami, Fla., 1997—2002, prof. dept. internat. and comparative studies, 2002—. Partipant exch. with Hungary and Poland, Internat. Rsch. and Exchs. Bd., 1976; cons. Inst. Pub. Policy Devel., Washington, 1977-79; assoc. Ctr. Advanced Study, U. Ill., 1981-82; mem. Coun. on Fgn. Rels., N.Y., 1991—; mem. Chgo. com. Chgo. Coun. on Fgn. Rels., 1993-97; chair internat. edn. panel Com. Instl. Coop. Big 10 & Chgo., 1993-96; co-founder Ill. Consortium for Internat. Edn. Editor: The Behavioral Revolution and Communist Studies, 1971, On the Road to Communism, 1972, The Soviet Union and the Developing Countries, 1974, Soviet and East European Policy, 1974, Soviet Economic and Political Relations with the Developing World, 1975, Background to Crisis: Policy and Politics in Gierek's Poland, 1981, Soviet Foreign Policy and East-West Relations, 1982, Soviet Foreign Policy in the 1980s, 1982, The Soviet Union, Eastern Europe and the Third World, 1987, Asia in Soviet Global Strategy, 1987, The Limits of Soviet Power in the Developing World: Thermidor in the Revolutionary Struggle, 1989, The Cold War as Cooperation: Superpower Cooperation in Regional Conflict Management, 1991, Soviet Foreign Policy in Transition, 1992, Regional Conflicts and Conflict Resolution, 1995, Coping with Conflict After the Cold War, 1996, Foreign Policy of the Russian Fed., 1997, Resolving Regional Conflicts, 1998; contbr. over 300 articles to scholarly jours. and books. Co-founder, pres. Kans. Parents Assn. Hearing-Handicapped Children, 1968-70. Recipient U.S. Dept. State Rsch. award, 1976, Excellence in Undergrad. Teaching award U. Ill., 1981, 84, Faculty Achievement award Burlington No. Found., 1989,U.S. Inst. Peace award, 1991; fellow NDEA, 1963-66, NATO, 1976, Internat. fellow Fed. Inst. for East European and Internat. Studies, Cologne, Fed. Republic of Germany, 1988; Am. Coun. Learned Socs. grantee, 1972-73, 78. Mem. Am. Assn. Advancement of Slavic Studies, Am. Polit. Sci. Assn., Assn. Internat. Edn. Adminstrs. (bd. dirs. 1994-99), Internat. Polit. Sci. Assn., Internat. Studies Assn. (chmn. Am.-Soviet rels. sect. 1990-92), Midwest Slavic Conf. (program chmn. 1980-81), Internat. Coun. for Ctrl. and Ea. European Studies (program chmn. 1st World Congress 1974), Ctrl. Slavic Conf. (pres., program chmn. 1966-67), Midwest Polit. Sci. Assn., Assn. Internat. Edn. Adminstrs., Midwest Univ. Consortium Internat. Activities (bd. dirs. 1989-97), Nat. Assn. State Univ. and Land Grant Colls. (internat. commn. 1992-97). Roman Catholic. Home: 9225 SW 142d St Miami FL 33176 Office: U Miami dept Internat Studies PO Box 248123 Miami FL 33124-2211 E-mail: rkanet@miami.edu.

KANE-VANNI, PATRICIA RUTH, lawyer, paleontology educator; b. Phila, Pa, Jan. 12, 1954; d. Joseph James and Ruth Marina (Ramirez) Kane; m. Francis William Vanni, Feb. 14, 1981; 1 child, Christian Michael. AB, Chestnut Hill Coll., 1975; JD, Temple U., 1985; postgrad., U. Pa. Bar: Pa. 1985, US Ct. Appeals (3d cir.) 1988. Freelance art illustrator, Phila., 1972-80; secondary edn. instr. Archdiocese of Phila., Pa., 1980-83; contract analyst CIGNA Corp., Phila., 1983-84; jud. aide Phila. Ct. of Common Pleas, Pa., 1984; assoc. atty. Anderson and Dougherty, Wayne, Pa., 1985-86; atty. cons. Bell Tele. Co. of Pa., Pa., 1986-87; sr. assoc. corp. counsel Independence Blue Cross, Phila., 1987-96; pvt. practice law, 1996-97; dinosaur educator Acad. Natural Scis., Phila., 1997—. Atty. cons., 1996-2003; counsel Reliance Ins. Co., Phila., 1998-2000, contract atty., 2000-2003; counsel Westmont Law Assoc., 2002; atty. Westmont Assocs., Haddonfield, NJ, 2002; legal counsel, Ho. Authority, Phila., Pa., 2003-; cons. Coll. Consortium on Drug and Alcohol Abuse, Chester, Pa., 1986-89; paleo-sci. educator Pa. Acad. Natural Sci., 1997—; paleontology field expdns. include Mont., 1999. 2000, Isle of Wight, Eng., 1999, Bahariya Oasis, Egypt, 2000; spkr. in field. Contbr. articles and illustrations to profl. mag.; performer Phila. Revels. Judge Del. Valley Sci. Fairs, Phila., 1986, 87, 98, 99; Dem. committeewomen, Lower Merion, Pa., 1983 87; ch. cantor, soloist, mem. choir Roman Cath. Ch.; bd. dir. Phila. Assn. Ch. Musicians. Recipient Legion of Honor award Chapel of the Four Chaplins, 1983. Mem. ABA, Pa. Bar Assn., Phila. Bar Assn. (Theatre Wing), Phila. Assn. Def. Counsel, Phila. Vol. Lawyers for Arts (bd. dir.), Nat. Health Lawyers Assn. (spkr. 1994 ann. conv.), Hispanic Bar Assn., Soc. Vertebrate Paleontology, Pa. Acad. Nat. Sci. (vol.), Delaware Valley Paleontol. Soc. (v.p. 1998—). Democrat. Avocations: choral and solo vocal music, portrait painting and illustrating, paleontology. Home: 119 Bryn Mawr Ave Bala Cynwyd PA 19004-3012 E-mail: pkv1@erols.com., Paleopatti@hotmail.com.

KANEYOSHI, TAKAHITO, physicist, educator; b. Otaru, Hokkaido, Japan, Aug. 24, 1940; s. Chukichi and Ine (Yoshikawa) K.; m. Yoshiko Yamashina, Mar. 24, 1968; children: Yoshitaka, Akihiro, Yukako. B Tech., Waseda U., Tokyo, 1963; MS, Kyoto (Japan) U., 1965, DSc, 1969. Rsch. assoc. Nagoya (Japan) U., 1968-92, assoc. prof., 1992-93, prof. physics, 1993—. Author: Amorphous Magnetism, 1984, Introduction to Surface Magnetism, 1991, Introduction to Amorphous Magnets, 1992. Mem. Phys. Soc. Japan, Applied Magnetic Soc. Japan, Am. Phys. Soc., Inst. Physics Office: Nagoya U Furoucho, Chikusaku Aichi Nagoya 464-8601 Japan E-mail: kaneyosi@phys.human.nagoya-u.ac.jp.

KANFER, JULIAN NORMAN, biochemist, educator; b. Bklyn., May 23, 1930; s. Benjamin N. and Clara (Lichtenberger) K.; m. Beverly Kanfer; children— Brian, Rachel, Addison Slaeton. BSc, Bklyn. Coll., 1954; MSc, George Washington U., 1958, PhD, 1961. Biochemist Mass. Gen. Hosp., Boston, 1969-75; dir. biochem. research E.K. Shriver Center, Waltham, Mass.; also dir. research W.E. Fernald State Sch., Waltham, 1969-75; adj. asso. prof. biochemistry Brandeis U., Waltham, 1969-75; asso. prof. neuropathology Harvard, 1969-75, prin. research assoc., 1974-75; prof. U. Man., Winnipeg, Can., 1975—, head dept. biochemistry, 1975—. Cons. Health Scis. Centre, Winnipeg, 1976—; mem. med. adv. bd. Nat. Tay-Sachs Found., N.Y.C., 1970—; mem. study sect. on pathobiol. chemistry NIH, 1974—; postdoctoral fellowship com. NRC, 1983—; mem. Grant Commn. Nutrition and Metabolism Med. Rsch. Coun., Can., 1992—; vis. prof. dept. psychiatry U. Pitts. Med. Ctr., 1993-94; vis. prof. Stetson U., Deland, Fla., 1998—. Contbr. articles to profl. jours. Bd. dirs. Winnipeg chpt. Multiple Sclerosis Soc. Can., 1976. Named Hon. Citizen of New Orleans, 1997, Fellow Inst. de la Sante et de la Recherche Medicale (France); mem. Am. Soc. Biol. Chemistry, Am., Internat. neurochemistry socs., Am. Chem. Soc., AAAS, Soc. for Complex Carbohydrates, Fedn. Am. Socs. for Exptl. Biology, Can. Fedn. Biol. Socs., Canadian Biochem. Soc. Office: 1415 Ocean Shore Blvd Ormond Beach FL 32176-3673

KANG, BANN C. immunologist; b. Kyungnam, Korea, Mar. 4, 1939; d. Daeryong and Buni (Chung) K.; came to U.S., 1964, naturalized, 1976; A.B., Kyungpook Nat. U., 1959, M.D., 1963; m. U. Yun Ryo, Mar. 30, 1963. Intern, L.I. Jewish Hosp.-Queens Hosp. Center, Jamaica, N.Y., 1964-65, resident in medicine, 1965-67; teaching assoc. Kyungpook U. Hosp., Taegu, Korea, 1967-70; fellow in allergy and chest Creighton U., Omaha, 1970-71; fellow in allergy Henry Ford Hosp., Detroit, 1971-72; clin. instr. medicine U. Mich. Hosp., Ann Arbor, 1972-73; asst. prof. Chgo. Med. Sch., 1973-74; chief allergy-immunology Mt. Sinai Hosp., Chgo., 1975—; asst. prof. Rush Med. Sch., Chgo. 1975-84, assoc. prof., 1984-86; assoc. prof. U. Ky. Coll. Medicine, 1987-92, prof., 1992-2002, prof. emeritus, 2003—; cons., 1976—, Nat. Heart, Lung, Blood Inst., 1979—; mem. Exptl. Transplantation Adv. Bd., Ill., 1985-86, Diagnostic and Therapeutic Tech. Assessment (AMA), 1987—, Gen. Clin. Rsch. Com. (NIH), 1989-93; adv. com. Ctr. for Biologics and Rsch., FDA, 1993-96; counselor Chgo. Med. Soc., 1984-86, mem. policy com., adv. com. to health dept. Chgo. and Cook County, 1984-86. Recipient NIH award U. Mich., 1972-73. Diplomate Am. Bd. Internal Medicine, Am. Bd. Allergy Immunology. Fellow ACP, Am. Acad. Allergy; mem. Am. Fedn. Clin. Research, AMA, Inter-Asthma Assn. Contbr. over 50 articles to profl. jours. Home: 2716 Martinique Ln Lexington KY 40509-9509 Office: U Ky Coll Medicine K528 Albert B Chandler Med Ctr 800 Rose St Lexington KY 40536-0001 E-mail: BCKang0@uky.edu.

KANG, BENJAMIN TOYEONG, writer, clergyman; b. Republic of Korea, Mar. 30, 1931; came to U.S., 1963, naturalized, 1979; s. Tae-Un and Kumjoo (Lee) K.; m. Katherine Chungcha Chung, Apr. 29, 1955; children: Jennifer, Mira, Gregory. BA, Yonsei U., Republic of Korea, 1954; MA, Kyungbuk U., Republic of Korea, 1959; BD, Temple U., 1967; ThD, Internat. Sem., 1981.)rdained to ministry Christian Ch., 1970. Instr. Yonsei U., 1956-58; exec. dir. Kyungju YMCA, Republic of Korea, 1958-59; asst. prof. Keimyoung U., Republic of Korea, 1959-61; pastor Korean Ch. of Lower Bucks, Levittown, Pa., 1974-84; pres. Korean Sch. of Lower Bucks, 1980-82; pastor Korean Gloria Ch., Phila., 1981-89; parish assoc. First Presbyn. Ch., Levittown, 1990—. Freelance writer, 1992—; columnist Dong-A Daily News, 1992-94, 99—. Author: (hymn) In a Strange Land, 1992. Trustee Presbytery of Phila., Presbyn. Ch. USA, 1982-88, Met. Christian Coun. Phila., 1984-88, Coun. Korean Chs. in Phila., 1985-89; comdr. Vol. Student Army Kyungju, Republic of Korea, 1950-51. Home: 3128 Benjamin Rush Ct Bensalem PA 19020-1903

KANG, ELIOT, advertising executive; b. Republic of Korea; m. Jennifer Kang; 4 children. BA in Social Psychology, Cornell U. Pres., CEO Kang & Lee Advt. divsn. Young & Rubicam, Inc., N.Y.C., 1985—. Named one of N.Y.'s 40 Under 40, Crain's N.Y. Bus., 1995, 100 Most Influential Asian Ams. in the Past 10 Yrs., A. Mag.: Inside Asia Am., 1999; named to Advt. Hall of Fame, Am. Advt. Fedn.; recipient Asian Businessman's award, N.Y.C. Mayor David Dinkins, 1992. Mem.: Am. Mktg. Assn. (bd. dirs.), Am. Assn. Advt. Agys. (mem. Asian task force diversity action com., 1st pl. O'Toole Multicultural Advt. Awards 1998), Asian Am. Advt. Fedn. (founding mem., pres.). Office: Kang and Lee Advt 20 Cooper Sq New York NY 10003*

KANG, EMIL J. orchestra executive; b. N.Y., 1969; BS in Econs., U. Rochester (N.Y.). Orch. mgr. Seattle Symphony Orch., 1996-99; v.p. ops. Detroit Symphony Orch., 1999-2000, pres., exec. dir., 2000—. Office: Detroit Symphony Orch 3663 Woodward Ave Ste 100 Detroit MI 48201-2444

KANG, KYUNGIN, electronics engineer, researcher; b. Taejon, Korea, July 1, 1967; s. Shinbong and Taebool (Chung) K.; m. Eunhee Cha, June 11, 1994; children: Sohyun, Jeehyun. BS, Kyungpook Nat. U., Taegu, Korea, 1991; MS in Info. and Comms., U. Taejon, 2001. Pres. Fuzzy Tech. Co., Taejon, 1991-94; rschr. SaTReC, KAIST, Taejon, 1995—; rsch. UN ESA-ESTEC, Noordwijk, Holland, The Netherlands, 1999-2000; team leader, head sect. SaTReC, KAIST, 2000—. Designer, developer MEIS payload contr. and solid state recorder of KITSAT3 satellite, 1995-99; design and devel. high data rate receiving sys. of ground sta. for remote sensing satellite, 1998, KAISTSAT4 satellite, 2000—. Contbr. articles to profl. jours. Recipient fellowship UN and European Space Agy., 1998. Avocations: swimming, skiing. Home: Narae Apt 101-105 Chonmin-dong Yusung Taejon 305-729 Republic of Korea Office: SaTReC KAIST 373-1 Kusung-Dong Taejon 305-701 Republic of Korea Fax: 82 42 861 0064. E-mail: Kyunginkang@hosanna.net., kikang@kaist.ac.kr.

KANG, SOON-YI, mathematician, educator; b. YangSan, KyungNam, Republic of Korea, Oct. 12, 1967; arrived in U.S., 1992; d. Boo-Ho Kang and Yoon-Kil Joo; m. Hong Seo Ryoo, Apr. 27, 1967; children: Rachel Hejung Ryoo, Helen E-Jung Ryoo. BS in Math., Pusan (Republic of Korea) Nat. U., 1990, M in Math. Edn., 1992; PhD in Math., U. Ill., 1999. Tchrs. cert. in secondary education Korea Bd. Edn., 1990. Ross asst. prof. dept. math. Ohio State U., Columbus, 2000—. Contbr. articles to profl. jours. Achievements include research in some theorems on the Rogers-Ramanujan Continued Fraction and Associated Theta Function Identities in Ramanujan's Lost Notebook; Ramanujan's formula for the explicit evaluation of the Rogers-Ramanujan continued fraction and theta functions; new proof of Winquist's identity. Office: Ohio State Univ 231 W 18th Ave Columbus OH 43210 E-mail: kang@math.ohio-state.edu.

KANG, SUNG KWON, materials scientist, researcher; b. Republic of Korea; m. Claire Won Kang; children: Esther, Elizabeth. BS, Seoul Nat. U., Korea, 1969; PhD, U. of Pa., 1973. Asst. prof. Stevens Inst. of Tech., Hoboken, NJ, 1977—80; sr. scientist INCO R&D Ctr., Sterling Forest, NY, 1980—84; rsch. staff mem. IBM T. J. Watson Rsch. Ctr., Yorktown Heights, NY, 1984—. Achievements include patents for 28 U.S. patents and 26 internat. patents; research in 80 tech. papers publ. on electronic materials, microelectronic packaging, materials sci. and metallurgy. Office: IBM Corp Thomas J Watson Rsch Ctr Yorktown Heights NY 10598

KANG, SUNG-MO (STEVE KANG), electrical engineering educator; b. Seoul, Korea, Feb. 25, 1945; came to U.S., 1969; s. Chang-Shik and Kyung-Ja (Lee) K.; m. Myoung-A Cha, June 10, 1972; children: Jennifer, Jeffrey. BSEE, Fairleigh Dickinson U., 1970; MSEE, SUNY, Buffalo, 1972; PhD in Elec. Engring., U. Calif., Berkeley, 1975. Asst. prof. Rutgers U., Piscataway, N.J., 1975-77; mem. tech. staff AT&T Bell Labs., Murray Hill, N.J., 1977-82, supr., 1982-85; prof. U. Ill., Urbana, 1985-2000, head dept. electrical and computer engring., 1995-2000, assoc. Ctr. for Advanced Study, 1991-92, assoc. dir. microelectronics lab., 1988-95; univ. scholar U. Ill., Urbana, 1995-96. Dir. Ctr. for ASIC R&D, dean sch. engring. U. Calif., Santa Cruz, 2001—; pres. Silicon Valley Engring. Coun., 2002-03. Author 9 books; contbr. over 350 papers to internat. jours. and confs.; 12 patents. Recipient Meritorious Svc. award Cirs. and Sys. Soc., 1994, Humboldt Rsch. award for Sr. U.S. Scientists, 1996, Grad. Teaching award IEEE, 1996, IEEE CAS Soc. Tech. Achievement award, 1997, KBS award in Sci. and Tech., 1998, SRC Tech. Excellence award, 1999, Alumnus award U. Calif., Berkeley, 2001. Fellow AAAS, ACM, IEEE (various offices in Circuits and Systems Soc. including pres. 1991, founding editor-in-chief Trans. on VSLI systems, Disting. lectr. 1994-97, Darlington award, SRC Inventor Recognition award 1993, 96, 99, 2001, 02, Meritorious Svc. award Compuer Soc. 1990, CAS Soc. Golden Jubilee medal 1999, Millennium medal 2000), Nat. Acad. Engring. of Korea (fgn. mem.). Presbyterian. Avocations: tennis, travel. Office: U Calif Baskin Sch Engring Santa Cruz CA 95064 E-mail: kang@soe.ucsc.edu.

KANG, YOOGOO, anesthesiologist, educator; b. Seoul, Apr. 10, 1946; s. Kiduk and Samkum (Koh) K.; m. Young H. Kim, Nov. 9, 1972; children: Michael N., David H. BS, Seoul (Korea) Nat. U., 1967, MD, 1971. Diplomate Am. Bd. Anesthesiology. Intern St. Raphael Hosp., New Haven, Conn., 1974-75; resident in surgery Albert Einstein Med. Ctr., Phila., 1975-76; resident in anesthesiology Thomas Jefferson U. Hosp., Phila., 1976-78; fellow in obstetric anesthesia Magee Women's Hosp., Pitts., 1978-79; asst. prof. U. Pitts., 1979-88, dir. hepatic transplantation anesthesiology, 1984-98, assoc. prof., 1989-93, prof., 1994-98; prof., chmn. dept. anesthesiology Tulane U. Med. Ctr., New Orleans, 1998-2000; prof. vice chmn. dept. anesthesiology Thomas Jefferson U., Phila., 2000—. Head Internat. Symposium in Liver Transplantation, Pitts., 1984-88. Editor: Hepatic Transplantation: Anesthetic Management and Perioperative Care, 1985, Anesthesia and Intensive Care for Patients with Liver Diseasae, 1995; assoc. editor Liver Surgery and Transplantation, 1993—; mem. editl. bd. Current Opinions in Organ Transplantation, 1996—. Med. officer Korean Army, 1971-74. Mem. Am. Soc. Anesthesiologists, Internat. Soc. Rsch. in Anesthesiology, Internat. Liver Transplantation Soc. (pres. 1989-93, mem. exec. coun. 1993-95, adv. bd. 1995—), Liver Intensive Care Group Europe. Avocations: woodwork, photography. Office: Thomas Jefferson U Dept Anesthesiology 111 S 11th St Ste 5480 Gibb Philadelphia PA 19107-5092 E-mail: yoogoo.kang@mail.tju.edu.

KANG, YOUNG WOO, special education educator, dean; b. Kyonggi, Republic of Korea, Jan. 16, 1944; arrived in U.S., 1972, naturalized; s. Myung Ki Kang and Lin Hee Lim; m. Kyoung Sook Suk, Feb. 26, 1972; children: Paul, Christopher. BA, Yonsei U., Seoul, Republic of Korea, 1972; MEd, U. Pitts., 1973, PhD, 1976. Cert. rehab. counselor; tchr. ESL, spl. edn. Spl. edn. cons. Gary (Ind.) Sch. Corp., 1976—. Prof., dean Taegu (Republic of Korea) U., 1978—; adj. prof. Northeastern Ill. U., Chgo., 1979—; vice-chmn. World Com. Disability, 1995—; sr. advisor Roosevelt Inst., 1996. Author: (book) A Light in My Heart, 1987, Love, Light, Liberty, 1989, Secrets to Success through Education, 1996, Dreams of a Father and His Sons, 1998, There is No Mountain That We Can Not Climb, 2000, Success is Inside Me: From Bad Luck to a Presidential Appointee, 2002; author: (with Kyoung Sook Kang) Two Candles Shining in the Darkness of the World, 1990. Apptd. mem. Nat. Coun. Disability, 2002—; bd. dirs. Nat. Orgn. Disability, 1995—, Goodwill Industries Internat., 1998—; pres. Edn. Rehab. Exch. Found. Internat., 1993—. Mem.: Internat. Coun. Exceptional Children, Rotary (bd. dirs., trustee Munster, Ind. chpt. 1982—, chmn. internat. svc. and youth svc. coms. dist. 6540 1983—85, presenter confs. 1983, 1987, 1988, one of 75 candles in 75th anniversary celebration 1992, Meritorious Svc. citation 1982, Pual Harris fellow 1987, scholar 1973). Presbyterian. Avocations: public speaking, writing, reading, travel, advocating rights of disabled. Home: 8912 Chestnut Ln Munster IN 46321-3224 Office: 1331 F StNW Ste 850 Washington DC 20004

KANGAS, MATTHEW ARVID, art critic, curator; b. Seattle, Sept. 18, 1949; s. Arvid Rudolph and Violet Loraine (Friedline) K. BA, Reed Coll., 1971; BA, MA, Oxford (Eng.) U., 1974. Editl. asst. Praeger Publs., N.Y.C., 1971-72, Vineyard Books, N.Y.C., 1974-75; adj. instr. U. Puget Sound, Seattle, 1976-85; N.Am. commr. World Ceramics Biennale, Republic of Korea, 2003. Contbr., contbg. editor Art in America, Washington DC, 1979—, Sculpture, N.Y., 1991—, Glass, 2000—; mem. adj. faculty Sch. Visual Concepts, Seattle, 1984-85. Author: Richard Fairbanks, American Potter, 1989, Jim Leedy: Artist Across Boundaries, 1997, Ryoji Koie, 2000, Robert Willson: Image-maker, 2002, William Ingham: Configuration of Forces, 2003, Bertil Vallien: Somna/Vakna, 2003; co-author (catalogs) Tales and Traditions, 1993, Expressions in Wood, 1997; author (catalogs) Breaking Barriers, 1995; contbg. writer The Seattle Times, Glass, La Revue de la Ceramique et du Verre. Mem. Ballard H.S. Found., 1997—. Recipient Everson medal Everson Mus. of Art, Syracuse, N.Y., 1990, Travel award Royal Norwegian Ministry Fgn. Affairs, 1996, Capt. William R. Ballard award, BHS Found., 2001. Mem. Coll. Art Assn., Internat. Assn. Art Critics, Am. Craft Coun., Glass Art Soc. Democrat. Avocations: playing piano, travel, collecting pottery, cooking, attending ballet. Home and Office: 3038 NW Market St Apt 4 Seattle WA 98107-4273 E-mail: mkangas@westernsafety.com.

KANGOVI, SACH, telecommunications industry executive; b. Bangalore, Karnataka, India, Aug. 25, 1948; s. Dhruva Rao Kongovi, S Rao Kongovi; m. Sita S Bhat; 1 child, Shreya. PhD, Rutgers U., 1977. Sr. scientist Boeing Computer Svcs., Phila.; prin. scientist Johnson & Johnson, New Brunswick, NJ, 1991—96; cons. AT&T/Lucent, Liberty Corner, 1996—2000; dir. rsch. & devel. ADC Telecomm., Cranbury, 2000—. Contbr. Mem. cable com. Princeton Junction Twp., Princeton Junction, NJ, 1996—2000. Recipient Minta Martin award, AIAA, 1975. Mem.: AAAS, ASME. Achievements include patents, publs. and copyrights in field. Home: 63 Saratoga Dr Princeton Junction NJ 08550

KANIN, DENNIS ROY, lawyer; b. Boston, Feb. 22, 1946; s. Irving Lynwood and Doris May (Small) K.; m. Carol Ann Licht, July 9, 1978; children: Zachary Joshua, Jonah Louis, Franklin Jacob. AB, Harvard U., 1968, JD, 1971. Bar: Mass. 1971, D.C. 1978. Assoc. Mahoney Atwood & Goldings, Boston, 1971-73; legis. asst. to congressman Frank Evans U.S. Ho. Reps., Washington, 1973-74, adminstrn. asst. to congressman Paul Tsongas, 1975-78; adminstrv. asst. to senator Paul Tsongas U.S. Senate, Washington, 1979-84; ptnr. Foley, Hoag & Eliot, Boston, 1985—. Mgr. campaign Tsongas for U.S. Senate, Boston, 1978; mem. Nat. Dem. Charter Commn., Washington, 1973-74, Nat. Commn. Dem. Platform Accountability, Washington, 1983-84; mem. exec. com. Mass. Ams. for Dem. Action, Boston, 1985-87; campaign mgr. Tsongas for pres.; nat. commr., regional vice chair New Eng. bd. Anti-Defamation League, 1985—; mem. bd. dirs. New Eng. Coun., 1993-98; bd. dirs. Concord Coalition Citizens Coun., 1995—; trustee, v.p. bd. dirs. Epiphany Sch., 1999—, Roxbury Latin Sch., 2000—; bd. overseers Children's Hosp., Boston, 1996—. Jewish. Home: 65 Stuart Rd Newton MA 02459-1210 Office: Foley Hoag & Eliot One Post Office Sq Boston MA 02109

KANIN, DORIS MAY, political scientist, consultant; b. Somerville, Mass., Mar. 28, 1928; d. Sidney J. and Ida Gail (Gelbsman) Small; m. Irving L. Kanin, June 11, 1944; children: Dennis, Erik, Lisa Hochheiser. BA in Govt., Boston U., 1966; MA in Govt., 1970; postgrad., Boston U., 1970-74. Dir. cultural activities Staff of George McGovern, 1972; legis. dir. to congressman Joe Moakley, 1972-74; nat. polit. dir. Frank Church for Pres., 1975-76; spl. asst. Paul Tsongas U.S. Senate campaign, Boston, 1977-78; dir. Human Svcs. Dept. Fed. State Rels., Mass., 1979-81; nat. dir. pub. affairs Physicians for Social Responsibility, 1981-82; exec. of Pub. Rels. and Comms. Lynwood Labs. Inc., 1982—; polit. adv. Paul Tsongas for pres. campaign, Mass., 1991—92. Inventor, creator: Spray-n-Starch aerosol, 1968; editor: Quincy Mass. Cmty. Ctr. Newsletter, 1956-58, Mass. Liberal Citizens of Mass. Bulletin; journalist Boston Daily Record, 1944; reporter Boston Daily Record-Am. Pres. LWV, Norwood, Mass., 1956—59, Mass. Citizens for Participation in Politics, Boston, 1973—74; chair, bd. dirs., mem., state bd. Mass. Civil Liberties Union, Boston, 1976—81; mem. steering com. women's caucus Capiol Hill Women's Polit. Caucus; elected del. to all Nat. Nominating Convs., 1972—92; del. Dem. Nat. Conv., 1972, 1976, 1980, 1982, 1986, 1992, Fla. Dem. Party Conf., 2002; dir. Mass. Cultural Affairs for Pres. Campaign, George McGovern; elected Dem. Nat. Committeewoman, Mass., 1972—76; mem. women's caucus, 1972—76; elected edn. and tng. coun. Dem. Nat. Com., 1976—80; bd. dirs. Mass. Ams. for Dem. Action, 1978—80, Mass. Pax; del. Mass. Dem. Party Conv., 2002. Named: Woodrow Wilson Semi-Finalist, 1972-76, Mass. Spelling Bee Champion, Boston Herald Traveler, 1939. Mem. Internat. Aerosol Congress. Democrat. Avocations: travel, painting, poetry writing, opera, ballet. Home: 501 Boylston St Brookline MA 02445-5701 also: 1289 Breakers West Blvd West Palm Beach FL 33411-1881

KANIN, FAY, screenwriter; b. N.Y.C. d. David and Bessie Mitchell; m. Michael Kanin (dec.); children: Joel (dec.), Josh. Student, Elmira Coll., LHD (hon.), 1981; BA, U. So. Calif. Mem. Western regional exec. bd., judge Am. Coll. Theatre Festival, 1975-76. Writer: (with Michael Kanin) screenplays including The Opposite Sex, Teacher's Pet; Broadway plays including Goodbye My Fancy, His and Hers, Rashomon, Grind (Tony nomination 1985); writer co-prodr. TV spls. including Friendly Fire, ABC-TV (Emmy award for best TV film, San Francisco Film Festival award, Peabody award), Hustling (Writers Guild award for best original drama), Tell Me Where It Hurts (Emmy award Christopher award); Heartsounds (Peabody award). Recipient Humanitas prize prestigious Kieser award, 2003. Mem. Writers guild Am. West (pres. screen br 1971-73, Val Davies award 1975, Morgan Cox award 1976), Am. Film Inst (trustee), Acad. Motion Picture Arts and Scis. (pres. 1979-82), Nat. Ctr. Film and Video Preservation (co-chmn.), Am. Film Preservation Bd. (chmn.).

KANIS, MERSH LUBEL, special education educator, writer; b. Montgomery Ala., June 26, 1960; d. William M. and Helena C. Lubel; m. Jack W. Kanis, June 22, 1988; 1 child, Daniel C. BA, Cambridge Coll., Mass., 1999; MEd, U. of Mass., Boston, 2001. Lic. tchr. Mass. Dept. of Edn., 2000. Spl. edn. tchr Dennis-Yarmouth Regional Sch. Dist., Yarmouth, Mass., 1999—. Yoga instr Nausett C.C., Orleans, Mass., 2002—. Contbr. poetry. Recipient Award for Outstanding Scholarship in Spl. Edn., U. of Mass./Boston-Grad. Sch. Edn. 2001. Mem.: Mass. Teachers Assn., Calif. Yoga Teachers Assn., Coun. for Exceptional Children. Home: PO Box 1419 Brewster MA 02631 Persona E-mail: emkan@aol.com.

KANJORSKI, PAUL EDMUND, congressman, lawyer; b. Nanticoke, Pa. Apr. 2, 1937; s. A. Peter and Wanda (Nedbalski) K.; m. Nancy Marie Hickerson Nov. 22, 1962; 1 child, Nancy Marie Student, Temple U., 1961, Dickinson Sch Law, 1965. Bar: Pa. Ptnr. Kanjorski & Kanjorski, Wilkes-Barre, Pa., 1966-84 mem. U.S. Congress from 11th Pa. dist., Washington, 1985—; mem. banking and fin. svcs., govt. reform coms. Acting solicitor City of Nanticoke, 1969-81 Pa. Workmen's Compensation referee, 1972-80; bd. dirs. Wyoming Valley Sanitary Authority, Wilkes-Barre, 1972-84; former trustee Wilkes U. Mem Wilkes-Barre Law Library Assn. Democrat. Roman Catholic. Avocation fishing. Office: 2353 Rayburn Ho Office Bldg Washington DC 20515-0001*

KANKEY, ROLAND DOYLE, educator; b. Batesville, Ark., Nov. 17, 1946 s. William Jasper Jr. and Verline Violet (Dockins) K.; m. Linda Grace Johnson July 6, 1974; children: Jason, Andrew, Adam. *Linda Kankey has dispatched fo the Enon Emergency Medical Service (EMS) since 1978, and is currently the head fire and EMS dispatcher and EMS Treasurer. A member of the Greenon Band Boosters 1989-2002, she served on their board as treasurer 1997-2002 Jason completed a Bachelor of Science degree in chemical engineering at the University of Dayton in 1999 and works for U.S. Gypsum. Andy started workin toward a degree in engineering at Ohio State University in 1998. Adam started an engineering/computer science degree program at Wright State U. in 2002* BS in Math, Wichita State U., 1968; MS in Math, Oklahoma State U. Stillwater, 1970; MA in Bus. Adminstrn., Ohio State U., Columbus, 1985, PhD in Bus. Adminstrn., 1988. Tech. mgr. Rome Air Devel. Ctr., Rome, N.Y. 1970-72; chief, mgmt. analysis 51st Air Base Wing, Osan, Korea, 1972-73 mgmt./cost analysis Headquarters USAF, Pentagon, 1973-77; faculty mem AFIT, Wright-Patterson, 1977-2000, dir. grad. cost analysis program, 1988-90 head dept. quantitative mgmt., 1990-93; sr. IMA to the commdr. Aerospace Guidance & Metrology Ctr., Newark AFB, 1995-96; sr. IMA to the compt Aero. Systems Ctr., Wright Patterson, 1996-99; head grad. acquisition mgmt dept. AFIT, Wright Patterson, 1993-98; head dept. contract pricing Midwes region Def. Acq. U., 2000—01, prof., 2001—. Mem. nat. bd. dirs. Soc. Cos Estimating & Analysis, Alexandria, Va., 1993-97, chmn. 1994 nat. conf. 1990-94, editor Jour. Cost Analysis, 1992-98; editor National Estimator Nat Estimating Soc., Alexandria, 1989-92. Editor: (book) Cost Analysis & Estimating, 1991; contbr. articles to profl. jours. Mem. Greenon H.S. Band Boosters Enon, 1995-2002, sec. 1995-97, pres. 2000-02. Capt. USAF, 1968-80. Mem Am. Soc. Military Comptrollers (chpt. pres. 1997-98), Wright-Patterson Ai Force Base Officers Club, Soc. Cost Estimating & Analysis, Beta Gamm Sigma Honor Soc., Phi Kappa Phi. Avocations: genealogy, golf, moderat running, military and air force memorabilia, family history. Home: 11 Cimmaron Trl Enon OH 45323-1653 Office: DAUW FP 2950 Hobson Wa Wright Patterson Afb OH 45433-7765 E-mail: Kankeyr@woh.rr.com.

KANN, PETER ROBERT, journalist, newspaper publishing executive; b N.Y.C., Dec. 13, 1942; s. Robert A. and Marie K. (Breuer); m. Francesca Mayer Apr. 12, 1969 (dec. 1983); m. Karen Elliot House, 1984; children: Hillar Francesca, Petra Elliot, Jason Elliot, Jade Elliott. BA, Harvard U., 1964. Wit The Wall St. Jour., 1964—; journalist N.Y.C., 1964-67, 1967-68, 1968-75; pub editor Asian edit., 1976-79; assoc. pub., 1979-88; asst. to chmn. and mem. exec com. Dow Jones & Co., 1986-89, pres. internat. and mag. groups, 1986-89, als chmn. bd. dirs., pres., COO, 1989-91, editl. dir., 1989—, chmn., CEO, 1991— pub., Wall St. Jour., 1989—2002. Chmn. bd. Far Ea. Econ. Rev., 1987—89 mem. Pulitzer Prize Bd., 1987—96. Trustee Asia Soc., 1989—94, Aspen Inst 1994—98, Spelman Coll., 1994—97, Inst. for Advanced Study, Princeton, N.J 1990—. Recipient Pulitzer prize for internat. reporting, 1972. Mem.: Spee Clu (Cambridge, Mass.). Office: Wall Street Journal Dow Jones & Co Inc 20 Liberty St New York NY 10281-1003

KANNANGARA, VIJITH JULIAN, entrepreneur; b. London, May 22, 196 s. Peter Vincent and Stella Marie (Jayawardhana) K.; m. Rochelle Marie Peiris Oct. 12, 1989. M.B.BS, North Colombo Med. Coll., Sri Lanka, 1991. Chmn. bd Q&E Advt. (Pvt.) Ltd., Sri Lanka, 1991—; chmn. Asia PrePress (Pvt) Ltd., Sr Lanka, 1994—, Smart Media Prodns. (Pvt) Ltd., Sri Lanka, 1994—; chmn CEO Affno (Pvt) Ltd., Sri Lanka, 2000—. Dir. Printel (Pvt) Ltd., Sri Lanka Mem. North Colombo Med. Coll. Alumni Assn. (pres. 1995-96), N.Y. Acad Sci., Computer Soc. of IEEE. Avocations: music, reading, badminton, swimming. Home: 56/4 Kynsey Rd Colombo 8 Sri Lanka Office: Smart Medi Prodns (Pvt) Ltd #100 Horton Pl Colombo 7 Sri Lanka

KANNE, MICHAEL STEPHEN, federal judge; b. Rensselaer, Ind., Dec. 2 1938; s. Allen Raymond and Jane (Robinson) Kanne; m. Judith Ann Stevens June 22, 1963; children: Anne, Katherine. Student, St. Joseph's Coll., Rensselaer, 1957—58; BS, Ind. U., 1962, JD, 1968; postgrad., Boston U., 1963, U Birmingham, Eng., 1975. Bar: Ind. 1968. Assoc. Nesbitt and Fisher, Rensselaer 1968—71; sole practice Rensselaer, 1971—72; atty. City of Rensselaer, 197 judge 30th Jud. Cir. of Ind., 1972—82, U.S. Dist. Ct. (no. dist.) Ind., Hammond 1982—87, U.S. Ct. Appeals (7th cir.), Chgo., 1987—; chmn. U.S. Cts. Desig Guide, 1988—95. Lectr. law St. Joseph's Coll., 1976—89, St. Frances Coll 1990—91; faculty Nat. Inst. for Trial Advocacy, South Bend, Ind., 1978—8 Bd. visitors Ind. U. Sch. Law, 1987—, Ind. U. Sch. Pub. and Environ. Affair 1991—; trustee St. Joseph's Coll., 1984—. 1st lt. USAF, 1962—65. Name Outstanding Alumnus, Today's Cath. Tchr., 1991; recipient Disting. Svc. award St. Joseph's Coll., 1973, Disting. Grad. award, Nat. Cath. Ednl. Assn. Mem FBA, Tippecanoe County Bar Assn., Jasper County Bar Assn. (pres. 1972—76 Ind. State Bar Assn. (bd. dirs. 1977—79, Presdl. citation 1979), Law Alumn Assn. Ind. U. (pres. 1980). Roman Catholic. Avocations: horseback riding weightlifting. Office: Charles A Halleck Federal Building 234 N Fourth Stre PO Box 1340 Lafayette IN 47902-1340 also: US Ct Appeals 219 S Dearborn Chicago IL 60604*

KANNEL, WILLIAM B. cardiologist, epidemiologist; b. Bklyn., Dec. 2 1913; s. Joseph Mayer and Sarah Molly Kannel; m. Rita Ruth Lefkowitz, Ma 29, 1943; children: Linda Isaacson, Stephen. MD, U. Ga., Augusta, 194 Diplomate Am. Bd. Internal Medicine. Dir. NHLBI Framingham (Mass.) Hea Study, 1966—79; prof. medicine Boston U. Sch. Medicine/Framingham Hea Study, 1979—. Chmn. sect. preventive medicine and epidemiology Boston U Sch. Medicine, 1979—90. Contbr. articles to profl. jours. Chmn. Coun. c Epidemiology, Am. Heart Assn., 1975. Capt. USPHS, 1949—79. Recipie Award for Pioneering Achievement in Health, Charles A. Dana Found., 198 Fellow: Am. Coll. Cardiology (life). Achievements include research in ris factors for cardiovascular disease. Office: Framingham Heart Study Suite 2 7 Mt Wayte Ave Framingham MA 01702-5827

KANNENBERG, LLOYD CHAMBERS, physicist, educator; b. Sarasot Fla., Mar. 23, 1939; s. Werner Frederick Ludwig Kannenberg and Nettie Louis Chambers; m. Susan Lippman, Aug. 10, 1963; 1 child, Susanna. SB, MIT, 196 MS, U. Fla., 1963; PhD, Northeastern U., 1967. Elec. engr. Electro-Mec Rsch., Inc., Sarasota, 1961-63; instr. physics Lowell (Mass.) Tech. Inst. (merge with Lowell State Coll.), 1966-67; from instr. to prof. physics U. Mas (formerly U. Lowell), 1968—; instr. physics Northeastern U., Boston, 1967-6 Translator: (by H. Grassmann) A New Branch of Mathematics, 1994, (by

rassman) Extension Theory, 2000, (by G. Peano) Geometric Calculus, 2000; ontbr. articles to profl. jours. Mem. Am. Phys. Soc. (life), Am. Math. Soc., Am. ssn. Physics Tchrs., Math. Assn. Am, Sigma Xi, Sigma Pi Sigma, Phi Kappa hi. Democrat. Office: U Mass-Lowell 1 University Ave Lowell MA 01854

ANNENSTINE, MARGARET LAMPE, artist; b. St. Louis, Apr. 1, 1938; d. ohn Avery and Elizabeth (Phillips) Lampe; m. Louis Fabian Kannenstine, Oct. , 1959; children: David Edward, Emily Ann. BFA, Washington U. St. Louis, 959; postgrad., Art Students League, N.Y.C., 1959-61. Bd. trustees Pentangle oun. Arts, 1982—88, 1993—96, chair, 1984—87, 1994, 95, hon. bd., 1997—; d. trustees Vt. Studio Ctr., 1989—94, chair, 1990—93; bd. trustees Vt. Coun. rts, 1994—2001, chair, 1994—98; bd. trustees Nat. Assembly Arts Agencies, 001—. One-woman shows include Vt. Artisans, Strafford, 1976, Gallery Two, Voodstock, Vt., 1974, 1977, 1985, Red Mill Gallery, Johnson, Vt., 1990, 1990, reen Mountain Power Corp., South Burlington, Vt., 1991, 1991, Vt. Coun. on rts, Montpelier, Vt., 1991, Woodstock Gallery Art, 1991, 1994, Beside Myself allery, Arlington, Vt., 1992, Taylor Gallery, Meriden, N.H., 1993, Kimball nion Acad., Dartmouth Coll., Hanover, N.H., 1993, 1999, Kent (Conn.) Sch., 993, Chittenden Bank, Burlington, Vt., 1994, Windy Bush Gallery, New Hope, a., 1995, N.H. Coll., Manchester, 1996, Flynn Theater Gallery, Burlington, 996, 1998, Nat. Wildlife Fedn. Gallery, Vienna, Va., 1996, McGowan Fine Art, oncord, N.H., 1997, Grayson Gallery, Woodstock, 1997, 1999, Spheris allery, Walpole, N.H., 1997, The Gallery at Johnny D's, Somerville, Mass., 997, AVA Gallery, Hanover, Lebanon, 1998, Main Street Mus. Art, Hartford, t., 1999, Collis Ctr., Dartmouth Coll., 1999, Gallery of Graphic Arts, N.Y.C., 999, Lyndon State Coll., Lyndonville, Vt., 1999, 2002, Supreme Ct., Mont- elier, 1999, Cushing Acad. Gallery, Ashburnham, Mass., 2001, Prince St. allery, N.Y.C., 2003, Woodstock Town Hall, Vt., 2002, Prince St. Gallery, .Y.C., 2003, one-man shows include Vt. Gov.'s Office Gallery, 2003, exhibited group shows at Gallery Two, 1973—88, Carl Battaglia Gallery, N.Y.C., 979—80, The Gallery, Williamstown, Mass., 1981—84, Vt. Coun. Arts, 1988, 996, AVA Gallery, Hanover, 1989—98, Woodstock Gallery Art, 1989, Beside Myself Gallery, 1990, Fleming Mus., U. Vt., Burlington, 1991, Bennington oll., 1992, Windy Bush Gallery, 1994, VCA, Woodstock, 1994, Riverfest, Vhite River Junction, Vt., 1995, Firehouse Gallery, Burlington, 1995, McGowan Fine Art, Concord, N.H., 1995, Chaffee Gallery, Rutland, Vt., 1997, elen Day Art Ctr., Stowe, Vt., 1997, Champion Internat., Stamford, Conn., 997, New Art New England, Newport, N.H., 1997, Gallery Graphic Art, .Y.C., 1998—2000, Grayson Gallery, Woodstock, Vt., 2000, Ute Stebich allery, Lenox, Mass., 1999—2001, Elsa Mott Ives Gallery, N.Y.C., 2000, Arts live Gallery, Burlington, 2001, G. Wilson Gallery, Stonington, Maine, 2001, atricia Carega Gallery, Sandwich, N.H., 2002, 2003, Woodstock (Vt.) Folk Art nd Prints, 2003, Represented in permanent collections The Hood Mus., anover, Robert Hull Fleming Mus., Burlington, Vt. Employees Credit Union, Montpelier, Champion Internat. Corp., Stamford, Conn., Union Mut. Ins. Co., Montpelier, Vt. Law Sch., South Royalton, Fletcher Allen Hosp., Burlington, t. Hist. Soc., Montpelier, Cushing Acad., Ashburnham, Mass. Apptd. by Sen. eahy to Millenium Commn. of Friends of Art and Preservation in Embassies, 999-2000; trustee New Eng. Found. for Arts, 1996-2001; incorporator Upper alley Cmty. Found., 1996-2000, trustee, 1999; founding dir. Woodstock Cty. ust, v.p. 1998, 99, pres., 2000, 01; charter mem. Creative Economy Coun. of ew Eng. Coun., Vt. Creative Economy Policy Coun., 2003—, Vt. Coun. ulture Innovation, 2003. Recipient Citation for achievement in arts, Vt. Arts oun., 2002; scholar Washington U. scholar, 1955. Mem. Cosmopolitan Club. vocations: music, gardening, hiking. E-mail: mlkannen@aol.com.

ANNER, EDWIN BENJAMIN, electrical manufacturing company execu- ve; b. N.Y.C., July 2, 1922; s. Charles and Grace (Edelson) K.; m. S. Barbara enenberg, Aug. 3, 1944; children: Jaimie Sue, Richard, Keith. BBA, CCNY, 943; MBA, Harvard U., 1947. Asst. West Coast mgr. Fairchild Publs., N.Y.C. nd L.A., 1948-50; gen. mgr. Dible Enterprises, L.A., 1951-53; sales mgr., gen. gr., pres. Western Insulated Wire Co. div. Teledyne, L.A., 1954-68; pres. Carol able Co. West div. Avnet, L.A., 1969-79; exec. v.p., COO Avnet Inc., N.Y.C., 980-83; pres. Pacific Electricord and Am. Ins. Wire Co., L.A., also Providence, 948—. Lt. USNR, 1943—47, PTO. Office: Pacific Electricord 747 W Redondo each Blvd Gardena CA 90247-4203

ANNER, GIDEON, lawyer; b. Lwów, Poland, Apr. 15, 1930; came to U.S., 947; s. Stanley and Claire Kanner; children: Jonathan, Jesse. B of Mech. ngring., The Cooper Union, 1954; JD, U. So. Calif., 1961. Bar: Calif. 1962, .S. Supreme Ct. 1967. Rocket engr. USN, N.J., 1954-55, Rocketdyne, Calif., 955-64; assoc. Fadem & Kanner, L.S., 1964-74; prof. law Loyola U., L.A., 974-90; assoc. Crosby, Heafey, Roach & May, L.A., 1990-95; lawyer Berger Norton, Santa Monica, Calif., 1995—. Cons. Calif. Law Revision Commn., 968-77, 97—. Co-editor: Nichols on Eminent Domain, Compensation for xpropriation-A Comparative Study, Vol. II, 1990, After Lucas: Land Use egulation and the Taking of Property Without Compensation, 1993; editor, ust Compensation, 1974—; contbr. articles and revs. to profl. law jours. ecipient Shattuck prize Am. Inst. Real Estate Appraisers, 1973, Harrison weed Spl. Merit award for continuing legal edn. Am. Law Inst.-ABA, 1999. ome: PO Box 1741 Burbank CA 91507-1741 Office: Berger & Norton 12121 ilshire Blvd Ste 1300 Los Angeles CA 90025 E-mail: anner@bergernorton.com.

ANNO, BRIAN M. state legislator, volunteer worker; b. Honolulu, Oct. 23, 961; s. Toshio and Kimiko (Takahashi) K. BA in Econs., Yale U., 1983. Group st. N.W. Ayer, N.Y.C., 1983-84; adminstrv. asst. Benton & Bowles, N.Y.C., 84-85; account exec. Ogilvy & Mather Hawaii, Honolulu, 1985-87, Starr igle McCombs, Honolulu, 1987; campaign office mgr. Patsy T. Mink mpaign com., Honolulu, 1988, 90; legis. asst. Rep. Patsy T. Mink, U.S. Ho. Reps., Washington, 1990-91; advt. mgr. Servco Pacific Inc., Honolulu, 988-90; youth vol. coord. Boys & Girls Club Waianae, 1991-92; mem. Hawaii enate, Dist. 20, Honolulu, 1992-. Father facilitator Parents and Children gether (PACT), 2000—. Mem. Yale Club of Hawaii (treas. 1987-90, bd. dirs. 87—). Office: Hawaii State Capitol 415 S Beretania St Rm 202 Honolulu HI 813-2407*

ANOF, NORMAN B. dermatologist; b. N.Y.C., May 31, 1920; AB, MD, eorge Washington U., 1941; D in Med. Sci., Columbia U., 1949. Diplomate m. Bd. Dermatology. Clin. prof. dermatology NYU Sch. of Medicine, N.Y.C. ome: 737 Park Ave New York NY 10021-4256 Office: 10 E 70th St New York Y 10021-4913

ANOFSKY, ALVIN SHELDON, physics educator; b. Phila., July 5, 1939; s. ilip and Mollie (Edelstein) K.; m. Donna Mikulik May 23, 1992; children om previous marriage: Robert, Nathan. BA, U. Pa., 1961, MS, 1962, PhD, 966. Rsch. asst. Johnson Found. Med. Physics, Phila., 1957-59, physics dept. Pa., 1960-66; faculty Lehigh U., Bethlehem, Pa., 1967—, prof. physics, 976—, dir. Lehigh Accelerator Lab., 1985—; pres. R&D Co., 1969—. Contbr. ticles to profl. jours. Fellow Am. Phys. Soc.; mem. AAAS, AAUP, Soc. hoto-Optical Intrumentation Engrs., Bethlehem C. of C., Sigma Xi. Jewish. odge: Rotary. Avocations: hiking, jogging, biking, piano, tennis. Office: high U Physics Dept Bldg 16 Bethlehem PA 18015

ANOVITZ, HOWARD, artist, educator; b. Fall River, Mass., Feb. 9, 1929; Meyer Julius and Dora (Rems) K. BS, Providence Coll., 1949; postgrad., R.I. h. Design, 1949-51, NYU, 1959-61. Instr. Bklyn. Coll., 1962-64, Pratt Inst., 64-66; prof. Southhampton Coll., 1977-78, Sch. Visual Arts, N.Y.C., 1981- . Artist, painter exhibited Tibor de Nagy Gallery, 1956, Stable Gallery, 1962, wish Mus., 1966, Waddell Gallery, 1969; one-man shows include U.S. and rope, Stefanotty Gallery, N.Y.C., 1975, Galerie Jöllenbeck, Cologne, 1977, nson Gallery, Bridgehampton, L.I., N.Y., 1977, Akademie der Kunste, Berlin, 79, Kestner Gesellschaft, Hannover, 1979, Alex Rosenberg Gallery, 1982, ge Baecker Gallery, 1987, 88, 91, Cologne, 1987, Marlborough Gallery, 1988, , Hokin-Kaufman Gallery, Chgo., 1989, Gana Art Gallery, Seoul, 1990, rich Gering Gallery, Frankfurt, 1997, Nabi Gallery, Sag Harbor, L.I., 1998; oup exhibits include Whitney Mus., N.Y.C., 1972, Dokumenta 5, Kassel, 72, Berlin Nat. Gallery, 1976, Guild Hall, East Hampton, L.I., 1976, okumenta 6, Kassel, 1977, Alex Rosenberg Gallery, 1978, Louise Himmelfarb allery, Watermill, L.I., 1979, L.A. Mus. Contemporary Art, 1984, Indpls. Mus. t, 1985, Ludwig Mus., Cologne, 1988, Parrish Art Mus., Southampton, L.I., 88, Fla. Internat. U., Miami, 1989, Met. Mus., N.Y.C., 1991, Weatherspoon t Gallery, Greensboro, N.C., 1991; represented in permanent collections Met. Mus., N.Y., Whitney Mus. Am. Art, N.Y., Hirshhorn Mus. and Sculpture Garden, Washington, L.A. County Mus. Modern Art, Guild Hall Mus., East Hampton, N.Y, Folkwang Mus., Essen, Germany. Studio: 361 N Sea Mecox Rd Southampton NY 11968-2829 E-mail: nero@optonline.net.

KANSAL, ACHIN SURESH, marketing professional, consultant; b. Meerut, India, Sept. 25, 1974; came to U.S., 1997; s. Suresh Kumar and Nirmal (Goel) K. BS, U. Pune, India, 1996; MS, U. Cin., 1999. Cons. Chemtex, Inc., Bombay, 1996-97; dir. tech. mgmt. and cons. Info. Resources, Inc., Cin., 2003—. Cons. Miller Brewing Co., Trenton, Ohio, 1997-98. Contbr. articles to profl. jours. including Internat. Jour. Indsl. Ergonomics, Internat. Jour. Indsl. Engring. U. Cin. fellow, 1997-98. Home: 4117 Fox Run Trl Apt 6 Cincinnati OH 45255 Office: Info Resources Inc 250 E 5th St Ste 700 Cincinnati OH 45202 E-mail: a_kansal@hotmail.com.

KANSFIELD, NORMAN J. seminary president; b. East Chgo., Ind., Mar. 24, 1940; s. Orval Russell and Margaret Jeannette (Norman) K.; m. Mary L. Klein, June 25, 1965; children: Ann Margaret, John Livingston. BA, Hope Coll., 1962; BD, Western Theol. Seminary, 1965; M of sacred theology, Union Theol. Seminary, 1967; MA, U. Chgo., 1970, PhD, 1981. Pastor Second Reformed Ch., Astoria, Queens, 1965-68; interim pastor First Reformed Ch., Berwin, Ill., 1968-69; assoc. pastor Ivanhoe Reformed Ch., Riverdale, Ill., 1969-70; libr., prof. theology Western Theol. Seminary, Holland, Mich., 1970-83; dir. libr. svcs., assoc. prof. ch. history Colgate Rochester (N.Y.) Divinty Sch., 1983-92; dir. libr. svcs. St. Bernard's Inst., Rochester, 1983-92; pres. New Brunswick (N.J.) Theol. Seminary, 1993—. Commn. on history, mem. Reformed Ch. in Am., 1969-74; A.J. Muste Meml. lectr. Hope Coll., Holland, Mich., 2000; St. Columba lectr., Oxford U., 2002; lectr. in field. Co-author: Evangelism: The Church's Proclamation, 1988; editor, contbr. (hymnbook) Rejoice in the Lord, 1985; mem. editl. bd. Perspectives, 1997—; contbr. articles to profl. jours. Chair Hist. Adv. Com., Holland, 1970—83; dir. New Brunswick Tomorrow, 1994—; pres. Mercersberg Soc., 2002—. Sealantic fellow Rockefeller Bros. Found., 1968-70, Conant fellow Episc. Ch. in USA, 1989-90; Rabbi Nathan Keller Meml. lectr. Temple Anshe Emeth, New Brunswick, 1995. Democrat. Avocations: book collecting, carpentry, fishing, gardening. Home: 25 Seminary Pl New Brunswick NJ 08901-1107 Office: New Brunswick Theol Seminary 17 Seminary Pl New Brunswick NJ 08901-1107 E-mail: njk@nbts.edu.

KANSTEIMER, WALTER H., II, federal agency administrator; M in Internat. Econ., Am. U.; M in Ethics, Va. Theol. Sem. Founding prin. Scowcroft Group; dir. african affairs Nat. Security Coun.; Africa specialist Sec.'s Policy Planning Staff; mem. strategic minerals task force Dept. of Def.; asst. sec. bur. african affairs U.S. Dept. State, Washington, 2001—. Author: South Africa: Revolution or Reconciliation. Mem.: Ctr. Strategic and Internat. Studies, Coun. Fgn. Rels. (sr. assoc.). Office: US Dept State Bur African Affairs 2201 C St NW Washington DC 20520 Office Fax: 202-647-6301.

KANSTOROOM, DAVID ARNOLD, real estate developer, entrepreneur; b. Washington, Oct. 20, 1964; s. Allen Roy and Sara Eta Kanstoroom; m. Cynthia Marie Martinez, May 19, 1996; children: Summer, Jared. BSBA, U. Fla., Gainesville, 1987, MBA, 1991. V.p. network svcs. W2COM LLC, Dayton, Ohio, 1999-2000; CFO, pres., chmn. bd. dirs. Intelicom Holding Corp., Tampa, Fla., 1991—2002, chief devel. officer U.S. local holdings, 2001—02; pres., chmn. Oasis Custom Homes, 2002—. Actor, stuntman live we. shows, 1978-84. Vol. Muscular Dystrophy Assn., Gainesville, Fla., 1984-89; pres. Bayport Colony Home Owners Assn., Tampa, 1999—; mem. Tampa Bay Performing Arts Ctr. Mem. Telecom Agent Assn., Ascent Assn. Comm. Enterprises, Tampa Bay C. of C., Sigma Chi (chmn. fundraising 1986-87, scholar 1987). Republican. Jewish. Avocations: football, basketball, boating, travel, snow skiing. Home: 10404 Double Bayou Way Tampa FL 33615 Fax: 813-854-4350. E-mail: dak1@tampabay.rr.com.

KANT, GLORIA JEAN, retired neuroscientist, researcher; b. Chgo., June 6, 1944; d. Hans Georg and Jo Sefa Kant; m. Philip Herbert Balcom, July 1, 1967 (div. 1976). BS in Chemistry, Mich. State U., 1965; PhD in Physiol. Chemistry, U. Wis., 1969. Chemist dept. psychiatry Walter Reed Army Inst. Rsch., Washington, 1970-71, neurochemist dept. microwave rsch., 1971-77, neurochemist dept. med. neurosci., 1977-87, chief dept. med. neurosci., 1987-95, dir. divsn. neurosci., 1995—2001; ret. Mem. editl. bd. Pharmacology, Biochemistry and Behavior, 1991—; contbr. over 80 articles to sci. jours. Mem. AAAS, Soc. for Neurosci., Internat. Behavioral Neurosci. Soc., Women in Neurosci. Avocation: golf. Home: 1124 Dennis Ave Silver Spring MD 20901-2171

KANT, LAURENCE HAROLD, religion historian; b. Brookline, Mass., Jan. 15, 1956; s. Arthur and Charlotte (Kaplan) K.; m. Dianne Marie Bazell. BA magna cum laude, Tufts U., 1978; MTS, Harvard U., 1981; MA, Yale U., 1983, PhD, 1993. Lectr. Cornell U., 1991-92, asst. prof. dept. Near Ea. studies and religious studies, 1992-95; asst. prof. divsn. humanities York U., North York, Ont., Can., 1995-96; vis. scholar dept. Nr. Ea. studies Cornell U., Ithaca, N.Y., 1996-97. Adj. prof. New Testament Greek Lexington Theol. Sem., 2000—01, vis. prof., 2001—02, asst. prof. religious studies, 2003—; chair Wisdom in the Pub. Sq., 2001—; presenter in field. Contbr. articles to profl. jours. Meml. Found. for Jewish Cultural doctoral dissertation fellow, 1987-88, Josephine de Kármán fellow for excellence in humanities, 1988-89, Deutscher Akademischer Austauschdienst fellow Goethe Inst. Berlin, summer 1988. Fellow Am. Acad. Rome (Rome prize in classics 1986-87); mem. Am. Acad. Religion, Am. Hist. Assn., Am. Philol. Assn., Arch. Inst. Am., Assn. Jewish Studies, N.Am. Patristic Soc., Soc. Ancient Historian, Soc. Biblical Lit., Soc. for Promotion Roman Studies. Office: Lexington Theol Sem 631 S Limestone Lexington KY 40508

KANTAR, ANDREW K. literature educator; b. Mpls., May 20, 1952; s. Bruce Leo and Sally (Dolf) Kantar; m. Fran Keleher, 1980; children: Sally Rebekah, Max Brendan, Emily Beth. BS with high distinction, U. Minn., 1975, MA, 1982, PhD, 1988. Prof. English Ferris State U., Big Rapids, Mich., 1986—. Fulbright scholar, English prof. Norwegian Inst. Sci. and Tech., Trondheim, Norway, 1991—93. Author: 29 Missing: The True and Tragic Story of the Disappearance of the S.S. Edmund Fitzgerald, 1998, (play) Brisket for Six, 2002; contbg. author: reference book Continuum Encyclopedia of Children's Literature. Sr. Fulbright Lectureship, Coun. for Internat. Exch. Scholars, 1991. Home: 18970 Winding Brook Rd Big Rapids MI 49307 Office: Ferris State Univ 820 Campus Dr ASC 3070 Big Rapids MI 49307

KANTER, CARL IRWIN, retired lawyer; b. Jersey City, Feb. 17, 1932; s. Morris and Beatrice (Wilson) K.; m. Gail Herman, Nov. 27, 1963; children—Deborah, David, Andrew, Aaron AB, Harvard U., 1953, LL.B., 1956. Bar: Calif. 1956, N.Y. 1959. Assoc. Stroock & Stroock & Lavan, N.Y.C., 1959-67, ptnr., 1967-92; sr. v.p., co-gen. counsel Merck-Medco Managed Care L.L.C., Montvale, N.J., 1992-97, spl. counsel, 1997-99; ret. Served with U.S. Army, 1957-58 Home: 19 Tompkins Rd Scarsdale NY 10583-2839 E-mail: kanterart@yahoo.com.

KANTER, L. ERICK, public relations executive; b. New Ulm, Tex., Dec. 15, 1942; s. Lawrence and Wilma A. (Kellner) K.; m. Mary Anne Meadows, Feb. 28, 1970. Staff reporter, Newsweek Mag., Houston, 1965-66, Newsweek Mag., Boston, 1970-71. Dir. media rels. U.S. Pay Bd. and Cost of Living Coun., Washington, 1971-74; dep. dir. pub. affairs NOAA, Washington, 1974-77; dir. pub. affairs White House Conf. on Econ. Devel., Washington, 1977-78, Presdl. Commn. on Coal Industry, Washington, 1978-80; cons. Energy Concepts, Inc., Washington, 1980-84; v.p. pub. info. and mktg. Investment Co. Inst., Washington, 1984-95; with Kanter & Assocs., Arlington, Va., 1995—. Co-author: Four Days, Forty Hours, 1970; editor: Final Report, White House Conference, 1978, Final Report, President's Commission on Coal, 1979. Lt. (j.g.) USN, 1967-69, Vietnam, the Pentagon. Mem. Nat. Press Club, Soc. Profl. Journalists, U.S. Navy Pub. Affairs Alumni Assn. Avocations: photography, fishing. Office: Kanter & Assocs 5313 Lee Hwy 2d Fl Arlington VA 22207-1607

KANTER, SEYMOUR, lawyer; b. Phila., Feb. 4, 1931; s. William and Elizabeth (Huberman) K.; m. Rhoda Rosen, Aug. 19, 1956; children: Cynthia, Gregg, Lawrence, Brad. BS, Temple U., 1953; LLB, U. Pa., 1956. Bar: Pa. 1957, U.S. Dist. Ct. (ea. dist.) Pa. 1957, U.S. Supreme Ct. 1965, U.S. Ct. Appeals (3rd cir.) 1980. Ptnr. Halbert & Kanter, Phila., 1958-74; sr. ptnr. Kanter, Bernstein, & Kardon, Phila., 1974—. Contbr. articles to profl. jours. Bd. dirs. Melrose (Pa.) Park Improvement Assn., Pa., 1967-72, Greater Basketball Assn., Melrose, 1966-70, Melrose Park Town Watch (treas. 1994-2000). Mem. ABA, Phila. Bar Assn. (chmn. fee disputes com. 1984, 87-91), Acad. of Advocacy (faculty 1981, 84), Pa. Bar Assn., Phila. Trial Lawyers Assn., Pa. Trial Lawyers Assn., Assn. Trial Lawyers Am., Pine Tree Rifle Club (sec., treas. 1970-75). Democrat. Jewish. Home: 1420 Locust St Apt 35K Philadelphia PA 19102-4222

KANTOR, FREDERICK WILLIAM, physicist; b. N.Y.C., July 19, 1942; s. Harry S. and Anne (Golden) K. AB, Columbia U., 1964, PhD in Physics, 1973. Ind. physicist, N.Y.C., 1973—. Founder Info. Mechanics. Author: Information Mechanics, also numerous publs. and computer programs. Mem. AAAS, Am. Phys. Soc. Achievements include patents in electronics, thermodynamics, vision, water pollution control, x-ray optics. Home: 523 W 112 St New York NY 10025-1619

KANTOR, HAL HALPERIN, lawyer; b. Chgo., Apr. 4, 1945; s. Philip and Jacqueline (Halperin) K.; m. Linda Schneider, Aug. 25, 1968; children: Lori, Jonathan. BBA, Tulane U., 1967; MBA, U. Calif.-Berkeley, 1969; JD U. Fla., 1972. Bar: Fla. 1972, U.S. Dist. Ct. (mid. dist.) Fla. 1972. Ptnr., Lowndes, Drosdick, Doster, Kantor & Reed P.A., Orlando, Fla., 1972—. Contbr. chpt. to book. Editor-in-chief U. Fla. Law Rev., 1971, The Briefs, 1974. Mem. Mcpl. Planning Bd., Orlando, 1975-79; chmn. Devel. Rev. Com., Orlando, 1975-79, Econ. Devel. Task Force, Orlando, 1980—; bd. dirs. Orlando Regional Med. Ctr., Fla. Symphony Orch.; mem. Leadership Fla. Mem. The Scribes (chmn.), Fla. Planning & Zoning Assn., Fla. Waterworks Assn., Phi Delta Phi. Democrat. Jewish. Club: Citrus. Office: Lowndes Drosdick Doster Kantor & Reed PA 215 N Eola Dr Orlando FL 32801-2095

KANTOR, HARVEY SHERWIN, retired medical educator; b. N.Y.C., Apr. 30, 1938; s. Jack and Henrietta (Feingold) K.; m. Elvia Frostick, Nov. 8, 1992; stepchildren: Harold, Eric Frostick. Student, U. Miami, 1955-58; MD, Washington U., 1962; postgrad., MIT, 1967-69. Diplomate Am. Bd. Internal Medicine, Am. Bd. Pathology certification in Medical Microbiology, Am. Bd. Infectious Diseases. Instr. U. Miami Sch. Medicine, 1969-71; asst. prof. medicine and microbiology U. Ill. Sch. Medicine, Chgo., 1971-75; assoc. prof. medicine and pathology Chgo. Med. Sch., North Chgo., Ill., 1975—93; dir. divsn. infectious diseases VA Med. Ctr., North Chicago, 1975-85, chief med. microbiology, 1985-92; prof. internal medicine Tex. Tech. U. Health Sci. Ctr., Odessa, 1993—2002, dir. divsn. infectious diseases, 1993—2002, interim chmn. dept. internal medicine, 2000—02; ret., 2002. Contbr. chpts. to textbooks, articles to profl. jours. Capt. U.S. Army, 1964-66. Recipient NIH postdoctoral fellowship in infectious diseases New Eng. Med. Ctr. Hosp., Boston, 1966-69, U. Health Scis./Chgo. Med. Sch. Bd. Trustees Rsch. award, 1977. Fellow ACP, Infectious Diseases Soc. Am.; mem. Am. Soc. Microbiology, Soc. Hosp. Epidemiology in Am. Avocations: cooking, photography, computers. E-mail: hkantormd@yahoo.com.

KANTOR, IGO, film and television producer; b. Vienna, Aug. 18, 1930; came to U.S., 1947; s. Samuel and Miriam (Sommerfreund) K.; m. Enid Lois Dershewitz, June 24, 1962; children: Loren, Mark, Lisa. AA, UCLA, 1950, BS, 1952, MS in Polit. Sci., 1954. Fgn. corr. Portuguese Mag. Flama, L.A., 1949-57; music supr., editor Screen Gems, Columbia, L.A., 1954 63; post-prodn. supr. various ind. cos. L.A., 1963-64; music supr.-editor Universal-MCA, L.A., 1964-66; pres., film editor Synchrofilm, Inc., L.A., 1966-74; pres., producer Duque Films, Inc., L.A., 1971-78; ind. producer Jerry Lewis Films, Film Ventures, L.A., 1979-84; pres., producer Laurelwood Prodns. Inc., L.A., 1984-87, Major Arts Corp., L.A., 1987—. Pres. Jubilee Holding Co., L.A., 1988—. Producer Legends of the West with Jack Palance (TV spl. series), 1992, United We Stand, 1988, Act of Piracy, 1987, The Golden Eagle Awards, 1986, It's A Wonderful World, 1986, The Grand Tour, 1985, Shaker Run, 1984, From Hawaii with Love, 1983, Night Shadows, 1983, Kill and Kill Again, 1981, Hardly Working, 1980, Good Luck, Miss Wyckoff, 1979, Holiday Classic Cartoons, 1994, Mom USA, 1996 (feature) Crazy Girls Undercover; writer, prodr., dir. Scope, 1999—. Named Emmy nominee, 1967, 68, 69, 70. Mem. Acad. Motion Picture Arts & Scis. (exec. sound bd. 1969-71), Dirs. Guild Am. (assoc. dir.). Democrat. Jewish. Avocations: swimming, chess, ping-pong, philately, collecting movie classics. Office: Major Arts Corp 11501 Duque Dr North Hollywood CA 91604-4279 Address: PO Box 1340 Studio City CA 91614-0340 E-mail: i.kantor@verizon.net.

KANTOR, ISAAC NORRIS, lawyer; b. Charleston, W.Va., Aug. 29, 1929; s. Israel and Rachel (Cohen) K.; m. Doris Sue Katz, June 17, 1956; children: Mark B., Cynthia Kantor Kraft, Beth Kantor Zachwieja. BA, Va. Mil. Inst., 1953; JD, W.Va. U., 1956. Bar: W.Va. 1956, U.S. Dist. Ct. (so. dist.) W.Va. 1956, U.S. Ct. Mil. Appeals 1957, U.S. Ct. Appeals (4th cir.) 1978, U.S. Dist. Ct. (no. dist.) W.Va. 1991, U.S. Ct. Fed. Claims 1996. Ptnr Katz Katz and Kantor, Bluefield, W.Va., 1958-70, Katz Kantor Katz Perkins and Cameron, Bluefield, W.Va., 1970-82, Katz Kantor and Perkins, Bluefield, 1982—. Town atty. Town of Bramwell, W.Va., 1970-75, Town of Petestown, W.Va., 1981-85; bd. dirs. First Cmty. Bank, First Cmty. Bancshares Inc., Bluefield, Va.; mem. vis. com. W.Va. U. Coll. Law, Morgantown, 1986-89; mem. dean's adv. coun. Appalachian Sch. of Law, Grundy, Va., 1998—. Parliamentarian W.Va. Dem. Exec. Com., 1964-68; co-chmn. W.Va. Gov.'s Jud. Selection Com., 1988-97; chmn. W.Va. Ethics Commn., 1998-2000; chmn. W.Va. divsn. Am. Cancer Soc., 1990-92, pres. New River Pkwy. Authority, 1996—; mem. adv. bd., chmn. Bluefield State Coll., 1997-2001, chmn. bd. govs. 2001—; vice-chair Governmental Affairs Bluefield C. of C., 1999-01; chmn. of bd., Greater Bluefield C. of C., 2002; chmn. Mercer County W.Va. Dem. Exec. Comm., 1966-70. Capt. JAGC, USAF, 1956-58; mem. USAFR, 1953-61. Paul Harris fellow Rotary Internat., 1999; recipient Citizen of Yr. award Greater Bluefield Jaycees, 1980, Boss of Yr. award, 1992, St. George medal, Nat. Divsnl. award Am. Cancer Soc., 1993. Mem. W.Va. Trial Lawyers Assn. (pres. 1980-81), B'nai B'rith (pres. W.Va. coun. 1975-76), Rotary Internat. Jewish. Avocations: golf, reading, travel, civic activities. Home: 231 Oakdell Ave Bluefield WV 24701-4840 Office: PO Box 727 Bluefield WV 24701-0727

KANTOR, JAMES GRAHAM, music educator, composer; b. Norwalk, Conn., Nov. 22, 1967; s. Geza and Barbara Kantor. MusB in Music Edn., Westminster Choir Coll., 1989, MusM in Conducting, 1990; MusD in Conducting, U. Ariz., 1997. Cert. Prekindergarten-12 tchr. Conn. Dir. of music French Am. Sch. of NY, Larchmont, 1993—95; head of fine arts Ridgefield (Conn.) Acad., 2000—. Condr. Norwalk Chorale, 1993—94. Composer: (composition for orchestra, chorus and ch) Venite Adoramus, 1997 (Commd. by the Reading Choral Soc.). Sponsor Interfaith Hospitality Network, Stamford, Conn., 1993—95. Mem.: Conn. Music Educator's Assn., Am. Choral Director's Assn., Pi Lambda Theta. Home: 3 Spruce Mountain Trail Miry Brook CT 06810 Office: Ridgefield Acad 223A West Mountain Rd Ridgefield CT 06877 Personal E-mail: jkantor@aol.com. E-mail: jkantor@ridgefieldacademy.com.

KANTOR, MARY LOUISE, music educator; d. Randall None and Jean Elizabeth Phillips; m. Michael Bruce Kantor, Feb. 15, 1974; children: Michael David, Jennifer Anne. BA in Music, U. Wash., 1980; Artist's Diploma, Acad. of Music and Performing Arts, Vienna, Austria, 1974. Applied music instr. Seattle U., 1986—92; clarinet instr. Northshore Sch. Dist., Kenmore, Wash., 1987—97; clarinet coach Seattle Youth Symphony, Seattle, Cascade Youth Symphony, Lynnwood, Wash.; adj. prof. of clarinet Seattle Pacific U., Seattle. Prin. clarinet Seattle Choral Co., Seattle, 1982—; clarinetist The Mazeltones, Seattle, 1983—87, Ensemble Vindobona, Seattle, 1996—, Shalom Ensemble, Seattle, 1996—; prin. clarinet Bellevue Philharm., Bellevue, Wash. Musician: (soloist) Clarinet Concerto by W.A. Mozart, Duet-Concertino for Clarinet and Bassoon by Richard Strauss; contbr. articles various profl. jours. Recipient Honors in Clarinet Performance, Acad. of Music in Vienna, 1974. Mem.: Music Educator's Nat. Conf., Internat. Clarinet Assn. Democrat-Npl. Christian. Avocations: cooking, yoga, mycology.

KANTOR, MEL LEWIS, dental educator, researcher; b. N.Y.C., 1956; s. Irving and Sarah Kantor. BA in Chemistry and Math., CUNY, 1977; DDS, U. N.C., 1981; MPH, U. Medicine and Dentistry N.J., Rutgers U., 1999. Diplomate Am. Bd. Oral and Maxillofacial Radiology. Resident Hennepin County Med. Ctr., Mpls., 1981-82, U. Conn. Health Ctr., Farmington, 1982-84; asst. prof. U. N.C. Sch. Dentistry, Chapel Hill, 1984-88, U. Conn. Sch. of Dental Medicine, Farmington, 1988-92; assoc. prof. N.J. Dental Sch., U. Medicine and Dentistry

N.J., Newark, 1993—2003; prof. N.J. Dental Sch. Um. Medicine and Dentistry, Newark, 2003—; clin. assoc. prof. N.J. Med. Sch. U. Medicine and Dentistry N.J., Newark, 1993-2000; health svcs. rsch. fellow Robert Wood Johnson Med. Sch., 1997-99. Cons. dental selection criteria panel FDA, 1985-87; test constructor Nat. Bd. Dental Exams., 1989-93, 96-99, 2002--; bd. dirs. Acad. Radiology Rsch., 2000—, Am. Bd. Oral and Maxillofacial Radiology, 2001—. Assoc. editor Jour. Dental Edn., 1986-2001, Radiology, 2003—; mem. editl. bd. Dentomaxillofacial Radiology, 1997—, Oral Surgery. Oral Pathology, Oral Medicine, Oral Radiology and Endodntics, 2003—; contbr. articles to Jour. Chem. Physics, Jour. ADA, Jour. Dental Rsch., Oral Surgery, Oral Medicine and Oral Pathology, Jour. Dental Edn., Dentomaxillofacial Radiology. Mem. Internat. Assn. Dental Rsch. (founding mem. diagnostic sys. group, group program chmn. 1993-97), Am. Acad. Oral and Maxillofacial Radiology (chair consitution and bylaws com., rsch. and tech. com.), Am. Assn. Dental Schs., Internat. Assn. Dentomaxillofacial Radiology, Radiol. Soc. N.Am., Soc. for Med. Decision Making, Soc. for Health Svcs. Rsch. in Radiology, Phi Beta Kappa, Sigma Xi, Omicron Kappa Upsilon. Office: UMDNJ-NJ Dental Sch 110 Bergen St Rm D860 Newark NJ 07101-1709

KANTOR, PAUL, information scientist, educator; b. Washington, Nov. 27, 1938; s. Harry S. and Anne (Golden) K.; m. Carole Kaplowitz, Feb., 1962; children: Michael, David. AB, Columbia U., 1959; PhD in Physics, Princeton U., 1963. Rsch. assoc. Brookhaven Nat. Lab., 1963-65; vis. asst. prof. physics SUNY, Stonybrook, 1965-67; asst. prof. physics Case-Western Res. U., 1967-68, assoc. prof. physics, 1968-72, program dir. Complex Systems Inst., lectr. systems engring., 1973; pres. Tantalus Inc., 1975—; mem. Ctr. for Ops. Rsch. Rutgers. U., 1990—, prof. Sch. Comm. Info. and Libr. Studies, 1991—; mem. DIMACS Ctr. for Discrete Math. and Computer Scis., 2002—. Disting. vis. scholar Online Computer Libr. Ctr., 1987, vis. prof. info. systems Rutgers U., 1990; mem. Ctr. for Discrete Math. and Computer Scis., 2002—; cons. in field. Contbr. articles to profl. jours. in physics, info. sci., mgmt. sci. Fulbright Rsch. scholar Oslo, Norway, 2000. Fellow AAAS; mem. IEEE, Am. Soc. Info. Sci.(Asst. Rsch. award), Am. Statis. Assn., Inst. for Ops. Rsch. and Mgmt. Scis. Home: 362 N 4th Ave Highland Park NJ 08904-2742 Office: SCILS Rutgers U 4 Huntington St New Brunswick NJ 08901-1071 E-mail: paul.kantor@ieee.org.

KANTOR, SIMON WILLIAM, chemistry educator; b. Brussels, Mar. 23, 1925; came to U.S., 1939, naturalized, 1946; s. Joseph Uszer and Josephine (Perez) K.; m. Karen Christine Duncan, 1989; children from previous marriage: Michael Bruce, Sharon Inez; stepchildren: Michael John Eisenbeiser, Jason James Eisenbeiser, Justin Ryan Eisenbeiser. BS, City Coll. N.Y., 1945; PhD, Duke U., 1949. Postdoctoral fellow Duke U., 1949-51; research asso. GE R & D Ctr., Schenectady, 1951-60, sect. mgr., 1960-65, br. mgr., 1965-72; v.p. R & D. GAF Corp., Wayne, N.J., 1972-82; prof. chemistry U. Mass., Amherst, 1982-2000, prof. emeritus, 2000—. Contbr. articles to chem. jours.; patentee in field. Mem. Am. Chem. Soc., AAAS, Soc. Chem. Industry, Indsl. Research Inst., Phi Beta Kappa, Phi Lambda Upsilon. Home: 153 Silver Lake Dr Agawam MA 01001-2351 E-mail: swkantor@polysci.umass.edu.

KANTROWITZ, ADRIAN, surgeon, educator; b. N.Y.C., Oct. 4, 1918; s. Bernard Abraham and Rose (Esserman) K.; m. Jean Rosensaft, Nov. 25, 1948; children: Niki, Lisa, Allen. AB, NYU, 1940; MD, L.I. Coll. Medicine, 1943; postgrad. physiology, Western Res. U., 1950. Diplomate: Am. Bd. Surgery, Am. Bd. Thoracic Surgery. Gen. rotating intern Jewish Hosp. Bklyn., 1944; asst. resident, then resident surgery Mt. Sinai Hosp., N.Y.C., 1947; asst. resident Montefiore Hosp., N.Y.C., 1948, asst. resident pathology, 1949, fellow cardiovascular rsch. group, 1949, chief resident surgery, 1950, adj. surg. svc., 1951-55; USPHS fellow cardiovascular rsch., dept. physiology Western Res. U., 1951-52; asst. prof. surgery SUNY Coll. Medicine, 1955-56, assoc. prof. surgery, 1957-64, prof., 1964-70; dir. cardiovascular surgery Maimonides Med. Ctr., Bklyn., 1955-64, dir. surgery, 1964-70; chmn. dept. surgery Sinai Hosp. Detroit, 1970-75, chmn. dept. cardiovascular surgery, 1975-85; prof. surgery Wayne State U. Sch. Medicine, 1970—. Contbr. articles profl. jours. 1st lt. to capt., M.C. AUS, 1944-46. Recipient H.L. Moses prize to Montefiore Alumnus for outstanding rsch. accomplishment, 1949; 1st prize sci. exhibit Conv. N.Y. State Med. Soc., 1952; Gold Plate award Am. Acad. Achievement, 1966; Max Berg award for outstanding achievement in prolonging human life, 1966; Theodore and Susan B. Cummings humanitarian award Am. Coll. Cardiology, 1967 Fellow ACS, N.Y. Acad. Sci.; mem. Internat. Soc. Angiology, Am. Soc. Artificial Internal Organs (pres. 1968-69, Barney Clark award 1993), N.Y. County Med. Soc., Harvey Soc., N.Y. Soc. Thoracic Surgery, N.Y. Soc. Cardiovascular Surgery, Am. Heart Assn., Am. Physiol. Soc., Am. Coll. Cardiology, Am. Coll. Chest Physicians, Bklyn. Thoracic Surgery Soc. (pres. 1967-68), Pan Am. Med. Assn., Soaring Soc. Am., Am. Ski Assn. Achievements include being pub. pioneer motion pictures taken inside living heart, 1950; contbr. to devel. pump- oxygenators for human heart surgey; pioneer devel. mech., artificial hearts; performed 1st permanent partial mech. heart surgery in humans, 1966; 1st use phase-shift intra-aortic balloon pump in patient in cardiogenic shock; 1st human heart transplant in U.S., Dec. 1967. Home: 70 Gallogly Rd Auburn Hills MI 48326-1227 Office: 300 River Place Dr Detroit MI 48207-4233 E-mail: adriank3ak@aol.com.

KANTROWITZ, JEAN, health products executive; b. Passaic, N.J., May 27, 1922; d. Nathan and Yetta (Applebaum) Rosensaft; m. Adrian Kantrowitz, Nov. 25, 1948; children: Niki, Lisa, Allen. BS, Rider Coll., 1942; MS, U. N.C., 1945; MPH, U. Mich., 1975. Adminstrv. asst. Maimonides Med. Ctr., Bklyn., 1961-70, Sinai Hosp., Detroit, 1970-78, '80-83; program coord., sr. clin. instr. child psyciatry divsn. Case Western Res. U. Sch. Medicine, Cleve., 1978-80; v.p., adminstrv. mgr. L.VAD Tech., Inc., Detroit, 1983—. Mgmt. cons. NIH, Washington, 1974— Mem. Am. Soc. Artificial Internal Organs (co-chairperson project bionics, history work group). Home: 70 Gallogly Rd Auburn Hills MI 48326-1227 Office: LVAD Tech Inc 300 River Place Dr Ste 6850 Detroit MI 48207-5095

KANTROWITZ, JONATHAN DANIEL, educational publishing and services company executive, lawyer; b. Bridgeport, Conn., Apr. 14, 1945; s. Ralph Samson and Beatrice (Schine) K.; m. Monica Victoria Fractenberg, Dec. 26, 1970; children: Bethany Eve, Ralph Richard. BA, Brown U., 1966; JD, Harvard U., 1969. Bar: Conn. 1969, N.Y. 1980. Ptnr. Kantrowitz & Kantrowitz, Bridgeport, 1969-74; atty. So. New Eng. Tel. Co., New Haven, 1975-76; asst. gen. counsel Touche Ross & Co., N.Y.C., 1977-81; founder, CEO Queue, Inc., Fairfield, Conn., 1981—. Adj. prof. Sch. Law Bridgeport, 1978-82. Author ednl. software Algebra Word Problems, 1984, How a Bill Becomes a Law, 1985. Vice chmn. Fairfield County Dem. Town Com., 1991-93, 96-2000; Dem. candidate for State Senate, 1972, 88, for U.S. Congress, 1994, 98; coach, mem. adv. bd. Fairfield Youth Soccer, 1985-90; coach Fairfield Little League, 1987, Joel Barlow H.S. Girls Varsity Soccer, 1991; mem. Fairfield Bd. Edn., 1991-93; chmn. bd. trustees Jewish Family Svcs., 1995-99; pres. bd. dirs. The Bridge Acad., 1997-99; mem. Fairfield Bd. Parks and Recreation, 1997-98; founder, pres. bd. Brooklawn Acad., 1998-99. Jewish. Avocations: soccer, tennis, biking, kayaking, books. Office: Queue Inc 1450 Barnum Ave Bridgeport CT 06610

KANTROWITZ, PAUL ALAN, gastroenterologist; b. Bklyn., July 10, 1933; s. Abraham R. and Anna A. (Abroff) K.; m. Judy Leopold, Feb. 1, 1959; children: Stephen D., Amy J., Jeffrey E. (dec.). BA with honors, Swarthmore Coll., 1954; MD, Columbia U., 1958. Diplomate Am. Bd. Internal Medicine, Am. Bd. Gastroenterology. Intern Mt. Sinai Hosp., N.Y.C., 1958-59, resident in pathology, 1959-60; asst. resident in medicine Boston City Hosp., 1962-63, Mass. Gen. Hosp., Boston, 1963-64, fellow in gastroenterology, 1964-66, asst. in medicine, 1966-67; instr. in medicine Harvard Med. Sch., Boston, 1967-69, asst. clin. prof. medicine, 1969—; asst. physician Mount Auburn Hosp., Cambridge, Mass., 1967-70, assoc. physician, 1970-73, chief gastroenterology, 1973—. Pres. med. staff Mount Auburn Hosp., 1991-92; mem. sci. adv. bd. Nat. Found. for Ileitis and Colitis, Boston, 1975-80; lectr., vis. prof., mem. faculty postgrad. courses at various instns., 1967—; tech. cons. gastroenterology Harvard Resource Based Relative Value Scale Study, 1988-92; invited mem. Diagnostic and Therapeutic Tech. Assessment Program, AMA, 1986—. Contbr. numerous articles to profl. jours. Elected mem. Brookline (Mass.) Town Meeting, 1974-86; mem. Emergency Med. Svcs. Rev. Com., Brookline, 1978-88. Capt. Med. Corps USAR, 1960-62. Fellow ACP; mem. Am. Gastroenterol. Assn. (Disting. Clinician award 2003), Am. Soc. for Gastrointestinal Endoscopy (councillor 1982-86, chmn. editl. bd. 1990-96, Disting. Svc. award 1992). Jewish. Avocations: travel, photography, music. Office: Mount Auburn Gastroenterol Assoc 300 Mount Auburn St Ste 404 Cambridge MA 02138-5600

KANTSYREV, VICTOR LEONIDOVICH, physicist; b. Moscow, Oct. 17, 1947; s. Leonid Petrovich and Vasilisa Petrovna (Kushnarenko) K. MS, Moscow Phys. Engring. Inst., 1972, PhD, 1981; DSc, Russian Acad. Sci., 1992. Rschr., tchg. asst. Moscow Phys. Engring. Inst., 1972-81; sr. sci. rschr., head of sector Rsch. Sci. Inst. Volna, Moscow, 1981-86; assoc. prof. Moscow Inst. Radiotech. Electr. Autom., 1983-91; head of sector, head of lab. Sci. Rsch. inst. Tech. Glass, Moscow, 1986-95; sci.-tech. expert Aviatech, Moscow, 1991-96; vis. scientist, lectr. dept. physics U. Nev., Reno, 1994-96, rsch. prof. dept. physics, 1996—. Contbr. numerous articles to profl. jours.; inventor in fields of x-ray capillary optics, x-ray microscopy, x-ray lithography, X-ray and EUV spectroscopy, Z-pinch, laser plasma x-ray source, others. Monbusho grantee, 1995; CAST grantee, 1995-96. Mem. IEEE, SPIE, Am. Phys. Soc., N.Y. Acad. Sci. Office: U Nev at Reno Physics Dept 220 Reno NV 89557-0001 E-mail: victor@physics.unr.edu.

KANUK, LESLIE LAZAR, management consultant, educator; b. NYC; d. Charles and Sylvia Lazar; m. Jack Lawrence Kanuk; children: Randi Kanuk Dauler, Alan Robert. MBA, Baruch Coll., 1964; PhD, CUNY, 1974; PhD (hon.), Mass. Maritime Acad., 1981, Maine Maritime Acad., 1988. Pres. Leslie Kanuk Assocs., NYC, 1965—78, 1981—; Lippert Disting. chair Baruch Coll., N.Y.C., 1981-84; prof. CUNY, 1981—99, prof. emeritus, 1999—. Bd. dirs. Cleve. Cliffs Inc.; mem. maritime transp. research bd. Nat. Acad. Scis., 1975-78; commr., vice chmn., chmn. Fed. Maritime Commn., 1978-81; chmn., pres., dir. Containerization and Intermodal Inst., 1981-93; panelist NRC-NAS, 1975-78, 91; vis. prof. grad. studies program Maine Maritime Acad., 1984-93. Author: Mail Questionnaire Response Behavior, 1974, Toward an Expanding U.S.M.M., 1976, Consumer Behavior, 1978, rev. edits., 1983, 87, 89, 94, 97, 2000; mem. editl. bd. Intermodal Forum, 1984-92. Trustee United Seamen's Svc., 1988—; bd. visitors Maine Maritime Acad., 1989-97. Recipient Connie award Containerization and Intermodal Inst., 1980, Diamond Superwoman award Harpers Bazaar mag., 1980, Person of Yr. award N.Y. Fgn. Freight Forwarders and Brokers Assn., 1981, Person of Yr. award Baruch Fgn. Trade Soc., 1981, Disting. Alumnus award CCNY, 1984, Disting. PhD Alumni award CUNY, 1988, Townsend Harris medal, 1986. Mem. Beta Gamma Sigma.

KANUTH, JAMES GORDAN, chemical engineer; b. Lexington, Ohio, June 18, 1953; s. John Gordon and Helena Jane (Castor) K.; m. Michelle Susan Cronk, Nov. 10, 2000; 1 child, Robert Gordon. BSChemE, U. Cin., 1976. Project engr. Joseph E. Seagram and Sons, Inc., Lawrenceburg, Ind., 1976-80; prodn. engr. Monsanto (name changed to Conoco), Alvin, Tex., 1980-81; sr. area engr. utilities Conoco (name changed to Oxy Chem), Alvin, 1981-89; regional mgr. Puckorius and Assocs., Inc. indsl. water treatment cons., League City, Tex., 1989-95; indsl. water treatment cons. Chemtreat, Inc., Nassau Bay, Tex., 1995—. Pres. Gulf Coast Energy Conservation Soc., Houston, 1988-89, Galveston County Mcpl. Utility Dist. 3, League City, 1983-88; city councilman City of League city, 1988-94; bd. dirs. Houston Galveston Area Coun., 1991; treas. Clear Lake Area Coun. of Cities, Webster, Tex., 1990-94. Mem. Nat. Assn. Corrosion Engrs. (com. mem. 1989—), Am. Inst. Chem. Engrs., Cooling Tower Inst. (water treatment com. 1981—). Presbyterian. Avocations: boating, reading. Home: 18124 Bal Harbour Dr Houston TX 77058 Office: Chemtreat Inc PO Box 412 League City TX 77574-0412 E-mail: jimk@chemtreat.com.

KANY, JUDY C(ASPERSON), health policy analyst, former state senator; b. June 29, 1937; d. Helmer C. and Florence P. Casperson; m. Robert Kany, Aug. 16, 1958; children: Kristin, Geoffrey, Daniel. BBA, U. Mich., 1959; MPA, U. Maine, Orono, 1976. Mem. Maine Ho. of Reps., 1975-82, Maine Senate, 1982-92; project dir. for health professions regulation Med. Care Devel., Augusta, Maine, 1993-97; mem. task force on health workforce regulation Pew Health Professions Commn., 1994-97; mayor Waterville, Maine, 1988-89; mem. issues and policy adv. com. Citizens Advocacy Ctr., Washington, 1994—; cmty. liaison Amity Found., Tucson, 2003—. Chmn. Maine's Adv. Commn. on Radioactive Waste, 1981-87, Joint Standing Com. Legal Affairs, 1987-88, Joint Standing Com. on State Govt., 1979-82, Joint Standing Com. Energy and Natural Resources, 1983-84, 89-90, Joint Standing Com. Banking and Ins., 1991-92, com. Maine Lakes, 1990-92, adv. com. on accountability to the Maine Health Care Reform Commn., 1994-95; mem. Commn. on Maine's Future, 1976, 87-89. Democrat. Home: 81 Lakeshore Dr PO Box 508 Belgrade Lakes ME 04918-0508 also: PO Box 508 Belgrade Lakes ME 04918-0508 Home: 36832 S Stoney Flower Dr Tucson AZ 85739 E-mail: jkany@aol.com.

KANZEG, DAVID GEORGE, radio station executive; b. Cleve., Apr. 9, 1948; s. George and Ida Marie Ada (Hienz) K. BA, Coll. Wooster (Ohio), 1970; MS, Syracuse (N.Y.) U., 1971; postgrad., SUNY, 1972. Cert. ESL lang. instr. Instr. English Meyer Lang. Ctr., Bogota, Colombia, 1969; grad. teaching asst. Syracuse U., 1971; instr. speech State U. Coll. at Buffalo, N.Y., 1971-73; exec. producer Sta. WCMU-FM Cen. Mich. U., Mt. Pleasant, 1973-76; radio program mgr. Sta. WLRH/Madison County Pub. Libr., Huntsville, Ala., 1976-77; radio program dir. Sta. WOUB-AM-FM Ohio U. Telecommunications, Athens, 1977-83; mgr. programming Sta. WNYC/N.Y. Pub. Radio, N.Y.C., 1983-86; sta. advisor Corp. for Pub. Broadcasting, Cleve., 1978-87; dir. programming Sta. WCPN/Cleve. Pub. Radio, 1987-99, v.p. programming divsn., 1999—2002; cons. Corp. for Pub. Broadcasting Mgmt. Consulting Svc., 1993—; dir. programing for TV, radio and web WCPN/Ideastream, 2002—; sr. dir., sr. dir. of programming WVIZ,903WLPN/Ideastream, 2002. Participant seminars on future pub. radio, San Francisco and Washington, 1984-85; panel mem. Airlie IV Seminar on Art of Radio, N.Y.C., 1983; radio organizer Nat. Assn. Ednl. Broadcasters, Washington, 1976-78; exec. producer Future Forward Nat. Radio Series, 1985. Author: Transit Revisions, 1988, Ever Young: Douglas Moore and the Persistence of Legend, 1993; contbr. articles to publs; author, co-creator website. Mem. Isabella County sub-com. on transp., Mt. Pleasant, Mich., 1975; incorporator Mid-Mich. Opera Assn., Mt. Pleasant, 1975, Tenn. Valley Opera Assn., Hunstville, 1976; mem. media panel Ohio Arts Coun., Columbus, Ohio, 1979-80; active Airlie II Seminar on Art of Radio, 1979. Recipient Tech. Prodn. award Ohio Ednl. Broadcasting, 1980, Ohio State award, 1986. Mem. Ohio Pub. Radio Programming (group chmn. 1978-80), Assn. Inds. in Radio, Sigma Delta Pi. Avocations: roller coasters, opera, traction, bicycling, travel. Home: 16253 Shurmer Rd Cleveland OH 44136-6115 Office: Sta WCPN/Cleve Pub Radio 3100 Chester Ave Ste 300 Cleveland OH 44114-4604

KANZER, LARRY, small business owner, food service director; b. Albany, N.Y., June 13, 1942; s. Sanford and Beatrice Helen (Strick) K.; m. Ginger Sherman, July 13, 1966 (div. 1983); 1 child, Glen Harris; m. Lynn Karen Trost, June 2, 1985. AAS in Culinary Arts, N.Y.C. Community Coll., 1962; Cert. Food Service supr., Auburn U., 1982-83; Master Locksmith, Foley Belsaw Inst., 1985. Food beverage controller Longchamps Restaurants, N.Y.C., 1962-65; dir. food service Laurelcrest Prep. Sch., Bristol, Conn., 1965-69; owner, operator Anze's Place Restaurant, Nashua, N.H., 1969-73; dir. food service Servend-Seilers, Waltham, Mass., 1973-76, Service Systems, Cambridge, Mass., 1976-78, ARA Services, White Plains, N.Y., 1978-88; owner Lots of Lock, Etc., 1988—. Com. chmn. Cub Scouts Am., Nashua, 1977-80; umpire Little League, Nashua, 1978-81; bd. dirs. Pike County C. of C., 2002. Served to sgt. USMCR, 1963-69. Recipient Otto Klitgord Meml. award N.Y.C. Community Coll., Bklyn., 1962, Student Govt. Service award, 1962, Cert. of Merit Jewish War Vets. of U.S., Bronx, N.Y., 1982, Cert. and Publ. Locksmith Ledger, Nat. Locksmith, Cert. Cmty. Svc., Pike County Sheriff's Office. Mem. Rte. 739 Bus. Coun. (treas. 1999, 2000), Pike County C. of C. (bd. dirs. 2002--). Democrat. Avocations: gunsmithing, clock repair, woodworking, antiques, gardening. Office: Lots of Lock Etc Locksmith Shop Hemlock Plz Rt 739 Hawley PA 18428 E-mail: lotslock@ptdprolog.net.

KANZLER, GEORGE, journalist, critic; b. Elizabeth, N.J., Mar. 30, 1939; s. George and Helen (Yorkunas) K.; m. Margaret A. Dudas, Dec. 31, 1978; children; Sarah Ella Dudas-Kanzler. BA, Seton Hall U., 1960; postgrad. Bread Loaf Sch. of English, Middlebury Coll., 1960; MA, NYU, 1969; postgrad., U. Wis., 1972. Reporter, editor Linden (N.J.) Leader, 1961-63; instr., asst. prof. Ibadan (Nigeria) Polytech., 1966-68; writer, pop and jazz critic Star Ledger, Newark, 1968-90, writer, jazz critic, 1990—2002, Newhouse News Svc., Washington, 1975—2002; contbg. editor Hot House Jazz mag., 2002—. Jazz disc jockey We. Nigeria Radio, Ibadan, 1966-68; instr. Essex C.C., Newark, 1970-73; elector Am. Jazz Hall of Fame, 1989—. Author: (TV show) One Wa to Heaven, 1967. Vice pres. bd. dirs. Newark Jazz Festival, 1991-93; vol. U.S Peace Corps., 1966-68. With U.S. Army, 1963-65, Congo. Fellow Newspap Fund, 1972, Music Critics Assn./Smithsonian Inst., 1974. Mem. Nat. Aca Recording Arts and Scis., Friends of Nigeria, Mbari Artists and Writers Clu (sec. pro-tem. 1966-68), Jazz Journalists Assn., N.Y. Jazz Critics Cir. Avoca tions: hiking, unicycling. Home: 406 Marseille Dr Simpsonville SC 2968 E-mail: gkjazz@usa.net.

KANZLER, KATHLEEN PATRICIA, kennel owner; b. Detroit, Apr. 1 1934; d. Vincent William and Helen Elizabeth (Murtagh) McGivney; r Norbert Alvin Kanzler, Dec. 21, 1954; children: Patricia, John, Sheila. Assoc in Animal Scis., Mich. State U., 1954. Owner Innisfree Kennel, Chateauga N.Y., 1948—; instr. Ecology Ferguson Found., Accokeek, Md., 1974-80. Judg Am. Kennel Club, 1970—; chair Morris Animal Found., Englewood, Colo 1986—98; cons. for episode on arctic dogs TV show Northern Exposure, 198 cons. mag. articles Nat. Geographic, 1986; hon. judge Japan Kennel Clu 1990—; internat. lectr. and judge on kennel mgmt. Author: A New Owner Guide to Siberian Huskies, 1996; author mag. column AKC Gazette, 199 2000; contbr. chpt. to: The Complete Siberian Husky, 1978, Medical ar Genetic Aspects of Purebred Dogs, 1983; contbr. articles to jours. in fiel Docent Nat. Zoo, 1970-73. Recipient Best in Show award Westminster Kenn Club, 1980, Asian Internat. Dog Show, 1996, Number One Siberian Husk Show Dog, 1992, 93, 97, Best in Show award Asian Internat. Dog Show, 199 Pedigree award for number one breed dog, 1997; named Breeder of Y Mexican Kennel Club, 1984. Mem.: Am. Kennel Club (apptd. del. 199 Siberian Husky Club (v.p. 1961—, Top Breeder award 1985, 1988, 1991—9 1996—2001, 63 Best in Show awards). Home and Office: Innisfree 94 Ryan F Chateaugay NY 12920-1711

KAO, CHARLES KUEN, electrical engineer, educator; b. Shanghai, Nov. 1933; s. Chun-Hsien and Tisung Fong K.; m. May Wan Wong, Sept. 19, 195 children— Simon M.T., Amanda M.C. B.Sc. in Elec. Engring., U. Londo 1957, PhD in Elec. Engring., 1965. Devel. engr. Standard Telephones & Cabl Ltd., London, 1957—60; prin. rsch. engr. Std. Telecomm. Lab. Ltd., Harlo England, 1960—70; prof. electronics, chmn. dept. Chinese U. Hong Kon 1970—74, vice chancellor, 1987—96; chief scientist Electro Optical Produc div./ITT, Roanoke, Va., 1974—81, v.p., dir. engring., 1981—83; exec. scienti dir. research ITT Advanced Tech. Ctr., Shelton, Conn., 1983—87; chmn., CE ITX Svcs. Ltd., Hong Kong, 2000—. Author: Optical Fiber Technology 1981, Optical Fibers Systems: Technology, Design and Applications, 198 Optical Fibre, 1988, A Choice Fulfilled--The Business of High Technolog 1991; contbr. articles to profl. jours.; patentee in field. Decorated Commdr. Br Empire, 1993; recipient Morey award Am. Ceramic Soc., 1976, Stewa Ballantine medal Franklin Inst., 1977, Rank prize Rank Trust Funds, 1978, L Ericsson Internat. prize, 1979, gold medal Armed Forces Comm. and Electro ics Assn., 1980, Internat. C & C prize Found. for C & C Promotion, Japa 1987, New Materials prize Am. Phys. Soc., 1989, Gold medal Internat. Soc. f Optical Engring., 1992, Japan prize The Sci. and Tech. Found. Japan, 199 Marconi Internat. fellow, 1985. Fellow: IEEE (Morris Liebmann Meml. awa 1978, Alexander Graham Bell medal 1985, Faraday medal 1989), Royal Aca Engring. (U.K.), Royal Soc. (U.K.), Chinese Acad. Scis.; mem.: NAE (M.S Charles Stark Draper prize 1999), Academia Sinica (Taiwan), Royal Swedi Acad. Engring. Scis. (fgn.). Office: Unit 1708 Office Tower 1 Harbor Rd Wa Chai Hong Kong Hong Kong

KAO, HUI-SHENG, mathematics educator; s. Yi-Lan Liu. MA in Math Queens Coll., CUNY, 2002; BS in Horticulture, Nat. Chung-Hsing U Taichung, Taiwan, 1999. Mem.: Am. Math. Soc. (corr.). Home: 35-15 167 Flushing NY 11358 Personal E-mail: pieceofmath@aol.com.

KAO, JOHN STERLING, mathematician, educator; b. Salt Lake City, Au 30, 1967; s. Shih Kung and Yasuko Watanabe Kao. BS, U. Utah, 1985; M. Princeton U., 1987, PhD, 1991. Asst. prof. U. San Francisco, 1991—97, assc prof., 1997—. Vis. assoc. prof. Princeton (N.J.) U., 1998—99. Assoc. edit Advances and Applications in Statistics, 2002—; contbr. articles to profl. jou Grad. fellow, NSF, 1985—91. Mem.: Math. Assn. Am., Inst. for Ops. Rsch. a the Mgmt. Scis., Soc. for Indsl. and Applied Math., Am. Math. Soc., Phi Be Kappa, Golden Key. Office: Univ San Francisco 2130 Fulton St San Francis CA 94117-1080

KAO, RACE LI-CHAN, medical educator; b. Chungking, China, Dec. 1943; s. Yu-Ho and Tsing (Tsou) K.; m. Lidia Wei Liu, Aug. 18, 1969; childre Elizabeth, Grace. BS, Nat. Tawian U., 1965; MS, U. Ill., 1971, PhD, 197 Rsch. assoc. U. Ill., Urbana, 1972, Pa. State U., Hershey, 1972-75, asst. pr physiology, 1976-77; asst. prof. surgery, psysiology, biophys. U. Tex. Med. B Galveston, 1977-82, dir. cardiothoracic rsch., 1977-82; assoc. prof. surge Washington U., St. Louis, 1982-83; dir. surg. rsch. Allegheny-Singer Rsc Inst., Pitts., 1983-92; prof. surgery Med. Coll. Pa., Phila., 1988-92; pro Carroll H. Long chair of excellence surg. rsch. East Tenn. State U., Johns City, 1992—. Reviewer, cons. Nat. Heart, Blood and Lung Inst., NIH, 1984- Contbr. numerous articles to profl. jours. Pres. U. Tex. Chinese Assn., 198 With ROTC, China, 1965-66. Nat. Taiwan U. scholar, 1962-65; grantee NI 1979—, Tex. Heart Assn., 1982-83, VA Merit Rev., 1995—. Mem. AAA Coun. Circulation, Coun. Basic Sci., Internat. Soc. Heart Rsch., Am. So Artificial Internal Organs, Am. Inst. Biol. Sci., Nat. Soc. Med. Rsch., N.Y. Aca Scis., Nutrition Today Soc. Home: 4 Blackberry Ct Johnson City TN 3760 1466 Office: East Tenn State U Dept Surgery JH Quillen Coll Medicine PO B 70575 Johnson City TN 37614-0575

KAO, SIMON C. radiologist, educator; b. Hong Kong; MBBS, U. Hong Kon 1976; Diploma in Med. Radiodiagnosis, London, 1982. Diplomate in radiolo and pediatric radiology Am. Bd. Radiology. Intern U. Hong Kong, 1976-7 med. and health officer Queen Elizabeth Hosp., Kowloon, Hong Kong, 1977-8 resident U. Iowa, Iowa City, 1985-87, assoc., 1987-88, asst. prof., 1988-9 assoc. prof., 1992-97, prof., 1997—. Fellow Royal Coll. Radiologists. Avoc tion: playing piano. Fax: 319-356-2220. E-mail: simon-kao@uiowa.edu.

KAO, TIMOTHY WU, civil engineering educator; b. Shanghai, July 20, 193 came to U.S., 1959; m. May Y.M. Lee, July 24, 1965; children: Michelle, Erik BS in Engring., U. Hong Kong, 1959; MS in Engring., U. Mich., 1960, Ph 1963. Registered profl. engr., D.C. Rsch. fellow W.M. Keck Lab. Hydrauli and Water Resources Calif. Inst. Tech., Pasadena, 1963-64; from asst. prof. prof. Sch. Engring. Cath. U. Am., Washington, 1964-70, prof., 1970—200 chmn. dept. civil engring., 1981—2003, assoc. dean, 1981-94, prof. emerit 2003—. Vis. oceanographer Goddard Space Flight Ctr., NASA, Greenbelt, M 1978-79. Contbr. over 70 articles to sci. jours. Rsch. grantee NSF, Office Naval Rsch., D.C. Water Resources Ctr.; named Eminent Engr., Tau Beta 1985. Fellow ASCE. Achievements include research in selective withdrawal water quality management of lakes and reservoirs, in solitary waves in coas oceans and oceanic fronts. Office: Cath Univ Am Dept Civil Eng Cardinal S Washington DC 20064-0001

KAO, YASUKO WATANABE, retired library administrator; b. Tokyo, M 30, 1930; came to U.S., 1957; d. Kichiji and Sato (Tanaka) Watanabe; Shih-Kung Kao, Apr. 1, 1959; children: John Sterling, Stephanie Margaret. B Tsuda Coll., 1950; BA in Lit., Waseda U., 1955; MSLS, U. So. Calif., 19 Instr., Takinogawa High Sch., Tokyo, 1950-57; catalog librarian U. U Library, 1960-67, Marriott Library, 1975-77, head catalog div., 1978-90; libr. Teikyo Loretto Heights U., 1991-95. Contbr. articles to profl. jours. V Utah Chinese Am. Community Sch., 1974-80, Asian Assn. Utah, 1981- Waseda U. fellow, 1958-59. Mem. ALA, Asian Pacific Librs. Assn., Assn. C and Rsch. Librs., Beta Phi Mu. Home: 2625 Yuba Ave El Cerrito 94530-1443

KAPADIA, ASHA SETH, education educator, consultant; arrived in U. 1963; d. Dev Raj and Sushila Seth; m. Bipin R. Kapadia, Dec. 17, 1966 (d Nov. 14, 1978); 1 child, Dev. BA in Math. (hons.), Delhi U., 1957, MA in Ma Stats., 1959; MS in indsl. mgmt., MIT, 1965; PhD in stats., Harvard U., 19 Mgmt. cons. Arthur D. Little Inc., Cambridge, 1969—71; asst. to assoc. prof. Houston, 1971—76; assoc. prof. U. Tex., 1976—; prof. biometry discipline Tex. Health Sci. Ctr., 1984—, prof. preventive dentistry, 1999—. Adj. ass

prof. math. sci. Rice U., Houston, 1977—80; cons. FAA, Washington, 1969—71, Veterans Adminstr., Little Rock, 1983—84, Tex. Inst. Rsch. and Rehab., Houston, 1983—92, U.S. Army Health Care Planning Divsn., 1993—. Author (with others): (book) A Study of Air Traffic Control System Capacity, 1970, Difference Equations with Public Health Applications, 2000; contbr. numerous articles to jours. Bd. dirs. Planned Parenthood, Houston, 1998—, India Culture Ctr., Houston, 1998—; mem. MIT Edn. Coun., Houston, 1988—. Recipient Disting. Svc. award, Sys. Rsch. Found., 1988, Outstanding Scholarly Contrb. award, 1988; Rsch. scholarship, Govt. India, 1959—63. Fellow: Am. Statis. Assn., Internat. Statis. Inst. Office: Univ Tex Sch of Pub Health 1200 Herman Pressler Houston TX 77030

KAPALCIK, MICHELE LIDA, therapist, guidance counselor; b. Drexel Hill, Pa., Jan. 23, 1961; d. John and Barbara Elizabeth Kapalcik. BA in German, Millersville (Pa.) U., 1982; MA in Counseling Psychology, Immaculata U., 2001. Cert. elem. and secondary sch. guidance counselor Pa. and Del., cognitive behavioral therapy 2003. Therapist and guidance counselor. Mem.: Am. Counseling Assn., Chi Sigma Iota.

KAPCSANDY, LOUIS ENDRE, building construction and manufacturing executive, chemical engineering consultant; b. Budapest, Hungary, June 5, 1936; came to U.S., 1957; s. Lajos Endre and Margit (Toth) K.; m. Roberta Marie Henson, Jan. 25, 1964; 1 son, Louis. BS in Chem. Engring., Tech. U. Hungary, 1956; postgrad. in law, U. San Francisco, 1963-64; MS in Petroleum Tech., U. Calif.-Berkeley, 1969. Freedom fighter Hungarian Revolution, Budapest, 1956; profl. football player San Diego Chargers, 1963-65; western regional mgr. Norton Co., San Francisco, 1965-72; product mgr. Koch Industries, Wichita, Kans., 1972-74; v.p., gen. mgr. Flow Systems, Inc., Seattle, 1974-78; pres. Fentron Bldg. Products, Inc., Seattle, 1978-85; CEO Baugh Enterprises Inc., Seattle, 1985—. Chem. engring. cons. HK Assocs., Seattle, 1974— Contbr. articles to profl. jours.; patentee vacuum fraction of crude oil, purification of hydrogen. Bd. dirs. Boy Scouts Chief Seattle, Seattle C. of C., Virginia Mason Med. Ctr.; active United for Wash., Seattle, 1982. With U.S. Army, 1959-62. Fellow AIChE; mem. Constrn. Specifications Inst., TAPPI, Columbia Tower Club, Rainier Club, Newcastle Golf Club, Seattle Rotary Lodge, PGA West. Republican. Roman Catholic.

KAPELAC, SAMUEL JAMES, writer, sales executive; b. Green Bay, Wis., Mar. 6, 1956; s. John Richard Sr. and Irene Alice (Rybicki) Kapelac. BAS in Comm. cum laude, U. Wis., Green Bay, 1977, MA in Comm., 1979. Loan officer Midwest Fed. Savings & Loan, Mpls., 1979—81; fin. aid adminstr. Control Data Inst., Mpls., 1981—83; quality control Control Data Corp., Mpls., 1987—90; customer svc. rep. Ceridian Corp., Mpls., 1990—97; retail salesman J. Oliver Antiques, Mpls., 1997—. Author: (novel) Roaches, 2000. Recipient Bright Idea award, Control Data Corp., 1981, Logo award, 1995. Mem.: Am. Mensa, Wis. Univ. Alumni. Bahai. Home: 3553 Dupont Ave S #2 Minneapolis MN 55408

KAPELMAN, BARBARA ANN, physician, educator; b. N.Y.C., Apr. 30, 1949; d. Leonard A. and Helen (Hass) K.; m. Lawrence William Koblenz, Mar. 24, 1979; 1 child, Adam. BA, Barnard Coll., 1970; MS in Microbiology, Yale U., 1972; MD, Albert Einstein Coll. Medicine, 1975. Diplomate Am. Bd. Internal Medicine, Am. Bd. Gastroenterology. Clin. asst. prof. hepatology and gastroenterology Mt. Sinai Sch. Medicine Mt. Sinai Hosp., 1981—82; intern Roosevelt Hosp.-Columbia U., N.Y.C., 1975-76, resident, 1976-78, fellow gastroenterology, 1978-80; fellow liver diseases Mt. Sinai Sch. Medicine-CUNY, N.Y.C., 1980-81; asst. attending physician in gastroenterology Beth Israel Hosp., N.Y.C., 1982-88, assoc. attending physician in medicine and gastroenterology, 1988-96, attending physician in medicine and gastroenterology, 1996—; clin. instr. in medicine Mt. Sinai Sch. of Medicine, N.Y.C., 1981-87, asst. clin. prof. medicine, 1987-94; bd. dirs. Beth Israel Med. Ctr., N.Y.C., 1984—, trustee, med. liaison, 1996-97; asst. clin. prof. medicine Albert Einstein Coll. Medicine, N.Y.C., 1994—. Trustee Med. Bd. Liaison, 1996-97; attending physician Beth Israel North, Beth Israel Med. Ctr., N.Y.C., 1982—, Hosp. for Joint Diseases-Orthopedic Inst., N.Y.C., 1982—; vis. clin. fellow Columbia U. Coll. Physicians and Surgeons, N.Y.C., 1975-80. Co-author: Gastroenterology for the House Officer, 1989; contbr. articles to profl. jours. Fellow ACP, Am. Coll. Gastroenterology; mem. Am. Women's Med. Assn., Women's Med. Assn. N.Y.C. (officer), Am. Gastroent. Assn., Am. Assn. for Study of Liver Diseases, Am. Soc. for Gastrointestinal Endoscopy, Am. Med. Informatics Assn., N.Y. Acad. Gastroenterology, N.Y. Soc. for Gastrointestinal Endoscopy. Avocations: computers, culinary arts, medical informatics, educational activities. Office: Ste 210A 133 E 73rd St New York NY 10021-3556

KAPELNER, DAVID ISRAEL, lawyer, educator; b. N.Y.C., Oct. 14, 1951; s. Samuel Myron and Rolayne (Kay) K.; B.A. in Math., U. Conn., 1973; M.A. (scholar), Tufts U., 1975; M.B.A., N.Y.U., 1982; JD Suffolk U., 1991. Bar: Mass. 1991, U.S. Dist. Ct. Mass. 1992. Fin. analyst IT&T, 1975-76, economist, 1976-78, mgr. analytical svcs., 1978-79; mgr. econ. analysis Continental Can Co., Stamford, Conn., 1979-80; corp. economist Smith Valve Corp., Westboro, Mass., 1980-84; dir. fin. Princeton Corp., Westboro, Mass., 1984-88; assoc. prof. mgmt. and bus. law Merrimack Coll., North Andover, Mass., 1985—; cons. pub. utility Columbia Group, Canton, Mass., 1988—. adj. instr. fin. and mgmt. Manchester (Conn.) Coll., 1982—, Anna Maria Coll., Paxton, Mass., 1982—, Worcester State Coll. (Mass.), 1982— . Cert. Equal Employment Adv. Council, Affirmative Action Program. Mem. ABA, Mass. Bar Assn., Boston Bar Assn., Worcester County Bar Assn., N.Am. Soc. Corp. Planners, Am. Econ. Assn., Nat. Assn. Bus. Economists, Am. Mgmt. Assn., Stamford Jaycees (past treas.). Home: 45 Manor Rd Shrewsbury MA 01545-2224 also: 37 Pierce St Northborough MA 01532-1935

KAPETANAKOS, CHRISTOS ANASTASIOS, science administrator, physics educator; b. Xirokabi, Lakonia, Greece, Jan. 2, 1936; s. Anastasios and Alexandra (Doukas) K.; m. Ioanna Plafoutzi, June 23, 1962 (div. 1993); children: Anastasios, Yula. Diploma, Nat. U. Greece, Athens, 1960; M in Nuclear Engring., MIT, 1964; PhD, U. Md., 1970. Rschr. U. Tex., Austin, 1970-71; br. head, sect. head, rschr. Naval Rsch. Lab., Washington, 1971-92; acting dir. Inst. Plasma Physics, U. Crete, Iraklion, Crete, Greece, 1993-95; prof. of physics U. Crete, Iraklion, 1993-96; pres. Leading Egde Tech. Corp., Washington, 1995—. Cons. Fuel and Mineral Resources, Reston, Va., Icarus Rsch. Inc. Bethesa MD., Naval Rsch. Lab., Washington, SFA. Inc., Largo, Md., FERMI Nat. Accelerator Lab. Patentee in field; contbr. over 110 articles and more than 50 tech. reports to profl. publs. 2d lt. Artillery, 1960-62, Greece. Grantee Dept. Def., Washington, Dept. Energy, Washington, Office of Naval Rsch. Def. Advanced Project Agy., Washington, ELINOIL, Athens, Naval System Command, Fermi Lab. Fellow Am. Phys. Soc., Washington Soc. Scis. Home: 4431 Macarthur Blvd NW Washington DC 20007-2564 E-mail: letkapetanakos@starpower.net.

KAPFER, MIRIAM BIERBAUM, technical documentation and training specialist; b. Atlantic, Iowa, May 8, 1935; d. Roy C. and Alma L. Bierbaum; m. Philip G. Kapfer, Aug. 21, 1960 (dec. 1988); children: Paul, Stephanie. B in Music Edn., Drake U., 1956; M in Music Edn., U. Kans., 1958; postgrad., U. Aberdeen, Scotland, 1958-59; PhD, Ohio State U., 1964. Tchr. cert. Iowa, Calif. Instr. Concordia Coll., Seward, Nebr., 1958, St. John's Coll., Winfield, Kans., 1959 61; tchr. Hamilton Local Sch., Columbus, Ohio, 1962-64; tchr., libr., curriculum staff Clark County Sch. Dist., Las Vegas, 1964-70; prof. project adminstrn. U. Utah, Salt Lake City, 1970-77; prof., tchr. U. North Iowa, Cedar Falls, 1977; tchr., analyst Arabian Am. Oil Co., Dhahran, Saudi Arabia, 1978-88; instrnl. designer Usertech/Canterbury, Medford, NJ, 1989—. Author, editor: Behavioral Objectives in Curriculum Development, 1971, Behavioral Objectives: Position of Pendulum, 1978; co-editor, author: Learning Packages in American Education, 1972; co-author: Inquiry ILPs, 1978, Project ILPs, 1978; contbr. articles to profl. jours. Mem. Soc. for Tech. Commn. (sr.), Music Educators Nat. Conf. (life), U. Kans. Alumni Assn. (life), Ohio State U. Alumni Assn. (life), Phi Delta Kappa (life). Avocations: traveling, hiking, reading. Office: Usertech/Canterbury 352 Stokes Rd Ste 200 Medford NJ 08055

KAPIKIAN, CATHERINE ANDREWS, artist; b. Cleve., Oct. 18, 1939; d. John Robert and Anne Alva (Cosgrove) Andrews; m. Albert Zaven Kapikian, Feb. 27, 1960; children: Albert, Thomas, Gregory. Student, Carnegie Mellon U., 1957-59; BA, U. Md., 1963; MTS summa cum laude, Wesley Theol. Sem., Washington, 1979. Gen. illustrator NIH, Bethesda, Md., 1959-61; artist-in-residence Wesley Theol. Sem., 1979—, mem. faculty, dir. Henry Luce III Ctr. for the Arts and Religion, 2001—. Designer, fabricator liturgical tapestries, banners, paraments and vestments; mem. commn. on worship and the arts Nat. Coun. Chrs., 1991-97. Works exhibited in group shows including Interfaith Forum on Religion, Art and Architecture, Phoenix, 1979, Chgo., 1981, Phila., 1987, Houston, 1989, Boston, 1990, St. Thomas More Newman Ctr. Liturg. Arts Exhibit, Bowling Green (Ohio) U., 1981, Archdiocese of Chgo., 1984, Biennial Exhbns. Liturg. Art Guild of Ohio, Columbus, 1985, 91, 93, 95, 97, 2001; author: Through the Christian Year: An Illustrated Guide, 1983; contbr. forward to (book) Full Circle, 1988; contbr. articles and images to profl. jours. Bd. dirs. Episcopal Ch. Visual Arts, 2002—. Mem. Arts and Religion Forum of Washington Theol. Consortium (founder, mem. steering com.), Interfaith Forum on Religion, Art and Architecture (bd. dirs. 1983-85, 87-90), Schuyler Inst. Worship and the Arts (bd. dirs. 1987-90). Democrat. Avocations: opera, remote control airplanes. Office: Wesley Theol Seminary Henry Luce III Ctr for Arts and Religion 4500 Massachusetts Ave NW Washington DC 20016-5632 E-mail: ckapikian@wesleysem.edu.

KAPITONOV, VLADIMIR V. molecular biologist; b. Novosibirsk, Russia, Sept. 13, 1958; arrived in US, 1994; s. Vyacheslav A. Kapitonov and Nadezhda I. Kapitonova. PhD, Inst. Cytology and Genetics, Novosibirsk; MD in Physics, Novosibirsk State Tech. U. Sr. scientist Inst. Cytology and Genetics, Novosibirsk, 1991—94; staff scientist Genetic Info. Rsch. Inst., Mountain View, Calif., 1996—. Business E-Mail: vladimir@ulam.girinst.org.

KAPLAN, ABNER J. social worker, public relations executive; b. Williamsport, Md., Dec. 27, 1910; s. Harry George and Annie Kaplan; m. Katharine Kirkpatrick Bowser; children: David, George, Douglas. B in Lit., Columbia U., 1932; MSW, U. Pa., 1942. Corr. Washington Times-Herald, 1933—36; caseworker, supr. exec. Washington County Social Svcs., Hagerstown, Md., 1936—46; chief divsn. stats. State Dept. Social Svcs., Balt., 1946—53, chief divsn. child welfare, 1953—70; dir. pub. rels. State Employees Credit Union, Balt., 1971—89, Towson, Md., 1971—89. Dir. pub. rels., bd. mem. Regional Mental Health Ctr., Balt., 1973—2001, Md. Rehab. Ctr., Balt., 1983—89. Contbr. articles to profl. jours. Active Childrens Def. Fund, Pub. Citizen, Common Cause; bd. mem., officer Md. Conf. Social Concern, Balt., 1961—98. Recipient award for svcs. to children, Nat. Foster Parents Assn., 1984, Humanitarian award, Md. State Employees Credit Union, 1986. Mem.: Soc. Profl. Journalists (life), Masons (life), Sigma Delta Chi (life). Democrat. Jewish. Avocations: computers, crossword puzzles, swimming, bowling, exercise. Home: 2402 E Strathmore Ave Baltimore MD 21214-2153

KAPLAN, ALAN I. film producer; b. Balt. s. Emanuel and Dora (Yaniger) K.; m. Gina Chiao, Feb. 17, 1991 (div. May 1994); 1 child, Daniel Victor. BA, MA, U. Md.; postgrad, Md. Inst. Art. Freelance photographer, N.Y.C., 1968-70; chmn. media dept. Antioch Coll., Balt., 1970-76; pres./owner Alan Kaplan Prodns., L.A., Calif., 1976-91; pres. Wavecrest, L.A., 1991-96, Cine L.A., 1998—. Co-prodr., dir., writer (PBS) including Harold Clurman: A Life of Theater (Cine Golden Eagle award 1989); (cable) What's Up America?; prodr. (film) Bad Manners, 1996, Felons, 1997, Lucky 13, 1998, Touched By a Killer, 1999, Snowbound, 2001, Fascination, 2002. Office: Cine LA 11693 San Vincente Blvd # 321 Los Angeles CA 90049-5105 Fax: 310-820-4415. E-mail: alan898@aol.com.

KAPLAN, ALAN LESLIE, gynecology educator, oncologist; b. Atlanta, Sept. 10, 1930; divorced; children: John, Robert. AB, Washington and Lee U., 1951; MD, Columbia U., 1955. Diplomate Am. Bd. Ob-Gyn. Intern Jackson Meml. Hosp., Miami, Fla., 1955-56; resident in ob-gyn Columbia-Presbyn. Med. Ctr., N.Y.C., 1956-59, 61-63; prof. dept. ob-gyn, dir. divsn. gynecologic oncology Baylor Coll. Medicine, Houston, 1963—. Med. dir. gynecologic oncology program Meth. Hosp., Houston, 1989—. Capt. M.C., U.S. Army, 1959-61. Mem. ACS, AMA, Am. Coll. Obstetricians and Gynecologists, Am. Cancer Soc., Am. Soc. Clin. Oncology, Soc. Gynecol. Oncology, Houston Gynecol. and Obstet. Soc. Office: Baylor Coll Medicine 6550 Fannin St Ste 801 Houston TX 77030-2738 E-mail: akaplan@bcm.tmc.edu.

KAPLAN, ALAN MICHAEL, lawyer; b. Chgo., May 2, 1951; s. Milton and Evelyn (Davis) K.; m. Madeline Lewis. BSE, Northwestern U., 1973, MA, 1975; JD, DePaul U., 1980. Bar: Ill. 1980, Ohio 1999, Ky. 1999, U.S. Dist. Ct. (no. dist.) Ill. 1984, U.S. Ct. Appeals (7th cir.) 1988, D.C. 2002, U.S. Ct. Appeals (11th cir.) 2002. Atty. NLRB, Washington, 1980-88; assoc. Brydges, Riseborough, Morris, Franke & Miller, Waukegan, Ill., 1988-93, Piper, Marbury, Rudnick & Wolfe, Waukegan, Ill., 1993-95; ptnr. Masuda, Funai, Eifert & Mitchell, Ltd., Chgo., 1995—. Contbr. articles to profl. jours. Mem. ABA, Ill. State Bar Assn. Home: 660 Carriage Way Deerfield IL 60015-4537

KAPLAN, ALLEN P. physician, educator, researcher; b. West New York, N.J., Oct. 27, 1940; m. Lee Kaplan, Aug. 22, 1965; children: Rachel, Seth. AB, Columbia U., 1961; MD, Downstate Med. Coll. Diplomate Am. Bd. Internal Medicine, Am. Bd. Rheumatology, Am. Bd. Allergy and Clin. Immunology; cert. in diagnostic lab. immunology. Head allergic disease sect. NIH, Bethesda, Md., 1972-78; prof. medicine, head divsn. allergy rheumatology & clin. immunology SUNY, Stony Brook, 1978-87, chmn. dept. medicine, 1987-94. Editor Allergy Clin. Immunol. Internat.; contbr. over some 250 articles to profl. jours. Lt. comdr. USPHS, 1972-78. Recipient Commendation medal USPHS, 1976. Mem. Am. Acad. Allergy & Immunology (pres. 1989-90), Clin. Immunology Soc. (pres. 1992-93), Internat. Assn. Allergology and Clin. Immunology (sec. gen. 1991-97, pres. elect 1997-2000, pres. 2000-2003). Office: Divsn Pulmonary-Allergy 96 Jonathan Lucas St Charleston SC 29425-8900 E-mail: Kaplana@musc.edu.

KAPLAN, ANDY, broadcast executive; Exec v.p. Columbia Tristar TV Group, Culver City, Calif., until 2000; CEO Hollywood Stock Exch., Santa Monica, Calif., 2000—. Office: Hollywood Stock Exch 8441 Santa Monica Blvd West Hollywood CA 90069-4220

KAPLAN, ANN LEOPOLD, lawyer; b. Harrisburg, Pa., Sept. 19, 1962; d. Marx S. and Joan (Yaverbaum) Leopold; m. Lawrence David Kaplan, Nov. 26, 1995; 1 child, Jeremy. BA magna cum laude, U. Pitts., 1984; JD, U. Pa., 1987. Bar: Pa. 1987, D.C. 1989. Assoc. Epstein, Becker & Green, P.C., Washington, 1987-96, ptnr., 1996—. Author: (with others) Health Law Handbook, 1993. Mem. young leadership cabinet United Jewish Cmtys., 1996—; mem. exec. coun. women's divsn. Jewish Fedn. Greater Washington, 1999—; chair Capital Polit. Action Com., Washington, 1994. Office: Epstein Becker & Green PC 1227 25th St NW Ste 700 Washington DC 20037-1175

KAPLAN, ARKADY, optical engineer, researcher; b. St. Petersburg, Russia, Mar. 17, 1969; s. Moris and Nadya Kaplan. MSc, cert. in physics and optical engring., Inst. Fine Mechanics and Optics, St. Petersburg, 1994; PhD, Tel Aviv U., 1999, cert. in electro-optics, 2000. Rsch. asst. Vavilov State Optical Inst., St. Petersburg, 1991—94, Tel-Aviv U., 1998—2000; physicist Elbit Systems Ltd., Haifa, Israel, 1999—2000; sr. mgr. integrated electro-optics CeLight Inc., Silver Spring, Md., 2000—. Contbr. articles to profl. jours. With USSR Air Force, 1987—89. Mem.: OSA, IEEE. Achievements include patents pending for integrated optics sensors. Home: 5 Lake Ave Apt 10A East Brunswick NJ 08816 Office: CeLight Inc 12200 Tech Rd Ste 300 Silver Spring MA 20904 Office Fax: 301-625-7001. Personal E-mail: arkady@ieee.org. E-mail: akaplan@celight.com.

KAPLAN, ARLINE RAY, editor, writer; b. South Gate, Calif., Oct. 13, 1942; d. Bernard and Annette Kaplan; children: Alysha Taylor, Robert Polgar. AB Journalism, U. So. Calif., Los Angeles, CA, 1964. Reporter Press Telegram, Long Beach, Calif., 1966—72; editor Kern Valley Sun, Kernville, Calif., 1973—74, World Dredging and Marine Constrn. Mag., San Pedro, Calif., 1974—76; pub. rels. specialist Am. Medicorp, Marina del Rey, Calif., 1976—77; med. editor Am. Assn. Gynecologic Laparoscopists, Downey, Calif., 1977—79; pub. affairs cons. Comprehensive Care Corp., Irvine, Calif., 1979—85; mng. editor Psychiat. Times, Irvine, Calif., 1992—95; sr. contbg editor Psychiat. Times / Geriatric Times, Irvine, Calif., 1996—; pres. ARK Comm., Huntington Beach, Calif., 1986—. Author: Thank You for My Life; editor: Endoscopy in Gynecology; contbr. Recipient Press Club Awards, Pacific Coast Press Club, 1970, Most Improved Publ., Mag. Publishers Assn., 1994. Mem.: Am. Med. Writers Assn., Long Beach - Sochi Sister City, Phi Beta Kappa. Avocations: travel, singing, lay counseling. Office: Psychiatric Times 2801 McGaw Ave Irvine CA 92614-5835 Personal E-mail: arlinerkaplan@aol.com.

KAPLAN, ARTHUR MITCHELL, lawyer; b. N.Y.C., May 5, 1945; s. George G. and Florence G. Kaplan. AB, U. Pa., 1967; JD, Harvard U., 1970. Bar: Pa. 1971, U.S. Dist. Ct. (ea. dist.) Pa. 1971, U.S. Ct. Appeals (3rd cir.) 1972, U.S. Ct. Appeals (4th cir.) 1987, U.S. Ct. Appeals (2d cir.) 1999, U.S. Supreme Ct. 1999, U.S. Ct. Appeals (7th and D.C. cirs.) 2001. Assoc. Ralph Nader, Washington, 1970—71, Harold E. Kohn, PA, Phila., 1971—75; ptnr. Fine, Kaplan & Black, R.P.C., Phila., 1975—. Pres. Com. to Support the Antitrust Laws, 1994—97; bd. advisors Am. Antitrust Inst.; mem. nat. bd. govs. Equality Forum, 2000—. Apptd. mem. Phila. Art Commn., 1993—2000. Mem.: Phila. ACLU (bd. dirs. 1990—, v.p. 1995—), Pa. ACLU (bd. dirs. 1993—97), Am. Law Inst. Office: Fine Kaplan & Black RPC 1845 Walnut St 23d Fl Philadelphia PA 19103-4708 Office Fax: 215-568-5872. E-mail: akaplan@finekaplan.com.

KAPLAN, BARRY MARTIN, lawyer; b. N.Y.C., Nov. 9, 1950; s. Stanley Seymour and Lillian (Schner) K.; m. Erica Green, July 26, 1981; children: Matthew Aaron, Elizabeth Rose, Andrew Nathan. BA, Colgate U., 1973; JD cum laude, U. Mich., 1976. Bar: Mich. 1976, Wash., 1978, U.S. Dist. (ea. dist.) Mich. 1976, U.S. Dist. Ct. (we. dist.) Wash. 1978, U.S. Dist. Ct. (ea. dist.) Wash. 1986, U.S. Tax Ct. 1983, U.S. Ct. Appeals (9th cir.) 1990. Law clk. to Hon. Charles W. Joiner U.S. Dist. Ct. (ea. dist.) Mich., Detroit, 1976-78; assoc. Perkins Coie, Seattle, 1978-85, ptnr., 1985—. Adj. prof. securities regulation U. Wash. Sch. Law; spkr. in field. Author: Washington Corporate Law, Corporations and LLCs, 2000; contbr. articles to legal jours. and procs. Mem. ABA (litigation sect., securities litigation com., bus. law sect., bus. and corp. litigation com., subcom. chmn. on control transactions 1993), Wash. State Bar Assn. (CLE spkr., bus. law sect., securities com., subcom. chair on dir.'s liability 1993), Wash. Athletic Club. Office: Perkins Coie 1201 3rd Ave Fl 40 Seattle WA 98101-3029 E-mail: bkaplan@perkinscole.com.

KAPLAN, BENJAMIN, judge; b. N.Y.C., Apr. 9, 1911; s. Morris and Mary (Berman) K.; m. Felicia Lamport, Apr. 16, 1942; children: James L., Nancy L. Mansbach. AB, CCNY, 1929; LL.B., Columbia, 1933; LL.D., Suffolk U., 1974, Harvard U., 1981, Northeastern U., 1981. Bar: N.Y. 1934, Mass. 1950. Assoc., then mem. firm Greenbaum, Wolff & Ernst, N.Y.C., 1933-42, 46; vis. prof. law Harvard, 1947, prof. law, 1948—, Royall prof. law, 1961-72, emeritus, 1972—; assoc. justice Supreme Jud. Ct. Mass., 1972-81; recalled to serve as judge Appeals Ct. Mass., 1983—. Reporter to adv. com. on civil rules Jud. Conf. U.S., 1960-66, mem., 1966-70; co-reporter restatement (2d) of judgments to Am. Law Inst., 1970-73 Served to lt. col. AUS, 1942-46. Mem. Am. Law Inst., Assn. Bar City of N.Y., Phi Beta Kappa. Achievements include assisting Justice Jackson on Nuremberg Trial, 1945. Home: 2 Bond St Cambridge MA 02138-2308 Office: Harvard Law Sch Cambridge MA 02138

KAPLAN, BETSY HESS, school board member; b. Bridgeton, N.J., Aug. 12, 1926; d. Alfred N. and Betsy (Bolton) Hess; m. Robert Leon Kaplan, June 11, 1953; children: Bruce Alfred, James Edward, Joan Ann. AB, Wesleyan Coll., 1947; BFA, Wesleyan Conservatory, 1948. Cert. tchr., Fla. Tchr. 4th grade Miami (Fla.)-Dade County Pub. Schs., 1950-53; edn. and cultural arts adv., 1961—88; instr. Miami Dade Cmty. Coll., 1979-81; adminrv. asst. to Ethel K. Beckham Miami-Dade County Sch. Bd., 1980-82, mem. sch. bd., 1988—, chair, 1993-95. Chair fed. rels. network Fla. Sch. Bds., Tallahassee, 1996-98; bd. dirs. New World Sch. of Arts, Miami; mem. Performing Arts Ctr. Trust, Miami, 1993—, student mentor. Mem. Emily's List, Washington, 1990—, Women's Emergency Network, Miami, 1990—, Women's Polit. Caucus, 1988—; cultural amb. Heart of the City cultural series Miami-Dade Park and Recreation Dept., 2002. Named Woman Worth Knowing, Miami Beach Commn. on Status of Women, 1994, Woman of Yr., King of Clubs, 2000; recipient Alumnae Disting. Achievement award, Wesleyan Coll., 1987, French Acad. Palms award, French Min. of Edn. of Youth and Sports, 1991, Co. of Women, Pioneer award, Miami-Dade County Pks. Dept., 1997, Ruth Wolkowsky Greenfield award, Am. Jewish Congress, 1993, Woman of Impact award, Cmty. Coalition for Women's History, 1995, Red Cross Spectrum award, Women in Edn., 1997, Trailblazer award, Women's Com. of 100, 1993, Lifetime Svc. to Music Edn. in Fla. and U.S., Fla. Music Educators Assn., 2000, Branches of Learning award, Women's Divsn. Greater Miami State of Israel Bonds Orgn., 2001. Mem.: AAUW (Phoenix award 1999), LWV, Alliance for Aging (mem. adv. bd. 1996—), Fla. Sch. Bds. Assn. (bd. dirs. 1990—99, Pres.'s award 2001), Phi Kappa Phi, Delta Kappa Gamma, Phi Delta Kappa. Democrat. Jewish. Avocations: studying art history, reading and interpreting poetry, studying and practicing French language, cooking. Home: 6790 SW 122d Dr Miami FL 33156-5459 Office: Miami Dade County Sch Bd 1450 NE 2d Ave Ste 700 Miami FL 33132 E-mail: bakaplan60@aol.com., bkaplan@sbab.dade.k-12.fl.us.

KAPLAN, BRADLEY S. corporate financial executive; b. Chgo., July 4, 1960; s. Irving and Gloria Lee (Hellerman) K.; m. Judith Ann Frei, Mar. 6, 1982; children: Patrick Marcus, Rachel Marie. BS in Acctg., Met. State Coll., 1982. CPA, Colo.; cert. mgmt. acct. Acct. Deloitte, Haskins & Sells, Denver, 1982-84; controller Internat. Tubular Supply, Englewood, Colo., 1984-85; fin. analyst U.S. West, Inc., Englewood, 1985—93, dir. exec. and internat. compensation, 1993—96, dir. fin. strategy, 1996—97, dir. human resources fin., 1997—98; dir. internat. audit svcs. Mediaone, 1998—2000; v.p., CFO Oreg. market Comcast Cable, Beaverton, Oreg., 2001—. Mem. AICPA, Inst. of Mgnt. Accts. (bd. dir. 1987-2000, chpt. pres. 1990-91, nat. dir. 1992-93), Colo. Soc. CPA's. Avocations: sports, reading, hiking. Office: 9605 SW Nimbus Ave Beaverton OR 97008

KAPLAN, CARL ELIOT, lawyer; b. N.Y.C., Apr. 17, 1939; s. Lawrence S. and Pearl (Eisenberg) K.; m. Diane L. Garvin, Dec. 16, 1965; children: Lynn, Jonathan. BA, Columbia Coll., 1959; LLB, 1962. Bar: U.S. Dist. Ct. (so. and ea. dists.) N.Y. 1964, U.S. Ct. Appeals (2nd cir.) 1966, U.S. Supreme Ct. 1970. Assoc. Fulbright & Jaworski L.L.P., N.Y.C., 1963-69; ptnr., 1969—. Bd. dirs. Bio Tech. Gen. Corp., East Brunswick, N.J. Bd. editors: Columbia Law Rev., 1961-62. Mem. ABA, N.Y. Bar Assn., Assn. of Bar City of N.Y., Am. Soc. Corp. Secs., Univ. Club (N.Y.C.), Phi Beta Kappa. Avocations: biking, jogging. Office: Fulbright & Jaworski LLP 666 5th Ave Fl 31 New York NY 10103-3198 E-mail: ckaplan@fulbright.com.

KAPLAN, DANIEL, lawyer; b. Memphis, Sept. 2, 1967; s. Steven Robert and Nancy Bonnie Kaplan. BA, U. Md., 1989; JD, Memphis State U., 1992. Bar: Fla. 1992, U.S. Dist. Ct. (so. dist.) Fla. 1995. Assoc. Rosenthal, Rosenthal and Rasco, Miami, 1992-97, Lawrence A. France, P.A., Miami, 1997-98; ptnr. Daniel Kaplan, P.A., Miami, 1998—. Mem. ABA, Dade County Bar Assn. (dir. 1995-98, Pro Bono Svc. awards), Fla. Bar Assn., North Dade Bar Assn. (bd. dirs. 1993—, chmn. family cts. com. 1998—). Office: Turnberry Plz Ste 500 2875 NE 191 St Aventura FL 33180

KAPLAN, DAVID JEREMY, research scientist, consultant; b. Honolulu, Hawaii, Oct. 8, 1934; s. Albert David and Lillian Kaplan; m. Dorothy Jane Spencer, July 14, 1979; children: Sharon Dee Rosman, Daniel Aaron, Ann B. MA, U. of Calif., Berkeley, 1958. Cons. ITT, Washington, 2002—; machine programming mathematician Ames Rsch. Ctr., NASA, Mountain View, 1958—60; mathematician Stanford Rsch. Inst., Menlo Park, Calif., 1960—69; ops. rsch. analyst Naval Rsch. Lab., Washington, 1969—. Mem. ACLU. Fellow: AAAS; mem.: Math. Assn. of Am., Ops. Rsch. Soc. of Am., Sigma Xi. Liberal. Achievements include development of processing graph method tool. Home: 2451 Windbreak Dr Alexandria VA 22306 Office: 2451 Windbreak Dr Alexandria VA 22306 E-mail: david.kaplan@verizon.net.

KAPLAN, DAVID K. emergency physician, educator; b. Amityville, N.Y., Sept. 15, 1953; s. Samuel and Evelyn Kaplan; m. Susan Jean Baker-Kaplan, June 22, 1990. BA, Hiram (Ohio) Coll., 1975; MD, U. London, 1980. Sr. lectr. U. London, 1988—94; cons. thoracic surgeon Brompton Hosp., London, 1988—94; emergency physician No. Maine Med. Ctr., Fort Kent, 1994—. Cons. Granada Health, Boston, 1994—96; adj. prof. biomed. humanities Hiram (Ohiho) Coll., 2002—. Assoc. editor Thorax, 1994; contbr. articles to profl. jours., chapters to books. Dir. Casco Bay Dist. Transit Authority, Portland,

Maine, 1999—2002. Fellow: Royal Coll. Surgeons; mem.: Gen. Thoracic Club. Home: 61 Crescent Ave Great Diamond Island Portland ME 04112 Office: Hiram Cottage Assocs PO Box 7308 Portland ME 04112 Personal E-mail: davegdi@earthlink.net.

KAPLAN, DAVID L. retired communications educator, actor, artist, sculptor; b. Chgo., Apr. 6, 1918; s. Maurice I and Emily (Seilin) Kaplan; m. Tea Stefancic, June 11, 1977. BS, Northwestern U., 1940, MA, 1941; postgrad., Stanford U., 1952-54. Actor, stage mgr. comml. Chicagoland theatre, Chgo. and Highland Park, 1953-76. Radio speech and theatre instr. Temple U., Phila., 1947—50; from instr. to prof. City Coll. Chgo., 1956—86; stage dir. Peninsula Players, Fish Creek, Wis., 1963—64; cmty. theatre dir., Wilmette, Lincolnwood, Wheaton, Winnetka, Ill., St. Joseph, Mich., 1965—70. Sculpture and paintings. Mem Equity Libr. Theatre, Chgo., 1953—99, pres., v.p., sec.-treas.; mem Skokie Art Guild, Ill., 1986—, Evanston Art Ctr, Ill. Recipient numerous artistic awards including Best Dir Award, Ill Community Theater Asn, 1970, Marge Dare Lifetime Achievment Award, Equity Library Theatre Chicago, 1999. Mem.: Actors Equity Assn., Chgo. Artists Coalition, Nat. Sculpture Soc.

KAPLAN, DAVID MARSHALL, psychologist, educator; b. Bklyn., Aug. 9, 1956; s. Ira and Gloria M. (Malden) K.; m. Vickie Voss, July 31, 1982. MA, MEd, Columbia U., 1979; PhD, U. N.C., 1985. Diplomate in counseling psychology Nat. Bd. Psychol. Splties.; lic. psychologist, N.Y.; nat. cert. counselor; nat. cert. career counselor; cert. family therapist. Asst. dir. Advising, Counseling & Career Devel. Ctr. Alma (Mich.) Coll., 1983-86; asst. dir. career and counseling svcs. Alfred (N.Y.) U., 1986-89, prof., dir. grad. program in counseling, 1989-2000; chair Dept. Counselor Edn. & Rehab. Programs Emporia (Kans.) State U., 2000—. Psychologist in pvt. practice Alfred Counseling Assocs., 1987-2000; pres. N.Y. State Assn. Marriage and Family Counselors, 1992-95; presenter in field. Contbr. articles to profl. jours. Strong Rsch. Adv. Bd. grantee, 1992. Mem. APA (cert. in the treatment of alcohol and other psychoactive substance use disorders), ACA (pres. 2002-03), Nat. Career Devel. Assn., Assn. Counselor Edn. Supr., Internat. Assn. Marriage and Family Counselors (pres. 1998-00, Disting. Svc. award 1992), N.Y. Counseling Assn. (pres. 1996-97, Disting. Legis. Svc. award 1997). Office: Emporia State U CERP Campus Box 4036 1200 Commercial St Emporia KS 66801-5087 E-mail: kaplanda@emporia.edu

KAPLAN, DORIS WEILER, social worker; b. Phila., Mar. 28, 1945; d. Edgar E. and Marianne S. (Gunzenhauser) Weiler; m. Daniel I. Kaplan, Apr. 15, 1967; children: Tammy G., Bradley E. BA in Sociology, U. Pitts., 1966; MA in Counseling, Social Work, Montclair State Coll., 1980. Social worker N.J. Div. Youth & Family Svcs., 1967-71, Union (N.J.) Twp. Bd. Edn., 1982—. Cons. Head Start Social Svc., Union, 1982-98. Treas. Livingston (N.J.) Coun. Girl Scouts U.S., 1977—2001; bd. dirs. Livingston H.S. PTA, 1985—89. Named Outstanding Vol., Essex County Coun., 1993. Mem.: N.J. Assn. Sch. Social Workers (treas. 1990—2001, bd. dirs. 1990—2002, pres. 2002—), Nat. Coun. Jewish Women, Crestmont Country Club. Avocations: skiing, golf, tennis, reading. Office: Union Twp Schs Morris Ave Union NJ 07083

KAPLAN, DOUGLAS ALLEN, financial care company executive; b. L.A., Aug. 14, 1956; s. Martin and Sally Kaplan. BA in Pub. Svc./Polit. Sci., U. Calif., Davis, 1978; cert., Solano (Calif.) Fire Acad., 1979. Cert. Calif. Pub. Guardians Assn., Nat. Guardianship Assn. Fire safety supr. Davis & Winter Fire Dept., 1979-80; asst. manpower analyst Yolo County, Woodland, Calif., 1980, voter outreach coord., 1980-82, pub. guardian, adminstr., 1983-2000; pres. Long Term Fin. Care Inc., Davis, 2000—. Tchr. U. Calif. Ext., 1992—; chair conservatorship adv. com. Am. River Coll., Sacramento, 1989-90. Mem. exec. bd. Calif. Dem. Party, Sacramento, 1987-88, 93-94, state ctrl. com., 1985-2000; bd. dirs. N.C.A. Ombudsman Adv. Bd., Sacramento, 1996-2000; bd. dirs., chair polit. action com. Sierra Club Yolano Group, 1999-2001. Recipient Grassroots Activism award Nat. Jewish Dem. Coun., Washington, 1993. Mem. Nat. Guardianship Assn. (legis. chair, bd. mem. 1988—, pres. 1994-96), Calif. Pub. Guardian Assn. (pres. 1988-89), Calif. State Bar (planning, probate and trust sect. com. 1995-2000). Jewish. Avocations: scuba diving, white water rafting. Office: Long Term Fin Care Inc 1411 W Covell Blvd #106-125 Davis CA 95616

KAPLAN, ERICA LYNN, typing and word processing service company executive, pianist, educator; b. Aug. 6, 1955; d. George William and Raylia (Eagle) Kaplan; m. James Laurence Kellermann, Feb. 26, 1982. B in Mus., Manhattan Sch. Music, N.Y.C., 1976, M in Mus., 1979. Pres. Erica Kaplan Typing/Word Processing/Music Svcs., N.Y.C., 1980—; from accompanist to tchr. Stuyvesant Adult Ctr., N.Y.C., 1988—97, tchr. performance singing, 1997—. Accompanist Literally Alive/Victory Theatrical, 2000—, mus. dir., 2001—. Transl., annotator with additional mus. examples: L'Anacrouse dans la Musique Moderne, 1978; composer: (songs) Four by Feiffer, 1978, Hey Boys, 1984, Unborn Child, 1988, Neighbor, 1991, Watch the Closing Doors, 2001; arranger Postcards from the Apple, 1993, Isn't It Romantic, 1996. Mem. Common Cause, Washington, 1983—, SANE/FREEZE, 1988—. Mem.: Am. Fedn. Musicians, Mensa. Democrat. Jewish. E-mail: ELKK@aol.com.

KAPLAN, EUGENE ALKEN, psychiatry educator, department chairman; b. Syracuse, N.Y., Dec. 24, 1933; s. David S. and Florence F. Kaplan; m. Sandra Ecker Kaplan, May 14, 1961; children: Susan Beth Kaplan Lue, Karen Lynn. BA magna cum laude, Syracuse U., 1954; MD, SUNY, Syracuse, 1957. Diplomate Nat. Bd. Med. Examiners, cert. Am. Bd. Psychiatry and Neurology. Med. intern Albert Einstein Med. Ctr., N.Y.C., 1957—58; psychiatry resident, chief resident SUNY Upstate Med. U., Syracuse, 1958—61, from instr. to prof., 1961—, prof., chair dept. psychiatry, 1987—99, prof., chair emeritus dept. psychiatry, 1999—. Cons. Peace Corps tng. programs Syracuse U., 1962—66; vis. prof. Sloan Sch. Cornell U., Ithaca, NY, 1967—82; lectr. Washington Sch. Psychiatry, 1967—69; vis. scientist The Tavistock Psychiat. Ctr., London, 1981; cons. psychiatrist Syracuse U. Health Svc., 1982—87. Co-editor: International Psychiatric Clinics, vol. 2 & 3, 1965; contbr. articles to profl. jours. Bd. dirs. Transitional Living Svc., Syracuse, 1975—82, Syracuse Opera, Syracuse, 1990—98, Syracuse Symphony, Syracuse, 1999—. Comdr. Med. Corps USN, 1967—69. Fellow: Am. Psychiat. Assn. (Disting. Life fellow); mem.: Am. Bd. Psychiatry and Neurology (sr. examiner 1974—98), Phi Kappa Alpha, Phi Beta Kappa. Avocations: sailing, piano. Home: 4804 West Lake Rd Cazenovia NY 13035 Office: SUNY Upstate Med Univ Dept Psychiatry 750 E Adams St Syracuse NY 13210

KAPLAN, GABRIELA DIANA, radiologist; b. Quito, Ecuador, Apr. 28, 1947; arrived in U.S., 1963; d. Isidor and Rosa Ortiz Kaplan. MD, U. Autonoma Guadalajara Sch.of Medicine, 1972; BA, Whittier Coll. Diplomate Am. Bd. Radiology. Fellow in body imaging Johns Hopkins U., Balt., 1980, fellow neuroradiology, 1982; fellow in whole body magnetic resonance U. Mich., Ann Arbor, Mich., 1989; asst. prof. Columbia U./Presbyn. Hosp., N.Y.C., 1979; lectr. diagnostic radiology Johns Hopkins Hosp., Balt., 1980—82; asst. prof. radiology U. Mich. Med. Ctr., Ann Arbor, 1988—89; pres. Lifewatch Group, Cleve. Author: Wealth, Hunger and Peace, 1989, (web page) www.arrowweb.com/life. Com. mem., organizer One Island One Govt., South Bass Island, 1999. Recipient Ptnrs. in Conservation award, World Wildlife Fund, 1999, Internat. award of Merit, Internat. Soc. Poetry, 2001, Rep. Presdl. Legion of Merit award. Mem.: Am. Coll. Radiology, P.I.B. Yacht Club (fleet surgeon). Republican. Roman Catholic. Achievements include invention of device to aid women in family planning. Avocations: environmental concerns, poetry, gardening.

KAPLAN, GARY, executive recruiter; b. Phila., Aug. 14, 1939; s. Morris and Minnie (Leve) K.; m. Linda Ann Wilson, May 30, 1968; children: Michael Warren, Marc Jonathan, Jeffrey Russell Wilson. BA in Polit. Sci., Pa. State U., 1961. Tchr. biology N.E. High Sch., Phila., 1962-63; coll. employment rep. Bell Telephone Labs., Murray Hill, N.J., 1966-67; supr. recruitment and placement Unisys, Blue Bell, Pa., 1967-69; pres. Electronic Systems Personnel, Phila., 1969-70; staff selection rep. Booz, Allen & Hamilton, N.Y.C., 1970-72; mgr. exec. recruitment M&T Chems., Rahway, N.J., 1972-74; dir. exec. recruitment IU Internat. Mgmt. Corp., Phila., 1974-78; v.p. personnel Crocker Bank, Los Angeles, 1978-79; mng. v.p. ptnr. western region Korn-Ferry Internat., Los Angeles, 1979-85; pres. Gary Kaplan & Assocs., Pasadena, Calif., 1985—. Bd. dirs. Ptnrs. in Care, Greater L.A. Zoo Assn., Coll. Liberal Arts, Pa. State U. Alumni Assn. Mgmt. columnist, Radio and Records newspaper, 1984-85. Mem. alumni coun. Pa. State U.; former bd. dirs. The Wellness Cmty., Pa. State U. Indsl./Orgn. Psychology Adv. Bd.; bd. dirs. Vis. Nurs Assn. L.A., Hme Pharmacy of Calif.; bd.dir. Calif. Exec. Recruiters Assn. Alumni fellow Pa. State U., 1998. Mem. World at Work, Soc. Human Resources Mgmt., Mount Nittany Soc. Pa. State U., Big Ten Club of So. Calif., Pa. State U. Alumni Soc., Big Ten Club of So. Calif. Home: 1735 Fairmount Ave La Canada Flintridge CA 91011-1632 Office: Gary Kaplan & Assocs 201 S Lake Ave Ste 600 Pasadena CA 91101-3018

KAPLAN, GEORGE WILLARD, urologist; b. Brownsville, Tex., Aug. 24, 1935; s. Hyman J. and Lillian (Bennett) K.; m. Susan Gail Solof, Dec. 17, 1961; children: Paula, Elizabeth, Julie, Alan. BA, U. Tex., 1955; MD, Northwestern U., 1959, MS, 1966. Diplomate Am. Bd. Urology. Intern Charity Hosp. of La. at New Orleans, 1959-60; resident Northwestern U., 1963-68, instr. Med. Sch., 1968-69; clin. prof. U. Calif., San Diego, 1970—, chief pediatric urology, 1970—98. Trustee Children's Hosp. and Health Ctr., San Diego, 1978-90, Am. Bd. Urology, Bingham Farms, Mich., 1991-96; del. Am. Bd. Med. Specialties, Evanston, Ill., 1992-96. Author: Genitourinary Problems in Pediatrics; asst. editor Jour. Urology, Balt., 1982-89, 98-2002; assoc. editor Child Nephrology and Urology, Milan, Italy, 1988-94; contbr. articles to profl. pubs. Pres. med. staff Children's Hosp., San Diego, 1980-82. Lt. USN, 1960-63. Recipient Joseph Capps prize Inst. of Medicine, 1967. Fellow ACS (pres. San Diego chpt. 1980-82), Am. Acad. Pediatrics (chmn. sect. on urology 1986); mem. AMA, Soc. for Pediatric Urology (pres. 1993), Am. Urol. Assn., Soc. Internat. Urologie, Soc. Univ. Urologists, Am. Assn. Genito-Urin. Surgeons. Republican. Jewish. Avocations: history of medicine, rare books. Office: Children's Specialists of San Diego Divsn Urology 7930 Frost St Ste 407 San Diego CA 92123-4286 E-mail: g-kaplan@chso.org.

KAPLAN, HARVEY L. lawyer; b. Kansas City, Mo., Nov. 11, 1942; BS in Pharmacy, U. Mich., 1965; JD, U. Mo., 1968. Bar: Mo. 1968, U.S. Tax Ct. 1971, U.S. Supreme Ct. 1971. Ptnr. Shook, Hardy & Bacon LLP, Kansas City. Faculty mem. NITA Advanced Advocacy Program, 1988-89; mem. Kansas City-St. Louis Panel, CPR Inst. Dispute Resolution, 1989—. Mem. bd. editors Mo. Law Rev., 1967-68. Fellow Internat. Acad. Trial Lawyers (bd. dirs. 1991-97, 98—, sec.-treas. 2001-02), Internat. Soc. Barristers, Am. Bar Found.; mem. Am. Soc. Pharmacy Law, Mo. Orgn. Def. Lawyers (bd. dirs. 1985-93), Internat. Assn. Def. Counsel (exec. com. 1991-94, def. counsel trial acad. 1989, dir.-elect 1992, dir. 1993, v.p., found. bd. dirs. 2001-03), Def. Rsch. Inst. (chmn. drug and med. device litigation com. 1991-94, bd. dirs. 1995-98, Law Inst. 1998-2001), Nat. Judicial Coll. (mem. adv. coun. 1993—),Phi Delta Phi. Office: Shook Hardy & Bacon LLP 1 Kansas City Pl 1200 Main St Ste 2700 Kansas City MO 64105-2118 E-mail: hkaplan@shb.com.

KAPLAN, HELENE LOIS, lawyer; b. N.Y.C., June 19, 1933; d. Jack and Shirley (Jacobs) Finkelstein; m. Mark N. Kaplan, Sept. 7, 1952; children: Marjorie Ellen, Sue Anne. AB cum laude, Barnard Coll., 1953; JD, NYU, 1967; LLD (hon.), Columbia U., 1990. Bar: N.Y. 1967. Pvt. practice, N.Y.C., 1967-78; ptnr. Webster & Sheffield, N.Y.C., 1978-86, counsel, 1986-90; of counsel Skadden, Arps, Slate, Meagher & Flom, N.Y.C., 1990—. Bd. dirs. The May Dept. Stores Co., Met. Life Ins. Co., JP Morgan Chase & Co., Inc. and Bank, Exxon Mobil Corp. Trustee N.Y. Coun. for Humanities, 1976-82, chmn., 1978-82; trustee Barnard Coll., 1973-99, chair bd. trustees, 1984-94, trustee and chair emerita, 1999—; trustee Columbia U. Press, 1977-80, MITRE Corp., 1978-95, N.Y. Found., 1976-86, John Simon Guggenheim Meml. Found., 1981-98, NYU Law Ctr. Found., 1985-87, Inst. for Advanced Study, 1986—, Neuroscis. Rsch. Found., 1986-92, Am. Mus. Natural History, 1989—, vice chair, 1993—; trustee Am. Trust for Brit. Libr., 1991-93, Com. for Econ. Devel., 1993-96, Commonwealth Fund, 1990—, vice chair, 1996—; trustee J. Paul Getty Trust, 1992—, vice chair 1997—; trustee Olive Free Libr.; trustee Carnegie Corp. N.Y., 1979—, vice-chair bd. trustees, 1981-84, 98—, chair bd. trustees, 1984-91, 2002—; chair, trustee Mt. Sinai Sch. Medicine, 1999-01, NYU Health, 1998—, vice-chair bd. trustees, 1993-99; trustee N.Y.C. Pub. Devel. Corp., 1978-83, vice-chair bd. trustees, 1978-82; adv. com. on South Africa, U.S. Sec. of State, 1986-88; mem. N.Y. State Gov.'s Task Force on Life and the Law, 1985-90, Women's Forum, Inc., 1982—, Rockefeller U. Coun., 1984-94, Bretton Woods Com., 1985-96, Carnegie Coun. on Adolescent Devel., 1986-96; chairperson task force on sci. and tech. and jud. decision making Carnegie Commn. on Sci., Tech. and Govt., 1988-93; ptnr. N.Y.C. Partnership, 1987-92; bd. dirs. Am. Arbitration Assn., 1978-82. Mem.: N.Y.C. Bar Assn. (treas. 1991—93, mem. com. on philanthropic orgns. 1975—81, mem. com. on recruitment of lawyers 1978—82, mem. com. on profl. responsibility 1980—83), Am. Philos. Soc., Am. Acad. Arts and Scis., Century Assn., Cosmopolitan Club.

KAPLAN, HENRY JERROLD, ophthalmologist, educator; b. N.Y.C., Dec. 29, 1942; s. Ralph and Henrietta (Davis) K.; m. Adele Lotner, June 26, 1966; children: Wendi Suzanne, Todd Daniel, Ariane Dev. AB, Columbia U., 1964; MD, Cornell U., 1968. Diplomate Am. Bd. Ophthalmology. Intern in medicine Lakeside Hosp., Univ. Hosps. Cleve., Case-Western Res. U., 1968-69; surg. resident Bellevue Hosp., NYU Med. Ctr., 1969-70; NIH rsch. fellow in immunology U. Tex. (Southwestern) Med. Sch., Dallas, 1972-74, asst. prof. dept. cell biology, 1974-75; resident in ophthalmology U. Iowa Hosps. and Clinics, Iowa City, 1975-78; retina-vitreous fellow dept. ophthalmology Med. Coll. Wis., Milw., 1978-79; assoc. prof. dept. ophthalmology Emory U. Sch. Medicine, Atlanta, 1979-84, prof., dir. rsch., 1984-88, assoc. prof. dept. microbiology, 1985-88; prof. dept. ophthalmology and visual scis. Washington U. Sch. Medicine, St. Louis, 1988-2000, chmn. dept. ophthalmology and visual scis., 1988-98; prof., chmn. dept. opthalmology and visual scis. U. Louisville (Ky.) Sch. Medicine, 2000—, William H. and Blondina F. Evans Prof. Ophthalmology, 2000—. Ophthalmologist in chief Barnes-Jewish Hosp., Washington U. Med. Ctr., 1988-98; affiliate scientist in pathology and immunology Yerkes Regional Primate Rsch. Ctr., Atlanta, 1981—; adj. prof. dept. small animal medicine U. Ga., Athens, 1985—; assoc. chief ophthalmology Emory U. Hosp., 1985-88; mem. visual scis. study sect. A-1 NIH, Bethesda, Md., 1985-89, chmn., 1987-89; pres. Barnes Eye Care Network, 1994-98; dir. Ky. Lions Eye Ctr., Louisville, 2000—. Author, co-author or editor, co-editor more than 200 med. textbooks, chpts. and articles on uveitis and macular degeneration and retinal degeneration pub. in refereed sci. and med. jours., 1974—; mem. sci. jour. rev. bds. Archives Ophthalmology, 1978—, Retina, 1982—, Am. Jour. Ophthalmology, 1983—, Ophthalmology, 1983—, Current Eye Rsch., 1986—, Exptl. Eye Rsch., 1986—; mem. sci. rev. bd. Investigative Ophthalmology and Visual Sci., 1983—, mem. editorial bd., 1990-92; co-editor Ocular Immunology and Inflammation, 1994-98; editor: Ocular Immunology and Inflammation, 1999—. Maj. M.C., USAF, 1970-72. Recipient sci. award Alcon Rsch. Inst., 1987; Olga Keith Weiss rsch. scholar to Prevent Blindness, Inc., N.Y.C., 1984. Fellow ACS, Am. Acad. Ophthalmology (Honor award 1984, Sr. Honor award 1994); mem. AMA, Assn. for Rsch. in Vision and Ophthalmology, Am. Assn. Immunologists, Macula Soc., Am. Uveitis Soc. (pres. 1997-99), Retina Soc., Louisville Ophthal. Soc., Ky. Acad. Eye Physicians and Surgeons. Jewish. Office: U Louisville Sch Medicine Dept Opthalmol & Visual Sci 301 E Muhammad Ali Blvd Louisville KY 40202-1511 E-mail: hank.kaplan@louisville.edu. *Faith in pursuit of one's own ideas and persistence in the face of adversity will bring success, but more importantly - personal satisfaction.*

KAPLAN, HOWARD GORDON, lawyer; b. June 1, 1941; s. David I. and Beverly Kaplan. BS, U. Ill., 1962; JD, John Marshall Law Sch., Chgo., Ill., 1967. CPA Ill.; bar: Ill. 1967, D.C. 1980, N.Y. 1982, Wis. 1983, U.S. Supreme Ct. 1971. CPA Ill. Acct., Chgo., 1962—67; sr. ptnr. The Kaplan Group Ltd., Chgo., 1967—, The Kaplan Ptnrs. L.L.P., Chgo., 1975—. Asst. prof. Chgo. City Colls., 1967—78. Contbr. articles to profl. jours. Treas. Ill. Devel. Fin. Authority. Mem.: ABA, AICPA, Ill. Soc. CPAs, Decalogue Soc., Bar Assn. 7th Cir., Chgo. Bar Assn., Ill. Bar Assn., B'nai B'rith, Friars Club (L.A.), Bryn Mawr Country Club (Chgo.), Standard Club, Chgo. Athletic Assn. Office: 180 N La Salle St 25th Fl Chicago IL 60601-2501

KAPLAN, HUETTE MYRA, business educator, training consultant; b. Chgo., July 11, 1933; d. Max and Jeannette (Smith) Lazan; m. Jerrold M. Kaplan, Feb. 14, 1954 (dec.); children: Lawrence, Jeffrey. BS in Bus. Edn., DePaul U., 1971. Instr. Pub. Svc. Careers Program State of Ill., Chgo., 1971-72; instr., dir. Patricia Stevens Bus. Sch., Chgo., 1972; relocation mgr., tng. specialist, dir. tng. and devel. Zurich-Am. Ins. Cos., Chgo. and Schaumburg, Ill., 1972-80; pres., tng. cons. H.K. & Assocs., Lansing, Ill., 1980—. Tng. dir. Calumet Area Lit. Coun., Hammond, Ind., 1985—; trainer Chgo. Literacy Coordinating Ctr., 1988-93; instr. Purdue U.-Calumet, Hammond, 1976—; substitute tchr. Sch. Dist. 171, Lansing, 1995-2002. Mem. task force Chgo. Coalition for Edn. and Tng. for Employment, 1984—86; literacy vol. tutor; candidate Dist. 215 Sch Bd., 1999; docent Chgo. Architecture Found., 2001—; bd. dirs. Temple Beth El, Hammond, 1986—88, Calumet Area Literacy Coun., 1990—92, 1994—95, pres., 1995—2002, 2003—. Jewish. Avocations: reading, pet therapy programs, travel. Home and Office: HK & Assocs 2843 192nd St Lansing IL 60438-3717 E-mail: huettek1@aol.com.

KAPLAN, ISAAC RAYMOND, chemistry educator, corporate executive; b. Baranowicze, Poland, July 10, 1929; came to U.S., 1957; s. Morris and Anny (Chait) K.; m. Helen Fagot, Sept. 4, 1955; children: Debora, David Joel. BS, Canterbury U., Christchurch, New Zealand, 1951, MS, 1953; PhD, U. So. Calif., 1961. Rsch. scientist Commonwealth Sci. and Indsl. Rsch. Orgn., Sydney, Australia, 1953-57; postdoctoral fellow Calif. Inst. Tech., Pasadena, 1961-62; guest lectr. Hebrew U., Jerusalem, 1962-65; assoc. prof. UCLA, 1965-69, prof., 1969-93, prof. emeritus, 1993—. Pres. Global Geochemistry Corp., Northridge, Calif., 1977-2003; cons. in field. Contbr. over 300 articles to profl. jours. Guggenheim Found. fellow, Sydney, 1970-71. Fellow: AAAS, Geol. Soc. Am., Am. Inst. Chemists; mem.: Am. Assn. Petroleum Geologists (Pres.'s award 2002, Pres. award 2002), Geochem. Soc. (Alfred Treibs medal 1993), Geophys. Union, Am. Chem. Soc., Russian Acad. Natural Sci. (fgn.) (Kapitsa medal 1998). Office: U Calif ESS Dept Plaza Circle Dr Los Angeles CA 90024

KAPLAN, JAMES LAMPORT, writer, editor, publisher; b. Washington, Mar. 6, 1944; s. Benjamin and Felicia (Lamport) K.; m. Jeanette Marie Muñoz, Mar. 25, 1967 (div. Aug. 1985); children: Benjamin, Matthew; m. Brooks Robards, June 25, 1988. BA, Yale U., 1966; MS in Journalism, Northwestern U., 1967. Staff writer Mpls. Star, 1967-70; reporter, writer Sports Illustrated, N.Y.C., 1970-86; editor Baseball Rsch. Jour., 1987-90; bridge columnist Daily Hampshire Gazette, Vineyard Gazette, Mass., 1990—; editor, polisher China Daily, Beijing, 1993-94; co-pub. Summerset Press, Northampton, Mass., 1986—. Freelance writer. Author: Pine-Tarred and Feathered: A Year on the Baseball Beat, 1985, Playing the Field: Why Defense Is the Most Fascinating Art in Major League Baseball, 1987, The Fielders, 1989, The Official Baseball Hall of Fame Book of Superstars, 1989, The Second Official Baseball Hall of Fame Book of Superstars, 1991, The Giants, 1991, Golden Years of Baseball, 1992, (with Ira Berkow) The Gospel According to Casey: Casey Stengel's Inimitable, Instructional, Historical Baseball Book, 1992, Raising Your Bridge: Valuable Tips for Improving Players, 1993, (with Brooks Robards) Sweet & Sour: One Woman's Chinese Adventure, One Man's Chinese Torture, 1995, Lefty Grove: American Original, 2000, Historic America: The Northwest, 2002, Historic America: New England, 2003; contbr. articles to numerous mags., newspapers. Mem. Conservation Commn., Northampton, 1997-2001. Mem. Nat. Writers Union, Rotary Internat. Democrat. Jewish. Avocations: golf, bridge. Home and Office: 20 Langworthy Rd Northampton MA 01060-2122 E-mail: jkaplan105@aol.com.

KAPLAN, JARED, lawyer; b. Chgo., Dec. 28, 1938; s. Jerome and Phyllis Enid (Rieber) K.; m. Rosellen Engstrom, Dec. 28, 1964 (div. 1978); children: Brian F., Philip B.; m. Maridee Quanbeck, June 2, 1990. AB, UCLA, 1960; LLB, Harvard, 1963. Bar: Ill. 1963, U.S. Dist. Ct. (no. dist.) Ill. 1969, U.S. Tax Ct. 1978. Assoc. Ross & Hardies, Chgo., 1963-69, ptnr., 1970, Roan & Grossman, Chgo., 1970-83, Keck, Mahin & Cate, Chgo., 1983-94, McDermott, Will & Emery, Chgo., 1994—. Bd. dirs. ESOP (Employee Stock Ownership Plan) Assn., Washington, 1987-90, Family Firm Inst., Boston, 1996-99; adv. coun. Ill. Employee-Owned Enterprise, Chgo., 1984-98; chmn. Ill. Adv. Task Force on Ownership Succession and Employee Ownership, 1994-95. Editor in chief: Callaghan's Fed. Tax Guide, 1988; author: Employee Stock Ownership Plans, 1999. Nat. pres. Ripon Soc., Washington, 1975-76; adv. council mem. Rep. Nat. Com., Washington, 1978-80; alt. delegate Rep. Nat. Conv., Detroit, 1980; bd. dirs. Family Firm Inst., 1996-99. Mem. ABA (chmn. section of taxation, administrv. practice com. 1978-80), City Club, Chgo. (bd. govs. 1982-92), Univ. Club, Met. Club. Republican. Jewish. Home: 105 W Delaware Pl Chicago IL 60610-3200 Office: McDermott Will & Emery 227 W Monroe St 47th Fl Chicago IL 60606-5018 E-mail: jkaplan@mwe.com., jkaplan0@aol.com.

KAPLAN, JEAN GAITHER (NORMA KAPLAN), reading specialist, retired educator; b. Cumberland, Md., Dec. 14, 1927; d. Frank Preston and Elizabeth (Mcneil) Gaither; m. Robert Lewis Kaplan, Dec. 4, 1959; 1 child, Benjamin Leigh. AB in Edn., Madison Coll., Harrisonburg, Va., 1950; MA in Edn., U. Va., 1956; postgrad., U. Va., William and Mary, 1958-61; reading specialist degree, U. Va., 1976. Tchr. Frederick County Sch. System, Winchester, Va., 1950-51, Washington County Sch. System, Hagerstown, Md., 1951-55, Charlottesville (Va.) Sch. System, 1955-60, York County (Va.) Sch. System, 1962, Newport News Sch. System, Denbigh, Va., 1963, Internat. Sch. Bangkok, 1965-67; tutor Reston Reading Ctr., Fairfax County, Va., 1972-74; tutor homebound, substitute tchr. Fairfax County Sch. Systems, 1974-78; pvt. practice pvt. tutor McLean/Middleburg, Va., 1978-89. Pres. Tutorial Svcs., Inc., McLean, 1985-87; sec. The Rumson Corp., Middleburg, 1981—. Mem. No. Va. Conservation Coun., Fairfax County, 1976-81; bd. dirs. Nat. Environ. Leadership Coun.; active Piedmont Environ. Coun. Mem. AAUW, LWV, Bangkok Am. Wives Assn., Tuesday Afternoon Club (pres. 1974-75, treas. 1995-96), Ayr Hill Garden Club, Soc. John Gaither Descs. Inc., Bluestone Soc., Kappa Delta Pi, Alpha Sigma Tau. Avocations: reading, theater, concerts, travel. Home and Office: PO Box 1943 Middleburg VA 20118-1943 E-mail: JK9600K@juno.com.

KAPLAN, JEROME, lawyer, accountant; b. Jersey City, Mar. 17, 1926; s. Julius and Leah (Levy) K.; m. Edith Jaffy, Sept. 6, 1953; 1 child, Paul L. BS, Temple U., 1947; JD, U. Mich., 1950. Bar: Mich. 1951, Pa. 1951; CPA. Assoc. Sklar & Pearl, Phila., 1951-53; atty. U.S. Treasury Dept., Phila., 1953-55; assoc. Abrahams & Lowenstein, Phila., 1955-57, ptnr., 1957-61, Kaplan Levy & Grodinsky, Phila., 1961-71, Abrahams & Lowenstein, Phila., 1971-88; of counsel Abrahams, Lowenstein & Bushman, Phila., 1988—. Contbr. articles to profl. jours. Bd. dirs. Phila. Jewis Cmty. Rels. Coun., Com. 70, Ams. for Dem Action; bd. dirs., nat. v.p. Am. Jewish Congress, Sr. Law. With AUS, 1944-45. Mem. ABA, Phila. Bar Assn. Democrat. Jewish. Avocations: skiing, playing music, reading, indoor gardening, bridge. Office: Abrahams Lowenstein et al 3 Parkway Ste 1300 Philadelphia PA 19102-7301

KAPLAN, JERRY, magazine publisher; Publisher, Country Home magazine, WOOD magzine Meredith Corp., Des Moines, Iowa, until 1989; v.p., group publisher Meredith Integrated Mktg., Better Homes and Gardens, Des Moines, Iowa, 1989—, Meredith Group Sales, New Media, N.Y.C., Iowa, 1989—. Office: Better Homes & Gardens 125 Park Ave New York NY 10017-5529

KAPLAN, JERRY (S. JERROLD KAPLAN), former electronics company executive; B in History and Philosophy of Sci., U. Chgo.; D in Computer and Info. Sci., U. Pa. Prin. technologist Lotus Devel. Corp.; co-founder, chmn. GO Corp.; co-founder, CEO ONSALE, Inc., Menlo Park, Calif., 1994—2000; CEO Egghead.com (merged with ONSALE, Inc.), Menlo Park, 2000. Author: Startup-A Silicon Valley Adventure, 1995.*

KAPLAN, JOEL A. dean; Sr. v.p. clin. affairs Mount Sinai Med. Ctr., NY dean, v.p. health affairs U. Louisville, Sch. Medicine, 1998—. Office: Abell Adminstrn Ctr U Louisville Louisville KY 40202

KAPLAN, JOEL HOWARD, psychiatrist; b. June 12, 1936; BA, Yeshiva U. MD, Albert Einstein Coll. Medicine, 1963. Lic. physician, N.Y. Resident in psychiatry Hillside Hosp., 1964-67; capt., chief psychiatrist Fitzsimmons Hosp. Denver, 1967-68; maj., chief 98th Med. Detachment U.S. Army, Nha Trang Vietnam; chief direct admissions Hillside Hosp., 1970-71; asst. clin. prof. psychiatry Mt. Sinai Med. Sch., N.Y.C., 1974-88; dir. psychiatry Franklin Gen Hosp., Woodmere, NY, 1980—, dir. emeritus, 1999—. Contbr. articles to profl. jours. Mem. AMA, Am. Psychiat. Assn. Office: 999 Central Ave Woodmere NY 11598-1205 Fax: (516) 374-4436.

KAPLAN, JOEL STUART, lawyer; b. Bklyn., Feb. 1, 1937; s. Abraham Larry and Phayne (Moses) K.; m. Joan Ruth Katz, June 19, 1960; children: Andrea Beth, Pamela Jill. BA, Bklyn. Coll., 1958; LLB, NYU, 1961. Bar: N.Y. 1962, U.S. Dist. Cts. (ea. and so. dists.) N.Y. 1964, U.S. Ct. Appeals (2d cir.) 1966, U.S. Supreme Ct. 1979, Fla. 1982, D.C. 1987. Asst. town atty. Town of Hempstead, Nassau County, N.Y., 1962-67; ptnr. Jaspan, Kaplan, Levin & Daniels and predecessors, Garden City, N.Y., 1970-83; sole practice Garden City, 1983-95; counsel Levin Belsky Ross and Daniels, Garden City, 1995—. Chmn. Hempstead Town Pub. Employment Rels. Bd., 1973-81; Rep. candidate for N.Y. State Senate, 1974. Mem. ABA, N.Y. State Bar Assn., Nassau County Bar Assn., B'nai B'rith Internat.(pres. 2002—). Office: 585 Stewart Ave Ste 700 Garden City NY 11530-4785

KAPLAN, JOHN, photojournalist, educator, consultant; b. Wilmington, Del., Aug. 21, 1959; s. Ralph Benjamin and Ruth Jillya (Denkin) Kaplan. BJ cum laude, Ohio U., Athens, 1982; MS in Journalism, Ohio U., 1998. Photojournalist, designer Spokesman Rev./Chronicle, Spokane, Wash., 1983—84; photojournalist, picture editor Pitts. Press, 1984—90; photojournalist Pitts. Post-Gazette, 1990—92; spl. corr. Block Newspapers, 1992—94. Tchr., lectr. numerous univs., seminars, profl. groups U.S., Can., 1984—; vis. lectr. Bradley U., Peoria, Ill., 1989; adj. prof. Syracuse U., London campus, 1993; assoc. prof. U. Fla., Gainesville, 1999—, dir. Media Alliance, cons., Pitts., 1990—2000; mem. Pulitzer Prize jury, 1994, 95; photojournalism mem. Ball State U., Muncie, 1998—99. Author: Mom and Me, 1996; contbr. to book series; work in permanent collection Carnegie Mus. Art, Pitts.; author: Photo Portfolio Success, 2003. Named Pitts. Photographer of Yr., News Photographers Assn. Greater Pitts., 1986, 1989, 1992, Photographer of Yr., Pa. Photographers Assn., 1989, No. Photographer of Yr., 1992; named to, Ohio U. Coll. Comm. Hall of Fame, 1993; recipient Golden Quill Journalism award, Pitts. Press Club, 1986, 1989, Robert F. Kennedy Journalism award, Kennedy Found., 1989, Pulitzer prize for feature photography, 1992, 2003, Matrix Mag. award, Women in Comm., 1992, Ohio U. Disting. Grad. award, 1993, Overseas Press Club award, 2023, award for feature photography, Overseas Press Club, 2003; Knight fellow, Ohio U., 1997—98. Mem.: Soc. Newspaper Design (Gold award 1989), Nat. Press Photographers Assn. (contest chmn. Region 3 1987—89, Regional Photographer of Yr. award 1985, 1986, 1987, 1989, Nat. Newspaper Photographer of Yr. award 1989, Nikon Documentary Sabbatical award 1990, Harry Chapin award 2023, others), Amnesty Internat. Avocations: racquet sports, furniture design, wines. Address: 3067 Weimer Hall Gainesville FL 32611-8400

KAPLAN, JONATHAN HARRIS, healthcare business transformation and information technology specialist; b. N.Y.C., Apr. 29, 1957; s. Bernard and Arlene (Lavender) K.; m. Lorraine Caryl Weiss, Aug. 6, 1983; children: Alexandra Lindsay, Elizabeth Sydney. AB, Cornell U., 1979; MPH, U. Pitts., 1980; grad. Exec. Program Kellogg Sch. Mgmt., Northwestern U. Cert. data processor, mgmt. cons., systems profl. Statistician Nat. Ctr. Health Stats., Hyattsville, Md., 1980; assoc. installation dir. Shared Med. Systems, N.Y.C., 1981, installation dir., 1981-82; cons. Ernst & Young, N.Y.C., 1982-83, sr. cons., 1984, supr., 1985, mgr., 1985-86, sr. mgr., 1986-90, ptnr., 1990—, regional dir. healthcare info. tech./performance improvement, 1991-95, Great Lakes area dir. Chgo., 1996-99, Midwest mng. dir. for health care consulting N.Y.C., 1999—, regional v.p. Midwest Health Care Consulting, Cap Gemini, 2000—, health practice solution leader, 2002—, bus. and tech. leader for svcs. industries, 2003—. Adj prof. health care adminstrn. Baruch Coll., CUNY; spkr. in field. Speaker in field. Bd. govs. Boy Scouts Am., exec. com. dinner com.; bd. govs. Arthritis Found., chmn. strategic planning com., mem. exec. com.; bd. govs. Larchmont Manor Park Soc.; bd. dirs. Juvenile Diabetes Found., Jr. Achievement; mem. long range planning com. Sukkot Shalom. Recipient Westinghouse Sci. award, Shared Med. Systems Field Svc. award; grantee USPHS, 1979, 80. Mem. Am. Coll. Healthcare Execs., Am. Assn. Healthcare Cons., Am. Med. Informatics Assn., Am. Hosp. Assn., Inst. Mgmt. Cons., Healthcare Info. and Mgmt. Sys. Soc., Healthcare Fin. Mgmt. Assn., N.Y. Acad. Scis., Inst. Cert. Computer Profls., Cornell U. Alumni Assn., U. Pitts. Alumni Assn., N.Y. Athletic Club, U.S. Rowing Assn., Lacrosse Found.. Met. Club., Econs. Club of Chgo., Execs. Club of Chgo., The Chgo. Club, Mich. Shores Club. Office: Cap Gemini Ernst & Young LLP Sears Tower 233 S Wacker Dr Chicago IL 60606-6306 E-mail: jonathan.kaplan@us.cgeyc.com.

KAPLAN, JUDITH HELENE, company executive; b. July 20, 1938; d. Abraham and Ruth (Kiffel) Letich; m. Warren Kaplan, Dec. 31, 1958; children: Ronald Scott, Elissa Aynn. BA, Hunter Coll., 1955; postgrad., New Sch. for Social Rsch., 1955-56. Registered rep. Herzfeld & Stern, N.Y.C., 1963; agt. New York Life Ins. Co., N.Y.C., 1964-69; registered rep. Scheinman, Hochstin & Trotta, N.Y.C., 1969-70; v.p. Alpha Capital Corp., N.Y.C., 1970-74; pres. Ipex, Inc., N.Y.C., 1966-84; v.p. Alpha Pub. Rels., N.Y.C., 1970-73; pres. Utopia Recreations Corp., N.Y.C., 1971-73, Howard Beach Recreation Corp., N.Y.C., 1972-73; chmn. bd. Alpha Exec. Planning Corp., N.Y.C., 1970-72; field underwriter N.Y. Life Ins. Co., N.Y.C., 1974-75; pres. Action Products Internat., Inc., N.Y.C., 1978-87, chairperson, 1980-95, dir., 1980—; chairperson Ronel Industries, Inc., N.Y.C., 1982-84; pres. Orlando (Fla.) Orange, Inc., 1995; ptnr. Kaplan Asset Mgmt., Ocala, Fla., 1997—. Participant White House Conv. on Small Bus., 1979; owner Orlando Orange, Inc. Profl. Baseball Team, 1995-96. Author: Woman Suffrage, 1977; co-author: Space Patches—From Mercury to the Space Shuttle, 1986; contbg. editor: Stamp Show News, M & H Philatelic Report; creator, prodr. Women's History series of First Day Covers, 1976-81; contbr. articles to profl. jours. Founder Women's History Mus., Judith Kaplan & Warren Kaplan's Women's History Collection Ctrl. Fla. C.C., Ocala, 1991; dir., trustee Feminist Scholarship Fund, Boca Raton, Fla., 1997—; advisor Kaplan Women's History Collection CFCC Found., Ocala, Fla.; adv. Nat. Women's History Mus., Washington, 1998-2000, dir. 2000—, sec., 2001--; active Wyo. adv. on woman suffrage, Vet. Feminists of Am., 2000—, dir.; trustee Found. for Innovative Lifelong Edn. Inc., 1986-88; bd. dirs. Ctrl. Fla. Regional Libr., 1996-97; mem. SPBCNOW, Boca Raton, Fla., 1997-2003, v.p., 2002-2003. Named Outstanding Young Citizen Manhattan Jaycees, Small Bus. Person of Yr. State of Fla., 1986. Mem. NOW (ns. coord. nat. task force on taxes, v.p. N.Y. Chpt., co-founder Ocala/Marion County chpt. 1982, bd. women's adv. coun. Ocala and Marion Counties 1986-88), Veteran Feminists of Am. (dir. 2001-), Nat. Women's Polit. Caucus, Women Leaders Round Table, Nat. Assn. Life Underwriters, Assn. Stamp Dealers Am., Am. First Day Cover Soc. (life), Am. Philatelic Soc. (life), Bus. and Profl. Women, AAUW. Home: 2842 Shadow View Cir Maitland FL 32751-7518 Office: Kaplan Asset Mgmt Div Ronel Mgmt Sys 2842 Shadow View Circle Boca Raton FL 33432

KAPLAN, JUSTIN, author; b. N.Y.C., Sept. 5, 1925; s. Tobias D. and Anna (Rudman) K.; m. Anne F. Bernays, July 29, 1954; children: Susanna Bernays, Hester Margaret, Polly Anne. BS, Harvard U., 1944, postgrad., 1944-46; D Humane Letters (hon.), Marlboro Coll., 1984. Free-lance editing, writing, N.Y.C., 1946-54; sr. editor Simon & Schuster, Inc., N.Y.C., 1954-59; lectr. English Harvard U., 1969, 73, 76, 78; prose writer in residence Emerson Coll., Boston, 1977-78. Vis. lectr. Griffith U., Brisbane, Australia, 1983; lectr. in field; judge Nat. Book Awards, 1968, 73, 78, 87, 93, Pulitzer prizes, 1989, 94, 97; resident Bellagio Study and Conf. Ctr., Italy, spring, 1990; Jenks prof. contemporary letters Coll. of Holy Cross, Worcester, Mass., 1992-95. Author: Mr. Clemens and Mark Twain, 1966, Lincoln Steffens, A Biography, 1974, Mark Twain and His World, 1974, Walt Whitman: A Life, 1980, (with Anne Bernays) The Language of Names, 1997, (with Bernays) Back Then, 2002; editor: Dialogues of Plato, 1948, With Malice Toward Women, 1949, The Pocket Aristotle, 1956, The Gilded Age, 1964, Great Short Works of Mark Twain, 1967, Mark Twain, A Profile, 1967, Walt Whitman: Complete Poetry and Collected Prose, 1982, The Harper American Literature, 1987, 94, Best American Essays, 1990; gen. editor: Bartlett's Familiar Quotations, 17th edit., 2002; contbr. to N.Y. Times, New Republic, Am. Scholar, Newsweek, Ploughshares, Yale Rev., others. Participant cultural programs USIA, Israel, Dominican Republic, Mex., 1985. Recipient Pulitzer prize for biography, 1967, Nat. Book award for arts and letters, 1967, Nat. Book award for biography, 1981, Guggenheim fellowship, 1975—76. Fellow: Mass. Hist. Soc., Soc. Am. Historians, Am. Acad. Arts and Scis.; mem.: Am. Acad. Arts and Letters, Harvard Club (NY), Phi Beta Kappa. Home: 16 Francis Ave Cambridge MA 02138-2010 E-mail: jknames@aol.com.

KAPLAN, KEITH JACOB, physician; b. Chicago, Illinois, Oct. 5, 1970; s. Martin and Adrienne (Shaffer) K.; m. Stephanie Jo (Schul), Apr. 20, 1996. BS cum laude(hon.), Mich. State U., 1992; MD, U. Ill., Northwestern, 1996. Intern Walter Reed Army Med. Ctr., Washington, 1996-97, resident, anatomic and clin. pathology, 1997-2001, staff pathologist. Asst. prof. pathology, Uniformed Svc. U. of Health Sci., Bethesda, Md., 2001—. Contbr. articles to sci. and profl. jours. Capt. M.C., U.S. Army, 1996. Mem.: Am. Soc. Clin. Pathologists; Coll. Am. Pathologists; U.S. and Can. Acad. Pathology, Am. Soc. Clin. Pathologists; Coll. Am. Pathologists (std. com.), Md. State Med. Soc. Avocations: fishing, boating, hockey, reading, stamp collecting, e-mail. Office: Walter Reed Army Med Ctr Dept Pathology 6900 Georgia Ave NW Washington DC 20307-5001 Home: 1032 Grand Oak Way Rockville MA 20852 E-mail: keith.kaplan@na.amedd.army.mil.

KAPLAN, KENNETH BARRY, psychologist; b. Boston, Mar. 15, 1947; s. Harold Irving and Eleanor (Miller) K.; m. Rhonda I. Sherer; children: David B., Rachel L., Howard D., Amy M. BA, U. Mass., Boston, 1969; EdM in Ednl. Counseling Psychology, Suffolk U., 1972; postgrad., Boston State Coll., 1974-76, Emmanuel Coll., 1974-76, Bridgewater State Coll., 1982-83, Fitchburg State Coll., 1989-90. Lic. cert. social worker, ednl. psychologist, sch. psychologist, tchr., secondary sch. prin. Asst. mgr. S.S. Pierce Co., 1970-71; tchr. Boston Pub. Schs., 1972-82; cons. svc. specialist for retarded individuals Wrentham State Sch., 1972-79; secondary sch. psychologist Bridgewater/Raynham (Mass.) Pub. Schs., 1982—. Bd. dirs. United Way of Greater Taunton, Mass., 1991—2000, chair edn. sector, 1991—98; bd. dirs. Taunton Family, 1991—98. Named Horace Mann Tchr., Mass. Dept. Edn., 1986-87; Alliance Against Drugs grantee, 1993. Mem.: NASP, NASW, NEA, Plymouth County Educators Assn., Bridgewater Raynham Edn. Assn., Bristol County Educators Assn., Raynham Edn. Assn. (pres. 1988—94), Mass. Tchrs. Assn., Mass. Assn. Social Workers, Mass. Sch. Counselors Assn., Mass. Soc. Psychol. Assn., Rotary (Sharon chpt., pres. 2000—01). Home: 2 Sherwood Cir Sharon MA 02067-2262 Office: Bridgewater Raynham Schs 420 Titicut Rd Raynham MA 02767-1561

KAPLAN, KENNETH FRANKLIN, manufacturing company financial executive; b. N.Y.C., July 14, 1945; s. Harold and Jeannette (Rubin) K.; m. Judith Zacharias, Aug. 26, 1967; children: Teri, Joshua. BS in Math., U. Mich., 1967; MBA in Mgmt., UCLA, 1969. Fin. analyst Northrop Corp., L.A., 1969-71; sr. fin. analyst Dart Industries, L.A., 1971-74; asst. controller consumer products group West Bend (Wis) Co., 1974-76, dir. fin. planning and analysis, 1976-77; controller Graham Co., Milw., 1977-81, v.p. fin. and adminstr., 1981-85; treas. Gehl Co., West Bend, 1986-96, corp. controller, 1985-87, v.p. fin., 1988-96; v.p., CFO Regal-Beloit Corp., Beloit, Wis., 1996—, sec., 1997—. Bd. dirs., chmn. fin. com. Kettle Moraine YMCA, West Bend, 1981-96; bd. dirs. West Bend C. of C., 1988-94. Mem. Fin. Execs. Inst., Greater Beloit C. of C. (bd. dirs. 1999-2003). Office: Regal-Beloit Corp 200 State St Beloit WI 53511-6254

KAPLAN, KERRY JOSEPH, internist, cardiologist; b. Louisville, June 23, 1950; s. Robert and Barbara Helen (Rudin) K.; m. Leslie Diamond, Dec. 31, 1973 (div.); 1 child, Lauren Elyse; m. Debra Jill Levine, Sept. 1, 1985; children: Zachary Aron, Jori Lee, Alyson Bari. BS, Northwestern U., Evanston, Ill., 1972; MD, Northwestern U., Chgo., 1974. Diplomate Am. Bd. Internal Medicine, Am. Bd. Cardiovascular Disease, Am. Bd. Critical Care Medicine. Intern Northwestern U. Med. Sch., 1974-75, resident in internal medicine, 1975-77, fellow in cardiology, 1977-79; pvt. practice Clearwater, Fla., 1988—; attending physician, assoc. dir. med. intensive care area Northwestern U. Med. Sch., Chgo., 1979-88. Pres. med. staff Mease Hosp., Dunedin, Fla., 1993; bd. dirs. Morton Plant Mease Hosp., Bay Care Med. Sys. Pres. Temple Ahavat Shalom, Palm Harbor, Fla., 1992-94. Fellow ACP, Am. Coll. Cardiology. Home: 1522 Silver Moon Ln Palm Harbor FL 34683-2108 Office: Heart & Vascular Inst of Fla 140 Mease Dr Office 201 Safety Harbor FL 34695

KAPLAN, LAURENCE SCOTT, computer engineer; b. Englewood, N.J., Sept. 23, 1962; s. Leonard and Vivian (Hacker) K. BA cum laude, Dartmouth Coll., 1984; MS, NYU, 1988. Software engr. Compugraphics Corp., Wilmington, Mass., 1984-86; rsch. asst. Ultracomputer Rsch. Project, N.Y.C., 1986-88; unix devel. engr. BBN Advanced Computers, Cambridge, Mass., 1988-91; sr. scientist oper. sys. Cray Inc., Seattle, 1991—. Courant Inst./NYU fellow, 1986, Army Rsch. Org./NYU fellow, 1987. Mem. IEEE Computer Soc.. Democrat. Jewish. Achievements include patents for techniques for interrupt free operating system; debugging in a multithreaded environment. Avocations: water-skiing, snow skiing, science fiction, scuba diving, ultimate Frisbee. Office: Cray Inc 411 1st Ave S Ste 600 Seattle WA 98104-3847

KAPLAN, LAWRENCE JAY, economist, educator; b. Oct. 28, 1915; s. Harris and Estelle (Wilner) Kaplan; m. Jeanne Leon, June 9, 1946; children: Harriet, Sanford S., Marcia. BA, Bklyn. Coll., 1937; MA, Columbia U., 1938, PhD, 1958. Chief info. officer Bur. Labor Stats., Dept. of Labor, N.Y.C., 1949—57; dir. planning and rsch. N.Y.C. Dept. City Planning, Dept. Relocation, 1957—65; prof. econs. John Jay Coll.. Criminal Justice, N.Y.C., 1965—86, prof. emeritus, 1986—; now lectr. and cons. Author: Elementary Statistics for Economics and Business, 1966, Ins and Outs of On-Track and Off-Track Betting, 1970, Retiring Right: Planning for A Successful Retirement, 2003; editor: An Economic Analysis of Crime, 1976. Vice-chmn., mem. profl. staff Congress-CUNY Welfare Fund, 1969—86, emeritus, 1986—; chmn. profl. staff Congress-CUNY Retirees chpt., 1991—2000; emeritus Coun. Mcpl. Retiree Orgns. N.Y.C., 2001—, chmn., 1995—, chmn. emeritus, 2003—. With mil. intelligence U.S. Army, 1942—45. Decorated NY State Conspcuous Svc. Cross, 5 Battle Stars; recipient citation, Republic of France. Mem.: Am. Statis. Assn., Am. Econ. Assn. Democrat. Jewish. Office: John Jay Coll Criminal Justice 899 10th Ave New York NY 10019-1104 E-mail: ljkjj@aol.com.

KAPLAN, LAWRENCE SAMUEL, historian, educator; b. Cambridge, Mass., Oct. 28, 1924; s. Jacob Copel Kaplan and Julia Starnfield; m. Janice Eyges Kaplan; children: Deborah Judith, Joshua Kopel. BS, Colby Coll., 1947; MA, Yale U., 1948, PhD, 1951. Historian hist. office Office Sec. Def., Washington, 1951—54; from instr. to prof. Kent State U., Ohio, 1954—77, univ. prof. history, 1977—93, dir. Lyman L. Lemnitzer Ctr. NATO and European Union studies, 1979—92; professorial lectr. history Georgetown U., Washington, 1993—. Cons. and rschr. hist. office Office Sec. Def., Washington, 1975—80, Washington, 1986—; Fulbright lectr. history U. Bonn, 1959—60, U. Louvain, 1964—65, U. Nice, 1965; lectr. history U. Coll. London, 1969—70; vis. prof. European U. Inst., Florence, Italy, 1978, Florence, 86; disting. Fulbright lectr. U. Malta, 1986. Author: Jefferson and France, 1967, The United States and NATO: The Formative Years, 1984, The Long Entanglement: NATO's First Fifty Years, 1999, Alexander Hamilton: Ambivalent Anglophile, 2002. Staff sgt. Army Signal Corps, 1943—46, Philippines. Fellow, Am. Coun. Learned Socs., 1950—51, Woodrow Wilson Internat. Ctr. Scholars, 1974; grantee, Am. Philos. Soc., 1969—70, 1980—81; Univ. fellow, Yale U., 1947—48, Rsch. fellow, NATO, 1980—81, Fulbright Rsch. grantee, NATO Archives, Brussels, 2002. Mem.: Soc. Historians Early Am. Republic (pres. 1991—92), So. Historians Am. Fgn. Rels. (pres. 1980—81), Cosmos Club. Home: 11400 Strand Dr # 314 Rockville MD 20852

KAPLAN, LEE LANDA, lawyer; b. Houston, Jan. 26, 1952; s. Charles Irving and Ara Celine (Seligman) K.; m. Diana Morton Hudson, Feb. 6, 1982. AB, Princeton U., 1973; JD, U. Tex., 1976. Bar: Tex., U.S. Dist. Ct. (no., wc., ea. and so. dists.) Tex., U.S. Ct. Appeals (5th, 11th and Fed. cirs.), U.S Supreme Ct. Law clk. to sr. cir. judge U.S. Ct. Appeals (5th cir.), Houston, 1976-77; assoc. Baker & Botts, L.L.P., Houston, 1977-84, ptnr., 1985-94, Smyser Kaplan & Veselka, L.L.P., Houston, 1995—. Mem. Tex. Aerospace Commn., 1994-99. Mem. ABA, State Bar Tex., Houston Bar Assn., Am. Bd. Trial Advs. (assoc.), Am. Intellectual Property Law Assn., Houston Intellectual Property Law Assn. Democrat. Jewish. Avocation: history. Office: Smyser Kaplan & Veselka LLP 700 Louisiana St Ste 2300 Houston TX 77002-2728 E-mail: lkaplan@skv.com.

KAPLAN, LEONARD EUGENE, accountant; b. Chgo., Mar. 3, 1940; s. David Solomon and Faye Gertrude (Grossman) K.; m. Myrna Dee Shellist, Dec. 20, 1959; children: Sheri Kaplan Mayes, Jodi Kaplan Hoffman, Jeffrey. Student, U. Ill., Chgo., 1958-59; BSC in Acctg., De Paul U., 1961. CPA, Tex., Ill.; cert. ins. counselor. Staff acct. Goldstein, Engerman & Shane, Chgo., 1960-63, BDO Seidman, Chgo., 1963-72, ptnr., 1972-79, Houston, 1979-95, regional tech. dir. region III, 1982-84, mng. ptnr., 1984-89, nat. dir. industry specialization, 1990-92; also bd. dirs.; exec. v.p., CFO Delta Ins. Group Corp., Houston, 1995—. Mem. adv. coun. dept. acctg. U. Tex., 1989-95. Contbr. articles to various publs. Bd. dirs. Chocolate Bayou Theater Co. Ill. State scholar, 1958-61, Jack Claitor Meml. scholar Tex. Surplus Lines Assn., 1998. Mem.: AICPA, Tex. Surplus Lines Assn. (bd. dirs., chmn. regulatory liaison com.), Bus. and Profl. Soc. of Jewish Fedn., Nat. Assn. Ind. Insurers, Am. Assn. Mng. Gen. Agts., Soc. of Cert. Ins. Counselors, Ill. CPA Soc., Tex. Soc. CPAs (vice chmn. com. on rels. with attys. Houston chpt. 1984—85), B'nai B'rith (newsletter editor 1971—72), Royal Oaks Country Club. Jewish. Avocations: golf, tennis, crossword puzzles. *Concern for what might have been is never productive. Yesterday is what it is. Today and the rest of your life are what you make them. Focus on the future and never look back.*

KAPLAN, LEWIS A. judge; b. S.I., Dec. 23, 1944; s. Alfred H. and Dorothy A. Kaplan; widowed; 1 child, Merrill. AB, U. Rochester, 1966; JD, Harvard U., 1969. Bar: N.Y. 1970, U.S. Ct. Appeals (1st and 2d cirs.) 1970, U.S. Dist. Ct. (so. and ea. dists.) N.Y. 1971, U.S. Ct. Appeals (3d cir.) 1973, U.S. Supreme Ct. 1973, U.S. Dist. Ct. (we. dist.) N.Y. 1975, U.S. Ct. Appeals (DC cir.) 1976, U.S. Dist. Ct. (no. dist.) Calif. 1980, U.S. Ct. Appeals (9th cir.) 1980, U.S. Dist. Ct. (ea. dist.) Mich. 1983, U.S. Ct. Appeals (6th cir.) 1983, DC 1985, U.S. Ct. Appeals (Fed. cir.) 1987, U.S. Dist. Ct. DC 1988. Law clk. to judge U.S. Ct. Appeals (1st cir.), 1969-70; assoc. Paul, Weiss, Rifkind, Wharton & Garrison, N.Y.C., 1970-77, ptnr., 1977-94; judge U.S. Dist. Ct. (so. dist.) N.Y., N.Y.C., 1994—, spl. master Westway litig., 1982. Trustee Lawyers Com. Civil Rights Under Law, 1992—94; mem. com. info. tech. Jud. Conf. U.S., 1997—; Brace Meml. lectr. Copyright Soc. U.S.A., 2001. Mem. trustees' coun. U. Rochester, 1982—88, mem. trustees' vis. com. William E. Simon Grad. Sch. Bus. Adminstrn., 1986—88; village trustee NY, 1988—91. Fellow: Am. Coll. Trial Lawyers; mem.: ABA, Fed. Judges Assn. (dir. 1995—2001, exec. com. 1999—2001), Am. Law Inst., Fed. Bar Coun., N.Y. State Bar Assn. Office: US Courthouse 500 Pearl St New York NY 10007-1316

KAPLAN, MADELINE, legal administrator; b. N.Y.C., June 20, 1944; d. Leo and Ethel (Finkelstein) Kahn; m. Theodore Norman Kaplan, Nov. 14, 1982. AS, Fashion Inst. Tech., N.Y.C., 1964; BA in English Lit. summa cum laude, CUNY, 1982; MBA, Baruch Coll., 1990. Free-lance fashion illustrator, N.Y.C., 1965-73; legal asst. Krause Hirsch & Gross, Esquires, N.Y.C., 1973-80; mgr. communications Stroock & Stroock & Lavan Esquires, N.Y.C., 1980-86; dir. adminstrn. Cooper Cohen Singer & Ecker Esquires, N.Y.C., 1986-87, Donovan Leisure Newton & Irvine Esquires, N.Y.C., 1987-93, Proskauer Rose Goetz & Mendelsohn, N.Y.C., 1993-95, Kaye Scholer LLP, N.Y.C., 1995—. Mem. adv. bd. Grad. Sch. Human Resources Mgmt. Mercy Coll., 1997—; bd. dirs. Suitability. Contbr. articles to profl. jours. Founder, pres. Knolls chpt. of Women's Am. Orgn. Rehab. Through Tng., Riverdale, N.Y., 1979 82, v.p. edn., Manhattan region, 1982-83; adv. bd. Suitability; vol. Starlight Found. Mem. ASTD, Assn. Legal Adminstrs. (program com.), MBA Alumni Assn. (bd. dirs.), Sigma Iota Epsilon (life). Office: 425 Park Ave New York NY 10022-3506

KAPLAN, MARC J. lawyer; b. Phila., Mar. 12, 1957; s. Ronald L. Kaplan and Sylvia B. (Meyers) Price; m. Mary J. Dulacki, Sept. 16, 1984; children: Alexandra Zoe, Rini Isadora. BA, Duke U., 1979; JD, U. Denver, 1983. Bar: Colo. 1984, Mont. 1999, U.S. Dist. Ct. Colo. 1984, U.S. Ct. Appeals (10th cir.) 1984; cert. civil trial advocate Nat. Bd. Trial Advocacy. Asst. for polit. ops. Dem. Nat. Com., Washington, 1979—80; asst. to spl. asst. to pres. White House, Washington, 1980—81; atty. Aisenberg & Kaplan, Denver, 1984—94, Rossi, Cox, Kiker & Inderwish, P.C., Denver, 1994—98; special counsel Gutterman, Carlton & Hockenbach LLP, 1998—2000; pvt. practice Denver, 2000—. Polit. cons. Washington, 1981, lawyering process adj. prof. U. Denver Coll. of Law, 1990-92, faculty basic civil litig. skills continuing legal edn. of Denver, 1990-92, Colo. Supreme Ct. Greivance Com. Hearing Bd., Denver, 1993-98; mem. Supreme Ct. Colo., com. county and dist. ct. cir. and jud. access issues, 1998-99. Contbr. Colo. Auto Litigator's Handbook. Pres. Duke Club of Denver, 1990-92, chmn. Children of Violence Com., Denver, 1993-94; bd. dirs. United Citizens of Arapahoe Neighborhoods, 1997-2001. Named Young Polit. Leader U.S. State Dept., Washington, 1979. Mem.: Am. Coll. of Master Advocates and Barristers (sr. coun. mem.), Faculty of Fed. Advocates, Thompson G. Marsh Inn of Ct., Denver and Arapahoe Bar Assn., Colo. Trial Lawyers Assn. (pres. 1998—99), Colo. Bar Assn. (gov. 1990—93, 2003—, Pro Bono award 1993), ATLA (state del. 1997—99, state del. family law sect. 2003—). Office: Kaplan Law LLC 2300 15th St Ste 200 Denver CO 80202 E-mail: marc@kaplan-law.com.

KAPLAN, MARK NORMAN, lawyer; b. N.Y.C., Mar. 7, 1930; s. Louis and Ruth (Hertzberg) K.; m. Helene L. Finkelstein, Sept. 7, 1952; children: Marjorie Ellen, Sue Anne. AB, Columbia, 1951, JD, 1953. Bar: N.Y. 1953. Assoc. Garey & Garey, N.Y.C., 1953; law clk. to Hon. William Bondy U.S. Dist. Ct. for So. Dist. N.Y., 1953-54; assoc. Columbia Law Sch., 1954-55, Wickes, Riddell, Bloomer, Jacobi & McGuire, N.Y.C., 1955-59; from assoc. to sr. ptnr. Marshall, Bratter, Greene, Allison & Tucker, N.Y.C., 1959-70; sr. ptnr. Burnham & Co., N.Y.C., 1970-71; pres. Drexel Burnham Lambert Inc., N.Y.C., 1972-77, also CEO, 1976-77; pres. Engelhard Minerals & Chem. Corp., N.Y.C., 1977-79; mem. firm Skadden, Arps, Slate, Meager & Flom, N.Y.C., 1979—. Bd. dirs. Am. Biltrite, Grey Advt., Inc., REFAC Tech. Devel. Corp., DRS Techs. Inc., Volt Info. Sci., Inc., Jim Pattison, Ltd., Internat. Creative Mgmt., Inc., Monte Carlo Grand Hotel, Congoleum Corp., World Wide Spl. Fund N.V.; vice-chmn. Am. Stock Exch., N.Y.C., 1974, bd. govs., 1975, vice-chmn. bd. govs., 1975-76; trustee Bard Coll.; chmn. audit com. City of N.Y. Co-chmn. audit adv. com. Bd. Edn. of City of N.Y.; chmn. Early Edn. Leadership Group; bd. dirs. New Alternatives for Children. Mem. Coun. Fgn. Rels., Century Assn., Econ. Club N.Y. Home: 146 Central Park W New York NY 10023-2005 Office: Skaden Arps 4 Times Sq Fl 24 New York NY 10036-6595 E-mail: mkaplan@skadden.com.

KAPLAN, MARSHALL MYLES, medical educator, researcher, gastroenterologist; b. Boston, Feb. 20, 1935; s. Harold and Ginda (Braverman) K.; m. Nancy Proger, June 5, 1960; children: Ginda, William, Thomas, Deborah. BS summa cum laude, Yale U., 1956; MD cum laude, Harvard U., 1960. Intern, resident Columbia-Presbyn., N.Y.C., 1960-62; clin. assoc. NIH, Bethesda, Md., 1962-65; trainee liver disease Yale U., New Haven, 1965-66; asst. prof. medicine Tufts-New England Med. Ctr., Boston, 1966-69, assoc. prof. medicine, 1969-75, prof. medicine, 1975—, chief divsn. gastroenterology, 1972—2002. Chmn. merit rev. com. VA Hosps., Washington, 1975-77; mem. gastroenterology bd. Am. Bd. Internal Medicine, 1983-89, chmn., 1987-89, bd. govs., 1987-89; manuscript reviewer Annals Internal Medicine, Am. Jour. Medicine, Archives of Internal Medicine, Gastroenterology, Hepatology, Digestive Diseases and Sci., Am. Jour. Gastroenterology, Jour. Hepatology. Assoc. editor New Eng. Jour. Medicine, 1993-2001; editor Tufts Family Health Guides, 1979-82; mem. editl. bd. Hepatology, 1988-92; contbr. over 280 articles to med. jours., chpts. to books. Lt. comdr. USPHS, 1962-65. Master ACP (chair sci. program com. 1990-93, gastroenterology med. knowledge self-assessment program); mem. Assn. Am. Physicians, Am. Soc. Clin. Investigation, Am. Gastroenterology Assn., Am. Assn. for Study of Liver Disease (com. chair 1984-86), Phi Beta Kappa, Alpha Omega Alpha (dir. 1983-89). Democrat. Jewish. Avocations: tennis, squash, golf, gardening, music. Home: 30 Oakridge Rd Wellesley MA 02481-2504 Office: New England Med Ctr 750 Washington St Boston MA 02111-1526

KAPLAN, MARTIN P. allergist, immunologist, pediatrician; b. Bklyn., Oct. 28, 1928; MD, SUNY Downstate. Diplomate Am. Bd. Allergy & Immunology, Am. Bd. Pediatrics. Resident Jewish Hosp., Bklyn., 1954-55, SUNY Upstate Med. Ctr., Syracuse, 1957-58; fellow Children's Hosp., Washington, 1958-59; active staff mem. dept. medicine St. Joseph Hosp., Lexington, Ky., 1959—; clin. assoc. prof. pediatrics and medicine U. Ky. Coll. Medicine, 1982-97. Mem. AAACI, ACAI, AMA, Ky. Med. Assn. Office: 166 Pasadena Ste 150 Lexington KY 40503-3014

KAPLAN, MITCHELL ALAN, sociologist, researcher; b. Bklyn., Jan. 26, 1954; s. Murray Robert and Claire (Meshnick) K. BA in Sociology and Psychology cum laude, L.I. U., 1976; MA in Sociology, New Sch. for Social Rsch., 1979; PhD in Sociology, CUNY, 1987. Cert. social rsch. specialist; cert. profl. sociol. practitioner Am. Acad. Profl. Sociol. Practitioners. Rsch. fellow Narcotic and Drug Rsch. Inc., N.Y.C., 1986-89, cons., 1989-90, Am. Found. for AIDS Rsch., N.Y.C., 1989-90; rsch. scientist Rsch. & Tng. Inst. Nat. Ctr. for Disability Svcs., Albertson, N.Y., 1991-92; acad. rsch. cons. Acad. Rsch. Consulting Svcs., Bklyn., 1993—2001; project mgr. dept. pain medicine and palliative care Beth Israel Med. Ctr., N.Y.C., 1999—2002; rsch. assoc. Acad.

Rsch. Con. Svcs., 1993—2001. Evaluations cons. office rsch. and ednl. assessment Bklyn. divsn. N.Y.C. Bd. Edn., 1992-93; devel. rschr. Am. Heart Assn. N.Y.C. Affiliate, 1994; sr. rsch. assoc., program evaluator Office Acad. Affairs, CUNY, Kennedy Fellows Program, 1994-95; evaluation cons. Mayor's Office on AIDS Policy Coordination, 1996, prin. investigator, 1996-98. Co-author: (chpt.) Days with Drug Distribution Which Drugs? How Many Transactions? With What Returns? 1990; contbr. articles to profl. jours. Nat. Inst. on Drug Abuse fellow, 1986-89. Mem. APHA, Nat. Rehab. Assn., Soc. for Disability Studies, N.Y. Acad. Scis., Am. Sociol. Assn. (cert. med. sociologist, social policy & evaluation rschr. law & social control rschr.), N.Y. State Sociol. Assn., Am. World Health Assn., Am. Assn. Sex Educators, Counselors and Therapists, Am. Assn. for Pub. Opinion Rsch., Nat. Rehab. Counseling Assn., Nat. Rehab. Assn. (job placement div. 1991), Pi Gamma Mu, Psi Chi, Phi Theta Kappa. Democrat. Jewish. Achievements include research in the areas of Aids and intravenous drug use, the relationship between drug use and criminal behavior, drug treatment methods, and vocational rehabilitation and the physically and emotionally disabled. Home and Office: 2560 Batchelder St Apt 8K Brooklyn NY 11235-1558

KAPLAN, MORTON A. political science and philosophy educator; b. Phila., May 9, 1921; s. Lewis J. and Anthea (Ginsberg) K.; m. Azie Mortimer, 1967. BS, Temple U., 1943; PhD, Columbia, 1951. Instr. Ohio State U., 1951-52; asst. prof. polit. sci. Haverford Coll., 1953-54; mem. staff Brookings Instn., Washington, 1954-55; asst. prof. polit. sci. U. Chgo., 1956-61, asso. prof., 1961-65, chmn. com. internat. relations, 1959-85, prof. polit. sci., 1965-89, Disting. Svc. prof., 1989-91, Disting. Svc. prof. emeritus, 1991—; editor, pub. The World & I, 1985—. Dir. Ford. workshop program in internat. relations, 1961-76, dir. faculty arms control and fgn. policy seminar, 1970-75; dir. Ctr. for Strategic and Fgn. Policy Studies, 1976-85; cons. Japan War Coll. and Defense Agy., 1979; rsch. assoc. Ctr. of Internat. Studies, Princeton, 1958-62; vis. assoc. prof. polit. sci. Yale U., 1961-62; mem. staff Hudson Inst., 1961-78, cons., 1978-80; lectr. Command and Gen. Staff Sch., 1965-67, Fgn. Svc. Inst., 1967, Air War Coll., 1967-69, NAt. Def. Coll. Can., 1970-72; bd. assocs. Fgn. Policy Rsch. Inst., 1967-90; Gabrielson Disting. lectr. Bowdoin Coll., 1968; Nulton Disting. lectr. Goucher Coll., 1969; cons. NEH, 1972-74; pres. Cetra Music Corp., 1962—, Moraz Prodns., Inc., 1963—; cons. Com. Econ. Devel., 1965, Braddock, Dunn and McDonald, 1969, 72, cons. USIA, 1972; sect. chmn. Internat. Confs. in Unity Scis., 1975, 76, 78, 79, chmn., 1980-83; bd. dirs. Univ. Ctrs. for Rational Alternatives, 1969-96; bd. govs., rsch. com. Stratis, Israeli Inst. Strategic Studies and Policy Analysis, 1974-79; trustee U. Bridgeport, 1992—. Author: System and Process in International Politics, 1957, Some Problems in the Strategic Analysis of International Politics, 1959, The Communist Coup in Czechoslovakia, 1960, (with Nicholas de B. Katzenbach) The Political Foundations of International Law, 1961, (with Reitzel and Coblenz) United States Foreign Policy, 1945-55, 1956, Macropolitics: Essays on the Philosophy and Science of Politics, 1969, On Historical and Political Knowing: An Inquiry into Some Problems of Universal Law and Human Freedom, 1971, Dissent and the State in Peace and War: An Essai on the Grounds of Public Morality, 1970, On Freedom and Human Dignity: The Importance of the Sacred in Politics, 1973, The Rationale for NATO: Past and Future, 1973, (with others) Vietnam Settlement: Why 1973, Not 1969?, 1973, Alienation and Identification, 1976, Towards Professionalism in International Theory: Macrosystem Analysis, 1979, Science, Language and the Human Condition, 1984, rev. edit., 1989, Law in A Democratic Society, 1993; editor: The Revolution in World Politics, 1962, The New Approaches to International Relations, 1968, SALT: Problems and Prospects, 1973, Strategic Thinking and Its Moral Implications, 1973; editor, contbg. author: Great Issues of International Politics, 1970, 74, Isolation or Interdependence? - Today's Choices for Tomorrow's World, 1975, NATO and Dissuasion, 1974, Global Policy: Challenge of the 80s, 1983, Character and Identity vol. 1: Philosophical Foundations of Political and Sociological Perspectives, 1998, vol 2: Historical and Literary Perspectives, 2000; co-author: The Life and Death of the Cold War: Selected Studies in Post-War Statecraft, 1976; co-editor, contbg. author: Japan, America, and the Future World Order, 1976, Justice, Human Nature, and Political Obligation, 1976; co-editor: The Soviet Union and the Challenge of the Future, 4 vols., 1988-89; mem. editl. bd. Jour. Conflict Resolution, 1961-79; mem. editorial bd. World Politics, 1961-71, ORBIS, 1967-90; editor, contbr. The Many Faces of Communism, 1978; editor, Consolidating Piece in Europe, 1987; co-editor: Morality and Religion, 1992, The World of 2044: Technological Development and The Future of Society, 1994. Bd. trustees U. Bridgeport, 1994—; pres. Profs. World Peace Acad., 1983—. With AUS, 1943-46. Fellow Center Internat. Studies Princeton, 1952-53; Center Advanced Study in Behavioral Scis., 1955-56; Carnegie fellow, 1959-60 Mem. AAAS, Am. Polit. Sci. Assn., Inst. Strategic Studies London, Instituto Mexicano de Cultura (corr.), Internat. Cultural Soc. Korea (hon.), Profs. World Peace Acad. Internat. (pres. 1983—). Address: 5446 S Ridgewood Ct Chicago IL 60615-5315 *Constantly to seek new ideas, not for their newness, but for their ability to illuminate the condition of man.*

KAPLAN, MURRAY LEE, nutritionist, educator; b. Weehawken, N.J., Jan. 9, 1941; s. Irving Wayne and Pearl (Masanoff) K.; m. Helene Joyce Soren, Nov. 25, 1965; children: Alissa Deborah, Cheryl Lynn. BA, Alfred U., 1962; PhD, CUNY, 1972. Lectr. Bklyn. Coll., 1966-71; rsch. fellow Mich. State U., East Lansing, 1971-74; asst. prof. Rutgers U., New Brunswick, N.J., 1974-81; assoc. prof. Iowa State U., Ames, 1981-85, prof., 1985—. Contbr. several articles to profl. jours. Bd. dirs. Ames Jewish Congregation. Mem. AAAS, Am. Soc. Nutritional Scis., Am. Oil Chemists Soc., N.Y. Acad. Scis., Sigma Xi. Avocations: music, trumpet, raquetball, theater. Office: Iowa State U Food Sci & Human Nutrition 1127 Human Nutrition Bldg Ames IA 50011 E-mail: mkaplan@iastate.edu.

KAPLAN, NADIA, writer; b. Chgo., Feb. 28, 1921; d. Peter and Aniela (Buchynska) Charydchak; m. Norman Kaplan, July 25, 1942 (dec. July 1989); children: Fawn Marie Stom, Norma Jean Martinez. BEd, Pestalozzi Froebel Tchrs. Coll, Chgo., 1948; postgrad., UCLA, 1947, L.A. City Coll., U. Hawaii, Pepperdine U., 1970, Santa Monica Coll., 1981-87. Cert. tchr., Calif. Photographer, mgr. Great Lakes (Ill.) Naval Tng. Sta., 1942-45; primary/kindergarten tchr. L.A. Unified Sch. Dist., 1946-81. Contbr. articles to profl. jours.; creator puzzles various mags. Vol. recreational tchr. Found. for Jr. Blind, L.A., 1956-75, vol. camp counselor Camp Bloomfield, Calif., camp dir., 1956-61, leader cross-country study tour for blind teenagers, 1962; mem. dem. Nat. Com., 1985—. Pestalozzi Froebel Tchrs. Coll. scholar, 1938-41; recipient Norman Kaplan Life Achievement award Found. UK Blind, 2003. Mem. AAUW, Women Writers West (membership chair 1982-84), United Tchrs. L.A., Calif. Ret. Tchrs. Assn., Assn. Ret. Tchrs. Ukrainian Orthodox. Avocations: writing, bonsai cultivation, doll collecting, travel, golf. Home: 1827 Fanning St Los Angeles CA 90026-1439

KAPLAN, PHYLLIS, artist, composer; b. Bklyn. d. Abraham and Ida (Heller) Kaplan. BFA, Cooper Union, 1972; postgrad., Domus Acad., Milan, 1985. Curator art exhibit Orgn. Ind. Artists, N.Y.C., 1995—96, Westside Arts Coalition, N.Y.C., 1997; artist in residence Hungarian Multicultural Ctr., Lake Balaton, 2002, F. J. Music Sch., Balatonfured, Hungary, 2002. Lectr., presenter in field. Exhibitions include Lever Ho., N.Y.C., 1969, Berkshire Mus., Pittsfield, Mass., 1970, L.I. U., N.Y.C., 1975, Biola U., La Miranda, Calif., Nat. Mus. Women in the Arts, Beijing, 1995, Three Rivers Arts Festival, Carnegie Mus., Pitts., 1995—96, Fine Arts Mus. L.I., Hempstead, 1996—97, Halpert Biennial, Boone, N.C., 1997, 1999, Cork Gallery, Lincoln Ctr., N.Y.C., 1997, Blue Mountain Gallery Invitationals, 1996—98, 2000, 2001, World Artists for Tibet at Blue Mountain, 1998, Trevi Flash Art Mus., Italy, 1998, City Hall, Balatonfured, 2002, Montgomery Coll. Gallery of Art, Rockville, Md., 2002, Canajoharie Libr. and Art Gallery Invitational, 1999, 2002 (Honorable Mention, 2002); contbr. paintings to various publs. including, ann. calendar. Recipient award for patriotism, U.S. Savs. Bond Dr., 1987, hon. mention award, Internat. Female Artist's Art Biennial, Stockholm, 1994, Halpert Biennial, Boone, N.C., 1999, Sharjah Art Mus., United Arab Emirates, 2000, Open Space Gallery, 2000, Mayfair, Allentown, Pa., 2000, Art Environ. Advocacy U. Oreg., Eugene, 2000, Virtue Coll. Visual Arts Gallery, St. Paul, Minn., 2000, Snapshot Contemporary Mus., Balt., 2000, 35th Internat. Exhbn., San Bernardino County Mus., Redlands, Calif., 2000—01, U. South Fla. Coll. Marine Sci., St. Petersburg, 2001, Sharjah Internat. Arts Biennial, United Arab Emirates, 2001, Univ. Place Gallery, Cambridge Art Assn. Nat. Prize Show, Mass., 2001, Three Rivers Arts Festival, Pitts., 2001, pub. project, bear sculpture painting project for Black Bear Film Festival, Milford, Pa., 2001, Hoboken (N.J.) Artists Studio Tour, 2001; grantee Artists Space/Ind. Project, 1999. Mem.: Greene County Coun. Arts, Monroe County Arts Coun. (instr. 2001). Avocations: travel, collecting antique tin toys, classical music. E-mail: phylliskaplan@mymailstation.com.

KAPLAN, RANDY KAYE, podiatrist; b. Detroit, Sept. 18, 1954; s. Earl Gene and Renee Joy (Sheftel) K. D of Podiatric Medicine, Ohio Coll., Cleve., 1979. Diplomate Am. Bd. Podiatric Surgery. Resident Kern Hosp., Warren, Mich., 1979-80; pvt. practice specializing in podiatric medicine, surgery Detroit, 1980—. Clin. instr., mem. staff Kern Hosp., Warren, 1980—; adj. prof. Ohio Coll. Podiatric Medicine, 1986—, Pa. Coll. Podiatric Medicine, 1986—; mem. staff, mem. resident tng. com. Providence Hosp., 1995; lectr. in field. Contbr. articles to profl. jours. Co-founder The Great Lakes Conf., 1988. Recipient Earl G. Kaplan award for polit. action excellence, 1994; Inspector Gen's. Integrity award U.S. HHS, 1995. Fellow Am. Coll. Foot Surgeons; mem. Am. Diabetes Assn., Am. Podiatric Med. Assn. (mem. continuing edn. com. 1988-94, mem. labor rels. com. 1990-94), Mich. Podiatric Med. Assn. (bd. dirs. 1985—, 2nd v.p. 1988-90, pres. 1990-91, 92-93, Podiatrist of Yr. Southeastern divsn. 1987-88, Shining Star award for excellence 1992), Kern Hosp. Resident Alumni Assn., Mich. Pub. Health Assn., Phi Alpha Pi (Man of Yr. 1979). Jewish. Office: 25725 Coolidge Hwy Oak Park MI 48237-1307 E-mail: rklions@aol.com.

KAPLAN, RICHARD, information technology executive; married; 3 children. BS in Computer Sci., Oreg. State U. With Hewlett-Packard Co.; from tech. specialist to corp. v.p. Microsoft, Redmond, Wash., 1990. Office: One Microsoft Way Redmond WA 98052-6399

KAPLAN, RICHARD ALAN, government official; b. San Francisco; s. Murray M. and Beatrice (Ray) K. AA, Canada Coll., 1973; BA, San Francisco State U., 1975, BA, 1976, MA, 1981; postgrad., U. London, 1978—80. Intelligence analyst US Govt., Washington, 1986—. Adv. bd. U.S. Congress, Washington, 1982—85; program mgr. Balance Tech. Initiative Office of Sec. of Def., 1988—89; office of dep. chief of staff intelligence Def. Intelligence Agy., 1988—89, mem. conv. arms control support group, 1987—88, mem. strategic def. intelligence working group, 1987—88, mem. change working group, 1987—88. Author: An Interdisciplinary Study of the International Law of Armed Conflict, 1981; author 62 intelligence documents and studies for Army and nat. intelligency cmty. With U.S. Army, 1968. Recipient Commdrs. award for civilian svc., Dept. of the Army, 1991, Superior Civilian Svc. award, 1991, Civilian award for humanitarian svc., 1992, Superior Civilian Svc. award, 1995, Meritorious Civilian Svc. award, 1996, Commdrs. award for civilian svc., 1996, others. Fellow Inter-Univ. Seminar on Armed Forces and Soc., Internat. Inst. Air and Space Law; mem. Am. Fgn. Law Assn., Internat. Law Assn. (com. on internat. terrorism 1983—, com. on armed conflict 1983—), Internat. Inst. Humanitarian Law, Am. Soc. Internat. Law, Royal Inst. Internat. Affairs. Home: Apt I 5701 Woodlawn Green Cir Alexandria VA 22309-4609

KAPLAN, RICHARD JAMES, producer, director, writer, educator, consultant; b. N.Y.C., Jan. 3, 1925; s. Benjamin David and Nathalie (Blaustein) K.; m. Blanche Beatrice Aanesen, Nov. 15, 1957 (div. 1981); children: Kjeld, Kirsti, Eve, Erica. BA in Polit. Sci., Antioch Coll., 1949; Diploma Cinema, U. So. Calif., 1951. Pres. Richard Kaplan Prodns., N.Y.C., 1957—; dir., promotional films Am. Film Theater, N.Y.C., 1973; media dir. Alternative Conf. on Environ., Stockholm, 1972; media cons. CUNY, 1974-75; dir. pub. programing Astoria Motion Picture and TV Studios, N.Y.C., 1979-80; assoc. dean Pratt Inst. Sch Art and Design, N.Y.C., 1984-85; producer ABC News, N.Y.C., 1986; pres., exec. producer The Exiles Project, Inc., N.Y.C., 1987-90. Cons. Harvard U., Cambridge, Mass., 1986-90; instr. NYU, CUNY, Parsons, Hunter Coll., U. Soc. Calif., U. Md., 1970-87; lectr., workshop dir. U.S. Info Svc., Arts Am., 1980, Israel, Egypt, India, Pakistan, Sri Lanka, Bangladesh, 1985; prof. Columbia U. Sch. of the Arts, 1991—; founder, dep. dir. Documentary Ctr. at Columbia U.; panelist NEH Pub. Media Program. Dir. documentary The Eleanor Roosevelt Story, 1965 (oscar 1966); producer documentary King: Montgomery to Memphis, 1970 (numerous awards 1970-71); writer, dir., producer TV film A Look at Liv, 1976, and others; dir., producer The Exiles, 1989 (Emmy award 1991), Assignment Rescue...The Story of Varian Fry and the Emergency Rescue Committee, 1997; exec. prodr./dir.: Varian and Putzi: A 20th Century Tale, 2001. Trustee Antioch Coll., Yellow Springs, Ohio, 1975-78; vice chmn. Rockland County Human Rights Commn., Rockland County, N.Y., 1968-71, Town of Ramapo (N.Y.) Housing Authority, 1972-76. Cpl. U.S. Army, 1943-46, ETO. Grantee NEH, Washington, 1987. Mem. Acad. Motion Picture Arts and Sci., Writers Guild of Am., Assn. Ind. Film and Video, N.Y. Film Video Council (bd. dirs.).

KAPLAN, RICHARD N. broadcast executive, cable; married; 2 children. Prodr. The CBS Evening News with Walter Cronkite, N.Y.C.; sr. prodr. World News Tonight, ABC, N.Y.C., 1979; exec. prodr. World News This Morning, Good Morning Am., Nightline, ABC, N.Y.C., 1984-89, Viewpoint, The Koppel Report; creator, exec. prodr. Capitol to Capitol; coord. ABC News; exec. prodr. PrimeTime Live, 1989-94, World News Tonight with Peter Jennings, 1994-96; exec. prodr. spl. projects ABC Television Network, 1996-97; pres. Cable News Network, Atlanta, 1997-. Recipient 32 Emmy awards, 4 Overseas Press Club awards, 3 George Foster Peabody awards, 2 George Polk awards, 4 Alfred I. du Pont-Columbia U. awards, 2 Gold Batons. Office: Cable News Network One CNN Ctr PO Box 105366 Atlanta GA 30348-5366

KAPLAN, ROBERT B. linguistics educator, consultant, researcher; b. N.Y.C., Sept. 20, 1929; s. Emanuel B. and Natalie K.; m. Audrey A. Lien, Apr. 21, 1951; children— Robin Ann Kaplan Gibson, Lisa Kaplan Morris, Robert Allen. Student, Champlain Coll., 1947-48, Syracuse U., 1948-49; BA, Willamette U., 1952; MA, U. So. Calif., 1957, PhD, 1962. Teaching asst. U. So. Calif., Los Angeles, 1955-57, instr. coordinator, asst. prof. English communication program for fgn. students, 1965-72, assoc. prof., dir. English communication program for fgn. students, 1972-76, assoc. dean continuing edn., 1973-76, prof. applied linguistics, 1976-95, prof. emeritus, 1995—, dir. Am. Lang. Inst., 1986-91; instr. U. Oreg., 1957-60. Cons. field service program Nat. Assn. Fgn. Student Affairs, 1964-84; pres.-elect faculty senate U. So. Calif., 1988-89, pres., 1989-90; adv. bd. internat. comparability study of standardized lang. exams. U. Cambridge Local Exams. Syndicate; vis. sr. prof. grad. sch. applied lang. studies Meikai U., Urayasu City, Chiba, Japan, 1998-2000. Author: Reading and Rhetoric: A Reader, 1963; (with V. Tufte, P. Cook and J. Aurbach) Transformational Grammar: A Guide for Teachers, 1968; (with R.D. Schoesler) Learning English Through Typewriting, 1969; The Anatomy of Rhetoric: Prolegomena to a Functional Theory of Rhetoric, 1971; On the Scope of Applied Linguistics, 1980; The Language Needs of Migrant Workers, 1980; (with P. Shaw) Exploring Academic English, 1984; (with U. Connor) Writing Across Languages: Analysis of L2 Text, 1987; (with W. Grabe) Introduction To Applied Linguistics, 1991, Writing Around the Pacific Rim, 1995, (with W. Grabe) Theory and Practice of Writing: An Applied Linguistics Perspective, 1996—, (with R.B. Baldauf) Language Policy from Practice to Theory, 1997, (with R.B. Baldauf) Language and Language-in-Education Planning in the Pacific Basin, 2003; co-editor: (with R.B. Baldauf) series The Language Situation in Malawi, Mozambique, The Philippines, 1998, Nepal, Taiwan, Sweden, 1999, Botswana, Côte d Ivoir, Hungary, Vanuatu, 2000, Paraguay, Tunisia, South Africa, European Union, 2001, Finland, 2002; editor: The Oxford Handbook of Applied Linguistics, 2002; editl. bd. Jour. Asian Pacific Comm., Internat. Educator, BBC English Dictionary, Second Lang. Instruction/Acquisition Abstracts, Jour. of Second Lang. Writing, Forensic Linguistics, Jour. Multilingual and Multicultural Devels., Asian Jour. of English Lang. Tchg., Current Issues in Lang. Planning. Bd. dirs. Internat. Bilingual Sch. L.A., 1986-91, Internat. Edn. Rsch. Found., 1986-94. Served with inf. U.S. Army, Korea. Fulbright sr. scholar, Australia, 1978, Hong Kong, 1986, New Zealand, 1992. Mem. AAAS, AAUP, Am. Anthrop. Assn., Am. Assn. Applied Linguistics (v.p., pres. 1992-94, award for disting. scholarship and svc. 1998), Assn. Internationale de Linguistique Appliquée, Assn. Internationale Pour La Researche et La Diffusion Des Methodes Audio-Visuelles et Structuro-Globales, Assn. Tchrs. English as Second Lang. (chmn. 1968-69), Calif. Assn. Tchrs. English to Speakers Other Langs. (pres. 1970-71), Can. Council Tchrs. English, Nat. Assn. Fgn. Student Affairs (nat. pres. 1983-84), Linguistics Soc. Am., Tchrs. English to Speakers of Other Langs. (1st v.p., pres. 1989-91). E-mail: rkaplan@olypen.com.

KAPLAN, ROBERT J. dermatologist; b. Englewood, N.J., Sept. 13, 1947; BS Franklin and Marshall Coll., Lancaster, Pa., 1969; MD, U. Tenn., Memphis 1973. Diplomate Am. Bd. Dermatology. Intern Geisinger Med. Ctr., Danville Pa., 1973-74; resident in dermatology U. Tenn. Ctr. Health Scis., Memphis 1974-77, chief resident, 1977; dermatologist in pvt. practice Memphis, 1979— Mem.: Alpha Omega Alpha. Office: 910 Madison Ave Ste 922 Memphis TN 38103-3483

KAPLAN, ROBERT SAMUEL, educator; b. N.Y.C., May 2, 1940; s. Bernard R. and Jeanette (Lieman) K.; m. Ellen F. Lasher, Dec. 25, 1965; children Jennifer Beth, Dina Rebecca. BSEE, MIT, 1961, MSEE, 1962; PhD, Cornell U. 1968; DPhil, U. Stuttgart, Germany, 1995. Prof. Carnegie-Mellon U., Pitts. 1968-84, dean bus. sch., 1977-83; prof. Harvard Bus. Sch., Boston, 1984—. Dir Pitts. Fed. Res. Bank, 1980-85, J.I. Kislak, Miami, Fla., 1986-97, Renaissance Solns, Lincoln, Mass., 1995-97, Balanced Scorecard Collaborative, Lincoln Mass., 1999—; trustee Technion Inst. Tech., Haifa, Israel, 1995-2001 chmn./bd. dirs. Balanced Scorecard Collaborative, Lincoln, Mass., Acorn Sys. Houston. Author: Relevance Lost, 1986, Measures for Manufacturing Excellence, 1989, The Balanced Scorecard, 1996, Cost and Effect, 1998, Strategy Focused Organization, 2000. Mem. Am. Acctg. Assn. (v.p. 1986-88), Am. Soc Tech. (bd. trustees 1994—). Jewish. Office: Harvard Bus Sch Soldiers Fld Boston MA 02163-1317 E-mail: rkaplan@hbs.edu.

KAPLAN, SAMUEL, pediatric cardiologist; b. Johannesburg, Mar. 28, 1922 came to U.S., 1950, naturalized, 1958; s. Aron Leib and Tema K.; m. Molly Eileen McKenzie, Oct. 17, 1952. MB, BcH., U. Witwatersrand, Johannesburg 1944, MD, 1949. Diplomate: Am. Bd. Pediatrics. Intern, Johannesburg, 1945 registrar in medicine, 1946; lectr. physiology and medicine U. Witwatersrand 1946-49; registrar in medicine U. London, 1949-50; fellow in cardiology, rsch assoc. U. Cin., 1950-54, asst. prof. pediat., 1954-61, assoc. prof. pediat. 1961-66, prof. pediat., 1967-87, asst. prof. medicine, 1954-67, assoc. prof medicine, 1967-82, prof. medicine, 1982-87; prof. pediat. UCLA, 1987-98 emeritus prof. pediat., 1997—. Cons. NIH; hon. prof. U. Santa Tomas, Manila Mem. editl. bd. Circulation, 1974-80, Am. Jour. Cardiology, 1976-81, Am Heart Jour., 1981-96, Jour. Electrocardiology, 1977-94, Clin. Cardiology 1979—, Jour. Am. Coll. Cardiology, 1983-87, Progress Pediat. Cardiology 1990—. Cecil John Adams fellow, 1949-50; grantee Heart, Lung and Blood Inst. of NIH, 1960-2000. Mem. Am. Pediatric Soc., Am. Soc. Pediatric Rsch. Am. Heart Assn. (med. adv. bd. sect. circulation), Am. Fedn. Clin. Rsch., Am Coll. Cardiology, Internat. Carviovascular Soc., Am. Acad. Pediatrics, Midwes Soc. Pediatric Rsch. (past pres.), Sigma Xi. Alpha Omega Alpha; hon. mem Peruvian Soc. Cardiology, Peruvian Soc. Angiology, Chilean Soc. Cardiology Burma MEd. Assn. Achievements include research and publications on cardio vascular physiology, diagnostic methods, cardiovascular complications o pediatric AIDS and heart disease in infants, children and adolescents. Office UCLA Sch Medicine Dept Pediatric Cardiology Los Angeles CA 90095-000

KAPLAN, SANFORD SANDY, geologist; b. N.Y.C., Oct. 2, 1950; s Lawrence J. and Jeanne (Leon) K.; m. Joanne Mandel Kaplan, June 5, 197 (dec. Sept. 1985); children: Elicia Anne, Shira Frieda; m. Connie Clark Kaplan, Jan. 19, 1989; stepchildren: Todd, Wendi, Bryan. AB, Lafayette Coll Easton, Pa., 1971; MS, Lehigh U., 1976; postgrad., U. Nebr., 1979; PhD, U Pitts., 1980; postgrad., U.S. Naval War Coll., 1986-87; MA in Internat. Rels Salve Regina Coll., 1987. Teaching asst. Lehigh U., Bethlehem, Pa., 1975-76 engr. U.S. Steel Corp., Monroeville, Pa., 1976; vis. instr. U. Nebr., Lincoln 1976-80, assoc. prof., 1989—; vis. prof. U. Pitts., 1980; geologist U.S. Dept Energy, Bruceton, Pa., 1979-80; geol. specialist Pennzoil Exploration, Denver 1980-86; pres. Earthsource Consulting, 1987—; assoc. prof. U. Nebr., Lincoln 1989—. Editor: Cenzoic Paleogeography of West Central U.S., 1985; assoc editor: Rocky Mountain Guidebook: Sandstone Reservoirs of the Rock Mountain Region, 1989; composer Trio Medieval Fantasy, 1979, Short Trio contbr. articles to profl. jours. Chmn. Citizens Against Jewell Ave Overpass Aurora, Colo., 1983-84; mem. Adoptive Families of Denver. Recipient Silver Acorn award Boy Scouts Am., 1986; James L. Dyson scholar Lafayette Coll 1970; rsch. grantee NSF, 1970, Sigma Xi, 1978. Mem. Am. Econ. Assn., Am Assn. Petroleum Geologists, Geol. Soc. Am. Soc. Econ. Paleontologists an Mineralogists (editor 1982-84), Rocky Mountain Assn. Geologists. Jewish Avocations: camping, skiing, gardening, tennis, piano. Home: 3720 Judith D Lincoln NE 68517 Office: U Nebr 214 Bessey Hall Lincoln NE 68588

KAPLAN, SEYMOUR H. allergist, immunologist, pediatrician; b. N.Y.C Sept. 28, 1924; Student, NYU, 1942-45; MD, U. Health Scis., 1950. Diplomat Am. Bd. Allergy and Immunology, Am. Bd. Pediats. Intern Harlem Hosp N.Y.C., 1949-50; resident pediats. Coney Is. Hosp., N.Y.C., 1950-51, Mai monides Hosp., N.Y.C., 1951, Beth-El Hosp., N.Y.C., 1953-54; attendin physician allergy, pediats. N. Shore U. Hosp., Manhasset, N.Y., 1955—, Lon Is. (N.Y.) Jewish Med. Ctr., New Hyde Park, 1955—; pvt. practice, 1955— Fellow Am. Acad. Allergy and Immunology, Am. Acad. Pediats., Am. Coll Allergy and Immunology. Office: 22 Chapel Pl Great Neck NY 11021-1428

KAPLAN, SHEILA, academic administrator; b. Bklyn. BA in History, Hunte Coll.; MA, The Johns Hopkins U.; PhD in History, CUNY. Instr. history CUN System; dir. spl. baccalaureate program CUNY; v.p. acad. affairs Winon (Minn.) State U.; vice-chancellor for acad. affairs Minn. State U. System chancellor U. Wis.-Parkside, Kenosha, 1986-93; pres. Met State Coll., Denve 1993—. Bd. dirs. Kenosha Area Devel. Corp., Racine County Econ. Deve Corp.; chmn. bd. Council for Adult and Experiential Learning. Office: Metr politan State Coll Office of President PO Box 173362 Denver CO 80217-336

KAPLAN, SHELDON, lawyer, director; b. Mpls., Feb. 16, 1915; s. Max Juliu and Harriet (Wolfson) K.; m. Helene Bamberger, Dec. 7, 1941; children— Ja Michael, Mary Jo, Jean Burton, Jeffrey Lee. BA summa cum laude, U. Minn 1935; LLB, Columbia U., 1939. Bar: N.Y. 1940, Minn. 1946. Pvt. practic N.Y.C., 1940-42, Mpls., 1946—; mem. firm Lauterstein, Spiller, Bergerman Dannett, N.Y.C., 1939-42; ptnr. Maslon, Kaplan, Edelman, Borman, Brand McNulty, Mpls., 1946-80. Chmn. Kaplan, Strangis and Kaplan, Mpls., 1980— bd. dirs. Stewart Enterprises Inc., Creative Ventures Inc. Decisions edit Columbia Law Review, 1939. Served to capt. AUS, 1942-46. Mem. Minn. B Assn., Hazeltime Nat. Golf Club, Mpls. Club, Phi Beta Kappa. Home: 295 Dean Pkwy Minneapolis MN 55416-4446 Office: Kaplan Strangis & Kapla 5500 Wells Fargo Ctr Minneapolis MN 55402

KAPLAN, SIDNEY MOUNTBATTEN, lawyer; b. Bombay, Jan. 31, 1939; Charles von Pickens Kaplan and Jennie (Churchill) Goldberg; m. Donn Darrow, Feb. 14, 1989; children: Gary, Michael, Rory Patel. BA cum laud Roosevelt U., 1960; JD, Ill. Inst. Tech., 1964. Bar: Ill., 1964, Minn., 197 Colo., 1982, U.S. Dist. Ct. Ill. (no. dist.) 1964. Ptnr. Hess & Kaplan, Chgo 1975-89, Baker & McKenzie, Chgo., 1989—. Bd. dirs. Jerome Gerson Mem Found.; advisor to Prince Faisl, U.S. Affairs Mem. Ill. Bar Assn., DuPag County Bar Assn., Cook County Bar Assn. Office: Baker & McKenzie 130 Randolph Dr 1 Prudential Plz Chicago IL 60601

KAPLAN, STEVEN F. business management executive; b. Bklyn., Feb. 1 1956; s. Allen J. and Hilda Kaplan; m. Anne Quirk; children: David, Michae BSEE, BS in Mgmt. Sci., MIT, 1977, MS in Mgmt., 1979. Engr. Data Ge Corp., Southboro, Mass., 1975-77; mgr., officer Strategic Planning Assocs Washington, 1979-83; v.p., dir. The Boston Consulting Group, 1983-87; pre Harris Graphics Web Press Group div. AM Internat., Dover, N.H., 1987-8 pres. AM ventures and chief strategic officer AM Internat., Chgo., 1989-9 exec. v.p., chief fin. officer, chief strategic officer, 1989-93, bd. dirs.; CF Marcam Corp., Newton, Mass., 1994-95; exec. v.p., CFO The Coleman Co Inc., 1996-98; pres., COO, CFO Favorite Brands Internat., Inc. Dir. Fibersen Tech. Corp., Indian Motorcycle Co., eHealth Direct, Pegasystems Inc.; pr CAF/Tex. Pacific Group; pres., COO, CFO Favorite Brands Internat., In Bannockburn, Ill.; mng. dir. The Audax Group, Boston. Office: 101 Huntingto Ave Boston MA 02199-7603

KAPLAN, STEVEN M. advertising executive; Pres., owner Sampling Cor Am., 1989-97; pres., CEO Bounty Sampling Corp. Am. Worldwide, Glenview Ill., 1997—. Spkr. Office: Bounty SCA Worldwide 4338 Di Paolo Ctr Glenvie IL 60025-5201

KAPLAN, STEVEN MARK, accountant; b. Bklyn., June 22, 1952; s. Irwin and Ruth Kaplan; m. Susan Lynn Rosenberg, Nov. 19, 1972; children: Eric, Corey, Shannon. BS in Acctg., Bklyn. Coll., 1973. CPA, N.Y. Staff acct. Morris Sherwood & May, N.Y.C., 1973-74; sr. acct. Slater & Slater, Rockville Centre, N.Y., 1974-75; ptnr. Kaplan and Roberts CPA, East Rockaway, N.Y., 1975-95; prin. Steven M. Kaplan, CPA, P.C., Merrick, N.Y., 1995—. Dir. investor rels. Healthaxis, Inc., Irving, Tex., 2000—03. Treas. Temple Beth Am., Merrick, 1989-94, Merrick-North Merrick Little League, 1984-97, v.p., 1989, treas., 1990-92, pres. 1993-97; bd. dirs. Merrick-North Merrick Police Athletic League, 1984-88; trustee Merrick Kiwanis Found., 2002. Mem. N.Y. State Soc. CPA's, Nat. Soc. Pub. Accts. Avocations: baseball, photography. Office: 25 Merrick Ave Ste 2 Merrick NY 11566-3416 E-mail: smkcpa@smkcpa.com.

KAPLAN, SUSAN, lawyer; BA summa cum laude, Hofstra U., 1971; JD, Columbia U., 1974. Bar: N.Y. 1975, U.S. Dist. Ct. (so. and ea. dists.) N.Y. 1975. Assoc. Patterson Belknap & Webb, N.Y.C., 1974-76; asst. dist. atty. Nassau County, N.Y., 1976-81; asst. chief prosecution Office Profl. Discipline, State of N.Y., 1981-83; dep. dir. prosecution Office Profl. Discipline State of N.Y., 1983-85; pvt. practice N.Y.C., 1985—. Mem. adv. bd. Employee Assistance Program Health Care Network, 1988-2002; lectr. in field. Contbr. articles to profl. jours. Mem. adminstrv. bd. Soc. Meml. Sloan-Kettering Cancer Ctr., 1975-78; mem. adv. coun. Nassau County Boy Scouts Am., 1977-87, v.p., 1981-84; sec., bd. dirs. Harkness Ballet Found., 1980-86. Assoc. fellow N.Y. Acad. Medicine 1990-91, fellow 1992—. Fellow N.Y. Bar Found.; mem. N.Y. State Bar Assn. (com. on pub. health 1975-78, com. on profl. discipline 1983-90, com. on health law 1985-88, 92-96, com. to confer with state med. soc. 1985-96, vice chair 1986-87, chair 1987-92, mem. health law sect. 1996—). Office: 165 W End Ave Ste 27P New York NY 10023-5515

KAPLAN, THEODORE NORMAN, insurance company executive; b. Newburgh, N.Y., July 23, 1935; s. Edward and Bella (Kesten) K.; m. Madeline Kahn, Nov. 14, 1982; children: Garrett, Judith. BS in Acctg., Syracuse U., 1957. CLU. Ins. sales Aetna Life, N.Y.C., 1959-67, Bankers Life, N.Y.C., 1967-73, Conn. Mut., N.Y.C., 1973-77; benefits cons. Theodore N. Kaplan Assocs., Inc., N.Y.C., 1977—. Mem. Life Underwriters Assn., Million Dollar Round Table (life and qualifying mem.). Office: Theodore N Kaplan Assoc Inc 515 Madison Ave New York NY 10022-5403

KAPLANSKY, IRVING, mathematician, educator, research institute director; b. Toronto, Ont., Can., Mar. 22, 1917; came to U.S., 1940, naturalized, 1955; s. Samuel and Anna (Zuckerman) K.; m. Rachelle Brenner, Mar. 16, 1951; children— Steven, Daniel, Lucille. BA, U. Toronto, 1938, MA, 1939; PhD, Harvard, 1941; LL.D. (hon.), Queen's U., 1969. Instr. math. Harvard, 1941-44; mem. faculty U. Chgo., 1945-84, prof. math., 1956-84, chmn. dept., 1962-67, George Herbert Mead Distinguished Service prof. math., 1969-84; dir. Math. Scis. Research Inst., Berkeley, Calif., 1984-92; dir. emeritus, 1992. Mem. exec. com. div. math. NRC, 1959-62 Author books, tech. papers. Mem. Nat. Acad. Scis., Am. Math. Soc. (pres. 1985-86) Office: Math Scis Rsch Inst 1000 Centennial Dr Berkeley CA 94720-5070 E-mail: kap@mahi.org.

KAPLEN, MICHAEL V. lawyer; b. NYC, June 17, 1955; BA, NYU, 1976; JD, Bklyn. Law Sch., 1979. Ptnr. De Caro & Kaplen LLP, NYC. Mem.: ATLA (chmn.-elect traumatic brain injury litigation 2002, vice-chmn. auto. liability sect. 2002), Brain Injury Assn. (pres. 1999—, Founders award 1978), Nat. Crime Victims Assn. (adv. bd. 2000—). Office: De Cardo and Kaplen LLP 20 Vesey St New York NY 10007

KAPLER, JEANNE MARIE, occupational therapist; b. St. Paul, June 21, 1951; d. Donald Eugene and Florence Marie (Berglund) Stanton; m. Leslie Steven Kapler, Nov. 6, 1976; children: Anne Marie, Emily Jeanne. BA in Occupl. Therapy, Coll. St. Catherine, St. Paul, 1974. Staff occupl. therapy St. Luke's Hosp., Cedar Rapids, Iowa, 1975-78, dir. occupl. therapy, 1978-80; staff occupl. therapy Linn County Orthopedics, Cedar Rapids, 1980-86; pvt. practice Cedar Rapids, 1986-90; staff occupl. therapist Ea. Iowa Therapeutics, Cedar Rapids, 1990-2001, Millennium Rehab. & Cons. Group, Ankeny, Iowa, 2001—. Cons. occupl. therapy WFR Aquaplast, Ramsey, N.J., 1982-89. Mem. Am. Occupl. Therapy Assn. (cert. com. 1978-80), Iowa Occupl. Therapy Assn. (sec. 1990-92). Democrat. Roman Catholic. Avocations: sewing, quilting, travel, reading, gardening. Home: 3333 Riverside Dr NE Cedar Rapids IA 52411-7403 Office: Millennium Rehab & Cons Group Inc PO Box 367 Ankeny IA 50021 Fax: (515) 963-9125. E-mail: jeankap@aol.com.

KAPLOVITZ, HARRY SAM, pediatric cardiologist; b. Cleve., Sept. 13, 1955; s. Isaac and Edith Kaplovitz. BA, Yeshiva U., 1977; MD, Albert Einstein Coll. Medicine, Yeshiva U., 1981. Bd. certified in pediat. cardiology; bd. cert. Nat. Bd. Med. Examiners, Am. Bd. Pediats. Attending physician, co-dir. pediat. cardiology Maimonides Med. Ctr., Bklyn., 1986—; asst. attending physician dept. pediats. Coney Island Hosp., Bklyn., 1987—; asst. prof. dept. pediats. Health Sci. Ctr. at SUNY, Bklyn., 1987—; asst. attending physician dept. pediats. Luth. Med. Ctr., Bklyn., 1988—; provisional staff dept. pediats. North Shore Univ. Hosp., Manhasset, N.Y., 1991—. Contbr. articles to profl. jours. Fellow Am. Acad. Pediats.; mem. Am. Heart Assn. (mem. coun. on cardiovasc. disease in the young), Pediat. Cardiology Soc. Greater N.Y. Office: Maimonides Med Ctr Dept Pediats 4802 10th Ave Dept Pediats Brooklyn NY 11219-2844

KAPLOW, HERBERT ELIAS, journalist; b. N.Y.C., Feb. 2, 1927; s. Solomon and Belle (Bernstein) K.; m. Betty Koplow, Aug. 10, 1952; children— Steven, Robert, Lawrence. BA, Queens Coll., N.Y.C., 1948; MS, Northwestern U., 1951. News corr. NBC, Washington, 1951-72, ABC, Washington, 1972-94. Served with AUS, 1945-46. Recipient Alumni awards Queens Coll., 1963, Alumni awards Northwestern U., 1959 Mem. Sigma Delta Chi. Jewish. Home: 211 N Van Buren St Falls Church VA 22046-3654 *Curiosity and an open, receptive mind are essential characteristics of good journalism. So too is a certain humility growing from the realization that peoples' lives can be affected by a journalist's work. It is a sobering responsibility.*

KAPLOW, LEONARD SAMUEL, pathologist, educator; b. N.Y.C., Feb. 11, 1920; s. Max and Rose (Augenstreich) Kaplowitz; m. Sheila Maureen Briscoe, July 10, 1955; children: Roberta Kit, David Ross. BS, Rutgers U., 1941; MS, U. Vt., 1955, MD, 1959; MA hon., Yale U., 1975. Diplomate Am. Bd. Pathology. Asst. prof. pathology Med. Coll. Va., Richmond, 1963-64; asst. clin. prof., then assoc. prof. pathology and lab. medicine Yale U., New Haven, 1964-75, prof., 1975-88, prof. emeritus, 1988; chief clin. pathology VA Med. Ctr., West Haven, Conn., 1966-74, acting assoc. chief of staff research, 1974-77, chief lab service, 1974-87; lab. dir. Community Health Care Program, New Haven, 1987-88; med. dir. med. lab. technician program Housatonic Community Coll., Bridgeport, Conn., 1977-87; mem. assoc. clin. faculty Quinnipiac Coll., Hamden, Conn., 1968-75; chmn. med. adv. com. New Haven chpt. ARC, 1967-74; mem. com. lab. regulation Conn. Health Dept., Hartford, 1977-84; del. Internat. Com. Standardization in Hematology, 1974-76; program specialist pathology reserach VA Med. Research Service, Washington, 1974-78. Mem. com. cytology automation Nat. Cancer Inst., NIH, 1977-81, acting chmn., 1979-81 Mem. editorial bd. Jour. Histochemistry and Cytochemistry, 1979-87; assoc. editor Jour. Soc. Analytical Cytology, 1983-87. Served to capt. AUS, 1942-46, PTO. Cited in Citation Classics Inst. Sci. Info., 1982 Mem. Histochem. Soc. (councilor 1975-80, pres. 1985), Assn. VA Chiefs of Lab. Services (pres. 1978-80), Sigma Xi, Alpha Omega Alpha Home: PO Box 929 Mink Hill Bradford VT 05033

KAPLOW, LOUIS, law educator; b. Chgo., June 17, 1956; s. Mortimer and Irene (Horwich) K.; m. Jody Ellen Forchheimer, July 11, 1982; children: Irene Miriam, Leah Rayna. BA, Northwestern U., 1977; AM, JD, Harvard U., 1981, PhD, 1987. Bar: Mass. 1983. Prof. law Harvard U., Cambridge, Mass., 1982—, assoc. dean for rsch. and spl. programs, 1989-91. Co-author: Antitrust Analysis, 1997, Fairness Versus Welfare, 2002; contbr. articles to profl. jours.; mem. editl. bd. Jour. of Law, Econs. and Orgn., 1989—. Nat. Tax Jour., 1995—, Legal Theory, 1995—, Jour. Pub. Econs., 2001—. Faculty rsch. assoc. Nat. Bur. Economic Rsch., Cambridge, Mass., 1985—. Mem. AAAS, Am. Acad. Arts and Scis., Am. Econ. Assn., Nat. Tax Assn., Am. Law and Econs. Assn. Jewish. Office: Harvard U 1575 Mass Ave Rm 322 Cambridge MA 02138-2801

KAPLOW, ROBERT DAVID, lawyer; b. Bklyn., Feb. 6, 1947; s. Herbert and Geraldine Rhoda Kaplow; m. Lois Susan Silverman, May 22, 1971; children: Julie, Jeffrey. BS, Cornell U., 1968; JD, U. Mich., 1971; LLM, Wayne State U., 1978. Bar: Mich. 1972, U.S. Dist. Ct. (ea. dist.) Mich. 1972, U.S. Tax Ct. 1976, U.S. Ct. Appeals (6th cir.) 1991. Assoc. Milton Y. Zussman, Birmingham, Mich., 1972-75, Rubenstein, Isaacs, Lax & Bordman, Southfield, Mich., 1975-89; ptnr. Maddin, Hauser, Wartell, Roth & Heller P.C., Southfield, 1989—. Mem. Fin. and Estate Planning Coun. Met. Detroit, Inc.; bd. dirs. Jewish Assn. Retarded Citizens. Mem.: ABA, Oakland County Bar Assn., Mich. Bar Assn., Cornell Club Mich. Office: Maddin Hauser Wartell Roth and Heller PC 28400 Northwestern Hwy Fl 3 Southfield MI 48034-1839 also: PO Box 215 Southfield MI 48037-0215 E-mail: rdk@maddinhauser.com.

KAPLOWITZ, KAREN (JILL), lawyer, business consultant; b. New Haven, Nov. 27, 1946; d. Charles Cohen and Estelle (Gerber) K.; m. Alan George Cohen, Aug. 17, 1980; children: Benjamin, Elizabeth. BA cum laude, Barnard Coll., 1968; JD, U. Chgo., 1971. Bar: Calif. 1971, U.S. Dist. Ct. (Cen. Dist.) Calif. 1971. Assoc. O'Melveny & Myers, L.A., 1971-74; ptnr. Bardeen, Bersch & Kaplowitz, L.A., 1974-80, Alschuler, Grossman & Pines, L.A., 1980-96, of counsel, 1997—. Contbr. articles to profl. jours. Mem. vis. com. U. Chgo. Law Sch., 1990-93. Mem. ABA (chmn. employer-employee rels. com. of tors and ins. practice sect.), Assn. Bus. Trial Lawyers (pres.), Calif. Women Lawyers (Fay Stender award 1982), Women Lawyers Assn. L.A. Home: 1 Woodside Ln New Hope PA 18938-9281 Office: 1620 26th St Fourth Fl N Tower Santa Monica CA 90404-4060 E-mail: kkaplowitz@newellis.com.

KAPLOWITZ, LISA GLAUSER, physician, educator; b. Phila., Apr. 18, 1951; d. Felix E. and Charlotte (Gordy) Glauser; m. Paul Bernard Kaplowitz, Dec. 28, 1970; children: Joshua Michael, Daniel Steven. BS, U. Mich., 1970; MD, U. Ill., Chgo., 1975; MS in Health Adminstrn., Va. Commonwealth U., 2002. Diplomate Am. Bd. Internal Medicine; Am. Bd. Infectious Diseases. Resident U. N.C., Chapel Hill, 1976—78, post grad. fellow, 1978—80, instr. dept. medicine, 1980—82; asst. prof., dept. medicine Med. Coll. Va., Richmond, 1982—89, assoc. prof., 1989—; dir. HIV/AIDS Ctr., Va. Commonwealth U., Richmond, 1993—2002, asst. v.p. fed. health policy; med. dir. ambulatory care Va. Commonwealth U. Health Sys., Richmond, 2000—02; dep. commr. for emergency preparedness and response Va. Dept. Health, Richmond, 2002—. Bd. dirs. AIDS Action Coun., Washington, 1995-96; mem., 1999-2000 class Exec. Leadership in Acad. Medicine Program for Women, MCP Hahnemann U. Contbg. (book chpt.) Conn's Current Therapy, 1985, 2d rev. edit., 1988, 3d edit., 1998; Principles of Critical Care Medicine, 1992. Mem. adv. bd. Va. League for Planned Parenthood, Richmond, 1993—, Richmond AIDS Ministry, 1988-92, Leadership Metro Richmond, 1992-93; grad. Exec. Leadership in Acad. Med. for Women, MCP-Hahnemann U., 2000. Named Woman of Yr. Va. Commonwealth U., 1995; mem. Va. Women's Hall of Fame; Coun. on Status of Women, 1992; health policy fellow, Inst. Medicine, 1996-97; fellow, Office of Senator Jay Rockefeller, 1997. Fellow ACP, Infectious Disease Soc. Am.; mem. APHA; Am. Soc. Microbiology. Avocation: piano. Office: Dept Commr Va Dept Health 1500 E Main St Richmond VA 23219 E-mail: lkaplowitz@vdh.state.va.us.

KAPNER, LEWIS, lawyer; b. West Palm Beach, Fla., May 21, 1937; s. Irving Michael and Mildred Leah (Pikelny) K.; m. Dawn Beth Grossman, Aug. 30, 1964; children: Steven, Kimberly, Michael, Allison. Student, Harvard U., 1956; BA, U. Fla., 1958, postgrad., George Washington U., 1961; JD, Stetson U., 1962; postgrad., Fla. Atlantic U., 1969-73. Bar: Fla. 1962, U.S. Dist. Ct. (so. dist.) Fla. 1963, U.S. Supreme Ct. 1968. Asst. county solicitor, West Palm Beach, 1962-65; ptnr. Kapner & Kapner, West Palm Beach, 1965-67; gen. counsel Palm Beach County Legis. Del., Tallahassee, 1967; judge Juvenile and Domestic Rels. Ct., West Palm Beach, 1967-73, Cir. Ct. West Palm Beach, 1973-81, chief judge, 1981-83; head marital and family law dept. Montgomery, Searcy & Denney and predecessor firm, West Palm Beach, 1984-88; pres. Lewis Kapner, P.A., West Palm Beach, 1988—. Faculty Nat. Jud. Coll., Reno, 1980-84, Fla. Jud. Coll., Gainesville, 1979-83, dean, 1982-83; adj. prof. law Nova U., 1982-84; mem. Supreme Ct. Commn. on Matrimonial Law, 1982-85. Contbr. articles to profl. jours. Pres. Internat. Found. Gifted Children, 1972-74; legal com. Am. Jewish Commn., 1998—. With USMC, 1959-60. Fellow Am. Acad. Matrimonial Lawyers (pres. Fla. chpt. 1983-84, bd. dirs. 1999-2000), Outstanding Fla. Judge in matrimonial law 1982), Fla. Bar (past chmn. family law sect.), Actors Equity. Republican. Jewish.

KAPNICK, RICHARD BRADSHAW, lawyer; b. Chgo., Aug. 21, 1955; s. Harvey E. and Jean (Bradshaw) Kapnick; m. Claudia Norris, Dec. 30, 1978; children: Sarah Bancroft, John Norris. BA with distinction, Stanford U., 1977; MPhil in Internat. Rels., U. Oxford, 1980; JD with honors, U. Chgo., 1982. Bar: Ill. 1982, N.Y. 1993. Law clk. to justice Ill. Supreme Ct., Chgo., 1982—84; law clk. to Justice John Paul Stevens U.S. Supreme Ct., Washington, 1984—85; assoc. Sidley, Austin, Brown & Wood, Chgo., 1985—89, ptnr., 1989—. Mng. editor: U. Chgo. Law Rev., 1981—82. Vestryman Christ Ch., Winnetka, Ill., 2000—03; trustee Chgo. Symphony Orch., 1995—, vice chmn., 2001—03; bd. dirs., chmn. Civic Orch. Chgo., 1999—2001; bd. dirs. Cabrini Green Legal Aid Clinic, 1990—94, chmn. bd., 1991—93; mem., advisor, bd. dirs. Stanford Inst. Econ. Policy Rsch., 1999—. Fellow, Leadership Greater Chgo., 1989—90; Marshall scholar, 1978—80. Mem.: Order Coif, Lawyers Club Chgo., Econ. Club Chgo., Chgo. Club, Phi Beta Kappa. Republican. Episcopalian.

KAPNICK, S. JASON, oncologist; b. Providence, Mar. 28, 1949; s. I.H. and Martha (Shaulson) K.; children: Senta Marie-Rose, Isrel Berndt-Stefan, Sesselja Edda, Finn MacComaill. BLS summa cum laude, boston U., 1974; MD, Harvard Med. Sch., 1981. Surg. rsch. assoc. Harvard Med. Sch., Boston, 1976-77, assoc. in ob/gyn., lectr., 1981-85, instr. in gynecology, 1985-87; cons. in gynecologic oncology Dana Farber Cancer Inst., Boston, 1985-87; clin. fellow Am. Cancer Soc., Boston, 1985-87; attending gynecologic oncologist West Palm Beach, Fla., 1989—; cert. gynecologic oncologist, 1991—. Asst. cons. prof. gynecol. oncology Duke U. Med. Ctr., Durham, N.C., 1994—; reviewer of rsch. submissions Cancer med. jour., Bethesda, Md., 1995—; invited lectr., 1995, Palm Beach County Hosps., 1990—, Am. Cancer Soc., Bethesda, 1995, also Switzerland, Germany, France and Eng., 1990—. Contbr. articles on colon, breast, and female pelvic cancers to profl. jours. Vol., contbr. Ctr. for Family Svcs., West Palm Beach, 1992—; mem., donor Bullfinch Soc., Mass. Gen. Hosp.; trustee, founder Helga Helgason BSRN Meml. Fund; mem., dean's coun. Med. Sch., Harvard U.; active Cath. Diocese children's programs, 1998—; mem., donor First Unitarian Ch., North Palm Beach, Fla.; bd. dirs. Palm Beach Opera, 1992—. Henry Merritt Wriston scholarship Brown U. Mem. Harvard Club of Palm Beach. Avocations: philosophy, music. Office: Farris Bldg Gynecol Oncology 1411 N Flagler Dr Ste 5000 West Palm Beach FL 33401-3410 Address: PO Box 30053 Palm Beach Gardens FL 33420-0053

KAPNICK, STEWART, investment banker; b. N.Y.C., Mar. 10, 1956; s. Charles and Ruth Kapnick; m. Alison Sue Cherry, 1988; children: Jordan Leigh, Michael Taylor. BA with honors, George Washington U., 1978; MBA, Baruch Coll., 1986. Summer internship IBM Corp., White Plains, NY, 1977—78; acct. exec. L & C Pub. Inc., LA, 1979—82, 3M Corp., N.Y.C., 1982—83; pres., fin. ops. prin. Ulysses Capital, N.Y.C., 1983—87, lease fin. cons. SK Capital, N.Y.C., 1987—; assoc. dir. product devel. and lease fin. Continental Info. Systems Corp., N.Y.C., 1987-89; dir. equity fin. Info. Processing Systems Inc. subs. USF&G Fin. Svcs. Corp., Hackensack, NJ, 1989—92; v.p. lease acquisitions The CIT Group, Livingston, NJ, 1992—94; sr. v.p. corp. banking-lease fin. HSBC Bank USA (formerly Republic Nat. Bank of N.Y.), N.Y.C., 1994—. Mem. Equipment Lessors Assn., Computer Dealers and Lessors Assn. Avocations: basketball, tennis, golf, playing options and foreign currency.

KAPOOR, ASHOK KUMAR, engineer; b. Allahabad, Uttar Pradesh, India, Feb. 7, 1952; s. Ram Nate and Sarla Kapoor; m. Nisha Malhotra, May 9, 1984; 1 child, Shweta. BTech, Indian Inst. Tech., 1973; MS, U. Cin., 1979, PhD, 1981. Illumination engr. Philips India Ltd., Bombay, 1973-76; with Fairchild Rsch. Ctr., Palo Alto, Calif., 1981-87; mgr. tech. devel. ASIC div. Nat. Semicondr., Santa Clara, Calif., 1987-88; sr. mem. tech. staff HP Labs., Palo Alto, 1988-91; dir. device tech. LSI Logic, Santa Clara, 1991—96, dir. advanced modeling group, 1998—2000; dir. rsch. Nat. Semiconductor Corp., Santa Clara, 1997—98; founder, chief tech. officer Sensitron, Inc., San Mateo, Calif., 2000—. Co-chair exec. tech. adv. bd. Semiconductor Rsch. Corp., 1995, mem. exec. tech. adv. bd., 1991-97; mem. tech. working group nat. tech. roadmap for Seminconductor Industry Assn., 1992, 94, mem. roadmap coord. group, 1996; spkr. at univs. Editor: Polysilicon Bipolar Transistors; contbr. tech. articles to profl. jours.; patentee in field. Mem. IEEE (sr.), IEEE Electron Devices Soc. (pres. Santa Clara Valley chpt. 1991-92), Sigma Xi. Hindu. Avocations: bicycling, swimming, reading poetry and lit. Home: 1056 Amarillo Ave Palo Alto CA 94303-3705

KAPOOR, NEERA, optometrist; b. Melfort, Sask., Can., June 25, 1966; arrived in U.S., 1990; d. Ajit and Prem Kapoor. BSc, U. Toronto, 1989; MS, SUNY, NYC, 1993, OD, 1994. Asst. clin. prof. SUNY-Optometry, NYC, 1995—2002, assoc. clin. prof., 2002—, dir. head trauma vision rehab. unit., 1996—2002, dir. Raymond J. Greenwald Rehab. Ctr., 2002—. Cons. neuro-optometry JFK Med. Ctr., NJ Neuro Sci. Inst., Edison, 2001—. Co-author, co-editor: Visual & Vestibular Consequences of Acquired Brain Injury, 2001. Recipient Founder's award, Brain Injury Assn. NY State, 2002. Fellow: Am. Acad. Optometry; mem.: Assn. Rsch. in Vision and Ophthalmology, Coll. Optometrists in Vision Devel. (assoc.). Office: SUNY 5th Fl 33 W 42nd St New York NY 10036

KAPOOR, VINOD KUMAR, electrical products executive; b. Lahore, Pakistan, May 2, 1943; came to U.S., 1966; s. Ascharaj Lal and Raj Kumari (Chopra) K.; m. Stanislawa Zareba, Dec. 7, 1974; children: Vijay, Sanjay. BS with honors in Mech. Engring., Indian Inst. Tech., Kharagpur, India, 1965; MS Indsl. Engring., U. Wis., 1968; MBA with honors, Northwestern U., 1972. Mfg. engr. Westinghouse Electric, Chgo., 1968-70, mfg. engring. mgr., 1970-76, mfg. mgr., 1976-79, plant mgr. Fayetteville, N.C., 1980-84, Asheville, N.C., 1984-87, total quality mgr. Pitts., 1989-90, mgr. Mexico ops., 1990-93, mng. dir. Ottermill Ltd. (subsidiary in U.K.), 1993-94, ops. mgr. Caribbean, 1995-96; divsn. ops. mgr., 1997-99; v.p. standard products Challenger Electric, Jackson, Miss., 1988-89; dir. mfg. ops. Lincoln Electric, Cleve., 2000—03, v.p. Cleve. ops., 2003—. Avocations: reading, arts, shell collecting, music, travel. Home: 7647 Herrick Park Dr Hudson OH 44236-2301 Office: Lincoln Electric 22801 St Clair Ave Cleveland OH 44117-1199

KAPP, C. TERRENCE, lawyer; b. Pine Bluff, Ark., Oct. 1, 1944; s. Robert Amos and Guenevere Patricia (DeVinne) Kapp; m. Betsy Langer, May 2, 1987. BA, Colgate U., 1966; JD, Cleve. State U., 1971; MA summa cum laude, Holy Apostles Coll., 1984. Bar: Ohio 1971, U.S. Dist. Ct. (no. dist.) Ohio 1973, U.S. Supreme Ct. 1980, U.S. Tax Ct. 1996. Ptnr. Kapp & Kapp, East Liverpool, Ohio, 1971-84; pvt. practice Cleve., 1984—; ptnr. Marshman, Snyder & Kapp, Cleve., 1991-93, Kapp Law Offices, Cleve., 1994—. Contbr. articles to profl. jours. Chair St. John's Cathedral Endowment Trust, Cleve., 1992—94; pres., bd. dirs. Lake Erie Nature and Sci. Ctr., Bay Village, Ohio, 1991—92. Mem.: ABA (judge finals nat. appellate adv. competition 1987, taxation com. exec. 1988—, nat. chmn. divorce laws and procedures com. family law sect. 1989—93, vice-chmn. step families com. 1991—93, task force client edn. 1991—, commr. presdl. commn. non-lawyer practice 1992—96, chmn. alternative funding com. 1992—, chair nat. symposium image family law atty-fact or myth 1993, domestic rels. taxatoin problems com. exec. tax sect., lit. sect., cert. Outstanding Svc. 1988, 1989, 1993, 1995), Cuyahoga County Bar Assn. (bar admissions com. exec. 1986—, cert. grievance com. 1990—, chair family law sect. 1991—92, jud. selection com. 1991—, unauthorized practice law com. 1992—, cert. Outstanding Leadership 1992), Ohio State Bar Assn. (family law com. exec. 1987—, family law curriculum com. Ohio CLE Inst. 1992—), Bay Men's Club, Cleve. Athletic Club (pres., bd.dirs.). Roman Catholic. Avocations: sailing, handball, racquet sports, dog training. Office: Kapp Law Offices PO Box 40447 Bay Village OH 44140-0447 Business E-Mail: kapplawoffices@ameritech.net.

KAPP, JOHN PAUL, lawyer, physician, educator; b. Galax, Va., Feb. 22, 1938; s. Paul Homer and Jesse Katherine (Vass) K.; m. Emily Lureese Evans, June 23, 1961; children: Paul Hardin, Emily Camille. MD, Duke U., 1963, BS, 1966, PhD in Anatomy, 1967; JD, Wake Forest U., 1990. Bar: N.C. 1990, Va. 1991, Fla. 1991. Intern Med. Coll. Va., Richmond, 1963; resident in surgery Duke U., Durham, N.C., 1964, resident in neurosurgery, 1964-69; asst. prof. neurosurgery U. Tenn., Memphis, 1971-72; attending neurosurgeon Bay Meml. Med. Ctr., Panama City, Fla., 1972-80, Gulf Coast Cmty. Hosp., 1977-80; assoc. prof. neurosurgery U. Miss., Jackson, 1980-83, prof., 1983-85; prof., chmn. dept. neurosurgery SUNY, Buffalo, 1985-87; pvt. practice as lawyer Galax, 1990—, Winston-Salem, NC, 1990—, Panama City, Fla., 1990—. Editor: The Cerebral Venous System and Its Disorders, 1984; contbr. articles to profl. jours. and chpts. to books; patentee arterial pressure control system, prosthetic vertebral body, cranial sensor attaching device. Major U.S. Army, 1969-71. USPHS Neurosurgy fellow, 1965-67; recipient Rsch. award Am. Acad. Neurol. Surgery, 1967. Republican. Methodist. Avocations: hunting, dog training. Office: 105 W Grayson St Galax VA 24333 E-mail: kappoffice@earthlink.net.

KAPP, MICHAEL KEITH, lawyer; b. Winston-Salem, N.C., Nov. 28, 1953; s. William Henry and Betty Jean (Minton) K.; m. Mary Jo Chancy McLean, Aug. 13, 1977; 1 child, Mary Katherine. AB with honors, U. N.C., 1976, JD with honors, 1979. Bar: N.C. 1979, U.S. Dist. Ct. (ea. dist.) N.C. 1980, U.S. Ct. Appeals (4th cir.) 1982, U.S. Dist. Ct. (mid. dist.) N.C. 1986, U.S. Supreme Ct. 1988. Law clk. to presiding justice N.C. Ct. Appeals, Raleigh, 1979-80, N.C. Supreme Ct., Raleigh, 1980-81; assoc. Maupin, Taylor & Ellis, Raleigh, 1981-85; ptnr. Maupin, Taylor P.A. (formerly Maupin, Taylor & Ellis, P.A.), Raleigh, 1985—, mng. dir., 2002—. Research editor U. N.C. Jour. Internat. Law and Comml. Regulation, 1978-79; editor Survey of Significant Decisions of North Carolina Court of Appeals and North Carolina Supreme Court, 1979-81, 2d vol., 1981-82. NC teen Dem. advisor, 1983-85; mem. exec. council NC Dem. Party, 1983-85; founding dir. NC Vol. Lawyers for Arts, Raleigh, 1982-85; counsel Moravian Music Found., Winston-Salem, 1982-85, trustee, 1985-90, pres., 1990-92; counsel Raleigh Little Theatre, 1996-98, bd. dir., 1998—, pres., 2003; bd. dir. Moravian Ch. Archives, Winston-Salem, 1984-89, Soc. for Preservation of Historic Oakwood, Raleigh, 1981-83, Carolina Charter Corp., 1990—, dir. 1995—. Morehead scholar U. N.C., 1972. Mem. ABA, N.C. Bar Assn. (chmn. young lawyer div. continuing legal edn. 1980-82, membership 1984-86, bd. govs. 1983-86), N.C. State Bar (ethics com. 1981-91, com. on professionalism 1986-87, jud. dist. councilor 2001—), Wake County Bar Assn. (bd. dirs. 1988-90, pres.-elect 1995, pres. 1996), Kiwanis (Raleigh Kiwanis Found. dir., 1996-98), Raleigh Execs. Club (pres. 1998-99), Phi Beta Kappa, Phi Delta Phi, Pi Lambda Phi. Avocations: historic preservation, hiking, gardening. Home: 1615 Craig St Raleigh NC 27608-2201 Office: Maupin Taylor PA Highwoods Tower One 3200 Beech Leaf Ct Ste 500 Raleigh NC 27604-1670 E-mail: KKapp@maupintaylor.com.

KAPPAGODA, SAMANTHA, economist, editor; b. Colombo, Sri Lanka, May 6, 1968; d. Nihal Malcolm and Subadra Kappagoda; m. David K.A. Mordecai, July 18, 1996. BSc in Math. with honors, U. London, 1989; MA in Econs., U. Toronto, 1992; MBA in Analytic Fin. and Stats., U. Chgo., 1996. Economist The World Bank, Washington, 1992-94, Caxton Assocs., N.Y.C., 1996—. Mng. editor Jour. of Risk Fin., 1999—. Mem.: Internat. Assn Fin. Engrs., Am. Econ. Assn., NY Assn. Bus. Economists, Nat. Assn. Bus. Economists. Office: Caxton Assocs 667 Madison Ave Fl 9 New York NY 10021-8029 E-mail: samkappa@aol.com.

KAPPAN, SANDRA JEAN, elementary education educator; b. Buffalo, N.Y., Sept. 25, 1961; d. Joseph Albert Sr. and Margaret Alice (Krupa) Savash; 1 child, Jason T. Cert. in dental assisting, Bd. of Coop. Ednl. Svcs., 1979; AAS in Secretarial Sci., Erie C.C., 1982; BS, Daemen Coll., 1997; MS in Edn. and Reading, St. Bonaventure U., 1998. Cert. spl. edn., pre-kindergarten, kindergarten, grades 1-6. Acctg. clk. Children's Hosp. of Buffalo, 1984-87; legal sec., receptionist Lofton, Savage, & Cain, Esqs., Charleston, S.C., 1987-88; sec., transciptionist Trident Regional Med. Ctr., Charleston, S.C., 1988-90; adminstrv. asst. Children's Hosp. of Buffalo, 1990-93; substitute tchr. Erie 1 Bd. Coop. Ednl. Svcs., Erie County, N.Y., 1996-97; resource room tchr. Lancaster (N.Y.) Ctrl. Sch. Dist., 1997; spl. edn. tchr. Erie I Bd. Ednl. Ednl. Svcs., Erie County, N.Y., 1997-98; elem. tchr. St. James Sch., Depew, N.Y., 1998-99, Amherst Ctrl. Sch. Dist., 1999 2000; spl. edn. tchr. Ctrl. Sch. Dist., West Seneca, N.Y., 2000—. Spl. edn. tchr. Erie I BOCES, summer 1999; presenter in field. Vol. PTA, Lancaster Ctrl. Sch. Dist., 1994—, Boy Scouts Am.; vol. after-sch. reading/math. program West Seneca Sch. Dist.; vol. Americare Kids Reading Program, 2000—; vol., mem. St. John's Luth. Ch., Sunday Sch. and

Choir, Lancaster, 1993—. Scholarship Lancaster Assn. of Svc. Pers., 1996. Mem.: Daemen Coll. Alumni Assn., Phi Delta Kappa. Democrat. Lutheran. Home: 479 Lake Ave Lancaster NY 14086-9666

KAPPAS, ATTALLAH, physician, medical scientist; b. Union City, N.J., Nov. 4, 1926; s. Attie and Sofia (Kozam) K.; m. Oct. 26, 1963; children: Peter, Michael, Nicholas. AB, Columbia U., 1947; MD with honors, U. Chgo., 1950; ScD, N.Y. Med. Coll., 1978. Diplomate: Am. Bd. Internal Medicine. Med. intern Univ. Service, Kings County Hosp., N.Y.C., 1950-51; ACS rsch. fellow Sloan Kettering Inst., N.Y.C., 1951-54; asst. resident physician and sr. asst. resident physician Peter Bent Brigham Hosp. Harvard Med. Sch., Boston, 1954-56; assoc. div. steroid biochemistry and metabolism Sloan Kettering Inst., 1956-57; from asst. prof. to assoc. prof. dept. medicine, head div. metabolism and arthritis U. Chgo. Med. Sch., 1957-67; Guggenheim fellow, guest investigator Rockefeller U., N.Y.C., 1966-67, assoc. prof., physician, 1967-71, sr. physician, 1971-74, prof., 1971-81, Sherman Fairchild prof., 1981—2004, v.p., 1983-91, physician-in-chief, 1974-91, physician-in-chief emeritus, 1991—, emeritus, 2004—. Contbr. articles to profl. jours. Bd. dirs. Vis. Nurse Service N.Y., 1982-86, 98—, Scenic Hudson, Inc., 2002—; dir. Theresa and Eugene Lane Ctr. for Rsch. and Edn. NY Hosp Queens Med. Sch., Weill-Cornell Med. Coll., 1998-2002, dir. emeritus, 2002; mem. gov.'s com. on rev. sci. studies and devel. pub. policy on problems resulting from hazardous wastes N.Y. State, 1980; mem. vis. com. Divsn. of Biological Sci. and the Pritzer Sch. of Medicine, Univ. of Chgo., 2003—; mem. bd. dirs. Beatrice Renfield Foundation, N.Y.C., 2003. Served with U.S. Army, 1945-46. Named named Sr. Henry Hallet Dale Meml. lectr. and vis. prof., Johns Hopkins Hosp., 1975, Pfizer lectr. clin. pharmacology, Peter Bent Brigham Hosp., Harvard Med. Sch., 1977, Pfizer lectr., Pa. State U., 1980, first Rolf Blomstrand lectr., Karolinska Inst., 1988, first Glaxo lectr., Cornell U. Med. Sch., Gunner and Lillian Nicholson Found. exch. prof., Karolinska Inst., Stockholm, 1985—86, Barowsky Meml. lectr., N.Y. Med. Coll., 1986, First Annual Lang Rsch. lectr., N.Y. Hosp. Med. Ctr., Queens, 2000; recipient Spl. award in clin. pharmacology, Burroghs Wellcome Fund, 1973, Disting. Svc. award in med. scis., U. Chgo. Sch. Medicine, 1975, Citation for profl. achievement, U. Chgo. Alumni Assn., 1995, 1st Ann. award for excellence in clin. rsch., NIH, 1989; fellow Commonwealth Fund, 1961—62, Guggenheim fellow, 1966—67. Fellow ACP; mem. Assn. Am. Physicians, Am. Soc. Clin. Investigation, Am. Clin. and Climatol. Assn., Am. Soc. Pharmacology and Exptl. Therapeutics (pub. affairs com., award for exptl. therapeutics 1978), Practitioners Soc. N.Y., Harvey Soc., Endocrine Soc., Interurban Clin. Club, Cosmos Club (Washington), N.Y. Athletic Club, Lotos Club, Univ. Club. Office: Rockefeller U Hosp 1230 York Ave New York NY 10021-6307 Office Fax: 212-327-8690.

KAPPAZ, MICHAEL H. engineering and energy executive; b. Cartagena, Colombia, May 14, 1942; came to the U.S., 1963; s. George and Elena (Hegel) K.; m. Chafica Maria Dau; children: George, Nur-Helene, Christine, Karen, William, Patricia. BS in Indsl. Engring. and Ops. Rsch., Poly. Inst. N.Y., 1970; MBA in Fin. Mgmt., Golden Gate U., 1976; cert. in Global Strategic Mgmt., U. Pa., 1984; cert. in exec. mgmt., Stanford U., 1986. Indsl. engr. for iron and steel Ramseyer and Miller, Inc., N.Y., 1964-71; v.p., gen. mgr. internat. ops. Bechtel Power Corp., Bechtel Group, Gaithersburg, Md. and San Francisco, 1971-86; v.p., mgr. Overseas Bechtel, Inc., Cairo, 1982-84; v.p., project mgr. Internat. Bechtel Corp., Inc., Venezuela, 1979-82; chmn., CEO K&M Engring. and Consulting Corp., Washington, 1987—; chmn. bd. dirs. KMR Power Corp., Arlington, Va., 1993-2000; chmn. K&M Interamerican Investment Corp., Arlington, 1993—2002, K&M Interamerican Energy Leasing, Arlington, 1993—2000, K&M Ventures, L.P., Arlington, 1993—2000, KMtel LLC, 1995—2000, K&M Global Constrn. LLC, 1995—, K&M Panam., LLC. Contbr. articles to various publs., papers to confs. and seminars. Mem. adv. bd. Rep. Nat. Com., 1993—; mem. Am. Rsch. Ctr. (Egyptology and Archeology), 1982-86; mem. engring. adv. com. Am. U., Cairo, 1982-86; co-chmn. coun. Latin Am. studies Johns Hopkins U., 1987-89, mem. adv. coun. 1987-97, mem. devel. com. 1993-98; bd. dirs. Washington Opera, Bus. Coun. for Internat. Understanding; chmn. U.S.-Colombia Bus. Partnership; trustee Latino Student Fund; vice chmn. US-Korea Com. Bus. Cooperation. Recipient Deal of Yr. award Project Fin. Internat. Yearbook, 1993, Infrastructure Fin. Mag., 1993, Blue Chip Enterprise award, 1995, Fast Track award, 1995, Inc 500 award, Nat. Tech. Fast 500 award, 1995, Fast 50 award 1996, Project Fin. Inter. 2000, Top 50 Hispanic High Tech Co. 2000. Mem. U.S. Energy Assn., Am. C. of C. (charter, Cairo), Am. Assn. Cost Engrs. (past v.p., dir. Capital chpt.), D.C. C. of C., Univ. Club, Georgetown Club, Avenel Country Club, Damascus Lodge, Group of 50, Bretton Woods Com., Cambridge Energy Rsch. Assoc. Republican. Roman Catholic. Avocations: opera, baseball, golf, bridge. Office: K & M Engring & Consulting Corp 1300 Wilson Blvd Ste 500 Arlington VA 22209-

KAPPENBERG, MARILYN KASCIUS, library director; b. Hicksville, N.Y., July 19, 1948; d. Adolf A. and Mary T. Kascius; m. Richard L. Kappenberg, Apr. 5, 1975; children: Neal, Glenn. BA, Molloy Coll., 1970; MLS, L.I. U., 1972. Children's libr. Hicksville (N.Y.) Pub. Libr., 1972-90; head ref. Hicksville Pub. Libr., 1990-95, asst. libr. dir., 1992-95; libr. dir. Wantagh (N.Y.) Pub. Libr., 1995—, Plainedge Pub. Libr., Massapequa, NY, 2001—. Sec. Hicksville Lions Club, 1990-95. Mem. ALA, Nassau County Libr. Assn., Wantagh C. of C. (mem.-at-large 1995—). Avocations: writing, volunteering. Home: 2873 Janet Ave North Bellmore NY 11710-2026 Office: Plainedge Pub Libr 1060 Hicksville Rd Massapequa NY 11758

KAPPES, PHILIP SPANGLER, lawyer; b. Detroit, Dec. 24, 1925; s. Philip Alexander and Wilma Fern (Spangler) K.; m. Glendora Galena Miles, Nov. 27, 1948; children: Susan Lea, Philip Miles, Mark William. Bar: Ind. 1948. Assoc. Armstrong and Gause, 1948-49, C.B. Dutton, 1950-51; ptnr. Dutton, Kappes & Overman, 1952-85, of counsel, 1983-85; ptnr. Lewis Kappes Fuller & Eads, Indpls., 1985-89, Lewis & Kappes, Indpls., 1989-92, Lewis & Kappes PC, Indpls., 1993—, Labeco Properties, Creston Group, Indpls.; pres., dir. K&K Realty, Inc., Indpls. Sec., dir., mem. Ind. Machine Works, Inc.(formerly named Laboratory Equipment Corp.), Mooresville, Ind.; instr. bus. law Butler U., 1948-49, chmn. bd. govs., 1965-66, bd. trustees, 1987-90; chmn. Ovid Butler Soc., 1982-83. Life bd. dirs. Crossroads Am. coun. Boy Scouts Am., 1965—, v.p. fin., mem. exec. com., pres., 1977-79, chmn. trustees endowment fund, 1987-92, trustee, 1987—, chmn. Gathering of Eagles dinner, 2000; bd. dirs. Fairbanks Hosp., Indpls., 1986-94, chmn. bd., 1988-91, exec. com., 1987-94, mem. audit and fin. com., 1992-94, life dir. emeritus, 1994—, chmn. nominating com., 1991; trustee Butler U., 1987-90, Children's Mus., Indpls., 1969-88, pres. bd. trustees, 1984-85, bd. disting. advisors, 1990-01, hon. trustee, 2001—; mem. First Meridian Heights Presbyn. Ch., 1933—, chmn. bd. trustees, 1958-61, 69-72, 1996— ruling elder 1982-85, 94-99, deacon, 1950-58; mem. planning com. and dir. Indpls. 32-Degree Masonic Learning Ctr. for Children, 1997-98, dir., 1998—, chmn. bd., 2002-2002, vice chmn., 2002—; chmn. Dyslexia Tutor Tng. Inst., 2000—. Recipient Paul H. Buchanan award of excellence Indpls. Bar Found. Mem. ABA (ho. of dels. 1970-71), Ind. State Bar Assn. (ho. dels. 1959—, chmn. pub. rels. exec. com. 1966-69, sec. 1973-74, bd. mgrs. 1975-77, chmn. law practice mgmt. com. 1991-92), Indpls. Bar Assn. (treas., 1st v.p. 1965, pres. 1970, bd. mgrs. 1968-71, 75-77, chmn. law day com. 1991-92, settlement week com. 1989-95, co-chair Family Law Study Commn., co-chmn. ct. liaison com. 1992-93, family law implementation com. 1993-97, exec. com. bd. mgrs. 1994-96, counsel bd. mgrs. 1994, chmn. sr. lawyers divsn. 1999-2000), Am. Judicature Soc., Indpls. Legal Aid Soc., Indpls. Jr. C. of C. (past 1st v.p., dir. ct. unification implementation com., chmn. 1995-98), Butler U. Alumni Assn. (past pres.), Mich. Alumni Assn., Meridian Hills Country Club, Lawyers Club, Gyro Club (pres. 1966), Masons (worshipful master 1975), Valley Scottish Rite (33d degree, most wise master 1982-84, trustee 1996-2002, chmn. bd. trustees 1998-99, 2001— pres. Indpls. Scottish Rite Cathedral Found., dir. 1996— chmn. 2001— dir. Indpls. Scottish Rite Found., 1996—, Shriners, Phi Delta Theta (chpt. advisor 1950-82), Tau Kappa Alpha. Republican. Presbyterian. Home: 624 Somerset Dr W Indianapolis IN 46260-2924 Office: 1 American Square PO Box 82053 Indianapolis IN 46282-0003 E-mail: pkappes@lewis-kappes.com.

KAPPLES, JOHN W. electronics executive; b. Boston, Sept. 1959; BA, Georgetown U., Washington, 1982; JD, Georgetown U., 1985. Atty. Sullivan & Worcester, Boston, 1985—94; sr. atty. Raytheon Co., Lexington, Mass., 1994—98, asst. corp. sec., 1996—2000, asst. gen. counsel, 1998—2000, v.p., sec., 2000—. Mem.: Mass. Bar Assn. Office: Raytheon Co 141 Spring St Lexington MA 02421*

KAPPNER, AUGUSTA SOUZA, academic administrator; b. Bronx, June 25, 1944; d. Augusto and Monica Thomasina (Fraser) Souza; m. Thomas Kappner, Aug. 14, 1965; children: Tania, Diana. AB, Barnard Coll., 1966; MSW, Hunter Coll., N.Y.C., 1968; DSW, Columbia U., 1984. Cert. social worker, N.Y. Lectr., community affairs specialist Dept. Urban Affairs, Grad. Div., Hunter Coll., 1968-70; adj. instr., field supr. N.Y.C. C.C., 1970-71; instr., coord. urban leadership unit Columbia U. Sch. Social Wk., 1970-72; asst. prof., dir. admissions and student svcs. SUNY, Stony Brook, 1973-74; assoc. prof., chmn. human svcs. divsn. LaGuardia C.C., 1974-78, prof., dean continuing edn., 1978-84; dean acad. affairs Adult & Continuing Edn., CUNY, 1984, dean acad. affairs, instructional rsch., adult learning, 1984-86; pres. Borough of Manhattan C.C./CUNY, 1986-92; asst. sec. of vocat. and adult edn. Dept. of Edn., Washington, 1993-95; pres. Bank Street Coll., N.Y.C., 1995—. Cons. in field; lectr. in field; mem. adv. bd. Fund for the Improvement of Post Secondary Edn., U.S. Dept. of Edn, Adult Literacy Media Alliance; mem. adv. panel Nat. Ctr. for Innovation in Governing Am. Edn., Nat. Writing Project; mem. N.Y.C. Bd. Edn. Adv. Bd. for Universal Pre-Kindergarten; former mem. Commn. for Nation of Lifelong Learners; commr., Commn. Higher Edn., Middle States Assn. Trustees Marymount Manhattan Coll.; mem. N.Y. State Edn. Commr.'s Task Force for the Edn. of Children and Youth at Risk, N.Y. State Gov.'s Coun. on Literacy, N.Y.C. Bd. Edn. Chancellor's U./Schs. Collaborative steering com.; appointed by Mayor of City of N.Y. to Joint Commn. on Integrity in Pub. Schs.; bd. dirs. N.Y. Urban Coalition; mem. N.Y.C. Coun. on Econ. Edn. Whitney M. Young Jr. fellow, 1982, USPHS awardee, 1981, Ford Found. fellow, 1973, Silverman Fund awardee, 1968, NIMH fellow, 1967, others; recipient Harlem Sch. Arts Humanitarian award, 1990, Am. Assn. Women in Community and Jr. Colls. Presdl. award, 1989, Asian Ams. for Equality Community Svc. award, 1989, Columbia U. Medal of Excellence, 1988, Barnard Coll. medal of distinction, 1988, Found. for Child Devel. Centennial award, 1999, Morris T. Keeton award Coun. for Adult and Exptl. Learning, others. Mem. Am. Coun. on Edn.

KAPPRAFF, JAY MARVIN, mathematics educator; b. N.Y.C., Nov. 4, 1937; s. Morris and Pearl (Morris) K.; m. Arlene Falkin, June 3, 1973; children: Sara, Jonah. BChemE, N.Y. Poly. Inst., 1958; MS, Iowa State U., 1960; MA, NYU, 1967, PhD, 1974. Nuclear engr. Westinghouse-Bettis Plant, Pitts., summer 1957, 58; chem. engr. DuPont de Nemours, Newport, Del., 1960-61; tchr. N.Y.C. Bd. Edn., 1961-62; aerospace engr. NASA-Lewis Rsch. Ctr., Cleve., 1962-65; rsch. assoc. Tchr.'s Coll. Columbia U., N.Y.C., 1967-68; instr. of math. Cooper Union Coll., N.Y.C., 1968-74; assoc. prof. math. N.J. Inst. Tech., Newark, 1974—. Physicist U.S. Dept. Energy, summer 1977; advisor, spkr. Chgo. Acad. Sci., Symposium on Art and Sci., 1993; vis. scholar JSPS, Japan, 2003. Author reference books: Connections, 1991 (Nat. Assn. Pubs. award), 2d edit., 2002, Beyond Measure, 2002, also workbook on math. of design, 1992; contbr. articles to profl. publs.; mem. editl. bd. Internat. Jour. Biol. Systems, 1991—, FORMA, 2003—. Organizer Ethical Culture Chamber Music Workshops, Maplewood, N.J., 1991—, Exptl. Math. and Comm. Precoll. Program (Dept. of Higher Edn. N.J. award, Excellence in Tchg. award 2002), 1983—; chmn. scientist and the arms race AAAS, N.Y.c., 1984. Grantee Naval Rsch. Lab., 1978-80, Schumann Found., 1983, 84, Graham Found., 1982, 87, 93, 2001, Nat. Endowment Arts, 1991. Mem. Math. Assn. Am. Avocations: violin, tennis, chamber music, tai chi. Office: NJ Inst Tech Math Dept University Heights Newark NJ 07102

KAPRAL, FRANK ALBERT, medical microbiology and immunology educator; b. Phila., Mar. 12, 1928; s. John and Erna Louise (Melching) K.; m. Marina Garay, Nov. 22, 1951; children: Frederick, Gloria, Robert; m. Esther McKenzie, May 10, 2003. BS, U. of the Scis. in Phila., 1952; Ph.D, U. Pa., 1956. With U. Pa., Phila., 1952-66, assoc. in microbiology, 1958-66; assoc. microbiologist Phila Gen. Hosp., 1962-64, chief microbiology research, 1964-66, chief microbiology, 1965-66; asst. chief microbiol. research VA Hosp., Phila, 1962-66; assoc. prof. med. microbiology Ohio State U., Columbus, 1966-69, prof. med. virology, immunology and med. genetics, 1969—95, prof. emeritus dept. molecular virology, immunology and med. genetics, 1995—. Cons. Ctr. Disease Control, Atlanta, 1980, Proctor and Gamble Co., 1981-87. Contbr. articles to profl. jours. Active Ctrl. Ohio Diabetes Assn., 1992-93. With AUS, 1946-47. Grantee, Ctrl. Ohio Diabetes Assn., 1992—93; Rsch. grant, NIH, 1959—95. Fellow Am. Acad. Microbiology, Infectious Diseases Soc. Am.; mem. AAAS, Am. Soc. for Microbiology, Am. Assn. for Immunologists, Sigma Xi. Democrat. Roman Catholic. Achievements include patents for implant chamber. Home: 873 Clubview Blvd S Columbus OH 43235-1771 Office: 2166B Graves Hall Columbus OH 43223-3226

KAPRIELIAN, VICTORIA SUSAN, medical educator; b. The Bronx, N.Y., June 30, 1959; d. Walter and Julia (Hachigian) K. BA, Brown U., 1981; MD, UCLA, 1985. Diplomate Am. Bd. Family Practice. Resident Duke-Watts Family Practice, Durham, N.C., 1985-88; fellow UCLA Family Medicine, L.A., 1988-89; asst. clin. prof. Duke U. Med. Ctr., Durham, N.C., 1989-98; chief, divsn. predoctoral edn. and faculty devel., dept cmty and family medicine Duke U., Durham, N.C., 1994-96; assoc. clin. prof. Duke U. Med. Ctr., Durham, NC, 1998—2003, clin. prof., 2003—; fellowship dir., dept. cmty. and family medicine Duke U., Durham, N.C., 1994-99, 2000—, dir. predoctoral edn. and faculty devel., 1996-99. Dir. inpatient svc. divsn. cmty. medicine Duke U., 1989-90, dir. sports medicine, 1989-94, dir. arts medicine, 1989-95, dir. predoctoral edn., 1990-2000; dir. quality improvement and continuing med. edn. dept. cmty. and family medicine, 1996—; dir. faculty devel. dept. cmty. and family medicine, Duke U., 2000—. Fellow Am. Acad. Family Physicians (pub. com. 1985, mental health com. 1986-88); mem. N.C. Acad. Family Physicians (bd. dirs. 1998-02, edn. com. 1989-90, med. sch. affairs 1990—2001, chair of com. 1991-97), Soc. Tchrs. Family Medicine (steering com., predoc. dir. working group 1995-98, chair 1998). Avocations: physical fitness, singing, science fiction, ethnic cooking. Office: Duke U Div Family Medicine PO Box 2914 Durham NC 27710-0001

KAPRIELIAN, WALTER, advertising executive; b. N.Y.C., June 2, 1934; s. Vartan and Shoushan (DerBargamian) K.; m. Julia Hachigian, July 7, 1957 (dec. Nov. 1983); children: Victoria Susan, Siran Marion, John Vartan; m. Dinaz Boga, May 20, 1988. AAS, SUNY, 1953. Licensed charterboat capt. Art dir. BBD&O, N.Y.C., 1953-64; group head, art dir. Grey Advt., N.Y.C., 1964-65; sr. art dir. Ketchum MacLeod & Grove, N.Y.C., 1965-66; v.p., head art dir., 1966-67; v.p., assoc. creative dir., 1967-71; sr. v.p., creative dir., 1971-77; exec. v.p., asst. gen. mgr., 1977-80; gen. mgr., 1980-81; pres., chief exec. officer Ketchum New York, 1981-82; ptnr., co-creative dir., vice chmn. Fearon O'Leary Kaprielian, Inc., 1983-84; chmn., creative dir. Kaprielian O'Leary Advt., 1984-95; pres. Walter Kaprielian & Co., East Hampton, N.Y., 1995—. Instr. N.Y.C. Tech. Coll., 1971-79, Sch. Visual Arts, 1982-88; mem. adv. bd. N.Y.C. Tech. Coll., 1980—; lectr. Graphic Arts Tech. Found., 1970-81; v.p. ADC Pub. Co., N.Y.C., 1986-88. Author/illustrator: The Captain's Cookbook, 1976, rev. edit., 1979; designer: Bliss in Chrysalis, 1968; designer/editor: The Consecration of a Cathedral, 1968; contbr. articles to profl. jours. V.p. Visual Communicators Scholarship Fund, 1986-88, pres., 1988-90; chmn. parish coun. Holy Cross Ch. of Armenia, 1965-66, Armenian Ch. of Holy Martyrs, 1968-69; bd. dirs. N.Y.C. Tech. Coll. Found., 1985-99, Fish Unlimited, 1994-2000.. Recipient awards Art Dirs. Club N.Y., awards Art Dirs. Club N.J., awards Soc. Illustrators, awards Am. Inst. Graphic Arts, awards Type Dirs. Club, awards Clio, awards Graphis, awards Advt. Club N.Y., awards Am. Advt. Fedn.; Theodore Rossevelt Meml. medal; St. Gauden's medal. Mem. Am. Inst. Graphic Arts, Art Dirs. Club (bd. dirs. 1974-76, 78-81, 91-93, pres. 1981-83, chmn. adv. bd. 1983-85, mem. adv. bd. 1984—, 1st v.p. 1993, pres. visual communicators scholarship fund 1988-90), U.S. Power Squadron, Nat. Party Boat Owners Alliance, Internat. Game Fish Assn., Maidstone Gun Club, Knights of Vartan. Republican. Avocations: seafood cooking, fishing. E-mail: wvkapriel@aol.com.

KAPSCH, ROBERT JAMES, engineering and architectural historian; b. Elizabeth, N.J., July 25, 1942; s. Joseph Michael and Mary Elizabeth Kapsch; m. Elizabeth Perry Kephart, Nov. 11, 2000. BS in Engring., Rutgers U., 1964; MS in Mgmt., George Washington U., 1974, MA in Am. Studies, 1978; PhD in Engring. and Arch., Cath. U. Am., 1983; PhD in Am. Studies, U. Md., 1993. Chief HABS/HAER, 1980—95; spl. asst. to dir. Nat. Park Svc., Washington, 1996-2000, sr. scholar in hist. arch. and hist. engring., 2001—. Mem. editl. bd. Bldgs. U.S. Publs. Series, 1991-94. Participant various hist. preservation activities, Washington, 1975—. Capt. USAR, 1964—68, Vietnam. Recipient Disting. Svc. medal, U.S. Dept. Interior, 2002. Mem.: AIA, ASCE (history and heritage com. 2000—), Constrn. History Soc., Nat. R.R. Hist. Assn., Nat. Bldg. Mus., Hist. Medley Dist., Nat. Trust for Hist. Preservation, Nat. Preservation Inst. (bd. dirs. 2001—), Am. Canal Soc., Vernacular Arch. Forum, Soc. Archtl. Historians, Soc. for Indsl. Archeology (bd. of dirs. 2001—), Newcomen Soc., Cosmo Club. Avocations: antique toy trains, travel. Home: 15220 DuFief Dr North Potomac MD 20878-2411 Office: Nat Park Svc 1100 Ohio Dr SW Washington DC 20242 Fax: 202-485-9705. E-mail: robert_kapsch@nps.gov.

KAPSON, JORDAN, automotive executive; b. 1923; Chmn. Jordan Motors, Inc. dba Jordan Ford, Mishawaka, Ind., 1947—, Jordan Toyota dba Jordan Volvo, Jordan Mitsubishi, 1981—, Jordan Motors, Inc. Office: Jordan Motors Inc 609 E Jefferson Blvd Mishawaka IN 46545-6524*

KAPSOS, PHILIP JOHN, anesthesiologist; b. Milw., Mar. 8, 1955; MD, Med. Coll. Wis., 1984. Diplomate Am. Bd. Anesthesiology; lic. staff anesthesiologist, Wis., Ariz., Calif. Intern Med. Coll. Wis. Affiliated Hosps., Milw., 1984-85, resident in anesthesiology, 1986-87; med. staff Casa Grande (Ariz.) Regional Med. Ctr., 2000—. Mem. Am. Soc. Anesthesiology, Internat. Anesthesia Rsch. Soc. Office: Casa Grande Regional Med Ctr 1800 E Florence Blvd Casa Grande AZ 85222 E-mail: pkapsos@aol.com.

KAPTEYN, HENRY CORNELIUS, physics and engineering educator; b. Oak Lawn, Ill., Jan. 21, 1963; m. Margaret Mary Murnane, 1988. BS, Harvey Mudd Coll., 1982; MA, Princeton U., 1984; PhD, U. Calif., Berkeley, 1989. Postdoctoral rschr. U. Calif., 1989-90; asst. prof. physics Wash. State U., Pullman, 1990-95, assoc. prof., 1995, U. Mich., Ann Arbor, 1996-99; prof. JILA, U. Colo., Boulder, 1999—. Contbr. articles to profl. jours. Regents fellow U. Calif., 1985, Sloan rsch. fellow, 1995. Fellow Optical Soc. Am. (Adolph Lomb medal 1993), Am. Phys. Soc.; mem. IEEE, Soc. Photo-Optical Instrumentation Engrs. (scholar 1988). Office: JILA Univ Colo Boulder CO 80309-0440 E-mail: kapteyn@jila.colorado.edu.

KAPTOPODIS, LOUIS, supermarket chain executive; CEO, pres. Fiesta Mart, Houston. Office: Fiesta Mart 5235 Katy Fwy Houston TX 77007-2210

KAPTUR, MARCIA CAROLYN, congresswoman; b. Toledo, Ohio, June 17, 1946; BA, U. Wis., 1968; M. Urban Planning, U. Mich., 1974; postgrad., U. Manchester, (Eng.), 1974, MIT; LLD (hon.), U. Toledo. Urban planner; asst. dir. urban affairs domestic policy staff White House, 1977-79; mem. U.S. Congress from 9th Ohio dist., Washington, 1983—; mem. appropriations com., Agr. subcom., D.C. subcom., VA, HUD, and indep. agys. subcom. Bd. dirs. Nat. Ctr. Urban Ethnic Affairs; adv. com. Gund Found.; exec. com. Lucas County Democratic Com.; mem. Dem. Women's Campaign Assn. Mem. Am. Planning Assn., Am. Inst. Cert. Planners, NAACP, Urban League, Polish Mus., U. Mich. Urban Planning Alumni Assn. (bd. dirs.), Polish Am. Hist. Assn. Clubs: Lucas County Dem. Bus. and Profl. Women's, Fulton County Dem. Women's. Democrat. Roman Catholic. Office: US House of Reps 2366 Rayburn Washington DC 20515-0001 also: One Maritime Pla 6th Fl Toledo OH 43604*

KAPUR, AJAY, systems engineer; b. Delhi, India, Feb. 22, 1970; arrived in U.S., 1993; s. Ashok and Rohini Kapur. BSc, St. Stephen's Coll., Delhi, 1991; MS, Indian Inst. Tech., New Delhi, 1993, Columbia U., 1994; PhD, Stanford U., 1999. Grad. rsch. asst. M.D. Anderson Cancer Ctr., Houston, 1994—95, Stanford (Calif.) U., 1995—99; sys. engr. GE Global Rsch., Schenectady, NY, 1999—. Chief editor: web forum Electronic Medical Physics World, 1997—, reviewer: jour. Physics in Medicine and Biology, 2001; contbr. articles to profl. jours. Recipient medal, Pres. India, New Delhi, 1988. Mem.: Internat. Orgn. Med. Physics, Soc. for Molecular Imaging, Am. Assn. Physicists in Medicine. Achievements include patents pending in field. Office: Gen Elec Global Rsch Rm KW C524 1 Research Cir Niskayuna NY 12309

KAPUR, KAILASH CHANDER, industrial engineering educator; b. Rawalpindi, Pakistan, Aug. 17, 1941; s. Gobind Ram and Vidya Vanti (Khanna) K.; m. Geraldine Palmer, May 15, 1969; children: Anjali Joy, Jay Palmer. BS, Delhi U., India, 1963; M of Tech., Indian Inst. Tech., Kharagpur, 1965; MS, U. Calif., Berkeley, 1968, PhD, 1969. Registered profl. engr., Mich. Sr. rsch. engr. Gen. Motors Rsch. Labs., Mich., 1969-70; sr. reliability engr. TACOM, U.S. Army, Mich., 1978-79; mem. faculty Wayne State U., Detroit, 1970-89, assoc. prof. indsl. engring. and ops., 1973-79, prof., 1979-89; prof., dir. Sch. Indsl. Engring. U. Okla., Norman, 1989-92; dir., indsl. engring. U. Wash., Seattle, 1992—. Vis. prof. U. Waterloo, Can., 1977-78; vis. scholar Ford Motor Co., Mich., summer 1973. Author: Reliability in Engineering Design, 1977; contbr. articles to profl. jours. Grantee GM, 1974-77, U.S. Army, 1978-79, U.S. Dept. Transp., 1980-82. Fellow Am. Soc. Quality Control; mem. Ops. Rsch. Soc. Am. (sr.), Inst. Indsl. Engrs. (assoc. editor 1980—). Home: 4484 E Mercer Way Mercer Island WA 98040-3828 Office: U Wash PO Box 352650 Seattle WA 98195-2650 E-mail: kkapur@attbi.com., kkapur@u.washington.edu.

KAPUSINSKI, ALBERT THOMAS, economist, educator; b. Greenport, N.Y., Oct. 16, 1937; s. Casimir Thomas and Anne Mary (Olbrys) K.; m. Margaret Catherine Eichler, Sept. 3, 1963 (dec. March, 1982); children: Albert J., George T., Frank P.; m. Theresa Tafuri, Dec. 27, 1987. BBA, St. Johns U., N.Y.C., 1961, MBA, 1966; PhD, NYU, 1981. Economist Lionel D. Edie & Co., 1962-64; mem. faculty Caldwell (N.J.) U., 1964-2000, from assoc. prof. to prof. econs., 1969-2000, chmn. bus. dept., 1970-79, prof. emeritus, 2000; owner Kapusinski Prodns. Mem. Faculty Senate, 1969-75; assoc. sr. economist Hans Klunder Assocs., Hanover, N.H., 1966-69, ENVICO, Windsor, Vt., 1969-73; owner, operator Albert T. Kapusinski & Assoc., 1966—; econ. cons. to various industries in N.Y. and Vt.; mem. faculty Adirondack Coll., 1966, NYU, 1970-71, Merrill-Lynch Tng. Ctr. for Brokers, N.Y.C., 1973-74. Author: The Economy of Greene County, New York, 1972; contbr. articles to profl. jours. Chmn. Pro-Life del. World Population Conf. Forum, Bucharest, Rumania, 1974; bd. advisors U.S. Coalition for Life, Export, Penn., Ednl. Opportunities Fund, 1973-75. Served with USAR, USNG, 1953-61. Recipient K.L. Kiernan award; Gen. Electric Faculty fellow U. Chgo., 1970, Found. for Econ. Edn. fellow, 1971. Mem. Am. Econ. Assn., AAUP, Assn. Social Econs., Inst. Social Rels. Newark (adv. bd. 1972-74), Univ. Devel. Inst. (pres. 1967-68), Omicron Delta Epsilon. Office: Eichler Dr PO Box 80 Huletts Landing NY 12841 E-mail: drcapp@aol.com.

KARA, PAUL MARK, corporate executive; b. Valparaiso, Ind., Mar. 7, 1954; s. Charles J. and June F. K.; m. Elizabeth Louise Smith, Aug. 18, 1979; children: Adeline M., Emily L., Charles J., Phillip H. BA, Ind. U., 1977, JD, 1980. Bar: Mich. 1980, U.S. Dist. Ct. (we. dist.) Mich. 1980, U.S. Ct. Appeals (6th cir.) 1985. Assoc. Landman, Luyendyk, Latimer Clink & Robb, Muskegon, Mich. 1980-84, ptnr., 1984-86, Varnum, Riddering, Schmidt & Howlett, Grand Rapids, Mich., 1986-2000; CEO SSW Holding Co, Inc., 2000—. Pres., bd. dirs Sr. Services of Muskegon, Inc., 1985-86, Cath. Social Services of Muskegon 1985-86. Glenn Peters fellow, Ind. U., 1977-79, Louden Meml. fellow Ind. U. 1977-79. Mem. ABA (labor law sect., litig. sect., com. on devels. under NLRA) Mich. Bar Assn. (labor rels. law sect. coun. 1985-96, chairperson 1995-96) Muskegon County Bar Assn. (pres. 1985-86), Grand Rapids Bar Assn., Univ Club Chgo. Republican. Home: 3905 Norton Hills Rd Muskegon MI 49441-4456

KARABACHEV, IVAN, otolaryngologist; b. Sofia, Bulgaria, Sept. 10, 1947 came to U.S., 1976; s. Dimitri and Anna K.; m. Jane Aimme Karabachev, May 24, 1989; children: Anna, Alexander. MD, U. Sofia, 1972; grad., U. Vt., 1980 Surgeon Ear, Nose and Throat Clin., Las Vegas, 1981—. Mem. Am. Acad Otolaryngology and Head and Neck Surgery, Am. Coll. Surgeons, Rotary Republican. Office: 3201 S Maryland Pkwy Ste 500 Las Vegas NV 89109-2427

KARABATSOS, ELIZABETH ANN, career counseling services executive; b Geneva, Nebr., Oct. 25, 1932; d. Karl Christian and Margaret Maurine (Emrich Brinkman; m. Kimon Tom Karabatsos, Apr. 21, 1957 (div. Feb. 1981); children Tom Kimon, Maurine Elizabeth, Karl Kimon. BS, U. Nebr., 1954; postgrad. Ariz. State U., 1980; Cert. contemporary exec. devel., George Washington U. 1985; M Orgnl. Mgmt., U. Phoenix, 1994; cert. tchg., Scottsdale (Ariz.) C.C. 1999. Myers Briggs Type Indicator Qualified Profl. Provider. Instr. bus Fairbury (Nebr.) H.S., 1954—55; staff asst. U.S. Congress, Washington 1955—60; with Karabatsos & Co. Pub. Rels., Washington, 1960—73; conf asst. to asst. adminstr. and dep. adminstr. Gen. Services Adminstrn., Washing

ton, 1973—76; dir. corr. Office Pres.-Elect, Washington, 1980; assoc. dir. adminstrv. svcs. Pres. Pers.-White House, Washington, 1981; dept. asst.to Sec. and Dep. Sec. Def., Washington, 1981—86, asst. to, 1987—89; dir. govt. and civic affairs McDonnell Douglas Helicopter Co., Mesa, Ariz., 1989—90, gen. mgr. gen. svcs., 1990—92, co. ombudsman, community rels. exec., 1992—95; exec. asst. to dir. adminstrn. State of Ariz., 1995—96; prin., owner Karabatsos & Assocs., bus. consulting and mediation svcs., Scottsdale, 1995—. Bur. chief Office Prevention and Health Promotion Ariz. Dept. Health Svcs., 1997-98. Mem. Nat. Mus. Women in Art, Washington; bd. dirs. U.S. C. of C. Com. on Labor & Tng.; mem. Gov.'s Sci. and Tech. Com.; mem. Ariz. Com. Employer Support the Guard and Res., 1991; active Gov. Com. for Ariz. Clean and Beautiful, World Affairs Coun. Ariz. Mem.: ASTD, AAUW, Ariz. Dispute Resolution Assn. (bd. dirs.), Assn. Conflict Resolution, Am. Arbitration Assn., Women in Def., U. Nebr. Cather Group, Internat. Friends Transformative Art, Order Ea. Star, Pi Beta Phi, Pi Omega Pi. Episcopalian. Home and Office: 4446 E Camelback Rd # 110 Phoenix AZ 85018 Fax: (602) 954-0225. E-mail: ebkarabats@aol.com.

KARABELL, ZACHARY, economic analyst; b. N.Y.C., July 6, 1967; s. David and Deena Karabell; m. Nicole Alger, Dec. 2002. BA, Columbia U., 1985—88; MPhil, Oxford U., Eng., 1988—90; PhD, Harvard U., 1990—96, MA, 1991. Sr. rschr. Kennedy Sch. of Govt., Cambridge, Mass., 1996—98; visting asst. prof. Dartmouth Coll., 1997; non-resident scholar Miller Ctr., U. of Va., Charlottesville, 1999—2001; v.p., sen. econ. analyst & futurist Fred Alger Mgmt., N.Y.C., 2001—. Shorenstein fellow in press/politics Kennedy Sch. of Govt., 1997. Author: (book) Parting the Desert: The Creation of the Suez Canal, A Visionary Nation: Four Centuries of Am. Dreams and What Lies Ahead, The Last Campaign: How Harry Truman Won the 1948 Presdl. Election (Chgo. Tribune Heartland Award for Best Non-Fiction Book, 2000), What's Coll. For? The Struggle to Define American Higher Edn., Architects of Intervention: The U.S., the Third World, and the Cold War. Recipient Tchg. Award, Derek Bok Ctr., Harvard, 1992, 1994; fellow Kellet Fellowship, Columbia U., 1988-1990, MacArthur Fellowship in Internat. Security, MacArthur Found., 1992-1993, Olin Inst., Harvard U., Olin Found./Ctr. for Internat. Affairs, 1993-1994, Grad. Fellowship, Eisenhower/Pappas Found., 1993-1994, Truman Libr. Inst. Fellowship, Truman Libr., 1994-1995; grantee Scholar's Award, 1998-1999. Mem.: Global Leaders of Tomorrow, World Econ. Forum, Coun. on Fgn. Rels.

KARADY, GEORGE GYORGY, electrical engineering educator, consultant; b. Budapest, Hungary, Aug. 17, 1930; came to U.S., 1976; s. Gyozo and Anna (Szamek) K.; 1 child, Gyuri. MSEE, Tech. U. Budapest, 1952, DEng, 1960, D (hon.), 1996. Registered profl. engr., N.Y., N.J., Que. From instr. to assoc. prof., docent Tech. U. Budapest, Hungary, 1952-66; lectr. U. Baghdad, Iraq, 1966-68, U. Salford, Eng., 1968-69; program mgr. Hydro Quebec Inst. of Rsch., Can., 1969-76; chief elec. cons. engr. Ebasco Svcs., N.Y.C., 1976-86; Salt River Project Chair prof. Ariz. State U., Tempe, 1986—. Adj. prof. McGill U., Montreal, 1972-76, Poly. Inst. N.Y., 1980-86; lectr. (part time) U. Montreal, 1970-76. Author: Operation of Electric Appliances and Network (in Hungarian), 1964; (with others) Advances in Electronics and Electron Physics, 1976; co-author: Electric Power Systems, Vol. V (in Hungarian), 1963, Electrical Power Systems and Networks (in Hungarian), 1964; contbr. more than 150 papers to tech. jours. Fellow IEEE (paper award 1982, working group achievement award 1986); mem. U.S. Nat. Com. of Internat. Conf. of Large Elec. Network (sec.-treas. 1978-94), Princeton Ski Club (bd. dirs. 1977-86). Avocations: skiing, sailing, tennis, opera. Home: 11836 N 134th Way Scottsdale AZ 85259-3642 Office: Ariz State U Coll Engring Applied Sci Dept Elec Engring Tempe AZ 85287-5706

KARAFA, JOSEPH A. psychology educator, consultant; b. Grand Rapids, Mich., Oct. 15, 1970; s. Joseph Andrew and Pamela Joy Karafa; m. Thuy Bich Pham, June 12, 1999. BS, Grand Valley State U., 1992; MS, Kans. State U., 1995, PhD, 1999. Rsch. asst. Kans. State U., Manhattan, 1995-97, instr. mktg., 1999-2000; asst. prof. psychology Ferris State U., Big Rapids, Mich., 2000—. Cons. SmartForce.com., Dublin, Ireland, 1999-2001. Contbr. articles to profl. jours., including Jour. Basic and Applied Social Psychology, Personality and Social Psychology Bull., others. Mem. APA (assoc.), Am. Psychol. Soc., Midwestern Psychol. Assn. Avocations: composing electronic music, camping, motorcycles. Office: Ferris State U 2090 ASC Big Rapids MI 49307 E-mail: karafaj@ferris.edu.

KARAGEORGE, THOMAS GEORGE, lawyer; b. Louisville, Sept. 26, 1950; s. George D. and Betty D. Karageorge. JD, U. Louisville, 1977. Bar: Ky. 1977. Assoc. Stallings & Stallings, Louisville, 1976-80; pvt. practice, Louisville, 1980-93; assoc. Borowitz & Goldsmith, Louisville, 1993—. Mem.: Louisville Bar Assn., Ky. Bar Assn., Am.Hellenic Ednl. Progressive Assn. (treas.). Office: Borowitz & Goldsmith 1 Riverfront Plz # 1100 Louisville KY 40202 E-mail: tkarageorge@bglaw.com.

KARAIAN, NORMA MAKSOODIAN, lawyer; b. Providence, Sept. 6, 1904; d. Mooseak and Tarvez (Aslanian) Maksoodian; m. Leo J. Karaian, Sept. 5, 1937; children: Lenore, John M., Marilyn A. Karaian Hollisian. LLB, Boston U., 1925, JD, 2002. Bar: Mass. 1927. Mem. Curtis H. Waterman, Elder, Whitman, Weyburn & Crocker, Boston, 1926—41; pvt. practice, 1942—71; mem. Rackemann, Sawyer & Brewster, Boston, 1971—72, Gaston, Snow, Ely & Bartlett, Boston, 1973—. Mem.: ABA, Mass. Bar Assn., Mass. Conveyancers Assn., Land Ct. Examiners, Mass. Assn. Women Lawyers (pres. 1954—55), Armenian Law Soc. Home: 289 Common St Watertown MA 02472-4937

KARAIM, BETTY JUNE, retired librarian; b. Devils Lake, N.D., May 27, 1936; d. Erick Henry and Anna Caroline (Steen) Keck; m. William James Karaim, Dec. 7, 1955 (dec. 1983); children: Reed, Lisa, Ryan, Lynn, Rachel, Lee, Lara. BS in Edn., Mayville (N.D.) State U., 1958; postgrad., U. N.D., summer 1961; MLS, U. Okla., 1972; postgrad., No. Mont. Coll., 1979, 81. Libr. Lando (N.D.) High Sch., 1960-62; asst. libr., tchr. Mayville State Coll., 1962-79; libr. Havre (Mont.) Pub. Schs., 1979-82; libr. dir. Mayville State U., 1982-99, ret., prof. emerita, 1999. Bd. dirs. Mayville (N.D.) Pub. Libr., 1991-97, 2000—, pres., 1994-97; bd. dirs. Goose River Heritage Ctr., Mayville, 2000—, pres., 2002—; bd. dirs. M300 Assn. (arm of Mayville State U. Found.), 2000—, sec., 2002—. Recipient Orville Johnson Meritorious Svc. award, 1992, Disting. Alumni award Mayville State U. Alumni Found., 1997. Democrat. Avocations: reading, travel. Home: 320 1st St NW Mayville ND 58257-1107 E-mail: bjkaraim@polarcomm.com.

KARAKASH, JOHN J. engineering educator; b. Istanbul, Turkey, June 14, 1914; came to U.S., 1936, naturalized, 1948; s. Joachim Theodore and Irene (Georges) K.; m. Marjorie Rutherford, June 21, 1945; 1 child, John Thomas. Student, Robert Coll., Istanbul, 1932-35; BS, Duke U., 1937; MS (Moore fellow), U. Pa., 1938; D Engring. (hon.), Lehigh U., 1971. Registered profl. engr., Pa. Instr. U. Pa., 1938 40; project engr. Moore Sch. Elec. Engring., 1944-46; rsch. engr. Am. TV Labs., Chgo., 1940-42; edn. dir. 6th Svc. Command Signal Corps Radar Sch., Chgo., 1942-44; from asst. prof. to assoc. prof. elec. engring. Lehigh U., 1946-55, prof., head dept., 1955-58, disting. prof., 1962-81; dean Lehigh U. Coll. Engring., 1965-81; project engr. UHF filters Lehigh U., 1950-54; project dir. active networks Signal Corps., 1954-60. Cons. Bell Telephone Labs., Murray Hill, N.J., 1950-56, Dept. Edn. Commonwealth P.R., 1972, IBM, 1980-93; bd. dirs. Komline & Sanderson Engring. Corp. Author: Transmission Line and Filter Networks, 1950, also articles. Mem. Gen. State Authority Commonwealth of Pa., 1974-81. Recipient Alfred Nobel Robinson award for svc. to univ., 1948, Hillman award for disting. svc. Lehigh, 1962, 81, Outstanding Tchr. award, 1968, Outstanding Prof. award Lehigh U. Alumni Assn., 1990, Pa. Profl. Engring. award for distinction, 1965; rebuilt north wing Packard Lab. dedicated in his honor, 1981. Fellow IEEE (life, co-founder Lehigh Valley chpt. 1963, Centennial medal award 1984); mem. Am. Soc. Engring. Edn. (life), Engring. Coun. for Profl. Devel. (nat. accreditation com. for engring.), Franklin Inst., Pergamon Inst. (hon. adv. bd.), Phi Beta Kappa, Sigma Xi, Phi Beta Delta, Tau Beta Pi, Omicron Delta Kappa, Eta Kappa Nu, Iota Gamma Pi. Home: 2112 Kirkland Village Cir Bethlehem PA 18017-4713 *In free societies, whenever rules and regulations, because of changing times, are in conflict with principles— it is the principles that need be conserved, and the conflicting rules and regulations summarily discarded.*

KARAKEY, SHERRY JOANNE, real estate company executive, interior designer; b. Wendall, Idaho, Apr. 16, 1942; d. John Donald and Vera Ella (Frost) Kingery; children: Artist Roxanne, Buddy (George II), Kami JoAnne, Launi JoElla. Student, Ariz. State U., 1960. Corp. sec., treas. Karbel Metals Co., Phoenix, 1963-67; sec. to pub. Scottsdale (Ariz.) Daily Progress, 1969-72; with D-Velco Mfg. of Ariz., Phoenix, 1959-62, dir., exec. v.p., sec., treas., 1972-87; mng. ptnr., financial and real estate investment Karitage, Ltd., Scottsdale, 1987—. E-mail: footnotes@cox.net.

KARALEKAS, ANNE, business executive; b. Boston, Nov. 6, 1946; d. Christus and Helen (Vogiantzis) K. AB, Wheaton Coll., Norton, Mass., 1968; AM, Harvard U., 1969, PhD, 1974. Chief project mgr. def. and arms control project Commn. on Orgn. of Govt. for Conduct of Fgn. Policy, Washington, 1974-75; sr. staff mem. Senate Select Com. on Intelligence, Washington, 1975-78; sr. assoc. McKinsey & Co., Washington, 1978-85; mktg. mgr. The Washington Post, 1985-87, dir. mktg., 1987-89; pub. Washington Post Mag., 1989-96, dir. specialty products group, 1993-96; gen. mgr. Washington Sidewalk, Microsoft Corp., Washington, 1996-99; bd. dirs. Digital Globe, Longmont, 1999—. Author: History of the CIA, 1976; contbr. articles and book revs. to profl. jours. Advisor fgn. policy Mondale-Ferraro Presdl. Campaign, Washington, 1984; trustee Wheaton Coll., Norton, 1985-88. Mem. Council on Fgn. Relations, Phi Beta Kappa. Greek Orthodox. Avocation: twentieth century art and lit.

KARALEKAS, GEORGE STEVEN, advertising agency executive, political consultant; b. Boston, Nov. 26, 1939; s. Steven George and Sotiria (Sarris) K. BS, Boston U., 1962. Vice pres., assoc. media dir. Grey Advt., Inc., N.Y.C., 1962-70; dir. advt. services Can. Dry Corp., N.Y.C., 1970-72, dir. mktg. N.Y. ops., 1972-74; exec. v.p., dir. media and mktg., mgmt. account dir. deGarmo Advt., Inc., N.Y.C., 1974-80; sr. v.p., exec. dir. media, mgmt. dir. D'Arcy-MacManus & Masius, N.Y.C., 1980-85; pres. Karalekas & Co., N.Y.C. and Washington, 1985—. Sr. v.p., exec. dir. media November Group, Pres. Nixon, N.Y.C., Washington, 1971-72; sr. v.p., spl. advt. cons. Campaign 76, Pres. Ford, N.Y.C., Washington, 1975-76; sr. v.p., exec. dir. media Campaign 80, Pres. Reagan, N.Y.C., Washington, 1979-80; spl. advt. cons. Nov. Co., President Bush, N.Y.C., Washington, 1992. Mem. Republican Nat. Com., 1970— . Mem. Internat. Radio and TV Soc., Am. Mgmt. Assn. Republican. Greek Orthodox. Home: Holiday Point 8 Circle Dr Sherman CT 06784-1643 Office: Karalekas & Co 360 E 72nd St New York NY 10021-4753 also: 1211 Connecticut Ave NW Washington DC 20036-2701

KARALIS, JOHN PETER, retired computer company executive, lawyer; b. Mpls., July 6, 1938; s. Peter John and Vivian Karalis; m. Mary Curtis, Sept. 7, 1963; children: Amy Curtis, Theodore Curtis. BA, U. Minn., 1960, JD, 1963. Bar: Minn. 1963, Mass. 1972, Ariz. 1983, N.Y. 1986, Pa. 1986. Pvt. practice, Mpls., 1963-70; assoc. gen. counsel Honeywell Inc., Mpls., 1970-83, v.p., 1982-83; pvt. practice Phoenix, 1983-85; sr. v.p., gen. counsel Sperry Corp., N.Y.C., 1985-87; v.p. gen. counsel Apple Computer Inc., Cupertino, Calif., 1987-89; of counsel Brown and Bain, Phoenix, 1989-92; sr. v.p. corp. devel. Tektronix, Inc., Portland, 1992-98; ret. Mem. bd. advisors Ctr. for Study of Law, Sci. and Tech., Ariz. State U. Coll. Law, Tempe, 1983-89, 2000—, adj. prof., 1990-91. Author: International Joint Ventures, A Practical Guide, 1992. Recipient Disting. Achievement award Ariz. State U., Tempe, 1985. Mem. Met. Club (N.Y.C.), Gainey Ranch Golf Club.

KARAM, ERNEST, chief magistrate; b. Cleve., Apr. 3, 1909; s. Henry Harvey and Frieda K.; m. Lucille Himebaugh, Nov. 23, 1934 (dec. 1985). BS in Bus. Adminstrn., Ohio State U., 1933; LLB, Chase Coll. Law, Cin., 1947; JD, Chase Coll. Law, 1968. Bar: Ohio, U.S. Ct. Mil. Appeals, 1955, U.S. Tax Ct., 1976, U.S. Supreme Ct., 1955. Circulation exec. Cin. Post, 1933-74; referee Hamilton County Domestic Rels. Ct., Cin., 1976-77, chief referee, 1977-97, dir., 1978-97, chief magistrate, 1997—. Lectr. Am. Press Inst., 1961-73; spl. counsel Atty. Gen. Ohio, 1983. Lt. cmdr. U.S. Navy, 1943-46, USNR, 1947-74. Named Citizen of Day and Citizen of Decade, Radio WLW-700, Cin., 1968, Ky. Col., 1969—, Hon. Col., Office of Gov. Okla.,1 969—; Ernest Karam Day named in his honor, Apr. 2, 1999, City of Cin. Mem. ABA, Assn. Trial Lawyers Am., Ohio State Bar Assn., Ohio Circulation Mgrs. Assn., Cin. Bar Assn. Home: 5105 Graves Rd Cincinnati OH 45243-3807

KARAM, LISA ROBERT, research chemist; b. Washington, Mar. 26, 1960; d. Robert Daniel and Margaret Ellen McCollom; m. Philippe Pierre Deroin, Nov. 25, 1989; children: Nathalie, Nicolas, Jacques. BSc, Berry Coll., Rome, Ga., 1982; MSc, American U., Washington, 1983, PhD, 1985. Tchg. asst. Berry Coll., 1979-82, Am. U., 1982-83; chemist Nat. Bur. Standards, Gaithersburg, Md., 1983-87; rsch. chemist Nat. Inst. Standards & Technology, Gaithersburg, 1987-97, supervisory rsch. chemist, 1997—. Mem. sci. com. Internat. Com. Radionuclide Metrology Internat., 1998—; mem. med. subcom. Coun. on Ionizing Radiation Measurements and Standards, 1993—. Mem. Sigma Xi. Home: 8105 Plum Creek Dr Gaithersburg MD 20882-4446 Office: Nat Inst Stds & Tech 100 Bureau Dr Stop 8462 Gaithersburg MD 20899-8462

KARAM-HAGE, MAHER A. psychiatrist, researcher; b. Kartaba, Lebanon, Aug. 31, 1964; s. Afif A. Karam, Yvonne T. Hage; m. Lina C. Boujaoude, Feb. 25, 2001. MD, U. Francisco Marroquin, Guatemala City, 1993. Cert. gen. psychiatry Am. Bd. Psychiatry and Neurology. House officer dept. psychiatry U. Mich., Ann Arbor, 1994—98, fellow in addiction psychiatry, 1998—99, rsch. fellow Addiction Rsch. Ctr., 1999—2000; med. dir. Chelsea Arbor Treatment Ctr., Ann Arbor, 2000—. Med. dir., dir. med. edn. U. Mich. and Chelsea Arbor Treatment Ctr., Ann Arbor, 2000—; clin. asst. prof. psychiatry Addiction Rsch. Ctr. U. Mich., Ann Arbor, 2000—. Contbr. articles to profl. jours. Fellow rsch. fellow, Am. Coll. Neuropsychopharmacology, 1998. Mem.: Am. Lebanese Med. Assn., Rsch. Soc. on Alcohol, Soc. Rsch. on Nicotine and Tobacco, Am. Soc. on Addiction Medicine, Am. Acad. Addiction Psychiatry, Collegio de Medicos de Guatemala, Am. Psychiat. Assn. Avocations: swimming, travel, bicycling. Office: U Mich Addiction Rsch Ctr Ste 2A 400 E Eisenhower Pkwy Ann Arbor MI 48108 Home Fax: 734-930-0727; Office Fax: 734-930-0727. Business E-Mail: maherakh@umich.edu.

KARAN, DONNA (DONNA FASKE), fashion designer; b. Forest Hills, N.Y., Oct. 2, 1948; m. Mark Karan, 1971 (div.); 1 child, Gabrielle; m. Stephan Weiss, 1983 (dec. June 2001) BFA, Parsons Sch. Design, 1987. With Addenda Co., to 1968; with Anne Klein & Co., N.Y.C., 1968-84, co-designer, 1971-74, designer, 1974-84; owner, designer, ptnr. Donna Karan Co., N.Y.C., 1984-96, chmn. bd., chief designer, 1996—. Showed first complete collection for Anne Klein & Co. in 1974; collaborator on Anne Klein collections with Louis dell'Olio; author: DKNY: NYC, 1994. Bd. dirs. Design Industries Found. for AIDS; co-chair Kids for Kids, 1993, Ovarian Cancer Rsch. Super Saturday, East Hampton, N.Y, summers 1998, 99. Recipient Coty award, 1977, Awards Coun. of Fashion Designers of Am., 1985, 86, 92, Frontrunner award Sara Lee Corp., 1992; co-recipient (with Louis dell'Olio) Coty Return award, 1981, Coty Hall of Fame citation, 1982, Coty award, 1984; named Menswear Designer of Yr. Coun. Fashion Designers Am., 1992. Mem. Fashion Designers Am. (bd. dirs.) Office: Donna Karan Co W 40th St New York NY 10018

KARAN, HIROKO ITO, organic chemistry educator; b. Osaka City, Japan, Jan. 7, 1942; arrived in US, 1965; d. Seito and Haruko Ito; m. Jeffrey David Karan, Dec. 28, 1972; 1 child, Elizabeth Mika. MS, Wilkes Coll., Wilkes-Barre, Pa., 1967; PhD, Brown U., 1972. Rsch. asst. Hoshi Coll. Pharmacy, Tokyo, 1964-65; rsch. assoc. Fels Rsch. Inst., Temple U., Phila., 1971-72; rsch. scientist NYU, N.Y.C., 1972-73, 76-77; vis. instr. Hoshi Coll. Pharmacy, Tokyo, 1973-74; asst. prof. organic chemistry Medgar Evers Coll. CUNY, Bklyn., 1977-85, assoc. prof. Medgar Evers Coll., 1985-90, prof. Medgar Evers Coll., 1990—; asst. dean Medgar Evers Coll., 1993-98, dean, 1998—. Contbr. articles to profl. jours. Recipient svc. award Medgar Evers Coll., 1984, 90; grantee NIH, 1979—. Mem. Am. Chem. Soc. (chmn., bd. dirs. Bklyn. subsect. 1982-88, chmn. metrowomen chemists com. 1989, bd. dirs. N.Y. sect. 1985, 89-90, sec. 1989-90, Outstanding Svc. award 1993), Sigma Xi. Office: CUNY Medgar Evers Coll 1150 Carroll St Brooklyn NY 11225-2201 E-mail: hiroko@mec.cuny.edu.

KARAN, PAUL RICHARD, lawyer; b. Providence, June 12, 1936; s. Aaron Arnold and Sadye (Persky) K.; m. Susan Clare Brody, Jan. 3, 1964 (dec. Apr. 1986); children: Jennifer Hilary, Steven Lee; m. Linda Doris Adler, July 2, 1987. BA, Brown U., 1957; JD, Columbia U., 1960. Bar: NY 1961, U.S. Dist. Ct. (so. dist.) N.Y. 1962, U.S. Supreme Ct. 1967, U.S. Tax Ct. 1975, U.S. Claims Ct. 1976. Assoc. Demov & Morris, N.Y.C., 1960—65, ptnr., 1966—85, Gordon Altman Weitzen Shalov & Wein, N.Y.C., 1985—2000, Tofel, Karan & Ptnrs., P.C., N.Y.C., 2000—03. Contbr. articles to profl. jours. Chmn. Bd. Assessment Rev., Greenburgh, N.Y., 1978-86; mem. Planning Bd., Greenburgh, 1975-78, Bd. Edn., Greenburgh, 1980-83. Fellow Am. Bar Found., Am. Coll. Trust and Estate Counsel (chmn. downstate N.Y. 1996-2001), N.Y. Bar Found.; mem. ABA, N.Y. State Bar Assn. (chmn. trusts and estates law sect. 1990-91), Assn. of Bar of City of N.Y. Avocation: golf. Office: Tofel Karan & Ptnrs PC 780 3d Ave New York NY 10017 E-mail: prkaran@tkplaw.com.

KARANDIKAR, NITIN J. physician, scientist, educator; b. Bombay, June 16, 1967; s. Jayant T. and Jayashree J. Karandikar; m. Ashwini Marathe, Dec. 1, 1997. MBBS, U. Poona, India, 1990; MD in Pathology, 1993; PhD, Northwestern U., 1997. Lectr., asst. prof. B.J. Med. Coll., U. Poona, 1993; pathology resident U. Tex., S.W. Med. Ctr., Dallas, 1997—99, hematopathology fellow, 1999-2000, asst. instr., 2000-01, postdoctoral rsch. fellow in immunology, 2000—01, chief resident, 2000—01, asst. prof. pathology and neurology, 2001—, dir. R&D, flow cytometry and immunology, dir. immunopathology fellowship, 2002—. Dir., actor Marathi plays, others; composer, singer Indian music (Best Composer awards, several awards for singing). Mem. various Indian orgns., Chgo. and Dallas, 1993—. Harry Weaver Neurosci. scholar Nat. MS Soc., 2003—; recipient Grad. Symposium award Chgo. chpt. Soc. Neurosci., 1996, Pres.'s Rsch. Coun. Disting. Young Rschr. award U. Tex. Southwestern Med. Ctr., 2002. Mem. Am. Soc. Clin. Pathology, Coll. Am. Pathologists, Am. Assn. Immunologists, Am. Soc. Hematology. Avocations: swimming, dramatics, music. Office: U Tex Southwestern Med Ctr 5323 Harry Hines Blvd Dallas TX 75390-9072 Fax: (214) 648-4070.

KARANIKAS, ALEXANDER, English language educator, author, actor; b. Manchester, NH, Oct. 5, 1916; s. Stephen and Vaia (Olgas) K.; m. Helen J. Karagianes, Jan. 2, 1949; children: Marianthe Vaia, Diana Christine, Cynthia Maria. Student, U. N.H., 1934-36; AB cum laude, Harvard, 1939; MA, Northwestern U., 1950, PhD in English, 1953. With N.H. Writers Project, 1940-41; editor Allegheny-Kiski Valley Edit. The CIO News, 1941-42; radio news commentator Sta. WMUR, Manchester, 1946; grad. asst. Northwestern U., Evanston, Ill., 1950-52; instr. Kendall Coll., Evanston, Ill., 1952-53, Northwestern U., Evanston, 1953-54, 57-58; mem. faculty U. Ill. at Chgo., 1954—, prof. English, 1974-82, prof. emeritus, 1982—; owner Deerhaven Orchard, 1974-96. Cons. in field. Author: When a Youth Gets Poetic, 1934, In Praise of Heroes, 1945, Tillers of a Myth: The Southern Agrarians as Social and Literary Critics, 1966 (Friends of Lit. award 1967), (with Helen Karanikas) Elias Venezis, 1969, Hellenes and Hellions: Modern Greek Characters in American Literature, 1981; (musical) Nashville Dreams, 1991; (screenplay) Marika (Neptune award Moondance Film Festival 2003); (poetry) Stepping Stones, 1994. Mem. nat. cabinet Am. Youth Congress, 1937-39; exec. sec. Mass. Youth Coun., 1939-40; co-chmn. Nat. Bicentennial Symposium on the Greek Experience in Am., 1976; Publicity dir. N.H. Ind. Voters, 1946; sec. Manchester Vets. Council, 1946; Candidate for Congress, 1948; exec. com. United Hellenic Am. Congress, 1983—; exec. sec. Am. Coun. for Dem. Greece, 1947. With USAAF, 1942-45, Alaska corr. YANK, 1943-45. Mem. Hellenic Profl. Soc. Ill., Modern Greek Studies Assn., Screen Actors Guild, Friends of Lit., Harvard Club Chgo., Phi Eta Sigma, Order Ahepa (dist. sec. 1946). Mem. Greek Orthodox Ch. Home: 618 N Harvey Ave Oak Park IL 60302-1740 Office: Univ of Ill at Chicago English Dept Chicago IL 60680

KARASA, NORMAN LUKAS, home builder, developer, geologist; b. Balt., June 10, 1951; s. Norman and Ona K.; m. Lois J. Hansen, Jan. 4, 1974; children: Andrew, Jane. AB in Geology, Rutgers Coll., 1973; MS in Geophysics, U. Wyo., 1976; MBA in Fin., U. Colo., Colorado Springs, 1990. Systems mgr. Brit. Petroleum, N.Y.C., 1973-74; seismic processing leader Phillips Petroleum, Bartlesville, Okla., 1976-79, geophysicist Houston, 1979-80; internat. spl. project geophysicist Marathon Oil, Findlay, Ohio, 1980-82, internat. exploration geophysicist Houston, 1982-85, internat. reservoir geologist/geophysicist, 1985-86; home builder, designer, owner D'signer Inc., Monument Homes, Colo., 1986—, developer, hydrologist, 1992—; owner Tri-Lakes Montessori Sch.; ind. broker (realtor), 1997—. Mem. Home Builder Assocs., Nat. Audubon Soc. Office: Monument Homes PO Box 1423 Monument CO 80132-1423

KARASIK, DAVID, anatomist, educator, genetic epidemiologist; b. Bryansk, Russia, Aug. 8, 1967; s. Yefim and Elizabeta Karasik; m. Elina Michailevitch, July 12, 1994; children: Yankel, Aaron. BA, Kalinin State Med. Acad., Tvjer, Russia, 1990; MSc, Tel Aviv U., 1995, PhD, 2000. Asst. prosector Forensic Inst., Tel Aviv, 1992-95; tchg. asst. Tel Aviv U., 1995-99, anatomy lectr., 1999-00; postgrad. fellow Harvard U., 2000—; rsch. asst. scientist Hebrew Rehab Ctr. Aged, Boston, 2001—. Cons. Israeli police, Tel Aviv, 1998-99; personal identification vol. Forensic Inst., 1995-98. Contbr. articles to profl. jours. With Soviet Army, 1985-87. Grantee, Brookdale Inst., Jerusalem, 1993, 1996, CARE Found. for Prehist. Studies, 1999—2000, NIA, Bethesda, Md., 2001, Am. Coll. Rheumatology, 2002, NIAMS, 2003. Mem.: Rsch. Edn. Found., Am. Soc. Bone Mineral Rsch., Human Biol. Assn., Am. Coll. Rheumatology. Avocations: stamp collecting, translation of verses. Office: Hebrew Rehab Ctr Aged 1200 Centre St Boston MA 02131-1011 Home: Apt 1 12 Grover St Malden MA 02148 E-mail: karasik@mail.hrca.harvard.edu.

KARASOV, PHYLLIS, lawyer; b. St. Paul, Oct. 3, 1951; d. Elliott and Doris (Unger) K.; m. Alan David Olstein, Sept. 2, 1979; children: Samuel Louis, Joshua Charles, Adam Bernard. Student, Eastman Sch. Music, Rochester, N.Y., 1969-73, U. Minn., 1972; BA with distinction, U. Rochester, 1973; JD, Emory U., 1976. Bar: Minn. 1976, Ga. 1976, U.S. Dist. Ct. Minn. 1976, U.S. Dist. Ct. (no. dist.) Ga. 1976. Field atty. NLRB, Mpls., 1976-81; assoc. Moore, Costello & Hart, St. Paul, 1981-84, ptnr., 1984—. Lectr. in field. Contbr. articles to profl. publs. Bd. dirs. Talmud Torah, St. Paul, 1982-86, pres., 1983-85; bd. dirs. U. Minn. Student Legal Svcs., 1982-85, United Arts Coun., 1994—; bd. dirs. Resources for Child Caring, Inc., St. Paul, 1985—, sec.-treas., 1992-95; bd. dirs. United Jewish Fund and Coun. St. Paul, 1999—, mem. exec. com., 2001—. Recipient Miriam Kaplan Young Leadership award United Jewish Fund and Coun. St. Paul, 1987. Mem. ABA, Nat. Assn. Coll. and Univ. Attys. (chair employment law sect. 1995—1997), Ramsey County Bar Assn. (pres. 1999-2000), Minn. Bar Assn. (mem. exec. com. 2001-2003, editor labor law sect. newsletter 1983-84, com. on non-criminal sexual harassment 1988-89, com. on rules profl. conduct 1989-92, chmn. com. on discrimination 1990-91), Minn. Women Lawyers (pres. 1979-80, trustee polit. action com. 1982-84), pres. Office: Moore Costello & Hart Suite 1400 55 5th St E Ste 1400 Saint Paul MN 55101-1792

KARASU, T(OKSOZ) BYRAM, psychiatry educator; b. Feb. 11, 1935; MD, U. Istanbul, Turkey, 1959. Jr. intern St. Jeanne D'Arc Hosp., Montreal, Can., 1963-64; sr. intern St. John Gen. Hosp., New Brunswick, Can., 1964-65; resident in psychiatry Yale-New Haven Med. Ctr., 1967-68, Conn. Mental Health Ctr., 1968-69; fellow in psychiatry Yale U., New Haven, 1969; dir. dept. psychiatry Jacobi Med. Ctr., N.Y., 1975-93; prof. psychiatry Albert Einstein Coll. Medicine, Bronx, NY, 1981—, Silverman prof., chmn. psychiatry, 1993—, univ. chmn., 1998—. Chmn. Albert Einstein Coll. Medicine, 1993—; psychiatrist-in-chief Montefiore Med. Ctr., 1993—. Author: Wisdom in the Practice of Psychotherapy, 1992, Deconstruction of Psychotherapy, 1996, The Psychotherapist's Interventions, 1998, The Psychotherapist as Healer, 2001, The Art of Serenity, 2003; editor: Psychotherapy Research, 1982, The Psychiatric Therapies, 1984, Treatments of Psychiatric Disorders, 1989, others; editor-in-chief: Am. Jour. Psychotherapy, 1994—; contbr. articles to profl. jours. Recipient Sigmund Freud award, 1997. Fellow: Am. Psychiat. Assn. (chmn. commn. 1979—83, task force 1981—90, practice guidelines in major depression 1993, revised 2000, disting. life, Disting. Svc. award 1983, Spl. Presdl. award 1988). Office: 2 E 88th St New York NY 10128-0555 Also: Albert Einstein Coll Medicine 1300 Morris Park Ave Bronx NY 10461 1975

KARATZ, BRUCE E. business executive; b. Chgo., Oct. 10, 1945; s. Robert Harry and Naomi Rae (Goldstein) K.; children: Elizabeth, Matthew, Theodore. BA, Boston U., 1967; JD, U. So. Calif., 1970. Bar: Calif. 1971. Assoc. Keatinge

& Sterling, Los Angeles, 1970-72; assoc. corp. counsel Kaufman and Broad, Inc., Los Angeles, 1972-73, dir. forward planning Irvine, Calif., 1973-74; pres. Kaufman and Broad Provence, Aix-en-Provence, France, 1974-76, Kaufman and Broad France, Paris, 1976-80, Kaufman and Broad Devel. Group, Los Angeles, 1980-86; chmn., pres., CEO KB Home (formerly Kaufman and Broad Home Corp.), Los Angeles, 1985—, also bd. dirs.; also chmn. bd. dirs. Kaufman and Broad Home Corp., Los Angeles, 1993. Bd. dirs. Avery Dennison, Edison Internat., Nat. Golf Properties, Inc., Honeywell Internat., Inc., Kroger Co.; trustee RAND Corp. Founder Mus. Contemporary Art, L.A., 1981; bd. councilors U. So. Calif. Law Ctr. Mem. Calif. Bus. Roundtable (chmn.), Coun. on Fgn. Rels., Pacific Coun. on Internat. Policy, L.A. World Affairs Coun. (chmn.). Democrat. Avocations: modern art, skiing, travel, golf. Office: KB Home 10990 Wilshire Blvd Fl 7 Los Angeles CA 90024-3913

KARATZ, WILLIAM WARREN, lawyer; b. Benton Harbor, Mich., Aug. 9, 1926; s. Harry E. and Grace M. (Campbell) K.; m. Barbara Lansburgh Low, May 25, 1989. Ph.B. (La Verne Noyes scholar), U. Chgo., 1948; postgrad., Sch. Pol. Sci., 1949; LL.B. (Harlan Fiske Stone scholar), Columbia U., 1952. Bar: N.Y. State 1953, U.S. Supreme Ct. 1960. Assoc. in law Columbia U. Sch. Law, N.Y.C., 1952-53; assoc. firm Winthrop, Stimson, Putnam & Roberts, N.Y.C., 1953-62, partner, 1963-86, sr. counsel, 1987-2000, Pillsbury Winthrop, 2001—. Bd. dirs. Burnham Fund., Inc. Bd. editors: Columbia Law Rev, 1950-52. Served with USN, 1944-46. Fellow Am. Bar Found. (life); mem. ABA, Am. Law Inst. (life), Bar Assn. City of N.Y. (mem. exec. com. 1969-73, chmn. 1972-73, v.p. 1973-74), N.Y. State Bar Assn., (mem. ho. of dels. 1972-77), Am. Coll. Trial Lawyers, Am. Judicature Soc., Century Assn., India House Club (N.Y.C.), Confrerie des Chevaliers du Tastevin (grand officer). Home: 100 E 50th St New York NY 10022-6805 Office: Pillsbury Winthrop 1 Battery Park Plz Fl 29 New York NY 10004-1405

KARAU, STEVEN JAMES, social psychologist, researcher; s. Emil and Karlene Karau. BS in psychology, Ariz. State U., 1983—87; PhD in soc. psychology, Purdue U., 1987—93. Vis. asst. prof. Clemson U., SC, 1993—94; asst. prof. Va. Commonwealth U., Richmond, Va., 1994—98; assoc. prof. of mgmt. So. Ill. U., 1998—. Cons. (various organizations), 1994—2002. Contbr. more than 20 articles to profl. jours. Mem.: Am. Psychol. Soc., Acad. of Mgmt. Achievements include development of collective effort model (co-developed with Kipling Williams) of individual motivation in groups; attentional focus model (co-developed with Janice Kelly) of group performance; role congruity theory (co-developed with Alice Eagly) of prejudice toward female leaders. Office: Southern Illinois University Dept of Mgmt Carbondale IL 62901-4627

KARAYANIS, PLATO STEVEN, opera company executive; b. Pitts., Dec. 24, 1928; BFA, Carnegie Mellon U., 1952; artist's diploma in performance, Curtis Inst. Singer, stage dir., Luzern and Zürich, Switzerland, 1958-65, Met. Opera Nat. Co., 1965-67; exec. v.p., treas. Affiliate Artists Inc., 1967-77; mgr. rehearsal dept. San Francisco Opera; gen. dir. The Dallas Opera, 1977-2000. Recipient creative arts award, Dallas Hist. Soc., TACA award for Excellence in Performing Arts, 1998; Performing scholar Berkshire Music Festival, 1952, Performing scholar, Curtis Inst., 1952-56, 1952—56. Mem.: Dallas Assembly, Opera Am. (chmn. bd. dirs. 1993—97), Sigma Alpha Iota. Office: The Dallas Opera 3102 Oak Lawn Ave Dallas TX 75219-4241

KARBEN, RYAN SCOTT, state legislator; b. Bronx, N.Y., Sept. 29, 1974; s. Barry Richard and Shelley Valerie (Gross) K.; m. Lauren Cheryl Bekritsky, June 23, 1996; children: Michal Fara, Hanna Meghan. BA in English, Yeshiva U., 1996; JD, Columbia U., 1999. Mem. planning bd. Town of Ramapo, Suffern, N.Y., 1992-97; county legislator County of Rockland, New City, NY, 1997—2003, maj. leader legislature, 2001—03; assoc. Simpson Thacher and Bartlett, N.Y.C., 1999—2001; ptnr. Kurtzman, Matera, Gurock & Karben LP, 2001—; mem. N.Y. State Assembly, 2003—. Bd. trustees United Jewish Appeal Fed., New Hempstead, N.Y., 1996—; adv. bd. Martin Luther King Ctr., Spring Valley, N.Y., 1993—, Big Bros./Big Sisters, New City, 1996—; mem. Arts Coun. Rockland. Mem. Spring Valley NAACP, Rockland County Conservation Assn. Jewish. Avocation: reading. Office: 1 Blue Hill Plz PO 13 1549 Pearl River NY 10965 E-mail: ryankarben@msn.com.

KARBOWITZ, STEPHEN R. physician; b. Bklyn., Feb. 19, 1948; MD, Albert Einstein, Bronx, 1971. Diplomate Am. Bd. Internal Medicine, Am. Bd. Pulmonary Diseases. Dir. Pulmonary Sect. N.Y. Hosp., Queens, 1976—. Fellow Am. Coll. Chest Physicians, Am. Thoracic Soc. Office: 56-45 Main Street Flushing NY 11355 Fax: 718-461-2943.

KARCH, JACQUELINE, artist; b. Newark, Jan. 17, 1946; d. Samuel Arthur and Miriam Francis K.; m. William Clinton Keach, June 27, 1991. Student, Art Students League, 1962—66; BFA, Syracuse U., 1968; MAT, R.I. Sch. of Design, 1971. Art tchr. Providence (R.I.) Pub. Schs., 1972-2000; artist, ceramic tile Ceramic Tiles, Providence, 1983-2000, LeLand, N.C., 2000—. One-woman shows include Gallery 401, Providence, RI, 1980, 1987, Gallery WHQR, Wilmington, NC, 2003, exhibited in group shows at San Regret Gallery, Boston, 1980, Am. Soc. on Aging, San Diego, 1988, Gallery 401, Providence, 1986, Bell St. Gallery, 1991—92, visual documentary, Trinity Square Repertory Theatre Productions, 1983—85, Jewish Home for the Aged, 1988; costume designer : (plays) The Charlatans, 1972; The Red Hat; author: Recipes Remembered, 1996. Mem. The Arts Students League (life). Avocations: animal rescue, calligraphy, costume design, cooking, gardening. Office: Ceramic Tiles-Jacqueline Karch 904 Woodridge Ct SE Leland NC 28451

KARCHER, BARBARA CORRENTI, sociologist, educator; b. New Orleans, Jan. 19, 1946; d. Alfred Francis and Betty Mae (Lockhart) Correnti; m. Charles Joseph Karcher, Aug. 31, 1968; 1 child, Elizabeth Marie. AB, Loyola U., New Orleans, 1967; MA, U. Ga., 1972, PhD, 1974. Instr. Ga. Inst. Tech., 1972-74; asst. prof. Kennesaw Coll., Marietta, Ga., 1974-79, assoc. prof. sociology, 1979-87, prof., 1987—; assoc. dir. Ctr. for Active Retirement Edn. Kennesaw State U., 2000—. Chair regent's acad. com. on sociology, anthropology and social work State of Ga. Univ. Sys., 1985—86, 1998—99. NSF trainee, 1967-68. Mem. Am. Sociol. Assn., So. Sociol. Soc., Ga. Sociol. Assn. (past pres., past sec.-treas.), Am. Soc. on Aging, Ga. Gerontology Soc., Phi Beta Kappa, Phi Kappa Phi (past chpt. pres.). Democrat. Roman Catholic. Home: 410 Arbor Trl Marietta GA 30067-6752 Office: Kennesaw State U 1000 Chastain Rd Kennesaw GA 30144 E-mail: bkarcher@kennesaw.edu.

KARCHIN, LOUIS SAMUEL, composer, educator; b. Sept. 8, 1951; s. Isadore David and Ida (Kessler) K. MusB, U. Rochester, 1973; MA, Harvard U., 1975, PhD, 1978. Asst. prof. music NYU, N.Y.C., 1979-85, assoc. prof. music, 1985-99, prof., 2000—. Pres. U.S. sect. Internat. Soc. for Contemporary Music, 1981-83, chmn., 1983-85; pub. C. F. Peters Corp. Composer: Capriccio for Violin and Seven Instruments, 1978, Duo for Violin and Cello, 1981, Viola Variations, 1982, Songs of John Keats, 1985, Canonic Mosaics, 1986, Sonata for Piano, 1987, Songs of Distance and Light, 1988, Sonata for Cello and Piano, 1989, Romulus, an Opera in One Act, 1990, String Quartet, 1991, Galactic Folds for chamber ensemble, 1993, Sonata da Camera, 1994, Summer Song, 1994, Rustic Dances, 1995, Rhapsody for Orchestra, 1996, Cascades, 1997, American Visions: Two Songs on Poems of Yevgeny Yevtushenko, 1998, Quartet for Percussion, 2000, Deux Poèmes de Mallarmé, 2001, Voyages for alto sax and piano, 2001, Carmen de Boheme, 2002, Orpheus, a Masque for baritone, instruments, and dance, 2003; commd. by Fromm Found., 1994, Koussevitzky Found., 1998, Barlow Found., 2001. Recipient Koussevitsky Composition prize Tanglewood, 1971, Joseph H. Bearns prize Columbia U., 1972, Composer award NEA, 1982, 83, Heckscher Found. prize, 1999, Goddard Lieberson prize AAAL, 2001. Office: NYU 24 Waverly Pl Rm 268 New York NY 10003-6757

KARCZ, ANDRZEJ, literature educator; b. Radom, Poland, Oct. 17, 1961; arrived in U.S., 1988; s. Jan and Ewa Karcz; m. Anna Karcz, July 20, 1996; 1 child, Agatha. MA, Cath. U. of Lublin, Poland, 1986; PhD, U. Chgo., 1999. Instr./rschr. Cath. U. of Lublin, 1986—88; asst. prof. U. Kans., Lawrence, 1999—. Author: (book) The Polish Formalist School and Russian Formalism, Teksty z daleka i bliska; contbr. articles and revs. to profl. jours., encys. Scholar, Stefan Batory Found., 1996. Mem.: Am. Assn. Advancement Slavic Studies, Am. Assn. Tchrs. Slavic and East European Langs., Polish Inst. Arts and Scis. of Am. Office: U Kans Slavic Dept 1445 Jayhawk Blvd Rm 2133 Lawrence KS 66045

KARCZMAR, MIECZYSLAW, economist; b. Lodz, Poland, Jan. 22, 1923; came to u.S., 1973; s. Henryk and Franciszka (Lubicz) K.; m. Gabriela Bogucka, Dec. 22, 1947; children: Thomas, Peter. MS in Econs. and Commerce, Acad. Commerce, Poznan, Poland, 1948; PhD in Econs., Main Sch. Planning Stats, Warsaw, Poland, 1960; postgrad., London Sch. Econs., 1958. With Nat. Bank Poland, Warsaw, 1949-62, dep. dir. planning dept., 1955-58, dep. dir. internat. dept., 1958-62; dir. fin. dept. Polish Ministry Fgn. Trade, Warsaw, 1962-69; trade commr., comml. counselor to Can. Montreal, 1969-73; sr. v.p., chief economist European Am. Bank & Trust Co., European Am. Banking Corp., N.Y.C., 1974-86; econ. advisor Deutsche Bank, N.Y.C., 1986—. Mem. supervisory bd. Bank Handlowy, Warsaw, 1962-69, Warta-Ins. Reins. Co., Warsaw, 1962-69; lectr., asst. prof. Main Sch. Planning Stats., Warsaw, 1951-68; lectr. vocat. courses in fin. planning and credit sys., 1950-56. Author: (with W. Pruss) Credit in Trade, 1956; (with others) Accountant's Guidebook, 1956, Money and Credit, 1960; contbr. articles to newspapers, mags., profl. jours.; rschr. in money, credit theory, internat. monetary system, banking.

KARDAN, MAHMOUD, chemist, educator; b. Iran, Mar. 25, 1955; s. Mohammad Taghi Kardan and Tahereh Mhajer; m. Soraya Kardan, Jan. 20, 1989; children: Kaveh, Kimia. Ph.D. in Chemistry, Seton Hall U., 1984. Projects mgr. Clifton Adhesive, Inc., Wayne, NJ, 1999—; spkr. in field. Contbr. articles to profl. jours. Grantee, U. Mass., 1984—86. Mem.: Fedn. Socs. for Coatings Tech. (assoc.). Achievements include research in latex durability and rubber conformation. Avocations: guitar, tennis. Home: 45 Walnut St Livingston NJ 07039 Office: Clifton Adhesive Inc Burgess Pl Wayne NJ 07470 E-mail: mkardan@juno.com.

KARDAUSKAS, MICHAEL JOHN, materials scientist, consultant; b. Elizabeth, N.J., 1953; s. Edmund and Agnes Kardauskas. BS in Engring. Sci., Pa. State U., 1980, MS in Engring. Sci., 1983, PhD in Solid State Sci., 1987. Sr. staff materials scientist Mobil Solar Energy Corp., Billerica, Mass., 1987-93; dept. v.p. engring. ASE Americas, Inc., Billerica, 1994-99; pres. Materials for Electronics, Billerica, 1999—, SunRay Techs., Inc., Billerica, 2002—. Cons. materials specialist 3M Touch Sys., Inc., Methuen, Mass., 1999—. Mem.: IEEE, Internat. Microelectronics and Packaging Soc., Electrochemical Soc., ASM Intnerat., Am. Chem. Soc., Am. Vacuum Soc. Achievements include patents in field of photovoltaic cells, solar modules and touch screen panels. Office: Materials for Electronics 8 River St Billerica MA 01821

KARDON, BRIAN, music company executive; m. Kara Silver, Mar. 23, 1991; children: Max, Elliot, Isabel. BS, U. Pa., 1979, MBA, 1987. V.p. corp. mktg. Cahners Pub. Co., Newton, Mass., 1995—97; sr. v.p. mktg. Cahners Bus. Info., Newton, 1997—99; exec. v.p. Home Portfolio Inc., Newton; pres. First Act Inc., Needham, Mass., 2000—. Office: 250 1st Ave Needham MA 02494-2814 E-mail: bkardon@firstact.com.

KARDON, DENNIS, artist, educator; BA cum laude, Yale U., 1973. Mem. faculty Sch. Fine Arts, N.Y.C. One-man shows include Barbara Toll Fine Arts, N.Y.C., 1981, 1984, 1984, 1986, 1989, Studio Space, 1990, Richard Anderson Fine Arts, 1996, exhibited in group shows at Mus. Modern Art, N.Y.C, 1983, 1986, List Art Ctr. MIT, Cambridge, Mass., 1985, Wellesley (Mass.) Coll. Mus., 1986, Indpls. Mus. Art, 1986, Bklyn. Mus., 1986, Barbara Toll Fine Arts, 1987, Lorence-Monk Gallery, N.Y.C., 1988, Nat. Gallery Art, Washington, 1989, Fernando Alcolea Gallery, Barcelona, Spain, 1989, Althea Viafora Gallery, N.Y.C., 1990, Marc Richards Gallery, L.A., 1990, Arts and Letters, N.Y.C., 1994, Aldrich Mus. Contempoirary Art, Ridgefield, Conn., 1995, Albright Gallery, Reading, Pa., 1995, 1996, Mus. Fine Arts, Boston, 1996, Jewish Mus., N.Y.C. (travelled to San Francisco, L.A., Balt.), Represented in permanent collections, J.V. Speed Mus., L.A. County Mus. Art, Boston Mus. Fine Art, Walker Art Mus., New Mus., Mus. Modern Art, Met. Mus., Des Moines Art Ctr., Ind. U. Art Mus., U. Iowa Mus. Art, Bklyn. Mus., Nat. Mus. Am. Art, Fogg Art Mus., N.Y. Pub. Libr., also pvt. and corp. collections, work reviewed and represented in newspapers and mags. Guggenheim fellow, 1998, grantee, N.Y. Found. Arts, Louis Comfort Tiffany Found., 1991. Office: Sch Visual Arts 209 E 23d St New York NY 10010

KARDON, JANET, museum director, curator, educator; b. Phila. d. Robert and Shirley (Drasin) Stolker; m. Robert Kardon, Nov. 19, 1955; children: Ross, Nina, Roy. BS in Edn., Temple U.; MA in Art History, U. Pa. Lectr. Phila. Coll. Art, 1968-75, dir. exhbns., 1975-78; dir. Inst. Contemporary Art, Phila., 1978-89, Am. Craft Mus., N.Y.C., 1989-95; ind. curator, 1996—. Adj. prof. Fashion Inst. of Tech., N.Y.C., Pratt Inst., Bklyn., Cooper Hewit; cons., panel mem. Nat. Endowment for Arts, 1975—; mus. panel mem. Pa. Coun. on Arts, Phila., 1988—; U.S. commr. Venice Biennale, Venice, 1980. Exhibitions include Labyrinths, Time, Artists SEts and Costumes, Laurie Anderson, Robert Mapplethorpe, David Salle, Gertrude and Otto Natzler; editor: Twentieth Century American Craft: A Centenary Project, The Ideal Home, 1900-1920, Revivals/Diverse Traditions, 1920-1945, Craft in the Machine Age, 1920-1945. Grantee Nat. Endowment for Arts, 1978. Home and Office: 150 E 69th St Apt 21J New York NY 10021-5704 E-mail: jakardon@aol.com.

KARDON, RANDY H. ophthalmologist, researcher; b. Des Moines, Feb. 17, 1954; s. Fred and Thelma (Sherman) K. BS, U. Iowa, 1975, MD, PhD, 1982. Diplomate Am. Bd. Ophthalmology; lic. physician, Iowa. Neuro-ophthalmology fellow U. Iowa Hosps., Iowa City, 1987-89, assoc. prof., 1989—; clin. scientist VA Hosp., Iowa City, 1995—. Dir. neuro-ophthalmology rsch. svc. U. Iowa, Iowa City, 1997; examiner Am. Bd. Opthalmology, Phila., 1997—; coord. com. Clin. Rsch. Ctr., 1997; grant review com. Fight for Sight Sci. Program, 1995. Co-author: Walsh & Hoyt Clinical Neuro-Ophthalmology, 1997, Atlas of Neuro-Ophthalmology, 1997; mem. editl. bd. Jour. Clin. Neuro-Ophthalmology, 1997. Recipient Lew Wasserman award Rsch. to Prevent Blindness, 1997, Career Devel. award VA, 1995-2000, Merit Review award 1993-98, 1999—. Jewish. Office: Univ Iowa Hosps and Clinics 200 Hawkins Dr Iowa City IA 52242-1009

KARDON, ROBERT, mortgage company executive; b. Phila., Mar. 8, 1922; s. Morris and Sophie (Winkleman) K.; m. Janet Stolker, Nov. 19, 1949; children—Roy, Nina, Ross. Student, U. Miami (Fla.), 1940-42, Shrivenham Am. U., Swindon, Eng., 1945-46. Chmn. bd. B.T. Babbitt Co., Inc., 1964-66, Pitts. Mortgage Corp., 1964-72, Murphree Mortgage Co., Nashville, 1966-72, Kardon Investment Co., 1945-75, Peoples Bond & Mortgage Co., Phila., 1950-72. Chmn. bd., v.p. United Container Co., Phila., 1938-75; pres., chief exec. officer Kardon Industries, Inc., 1974—, also chmn. Trustee Phila. Mus. Art. Served with AUS, 1942-46. Mem. Young Pres. Orgn., World Bus. Council. Home: 150 E 69th St # 12G New York NY 10021-5704 Office: Kardon Industries Inc 150 E 69th St Apt 12G New York NY 10021-5704

KARDOS, MEL D. lawyer, educator; b. Phila., Feb. 6, 1947; s. Julius S. and Rose (Klein) K.; children: Lindsay Dara, Matthew Daniel. BS, Temple U., 1970; MEd, Trenton State Coll., 1972; JD, U. Balt., 1975. Bar: Pa. 1975, N.J. 1975, U.S. Dist. Ct. (ea. dist.) Pa. 1975, U.S. Dist. Ct. N.J. 1975, U.S. Supreme Ct. 1984. Asst. pub. defender Bucks County, Doylestown, Pa., 1975-80; ptnr. Kardos & Lynch, Newtown, Pa., 1980, Kardos & Heley, Newtown, 1980-87, Kardos, Rickles, Sellers & Hand, Newtown, 1988-. Adj. prof. Temple U., Phila., 1987, Bucks County C.C., 1995. Sec., bd. dirs. Lower Bucks County Pa. chpt. ARC; mem. exec. bd. Bucks chpt. ARC; supr. Middletown Twp., Bucks County, 1998-2003, chmn. Mem. ABA, Bucks County Bar Assn., Assn. Trial Lawyers Am., Soc. for Am. Baseball Research. Democrat. Avocations: sports broadcasting, sports, history, politics. Office: Kardos Rickles Sellers & Hand 626 S State St Newtown PA 18940-1509 also: 194 S Broad St Trenton NJ 08608-2405

KAREEM, A'ISHA, educational consultant, counselor; b. Dallas, Jan. 11, 1947; d. James and Henrietta Payton; m. Thomas Abdul-Salaam; 1 child, Dawn Ali. BEd, U. of Pacific, 1971, MEd, 1976; PhD, Universal Life, Modesto, Calif., 1985, U. Santa Barbara, 2002. Cert. counselor, ednl. adminstr., in behavioral edn. Gen. edn. instr. Stockton (Calif.) Unified Sch. Dist., 1971—85; ednl. rschr. for behaviorally-challenged students Acad. Human Devel., Stockton, 1985—97; ednl. rschr. Clara Mohammed Schs., Stockton, 1998—2002; counselor, field advisor Calif. Dept. Corrections, Stockton, 1998—2002. Ednl. cons. U. of Pacific, Stockton, 1996—2002, adj. prof., 1998—2002; advisor San Joaquin County A+, Stockton, Calif.; mem. MAS Edn. Monitoring Team, Chgo., 1998—2002; bd. dirs. San Joaquin County Mental Health, Stockton, U. Calif. Affirmative Action, Oakland, 1990—95; program devel. Bush's New Am. Schools, Stockton, 1989—90; facilitator Rotary Read In, Stockton, 1994—2002; participant Black Pedagogy Group, San Francisco, 1982, Pacific Sociology of Edn., Monterey, Calif., 1984; rschr. U. Santa Barbara, 2000. Contbr. (book of poetry) Save Our Children: An Appeal to American Families, 1998; dir.: (ednl. video) Thriller Time, 1985 (Cable Showcase, 1986); composer, dir. Youth Excellence Showcase, 1990 ("Save Our Children" Proclamation, 1995), contbr. (performance theater) Children's Vision Theater, 1994; editor: (newsletter) PEACE, 1999. Mem. Haggin Mus., Stockton, 1996—2002; facilitator Am. Muslim Alliance, Fremont, Calif., 1994—2002, Drug Task Force, Stockton, 1987—92, We Are Family, Stockton, 1995—2002; state rep. Miller Family Genealogy, Dallas, 1972—2002; mem. Good Govt., Chgo., 1996—2002; elected area rep. Rep. Ctrl. Com., Stockton, 1996—98; mem. Profl. Bus. Women, Stockton, 1989—92, NAACP, Stockton, 1988—98. Nominee Stocktonian Of Yr., Am. Friends Assn., 1989, Jefferson award, 1990; named Valley Woman In History, Commn. On Status Of Women, 1989—2002; named to Hall of Fame, Stockton Unified Sch. Dist., 1994. Fellow: Am. Muslim Assn. (scholar 1985); mem.: Black Educators Assn., U. Pacific Alumni Assn., Muslim Am. Soc. (life), Stockton Metro Ministry. Achievements include research in significance of culture in education especially among student of African descent; the significance of rewards in behavior modification program. Home: 1242 W Rose St Stockton CA 95203 Office: Calif Dept Corrections 7150 E Arch Rd Stockton CA 95213-9006 Home Fax: 209-462-0183; Office Fax: 209-462-0183. Personal E-mail: habi@gotnet.net. Business E-Mail: habi@gotnet.com.

KARELIS, CHARLES HOWARD, former academic administrator; b. Denver, July 7, 1945; s. Lloyd Howard and Annabelle (Weinberg) Karelis; m. Judith Theodora Johanna Johnston, June 10, 1972 (div. 1991); children: Alexander O. Oliver L. BA, Williams Coll., 1966; PhD, Oxford (Eng.) U., 1972; LHD, Phillips U., Okla., 1990; HHD, Marietta Coll., 1993. Assoc. producer WGBH-FM, WGBH-TV, Boston, 1967—68; lectr. in philosophy Williams Coll., Williamstown, Mass., 1972—73, asst. prof., 1977—79, assoc. prof., 1979—85, prof., 1985—99; spl. asst. to sec. Dept. Edn., Washington, 1985, dir. Fund for Improvement of Postsecondary edn., 1985—99; pres. Colgate U., Hamilton, 1999—2001; vis. prof. philosophy George Washington U., Washington, 2001—02. Vis. assoc. prof. philosophy Wesleyan U., Middleton, Conn., 1980—81; bd. dirs. (sec.) Charter Schools Develop. Corp.; mem. of governing bd. U.S. Dept. of Agrl. Contbr. articles to profl. jours. Mem.: Phi Beta Kappa. Office: Colgate U 13 Oak Dr Hamilton NY 13346-1383 also: 1090 Vemont Ave NW Ste 800 Washington DC 20005

KARELITZ, RICHARD ALAN, financial executive, lawyer; b. Elizabeth, N.J., Nov. 1, 1949; s. David Karelitz and Doris Frances (Tuck) Kahn; m. Virginia Lee Harris, Aug. 18, 1974; children: David Benjamin, Daniel Seth. AB, Coll. William and Mary, 1971; JD, Boston U., 1974, LLM, 1977. Bar: Mass. 1974, U.S. Supreme Ct. 1979; notary pub., Mass. Tax atty. Coopers & Lybrand, Boston, 1974-75; comptr. Internat. Forest Products Corp., Boston, 1975-79, treas., 1979-91, sr. v.p., 1991—. Treas. New Eng. TV Corp., 1987-91, Sta. WHDH-TV, Inc., 1987-91; gen. coun., New Eng. Patriots (NFL) Football Club, 1994—, Foxboro Stadium Assocs. L.P., Foxboro, Mass., 1989-2000, New England Revolution (Major League Soccer Team), Foxboro, 1996—, NPS LLC, Foxboro, 2000—; dir. Carmel Container System, Ltd., Tel Aviv, 1988—, chmn. audit com., 1992—; treas. Chestnut Hill Mgmt. Corp., Boston, 1991—. Trustee Kraft Found., Boston, 1979-2002; bd. dirs. Temple Sinai, Sharon, Mass., 1995-99, Caritas Norwood (Mass.) Hosp., 2002—. Mem. ABA, Mass. Bar Assn. Jewish. Avocations: travel, family activities. Home: 31 Sunset Dr Sharon MA 02067-1738 Office: Internat Forest Products Corp Gillette Stadium One Patriot Pl Foxboro MA 02035

KAREN, JOEL S. plastic surgeon; b. N.Y.C., Mar. 28, 1938; s. Abraham and Frieda (Draisin) K.; m. Gudrun Elisabeth Elmqvist, June 25, 1967; children: Allison, Anders. BA, Columbia Coll., 1959; MD, Chgo. Med. Sch., 1963. Diplomate Am. Bd. Surgery, Am. Bd. Plastic Surgery. Internship Jersey City Med. Ctr., 1963-64; residency New England Med. Ctr., 1964-66, 67-69; fellowship in surgery Malmö (Sweden) Gen. Hosp., 1966-67; residency in plastic surgery U. Tex. Med. Br., Galveston, 1969-72; pvt. practice plastic surgery Plainview, NY, 1972—2003. Chief divsn. plastic surgery North Shore U. Hosp., Plainview, 1988-2003. Mem. AMA, Am. Soc. Plastic and Reconstructive Surgeons, N.Y. State Med. Soc., Nassau County Med. Soc.

KAREN, LINDA TRICARICO, interior designer; b. Bklyn., June 8, 1961; d. John William and Phyllis Jean (D'Addario) T. Student, Bucks County Community Coll., 1978-79; AAS, Fashion Inst. Tech., 1992. Retail mgr. Canadians, Brooks, Casual Corner, 1980—83; coord. sales and design Sure Snap Corp., NYC, 1983—84; asst. designer E.S. Sutton Inc., NYC, 1984—86; designer Good 'N Plenty Inc., NYC, 1986—90; sr. designer, merchandiser Leonard A. Feinberg, Inc., NYC, 1991—98; freelance designer, ind. contractor, 1998—; mem. retail sales staff Oilily, 1999—; children's interior design cons. BOCES N.Y. Interior Decorating, 2000—, Sheffield Sch. Interior Design, 2001—; sales and design cons. Furniture Options, Goshen, NY, 2001—; interior designer Suffern (N.Y.) Furniture, 2002—; decorating cons. Gervic Paint & Decorating Ctr., Monroe, NY. Free-lance illustrator, designer; children's designer, party planner, 1999—; seminar spkr. in field. Contbr. fashion trend reports, Milan, Italy, 1984, Rome, 1985, Milan and Florence, Italy, 1986, London and Paris, 1987, Montreal, 1988, 94, 95, L.A., 1993, 95, 96. Mem. Fashion Soc., Women of the Monroe Area, Orange County C. of C., Warsick Valley C. of C. Republican. Roman Catholic. Avocations: fashion design, illustration, travel. Home: 124 Dug Rd Chester NY 10918-2620

KARETZKY, STEPHEN, library director, educator, researcher; b. Bklyn., Aug. 29, 1946; s. Harry and Lillian Dorothy (Abrams) K.; m. Deborah Ann Shaw, Apr. 12, 1970 (div. July 1972); Joanne Louise Ballestrasse, Mar. 17, 1985. BA, CUNY, Flushing, 1967; MLS, Columbia U., 1969, DLS, 1978; MA, Calif. State U., Dominguez Hills, 1991. Libr. Bklyn. Pub. Libr., 1969-70; asst. prof. SUNY, Buffalo, 1974-76, Geneseo, 1977-78; assoc. prof. U. Haifa, Israel, 1978-81, San Jose (Calif.) State U., 1982-85; researcher, editor Shapolsky/Steimatzky Pub., N.Y.C., 1981-82; sr. editor Shapolsky Pubs., N.Y.C., 1985-86; libr. dir. Felician Coll., Lodi, N.J., 1986—. Author: Reading Research and Librarianship: A History and Analysis, 1982 (2d place award for Best Book of Yr. Am. Soc. Info. Sci 1983), The "Cannons" of Journalism, 1984; editor: The Media's War Against Israel, 1985, The Media's Coverage of the Arab-Israeli Conflict, 1989, Not Seeing Red: American Librarianship and the Soviet Union, 2002; bd. advisors Directory of American Scholars, 1999-2001; contbr. articles to profl. jours. Exec. dir. Ams. for a Safe Israel, N.Y.C., 1985-86. Mem.: Author's Guild, Orgn. Am. Historians, Am. Hist. Assn., Am. Soc. Info. Sci. and Tech. Jewish. Avocation: book collecting. Office: Felician Coll Libr 262 S Main St Lodi NJ 07644-2117

KARFF, SAMUEL EGAL, rabbi; b. Phila., Sept. 19, 1931; s. Louis and Reb (Margalit) K.; m. Joan Mag, June 29, 1959; children: Rachel Karff Weissenstein, Amy Karff Halevy, Elizabeth Karff Kampf. AB magna cum laude, Harvard U., 1953; MAHL, DHL, Hebrew Union Coll., 1956. Rabbi Congregation Beth Israel, Hartford, Conn., 1958-60, Temple Beth El, Flint, Mich., 1960-62, Chgo. Sinai Congregation, 1962-74; sr. rabbi Congregation Beth Israel, Houston, 1975-99, rabbi emeritus, 1999—; vis. prof. soc. and health U. Tex. Health Sci. Ctr., Houston, 1999—. Lectr. U. Chgo. Divinity Sch., 1968-75; vis. assoc. prof. U. Notre Dame, 1966-67; adj. prof. religious studies Rice U., Houston, 1976—. Author: Agada: The Language of Jewish Faith, 1970; editor Centennial Vol. Hebrew Union Coll.-Jewish Inst. of Religion, 1981-84; contbr. chpts. Judaism Religions of the World, 1982. Bd. dirs. United Way, Houston, 1991—, Inst. Religion, Houston, 1990—. Recipient Homiletics award HUC-JIR, Cin., 1956; John Harvard scholar Harvard U., 1951-52. Mem. Cen. Conf. Am. Rabbis (pres. 1989-91), Houston Philos. Soc., Phi Beta Kappa, Kiwanis. Jewish. Avocations: tennis, walking, movies, reading. Office: Congregation Beth Israel 5600 N Braeswood Blvd Houston TX 77096-2901 E-mail: skarff@sph.uth.tmc.edu.

KARGBO, RANYA, educational association administrator; b. Freetown, Sierra Leone, Feb. 26, 1974; arrived in U.S., 1991; d. Thomas K. and Aminata S. Kargbo. BA, Spelman Coll., 1996; MPA, Am. U., 2002. Cons. IBM Corp., Dallas, 1997—2001; founder, dir., exec. dir. Orgn. for the Advancement of Literacy, Alexandria, Va., 2001—; dir. implementations Be Home Wise, Inc., McLean, Va., 2002—. Avocations: writing, reading. Office: OFAL PO Box 11358 Mc Lean VA 22102

KARGER, WALTER, mechanical engineer; b. Berlin, June 7, 1926; came to U.S., 1949; s. Alfred and Anna Karger; m. Ruth Susskind, Oct. 9, 1965; 1 child, Allen J. BME magna cum laude, NYU, 1954; MS, Purdue U., 1955. Registered profl. engr., Tex., N.Y. Internat. engring. supr. indsl. equipment Carrier Corp., N.Y.C., 1955-67; asst. to v.p. Elliott Overseas Corp., N.Y.C., 1967-69, European engring. mgr. London, 1969-74; regional mgr. application engring. Elliott Co., Jeannette, Pa., 1974-83, Elliott Co. divsn. United Techs., Houston, 1983-87; sr. power engr. Falcon Seaboard Oil Co., Houston, 1987-89; sr. prin. engr. Stone & Webster Engring. Corp., Houston, 1989—. Author: Modern International Units of Measurement, 1974, 77; designer metrication slide rule. Cpl. U.S. Army, 1950-52. Mem. ASME, ASHRAE, Sigma Xi, Tau Beta Pi, Pi Tau Sigma. Office: Stone & Webster Engring Corp A Shaw Group Co 1430 Enclave Pkwy Houston TX 77077-2023

KARGLEDER, CHARLES LEONARD, language educator; b. Milbank, SD, July 19, 1939; s. George Leonard Kargleder and Ruby Teresa Gulck. BA, U. SD, 1960; MA, U. Ala., 1962, PhD, 1968; MS, U. South Ala., 1986. From instr. to prof. Spring Hill Coll., Mobile, Ala., 1963—83, prof., 1983—, chair dept. fgn. lang., 1971—, chair divsn. lang. and lit., 1992—99. Grad. asst. U. Ala., Tuscaloosa, 1965—67. Grantee Nat. Def. Edn. grant, US Govt., 1960—63. Mem.: South Ea. Coun. Latin Am. Studies, Am. Assn. Tchrs. Spanish and Portuguese, Kappa Delta Pi. Roman Catholic. Avocations: travel, reading, music, sports. Home: 1251 Henckley Ave # 207 Mobile AL 36609 Office: Spring Hill Coll 4000 Dauphin St Mobile AL 36608

KARGMAN, MARIE WITKIN, marriage counselor, consultant; b. Chgo., Aug. 28, 1914; d. Joseph and Clara (Zucker) Witkin; married, 1935; children: Donna, William, Robert. JD, DePaul U., 1936; MA, Radcliffe Coll., 1951. Pub. defender Boys' Court, Chgo., 1936-37; ptnr. Kargman & Kargman, Chgo., 1937-44, Boston, 1953-54; pvt. practice marriage counselor, family mediator Boston, 1953—. Chmn. gov.'s council on home and family, Commonwealth of Mass., Boston, 1966-76. Author: How to Manage a Marriage, 1985; contbr. articles to profl. jours. Mem. Assn. of Practicing Sociologists (cited outstanding contbr.), Nat. Council on Family Relations, DePaul U. Law Sch. Alumni Assn. (outstanding alumnae, 1977). Avocations: tennis, tv appearances. Home: 115 Rutledge Rd Belmont MA 02478-2631

KARI, DAVEN MICHAEL, religious studies educator; b. Hot Springs, S.D., Sept. 24, 1953; s. John Nelson and Corinna Nicolls (Morse) K.; m. Priya Perianayakam, Apr. 4, 1988; children: David Prem, Daniel Michael, Dante Gabriel. BA in English, Bibl. Studies, History, Fresno Pacific Coll., 1975, BA in Music, 1977; MA in English, Baylor U., 1983; MA, PhD in English, Purdue U., 1985, 86; MDiv, PhD, So. Bapt. Theol. Sem., 1988, 91. Lic. to ministry So. Bapt. Ch., 1971, ordained to ministry, 1996. Photography studio technician Johnson's Studio, Manteca, Calif., 1975-77; grad. teaching asst. Baylor U., Waco, Tex., 1978-79; minister of music Calvary Bapt. Ch., West Lafayette, Ind., 1984-85; grad. teaching asst. Purdue U., West Lafayette, Ind., 1979-85; lectr. in English Jefferson C.C., Louisville, 1987-90, Spalding U., Louisville, 1986-90, U. Louisville, 1986-90; asst. prof. English Mo. Bapt. Coll., St. Louis, 1991; assoc. prof. English Calif. Bapt. Coll., Riverside, 1991-93, assoc. prof. English, dir., Christian Ministry and Fine Arts, 1993-98; prof. Christian Studies and English Calif. Baptist U., 1998; acad. dean Washington Bible Coll., Lanham, Md., 1998-2000; adminstr., min. Bapt. Christian Sch., Hemet, Calif., 2000—01; freelance writer, 2001—02; assoc. prof. English Vanguard U. So. Calif., 2002—. Author: T. S. Eliot's Dramatic Pilgrimage, 1990, Bibliography of Sources in Christianity and the Arts, 1995; co-editor: Baptist Reflections on Christianity and the Arts: Learning from Beauty, 1997, Contemporary Authors, 1997. Founder, co-dir. local Boys Brigade, Linden, Calif., 1969-71; asst. pastor Linden (Calif.) First Bapt. Ch., 1971; chair transp. com. Calvary Bapt. Ch., West Lafayette, 1982-83, dir. singles ministry, 1983-85; moderator Scholar's Bowl Quiz Contest, Riverside, 1993-94; min. First Bapt. Ch. Hemet, 2000-01. Recipient Lit. Criticism award Purdue U., 1983; named to Outstanding Young Men Am., 1985; named Faculty Mem. of Yr., Calif. Bapt. Coll., 1993; named to Contemporary Authors, 1997. Mem. Am. Acad. Religion, Conf. on Christianity and Lit., Evang. Theol. Soc. Democrat. Baptist. Avocations: poetry, stained glass windows, sculpture, photography, painting, music. E-mail: davenmkari@aol.com.

KARI, JOUKO, education educator; b. Lehtimäki, Finland, Mar. 18, 1939; s. Väinö and Lyyli Wilhelmiina (Saarenpää) K.; m. Pirkko Kaarina Hautamäki, June 25, 1960; children: Tuulikki, Hannu, Aila, Elina. PhD, U. Jyväskylä, 1972. Headmaster of secondary sch., Soini, Finland, 1966-70; rschr. Inst. of Edn., Jyväskylä, 1970-76, prof., 1980-93; assoc. prof. U. Jyväskylä, Finland, 1977-80, prof. dept. tchr. edn., 1993—. Docent U. Tampere, Finland, 1980—. Editor Scandinavian Jour. of Ednl. Rsch., 1983-91; author: Opetus-ja kasvatustyö ammattina, 1986, Opettajan ammatti ja kasvatustietoisuus, 1996. Mem. Finnish Assn. of Ednl. Rsch. (head 1978, 86). Home: Korkeakatu 7 SF-40630 Jyväskylä Finland Office: PO Box 35 SF-40351 Jyväskylä Finland E-mail: kari@edu.jyu.fi.

KARI, ROSS, banking executive; BA in Math., U. Oreg., 1980, MBA in. Fin., 1983. Analyst in fin. Wells Fargo, 1983, v.p., 1987, sr. v.p. fin. and planning, gen. auditor, exec. v.p., 1995, head fin., mgr. controller's divsn./corp. tax., 1997, CFO, v.p., 1998—. Office: Wells Fargo Bank 420 Montgomery St San Francisco CA 94163

KARIMI-NEJAD, ABBAS, retired neurosurgeon, educator; b. Said-Abad, Kirman, Iran, Dec. 28, 1931; arrived in Germany, 1952; s. Mohammad-Ali and Fatimah K.; div. 1978; children: Yasmin, Darius, Sussan. MD, Götting U., Göttingen, Germany, 1957. Med. resident Max-Planck Inst., Göttingen, 1957-60; resident Duisburg (Germany) Hosp., 1960-61; neurosurg. resident Cologne (Germany) Hosp., 1961-70; assoc. prof. neurosurg. dept. Cologne U., 1970-74, prof. neurosurg. dept., 1974-97; ret., 1997. Mem. exec. com. German Interdisciplinary Assn. Critical Care Medicine, 1982, European Brain Injury Consortium, 1989; dep. chmn. Emergency and Disaster Medicine, Germany, 1988. Author: Traumatic and Non-traumatic Emergency Medicine, 1987; contbr. over 150 articles to med. and profl. jours. Avocations: horseback riding, golf, music. Home: Koppensteinstr 1 50935 Cologne Germany Fax: 49221-436328. E-mail: a.karimi@uni-koeln.de.

KARIN, SIDNEY, computer science and engineering educator; b. Balt., July 8, 1943; BSME, CCNY, 1966; MS in Nuclear Engring., U. Mich., 1967, PhD in Nuclear Engring., 1973. Registered profl. engr., Mich. Computer programmer, nuc. engr. ESZ Assocs., Inc., Ann Arbor, Mich., 1968-72; sr. engr., sect. leader Gen. Atomics (formerly GA Techs., Inc.), San Diego, 1973-75, mgr. fusion divsn. Computer Ctr., 1975-82, dir. info. sys. divsn., 1982-85; dir. San Diego Supercomputer Ctr., 1985-2001, Nat. Partnership for Advanced Computational Infrastructure, 1997-98. Bd. dirs. Corp. for Ednl. Network Initiatives in Calif.; prof. computer sci. and engring., 1986—; chair Fed. Networking Adv. Com., 1991-97; mem. adv. com. CISE Directorate, NSF. Contbr. articles to profl. jours. NDEA fellow, AEC fellow. Fellow AAAS, Assn. for Computing Machinery; mem. IEEE Computer Soc., Computing Rsch. Assn. (bd. dirs. 1998—). Avocations: flying, technical rock climbing, motorcycle riding, alpine skiing, reading. Home: 748 Avocado Ct Del Mar CA 92014-3911 Office: U Calif San Diego Supercomputer Ctr 9500 Gilman Dr La Jolla CA 92093-5003 E-mail: skarin@ucsd.edu.

KARIYA, PAUL, professional hockey player; b. Vancouver, Oct. 16, 1974; Forward/hockey player Anaheim Mighty Ducks, 1994—. Mem. Can. Olympic Hockey Team, 1994. Recipient Lady Byng Meml. Trophy for Sportsmanship and Gentlemanly Conduct, 1995—96, Silver medal, Olympic Games, 1994. Office: Anaheim Mighty Ducks PO Box 61077 2695 E Katella Ave Anaheim CA 92803-6177

KARKANIAS, GEORGE B. neurologist, educator; BS in Biology, Rutgers U., 1987; MS with honors, Albert Einstein Coll. Medicine, 1991, PhD, 1993. Postdoctoral fellow dept. neurosci. Albert Einstein Coll. Medicine, 1993—94, instr., 1994—95, asst. prof. neurosci., 1995—. Contbr. articles to profl. jours. Grantee rsch. grantee, Juvenile Diabetes Found. Mem.: AAAS, Soc. Neurosci., Internat. Brain Rsch. Orgn., N.Y. Acad. Scis., Am. Diabetes Assn. (rsch. grantee 1995). Office: Albert Einstein Coll Medicine 1300 Morris Park Ave U103A Bronx NY 10461-1926

KARKHANIS, SHARAD, librarian, political science educator; b. Khopoli, India, Mar. 8, 1935; came to U.S., 1959; s. Dwarkanath D. and Indira (D.) K. BA in Econs., U. Bombay, 1958; MLS, Rutgers U., 1962; MA in Polit. Sci., CUNY, 1967; PhD in Polit. Sci., NYU, 1978. Libr. U.S. Info. Svc., Bombay, 1955-58; libr. trainee Leyton Pub. Libr., Layton, Eng., 1958-59, Montclair (N.J.) Pub. Libr., 1959-60; libr. East Orange (N.J.) Pub. Libr., 1960-63, CUNY, Bklyn., 1963-64; prof. libr. and polit. sci. depts. Kingsborough C.C., Bklyn., 1964—. Author: Indian Politics and the Role of the Press,1981, Jewish Heritage in America, 1988; editor How to Avoid Dead End in Your Career, 1988; Educational Excellence of Asian Americans, 1989. Mem. Ethnic Task Force borough pres., Bklyn., 1987-2000. Mem. ALA, Asian/Pacific Am. Librs. Assn. (pres. 1980-82), Libr. Assn. CUNY pres. 1967-69). Republican. Hindu. Avocations: political biographies, movies. Office: Kingsborough CC Oriental Blvd Brooklyn NY 11235 E-mail: s.karkhanis@worldnet.att.net.

KARKHECK, JOHN PETER, physics educator, researcher; b. N.Y.C., Apr. 26, 1945; s. John Henry and Dorothy Cecilia (Riebling) K.; m. Kathleen Mary Shiels, Nov. 8, 1969; children: Lorraine, Michelle, Eric. BS, LeMoyne Coll., 1966; MA, SUNY, Buffalo, 1972; PhD, SUNY, Stony Brook, 1978. Various positions Grumman Corp., Bethpage, N.Y., 1964-68; grad. asst. SUNY, Buffalo, 1968-70; tchr. secondary schs. Mattituck (N.Y.) Sch. Dist., 1970-71, Shelter Island (N.Y.) Sch. Dist., 1971-73; grad. asst. SUNY, Stony Brook, 1973-78, postdoctoral fellow, 1978-79, rsch. assoc., 1979-81; asst. prof. physics GMI Engring. and Mgmt. Inst., Flint, Mich., 1981-84, assoc. prof., 1984, prof., dir. physics, 1988-89, head. dept. sci. and math., 1989-93; prof., chmn. dept. physics Marquette U., Milw., 1993—2003, dir. physics for medicine program, 2003—. Physics assoc. Brookhaven Nat. Lab., Upton, N.Y., 1975-79, cons., 1979-85, STS, Hauppauge, N.Y., 1983, BID Ctr., Flint, 1985-90; acad. assoc. Mich. State U., 1988, 90, vis. scholar, 1989, vis. scientist, 1991; reviewer Addison-Wesley Pub., 1990, 93; regional dir. Mich. Sci. Olympiad, 1991-92, 92-93; co-dir. NATO Advanced Study Inst., 1998, editor, 1999-2000. Contbr. numerous articles to profl. jours. Den leader Cub Scouts Am., Flint, 1987-91; leader Boy Scouts Am., 1991-98; bd. dirs. Flint Area Sci. Fair, 1991-93; mem. sci. curriculum adv. com. Milw. Acad. Sci., 2000-; judge local sci. fairs. Dept. Energy rsch. grantee, 1977-79, NATO travel grantee, 1983-86, 89, NATO ASI grantee, 1998. Mem. Am. Phys. Soc., AAAS, AAPT, Sigma Xi (v.p. Marquette U. chpt. 1998-99, pres., 1999-2000). Roman Catholic. Avocations: swimming, reading, bicycling, travel, learning german. Home: 6592 N Bethmaur Ln Glendale WI 53209-3320 Office: Marquette Univ Dept Physics PO Box 1881 Milwaukee WI 53201-1881 E-mail: John.Karkheck@marquette.edu.

KARKUT, RICHARD THEODORE, clinical psychologist; b. Derby, Conn., Apr. 28, 1948; s. Harry Chester and Mary K. AB, William Jewell Coll., 1971; MA, U. Mo., Kansas City, 1976; D Psychology, Forest Inst. Profl. Psychology, 1988. Lic. psychologist, Ind.; cert. in biofeedback. Psychology intern Burrell Mental Health Ctr., Springfield, Mo., 1987-88; clin. psychologist Wabash Valley Hosp., Lafayette, Ind., 1989-91, Quinco Cons., North Vernon, Ind., 1991-93; CEO Adkar Assocs., Inc., Bloomington, Ind., 1993—. Cons. Div. Family Svcs., Lafayette, 1989-90. Guest editor jour. Ind. Psychologist; contbr. articles to profl. jours. Mem. Assn. Applied Psychophysiology and Biofeedback, Am. Counseling Assn. Anglican. Home: Box 349 Salem IN 47167

KARL, GABRIEL, physics educator; b. Cluj, Romania, Apr. 30, 1937; came to Can., 1960; s. Alexander and Frida (Izsak) K.; m. Dorothy Rose Searle, Apr. 10, 1965; 1 child, Alexandra PhD, U. Toronto, Ont., Can., 1964. Research assoc. Oxford U., Eng., 1966-69; prof. physics U. Guelph, Ont., Can., 1969—. Contbr. articles to profl. jours. German-Canadian Research Prize (Deutsch-Kanadischer Forschungspreis). Fellow Royal Soc. Can.; mem. Am. Phys. Soc., Can. Assn. Physicists (CAP medal 1991). Office: U Guelph Macnaughton Bldg 50 Stone Rd E Guelph ON Canada N1G 2W1 E-mail: gk@physics.uoguelph.ca.

KARL, GEORGE, professional basketball coach; b. Penn Hills, Pa., May 12, 1951; children: Kelci Ryanne, Coby Joseph. Grad., U. N.C., 1973. Guard San Antonio Spurs, NBA, 1973-78, asst. coach, head scout, 1978-80; coach Mont. Golden Nuggets, Continental Basketball Assn., 1980-83; dir. player acquisition Cleve. Cavaliers, 1983-84, coach, 1984-86; head coach Golden State Warriors, Oakland, Calif., from 1986, Albany (N.Y.) Patrons, 1988-89, 90-91, Real Madrid, Spain, 1991-92, Seattle Supersonics, 1992-98, Milwaukee Bucks, 1998—2003. Named Coach of Yr., Continental Basketball Assn., 1981, 83. Mem. Continental Basketball Assn.

KARL, HELEN WEIST, pediatric anesthesia and pain management educator, researcher; b. NYC, Oct. 28, 1948; d. Edward C. and Louise (Stursberg) Weist; m. Stephen R. Karl, June 1, 1974 (div. 1990); children: Katherine L., Thomas R., John W. BA in Philosophy, Smith Coll., 1970; MD, U. Va., 1976. Diplomate Am. Bd. Anesthesiology, Nat. Bd. Med. Examiners. Intern Hartford (Conn.) Hosp., 1976-77, resident in anesthesia, 1977-79; fellow pediat. anesthesiology Children's Hosp. of Phila., 1979-81; staff anesthesiologist St. Christopher's Hosp. for Children, Phila., 1981; asst. prof. anesthesiology and pediatrics Pa. State U., Hershey, 1981-90; asst. prof. anesthesiology U. Washington, 1990-97, assoc. prof. anesthesiology, 1997—; Parker B. Francis fellow in pulmonary rsch. Pa. State U., Hershey, 1986-88; dir. pain mgmt. Children's Hosp., Seattle, 1994-99. Adj. assoc. prof. dental pub. health scis., U. Wash., 1997-2000. Contbr. articles to profl. jours. Mem.: AAUW, Wash. Soc. Anesthesiologists, Am. Med. Women's Assn., Am. Soc. Anesthesiologists. Avocations: swimming, trumpet. Office: Children's Hosp & Med Ctr 4800 Sand Point Way NE Seattle WA 98105-3901 E-mail: helen.karl@seattlechildrens.org.

KARL, KURT ERSKINE, economist; b. Eugene, Oreg., Jan. 23, 1952; s. Emil William and Margaret Ann (McClymonds) K.; m. Ida Louise Green, May 27, 1988; children: Zoe Thandiwe, Julia Louise. BA with honors, U. Oreg., 1974; MSc, London Sch. Econs., 1975; PhD, Princeton U., 1992. Rsch. assoc. Birkbeck Coll., London, 1975-77; statistician Cen. Stats. Office, Mbabane, Swaziland, 1977-80; dir. long term svc. Wharton Econometrics, Phila., 1981-86; cons. WEFA Group, Bala Cynwyd, Pa., 1986-90, v.p. U.S. ops., 1990-94, sr. v.p. U.S. macroeconomic svcs., 1994—2000; head econ. rsch. and cons. Swiss Re, N.Y.C., 2000—. Author: two papers on Thailand, 1992, (with others) Third Five Year Development Plan-Swaziland, 1976, Report on Population Development-Swaziland, Analysis of the Treasury's Tax Reform Proposal, 1983. Mem. Am. Econ. Assn., Nat. Assn. Bus. Economists, Phi Beta Kappa. Avocations: carpentry, swimming. Office: Swiss Re 55 E 52d St New York NY 10055

KARL, ROBERT HARRY, cardiologist; b. Milw., Sept. 4, 1947; s. Max Henry and Anita Rene (Davis) K.; m. Nilza Maria Secomandi, Jan. 14, 1979; children: Daniel, Lara, Kevin. BA, Northwestern U., Evanston, Ill., 1969; MD, Washington U., St. Louis, 1973. Diplomate in internal medicine and in cardiovasc. disease Am. Bd. Internal Medicine. Intern internal medicine U. Miami (Fla.), 1973-74, resident internal medicine, 1974-76, cardiology fellow, 1976-78; pvt. practice cardiology Miami, 1978—. Asst. clin. prof. U. Miami Med. Sch., 1978-2002; chief cardiology Bapt. Hosp. Miami, 1986-88; asst. chief of medicine Bapt. Hosp., 1992-94, chief of medicine, 1994-97; pres. Medicard Am., Inc., Miami, 1992-97, Biocard Corp., Miami, 1997--; v.p. Schoolink, Inc., Miami, 1996-97. Mem. exec. com. South Dade Jewish Fedn., Miami, 1986-89; bd. dirs. Beth David Congregation, Miami, 1985-87, Bet Shira Synagogue, Miami, 1987-88, Child Abuse Prevention Project, 1986—, Aish Hatorah, Miami, 1991—, Ohr Samayach, Miami, 1995—, David and Mary Alper JCC, 1997-2001, Hebrew Acad. of Miami Beach, 1997—, The Ctr. of Life Food Bank, 1998—, The Gesher Inst. Miami, v.p., 1997-2000, pres., 2000—; bd. trustees Collegiate Learning Exch., 2002—. Fellow Am. Coll. Cardiology (dist. councillor Fla. chpt. 1995—), Coun. Clin. Cardiology of Am. Heart Assn.; mem. ACP, Fla. Med. Assn., Dade County Med. Assn. (peer rev. com. 1980-82), Young Israel of Kendall (v.p. 1995—). Avocations: piano, golf, reading, travel, skiing. Office: 8950 N Kendall Dr Ste 601 Miami FL 33176-2139

KARLAN, ANDREW WARREN (DREW KARLAN), pharmaceutical company executive; b. N.Y.C., May 2, 1944; s. Laurence Jack and Isabelle (Kerner) K.; m. Rosalyn Silverberg, Mar. 1, 1969; children: Mara Lisa, Adam Jason. BA in Biology, Hofstra U., Hempstead, N.Y., 1967; MS in Biology, Adelphi U., Garden City, N.Y., 1972; MBA in Pharm. Mktg., Fairleigh Dickinson U., Teaneck, N.J., 1982. Rsch. assoc. Worthington Biochem. Corp., Freehold, N.J., 1972-73; supr. E.R. Squibb & Sons, Inc., New Brunswick, N.J., 1973-79, sect. head, 1979-82, asst. mgr. of investigational data, 1982-88, regulatory mgr., 1988-89, sr. regulatory mgr., 1989-91; dir. regulatory affairs Roberts Pharm. Corp., Eatontown, N.J., 1991-94, v.p. worldwide regulatory affairs, 1994—98, exec. dir. R&D program mgmt., 1998—2000; v.p. regulatory and quality affairs and project mgmt. WellSpring Pharm. Corp., Neptune, NJ, 2000—. Bd. dirs. Howell (N.J.) Jewish Cmty. Ctr., 1980—91, pres. Men's Club; vice chmn. United Way-Squibb, New Brunswick, 1982; chmn. Jewish com. on Scouting, 1983—91, 1998—, dist. vice chmn., 1983—87; cubmaster Monmouth Coun. (N.J.) Boy Scouts Am., 1989—92. 1st lt. U.S. Army, 1969—71, LTC USAR, 1967—94. Mem. Res. Officers Assn., Parenteral Drug Assn., Regulatory Affairs Profl. Soc., Drug Info. Assn., Delta Mu Delta. Home: 121 Sargent Rd Freehold NJ 07728-2842 Office: WellSpring Pharm Corp Neptune NJ 07753-

KARLAN, SANDY ELLEN, judge; b. N.Y.C. d. Bernard and Muriel (Richter) K. BA, U. Miami, 1971; JD cum laude, Nova Southeastern U., 1978. Bar: Fla. 1978, U.S. Ct. Appeals (5th and 11th cirs.) 1981, U.S. Bankruptcy Ct. 1985, U.S. Dist. Ct. (so. dist.) Fla. 1988; cert. in matrimonial law, Fla. Law clk. to Hon. Alan R. Schwartz Third Dist. Ct. Appeals, Miami, Fla., 1978-80; assoc. Gars, Dixon & Shapiro, Miami, 1980-82; ptnr. Chaykin, Karlan & Jacobs, Coral Gables, Fla., 1982-85; sr. ptnr. Sandy Karlan, P.A., Miami, 1985-95; judge 11th Jud. Cir. Ct., Miami, 1995—. Chair steering com. gender bias commn. Fla. Supreme Ct., 1987, mem. family ct. steering com., 1994, Conf. Cir. Ct. Judges, 1995—, Supreme Ct. steering com. on Families and Children, 2002—; chair on legal needs of children Fla. Bar Commn., 1999—. Author: (with others) Florida Family Law, 1986; contbr. articles to profl. jours. Bd. govs. Shepard Broad Sch. Law Nova Southeastern U., Ft. Lauderdale, Fla.; trustee Dade Marine Inst., Miami, 1993—, pres., 1999—. Recipient Sojourner Truth award NOW, 1989. Fellow ABA; mem. Nat. Assn. Women Judges, Fla. Bar (mem. legislation com. 184-88, grievance com. 11J 1985-87, vice chair disciplinary rev. com. 1987-89, vice chair access com. 1988-89, bd. govs. 1988-92, chair pub. rels. com. 1989-92, mem. gender equality com. 1994, mem. rules of civil procedure com. 1998—), Fla. Assn. Women Lawyers (pres. Dade County chpt. 1984-85), Dade County Bar Assn. (bd. dirs. 1986-89), Bankruptcy Bar Assn. (bd. dirs. 1991-94), Leadership Miami Alumni Assn. Address: 175 NW 1st Ave Ste 2327 Miami FL 33128-1846

KARLE, ISABELLA L. chemist; b. Detroit, Dec. 2, 1921; d. Zygmunt Apolonaris and Elizabeth (Graczyk) Lugoski; m. Jerome Karle, June 4, 1942; children: Louise Hanson, Jean Marianne, Madeleine Tawney. BS in Chemistry, U. Mich., 1941, MS in Chemistry, 1942, PhD, 1944, DSc (hon.), 1976; DSc (hon.), Wayne State U., 1979, U. Md., 1986, Athens (Greece) U., 1997, U. Pa., 1999; LHD (hon.), Georgetown U., 1984; DSc (hon.), Harvard U., 2001; Doctor honoris causa, Jagiellonian U., Cracow, Poland, 2002. Assoc. chemist U. Chgo., 1944; instr. chemistry U. Mich., Ann Arbor, 1944—46; physicist Naval Rsch. Lab., Washington, 1946—. Paul Ehrlich lectr. NIH, 1991; exec. com. Am. Peptide Symposium, 1975—81; adv. bd. Chem. and Engring. News, 1986—89. Mem. editl. bd.: Biopolymers Jour., 1975—, Internat. Jour. Peptide Rsch., 1981—; contbr. articles to profl. jours. Named to Mich. Women's Hall of Fame, 1989; recipient Superior Civilian Svc. award, USN, 1965, Fed. Women's award, U.S. Govt., 1973, Annual Achievement award, Soc. Women Engrs., 1968, U. Mich., 1987, Dexter Conrad award, Office Naval Rsch., 1980, WISE Lifetime Achievement award, Women in Sci. and Engring., 1986, award for disting. achievement in sci., Sec. of Navy, 1987, Gregori Aminoff prize, Swedish Royal Acad. Scis., 1988, Adm. Parsons award, Navy League U.S., 1988, Ann. Achievement award, CCNY, 1989, Bijvoet medal, U. Utrecht, The Netherlands, 1990, Vincent du Vigneaud award, Gordon Conf. (Peptides), 1992, Bower Sci. award, Franklin Inst., 1993, Nat. medal of sci., Pres. of the U.S., 1995. Fellow: Am. Inst. Chemists (Chem. Pioneer award 1984), Am. Acad. Arts Scis.; mem.: NAS (Chem. Scis. award 1995), Biophys. Soc., Am. Philos. Soc., Am. Phys. Soc., Am. Chem. Soc. (Garvan award 1976, Hillebrand award 1970, Ralph Hirschmann award in peptide chemistry 1998), Am. Crystallographic Assn. (pres. 1976). Home: 6304 Lakeview Dr Falls Church VA 22041-1309 Office: Naval Rsch Lab Code 6030 Washington DC 20375-5341

KARLE, JEROME, physicist, researcher; b. NYC, June 18, 1918; married, 1942; 3 children. BS, CCNY, 1937; AM, Harvard U., 1938; MS, U. Mich., 1942, PhD in Phys. Chemistry, 1943. Rsch. assoc. Manhattan project, Chgo., 1943—44, U.S. Navy Project, Mich., 1944—46; head electron diffraction sect. Naval Rsch. Lab., Washington, 1946—58, head diffraction br., 1958—68, now head lab. for structure matter, 1968—. Mem. NRC, 1954—56, 1967—75, 1978—87; chmn. U.S. Nat. Com. for Crystallography, 1973—75. Recipient Nobel prize in Chemistry, 1985. Fellow: Am. Phys. Soc.; mem.: NAS (chair chemistry sect. 1988—91), Internat. Union Crystallography (mem. exec. com. 1978—87, pres. 1981—84), Am. Crystallograph Assn. (treas. 1950—52, pres. 1971—73), Am. Math. Soc., Am. Chem. Soc. Office: US Naval Rsch Lab Lab for Structure of Matter Code # 6030 Washington DC 20375-5341 E-mail: williams@harker.nrl.navy.mil. *There is too much administration of everything creative. It distorts our society and its character. The solution is to select competent, well-qualified people and give them freedom and support to pursue their creative gifts.*

KARLEN, DOUGLAS LAWRENCE, soil scientist; b. Monroe, Wis., Aug. 28, 1951; s. Lawrence Herman and Marian Bertha (Trumpy) K.; m. Linda Sue Bender, June 9, 1973; children: Sarah Jean, Steven Douglas, Holly Lin. BS, U. Wis., 1973; MS, Mich. State U., 1975; PhD, Kans. State U., 1978. Rsch. soil scientist Coastal Plains Soil, Water Conservation Rsch. Ctr., USDA-ARS, Florence, S.C., 1978-88, Nat. Soil Tilth Lab. USDA-ARS, Ames, Iowa, 1988—. Team leader Leopold Ctr. for Sustainable Agr., Ames, 1989—94. Asst. scoutmaster, com. chmn. Boy Scouts Am., Ankeny, Iowa, 1991—. Fellow Am. Soc. Agronomy (bd. rep. Ag sys. 1997-99, Agronomic Rsch. award 2001, Werner L. Nelson award for diagnosis of Yeild limiting factors 2001), Crop Sci. Soc. Am. (assoc. editor 1988-93, tech. editor 1994-99), Soil Sci. Soc. Am. (bd. rep. divsn. S6, 2002—, Agronomic Achievement award-soils 1996), Applied Soil Sci. Rsch. award 2002); mem. Coun. Agrl. Sci. and Tech., Soil and Water Conservation Soc. Am., Internat. Soil Tillage Rsch. Orgn. Episcopalian. Office: USDA-ARS-MWA-NSTL 2150 Pammel Ct Ames IA 50011-4420 E-mail: karlen@nstl.gov.

KARLGAARD, RICH, publishing executive; Co-founder Upside, 1989—92, editor, 1989—92, Forbes ASAP, 1992—98; pub. Forbes Mag., N.Y.C., 1998—. Office: Forbes 60 5th Ave New York NY 10011-8882 also: 555 Airport Blvd 5th Fl Burlingame CA 94010*

KARLIN, CALVIN JOSEPH, lawyer; b. Hutchinson, Kans., Oct. 31, 1952; s. Norman Joseph and Edith Lucille (Biggs) K.; m. Janice Miller, May 25, 1975. BA, U. Kans., 1974, JD, 1977. Bar: Kans. 1977, U.S. Dist. Ct. Kans. 1977. Mem. Barber, Emerson, Springer, Zinn & Murray, L.C., Lawrence, Kans., 1977—. Adj. faculty Sch. Law U. Kans. Note and comments editor U. Kans. Law Rev.; contbr. articles to profl. jours. Bd. dirs. United Way, Lawrence, 1983-85, drive chair, 1993, pres., 1995-96; bd. dirs. Kaw Valley Dance Theatre, Lawrence, 1982-85, Vis. Nurses Assn., 1987-93, Lawrence Pub. Libr., 1989-94; coun. pres. Lawrence Free State H.S. Site, 2001-03. Mem. Am. Coll. Trust and Estate Counsel, Kans. Bar Assn. (exec. com. corp. bus. and banking law sect. 1985-88, exec. com. real estate, probate and trust law sect. 1998—), Douglas County Bar Assn. (sec. 1982-83, v.p. 1986-87, pres. 1987-88, chair ethics com. 2002—), Lawrence C. of C. (bd. dirs. 1997-2000), Swarthout Soc. (corp. and bus. com. 1983-91), Order of Coif, Phi Beta Kappa. Democrat. Avocations: travel, biking. Office: Barber Emerson Springer Zinn & Murray LC PO Box 667 Lawrence KS 66044-0667 E-mail: ckarlin@beszm.com.

KARLIN, GARY LEE, insurance executive; b. Chgo., Jan. 18, 1934; s. Jack and Pearl (Malin-Weiss) K.; children: David, Paige; m. Cheryl Daneman; stepchildren: Chad, Brooke. Student, U. Ill., 1951-52, Roosevelt U., 1952. With Mut. of N.Y., 1956-62, sales mgr., 1958-62, regional trainer, 1962-63; pres. Exec. Motivation, Inc., Chgo., 1964—; fin. planner, 1980—; chmn. field underwriters benefits/contracts com. MONY, 1974-85; v.p. Exec. Planning Svcs. divsn. Alexander & Alexander, Inc., 1990-96; dir., chmn. compensation com. Vasocor, Inc., Charleston, SC, 1990—2003; dir., chmn. audit com. Perception, Inc., Miami, 1993-98; v.p., treas. Exec. Fin. Group divsn. F.P.I.S., Inc., 1993-99. Pres. Karlin Bus. Group, 1998—; cons. in field; speaker numerous ins. seminars. Contbg. editor Profl. Mgmt. mag., 1965-67; subject of poem There Are No Heroes Anymore; contbr. articles to profl. jours.; subject of ins. film Impressions of Life. Named to MONY Hall of Fame, 1966; featured in Time mag., 1967. Mem. Internat. Assn. Fin. Planners, Chgo. Assn. Life Underwriters, (past bd. dirs.) Nat. Assn. Life Underwriters (life), Million Dollar Round Table (Top of Table), Ill. Leaders Round Table (past pres.), Emil Verban Soc., The Point Lake and Golf Club. Home: 130 Rehoboth Ln Mooresville NC 28117

KARLIN, MURIEL SCHLOSBERG, information technology manager, consultant; b. Mt. Vernon, N.Y., Dec. 19, 1940; d. Nat and Lee (Karlin) Schlosberg; children: Leeza Beth Watstein, David Michael Watstein. BA in Psychology, Clark U., 1962; MS in Computer Sci., NYU, 1986. Cert. project mgr., Java SE. Programming cons. N.Y.C. Bd. Edn., Bklyn., 1983; systems engr. Electronic Data Systems, Woodbury, N.Y., 1983-84; documentation mgr., systems adminstrn. mgr. Instinet Corp., N.Y.C., 1987-91; cons. Bellcore, NYNEX, 1991-92; project mgr. N.Y.C. Dept. Probation, 1992-94; cons. Bantam, Doubleday, Dell, Neuberger & Berman, AT&T, Merrill Lynch, 1994-2000; sr. program mgr. Golobix Corp., 2001. Instr. Info. Techs. Inst., NYU, N.Y.C., 1987. Enrichment coordinator, v.p. Ridge Rd. Elem. Sch. PTA, North Haven, Conn.; mem. North Haven Ednl. Council. Mem.: Project Mgmt. Inst. N.Y.C., Assn. Computing Machinery, IEEE, NAFE. Home and Office: 77 Bleecker St New York NY 10012-1547

KARLIN, SAMUEL, mathematics educator, researcher; b. Yonova, Poland, June 8, 1924; s. Morris Karlin; m. Elsie Karlin (div.); children: Kenneth, Manuel, Anna. BS in Math., Ill. Inst. Tech., 1944; PhD in Math., Princeton U., 1947; DSc (hon.), Technion Israel Inst. Tech., Haifa, 1986. Instr. math. Calif. Inst. Tech., Pasadena, 1948—49, asst. prof., 1949—52, assoc. prof., 1952—55, prof., 1955—56; vis. asst. prof. Princeton U., 1950—51; prof. Stanford U., Calif., 1956—. Wald lectr., 1957; Andrew D. White prof.-at-large Cornell U., 1975—81; Wilks lectr. Princeton U., 1977; pres. Inst. Math. Stats., 1978—79; Commonwealth lectr. U. Mass., 1980; 1st Mahalanobis meml. lectr. Indian Statis. Inst., 1983; prin. invited spkr. XII Internat. Biometrics Meeting, Japan; prin. lectr. Que. Math. Soc., 1984; adv. dean math. dept. Weizmann Inst. Sci., Israel, 1970—77; Britton lectr. McMaster U., Hamilton, Ont., Canada, 1990; Cockerham lectr. N.C. State U., 1996. Author: Mathematical Methods and Theory in Games, Programming, Economics, Vol. I: Matrix Games, Programming and Mathematical Economics, 1959, Mathematical Methods and Theory in Games, Programming, Economics, Vol. II: The Theory of Infinite Games, 1959, A First Course in Stochastic Processes, 1966, Total Positivity Vol. I, 1968; author: (with K. Arrow and H. Scarf) Studies in the Mathematical Theory of Inventory and Production, 1958; author: (with W.J. Sudden) Tchebycheff Systems: With Applications in Analysis and Statistics, 1966; author: (with H.Taylor) A First Course in Stochastic Processes, 2d edit., 1975; author: A Second Course in Stochastic Processes, 1980, An Introduction to Stochastic Modeling, 1984; author: (with C.a. Michelli, A. Pinkus, I.I. Schoenberg) Studies in Spline Functions and Approximation Theory, 1976. Recipient Lester R. Ford award, Am. Math. Monthly, 1973, Robert Grimmett Chair Math., Stanford U., 1978, The John Von Neumann Theory prize, 1987, award, U.S. Nat. Medal Sci., 1989, The Karlin prize in Math. Biology named in honor, Stanford U. Dept. Biol. Scis., 1992; fellow Proctor, 1945, Bateman Rsch., 1947—48, Guggenheim Found., 1959—60, NSF, 1960—61. Fellow: AAAS, Inst. Math. Statis., Internat. Statis. Inst.; mem.: NAS (award in applied math. 1973), Am. Philos. Soc., Human Genome Orgn., Am. Naturalist Soc., London Math. Soc. (hon.), Genetics Soc. Am., Am. Soc. Human Genetics, Am. Acad. Arts and Scis., Am. Math. Soc. Office: Stanford U Bldg 380 Stanford CA 94305-2125 E-mail: karlin@math.stanford.edu.

KARLIN, WAYNE, writer; b. L.A., June 13, 1945; s. Louis and Rhoda (Brickman) K.; m. Ohnmar Thein, Oct. 27, 1977; 1 child, Adam. Student, L.A. Pierce Coll., 1968-69; BA, Am. Coll., Jerusalem, 1972; MA in Creative Writing, Goddard Coll., 1976. Reporter Reporter Dispatch, White Plains, N.Y., 1972; pres. and co-editor First Casualty Press, 1972-73; free-lance writer Israel, 1973-75; instr. English Montgomery Coll., Rockville, Md., 1982-84, 1982-84; prof. lang. and lit. Coll. of So. Md., LaPlata, Md., 1984—. Vis. writer William Joiner Ctr. for Study of War and Social Consequences, U. Mass., Boston, 1989, tchg. faculty, 1990-93; dir., tchr. fiction workshop St. Mary's Coll. of Md. Lit. Festival, summer, 1993—; dir., coord. Connections Reading Series, Coll. So. Md., 1989—. Author: Crossover, 1984, Lost Armies, 1988, The Extras, 1989, Us, 1993, Rumors and Stones, 1996, Prisoners, 1998, The Wished-For Country, 2002; co-editor: (with Ho Anh Thai) Love After War: Contemporary Fiction from Vietnam, 2003; editor and contbr. (with Le Minh Khue and Truong Vu) The Other Side of Heaven: Postwar Fiction by Vietnamese and American Writers, 1995; co-editor and contbr.: Free Fire Zone: Short Stories by Vietnam Veterans, 1973, Contemporary American Fiction, 1997; contbr. short stories various publs.; translator, editor The Stars, The Earth, The River:, 1997, Behind the Red Mist, 1998, Against the Flood, 2000, The Women on the Island, 2001, Past Continuous, 2001; writer feature film Song of the Stork, 2002. Mem. lit. panel Md. State Arts Coun., 1986-88; mem. St. Mary's County Arts Coun., 1989-90. Sgt. USMC, 1963-67. Decorated Air Medal w/combat aircrew insignia; recipient State of Md. Individual Artist award for fiction, 1988, 91, 93, 97, 2001; recipient Gov.'s Citation, State of Md., 1991, Cert. of Recognition for outstanding svc. to City of Boston, 1992, Critics Choice award, 1995-96, Paterson prize in Fiction, 1999; Nat. Endowment for the Arts fellow, 1993. Mem. PEN, Washington Writers' Ctr., Assoc. Writing Programs. Home: PO Box 239 Saint Marys City MD 20686-0239 E-mail: waynek@csmd.edu., waynekarlin@hotmail.com.

KARLINS, M(ARTIN) WILLIAM, composer, educator; b. NYC, Feb. 25, 1932; s. Theodore and Gertrude Bertha (Leifer) K.; m. Mickey Cutler, Apr. 6, 1952; children: Wayne, Laura. MusB, MusM, Manhattan Sch. Music, 1961; PhD in Composition, U. Iowa, Iowa City, 1965; studied with, Frederick Piket, Vittorio Giannini, Stefan Wolpe, Philip Bezanson, Richard Hervig. Asst. prof. music Western Ill. U., 1965-67; assoc. prof. theory and composition Northwestern U. Sch. Music, Evanston, Ill., 1967-73, prof., 1973—, dir., co-dir. Contemporary Music Ensemble, 1967—, apptd. Harry N./Ruth F. Wyatt prof. music theory/composition, 1998—2002, prof. emeritus, 2003—. Vis. guest composer Ariz. State U., 1978, Ill. Wesleyan U., 1978; guest composer Nazareth Coll., Rochester, NY, 1978, Bowling Green State U., 1982, 89, Navy Band, Washington, 1988, Nat. Conf. for Condrs., Chgo., Ball State U., Bloomington, Composer's Symposium U. N.Mex., Albuquerque, 1991, Alta. (Can.) Coll. Conservatory Music, 1991, Sigma Alpha Iota Internat. Am. Music Awards Competition, 1993, U. Fla., Gainesville, 2003; featured guest composer We. Ill. U., Macomb, 1994; participant Coll. Band Dirs. Nat. Assn. Nat. Conf., Northwestern U., 1987; coord. composers workshops Internat. World Congress Saxophones, London; lectr., composer-in-residence World Saxophone Congress, Bordeaux, France, 1974, Nat. Saxophone Tng. Course, Duras, France, 6th Stage de Saxophone, Duras, France, 1991; panelist Nat. Conf. Am. Symphony Orch. League; lectr., guest composer Franz Liszt Acad. Music, Budapest, Franz Liszt Musical Coll., Györ, Hungary, 1995; vis. composer U. Fla., Gainesville, 2003; composer, coord. Stefan Wolpe Festival, Northwestern U., 2001; guest composer Budapest Spring Festival, 1999; honored composer, Sofia, Bulgaria, 1997; guest lectr., composer Vienna, Austria, 1999, Bowdoin Coll., Maine, 1999. Composer: Concert Music 1 through 5, Lamentations-In Memoriam, Elegy for Orchestra, Reflux (concerto for double bass and wind ensemble), Symphony No. 1, Concerto Grosso I and II, Academic Festival Fanfare for wind ensemble, Woodwind Quintet I and II, Saxophone Quartet I and II, Night Light Quartet No. 3 for Saxophones, 3 Plano Sonatas, Outgrowths-Variations for Piano, Suite of Preludes for piano, Humble Harvest for piano, Catena I (clarinet and chamber orch.), Catena II (soprano saxophone and brass quintet), Catena III (concerto for horn and orch.), Birthday Music I (flute, bass clarinet/clarinet and double bass) and II (flute and double bass), Under and Over (flute and double bass), Variations on Obiter Dictum (cello, piano and percussion), Music for Cello Alone I and II, Music for Oboe, Bass Clarinet and Piano, Music for Tenor Saxophone and Piano, Music for Alto Saxophone and Piano, Music for English Horn and Piano, Four Inventions and a Fugue for Bassoon, Piano and Female Voice, Infinity for Oboe d'amore, clarinet, viola and female voice, Song for Soprano with Alto Flute, Cello, Three Songs for Soprano, Flute and Piano, Chameleon for Harpsichord, Drei Kleine Cembalostücke (harpsichord), Celebration for Flute, Oboe and Harpsichord, Kindred Spirits for mandolin, guitar and harp, Quintet for Alto Saxophone and String Quartet, Impromptu for Saxophone and Organ, Nostalgie for 12 Saxophones Ensemble, Introduction and Passacaglia for 2 Saxophones and Piano, Just A Line From Chameleon, for 2 clarinets, Fantasia for tenor saxophone and percussion, Saxtuper for Saxophone, Tuba, and Percussion, Seasons for solo saxophonist, Concerto for Alto Saxophone and Orch., String Quartet with soprano in the last movement, Chidlren's Bedtime Songs for mixed chorus, Three Love Songs for male chorus, Three Poems for mixed chorus, Looking Out My Window for Treble Chorus and viola; (solo bass clarinet) Improvisations on Lines Where Beauty Lingers; recs. include Music for Tenor Saxophone and Piano, Music for Alto Saxophone and Piano, Variations on Obiter Dictum for cello, piano and percussion, Introduction and Passsacaglia for 2 saxophones and piano, Solo Piece with Passacaglia for clarinet, Sonata No. 2, Sonata No. 3 for piano and Outgrowth Variations for Piano, Saxophone Quartets Nos. 1 and 2, Chameleon for harpischord, Drei Kleine Cembalostücke (harpischord), Quintet for alto saxophone and string quartet, Nostalgie for 12 saxophone ensemble, Impromptu for alto saxophone and organ, Reflux (concerto for amplified double bass and winds), Quartet for Strings with soprano in the last movement, Song for Soprano, with alto flute and cello, Four Inventions and a Fugue for bassoon, piano, and soprano, Kindred Spirits for mandolin, guitar and harp, Concerto Grosso # 1 for 9 instruments, Catena II for soprano saxophone and brass quintet; CDs include Klecka Plays Broege and Karlins, Nostalgie, Salvatore Spina Piano Music By Karlins, Lombardo and Stout, M. William Karlins, Works by M. William Karlins, Howard Sandroff, Charles Tomlinson Griffes, Carl Ruggles, Chicago Saxophone Quartet, Joseph Wytko Saxophones-Wytko Saxophone Quartet, Midwest Composers-Music for Winds, American Millennium Tribute to Adolphe Sax, Vol II, Lifting the Veil, Mixed Company, Héliosaxo, Shaking the Pumpkin, Conicality. Grantee MacDowell Colony, Nat. Endowment for Arts, 1979, 85, Meet the Composer, 1980, 84-85, 90, 95, Ill. Arts Coun., 1985, 87, 90, 96, 98, 2003. Mem. Am. Music Ctr., Broadcast Music, Inc., Am. Woman Composers (trustee Chgo. chpt.), Pi Kappa Lambda, Sigma Alpha Iota (nat. arts. assoc.). Office: Northwestern U Sch Music Evanston IL 60208-1200 E-mail: m-karlins@northwestern.edu.

KARLINSKY, SIMON, language educator, writer; b. Harbin, Manchuria, Sept. 22, 1924; came to U.S., 1938, naturalized, 1944; s. Aron and Sophie (Levitin) K. BA, U. Calif., Berkeley, 1960, PhD, 1964; MA, Harvard U., 1961. Conf. interpreter, music student, Europe, 1947-57; teaching fellow Harvard U., Cambridge, Mass., 1960-61; asst. prof. Slavic langs. and lits. U. Calif., Berkeley, 1963-65, prof., 1967-91, prof. emeritus, 1991—, chmn. dept., 1967-69. Vis. asso. prof. Harvard, 1966 Author: Marina Cvetaeva: Her Life and Her Art, 1966, The Sexual Labyrinth of Nikolai Gogol, 1976, 2d edit., 1992, Russian Drama from Its Beginnings to the Age of Pushkin, 1985, Marina Tsvetaeva: The Woman, Her World and Her Poetry, 1986, 2nd edit., 1988, Italian edit., 1989, Spanish edit., 1990, Japanese edit., 1991; editor: The Bitter Air of Exile, 1977; editor, annotator: Anton Chekhov's Life and Thought, 1974, 2d edit. 1997, The Nabokov-Wilson Letters, 1979, 2nd edit., 2001, French edit., 1988, German edit., 1995, Japanese edit., 2002; co-editor: Language, Literature, Linguistics, 1987, O RUS! Studia literaria slavica in honorem Hugh McLean, 1995; contbr. articles to nat. and profl. jours. Served with AUS, 1944-46. Woodrow Wilson fellow, 1960-61; Guggenheim fellow, 1969-70, 77-78 Mem. Phi Beta Kappa. Office: U Calif Dept Slavic Lang & Lit Berkeley CA 94720-0001

KARLL, JO ANN, state administrative law judge, lawyer; b. St. Louis, Nov. 16, 1948; d. Joseph H. and Dorothy Olga (Pyle) K.; m. William Austin Hernlund, Sept. 9, 1990. BS magna cum laude, Maryville U.; JD, St. Louis U. Bar: Mo. 1993. Ins. claims adjuster, 1967-88; mem. Mo. Gen. Assembly dist. 104, 1991-93; dir. Mo. State Divsn. Workers' Compensation, Jefferson City, 1993-2000, adminstrv. law judge, 2000—; sch. bd. Gwinnett County, 2003—. Founder, 1st pres. scholarship fund Mo. Kids' Chance, Inc., 1995-96, bd. dirs., 1995—. Internat. Assn. of Indsl. Accident Bds. and Commns. (past pres.). Office: Mo St Divsn Worker's Compensation 3737 Harry S Truman Blvd Saint Charles MO 63301

KARLS, JOHN SPENCER, lawyer, accountant; b. Saginaw, Mich., Feb. 26, 1942; s. Harold M. and Mary Ellen (Spencer) K.; div.; children: Michael Berens, Hilary Marie. BA in Econs., U. Mich., 1964; JD, Harvard U., 1967; LLM in Taxation, NYU, 1973; MS in Acctg., Northwestern U., 1971. Bar: N.Y. 1967, Conn. 1978. Acct. Arthur Young & Co., N.Y.C., 1969-74; sr. tax atty., dir. tax planning Texaco Inc., White Plains, N.Y., 1974-87; tax ptnr. Ernst and Young, N.Y.C., 1987—. Prof. taxation Fordham U. MBA program, N.Y.C., 1988—; lectr. NYU Law Sch. Tax Inst., 1994—. Editor: Effective Tax Strategies for International Corporate Acquisitions: assoc. editor Federal Income Taxation of Oil and Gas; adv. bd. Jour. Internat. Taxation; editl. asst. Oil and Gas: Federal Income Taxation (CCH), 1971-74. Deacon First Congregational Ch., Greenwich, Conn.; pres. I Have A Dream Found. of Stamford, Inc., 1991—; treas. Nat. I Have a Dream Found., 1995—; co-founder first homeless shelter in Fairfield County, Conn., 1983; dir. Kids to Coll. Found., 1997—. Lt. USN, 1967-69. Recipient Elijah Watt Sells Silver medal AICPA, 1971; named Citizen of Yr., Fairfield County, Conn., 1998. Mem. ABA (tax sec. fgn. tax com., chmn.), Tax Execs. Inst., Westchester-Fairfield County Corp. Counsel Assn., YMCA, Harvard (N.Y.C.). Home: Harvard Club Box 126 27 W 44th St New York NY 10036-6613 Office: 75 Wall St New York NY 10005-2833

KARLS, NICHOLAS JAMES, engineering executive; b. Mandan, N.D., Nov. 19, 1951; s. Clarence Joseph and Irene (Kallberg) K. Student, U. Minn., 1982—. Inventory contr. Brown Boveri Turbomachinery, St. Cloud, Minn., 1972—78, mfg. engr., 1978—82; engring. documentation coord. Check Tech. Corp., Minnetonka, Minn., 1982—2000; sr. documentation specialist Phys. Electronics, Eden Prairie, Minn., 2000—02; documentation control adminstr. Compex Techs., New Brighton, Minn., 2002—. Mem. Soc. Engring. Systems Mgmt. (v.p. 1987-88, exec. v.p. 1988-89, pres. 1989-91, planning dir. 1991-92, Disting. Svc. award 1990, Appreciation award 1989, Honor award 1991), KC (Grand Knight). Roman Catholic. Avocations: fishing, golf, downhill and cross country skiing, trapshooting, vocal music. Home: 26065 Wildrose Ln Excelsior MN 55331-7936 Office: 1811 Old Hwy 8 New Brighton MN 55112 E-mail: Nick.Karls@compextechnologies.com.

KARLSON, DONNA MAE, clinical social worker; b. Holden, Mass., Mar. 25, 1951; d. Gustaf Andrew and Myrtle Stebbins (Gary) Karlson; m. Geoffrey William Johnson Heath, Oct. 21, 1973 (div. Oct. 1983); m. Arthur John Greif, June 21, 1986. BA cum laude, Elmira (N.Y.) Coll., 1973; student, U. St. Andrews, Scotland, 1971-72; MEd magna cum laude, U. Maine, 1980; MSW, U. Conn., 1988. Lic. clin. social worker; nat. cert. social worker. Instr. Outward Bound. and Nat. Outdoor Leadership Sch., Wyo., Colo., Maine, 1974, Bancroft North, Owlshead, Maine, 1976-78; tchr. Cushing (Maine) Sch., 1980-81, Region 8 Vocat. Sch., Rockland, Maine, 1981-82, Projects, Inc., Rockport, Maine, 1981-82; family counselor Home Counselors, Inc., Rockland, 1982-86; clin. social worker Casey Family Svcs., Portland, Maine, 1989-93; family therapist St. Michael's Ctr., Bangor, Maine, 1993-94; med. social worker Bangor Area Vis. Nurses, 1994-95; pvt. practice clin. social worker Bangor, 1995—. Mem. Nat. Assn. Social Workers. Democrat. Congregationalist. Avocations: travel, bicycling, hiking, sea kayaking, cross-country skiing. Home: 551 Main Rd N Hampden ME 04444-1804 Office: 551 Main Rd N Hampden ME 04444

KARLSSON, ANETTE M. aerospace engineer, educator; came to U.S., 1992; d. Lennart and Katie Karlsson; m. Richard L. Lehman, Jan 5, 1996. BS, Linkoping (Sweden) U., 1989, MS, 1990; PhD, Rutgers U., 1999. Structural engr. Saab Aerospace, Linkoping, 1982-87; rsch. engr. Saab Missiles, Linkoping, 1987-92; tech. attache Embassy of Sweden, Washington, 1992-94; rschr. Princeton (N.J.) U., 1999—2002; prof. U. Del., Newark, 2002—. Mem. AIAA, ASME, Am. Ceramic Soc., Sigma Xi. Office: Univ Del Dept Mech Engring Newark DE 19716 E-mail: karlsson@me.udel.edu.

KARLSSON, MAGNUS, computer engineer/scientist, researcher; b. Karlskrona, Blekinge, Sweden, June 25, 1969; s. Ove and Ulla K. BSc, Lund (Sweden) U. Tech., 1991, MSc, 1992; PhD, Chalmers U. Tech., Gothenburg, Sweden, 1999. Software engr. HP Labs, Palo Alto, Calif., 2000. Avocations: wine, good food, travel, friends. Home: 481C Thompson Ave Mountain View CA 94043 Office: HP Labs 1501 Page Mill Rd 1134 Palo Alto CA 94304

KARLSTROM, PAUL JOHNSON, art historian; b. Seattle, Jan. 22, 1941; s. Paul Isadore and Eleanor (Johnson) K.; m. Ann Heath, Dec. 29, 1964; 1 dau., Clea Heath. BA in English Lit, Stanford U., 1964; MA, UCLA, 1969, PhD (Samuel H. Kress fellow), 1973. Asst. curator Grunwald Center for Graphic Arts, UCLA, 1967-70; Samuel H. Kress fellow Nat. Gallery Art, Washington, 1970-71; instr. Calif. State U., Northridge, 1972-73; West Coast regional dir. Archives Am. Art, Smithsonian Instn. at De Young Mus., San Francisco, 1973-91, Huntington Libr., San Marino, Calif., 1991—2003. Guest curator Hirshhorn Mus., Washington, 1977; writer, curator art and cultural history, 2003--. Author: Louis M. Eilshemius, 1978, Los Angeles in the 1940s-Post Modernism and the Visual Arts, 1987, The Visionary Art of James M. Washington, Jr., 1989, Turning the Tide: Early Los Angeles Modernists, 1920-1956, 1990; editor: On the Edge of America: California Modernist Art, 1900-1950, 1996; contbg. author: Diego Rivera: Art and Revolution, 1999, Reading California, 2000, Over the Line: The Art and Life of Jacob Lawrence, 2000, Eros in the Studio in Art and the Performance of Memory: Sounds and Gestures of Recollection, 2002; prodr. (video) David Hockney, 1984, 1993, George Tsutakawa in Japan, 1988, Richard Shaw, 1998, editor, co-project dir. Calif. Asian Am. Artist Biog. Survey; contbr. articles to profl. jours. Mem. adv. bd. Humanities West, Jacob Lawrence Catalogue Raisonné Project; former bd. dirs. S.W. Art History Coun., Bay Area Video Coalition; sec. Va. Steele Scott Found; v.p. Noah Purifoy Found. E-mail: pkarlstrom@sbcglobal.net.

KARLUK, LORI JEAN, craft designer, copy editor; b. Scranton, Pa., Aug. 29, 1958; d. Edward Julius and Josephine Anne (Cuozzo) K. Grad., high sch., 1976. Consignor, designer various shops, Pa., 1982-85; owner mail order bus. Loveables, 1983-85; staff designer Tradition Today, Roselle, Ill., 1985-86; designer All Occasion Crafts, Sparks, Nev., 1986-88; copy editor McCalls, N.Y.C., 1987-90; copy editor, product designer Herrschners, Inc., Schaumburg, Ill., 1988-92; designer Banar Designs, Fallbrook, Calif., 1991-92, Yarn Kits, Inc., N.Y.C., 1992-94; freelance designer, 1984-99; prin., owner Josie's Inspiration Studio, 1999—. Author: Safari Friends, 1987, Bear-E-Tale Bears, 1991. Sec. MADD, Lackawanna County, 1991. Recipient numerous spl. awards for designs. Mem. NOW, Soc. Craft Designers, People for the Ethical Treatment of Animals, United Friends of the Children, Internat. Soc. for Animal Rights, Teddy Bear Artists Assn., Good Bears of the World. Avocations: travel, reading, art. Home and Office: PO Box 68 Jessup PA 18434-0068 E-mail: ljkbears@aol.com.

KARMALI, RASHIDA ALIMAHOMED, lawyer; b. Uganda, May 12, 1948; came to U.S., 1978; d. Alimahomed and Sakina (Govani) K. BSc, MakerereU., 1971; MSc, Aberdeen U., 1973; PhD, U. Newcastle Upon Tyne, 1976; JD, Rutgers U., 1993. Bar: N.Y. 1994; registered to practice U.S. Patent Office. Fellow Clin. Rsch. Inst., Montreal, 1976-78; rsch. assoc. E. Carolina U., Greenville, N.C., 1978-80, Meml. Sloan-Kettering Inst., N.Y.C., 1980-84; adj. assoc. prof. Cook Coll., New Brunswick, N.J., 1984-90; practice in tech. law N.Y.C., 1991—. Bd. dirs. Skin Rsch. Found., N.Y.C. Grantee NIH, Am. Cancer Soc. Mem. ABA, Assn. Bar City N.Y. (com. on patents), Am. Intellectual Property Law Assn. (internat. and fgn. law com.), Licensing Execs. Soc. Office: 99 Wall St 13th Fl New York NY 10005 E-mail: karmali@aol.com.

KARMANOS, PETER, JR., computer software company executive, professional sports team executive; m. Debra Karmanos; children: Peter III, Nick, Jason. Grad., Wayne State U. CEO, gov. Hartford Whalers, 1994—96; corp. chmn., CEO Compuware, Detroit, 1973—; CEO, gov. Carolina Hurricanes, 1996—. Sponsor youth hockey Detroit Jr. Whalers; Sponsor youth hockey programs New Eng. Jr. Whalers, Conn. Named Named Entrepreneur of Yr., Inst. Am. Entrepreneurs, 1989. Address: Compuware 31440 Northwestern Hwy Farmington Hills MI 48334 Office: Carolina Hurricanes 1400 Edwards Mill Rd Raleigh NC 27607-3624

KARMANOVA, TATIANA VICTOROVNA, language educator; b. Moscow; arrived in U.S., 1988; d. Victor Grigorievich Karmanov. BA, U. Tex., 1991, MA, 1995, PhD, 2002. Lectr. U. Tex., Austin, 1989, asst. instr., 1992—96; asst. prof. Mo. So. State Coll., Joplin, 1996—2002, dir. lang. resource ctr., 1996—2002, assoc. prof., 2002—. Instr. NEH Russian Inst., Austin, 1993. Grantee, Mo. Dept. Elem. and Secondary Edn., 1996—97. Mem.: MLA, Am. Coun. Tchg. Fgn. Lang., Am. Assn. Tchrs. Slavic and East European Lang. Office: Mo So State Coll 3950 E Newman Rd Joplin MO 64801 Office Fax: 417-625-9580. Business E-Mail: karmanova-t@mail.mssc.edu.

KARMARKAR, UDAY SADASHIV, management educator; b. Mumbai (Bombay), India, Feb. 2, 1947; s. Sadashiv Ganesh and Kamal Karmarkar; m. Reeta Gidwani, Sept. 9, 1971; children: Uma Reeta, Harsh Uday. B.Tech., IIT Bombay, Mumbai, India, 1963—68; PhD, Sloan Sch., MIT, Cambridge, MA, 1970—75. Asst. prof. GSB, U. of Chgo., Chicago, Ill., 1975—79, U. of Rochester, Rochester, NY, 1979—82; assoc. prof. Simon Sch., U. of Rochester, 1982—87, prof., 1987—88, xerox prof. of ops. mgmt., 1988—94, dir., ctr. for mfg. and ops., 1985—94; times mirror prof. of mgmt. strategy Anderson Sch. at UCLA, Los Angeles, Calif., 1994—, dir., ctr. for ops. and tech. mgmt., 1994—99, dir., ctr. for mgmt. in the info. economy, 1999—. Dir. iSeva.com, Philadelphia, Pa., 2000—01; adv. Aditya Birla Group, Mumbai, India, 2001—, Indiaco.com, Pune, India, 2001—; dir. Xoriant Corp, San Jose, Calif., 2002—. Recipient Disting. Alumnus, I.I.T.Bombay, Powai, India, 1997, U. Mentor, U. of Rochester, 1984-1985. Mem.: INFORMS. Office: Anderson Sch Mgmt at UCLA 110 Westwood Plaza Box 951481 Los Angeles CA 90095-1481

KARMAZIN, MEL, broadcast executive; b. 1944; Past sta. mgr. CBS radio, N.Y.C., 1960—70; v.p., gen. mgr. Metromedia Inc., N.Y.C., 1970—81; pres. Infinity Broadcasting Corp., N.Y.C., 1981—96; CEO Infinity Broadcasting Corp. Md, 1988—96; pres., CEO CBS Sta. Group (Viacom), 1996—. Office: CBS Corp 51 W 52d St New York NY 10019-4001

KARMEIER, DELBERT FRED, consulting engineer, realtor; b. Okawville, Ill., Apr. 2, 1935; s. Wilbert and Ida (Harre) K.; m. Naomi Firnhaber, Oct. 18, 1958; children: Kenton Howard, Dianne Jill. BSCE, U. Ill., 1957, MS in Transp. Engring., 1959. Rsch. assoc. U. Ill., 1958-59; traffic engr. St. Louis County, Mo., 1959-65, traffic commr., 1965-69; dir. transp. City of Kansas City, Mo., 1969-74, dir. aviation and transp., 1974-90; dir. pub. works City of Hartford, Conn., 1990-92; assoc. exec. dir. Am. Pub. Works Assn., Chgo., 1992-94; cons. Torres Cons. Engrs., Kansas City, Mo., 1994-95; assoc. J.D. Reece, Leawood, Kans., 1995—. Mem. Nat. Com. on Uniform Traffic Control Devices, 1971-85 Automotive Safety Found. fellow U. Ill., 1959. Mem. Inst. Transp. Engrs. (pres. Missouri Valley sect. 1965-66), Airport Operator's Coun. Internat., Am. Rd. and Transp. Builder's Assn. (dir. 1973-83, chmn. pub. transit adv. coun. 1980-83), Transp. Rsch. Bd., Am. Pub. Works Assn., U. Ill. Alumni Club Kansas City (pres. 1996—), Thrivent Fin. for Lutherans (v.p. West Jackson County chpt. 2003—), Beta Sigma Psi (nat. editor 1963-69, pres. Kansas City alumni 1981-82, Disting. Alumnus award 1971, nat pres. 1986-88, nat. treas. 1996—). Lutheran. Home: 12206 Avila Dr Kansas City MO 64145-1750 Office: Reece & Nichols 13002 State Line Rd Leawood KS 66209-1756 E-mail: delkarm@aol.com.

KARMEL, PHILIP ELIAS, lawyer; b. N.Y.C., Dec. 6, 1963; s. Paul R. and Roberta S. (Segal) K.; m. Barbara A. Landress, June 12, 1994. BA in Econs., U. Pa., 1984; MPhil in Econs., U. Cambridge, Eng., 1985; JD, U. Chgo., 1988. Bar: N.Y. 1989. Law clk. to Hon. Edward R. Becker U.S. Ct. Appeals (3rd cir.), 1988-89; trial atty. U.S. Dept. of Justice, Environtl. Enforcement Sect., Washington, 1989-94; ptnr. Bryan Cave LLP, N.Y.C., 2002—. Recipient Spl. Achievement award for Superior Performance of Duty U.S. Dept. of Justice, 1992. Office: Bryan Cave LLP 1290 Avenue Of The Americas New York NY 10104-3300 E-mail: pekarmel@bryancave.com.

KARMEL, ROBERTA SEGAL, lawyer, educator; b. Chgo., May 4, 1937; d. J. Herzl and Eva E. (Elin) Segal; m. Paul R. Karmel, June 9, 1957 (dec. Aug. 1994); children: Philip, Solomon, Jonathan, Miriam; m. S. David Harrison, Oct. 29, 1995. BA, Radcliffe Coll.; LLB, NYU, 1962; HHD (hon.), King's Coll., 1998. Bar: N.Y. 1962, U.S. Dist. Ct. (so. and ea. dists.) N.Y. 1964, U.S. Ct. Appeals (2d cir.) 1968, U.S. Supreme Ct. 1968, U.S. Ct. Appeals (3d cir.) 1987. Asst. regional adminstr. SEC, Washington, 1962-69, commr., 1977-80; assoc. Willkie Farr & Gallagher, N.Y.C., 1969-72; ptnr. Rogers & Wells, N.Y.C., 1972-77, of counsel, 1980-85; ptnr. Kelley Drye & Warren, N.Y.C., 1987-94, of counsel, 1995—2002. Adj. prof. law Bklyn. Law Sch., 1973-77, 82-85, prof., 1985—, co-dir. Ctr. for Study of Internat. Bus. Law; bd. dirs. Kemper Ins Cos.; trustee Practicing Law Inst. Author: Regulation by Prosecution, 1982; contbr. articles to profl. jours. Fellow Am. Bar Found.; mem. ABA, Assn. Bar City N.Y., Am. Law Inst., Fin. Women's Assn. Home: 66 Summit Dr Hastings On Hudson NY 10706-1215 Office: Bklyn Law Sch 250 Joralemon St Brooklyn NY 11201-3700 E-mail: roberta.karmel@brooklaw.edu.

KARMELIN, MICHAEL ALLEN, financial executive; b. Bronx, N.Y., Feb. 26, 1947; s. Samuel and Fannie (Levine) K.; m. Risa G. Kaplan, Apr. 2, 1966. BBA, Baruch Coll. CUNY, 1972; MBA, NYU, 1979. CPA, N.Y. Staff acct. Allied Chem. Corp., N.Y.C., 1965-69; dir. of financial mgmt. analysis Avco Corp., Greenwich, Conn., 1969—85; CFO of various sub divsn. and bus. divsn. Merrill Lynch & Co., N.Y.C., 1985—98; v.p., treas. Ocwen Fin. Corp., West Palm Beach, Fla., 1998-99; CFO, CEO, dir. Touch Tone Techs., Inc., Boca Raton, Fla., 1999—2000; CFO BarPoint.com, Inc., Deerfield Beach, Fla., 2000—02; fin. adv. AXA Advisors, Boca Raton, Fla., 2002—. Mem.: Strategic Leadership Forum, Inst. Mgmt. Accts., Assn. of Financial Prof. Home: 132 Banyan Isle Dr Palm Bch Gdns FL 33418-4601 Office: AXA Advisors LLC 2255 Glades Rd Boca Raton FL 33431

KARNAS, FRED G., JR., non-profit organization executive; b. Olean, N.Y., Sept. 9, 1948; BCP, U. Va., 1971; MSW, Va. Commonwealth U., 1980; PhD, Va. Tech. U., 1984. Gen. program dir. Cmty. Coun., Phoenix, 1983-87; exec. dir. Cmty. Housing Partnership, Phoenix, 1987-89, Ctrl. Fla. Coalition for the Homeless, Orlando, Fla., 1989-91, Nat. Coalition for the Homeless, Washington, 1991-95; with HUD, Washington, 1995-2000, dep. asst. sec., 1997-2000; cons. on homelessness, AIDS, housing policies, 2000—; pres. Ariz. Family Housing Fund, Phoenix, 2002—. Office: 5 E Loma Ln Phoenix AZ 85020 also: Ariz Family Housing Fund 6730 N Scottsdale Rd #235 Scottsdale AZ 85253 E-mail: fkarnas1@msn.com.

KARNAUGH, MAURICE, computer scientist, educator; b. N.Y.C., Oct. 4, 1924; s. George Victor and Fannie (Weinstein) K.; m. Linn Blank; children: Robert Victor, Paul Joseph. BS, CCNY, 1948; MS, Yale U., 1950, PhD, 1952. Mem. tech. staff Bell Telephone Labs., Murray Hill, N.J., 1952-56, mgr. digital techs., 1956-66; chief scientist exploratory systems ctr., fed. system ctr. IBM, Gaithersberg, Md., 1966-70; mem. rsch. staff IBM Watson Rsch. Ctr., Yorktown Heights, N.Y., 1970-93. Disting. adj. prof. Poly. U., Bklyn., 1981-99. Contbr. articles on digital switching and artificial intelligence to profl. jours.; patentee in field. With U.S. Army, 1943-46, ETO. Fellow IEEE; mem. Internat. Coun. Computer Communications (gov. emeritus 1988—).

KARNES, KEITH DALE, portfolio manager; b. Tyler, Tex., Aug. 20, 1953; s. Ralph Dale and Gloria Anne Karnes; m. Mary Ellis, 1999; children: Kathryn, Kristofferstepchildren: Will, Stephen, Emily. BBA, Tex. Christian U., Ft. Worth; diploma of grad., Stonier Grad. Sch. of Banking of Am. Banking Assn., 1987. Dir., cashier Royal Nat. Bank, Palestine, Tex., 1984—93; fin. advisor Merrill Lynch, Ft. Worth, 1993—97; v.p., investment officer, portfolio mgr. Wachovia Securities (formerly First Union Securities), Ft. Worth, 1997—. Mem. Jewels Charity Ball; mem. dirs. coun. Modern Art Mus. Mem.: Houston Tex. Angel Group, Ft. Worth Angels Group, Rivercrest Club, Ridglea Country Club, Ft. Worth Rotary. Episcopalian. Office: Wachovia Securities 777 Taylor St Ste 850 Fort Worth TX 76102-4915

KARNES, LUCIA ROONEY, psychologist; b. Moncton, N.B., Can., Mar. 9, 1921; d. Charles William and Jean Waring (Robson) Rooney; m. Thomas Campbell Karnes, June 7, 1946; children; Eleanore, Campbell, Timothy. Charles. BS, Ga. State Coll., 1942; MA, Emory U., 1946; PhD, U. N.C., 1967. Tchr. Decatur Girls High, Decatur, Ga., 1942-46; tchr. Summit Sch., Winston-Salem, N.C., 1947; prof. Salem Coll., Winston-Salem, 1949-54, 60-77; lang. therapist Bowman Grey Sch. Medicine, Winston-Salem, 1950-57, Orton Reading Ctr., Winston-Salem, 1957-72; dir. Ctr. for Spl. Edn., Salem Coll., Winston-Salem, 1972-77; pvt. practice psychology Winston-Salem, 1977—. Dyslexic cons. Jefferson Acad., Winston-Salem, 1980—, Greenfield Sch., Wilson, 1986—. Wingate (N.C.) U., 1988—. Creator Using Computers in Psychology courses, 1972; author (video) Teaching Dyslexics, 1975. Founder, pres. state bd. LWV, Winston-Salem, 1953; pres. state bd. AAUW, Winston-Salem, 1950-54; bd. dirs. YWCA, Winston-Salem, 1950-54; v.p. bd. dirs. Arts Coun., Winston-Salem, 1954-60. Named Outstanding Reading Tchr., Reading Assn., Winston-Salem, 1982; fellow Orton-Gillingham Acad. Mem. APA, Orton Dyslexia Soc. (v.p. bd. dirs. 1960-77), N.C. Psychol. Assn., Assn. for Children with Learning Disabilities (v.p. bd. dirs. 1972—, Orton-Gillingham Acad. fellow), Sorosis Club, Delta Kappa Gamma. Democrat. Presbyterian. Avocation: travel. Home: 131 Lamplighter Cir Winston Salem NC 27104-3419

KARNETTE, BETTY, state senator; b. Paduch, Ky., Sept. 13, 1931; m. Richard Karnette; 1 child, Mary. BA, MA, Calif. State U. Sec, office mgr. Terminal Island; tchr. L.A. Unified Sch. Dist., 1961—92; mem. Calif. State Assembly, 1992—94, dist. 27, Calif. State Senate, 1996—. Cons. edn., 1994—96; subs. tchr., 1994—96; mem. Banking, Commerce and Internat. Trade, Edn. Com., Govt. Orgn. Com., Pub. Employment and Retirement Com., Rules Com., Transp. Com. Mem. Long Beach Meml. Hosp. Children's Clinic; mem. assoc. bd. Sage House in San Pedro; bd. dirs. Young Horizon. Democrat. Mailing: State Capitol Rm 5066 Sacramento CA 95814 Office: 3711 Long Beach Blvd Ste 801 Long Beach CA 90807*

KARNEY, IRVING HYMAN, construction company executive; b. Bklyn., Dec. 1, 1923; s. Meyer and Lena (Feldman) K.; m. Reba Krell, June 21, 1947; children: Robert Lloyd, Mark Howard. BS in Constrn. Mgmt., Columbia U., 1956. Archl. draftsman Kahn & Jacobs, Archs., N.Y.C., 1946-52; asst. arch. N.Y.C. Bd. Edn., 1952-54; constrn. adminstr. Uris Bldgs. Corp., N.Y.C., 1954-63; v.p. constrn. Goodrich Constrn. Corp., N.Y.C., 1963-67; constrn. project mgr. Tishman Realty & Constrn. Corp., N.Y.C., 1967-69; v.p. constrn. The Frouge Corp., N.Y.C., 1969-72; constrn. project mgr. Litwin & Swarzman, Owner-Builders, N.Y.C., 1972-75; v.p. constrn. Cohen Bros. Realty & Constrn., Inc., N.Y.C., 1975-77, 79-91; constrn. project mgr. Rose Assocs., Inc., N.Y.C., 1977-79. Adv. bd. The Frouge Corp., N.Y.C., 1970-72. With U.S. Army, 1943-46. Recipient Master Builder award Builders Assn. Greater N.Y., 1960, Excellence in Constrn. award N.Y. Soc. Archs., 1977; completion of tallest apt. building in N.Y.C., Park Ave. Assocs., 1979. Avocations: tennis, biking, swimming, arts and crafts, handball. Home: 1317 E 23rd St Brooklyn NY 11210-5112 E-mail: ihkarney@webtv.net.

KARNI, EDI, economics educator; b. Tel Aviv, Mar. 20, 1944; s. Eliezer and Sara (Vitis) K.; m. Barbara Shapiro, Mar. 16, 1980; children: Anat, Anna. BA in Econs., Hebrew U., 1965, MA in Econs., 1970, U. Chgo., 1970, PhD in Econs., 1971. Asst. prof. Ohio State U., Columbus, 1971-72; fellow Inst. for Advanced Studies/Hebrew U., Jerusalem, Israel, 1976-77; vis. prof. U. Chgo., 1977-79; assoc. prof. Tel Aviv U., 1972-81; prof. econs. Johns Hopkins U., Balt., 1981—. Disting. vis. prof. Vanderbilt U., 1987. Author: Decision Making Under Uncertainty, 1985; contbr. articles to profl. jours. Fellow: Econometric Soc.; mem.: Am. Econ. Assn. Jewish. Home: 6208 Sareva Dr Baltimore MD 21209-3530 Office: Johns Hopkins U Dept Econs Baltimore MD 21218

KARNIOTIS, STEPHEN PAUL, computer scientist; b. Detroit, July 27, 1963; s. Christ Emmanuel and Mary (Zangkas) K. BA in Computer Sci., Wayne State U., 1985, MBA in Mgmt. Info. Systems, 1994. Cert. Oracle database adminstr., cert. Oracle 7 database adminstr. Computer lab. mgr. Wayne State U., Detroit, 1982-85; programmer, analyst A.J. Foland & Co., Dearborn and Livonia, Mich., 1984-85; ednl. cons. Compuware Corp., Farmington Hills, Mich., 1985-88, programmer, analyst, 1989-92; oracle database adminstr. Compuware Copr., Farmington Hills, Mich., 1990—, mgr. oracle tech., 1993—; product mgr. Compuware Corp., Farmington, Mich., 2001—; assoc. prof. Walsh Coll., Troy, Mich., 1997-2000. V.p. Detroit Oracle Users Group, 1994—96; tech. advisor Oracle VMS Spl. Interest Group, 1991—96, Midwest Oracle User Group, 1992—2001; v.p., advisor Oracle for MVS Spl. Interest Group, Redwood Shores, Calif., 1990—93; tech. judge Ednl. Testing Svc., Princeton, NJ, 1995; adj. prof. Walsh Coll., Troy, Mich., 1997—2001, Lawrence Technol. U., Southfield, Mich., 2002—. Contbr. articles to jours. and newsletters. Treas., bd. dirs. Greek Orthodox Young Adult League Detroit Diocese, 1991-96. Recipient Peer Recognition award Ford Motor Co. Powertrain Ops., 1994. Mem. Alpha Kappa Psi (life, pres. Wayne State U. chpt. 1984-85). Avocations: fine dining, international travel, racquetball, rollerblading. Office: Compuware Corp 31440 Northwestern Hwy Farmington Hills MI 48334-2564 E-mail: stephen.karniotis@compuware.com.

KARNOFSKY, MOLLYNE, artist, poet; b. New Orleans, July 19, 1932; d. Samuel and Lena (Gaethe) Finegold; m. Dave E. Winston, Sept. 17, 1952 (div. Sept. 1975); children: Craig T. Winston, Janelle R. Winston Lewis. BBS in Bus. Adminstrn., Tulane U., New Orleans, 1966; student in Art Studio Courses, Tulane, Newcomb Coll., New Orleans, 1966-70; MAT in Painting and Teaching, Tulane U., New Orleans, 1972. Lic. teaching La., 1972, N.Y.C. Bd. Edn., 1986. Dir., owner La. Lic. Art Sch., New Orleans, 1972-77; art tchr., art workshops N.Y.C., 1977—. Mem. univ. course and policy study com. Tulane U., 1952; panelist Artists Talk on Art, N.Y.C., 1993, 94; guide to internat. artists, Mid. Am. Arts Alliance, N.Y.C., 1994. One-woman shows include Vincent Mann Gallery, New Orleans, 1974, Spirit of New Orleans, 1976, Viridian Gallery, N.Y.C., 1977, 79, Spring St. Performance Painting for Artists' Day, N.Y.C., 1977, PS1 Inst. Art and Urban Resources, Long Island City, N.Y., 1978, Contemporary Art Ctr., New Orleans, 1978, Galerie Forum, Stockholm, 1980, Satellite gallery Bronx Mus. Art, N.Y., 1980, Galerie Leger, Malmö, Sweden, 1980, Ave. B Gallery, 1985, Asphalt Green Cmty. Ctr., N.Y.C., 1988, N.Y. Pub. Libr., 1988, Leonard Stern Bldg. NYU, 1994, Galerie Lafitte, New Orleans, La., 2001, (Site Specific: Found Spaces and Other Places) Eclectic Properties, 1979, Rudolph Bass Power Tool Co., N.Y.C., 1982, Galeriex, Istanbul, Turkey, 2003; exhibited in group shows at Judson Poets Theater, N.Y.C., 1977, World Trade Ctr., N.Y.C., 1979, Ear Inn, N.Y.C., 1979, Artists' Day Art Parade, 1979, 83, Bklyn., Atlantic Ave. Galleries, Bklyn., 1979, Bklyn. Arts Cultural Assn., 1981, Emily Harvey Gallery, N.Y.C., 1983, WPA Gallery, Washington, 1983, Jack Tilton Gallery, N.Y.C., 1983, Jon Leon Gallery, N.Y.C., 1984, Franklin Furnace, N.Y.C., 1984, Minor Injury Gallery, Williamsburg, Bklyn., 1989, World Congress Arts and Medicine, N.Y.C., 1992, Tribeca 148, N.Y.C., 1993, 94, Printmaking Workshop, N.Y.C., 1997, Chuck Levitan Gallery, N.Y.C., 1998, Broome St. Gallery, N.Y.C., 2000, Lyman-Eyer Gallery, Newton, Mass., 2001, 2002, Gallery X, N.Y.C., 2002, Lyman Eyer Gallery, Provincetown, Mass., 2001-02, Ch. of All Sts., 2002, Extreme Exteriors, 2002, Lyman Eyer Gallery, Newton and Provincetown, Mass., 2001-02, Ch. of All Souls, N.Y.C., 2002; permanent collections include Cigna, Insurance Co. of N.Am., Mollyne Karnofsky Papers, NYU Library, Anthology Film Archives, N.Y.C., 1996, Chuck Levitan Gallery, N.Y.C, 1998; subject of art Coll. Art Assn., N.Y.C., 1980; documentary video of art exhbn. Vesteras Mus., Sweden, 1981; documentary video of art ehbn. and interview Fuji Network, Japan, 1981; contbr. articles to profl. jours. Pres. Tulane Commerce Women's Club, New Orleans, 1951; publicity dir. Chevra Thilim Sisterhood, New Orleans, 1960-63; com. mem. Coun. of Jewish Women, New Orleans, 1965-70; tour dir. Spring Fiesta Assn., New Orleans, 1965. Grantee for performance poetry, Poets and Writers, N.Y.C., 1982, 92, 98; named Artist in Residence Avenue B. Gallery, N.Y.C., 1985, honorarium, spl. project, Coal Bin PSI Inst. for Arts and Urban Resources, Queens, N.Y., 1978, Contemporary Art Ctr., New Orleans, 1978. Mem. Tulane Alumni Assn. (bd. dirs. 1970-71, editor bus. review 1971), Artists Equity, Mcpl. Art Soc. Avocations: writing, music, urban archaeology. E-mail: MKarnArt@aol.com.

KARNOW, STANLEY, journalist, writer; b. N.Y.C., Feb. 4, 1925; s. Harry and Henriette (Koeppel) Karnow; m. Claude Sarraute, July 15, 1948 (div. 1955); m. Annette Kline, Apr. 21, 1959; children: Curtis Edward, Catherine Anne, Michael Franklin. BA, Harvard U., 1947; student, U. Paris, France, 1948—49; postgrad., Inst. d'Etudes Politiques, U. Paris, Paris, 1949—50. Corr. Time mag., Paris, 1950—57; bur. chief North Africa Time-Life, 1958—59, 1959—62; spl. corr. London Observer, 1961—65, Time, Inc., 1962—63; Far East corr. Sat. Eve. Post, 1963—65, Washington Post, 1965—71, diplomatic corr., 1971—72, spl. corr. NBC News, 1973—75; assoc. editor The New Republic, 1973—75; columnist King Features, 1975—88, Le Point, Paris, 1976—83, Newsweek Internat., 1977—81; editor Internat. Writers Service, 1976—86; chief corr. PBS series Vietnam: A TV History, 1983; chief corr., narrator PBS Series The U.S. and the Philippines: In Our Image, 1989. Author: (book) Southeast Asia, 1963, Mao and China: From Revolution to Revolution, 1972, Vietnam: A History, 1983 (Emmy award, 1984, DuPont award, 1984, Polk award, 1984, Peabody award, 1984), In Our Image: America's Empire in the Philippines, 1989 (Pulitzer Prize for history, 1990), Paris in the Fifties, 1997; co-author: Asian Americans in transition, 1992; contbg. author (book) Passage to Vietnam, 1994, Mekong, 1995, Historical Atlas of the Vietnam War, 1995, Past Imperfect: History According to the Movies, 1995. Bd. advisors Vietnam Vets. Meml. Wall. With USAF, 1943—46. Recipient citation, Overseas Press Club, 1966, Ann. award for best newspaper interpretation of fgn. affairs, 1968, Lifetime Achievement award for coverage of Asia, Shorenstein Ctr. for Press and Politics, Harvard and Stanford Univs., 2002; fellow Neiman fellow, Harvard U., 1957—58; Inst. Politics John F. Kennedy Sch. Govt. fellow, East Asian Rsch. Ctr. fellow, 1970—71. Mem.: Soc. Am. Historians, Asia Soc., Coun. Fgn. Rels., PEN Am. Ctr., Signet Soc., Century Assn., Shek-O Club (Hong Kong). Home: 10850 Spring Knoll Dr Potomac MD 20854-1550

KARODE, SANDEEP KISHOR, chemical engineer, researcher; b. Gauhati, Assam, India, Dec. 19, 1970; s. Kishor T. and Neela Karode; m. Madhuri Joshi, Dec. 19, 1997. PhD, Indian Inst. Tech., Mumbai, 1994. Cert. in chem. engring. Sr. process cons. water treatment divsn. Thermax Ltd., Pune, India, 1998-99; asst. rsch. officer NRC Can., Ottawa, Canada, 2000—02; applications engr. Air Liquide/MEDAL, Newport, Del., 2002—. Postdoctoral fellow U. Belfort, France, 1998-99. Contbr. rsch. articles to profl. jours. Sr. rsch. fellow Coun. Sci. and Engring. Rsch. Mem.: N.Am. Membrane Soc., Indian Membrane Soc. Office: Air Liquide/MEDAL 305 Water Street Newport DE 19804 Home: 3014 Larkin Rd Boothwyn PA 19061 Business E-Mail: Sandeep.Karode@Airliquide.com. E-mail: sandeepkarode@yahoo.com.

KAROFSKY, PETER STUART, pediatrician, medical educator; b. Boston, Nov. 11, 1939; s. Sydney Bernard Karofsky, Sylvia Ruth Karofsky; divorced; children: Jill, Amy, Andrew; m. Kathryn Jean Anderson, 2000. AB, Bowdoin Coll., 1962; MD, Tufts U., 1966. Pediatrician Jackson Clinic, Madison, Wis., 1971—79; chief pediat. Meth. Hosp., Madison, 1975—76; dir. Gen. Pediat. and Adolescent Clinic U. Hosp., Madison, 1979—86; prof. U. Wis. Med. Sch., Madison, 1979—. Cons. to the Gov. on health care issues State of Wis., Madison, 1975—76; pres. Dane County Pediat. Assn., Madison, 1976—77; med. cons. to Nicaragua U. Wis., Pearl Lagoon, Nicaragua, 1976; cons. on health care issues Bowdoin Coll., Brunswick, Maine, 1979. Radio broadcaster Second Opinion, 1975 (Wis. Outstanding Pub. Svc. Radio Program, 1976); contbr. articles to profl. jours. Team physician Middleton H.S., 1980—91; baseball and softball coach Middleton Youth Baseball and Softball Leagues, 1976—85; founding bd. mem. Emergency Med. Svcs., Middleton, 1975—77. Capt. USAF, 1968—70. Named Olympian of Yr., Service Clubs of Dane County, 1992; recipient Disting. Service to Youth award, Middleton-Cross-Plains Sch. Dist., 1992, Ann. Mason's award, 1993, award, Wis. Assn. Athletic Dirs., 1994. Fellow: Am. Acad. Pediat. Jewish. Avocations: travel, tennis, bicycling, golf. Home: 1406 Shady Oak Cir Middleton WI 53562 Office: U Wis Health-Westside Clinic 451 Junction Rd Madison WI 53717

KAROL, CECILIA, psychiatrist, psychoanalyst; b. Mohilof, Ukraine, Jan. 28, 1926; came to U.S., 1958; d. Mendel and Ethel; m. Morris T. Karol; 1 child, Peter Douglas. B of Pre-Medicine, Instituto Vasquez Acevedo, 1942; MD in Medicine and Surgery, Facultad de Medicina, Montevideo, Uruguay, 1953. Diplomate Am. Bd. Psychiatry and Neurology; bd. cert. child-adolescent and adult psychoanalysis. Grad. in child, adolescent, and adult psychoanalysis N.Y. Downstate Med. Sch., 1969; grad. in forensic psychiatry Albert Einstein Sch. Medicine, 1991; past dir. child and adolescent psychiatry Hackensack Hosp. U. Med. Ctr.; past pres. N.J. Coun. Child and Adolescent Psychiatry. Clin. instr. psychiatry NYU Med. Ctr., 1980. Author: Psychosomatic Symptoms, 1989, The Role of Primal Scene and Sadomasochistic Fantasies in Asthma, 1981; contbr. articles to profl. jours. Fellow Am. Psychiat. Assn. (life), AMA (life); mem. Am. Psychoanalytic Assn. (life), N.J. Psychiat. Assn. (mem. coms.), N.J. Psychoanalytic Assn. (past pres.), Psychoanalytic Assn. of N.Y. Avocations: travel, reading, cinematography. Home: 1055 River Rd Apt 511S Edgewater NJ 07020-1360

KAROL, EUGENE MICHAEL, school system administrator; b. Mifflinville, Pa., Nov. 28, 1933; s. Michael F. and Catherine R. K.; m. Victoria Diane Karol, Aug. 9, 1996; children: Paul Eugene, Eugene Michael, Theodore Lee. BS, U. Md., 1955; MEd, Western Md. Coll., 1964; EdD, Nova U., EdD, 1975; postgrad., Vanderbilt U. Cert. elem. and secondary tchr., Md. Tchr., bldg. level. adminstr. Balt. County Pub. Schs., Towson, Md.; exec. asst. to state supt. Md. State Dept. Edn., Balt.; supt. Somerset County Pub. Sch., Princess Anne, Md., Calvert County Pub. Schs., Prince Frederick, Md., 1980-93; dir. So. Md. Higher Edn. Ctr., 1994-96; campus dean Strayer U., Washington, 1996—. Coord. nat. EdD program for ednl. leaders Nova U., 1970—. Contbr. articles to profl. jours. Recipient Meritorious Svc. award Md. Tchrs. Assn., 1970, Disting. Svc. award NEA, 1971, Golden Apple award Md. PTA. Mem. NAESP, ASCD, Am. Assn. Sch. Adminstrs. (Supt. of Yr. award 1991), Assn. Sch. Bus. Ofcls., Coun. for Exceptional Children, Coun. Ednl. Adminstrv. and Supervisory Orgns. Md. (past pres.), Nat. Assn. Elem. Sch. Adminstrs., Balt. Coun. on Fgn. Affairs. Home: 2410 Vern Rd Port Republic MD 20676-2382

KAROL, FREDERICK JOHN, industrial chemist; b. Norton, Mass., Feb. 28, 1933; s. John and Valeria (Bzdula) K.; m. Ruth Helen Lindbom, May 31, 1958; children: Mark, Donald, Cynthia. BA, Boston U., 1954; PhD in Chemistry, MIT, 1962. With Union Carbide Corp., Bound Brook, N.J., 1956—, chemist, 1956-59, 62-65, project scientist, 1965-67, rsch. scientist, 1967-72, sr. rsch. scientist, 1972-76, rsch. assoc., 1976-80, corp. fellow, 1980-84, sr. corp. fellow, 1984-2000; ret/. Contbr. numerous articles to profl. jours. With U.S. Army, 1954-56. Recipient Thomas Edison award R&D Coun. N.J., 1982, 99, Excellence in Catalysis award Met. N.Y. Catalysis Soc., 1987, Perkin Medal Soc. Chem. Industry, N.Y., 1989, ACS award for Creative Invention, 1991; named to Nat. Plastics Hall of Fame, 1997. Fellow: Soc. Plastic Engrs. (S.P.E. Conley award 1989, Internat. Gold medal 1990); mem.: Am. Chem. Soc., Nat. Assn. Engrs., Am. Inst. Chemists (Chem. Pioneer award 1988). Achievements include patents for 106 U.S. Home: 157 Skyline Dr Lakewood NJ 08701-5739 E-mail: fkarol@optonline.net.

KAROL, JOHN J., JR., producer, filmmaker; b. Mt. Kisco, N.Y., Apr. 1, 1935; s. John J. and Ann (Hale) K.; m. Georgina P. Forbes, Oct. 1963 (div. 1977); children: Angelisse F., Christopher H.; m. Portia L. Fitzhugh, June 21, 1980; 1 child, Fitzhugh B. BA, Williams Coll., 1958; LLB, Yale U., 1962. Assoc. Lord, Day & Lord, N.Y.C., 1962-64; parliamentary draftsman Atty. Gens. Chambers, Zomba, Malawi, Africa, 1964-67; dep. commr., gen. counsel State of Vt. Dept. Taxes, Montpelier, Vt., 1967-69; prodr., filmmaker Apertura, Orford, N.H., 1969—. Prodns. include (films) Brush Dance, 1985, Ben's Mill, 1982 (Acad. award nomination 1982, Golden Eagle award 1982), Main Street, 1979, A Place in Time, 1977 (Golden Eagle award 1977), Settling In, 1974, (video) Photographing with Fred Picker, 1991 (Telly award 1992), Printing with Fred Picker, 1990 (Golden Eagle award 1990, Telly award 1990), Ben's Water Tub, 1990. Dir. Inherit N.H., Concord, 1984-90; trustee Upper Valley Land Trust, Norwich, Vt., 1987-90, mem. exec. bd. St. Martin's Ch., Fairlee, Vt., 1976-79, jr. warden, 1978. Mem. Soc. Motion Picture and TV Engrs., Century Assn. (N.Y.C.), Tavern Club (Boston). Home and Office: Apertura Main St Orford NH 03777 E-mail: karol@apertura.org.

KAROL, MERYL HELENE, medical educator, researcher; b. N.Y.C., Aug. 10, 1940; m. Paul Jason; children: Darcie, Deverin, Meredith. BS, Cornell U., 1961; PhD, Columbia U., 1967. Rsch. asst. SUNY, Stony Brook, 1976-79, assoc. prof., 1979-85, prof. environ. and indsl. health, 1985—, assoc. dept. chair, 1993-2000; prof. environ. and indsl. health U. Pitts., 1985—, assoc. dean rsch., 2002, assoc. dean acad. affairs, 2002—. Sec.-gen. Internat. Union Toxicologists, 1998—; advisor numerous govt. health adv. bds., agys.; lectr. in field; advisor to sec. U.S. Dept. HHS; mem. adv. panel FDA, CDC, 2003; chair sci. adv. panel Mickey Leland Ctr., 2001—03. Assoc. editor Toxicology Sci., mem. editl. bd.: Inhalation Toxicology, Environ. Health, Toxicology and Ecotoxicology News, Biomed. and Environ. Scis.; contbr. articles to profl. jours. Recipient Women in Sci. award, U. Mich., 1986, Rachel Carson award, 1993, Outstanding Contbns. to Pub. Health, 1999; fellow NIH, SUNY, 1967—68. Mem.: AAAS, Soc. Toxicology (v.p. 1993, pres. 1994, Frank R. Blood award), Internat. Union Toxicologists (sec.-gen. 1998—2001), N.Y. Acad. Scis., Am. Conf. Govt. Indsl. Hygienists, Am. Assn. Immunologists, Am. Thoracic Soc., Am. Chem. Soc. Avocations: sports, design, travel, biotechnology. Office: U Pitts Dept Env & Occupl Health 130 DeSoto St Pittsburgh PA 15261 E-mail: mhk@pitt.edu.

KAROL, MICHAEL ALAN, editor; b. New Brunswick, NJ, Mar. 1, 1953; s. Reuben Hirsch and Sylvia (Gross) K. BA in Sociology and Comm., U. Pa., 1975; MS in Comm./TV Broadcasting, Boston U., 1977. Rhythm and blues editor Pop Top Mag. Little Face, Inc., Boston, 1976-78; staff photographer, prodn. editor Nat. Jewel Mag., N.Y.C., 1978-79; assoc. editor Gift and Stationery Bus. Gralla Publs., N.Y.C., 1979; mng. editor Modern Floor Coverings Charleson Pub. Co., N.Y.C., 1979-82; editor-in-chief Floor Covering Bus. Thomson Retail Press, N.Y.C., 1982-89; mng. editor Graphic Arts Monthly Cahners Pub.Co., N.Y.C., 1990-96; copy chief Computer Shopper, Ziff-Davis, Inc., N.Y.C., 1996-98; copy flow mgr. CMP, Inc., N.Y.C., 1998-2000; spl. projects editor CNET Networks, 2001—; editl. cons. Martha Stewart Living Omnimedia, 2002—03. Author: Lucy A to Z, 2001, Kiss Me, Kill Me, 2003, Lucy in Print, 2003; copy chief Soap Opera Weekly, 2003—. Recipient Silver awards for graphic excellence Modern Floor Coverings, MFC Mkt. Report, 1981, 84, Regional Design awards for Modern Floor Coverings covers Print Mag., 1985, 88, 65th Ann. Exhbn. Merit award Art Dirs. Club, 1986, Cert. of Distinction in editl. design for Elvis Lives!, Art Direction mag., 1992, Cert. of Merit, Cmty. Action Network, 1992, Bronze Editl. Medal of Excellence for How'd They Print That?, Cahners Pub. Co., 1995. Democrat. Avocations: travel, biking, reading, writing.

KAROL, NATHANIEL H. lawyer, consultant; b. N.Y.C., Feb. 16, 1929; s. Isidore and Lillian (Orlow) K.; m. Liliane Leser, July 20, 1967; children: David, Jordan. BS in Social Sci, CCNY, 1949; MA (fellow), Yale U., 1950; LL.B., N.Y. U., 1957, LL.M., 1959, JD, 1966. Bar: N.Y. 1957. Mgmt. trainee Curtiss Wright Corp., Wood-Ridge, N.J., 1956-57; practiced in N.Y.C., 1957-58; contracting officer USAF, N.Y.C., 1958-62; chief contract mgmt. survey and cost adminstrn. Office of Procurement, NASA, Washington, 1962-64; asst. dir. cost reduction, 1964-66; dep. asst. sec. Grants Adminstrn., HEW, Washington, 1966-69; univ. dean City U. N.Y.; exec. dir. Research Found., 1969-73; v.p. Hebrew Union Coll., Cin., 1973-75; partner, nat. chmn. cons. services for edn. Coopers & Lybrand (C.P.A.s), Chgo., 1975-81; pres. Nathaniel H. Karol & Assocs. Ltd., 1981—. Cons. to govt. agys. and ednl. instns. Author: Managing the Higher Education Enterprise. Served with U.S. Army, 1953-56. Recipient Outstanding Performance award HEW, 1968, Superior Performance award, 1969 Mem. N.Y. Bar, Nat. Assn. Coll. and Univ. Bus. Officers, Nat. Assn. Coll. and Univ. Attys. Home and Office: 1228 Cambridge Ct Highland Park IL 60035-1014 *What one is, is as important as what one does. I regard as successful the man who is able to establish a set of values and to observe them consistently. If there is a single thing for which I would wish to be remembered, it is that I was a man whose word was his bond.*

KAROL, VICTORIA DIANE, educational administrator; b. Bremerhaven, Germany, Sept. 22, 1956; d. Arthur Lee and Esther Marie Stephens; m. Eugene Karol; 1 child: Theodore L. BS in Elem. Edn. magna cum laude, Towson State U., 1978; M Adminstrn. and Supervision, Bowie State U., 1992; EdD in Ednl. Leadership, Nova Southeastern U., Fla., 1996. Cert. tchr., Md. Tchr. Calvert County Pub. Schs., Prince Frederick, Md., 1978-89, asst. dir. staff devel. and art and dance Title IV, Tchr. Ctr., student tchrs., media svcs., 1989—. Cons. coop. learning strategies, adult learners, team-building strategies, dimensions of learning, supervision, sch. to work, Internet, multicultural edn., 1990—; adv. com. Bowie (Md.) State U., 1990-91. Bd. dirs. St. Mary's Elem. Sch., sec., 1990—; mem. adv. coun. on Multicultural Edn. Md. State Dept. of Edn. Mem. Calvert Assn. Suprs. and Adminstrs. (pres.), Calvert County Pub. Sch. Ctrl.

Office Social Com. (chairperson), So. Md. Tri-County Staff Devel. Consortium. Roman Catholic. Avocations: dance, sports, baton twirling, gardening. Office: Calvert County Pub Schs 1305 Dares Beach Rd Prince Frederick MD 20678-4208

KAROLL, BRAD R. psychotherapist, researcher; b. Syracuse, N.Y., Dec. 8, 1953; s. Seymour and Lillian Karoll; m. Denise Reilman, Mar. 21, 1976 (div. Aug. 1989); 1 child, Jori Lee. BSW, U. Mo., St. Louis, 1995; MSW, St. Louis U., 1997; postgrad. in doctoral program, U. Ill., 1998—. LCSW Mo., Ill. Residential technician Bridgeway Counseling Svc., Troy, Mo., 1993—94; addictions counselor Christian Hosp. NW, Florissant, Mo., 1994—98; ind. contractor, assessor, facilitator Safety Coun. Greater St. Louis, St. Louis, 2000; regional case mgr.-therapist Mo. Physicians Health Program, St. Louis, 2000—; pvt. practice therapist Mo. and Ill., 2001—; therapist Assisted Recovery Ctr. Am., St. Louis, 2002—. Mem. bd. F.R.E.S.H. Renewal Ctr., Augusta, Mo., 1997—2001; bd. mem., various offices Coalition on Addiction, St. Louis, 1992—99; mem. advocacy team Dept. Mental Health, Divsn. Alcohol and Drug Abuse, St. Louis, 1994—97. Contbr. articles to profl. jours. Mem.: NASW. Eckankar. Avocation: billiards. Office: Mo Physicians Health Program 3839 Lindell Blvd Saint Louis MO 63108

KARP, DONALD MATHEW, lawyer, banker; b. Newark, N.J., Jan. 15, 1937; s. Michael N. and Beatrice (Laufer) K.; m. Margery Paula Lesnik, June 28, 1962; children: Jonathan David, Kathryn Jill. BA, U. Vt., 1958; JD, Cornell U., 1961. Bar: N.J. 1961, N.Y. 1981. With Broad Nat. Bank and Broad Nat. Bancorp., Newark, N.J., chmn. bd., 1985—, CEO, 1991; regional counsel SBA, N.J., 1966. Vice chmn., dir. Independence Cmty. Bank, 1999. Mem. coun. trustees NJ Performing Arts Ctr.; mem. adv. com. Greater Newark Conservancy; bd. dirs. Ind. Cmty. Found., Newark Hist. Soc., Friends of Newark Pub Libr., Newark Preservation and Landmarks Commn., Local Initiatives Support Corp., Newark Mus.; mem. adv. bd. NJ Coll. Medicine and Dentistry; bd. dirs. Friends of Thirteen, Inc. Recipient CEO of the Yr. Bronze award Fin. World mag., 1994, Businessman of the Yr. award City of Newark, 1999; named City News 100 Most Influential, Newark, Rotary Club Person of the Yr., St. Philip's Acad. Role Model, 1998. Mem. ABA, N.J. Bar Assn., N.Y. State Bar Assn., Fed. Bar Assn., Assn. Bar City of N.Y., Essex County Bar Assn. Clubs: Mountain Ridge Country (West Caldwell). Office: Independence Community Bank 905 Broad St Ste 2 Newark NJ 07102-2095 E-mail: dkarp@icbny.com.

KARP, GERALD CHARLES, biologist, educator, writer; b. L.A., Dec. 24, 1942; s. Harry and Sally Karp; m. Patrice Marie Patrick, Nov. 21, 1973; 1 child, Jennifer. BS, UCLA, 1964; PhD, U. Wash., 1970. Postdoctoral rschr. U. Colo. Med. Ctr., Denver, 1970-71; prof. biology U. Fla., Gainesville, 1971-84; vis. scientist U. Iowa, Iowa City, 1984, U. Calif., San Francisco, 1988-89; freelance writer Cin., 1990—. Mem. ad hoc com. med. grants rsch. NIH, Bethesda, Md., 1976; cons. Morrison and Foerster, San Francicso, 1988, Wiley and Sons Publs., N.Y.C., 1990—. Author: Development, 1976, Development, 2d edit., 1981, Cell Biology, 1979, Cell Biology, 2d edit., 1984, Cell and Molecular Biology, 1996, Cell and Molecular Biology, 2d edit., 1999, Cell and Molecular Biology, 3d edit., 2002. Predoctoral fellow NSF, 1964-69, Postdoctoral fellow NIH, 1970-71. Mem. AAAS, Phi Beta Kappa.

KARP, HARVEY L. metal products manufacturing executive; Pres., founder Monogram Industries Inc., L.A.; chmn. bd. Mueller Industries, Memhis, 1991—. Office: Mueller Industries 8285 Tournament Dr Ste 150 Memphis TN 38125

KARP, HARVEY LAWRENCE, metal products manufacturing company executive; b. N.Y.C., Nov. 26, 1927; s. Harry and Sadie (Zimmerman) K.; children: David, Nicholas. BA, Coll. City N.Y., 1949; LLB, Yale U., 1952. Bar: N.Y. 1952, Calif. 1954. Lawyer Chesapeake Industries, Inc., N.Y.C., 1952-54; gen. counsel, v.p. Houston Fearless Corp., Los Angeles, 1955-60; founder, vice-chmn. bd. dirs., pres. Monogram Industries, N.Y.C., 1960-83; chmn. bd. Mueller Industries, Inc., 1991—. Served with USNR, 1945. With USNR, 1945. Mem. Atlantic Golf Club, Bel Air Country Club. Home: PO Box 30 East Hampton NY 11937-0030 also: 101 Park Ave Fl 48 New York NY 10178-0002 E-mail: harvey@karp.com.

KARP, HERBERT RUBIN, neurologist, educator; b. Atlanta, Apr. 13, 1921; s. Louis and Sadie (Fischer) K.; m. Hazel Berman, June 16, 1948; children—Eleanor Beth, Miriam Sarah, Benjamin Chaim. BA, Emory U., 1943, MD, 1951. Diplomate Am. Bd. Psychiatry and Neurology. Intern then resident in internal medicine Grady Meml. Hosp., 1951-54; resident in neurology Duke U. Med. Center, 1954-56; clin. and research fellow in neurology and neuropathology Harvard U.-Mass. Gen. Hosp., 1956-58; asst. prof. neurology Emory U., Atlanta, 1958-63, prof., 1963-91, prof. emeritus, 1991—, prof. medicine, 1983-91, prof. emeritus, 1991—, chmn. dept. neurology, 1974-83, dir. geriatrics program dept. medicine, 1983-90; dir. med. services Wesley Woods Geriatric Ctr., 1983-91, med. dir. emeritus, 1991—. Assoc. med. dir., prin. clin. coord. Ga. Med. Care Found.; trustee Atlanta Symphony Orch., 1975-95, bd. counselors 1996—, sec., 1979-80; pres. Ahavath Achim Synagogue, 1980-82; trustee Nat. Found. Jewish Culture, 1976-84, mem. bd. overseers, 1984-90. Served with USNR, 1943-46. Recipient Thomas Jefferson award Emory U., 1984, Outstanding Med. Alumnus award, 1986, Disting. Med. Achievement award, 2001; Eternal Light award Jewish Theol. Sem. Am., 1985, Civic Endeavor award Med. Assn. Ga., 1989, Myrtle Wreath award Hadassah, 1990, Wakeman award Duke U., 1990; spl. fellow Nat. Inst. Neurol. Diseases, 1956-58; Herbert R. Karp Leadership award established in his name Dept. of Neurology, Emory U., 1999. Fellow Am. Acad. Neurology; mem. Am. Neurol. Assn. (mem. coun.), Assn. Univ. Profs. Neurology, Atlanta Interfaith Broadcasters (bd. dirs. 1991—, sec. 1997—), Alpha Omega Alpha. Democrat. Home: 880 Somerset Dr NW Atlanta GA 30327-3732 Office: Ga Med Care Found 1455 Lincoln Pkwy E Ste 800 Atlanta GA 30346 E-mail: hkarp02@emory.edu.

KARP, JUDITH ESTHER, oncologist, science administrator; b. San Diego, July 15, 1946; d. Louis Moses and Bella Sarah (Perlman) K.; m. Stanley Howard Freedman, Sept. 21, 1975. BS in Chemistry, Mills Coll., Oakland, Calif., 1966; MD, Stanford U., 1971. Diplomate Am. Bd. Internal Medicine. Intern in medicine, jr. resident in medicine Stanford Hosps., 1971-72; asst. resident in medicine Johns Hopkins Hosp., 1972-73; clin. and rsch. fellow oncology Johns Hopkins Med. Sch., 1973-75, instr. oncology and medicine, 1975-78, asst. prof., 1978-85, assoc. prof., 1985-92; spl. asst. to dir. Nat. Cancer Inst., NIH, 1990-94, asst. dir. applied sci., 1995-96; prof. medicine and oncology, dept. medicine U. Md. Cancer Ctr., U. Md. Sch. Medicine, 1996—2002; dir. hematology-oncology fellowship program U. Md. Cancer Ctr., 1997—2002, head hematologic malignancies program, 1998—2002, assoc. dir. for clin. rsch., 2001—02; prof. oncology Johns Hopkins U. Sch. Medicine, 2002—, dir. adult leukemia program, 2002—. Mem. census com. Immuno-compromised Host Soc., 1987-88. 010Mem. editl. bd. Exptl. Hematology, 1998—. Mem. med. and sci. affairs com. Leukemia Soc. Am., 1995—, trustee, 1998—, vice chair clin. rsch., med. and sci. affairs com., 1998—2002. Am. Cancer Soc. Jr. clin. faculty fellow, 1976-79; San Diego Heart Assn. grantee, 1965-67; recipient Aurelia Henry Reinhardt prize Mills Coll., 1966, Cancer Rsch. award Washington chpt. Awards for Rsch. Coll. Scientists, 1975, Resolution of Commendation award State of Md., 1982, Recognition award City of Balt., 1984, NIH Dirs. award, 1995, de Villiers Soc. award Md. chpt. Leukemia Lymphoma Soc., 2003; named Eminent Scientist of Yr., Internat. Rsch. Promotion Coun., Asia, 2002; named among Hematology-Oncology Top Docs, Balt. Mag., 2002. Mem. Am. Soc. Hematology, Am. Soc. Clin. Oncology, Cell Kinetics Soc. (clin. counselor governing council 1985-87), Am. Soc. Microbiology, Immunocompromised Host Soc., Internat. Soc. Exptl. Hematology, Nat. Bd. Med. Examiners, Phi Beta Kappa. Democrat. Jewish. Home: 3422 Manor Hill Rd Baltimore MD 21208-1824 Office: Sidney Kimmel Cancer Ctr Bunting Blaustein Bldg Rm 289 1650 Orleans St Baltimore MD 21231-1000 E-mail: jkarp2@jhmi.edu.

KARP, MARTIN EVERETT, management consultant; b. N.Y.C., Apr. 30, 1922; s. Albert and Bessie (Orenstein) K.; m. Naomi Joslyn Kaplan, Mar. 14, 1948; children: Betsy, Leslie Karp Goldenberg, Jonathan. B.M.E., CCNY, 1942; student, Harvard U., 1944, MIT, 1945, Northeastern U., 1951-52. Lab. engr. Gen. Electric Co., Lynn, Mass., 1942-44; mgr. research and devel. Nat. Pneumatic Co., Boston, 1946-52; dir. product planning, engring. Remington Office Machine div. Sperry Rand Co., 1953-66, dir. mfg., 1966-68; staff asst. to office of pres. ITT, 1968-69, v.p., group gen. mgr., 1969-82, group exec., 1977-82, dir. product and mktg. strategy, 1980-82; mgmt. cons. Adj. prof. Stevens Inst. Grad. Sch. Mgmt., 1984—87. Contbr. articles to tech. jours.; patentee control systems. Dir. Coun. N.Y. Coops. Served as lt. (j.g.) USNR, 1944-46. Mem. ASME, Tau Beta Pi. Jewish (pres. congregation 1961-63). Home and Office: 250 E 87th St New York NY 10128-3115 E-mail: nitram1@ix.netcom.com.

KARP, MARVIN LOUIS, lawyer; b. Milo, Maine, June 12, 1934; s. Harry and Rose Helen (Kiersh) K.; m. Lesley M. Ulevitch, Aug. 11, 1963; children: Harlan, Elissa, Douglas. BA, Yale Coll., 1955, JD, 1958. Bar: Ohio 1958, U.S. Dist. Ct. (no. dist.) Ohio 1960, U.S. Ct. Appeals (6th cir.) 1963, U.S. Supreme Ct. 1974. Ptnr. Ulmer & Berne, Cleve., 1958—, head litigation dept., 1968—. Pres. Park Synagogue. Fellow Internat. Acad. Trial Lawyers, Am. Coll. Trial Lawyers; mem. ABA (chmn. torts and ins. practice sects., ins. law commn.), Cleve. Bar Assn. (trustee 1981-84, pres. 1988-89, professionalism award, 2001), Fedn. Ins. and Corp. Counsel (pres., chmn. standing com. on ethics), Am. Judicature Soc., Def. Rsch. Inst. Home: 3180 Lander Rd Cleveland OH 44124 Office: 900 Bond Court Blvd Cleveland OH 44114

KARP, MICHAEL ALAN, physician; b. Kittanning, Pa., June 29, 1962; s. Norman and Nancy Elaine (Friedman) K.; children: Avi Jefferson, Zachary Elijah, Arielle Chaia. BS, Allegheny Coll., 1984; MD, Temple U., 1988. Diplomate Am. Bd. Family Practice. Family physician/clinic chief, Patterson Army Cmty. Hosp. U.S. Army, Ft. Monmouth, N.J., 1991-95; family physician, med. dir. Sewickley Valley Med. Group, Wexford, Pa., 1995-98, Ambridge (Pa.) Area Healthcare Svcs., 1998—. Trustee Sewickley Valley Med. Group, 1995—; med. dir. Windwood Health and Sports Club, Bradford Woods, Pa., 1995—; chair dept. family practice Sewickley Valley Hosp., 1997-2002. Bd. dirs. Brothers Brother Found., 2001—; Every Child, Inc., 2000—. Maj. U.S. Army, 1988-95. Fellow Am. Acad. Family Physicians; mem. AMA, Pa. Med. Soc., Allegheny County Med. Soc., Pa. Acad. Family Physicians, Allegheny County Acad. Family Physicians. Avocations: weightlifting, walking, tennis, reading. Office: Ambridge Area Healthcare Svcs 72 First St Ambridge PA 15003-2413 E-mail: drkarp@nauticom.net., mkarp@hvhs.org.

KARP, PETER SIMON, marketing executive; b. New City, N.Y., Dec. 9, 1935; s. Joseph Bernard and Esther (Wexler) K.; m. Mona Leea Pecheux; children: Matthew Henry, Mark Andrew. BA, Hobart Coll., 1954, MBA, Columbia U., 1957. Rschr. Bur. Advt., Am. Newspaper Pubs. Assn., N.Y.C., 1954-56; media dir. Smith, Hagl & Knudsen, Inc., N.Y.C., 1957-59; media and rsch. dir. CAG Advt., Inc., N.Y.C., 1960-62; exec. v.p. Bennett-Chaiken, Inc., N.Y.C., 1963-66; founder, CEO BSI/Bus. Sci. Internat., N.Y.C., 1967—; mng. dir. The Concept Testing Inst., N.Y.C., 1972—; chairperson, CEO Pimi. Inc., N.Y.C., 1986—. Dir. Office of the Future Panel, N.Y.C., 1976—; co-dir. The Genesis Group, N.Y.C., 1983—. Co-author: Customer Satisfaction: How to Maximize, Measure and Market your Company's Ultimate Product, 1989, Competing on Value, 1991; creator BSI Tech. Value Assessments, 1989-90; editor BSI Newsletter, 1976—. Pollster Ken Keating Campaign, State of New York, 1964; vol. Grand Cen. YMCA, N.Y.C., 1964-82. Fellow Inst. Dirs. (London); mem. Am. Mktg. Assn., Advt. Rsch. Found., Artificial Intelligence Assn., N.Y. Acad. Scis., Palisades Tennis Club. Jewish. Avocations: art, sculpture, travel, music. Home: 159 Tweed Blvd Nyack NY 10960-4913

KARP, RICHARD M. advertising and communication executive; b. N.Y.C., Aug. 17, 1929; s. Harry and Jo Golden (Bosk) K.; m. Jane Hausman, Nov. 26, 1978; 1 son, David. BS, BA, N.Y. U., 1950; postgrad., Boston U. Publicist 20th Century Fox Film Corp., 1954-56; sr. writer Donahue & Coe Advt., N.Y.C., 1956-58; asso. creative dir., account supr. Reach, McClinton Advt., N.Y.C., 1958-63; exec. v.p., creative dir. Grey Advt. Inc., N.Y.C., 1963-93, ret., 1993—; v.p. Karp Devel. Co., 1993—; guest lectr. Baruch U., 1977-79; chmn. bd. L.A. Weekly, 1993-95; dir. Hitthebeach.com., Inc., 1999—. Author: monograph The Films of Buster Keaton, 1949. Mem. coun. of trustees Am. Friends of the Hebrew U., 1998. With AUS, 1950-51, USAF, 1951-54. Recipient Clio award, Internat. Advt. award, Screen Advt. award, Copywriters Club award. Mem. Brit. Inst. Practitioners in Advt. Office: 44 Cocoanut Row Ste 118B Palm Beach FL 33480-4069 E-mail: rkarp@webtv.net.

KARP, RICHARD MANNING, computer sciences educator; b. Boston, Jan. 3, 1935; s. Abraham Louis and Rose (Nanes) Karp; m. Diana Leigh Grand; 1 child, Jeremy Alexander. AB, Harvard U., 1955, SM, 1956, PhD in Applied Math., 1959; DSc (hon.), U. Pa., 1986, Technion, 1989, U. Mass., 1990, Georgetown U., 1992, U. Ctrl. Fla., 2000. Rsch. staff mem. IBM Watson Rsch. Ctr., Yorktown Heights, NY, 1959—68; visiting assoc. prof. elec. engring. U. Mich., Ann Arbor, 1964—65; prof. computer sci., indsl. engring., ops. rsch. U. Calif., Berkeley, 1968—96, assoc. chmn. elec. engring., computer sci., 1973—75, prof. math., 1980—95; co-chmn. program in computational complexity Math. Sci. Rsch. Inst., Berkeley, 1985—86; rsch. scientist Internat. Computer Sci. Inst., Berkeley, 1988—96; prof. computer sci. U. Wash., Seattle, 1995—99, adj. prof. molecular biotech., 1996—2000; univ. prof. U. Calif., Berkeley, 1999—; Hewlett-Packard vis. prof. Math Sci. Rsch. Inst., Berkeley, 1999—2000. Bd. govs. Weizmann Inst. Soc.; adv. bd. Computer Profsns. for Social Responsibility; faculty rsch. lectr., Berkeley, 1981—82; Miller rsch. prof., Berkeley, 1980—81. Contbr. articles to profl. jours. Recipient Fulkerson prize in Discrete Math., 1979, Lanchester prize in Ops. Rsch., 1977, ORSA/TIS von Neumann Theory prize, 1990, ACM Turing award, 1985, Babbage prize, 1995, Nat. medal of Sci. award, NSF, 1996, Harvey prize, 1998; fellow Einstein, Technion, 1983, Lady Davis, 1983. Fellow: ACM; mem.: NAS, NAE, Am. Philos. Soc., Am. Acad. Arts and Scis., Inst. Combinatorics and Applications. Office: U Calif Computer Sci Divsn 387 Soda Hall # 1776 Berkeley CA 94720 E-mail: karp@icsi.berkeley.edu.*

KARP, RONALD ALVIN, lawyer; b. Bklyn., Feb. 12, 1945; BA, U. Md., 1967; JD, Washington Coll. Law, 1971. Bar: D.C. 1972, Md. 1972, U.S. Dist. Ct. Md. 1972, U.S. Dist. Ct. D.C. 1972, U.S. Ct. Appeals (D.C. cir.) 1972, U.S. Supreme Ct. 1975. Ptnr. Chalkin & Karp, P.C., Washington, 1971-96; mng. ptnr. Karp, Frosh, Lapidus, Wigodsky & Norwind, P.A., Washington, 1996—. Faculty Nat. Coll. Advocacy, Georgetown U., Washington, 1983. Producer, moderator legal programs for NBC Radio, 1974-79, pub. TV programs, 1986—. Trustee McLean Sch. Md., 1985-88; bd. govs. Washington Regional Bd., ADL, 1988—, co-chair, 1996-2000. Mem.: ATLA (del. D.C. 1986—88), ABA (litigation sect.), George Washington Am. Inn. of Ct. (pres. 1994—95), Am. Bd. Trial Advocates (pres. Washington chpt. 2002—), Trial Lawyers Assn. Met. Washington D.C. (bd. govs. 1980—82, pres. 1985, named Trial Lawyer of Yr. 1988), Montgomery County Bar Assn. (chair personal injury sect. 1997—99), Md. Bar Assn., D.C. Bar Assn. Office: Karp Frosh et al 1370 Piccard Dr Rockville MD 20850-4304 also: 1133 Connecticut Ave NW Washington DC 20036-4104 E-mail: ronk@karpfrosh.com.

KARP, ROSANNE, oncology and women's health nurse; b. Lynn, Mass., Oct. 8, 1946; d. Max and Dorothy (Cohen) Sidman; children: Stacy, Matthew. ADN, Northeastern U., 1967; postgrad., Lesley Coll., 1990—2002. RN, Mass. Staff nurse Holy Family Hosp., Methuen, Mass., 1969-90; staff nurse Mass. Gen. Hosp., Boston, 1990-96, case mgr. gynecology/oncology svc., 1996—. Chair, prof. edn. Greater Lawrence unit Am. Cancer Soc., bd. dirs. Mass. div., 1990-92. Recipient Excellence in Med./Surg. Nursing award Merrimack Valley Area Health Edn. Ctr., 1988, Award for Disting. Vol. Leadership Greater Lawrence unit ACS, 1995, nat. leadership award Hadassah, 1997. Ptnrs. award Ptnrs. Healthcare Sys., Inc., 1999.

KARP, SANDER NEIL, lawyer; b. Milw., July 4, 1943; s. Harry and Rosalind (Schewitz) K.; m. Lana Faye Thering, June 16, 1968; children: Grady Thomas, Milu Su. BS, U. Wis., Madison, 1965, JD, 1968. Bar: Wis. 1968, Colo. 1973, U.S. Supreme Ct., U.S. Ct. Appeals (7th and 10th cirs.), U.S. Dist. Ct. Ohio, U.S. Dist. Ct. Nebr., U.S. Dist. Ct. (ea. and we. dists.) Wis., U.S. Dist. Ct. (no. and ea. dists.) Ill. Ptnr. Greenberg & Karp, Milw. and Madison, 1968-71, Law Office of Rudolph Schware, Denver, 1973-78, Karp, Goldstein & Stern, Denver, 1978-84, Karp & Dodge, Denver, 1984-89; atty. mil. law office Nat. Lawyers Guild, Angeles City, Olongapo, Philippines, 1971-73; pvt. practice Denver, 1989-2000; ptnr. Leavenworth & Karp, P.C., Glenwood Springs, Colo., 2000—. Vis. prof. Denver U. Sch. Law, 1989-90; lectr. profl. and ednl. seminars; atty. Am. Coll. Labor and Employment, 2000. Pres. Community Resources, Inc., Denver, 1988-90. Mem. Assn. Trial Lawyers Am., Colo. Trial Lawyers Assn., Denver Bar Assn., Colo. Bar Assn., Plaintiff's Employment Lawyers Assn., Nat. Lawyers Guild (exec. bd. Colo. chpt. 1987-90, reg. v.p. 1992—). Avocations: fly-fishing, hiking, reading, climbing. Office: 1011 Grand Ave Glenwood Springs CO 81601-3603 E-mail: snk@lklawfirm.com.

KARP, STEVE, producing director; b. Mt. Vernon, N.Y., Apr. 5, 1943; s. Mortimer Lester and Pearl Marion (Radding) K. BA, Tufts U., 1965; postgrad., Boston U., 1965-66, Am. Acad. Dramatic Arts, 1968. Actor Light Opera Manhattan, N.Y.C., 1969-70, Am. Shakespeare Festival, Stratford, Conn., 1972, Long Wharf Theatre, New Haven, Conn., 1972-74, N.Y. Shakespeare Festival, N.Y.C., 1974-75; founder, pres. Perk Prodns. Ltd., N.Y.C., 1974-88; artistic dir. Maxwell Anderson Playwrights Series, Stamford, Conn., 1986-87; founder, producing dir. Stamford Theatre Works, 1988—. Tchr. playwriting Westport (Conn.) Playhouse Theatre Sch., 1986-87; tchr. screenwriting Fairfield (Conn.) U., 1986-87; cons. Perk Prodns. Ltd., N.Y.C., 1988—. Appeared in Broadway plays The Changing Room, 1973, Hertzl, 1975-76; writer, dir., prodr. (dramatic short films) The Tennis Lesson, 1976 (Silver medallion V.I. Film Festival 1976-77, Achievement award Am. Film Festival 1976-77, Achievement award Chgo. Film Festival 1976-77), Inside The Jogger, 1977 (Nat. Film Collection Libr. Congress 1979, Gold medallion V.I. Film Festival 1977-78, Excellent Achievement award Melbourne Film Festival 1977-78), The Tennis Match, 1978 (Nat. Film Collection Libr. Congress 1979, Achievement award Am. Film Festival 1978); playwright, dir. The Warehouse, 1991. Recipient Best Dir. Theatre award Conn. Critics Cir., 1991-92, Outstanding Contribution to Conn. Theatre award, 1996-97; Film Prodn. grantee Am. Film Inst.-Nat. Endowment, 1976. Avocations: jogging, tennis. Office: Stamford Theatre Works 95 Atlantic St Stamford CT 06901-2403

KARPATKIN, RHODA HENDRICK, consumer information organization executive, lawyer; b. N.Y.C., June 7, 1930; d. Charles and Augusta (Arkin) Hendrick; m. Marvin Karpatkin, June 16, 1951 (dec.); children: Deborah Hendrick, Herbert Isaac, Jeremy Charles. BA, Bklyn. Coll., 1951; LLB, Yale U., 1953. Bar: N.Y. 1954. Pvt. practice law, 1954-74; ptnr. Karpatkin & Karpatkin, 1958-61, Karpatkin, Ohrenstein & Karpatkin, N.Y.C., 1961-74; pres. Consumers Union of U.S. Inc., Yonkers, N.Y., 1974—, Internat. Orgn. Consumers Unions (name changed to Consumers Internat.), 1984-91, v.p., 1994-97; pres. Consumers Union U.S., Inc., 1994—; hon. sec. Consumers Internat., 1997—, also bd. dirs. Spl. counsel for decentralization N.Y.C. Bd. Edn., 1969-70; adj. prof. dept. urban studies Queens Coll., 1972-74; commr. Nat. Commn. on New Tech. Uses of Copyrighted Works, 1975-78; mem. Pres.'s Com. Trade Policy and Negotiation, 1993—; mem. Pres.'s Trade and Environ. Policy Adv. Com., 1995—. Contbg. author: Current School Problems, 1971, Consumer Education in the Human Services; contbr. articles to profl. publs. Mem. Local Sch. Bd. 5, N.Y.C., 1966-70, chmn., 1967-69; mem. Community Sch. Bd. 3, N.Y.C., 1970-71; mem. com. acad. freedom ACLU, 1973-84; mem. Pres.'s Comm. for Nat. Agenda for the Eighties., 1979-80; trustee Pub. Edn. Assn., 1972-85. Mem. ABA (commn. on law and the economy 1976-79, commn. to reduce costs and delay 1978-84, commn. access to justice 2000 1993—), Assn. of Bar of City of N.Y. (com. consumer affairs 1969-80, chmn. 1974-79, com. on internat. human rights 1987-90, audit com. 1982-83, com. Ea. European affairs), Nat. Inst. for Dispute Resolution (bd. dirs. 1982-89), Helsinki Watch (mem. adv. bd.), Assn. Yale Alumni (rep.-at-large 1982-85). Office: Consumers Union of US Inc 101 Truman Ave Yonkers NY 10703-1057

KARPEL, CRAIG S. journalist, editor; b. Midland, Tex., 1944; married. AB, Columbia U., 1965. Contbg. editor Harper's mag., N.Y.C., 1985-92. Author: The Rite of Exorcism, 1974, The Retirement Myth, 1995; contbr. numerous articles to mags. and newspapers, U.S., S.Am., Europe, Africa, Asia. Office: c/o Don Congdon Assocs 156 5th Ave Ste 625 New York NY 10010-7002 E-mail: karpel@aol.com.

KARPELES, DAVID, museum director; b. Santa Barbara, Calif., Jan. 26, 1936; s. Leon and Betty (Friedman) Karpeles; m. Marsha Mirsky, June 29, 1958; children: Mark, Leslie, Cheryl, Jason. BS, U. Minn., 1956, postgrad., 1956-59; MA, San Diego State U., 1962; postgrad., U. Calif., Santa Barbara, 1965-69; PhD, Atlantic Internat. U., 2003. Founder Karpeles Manuscript Libr. Mus., Montecito, Calif., 1983—, dir., founder Santa Barbara, Calif., 1988—, N.Y.C., 1990—, Tacoma, 1991—, Jacksonville, Fla., 1992—, Duluth, Minn., 1993—, Charleston, SC, 1995—, Buffalo, 1995—, Newburgh, NY, 1999—, Wichita, 2001—. Dir. 202 mini-museums throughout U.S. and Can.; established the 1st cultural literacy program, presented to schs. by respective mus. staffs, 1993—; tchg. fellow Buffalo State U., 2001—. Creator program to provide ownership of homes to low-income families, 1981. Named commencement spkr. to graduating class, U. Minn., 1996, hon. inductee, Acad. Sci. and Engring., U. Minn., 2002; recipient Affordable Housing Competition award, Gov. Edmund G. Brown Jr., State of Calif., Dept. Housing and Cmty. Devel., 1981, Disting. Alumni award, U. Minn., 1996. Jewish. Home: 465 Hot Springs Rd Santa Barbara CA 93108-2029 E-mail: kmuseumsb@aol.com.

KARPEN, MARIAN JOAN, financial executive; b. June 16, 1944; d. Cass John and Mary (Jagiello) Karpen. BA, Vassar Coll.; postgrad., Sorbonne, Paris, NYU, 1974—77. New England corr. Women's Wear Daily, 1966—68; Paris fashion editor Capital Cities Network, 1966—69; syndicated newspaper columnist, photojournalist Queen Features Syndicate, N.Y.C., 1971—73; acct. exec. Blyth Eastman Dillon (merged into Paine Webber), 1973—75, Oppenheimer, N.Y.C., 1975—76; v.p. mcpl. bond coord. Faulkner Dawkins & Sullivan (merged into Shearson Hayden Stone Smith Barney et al), 1976—77; mgr. retail mcpl. bond dept., nat. fin. lectr. Warburg Paribas Becker-A.G. Becker (merged into Merrill LYnch), sr. v.p., prin., 1977—84; sr. v.p., ltg. ptnr. Bear Stearns & Co., 1984—87, assoc. dir., 1987—90; pres., prin., CEO EuroEast® Group, Inc., N.Y.C., 1990—92; writer, creator newsletter Ea. European News; founder, pres., CEO Work Talk, The Forum Work Talk, Inc., N.Y.C., 1992—; creator, writer newsletter The WorkTalk Times website; pres., founder, CEO Career Renewal Ctr.®, Inc. Writer, lectr., seminar organizer and leader; ormer mem. Bus. Adv. Coun. U.S. Senate. Contbr.: articles, photographs to newspapers and mags.; author: Career Crossroads: Ideas and Inspiration for Your Work/Life Journey. Mem. benefit com. March of Dimes, 1983; mem. Torchlight Ball com. Internat. Games for Disabled, 1984; vol. Whitney Mus. Am. Art. Named New Yorker of Week, Channel One, 1996. Mem.: Vassar Club NY (bd. dirs., exec. com., ex-officio chmn. corp. devel. com., chmn. benefit holiday open house 1989, chmn. major scholarship benefit 1991, chmn. scholarship fundraising raffle benefit 1992). Office: WorkTalk® E 76th St at Lexington Ave New York NY 10021 Home: 233 E 69th St New York NY 10021-5414 E-mail: mjkarpen@aol.com.

KARPF, MICHAEL, health facility administrator, director; b. Poland; grad., MD, U. Pa. Intern Johns Hopkins Hosp.; rsch. assoc. immunology lab. NIH; resident U. Pa., fellow, chief resident; with divsn. gen. internal medicine VA Hosp, Miami, 1978-79, U. Pitts., 1979-1985, Falk Chair in gen. medicine, vice chair dept. medicine, 1985-94; sr. v.p. clin. affairs Allegheny Gen. Hosp. Allegheny Health Systems, 1994-95; sr. v.p. clin. affairs Allegheny Integrated Health Group, 1994-95; dir., vice provost hosp. systems UCLA Med. Ctr., 1995—. Bd. dirs. So. Calif. Organ Procurement Ctr. Contbr., reviewer numerous jours. in field. Chmn. Statewide Healthcare Coord. Com., Pa., 1993; mem. gov.'s task force evaluating managed care, Calif., 1997-98. Mem. Hosp. Assn. So. Calif. (bd. dirs.), AMA (bd. dirs.). Office: UCLA Med Ctr Box 951730 Los Angeles CA 90095-1730

KARPICK, RONALD JOHN, pulmonologist, internist, geriatrician; b. Buffalo, May 24, 1940; s. John Andrew and Grace Ruth K.; m. Jane Elizabeth Carey, Sept. 25, 1971; children: Jonathan Keith, Carey Anne. BA, U. Rochester, 1961; MD, Yale U., 1965. Diplomate Am. Bd. Internal Medicine, Am. Bd. Pulmonary Disease, Am. Bd. Critical Care, Am. Bd. Geriatrics. Resident in internal medicine Duke U. Med. Ctr., Durham, N.C., 1965-67, fellow in pulmonary disease, 1967-69; assoc. prof. medicine George Washington Med. Ctr., Washington, 1971-73; v.p. Pulmonary Assocs., Alexandria, Va., 1973-2000, Genesis Physicians Svcs., Alexandria, 2002—03; tuberculosis cons. Fairfax (Va.) County Dept. Health, 2003—. Med. cons. Emphysema Found. for Our Right to Survive; assoc. prof. respiratory therapy No. Va. C.C., 2000—. Contbr. articles to profl. jours. Lt. cmmdr. USNR, 1969-71. Fellow ACP, Am.

Coll. Chest Physicians, Am. Lung Assn. Va. (vol. bd. mem 2000-03), Phi Beta Kappa, Alpha Omega Alpha. Roman Catholic. Avocations: gardening, hiking, canoeing. Home: 3413 Rusticway Ln Falls Church VA 22044-1242 E-mail: ronkarpick@cs.com.

KARPINOS, ROBERT DOUGLAS, anesthesiologist; b. Oscoda, Mich., July 8, 1965; s. Stewart Harvey and Karyl Mae (Schatz) K.; m. Deborah Sue Haizen, Aug. 13, 1989; children: Marc, Brett, Rebecca. BA, U. Mich., 1987, MD, Sackler Sch. Medicine, Tel Aviv, 1991. Diplomate Am. Bd. Anesthesiologists; cert. Basic Life Support, Neonatal ACLS, ACLS, ATLS instr. Intern in internal medicine Northshore Univ. Hosp.-Meml. Sloan-Kettering Cancer Ctr., Manhassett, N.Y., 1991-92; resident in anesthesia NYU Med. Ctr., N.Y.C., 1992-95; attending anesthesiologist Hackensack (N.J.) U. Med. Ctr., 1995—, dir. divsn. critical care anesthesia, 1995—. Tacticle physician Bergan County S.W.A.T. Team. Contbr. articles to profl. jours. Mem. AMA, Am. Soc. Critical Care Anesthesiologists, Am. Soc. Anesthesiologists, N.J. State Med. Soc., N.J. State Soc. Anesthesiologists, Bergan County Med. Soc.

KARPINSKI, GENE BRIEN, non-profit group administrator, think tank executive; b. Bridgeport, Conn., Jan. 14, 1952; s. Eugene Daniel and Madlyn Ann (Capasso) K.; m. Elizabeth Collaton, Sept. 28, 1991; children: Andrew Hunter., Lauren Gail. BA, Brown U., 1974; JD, Georgetown U., 1977. Field dir. Pub. Citizen's Congress Watch, Washington, 1977-81; exec. dir. Colo. Pub. Interest Rsch. Group, Boulder, 1981; field dir. People for the Am. Way, Washington, 1982-84; exec. dir. U.S. Pub. Interest Rsch. Group, Washington, 1984—. Bd. dirs. League of Conservation Voters, Washington, 1993—, Beldon Fund, 1999—, Nat. Assn. for Pub. Interest Law, Washington, 1987-99, Earthshare, Washington, 1992-95. Contbr. chpts. to books, articles to profl. jours.; appeared on four maj. TV news networks. Home: 807 N Irving St Arlington VA 22201-2007 Office: US Pub Interest Rsch Group 218 D St SE Washington DC 20003-1900 E-mail: genek@pirg.org.

KARPINSKI, HUBERTA ELAINE, library trustee; b. Cato, N.Y., Jan. 4, 1925; d. Alfred Raymond and Lena Margaret (Fuller) Tuxill; m. Edward Karpinski, Nov. 17, 1956; children: Susan Tanielian, Rebecca Hitch, Amy Jaward. Student, U. Mich., 1943-45, Wayne U., 1949-50; grad., N.Y. Art Acad. Design, 1972. Operator to svc. observer supr. Mich. Bell Telephone Co., Detroit, 1946-57; tchr. art Birmingham (Mich.) Pub. Sch., 1977-87; libr. trustee Redford (Mich.) Twp. Dist. Libr., 1971—. Chmn. Lola Valley Civic Assn., Redford, 1960-70; vice chmn. Redford Twp. Coun. Civic Assn., 1967-71; bd. dirs. 17th Dist. Mich. Dem. Party, Redford, 1968-71. Mem. Nat. Mus. Women in arts (charter), Mich. Porcelain Artists, Internat. Porcelain Art Tchrs. Avocations: portrait painting in colored pencil, pastel, oil or on porcelain. Home: 17418 Macarthur Redford MI 48240-2241

KARPINSKI, IRENA IZABELLA, lawyer; b. Phila., July 6, 1950; d. Zygmunt Karpinski and Izabella Styczek; m. Walter Charles Johnston, Sept. 17, 1988; 1 child, Aleksander Styczek Johnston. BA, Manhattanville Coll., 1968-72; JD, Temple U., 1972-75; student, Leningrad (USSR) State U., 1970, U. Fribourg, Switzerland, 1970-71. Bar: Pa., 1975, D.C., 1976, N.Y., 1982, Md., 1982; U.S. Dist. Ct. D.C., 1977, U.S. Dist. Ct. (ea. dist.) Pa., 1978, U.S. Dist. Ct. Md., 1986. Spl. asst. to E.G. Biester U.S. Congress, Washington, 1975-76; assoc. atty. Samuel J. Levine, Esq., Washington, 1976-77; pvt. practice Washington, 1977—. Chairperson D.C. Bd. Appeals Rev., Washington, 1984-91; cons. bd. govs. Fed. Res., Washington, 1992-94. Mem. Women's Bar Assn. (chair standing com. 1993—). Avocations: languages, traveling, bridge, chess, tennis. Office: # 111 1330 New Hampshire Ave NW Washington DC 20036

KARPMAN, HAROLD LEW, cardiologist, educator, writer; b. Belvedere, Calif., Aug. 23, 1927; s. Samuel and Dora (Kastleman) K.; m. Molinda Karpman. Student, UCLA, 1945-46; BA, U. Calif., Berkeley, 1950; MD, U. Calif., San Francisco, 1954. Diplomate Am. Bd. Internal Medicine. Rotating intern L.A. County Gen. Hosp., L.A., 1954-55; cardiovascular trainee Nat. Heart Inst., L.A., 1957-58; asst. resident Beth Israel Hosp., Boston, 1955-57; fellow Wyley Winsor Rsch. Found., L.A., 1958-59; pvt. practice Beverly Hills, Calif., 1958—; clin. instr. medicine U. So. Calif., L.A., 1958-64, asst. clin. prof., 1964-71, assoc. clin. prof., 1971-72; assoc. clin. prof. medicine UCLA Sch. Medicine, 1972-92, clin. prof. medicine, 1992—. Attending physician, bd. govs. Cedars-Sinai Med. Ctr., L.A.; attending physician UCLA Med. Ctr., Westside Hosp., L.A., Brotman Med. Ctr., Culver City, Calif.; examiner in cardiovascular diseases Calif. Indsl. Accident Commn., Calif. Dept. Vocat. Rehab.; founder, bd. dirs., chmn. bd. Cardio-Dynamics Labs., Inc., 1969-82; gen. ptnr. Camden Med. Bldg., L.A., 1970-86; bd. dirs. Mcht. Bank Calif.; bd. dirs. med. rsch. Faberge, Inc., N.Y.C., 1980-84; cardiovascular cons. Delta Air Lines, 1992-94; founder, bd. dirs., chmn. bd., chief med. officer CORDA Med. Care, Inc., 1995-2000; chmn., founder, dir. Integrated Diagnostic Ctrs., Inc., 2000—. Author: Your Second Life, 1979, Preventing Silent Heart Disease, 1989; assoc. editor Internat. Medicine Alert, 1992—; contbr. numerous articles to med. jours. Fellow ACP, Am. Coll. Cardiology, Am. Coll. Chest Physicians, Internat. Cardiovascular Soc., Am. Coll. Angiology, Internat. Coll. Angiology, Am. Thermographic Soc. (charter, pres. 1971-72), Am. Acad. Thermology; mem. AMA, Calif. Med. Assn., L.A. Med. Assn., Nat. Cardiovascular Network (exec. com., bd. dirs. 1994-98), Western Cardiovascular Network (chmn., med. dir. 1993-96), Am. Soc. Internal Medicine, Am. Heart Assn., Calif. Heart Assn., L.A. County Heart Assn. Office: 414 N Camden Dr #1100 Beverly Hills CA 90210-4532

KARR, CHARLES, lawyer; b. Coal Hill, Ark., Aug. 3, 1941; s. William Joe and Doris Jane (Coats) K.; m. Suzanne Mary Stoner, Dec. 23, 1962; children: Stephanie, Jennifer, Jeffrey. BA, U. Ark., 1965, LLB, 1967. Bar: Ark. 1968, U.S. Dist. Ct. (we. dist.) Ark. 1979, U.S. Ct. Appeals (8th cir.), 1982, U.S. Supreme Ct. 1985. Law clk. to assoc. justice Ark. Supreme Ct., Little Rock, 1968; dep. pros. atty. Sebastian County, Fort Smith, Ark., 1969-72; pros. atty. 12th Jud. Cir., Fort Smith, 1973-78; ptnr. Law Offices Charles Karr, PA, Fort Smith, 1979—. Mem. staff Ark. Constl. Revision Study Commn. Mem. Criminal Detention Facilities Bd., Pine Bluff, Ark., 1976-78, Gov.'s Commn. on Prisons, Little Rock, 1977; bd. dirs. United Way Fort Smith, Inc., 1977-79, Bost Human Devel. Svcs., Inc., Fort Smith, 1983-88. Mem.: ATLA, ABA (speedy trial com. 1976—77, prosecution discretion com. 1983—84), Ark. Pros. Attys. Assn. (pres. 1977), Ark. Bar Assn. (chmn. criminal law sect. 1976—77), W.B. Putman Am. Inn of Ct. (pres. 1999). Democrat. Mem. Ch. of Christ. Home: 7415 Westminister Pl Fort Smith AR 72903-4250 Office: Law Offices Charles Karr PA 1st Nat Bank Bldg 602 Garrison Ave Ste 650 Fort Smith AR 72901-2535 E-mail: karrlawfirm@aol.com.

KARR, DAVID DEAN, lawyer; b. Denver, Sept. 3, 1953; s. Dean Speece and Jean (Ransbottom) K.; m. Laura A. Foster, Apr. 10, 1982; children: Emily Ann, Bradley Foster. BA, U. Puget Sound, 1975; JD, Loyola U., 1979. Bar: Colo. 1979, U.S. Dist. Ct. 1979, U.S. Ct. Appeals (10th cir.) 1981, U.S. Supreme Ct. 1983. Assoc. Pryor Carney & Johnson, P.C., Englewood, Colo., 1979-84, ptnr., 1984-95, Pryor, Johnson, Montoya, Carney and Karr, P.C., Englewood, Colo., 1995—. Mem. ABA (lead atty. pro bono team death penalty project Tex. chpt. 1988—), Colo. Bar Assn. (interprofl. com. 1990—), Arapahoe County Bar Assn.. Denver Bar Assn., Def. Rsch. Inst., Colo. Def. Lawyers Assn. Home: 5474 E Hinsdale Cir Littleton CO 80122-2538 Office: Pryor Johnson Montoya Carney and Karr PC 5619 DTC Pkwy Ste 1200 Greenwood Village CO 80111-

KARR, GERALD LEE, agricultural economist, state senator; b. Emporia, Kans., Oct. 15, 1936; s. Orren L. and Kathleen M. (Keller) K.; B.S., Kans. State U., 1959; M.S. in Agrl. Econs., So. Ill. U., 1962, Ph.D. in Econs., 1966; m. Sharon Kay Studer, Oct. 18, 1959; children: Kevin Lee, Kelly Jolleen. Livestock mgr. Eckert Orchards Inc., Belleville, Ill., 1959-64; grad. asst. So. Ill. U., Carbondale, 1960-64; asst. prof. econs. Central Mo. State U., Warrensburg, 1964-67; asst. prof. agrl. econs., head dept. Njala U., Sierra Leone, West Africa, 1967-70; asst. prof. agrl. econs. U. Ill., Urbana, 1970-72; asso. prof. agrl. econs., chmn. dept., mgr. coll. farms Wilmington (Ohio) Coll., 1972-76; farmer, Emporia, Kans., 1976— ; mem. Kans. Senate, 1981-98, minority leader, 1991-96; rsch. advisor Bank of Sierra Leone, Freetown, summer 1967; agrl. sector cons. Econ. Mission to Sierra Leone, IBRD, 1973. Mem. Lyon County Farmer Union, Lyon County Livestock Assn., Omicron Delta Epsilon, Farm House. Contbr. articles to profl. jours. Democrat. Methodist. Club: Kiwanis.

KARR, JAMES RICHARD, ecologist, educator, research director; b. Shelby, Ohio, Dec. 26, 1943; s. Rodney Joll and Marjorie Ladonna (Copeland) K.; m. Kathleen Ann Reynolds, Mar. 23, 1963 (div. Nov. 1982); children: Elizabeth Ann, Eric Leigh; m. Helen Marie Herbst Serrano, Dec. 22, 1984. BS, Iowa State U., 1965; MS, U. Ill., 1967, PhD, 1970. Fellow in biology Princeton (N.J.) U., 1970-71, Smithsonian Tropical Rsch. Inst., Balboa, Panama, 1971-72, dep. dir., 1984-87, acting dir., 1987-88; asst. prof. biology Purdue U., Lafayette, Ind., 1972-75; assoc. prof. U. Ill., Urbana, 1975-80, prof., 1980-84; Harold H. Bailey prof. biology Va. Poly. Inst. and State U., Blacksburg, 1988-91; prof. zoology, fisheries, environ. health, civil engring. and pub. affairs U. Wash., Seattle, 1991—, dir. Inst. Environ. Studies, 1991-95. Cons. on water resources EPA, 1978—, OAS, Washington, 1980, South Fla. Water Mgmt. Dist., West Palm Beach, 1989—; cons., gen. counsel Fla. Dept. Environ. Protection, 2002-03. Grantee EPA, 1972-85, 93-2000, U.S. Forest Svc., 1980-81, 90-91, U.S. Fish and Wildlife Svc., 1979-82, NSF, 1982-84, 1997-2000, TVA, 1990-93, Dept. Energy, 1995-2002. Fellow AAAS, Am. Ornithologists Union. Achievements include development of Index of Biotic Integrity, now used in North and South America, Asia, Australia, and Europe to assess directly the quality of water resources. Office: U Wash PO Box 355020 Seattle WA 98195-5020

KARR, NORMAN, communications consultant, public relations executive; b. N.Y.C., July 30, 1927; s. Arnold and Hilda (Horowitz) K.; m. Selma Butter, June 17, 1951; children: Arnold J., Joanne Karr Skop. BA, CCNY, 1950. Textile editor Jour. of Commerce, 1950—55; editor Driver's Digest, 1955-56; exec. dir. Am. Inst. Men's and Boy's Wear (now The Fashion Assn. Am.), N.Y.C., 1956—95, Internat. Assn. Clothing Designers and Execs., 1986-98, Jeanswear Comm., 1991—2001. Adv. com. H.S. of Fashion Industries; bd. dirs. Father's Day Coun., Young Menswear Assn. Bd. dirs. menswear divsn. UJA/Fedn., NCCJ; appointed nat. office vols. March of Dimes, 1997. With U.S. Army, 1945-46.

KARR, RONALD DALE, librarian, historian; b. Pitts., Apr. 19, 1948; s. Emil and Vera J. Karr; m. Diane M. Beaudoin, July 13, 1974; children: Emilie R., Matthew B., Jeannine M. AB, Bucknell U., 1970; MA, Boston U., 1972, PhD, 1981; MS, Simmons Coll., 1978. Lectr. history Northeastern U., Boston, 1974—79; tech. editor Transp. Systems Ctr., U.S. Dept. Transp., Cambridge, Mass., 1974—77, libr., 1977—79; pub. svcs. libr. Transp. Libr. Northwestern U., Evanston, Ill., 1979—85; reference libr. U. Mass., Lowell, 1985—. Adj. faculty history dept. U. Mass., Lowell, 1997—. Editor: (book) Indian New England, 1524-1674, 1999; author: Lost Railroads of New England, 1996, The Rail Lines of Southern New England, 1995; contbr. encyclopedia. Mem., chmn. Planning Bd., Pepperell, Mass., 1989—2001; commr. No. Middlesex Coun. Govts., Lowell, 1989—95. Mem.: Urban History Assn., Orgn. Am. Historians, Am. Hist. Assn., Beta Phi Mu. Home: 13 Cross St Pepperell MA 01463 Office: Univ Mass Lowell 61 Wilder St Lowell MA 01854 Office Fax: 978-934-3015. E-mail: ronald_karr@uml.edu.

KARRAKER, LOUIS RENDLEMAN, retired corporate executive; b. Jonesboro, Ill., Aug. 2, 1927; s. Ira Oliver and Helen Elsie (Rendleman) K.; m. Patricia Grace Stahlheber, June 20, 1952; children: Alan Louis, Sharon Elaine Cohen. BA, So. Ill. U., 1949, MA, 1952; postgrad., U. Wis., 1951-52, Washington U., St. Louis, 1954-56. V.p. personnel Am. Appraisal Assocs., Inc., Milw., 1969-73, v.p. adminstrn., 1973-74, group v.p., dir., 1974-77, exec. v.p., dir., 1977-79, pres., dir., 1979-82; bus. mgr. Concordia Coll., Ann Arbor, Mich., 1986-91. Cons. in field, 1982-86, asst. to chmn. Parker Pen Co., Janesville, Wis., 1967-69, personnel mgr., 1966-67; asst. to pres. Augustana Coll., Sioux Falls, S.D., 1962-64, acting chmn., dept. social scis., 1960-61, asst. prof. history, 1956-60. Columnist The Jour. Times, Racine, Wis., 1993-99; speaker Rep. and civic groups, Wis., 1993—. Trustee Better Bus. Bur., Milw., 1979-82, Citizens Govtl. Rsch. Bur., Milw., 1979-82; speaker, canvasser Rep. Party, S.D., 1956-60. With USNR, 1952-53, Korea. Mem. The Heritage Found., Hoover Presdl. Libr. Assn., Am. Legion. Lutheran. Avocations: church activities, travel, family activities, fishing. Home: 217 S 7th St Apt 11 Waterford WI 53185-4500 E-mail: karr217@webtv.net.

KARRAS, ALEX, actor, former professional football player; b. Gary, Ind., July 15, 1935; m. Susan Clark Player Detroit Lions, 1958-71; host NFL Monday Night Football Preview WLS-TV, Chgo. Co-owner Georgian Bay Prodns. Former commentator Monday Night Football, ABC TV; numerous TV appearances including Tonight Show, TV movies: Paper Lion, The 500 lb. Jerk, Mad Bull, Mighty Moose & The Quarterback Kid, Babe, 1975, Mulligan's Stew, 1977, Centennial, 1978, Jimmy B. and Andre, 1979, Alcatraz: The Whole Shocking Story, When Fame Ran Out, 1980, Maid in America, 1982, Fudge-A-Mania, 1994; star TV series Webster, ABC-TV, 1983-86; films include: Blazing Saddles, 1974, Win, Place or Steal, 1977, FM, 1978, Nobody's Perfect, 1981, Victor, Victoria, 1982, Porky's, 1982, Against All Odds, 1984; author: (with Herb Gluck) Even Big Guys Cry, 1977, Alex Karras: My Life in Football, 1979, Tuesday Night Football, 1991. Named All-Pro, 1960, 61, 63, 65; recipient Outland Trophy, 1957, 79. Office: Georgian Bay Prodns 13400 Riverside Dr Ste 308 Sherman Oaks CA 91423-2541

KARRER, RATHE STEVENS, psychophysiologist; b. Cleve., Mar. 8, 1930; s. Enoch and Ethel (Walther) K.; m. Nancy Donaldson, Apr. 15, 1951 (div. 1971); children: Dana, Tana; m. Betty MacKune, Aug. 15, 1971 (div. 1991); m. Jennifer West, Nov. 30, 1991. BA, La. State U., 1953; MA, New Sch. for Social Rsch., 1957, PhD, 1966. Lic. psychologist, Ill. Rsch. psychologist Tng. Sch. at Vineland, N.J., 1960-66; sr. rsch. scientist Pediatric Inst., Chgo., 1966-78; assoc. rsch. dir. Ill. Inst. Devel. Disabilities, Chgo., 1979-82, dir. behavioral scis., 1982-94; asst. prof. dept. psychiatry U. Ill., Chgo., 1967-73, prof. dept. psychology, 1975-94, prof. emeritus, 1994—; rsch. prof., sr. scientist Life Span Inst. U. Kans., Kansas City, 1994—. Assoc. divsn. psychology and psychiatry Northwestern U., Chgo., 1967-85. Author, editor: Developmental Psychophysiology of Mental Retardation, 1976, Brain and Information, 1984; contbr. articles to profl. jours. Nat. Inst. Child Health grantee, 1971-91, 94—, March of Dimes Found. grantee, 1982, 88. Fellow AASS, APA, APS; mem. Soc. Psychopysiol. Rsch., Soc. Neurosci., Soc. Rsch. Child Devel., Sigma Xi. Office: U Kans Med Ctr Smith Rsch Ctr Cognitive Neurosci Labs 39th & Rainbow Kansas City KS 66103

KARSCH, JAY HARRIS, lawyer; b. Phila., May 11, 1942; s. Eli and Pearl (Parris) K.; m. Mary Lynn Dean, June 30, 1962; 1 child, Tamara Lynn. BA, Temple U., 1964, JD, 1974. Bar: Pa. 1974, U.S. Dist. Ct. (ea. dist.) Pa. 1974, U.S. Dist. Ct. (mid. dist.) Pa. 1986, U.S. Ct. Appeals (3rd cir.) 1982, U.S. Supreme Ct. 1998. Assoc. Eastburn & Gray, Doylestown, Pa., 1974-80, ptnr., 1980—. Chmn. disciplinary hearing com. 2.07 Pa. Supreme Ct., 2001. Bd. dirs. ARC, Doylestown, 1979-81. Fellow Am. Bar Found. (life); mem. ABA, Pa. Bar Assn., Bucks County Bar Assn. (bd. dirs. 1988-90, v.p., pres.-elect 1991 92, pres. 1992-93). Avocations: running, golf, reading. Home: 148 Wagon Wheel Ln Doylestown PA 18901 Office: Eastburn & Gray 60 E Court St Doylestown PA 18901-4350 E-mail: jkarsch@eastburngray.com., ljkar@voicenet.com.

KARSCH, STEPHEN E. store executive, lawyer; b. N.Y.C., Nov. 23, 1939; s. Samuel and Bertha (Delman) K.; m. Phyllis Sloan, Mar. 20, 1965; children—Roxanne C., Michael A. B.S. in Bus. Adminstrn., Am. U., 1961; LL.B., George Washington U., 1964. Bar: D.C., N.Y. Trial atty. SEC, Washington, 1964-66; sr. v.p. Sloan's Supermarkets, Inc., N.Y.C., 1966— ; sr. ptnr. Karsch & Meyer, N.Y.C., 1966— ; pres. Hunts Point Terminal Produce Coop., Bronx, N.Y. Chmn. Citizen Budget Com. Long Beach Sch. Dist., N.Y., 1981-82, active sch. reorgn. com., 1983. Recipient Nat. Retinitis Pigmentosa Found. award, 1980; Man of Yr. award Congregation Beth Shalom, 1982. Mem. N.Y. County Lawyers Assn., Phi Delta Phi. Democrat. Jewish. Office: Karsch & Meyer 108 Greenwich St New York NY 10006-1821

KARSEN, SONJA PETRA, retired American-Hispanic literature educator; b. Berlin, Apr. 11, 1919; came to U.S., 1938, naturalized, 1945; d. Fritz and Erna (Heidermann) K. Titulo de Bachiller, 1937; BA, Carleton Coll., 1939; MA (scholar in French), Bryn Mawr Coll., 1941; PhD, Columbia U., 1950. Instr. Spanish Lake Erie Coll., Painesville, Ohio, 1943-45; instr. modern langs. U. P.R., 1945-46; instr. Spanish Syracuse U., 1947-50, Bklyn. Coll., 1950-51; asst. to dep. dir. gen. UNESCO, 1951-52, Latin Am. Desk, tech. assistance dept., 1952-53, mem. tech. assistance mission Costa Rica, 1954; asst. prof. Spanish Sweet Briar Coll., Va., 1955-57; assoc. prof., chmn. dept. Romance langs. Skidmore Coll., Saratoga Springs, N.Y., 1957-61, chmn. dept. modern langs. and lits., 1961-79, prof. Spanish, 1961-87, prof. emerita, 1987; cons. Hudson-Mohawk Assn. Colls. and Univs., 1990. Faculty rsch. lectr. Skidmore Coll., 1963; mem. adv. and nominating com. Books Abroad, 1965-67; Fulbright lectr. Free U. Berlin, 1968; lectr. U. Gesamthochschule, Paderborn, Germany, 1995, 99. Author: Guillermo Valencia, Colombian Poet, 1951, Educational Development in Costa Rica with UNESCO's Technical Assistance, 1951-54, 1954, Jaime Torres Bodet: A Poet in a Changing World, 1963, Selected Poems of Jaime Torres Bodet, 1964, Versos y prosas de Jaime Torres Bodet, 1966, Jaime Torres Bodet, 1971, Ensayos de Literatura E Historia Iberoamericana/Essays on Iberoamerican Literature and History, 1988, Papers on Foreign Languages, Literature and Culture, 1982-87, 88, Bericht Über Den Vater: Fritz Karsen 1885-1951, 1993; translator: The Role of the Americas in History (Leopoldo Zea), 1992; editor Lang. Assn. Bull., 1980-83; mem. editl. adv. bd. Modern Lang. Studies, 1977-93; contbr. articles to profl. jours. Decorated Chevalier dans l'Ordre des Palmes Académiques, 1964; recipient Leadership award N.Y. State Assn. Fgn. Lang. Tchrs., 1973, 76, 78, Nat. Disting. Leadership award, 1979, Disting. Service award, 1983, 86, Capital Dist. Fgn. Language Disting. Service award, 1987; recipient Spanish Heritage award, 1981, Alumni Achievement award Carleton Coll., 1982; exchange student auspices Inst. Internat. Ednl. at Carleton Coll., 1938-39; Buenos Aires Conv. grantee for research in Colombia, 1946-47; faculty research grantee Skidmore Coll., summer 1959, 61, 63, 64, 67, 69, 70, 73, ad hoc faculty grantee, 71, 78, 85. Mem. Am. Assn. Tchrs. Spanish and Portuguese, Nat. Assn. Self-Instructional Lang. Programs (v.p. 1981-82,pres. 1982-83), AAUW (life), AAUP (life), MLA (del. assembly 1976-78, Mildenberger medal selection com 1984-86), El Ateneo Doctor Jaime Torres Bodet (founding mem.), Nat. Geog. Soc., Asociación Internacional de Hispanistas, UN Assn. U.S.A., Am. Soc. French Acad. Palms, Fulbright Alumni, Phi Sigma Iota, Sigma Delta Pi. Home: 1755 York Ave Apt 37A New York NY 10128-6875 *Perseverance, hard work and high ethical standards coupled with the opportunities for fulfilling one's potential, available in the United States to a greater extent than anywhere else in the world, have made my life what it is today.*

KARSH, PHILIP HOWARD, advertising executive; b. Salt Lake City, Sept. 19, 1935; s. Sol and Ruth (Marks) K.; m. Carol Hyman, July 3, 1962 (div. Sept. 1973); children: Michael David, Jill Ann; m. Linda Love, Sept. 7, 1984. BA, U. Colo., 1957. Account exec. Ted Levy/Richard Lane & Co., Denver, 1957-59; v.p. Jerome/Philip Advt., Denver, 1959-62, pres., 1962-65; v.p. Frye Sills Advt., Denver, 1966-77; pres. Karsh & Hagan Advt. Inc., Denver, 1977-85, chmn., 1985-97; ret., 1998. Trustee Nat. Jewish Ctr. Immunology and Respiratory Medicine, Denver, 1963—, chmn. 1991-95, Kern Rsch. Found., Denver, 1984—, Mile High United Way, Denver, 1986-92; mem. Denver Metro Conv. and Visitors Bur., 1994—, chmn., 1997. Mem. Worldwide Ptnrs. (internat. chmn. 1986-87), Denver Advt. Fedn. (bd. dirs. 1968-69, 87-88), Rotary (pres. S.E. Denver club 1989-90), Colo. Hist. Soc. (vice chair 2001—). Democrat. Jewish. Avocations: skiing, travel, golf. Home: 11704 W Auburn Dr Denver CO 80228-4758 Office: 2399 Blake St # 160 Denver CO 80205-2108 E-mail: philkarsh@aol.com.

KARSON, BURTON LEWIS, musician, educator; b. L.A., Nov. 10, 1934; s. Harry L. and Cecilia K. BA, U. So. Calif., 1956, MA, 1959, D.MA, 1964. Instr. music Univ. Coll., U. So. Calif., Los Angeles, 1958-59, univ. chapel organist, 1960-61; instr. music Glendale (Calif.) Coll., 1960-65; asst. prof. music Calif. State U., Fullerton, 1965-69, assoc. prof., 1969-74, prof., 1974-97, prof. emeritus, 1997—; writer, critic Los Angeles Times, 1966-71. Founder, condr., artistic dir., Baroque Music Festival, Corona del Mar, Calif., 1980— ; concert preview lectr. Los Angeles Philharm. Orch., Carmel Bach Festival, Pacific Symphony and Pacific Chorale, Orange County Phil. Soc., others; editor: Festival Essays for Pauline Alderman, Brigham Young Univ. Press, 1976; contbr. articles to profl. jours. including Mus. Quar. Pianist, harpsichordist, organist, choirmaster St. Joachim Ch., Costa Mesa, Calif., 1974—82, St. Michael and All Angels Episc. Ch., Corona del Mar, Calif., 1982—2000, organist-choirmaster emeritus, 2000—; choral condr. Luth. Chorale L.A., 1979—83. Mem. Am. Musicol. Soc., Am. Guild Organists, Phi Mu Alpha Sinfonia (province gov. 1976-81, chair nat. com.), Pi Kappa Lambda. Achievements include profl. rsch. on music history and criticism in early Calif., German, Czech and English Baroque, cantatas and concertos; conductor first American performances. Home: 404 De Sola Terr Corona Del Mar CA 92625-2650

KARSON, CATHERINE JUNE, database administrator; b. Salt Lake City, Jan. 26, 1956; d. Gary George and Sylvia June (Naylor) Anderson; m. Mitchell Reed Karson, June 14, 1987; 1 child, Rhonda. A in Gen. Studies, Pima C.C., Tucson, 1989, AAS in Computer Sci., 1990. Night supr. F.G. Ferre & Son, Inc., Salt Lake City, 1973-76, exec. sec., 1977-79; operating room technician Cottonwood Hosp., Salt Lake City, 1976-77; customer svc. rep., System One rep. Ea. Airlines, Inc., Salt Lake City and Tucson, 1979-88; edn. specialist Radio Shack Computer Ctr., Tucson, 1988-89; programmer/analyst Pinal County DPIS, Florence, Ariz., 1989-90; systems analyst Carondelet Health Svcs., Tucson, 1990; programmer/analyst Misys Healthcare Sys., Tucson, 1990-94, sr. tech. proposal specialist, 1994-95, software developer, 1995-97, sr. sys. software specialist/dba, 1997—99; cons. Tucson Hebrew Acad., 2002—03. Cons. Pinal County Pub. Fiduciary, Florence, 1990, UBET, Barbados, W.I., 1990-96, numerous clients, Tucson, 1990-93. Mem. bus. adv. coun. Portable Practical Ednl. Preparation, Inc., Tucson, 1990-91. Mem. Nat. Sys. Programmer Assn. Republican. Jewish. Avocations: reading, painting, music, light opera performance, dance classes. Home: 5413 N Ventana Vista Rd Tucson AZ 85750-7203

KARSON, EMILE, international business executive; b. Berlin, Sept. 10, 1921; came to U.S., 1948, naturalized, 1955; s. Bogdan and Zorka (Natowa) Karastoyanoff; m. Lilia Usunowa, Dec. 31, 1944; 1 child, Danielle. LLB, U. Sofia, 1946, U. PAris, 1946; Docteur-en-Droit, U. Paris, 1948; LLM, Yale U., 1951, JSD, 1953; postgrad., U. So. Calif., 1953-54, U. Pa., 1978, Harvard U., 1978, Cornell U., 1991. Internat. atty. World Bank, Washington, 1951—53; gen. counsel Coast Fed. Savs., Great We. Savs., L.A., 1954—58; F-104 exec. Lockheed Aircraft Internat., L.A., 1959—63; treas. Europe, Zurich, Switzerland Litton Industries, Inc., 1964-69; corp. treas. Continental Grain Co., N.Y.C., 1969-72; v.p. fin. & adminstrn. Loctite Corp., Newington, Conn., 1972-81; founder, CEO, INTECH (internat. high tech. venture capital), Washington, 1981-85; internat. atty., 1998—. Vis. prof. law U. P.R., 1957; organizer 1st symposium on atomic energy and law for L.A.m.; lectr. Naval War Coll., Fgn. Svc. Inst., U. So. Calif., Ind. U., U. Pitts.; mem. Rep. Assocs., 1954-56; Bus. Internat. Round Table, 1960-65; cons. Dept. State, 1983, U.S. Dept. Labor internat. programs, 1991, 92. Dir. 2 documentary films shown at Cannes and Venice Film Festivals, 1947. Mem. adv. bd. Genetics Unique Fund, 1985-87; broadcaster Voice of Am., 1949-51; pres. Ea. European Orphans, Washington; steering com. Am. U. in Bulgaria, 1992-96; chmn., pres. Bulgarian-Am. Charitable and Ednl. Ctr., 1989-98. Fellow French Govt., 1946-48. Mem. State Bar Calif., Bar U.S. Supreme Ct., World Affairs Coun., Yale Club (Calif.), Yale Law Sch. Club (Calif.). Home: 10025 Gable Manor Ct Potomac MD 20854

KARSON, SAMUEL, psychologist, educator; b. Baltimore, Md., Jan. 3, 1924; s. Norman Jacobson and Annie (Raskin) K.; m. Dorothy Faye Libert, Sept. 6, 1946; children: Linda Catherine, Michael Craig. BS, L.I. U., 1948; PhD, Washington U., St. Louis, 1952. Diplomate Clin. Psychology Am. Bd. Profl. Psychology. With psychiatric unit U.S. Naval Tng. Ctr., San Diego, 1952-55; asst. prof. dept. psychology U. N.H., 1957-58; chief psychologist, dir. rsch. Dade County Child Guidance Clinic, Miami, Fla., 1958-62; rsch. asst. prof. dept. nursing U. Miami, Fla., 1959-62; chief clin. psychologist, office aviation medicine FAA, Washington, 1962-66; prof., head dept. psychology Ea. Mich. U., Ypsilanti, 1966-77; chief psychologist, adminstr. overseas mental health program Dept. State, Washington, 1977-81; regional psychologist Southeast Asia Am. Embassy, Bangkok, Thailand, 1981-83; prof. clin. psychology Sch. Psychology Fla. Inst. Tech., Melbourne, 1983-85, prof., dir. grad. clin. tng., 1985-89; prin. investigator Second Genesis, Inc., Bethesda, Md., 1990-95. Cons. clin. psychology to office aviation medicine FAA, Washington, 1966-75. Author: (with J. O'Dell and M. Karson) 16PF Interpretation in Clinical Practice, 1997, The Karson Clinical Report; contbr. articles to profl. jours. Served with USAAF, 1942-45, with USAF, 1955-57. Recipient Appreciation certificate Sec. State Alexander Haig, 1981, Personality Assessment award Thai Psychol. Assn.,

1983, Disting. Profl. Contbns. award Md. Psychol. Assn., 1987. Fellow APA, Soc. Personality Assessment (life); mem. Soc. Multivariate Exptl. Psychology, Assn. Aviation Psychologists (pres. 1973-74). E-mail: SamKarson16pf@aol.com.

KARST, GARY GENE, retired architect; b. Barton County, Kans., Sept. 2, 1936; s. Emil and Clara (Nuss) K.; m. Loretta Marie Staub, Nov. 30, 1957; children: Kevin Gene, Sheri Lynn, Stacey Marie. BArch, Kans. State U., 1960. Registered profl. arch., Kans. Staff architect Horst & Terrill Architects, Topeka, 1960—64; ptnr. Horst, Terrill & Karst Architects, Topeka, 1965—2001, dir. design, 1965—2001, sec., 1973—78, v.p., treas., 1978—92, v.p., 1992—99; pres., 1999—2001; ret., 2001; design architect Ruhnau, Evans, Brown & Steinman Architects, Riverside, Calif., 1964—65. Mem. Capital City Redevel. Agy., Topeka, 1978-86; mem. adv. bd. dept. architecture Kans. State U., Manhattan, 1986-87. Prin. works include Emporia (Kans.) H.S., 1972, (Kans. Soc. Architects award 1975), S.W. Bell Telephone Co. Equipment Bldg., 1974 (Bell Sys. award 1976), Durland Hall-Univ. Engring. Bldg., 1981 (Kans. Soc. Architects award 1983), Kans. State Prison Medium Security Facility, 1983 (Kans. Soc. Architects award 1985), Lansing H.S., 1988 (William W. Caudill citation Am. Sch. and Univ. Mag.), Leavenworth H.S., 1990 (citation Am. Sch. and Univ. Mag.), Plant Scis. Bldg., Kans. State U., 1994, Tomanek Hall, Ft. Hays State U., 1995; featured in publs. including Archtl. Record Mag. Recipient citation Am. Sch. and Univ. Mag.; Bales Organ Recital Hall, U. Kans., 1995, Weigel scholar Kans. State U., 1958-60. Mem. AIA, Kans. Soc. Architects (pres. 1981-82), Future Heritage Topeka, Optimists (pres. Topeka breakfast club 1970-71, lt. gov. Kans. dist. 1981-82). Avocations: woodworking, photography, sculpting. Home: 3535 SW Macvicar Ave Topeka KS 66611-1841 E-mail: gkarst@cox.net.

KARST, KENNETH LESLIE, law educator; b. Los Angeles, June 26, 1929; s. Harry Everett and Sydnie Pauline (Bush) K.; m. Smiley Cook, Aug. 12, 1950; children— Kenneth Robert, Richard Eugene, Leslie Jeanne, Laura Smiley AB, UCLA, 1950; LL.B., Harvard U., 1953. Bar: Calif. 1954, U.S. Dist. Ct. (cen. dist.) Calif. 1954, U.S. Ct. Appeals (9th cir.) 1954, U.S. Supreme Ct. 1970. Assoc. Latham & Watkins, Los Angeles, 1954, 56-57; teaching fellow law Harvard U. Law Sch., 1957-58; asst. prof. Ohio State U. Coll. Law, Columbus, 1958-60, assoc. prof., 1960-62, prof., 1962-65; prof. law UCLA, 1965-90, David G. Price and Dallas P. Price prof. law, 1990—. Author: (with Harold W. Horowitz) Law, Lawyers and Social Change, 1969, (with Keith S. Rosenn) Law and Development in Latin America, 1975, Belonging to America: Equal Citizenship and the Constitution, 1989, Law's Promise, Law's Expression: Visions of Power in the Politics of Gender, Race, and Religion, 1993; assoc. editor Ency. of Am. Constn., 1986, co-editor-in-chief, 2d edit., 2000; contbr. articles to profl. jours. Served to 1st lt. JAGC, USAF, 1954-56 Law faculty fellow Ford Found., 1962-63 Fellow Am. Acad. Arts and Scis.; mem. State Bar Calif. Office: UCLA Law Sch PO Box 951476 Los Angeles CA 90095-1476 E-mail: karst@law.ucla.edu.

KARSTAEDT, ARTHUR R., III, lawyer; b. Madison, Wis., Sept. 15, 1951; BA, U. Wis., 1972; JD, U. Denver, 1975. Bar: Colo. 1976. Formerly lawyer Hall & Evans, Denver; ptnr. Harris, Karstaedt, Jamison & Powers, P.C., Englewood, Colo., 1995—. Office: Harris Karstaedt Jamison & Powers PC 383 Inverness Pkwy S Ste 400 Englewood CO 80112-5816

KARSTEN, PHILIP, air traffic control automation system designer; b. NYC, July 27, 1920; s. Morris and Gussie (Weinberg) K.; m. Dorothy Leibowitz, Oct. 11, 1942; 1 child, Gloria. BS, Stockton State Coll., 1975. Cert. air traffic controller. Supervisory air traffic control, air traffic control automation coord. CAA/FAA, N.Y.C., 1949-60; tech. program mgr. air traffic control automation Nat. Aviation Facilities Exptl. Ctr., FAA Tech. Ctr., Pomona, N.J., 1960-81; pres., air traffic control system automation cons. Karsten Assoc., Margate, N.J., 1984—; planner air traffic control automation-system test and evaluation. Lt. Col. USAF, 1942-45, 51-52. Mem. Air Traffic Control Assn. (hon., nat. councilor 1958-70, citation of merit l980), Air Force Assn. (chpt. pres.), AIAA (sr.). Home: 8097 Amherst Ave Margate City NJ 08402-1621

KARTHA, KUTTY KRISHNAN, plant pathologist; b. Shertallai, India, Aug. 9, 1941; married, 1972; 2 children. BSc, Saugar U., India, 1962; MSc, Jawaharal Nehru Agrl. U., India, 1965; PhD in Plant Pathology, India Agrl. Rsch. Inst., 1969. Fellow Nat. Inst. Agrl. Rsch., France, 1970-72; vis. scientist Prairie Regional Lab., Nat. Rsch. Coun., Saskatoon, Can., 1973-74; asst. rsch. officer Plant Biotechnology Inst., 1974-76, assoc. rsch. officer, 1976-81, head cell tech. sect., 1985-87; sr. rsch. officer Plant Biotech. Inst., Nat. Rsch. Coun., Saskatoon, 1981, group leader cereal biotech., 1985-93, acting rsch. dir., 1993-95, dir. gen., 1995—. Adj. prof. U. Sask., Saskatoon, 1987—; mem. Can. Agrl. Rsch. Coun., 1990-94. Editor Jour. Plant Physiology, 1987, Cyropreservation Plant Cells and Organs, 1985. Recipient George M. Darrow award Am. Soc. Hort. Sci., 1981, C.J. Bishop award Can. Soc. Hort. Sci., 1992, Excellence in Rsch. award Treasury Bd. Can., 1992, Commemorative medal for 125th anniversary of Confedn. Can., 1992, Queen Elizabeth II Golden Jubilee medal, 2002. Mem. Internat. Assn. Plant Tissue Culture (nat. corr. 1982-86), Can. Soc. Plant Physiologists, Can. Phytopathol. Soc. Achievements include research in plant biotechnology, cryopreservation of plant cells and organs, plant tissue culture. Office: Plant Biotech Inst 110 Gymnasium Pl Saskatoon SK Canada S7N OW9 E-mail: kutty.kartha@nrc-cnrc.ca.

KARTIGANER, JOSEPH, retired lawyer; b. Berlin, June 5, 1935; came to U.S., 1939; s. Harold and Lilly (Wolkowitz) K.; m. Audrey Gertsman Amdursky; children: Deborah Lynn, Alison Beth. AB, CCNY, 1955; LL.B., Columbia U., 1958. Bar: N.Y. 1960, Fla. 1978, D.C. 1979. Assoc. White & Case, N.Y.C., 1960-69, ptnr., 1969-88, Simpson Thacher & Bartlett, N.Y.C., 1988-99; ret., 1999. Lectr. law Columbia Law Sch., N.Y.C., 1973-80; vis. lectr. Sch. Law Yale U., 1997-2000; mem adv. com. N.Y. Estates, Powers and Trust Law-Surrogate's Ct. Procedure Act, 1997—. Mem.: Columbia Law Rev. Fellow Am. Bar Found., Am. Coll. Trust and Estate Counsel (regent 1978-84), Am. Coll. Tax Counsel, N.Y. State Bar Found.; mem. ABA (chmn. real property, probate and trust law sect. 1986-87, co-chair sect. standing com. on govt. submissions 1995—), N.Y. State Bar Assn., Assn. of Bar of City of N.Y. (chmn. com. on trusts, estates and surrogate's cts. 1990-92), Nat. Conf. Lawyers and Corp. Fiduciaries (co-chair 1991-93), Am. Law Inst., Internat. Acad. Estate and Trust Law (exec. coun. 1980-94, 98-2002), Scarsdale Golf Club (Hartsdale, N.Y.). Home: 812 5th Ave # 5B New York NY 10021-7253 Office: Simpson Thacher & Bartlett 425 Lexington Ave Fl 15 New York NY 10017-3954 E-mail: joekart@yahoo.com.

KARTTUNEN, FRANCES ESTHER, retired linguist, research scientist; b. Boston, Apr. 16, 1942; d. Eugene Joseph and Charlotte Hamblen (Gibbs) Ruley; m. Lauri Juhani Karttunen, Apr. 1965 (div. 1982); m. Alfred W. Crosby, May, 1983; children: Jaana Terhikki Karttunen-Lehner, Suvi Aika. AB, Harvard U., 1964; MA, Ind. U., 1968, PhD, 1970. NSF rsch. fellow Rand Corp., Santa Monica, Calif., 1967-68; rsch. assoc. U. Tex., Austin, 1968-78, sr. rsch. scientist, 1978-2000; program dir. for linguistics NSF, Washington, 1987-88. Vis. prof. linguistics Umeå (Sweden) U., 1999. Author: An Analytical Dictionary of Nahuatl, 1983, 2d edit., 1992, Between Worlds, 1994, The Other Islanders, 2002; contbr. articles and revs. to profl. publs. Assoc. Mexic-Arte Mus., Austin, 1992-98; bd. dirs. Estudios de Cultura Nahuatl, Mexico City, 1987—, Friends of Nantucket Atheneum, 2000-2002. Recipient awards NEH, 1977, 86, 88-89, 91-92, NSF, 1978-85; rsch. grantee Fulbright Commn., 1972, 85-86; Bicentennial prof. N.Am. studies Fulbright Commn., Helsinki, Finland, 1997-98; James Bradford Ames fellow, 2000-01. Mem. Soc. for Study of Indigenous Langs. of the Ams., Am. Soc. Ethnohistory, Hawaiian Hist. Soc., Nantucket Hist. Assn.

KARU, GILDA M(ALL), lawyer, federal agency administrator; b. Oceanport, N.J., Dec. 1, 1951; d. Harold and Ilvy (Meriloo) Karu; m. Frederick F. Foy, May 23, 1981. AB, Vassar Coll., 1974; JD, Ill. Inst. Tech., 1987. Bar: Ill. 1987, U.S. Dist. Ct. (no. dist.) Ill. 1987. Quality control reviewer Food and Nutrition Svc. USDA, Robbinsville, NJ, 1974-77, team leader, 1977-78, supr., 1978-81, sect. chief Food and Nutrition Svc. Chgo., 1991-2000, acting dir. field ops., 1998, acting dir. food stamp program, 1999, regional dir. civil rights/EEO for midwest region Food and Nutrition Svc., 2000—. Employer adviser Ctr. Rehab. and Tng. Disable Persons, Chgo., 1986—93; chief mgmt. negotiator collective bargaining agreement Nat. Treasury Employees Union, 1990; acting regional dir. Food Stamp program, 1999, 2000; chair. diversity adv. com. Chgo. Fed. Exec. Bd., 2001—, co-mediator shared neutrals ADR program, 2003—. Mem. Chgo. Vol. Legal Svcs., Friends Arlington Heights Meml. Libr.; vol. dep. voter registration officer Cook County, Ill.; v.p. 1st Estonian Evang. Luth. Ch., Chgo., treas., 1994—; bd. dirs., legal counsel, regional dir. N. Ctrl. Estonian Am. Nat. Coun., N.Y.C. Recipient cert. of recognition, William A. Jump Meml. Found., 1987, Arthur S. Flemming award, Washington Downtown Jaycees, 1987, Ill. Dem. Ethnic Heritage award, 1989, cert. of appreciation, Assn. Persons with Disabilities Agr., 1992. Mem.: LWV (bd. dirs. 1992—, v.p. chpt. 2000—, newsletter editor), AAUW, ABA, United Coun. Welfare Fraud, Baltic Bar Assn., Chgo. Bar Assn., Ill. Bar Assn., Mensa, Chgo. Area Seven Sisters Coll. Consortium (sec. 1995—), Vassar Club (chpt. treas. 1988—90, v.p. 1990—91, coord. pub. rels. 1991—2000). Avocations: photography, reading, travel, crafts. Office: USDA Food and Nutrition Svc 77 W Jackson Blvd Fl 20 Chicago IL 60604-3591

KARWA, GATTU LAL, urologist; b. Karimnagar, India, Aug. 19, 1935; came to U.S., 1974; s. Devikishan and Kamala Bai Karwa; widowed; children: Neeta, Manoj, Sangeeta. MD, Osmania Med. Coll., Hyderabad, India, 1957. Intern Osmania Gen. Hosp., Hyderabad, 1957-58; resident in urology Boston City Hosp., 1968-71; resident in surgery Lancaster (Eng.) Royal Infirmary, 1959-60, Montefiore Hosp., Pitts., 1966-67, Columbia (S.C.) Hosp., 1967-68; assoc. prof. urology Einstein Med. Sch., Bronx, N.Y.; attending urologist Montefiore Hosp., Bronx. Fellow Royal Coll. Surgeons Edinburgh, Royal Coll. Surgeons Urology Can., Am. Coll. Surgeons. Office: 3130 Grand Concourse Ste 1S Bronx NY 10458 Fax: 718-295-8004.

KARWAN, MARK HENRY, engineering educator, dean; b. Cleve., Nov. 16, 1951; B in Engring. Scis. with full honors, MS in Engring., Johns Hopkins U., 1974; PhD, Ga. Inst. Tech., 1976. From asst. prof. to assoc. prof. dept. indsl. engring. Univ. at Buffalo, SUNY, 1976-86, prof. dept. indsl. engring., 1986—, prof., chair dept. indsl. engring., 1987-92, prof., assoc. dean grad. edn. Sch. Engring. & Applied Scis., 1992-94, prof., acting dean Sch. Engring. & Applied Scis., 1994-95, dean Sch. Engring. & Applied Scis., 1996—. Chair U. at Buffalo Bus. Alliance, 1998-2001; cons. Mgmt. Adv. Svcs., Inc., Columbia, Md., 1974, Health Care Plan, Inc., Buffalo, 1984-87, Praxair, Inc., Tonawanda, N.Y., 1987—; faculty advisor student chpt. Inst. Indsl. Engrs. 849, 1977-83; proposal reviewer NSF-Sys. Theory and Ops. Rsch., NSF-Applied Math.; cluster chmn. ORSA/TIMS joint nat. meeting, 1986, chmn. numerous sessions, 1977—; mem. grad. sch. fellowship com. SUNY, Buffalo, 1980-82, grad. sch. exec. com., 1982-85, 92-94, grad. sch. polyc rev. com., 1984-91, chmn., 1984-88, honors coun., 1992-98, mem. Sch. Engring. and Applied Scis. divisional com. of grad. sch., 1976-79, Sch. Engring. and Applied Scis. acad. programs com., 1981-87, chmn. Sch. Engring. and Applied Scis. acad. programs com., 1982-85, 89-90, 93-95, dir. Ctr. for Indsl. Effectiveness, 1993-98, undergrad. affairs com., 1976-78, grad. affairs com., 1979-87, dir. grad. studies, 1982-87. Assoc. editor: Naval Research Logistics, 1987—, IIE Transactions, 1991-93; co-editor spl. issue Naval Rsch. Logistics, 1988; mem. editl. adv. bd. Computers & Ops. Rsch., 1984—; contbr. refereed papers to profl. jours. including Annals of Discrete Math., European Jour. Operational Rsch., IEEE Transactions on Automatic Control, Jour. Mechanics Design, Mgmt. Sci., Math. Programming, Networks, Ops. Rsch., Water Resources Rsch.; contbr. over 70 articles to profl. publs.; patentee two-phase method for real time process control. Pres.'s fellow Ga. Tech. U., 1974-75. Mem. Alpha Pi Mu, Omega Rho (regional dir. N.E. U.S. chpt. 1982-84). Office: Univ at Buffalo Sch Engring And Appld Scis Buffalo NY 14260-1900 E-mail: mkarwan@buffalo.edu.

KARWECKI, MARGARET, nurse practitioner, consultant; b. Elblag, Poland, Apr. 5, 1966; d. Stefan and Teresa Karwecki; m. John Carl Perrotta, Aug. 22, 1992. MSN, UCLA, 1999. Clin. III staff nurse Centinela Hosp., Inglewood, Calif., 1988—99, nurse practitioner electrophysiology, 1999—. Cons. Heartcare, L.A., 1999—; rsch. coord. various lipid studies. Author: (newsletter) Lipid Clinic Update; author: (contbg.) Mosby's Handbook of Patient Teaching, 3d edit. Mem.: AACN, Preventive Cardiovasc. Nurses Assn., Am. Heart Assn., Nat. Wildlife Fedn. Avocations: reading, travel, cycling, piano, music. Personal E-mail: mrijohn@aol.com.

KARWIC, RICHARD A. management consultant, educator; b. Hartford, Conn., Dec. 16, 1946; m. Kathleen A. Bassell. BS in Accounting, Ctrl. Conn. State U., 1971; MBA, Western New England Coll., 1995. Staff acct. Soc. for Savings, Hartford, Conn., 1971-72; contr. The Stanley Works, New Britain, Conn., 1972-80; staff cons. Emhart Corp., Farmington, Conn., 1980—84; divsn. contr., CFO EIS Brake Parts, Berlin, Conn., 1984-90; v.p., dir. Linatex Corp. of Am., Stafford Springs, Conn., 1990—93; priv. practice Wethersfield, Conn., 1993—95; v.p. Technicarbon Co. L.P., Springfield, Mass., 1996-97; v.p. mergers and acquisitions Valufinder Group Inc., 1998—99; pvt. practice, 2000—. Prof. Western New England Coll., Springfield, Mass., 1996-98; seminar leader, Ctr. Profl. Edn., 1999—. Mem. Berlin (Conn.) C. of C., dir. 1984-90, treas. 1988-90. Mem. Inst. Mgmt. Accts. Home: 100 Lantern Ln Wethersfield CT 06109-4047 Office: Indepco Inc 100 Lantern Ln Wethersfield CT 06109-4047

KASAKOVE, SUSAN, interior designer; b. Newark, N.J., Nov. 11, 1938; BFA, U. Buffalo, 1958, Hunter Coll., 1960; postgrad., N.Y. Sch. of Interior Design, 1960-64, New Sch. for Social Rsch., 1967-68, Pratt Inst., 1968-69. Asst. interior designer Rodgers Assocs., N.Y.C., 1964-66; interior designer Walter Dorwin Teague Assocs., N.Y.C., 1966-70; sr. interior designer N.Y. State Facilities Devel. Corp., N.Y.C., 1970-95; Dormitory Authority for the State of N.Y., 1995—. Reading tutor Vols. for Children's Svcs., N.Y.C., 1976-82; chair Friends of White Plains (N.Y.) Symphony, 1981-83, Met. Mus. Art; vol. dept. Asian Dept. Work Endod, 1995, vol. guide edn. dept., 1978—; Rep. treas. 11th Ward, Yonkers, N.Y., 1979-81. Recipient Outstanding Svc. to Sch. award Rockland County (N.Y.) Lions Club, 1955. Mem. Environ. Design Rsch. Assn. Avocations: photography, history of art and architecture, golf, swimming. Home: 793 Palmer Rd Apt 3F Bronxville NY 10708-3337 Office: 1 Penn Plz Fl 52 New York NY 10119-5299

KASAMA, HIDETO PETER, international business and investment advisor; b. Tokyo, Nov. 21, 1946; came to U.S., 1969; s. Toshiyoshi and Hamako (Yoshioka) K.; m. Evelyn P. Cruz (div. Apr. 1990); children: Jennifer, Nicole, Leona; m. Heidi W. Snare, June 29, 1991; 1 child, Serena. BABA, Seattle U., 1971, MBA, 1973. CPA. Mgmt. trainee Bank of Am., Seattle, 1972-74; audit supr. Ernst & Young, Seattle, 1974-79; pres. KASPAC Corp., Seattle, 1979-89; mng. ptnr. Kasama & Co., Seattle, 1980-98; shareholder AZ & Co., Seattle, 2000; pres. Kasama Internat., Edmonds, Wash., 2000—. Contbr. articles to newspapers and mags. Mem. AICPA, Wash. Soc. CPA's, Wash. Assn. Realtors, Columbia Tower Club (founder). Avocations: golf, classical guitar, gardening. Office: 9792 Edmonds Way # 415 Edmonds WA 98135 E-mail: peterkasama@hotmail.com.

KASAMI, TADAO, information science educator; b. Kobe, Hyogo, Japan, Apr. 12, 1930; m. Fumiko Okada, May 9, 1964; children: Yuuko, Ryuichi. B in Engring., Osaka (Japan) U., 1958, M in Engring., 1960, D in Engring., 1963. Assoc. prof. engring. Osaka (Japan) U., 1963-66, prof. engring. sci., 1966-94, dean engring. sci., 1990-92, prof. emeritus, 1994—; prof., Grad. Sch. Info. Sci. Nara (Japan) Inst. Sci. and Tech., 1992-98, dean, Grad. Sch. Info. Sci., 1992-94, dir. libr., 1994-98, prof. emeritus, 1998—; prof. Hiroshima (Japan) City U. Sch. Info. Sci., 1998—2003, prof. emeritus, 2003—. Adj. prof. U. Hawaii Grad. Sch., Honolulu, 1992—97; guest prof. Nara Inst. Sci. and Tech., 2003—. Author: Coding Theory, 1978, Discrete Structure II, 1983, Formal Language Theory, 1988, Introduction to Information and Coding Theory, 1989, Trellises and Trellis-based Decoding Algorithms for Linear Block Codes, 1998. Fellow IEEE (life), Inst. Electronics, Info. and Comm. Engrs. (hon., Achievement award 1987, Disting. Svc. award 2001); mem. Soc. Info. and Its Applications (hon., pres. 1993), IEEE Info. Theory Soc. (Claude E. Shannon award 1999). Office: Nara Inst Sci and Tech Ikoma Takayama-cho 8916-5 Nara 630-0101 Japan Personal E-mail: kasami@is.aist-nara.ac.jp.

KASANIN, MARK OWEN, lawyer; b. Boston, June 28, 1929; s. Jacob Sergei and Elizabeth Owen (Knight) K.; m. Anne Camilla Wimbish, Dec. 18, 1960; children: Marc S., James W. BA, Stanford U., 1951; LL.B., Yale U., 1954. Bar: Calif. Assoc. Brigham McCutchen, San Francisco, 1957-62, 63-67; ptnr. McCutchen, Doyle, Brown & Enersen, 1967—. Mem. planning commn. City of Belvedere, Calif., 1974-76; chair tech. adv. com. San Francisco Bay Area Water Transit Authority, 2001-. Served with USNR, 1955-57 Named among Best Lawyers in Am., 2001—02. Fellow Am. Coll. Trial Lawyers; mem. Maritime Law Assn. U.S. (exec. com. 1984-87), Product Liability Adv. Coun. Found. (trustee 1990—), Jud. Conf. U.S. (mem. fed. civil rules adv. com. 1992-2002). Home: PO Box 698 Belvedere Tiburon CA 94920-0698 Office: Bingham McCutchen 3 Embarcadero Ctr San Francisco CA 94111-4003 Fax: 415-393-2286.

KASARJIAN, LEVON, JR., lawyer; b. Boston, Nov. 27, 1937; s. Levon and Olga Mary (Moses) K.; m. Nancy Elizabeth Sexton, Oct. 12, 1963; children: David, Laurie, Kevin. AB, Harvard Coll., 1959; JD, Boston U., 1962. Bar: Mass. 1962, N.Y. 1974. Trial atty. tax div. U.S. Dept. Justice, Washington, 1963-68; gen. counsel, sec. EDP Resources, Inc., White Plains, N.Y., 1968-74; v.p., corp. counsel Greyhound Capital Corp., Phoenix, 1975-86; sr. v.p., corp. counsel Greyhound Leasing & Fin. Corp., Phoenix, 1986; sr. v.p., corp. counsel Bell Atlantic Systems Leasing Internat., Inc., Phoenix, 1986—. Exec. v.p. Ariz. Assn. for Children and Adults with Learning Disabilities, Phoenix, 1979-82; pres. Valley of the Sun Kiwanis, Phoenix, 1983-84. With U.S. Army, 1962. Recipient Sustained Superior Performance award Tax div. Dept. Justice, Washington, 1967. Methodist. Office: Bell Atlantic Systems Leasing Internat Inc 11811 N Tatum Blvd Phoenix AZ 85028-1614

KASCHAK, DAVID JAMES, accountant; b. South Weymouth, Mass., Nov. 8, 1960; s. Thomas John and Joan Marie (Holahan) K. Student, Rider U., 1979-81; BS in Acctg., Pa. State U., 1983. CPA, N.J. Prin. auditor Office of State Auditor, Trenton, N.J., 1984—. Baseball coach Lawrence Twp. (N.J.) Babe Ruth, 1992-94. Mem. AICPA, Assn. Govt. Accts. (officer 1995-99, scholar 1982, Chpt. Svc. award 1997, exec. bd. 1998—, v.p. 2000-03, pres. 2003—), Alpha Chi Rho (nat. treas. 1989-95). Avocations: jogging, softball, golf, ice hockey, collectibles. Home: 17 Rail Rd Pl Pennington NJ 08534

KASDAN, LAWRENCE EDWARD, film director, screenwriter; b. Miami Beach, Fla., Jan. 14, 1949; s. Clarence Norman and Sylvia Sarah (Landau) K.; m. Meg Goldman, Nov. 28, 1971; children: Jacob, Jonathan. BA, U. Mich., 1970, MA in Edn., 1972. Copywriter W.B. Doner & Co. (Advt.), Detroit, 1972-75, Doyle, Dane Bernbach, Los Angeles, 1975-77; freelance screenwriter, 1977-80; motion picture dir., screenwriter, 1980—. Co-screenwriter: The Empire Strikes Back, 1980, Return of the Jedi, 1982; screenwriter: Continental Divide, 1981, Raiders of the Lost Ark, 1981, writer, dir.: Body Heat, 1981, Grand Canyon, 1992; co-screenwriter, dir., exec. prodr.: The Big Chill, 1983; co-screenwriter, dir., prodr.: Silverado, 1985, The Accidental Tourist, 1988; prodr. Cross My Heart, 1987; dir. I Love You to Death, 1989; co-screenwriter, dir. Wyatt Earp, 1994; screenwriter, co-prodr. The Bodyguard, 1992; exec. prodr. Jumpin at the Boneyard, 1992; dir. French Kiss, 1995, Mumford, 1999. Recipient Clio awards for advt., Writers Guild Am. award for the Big Chill, 1983, New York Film Critics Circle award for The Accidental Tourist, 1988; nominated 4 Acad. Awards. Mem. Writers Guild Am. West, Dirs. Guild Am. West.

KASE-JANOWSKI, KRISTEN MARIAN, healthcare educator; b. Cleve., Jan. 23, 1978; d. Fredrick Alan and Florence Ann Janowski. BA, Ohio State U., 2000; MPA, Ga. State U., 2001. Peer counselor Children's Resource Ctr., Bowling Green, Ohio, 1997—98; tchr. Young Friends of Brecksville, Ohio, 1998—99; adminstr. Inman Pk. Coop. Preschool, Atlanta, 2000—01; cmty. dir. March of Dimes, Cleve., 2002—; educator pub. health Summit County Combined Gen. Health Dist., Stow, Ohio. Mem.: ASPA, Alpha Lambda Delta, Phi Eta Sigma, Kappa Delta. Democrat. Avocations: dancing, choreography, travel, reading. Office: Summit County Combined Gen Health Dist 1100 Graham Road Cir Stow OH 44125 Personal E-mail: krisja23@hotmail.com.

KASER, DAVID, retired librarian, educator, consultant; b. Mishawaka, Ind., Mar. 12, 1924; s. Arthur Leroy and Loah (Steele) K.; m. Jane Jewell, Sept. 1, 1950; children: John Andrew, Kathleen Jewell. AB, Houghton Coll., 1949; MA, U. Notre Dame, 1950; A.M. in L.S, U. Mich., 1952, PhD, 1956. Serials librarian, instr. library sci. Ball State U., 1952-54; asst. in exchanges U. Mich. Library, 1954-56; chief acquisitions Washington U. Libraries, St. Louis, 1956-59, asst. dir., 1959-60; prof. library sci. Peabody Coll. and dir. libraries Vanderbilt U., 1960-68; dir. libraries Cornell U., 1968-73; prof. library sci. Ind. U., Bloomington, 1973-86, Disting. prof., 1986-91, Disting. prof. emeritus, 1991—; pres. Kaser Assocs., Inc., libr. bldg. cons., Bloomington, 1988-95. Fgn. assignments in Ireland, 1960, Korea, 1965, 81, 93, Laos, 1966, Taiwan, 1967, 79, 81, 88, 89, 93, S.E. Asia, 1969, Eng., 1971, France, 1972, Saudi Arabia, 1975-76, 83, Nigeria, 1978, Indonesia, 1978, Malaysia, 1992. Author: Messrs. Carey & Lea of Philadelphia, 1957, Washington University Manuscripts, 1958, Cost Book of Carey & Lea, 1825-1838, 1963, Joseph Charless, Printer in the Western Country, 1963, Books in America's Past, 1966, Book Pirating in Taiwan, 1969, Library Development in Eight Asian Countries, 1969, Book for a Sixpence, 1980, Books and Libraries in Camp and Battle, 1984, The Evolution of the American Academic Library Building, 1997, Just Lucky I Guess, 2000; editor Mo. Libr. Assn. Quar., 1958-60, Coll. and Rsch. Librs., 1963-69. Guggenheim fellow, 1967 Mem. ALA (councilor 1965-69, 75-79), Assn. Coll. and Research Libraries (pres. 1968-69), Assn. Southeastern Research Libraries (chmn. 1966-68), Tenn. Library Assn. (pres. 1968-69), Am. Antiquarian Soc., Phi Beta Kappa, Beta Phi Mu (internat. pres. 1975)

KASER, MICHAEL CHARLES, economist, educator; b. London, May 2, 1926; s. Charles Joseph and Mabel Lucina Ella (Blunden) Kaser; m. Elizabeth Anne Mary Piggford, 1954; children: Gregory, Matthew, Benet, Thomas, Lucy. BA, Cambridge (Eng.) U., 1946; MA, Oxford (Eng.) U., 1960, DLitt, 1993; DSocSc (hon.), Birmingham (Eng.) U., 1994. Economist Brit. Ministry of Works, 1946-47, Fgn. Office, 1947-51, UN Econ. Commn. Europe, 1951-63; lectr. U. Oxford, 1963-72, reader econ., 1972-93, dir. Inst. Russian, Soviet and East European Studies, 1988-93; sr. rsch. fellow Inst. for German Studies Birmingham U., 1994—, hon. prof., 1994—. Prof. econs. U. Mich., 1966; professorial fellow St. Anthony's Coll., emeritus fellow, 1993—; prin. Charlemagne Inst., Edingburgh, Scotland, 1993—94; sr. rsch. assoc. Inst. Slavonic Studies Oxford U., 1997—. Author: 7 books; editor: 14 books; contbr. articles to profl. jours., chapters to books. Trustee Found. King George VI and Queen Elizabeth, past chair acad. com. Decorated knight's cross Polish Order of Merit, Order of Naum Frashëri, Albania. Mem.: Internat. Econ. Assn. (gen. editor), European Econ. Assn. (past chair com. East European affairs), Royal Inst. Internat. Affairs (past coun., chmn. adv. bd. caucuses and ctrl. Asia), Royal Econ. Soc. (past coun.), Brit. Assn. Former UN Civil Servants, Kesten Inst. (past chmn.), Brit. Assn. Soviet Slavonic and Ea. European Studies (past pres.), Albania Soc. Britain (past pres.), Order of St. Gregory (papal knighthood 1990). Roman Catholic. Home and Office: 31 Capel Close Oxford OX2 7LA England

KASH, DON ELDON, political science educator; b. Macedonia, Iowa, May 29, 1934; s. Albert W. and Blanche Opal (Smith) K.; m. Elizabeth Gunn; children: Kelli Denise, Jeffrey Paul. BA, U. Iowa, 1959, MA, 1960, PhD, 1963. Instr. Tex. Tech. U., 1960-61; asst. prof. Ariz. State U., 1963-65, U. Mo., Kansas City, 1965-66; assoc. prof. Purdue U., West Lafayette, Ind., 1966-70; prof. polit. sci. U. Okla., Norman, 1970-91, George Lynn Cross rsch. prof. polit. sci., 1975-91, dir. Sci. and Pub. Policy Program, 1970-78; John T. Hazel Sr. and Ruth D. Hazel chair in pub. policy George Mason U., Fairfax, Va., 1991—. Vis. assoc. prof. Ind. U., 1969-70; chief conservation div. U.S. Geol. Survey, 1978-81; mem. Assembly Engring., Marine Bd. NRC; prof. Tsinghua U., Beijing. Author: The Politics of Space Cooperation, 1967, Energy Under the Oceans: A Technology Assessment of Outer Continental Shelf Oil and Gas Operations, 1973, North Sea Oil and Gas: Implication for Future U.S. Development, 1973, Energy Alternatives: A Comparative Analysis, 1975, Our Energy Future, 1976, U.S. Energy Policy: Crisis and Complacency, 1983, Perpetual Innovation: The New World of Competition, 1989, The Complexity Challenge: Technological Innovation in the 21st Century, 1999; contbr. articles to profl. jours. With AUS, 1952-54. Recipient Disting. Alumni award U. Iowa, 1988. Fellow AAAS. Office: George Mason U Sch Public Policy 4400 University Dr Fairfax VA 22030-4444 E-mail: dkash@gmu.edu.

KASHA, KENNETH JOHN, agriculturist, educator; b. Lacombe, Alta., Can., May 6, 1933; s. John Clarence and Mary Jennette (Proudfoot) K.; m. Marion Eileen Lenz, Aug. 14, 1958, children: Lorelei Marion, David John. BSc in Agr., U. Alta., Edmonton, 1957, MSc, 1958; PhD, U. Minn., 1962; LLD (hon.), U. Calgary, Alta., 1986. Rsch. asst. U. Minn., Mpls., 1958-61, fellow rsch.

agronomy and plant genetics, 1961-62; rsch. scientist forages Agr. Can. Rsch. Sta., Ottawa, Ont., 1962-66; asst. prof. crop sci. dept. U. Guelph, Ont., 1966-69, assoc. prof. crop sci. dept., 1969-74, prof. crop sci. dept., 1974-98—, Univ. prof. emeritus, 1998—. Cons. Ciba Geigy Seeds Ltd., Ailsa Craig, Ont., 1974-81, Monsanto Co., St. Louis, 1997-2002; organizing chair and editor 1st Internat. Symposium on Haploids in Plants, Guelph, 1974; dir. Plant Biotech Centre, Guelph Waterloo Biotech, 1984-87; program chmn. XVI Internat. Congress Genetics, Toronto, 1988. Editor: Haploids in Higher Plants, 1974, Plant Cell Culture in Agriculture and Forestry, 1980, Mutation, In Vitro and Molecular Techniques for Environmentally Sustainable Crop Improvement, 2002, Doubled Haploid Production in Crop Plants, A Manual, 2003; contbr. articles to profl. jours.; mem. numerous jour. editl. bds. Decorated officer Order of Can., 1994; recipient Agrl. Inst. Can. Grindley medal, 1970; Can. Award of Excellence EC Manning Found., 1983, Disting. Rsch. award Ont. Agr. Coll. Alumni, 1984, Outstanding Achievement award U. Minn., 1999, Queen Elizabeth Golden Jubilee medal, 2002. Fellow Royal Soc. Can. (fellow selection com., life scis. 2000-02); mem. Sigma Xi (Disting. Researcher award Guelph chpt. 1974), Genetics Soc. Can. (pres. 1976-77, sec. 1966 69, award of Excellence 1994), Internat. Assn. Plant Tissue Culture (nat. corr. 1990-94), Can. Soc. Plant Molecular Biology (founding mem.), Genetics Soc. Am., Am. Soc. Agronomy, Sigma Xi. Home: 28 Halesmanor Ct Guelph ON Canada N1G 4E2 Office: U Guelph Dept Plant Agr Guelph ON Canada N1G 2W1 E-mail: KKasha@uoguelph.ca.

KASHANI, HAMID REZA, lawyer, computer consultant; b. Tehran, Iran, May 1, 1955; came to U.S., 1976; s. Javad K. BSEE with highest distinction, Purdue U., 1978, MSEE, 1979; JD, Ind. U., 1986. Bar: Ind. 1986, U.S. Dist. Ct. (so. and no. dists.) 1986, U.S. Ct. Appeals (7th cir.) 1986, U.S. Supreme Ct. 1994, U.S. Ct. Appeals (9th cir.) 1996. Rsch. asst. Purdue U., West Lafayette, Ind., 1978-79, 80-81; engr. Cummins Engine Co., Columbus, Ind., 1981-82; assoc. faculty Ind. U.-Purdue U., Indpls., 1983-84; sr. software engr. Engineered System Devel., Indpls., 1985-87; computer cons. Hamid R. Kashani, Indpls., 1986—; pvt. practice law Indpls., 1986—; cons. Good Techs., Indpls., 1987-90; pres. Virtual Media Techs., Inc., 1998—. Cons. Prism Imaging, Denver, 1990-93, Ind. Bar Assn., 1989-95. Editor: Computer Law Desktop Guide, 1995. Mem., bd. dirs. ACLU, 1997—, Ind. Civil Liberties Union, Indpls., 1987—, mem. legis. com., 1987—, mem. screening com., 1985—, del., 1989, 91, 93, 95, 97, 99, 2001, acting v.p. fundraising, 1995-96, v.p. edn., 1996—, chair long-range planning com., 1991-92, 96—, chmn. nominating com., 1997—, pres., 1999—; bd. dirs. ACLU, 1997—. Fellow Ind. U. Sch. Law, 1984; recipient Cert. of Appreciation Ind. Correctional Assn., 1988; named Cooperating Atty. of Yr. Ind. Civil Liberties Union, 1990, 95, 98. Mem. ABA (vice chmn. YLD computer law com. 1990-91, chmn. computer law exec. com. 1991-93, litigation exec. com. 1987-89, 90-93, YLD liaison standing com. on jud. selection, tenure and compensation 1992-94, 95-96, sci. and tech. co-chair first amendment rights in the digital age com. 1997—, vice chair com. on opportunities for minorities and women 1997-99, YLD liaison to ABA tech. coun. 1992-93, vice chmn. nat. info. infrastructure com. sect. sci. and tech. 1993-97, chair privacy info. and civil liberties ABA sect. of individual rights and responsibilities 1998-2002, co-chair technology com., mem. standing com. on jud. selection, tenure and compensation 1995-96, chair privacy info. and civil liberties sect. of individual rights and responsibilities 1998-2002), IEEE (Outstanding Contbns. award 1983), Indpls. Bar Assn. (chmn. articles and bylaws coms. 1994-95), Ind. State Bar Assn. (vice chair computer comms. com. 1995-98, chair computer comms. com. 1998—, chair computer comm. com. 1998—), Eta Kappa Nu, Tau Beta Pi, Phi Kappa Phi, Phi Eta Sigma. Office: 445 N Pennsylvania St Ste 600 Indianapolis IN 46204-1818 E-mail: hkashani@kashanilaw.com.

KASHANI-SABET, MOHAMMED, physician; Diplomate Dermatology Am. Bd. Dermatology. Dir. Melanoma Ctr., Zackheim endowed chair in cutaneous oncology U. Calif., San Francisco, 1998—. Mem. editl. bd. Cancer Gene Therapy, San Diego. Recipient Health Caring award, William S. Graham Found., 2000. Mem.: AAAS. Office: Melanoma Ctr Univ Calif San Francisco Cancer Ctr 1600 Divisadero St Box 1706 San Francisco CA 94115 Office Fax: 415-353-9505.

KASHDIN, GLADYS SHAFRAN, painter, educator; b. Dec. 15, 1921; d. Edward M. and Miriam P. Shafran; m. Manville E. Kashdin, Oct. 11, 1942 (dec.). BA magna cum laude, U. Miami, 1960; MA, Fla. State U., 1962, PhD, 1965. Photographer, N.Y.C. and Fla., 1938-60; tchr. art Fla. and Ga., 1956-63; from asst. prof. humanities to assoc. prof. to prof. U. South Fla., Tampa, 1965-87, prof. emerita, 1987—. Lectr., adv. bd. Hillsborough County Mus., 1975—84. Exhibitions include 68 one-woman shows, 55 group exhbns., The Everglades, 1972—75, Aspects of the River, 1975—80, Processes of Time, 1981—91, Retrospective, 1941—96, Tampa Mus. Art, 1996, Appleton Mus. Art, Ocala, 1999, 2001—02, Mus. Sci. and Industry, Tampa, 2003, Represented in permanent collections, Taiwan, China, Columbus Mus. Arts, LeMoyne Art Found., Tampa Internat. Airport, Tampa Mus. Art, Appleton Mus. Art, Ocala, Mus. Sci. and Industry, Tampa, Miss. Mus. Art, Jackson, Jan Kaminis Platt Libr., Tampa. Mem. U.S. Fla. Status of Women Com., 1971-76, chmn., 1975-76. Recipient Women Helping Women in Art award Soroptomist Internat., 1979, Citizens Hon. award Hillsborough Bd. County Commrs., 1984, Mortar Bd. award for tchg. excellence, 1986, Recognition award for lifetime achievement in arts and scis. So. Acad. Letters, Arts and Scis., 2002. Mem. AAUW (1st v.p. Tampa br. 1971-72), Phi Kappa Phi (chpt.-pres. 1981-83, artist/scholar award 1987). Home: 441 Biltmore Ave Temple Terrace FL 33617-7207

KASHEF, ALI EBRAHIM, industrial technology educator; b. Tehran, June 28, 1957; came to U.S., 1976, naturalized, 1986. s. Iraj Ebrahimi and Kokab (Amini) K.; m. Farah L. Kashef, July 17, 1990; children: Omeed Ebrahimi, Raud Ebrahimi. BS, Lincoln U., Jefferson City, Mo., 1980; MS in Indsl. Mgmt., Ctrl. Mo. State U., Warrensburg, 1981; PhD in Vocat. Edn. Studies, So. Ill. U., 1990. Nuc. power plant engr. Sys. Coordination Inc., Fulton, Mo., 1981—84; instr. Ea. Ill. U., Charleston, 1984—85; program dir. W.Va. State Coll., Institute, 1985—88; asst. prof. Montclair State U., Upper Montclair, NJ, 1988—92; asst. prof. dept. indsl. tech. U. No. Iowa, Cedar Falls, 1992—96, assoc. prof. dept. indsl. tech., 1996—2001, prof., 2001—, coop. edn. coord., 2001—, tech. mgmt. coord., 2003—. Acad. specialist Montclair State Coll., 1990-91; cons. Charleston (W.Va.) Job Corps Ctr., 1987-88. Contbr. articles to nat. and internat. profl. jours. UN devel. program grantee, 1994. UN Devel. Programme grantee, 1994. Avocations: soccer, volleyball, travel. Office: U No Iowa Dept Indsl Tech Cedar Falls IA 50614-0001 E-mail: kashef@uni.edu.

KASHEM, M. ABUL, medical researcher; b. Dhaka, Bangladesh, Jan. 10, 1962; s. M. Wali Ullah and Sufia Begum; m. Sarmina Hassan; children: Sakeen, Abyaad. B Medicine and Surgery, U. Dhaka, 1985; PhD, Kobe (Japan) U., 1996. Clin. and rsch. fellow Kobe (Japan) U. Sch. Medicine, 1991—96; postdoctoral rsch. fellow U. Louisville, 1997—99; rsch. assoc. Temple U., Phila., 1999—. Mem. sci. adv. bd. CardioClasp Inc., Pine Brook, NJ, 2000—. Pres. Kansai Bangladesh Students Assn., Kobe, 1992—96, Kobe-Dhaka Friendship Hosp., Dhaka, 1996—. Recipient Best Trainee Young Investigator award, Mid-Western Soc. of Am. Fedn. Med. Rsch., 1999; grantee, 3rd Heart Failure Soc. Meeting, 1999, 2001; scholar, Ministry of Edn., Govt. Bangladesh, 1972—76, 1976—98, 1978—84, Monbusho, Edn. Ministry of Japan, 1991—96. Fellow: Am. Coll. Angiology; mem.: Am. Soc. Artificial Internal Organs, Am. Coll. Internat. Physicians, Bangladesh Med. and Dental Coun., Japanese Soc. Artificial Organ Transplantation, Japanese Soc. Cardiovasc. Surgery, Heart Failure Soc. Am., Coun. Thoracic and Cardiovasc. Surgery, Am. Heart Assn. (Trainee Young Investigator award and stipend 1998), Internat. Soc. Cardiovasc. Surgery, Internat. Soc. Heart and Lung Transplantation. Avocations: travel, swimming, tennis. Home: 4407 Waterperry Ct Mount Laurel NJ 08054 Office: Temple U 3420 N Broad St MRB Rm 800A Philadelphia PA 19140 Home Fax: 856-914-1545; Office Fax: 215-707-5737. Personal E-mail: kashem1@comcast.net. E-mail: mkashem@temple.edu.

KASHGARIAN, MICHAEL, pathologist, physician; b. N.Y.C., Sept. 20, 1933; s. Toros and Arax (Almasian) K.; m. Jean Gaylor Caldwell, July 2, 1960; children: Michaele, Thea. AB, N.Y. U., 1954; MD, Yale U., 1958. Diplomate Am. Bd. Pathology. Intern Barnes Hosp., St. Louis, 1958-59; asst. in medicine Washington U., St. Louis, 1958-59; asst. resident in pathology Yale New Haven Med. Center, 1959-61, resident in pathology, 1962-63; research fellow in renal physiology (U. Goettingen), Germany, 1961-62; practice medicine specializing in pathology New Haven, 1962—. Instr. Yale U., 1962-64, asst. prof., 1964-67, asso. prof., 1967-74, prof., 1974—, vice chmn. dept., 1976-89, chmn., 1990— assoc. pathologist Yale New Haven Hosp., 1964-66, asst. attending pathologist, 1966-69, attending pathologist, 1969—, pres. med. staff, 1983-84; cons. in pathology, 1962—. Author: (with J.P. Hayslett, B.H. Spargo) Renal Disease, 1974, (with G.N. Burrow) The Endocrine Glands; editor: Yearbook of Nephrology, Yale Medicine, Current Opinion in Nephrology; mem. editorial bd. Nephron, 1970—, Am. Jour. Pathology, 1975—, Am. Jour. Kidney Diseases; contbr. articles to med. jours. Chmn. ednl. adv. council North Haven Bd. Edn., 1971; chmn. Christian edn. com. Ch. of Christ, Yale, 1970; bd. dirs. New Haven Symphony Orch.; v.p. Conn. Fund for Environ. 1st lt., M.C. USAR, 1954-65. USPHS fellow, 1963-65; research career devel. awardee, 1965-75 Fellow AAAS, Am. Soc. Clin. Pathologists, Coll. Am. Pathologists; mem. AMA, Am. Soc. Nephrology, Internat. Acad. Pathology, Conn. State Med. Soc. (chmn. com. on organ and tissue transfer), New Haven County Med. Assn. (pres. bd. govs.), Am. Soc. Investigative Pathologists, Conn. Soc. Pathologists (pres. 1975), Am. Heart Assn., Am. Physiol. Soc., Gesellshaft Nephrologie (hon.), Sigma Xi, Alpha Omega Alpha, Alpha Kappa Kappa. Home: 22 Old Orchard Rd North Haven CT 06473-3022 Office: 310 Cedar St PO Box 208023 New Haven CT 06520-8023

KASHIKHIN, VADIM, electrical engineer, researcher; b. St. Petersburg, Russia, Sept. 8, 1974; arrived in U.S., 1998; PhD in Electrophys., Tech. U. St. Petersburg, 2002. Rschr. Efremov Inst., St. Petersburg, Russia, 1995—98; guest scientist Fermi Nat. Accelerator Lab., Batavia, Ill., 1998—2001, engr., 2001—.

KASHIWA, RUSSELL H. communication executive; b. Honolulu, July 30, 1957; s. George K. and Grace K. Kashiwa; m. Lori K. Marumoto, May 17, 1997. BA in Radio, TV, U. Ariz., 1982. News asst. Sta. KOLD-TV, Tucson, 1982; news photographer Sta. KBIM-TV, Roswell, N.Mex., 1982-83; stringer Sta. KOAT-TV, Albuquerque, 1983-84; founder, producer RHK Prodns., Roswell, 1983-85; producer Honolulu, 1985—; news photographer, editor Sta. KITV-TV, Honolulu, 1988—. Cons. City of Roswell, 1984-85. Editor (newsletter) Tropic Topics, 1981; prodr. (video) Roswell A City That Works, 1984. Bd. dirs. Syracuse (NY) U. Jud. Bd., 1976-77; active Leadership Roswell, 1985; producer Chaves County United Way, Roswell; active Boy Scouts Am., 1969-75; tutor Haihaione Sch., 2002-03. Mem. Internat. TV Assn., Jaycees, (Honolulu chpt., Fall bd. 1981). Office: RHK Prodns PO Box 23032 Honolulu HI 96823-3032

KASHMERI, SARWAR AGHAJANI, internet publishing company executive; b. Nov. 2, 1942; came to U.S., 1964; s. Aghajani and Khursheed (Kazi) K.; m. Deborah Kellogg Ellis, May 23, 1981. BS, Parks Coll., St. Louis U., 1967; MS, St. Louis U., 1971. Faculty St. Louis U., 1967-72, pvt. practice info. systems mgmt., 1972-73; co-founder, dir. REJIS Commn., St. Louis, 1973-76; spl. cons. info. tech. dep. mayor criminal justice N.Y.C., 1976-78, Divsn. Criminal Justice Svcs., State of N.Y., 1978-82; founder, pres. Sabzevar, Inc., N.Y.C., 1982-85; founder, CEO Niche Systems Inc. Corp. Cons., N.Y.C., 1985-98; founder, pub., CEO ebizChronicle.com, 1999—. Mem. adv. coun. Am. Ditchely Found. Fellow Fgn. Policy Assn.; mem. Union League Club (N.Y.C.), Carlton Club (London), Pilgrims of the U.S., Econ. Club NY. Home: 1 Leonard St Mount Kisco NY 10549-2913 Office: ebizChronicle dot com Inc 274 Madison Ave New York NY 10016-0701 E-mail: skashmeri@aol.com., sarwar.kashmeri@ebizchronicle.com.

KASHTAN, CLIFFORD ELLIOT, physician; b. Detroit, Nov. 2, 1952; s. Harry Aaron and Doris Bernice (Rabinowitz) K.; m. Judith Finkelstein, Dec. 11, 1977; children: Aaron, Paula, Sarah. BS, U. Mich., 1974; MD, Wayne State U., 1978. Diplomate Am. Bd. Pediatrics; cert. in pediatrics and pediatric nephrology. Resident in pediatrics Boston City Hosp., 1978-81; staff pediatrician Columbia Point Health Ctr., Dorchester, Mass., 1981-83; fellow pediatric nephrology Mass. Gen. Hosp., Boston, 1983-84, U. Minn., Mpls., 1984-87, instr. in pediatrics, 1987-89, asst. prof. pediatrics, 1989-95, assoc. prof. pediatrics, 1995—2000, prof., 2000—. Contbr. articles to profl. jours., book chpts. Mem. Am. Pediat. Soc., Soc. for Pediatric Rsch., Internat. Soc. Nephrology, Internat. Pediatric Nephrology Assn., Am. Soc. Nephrology, Am. Soc. Pediatric nephrology. Office: U Minn Med Sch MMC 491 420 Delaware St SE Minneapolis MN 55455-0348

KASHYAP, VIKRAM S. vascular surgeon, military officer; b. Mysore, India, Jan. 25, 1966; s. Shantaram and Lakshmi Kashyap; m. Sangeeta Rao, June 18, 1995; children: Tejas, Anjali. BS, Pa. State U., 1984; MD, Jefferson Med. Coll., Phila., 1990. Cert. Surgery Am. Bd. of Surgery, 1999, Vascular Surgery Am. Bd. of Surgery, 2000. Resident gen. surgery Mass. Gen. Hosp., Boston, 1990—97; fellow vascular surgery UCLA, 1997—99; chief vascular surgery Wilford Hall Med. Ctr., San Antonio, 1999—. Presdl. med. support team mem. White Ho. Med. Unit, USAF. Author: (over 30 articles and book chpts.) various subjects in Vascular Surgery/atherosclerosis (ISET award, 2002). Lt col. USAF, 1986—2002. Recipient Cert. of Appreciation, Cert. of Commendation, White Ho. Med. Unit, 2000; fellow Surg. Rsch. Fellow, Nat. Heart Lung and Blood Inst., 1993—95; scholar Health Professions Scholarship, USAF, 1986. Fellow: ACS; mem.: The Am. Assn. for Vascular Surgery, Alpha Omega Alpha (v.p. 1989—90). Achievements include research in Novel Thrombolytic Regimen, gene therapy findings. Avocations: travel, tennis, skiing. Home: 2530 Slickrock Way San Antonio TX 78258 Office: Wilford Hall Med Ctr 2200 Bergquist Dr Lackland A F B TX 78236 Personal E-mail: viksang@yahoo.com.

KASI, LEELA PESHKAR, pharmaceutical chemist; b. Bombay, July 15, 1939; came to U.S., 1971; d. Subbaraman and Lakshmi (Shastri) Peshkar; m. Kalli R. Kasi, June l0, l97l. BS, U. Bombay, India, 1958; PhD, U. Marburg, W. Germany, 1968. Jr. chemist Khandelwal Labs., Bombay, India, 1958-59; trainee Farbwerke Hoechst, Frankfurt, W. Germany, 1960; teaching asst. U. of Marburg, W. Germany, 1967-68; sr. chemist Boehringer-Knoll Ltd., Bombay, India, 1969-71; mgr. quality control Health Care Ind., Michigan City, Ind., 1972-77, U. Tex.-M.D. Anderson Cancer Ctr., Houston, 1979-95, assoc. prof. nuclear medicine, faculty mem., 1990-95, dir. Exptl. Nuclear Medicine Lab., 1979-95; cons. Radiopharms. Devel., Houston, 1995—. Mem. grad. faculty U. Tex., 1984-90. Asst. editor Jour. Nuclear Medicine, 1984-89. Mem. AAAS, Am. Assn. Cancer Rsch., Soc. of Nuclear Medicine. Home and Office: 4710 Mcdermed Dr Houston TX 77035-3706 E-mail: lkasi@hal-pc.org.

KASICA, GEORGE RAYMOND, computer technician, consultant, emergency medical technician; b. Milw., Apr. 30, 1966; s. Raymond Stanley Kasica and Dorothy Marie Abraham; m. Rachel Budowle, Feb. 23, 1991. BBA in Mgmt. Info. Sys., U. Wis., Milw., 1989. Cert. network engr. Novell Inc., 1994, sys. engr. Microsoft Corp., 1995; registered EMT Wis., 2001. Telecom. analyst U. Wis., Milw., 1987—89; tech. support rep., PC programmer ARI Network, Milw., 1989—90; telecom. mgr. First Bank, Milw., 1990—92; microcomputer support/network analyst United Wis. Svcs./Blue Cross-Blue Shield, Milw., 1992—94; ind. computer cons. Netwrx Consulting Inc., Jackson, Wis., 1995—; EMT Village of Jackson, 2001—; networking and computer instr. Moraine Pk. Tech. Coll., Fond du Lac, Wis., 2001—02. With USNR, 2002—03. Home: N165 W20901 Glencoe Ln Jackson WI 53037 Office: Netwrx Consulting Inc N165 W20901 Glencoe Ln Jackson WI 53037 Personal E-mail: georgek@netwrx1.com. E-mail: georgek@netwrx1.com.

KASICH, JOHN R. former congressman; b. McKees Rocks, Pa., May 13, 1952; BA, Ohio State U., 1974. Administrv. asst. Ohio State Senate, 1975-77; mem. Ohio Legislature, 1979-82, 98th-106th Congresses from 12th Ohio dist., Washington, 1983-2001; mem. nat. security com., armed svc. com.; mem. house budget com., chmn.; chmn. New Century Project, Columbus, 2001—.

KASIMIS, BASIL S. oncologist; b. Athens, 1946; MD, Athens U., 1970, DSc, 1974. Diplomate Am. Bd. Internal Medicine, Am. Bd. Oncology. Resident internal medicine South Balt. Gen. Hosp., 1974—77; fellow in med. oncology Boston U. Hosp., 1977-79, fellow in hematology, 1979-80; sr. staff physician Long Beach (Calif.) Vet. Affairs Med. Ctr., 1980-84; asst. prof. medicine U. Calif., Irvine, 1980—84; chief hematol. oncology St. Peters Med. Ctr., 1984-86; sr. attending physician U. Hosp., Newark, 1986; chief hematol. oncology N.J. Vet. Health Care Sys., East Orange, NJ, 1986—; assoc. prof. medicine N.J. Med. Sch. U. Medicine and Dentistry N.J., 1986—2001. Adj. prof. Rutgers U., NJ; prof. medicine NJ Med. Sch., 2001—. Mem. ACP, AMA, Am. Soc. Clin. Oncology, Ea. Coop. Oncology Group, Radiation Therapy Oncology Group. E-mail: Basil.Kasimis@med.va.gov.

KASIMOS, JOHN NICHOLAS, pathologist; b. Chgo., Jan. 26, 1955; s. Nicholas John and Mia (Panos) K.; m. Helen Papadakis, July 10, 1994; children: Nicholas John II, Anastasia Eleni. BS in Biology, Loyola U., Chgo., 1978; MS in Biology, Ill. Inst. Tech., 1980; DO, Chgo. Coll. Osteopathic Med., 1984. Diplomate Nat. Bd. Examiners for Osteo. Physicians and Surgeons, Am. Osteo. Bd. Pathologists, Anatomic Pathology and Lab. Medicine, Am. Osteopathic Bd. of Family Physicians, Family Medcine. Intern Chgo. Osteo. Health Systems, 1984-85, resident pathology, 1985-89, pathologist, 1989—, resident in family medicine, 1997-2000; asst. prof. pathology Chgo. Coll. Osteo. Medicine, 1989-93; assoc. prof. pathology Midwestern U., 1993-98, prof. pathology, 1998—; acad. mentor, advisor Chgo. Coll. Osteo. Medicine, 1989—, dir. residence tng. dept. pathology, dir. deptl. edn./rsch., vice chmn. dept. pathology, 1993-96, acting chmn. dept. pathology, 1996-97, chmn. dept. pathology, 1997—. Fellow Coll. Am. Pathologists, Am. Soc. Clin. Pathologists, Am. Osteo. Coll. Pathologists; mem. Am. Coll. Osteo. Family Physicians, Am. Osteo. Assn., U.S. and Can. Acad. Pathologists, Ill. Assn. Osteo. Physicans and Surgeons, Ill. Pathology Soc., Chgo. Pathology Soc., Am. Acad. of Osteopathy. Greek Orthodox. Achievements include research in nuclear magnetic resonance spectroscopy of tumors and pathophysiologic development of disease. Office: St James Hosp Dept Pathology 20201 Crawford Ave Olympia Fields IL 60461-1010

KASINEC, EDWARD JOSEPH, library administrator; b. N.Y.C., Oct. 10, 1945; s. Ignac A. Kasinec and Justina I. Kasinac. BA cum laude, St. John's U., Jamaica, N.Y., 1963; MA, Columbia U., 1966, M in Philology, 1979; MLS, Simmons Coll., 1976. Rsch. bibliographer, libr. Harvard U. Libr., Cambridge, Mass., 1973-80; libr. Slavic collection U. Calif., Berkeley, 1980-84; chief Slavic and Baltic div. N.Y. Pub. Libr., N.Y.C., 1984—. Cons. Nat. Library Can., Ottawa, Soviet and E. European Ctr., U. Pa., U. Tex. Author: Slavic Books and Bookmen: Papers and Essays, 1984 Russian Inst. fellow Columbia U., 1972-73, Astor fellow N.Y. Pub. Libr., 1989—; Can. Inst. Ukrainian Studies grantee U. Alta, 1979; vis. fellow grantee Newberry Libr., Chgo., 1980, Kennan Inst., Washington, 1980, Aitken fellow, 1991-92; rsch. grantee Libr.'s Assembly, U. Calif., 1981-83. Mem. Am. Assn. for Advancement Slavic Studies (co-chmn. bibliography and documentation com. 1983-89) Office: NY Pub Libr Slavic & Baltic Div Central Bldg Rm 217 Fifth Ave and 42d St New York NY 10018-2788 E-mail: ekasinec@nypl.org.

KASINITZ, PHILIP, sociologist, educator; b. Chgo., Sept. 18, 1957; s. Julius and Margaret Rose Kasinitz; m. Lisa Jane Gibbs, Aug. 16, 1987; children: Basya, Mira. BA magna cum laude, Boston U., 1979; MA, NYU, 1982, PhD, 1987. Asst. prof. Williams Coll., Williamstown, Mass., 1987—93; assoc. prof. Hunter Coll., N.Y.C., 1993—99, prof. sociology, 1992—; prof., chair sociology CUNY Grad. Ctr., N.Y.C., 2001—. Assoc. dir. CUNY Ctr. for Urban Rsch., 1998—; mem. com. on migration Social Sci. Rsch. Coun., 2000—; vis. scholar Russell Sage Found., N.Y.C., 2000—01. Author: Caribbean New York, 1992; editor. Metropolis, 1995; editor: Handbook on Immigration, 1999; co-editor: Handbook on International Migration, 1999. Vis. scholar, Wagner Sch. NYU, 1990—91, Russell Sage Found., 2000 01, fellow, NEH, 1990—91. Mem.: Families of Children from China, Am. Sociol. Assn. (chair sect. on internat. migration 1998—99, Thomas and Znanieki award 1996, 2000). Democrat. Jewish. Office: CUNY Grad Ctr Sociology 365 Fifth Ave New York NY 10016 E-mail: pkasinitz@gc.cuny.edu.

KASIRAJAN, KARTHIKESHWAR, surgeon, researcher; b. Madurai, Tamil Nadu, India, Feb. 26, 1967; s. Kasirajan Natarajan and Meenakshi Kasirajan; m. Stephanie Sandor, Dec. 17, 1995. MBBS, Madras (India) U., 1990. Diplomate. Asst. prof. U. of N.Mex, Albuquerque, N.Mex., 1999—. Contbr. articles to profl. jours., chapters to books. Fellow: ACS, ICS, AOA. Office: University of New Mexico 915 camino de Salud NE Rio Rancho NM 87131 Office Fax: 505-272-4851. Personal E-mail: kkasirajan@aol.com. E-mail: kkasirajan@salud.unm.edu.

KASISCHKE, LOUIS WALTER, lawyer; b. Bay City, Mich., July 18, 1942; s. Emil Ernst and Gladys Ann (Stuady) K.; m. Sandra Ann Colosimo, Sept. 30, 1967; children: Douglas, Gregg. BA, Mich. State U., 1964, JD, 1967; LLM, Wayne State U., 1971. Bar: Mich. 1968, U.S. Dist. Ct. (southeastern dist.) Mich. 1968; CPA. Acct. Touche Ross & Co., Detroit, 1967-71; atty. Dykema Gossett, Detroit, 1971—; pres. Pella Window and Door Co., West Bloomfield, Mich., 1990-98. Bd. dirs. Barton Malow Co., Southfield. Author: Michigan Closely Held Corporations, 1986; contbr. articles to profl. jours. Mem. ABA, AICPA, State Bar Mich. (editor column Mich. Bar Jour. 1971-83), Mich. Assn. CPAs, Am. Coll. Tax Counsel Republican. Lutheran. Avocations: mountaineering, skiing, running, squash, golf. Home: 3491 N Lakeshore Harbor Springs MI 49740 Office: Dykema Gossett 39577 Woodward Ave Ste 300 Bloomfield Hills MI 48304-5086

KASKELL, PETER HOWARD, association executive, lawyer; b. Berlin, Mar. 29, 1924; s. Joseph and Lilo (Schaeffer) K.; m. Joan Folsom Macy, Nov. 30, 1968; stepchildren: Bryn, Alison. Grad., Horace Mann Sch., N.Y.C., 1940; BA, Columbia U., 1943, LLB, 1948. Bar: N.Y. 1948. Assoc. White & Case, N.Y.C., 1948-51; atty. Nat. Prodn. Authority, Washington, 1951-52, W.R. Grace & Co., N.Y.C., 1952-54; div. counsel Curtiss-Wright Corp., Buffalo, 1954-56; with Olin Corp., Stamford, Conn., 1956-83, v.p. legal affairs, 1971-83; sr. v.p. CPR Inst. for Dispute Resolution, N.Y.C., 1983-99, sr. fellow, 2000—. Former dir. CARE; former mem. adv. com. U.S. Dist. Ct. (ea. dist.) N.Y. Former trustee Aldrich Mus. Contemporary Art, Ridgefield, Conn., Boys' Athletic League, N.Y.C.; vice chmn. Conn. Humanities Coun.; organizer, chmn. Lawyers Com. for U.N. Conv. on Contracts for Internat. Sale of Goods. With Intelligence Svc., AUS, 1943-45, ETO. Decorated Bronze Star. Mem. Assn. of Bar of City of N.Y., Am. Arbitration Assn. (comml. arbitration panel), Wilton Riding Club (past gov.), Century Assn. Home: 226 Nod Hill Rd Wilton CT 06897-1717 Office: 366 Madison Ave New York NY 10017-3122

KASKINEN, BARBARA KAY, author, composer, songwriter, musician, music educator; d. Norman Ferdinand and Martha Agnes (Harju) Kaskinen. AA, Broward C.C., Coconut Creek, Fla., 1978; BA with honors, Fla. Atlantic U., 1981, MA, 1995; postgrad., U. Miami, 2000—. Instr. adult piano Atlantic H.S., Delray Beach, Fla., 1981-82; organist, combo dir. Affirmation Luth. Ch., Boca Raton, Fla., 1981-86; studio musician, composer/arranger Electric Rize Prodns., Margate, Fla., 1982-94; ind. instr. piano, electronic keyboard and guitar. Margate, 1979-91. Co-founder Oasis Coffee House, Boca Raton, Fla., 1990—92; co-owner Electric Rize Publ, 1991; mem adj faculty Fla Atlantic Univ, 1995—; asst dir TOPS Piano Camp, 1994—96; mem. adj faculty Broward C.C., Coconut Creek, 1996—. Musician (bass, keyboard player): Electric Rize Band, 1982—91, composer: Hansen House, 1987—88; author: Adult Electronic Keyboard Course Book I, 1988, Adult Electronic Keyboard Course Books II and III, 1989. Mem.: ASCAP, Nat. Piano Found., Music Guild Boca Raton, Broward County Music Tchr's Asn (treas), Fla State Music Tchr's Asn, Nat Guild Piano Tchrs, Fla Atlantic Univ Alumni Asn. Home: 6601 NW 22nd St Pompano Beach FL 33063-2117 Address: 6601 NW 22 St Margate FL 33063 E-mail: neniksa@aol.com.

KASKOWITZ, EDWIN, social services executive; b. St. Louis, May 15, 1936; s. Nathan and Fannie K.; children: Joy, Sara, Naomi. BA, Washington U., St. Louis, 1958, MSW. (grad. scholar), 1961. Lic. clin. social worker. Sr. social worker St. Louis County Health Dept., 1965-67; exec. dir. Gerontol. Soc. Am., 1967-80; pres. Business Radio Corp., Atlanta, 1981 82; pres., chief exec. officer The Association Mgmt. Group, Chevy Chase, Md., 1982-86; dir. JCCA Sr. Adult Services, Creve Coeur, Mo., 1986-89, The Forum on Aging Consumers and Employees, St. Louis U., 1989-90; pres. Gerontology Svcs. of Mo., 1991—; CEO, pres. People Sculptures Inc., 2002—. Pres. B'nai-Brith-Habirah, Washington, 1974-75; adv. bd. Over Easy program Sta. KQED-TV, 1977-81. With USAR, 1954-62. Fellow Royal Soc. Health; mem. Gerontol. Soc. Am., Am. Soc. Assn. Execs. (cert. assn. exec.), Nat. Assn. Social Workers, Acad. Cert. Social Workers.

KASLICK, RALPH SIDNEY, dentist, educator; b. Bklyn., Oct. 17, 1935; s. John J. and Dorothy K.; m. Jessica Hellinger, Oct. 24, 1976; 1 child, Andrew AB, Columbia U., 1956, D.D.S., 1959, cert. in periodontology, 1962. Instr. Fairleigh Dickinson U., Coll. Dental Medicine, Hackensack, N.J., 1965-67, asst. prof., 1967-70, assoc. prof., 1970-74, prof., 1974-88, asst. dean for acad. affairs, 1973-75, acting dean, 1975-76, dean, 1976-88, acting provost, Teaneck-Hackensack campus, 1983-85, sr. dean Teaneck-Hackensack campus, 1985-88; chief dentistry Coler-Goldwater Splty. Hosp., Roosevelt Island, NY, 1988—; pres. med. staff Coler-Goldwater Meml. Hosp., Roosevelt Island, N.Y., 1992-94, 97-99, dir. consultative svcs., 1995—. Clin. prof. periodontics Coll. Dentistry, NYU, 1988—; cons. in field. Contbr. chpts. to textbooks, articles to profl. jours. Served to capt. U.S. Army, 1962-64. Recipient Journalism award of the Internat. Coll. of Dentists, 1972, medal of Japan Stomatological Soc., 1977, Stanley S. Bergen award for contbn. to dental edn. Seton Hall U., 1982, Disting. Alumnus award Columbia U. Periodontal Alumni Assn., 1984, Achievement award Fairleigh Dickinson U. Periodontal Alumni Assn., 1984, Hirschfeld Meml. medal and cert. Northeastern Soc. Periodontists, 1987, Disting. Practitioner medallion Nat. Acad. Practice, 1999 Fellow Am. Coll. Dentists, N.Y. Acad. Dentistry; mem. ADA, Am. Assn. Dental Schs., Internat. Assn. Dental Rsch. (past pres. N.J. sect.), Am. Acad. Periodontology, Fedn. Spl. Care Orgns. in Dentistry, Sigma Xi, Omicron Kappa Upsilon. Office: Roosevelt Island Coler-Goldwater Splty Hosp New York NY 10044

KASLOW, FLORENCE WHITEMAN, psychologist, educator, family business consultant; b. Phila., Jan. 06; d. Irving and Rose (Tarin) Whiteman; m. Solis Kaslow; children: Nadine Joy, Howard Ian. AB in Sociology with distinction, Temple U., 1952; MA, Ohio State U., 1954; PhD, Bryn Mawr Coll., 1969. Lic. psychologist, marriage and family therapist, Fla., diplomate Am. Bd. Clin. Psychology, Am. Bd. Forensic Psychology, Am. Bd. Family Psychology (pres. 1996-2000). Pvt. practice, Palm Beach Gardens, Fla., 1964—; dir. Fla. Couples and Family Inst., Palm Beach Gardens, 1982—; adj. prof. med. psychology Duke U. Med. Ctr., Durham, N.C., 1982—; vis. prof. psychology Fla. Inst. Tech., Melbourne, 1985—; disting. vis. prof. Calif. Grad. Sch. Family Psychology, 1989-92. Cons. USN Dept. Psychiatry Residency Tng. Programs, San Diego, Portsmouth, Va., Phila., 1976-88, Palm Beach Inst., 1983-90; weekly radio guest Voice of Am., Focus on Families, 1993—. Editor: Voices in Family Psychology, 1990; author: (with L.L. Schwartz) Dynamics of Divorce: A Life Cycle Perspective, 1987, The Military Family in Peace and War, 1993, Handbook of Relational Diagnoses and Dysfunctional Family Patterns, 1996, Painful Partings, 1997, Handbook of Couple and Family Forensics, 1999, Comprehensive Handbook of Psychotherapy, 4 vols., 2002, Welcome Home: an Internat. and Non Traditional adaption reader, 2003; contbr. articles to profl. jours., chpts. to books; mem. editl. bd. Jour. Marital and Family Therapy, 1976—, Marriage and Family Rev., 1977-92, Jour. Sex and Marital Therapy, 1984—, Jour. Clin. Child Psychology, 1986—. Jour. Psychotherapy, 1988—. Recipient Disting. Psychology Contbn. award Am. Bd. Profl. Psychology, 1994, Outstanding Family Therapy Contbn. award Am. Assn. Marriage and Family Therapy, 1991; NIMH trainee, 1969. Mem. APA (divsn. family psychology pres. 1987, sec. 1983-85, com. mem. 1987—, pres. divsn. media psychology 1993. Disting. Contbn. to Internat. Psychology award 2000, 03), Am. Bd. Forensic Psychology (pres. 1978-80, bd. dirs. 1978-81), Am. Assn. Marital and Family Therapy, Am. Family Therapy Acad., Coalition Family Diagnosis (chmn. 1989-93), Am. Assn. Sex Educators, Counselors and Therapists, Internat. Family Therapy Assn. (founding pres. 1987-90), Acad. Family Mediators (bd. dirs. 1982-88, treas. 1985-87). E-mail: kaslowfs@worldnet.att.net.

KASMAI, HAMID SALEH, chemistry educator, researcher, consultant; b. Tabriz, Azarbaijan, Iran, May 28, 1939; came to U.S., 1962; s. Hoseinguli Saleh-Kasmai and Aameneh Aalemrajabi; m. Roselyn Mae Senior, July 18, 1971; children: Armon, Nikoo. BSc in Chemistry, Tchrs. Coll., Tehran, Iran, 1961; PhD in Chemistry, U. Wis., 1969; postdoctoral, Syracuse U., 1973-74, 78-79. Asst. prof. Pahlavi U., Shiraz, Iran, 1968-74, assoc. prof., 1974-80; adj. prof. Syracuse U., 1980-82; asst. prof. Hamilton Coll., Clinton, N.Y., 1982-87, East Tenn. State U., Johnson City, 1987-91, assoc. prof., 1991-99, prof., 1999—. Cons. chem. industries, 1987—; spkr. in field. Author: (with others) Advances in Heterocyclic Chemistry, 1978, Trends in Organic Chemistry, 1993; contbr. articles to profl. jours. Fulbright-Hays travel grant Fulbright Found., 1973; Cottrell Coll. Sci. grant Rsch. Corp., 1982-84, type B grants Am. Chem. Soc., 1986-88, 89-91, various grants Hamilton Coll. and East Tenn. State U., 1982-94. Mem. AAAS, AAUP, Am. Chem. Soc. (Spkr. of Yr. N.E. sect. 1994), Internat. Soc. Heterocyclic Chemistry, Tenn. Acad. Scis., Sigma Xi. Avocations: woodworking, swimming, hiking, music, stamp and coin collecting. Office: East Tenn State U PO Box 70695 Johnson City TN 37614-1710

KASMERIDI, SOFIA, translator, researcher; d. Ivan and Elena Kasmeridi; m. Matthew S Lenco, Mar. 2, 2001. MA, George Mason U., Fairfax, VA, 2002—03. Pres. Palmyra Comm. Co., Arlington, Va., 1994—. Mem.: Nat. Chpt. of Am. Translators Assn., MLA, Am. Translators Assn. (assoc.). Office: Palmyra Comm Co PO Box 9471 McLean VA 22102 E-mail: linguistworks@yahoo.com.

KASNOWSKI, CHESTER NELSON, artist, educator; b. Perth Amboy, N.J., Jan. 23, 1944; BFA, Dayton Art Inst., 1971; MFA, Tulane U., 1973. Curator New Orleans Mus. Art, 1971-74; tchr. So. Vt. Art Ctr., Manchester, 1981—. One-man show includes Bertha Undang Gallery, N.Y.C., 1984, 85, 87, 91, 93, Carmen Llewellyn Gallery, New Orleans, 1996; group exhbns. at Dartmouth Coll., 1978, Robert Hall Fleming Mus., 1981, Franklin Furnace, 1982, 84, Bertha Undang Gallery, 1983, Hand Gallery, 1985; permanent collections include Bklyn. Mus., Franklin Furnace, Solomon R. Guggenheim Mus., Stedelijk Mus., Tate Gallery, Mus. Modern Art. Grantee Nat. Endowment Arts, 1974, 78. Mem. Coll. Art Assn. Home: PO Box 1 Weston VT 05161-0001

KASOUF, JOSEPH CHICKERY, lawyer, consultant; b. Syracuse, N.Y., July 3, 1954; s. Herbert Chickery and Helen (Hawa) K.; m. Nancy A. Middleton, Sept. 10, 1977; children: Jennifer C., Lauren E., Joseph P. A, Onondaga C.C., 1976; BA, Syracuse U., 1987, MS, JD, Syracuse U., 1990. Police officer, detective Syracuse Polic Dept., 1977-87; asst. gen. counsel The Pyramid Co., 1988-91; mgr. claims counsel Nationwide Mutual Ins. Co., 1991—2001, sr. counsel, office of gen. counsel, 2001—. Adj. prof. Syracuse U., 1991-2001. Contbr. articles to profl. jour. Mem. Civic Action Program, Syracuse, 1991—. Mem. N.Y. State Bar Assn. sect. torts, ins. and compensation law), Def. Assn. N.Y., Onondaga County Bar Assn., Def. Rsch. Inst., Am. Corp. Counsel Assn. Avocations: golf, skiing. Office: Nationwide Mutual Ins Co 7th Fl Office of Claims 1 Nationwide Plz Columbus OH 43215 Home: 4228 Hertford Ln Dublin OH 43017

KASPAR, FRANCES WOLF, music educator; b. Rome, N.Y., Jan. 10, 1944; d. E. Mark Wolf and Christine Wilma Smith Wolf; m. Frederick Rudolph Kaspar, Feb. 15, 1969; children: Christina Marie Lemaire, Michael Todd. BS, SUNY, Potsdam, 1968; postgrad., Ariz. State U., 1998—. Gen. music tchr. Chandler (Ariz.) Pub. Sch. Dist., 1968—69; choral and gen. music tchr. Dysart Unified Sch. Dist., El Mirage, Ariz., 1969—72; piano instr. Kaspar Piano Studio, Glendale, Ariz., 1970—74, Mesa, Ariz., 1974—; profl. accompanist Cassilons Choral Soc., Avondale, Ariz., 1971—74; instr. Yamaha Music Sch., Mesa, 1975—78; music coord. Christ the King Cath. Ch., Mesa, 1976—81. Chmn. Ariz. study program Ariz. State Music Tchrs. Assn., 1991—99. Recipient Honored Tchr. award, Ariz. State Music Tchrs. Assn., 1991; scholar, Piano Technicians Guild Found., 2000; Janice McCurnin Tchr. Enrichment grantee, Ariz. Study Program, 2000, 2001. Mem.: Music Tchrs. Nat. Assn. (nat. cert. tchr. of music), Sigma Alpha Iota. Roman Catholic. Achievements include development of series of 12 workbooks for Ariz. State Music Tchrs. Assn., now used statewide by approximately 3000 students each year. Personal E-mail: frfwkaspar@aol.com.

KASPAR, VICTORIA ANN, school administrator; d. Rudolph Hans and Rose Marie Boysen; m. Ronald Michael Kaspar, 1948; children: Ron Jr., John, Jim. BS in Secondary Edn., U. Nebr., Omaha, 1974, MS in Secondary Adminstrn., 1995; EdD, U. Nebr., 2003. Tchr. English Bellevue (Nebr.) Pub. Schs., 1974-75; dir. daycare pvt. practice, Omaha, 1978-88; tchr. English Millard South H.S., Omaha, 1988-98, chair dept. English, 1995-98, asst. prin., 1998—. Author of poems. Mem. Friends of Omaha Pub. Libr. Mem. LWV, Internat. Soc. for Tech. in Edn., Nat. Coun. Sch. Adminstrs., Nat. Assn. Secondary Sch. Prins., Nebr. Assn. Secondary Sch. Adminstrn. (Region II), Nat. Coun. Staff Devel., Alpha Xi Delta, Phi Delta Kappa. Avocations: reading, gardening, writing.

KASPAROV, ANDREY R. composer, pianist, conductor, educator; b. Baku, The Former USSR, Apr. 6, 1966; s. Rafail Kasparov and Nigiar Kasparova; m. Oksana Lutsyshyn, Nov. 1, 1991. M in Music Composition (hons.), The Moscow State Conservatory, 1989, M in Piano Performance (hons.), 1990; Mus D in Composition, Ind. U. Sch. of Music, 1999. Assoc. instr. music composition Ind. U., Bloomington, 1994—96; dir., condr. CREO, the Old Dominion U. Contemporary Music Ensemble, Norfolk, Va., 1998—; asst. prof. music Old Dominion U., Norfolk, 1997—2003, assoc. prof. music, 2003—. Organist, pianist St. Paul's Luth. Ch., Hampton, Va., 2002—. Composer: (musical composition on CD) Toccata for piano, 1983 (1st prize Contemporary Record Soc. Composition Competition, 1997, 3d prize All-U.S.S.R. Composition Competition, 1985), (musical composition) Piano Sonata No. 1 in tre canti ostinati., 1988, Symphony of Three Cycles for symphony orch, 1988—89, Traumes-Wirren for flute, clarinet, bassoon and percussion, 1992, Three Prayers for string quartet, 1992—93, Cadenza for solo euphonium, 1994, Auction for electronic tape, 1995—96, Nocturne for bassoon, harp, double bass and piano, 1998, Michal for solo clarinet, 1999—2000 (Selected by Soc. of Composers Inc. for publ. by European Am. Music in the Soc. Composers, Inc. Jour. of Music Scores, 2002), Variations on a Theme by Mark Schultz for horn and piano, 2000—01, Three Aphorisms for flute, violin and cello (2d prize at the All-U.S.S.R. Composition Competition, 1987), Verses and Interludes for mezzo soprano, clarinet, percussion and piano/harpsichord, Syllables for three percussion instruments, Chamber Sonata for chamber orch. and piano, (musical composition on CD) Piano Sonata No. 2, 1993—94 (2d prize at the Prokofiev Internat. Composition Competition in Moscow, 1997); composer: (pianist) Perestroika for symphony orchestra, 1996—99; pianist Concert Tours in the U.S., France, Ukraine, Argentina and Russia, The world premiere of the new edit. of Béla Bartók's Third Piano Concerto with newly-discovered revisions by the composer himself. Columbus Indiana Philharmonic under David Bowden, conductor (ensemble performance) World and Am. premieres of works by composers from Argentina, Armenia, Holland, Latvia, Serbia, Ukraine and the U.S., 1998—2003; author: (article) Hungarian Music Quar., Vol. XI. Recipient Individual award, Yvar Mikhashoff Trust for New Music, 1997, Albert Roussel prize, Internat. Piano Competition for 20th-Century Music in Orléans, France, 1998; fellow Ind. Arts Commn. Fellowship, Ind. Arts Commn., 1996—97. Mem.: Southeastern Composers League, Soc. of Composers, Inc., ASCAP (Std. awards 1999—2002). Home: 1460 Harmott Ave Norfolk VA 23509 Office: Old Dominion Univ Dept of Music 4810 Elkhorn Ave Norfolk VA 23529-0187 Home Fax: 757-852-9072; Office Fax: 757-683-5056. Personal E-mail: akasparo@odu.edu.

KASPER, DENNIS LEE, health facility administrator, educator; William Ellery Channing prof. med. Harvard Med. Sch., prof. microbiology and molecular genetics; sr. phys. Channing Lab. Brigham and Women's Hosp., Boston. Mem.: Inst. Medicine. Office: Brigham and Women's Hosp Channing Lab 181 Longwood Ave Boston MA 02115-5804 E-mail: dennis_kasper@hms.harvard.edu.

KASPER, HORST MANFRED, lawyer; b. Dusseldorf, Germany, June 3, 1939; s. Rudolf Ferdinand and Lilli Helene (Krieger) K.; 1 child, Olaf Jan. Diploma in chemistry, U. Bonn, 1963, D. in Natural Scis., 1965; JD, Seton Hall U., 1978. Bar: N.J. 1978, U.S. Patent Office 1977. Mem. staff Lincoln Lab., MIT, Lexington, 1967-69; mem. tech. staff Bell Tel. Labs., Murray Hill, N.J., 1970-76; assoc. Kirschstein, Kirschstein, Ottinger & Frank, N.Y.C., 1976-77; patent atty. Allied Chem. Corp., Morristown, N.J., 1977-79; pvt. practice Warren, N.J., 1980-83; with Kasper and Weick, Warren, 1983-85, Kasper and Laughlin, 1985—. Contbr. numerous articles to profl. jours.; patentee semicondr. field. Mem. ABA, AAAS, N.J. Bar Assn., Internat. Patent and Trademark Assn., Am. Patent Law Assn., N.J. Patent Law Assn., Am. Chem. Soc., Electrochem. Soc., Am. Phys. Soc., N.Y. Acad. Scis. Home and Office: 13 Forest Dr Warren NJ 07059-5832 Office: ul Na Grzgdkach 9 30421 Cracow Poland

KASPER, LARRY JOHN, accountant, litigation support consultant; b. Springfield, Ohio, Apr. 17, 1947; s. Billy D. and Phyllis M. (McCauley) K.; m. Helen L. Harrison, Dec. 22, 1976. BSBA, Ohio State U., 1969, M in Acctg., 1975; MBA in Ops. Rsch., U. Mich., 1971. CPA, Ohio. Econometrician Dean Witter, N.Y.C., 1971; economist Battelle Meml. Inst., Columbus, Ohio, 1971-75; acct. Touche Ross, Columbus, Ohio, 1975-76; pvt. practice Larry J. Kasper, CPA, Columbus, Ohio, 1976—. Treas. Inst. Mgmt. Accts., Columbus, 1981-82. Author: Business Valuations: Advanced Topics, 1997; contbr. articles to profl. jours. Mem. Ohio Child Support Guidelines Adv. Commn., Columbus, 1991-93. Featured in Acctg. Today, 1992, The Street.com, 2000. Mem. Ohio Soc. CPAs (litigation support com. 1976—, seminar writer 1990—), Inst. Bus. Appraisers (Publ. of the Yr. award 2000), Nat. Assn. Cert. Valuation Analysts (cert. value analyst). Avocation: weight training. Office: Larry J Kasper CPA 773 Dennison Ave Columbus OH 43215-1364

KASPER, VICTOR, JR., economics educator; b. Rochester, N.Y., Apr. 12, 1947; BS in Agrl. Econs., Rutgers U., 1969, MS in Agrl. Econs., 1972, PhD in Econs., 1983. Instr. dept. agrl. econs. and mktg. Rutgers U., 1980-84; asst. prof. econs. St. John Fisher Coll., Rochester, N.Y., 1985-86; asst. prof. Rochester (N.Y.) Inst. Tech., 1986-90; asst. prof. econs. Elmira (N.Y.) Coll., 1990-97, Buffalo State Coll., 1997-98, Ramapo Coll., Mahwah, N.J., 1998-99, Wagner Coll., 2000; asst. prof. St. Francis Coll., 2001, Bklyn. (N.Y.) Polytechnic Inst., 2000—01; asst. prof. econs. Buffalo (N.Y.) State Coll., 2001—. Contbr. articles to profl. jours. Mem. AAUP, Am. Econs. Assn., Eastern Econs. Assn., Assn. for Econ. and Social Analysis, Sci. Soc. E-mail: kasperv@buffalostate.edu.

KASPERSON, JEANNE XANTHAKOS, librarian, editor, educator; b. Feb. 3, 1938; d. James and Mary (Mitsakos) Xanthakos; m. Roger Eugene Kasperson, Sept. 6, 1959; children: Demetri Alexander, Kyra Eleni. BA in English with honors, Clark U., 1959; postgrad. in L.S., U. Chgo., 1959-60, MA in English, 1962; MLS, Simmons Coll., 1967. Asst. libr. circulation and reference Edn. Libr. U. Chgo., 1959-60; asst. acquisitions libr. Wilbur Cross Libr. U. Conn., Storrs, 1964-66; asst. to chief bibliographer Mich. State U. Libr., East Lansing, 1966-67; rsch. libr. Hazard Assessment Group Clark U., Worcester, Mass., 1977-78; rsch. libr. Ctr. Tech., Environ., and Devel., Worcester, 1979-90; rsch. libr. George Perkins Marsh Inst. Marsh Libr., Worcester, 1991—2002; rsch. libr. Jeanne X. Kasperson Rsch. Libr., Clark U., Worcester, Mass., 2002—. Rsch. assoc. prof. Clark U., 1993—; sr. rsch. assoc. World Hunger Program Brown U., 1986-96. Editor Aquarius Project, 1972-73; dir. publs. CENTED, 1983—; co-editor: Water Re-use and the Cities (best sci. book award 1977), 1977, Risk in the Technological Society, 1982; co-author, co-editor: Natural Hazards Observer, 1984, Perilous Progress: Managing the Hazards of Technology, 1985 (Choice Outstanding Acad. Books 1987), Nuclear Risk Analysis in Comparative Perspective, 1986, Corporate Management of Health and Safety Hazards, 1988, Global Environmental Change: The Contributions of Risk Analysis and Management, 1990, Managing Nuclear Accidents: A Model Emergency Plan for Power Plants and Communities, 1992, Preparing for Nuclear Power Plant Accidents, 1995, Regions at Risk: Comparisons of Threatened Environments, 1995, Global Environmental Risk, 2001; contbg. editor Environment, 1987-92; bd. editors Risk Abstracts, 1988—, book rev. editor, 1990—; co-editor nature and soc. sect. Annals Assn. Am. Geographers, 2000—; contbr. articles to profl. jours. Exec. bd. Woodstock Libr. Assn., 1974-75, v.p., 1975-77, pres., 1978-80, book selection com., 1980-85; pres. N. Woodstock Libr. Assn., 1977-82. Mem. ALA, N.Y. Acad. Sci., Soc. Risk Analysis, Union of Concerned Scientists, Rsch. Com. Disasters, Risk Assessment and Policy Assn., Internat. Disaster Inst., Internat. Assn. Impact Analysis, Spl. Librs. Assn., Am. Soc. Environ. History, U.S. Agrl. Info. Network, Assn. Population Family Planning Librs. Info. Ctrs. Internat., Nat. Hazards Soc. Democrat. Greek Orthodox.

KASPIN, JEFFREY MARC, floor covering professional; b. Bklyn., May 30, 1948; s. Seymour and Frances (Babad) K.; m. Susan Jane Engel, Apr. 17, 1977; children: Jodi-Anne, Stacey, Melanie. BA, Am. U., 1970. Cert. tchr., Va.; cert. archtl. carpet rep.; cert. tech. carpet rep. Tchr. Fairfax (Va.) Sch. System, 1970-72; exec. v.p. sales and mktg. Atlantic Distbrs., S.I., 1972-88; sales and ter. mgr. Norman D. Lifton Co., Mt. Vernon, N.Y., 1988-89, mgr. customer svc. Yonkers, N.Y., 1990-92, gen. adminstrv. mgr., 1992-93; gen. mgr. Western Carpet Distbrs., Bklyn., 1989-90; sales and ter. mgr. Columbus (Ga.) Carpet Mills, 1990; gen. mgr. Norman D. Lifton Co., Yonkers, N.Y., 1992-97; territory mgr. Aladdin Carpet Mills divsn. Mohawk Industries, 1997—2002; mgr. Nick's Floor Covering, Morristown, NJ, 2002—. Floor convering cons. to architects, contractors, builders, retailers, publs.; floor convering profl. speaker, 1984-90. Vol. Spl. Olympics, Washington, 1968-69; bd. dirs. Country Swim Club, East Brunswick, N.J., 1982-92; fundraising chmn. Am. Cancer Soc., Middlesex County, N.J., 1984-96, 93-94; trustee Temple B'nai Shalom, East Brunswick, 1986-89; v.p. U.S. Jaycees, 1978-85; mem. Ctrl. N.J. bd. advisors Am. Cancer Soc., 2000—. Mem. L.I. Carpet Club, Nat. Assn. Floor Covering Distbrs., N.J. Carpet Club. Avocations: running, swimming, reading, camping, swim coaching.

KASPIN, SUSAN JANE, child care specialist; b. Bklyn., May 28, 1950; d. Stanley Engel and Thelma Rosenblum; m. Jeffrey Marc Kaspin, Apr. 17, 1977; children: Jodi-Anne, Stacey, Melanie. BA, Bklyn. Coll., 1972. Cert. tchr. N.J. Adminstrv. asst. Stone & Webster Mgmt. Cons., N.Y.C., 1972-74, Am. Electric Power Co. (formerly in N.Y.C.), Columbus, Ohio, 1974-78; program dir. Office for Youth/Sch. Age Child Care Twp. of East Brunswick, NJ, 1989—98; mgr. Sch. Age Child Care/Alliance, 1999—. Staff liaison East Brunswick Alliance for the Prevention of Alcoholism and Drug Abuse, 1990—. Mem. twp. ad-hoc com., N.J. tpk. expansion, East Brunswick, 1985-90; mem. adv. bd. Local Law Enforcement Block Grant Program. Mem. N.J. Sch. Age Child Care Coalition, Nat. Sch. Age Care Alliance, Assn. for Children of N.J. (John Alexander Outstanding Project award 1992), Middlesex County Mcpl. Alliance Network.

KASPROW, BARBARA ANNE, biomedical scientist, writer; b. Hartford, Conn., Apr. 23, 1936; d. Stephen G. and Anna M. Kasprow. AB cum laude, Albertus Magnus Coll., 1958; postgrad., Laval U., 1958, Yale U., 1958-61; PhD, Loyola U., Chgo., 1969. Staff microbiology dept. Conn. State Dept. Health, 1957; lab. asst. dept. microbiology Yale U., New Haven, 1958—59; tng. scholar USPHS, 1959—60; asst. rsch. and editl. dept. anatomy Yale U., New Haven, 1961; rsch. assoc. N.Y. Med. Coll., 1961—62; rsch. assoc. to sr. rsch. assoc. and adminstrv. assoc. Inst. for Study Human Reprodn. St. Ann Ob-Gyn. Hosp., Cleve., 1962—67, asst. to dir. grad. med. edn., asst. dir. adminstrn. grad. rsch. endocrinology, Inst. for Study Human Reprodn., 1962—67; sr. rsch. assoc. dept. anatomy Stritch Sch. Medicine, Chgo., Hines, Ill., 1967—69; asst. prof. anatomy Loyola U., Chgo., 1969—75, asst. to v.p. University Rsch. Sys., 1975-79; v.p. med. topics Univ. Rsch. Sys., 1979—; asst. to pres. Internat. Basic and Biol.-Biomed. Curricula, Lombard, Ill., 1979—. Lectr. in field; invited U.S. del. on reprodn. to Vatican, 1964; round table leader Brazil-Israel Congress on Fertility and Sterility, Brazil Soc. Human Reprodn., São Paulo, 1972. Editl. asst. vol. VIII/3 Handbuch der Histochemie, Gustav Fischer Verlag, 1963; prodn. aide ednl. med. film The Soft Anvil, 1965-66; co-editor: Biology of Reproduction, Basic and Clinical Studies, 1973; contbr. articles to profl. jours. Recipient Certificate of Outstanding Achievement and Scholarship award Am. Assn. German Tchrs. and New Britain German Assn., 1954; named Honorary Citizen São Paulo, 1972. Mem. AAAS (life), Am. Assn. Anatomists, Am. Soc. Zoologists-The Soc. Integrative and Comparative Biology, Pan Am. Assn. Anatomy (co-organizer symposium on reproduction New Orleans 1972), Midwest Anatomists Assn. (program officer ann. meeting Chgo. 1974), Sigma Xi (life). Roman Catholic. Achievements include biological elucidation of growth horizons in uterine development, growth, and maturity; perfection of a hormonal model-system in highly controlled (surgerized) animals to ascertain quantitative relationships of purified estradiol-17beta and progesterone required for promotion of and duplication of these uterine growth horizons; development of experimental paradigms for the biomorphological elucidation of hormonally stimulated growth responses in endocrine target organs, and cyto- and histochemical elucidation of growth stimulants. Office: 607 E Wilson Ave Lombard IL 60148-4062

KASPRZAK, LUCIAN ALEXANDER, physicist, researcher, technical manager; b. Scranton, Pa., July 22, 1943; s. Alexander Lucian and Helen Frances (Skubic) K.; m. Carole Anne Nowakowski, July 22, 1967; children: Brian, Dawn. BS in Physics, Stevens Inst. Tech., 1965, PhD in Materials, 1972; MS in Physics, Syracuse U., 1970. Engr. failure analysis IBM East Fishkill, Hopewell Junction, N.Y., 1965-69, engr. reliability Large Scale Integration, 1972-77, mgr. Very Large Scale Integration devel., 1977-81; mgr. vendor memory IBM Gen. Tech. Div. Assurance, Poughkeepsie, N.Y., 1981-82; tech. asst. to corp. v.p. IBM Corp. Hdqrs., White Plains, N.Y., 1982-83, mgr. memory tech., Gen. Tech. Div., 1983-84; program mgr., tech. support IBM Data Systems Div. Assurance, Poughkeepsie, 1984-85; program mgr. tech. profl. relations IBM Corp. Hdqrs., Thornwood, N.Y., 1985-92; assoc. prof. physics and engring. sci. Franciscan U. Steubenville, Ohio, 1992-96; reliability mgr. direct radiography Sterling Diagnostic Imaging, Newark, Del., 1996-97; dir. reliability Direct Radiography Corp., Newark, Del., 1997—2001; reliability cons., 2001—. Bd. dirs. Internat. Reliability Physics Symposium, 1985—, chmn. 1986-87. Contbr. articles to profl. jours.; co-discoverer hot electron effect in Metal Oxide Semiconductor Field Effect Transistor; patentee in field. Mem. Environ. Bd., Wappingers Falls, N.Y., 1973; coach East Fishkill Youth Soccer League, 1974-82; coun. mem. St. Columba Parish, Hopewell Junction, 1985-91. Recipient Benefactors award Franciscan U. of Steubenville, 1989; IBM resident fellow, Yorktown and Hoboken, N.J., 1969-72 Fellow IEEE (chmn. adv. bd. transactions on device and materials reliability); mem. Electron Devices Soc. of IEEE (adminstrv. com. 1986—, treas. 1988-99, adv. bd. Circuits and Devices mag. 1987-98, treas. trans. of semiconductor mfg. 1992—, chmn. device reliability com. 1983-97, treas. Device Rsch. Conf. 1989-92, chmn. device reliability physics com. 1997—), Am. Phys. Soc. Roman Catholic. Avocations: music, astronomy, philosophy, theology, art. E-mail: l.kasprzak@ieee.org.

KASPUTYS, JOSEPH EDWARD, corporate executive, economist; b. Jamaica, N.Y., Aug. 12, 1936; s. Joseph John and Henrietta Viola (Derenthall) K.; m. Marilyn Patricia Kennedy, Oct. 29, 1953; children: Clare Victoria, Patricia Jeanne, Jacqueline Ann, Veronica Joy. BA magna cum laude, Bklyn. Coll., 1959; MBA with high distinction, Harvard U., 1967, DBA, 1972. U.S. Dept. Def., Washington, 1967-70; asst. adminstr. U.S. Maritime Adminstrn., Washington, 1972-75; asst. sec. U.S. Dept. Commerce, Washington, 1975-77; exec. v.p., COO Data Resources, Inc., Lexington, Mass., 1977-81, pres., CEO, 1981-84; exec. v.p. McGraw-Hill, Inc., N.Y.C., 1984-87; pres., COO Primark Corp. Inc., Waltham, Mass., 1987-88, chmn., CEO, 1988-2000; chmn. Thomson Fin., 2000-01; chmn., CEO, pres. Global Insight, Inc., Waltham, 2001—. Lectr. Am. U., Washington, 1967-68, Bentley Coll., Boston, 1971-72; assoc. prof., lectr. George Washington U., Washington, 1967-77; bd. dirs. Lifeline Systems, Inc., Boston, Logistics Mgmt. Inst., Washington. Chmn. Hitachi Found., Washington, Coun. for Excellence in Govt., Washington; mem. Com. for Econ. Devel., Washington. Comdr. USN, 1956-76. Decorated Legion of Merit; Warren G. Harding Aerospace fellow, 1971 Mem. Phi Beta Kappa. Clubs: Harvard Bus. Sch. (Boston); Capitol Hill (Washington). Republican. Roman Catholic. Home: 398 Simon Willard Rd Concord MA 01742-1624 Office: Global Insight Inc 1000 Winter St Waltham MA 02451

KASS, BENNY LEE, lawyer; b. Chgo., Aug. 20, 1936; s. Herman and Ethel (Lome) K.; m. Salme Lundstrom, Aug. 30, 1963; children: Gale, Brian. BS, Northwestern U., 1957; LLB, U. Mich., 1960; LLM, George Washington U., 1967. Bar: D.C. 1960. Atty. Maritime Adminstrn., 1960-61; counsel House Info. Subcom., 1962-65; asst. counsel Senate Adminstrv. Practice Subcom., Washington, 1965-69; pvt. practice law Washington, 1969—; mem. Kass, Mitek & Kass, PLLC, 2001; prof. communication law Am. U.; pub. mem. Nat. Advt. Rev. Bd., 1971-74. Life mem. Conf. on Uniform State Laws. Columnist Washington Post, L.A. Times; contbr. articles to profl. jours. Chmn. consumer affairs subcom. Mayors Econ. Devel. Com., 1968-70; chmn. Ad Hoc Com. on Consumer Protection, 1965—. With USAF, 1961-62. Am. Polit. Sci. Assn. Congl. fellow, 1966. Mem. ABA, FBA, Am. Polit. Sci. Assn., Sigma Delta Chi. Office: Kass & Skalet PLLC 1050 17th St NW Ste 1100 Washington DC 20036-5596 E-mail: bkass@kmklawyers.com.

KASS, DAVID NORMAN, accountant, lawyer; b. N.Y.C., Mar. 8, 1951; s. Joseph Zane and Rosalind (Sperber) K.; m. Esta Gail Millman, Nov. 26, 1977; children: Sean N., Joshua A. BS in Acctg., SUNY, Albany, 1973; JD, St. John's U., Jamaica, N.Y., 1982. Bar: N.Y. 1983. Staff acct. Touche Ross & Co., N.Y.C., 1972-74; sr. acct. Reich Weiner & Co., N.Y.C., 1974-76; ptnr. Brandt, Pollack, Kass & Wilkins, N.Y.C., 1976-79, Kass & Kass CPAs PC, Roslyn, N.Y., 1979—; pvt. practice Roslyn, 1983—. Seminar leader Nassau Acad. Law,

Mineola, N.Y., 1993, seminar leader/lectr., 1995. Contbr. articles to The Nassau Lawyer. Baseball coach Roslyn Little League, 1990-95; active in alumni fund campaign SUNY, Albany, 1994. Mem. Am. Arbitration Assn. (comml. law arbitrator), N.Y. State Bar Assn., Nassau County Bar Assn. (mentor), Nat. Assn. CPA Practitioners, N.Y. State Soc. CPAs. E-mail: dkass@mindspring.com.

KASS, JEROME ALLAN, writer; b. Chgo., Apr. 21, 1937; s. Sidney J. and Celia (Gorman) K.; children from previous marriage: Julie, Adam; m. Della Ephron, May 21, 1982. BA, NYU, 1958, MA, 1959. Adj. prof. Columbia U. Film Sch. Playwright: Monopoly, 1965, Saturday Night, 1968, (mus.) Ballroom, 1978 (Tony nomination), (mus.) Norman's Ark, Montclair U., 2002, (TV) A Brand New Life, 1973, Queen of the Stardust Ballroom, 1975 (Writers Guild Am. award, Emmy nomination), My Old Man, 1979, The Fighter, 1982, Scorned and Swindled, 1984, Crossing to Freedom (aka Pied Piper), 1989, Last Wish, 1991, The Only Way Out, 1993, Secrets, 1995; screenwriter: The Black Stallion Returns, 1981, (miniseries) Evergreen, 1985; author: Four Short Plays by Jerome Kass, 1966, Saturday Night, 1969; adapted to concert form Finian's Rainbow, L.A., 1997, Pajama Game, L.A., 1998, Fiorello, L.A., 1999; musical version Queen of the Stardust Ballroom, Chgo., 1998. Mem. Dramatists Guild, Writers Guild Am., Actors Studio, Phi Beta Kappa.

KASS, LAWRENCE, hematologist, oncologist, hematopathologist; b. Toledo, Ohio, Sept. 30, 1938; AB magna cum laude, U. Mich., 1960; MD with hons., MS Anatomy, U. Chgo., 1964. Diplomate Nat. Bd. Med. Examiners, Am. Bd. Internal Medicine/Internal Medicine and Hematology, Med. Oncology, Am. Bd. Pathology/Hematology. Intern Peter Bent Brigham Hosp., Boston, 1964-65, asst. resident internal medicine, 1965-66; sr. asst. resident internal medicine U. Hosps. of Cleve., 1966-68; Elliott Hoyt fellow in hematology Univ. Hosps. of Cleve., 1967-68; various to rsch. assoc. U. Chgo., 1968-70; asst. prof. internal medicine U. Mich. Med. Sch., Ann Arbor, 1970-73, assoc. prof. internal medicine, 1973-78; prof. path., medicine Case Western Res. U. Sch. Medicine, Cleve., 1978—; head hematopathology MetroHealth Med. Ctr., Cleve., 1978—. Cons. in medicine, VA Hosp., Ann Arbor; editorial cons. Williams and Wilkins Pubs., Balt., 1974—. Archives of Pathology and Lab. Medicine Blood, The Jour. of Hematology, The Jour. of Histochemistry and Cytochemistry, Western Jour. of Medicine, Am. Jour. of Hematology, Biotechnic & Histochemistry, 1975—, Rsch. Career Selection Rev. Com., VA, Washington, 1976—; active numerous coms. in field. Contbr. articles to profl. jours. Maj. med corps. U.S. Army, 1968-70. Recipient Internat. Giovanni DiGuglielmo prize, Giovanni DiGuglielmo Found., Accademia Nazionale Die Lincei, Rome, 1976, Diamond Cover award Nat. Soc. Histotechnologists and Jour. of Histotechnology, 1988, C.V. Mosby award, 1964, Merck award 1964. Fellow Am. Coll. Phys., Coll. Am. Pathologists; mem. AAAS, Am. Soc. Hematology, Am. Fedn. Clin. Rsch., Am. Soc. Clin. Oncology, Soc. Exptl. Biology and Medicine, Cen. Soc. Clin. Rsch., Histochem. Soc., Biol. Stain Commn., Am. Soc. Clin. Path., Phi Eta Sigma, Phi Beta Kappa, Alpha Omega Alpha. Office: MetroHealth Med Ctr 2500 Metrohealth Dr Cleveland OH 44109-1900 Fax: (216) 778-5701. E-mail: lkass@metrohealth.org.

KASS, LEON RICHARD, science educator; b. Chgo., Feb. 12, 1939; s. Samuel and Anna (Shoichet) K.; m. Amy Judith Apfel, June 22, 1961; children: Sarah, Miriam. BS, U. Chgo., 1958, MD, 1962; PhD in Biochemistry, Harvard U., 1967. Intern Beth Israel Hosp., Boston, 1962-63; staff assoc. Lab. Molecular Biology, Nat. Inst. Arthritis and Metabolic Diseases, NIH, Bethesda, Md., 1967-69, staff fellow, 1969-70, sr. staff fellow, 1970; exec. sec. com. on life scis. and social policy NRC-NAS, Washington, 1970-72; tutor St. John's Coll., Annapolis, Md., 1972-76; Joseph P. Kennedy Sr. research prof. in bioethics Kennedy Inst., Georgetown U., 1974-76; Henry R. Luce prof. liberal arts of human biology in coll. U. Chgo., 1976-84, prof. com. on social thought, 1984-90, Addie Clark Harding prof. in coll. and com. on social thought, 1990—; Hertog fellow Am. Enterprise Inst., Washington, 2002—. Founding fellow, bd. dirs. Hastings Ctr., 1969-96; bd. govs. U.S.-Israel Binat. Sci. Found., 1982-88; mem. coun. Nat. Humanities Coun., 1984-91, vice chmn. 1987-89; chmn. Pres.'s Coun. Bioethics, 2001-. Author: Toward a More Natural Science: Biology and Human Affairs, 1985, The Hungry Soul: Eating and the Perfecting of Our Nature, 1994, (James Q. Wilson) The Ethics of Human Cloning, 1998, (Amy A. Kass) Wing to Wing, Oar to Oar: Readings on Courting and Marrying, 2000, Life, Liberty, and The Defense of Dignity: The Challenge for Bioethics, 2002, The Beginning of Wisdom: Reading Genesis, 2003; contbr. articles to profl. jours. Served with USPHS, 1967-69. NIH postdoctoral fellow, 1963-67, John Simon Guggenheim Meml. Found. fellow, 1972-73, Nat. Humanities Ctr. fellow, 1984-85, W.H. Brady, Jr. Disting. fellow Am. Enterprise Inst., 1991-92, 98-99; NEH grantee, 1973-74. Mem. Phi Beta Kappa, Alpha Omega Alpha. Jewish. Office: American Enterprise Inst 1150 17th St NW Washington DC 20036-4603

KASSAL, ROBERT JAMES, polymer research scientist; b. Berwick, Pa., Oct. 23, 1936; s. Joseph P. and Isabel Kassal; m. Barbara H. Swanson, Aug. 1, 1958; children: Christopher, Kenneth, Cynthia, Richard. BA, Hofstra U., 1958; postgrad., Poly. Inst. Bklyn., 1958-60; PhD, U. Fla., 1964. Chemist Am. Cyanamid, Stamford, Conn., 1958-60; rsch. chemist DuPont Plastics, Wilmington, Del., 1963-68, sr. rsch. chemist, 1968-69, rsch. supr., 1969-72, Parkersburg, W.Va., 1972-75; sr. rsch. chemist DuPont Elastomers, Wilmington, 1975-79; rsch. assoc. high performance composite matrix devel. DuPont Elastomers and Polymers, Wilmington, 1979-84; sr. rsch. assoc. DuPont Polymers, Wilmington, 1984-90; rsch. fellow R&D DuPont Engring. Resins, Wilmington, 1990-99, sr. rsch. fellow, 1999—2002; ret., 2002; cons. plastics litigation and trial support. Tech. expert polybutylene plumbing systems, plastic pipe, failure analysis, accelerated test method devel., engring. resin product devel., tribology, enhanced molding performance, sr. rsch. fellow, 1999; expert witness in field; cons. in field. E-mail: robert.j.kassal@att.net.

KASSAPOGLOU, CHRISTOS, aeronautical engineer; b. Athens, Nov. 27, 1959; came to U.S., 1978; s. George and Dia (Alexis) K.; m. Annie Karaoulani, June 2002. BS, MIT, 1982, MS in Aeros. and Astronautics, MSME, 1984. Stress analyst Beech Aircraft Corp., Wichita, Kans., 1984-87; sr. structures researcher Sikorsky Aircraft, Stratford, Conn., 1987—. Seminar speaker on cert. of civil composite aircraft in Milan (Italy), Toronto, and Ottawa (Can.); seminar spkr. applicatiohs of compsites Aristotle U. of Thessaloniki, Greece, Advance Tech. Svcs. Internat., Wichita, 1987—. Recipient Salisbury Webb award MIT, 1982, R. DuPont fellow, 1983. Mem. AIAA, Am. Helicopter Soc., Soc. for Advancement of Material and Process Engring., Phi Beta Kappa, Tau Beta Pi, Sigma Gamma Tau. Achievements include patents for transmission support structure for a rotary wing aircraft. Avocations: snow skiing, tennis.

KASSEBAUM, JOHN PHILIP, lawyer; b. Oct. 24, 1932; s. Leonard Charles and Helen Nancy (Horn) K.; m. Nancy Josephine Landon, June 8, 1955; children: John Philip, Richard L., William A., Linda J. Johnson; m. Llewellyn Hood Sinkler, Aug. 4, 1979; stepchildren: G. Dana, J. Marshall, Huger II, Llewellyn H. Sinkler. AB, U. Kans., 1953; JD, U. Mich., 1956. Bar: Kans. 1956, U.S. Supreme Ct. 1971, U.S. Ct. Appeals (2d, 4th, 10th, D.C. cirs.), U.S. Tax Ct. 1976, N.Y., 1979. Ptnr. Kassebaum & Johnson, N.Y.C. Bd. dirs. Wichita Eagle-Beacon Pub. Co.. pres. Wyoming-Paris, Ltd. Author: Kassebaum Collection Vol I, 1981. Spl. asst. atty. gen., Kansas, 1970; chmn. Gov.'s Adv. Commn. Kansas Instl. Mgmt., 1961-69, bd. dirs., pres. Wichita Art Mus. Members; chmn. Kans. Assn. for Mental Health; trustee Price R. and Flora A. Reid Charitable Trust; chmn., bd. dirs. Skowhegan (Maine) Sch. Painting and Sculpture; bd. dirs., pres. Carolina Art Assn. and Gibbes Art Gallery, Charleston S.C.; pres. Spoleta Festival U.S.A., Chaleston; treas. Am. Arts Alliance, Washington; bd. dirs. Nat. Inst. for Music Theater; mem. endowment art com. Ulrich Mus. Art, Wichita; chmn. adv. com Spencer Mus. Art, U. Kans. Hon. curator of ceramics Spencer Mus. Art. Mem. ABA (sect. dispute resolution), ATLA, Am. Arbitration Assn., Nat. Inst. Dispute Resolution, Conflict Resolution Edn. Network, Assn. of Bar of City of New York, Kans. Trial Lawyers Assn., Kans. Assn. Def. Counsel, Fedn. Ins. Counsel, Union Club, (NYC), Met Club (Washington), Phi Delta Theta, Omicron Delta Kappa, Phi Delta Phi. Republican. Episcopalian. Home: 2065 Pettigrew St Sullivans Island SC 29482-8760 Office: 652 Hudson St Fl 5 New York NY 10014-1619 also: Ste 585 River Park Pl 727 N Waco St Wichita KS 67203-3951

KASSEBAUM, NANCY See BAKER, NANCY KASSEBAUM

KASSEL, CATHERINE M. community, maternal, and women's health nurse, consultant; b. Bklyn., Dec. 18, 1953; d. Christopher Frank and Ana Rosa (Sousa) Pannone; m. David L. Kassel, Dec. 27, 1979. Diploma in nursing, Kings County Hosp., Bklyn., 1974; BA in Cmty. Health, CUNY, 1979; BSN with honors, Columbia U., 1989. RN, N.Y. V.p. Kassel Mgmt. Co., N.Y.C., 1985—; pres. Kassel & Co., LLC, N.Y.C. Bd. dirs., co-chair legis. com. N.Y. Counties of RNs, Dist. 13, trustee, treas. polit. action com.; past bd. dirs. Nat Abortion Rights Action League; bd. dirs., treas., chmn. fundraising, nominating com., adv. coun., Global Kids Inc.; mem. Women's Leadership Forum of Dem. Nat. Com. Mem. ANA (polit. action com.), ANA Found. (founding mem.), N.Y. State Nurses Assn., PAC. Home: 145 W 67th St Apt 7H New York NY 10023

KASSEL, DANIEL BRIAN, biotechnologist, researcher; b. Midland, Mich., July 30, 1961; s. Fred L. and Dorothy L. Kassel; m. Nancy N. Kassel, Sept. 11, 1993. BA in Chemistry, Ohio State U., 1983; PhD in Chemistry, Mich. State U., 1988. Postdoctoral fellow MIT, Cambridge, Mass., 1988—89; NIH NRSA fellow Harvard U., Boston, 1989—91; rsch. investigator, various projects Glaxo, Inc., Research Triangle Park, NC, 1991—95; dir., analytical chemistry Combichem, Inc., San Diego, 1995—99; sr. dir., analytical tech. DuPont Pharms., San Diego, 1998—2002; sr. dir., drug discovery Syrrx, Inc., San Diego, 2002—. Scientific adv. bd. Syagen Techs., Tustin, Calif., 1999—, Sepiatec, Inc., Berlin, 2002—. Contbr. articles to profl. jours. Recipient honor, Am. Registry Profls., 2002; grantee NIH, 1989—91. Mem.: Am. Soc. Mass Spectrometry (short course coord. 1985—, invited plenary lectr. 1997—), Am. Chem. Soc. (invited plenary lectr. 1997—), Am. Assn. Pharm. Scis. Achievements include patents in field of parallel spray mass spectrometry; on-line quantitation; first to fast protein analysis using perfusion chromatography coupled with a mass spectrometer; concept and application of "mass-directed" purification of compound libraries. Avocations: golf, musical theater, international travel, skiing. Office: Syrrx Inc 10410 Science Ctr Dr San Diego CA 92121 E-mail: daniel.kassel@syrrx.com.

KASSEL, VIRGINIA WELTMER, television producer, writer; b. Omaha; d. Tyler and Inez (Willard) Weltmer. BA, Bryn Mawr Coll. Producer Sta. WGBH-TV, Boston; producer NET, N.Y.C., coordinator nat. programs; mgr. spl. projects, exec. prodr. humanities programs WNET, N.Y.C.; sr. producer CBS Cable, N.Y.C., 1981-83; dir. devel. and prodn. East Coast Primetime Entertainment, Inc., 1983-87; v.p. East Coast Primetime Entertainment, Inc., 1987-89; assoc. dir. performance programs, prodn. exec. Great Performances Sta. WNET-TV, N.Y.C., 1989-91; producer, dir., writer Potter Prodns., 1991-92; dir. devel. Internat. Cultural Programming, 1992-94. Creator, prodr.: The Adams Chronicles, Sta. WNET, N.Y.C.; prodr.: The Soong Connection, 1995; contbr. articles to profl. publs. Recipient George Foster Peabody award, 1977, 2 Ohio State awards, 1977, Spl. Achievement award Nat. Assn. Ednl. Broadcasters, 1977, Triangle award, 1986, NEH, Mellon Found. grants. Mem.: NATAS, N.Y. Women in TV and Film, Brit. acad. Film and TV Arts, Brit. Acad. Film and TV Arts (N.Y. and London, mem. U.S./China rels. com.), Am. Acad. TV Arts and Scis., Writers Guild Am. East, Women's City Club N.Y. (bd. dirs.), Princeton Club (N.Y.). Home: 4 E 89th St New York NY 10128 0636

KASSELL, NEAL FREDERIC, neurosurgery educator; b. Phila., Mar. 17, 1946; s. Martin Buddy and Evelyn Abigail (Block) K.; m. Nancy Coffin, Dec. 14, 1967 (div.), children: Natasha Lynn, Lauren Tamara, Nicole Tristan; m. Denise Etheridge, Aug. 30, 1986 (div. 1987); m. Lynn Haire, Mar. 12, 1994 (div. 2000). MD, U. Pa., 1972. Diplomate Am. Bd. Neurol. Surgery. Intern Pa. Hosp., Phila., 1972-73, resident in neurology, 1973-74, resident in neurosurgery, 1974-75, U. Western Ont., London, 1975-77; asst. prof. neurosurgery U. Iowa, Iowa City, 1977-81, assoc. prof. neurosurgery, 1981-82, prof. neurosurgery, 1982-84; prof. and vice chmn. neurosurgery U. Va. Sch. Medicine, Charlottesville, 1984-97, prof., co-chmn. neurosurgery, 1997—; pres. Va. Neurol. Inst., 1993—2000; mem. staff U. Va. Hosp., Charlottesville. Chmn. bd., founder Multimedia Med. Sys., Inc., 1995-2000—; chmn., founder Med. Specialists, 1999; bd. dirs. Va. Nat. Bank; dir. NIH-Nat. Inst. Neurol. Disorders and Stroke study sects., 1984—. Reviewer Neurosurgery, Jour. Cerebral Blood Flow and Metabolism, 1977—; mem. editl. bd. Stroke, Surg. Neurology; contbr. over 450 papers to profl. jours. Recipient numerous rsch. grants and contracts; recipient McKenzie Meml. award, 1977, Grass award. Republican. Avocations: riding, classical music, hiking. Home: Wingate 2154 Garth Rd Charlottesville VA 22901-5412 Office: U Va Health Sys PO Box 800212 Charlottesville VA 22908-0212 E-mail: neal@virginia.edu.

KASSELL, PAULA SALLY, editor, publisher; b. N.Y.C., Dec. 5, 1917; d. Daniel Herman and Bertha Blanche (Jaret) K.; m. Gerson Gustav Friedman, Aug. 16, 1941 (dec.); children: Daniel Kassell, Claire Florence Friedman. BA, Barnard Coll., 1939. Tech. editor Bell Labs., Whippany, N.J., 1955-65, methods analyst Murray Hill, N.J., 1965-70; founder, editor, pub. New Directions for Women, Dover, N.J., 1971-77, assoc. editor Englewood, N.J., 1977-87, sr. editor, 1987-93, index editor Dover, 1993-98. V.p., UN rep. Women's Inst. for Freedom of Press, Washington, 1990—; convenor, mem. media task force Com. on Status of Women, UN, 1990-98. Contrubutor chapters to books: "Planning an International Communications System for Women" in Communications at the Crossroads: The Gender Gap Connection (Ablex Publishing Corporation, 1989). "The Birth, Success, Death and Lasting Influence of a Feminist Periodical: New Directions for Women (1972-1993-?)" in Women Transforming Communications: Global Intersections (Sage Publications, 1996). "New Directions for Women" in Women's Periodicals in the United States: Social and Political Issues (Greenwood Press, 1996); featured exhibit NJ feminism "Womens Work is Never Done", 2000-2001. Co-convenor Lakeland chpt. NOW, Dover, 1970; v.p. Dover (N.J.) Child Care Ctr., 1979-91; bd. dirs. Nat. Woman's Party, Washington, 1991-98; mem. media com. Forum 95, UN, N.Y.C., 1994-95; mem. adv. bd. Vet. Feminists Am., Lafayette, La., 1995—; mem. TV task force Morris County NOW, Morristown, N.J., 1995—; trustee Women's Media Initiative, 1997. Recipient First Feminist Action award NOW NJ, 1985, Women Making Herstory award, 1995, Elizabeth Cady Stanton award Women's Rights Info. Ctr., 1993, Woman of Achievement award Douglass Coll., 1994, Medal of Honor, Vet. Feminists Am., 1998, Featured in exhibit on NJ feminists by Morris County (NJ) Hist. Soc., September 17, 2000 to March 18, 2001, Journalist of Month, on women's e-news, www.womensenews.org, 2002. Mem. Am. Journalism Historians Assn., Internat. Women's Media Found., Journalism & Women Symposium. Avocations: attending opera, concerts, ballet performances, visiting museums, travelling. Home: 25 W Fairview Ave Dover NJ 07801-3417

KASSENS, ALICE LOUISE, economist, educator; b. Wilmington, N.C., Dec. 24, 1974; d. William D. and Catherine H. Kassens. BA, Coll. William and Mary, 1998; PhD in Econs., NC State U., 2003. Rsch. asst. Citizens Conservation Svcs., Chapel Hill, NC, 1999—2001; tchg. asst. N.C. State U., Raleigh, 2000—03; instr. econs. U. N.C., Pembroke, NC, 2003—. Avocation: running. Office: U NC Pembroke Sch Bus PO Box 1510 Pembroke NC 28372

KASSIDAY, JOEL DAVID, legislative staff member; b. Chgo., Sept. 1, 1952; m. Zmira Alfie. BA with high distinction, Colo. State U., 1973. Staff writer, assoc. editor, mng. editor Ft. Collins Rev. newspaper, 1974-79; legis. asst., press sec. U.S. Rep. James P. Johnson, 1979-81; adminstrv. asst., press sec. U.S. Rep. then U.S. Senator Hank Brown, 1982-94; chief of staff U.S. Rep. Rick Lazio, 1994-97; press sec. U.S. Senator Kay Bailey Hutchinson, 1997-98; chief of staff Congressman Elton Gallegly, Washington, 1998—. Mem. Phi Beta Kappa, Phi Kappa Phi. Republican. Office: Hon Elton Gallegly US Ho Reps 2427 Rayburn Hob Washington DC 20515-0001

KASSIMATIS, LORETTA EILEEN, clinical social worker; b. Flushing, N.Y., Sept. 30, 1955; d. Thomas Aloyious and Eleanor Cecile (Hoar) Fitzpatrick; m. Peter Kassimatis, Aug. 4, 1979; children: Peter, Melissa, Vanessa. BA in Sociology magna cum laude, BA in Psychology, BA in Sociology, St. John's U., Jamaica, N.Y., 1977; MSW, Fordham U., 1979. Diplomate Am. Bd. Examiners in Clin. Social Work. Clin. social worker Skills Unltd. Vocat. Rehab. Program, Oakdale, N.Y., 1979-81, West Nassau Mental Health Ctr., Franklin Square, N.Y., 1981-83; coord. clin. svcs. South Shore Svcs. for Handicapped-Peninsula Counseling Ctr., Woodmere, N.Y., 1984-98; pvt. practice Lynbrook, N.Y., 1998—. Contbr. articles and poetry to profl. jours. Fellow N.Y. State Soc. for Clin. Social Workers; Mem. NASW, Amnesty Internat., Acad. Cert. Social Workers. Roman Catholic. Avocations: creative writing, historical research, political advocacy, boating, fishing, creative writing. Home: 168 Loines Ave Merrick NY 11566-3212 Office: 7 Franklin Ave Lynbrook NY 11563-1251

KASSIN, SAUL, psychology educator; b. N.Y.C., Apr. 25, 1953; s. Mordy and Betty (Ashear) K.; m. Carol Beth Goldner, Sept. 19, 1952; children: Briana Rachel, Marc Joseph. BS, Bklyn. Coll., 1974; MA, U. Conn., 1976, PhD, 1978. NIH postdoctoral fellow U. Kans., Lawrence, 1978-79; asst. prof. Purdue U., West Lafayette, Ind., 1979-81, Williams Coll., Williamstown, Mass., 1981-84; rsch. assoc. Fed. Jud. Ctr., Washington, 1984-85; NIH postdoctoral fellow Stanford (Calif.) U., 1985-86; from assoc. to full prof. Williams Coll., Williamstown, 1986—. Jury cons., expert witness. Author: Psychology, 1995, 4th edit., 2004; co-author: The American Jury on Trial, 1988, Confessions in the Courtroom, 1993, Social Psychology, 1990, 5th edit., 2002; co-editor: Developmental Social Psychology: Theory and Research, 1981, The Psychology of Evidence and Trial Procedure, 1985, On The Witness Stand: Controversies in the Courtroom, 1987, In the Jury Box: Controversies in the Courtroom, 1987, Readings in Social Psychology, 2002; cons. editor Jour. Exptl. Social Psychology, 1982-87, Jour. Personality and Social Psychology: Attitudes and Social Cognition, 1992-94; editl. cons. Law and Human Behavior, 1986—; ad hoc reviewer in field; contbr. articles to profl. jours. Recipient MacArthur Found. Rsch. Network, 2003—; Rsch. grantee Found. Child Devel., 1984—85, Jud. fellow U.S. Supreme Ct., Washington, 1984—85. Fellow APA, Am. Psychol. Soc.; mem. Am. Psychology-Law Soc., Soc. for Exptl. Social Psychology, Phi Beta Kappa. Office: Williams Coll Bronfman Sci Ctr Williamstown MA 01267 E-mail: skassin@williams.edu.

KASSINGER, THEODORE WILLIAM, federal agency administrator; b. Atlanta, Jan. 26, 1953; s. Edward Theodore and Sarah Mell (Laurent) K.; m. Ruth Lynn Good, Oct. 13, 1984; children: Anna Laurent, Austen Elizabeth, Alice Caroline. BLA, U. Ga., 1975, JD, 1978. Bar: Ga. 1978, D.C. 1986. Atty.-advisor U.S. Internat. Trade Commn., Washington, 1978-80; atty., advisor U.S. Dept. State, Washington, 1980-81; internat. trade counsel com. on fin. U.S. Senate, Washington, 1981-85, assoc., 1985-89; ptnr. Vinson & Elkins L.L.P., Washington, 1990—2001; gen. counsel U.S. Dept. Commerce, Washington, 2001—. Co-author: U.S. Regulation of International Trade, 1987, Basic Documents in International Economic Law, 1989. Mem. ABA. Republican. Roman Catholic. Office: US Dept Commerce General Counsel 14th & Constitution Ave NW Washington DC 20230

KASSINOVE, JEFFREY IAN, psychologist, educator, research scientist; s. Howard and Tina Kassinove. PhD, Hofstra U., 1993—98. Vis. asst. prof. Adelphi U., Garden City, NY, 1999—2001; asst. prof. Monmouth U., West Long Br., NJ, 2001. Clin. psychologist UNITAS, NYC, 1999—. Contbr. articles to profl. jours. Crisis counselor Project Liberty, NYC, 2001. Recipient Harold E. Yuker Rsch. prize, Hofstra U., 1998, Ted Bernstein award, NY Assn. of Sch. Psychologists, 1996; Arnold Horowitz scholarship, Hofstra U., 1997, Robert Vane Meml. scholarship, 1995. Mem.: APA.

KASSIRER, JEROME PAUL, medical educator, editor-in-chief; b. Buffalo, Dec. 19, 1932; Grad., U. Buffalo, 1953, MD magna cum laude, 1957; DS (hon.), U. Mass., 1992; D honoris causa, L'Universite Rene Descartes, Paris, 1992; DS (hon.), Thomas Jefferson U., 1994, SUNY, 1995. Diplomate Am. Bd. Internal Medicine (mem. certifying examination com. 1987 89, bd. dirs. 1989-96, mem. exec. com. 1993-96, chmn. 1995-96). Intern, asst. resident in medicine Buffalo Gen. Hosp., Buffalo, 1957—59; fellow in nephrology New Eng. Med. Ctr., Boston, 1959—61, sr. resident in medicine, 1961—62, asst. physician, 1961—65, physician renal svc., 1969-74, assoc. physician-in-chief, 1971—91, acting physician-in-chief, 1976—77; instr. medicine Sch. Medicine, Tufts U., Medford, Mass., 1961-65, asst. prof. medicine, 1965—69, assoc. prof., 1969—74, vice chmn. dept. medicine, 1971—91, acting chmn. dept. medicine, 1974—75, prof. medicine, 1974—. Sara Murray Jordan Prof. Medicine, 1987—91; editor-in-chief New Eng. Jour. Medicine, Boston, 1991—99. Lectr. in medicine Harvard U., 1991—; bd. dirs. Postgrad. Med. Inst. Mass. Med. Soc., 1988—91. Editor in chief: Current Therapy in Internal Medicine, 1990; co-editor: Clin. Problem Solving, Hosp. Practice, 1985—91; cons. editor. Am. Jour. Medicine, 1976—86, mem. editl. bd.: New Eng. Jour. Medicine, 1972—75; co-editor: Nephrology Forum, Kidney Internat, 1978—91, ed. Decision Making, 1987—89; editl. advisor: Outline of Knowledge, Part 4: Human Life, The New Encyclopaedia Britannica, 1989. Recipient Ednl. Rsch. Found. award, AMA, 1993. Master: ACP (chmn. 1985—88, gov. Mass. 1985—89, mem. exec. com. bd. govs. 1988—89, mem. health and pub. policy com. 1989—91, bd. regents 1990—91, chmn. sci.); fellow: AAAS; mem.: Soc. Clin. Decision Making (charter mem.), Buffalo Acad. Medicine, Mass. Med. Soc. (hon. life), Nat. Libr. Medicine (chmn. bd. sci. counselors 1989—90, mem. biomed. journalism award com. 1992—), Assn of Am. Physicians, Inst. Medicine NAS, Am. Fedn. Clin. Rsch., Am. Soc. Nephrology. Jewish. Avocation: photography. Office: New Eng Jour Medicine 10 Shattuck St Boston MA 02115-6011

KASSLER, HASKELL A. lawyer; b. Boston, Feb. 8, 1936; s. Harry and Natalie (Steinberg) K.; m. Mary Elizabeth Kelligrew, May 30, 1965; children: Marion Adelaide, Sarah Elizabeth. BA, Tufts U., 1957; JD, Boston U., 1960. Bar: Mass. 1960, U.S. Dist. Ct. Mass. 1961, U.S. Dist. Ct. (no. dist.) Miss. 1964, U.S. Dist. Ct. (so. dist.) La. 1965, U.S. Ct. Appeals (5th cir.) 1965, U.S. Ct. Appeals (1st cir.) 1969, U.S. Supreme Ct. 1967. Assoc. Poster, Wilinsky & Goldstein, Boston, 1960-64; pvt. practice law Boston, 1964-66, 69-71; asst. dir. Vol. Defenders Com., Inc., Boston, 1967-68; ptnr. Kassler & Feuer (formerly Richmond, Kassler, Feinberg & Feuer), Boston, 1971-99, Casner & Edwards, LLP, Boston, 1999—. Regional counsel New Eng. Region, Am. Jewish Congress, 1965-67; counsel Civil Liberties Union Mass., 1968-70; asst. prof. criminal justice Northeastern U., Boston, 1969-76; chmn. Mass. Jud. Nominating Coun., 1987-90; mem. Lawyers Constl. Def. Commn., 1964-65. Trustee U. Mass., 1977-81, U. Mass. Bldg. Authority, 1980-81, Mus. Transp., 1981—; selectman Town of Brookline, 1971-74, elected town meeting mem., 1959-84; mem. Local Redistricting Rev. Commn., 1976-78. Fellow Am. Acad. Matrimonial Lawyers (chpt. bd. mgrs. 1980-90, v.p. 1981-82, pres. 1984-86, Judge Haskell Freedman award Mass. chpt. 1984, Mass. Jurisprudence award 1999); mem. ABA, Mass. Bar Assn., Norfolk County Bar Assn., Tufts U. Alumni Coun. Office: Casner & Edwards LLP 303 Congress St Boston MA 02210 E-mail: kassler@casneredwards.com.

KASSMAN, ANDREW LANCE, orthodontist; b. N.Y.C., Nov. 14, 1950; s. David and Phyllis Ivy (Einhorn) K.; children: Stacey Arielle, Alexandria Devin; m. Laurie Ann Kassman, July 7, 1997; 1 child, Dylan Nathaniel BS in Engring., Tulane U., 1972; DMD, Tufts U., 1975; cert. orthodontics, Columbia U., 1978. Lab. technician Tufts Med. Ctr., Boston, 1973-75; resident VA Hosp., Northport, N.Y., 1975-76; pvt. practice Astoria, NY, 1976-78, Phila., 1978—79, East Patchogue, NY, 1979-80; pvt. practice dentistry specializing in orthodontics Tucson, 1980—. Chief orthodontia Crippled Children's Ctr., Tucson, 1980—; assoc. staff Tucson Med. Ctr., 1980—. Bd. dirs. Comstock Found., Tucson, 1980—; active Congregation Or Chadash, Tucson, 1996—, Alta Vista Assn., 1996—, Tucson Boys Club, 1988—, Jewish Cmty. Ctr., Tucson, 1988—. Mem. ADA, Am. Assn. Orthodontists, Pacific Coast Soc. Orthodontists, Tucson Orthodontist Soc., Tucson C. of C. Avocations: baseball, football, tennis, travel. Home: 6501 N Placita Alta Reposa Tucson AZ 85750-4204 Office: 6700 N Oracle Rd Ste 327 Tucson AZ 85704-7740 E-mail: drkaz@mindspring.com.

KASSNER, HERBERT SEYMORE, lawyer; b. N.Y.C., Dec. 3, 1931; s. Abraham and Rose (Rosenblatt) K.; m. Sheilah Goodwin, 1957 (div. 1965); children: Andrew, Kenneth; m. Marjorie Fern Golding, 1974 (div. 1992); children: Robin, Jeffrey; m. Linda Rubinstein Finder, 1993. BA (hon.), Franklin and Marshall U., 1952; cert., Hague (Netherlands) Acad. of Internat. Law, 1953; MA, NYU, 1955; LLB (hon.), Harvard U., 1955. Bar: N.Y. 1955, Conn. 1986. Atty. Gallap, Climenko & Gould, N.Y.C., 1955, Otterbourg, Steindler, Huston & Rosen, N.Y.C., 1956; pvt. practice law N.Y.C., 1957-65, 1969; atty. Dryer & Traub, N.Y.C., 1966-68, Kassner & Detsky, N.Y.C., 1970-80, Kassner & Haigney, N.Y.C., 1981-90. Instr. Ohio State U., Columbus, 1956-57; asst. prof. Ark. State U., Pine Bluff, 1965. Contbr. articles to profl. jours. on 1st amendment law. Mem. Phi Beta Kappa. Home: 7221 Montrico Dr Boca Raton FL 33433-6931

KASSNER, MICHAEL ERNEST, materials science educator, researcher; b. Osaka, Japan, Nov. 22, 1950; (parents Am. citizens); s. Ernest and Clara (Christa) K.; m. Marcia J. Wright, Aug. 19, 1972 (div. Dec. 1976). BS, Northwestern U., 1972; MS, Stanford U., 1979, PhD, 1981. Metallurgist Sargent and Lundy Engrs., Chgo., 1977, Lawrence Livermore (Calif.) Nat. Lab., 1981-90, head phys. metallurgy and joining sect., 1988-90; lectr. San Francisco State U., 1983; prof. Naval Postgrad. Sch., Monterey, Calif., 1984-86; prof., dir. grad. program in materials sci. Oreg. State U., Corvallis, 1990—, Chevron endowed prof., 1996, Northwest Aluminuim prof., 1997—. Temporary assignment as project mgr. Office Basic Energy Scis., U.S. Dept. Energy, 1991-96, 2000-03; vis. scholar dept. physics U. Groningen, Netherlands, 1985-87; vis. scholar dept. materials, sci. and engring. Stanford U., 1981-83; adj. prof. dept. mech. and aerospace engring. U. Calif., San Diego, 1999—. Author over 160 articles; author book on binary phase diagrams; editor various sci. jours. Lt. USN, 1972-76; lt. comdr. USNR, 1976-81. Fulbright scholar, The Netherlands; fellow ASM Internat., 1998. Mem. ASME, Am. Soc. Metals, The Metall. Soc., Materials Research Soc., Sigma Xi. Home: PO Box 269 Otter Rock OR 97369-0269

KASSOF, ALLEN H. foundation administrator; b. N.Y.C., Dec. 17, 1930; s. Morris and Sophia B. Kassof; m. Arianne Scholz, 1953; children: Andrea, Arlen, Anita. BA, Rutgers U., 1952; AM, Harvard U., 1954, PhD, 1960. Asst. prof. Smith Coll., Northampton, Mass., 1957-60, Princeton (N.J.) U., 1961-65, assoc. prof., asst. dean coll., 1965-68; founder, exec. dir. Internat. Rsch. and Exchs. Bd., N.Y.C. and Princeton, 1968-92; pres. Project on Ethnic Rels. in Ea. Europe, Carnegie Corp. N.Y., Princeton, 1991—. Cons. conf. security and cooperation Europe, Hamburg, Germany, Budapest, Hungary, 1980, 85, Warsaw, Poland, 1993; mem. pres. com. fgn. lang., Washington, 1978-79; mem. U.S. task force Romania, Bucharest, 1990-92; prin. mediator between Govt. of Romania and Dem. Union Hungarians in Romania, 1993—; mem. Coun. for Ethnic Accord, 1992—; chair roundtable talks between Slovak and Ethnic Hungarian parliamentary parties of Slovakia, 1995—, Serb-Albanian Roundtable on Future of Kosovo, N.Y.C., 1997; chmn. Regional Roundtable of Polit. Leaders from Southeast Europe on Rels. between Albanians and their Neighbors, Budapest and Athens, 2000, Lucerne, 2002; co-chmn. Euro-Atlantic group on interethnic conflicts NATO, Brussels, 1998. Decorated Grand Officer Nat. Order of Faithful Svc., Pres. of Romania. Mem.: Coun. Fgn. Rels., Am. Assn. Advancement Slavic Studies. Avocation: photography. Home: 949 Mercer Rd Princeton NJ 08540-4823 Office: Project on Ethnic Rels 15 Chambers St Princeton NJ 08542-3707 E-mail: aakassof@cs.com., allen.kassof@per-usa.org.

KASSON, JAMES MATTHEWS, electronics executive; b. Muncie, Ind., Mar. 19, 1943; s. Robert Edwin and Mary Louise K.; m. Betty Roseman, Aug. 14, 1976. BSE.E., Stanford U., 1964; MSE.E., U. Ill., 1965. Engring. mgr. Santa Rita Tech., Santa Clara, Calif., 1963-69; engring. sect. mgr. Hewlett-Packard, Palo Alto, Calif., 1969-73; v.p. research and devel. ROLM Corp., Santa Clara, 1973-88; fellow IBM Corp., San Jose, Calif., 1988-95; v.p. engring. Echelon Corp., Palo Alto, Calif., 1995-98, CIO, 1998-2000. Patentee in field. Trustee Choate Rosemary Hall, Wallingford, Conn., 1990-96, Ctr. Photographic Art, Carmel, Calif., 2001—. Mem. IEEE (citation for contbn. 1981). Home: 33732 E Carmel Valley Rd Carmel Valley CA 93924 E-mail: jim@kasson.com.

KASSOUF, GERARD JOSEPH, accountant; b. Birmingham, Ala., Nov. 2, 1953; s. Louis Paul and Naomi Hawie; m. Nazha Mary Boohaker, Feb. 23, 1953; children: Michelle, Jonathan, Jason. BS, U. Ala., Tuscaloosa, 1974, MA, 1976, M in Tax Acctg., 1980. CPA, Ala.; CFP; accredited estate planner. Pres. L. Paul Kassouf & Co., P.C., Birmingham, 1989—. Pres. Ctr. Mgmt. Inc., Birmingham, 1999-2000. Mem. AICPA, Rotary (sgt.-at-arms 1999-2000). Home: 1710 Somerset Cir Birmingham AL 35213 Fax: 205-443-2501. E-mail: gkassouf@kassouf.com.

KASSOY, HORTENSE (HONEY KASSOY), artist, sculptor, painter, printmaker; b. N.Y.C., Feb. 14, 1917; d. Adolph and Mary (Apfel) Blumenkranz; m. Bernard Kassoy, June 30, 1946; children: Meredith, Sheila. Diploma, Pratt Inst., 1936; BS, Columbia U., 1938, MA, 1939; student, Parsons Sch. Design, Paris, U. Colo., 1966, NYU, 1966-67; studied sculpture with Sahl Swarz, Chaim Gross & Oronzio Maldarelli. Solo exhbns. include Caravan House Gallery, 1974, Women in the Arts Gallery, 1978, Ward-Nasse Gallery, 1986, Pioneer Gallery, Cooperstown, N.Y., 1987, 91, 97, 80th Birthday Retrospective Solo of Wood Sculpture Prints and Watercolors, Vladeck Hall Gallery, N.Y., 1997, 2002, Pioneer Gallery, Cooperstown, 1997, 2002; group exhbns. include Bronx (N.Y.) Mus., 1971, 75, 85-86, Toledo Mus. Art, Toronto Mus. Art, Hudson River Mus., Bklyn. Mus., New Age Gallery, Lever House, Bklyn. Coll., Fordham U., Lehman Coll., Cork Gallery, Nat. Acad. Design; permanent collections include Slater Meml. Mus. Co-chair visual arts Bronx (N.Y.) Coun. on Arts, 1973-76. Fellow Va. Ctr. for Creative Arts, 1986, 88, 89, 92, 95, 97; recipient 1st prize in watercolor Painters Day at N.Y. World's Fair, 1940, ASCA award in sculpture, 2002, Walker prize for sculpture, Oneonta, NY, 2002. Mem. Am. Soc. Contemporary Artists (v.p. 1989-94, 99—, awards in sculpture 1979, 80, 83, 90, 92, 96, 2000, 02), N.Y. Artists Equity Assn. (v.p., bd. dirs. 1971-83), Internation Assn. Art (corr. sec. 1979-93), del. to 10th Congress 1983), Contemporary Arts Guild (rec. sec. 1981-89), Fedn. Modern Painters and Sculptors. Home: 130 Gale Pl Apt 6B Bronx NY 10463-2853 also: Butternut Hill Studio 1577 County Route 16 Burlington Flats NY 13315-3211

KASSULKE, PAUL ROBERT, secondary school educator; b. Milw., July 20, 1954; children: Joel Richard, Rachel Elaine, Elizabeth Louise, Jared Donald, Abigail Jean, Jacob Arthur. BS in Edn., Dr. Martin Luther Coll., 1976; MS in Fine Arts, So. Oreg. U., 1994. Cert. tchr. Wis. Evang. Luth. Synod, 1976. Tchr. First German Evang. Luth. Ch., Manitowoc, Wis., 1976—79, Manitowoc Luth. H.S., 1979—88; tchr., chmn. music dept. St. Croix Luth H.S., West St. Paul, Minn., 1988. Grad. staff Am. Band Coll. So. Oreg. U., Ashland, 1998—; mgr. concert. clinician Western Internat. Band Clinic, Seattle, 2002—. Stewardship chmn. Emanuel Evang. Luth. Ch., St. Paul, 1997—2002. Mem.: Music Educators Nat. Conf. (corr.), Minn. Music Educators (assoc.), Am. Choral Dirs. Assn. (assoc.), VoiceCare Network (life). Lutheran. Home: 7531 Banning Way Inver Grove Heights MN 55077 Office: St Croix Lutheran High School 1200 Oakdale Avenue West Saint Paul MN 55118 Home Fax: 651-451-3968; Office Fax: 651-451-3968. Personal E-mail: kassulke@aol.com. E-mail: pkassulke@sclhs.org.

KAST, W. MARTIN, microbiology and immunology educator; b. Haarlem, North Holland, The Netherlands, Mar. 24, 1958; came to U.S., 1996; s. Hendrikus Martinus Kast and Dina Scholte; m. Sylvia Martha Helene Ferkranus, Oct. 7, 1983; children: Dieuwertje Jasmijn, Hinde Rozemarijn, Harold Martin. BS, U. Amsterdam, 1980, MS, 1983, PhD, 1987. Cert. immunologist, The Netherlands. Postdoctoral fellow immunology The Netherlands Cancer Inst., Amsterdam, 1987-90, asst. prof. immunology, 1990-91; assoc. prof. immunohematology Leiden (The Netherlands) U. Med. Ctr., 1991-96; prof. microbiology and immunology and pharmacology Loyola U., Chgo., 1996—2003, interim dir. Oncology Inst., 2001—03; prof. molecular microbiology and immunology U. So. Calif., L.A., 2003—; Walter A. Richter chair for cancer rsch. Norris Comprehensive Cancer Ctr., L.A., 2003—. Vis. sr. scientist immunochemistry Cytel Corp., San Diego, 1992-93; vis. prof. molecular genetics Pitts. Cancer Inst., 1994; cons. Wyeth, Pearl River, N.Y., 1996—, Genencor, Palo Alto, Calif., 2002—; mem. NIH Study Sect. Exptl. Immunology, Washington, 1998-2002; cons. Nat. Gynecol. Oncology Group, 2000—; Walter A. Richter chair for cancer rsch. Norris Comprehensive Cancer Ctr., L.A., 2003—. Editor: Peptide Based Cancer Vaccines, 2000; sect. editor: Leukemia, 1999-2001, YourDoctor.com, 2000; contbr. articles to profl. jours. Recipient Career award Royal Netherlands Acad. Arts and Scis., 1991-96, Antoni Van Leeuwenhoek Rsch. award, 1991. Mem. Am. Assn. Immunologists, Am. Assn. for Cancer Rsch., Dutch Soc. Immunology, Chgo. Assn. Immunology (pres. 1999-2001). Avocation: long distance swimming. Office: Univ So Calif Comp Cancer Ctr Zilkha Inst Bldg Rm 245 1501 San Pablo St MC 2821 Los Angeles CA 90089-2021 E-mail: kast@usc.edu.

KASTAN, DAVID SCOTT, university educator, writer; b. N.Y.C., Jan. 4, 1946; s. Peter Lewis and Audrey Brown (Kastan); m. Susan Elise, March 20, 1983; children: Marina Claire. AB, Princeton U., 1967; MA, U. Chgo., 1968, PhD, 1974. Asst. prof. Dartmouth Coll., 1973-79, 1973-79, assoc. prof., 1979-86; prof. Columbia U., 1987—. Disting. vis. prof. Am. U., Cairo, 1995, Copenhagen U., 1998; vis. prof., hon. rsch. prof. Univ. Coll. London, 1999—. Gen. editor: Arden Shakespeare, 1995, assoc. editor: Bantam Shakespeare, 1988; author: Shakespeare and the Shapes of Time, 1982, Shakespeare after Theory, 1999, Shakespeare and the Book, 2001; editor (with Marina Kastan): Poetry for Young People: William Shakespeare, 2000; editor: Staging the Renaissance, 1991, Critical Essays on Shakespeare's Hamlet, 1995, New History of Early English Drama, 1997, A Companion to Shakespeare, 1999, 1 Henry IV (Arden Shakespeare), 2002. Woodrow Wilson fellow, 1968, Folger Libr. fellow, 1994, Huntington Libr. Mellon fellow, 1995, Burke Libr. fellow, 2003. Mem. MLA (divisional exec. com.), Renaissance English Text Soc. (coun. mem.), Shakespeare Assn. Am., Renaissance Soc. Am., Phi Beta Kappa. Office: Columbia Univ Dept English 116th St & Broadway New York NY 10027 E-mail: dsk1@columbia.edu.

KASTE, SUE CREVISTON, pediatric radiologist, researcher; b. Lakewood, Ohio, Feb. 25, 1952; d. Donald P. and Marion S. Creviston; m. Ronald H. Kaste, Apr. 28, 1984; children: Rebecca, Steven, Matthew. BA, Lake Erie Coll., 1974; AAS Physicians Asst., Cuyahoga C.C. and Cleve. Clin., 1977; DO, Chgo. Coll. Osteo. Medicine, 1981. Diplomate Am. Bd. Radiology cert. added qualifications pediat. radiology; cert. osteopath Osteo. Nat. Bd. Med. Examiners. Intern Chgo. Coll. Osteo. Medicine, Ill., 1981-82; diagnostic radiology U. Hosps. Cleve., 1982-86, fellow pediat. radiology, 1986-87; officer in charge pediat. radiology KTTCMC, Keesler AFB, Biloxi, Miss., 1987-90, chief diagnostic radiology, 1990-91; cons. dept. radiology LeBonheur Children's Med. Ctr., Memphis, 1991—2003; assoc. prof. dept. radiology U. Tenn. Coll. Medicine, Memphis, 1991—2003, prof., 2003—; full mem. dept. diagnostic imaging St. Jude Children's Rsch. Hosp., Memphis, 1991—. Reviewer Am. Jour. Roentgenology, 1994—, Pediat. Radiology, 1997—, Cancer, 1997—; contbr. articles to profl. jours. Leader/asst. leader Girl Scouts Am., Cordova, Tenn., 1992-99; youth club asst. Advent Presbyn. Ch., Cordova, 1993-98, mem. ch. orch. Maj. USAF Med. Corps, 1977-91. Grantee, Soc. Pediat. Radiology, 1998. Mem. Children's Oncology Group, Am. Coll. Radiology, Radiologic Soc. N.Am., Midwest Soc. Pediat. Radiology. Avocations: flute, painting, drawing, swimming. Office: St Jude Childrens Rsch Hosp Dept Diagnostic Imaging 332 N Lauderdale St Memphis TN 38105-2729 Fax: 901-495-3962. E-mail: sue.kaste@stjude.org.

KASTELIC, ROBERT FRANK, aerospace company executive; b. Granite City, Ill., July 17, 1934; s. Joseph and Anna Marie (Kries) K.; m. Patricia Ann Dalton, Apr. 8, 1961; children: Michael J., Constance A., Robert J., Kirsten S. BS in Acctg., U. Ill., 1956. Sr. acct. Price Waterhouse & Co., St. Louis, 1956-63; v.p., CFO, comptroller Merc. Bancorp., St. Louis, 1963-72; exec. v.p., CFO Equimark Corp. and Equibank, Pitts., 1972-83, vice-chmn. bd., 1983-84; pres., COO Astrotech Internat. Corp., Pitts., 1986—; chmn., CEO X-Mark Industries, Washington, Pa., 1988—. Bd. dirs. Glenshaw (Pa.) Glass Co., Quasitronics, Inc., X-Mark Industries, Astrotech Internat., Pitts., Fidelity Savs. Bank; chmn. St. Francis Fin. Corp. Mem. rev. com. United Way, Pitts., 1977-78; bd. dirs. St. Francis Hosp., Civic Light Opera. Served with U.S. Army, 1956-58. Mem. AICPA, Am. Mgmt. Assn., Am. Soc. Corp. Secs., Mo., Pa. insts. CPAs, Bank Adminstrn. Inst., Fin. Execs. Inst., Nat. Investor Relations Inst. Clubs: Duquesne. Home: 825 Fox Chapel Rd Pittsburgh PA 15238-2003 Office: X-Mark Industries 2001 N Main St Washington PA 15301-6180 E-mail: rfkastelic@netscape.net.

KASTEN, G. FREDERICK, JR., investment company executive; Pres., CEO, now chmn. Baird Fin. Corp., Milw. Office: Baird Fin Corp 777 E Wisconsin Ave Milwaukee WI 53202-5300

KASTEN, KARL ALBERT, painter, printmaker, educator; b. San Francisco, Mar. 5, 1916; s. Ferdin and Barbara Anna Kasten; m. Georgette Gautier, Mar. 29, 1958; children: Ross, Lee, Beatrix, Joellen, Cho-An. MA, U. Calif., 1939; postgrad., U. Iowa, 1949; student, Hans Hofmann Sch. Fine Arts, 1951. Instr. Calif. Sch. Fine Arts, 1941, U. Mich., 1946-47; asst. prof. art San Francisco State U., 1947-50; prof. U. Calif., Berkeley, 1950-83. Bibliography appears in Etching (Edmondson), 1973, Collage and Assemblage (Meilach and Ten Hoor), 1973, Modern Woodcut Techniques (Kuroski), 1977, California Style (McClelland and Last), 1985, Art in the San Francisco Bay Area (Albright), 1985, Breaking Type: The Art of Karl Kasten (Landauer), 1999, The Stamp of Impulse, Abstract Expressionist Prints (David Acton), 2001; group shows include San Francisco Mus. Art, 1939, Chgo. Art Inst., 1946, Whitney Mus., 1952, Sao Paolo Internat. Biennials, 1955, 61, Achenbach Found., 1976, World Print III Traveling Exhbn., 1980-83, Gallery Sho, Tokyo, 1994, Inst. Franco-Americain, Rennes, 1995, Calif. Heritage Gallery, 1999, Robert Green Fine Arts Gallery, 2002; patentee etching press. Capt. U.S. Army, 1942-46. Decorated 4 battle stars; fellow Creative Arts Inst., 1964, 71, Tamarind Lithography Artist Fellowship, 1968, Regents Humanities, 1977. Mem. Berkeley Art Ctr. Assn. (bd. dirs. 1987-92), Calif. Soc. Printmakers (Disting. Artist award 1997), Univ. Faculty Club, Univ. Arts Club. Home: 1884 San Lorenzo Ave Berkeley CA 94707-1841 Office: Univ Calif Berkeley Art Dept Berkeley CA 94707

KASTEN, WENDY CHRISTINA, literacy educator, writer, consultant; b. Neptune, N.J., Jan. 13, 1951; d. Henry and Mary H. Overeem; 1 child, Tiara Denise. BA, Rowan U., 1973; MEd, U. Maine, 1981; PhD, U. Ariz., 1984. Tchr. St. Mary's Sch., Bangor, Maine, 1974-76, Searsport (Maine) Elem. Sch., 1977-80; asst. prof. U. So. Fla., Sarasota, 1984-90, assoc. prof., 1990-94, Kent State U., Kent, Ohio, 1995-99, prof., 1999—. Pres. Ctr. for Expansion of Lang. and Thinking, 1996-01; bd. dirs. Children's Lit. Spl. Interest Group of Internat. Reading Assn., Newark, Delaware. Co-author: The Multiage Classroom, 1993, Implementing Multiage Education, 1998, Action Research for Teachers: Traveling the Yellow Brick Road, 2001, Living Literature, 2004; assoc. editor Reading and Writing Quar. Mem., bd. dirs. Friends of Selby Libr., Sarasota, Fla., 1987-89. Recipient Literacy award Sarasota Reading Coun., 1986. Mem. Internat. Reading Assn. (editorial review bd. 1995—), Nat. Coun. Tchrs. English (editorial review bd. 1999—), Nat. Reading Conf. (mem. ethics com.). Democrat. Buddhist. Avocations: travel, walking, pets, craft shows, music. Office: Kent State U 402 White Hall Kent OH 44242-0001 E-mail: wkasten@kent.edu.

KASTENBERG, WILLIAM EDWARD, engineering educator, science educator; b. N.Y.C., June 25, 1939; s. Murray and Lillian Kastenberg; m. Berna R. Miller, Aug. 18, 1963; children: Andrew, Joshua, Lillian; m. Gloria Hauser, May 3, 1992. BS, UCLA, 1962, MS, 1963; PhD, U. Calif., Berkeley, 1966. Asst. prof. Sch. Engring. and Applied Sci. UCLA, 1966-71, assoc. prof., 1971-75, assoc. dean Sch. Engring. and Applied Sci., 1981-85, chmn. mech. aerospace and nuc. engring., 1985-88, prof. mech., aerospace and nuc. engring. dept., 1975-94; sr. fellow U.S. NRC, Washington, 1979-80; prof. nuc. engring. dept. U. Calif., Berkeley, 1995—, chmn. nuc. engring. dept., 1995-2000, Chancellor's prof., 1996—99, Daniel Tellep disting. prof. engring., 1999—. Guest scientist Karlsruhe (Fed. Republic Germany) Nuc. Rsch., 1972—73; mem. Nat. Rsch. Com. Reactor Safety, 1985—86; chmn. peer rev. com. U.S. NRC, Washington, 1987—88; mem. adv. com. nuc. facility safety Dept. of Energy, 1988—92; mem. adv. com. Diablo Canyon Nuc. Power Plant, 1999—2000; dir. risk and sys. analysis control toxics program UCLA, 1989—95, chmn. Ctr. Clean Tech., 1992—94; project dir. Ctr. Nuc. and Toxic Waste Mgmt. U. Calif., Berkley, 1995—2000. Contbr. articles to profl. jours. Recipient Disting. Tchg. award, Am. Soc. Engring. Edn., 1973. Fellow: AAAS, Am. Nuc. Soc. (chmn. nuc. safety 1984—85, Arthur Holly Compton award); mem.: NAE. Office: Univ Calif Nuclear Engring Dept 4155 Etcheverry Hall Berkeley CA 94720-1731

KASTER, LAURA A. lawyer; b. N.Y.C., May 24, 1948; BA, Tufts U., 1970; JD magna cum laude, Boston U., 1973. Bar: Mass. 1973, Ill. 1975. Law clk. to Hon. Frank M. Coffin, U.S. Ct. Appeals for 1st circuit, Boston, 1973-75; assoc. Jenner & Block, Chgo., 1975-81, ptnr., 1981-97; gen. atty. law and govt. affairs AT&T Corp., Bedminster, NJ, 1997—. Co-author: Sanctions in Federal Litigation, 1991; co-editor: The Attorneys' Guide to the Seventh Circuit Court of Appeals, 1987; note editor Law Rev. Boston U., 1973-72; contbr. chpt. to book and articles to profl. jours. Fellow Am. Bar Found. (life); mem. ABA, Ill. Bar Assn., 7th Circuit Bar Assn., Fed. Cir. Bar Assn. E-mail: lkaster@att.com.

KASTING, JAMES FRASER, research meteorologist, physicist; b. Schenectady, N.Y., Jan. 2, 1953; married; 3 children. AB, Harvard U., 1975; MS in Physics and Atmospheric Sci., U. Mich., 1978, PhD in Atmospheric Sci., 1979. Rsch. fellow Nat. Ctr. Atmospheric Rsch., 1979-81, Ames Rsch. Ctr., NASA, 1981-83, rsch. scientist, 1983-88; prof. geosci., meteorology Pa. State U., State College, 1988—. Fellow AAAS; mem. Am. Geophys. Union, Internat. Soc. Study of Origin of Life. Achievements include research on evolution of planetary atmospheres; history of the earth and why it is different from that of Mars and Venus. Office: Pa State U Dept Geo Scis 443 Deike Bldg University Park PA 16802-2713 E-mail: kasting@essc.psu.edu.

KASTNER, MARC AARON, physics educator; b. Toronto, Ont., Can., Nov. 20, 1945; came to U.S., 1952; s. Jacob and Ida Pearl (Shidlowsky) K.; m. Marcia Jill Paul, Aug. 27, 1967; 2 children. BS in Chemistry, U. Chgo., 1967, MS, 1969, PhD in Physics, 1972. Rsch. fellow Harvard U., Cambridge, Mass., 1972-73; asst. prof. physics MIT, Cambridge, 1973-77, assoc. prof., 1977-83, prof., 1983-89, Donner prof. of physics, 1989—. Dir. Consortium for Superconducting Electronics, 1989-91, Ctr. for Materials Sci. and Engring, 1993-98; head MIT Dept. Physics, 1998—. Recipient David Adler Lectureship award Am. Physical Society, 1995 Fellow AAAS, Am. Phys. Soc. (councillor at large 1991-94, Oliver E. Buckley prize 2000). Achievements include discovery of single electron effects in nanostructures and research in electronic, optical and magnetic properties of condensed matter, including semiconductors and high temperature superconductors.

KASTNER, MICHAEL JAMES, dentist; b. Huntington, Ind., Oct. 20, 1954; s. James H. and Barbara A. (Bartrom) K.; m. Kimberly A. Ricke, June 18, 1983; children: Kevin Michael, Ryan James, Derek Edward. BS in Biology and Chemistry, Manchester Coll., 1977; DDS, Ind. U., Indpls., 1981; postgrad., Armed Forces Inst. Pathology, 1989. Gen. practice dentistry, Toledo, 1981—. Asst. dentist Toledo Zoo, 1991—; mem. Ohio Mass Disaster Team, 1995—, team capt., 2001—; asst. Lucas County Coroner's Office, 1987—; asst. to N.Y. Med. Examiners Office in dental forensic identification of World Trade Ctr. victims, 2001. Bd. trustees Dental Ctr. Northwest Ohio, 1995-98, 2000, nominating com., 1995-2001, long range planning com., 1999-2001, dental com., 1995-98, 2000; mem. Lucas County Oral Health Coalition. Recipent Alumni Honor award Manchester Coll., 1997, Recognition for Honor award Ohio State Senate Resolution, 1997, Honoring Am. Spirit award Gov. Ohio, 2002. Mem. ADA (chmn. local chpt., chmn. area grass roots membership initiative, Recognition for Vol. Svc. Fgn. Country award in Dominican Republic 1984, 87, in Costa Rica 1990, in Nepal 1994, Nicaragua 2000, 01), Ohio Dental Assn. (state del. 2002, 03, alt. del. 1999, 2000, 01, statewide subcom. on peer rev. 2000—, dental options program, 1999—, Humanitarian of Yr. 1995, 2002), Toledo Dental Soc. (bd. dirs. 1996-99, peer rev. com. 1998—, nominating com. 1999—2003, chmn. 2003,, program and continuing edn. com. 1999—, fin. com. 2000, constitution by-laws com., 2002—, exec. office com. 2000—03, exec. bd. sec./treas. 2000, v.p. 2001, pres. 2002, long range planning com. 2000, relief fund subcom. 1999), Am. Acad. Cosmetic Dentistry, Am. Soc. Forensic Odontology, Am. Coll. Oral Implantology, Am. Soc. Osseointegration Internat. Congress Oral Implantologists, Mensa. Roman Catholic. Avocations: photography, basketball, travel, outdoor activities, oenology. Home: 4616 Waterford Ct Toledo OH 43623-2988

KASTOR, FRANK SULLIVAN, English language educator; b. Evanston, Ill., Aug. 19, 1933; s. Herman Walker and Rebecca (Sullivan) K.; m. Tina Bennett, Oct. 28, 1979; children: Jeffrey, Mark, Harlan, Kristina, Patrick, Liam, Mary Elisabeth, Caroline. BA, U. Ill., 1955, MA, 1956; PhD, U. Calif., Berkeley, 1963. Teaching asst. U. Ill., 1955-56, U. Calif., Berkeley, 1960-63; asst. prof. English U. So. Calif., 1964-66, 67-68; assoc. prof. English No. Ill. U., 1968-69; prof. English, Wichita State U., 1969—, chmn. dept., 1969-75, prof. emeritus, 1998, ret., 1998. Contbr. to: The Milton Ency., The Dictionary of Literary Biography; author books, articles, revs., TV documentaries, C.S. Lewis study guides. Served with USAF, 1956-59. Rsch. grantee U. Calif., Berkeley, 1962, U. So. Calif., 1964, No. Ill. U., 1969, Wichita State U., 1970, 72, 73, 74, 84, 86, 92; Fulbright lectr., Spain, 1966-67; Kans. Com. for Humanities grantee, 1973, 74, 94; recipient NEH award, 1971, 84. Mem. MLA, Milton Soc. Am., Conf. on Christianity and Lit., AAUP, N.Y. C.S. Lewis Soc., C.S. Lewis Soc. of Kans. (founder, pres.), Phi Kappa Phi. Christian Ch. E-mail: fskdr3@aol.com.

KASTOR, JOHN ALFRED, cardiologist, educator; b. N.Y.C., Sept. 15, 1931; s. Alfred Bernard and Ellen Voigt Bentley; m. Mae Belle Eisenberg, July 4, 1954; children: Elizabeth Mae, Anne Sarah, Peter John. BA, U. Pa., 1953; MD, NYU, 1962. With NBC, N.Y.C., 1956-58; intern, asst. resident in medicine Bellevue Hosp., N.Y.C., 1962-64; chief resident physician N.Y. U. Hosp., N.Y.C., 1964-65; clin. and research fellow in medicine Mass. Gen. Hosp., Boston, 1965-68, clin. asst. and asst. in medicine, 1968-69; instr. in medicine Harvard Med. Sch., 1968-69; dir. med. intensive care unit Hosp. U. Pa., Phila., 1969-72, assoc. chief cardiovascular sect., 1972-77, chief, 1977-81; physician-in-chief U. Md. Hosp., 1984-97; prof. medicine U. Pa. Sch. Medicine, Phila., 1976-83; Theodore E. Woodward prof. medicine U. Md. Sch. Medicine, 1984-97, chmn. dept. medicine, 1984-97, prof. medicine, 1997—. Vis. prin. fellow Nat. Heart and Lung Inst., London, 1995. Author: Arrhythmias, 1994, 2nd edit. 2000, Mergers of Teaching Hospitals in Boston, New York and Northern California, 2001, Governance of Teaching Hospitals: Turmoil at Penn and Hopkins, 2003; founding editor Internat. Jour. Cardiology, 1981-84; contbr. numerous articles on cardiac electrophysiology and gen. cardiology to med. jours. Served with U.S. Army, 1953-55. Fellow ACP, Am. Coll. Cardiology, Coun. Clin. Cardiology Am. Heart Assn.; mem. Am. Fedn. Clin. Rsch., Am. Heart Assn. (bd. govs. Southeastern Pa. chpt. 1975-81, bd. govs. Md. affiliate 1990-93), Assn. Am. Physicians, Assn. Univ. Cardiologists, Venezuelan Soc. Internal Medicine, Paul Dudley White Soc. (dir. 1977-86), Alpha Omega Alpha. Home: 2415 Boston St Baltimore MD 21224-4733 Office: U Md Hosp 22 S Greene St Baltimore MD 21201-1544

KASTRUP, DIETER, diplomat; Mem. German permanent mission to UN, N.Y.C.

KASTURIARACHI, ALOYSIUS BATHI, mathematician, educator, mathematician, researcher; arrived in U.S., 1987; s. Edward Weerasinghe and Charlotte Kasturiarachi; m. Sharon Ann Kasturiarachi, Aug. 20, 1988; children: Brittany Marie, Naomi Sonali, Courtney Minoli. BSc with honors, U. Peradeniya, Sri Lanka, 1985; PhD, U. N.C., 1993. Post doctoral instr. Duke U., Durham, NC, 1993—94; asst. prof. Occidental Coll., L.A., 1994—95; assoc. prof. Kent State U., Canton, Ohio, 1995—. Dir. academic mastery program in math. Occidental Coll., L.A., 1994—95; vis. asst. prof. U. N.C., Chapel Hill, 1994—95. Mem.: Math. Assn. Am. Office: Kent State Univ-Stark Campus 6000 Frank Ave NW Canton OH 44720 Office Fax: 330-494-6121. E-mail: bathi@stark.kent.edu.

KASULIS, THOMAS PATRICK, humanities educator; b. Bridgeport, Conn., Mar. 5, 1948; s. Joseph John and Albina Anna (Checkanouskas) K.; m. Ellen Elizabeth Sponheimer, June 5, 1970; children: Telemachus, Matthias, Benedict. BA, Yale U., 1970, MPh, 1972, PhD, 1975; MA, U. Hawaii, 1973. Asst. prof. philosophy U. Hawaii, Honolulu, 1975-80; from asst. prof. to prof. philosophy and religion Northland Coll., Ashland, Wis., 1981-91; prof. comparative studies The Ohio State U., Columbus, 1991—, chair East Asian langs. and lit., 1993-95, chair comparative studies, 1995-98. Mellon faculty fellow in humanities Harvard U., Cambridge, Mass., 1979-80; vis. facility rschr. Osaka (Japan) U., 1982-83; Numata vis. prof. U. Chgo., Ill., 1988. Author: Zen Action/Zen Person, 1981, Intimacy or Integrity: Philosophy and Cultural Difference, 2002; editor, co-translator: The Body: Toward an Eastern Mind-Body Theory, 1987; co-editor: Self as Body in Asian Theory and Practice, 1993, Self as Person in Asian Theory and Practice, 1994; contbr. chpts. to books and articles to profl. jours. Fellow Japan Found., 1982-83; NEH fellow for Coll. Tchrs., NEH, 1986-87; Sr. Rsch. fellow East West Ctr., Honolulu, 1988. Mem. Soc. for Asian and Comparative Philosophy (pres. 1988-91), Am. Soc. for the Study of Religion (pres. 1999-2002), Soc. for Values in Higher Edn. Home: 1465 Montcalm Rd Upper Arlington OH 43221-3450 Office: Comparative Studies Ohio State Univ 230 W 17th Ave Columbus OH 43210-1361 E-mail: kasulis.1@osu.edu.

KASUM, MICHAEL, humanities educator, writer; b. Milw., Wis., Oct. 22, 1934; s. Anton Kasum and Olive Sarah Elmer; m. Patricia W. Kasum, June 17, 1994. BA, U. State NY, Albany, 1998; MFA, Vt. Coll. Norwich U., 1998; PhD, U. Wis., Milw., 2001. Pub. Curay (Colo.) County Herald, 1966—68; co. exec. Kas-Com Inc., Boise, Idaho, 1969—78; internat. currency cons. Assn.: Amb. Eusebio A. Morales, Harry D. Schultz, PhD, PaulEinzig, PhD, Robert Z. Aliber, PhD, 1974—83; newspaper co. exec. Metro-News Features Inc., Portland,

Maine, 1978—94; prof. english Cardinal Stritch U., Milwaukee, Wis., 2000—01, U. Wis., Milwaukee, Wis., 2000—01, U. South Fla., Tampa, Fla., 2001—. Author: Coney Island of the Mind, (novels) The Last Truth, Islands Below the Wind; contbr. articles to profl. jours. Pres. Phoenix Found., Carson City, Nev., 1964—66. Mem.: MLA, Associated Writing Programs, Valdimir Nabokov Soc., Samuel Beckett Soc. Achievements include experimental work in hyperfiction. Avocations: sailing, racquetball, scuba diving, skydiving. Home: 19046 Bruce B Downs Boulevard 145 Tampa FL 33647

KASZAS, WILLIAM JOSEPH, technology educator; b. N.Y.C., Aug. 14, 1944; s. Thomas and Ruth (Trub) Kaszas; m. Ann M. Budnik, Aug. 12, 1966 (div. Dec. 14, 1987). BS, NYU, 1966, MA, 1970. Tchr. indsl. arts Eldred (N.Y.) Cen. Sch., 1966—68, Monticello (N.Y.) Cen. Sch., 1968—81, tchr. tech. edn., 1981—2000. Exhibit designer Lower Hudson Interactive Mus., Middletown, NY, 2000—; presenter in field. Contbr. Scholar NYU scholar, Hebrew Tech. Inst., 1970—2000. Achievements include invention of magnetic levitation track; design of knee brace. Avocations: playing harmonica, reading, Karate. Home: 374 Glen Wild Rd Glen Wild NY 12738

KASZNIAK, ALFRED WAYNE, neuropsychologist; b. Chgo., June 2, 1949; s. Alfred H. and Ann Virginia (Simonsen) K.; m. Mary Ellen Beaurain, Aug. 26, 1973; children: Jesse, Elizabeth. BS with honors, U. Ill., 1970, MA, 1973, PhD, 1976. Instr. dept. psychology Rush Med. Coll., Chgo., 1974-76, asst. prof. dept. psychology, 1976-79; from asst. prof. to assoc. prof. dept. psychiatry U. Ariz. Coll. Medicine, Tucson, 1979-82, assoc. prof. dept. psychology and psychiatry, 1982-87, prof. dept. psychology, neurology and psychiatry, 1987—; chmn. U. Ariz. Commn. on Gerontology, Tucson, 1990-93; acting head dept. psychology U. Ariz., 1992-93, assoc. head dept. psychology, 1999—2002, head dept. psychology, 2002—. Dir. U. Ariz. Coordinated Clin. Neuropsychology Program, dir. Ctr. Consciousness Studies, 1998-2002; staff psychologist Presbyn.-St. Luke's Hosp., Chgo., 1976-79, Univ.Hosp., Tucson, 1979—; mem. human devel. and aging study sect. divsn. rsch. grants, NIH, 1981-86. Author 6 books; mem. editl. bd. Psychology and Aging, 1984-87, The Clin. Neuropsychologist, 1986-96, Clin. Geropsychology, 1994-2003, Jour. Clin. and Exptl. Neuropsychology, 1987-90, Jour. Gerontology, 1988-92, Neuropsychology, 1992-93, Psychological Bull., 1998-2003, Aging, Neuropsychology, and Cognition, 1999—, Consciousness and Emotion, 2000—; contbr. articles to profl. jours. Trustee So. Ariz. chpt. Nat. Multiple Sclerosis Soc., 1980-82; mem. med. and sci. adv. bd. Nat. Alzheimer's Disease and Related Disorders Assn., 1981-84; mem. VA Geriatrics and Gerontology Adv. Com., 1986-89, Ariz. Gov.'s Adv. Com. on Alzheimer's Disease, 1988-92; mem. med. adv bd. Fan Kane Fund for Brain-Injured Children, Tucson, 1980-92. Grantee Nat. Inst. Aging, 1978—83, 1989—94, 2001—, NIMH, 1984—94, 2002—, Robert Wood Johnson Found., 1986—89, Fetzer Inst., 1997—, Flinn Found., 1998—99. Fellow Am. Psychol. Assn. (Disting. Contbr. award div. 20 1978, pres. clin. geropsychology sect. 1995), Am. Psychol. Soc.; mem. Internat. Neuropsychol. Soc. (bd. govs. 1994-97), Gerontol. Soc. (rsch. fellow 1980). Home: 2327 E Hawthorne St Tucson AZ 85719-4944 Office: U Ariz Dept Psychology 1503 E University Tucson AZ 85721-0001 E-mail: kaszniak@u.arizona.edu.

KATAI, ANDREW ANDRAS, chemical company executive; b. Gyor, Hungary, Sept. 17, 1937; came to U.S., 1956; s. Ivan and Clara (Szel) K.; m. Debbie Judwin, May 12, 1963 (div. 1970); children: Alisa, Gregory; m. Joan Eleanor Klein, July 30, 1972; children: Peter, Daniel. BS, Juniata Coll., 1960; MS, PhD, Syracuse U., 1965; MS, PhD in Chemistry, SUNY, Syracuse, 1965. Internat. mktg. asst. Esso chem. Co., N.Y.C., 1965-66; asst. prof. Hunter-Lehman Coll. N.Y.C., 1965-70; research chemist Union Carbide Corp., Tarrytown, N.Y., 1966-67, internat. assoc. prodn. mgr. N.Y.C., 1967-69, internat. product mgr., 1969-71; new bus. devel. mgr. W.R. Grace Constrn. Co., Cambridge, Mass., 1971-73; bus. mgr. internat. div. Inolex Corp., Chgo., 1973-77; Far East devel mgr. Eschem (Swift) Inc., Chgo., 1977, gen. mgr. internat. div., 1977-81, dir. internat. div., 1981-82, v.p. internat. div., 1982-83; pres. Swift Adhesives subs. Reichhold Chem. Co., Downers Grove, Ill., 1983-93; sr. Corridor fellow, assoc. prof. internat. bus. North Ctrl. Coll., Naperville, Ill., 1994-2000. Contbr. articles to profl. jours. Chmn. coll. fundraising dr., Westchester County, N.Y., 1969; co-chmn. Homeowners' Assn., Flossmoor, Ill., 1981-82. Mem. Adhesive Mfrs. Assn. (treas. 1986-88, pres.-elect 1988, pres. 1990), East West Corp. Corridor Assn. (v.p. 1992-94), Am. Chem. Soc., Sigma Xi, Phi Lambda Upsilon. Avocations: bridge, classical music, kayaking, photography, travel. Home: 1105 E Johnson Dr Naperville IL 60540-8245

KATAKKAR, SURESH BALAJI, hematologist, oncologist; b. Poona, India, Feb. 9, 1944; s. Balaji Vasudeo Katakkar and Padmavati (Gangadhar) Varavandkar; m. Sunila Moghe; children: Smita, Sucheta, Swati. MB, BS, Poona U., India, 1969; grad., Ednl. Coun. Fgn. Med., 1970. Lic. Med. Coun. Can., diplomate in internal medicine and oncology Am. Bd. Internal Medicine, Am. Bd. Quality Assurance and Utilization Rev., Am. Bd. Forensic Medicine, Am. Bd. Thrombosis and Vascular Medicine, European Soc. Med. Oncology. Intern, then resident St. Paul's Hosp., Saskatoon, 1969-71; resident U. Hosp., Saskatoon, 1971-72; resident clin. hematology Gen. Hosp., Ottawa, 1973-74; fellow in med. oncology W.W. Cross Cancer Inst., Edmonton, Can., 1974-75; sr. cancer clin. assoc. Saskatchewan Cancer Commn., 1975-78; clin. investigator NCI, USA, 1975—; med. oncologist Madigan Army Med. Ctr., 1978-80; pvt. practice Tucson, Ariz., 1980—; med. dir., chmn. cancer com. N.W. Cancer Ctr., 1991—. Chmn. tumor bd. St. Mary's Hosp., Tucson, 1981-83, chmn. transfusion com., 1982-97; chmn. dept. med. Northwest Hosp., 1983-84, chief of staff, 1984-86, trustee, 1984-96, clin. lectr. Univ. Med. Ctr., Ariz. Cancer Ctr., 1989—. Contbr. articles to profl. jours.; spkr, presenter, abstracts in field. W.W. Cross Cancer Inst. fellow, 1974-75. Fellow ACP, Royal Coll. Physicians Can., Internat. Acad. Thrombosis/Hemostasis; mem. AMA, Am. Soc. Clin. Oncology, Internat. Soc. Preventive Oncology, Am. Geriatrics Soc., Am. Hosp. Assn., Am. Assn. Blood Banks, Am. Bd. Med. Dirs., Am. Coll. Med. Quality, N.Y. Acad. Scis., European Soc. Med. Oncology, European Assn. Cancer Rsch. Home: 1391 E Placita Mapache Tucson AZ 85718-3929 Office: NW Cancer Ctr 1845 W Orange Grove Rd Bldg 2 Tucson AZ 85704-1144 E-mail: azhemonc@aol.com.

KATAVOLOS, WILLIAM, architecture educator, furniture designer; b. N.Y.C., Mar. 14, 1924; s. Peter and Sophia Katavolos; m. Terenia Lombard Katavolos, Dec. 13, 1960. B in Indsl. Design, Pratt Inst., 1949. Fine arts painter John Nichols Residency, Woodstock, NY, 1940—42; designer furniture line Frankel/Robert John, N.Y.C., 1946—; designer Luss Design Office, N.Y.C., 1954—59; designer furniture line Geo. Nelson Office, N.Y.C., 1955—57; tchr. design, chair indsl. design Parson Sch., N.Y.C., 1955—71; tchr. design Pratt Inst., Bklyn., 1957—. Co-dir. Ctr. Exptl. Structures, 1985—; lectr. USIS-USIA. Author: Organics, 1960, Manifestos of Twentieth Century, 1970, Chemical City, 1990. Sgt. USAF, 1942—46. Recipient 1st prize furniture design, Mus. Modern Art, N.Y.C., 1952, 1953, 1st prize furniture, Am. Inst. Design, N.Y.C., 1953—54. Mem.: N.Y. Acad. Sci. Achievements include patents for hydronic and building systems; development of theory of quantum numerodynamics. Avocation: golf. Office: Pratt Inst Ctr Exptl Structures N Higgins Hall 200 Willoughby Ave Brooklyn NY 11205

KATAYAMA, ROBERT NOBUICHI, lawyer; b. Honolulu, Oct. 11, 1924; s. Sanji K.; married; children: Alyce A. Katayama Jenkins, Robert Nobuichi, Kent J., Susan H. Ono, Carole Y. Kaneshiro, Wendy L. Lee. BA, U. Hawaii, 1950; LLB, Yale U., 1955; grad., Command and Gen. Staff Coll., 1964; LLM, George Washington U., 1967; grad., Indsl. Coll. Armed Forces, 1971. Bar: Calif. 1956, Ill. 1973, Hawaii 1989. Commd. 1st lt. JAGC U.S. Army, 1958, advanced through grades to col., 1973, ret., 1973; gen. counsel Overseas Mdse. Inspection Co., San Francisco, 1956-58, Army Contract Adjustment Bd., Washington, 1964-68; prof. law JAG Sch. U. Va., 1968-70; from assoc. to ptnr. Baker & McKenzie, Chgo., Tokyo and San Francisco, 1973-85; ptnr. Seki & Jarvis, San Francisco and San Jose, 1985-86, Nutter, McClennen & Fish, San Francisco, 1986-88; spl. counsel, sr. advisor Crosby, Heafey, Roach & May, Oakland, Calif., 1988; ptnr. Carlsmith Ball, Honolulu, 1988-95, counsel, 1995—. Chmn., CEO Kapolei People's Inc. dba Kapolei Golf Course, Honolulu, 1996-99, Kapolei Holding Corp. Trustee Nat. Japanese Am. Meml. Found., 1995—97, gov., 1997—; mem. Hawaii Adv. Coun. to Japanese Am. Nat. Mus., 2001—03; bd. dirs. Japanese Cultural Ctr. Hawaii, 1997—98, bd. govs., 1998—. Named Real Dean, U. Hawaii, Honolulu, 1950; recipient Disting. Alumni award, 2001. Mem.: ABA, Ill. Bar Assn., 442d Regimental Combat Team Found. (trustee 1993—2003, pres. 1999—2002), Hawaii Army Mus. Soc. (trustee 2001—03), Ret. Officers Assn., Japanese Am. Soc. Legal Studies, Nat. Japanese Am. Hist. Soc. (legal officer 1984—89), Japan Am. Soc. Hawaii, Hawaii Bar Assn., Calif. Bar Assn., Oahu AJA Vets. Coun. (pres. 1997), Japanese C. of C. of No. Calif. (bd. dirs. 1987—89), 442d Vets. Club (legal advisor 1994—95, pres.-elect 1996, pres. 1997—98, legal advisor 2000—). Democrat. Buddhist. Office: Carlsmith Ball ASB Tower Ste 2200 1001 Bishop St Honolulu HI 96813-3676

KATCHEN, AARON L, historian; b. Burlington, Vt., July 20, 1942; s. Jacob and Jean Perelman Katchen; m. Rosalie Ethel Landesman, May 25, 1969 (dec. Sept. 11, 2000); children: Yonatan Mayer, Medinah Anne Korn, Hillel Hayim. AB, Bklyn Coll., CUNY, 1960—64; PhD, Harvard U., 1979. Lectr. U. of Toronto, 1971—73, Ind. U., Bloomington, Ind., 1974—77; asst. prof. Brandeis U., Waltham, Mass., 1977—87; project dir. Brandeis U. Libr., Waltham, Mass., 1992—93; exec. dir. Assn. for Jewish Studies, Waltham, 1994—. Dissertation Fellowship, Meml. Found. for Jewish Culture, 1970—71, Dissertation fellowship, Nat. Found. for Jewish Culture, 1973—74, Regents Coll. Tchg. fellowship, NY State, 1964—66, 1967—68. Avocations: music, travel, cycling, swimming. Home: 44 Ellison Rd Newton Center MA 02459 Office: Assn for Jewish Studies MS 011 Brandeis University Waltham MA 02454 Office Fax: 781-736-2982. E-mail: katchen@brandeis.edu.

KATCHER, RICHARD, lawyer; b. N.Y.C., Dec. 17, 1918; s. Samuel and Gussie (Applebaum) K.; m. Shirley Ruth Rifkin, Sept. 24, 1944; children: Douglas P., Robert A., Patti L. BA, U. Mich., 1941, JD, 1943. Bar: Mich. 1943, N.Y. 1944, Ohio 1946. Assoc. Noonan, Kaufman & Eagan, N.Y.C., 1943-46; from assoc. to ptnr. Ulmer, Berne & Laronge, Cleve., 1946-72; ptnr. Baker & Hostetler, Cleve., 1972-95. Lectr. in fed. income taxation Case Western Res. U. Sch. Law, Cleve., 1953-69, 71-72; mem. bd. in control of intercollegiate athletics, U. Mich., 2001—. Contbr. articles on fed. tax to profl. jours. Recipient Disting. Alumni Service award U. Mich., 1987, Leadership medal Pres.' Soc. of U. Mich., 1991. Fellow ABA (coun. sect. taxation 1973-76), Am. Coll. Tax Counsel (regent); mem. Am. Bar Retirement Assn. (bd. dirs., v.p. 1986-87, pres. 1987-88), U. Mich. Pres. Soc. (chmn. exec. com. 1987-90), U. Mich. Cleve. Club (pres. 1959, Outstanding Alumnus award 1987), U. Mich. Alumni Assn. (dir. 1994-98, sec. 1997-98). Avocation: tennis. Home: 26150 Village Ln Apt 104 Beachwood OH 44122-7527 Office: Baker & Hostetler 3200 National City Ctr 1900 E 9th St Ste 3200 Cleveland OH 44114-3475 E-mail: RKatcher@baker-hostetler.com.

KATCHOR, BEN, cartoonist, artist, writer; b. Bkyln., Nov. 19, 1951; BA, Bklyn. Coll., 1975. Author: Cheap Novelties, 1991, Julius Knipl, Real Estate Photographer, 1996, The Jew of New York, 1999, The Beauty Supply District, 2000. Fellow Guggenheim fellowship, 1995, MacArthur Found., 2000. E-mail: ben@katchor.com.

KATCHUR, MARLENE MARTHA, nursing administrator; b. Belleville, Ill., Dec. 20, 1946; d. Elmer E. and Hilda B. (Gutherz) Wilde; m. Raymond J. Katchur, Feb. 22, 1969; 1 child, Nickolas Phillip. BSN, So. Ill. U., 1968; MS in Health Care Adminstrn., Calif. State U., L.A., 1982. RN; cert. critical care nurse. Staff nurse, head nurse, nursing supr. U. So. Calif Med. Ctr. LA County, 1968-81, assoc. dir. nursing, internal medicine nursing, 1981-83, internal medicine nursing info. systems coord., 1983-89, patient-centered info. systems cons., 1989-90, nursing info. systems cons. for pediatrics, psychiatry and ICU, 1990-92, psychiat. nursing svcs. human resources and info. systems, 1992-94; nursing supr. adminstrv. nursing office, 1994-95; nurse mgr. Gen. Hosp., 1995-2000, assoc. dir. patient care svcs., 2000—. Mem. Sheriff's Relief Assn. Mem. AACN, NAFE, AAUW, Am. Heart Assn., So. Ill. U. Alumni Assn. (life), Health Svcs. Mgmt. Forum, Am. Orgn. Nurse Execs., Am. Soc. Profl. and Exec. Women, Soc. Clin. Data Mgmt. Systems (bd. dirs. 1990-91), Soc. Med. Computer Observers (charter), Am. Legion Aux., Nat. Hist. Soc., Job's Daus. (past honor queen). Avocations: reading, crocheting, embroidering, gardening, travel. Office: LA County U So Calif Med Ct 1200 N State St Los Angeles CA 90033-1029

KATDARE, ASHOK V. science administrator; b. Mumbai, India, May 29, 1950; arrived in US, 1975; s. Vishwanath A. and Sudha V. Katdare. BS in Pharmacy, U. Bombay, 1971, MS, 1973; PhD, U. Mich., 1986. Scientist, mgr. Burroughts Welcome, Mumbai, 1973—75; scientist Merck & Co., West Point, Pa., 1982—86, dir., 1986—99; sr. dir. Delsys Pharma, Princeton, NJ, 1999—2000; dir. Abbott Labs., Chgo., 2000—. Steering com. Product Quality Rsch. Inst.; expert USP; chair-elect Internat. Pharm. Excipients Coun. Am., DC, 1999—2001, chair, 2001—02, past chair, 2003—. Achievements include patents for drug formulations. Avocations: music, theater. Office: Abbott Labs 1441 Sheridan Rd North Chicago IL 60064

KATEB, GEORGE ANTHONY, political science educator; b. Bklyn., Feb. 27, 1931; s. Anthony Francis and Victoria Anna (Mesnooh) K. AB, Columbia U., 1952, A.M., 1953, PhD, 1960; D.H.L. (hon.), Amherst, 1989. Mem. faculty Amherst Coll., 1957, prof., 1967-87, Kenan prof. polit. sci., 1974-78, Joseph B. Eastman prof. polit. sci., 1980-87; prof. politics Princeton U., 1987—, William Nelson Cromwell prof. politics, 1999—2002, William Nelson Cromwell prof. politics emeritus, 2002—. Vis. lectr. Mt. Holyoke Coll., 1958, Yale U., 1973, Harvard U., 1986. Author: Utopia and Its Enemies, 2d edit., 1972, Political Theory: Its Nature and Uses, 1968, Utopia, 1971, Hannah Arendt: Politics, Conscience, Evil, 1984, The Inner Ocean: Individualism and Democratic Culture, 1992 (Spitz prize Conf. for Study Polit. Thought 1994), Emerson and Self-Reliance, 1994; co-editor: (with David Bromwich) John Stuart Mill, On Liberty; mem. editl. bd. Mass. Rev., 1961-70, Polit. Theory, 1972—, Am. Polit. Sci. Rev., 1976-81, Jour. History Ideas, 1976—, Jour. Utopian Studies, 1977-80, Raritan, 1980-2002; cons. editor: Polit. Theory, 1983-2000. Univ. fellow Columbia U., 1953-54; fellow Soc. Fellows, Harvard U., 1954-57; Guggenheim fellow, 1971-72 Mem. AAUP, Am. Acad. Arts and Scis., New Eng. Polit. Sci. Assn. (exec. com. 1965-66, pres. 1978-79), Am. Soc. Polit. and Legal Philosophy (v.p. 1972-74), Conf. for Study of Polit. Thought, ACLU, Phi Beta Kappa. Office: Princeton U Dept Politics Princeton NJ 08544-0001

KATEN, JOAN ALICE, political scientist, educator; d. Frederick J. Maliha and Alice H. Haddad; m. Ronald N. Katen, Nov. 22, 1969; children: John, Laura, Allison. MA, Columbia U., 1971. Cons. on Middle East politics Am. Friends Svc. Com., Boston, 1973; pvt. cons. on Middle East politics, 1973—. Instr. Cambridge (Mass.) Ctr. for Adult Edn., Mass., 1974—76; prof. polit. sci. Pace U., Pleasantville, NY, 1999—; v.p. UN Assn. Westchester County, N.Y.C., 2003—. Commr. health Village of Mamik, NY, 1985; pres. Friends of Florence Park, Mamk, 1985—. Mem.: LWV (pres. 1985), Acad. Polit. Sci., Pi Gamma Mu, Pi Sigma Alpha, Phi Beta Kappa. Office: Dept Social Sci 861 Bedford Rd Pleasantville NY 10570-2700

KATEN, KAREN L. pharmaceutical company executive; From mem. mktg. ops. to pres. Pfizer Inc., N.Y.C., 1975-95, pres., 1995—, exec. v.p., PPG, 1997—. Office: Pfizer Inc 235 E 42nd St New York NY 10017-5755

KATES, BRIAN C. newspaper editor; b. N.Y.C., Mar. 15, 1946; s. Charles Oliver Kates and Elmyra Von Winkle; 1 child, Elizabeth. BA, Pa. Mil. Coll., 1968. Tchr. English and French Gunning-Bedford High, Delaware City, Del., 1968-69; reporter, editor Herald Statesman, Yonkers, N.Y., 1972-74; from reporter to spl. projects writer Daily News, N.Y.C., 1974—2001, spl. projects writer, 2001—. Adj. prof. NYU, 1976-83, Columbia Grad. Sch. Journalism, N.Y.C., 1980-83. Author: The Murder of a Shopping Bag Lady, 1985 (Spl. Edgar Allan Poe award Mystery Writers of Am. 1985, named one of 25 Books to Remember, N.Y. Pub. Libr. 1985). Capt. mil. police, 1968-72. Recipient 1st pl. prize deadline reporting AP, N.Y. State, 1983, 1st prize editl. writing, 1998; Gold Typewriter award N.Y. Press Club, 1985, 89, Pulitzer prize Columbia U., 1999, George Polk award L.I. U., 1999. Office: NY Daily News 450 W 33d St New York NY 10001

KATES, CHERYL L. legal nursing consultant; b. Rochester, N.Y., July 4, 1970; d. John Edward Leavy and Jean Ellen (Boyle) Leavy-Ellis; 1 child, Markas J. LPN, SUNY, Brockport, 1991; AA, Monroe C.C., Rochester, 1998; BA, St. John Fisher Coll. Cert. EMT; LPN. LPN Unique Staffing, Rochester, 1991—94. Tutor Literacy Vols., Rochester, 1996—; co-dir. Edge of Justice; bd. dirs. legal com. NYCLU, Rochester. Avocations: ceramics, African American studies. Home: PO Box 11078 Rochester NY 14611

KATES, MORRIS, biochemist, educator; b. Galati, Romania, Sept. 30, 1923; arrived in Can., 1924, naturalized, 1944; s. Samuel and Toby (Cohen) K.; m. Pirkko Helena Sofia Makinen, June 14, 1957; children: Anna-Lisa, Marja Helena, Ilona Sylvia. Student, Parkdale Coll., 1936-41; BA, U. Toronto, Ont., Can., 1945, MA, 1946, PhD, 1948. Research asst. Banting Inst., U. Toronto, 1948-49; postdoctoral fellow Nat. Research Council Can., Ottawa, Ont., 1949-51, research officer bioscis. div., 1951-68; prof. chemistry U. Ottawa, 1968-69, prof. biochemistry, 1969-89, prof. emeritus, 1989—, vice-dean research Faculty Sci. and Engring., 1978-82, staff research lectr., 1981, chmn. dept. biochemistry, 1982-85. Author: Techniques of Lipidology, 1972, 2d edit., 1986; co-editor: Metabolic Inhibitors vols. II and IV, 1972, 73, Biomembranes vol. 12, 1984, Handbook of Lipid Rsch., vol. 6, 1990, Biochemistry of Archaea (Archaebacteria), 1993; co-editor: Can. Jour. Biochemistry, 1974-84; contbr. numerous articles on lipid rsch. to profl. jours. Fellow Chem. Inst. Can., Royal Soc. Can.; mem. Can. Biochem. Soc. (pres. 1987-88), Am. Chem. Soc., Am. Soc. Biol. Chemists, Biochem. Soc. (London, Morton lectr. 1995), Am. Oil Chemists Soc. (Supelco rsch. award 1984), Ottawa Biol. and Biochem. Soc. (Sci. prize 1977, pres. 1974-75). Achievements include rsch. on lipid biochemistry. Home: 1723 Rhodes Crescent Ottawa ON Canada K1H 5T1 Office: U Ottawa Dept Biochemistry 40 Marie Curie Ottawa ON Canada KIN 6N5 E-mail: mkates@science.uottawa.ca.

KATES, ROBERT WILLIAM, geographer, educator; b. Bklyn., N.Y., Jan. 31, 1929; m. Eleanor Hackman Kates, Feb. 9, 1948. Student, NYU, 1946—48, U. Ind., 1957; AM, U. Chgo., 1960, PhD, 1962; Doctorate (hon.), Clark U. Mem. faculty grad. sch. geography Clark U., Worcester, Mass., 1962—, prof., 1968—92, univ. prof., 1974—88; univ. prof., dir. Alan Shawn Feinstein World Hunger Program, Brown U., Providence, 1986—92, univ. prof. emeritus, 1992—. Dir. Bur. Resource Assessment and Land Use Planning, U. Coll., Dar es Salaam, Tanzania, 1967—69; hon. rsch. prof. U. Dar es Salaam, 1970—71. Author: Risk Assessment of Environmental Hazard, 1978; co-author (with Ian Burton and Gilbert F. White): The Environment as Hazard, 1978; co-editor: Climact Impact Assessment, 1985, Hunger in History, 1990, The Earth as Transformed by Human Action, 1990; contbr. articles to profl. jours. Recipient Nat. Medal Sci., Pres. Bush, NSF, 1991; fellow Prize fellow, MacArthur Found. Mem.: AAAS, NAS, Am. Acad. Arts and Scis., Tanzania Soc., Academia Europaea, Assn. Am. Geographers (pres. 1993—94). Office: C/O Brown U 182 George St Providence RI 02912-9056

KATHAN, DEBRA, personnel director, educator; b. Viroqua, Wis., May 26, 1953; d. Bennorris I. and Margaret L. Sovde; m. Richard L. Kathan, Aug. 1, 1975; children: Scott, Angela, Andrew. BS, U. Wis., LaCrosse, 1975, MS, 1977; postgrad., U. Minn., 1983—. Pers. dir. St. Croix County, Hudson, Wis., 1981—. Adj. faculty U. Wis., River Falls, 1998—. Office: St Croix County 1101 Carmichael Rd Hudson WI 54016-7713 Home: 2224 Jodi Cir Hudson WI 54016-5854

KATHER, GERHARD, retired federal administrator; b. Allenstein, Germany, Jan. 30, 1939; arrived in U.S., 1952, naturalized, 1959; s. Ernst and Maria (Kempa) K.; m. Carol Anne Knutsen, Aug. 18, 1962; children: Scott T., Cynthia M., Tracey S., Chris A.; m. Mary Elsie Frank, Oct. 25, 1980. BA in Govt., U. Ariz., 1964; MPA, U. So. Calif., 1971; cert. in pers. adminstrn., U. N.Mex., 1987. Tchr. social studies, Covina, Calif., 1965-67; tng. officer Civil Pers., Ft. MacArthur, Calif., 1967-70; chief employee tng. and devel. Corps Engrs., L.A., 1970-72, Frankfurt Area Army Pers. Office, 1972-73; chief employee rels. and tng. brs. Corps Engrs., L.A., 1973-74; chief employee devel. and tng. Kirtland AFB, N.Mex., 1974-87; labor rels. officer Kirtland AFB and detachments in 13 U.S. cities, 1987-90; project coord., adv. Protection and Advocacy Sys., 1991-96; ret., 1996. Mem. adv. com. Albuquerque Tech.-Vocat. Inst., 1982-92, U. N.Mex. Valencia Campus, 1985-92; mem. Coalition for Disability Rights, 1988-96; chmn. Comprehensive Accessibility Network, 1990-96; adv. coun. N.Mex. Disability Prevention, 1992-96; rec. sec. N.Mex. Commn. Blind State Rehab. Adv. Coun., 1993-96. With USAF, 1958—64. Named Prominent Tng. and Devel. Profl., H. Whitney McMillan Co., 1984; recipient GEICO Pub. Svc. Phys. Rehab. award, 1988. Mem. ASTD (treas. chpt. 1984-85), Paralyzed Vets. Am. (bd. dirs. 1986-87, pres. local chpt. 1986-87, 90-92), Toastmasters Internat. (chpt. treas., v.p., pres. 1967-70), Vietnam Vets. Am. (chpt. newsletter editor 1994-95), Phi Delta Kappa. Democrat. Roman Catholic.

KATHERINE, ROBERT ANDREW, chemical company executive; b. Phila., May 26, 1941; s. John and Winifred Irene (Smith) K.; m. Lynda Ann Ketchell, Dec. 27, 1988. BSCh.E., Drexel Inst. Tech., 1964, MBA, 1968; P.MD, Harvard U. Grad. Sch. Bus., 1977. Plant mgr. synthetic phenol plastics div. Allied Chem. Corp., 1964-66; asst. to dir. Far East sales Air Products & Chems., Phila., 1966-70; product group mgr. corp. devel. P.Q. Corp., 1970-72, div. sales mgr. splty. chems., 1972-74; bus. dir. polymers Hooker Chem. & Plastics div. Occidental Petroleum Corp., Burlington, N.J., 1974-78, v.p., gen. mgr. Ruco div., 1978-80, v.p., gen. mgr. fabricated products div., 1980-81; pres. The McCloskey Corp., 1981-83, chmn. bd., chief exec. officer, 1983—. Chmn. bd. McCloskey Corp. (Calif.), McCloskey Corp. (Oreg.); instr. Villanova U., 1973-75; asst. prof. Phila. Coll. Textiles and Sci., 1969-75 Mem. adv. bd. Modern Paint & Coatings Mag.; contbr. numerous articles to profl. jours. and newspapers. Bd. dirs. Inter-Sci. Found., UCLA Med. Sch., 1983-86; bd. dirs., chmn. fin. com., exec. compensation com., mem. exec. com. Hahnemann U.; corp. adv. bd. Huntington's Disease of Am. Mem. Soc. Plastics Industry (chmn. vinyl film group, exec. com. plastic bottle inst.), Nat. Paint and Coatings Assn. (bd. dirs., indsl. coatings steering com.), Young Pres. Orgn., Am. Chem. Soc., Am. Mgmt. Assn. (pres.' assn.), Pa. Soc. Clubs: Harvard Bus. Sch. (Phila., N.Y.C.); Union League (Phila.); Aronimink. Republican. Baptist. Home: 4102 Battles Ln Newtown Square PA 19073-1602 Office: 7600 State Rd Philadelphia PA 19136-3404

KATHOL, ANTHONY LOUIS, real estate executive; b. San Diego, June 12, 1964; s. Cletus Louis and Regina Antoinette (Ellrott) K.; m. Kathleen Marie Moore, Jan. 23, 1988; children: Nicole Kathleen, Natalie Antoinette, Holly Rose. BS, U. So. Calif., 1986; MBA, U. San Diego, 1988. Fin. aid analyst U. San Diego, 1986-87; bookkeeper Golden Lion Tavern, San Diego, 1987-88; fin. and budget coord. Santa Fe Pacific Realty Corp. (name now Catellus Devel. Corp.), Brea, Calif., 1988-91; mgr. fin. analysis SW U.S. Catellus Devel. Corp., Anaheim, Calif., 1992-93; mgr. leasing Pacific Design Ctr., West Hollywood, Calif., 1994-95, dir. fin. and policy, 1995-96, v.p. asset mgmt., 1996-97; project mgr. Spieker Properties, Orange, Calif., 1997-2001; sr. property mgr. Equity Office Properties, Cerritos, Calif., 2001—02, gen. mgr. Pasadena, Calif., 2002—. Bd. dirs. Pasadena Playhouse Dist. Assn., 2002—. Calif. Bldg. Industry Assn. fellow, 1986, U. San Diego fellow, 1987. Mem. U. San Diego Grad. Bus. Students Assn., K.C. (fin. sec. 1990-91), Tau Kappa Epsilon. Republican. Roman Catholic. Avocations: civil war history, collecting commerative plates and coins, reading, basketball, golf. Home: 12170 Orgren Ave Chino CA 91710-2115 Office: Equity Office Properties 550 S Hope St # 2200 Pasadena CA 90017 E-mail: tony_kathol@equityoffice.com., a.kathol@att.net.

KATHREIN, REED RICHARD, lawyer; b. Cadillac, Mich., Aug. 14, 1954; s. John Anton and Jean Ann (Reeder) K.; m. Margaret Ann McClellan, Aug. 24, 1980; children: Jonathan, Michael, Eric. Student Universidad Nacional Autonomo de Mexico, Mexico City, 1971, 73; BA, U. Miami, 1974, JD, 1977. Bar: Ill. 1977, Fla. 1978, Calif. 1988. Clk. Racal-Milgo Corp., Miami, Fla., 1976-77; assoc. W. Yale Matheson, Chgo., 1977-79; assoc. Arnstein & Lehr, 1979-85, ptnr., 1985-88; prin. Gold & Bennett, San Francisco, 1988-94; ptnr. Milberg Weiss Bershad Hynes & Lerech LLP, 1994-. Author newsletter Internat. Bus. Council Midamerica Update, 1981-88; editor-in-chief Lawyer of the Americas, 1976-77; co-editor Internat. Sales Handbook, 1987. Mem. ABA (sect. internat. law and practice, chmn. pvt. internat. law com. 1984—), Chgo. Bar Assn. (chmn. internat. and fgn. law com. 1983-84), Ill. Bar Assn. (council mem., internat. and immigration law sect.), Internat. Bus. Coun. MidAm. (vice-chmn. policy com. 1982-86, bd. dirs. 1983-88, sec. 1985-87, v.p. 1987-88), Nat. Assn. Securities and Comml. Law Attys. (exec. com. 1994-), Consumer Atty. Calif. (bd. govs. 1998-), Phi Kappa Phi., Omicron Delta Kappa, Sigma Alpha Epsilon. Republican. Home: 1098 Idylberry Rd San Rafael CA 94903-1144 E-mail: reedk@mwbhl.com.

KATIN, PETER ROY, pianist; b. Nov. 14, 1930; m. Eva Zweig, 1954;2 children. Ed., Royal Acad. Music.; DMus (hon.), De Montfort U., 1994. Prof. Royal Acad. Music, 1956-60; prof. piano U. Western Ont., Can., 1978-84; prof.

Royal Coll. Music, 1992—2001, Thames Valley Univ., 2001—. Made 1st London appearance Wigmore Hall, 1948; leading interpreter of Chopin; concerts include Europe, Africa, Japan, Can., U.S., Hong Kong, India, New Zealand, Singapore, Malaysia; rec. artist for Athene, Decca, Everest, Unicorn, HMV, Philips, Lyrita, MFP, Carlton, Simax, Claudio, Olympia; formed The Katin Piano Trio, 1997. Pres. Camerata of London; v.p. Bridgwater Arts Centre. Recipient Chopin Arts award, NYC, 1977. Fellow Royal Acad. Music; assoc. Royal Coll. Music; mem. Inc. Soc. Musicians, Royal Soc. Musicians. Avocations: reading, writing, theatre, tape recording, photography. Office: 4 Clarence Rd Croydon CR0 2EN England E-mail: pkatin@compuserve.com., tonypurkiss@supanet.com.

KATINSKY, STEVEN, communications company executive; b. Phila., Feb. 6, 1959; BS, Rutgers Coll., 1981. CEO, pres. Supertuner.com, Santa Monica, Calif.; co-founder, former CEO Hollywood Online, Santa Monica.

KATKIN, EDWARD SAMUEL, psychology educator; b. N.Y.C., Aug. 15, 1937; s. Nathan and Rosalind (Davis) K.; m. Felice Lapin, Aug. 10, 1958 (dec. 1961); m. 2d Wendy Sue Freedman, Feb. 3, 1963; children: Kenneth, Elizabeth. BA, CCNY, 1958; PhD, Duke U., 1963. Asst. prof. SUNY, Buffalo, 1963-66, assoc. prof., 1966-70, prof. dept. psychology, 1970-86 (chmn. 1980-86), Stony Brook, 1986—, chmn. dept. psychology, 1986-92, dean divsn. social and behavioral scis., 1993—96, prof. emer., 2000—. Fellow Am. Psychol. Soc.; mem. Soc. Psychophysiol. Rsch. (pres. 1983-84), Am. Psychosomatic Soc. Home: 11 Bayview Ave East Setauket NY 11733-3903 Office: SUNY Dept Psychology Stony Brook NY 11794-2500

KATLIC, JOHN EDWARD, management consultant; b. Washington, Pa., Nov. 3, 1928; s. Frederick John and Dorothy Ann (Gideon) K.; m. Nancy Jean Nicely, Aug. 26, 1950; children: Mark Richard, Kerry Leigh, Kevin Edward, Kathleen Diane, Nancy Ellen. BS in Engring. of Mines, W.Va. U., 1955, MS in Engring. of Mines, 1961. Mine surveyor Rochester & Pittsburgh Coal Co., Indiana, Pa., 1948-49; mine supt. Consolidation Coal Co., Morgantown, W.Va., 1959-62, gen. supt., 1962-66, v.p. Pitts., 1973-75; sr. mining engr. Ea. Assn. Coal, Pitts., 1967-68, divsn. mgr., 1969, v.p. pers. safety and indsl. rels., 1970, v.p. gen. mgr. Semet-Solvay divsn. Allied Chem., 1970-73; exec.v.p. adminstrn. engring. and govt. rels. Island Creek Coal Co., Lexington, Ky., 1975-83; sr. v.p. fuel supply Am. Electric Power Svc. Corp., 1983-93; pres. So. Ohio Coal, Cen. Ohio Coal, Windsor Coal, Conesville Coal (all subs.), 1983-93. Mem. negotiating team Nat. Bituminous Coal Wage Agreement, Joint Industry Devel. Com., 1978; cons. projects in Russia, Siberia, Kazakhstan, S. Africa. Patentee mining machine indicator, dust control in longwall mining. Mem. Morgantown City Coun., 1964-66, Marshall U. Found., 1979; bd. dirs. W.Va. Edn. Found., 1983-90, Inland Waterways Users Bd., 1992-93, Fairfield County Found.; mem. Steering com. W.Va. U.; chmn. bd. trustees Lancaster Fairfield Community Hosp., 1990-91. With inf. U.S. Army, 1946-47, C.E., 1950-52. Named Man of Yr., Coal Age Mag., 1987, Ohio Mining and Reclamation Assn., 1988; recipient Erskine Ramsay medal AIME, 1995, Kingery Safety award Pa. Coal Mining Inst. Am., 1995; named to W.Va. Coal Hall of Fame, 2000. Mem. AIME, VFW, Soc. Mining Engrs., Nat. Mine Rescue Assn., Nat. Mining Assn. (chmn. 1990-92), Mine Rescue Vets. of Pitts. Dist., Lancaster Fairfield C. of C. (pres. 1989), Symposiarchs, King Coal Club, Ky. Cols., Cherry River Navy Club, Buckeye Lake Yacht Club, Masons, Shriners. Republican. Presbyterian. Home: 1233 Ridgewood Way Lancaster OH 43130-1154 E-mail: minerjack@aol.com.

KATO, IKUKO, epidemiologist; b. Nagoya, Aichi, Japan, Nov. 13, 1957; d. Hiroshi and Sonoko (Ando) K. MD, Nagoya Health U., Toyoake, Japan, 1982; PhD, Fujuta-Gakuen Health U., Japan, 1987. Med. officer Aichi Prefecture Dept. Health, Nagoya, 1982-83; rsch. staff Aichi Cancer Ctr., Nagoya, 1983-90, sr. rschr., 1991-92; postdoctoral scientist Internat. Agy. for Rsch. on Cancer, Lyon, France, 1992-93, scientist, 1993-94; rsch. assoc. prof. NYU, 1994-99; assoc. prof. La. State U. Health Sci. Ctr., Shreveport, 1999—2000, Wayne State U. Sch. Medicine, Detroit, 2000—. Vis. scientist Japan-Hawaii Cancer Study, Honolulu, 1990-91. Author: (book) Alcohol and the Gastrointestinal Tract, 1996. Grantee NIH, 1996. Achievements include rsch. findings showing individuals with lower levels of serum folate are more likely to develop colorectal cancer. Office: Wayne St U Sch Medicine 110 E Warren Ave Detroit MI 48201

KATO, SHUICHI, information engineering educator; b. Agematsu, Nagano, Japan, Sept. 4, 1943; BS in Elec. Engring., Nagoya (Japan) Inst. Tech., 1969; MS, Chiba (Japan) U., 1976; Dr of Med. Sci., Tokyo U., 1981. Cert. in biomed. engring., neurophysiology. Staff Devel. Ctr. of Abilities, Seiko Co. Ltd., Tokyo, 1971-73; vis. rschr. Physiol. Lab., Cambridge (Eng.) U., 1981-82; vis. rschr. dept. electronics and computer sci. U. Calif., Berkeley, 1982-83; prof. faculty informatics Teikyo Heisei U. (formerly Teikyo U. Tech.), 1988—, prof. Grad. Sch. Informatics, 1999—; lectr. dept. materials sci. Chiba U., 1989—. Pre-reviewer New Energy and Indsl. Tech. Develop. Orgn. Japan, 2001—. Author: Physiological Base of Creativity, 1988, Application of Microprocessor to Monitor and Conditioning during Sleep, 1979, Design of a Life Support Computer Network System for Aged People, 1998, Nonlinearity of the ABR frequency characteristic, 1998; cons. editor Contemporary WHO's WHO, 2002—. Recipient Internat. Educator of Yr., Internat. Biog. Centre, Cambridge, Eng., 2003. Mem. IEEE, N.Y. Acad. Sci., Physiol. Soc. Japan (nominated Internat. Educator of Yr., Internat. Biographical Centre Cambridge, 2003, Japan Soc. Med. Electronics and Biol. Engring., Japan Soc. EEG and EMG, Inst. Electronics, Info. and Comm. Engrs., Welfare and Med. Soc. Chiba (vice-chmn. 2002—). Home: 3-12-11-206 Yamadabashi Ichihara 290-0021 Japan Office: Tokyo Met Ctrl Libr 5-7-13 Minami-Azabu Minato-ku Tokyo 106 Japan Fax: 0436-42-1496. E-mail: kato@grape.plala.or.jp., kato@ieee.org.

KATO, TERRI EMI, elementary school and gifted and talented educator; b. Gardena, Calif., Sept. 1, 1953; d. Shunji James and Ruby Miyo (Sumi) K. BA, Calif. State U., Long Beach, 1976; MA, U.S. Internat. U., 1987. Cert. tchr. multiple subjects, learning handicapped, severely handicapped, resource specialist, lang. devel. specialist, c.c.'s, Calif. Learning disabled group specialist Montebello (Calif.) Unified Sch. Dist., 1979-81; resource specialist ABC Unified Sch. Dist., Cerritos, Calif., 1981-82; spl. day class tchr. Santa Ana (Calif.) Unified Sch. Dist., 1982—; math. resource tchr., 1990-98; 1st and 2nd grade tchr. Santa Ana (Calif.) Unified Sch. Dist., 1996-98, kindergarten tchr., 1999—. Mem. NEA, Calif. Tchrs. Assn., Santa Ana Educators Assn. (mem. spl. edn. task force rules and election com., bldg. rep. 1992—, mem. supt.'s cabinet 1995—), Coun. for Exceptional Children, Orange County Math. Coun. Avocations: travel, reading, hiking, dog grooming, golf. Office: James Monroe Elem 417 E Central Ave Santa Ana CA 92707-3501

KATO, TOMIKO, artist; b. Tokyo, Nov. 16, 1936; d. Seiji and Yae Suzuki; m. Yasuo Kato, Mar. 7, 1958; 1 child, Yuka. BFA, Tokyo Nat. U. Fine Arts/Music, 1959. Cert. secondary and univ. tchr. Artist in Nihon-ga (Japanese style painting). Solo exhbns. of works at Shiseido Ginza Gallery, Tokyo, Matsuya Ginza Gallery, Tokyo, 1983, 86, 90, 93, Bill Hodges Gallery, N.Y.C., 1996-98, 2002, Takashimaya Art Gallery, Tokyo, 1997, Hammond Mus. and Japanese Stroll Garden, N.Y.C., 2000; group exhbns. at Yamatane Art Mus., Tokyo, 1977, 79, 81, Saitama Prefectural Modern Art Mus., 1988, Takashimaya Gallery, Tokyo, 1981-98, Mitsukoshi Gallery, Tokyo, 1992-96, numerous others; author: Sakura no mori no mankai no shita (Beneath Blossoming Cherry Trees), 1993; dancer, choreographer Performance Art: Dances of My Paintings in Real Space, 1986; guest on TV program; subject of numerous revs. Recipient honorable mention Yamatane Art Mus. Award, 1981. Avocations: japanese dance, shamisen, theater, music. Home: 1184-63 Hamanogo Chigasaki-Shi Kanagawa 253-0086 Japan

KATO, YOSHIKI, international economics educator; b. Midori-cho, Hiroshima, Japan, Oct. 23, 1930; s. Ryuichi and Fusano Kato; m. Kyoko Soeda, Aug. 16, 1956; children: Takako, Noriko. BA, Waseda U., Tokyo, 1955, MA, 1958; PhD, Nihon U., Tokyo, 1986. Rschr. The Inst. of World Economy, Tokyo, 1958-65, sr. rschr., 1965-69; assoc. prof. Nihon U., 1969-73, prof. internat. econs., 1973—2001, dean corr. divsn., 1998—2001; assoc. rschr. The Inst. of World Economy, 1969-94; prof. emeritus Nihon U., 2001—. Author: Economic Development and Trade in Underdeveloped Countries, 1969, Political Economy of National Character, 1986. Fellow Japan Assn. for Asian Polit. and Econ. Studies; mem. Japan Soc. Internat. Econs., Japan Soc. Internat. Devel., Sci. Coun. Japan. Avocations: reading, hiking, fine art. Home: 7-7-13 Kokuryo-cho, Chofu-shi Tokyo 182 Japan Office: Nihon U Coll Econs 1-3-2 Misaki-cho Tokyo Japan

KATO, YVONNE MARIE, lawyer; b. Oak Park, Ill., Dec. 15, 1973; d. Theodore Toshihiko Kato and Claudette Louise Desiron. BA in Eng. Lang. and Lit., U. Chgo., 1995; JD, Chgo.-Kent Coll. Law, 1998. Bar: Ill. 1999, (U.S. Ct. Appeals (7th cir.)) 2002, U.S. Dist. Ct. (7th dist.) 1999. Atty. Hartigan & Cuisinier, Chgo., 1999—. Mem.: Chgo. Bar Assn., Ill. State Bar Assn. (editor Challenge 2000—03), Alpha Omicron Pi. Republican. Avocations: rowing, travel, Japanese dance. Home: 2836 N Damen Chicago IL 60618 Office: Hartigan & Cuisinier 222 N LaSalle #2150 Chicago IL 60601 Office Fax: 312-201-8905. E-mail: ykato@hartiganlaw.com.

KATONA, MICHAEL GEORGE, civil engineer, educator; b. Bridgeport, Conn., Apr. 28, 1940; s. George and Ruth Elanor (Schenk) K.; m. Patty Lou Sullivan, Aug. 22, 1959 (div. Sept. 1997); children: Michele Joy Katona Lankford, Teresa Noelle Katona Wickstrom. BA in Math., BSCE, U. Mich., 1967, MS in Structures, 1968; PhD in Structural Mechanics, U. Calif., Berkeley, 1976. Sr. rsch. engr. Naval Civil Engring. Lab., Port Hueneme, Calif., 1968-77; prof. civil engring. U. Notre Dame, South Bend, Ind., 1977-86; sr. sect. head TRW, Ballistic Missiles Divsn., San Bernardino, Calif., 1986-89; chief scientist Air Force Civil Engring. Lab., Panama City, Fla., 1989-97; prof., chair civil engring. Wash. State U., Pullman, Wash., 1997—. Group II chmn. Transp. Rsch. Bd., 1994-97; U.S. rep. NATO Com. Protective Structures, 1990-93; sci. advisor EPA Mid-Atlantic Ctr., Ann Arbor, Mich., 1994—; Air Force prin. mem. Joint Engrs. Mgmt., Dept. Def., 1992-97; chmn. Nat. Coop. Hwy Rsch. Program panel Transp. Rsch. Bd., Washington, 1995-98; v.p. Acad. Rsch. Coun. of Civil Engring.-Rsch. Found., 1998—. Mem. editl. bd. Internat. Jour. Numerical Methods, 1985—; contbr. more than 60 articles to profl. jours. With USN, 1959-62. Recipient Presdl. Young Investigator award NSF, 1984, Naval Civil Engring. award USN, 1970, Outstanding Civilan Career award USAF, 1998. Fellow ASCE; mem. Marina Club Home Owners Assn. (pres. 1995-97). Achievements include CANDE computer software program used for the design and analysis of buried structures such as culverts, pressure pipes, conduits, and soil bridges. Office: Wash State U Dept Civil Engring Pullman WA 99164-0001 E-mail: mgk@wsu.edu

KATONA, PETER GEZA, biomedical engineer, educator; b. Budapest, Hungary, June 25, 1937; came to U.S., 1956, naturalized, 1962; s. Stephan and Irene (Renner) K.; m. Jaroslava Blanar, Aug. 27, 1966; children— Catherine Iris, Andrew George. BS in Elec. Engring, U. Mich., 1960; S.M. in Elec. Engring. (Sloan fellow, 1960-62), M.I.T., 1962, Sc.D. in Elec. Engring, 1965. Asst. prof. elec. engring. M.I.T., 1965-69; assoc. prof. biomed. engring. Case Western Res. U., Cleve., 1969-78, prof., 1978-92, chmn. dept., 1980-87. Program dir. biomed. engring. and aiding the disabled NSF, 1989—91; v.p. biomed. engring. The Whitaker Found., 1991—95, exec. v.p. biomed engring., 1995—98, pres. biomed. engring., 1998—2000, pres., CEO, 2000—. Editorial bd.: American Jour. Physiology, 1975-81; contbr. articles on cardio-respiratory control and automated drug delivery to profl. jours. Recipient Alexander von Humboldt award, 1987-88. Fellow AAAS, Am. Inst. Med. & Biol. Engring. (founding); sr. mem. IEEE, Am. Physiol. Soc., Biomed. Engring. Soc. (bd. dirs. 1977-80, pres. 1984-85), Am. Soc. Engring. Edn. Office: The Whitaker Found 1700 N Moore St Ste 2200 Arlington VA 22209-1923 E-mail: katona@whitaker.org.

KATOPE, CHRISTOPHER GEORGE, English language educator; b. Lowell, Mass., Apr. 1, 1918; s. George and Bessie (Savas) K.; m. Marjorie Spencer King, June 6, 1942; children: Theodora Katope Rowland, Christopher Lawrence. Student, U. Louisville, 1939-41; MA, U. Chgo., 1947; PhD, Vanderbilt U., 1954. Instr. English Westminster Coll., 1947-50; instr. English Allegheny Coll., 1952-54, asst. prof., 1954-62, asso. prof., 1962-69, prof. English, 1969-83, prof. emeritus, 1983—. Fulbright prof. Athens Coll., 1959-60, Anatolia Coll., Greece, 1960-61. Author, editor: (with P. Zolbrod) Beyond Berkeley, 1966, Rhetoric of Revolution, 1970; Contbr. articles to profl. jours. Served with USNR, 1941-45. Home: Meadville, Pa. Died Oct. 28, 2002.

KATOPIS, GEORGE A. electrical engineer; b. Athens, Greece, Apr. 30, 1944; came to U.S., 1970; s. Alexander G. and Emilia A. K.; m. Angela G. Economopoulou, May 31, 1977; 1 child, Alexander. M in Elect. Engring. and Mech. Engring., Poly. U., Athens, 1967; MS in Elec. Engring., Columbia U., 1972, MPH in Elec. Engring., 1980. From sr. assoc. engr. to sr. engring. mgr. IBM Semiconductor Devel. Lab., East Fishkill, N.Y., 1974-92; sr. engr. IBM S/390 Devel. Lab., Poughkeepsie, N.Y., 1992-98, sr. tech. staff, 1997-2000; disting. engr. IBM ESG Devel. Lab., Poughkeepsie, N.Y., 2000—. Indsl. mentor SRC, Ariz., 1984-94; lectr. U. Ga., 1997; instr. CEI-Europe/Elsevier, Germany, Italy, 1988-90. Co-author: Microelectronic Packaging Handbook, 1989; patentee in field; contbr. articles to profl. jours. Bd. dirs. Kimisis Greek Orthodox Ch., Poughkeepsie, 1988, v.p. bd. dirs., 1989; Greek rep. YMCA, Holland, 1964. Mem. IEEE (sr.). Avocations: sailing, chess, bridge, table tennis, photography. Home: 11 Fair Oaks Dr Poughkeepsie NY 12603 Office: IBM 2455 South Rd Poughkeepsie NY 12601 E-mail: katopis@us.ibm.com.

KATRANA, DAVID JOHN, plastic and reconstructive surgeon; b. Moline, Ill., Oct. 16, 1945; s. Nicholas John and Marilyn Ann Katrana; children: Nicole Elaine, Kimberly Ann. BA in Biology, Northwestern U., Evanston, Ill., 1967; DDS, Northwestern U., Chgo., 1971, MD, 1974. Diplomate Am. Bd. Plastic and Reconstructive Surgery. Resident oral surgery Northwestern U. Dental Sch., Chgo., 1971-72; intern surgery Northwestern U. McGraw Med. Ctr., Chgo., 1974-75, resident gen. surgery, 1975-77, resident plastic and reconstructive surgery, 1977-79; assoc. Houston Plastic Surgery Assocs., 1979-91; pvt. practice plastic surgery, 1991—; asst. clin. prof. plastic surgery Baylor Coll. Medicine, Houston, 1980—. Pres. Hyperbaric Mgmt. Assocs. Inc., 1997-2000; dental cons. The Chgo. Bulls, 1977-79; instr. surgery, dental cons. Northwestern U. Med. Sch., Chgo., 1978-79; dir. burn unit Humana Hosp. Southmore, Pasadena, Tex., 1982-88; div. chief surgery Rosewood Hosp., Houston, 1984-86, pres. med. staff, 1988-89; plastic surg. cons. Houston Gamblers Profl. Football Team, 1984; mem. courtesy staff St. Luke's Episcopal Hosp., West Houston Med. Ctr., Meml. Hosp. at Memorial City, also others; lectr. various univs. and hosps. Contbr. articles to profl. jours. Trustee Rosewood Med. Ctr., Houston, 1989—96, chmn. bd., 1995—2000; dir. Ctr. for Wound Care and Hyperbaic Med., Spring Br. Med. Ctr., 1991—2001. Fellow ACS; mem. Undersea and Hyperbaric Med. Soc., Internat. Soc. Burn Injuries, Am. Burn Assn., Am. Soc. Plastic and Reconstructive Surgeons, Tex. Soc. Plastic Surgeons, Tex. Med. Assn., Harris County Med. Soc., Houston Soc. Plastic Surgeons, Wound Healing Soc. Home: 5035 A Tangle Ln Houston TX 77056-2113 Office: 909 Frostwood # 260 Houston TX 77024 E-mail: dj2870@aol.com.

KATRICHIS, JEROME M. business educator, consultant; b. Milw., Aug. 2, 1954; s. Peter J. and Martha E. K.; m. Christine G. Katrichis, Aug. 7, 1993; 1 child, Katharine Griffin. BSBA, U. Wis., LaCrosse, 1977, MBA, 1979; MA in Psychology, U. Mich., 1986, PhD in Bus. Adminstrn., 1990. Lectr. mgmt. and mktg. U. Wis., LaCrosse, 1979-81; sr. account exec. Din and Bradstreet, N.Y.C., 1981-84; asst. prof. mktg. U. Mich., Ann Arbor, 1987-88, 90-91, Temple U., Phila., 1988-95, U. Hartford, Conn., 1995—. Cons. numerous orgns. Contbr. articles to profl. jours. Maynard Phelps scholar U. Mich., 1984-87; Albert Haring fellow Ind. U., 1986. Mem. Am. Mktg. Assn. (Doctoral fellow 1987), Assn. Consumer Rsch., Acad. Mktg. Sci., Soc. Consumer Psychology, Inst. Mgmt. Sci. Avocations: music, sports, literature, theater. Office: U Hartford Barney Sch Bus West Hartford CT 06117

KATRITZKY, ALAN ROY, chemistry educator, consultant; b. London, Eng., Aug. 18, 1928; s. Frederick Charles and Emily Gertrude (Lane) K.; m. Agnes Juliane Dietlinde Kilian, Aug. 5, 1952; children: Margaret, Erika, Rupert, Freda. BA, Oxford U., 1951, BSc, 1952, MA, DPhil, Oxford U., 1954; PhD, Cambridge U., 1958, ScD, 1963, U. Nac. Madrid, 1986, U. Poznan, Poland, 1990, U. Gdansk, 1994, U. East Anglia, U.K., 1995, U. Toulouse, France, 1996; Prof. (hon.), Xian Modern U., 1995, Beijing Inst. Tech., 1995; ScD (hon.), U. St. Petersburg, Russia, 1997, U. Bucharest, Romania, 1998, U. Rostov, Russia, 2000, U. Ghent, Belgium, 2001, Bundelkhand U., India, 2001, U. Timisoara, Romania, 2003. ICI fellow U. Oxford, 1956-58; lectr. chemistry U. Cambridge, 1958-63; fellow Churchill Coll.; prof. chemistry U. East Anglia, 1963-80; dean U. East Anglia (Sch. Chem. Scis.), 1963-70, 76-80; Kenan prof. organic chemistry U. Fla., Gainesville, 1980—. Dir. Fla. Inst. Het. Cpds., 1986—. Editor: Advances in Heterocyclic Chemistry, vols. 1-81, 1963—; regional editor: Tetrahedron, 1980-98; chmn. editl. bd. Comprehensive Heterocyclic Chemistry, 1st edit., 9 vols., 1985, 2d edit., 10 vols., 1996, Comprehensive Organic Functional Group Transformations, 7 vols., 1995. Decorated Cavaliere Ufficiale. Fellow Royal Soc.; mem. Am., Brit., Japanese, Italian (hon. mem.), Polish (hon. mem.) Chem. Socs., Internat. Soc. Het. Chem., Polish Acad. Sci. (fgn. mem.), Real Catalan Acad., Slovenian Acad., Russian Acad. Sci. (fgn. mem. Siberian br.). Home: 1221 SW 21st Ave Gainesville FL 32601-8417 Office: U Fla Dept Chemistry Gainesville FL 32611 E-mail: katritzky@chem.ufl.edu.

KATSAKIORES, GEORGE NICHOLAS, state legislator, retired restaurateur; b. Derry, N.H., Dec. 11, 1924; s. Nicholas G. and Agoristа (Siatravinos) K.; m. Lucille Brunelle, Nov. 11, 1963 (div. July 1980); children: Sheila, Glen, Greg, Karen, Gary; m. Phyllis M. Harrie, Oct. 9, 1983. Student, U. N.H., 1946-48. Owner White's Restaurant, Derry, 1948-88, ret.; mem. N.H. Ho. of Reps., 1982—, chair transp. com., chmn. emeritus. Dir. Derry Devel. and Preservation Corp.; vice chmn. Airport Access Hwy. Task Force, Manchester, N.H.; mem. transp. task force Am. Legis. Exch. Coun., Washington.; appointed to N.H. Integrated Trans. and Railroad Coun. Dir. Northeast Corridor Initiative, Boston, Greater Derry/Saleit Transp. Coun., Nutfield Sr. Devel. Corp.; mem. Rockingham County Com., Brentwood, N.H., chmn. Rock City Del., Rep. Nat. Party, N.H. Rep. Com. Cpl. Med. Corps. U.S. Army, 1943-45, ETO. Inducted into Pinkerton Acad. Hall of Fame, 1999. Mem. Am. Legion #9, VFW (Post 1617), AARP, N.H. Transp. and Hwy. Users Coalition, N.H. R.R. Revitalization Assn., Hoodkroft County Club (Derry). Greek Orthodox. Avocations: golf, politics. Home: 1 Bradford St Derry NH 03038-4258

KATSAPIS, CHRISTINE C. A. university research administrator; d. Robert C. and Catherine A. Rossi; m. Tim Katsapis, Sept. 9, 1995; 1 child, Georgia C. BA in Lt., Am. U., Washington, D.C., 1992; postgrad., Am. U., 2003—; MA in Edn. and Human Devel., George Wash. U., Washington, D.C., 1999. Program mgr. Sch. Bus. and Pub. Mgmt.George Wash. U., Washington, 1998—99; grants and contracts specialist Gallaudet U., Washington, 1998—2000, asst. dir., office of sponsored programs, 2000—03, dir., office of sponsored programs, 2003— Founders Scholarship, Am. U., 1990. Mem.: Nat. Coun. U. Rsch. Adminstrs. (mem. evaln. task force 2001—02), Phi Delta Kappa Internat., Golden Key Nat. Honor Soc. (life Meritorious Recgognition 1998). Republican. Greek Orthodox And Roman Catholic. Avocations: camping, Nova Scotia duck tolling retrievers, painting. Office: Gallaudet U 800 Florida Ave NE Washington DC 20002-3695 E-mail: christine.katsapis@gallaudet.edu.

KATSENELINBOIGEN, ARON JOSEF, economist; b. Isaslavl, Ukraine, Sept. 2, 1927; came to U.S., 1973, naturalized, 1980; m. Josef Jacob and Ida Gersh (Feldman) K.; C.A., Moscow State Econ. Inst., 1946; Ph.D., Inst. Econs., USSR Acad. Scis., 1957; D.Econ. Scis., Inst. Nat. Economy, 1966; m. Gena L. Gabin, Jan. 31, 1954; children— Gregory, Alexander. Head dept. complex systems Central Econ. Math. Inst., USSR Acad. Scis., 1966-73; prof. econs. Moscow State U., 1970-73; vis. lectr. econs. U. Pa., 1974-78, prof. social systems scis., 1978-87, prof. decision scis., 1988—, chmn. social systems scis., 1984-86. Bd. dirs. Hebrew Immigrants Aid Soc., 1980-83. Grantee Ford Found., 1975-77, Am. Council Learned Socs., 1978, Nat. Council Soviet Studies, 1980-82. Mem. Soc. Gen. Systems Research. Author, editor books in field. Office: U Pa 500 Jon Huntsman Hall Philadelphia PA 19104 Home: 250 Gorge R #17J Cliffside Park NJ 07010

KATSH, M. ETHAN, law educator; b. N.Y.C., Sept. 3, 1945; s. Abraham Isaac and Estelle (Wachtell) Katsh; m. Beverly Schwartz; children: Rebecca, Gabriel, Gideon. BA, NYU, 1967; JD, Yale U., 1970. Bar: NY 1970. Asst. prof. legal studies U. Mass., Amherst, 1970—76, assoc. prof., 1977—88, prof., 1988—, chair legal studies dept., 1993—94, dir. Ctr. Info. Tech. and Dispute Resolution, 1997—. Author: The Electronic Media and the Transformation of Law, 1989, Law in a Digital World, 1995, Online Dispute Resolution, 2001; co-author: Before the Law, 6th edit., 1998; editor: Taking Sides: Clashing Views on Controversial Legal Issues, 1982, 10th edit., 2002; bd. of editors Cyberspace Law Abstracts; contbr. articles on law, media and computers to profl. jours. and mags. Chair Europe online dispute resolution expert group UN Econ. Commn., 2002—; co-founder U. Mass. Mediation Project, 1980; founder, dir. Online Ombuds Office, 1996—. Office: U Mass Dept Legal Studies Amherst MA 01003 E-mail: katsh@legal.umass.edu.

KATSH, SALEM MICHAEL, lawyer; b. NYC, May 5, 1948; s. Abraham Isaac and Estelle (Wachtell) K.; m. Jennette Williams, Sept. 4, 1983; children: Halley Rachel, Emmet Walker. BA, NYU, 1970, JD cum laude, 1972. Bar: N.Y. 1973, U.S. Dist. Ct. (so., ea., no. dists. N.Y.) 1975, U.S. Ct. of Appeals (2d cir.) 1975, U.S. Ct. of Appeals (9th cir.) 1977, U.S. Supreme Ct. 1983, U.S. Ct. Appeals (fed. cir.) 1990, U.S. Dist. Ct. (no. dist.) Calif. 1993. Assoc. Weil, Gotshal & Manges, N.Y.C., 1972-80, ptnr., 1980-97, Shearman & Sterling, N.Y.C., 1997—. Adj. prof. New York Law Sch., 1980-84. Author: Industrial Power and the Law, 1980, (with others) The Limits of Corporate Power, 1981; founder Jour. Proprietary Rights; contbr. articles to profl. jours. Mem.: ABA, NY State Bar Assn., Order of Coif. Office: 599 Lexington Ave New York NY 10022-6030

KATSIANIS, JOHN NICK, financial executive; b. Chgo., Oct. 27, 1960; s. John Nick and Rosalie A. (Kitzberger) K. BS in Acctg. and Fin., U. Ill., Chgo., 1982. CPA, Ill. Staff acct. gen. acctg. Svc. Master Industries, Inc., Downers Grove, Ill., 1983-84, staff acct. spl. projects, 1984-85, staff acct., 1985, controller, 1985-89; dir. fin., asst. treas. Rush-Presbyn.-St. Luke's Med. Ctr., Chgo., 1989-93; sr. v.p., CFO NYLCare Health Plans of the Midwest, Oak Brook, 1993-98; regional pres. Avanti Health Sys. Ill., Inc., 1995-96; dir. fin. Elmhurst Meml. Health Sys., 1998—2002; v.p., CFO Caritas Health Svcs., 2002—. Vice pres. Countryside (Ill.) Police Pension Bd., 1987-2001, pres. 2001-2002. Mem.: AICPA, Chgo. Healthcare Exec. Forum, Healthcare Fin. Mgmt. Assn. (bd. dirs. 2000—, treas. 2001—02), Ill. CPA Soc. Baptist. Avocations: golf, snow skiing, swimming, softball. Home: 12805 Crestview Cir Prospect KY 40059

KATSIFF, BRUCE, artist; b. Phila., Dec. 10, 1945; s. Myer and Rose (August) K.; m. Joane Mitnick, Dec. 30, 1965; 1 child, Timothy. BFA, Rochester Inst. Tech., 1968; MFA, Pratt Inst., 1973; postgrad., Oxford (Eng.) U., 1987. Film producer Eastman Kodak Co., Rochester, N.Y., 1968; adj. prof. Thomas Edison Coll., Trenton, N.J., 1970-74; chmn. fine art Bucks County Coll., Newtown, Pa., 1973-84, prof., 1984-88; chmn. art and music Bucks Coll., Newtown, 1988-89; dir. James A. Michener Art Mus., 1990—. Mng. bd. dirs. Photography Sesquicentennial, Phila., 1988-90. Exhibited at Mus. Modern Art, N.Y.C., 1968, Internat. Mus. Photography, Rochester, N.Y., 1969, Phila. Art Mus., 1970, Am. Arts Ctr., Exeter, Eng., 1970, Tainjan Inst., China, 1987, Pa. Acad. Fine Arts, 1990, Washington Photography Ctr., 1993. Grantee NEA, 1973; fellowship Pa. Arts Coun., 1990. Fellow Soc. Photographic Educators; mem. Pa. Coun. on Arts (mus. panel 1982-85, visual arts panel 1987-90). Home: PO Box 28 Lumberville PA 18933-0028

KATSMAN, ZINAIDA, musician, music educator; b. Minsk, Belarus, Dec. 5, 1972; arrived in U.S., 1996; d. Abram R. and Maria Z. Katsman. B in Music and Piano, State Music Sch., Minsk, 1992; postgrad., DePaul U., Chgo., 1999—2000. Pianist for ballet, music tchr. State Ballet Sch., Minsk, 1992—94; pianist Chgo. Ballet Arts, 1998—, North Shore Sch., Chgo., 1998—; pvt. piano tchr. Chgo., 1998—; freelance piano accompanist, 1999—; pianist Hubbard Street Dance Co., Chgo., 2002—. Performance pianist, voice coach Oberlin in Italy, Urbania, 2000. Mem.: Suzuki Assn. of the Ams., Music Tchrs. Nat. Assn. Avocations: reading, dancing, art, travel. Home: Apt 109 2541 W Fitch Ave Chicago IL 60645

KATSORIS, CONSTANTINE NICHOLAS, lawyer, consultant; b. Bklyn., Dec. 5, 1932; s. Nicholas C. and Nafsika (Klonis) K.; m. Ann Kanganis, Feb. 19; children: Nancy, Nicholas, Louis. BS in Acctg., Fordham U., 1953; JD cum laude, 1957; LLM, NYU, 1963. Bar: N.Y. 1957, U.S. Dist. Ct. (so. and ea. dist.) N.Y. 1959, U.S. Tax. Ct. 1959, U.S. Ct. Appeals (2nd cir.) 1959, U.S. Supreme

Ct. 1961. Assoc. Cahill, Gordon, Reindel & Ohl, N.Y.C., 1958-64; asst. prof. Law Sch. Fordham U., N.Y.C., 1964-66, assoc. prof., 1966-69; prof., 1969—; apptd. Wilkinson prof. law, 1991. Cons. N.Y. State Temporary Commn. on Estates, 1964-67; arbitration panelist N.Y. Stock Exchange, 1971—, Nat. Assn. Securities Dealers, 1968—, 1st Jud. Dept., 1972—; pub. mem. Securities Industry Conf. on Arbitration, 1977-97, 2003-, chairperson, 2003-; pvt. judge adjudication ctr. Duke U. Law Sch., 1989—. Contbr. articles to profl. jours. Mem. sch. bd. Greek Orthodox Parochial Sch. St. Spyridon, 1975-89, chmn. sch. bd., 1983-89. With U.S. Army, 1963. Recipient Cert. Appreciation Nat. Assn. Securities Dealers, 1982, Ellis Is. Medal of Honor award, 1999. Mem. ABA (fed. estate and gift tax com. 1966-68), N.Y. State Bar Assn. (sect. on trust and estates 1969—), Assn. Bar City of N.Y. (trusts, estates and surrogates' cts. com. 1968-70, legal assistance com. 1965-67), Fordham U. Law Alumni Assn. (bd. dirs. 1972—), Fordham U. Law Rev. Alumni Assn. (pres. 1962-64). Republican. Greek Orthodox. Office: 140 W 62nd St New York NY 10023-7407

KATSOS, BARBARA HELENE, lawyer; b. N.Y.C. MA, NYU; JD, U. of City of N.Y.; PhD, NYU. Bar: N.Y., U.S. Dist. Ct. (so. dist.) N.Y., U.S. Dist. Ct. (ea. dist.) N.Y. Pvt. practice, N.Y.C. Office: Ste 3200 777 3d Ave New York NY 10017

KATSOV, KIRILL, education educator, researcher; b. Vologda, Russia, May 24, 1972; s. Mikhail Grigorjevich Katsov and Zhanna Nikolaevna Katsova. BS, MS, Moscow State Univ., Moscow, Russia, 1994; PhD, U. Md., Coll. Pk., Md., 2000. Rsch. asst. Moscow State U., Moscow, 1993—94; rsch. and tchg. asst. U. Md., Coll. Pk., Md., 1994—2000; rsch. assoc. U. Wash., Seattle, 2000—. Recipient Gold Medal, Moscow State U., 1989. Mem.: Am. Biophysical Soc., Am. Phys. Soc. Office: Dept of Physics Univ Wash Box 351560 Seattle WA 98195-1560

KATSOYANNIS, PANAYOTIS GEORGE, biochemist, educator; b. Greece, Jan. 7, 1924; came to U.S., 1952; naturalized U.S. citizen, 1961. MS in Organic Chemistry, U. Athens, Greece, 1948, PhD in Organic Chemistry, 1952; Dsc honoris causa, U. Patras, Greece. Rsch. asst. Lab. Organic Chemistry U. Athens, 1947-50, vis. scientist Lab. Organic Chemistry, 1957-58; rsch. assoc. dept. biochemistry Cornell U. Med. Coll., 1952-56, asst. prof. biochemistry, 1956-57; assoc. prof. biochemistry U. Pitts. Sch. Medicine, 1958-64; head divsn. biochemistry Med. Rsch. Ctr. Brookhaven Nat. Lab., Upton, N.Y., 1964-68; Dorothy H. and Lewis Rosensteil prof. biochemistry Mt. Sinai Sch. Medicine, CUNY, 1968-98, prof. biochemistry and molecular biology, 1998—, head chmn. dept. biochemistry, 1968-99. Edwin J. Meml. lectr. Harvard U., 1963. Patentee in field; contbr. over 130 articles to profl. jours., chpts. to books. Fellow State Scholarship Found. of Greece, 1952-54, sr. rsch. fellow USPHS, 1958-63; recipient Commemorative medallion Am. Diabetes Assn., 1972, Jacobi Medallion Mt. Sinai Alumni, 1995, Rsch. Career Devel. award USPHS, 1963. Fellow AAAS, N.Y. Acad. Scis.; mem. Am. Chem. Soc., Royal Soc. Chemistry., Nat. Acad. Greece (corr.), Biochem. Soc., Am. Soc. Biochemistry and Molecular Biology, Pharm. Soc. Japan. Office: Mt Sinai Sch Medicine CUNY Box 1020 Dept Biochemistry One Gustave L Levy Pl New York NY 10029 Home: 69 Drake Ln Manhasset NY 11030-1229

KATSURINIS, STEPHEN AVERY, lawyer; b. Houston, Aug. 4, 1966; s. Ted and JoAnn Katsurinis. BA, Southwestern U., 1988; JD, Franklin Pierce Law Ctr., 1991. Bar: Va. 1992, U.S. Ct. Appeals (4th cir.) 1992, U.S. Dist. Ct. (ea. dist.) Va. 1995, D.C. 1999. Legis. counsel to Rep. Dana Rohrabacher, Washington, 1991-94; policy analyst Dept. of Planning and Budget, Richmond, Va., 1994-95; of counsel Magenheim, Bateman, Houston, 1995-97; staff atty. McGuireWoods LLP, Washington, 1997—2003; spl. asst. to dir. Office Nat. Drug Control Policy, 2003—. Alt. del. Rep. Nat. Conv., San Diego, 1996; election judge State of Tex., Georgetown, 1986; mem. Alexandria City Rep. com.; Alexandria City chair Bush for Pres., 2000, Earley for Gov., 2001; vice chair Alexandria Electoral Bd., 2001—03; chair Va. Task Force on Mil. and Overseas Voting, 2002—03. Recipient Am. Citizenship award, DAR, 1980. Mem.: Alexandria Bar Assn., Federalist Soc. Law and Pub. Policy, Am. Hellenic Progressive Assn. (chpt. sec. 1990—91), Charles Fahy Am. Inn of Cts. (barrister). Greek Orthodox. Office: White Ho Drug Policy Office 750 17th St Washington DC 20503

KATTI, SHRINIWAS K. retired statistician, consultant; b. Bijapur, India, June 20, 1936; s. Keshav Narasinha and Yamuna K. Katti; m. Pramila S. Chivate, Nov. 8, 1938; children: Romney Rajeev, Anita M. PhD, Iowa State U., 1960. Asst/assoc prof. Fla. State U., Tallahassee, 1960—69, dir. grad. studies, 1960—69; prof. U. Mo., Columbia, 1969—95; biostatistical cons. Lilly, Tyco, Hoffman La Roche and others, Indpls., 1995—2002; dir. biostatistics Biodam inc., N.Y.C., 2002—. Fellow: Am. Statis. Assn. Home: 276D Branch Brook Dr Belleville NJ 07109 Office: Biodam Inc 5th Fl 116 West 23rd St New York NY 10011 Office Fax: 646-374-2353. Personal E-mail: skatti@worldnet.att.net. E-mail: skatti@biodam.com.

KATTLOVE, HERMAN ELY, oncologist; b. Chgo., 1937; MD, U. Chgo., 1962; MPH, UCLA, 1992. Cert. Internal Medicine, 1972, Hematology, 1973, Med. Oncology, 1975. Intern U. Chgo. Clinics, 1962-63; resident in medicine Montefiore Hosp., Bronx, N.Y., 1965-67, resident in hematology, 1967-69; assoc. clin. prof. medicine UCLA; med. editor Am. Cancer Soc., L.A., 1999—. Fellow Am. Coll. Physicians; mem. Am. Soc. Clin. Oncology, Am. Soc. Hematology. Office: American Cancer Soc 3300 Wilshire Blvd Los Angeles CA 90010-1404

KATTOUF, THEODORE E. ambassador; b. Altoona, Pa., 1946; Grad., Pa. State U. With U.S. Fgn. Svc., 1972—, econ. and comml. officer, 1973-75, polit. officer, Middle East analyst Bur. of Intelligence and Rsch. Washington, internat. relations officer Near East Bur., dep. chief of mission Baghdad, 1983, Sanaa, dep. dir. Office of Arab North Affairs Washington, 1988, dir. Office of Arab North Affairs, dep. chief of mission Damascus, Riyadh, Saudi Arabia, amb. United Arab Emirates, 1998—. With U.S. Army. Office: American Embassy Abu Dhabi Dept Ofstate Washington DC 20521-0001

KATTWINKEL, JOHN, physician, pediatrics educator; b. Newton, Mass., June 24, 1941; s. Egon Emil and Dorothy Lucile (Fish) K.; m. Phyllis Ann Denton, Sept. 14, 1963; children: Susan, Linda. BS, Rensselaer Poly. Inst., 1964; B in Med. Sci., Dartmouth Coll., 1966; MD, Harvard U., 1968. Diplomate Am. Bd. Pediatrics, Am. Bd. Neonatology (bd. dirs. 1981-86). Resident in pediatrics Duke Med. Ctr., Durham, N.C., 1968-70; clin. assoc. NIH, Bethesda, Md., 1970-72; neonatology fellow Case Western Res. U., Cleve., 1972-74; asst. prof. pediatrics U. Va., Charlottesville, 1974-78, assoc. prof., 1978-84, prof., 1984—, dir. neonatology, 1974—, Charles Fuller chair in neonatology, 1998—. Founder Perinatal Edn. Ctr., Charlottesville, 1976—; Poland and China cons. Project HOPE, Milwood, Va., 1979-92; hon. prof. Zhejiang Med. U., Hangzhou, People's Republic of China, 1985. Mem. editl. bd. Pediatrics, 1999—; contbr. articles on newborn respiration and med. edn. to profl. jours.; inventor device for nasal ventilation of infants. Lt. comdr. USPHS, 1970-72. Fellow: Am. Acad. Pediat. (fetus and newborn com. 1983—89, neonatal resuscitation program steering com. 1989—98, chair SIDS task force 1992—, chair 1994—98, editor 1999—, Ross Profl. Edn. award 1989); mem.: Soc. Pediat. Rsch., Am. Pediat. Soc. Avocation: tennis. Home: 920 Charter Oaks Dr Charlottesville VA 22901-0629 Office: U Va Dept Pediatrics Charlottesville VA 22908-0001 E-mail: jk3f@virginia.edu.

KATZ, ABRAHAM, retired foreign service officer; b. Bklyn., Dec. 4, 1926; s. Alexander and Zina (Rabinowitz) K.; children: Tamar, Jonathan, Naomi; m. Marion Scheinberger, July 29, 1996. BA cum laude, Bklyn. Coll., 1948; M.I.A., Columbia U., 1950; PhD, Harvard U., 1968. Commd. fgn. service officer Dept. State, 1951; vice-consul, prin. officer Am. Consulate, Merida, Mexico, 1951—53; 2d sec. Am. Embassy, Mexico, 1953—56; chief Soviet fgn. econ. Bur. Intelligence Rsch., Washington, 1957—59; 1st sec. U.S. missions to NATO, OECD, Paris, 1959-64; counselor Am. Embassy, Moscow, 1964-66; dir. office of OECD European Communities and Atlantic Polit. Econ. Affairs, Washington, 1967-74; dep. chief of mission OECD, Paris, 1974-78; dep. asst. sec. for internat. econ. policy and research Dept. Commerce, Washington, 1978-80, asst. sec. internat. econ. policy, 1980-81; U.S. rep., ambassador OECD, Paris, 1981-84; pres. U.S. Coun. Internat. Bus., 1984-99, pres. emeritus, 1999—. Employer mem. gov. body Internat. Labor Orgn., 1984-99; v.p. Internat. Orgn. Employers, 1984-99. Author: The Politics of Economic Reform in the Soviet Union, 1972. Decorated grand officier Ordre National du Merite (France); recipient U.S. Coun. Internat. Bus. Internat. Leadership award. Mem. Am. Polit. Sci. Assn., Assn. Advancement Slavic Studies, Am. Fgn. Svc. Assn., Am. Assn. Comparative Econ. Studies, Coun. of Fgn. Rels., Cosmos Club, Harvard Club, B'nai Brith, Century Assn. Office: US Coun Internat Bus 1212 Avenue Of The Americas New York NY 10036-1602

KATZ, ADRIAN IZHACK, physician, educator; b. Bucharest, Romania, Aug. 3, 1932; came to U.S., 1965, naturalized, 1976; s. Ferdinand and Helen (Lustig) K.; m. Miriam Lesser, Mar. 31, 1965; children— Ron, Iris. MD, Hebrew U., 1961. Research fellow Yale U., 1965-67, Harvard U., 1967-68; intern Belinson Med. Center, Israel, 1961, resident, 1962-65; practice medicine specializing in internal medicine and nephrology New Haven, 1966-67, Boston, 1967-68, Chgo., 1968—; attending physician U. Chgo. Hosps., 1968—, head nephrology sect., 1973-82; asst. prof. medicine U. Chgo., 1968-71, assoc. prof., 1971-74, prof., 1975—2002, prof. emeritus, 2002—. Fogarty sr. internat. fellow, vis. scientist Lab Cell Physiology, Coll. de France, Paris, 1977-78; vis. prof. cellular and molecular physiology Yale U., 1988; vis. scientist dept. molecular medicine Karolinska Inst., Stockholm, 1994— Co-author: Kidney Function and Disease in Pregnancy; contbr. chpts. to books, articles to profl. jours. Fellow A.C.P.; mem. Am. Physiol. Soc., Am. Soc. Clin. Investigation, Assn. Am. Physicians, Am. Soc. Nephrology, Internat. Soc. Nephrology, Central Soc. Clin. Research, N.Y. Acad. Scis. Home: 1125 E 53rd St Chicago IL 60615-4410 Office: U Chgo 5841 S Maryland Ave Chicago IL 60637-1463 E-mail: akatz@medicine.bsd.uchicago.edu.

KATZ, ALAN CHARLES, toxicologist; b. Kearny, N.J., Nov. 10, 1946; s. Edward Myron and Margaret Ellen Katz; m. Marcia Anne Ellenwood, July 26, 1974; children: Bryan Jeffrey, Jeffrey Alan. BS in Biology, Fairleigh Dickinson U., 1970, MS in Human Physiology, 1977; Cert. in Mgmt., Ctrl. Conn. State U., 1981. Diplomate Am. Bd. Toxicology, Am. Bd. Forensic Examiners. Chemist Union Carbide Corp., Bound Brook, N.J., 1965-70; toxicologist Ortho Pharm. Corp., Raritan, N.J., 1971-74; sr. ophthalmic pharmacologist Cooper Labs., Cedar Knolls, N.J., 1974-76; sr. assoc. toxicologist J&J Rsch. Found., North Brunswick, N.J., 1976-79; study dir. Stauffer Chem. Co., Farmington, Conn., 1979-84; sr. toxicologist EPA, Washington, 1984-87; exec. dir. TAS, Inc., Washington, 1987-97; mgr. tech. affairs Sanachem USA, Inc., 1997-98; pres. TOXCEL, 1999—; prin. Katz Assocs., 1985—, TOXCEL, LLC, 1999—; dir. TOXCEL, Internat., Ltd., 2000—. Contbg. editor Acute Toxicity, 1991-97; editl. bd. Jour. Applied Toxicology. Fellow Am. Coll. Forensic Examiners; mem. N.Y. Acad. Scis., Soc. Comparative Ophthalmology (past pres.), Soc. Toxicology, Am. Coll. Toxicology, Am. Chem. Soc., Soc. Toxicologie du Can., Roundtable Toxicology Cons. Home: 16090 Simon Kenton Rd Haymarket VA 20169-2109 E-mail: akatz@toxcel.com.

KATZ, ALAN ROY, public health educator; b. Pitts., Aug. 21, 1954; s. Leon B. and Bernice Sonia (Glass) K.; m. Donna Marie Crandall, Jan. 19, 1986; 1 child, Sarah Elizabeth. BA, U. Calif., San Diego, 1976; MD, U. Calif., Irvine, 1980; MPH, U. Hawaii, 1987; postgrad., U. So. Calif., 1980-81, U. Hawaii, 1982-83. Staff physician emergency medicine L.A. County U. So. Calif. Med. Ctr., 1981-82; staff physician, med. dir. Waikiki Health Ctr., Honolulu, 1983-87; dir. AIDS/STD prevention program Hawaii State Dept. of Health, Honolulu, 1987-88; asst. prof. dept. pub. health scis. U. Hawaii, Honolulu, 1988-94, assoc. prof., 1994—. Dir. preventive medicine residency program U. Hawaii, Honolulu, 1994-99; com. mem. Chlamydia control workgroup USPHS, 1985-87, sci. adv. bd. Hawaii AIDS Clin. Trials Rsch. Program, staff physician, lab. dir. Diamond Head STD Clinic, Hawaii State Dept. Health, 1998—. Contbr. articles to profl. jours. Leptospirosis ad hoc com. Hawaii State Dept. Health, Honolulu, 1988—; mem. com. human subjects U. Hawaii, 1989—. USPHS Chlamydia Prevalence Survey grantee, Hawaii, 1986, Tuberculosis Survey grantee U. Hawaii, 1991; recipient presdl. citation for meritorious teaching, U. Hawaii, 1989, Regents medal excellence in teaching, 1992. Fellow Am. Coll. Preventive Medicine; mem. Am. Pub. Health Assn., Soc. Epidemiologic Rsch., Delta Omega. Office: U Hawaii Medicine Dept Pub Health Sci 1960 E West Rd Honolulu HI 96822-2319 E-mail: katz@hawaii.edu.

KATZ, ALEX, artist; b. Bklyn., July 24, 1927; s. Isaac and Ella (Marion) K.; m. Ada Del Moro, Feb. 1, 1958; 1 child, Vincent. Degree in fine arts, Cooper Union, 1949; DFA (hon.), Colby Coll., 1984; PhD (hon.), 1986. One-man exhbns. include Roko Gallery, N.Y.C., 1954, 57, Fischbach Gallery, N.Y.C., 1964, 65, 67, 68, 70, 71, Stable Gallery, N.Y.C., 1960-61, Tanager Gallery, N.Y.C., 1959, 62, Martha Jackson Gallery, N.Y.C., 1962, Grinnell Gallery, Detroit, 1964, Sun Gallery, Provincetown, Mass., 1958, 59, Pa. State Coll., 1957, David Stuart Gallery, L.A., 1966, Bertha Eccles Art Center, Ogden, Utah, 1968, Towson State Coll., Balt., 1968, Phyllis Kind Gallery, Chgo., 1969, 71, W.Va. U., 1969, Galerie Dieter Brusberg, Hanover, Germany, 1971, Thelen Galerie, Cologne, Germany, 1971, Reed Coll., Portland, 1972, Sloan-O'Sickey Gallery, Cleve., 1972, Carlton Gallery, N.Y.C., 1973, Marlborough Gallery, N.Y.C., 1973, 75, 76, Whitney Mus. Am. Art, N.Y.C., 1974-75, Va. Mus. Fine Arts, Richmond, 1974-75, Santa Barbara (Calif.) Mus. Art, 1974-75, U. Minn., 1974-75, Indpls. Mus. Art, 1975, Marlborough Fine Art, London, 1975, Galerie Marguerite Lamy, Paris, 1975, Galerie Roger d'Amé court, Paris, 1977, traveling show Fresno Arts Center, Art Galleries Calif. State U., Seattle Art Mus., Vancouver Art Gallery, 1977-78, Marlborough Galerie, A.G., Zurich, 1977, Rose Art Mus., Brandeis U., Waltham, Mass., Balt. Art Mus., 1978, Brooke Alexander Gallery, N.Y.C., 1979, Robert Miller Gallery, N.Y.C., 1987, Inge Baecker Galerie, Cologne, Germany, 1987, Hokin Gallery, Chgo., 1987, Bklyn. Mus., 1988, Galerie Daniel Templon, Paris Marlborough Gallery, N.Y., 1988, Seibu Mus., Tokyo and Osaka, 1988, Cleve. Mus. Art, 1988, Bernd Kluser, Munich, 1989, Mario Diacono, Boston, 1989, Michael Kohn, L.A., Moscow-USSR CAT, 1989, Palma de Malorca, Spain, 1989, I.C.A., London, 1991, Turin, Italy, 1992, Marlborough Gallery N.Y. CAT, 1992, Munson-Williams-Proctor Inst., 1992, Colby Coll. Art Mus., 1992, Robert Miller Gallery, N.Y.C., 1993, Betsy Senior Gallery, N.Y.C., 1993, Rubenstein/Diacono Gallery, 1993, Marlborough Gallery, N.Y.C., 1993, 95, Ark. Art Mus., 1993, 94, Robert Mullen Gallery, 1994, Staatliche Kunsthalle, Baden-Baden, Germany, 1995, Peter Blum, N.Y.C., 1996, Balt. Mus. Fine Arts, 1996, Inst. Valencia de Arte Moderna Mus., Valencia, Spain, 1996, Fred Hoffman, L.A., 1996, Galerie Jablonka, Cologne, Germany, 1997, Saatchi Gallery, London, 1998, The Cultural Found., Germany, 1998, Galerie Thaddaeus Ropac, Paris, 1998, Galerie Barbara Thumm, Berlin, 1998, P.S.I. Contemporary Art Ctr., N.Y., 1998, Centro Cultural Recoleta, Buenos Aires, 1998, Arts Club Chgo., 2000, Carnegie Mes. Art, Pitt., Pa., 2000, Pace Wildenstein Gallery, N.Y.C., 2001, Timothy Tyler Gallery, London, 2002, Peter Blum Gallery, N.Y.C., 2001-2002, Addison Gallery of Am. Art, Andover, Mass., 2001, Whitney Mus. Am. Art, N.Y.C., 2001, Kemper Mus. Contemporary Art, Kansas City, Mo., 2002, Albright-Knox Mus., Buffalo, 2002, Seattle Mus., 2002, Galeria Mario Sequeira, Braga, Portugal, 2002, others; retrospective exhbn. at Utah Mus. Fine Arts, Salt Lake City, U. Calif. at San Diego, Mpls. Mus. Art, Wadsworth Atheneum, Hartford, Conn., 1971, Am. Found. Arts, Miami, Fla., 1976, Whitney Mus. Am. Art, N.Y.C., 1986 (paintings), Bklyn. Mus., 1980 (prints), 1986, 88, Galerie Templon, Paris (paintings), Marlborough Gallery, N.Y.C., Massimo Audiello, N.Y.C., Seibu Mus. at Tokyo, Osaka, Japan, 1988 (paintings, cutouts); group shows include Pa. Acad. Fine Arts, 1960, Va. Mus., Richmond, 1960, Whitney Mus. Am. Art, N.Y.C., 1960, 67-68, 72 (Ann.), 73 (Biennial), 79, 86 (traveling show), 88 (Philip Morris), 91 (Biennial), Art Inst. Chgo., 1961, 62, 64, 72, Yale Mus., 1962, Colby Coll., 1961, 63, 64, 70, 85, Am. Fedn. Art., 1964-65, Mus. Modern Art, N.Y.C., 1964, 65, 66, 68, 69, 91, 93 (Pfizer), Milw. Arts Center, 1966, 69, 75, R.I. Sch. Design, 1966, Cin. Art Mus., 1968, Am. Acad. Design, 1968, U. Calif. at LaJolla, 1969, N.Y. Acad. Design, N.Y.C., 1973, Marlborough Gallery, N.Y.C., 1976, Cleve. Mus. Art, 1974, DeCordova Mus., Mass., 1975, Mus. Fine Arts, St. Petersburg, 1975-76, U. Mo., 1979, Bowdoin Coll., Maine, 1985, Wichita State Mus., Kans., 1985, Found. Daniel Templon, 1989, France Madison (Wis.) Art Ctr., 1989, Walker Art Ctr, Mpls., 1989, Whitney Mus. at Equitable Ctr., N.Y.C., P.S. 1 Mus., Kuznetsky Most Exhibition, Moscow, 1990, Nassau County Art Mus., 1991, Art Contemporaire, Lyon, France, 1993, Mus. Contemporary Art, São Paulo, Brazil, 1993, Nat. Gallery Art, Washington, 1993, Nat. Portrait Gallery, Washington, 1993, Whitney Mus., N.Y.C., 1994, Mus. Modern Art, N.Y.C., 1994, 1995, Am. Acad. in Rome, 2001, Pompidou Ctr., Paris, 2002, Schinn Kunsthalle, Frankfurt, Germany, 2002, travelling exhibitions solo, 1996—; Krusthalle, Baden-Baden, Germany; Alex Katz, American Landscape, 1996; N.Y. Inst. Contemporary Art, 1998, Galleria Civica di Arte Contemporanea Trento, 1999, numerous others; exhibited in group shows at Mus. fur Moderne Kuust, Frankfurt, Germany, 1996, Deichtorhallen, Hamburg, Germany, 1996, Kunsthaus, Zurich, Switzerland, 1997; represented in permanent collections Whitney Mus., Mus. Modern Art, Met. Mus. Art, Brandeis U., N.Y.U., Bowdoin Coll., Detroit Mus., Allentown (Pa.) Art Mus., Weatherspoon Gallery of Art, Greensboro, N.C., Tokyo (Japan) Gallery, Allen Meml. Art Mus., Oberlin, Ohio, Houston Mus., Tate Gallery, London, The Israel Mus., Jerusalem, Iwaki City Mus., Japan, Hiroshima Mus., Museo Rufino Tamayo, Mex., Honolulu Acad. Art, Reina Sofia, Madrid, Valencia Mus., numerous others; vis. critic Yale U., 1960-63; Marshall Crogan vis. artist Harvard U., 1991-92. Subject of books: Alex Katz (Irving Sandler), 1979, Alex Katz: The Complete Prints (Nick Maravell), 1983, Alex Katz (Marshall and Rosenblum), 1986; also contbr. prints to Give Me Tomorrow (Ratcliff), 1984, A Tremor in the Morning (Vincent Katz), 1986, Alex Katz (Ann Beattie), Alex Katz Night Paintings (Donald Kuspit), Alex Katz (Sam Hunter), 1992; represented in permanent wing for Alex Katz Colby (Me.) Coll. Mus. Art. Recipient award New Eng. Art, Provincetown, Mass., 1971, Art in Pub. Places award, Harlem Station, Chgo., 1985, Profl. Achievement citation Cooper Union, 1974, alumni medal for achievement, 1980, Augustus St. Gaudens award for professionalism in art, 1980, medal for achievement in painting Skowhegan Sch., 1980; Guggenheim fellow, 1972; U.S.-USSR cultural exch. gurantee 1978; resident Am. Acad. in Rome, 1983; inducted into Am. Acad. and Inst. of Arts and Letters; opening of Paul J. Schupf wing for the Alex Katz collection Colby Coll. Mus., 1996. Address: 435 W Broadway New York NY 10012-5902

KATZ, ALEXANDER, chemical engineering educator; s. Marat G. and Sophia E. Katz; m. Julia Katz. BS of Chem. Engring., Cum Laude, U. of Minn., Twin Cities, 1992, MS in Chem. Engring., 1994; PhD in Chem. Engring., Calif. Inst. of Tech., 1999. Postdoctoral assoc. U. Louis Pasteur, Strasbourg, France, 1989—2000; asst. prof. U. of Calif., Berkeley, 2000—. Recipient NSF Internat. Awards fellowship, 1989—2000. Mem.: Am. Chem. Soc. (assoc.). Achievements include development of templated materials with nanoscale structure for specific adsorption and selective catalysis.

KATZ, ALIX MARTHA, respiratory care practitioner; b. Newark, Dec. 7, 1948; d. Leo F. and Anne (Chase) K. AS, Passaic County Community Coll., Paterson, N.J., 1982. Cert. respiratory therapy technician. Staff respiratory therapist Hosp. Ctr. at Orange, N.J., 1979-82; home care respiratory practitioner Homed Convalescent Equipment, Mountain Lakes, N.J., 1982-85; clin. respiratory supr. Elizabeth (N.J.) Gen. Med. Ctr., 1985-86; dir. respiratory therapy Paramed. Splty., Inc., Fairfield, NJ, 1986-88; respiratory therapist Ultra-Care Health Care Svcs., West Orange, NJ, 1988-94, Rahway Hosp., Rahway, NJ, 1994—2003, Advanced Life Svcs., Louisville, 2003—. Drug and Hosp. Union scholar, 1980. Mem. Am. Assn. for Respiratory Care, Nat. Soc. Cardio-Pulmonary Technologists, Respiratory Therapy Hist. Soc., Methaphys. Ctr. N.J. Democrat. Jewish. Avocations: science, medicine, language, religion, philosophy. Home: 230 Clarken Dr West Orange NJ 07052-3400

KATZ, ANNE HARRIS, biologist, educator, writer, aviator; b. Long Branch, N.J; BS, Ursinus Coll., Collegeville, Pa., 1966; MS, U. Mass., 1974, PhD, 1976. Cert. pvt. pilot. Tchr. biology Middletown (N.J.) Twp. High Sch., 1966-69; instr. biology Holyoke (Mass.) Community Coll., 1969; teaching and research assoc. U. Mass., 1969-76; asst. prof. biology Fordham U., N.Y.C., 1977-83; assoc. prof. biology, asst. dean Coll. St. Elizabeth, Convent Station, N.J., 1983-86; assoc. dean Coll. Natural Scis. and Math. Ind. U. Pa., 1987-91, interim dean Coll. Natural Scis. and Math., 1988-89; dean of the coll., prof. biology Lycoming Coll., Williamsport, Pa., 1991-93. Cert. pvt. pilot; cert. ecologist. Founder, editor, pub. Aviation Mus. & Event News, 1993; contbr. abstracts and articles to profl. jours. Vis. scholar Drew U., Madison, N.J., 1984-87; grantee Ctr. Field Rsch., Watertown, Mass., 1981-82, Geraldine R. Dodge Found., Morristown, N.J., 1981-83, N.J. DEP, 1983, Pa. Dept. Edn., 1989, GTE, 1990, CDC, 1991. Mem. AAAS, Ecol. Soc. Am., Aircraft Owners and Pilots Assn., Ninety Nines (aerospace edn.), Civil Air Patrol (aerospace edn. officer, pub. affairs officer), Soc. Study Reprodn., Am. Inst. Biol. Scis., N.Y. Acad. Sci., N.J. Acad. Sci., Pa. Acad. Sci., Ecol. Soc. Am. Avocations: hiking, traveling, writing, flying small airplanes.

KATZ, ARNOLD MARTIN, medical educator; b. Chgo., July 30, 1932; s. Louis Nelson and Aline (Grossner) K.; m. Phyllis Beck, Apr. 18, 1959; children: Paul, Sarah, Amy, Laura. BA with honors, U. Chgo., 1952; MD cum laude, Harvard U., 1956; D.Med. (hon.), Carol Davila U., 1994. Diplomate Nat. Bd. Med. Examiners. Intern Mass. Gen. Hosp., Boston, 1956-57, asst. res., 1959-60; rsch. assoc. NIH, Bethesda, Md., 1957-59; asst. registrar Inst. Cardiology, London, 1960-61; rsch. fellow dept. medicine UCLA, 1961-64; asst. prof. physiology Columbia U., N.Y.C., 1963-67; assoc. prof. medicine and physiology U. Chgo., 1967-69; Philip J. and Harriet L. Goodhart prof. cardiology Mt. Sinai Sch. Medicine, N.Y.C., 1969-77; prof. medicine U. Conn., Farmington, 1977—2000, prof. medicine emeritus, 2000—, head cardiology divsn., 1977—95; vis. prof. medicine Dartmouth Med. Sch., 1990—2001, vis. prof. medicine and physiology, 2001—. Cons. VA, 1970; coord. Problem Area #3, US-USSR Collaboration in Cardiovasc. Rsch., 1983—86; mem. adv. com. Chinese Acad. Med. Sci., 1982—89; R.T. Hall lectr. Cardiac Soc., Australia, 1991, New Zealand, 91; chair sci. bd. Stanley J. Sarnoff Endowment Cardiovasc. Sci. Inc., 1992—93; chair, sci. adv. bd. Patrick, Catherine, Weldon, Donaghue Med. Rsch. Found., 1994—97; mem. bd. sci. counsellors Nat. Heart Lung Inst., 1989—92. Author: Physiology of the Heart, 1977, Physiology of the Heart, 3rd edit., 2001, Heart Failure: Pathophysiology, Molecular Biology and Clinical Management, 2000; editor: The Heart and Cardiovascular System, 1986, 1991; Am. Jour. Physiology, 1966—72, mem. editl. bd.: Jour. Molecular and Cellular Cardiology, 1970—92, editor-in-chief:, 1986—92, mem. editl. bd.: Am. Jour. Cardiology, 1970—75, Jour. Mechanochemistry and Cell Motility, 1970—72, Am. Jour. Medicine, 1971—77, Jour. Clin. Investigation, 1971—76, Circulation Rsch., 1974—80, Physiol. Rev., 1976—80, Cardiovasc. Pharmacol., 1979—88, Life Scis., 1979—88, Cardiology, 1980—85, Jour. Am. Coll. Cardiology, 1983—87, Can. Jour. Cardiology, 1988—91, Cardioscience, 1988—95, Circulation, 1992—, reviewer : several profl. jours.; contbr. articles to profl. jours. Served with USPHS, 1957-59. Humboldt fellow Alexander von Humboldt Found., 1975-76, Moseley traveling fellow Harvard U., 1960-61. Fellow ACP, Am. Coll. Cardiology (gov. Conn. 1984-87), Coun. on Basic Cardvasc. Sci. (charter); mem. Am. Heart assn. (advanced rsch. fellow 1961-63, established investigator 1963-68, v.p. couns. 1992-94, bd. dirs. 1992-94, chmn. coun. affairs com. 1992-94, chmn. exec. com. basic sci. coun. 1990-92, Conn. affiliate bd. dirs. 1986-94, Greater Hartford chpt. bd. dirs. 1977-84, sec. 1982-84, v.p. 1984-86, pres. 1986-88, Rsch. Achievement award 1989, Disting. Achievement award Basic Sci. Coun. 1991, award of Meritorious Achievement 1995, Honoree Louis N. and Arnold M. Katz prize Basic Sci. Coun. 1995), N.Y. Heart Assn. (bd. dirs. 1971-74, 75-77), Am. Physiol. Soc., Cardiac Muscle Soc. (pres. 1969-71), Assn. Am. Physicians, Internat. Soc. Heart Rsch. (pres. Am. sect. 1985, founding fellow 2000), Assn. Univ. Cardiologists, Alpha Omega Alpha. Home: PO Box 1048 1592 New Boston Rd Norwich VT 05055-1048

KATZ, ARNOLD MARTIN, insurance brokerage firm executive; b. Schenectady, N.Y., Mar. 22, 1940; s. David and Minna Katz; 1 child, Sharon. BS in Pub. Relations, Boston U., 1962. Cert. life underwriter, Pa. Sales rep. Mass. Gen. Life Ins. Co., Hartford, Conn., 1964-66, sr. sales rep., 1966-67, asst. mgr., 1967; mgr. Phila., 1967-72; v.p. Boston, 1972-76; pres. Brokerage Concepts, Inc., Phila., 1977—. Chmn. bd. dirs. Brokers Svc. Inc., N.Y.; pres. BCI Holdings Inc., Atlantic Adminstrs., Waltham, Mass., Group Source, Phila., Am. Ind. Life Ins. Co. Contbr. articles to profl. jours. Bd. dirs. Moss Rehab. Hosp., Phila., 1985-93, Police Athletic League, Phila., 1986—; vice chmn. Einstein Health Care Found., Phila., 1987—; chmn., mem. bd. Belmont Hosp. 1987—. Served to maj. U.S. Army, 1962-73. Mem. Life Underwriter Assn., CLU (bd. dirs. Phila. chpt.), Assn. Health Ins. Agts. (pres.). Jewish. Office: Brokerage Concepts Inc 1021 8th Ave King Of Prussia PA 19406 E-mail: arnold.katz@bcitpa.com.

KATZ, AVRUM SIDNEY, lawyer; b. Melrose Park, Ill., Oct. 10, 1939; s. Joseph George and Bessie Goldie (Ancel) K.; m. Sheela Cara Cooperman, Sept. 1, 1963; children: Julie Anne, Aaron Richard, Michele Sharon. BSEE, Ill. Inst. Tech., 1962; JD, George Washington U., 1966. Bar: Ill. 1966, U.S. Dist. Ct. (no. dist.) Ill. 1967, U.S. Patent Office 1967, U.S. Supreme Ct. 1977, U.S. Ct. Appeals (7th cir.) 1978, D.C. 1991, cert.: U.S. Patent Office (examiner). Assoc. Leonard G. Nierman, Chgo., 1966—67, Fitch, Even, Tabin, Flannery & Welsh

and predecessor firms, Chgo., 1967—70, ptnr., 1971—82, Welsh & Katz, Chgo., 1983—. Author (with others): Effective Litigation Against Knockoffs, 1984; author: Chip, Mask and Program Protection, 1985, Electronics and Computer Patent and Copyright Practice, 1988, 2d edit., 1990; mem. editl. bd. Mealey's Litig. Report on Intellectual Property, 1992—, mem. adv. bd. Licensing Jour., 1987—, The IP Litigator, 2000—. Mem. ad hoc com. Lake Forest (Ill.) City Coun., 1970; mem. intellectual property adv. bd. George Washington U. Law Sch., 2000—; bd. dirs., mem. exec. com. Midwest region Am. Friends of Hebrew U., 1999—. Recipient award of distinction, Patent Resources Group, 1983. Mem.: ABA, IEEE, Assn. Patent Law Firms (pres. 1998—99), Licensing Exec. Soc., Internat. Trademark Assn., Intellectual Property Law Assn. Chgo., Chgo. Bar Assn., Ill. Bar Assn., Std. Club Chgo., Union League Club Chgo., Sigma Iota Epsilon, Eta Kappa Nu, Tau Beta Pi, Delta Theta Phi. Home: 475 Turicum Rd Lake Forest IL 60045-3363 Office: Welsh & Katz Ltd 120 S Riverside Plz Fl 22 Chicago IL 60606-3913 Business E-Mail: askatz@welshkatz.com.

KATZ, BARBARA S. special education educator; b. Springfield, Mass., July 22, 1933; d. Harry and Pearl (Black) Stein; m. Charles Murry Katz, July 14, 1957; children: Helen Lee, Robert Alan. BS, Am. Internat. Coll., Springfield, 1956, MA in Ednl. Psychology in Learning Disabilities, 1979. Cert. in elem. edn., moderate spl. needs, Mass. Elem. tchr. Springfield Pub. Schs., 1956-60; Jr. Great Books discussion leader, 1968-69; Gillingham remedial tchr. Pub. Schs., Longmeadow, Mass., 1975-78, spl. edn. tchr. Chicopee, Mass., 1978-98, reader, 1998—. Reader Pioneer Valley Collaborative, East Longmeadow, Mass., 1998—. Pres. Kodimoh Synagogue Women's Group, Springfield, 1972-74; troop leader Girl Scouts U.S., Longmeadow, 1967-70. Horace Mann grantee, 1988. Mem. NEA, Mass. Tchrs. Assn. Avocations: painting, reading, walking, swimming. Home: 407 Bliss Rd Longmeadow MA 01106-1538

KATZ, BEN Z. pediatrician, educator; BA, Touro Coll., 1976; MD, NYU, 1980. Diplomate Am. Bd. Pediat., Am. Bd. Pediat. Infectious Diseases. Intern, resident NYU, N.Y.C., 1983; asst. prof. pediat. Yale U. Sch. Medicine, New Haven, 1987—91; assoc. prof. pediat. Northwestern U. Feinberg Sch. Medicine, Chgo., 1996—. Dir. travel clinic Children's Meml. Hosp., Chgo., 1997—. Contbr. articles to profl. jours. Grantee, NIH, 1988. Fellow: Soc. for Pediat. Rsch., Infectious Disease Soc. Am. Jewish. Avocation: Karate. Office: Childrens Meml Hosp 2300 Childrens Plaza Chicago IL 60614

KATZ, BRIAN PHILIP, language educator, writer; s. Linda Ellen Timpone and Arnold Ivan Katz; m. Maria L. Rosenblum, Sept. 6, 1997. BA, Bennington Coll., 1992; MFA, Columbia U., 1997. Creative writing instr. Hofstra U., Hempstead, NY, 1998—2000; English educator Yeshiva U. L.A., 2001—. Editor Anthropophagy.com, L.A., 2001—. Democrat. Home: 222 Bernard Ave Venice CA 90291 Personal E-mail: bpkatz@aol.com.

KATZ, CHERYL ANN, human services manager, social worker; b. Bklyn., Apr. 11, 1955; d. Henry and Esther (Rosenberg) Borenstein; m. Yuri Katz (div.); children: Michael Philip, Daniel Evan. BS, Jewish Theol. Sem., 1977; BSW, Columbia U., 1977, MSSW, 1979; MPA, Pace U., 1994. Youth group dir. United Synagogue Youth, 1973-77; tchr. Hebrew Sch. Conservative Synagogues, 1973-77; social worker N.Y. Assn. New Ams., 1979-81, St. Vincent's Med. Ctr. Richmond, 1981-87; pvt. practice psychotherapy N.Y.C., 1984-86; adminstr. Mt. Sinai Med. Ctr., NYC, 1994-96, Lippman Eye Inst., 1996-97, Comprehensive Health Mgmt. Svcs., 1997-98; adminstr. dept. ob-gyn. Westchester Med. Ctr./N.Y. Med. Coll., Valhalla, 1998—2003; adminstr. primary care divsn. Weill Cornell Med. Coll., N.Y., 2003—. Mem.: ACSW, Med. Group Mgmt. Assn., Women's Healthcare Network Westchester. Home: 5 Hemlock Rd Briarcliff Manor NY 10510-1606 Office: Weill Cornell Med College 201 East 80th St New York NY 10021 E-mail: cabkatz@hotmail.com.

KATZ, CLEO, real estate educator; b. Cleve. d. Joseph and Edith Hoffman; children: Darlene Katz Weiner, David. Student, Lumbleau Real Estate Sch., L.A., 1998. Lic. real estate agt. Calif., 98. Real estate specialist, 1979—; seminar spkr., instr. Real Estate Profits and Secrets Seminars, 1982—90; condr. in-house seminars, spkr. title, escros and real estate cos., 1990—. Host weekly radio program KIEV, K Money Radio; various TV guest appearances. Author: Foreclosure Secrets, 1979, How to Buy and Sell Foreclosure Property, 1982, (column) Foreclosure Secrets in Daily Commerce newspaper, 2001—; author: (author and guest spkr.) Foreclosure Properties, —. Mem.: NAFE. Avocations: painting, dancing, travel. Office: Cleo Katz Seminars 22704 Ventura Blvd # 501 Woodland Hills CA 91364

KATZ, COLLEEN, publisher; b. Newark; BA in Math., Montclair (N.J.) Coll.; cert., Ctr. Linguistique Etrangers, Tours, France. Assoc. editor Fawcett Publs., N.Y.C., 1972-73, editor, 1973-76; editorial dir. Butterick Fashion Mktg. Co., N.Y.C., 1976-77; editor Ency. of Textiles, N.Y.C., 1979; editor in chief N.J. Monthly, Morristown, 1982-85; dir. publs. Ins. Info. Inst., N.Y.C., 1985-88; pub., editor-in-chief Journal of Accountancy, N.Y.C., 1988—. Adj. prof. Audrey Cohen Coll., 2000. Editor Ins. Rev., 1985-88; pub. mags. and newsletters AICPA, 1997—; editor Huguenot Heritage, 1999. Vol. tchr. Elizabeth (N.J.) Sch. System; vol. editor Nat. Council Jewish Women, NJ, 1967—71; vol. pub. relations worker Essex County Mental Health Assn., NJ, 1980—81. Named Woman of Yr., Cen. N.J. March of Dimes, 1984, Outstanding Alumnus, Montclair Coll., 1984; recipient Gold Cir. award Am. Soc. Assn. Execs., 1989, award for pub. excellence Comm. Concepts, 1990, Pub. Excellence award Mag. Week, 1990, Gen. Excellence award Soc. Nat. Assn. Publs., 1991, Golden Page award, 2000-01. Mem.: Conf. des Vins du Cahors, Soc. Nat. Assn. Publs. (Silver medal for gen. excellence 1997), Am. Soc. Mag. Editors, Soc. Profl. Journalists, Nat. Arts Club. Avocation: foreign languages. Office: Jour of Accountancy Harborside III Jersey City NJ 07311

KATZ, DAVID, gastroenterologist, educator; b. Harrisburg, Pa., Nov. 28, 1928; s. William Meyer and Fanny (Zwick) Katz; m. Shirley Eileen Love, Sept. 17, 1987; children: Jonathan, Peter, Jeremy. BS, Tulane U., 1946, MD, 1950. Intern Kings County Hosp., Bklyn., 1950-52; resident in internal medicine VA Hosp., Newington, Conn., 1952-53, West Haven, Conn., 1955, fellow in gastroenterology, 1955-56; asst. prof N.Y. Med., N.Y.C., 1958-62, assoc. prof., 1962-68, prof., 1968—, Valhalla, 1974—. Home: 100 E Hartsdale Ave Apt 6jw Hartsdale NY 10530-3846

KATZ, DOUGLAS JEFFREY, retired naval officer, consultant; b. Madison, Wis., May 1, 1942; s. Harold Leroy and Lois Wayne (Hoops) K.; m. Sharon Lynne Mustard, June 11, 1965; children: Robert Douglas, Erica Lynne. BS in Engring., U.S. Naval Acad., 1965; MS in Material Mgmt., Naval Postgrad. Sch., 1973. Commd. ensign USN, 1965, advanced through grades to vice adm., mil. advisor Fleet Adv. Unit, 1971-72, exec. officer USS Mahan, 1977-79, surface ops. office Cruiser-Destroyer Group 2, 1979-80, plans/budget officer Chief of Naval Ops. Washington, 1980-83, comdg. officer USS Deyo Charleston, S.C., 1983-85, dir. prof. devel. U.S. Naval Acad. Annapolis, Md., 1985-87, comdg. officer USS New Jersey Long Beach, Calif., 1987-89, dir. surface warfare Chief of Naval Ops. Washington, 1989-90, comdr. Cruiser-Destroyer Group 2 Charleston, S.C., 1990-92; comdr. Naval Forces Ctrl. Command, 1992-94, Naval Surface Forces Atlantic, 1994-97, ret., 1997, cons., 1997—. Decorated Disting. Svc. medal with two gold stars, Legion of Merit with three gold stars, Bronze Star with combat V, Meritorious Svc. medal with two gold stars, Navy commendation medal with one gold star. Mem. U.S. Naval Inst., U.S. Naval Acad. Alumni Assn., Surface Navy Assn. (bd. dirs.), U.S. Naval Sailing Assn. (commodore). Avocation: athletics. Home and Office: 1530 Gordon Cove Dr Annapolis MD 21403-5004

KATZ, EDWARD MORRIS, banker; b. Passaic, N.J., Apr. 18, 1921; s. David and Badane (Gubersky) K.; m. Phyllis Kushner, June 20, 1948; children—David, Alan, Michael. BA, Bklyn. Coll., 1947; MA, NYU, 1948. Auditor Amalgamated Bank N.Y., N.Y.C., 1951-55, cashier, 1955-73, v.p., 1957-61, sr. v.p., 1961-71, exec. v.p., 1971-78, pres., chief exec. officer, 1978-89, dir., 1966-89, ret., 1989. Home: 48 Windsor Rd Great Neck NY 11021-2740 E-mail: phyllisedkat@aol.com.

KATZ, ELIHU, sociologist, communications educator; b. NYC, May 31, 1926; s. Maurice Lionel and Rose (Lefkowitz) Katz; m. Ruth Torgovnik, Sept. 16, 1951; children: Matthew Joseph, Nathaniel Zvi. BA, Columbia U., 1948, MA, 1950, PhD, 1956; cert. in Japan studies, U. Chgo., 1945; D (hon.), U. Ghent, Belgium, 1989, U. Montreal, Can., 1990, U. Paris 2, 2000, U. Haifa, Israel, 2000. Rsch. assoc. Bur. Applied Social Rsch. Columbia U., N.Y.C., 1951-54; from asst. to assoc. prof. U. Chgo., 1954-69; prof. Hebrew U., Jerusalem, 1963-93; trustee prof. U. Pa., Phila., 1993—. Sci. adv. com. NSF, Washington, 1960—62; founding dir. Israel TV, Jerusalem, 1967—69; cons. Office Social Rsch. CBS, N.Y.C., 1969, BBC, London, 1970—71, London, 1975—77; disting. vis. prof. U. So. Calif., L.A., 1978—92, U. Padua, Italy, 1985, Keio U., Tokyo, 1988, PUC, Porte Alegre, Brazil, 1999, U. Vienna, 2002; sci. dir. Israel Inst. Applied Social Rsch., Jerusalem, 1988—95, rsch. assoc., 1996—; Wilbur Schramm Meml. lectr. U. Ill., 1990; Wayne Danielson lectr. U. Tex., 1995. Co-author: (book) Personal Influence, 1955, Medical Innovation: A Diffusion Study, 1966, Politics of Community Conflict: The Fluoridation Decision, 1969, Secularization of Leisure, 1976, Broadcasting in the Third World, 1977, Social Research on Broadcasting: Proposals for Further Development, 1977, Almost Midnight: Reforming the Late Night News, 1980, Mass Media and Social Change, 1981, Export of Meaning, 1990, Media Events, 1992, Jewishness of Israelis, 1997, Election Studies: What's Their Use, 2001, Canonic Texts in Media Research, 2003; contbr. articles to profl. jours. Active Israel Coun. Culture and Arts, 1970—73, Israel Film Coun., 1972—76; chmn. U.S. Ednl. Found. Isreal, 1976; bd. dirs. U.S. Ednl. Found. Israel, 1971—75, chmn., 1976. Recipient prize in media rsch., Germany, 1977, McLuhan-Teleglobe Can. award, 1987, Israel prize, Govt. of Israel, 1989, Murray Edelman award, Am. Polit. Sci. Assn., 1991, Friedrich Albert Lange prize, German Soc. Leisure Study, Helen Dinerman award, Internat. Assn. Pub. Opinion Rsch., 1992. Fellow: Internat. Commn. Assn., Am. Sociol. Assn.; mem.: Internat. Inst. Comm. (trustee 1977—81), World Assn. Pub. Opinion Rsch., Am. Assn. Pub. Opnion Rsch., Israel Sociol. Soc. (chmn. 1977—81), Internat. Sociol. Assn., Am. Acad. Arts and Scis., Penn Club (N.Y.). Jewish. Home: Hagdud Haivri 15 Jerusalem Israel Office: U Pa Annenberg Sch Comm Philadelphia PA 19104

KATZ, GEORGE GERSHON, psychologist; b. Aug. 3, 1927; s. Abraham Michael and Dora K.; 1 child, Esti Goodman. BA, Brooklyn Coll., 1950; JD with honors, Calif. Coll. Law, 1978; PhD with honors, N.Y. U., 1956. Diplomate Am. Bd. Clinical Psychology, Am. Bd. Forensic Psychology, Am. Bd. Profl. Psychology. Clin. assoc. U. So. Calif., Los Angeles, 1971-89; instr. Northwestern U., Evanston, Ill., 1960-64, assoc. prof. Calif. State U., Los Angeles, 1969-72; adj. prof. Fuller Inst., Pasadena, Calif., 1982-86; clin. prof. U. Calif., Los Angeles, 1974-94; dir. clin. tng. VAMC, Los Angeles, 1984-93, asst. chief psychology, 1984-94. Mem. pres.'s com. mental health edn., White House, Washington, 1972; cons. senate com. on Vets. Affairs, Washington, 1972-74, Hathaway Sch. for Children:, Calif., 1969-74; co-dir./cons. Project NOVA, L.A., 1971-72; author/presenter papers in field. Co-initiator of the unit system within VA; introduced the first ombudsman program in the VA. Oral commr. Bd. of Psychology, State of Calif., 1992—. With USCG, 1944-46. Grantee NIMH, Va., 1971-75; patient advocate VISTA program, 1973. Fellow: APA, Am. Acad. Forensic Psychology, Am. Psychol. Soc.; mem.: State Bar Calif. (chair, legal profl. com. 1998—), Am. Bd. Profl. Psychology (treas. 1992—2001, v.p. 2001—), Acad. Clin. Psychology, Am. OrthoPsychiatric Assn. Office: Forensic Psych Assocs 17337 Tramonto Dr Pacific Palisades CA 90272-3121 E-mail: bb283@lafh.org.

KATZ, HADRIAN RONALD, lawyer; b. Cambridge, Mass., Aug. 12, 1949; s. Samuel and Alice (Greenstein) K.; m. Candace Kay Kaufman, Apr. 1, 1977; children: Gwendlyn Rebecca, Jonathan Harold. AB, Harvard U., 1969, JD, 1976; MA, U. Calif., Berkeley, 1973. Bar: D.C. 1977, Mass. 1977, U.S. Dist. Ct. D.C. 1977, U.S. Ct. Appeals (D.C. cir.) 1979, U.S. Supreme Ct. 1983, U.S. Ct. Appeals (6th cir.) 1985, U.S. Ct. Appeals (4th cir.) 1989. Ptnr. Arnold & Porter, Washington, 1976—. Mem. ABA, IEEE, Am. Phys. Soc., Assn. for Computing Machinery, Math. Assn. Am. Democrat. Avocation: computer. Home: 1324 Lancia Dr Mc Lean VA 22102-2204 Office: Arnold & Porter 555 12th St NW Washington DC 20004-1206

KATZ, HAROLD AMBROSE, lawyer, former state legislator; b. Shelbyville, Tenn., Nov. 2, 1921; s. Maurice W. and Gertrude Evelyn (Cohen) K.; m. Ethel Mae Lewison, July 21, 1945; children: Alan, Barbara, Julia, Joel. AB, Vanderbilt U., 1943; JD, U. Chgo., 1948, MA, 1958. Bar: Ill. 1948. Ptnr. Katz, Friedman, Eagle Eisenstein & Johnson, Chgo., 1948—; spl. legal cons. to Gov. of Ill., 1961-63; master-in-chancery, circuit ct. Cook County, Ill., 1963-67; mem. Ill. Ho. of Reps., 1965-83, chmn. judiciary com., co-chmn. rules com. Lectr. U. Coll., U. Chgo., 1959-64; Chmn. Ill. Commn. on Orgn. of Gen. Assembly, 1966-82; del. nat. Democratic conv., 1972 Author: Liability of Auto Manufacturers for Unsafe Design of Passenger Cars, 1956; (with Charles O. Gregory) Labor Law: Cases, Materials and Comments, 1948, Labor and the Law, 1979, Harold A. Katz Memoirs, 1988; editor: Improving the State Legislature, 1967; contbr. articles to mags. Recipient Jurisprudence award, Chgo. Am. Orgn. for Rehab. through Tng., 2000, Laureate, Ill. Acad. Lawyers, 2001. Fellow Coll. Labor and Employment Lawyers; mem. ABA, Ill. Bar Assn. (chmn. labor law sect. 1979-80), Internat. Soc. for Labor Law and Social Legislation (U.S. chmn. 1961-67), Am. Trial Lawyers Assn. (chmn. workmen's compensation sect. 1963-64. Jewish. Home: 1180 Terrace Ct Glencoe IL 60022-1241 Office: Katz Friedman Eagle Eisenstein & Johnson 77 W Washington St Fl 20 Chicago IL 60602-2904

KATZ, HARRIET MARX, retired social worker; b. Cleve., Jan. 7, 1941; d. Sylvester and Lucile (Kline) Marx; m. Ronald Glickman, Aug. 28, 1960 (div. Aug. 1982); children: Mark, Lawrence, James; m. Joel Samuel Katz, Feb. 19, 1989. BA, Miami U., 1962; MSW, U. Ill., Chgo., 1978. Lic. ind. clin. social worker, Minn.; diplomate Am. Bd. Examiners Clin. Social Work. Social worker Coun. for Jewish Elderly, Evanston, Ill., 1978-79, N.W. Suburban Spl. Edn. Assn., Arlington Heights, Ill., 1978-79, Northbrook (Ill.) Dist. 30, 1979-81, Winnetka (Ill.) Pub. Schs., 1980-88, Anoka-Hennepin Dist. 11, Coon Rapids, Minn., 1988-89, Mpls. Pub. Schs., 1989—2001; ret., 2001. Mem. Midwest Sch. Social Work Coun., 1993-95. Mem. NASW (ACSW cert.; mem. sch. social work steering com. 1999-2001), Ill. Assn. Sch. Social Workers (bd. dirs. 1985-86, 86-87), Minn. Sch. Social Workers Assn. (co-chair ann. mtg. 1990, 91, rec. sec. 1991-93, pres.-elect 1993-94, pres. 1994-95). Jewish. Avocations: music, chamber music, flute, needlework, travel. E-mail: jandhkatz@mn.rr.com.

KATZ, HILLIARD JOEL, physician; b. Stockton, Calif., May 26, 1918; s. Nelson and Pauline (Landman) K.; m. Jeanette Lillian Gordon, Aug. 18, 1946; children: Stephanie, Steven Nelson, Hilary. AB, U. Calif. at Berkeley, 1939; MD, U. Calif. at San Francisco, 1942. Diplomate: Am. Bd. Internal Medicine. Intern U. Calif. Hosps., San Francisco, 1942-43, asst. resident internal medicine, 1943-44, attending physician, electrocardiographer, 1958—95, chief staff, 1964-66, physician charge CCU, 1966-73; resident, sr. resident in internal medicine San Francisco VA Hosp., 1946-48; practice medicine specializing in cardiology San Francisco, 1948—95; clin. instr. medicine U. Calif. Sch. Medicine, San Francisco, 1948-53, asst. clin. prof., 1953-61, asso. clin. prof., 1961-70, clin. prof. cardiovascular div., 1970—95, clin. prof. emeritus, 1996—, asst. to chancellor for spl. events. Chmn. Nat. Com. Emergency Coronary Care, 1974-76; mem. rsch. coun., Am. Wine Alliance for Rsch. and Edn. Served to capt. M.C. AUS, 1944-46. Fellow ACP, Am. Coll. Cardiology, Am. Heart Assn. (coun. clin. cardiology 1963, Disting. Svc. award 1963, Svc. Recognition award 1964); mem. Calif. Heart Assn. (dir. 1956-71), San Francisco Heart Assn. (pres. 1955-57, Disting. Svc. cert. 1959), Calif. Acad. Medicine (pres. 1965), U. Calif. Sch. Medicine Alumni-Faculty Assn. (pres. 1961-62), Soc. Med. Friends Wine (pres. 1968, bd. govs.), Wine and Food Soc., San Francisco (chmn. 1997-99), Club Culinaire Francais de Californie, Commanderie du Bontemps de Medoc et des graves, Commanderie de Bordeaux de San Francisco, Cercle de l'Union, Phi Beta Kappa, Alpha Omega Alpha. Home: 223 Cherry St San Francisco CA 94118-1606

KATZ, IRWIN, marketing executive; b. N.Y.C., Oct. 6, 1942; s. Sam and Ethel (Weinstein) K.; m. Beatrice Eva Kraus, July 11, 1965; children: Ivan Todd, Andrew Craig. BBA, Ohio U., 1964. Sales analyst J.B. Williams Co., N.Y.C., 1964-67; product mgr. Thayer Knomark div. Revlon Co., N.Y.C., 1967-69; supr. accounts Rumrill-Hoyt Advt. Agy., N.Y.C., 1969-71; exec. v.p., ptnr. Popofsky Advt. Agy., N.Y.C., 1971-78; v.p. mktg. Commerce Drug Co. div. Del Labs. Inc., Plainview, N.Y., 1979-81; v.p. strategic planning Del Labs Inc., Farmingdale, N.Y., 1981-83; sr. v.p. Ansell-Ams. Inc., Tinton Falls, N.J., 1983-89, Eatontown, N.J., 1989; pres. Irwin Katz and Assocs., Marlboro, N.J., 1989—. Mem.: Free Sons. Jewish. Avocation: Karate. Office: 746 Highway 34 Ste 1 Matawan NJ 07747-6680 E-mail: info@irwinkatz.com.

KATZ, JAMES E. communications educator; PhD, Rutgers U., 1974. Post doctoral fellow Kennedy Sch. Govt. Harvard U.; post doctoral fellow Ctr. for Policy Alternatives MIT; assoc. prof. Clarkson U.; asst. prof. Lyndon B. Johnson Sch. Pub. Affairs U. Tex., Austin; disting. mem. staff Bell. Comms. Rsch.; prof. comm. Rutgers U., New Brunswick, NJ, 1997—. Editl. bd. Info: An Internat. Jour. Policy and Rsch., 1998—, Info., Comm. & Soc. (jour.), 1997—, Internet Rsch. Jour.: Tech., Policy and Applications, 1996—2001, Personal and Ubiquitous Computing, 1996—2001, Personal Tech., 2001—. Assoc. editor The Information Society, 1996—2001; author: Social Science and Public Policy in the United States, 1975, Presidential Politics and Science Policy, 1978, Congress and National Energy Policy, 1984, Sowing the Serpents' Teeth: The Implications of Third World Military Industrialization, 1986, Connections: Social and Cultural Studies of the Telephone in American Life, 1999; editor: Arms Production in Developing Countries, 1984, People in Space: Policy Perspectives for a Star Wars Century, 1985, Machines that Become Us: The Social Context of Personal Communication Technology, 2002; co-editor: Internet and Health Communication: Experience and Expectations, 2000, Perpetual Contact: Mobile Communication, Private Talk, Public Performance, 2002, Corpo Futuro: Il Corpo Umano Tra Tecnologie, Communicazione e moda, 2002; co-author: Social Consequences of Internet Use: Access, Involvement and Expression, 2002. Office: Rutgers U 4 Huntington Street New Brunswick NJ 08910

KATZ, JANE, swimming educator; b. Sharon, Pa., Apr. 16, 1943; d. Leon and Dorthea (Oberkewitz) Katz BS in Edn., CCNY, 1963; MA, NYU, 1966; MEd, Columbia Tchrs. Coll., 1972, EdD, 1978. Faculty Bronx C.C., CUNY, 1964—, prof. phys. edn., 1972—. Mem. U.S. Round-the-World Synchronized Swim Team, 1964; synchronized swimming solo tour of Eng., 1969; founding co-organizer, coach 1st Internat. Israeli Youth Festival Games, 1970; mem. winning U.S. Maccabiah Swim Team, 1957; vice-chair U.S. Masters All-Am. Swim Team, 1974—; mem. Nat. Masters All-Am. Swim Team, 1974—, synchronized swimming solo champion, 1975; spkr. judge in field. Author: Swimming for Total Fitness, A Progressive Aerobic Program, 1981, rev. ed. 1993, Swimming Through Your Pregnancy, 1983, W.E.T. Workouts: Water Exercises and Techniques to Help You and Tone Up Aerobically, 1985, Fitness Works: Blueprint for Lifelong Fitness, 1988, Swim 30 Laps in 30 Days, 1991, The Workstation Workout, 1994, Aquatic Handbook for Lifetime Fitness, 1996; author: (video) The New W.E.T. Workout, 1994, The All-American Aquatic Handbook: Your Passport to Lifetime Fitness, 1996, The W.E.T. Workout, 1996; contbr. Encyclopedia Britannica Med. and Health Ann., 1997, Swim Basics Video, 2001, Synchro Video, 2003, Aqua Fit Book, 2003; papers in field. Trainee Fed. Adminstrn. Aging, 1971-72; mem. Internat. Hall of Fame, Ft. Lauderdale. Named Healthy Am. Fitness Leader U.S. Jaycees and the Pres.'s. Coun. on Phys. Fitness, 1987, Outstanding Masters Synchronized Swimming, 1987; recipient CCNY Towsend Harris Acad. medal, 1989, Outstanding Lifetime Leadership award Fedn. Internat. Nat. Amateur, 1999, cert. of merit Fedn. Internat. de Natation Amateur (FINA), Sydney, Australia, 2000, Lifetime Contbrn. to Swimming award Internat. Olympic Com., 2000. Mem.: AAHPER, Internat. Aquatics (Hall of Fame Paragon award), U.S. Com. Sports for Israel (co-chmn. women's swimming com. 1970—, dir.), Internat. Swimming Hall of Fame (bd. of dir. 2002—). Address: 400 2nd Ave Apt 23B New York NY 10010-4052 E-mail: jkatz@jjay.cuny.edu.

KATZ, JASON LAWRENCE, lawyer, insurance executive; b. Chgo., Sept. 28, 1947; s. Irving and Goldie (Medress) K.; 2 children. B.A., Northeastern Ill. U., 1969; J.D., DePaul U., 1973. Bar: Calif. 1976, Ariz. 1973, U.S. Ct. Appeals (9th cir.) 1976. Sole practice, Scottsdale, Ariz., 1973-76; v.p., corp. counsel Mission Ins. Group, Inc., Los Angeles, 1976-84; exec. v.p., gen. counsel Farmers Group, Inc., Los Angeles, 1984—, bd. dirs., 1986—; v.p., bd. dirs. Calif. Def. Counsel, 1986-88. Mem. Calif. Bar Assn. (exec. bd. ins. law subcom. 1991-94), Los Angeles County Bar Assn. (mem. exec. bd. corp. law sect. 1993—), Conf. Ins. Counsel (v.p., pres. L.A. chpt. 1981-82), Assn. Calif. Tort Reform (bd. dirs. 1990—), The Ins. Coun. So. Calif. (City of Hope chpt. 1991—). Office: Farmers Group Inc 4680 Wilshire Blvd Los Angeles CA 90010-3807

KATZ, JEFFREY IVAN, urologist; b. Aug. 21, 1943; s. David and Rebecca (Shapiro) K.; m. Ethelinda Spiegel, Sept. 29, 1973; children: David, Jennifer. BA, Pa. State U., 1965; MD, U. Bologna (Italy), 1970. Diplomate AM. Bd. Urology. Intern N.Y. Med. Coll., 1971-72; resident in surgery Mt. Sinai Hosp., Miami, Fla., 1972-73; resident in urology Albert Einstein Med. Coll., Bronx, N.Y., 1973-76; pvt practice specializing in urology West Orange, N.J., 1976—. Mem. staff St. Barnabas Med. tr., Livingston, N.J., chief urology, 1984-89, 98—; chief of surgery Irvington (N.J.) Gen. Hosp., 1989-95. Rschr. in field. Fellow ACS.l mem. AMA, N.J. Med. Assn., Essecx County Med. Assn., Am. Assn. Clin. Urologists, Am. Urology Assn., N.J. Urology Assn. Jewish. Office: 101 Old Short Hills Rd West Orange NJ 07052-1000

KATZ, JEROME CHARLES, lawyer; b. Boston, Sept. 25, 1950; s. Ralph and Thelma M. (Clark) K.; m. Nancy M. Green, Aug. 29, 1976; children: Jonathan Green, Elizabeth Rachel. AB magna cum laude, Duke U., 1972; JD, Columbia U., 1975. Bar: N.Y. 1976, U.S. Dist. Ct. (so. and ea. dists.) N.Y. 1976, U.S. Supreme Ct. 1979, U.S. Ct. Appeals (2d cir.) 1981, U.S. Dist. Ct. (we. dist.) N.Y. 1990. Assoc. Chadbourne & Parke, N.Y.C., 1975-83, ptnr., 1983—. Ct.-apptd. neutral mediator U.S. Dist. Ct. (so. dist.) N.Y., 2001—; bd. dirs. The Legal Aid Soc., 2002--. Assoc. editor Columbia Jour. Transnat. Law, 1974-75. Harlan Fiske Stone scholar Columbia U., 1974. Mem. ABA, Assn. of the Bar of the City of N.Y., Phi Beta Kappa. Home: 77 E 12th St New York NY 10003-5002 Office: Chadbourne & Parke 30 Rockefeller Plz Fl 31 New York NY 10112-0129 E-mail: jkatz@chadbourne.com.

KATZ, JOEL ABRAHAM, lawyer, music consultant; b. Bronx, N.Y., May 27, 1944; s. Harry and Hilda (Wiesenthal) K.; Kane Swims, 1994; children from previous marriage: Leslie Helaine, Jeni Michelle. BA in Econs., Hunter Coll., 1966; JD, U. Tenn., 1969. Bar: Tenn. 1969, D.C. 1970, Ga. 1971, U.S. Dist. Ct. (ea. dist.) Tenn. 1970, U.S. Dist. Ct. Appeals (11th cir.) 1971. Co-mng. shareholder, chair entertainment practice Greenberg Traurig, Atlanta. Gen. coun., bd. dirs. Farm Aid Inc., T.J. Martell Found.; bd. contbg. editors Entertainment Law & Finance. Mem. exec. coun. T.J. Martell Found. for Leukemia Rsch., N.Y.C.; mem. Ga. Music Hall of Fame Authority; bd. dirs. Very Special Arts. Mem. NARAS (gen. counsel, past v.p., past nat. trustee, dir. found. bd., nat. chmn. bd. trustees, trustee Atlanta chpt., chmn. emeritus), ABA, Fed. Bar Assn., Ga. Bar Assn., Tenn. Bar Assn., Atlanta C. of C. (bd. advisors), D.C. Bar Assn., Atlanta Bar Assn. Home: 675-8 W Paces Ferry Rd Atlanta GA 30327 Office: 3290 Northside Pkwy Ste 400 Atlanta GA 30327 E-mail: katzj@gtlaw.com.

KATZ, JOETTE, state supreme court justice; b. Bklyn., Feb. 3, 1953; BA, Brandeis U., 1974; JD, U. Conn., 1977. Bar: Conn. 1977. Pvt. practice, 1977-78; asst. pub. defender Office Chief Pub. Defender, 1978-83; chief legal svcs. Pub. Defender Svcs., 1983-89; judge Superior Ct., 1989-92; assoc. justice Conn. Supreme Ct., Hartford, 1992—; adminstrv. judge Appellate Sys., Hartford, 1994-2000. Instr. U. Conn. Sch. Law, 1981-84; instr. ethics and criminal law Quinnipiac Coll. Sch. Law, 1999—. Mem. Justice Edn. Ctr. Mem. Am. Law Inst.; Chair Evidence Code Drafting Com., Chair Adv. Com. for Appellate Rules; Am. Inns Ct. (past pres. Fairfield County br.), Assn. Reproductive Tech. (mem. com.). Office: Conn Supreme Ct Drawer N Sta A 231 Capital Ave Hartford CT 06106-1548

KATZ, JOHN, investment banker; b. Washington, Aug. 2, 1938; s. Milton and Vivian (Greenberg) K.; divorced; children: Ellen, Allison; m. Laura Cherkis, May 29, 1988; stepchildren: Ann Cherkis, Nancy Gernstetter. AB, Harvard U., 1960, JD, 1963. Bar: N.Y. 1964. With Hall, Casey, Dickler & Howley, 1963-67; asst. corp. counsel City of N.Y., 1967-69; spl. asst. to Congressman Richard L. Ottinger, 1969; with Poletti, Freidin, Prashker, Feldman & Gartner, 1969-75; atty. Equitable Life Assurance Soc. of U.S., 1975-79, v.p., counsel, 1979-82, v.p. Office of Chief Investment Officer, 1982-86; sr. v.p. Equitable Investment Corp., 1986-88, exec. v.p., 1989-91; chmn., CEO Sam's Restaurant Group, Inc., N.Y.C., 1991-92, investment banker, 1992-2000; mng. ptnr. Associated Mezzanine Investors, LLC, 2000—. Bd. dirs. The Legends Fund, Inc. Mem. Greater

N.Y.C. Com. of Harvard Law Sch. Fund; chmn. admissions com. Harvard Club N.Y.C., 1988-89; bd. dirs. Resources for Children with Spl. Needs, Inc., 1985-98; bd. dirs. My Sisters' Place, 1995—, co-chmn., 1996-99, chmn., 1999-2000. Home and Office: 10 Hemlock Rd Hartsdale NY 10530-2951 E-mail: johnkatz@cloud9.net.

KATZ, JOHN W. lawyer, state official; b. Balt., Md., June 3, 1943; s. Leonard Wallach and Jean W. (Kane) Katz; m. Joan Katz, June 11, 1969 (div. 1982); 1 child, Kimberly Erin. BA, Johns Hopkins U., Balt., 1965; JD, U. Calif., Berkeley, 1969; DDL (hon.), U. Alaska, 1994. Bar: Alaska 1971, Pa. 1971, U.S. Dist. Ct. D.C. 1971, U.S. Ct. Appeals (D.C. cir.), U.S. Tax Ct., U.S. Ct. Claims, U.S. Ct. Mil. Justice, U.S. Supreme Ct. Legis. and adminstrv. asst. to Congressman Howard W. Pollock of AK, Wash., 1969—70; legis. asst. US Sen. Ted Stevens of AK, Wash., 1971; assoc. McGrath and Flint, Anchorage, 1972; gen. counsel Joint Fed. State Land Use Planning Commn. for AK, Anchorage, 1972—79; spl. counsel Gov. Jay S. Hammond of AK, Anchorage and Washington, 1979—81; commr. AK Dept. Natural Resources, Juneau, Alaska, 1981—83; dir. state fed. rels. and spl. counsel Gov. Bill Sheffield of AK, Wash. and Juneau, 1983—86; dir. state-fed. rels., spl. counsel to Gov. Steve Cowper of AK, Wash., 1986—90, Gov. Walter J. Hickel of AK, Wash., 1990—94, Gov. Tony Knowles, 1994—2002, Gov. Frank Murkowski, 2002—. Mem. Alaska Power Survey Exec. Adv. Com. of FPC, Anchorage, 1972—74; com. hard rock minerals Gov.'s Coun. of Sci. and Tech., Anchorage, 1979—80; guest lectr. on natural resources U. Alaska, U. Denver. Contbr. articles to profl. jours.; columnist (Anchorage Times), 1991. Acad. supr. Alaska Externship Program, U. Denver Coll. Law, 1976—79; mem. Reagan-Bush transition team, U.S. Dept. Justice, 1980. Recipient Superior Sustained Performance award, Joint Fed. State Land Use Planning Commn. for Alaska, 1978, Resolution of Commendation award, Alaska Legis., 1988, Citation for svc. to people of Alaska, 2003. Republican. Office: State of Alaska Office of Gov 444 N Capitol St NW Ste 336 Washington DC 20001-1529

KATZ, JONATHAN L. lawyer; b. Bridgeport, Conn., Apr. 1, 1963; married. JD, George Washington Law Sch., Washington, 1989. Bar: Md. 1989, D.C. 1990, Va. 1997. Ptnr. Marks & Katz, LLC, Silver Spring, Md., 1998—. Pres. Free Speech Coalition of DC, MD and VA, Silver Spring, Md., 2001—; bd. dirs. American Civil Liberties Union - NCA Affiliate, Washington, 1992—95. Mem.: Philippine-Am. Bar Assn. (v.p. ops. 1999—2001), Nat. Assn. Criminal Defense Lawyers (mem. adv. bd. Champion Magazine 1996—2002). Office: Marks & Katz, LLC 1400 Spring St Ste 410 Silver Spring MD 20910 Office Fax: 301-495-8815. Business E-Mail: justice@markskatz.com.

KATZ, JOSE, cardiologist, theoretical physicist, educator; b. Havana, Cuba, June 6, 1944; s. Lipa and Victoria (Masson) K.; m. Anke Ebsen; children: Susan, David, Rachel, Hannah. BS, U. Ill., 1963, MS, 1964, PhD, 1967; MD, F.U., Berlin, 1980. Rsch. assoc. physicist U. Hamburg, Fed. Republic Germany, 1967-69; instr. physics Purdue U., Lafayette, Ind., 1969-71; asst. prof. physics Free U., West Berlin, Fed. Republic Germany, 1971-74, prof. physics, 1974-82; resident in internal medicine Cleve. Met. Gen. Hosp., Mt. Sinai Med. Ctr., Cleve., 1982-85; cardiology fellow Southwestern Med. Sch., Dallas, 1985-88; asst. prof. medicine and radiology Columbia U. Coll. Physicians and Surgeons, N.Y.C., 1988-94, assoc. prof. medicine and radiology, 1994—; dir. cardiovascular MRI and spectroscopy Columbia-Presbyn. Med. Ctr., N.Y.C., 1988—, co-dir. EKG lab., 1999—. Staff attending Columbia-Presbyn. Med. Ctr., N.Y.C., 1988—. Contbr. articles to profl. jours., chpts. to books. Fellow Am. Coll. Physicians, Am. Coll. Cardiology, Am. Coll. Chest Physicians, Am. Coll. Angiology, Am. Heart Assn. (coun. clin. cardiology, coun. on cardiovascular radiology, coun. on basic scis.), Internat. Soc. Magnetic Resonance in Medicine; mem. AMA, Radiol. Soc. N.Am., Soc. Nuclear Medicine, N.Am. Soc. Cardiac Imaging, Sigma Xi, Phi Kappa Phi, Sigma Tau, Pi Mu Epsilon, Tau Beta Pi. Office: Columbia U Dept of Med Divsn Cardiology 630 W 168th St New York NY 10032-3702

KATZ, JOSEPH, research and development executive; b. Tel Aviv, June 6, 1952; came to U.S., 1978, naturalized, 1988; s. David and Dvora (Kuint) K.; m. Yael Schapira, Aug. 12, 1974; children: Yariv C., Tamir B., Hila E. BSEE with honors, Technion, Israel Inst. Tech., Haifa, 1973; MSEE with high honors, Tel Aviv U., 1976; PhD, Calif. Inst. Tech., 1981. Project engr. Ministry of Def., Tel Aviv, 1974-78; sr. engr. Jet Propulsion Lab., Pasadena, Calif., 1979-81, mem. tech. staff, 1981-84, tech. group leader, 1984-86, group supr., 1986-89; dir. R&D Symbol Techs., Inc., Holtsville, N.Y., 1989-90, sr. dir., 1991-94, v.p. R&D, 1994-96, sr. v.p. R&D, 1996—. Lectr. Calif. State U., Los Angeles, 1982-88, SUNY, Stony Brook, 1990-91; cons. Gen. Electric Co., Syracuse, N.Y., 1984-86. Contbr. articles to profl. jours.; patentee in field. Recipient Cert. Recognition, NASA, 1982-92, JPL Dir.'s Research Achievement award, 1987; Northrop Corp. fellow, 1979; U.S.-Israel Ednl. Found. scholar, 1978. Fellow Optical Soc. Am., IEEE; mem. Tau Beta Pi. Office: Symbol Tech Inc 1 Symbol Plz Holtsville NY 11742-1300 E-mail: katz@symbol.com.

KATZ, JOSEPH JACOB, retired chemist, educator; b. Apr. 19, 1912; s. Abraham and Stella (Asnin) K.; m. Celia S. Weiner, Oct. 1, 1944; children: Anna, Elizabeth, Mary, Abram. BSc, Wayne U., 1932; PhD, U. Chgo., 1942. Research asso. chemistry U. Chgo., 1942-43, asso. chemist metall. lab., 1943-45; sr. chemist Argonne Nat. Lab., Ill., 1945—92, ret., 1992; Tech. adviser U.S. delegation UN Conf. on Peaceful Uses Atomic Energy, Geneva, 1955; chmn. AAAS Gordon Research Conf. on Inorganic Chemistry, 1953-54. Am. editor Jour. Inorganic and Nuclear Chemistry, 1955-82. Recipient Distinguished Alumnus award Wayne U., 1955, Profl. Achievement award U. Chgo. Alumni Assn., 1983, Rumford Premium Am. Acad. Arts & Scis., 1992; Guggenheim fellow, 1956-57 Mem. Am. Chem. Soc. (award for nuclear applications in chemistry 1961, sec.-treas. div. phys. chemistry 1966-76), Nat. Acad. Scis., Phi Beta Kappa, Sigma Xi. Home: 1700 E 56th St Apt 1901 Chicago IL 60637-5085 Office: Argonne Nat Lab 9700 Cass Ave Argonne IL 60439-4803 E-mail: jjkatz@worldnet.att.net.

KATZ, JOSEPH LOUIS, chemical engineer, educator; b. Colon, Panama, Aug. 4, 1938; naturalized, 1970; s. Adolfo and Margarita (Eisen) K.; m. Liliane Capelluto, Apr. 10, 1965; children: Daniel P., Alan R. BS, U. Chgo., 1960, PhD, 1963. Amanuensis U. Copenhagen Chem. Lab. III, 1963-64; mem. tech. staff N.Am. Aviation Sci. Ctr., Thousand Oaks, Calif., 1964-70; assoc. prof. chem. engring. Clarkson Coll. Tech., Potsdam, N.Y., 1970-75, prof., 1975-79, Johns Hopkins U., Balt., 1979—, chmn. dept. chem. engring., 1981-84; dir. Energy Rsch. Inst., 1981-83. Prof. U. Aix-Marseille, France, 1976; vis. prof. MIT, Cambridge, 1977. Recipient John W. Graham Rsch. prize, Clarkson U., 1975; John Simon Guggenheim Meml. Found. fellow, 1976-77. Fellow AAAS, Am. Phys. Soc.; mem. AIChE, Am. Chem. Soc. (Md. sect. Chemist of Yr. 1982), Sigma Xi. Home: 5600 Greenspring Ave Baltimore MD 21209-4308 Office: Johns Hopkins U Dept Chem Engring Baltimore MD 21218

KATZ, JULIAN, gastroenterologist, educator; b. N.Y.C., Apr. 3, 1937; s. Abraham M. and Fay (Sher) K.; m. Sheila Moriber, Aug. 18, 1963; children: Jonathan Peter, Sara Katherine. AB, Columbia U., 1958; MD, U. Chgo., 1962. Diplomate Am. Bd. Internal Medicine. Intern U. Chgo. Hosps., 1962-63; resident in medicine Duke U., 1963-65; fellow in gastroenterology Yale U., 1965-67; practice medicine specializing in gastroenterology, internal medicine and geriatrics Phila., 1969—; prof. medicine, lectr. in physiology and biochemistry Med. Coll. Pa., 1970—; prof. medicine Jefferson Med. Coll., 1988-2001. Chief clin. gastroenterology Med. Coll. Pa.; lectr. in field. Editor profl. jours. and books; contbr. articles to profl. jours. and books. Mem. Bd. Health, City of Phila. With USN, 1967-69. Fellow ACP, Am. Coll. Gastroenterology; mem. Am. Soc. Gastrointestinal Endoscopy, Am. Soc. Study Liver Disease, Am. Gastroent. Assn., Phila. County Med. Soc. (pres. 1997-98), Pa. Soc. Gastroent. (pres. 1999-2001). Home: 701 Dodds Ln Gladwyne PA 19035-1516 Office: Med Coll of Pa 3300 Henry Ave Philadelphia PA 19129-1191 E-mail: jkatz@icdc.com.

KATZ, LAUREN FREIDUS, psychiatrist; b. Hillside, N.J., Apr. 4, 1957; BA, Brandeis U., 1978; MD, Hahnemann U., 1982. Diplomate Am. Bd. Psychiatry and Neurology. Intern Hahnemann U.; resident Inst. Pa. Hosp.; mem. faculty creative arts therapy dept. Drexel U., 1997—. Vol. faculty Widener U., Pa. Mem. Am. Psychiat. Assn., Am. Psychoanalytic Assn., Psychoanalytic Ctr. of Phila. Office: 110 Park Ave Swarthmore PA 19081-1724

KATZ, LAURENCE M. legal educator; b. 1940. J.D., U. Md., 1963. Bar: Md. 1963, Fla. 1963. Law clk. presiding justice U.S. Ct. Appeals (4th cir.), 1963-64; assoc. Frank, Bernstein, Conaway and Goldman, Balt., 1964-66; asst. prof. U. Md., 1966-69, assoc. prof., 1969-72, prof., assoc. dean, 1972-78; prof., dean U. Balt., 1978-93, prof., 1993—. Case note editor Md. Law Rev. Mem. Order of Coif. Office: U Balt Sch Law 1420 N Charles St Baltimore MD 21201-5720

KATZ, LAWRENCE EDWARD, lawyer; b. Norfolk, Va., Sept. 15, 1947; s. Hyman and Beatrice (Kellert) K.; m. Susan Dubick, Mar. 24, 2002. BA, U. Richmond, Va., 1969; JD, U. Balt., 1973. Contract specialist U.S. Dept. Energy, Washington, 1979-80; law clk. various attys., Fla., 1980-86; atty. Richard M. Labovitz, Balt., 1986-87; pvt. practice law Balt., 1987—. Movie critic Sta. WTTR, Westminster, Md., 1987—, Prestige Cablevision, Westminster, 1988—, Montgomery County Cable TV, 1991—, Crix Pix Variety, 1991, Labor Herald Weekly mag., 1991, Norfolk City News, L.A., Navy Voice, North Orange County News; entertainment critic Landmark News, Reisterstown, Md., 1987—; host Pro Wrestling Talk, Radio Sta. WCAO, Balt., 1989-92 Fundraiser Jewish Nat. Fund, Balt., 1988, vol. Assoc. Jewish Charities, Balt., 1985—, Zionist Orgn. Am., Balt., 1987—. With U.S. Army Res., 1969-75. Mem. B'nai B'rith. Home and Office: PO Box 32060 Baltimore MD 21282-2060

KATZ, LAWRENCE FRANCIS, economics educator; b. Ann Arbor, Mich., Apr. 21, 1959; s. Robert and Vera (Reichenfeld) Gantz. AB, U. Calif., Berkeley, 1981; PhD, MIT, 1986; MA (hon.), Harvard U., 1991. Asst. prof. U. Calif., Berkeley, 1985-86; asst. prof. econs. Harvard U., Cambridge, 1986-90, prof. econs., 1991—; chief economist U.S. Dept. Labor, Washington, 1993-94; rsch. assoc. Nat. Bur. of Econ. Rsch., Cambridge, 1985—. Project dir., Project on the Well-Being of Children and Econs. of the Family, Nat. Bur. Econ. Rsch., 1994-96. Co-editor: Differences and Changes in Wage Structures, 1995; editor Quar. Jour. of Econs., 1991—; contbr. numerous articles to profl. jours. Named Global Leader for Tomorrow World Econ. Forum, 1993; grantee NSF, 1988-90, 90-92, 96-99, Russell Sage Found. grantee, 1988-90, Spencer Found., 2001—; Olin fellow in econs., 1988-89, NSF fellow, 1981-84. Fellow Econometric Soc., Am. Acad. Arts and Scis.; mem. Am. Econs. Assn. Avocations: hiking, bird watching. Home: 14 Scott St Cambridge MA 02138-2016 Office: Harvard Univ Dept of Econs Cambridge MA 02138 E-mail: lkatz@harvard.edu.

KATZ, LAWRENCE SHELDON, lawyer; b. Newark, N.J., Jan. 30, 1943; s. Edward and Pearl (Weiss) K.; married; 1 child, Scott. BBA in Govt., U. Miami, 1965, JD, 1968. Assoc. Hoffman & St. Jean, Miami Beach, Fla., 1968-70, Jack R. Nageley Law Office, Miami Beach, Fla., 1970-72, Swickle, Katz & Brotman, Miami Beach, Fla., 1972-77; pvt. practice Miami Beach, Fla., 1977—90, Coconut Grove, Fla., 1990—2001, Miami, 2001—. Gen. counsel Fraternal Order of Police, Hialeah, Fla., 1972-89; gen. counsel U.S. Shooting Team Found., Colorado Springs, 1978-95, chmn., 1978-83; mem. U.S. Olympic Com. Ho. Dels., 1978-83. 2d lt. U.S. Army, 1965-69. Recipient Pres.'s award Nat. Assn. Criminal Def. Atty.'s, 1977. Mem. ABA (com. on internat. criminal law 1971-94, criminal def. function com. 1989-98, family law sect. com. on internat. law and procedure, 1996-, internat. child abduction atty. network 1997-, 11th Cir. Pro Bono Award), NRA (bd. dirs. 1977-83), Fla. Sportshooting Assn. (pres. 1985), The Fla. Bar (narcotics practice com. 1988-92, mental health profl. in litigation com. 1994-96, domestic violence com. 1994-98, legislation com. 1998-2003), Acad. Fla. Trial Lawyers (vice chmn. criminal law sect.), Fla. Assn. Criminal Def. Attys. (sec. 1978-79, v.p. 1979-80), Fla. Smallbore Rifle Assn. (pres. 1968-70), Safari Club Internat. Found. (v.p. 1992-98, sec. 1997-98, pres.-elect 1998-99, pres. 1999-2000, pres. Miami chpt. 2001-2003, Mem. of Yr. award 1999-2000, Presdl. award 1996, 98), Phi Epsilon Pi (pres. 1964), Phi Alpha Delta, World Forum for Future of Sportshooting (v.p. 2000-01). Jewish. Avocations: flying, photography, scuba, skiing, hunting. Office: 1 Datran Ctr Penthouse 1-Ste 1702 9100 S Dadeland Blvd Miami FL 33156-7814 Office Fax: 305-670-1314.

KATZ, LEANDRO, artist, filmmaker; b. Buenos Aires, June 6, 1938; came to U.S., 1965; s. Mauricio and Elisa K. BFA, U. Nacional, Buenos Aires, 1961; student, Pratt Graphic Arts Inst., N.Y.C., 1967. Faculty Sch. Visual Arts, N.Y.C., 1971—; asst. prof. Brown U., Providence, 1980-84; prof. William Paterson U., Wayne, N.J., 1987—. One person shows include Museo del Barrio, 1996, Betty Rymer Gallery/Sch. Art Inst. Chgo., 1998, Museo de Arte Moderno, Buenos Aires, 2003; exhibited in group shows Whitney Mus. Am. Art, 1982, R.I. Sch. Design Mus., 1984, Bronx Mus. Art, 1988, New Mus. Contemporary Art, 1990; author: Es Una Ola, 1965, others; filmmaker numerous titles. Recipient Coral prize for The Day You'll Love Me, Havana L.Am. Film Festival, 1997; Meml. fellow Guggenheim Found., 1979-80, fellow NEA, 1979, 91, 94, N.Y. State Coun. on Arts, 1990, 98, Rockefeller Found., 1993; grantee Jerome Found., 1982, 90, N.Y. Found. for Arts, 1989. Home: 25 E 4th St New York NY 10003-7061 Office: William Paterson Univ Wayne NJ 07470 E-mail: leandrok@rcn.com.

KATZ, LEONARD, psychology educator; b. Boston, Mar. 6, 1938; s. William and Ruth K.; m. Barbara A. Mahoney, May 28, 1962; children: Nicholas, Stephen, Alexis. BS, U. Mass., 1959, PhD, 1963. Postdoctoral fellow Stanford (Calif.) U., 1963-65; prof. psychology U. Conn., Storrs, 1965—; researcher Haskins Labs., New Haven, 1974—. Contbr. articles to profl. jours. Fulbright fellow, Yugoslavia, 1986. Fellow Am. Psychol. Soc., Am. Assn. Advancement of Sci. Office: U Conn Dept Psychology Wab U 20 Mansfield CT 06269-1020

KATZ, LEWIS ROBERT, law educator; b. NYC, Nov. 15, 1938; s. Samuel and Rose (Turoff) K.; m. Jan Karen Daugherty, Jan. 14, 1964; children: Brett Elizabeth, Adam Kenneth, Tyler Jessica. AB, Queens Coll., 1959; JD, Ind. U., 1963. Bar: Ind 1963, Ohio 1971. Assoc. Snyder, Bunger, Cotner & Harrell, Bloomington, Ind., 1963-65; instr. U. Mich. Law Sch., Ann Arbor, 1965-66; asst. prof. Case Western Res. U. Law Sch., Cleve., 1966-68, assoc. prof., 1968-71, prof., 1971—, John C. Hutchins prof. law, 1973—. Dir. Ctr. for Criminal Justice, Case Western Res. U., 1973-91, dir. fgn. grad. studies, 1992—; cons. criminal justice agys. Author: Justice is the Crime, 1972, The Justice Imperative: Introduction to Criminal Justice, 1979, Ohio Arrest Search and Seizure, 2003; (with J. Shapiro) New York Suppression Manual, 1991, Know Your Rights, 1994; (with P.C. Giannelli, B. Blair, J. Lipton) Ohio Criminal Law, 2d edit., 2003; (with P.C. Giannelli) Ohio Criminal Justice, 2003; (with B.W. Griffin) Ohio Felony Sentencing Law, 2002. Mem. regional bd. Anti-Defamation League; trustee Women's Law Fund. Recipient Disting. Tchr. award Case West Res. U. Law Alumni Assn., Tchr. of Yr. award Case Western Res. U., 1999; Nat. Defender Project of Nat. Legal Aid and Defender Assn. fellow, 1968 Mem. ABA. Home: 29550 S Woodland Rd Pepper Pike OH 44124-5743 Office: Case Western Res U Law Sch Law Sch Cleveland OH 44106

KATZ, LOIS ANNE, internist, nephrologist; b. Rockville Centre, N.Y., Dec. 1, 1941; d. Irvin Martin and Frances (Berenstein) Fradkin; m. Arthur A. Katz, Aug. 18, 1962; children: David, Brian. BA, Wellesley Coll., 1962; MD, NYU, 1966. Diplomate Am. Bd. Internal Medicine, Am. Bd. Nephrology. Intern medicine Bellevue Hosp., NYU, N.Y.C., 1966-67, resident medicine, 1967-68; sr. resident medicine N.Y. Hosp., N.Y.C., 1968-69, from chief resident medicine to assoc. chief staff N.Y. VA Med. Ctr., N.Y.C., 1969—2000, assoc. chief of staff spl. emphasis programs and quality mgmt., 2000—; asst. prof. clin. medicine NYU Sch. Medicine, N.Y.C., 1974-79, assoc. prof., 1979-94, prof. clin. medicine, 1994—. Fellow: ACP; mem.: Am. Soc. Hypertension, Women in Nephrology (treas. 1985—89), Soc. Gen. Internal Medicine, Am. Med. Women's Assn., Am. Soc. Nephrology, Wellesley Coll. Alumnae Assn. (region 2 admission rep. 1997—2001), Sigma Xi, Alpha Omega Alpha. Jewish. Avocations: reading, swimming, cooking, music. Office: Dept Vets Affairs NY Harbor Healthcare System 423 E 23rd St New York NY 10010-5013

KATZ, MANFRED, research scientist, consultant; b. Giesen, Germany, Feb. 16, 1929; came to U.S., 1938; s. Karl and Jettchen (Oppenheimer) K.; m. Edith Schiff, Mar. 20, 1953 (dec. June 1958); 1 child, Harold; m. Barbara A. Ehrlich, Apr. 4, 1965; children: Anita, Carl, Daniel. BS, Okla. State U., 1950, MS, 1951; PhD, U. Del., 1961. Rschr. E.I. DuPont de Nemours & Co., Inc., Wilmington, Del., 1951-54, 55-92; prof. Howard U., Washington, 1992-94; cons. Wilmington, 1994—. Patentee in field; contbr. chpt. in book and articles to profl. jours. With U.S. Army, 1954-55. Mem. AAAS, Am. Chem. Soc., N.Y. Acad. Scis., Sigma Xi. Home: 310 Brockton Rd Wilmington DE 19803-2412

KATZ, MARCIA, public relations company executive; b. N.Y.C., Mar. 20, 1950; d. Alexander and Dorothy Harriet (Frank) K.; m. R. Glenn Brode, Oct. 3, 1982; 1 child, Richard Gregory. BS magna cum laude, CUNY, 1972, MS, 1975. Tchr. N.Y.C. Bd. Edn., 1972-76; exec. v.p. worldwide Burson-Marsteller, N.Y.C., 1976-91; exec. v.p. U.S.A. Hill and Knowlton, N.Y.C., 1991-92; pres., CEO InterScience, N.Y.C., 1993—. Cons. Nat. Coun. on Patient Inf. and Edn., Washington, 1985—, Am. Health Found., N.Y.C., 1991—. Editor: Perspectives on Aging Worldwide, 1989; contbr. articles to profl. jours. Cons. Nat. Neurofibromatosis Soc., 1988-90; mktg. counselor Nat. Multiple Sclerosis Soc., 1990—. Named to Acad. Women Achievers, YWCA, N.Y.C., 1985. Mem. Healthcare Bus. Women's Assn., Healthcare Comms. Council (pub. rels. chair 1985), Phi Beta Kappa. Office: InterScience 1675 Broadway New York NY 10019-5820

KATZ, MARK DAVID, lawyer; b. N.Y.C., Apr. 26, 1949; s. Irving and Belle (Bilinkoff) K.; m. Deborah Jane Exler, Aug. 25, 1974; children: Megan Diane, Craig Edward. BA, SUNY, Buffalo, 1971; JD, Case Western Res. U., 1974. Bar: Ohio, 1974, U.S. Dist. Ct. (no. dist.) Ohio, 1975, U.S. Supreme Ct. 1980, U.S. Ct. Appeals (3d, 6th, 7th and D.C. cirs.). Assoc. Consiglio & Katz, Cleve., 1974-75; trial atty. Dept. Labor, Cleve., 1975-85; asst. group counsel LTV Steel Co., Inc., Cleve., 1985-97; assoc. Ulmer & Berne, LLP, Cleve., 1997—. Mem. ABA, Ohio Bar Assn. Home: 5043 Boulder Creek Dr Cleveland OH 44139-1379 Office: 1300 E 9th St Cleveland OH 44114-1501 E-mail: mkatz@ulmer.com.

KATZ, MARK NORMAN, international relations educator, consultant, author; b. Riverside, Calif., Nov. 11, 1954; s. Norman Nathan Katz and Eithne Dolores (Dorney) Scott; m. Nancy Virginia Yinger, Sept. 9, 1978; 1 child, Melissa. BA, U. Calif., Riverside, 1976; MA, Johns Hopkins U., 1978; PhD, MIT, 1982. Soviet Affairs analyst Dept. State, Washington, 1982; guest scholar The Brookings Instn., Washington, 1982-84; Professorial lectr. Am. U., Washington, 1985; rsch. assoc. Woodrow Wilson Internat. Ctr. for Scholars, Washington, 1985-87; adj. prof. Georgetown U., Washington, 1986-87; asst. prof. dept. pub. affairs George Mason U., Fairfax, Va., 1988-92, assoc. prof. dept. pub. and internat. affairs, 1992-98, prof. dept. pub. and internat affairs, 1998—. Cons. in field. Author: The Third World in Soviet Military Thought, 1982, Russia and Arabia, 1986, Gorbachev's Military Policy in the Third World, 1989, Middle Eastern Sketches, 1997, Revolutions and Revolutionary Waves, 1997, Reflections on Revolutions, 1999; editor: The USSR and Marxist Revolutions in the Third World, 1990, Soviet-American Conflict Resolution in the Third World, 1991, Revolution: International Dimensions, 2001. Rsch. fellow Brookings Instn., 1980-81, Internat. Rels. fellow Rockefeller Found., N.Y.C., 1982-84, Jennings Randolph Peace fellow U.S. Inst. Peace, Washington, 1989-90; Rsch. scholar Kennan Inst., Washington, 1985; U.S. Inst. of Peace grantee, 1994-95. Mem. Internat. Inst. Strategic Studies, Internat. Studies Assn., Am. Polit. Sci. Assn., Nat. Capital Area Polit. Sci. Assn. (pres. 1999-2000). Avocations: traveling, bicycling, cats, writing. Home: 10612 Samaga Dr Oakton VA 22124-1631 Office: Dept Pub-Internat Affairs MS 3F4 George Mason Univ Fairfax VA 22030 E-mail: mkatz@gmu.edu.

KATZ, MARYANNE, artist, educator; b. Buffalo, Feb. 5, 1931; d. Samuel Sulim and Elma Burns (Aitken) Vineberg; m. David Robert Katz, Feb. 7, 1953; children: Avery Myron, Regina, Samuel Ellis, Sarah Beth Gonta. Student, SUNY, Buffalo, 1948-51, Academie Julien, Paris, 1951-53; BS in Art, Daemen Coll., Amherst, N.Y., 1973; MS in Art Edn., State U. Coll., Buffalo, 1983. Cert. tchr., N.Y., N.J., Va. Art dir. Herald Plastics, Tonawanda, N.Y., 1979-80; substitute tchr. Williamsville (N.Y.) Ctrl. Sch., 1981-86; substitute art tchr. Warren County Vocat.-Tech. Sch., Washington, N.J., 1987-88, Hackettstown (N.J.) H.S., 1994; substitute tchr. Mt. Olive (N.J.) Schs., 1986-94, Chesapeake (Va.) Ctrl. Sch. Sys., 1996—. Adj. prof. State U. Coll., Buffalo, 1982-85; art demo, lectr. Associated Art Orgn., Buffalo, 1975-85, art show judge, 1980; art show judge Sr. Citizens Coun., Chesapeake, Va., 1996; tchr. watercolor painting Chesapeake Parks & Recreation Dept. 6 one-woman shows pub. and pvt. galleries, N.Y., N.J., Va., 1976-97; author: Fezants and Other Bird Wirds, 1983; artist (book) To Life: Stories of Courage and Survival, 2002; artist paintings, drawings, lithographs, miniatures, illustrations, 1950—. Docent Chrysler Mus. Art, Norfolk, Va., 1996—. Recipient artist-in-sch. award Allentown Art Soc., Buffalo, 1983; featured artist Watercolor mag., N.Y.C., 1996. Mem. Tidewater Artists Assn., Va. Watercolor Soc. Avocations: indoor gardening, floral design. Home: 828 Fallcreek Run Chesapeake VA 23322-2147

KATZ, MICHAEL, pediatrician, educator; b. Lwow, Poland, Feb. 13, 1928; arrived in U.S., 1946, naturalized, 1951; s. Edward and Rita (Gluzman) Katz; m. Robin J. Roy, July 19, 1986; 1 child, Edward Alexander. AB, U. Pa., 1949, postgrad. (Harrison fellow), 1950—51; MD, SUNY, Bklyn., 1956; MS, Columbia U. Sch. Public Health, 1968. Intern UCLA Med. Ctr., 1956—57; resident Presbyn. Hosp. (Babies Hosp.), N.Y.C., 1960—62, dir. pediatric svc., 1977—92, cons., 1992—; hon. lectr. pediat. Makerere U. Coll., Kampala, Uganda, 1963—64; instr. in pediat. Columbia U., 1964—65, prof. tropical medicine Sch. Pub. Health, 1971—92, prof. pub. health emeritus, 1992—, prof. pediat. Coll. Physicians and Surgeons, 1972—77, prof. pub. health, 1977—92, Reuben S. Carpentier prof., 1977—92, Reuben S. Carpentier prof. emeritus, 1992—; sr. v.p. for rsch. and global programs March of Dimes Birth Defects Found., White Plains, NY, 1992—. Assoc. mem. Wistar Inst., Phila., 1965—71; asst. prof. pediat. U. Pa., 1966—77; cons. WHO, Guatemala, Venezuela, Egypt, Yemen; mem. U.S. del. 32d World Health Assembly, Geneva, 1979; cons. UNICEF, N.Y.C., Tokyo, USAID, Egypt, 1982, Poland, 87; mem. bd. sci. councillors Nat. Inst. Dental Rsch., 1986—90, chmn., 1990—92; vis. prof. U. Würzburg, Germany, 1988; vis. prof. pediat. U. Negev, Beer Sheva, Israel, 1996. Author (with others): Parasitic Diseases, 1982, 2d edit., 1989; editor (with Volker ter Meulen): Slow Virus Infections of the Central Nervous System, 1977; mem. editl. bd.: Med. Microbiology and Immunology, 1975—90, Pediatric Infectious Diseases Jour., 1981—92, Vaccines, 1983—94; co-editor: Manuals in Pediatrics; contbr. articles to profl. jours. Pres. World Allaince of Orgns. for the Prevention of Birth Defects, Inc., 1995—. Lt. M.C. USNR, 1957—59. Recipient Jurzykowski Found. award in Medicine, 1983, Alexander von Humboldt Sr. U.S. Scientist award, 1988; grantee, NIH, 1968—76, WHO, 1972—76. Fellow: AAAS, Am. Acad. Pediat., Infectious Diseases Soc. Am.; mem.: Eastern Soc. for Pediatric Rsch., Inst. Medicine of NAS, World Alliance of Orgns. for the Prevention of Birth Defects (pres. 1995—), Pediatric Infectious Disease Soc., Royal Soc. Tropical Medicine and Hygiene (London), Deutsche Gesellschaft für Neuropathologie und Neuroanatomie E.V. (corr.), N.Y. Soc. Tropical Medicine (pres. 1976—77), Am. Soc. Tropical Medicine and Hygiene, Am. Soc. Microbiology, Harvey Soc., Am. Pediatric Soc., Soc. Pediatric Rsch., Sigma Xi. Home: 1 Griggs Ln Chappaqua NY 10514-1404 Office: March of Dimes Birth Defects Fdn 1275 Mamaroneck Ave White Plains NY 10605-5298 E-mail: robinroy@optonline.net., mkatz@marchofdimes.com.

KATZ, MICHAEL ALBERT, lawyer; b. Bklyn., May 8, 1942; s. Emanuel and Miriam (Fassler) K.; 1 child, Nathaniel P. BS, Bklyn. Coll., 1963; LLB, NYU, 1966; LLM, George Washington U., 1973. Bar: N.Y. 1966, D.C. 1970, Ill. 1976, N.J. 1995, U.S. Supreme Ct. 1975. Asst. U.S. atty., D.C., 1971-75; trial atty. United Airlines, Chgo., 1975-78; div. counsel ea. divsn. N.Y.C., 1978-81; counsel indsl. rels. Trans World Airlines, Inc., N.Y.C., 1981-86, asst. gen. counsel, 1986-91, assoc. gen. counsel, 1991-94; assoc. gen. counsel GAF/ISP Corp., Wayne, N.J., 1994-96; of counsel Pfaltz & Woller PA, Summit, N.J., 1996—. Capt. JAGC, U.S. Army, 1967-71, ret. col. res. Decorated Bronze Star. Home: 94 Canterbury Rd Chatham NJ 07928-1771 Office: 382 Springfield Ave Ste 217 Summit NJ 07901-2707 E-mail: makatz@att.net.

KATZ, MICHAEL BARRY, humanities educator; b. Wilmington, Del., Apr. 13, 1939; s. George Joseph and Beatrice Katz; m. Edda Britt Katz; children: Paul, Rebecca, Sarah. BA, Harvard U., 1961, MAT, 1962, EdD, 1966. Prof. OISE and U. of Toronto, 1966—73, York U., Toronto, 1973—78; Walter H. Annenberg prof. history U. of Pa., 1978—. Archivist Social Sci. Rsch. Coun. Com. for Rsch. on the Urban Underclass, N.Y.C., 1990—95; chair History Dept. U. of Pa., 1991—95; mem. Social Sci. Rsch. Coun. Com. on Philanthropy and Non-Profits, N.Y.C., 2000—. Author: (book) The Irony of Early School Reform: Educational Innovation in Mid-Nineteenth Century Massachusetts, The Price of Citizenship: Redefining the American Welfare State, Class, Bureaucracy, and Schools: The Illusion of Educational Change in America, The People of Hamilton, Canada West: Family and Class in a Mid-Nineteenth Century City (Albert C. Corey award, 1976), Poverty and Policy in American

History, The Undeserving Poor: From the War on Poverty to the War on Welfare, Reconstructing American Education, In the Shadow of the Poorhouse: A Social History of Welfare in America, Improving Poor People: The Welfare State, the Underclass, and Urban Schools as History; co-author: The Social Organization of Early Industrial Capitalism; editor: The Underclass Debate: Views from History; co-editor: W.E.B. DuBois, Race, and the City: The Philadelphia Negro and its Legacy. Mem. Rsch. for Action, Phila., 1996—2002; v.p. Haines Landing Cottage Assn., Oquossoc, Maine, 2001—02. Fellow, Inst. for Advanced Study, 1973—74, Guggenheim Found., 1975—76, Shelby Cullom Davis Ctr., 1984—85, Russell Sage Found., 1988—89, Open Soc. Inst., 1998—99. Mem.: Pa. Hist. Soc., Urban History Assn., Social Sci. History Assn., Organ. of Am. Historians, History of Edn. Assn. (pres. 1975—76), Am. Hist. Assn., U. City Hist. Soc., Appalaichan Mountain Club, Am. Canoe Assn. Avocations: kayaking, hiking, bicycling. Office: U of Pa History Dept Philadelphia PA 19104 E-mail: mkatz@sas.upenn.edu.

KATZ, MICHAEL JEFFERY, lawyer; b. Detroit, May 11, 1950; s. Wilfred Lester and Bernice (Ackerman) K. BE with honors, U. Mich., 1972; JD, U. Colo., 1976; cert. mgmt., U. Denver, 1985, cert. fin. mgmt., 1990. Bar: Colo. 1978. Rsch. atty., immigration specialist Colo. Rural Legal Svcs., Denver, 1976-77, supervising atty. migrant farm lab., 1977-78; ind. contractor Colo. Sch. Fin., Denver, 1978-79; sole practice Denver, 1978-86; assoc. Levine and Pitler, P.C., Denver, 1986-88; gen. counsel, sec. Grease Monkey Internat., Inc., Denver, 1988-92; prin. Katz & Co., Denver, 1992—; ptnr. Corprorn, Eyler & Katz LLC, Denver, 1999—. Lectr. on incorporating small bus. and real estate purchase agreements Front Range Coll., 1986—, condr. various seminars on real estate and landlord/tenant law, 1980—; lectr. on real estate Lorman Ednl. Svcs., Inc., 2001-; of counsel Levine and Pitler, P.C., Englewood, Colo., 1985—. Contbr. Action Line column Rocky Mountain News; contbr. articles to profl. jours. Mem. ATLA, Am. Arbitration Assn. (mem. panel of arbitrators 1989), Denver Bar Assn. (mem. law day com. 1985—, mem. real estate com. 1980—, mem. pro bono svcs. com. 1984—), Colo. Assn. Bus. Intermediaries, U.S. Yacht Racing Assn., Dillon Yacht Club. Avocations: sailing, bicycling, swimming, art collecting, reading. Office: 13710 E Rice Pl Aurora CO 80015-1058 Fax: 303-790-0927. E-mail: bizlaw@ix.netcom.com.

KATZ, MICHAEL RAY, Slavic languages educator; b. N.Y.C., Dec. 9, 1944; s. Louis M. and Alice (Gordon) K.; m. Mary K. Dodge, Nov. 19, 1978; 1 child, Rebecca Marie Dodge-Katz BA, Williams Coll., 1966; MA, Oxford U., 1968, PhD, 1972. From asst. to assoc. prof. Williams Coll., Williamstown, Mass., 1972-83; prof., chmn. dept. Slavic langs. U. Tex., Austin, 1984-97, dir. Russian, East European and Eurasian studies; dean lang. schs. and schs. abroad Middlebury (Vt.) Coll., 1998—. Author: The Literary Ballad in Early 19th Century Russian Literature, 1976, Dreams and the Unconscious in Russian Literature, 1984; translator: Who Is To Blame? (A. Herzen), 1984, Notes from Underground (Dostoevsky), 1989, What Is To Be Done: (Chernyshevsky), 1989, Tolstoy's Short Fiction, 1991, Devils (Dostoevsky), 1992, Polina Saks (Druzhinin), 1992, Fathers and Sons (Turgenev), 1994, Antonina (Turgenev), 1997, Prologue (Chernyshevsky), 1995, Antonina (Tur), 1997, Sanin (Artsybashev), 2001. NEH grant, 1981-82; recipient Max Haywood Translation prize, 1982. Mem. Am. Assn. Advancement Slavic Studies, Am. Assn. Tchrs. Slavic and East European Langs. (v.p. 1989-92, pres.-elect 1995-96, pres. 1997-98, past pres. 1999-2000), Am. Coun. Tchrs. of Russian (bd. dirs. 1984-2001), Assn. Dept. of Fgn. Langs. (exec. com. 2000-02). Avocations: flute, jogging. Home: 1712 Sperry Rd Middlebury VT 05753-9442 Office: Middlebury Coll 209 Sunderland Middlebury VT 05753

KATZ, MIRA LYNN, vascular ultrasound technologist, medical educator; b. Erie, Pa., June 1, 1954; d. Morris and Ada (Gold) K. BS in Biology, U. Cin., 1976; MLA, Temple U., 1990, MPH, 1999, PhD, 2000. Registered vascular technologist, Am. Registry Diagnostic Med. Sonographers (bd. dirs. 1985-91, vice chmn. bd. dirs. 1991-93). Vascular technologist Good Samaritan Hosp., Cin., 1977-81; rsch. instr. surgery, tech. dir. vascular lab. Sch. Medicine Temple U., Phila., 1981-98; mem. staff dept. radiology Children's Hosp. Phila., 1998-2000; fellow cancer prevention edn. U. N.C., Chapel Hill, 2000—02; asst. prof. Sch. Pub. Health Ohio State U., Columbus, 2002—. Mem. editl. rev. bd. Jour. Vascular Tech., 1986-92, assoc. editor, 1993-96; contbr. over 40 articles to med. jours. Mem. APHA, Soc. Vascular Tech. (sec. 1982-83, bd. dirs. 1982-84, Disting. Svc. award 1990). E-mail: katz-4@medctr.osu.edu.

KATZ, PEARL, anthropoligist, public health analyst; b. Chgo., Sept. 7, 1940; d. Harry H. and Esther Gottlieb; m. Oscar Wallace Greenberg; children: Michael Robinson, Dvora Robinson, Liat. PhD, SUNY, Buffalo, 1974. Lectr. dept. psychiatry Johns Hopkins U. Sch. Medicine, Balt., 1985—; pub. health analyst Dept. Health and Human Svcs., Rockville, Md., 1991—2003. Author: The Scalpel's Edge: The Culture of Surgeons, 1999. Home: 9404 St Andrews Way Silver Spring MD 20901

KATZ, RICHARD JON, marketing and advertising company executive; b. Bklyn., Feb. 26, 1932; s. Irving Paul and Lillian Katz; m. Helen Borow, June 7, 1953; children: Robin Lee, Juli Beth, Jennifer Sue. AAS, Bklyn. Coll., 1960. Pres., creative dir. Katz, Jacobs & Douglas Advt., N.Y.C., 1960-75, KLN Advt., N.Y.C., 1975-78, Ric Catz & Assocs. Inc., N.Y.C., 1978—. Pres., chief exec. officer Rams Mktg. Inc., N.Y.C., 1978-90; pres., creative dir. The Ramstar Group Advt., 1986-95; cons. Pinnacle Mktg. & Resources, Inc., 1990; COB Fitness Clinic for Ageless Dynamics; CEO World Digital Deliverance Techs., LLC, 1997; lectr. Fashion Inst. Tech., NYU; bd. dirs. Palletnet. Author: Professional Guidelines for Effective Advertising. Trustee inst. geriatric care New Sch. for Rsch., Hunter, N.Y., The Parker Jewish Inst. Geriatric Care; bd. dirs. Palletnet. Served with USAF, 1951-55. Recipient awards for creativity, graphics, design and mktg. Mem. Am. Mgmt. Assn., Presidents Club. Home: 7227 Montrico Dr Boca Raton FL 33433-6931

KATZ, ROBERT NATHAN, ceramic engineer, educator; b. Williamsport, Pa., Sept. 2, 1939; s. Louis and Rose Bernice (Golbitz) K.; m. Barbara Kurn Rubin, June 15, 1986; children: Pamela Lynn, Jonathan Adam. SB, MIT, 1961, PHD, 1969; MS, U. Mich., 1963. Rsch. asst. U. Mich., 1961-62; metallurgist Army Materials Rsch. Agy., Watertown, Mass., 1962-65; ceramic engr. Army Materials Tech. Lab., Watertown, 1965-70, chief ceramics rsch. divsn., 1970-87, chief materials technologist, 1987-95; prin. R. Nathan Katz Assocs., 1995—. Norton assoc. prof. mech. engring. Worcester (Mass.) Poly. Inst., 1990—91, Norton rsch. prof., 1991—93, rsch. prof., 2003—; apptd. spl. mem. grad. faculty U. Med., 2000—02; liaison mem. various coms. Nat. Materials Adv. Bd.; participant Nat. Rsch. Coun., Bd. of Army Sci. and Tech., Star-21, Strategic Techs. for the Army of the 21st Century study, 1988—92, Nat. Acad. Sci. Naval Studies Bd., Future Carrier Tech. Study, 1990—91, Nat. Acad. Sci., Nat. Materials Adv. Bd., Materials Rsch. for Def.-After-Next study, 2001—02; external examiner Bd. Grad. Studies, U. Cambridge, England, 1979; cons. Dept. Def., Dept. Energy, Congl. Office of Tech. Assessment; mem. U.S. del. NATO Com. on Challenges of Modern Soc., 1974; mem. organizing com., lectr. NATO Advanced Study Inst. Nitrogen Ceramics, 1976, 81. Editor: Ceramics for High Performance Applications, 1974, Vol. II, 1978, Vol. III, 1983; mem. editl. bd. Internat. Jour. High Tech. Ceramics, 1984-89, Jour. European Ceramic Soc., 1989-; columnist Ceramic Industry Mag., 1999-2001; contbr. articles to tech. publs. Trustee Temple Israel of Natick, 1979-80, Temple Beth Zion, Brookline, 1998-, chmn., 1999-2003; Eagle Scout, BSA, Troop 65, Scranton, Pa., 1956. Recipient Tech. Writing award, Dept. Army, 1981, Mass. Rep. of Yr. award, Nat. Rep. Congl. Com., 2002. Fellow Am. Ceramic Soc.; mem. Nat. Inst. Ceramic Engrs., New Eng. Ceramic Soc. (F.H. Norton award 1978), Am. Soc. Metals, Sigma Xi. Home: 1731 Beacon St Apt 1403 Brookline MA 02445-5329 Office: Dept Mech Engring Worcester Polytechnic Inst Worcester MA 01609 E-mail: katz@wpi.edu.

KATZ, RONALD ALAN, dermatologist; b. St. Joseph, Mo., July 13, 1942; s. Walter and Mildred (Talman) K.; m. Jane Ellen Markin, Dec. 26, 1968; children: Jennifer Lynn, Hilary Beth. BS, U. Cin., 1964; MD, U. Md., 1969. Diplomate Am. Bd. Dermatology. Intern Childrens Nat. Med. Ctr., Washington, 1969-70; resident Yale U., New Haven, Conn., 1972-75, chief resident in dermatology, 1974-75; pvt. practice College Park, Md., 1975—. Clin. prof. dermatology and pediats. George Washington U., 1975—. Contbr. articles to profl. jours. Founding vol. U.S. Meml. Holocaust Mus., Washington, 1993-96. Lt. comdr. USPHS, 1970-72. Named Outstanding Physician Specialist, Consumer Checkbook, 1998, 2002; named one of Top Doctors, Washingtonian, 1993, 1995, 1999, 2002, Best Doctors in Am., 2001, 2002. Mem. AMA, Md. State Med. Soc., Prince George's County Med. Soc., Washington Dermatol. Soc. pres. 1990-91), Am. Acad. Dermatology, Soc. for Pediatric Dermatology, Soc. for Investigative Dermatology, Alpha Omega Alpha. Democrat. Jewish. Avocations: photography, running marathons. Home: 9304 Sprinklewood Ln Potomac MD 20854-2257 Office: 6201 Greenbelt Rd College Park MD 20740-2354 E-mail: ronaldk204@aol.com.

KATZ, RONALD LEWIS, physician, educator; b. Bklyn., Apr. 22, 1932; s. Joseph and Belle (Charnis) K.; children: Richard Ian, Laura Susan, Margaret Karen. BA, U. Wis.-Madison, 1952; MD, Boston U., 1956; postgrad. in Pharmacology (NIH fellow), Coll. Physicians and Surgeons, Columbia U., 1959-60; postgrad. (John Simon Guggenheim fellow), Royal Postgrad. Med. Sch., U. London, 1968-69. Intern USPHS Hosp., S.I., 1956-57; resident Columbia-Presbyn. Med. Center, 1957-60; asst. prof. anesthesiology Coll. Physicians and Surgeons, Columbia U., 1960-66, assoc. prof., 1966-70, prof., 1970-73; prof., chmn. dept. anesthesiology UCLA, 1973-90, prof. anesthesiology, 1990-94, chief staff Med. Ctr., 1984-86; prof., chmn. dept. anesthesiology U. So. Calif., L.A., 1995—2000, prof., 1995—. Cons. NIH, FDA, numerous state agys. Author, editor: Muscle Relaxants, 1975; Contbr. numerous articles to profl. jours.; Mem. editorial bd.: Handbook of Anesthesiology, 1972—, Progress in Anesthesiology, 1973—; editor in chief Seminars in Anesthesia, 1982—. Mem. Am. Soc. Anesthesiologists, Am. Physiol. Soc., Am. Soc. Pharmacology and Exptl. Therapeutics, N.Y. Acad. Medicine; Faculty Anaesthetists of Royal Coll. Surgeons of Eng. Achievements include inventor peripheral nerve stimulator. Home: 2910 Neilson Way Apt 407 Santa Monica CA 90405-5323 Office: U So Calif Dept Anesthesiology Health Sci Campus 1200 N State St Rm 14901 Los Angeles CA 90033-1029

KATZ, RONALD SCOTT, lawyer; b. Norwich, Conn., Dec. 14, 1946; s. Irving David and Joan (Lebovitz) K.; m. Ann Lisa Mark, Dec. 27, 1969; children: Benjamin, Cynthia. BA, Johns Hopkins U., 1968; JD, Columbia U., 1972. Bar: N.Y. 1972, U.S. Ct. Appeals (2d cir.) 1974, U.S. Ct. Appeals (4th cir.) 1993. Assoc. Golenbock & Barell, N.Y.C., 1972—80, ptnr., 1981—89, Whitman & Ransom, N.Y.C., 1990—93; shareholder, dir. Shack Siegel Katz & Flaherty PC, N.Y.C., 1993—. Mem. ABA, N.Y. State Bar Assn. Home: 16 Paxford Ln Scarsdale NY 10583-3318 Office: Shack Siegel Katz & Flaherty PC 530 5th Ave New York NY 10036-5101 E-mail: rkatz@sskfny.com

KATZ, SAMUEL, geophysics educator; b. Berlin, Feb. 13, 1923; came to U.S., 1934, naturalized, 1940; s. Herman and Bertha (Low) K.; m. Jean Barbara Parker, July 10, 1953; children— David R., Daniel M., Miriam E. BS, U. Mich., 1943; A.M., Columbia, 1947, PhD, 1955. With radiation lab. Mass. Inst. Tech., 1943-46; mem. sci. staff Lamont Geol. Obs., Columbia, 1948-53; sr. physicist Stanford Research Inst., 1953-57; mem. faculty Rensselaer Poly Inst., 1957—, prof. geophysics, 1962-86, prof. emeritus, 1986—, chmn. dept. geology, 1964-69. Contbr. articles in field to profl. jours. Mem. Am. Geophys. Union, AAAS, Sigma Xi. Home: 908 Karenwald Ln Niskayuna NY 12309-6416

KATZ, SAMUEL LAWRENCE, pediatrician, scientist; b. Manchester, N.H., May 29, 1927; s. Morris and Ethel (Lawrence) Katz; m. Betsy Jane Cohan, June 27, 1950; children: Samuel Lawrence Jr.(dec.), John S.L., David L., Deborah Susan, William L., Susan Johanna, Penelope Jennifer; m. Catherine Minock Wilfert, July 23, 1971; stepchildren: Rachel Ann, Katie Claiborne. AB magna cum laude, Dartmouth Coll., 1948; MD cum laude, Harvard U., 1952; DSc (hon.), Georgetown U., 1996, Dartmouth Coll., 1998. Intern Beth Israel Hosp., Boston, 1952—53; resident Children's Hosp., Boston, 1953—54, 1955—56, Mass. Gen. Hosp., 1954—55; from rsch. fellow to asst. prof. Harvard Med. Sch., 1956—68; prof., chmn. dept. pediat. Duke Med. Sch., 1968—90, Wilburt C. Davison prof., 1972—97. Mem. sci. adv. bd. Hasbro Children's Found., St. Jude's Children's Rsch. Hosp., Pediat. AIDS Found.; rschr. on virology, virus vaccines and immunization NIH couns. and study sects. WHO; chmn. India-U.S. Vaccine Action Program (VAP), 1999—; chmn. adv. com. immunization practice Ctrs. for Disease Control, Atlanta, 1985—93. Developer (with John F. Enders) attenuated live measles-virus vaccine; contbr. chapters to books, articles to profl. jours. Bd. trustees Internat. Vaccine Inst., Seoul, Republic of Korea. With USNR, 1945—46. Recipient Rsch. Career Devel. award, NIH, 1965—68, Presdl. medal of achievement, Dartmouth Coll., 1991, Sabin Gold medal, Albert Sabin Vaccine Inst., 2003; fellow, Nat. Found., 1956—58. Mem.: APHA (Needleman medal and award 1997), Inst. Medicine of NAS, Pediat. Infectious Diseases Soc. (Disting. Physician award 1991), Assn. Med. Sch. Pediat. Dept. Chmn. (pres. 1977—79), Am. Acad. Pediat. (Grulee award 1975, Jacobi award 1986), Am. Assn. Immunologists, Infectious Diseases Soc. Am. (co-chmn. vaccine initiative 1998—99, co-chmn. nat. network for immunization info. 1999—, Bristol award 1988, Soc. citation 1993), New Eng. Pediat. Soc., Am. Pediat. Soc. (pres. 1986—87, St. Geme award 1988, Howland award 2000), Soc. Pediat. Rsch., Am. Soc. Clin. Investigation, Am. Fedn. Clin. Rsch. Home: 1917 Wildcat Creek Rd Chapel Hill NC 27516-9786 Office: Duke U Med Ctr PO Box 2925 Durham NC 27710-0001

KATZ, SANFORD NOAH, lawyer, educator; b. Holyoke, Mass., Dec. 23, 1933; m. Joan Raphael; children: Daniel, Andrew. BA in History with distinction, Boston U., 1955; JD, U. Chgo., 1958; postgrad., Yale U., 1963-64. Bar: D.C. 1959, U.S. Supreme Ct. 1963, Mass. 1970. Law clk. to chief judge U.S Ct. Claims, Washington, 1958-59; instr. Sch. of Law Cath. U., 1959-60; asst. prof. law Cath. U., 1960-62; assoc. prof. Am. Sch. Law, Cath. U., 1962-64, U. Fla., 1964-66, prof., 1966-68, Boston Coll., 1968-2000, Libby prof. law, 2000—. Vis. prof. U. Mich., summer 1967; lectr. in law and social work Smith Coll., summers 1965-69; assoc. Clare Hall, Cambridge (Eng.) U., 1973; mem. Faculty of Laws, 1973; vis. fellow Hampstead Child Therapy Clinic, London, 1973, All Souls Coll., Oxford U., 1997, Pembroke Coll., Oxford U., 2000; del. White House Conf. on Children, 1970; mem. Spl. Adv. Com. Atty. Gen. Mass., 1974; Joint Mass. House and Senate Commn. on Family, 1977, Mass. Jud. Nominating Commn., 1977-79; chief drafter HEW model acts; research on child abuse and neglect, marriage, child custody in divorce, model legislation, contract law. Author: When Parents Fail, 1971, Adoptions Without Agencies: A Study of Independent Adoptions, 1978, Child Snatching-The Legal Response to the Abduction of Children, 1981, (with Weyrauch) American Family Law in Transition, 1983, (with Weyrauch) Cases and Materials on Family Law-Legal Concepts and Changing Human Relationships, 1994, (with Eekelaar and Maclean) Cross Currents, 2000, Family Law in America, 2003, also others; also monographs, book introductions; editor: The Youngest Minority: Lawyers in Defense of Children, vols. I and II, 1974, (with John Eekelaar) Family Violence: An International and Interdisciplinary Study, 1978, Marriage and Cohabitation in Contemporary Societies, 1980; editor-in-chief Family Law Quar., 1970-83; contbr. articles, revs. to profl. publs. Chmn. Lydia Rapoport Endowment Fund Smith Coll. Grantee Field Found., 1968-69, Grant Found., 1971-75, HEW, 1973-78. Mem. Internat. Soc. Family Law (pres. 1981-84), Mass. Bar Assn., ABA (chmn. family law sect. 1980-81).

KATZ, SHERMAN E. lawyer; b. Pitts., July 13, 1943; s. Saul H. Katz and Ann (Sklov) Cohen; m. Maureen Murphy, Jan. 26, 1980; 1 child, Barnaby Simon. Student, U. Stockholm, 1963-64; BA cum laude, Amherst Coll., 1965; JD, MA in Internat. Affairs, Columbia U., 1969; diploma in European Law, Oxford U., 1992. Bar: N.Y. 1969, D.C. 1969, U.S. Ct. Appeals D.C. 1970, U.S. Supreme Ct. 1973, U.S. Ct. Internat. Trade 1984. Ptnr. Coudert Bros., Washington, 1977-94, Squire, Sanders & Dempsey, Washington, 1994-98, Kelley, Drye & Warren, Washington, 1998—, of counsel; William Scholl chair internat. bus. Ctr. For Strategic and Internat. Studies, Washington. Contbr. articles to profl. jours. Commr. D.C. Commn. on Arts & Humanities, Washington, 1987—; chmn. exec. com., hon. dir. Washington Performing Arts Soc., 1981—; bd. dirs. The Washington Opera, 1988—. The Source Theatre, Folger Poetry Series. Decorated Knight of the Royal Polar Star by King of Sweden. Mem. ABA (chmn. svcs. trade com. 1987-89, vice-chair internat. bus. transactions com. 1999), N.Y. State Bar Assn., Assn. of Bar of City of N.Y., D.C. Bar Assn., Am. Soc. Internat. Law (chmn. publs. com. 1984-87), Nat. Fgn. Trade Coun. (chmn. internat. trade com. 1986), Coun. Fgn. Rels., Washington Fgn. Law Soc., Cosmos Club. Office: Ctr for Strategic & Internat Studies 1800 K St NW Washington DC 20006-2202 E-mail: skatz@osis.org.

KATZ, SHMUEL, surgeon; b. Debrecen, Hungary, 1946; MD, U. Milano, 1973. Diplomate Am. Bd. Surgery. Intern Mt. Sinai Med. Ctr., Miami, 1982-83; resident Soroka Med. Ctr. - Shaare Zedek, 1974-80; resident in gen. surgery Mt. Sinai Med. Ctr., 1982-85, Maimonides Med. Ctr., Bklyn., 1988-90; fellow in pediat. surgery Miami Children's Hosp., 1985-86. Fellow Am. Coll. Surgeons; mem. AMA, Fla. Med. Assn., Italian Med. Assn., Israeli Med. Assn., Israeli Surg. Soc., Dade County Med. Assn. Office: 10185 Collins Ave Apt 419 Bal Harbour FL 33154-1606

KATZ, SIDNEY FRANKLIN, obstetrician, gynecologist; b. Detroit, Sept. 5, 1928; m. Sally R. Katz. BS, Wayne State U., 1949; MD, U. Mich., 1953. Diplomate Am. Bd. Ob-Gyn. Intern Wayne County Gen. Hosp., Detroit; resident Grace Hosp., Detroit, 1956—57; pvt. practice, Dearborn, Mich., 1959—. Capt. USAF, 1954—56. Fellow: ACS, ACOG; mem.: So. Mich. Surg. Soc., Mich. Soc. Gynecologists, Am. Soc. for Reproductive Medicine. Office: Ste 150 31500 Telegraph Rd Bingham Farms MI 48025-4313

KATZ, STANLEY NIDER, law history educator; b. Chgo., Apr. 23, 1934; s. William Stephen and Florence (Nider) K.; m. Adria Holmes, Jan. 16, 1960; children: Derek Holmes, Marion Holmes. AB, Harvard U., 1955, MA, 1959, PhD, 1961; LLD (hon.), Stockton State Coll., 1981; DHL (hon.), U. Puget Sound, 1994, C.W. Post/L.I. U., 1997, Sacred Heart U., 1997; LLD, Ohio State U., 1998, U. Hartford, 1998; DHL (hon.), Roosevelt U., 2003, Ursinus Coll., 2003; DLA (hon.), Dickinson Coll., 2003. Asst. prof. history Harvard U., 1961-65, U. Wis., Madison, 1965-71; prof. legal history Law Sch. U. Chgo., 1971-78; Class of 1921 Bicentennial prof. history Am. law and liberty Princeton U., 1978-86, sr. fellow Woodrow Wilson Sch., 1986-97, lectr. with rank of prof. Woodrow Wilson Sch., 1997—; pres. Am. Council Learned Socs., N.Y.C., 1986-97; dir. Ctr. for Arts and Cultural Policy Rsch./Woodrow Wilson Sch., 1998—. Vis. prof. law U. Pa., 1978-86; mem. Oliver Wendell Holmes Devise, Washington, 1976-84; bd. govs. Inst. European Studies, Chgo., 1976—; chmn. Coun. on Internat. Exchange Scholars, Washington, 1981-85; adj. prof. Cardozo Law Sch., 1999-2000. Author: Newcastle's New York, 1968; editor: The Case and Tryal of John Peter Zenger, 1963, rev. edit., 1972, Oliver Wendell Holmes Devise History of U.S. Supreme Court, 1984—, Colonial America, 1971, 76, 83, 92, 2000, American History: Promise and Progress, 1983, Constitutionalism and Democracy, 1993, The Life of Learning, 1994, Philanthropy in the World's Traditions, 1998, Mobilizing for Peace, 2002. Active N.J. Com. for Humanities, 1978—84, 1996—; trustee So. Meth. U., 1988—2000, Nat. Cultural Alliance, 1990—97, chmn., 1997—98; trustee Rsch. Librs. Group, 1991—93, 1997—99, Brit.-Am. Arts Assn., 1991—, Newberry Libr., Chgo., ind. sector, 1989—92, Toynbee Prize Found., 1994—97, pres., 1995—97, Nat. Faculty, 1995—2001, Fulbright Internat. Ctr., 1995—, Copyright Clearance Ctr., 1997—, civic edn. project, 1997—; bd. dirs. Social Sci. Rsch. Coun., N.Y.C., 2002—; v.p. Friends of the Law Libr., Libr. of Congress, 1991—, Surpeme Ct. N.J., disciplinary oversight com., 1994—2000, N.J. Ethics Commn., 1991—94, com. model rules of profl. conduct, 1982—83, com. sale of law practices, 1983—84, 1989. Fellow Am. Soc. Legal History (pres. 1978-81); mem. AAAS, Papers of the Founding Fathers (chair 1985—), Inst. Early Am. History and Culture (coun. 1974-76, 90-93, 97-98), Am. Hist. Assn. (v.p. rsch. 1997-2000), Orgn. Am. Historians (exec. com. 1976-79, pres. elect 1986-87, pres. 1987-88), Am. Antiquarian Soc., Mass. Hist. Soc., Am. Philos. Soc., Soc. Am. Historians, Coun. Fgn. Rels., Phi Beta Kappa. Clubs: Princeton (N.Y.C.). Democrat. Jewish. Office: Princeton U Woodrow Wilson Sch Princeton NJ 08544-0001 E-mail: snkatz@princeton.edu.

KATZ, STEPHEN IRA, dermatologist; b. Bklyn., Jan. 26, 1941; BA with honors, U. Md., 1962; MD with honors, Tulane U., 1966; PhD in Immunology, U. London, 1974. Diplomate Am. Bd. Dermatology. Chief dermatologist Nat. Cancer Inst./NIH, Bethesda, Md., 1974-95; v.p., rschr. March of Dimes, Fla., 1995—; asst. dermatology Walter Reed Gen. Hosp., Washington, 1970-72; rsch. fellow dept. pathology Royal Coll. Surgeons Eng., London, 1972-74; sr. investigator dermatology Nat. Cancer Inst./NIH, Bethesda, Md., 1974-77, acting chief dermatology br., 1977-80, chief dermatology br., 1980—2001; dir, Nat. Inst. Arthritis and Musculoskeletal and Skin Diseases, 1995—. Marion B. Sulzberger prof. dermatology Uniformed Svcs. U. Health Scis., Bethesda, 1989-95, acting chmn. dermatology dept., 1993-95; dir. Nat. Inst. Arthritis and Musculoskelatal and Skin Diseases; cons. Georgetown U., 1970-72, Walter Reed Army Hosp., 1975-79, Nat. Naval Med. Ctr., 1976-95, Washington Dermatol. Soc., 1980-81. Editl. bd. Internat. Jour. Dermatology, 1977-81, Jour. Investigative Dermatology, 1979-82, Jour. Am. Acad. Dermatology, 1979-83, Jour. Immunology, 1981-85, Am. Jour. Dermatopathology, Epithelia, 1986-88, Regional Immunology, 1988-95, Medicine, 1992—, Am. Jour. Contact Dermatitis, 1992—, Dermatology Internat., 1992—, Proceedings Assn. Am. Physicians, 1995—, others. Goldberger Summer fellow AMA, 1965, Advanced Tng. fellow Dermatology Found., 1972-74. Mem. Inst. Med.-Nat. Acad. Sci. Office: NIH Bldg 31, Rm 4C32D Bethesda MD 20892-2350

KATZ, STEVEN MARTIN, lawyer, accountant; b. Washington, Feb. 8, 1941; s. Joseph and Pauline (Weinberg) K.; m. Lauri Gail Berman, Aug. 23, 1964; children: Benjamin, Aaron, Rebecca, Joshua. BS, U. Md., College Park, 1962; JD, George Washington U., 1965. Bar: D.C. 1966, Md. 1971; CPA, Md. Ptnr. Euzent, Katz & Katz, Washington, 1969-72; sr. ptnr. Katz, Frome & Bleecker, P.A., and predecessors, Rockville, Md., 1972-95; pvt. practice Rockville, 1995—. Mem. Md. State Grievance Commn., 1991—. Mem. Am. Soc. Atty.-CPAs, Md. Bar Assn., Md. Assn. CPAs, D.C. Bar, Montgomery County Bar Assn., Md. Soc. Accts., Md. State Bar Found. Jewish. Office: 401 E Jefferson St Ste 208 Rockville MD 20850-2613 Fax: 301-294-9484. E-mail: smkatz@intr.net.

KATZ, STEVEN THEODORE, religious studies educator; b. Jersey City, Aug. 24, 1944; s. Abraham and Mary (Bell) K.; m. Rebecca Anne Horwich, Jan. 5, 1969; children: Shira, Tamar, Yehuda. BA, Rutgers U., 1966; MA, NYU, 1967; PhD, Cambridge (Eng.) U., 1972; DHL, Gratz Coll., 1987; BD, Cambridge U., Eng., 1991. From asst. to assoc. to full prof. Dartmouth Coll., Hanover, N.H., 1972-84; prof. Near Ea. studies Cornell U., Ithaca, N.Y., 1985-96, chmn. dept., 1985-88; dir. program in Judaic Studies, prof. religion Boston U., 1996—. Vis. prof. Hebrew U., Jerusalem, 1971, U. Lancaster, Eng., 1974, U. Toronto, Ont., Can., 1978, 80, U. Calif., Santa Barbara, 1981, Harvard U., Cambridge, Mass., 1982-84, Brandeis U., Waltham, Mass., 1983, Yale U., New Haven, 1983, Yeshiva U., 1995-96; Mason prof. Coll. William and Mary, 1983; Meyerhoff prof. U. Pa., 1989. Author: Jewish Philosophers, 1975, Jewish Ideas and Concepts, 1977, Mysticism and Philosophical Analysis, 1978, Mysticism and Religious Traditions, 1983, Post-Holocaust Dialogues, 1984 (Nat. Jewish Book award 1984), Historicism, The Holocaust and Zionism, 1992, Mysticism and Language, 1992, Frontiers of Jewish Thought, 1992, Interpreters of Judaism, 1993, The Holocaust in Historical Context, 4 vols., 1994 (Outstanding Book in Philosophy and Religion, Am. Assn. Pubs. 1994), American Rabbi, 1997, The Essential Agus, 1997, Mysticism and Sacred Scripture, 2000; editor: Modern Jewish Masters Series, 1984—, Johns Hopkins Studies in Judaica Series, 1987—; editor Modern Judaism, 1981; mem. editl. bd. Ency. of Holocaust, 1986—, Ency. of Spirituality, 1986—. Recipient Lakrits prize Hebrew U., 1978, Leopold Lucas prize U. Tübingen, 1999; NEH fellow, 1981, 2001—, David Baumgardt fellow Am. Philos. Assn., 1984. Fellow Am. Soc. Study Religion, Am. Acad. Jewish Philosophy, Assn. Jewish Studies (v.p. 1980-86), Am. Acad. Religion, Am. Acad. Jewish Rsch.; mem. Internat. Metaphys. Soc. Avocations: book collecting, travel, photography. Home: 842 Commonwealth Ave Newton MA 02459-1043 Office: Boston Univ Dept Religion Boston MA 02215 E-mail: stk1@bu.edu.

KATZ, STUART CHARLES, lawyer, jazz musician; b. Chgo., June 9, 1937; s. Jerome H. and Sylvia L. (Singer) K.; m. Penny Schatz, Jan. 23, 1959; children: Steven, Lauren. BA, Roosevelt U., Chgo., 1959; JD with distinction, John Marshall Law Sch., 1964. Bar: Ill. 1964, U.S. Dist. Ct. (no. dist.) Ill. 1965, U.S. Supreme Ct. 1967. Exec. v.p. Heitman LLC, Chgo., 1972—. Jazz pianist and vibraphonist, appeared in concerts with Benny Goodman, Gene Krupa, Bud Freeman. Mem. ABA, Ill. Bar Assn., Chgo. Bar Assn. Jewish. Office: 191 N Wacker Dr Ste 2500 Chicago IL 60606-1885

KATZ, STUART Z. lawyer; b. N.Y.C., July 14, 1942; s. David B. and Sally K.; m. Jane Martin, Sept. 10, 1977; children: Amanda, Sally; children from a previous marriage: Jennifer, Emily. BA, CCNY, 1964; JD, NYU, 1968. Bar: N.Y. 1968. Ptnr. Fried, Frank, Harris, Shriver & Jacobson, N.Y.C., 1968—. Lectr. Practicing Law Inst., Prentice Hall, N.Y.C. and Mile, Minn., 1984-92. Mem.: ABA. Office: Fried Frank Harris Shriver & Jacobson 1 New York Plz Fl 27 New York NY 10004-1980

KATZ, SUSAN ARONS, language arts specialist, author, poet; b. N.Y.C., Dec. 3, 1939; d. Edward Maurice and Selma (Stark) Arons; m. Donald Ira Katz, June 20, 1961; children: David Lawrence, Elizabeth Cheryl. BFA, Ohio U., 1961. Poet-in-residence N.Y. State Poets in Pub. Svc., N.Y.C., 1975-96; book rev. editor Bitterroot Internat. Lit. Mag., 1985-91. Workshop dir. Lang. Arts Nat.-Internat. Workshops, U.S. and Can., 1995—; mem. reading panel Poets in Pub. Svc.; workshop coord. sr. citizen and intergenerational workshops Finklestein Meml. Libr., Spring Valley, NY, 1989; cons. Disney Interactive, 1996; invited guest poet Donnell Libr. Ctr., N.Y. Pub. Libr., 1980—90; presenter in field. Author: Teaching Creatively by Working the Word, 2d edit., 1996, The Word in Play, 2003, (poetry books) The Separate Sides of Need, 1984, Two Halves of the Same Silence, 1985, An Eye for Resemblances, 1991. Recipient Henry V. Larom prize Rockland C.C., 1976, Blue Ribbon award So. Poetry Assn., 1988; nominee Pushcart prize, 1976. Mem. Poetry Soc. Am., Conservatory of Am. Letters, Ga. Poetry Soc., Ariz. State Poetry Soc. (judge). Avocations: skiing, hiking, bike and horseback riding, sailing, gardening. E-mail: poetlady@earthlink.net.

KATZ, THOMAS J. chemistry educator; b. Prague, Czechoslovakia, Mar. 21, 1936; m. Meta Oehmsen, 1963; 1 child, Joshua. BA, U. Wis., 1956; MA, Harvard U., 1957, PhD in Chemistry, 1959. Instr. Columbia U., 1959-61, from asst. prof. to assoc. prof., 1961-68, prof. chemistry, 1968—; Sloan fellow, 1962-66; Guggenheim fellow, 1967-68. Recipient Arthur C. Cope Scholar award Am. Chemical Soc., 1995. Fellow AAAS; mem. Am. Chem. Soc., Royal Soc. Chem. Office: Columbia U mail code 3112 3000 Broadway New York NY 10027-6941

KATZ, THOMAS OWEN, lawyer; b. Killeen, Tex., Jan. 15, 1958; s. Herbert D. and Eleanor (Meyerhoff) K.; m. Elissa Ellant, Nov. 6, 1983; children: Joseph, Peyton, Jacob. BS in Econs., U. Pa., 1979; JD, Georgetown U., 1982. Bar: Fla. 1982, U.S. Tax Ct. 1983. Shareholder, chair income tax dept. Ruden, McClosky, Smith, Schuster & Russell, P.A., Ft. Lauderdale, Fla., 1982—. Bd. dirs. CLAL-Ctr. for Jewish Learning and Leadership, N.Y., 1993—, chmn., 2002—, Donors Forum S.Fla., 1998—, Cmty. Found. of Broward, 2000—; bd. overseers Ctr. Advanced Judaic Studies U. Pa., 2001—. Office: Ruden McClosky Smith Sch PO Box 1900 Fort Lauderdale FL 33302-1900 E-mail: thomas.katz@ruden.com.

KATZ, TONNIE, newspaper editor; BA, Barnard Coll., 1966; MSc, Columbia U., 1967. Editor, reporter newspapers including The Quincy Patriot Ledger, Boston Herald Am., Boston Globe; Sunday/projects editor Newsday; mng. editor Balt. News Am., 1983-86, The Sun, San Bernardino, Calif., 1986 88; asst. mng. editor for news The Orange County Register, Santa Ana, Calif., 1988-89, mng. editor, 1989-92, editor, sr. v.p., 1992-98, editor, 1998—. Office: Orange County Register 625 N Grand Ave Santa Ana CA 92701-4347

KATZ, VERA, mayor, former college administrator, state legislator; b. Dusseldorf, Germany, Aug. 3, 1933; came to U.S., 1940; d. Lazar Pistrak and Raissa Goodman; m. Mel Katz (div. 1985); 1 child, Jesse. BA, Bklyn. Coll., 1955, postgrad., 1955-57; PhD (hon.), Lewis & Clark Coll., Portland (Oreg.) State U. Market research analyst TIMEX, B.T. Babbitt, N.Y.C., 1957-62; mem. Oreg. Ho. of Reps., Salem; former dir. devel. Portland Community Coll., from 1982; mayor City of Portland, Oreg., 1992—. Mem. Gov.'s Council on Alcohol and Drug Abuse Programs, Oreg. Legis., Salem, 1985—; mem. adv. com. Gov.'s Council on Health, Fitness and Sports, Oreg. Legis., 1985—; mem. Gov.'s Commn. on Sch. Funding Reform; mem. Carnegie task Force on Teaching as Profession, Washington, 1985-87; vice-chair assembly Nat. Conf. State Legis., Denver, 1986—2003. Recipient Abigail Scott Duniway award Women in Communications, Inc., Portland, 1985, Jeanette Rankin First Woman award Oreg. Women's Polit. Caucus, Portland, 1985, Leadership award The Neighborhood newspaper Portland, 1985, Woman of Achievement award Commn. for Women, 1985, Outstanding Legis. Advocacy award Oreg. Primary Care Assn., 1985, Service to Portland Pub. Sch. Children award Portland Pub. Schs., 1985, Visionary Leadership award, 1998, Legal Citizen of Yr. award, 2002. Fellow Am. Leadership Forum (founder Oreg. chpt.); mem. Dem. Legis. Leaders Assn., Nat. Bd. for Profl. Teaching Standards. Democrat. Jewish. Avocations: camping, jogging, dancing. Office: Office of the Mayor City Hall 1221 SW 4th Ave Rm 340 Portland OR 97204-1995*

KATZ, VINCENT ISAAC, writer; b. N.Y.C., June 4, 1960; s. Alex and Ada Katz; m. Vivien Taques Bittencourt, Nov. 16, 1987; children: Isaac, Oliver. BA, U. Chgo., 1982; BA, MA, Oxford (Eng.) U., 1985. Assoc. editor Print Collector's Newsletter, N.Y.C., 1988-91. Exhbn. curator Rudy Burckhardt exhbn. Grey Art Gallery, NYU, 2000, Black Mountain Coll. exhbn. Reina Sofia Mus., Madrid, 2002. Author: (poems) Boulevard Transportation, 1997, Pearl, 1998, Understanding Objects, 2000; (art criticism) Life Is Paradise, 1999, Janet Fish, 2002. Home: 211 W 19th St 5th Fl New York NY 10011 E-mail: vincent@el.net.

KATZ, WILLIAM A. library science educator; b. Seattle, July 6, 1932; m. Linda Sternberg, Dec. 11, 1970; children: Randy, Janet. BA, U. Wash., 1953, MA, 1955; PhD, U. Chgo., 1965. Librarian King County Pub. Library, Seattle, 1955-60; asst. to dir. publishing dept. ALA, 1960-63; asso. prof. U. Ky., 1963-66; prof. Sch. Library and Info. Sci., State U. N.Y., Albany, 1966—. Cons. in field. Author: Introduction to Reference Work, 2 vols., 8th edit., 2002, Magazines for Libraries, 11th edit., 2002, Writer's Choice, 1983, The Columbia Granger's Guide to Poetry Anthologies, 1990, Magazines for Young People, 1991, Community Colleges Reference Services., 1993, A History of Book Illustration, 1994, Dahl's History of the Book, 1995, Cuneiform to Computer, 1998, Long Live Old Reference Services, 2001; editor: Jour. Edn. for Librarianship, 1964-72, Reference Quar., 1963-73, Best of Libr. Lit., 1970-91, The Reference Libr., 1981, The Acquistions Libr., 1987; contbr. to Ency. Brit. Yearbook, 1970—. Recipient award of merit Seattle Hist. Soc., 1965, Shores-Oryx Press award, 1993. Mem. ALA (Isadore G. Mudge citation 1973) Address: SUNY Sch Info Sci and Policy 855 Mercer St Albany NY 12208-2206 E-mail: katzwilliam@hotmail.com.

KATZ, WILLIAM EMANUEL, chemical engineer; b. Honesdale, Pa., June 12, 1924; s. Edward David and Aimee Helen (Rosenfelder) K.; m. Martha Elizabeth Legg, Feb. 13, 1960; children: Susan Katz Miller, Martha Katz Laserson, E. David II, James A.L. BSChE, MIT, 1948, MSChE, 1949. Chem. engr. Ionics Inc., Watertown, Mass., 1949-51, asst. treas., 1951-53, treas., 1953-58, v.p. and dir., 1958-81, exec. v.p. and dir., 1981—2003. Author chapter in AWWA Manual of Water Quality and Treatment, 1964, and 30 articles on water and waste treatment; patentee in field. With U.S. Army, 1942-46, PTO. Recipient Life Achievement award Internat. Desalination Assn., 1999. Mem. Am. Inst. Chem. Engrs., Am. Water Works Assn., Am. Desalting Assn. (Water Quality Person of Yr. 1992), Internat. Desalination Assn. Avocations: piano, composing. Home: 11 Sunset Rd Weston MA 02493-1623

KATZ, WILLIAM LOREN, author; b. Bklyn., June 2, 1927; s. Bernard and Madeline (Simon) K.; m. Laurie Lehman, Sept. 10, 1994. BA, Syracuse U., 1950; MA, NYU, 1952. Tchr. Am. history, N.Y.C., 1954-60, Hartsdale, N.Y., 1960-67; author, 1967—. Cons. N.Y. State Edn. Dept., 1967-68, 83-84, USAF Sch. in Eng., Belgium and Holland, 1974-75; scholar in residence Tchrs. Coll. Columbia, 1971-73, NYU, 1987-91; tchr. Black history Tombs Prison, N.Y.C., 1973, N.Y. U. Afro-Am. Inst., 1973; faculty Inst. Urban and Minority Edn., Gen. Assistance Ctr., Tchrs. Coll. Columbia U., 1976; tchr. Am. history New Sch. for Social Rsch., N.Y.C., 1977-83; pres. Ethrac Publs., 1971—. Author: Eyewitness: The Negro in American History, 1967 (Gold medal for nonfiction NCCJ), Teachers' Guide to American Negro History, 1968; author: (with Warren J. Halliburton) American Majorities and Minorities: A Syllabus of United States History for Secondary Schools, 1970, A History of Black Americans, 1973; author: The Black West: A Documentary and Pictorial History, 1971 (Mark Twain award for non-fiction); 4th edit., 1996, Teaching Approaches to Black History in the Classroom, 1973, The Constitutional Amendments, 1974, An Album of Reconstruction, 1974, An Album of the Civil War, 1974, Minorities in American History, Vols. I-VI, 1974—75, Making Our Way, 1975, Black People Who Made the Old West, 1977, 2d edit., 1994, An Album of the Great Depression, 1978, Black Indians: A Hidden Heritage, 1986, 2d edit., 1997, The Invisible Empire: The Ku Klux Klan Impact on History, 1986, A History of Multicultural America, Vols I-VIII, 1993—94, Eyewitness: The Negro in American History, 4th edit., 1996, The Black West: A Documentary and Pictorial History, 4th edit., 1996; author: (with Marc Crawford) The Lincoln Brigade: A Picture History, 1989, 2d edit., 2002, Proudly Red and Black, 1993, Black Women of the Old West, 1995, Flight From the Devil: Six Slave Narratives, 1996, Black Legacy: A History of New York's African Americans, 1997, Black Pioneers: An Untold Story, 1999, The Cruel Years: American Voices at the Turn of the 20th Century, 2002; author: (with Laurie R. Lehman) 2d edit., 2003; editor: The American Negro: History and Literature, 1968—71; editor: (with James M. McPherson) The Anti-Slavery Crusade in America, 1969; editor: (with Henry Steele Commager and Arthur Schlesinger Jr.) Vital Sources in American History for High School Students, 1980; columnist: NY Daily Challenge, 1986—; contbr. articles to profl. jours. Exec. bd. Art Against Apartheid, 1984; nat. coun. Nat. Emergency Civil Liberties Com., 1983-85; curator Black West Exhibit, Schomburg Ctr. for Rsch. in Black Culture, NYC, 1985-86. With USNR, 1945-46. Recipient Imani White Dove Peace award, 2000. E-mail: wlkatz@aol.com. *If you believe that people have no history worth mentioning, it's easy to assume they have no humanity worth defending.*

KATZ, WILLIAM MICHAEL, writer; b. NYC, Mar. 18, 1940; s. Herbert and Sylvia (Dulberg) K.; m. Jane Louise Reckseit, Dec. 11, 1966; children: Sharon Elizabeth, Abigail Eve. BA, U. Chgo., 1961; MS, Columbia U., 1962. Officer CIA, Washington, 1962-63; asst. to dir. Hudson Inst., Harmon, N.Y., 1964-65; mem. editl. staff N.Y. Times, N.Y.C., 1965-70; staff editor N.Y. Times Mag., 1968-70. Adj. instr. writing and speech SUNY, Westchester; spkr., presenter in field. Author: North Star Crusade, 1976, Death Dreams, 1979, Ghostflight, 1980, Visions of Terror, 1981, Copperhead, 1982, Surprise party, 1984, Open House, 1985, Facemaker, 1988, After Dark, 1988, Double Wedding, 1990, A Very Private Act, 2002; TV dramas include Nicky's World, 1974, Nightmare at 43 Hillcrest, 1974, Death Dreams, 1991, Please Forgive Me, 1996.

KATZANEK, ROBIN JEAN, physical therapy educator; b. N.Y.C., Jan. 19, 1957; d. Reynold and Gertrude (Kupetzky) K. BS in Phys. Therapy, Boston U., 1979; MA in Sport Scis., U. Denver, 1987, PhD in Edn., 2000. Lic. phys. therapist, R.I., Colo. Phys. therapist Rose Med. Ctr., Denver, 1979-86; lab. asst. Sport Sci. Lab. U. Denver, 1987-90; phys. therapist III, Nat. Jewish Ctr. for Immunology and Respiratory Medicine, Denver, 1989-93; phys. therapist Colo. Easter Seal Soc., Lakewood, 1989-93, dir. phys. therapy, 1993-96; clin. asst. prof. U. R.I., Kingston, 1996—, acad. coord. clin. edn. phys. therapy program, 1996—. Clin. instr. phys. therapy program U. Colo. Health Scis. Ctr., Denver, 1987-88; phys. therapist Gaylord Street Phys. Therapy, Denver, 1988-89. Contbr. articles and abstracts to sci. jours. Alumni mentor U. Denver, 1988—, Boston U., 1988—, planning com., First Swing R.I., 2001—; asst. leader Brownie troop Mile Hi coun. Girl Scouts U.S.A., 1994-96. Mem. Am. Phys. Therapy Assn. (Advocates for the Disabled and Access spl. interest group, health policy, legis. and regulation sect., chmn. nominating com. 1994-2000, sec. R.I. chpt. 1997—, newsletter advt. editor R.I. chpt. 1996—), Am. Coll. Sports Medicine, Am. Coll. Rheumatology, Assn.-Assn. Rheumatology Health Profls. Avocations: needlepoint, baseball, photography. Office: U RI Phys Therapy Program 25 W Independence Way Kingston RI 02881-0810

KATZBERG, JANE MICHAELS, health care administrator, consultant, educator; b. Bklyn., Apr. 17, 1940; d. David Donn and Shirley (Ingram) Michaels; m. Mitchell Ronald Katzberg, Jan. 19, 1959; children: L. Michael, Todd Alexander. BS, Adelphi U., 1961; M of Profl. Studies in Health Care Adminstrn., L.I. U., 1975. Cert. home economist, tchr., N.Y. Mgr. quality assurance Suffolk Physicians Rev. Orgn., Central Islip, N.Y., 1979-81; dir. quality assurance and utilization rev. Cmty. Hosp. of Glen Cove, N.Y., 1982-84; dir. intermediate care facilities program United Cerebral Palsy, Commack, N.Y., 1985-86; dir. svcs. for handicapped Town of Huntington, L.I., N.Y., 1986-95; tchr. DayCare Town of Smithtown, L.I., 1995-96; ret., 1999. Pres., cons. Images, Dix Hills, N.Y., 1985-88; cons. JMK Cons., pres., 1994-99; lectr. in field. Mem. Citizen's Adv. Com. for Handicapped, Town of Huntington, 1985-86; mem. selection and steering com. C. of C. Found., 1993-97, Leadership Round Table, Huntington Health and Human Svcs. steering com., 1992-97, Huntington Hosp. Dolan Cmty. Health Ctr. Bd., 1992-97; mem. adv. bd. Dept. Social Svcs., Huntington, L.I., 1986-97, Devel. Ctr., Melville Estates, 1989-97; facilitator Nat. Orgn. Disability award N.Y. State Eleanor Roosevelt award for Town Huntington; pres. Howell Rd. Sch. PTA, North Valley Stream, N.Y., 1973; meeting rep. N.Y. State Advocate for Disabled, 1986-95; mem. divsn. dirs. Cmty. Resource Dept., 1986-89, divsn. dirs. human svcs., 1989-95. Acad. scholar C.W. Post Coll., Greenvale, N.Y., 1974. Mem. Assn. Local Govt. Advocates for Disabled. Republican. Jewish. Avocations: reading, stock market, oil painting, clothing design, jewelry design and manufacturing. Home: 81 Buttonwood Dr Dix Hills NY 11746-4804 E-mail: JKatzber@suffolk.lib.ny.us.

KATZEN, JAY KENNETH, foundation administrator, consultant, former foreign service officer; b. N.Y.C., Aug. 23, 1936; s. Perry and Minerva (Rich) K.; m. Patricia Anne Morse, May 30, 1963; children: John Timothy Rich, David Mark Nicholas, James Alexander Scott. BA magna cum laude, Princeton U., 1958; MA, Yale U., 1959. Joined U.S. Fgn. Svc., 1959; fgn. svc. officer Dept. State, Washington, 1959-60, 62-63, 66-69; consular-comml. officer Am. consulate gen. Sydney, Australia, 1960-62; econ. officer Am. embassy Bujumbura, Burundi, 1963-64; labor attaché Am. Embassy, Kinshasa, 1964-66, polit. officer Bucharest, Rumania, 1969-71, counselor of embassy Bamako, Mali, 1971—73; adviser U.S. Mission to UN, N.Y.C., 1973-77; with Office of Vice Pres., Washington, 1977, Nat. War Coll., 1977; chargé d'affaires Am. Embassy, Brazzaville, Congo, 1977-78; polit. adv. to U.S. del. World Adminstrv. Radio Conf., 1979; pres., CEO Victims of Communism Meml. Found. Vis. prof. Boston Coll. Grad. Sch. Mgmt., 1978-79; vice-chmn. bd. dirs. African Devel. Found., 1988-90; bd. advisers Patterson Sch. Diplomacy and Internat. Commerce, U. Ky., 1989—, Duke U. Primate Ctr., 1986—. Chmn. Fauquier County (Va.) Rep. Com., 1992-94; elected to Ho. of Dels. of Va. Gen. Assembly, 1993, 95, 97, 99; Republican candidate lt. gov., Va., 2001; Republican candidate U.S. Congress, 2002. Mem. Princeton Quadrangle Club, Army and Navy Club, Dacor House Club, Lions Internat. Address: PO Box 9917 Arlington VA 22219

KATZEN, RAPHAEL, consulting chemical engineer; b. Balt., July 28, 1915; s. Isidor and Esther (Stein) K.; m. Selma M. Siegel, June 19, 1938; 1 child, Nancy Katzen Riedel. B.Chem. Engring., Poly. U. Bklyn., 1936, M.Chem. Engring., 1938, D.Chem. Engring., 1942. Registered profl. engr. in 16 states. Tech. dir. Northwood Chem. Co., Phelps, Wis., 1938-42; project mgr. Diamond Alkali Co., Painesville, Ohio, 1942-44; mgr. engring. divsn. Vulcan, Cin., 1944-53; mng. partner Raphael Katzen Assos., Cin., 1953-80; chmn. Raphael Katzen Assos. Internat., Inc., 1956—97. Contbr. articles to profl. jours; patentee in field. Mem. Cin. Air Pollution Bd., 1972-75. Recipient Disting. Alumnus award Poly. Inst. Bklyn., 1970, Dedicated Alumnus award, 1977; Disting. cons. award Ohio Assn. Cons. Engrs., 1978; Profl. Accomplishment, Disting. Engr. award Tech. and Sci. Socs. Coun., 1978, 79, Personal Achievement in Chem. Engring. award Chem. Engring., McGraw Hill, 1988, Renewable Fuels Assn. Lifetime Achievement award, 1999, 16th Ann. Fuel Ethanol Workshop award of excellence, 2000, others; Poly. U. fellow, 1981. Fellow AIChE (Chem. Engring. Practice award 1986, Robert L. Jacks Meml. award 1990, Founders award 2001), Am. Inst. Chemists; mem. NAE (elected), TAPPI, PAPTAC, Am. Chem. Soc. (Spl. Lifetime Achievement award 2000), Am. Arbitration Assn., Am. Club Miami, Fla., Sigma Xi, Tau Beta Pi, Phi Lambda Upsilon. Home: 27901 Riverwalk Way Bonita Springs FL 34134-8692 Office: 9220 Bonita Beach Rd Ste 200 Bonita Springs FL 34135-4231 E-mail: rkatzenpe@aol.com. *We are put on this earth to produce to the best of our ability to improve the lot of mankind, and our talents should not be wasted through lack of effort or misguided direction.*

KATZEN, SALLY, lawyer, educator; b. Pitts., Nov. 22, 1942; d. Nathan and Hilda (Schwartz) K.; m. Timothy B. Dyk, Oct. 31, 1981; 1 child, Abraham Benjamin BA magna cum laude, Smith Coll., 1964; JD magna cum laude, U. Mich., 1967. Bar: D.C. 1968, U.S. Supreme Ct. 1971. Congl. intern Sente Subcom. on Constl. Rights, Washington, 1963; legal rsch. asst. civil rights div. Dept. Justice, Washington, 1965; law clk. to Judge J. Skelly Wright U.S. Ct. Appeals (D.C. cir.), 1967-68; assoc. Wilmer, Cutler & Pickering, Washington, 1968-75, ptnr., 1975-79, 81-93; gen. counsel Coun. on Wage and Price Stability, 1979-80; dep. dir. for policy, 1980-81; adminstr. Office of Info. and Regulatory Affairs, Office of Mgmt. and Budget, Washington, 1993-98; dep. dir. Nat. Econ. Coun., The White House, Washington, 1998-99; counsellor to the dir. Office Mgmt. and Budget, Washington, 1999-2000, dep. dir. mgmt., 2000-2001. Adj. prof. Georgetown U. Law Ctr., 1988, 1990—92; resident scholar and lectr. Smith Coll., 2001—; vis. lectr. Johns Hopkins U., 2002—03, U. Pa. Law Sch., 2003; pub. mem. Adminstrv. Conf. U.S., 1988, govt. mem. and vice chair, 1993—95; mem. exec. com. Prettyman-Leventhal Inn of Ct., 1988—90, counselor, 1990—91; mem. Jud. Conf. for D.C. Cir., 1972—91. Editor-in-chief U. Mich. Law Rev., 1966-67 Mem. com. visitors U. Mich. Law Sch., 1972—. Fellow ABA (ho. of dels. 1978-80, 89-91, coun. adminstrv. law sect. 1979-82, chmn. adminstrv. law and regulatory practice sect. 1988-89, governing com. forum com. communications law 1979-82, chmn. standing com. Nat. Conf. Groups 1989-92); mem. D.C. Bar Assn., Women's Bar Assn., FCC Bar Assn. (exec. com. 1984-87, pres. 1990-91), Women's Legal Def. Fund (pres. 1977, v.p. 1978), Order of Coif. Home: 4638 30th St NW Washington DC 20008-2127

KATZENBACH, NICHOLAS DEBELLEVILLE, lawyer; b. Phila., Jan. 17, 1922; s. Edward Lawrence and Marie Louise (Hilson) K.; m. Lydia King Phelps Stokes, June 8, 1946; children— Christopher Wolcott, John Strong Minor, Maria Louise Hiltson, Anne deBelleville. BA, Princeton U., 1945; LL.B., Yale U., 1947; Rhodes scholar, Balliol Coll., Oxford (Eng.) U., 1947-49. Bar: N.J. 1950, Conn. 1955, N.Y. 1972. With firm Katzenbach, Gildea & Rudner, Trenton, N.J., 1950; atty.-adviser Office Gen. Counsel Air Force, 1950-52, part-time cons., 1952-56; asso. prof. law Yale Law Sch., 1952-56; prof. law U. Chgo. Law Sch., 1956-60; asst. atty. gen. Dept. Justice, 1961-62; dep. atty. gen., 1962-64; acting atty. gen., 1964; atty. gen., 1965-66; under sec. state, 1966-69; sr. v.p., gen. counsel IBM Corp., 1969-84, sr. v.p. law and external relations, 1984-86, also bd. dirs.; ptnr. Riker, Danzig, Scherer, Hyland & Perretti, Morristown, N.J., 1986-91. Author: (with Morton A. Kaplan) The Political Foundations of International Law, 1961; editor-in-chief: Yale Law Jour, 1947; contbr. articles to profl. jours. Served to 1st lt. USAAF, 1941-45. Decorated Air medal with three clusters; Ford Found. fellow, 1960-61 Mem. AAAS, Am. Law Inst. (mem. coun.), Am. Bar Assn., Am. Judicature Soc., Am. Philos. Soc. Democrat. Episcopalian. Home: 33 Greenhouse Dr Princeton NJ 08540-4802 E-mail: nkatzenbac@aol.com.

KATZENBERG, JEFFREY, motion picture studio executive; b. Dec. 21, 1950; m. Marilyn Siegel; children: Laura, David. Asst. to chmn., chief exec. officer Paramount Pictures, N.Y.C, 1975-77, exec. dir. mktg., 1977; then v.p. programming Paramount TV, Calif., 1977-78; v.p., feature prodn. Paramount Pictures, 1978-80, sr. v.p., prodn. motion picture div., 1980-82, pres. prodn., motion pictures & TV, 1982-94; chmn. Walt Disney Studios, Burbank, Calif., 1994; chmn., founding ptnr. DreamWorks SKG, 1994—. Co-prodr.: Nightmare Before Christmas, 1993, exec. prodr.: Prince of Egypt, 1998, Road to El Dorado, 2000, Chicken Run, 2000, Joseph: King of Dreams, 2000; prodr.: (films) Shrek, 2001, Spirit: Stallion of the Cimarron, 2002, Sinbad: Legend of the Seven Seas, 2003; exec. prodr.: TV series Father of the Pride, 2003. Office: Dreamworks SKG 1000 Flower St Glendale CA 91201-7500*

KATZEN-GUTHRIE, JOY, performance artist, engineering services executive; b. Memphis, Nov. 11, 1958; d. Eli and Bess (Bloomfield) Katzen; m. Mark C. Guthrie, Aug. 7, 1983. BFA in Music cum laude, BA in Comms. magna cum laude, Stephens Coll., Columbia, Mo., 1980. Traffic dir. WPLP News/Talk Radio, Pinellas Park, Fla., 1981-83, ops. mgr., 1982-83; traffic reporter WUSA-FM and WDAE-AM, Tampa, Fla., 1985-86; announcer, programmer, pub. rels. mgr. WXCR-FM Classics 92, Safety Harbor, Fla., 1983-87; v.p., dir. Katzen and Guthrie Assocs., Inc., Palm Harbor, Fla., 1987—; pres. Tune-of-the-Century Music, 1989—. Creator, designer, owner website www.JoyfulNoise.net, 1998—. Co-author, composer musical comedy Once Around Manhattan, 1985; author: (one-act play) A Murder in Pine County, 1987; composer, lyricist some 600 songs; performance artist CD/Cassette albums Seasons of Joy, 1989, Heart of Ancient Promise, 1993, New State of Mind, 1993, How Good and Pleasant, 1996, Passages, 1998; studio vocalist Jeff Arthur Prodns., St. Petersburg, Fla., 1985, 86, Studio C. Prodns., Tampa, 1991-92; studio vocalist, jingle writer West End Rec., Tampa, 1989, 90; session musician Hurricane Pass Studios, Clearwater, Fla., 1993—. Music dir. religious sch. Temple B'nai Israel, Clearwater, 1988-89; music dir. Perry-Mansfield Performing Arts Camp, Steamboat Springs, Colo., 1987; cantorial soloist B'nai B'rith Hillel Found., Tampa, 1990-93, Temple Shir Shalom, Gainesville, 1994-99, Congregation B'nai Emmunah, Tarpon Springs, 1996-99, Congregation Aliyah, Clearwater, 1999-2000, Temple B'nai Israel, Clearwater, 2000—. Recipient 1st and 3d place awards Memphis Songwriters Assn. Competition, 1988, others; Pinellas County Arts Coun. grantee, 1997. Mem. AAUW (dir. pub. rels. 1985-97), ASCAP, Songwriters Guild Am., Dramatists Guild, Nat. Acad. Songwriters, Nashville Songwriters Assn. Internat., Guild of Temple Musicians, Fla. Music Assn., Women's Musicians' Alliance (bd. dirs. 1998—), Hadassah (life). Democrat. Jewish. Avocations: photography, travel, music, theatre, film, books. Home and Office: 2487 Indian Trl E Palm Harbor FL 34683-2806 E-mail: joyfulnoise@earthlink.net.

KATZENSTEIN, ROBERT JOHN, lawyer; b. Phila., May 2, 1951; s. Lawrence and Joan I. (Hassall) K.; children: Jeffrey Hunt, Erick Hill. BA, Yale U., 1973; JD, U. Pa., 1976. Bar: Del. 1976, DC 1979. Trial atty. antitrust div. U.S. Dept. of Justice, Washington, 1976-78; assoc. Richards, Layton & Finger, Wilmington, Del., 1978-84; ptnr. Katzenstein & Furlow, Wilmington, 1984-85, Lassen, Smith, Katzenstein & Furlow, Wilmington, 1985-91, Smith, Katzenstein & Furlow LLP, Wilmington, 1992—. Asst. disciplinary counsel to Del. Bd. Profl. Responsibility, 1986-92; mem. Richard S. Rodney Inn of Court, 1993—, Product Liability Adv. Coun.; mem. bd. bar examiners Del. Supreme Ct., 2003--. Mem. ABA (litig. sect., bus. law sect.), Del. State Bar Assn. (jud. appts. com. 1991—, co-chair 1999—, corp. law, litig. sect.), Internat. Assn. Def. Coun., Def. Counsel of Del. (pres. 1997-99), Yale Club of Del., ARC (bd. dirs. Delmarva peninsula, sec. 1998-99, vice chair 1999-2001, chair 2001-03), Mass for the Homeless Inc. (pres. 1998—). Democrat. Office: Smith Katzenstein & Furlow LLP PO Box 410 800 Delaware Ave The Corp Plz Wilmington DE 19899-0410 Home: 2522 W 18th St Wilmington DE 19806-1208 E-mail: rjk@skfdelaware.com.

KATZENSTEIN, THEA, retail executive, jewelry designer; b. N.Y.C., Mar. 30, 1927; d. Carl E. and Lillian (Rosenblatt) Schustak; m. William Katzenstein, Sept. 10, 1950; children: Leo, Ranee. Student, Sarah Lawrence Coll., 1948-50; BS, Columbia U., 1962, MA, 1967. Pres. Gallery A., N.Y.C., 1967-71, Melita, N.Y.C., 1972-77, TK Studio, Miami Beach, Fla., 1977—. Adj. prof. of jewelry Fla. Internat. U., 1989-90; enamelling instr. U. Miami, 1991. Author: Early Chinese Art and The Pacific Basin, 1967; painting, graphics and jewelry represented in numerous pvt. collections. Trustee Miami Metro Zoo, 1994-2000, dir. 2000—; founder Mt. Sinai Hosp., 1996—, U. Miami, 1999; dir. Circle Lowe Mus., U. Miami, 1999. Mem. Soc. N.Am. Goldsmiths, Enamel Guild South (sec. 2001—), Nat. Enamelist Guild, Fla. Soc. Goldsmiths (pres. S.E. chpt. 1988-91, 94-98, v.p. state bd. 1998-2000, treas. 2000—), Fla. Craftsmen, Zonta (sec. Coral Gables chpt. 1989-90), Women in the Visual Arts, Womens Jewelry Assn. Democrat. Jewish. Home: Apt 1423 19333 W Country Club Dr Aventura FL 33180

KATZIN, CAROLYN FERNANDA, nutritionist, consultant; b. London, July 21, 1946; came to U.S., 1983; d. John Mourier and Shelagh B. A. (Tighe) Lade; m. Anthony Arthur Speelman, Mar. 18, 1968 (div. Dec. 1984); 1 child, Zara Jane; m. David Brandeis Katzin (div. Mar. 1999). BS with honors, U. London, 1983; MS in Pub. Health, UCLA, 1988. Nutritionist, L.A., 1985—. Chair dean's adv. bd. UCLA Sch. Pub. Health, 1997—; mem. profl. adv. bd. The Wellness Cmty., L.A., 1998—; pres. Am. Cancer Soc., L.A., Coastal Cities U., 1999-2002. Author: The Advanced Energy Guide, 1994, The Good Eating Guide and Cookbook, 1996, The Cancer Nutrition Ctr. Handbook, 2001, 2d edit., 2003. Democrat. Jewish. Office: 12011 San Vicente Blvd Ste 402 Los Angeles CA 90049-4946 E-mail: cfk@aol.com.

KATZKE, MARY ROSANNE, filmmaker, scriptwriter; b. Moorhead, Minn., Mar. 12, 1962; d. August Floyd Katzke and Carola Clara Thornberg. MFA in Film Writing and Direction, NYU, 1992. Dir. Affinityfilms, Inc., Anchorage, 1980—, N.Y.C., 1980—. Prodr. Paraview Prodns., N.Y.C., 1996—97. Prodr.: (documentaries) Sea Of Oil (POV Nat. Airing, Sundance Film Festival, MOMA exhbn., 1991). Bd. mem. Alaska Film Group, Anchorage, 2002. Mem.: N.Y. Women in Film. Office: Affinityfilms Inc Anchorage AK 99503 Personal E-mail: arcapple@aol.com.

KATZMAN, CHAIM, finance company executive; Chmn. bd., CEO Equity One, Inc., Miami Beach, Fla. Office: Ste 200 1696 NE Miami Gardens Dr North Miami Beach FL 33179 Office Fax: 305-947-1734.

KATZMAN, IRWIN, lawyer; b. Windsor, Ont., Can., June 29, 1931; s. Aaron and Rose (Tarnow) K.; m. Helen Frances Blecher, Dec. 20, 1952 (dec. Feb. 1998); children: Barry, Harriet, Kenneth, Rhonda, Aaron; m. Toby Lyman, Aug. 15, 1999. BS, Wayne State U., 1953, MBA, 1963; JD cum laude, Loyola U., L.A., 1974. Bar: Calif. 1974, U.S. Dist. Ct. (cen. dist.) Calif. 1974, U.S. Ct. Appeals (9th cir.) 1980, U.S. Supreme Ct. 1980, U.S. Tax Ct. 1988. Chemist E.I. Dupont de Nemours, Phila., 1953-54; asst. quality mgr. Chrysler Corp., Detroit, 1956-63; mfg. plans mgr. Ford Motor Co., Newport Beach, Calif., 1963-70; prodn. control mgr. Dresser Industries, Huntington Park, Calif., 1970-73; purchasing mgr. Hughes Aircraft Co., Inglewood, Calif., 1973-74; v.p. First Alliance Mortgage Co., Santa Ana, Calif., 1976-77; pvt. practice Anaheim, Calif., 1975-94, San Jose, Calif., 1995—. Pres. Temple Beth Emet, Anaheim, 1988-90. With U.S. Army, 1953-56. Mem. State Bar of Calif., Orange County Bar Assn., Santa Clara County Bar Assn., Alpha Epsilon Pi (life). Avocations: sailing, golf, amateur radio. Office: 8346 Riesling Way San Jose CA 95135-1435

KATZMAN, MERLE HERSHEL, retired orthopaedic surgeon; b. Hartford, Conn., Aug. 28, 1928; s. Samuel Sidney and Bertha (Hirshberg) K.; m. Charna Lytell, June 26, 1955; children: Beth, Amy, Sam, Robert. BS, Trinity Coll., 1950; MD, Jefferson Med. Coll., 1954. Diplomate Am. Bd. Orthop. Surgery. Intern Hartford (Conn.) Hosp., 1954-55, resident in surgery, 1957-58; surgeon N.Y. Orthop. Hosp., 1958-61; attending orthop. surgeon, chief orthop. dept. Englewood Hosp., 1965-94, attending orthop. surgeon, 1980-94; asst. attending orthopedic surgeon Presbyn. Hosp., N.Y.C., 1963-94; asst. clin. prof. orthopedic surgery Columbia U. Med. Sch., 1975-94; pres. Katzman, Tarsney & Feldman, Tenafly, N.J., 1994; ret., 1994. Mem. credentials com., exec. com., chmn. future devel. com., Englewood Hosp.; asst. attending orthopedic surgeon Presbyn. Hosp., N.Y.C., until 1994; asst. clin. prof. orthopedic surgery Columbia U. Coll. Physicians & Surgeons, N.Y.C., until 1994. Lt. USNR, 1955-57. Fellow ACS, Am. Acad. Orthopaedic Surgeons, Bergen County Med. Soc. (del., health ins. review com. mem.), N.J. State Med. Soc., N.J. Orthopaedic Soc. (exec. com. pres. 1977-78), Stannard Beach Assn. (exec. com. mem., pres. 1996-98).

KATZMAN, RICHARD A. cardiologist, internist, consultant; b. Cleve., Mar. 22, 1931; s. Abraham N. and Anne Ruth (Kustin) K.; m. Roberta Brown, July 28, 1962; children: Audrey, Sharon, Naomi, Noah. BS, Case Western Reserve U., 1952; MD, U. Chgo., 1955. Diplomate Am. Bd. Internal Medicine. Prin. Richard A. Katzman M.D., Cleve., 1963—; dir. electrocardiography, dept. cardiology Metro Health Med. Ctr., 1992-97; staff cardiologist Mt. Sinai Hosp., Cleve., 1998-2000. Assoc. clin. prof. medicine Case Western Reserve U. V.p. Cleve. Coll. Jewish Studies, 1985-88. Capt. U.S. Army Med. Corps., 1956-58. Fellow Am. Coll. Physicians, Am. Coll. Chest Physicians. Home: 28950 Gates Mills Blvd Pepper Pike OH 44124-4744 Office: Parkway Med Bldg 24755 Chagrin Blvd Beachwood OH 44122

KATZMAN, RICHARD ALAN, lawyer, arbitrator; b. N.Y.C., N.Y., Sept. 3, 1953; s. George and Ellen Delyse (Shure) K.; 1 child, Braden Michael Harris Katzman. AA, Miami-Dade Jr. Coll., 1972; BA, Fla. Internat. U., 1973; JD, U. Miami, 1976; MA, U. So. Calif., 1981. Bar: Fla. 1976, N.J. 1977, Calif. 1980, U.S. Dist. Ct. (so. dist.) Fla. 1976, U.S. Dist. Ct. N.J. 1977, U.S. Dist. Ct. (cent. dist.) Calif. 1980, U.S. Ct. Appeals (9th cir.) 1980, U.S. Ct. Appeals (5th and 11th cirs.) 1981, U.S. Supreme Ct. 1979, U.S. Dist. Ct. (no. dist.) Calif. 1996. Of counsel Black and Denaro, Miami, 1976-78; rsch. atty. 3d Dist. Ct. Appeal, Miami, 1978; labor atty. Pomona (Calif.) divsn. Gen. Dynamics, 1980-82; assoc. atty. Balowitz & Wolf, Santa Ana, Calif., 1982-84; sr. assoc. Petersen & Ferguson, Santa Ana, Calif., 1984-86; sr. litig. L.A. County Met. Transp. Authority, L.A., 1986-94; prin. dep. county counsel County of L.A., L.A., 1994-96; asst. gen. counsel Santa Clara Valley Transp. Authority, 1996—. Jud. arbitrator L.A. County Superior Ct., 1986-96, Orange County Superior Ct., Santa Ana, Calif., 1988-96. Judge Pro Tempore West Orange County Mun. Ct., Westminster, Calif., 1985-96. Mem. Amer. Coll. of Legal Medicine (assoc.-in-law). Avocations: boating, skiing, rv. Home: 310 N 1st St Apt 2 Campbell CA 95008-1341 Office: 3331 N 1st St Fl 2 San Jose CA 95134-1906

KATZMAN, ROBERT, medical educator, neurologist; b. Denver, Nov. 29, 1925; s. Maurice and Leah K. (Schnitt) K.; m. Nancy Bernstein, Sept. 2, 1947; children: David Jonathan, Daniel Mark. BS, U. Chgo., 1949, MS, 1951; MD cum laude, Harvard U., 1953. Diplomate Am. Bd. Psychiatry and Neurology. Intern Boston City Hosp., 1953-54; chief resident Neurol. Inst. Columbia Presbyn. Hosp., N.Y.C., 1956-57; faculty mem. Albert Einstein Coll. Medicine, N.Y.C., 1957-84, prof., chmn. neurology dept., 1964-84, dir. Resnick Gerontology Ctr., 1979-84; chmn. dept. neurosci. U. Calif., San Diego, 1984-90, Florence Riford prof. neurosci. and rsch. in Alzheimer's disease, 1984-94, rsch. prof. neurosci., 1994—2002, prof. emeritus neurosci., 2003—. Mem. clin. rsch. adv. com. Nat. Found. March of Dimes, 1975-76; mem. adv. coun. Nat. Inst. on Aging, 1982-85; chmn. med. and sci. bd. Alzheimer Disease and Related Disorders Assn., Chgo., 1979-85; mem. adv. panel on Alzheimer's disease HHS, 1987-93. Co-author: Brain Electrolytes and Fluid Metabolism, 1973, Neurology of Aging, 1983, Alzheimer Disease: The Changing View, 2000; co-editor: Basic Neurochemistry, 1972-81, Principles of Geriatric Neurology, 1992, Alzheimer Disease, 1994, Alzheimers Disease, 2d edit., 1999; mem. editl. bd. Clin. Neuroscience Rsch. Jour., ARNMD, 2001--. With USN, 1944-46, PTO. Recipient Humanitarian Award Alzheimer's Disease and Related Disorders Assn., 1985, Disting. Svc. award, 1989, Allied Achievement in Aging award Allied Signal Corp., 1985, Henderson Meml. award Am. Geriatric Soc., 1986, 7th Ann. Chgo. Rita Hayworth Gala award recipient, Alzheimer's Assn., 1994, Crystal Tower award Alzheimer's Assn., 1998. Fellow Am. Acad. Neurology (S. Weir Mitchell award 1960, George W. Jacoby award 1989, co-recipient Potamkin prize for Alzheimer's disease rsch. 1992); mem. Assn. for Rsch. in Nervous and Mental Disorders (pres. 1977), Am. Physiol. Soc., Inst. Medicine NAS, Am. Neurol. Assn. (pres. 1985-86), Internat. Soc. for Alzheimer's Disease Rsch. (pres. 1996—), Alpha Omega Alpha. Office: U Calif San Diego Sch Medicine 9500 Gilman Dr Dept 0949 La Jolla CA 92093-0949 E-mail: rkatzman@ucsd.edu.

KATZMANN, GARY STEPHEN, lawyer; b. N.Y.C., Apr. 22, 1953; s. John and Sylvia Katzmann. AB summa cum laude, Columbia U., 1973; MLitt, Oxford U., 1976; MPPM, JD, Yale U., 1979. Bar: Mass. 1982, U.S. Dist. Ct. Mass. 1983, U.S. Ct. Appeals (1st cir.) 1983, D.C. 1984, U.S. Ct. Appeals (2d cir.) 1987, N.Y. 1990, U.S. Ct. Appeals (fed. cir.) 1991. Law clk. to judge U.S. Dist. Ct. (so. dist.) N.Y., N.Y.C., 1979-80; law clk. to Hon. Stephen Breyer U.S. Ct. Appeals (1st cir.), Boston, 1980-81; rsch. assoc. ctr. criminal justice Law Sch. Harvard U., Cambridge, Mass., 1981-83; asst. U.S. atty., chief appellate atty., dep. chief criminal div., chief legal counsel U.S. Atty.'s Office, Mass., 1983—; assoc. dep. atty. gen. U.S. Dept. Justice, Washington, 1993-94. Lectr. Harvard U. Law Sch., 1989—; project dir. J.F. Kennedy Sch. Govt., Harvard U., 1997—; participant Yale Law Sch. Sentencing Seminar, 1999—. Author: Inside the Criminal Process, 1991, Securing Our Children's Future: New Approaches to Juvenile Justice and Youth Violence, 2002. Recipient Dir's. Superior Performance award U.S. Dept. Justice, 1993; fellow Harvard U., 1997—, Governance Inst. Mem. ABA, Phi Beta Kappa. Office: US Attys Offci US Courthouse 1 Courthouse Way Ste 9200 Boston MA 02210-3011

KATZMANN, ROBERT ALLEN, judge; b. N.Y.C., 1953; AB summa cum laude, Columbia U., 1973; MA in Govt., Harvard U., 1975, PhD in Govt., 1978; JD, Yale U., 1980. Bar: Mass. 1982, U.S. Ct. Appeals (1st cir.) 1983, D.C. 1984, U.S. Dist. Ct. Mass. 1984, N.Y. Law clk. to judge U.S. Ct. Appeals (1st cir.), Concord, N.H., 1980-81; rsch. assoc. Brookings Instn., Washington, 1981-85, fellow, 1985-99; adj. prof. law, pub. policy Georgetown U., Washington, 1984-92, William J. Walsh prof. govt., prof. law, 1992-99; pres. Governance Inst., Washington, 1986-99; acting dir. govt. studies Brookings Instn., Washington, 1998; judge U.S. Ct. Appeals (2nd cir.), 1999—; adjunct prof. of Law New York University, New York, 2001—. Vis. prof. polit. sci. UCLA, Washington program, 1990-92; vis. chair, Wayne Morse prof. law and politics U. Oreg., 1992; cons. Fed. Cts. Study Com., 1990; adj. prof. law N.Y. U., 2001-. Author: Regulatory Bureaucracy: The Federal Trade Commission and Antitrust Policy, 1980, Institutional Disability, 1986, Courts and Congress, 1997; co-editor: Managing Appeals in Federal Courts, 1988; editor: Judges and Legislators, 1988, The Law Firm and the Public Good, 1995; article and book editor Yale U. Law Jour., 1979-80. Fellow: Am. Acad. Arts and Scis.; mem.: ABA (adminstrv. law sect., vice chair com. on govt. ops. and separation of powers 1991—94, pub. mem. adminstrn. conf. 1992—95), Am. Polit. Sci. Assn. (Charles E. Merriam award 2001), Am. Judicature Soc. (bd. dirs. 1992—98), Phi Beta Kappa. Office: US Ct Appeals 2d Cir 40 Foley Sq New York NY 10007-1502

KATZMAN-TELLER, SHARON M. writer; b. Bridgeport, Conn., Oct. 11, 1966; d. Edward E. and Eileen S. Katzman; m. Bruce S. Teller, May 4, 2002. BS in Biochemistry, Rutgers U., 1991; MS in Profl. and Tech. Comm., N.J. Inst. Tech., 1999. Rsch. assoc. Enzon, Inc., South Plainfield, NJ, 1989—92; sr. rsch. technologist Internat. Technidyne Corp., Edison, NJ, 1993—98; tech. writer Glenwood, LLC, Piscataway, NJ, 1998—99; freelance tech. writer various, 2000—02; med. writer Covance, Inc., Princeton, NJ, 2002—. Rec. sec. Or Chadash, The Reform Temple of Hunterdon County, Flemington, NJ, 2000, newsletter pub., 2000. Mem.: Am. Med. Writer's Assn. Home: 21 Plantation Rd Whitehouse Station NJ 08889 Office: Covance Inc Princeton NJ Personal E-mail: smkt@earthlink.net. E-mail: sharon.katzman-teller@covance.com.

KATZOWITZ SHENFIELD, LAUREN, philanthropic consultant, foundation executive; m. Marc Shenfield. BS in Comparative Lit. with honors, Brandeis U., 1970; MS with honors, Columbia U., 1971. With Newsweek mag.; then with Phila. Bull.; freelance writer, editor, cons., until 1975; cons. Ford Found., 1972-75; mgr. PBS programs Exxon Corp., 1978-81; mgr. Exxon Rsch. and Engring. Co., 1981-84; regional liaison for Europe and Africa, Exxon Corp., 1984-86; exec. dir. Found. Svc., 1986—; pres. Lauren Katzowitz Cons., Croton on Hudson, N.Y., 1986—. Mem. profl. adv. coun. Met. Mus. of Art, 2000—, Central Park Conservancy, 2001—; bd. dirs. N.Y. Regional Assn. of Grantmakers, 2000—, Women and Philanthropy, 2003—. Named one of 12 Women to Watch in the Eighties, Ladies' Home Jour., 1979. Office: Lauren Katzowitz Consulting 4 Hamilton Ave Croton On Hudson NY 10520-2521

KATZPER, MEYER, analyst; b. Ramat-Gan, Israel, July 31, 1936; came to U.S., 1937; s. Moses and Lillian (Gincenberg) K.; m. Linda Beryl Schwartz, Aug. 19, 1973; children: Moshe Ariel, Margalit Ahuvah, David Evan. BA, BRE, Yeshiva U., 1957; PhD, NYU, 1967. Asst. prof. L.I. U., N.Y.C., 1966-67; sr. rsch. scientist Nat. Biomed. Rsch. Found., Silver Spring, Md., 1967-70, asst. prof. SUNY, Plattsburgh, 1970-73; tech. assoc. Ocean Data Systems, Inc., Rockville, Md., 1974-76; assoc. prof. George Washington U. Med. Sch., Washington, 1978-84; ind. cons. systems and info. analysis Rockville, Md., 1976-89; sr. staff fellow Ctr. for Drug Evaluation and Rsch., FDA, Rockville, 1989—. Author: Fortran Programming Through Examples, 1973; co-author: Modeling and Simulation of Alcohol Utilization, 1976; (with others) Brain Oxygen Supply and Electrical Act, 1969; author: (monograph) Modeling of Long Term Care, 1980; editor: Social and Environmental Analysis, 1970; co-editor: Simulation in Health Sciences and Services, 1993, Proceedings of the Simulation in Health Sciences Conference, 1994, Health Sciences, Physiological and Pharmacological Simulation Studies, 1995, Simulation in the Medical Sciences, 1996, Medical Sciences Simulation, 1997, Medical Sciences Simulation Conference Proceedings, 1998, Health Sciences Simulation, 1999, 2000, Simulation in the Health and Medical Sciences, 2001, Health Sciences Simulation, 2003. Dir. Beth Sholom Beth Hamedrash Series, Rockville, 1977-78; faculty advisor Hillel, Plattsburgh, 1972-73; faculty Lehrhaus, Washington, 1975-76. NSF fellow, 1958; Miner Inst. Environ. grantee SUNY, 1972. Achievements include design of pharmacoscope and pharmacofit. E-mail: katzper@cder.fda.gov.

KATZUNG, BERTRAM GEORGE, pharmacologist; b. Mineola, N.Y., June 11, 1932; m. Alice V. Camp; children: Katharine Blanche, Brian Lee. BA, Syracuse U., 1953; MD, SUNY, Syracuse, 1957; PhD, U. Calif., San Francisco, 1962. Prof. U. Calif., San Francisco, 1958—. Author: Drug Therapy, 1991, Pharmacology, Examination and Board Review, 2002, Basic and Clinical Pharmacology, 2003; contbr. to profl. jours. Markle scholar. Mem. AAAS, AAUP, Am. Soc. Pharmacology and Exptl. Therapeutics, Biophysical Soc., Fed. Am. Scientists, Internat. Soc. Heart Rsch., Soc. Gen. Physiologists, Western Pharmacology Soc., N.Y. Acad. Sci., Astron. Soc. of Pacific, Internat. Dark-Sky Assn., Nat. Deep Sky Observers Soc., Planetary Soc., Royal Astron. Soc. of Canada, San Francisco Amateur Astronomers Soc., Sonoma County Astron. Soc., Phi Beta Kappa, Alpha Omega Alpha, Golden Gate Computer Soc. Office: U Calif San Francisco Dept Cellular/Molec Pharm PO Box 450 San Francisco CA 94143-0450

KAUCHER, JAMES WILLIAM, lawyer; b. Belleville, Ill., Oct. 20, 1958; s. Robert Frederick and Mary Ellen (Shepard) K.; m. Janine Kaucher, Oct. 24, 1993. BA, U. Colo., 1980; JD, U. Ill., 1983. Bar: Ariz. 1983, U.S. Dist. Ct. Ariz. 1983. Assoc. Evans, Kitchel & Jenckes, Phoenix, 1983—85, Teilborg, Sanders & Parks, Phoenix, 1985—92; ptnr. Cavett and Kaucher, Tucson, 1992—98; dir. Goodwin Raup PC, Tucson, 1998—2002, Shughart, Thomson, Kilroy, P.C., Tucson, 2002—. Chmn. human rsch. rev. bd. Humana Hosp., Phoenix, 1989-94. Mem. bioethics com. Northwest Hosp., Tucson, 1993—. Mem. Am. Assn. Health Lawyers, Maricopa Bar Assn., Def. Rsch. Inst., Forum on Health Law, Ariz. Soc. Health Care Risk Mgrs. (bd. dirs. 1989-91), Ariz. Assn. Def. Counsel, Ariz. Mountaineering Club, Am. Alpine Club. Avocations: mountaineering, flying, bicycle racing. Office: Shughart Thomson & Kilroy PC Ste 2130 One S Church Ave Tucson AZ 85701 E-mail: jamesw@kaucher.com.

KAUDERER, BERNARD MARVIN, retired naval officer, consultant; b. Phila., July 21, 1931; s. Harry Thau and Anne Mae (Mandell) K.; m. Myra Frances Weissman, Mar. 21, 1954; children: Howard Todd, Heidi Susanne, Robin Beth. BS, U.S. Naval Acad., 1953. Commd. ensign U.S. Navy, 1953, advanced through grades to vice adm., 1983; comdr. Submarine Group Five, 1977-79; dep. dir. research, devel., test and evaluation Office Chief Naval Ops., Navy Dept., Washington, 1979-81; comdr. submarine forces U.S. Pacific Fleet, 1981-83; comdr. submarine force U.S. Atlantic Fleet, 1983-86; ret. U.S. Navy, 1986. Cons. to industry and govt. Decorated D.S.M., Legion of Merit, Meritorious Service medal, Navy Commendation medal, Navy Expeditionary medal. Mem. Naval Submarine League (dir.), Masons, Shriners. Home: 7025 Ibis Pl Carlsbad CA 92009-5011

KAUFER, CONNIE TENORIO, retired reading specialist; b. Saipan, No. Mariana Islands, June 12, 1945; d. Lino Pangelinan and Magdalena Faosto (Arriola) Tenorio; m. Leonard James Kaufer, Jan. 20, 1974; 1 child, Lucile Tenorio. AA in Elem. Edn., Chaffey Coll., 1968; BS in Lang. Arts, Calif. State Poly. U., 1971; MA in Edn., San Jose State U., 1983. Cert. tchr., Calif., Mariana Islands. Elem. tchr. Marianas Dept. Edn., Chalan Kanoa, Saipan, Mariana Islands, 1964-66, 74-76, 80-84, elem. and h.s. tchr., 1970-71, elem. sch. supr. Lower Base, Saipan, 1971-74, elem. sch. prin. Tanapag Village, Saipan, 1979-80; comprehensive lang. arts skills project dir. Pub. Sch. Sys., Lower Base, Saipan, 1984-87, reading specialist, 1984-94, trainer Marianas instrument for obs. of tchr. activities, 1986—94, trainer onward to excellence, 1988—94; ret., 1994. Part-time instr. U. Guam Ext., No. Marianas Coll., Saipan, 1993—; sec. Diocesan Bd. Edn. Saipan, 1985-90; trainer pacific region pacific effective schs. Pacific Region Edn. Lab., Honolulu and Saipan, 1991-93; presenter in field. Mem. Mariana Islands rep. Trust Ter. Curriculum Coun., Saipan, 1970-72; coord. cross cultural Peace Corps, Saipan, 1973, coord. Chamorro lang., 1975; pres. Chalan Kanoa Sch. Saipan Tchrs. Assn., 1981-83. Scholar Marianas Edn. Found., 1966-70, Bilingual Edn. scholar Trust Ter. Dept. Edn., 1975. Mem. ASCD, AAUW, Internat. Reading Assn. (Saipan chpt. pres. 1975-76), Pacific Islands Bilingual/Bicultural Assn., Phi Delta Kappa. Roman Catholic. Avocations: raising orchids, cooking, baking. Home: PO Box 7611 Saipan MP 96950

KAUFER, SHIRLEY HELEN, artist, painter; b. Bklyn., Oct. 3, 1920; m. Bernard Goldberg, Apr. 18, 1943; children: Alice, Marjorie. Student in art studies, Pratt Inst.; student, Bklyn. Mus., Art Students League, N.Y.C. Art dir. Advt. Agys., N.Y.C., 1938-63; art cons. N.Y.C., 1964-73; sculptor Vero Beach, Fla., 1973-77; graphic designer Jewish Fedn. Coun., L.A., 1977-82. With Haystack Mt. Art Colony, Deer Isle, Maine, summers 1959-65; instr. advt., design, illustration Pels Art Sch., N.Y.C., 1968-71; instr. painting Indian River C.C., Vero Beach, 1973-77. Represented in permanent art collection pf UCLA Med. Ctr., L.A.; exhibited in numerous nat. and internat. galleries; 2 films produced on her life and works. Home: 1029 Via De La Paz Pacific Palisades CA 90272-3534

KAUFFMAN, AMY, political organization worker; b. Ardmore, Pa., Sept. 14, 1963; d. William J. Kauffman, Joanne Solomon Kauffman; m. Kenneth R. Weinstein; children: Eden Weinstein children: Raina Weinstein, Harrison Weinstein. BA, U.Pa., 1985; MBA, Georgetown U., 1996. Political cons. Senators John Heinz, Arlen Specter, Dick Thornburgh, Mike Dewine, various, DC, 1986—94; dir. Campaign for Am., Washington, 1996—99; dir. campaign & election law project Hudson Inst., Washington, 1999—. Office: Hudson Institute 1015 18th Street NW; Suite 300 Washington DC 20036-5200

KAUFFMAN, CHARLES WILLIAM, aerospace engineer; b. Waynesboro, Pa., Dec. 6, 1939; s. Charles Edgar and Florence Evelyn (Neibert) K.; m. Carol Ann Dussinger, Sept. 12, 1964. MS, Pa. State U., 1963; PhD, U. Mich., 1971. Engr. Martin Aircraft Co., Balt., 1961-62; physicist HRB-Singer Inc., State College, Pa., 1963-65; asst. prof. U. Cin., 1971-75, assoc. prof., 1975-77; rsch. scientist U. Mich., Ann Arbor, 1977-85, assoc. prof., 1986-95, prof., 1995—. Pres. Explosion Rsch., Whitmore Lake, Mich., 1981—; bd. dirs. ViewNet, Virtual Interactive East West Network for Engring. and Tech.; cons. OSHA, Washington, 1979—, EPA, Washington, 1997—; mem. aero. regulatory adv. commn. FAA, Excom and Fuel Tank Inerting. Contbr. articles to profl. jours. Recipient Smolenski medal Polish Acad. of Sci., 1988, Computerworld Smithsonian award 1998. Mem. ASME, AIAA, Combustion Inst. (pres. ctrl. state sect. 1991-95), Soc. Automotive Engrs. Episcopalian. Home: 9669 Hermitage Way Whitmore Lake MI 48189-9624 Office: U Mich Dept Aerospace Engring Ann Arbor MI 48109-2140 E-mail: cwkauff@engin.umich.edu.

KAUFFMAN, DAGMAR ELISABETH, writer, researcher; b. Hamburg, Federal Republic of Germany, Feb. 24, 1961; came to U.S., 1983; d. Gustav Ewald and Margot Hildegard (Holz) Franke; m. Bruce Alan Kauffman, July 25, 1986; children: Philip Uwe, Patrick Axel. BA, U. Hamburg, 1984; MA, U. Md., 1987, postgrad., 1987-90. Rschr., teaching asst. U. Hamburg, Germany, 1982-83; edit./ mktg. asst. Ednl. Svc. USA Today, Arlington, Va., 1983-84; adminstrv. asst. U. Md., Coll. Pk., Md., 1985-86; rschr., info. program assoc. Am. Assn. Coll. for Tchr. Edn., Washington, 1986-89; freelance rschr., edn. writer Columbia, Md., 1989-97; PTA pres., substitute tchr. Internat. Sch. Hamburg, Germany, 1998-99; freelance writer/rschr. Hamburg, Germany, 1997-99. Editl. cons. Morgan Fin. Group, Balt., 1993-95. Author, rschr.: A Practical Guide to Recruiting Minority Teachers, 1989, Comprehensive Services Guide, 1995; editor: Minority Teacher Recruitment and Retention: A Public Policy Issue, 1987; contbr. articles to profl. jours. Pres. PTA, Internat. Sch. of Hamburg. German Acad. Exch. Svc. scholar, 1983-84. Mem.: Chgo. Coun. on Fgn. Affairs, Am. Studies Assn., Sister Cities Internat., Mothers and More, Am. Women's Club Hamburg. Democrat. Lutheran. Avocations: travel, literature, sports, politics. E-mail: dkauffman@wideopenwest.com.

KAUFFMAN, GEORGE BERNARD, chemistry educator; b. Phila., Sept. 4, 1930; s. Philip Joseph and Laura (Fisher) K.; m. Ingeborg Salomon, June 5, 1952 (div. Dec. 1969); children: Ruth Deborah (Mrs. Martin H. Bryskier), Judith Miriam (Mrs. Mario L. Reposo); m. Laurie Marks Papazian, Dec. 21, 1969; stepchildren: Stanley Robert Papazian, Teresa Lynn Papazian Baron, Mary Ellen Papazian. BA with honors, U. Pa., 1951; PhD, U. Fla., 1956. Grad. asst. U. Fla., 1951-55; rsch. participant Oak Ridge Nat. Lab., 1955; instr. U. Tex., Austin, 1955-56; rsch. chemist Humble Oil & Refining Co., Baytown, Tex., 1956, GE, Cin., 1957, 59; asst. prof. chemistry Calif. State U., Fresno, 1956-61, assoc. prof., 1961-66, prof., 1966—. Guest lectr. coop. lecture tours Am. Chem. Soc., 1971; vis. scholar U. Calif., Berkeley, 1976, U. Puget Sound, 1978; dir. undergrad. rsch. participation program NSF, 1972. Author: Alfred Werner— Founder of Coordination Chemistry, 1966, Classics in Coordination Chemistry, Part I, 1968, Part II, 1976, Part III, 1978, Werner Centennial, 1967, Teaching the History of Chemistry, 1971, Coordination Chemistry: Its History through the Time of Werner, 1977, Inorganic Coordination Compounds, 1981, The Central Science: Essays on the Uses of Chemistry, 1984, Frederick Soddy (1877-1956): Early Pioneer in Radiochemistry, 1986, Aleksandr Porfirevich Borodin: A Chemist's Biography, 1988, Coordination Chemistry: A Century of Progress, 1994, Classics in Coordination Chemistry, 1995, Metal and Nonmetal Biguanide Complexes, 1999; contbr. articles to profl. jours.; contbg. editor: Jour. Coll. Sci. Tchg., 1973—, The Hexagon, 1980—, Polyhedron, 1983-85, Industrial Chemist, 1985-88, Jour. Chem. Edn., 1987—, Today's Chemist, 1989-91, The Chemical Intelligencer, 1994-2000, Today's Chemist at Work, 1995—, Chemical Heritage, 1996—, The Chemical Educator, 1998—, Chem. 13 News, 1998—; guest editor: Coodination Chemistry Centennial Symposium (C3S) issue, Polyhedron, 1994; editor tape lecture series: Am. Chem. Soc, 1975-81. Named Outstanding Prof., Calif. State U. and Colls. Sys., 1973; recipient Exceptional Merit Svc. award, 1984, Meritorious Performance and Profl. Promise award, 1986-87, 88-89, Coll. Chemistry Tchr. Excellence award Mfg. Chemists Assn., 1976, Chugaev medal, 1976, Kurnakov medal, 1990, Chernyaev medal, 1991, USSR Acad. Sci., George C. Pimentel award in chem. edn. Am. Chem. Soc., 1993, Dexter award in history of chemistry, 1978, Marc-Auguste Pictet medal Soc. Physique et d'Histoire Naturelle de Genève, 1992, Pres.'s medal of Distinction, Calif. State U., Fresno, 1994, Rsch. award at an Undergraduate Instn., Am. Chem. Soc., 2000, Laudatory Decree Inst. History of Sci. and Tech. Russian Acad. Sci., 2000; Rsch. Corp. grantee, 1956-57, 57-59, 59-61, Am. Chem. Soc. Petroleum Rsch. Fund grantee, 1963-64, 69-70, NSF grantee, 1960-61, 63-64, 67-69, 76-77, NEH grantee, 1982-83; John Simon Guggenheim Meml. Found. fellow, 1972-73, grantee, 1975; Strindberg fellow Swedish Inst., Stockholm, 1983. Fellow: AAAS; mem.: Mensa, Am. Chem. Soc. (chmn. divsn. history of chemistry 1969, mem. exec. com. 1970, councilor 1976—78, George C. Pimentel award in chem. edn. 1993, Helen M. Free Pub. Outreach award 2002), Soc. History Alchemy and Chemistry, History of Sci. Soc., Assn. Univ. Pa. Chemists, AAUP, Gamma Sigma Epsilon, Alpha Chi Sigma, Phi Kappa Phi, Phi Lambda Upsilon, Sigma Xi. Home: 1609 E Quincy Ave Fresno CA 93720-2309 Office: Calif State U Dept Chemistry Fresno CA 93740-8034 E-mail: georgek@csufresno.edu.

KAUFFMAN, JOEL MERVIN, chemistry educator, researcher, consultant; b. Phila., Jan. 3, 1937; s. david and Mathilde (Goldstein) K.; m. Thea Barbara Feldman, June 20, 1967 (div. Mar. 1980); m. Helen Ehrlich Plotkin, June 6, 1981 (dec. Sept. 20, 2000); children; Michael, Alec. BS in Chemistry, Phila. Coll. Pharmacy and Sci., 1958; PhD in Organic Chemistry, MIT, 1963. Sr. develop. chemist I.C.I. Organics Inc., Dighton, Mass., 1964-66; rsch. assoc. Mass. Coll. Pharmacy and Sci., Boston, 1966-67, 77-79; dir. R & D div. pilot chems. New England Nuclear Corp., Watertown, Mass., 1969-76; from asst. to assoc. prof. chemistry Phila. Coll. Pharmacy and Sci., 1979—92, prof., 1992—97; rsch. prof. U. of Scis. Phila. (formerly Phila. Coll. Pharmacy and Sci.), 1997—2001, ret., 2001, prof. chemistry emeritus, 2002—. Cons. Franklin Rsch. Ctr., Phila., 1982-90. Contbr. chpts. to books, articles to profl. jours. including Jour. Organic Chemistry, Jour. Pharm. Scis., Jour. Chem. Engring. Data, Optics Communus, Jour. Chem. Edn., Jour. Sci. Exploration, Pharmacotherapy, Science, Jour. Am. Phys. Surgery, numerous others. Mem. Ams. for Legal Reform, Washington, 1985—; assoc. Consumers Union, Yonkers, N.Y., 1991-2002, CSICOP, 1993-98, The Skeptic Soc., 1998—; mem. Am. United Separation Ch. of State, 1994—. Recipient Am. Inst. Chemists medal, 1958, Merck Chemistry award, Alumni medal Phila. Coll. Pharmacy and Sci.; grantee NSF, NIH, Dept. of Energy. Mem. Am. Chem. Soc. (award), Nat. Motorists Assn., Planned Parenthood, Soc. of Sci. Exploration, 1998—, www.thincs.org. Achievements include patents in Process of Preparing Nitrosocarborane Monomers, Process for Preparing a Thiodiacyl Halide, Compositions and Process for Liquid Scintillation Counting, o,o-Bridged Oligophenylene Laser Dyes, and Dyestuff Lasers, and Methods of lasing Therewith, Radiation Hard Plastic Scintillator, Porton-Transfer Fluors; AntipTuberculosis Drugs; Halogenated Antituberculosis Agents; research in antineoplastic drugs, direct synthesis of heterocyclic thiols, bridged quarterphenyls as flashlamp-pumpable laser dyes, new high efficiency fluors for liquid scintillation counting and bichemical staining, glycosides and pseudoglycosides of 1,2,4-triazines as potential immunogenetic anticancer drugs, antituberculosis drugs, design of radiation-hard fluors, development of oligophenylene laser dyes, photophysical properties of some new protein-transfer fluors, others. Home: 65 Meadowbrook Rd Wayne PA 19087-2510 E-mail: kauffman@hslc.org.

KAUFFMAN, KAETHE COVENTON, art educator, artist, author; b. Washington, Aug. 12, 1948; d. Richard G. and Kathleen B. (Coventon) K.; m. James William Hite, Oct. 23, 1983; children: James Haydn, Kauffman Hite. BA, U. Wash., 1970, U. Nev., 1975; MFA, U. Calif., Irvine, 1978; PhD, Union Inst. Cin., 1989. Art dept. faculty U. Nev., Las Vegas, Mount St. Mary's Coll., L.A.;

chmn. art dept. Sierra Nevada Coll., Incline Village, 1989-91, assoc. prof., 1991-2001, Chaminade U., Honolulu, 2001—, adj. faculty, 2001—. Faculty dept. art U. Calif., Irvine; bd. dirs. Buddhist Studies Ctr. Press. Author: Sex and the Avant-Garde: A Gender Revolution in the Visual Arts 1830-1993, Female Forms of Originality and the New, Women Artists in the Avant-Garde, How Art Professors Teach Avant-Garde Values, Women Artists Deconstruct the Male Avant-Garde, A Modern Renaissance of the Arts; columnist: Lake Tahoe World newspapers; art exhibited at Utrecht, Holland, 1977, Inst. Modern Art, Brisbane, Australia, 1978, George Patton Gallery U. Melbourne, Australia, 1979, Newport Harbor Art Mus., Calif., 1980, Fiberworks Gallery, Berkeley, Calif., 1981, Galerie Triangle, Washington, 1982, Nev. Mus., Reno, 1983, Schoharie Nat., Cobleskill, N.Y., 1984, Pinnacle Gallery, N.Y., 1986, Space Gallery, Las Vegas, Nev., 1988, Manville Gallery, U. Nev., Reno, 1989, Galerie Art-Jeunesse, Montreal, Que., 1990, Kleinert Gallery, N.Y., 1991, West Gallery, Claremont Grad. Sch., 1992, Sierra Nev. Coll. Art Gallery, Lake Tahoe, Nev., 1995, Exhbn. Hall U. Prague, Czech Republic, CERES Gallery, N.Y., Women's UN Conf., Beijing, Nat. Mus. Women in Arts, Washington, Gallery of the Pali, Honolulu, Czech Mus. Fine Arts, Prague; represented in permanent collections Women's Studio Workshop, N.Y.C., Calif. Mus. Photography, L.A., Fluor Corp., L.A., Harris Found., Las Vegas, Nev., Computer Scis. Corp., L.A., Sheraton Plaza Inn, L.A., Glendale Fed. Bank, L.A.; mem. editl. bd. Collegiate Press. Juror 3d biennial Nev. Craft Show. Recipient Max H. Block award for Humanism, Juror's award Am. Pen Women Bienniale, Dr. Wu and Elsie Ject-Key meml. award for photography Nat. Assn. Women Artists, N.Y.; Laguna Beach Festival of the Arts fellow; TOSCO Corp. grantee; Artists grantee Sierra Arts Found. Mem. Nat. Mus. Women in Arts, Women's Caucus for Art, Nat. Assn. for Women Artists (medal of honor for works on paper, Elizabeth Morse Genius Found. award), Ceres Gallery, Am. Pen Women (3 awards for non-fiction writing nat. competition), Arts and Letters, Natl. Assn. for Women Artists.

KAUFFMAN, KENT DAVID, law educator; b. Portland, Oreg., Sept. 9, 1967; s. Luke Edward and Sandy Jean Kauffman; m. Karen Lynn Kauffman. BA summa cum laude, Temple U., 1989; JD, Pa. State U., 1992. Bar: Ind. 1996, cert.: (civil mediation) 1997, (domestic mediation) 1998. Program chair Ivy Tech State Coll., Fort Wayne, Ind., 1995—; adj. prof. Ind. U.-Purdue U., Fort Wayne, 1996—. Seminar spkr. Half Moon Seminars, LLC, Eau Claire, Wis., N.E. Ind. Paralegal Assn., Fort Wayne. Author: (textbook and instr. manual) Legal Ethics, 2002; contbr. articles to profl. jours. Mem.: NRA, AAUP, ABA, Ind. State Bar Assn. (seminar spkr.), BMW Car Club Am. Avocations: guitar, investing. Home: 740 Ireland Dr Warsaw IN 46580 Office: Ivy Tech State Coll 3800 N Anthony Blvd Fort Wayne IN 46805 Office Fax: 260-480-2051. Personal E-mail: double67@kconline.com. Business E-Mail: kkauffma@ivytech.edu.

KAUFFMAN, KREG ARLEN, lawyer; b. Des Moines, May 24, 1950; s. Arlo B. and Helen M. (Crouse) Kauffman; m. Georgia Ann Millhollin, Aug. 11, 1973; children: Katherine Elizabeth, Alex Kreg. BA, U. Iowa, 1972, JD, 1977. Bar: Minn. 1977, U.S. Dist. Ct. Minn. 1978, Iowa 1982, U.S. Dist. Ct. (no. and so. dists.) Iowa 1986, Wis. 1992. Law clk. to presiding justice Minn. 3d Jud. Dist. Ct., Faribault, 1977—78; assoc. Dunlap, Keith, Finseth, Berndt & Sandberg, Rochester, Minn., 1978—82, asst. atty. gen. State of Iowa, Des Moines, 1982—85; atty. Dingle, Wendland & Kauffman, Ltd., Rochester, 1985—93; prin. Kauffman Law Firm, Rochester, 1993—. Legal advisor Delta Chi, Iowa City, 1978—90; civil trial advocate Nat. Bd. Trial Advocates. Bd. dirs. mayor's adv. com on alcohol and drug abuse, Rochester, 1978—90; mem. Rochester brain injury com. Brain Injury Assn.; bd. dirs., past pres. Southeastern Minn. Ctr. Ind. Living. Mem.: ABA, Acad. Cert. Trial Lawyers Assn. (treas., sec., past dean), Minn. State Bar Assn. (cert. civil trial specialist, civil litigation sect. coun.), Minn. Trial Lawyers Assn. (bd. govs., mem. exec. com.), Olmsted County Bar Assn. Home: 734 11th St SW Rochester MN 55902-6339

KAUFFMAN, MARVIN EARL, geoscience consultant; b. Lancaster, Pa., Aug. 31, 1933; s. D. Ivan and Leah Kauffman; m. Sue Cox (Pilgrim); children: Dorinda, Barbara, Douglas, Betsy, Ruth, Peter, Philip. BS, Franklin and Marshall Coll., 1955; MS, Northwestern U., 1957; PhD, Princeton U., 1960. Prof. and past chmn. dept. geology Franklin & Marshall Coll., Lancaster, Pa., 1959-84; exec. dir. Am. Geol. Inst., Alexandria, Va., 1985-90; program dir. Nat. Sci. Found., Washington, 1990-94; cons., 1994—. Cons. Martin Marietta Corp., Balt., 1964-65, R.E. Wright Assocs., Middletown, Pa., 1978-81, 1990-91, Meiser & Earl Assocs., State Coll., Pa., 1981-84; vis. prof. U. Christchurch & Dunedin, New Zealand, 1994-95; adj. prof. geoscis. Mont. State U., Western Mont. Coll., Dillon, U. Mont., Billings. Author: (with others) Physical Geology, 1978, 5th, 6th edit., 1982, 7th edit., 1987, 8th edit., 1990. NSF Grad. fellow, 1955-59, sci. faculty fellow 1965-66. Fellow Geol. Soc. Am.; mem. Nat. Assn. Geology Tchrs. (pres. 1983-84). Methodist. Home and Office: 540 Upper Continental Dr PO Box 833 Red Lodge MT 59068-0833

KAUFFMAN, ROBERT PORTER, gynecologist, educator; b. Houston, Tex., Apr. 8, 1954; s. Arnold Edwin and Elizabeth Siler Kauffman; m. Rosalie Michele Milburn, Apr. 19, 1988; children: Elisabeth Frances Milburn, Mary Katherine Milburn. BA, U. Tex., Austin, 1976; MD, U. Tex., Houston, 1979. Diplomate Am. Bd. Ob-Gyn. Clin. asst. prof. U. Tex. Southwestern Med. Sch., Dallas, 1983—97; pvt. practice North Dallas Ob-Gyn. Assocs., Dallas, 1983—97; asst. prof. ob-gyn. Tex. Tech U. Sch. of Medicine, Amarillo, Tex., 1999—. Dir., reproductive medicine and infertility, dept ob-gyn. Tex. Tech U. Sch. of Medicine, Amarillo, Tex., 1999—. Contbr. articles and revs. to profl. jours. Mem. physician health and rehab. com. Tex. Tech U. Med. Sch., Amarillo, Tex., 2002—03; bd. trustees Parish Episc. Sch. Dallas, Dallas, 1985—88; vestryman Episcopal Ch. of the Transfiguration, Dallas, 1989—91. Fellow: ACOG, Am. Soc. Reproductive Medicine, Tex. Assn. of Obstetricians and Gynecologists; mem.: Potter-Randall County Med. Soc. (editor Panhandle Health 2002—, editl. bd. 2001—02), N.Y. Acad. Scis., Am. Soc. Reproductive Immunology, European Soc. for Human Reproduction and Embryology, Endocrine Soc., Amarillo Country Club. Episcopal. Achievements include research in Mexican American women with polycystic ovary disease. Avocations: swimming, piano, opera. Office: Texas Tech Univ Health Sci Ctr 1400 Coulter Amarillo TX 79106 Office Fax: 806-354-5516. E-mail: robertk@ama.ttuhsc.edu.

KAUFFMAN, TERRY, broadcast and creative arts communication educator, artist; b. San Francisco, Aug. 24, 1951; d. Raymond Roger and Patricia Virginia Kauffman. BA in Journalism with hons., U. Calif., Berkeley, 1974; MA in Comm. summa cum laude, U. Tex., 1980; PhD in Psychology, Comm., and Creative Expression with distinction, Union Inst., 1996. With Alta. Ednl. TV, 1976; sr. writer, prodr. and dir. Ampex Corp., Calif., 1980; writer, news prodr., reporter, anchor ABC, Tex., 1974-75; mem. faculty dept. radio, TV and motion pictures U. N.C., Chapel Hill, 1985; mem. faculty dept. comm. N.C. State U., Raleigh, 1986—2001; founder, artist Cozy Cards, Cards by Terry, 2000—. Adj. prof. music, theatre and comm. dept. Meredith Coll., Raleigh, 1990—; adv. bd. chmn. publicity Raleigh Conservatory Music; v.p. Wake Visual Arts Assn. and Gallery; tchr. art Meredith Coll., 1995—, founder, owner Creative Spaces; expressive art therapist at psychit. hosps. and pvt., 1994—. Author: I'm Clueless, Confessions of a College Teacher, The Script as Blueprint, 1994, 8 vol. set poetry including Psalms of Teresa, Secret Place, Just Visiting, others; author numerous poems; composer, prodr., dir. When the Wind Blows, The Rainbow, The Seasons of Change, PBS, Women Today, Profiles in Leadership, Little Miss Puppet Talks to the Angels, I'm One Person or Another, One; commd. and exhibited in solo shows (1st place painting), San Francisco, Raleigh; artist for documentary series, rschr., writer, Alta., Can., 1976; prodr., dir., writer, composer I'm One Person...Or The Other, Thanksgiving (PBS), 1980—; writer, prodr. Consumer Hotline, PBS, Customs Operations at the Border; main character, vocalist, composer Little Miss Puppet Talks to the Angels; pub. music book: Songs by Terry Kauffman. Singer/composer for chs. and retirement homes; past bd. dirs. Tex. Consumer Assn., Wake visual Arts. Named Outstanding Lectr. of Yr., Coll. of Humanities and Social Scis., N.C. State U., 1996; recipient Emmy nomination for documentary Otters from Oiled Waters, 1991, more than 15 1st place nat. awards in TV, including writing, producing, directing, music composition, acting, art and photography, vrious art and music shows. Mem. APA, NATAS, Internat. TV Assn. (judge nat. contests), Nat. Broadcasting Soc. (8 1st place nat. awards 1973—, named Outstanding Mem., 1993-94, Profl. Mem. of Yr. 1994), Internat. Expressive Art Therapists Assn., Calif. Scholastic Fedn. (life), Calif. Scholastic Assn., Berkeley Honor Soc., Am. Psychol. Assn., Phi Kappa Phi. Home: 407 Furches St Raleigh NC 27607-4017

KAUFFMAN, TIM L. physical therapist, educator; b. Lancaster, Pa., Apr. 23, 1948; s. Walter L. Kauffman and Lillian J. Geisler; m. Brenda Gene Shrum, Mar. 13, 1971; children: Benjamin W., Emily S. BA, Gettysburg (Pa.) Coll., 1970; MS, Med. Coll. of Va., Richmond, 1979; PhD, LaSalle U., Mandeville, La., 1998. Cert. physical therapy U. Pa., 1971, Wash., 1971, Va., 1977, Pa., 1981. Staff phys. therapist Madigan Army Med. Ctr., Tacoma, 1971—74; chief phys. therapist 56 Sta. Hosp., Bad Kahnstadt, Germany, 1974—77, Va. Rehab., Richmond, 1979—81; pvt. practice Kauffman Gamber, Lancaster, Pa., 1981—; adj. faculty Hahnemann U., Phila., 1987—, Lebanon Valley Coll., Annville, Pa., 2001—. Bd. dir. sect. on geriat. Am. Phys. Therapy Assn., Washington, 2000—; editl. bd. Physiotherapy Theory and Practice, 1984—, Jour. Geriat. Phys. Therapy, 1994—; vis. prof. Health Vols. Overseas, Paramaribo, Suriname, 2000. Editor: Geriat. Rehab. Manual, 1999; co-editor: (journal) History of Sect. on Geriat., 2003; contbr. articles to profl. jours. Referee Ea. Pa. Rugby Referee Soc., Phila., 1995—; coach Lancaster Youth Soccer, 1988—94; dir. adult Sunday sch. Grandview Heights United Meth. Ch., Lancaster, 1985—94. With USAR, 1968—, lt. col. USAR, 1983—. Recipient Joan Mille award, Sect. on Geriat., 1990, Lucy Blair award, Am. Physiotherapy Assn., 1990. Mem.: Gerontology Assn. Am, Sports Medicine sect. Am. Phys. Therapy Assn. Independent. Methodist. Avocations: rugby, soccer, mountain climbing, scuba diving, travel.

KAUFFMAN, WILLIAM JOSEPH, writer, editor; b. Batavia, N.Y., Nov. 15, 1959; s. Edward Joseph and Sandra Jean (Baker) K.; m. Lucine Margaret Andonian, May 22, 1987; 1 child, Gretel. BA, U. Rochester, 1981. Rsch. asst. Senator D.P. Moynihan, Washington, 1981-82, legis. asst., 1982-83; asst. editor Reason, Santa Barbara, Calif., 1985-86, Washington, 1986-87; assoc. editor The Am. Enterprise, Washington, 1994—. Author: Every Man a King, 1989, Country Towns of New York, 1994, America First! Its History, Culture and Politics, 1995, With Good Intentions? Reflections on the Myth of Progress in America, 1998, Dispatches from the Muckdog Gazette, 2003. Dir. Genesee Landmark Soc., 1993—, Holland Purchase Hist. Soc., 1993—, Friends of the Richmond Meml. Libr., 1995—. Roman Catholic. Avocations: astronomy, music, collecting coins and political campaign items. Home: 28 Chapel St PO Box 266 Elba NY 14058-0266 E-mail: bkauffman@2ki.net.

KAUFFMANN, ROBERT FREDRICK, software engineer; b. Willingboro, N.J., Dec. 13, 1963; s. Robert Albert and Lori Kathleen (Mastroni) K. AS in Computer Sci., Burlington County Coll., Pemberton, N.J., 1984; BA in Computer Sci., Rutgers U., 1987; postgrad., N.J. Inst. Tech., 1995. Engr. software Computer Scis. Corp., Moorestown, N.J., 1989—. Illustrator Robert's Rhymes, 1988; filmmaker Animated Shorts, 1995, Mask of Ollock, 1999; author: The Mask of Ollock, 2000. Recipient Silver award Artist's Guild of Delaware Valley, 1997, Bronze award Worldfest Houston, 1997, Benton Spruance award Phila. Watercolor Club, 2000, cert. merit Rochester Internat. Film Festival, 2000. Mem. IEEE Computer Soc., Internat. Animated Film Assn. Avocations: Karate, poetry. Home: 2401 Arden Rd Cinnaminson NJ 08077-3601 E-mail: rkauffmann@csc.com.

KAUFFMANN, STANLEY JULES, author; b. N.Y.C., Apr. 24, 1916; s. Joseph H. and Jeannette (Steiner) K.; m. Laura Cohen, Feb. 5, 1943. B.F.A., NYU, 1935. Mem. Washington Sq. Players, 1931-41; assoc. editor Bantam Books, 1949-52; editor-in-chief Ballantine Books, 1952-56, consulting editor, 1957-59; editor Alfred A. Knopf, 1959-60; film critic New Republic, N.Y.C., 1958-65, 67—, assoc. lit. editor, 1966-67; theater critic New York Times, 1966, New Republic, N.Y.C., 1969-79, Saturday Rev., 1979-85. Condr. program The Art of Film, Channel 13, N.Y.C., 1963-67; vis. prof. Sch. of Drama, Yale U., 1967-86, 95, 97; vis. prof. CUNY, 1973-76, 77-92, Hunter Coll, 1993—; Disting. vis. prof. Adelphi U., 1992-94, profl. performing arts, 1994-96. Author: The Hidden Hero, 1949, The Tightrope, 1952, A Change of Climate, 1954, Man of the World, 1956, A World on Film, 1966, Figures of Light, 1971, editor: (with Bruce Henstell) American Film Criticism: from the Beginnings to Citizen Kane, 1973, Living Images, 1975, Persons of The Drama, 1976, Before My Eyes, 1980, Albums of Early Life, 1980, Theater Criticisms, 1983, Field of View, 1986, Distinguishing Features, 1994, Regarding Film, 2001. Recipient George Jean Nathan award for dramatic criticism, 1972-73, George Polk award for criticism, 1982, Outstanding Tchr. award Assn. for Theater in Higher Edn., 1995, Telluride Film Festival medal, 1998; Ford Found. fellow for study abroad, 1964, 71, hon. fellow Morse Coll., Yale U., 1964, Guggenheim fellow, 1979-80. Address: 10 W 15th St New York NY 10011-6838

KAUFFOLD, RUTH ELIZABETH, clinical psychologist; b. Decatur, Ill., Sept. 5, 1946; d. James Henry and Elizabeth Opal Kauffold; m. Paul Dwight Entner, Aug. 23, 1968; 1 child, James Paul. BA, Cedarville (Ohio) Coll., 1968; MEd, Wright State U., 1972; MS, U. Dayton, 1986; Ph.D, The Union Inst., 1997. Tchr. Springfield (Ohio) Pub. Schs., 1968-72, Pomona (Calif.) Unified Sch. Dist., 1973-76, Bethel Sch. Dist., New Carlisle, Ohio, 1977-81; practicum Sycamore Hosp., Miamisburg, Ohio, 1994; intern, resident clin. psychology Agape Counseling Ctr., Centerville, 1995-2000. Co-hostess radio talk show WHIO Radio Sta., Dayton, 1998; lectr. nat. and internat. profl. convs.; spkr. AACC World Conf., 2001. Lectr., missionary Project Ptnr., Lima, Peru, 1986; lectr., tchr. For Hills Bapt. Ch., Dayton, Ohio, 1997; lectr., tchr. Fair Haven Ch., 2000. Jennings scholar Martha Holden Jennings Found., 1972. Mem. APA, Dayton Area Psychol. Assn. Avocations: interior design, architecture, gardening, reading, walking. Office: Agape Counseling Ctr 175 S Main St Centerville OH 45458-2372

KAUFMAN, ALAN, internist, allergist; b. Lakewood, NJ, Oct. 22; 1958; MD, Ross U., Roseau, 1984. Diplomate Am. Bd. Allergy and Immunology, Am. Bd. Internal Medicine. Resident in internal medicine Metro Hosp. Ctr., NYC, 1984—87; fellow allergy and immunology Albert Einstein Coll. Medicine, Bronx, N.Y., 1987-89; internist Westchester Sq. Hosp. Ctr., Bronx, 1989—; cons. Lawrence Hosp. Ctr., Bronxville, NY, 2002—. Dir. adult allergy clinic Our Lady Mercy Med. Ctr., Bronx; dir. allergy clinic Terence Cardinal Cooke Health Care Ctr., NY. Fellow: Am. Coll. Allergy, Asthma and Immunology, Am. Acad. Allergy, Asthma and Immunology; mem.: ACP, Westchester Allergy Soc., NY Allergy Soc. Office: 559 Gramatan Ave Mount Vernon NY 10552-2155 also: Lauren Profl Bldg 3626 E Tremont Ave Bronx NY 10465-2030

KAUFMAN, ALAN STEPHEN, psychologist, educator; b. NYC, Apr. 21, 1944; s. Max and Blanche (Levine) K.; m. Nadeen Laurie Bengels, Dec. 20, 1964; children: Jennie Lynn, David Scott, James Corey. BA, U. Pa., 1965; MA, Columbia U., 1967, PhD, 1970. Assoc. prof. psychology U. Ga., Athens, 1974-79, U. Ill., Chgo., 1979-80; prof. psychology Nat. Coll. Edn., Evanston, Ill., 1980-82, Calif. Sch. Profl. Psychology, San Diego, 1982-84; rsch. prof. U. Ala., Tuscaloosa, 1984-95; sr. rsch. scientist Psychol. Assessment Resources, Inc., Odessa, Fla., 1995-97; clin. prof. psychology Yale U. Sch. Medicine, New Haven, 1997—. Author: Intelligent Testing with the WISC R, 1979, Assessing Adolescent and Adult Intelligence, 1990, Intelligent Testing with the WISC-III, 1994, (with Nadeen Kaufman) Clinical Evaluation of Young Children, 1977, Specific Learning Disabiities in Children and Adolescents, 2001; (with E. Lichtenberger) Essentials of WAIS-III Assessment, 1999, Assessing Adolscent and Adult Intelligence, 2d edit., 2002; writer tests (with Nadeen Kaufman) including K-ABC and others; co-editor: Research in the Schools; mem. editl. bd. Sch. Psychology Quar., Archives Clin. Neuropsychology, Psychology in Schs., Jour. Psychoednl. Assessment, Ednl. and Psychol. Measurement; patentee psychol. testing device. Recipient Outstanding Rsch. award Ariz. Assn. Sch. Psychologists, 1980, Award for Excellence, Mensa Edn. and Rsch. Found., 1989. Fellow APA (Sr. Scientist award divsn. 16, 1997), Am. Psychol. Soc.; mem. Nat. Assn. Sch. Psychologists, Nat. Coun. Measurement in Edn., Coun. for Exceptional Children, Am. Ednl. Rsch. Assn., Mid-South Ednl. Rsch. Assn. (Outstanding Rsch. award 1988, 93), Phi Beta Kappa, Sigma Xi. Avocation: researching baseball. Home: 8721 Sherwood Forest Ct Escondido CA 92026 Office: Yale Child Study Ctr PO Box 207900 New Haven CT 06520-7900 E-mail: alanadeen@att.net.

KAUFMAN, ALBERT I. lawyer; b. N.Y.C., Oct. 2, 1936; s. Israel and Pauline (Pardes) K.; m. Ruth Feldman, Jan. 25, 1959; 1 son, Michael Paul. AA, L.A. City Coll., 1957; BA, U. San Fernando Valley, 1964, JD, 1966. Bar: Calif. 1967, U.S. Ct. Appeals (9th cir.) 1968, U.S. Supreme Ct. 1971, U.S. Dist. Ct. (cen. dist.) Calif. 1967, U.S. Tax Ct. 1971, U.S. Ct. Internat. Trade 1981. Sole practice, Woodland Hills, Calif., 1967—; judge pro tem L.A. Mcpl. Ct., 1980—, L.A. Superior Ct., 1991—; family law mediator L.A. Superior Ct., 1980—. Mem. Pacific S.W. regional bd. Anti-Defamation league of B'nai B'rith, 1970-91. Served with USAF, 1959-65, to col. CAP, 1956—. Recipient Disting. Svc. award B'nai B'rith, 1969; Exceptional Svc. award CAP, 1977, 95. Mem. ABA, L.A. County Bar Assn., San Fernando Valley Bar Assn., Consumer Atty. of Calif., Consumer Atty. Assn. L.A. Republican. Clubs: Toastmasters, Westerners 1117 (pres. 1969), B'nai B'rith (pres. 1971-72), Santa Monica Yacht (judge adv.) Office: 22900 Ventura Blvd Ste 205 Woodland Hills CA 91364 E-mail: lawyer4@earthlink.net.

KAUFMAN, ANDREW LEE, law educator; b. Newark, Feb. 1, 1931; s. Samuel and Sylvia (Meltzer) K.; m. Linda P. Sonnenschein, June 14, 1959; children: Anne, David, Elizabeth, Daniel. AB, Harvard U., 1951, LL.B., 1954. Bar: D.C. 1954, Mass. 1979, U.S. Supreme Ct. 1961. Assoc. Bilder, Bilder & Kaufman, Newark, 1954-55; law clk. to Justice Felix Frankfurter U.S Supreme Ct., 1955-57; ptnr. Kaufman, Kaufman & Kaufman, Newark, 1957-65; lectr. in law Harvard U., Cambridge, Mass., 1965-66, prof., 1966-81, Charles Stebbins Fairchild prof. law, 1981—, assoc. dean, 1986-89. Author: (with others) Commercial Law, 1971, 82, Problems in Professional Responsibility, 1976, 84, 89, 2002, Cardozo, 1998. Treas. Shady Hill Sch., 1969-76; treas. Hillel Found. Cambridge, Inc., 1977-86. Mem. Mass. Bar Assn. (chmn. com. profl. ethics 1982—). Office: Harvard U Law Sch Cambridge MA 02138 E-mail: kaufman@law.harvard.edu.

KAUFMAN, ANDREW MICHAEL, lawyer; b. Boston, Feb. 19, 1949; s. Earle Bertram and Miriam (Halpern) K.; m. Michele Moselle, Aug. 24, 1975; children: Peter Moselle, Melissa Lanes, Caroline Raney. BA cum laude, Yale U., 1971; JD, Vanderbilt U., 1974. Bar: Tex. 1974, Ga. 1976, Ill. 1993, U.S. Ct. Appeals (5th and 11th cirs.) 1981. Assoc. Vinson & Elkins, Houston, 1974-76, ptnr., 1982-83, Austin, 1983-92, Dallas, 1992; assoc. Sutherland, Asbill & Brennan, Atlanta, 1976-80, ptnr., 1980-81, Kirkland & Ellis, Chgo., 1993—. Editor in chief Vanderbilt U. Law Rev., 1973-74. Mem. nat. alumni bd. Vanderbilt U.Law Sch., 1994—2000; Alumni fund raiser Yale U., 1971—; mem. Alumni Schs. Com. Yale U., 1986—92; mem. med. ethics coun. Seton Hosp., 1988—92; participant Leadership Austin, 1987—88; bd. dirs. KLRU-TV, 1989—93; mem. Austin (Tex.) Entrepreneurs Coun., 1991—92; mem. adv. bd. Dallas Bus. Com. Arts Leadership Inst., 1992—93; governing bd. mem. Chgo. Symphony Orch.; bd. dirs. United Way, Austin, Tex.; pub. TV Ballet Austin, Tex., 1986—92; mem. adv. bd. Austin Tech. Incubator, 1989—93. Mem. ABA (bus. law sect. 1978—, chmn. lease financing and secured transactions subcom. of com. devels. in bus. financing 1993-99, UCC com., legal opinions com., comml. fin. svcs. com.), Tex. Bar Assn., Yale U. Alumni Assn., Order of Coif, Headliners Club, Yale Club, N.Y.C. and Chgo., Knights of the Symphony Austin. Avocation: sailing. Office: Kirkland & Ellis 200 E Randolph St Fl 54 Chicago IL 60601-6636 E-mail: Andrew.Kaufman@chicago.kirkland.com.

KAUFMAN, ANGELA J. music educator; b. Freeman, S.D., Jan. 29, 1962; d. Larry Duane and Lois Marie Kaufman; m. Robert Ronald Perkinson, Sept. 20, 1991; children: Robert, Nyshie, Shane. AA, Freeman Jr. Coll., 1982; BA in Music Edn., U. Sioux Falls, 1984. 5-12 grade band instr. Montrose (S.D.) H.S., 1984—86; 9-12 grade band instr. Freeman Acad., 1986—87; 4-6 grade vocal/band tchr. Sioux Falls (S.D.) Pub. Schs., 1986-96, K-5 grade vocal/band tchr., 1996-97; music tchr. Angela's Sch. Music, Canton, SD, 1998—2001; tchr. K-4 gen. music, h.s. jazz band Canton (S.D.) Schs., 2001—02. Vocal judge vocal contest and all state chorus, various cities, S.D., 1989-97. Musician (CD) God Talks, 1999, (CD) Peace Will Come, 2002; co-creator (original music/drama duo) Are You Listening?, 1989. Recipient John Philip Sousa award. Mem. NEA, Music Tchrs. Nat. Assn., Am. Choral Dirs. Assn., Music Educators Assn., S.D. Bandmasters Assn. Home: 1026 E 1st St Canton SD 57013 also: PO Box 159 Canton SD 57013-0159

KAUFMAN, ANTOINETTE D. business services company executive; b. Phila., Mar. 10, 1939; d. Joseph and Maria Falcone; m. John R. Kaufman, Apr. 30, 1988. Ed., St. Joseph's U., 1968. With N.W. Ayer & Son, Inc., N.Y.C., 1956-81; adminstrv. asst. N.W. Ayer ABH Internat., 1960, asst. corp. sec., 1977, corp. sec., 1978-79, stock transfer agt., 1969-79, info. specialist, 1979-81; exec. v.p., sec., creative dir., chief oper. officer Help Bus. Svcs., Inc., Swarthmore, Pa., 1981—. Avocations: ballroom dancing, cooking, violin, piano, gardening. Office: Help Bus Svcs Inc 110 Park Ave HBS Bldg Swarthmore PA 19081

KAUFMAN, ARTHUR STEPHEN, lawyer; b. N.Y.C., July 27, 1946; s. Jacob and Helen (Chalphin) K.; m. Susan Werner, Jan. 31, 1971; children: Lewis Scott, Jonathan Charles. AB, Columbia Coll., 1968, JD, 1971. Bar: N.Y. 1972. Assoc. Dewey, Ballantine, Bushby, Palmer & Wood, N.Y.C., 1971-79; ptnr. Shea & Gould, N.Y.C., 1980-85, Fried, Frank, Harris, Shriver & Jacobson, N.Y.C., 1985—. Home: 17 Withington Rd Scarsdale NY 10583-3305 Office: Fried Frank Harris Shriver & Jacobson 1 New York Plz Fl 22 New York NY 10004-1980

KAUFMAN, BARTON LOWELL, financial services company executive; b. Shelbyville, Ind., Mar. 28, 1941; s. Nathan and Hortense (Schwartz) K.; m. Judy Dorman, June 17, 1962; children: Grant, Wendy Kaufman Siegel, Emily Kaufman Frank, Hannah. BS, Ind. U., 1962, JD, 1965. Bar: Ind. 1965. Agt. Kaufman Multi-Million Dollar Agy., Indpls., 1965-70; pres., CEO Kaufman Fin. Corp., Indpls., 1970—. Pres. Twenty-Five Million Dollar Internat. Forum, Chgo., 1989. Republican. Jewish. Office: Kaufman Fin Corp 201 W 103rd St Ste 630 Indianapolis IN 46290-1126 E-mail: bartk@kaufin.com.

KAUFMAN, BEL, author, educator; b. Berlin; d. Michael J. and Lala (Rabinowitz) K.; divorced; children: Jonathan Goldstine, Thea Goldstine. BA magna cum laude, Hunter Coll., 1934; DHL, Hunter Coll, 2001; MA with highest honors, Columbia U., 1936; LLD honors, Nasson Coll., Maine, 1965. Adj. prof. English CUNY; lectr. throughout country, also appearances on TV and radio. Mem. Commn. Performing Arts. Editorial bd., Phi Delta Kappan.; Author: Up the Down Staircase, 1965, Love, etc, 1979; also short stories, articles, TV play, translations from Russian, lyrics for musicals. Bd. dirs. Shalom Aleichem Found.; adv. council Town Hall Found. Recipient plaque Anti-Defamation League, award and plaque United Jewish Appeal, Paperback of Year award, Ky. Col. award, Bell Movie award; also ednl. journalism awards; named to Hall of Fame Hunter Coll., winner short story contest sponsored by NEA and PEN, 1983. Mem. Author's Guild, Dramatists Guild, P.E.N., English Grad. Union, Phi Beta Kappa. Address: 1020 Park Ave New York NY 10028-0913 E-mail: belkau@aol.com.

KAUFMAN, CHARLOTTE S. communications executive; b. Bridgeport, Conn., Mar. 8, 1918; d. Samuel N. and S. Elizabeth (Cohen) Schnee; m. William Kaufman, May 9, 1940. BA, U. Mich., 1938. Med. office assoc., 1941-63; dir. pub. rels. Parents and Friends of Retarded Children, Bridgeport, 1965-66; founder, exec. dir. Family Life Film Ctr. of Conn., Fairfield, Conn., 1967-74; exec. producer Topic '69/WNHC-TV, New Haven, Conn., 1969; project dir. pilot project with Social/Rehab. Svc. U.S. Dept. HEW, 1969-70; pub. rels. chmn. Friendship Fair of Aux./Bridgeport Regional Ctr. Retarded, 1979. Founder CAT-TV, pub. access channel, Winston-Salem and Forsyth County, 1994; coord. five annual Film Day Workshops, Fairfield U., 1967-71; coord. coms. of jurors for Am. Film Festival, N.Y.C., 1968-74; chmn./mem. planning and adv. bd. Bridgeport Regional Ctr. for the Retarded; exec. bd. Bd. of Assocs., U. Bridgeport, others; film use cons. to many local and state orgns. Author: Film Discussion: A Technique to Communicate Information About Rehabilitation, 1970; exec. producer: A Day in the Life of P.T. Barnum, 1971; author publs. in field. Vol. patient advocate for nursing homes, Southwestern Conn. Area Agy. on Aging, 1976-78; v.p. Oronoque Village Improvement Assn., 1986-88. Mem.: Kappa Tau Alpha, Theta Sigma Phi. Home: 3180 Grady St Winston Salem NC 27104-4008 E-mail: wkaufman@pol.net.

KAUFMAN, CHRISTOPHER LEE, lawyer; b. Chgo., Mar. 17, 1945; s. Charles R. and Violet-Page (Koteen) K.; m. Carlyn A. Clement, Jan. 25, 1986; children: Charles Alexander, Caroline Clement. BA, Amherst Coll., 1967; JD, Harvard U., 1970. Bar: Ill. 1970, Calif. 1972. Law clk. to judge U.S. Ct. Appeals (2d cir.), N.Y.C., 1970-71; from assoc. to ptnr. Heller, Ehrman, White and McAuliffe, San Francisco, Palo Alto, Calif., 1974-90; ptnr. Latham & Watkins, Menlo Park, Calif., 1990—. Editor: Harvard Law Review., 1968-70. Mem. ABA (com. on negotiated acquisitions, com. on fed. regulation of securities). Office: Latham & Watkins 135 Commonwealth Dr Menlo Park CA 94025-1105 E-mail: christopher.kaufman@lw.com.

KAUFMAN, DAVID GRAHAM, construction executive; b. North Canton, Ohio, Mar. 20, 1937; s. DeVere and Josephine Grace (Graham) Kaufman; m. Carol Jean Monzione, Oct. 5, 1957 (div. Aug. 1980); children: Gregory Allan, Christopher Patrick. Student, Kent State U., 1956; grad., Internat. Corr. Schs., 1965, N.Y. Inst. Photography, 1983; postgrad., Calif. Coast U. Cert. constrn. insp., constrn. project mgr., asbestos insp., lead insp., lead risk assessor, asbestos project designer, lock-out/tag-out, environ. insp., environ. specialist, environ. mgr., EPA cert. lead insp. and risk assessor. Machinist apprentice Hoover Co., North Canton, Ohio, 1955-57; draftsman-designer Goodyear Aircraft Corp., Akron, Ohio, 1957-60, Boeing Co., Seattle, 1960-61; designer Berger Industries, Seattle, 1961-62, Puget Sound Bridge & Drydock, Seattle, 1963, C.M. Lovsted, Seattle, 1963-64, Tracy, Brunstrom & Dudley, Seattle, 1964, Rubens & Pratt Engrs., Seattle, 1965-66; founder, owner Profl. Drafting Svcs., Seattle, 1965, Profl. Take-Off Svcs., Seattle, 1966, Profl. Representation Svcs., Seattle, 1967; pres. Kaufman Inc., Seattle, 1967-83, Kaufman-Alaska Inc., Juneau, 1975-83, Kaufman-Alaska Constructors, Inc., Juneau, 1975-83; constrn. mgr. U. Alaska, 1979-84; constrn. cons. Alaskan Native and Eskimo Village Corps., 1984—; prin. Kaufman S.W. Assocs., N.Mex., 1984—, Graham Internat., 1992—, Parsons-Brinckernoff, Santa Fe, 2000—. Trustee advisor Kaufman Internat., Kaufman Group, Kaufman Enterprises. Mem.: Prodrs. Coun. Alaska, Prodrs. Coun. Hawaii, Prodrs. Coun. Idaho, Prodrs. Coun. Wash., Prodrs. Coun. Oreg., Associated Gen. Contractors Seattle Constrn. Coun., Internat. Conf. Bldgs. Ofcls., Assn. Constrn. Insps., Constrn. Specifications Inst., Toastmasters (past gov.), Portland C. of C., Nat. Eagle Scout Assn., Lions. Republican. Roman Catholic. Office: PO Box 458 Haines AK 99827-0458 also: PO Box 1781 Santa Fe NM 87504 Home: # 409 505 Oppenheimer Los Alamos NM 87544

KAUFMAN, DAVID JOSEPH, lawyer; b. Harrisburg, Pa., Apr. 7, 1931; s. S. Herbert and Bessie (Claster) K.; m. Virginia Stern, Aug. 30, 1959; children: David J. Jr., James H. BS in Econs. cum laude, Franklin and Marshall Coll., 1952; JD cum laude, U. Pa., 1955. Bar: Pa. 1955. First assoc., to ptnr., then of counsel Wolf, Block, Schorr & Solis-Cohen, Phila., 1957—; chmn., exec. com., 1979, 83. Trustee Abington (Pa.) Meml. Hosp., 1981—, chmn. bd. trustees, 1992-94; pres. Congregation Rodeph Shalom, Phila., 1983-86; mem. adv. com. on decedents estates laws Pa. Joint State Govt. Commn., 1985-. Fellow Am. Coll. Trust and Estate Counsel; mem. ABA, Pa. Bar Assn. (chmn. real property, probate and trust sect. 1986-87), Phila. Bar Assn. (chmn. probate sect. 1977), Order of Coif. Republican. Home: 1770 Oak Hill Dr Huntingdon Valley PA 19006-5817

KAUFMAN, DONALD LEROY, building products executive; b. Erie, Pa., May 9, 1931; s. Isadore H. and Lena (Sandler) K.; m. Estelle Friedman, Aug. 15, 1954; children: Craig Ivan, Susan Beth, Carrie Ellen. BS in Bus. Adminstrn, Ohio State U., 1953, LL.B., 1955. Bar: Ohio 1955. Pres. Alside, Inc., Akron, Ohio, 1974—, chief exec. officer, 1982—. V.p., bd. dirs. Assoc. Materials Inc. Mem. adv. com. U. Akron; trustee Jewish Welfare Fund, Akron, 1958-65, young leaders div., 1961-65; trustee Akron City Hosp. Found., 1984-91, Menorah Park Home for Aged, Akron Children's Hosp. Found. Mem. Akron Bar Assn., Sigma Alpha Mu, Tau Epsilon Rho. Home: 2825 Roundhill Rd Akron OH 44333-2273 Office: PO Box 2010 Akron OH 44309-2010

KAUFMAN, DONALD WAYNE, research ecologist; b. Abilene, Tex., June 7, 1943; s. Leo Fred and Marcella Genevieve (Hobbie) K.; m. Glennis Ann Schroeder, Aug. 5, 1967; 1 child, Dawn. BS, Ft. Hays Kans. State Coll., 1965, MS, 1967; PhD, U. Ga., 1972. Postdoctoral fellow U. Tex., Austin, 1971-73; asst. prof. U. Ark., Fayetteville, 1974-75, SUNY, Binghamton, 1975-77; assoc. program dir. Population Biology, NSF, Washington, 1977-80; asst. prof. biology Kans. State U., Manhattan, 1980-84, assoc. prof. biology, 1984-91, prof. biology, 1991—; adj. curator mammals Sternberg Mus. Nat. History Ft. Hays State U., Hays, Kans., 2000—. Adj. prof. biology U. N.Mex., 1998; vis. scientist Savannah River Ecology Lab., Aiken, S.C., 1973-74; acting dir. Konza Prairie Rsch. Natural Area, 1986-87, coord., 1990-91; dir. Konza Prairie Long-Term Ecol. Rsch. Program, 1985-90; grant rev. panelist EPA, 1981-85, USDA, 1995-96; cons. NSF, 1984, Nat. Pk. Svc., 2000. Contbr. articles to profl. jours. Fellow NDEA, 1967—69. Mem. AAAS, Am. Soc. Mammalogists (award 1972, bd. dirs. 1989-92), Ecol. Soc. Am., Am. Inst. Biol. Scis., Soc. for the Study Evolution, The Wildlife Soc. (pres. elect Kans. chpt. 2003-), Soc. Conservation Biology, Ctrl. Plains Soc. Mammalogists (bd. govs. 2000—), Sigma Xi. Office: Kans State U Div Biology Ackert Hall Manhattan KS 66506 E-mail: dwkaufma@ksu.edu.

KAUFMAN, DONNA S. lawyer; m. Fred Kaufman; 2 children. BCL, McGill U.; LLM, U. Montreal. Bar: Quebec, (Ontario). Former broadcast exec. Sta. CHCH-TV, Hamilton and Toronto, Canada; former chmn., CEO Selkirk Comm. Ltd.; former ptnr. Stikeman Ellliott; profl. corp. dir. BCS Comm., Montreal, Canada. Bd. dirs. BCE Inc., Bell Can. Internat. Inc., TransAlta Corp., 1989—, Pub. Sector Pension Investment Bd.; gov. Coun. for Can. Unity, Baycrest Centre for Geriatric Care. Author: Broadcasting Law in Canada: Fairness in the Administrative Process; contbr. articles. Recipient Award of Distinction, Faculty of Commerce, Concordia U., Montreal, 1995. Office: BCE Comm Ste 3700 1000 de la Gauchetiere St W Montreal QC H3B 4Y7 Canada Address: Bell Can Internat Inc Bur 1100 1000 rue de la Gauchetiere Quest Montreal QC H3B 4YB Canada Office Fax: 514-392-2266. E-mail: bcecomms@bce.co.

KAUFMAN, GLEN FRANK, art educator, artist; b. Fort Atkinson, Wis., Oct. 28, 1932; s. Eli J. and Elynor B. (Jensik) K. BS with honors, U. Wis., 1954; MFA, Cranbrook Acad. Art, 1959; cert., State Sch. Arts and Crafts, Copenhagen, 1960. Head fibers dept. Cranbrook Acad. Art, Bloomfield Hills, Mich., 1961-67; assoc. prof. art U. Ga., Athens, 1967-72, prof. art, 1972—, prof. in charge, fabric design, 1967—, grad. faculty, 1969—. Staff designer Dorothy Liebes Design Studio, N.Y.C., 1960-61; designer Regal Rugs, Inc., North Vernon, Ind., 1966-82; vis. artist Sch. Textiles, Royal Coll. Art, London, 1976; juror The Albuquerque (N.Mex.) Mus., 1981, Midland (Mich.) Art Coun., 1985, Itami Craft Ctr., Osaka, Japan, 1991, others; panelist Visual Artists Fellowship/Crafts, Nat. Endowment for the Arts, Washington, 1992—; cons. in field; lectr. and workshop presenter in field. One-man shows include Gallery Maronie, Kyoto, Japan, 1984, Sembikiya Gallery, Tokyo, 1985, Arrowmont Sch. Arts and Crafts, Gatlinburg, Tenn., 1986, Fiberworks, Berkeley, Calif., 1987, Madison (Ga.)-Morgan Cultural Ctr., 1988, Fuji Gallery, Osaka, Japan, 1988, Wacoal Ginza Art Space, Tokyo, 1989, Allrich Gallery, San Francisco, 1990, Azabu Mus. of Arts and Crafts, Tokyo, 1991, Lamar Dodd Art Ctr., LaGrange (Ga.) Coll., 1992, Gallery Gallery, Japan, 1992, Wacoal Ginza Art Space, Tokyo, 1994, Gallery Nouveau, Pusan, Korea, 1994, Ba Tang Gol Arts Ctr., Seoul, korea, 1994, Wacoal Ginza Art Space, Tokyo, 1996, Gallery Gallery, Kyoto, Japan, 1996, many others; exhibited in group shows at Columbia Mus. Art, S.C., 1980, No. Ill. U., DeKalb, 1981, Visual Arts Ctr. Alaska, Anchorage, 1982, Robert L. Kidd Gallery, Birmingham, 1983, Am. Craft Mus., N.Y., 1986, Denki Kaikan Gallery, Nagoya, Japan, 1987, Gayle Wilson Gallery, Southampton, N.Y., 1988, Sch. Visual Arts, N.Y., 1989, Itami Craft Ctr., Osaka, 1989 (Silver prize), Farrell Collection, Washington, 1991, Allrich Gallery, San Francisco, 1991, Nagoya Trade and Industry Ctr., 1991, New Visions Gallery Contemporary Art, Atlanta, 1992, Mus. Kyoto, 1992, Smithsonian Instn., Washington, 1992-93, Atlanta (Ga.) Fin. Ctr., 1993, The Nat. Mus. Modern Art, Kyoto, Japan, 1993, Art Inst. Chgo., Ill., 1993, Brenau U. Gallery, Gainesville, Ga., 1993, Mus. Kyoto, 1994, Asian Arts Ctr. Towson (Md.) State U., 1994, Am. Craft Museum, N.Y., 1995, Nogaya and Trade Industry Ctr., Japan, 1995, Gallery, Gallery, Kyota, Japan, 1995, Harbourfront Ctr., Toronto Can., 1995, Museé Marsil, Montreal, Can., 1995, The Brown/Grotta Gallery, Wilton, Conn., 1995, New Jersey Ctr. for Visual Arts, Summit, 1997, Georgia State U. Gallery, Atlanta, 1997, Brown/Grotta Gallery, Wilton, Conn. 12997, Vanderbilt U. Sarratt Gallery, Nashville, 1997, Georgia Museum of Art, Athens, 1997, others; represented in permanent collections Am. Craft Mus., N.Y.C., Juraku Mus, Kyoto, Cleve. Mus. Art, Art Inst. Chgo., U. Wis., Madison, Itami City Craft Ctr., Hyogo Prefecture, Japan, Ithaca (N.Y.) Coll. Mus. Art, Long House Found., L.I., N.Y., Nat. Mus. Modern Art, Kyoto, Smithsonian Instn., Rockford Art Assn., Ill., S.C. Johnson Collection, U.S.A. Collection Contemporary Crafts, SUNY, Oneonta, Wichita Art Assn., Kans., pvt. collections; works illustrated in many books; contbr. articles to jours. Recipient Fulbright grant to Denmark, 1959-60, Grant for rsch. and travel to Europe, U. Ga., Dept. Art, 1973, Nat. Endowment for the Arts Craftsmen's Fellowship grant, 1976, Nat. Endowment for the Arts Svcs. to the Field grant, 1980-81, 81-82, Faculty Rsch. grant U. Ga. Athens Office of V.P. for Rsch., 1983-96, Nat. Endowment for the Arts Visual Artist's Fellowship grant, 1990, Ga. Coun. for the Arts Individual Artist grant, 1991, Sr. Faculty Rsch. grant U. Ga. Athens Rsch. Found., 1992, others. Fellow Am. Craft Coun.; mem. World Craft Coun., Surface Design Assn. (S.E. regional rep. 1977-80, pres. 1980-82, named hon. life mem. 1983), Phi Beta Delta. Office: Sch of Art Univ Ga Athens GA 30602

KAUFMAN, GORDON DESTER, theology educator; b. Newton, Kans., June 22, 1925; s. Edmund George and Hazel (Dester) K.; m. Dorothy Wedel, June 11, 1947; children: David W., Gretchen E., Anne Louisa, Edmund G. AB with highest distinction, Bethel (Kans.) Coll., 1947, LHD (hon.), 1973; MA in Sociology, Northwestern U., 1948; BD magna cum laude, Yale U., 1951, PhD in Philos. Theology, 1955. Ordained to ministry Mennonite Ch., 1953. Asst. prof. religion Pomona Coll., 1953-58; asso. prof. theology Vanderbilt U., 1958-63; prof. theology Harvard U. Div. Sch., Cambridge, Mass., 1963-95, Edward MallincKrodt Jr. prof. div., 1969-95, prof. emeritus, 1995—. Vis. prof. United Theol. Coll., Bangalore, India, 1976-77, Doshisha U., Kyoto, Japan, 1983, U. South Africa, Pretoria, 1984; vis. lectr. Oxford U., 1986, Chinese U. Hong Kong, 1991. Author: Relativism, Knowledge and Faith, 1960, The Context of Decision, 1961, Systematic Theology: a Historicist Perspective, 1968, God the Problem, 1972, An Essay on Theological Method, 1975, 3d edit., 1995, Nonresistance and Responsibility and other Mennonite Essays, 1979, The Theological Imagination: Constructing the Concept of God, 1981, Theology for a Nuclear Age, 1985, In Face of Mystery: A Constructive Theology, 1993, God—Mystery—Diversity: Christian Theology in a Pluralistic World, 1996. Mem. Am. Acad. Religion (pres. 1981-82), Am. Theol. Soc. (pres. 1979-80) Democrat. Home: 6 Longfellow Rd Cambridge MA 02138-4736 Office: 45 Francis Ave Cambridge MA 02138-1911

KAUFMAN, HAROLD RICHARD, mechanical engineer and physics educator; b. Audubon, Iowa, Nov. 24, 1926; s. Walter Richard and Hazel (Steere) K.; m. Elinor Mae Wheat, June 25, 1948; children: Brian, Karin, Bruce, Cynthia. Student, Evanston Community Coll., 1947-49; BSM.E., Northwestern U., 1951; PhD, Colo. State U., 1971. Researcher in aerospace propulsion NACA, Cleve., 1951-58; mgr. space propulsion research NASA, Cleve., 1958-74; prof. physics and mech. engring. Colo. State U., Ft. Collins, 1974-84, prof. emeritus, 1984—, chmn. dept. physics, 1979-84; pres. Kaufman & Robinson, Inc., Ft. Collins, 1984—; v.p. R&D Commonwealth Sci. Corp., Alexandria, Va., 1984-96. Pioneer in field of electron bombardment ion thruster, 1960; cons. ion source design and applications. Contbr. over 140 publs. and 30 patents in field. Served with USNR, 1944-46. Recipient NASA medal for exceptional sci. achievement, 1971. Fellow Am. Vacuum Soc. (Albert Nerken award 1991), AIAA (assoc. fellow, James H. Wyld Propulsion award 1969); mem. Tau Beta Pi, Pi Tau Sigma. Office: Kaufman & Robinson Inc 1306 Blue Spruce Dr Ste 2A Fort Collins CO 80524-2067

KAUFMAN, HARRY, retail executive; b. Altoona, Pa., July 16, 1937; s. Nathan and Ethel (Ritchin) K.; m. Margaret Anne Weiss; children: Ira, David. BBA, U. Pitts., 1959, M.Bus. Retailing, 1960. Owner, chief exec. officer Kaufman's & Sons Stores and Wedding World Stores, Altoona, Pa., 1970—, Kaufman's Real Estate & Devel., Altoona, 1980—. Developer The Kaufman Gallery, Altoona, 1987. Chmn. Pa. Retailers Polit. Action Com., 1987—; nat. bd. dirs. Union Am. Hebrew Congregations-N.Am., 1987—, regional pres., 1993-97; pres. Temple Beth Israel, Altoona, 1977-79; bd. dirs. Jewish Meml. Ctr., Altoona, 1989—; pres. Greater Altoona Econ. Devel. Corp., 1991-93, chmn. bd. dirs., 1993-95; mem. Sesquicentennial Com., Altoona, 1989; vice chmn. Altoona Redevel. Authority, 1989-94, chmn., 1996-99; bd. dirs. Am. Heart Assn., Altoona, 1992-98; nat. bd. dirs. ARZA/World Union Progressive Judaism, 2001—. Named Retailer of Yr., Pa. Retailers Assn., 1987. Mem. Pa. Retailers Assn. (v.p. 1986—), Kiwanis. Home: 3509 Baker Blvd Altoona PA 16602-1827 Office: Kaufman's & Sons Stores 1301 11th Ave Altoona PA 16601-3301

KAUFMAN, HARVEY ISIDORE, neuropsychology consultant; b. Virginia, Minn., May 13, 1937; s. Carl and Marcia (Borkon) K.; m. Glenda Kaufman, Oct. 16, 1971; children: Jason Alexis, Justin Bram. BA, U. Minn., Duluth, 1959, BS cum laude, 1960; MA, U. Minn., Mpls., 1961; PhD, Marquette U., 1967, Southwest U., 1992. Fellow and diplomate Am. Bd. Neuropsychology, Am. Bd. Med. Psychotherapists; Diplomate Internat. Acad. of Behavioral Medicine; cert. in clin. hypnosis. Psychology supr. Winnebago (Wis.) Mental Health Inst., 1971-75; dir. outpatient svcs. Health Care Ctr., Fond du Lac, Wis., 1975-81; neuropsychologist Sharpe Clinic, Fond du Lac, 1983-89, St. Mary's Hosp., Milw., 1986-89; cons. Fond du Lac, 1990—; cons. in neurology Racine, 1992—. Fellow dept. neurology med. sch. U. Wis., 1981-82. Mem. Am. Psychol. Assn., Wis. Psychol. Assn., Nat. Acad. Neuropyschologists, Am. Soc. Clin. Hypnosis, Internat. Soc. Clin. Hypnosis, Internat. Neuropsychol. Soc. Home and Office: 8530 N Fielding Rd Bayside WI 53217

KAUFMAN, HELENE, legal secretary; b. N.Y., June 16, 1939; d. Jack and Faye Kaufman. Student, San Diego Jr. Coll., 1959-60, San Diego State Coll., 1960-62; BA, U. Calif., Berkeley, 1963. Legal sec., San Diego, 1965-77, City of San Diego, 1980-87, sr. legal sec., 1987—. Avocations: gardening, decorating, investing. E-mail: HLNKFMN@aol.com.

KAUFMAN, HERBERT MARK, finance educator; b. Bronx, N.Y., Nov. 1, 1946; s. Henry and Betty (Fried) K.; m. Helen Laurie Fox, July 23, 1967; 1 child, Jonathan Hart. BA, SUNY, Binghamton, 1967; PhD, Pa. State U., 1972. Economist Fed. Nat. Mortgage Assn., Washington, 1972-73; asst. prof. Ariz. State U., Tempe, 1973-76, econs. prof., 1980-88, fin. prof., 1988—, chair dept. fin., 1991—, exec. dir. Ctr. for Fin. System, 1988—. Cons. World Bank, Washington, 1985-86, Gen. Acctg. Office, Washington, 1985, Congl. Budget Office, Washington, 1980, N.Y. Stock Exch., 1995—. Author: Financial Markets, Financial Institutions and Money, 1983, (with others) The Political Economy of Policy Making, 1979, Money and Banking, 1991; contbr. articles to profl. jours. Mem. Am. Econ. Assn., Am. Fin. Assn., Nat. Assn. of Bus. Economists. Avocations: golf, piano. Home: 1847 E Calle De Caballos Tempe AZ 85284-2505 Office: Ariz State U Dept Fin Tempe AZ 85287 Business E-Mail: herbert.kaufman@asu.edu.

KAUFMAN, IRA GLADSTONE, judge; b. N.Y.C., Dec. 13, 1909; s. Joseph and Esther K.; m. Margaret Kaufman, Sept., 1988; children: Harvey David, Sylvia Kaufman Delin. BS, NYU, 1933, JD, 1936; DSc in Bus. Adminstrn. (hon.), Cleary Coll., Ypsilanti, Mich., 1976. Bar: Mich. 1939. Pvt. practice law, Detroit, 1939-59; judge of brobate Wayne County Probate Ct., Detroit, 1958-84, presiding judge, 1962-63, 66-67, 72-73, 77-85; chief judge pro tem Wayne County Probate and Juvenile Ct., 1981-85; Moot Ct. judge U. Detroit, 1966-72; lectr. Trustee Children's Hosp. of Detroit, chmn. devel., 1980-83, hon. chmn. ann. concert 1983, chmn. ad hoc com. alcoholism Detroit United Cmtys. Svcs., 1967-68; chmn. Detroit Com. Fgn. Rels., 1974-76; trustee Mich. Cancer Found., 1973, hon. life trustee emeritus, 1985; trustee Detroit Inst. Tech., 1962-72, Park Cmty. Hosp., 1962-73; pres. Inter-Agy. Council on Alcoholism, 1967; pres., chmn. bd. Met. Soc. for Blind, 1966-70, bd. dirs., 1960—; mem. Gov.'s Com. Mental Health Statute Rev. Commn., 1970-72, Mich. Soc. Mental Health, 1960—; hon. life mem. Children's Charter Mich., 1965-75; exec. bd. League Handicapped-Goodwill 1949-60; bd. overseers Dropsie Coll., 1973-75; bd. dirs. Hebrew Free Loan Soc., Detroit, 1979-84, Jewish Nat. Fund Bd.; v.p. United Hebrew Schs. Detroit, 1947-58; founding sec. Midrasha Coll. Hebrew Studies, 1948-58; pres. Adat Shalom Synagogue, 1945-51, founder cemetery, 1948, hon. life pres. 1953; founding chmn. Einstein Luncheon Forum, 1986—. Fellow Mich. State Bar Found. (life mem.); mem. ABA, Mich. Probate and Juvenile Ct. Assn. (exec. bd. 1969-72, pres. 1970-71), Mich. Bar Assn., Detroit Bar Assn., Supreme Ct. Hist. Soc., Mental Health Assn. Mich. (Advocacy award 1989), U.S. Air Force Assn. (ann. installing officer 1983-84), B'nai B'rith (hon. pres. Tikvah Lodge 1974), Valley of Detroit, Masons (33 degree, sovereign prince), Shriners, Jesters. Contbr. biog. sketches of Mich. judges to Jewish Hist. Soc. publ., 1983-84. Home: 1285 Ruffner Ave Birmingham MI 48009-7173

KAUFMAN, IRVING, retired engineering educator; b. Geinsheim, Germany, Jan. 11, 1925; came to U.S., 1938, naturalized, 1945; s. Albert and Hedwig Kaufmann; m. Ruby Lee Dordek, Sept. 10, 1950; children— Eve Deborah, Sharon Anne, Julie Ellen. BE, Vanderbilt U., 1945; MS, U. Ill., 1949, PhD, 1957. Engr. RCA Victor, Indpls., Ind. and Camden, N.J., 1945-48; instr., research assoc. U. Ill., Urbana, 1949-56; sr. mem. tech. staff Ramo-Wooldridge & Space Tech. Labs., Calif., 1957-64; prof. engring. Ariz. State U., 1965-94, ret., 1994; founder, dir. Solid State Research Lab., 1968-78. Collaborator Los Alamos Nat. Lab., 1989, 91; vis. scientist Consiglio Nazionale delle Ricerche, Italy, 1973-74; vis. prof. U. Auckland, N.Z., 1974; liaison scientist U.S. Office Naval Rsch., London, 1978-80; lectr. and cons. elec. engring. Contbr. articles to profl. jours. and encys.; patentee in field. Recipient Disting. Research award Ariz. State U. Grad. Coll., 1986-87; Sr. Fulbright research fellow Italy, 1964-65, 73-74, Am. Soc. for Engring. Edn./Naval Rsch. Lab. fellow, 1988. Fellow IEEE (life, Phoenix sect. leadership award 1994); mem. Electromagnetics Acad., Gold Key (hon.), Sigma Xi, Tau Beta Pi, Eta Kappa Nu, Pi Mu Epsilon. Jewish. E-mail: rubyirv@earthlink.net.

KAUFMAN, JANICE HORNER, foreign language educator, women's and gender studies educator; b. Mattoon, Ill., Apr. 30, 1949; d. Daniel Ogden and Julia Betty (McDermid) Horner; m. Richard Boucher Kaufman, June 24, 1972 (div. Mar. 27, 2002); children: Julia Ogden, Richard Pearse. AB, Duke U., 1971; MA in Liberal Studies, Hollins Coll., 1979; postgrad., NYU, 1986; PhD in French, U. Va., Charlottesville, 1997. Tchr. in French Roanoke (Va.) City Pub. Schs., 1971-72, North Cross Sch., Roanoke, Va., 1974-82; instr. French Va. Poly. Inst. and State U., Blacksburg, 1984-86, 88, 90, 94, 98, asst. dir. fgn. lang. camps, 1984-85, administrv. dir., 1986; French, English interpreter, translator Coll. Architecture and Urban Studies, Blacksburg, 1988; instr. ESL U. Cmty. Internat. Coun., Cranwell Internat. Ctr., Blacksburg, 1987-89; instr. French Hollins Coll., Roanoke, Va., 1989-90, Radford (Va.) U., 1989-90; grad. tchg. asst. U. Va., Charlottesville, 1992; adj. assoc. prof. French No. Va. C.C., Woodbridge and Alexandria, 1997-99; asst. prof. French and women's and gender studies SUNY-Oneonta, 2000—. Student counselor Am. Inst. Fgn. Study, Greenwich, Conn., 1977; session leader Russell County Pub. Schs., Lebanon, Va., 1985, Va. Assn. Ind. Schs., Richmond, 1986; asst. tchr. Am. Coun. for Internat. Studies "Toujours en France," 1995; faculty cons. advanced placement exam in French, Ednl. Testing Svc., Trenton State Coll., 1991-95, 97-98; adj. prof. French, George Mason U., Fairfax, Va., 1999-2000; acad. dir. study abroad in Strasbourg, France, George Mason U. Ctr. for Global Edn., summer 2000; presenter in field. Contbr. articles to profl. jours. Mem. MLA, Am. Assn. Tchrs. French, African Lit. Assn., Women in French, Pi Delta Phi, Phi Sigma Iota. Avocations: reading, travel, hiking. E-mail: kaufmajh@oneonta.edu.

KAUFMAN, JEFFREY ALLEN, publisher; b. Mpls., May 28, 1952; s. Theodore and Jean Louise (Tiegs) K. Student, Mankato State U., 1970-71, Ariz. State U., 1971-72; BA, U. Minn., 1975. Pres. Creative Resources, Inc., Mpls., 1976-80; sr. v.p. Literary Resources, Inc., Phoenix, 1980-81; pres. Multi-Media, Phoenix, 1981-83, Where To Go, Inc., Excelsior, Minn., 1983-86; v.p. The Old Utica Co., Mpls., 1986-88; chmn. Actif, Inc., Wayzata, Minn., 1988-89; ptnr. S&K Group, Mpls., 1989-90; editor in chief Spl. Events Pub., Inc., Mpls., 1990-92; founder Electronic Claims Processing, Inc., Edina, Minn., 1992-96; co-owner BIO-Works, Inc., 1994—, Kaufman Capital Funding, 1997—; pres. Comfort Mobility, Inc., Phoenix, 2002—. Cons. Control Data Corp. Mpls., 1978-81; dir. Nexus Inc. Mpls., 1978-81; founder ECP Inc., 1992. Author: (books) Where To Go in Minneapolis and Saint Paul, 1984, Where To Go in Los Angeles, 1985, (screenplay) Born To Be Chief, 1985. Avocations: golf, flying, equestrian. Home: PO Box 475 Scottsdale AZ 85252-0475 E-mail: Jeffrey_Kaufman@msn.com.

KAUFMAN, JEROME BENZION, neurosurgeon; b. Waterloo, Iowa, July 22, 1934; s. Louis and Dorothy (Rosenbloom) K.; m. Judith Ellen Lasker, June 29, 1967; children: David, Jonathan, Jefferey. BA, Wayne State U., 1955, MD, 1961; postgrad., U. Madrid. Diplomate Am. Bd. Neurol. Surgery, 1975. Rotating intern Michael Reese Hosp. and Med. Ctr., Chgo., 1961-62; resident in internal med. Michael Reese Hosp. and Med. Ctr., Chgo., 1962-63; resident in gen. surgery VA Hosp., Bronx, 1965-66, resident in neurology, 1966, resident in neurosurgery, 1967, from sr. to chief resident neurosurgery, 1969-70; resident neurosurgery Neurol. Inst. N.Y., Columbia Presbyn. Hosp., 1968; resident neuropathology Mt. Sinai Hosp. and Med. Sch., N.Y.C., 1968; chief resident neurosurgery City Hosp., Elmhurst, N.Y., 1969; chmn. dept. neurosurgery Carle Clinic Assn. and Found. Hosp., Urbana, Ill., 1972—96. Cons. neurosurgery McKinley Hosp., Urbana, Covenant Hosp., Urbana; asst. instr. internal medicine Chgo. Med. Sch., 1963; clin. assoc. prof. neurosurgery U. Ill. Coll. Medicine, Urbana, 1982-96, clin. prof., chmn. neurosurgery. Contbr. articles to profl. jours. Served to capt. USAF, 1963-65. Named one of Best Drs. in Am.-Midwest (Ill.). Fellow ACS, Am. Assn. Neurol. Surgeons (Continuing Edn. award in neurosurgery 1980, 83, 85, 87, 89, 93, 96), Internat. Coll. Surgeons (vice regent) N.Y. Acad. Scis.; mem. AMA (Physicians Recognition award 1980, 82, 85, 89, 93), Ill. Med. Soc., Champaign County Med. Soc., Congress Neurol. Surgeons, Ctrl. Neurosurg. Soc., Assn. Mil. Surgeons U.S., Chgo. Neurol. Soc. (Best Doctors in Am. Midwest). Home: 2104 Zuppke Dr Urbana IL 61801-6706 E-mail: jkauf@uiuc.edu.

KAUFMAN, JEROME SEYMOUR, retired ophthalmologist; b. Detroit, June 13, 1929; s. Sam and Libby Friedman K.; m. Melinda Soble; four children from previous marriage. DO, Kans. City Coll. Osteopathy, 1954. Pvt. practice ophthalmology, Garden City, Mich., 1957-90. Nat. sec. Zionist Orgn. Am., 1996—. Fellow Am. Coll. Ophthalmology. Jewish. Avocations: politics, golf, tennis, tournament bridge. Home: 1728 Saint Johns Ct Bloomfield Hills MI 48302-1776 E-mail: jkaufman253469MI@comcast.net.

KAUFMAN, JOHN ROBERT, marketing and information management consultant; b. New Cumberland, Pa., Dec. 13, 1931; s. Jean Coulson and Mercedes Katherine (Beshore) K.; m. Antoinette Anna Dolores Falcone, Apr. 30, 1988. AB, Pa. State U., 1953; MBA, U. Pa., 1955. V.p. N.W. Ayer & Son, Inc., Phila., 1965-80; pres. HBS, Inc. (Help Bus. Services, Inc.), Swarthmore, Pa., 1980—, Swarthmore Bus. Dist. Authority, 1991—93. Pres. Swarthmore Bus. Dist. Authority, 1991-93. Capt. USNR, ret. Mem. Am. Mktg. Assn. (nat. v.p., publisher 1975-80), Am. Mktg. Assn (pres. Phila. chpt. 1968), Parlin Bd. Govs. (chmn. 1982-84), Soc. Competitor Intelligence Profls., Navy League, Mil. Officers Assn., Destroyer Escort Assn., Am. Legion, Univ. Club (N.Y.C.), ACACIA Fraternity, Rotary (local pres. 1985, bd. dirs., sec. Rotary Trust Found. 2002), Masons. Avocations: reading, gourmet cooking, tennis, outdoor landscape design. Home: Villa Fontana 112 Park Ave Swarthmore PA 19081-1724 Office: HBS Inc HBS Bldg 110 Park Ave Swarthmore PA 19081

KAUFMAN, JONATHAN ALLAN (JON KAUFMAN), public relations executive; b. N.Y.C., May 31, 1943; s. Stephen Allan (dec.) and Jean (Friedman) K.; m. Jill J. Horowitz, July 17, 1983. BA, Carleton Coll., 1966; MA, Syracuse U., 1967. Vol. VISTA, N.Y.C., 1967-69; rsch. dir. Nat. Welfare Rights Orgn., Washington, 1969-71; polit. campaign mgr. various, San Francisco, 1971-77; exec. dir. Calif. Tax Reform Assn., San Francisco, 1972-77; asst. mgr. Household Fin. Corp., San Francisco, 1977-79; account exec. Solem & Assocs., San Francisco, 1979-84, v.p., 1984-86, exec. v.p., 1986—; rsch. dir. SA Opinion Rsch., San Francisco, 2000—. Contbr. articles to profl. jours. Bd. dirs. Jewish Bull. No. Calif. Andrew W. Mellon Fellow, Syracuse U., 1966, Max Bondy Citizenship award Windsor Mt. Sch., Lenox, Mass., 1962. Mem. Am. Assn. Polit. Cons., Am. Mktg. Assn. Jewish. Avocations: hiking, travel, food. Home: 107 Alvarado Rd Berkeley CA 94705-1510 Office: Solem & Assocs 550 Kearny St Ste 1010 San Francisco CA 94108-2570 E-mail: jon_kaufman@solem.com.

KAUFMAN, JULIAN MORTIMER, broadcasting company executive, consultant; b. Detroit, Apr. 3, 1918; s. Anton and Fannie (Newman) K.; m. Katherine LaVerne Likins, May 6, 1942; children: Nikki, Keith Anthony. Grad. high sch., Newark. Pub. Elizabeth (N.J.) Sunday Sun, Inc., 1937-39; account exec. Tolle Advt. Agy., San Diego, 1947-49; pub. Tucson Shopper, 1948-50; account exec. ABC, San Francisco, 1949-50; mgr. Sta. KPHO-TV, Phoenix,

1950-52; gen. mgr., v.p. Bay City TV Corp., San Diego, 1952-95; v.p. Jai Alai Films, Inc., San Diego, 1961—; TV cons. Julian Kaufman, Inc., San Diego, 1985—. Dir. Spanish Internat. Broadcasting, Inc., L.A.; chmn. bd. dirs. Bay City TV Inc. Contbr. articles to profl. jours.; producer (TV show) Pick a Winner. Mem. Gov.'s adv. bd., Mental Health Assn., 1958—; bd. dirs. Francis Parker Sch., San Diego Better Bus. Bur., 1979-84, San Diego Conv. and Visitors Bur., World Affairs Coun., Pala Indian Mission. Served with USAAF, 1942-46. Recipient Peabody award, 1975, Emmy award, 1980. Mem. San Diego C. of C., Advt. and Sales Club, Sigma Delta Chi. Clubs: San Diego Press, University (San Diego). Republican. Home: 3125 Montesano Rd Escondido CA 92029-7302 Office: 7677 Ronson Rd Ste 210 San Diego CA 92111-1538 E-mail: consultingjmk@aol.com.

KAUFMAN, KENNETH ROLAND, psychiatrist, educator; s. Jerome and Rebecca Kaufman; m. Christine Hanson Adams; children: Sarah Jennifer, Deborah Anne, Eliot Michael, Noah Shimon, Nathaniel David. BA (summa cum laude), Columbia U., N.Y.C., 1968; MA in Chemistry, Harvard U., 1970; MD, Wash. U. Sch. of Medicine, St. Louis, 1974. Cert. Bd. Med. Examiners Mo., 1977, Pa., 1977, N.Y., 1978, Calif., 1978, N.J., 1995; Psychiatry Bd. Am. Bd. of Psychiatry and Neurology, 1981. Rsch. asst. Dept. of Chem. Pathology, St. George's Hosp. U. of London, 1966; tchg. fellow Dept. of Chemistry Harvard U., Cambridge, 1968—70; tutor in chemistry Quincy House, Harvard U., Cambridge, 1969—70; asst. instr. psychiatry, NIMH trainee in psychiatry Washington U. Med. Ctr. (Barnes and Renard Hosp.), St Louis, 1974—77; psychiatry resident Washington U. Sch. of Medicine, St. Louis, 1974—77; hon. clin. neurophysiologist Maudsley Hosp., London, 1976; rsch. fellow Inst. of Psychiatry, U. of London, 1976; advanced rsch. fellow Western Psychiat. Inst. and Clinic, U. of Pitts., 1977, asst. prof. of clin. psychiatry, 1977—79; rsch. fellow Dept. of Child and Adolescent Psychiatry Inst. of Psychiatry U. of London, 1976; asst. prof. psychiatry U. of So. Calif. Sch. of Medicine, LA, 1979—82, asst. prof. neurology, 1980—82, clin. asst. prof. psychiatry, 1982—84, clin. asst. prof. neurology, 1982—99; asst. clin. prof. of psychiatry and biobehavioral scis. UCLA, LA, 1984—96; pvt. practitioner Kenneth R Kaufman, MD Inc., LA, 1982—96; vis. asst. prof. psychiatry Columbia U. Coll. of Physicians and Surgeons, N.Y.C., 1986—86; assoc. prof. clin. psychiatry U. of Medicine and Dentistry of N.J., Robert Wood Johnson Med. Sch., New Brunswick, 1995—98, assoc. prof. clin. neurology, 1996—98, assoc. prof. psychiatry, 1998—2002, prof. neurology, 2003—, assoc. prof. neurology, 1998—2003, prof. psychiatry, 2002—; attending psychiatrist U. Behavioral Health Care U. of Medicine and Dentistry of N.J., Robert Wood Johnson Med. Sch., New Brunswick, 1997—98, Cmty. Mental Health Ctr. at Piscataway U. of Medicine and Dentistry of N.J., Robert Wood Johnson Med. Sch., New Brunswick, 1996—97, Consultation Liaison Svc., Robert Wood Johnson U. Hosp., New Brunswick, NJ, 1997—, Splty. Psychopharmacology Clinics, New Brunswick, NJ, 1998—. Editl. bd. Annals of Clin. Psychiatry, 1988—2003, contr. editor editl. bd. Mt. Sinai Jour. Medicine, 1986—89, reviewer (9 profl. jours.); author: numerous articles, chpts., abstracts and internat. presentations in field. Team psychiatrist Mem. U.S. Med. Team, 16th Maccabiah Games, Tel Aviv, 2001. Recipient Gold medal in Cricket, 13th Maccabiah Games, 1989, Humanitarian award, Women's Am. O.R.T., 1993; fellow The Harvard Fellowship, Harvard U., 1968—69. Fellow: Am. Psychiat. Assn.; mem.: The Am. Epilepsy Soc., Am. Chem. Soc., Am. Psychopathological Assn., Assn. of European Psychiatrists, Am. Acad. of Clin. Psychiatrists (treas. 1997—99, program chair 1999—2001, v.p. 2001—02), Royal Coll. of Psychiatry, AMA. Jewish. Avocations: travel, cricket, golf, theater, reading. Home: 8 Villa Dr Princeton Junction NJ 08550 Office: UMDNJ-Robert Wood Johnson Medical School 125 Paterson St Ste #2200 New Brunswick NJ 08901 Personal E-mail: adamskaufman@comcast.net. E-mail: kaufmakr@umdnj.edu.

KAUFMAN, LAWRENCE JESSE, computer engineer; b. Newark, Sept. 13, 1959; s. David and Honora (Cowen) Kaufman; m. Melissa F. Crespy, Aug. 10, 1992; 1 child, Avigdor. BS Computer Sci. and Engr., MA Inst. of Tech., Cambridge, MA, 1977—83; MS Sys. Sgmt., U of S CA, Stuttgart, Germany, 1986—87. Software engr. Bolt Beranek and Newman, Inc., Cambridge, Mass., 1983—85, BBNCC, Stuttgart-Vaihingen, Germany, 1985—87, Bolt Beranek and Newman, Inc., Columbia, Md., 1987—92; pres. Kaufman.COM, Inc., New York, NY, 1992—94; prin. Goldman Sachs & Co., New York, NY, 1994—95, VP, 1995—. Pres. MAXM Users Group, Arlington, Va., 1995—98. Mem.: NY Acad. of Sci., IEEE, Assoc. for Computing Machinery, MIT Sci. Fiction Soc. (mem. 1983—2000), Alpha Phi Omega/ Leadership Devel. Staff. Office: Goldman Sachs & Co 180 Maiden Lane New York NY 10038

KAUFMAN, LUNA AMALIA, musicologist; b. Nov. 28, 1926; came to U.S., 1952; Musicologist, Jagellonain U., Cracow, Poland, 1949. Pres. Temple Sholom, Plainfield, N.J., 1980-82; chmn. Liberty State Park (N.J.) Monument, 1982-85; pres., mgr. N.J. State Opera, Newark, 1987-94; exec. bd. mem. endowment for Judeo-Christian edn. Seton Hall U., West Orange, N.J., 1984—. Pub. spkr. on the Holocaust, 1976—; exec. bd. Anti-Defamation League of N.Y. Charter mem. Gov.'s Coun. on Holocaust Edn., 1982-92, Trenton, N.J.

KAUFMAN, MARK DAVID, lawyer; b. St. Louis, Feb. 24, 1949; s. Rudolf Ernst and Edith (Greiderer) K.; m. Margaret Taylor James, June 1, 2002; 1 child, Mark David. BA, Northwestern U., 1971; JD, Duke U., 1974. Bar: Ga. 1974, U.S. Ct. Appeals (11th cir.) 1974, U.S. Dist. Ct. (no. dist.) Ga. 1974. Assoc. Sutherland Asbill & Brennan LLP, Atlanta, 1974-81, ptnr., 1981—, exec. com., 1996-2000. Contbr. articles to profl. jours. Mem. ABA, Ga. Bar Assn., Atlanta Bar Assn. (legal counsel 1979-2000, Exceptional Svc. award 1987, Pres.'s Disting. Svc. award 1979-80, Charles E. Watkins Jr. award 1989), Atlanta Bar Found. (legal counsel 1985-2000), Order of Coif. Lutheran. Home: 3181 Habersham Rd NW Atlanta GA 30305

KAUFMAN, MICHELE BETH, clinical pharmacist, educator; b. Perth Amboy, N.J., May 13, 1963; d. Harold Alexander and Elaine Sue (Sommers) K. BS in Pharmacy, U. R.I., 1986; PharmD, Mass. Coll. Pharmacy, 1991. RPh, Mass., N.J., N.Y. Staff pharmacist Robert Wood Johnson U. Hosp., New Brunswick, N.J., 1986-91; product devel. pharmacist Reed & Carnrick Pharm. Co., Piscataway, N.J., 1987-89; poison info. specialist Mass. Poison Control System Children's Hosp., Boston, 1990-92; drug info. specialist U. R.I. Drug Info. Ctr., Providence, 1991-92; asst. clin. prof. pharmacy St. John's U., Jamaica, N.Y., 1992-96. Clin. coord. internal medicine, drug info. specialist L.I. Jewish Med. Ctr., New Hyde Park, N.Y., 1992-96; clin. pharmacy coord., drug info. specialist HIP Health Plan of N.Y., N.Y.C., 1996-2001, project leader clin. pharmacy programs, 2001—; drug info. cons., med. writer, 1996—; reviewer Micromedex Info. Sys. Mem. editl. bd. Formulary; contbr. articles and revs. to profl. jours.; patent pending for pineapple colon electrolyte lavage solution. Player tenor sax St. John's Univ. Jazz Ensemble, 1992-97, player tenor and baritone sax Big Apple Corps Band, N.Y.C., 1997—. Fellow Drug Info., 1997. Mem. Acad. Managed Care Pharmacy, Am. Soc. Health Sys. Pharmacists, Am. Coll. Clin. Pharmacy, Am. Diabetes Assn. (profl. divsn. 1999—), Am. Coll. Rheumatology (health professions divsn. 1999—), Am. Med. Writers Assn., Am. Assn. Diabetes Educators, N.Y. State Coun. Health Sys. Pharmacists, N.Y.C. Soc. Health Sys. Pharmacists (membership chair 1998-99, bull. editor 1999-2003), Lambda Kappa Sigma. Avocations: travel, cultural events, racquet sports, postcard collecting, playing tenor sax. Home: 97 Preusser Rd Craryville NY 12521-5218 Address: 445 W 23rd St Apt 14E New York NY 10011-1450 E-mail: mkaufman@hipusa.com.

KAUFMAN, NATHAN, pathology educator, physician; b. Lachine, Que., Can., Aug. 3, 1915; s. Solomon and Anna (Sabesinsky) K.; m. Rita Friendly, Sept. 10, 1946; children: Naomi, Michael, Miriam, Hannah, Judith. B.Sc., McGill U., Montreal, 1937, MD, C.M., 1941. Mem. faculty Western Res. U. Med. Sch., 1948-60, asst. prof., 1952-54, asso. prof., 1954-60; pathologist-in-charge Cleve. Met. Gen. Hosp., 1952-60; prof. pathology Duke Sch. Medicine, 1960-67; prof. dept. pathology Queen's U. Med. Sch., Kingston, Ont., Can., 1967-81, prof. emeritus, 1981—, head dept., 1967-79; clin. prof. office of humanities Med. Coll. Ga., Augusta, 1980-85. Pathologist-in-chief Kingston Gen. Hosp., 1967-79; past cons. Hotel Dieu Hosp., St. Mary's of the Lake Hosp., Kingston Clinic, Ont. Cancer Treatment and Research Found.; asso. editor Lab. Investigation Jour., 1952-66, editor, 1972-75, mem. editorial bd., 1975— ; asso. editor Am. Jour. Pathology, 1967, mem. editorial bd., 1967-71; Mem. grants panel Med. Research Council Can., 1970-74, mem. council, 1971-77, exec. com., 1971-74; active coms. Ont. Council Health, 1968-79, chmn. provincial rev. ednl. subcom., 1972-75 Editor Modern Pathology, 1988, mem. editl. bd., 1989-95. Served to capt. M.C., Royal Can. Army, 1942-46, Medical Corps. Decorated mem. Order Brit. Empire; recipient Disting. Alumni award Duke U., 1975, Internat. Acad. Pathology Gold medal, 1996. Mem. Internat. Acad. Pathology (v.p. 1972-74, pres. elect 1974, pres. 1976-78, pres. U.S.-Can. div. 1973-75, sec.-treas. 1979-91, F.K. Mostofi Disting. Svc. award U.S.-Can. div. 1990), U.S. and Can. Acad. Pathology, Royal Coll. Physicians and Surgeons Can. (com. on exams. 1972), Cleve. Soc. Pathologists (past pres.), Am. Assn. Pathologists (editor Symposium series 1970-71), Am. Soc. for Investigative Pathology, Am. Soc. Clin. Pathologists, Am. Assn. Cancer Research, Am. Soc. Cytology, Coll. Am. Pathologists, Canadian Med. Assn., Can., Ont. assns. pathologists, Ont. Med. Assn., Can. Soc. Cytology. Home: 185 Ontario St # 704 Kingston ON Canada K7L 2Y7

KAUFMAN, PETER BISHOP, biological sciences educator; b. San Francisco, Feb. 25, 1928; s. Earle Francis and Gwendolyn Bishop (Morris) K.; m. Hazel Elizabeth Snyder, Apr. 5, 1958; children— Linda Myrl, Laura Irene BS, Cornell U., 1949; PhD in Botany, U. Calif.-Davis, 1954. Instr. botany U. Mich., Ann Arbor, 1956-58, asst. prof., 1958-62, assoc. prof., 1962-72, prof. botany, cellular and molecular biology and bioengring. program, 1972-97, emeritus prof. dept. biology, 1998—, 1st yr. seminar Residential Coll., 1997—2002. Cons. NASA Space Biology Program; vis. prof. U. Lund, Sweden, 1964-65, U. Colo., Boulder, 1973-74; mem. faculty agr. Nagoya U., Japan, 1981 Author: Laboratory Experiments in Plant Physiology, 1975, Plants, People and Environment, 1979, Botany Illustrated, 1983, Practical Botany, 1983, Plants: Their Biology and Importance, 1989; co-author: Handbook of Molecular and Cellular Methods in Biology and Medicine, 1995, 2d edit., 2003, Methods in Gene Biotechnology, 1997, 2d edit., 2003, Natural Products from Plants, 1998, Creating a Sustainable Future Living in Harmony with the Earth, 2002. Mem. Mich. Natural Areas Coun.; mem. exec. com. U. Mich. Program in Scholarly Rsch. for Urban Minority Students. Grantee NIH, NSF, NASA Fellow AAAS; mem. Am. Inst. Biol. Scis., Am. Soc. Plant Biologists, Am. Soc. Gravitational and Space Biology (sec.-treas., 1985-1993), Internat. Soc. Plant Molecular Biologists, Bot. Soc. Am., Mich. Bot. Club (pres. 1985-89), Sigma Xi. Democrat. Presbyterian. Home: 8040 Huron River Dr Dexter MI 48130-9322 Office: U Mich 1270 Natural Sci Bldg 830 N University Ave Ann Arbor MI 48109-1048 E-mail: pbk@umich.edu.

KAUFMAN, RAYMOND HENRY, physician; b. Bklyn., Nov. 24, 1925; s. Morris and Anne (Markewich) K.; m. Patricia Ann Judson, June 23, 1946; children: Susan Jo (Mrs. Edward B. Kahn), Wendy Beth (Mrs. Seth Katzman), Murri Ellen (Mrs. Raymond Simonetti), Elisabeth Ann. Student, Coll. William and Mary, 1942-43, U. N.C., 1943-44; MD, U. Md., 1948. Diplomate: Am. Bd. Obstetrics and Gynecology. Intern Beth Israel Hosp., N.Y.C., 1948-49, resident obstetrics and gynecology, 1949-53; fellow pathology Meth. Hosp., Houston, 1955-58; asst. prof. obstetrics, gynecology, pathology Baylor Coll. Medicine, Houston, 1959-65, assoc. prof., 1965-72, acting chmn. dept., 1968-72, prof., chmn. dept. ob-gyn, 1973-93, prof. pathology, 1973—, prof. dept. ob-gyn., 1973—. Author: (with H.L. Gardner) Benign Diseases of Vulva and Vagina, 1969, 4th edit. (with S. Faro, E. Friedrich and Gardner), 1994; contbr. over 200 articles to profl. jours. Served with USNR, 1943-45; to capt. USAF, 1953-55. Mem. Am. Coll. Obstetrics and Gynecology, ACS, Cen. Assn. Obstetrics and Gynecology (chmn. com. for cons. gynecol. pathology 1968-87, pres. 1976), Tex. Assn. Obstetrics and Gynecology (v.p. 1971, 81, pres. 1983), Am. Gynecol. and Obstet. Soc. (v.p. 1985-86), Houston Obstet. and Gynecol. Soc. (pres. 1971-72), Soc. Gynecol. Oncology (v.p. 1983-84), Am. Cytology Soc., Am. Fertility Soc., Am. Soc. Colposcopy, Internat. Soc. Vulvar Disease (pres. 1978-79), Phi Delta Epsilon (nat. sec. 1970-75). Office: Baylor Coll Med 1 Baylor Plz Houston TX 77030-3411

KAUFMAN, RICHARD STUART, conductor, music director; b. LA, Nov. 20, 1947; s. Walter S. and Margye L. (Whisler) Kaufman; 1 child, Whitney Claire. BA, Calif. State U., Northridge, 1970. Music dir., condr. Sweet Charity, Two Gentlemen of Verona, Company, nat. tours, 1970-74, LA Civic Light Opera, 1975—80; condr. for various performers including Burt Bacharach, Juliet Prowse, Andy Williams, John Denver, nationwide, 1976—; music assoc. 20th Century Fox Studios, LA, 1982—84; music coordinator Metro Goldwyn Mayer/United Artists Communications, Culver City, Calif., 1984-87; dir. music for TV Metro Goldwyn Mayer/United Artists Comm., Culver City, Calif., 1988—; prin. condr. Dallas Symphony Orch., 1997—; condr. Pacific Symphony, 1990—. Composer: Alma Mater for Calif. State U., 1969. Fellow, Berkshire Music Festival, 1969, Tanglewood, 1969. Mem.: Phi Mu Alpha. Avocations: baseball, racquetball. Office: MGM/UA Communications Inc 10000 Washington Blvd Suite 2091 Culver City CA 90232 also: Dallas Symphony 2301 Flora St Dallas TX 75201 also: Pacific Symphony Ste 100 3631 S Harbor Blvd Santa Ana CA 92704*

KAUFMAN, ROBERT JULES, communications consultant, lawyer; b. N.Y.C., Jan. 21, 1921; s. Ernst B. and Gertrude S. (Popper) K.; m. Susan H. Sanger, Feb. 22, 1951; children— Peter S., James H. Student, Columbia Coll., 1942, Yale U. Law Sch., 1948. Bar: N.Y. bar 1949. Assoc. Gale, Bernays, Falk & Eisner, N.Y.C., 1948-53; ptnr. Gale & Falk, 1953-55; asst. gen. counsel DuMont TV Network, 1953-55; with ABC, N.Y.C., 1955-86, v.p., gen. atty. network govtl. regulation, 1968-86; comm. cons. Scarsdale, N.Y., 1986—. Mem. internat. copyright panel Dept. State; guest speaker on radio and television matters at Practicing Law Inst. and N.Y. U. Law Sch. Served to lt. USN, 1942-46. Mem. Bar Assn. City N.Y. (communications com.), Copyright Soc. U.S.A., Nat. Acad. TV Arts and Scis. (mem. U.S. Olympic job opportunity program com.), Phi Beta Kappa. Home and Office: 33 Clarendon Rd Scarsdale NY 10583-2452

KAUFMAN, ROBERT MAX, lawyer, director; b. Vienna, Nov. 17, 1929; came to U.S., 1939, naturalized, 1945; s. Paul M. and Bertha (Hirsch) K.; m. Sheila Seymour Kelley. BA with honors, Bklyn. Coll., 1951; MA, NYU, 1954; JD magna cum laude, Bklyn. Law Sch., 1957. Bar: N.Y. 1957, U.S. Supreme Ct. 1961. Successively jr. economist, economist, sr. economist N.Y. State Div. Housing, 1953-57; atty. antitrust div. U.S. Dept. Justice, 1957-58; legis. asst. to U.S. Senator Jacob K. Javits, 1958-61; assoc. Proskauer Rose LLP, N.Y.C., 1961-69, ptnr., 1969—. Past chmn. bd. Pirelli Cables & Systems, LLC, Pirelli Tires LLC; chmn. bd. Old Westbury Funds, Inc.; bd. dirs. Roytex Inc., Meadowbrook Equity Fund, L.L.C.; mem. N.Y. State Legis. Adv. Com. on Election Law, 1973-74; chmn. adv. com. N.Y. State Bd. Elections, 1974-78; chmn. N.Y. State Bd. Pub. Disclosure, 1981-82, U.S. Army Chief of Staff's Spl. Commn. on Honor System, 1988-89, N.Y. Chief Judge's Com. on Availability of Legal Svcs., 1988-90; referee Commn. on Jud. Conduct; spl. master N.Y. Supreme Ct. Appellate Divsn., 1999—; mem. Adminstrv. Conf. U.S. (chair com. regulations), 1988-95; chmn. Fund for Modern Cts., 1990-95; mem. Def. Adv. Com. on Women in the Svcs., 1997-99, vice chair com. on equality mgmt., mem. exec. com. 1998. Co-author: Congress and the Public Trust, 1970, Disorder in the Court, 1973; co-gen. editor: Matthew Bender Treatise on Health Care Law, 4 vols., 1992—. Bd. dirs., mem. exec. com. Lawrence M. Gelb Found., Inc., Lawyers in Pub. Interest, 1986—95, Am. Judicature Soc., pres., 1995—97; bd. dirs. NOW Legal Def. and Edn. Fund; bd. dirs., chmn. exec. com. Cmty. Action Legal Svcs., Inc., 1976—78; dir., mem. exec. com. Legal Aid Soc., 1985—90, mem. exec. com. Vols. of Legal Svc., 1986—94; mem. platform com. N.Y. Rep. State Com.; mem. jud. selection adv. coms. Senator Javits, 1972—80, Senator Moynahan, 1977—2000, N.Y.C. Quadrennial Comm. on compensation of elected officials, 1995, 1999, mem. distbn. com., vice chair, 2001—, N.Y. Cmty. Trust; bd. dirs. N.Y. Cmty. Funds., James Found.; bd. vis. U. S. Mil. Acad., 1976—79; dir., mem. exec. com., past chmn. bd. Times Sq. Bus. Improvement Dist.; trustee Bklyn. Law Sch.; pres. Citizen's Union Found., 1993—. With U.S. Army, 1957—58. Fellow Am. Bar Found., N.Y. State Bar Found.; mem. ABA, Assn. of Bar of City N.Y. (pres. 1986-88, chmn. house com., co-chmn. com. on campaign fin. reform 1997-2001, past chmn. com. on 2d Century; past chmn. exec. com., past chmn. com. profl. responsibility, past chmn. spl. com. on campaign expenditures, past chmn. com. civil rights, past vice chmn. com. grievances, past chmn. delegation to state bar ho. dels.), N.Y. State Bar Assn. (ho. of dels. 1978, 86-90), N.Y. County Lawyers Assn. (past chmn. com. on civil rights), Am. Law Inst. Office: Proskauer Rose LLP 1585 Broadway New York NY 10036-8299 E-mail: kaufman@proskauer.com.

KAUFMAN, RUSSEL EUGENE, hematologist, oncologist; b. Kenton, Ohio, Mar. 7, 1946; s. George W. and Eileen M. (Risner) K.; m. Jane Ann Steinman, Sept. 25, 1948; children: Jonathon R., Emily J. BS, Ohio State U., 1968, MD cum laude, 1973. Diplomate Am. Bd. Internal Medicine. Resident medicine Duke U. Med. Ctr., Durham, N.C., 1973-77, chief resident medicine, 1977; rsch. hematologist NIH, Bethesda, Md., 1978-80; asst. prof. medicine Duke U. Med. Ctr., Durham, 1980-86, from asst. prof. to assoc. prof. biochemistry, 1985—2001, from assoc. prof. to prof. medicine, 1986—, prof. dept. biochemistry, 2000—02, prof. emeritus, 2002—, chief divsn. hematology and oncology, 1989-96, chief divsn. med. oncology & transplantation, 1996-98, vice chair dept. medicine, 1995-99, assoc. dean Sch. of Medicine, 1998-99, vice dean for edn. & acad. affairs, 1999—2002, assoc. vic chancellor acad. affairs, 2000—02; dir., CEO Wistar Inst., 2002—; dir. Wistar NCI Cancer Ctr. Mem. sci. adv. com. Am. Cancer Soc., Atlanta, N.Y.C., 1987—; mem. com. Nat. Acad. Sci., Washington, 1983-86; mem. sci. rev. coms. NIH, Bethesda, Md., 1985—; assoc. chief of staff edn. Durham VA Med. Ctr., 1998-99. Contbr. articles to profl. jours., chpts. to books. Searle Found. scholar, 1983-86, Leukemia Soc. scholar, N.Y.C., 1986-90. Fellow ACP; mem. AAAS, Am. Soc. Biochemistry, Am. Soc. Hematology (head subcom. on red cell 1985-88, chmn. com. on tng. programs 1995-98), Assn. Subsplty. Profs. (exec. coun. 1994, treas. 1997-98, pres.-elect 1998-99, pres. 1999-2000, past pres. 2000-01), Assn. Hematology/Oncology Program Dirs. (chair 1997-98). Presbyterian. Avocations: golf, tennis. Office: The Wistar Inst 3601 Spruce St Philadelphia PA 19104-4268 Fax: 215-573-2097. E mail: kaufman@wistar.upenn.edu.

KAUFMAN, SANFORD PAUL, lawyer; b. N.Y.C., Jan. 4, 1928; s. Max and Rose (Kornitzky) K.; m. Bernice R. Sulkis, June 17, 1956; children— Leslie Keith, Brad Leigh, Rona Sheryl, Jeffrey Scott, Adam Ira. BBA in Accounting, Coll. City N.Y., 1948; LL.B., N.Y. U., 1952, LL.M. in Taxation, 1957. Bar: N.Y. bar 1953, Calif. bar 1962. With firm Garey & Garey, N.Y.C., 1953-55; asst. gen. counsel Olympic Radio & TV, L.I. City, 1961-63; sec., gen. counsel Tel-Autograph Corp., L.A., 1961-63; asst. gen. counsel Nat. Gen. Corp., L.A., 1963-74; sec., gen. counsel Familian Corp., L.A., 1974-77; pvt. practice Torrance, Calif., 1977—. Bd. dirs. Temple Ner Tamid, S. Bay, Calif. Mem. Am. Soc. Corporate Secs., Los Angeles County Bar Assn., Beverly Hills Bus. Men's Assn. Clubs: K.P. (past chancellor). Home: 28412 Golden Meadow Dr Rancho Palos Verdes CA 90275-2926 Office: 23505 Crenshaw Blvd Ste 246 Torrance CA 90505-5223 *A person's finest attributes: honesty, integrity, loyalty, dependability and reliability, and the fear of God.*

KAUFMAN, STEPHEN EDWARD, lawyer; b. N.Y.C., Feb. 16, 1932; s. Herbert and Gertrude Kaufman; m. Marina Pinto, June 22, 1967; children: Andrew H. and Douglas P. BA, Williams Coll., 1953; LLB, Columbia U., 1957. Bar: N.Y. 1958, U.S. Ct. Appeals (2d cir.) 1958, U.S. Dist. Ct. (so. and ea. dists.) N.Y. 1960, U.S. Supreme Ct. 1963. Asst. U.S. Atty. U.S. Attys. Office, So. Dist., N.Y., 1964-69, chief of criminal div., 1964-69; pres. Stephen E. Kaufman, P.C., N.Y.C., 1976—. Bd. dirs. Smith Barney Mut. Funds. Trustee Mus. Jewish Heritage; dir. Police Athletic League. Fellow Am. Coll. Trial Lawyers; mem. ABA, N.Y. State Bar Assn., Assn. of Bar of City of N.Y. Office: 277 Park Ave New York NY 10172-0003

KAUFMAN, STEPHEN LAWRENCE, radiologist, educator; b. Phila., Nov. 7, 1942; s. Abraham S. and Genevieve (Finestone) K.; m. Linda S. Brier, Feb. 14, 1996. BA, U. Pa., 1963, MD, 1967. Resident in radiology, then fellow cardiovasc. radiology Johns Hopkins Med. Ctr., Balt., 1970-75, asst. prof. radiology, 1975-79, assoc. prof., 1980-88; prof. radiology, dir. cardiovasc. & interventional radiology Emory U., Atlanta, 1988—2003, prof. emeritus radiology, 2003—. Author: Techniques in Interventional Radiology, 1982; editor: Biliary Radiology, 1992; contbr. articles to med. jours. Lt. comdr. USPHS, 1968-70. Fellow Soc. Cardiovasc. and Interventional Radiology, Am. Heart Assn.; mem. Radiol. Soc. N.Am., Am. Coll. Radiology. Avocations: hiking, white-water rafting, golf, computers.

KAUFMAN, STEPHEN P. former electronics company executive, business educator; b. Cambridge, Mass., Nov. 19, 1941; s. Arthur Samuel and Dorothy Ethel (Birman) Kaufman; m. Sharon Kay Malin, Sept. 28, 1969 (div.); 1 child, Jeremy Scott. BS, MIT, 1963; MBA, Harvard U., 1965; D (hon.), Dowling Coll., 1995. Asst. to pres. Grand Steel & Mfg. Co., Clawson, Mich., 1965—67; group controller Chase, Brass & Copper Co., Cleve., 1967—69; assoc. McKinsey & Co., Cleve., 1969—75, ptnr., 1976—80; group v.p. Midland Ross Corp., Cleve., 1980—82; exec. v.p. Arrow Electronics, Inc., Melville, NY, 1982—84, pres., 1984—2000, COO, 1984—86, CEO, 1986—2000, chmn., 1994—2002; also bd. dirs.; sr. lectr. Harvard Bus. Sch., 2001—. Bd. dirs. Harris Corp., Indigo Systems, 2003—. Trustee L.I. U., Brookville, 1985—. Recipient Corp. Leadership award, MIT, 1987, Disting. Alumni award, Harvard Bus. Sch., 1998. Mem.: Useppa (Fla.) Yacht Club, Harvard Club (Boston and N.Y.C.), Mill River Club (Oyster Bay, N.Y.). Avocations: sailing, tennis. Office: Arrow Electronics Inc 25 Hub Dr Melville NY 11747-3509

KAUFMAN, STEVEN MICHAEL, lawyer; b. Spokane, Wash., July 2, 1951; s. Gordon Leonard and Terri (Thal) K.; m. Connie Hoopes, June 7, 1973; children: Kristopher, Shana. BS magna cum laude, U. Utah, 1973; JD cum laude, Gonzaga U., 1977. Bar: Utah 1977, U.S. Dist. Ct. Utah 1977, U.S. Ct. Appeals (10th cir.) 1977, U.S. Supreme Ct. 1985. Founding ptnr. Farr, Kaufman, and Hamilton, 1979-89; mng. ptnr. Farr, Kaufman, Sullivan, Gorman, Jensen, Medsker, Nichols & Perkins, 1989—; judge pro tem, 1981-98; bar commr. Utah State Bar Commn., 1991-98. Chmn. Commn. on Pub. Defenders, Ogden, 1984. Mem. ATLA, ABA, Utah Bar Assn. (pres.-elect 1995-96, pres., 1996-97, bar commr. 1992-98, rep. Utah Jud. Coun. 1998-99), Weber County Bar Assn. (pres. 1981-82), Rex E. Lee Inn of Ct. (master), Utah Jud. Coun. Jewish. Home: 5878 S 1050 E Ogden UT 84405-4959 Office: Farr Kaufman Sullivan Gorman Jensen Medsker Nichols & Perkins 205 26th St Ste 34 Ogden UT 84401-3109

KAUFMAN, VICTOR A. entertainment executive, former film company executive; b. 1943; Various sr. positions Columbia, 1974—87; founding chmn., CEO Tri-Star Pictures, 1987—89; pres. CEO Columbia Pictures Entertainment, Inc., 1987—89; chmn. Savoy Pictures Entertainment, N.Y.C., 1990—96; CFO, chmn. HSN, Inc., 1996—98, USA Networks, Inc., N.Y.C., 1998—, vice chmn. and Office Chmn., 1999—. Office: USA Networks Inc 42d Fl 152 W 57th St New York NY 10019-3310

KAUFMAN, VICTOR SCOTT, historian, educator; b. Slidell, La., Feb. 22, 1969; s. Burton Ira and Diane Beatrice (Kallison) Kaufman. BA cum laude, Kans. State U., Manhattan, 1991; MA, Ohio U., Athens, 1994, PhD, 1998. Instr. Va. Tech. U., Blacksburg, 1997—98, Geo. State U., Atlanta, 1998—99, Kennesaw State U., Ga., 1998—99; lectr. Southwest Mo. State U., Springfield, 1999—2001; asst. prof. Francis Marion U., Florence, SC, 2001—. Sec. faculty support com. Francis Marion U., mem. bookstore adv. com. Author: (Book) Confronting Communism, 2001; contbr. articles to profl. jours.and numerous papers to confs. and workshops. Mem.Francis Marion U. chpt. Habitat for Humanity. Fellow Contemporary History Inst. fellowship, 1992, 1993; grantee Moody grant, Lyndon Baines Johnson Found., 1996, Eisenhower Presdl. Libr. travel grant, 1999; scholar Kelce Found. Scholarship, 1990, Golda Crawford Scholarship, 1990. Mem.: AAUP (editor newsletter S.C chpt.), Soc. for Historians of Am. Fgn. Rels., Phi Alpha Theta (faculty advisor Francis Marion U. chpt.), Phi Kappa Phi, Phi Beta Kappa, Golden Key. Office: Dept History Francis Marion Univ Florence SC 29501 E-mail: vkaufman@fmarion.edu.

KAUFMAN, WILLIAM MORRIS, engineer consultant; b. Pitts., Dec. 31, 1931; s. Nathan and Sarah M. (Paper) K.; m. Iris F. Picovsky, June 21, 1953; children: Nathan E., Marjorie L., Emily M. BSEE, Carnegie Inst. Tech., 1953, MSEE, PhD in EE, Carnegie Inst. Tech. Registered profl. engr. Supr. Westinghouse Electric Corp., Pitts., 1955-62; dir. rsch. Gen. Instrument Corp., Newark, 1962-65; cons. engr. GE, Valley Forge, Pa., 1965-66; mgr. med. engr. dept. Hittman Assocs. Inc., Columbia, Md., 1966-71; v.p. engring. ENSCO, Springfield, Va., 1971-83; v.p. Ocean Data Systems Inc., Rockville, Md., 1984-85; v.p. applied rsch., dir. Carnegie Mellon Rsch. Inst. Carnegie Mellon U., Pitts., 1985-97, mem. tech. transfer bd., 1989-94, mem. employee retirement and welfare benefit plan com., 1988-97. Chmn. tech. adv. group Fostin Capital, Pitts., 1986-95; mem. adv. bd. Pitts. Seed Fund, 1986-97; bd. dirs. Mellon Pitt Carnegie Corp., Maglev, Inc., Tech. Devel. and Edn. Corp. Patentee in field. Mem. adv coun. on regional devel. U. Pitts., 1986; bd. dirs. Ben Franklin Tech. Ctr. of Western Pa., 1988-97, treas., 1997; cons. tech. acquisition. Fellow IEEE (life); mem. Sigma Xi, Tau Beta Pi, Eta Kappa Nu. Home and Office: 38 Sheridan Rd Swampscott MA 01907-2045 E-mail: billkaufman@cmu.edu.

KAUFMANN, ANDREW STONE, music journalist; b. Boston, Feb. 4, 1973; s. John William and Katherine Stone Kaufmann. BA, Sarah Lawrence Coll., 1995. Freelance writer, 1999—. Contbr. articles to Music.com, Riffage.com, Microsoft Network, Music Connection, Rhythm mag., Meanstreet, Perfect Sound Forever. Mem. Soc. Profl. Journalists, Assn. Music Writers and Photographers. Unitarian Universalist. Avocations: video games, movies, internet, comedy. Home: 193 Oak St Apt 501E Newton Upper Falls MA 02464 E-mail: andy.kaufmann@rcn.com.

KAUFMANN, HENRY MARK, mortgage banker; b. Basel, Switzerland, May 23, 1929; came to U.S. 1940; s. Ferdinand and Carola (Levy) K.; m. Barbara Lurie, Dec. 23, 1961; children: Frederic, Nancy. Student, Univ. Geneva, Switzerland, 1948; BA in Economics, Oberlin Coll., 1951; JD, Harvard U., 1954. Bar: N.Y. 1957, U.S. Ct. Appeals 1960, U.S. Supreme Ct. 1960, U.S. Tax Ct. 1974. V.p. Pearce Mayer & Greer, N.Y.C., 1958-70, I.F.C. Capital Resources, N.Y.C., 1970-75, Smith Barney Real Estate Corp., N.Y.C., 1975-80; pres., chmn. Henry Kaufmann Assocs., Larchmont, N.Y., 1980—. With Mil. Intelligence Europe 1955-57. Mem. New Rochelle Bar Assn., N.Y. Bar Assn., New York County Lawyers Assn., Harvard Club. Avocations: numismatist, world travel. Home: 64 Greentree Dr Scarsdale NY 10583-7029 Office: Henry Kaufmann Assocs 2 East Ave Larchmont NY 10538-2462

KAUFMANN, JEFFREY BAER, business educator, lawyer; b. St. Louis Park, Minn., Aug. 27, 1959; s. Harold Ralph and Nora Jane (Baer) K.; m. Peggy Alicia Rouleau, May 9, 1994. BBA cum laude, James Madison U., 1987; JD, Coll. William and Mary, 1990; PhD, U. N.C., 1999. Bar: Va. 1990, U.S. Ct. Appeals (4th cir.) 1990. Summer assoc. Jeremiah Denton and Assoc., Virginia Beach, Va., summer 1989; rsch. asst. Coll. of William and Mary, Williamsburg, Va., 1988-90; instr. U. N.C., Chapel Hill, 1990-94; instr./asst. prof. corp. strategy and internat. bus. St. Mary's U., Winona, Minn., 1995-97; vis. asst. prof. mgmt. U. Ill., Urbana-Champaign, 1997—2001; asst. prof. mgmt. Iowa St. U., Ames, 2001—. Mem. Nat. Moot Ct. Team, Coll. William and Mary, Williamsburg, 1989; adj. assoc. prof. Ctrl. Mich. U., Mt. Pleasant, 1995, 1997. Mng. editor Adminstrv. Law Rev., 1989-90; contbr. chpt. to book and articles to profl. jours.; reviewer profl. jours. and assns. With USN, 1978-82. Decorated Expeditionary Forces medals (2); Richard D. Irwin Doctoral Dissertation fellow Richard D. Irwin Co., 1993-94, Nat. Doctoral Bus. Fellow Am. Assn. Colls. and Schs. of Bus, finalist Free Press Doctoral Dissertation award, Acad. Mgmt. Mem. ABA (vice chmn. internat. law com., sect. adminstrv. law), Va. Bar Assn., Acad. Mgmt. (3 Outstanding Reviewer awards), Strategic Mgmt. Soc., VFW, Phi Kappa Phi, Beta Gamma Sigma. Avocations: hiking, exercise, reading, history. Office: Iowa St U Coll of Business 343 Carver Hall Ames IA 50011

KAUFMANN, MARK STEINER, banker; b. N.Y.C., Dec. 3, 1932; s. Milton L. and Elsa S. (Steiner) K.; m. Carole Richard, June 16, 1957; children: Jon Richard, Susan Helen. BS cum laude in Bus. Adminstrn., Lehigh U., 1953. V.p., dir. mktg. Standard Fin. Corp., N.Y.C., 1958-64; sr. v.p., dir. Milberg Factors, Inc., N.Y.C., 1964-73; dir. corp. devel. Chase Manhattan Bank, N.Y.C., 1973-87, sr. v.p., 1987-96; chmn. Kaufmann & Ptnrs., LLC, N.Y.C., 1996—. Past chmn. banking divsn. UJA/Fedn.; chmn. bd. dirs. Industry Leaders Fund. Hon. trustee Calhoun Sch., N.Y.C.; hon. dir. Lower Manhattan Cultural Coun.; former chmn. bd. Temple Israel, N.Y.C.; mem. bus. adv. coun. Lehigh U. Served as 1st lt. USAF, 1953-55. Recipient human rels. award Anti-Defamation League, 1973, Am. Jewish Com., 1987. Mem. Harmonie Club, Old Oaks Country Club (bd. mem.), Beta Gamma Sigma, Lambda Mu Sigma, Pi Gamma Mu, Omicron Delta Kappa. Home: 124 W 79th St New York NY 10024-6446 Office: Kaufmann and Ptnrs LLC 124 W 79th St New York NY 10024-6446 E-mail: mskaufmann@aol.com.

KAUFMANN, RACHEL NORSWORTHY, educator; b. Los Angeles, Feb. 12, 1964; d. Ralph Henry and Audely (Gutierrez) N.; m. Karl Alexander Kaufmann, May 28, 1988. BA, Scripps Coll., 1988; MA, Webster U., 1997. Pharmacy tech. Torrance (Calif.) Meml. Hosp., 1982-88, St. Mary Med. Ctr., Long Beach, Calif., 1987-88; asst. area mgr. AutoFuel Co., Abilene, Tex., 1989-90; adminstrv. asst. McMurry U., Abilene, 1990-92; 911 tech. asst. West Cen. Tex. Coun. of Govts., Abilene, 1992-94; adminstrv. asst. Piedmont Natural Gas, Greenville, S.C., 1995-97; gen. psychology and devel. psychology tchr. Sandhills C.C., Pinehurst, NC, 1998—2001; marriage and family counselor pvt. practice, 1999—2002; dir. counseling svcs. St. Andrews Presbyn. Coll., 2001—. Auction com. Am. Cancer Soc., Abilene, 1994; bd. dirs. West Tex. Girl Scout Coun., Abilene, 1992-94. Mem. AAUW (bd. dirs. 1989-94). Presbyterian. Avocations: sewing, cooking, travel, music. Home: 565 S Bethesda Rd Southern Pines NC 28387-6401

KAUGER, YVONNE, state supreme court justice; b. Cordell, Okla., Aug. 3, 1937; d. John and Alice (Bottom) K.; m. Ned Bastow, May 8, 1982; 1 child, Jonna Kauger Kirschner. BS magna cum laude, Southwestern State U., Weatherford, Okla., 1958; cert. med. technologist, St. Anthony's Hosp., 1959; JD, Oklahoma City U., 1969, LLD (hon.), 1992. Med. technologist Med. Arts Lab., 1959-68; assoc. Rogers, Travis & Jordan, 1970-72; jud. asst. Okla. Supreme Ct., Oklahoma City, 1972-84, justice, 1984-94, vice chief justice, 1994-96, chief justice, 1997-98, justice, 1998—. Mem. appellate div. Ct. on Judiciary; mem. State Capitol Preservation Commn., 1983-84; mem. dean's adv. com. Oklahoma City U. Sch. Law; lectr. William O. Douglas Lecture Series Gonzaga U., 1990. Founder Gallery of Plains Indian, Colony, Okla., Red Earth (Down Towner award 1990), 1987; active Jud. Day, Girl's State, 1976-80; keynote speaker Girl's State Hall of Fame Banquet, 1984; bd. dirs. Lyric Theatre, Inc., 1966—, pres. bd. dirs., 1981; past mem. bd. dirs. Civic Music Soc., Okla. Theatre Ctr., Canterbury Choral Soc.; mem. First Lady of Okla.'s Artisans' Alliance Com. Named Panhellenic Woman of Yr., 1990, Woman of Yr. Red Lands Coun. Girl Scouts, 1990, Washita County Hall of Fame, 1992. Mem. ABA (law sch. accreditation com.), Okla. Bar Assn. (law schs. com. 1977—), Washita County Bar Assn., Washita County Hist. Soc. (life), St. Paul's Music Soc., Iota Tau Tau, Delta Zeta (Disting. Alumna award 1988, State Delta Zeta of Yr. 1987, Nat. Woman of Yr. 1988). Episcopalian.

KAUL, ALAN FRANKLIN, healthcare consultant, pharmacist; b. Wilkes Barre, Pa., July 15, 1947; s. Benjamin B. Kaul and Julia Trachtenberg. BS in Pharmacy, Northeastern U., Boston, 1970, MS in Pharmacology, 1976; MBA, Suffolk U., Boston, 1980; PharmD, U. Ark., 2002. Registered pharmacist, Mass., N.Y. Dir. pharmacy svcs. Boston Hosp. for Women, 1974-79; assoc. dir. pharmacy svcs. Brigham Women's Hosp., Boston, 1979-81, dir. pharmacy svcs., 1981-88; v.p. clin. and quality assurance Nat. Med. Care Homecare Divsn., Waltham, Mass., 1988-89; pres. Alan Kaul & Assocs., Sharon, Mass., 1989-90; project mgr. Lewin/ICF, Wash., 1990-91; pres., CEO Med. Outcomes Mgmt., Foxborough, Mass., 1991—. Adj. prof. clin. pharmacy Mass. Coll. Pharmacy, 1982-88, 2002—; lectr. in ob/gyn. Harvard U. Faculty Medicine, 1986-88; clin. assoc. prof. pharmacy Northeastern U. Coll. Pharmacy and Allied Health Scis., 1986-88; adj. prof. pharmacy practice U. R.I., Kingston, 1997—; presenter in field. Contbr. articles to profl. jours.; chair editl. bd. Annals of Pharmacotheory for Ob/gyn. Recipient Outstanding Alumni in Health Scis. award Northeastern U., 1986. Fellow: Am. Coll. Clin. Pharmacy; mem.: Internat. Soc. for Pharmacoecons. and Outcomes Rsch., Inst. Mgmt. Cons. New Eng., Am. Soc. Health Sys. Pharmacists, Acad. Managed Care Pharmacy, Rho Chi, Delta Mu Delta. Office: Med Outcomes Mgmt Inc 132 Central St Ste 106 Foxboro MA 02035-2422 E-mail: alan@mom-inc.com.

KAUL, ANTON, mathematician, educator; b. Sacramento, Calif., July 31, 1970; s. David W. Kaul and Michele R Morgan. PhD, Oreg. State U., Corvallis, 2000. Instr. dept. math. U. South Fla., Tampa, 2000—01; asst. prof. dept. math. Tufts U., Medford, Mass., 2001—. Home: 80 Packard Ave #1 Somerville MA 02144 Office: Tufts Univ Dept Math Medford MA 02155 E-mail: anton.kaul@tufts.edu.

KAUL, MOHAN LAL, social worker, educator; arrived in U.S., 1969, naturalized, 1976; s. Mahanand and Tarawati Kaul; m. Jaya Nagari, Aug. 8, 1950; children: Rajiv M., Sanjiv M., Prerna J. Kvalvik. BSc, Panjab U., India, 1947; Social Work, Delhi (India) Sch. of Social Work, 1958; MSW, U. Pitts., 1967; PhD, Case Western Reserve U., Cleve., 1977. Lic. ind. social worker Ohio. Warden Social Edn. Ctr., Delhi, India, 1950—59; comty. organizer Dept. Urban Comty. Devel., Delhi, 1959, chief comty. organizer, 1959—63, dir., 1963—65; asst. dir. Dept. Comty. Svcs., Delhi, 1967—69, East Akron (Ohio) Comty. House, 1969—71; asst. prof. Kent (Ohio) State U., 1971—77, assoc. prof., 1977—94. Mem. editl. bd. Pediatric Social Work, 1984—88. Contbr. articles to profl. jours.; author: First Account, Family Edition, 2003. Active Portage County Housing Advocates, 1985—86; coord. Citizens Effort to Close Lucky Shoe Cafe, Akron, Ohio, 1972. Fellow, Ford Found., 1965—67; grantee Delhi Sch. of Social Work grant, Govt. India, 1957—58, NIMH, 1974—75. Mem.: NASW (Gold Card mem., cert.), Assn. for Advancement of Social Work with Groups, Ohio Ret. Tchrs. Assn. (life), Coun. East Akron Block Club Pres. (founder 1972). Hindu. Achievements include development of of two centers in India; one for the minorities, 1950; the other for lower caste, 1954. Avocations: gardening, mall walking, Experience-related writing. Home: 1158 Morningview Dr Tallmadge OH 44278

KAUL, PUSHKAR NATH, s. Radha Krishen Kaul and Prabhawati Dhar; m. Leela Kaul, Feb. 23, 1942; children: Meena Javier, Venita Kaul-Bules, Reena. PhD, U. Calif., San Francisco, 1960; cert. Inst. Ednl. Mgmt., Harvard U., 1988. Prof. pharmacodynamics, medicine and pediat. U. Okla., Oklahoma City, 1968—81; dir. Drug Metabolism Labs. Dnaghue Mental Health Ctr., Norman, Okla., 1971—81; assoc. v.p. rsch., acad. affairs and devel. Atlanta U., 1984—87; assoc. v.p. rsch. adminstrn. Wichita State U., Kans., 1987—89; prof. biol. scis. Clark Atlanta U., 1989—. Chair pharmacology and dir. rsch. adminstrn. Morehouse Sch. Medicine, Atlanta, 1981—84; vis. prof. various instns.; spkr. in field. Author: (book) Drugs and Food From the Sea, 1978; mem. editl. adv. bd.: Progress in Drug Rsch., 1998—; contbr. articles to profl. jours. Bd. dirs. India-America Cultural Assn., Atlanta, 1995—96; co-founder U.S. Nat. Soccer Found.; capt. U.S. Nat. Field Hockey Team, 1959. Recipient Lunsford Richardson award, Drug Cos. Am., 1960, Ebert prize, Am. Pharm. Assn., 1962, Alumni Rsch. award, U. Okla., 1968, 1969, Career Devel. award, NIH, 1972, Maharishi Rsch. award, Maharishi Maheshyogi Found., 1977, Nat. Rsch. Svc. award, NIMH, 1975, Acharya Gold medal, Pharmacology Soc. India, 1997, Prof. Dandiya Oration award, Indian Pharm. Soc., 1999; fellow Smith Kine & French Found. fellow, U. Calif. at Berkeley, 1958; grantee several rsch. grant awards, NIMH, Nat. Sea Grant Agy., NIH, others, 1970—87. Home: 385 Longwood Pl Jonesboro GA 30236 Office: Clark Atlanta Univ 223 J P Brawley Dr SW Atlanta GA 30314 Office Fax: 404-880-8647. Business E-Mail: pkaul@cau.edu.

KAULAKIS, ARNOLD FRANCIS, management consultant; b. Lewiston, Maine, Oct. 6, 1916; s. Frank Kaulakis and Amelia (Vilaniskis) K.; m. Marguerite Marie Adams, Oct. 18, 1940; children: Bernadette, Robert, Michael, Marguerite. BS in Chem. Engring., MIT, 1938. V.p., dir. Exxon Research & Engring. co., Linden, N.J., 1961-66; dep. refining coordinator Exxon Corp., N.Y.C., 1966-68; exec. chmn., chief exec. officer BOC-Airco Cryogenic Plant Ltd., London, 1968-71; mng. dir. Cryoplants Ltd., London, 1971-72; v.p. energy devel. The Pittston Co., Greenwich, Conn., 1972-81; chmn. bd., chief exec. officer Pittston Petroleum Inc., Montvale, N.J., 1977-83; mng. ptnr. Kensyntar Project Co., Greenwich, Conn., 1981-83; pres. Afkay Assocs., Rye, N.Y., 1983—. Patentee in field; contbr. articles to profl. jours. Mem. Welding Research Council (vice chmn. exec. com. 1964-68), Jr. Engring. Tech. Soc. (dir. 1962-68), Am. Petroleum Inst., Am. Mining Congress (synthetic fuels com.) Address: 5005 Theall Rd Rye NY 10580-1445

KAUNE, JAMES EDWARD, ship repair company executive, former naval officer; b. Santa Fe, N.Mex., Mar. 4, 1927; s. Henry Eugene and Lucile (Carter) K.; m. Pauline Stamatos, June 24, 1956; children: Bradford Scott, Audrey Lynn, Jason Douglas. BS, U.S. Naval Acad., 1950; Naval engr. degree, MIT, 1955; BS in Metallurgy, Carnegie-Mellon U., 1960. Commd. ensign USN, 1950, advanced through grades to capt., 1970, ast. gunnery officer U.S.S. Floyd B. Parks, 1950-52; project officer U.S.S. Gyatt Boston Naval Shipyard, 1955-57; main propulsion officer U.S.S. Tarwa USN, 1957-58; asst. planning officer Her Majesty's Can. Dockyard, Halifax, N.S., 1960-62, repair officer U.S.S. Cadmas, 1962-64; fleet maintenance officer Naval Boller and Turbine Lab., 1964-68; project officer USS Midway CV41, Hunters Point Shipyard, 1968-70; material staff officer U.S. Naval Air Forces Atlantic Fleet, 1971-74; prodn. officer Phila. Naval Shipyard, 1974-79; comdr. Long Beach Naval Shipyard, Calif.; exec. v.p. Am. Metal Bearing Co., Garden Grove, Calif., from 1979; gen. mgr. San Francisco divsn. Topp Shipyards, Alameda, Calif.; v.p. engring. Point Richmond Shipyard, Calif., 1983-84; v.p. engring., mktg. Svc. Engring. Corp., San Francisco, 1984-92; CEO Am. Modular Power Sys., Walnut Creek, Calif., 1992—. Pres., CEO BioLumber, Inc. Contbr. articles to profl. jours. Mem. Am. Soc. Naval Engrs., Am. Soc. Quality Control, Soc. Naval Architects and Marine Engrs., U.S. Naval Inst., Am. Soc. Metals, Masons. Episcopalian. Home: 403 Camino Sobrante Orinda CA 94563-1844 Office: BioLumber Inc 5500 Muddy Creek Rd Cincinnati OH 45238

KAUNITZ, JONATHAN DAVIDSON, physician; b. N.Y.C., Nov. 6, 1950; s. Paul Ehrlich and Rita (Davidson) K.; m. Christine Lee, July 31, 1983; children: Justin Lee, Genevieve Jung. BA in Molecular Biology, Columbia Coll., 1972, MD, 1976. Diplomate Am. Bd. Internal Medicine, Am. Bd. Gastroenterology. Intern in medicine Presbyn. Hosp., N.Y.C., 1976-77, resident in medicine, 1977-79; gastroenterology fellow U. Calif., San Francisco, 1979-80, gastrointestinal rsch. fellow, 1980-81, L.A., 1981-82; asst. prof. medicine U. Calif. L.A. Sch. Medicine, 1983-91; assoc. investigator VA Career Devel. Series, 1984-85, rsch. assoc., 1985-88, clin. investigator, 1990-95; assoc. dir. UCLA Integrated Tng. Program in Digestive Diseases, 1986-90, co-dir., 1996-98, dir., 1998-2001; assoc. prof. dept. medicine Sch. Medicine UCLA, 1991-97, prof. dept. medicine Sch. Medicine, 1997—. Assoc. chief med. svc. gastrointestinal sect. Wadsworth VA Med. Ctr., 1993—; mem. legis. assembly UCLA, 1991-94, com. on appointments and promotions, 1991—; mem. gastrointestinal bd. Med. Rsch. Svc., Dept. Vet. Affairs, 1993-96, chair, 1995, mem. coun., 1996; mem. NIH study sects.; vis. lectr. Keio U. Med. Soc., Tokyo, 1994, 97, 2000. Editl. bd. Am. Jour. of Physiology. Recipient numerous rsch. grants. Fellow Am. Coll. Gastroenterology; mem. Am. Gastroenterol. Assn., Am. Physiol. Soc., Columbia Coll. Physicians and Surgeons (alumni dir. 1976-86), Soc. for Auditory Integration Tng. (bd. dirs., v.p. 1994-95), Cure Autism Now (bd. dirs., mem. sci. adv. group 1995—, chair 1996, mem. sci. rsch. coun. 2000—), Brentwood Biomed. Rsch. Inst. (bd. dirs. 2002—, chair, 2003—), West Coast Salt and Water Club (program chmn. 1989, treas. 1989-98, pres. 1998—), Alpha Omega Alpha. Avocations: sailing, soccer, bicycling, travel, collecting books. Office: CURE Wadsworth VA Med Ctr Los Angeles CA 90073 E-mail: jake@ucla.edu.

KAUNITZ, KAREN ROSE KOPPEL, retired lawyer; b. Richmond, Va., July 17, 1951; d. Leopold and Lore (Baer) Koppel; m. Andrew Moss Kaunitz, Sept. 10, 1978; children: Kate Baer, David Koppel. AB, Goucher Coll., 1973; JD, Albany Law Sch., 1976. Bar: N.Y. 1977, Ill. 1978, Fla. 1980, D.C. 1980, Ga. 1982, U.S. Dist. Ct. (no. dist.) N.Y. 1977, U.S. Dist. Ct. (no. dist.) Ga. 1983, U.S. Ct. Appeals (5th cir.) 1980, U.S. Ct. Appeals (9th cir.) 1980, U.S. Ct. Appeals (D.C. cir.) 1980. Gen. counsel N.Y. Farm Bur., Albany, 1976-78; sr. staff atty. Am. Hosp. Assn., Chgo., 1978-82; atty., advisor Ctrs. for Disease Control USPHS/HHS, Atlanta, 1982-84; v.p. legal affairs Meth. Med. Ctr., Jacksonville, Fla., 1984-92; assoc. gen. counsel Bapt. Health Sys., Jacksonville, Fla., 1992-2000; ret., 2000. Contbr. articles to profl. jours.; chpt. to book. Mem. ABA (health law forum com.), Ga. Bar Assn., Fla. Bar Assn. (health law com.), D.C. Bar Assn., Am. Acad. Hosp. Attys., Am. Soc. Law and Medicine, Nat. Health Lawyers Assn., Phi Beta Kappa. Jewish. Home: 2966 Forest Cir Jacksonville FL 32257-5618 E-mail: krkk51@aol.com.

KAUPINS, GUNDARS EGONS, education educator; b. Mpls., Dec. 29, 1956; s. Alfreds and Skaidrite Kaupins; m. Debra Ann Queen, Mar. 27, 1998; children: Amanda, Kyle. BA, Wartburg Coll., 1979; MBA, U. No. Iowa, 1981; PhD, U. Iowa, 1986. Sr. prof. in human resources. Grad. asst. U. No. Iowa, Cedar Falls, 1979-81; employee rels. asst. Norand Corp., Cedar Rapids, 1983; grad. asst. Univ. Iowa, Iowa City, 1981-86; prof. Boise (Idaho) State U., 1986—. Cons. in field. Contbr. articles to profl. jours. Recipient rsch. grants Boise State U., 1987-2001, Ponder scholarship U. Iowa, 1983-85; named Adv. of the Yr., Boise State U., 1989. Mem. Soc. for Human Resource Mgmt. (faculty advisor 1986—), Assn. for Advancement of Baltic Studies, Acad. of Mgmt. Avocations: racewalking, golf, racquetball, tennis, skiing. Home: 8475 W Beachside Ct Boise ID 83714 Office: Boise State U Dept Mgmt Boise ID 83725-0001

KAUR, HARMINDER, language educator; b. Delhi, India, Jan. 12, 1971; d. Rajinder Pal Singh and Charanjit Kaur. BA in English, U. Delhi, India, 1989—92, diploma in Spanish lang., 1992—93, MA in Spanish Studies, 1993—95; MA in Spanish Edn., U. Alcala, Madrid, 1996—98. Guest lectr. Indraprastha Coll., Delhi, India, 1995—99; adj. lectr. Medger Evers Coll., CUNY, N.Y.C., 1999, York Coll., CUNY, N.Y.C., 1999—, Pace U., N.Y.C., 2000—. Aux. prof. Spanish Madrid Plus, N.Y.C., 1998; univ. supr. Pace U., N.Y.C., 2002—03; Spanish instr. for health profls. York Coll., N.Y.C., 2003—. Recipient First Prize in Essay Competition, Ministry of Cuba in Delhi, 1995; scholar, Ministry of External Affairs, Madrid, 1996—98; grad. tchg. fellow, City U. Grad. Ctr., N.Y.C., 1999—2002. Mem.: Network Indian Profls. N.Am., Profl. Staff Congress. Avocations: reading, walking, travel, cooking. Home: 122-06 135th Ave South Ozone Park NY 11420 Office: York Coll 94-20 Guy R Brewer Blvd New York NY 11433 E-mail: HKaur12@hotmail.com.

KAUSHIK, SURENDRA KUMAR, economist; b. Malsisar, India, June 21, 1944; came to U.S., 1970; naturalized, 1980; s. Lakminarain Sharma and Rathi Chaturvedy; m. Helena Pokornicki, Sept. 12, 1973. BS in Commerce, U. Rajasthan, India, 1965, MA in Econs., 1967; PhD in Econs., Boston U., 1976. Rsch. asst., instr. Inst. Econ. Growth, Delhi, India, 1968-70; tchg. fellow, rsch. asst., then sr. tchg. fellow and lect. Boston U., 1971-75; lectr. Lowell Tech. Inst. Boston State Coll., 1973-74; asst. prof. Babson Coll., Wellesley, Mass., 1976-81; dir. Inst. Internat. Banking Lubin Grad. Sch. Bus., 1981—; prof. Pace U., White Plains, 1984—. Instr. Northeastern U., Bosron, 1972-73; cons. UN, 1976-77; founder Mrs. Helena Kaushik Women's Coll., Malsisar, India, 1999. Condr. rsch. internat. banking and fin.; editor: Banking, Money Markets and Monetary Policy, 1980, International Banking and Global Financing, 1983, Debt Crisis and Financial Stability: The Future, 1985, Internal Banking and World Economic Growth, 1987, The Practical Financial Manager, 1988; co-author: The Practical Financial Manager, 1988, Multinational Financial Management, 1989. Mem. AAUP, Am. Econ. Assn., Am. Fin. Assn., Western Econ. Assn., Ea. Econ. Assn., Atlantic Econ. Soc. Office: Pace U Lubin Grad Sch Bus 1 Martine Ave White Plains NY 10606-1932

KAUTH, BENJAMIN, podiatry consultant; b. N.Y.C., Oct. 20, 1913; m. Bertha Locke (dec.); m. Yvonne Riley. Student, CCNY, 1936-39; D in Podiatric Medicine, N.Y. Coll. Podiatric Medicine, 1939, postgrad., 1944-45, HHD (hon.), 1981. Pvt. practice, N.Y.C., 1939-78; podiatric cons., 1960—. Co-chief podiatry staff St. Clare's Hosp., N.Y.C.; chief of staff podiatry Jewish Home and Hosp. for Aged, Village Nursing Home of St. Vincents Hosp.; mem. staff French Polyclinic; chief podiatry panel 1199 Nat. Fund; coord. podiatry panel 32 B-J Health Ctr.; mem. med. panel Med. Malpractice Bronx County; trustee, mem. exec. coun. N.Y. Coll. Podiatric Medicine, cons. Podiatrist Local 1199 Health Fund, Equitable Life Assurance Co., various other third-party insurers, pub. rels. firms. Editorial asst. N.Y. Podiatrist Del. to Nat. Conv.; contbr. articles to profl. jours. Bd. dirs. Adams Sch. for Retarded Children, Am. Jewish Distbn. Com. Fellow Nat. Assn. of Professions; mem. Am. Coll. Foot Surgeons (assoc.), Am. Podiatric Med. Assn. (pub. affairs com., editorial asst.), Podiatry soc. of the State N.Y. (spl. asst. to pres., editorial asst. ann. meeting), N.Y. County Podiatry Soc. (sec., exec. bd.), Fair Harbor Yacht Club (sec.), Friars. Home and Office: 302 W 12th St Apt 5F New York NY 10014

KAUTT, GLENN GREGORY, financial planner, consultant; b. Arlington, Va., Jan. 25, 1948; s. Elmer Curtis and Phyllis Ruth (Schmalz) K.; m. Elisabeth B. Emerson, Aug. 19, 1971 (div. 1975); 1 child, Christopher Curtis; m. Elizabeth M. Dansereau, Dec. 22, 1989. BS, Purdue U., 1973; MBA, Harvard U., 1979. Cert. fin. planner; enrolled agt., admitted to practice before IRS. Commd. lt. USN, 1969, resigned, 1977; sr. assoc. ICF, Inc., Washington, 1979-81; mng. dir. The Challenger Group, Silver Spring, Md., 1981-85; sr. planner Fin. Svc. Group, Vienna, Va., 1985-87; prin., dir. Capitol Fin. Cons., Inc., Vienna, 1987-91; pres. Kautt Fin. Svcs., Inc., Vienna, 1991-99, The Monitor Group, Inc., Fairfax, Va., 1999—, chmn. bd., 2003—. Lectr. ADA, FPA, Am. Mgmt. Assn., US SBA, also maj. corps. Author: Stochastic Modeling: A New Way to Predict Your Financial Future, 2001; co-author: The Invincibility Shield for Investors, 2003; co-author, editor Inside the Real Estate Business, 1981; mem. editl. adv. bd. Jour. Fin. Planning, 1999-2002; contbr. articles to profl. mags. Mem. Registry Fin. Planning Practitioners, Fin. Planning Assn. Nat. Capitol Area (bd. dirs., pres. 1999, co-chair 2000, nat. chpt. leadership resource coun.2000-02). Republican. Avocations: flying, skiing, scuba diving, singing. Office: 12450 Fair Lakes Cir Fairfax VA 22033-3810 E-mail: kautt@themonitorgroup.com.

KAUTTER, DAVID JOHN, lawyer; b. Wilkes-Barre, Pa., Mar. 20, 1948; s. William George and Mary (Flanagan) K.; m. Kathy Jane Price, May 22, 1976; children: Hilary, David Jr. BBA, Notre Dame U., 1971; JD, Georgetown U., 1974. Bar: D.C. 1975, U.S. Dist. Ct. D.C. 1981, U.S. Tax Ct. 1981, U.S. Supreme Ct. 1981. Staff acct. Coopers & Lybrand, Washington, 1971-74; mgr. Arthur Young and Co., Washington, 1974-78; legis. asst. Senator John Danforth, Washington, 1979-82; ptnr. Arthur Young and Co., Washington, 1982-89, dir. Wash. Nat. Tax Group, 1986-89; nat. dir. compensation and benefits tax svcs. Ernst & Young, Washington, 1989-98, mem. ptnrs. adv. coun., 1993-96, nat. dir. human resource svcs., 1998-2001, dir. nat. tax, 2001—. Contbr. articles to profl. jours. Mem. ABA, Fed. Bar Assn., AICPA's. Republican. Roman Catholic. Avocation: cabinet making. Home: 8312 Summerwood Dr Mc Lean VA 22102-2212 Office: Ernst & Young 1225 Connecticut Ave NW Ste 700 Washington DC 20036-2621

KAUTZMAN, JOHN FREDRICK, lawyer; b. Indpls., Aug. 23, 1959; s. Fred L. and Barbara J. (Seeger) K. BA, Ind. U., 1981; JD, Ind. U., Indpls., 1984. Bar: Ind. 1985, U.S. Dist. Ct. (no. and so. dists.) Ind. 1985, U.S. Ct. Appeals (7th cir.) 1992. Law clk. Marion County Pros. Office, Indpls., 1981; bailiff Marion County Cir. Ct., Indpls., 1981-84, commr., judge pro tempore, 1985-89; assoc. Ruckelshaus, Roland, Hasbrook & O'Connor, Indpls., 1985-89, ptnr., 1990-98, Ruckelshaus, Roland, Kautzman, Blackwell & Hasbrook, Indpls., 1998—. Mem. faculty Ind. Trial Advocacy Coll., 1998—. Contbg. author The Indiana Lawyer newspaper, 1991—. Mem. bd. assocs. Ind. U. Found., Bloomington, 1993—, v.p. 1997-99, pres., 2000—; precinct commiteeman Marion County Rep. Party, Indpls., 1994-96. Mem.: ABA, Indpls. Bar Assn. (chmn. young lawyers divsn. 1988—89, bd. mgrs. 1994—2002, v.p. 1998, first v.p. 2003, Disting. fellow 1993), Ind. State Bar Assn., Phi Delta Phi. Methodist. Avocations: professional piano, golf. Office: Ruckelshaus Roland Kautzman Blackwell & Hasbrook Ste 900 107 N Pennsylvania St Indianapolis IN 46204-2424 Fax: (317) 634-8635.

KAUVAR, ABRAHAM J. gastroenterologist, medical administrator; b. Denver, May 8, 1915; s. Charles Hillel and Belle Gertrude (Bluestone) K.; m. Jean Bayer, Aug. 22, 1943; children: Kenneth B., Jane Kauvar Athens, Lawrence, David. BA, U. Denver, 1935; MD, U. Chgo., 1939; Sc.D. (hon.), Hawthorne Coll., 1981; LHD (hon.), U. Denver, 2000. Diplomate: Am. Bd. Internal Medicine. Intern Billings Hosp., U. Chgo., 1939-40; resident Peter Bent Brigham Hosp., Boston, 1940-41, Mayo Clinic, Rochester, Minn., 1941-42; practice medicine specializing in gastroenterology Denver, 1946-74; mgr., chief exec. officer Health and Hosps. Agy., City and County of Denver, 1974-80; pres. Health and Hosp. Corp., N.Y.C., 1980-81. Spl. cons. med. Care and Rsch. Found., Denver; Goodstein Disting. prof. emeritus medicine and geriatrics U. Colo. Med. Sch.; adj. prof. Health Policy Univ. Colo. at Denver; health cons. govts., Ireland, Israel; mem. Social Security Appeals Coun., Dept. Health and Human Svcs.; pres. med. staffs Colo. Gen. Hosp., 1954-55, Rose Meml. Hosp., 1955-56; dir. Nat. Jewish Hosp., 1957—; pres. Tchrs. Award Found., 1957. Contbr. articles to profl. jours.; lectr.: hypoglycemia Am. Lecture Series, 1954. Bd. dirs. Salvation Army, 1957— . Served to maj. U.S. Army, 1942-46. Recipient Disting. award, Denver Med. Soc., 1975, Disting. Humanitarian award, U. Chgo. Alumni Assn., 1981, Disting. Svc. award, U. Colo., 1987, award for profl. achievement, U. Denver, 1994, Lifetime Achievement award, Denver Med. Soc., 1996, U. Colo., 2001. Mem. Am. Fedn. Clin. Research, ACP, Am. Gastroent. Assn., Am. Endoscopic Soc., Am. Geriatric Soc., Soc. Med. Adminstrs., Am. Coll. Gastroenterology (v.p. 1976-77) Clubs: Denver, Denver Tennis, U. Club, Rotary. Jewish. Home and Office: 70 S Ash St Denver CO 80246-1004 *Seize the opportunities that are presented whether it be in terms of work, family, friends.*

KAUZLARICH, RICHARD DALE, retired ambassador, political scientist, consultant; b. Moline, Ill., Aug. 18, 1944; s. Victor and Eva Marie (Kronfeld) Kauzlarich; m. Anne Elizabeth Bregstone, Aug. 26, 1967; children: Richard Dale, Jr., Terri Lynne. AA, Black Hawk Coll., Moline, Ill., 1964; BA, Valparaiso U., 1966; MA, Ind. U., 1967, U. Mich., 1976. 2d sec. Am. Embassy, Addis Ababa, Ethiopia, 1973-75; fin. economist Office Devel. Fin., Dept. State,

Washington, 1976-77, dep. office dir. Office Investment Affairs, 1977-80; counselor for econ. affairs Am. Embassy, Tel Aviv, 1980-83; office dir. ops. ctr. Dept. State, Washington, 1983-84, dep. asst. sec. internat. orgn. affairs, 1984-86, dep. dir. policy planning staff, 1986-89, office dir. regional polit.-econ. affairs, 1989-91, dep. asst. sec. Bur. European Affairs, 1991-93; prin. dep. to the amb.-at-large and spl. adviser S/NIS Dept State, Washington; U.S. amb. to Republic of Azerbaijan, 1994-97, Bosnia and Herzegovina, 1997-99; sr. advisor to undersec. state econ., bus. and agrl. affairs Dept. State, Washington, 1999-2001; pres. Kauzlarich Cons. Inc., Falls Church, Va., 2001—02; dir. spl. initiative on Muslim world U.S. Inst. Peace, Washington, 2002—. Mem. Am. Internat. Sch. Bd., Tel Aviv, 1981—83. Named Internat. Person of the Yr., Dnevi Avaz, 1997; recipient Presdl. Meritorious Svc. award, 1993, Hall of Fame award, Black Hawk Coll. Alumni Assn., 1993, Disting. Alumnus award, Valparaiso U., 1999. Lutheran. Home: 7019 Ted Dr Falls Church VA 22042-3943 Office: US Inst Peace 1200 17th St NW Washington DC 20036-3001 Business E-Mail: rkauzlarich@usip.org. E-mail: rkauzlarich@cox.net.

KAUZMANN, WALTER JOSEPH, chemistry educator; b. Mt. Vernon, N.Y., Aug. 18, 1916; s. Albert and Julia Maria (Kahle) K.; m. Elizabeth Alice Flagler, Apr. 1, 1951; children: Charles Peter, Eric Flagler, Katherine Elizabeth Julia Kauzmann Pacala. BA, Cornell U., 1937; PhD, Princeton U., 1940; PhD (hon.), U. Stockholm, 1992. Westinghouse research fellow Westinghouse Mfg. Co., E. Pittsburgh, Pa., 1940-42; mem. staff Explosives Research Lab., Bruceton, Pa., 1942-44, Los Alamos Lab., 1944-46; asst. prof. Princeton U., 1946-51, assoc. prof., 1951-60, prof. chemistry, 1960-82, chmn. dept., 1964-68, David B. Jones prof. chemistry, 1963-82, chmn. biochem. sci. dept., 1980-81; vis. scientist Atlantic Research Lab., NRC Can., 1983. Vis. lectr. Kyoto U., 1974; vis. prof. U. Ibadan, 1975 Author: Quantum Chemistry, 1957, Kinetic Theory of Gases, 1966, Thermal Properties of Matter, 1967, (with D. Eisenberg) Structure and Properties of Water, 1969. Recipient Linderstrom-Lang medal, 1966, Stein and Moore award, 1993; Jr. fellow Soc. Fellows, Harvard U., 1942. Fellow: AAAS, Am. Phys. Soc., Am. Acad. Arts and Scis.; mem.: NAS, Royal Astron. Soc. Can., Fedn. Am. Scientists, Am. Chem. Soc., Am. Geophys. Union, Protein Soc., Am. Soc. Biochemistry and Molecular Biology, Sigma Xi. Home and Office: 301 N Harrison St PMB 152 Princeton NJ 08540-3512

KAVADAS-PAPPAS, IPHIGENIA KATHERINE, preschool administrator, educator, consultant; b. Manchester, N.H., Oct. 24, 1958; d. Demetrios Stefanos and Rodothea (Palaiologou) K.; m. Constantine George Pappas, July 29, 1979; children: George Demetrios, Rodothea Constance. BA magna cum laude, U. Detroit, 1980; MAT summa cum laude, Oakland U., 1985. Cert. tchr., Mich. Pre-sch. tchr. Assumption Nursery Sch., St. Clair Shores, Mich., 1977-80, interim dir., 1984, bd. dirs., 1980—; Sunday sch. tchr. Assumption Greek Orthodox Ch., St. Clair Shores, 1985—; chairperson pre-sch. curriculum com. Greek Orthodox Archdiocese Dept. Religious Edn., Brookline, Mass., 1987—. Cons. Assumption Nursery Sch., 1985—; validator preschs. program for cert. Co-author: Pre-school Curriculum Manual for Greek Orthodox Archdiocese, 1990, Pre-School Curriculum for National Use, 1991. Mem. Assumption Greek Orthodox Ch. Philoptochos Soc., 1978-87; trustee Assumption Nursery Sch., 1979—, Sunday sch. presch. tchr., 1985—; spl. events coord. Assumption Sunday Sch., 1999—; vol. svcs. Bemis Elem. Sch., Boulan Park Mid. Sch., 1991-96; mem. Nat. Ctr. for the Early Childhood Work Force; vol. Troy H.S., 1996—, Rainbow Connection Orgn. Recipient Vol. Svc. award Angus Elem. Sch., 1989. Mem. AAUW, Nat. Assn. for the Edn. Young Children (validator presch. programs for accreditation), Nat. Multiple Sclerosis (adv. bd. 2000). Office: Assumption Greek Orthodox 21800 Marter Rd Saint Clair Shores MI 48080-2464

KAVALEK, LUBOMIR, chess expert; b. Prague, Czechoslovakia, Aug. 9, 1943; came to U.S., 1970; s. Lubomir and Stepanka (Kavalkova) K.; m. Irena Koritsanska, Nov. 24, 1971; 1 child, Steven. Student, Faculty of Transp., U. Zilina, 1960-65, Faculty of Journalism, Charles U., Prague, 1967-68, George Washington U., 1970-71. Journalist Voice of Am., USIA, 1971-72; chief editor RHM Chess Pub., Great Neck, N.Y., 1973-89; mem. German chess team, Solingen, 1969-89, U.S. chess team in chess Olympiad, 1972, 74, 76, 78, 82, 84, 86; reporter world chess championship, chess columnist Washington Post, 1986—; exec. dir. Grandmaster Assn., Brussels, 1987-91, key organizer world cup, 1988-89; coach world championship Challenger, N. Short, 1990-93. Recipient Cramer award, 1999; inductee World and U.S. Chess Hall of Fame, 2001. Mem. Internat. Assn. Chess Journalists, U.S. Chess Fedn. Achievements include being the German chess team champion, 1969, 71, 72, 73, 74, 75, 80, 81, 86, SS Dutch Open champion, 1969, Czechoslovakian champion, 1962, 68, Internat. Grandmaster, 1965—, U.S. co-champion, 1972, 73; U.S. champion, 1978, European Cup team champion, 1976, Olympic champion, 1976, German Internat. champion, 1981; winner 30 internat. all-play-all tournaments. E-mail: lkavalek@att.net.

KAVALER, THOMAS J. lawyer; b. N.Y.C., Dec. 10, 1948; BA, CCNY, 1969; JD, Fordham U., 1972; LLM, NYU, 1975. Bar: N.Y., U.S. Dist. Ct. (so., ea., we. and no. dists.) N.Y., U.S. Ct. Appeals (2d, 3d, 4th, 5th, 6th, 7th, 8th, 10th, 11th and fed. cirs.), U.S. Supreme Ct., U.S. Tax Ct. Law clk. to judge U.S. Dist. Ct. N.Y., N.Y.C., 1972-74; assoc. Cravath, Swaine & Moore, N.Y.C., 1974-75, Cahill Gordon & Reindel, N.Y.C., 1975-80, ptnr., 1980—. Served to capt. USAR, 1969-77. Fellow Am. Bar Found., Internat. Acad. Trial Lawyers, N.Y. Bar Found.; mem. Fordham Law Alumni Assn. (pres. 2000-02), Fed. Bar. Coun. (v.p. 2002—). Office: Cahill Gordon & Reindel LLP 80 Pine St Fl 17 New York NY 10005-1790

KAVALER-ADLER, SUSAN, clinical psychologist; b. N.Y.C., Jan. 31, 1950; d. Solomon and Alice (Zelikow) Weiss; m. Thomas Kavaler, July 12, 1970 (div. 1975); m. Saul Michael Adler, Aug. 14, 1983. PhD in Clin. Psychology, Adelphi U., 1974. Cert. in psychotherapy/psychoanalysis. Psychologist Beth Israel Hosp., N.Y.C., 1974-76, Manhattan Psychiat. Children's Ctr., N.Y.C., 1977-80; pvt. practice psychotherapy-psychoanalysis N.Y.C., 1976—; founder, exec. dir. Object Rels. Inst. Psychotherapy and Psychoanalysis, 1991. Condr. writing and mourning groups; founding dir., supr. faculty, tng. analyst Object Rels. Inst. for Psychotherapy and Psychoanalysis, 1991—; mem. faculty Postgrad. Ctr. Mental Health, N.Y.C., 1984-86, 90; mem. faculty, supr. Nat. Inst. Psychotherapies, N.Y.C., 1985-91; bd. dirs., supr. Bklyn. Inst. Psychotherapy and Psychoanalysis; adj. prof. Fordham U.; founding exec. dir. Object Rels. Inst. Psychotherapy and Psychoanalysis, 1991—; spkr pvt. seminars, writing groups. Author: The Compulsion to Create, 1993, 2d edit., 2000, Women Writers and Their Demon Lovers, 1993, rev. edit., 2000, The Creative Mystique: From Red Shoes Frenzy to Love and Creativity, 1996, International Forum of Psychoanalysis, 1999, The Divine, the Deviant and the Diabolical: A Female Artist's Developmental Journey from Self Fragmentation to Self Integration in a Creative Process Group, 2000, Mourning, Spirituality and Psychic Change, 2003; contbr. over 45 articles to profl. jours.; editor: book chpts. Recipient 6 writing awards, Postgrad. Ctr. for Mental Health. Office: 115 E 9th St Apt 12P New York NY 10003-5420 also: 41 Central Park West New York NY 10023 E-mail: suska674@aol.com.

KAVALERCHIK, BORIS YAKOVLEVICH, information technology developer, researcher; b. Luban, Minsk, USSR, May 26, 1948, came to U.S., 1992; s. Yakov I. Kavalerchik and Liliya S. Rosnegaus; m. Bella K. Kavalerchik, Dec. 27, 1979; 1 child, Inna. MS in Applied Mechanics with honors, Moscow Inst. Physics & Tech., 1969, PhD in Applied Math., 1972; DSc in Computer Sci., Glushkov Inst. Cybernetics, Kiev, Ukraine, 1990. Project leader Belorussian Rsch. Inst. for Mgmt. Info. Systems, Minsk, USSR (Belarus), 1972-77, head system software dept., 1977-79, head systems devel. dept., 1979-90, prin. rschr., 1990-92; tech. specialist, cons., mgr. info. tech. Guardian Life Ins. Co. of Am., NYC, 1992—. Assoc. prof. Belorussian Polytech. Inst., Minsk, 1975-78; leader of many nat. computer projects. Contbr. numerous articles to Russian, Am. and German profl. jours. Recipient Outstanding Sci. and Engring. Rsch. prize USSR Coun. Ministers, Moscow, 1984. Mem. IEEE, Assn. for Computing Machinery. Achievements include research in the fields of data and image compression; reliability and performance of data processing; operations research and its business and engineering applications. Home: 1 Grover Ter Fair Lawn NJ 07410-4506 Office: Guardian Life Ins Co 7 Hanover Sq New York NY 10004-2616

KAVAN, JAN, UN General Assembly official, former Czech Republic government official; b. London, Oct. 17, 1946; married, 1991; 4 children. Degree in internat. rels., London Sch. Econs. and Polit. Sch., 1974; postgrad., St. Anthony's Coll., Oxford, England, U. Reading. Polit. writer, asst. editor; head Czechoslovak sect. East European Reporter jour., 1985—90; founder, Policy Centre for the Promotion of Democracy in the Czech Rep., 1993—; member, Czech Social Democratic Party, 1993—; chmn. fgn. affairs comm., 1994—98; v.p. East European Cultural Found.; mem. Civic Forum Coord. Ctr. Coun., Czech Republic; mem. fed. assembly Czech Republic Parliament, mem. senate, 1996—2000; min. fgn. affairs Govt. of Czech Republic, 1998—2002, dep. prime min. for foreign and security policy, 1999—2002; pres. 57th U.N. Gen. Assembly, New York, 2002—. Vis. prof. Adelphi U., NY, 1992—93; Karl Loewenstein fellow Amherst Coll., Mass., 1993—94. Mem. Helsinki Civic Coun. Presidium; sec. Peace Groups Info. Ctr.; vice chmn. regional com. for Ctrl. and Ea. Europe Socialist Internat. Office: Pres of UN Gen Assembly United Nations New York NY 10017

KAVANAGH, EILEEN J. librarian; BA, Ladycliff Coll.; MS in Libr. Sci., Columbia U., 1969; MA in Liberal Studies, SUNY, Stonybrook, 1980. Reference libr. Farmingdale (N.Y.) Pub. Libr., 1969-70; from reference libr. to libr. dir. Bay Shore-Brightwaters (N.Y.) Pub. Libr., 1970—. Office: Bay Shore-Brightwaters Pub Libr 1 S Country Rd Brightwaters NY 11718 1513 E-mail: ekavanag@suffolk.lib.ny.us.

KAVANAGH, FREDERICK GRAHAM, Japanese language educator; s. Frederick Joseph Kavanagh and Jeannette Graham; m. Ragnhild Marie Greenhagen, Sept. 9, 1988; m. Sue Agnes Lozeau, 1974 (div. 1986). BA in French, Middlebury Coll., Vt., 1966; MA in Russian, U. of Va., 1970; PhD in Japanese, U. of Hawaii, Manoa, Honolulu, 1985. Photo-offset cameraman Kavanagh Assocs., Inc., Huntington Station, NY, 1961—66; tchg. asst. Russian U. of Va., Charlottesville, Va., 1967—70; intelligence translator, russian Leo Kanner Assocs., Redwood City, Calif., 1971—73; asst. prof. Japanese U. of Kans., Lawrence, Ohio State U., Columbus, 1985—86; assoc. prof. Japanese Valparaiso U., Ind., 1987—. Author: (translation) Shinkokinshu; contbr. Fellow Woodrow Wilson fellow, Woodrow Wilson Found., 1966, Mombusho fellow, Japan Ministry of Edn. (Mombusho), 1977—79, Summer Inst. on Modern Chinese Art and Culture fellow, NEH, 1991, Hasegawa Cross-Cultural Comm. fellow, Kiyoshi Hasegawa, Yokahama, Japan, 1994. Mem.: Assn. for Asian Studies. Office: Valparaiso University 1800 Chapel Drive Valparaiso IN 46383 Office Fax: 1-219-464-6952. E-mail: fred.kavanagh@valpo.com.

KAVANAUGH, BONNIE B. corporate communications executive; b. Dayton, Ohio, July 22, 1948; d. Joseph Edward and Phyllis Jean (Shook) Smith. BS in Journalism, Ohio U., 1970. Accredited bus. communicator. Reporter Piqua (Ohio) Daily Call, 1970—71; asst. dir. pub. rels. Bethesda Hosps., Cin., 1971—76; dir. comm. St. Joseph's Hosp., Ft. Wayne, Ind., 1976—81; publs. editor E. Ohio Gas Co., Cleve., 1981—88; coord. customer comm. East Ohio Gas Co., Cleve., 1988—90; mgr. employee comm. Picker Internat., Inc., Highland Heights, Ohio, 1990—96; mgr. internal comm. Prudential Health-Care, Roseland, NJ, 1996—97; comm. mgr. human resources Prudential Ins., Newark, 1997—99, dir. human resources comm., 1999—2002. Speaker, seminar leader various hosps., bus. and profl. orgns., 1975—. Outreach vol. Cleve. Children's Mus., 1986-88, co-chmn. outreach program, mem. speaker's bur., 1988-89, mem. pub. rels. task force, 1989-92. Recipient numerous awards Ohio Hosp. Assn., Ohio Press Women, Acad. Hosp. Pub. Rels., Cin. Editors Assn., also others. Mem. Internat. Assn. Bus. Communicators (dir. mem. svcs. internal communications coun. 1985-88, chmn. directory mktg. coun. 1988-90, dir. examiners accreditation bd. 1986-88, pres. Greater Cin. chpt., 2003—), numerous awards 1975—). Avocations: needlepoint, reading, gardening. E-mail: bbkavanaugh@aol.com.

KAVANAUGH, EVERETT EDWARD, JR., trade association executive; b. New Haven, June 9, 1941; s. Everett Edward and Marion (Gallagher) K.; m. Martha Gamble Murphy, Feb. 23, 1963; 1 son, Brett Michael. AB, Georgetown U., 1963; MBA, George Washington U., 1970; JD, Am. U., 1978. Bar: Md. 1979, D.C. 1990. Sales rep. Northwestern Mut. Ins. Co., Washington, 1963-68; asst. to exec. offices U.S. C. of C., Washington, 1970-72; pres. Cosmetic, Toiletry and Fragrance Assn., Washington, 1972—. Mem.: Congressional Country, Burning Tree (Bethesda, Md.). Roman Catholic. Home: # 12 8500 River Rd Bethesda MD 20817 Office: Cosmetic Toiletry & Fragrance Assn 1101 17th St NW Ste 300 Washington DC 20036-4702 E-mail: kavanaughe@ctfa.org.

KAVANAUGH, FRANK JAMES, film producer, educator; b. Chgo., Sept. 12, 1934; s. Kenneth James and Carol Mae (Wilkey) K.; m. Barbara Ann Barrett, Nov. 16, 1957; children: Franklin James Jr., Christopher Barrett, Kenneth Wilkey. BA, Lake Forest Coll., 1956; PhD, Union Inst., 1982. Producer, dir., exec. ABC-TV, Chgo., N.Y.C., 1956-67; pres. Ravens Hollow Ltd., Warrenton, Va., 1967-69; exec. producer Airlie Prodns., Warrenton, 1979-89; prof. comm., prof. med. and pub. affairs, comm. chair George Washington U., Washington, 1983-89. V.p. Airlie Found., 1979—; adj. prof. Union Inst. Grad. Sch., 1987—; pres. Kavanaugh Assocs., Inc., 1989—; mentor Capella U.; pres. Internat. Acad. for Preventive Medicine. Asst. dir. TV Kukla, Fran & Ollie, 1958; producer film The Saving of the President, 1982 (Emmy award 1982); producer dir. films A Moveable Scene, 1968 (Emmy award nominee 1969), Flowers of Darkness, 1969 (Emmy award 1969), Bridge From No Place, 1970 (Emmy award 1970), The Possible Dream, 1970 (Emmy award 1970), More Than a Paycheck, 1978 (Emmy award nominee 1978), others; producer, dir., writer film Each Child Loved, 1972 (Emmy award 1972), others. Bd. dirs. Performing Arts Trust. Recipient Cup of Italy Italian Film Festival, Salerno, 1982, highest award Edinburgh Film Festival, Scotland, 1982, Blue Ribbon Am. Film Festival, N.Y.C., 1983, Gold medal Houston Internat. Film Festival, 1983. Mem. Nat. Acad. TV Arts and Scis. (life), C.I.N.E., Inc. (life), Dirs. Guild Am., Radio and TV Dirs. Guild, Mensa, Nat. Assn. TV Program Execs. (Iris award 1983), Broadcast Pioneers. Avocations: photography, scuba, boating, motorcycling.

KAVANAUGH, JAMES FRANCIS, JR., lawyer; b. New Bedford, Mass., Feb. 20, 1949; s. James Francis and Catherine Mary (Loughlin) K.; m. Cynthia Louise Ward, July 4, 1968; 1 child, James F. III. BA, Coll. of the Holy Cross, 1970; JD magna cum laude, Boston Coll., 1977. Bar: Mass. 1977, U.S. Dist. Ct. Mass., 1978, U.S. Ct. Appeals (1st cir.) 1978, U.S. Supreme Ct. 1990. Law clk. to assoc. justice Mass. Supreme Jud. Ct., Boston, 1977-78; assoc. Burns & Levinson, Boston, 1978-82, ptnr., 1983-88, Conn, Kavanaugh, Rosenthal, Peisch & Ford, Boston, 1988—. Adj. lectr., litig. specialist Boston Coll. Law Sch., 1994-99. Editor, contbr. Boston Coll. Law Rev., 1975-77. Mem.: ABA, Boston Bar Assn., Mass. Bar Assn., Boston Coll. Law Sch. Alumni Assn. (pres. 1999—2001), Winchester Country, New Bedford Country. Democrat. Roman Catholic. Avocations: golf, skiing, reading fiction and history. Office: Conn Kavanaugh Rosenthal Peisch & Ford Ten Post Office Sq Boston MA 02109

KAVANAUGH, WALTER J. state legislator; b. Bound Brook, N.J., June 30, 1933; m. Carole Pahler; children: Mary Jo, Kathryn. Grad., U. Notre Dame, 1955. Assoc. Kavanaugh Brothers, 1958 86, gen. ptnr., 1986—; mem. N.J. Gen. Assembly, Trenton, 1976-98, N.J. Senate, Dist. 16, Trenton, 1998—. Assoc. Kavanaugh Inc. Fuel Oil Distbrs., 1958-86, exec. v.p., 1986—; asst. minority whip N.J. Gen. Assembly, 1977-78, minority whip, 1978-80, dep. asst. minority leader, 1980-81, asst. minority leader, 1985, asst. majority leader, 1986-89, dean rep. assembly, 1991, trustee Jud. Retirement Sys., revenue, fin. and appropriations com., state house commn.; exec. com. Nat. Conf. State Legis., 1978-82, fgn. trade task force, 1986-87, exec. com., 1986-87, grants com., 1986-87, legis. svc. commn., 1988—, Gov.'s Commn. on Drunk Driving. Chmn. parent's coun. St. Mary's Coll., 1986—, bd. regents, 1988—; bd. dirs. Somerset Alcoholism Coun., 1983—; life mem., past pres. Somerset First Aid & Rescue Squad; mem. Somerville (N.J.) Bd. Edn., 1962-75; pres. Somerset County Mental Health Bd., 1965-68; bd. dirs. Somerset County Park Commn., 1968-75. Address: 76 N Bridge St Somerville NJ 08876-1919*

KAVARNOS, GEORGE JAMES, research chemist; b. New London, Conn., Feb. 25, 1942; s. James Spiros and Mary Pantelis Kavarnos. BA, Clark U., 1964; PhD, U. R.I., 1968. Postdoctoral fellow Columbia U., N.Y.C., 1968-70; postdoctoral rschr. Albert Einstein Coll. Medicine, N.Y.C., 1971; clin. chemist Cyto-Roche, Norwich, Conn., 1971-89; chemist Naval Undersea Warfare Ctr., Newport, R.I., 1989-97; scientist Analysis and Tech., Stonington, Conn., 1997, EG&G Inc., Groton, Conn., 1998—. Adj. prof. U. R.I., Kingston, 1978—, Pa. State U., 2000—01; mem. electroactive polymer team Office of Naval Rsch.; cons. Pfizer, Inc., Groton, 1996—. Address: 121 Riverview Ave New London CT 06320-5440 Office: Pfizer PGM MS9-178-2 Groton CT 06340

KAVDIA, MAHENDRA, chemical engineer, researcher; B, Indian Inst. of Tech., 1988—92, M, 1993—94; D, Okla. State U., 1996—2000. Post doctoral fellow Johns Hopkins U., Balt., 2000—03. Contbr. articles to profl. jours. Office: Johns Hopkins University 720 Rutland Baltimore MD 21205

KAVERIPATNAM, SANDESH, venture capitalist; s. Shantha Kumar and Shanthala Kaveripatnam; m. Divya Kaveripatnam. BS(hon.), U. Rochester, 1996. Design engr. Silicon Graphics, Mountain View, Calif., 1996—99; product mktg. and applications Malleable Techs., San Jose, Calif., 1999—2000; product mktg. PMC- Sierra, San Jose, Calif., 2000; sr. assoc. Telesoft Ptnrs., San Mateo, Afghanistan, 2000—. Scholar Genesee, U. Rochester, 1992-1996. Mem.: IEEE, N.Y. Acad. Scis. Achievements include development of Next gen cutting edge Multi threaded 4 way super scalar microprocessor architecture.

KAVESH, ROBERT A. economist, educator; b. N.Y.C., Sept. 12, 1927; s. Samuel and Pearl (Berlin) K.; m. Ruth Freidson, 1951 (div. 1980); children: Richard, Laura, Andrew, Joseph; m. Danielle Nisivoccia, July 11, 1990. BS, NYU, 1949; MA, Harvard U., 1950, PhD, 1954. Asst. prof. econs. Dartmouth Coll., 1953-56; bus. economist Chase Manhattan Bank, N.Y.C., 1956-58; prof. econs. and fin. NYU Grad. Sch. Bus. Adminstrn., 1958-74, Marcus Nadler prof. fin. and econs., 1974—, chmn. dept. econs., 1968-83. Bd. dirs. Del Labs., Inc.; dir. The Caring Cmty. Neuberger Berman Mutual Funds; econ. adv. bd. U.S. Dept. Commerce, 1968-70; investment adv. com. N.Y. State Compt., 1976-86; pres. The Money Marketeers, 1983-84. Author: Businessmen in Fiction, 1955, How Business Economists Forecast, 1966, Methods and Techniques of Business Forecasting, 1974; contbr. articles to profl. jours.; mem. editl. bd. Bus. Economics, 1965-99. Bd. dirs. Thomas A. Edison Coll. N.J., 1973-78. With U.S. Navy, WWII. Recipient Danforth Found. prize disting. teaching, 1968, Madden Meml. award for profl. achievement NYU, 1979, Gt. Tchr. award NYU, 1983. Fellow Nat. Assn. Bus. Economists (council 1973-76); mem. Am. Fin. Assn. (exec. sec.-treas. 1961-79), Regional Sci. Assn. (past sec.), Am. Econ. Assn. Home: 110 Bleecker St New York NY 10012-2101 Office: 44 W 4th St New York NY 10012-1106

KAVEY, RAE-ELLEN WEBB, pediatric cardiologist; b. Winnipeg, Man., Can., Jan. 9, 1948; came to U.S., 1969; d. Roy S. and Edna Rae Webb; 1 child, Allison Brooke. BSc, McGill U., 1968; MD, SUNY, Bklyn., 1972; MPH, U. Rochester, 1995. Cert. in pediats., pediat. cardiology. From asst. prof. to assoc. prof. SUNY-Health Sci. Ctr. at Syracuse, 1977-92, prof. pediats., 1992-2001; chief pediatric cardiology Children's Meml. Hosp., Northwestern U Med. Sch., Chgo., 2001—. Pediat. rep. N.Y. State Cardiac Adv. Com., 1989—. Recipient Preventive Cardiology Acad. award NIH, 1991-96. Fellow Am. Coll. Cardiology, Am. Acad. Pediats.; mem. Am. Heart Assn. (chairperson coun. for cardiovasc. disease in the young 1996-98, chmn., bd. dirs. upstate region 1992-93), Alpha Omega Alpha (bd. dirs. 1999—). Office: Childrens Meml Hosp Pediat Cardiology 2300 Children's Plaza Chicago IL 60614

KAVIS, GEORGE, engineer, photographer; b. Chgo., Feb. 2, 1935; s. Theodore and Margaret Marie Kavis; m. Patricia Marie Hewison, Dec. 17, 1978 (div. 1989); 1 child, Sherri Lynn. Design draftsman Pullman R.R. Car Mfg. Co., Chgo., 1953—55. Cons. for design of prodn. machinery. Furniture design and mfg. With U.S. Army, 1955—57. Achievements include patents in field. Avocations: invention, art, photography, writing, collecting. Office: FH Ayer Mfg Co Box 247 Chicago Heights IL 60411 Office Fax: 708-755-9445.

KAVLI, FRED, retired manufacturing executive, retired engineering executive; b. Norway, Aug. 20, 1927; came to U.S., 1956; Grad. in physics, Norwegian Inst. Tech., 1955. Founder, CEO automotive and aerospace sensor engring.-mfg. Kavlico Corp., 1958—2000; ret. Bd. dirs. The Found. for Santa Barbara City Coll.; trustee Found. for U. Calif., Santa Barbara; founder, chmn The Kavli Found./The Kavli Inst.; mem. pres. adv. bd. U. Calif. Office: Ste 250 1801 Solar Dr Oxnard CA 93030

KAVOUKJIAN, MICHAEL EDWARD, lawyer; b. Mpls., Apr. 19, 1958; s. Antranik M. and Leikny Dorthea (Oines) K. AB with distinction, Stanford U., 1980; JD cum laude, Harvard U., 1984. Bar: Minn. 1984, N.Y. 1986, U.S. Dist. Ct. Minn. 1985, U.S. Dist. Ct. (so. dist.) N.Y. 1988, Fla. 1999. From assoc. to ptnr. White & Case, N.Y.C. and Miami, Fla., 1985—. Mem.: ABA (chmn. com. estate planning and drafting 1992—94), Soc. Trust and Estate Practitioners (UK), Assn. Bar City N.Y., The Fla. Bar, Minn. State Bar Assn., Lincoln's Inn Soc. of Harvard Law Sch. (bd. govs. 1982—84), Nat. Press Club (Washington), Harvard Club (N.Y.C., Washington, Boston). Republican. Presbyterian. Office: White & Case 1155 Avenue Of The Americas New York NY 10036-2787 also: White & Case 200 S Biscayne Blvd Miami FL 33131-2352

KAVULICH, JOHN STEVEN, II, international marketing executive; b. Buffalo, Sept. 2, 1961; s. John Sr. and Emily Helen Anne (Kloc) K. BBA, George Washington U., 1983. Pres. U.S.-Cuba Trade and Econ. Coun., Inc., 1994—.

KAVVAS, M. LEVENT, civil engineering educator; b. Ankara, Turkey, May 24; s. A.C. and A. Kavvas; m. Jale C. Kavvas, Apr. 28, 1976; children: Ercan (Dec.), Eren B., Erol. BSc in Civil Engring., M.E.T.U., Ankara, 1970; MSc in Water Resource Engring., Colo. State U., 1972; PhD, Purdue U., 1975. Assoc. prof. civil engring. U. Ky., Lexington, 1981-85, U. Calif., Davis, 1985-90, prof. civil engring., 1990—. Editor: New Directions for Surface Water Modeling, 1989; editor ASCE Jour. Hydrologic Engring., 1995—; contbr. nearly 100 articles to profl. jours. Recipient ASCE Arid Lands Hydraulic Engring. Awd., 2001, Fulbright scholar, 1970-75. Mem. (Richard R. Torrens award 1999, Arid Lands Hydraulic Engring. award 2001). Home: 526 Isla Pl Davis CA 95616-0137 Office: U Calif Dept Civil/Environ Engring Davis CA 95616

KAW, AUTAR KRISHEN, mechanical engineer, educator; b. Srinagar, India, Feb. 15, 1960; came to U.S., 1982; s. Radha Krishen and Chuni Devi (Mattoo) K.; m. Sherrie Lynn Phillips, May 16, 1986; children: Candace Sandhya, Angelie Kristen. BE with honors, Birla Inst. Tech. & Sci., Pilani, India, 1981; MS, Clemson U., 1984, PhD, 1987. Student trainee Nat. Thermal Power Corp., New Delhi, 1980; maintenance engr. Escorts Tractors Ltd., Faridabad, India, 1981-82; grad. rsch. asst. Clemson (S.C.) U., 1982-83, prin. grad. asst., 1984-87; asst. prof. mech. engring. U. South Fla., Tampa, 1987-92, assoc. prof., 1992-96, prof., 1996—. Author: Mechanics of Composite Materials, 1997; contbr. articles to profl. publs. Recipient Ralph Teetor award Soc. Automotive Engrs., 1991, Tchg. Incentive Program award State of Fla., 1994, 96. Mem. ASME (assoc., chpt. exec. com. 1989-90), Mech. Engring. Assn. India (pres. local chpt. 1982), Am. Soc. Engring. Edn. (New Mechanics Educator award 1992, Archie Higdon Mechanics Educator award 2002), Soc. Engring. Sci., Am. Acad. Mechanics. Christian. Avocations: music, bicycling, movies. Office: U South Fla Mech Engring ENB 118 4202 E Fowler Ave Tampa FL 33620-5350

KAWACHIKA, JAMES AKIO, lawyer; b. Honolulu, Dec. 5, 1947; s. Shinichi and Tsuyuko (Murashige) K.; m. Karen Keiko Takahashi, Sept. 1, 1973; 1 child, Robyn Mari. BA, U. Hawaii, Honolulu, 1969; JD, U. Calif., Berkeley, 1973. Bar: Hawaii 1973, U.S. Dist. Ct. Hawaii 1973, U.S. Ct. Appeals (9th cir.) 1974, U.S. Supreme Ct. 1992. Dep. atty. gen. Office of Atty. Gen. State of Hawaii, Honolulu, 1973-74; assoc. Padgett, Greeley & Marumoto, Honolulu, 1974-75, Law Office of Frank D. Padgett, Honolulu, 1975-77, Kobayashi, Watanabe, Sugita & Kawashima, Honolulu, 1977-82; ptnr. Carlsmith, Wichman, Case, Mukai & Ichiki, Honolulu, 1982-86, Bays, Deaver, Hiatt, Kawachika & Lezak, Honolulu, 1986-95; propr. Law Offices of James A. Kawachika, Honolulu, 1996—2002; ptnr. Reinwald, O'Connor & Playdon LLP, Honolulu, 2002—. Mem. Hawaii Bd. of Bar Examiners, Honolulu; arbitrator Cir. Ct. Arbitration Program State of Hawaii, Honolulu, 1986—. Chmn. Disciplinary Bd. Hawaii Supreme Ct., 1991-97; mem. U.S. Dist. Ct. Adv. Com. on the Civil Justice Reform Act of 1990, 1991—. Mem. ABA, ATLA, Am. Judicature Soc. (bd. dirs. Hawaii chpt. 2003-), Hawaii State Bar Assn. (bd. dirs. 1975-76, young lawyers

sect. 1983-84, 92-93, treas. 1987-88, v.p./pres.-elect 1997-98, pres. 1998-99), 9th Cir. Jud. Conf. (lawyer rep. Honolulu chpt. 1988-90). Avocations: running, tennis, skiing. Office: Pacific Guardian Ctr Makai Tower 733 Bishop St 24th Flr Honolulu HI 96813-4070

KAWADA, JANET HANSEN, artist, educator; b. Newton, Mass., June 20, 1953; m. Charles Y. Kawada; children: Taylor Hansen, Russell Hansen. AS, Lasell Jr. Coll., Newton, Mass., 1973; BFA, Mass. Coll. Art, 1992; MFA, Vermont Coll., 1998. Studio mgr. Mass. Coll. Art., Boston, 1992-2001. Mem. adj. faculty Mass. Coll. Art, 1996—, New Eng. Sch. Art and Design, Boston, 1997—; dir. Kingston Gallery, Boston, 1999-2003; tech. dir. Devotion Pub. Sch., Brookline, Mass., 1985-92. Martin Godine fellow Mass. Coll. Art, 1992. Home: 197 Fuller St Brookline MA 02446-5774 E-mail: jkawada@usa.net.

KAWAGUCHI, MEREDITH FERGUSON, lawyer; b. Dallas, Feb. 5, 1940; d. Hugh William Ferguson and Ruth Virginia (Perdue) Drewery; m. Harry H. Kawaguchi, Apr. 22, 1977. BA, U. Tex., 1962, MA, 1968; JD, So. Meth. U., 1977. Bar: Tex. 1977. Legal examiner gas utilities div. Tex. Railroad Commn., Austin, 1977-84, legal examiner oil and gas div., 1984-89, asst. dir. gas utilities and liquified petroleum gas sect. of legal div., 1989-90, legal examiner legal div., 1990—; cons. in law, lectr. to profl. confs. Author position paper Tex. Energy Natural Resources Adv. Council. Mem., Sorority Adv. Coun., Austin, 1980-88, Japanese-Am. Citizens League, Houston, 1981—, Exec. Women in Tex. Govt., Austin, 1984. Recipient Cert. of Recognition Tex. Railroad Commn., 1982, Outstanding Svc. award, 1987. Mem. ABA, Tex. Bar Assn., Travis County Bar Assn. (oil gas and mineral law sect.), Travis County Women Lawyers Assn., Exec. Women in Tex., Internat. Platform Assn. Home: 5009 Westview Dr Austin TX 78731-4741 Office: Tex Railroad Commn 1701 Congress Ave Austin TX 78701-1402

KAWAHARA, FRED KATSUMI, research chemist; b. Penngrove, Calif., Feb. 26, 1921; s. Kentaro and Kiku (Seo) K.; m. Sumiko Hayami, May 5, 1952; children: Robert Katsumi, Kiku Seo, Richard Hojo; m. Andrea L. Eary, June 29, 1991. BS with honors, U. Tex., 1944; PhD, U. Wis., 1948. Assoc. chemist USDA, Peoria, Ill., 1948-51; fellow U. Chgo., 1951-53; sr. rsch. scientist Amoco Corp. (formerly Standard Oil of Ind.), Whiting, 1953-65; rsch. chemist EPA, Cin., 1965—. Cons., expert witness U.S. Dept. Def., U.S. Dept. Air Force, U.S. Dept. Justice, State of Pa., State of N.J.; mentor EPA, others, 1965—; patent reviewer in field; lectr. in field. Co-author: Fossil Energy Extraction, 1983, Innovative Site Remediation Technology, Chemical Treatment, vol. 2, 1994; contbr. 8 chpts. to books, over 70 articles to profl. jours. Recipient Superior Svc. award Bur. Indsl. and Agrl. Chemistry, Dept. Agr., 1952. Fellow Am. Inst. Chemists. rsch. scientist EPA. Home: 1632 Cumberland St Covington KY 41011-3716 Office: US EPA 26 Martin Luther King Dr W Cincinnati OH 45220-2242

KAWAKAMI, BERTHA C. state representative; b. Honolulu, July 28, 1931; children: Wendall, Lyndall. BA in Edn., U. of Hawaii, 1953; MA in Edn., NYU, 1962. Elem., resource tchr. Eleele Pearl Harbor Internat., Nanaikapono, 1954—61; lang. arts dist. team, 1962—65; prin., elem. intermediate Eleele and Kekaha Schs., 1965—79; ednl. specialist Kauai Dist. Office, 1980—87, dep. dist. supr. dept. edn., 1987; asst. majority fl. leader, 1987—. Bd. trustees Blood Bank of Hawaii, 1992—; adv. com. Cmty. Health Nursing Divsn., 1991—; quality assurance com. Kauai Vets. Meml. Hosp., 1991—; bd. dirs., v.p. Comml. Properties Inc., 1988—; mem. Waimea United Chs. of Christ, 1989—. Mem.: Japanese Am. Nat. Mus. (hon. chairperson), Hawaii State Found. on Culture and Arts, Delta Kappa Gamma Soc. Internat. Democrat. Office: State Capitol Rm 434 415 S Beretania St Honolulu HI 96813 Fax: 808-586-6281. E-mail: repkawakami@capitol.hawaii.gov.*

KAWAMOTO, CALVIN KAZUO, state legislator; b. Pepeekeo, Hawaii, Apr. 14, 1940; m. Carolyn Kawamoto; children: Walter, Nina. BA, U. Hawaii, 1963; postgrad., No. Mich. U.; D, Oreg. State U. Mem. Hawaii Senate, Dist. 18, Honolulu, 1994—; chair transp. and mil. affairs, govt. ops. Hawaii Senate, Honolulu, 1996—, mem. ways and means com., mem. econ. devel. com., 1994—, sen. mil. liaison, 1994—, mem. edn. com., agrl. com., labor com., majority fl. leader. Exec. dir. Waipahu Cmty. Found.; dir. Waipahu Bus. Assn., Wahiawa Hosp. Bd., Rural Oahu Family Bd., Waianae Coast Comprehensive Ctr., Am. Box Car Racing Internat.; mem. Pearl City H.S., Manana Elem. PTA, Kanoelani Elem. PTA, Aiea/Pearl City Bus. Assn., Waipahu H.S.; mem. mgmt. com. Waipahu H.S. Budget Com.; exec. dir. Waipahu Cmty. Adult Day Health Ctr. and Youth Ctr.; exec. dir., v.p. Waipahu Cmty. Found. With USAF. Recipient award Waipahu Pride, Eagle Scout, 1958; decorated Disting. Flying Cross, thirteen air medals. Mem. VFW (judge advocate). Democrat. Office: State Capitol 415 S Beretania St Honolulu HI 96813-2407

KAWAMOTO, HENRY K. plastic surgeon; b. Long Beach, Calif., 1937; Intern U. Calif. Hosp., L.A., 1965; resident gen. surgery Columbia Presbyn. Med. Ctr., N.Y., 1969-71; resident plastic surgery NYU, 1971-73; fellow crano-facial surgery Dr. Paul Tessier, Paris, 1973-74; clin. prof. plastic surgery U. Calif., L.A. Mem. Am. Assn. Plastic Surgeons, Am. Soc. Plastic Surgeons, ASMS, AOA. Office: 1301 20th St Ste 460 Santa Monica CA 90404-2054

KAWAMOTO, WALTER, family life educator, consultant; PhD in Family Studies, Oreg. State U. Cert. family life educator Nat. Coun. on Family Rels., 2000. Asst. prof. Syracuse U., NY, 1997—98, Calif. State U., Sacramento, 1998—2003; prin. cons. survey on the lifestyle and health of Japanese Ams. Gakugei U., Tokyo, 2001; nat. cons. panel mem. ORC Macro Inc., Washington D.C., 2002. Singer George Brunis Band, Tommy Dorsay. Contbr. Pres. Japanese Am. Citizens League, Florin, Calif., 2002—03, Multicultural Assistance Program, Corvallis, Oreg., 1994—95; bd. dirs. Associacion Cultural Latinoamericana, Corvallis, Oreg., 1995—96. Fellow Sasakawa fellow, Nippon Found., 2001; grantee Rsch. grantee, NIMH, 1992—94. Mem.: Econ. and Social Rsch. Coun. (assoc.; grant application reviewer 2000—00), Nat. Assn. for Chicano Studies (assoc.), Calif. Coun. on Family Rels. (assoc.; pres. 2000—01), Nat. Coun. on Family Rels. (assoc.; pub. policy com. vice chair 2001—01, mem. ethnic minority sect.). Home: 3604 Pinell St Sacramento CA 95838 Personal E-mail: waltertk@yahoo.com.

KAWANO, ARNOLD HUBERT, lawyer; b. Phila., Mar. 27, 1948; s. James Tadao and Shigeko (Sakamoto) K.; m. Sandra K. Lee, July 1, 1970; children: Thomas L., Mark L. BS magna cum laude, Columbia U., 1975, JD, 1977. Bar: N.Y. 1978, D.C. 1979, Pa. 1981, U.S. Dist. Ct. (ea. and so. dists.) N.Y. 1978, U.S. Ct. Appeals (fed. cir.) 1992, U.S. Ct. Internat. Trade 1992, U.S. Supreme Ct. 1981. Assoc. Reid & Priest, N.Y.C., 1977-80, Weil, Gotshal & Manges, N.Y.C., 1980-81; counsel Sumitomo Corp. of Am., N.Y.C., 1981-84; pvt. practice N.Y.C., Mineola, N.Y., 1984-87; v.p. J.P. Morgan, N.Y.C., 1987-91; ptnr. Inouye & Ogden, N.Y.C., 1992-93; sr. v.p., gen. counsel ORIX USA Corp., N.Y.C., 1993-98; mng. dir. Harold L. Lee & Sons, Inc., N.Y.C., 1999—. Bd. dirs. Harold L. Lee & Sons, Inc., N.Y.C. Bd. dirs. Asian-Am. Legal Def. and Edn. Fund, N.Y.C., 1977-88, N.Y. Civil Liberties Union, 1992-94. Harlan Fiske Stone scholar Columbia Law Sch., 1976, Internat. fellow Columbia U. Sch. Internat. Affairs, 1976. Fellow Am. Coll. Investment Counsel; mem. ABA, NAACP, N.Y. State Bar Assn., D.C. Bar, Assn. of Bar City N.Y., Asian Pacific Am. Bar Assn. N.Y. (bd. dirs. 1992-93), Am. Corp. Counsel Assn., Computer Law Assn., Internat Wine Law Assn., Assn. for Computing Machinery, Nat. Press Photographers Assn., Evidence Photographers Internat. Coun., Japanese Am. Citizens League, Phi Beta Kappa. Avocations: photography, skiing. Office: 31 Pell St New York NY 10013-5148 E-mail: kawano@abanet.org.

KAWANO, JAMES CONRAD, investment analyst; Student, U. Calif., Berkeley, 1972-73; PharmD, U. Calif., San Francisco, 1978; postgrad., U. Pa., 1986—. Registered pharmacist, Calif., Pa. Clin. pharmacist Med. Coll. Pa. and Hosp., Phila., 1978-82; med. devel. coord. E.R. Squibb and Sons, U.S., Princeton, N.J., 1982-84, mktg. rsch. supr., 1984-85, mktg. rsch. mgr., 1985-86; mgr. strategic planning and bus. analysis Squibb U.S., Princeton, 1986-87, bus. devel. mgr., 1987-88; mgr. product planning worldwide bus. devel. Squibb Pharms. Group, Princeton, 1988-89; mgr. product planning pravastatin, worldwide strategic product planning Bristol-Myers Squibb Pharm. Group, Princeton, 1989-90, sr. product planning mgr., strategic product planning, 1990-91; cons. mktg. Narberth, Pa., 1991-94; investment analyst, 1991—; pres. Riverfield Investment Rsch., Wynnewood, Pa., 1994—. Pub., editor: The Optimer Report, 1994—; patentee in field. Mem. Japanese Am. Citizens League (bd. dirs. Phila. chpt. 1997-98, treas. Phila. chpt. 1998—, vice-gov. Ea. dist. coun. 1998-99, treas. Ea. dist. coun. 1999—), Calif. Pharmacists Assn., Phila. Skating Club, Humane Soc. (bd. dirs. 2002-).

KAWANO, TOSHIAKI, retired economics educator; b. Shintomi-machi, Miyazaki, Japan, Jan. 25, 1933; s. Yoshimatsu and Kesazuru (Hiezima) K.; m. Miho Kanai, Dec. 8, 1967 (dec. May 1979); children: Chiho, Toshihide, Toshifumi. Bachelor, Miyazaki (Japan) U., 1955; M in Agr., U. Tokyo Grad. Sch., 1958, PhD in Agr., 1982. Rsch. fellow Internat. Christian U., Tokyo, 1955-56; rschr. Nat. Inst. of Agrl. Sci., Tokyo, 1960-73, chief mktg. lab., 1974-80; prof. economic geography Hitotsubashi U., Tokyo, 1983-96; prof. agrl. econ. Ryutsu Keizai U., Ryugasaki, Japan, 1996—2003. Vis. lectr. Chiba U. Sch. Horticulture, Matsudo, Japan, 1980-98, Tokyo U. Agr. and Engring., 1988-91; lectr. fgn. agrl. trainees Japan Internat. Coop. Agy., 1990--; cons. Nat. Rural Devel. Assn., others, Tokyo, 1960-1990; del. to internat. congresses Asian Productivity Orgn., Tokyo, 1970-90; sec. gen. Farm Mgmt. Assn. Japan, Tsukuba, 1982-83; lectr. in field. Author, editor books; editor Agrl. Econ. Soc. of Japan, 1976-77; contbr. articles to profl. jours. FAO fellow UN, Mich. State U., 1964-65. Mem. Internat. Soc. Horticultural Sci. (corr. economic newsletter 1970-80), Internat. Assn. Agrl. Economists. Buddist. Avocations: gardening, folkmusic. Home: 381-13 Myojin Tsukuba Ibaraki 300-1257 Japan E-mail: fwny6056@mb.infoweb.ne.jp.

KAWARSKY, JAY A. music educator, conductor, composer; b. Des Moines, Iowa, Aug. 29, 1959; s. Irvin Kalman and Eloise Ann Kawarsky. DMA, Northwestern U., Evanston, IL, 1983—85, MM, 1981—82; MusB, Iowa State U., Ames, IA, 1978—81. Asst. prof. Ft. Hays State U., Hays, Kans., 1985—86; instr. Univ. of Wis.-Marathon, Wausau, Wis., 1986—87; asst. prof. Moraine Valley Comm. Coll., Palos Hills, Ill., 1987—89; prof. Westminster Choir Coll. of Rider Univ., Princeton, NJ, 1989—. Condr. NJ. Gay Men's Chorus, Princeton, NJ, 1991—97; artistic dir. Lehigh Valley Gay Men's Chorus, Allentown, Pa., 1997—. Composer: (choral/orchestral) Prayers for Bobby, (choral) I Dreamed in a Dream, Magnificat, Ocho Kandelikas, The Final Word, Blessed is the Match, Life Doesn't Frighten Me, Civil War Voices, Freedom, Erev Shel Shoshanim, As a Driven Leaf, (orchestral) Episodes, (instrumental) Observation I, (choral) Al Hanissim, (choral/orchestral) Alec Baldwin Doesn't Love Me; musician: Sing for the Cure; composer: (choral) Adon Olam, Creed, (instrumental) Rejoice, O Young Man, Awake, North Wind, (orchestral) Grace Dances. Recipient ASCAP award, ASCAP, 1998, 1999, 2000, 2001, 2002, 2003; fellow Summer Fellowships, Rider U., 2000, 2002. Mem.: AAUP (hon.; president-rider univ. chpt. 2002—03). D-Liberal. Jewish. Avocations: theater, travel, weightlifting. Home: PO Box 213 New Hope PA 18938 Office: Westminster Choir Coll of Rider Univ 101 Walnut Lane Princeton NJ 08540 Personal E-mail: jaktg@verizon.net. E-mail: jkawarsky@rider.edu.

KAWCZAK, JANUSZ, mathematician, educator; b. Gorowo Ilaweckie, Poland, Dec. 2, 1963; arrived in U.S., 1998, permanent resident; s. Grzegorz and Anna Kawczak; m. Pauline To, Sept. 17, 2000. BSc with hons., U.Man., Winnipeg,Can., 1992—92; MSc, U. Man., Winnipeg, Can., 1993; PhD, U Western Ont., London, Ontario, Can., 1998. Lectr. U. Western Ont., London, Canada, 1997—98; prof. of math. U. N.C., Charlotte, 1998—. Cons. Act Stats Consulting, Charlotte, NC, 2001—. Grantee Scholarship, NSERC, 1995-97, rsch. in probability, stats. and finance, NSF, 2002—. Office: Univ NC Math Dept 9201 University City Blvd Charlotte NC 28223 Office Fax: 704-687-6415. E-mail: jkawczak@math.uncc.edu.

KAWCZYNSKI, DIANE MARIE, elementary and middle school educator, composer; b. Milw., Jan. 22, 1959; d. Adalbert Lawrence and Joan (Zernia) K. BMus, Lawrence U., 1981; MMus, U. Wis., 1985. Cert. music tchr. Va., adminstrn. and supervision pre-K-12 Va. Suzuki violin instr., string methods instr. Brandon (Manitoba, Can.) Univ. Sch. Music, 1982-83; violin/viola instr., univ. prep program U. Wis. Sch. of Music, Madison, 1983-85; elem. and middle sch. string instr. Albuquerque Pub. Schs., 1985-86; middle sch. string and chorus instr. Ft. Morgan (Colo.) Pub. Schs., 1986-87; elem. string instr., middle sch. orchestra instr. Norfolk Pub. Schs., 1987—. Mem. NEA, Am. String Tchr. Assn., Music Educators Nat. Conf. Avocations: knitting, walking, crafts. Home: 860 Gaslight Ln Virginia Beach VA 23462-1232 E-mail: dkawczynksi@blairms.nps.k12.va.us.

KAWEWE, SALIWE MOYO, social work educator, researcher; children: Neo Jomo, Rujeko. BSW, University Of Zambia, Lusaka, Zambia, 1970—74; MSW, Washington U., St. Louis, Mo., 1977—79; PhD, St. Louis U., 1981—85. Cert. edn. accreditation reaffirmation Coun. on Social Work, 2001. Adminstrv. asst. University of Zambia, Lusaka, Zambia, 1974—77; social svcs. officer, probation officer Dept. Social Svcs., Bulawayo, Zimbabwe, 1979—81; instr. Bd. Edn. St. Louis Public Schools, Saint Louis, Mo., 1981—83; social service worker II Mo. Div. of Family Services, St. Louis, 1984—85; asst. prof. Southeastern La. U., Hammond, La., 1985—88, Central State U., Wilberforce, Ohio, 1989, James Madison U., Harrisonburg, Va., 1989—91, Wichita State U., Wichita, Kans., 1991—96; assoc. prof. Southern Ill. U., Carbondale, Ill., 1996—2001, grad. program dir., 1996—98, prof., 2002—. Chair Coun. on Social Work Edn. Internat. Commn.'s Internat.l Issues Symposium, Alexandria, 1999—; contract bargaining team mem. Southern Ill. U. Faculty Assn., IEA-NEA, Carbondale, 1998—2003, dept. rep., 1998—99. Contbr. chapters to books, ; editl. bd. mem.: Social Devel. Issues, 1998—, guest editl. bd. mem.: Nat. Women Studies Jour., 1997—98; contbr. articles and conf. proceedings. Mem. Nat. Assn. Social Workers, Bulawayo, Zimbabwe, 1980—82; Africa regional rep. Inter-Univ. Consortium for Internat. Social Devel., Wichita, 1992—94; mem. Tangipohoa Parish Mayor's commn. on Needs of Women, Hammond, La., 1985—88, Inter-Univ. Consortium for Internat. Social Devel., Carbondale, 1995—, Ill. Hunger Coalition, Chgo., 1998—; sec. Kans. Coun. on Social Work Edn., Topeka, 1992—93; mem. Com. to Enhance Minority, Human and Civil Rights, Springfield, 2000—. Recipient Outstanding Scholastic Achievement award, George Warren Brown Sch. of Social Work, Wash. U., 1979, Superior Acad. Achievement award, St. Louis U. Internat. Student Assn., 1984, Appreciation for Continuing Svc. as a Faculty Advisor, Nat. Assn. Black Social Workers, 2001, Appreciation as Faculty Advisor, 2000, certificate of Dedication, African Student Coun. So. Ill. U. at Carbondale, 2001, Internat. Student Coun So. Ill. U. at Carbondale, 2001, Award of Appreciation of Svc., Nat. Assn. Black Social Workers, 2000, Recognition of Dedicated Svc., African Student Coun. So. Ill. U. at Carbondale, 1998, Dedication of Svc., African Student Coun., So. Ill. U. at Carbondale, 1997, Outstanding Leadership and Guidance, Student Orgn. of Social Work, Wichita State U., 1996, Outstanding Multilateral Study Del. award, World Congress on the Family, 1992; grantee Summer Rsch. Travel Grant, Wichita State U., 1994. Mem.: NASW (asst. dist. chair 1997—99), Internat. Coun. on Social Welfare, Internat. Assn. for Schs. of Social Work, Soc. for Study of Social Problems, Peace and Social Justice Ctr. of So. Ctrl. Kans., Inter-U. Consortium for Internat. Social Devel., Coun. on Social Work Edn., Coun. on Social Work Edn. Internat. Commn., Internat. Assn. Feminist Econs., So. Ill. U. Women's Caucus, Nat. Women Studies Assn., So. Ill. HIV Care Consortium (bd. mem. 1997—2001), Internat. Fedn. Social Workers (life), Beta Delta of Phi Alpha (hon.). Office: So Ill U Sch Of Social Work Mailcode 4329 Carbondale IL 62901 Office Fax: 618-457-1219. Business E-mail: smkawewe@siu.edu.

KAWITT, ALAN, lawyer; JD, Chgo.-Kent Coll. Law, 1965; postgrad. Lawyers Inst., John Marshall Law Sch., 1966-68. Bar: Ill. 1966, U.S. Dist. Ct. (no. dist.) Ill. 1967, U.S. Ct. Appeals (7th cir.) 1971, U.S. Supreme Ct. 1971. Sole practice, 1970—. Mem. Am. Arbitration Assn. (arbitrator). Office: 226 S Wabash Ave Ste 905 Chicago IL 60604-2319

KAY, ALBERT JOSEPH, textile executive; b. Cleve., June 3, 1920; s. Simon and Eszter (Rosenzweig) K.; m. Irene Pramisloff, June 11, 1944; children: Leslie Andrzejewski, Stephen, Adrienne Gallagher. Student, Cuyahoga Community Coll., 1961. Sales rep. The Carnegie Textile Co., Cleve., 1938-68, v.p., gen. mgr., 1968-94, pres., 1994—. Mem. citizens adv. com. Centerior Energy, 1991-97; adv. bd. ARC, 1988-93. Pres. Mayfield H.S. PTA, 1968-69, Friends Mayfield Regional Libr., 1998-99; former pres. Mayfield Boys Baseball League; past. sect. chmn. United Way; founder Mayfield Heights Bicentennial Com., Mayfield Area Recreation Coun.; mem. Citizens Com. for Edn., 1968; chmn. Citizens for Honest Govt., 1965; past pres. Friends of Hillcrest Libr.; coun. mem. City Mayfield Heights, 1969-97, coun. pres., 1981-85, 1996-97; campaign co-chmn. Aveni for State Rep., Ohio, 1975; chmn. levy renewal com. Cuyahoga County Pub. Libr., 1989; past. mem. exec. com. Hillcrest Dem. Caucus, Mayfield Schs. Acad. Booster's Club; former chmn. planning and zoning commn. City Mayfield Heights; trustee Schnurmann House, 1970-2001, Assn. Retarded Citizens, 1992-94; cmty. coord. Clinton-Gore campaign, 1992; mem., founder Edn.-Bus. Cmty. Alliance, Mayfield City Schs., 1994—; former pres. Hillcrest Coun. of Couns., 1977; mem. Cuyahoga County Dem. Exec. Com.; mem. Mayfield Heights Planning Commn., 1998—; founder, chmn. Mayfield Dist. Millenium Celebration, 2000; gov. Cuyahoga County Bd. Mental Health, 2001—. With U.S. Army, 1943. Recipient Cmty. Svcs. award Hillcrest Cleve. Exch., 1977, Civic Svcs. award Citizens League of Cleve., 1996, Cmty. Svc. award Nat. Exch. Club, 1984, Outstanding Svc. award Mayfield Heights C. of C., 1979, Citizenship award VFW, 1976, Disting. Svc. award Assn. for Retarded Citizens, 1991, Citizen of Yr. award (with wife) Mayfield City Schs., 1995, Award for Disting. Svc., Citizens League of Cleve., 1996, Cert. of Appreciation for Pub. Svc., Gov. Ohio, 1997, Cuyahoga County Commrs., 1997, Ohio Ho. of Reps., 1997, Ohio State Senate, 1997; commendation Ohio State Sen. for Disting. Cmty. Svc., 1997; named Mayfield Schs. Citizen of Yr., 1995—. Mem. Mayfield Heights Planning Commn., 1998, Friends of Mayfield Regional Libr. (pres. 1998-2000), Internat. Assn. Wiping Cloth Mfrs. (bd.dirs. 1981-85, 89-93, Outstanding and Dedicated Svc. award 1985), Am. Assn. Ret. Persons (bd. dirs. East Suburban Cuyahoga County chpt. 371 1993-95), Secondary/Materials and Recycled Textiles, Jewish Vets Cleve. (comdr. 1946-48), East Cleve. Bus. Alliance (pres.), Masons. Democrat. Jewish. Avocations: polit. activity, piano. Home: 1835 Beham Dr Cleveland OH 44124-3121 Office: The Carnegie Textile Co 1734 Ivanhoe Rd Cleveland OH 44112-1623 E-mail: cartex@stratos.net., alandirene2@netzero.net.

KAY, CHARLES D. philosophy educator; b. Paterson, N.J., June 25, 1950; s. Herbert and Adrienne (Spruit) K.; m. Margaret M. Trageser, Dec. 29, 1972; children: Ian, Peter, Thomas. AB, Princeton U., 1972; MA, U. Pitts., 1975, PhD, 1981. Asst. prof. Hampden-Sydney Coll., 1981-84; vis. asst. prof. Coll. Charleston, 1984-86; assoc. prof. Wofford Coll., Spartanburg, S.C., 1986-2000, prof., 2000—. Contbr. essays and revs. to profl. jours. Chmn. bd. dirs. Spartanburg Campuses chpt. Habitat for Humanity, 1988-91; mem. ethics com. Spartanburg Regional Med. Ctr., 1996—; v.p. Friends Spartanburg County Pub. Librs., 1998-99, pres., 1999-2000; exec. dir. Spartanburg County Character Edn. Acad., 1999—, Leadership Spartanburg, 2001-02, mem. Princeton U. Alumni Schs. Com.; mem. ethics com. S.C. Med. Assn., 2003—. Mem. S.C. Soc. for Philosophy (v.p. 1987-88, pres. 1988-89), Soc. Christian Philosophers, Philosophy Sci. Assn., Am. Philos. Assn. Office: Wofford Coll Philosophy Dept Spartanburg SC 29303

KAY, CYRIL MAX, biochemist, educator; b. Calgary, Alta., Can., Oct. 3, 1931; s. Louis and Fanny (Pearlmutter) K.; m. Faye Bloomenthal, Dec. 30, 1953; children: Lewis Edward, Lisa Franci. B.Sc. in Biochemistry with honors (J.W. McConnell Meml. scholar), McGill U., 1952; PhD in Biochemistry (Life Ins. Med. Research Fund fellow), Harvard U., 1956; postgrad., Cambridge (Eng.) U., 1956-57. Phys. biochemist Eli Lilly & Co., Indpls., 1957-58; asst. prof. biochemistry U. Alta., Edmonton, 1958-61, assoc. prof., 1961-67, prof., 1967—, co-dir. Med. Rsch. Coun. Group on Protein Structure and Function, 1974-95, mem. protein engring. network Centre of Excellence, 1990—, chmn. internat. rsch. adv. com. to protein engring. network Centre of Excellence, 2000—; v.p. rsch. Alta. Cancer Bd., 1999—. Med. Rsch. Coun. vis. scientist in biophysics Weizmann Inst., Israel, 1969-70, summer vis. prof. biophysics, 1975, summer vis. prof. chem. physics, 1977, 80; mem. biochemistry grants com. Med. Research Council, 1970-73; mem. Med. Rsch. Coun. Can., 1982-88; Can. rep. Pan Am. Assn. Biochem. Socs., 1971-76; mem. exec. planning com. XI Internat. Congress Biochemistry, Toronto, Ont., Can., 1979; mem. med. adv. bd. Gairdner Found. for Internat. awards in Med. Sci., 1980-89; chmn. Internat. Scientific adv. com. on protein engring., 2000—. Contbr. numerous articles to profl. publs.; asso. editor Can. Jour. Biochemistry, 1968-82; editor-in-chief Pan Am. Assn. Biochem. Socs. Revista, 1971-76. Decorated Order of Can.; recipient Ayerst award in biochemistry Can. Biochem. Soc., 1970, Disting. Scientist award U. Alta. Med. Sch., 1988. Fellow N.Y. Acad. Scis., Royal Soc. Can.; mem. Order of Can., Can. Biochem. Soc. (coun. 1971—, v.p. 1976-77, pres. 1978-79). Home: 9408-143d St Edmonton AB Canada T5R 0P7 Office: U Alta Dept Biochemistry Med Scis Bldg Edmonton AB Canada T6G 2H7 E-mail: ckay@gpu.srv.ualberta.ca.

KAY, DENNIS MATTHEW, retired publishing company official; b. Chgo., Sept. 20, 1936; s. Edward Francis and Rose Anne (Koziel) Kolodzinski; m. Judy R. Kalinsky, Jan. 9, 1965; 1 child, Alan Edward. BBA, Loyola U., 1976. Customer svc. agt. Am. Airlines, Chgo., 1959-69; expeditor Time Inc., Chgo., 1969-73, traffic mgr. People mag., 1973-75, Time mag. traffic mgr., 1975-78, ops. mgr., 1978-81, electronic data mgr., 1981-83, plant mgr. Waterloo, Wis., 1983-88, field ops. mgr., 1988-95, nat. prodn. analyst, 1995-96, field ops. mgr., 1996-99; ret., 2000. With U.S. Army, 1959-61. Recipient MM&D Excellence award Time Inc., 1989, Prodn. Excellence awards, 1993, 94, Pres. award, 1993. Mem. Moose Lodge River Grove 378 (gov. 1982-83). Roman Catholic. Avocations: stamp collecting, piano, model building. Home: 604 Long Cove Dr Lake In The Hills IL 60156 E-mail: dennykay@worldnet.att.net.

KAY, GEORGE PAUL, environmental engineer; b. McKeesport, Pa., Sept. 25, 1954; s. George and Darlene Ann (Snyder) K.; m. Rosemary Ann Lynam, July 19, 1986; children: Brittany Elaine, Hope Elise, George Prescott. BS in Biology, U. Pitts., 1975, MS in Environ. Health, 1976, MSCE, 1982. Registered profl. engr., Pa., Ohio; cert. sewage treatment plant and waterworks operator, Pa. Rsch. asst. U. Pitts., 1976-79; from asst. aquatic ecologist to sr. environ. engr. Michael Baker Corp., Beaver, Pa., 1979-87, sect. mgr. water and wastewater Coraopolis, Pa., 1987-89; sr. engr. water and wastewater AK Steel Corp. (formerly Armco, Inc.), Butler, Pa., 1989-2000; mgr. water quality engring. Michael Baker Jr. Inc., Coraopolis, Pa., 2000—02, mgr. civil and environ. engring., 2002—. Contbr. articles to profl. jours. Mem. Pa. Water Environ. Assn., Water Environ. Fedn., World Aquaculture Soc., Aquacultural Engring. Soc. Avocations: traditional archery, bonsai, rock guitar, aquarium science. Home: 4596 Bucktail Dr Allison Park PA 15101-2120 Office: Michael Baker Jr Inc 100 Airside Dr Coraopolis PA 15108 E-mail: gkay@mbakercorp.com.

KAY, HAZEL T. local commissioner; b. Muskegon, Mich., Sept. 21, 1924; d. Alonzo Stansell and Laura Estelle Gasaway; m. Heinz Theodore Kay, Nov. 21, 1951 (widowed, Dec. 3, 1992); children: Joanne, Carolyn, Cezane, Ben. BS, Mich. State U., 1945; postgrad, UCLA, 1949, U. So. Calif., 1949. Lab. tech. Vets. Administrn, L.A., 1946-48; mgr. hosp. lab, x-ray Trans-Arabian Pipeline, Ras El Mishab, Saudia Arabia, 1948-50; chief technologist Bio-Science Lab., L.A., 1950-54; manufacturing chemist Cyclo-Chemical Co., L.A., 1954-58; petroleum chemist Petroleum Technology, Inc., Montebello, Calif., 1958-60; chief tech., lab. tech. Santa Paula Meml. Hosp., Calif., 1968-90; commr. Housing Authority, Santa Paula, 1992—. Woman's activity coun. Interface Children Svc., Santa Paula, 1997—, dir. Interface-Ventura County, Camarillo, Calif., 1998—; pres. Woman's Adv. Coun. Mem. Kiwanis Internat., Santa Paula, 1988-91; officer (all posiitons) Assn. Retarded, Ventura, Calif., 1966—; pres., v.p., treas. Tri-Counties Regional Ctr., Santa Barbara, Calif., 1998—; trustee Unitarian Universalist Ch., Santa Paula, 1986-88. Recipient Lifetime Achievement award Girl Scouts of Am., 1965, Bus. Woman of Yr. award Soroptimists Internat., 1972, Woman of Dist. award, 1980-90, Cmty. Svc. award C. of C., Santa Paula, 1994, Calif. State Vol. of Yr. award ARC-Calif., 2000. Mem. C. of C. Santa Paula, Assn. Retarded Citizens of Calif., Assn. Retarded Citizens of Ventura County, Soropimist Internat., Interface Children and Family, Ventura County Greenline Parents, Found. for the Retarded of the Desert, Sacramento Assn. for the Retarded. Democrat. Universalist Unitarian. Avocations: duplicate bridge, coin collector, swimming, philately, photography, traveling, reading, community service. Home: 514 Anacapa Ter Santa Paula CA 93060-1902

KAY, HERBERT, retired natural resources company executive; b. Johnsonburg, Pa., Mar. 19, 1924; s. Alexander S. and Carla Z. Racusin; m. Rita Inge Schmidt, May 4, 1956; children: Peter, Darcy, Philip. BS in Chem. Engring., Pa. State U., 1944; S.M., MIT, 1947; postgrad., Sloan Sch., 1968. Process engr. Stanolind Oil & Gas Co., Tulsa, 1947-49; group supr. Consolidation Coal Co., Library, Pa., 1949-55; sr. v.p. Climax Molybdenum Co., 1955-77; v.p. Amax Inc., 1977-85; also dir. U.K., Holland, Italy, France, Japan. Patentee in field.

Served with USNR, 1944-45. Mem. AIChE, Univ. Club (N.Y.), Madison Beach and Country Clubs (Conn.), Audubon Country Club (Fla.). Home: 1 E Wharf Rd PO Box 687 Madison CT 06443-0687

KAY, HERMA HILL, education educator; b. Orangeburg, S.C., Aug. 18, 1934; d. Charles Esdorn and Herma Lee (Crawford) Hill. BA, So. Meth. U., 1956; JD, U. Chgo., 1959. Bar: Calif. 1960, U.S. Supreme Ct. 1978. Law clk. to Hon. Roger Traynor Calif. Supreme Ct., 1959-60; from asst. prof. to assoc. prof. law U. Calif., Berkeley, 1960-62, prof., 1963, dir. family law project, 1964-67, Jennings prof., 1987-96, dean, 1992-2000, Armstrong prof., 1996—; co-reporter uniform marriage and div. act Nat. Conf. Commrs. on Uniform State Laws, 1968-70. Vis. prof. U. Manchester, England, 1972, Harvard U., 1976; mem. Gov.'s Commn. Family, 1966. Author (with Martha S. West): (book) Text Cases and Materials on Sex-Based Discrimination, 5th edit., 2002; author: (with D. Currie and L. Kramer) Conflict of Laws: Cases, Comments, Questions, 6th edit., 2001; contbr. articles to profl. jours. Trustee Russell Sage Found., NY, 1972—87, chmn. bd. trustees, 1980—84; trustee, bd. dirs. Equal Rights Advs., Calif., 1987—88, chmn., 1976—83; pres. bd. dirs. Rosenberg Found., Calif., 1987—88, bd. dirs., 1978—. Recipient Rsch. award, Am. Bar Found., 1990, Margaret Brent award, ABA Commn. Women in Profession, 1992, Marshall-Wythe medal, 1995; fellow, Ctr. Advanced Study Behavioral Sci., Palo Alto, Calif., 1963. Mem.: ABA (sect. legal edn. and admissions to bar coun. 1992—99, sec. 1999—2001), Order of Coif (nat. pres. 1983—85), Am. Philos. Soc., Am. Acad. Arts and Scis., Assn. Am. Law Schs. (exec. com. 1986—87, pres.-elect 1988, pres. 1989, past pres. 1990), Am. Law Inst. (mem. coun. 1985—), Calif. Women Lawyers (bd. govs. 1975—77), Bar U.S. Supreme Ct., Calif. Bar Assn. Democrat. Office: U Calif Law Sch Boalt Hall Berkeley CA 94720-7200 E-mail: kayh@law.berkeley.edu.

KAY, IRENE PRAMISLOFF, school system administrator; b. Cleve., Mar. 26, 1920; d. Benjamin and Anna Esther (Kahan) Pramisloff; m. Albert Joseph Kay, June 11, 1944; children: Leslie Kay Andrzejewski, Stephen W., Adrienne Kay Gallagher. AA in Bus., Cuyahoga C.C., 1971. Sec. Cleve. Job Corps Ctr., 1970-88, Soc. for Prevention Violence, Auctor Assoc., Inc., Cleveland Heights, Ohio, 1988-95; mem., past v.p., past pres. Mayfield (Ohio) City Sch. Bd., 1965-91, mem. emeritus, 1992—; mem. All N.E. Region Sch. Bd., 1975, 83, All Ohio Sch. Bd., 1983. Past adv. com. mem. Star Bank (now US Bank), Mayfield Heights, Ohio; past legis. com., mem. Cuyahoga County Auditor Citizens Adv. Bd., pres. 2000—02, pres. emeritus, 2002-; past mem. health care/human svcs. com.; custody rev. bd. mem. Cuyahoga County Juvenile Ct., 1981-83; mem. adv. coun. Sun Newspapers, 2002-. Chmn. Whale of a Sale book fair Cuyahoga County Libr. Sys., 1993; mem. planning com. Cuyahoga County Pub. Libr. 75th Anniversary; founder, past pres., past treas. Mayfield Area Recreation Coun.; appointee Ohio Lottery Commn., 1983—92, chmn., 1986—92; past mem. mayor's adv. com. City Mayfield Heights, 17 yrs.; mem. Cuyahoga County Adv. Coun. for Sr. and Adult Svcs., 1993—97, reapptd., 1999—; chmn. Mayfield Heights Gold Residents, 2001—02, mem., 2003—, Mayfield Heights Commn. on Aging, 1993—, Cuyahoga County Office on Aging Com., 1995—; former mem. Cuyahoga County Urban County Cmty. Devel. Block Grant Com.; mem. exec. bd. Mayfield Heights Bicentennial Com., 1974—76; former adv. com. East Shore divsn. ARC; mem. cmty.-wide svcs. panel United Way, 1983—86, also former chmn.; mem. edn. com. Cleve. Bicentennial Commn., 1993—96; cmty. capt. Mayfield City Schs. Bond/Levy campaign, 1994; chmn. Tell the People the Truth Com. City of Mayfield Heights, 1996; mem. adv. bd. Oakville Park Com., 1993—99; mem. Mayfield Heights History Book Com., 1997; mem. East Metro leadership com. Am. Heart Assn., 1997—98; mem. cmty. rels. coun. Cleve. Job Corps Ctr., 1998—; v.chmn. Cuyahoga County Adv. Coun. for Sr. and Adult Svcs., 2001—; mem. Cuyahoga County Dem. Exec. Com.; precinct committeeperson Mayfield Heights; Mayfield Heights co-coord. Clinton-Gore-Glenn campaign, 1992; coord. 2 campaigns Mayfield Heights Richard Celeste for Gov.; mem. Congressman LaTourette's Sr. Task Force, 1995—; trustee Schnurmann House, Mayfield Heights, 1984—2002, reapptd., 2002—; trustee Friends of Mayfield Regional Libr., trustee, past pres., chmn. levy replacement campaign, 1984, 1989; former bd. trustees, cmty. rep. WomenSpace. Honored in resolutions Ohio Senate, Ohio Ho. Reps., govs. spl. recognition; recipient commendation U.S. Congress, 1990, Cuyahoga County Auditor, 1992, Cert. Recognition Ohio Atty. Gen., 1992, Spl. Friend award Cuyahoga East Vocat. Edn. Consortium, 1992, Cert. of Appreciation, Cuyahoga County Auditor, 1996; named (with Albert Kay) Citizen of Yr. Mayfield City Schs., 1995; nominated Keeper of Flame award Ohio Sec. State, 1990, Resolution, Mayfield Bd. Edn., 1990, City Mayfield Heights, 1990, nominated Ohio Women's Hall Fame, 1986, 92, nominated CitiSun of Yr. Sun Newspapers, 1992, Citizens League of Greater Cleve. award for civic svc. (with Albert Kay), 1996, awarded Key to City of Mayfield Hgts. by Mayor, 2002. Mem.: AARP (chpt. 371) (program chmn. 1991—94, bd. dirs. 1995—97, pres. 2001—02, mem. coalition for affordable prescription drugs 2001—, past legis. chmn., pres. 1993—94, Outstanding Svcs. award 1994), LWV (past pres. 1992—93, v.p. Cuyahoga County unit bd. dirs., bd. dirs. Hillcrest Area unit), Mayfield Hts. Dem. Club (pres. 2001—02). Avocations: cmty. activist, politics. Home: 1835 Beham Dr Cleveland OH 44124-3121 E-mail: alandirene2@netzero.net.

KAY, JERALD, psychiatry educator, researcher; b. Washington, Mar. 26, 1945; s. Max and Miriam (Schwartz) K.; m. Rena Lynn Victor, Aug. 17, 1968; children: Sarah Jennifer, Rachel Hannah, Jonathan Emile. BA, Washington U., 1967; MD, U. Md., 1971; diploma, Cin. Psychoanalytic Inst., 1984. Diplomate Am. Bd. Psychiatry and Neurology. Resident in psychiatry Cin. Gen. Hosp., 1971-73, fellow in child psychiatry, 1973-75; instr. child psychiatry U. Cin. Coll. Medicine, 1971-77, asst. prof. child psychiatry, 1977-82, assoc. prof. child psychiatry, 1982-89, prof. child psychiatry, 1989-90; prof., chair dept. psychiatry Wright State U. Sch. Medicine, Dayton, Ohio, 1990—. Dir. med. student edn. U. Cin. Dept. Psychiatry, 1975-82, dir. residency tng., 1982—; mem. psychiatry com. Nat. Bd. Med. Examiners, 1988-90; specialist site visitor Accreditation Coun. Grad. Med. Edn., 1986—, mem. residency rev. com., 2001—. Editor Jour. Psychotherapy Practice and Rsch., 1990-2001; assoc. editor, Am. Jour Psychotherapy, 2001-; mem. editorial cons. bd. Am. Psychiat. Press, Inc., 1987, mem. editorial bd. Acad. Psychiatry; contbr. articles on child and adult psychiatry, psychoanalysis, psychotherapy, ethics, psychiat. and cardiac transplantation edn. to profl. jours. Chair Ohio Commn. on Mental Health, 1999—. Recipient Golden Apple Teaching award U. Cin. Coll. Medicine, 1979; named Exemplary Psychiatrist, Nat. Alliance for the Mentally Ill, 1994, Educator of Yr. Assn. Acad. Psychiatry, 1996. Fellow Am. Psychiat. Assn. (Disting. fellow, chmn. med. studies edn. com. 1982-86, coun. med. edn. 1989, career devel. 1986—, chmn. 1989, mem. com. on psychotherapy, program com., commn. on practice of psychotherapy 1996—, rsch. on psychiat. treatments 1996—), Am. Coll. Psychiatrists; mem. Am. Psychoanalytic Assn., Am. Acad. Child and Adolescent Psychiatry, Am. Assn. Chmn. Depts. of Psychiatry, Alpha Omega Alpha. Avocations: playing jazz drums, tuba, reading. Home: 4192 Rose Hill Ave Cincinnati OH 45229-1421 Office: Wright State U Sch Medicine PO Box 927 Dayton OH 45401-0927

KAY, JOEL PHILLIP, lawyer; b. Corsicana, Tex., Aug. 27, 1936; m. Marilyn Soltz, July 9, 1961; children: Arthur Hyman, Sarah Anne, Leslie Anette. BS in Econs., Wharton Sch., U. Pa., 1958; LLB, U. Tex., 1961; LL.M., Georgetown U., 1967. Bar: Tex. 1961, U.S. Dist. Ct. (so. and we. dists.) Tex., U.S. Dist. Ct (so. dist.) Ala., U.S. Ct. Appeals (5th cir.), U.S. Supreme Ct. Trial atty. tax div. Dept. Justice, 1963-67; U.S. atty. So. Dist. Tex., 1967-69; ptnr. Sheinfeld, Maley & Kay, P.C., Houston, 1969—2001; of counsel Hughes, Watters & Askanase, LLP, Houston, 2001—. Mem. Tex. Bd. Pub. Accountancy, 1984-85, quality rev. oversight bd., 1992-93; speaker at numerous institutes on comml. and bankruptcy law. With AUS, 1961-63. Fellow Am. Bar Found., Am. Coll. Bankruptcy (5th cir. regent 1998-2003); mem. ABA, Tex. Bar Assn. (dir. 1979-81, chmn. bd. 1981-82), Houston Bar Assn., Tex. Bar Found. (trustee 1983-86), Houston Bar Found. (dir. 1995-98), Tex. Supreme Ct. (grievance oversight com. 1987-94). Office: 1415 Louisiana 37th Fl Houston TX 77002-6709

KAY, KENNETH JEFFREY, real estate company executive; b. L.A., Apr. 2, 1955; s. Morton M. and Beverly J. Kay; m. Lisa Ellen, July 24, 1982. BS in Acctg., U. So. Calif., 1978, MBA in Fin., 1980. CPA, Calif. Staff acct. in charge Price Waterhouse and Co. (now PriceWaterhouse Coopers LLP), Century City, Calif., 1980-82; mgr. acctg. TRW-Fujitsu Co., L.A., 1982-83; corp. controller Ameron, Internat., Pasadena, Calif., 1983-88, sr. v.p. fin. and adminstrn., CFO, 1990-92; group v.p. Ameron, Inc., Pasadena, Calif., 1992-94; pres., CEO, dir. Bishop, Inc., Westlake Village, Calif., 1988-90; sr. v.p. fin. and adminstrn., CFO Systemed, Inc., Torrance, Calif., 1994-96; sr. v.p., CFO Playmates Inc., Costa Mesa, Calif., 1997; exec. v.p., CFO Universal Studios Consumer Products Group, Universal City, Calif., 1998-99; v.p., CFO, Dole Food Co., Inc., Westlake Village, Calif., 1999—2002; sr. exec. v.p., CFO CB Richard Ellis, Inc., L.A., 2002—. Chmn. supervisory com. Ameron Fed. Credit Union, South Gate, Calif., 1986. Bd. govs. Cedars-Sinai Med. Ctr.; mem. exec. com. Friends for Life, L.A.; mem. bd. dirs. Paralysis Project Am. Mem. AICPA, Am. Mgmt. Assn., Calif. Soc. CPAs, Assn. for Strategic Planning, Fin. Execs. Inst., USC Marshall Sch. Alumni. Office: CB Richard Ellis Inc 355 S Grand Ave Ste 3100 Los Angeles CA 90071

KAY, MARGARITA, anthropologist, consultant, nurse; b. Washington, D.C., Nov. 15, 1926; s. Ernst Friedrich and Eugenia (Brodsky) Artschwager; m. Arthur M. Kay, Jan. 29, 1949; children: Laura Kay Malone, Julie Eugenia Powers. AB, Stanford U., 1948; MSN, U. Calif., San Francisco, 1961; MA, U. Ariz., Tucson, 1970, PhD in Anthropology, 1972. RN Calif., N.Y., Ariz. Staff nurse Vis. Nurse Svc. N.Y., N.Y.C., 1949—53; instr. St. Mary's Sch. Nursing, Tucson, 1957—65; asst. prof. to prof. nursing and anthropology Coll. Nursing, U. Ariz., Tucson, 1972—92. Reviewer proposals NIMH ADAHMA, Washington, 1988—90; reviewer submissions Jour. Transcultural Nursing, Palo Alto, Calif., 1998—; established Women's Health Clinic, Tucson, 1972; site visitor Am. Acad. Pediat., San Juan, P.R., and Carson City, Nev.; mem. exec. bd. numerous rsch. jours., including Jour. Transcultural Nursing, Med. Anthropology Quarterly, others. Author: Healing with Plants in the American and Mexican West, 1986, Southwestern Medical Dictionary, Spanish-English, English-Spanish, 2d edit., 2001; editor: Anthropology of Human Birth, 1981. Exec. bd. La Leche Internat., War On Poverty. Grantee HHS, 1974—75, HUD, 1984—87, numerous others. Fellow: Am. Acad. Nursing, Am. Assn. Anthropologists (bd. med. anthropology 1978—81, 1981—). Democrat. Unitarian-Universalist. Achievements include research in history of medicine in New Spain. Avocations: writing, reading, gardening, drawing. Home: 8861 E Calle Bolivar Tucson AZ 85715 E-mail: kartrita@opus1.com.

KAY, PATRICIA KREMER, business owner; b. Arlington, Va., July 10, 1957; d. George Andrew and Eileen Lois (Ludwig) Kremer; m. Jimmy Lamar Kay, Dec. 4, 1989; children: Sabrina Lea, Kelly Marie. Purchasing agt. Medisorb Tech., Wilmington, Ohio, 1994-96, mgr.; owner JP Resources Inc, Middletown, OH, 1995—; employment specialist Dept. VA Job Coaching Svcs., Middletown, 1996—. Avocations: boating, skiing. Office: Job Coaching Svcs 4576 Yankee Rd Middletown OH 45044

KAY, PAUL DE YOUNG, linguist; b. N.Y.C., Nov. 7, 1934; s. William de Young and Alice Sarah Kay; m. Patricia Boehm, Feb. 13, 1934; children: Yvette, Suzanne de Young. BA in Econs., Tulane U., 1955; PhD in Anthropology, Harvard U., 1963. Asst. prof. MIT, Cambridge, Mass., 1964-65; asst prof., prof. dept. anthropology U. Calif., Berkeley, 1966-83, prof. dept. linguistics, 1983—, chmn. dept., 1986-91. Author: Words and the Grammar of Context, 1997; editor: Explorations in Mathematical Anthropology, 1971; co-author: Basic Color Terms, 1969; contbr. articles to Language, Linguistic Inquiry, Foundations of Language, Linguistics and Philosophy, Language and Society, Am. Anthropologist, Current Anthropology, Jour. of Linguistic Anthrop. Fellow Ctr. Advanced Study in Behavioral Scis., Stanford, Calif., 1965-66, Guggenheim Found., U. Hawaii, Oahu, 1972-73. Mem.: NAS, Soc. for Linguistic Anthropology (pres. 1988—89), Am. Anthrop. Assn., Linguistic Soc. Am. Office: Internat Computer Sci Inst 1947 Center St Berkeley CA 94704-1198 E-mail: kay@cogsi.berkeley.edu.

KAY, REED, artist, educator; b. Boston, Mar. 29, 1925; s. Israel and Leah (Shalman) K.; m. Frieda Hymowitz, Feb. 19, 1946; children: Jonathan, Susannah. Diploma, Sch. Mus. Fine Arts, Boston, 1949. Instr. painting Sch. Mus. Fine Arts, Boston, 1951-55, Sch. Painting and Sculpture, Skowhegan, Maine, 1952, 54-60; mem. studio faculty Sch. Visual Art, Boston U., 1956—, prof. art, 1968—. Lectr. Amherst Coll., 1975, Md. Inst. Coll. Art, 1975, Yale U., 1977, RISD, 1978, Harvard U. Fogg Mus., 1978, U. N.H., 1983, Columbus Coll. Art and Design, 1985, Columbia U., 1986, Washington Studio Sch., 1986, Swarthmore Coll., 1988, Yale U., 1989, Harvard U., 1989, Dartmouth Coll., 1995. Exhibited in group shows at Kanegis Gallery, Boston, 1956, Boris Mirski Gallery, Boston, 1965, Fitchburg Art Mus., Mass., 1967, Amherst Coll., 1973, 94, Queens Mus., N.Y.C., 1976, Mus. Fine Arts, Boston, 1977, Alpha Gallery, Boston, 1978, 83, 90, Boston U. Gallery, 1956-79, 2002, Circle Gallery, Washington, 1986, DeCordova Mus., Mass., 1987, 2001, Boston Archtl. Ctr., 1994, Danforth Mus., Framingham, 1995, Alpha Gallery, Boston, 1996, Boston Athenaeum, 1996, Cape Ann Hist. Mus., Gloucester, Mass., 1997, 2002, Nat. Acad. Mus., N.Y.C., 1998, Wiggin Gallery, Boston, 1998-99, U. NH, 2000, Alpha Gallery, Boston, 2000, 02; author: The Painter's Companion, 1961, The Painter's Guide to Studio Methods and Materials, 1983; contbr. articles to profl. jours. With AUS, 1943-45, ETO. Decorated Purple Heart; James Paige traveling fellow Sch. Mus. Fine Arts Boston, 1950-51; grantee Nat. Endowment Arts, 1981-82. Home and Office: 109 Rawson Rd Brookline MA 02445-4509

KAY, RICHARD BROUGHTON, lawyer; b. Cleve., Apr. 7, 1918; s. Joseph Stanley and Frances Anna (Broughton) Kay; m. Ellen Fletcher, June 7, 1992. BBA, Miami U. of Ohio, 1939; LLB, Case Western Res. U., 1948. Bar: Fla., U.S. Supreme Ct. Pvt. practice, Tequesta, Fla. Field organizer Eisenhower for Pres., N.Y.C., 1952; exec. sec. Stassen for Pres., Cleve., 1948; nat. v.p. Wilkie Young Voters, N.Y.C., 1940. Lt. USNR, 1941-61. Mem.: Attys. Bar of Palm Beach County, North Palm Beach County Bar Assn. (pres. 1988), Palm Beach County Bar Assn., Fla. Bar Assn., Am. Legion, VFW, Elks. Avocation: travel. Home: 19800 Us Highway 1 Apt 506 Tequesta FL 33469-2357 Office: 222 US Hwy # 208 Tequesta FL 33469

KAY, SAUL, retired pathologist; b. N.Y.C., Feb. 13, 1914; s. Wolf and Rose (Savitzky) Kossovsky; m. Grace Calef, Aug. 15, 1940; 1 dau., Deborah. BA, N.Y. U., 1936; MD, N.Y. Med. Coll., 1939. Intern Harlem Hosp., N.Y.C., 1939-41; resident Fordham Hosp., 1941-42, N.Y. Postgrad. Med. Sch. and Hosp., 1946-48, Columbia Presbyn. Med. Center, 1948-50; practice medicine specializing in pathology Richmond, Va., 1950-96; ret., 1996. Prof. dept. surg. pathology Med. Coll. Va., 1952-78, emeritus prof., 1978— Served to maj. AUS, 1942-45. Decorated Bronze Star. Mem. AMA, Coll. Am. Pathology, Va. Med. Soc., Richmond Acad. Medicine, Am. Soc. Clin. Pathology, Internat. Acad. Pathology, Va. Path. Soc. Home and Office: 322 Charmian Rd Richmond VA 23226-1705

KAY, SEAN I. politics and government educator; b. Oakland, Calif., Sept. 7, 1967; s. David Alan and Jennifer Grimes Kay; m. Anna-Marie Kay, July 25, 1992; children: Cria Anne Madigan Kay, Siobhan Mattie Madigan Kay, Alana Rose Kay. BA in Polit. Sci., Kent State U., 1989, MA in Polit. Sci., 1991; postgrad., Johns Hopkins U., 1991; MA, Free U. Brussels, 1992; PhD with honors, U. Mass., Amherst, 1997. Rsch. and tchg. asst. dept. polit. sci. Kent (Ohio) State U., 1989-91; rschr. North Atlantic Assembly, Brussels, 1991-92; tchg. fellow, then instr. dept. polit. sci. U. Mass., Amherst, 1992-96; rsch. fellow Nat. Def. U., Washington, 1996-97; vis. asst. prof. Dartmouth Coll., Hanover, N.H., 1997-98; asst. prof. Rhodes Coll., Memphis, 1998-99; assoc. prof. of politcs and govt. Ohio Wesleyan U., Delaware, 1999—2002, chmn. internat. studies, 1999—. Corr. assoc. Lemnitzer Ctr. for NATO and EU Studies, Kent, Ohio, 1992—; non-resident fellow The Eisenhower Inst., Washington, 2002—; spkr. in field. Author: NATO and the Future of European Security, 1998; co-editor: NATO After 50 Years, 2001, Limit Institutions: The Challenge of Eurasian Security Government; contbr. articles to profl. jours., chpts. to books. NATO co-fellow, 1992-93; TEW presdl. grantee Ohio Wesleyan U., 2001. Mem. Internat. Inst. Strategic Studies, Am. Polit. Sci. Assn., Internat. Studies Assn. Democrat. Avocations: guitar, jogging, basketball, river rafting, outdoor activities.

KAY, THOMAS OLIVER, agricultural consultant; b. Anderson, S.C., Sept. 29, 1929; s. Thomas Crayton and Gertrude (Whitworth) K.; m. Rebecca Moore, Aug. 29, 1954 (div. 1965); children— Michael (dec.), Mitchell; m. Bette Hutto, Oct. 1, 1966 (dec. Nov. 1991); stepchildren— Dallon Weathers, Bruce Weathers BA, Furman U., 1950, LL.D. (hon.), John Marshall Law Sch., Atlanta, 1960. Adminstrv. asst. U.S. Congress, Washington, 1966-73; legis. officer USDA, Washington, 1973-77; exec. asst. U.S. Senate, Washington, 1977-79; lobbyist Nat. Assn. Realtors, Washington, 1979-80; asst. to adminstr. Fgn. Agrl. Service USDA, Washington, 1981-82, dir. congl. relations, 1982-83, dep. asst. sec. govtl. and pub. affairs, 1983-85, dep. undersec. internat. affairs and commodity programs, 1985-86, adminstr. fgn. agrl. svc., 1986-90; pres. Kay Assoc., 1989-94. Mem. Litchfield Country Club (Pawleys Island, S.C.). Avocations: golf, swimming. Home: 17 Goodson Loop Pawleys Island SC 29585-8037

KAYAFAS, STEPHANIE ANN, special education educator, consultant, supervisor, actress; b. Pitts., Oct. 18, 1957; d. Nicholas and Helen Kayafas. BS, Rutgers U., 1979; MA, Georgian Ct. Coll., Lakewood, N.J., 1996. Cert. tchr. handicapped, elem. tchr., supr., prin., sch. bus. adminstr. N.J. N.J. spl. edn. tchr. Old Farmers Rd. Elem. Sch., Long Valley, NJ, 1979—82; spl. edn. tchr. Tinton Falls (N.J.) Mid. Sch., 1982-83, Rugby Sch., Wall, NJ, 1982—83; owner, operator Charlie's Auto Body Facility, Asbury Park, NJ, 1983—86; computer trainer Dendrite Internat. Inc., Morristown, N.J., 1998-99; actress Actor's Reps, N.Y.C., 1998—; real estate referral cons. Ind. Referral Cons., Woodstown, N.J., 1999—; spl. edn. tchr. Marlboro (NJ) HS, 1987—2000, supr. spl. edn., 2002—. Mem. People to People Internat., 2001—; del. People's Republic of China Amb. Program, 2001. Mem.: ASCD (vol. tchr. reading to adults), Am. Coun. Exercise, Rutgers Alumni Assn. Avocations: reading, writing poetry, weight training. Home: Riverview Twrs 28 Riverside Ave Unit 10G Red Bank NJ 07701 Office: Marlboro HS 95 N Main St Marlboro NJ 07746 E-mail: stephaniekni@aol.com.

KAYDEN, JEROLD S. lawyer, urban planner; b. N.Y.C., Sept. 12, 1953; AB, Harvard U., 1975, JD, MCRP, Harvard U., 1979. Bar: Mass. 1985, D.C. 1991, N.Y. 1992. Law clk. to judge U.S. Ct. Appeals for 2nd Cir., 1979-80; law clk. to Justice William J. Brennan, Jr. U.S. Supreme Ct., Washington, 1980-81; lectr. Harvard Grad. Sch. Design, Cambridge, Mass., 1981-84, assoc. prof. urban planning, 1995—, dir M. in Urban Planning program, 1998—2000; of counsel Warner & Stackpole, Boston, 1987—99. Gerald D. Hines lectr. Harvard Grad. Sch. Design, 1986-87; sr. fellow Lincoln Inst. Land Policy, Cambridge, 1988-92; sr. advisor on land reform PADCO/U.S. Agy. for Internat. Devel., 1992-94; pres. Masterclass, Inc., L.A., 1976—; bd. dirs. PADCO, Inc. Co-author: Landmark Justice, 1989, Privately Owned Public Space, 2000; co-editor: Zoning and the American Dream, 1989; contbr. articles to profl. jours. Bd. dirs. Kathmandu Valley Pres. Trust. Guggenheim fellow, 1989-90; grantee Nat. Endowment for Arts, 1979, 88, 20th Century Fund, 1989-92. Home: 11 Clement Cir Cambridge MA 02138-2205 Office: Harvard U Grad Sch Design 48 Quincy St Cambridge MA 02138 E-mail: jkayden@gsd.harvard.edu.

KAYE, ALAN DAVID, anesthesiologist, researcher; b. L.I., N.Y., Mar. 21, 1962; s. Joel and Florence Susan (Feldman) K.; m. Kim Sutker, May 26, 1990; children: Aaron, Rachel. BS in Biology, U. Ariz., 1984, BS in Psychology, 1985, MD, 1989; PhD in Pharmacology, Tulane U., 1997. Diplomate Am. Bd. Anesthesiology, Nat. Bd. Med. Examiners; lic. physician, La.; cert. ACLS. Intern Alton Ochsner Med. Found. and Clinic, New Orleans, 1989-90; resident in anesthesiology Mass. Gen. Hosp., Boston, 1990-91, Tulane Med. Ctr., New Orleans, 1991-93, asst. prof. anesthesiology/attending staff, 1993-97, assoc. prof., 1997-99; attending staff/vice med. dir. Greater New Orleans Surg. Ctr., 1995-97, med. dir., 1997-2000; chmn., prof. dept. of anesthesia Tex. Tech U. Med. Ctr., Lubbock, 1999—, prof. dept. pharmacology, 1999—. Lectr. in field. Contbr. articles and abstracts to profl. jours., chpts. to books; mem. editl. adv. bd. OR Reports, 1997—; co-editor: JASA Mfg. Book, 1986—, JASA Contractor's Book, 1986—; mem. editl. bd. Current Drugs, Anesthesia News. Capt. U.S. Army Med. Res., 1990—, maj., 1997. Recipient Nat. Student Rsch. Forum 1st place Roche Labs. award for excellence in basic sci. rsch., 1992, Baxter Clin. Rsch. award of Excellence, 1999; Ariz. Med. Assn. scholar, 1987-89, U. Utah Joshua Millbank Scholars Program scholar, 1987, E. Blois du Bois scholar, 1981-89; Tulane Sch. Medicine grantee, 1993-94, 94, 95—, 97—. Fellow N.Y. Acad. Sci., Am. Physiol. Soc.; mem. Bd. Examiners in Anesthesia (nat. assoc.), Am. Soc. Anesthesiology (pres. 1992-93), Am. Heart Assn., Mass. Gen. Hosp. Anesthesia Alumni Assn., Soc. Critical Care Medicine, Soc. Cardiovascular Anesthesiologists, Internat. Anesthesia Rsch. Soc., La. Soc. Anesthesiologists, New Orleans Anesthesia Soc., Tulane Med. Ctr. Anesthesia Alumni Assn., Golden Key, Blue Key, Phi Beta Kappa, Phi Eta Sigma (pres. 1982-83, Baxter award of appreciation 1999). Office: Tex Tech U Health Sci Ctr Sch Medicine 3601 4th St Rm 1c282 Lubbock TX 79430-0001 Fax: 806-743-2984. E-mail: aneadk@ttuhsc.edu.

KAYE, BARRY, insurance company executive; b. N.Y.C., May 20, 1928; s. Herbert and Blanche (Sabin) K.; m. Carole Golison, Mar. 16, 1962; children: Fern L., Alan L., Howard S. CLU, Am. Coll. Life Underwriters. Pres. Barry Kaye, Inc., 1960—; owner Barry Kaye Assocs., Century City, Calif., 1970—; founder, chmn. Wealth Creation Ctrs., L.A., 1980; mem. faculty Practicing Law Inst., 1969—; lectr. UCLA, 1970—. Co-owner, Carole & Barry Kaye Museum of Miniatures. Author: How to Save a Fortune on Your Life Insurance, 1980, rev. edit., 1991, Save a Fortune on Your Estate Taxes, 1990, (tape and audio book) Save a Fortune on Your Estate Taxes, (tape) Wealth Creation and Preservation, Die Rich and Tax Free!, 1995, Live Rich, 1996, The Investment Alternative, 1997, Die Rich 2, 2000, All New Investment Alternative, Give Your Estate Away Twice, 2003. Mem. bd. govs. Diamond Cir. of Hope; trustee City of Hope; fellow Ben Gurion Soc., Ben Gurion Soc. of the Negev; chmn. Love and Hope Ball Inst. Diabetic Rsch., U. Miami, 2002. Recipient Founders award Diamond Cir. City of Hope, 1972, Lifetime Achievement award Ben Gurion U. of the Negev, 1987, Man of Yr. award Gen. Agts. and Mgrs. Conf., 1965, 66, 67, Fin. Advisor of Yr. award Fin. Svcs. Advisor Mag., 1999; named Man of Yr. Anti-Defamation League, 2002, named Man or Yr. Jewish Fedn. Palm Beach County, 2002. Mem. NCCJ (trustee, bd. dirs.), Am. Soc. CLUs, B'nai B-rith (Pres. Club), Uncles of Vista del Mar, Internat. Forum. Office: Barry Kaye Assocs 5100 Town Center Tower II #440 Boca Raton FL 33486 E-mail: barrykaye@barrykaye.com.

KAYE, CELIA ILENE, pediatrics educator; b. July 12, 1943; m. Tod B. Sloan. BS, Wayne State U., 1965, MS, 1968, MD, 1969; PhD, Northwestern U., 1975. Diplomate Am. Bd. Pediatrics, Am. Bd. Med. Genetics; lic. physician, Mich., Ill., Tex. Resident in pediat. Bronx (N.Y.) Mcpl. Hosp. Ctr., 1969-71, U. Ill. Hosp., Chgo., 1971-72; fellow in biochem. genetics Children's Meml. Hosp., Chgo., 1972-75; instr. pediat. Northwestern U. Coll. Medicine, Chgo., 1974-75; from asst. prof. to assoc. prof. pediat. U. Ill. Coll. Medicine, Chgo., 1975-89; chmn. divsn. genetics dept. pediat. Cook County Hosp., Chgo., 1975-80, attending physician divsn. genetics dept. pediat., 1980-89; dir. sect. genetics and genetics lab. divsn. pediat. Luth. Gen. Hosp., Park Ridge, Ill., 1980-89, co-med. dir. perinatal ctr., 1986-89; dep. chmn. Santa Rosa Children's Hosp. Activities, co-dir. clin. cytogenics lab. U. Tex. Health Sci. Ctr., San Antonio, 1990-97, prof. depts. pediat. and cellular and structural biology, 1990—, chief sect. metabolism, 1990—99, vice-chmn. dept. pediat., 1993-97, chmn. dept. pediat., 1997—2002, vice dean med. sch., 2001—, co-dir. cytogenetics lab., 1990—98. Mem. quality assurance com. cytogenetics lab. dept. cellular and structural biology U. Tex. Health Sci. Ctr., 1991-97, chair clin. faculty promotions com. dept. pediats., 1991-97, chair com. for devel. plan for selection, evaluation and promotion of clin. faculty dept. pediats., 1990-91, mem. perinatal mktg. com. dept. pediats., 1990-91, mem. residency adv. com. dept. pediats., 1990-2002, mem. faculty tenure and promotions com., 1995-97, mem. search com., chmn. dept. pathology, 1995-96, mem. dual degree program com., 1995-98, vice-chmn. bd. dirs. Univ. Physicians Group, 1995-97, 2001—, chmn. fin. com., 2000—, exec. com. mem, 2000—, mem. contract rev. com. 1995-97, bd. dirs.; mem. clin. coord. com., 1990-92, 2000, ad hoc clin. care com., 1990—, MSRDP adv. bd., 1991-93, 97—, search com. chmn. dept. medicine, 1992-93; chmn. program comm. sect. on genetics and birth defects Am. Acad. Pediat., 1995-99; dir. sect. genetics, Ctr. Craniofacial Anomalies, U. Ill. Coll. Medicine, Chgo., 1975-85; mem. med. adv. bd. Santa Rosa Children's Hosp., 1990-91, mem. exec. com. sect. on genetics and birth defects, Am. Acad. Pediat., 1995-2001, dir. med. edn., 1991-97, exec. com., 1992-2002, medicine policy com., 1992-97, chair med. edn. com., 1992-94; assoc. med. dir. cytogenetics lab. Santa Rosa Med. Ctr., San Antonio, 1991-98; vis. assoc. prof. pediats. Rush-Presbyn.-St. Luke's Med. Ctr., Chgo., 1979-89; mem. Genetics Task Force Ill., 1981-89, sec., 1981-83, pres., 1983-85; mem. genetics svc. com. Tex. Genetics Network, 1989-94, chmn. steering com., 1992-2000, mem. data com., 1995-2002; chmn. sci. adv. com. on birth defects Tex. Dept. Health, 1995-97; del. Nat. Coun. Regional Genetics Networks, 1992-99, mem. exec. com., 1993-97, bd. dirs., 1997-99; mem. Ill. Genetic and Metabolic Diseases Adv. Bd., 1984-89, chmn. lab. subcom., 1985-89; mem. sci. adv. com. Tex. Dept. Health, 1992-2000; sr. advisor Nat. Newborn Screening and Genetics Resource Ctr., 1998—; chmn. exec. com. Pub. Health Spl. Interest Group Am. Coll. Med.

Genetics, 2002—; mem. steering com. Children's Regional Health Care Network, San Antonio, 1993-94; mem. mgmt. com. Children's Regional Health Care Sys., San Antonio, 1993-94; mem. instl. rev. bd. Cook County Hosp., Chgo., 1975-80, Luth. Gen. Health Care Sys., Park Ridge, Ill., 1988-89; chmn. pediat. edn. com. Luth. Gen. Hosp., Park Ridge, 1981-86, chmn. pediat. bioethics com., mem. faculty adv. com., 1986-89; mem. faculty com. tenure and promotion com., 1995, mem. search com. chmn. dept. pathology, 1995-96, mem. cons. Med. Ctr. Hosp. Ward and Nursery, Bapt. Hosp. Sys., Santa Rosa Children's Hosp., Meth. Hosp., Humana Women's Hosp.; mem. by laws com. Santa Rosa Healthcare, San Antonio, 1995-97. Mem. adv. bd. Am. Jour. Med. Genetics; reviewer Am. Jour. Human Genetics, Pediatric Dermatology; contbr. articles to profl. jours., chpts. to books. Mem. program planning com. March of Dimes Defects Found., Chgo., 1985-89, mem. health profl. adv. com., 1983-89, chmn., 1981-83; mem. health profl. adv. com. South Ctrl. Tex. chpt., 1989-90; bd. dirs., mem. exec. com. Harkness House for Children, Winnetka, Ill., 1988-89; mem. Ill. Spina Bifida Assn., 1983-89; mem. exec. bd. El Valor Corp. for Handicapped Children, Chgo., 1980-81; mem. med. adv. com. Tex. Sickle Cell Assn., 1990-91. Fellow Am. Coll. Med. Genetics (founding, edn. com. 1993-97, pub. health com., moderator pub. health and delivery of svcs. sect. ann. meeting 1994); mem. AMA, Am. Soc. Human Genetics (info. and edn. com. 1990-94), Am. Acad. Pediats. (genetics sect., com. on genetics, liaison to bone and joint decade 2002, judge sci. awards uniformed svcs. sect. 1992-93, chair program com. sect. on genetics and birth defects 1995—, mem. exec. com. sect. on genetics and birth defects 1995—), Soc. for Pediat. Rsch., Soc. for Inherited Metabolic Diseases, So. Soc. for Pediat. Rsch. (moderator genetics sect. ann. meeting 1993), Tex. Med. Soc., Tex. Genetics Soc., Tex. Pediat. Soc., Bexar County Med. Soc., San Antonio Pediat. Soc. Office: U Tex Health Sci Ctr Med Dean's OFfice 7703 Floyd Curl Dr San Antonio TX 78229-3900

KAYE, DANIEL THEODORE, editor; b. Chgo., Ill., Aug. 16, 1946; s. Theodore W. and Dorothy L. Kaye; m. Susan Jane Sargent, Apr. 11, 1981; children: Jeffrey Daniel, Kristin Dollyne. BA, Principia Coll., 1968. Tchr. Sch. Dist. No. 28, Northbrook, Ill., 1968—74; sports reporter & editor Pioneer Press Newspapers, Wilmette, Ill., 1975—78; news reporter Wilmette Life, Wilmette, 1979—80; asst. mng. editor Highland Park News, Highland Park, Ill., 1980—81; assoc. editor McDougal, Littell & Co., Evanston, Ill., 1981—84; copy editor Chgo. Sun Times, Chgo., 1984—. Co-author, co-editor: Northbrook, Illinois: The Fabric of Our History, 2000 (Superior Achievement award Ill. State Hist. Soc., 2001, Spl. Merit award Northbrook Civic Found., 2001). Mem.: Northbrook Hist. Soc. (bd. dir. 2000—).

KAYE, DAVID L. psychiatrist; b. Chgo., Sept. 16, 1951; s. Bernard M. and Edith C. (Seder) K.; m. Emily G. Ets-Hokin. BA in Natural Scis., Johns Hopkins U., 1973; MD, U. Vt., 1977. Diplomate Am. Bd. Psychiatry and Neurology (bd. examiner 1992—), Am. Bd. Child and Adolescent Psychiatry. Resident in gen. psychiatry U. Wis., Madison, 1977-80, fellow in child psychiatry, 1980-82; dir. outpatient svcs. dept. child psychiatry Children's Hosp. Buffalo, 1982-85; dir. tng. & edn. in child psychiatry, clin. asst. prof. psychiatry SUNY, Buffalo, 1985-98, assoc. prof. clin. psychiatry, 1998—. Psychiat. cons. Therapeutic Presch. Program, Children's Hosp. Buffalo, 1982-91, Day Sch. Program, Gateway Youth and Family Svcs., 1988-91, Renaissance House, 1992—; acting dir. child & adolescent psychiatry consultation/liaison svc. Children's Hosp. Buffalo, 1994-96; lectr. in field; presenter in field. Editor Western N.Y. Psychiat. Soc. Newsletter, 1985-88; mem. editl. bd. Psychiatry Resident In-Tng. Exam, 1997—; contbr. articles to profl. jours., chpts. to books. Bd. dirs. Buffalo Family Sys. Program, 1984—86, Anorexia Bulimia Buffalo Assn., 1986—88, Gateway Youth & Family Svcs., 1992—96, Buffalo Fin. Planning Commn. rev. Buffalo Pub. Schs., 1994—95, City Honors Found., 2000—, Jewish Family Svcs., 2001—; pres. U. Wis. House Staff Assn., 1981—82. Fellow: Am. Coll. Psychiatrists; mem.: Western N.Y. Coun. Child and Adolescent Psychiatry (pres. 1991—94, v.p. 1994—), Am. Assn. Dirs. Psychiat. Residency Tng. (Peter Henderson, MD award com. 1993—, chair region II child psychiatry caucus 1995—2000, charter fellow award com. 1995—, exec. com. 2001—), Am. Acad. Child and Adolescent Psychiatry (family com.), Am. Psychiat. Assn. (disting.). Office: SUNY Dept Psychiatry Divsn Child & Adolescent Psychiatry Childrens Hosp 219 Bryant St Buffalo NY 14222-2006 E-mail: dlkaye@acsu.buffalo.edu.

KAYE, DINA LYNN, librarian; b. West Allis, Wis., Feb. 11, 1966; d. James Briggs and Ruth J. Kaye. BFA, U. Wis., Milw., 1990, M in Libr. and Info. Sci., 1994, MusM, 1997. Sr. academic libr. U. Wis. Parkside, Kenosha, 1994—. Mem. Friends of the U. Wis.-Parkside Libr., Kenosha, 1997—2002. Mem.: AMS, MLA, WLA. Democrat. Lutheran. Avocation: singing. Office: Univ Wis-Parkside 900 Wood Rd Kenosha WI 53144 Personal E-mail: kaye@uwp.edu. E-mail: kaye@uwp.edu.

KAYE, DONALD, physician, educator; b. N.Y.C., Aug. 12, 1931; s. Morris and Rose (Hirschtritt) K.; m. Janet Miriam Sovitsky, June 26, 1955; children: Kenneth Marc, Karen Lynne, Kendra Beth, Keith Steven. AB, Yale, 1953; MD, NYU, 1957. Diplomate Am. Bd. Internal Medicine, Am. Bd. Infectious Disease. Intern N.Y. Hosp., 1957-58, resident, 1958-60, fellow infectious diseases, 1960—63, asso. attending physician, 1961-69; physician-in-chief Hosp. Med. Coll. Pa., 1969-95; instr. medicine Cornell U. Med. Coll., 1961-63, asst. prof., 1963-66, asso. prof., 1966-69; prof., chmn. dept. medicine Med. Coll. Pa., Phila., 1969-94, Med. Coll. Pa. and Hahnemann U. Sch. Medicine, 1994-95, prof., 1995-96, Allegheny U. of Health Scis., 1996-98, MCP Hahnemann Sch. Medicine, 1998—2002, Drexel U. Coll. Medicine, 2002—. Cons. Phila. VA Hosp., 1969-95; CEO, pres. Med. Coll. Hosp., 1991-94, Med. Coll. Pa. and Hahnemann U. Hosp. Sys., 1994-96, Allegheny U. Hosps., 1996-98, Allegheny Integrated Health Group, 1996-97, Allegheny U. Health Scis., 1998; mem. revision com. U.S. Pharmacopeia, 1975-95; mem. VA Merit Rev. Bd. in Infectious Diseases, 1976-78; mem. com. on infectious diseases Am. Bd. Internal Medicine, 1976-84, cons., 1984-86. Author: Urinary Tract Infection and Its Management, 1972, Infective Endocarditis, 1976, Fundamentals of Internal Medicine, 1983, Internal Medicine for Dentists, 1983, 2d edit., 1990, Endocarditis, 1984, Infective Endocarditis, 1992; mem. editorial bd. Aging: Immunology and Infectious Diseases, Gerontology: Med. Sci., 1987-98, Antimicrobial Agts. Chemotherapy, 1972-98, Clinical Infectious Diseases, 2001-; contbr. articles to med. jours. Recipient Disting. Tchg. award Lindback Found., 1972; NIH grantee, 1967-76, 82-96; Pharm. Industry grantee, 1965-96, Emilio Ribas medal for disting svc. Brazilian Soc. of Infectious Diseases, 1994, Disting. Achievement award N.Y. Hosp.-Cornell Med. Ctr. Alumni Coun., 1994, Solomon A. Berson Alumni Achievement award NYU Sch. Medicine, 1996, Strittmatter award Philadelphia County Med. Soc., 1997. Master ACP (gov. Ea. Pa. region 1983-88, pres. Pa. chpt. 1987); fellow Gerontol. Soc. Am., Infectious Disease Soc. Am.; mem. AMA, Pa. Med. Soc. (alt. del to AMA 1991-92), Phila. County Med. Soc. (pres. 1991-92), Am. Soc. for Microbiology, Am. Fedn. for Clin. Rsch., Am. Soc. for Clin. Investigation, Assn. Am. Physicians, Am. Clin. and Climatol. Assn., Phi Beta Kappa, Alpha Omega Alpha, Sigma Xi. Home: 1535 Sweet Briar Rd Gladwyne PA 19035-1216 E-mail: donjank@aol.com.

KAYE, GAIL LESLIE, healthcare consultant, educator; b. Upland, Pa., Aug. 6, 1955; d. Ronald E. and Doris T. (Welfley) K. BS, W.Va. Welseyan Coll., 1977; MS, Ohio State U., 1982, PhD, 1989. Lic. profl. clin. counselor; registered dietitian. Asst. dir. food svc., chief clin. dietitian Albert Einstein Med. Ctr., Phila., 1983; asst. prof. Ind. State U., Terre Haute, 1983-85; nutrition cons. Ohio State U. Hosp. Clinics, Columbus, 1986-88, grad. rsch. asst., 1986-89; legis. rep. Ohio Assocs. Counseling and Devel., Columbus, 1988-89; rsch. cons. State Dept. Edn., Columbus, 1988-89; lectr. counselor edn. Ohio State U., Columbus, 1989-93; program devel. and clin. rschr. Ross Labs., Columbus, 1990-94; pres. Kaye Consultation Svcs., Inc., 1994—. Mem. faculty dept. human nutrition Ohio State U., 1998—, dir. MS/DI program in diebetics. Inventor in field; contbr. articles to profl. jours. Recipient Pres. award Ohio Mental Health Counselors Assn., 1990. Mem. Am. Dietetics Assn., Ohio Dietetics Assn. Avocations: swimming, piano, reading, hiking, painting, theatre. Home and Office: 365 Helmbright Dr Gahanna OH 43230-3290

KAYE, GORDON ISRAEL, pathologist, anatomist, educator; b. N.Y.C., Aug. 13, 1935; s. Oscar Swarz and Rebecca (Schachman) K.; m. Nancy Elizabeth Weber, June 4, 1956; children: Jacqueline Elizabeth, Vivienne Rebecca. AB, Columbia U., 1955, AM, 1957, PhD, 1961. From rsch. asst. cytology to dir. Columbia U., N.Y.C., 1953—63, dir. F. Higginson Cabot Lab. Electron Microscopy, 1963—76; rsch. and tchg. asst. cytology Rockefeller Inst., N.Y.C., 1957-58; from Alden March prof. to prof. emeritus Albany Med. Coll., N.Y.C., 1976—99, prof. emeritus pathology, 1999—; prof. biomed. sci. SUNY Sch. Pub. Health, 1986-99; pres., CEO Waste Reduction by Waste Reduction, Inc., Troy, NY, 1993-98, chmn., 1998—, exec. v.p., 2002—. Mem. seminar on creative process Wenner-Gren Found., 1964-65; cons. electron microscopy dept. pathology N.Y. VA Hosp., 1965—; Raymond C. Truex Disting. lectr. Hahnemann U., 1987. Co-author: Key Facts in Histology, 1985, Histology: A Text and Atlas, 1995, 4th edit., 2003; co-author: (in German) Atlas der Histologie, 1995; co-author: Histology, nat. med. series rev. series, 1997; editor: Current Topics in Cellular Anatomy, 1981; assoc. editor The Anat. Reocrd, 1972—98, editl. reviewer Exptl. Eye Rsch., 1964, Cancer, 1972—, Investigative Ophthalmology, 1973—, Gastroenterology, 1969—. Trustee Palisades free Libr., 1965-71; mem. Citizens Adv. Com., Sparkill Palisades Fire Dist., 1968-69; pres. Palisades Free Libr., 1969-71; trustee Orangetown Pub. Libr., 1971-73, Friends of Chamber Music, Troy, N.Y., 1988—; mem. citizens adv. com. Title III Program, S. Orangetown Ctrl. Sch. Dist., 1972-75; chmn. N.Y. State Low Level Waste Group, 1986-95; trustee Rockland Country Day Sch., 1974-78. Recipient Charles Huebschman prize in zoology Columbia U., 1954, Career Scientist award Health Rsch. Coun. N.Y.C., 1963-72, Rsch. Career Devel. award Nat. Inst. Arthritis and Metabolic Diseases, NIH, USPHS, 1972-76, Tousimis prize in biology, 1984; Ford Found. scholar, 1951-55; NSF predoctoral fellow, 1955-56, Nat. Inst. Neurol. Diseases and Blindness predoctoral fellow, 1959-61 Mem.: N.Y. Soc. Electron Microscopists (dir. 1964—67), Internat. Soc. Eye Rsch., Assn. Career Scientists Health Rsch. Coun., Harvey Soc., Am. Soc. Cell Biology, Am. Assn. Anatomists, Assn. Am. Med. Colls. (rep. con. acad. socs. 1979—2002, mem. adminstrn. bd. CAS 1985—86), Assn. Anatomy Chmn. (pres. 1980—81), Arthur Purdy Stout Soc. Surg. Pathologists (hon.), Waquoit Bay Yacht, Sigma Xi. Achievements include patents for (with Dr. Peter B. Weber) Method for disposal of radioactively labeled animal carcasses; methods for treatment and disposal of regualted med. waste; in field. Office: Waste Reduction by Waste Reduction 5711 W Minnesota St Indianapolis IN 46241-3825 E-mail: wr2kaye@aol.com.

KAYE, JHANI, radio station manager, owner production company; b. Maywood, Calif., June 18, 1949; s. Jimmie Eccak and Betty Jo (Holland) Kazaroff. BA, UCLA, 1971. Lic. 1st class radio. Music dir. Sta. KFXM, San Bernardino, Calif., 1969-73; announcer Stas. KUTE FM/KKDJ FM, L.A., 1972-74; asst. program dir. Sta. KROQ, L.A., 1973-74, Sta. WCFL, Chgo., 1980-82, Sta. KFI, L.A., 1982; program dir. Sta. KINT-FM, El Paso, Tex., 1975-80; sta. mgr., program dir. Sta. KOST-FM, L.A., 1982-99; program dir. Sta. KBIG-FM, Glendale, Calif, 1999—. Dir. adult contemporary programming Clear Channel Radio, 1999—; owner Los Feliz Post Prodn. Video Svcs.; sta. mgr. KBIG/KOST, 2001—. Appeared in TV series Falcon Crest, 1985, Drew Carey Show, 1998; dir. TV commls., 1986—; voice-over motion picture The Couch Trip, 1987; dir., video editor Dick Clark TV Commls. Recipient Marconi Radio awards Nat. Assn. Broadcasters, 1990, 91. Avocation: video production. Office: Sta KBIG-FM 330 N Brand Blvd Ste 800 Glendale CA 91203-2318

KAYE, JUDITH SMITH, state court chief justice; b. Monticello, N.Y., Aug. 4, 1938; d. Benjamin and Lena (Cohen) Smith; m. Stephen Rackow Kaye, Feb. 11, 1964; children: Luisa Marian, Jonathan Mackey, Gordon Bernard BA, Barnard Coll., 1958; LLB cum laude, NYU, 1962; LLD (hon.), St. Lawrence U., 1985, Union U., 1985, Pace U., 1985, Syracuse U., 1988, L.I. U., 1989. Assoc. Sullivan & Cromwell, N.Y.C., 1962-64; staff atty. IBM, Armonk, N.Y., 1964-65; asst. to dean Sch. Law NYU, 1965-68; ptnr. Connelly Chase O'Donnell & Weyher, N.Y.C., 1969-83; assoc. judge N.Y. State Ct. Appeals, N.Y.C., 1983-93, chief justice, 1993—. Bd. dir. Sterling Nat. Bank. Contbr. articles to profl. jours. Former bd. dirs. Legal Aid Soc. Recipient Vanderbilt medal NYU Sch. of Law, 1983, Medal of Distinction, Barnard Coll, 1987. Fellow Am. Bar Found.; mem. Am. Law Inst., Am. Coll. Trial Lawyers, Am. Judicature Soc. (bd. dirs. 1980-83). Democrat. Office: NY Court of Appeals Court of Appeals Hall 20 Eagle St Albany NY 12207-1009 also: NY Court of Appeals 230 Park Ave Rm 826 New York NY 10169-0007*

KAYE, KENNETH MARC, physician, educator, scientist; b. N.Y.C., Feb. 5, 1960; s. Donald and Janet Kaye; m. Elaine Tracy, Jul. 4, 1985; 3 children. AB summa cum laude, Harvard U., 1982, MD, 1986. Diplomate Am. Bd. Internal Medicine, also sub-bd. Infectious Disease. Resident in internal medicine Mass. Gen. Hosp., Boston, 1986-89; fellow in infectious disease Dana Farber Cancer Inst. Brigham & Women's Hosp., Beth Israel Hosp., Boston, 1989-91; instr. Med. Sch. Harvard U., Boston, 1991-95; asst. prof. of medicine Boston, 1995—; assoc. physician Brigham & Women's Hosp., Boston, 1991—. Contbr. articles to profl. jours. Recipient Edward H. Kass award for Clin. Excellence, Mass. Infectious Diseases Soc., 1991; Howard Hughes Med. Inst. postdoctoral fellow, 1991-92, Physician Scientist awardee NIH, 1992-97. Fellow ACP; mem. AAAS, IDSA, Phi Beta Kappa. Office: Brigham & Womens Hosp Divsn Infectious Diseases 75 Francis St Boston MA 02115-6106

KAYE, MARC MENDELL, lawyer; b. Irvington, N.J., Nov. 25, 1959; s. Aaron Morton and Sandra (Hoch) K. AA, BA, Rutgers U., 1980; JD, U. Toledo, 1983. Bar: N.J. 1984, Fla. 1987, D.C. 1991, N.Y. 1998, U.S. Dist. Ct. N.J. 1984, U.S. Supreme Ct. 1992; cert. civil trial atty. 1991. Trial atty. Shevick, Ravich, Koster et al, Rahway, N.J., 1984-85, Greenberg, Margolis et al, Roseland, N.J., 1985-86, Brian Granstrand, Fairfield, N.J., 1986-90; pvt. practice Livingston, N.J., 1986-94, Short Hills, 1994—. Counsel CNA Ins. Co., Fairfield, 1986-90; apptd. arbitrator Union County Arbitration Program, 1993, Essex County Arbitrator and Mediator Programs, 1995, Millburn Citizen Budget Com., 1998—; adv. coun. mem. Chmn.'s Club Summit Bank, 1989-91. Mem. exec. com. Young Leadership div. United Jewish Appeal, Metrowest, N.J, 1988-91; bd. dirs. Jewish Cmty. Ctr. of MetroWest, 1998—, Opera Music Theatre Internat., 1999—. Mem. N.J. Bar Assn., Essex County Bar Assn. (subcom. chmn. legal med. com. 1992-94), Union County Bar Assn., Fla. Bar Assn., D.C. Bar Assn., Assn. Trial Lawyers Am., N.J. Trial Lawyers Assn., Lions Club (v.p. 1993-95), Prime Ministers Club, Israel Bonds. Avocations: golf, swimming, scuba diving, travel. Office: One N Brook Dr at S Orange Ave Short Hills NJ 07078-3126 E-mail: Kayemarc@hotmail.com.

KAYE, RICHARD PAUL, lawyer; b. East Meadow, N.Y., June 11, 1953; s. Maurice and Sarah (Chanin) K.; m. Susan Ann Strickler, April 21, 1985. BA magna cum laude, Clark U., 1975; JD, George Washington U., 1978. Bar: N.Y. 1979, U.S. Dist. Ct. (so. dist.) 1979, (ea. dist) 1982, U.S. Ct. Appeals (2d cir.) 1998. Asst. dist. atty. N.Y. County, State of N.Y., 1978-81; assoc. Burlingham Underwood & Lord, N.Y.C., 1981-83, Danziger Bangser Klipstein Goldsmith Greenwald & Weiss, N.Y.C., 1983-86; ptnr. Carb, Luria, Glassner, Cook & Kufeld, N.Y.C., 1986-95, Bangser Klein Rocca & Blum, N.Y.C., 1995-97, Berger & Kaye LLP, N.Y.C., 1997—2001, Ellenoff Grossman & Schole, LLP, N.Y.C., 2001—. Arbitrator small claims Civil Ct. City of N.Y.C., 1986-90. Mem. ABA, N.Y. State Bar Assn., Assn. Bar City N.Y., Phi Beta Kappa, Phi Delta Phi. Office: Grossman & Schole 370 Lexington Ave New York NY 10017 E-mail: rkaye@egsllp.com.

KAYE, RICHARD WILLIAM, labor economist; b. Chgo., May 14, 1939; s. Albert Louis and Helen (Beckman) K.; m. Betty Ann Terry, Aug. 7, 1964; children: Ronald, William, Richard, Timothy. AB, Cornell U., 1960; MBA, Columbia U., 1962. Various fin. positions Inland Steel Co., Chgo., 1964-81; dir. info. svcs. No. Ind. Pub. Svc. Co., Hammond, 1981-86, dir. econ. analysis, 1986-98. Sis. dir. Purdue U., 1988; cons., ct. appointed receiver, 1989—; mgmt./fin. cons., 1990—. Advisor Calumet Coll., Whiting, Ind., 1985—; active Village Planning Commn., village trustee. Lt. (j.g.) USNR. Mem. Am. Mgmt. Assn., Cornell U. Alumni Assn., Columbia U. Alumni Assn., Rotary. Avocations: tennis, golf. Home: 2801 Cherrywood Ln Hazel Crest IL 60429-2126 Office: IDES 401 S State St Chicago IL 60605-1229

KAYE, ROBERT, pediatrics educator; b. NYC, July 17, 1917; s. Harry and Anna (Brisk) K.; m. Ellen Eskin, Nov. 16, 1960; children: Elizabeth, Margaret, Hillary, Sanford, Anthony. BA, Johns Hopkins U., 1939, MD, 1943. Intern Johns Hopkins Hosp., Balt., 1943, resident, 1944-45; instr. pediatrics Johns Hopkins Med. Sch., Balt., 1945; assoc. physiology Harvard Sch. Pub. Health, 1946-48; prof. pediatrics U. Pa., 1964-73, 86-88; prof., chmn. pediatrics Hahnemann Med. Coll. and Hosp., Phila., 1973-86; chmn. dept. pediatrics Med. Coll. Pa., Phila., 1988-92, prof., 1992-95; prof. emeritus Med. Coll. Pa., U. Pa., Hahnemann Med Coll., Phila. Contbr. articles to profl. jours. With U.S. Army, 1942—46. Nat. Found. Infantile Paralysis fellow, 1946-48. Mem. AAAS, Am. Pediatric Soc., Soc. Pediatric Rsch., Am. Diabetes Assn., Brodhead Forest and Stream Assn., Bala Golf Club. Jewish. Home: 200 Locust St Apt 22bc Philadelphia PA 19106-3914

KAYE, STEPHEN RACKOW, lawyer; b. Nyack, N.Y., May 4, 1931; s. Edward and Florence (Karp) K.; m. Judith Smith, Feb. 11, 1964; children: Luisa Marian, Jonathan Mackey, Gordon Bernard. AB, Cornell U., 1952, LL.B. with honors, 1956. Bar: N.Y. 1956, U.S. Supreme Ct. 1961. Assoc. Sullivan & Cromwell, N.Y.C., 1956-63, Proskauer Rose Goetz & Mendelsohn, N.Y.C., 1964-68, ptnr., past chair, co-chmn. lit. dept., 1968—. Mem. Judicial Inst. on Professionalism in the Law, 1999—. Author treatise texts on trials and appeals of comml. cases; mng. editor Cornell Law Quar.; contbr. to profl. publs. Served to 1st lt. AUS, 1952-54, Korea. Mem. ABA, N.Y. State Bar Assn., Assn. of Bar of City of N.Y. (past chmn. com. on profl. and jud. ethics, chmn. com. on profl. discipline), N.Y. County Lawyers Assn. (past vice chmn. com. on Supreme Ct.), 1st Dept. Disciplinary Commn. (hearing panel chair, policy com. 1991-96, 1999-2002), Order of Coif, Phi Kappa Phi. Office: Proskauer Rose LLP 1585 Broadway New York NY 10036-8299

KAYE, STUART MARTIN, lawyer; b. Bronx, N.Y., Dec. 2, 1946; s. Jules Krupnikoff and Gussie (Lipchinsky) Kaye; m. Nancy Elaine Carter, Oct. 19, 1967 (div. 1970); m. Christine Marie Heitkam, Sept. 25, 1970 (div. 1983); children: Joshua Brandon, Jeremy Jason; m. Eve C. Farkas, Apr. 2, 1988 (div. 1991); 1 child, Kimberly I. Morlan; m. Patricia S. Cruise, Mar. 3, 1996; 1 child, Trina S. Cruise. AA, Glendale Community Coll., 1971; BS in Polit. Sci., Ariz. State U., 1974; JD, Western State U., 1978. Bar: Calif. 1980, U.S. Dist. Ct. (no. dist.) Calif. 1980, (so. dist.) Calif. 1985, (cen. dist.) Calif. 1987. Assoc. mgmt. analyst State of Calif., Sacramento, 1978-84; pvt. practice Shingle Springs, 1981-84; legal counsel State of Calif., Sacramento, 1984-85, indsl. relations counsel San Diego, 1985-92; legal asst. Ariz. Atty. Gen., Phoenix, 1992-93; indsl. rels. coun. State of Calif., Santa Ana, 1993-95; atty. Don D. Sessions, APLC, Mission Viejo, 1995-98; pvt. practice La Mesa, 1998-2001; indsl. rels. coun. State of Calif., San Diego, 2001—. With U.S. Army, 1964-68. Democrat. Jewish. Avocation: camping. E-mail: stuart7@msn.com.

KAYE, WALTER, financial executive; b. Bklyn., Aug. 22, 1927; s. Jack and Ida (Shapiro) K.; m. Bernice Glatzer, May 6, 1952; children: Steven Mark, Russell Stuart. Student, CCNY, 1950-53; postgrad. (fellow), N.Y. Inst. Credit, 1956. Credit mgr., treas. A. Steinam Co., Inc., N.Y.C., 1951-68; v.p. Ambassador Factors Corp., N.Y.C., 1968-74; sr. v.p. Congress Factors Corp., N.Y.C., 1974-84; pres., chief exec. officer Mcht. Factors Corp., N.Y.C., 1985—. Bd. dirs. The Crossing Homeowners Assn., Trump Plaza, N.Y.C. Served with U.S. Army, 1944-46. Recipient Yitzak Rabin award B'nai B'rith, 1982, plaque Manhattan Credit, 1979; named Needlers Man of Yr., 2000; honoree NY Inst. Credit, 2003. Mem. N.Y. Inst. Credit, N.Y. Credit and Fin. Mgmt., Nat. Comml. Fin. Assn., Manhattan Credit (pres. 1978-79) Empire Credit (pres. 1971-74), The Financemen's Group Club, 475 Club, N.Y. Friars Club. Home: 18 The Crossing At Blind Brk Purchase NY 10577-2200 Office: Mcht Factors Corp 1430 Broadway New York NY 10018-3308

KAYFETZ, VICTOR JOEL, writer, editor, translator; b. N.Y.C., July 20, 1945; s. Daniel Osler and Selma Harriet (Walowitz) K. BA, Columbia U., 1966; postgrad., U. Stockholm, Sweden, 1966—67; MA History, U. Calif., Berkeley, 1969. Tchg. asst. in Swedish U. Calif., Berkeley, 1969-70, tchr., adminstr. Swedish adult edn. programs, 1970-75; corr. Reuters, Stockholm, 1975-78; sub-editor Reuters World Svc., London, 1978; corr. London Fin. Times, Stockholm, 1979-80; freelance translator Swedish, Danish, Norwegian, 1967—; freelance editor Swedish and Am. mags., 1980—. Author: Sweden in Brief, 1974, 80; Invest in Sweden, 1984; Skanska, The First Century, 1987; editor, translator numerous books, ann. reports, mags. for Swedish govt. agys., interest orgns., univs., indsl. corps., banks. Henry Evans traveling fellow, 1966-67; Nat. Def. Fgn. Lang. fellow, 1967-69; Thord Gray fellow Am.-Scandinavian Found., 1970. Mem. Swedish Am. C. of C., Soc. Advancement Scandinavian Study, Am. Scandinavian Found., Swedish Assn. Profl. Translators, World Affairs Council No. Calif., Sierra Club, Phi Beta Kappa.

KAYLAN, HOWARD LAWRENCE, musical entertainer, screenwriter, composer; b. N.Y.C., June 22, 1947; s. Sidney and Sally Joyce (Berlin) Kaylan; m. Mary Melita Pepper, June 10, 1967 (div. Sept. 1971); 1 child, Emily Anne; m. Susan Karen Olsen, Apr. 18, 1982 (div. June 1996); 1 child, Alexandra Leigh. Student, UCLA; PhD in Philosophy, Am. Coll. Metaphys. Theology, St. Paul, Minn., 2000. Lead singer and founder rock group The Turtles, Los Angeles, 1965—; lead singer rock group Mothers of Invention, Los Angeles, 1970-72, Flo and Eddie, 1972-83; radio, TV, recording entertainer various broadcast organizations, Los Angeles, 1972—; screenwriter Larry Gelbart, Carl Gotleib prodns., Los Angeles, 1979-85; prodr. children's records Kidstuff Records, Hollywood, Fla., 1980-83; singer, prodr. rock band Flo and Eddie, Los Angeles, 1976-83; singer, prodr. The Turtles (reunion of original band), Los Angeles, 1980—; actor, TV and film Screen Actors Guild, Los Angeles, 1983—. Background vocalist various albums for numerous performers; syndicated talk show host Unistar Radio Network, 1989—; radio personality Sta. WXRK-FM, N.Y.C., 1990—91, KLOU, St. Louis, 1993, WGRR, Cin., 1995—97. Author: Hi Bob, 1995, The Energy Pals, 1995; contbr. ; actor: (films) 200 Motels, 1971, Get Crazy, 1985, General Hospital, Suddenly Susan, 1999; performer: at White House, 1970; exec. prodr.(radio): Down Eerie Street, 1998; singer: numerous top ten hit songs with Turtles, Bruce Springstein, The Ramones, Duran Duran, T. Rex, John Lennon and others, commls. for Chevrolet, Pepsi, Bruger King and NFL, 1970— (awards); screenwriter My Dinner With Jimi, 2003. Recipient 10 Gold and Platinum LP album awards while lead singer, 1995—, Fine Arts award, Bank of Am., 1965, Spl. award, Billboard Mag., 1992, Best Script award, Slam Dunk Film Festival, 2003, Bubblegum award, 2003. Mem.: AGVA, AFRTA, Am. Fedn. Musicians, Screen Actors Guild.

KAYNE, JON BARRY, industrial psychologist; b. Sioux City, Iowa, Oct. 20, 1943; s. Harry Aaron and Barbara Valentine (Daniel) K.; m. Bunee Ellen Price, July 25, 1965; children: Nika Jenine, Abraham; m. Sandra Kay Fossbender, Jan. 5, 1985; 1 child, Shay-Marie Kathryn. BA, U. Colo., 1973; MSW, U. Denver, 1975; PhD, U. No. Colo., 1978. With spl. svcs. Weld County Sch. Dist. 6, Greeley, Colo., 1975-77; forensic diagnostician Jefferson County (Colo.) Diagnostic Unit, 1977-78; assoc., dir. mktg. 1 Dow Ctr., assoc. prof. psychology Hillsdale (Mich.) Coll., 1978-87; pres. Jon B. Kayne, P.C., Hillsdale, 1980-87; pres. bd. dirs. Lang. Learners in Partnership of Omaha, 1989-93; chmn. bd. dirs., CEO Am. Internat. Mgmt. Assocs., Ltd., Denver, 1984-87; prof. bus. adminstrn. and psychology Bellevue (Neb.) U., 1987—, v.p. profl. and continuing edn. studies, 1987-93, v.p. acad. affairs, 1993—. Chmn. bd. dirs. Domestic Harmony, 1979-82; bd. dir. religious sch., Greeley, 1975-77; candidate for sheriff of Boulder County, 1974. With USAR, 1962. Mem. Am. Psychol. Assn., Am. Soc. Clin. Hypnosis, Am. Statis. Assn., Internat. Neuropsychol. Soc., Mich. Soc. Investigative and Forensic Hypnosis (chmn. bd., pres. 1982), N.Y. Acad. Scis., Phi Delta Kappa, Psi Chi, Alpha Gamma Sigma. Office: Bellevue U 1000 Galvin Rd S Bellevue NE 68005-3098

KAYNE, MICHELE S. lawyer; b. Pequannock, N.J., Apr. 25, 1972; d. Martin Robert and Cecile Sasson Kayne BA in English, cert. tchr. handicapped, Rutgers Coll., 1994; JD, Rutgers U., 1997. Bar: N.J. 1997, U.S. Dist. Ct. N.J. 1997, N.Y. 1998, U.S. Dist. Ct. (so. and ea. dists.) N.Y. 1999. Respite cons. New Horizons in Autism, Cranbury, N.J., 1991-97; jud. clk. N.J. Superior Ct., Chancery N.J., Elizabeth, 1997-98; assoc. Wolff & Samson, P.A., Roseland, N.J., 1998—. Ct.-apptd. mediator N.J. Jud. of Morris County, Morristown, 1999—. Mem. ABA, N.Y. State Bar Assn., N.J. State Bar Assn., Essex County Bar Assn. (employment law divsn. 1998—, young lawyer's divsn.). Avocations: marathon running, ultimate race competition, playing field hockey. Home: 417 3rd Ave Apt 3A New York NY 10016-8189 Office: Wolff & Samson PA 5 Becker Farm Rd Roseland NJ 07068-1727 E-mail: mkayne@wolffsamson.com.

KAYO, IDE, research scientist; PhD, Calif. Inst. Tech. Rschr. UCLA, Los Angeles, Calif., 1995.

KAYS, WILLIAM MORROW, university administrator, mechanical engineer; b. Norfolk, Va., July 29, 1920; s. Herbert Emery and Margaret (Fechteler) K.; m. Alma Campbell, Sept. 14, 1947 (dec. June 1982); children: Nancy,

Leslie, Margaret, Elizabeth.; m. Judith Scholtz, July 17, 1983. AB, Stanford U., 1942, MS, 1947, PhD in Mech. Engring., 1951. Asst. prof. mech. engring. Stanford U., 1951-54, assoc. prof., 1954-57, prof., 1957-90, prof. emeritus, 1990—, chmn. dept. mech. engring, 1961-72, dean engring., 1972-84. Dir. Acurex Corp., Alcohol Energy Systems; cons. to numerous firms. Author: Compact Heat Exchangers, 1964, 93, Convective Heat and Mass Transfer, 1966, 80. Hon. editorial adv. bd.: Internat. Jour. Heat and Mass Transfer. Served with U.S. Army, 1942-46. Fulbright fellow, 1959-60; NSF sr. postdoctoral fellow, 1966-67 Fellow ASME (Heat Transfer Divsn. Meml. award 1965, Max Jacob award 1992); mem. Am. Soc. Engring. Edn., Nat. Acad. Engring. Office: Stanford U Dept Mech Engring Stanford CA 94305

KAYSE, KATHLEEN, publishing executive; b. Chgo, Ill, 1959; Grad., Univ. of Ill. Media planning Wells, Rich, Greene and J. Walter Thompson, Chgo., 1980—83; sales trainee Time, 1983; midwest advt. mgr. Time Mag., Chgo.; nat. advt. dir. Time for Kids; pub. Fortune Small Bus. (FSB), Time Mag., NYC, 1998—2001, Money mag., 2001—02, People mag., 2002—. Named Most powerful women in the US, Fortune. Mem.: Fin. Comm. Soc., Advertising Women of NY. Achievements include She is the only woman in the position of publisher within AOL/Time/Warner. Office: People Mag 1271 Ave of the Americas New York NY 10020-1393

KAYSEN, CARL, economics educator; b. Phila., Mar. 5, 1920; s. Samuel and Elizabeth (Resnick) K.; m. Annette Neutra, Sept. 13, 1940 (dec. 1990); children: Susanna, Laura; m. Ruth Butler, 1994. AB, U. Pa., 1940; PhD, Harvard U., 1954. Rschr. Nat. Bur. Econ. Rsch., 1940-42; economist OSS, 1942; mem. faculty Harvard U., 1950—66; jr. fellow Harvard U. (Soc. Fellows), 1947-50, asst. prof. econs., 1950-55, assoc. prof., 1955-57, prof., 1957-66, Lucius N. Littauer prof. polit. economy, 1964-66; assoc. dean Harvard U. (Grad. Sch. Public Adminstrn.), 1960-66; dir. Inst. Advanced Study, Princeton, N.J., 1966-76, prof., 1966-77; David W. Skinner prof. polit. economy MIT, 1977-90, dir. program in sci., tech. and soc., 1981-87, prof. emeritus, 1990—. Clk. to Judge C. E. Wyzanski, U.S. Dist. C., 1950-52; dep. spl. asst. to Pres. Kennedy for nat. security affairs, 1961-63; mem. Carnegie Commn. on Higher Edn.; vice chmn., dir. research Sloan Commn. on Govt. and Higher Edn.; faculty lectr. London Sch. Econs., 1956; Haynes lectr. Calif. Inst. Tech., 1966; Stafford Little lectr. Princeton U., 1968; Oliver W. Holmes lectr. Harvard Law Sch., 1969; Paley lectr. Hebrew U., Jerusalem, 1970; Godkin lectr. Harvard U., 1976; Bernard Brodie lectr., U.C.L.A., 1994; dir. Charles River Assocs. Life trustee U. Pa. Served to capt. air intelligence AUS, 1942-45. Fulbright scholar London Sch. Econs., 1955-56; Guggenheim fellow, 1955-56; Ford Found. fellow Greece, 1959-60 Mem. Am. Philos. Soc., Am. Acad. Arts and Scis., Phi Beta Kappa. Clubs: Century (N.Y.C.). Office: MIT Security Studies Program E 38-614 Cambridge MA 02139

KAYSER, KENNETH WAYNE, lawyer; b. N.Y.C., Apr. 28, 1947; s. William Gilbert and Joan Phyliss (Bach) K.; m. Linda Calcote, Apr. 13, 1968; 1 child, Christopher R. BA, Syracuse U., 1969; JD, Seton Hall, 1977. Bar: N.J. 1977, U.S. Dist. Ct. N.J. 1977, U.S. Cir. Ct. (3d cir.) 1988, U.S. Ct. Internat. Trade 1990. Asst. prosecutor Essex County Prosecutor's Office, Newark, 1978-82; assoc. Brach, Eichler, Rosenberg, Silver, Bernstein & Hammer, Roseland, N.J., 1982-83; sole practice West Orange, N.J., 1984—. Mem. ABA, N.J. State Bar Assn., Essex County Bar Assn., Assn. Criminal Def. Lawyers N.J. Democrat. Home: PO Box 2087 Livingston NJ 07039 Office: 120 Eagle Rock Ave East Hanover NJ 07936-3105 E-mail: kenkayser@cs.com.

KAYTON, MYRON, engineering company executive; b. N.Y.C., Apr. 26, 1934; s. Albert Louis and Rae (Danoff) K.; m. Paula Erde, Sept. 5, 1954; children: Elizabeth Kayton Kerns, Susan Kayton Barclay. BS, The Cooper Union, 1955; MS, Harvard U., 1956; PhD, MIT, 1960. Registered engr., Calif. Sect. head Litton Industries, Woodland Hills, Calif., 1960-65; dep. mgr. NASA, Houston, 1965-69; mem. sr. staff TRW, Inc., Redondo Beach, Calif., 1969-81; pres. Kayton Engring. Co., Inc., Santa Monica, Calif., 1981—. Chmn. bd. dirs. WINCON Conf., L.A., 1985-92; founding dir. Caltech-MIT Enterprise Forum, Pasadena, Calif., 1984—; dir. Electronic Convs., Inc., 2000-01; tchr. tech. courses UCLA Extension, 1969-88. Author: Avionic Navigation Systems, 1966, 2d edit., 1997, Navigation: Land, Sea, Air and Space, 1990; contbr. numerous articles on engring., econs. and other profl. subjects. Founding dir. UCLA Friends of Humanities, 1971-75; West coast chmn. Cooper Union Fund Campaign, 1989-93. Fellow NSF, Washington, 1956-57, 58-60; recipient Gano Dunn medal The Cooper Union, N.Y.C., 1975. Fellow IEEE (life; nominating com. 1999—, corp. bd. dirs. 1996-97, pres. aerospace 1993-94, exec. v.p. aerospace 1991-92, v.p. tech. ops. 1988-90, nat. bd. govs. 1983—, vice-chmn. L.A. coun. 1983-84, avionics editor Aerospace Transactions 2002—, M.B. Carlton award 1988, Disting. lectr., Millennium medal 2000); mem. ASME, Harvard Grad. Soc. (coun. mem. chmn. nominating com. 1988-91, Inst. Navigation, Soc. Automotive Engr., Harvard Club So. Calif. (pres. 1979-80), MIT Club (L.A.). Avocations: tennis, history, languages, flying. Office: Kayton Engring Co PO Box 802 Santa Monica CA 90406-0802

KAYWELL, JOAN, education educator; b. West Palm Beach, Fla., Mar. 1, 1956; d. Bernard E. and Grace H. Kaywell; 1 child, Stephen Matthew. BA in Edn., U. Fla., 1979, MEd, 1980, PhD, 1987. Prof. U. South Fla. Coll. Edn., Tampa, 1988—, interim chair secondary edn. Award winning tchr. and presenter in field. Author: Adolescent Literature as a Complement to the Classics (4 vols. 1993, 95, 97, 2000), Adolescents At Risk: A Guide to Fiction & Nonfiction for Young Adults, Parents and Professionals, 1993; series editor Using Literature to Help Troubled Teenagers Cope, 6-book series, 1999, 2000, 2001. Mem.: ASCD, Assembly on Lit. for Adolescents (past pres.), Fla. Coun. Tchrs. English (past pres., Honor award 2000), Eastern Ednl. Rsch. Assn., Am. Ednl. Rsch. Assn., Nat. Coun. Tchrs. English, Tau Beta Sigma, Phi Delta Kappa. Avocations: cooking, boating, writing, reading. Office: U South Fla Coll Edn 162 Tampa FL 33620-5650

KAZA, GREG JOHN, economist, educator; b. Wyandotte, Mich., Nov. 11, 1960; s. John J. and Mary A. (Lazurek) K. BA in Econs., U. Detroit, 1989; MSF in Internat. Fin., Walsh Coll., Troy, Mich., 1998. V.p. policy rsch. The Mackinac Ctr., Midland, Mich., 1989-91; adj. prof. Northwood Inst. and Walsh Coll., Troy, Mich., 1998—; state rep. State of Mich., 1993-98; exec. dir. Citizen Legislators' Caucus Found., Washington, 1999-2000, Ark. Policy Found., Little Rock, 2001—. Author 9 state laws. Named Nat. Legislator of Yr., Rep. Liberty Caucus, 1994, Fellow Nat. Journalism Ctr.; mem. Highpointers Mountaineering Club. Republican. Roman Catholic. Office: Ark Policy Found 111 Center St Ste 1310 Little Rock AR 72201

KAZAL, LOUIS ANTHONY, JR., health facility administrator; s. Louis Anthony and Marie Barry Kazal; m. Rebecca Charlotte Kaesmeyer. BS, Muhlenberg Coll., 1980; MD, Jefferson Med. Coll., 1984. Diplomate Am. Bd. of Family Practice. Staff physician Star Valley Hosp., Afton, Wyo., 1987—89; faculty devel. fellow Baylor Coll. of Medicine, Houston, 1989—90, asst. prof., 1990—92; staff physician Navajo Health Found., Ganado, Ariz., 1992—2001, med. dir., 1996—99, chief med. officer, 1999—2002; med. dir. Dartmouth-Hitchcock Cmty. Health Ctr., Lebanon, NH, 2002—. Med. registrar Lincoln County, Afton, 1987—89. Contbr. articles to profl. jours., chpts. to books. Mem. Mental Health, Afton, 1987—89; physician cons. Navajo Reach Out and Read, Ganado, 1995—2001. Named Ariz. Family Physician of the Yr., Ariz. Acad. of Family Physicians, 2000; Robert Wood Johnson Health Policy fellow, Inst. of Medicine, 2001—02. Fellow: Am. Acad. of Family Physicians (award 2001). E-mail: rkazal@hotmail.com.

KAZALIA, MARIE ANN, writer; b. Toledo, Feb. 12, 1954; d. Charles and Lois Jean (Gelvin) K.; children: Sarah Jean Richards, Jason Samuel Williams. BFA, Calif. Coll. Arts & Crafts, 1981; MA, Ctr. Mus. Studies, 1983. Mus. registrar City & County Arts Commn., San Francisco, 1982-83. Author: (book of poetry) Erratic Sleep in a Cold Hotel, 1999, All-Purpose Tragedy, 2000, (novels) Minden Row, 2002. Office: PO Box 422344 San Francisco CA 94142-2344 E-mail: makazalia@aol.com.

KAZAN, ALEXANDRA KHAN, photographer, web site designer; d. Pat Anna Landon-Robbins-Taylor and C. Richard Taylor; m. Edgar Rolf Schneider, June 26, 1999. Web designer Garfield Images and Design, Ft. Lauderdale, Fla., 1998—. Recipient Golden Web award, Internat. Assn. Web Masters and Designers, 2002, 2003. Mem.: ASPCA, Humane Soc. Republican. Episcopalian. Avocations: photography, painting, writing, reading, animal welfare.

KAZAN, BENJAMIN, research engineer; b. N.Y.C., May 8, 1917; s. Abraham Eli and Esther (Bookbinder) K.; m. Gerda B. Mosse, Nov. 4, 1988; 1 child from previous marriage, David Louis. BS in Physics, Calif. Inst. Tech., 1938; MA in Physics, Columbia U., 1940; PhD in Physics, Tech. U. Munich, 1961. Radio engr. Dept. Def., Ft. Monmouth, N.J., 1940-50; rsch. engr. RCA Labs., Princeton, N.J., 1950-58; head solid state display group Hughes Rsch. Lab., Malibu, Calif., 1958-61; head imaging sect. Electro-Optical Sys., Pasadena, Calif., 1961-68; head exploratory display group T.J. Watson Rsch. Ctr., Yorktown Heights, N.Y., 1968-74; prin. scientist Xerox Rsch. Ctr., Palo Alto, Calif., 1974-85; cons. display and imaging tech., 1985—. Cons. Advisory Group Electron Devices, Dept. Def., 1973-82; adj. prof. U. R.I., Kingston, 1970-74. Author: (with others) Storage Tubes, 1952, Electronic Image Storage, 1968; editor: Advances in Image Storage, 1968, Advances in Image Pickup and Display series, 1972-84, assoc. editor Advances in Imaging and electron Physics series, 1984—; contbr. articles to profl. jours., patentee in field. Recipient silver medal Am. Roentgen Ray Soc., 1957. Fellow IEEE (assoc. editor Jour. Electron Devices 1979-83), Soc. Info. Display (editor jour. 1974-78); mem. Am. Phys. Soc., Sigma Xi, Tau Beta Pi. Home: 800 Blossom Hill Rd Unit P394 Los Gatos CA 95032-3575 E-mail: bkazan@earthlink.net.

KAZAN, ROBERT PETER, neurosurgeon; b. Chgo., Mar. 29, 1947; s. Peter Joseph and Genevieve (Pauga) K.; m. Janet Rae Hoiland, June 21, 1975. BS, Loyola U., Chgo., 1969, MD, 1973. Diplomate Am. Bd. Neurol. Surgeons; lic. physician Ill. Intern Mayo Clinic, Rochester, Minn., 1973-74, resident in neurosurgery, 1974-78; neurosurg. cons. West Suburban Neurosurg. Assocs., Hinsdale, Ill., 1978—; med. dir. neurosci. dept. Hinsdale Hosp., 1992. Clin. asst. prof. neurosurgery U. Ill., Chgo., 1983—; various teaching appointments West Suburban Hosp. Dept. Surgery, Chgo. Med. Soc. Midwest Conf., Northwestern U.; staff neurosurgeon Hinsdale Hosp., vice-chmn. surgery, 1988-90, chmn. dept. surgery, 1990—, med. dir. neuroscis., 1992. Contbr. articles to profl. jours. Named one of best neurosurgeons in Chgo., Chicago Mag., 2001. Fellow: ACS; mem.: AMA, Ill. State Neurosurg. Soc. (membership chmn. 1995, treas. 1996, sec.-treas. 1997, v.p. 1998, pres. 1999—2000), Internat.Skullbase Soc., Congress Neurol. Surgeons (joint sect. trauma and disorders of spine and peripheal nerves), Am. Assn. Neurol. Surgeons, Soc. Med. Cons. Armed Forces US, Cen. Neurosurg. Soc., Am. Assn. Neurol. Surgeons (joint sect. trauma and disorders of spine and peripheal nerves), Congress Neurosurg. Surgeons, Mayo Clin. Neurosurg. Soc., Ill. Med. Soc., DuPage County Med. Soc., The Explorers Club. Republican. Roman Catholic. Office: West Suburban Neurosurg Assocs 20 E Ogden Ave Hinsdale IL 60521-3543 E-mail: wsna@mindspring.com.

KAZANJIAN, PHILLIP CARL, lawyer; b. Visalia, Calif., May 15, 1945; s. John Casey and Sat-ten Arlene K.; m. Wendy Coffelt, Feb. 5, 1972; 1 child, John. BA with honors, U. So. Calif., 1967; JD with honors, Lincoln U., 1973. Bar: Calif. 1979, U.S. Dist. Ct. (ctrl. dist.) Calif. 1980, U.S. Tax Ct. 1980, U.S. Ct. Appeals (9th cir.) 1980, U.S. Mil. Ct. Appeals 1980, U.S. Supreme Ct. 1983. Ptnr. Brakefield & Kazanjian, Glendale, Calif., 1981-87; sr. ptnr. Kazanjian & Martinetti, Glendale, Calif., 1987—. Judge pro tem L.A. County Superior Ct., 1993—; instr. U.S. Naval Acad., Annapolis, Md., 1981; adj. prof. Glendale C.C., 1997—. Author: The Circuit Governor, 1972; editor-in-chief Lincoln Law Rev., 1973. Mem. Calif. Atty. Gen.'s Adv. Commn. on Cmty.-Police Rels., 1973; bd. dirs. L.A. County Naval Meml. Found., Inc., 1981-85; pres., bd. trustees Glendale C.C. Dist., 1981-97, L.A. World Affairs Coun., Town Hall Calif., Rep. Assocs. (dir.), Rep. Lincoln Club; vice chmn. bd. govs. Calif. Maritime Acad., 1986-94. Capt. USNR, 1969-99. Decorated Navy Commendation medal, Navy Achievement medal, knight Order of Knights Templar, 1990; recipient Patrick Henry medal Am. Legion, 1963, Congl. Record tribute U.S. Ho. of Reps., 1974, Centurion award Chief of Naval Ops., 1978; commendatory resolutions Mayor of L.A., L.A. City Coun., L.A. County Bd. Suprs., Calif. State Assembly and Senate, and Govt. of Calif., 1982, 2003, Justice award Calif. Law Student Assn., 1973. Mem. ABA (Gold Key 1972), Calif. Bar Assn., L.A. County Bar Assn., Am. Judicature Soc., ATLA, Glendale C. of C. (bd. dirs., Patriot Yr. 1986), Res. Officers Assn. (nat. judge adv., award 1981), Naval Res. Assn. (nat. adv. com.), U.S. Naval Inst., Interallied Confedn. Res. Officers (internat. chmn. 1987-94), Explorers Club, Commonwealth of Calif. Club. Republican. Episcopalian. Office: Kazanjian & Martinetti 520 E Wilson Ave Ste 250 Glendale CA 91206-4346

KAZARIAN, POGHOS F. physicist, researcher, educator; b. Yerevan, USSR, Armenia, Sept. 2, 1973; arrived in USA, 1998; s. Frunzik H. and Tamara G. (Movsesyan) Kazarian. PhD physics, Yerevan State Univ., Yerevan, Armenia, 1997, MS physics, 1994. Post grad. rsch. asst. Dept. of Theory Physics, Yerevan State Univ., Yerevan, Armenia, 1994—97, rsch. assoc., 1997—2000; instr. physics dept., Glendale Cmty. Coll., Glendale, Calif., 2000—. Author: (Theory) Astrophysics, 1994—99, 8th Internat. Symposium on Light Sources, 1998, (book) Concepts in Physics: Classical Mechanics, 2003. Recipient Diploma with Honors, Faculty of Physics, Yerevan State Univ./Yerevan Armenia, 1994, Scholarship for Excellence, Yerevan State Univ./Yerevan Armenia, 1989—94, Diploma with Honors & Medal, AS Pushkin, Secondary Sch./Yerevan, Armenia, 1989. Mem.: Am. Assoc. for the Advancement of Sci., NY Acad. of Sci. Bimetric scalar-tensor theory of gravitation-construction of pre-stellar objects of V. Ambartsumian's cosmogony concept, and full agreement with gen. relativity (GR included as partial case), 1993-1999; Abnormally intense radiation from dielectric, 1998. Home: 122 N Adams, #22 Glendale CA 91206 Office: Glendale Cmty Coll 1500 N Verdugo Rd Glendale CA 91208

KAZAZIAN, HAIG HAGOP, JR., medical scientist, physician, educator; b. Toledo, July 30, 1937; s. Haig Hagop and Hermine Adriene (Papelian) K.; m. Lillian Agnes Cleaver, Oct. 13, 1962; children: Haig Hagop III, Sonya Elizabeth. AB, Dartmouth Coll., 1959; MD, Johns Hopkins U., 1962. Diplomate Am. Bd. Pediatrics, Am. Bd. Medical Genetics (pres. 2000). Asst. prof. pediatrics Johns Hopkins U., Balt., 1969-74, assoc. prof. pediatrics, 1974-77, prof. pediats., 1977-94, prof. biology, 1979-94, prof. ob-gyn., 1985-94, prof. medicine, 1989-94, dir. Ctr. Med. Genetics, 1989-94, Sutland prof. pediat. genetics, 1991-94; chmn. dept. genetics U. Pa. Sch. Medicine, Phila., 1994—. Mem. mammalian genetics study sect. NIH, Bethesda, Md., 1981-85; pres. bd. dirs. Citizens for Good Govt., Balt., 1973-75; bd. dirs. Am. Bd. Med. Genetics. Author more than 250 sci. papers; editor jour. Human Mutation, 1992. Sr. surgeon USPHS, 1966-68. Grantee NIH, 1968—; recipient Mead Johnson award Am. Acad. Pediatrics, 1976. Mem. Inst. of Medicine, Am. Pediat. Soc., Am. Soc. Human Genetics (bd. dirs. 1982-85), Am. Soc. Clin. Investigation, Assn. Am. Physicians, Alpha Omega Alpha. Democrat. Episcopalian. Avocations: jogging, tennis, classical music. Home: 1015 Winding Way Baltimore MD 21210-1232 Office: U Pa Sch Medicine 475 Clinical Research Bldg 415 Curie Blvd Philadelphia PA 19104-4218

KAZDIN, ALAN E. psychology educator; b. Chi., Jan. 24, 1945; s. Leon Nathan Kazdin and Eva Edith Shapira; m. Joann M. DiDonato, June 29, 1969; children: Nicole, Michelle. BA, San Jose State U., 1967; MA, Northwestern U., 1968, PhD, 1970. Diplomate Am. Bd. Profl. Psychology, Am. Bd. Assessment Psychology. Asst. prof. psychology Northwestern U., Evanston, Ill., 1971; from asst. prof. to assoc. prof. Pa. State U., University Park, 1971-77, prof. psychology, 1977-81; vis. prof. U. Pitts. Sch. Medicine, 1979-80, prof. psychiatry and psychology, 1981-89; program/rsch. dir. Children's Psychiat. Intensive Care Svc. Western Psychiat. Inst. and Clinic, 1981-89; dir. clin. tng. dept. psychology Yale U., New Haven, 1991-95, chmn. dept. psychology, 1997—2000; chmn. dept. child psychiatry Yale U. Sch. Medicine, New Haven, 2000—. Author 35 books, including Psychotherapy for Children and Adolescents: Directions for Research and Practice, 2000, The Encyclopedia of Psychology, Vols. 1-8, 2000, Behavior Modification in Applied Settings, 6th edit., 2001; editor: (jours.) Behavior Therapy, 1979-83, Jour. Consulting and Clin. Psychology, 1985-90, Psychol. Assessment, 1989-91, Clin. Psychology: Sci. and Practice, 1994-98, Current Directions in Psychol. Sci., 1999—. Recipient Nat. Inst. Mental Health MERIT Award, 1987, award for disting. profl. contbn. to clin. child psychology divsn. 12 APA, 1995, Outstanding Rsch. Contbn. by an Individual award Assn. for Advancement of Behavior Therapy, 1998, Disting. Scientist award Soc. for Sci. of Clin. Psychology, divsn. 12 APA, 1999; fellow Ctr. for Advanced Study in Behavioral Scis., 1976-77; grantee Leon Lowenstein Found., Nat. Inst. Mental Health, State of Conn., Dept. Social Svcs., Behavioral Mental Health Outcomes of Psychotherapy for Children and Adolescents. Office: Yale U Sch of Medicine Child Study Ctr 230 S Frontage Rd New Haven CT 06520-7900 Office Fax: 203-785-7402.

KAZELL, DORIS LILLIAN, librarian; b. Chaffee, N.D., Dec. 2, 1917; d. John Frederick and Lillian Henrietta Paulina (Kopischke) Martin; m. Josef Kazell, June 9, 1951; children: David, Marla, Susan, Alan. BS in Edn., State Tchrs. Coll., 1940; BSLS, U. Minn., 1948; MSLS, U. Wis., 1977, cert. profl. devel., 1988. Tchr., libr. Beltrami (Minn.) Sch., 1940-41, Beaver Creek (Minn.) Sch., 1941-42, Atwater (Minn.) Sch., 1942-43; hosp. recreation worker ARC, Kansas, Ill., 1943-46; tchr., libr. Ferry Hall, Lake Forest, Ill., 1946-47; jr. high tchr., libr. Cleveland Hts. Ohio, 1948-49; ref. libr. GM Simmons Libr., Kenosha, Wis., 1950-52; elem. sch. libr. Unified Sch. Dist. 1, Kenosha, Wis., 1966-88. Presenter early childhood conf. U. Wis., Menominee. Reader EARS tapes for blind and legally blind, Kenosha, 1991-96. Recipient Literacy award Racine Kenosha Reading Coun., 1993; Doris Lillian Kazell gift named in her honor to Wis. Edn. Found., AAUW, 1990-91. Mem. AAUW (edn. chair local br. 1993, cmty. network chair 1998—), Internat. Reading Assn. (publ. com. 1994—), Assn. for Childhood Edn. Internat. (internat. publ. com. 1991-94), Wis. Libr. Assn. (awards com. 1994-97), Wis. State Libr. Assn. (awards and honors com. 1994—), Wis. State Reading Assn., Coop. Children's Book Ctr. Lutheran. Avocations: gardening, childrens literature. Home: 6502 47th Ave Kenosha WI 53142-3112

KAZEMI, FARHAD, political scientist, educator; b. Tehran, Iran, Jan. 7, 1943; came to U.S., 1960; s. Parviz and Irandokht (Ehteshami) K.; m. Tina A. Garber, July 9, 1966 (div. 1975); children: Shirin, Sara; m. Jane Opper, Apr. 28, 1977; stepchildren: Lygeia, Maude. BA, Colgate U., 1964; MA, George Washington U., 1966, Harvard U., 1968; PhD, U. Mich., 1973. Teaching fellow U. Mich., Ann Arbor, 1968-70; from instr., asst. prof., assoc. prof. to prof. pol. sci. NYU, 1971-88, acting dean Grad. Sch. Arts and Sci., 1989-91, vice provost, 1999—2003. Vis. lectr. U. Pa., 1979; cons. U.S. Govt., 1980—; dir. Kevorkian Ctr., NYU, 1982—85, chmn. dept. polit. sci., 1985—89, 1992—93, 1996—97; vis. prof. Princeton U., 1996; vis. sr. fellow Oxford (Eng.) U., 1997. Author: Poverty and Revolution in Iran, 1980, Politics and Culture in Iran, 1988; author, editor: Iranian Revolution, 1980, Civil Society in Iran, 1995-96; co-editor: A Way Prepared: Studies on Islamic Culture, 1987, Peasants and Politics in the Modern Middle East, 1991, other books and articles. Grantee NSF, 1973, Social Sci. Rsch. Coun., 1974-75, 84-85, Kervorkian Fund, 1985, Ford Found., 1992-93, 94-95, Rockefeller Found., 1993, 94. Fellow Middle East Studies Assn. (bd. dirs. 1985-88, pres. 1995-96); mem. Am. Polit. Sci. Assn., Internat. Polit. Sci. Assn., Internat. Studies Assn., Middle East Inst., Soc. Iranian Studies (mem. coun., editor 1982-86, pres. 1998-99), Internat. Soc. Polit. Psychology, Coun. Fgn. Rels., Atlantic Coun. Washington (acad. assoc. 1985-98). Democrat. Avocations: tennis, biking, sailing. Office: NYU Dept Politics 726 Broadway New York NY 10003-6860

KAZEMI, HOMAYOUN, physician, medical educator; b. Teheran, Iran, Sept. 28, 1934; came to U.S., 1953, naturalized, 1970; s. Parviz and Irandokht K.; m. Katheryne McNulty, June 7, 1958; children: Paul, Laili. BA, Lafayette Coll., 1954; MD, Columbia U., 1958; MSc (hon.), Harvard U., 1990. Diplomate: Am. Bd. Internal Medicine. Intern M.I. Bassett Hosp., Cooperstown, N.Y., 1958-59; resident in medicine Mass. Gen. Hosp., Boston, 1963, chief pulmonary unit, 1967-89, chief pulmonary and critical care unit, 1989-98, chief emeritus, 1998—; assoc. prof. medicine Harvard U., 1971-78, prof., 1979—, prof. medicine Harvard/MIT program in health sci. and tech., 1980—. Hon. cons. in intrenal medicine Shanghai 1st People's Hosp., 1992—; vis. scholar dept. medicine, U. Calif., San Diego, 1998-99; bd. dirs. Boston Tb Assn.; vis. prof. U. Ghent, 1975-76, Peking Union Med. Coll., China, 1992; dir. U.S. Beryllium Case Registry, 1968-78; vis. fellow Hammersmith Hosp., London, 1965; cons. Fed. Aviation Agy., 1987. Author: (book) Poon C-S and Kazemi, H Editors, Frontiers in Modeling and Control of Breathing, 2001, Disorder of the Respiratory System, 1976, (with L.G. Miller) Manual of Pulmonary Medicine, 1982—, Acute Lung Injury, 1986; mem. editl. bd. New Eng. Jour. Medicine, 1981-90, Respiratory Mgmt., 1989-93, Current Opinion in Pulmonary Medicine, 1993-99, Current Opinion in Critical Care, 1993-2000; guest editor Respiration Physiology, 2000. Dir. Am. Lung Assn. Boston; mem. rsch. evaluation subcom. Am. Heart Assn., mem. cardiopulmonary coun., 1979—, v.p. 1985-87, pres. 1987-89, mem. rsch. rev. com.; bd. trustees Dublin (N.H.) Sch., 1987-97. Fellow Am. Heart Assn. 1961-63; named Dickinson Richards lectr., 1996; recipient Chadwick medal Mass. Thoracic Soc., 1988, Lifetime achievement award AMA, 2000. Fellow ACP; mem. Am. Fedn. Clin. Rsch., Am. Thoracic Soc. (pres. Ea. sect. 1974-75), Mass. Med. Soc., Am. Physiol. Soc, Am. Soc. Clin. INvestigation, Soc. Occupl. and Environ. Health, Sigma Xi. Office: Mass Gen Hosp Boston MA 02114 E-mail: Hkazemi@partners.org.

KAZEMZADEH, MASOUD, political scientist, educator; b. Tehran, Iran; arrived in U.S., 1978; MA, U. So. Calif., L.A., PhD, 1995. Postdoctoral fellow Harvard U., Cambridge, Mass., 1998; asst. prof. Utah Valley State Coll., Orem, Utah, 1999—. Home: 338 W 1450 S Orem UT 84058 Office: Utah Valley State Coll Dept Polit Sci Orem UT 84058-5999

KAZHDAN, DAVID, mathematician, educator; b. Moscow, June 20, 1946; came to U.S., 1975; s. Alexander and Rimma (Ivanskaya) K.; m. Helena Slobodkina, Mar. 22, 1968; children: Eli, Dina, Misha, Daniel. MA, Moscow State U., 1967, PhD, 1969; BA (hon), Harvard U., 1977. Researcher Moscow State U., 1969-75, vis. prof., 1975-77; prof. Harvard U., Cambridge, Mass., 1977—. MacArthur fellow. Mem. NAS. Office: Harvard U 1 Oxford St Cambridge MA 02138-2901

KAZIM, VICTOR, accountant; b. May 6, 1942; s. Kani and Margaret (Demirs) K.; m. Loretta Ann Giannusa, Aug. 30, 1964; children: Victor P., Jennifer M., Christopher T. Student, Pace U., 1961-64; BS, Fairleigh Dickinson U., 1967, MBA, 1968. CPA, N.J. Fin. and credit analyst Burlington Industries, N.Y.C., 1963-66; acct. Deloitte Touche, CPA, N.Y.C., 1966-71; asst. v.p. fin. and contr. Health Ins. Plan N.Y., N.Y.C., 1971-73; dir. fin. and adminstrn. Univ. Health Ctr., Inc., Burlington, Vt., 1973-87. V.p., exec. dir., Mt. Sinai Med. Ctr., N.Y.C., Faculty Practice Assocs.; exec. dir. La. State U. Med. Ctr. Clinics, New Orleans; adminstrv. dir. faculty practice plan Monmouth Med. Ctr., Long Branch, N.J.; sr. v.p. fin. Nat. Health Plan Plus Inc. With U.S. Army, 1960-61. Mem. AICPA, N.J. Soc. CPA, Med. Group Mgmt. Assn. Home: 47 Quaker Hill Dr Croton On Hudson NY 10520-3520

KAZIMI, MUJID SULIMAN, nuclear engineer, educator; b. Jerusalem, Nov. 20, 1947; came to U.S., 1969; s. Suliman Ishak Kazimi and Fikrat Nuseibeh; m. Nazik D. Denny, Sept. 1, 1973. B. Engring., Alexandria U., Arab Republic of Egypt, 1969; MS, MIT, 1971, PhD, 1973. Sr. engr. Westinghouse Electric Corp., Madison, Pa., 1973-74; assoc. scientist Brookhaven Nat. Lab., Upton, N.Y., 1974-76; asst. prof. MIT, Cambridge, 1976-79, assoc. prof., 1979-86, prof., 1986—, head dept. nuclear engring., 1989-97. Tokyo Elec. Power Co (TEPCO) chair for nuc. engring. at MIT, 2000—; dir. Ctr. Advanced Nuc. Energy Systems, 2000—; chmn. high-level waste tank safety adv. panel U.S. Dept. Energy, Washington, 1990-95, chmn. new prodn. reactor severe accident group, 1990-91. Co-author: (with Neil Todreas) Nuclear Systems: Volume I: Thermal Hydraulic Fundamentals, 1990, Nuclear Systems: Volume II: Elements of Thermal Hydraulic Design, 1990; editor: Perspectives on Technological Development in the Arab World, 1978. Pres. Assn. Arab-Am. Univ. Grads., Belmont, Mass., 1980, 87. Fellow Am. Nuclear Soc. (bd. dirs. N.E. chpt. 1978, 80, exec. com. thermal hydraulics divsn. 1988-90); mem. ASME, AAAS, AIChE (chmn. nuclear heat transfer com. 1980-83), Am. Soc. for Engring. Edn. (exec. com. nuclear engring. divsn. 1995-97). Office: MIT Dept Nuc Engring 77 Massachusetts Ave Rm 24-215 Cambridge MA 02139-4307 E-mail: kazimi@mit.edu.

KAZIMIERCZUK, MARIAN KAZIMIERCZUK, electrical engineer, educator; b. Smolugi, Poland, Mar. 3, 1948; came to U.S., 1984; s. Stanislaw and Stanislawa (Tomaszewska) K.; m. Alicja Nowowiejska, July 5, 1973; children: Andrzej, Anna. MS, Tech. U. of Warsaw, Poland, 1971, PhD, 1978, DSc, 1984. Instr. elec. engring. Tech. U. of Warsaw, Poland, 1972-78, assoc. prof., 1978-84; project engr. Design Automation, Inc., Lexington, Mass., 1984; vis. prof. Va. Poly. Inst., Blacksburg, 1984-85, Wright State U., Dayton, Ohio, 1985—. Author: Resonant Power Converters, 1995, Electronic Devices: A Design Approach, 2003; contbr. numerous articles to profl. jours. Recipient Univ. Edn.

and Tech. award Polish Ministry of Sci. award, 1981, 84, 85, Polish Acad. Sci. award, 1983. Mem. IEEE (Harrel V. Noble award 1990), Assn. Polish Engrs., Polish Soc. Theoretical and Applied Elec. Scis. Roman Catholic. Home: 3620 Cypress Ct Dayton OH 45440-4515 Office: Wright State U Dept Elec Engring Dayton OH 45435

KAZIN, MICHAEL, history educator, writer; b. N.Y.C., June 6, 1948; s. Alfred and Carol Bookman (Salvadori) K.; m. Beth Horowitz, Aug. 24, 1980; children: Daniel, Maia. BA, Harvard U., 1972; PhD, Stanford U., 1983. Instr. history San Francisco State U., 1978-82; asst. prof. history Stanford (Calif.) U., 1983-85; prof. history Am. U., Washington, 1986-99, Georgetown U., 1999—. Author: The Populist Persuasion, 1995, 96, revised edit., 1998, Barons of Labor, 1987, 89 (Gutman award 1988), America Divided, 1999, rev. edit. 2003; contbr. articles to profl. hist. jours., popular mags. and newspapers; book editor Tikkun, San Francisco/N.Y.C., 1987-96; assoc. editor Socialist Rev., San Francisco, 1978-84; hist. advisor several documentaries, 1982—. Mem. steering com. Com. for a Teach-In with Labor, N.Y.C., 1996-97; spkr., local leader Nuc. Freeze Campaign, San Francisco, 1982-84. John Adams chair Am. Studies, Fulbright program, Utrecht, The Netherlands, 1996; Fulbright lectr. Ritsumeikan U., Tokyo/Kyoto, 1997; sr. fellow William and Mary Coll. Commonwealth Ctr., Williamsburg, Va., 1990-91; postdoctoral fellow Smithsonian Instn., Washington, 1988-89; NEH fellow, 1998-99; Woodrow Wilson Ctr. fellow, 1998-99. Mem. Am. Hist. Assn., Orgn. Am. Historians (chair com. for Ellis Hawley award). Democrat. Jewish. Avocations: baseball, fiction. Office: Georgetown U Dept History Washington DC 20057-0001 E-mail: mk8@georgetown.edu.

KAZLE, ELYNMARIE, producer, performing arts executive; b. St. Paul, June 22, 1958; d. Victor Anton and Marylu (Gardner) K. BFA, U. Minn., Duluth, 1982; MFA, Ohio U., 1984. Prodn. mgr. Great Lakes Shakespeare, Cleve., 1983; prodn. stage mgr. San Diego (Calif.) Opera, 1984, PCPA Theaterfest, Santa Maria, Calif., 1985-86; stage mgr. Bklyn. Acad. Music, 1987; assoc. producer Assn. Am. Theater Actors, N.Y.C., 1988-89; prodn. stage mgr. Time Flies When You're Alive, West Hollywood, Calif., 1988—; asst. advt. display Wall St. Jour., L.A., 1988-89; West Coast adminstr. Soc. Stage Dirs. and Choreographers, 1991-93, assoc. mng. dir. Actors Alley, North Hollywood, Calif., 1993-96; mng. ptnr., AIW Prodns., 1987—; founder, stage mgr. mentoring project U.S. Inst. Theatre Tech., 1991—, project dir., 1991-96, v.p. for membership devel., bd. dirs., 2000—; exec. dir. Weathervane Playhouse, Akron, Ohio, 1997—. Editor, pub. The Ohio Network newsletter, 1984-90; prodr. Santa Monica Playhouse, 1988-94. Trustee Theatre/L.A., 1992-94. Mem.: Ohio Cmty. Theatre Assn. (del. 1997—2001), Akron Area Arts Alliance (v.p. 2002—), Actors Equity Assn., Stage Mgrs. Assn. LA, Stage Mgrs. Assn., US Inst. Theatre Tech. (bd. dir. 1990—96, vice commr. 1992—2000, v.p. membership and devel. 2000—), North Hollywood/Universal City C. of C. (bd. dir. 1994—96), Delta Chi Omega (pres. 1978), Phi Kappa Phi (v.p.). Avocations: poetry, journalism, flying, rowing, rugby. Office: Weathervane Playhouse 1301 Weathervane Ln Akron OH 44313-5186 Fax: 330-873-2150. E-mail: emk2u@aol.com.

KAZMAREK, LINDA ADAMS, secondary education educator; b. Crisfield, Md., Jan. 18, 1945; d. Gordon I. Sr. and Annie Ruby (Sommers) Adams; m. Stephen Kazmarek, Jr., Aug. 2, 1981. B of Music Edn., Peabody Conservatory of Music, 1967; postgrad., Morgan U., Towson U. Cert. advanced profl. tchr., K-12, Md.; nat. cert. tchr. Mayron Cole piano method. Organist, choir dir. Halethorpe United Meth. Ch., Balt., min. music, 1978-92, 93-99; organist, choir dir. Olive Branch United Meth. Ch., 1973-77, 1978-83, 93—; piano tchr. Modal Cities Program, Balt., Balt. Community Schs; tchr. vocal music Balt. City Schs., 1967-99; min. music Halethorpe Meth. Ch., 1978-92, 93-99, St. John's Episcopal Parish Day Sch., 1999-2001; music specialist. Piano accompanist Witness Sing, 2000, Christian Choir, 2000-01; pianist Chestnut Ridge Bapt. Ch., 2001; pianist and performer Joppa Gospel Tabernacle, 2002-; pvt. tchr. piano and organ, concert artist. Composer, arranger: A Family of Care (award, 1991, Praise Song, 1992, Thy Way, Lord, 1993, Peace and Rest, 1994, Sing Praise to Jesus, 1994, Trilogy for piano solo, 1994, Shine Your Light, 1994, Resurrection, 1995, 1-800-Heaven, 1995, God Has A Plan for You, 1995, Christmas Joy, 1998, His Name is Jesus, 1998, Only Love, 1999, Be Still and Listen, 1999, Awesome Love, 2001, The Gifts of the Vine, 2002, (piano arrangements) The First Noel, Angels We Have Heard on High, O Come All Ye Faithful, All Through the Night/Lullaby, I Heard the Bells on Christmas Day/Silent Night Christmas Medley, I Saw Three Ships; rec. Christmas CD His Name is Jesus, 2000, Gifts of the Vine, 2002; guest performer S.W. Emergency Svcs., 1999, Joppa Gospel Tabernacle; CD Praise, Peace and Promise, 2002; rec. America the Beautiful/America, Jesus Loves Me, The Promise, Blessings, His Eye Is on the Sparrow, I Bowed on My Knees and Cried Holy, Praising My Saviour, 2002. Concert perfomer for Halethorpe Meth. Ch., 1994, Meth. Bd. Child Care, 1989, Balt. S.W. Emergency Svcs., 1991; guest performer Balt. City Tchrs. Appreciation Banquet, 1991, S.W.E.S. 18th Yr. Celebration, 1999; concert artist and performer, 2001—. Recipient vol. award for music enrichment summer program, 1973, award for voluntarism Fund. for Ednl. Excellence, 1985; Fund for Ednl. Excellence grantee, 1988. Mem. NEA, Md. State Tchrs. Assn., Balt. City Tchrs. Assn., Md. Music Educators Assn. (award for 30 yrs. of svc. in music and music edn. 1997), Music Educators Nat. Conf., Md. State Music Tchrs. Assn., Nat. Music Tchrs. Assn., Gospel Music Assn., Peabody Alumni Assn. E-mail: Kazmarekl@comcast.net.

KAZMER, DAVID OWEN, engineering educator; s. Andrew James and Dawn (Gildersleeve) Kazmer; m. Nancy McLaughlin, Sept. 4, 1993; children: Laura, Julia, Elizabeth. BSME, Cornell U., 1989; MSME, Rensselaer Poly. Inst., 1991; PhD, Stanford U., 1995. Cert. profl. engr., Calif. Engr. GE, Schenectady, 1988—92; from asst. prof. to assoc. prof. U. Mass., Amherst, 1995—2000, assoc. prof. Lowell, 2002—; dir. R&D Synventive Molding Solutions, Peabody, Mass., 2001. Bd. dirs. Thermociramix LLC, Leominster, Mass.; lectr. in field. Contbr. articles to profl. jours. Recipient Best Design award, Lincoln Electric, 1995; Tchg. fellow, U. Mass., 2000. Mem.: ASME (chmn. design for mfg. conf. 2000, 2003—), Soc. Plastics Engrs. Democrat. Roman Catholic. Achievements include patents for dynamic feed control. Office: Univ Mass Dept Plastics Engring 1 University Ave Lowell MA 01854

KAZMIERCZAK, ELZBIETA TERESA, graphic designer, illustrator, educator, semiotician; b. Lodz, Poland, Dec. 30, 1959; came to U.S., 1990; d. Leon Antoni and Krystyna Irena (Grabowska) K.; div. BFA, Acad. Fine Arts, Lodz, 1984; MFA, U. Ill., 1993, MA, 1995. Instr. U. Ill., Urbana-Champaign, 1990-93, Capilano Coll., North Vancouver, B.C., Can., 1995-96; asst. prof. SUNY, Buffalo, 1996—, head illustration program, 1996—. Cons., U.S., Can. and Poland. Contbr. articles to profl. jours. Creative and Performing Arts fellow, 1991-92; Poland Ministry of Culture and Art scholar, 1987-88. Mem.: Internat. Inst. for Info. Design (co-chair knowledge presentation, expert group), Internat. Assn. for Semiotic Studies, Semiotic Soc. Am. (exec. bd.). Avocations: meditation, reading, movies, classical music, jazz. Home: 22 Claremont Ave # 2 Buffalo NY 14222-1123 Office: SUNY Buffalo Dept Art 202 Center For The Arts Buffalo NY 14260-6010

KAZMIERCZAK, MATTHEW, economist, researcher; b. Calif. s. Fred and Jerri K. B in Econ. and Polit. Sci., U. Calif., Irvine, 1993; M in Pub. Policy, Georgetown U., 1997. With Congressman Mineta, Washington, 1993-95; sr. mgr. rsch. Am. Electronics Assn., Washington, 1996—. Author: Cyberstates 2002, 2002, Cyber Education, 2002, Broadband in the States, 2002. Home: 1114 P St NW Washington DC 20005-4408 Office: Am Electronics Assn N Bldg 601 Penn Ave NW Ste 600 Washington DC 20004-3609 Fax: 202-216-2675. E-mail: matthew_kazmierczak@aeanet.org.

KAZUYA, TETSUJI, business educator; b. Kure, Japan, Mar. 20, 1944; s. Kengiro and Yotsue (Tatebe) K.; m. Keiko Matsushita, Nov. 11, 1973. MEcon, U. Osaka Prefecture, Japan, 1969. Lectr. Osaka Shogyo U., Higashi, Japan, 1973-78, assoc. prof., 1973-90, prof. bus. orgn., 1990—. Author: Organization Theory of Business, 1980, Organization Theory of Modern Business, 1985. Mem. mediation com. Higashi-Osaka Ct., 1992; adminstrv. monitor Nara Prefecture, Japan, 1993-94l mem. com. adminstrv. change Haibara, Japan, 1997—. Mem. Assn. Organizational Sci. (bd. dirs. 1993-96). Home: Akanedai 2-13-8 Nara Haibara 633 0256 Japan Office: Osaka Shogyo U Fac Commerce Mikuriya Sakae Machi 4-1-10 Osaka Higashi-Osaka 577 8505 Japan

KE, YONG, medical educator, researcher; b. Huang Shi, Hubei, China, Jan. 31, 1956; s. Zheng Dong Ke and You Ru Chen; m. Manqiu Yang, Sept. 9, 1957; children: William, Max. MS in Physics, Mont. State U., 1988; PhD in Physics, U. of Minn., 1993. Rschr. UCLA, 1997—98; instr. McLean Hosp., Harvard Med. Sch., Belmont, Mass., 1998—. Mem. sci. com. 2nd Internat. Conf. on Biomed. Spectroscopy, London, 2002—. Contbr. scientific papers to profl. publs. (NARSAD Young Investigator award, 1999). Recipient Young Investigator award, NARSAD, 1999, Nat. Rsch. Svc. award, NIH, 1996. Mem.: Am. Psychiat. Assn., Internat. Soc. for Magnetic Resonance in Medicine. Achievements include invention of A new method for quantification of 2D magnetic resonance spectroscopy; discovery of Creatine and phosphocreatine in vivo have different transverse relaxation times in proton MRS. Office: McLean Hosp Harvard Med Sch 115 Mill St Belmont MA 02478 Office Fax: 617-855-2770. E-mail: yke@mclean.harvard.edu.

KEA, JONATHAN GUY, instrumental music educator; b. Honolulu, June 2, 1960; s. Gilbert Halemano and Goldie Lee Gum (Chun) K. BMus, cert. teaching, Coe Coll., Cedar Rapids, Iowa, 1982. Band dir. James Campbell High Sch., Ewa Beach, Hawaii, 1982—. Asst. condr. Honolulu Cmty. Band, 1988-94; dir. Honolulu Cmty. Jazz Band, 1993—. Mem. NEA, Oahu Band Dirs. Assn., Hawaii Music Educators Assn., Music Educators Nat. Conf., Phi Mu Alpha. Office: James Campbell High Sch 91-980 North Rd Ewa Beach HI 96706-2746

KEACH, STACY, JR., actor, director, producer, writer, musician, composer; b. Savannah, Ga., June 2, 1941; s. Stacy and Mary Cain (Peckham) K.; m. Malgosia Tomassi, 1986; children: Shannon and Karolina. AB in English and Drama, U. Calif. at Berkeley, 1963; student, Yale Drama Sch., 1963-64, London Acad. Dramatic Art, 1964-65. Assoc. prof. drama Yale, 1967-68. Pres. Positron Prodns. Ltd. Contbr. articles to newspapers and mags.; mem. Lincoln Ctr. Repertory Co., Long Wharf Theatre, Washington Shakespeare Theatre, Williamstown Summer Theatre, Oreg. Shakespeare Festival, Tufts Arena Theatre; charter mem. The Yale Theatre Circle, 1986; Broadway debut in Indians, 1969; appeared in Broadway prodn. Deathtrap, 1979, Solitary Confinement, 1992, The Kentucky Circle, 1993 (Helen Hayes award for Best Actor 1993, Outstanding Performance award Drama League); off-Broadway appearances in Macbird, 1966-67, The Niggerlovers, 1967, Peer Gynt, 1969, Henry IV, 1 and 2, 1968, Hamlet, 1972, King Lear, 1968, Long Day's Journey Into Night, 1971, Cyrano de Bergerac, 1978, Hughie, London, 1980; Nat. Touring Co., Barnum, 1981; Kennedy Ctr. Prodn. of Idiot's Delight, 1986, Nat. Touring Co., Sleuth, 1988, The King & I, 1989, Love Letters, 1990-93, Richard III, 1991, Stieglitz Loves O'Keefe, 1995, MacBeth, 1995, The Ten Unknowns, 2003; film appearances include: The Heart is a Lonely Hunter, 1968, End of the Road, 1969, Doc, 1970, The Traveling Executioner, 1970, The New Centurions, 1971, Fat City, 1971, Brewster McCloud, 1970, Luther, 1972, The Dion Brothers, 1973, Conduct Unbecoming, 1974, Jesus of Nazareth, 1967, The Killer Inside Me, 1974, The Squeeze, 1976, Gray Lady Down, 1976, The Greatest Battle, 1977, Two Solitudes, 1977, Cheech & Chong's Up in Smoke, 1977, The Ninth Configuration, 1978, The Long Riders, 1979, Road Games, 1980, Butterfly, 1980, Cheech & Chong's Nice Dreams, 1981, That Championship Season, 1982, Butterfly, 1982, The Class of 1999, 1990, The Forgotten, Milena, 1989, Escape from L.A., 1996, The Sea Wolf, 1996, Die Gang, 1996, American History X, 1998; TV appearances in: Orville and Wilbur, 1971, Particular Men, 1972, Classics For Today, 1972, Man of Destiny, 1973, all PBS, All the Kind Strangers, 1974, Caribe, 1974-75, both ABC, The Michener Dynasty, NBC, 1975, A Rumor of War, CBS, 1979, The Blue and the Gray, 1981, Wait Until Dark, 1982, Murder Me, Murder You, 1983, Princess Daisy, 1983, Mistral's Daughter, 1984, Intimate Strangers, 1986, More Than Murder, 1983, Mickey Spillane's Mike Hammer series, 1983, 86-87, Return of Mickey Spillane's Mike Hammer, 1986, starring role 6 hour mini-series on life of Ernest Hemingway, 1988 (Best Actor award Golden Globes 1988), Murder Takes All, 1989 (Emmy nominee Best Actor in Special or Miniseries), Body Bags, 1992 (Cable Ace Award nominee Best Actor), Against Their Will, 1994, Texas, 1995, Titus, 2000, The Santa Trap, 2002, The Simpsons, 2002-03 Frozen Impact, 2003; host TV programs Missing/Reward, 1988, Arts and Entertainment Stage Series, 1988-89, Circus of Stars, 1991, Case-Closed, 1993-94; dir.: Pullman Car Hiawatha, 1964-65, The Stronger, 1964-65, The Maids, 1964-65, The Repeater, 1971 (Cine Golden Eagle award, London Film Festival outstanding film), Incident at Vichy, 1974, Six Characters in Search of an Author, 1976, A Blinding Fear (episode of The New Mike Hammer), 1987; host PBS July 4th Festivities, 1995; narrator (TV documentary) Nova, Nat. Geographic, Am. Experience, Discover Channel Flight Over the Equator, 1995, Planet of Life, 1995, Stupid Behavior Caught on Tape, 2003; (books on tape) Hardboiled, 1994, Mickey Spillane's Works, 1990, CD-ROM, 1994, Ten Lost Tribes of Israel, Shakespeare's Sonnets; screen writer, producer The Long Riders, 1979. Sponsor Nat. Repertory Theatre Found. (Nat. Play Award Com.), 1986; hon. chair Cleft Palate Assn., 1995; spokesman United Indian Devel. Assn.; mem. Nat. Citizens Comm. Lobby, Entertainment Industries Coun. before House Select Com. on Drug Abuse, 1985; panelist Am. TV, Arts and Scis. Substance Abuse Conf., 1986, Artists Com. Kennedy Ctr. Honors, 1986—; mem. Players Club; charter mem. L.A. Classic Theatre Works, Artists Rights Found.; mem. artistic adv. bd. Nat. Found. for Advancement in Arts; mem. Helen Hayes Honorary Com. Fulbright award, 1964-65; recipient Best Actor award U. Calif., 1963, Best Actor award Oreg. Shakespeare award, 1963, Obie award, 1967, 71, 73, Vernon Rice Drama Desk award, 1967, 71, 72, Saturday Rev. award, 1967, Helen Hayes Best Actor award, 1994, Hon. chmn. Am. Cleft Palate Found., 1995—, Celebrity Outreach honoree, 1995, Master of Ceremonies, Capitol Mall, 1995. Address: c/o Jim Palmer 24800 Pacific Coast Hwy Malibu CA 90265 *The fundamental virtue of success is making your dreams come true. But without loved ones to share it with it means little or nothing.*

KEADY, GEORGE CREGAN, JR., judge; b. Bklyn., June 16, 1924; s. George Cregan and Marie (Lussier) K.; m. Patricia Drake, Sept. 2, 1950; children: Margaret Keady Goldberg, Marie E., George Cregan, Catherine A. Keady Dunn, Kathleen V. Student, U. Kans., 1943-44; BS, Fordham U., 1949; JD, Columbia U., 1950; LL.D., Western New Eng. Coll., 1973. Bar: Mass. 1950. Since practiced in, Springfield, Mass.; asso. firm Ganley & Crook, 1950-53; assoc. firm Peter D. Wilson, 1953-57; partner firm Wilson, Keady & Ratner, 1958-79; justice Dist. Ct., Springfield, 1979-82; assoc. justice Superior Ct., Springfield, 1982-93; ret., 1993; freelance mediator and arbitrator, 1993—. Dean Western New Eng. Coll. Law Sch., 1970-73; dir. Western Mass. Bar Rev., 1956-63, Western New Eng. Coll. Bar Rev., 1965-72; chmn. Mass. Continuing Legal Edn., Inc., 1977-80; mem. Mass. Commn. on Jud. Conduct, 1988, chmn., 1990-93. Active United Fund, Springfield, 1950-72, Joint Civic Agys.; chmn. fund drive Am. Cancer Soc., 1962, selectman, Longmeadow, Mass., 1958-68, chmn. selectmen, 1960-61, 63-64, 66-68, moderator, 1968-73; vice chmn. Rep. Town Com., Longmeadow, 1956-60; alt. del. Rep. Nat. Conv., 1960, del., 1964; pres. Hampden Dist. Mental Health Clinic, Inc., 1968-71, Child Guidance Clinic, Springfield, 1962-64; corporator, trustee, chmn. bd. Baystate Med. Center, 1985-87, trustee, 1984-92, 94-99; chmn. bd. Baystate Health System, 1987-90; trustee Western New Eng. Coll., 1978-84, Baypath Jr. Coll., 1972-87, Baystate Health Systems, 1993-98; dir. BHIC, 1993—. Served with AUS, 1943-46. Decorated Bronze star. Mem. Am. Law Inst., Mass. Bar Assn., Hampden County Bar Assn. (exec. com. 1960-79, pres. 1965-67), Supreme Ct. Hist. Soc., Longmeadow Country Club, Phi Delta Phi. Roman Catholic. Home: 16 Meadowbrook Rd Longmeadow MA 01106-1341

KEADY, WALTER JAMES, writer; b. Castlebar, Ireland, Nov. 21, 1934; came to U.S., 1967; s. Thomas and Margaret (Murray) K.; m. Patricia Anne Elkins, Feb. 14, 1970; children: Kate Keady-Dooley, Marygrace Keady Petoff, Juliette. BA in Philosphy, Nat. U. Ireland, 1960. Ordained priest Roman Cath. Ch., 1963. Auditor Civil Svc., Dublin, Ireland, 1952-56; priest Holy Ghost Missionary Congregation, Florida Paulista, Brazil, 1964-67; software engr. IBM, Poughkeepsie, N.Y., 1968-94. Author: Celibates and Other Lovers, 1997 (Discover Great New Writers award Barnes and Nobel 1997), Mary McGreevy, 1998, The Altruist, 2003. Bd. dirs., newsletter editor Coalition Against Domestic Violence and Sexual Assault, Poughkeepsie, 1987-2003. Avocations: choral singing, raquetball, reading.

KEALA, FRANCIS AHLOY, security executive; b. Honolulu, June 1, 1930; s. Samuel Louis and Rose (Ahloy) K.; m. Betty Ann Lyman, Nov. 28, 1952; children— Frances Ann, John Richard, Robert Mark. BA in Sociology, U. Hawaii, 1953. Patrolman Honolulu Police Dept., 1956-62, detective, 1962-65, lt., 1965-68, capt., 1968-69, chief of police, 1969-83; dir. security Hawaiian Telephone Co., 1983-93. Bd. dirs. Liliuokalani Trust; trustee St. Louis Sch., 1980-87, S. Keala Trust, 1989—, Kamehameha Schs. Bishop Estate, 1999-2001. Bd. dirs. Aloha coun. Boy Scouts Am., 200 Club, Sex Abuse Treatment Center, Am. Automobile Assn. of Hawaii, Hawaii Meml. Park Assn., St. Louis Found., ARC-Hawaii chpt., St. Francis Med. Ctr.-West; bd. govs. Boys and Girls Clubs of Honolulu; mem. Civilian Adv. Group U.S. Army; mem. Commn. on Jud. Discipline; v.p., dir. Hawaiian Music Hall of Fame and Mus.; mem. Honolulu City and County Ethics Commn. Served with U.S. Army, 1953-55. Mem. Internat. Assn. Chiefs of Police, Hawaii State Law Enforcement Ofcls. Assn., FBI Nat. Acad. Assocs. Clubs: Oahu Country, Pacific.

KEAN, HAMILTON FISH, lawyer; b. NYC, Mar. 1, 1925; s. Robert Winthrop and Elizabeth Stuyvesant (Howard) K.; m. Ellen Shaw Garrison, Mar. 25, 1950 (div. 1976); children: Leslie K. McKim, Elizabeth Douglas, Lloyd Garrison, Lewis Morris; m. Alice Kay Newcomer, July 6, 1981 (dec. 1986); m. Edith Williamson Bacon, Sept. 23, 1989. AB cum laude, Princeton U., 1949; JD, Columbia U., 1954. Bar: NY 1954, NJ 1955. Asst. counsel Waterfront Commn. NY Harbor, 1954; law sec. NJ Supreme Ct., 1954-55; asst. U.S. atty. NJ Dist., 1955-57; ptnr. Clapp and Eisenberg and predecessors, Newark, 1957-62; trustee various funds, 1963—; lectr. law Rutgers U. Sch. Law, 1960; lectr. environ. law SUNY at Purchase, Westchester Cmty. Coll., 1974-76. Supervising atty. clin. program environ. law NYU Sch. Law, 1972-76; chmn. Livingston Nat. Bank, 1984; bd. dir. Realty Transfer Co. Bd. dir. Morris County Urban League, 1956-51; mem. Urban Crisis Task Force, 1976; bd. dir. Youth Counseling League, 1969-93, pres., 1979-83, hon. dir.; bd. dir. Citizens Com. for Children NY, 1971-2002, now hon. dir., pres., 1972-77, Eleanor Roosevelt award, 2001; chmn. Joint Action for Children, 1976; trustee Natural Resources Def. Coun., 1973-2002, hon. trustee, 2002—, treas., 1973-76; bd. dir., sec. Environ. Advocates, 1972-78, hon. bd. dir., 1999--; bd. dir. Fountain House, 1966—, pres., 1975-78; mem. Adv. Coun. to NY State Office Mental Health, 1979-83; mem. Mental Health Svc. Coun., 1983-90; trustee Coro Found., 1979-85; mem. NY State Mental Hygiene Planning Coun., 1981-85; trustee Alice Desmond and Hamilton Fish Libr., 1981-98; trustee Schuyler Ctr. for Analysis and Avocacy, 1982—, pres., 1985-92; mem. adminstrv. bd. Lab. Ornithology Cornell U., 1982-87; trustee Hancock Shaker Village, 1986-92; mem. adv. bd. Panel of Ams., 1986—; bd. dir., sec. Episc. Charities, 1995-2002; trustee World Federalist Assn. Endowment Fund, 1998—, chmn., 2001—. 2d lt. US Army, 1943-46. Decorated Purple Heart Mem.: ABA, Assn. Bar City NY, NY State Bar Assn. (chmn. conf. on pub. interest law 1975), Columbia Law Sch. Alumni Assn. (treas. 1958—62), New Bedford Yacht Club, Millbrook Golf and Tennis Club, NY Health and Racquet Club, Princeton Club, Knickerbocker Club, Century Assn. Home: 130 East End Ave New York NY 10028-7553 Office: 120 E 56th St New York NY 10022

KEAN, JOHN VAUGHAN, retired lawyer; b. Providence, Mar. 12, 1917; s. Otho Vaughan and Mary (Duell) Kean. AB cum laude, Harvard U., 1938, JD, 1941; grad., U.S. Army War Coll., 1970. Bar: R.I. 1942, U.S. Dist. Ct. R.I. 1946, U.S. Ct. Appeals (1st cir.) 1950, U.S. Ct. Appeals (4th cir.) 1955, U.S. Ct. Claims 1963, U.S. Supreme Ct. 1982. With Edwards & Angell, Providence, 1941—, ptnr., 1954-87, ret. ptnr., 1987—. Bd. dirs. Greater Providence YMCA, 1964—76; chmn. Downtown Providence YMCA, 1964—67, Providence Com. on Fgn. Rels., 1994—2000. Capt. AUS U.S. Army, 1943—46, capt. AUS U.S. Army, 1950—52, brig. gen. R.I. Nat. Guard U.S. Army, 1964—72. Decorated Legion of Merit. Mem.: ABA, R.I. Bar Assn., Res. Officers Assn., N.G. Assn., Soc. Cin. (hon.; R.I.), The Robbins Co. (bd. dirs. 1988—2000), Assn. U.S. Army, Nature Conservancy (hon.), Urban League R.I., Alexis de Tocqueville Soc. R.I., Soc. Colonial Wars in R.I., Harvard Club R.I. (pres. 1964—66), Sakonnet Golf Club (Little Compton, R.I..), Army and Navy Club (Washington), Hope Club (bd. govs. 1996—2000, v.p.), Agawam Hunt Club. Home: 2 Angell St Providence RI 02903 Office: c/o Edwards & Angell 2800 Financial Plz Providence RI 02903-2499

KEAN, ORVILLE, academic administrator; Pres. U. V.I., St. Thomas. Office: Univ Virgin Islands Office of President 2 John Brewers Bay St Thomas VI 00802

KEANE, JAMES IGNATIUS, lawyer, consultant; b. Oct. 28, 1944; s. Ignatius James and Anna Mae (Rover) Keane. BA magna cum laude, Marquette U., 1966; JD, Georgetown U., 1970. Bar: Md. 71, U.S. Dist. Ct. Md. 74, U.S. Ct. Appeals (4th cir.) 74, U.S. Supreme Ct. 74. Dep. ct. clk. Prince George's County Cir. Ct., Md., 1963—65, law clk., 1968—70, Md. Ct. Appeals, Annapolis, 1970—71; assoc. DePaul, Willoner & Kenkel P.A., College Park, Md., 1971—73; asst. atty. gen. Md. Atty. Gen.'s Office, Balt., 1973—75; dir. rsch. Aspens Sys. Corp., Germantown, Md., 1976—78; dir. litigation svcs. Coopers & Lybrand, L.A. and N.Y.C., 1978—84; nat. dir. legal info. sys., assoc. gen. counsel Arthur Young & Co., 1984—85; pres. James Keane Co., North Potomac, Md., 1985—. Cons. in field of litigation sys. Author: Litigation Support Systems: An Attorney's Guide, 2d edit., 1992; author, editor (with others): Conflicts of Interest, 1984. Fellow, NDEA, U. Va., 1966—67. Mem.: ABA, Md. Bar Assn. (chmn. spl. com. on tech.), Rio. Democrat. Avocation: windsurfing. Office: Ikeane Law Pro 20 Esworthy Ter North Potomac MD 20878-8724

KEANE, JAMES R. neurologist; MD, Harvard U., 1961. Intern Cornell Med. Divsn./Bellevue Hosp., N.Y.C., 1961—62; resident in neurology U. Calif., San Francisco, 1964—65; resident Columbia-Presbyn. Hosp., N.Y.C., 1965—67; fellow in neurology Mt. Sinai Hosp., N.Y.C., 1967—68, U. Calif., San Francisco, 1968—69; staff Los Angeles County/U. So. Calif. Med. Ctr., 1970—; prof. neurology U. So. Calif., L.A., 1982—. Contbr. more than 100 articles to profl. jours.

KEANE, JOHN MICHAEL, career officer; b. N.Y.C., Feb. 1, 1943; B.S., Fordham U., 1966; M.A., Western Kentucky U. Commd. officer U.S. Army, advanced through grades to gen.; commdg. gen. 101st Airborne Div., Fort Campbell, Ky., 1993—96, XVIII Airborne Corps, Fort Bragg, NC, 1996—98; dep. comdr., chief of staff U.S. Atlantic Command, Norfolk, Va., 1998—99; vice chief of staff U.S. Army, Washington, 1999—, acting chief of staff, 2003.

KEANE, JOHN PATRICK, retired secondary education educator; b. N.Y.C., Nov. 28, 1931; s. John and Mary (Walsh) K.; m. Lucille Ann Dunn, Apr. 3, 1976. BA in English, Iona Coll., 1954; JD, Fordham U., 1963, MS in Edn., 1965; EdM, Columbia U., 1973; MA in English, CUNY, 1984. Cert. secondary tchr. (English), adminstr., N.Y.C., N.Y. State. Tchr. area jr. h.s., N.Y.C., 1962-65; tchr. h.s. English N.Y.C. Bd. Edn., Bklyn., 1965-93; dean of boys W.H. Taft H.S., Bronx, 1969-72; reading, writing coord. John F. Kennedy H.S., Bronx, 1985-91; tchr. English advanced placement John F. Kennedy H.S., Manhattan Coll., Bronx, 1991-93, retired, 1993. Editor, compiler: (manual) Handbook for Teachers of Reading and Writing, 1987, Writing Sampler (student's work), 1989-91 biannual. Founder Hamilton Heights Dems., 1965-69; candidate N.Y. State Assembly, 1965; Dem. candidate 1st Selectman, North Stonington, 1997; past mem. North Stonington, Conn. Bd. Edn; justice of peace North Stonington; chmn. North Stonington Dem. Town Com.; music min. St. Mary's Ch., Groton. MA thesis placed on permanent display as model, Lehman Coll., CUNY, Bronx, 1984. Mem. NEA (del. local 2), Am. Fedn. Tchrs. (del. local 2), United Fedn. Tchrs. (del N.Y. State, chpt. leader, unity com.), N.Y. State United Tchrs., Delta Kappa Pi, Phi Delta Kappa. Roman Catholic. Avocations: poetry, drama, environmentalist. Home: 6 Wyassup Lake Rd North Stonington CT 06359-1124

KEANE, KEVIN, federal agency administrator; Grad., U. Wis., Eau Claire, 1987. Reporter Fond du Lac (Wis.) Reporter Newspaper; asst. city editor Waukesha (Wis.) Freeman Newspaper; Washington corr. Thompson Newspapers, 1992—94; dir. comm., exec. asst. Gov. Tommy G. Thompson; asst. sec. for pub. affairs Dept. HHS, Washington, 2001—. Fellow Paul Miller fellow, Freedom Forum. Office: Dept HHS Pub Affairs 200 Independence Ave SW Washington DC 20201

KEANE, MICHAEL J. lawyer; b. Boston, Aug. 27, 1953; BA, U. Md., 1974; JD magna cum laude, Stetson U., 1978. Bar: Fla. 1978, U.S. Dist. Ct. (no. and mid. dists.) Fla. 1979, U.S. Dist. Ct. (so. dist.) Fla. 1981; bd. cert. bus. litig and civil trial lawyer, Nat. Bd. Trial Advocacy; cert. mediator, Fla. Law clk. to Hon. Ben F. Overton Fla. Supreme Ct., 1978-79; atty. Keane, Reese & Vesely, P.A.,

St. Petersburg, 1979—. Adj. prof. Stetson U.; chmn. Fla. Bd. Bar Examiners, 2002—03. Editor-in-chief Stetson Law Rev., 1977—78. Office: Northtrust Bank Building 100 2nd Ave S Ste 1201 Saint Petersburg FL 33701-4338

KEANE, THOMAS J. lawyer; b. N.Y.C., Mar. 12, 1953; s. Raymond T. and Catherine (Mcloughlin) K.; m. Alyson M. Krohne, July 24, 1976; children: Raymond G., Kristen M., Danielle M. BA, St. Anselm Coll., Manchester, N.H., 1975; JD magna cum laude, Western New Eng. Coll., Springfield, Mass., 1980. Bar: Mass. 1980, NY 1981, U.S. Dist. Ct. (so. and ea. dists.) NY 1983. Claims Royal Globe Ins. Cos., White Plains, NY, 1975—76; staff atty. Ins. Co. N.Am., Springfield, Mass., 1980—82; assoc. Law Offices of Joseph Conklin, N.Y.C., 1982—84; in house assoc. Cigna Corp., N.Y.C., 1982—84; asst. gen. counsel Liberty Lines Cos., Yonkers, NY, 1984—93; atty., ptnr. Nesci, Keane, Piekarski, Keogh & Corrigan, White Plains, 1993—. V.p. Specialized Risk Mgmt. Inc., White Plains, 1993—. Mem. Mass. Jud. Internship Program, Boston, 1980; mem. Rep. Congl. Task Force, Washington, 1995-96. Mem. N.Y. State Bar Assn., Westchester County Bar Assn., Soc. Friendly Sons of St. Patrick in the County of Westchester. Avocations: history, golf. Home: 348 Fort Washington Ave Hawthorne NY 10532-1457 Office: Nesci Keane et al 245 Main St Ste 600 White Plains NY 10601 E-mail: tjkeane@nesci-keane.com.

KEANEY, WILLIAM REGIS, engineering and construction services executive, consultant; b. Pitts., Nov. 2, 1937; s. William Regis Sr. and Emily Elizabeth (Campi) K.; m. Sharon Lee Robinson, Feb. 23, 1956; children: William R., James A., Robert E., Susan Elizabeth. BBA in Mktg. and Internat. Mktg., Ohio State U., 1961. Sales engr. Burdett Oxygen Co., Cleve., 1961-64, A.O. Smith Co., Milw., 1964-66; pres. W.R. Keaney & Co., Columbus, Ohio, 1966-71, Power Equipment Service Corp., Columbus, 1971-80, Gen. Assocs. Corp., Worthington, Ohio, 1980—. Cons. Mannesmann, Houston, 1984-85, TVA, Knoxville, 1984-86, Power Authority of N.Y., White Plains, 1985-86, Utility Power Corp., Atlanta, 1985-86; mem. various task forces in the field. Vol. Cen. Ohio Lung Assn., Columbus, 1984-86. Mem. ASME (subgroups on nonferrous alloys, strenght/nonferrous alloys), ASTM (B2 com.), Am. Welding Soc., Welding Rsch. Coun., Worthington C. of C. (leadership program 1991-92), Mil. Vehicle Collectors Club, Masons. Democrat. Methodist. Avocations: antique cars, genealogy, camping, photography. Home: 1314 Oakview Dr Columbus OH 43235-1135 Office: Keaney & Co PO Box 762 Columbus OH 43085-0762 E-mail: bKEANEY@aol.com.

KEANINI, RUSSELL GUY, mechanical engineering educator, researcher; b. Denver, June 29, 1959; s. Russell Eldridge and Patricia Ann (Regan) K.; m. Tracy Jo. BS, Colo. Sch. of Mines, Golden, 1983; MS, U. Colo., Denver, 1987; PhD, U. Calif., Berkeley, 1992. Bldg. specialist Nicor Exploration, Golden, 1984-85; structural designer Commerce City Supply, 1985-86; grad. rsch. asst. U. of Colo., Denver, 1985-87, U. of Calif., Berkeley, Calif., 1987-92; asst. prof. U. N.C., Charlotte, 1992-98, assoc. prof., 1998—. Contbr. articles to profl. jours. Recipient Engrng. Found. Rsch. Initiation award Engrng. Found. and ASME, 1993-94, Alcoa Found. award, 1995, Jr. Faculty Enhancement award Oak Ridge Assoc. Univs., 1995; Colo. Sch. Mines scholar, 1982-83; NASA grad. rsch. fellow, 1988-89. Mem. AIAA, ASME, Am. Phys. Soc. Office: U NC Charlotte Dept Mech Engring Charlotte NC 28223 Home: 16014 Woodcote Drive Huntersville NC 28078 E-mail: rkeanini@uncc.edu.

KEARFOTT, JOSEPH CONRAD, lawyer; b. Martinsville, Va., Sept. 24, 1947; s. Clarence P. and Elizabeth (Kelly) K.; m. Mary Jo Veatch, Feb.10, 1969; children: Kelly, David. BA, Davidson Coll., 1969; JD, U. Va., 1972. Bar: Va. 1972, U.S. Dist. Ct. (ea. and we. dists.) Va. 1973, U.S. Ct. Appeals (4th cir.) 1973, U.S. Tax Ct. 1979, U.S. Ct. Appeals (1st cir.) 1981, U.S. Ct. Appeals (5th cir.) 1982. Law clk. to presiding judge U.S. Dist. Ct. (ea. dist.) Va., Richmond, 1972-73; assoc. Hunton & Williams, Richmond, 1973-80, ptnr., 1980—. Lectr. NITA program, Washington and Lee U., 1982-83, Va. Com. on Continuing Legal Edn., 1984—; mem. 4th Cir. Jud. conf. Co-author: Virginia Evidentiary Foundations, 1998. Mem. Richmond Bd. Housing, 1977-85, Richmond Dem. Com., 1978-82; trustee Libr. Va. Found., 1994—, William Byrd Cmty. House, 1978-84, chmn., 1982-84; trustee United Way Svcs., Richmond, 1989-95, treas., 1993-95; trustee Libr. Va., 1989-94, vice chmn., 1990-91, chmn., 1991-92; trustee Trinity Episcopal Sch., 1986-94, treas., 1989-92, chmn., 1993-94; mem. Richmond Regional Bd., Thomas C. Sorensen Inst. Polit. Leadership.; treas. St. Paul's Episcopal Ch., 2003—. Mem.: ABA, Richmond Bar Assn., Va. Bar Assn. (Boyd Graves conf. chmn. 1999—2001), Order of Coif, Country Club Va. Avocations: golf, skiing. Home: 4436 Custis Rd Richmond VA 23225-1012 Office: Hunton & Williams East Tower Riverfront Pla 951 E Byrd St Richmond VA 23219-4074

KEARNEY, ANNA ROSE, history educator; b. Mount Pleasant, Pa., Mar. 1, 1940; d. John Joseph and Marguerite Costello (Gettings) K. BA, St. Mary's Coll., Notre Dame, Ind., 1962; MA, U. Notre Dame, 1967, PhD, 1975; MLS, Ind. U., 1983; JD, U. Louisville, 2002. Cert. tchr., Pa. Tchr. Hempfield Area Schs., Greensburg, Pa., 1962-66, Mishawaka (Ind.) Sch. Dist., 1967-68; teaching asst. U. Notre Dame, 1968-70, libr. clk., 1974-76, libr. assoc., 1976-86; divsn. chair gen. edn. Ind. Vo-Tech. Coll., South Bend, 1970-72; asst. to univ. libr. U. Louisville, 1986-89; prof. Am. history Jefferson C.C./Ky. Tech. and C.C., Louisville, 1989—. Faculty cons. Ednl. Testing Svc., San Antonio, 1993, 96, 2000, 01. Contbr. articles to profl. jours. Judge Nat. History Day, Louisville and Indpls., 1990-94; exec. on loan United Way of St. Joseph County, South Bend, 1982; food coord. Ethnic Festival, South Bend, 1974; lector Our Lady of Lourdes Ch., Louisville, 1987—. Grantee U. Louisville, 1987, U. Notre Dame, 1988, Ky. Libr. Assn., 1988, NEH, 1990-92, 95. Mem. Assn. of Coll. and Rsch. Librs. (exec. com. for 5th nat. conf. 1987-89), Orgn. Am. Historians, So. Hist. Assn., Cath. Hist. Assn., Ky. Assn. Tchrs. History, Nat. Coun. of Women's Studies Assn., St. Mary's Coll. South Bend Alumnae Assn. (pres. 1984-85), Phi Alpha Theta. Democrat. Roman Catholic. Avocations: knitting, sewing, reading, computers. Home: 3316 Cawein Way Louisville KY 40220-1908 Office: Jefferson Cmty Coll/KCTCS 109 E Broadway Louisville KY 40202-2005

KEARNEY, COLLEEN ANN, occupational therapist; b. Lakewood, N.J., Dec. 14, 1972; d. James Phillip and Patricia Lynn Kearney. BS in Occupl. Therapy, U. Ala., Birmingham, 1995. Modality cert. Ga. Occupl. therapist Wellstar Kennestone, Marietta, Ga., 1995—, Kids Connection, Kennesaw, Ga., 2001—. Co-leader Impact Adventures, Ch. of Apostles, 2001—. Mem.: Ga. Brain Injury Assn. (co-chair profl. prouders 1997), Occupl. Therapy Nat. Honor Soc. Office: Wellstar Kennestone Hosp 100 Lacy St Marietta GA 30060

KEARNEY, DOUGLAS CHARLES, lawyer, journalist; b. Gloucester, Mass., June 24, 1945; s. Charles Matthew Kearney and Jean (Tarr) Thomas. Student, Brown U., 1963-64; BA, Fla. State U., 1971, JD with high honors, 1973. Bar: Fla. 1974, Calif. 1976, U.S. Ct. Appeals (5th cir.) 1977, U.S. Dist. Ct. (mid. and so. dists.) Fla. 1978, U.S. Ct. Appeals (11th cir.) 1981, U.S. Supreme Ct. 1982, U.S. Dist. Ct. (no. dist.) Tex. 1985, Tex. 1986. Asst. pub. defender Office of Pub. Defender 2d Jud. Cir., Tallahassee, 1973-76; asst. atty. gen. Atty. Gen.'s Office State of Fla., Tallahassee, 1977-78, chief antitrust enforcement unit Atty. Gen.'s Office, 1978-79; prin. Law Offices of Douglas C. Kearney, Tallahassee, 1979-85; assoc. Brice & Mankoff, P.C., Dallas, 1985-87, mem., 1987-89, Choate & Lilly, P.C., Dallas, 1989-92; prin. Kearney & Assocs., Dallas, 1992—. Pres. Legal Aid Found. of Tallahassee, Inc., 1984. With U.S. Army, 1965-68, Vietnam. Mem. Fla. Bar Assn., Tex. Bar Assn., Calif. Bar Assn. Episcopalian. Avocations: sailing, tennis, swimming, gardening. Office: Kearney & Assocs 15105 Cypress Hills Dr Dallas TX 75248-4914

KEARNEY, JOHN FRANCIS, III, lawyer; b. Phila., July 27, 1947; s. John Francis and Adria B. (Linder) K.; m. Roseanne M. McAnally, Feb. 25, 1967 (dec. 1983); children: Jennifer F. Kearney Johnstone, Aileen M. Kearney Jones, John F. IV, Anne L.; m. Andrea D. Zaneski, Mar. 20, 2000. BBA, Temple U., 1970; JD cum laude, Rutgers U., 1973. Bar: N.J. 1973, U.S. Dist. Ct. N.J. 1973, U.S. Supreme Ct. 1977; cert. criminal trial atty. N.J. Supreme Ct. 1984. Assoc. Tomar, Parks, Seliger, Simonoff & Adourian, Camden, N.J., 1973-74; sr. trial atty. Office of Pub. Defender, Mt. Holly, N.J., 1974-83; pvt. practice Moorestown, N.J., 1983—; judge mcpl. ct. City of Bordentown, Twp. of Delran and Borough of Palmyra, N.J., 1993-97. Counsel Burlington County Bd. Social Svcs., Mt. Holly, 1984—; prosecutor Borough of Palmyra, 1992-93; pub. defender Woodland Twp., Chatsworth, N.J., 1990-93, Borough of Riverton, N.J., 1984-93; adj. faculty Burlington County Coll., Pemberton, N.J., 1981; pub. defender Twp. of Mt. Holly and Westampton, 1986-90. Editorial bd. Rutgers Law Jour., 1972-73. Bd. dirs. Camden Regional Legal Svcs., Inc., 1972-74; bd. trustees Burlington County Community Action Program, 1971-74; arbitrator Personal Injury and Comml. Arbitration Programs, Superior Ct. of N.J., Burlington County, 1990—; mem. local bd. # 2, Selective Svc. Sys., 2002-. 1st Lt. U.S. Army, 1973. Recipient Am. Jurisprudence award LCP Pub. Co., 1971. Mem. N.J. Assn. County Welfare Attys., Burlington County Mcpl. Judges Assn., Burlington County Bar Assn (sec. 1998 99, treas. 1999-2000, v.p. 2000-01, pres.-elect 2001-02, pres. 2002-03), Trial Attys. of N.J., Assn. Trial Lawyers of Am., N.J. State Bar Assn. (gen. coun.). Republican. Roman Catholic. Avocations: wildlife and underwater photography, boating, travel, hiking and climbing, collecting inuit and native american art. Office: 720 E Main St Ste 2S Moorestown NJ 08057-3058

KEARNEY, JOHN WALTER, sculptor, painter; b. Omaha, Aug. 31, 1924; m. Lynn Haigh, June 2, 1951; children: Daniel Raymond, Jill Ann. Student, Cranbrook Acad. Art, 1946-48. Tchr., 1948—; co-founder, 1949; since co-dir. Contemporary Art Workshop Chgo. Mem. adv. bd. Art Inst. Chgo., A.R.S.G., Fine Arts Work Ctr., Provincetown, Mass., Chgo. Coun. on Fine Arts; vis. artist Am. Acad. in Rome, 1985, 92, 98, 03—; mem. summer faculty Fine Arts Work Ctr., Provincetown, 1996. Numerous one-man shows including A.C.A. Gallery, N.Y.C., (5 shows) 1964-79, 03—, Ft. Wayne (Ind.) Mus., 1966, Galleria Schneider, Rome, 1969, Ill. Inst. Tech., 1976, 91, Ulrich Mus. Art, Wichita State U., 1976, Dirksen Fed. Bldg., Chgo., 1979, Cherrystone Gallery, Wellfleet, Mass., 1980, 92, Contemporary Art Workshop, 1981, 84, Goldman-Kraft Gallery, Chgo., 1985, others in N.Y.C., 1964-79, Venice, 1964, Rome, 1964, 68, Chgo., 1966-85, Berta Walker Gallery, Provincetown, Mass., 1992, 93, 95, 97, Mitchell Mus., Mt. Vernon, Ill., 1994; sculpture show 1998, Thomas McCormick Fine Art, Chicago, 1998. 2-person show, Art Inst. Chgo., A.R.S.G., 1977; represented in permanent collections, Mus. Contemporary Art, Chgo., Standard Oil Bldg., Chgo., Lawrence U., Appleton, Wis., Interfirst Plaza, Dalla, Mundelein Coll., Chgo., Chrysler Art Mus., Norfolk (Va.) Art Mus., Ulrich Mus. Art of Wichita State U., Canton Art Inst., Capitol Bldg. Complex State Ill., Springfield, 1993, Detroit Children's Mus., Ft. Wayne Art Mus., Minn. Mus., St. Paul, New Sch. Social Research, N.Y.C., City of Chgo. Park Dist., Northwestern U., Roosevelt U., Chgo., U. Wyo. Art Mus., St. Lawrence U., Canton, N.Y., Wichita Art Mus., Peace Mus., Chgo., Chgo. Mus. Sci. and Industry, Lincoln Park Zoo, Chgo., Kans. Coliseum, Wichita, Fourth Fin. Ctr., Wichita, Kresgc Collection, Troy, Mich., Spertus Mus., Chgo., Ill. State Mus., Ill. Capitol Bldg. Mitchell Mus., Mt. Vernon, Ill., Cranbrook Acad. Art, Bloomfield Hills., Mich., Oakton Coll., Des Plaines, Ill., Oz Park, Chgo., Tin Man and Cowardly Lion, Goudy Sch., Chgo.; also pvt. collections including, John D. Rockefeller IV collection, Robert Mayer collection, spl. sculpture in bronze and silver, Sculpture Park (4 works) Munster Ind., 2000, steel bumpers sculpture, others. Trustee Ill. Com. for Handgun Control. Served with USN, World War II, PTO. Named Man of Year in Arts in Chgo., 1963; Fulbright grantee, 1963-64; Italian Govt. grantee, 1963-64; grantee Nat. Endowment Arts, 1968 Mem. Provincetown Art Assn. (former v.p. and trustee) Home: 830 W Castlewood Ter Chicago IL 60640-4217 Studio: (summer) 638 Commercial St Provincetown MA 02657 Home: 830 W Castlewood Ter Chicago IL 60640-4217 E-mail: jaklynk830@aol.com.

KEARNEY, JOSEPH LAURENCE, retired athletic conference administrator; b. Pitts., Apr. 28, 1927; s. Joseph L. and Iva M. (Nikirk) K.; m. Dorothea Hurst, May 13, 1950; children: Jan Marie, Kevin Robert, Erin Lynn, Shawn Alane, Robin James. BA, Seattle Pacific U., 1952, LL.D., 1979; MA, San Jose State U., 1964; Ed.D., U. Wash., 1970. Tchr., coach Paradise (Calif.) High Sch., 1952-53; asst. basketball coach U. Wash., 1953-54; coach, tchr. Sunnyside (Wash.) High Sch., 1954-57; prin. high sch., coach Onalaska (Wash.) High Sch., 1957-61; prin. Tumwater (Wash.) High Sch., 1961-63; asst. dir. Wash. High Sch. Activities Assn., 1963-64; athletic dir., assoc. dir. U. Wash., 1964-76; athletic dir. intercollegiate athletics Mich. State U., East Lansing, 1976-80, Ariz. State U., Tempe, 1980; commr. Western Athletic Conf., Denver, 1980-95. Hon. chmn. Holiday Bowl, 1994, commr. emeritus, 1994. Pres. Cmty. Devel. Assn., 1957-61; bd. dirs. U.S. Olympic Com., 1985-94, chmn. games preparation com., 1985-2001. With USN, 1945—47. Recipient Disting. Service award Mich. Assn. Professions, 1979, Citation for Disting. Svc., Colo. Sports Hall of Fame, U.S. Olympic Com. Order of Olympic Shield, 1996. Mem. Nat. Football Found. (ct. of honors com., Western Regional Leadership award 1999), Nat. Collegiate Athletic Assn., Nat. Assn. Collegiate Dirs. Athletics (Corbett award 1991, Adminstr. Excellence award), Collegiate Commrs. Assn. (pres., award of Merit 1998), Am. Football Assn. (Commrs. award 1996, Athletic Dir.'s award 1998). Home: 2810 W Magee Rd Tucson AZ 85742-1500 E-mail: josephlkea@msn.com.

KEARNEY, LYNN MARILYN HAIGH, arts administrator, curator; b. Chgo., Nov. 16, 1927; d. Raymond Haigh and Agnes (Dahl Haigh) Thompson; m. John W. Kearney, June 2, 1951; children: Daniel R., Jill Kearney McDonnell. BA, Northwestern U., 1949; cert. in arts adminstrn., Harvard U., 1978. Adminstr. Contemporary Art Workshop, 1951-67; dir. Contemporary Art Workshop, Inc., Chgo., 1967—. Juror Sch. Art Inst. Chgo., 1986, So. Ill. Artists Open, Mitchell Mus., Mt. Vernon, Ill., 1991, St. Louis Art Assn. Ann., 1989, Women's Caucus for Art, Millenium Exhib., 1999, Chgo., 2000; lectr. Columbia Coll., Chgo., 1970; vis. artist Am. Acad. in Rome, 1992, 98, 03. Exhibited weaving works Art Inst. Chgo., 1954. Trustee Dedalus Found., Robert Motherwell Found., N.Y.C., 1991—, Francis Parker Sch., Chgo., 1981-84, Provincetown (Mass.) Art Assn. and Mus., 1982-85, Mid-North Assn., Chgo., 1981-84; mem. adv. bd. Oriana Singers, Chgo., 1985—, Lincoln Park Conservation Assn., Chgo., 1994—, Art Rental and Sales Gallery, Art Inst. Chgo., 1984-87; active Ill. Coun. Against Handgun Violence, 1977-97. Grantee Ill. Arts Coun., 1982. Mem. Midwest Designer Craftsmen Orgn. Home: 830 W Castlewood Ter Chicago IL 60640-4217 Office: Contemporary Art Workshop 542 W Grant Pl Chicago IL 60614-3706 Home (Summer): 638 Commercial St Provincetown MA 02657

KEARNEY, NANCY JEAN, artist; b. Denver, Aug. 26, 1941; d. Fred Leslie and Florence Marguerite Bennett; divorced; children: Jennifer, Susan. BFA, Brigham Young U., 1971; MA, Calif. State U., Long Beach, 1975. Cert. tchr. substitute, K-12. Artist Galleria Tubac, Ariz., 1998—, Mo's Gallery and Fine Framing Inc., Tucson, 2002. Art tchr. Tucson Mus. of Art, 1994. Artist: oil painting Ariz. Bank Commn., 1997, murals Hacienda Del Sol Guest Ranch, 1996, Starr Learning Ctr., other paintings. Mem. Lds Ch. Avocations: music, reading, exercise.

KEARNEY, STEPHEN MICHAEL, corporate executive; b. Washington, Apr. 8, 1956; s. John James and Helen Joan (Gaffney) K.; m. Julie Elizabeth Mosio, June 30, 1984; children: Justin Samuel, Caitlin Elizabeth. BA, McGill U., 1978; MBA, George Washington U., 1985; AMP, Harvard Bus. Sch., 2000. CFA, cert. cash mgr. Fin. economist US Treasury Dept., Washington, 1978-80; investment officer US Postal Svc., Washington, 1980-81, investment mgr., 1981-90, treas., 1990-99, v.p., treas., 1999—2000, sr. v.p. corp./bus. devel., 2000—01, v.p. pricing, 2001—. Mem. sch. bd. of advisors, chmn. endowment com. St. Anselm's Abbey. First class honors, Univ. scholar McGill U., 1978; recipient Alexander Hamilton award for Excellence in Treasury Mgmt., 1996, 98, 99, Postmaster Gen. award, 1997, 99. Mem.: Assn. for Fin. Profl., Washington Soc. Investment Analysts, Washington Assn. Money Mgr. (pres. 1985—86), Assn. for Investment Mgmt. and Rsch., Fin. Execs. Internat., Beta Gamma Sigma. Democrat. Roman Catholic. Office: US Postal Svc 1735 N Lynn St Arlington VA 22209-6001 E-mail: skearney@usps.com.

KEARNEY-NUNNERY, ROSE, nursing administrator, educator, consultant; b. Glen Falls, NY, July 8, 1951; d. James J. and Helen F. (Oprandy) K.; m. Jimmie E. Nunnery. BS(hon.), Keuka Coll., 1973; M of nursing, U. Fla., 1976, PhD, 1987. Asst. prof. La. State U. Med. Ctr., New Orleans, 1976-87; project coord., indigent health care U. Fla., Gainesville, 1984-85; asst. prof. U. of South Fla., Tampa, Fla., 1987-88; dir. nursing programs State Univ. of N.Y., New Paltz, NY, 1988-94; project dir. MS in gerontol. nursing advanced nursing edn. grant U.S. Health Resources and Svc. Adminstrn. Div. Nursing, 1992-94; head nursing dept. Tech. Coll. of the Low Country, Beaufort, SC, 1995-97, v.p. acad. affairs, 1997—. Author: Advancing Your Profession Concepts for Profl. Nursing, 1997, Advancing Your Profession: Concepts for Profl. Nursing, 2001. Bd. dir. Beaufort Co. First Steps, 2000-01; Ulster County unit Am. Cancer Soc., 1991-94; nursing edn. com., 1990-92; bd. dir. Mid-Hudson Consortium for Advancement Edn. for Health Profl., 1988-94; nursing edn. com., 1988-92; scholarship com., 1989-93; com. chmn., 1990-93, treas., 1992-94; prof. devel. program SUNY, Albany, 1989-92; adv. coun. Ulster CC, 1989-94; adv. regional planning group for early intervention svc. United Cerebral Palsy Ulster County Inc., Children's Rehab. Ctr., 1989-91; mem. Ulster County adv. com. Office for Aging, 1991-94; state del. S.C. Conf. on Aging, 1995; bd. dir. Beaufort County Coun. on Aging, 1995; cmty. adv. bd. Hilton Head Med. Ctr. and Clinics, 1996-2000; mem. SC Bd. Nursing, 2000—, pres. 2000-03; mem. practice, regulation, and edn. com. Nat. Coun. State Bd. of Nursing, 2001-03; accreditation evaluator So. Assn. Coll. and Sch. Commn. on Coll. Mem. ANA, S.C. Nurses Assn. (editl. bd. 1994-99, chair 1996-99); Nat. Coun. of State Bd. of Nursing (mem. practice, regulation, and edn. com. 2001—); Sigma Theta Tau. Roman Catholic. Home: 80 Peninsula Dr Hilton Head Island SC 29926-1119

KEARNS, ELLEN VERONICA, artist; b. Washington, Apr. 29, 1964; d. Francis E. and Ann P. Kearns AB cum laude, Smith Coll., 1986; PhD, Mich. State U., 1991. Grad. fellow Mich. State U., East Lansing, Mich., 1986-91; fellow Harvard U., Cambridge, 1992-93; USDA fellow Mass. Inst. Tech., Cambridge, 1993-95; vis. fellow Max-Planck-Inst., Golm, Germany, 1995-96; rsch. assoc. Dartmouth Coll., Hanover, NH, 1996-98; asst. mgr. Starbucks Coffee Co., Ridgefield, Conn., 1999—2000; assoc. mgr. Banana Republic, Mt. Kisco, NY, 2000—01; tng. specialist Fleet Boston Fin., NYC, 2001—. Avocations: oil painting, gardening, cats, knitting, art cars.

KEARNS, GARY P. finance company executive; b. DuBois, Pa., Oct. 29, 1956; s. Philip F. Kearns, Arlene Allen. BS, Georgetown U., Washington, 1979. Pres., CEO Kearns Assocs., Washington, 1979—82; asst. v.p. Irving Trust Co., N.Y.C., 1982—86; v.p. Chemical Bank Corp., N.Y.C., 1986—88, Mellon Bank Corp., Phila., 1988—93; exec. v.p. FleetBoston Fin. Corp., Boston, 1993—2000; COO Bank Austria Creditanstalt, Greenwich, Conn., 2000—01; pres., CEO Kearns Venture Assoc., New Canaan, Conn., 2001—; mng. dir. Std. & Poor's Risk Solution, 2003—. Contbr. Book. Treas., exec. com., bd. dirs. Stamford Cultural Devel. Corp., 1998—; chmn. Stamford United Way Ann. Campaign, 1997; bd. dirs. Stamford Ctr. for the Arts, 1995—2000. Fellow Rotary fellow, Rotary Club of DuBois, Pa., 1974. Mem.: Field Club of New Canaan. Avocations: triathlete, jazz piano. Home: 26 Shagbark Dr New Canaan CT 06840

KEARNS, JAMES JOSEPH, artist; b. Scranton, Pa., Aug. 7, 1924; s. David Joseph and Ann Mary (Keller) K.; m. Betty Ione Hough, June 19, 1948; children: David, Diane, Mark, Aaron, Lisa. B.F.A., Sch. Art Inst. Chgo., 1950. Instr. Sch. Visual Arts, N.Y.C., 1960-90, Skowhegan (Maine) Sch. Painting, summers 1961-64. Illustrator: Can These Bones Live (E. Dahlberg), 1962, The Heart of Beethoven (S. Rodman), 1969; One-man shows include, Grippi Gallery, N.Y.C., 1956, 57, 60, 62, 68, Bloomfield (N.J.) Coll., 1967, 72, Sculpture Center, N.Y.C., 1973, Caldwell (N.J.) Coll., 1976, Trenton (N.J.) State Mus., 1984, group shows include, Whitney Mus. Am. Art, 1959, 60, 61, 80, Am. Fedn. Art, Art Inst. Chgo., 1979, traveling exhbns., Pa. Acad. Fine Arts, Phila., 1964, 65, Butler Inst. Am. Art, Youngstown, Ohio, 1964, Monmouth (N.J.) Mus., 1969, Squibb Gallery, Princeton, N.J., 1974, sculpture, Schenectady Mus., 1976, 35th Audubon Artists, N.Y.C., 1977, Whitney Mus. Am. Art, N.Y.C., 1980, represented in permanent collections, Mus. Modern Art, N.Y.C., Whitney Mus. Am. Art, Newark Mus. Art, Montclair (N.J.) Mus., Topeka Pub. Library, Smithsonian Nat. Collection Fine Arts, Washington, Hirshhorn Mus., Washington, also numerous pvt. collections. Served with U.S. Army, 1943-46. Recipient Ann. Disting. Artist-Tchr. award Sch. Visual Arts, 1990; Nat. Inst. Arts and Letters grantee, 1959 E-mail: jbkearns@ix.netcom.com.

KEARNS, JOHN J., III, lawyer; b. Jersey City, Apr. 24, 1951; s. John J. Jr. and Beverly (Bailey) K.; m. Maria C. DelFemine, May 15, 1976. AB, Columbia U., 1972; JD cum laude, Fordham U., 1976. Bar: N.J. 1976, N.Y. 1977, Pa. 1985. Assoc. firm White and Case, N.Y.C., 1976-84; mem. firm Eckert, Seamans, Cherin and Mellott, LLC, Pitts., 1984—, mem. exec. com., 1989-93, chmn. tax dept., 1994-96, mem. fin. com., 1994—, CFO, 2000—01. Contbr. articles to profl. publs. Mem. ABA, Pitts. Tax Club. Avocations: thoroughbred racing, softball, reading. Office: Eckert Seamans Cherin & Mellot 600 Grant St Ste 4400 Pittsburgh PA 15219-2702 E-mail: jjk@escm.com.

KEARNS, JOHN W. lawyer; b. Sept. 9, 1933; s. John W. and Frances R. (Forch) Kearns; m. Karen E. Swanson, May 3, 1960 (div. 1979); children: Jennifer F., John W., Charles S. BA, Yale U., 1955; JD, Harvard U., 1958. Bar: Ill. 58, Fla. 70, U.S. Dist. Ct. (no. dist.) Ill. 58, U.S. Ct. Appeals (7th, 5th., 3d and 11th cirs.), U.S. Supreme Ct. 71. With Peterson, Ross, Rall, Barber & Seidel, Chgo., 1958—61, Kirkland & Ellis, Chgo., 1961—69, Paul & Thompson, Miami, Fla., 1969—73; pvt. practice Miami, 1973—. Bd. dirs. Fla. Zool. Soc., 1974—79. Mem.: ABA, Chgo. Bar Assn., Dade County Bar Assn., Fla. Bar Assn., Coral Feef Yacht Club, Chgo. Yacht Club. Office: 431 Gerona Ave Coral Gables FL 33146-2807

KEARNS, JOHN WILLIAM (BILL KEARNS), electronics inventor and executive; b. Salem, W.Va., Oct. 30, 1935; s. John D. and Mary Agnes (Nutter) K.; m. Kathleen E. McIntyre, June 10, 1946; children: Mary A., John W. Jr., Chester Paul. BS, St. Mary Coll., Xavier, Kans., 1970; M., U. Mich., Lansing, 1978. Commd. 2d lt. U.S. Army, 1952; advanced through grades to lt. col. U. S. Army, 1973; ret. U.S. Army, various places, 1973; v.p. United Banking Group, W. Palm Beach, Fla., 1973-76; gen. agt. Mass. Mutual Life Ins. Co., Nashville, 1976-79; pres., owner Bill Kearns & Assocs. Inc., Brentwood, Tenn., 1979-88; pres., CEO Adcom, Paxton, Fla., 1988-91, Elecom Inc., Paxton, 1988—91; owner Ed Smith's Antique Old Time Ice Cream Parlor & Fillin Sta., 1992—; co-owner Tri Cities Emporium, Fla., 1998—. Bd. dirs. Sister Cities Internat., Washington. Contbr. articles to profl. jours.; inventor T Ball for children, elevator audio machine, Talking Info. Madallion, 1999. Vice mayor City of Brentwood, 1983-85, commr. 1981-85; planning commr. 1981-83. Decorated Vietnamese Cross of Gallantry, Bronze Star, Air medal. Mem. Gideons Internat., Fla. C. of C., Tri-Cities C. of C. (past pres.), VFW, Rotary (past pres., lt. gov., zone gov.), Paxton Ruritan Club (pres. lt. gov., zone gov. dist. 27). Republican. Baptist. Avocation: piloting (comml. fixed and rotary wing lic. with instrument rating). Home and Office: PO Box 5240 Paxton FL 32538-5240 E-mail: kearns1@gdsys.net.

KEARNS, KEVIN LAWRENCE, political association executive, lawyer; b. Bklyn., Sept. 5, 1947; s. John C. and Alice C. (Kelleher) K.; children: Kathleen, Christopher, Kevin Michael. BA, Fordham U., 1969; MA, SUNY, Stony Brook, 1970; JD, Bklyn. Law Sch., 1976. Bar: N.Y. 1977, D.C. 1977. Legis. counsel State Senator Sheldon Farber, Queens, N.Y., 1976-77; fgn. svc. officer U.S. Dept. State, Washington, 1977-90; assigned to Am. Consulate Gen., Frankfurt, Germany, 1977-79, Am. Embassy, Bonn, Germany, 1979—80, Seoul, 1981-83, Tokyo, 1986-88; congrl. fellow Senate Fgn. Rels. Com., 1988—89; dir. Office Strategic Trade, 1989—90; sr. rsch. fellow Econ. Strategy Inst., Washington, 1990-92, Mfg. Policy Project, Washington, 1992-93; pres. U.S. Bus. and Industry Coun., Washington, 1993—. Roman Catholic. Office: US Bus & Industry Coun 910 16th St NW Ste 300 Washington DC 20006 2903 E-mail: kearns@usbusiness.org.

KEARNS, MERLE GRACE, state representative; b. Bellefonte, Pa., May 19, 1938; d. Robert John and Mary Katharine (Fitzgerald) Grace; m. Thomas Raymond Kearns, June 27, 1959; children: Thomas, Michael, Timothy, Matthew. BS, Ohio State U., 1960. Tchr. St. Raphael Elem. Sch., Springfield, Ohio, 1960-62; substitute tchr. Mad River Green Dist., Springfield, 1972-78; instr. Clark Tech. Coll., Springfield, 1978-80; commr. Clark County, Ohio, 1981-91; mem. Ohio Senate, Columbus, 1991-2000, Ohio Ho. of Reps., Columbus, 2001—. Mem. fin. and appropriations, edn. com. Ohio Ho. of Reps., chair human svcs. subcom. of fin & app, mem. health com., mem. jt. com. agy. rule rev.; co-chair-domestic violence com. Ohio Supreme Ct.; pres. bd. county commrs., 1982, 83, 86, 87, 90; v.p., 85, 88, 89. Sec. County Commrs. Assn. Ohio, 1988, 2d v.p., 1989—90, 1st v.p., 1990; mem. exec. com. Springfield Reps., 1984—2001; chair Ohio Children's Trust Fund, 1995—2000, Legis. Office of Edn. Oversight; mem. NCSL Welfare Reform Task Force, 2001—; vice-chair Policy Consensus Initiative Bd., 2002—; bd. dirs. Springfield Symphony, 1980—86, Arts Coun., 1980—85, County Commrs. Assn. Ohio; bd. dirs., mem. exec. bd. Nat. Conf. State Legislatures, 2000—03. Named Woman of the Yr., Springfield Pilot Club, 1981, Wittenburg Woman of Accomplishment, 1991, Watchdog of Treasury, 1991, 1996, 2000, Legislator of the Yr., Assn. Mental Health and Drug Addition Svcs. Bds., 1996, Pub. Childrens Svcs.

Agys. Ohio, 1999, Ohio Cmty. Colls., 1997, Ohio Disting. Nurses, 2000, Advance Practice Nurse Assn., 2002, Legis. Co-Person of the Yr., Assn. Joint Vocat. Sch. Supts., 1996, Mental Health Adv. of the Yr., 2002, Outstanding Head Start Legislator of the Yr., Miami Valley, 2002, Legislator of Yr., Ohio Fedn. Tchrs., 2003; recipient Pub. Policy Leadership award, 1997, Disting. Svc. Pub. Ofcls. award, Assn. Ohio Philanthropic Homes, 1999, 1st Ann. Jane Swart Disting. Svcs. to Nursing, 2000, Citizenship award, Ohio State U. Coll. Human Ecology, 2000; scholar, Ohio State U., 1957—59. Mem.: LWV (bd. dirs. 1964—78, pres. 1975—78), Ohio Nurses Assn. (Legislator of the Yr. 1995, 1999), Rotary, Omicron Nu. Roman Catholic. Avocation: reading. Office: Ohio Ho of Reps 72d Dist 77 S High St Columbus OH 43215

KEARNS, MICHAEL SHAWN, career officer; b. Balt., Apr. 14, 1958; s. Richard Anthony and Janet Elaine (Horn) K.; m. Mimi Corcoran, Dec. 31, 1991. AAS, C.C. Air Force, 1980; BSc, U. Md., 1982; MA, Gonzaga U., 1991; DDiv, ULC Seminary, 2000. Commd. 2d lt. USAF, 1977; chief internat. co-prodr. divsn. Def. Mapping Agy., Ft. Belvoir, Va., 1993-94; command historian Naval Spl. Warfare, Coronado, Calif., 1996-97; sr. mktg. mgr. Silicon Graphics, Inc., Mountain View, Calif., 1997-99; dir. fed. programs Terrain Experts, Inc., San Jose, Calif., 1999-2000; pres. Meta Matics, Inc., Warrenton, Va., 2000—. Owner Kearns & Assoc. Pvt. Investigators, Coronado, 1994-96. Decorated Achievement medal for heroism USAF; Air Force ROTC scholar U. Md., College Park, 1980-82. Mem. Assn. Former Intelligence Officers, Nat. Mil. Intelligence Assn. Avocations: skydiving, parachuting. E-mail: msk@metamatics.com.

KEARNS, NANCY J. language educator; b. Huntsville, Ala. d. Wiley Thomas and Lillian Estelle Jones; m. William Thomas Kearns (dec.); 1 child, Michael Thomas. BA, Athens Coll., 1966; MA, U. North Ala., 1979, U. Valencia, 1980, Middlesex U., 2000. Tchr. Hartselle H.S., Ala., 1966—68, Decatur H.S., Ala., 1968—82; adj. faculty Okaloosa-Walton C.C., Niceville, Fla., 1983—90, U. Ala.-Huntsville, 1990—93; asst. prof. Ala. A&M U., Normal, 1993—. Contbr. Mem.: Nat. Coun. Tchrs. English, Delta Kappa Gamma Beta chpt. Republican. Avocations: writing, poetry. Home: Box 253 5462 Winchester Rd New Market AL 35761*

KEARNS, SHARON ELAINE JOHNSON, retired benefits specialist; b. Buffalo, N.Y., Mar. 11, 1942; d. William Allen and Alice Lillian (Krohn) Johnson; m. James Walton Kearns, Sr., Feb. 3, 1962 (div. June 1967); 1 child, James Walton Jr. 401-K benefits specialist GTE, Camillus, N.Y., 1968-93. Pres. Guiding Light Fan Club, Springfield Jour., 1988-99. Mem. Guiding Light Fan Club (pres. Springfield Jour. 1988-99). Democrat. Methodist. Avocations: reading, computers, travel. Home: 20-2 Queens Way Camillus NY 13031-1720

KEARNS, WARREN KENNETH, business executive; b. Wilmington, Ohio, July 15, 1929; s. Roy William and Marie (Kay) K. BS in Civil Engring., Case Western Res. U., 1951. Registered profl. engr., Ohio, Pa. Supr. Pa. R.R. Co., 1951-56; exec. v.p. Pitts. & W.Va. Rwy. Co., 1956-64; mgr. mfg. services Wheeling Steel Corp., W.Va., 1964-67; v.p. L. B. Foster Co., Pitts., 1967-70, pres., 1979-85; v.p. Sharon Steel Co., Pa., 1970-73; pres. Ogden Steel Co., Cleve., 1973-79, Warren Kearns Assocs., 1985—. Bd. dirs. N.W. Pipe & Casing Co., Portland, Oreg., Erie (Pa.) Forge & Steel Co. Mem.: Sigma Xi, Tau Beta Pi. Avocation: music. Home: 2 High St Hudson OH 44236-2912 Office: Warren Kearns Assocs 1507 Guenevere St Streetsboro OH 44241-5025

KEARNS, WILLIAM MICHAEL, JR., investment banker; b. Orange, N.J., June 26, 1935; s. William Michael and Doris Mae (Hodgkinson) K.; m. Patricia Anne Wright, Aug. 17, 1957; children: William Michael III, Susan Elizabeth (Mrs. Eric R. Hubbard), Kathleen Anne, Michael Patrick, Elizabeth Anne (Mrs. James P. Leonard). AB, U. Maine, 1957; AM, NYU, 1960; postgrad., Boston Coll. Law, 1957-58, NYU, 1960-64; LLD (hon.), Gonzaga U., 1988. With Chase Manhattan Bank, 1958-59; security analyst Hayden, Stone & Co., Inc., N.Y.C., 1960-62; assoc. instl. sales and syndicate dept. Kuhn, Loeb & Co., N.Y.C., 1962-64, asst. v.p., 1964-66, v.p., 1966-68, sales mgr., 1969-68, gen. ptnr., 1970-75; mng. dir. Kuhn, Loeb & Co., Inc., 1976-77, Lehman Bros. Kuhn Loeb Inc., 1977-84, Shearson Lehman Bros. Inc., N.Y.C., 1984—92; adv. dir. Lehman Bros., N.Y.C., 1993; pres. W. M. Kearns & Co. Inc., Morristown, N.J., 1994—; vice chmn. Keefe Mgrs., LLC, N.Y.C., 1998—2002, chmn., co-CEO, 2002—. Bd. dirs. Selective Ins. Group, Inc., Branchville, N.J., Transistor Devices, Inc., Cedar Knolls, N.J.; trustee EQ Advisors Trust (Equitable Life Assurance Soc. U.S.), N.Y.C.; dir. U.S. Shipping LLC, Edison, N.J.; sr. adv. Proudfoot Cons., Plc., London, 1997—; adv. dir. Gridley and Co. LLC, N.Y.C., 2001—; investment adv. Young Nichols Gilstrap, Inc., Phoenix, 1982-1992; sr. cons. Ing Baring Furman Selz LLC, N.Y.C., 1994-98; mem. faculty Fairleigh Dickinson U. Coll. Bus. Adminstrn., 1959-68; instr. security analysis N.Y. Inst. Fin. 1961-67; adj. prof. Grad. Sch. Bus. Adminstrn., NYU, 1971-72, chmn. NYU Forum Fin., 1971; lectr. Columbia U., Fairleigh Dickinson U., U. Rochester, NYU. Trustee Drumthwacket Found., Inc., 1985-95, Morristown-Beard Sch., 1982-88, Rider Univ., 1982-88, Morristown Meml. Health Found., 1999—; trustee Morris Mus., 1968-86, mem. adv. bd., 1987—; trustee Tri-County Scholarship Fund, 1982—, v.p., 1985-86, pres., 1987-89, pres. emeritus, 1990—; bd. dirs. Greater N.Y. coun. Boy Scouts Am., 1986—, exec. v.p., 1990—; bd. dirs. The Am. Friends of Covent Garden and the Royal Ballet, London, 1989—; mem. N.Y. Spl. Rep. Fin. Com., 1978-84; adv. bd. Intrnat. Tennis Hall of Fame, 1984-86, bd. dirs., 1986-95, internat. coun., 1995-97; mem. adv. bd. Templeton Prize, Lyford Cay, Nassau, Bahammas, 1990—; exec. com. William E. Simon Grad. Sch., Bus. Adminstrn., U. Rochester, 1986—; devel. com. U. Maine, 1990-96, diocesan investment com., Diocese of Paterson N.J., 1986—; mem. Cardinal's Com. of Laity, N.Y.C.; mem. 1910 Soc., Boy Scouts Am., 2000. Decorated Am. Assn. Master Knights Sovereign Mil. Order Malta; Pontifical Order of St. Gregory The Great; recipient Leadership award Tri-County Scholarship Fund, 1990, Leadership award Morristown Meml. Hosp., 1998, Augusta Stone award Morristown Meml. Health Found., 1999. Mem. Nat. Assn. Security Dealers (corp. fin. com. 1976-80), Securities Industry Assn. (minority capital com. 1978-86, exec. com. N.Y. dist. 1970, vice chmn. 1973, chmn. 1974), New Eng. Soc., Soc. Friendly Sons St. Patrick City of N.Y., Univ. Club (N.Y., trustee 1978-81), Bond Club N.Y., Econ. Club (N.Y.), Morris County Golf Club (Convent, N.J. gov. 1976-82), Green Jacket Club (Homestead, Va., founder 1991—), Morristown (N.J.) Club, Log Cabin Gun Club (Sterling, N.J.), Rolling Rock Club (Ligonier, Pa.), Mid-Ocean Club (Bermuda), Palm Beach (Fla.) Polo and Country Club, Beta Theta Pi, Kappa Phi Kappa. Roman Catholic. Office: W M Kearns & Co Inc 310 South St Morristown NJ 07960-7301

KEARSE, AMALYA LYLE, federal judge; b. Vauxhall, N.J., June 11, 1937; d. Robert Freeman and Myra Lyle (Smith) K.. BA, Wellesley Coll., 1959; JD cum laude, U. Mich., 1962. Bar: N.Y. 1963, U.S. Supreme Ct. 1967. Assoc. Hughes, Hubbard & Reed, N.Y.C., 1962—69, ptnr., 1969—79; judge U.S. Ct. Appeals (2d cir.), 1979—. Lectr. evidence NYU Law Sch., 1968—69. Author: Bridge Conventions Complete, 1975, Bridge Conventions Complete, 3d edit., 1990, Bridge at Your Fingertips, 1980; transl., editor: Bridge Analysis, 1979; editor: Ofcl. Ency. of Bridge, 3d edit., 1976; mem. editl. bd.: Charles Goren, 1974—. Trustee N.Y.C. YWCA, 1976—79, Am. Contract Bridge League Nat. Laws Commn., 1975—; mem. Pres.'s Com. on Selection of Fed. Jud. Officers, 1977—78; bd. dirs. NAACP Legal Def. and Endl. Fund, 1977—79, Nat. Urban League, 1978—79. Named Women's Pairs Bridge Champion Nat. div., 1971, 1972, World div., 1986, Nat. Women's Teams Bridge Champion, 1987, 1990, 1991. Mem.: ABA, Lawyers Com. for Civil Rights Under Law (mem. exec. com. 1970—79), Am. Law Inst., Assn. of Bar of City of N.Y. Office: US Ct Appeals US Courthouse 40 Foley SqRm 2001 New York NY 10007

KEARSE, JEVON, football player; b. Ft. Myers, Fla., Sept. 3, 1976; Student, U. Fla. Defensive end Tennessee Titans, Nashville, 1999—. Named All-Pro, AP, Pro Football Weekly, Dr. Z of Sports Illustrated, 1999, Defensive Rookie of Yr., AP, Football News, Football Digest, Pro Football Weekly/Pro Football Writers Assn. of Am., 1999, AFC Defensive Player of Month of Dec., 1999, NFL Rookie of Month of Sept., Nov., Dec., 1999, NFL Pass Rusher of Yr., NFL Alumni group, All-AFC and All-Rookie, Football News, Pro Football Weekly, 1999, All-Pro, All-Rookie, Football News, Coll. and Pro Football Weekly, 1999. Office: 460 Great Circle Rd Nashville TN 37228

KEARY, DAVID, artistic director; BA, Millsaps Coll.; JD, Miss. Coll. Sch. Law. Law clk. to justice James W. Smith Jr. Miss. Supreme Ct.; with N.Y.C. Ballet; prin. dancer Ft. Worth Ballet; artistic dir. Ballet Miss., Jackson, 1994—. Asst. stage mgr. Internat. Ballet Competition, Jackson. Performed in honor of Princess Grace of Monaco; with Markarova and Co. at Uris Theatre, N.Y.C.; in ednl. lecture series; prin. dancer, dance capt. musical drama Texas at Palo Duro Canyon, Canyon, Tex.; prin. dancer in numerous ballets by George Balanchine, including Scotch Symphony, Square Dance, Donizetti Variations, Rubies, Raymonda Variations, Allegro Brilliante; also classical ballets The Sleeping Beauty, The Nutcracker, Le Fille Mal Garde, Romeo and Juliet Pas de Deux. Ford Found. scholar Sch. Am. Ballet. Office: Ballet Miss PO Box 1787 Jackson MS 39215-1787

KEASLING, GERALD FRANK, obstetrician-gynecologist, educator; b. Hastings, Nebr., Mar. 6, 1950; s. Dean Albert and Clare Ellen Keasling; m. Barbara Joan Behling, May 27, 1972; children: Susan, Thomas, Anne, Katherine, Amanda, Emily. BSChemE with high distinction, U. Nebr., 1972, MD with distinction, 1975. Cert. in ob-gyn. Resident in ob-gyn. U. Kans. Hosp., Wichita, 1975-78; with Fremont (Nebr.) Area Med. Ctr.; clin. asst. prof. U. Nebr. Med. Ctr. Pres. Fremont Area Med. Ctr., 1989. Fellow ACOG, Am. Soc. Gynecologic Lapararscopists; mem. Cen. Assn. Obstetricians and Gynecologists, Fremont Med. Assn. (pres. 1996-97), Alpha Omega Alpha. Office: Health Care for Women 700 E 29th St Fremont NE 68025

KEATING, ANALOUISE, educator, author; b. Chgo., June 24, 1961; PhD, U. Ill., 1990. Assoc. prof. Ea. N.Mex. U., 1990-99, Aquinas Coll., 1999—2001, Tex. Woman's U., 2001—. Author: Women Reading Women Writing: Self-Invention in Paula Gunn Allen, Gloria Anzaldúa and Audre Lorde, 1996 (Choice Outstanding Acad. book 1996); editor: Perspectives: Gender Studies, 1999; editor Interviews/Entrevistas by Gloria E. Anzaldúa, 2000 (Susan Koppelman award 2001); co-editor (with Gloria E. Anzaldua) This Bridge We Call Home: Radical Visions for Transformation; contbr. articles to profl. jours. Grad. fellowship U. Ill., 1984, 86, Rockefeller Summer Rsch. fellowship S.W. Inst. for Rsch. on Women U. Ariz., 1992; Irene Kogan scholarship U. Ill., 1989; Tchg. Excellence Faculty Round Table grantee N.Mex. Ctr. for Tchg. Excellence, 1995-96. Mem. MLA, Nat. Women's Studies Assn., Am. Studies Assn., Soc. for the Study of Multi Ethnic Lit. of the U.S. Avocation: swimming. Office: Tex Woman's U Women's Studies Program PO Box 425557 Denton TX 76204-5557 Fax: 616-732-4487. E-mail: aKeating@twu.edu.

KEATING, BERN, writer, journalist; b. Fassett, Can., May 14, 1915; came to U.S., 1920; s. John Julian Keating and Laure Lalonde; m. Marian West, June 10, 1939; 1 child, John G. BA magna cum laude, U. Ark., 1938. Reporter, relief editor Palm Beach (Fla.) Post Times, 1938-41; news editor Utica N.Y. Radio, 1941; freelance journalist, writer Greenville, Miss., 1945—. Author over 25 books, 800 mag. articles, 1 documentary movie. With U.S. Navy, 1942-45. Recipient Lifetime Achievement award Miss. Inst. Arts Letters, 1995. Mem. Travel Journalists Guild (founder, pres.), Authors Guild, Soc. Am. Travel Writers, Am. Soc. Journalists Authors. Home and Office: 141 Bayou Rd Greenville MS 38701-7732 E-mail: bkeating@tecinfo.com.

KEATING, CHRISTOPHER PATRICK, reporter; b. N.Y.C., Sept. 2, 1960; s. Francis A. and Jeanne Gertrude (Scully) K.; m. Margaret Grottola, June 20, 1987. BA, Fordham U., 1982; MS, Columbia U., 1984. Filer, lister, rschr. Newsweek mag., N.Y.C., 1981-84; reporter Greenwich (Conn.) Time, 1984-90, The Hartford (Conn.) Courant, 1990—, capitol bur. chief, 1995—2000, The Hartford (Conn.) Couran, 2002—; ct. reporter, 2001—02. Recipient 1st prize for news in depth Conn. chpt. Soc. Profl. Journalists, 1987, for feature writing, 1990, 2d pl. bus. reporting, 1999; hon. mention New Eng. AP Newspapers Editors Assn., 1990, 1st place, 1997. Office: The Hartford Courant 285 Broad St Hartford CT 06115-2510

KEATING, DAVID, photographer; b. Rye, N.Y., Sept. 5, 1962; BA in Philosophy, Yale U., 1985; MA in Studio Art with distinction, U. N.Mex., 1991; student, Calif. Inst. Arts, Santa Clarita, 1992; MFA in Studio Art with distinction, U. N.Mex., 1994. Solo exhbns. include U. N.Mex., 1990 (traveled to Pace U., N.Y.C., Nat. Coun. Alcoholism Conf. of Affiliates, Nashville), 91, Calif. Inst. Arts, 1992, Graham Gallery, Albuquerque, 1994, Univ. Art Mus. Downtown, Albuquerque, 1995-96, George Eastman House, Rochester, N.Y., 1997, others; group exhbns. include Raw Space Gallery, Albuquerque, 1990, Betty Rymer Gallery, Sch. Art Inst. Chgo., 1991, 92, Randolph St. Gallery, Chgo., 1992, Atlanta Gallery Photography, 1992, San Jose (Calif.) Inst. Contemporary Art, 1992, Univ. Art Mus., Albuquerque, 1993, Ctr. African Am. History and Culture, Smithsonian Instn., Washington, 1994-95, Mus. Photographic Arts, San Diego, 1996-97, SF Camerawork, San Francisco, 1993, 98, others; represented in pub. collections, including Univ. Art Mus., Albuquerque; subject of various articles and catalogs, 1992—. NEA Visual Artists fellow in photography, 1994, Van Deren Coke fellow, U. N.Mex., 1991; recipient award Photographers and Friends United Against AIDS/Art Matters Inc., 1992. Home: 1410 Central Ave SW Apt 38 Albuquerque NM 87104-1166

KEATING, EUGENE KNEELAND, animal scientist, educator; b. Liberal, Kans., Feb. 15, 1928; s. Arthur Hitch and Nilie Charlotte (Kneeland) K.; m. Iris Louise Myers, Aug. 12, 1951; children— Denise Keating Schnagl, Kimberly Alan. BS, Kans. State U., 1953, MS, 1954; PhD, U. Ariz., 1964. Owner, mgr. ranch, Kans., 1954—; instr., farm mgr. Midwestern U., Wichita Falls, Tex., 1957-60; rsch. asst. U. Ariz., Tucson, 1960-64; prof. animal sci. Calif. State Poly. U., Pomona, 1964-98, prof. emeritus, 1998—, chmn. dept., 1971-78. Contbr. articles to profl. jours. Bd. dirs. Los Angeles County Jr. Livestock Fair, 1971-79, chmn., 1975. With USAAF, 1946-49. Recipient Farm Bur. Century award, 2000. Fellow: Am. Inst. Chemists; mem.: NRA Whittington Ctr. Founders Club, NRA (benefactor), Brit. Soc. Animal Prodn., Am. Soc. Lab. Animal Sci., Coun. for Agrl. Sci. and Tech. (life), Am. Soc. Animal Sci. (life), Nat. Intercollegiate Rodeo Assn. (West Coast regional faculty dir. 1972—76), Western Heritage Ctr., Rep. Nat. Com. (life), Calif Rifle and Pistol Assn. (Gold Eagle), Am. Legion, Block and Bridle Club, Santa Fe Trail and Gun Club (life), Ind. Order Foresters, Sigma Xi, Alpha Zeta, Gamma Sigma Delta, Phi Lambda Upsilon. Presbyterian. Home: 149 W Loretto Ct Claremont CA 91711-1739 Office: 3801 W Temple Ave Pomona CA 91768-2557

KEATING, FRANCIS ANTHONY, II, former governor, lawyer; b. St. Louis, Feb. 10, 1944; s. Anthony Francis and Anne (Martin) K.; m. Catherine Dunn Heller, 1972; children: Carissa Herndon, Kelly Martin, Anthony Francis III. AB, Georgetown U., 1966; JD, U. Okla., 1969. Bar: Okla. 1969. Spl. agt. FBI, 1969-71; asst. dist. atty. Tulsa County, 1971-72; mem. Okla. Ho. of Reps., 1972-74, Okla. Senate, 1974-81; U.S. atty. No. Dist. Okla., 1981-84; asst. sec. U.S. Treasury Dept., Washington, 1985-88; assoc. atty. gen. Dept. Justice, 1988-89; gen. counsel, acting dep. sec. Dept. Housing and Urban Devel., Washington, 1989-93; gov. State of Okla., 1995—2003; pres. Am. Coun. Life Insurers, Washington, 2003—. Mem. Okla. Bar Assn. Republican. Office: Am Coun Life Insurers 101 Constitution Ave NW Washington DC 20001*

KEATING, MARGARET MARY, entrepreneur, business consultant; b. Chgo., Feb. 18, 1950; d. Jeremiah Joseph and Margaret Mary (Donnelly) K. Cert. in law, U. Mass., 1993; BS, Emmanuel Coll., 1994; MBA, Simmons Coll., 1996. Sr. merchandiser J.C. Penney Co., Chgo., 1971-73, dist. mgr. fashions, 1973-75, regional mgr., 1976-78, gen. mgr. merchandise Aurora, Ill., 1978-82; co-founder, exec. v.p., dir. mktg. The Pres. Mgmt. Group, Inc., Hingham, Mass., 1984-88; pres., CFO Keating Konsult, Inc., Scituate, Mass., 1988—. V.p., co-founder Video Tours, Inc., Hartford, Conn., 1986-87. Founder Advocates for Moral and Ethical Treatment by Divorce Attys., Accord, Mass., 1991—. Mem. NAFE, LWV, Nat. Assn. for Women in Careers, Nat. Womens Polit. Caucus, Am. Mgmt. Assn., Ctr. for Entrepreneurial Mgmt. Democrat. Avocation: political and community drives. Office: Keating Konsult 55 Richfield Rd Scituate MA 02066-3425

KEATING, MICHAEL BURNS, lawyer, educator; b. Cambridge, Mass., May 17, 1940; s. John Stuart and Anne Veronica (Burns) K.; m. Martha Harrison McGuire, OCt. 12, 1974; children: Michael Burns, Andrew Wade, Lucy Harrison. BA, Williams Coll., 1962; LLB, Harvard U., 1965. Bar: Mass. 1965, U.S. District Ct. Mass. 1966. Law clk. to presiding justice Superior Ct. Mass., Boston, 1965-66, U.S. Dist. Ct. Mass., Boston, 1966-67; assoc. Foley Hoag, Boston, 1967-74, ptnr., 1974—. Adj. prof. trial practice Northeastern Law Sch., Boston, 1985—. Trustee Brooks Sch., North Andover, Mas., 1978—, Foley, Hoag & Eliot Found., Boston, 1981-89, Williams Coll., Williamstown, Mass., 1996—; pres. Crime & Justice Found., Boston, 1985-94; bd. dirs. Navy Meml. Found., 1994—. Lt. (j.g.) USNR, 1967-72. Fellow Am. Coll. Trial Lawyers, Harvard Club; mem. Boston Bar Assn. (pres. 2001-02). Democrat. Roman Catholic. Avocations: tennis, squash, skiing, sailing. Home: 3 W Cedar St Boston MA 02108-3535 Office: Foley Hoag 155 Seaport Blvd Boston MA 02210-2600

KEATING, MICHAEL JOSEPH, lawyer; b. St. Louis, June 8, 1954; s. John David and Patricia Ann (Sullivan) K.; m. Maureen Ann Moder, Aug. 28, 1981; children: Sarah Kathleen, Brendan Michael. AB, Washington U., St. Louis, 1976; JD, St. Louis U., 1979. Bar: Mo. 1979, Ill. 1980. Law clk. Mo. Ct. Appeals, St. Louis, 1979-80, U.S. Dist. Ct. Ea. Dist., St. Louis, 1980-81; assoc. Bryan, Cave, McPheeters & McRoberts, St. Louis, 1981-83; corp. atty. Emerson Electric Co., St. Louis, 1983-85, sr. atty., 1985-87, asst. gen. counsel product liability, 1987—. Author: Designing an Effective Product Liability Corporate Compliance Program, 2002; contbr. articles to profl. jours. Mem. Am. Law Inst., Mo. Athletic Club, Sigma Alpha Epsilon, Phi Delta Phi, Pi Sigma Alpha. Roman Catholic. Home: 11117 Apache Trl Saint Louis MO 63146-5627 Office: Emerson Electric Co PO Box 4100 8100 W Florissant Ave Saint Louis MO 63136-1494 E-mail: michael.keating@emrsn.com.

KEATING, REGINA G. computer analyst consultant; b. Bryn Mawr, Pa., Mar. 20, 1940; d. Francis Stanislaus and Frances Mulligan Gear; m. Frank J. Keating, Mar. 4, 1972 (div. Dec. 1978); 1 child, Frank. BBA, Temple U., 1981, MBA, 1982. Sr. staff local govt. com. Pa. Constnl. Conv., 1967-68; adminstr. Blank Rome Comisky & McCauley, Phila., 1968-72; computer programmer Lee Tire & Rubber Co., Valley Forge, Pa., 1984-86; programmer, analyst Amerigas Corp., Valley Forge, 1986-88, Am. Electronic Labs., Lansdale, Pa., 1988-93; cons. computer analyst Polin Assocs., Richboro, Pa., 1993—. Instr., adj. lectr. Temple U., Phila., 1981, 85. Sec., registration chmn. Dem. Com., Haverford Twp., Pa., 1964-71, com. woman, Abington Twp., 1978—. Mem. NAACP, NOW, NAFE, ACLU, World Affairs Coun.-Phila., So. Poverty Law Ctr., Pub. Citizen.

KEATING, ROBERT B. ambassador; b. Medford, Mass., May 7, 1924, married, 1 child BS, U.S. Naval Acad., 1946; M.E.A., George Washington U., 1961. Chmn. com. on transport tech. for developing countries U.S. Dept. State, 1961-62; dir. Chile-Calif. Program for Tech. Coop., 1964-67; sr. adviser Inter-Am. Devel. Bank, 1967-69; dir. gen. Bur. Roads, Ministry Pub. Works, Rep. of Zaire, 1970-73; cons., 1973-79; v.p. Pure Water Systems Inc., 1979-81; cons. on internat. security affairs Office Sec. Def., 1981-82; cons. Office Gen. Counsel, Dept. Navy, 1982-83; ambassador to Madagascar, 1983-86; ambassador to Comoros, 1983-86; U.S. exec. dir. The World Bank and Affiliates, Washington, 1986-89; sr. adviser internat. affairs Pepper, Hamilton & Scheetz, Washington, 1989—. Mem. U.S. del. to Law of Sea Conf., Geneva, 1981, N.Y.C., 1982; chmn. Presdl. Study of Third World Hunger, 1984 Author: Food For Progress Initiative. Vet., Korean War, 1952-53, Minesweeping (combat action ribbon, LCDR USNR). Decorated Nat. Order of Leopard, Republic of Zaire, Nat. Order of Madagascar, Dem. Republic Madagascar, Nat. Order of Star of Anjouan, Fed. Republic of Comoros. Office: Hamilton Square 600 14th St NW Washington DC 20005-2004

KEATING, THOMAS PATRICK, health care administrator, educator; b. Cleve., Jan. 5, 1949; s. Thomas Wilbur and Margaret (Gahllagher) K.; m. Carolyn Elizabeth Kraft, Sept. 4, 1976; children: Jerrod Patrick, Kerri Ann, Zane, Kriste, Marite. BS in Bus., Cleve. State U., 1971; MS in Bus., U. Toledo, 1973. Cert. health care exec. Asst. dir. facilities U. Kans. Med. Ctr., Kansas City, 1977-80; dir. mgmt. svcs. Charleston (S.C.) County Park and Recreation Commn., 1980-84; adminstr. Children's Health Sys., Med. U. of S.C., Charleston, 1984-2001, instr., 1987-2001, preceptor adminstrv. residency, master health svcs. adminstrn., 1990-93; asst. supt. Bibb County Schs., 2001—. Adj. instr. Cen. Mich. U., Mt. Pleasant, 1979—, Rockhurst Coll., Kansas City, 1979-80, Kansas City (Kans.) Cmty. Jr. Coll., 1978-80, Fayetteville (N.C.) Tech. Inst., 1974-75; accredited cons. SBA, Charleston, 1980-91; adj. prof. Webster U., St. Louis, 1981-2000, faculty U. Ala., New Coll., 1974; nursing home cons. Charleston County Mental Retardation Bd., Charleston, 1987-88. Contbr. articles to profl. jours. Vol. Driftwood Health Care Ctr., Charleston, 1981-83. Capt. U.S. Army, 1973-77, lt. col. USAR ret. Fellow Am. Coll. Health Care Execs., Am. Acad. Med. Adminstrs.; mem. Toastmasters (adminstrv. v.p. 1985-86), Sigma Phi Epsilon (com. chmn. 1970-71), Alpha Kappa Psi (com. chmn. 1972-73), KC. Roman Catholic. Home: 110 Trophy Ct Macon GA 31211-6042

KEATING, TIM, chef; Studied with. Chief La Reserve Omni Hotel; cook Rancho Mirage, Ritz-Carlton Resort, Le Meridien; owner Catering Co., San Diego; chief DeVille Four Seasons, Houston, 2002—. Serves regional steering com. Chefs Collaborative; mem. Houston chpt. Am. Heart Assn. Com. Office: Deville Restaurant Four Seasons Hotel 1300 Lamar St Houston TX 77001

KEATINGE, ROBERT REED, lawyer; b. Berkeley, Calif., Apr. 22, 1948; s. Gerald Robert and Elizabeth Jean (Benedict) K.; m. Katherine Lou Carr, Feb. 1, 1969 (div. Dec. 1981); 1 child, Michael Towne; m. Cornelia Elizabeth Wyma, Aug. 21, 1982; 1 child, Courtney Elizabeth. BA, U. Colo., 1970; JD, U. Denver, 1973, LLM, 1982. Bar: Colo. 1974, U.S. Dist. Ct. Colo. 1974, U.S. Ct. Appeals (10th cir.) 1977, U.S. Tax Ct. 1980. Ptnr. Kubie & Keatinge, Denver, 1974-76; pvt. practice Denver, 1976; assoc. Richard Young, Denver, 1977-86; counsel Durham & Assoc. P.C., Denver, 1986-89, Durham & Baron, Denver, 1989-90; project editor taxation Shepard's/McGraw-Hill, Colorado Springs, Colo., 1990-96; of counsel Holland & Hart, LLP, Denver, 1992—. Lectr. law U. Denver, 1982-92, adj. prof. grad. tax program, 1983-94. Author, cons. (CD-ROM) Entity Expert, 1996; co-author: Ribstein and Keatinge on Limited Liability Companies, 1992; contbr. articles to profl. jours. and treatises. Spkr. to profl. soc. and univ. including AICPA, ALI-ABA, U. Tex., 1984—. Recipient Law Week award U. Denver Bur. Nat. Affairs, 1974. Fellow: Am. Coll. of Tax Counsel; mem.: Am. Law Inst., Denver Bar Assn., Colo. Bar Assn. (taxation sect. exec. coun. 1988—94, sec.-treas. 1991—92, chmn. 1993—94, bd. govs. 1996—, bus. law sect. sec 2001—03, vice chair 2003—, ethics com., corp. code revision com., co-chmn. ltd. liability co. revision com.), ABA (chmn. subcom. ltd. liability cos. of com. on partnerships 1990—95, ABA adviser to Uniform Ltd. Liability Co. Act 1995, chmn. com. on taxation 1995—99, mem. ho. of dels. 1996—2002, ABA/Nat. Conf. Commrs. on Uniform State Laws joint editl. bd. on uninc 1996—, editl. bd. ABA/BNA Lawyer's Manual on Professional Conduct 1998—2002, chmn. com. on partnerships 2000—02, ABA adviser to Revision of Uniform Ltd. Partnership Act 2001). Home: 460 S Marion Pky Apt 1904 Denver CO 80209-2544 E-mail: rkeatinge@hollandhart.com.

KEATON, DIANE, actress; b. Santa Ana, Calif., Jan. 5, 1946; Student, Neighborhood Playhouse, N.Y.C., 1968. Appeared on N.Y. stage in Hair, 1968, Play It Again Sam, 1969, The Primary English Class, 1976; appeared in numerous films including Lovers and Other Strangers, 1970, Play It Again Sam, 1972, The Godfather, 1972, Sleeper, 1973, The Godfather Part II, 1974, Love and Death, 1975, I Will, I Will...For Now, 1975, Harry and Walter Go To New York, 1976, Annie Hall, 1977 (Best Actress Acad. award 1978, Brit. Acad. Best Actress award 1978, N.Y. Film Critics Circle award 1978, Nat. Soc. Film Critics award 1978), Looking for Mr. Goodbar, 1977, Interiors, 1978, Manhattan, 1979, Reds, 1981 (Acad. award nominee), Shoot the Moon, 1982, Little Drummer Girl, 1984, Mrs. Soffel, 1984, Crimes of the Heart, 1986, Radio Days, 1987, Baby Boom, 1987, The Good Mother, 1988, The Lemon Sisters, 1990, The Godfather Part III, 1990, Father of the Bride, 1991, Manhattan Murder Mystery, 1993, Look Who's Talking Now, 1993 (voice), Father of the Bride 2, 1995, Marvin's Room, 1996, First Wives Club, 1996, The Only Thrill, 1997, The Other Sister, 1999, Hanging Up, 2000, Town and Country, 2001; (TV movie) Running Mates, 1992, Amelia Earhart, 1994, Sister Mary Explains It All, 2001; dir. film: Heaven, 1987, Wildflower, 1991, Unstrung Heroes, 1995; accomplished artist and singer; author book of photographs: Reservations, 1980; editor: (with Marvin Heiferman) Still Life, 1983, Mr. Salesman, 1994; prodr.: The Lemon Sisters, 1990; exec. prodr.: Northern Lights (TV), 1997. Recipient Golden Globe award, 1978 Office: John Burnham William Morris Agy 151 S El Camino Dr Beverly Hills CA 90212-2704

KEATON, FRANCES MARLENE, insurance sales representative; b. Redfield, Ark., July 1, 1944; d. John Thomas and Pauline (Hilliard) Wells; m. Larry Ronald Keaton, Sept. 17, 1946. Cert. in acctg., Draughon's Sch. Bus., 1972. Lic. ins. agt. Acctg. supr. Home Ins. Co., Little Rock, 1962-70; auditor St. Paul Ins. Co., Little Rock, 1970-74; spl. agt. Continental Ins. Co., Little Rock, 1974—. Vol. Ark. Sch. for the Blind, Little Rock, 1968. Mem. Little Rock Field Club, Casualty Roundtable, Auditor's Assn., Ins. Women, Underwriters Roundtable, The Executive Female, Ind. Ins. Agts. Assn., Profl. Ins. Assn. Democrat. Methodist. Avocations: golf, tennis, racquetball, travel. Home and Office: 111 Red River Rd Sherwood AR 72120-5851

KEATON, LAWRENCE CLUER, safety engineer, consultant; b. Gainesville, Tex., Nov. 24, 1924; s. William Lenard and Lettie (Phipps) K.; m. Emalee Prichard, Feb. 22, 1947; children: Lawrel Larsen, L.C. Jr., T.E. BSME, U. Okla., 1945; MS in Safety Mgmt. (hon.), PhD in Bus. Adminstrn. (hon.), Western States U., 1989. Registered profl. engr., Tex.; cert. lightning protection inspector; diplomate Coun. of Engring. Specialty Bds. In various engring. positions Phillips Petroleum Co., Borger, Tex., 1946-65, project devel. engr. N.Y.C., 1964-65; mng. dir. Nordisk Philback AB, Malmo, Sweden, 1965-73; dir. carbon black ops. Europe and Africa Phillips Petroleum Co., 1973-74, world-wide dir. carbon black ops., 1974-76; mng. dir. Sevalco Ltd., Bristol, Eng., 1976-81; ind. cons., 1981-85; mng. ptnr. System Engring. and Labs. Northwest Tex., Amarillo, 1985—. 5 patents in petrochem. processes. Lt. (j.g.) USN, 1943-45, PTO. Mem. ASME, Am. Soc. Safety Engrs., Lightning Protection Inst., Nat. Assn. Corrosion Engrs., Nat. Acad. Forensic Engrs., Nat. Assn. Fire Investigators, Nat. Assn. Profl. Accident Reconstruction Specialists, Nat. Soc. Profl. Engrs., Soc. Am. Mil. Engrs., Tex. Soc. Profl. Engrs., Amarillo Rotary, Shriners, Masons, Amarillo Club, Am. Legion, Tenn. Squires. Methodist. Avocations: gourmet cooking, gardening. Home: 7720 Baughman Dr Amarillo TX 79121-1752 Office: System Engring and Labs NW Tex PO Box 1506 Amarillo TX 79105-1506 E-mail: lkeaton@am.net.

KEATOR, DAVID P. G. stockbroker, financial consultant; b. New Haven, Conn., Dec. 8, 1962; s. George and Sheila Nesbit K.; m. Joanne Marie Sheehan, June 18, 1994; children: Daley Boucher, Ehan O'Donnell. BA in Economics, Fordham U., 1985; MA in Orgn. Comm., SUNY, 1991. Sr. exec. Macy's, N.Y.C., 1985-89; dir. devel. Hillcrest Edn. Ctrs., Pittsfield, Mass., 1990-93; v.p. NCI, N.Y.C., 1993-97; investment cons. First Albany Co., Albany, N.Y., 1997-2000; assoc. v.p. Wachovia Securities, Pittfield, Mass., 2000—. Lectr. in field. Home: PO Box 2431 Lenox MA 01240-5431 Office: 66 West St Pittsfield MA 01201-5790

KEATOR, MARGARET WHITLEY, legislative aide; b. Suffolk, Va., Oct. 27, 1945; d. Jacob Jordan and Margaret Mitchell Whitley; m. Philip John Keator, Sept. 2, 1967; 1 child, Jennifer. AB in Govt., Coll. William and Mary, 1968. Tchr. Newport News (Va.) Pub. Sch., 1968-69, 72-84; rsch. asst. Marine Corps. Ops. Analysis Group, Arlington, Va., 1969-72; v.p. Keator Signs, Inc., Newport News, 1990-93; sr. legis. asst. Congressman Bobby Scott, Newport News, 1993—. Polit. cons., Newport News, 1990-93. Mem. Newport News City Coun., 1982-90, Peninsula planning dist. com., 1982-90, Newport News planning com., 1982-87; exec. bd. Va. Peninsula Econ. Devel. Com., Newport News, 1986-90; vice chmn. environ. quality policy com. Va. Mcpl. League, 1988-90; bd. trustees Peninsula Marine Inst., 1992—; citizen adv. bd. Newport News Healthy Famililes Initiative, 1997—. Mem. AAUW (Newport News br.), Soroptimist Club (pres. 1996-98), Monitor Club (pres.-elect), Visionarics (recording sec. 1997—), Church Women United (chair citizen action 1994—), Kiwanis. Democrat. Methodist. Office: Congressman Bobby Scott 2600 Washington Ave Ste 1010 Newport News VA 23607-4333 E-mail: maggiekeator@netscape.net.

KEATS, DONALD HOWARD, composer, educator; b. N.Y.C., May 27, 1929; s. Bernard and Lillian K.; m. Eleanor Steinholz, Dec. 13, 1953; children: Jeremy, Jennifer, Jeffrey, Jocelyn. MusB, Yale U., 1949; MA, Columbia U., 1951; PhD, U. Minn., 1962; student, Staatliche Hochschule fur Musik, Hamburg, Germany, 1954-56. Teaching fellow Yale U. Sch. Music, New Haven, Conn., 1948-49; instr. music theory U.S. Naval Sch. Music, Washington, 1953-54; post music dir. Ft. Dix, N.J., 1956-57; faculty Antioch Coll., Yellow Springs, Ohio, 1957-76, prof., 1967-76, chmn. music dept., 1967-71; vis. prof. music U. Wash. Sch. Music, 1969-70, Lamont Sch. Music, U. Denver, 1975-76; composer-in-residence Colo. Music Festival, 1980, Arcosanti, 1986; vis. composer Aspen Music Festival, 1987; prof. music, composer-in-residence Lamont Sch. Music, U. Denver, 1975-99, Phipps Prof. in the humanities, 1982-85, prof. emeritus, 1999—. Concerts devoted solely to his music often with his participation as pianist, London, 1973, Tel Aviv, 1973, Jerusalem, 1973, N.Y.C., 1975, Denver, 1984, 91; Composer: Sonata for Clarinet and Piano, 1948, String Trio, 1948, Divertimento for Winds and Strings, 1949, The Naming of Cats, 1951, The Hollow Men, 1951, String Quartet 1, 1952, Concert Piece for Orchestra, 1952, Variations for Piano, 1955, First Symphony, 1957, Piano Sonata, 1960, An Elegiac Symphony, 1962, Anyone Lived in a Pretty How Town, 1965, String Quartet 2, 1965; ballet New Work, 1966; Polarities for Violin and Piano, 1968-70, A Love Triptych, 1970, Dialogue for Piano, and Winds, 1973, Diptych for Cello and Piano, 1975, Upon the Intimation of Love's Mortality, 1975, Branchings for Orch., 1976, Four Puerto Rican Love Songs: Tierras del Alma for soprano, flute and guitar, 1978, Musica Instrumentalis for chamber group, 1980, Concerto for Piano and Orch., 1990, Revisitations for Violin, Cello and Piano, 1992, Elegy for chamber orch., 1995, Fanfare for Brass, 1996, String Quartet No. 3, 2001. Served with U.S. Army, 1952-54. Recipient ASCAP awards, 1964— ; awards from Ford, Danforth and Lilly founds., Nat. Endowment for Arts; winner Rockefeller Found. Symphonic Competitions, 1965, 66; Guggenheim fellow Europe, 1964-65, 72-73; Nat. Endowment for Arts grantee, fellow, 1975; Fulbright Scholar, 1954-56. Mem. ASCAP, Am. Music Ctr., Phi Beta Kappa. Home: 12854 Buckhorn Rd Littleton CO 80127 E-mail: dkeats@du.edu.

KEATS, GLENN ARTHUR, manufacturing company executive; b. Chgo., July 1, 1920; s. Herbert J. and Agnes H. (Streich) K.; m. Olga Maria Loor Hurtado, Feb. 13, 1946; children; Maria Susana Keats Eggemeyer, Allwyn Dolores Keats Nagel. BS in Commerce, Northwestern U., 1941. Sales exec. Keats-Lorenz Spring Co., Chgo., 1947-56; contr., auditor Plantaciones Ecuatorianas, S.A., Guayaquil, Ecuador, 1956-58; co-founder Keats Mfg. Co., Wheeling, Ill., 1958—. Lt. comdr. USN, 1941—47. Mem. Spring Mfrs. Inst., Northwestern U. Alumni Assn., Sigma Nu. Clubs: Evanston Golf, Amelia Island (Fla.). Republican. Lutheran. Home: 368 Woodland Rd Highland Park IL 60035-5055 Office: 350 Holbrook Dr Wheeling IL 60090-5812 E-mail: gkeats@keatsmfg.com.

KEATS, JONATHON, writer; b. N.Y.C., Oct. 2, 1971; s. Andrew Terry Keats, Adrienne Schlossberg. BA, Amherst Coll., Mass., 1994. Art critic San Francisco Mag., 1997—; books columnist San Francisco Examiner, 2002—. Writer-in-residence Ucross Found., Clearmont, Wyo., 2002, U. Ariz. Poetry Ctr., Tucson, 2000, Yaddo, Saratoga Springs, NY, 2003. Author: (novels) The Pathology of Lies, 1999, The Salon.com Reader's Guide to Contemporary Authors, 2000; contbr. book (nonfiction); creator: Twenty Four Hour Cogito, 2000, Every Entity Is Identical to Itself, 2002; composer: 1,001 Concertos for Tuning Forks and Audience, 2002; contbr. Mem.: The Last Supper Soc., The Philos. Soc. of San Francisco (Founding Member), Nat. Book Critics Cir. (bd. dirs.). Home: 1276 Jackson St #3 San Francisco CA 94109 Personal E-mail: jonathon_keats@yahoo.com.

KEATS, THEODORE ELIOT, physician, radiology educator; b. New Brunswick, N.J., June 26, 1924; m. Margaret E. McNamara, Aug. 27, 1949 (dec.); children: Matthew Mason, Ian Stuart B.; m. Patricia L. Hart, Mar. 30, 1974. BS, Rutgers U., 1945; MD, U. Pa., 1947. Diplomate: Am. Bd. Radiology (trustee). Intern U. Pa. Hosp., Phila., 1947-48; resident U. Mich. Hosp., Ann Arbor, 1948-51; instr. U. Calif. Sch. Medicine, San Francisco, 1953-54, asst. prof., 1954-56; assoc. prof. U. Mo. Sch. Medicine, Columbia, 1956-59, prof. radiology, 1959-63, U. Va. Sch. Medicine, Charlottesville, 1963—, chmn. dept. radiology, 1963-92, alumni prof. radiology, 1992—. Vis. prof. Karolinska Hosp., Stockholm, 1963-64. Author: Atlas of Roentgenographic Measurement, 7th edit., 2001 (with Christopher Sistrom), An Atlas of Normal Roentgen Variants That May Simulate Disease, 7th edit., 2001, Self-Assessment of Current Knowledge in Diagnostic Radiology, 2d edit., 1980, An Atlas of Normal Developmental Roentgen Anatomy, 1978, 2d edit., 1988, (with Thomas H. Smith) Radiology of Musculoskeletal Injury, 1990; editor-in-chief Current Problems in Diagnostic Radiology, 1981, 2001, Emergency Radiology, 1984, 2d edit., 1989, Applied Radiology, 1989-2001; Am. editor Skeletal Radiology, 1987-97; editor Emergency Radiology, 1993-2001. Served with AUS, 1943-47; to capt., M.C. AUS, 1951-53. Fellow Am. Coll. Radiology (Gold medal 1995); mem. AMA, Am. Roentgen Ray Soc., Radiol. Soc. N.Am., Soc. Pediatric Radiology (hon.), So. Med. Assn., Internat. Skeletal Soc. (medal 1995), Soc. Emergency Radiology (gold medal 1999), Phi Beta Kappa, Sigma Xi, Alpha Omega Alpha. Home: 421 Key West Dr Charlottesville VA 22911-8423 Office: U Va Hosps Lee St Rm 1831 Charlottesville VA 22911 also: U Va Sch Medicine Dept Radiology Charlottesville VA 22908-0001 E-mail: ted@averymed.virginia.edu.

KEATY, ROBERT BURKE, business consultant; b. Baton Rouge, July 7, 1949; s. Thomas St. Paul and Alicia (Armshaw) K.; m. Erin Kenny, July 6, 1973; children: Kellen Elizabeth, Kathryn Ellen, Robert Burke II, Kaneil Erin, Rory Bridgette-Anne. BS, U. La., 1971; JD, Tulane U., 1974. Law clk. to judge U.S. Dist. Ct. for Ea. Dist. La., New Orleans, 1974-76. Mem. pres.'s com. Offshore Tng. and Survival Ctr., U. Lafayette, 1988-89; co-chmn. United Giver Fund Jud. Legal, 1994, Bishops Charity Ball Legal Com., 1995. Member dean's adv. com. Tulane U. Law Sch., New Orleans, 1987; mem. dean's exec. adv. com. Coll. Bus. Adminstrn., U. La., Lafayette, 1991. Sears scholar, 1971, Teagle scholar, 1973; recipient Most Outstanding Alumnus award U. La. Coll. Bus., Lafayette, 1991. Fellow La. Bar Found. (lifetime charter mem.). Avocations: reading, woodworking, tennis, fishing, carpentry.

KEAY, CHARLES LLOYD, elementary school educator; b. Cleve., Dec. 12, 1959; s. Richard Thomas and Betty Eleanor (Dixon) K. BS, Kent (Ohio) State U., 1984; postgrad., U. West L.A., 1984-86; MS, Nat. U., San Diego, 1990. Tchr. L.A. Unified Sch. Dist., 1985-90, Euclid (Ohio) Pub. Schs., 1990—. Exch. tchr. Nahara-Machi, Japan, 1998-99. With U.S. Army, 1978-82. Mem. ASCD, NEA, Ohio Edn. Assn., Soka GAkki Internat. (culture dept.), Euclid Tchrs. Assn., United Tchrs. L.A. (co-chmn. local chpt.). Home: 23651 Glenbrook Blvd Euclid OH 44117-1960 also: 2-1 Aza Kanetsukido Ohaza-Kitada Naraha-Machi Fukushima-ken 979-06 Japan E-mail: ckeay@aol.com.

KEBBEDE, ANTENEH, materials scientist, researcher; s. Kebbede Tiku and HaregeWein Kebede; m. Kidist M. Mekonnen; 1 child, Maraki A. BSc, Addis Ababa (Ethiopia) U., 1988; MS, Queen's U., Kingston, Ont., Can., 1994; PhD, Pa. State U., 1999. Asst. lectr. Addis Ababa U., 1988—92; grad./tchg. asst. Queen's U., Kingston, 1992—94, Pa. State U., University Park, 1995—99; staff scientist Gen. Electric Global Rsch., Niskayuna, NY, 1999—. Fellow, Queen's U. and Can. Internat. Devel. Agy., 1992—94. Mem.: The Am. Ceramic Soc., Sima Xi (assoc.). Achievements include patents pending for ceramic short arc lamp (2); Repair technology for ceramic matrix composites; research in Grain Boundary Microstructure in Titania-Doped Alpha-Alumina; Microstructural Evolution in Alpha-Alumina with Small Titania and Silica Additions. Office: General Electric Global Research One Research Circle Niskayuna NY 12309

KEBBLISH, JOHN BASIL, retired coal company executive, consultant; b. Gray, Pa., Jan. 14, 1925; s. Joseph and Catherine (Benya) K.; m. Ruth L. Mueller, Oct. 14, 1955; children: John J., Heather R. BS in Mining Engring., Pa. State U., 1947, BSEE, 1948. With Consol. Coal Co. (and subs. cos.), various locations, 1948-71; pres. Pocahontas Fuel Co. divsn. Consol. Coal Co., Bluefield, W. Va., 1966-70; v.p. Consol. Coal Co., Pitts., 1970-71; exec. v.p. The Pittston Co., N.Y.C., 1971-73; pres., CEO Ashland (Ky.) Coal, Inc. subs. Ashland, Coal, 1974-87, also bd. dirs.; v.p., exec. officer Ashland Oil, Inc., 1976-87. Cons. in field. With AUS, 1944-46.

KECECIOGLU, DIMITRI BASIL, reliability engineering educator, consultant; b. Istanbul, Turkey, Dec. 26, 1922; came to U.S., 1946, naturalized, 1956; s. Basil C. and Mary (Melayios) K.; m. Lorene June Legan, Dec. 22, 1951; children: Zoe Diana Kececioglu Draelos, John Dimitri. BS, Robert Coll., Istanbul, 1942; MS, Purdue U., 1948, PhD, 1953. Asst. instr. Purdue U., Lafayette, Ind., 1943-47, instr., 1947-52; engring. scientist in charge mech. research labs. Allis-Chalmers Mfg. Co., Milw., 1952-57, asst. to dir. mech. engring. industries group, 1957-60, cons. engr. industries group, 1960-63, dir. corp. reliability program, 1960-63; prof. aerospace and mech. engring. U. Ariz., Tucson, 1963—, prof.-in-charge reliability engring. program, 1963—. Reliability and maintainability engring. cons., Tucson, 1963— ; dir. Reliability Engring. and Mgmt. Inst., 1963—, Reliability Testing Inst., 1975— ; applied reliability engring. and product assurance cons. Northrop Space Labs., Gen. Elec. Co., Center for Mgmt. and Indsl. Devel., Rotterdam, Netherlands, Delco Radio div. Gen. Motors Corp., Aerojet-Gen. Corp., Westinghouse Elec. Co., U.S. Army Mgmt. Engring. Tng. Agy., Allied Signal, Data General, Polaroid, Storage Tek, Motorola, Digital Equipment, ITT, B.F. Goodrich, Gen. Dynamics, Xerox, Ford, JPL, Bendix, Cummins Engine, MOOG, Copeland, Eastman Kodak, Allied Chem. and many others; Fulbright lectr. Nat. Tech. U., Athens, 1971-72; sr. extension tchr. UCLA, 1983; hon. prof. Shanghai U. Tech., 1984; assoc. prof. Tech. U. Bordeaux, France; vis. prof. reliability engring. UCLA. Author: Bibliography on Plasticity, 1950, Introduction to Probabilistic Design for Reliability, 1975, Manual of Product Assurance Films and Videotapes, 1980, Reliability Engineering Handbook, Vols. 1-2, 1991, 7th printing, 1997, The 1992-94 Reliability Maintainability and Availability Software Handbook, 1992, Reliability and Life Testing Handbook, Vols. 1-2, 1993, 94, 2nd printing, 1997, Environmental Stress Screening, 1995, Burn-in Testing, 1997, Maintainability, Availability and Operational Readiness Engineering Handbook Vol. 1, 1995, Robust Engineering Design by Reliability, Vol. 1, 2002; contbr. more than 148 articles to profl. jours.; patentee in field. Founder, fund raiser Dr. Dimitri Basil Kececioglu Reliability Engring. Rsch. Fellowships Endowment Fund, 1987. Recipient Presidency award Milw. Tech. Coun., 1962, Automotive Industries Author award, 1963, Ralph E. Teetor Outstanding Engring. Educator award Soc. Automotive Engrs., 1977, Anderson prize U. Ariz., 1983, U. Ariz. Scholarship Devel. Office award, 1991, Acad. of Achievement award in edn. Am. Hellenic Ednl. Progressive Assn., 1991-92. Fellow Soc. Automotive Engrs. (Disting. Probabilistic Methods Educator award 1997), Am. Soc. for Quality, Soc. Reliability Engrs. (founder, pres. Tucson chpt. 1974-77); mem. ASME (chmn. Milw. sect. 1960), IEEE, Soc. Exptl. Stress Analysis (chmn. Milw. sect. 1957), Am. Hellenic Ednl. Progressive Assn. (Acad. Achievement award in edn. 1992), Am. Soc. Engring. Edn., Am. Soc. Quality Control (Reliability Edn. Advancement award 1980, Allen Chop award for outstanding contbns. to reliability 1981), Hellenic Ops. Rsch. Soc. Greece, Phi Beta Kappa (hon.), Sigma Xi (pres. Univ. chpt. 1990-91), Tau Beta Pi, Phi Kappa Phi (pres. U. Ariz. chpt. 1988-89), Nat. Golden Key Soc. (hon.). Home: 7340 N La Oesta Ave Tucson AZ 85704-3119

KECHIJIAN, PAUL, dermatologist, educator; b. Providence, Mar. 17, 1940; s. Harry Maderos and Annette (Rhia) Paré; m. Janice Ann Kechijian, July 31, 1976; children: Douglas Paul, Lisa Ann. AB in Psychology, Brown U., 1961, ScM in Biology, 1964; MD, Albany Med. Coll., 1968. Lic. Nat. Bd. Med. Examiners, N.Y. State Med. Lic.; diplomate Am. Bd. Dermatology, diplomate Dermatopathology Am. Bds. of Dermatology and Pathology. Med. intern, med. resident Barnes Hosp., St. Louis, 1968-69, 69-70; dermatology resident Mass. Gen. Hosp., Boston, 1970, Univ. Miami (Fla.) Sch. of Medicine, 1973-75; dermatopathology fellow NYU Med. Ctr., N.Y.C., 1975-76; instr. clin. dermatology NYU Sch. of Medicine, N.Y.C., 1975-78, clin. asst. prof. dermatology, 1978-84, clin. assoc. prof., 1984—2002; asst. attending physician to assoc. attending physician Bellevue Hosp., 1976-81, 81—, NYU Med. Ctr., 1976-84, 84—; asst. attending dermatologist to sr. asst. North Shore Univ. Hosp., 1978-87, 87—. Chief inpatient dermatology svc. Bellevue Hosp., 1976—86; cons. Holy Martyrs Armenian Day Sch., 1976—; hon. surgeon (dermatology) N.Y.C. Police Dept., 1981—; chief nail sect. NYU Med. Ctr., 1983—2002; presenter and lectr. in field. Contbg. editor: Jour. Dermatologic Surgery and Oncology, 1983-85; contbr. reports and articles to profl. jours. and chpt. to books. Fellow ACP, Am. Acad. Dermatology (com. on evaluation 1980-84, coun. on govtl. liaison key contact program 1986—), Am. Soc. Dermatopathology; mem. AMA, N.Y. Acad. Scis., Dermatology Found., Soc. for Investigative Dermatology, Nassau County Med. Soc., L.I. Dermatol. Soc., Soc. for Dermatol. Surgery, Internat. Soc. for Tropical Dermatology, Internat. Soc. Dermatol. Surgery, others. Office: 935 Northern Blvd Great Neck NY 11021-5309 E-mail: kech1@optonline.net.

KECK, DONALD BRUCE, physicist; b. Lansing, Mich., Jan. 2, 1941; s. William G. and Zelda D. Keck; m. Ruth A. Moilanen, July 10, 1965; children: Lynne Ann Vaia, Brian William. BS, Mich. State U., 1962, MS, 1964, PhD, 1967. With Corning (N.Y.) Glass Works, 1968-76, mgr. applied physics, 1976-86; dir. optics and photonics Corning, Inc., 1986-91, v.p., dir. optics and photonics, 1997—2000, v.p., exec. dir. rsch., 2000—02; chief tech. officer Infotonic Tech. Cu., 2002—. Bd. dirs. PCO, Inc., L.A.; lectr. in field. Editor: Jour. Lightwave Tech., 1989—94, co-author (5 books on optical fibers) ; contbr. more than 150 to profl. jours. Chmn. planning bd. Town of Corning, 1990—; mem. adv. bd. Corning Salvation Army; moderator 1st Congl. Ch., Corning, 1986—87, 1991—92; bd. dirs. ARC-Corning chpt., 1995—, Cmty. Found., 2000—; chmn. troop com. Boy Scouts Am., Corning, 1968—71; pres. Civic Music Assn., Corning, 1971—75; bd. dirs. Nat. Inventors Hall of Fame Found., 1994—, pres., 2001—02; bd. dirs. Nat. Inventors Hall of Fame, 2000—, sec., 2002, vice chair, 2003. Recipient Tech. Achievement award Internat. Soc. Optical Engring., 1981, IR-100 award Indsl. Rsch., 1981, Engring. Achievement award Am. Soc. Metals, 1983, Am. Innovator award, 1995, John Tyndall award IEEE/Optical Soc. Am., 1992, Disting. Alumni award Mich. State U., 1996, Lauren Publishing, "Distinction in Photonics" award, 2002, Nat. medal of Tech., U.S. Pres., 2000; inductee Nat. Innovators Hall of Fame, 1993; Paul Harris fellow Rotary Internat., 1998. Fellow IEEE, OSA, Optical Soc. Am. (bd. dirs. 1994-96), Nat. Acad. Engring., Opto-Electronics Industry Devel. Assn. (bd. chmn. 1999-2002). Achievements include 36 patents in field. Avocations: water and snow skiing, music, woodworking. Home: 2877 Chequers Cir Big Flats NY 14814-9610 E-mail: dkeck@stny.rr.com.

KECK, JUDITH MARIE BURKE, business owner, retired career officer; b. Springfield, Ohio, Feb. 24, 1938; d. John T. and Mary Elizabeth (Kaliher) Burke; m. Henry J. Reinhardt, Feb. 22, 1958 (div.); 1 child, Lucy L.; m. James E. Keck, Feb. 18, 1978. BS in Mgmt., Park Coll., 1983; MA in Mgmt., Cen. Mich. U., 1985; postgrad., Def. Systems Mgmt. Coll., 1986, Air War Coll., 1989; PhD, Pacific Western U., 1990. Commd. GM-14 USAF, 1969, billeting officer, 1969-72; commissary officer Edwards AFB, Calif., 1972-74; procurement agt. George AFB, Calif., 1974-76; chief contract adminstrn. Nellis AFB, Nev., 1976-78; chief svcs. contracting Grand Forks AFB, N.D., 1978-81; contracting officer aero. systems div./air launched cruise missile div. Wright Patterson AFB, Ohio, 1981-85; program mgr. aero. sys. divsn./B-1 Bomber, 1985-87; program mgr. aero. sys. divsn. project Tomorrow, 1987-94; chief acquisition mgmt. HQ. aero. sys. divsn., 1990-94; pres., CEO Thread Bear Monograms, San Antonio. Instr. systems mgmt. Air Force Inst. Tech., Wright Patterson AFB, 1985, quality assurance, 1981; dir. fed. women's program George AFB, 1976. Mem. aero. systems divsn. Exec. Combined Fed. Campaign, 1989—. Mem. Am. Assn. for Artificial Intelligence, Nat. Contract Mgmt. Assn., Air Force Assn., Nat. Assn. Mil. Comptrollers, NAFE, Sigma Iota Epsilon. Democrat. Avocations: hunting, fishing, gardening. Home: 9139 Powhatan Dr San Antonio TX 78230-4401 Fax: 210-340-5616. E-mail: jthreadbear@swbell.com.

KECK, RAY MARVIN, III, academic administrator; b. San Antonio, Feb. 20, 1948; s. Ray Marvin, Jr. and Joyce Littlepage Keck; m. Patricia Cigarroa, Mar. 25, 1977; children: Teresa Cigarroa, Joyce Cigarroa, Lacey Cigarroa. BA, Princeton U., N.J., 1969, PhD, 1978. Instr. in Spanish, chair dept. of modern lang. The Hotchkiss Sch., Lakeville, Conn., 1970—78; internat. banking officer Union Nat. Bank, Laredo, Tex., 1978—79; asst. prof. spanish, asst. to the pres. Laredo State U., Tex., 1979—83; chair fgn. lang. dept. Episcopal HS, Alexandria, Va., 1983—87, Potomac Sch., McLean, Va., 1987—89; dir. upper sch. St. Anne's Belfield Sch., Charlottesville, Va., 1989—93; assoc. prof. Spanish Tex. A&M Internat. U., Laredo, Tex., 1994—99, assoc. prof. Spanish, chair dept. of lnaguage, lit. and arts, 1997—99, provost and v.p. academic affairs, 1999—2001, pres., 2001—. Author: (book) Love's Dialect, (jour. article) Jour. of Higher Edn. Vol. I, No. I. Mem.: Am. Assn. of State Colls. and Univs., Assn. of Tex. Colls. and Univs., Tex. Higher Edn. Coun. of Pres., Laredo Rotary Club. Office: Texas A & M Internat U 5201 Univ Blvd Laredo TX 78041 Office Fax: 956-326-2319. E-mail: president@tamiu.edu.

KECKEL, PETER J. advertising executive; b. Berlin, Dec. 13, 1942; came to U.S., 1956; s. F. Paul and Frieda G. (Schmidt) K.; m. Katherine Alice Brown, Nov. 27, 1971. BS in Polit. Sci., postgrad., U. Md., 1966; grad., U.S. Infantry Sch., Ft. Benning, Ga., 1967; grad. advanced officers course, Adjutant Gens. Sch., Ft. Ben Harrison, Ind., 1971. Exec. dir. Med. Personnel Pool, Oklahoma City, 1973-74; regional dir. Medox div. Drake Internat., Oklahoma City, 1974-78; pres., owner Okla. Communities, Inc., Edmond, 1978—, Okla. Gold Jewelry, Inc., Edmond, 1982—. Mktg. cons. to various orgns. and groups, 1978—. Bd. dirs. Edmond YMCA, 1980-81, Okla. Disaster Edn. Fund, 1995—. Served to capt. U.S. Army, 1966-73, Vietnam. Decorated Bronze Star; recipient Presdl. Vietnam Veterans Outstanding Community Achievement award Pres. Carter, 1979; received Key to the City of Garland, Tex. Mem. Am. Bus. Clubs (life; bd. dirs. 1979—, pres. 1985-86, chmn. bd. dirs. 1986-87, regional big hat chmn. 1986-87, 2d dist. gov. 1989-90, nat. big hat pres. 1991-92, mem. nat. new club bldg. com., Mr. Ambuc awards 1980-81, 83-84, 87-88, dist. 1987-88, Nat. Ambuc of Yr. 1988-89, top nat. mem. recruiter 1982—, top nat. fundraiser, excellence award 1982-83, #1 club pres. in country 1985-86, chartered New Ambucs chpt., 1988), U. Md. Alumni Assn. (life.), POW-MIA Orgn., Edmond C. of C. (life; officer, awards), Rep. Presdl. Task Force (life) and others. Clubs: Edmond Soccer (v.p., bd. dirs. 1977-79, coach, referee 1976-82). Republican. Lutheran. Avocations: sports, travel, music, community activities, foreign languages. Home: 908 E 10th St Edmond OK 73034-5451 Office: Okla Communities Inc 222 E 10th St Plz Edmond OK 73034-4737

KECSKES, ISTVAN, linguist, educator; b. Miskolc, Hungary, Sept. 20, 1947; s. Istvan Kecskes and Ilona Juhasz; m. Tunde Papp, July 11, 1970; children: Andras Istvan, Tunde Kinga. MA in English Lang. and Lit., Kossuth U., Debrecen, Hungary, 1972, PhD in Comparative Linguistics, 1977; degree in applied linguistics, Hungarian Acad. Scis., Budapest, Hungary, 1986. Founding chair, prof. English linguistics Berzsenyi Coll., Szombathely, Hungary, 1990—93; prof. English linguistics U. of Mont., Missoula, 1993—99; dir. TESOL grad. programs SUNY, Albany, 1999—, chmn. acad. coun. Sch. Edn., 2001—. Fulbright prof. Brigham Young U., Provo, Utah, 1989, U. Mont., 1991—93; Charles Culpepper prof. Duke U., Durham, NC, 1991; vis. prof. U. St. Louis, 1997, Internat. Christian U., Tokyo, 1995, U. Autonoma Barcelona, Barcelona, 2001; established Ctr. European Computer Assisted Learning Lang. Learning Ctr. Berzsenyi Coll., Szombathely, 1991. Author: (book) Let's Talk it Over (in Hungarian), 1989 (Publishers' Prize, 1989), English for Computer Users, 1990, Theoretical Linguistics, Applied Linguistics, Language Teaching, 1991, Situation-Bound Utterances in L1 and L2, 2002; co-author (book) Foreign Language and Mother Tongue, 2000; editor: (book) New Technology Supporting Language Teaching, 1994; editor-in-chief: jour. Intercultural Pragmatics, 2004. Mem.: Am. Assn. of Applied Linguists, TESOL, Internat. Pragmatics Assn. Avocations: tennis, travel, classical music. Home: 4 Meadow Lane Latham NY 12110 Office: SUNY Albany 1400 Washington Ave Albany NY 12222 Office Fax: 518-442-5008. E-mail: ikecskes@uamail.albany.edu.

KEDDIE, NIKKI R. education educator; b. N.Y.C., Aug. 30, 1930; d. Harry and Sarra Ragozin; m. Wells H. Keddie, 1953 (div. 1960). BA, Radcliffe Coll., 1951; MA, Stanford U., 1951; PhD, U. Calif., Berkeley, 1955. Instr. U. Ariz., Tucson, 1957; instr.-asst. prof. Scripps Coll., Claremont, Calif., 1957-61; asst. prof. UCLA, 1961-67, assoc. prof., 1967-72, prof., 1972—. Author: An Islamic Response to Imperialism, 1968, Iran and the Muslim World, 1995, Modern Iran: Roots and Results of Revolution, 2003; co-editor: Women in the Muslim World, 1978, Women in Middle Eastern History, 1991, Iran and the Surrounding World, 2002. Rockefeller fellow Rockefeller Found., Bellagio, 1992, Washington, 1980, 82, fellow Social Sci. Rsch. Coun., Iran, 1966, Guggenheim Found., Iran, 1963-64, Europe, 1959-60; recipient Persian History award Ency. Iranica Found., 2002. Fellow AAAS; mem. Am. Hist. Assn. (award for scholarly distinction 2001), Middle East Studies Assn. (Mentoring award 2001—), Soc. for Iranian Studies. Avocations: art, politics. Office: UCLA Dept Of History Los Angeles CA 90095-0001

KEDDIE, ROLAND THOMAS, physician, hospital administrator, lawyer; b. Altoona, Pa., Oct. 21, 1928; s. John Barkeley and Jessie E. (Keddie) Isenberg; m. Suzanne M. Seno, Feb. 6, 1978; 1 child, Dawn Michelle; children by previous marriage: Roland, Thomas, Francis, Robert, Michael, Karen, Andrew, Rosemary. BS cum laude, U. Pitts., 1956, MD, 1957, JD, 1970. Diplomate Am.

Bd. Family Practice. Bar: Pa. 1970. Intern St. Josephs Hosp., Pitts., 1958; practice medicine specializing in emergency medicine and family practice. Med. dir. Westmoreland Manor, Greensburg, Pa., 1971; dir. emergency dept. Connemaugh Valley Meml. Hosp., Johnston, Pa., 1976-77, Shadyside Hosp., Pitts., 1978-80, chmn. dept. emergency services McKeesport (Pa.) Hosp., 1980-83, dir. emergency medicine residency program; pres. EmergiCenters Inc., 1983-97; chmn. dept. family practice St. Clair Hosp., Pitts., 1990-93; pres. Emergency Med. Svcs. Inst., 1982-85; adj. prof. U. Pitts. Sch. Nursing; cons. in field. Served with USN, 1946-47, 50-52. Mem. Am. Coll. Emergency Physicians (life, bd. dirs. Pa. chpt. 1977-81, 83-86, v.p. 1980-81, pres. 1985-86), Pa. Med. Soc., Hosp. Assn. Pa. (mem. profl. practice com. 1981-82), Allegheny County Bar Assn., AMA (Physicians Recognition award 1974, 77, 80), Allegheny County Med. Soc., Pa. Emergency Health Services Council (dir. 1980), Soc. Tchrs. Emergency Medicine, Beta Beta Beta. Roman Catholic. Home and Office: 45 Meadowcrest Dr Cecil PA 15321-1118 E-mail: RTKeddie@msn.com.

KEE, BRENDA ELTRINE, music educator, concert pianist; b. Raleigh, NC, July 25, 1944; d. Thomas Edward Kee, Sr. and Elnora McCrimmon Kee; m. Wayne Stanley Brown, June 6, 1981; children: Alanna Kee Brown, Colin Kee Brown. MusB, Oberlin Coll. Conservatory Music, 1962—66; MusM, U. Ill., Urbana, 1968—70; D Mus. Arts, U. Mich., Ann Arbor, 1972—77. Music tchr. Sch. Dist. Phila., 1966—68; instr. music Bennett Coll., Greensboro, NC, 1970—72; asst. prof. music Norfolk State U., Va., 1978—81; asst. prof. piano Mt. Holyoke Coll., South Hadley, Mass., 1981—86, U. Louisville, 1987—90, assoc. prof. piano, 1990—98, prof. piano and chair keyboard/vocal performance dept., 1998—. Bd. dirs. Chamber Music Soc. Louisville, 1988—, dir. Macauley Chamber Music Competition, 1995—; classical roots com. Louisville Orch., 1990—96. Musician piano and chamber music recitals, lecture-recitals, piano workshops and master classes. Elder Highland Presbyn. Ch., Louisville, 2001—. Named one of Outstanding Young Women of Am., 1980; recipient Disting. Tchg. Fellow Award, U. Mich., 1975; fellow John Hay Whitney Fellowship, John Hay Whitney Found., 1968. Mem.: Greater Louisville Music Teachers Assn. (v.p. programs 1988—90, pres. 1990—92, exec. bd. 1988—94), Ky. Music Teachers Assn. (certification chair 2000—, exec. bd. 1990—94, 2000—), Music Teachers Nat. Assn., Louisville Chpt. Jack and Jill Am., Inc. (v.p. 1996—2000), Louisville Chpt. The Links, Inc., Pi Kappa Lambda, Delta Sigma Theta. Home: 2904 Carlingford Dr Louisville KY 40222 Office: Uf Louisville Sch Music Louisville KY 40292 Office Fax: 502-852-0520. E-mail: bekee001@louisville.edu.

KEE, HOWARD CLARK, religion educator; b. Beverly, N.J., July 28, 1920; s. Walter Leslie and Regina (Corcoran) K.; m. Janet Burrell, Dec. 15, 1951; children: Howard Clark III, Christopher Andrew, Sarah Leslie. AB, Bryan (Tenn.) Coll., 1940; Th.M., Dallas Theol. Sem., 1944; postgrad., Am. Sch. Oriental Research, Jerusalem, 1949-50; PhD (Two Bros. fellow), Yale, 1951. Instr. religion and classics U. Pa., 1951-53; from asst. prof. to prof. N.T. Drew U., 1953-68; Rufus Jones prof. history of religion, chmn. dept. history of religion Bryn Mawr (Pa.) Coll., 1968-77; William Goodwin Aurelio prof. Biblical studies Boston U., 1977-89, chmn. grad. div. religious studies, 1977-86; sr. rsch. fellow U. Pa., 1987—. Vis. prof. religion Princeton U., 1954-55, Brown U., 1985; vis. lectr. U. of Durham, 1987, Claremont Sch. of Theology, 1991; Rsch. scholar, Miss. state U., 1992, vis. scholar, Princeton Theological Seminary, 1993; mem. archaeol. teams at Roman Jericho, 1950, Shechem, 1957, Mt. Gerizim, 1966, Pella, Jordan, 1967, Ashdod, Israel, 1968; chmn. Coun. on Grad. Studies in Religion; cons. for transls. Am. Bible Soc., 1989—. Author: Understanding the New Testament, 1957, 4th edit., 1983, 5th edit., 1992, Making Ethical Decisions, 1958, The Renewal of Hope, 1959, Jesus and God's New People, 1959, Jesus in History, 1970, 3d edit., 1995, The Origins of Christianity: Sources and Documents, 1973, The Community of the New Age, 1977, Christianity: An Historical Approach, 1979, Christian Origins in Sociological Perspective, 1980, Miracle in the Early Christian World, 1983, The New Testament in Context: Sources and Documents, 1984, Medicine, Miracle and Magic in New Testament Times, 1986, Knowing the Truth: A Sociological Approach to New Testament Interpretation, 1989, What Can We Know About Jesus?, 1990, Good News to the Ends of the Earth: The Theology of Acts, 1990, Christianity: A Social and Cultural History, 1991, 2d edit., 1998, Who Are the People of God? Early Christian Models of Community, 1995, To Every Nation Under Heaven: The Acts of the Apostles, 1997; editor: Biblical Perspectives on Current Issues, 1976-83, Understanding Jesus Today, 1985—; editor Cambridge UP Annotated Study Bible, 1993, Cambridge Annotated Study Apocrypha, 1994, Cambridge Companion to the Bible, 1997, Removing Anti-Judaism From the New Testament, 1996, Removing Anti-Judaism From the Pulpit, 1998, The Evollution of the Synagogue, 1999; librettist: New Land, New Covenant (Howard Hanson), 1976; contbr.: Interpreter's Dictionary of the Bible, 1962, supplement, 1976, Harper's Bible Dictionary, Dictionary of Bible and Religion, The Books of the Bible, Anchor Bible Dictionary. Bd. mgrs. Am. Bible Soc., 1956-89, chmn. transls. com., 1985-89; chmn. transls. com. United Bible Socs., 1985-89; bd. dirs. Mohawk Trail Concerts, Inc., Charlemont, Mass.; mem. adv. bd. Yale U. Inst. Sacred Music; exec. bd. Liberty Mus. Am. Assn. Theol. Schs. fellow Germany, 1960; Guggenheim fellow Israel, 1966-67; Nat. Endowment Humanities grantee Eng., 1984 Mem. Soc. Values in Higher Edn., Phila. Seminar on Christian Origins, Am. Acad. Religion, Soc. Bibl. Lit., Bibl. Theologians, Studiorum Novi Testamenti Societas, New Haven Theol. Discussion Group, Assn. for Sociology of Religion (pres.), Am. Interfaith Inst. (pres.). Presbyterian. Home: 3300 Darby Rd Haverford PA 19041-1061 *Life is a gift from the Creator. It is mediated to us through parents, family, friends, teachers. It is conveyed through love and learning, through challenge and conflict, through accomplishment and disappointment. The gift must be shared, not jealously guarded or proudly prized. By sharing life, we can approach others with candor and honesty, with joy and sympathy, with wonder and understanding. The shared gift brings gratitude and fulfillment.*

KEE, LEE SHAU, real estate developer; married; 5 children. With Henderson Land Devel., Hong Kong; chmn. Hong Kong & China Gas. Avocation: golfing. Office: 23d Fl 363 Java Rd Northpoint Hong Kong China

KEE, WALTER ANDREW, former government official; b. Phila., July 12, 1914; s. Walter Leslie and Regina Veronica (Corcoran) K.; m. Genevieve O'Hair, Dec. 2, 1943; children: Kathleen, Sheila. BS, Purdue U., 1949; M.L.S., Columbia U., 1950. Engring. and phys. sci. librarian N.Y. U., N.Y.C., 1950-51; librarian E.I. DuPont de Nemours, Savannah River Lab., Aiken, S.C., 1951-55; head library and documents sect. Martin Co., Balt., 1955-59; chief library br. AEC, Washington, 1959-74; librarian ERDA, Washington, 1975-76, asst. to dir. div. adminstrv. services, 1976-77, also Freedom of Info. and Privacy Act officer, 1975-77; dir. div. publs. mgmt. Dept. Energy, 1977-78; ret., 1978. Chmn. AEC-Dept. of Def. Joint Atomic Weapon Tech. Info. Group, 1962-72. Contbr.: chpt. to Special Librarianship: A New Reader (Eugene Jackson), 1980. Asst. to chief So. Shores Fire Dept.; sec. Dare County Firemen's Assn., 1980—83; historian So. Shores Civic Assn.; legis. officer Alamance County, N.C. fedn. Nat. Assn. Ret. Fed. Employees, 1994—2002; bd. dirs. Friends Alamance County Librs. Mem. Fed. Library Com., Com. on Sci. and Tech. Info., Spl. Libraries Assn. (cons., pres. nuclear sci. divsn. and info. tech. divsn., pres. Balt. chpt.), Am. Soc. Info. Sci. Home: 1652 Wycliff Ct Burlington NC 27215-8739

KEEBAUGH, MICHAEL D. electronics executive; b. Nov. 1945; m. Andree Keebaugh; 1 child. BA, Pa. State U., 1967, MS, 1971. With HRB Systems, 1976—95; v.p., gen. mgr. Garland operation GRaytheon Co., 1996—98; v.p., gen. mgr. imagery and geospatial systems for the command, control, comm. and info. systems Raytheon Co., Garland, Tex., 1998—2002, pres. intelligence and info. systems, 2002—. Office: Raytheon Co 1200 S Jupiter Rd Garland TX 75042*

KEEBLER, LOIS MARIE, elementary school educator; b. Jasper, Ala., Nov. 24, 1955; d. Roosevelt T. and Marie (Smiley) K. Student, Cen. State U., Wilberforce, Ohio; cert., North Ala. Regional Hosps., 1981. Cert. tchr., Ala. Tchr. Mamani Vallied Children Devel. Ctr., Dayton, Ohio. Vol. pub. schs. Democrat. Baptist. Avocation: bowling.

KEECH, ELOWYN ANN, interior designer; b. Berrien County, Mich., Oct. 5, 1937; d. Earl Docker and Elizabeth Hall (Paullin) Stephenson; 1 child, Robert Earl Stephenson. Contract and residential interior designer. Print designer, 1957-75; freelance interior designer, photoset and video set designer, 1975—; owner Fog Horn Records & Tapes. Trustee Mich. Maritime Mus., 1994—97; bd. dirs., mem. steering and long-range planning coms. United Way Mich., 1980—87; bd. dirs. Blossomland United Way, 1981—86. Mem.: Internat. Interior Design Assn., Miami Heritage Soc., New Territory Arts Alliance, Econ. Club S.W. Mich., Nature Conservancy, Am. Rottweiler Club, Rotary Club.

KEECH, PAMELA, artist, curator; b. Elyria, Ohio, Sept. 21, 1947; d. Paul and Mildred Sievert. BFA, Ohio State U., 1978, MFA, 1980. Asst. prof. U. Akron, Ohio, 1989-90; cons. curator Lower E. Side Tenement Mus., N.Y.C., 1994—; sr. exhbn. preparator Am. Mus. Nat. History, N.Y.C., 1997-98; curator The Women's Mus., Dallas, Tex., 2000—; co-founder cons. firm Curious Curators, 2000. Artist-in-residence The John Kohler Arts Ctr., Sheboygan, Wis., 1993, 2003, The Muse Machine, Dayton, Ohio, 1995; project dir. centennial block N.Y.C. Dept. Transp., 1998, Lower E. Side Tenement Mus., N.Y.C., 1998. One-woman shows include Broadway Windows, N.Y.C., 1992, Antioch Coll., 1995, Lower E. Side Tenement Mus., 1996, U. Conn., 1996, Lower East Side Tenement Mus., 2001. Recipient Rome prize in sculpture Am. Acad. Rome, 1982, Urban Pioneer award Lower E. Side Tenement Mus.; fellow Nat. Endowments Arts, 1982; Rsch. fellow Am. Antiquarian Soc., 1997; Architecture and Design Rsch. grantee N.Y. State Coun. Arts, 1997. Mem.: Am. Assn. Mus., Am. Assn. State and Local History, Soc. Fellows Am. Acad. Rome (v.p. 1993—2000, pres. 2000—, coun. mem.). Office: PKM Studios 451 Greenwich St New York NY 10013-1757 E-mail: pakeech@earthlink.net.

KEEDY, CHRISTIAN DAVID, lawyer; b. Worcester, Mass., Jan. 9, 1945; BBA, Tulane U. La., 1967, JD, 1972. Bar: Fla. 1972; bd. cert. in admiralty and maritime law, Fla. Pvt. practice Christian D. Keedy, P.A., Miami, Fla., 1981—. Mem. ABA, Maritime Law Assn. U.S., Southeastern Admiralty Law Inst. (dir. 1982-83), The Fla. Bar (chmn. 1981-82, 2003—, admiralty law com.), Miami Maritime Arbitration Coun. (dir.). Office: Christian D Keedy PA 7931 SW 59th Ave South Miami FL 33143-5513

KEEFE, ARTHUR THOMAS, III, non-profit fund raising executive; b. N.Y.C., Mar. 1, 1953; s. Arthur Thomas and Marie Lorraine (Bernard) K.; m. Lorene Ann Lion, Aug. 7, 1981; children: Ryan Arthur, Garrett Thomas. BA in Econs., Yale U., 1975. Assoc. dir. The Campaign for Yale U., New Haven, 1976-79; dir. devel. Georgetown Prep., Rockville, Md., 1980-84; dir. resource devel. Greater S.E. Community Hosp., Washington, 1984-86, United Svcs. Orgn., Washington, 1987; dir. devel. Franklin Square Hosp., Balt., 1988-89, The Humane Soc. U.S., Washington, 1990-95; v.p. devel. AOPA Air Safety Found., Frederick, Md., 1995—. Bd. dirs., corp. sec. Nat. Catholic Cmty. Found.; bd. dirs. Allegheny Planned Giving Alliance. Named NCAA All-Am., Inter Collegiate Yacht Racing Assn. N. Am., 1973; recipient Gold Maxi, Direct Mktg. Assn. D.C., 1989. Mem. Nat. Soc. Fund Raising Execs. (cert.), The Planned Giving Study Group Washington, D.C. (pres. 1990-94), Nat. Com. on Planned Giving (bd. com. mem.), Aircraft Owners and Pilots Assn. Republican. Roman Catholic. Avocations: yacht racing, duplicate bridge, numismatics, art collecting. Home: 9017 Willow Valley Dr Potomac MD 20854 Office: AOPA/Air Safety Found 421 Aviation Way Frederick MD 21701-4798 E-mail: arthur.keefe@aopa.org.

KEEFE, CAROLYN JOAN, tax accountant; b. Huntington Park, Oct. 11, 1926; d. Paul Dewey and Mary Jane (Parmater) K. AA, Pasadena (Calif.) City Coll., 1947; BA, U. So. Calif., 1950. Tax acct. Shell Oil Co., L.A., 1950-71, Houston, 1971-91, ret., 1991. Advisor Midwest Mus. of Am. Art, 1993—; vol. Houston Mus. of Fine Arts, 1991—; vol. docent Houston Mus. of Natural Sci., 1991—, Theatre Under the Stars, 1991—, Houston Pub. TV Channel 8, Houston, 1989—; donor 2 ann. coll. scholarships in memory of Paul Dewey and Mary Jane Keefe. Mem. LWV, Inst. Mgmt. Accts. (emeritus life mem.), Desk and Derrick Club (bd. dirs. 1994-95), Houston Alumni Club of Alpha Gamma Delta, USC Houston Alumni Club. Christian Scientist. Avocation: travel. Home: 1814 Auburn Trl Sugar Land TX 77479-6333

KEEFE, JAMES WASHBURN, educational writer, researcher, consultant; b. L.A., Oct. 23, 1931; s. James E. and Leah M. (Washburn) K.; m. Jean Showalter, Dec. 6, 1980. BA Maxima Cum Laude, St. Ambrose Coll., 1953; MusB, Mt. St. Mary's Coll., 1965, MA in Edn., 1966; EdD, U. So. Calif., L.A., 1973. Cert. tchr./adminstr., Calif. Dean of studies Pius X High Sch., Downey, Calif., 1962-67, prin., 1967-75; instr. U. So. Calif., 1972-75; lectr. Loyola Marymount U., L.A., 1975-77, adj. prof. edn., 1977-78; coord. rsch. Nat. Assn. Secondary Sch. Prins., Reston, Va., 1978-80, dir. rsch., 1980-95. Mem. various nat. adv. bds. including Dept. of Edn. Ctr. on Orgn. and Restructuring of Schs., NSSE Evaluative Criteria, Sizer Coalition of Essential Schs. Author: Take Five: A Metholdolgy for the Humane School, 1979, Student Learning Styles: Diagnosing and Prescribing Programs, 1979, Middle Level Principalship, 1981, 83, Student Learning Styles and Brain Behavior, 1982, High School Leaders and their Schools, 1988, 90, Instructional Leadership Handbook, 1984, 91, Learning Style Profile Handbook, 1989, The CASE-IMS School Improvement Process, 1991, Teaching for Thinking, 1992, Leadership in Middle Level Education, 1993, Instruction and the Learning Environment, 1996, Redesigning Schools for the New Century, 1997, Personalized Instruction: Changing Classroom Practice, 2000, Changing the School Learning Environment, 2003. Recipient Disting. Achievement award City of Downey, 1975, Award for Outstanding Ednl. Rsch. Calif. State U., Fullerton, 1992-93, Disting. Svc. award Nat. Cath. Edn. Assn., 1981. Mem. ASCD, Learning Environs. Consortium (pres., forum coord.), Nat. Assn. Secondary Sch. Prins., Nat. Cath. Honor Soc., Phi Delta Kappa. Office: JK Cons Ltd 1419 Belcastle Ct Reston VA 20194-1245

KEEFE, MARGARET JOHNSON, librarian; b. New Britain, Conn., Dec. 10, 1941; d. Edward J. and Margaret Helen (Naczi) Johnson; m. Thomas J. Keefe Jr., Oct. 27, 1966; children: Thomas E., Michael S. AB, Albertus Magnus Coll., New Haven, 1963; MLS, Rutgers U., 1964. Asst. libr.-reference U. R.I., Kingston, 1964-67, head reference dept., 1968-73, coord. pub. svcs., 1974-82, chair pub. svcs. dept., 1982-88, asst. to provost, 1988-89, reference/bibliographer social scis. libr., 1989—, asst. prof., 1971-75, assoc. prof., 1975—, head ref. dept., 2003—. Lectr. libr. techniques cert. program U. R.I., Kingston, 1969-72, lectr. Grad. sch. L.S., 1972-76. Clk., Dist. 4, South Kingston, R.I., 1988-92, moderator, 1992—; sec. South County Youth Soccer Club, South Kingston, 1987—. Mem. ALA, R.I. Libr. Assn., Assn. Coll. and Rsch. Librs. Democrat. Roman Catholic. Avocations: reading, handcrafts (knitting, embroidery), soccer. Home: PO Box 283 Kingston RI 02881-0283

KEEFE, MARY, architectural firm executive; BA, Newton Coll., 1975; MBA, U. of Pa., 1981. Assoc. MGA Ptnrs., Phila., 1991—. Bd. mem. Ctrl. Phila. Devel. Corp., 1997—, exec. com., 2001—02; founding mem. The Salon, 2001—. Mem.: Wharton Alumni Club (bd. mem. 1997—, chair liaison com. 1997—2002). Office: MGA Ptnrs Architects 234 Market St Philadelphia PA 19106 E-mail: mkeefe@mgapartners.com.*

KEEFE, WILLIAM JOSEPH, political science educator; b. Piper City, Ill., Nov. 28, 1925; s. Joseph and Elfreda (Huxtable) K.; m. Martha Marie Schneider, Dec. 22, 1948; children: Kathryn, Robert, Nancy, Mary Jo, John. BS, Ill. State U., 1948; MA, Wayne State U., 1949; PhD, Northwestern U., 1951. Asst. prof. polit. sci. U. Ala., 1951-52; mem. faculty Chatham Coll., Pitts., 1952-68, asso. prof., 1955-61, prof., 1961-68; prof. dept. polit. sci. U. Pitts., 1968—2002, prof. emeritus, 2002—, chmn. dept., 1968-75. Mem. adv. com. Eagleton Inst. Politics, Rutgers U., 1965— Author: (with Morris Ogul) The American Legislative Process: Congress and the States, 10th edit., 2001, Parties, Politics and Public Policy in America, 1972, 9th edit., 2003, Congress and the American People, 1980, 3d edit., 1988, American Democracy, 3d edit., 1990; contbr. articles to profl. jours. Del. Democratic Nat. Conv., 1976. Served with USNR, 1944-46. Mem. Am. Polit. Sci. Assn. (chmn. program com. 1975—, chmn. Congl. fellowship program 1968-75, chmn. Woodrow Wilson award com. 1977, treas. 1981, trustee trust and devel. bd. 1981-85, 90-93), Pi Sigma Alpha (pres. 1998—, mem. exec. coun. 1992-96, pres.-elect 1996-98). Home: 838 7th St Oakmont PA 15139-1429 Office: U Pitts Dept Polit Sci Pittsburgh PA 15260

KEEFER, ELIZABETH J. general counsel; b. New London, Conn., July 3, 1948; d. Edward Boyd and Elizabeth Keefer; m. Richard A. Brown, May 13, 1978; 1 child, Andrew Boyd Keefer Brown. BA cum laude, Barnard Coll., 1969—71; JD mem. Order of Coif, U. Colo., 1966—67, George Wash. U., 1977. Trial atty. Fed. Trade Commn., Wash., DC, 1977—79; assoc. Bergson Borkland Margolis & Adler, Wash., DC, 1979—82; atty. adv. Dept. State, Wash., DC, 1982—86, asst. legal adv., 1986—89; dep. under sec. Internat. Affairs, U.S. Air Force, Wash., DC, 1989—92; ptnr. Hughes Hubbard & Reed, Wash., DC, 1992; dep. gen. counsel Teledyne, L.A., 1995—97; gen. counsel Columbia U., N.Y.C., 1997—. Bd. trustees Mitre Corp., McLean, Va., 2001—. Mem. bd. dirs. Women's Commn. for Women Refugee and Children, N.Y.C., 2003—. Mem.: Am. Corp. Counsel Assn. (mem. bd. dirs. 2001—). Avocations: hiking, theater, tennis. Office: Columbia U 412 Low Libr 535 W 116th St New York NY 10027 Office Fax: 212-864-4947. Business E-Mail: ejk27@columbia.edu.

KEEFER, J(AMES) MICHAEL, lawyer; b. Ft. Wayne, Ind., July 16, 1947; s. James Martin and Helen Patricia (Smith) K.; m. Jan Elaine McDonald, June 3, 1972; children: Christopher, Sean, Alison. AB in Hist., U. Notre Dame, 1969, JD, 1972. Bar: Ind. 1972, U.S. Dist. Ct. (no. and so. dists.) Ind. 1972. With legal dept. Lincoln Nat. Corp., Ft. Wayne, Ind., 1972—2002; 2d v.p., assoc. gen. counsel Lincoln Nat. Corp. and Lincoln Nat. Life Ins. Co., 1982-88, v.p., assoc. gen. counsel, 1988—2002; v.p., gen. counsel and dir. Lincoln Investment Mgmt., Inc., Ft. Wayne, 1997-2000; v.p., dep. gen. counsel Lincoln Nat. Reassurance Co., 2001—02; of counsel Barnes & Thornburg, Ft. Wayne, 2002—03; sr. v.p., gen. counsel, sec. Security Benefit Group, Topeka, 2003—. Bd. dirs. Allen County unit Am. Cancer Soc., Ft. Wayne, 1975-82, Embassy Theatre Found., 1998-2003, The Lincoln Mus., 1996—2000, Ft. Wayne-Allen County Hist. Soc., pres., 1993-95, Ft. Wayne Mus. Art, 1999-2003. Fellow: Ind. Bar Found., Am. Coll. Investment Counsel; mem.: Assn. Life Ins. Counsel (sec.-treas. 1994—2000, bd. govs. 2000—, pres.-elect 2003—), Am. Corp. Counsel Assn., Am. Coun. Life Ins. (various task forces), Allen County Bar Assn. (bd. dirs., pres. 1996—97), Ind. Bar Assn. Roman Catholic. Home: 1130 Woodland Xing Fort Wayne IN 46825-7239 Office: Security Benefit Group One Security Benefit Plaza Topeka KS 66636 E-mail: michael.keefer@securitybenefit.com.

KEEGAN, JAMES JOSEPH, financial executive; b. Phila., Sept. 6, 1947; s. George Washington and Kathryn Margaret (Eckels) K.; m. Martha Jana Pettinga, Apr. 27, 1984. BBA in Acctg. cum laude, Tex. Christian U., 1969; MBA in Internat. Fin., U. Mich., 1970. CPA, Colo. Supervising sr. acct. Peat Marwick Mitchell, Denver, 1974-79; pvt. practice acctg. Englewood, Colo., 1979-81; pres. Trinity Securities, Englewood, 1981-83, Keegan Capital Devel., Englewood, 1983-89, Fairway Sys., Inc., Englewood, 1989—. CPA Small Bus. Adv. Coun., 1984-85; vol. Internat. Golf Tournament, 1986; mem. rules and course rating coms. Colo. Golf Assn., committeeman, 1986-2002; mem. sectional affairs com. USGA, 1996-97, Golf Mag. course rater, 2002—; mem. Fellowship Christian Athletes. Capt. USAF, 1971-74. Mem. AICPA, Colo. Soc. CPAs, Beta Gamma Sigma, Beta Alpha Psi, Delta Sigma Pi. Republican. Roman Catholic. Home: 8101 E Dartmouth Ave Apt 36 Denver CO 80231-4259 Office: Fairway Systems Inc 6 Inverness Ct E Ste 120 Englewood CO 80112-5517 E-mail: JKeegan@fairway.com.

KEEGAN, JANE ANN, insurance executive, consultant; b. Watertown, N.Y., Sept. 1, 1950; d. Richard Isidor and Kathleen (McKinley) K. BA cum laude, SUNY, Potsdam, 1972; MBA in Risk Mgmt., Golden State U., 1986. CPCU. Comml. lines mgr. Lithgow & Rayhill, San Francisco, 1977-80; risk mgmt. account coord. Dinner Levison Co., San Francisco, 1980-83; ins. cons. San Francisco, 1983-84; account mgr. Rollins Burdick Hunter, San Francisco, 1984-85; account exec. Jardine Ins. Brokers, San Francisco, 1985-86; ins. cons. San Francisco, 1986-87; ins. adminstr. Port of Oakland, 1987—, risk mgr., 1989—, mgr. accts. payable, 1996—. Vol. San Francisco Ballet vol. orgn., 1981-96, Bay Area Bus., Govt. ARC disaster conf. steering com., 1987-88, 89, 90, 91-92; mem. Nob Hill Neighbors Assn., 1982—, City of Oakland Emergency Mgmt. Bd., 1990—. Mem. Safety Mgmt. Soc., CPCU Soc. (spl. events chairperson 1982-84, continuing profl. devel. program award 1985, 88, chair loss prevention), Calif. Assn. of Port Authorities (ins. chair 1998—), Risk and Ins. Mgr. Soc. (dep., sec. 1990—, dir. legis. 1993, dir. conf.). Democrat. Roman Catholic. Home: 17 Calafia Ct San Rafael CA 94903-2464

KEEGAN, JOHN E. lawyer; b. Spokane, Wash., Apr. 29, 1943; BA, Gonzaga U., 1965; LLB, Harvard U., 1968. Bar: Wash. 1968, U.S. Ct. Appeals (9th cir.) 1976, U.S. Supreme Ct. Gen. counsel Dept. Housing and Urban Devel., Washington, 1968-70; instr. in bus. sch. and inst. environ. studies U. Wash., 1973-76, instr. land use and environ. law, 1976-78; now ptnr. Davis, Wright & Tremaine, Seattle. Author: (novels) Clearwater Summer, 1994, Piper, 2001. Office: Davis Wright Tremaine 2600 Century Sq 1501 4th Ave Seattle WA 98101-1688

KEEGAN, JOHN ROBERT, lawyer, educator; b. Boston, Aug. 22, 1950; s. Francis Harold and Margaret (Huntley) K.; children: Kathleen Elizabeth, Margaret Mary, John Takao. BBA cum laude, Suffolk U., 1972, JD cum laude, 1976; LLM in Taxation, Boston U., 1980; chtd. fin. cons., CLU, Am. Coll., 1985. Bar: Mass. 1977. Group pension adminstr. New Eng. Life Ins. Co., Boston, 1972-75, pension legal specialist, 1975-78, group pension atty., 1978-80, pension atty., 1980-81; asst. counsel Sun Life Assurance Co. of Can., Wellesley Hills, Mass., 1981-83, advanced underwriting officer, 1983-87; assoc. Flynn, Joyce and Sheridan, Boston, 1987, R.W. Joyce PC, Boston, 1988-89; sr. pension atty. New Eng. Life Ins. Co., Boston, 1989-90; sr. rsch. atty. The Alexander Consulting Group, Boston, 1990-97; sr. cons. Coopers & Lybrand, Boston, 1997-98, Pricewaterhouse Coopers, Boston, 1998—2003; ptnr. Wagner Law Group, 2003—. Instr. Bentley Coll., Waltham, Mass., 1981-88, adv. bd. 1984-88; Northeastern U., Boston, 1985-86, Mass. Soc. CPAs, Boston, 1984-87. Mem. editl. bd. Jour. Deferred Compensation, 1996—; contbr. articles to profl. publs. Mem. ABA, Boston Bar Assn. Roman Catholic. Avocations: softball, tennis, skiing. E-mail: jkeegan@mwagner.net.

KEEGAN, RICHARD, federal agency administrator; Degree in biol. scis. and secondary edn., U. Md. Jr. H.S. sci. tchr.; various positions Dept. Energy; exec. asst. assoc. dep. adminstr. NASA, Washington, dir. bus. divsn. Office Earth Sci., 2002—. Office: NASA Hdqrs Mail Code Y 300 E St SW Washington DC 20546

KEEGAN, ROBERT J. manufacturing executive; b. NY, July 27, 1947; BS in Math., LeMoyne Coll.; MBA in Fin., U. Rochester, 1972. With Kodak, Rochester, NY, 1972—95; gen. mgr. Kodak New Zealand, 1986—87; dir. fin. photographic products group Kodak, Rochester, NY, 1987—90; gen. mgr. Kodak Spain, 1990—91; gen. mgr. consumer imaging Kodak European Middle Ea. African Region, 1991—93; exec. v.p., global strategy officer Avery Dennison Corp., Pasadena, Calif., 1995—97; pres. Kodak Profl., 1997; corp. v.p. Kodak, Rochester, 1997—2000, pres. consumer imaging, sr. v.p., 1997—2000, exec. v.p., 2000; pres., COO, dir. Goodyear Tire & Rubber Co., 2000—03, chmn., CEO, 2003—. Office: Goodyear Tire & Rubber Co 1144 E Market St Akron OH 44316*

KEEGAN, WARREN JOSEPH, business educator, consultant; b. Junction City, Kans., Oct. 19, 1936; s. Donald and Edla (Polson) K.; m. Maryann Bergin, June 17, 1961 (div. July 1975); children: Donald, Mark, Tracy. BS, Kans. State U., 1958, MS, 1959; MBA, Harvard U., 1961, DBA, 1967. Assoc. prof. Columbia Bus. Sch., N.Y.C., 1967—74, Baruch Coll., N.Y.C., 1974—76; prof. George Washington U., Washington, 1976—80, Pace U., N.Y.C. and Westchester County, NY, 1982—2001, disting. prof., 2002—; pres. Warren Keegan Assocs., Inc., Rye, NY. Vis. prof. NYU, 1980-82; ind. commr. P.T. Indoofood, Jakarta, Indonesia; vis. univ. prof. Cranfield U. Sch. Mgmt., U.K., 1999—. Author: Global Marketing Management, 7th edit., 2002, Marketing, 2d edit., 2002, Global Marketing, 3d edit., 2003, Marketing Plans That Work, 1997, 2d edit., 2002. Fellow Acad. Internat. Bus.; mem. Am. Mktg. Assn. (v.p.) Presbyterian. Avocations: tennis, running, motorcycle riding, skiing. Home: 210 Stuyvesant Ave Rye NY 10580-3115 Office: Pace U 1 Martine Ave White Plains NY 10606-1932 E-mail: wkeegan@pace.edu.

KEEHN, RICHARD H. economics educator emeritus; b. Cedar Rapids, Iowa, Jan. 10, 1934; s. Percy F. and Dorothy D. Keehn; m. Audrey DeWitz, Nov. 12, 1960; children: Stephen, Peter, James, Kathryn. BSc in Econs., U. Iowa, 1956; MBA, U. Chgo., 1959; MA, U. Wis., 1968, PhD in Econs., 1972. With treasury dept. U.S. Steel Corp., Chgo., 1956-65; from asst. prof. to assoc. prof. to prof. U. Wis., Parkside, 1969-2000, dept. chair econs., 1987-89, 96-00. Contbr.

articles and essays to profl. jours. Dir. Racine (Wis.) Heritage Mus., 1987-90; dir., coord. Parkside Econ. Edn. and Rsch. Inst., Kenosha, Wis., 1977-89; cons. Kenosha/Racine Econ. Devel. Com., 1978-82; curriculum advisor Wis. Bankers Assn., Madison, 1974-76. Recipient Newcomen Spl. award, 1974; grantee Grad. Sch. Banking, 1973, 78. Mem. Am. Econ. Assn., Bus. History Conf., Econ. and Bus. Hist. Soc. (trustee 1992-95, 99—, pres., program chair 2000), Econ. History Assn., Cliometric Soc., Univ. Ins. Assn. (pres. 1994-2000). Avocations: biking, hiking, reading. Home: 3333 S Green Bay Rd Racine WI 53403 E-mail: keehnr@uwp.edu.

KEEHN, SILAS, retired bank executive; b. New Rochelle, N.Y., June 30, 1930; s. Grant and Marjorie (Burchard) K.; m. Marcia June Lindquist, Mar. 26, 1955; children: Elisabeth Keehn Lewis, Britta Keehn Scott, Peter. AB in Econs, Hamilton Coll., Clinton, N.Y., 1952; MBA in Fin, Harvard U., 1957. With Mellon Bank N.A., Pitts., 1957-80, v.p., then sr. v.p., 1967-78, exec. v.p., 1978-79, vice-chmn., 1980; v.p. Mellon Nat. Corp., 1979-80, vice-chmn., 1980; chmn. bd. Pullman, Inc., Chgo., 1980; pres. Fed. Res. Bank Chgo., 1981-94; ret., 1994. Bd. dirs. Kewaunee Sci. Corp., Nat. Futures Assn., Chgo. Bd. Options Exch., Inc. Trustee Rush-Presbyn.-St. Luke's Med. Ctr., Hamilton Coll., Clinton, N.Y. With USNR, 1953-56. Mem. Chgo. Club, Comml. Club Chgo., Econ. Club Chgo., Fox Chapel Golf Club (Pitts.), U. Club, Links Club (N.Y.C.), Rolling Rock Club (Ligonier, Pa.), Indian Hill Club. Office: 707 Skokie Blvd Ste 600 Northbrook IL 60062-2841

KEEHNER, MICHAEL ARTHUR MILLER, investment bank executive; b. Cedar Rapids, Iowa, Nov. 15, 1943; BS in Nuclear Physics, MIT, 1965; MBA in Fin. with high distinction, Harvard U., 1971. Registered securities rep. Engring. mgr. Gen. Dynamics Corp., Quincy, Mass., 1965-69; investment banking mgr. Kidder Peabody & Co., 1971-89, exec. mng. dir. individual investor svcs., 1991-94; chmn., dir. Kidder Peabody Internat. Corp., N.Y.C., 1989-91; pres., chief exec. officer K P Exploration. Inc., N.Y.C., 1982-88; mng. dir., mem. exec. com., bd. mem. Kidder Peabody Group, Inc., N.Y.C., 1987-94; mng. ptnr. The Keehner Group, LLC, N.Y.C., 1994—. Bd. dirs. Cross Border LLC, LDMI Telecom. Inc. Trustee Bklyn. Mus. Baker scholar Harvard U.; Loeb Rhodes fellow Harvard U. Mem. India House (N.Y.C.), Rembrandt Club (Bklyn.), Long Island Wyandanch Club (N.Y.), Lake Waramug Country Club. Address: PO Box 99 South Kent CT 06785-0099

KEEL, ALTON GOLD, JR., ambassador; b. Newport News, Va., Sept. 8, 1943; s. Alton Gold and Ella Clare (Kennedy) K.; 1 child, Kristen Ann; m. Lynn (Matti) K. BS in Aerospace Engring., U. Va., 1966, PhD in Engring. Physics, 1970; postdoctoral scholar, U. Calif., Berkeley, 1971. Staff Naval Surface Weapons Ctr., Silver Springs, Md., 1971-77; congl. sci. fellow Senate Armed Services Com., Washington, 1977-79, staff mem., 1977-81; asst. sec. for research, devel. and logistics USAF, Washington, 1981-82; assoc. dir., nat. sec. internat. affairs Office Mgmt. and Budget, Washington, 1982-86; exec. dir. Pres.' Commn. on Challenger Accident, Washington, 1986; acting asst. to pres. for nat. security affairs The White House, Washington, 1986; U.S. permanent rep. NATO, Brussels, 1987-89; dep. chmn. The Riggs Nat. Bank, Washington, 1989-92; pres., mng. dir. Carlyle Internat. The Carlyle Group, Washington, 1992-94; chmn. Carlyle SEAG, 1994-95; chmn., mng. dir. Atlantic Ptnrs., L.L.C., Washington, 1992—; chmn., CEO Land-5 Corp., 1999—2002; CEO, InoStor Corp., 2002—. Chmn. F-16 fighter aircraft multinat. steering com.; nat. del., bd. dirs. Adv. Group for Aerospace R & D, 1982; bd. dirs. Tandberg Data, Inc. (InoStor), Digital Atlantic. Bd. dirs. Fondation pour la Promotion de la Recherche Fundamentale en Cancerologie, Belgium, 1988; mem. dean's adv. bd. U. Va., 1996—. Recipient research award NRC, 1970; Nat. Congl. Sci. fellow AIAA, 1976; recipient Young Engr.-Scientist award AIAA, 1978, Air Force Exceptional Civilian Service award, 1982, NASA Group Achievement award, 1986, Disting. Alumni award U. Va., 1988. Fellow AIAA, Sigma Xi; mem. French Am. C. of C. (mem. sr. adv. group 1990-95), Belgian Am. Assn. (bd. dirs. 1990-94), Phi Eta Sigma, Tau Beta Pi. Office: Atlantic Ptnrs 2891 S River Rd Stanardsville VA 22973-2416

KEELE, JEAN A. medical, surgical, geriatrics and home health nurse; b. Tullahoma, Tenn., Jan. 2, 1955; d. Sam Allen and Helen Virginia Keele; children: William Adam Keele, Mark Allen Keele. AS, Motlow State Community Coll., Tullahoma, 1984, Cleve. State Community Coll., 1980. Staff and charge nurse Coffee Med. Ctr., Manchester, Tenn., 1985-86; staff nurse Elk Valley Home Health, Tullahoma, 1986-87; charge and staff nurse Bedford County Nursing Home, Shelbyville, Tenn., 1987-88; asst. dir. nursing Geriatrics Nursing Ctr., Heber Springs, Ark., 1990-93; geriatric psychiat. nurse Coffee Med. Ctr. Sr. Care, Manchester, Tenn., 1997; geriatric nurse Glen Oak sConvalesce Ctr., Shelbyville, Tenn., 1999—. Owner, operator Jean's Feline & Canine Emporium, Tullahoma, Tenn., 1995—2001. Home: 441 Smith Ln Tullahoma TN 37388-6272

KEELE, LYNDON ALAN, electronics executive; b. Clyde, Tex., Nov. 3, 1928; s. Theodore Fannin and Zada (Sikes) Keele; m. Muriel Alice Murphy, June 1, 1968; children: Carolyn Chase, Tiffany Ames. BBA, U. Tex., 1951. With York (Pa.) divsn. Borg-Warner Co., 1953—58, asst. gen. plant mgr., 1956—58; program mgr. Sylvania Elec. Sys. divsn. GTE, Needham, Mass., 1958—62, ITT Fed. Labs., Nutley, NJ, 1962—68; exec. v.p. TeleScience, Inc., Moorestown, NJ, 1968—73; pres. and chmn. Sci. Dynamics Corp., Cherry Hill, NJ, 1973—99; chmn. Venture Scis. Corp., Moorestown, 1999—. With AUS, 1946—47, with USAF, 1951—53. Mem.: IEEE, Riverton Country. Office: Venture Scis Corp 5 Dover Ln Medford NJ 08055 E-mail: lakx@msn.com.

KEELER, JAMES LEONARD, food products company executive; b. Richmond, Va., Jan. 31, 1935; s. Joseph McCauley and Nora Elizabeth (Thomas) K.; m. Joan Sandra Barnhart, Aug. 14, 1954; children: Mark Leonard, Tracy Ann, Steven James, Gregory Wayne. BS, Bridgewater Coll., 1957; JD, U. Va., 1983. Bar: Va. 1983; CPA, Va. Ptnr., acct. Hueston & Keeler, CPAs, Harrisonburg, Va., 1958-63; mng. ptnr., acct. Keeler, Phibbs & Co., CPAs, Harrisonburg, 1963-80; ptnr., atty. Wharton, Aldhizer & Weaver, Harrisonburg, 1983-88; chief exec. officer WLR Foods, Inc., Broadway, Va., 1988-01, pres., 1990-01, Wampler Foods, Inc., Broadway, 1997-01. Vice chmn. Bridgewater (Va.) Coll., 1974-91, mem. exec. com., trustee, 1974—; exec. adv. coun. James Madison U. Coll. Bus., Harrisonburg, 1989-95; bd. dirs. Valley of Va. Partnership for Edn., James Madison U., Rockingham Meml. Hosp., 1994-98, Va. Econ. Devel. Partnership, 1995-2001, Massanutten Regional Libr.; mem. Va. Bus. Coun., 1995-2001, vice-chmn., 1999-01; mem. Gov.'s Adv. Com. on Va.'s Strategy, 1998. Recipient disting. alumnus award Bridgewater Coll., 1990; named outstanding bus. person award Harrisonburg-Rockingham C. of C., 1995. Fellow Va. Soc. CPAs (pres. 1970-71, hon. chmn., Outstanding Mem. 1977); mem. ABA, AICPA (governing coun. 1969-70, 74-75, 76-77), Va. Bar Assn., Va. C. of C. (vice chmn. 1994-96, chmn. 1997-98, exec. com., bd. dirs. 1994-98). Republican. Mem. Brethren Ch. Avocation: boating. E-mail: jkeeler@shentel.net.

KEELER, KATHLEEN HOWARD, biological sciences educator, ecologist; b. Hackensack, N.J., Jan. 17, 1947; d. James Howard and Irene (Krantz) K.; m. Richard Karl Anderson, Dec. 24, 1975. BS, U. Mich., 1969; PhD, U. Calif., Berkeley, 1975. Asst. prof. U. Nebr., Lincoln, 1975-81, assoc. prof., 1981-91, prof., 1991—. Chair ecology sect. biol. scis. U. Nebr., 1985-88, dir. Cedar Point Biol. Sta., Ogallala, Nebr., 1991-94; biotech. cons. Nat. Audubon Soc., N.Y.C., 1988-89; mem. adv. panel for biotech. in environment U.S. EPA, 1992-98. Contbr. over 50 articles to profl. jours. Babcock scholar U. Calif., 1969-71. Fellow Ctr. for Great Plains Studies; mem. Ecol. Soc. Am., Soc. for the Study of Evolution, Botanical Soc. Am., Soc. for Conservation Biology. Achievements include synthetic work on ecology of mutualism; application of flow cytometry to plant population biology; contributions to safe release of genetically engineered plants; prairie population biology. Home: 3633 Washington St Lincoln NE 68506-1054 Office: U Nebr Sch Biol Scis 412 Manter Hall Lincoln NE 68588

KEELER, ROSS VINCENT, securities company executive; b. Evansville, Ind., Nov. 28, 1948; s. Mark V. and Lola (Saunders) K.; m. Pamela Person, Jan. 24, 1981; children: Margo, Eric. BS with honors, U. Fla., 1970; MBA with honors, U. So. Calif., 1971. Asst. v.p. SE Banks, Miami, Fla., 1972-74; exec. v.p. Barnett Leasing, Ft. Lauderdale, Fla., 1975-78, lst Capital, Chgo., 1979-84; pres. Berkshire Investment Advisors (formerly Krupp Securities), Boston, 1984-96; ptnr. various Berkshire Cos., Boston, 1997—, also bd. dirs.; mng. gen. ptnr. First Coast Hedge Fund, Ponte Vedra, Fla., 1997—. Contbr. articles on fin. to profl. publs. Mem. Investors Program Assn. (trustee, chmn. 1988-93), Pension Real Estate Assn., Marsh Landing C.C., Ponte Vedra Inn and Club, Phi Kappa Phi, Beta Gamma Sigma. Home: 108 Teal Nest Ct Ponte Vedra Beach FL 32082-1944

KEELER, WILLIAM H. archbishop; b. San Antonio, Mar. 4, 1931; s. Thomas Love and Margaret T. (Conway) Keeler. BA, St. Charles Borromeo Sem., 1952; STL, Pontifical Gregorian U., Rome, 1956, JCD, 1961; DD (hon.), Lebanon Valley Coll., 1984, Gettysburg Coll., 1986, Susquehanna U., 1989; LHD (hon.), Mt. St. Mary's Coll., 1985; LLD (hon.), Gannon U., 1993; LHD (hon.), Loyola Coll., 1995, Shippensburg State U., 1995; DD (hon.), St. Mary's U., Winona, Minn., 1995, Elizabeth Coll., 1996, Western Md. Coll., 1996, St. Vincent Sem., 1996, Coll. of Notre Dame of Md., 1997, U. Notre Dame, 1998, Ateneo de Manila U., 1998, Sacred Heart U., 2000, Cath. U., Lublin, Poland, 2000. Ordained priest Roman Catholic Ch., 1955, consecrated bishop, 1979. Asst. pastor Our Lady of Good Counsel Ch., Marysville, Pa., 1956—58; sec. diocesan tribunal Diocese of Harrisburg, Pa., 1956—58, defender of the bond, 1961—66, vice-chancellor, 1965—69, chancellor, 1969—79, aux. bishop and vicar gen., 1979—83, bishop of Harrisburg, 1984—89; archbishop of Balt., 1989—94; cardinal, 1994—; chmn. Md. Cath. Conf., 1989—. Newspaper publ. The Cath. Rev.; co-chmn. Pa. Conf. Inter-Ch. Coop., 1981—89; pres. Pa. Cath. Conf., 1983—89; chmn. com. on ecumenical and inter-religious affairs Nat. Conf. Cath. Bishops, 1984—87, mem., 1984—, sec., 1988—89, Episcopal moderator Cath.-Jewish rels., 1988—92, 1995—, v.p., 1989—92, pres., 1992—95; chmn. World Youth Day Celebration, Denver, 1993; cons. Com. Comm., 1995—; past pastor Marysville Parish; chmn. Com. Pro-Life Activities, 1998—2001; past titular bishop Ulcinium (Dulcigno); mem. Internat. Joint Com. for Cath.-Orthodox Theol. Dialogue, 1986—. Internat. Liaison Com. Caths. and Jews, 1987—, Synod of Bishops for Africa, 1994, World Synod of Bishops for the Consecrated Life, 1994, Synod of Bishops for Am., 1996; sec., spl. advisor 2d Vatican Coun., 1962—65; staff Coun. Digest, 1963—65; apptd. mem. Coun. for Assembly of Synod Bishops, 1997—. Active Black and Native Am. Missions Bd.; exec. bd. Keystone Area coun. Boy Scouts Am., 1979—89; trustee Cath. U. Am.; chancellor, chmn. bd. trustees St. Mary's Sem. and Univ., 1989—; chancellor Mt. St. Mary's Sem., 1989—; vice-chair North Am. Coll. Bd. Govs., 1998—; trustee Basilica of Nat. Shrine of Immaculate Conception, Washington, 1989—; active Interreligious Forum Greater Harrisburg, 1968—89; Pontifical coun. Promoting Christian Unity, 1994—; active Congregation for the Oriental Chs., 1994—; chmn. bd. trustees Associated Cath. Charities, 1989—, Basilica of Nat. Shrine of Assumption of the Blessed Virgin Mary, 1989—; v.p. Cath. Near East Welfare Assn. Named papal chamberlain, Pope Paul VI, 1965, prelate of honor, 1970, Marylander of Yr., Md. Colonial Soc., 1986, The Balt. Sun, 1994, Media Person of Yr., Md. Press Assn., 1994; recipient Gold medal, Pope John XXIII, 1961, John Baum Humanitarian award, Dauphin County unit Am. Cancer Soc., 1984, Americanism award, Anti-Defamation League, 1985, De Tocqueville Soc. award, 1988, Nat. award, Boy Scouts of Am., 1990, Disting. Citizen award, 1998, Weil medal, Jewish Chataqua Soc., 1993, Salvation Army award, 1995, Shaw award, Rotary Internat., 1995, Mahmoud Abu Sand Excellence award, Am. Muslim Coun., 1995, Nostra Aetate award, Inst. Christian Jewish Understanding, 1997, Silver St. George medal, Nat. Cath. Com. Scouting, 1998, Lifetime Achievement award, Shaare Zedek Med. Ctr., Jerusalem, 1999, Disting. Citizens award, Balt. coun. Boy Scouts Am., 1999. Mem.: Cath. Extension Soc. Govs., Am. Cath. Hist. Soc., Canon Law Soc. Am. Roman Catholic.

KEELEY, ETHEL S. workforce development trainer; b. Dickinson, N.D., Jan. 2, 1946; d. Clarence and Pauline (Heck) Schmitz; m. Ronald P. Keeley, July 18, 1970; children: Patrick, Ryan, Janine. BEd, Dickinson State U., 1969; MS, No. State U., 1980. Nat. field rep. Alpha Sigma Alpha, Springfield, Mo., 1969-70; instr. English Bismarck (N.D.) Pub. Schs., 1971-94, spl. projects coord., 1994-2000. Prin. Keeley Cons., Bismarck, 1994—; mem. N.D. Tech. Prep. Adv. Coun., Bismarck, 1994—2000, N.D. Workforce Devel. Coun., 1997—2001. Author: 10 Steps to Writing a Research Paper, 1990; co-author: Essay Writing, 1995. Mem. N.D. Youth Coun., 2001—; Bd. dirs. Dakota Jr. Golf Assn. Recipient Educator award Greater N.D. Assn.; named Tchr. of yr. Bismarck-Mandan C. of C., 1995. Mem. ASCD, Assn. for Careers and Tech. Edn., Phi Delta Kappa. Avocations: reading, music, golf. Home and Office: 7710 Greenbrier Cir Port Saint Lucie FL 34986-3301 E-mail: ethelskeeley@earthlink.net.

KEELEY, MICHAEL CLARK, economist; b. Kearney, Nebr., May 5, 1947; s. Benjamin J. and Helen I. (Moon) K.; m. Maryann Bezich, June 24, 1973. BS, MIT, 1969; MA, U. Chgo., 1971, PhD, 1974. Economist GE TEMPO, Washington, 1973—75; mgr., antitrust cons. Stanford Rsch. Inst., Menlo Park, Calif., 1975-83; rsch. officer Fed. Res. Bank San Francisco, 1983-89; sr. v.p. Cornerstone Rsch., Menlo Park, 1989—. Author: Labor Supply and Public Policy, 1981; editor: Population, Public Policy and Economic Development, 1976; contbr. numerous articles to profl. jours.; chpts. to books. Mem. Am. Econs. Assn., Western Econs. Assn., Nat. Assn. Bus. Economists. Avocation: boating. Office: Cornerstone Rsch 1000 El Camino Real Ste 250 Menlo Park CA 94025-4315

KEELEY, ROBERT VOSSLER, retired academic administrator, retired ambassador; b. Beirut, Sept. 4, 1929; s. James Hugh and Mathilde Julia (Vossler) K.; m. Louise Schoonmaker, June 23, 1951; children: Michal M., Christopher J. AB, Princeton U., 1951, postgrad., 1951-53; postgrad. (Princeton fellow in pub. affairs), 1970-71; postgrad. (Nat. Inst. Pub. Affairs fellow), Stanford U., 1965-66. With Fgn. Service, Dept. State, Washington, 1956-89; officer in charge Congo (Leopoldville) external affairs Washington, 1963-64; officer-in-charge Congo (Brazzaville), Rwanda and Burundi affairs, 1964-65; polit. officer, 1966-70; detailed Woodrow Wilson fellow Princeton U., 1970; dep. chief mission Kampala, Uganda, 1971-73; alt. dir. E. African affairs Washington, 1974; dep. chief mission Phnom Penh, Khmer Republic, 1974-75; dep. dir. Interagency Task Force for Indochina Refugees, 1975-76; ambassador Mauritius, 1976-78; dep. asst. sec. for African Affairs Dept. State, Washington, 1978-80; ambassador to Zimbabwe, 1980-84; sr. fellow Ctr. for Study Fgn. Affairs, Fgn. Service Inst., Washington, 1984-85; ambassador to Greece, 1985-89. Pres. Middle East Inst., Washington, 1990-95; writer, lectr., cons. Pub. Five and Ten Press, 1995—. Bd. mem. Middle East Inst. Lt. (j.g.) USCGR, 1953-55. Mem. Am. Fgn. Svc. Assn., Washington Inst. Fgn. Affairs, Am. Acad. Diplomacy, Cosmos Club. Home: 3814 Livingston St NW Washington DC 20015-2803

KEELING, GERALDINE ANN, musicologist, educator; b. Mason City, Iowa, Aug. 10, 1946; d. John Odell and Marie Christine (Birkedal) Field; m. Steven R. Keeling, Aug. 17, 1974 (dec. Jan. 1998). BA in Music with honors cum laude, St. Olaf Coll., 1968; MMus. with high distinction, Ind. U., 1973; postgrad., UCLA, 1982. Assoc. instr. music Ind. U., Bloomington, 1968-70; asst. prof. music Valley City (N.D.) State U., 1970-78; teaching fellow UCLA, 1980-83; pvt. piano tchr. San Gabriel, Calif., 1980—; ch. organist Trinity United Meth. Ch., Pomona, Calif., 1981-90; instr. music. Calif. State U., Fullerton, 1985-86, 2001; with First Congrl. Ch. of Glendale, 1999—. Performer, lectr. U.S., Can., Hungary, Germany, Austria, Sweden, Japan. Contbr. articles to profl. jours. Recipient Gurtha Olin Rodda Disting. Svc. award, 1997; NEH fellow, 1977-78; grantee Internat. Edn. Program Alpha Delta Kappa, 1983-84; recipient John Lennon award, 1982, Atwater Kent award in Musicology, UCLA, 1980, Franz Liszt medal Hungarian Liszt Soc., 1995. Mem. Music Tchrs. Assn. Calif. (state solo and concerto chmn. 1991-94, br. v.p. 1991-92, br. pres. 1992-94, br. piano chmn. 1995-2002, br. treas. 1998-2000, cert. merit chmn. 1985-88), Am. Musicol. Soc., Am. Liszt Soc. (editl. assoc. 1987-91, bd. dirs. 1988—), Music Tchrs.' Nat. Assn. (editl. com. 1997-99, chmn. state ensemble 2001-03), Am. Guild Organists (chpt. sec. 1987-90), L.A. Liszt Competition (founder, dir. 1990—), Nat. Fedn. Music Clubs (Pasadena area Jr. Festival chair 1991—), Pi Kappa Lambda. Home: 8260 Youngdale St San Gabriel CA 91775-1744

KEELING, JOE KEITH, religion educator, college official and dean; b. Muskogee, Okla., Apr. 21, 1936; s. William Lytle and Anna Madge (Watts) K.; m. Marjorie Ann Brotherton, 1957; children: Kara Kay, William Kent. BA in History, Northeastern State U., 1958; BD in Theology, So. Meth. U., 1962; MA in Theology, U. Chgo., 1967, PhD, 1974. Ordained to ministry United Meth. Ch., 1962. Dir. orientation, acad. advisor U. Chgo., 1964-68; asst. prof. religion Augustana Coll., Sioux Falls, SD, 1968-72; from asst. to assoc. prof. philosophy and religion Rockford (Ill.) Coll., 1972-86, dean of spl. acad. programming, assoc. dean of coll., 1981-86; adj. assoc. prof. dept. medicine U. Ill. Coll of Medicine at Rockford, 1984-86; provost, dean, prof. religion and philosophy Baker U., Baldwin City, Kans., 1986-96; v.p., dean Ctrl. Meth. Coll., Fayette, Mo., 1996—2002, prof. emeritus philosophy and religion, 2002—. Mem. bd. ordained ministry Kans. Ea. Conf. United Meth. Ch., 1987-96; cons., evaluator, mem. accreditation rev. coun. North Ctrl. Assn. Colls. and Schs., Am. Conf. Acad. Deans, Midwest Bioethics Ctr. Author and lectr. in field. Mem. Kansas City Regional Coun. Higher Edn., 1986-94; mem. instnl. rev. com. Swedish-Am. Hosp., Rockford, 1981-86. Mem. Am. Acad. Religion (v.p., program chmn. Midwest region 1981-82, pres. 1982-83), Rockford C. of C. (bd. dirs. 1983-86), AAUP (Ill. state coun. mem. 1979-81), Archael. Inst. Am. (bd. dirs. Rockford chpt. 1984-86), Rotary. Democrat. Avocations: fishing, camping, canoeing. Home: PO Box 429 878 Highway 5 And 240 Fayette MO 65248-9509 Office: Ctrl Meth Coll Stedman 313 411 Central Methodist Sq Fayette MO 65248-1129

KEELING, J(OHN) MICHAEL, lawyer, trade association administrator; b. Kilgore, Tex., Feb. 24, 1947; s. Frank Marion and Eva Mae (Buse) K.; m. Michaela Eleanora Halik, Aug. 2, 1969; children: Alexandra Halik, J. Michael Jr. BA, Yale U., 1969; JD, U. Tex., 1971. Bar: Tex. 1972, D.C. 1982. Rsch. dir. Tex. Legislature Interim Com. on Ad Valorem Taxation, Austin, 1971; rsch. dir. gubernatorial gov. campaign Frances T. Farenthold, Austin, 1972; legis. dir. office congressman J.J. Pickle 10th Jud. Dist. Tex., Washington, 1972-73, chief staff office congressman J.J. Pickle, 1973-81; prin. David P. Stang, P.C., Washington, 1981-88; counsel Zuckert, Scott & Rasenberger, Washington, 1988-91; gen. counsel Employee Stock Ownership Plan Assn., Washington, 1984-91, pres., 1991—. Host Employee Ownership Talk Radio. Recipient Disting. Svc. award Small Bus. Coun. Am., 1993. Mem. ABA, Nat. Assn. Royalty Owners (life), Am. Soc. Assn. Execs. (cert.). Democrat. Baptist. Avocation: civil war history.

KEELING, LARRY DALE, journalist; b. Anderson County, Ky., May 5, 1947; s. Elmer Pascal and Ida Elizabeth (Gregory) K.; m. Cynthia Maria Taylor, Nov. 28, 1987 (div. Feb. 2001); m. Dorothy Elizabeth Cayce Wilson, Sept. 18, 2002. BA, U. Ky., 1969. Reporter Henry County Jour., Bassett, Va., 1972, Martinsville (Va.) Bull., 1972-74, Bradenton (Fla.) Herald, 1974-75, Lexington (Ky.) Herald, 1975-79; editl. writer Lexington Herald-Leader, 1979—. 1st lt. USAF, 1969-72, Taiwan. Recipient Sigma Delta Chi award for editl. writing, 1993, Nat. Headliner award for editl. writing, 1994, Green Eyeshade award for editl. writing, 1995, 97, spl. citation for opinion Nat. Awards for Edn. Reporting, 1997; fellow Knight Ctr. for Specialized Journalism, 1997. Mem. Soc. Profl. Journalists (Bluegrass chpt.), Nat. Conf. Editorial Writers. Office: Lexington Herald-Leader 100 Midland Ave Lexington KY 40508-1999

KEELING, ROBERT E. secondary school educator; b. St. Louis, Feb. 22, 1957; s. Robert Eugene Keeling and Janet Freukes; m. Verna Melton Keeling, June 28, 1980 (div. July 1987); m. Kathy Kline Mercille, Apr. 3, 1992. BS in Edn., S.E. Mo. State U., 1979; MA in English, U. Mo., St. Louis, 1989. Tchr. Hancock Pl. Sch. Dist., St. Louis, 1979—; chair dept. English Hancock Pl. Sr. H.S., 1997—. Recipient Emerson Elec. Excellence in Tchg. award, Emerson Elec. Co., 1998, Outstanding Educator award, Lemay C. of C., 2002. Democrat. Roman Catholic. Avocations: golf, reading, sports. Home: 9 Deer Lodge Fenton MO 63026 Office: Hancock Place Sch Dist 229 W Ripa Saint Louis MO 63125

KEELING,SR. KENNETH AUGUSTUS, music educator, headmaster; b. Norfolk, Va., May 29, 1938; d. Willis Eugene and Helen Ballard Keeling; m. Jean Ellis Keeling, June 10; children: Kenneth, Jr. Augustus Keeling, Anthony Charles Keeling. Mus D Musical Arts, Cath. U., Washington, D.C., 1969—72. Prof. of music Carnegie Mellon Univ., Pitts., 1996—, head, sch. of music, 1996—2001. Musician: (conductor, clarinetist) Performing Musician. Bd. mem. Gateway to the Arts, Pitts., 1997—2003. Lt. comdr. U.S. Naval Res., 1977—87, Columbia, MD. Liberal. Baptist. Achievements include Recording Artist. Avocations: training, travel, reading. Home: 101 Country Club Drive Pittsburgh PA 15235 Office: Carnegie Mellon Univ Sch of Music 5000 Forbes Ave Pittsburgh PA 15213 Personal E-mail: kak@andrew.cmu.edu.

KEEM, MICHAEL DENNIS, veterinarian; b. Buffalo, July 29, 1950; s. Sanford Joseph and Clara C. (Chmiel) K.; m. Mary Beth Fix, June 1, 1973 (div. 1993); children: Chelsey, Erin, Daniel, Ryan. BS, Niagara U., 1972; MS, U. Wyo., 1974; DVM, Cornell U., 1979. Assoc. veterinarian Spink Vet. Assn., Attica, N.Y., 1979-80, Cheektowaga (N.Y.) Vet. Hosp., 1980-1984, vet., owner, pres., 1985—, Amclare Vet. Hosp., P.C., Williamsville, N.Y., 1987—. Pun. Greater Buffalo Vet. Emergency Svcs., P.C., 1985—, also bd. dirs. Com. chmn. pack 601 Boy Scouts Am., 1989-91, Webelos den leader, 1991-92, asst. scoutmaster troop 601, 1992-96, com. mem. 1996—. Mem. AVMA, Animal Birth Control Soc. (bd. dirs. 1981—), N.Y. State Vet. Med. Soc., Am. Animal Hosp. Assn., Western N.Y. Vet. Med. Assn. (pres.-elect 1988, pres. 1989, past pres. 1990, bd. dirs. 1991-94), Niagara Frontier Vet. Soc. (bd. dirs. 1986-96, 00—), Buffalo Acad. Vet. Medicine (sgt.-at-arms 1995-96, sec./treas. 1996-97, v.p. 1997-98, pres. 1998-99), Phi Kappa Phi, Phi Zeta, Omega Tau Sigma. Republican. Roman Catholic. Office: Cheektowaga Vet Hosp PC 957 Dick Rd Cheektowaga NY 14225-3554 also: Amclare Vet Hosp PC 895 Hopkins Rd Williamsville NY 14221-1728

KEEN, BRENDA DENNISTON, lawyer; b. Ft. Smith, Ark., Dec. 5, 1949; d. James Pritchard and Era Erline (Jones) Denniston; m. Dean Edward Keen, June 23, 1973 (dec. June 1990); 1 child, Duncan Denniston Keen; m. Sylvan Schwartz, Jr., Apr. 26, 1992 (dec. Mar. 2003). BA, U. Houston, 1972, JD magna cum laude, 1975. Bar: Tex. 1975, U.S. Dist. Ct. (so. dist.) Tex. 1975. Assoc. Haynes & Fullenweider, P.L.C., Houston, 1975-79, v.p., ptnr., 1979-87; ptnr., officer Wallis & Keen, P.C., Houston, 1988-92; prin. Brenda D. Keen P.C., Houston, 1992—. Contbr. articles to legal publs. Fellow Am. Acad. Matrimonial Lawyers (pres. Tex. chpt. 1996-97), Tex. Acad. Family Law Specialists (pres. 2003—), Tex. Bar Found., Houston Bar Found.; mem. State Bar Tex. (family law coun. 1989-93). Roman Catholic. Office: 1800 Bering Dr Ste 690 Houston TX 77057-3169

KEEN, CHARLOTTE ELIZABETH, marine geophysicist, researcher; b. Halifax, N.S., Can., June 22, 1943; d. Murray Alexander and Elizabeth Randell (Cobb) Davidson; m. Michael J. Keen, May 11, 1963 (div.). BSc with 1st class honors, Dalhousie U., Halifax, 1964, MSc with 1st class honors, 1966; PhD, Cambridge U., Eng., 1970, LLD honoris causa, 2003. Research scientist Atlantic Oceanographic Lab., Energy, Mines, Resources, Dartmouth, N.S., 1970-74, Geol. Survey of Can., Atlantic Geosci. Centre, Dartmouth, 1972—. Chmn. Can. Nat. Com. Lithosphere; mem. Can. Nat. Com. Internat. Union Geol. Scis., Geodesy and Geophysics, Iternat. Commn. Marine Geology Contbr. articles to sci. jours. Recipient Young Scientist medal Atlantic Provinces Inter-Univ. Commn. Sci., 1977 Fellow Royal Soc. Can., Geol. Soc. Can. (Past Pres.'s medal 1979, Keen medal 1993), Geol. Soc. Am. (Woolard award 1994), Can. Soc. Exploration Geophys. (hon.), Am. Geophysics Unions; mem. Can. Geophys. Union (Wilson medal 1995). Buddhist. Home: 9 Wenlock Grove Halifax NS Canada B3P 1P6 Office: Atlantic Geosci Ctr Bedford Inst Oceanography Dartmouth NS Canada B2Y 4A2 E-mail: ckeen@agc.bio.ns.ca.

KEEN, CONSTANTINE, retired manufacturing company executive; b. N.Y.C., Jan. 1, 1925; s. Andrew and Sophie (Findani) K.; m. Kally Carajikis, Sept. 23, 1951; children: Katherine, Andrew. BA, NYU, 1952. Asst. treas. Sandz Indsl. Corp., N.Y.C., 1951-55; with Fedders Corp., Edison, N.J., 1955—, asst. credit mgr., 1955-57, credit mgr., 1957-60, dir. credit, 1960-68, v.p., dir. credit, 1968-75, v.p., dir. distbr. relations, 1975-77, v.p., treas., 1980-87, v.p. internat., 1984-86; pres. Fedders Internat. Corp., 1987-93, dir., 1996—. With USAAF, 1942-45. Decorated D.F.C., Air medal. Mem.: Ahepa, Masons. Greek Orthodox. Home: 55 Cardinal Rd Manhasset NY 11030-1204

KEEN, M. WHITNEY, ink manufacturing company executive; b. Englewood, N.J., Jan. 28, 1938; d. Frederick Snare and Mary Carolyn Peters; m. Howard William Kelting, April 4, 1959 (div. 1973); children: Anne Kelting Kronenberg, Jeannette Kelting Sacchini, Mary Whitney Kelting Runge, m. Fred Jacob Keen, June 7, 1975. BA in history, Columbia U., 1973. CFRE, Nat. Soc. Fundraising Execs. Alumni ofc. dir. Columbia U./Sch. of Gen. Studies, N.Y., N.Y., 1976-80; dir. ann. & planned giving Marymount Coll., Tarrytown, N.Y., 1980-86; dir. devel. Arthritis Found., N.J., Iselin, 1986-88; mgr. annual giving N.Y. Botanical

Garden, Bronx, 1988-89; self employed fundraising cons. Tenafly, N.J., 1989-97; treas., CFO Repeat-O-Type Mfg., Wayne, N.J., 1997-98, pres., treas., CEO/CFO, 1998—. Cons. Brakeley John Price Jones, Stamford, Conn., 1990-93, Pierpont & Wilkerson, Garrison, N.Y., 1993-95. Bd. dirs. Tenafly Nature Ctr., 1990—, inksite.inc, Ringwood, N.J.; com. mem., treas., pres. Women's Coun. of the N.Y. Bot. Garden, Bronx, 1997—. Mem.: Soc. Archaeol. Inst. Am. (sec. 2001—), Quissett Yacht Club, Englewood Field Club, Garden Club of Englewood (treas. 1995—2000, bd. dirs.), Phi Beta Kappa. Democrat. Christian. Avocations: gardening, archaeology, sailing. Office: Repeat O Type Mfg 665 State Hwy 23 Wayne NJ 07470 Fax: (973) 694-7287. E-mail: wkeen@repeatotype.com.

KEENAN, ANTHONY LEE, trucking company executive; b. Greenwood, S.C., Mar. 18, 1949; s. Arthur Lee and Betty (Hart) K.; m. Cheryl Toney, Dec. 31, 1985; children: Andrew Lee, Anthony LeBrett, Aric Lane. BA, W.Ga. Coll., 1973; postgrad., Woodrow Wilson Coll. Law, 1975-79. Pres. Keenan, Inc., Decatur, Ga., 1975—; v.p. All Day Leasing Co., Decatur, 1977—; pres. United Trucker's Svcs., Conyers, Ga., 1978—; exec. dir. Ind. Trucker's United Co., Conley, Ga., 1979-80; pres. Southeastern Gen. Agy., Inc., 1983—; CEO Getaway Travel, 1996—. Pres. Am. Risk Reduction, Inc.; CEO, Am. Commerce and Shipping Assn.; mem. adv. bd. Rockdale Nat. Bank. Mem. White House Task Force To Develop Motor Carrier Act of 1980, 1979-80; com. chmn. Am. Mem. Profl. Truck Svcs. Assn., pres. 1987-89, chmn. bd. 1990; com. chmn. 354 Cub Scouts Am., Ga. Suplus Lines Assn., 1982—, Assn. Transp. Practitioners, 1992—, Aircraft Owners and Pilots Assn., Am. Commerce and Shipping Assn. (CEO 1991—).

KEENAN, BARBARA MILANO, judge; Judge Gen. Dist. Ct., Fairfax County, Va., 1980-82, Circuit Ct., Fairfax County, Va., 1982-85, Court of Appeals of Va., 1985-91; justice Supreme Court Va., Richmond, 1991—. Office: Ste 425 200 Golden Oak Ct Virginia Beach VA 23452-8509

KEENAN, BOB, state legislator; b. Salem, Mass., Mar. 11, 1952; m. Suzie Keenan. Grad., U. Mass. Owner Bigfork Inn; ptnr. Internat. Newspaper Network; self-employed entrepreneur; mem. Mont. Ho. of Reps., 1995-98, Mont. Senate, Dist. 38, 1998—; mem. fin. and claims com., labor and employment rels. com.; mem. joint appropriations subcom. on health and human svcs.; mem. edn. and cultural resources com.; pres. Mont. Senate, Dist. 38, 2002—. Trustee Bigfork Cmty. Fund, Bigfork Lighting Dist.; mem. Mont. Food Code Task Force; mem. adv. coun. Swan River Correctional Tng. Ctr., Mont. Dept. Corrections. Mem. Bigfork C. of C. (bd. dirs.). Republican. Home: PO Box 697 Bigfork MT 59911-0697 E-mail: inn1@digisys.net.*

KEENAN, EDWARD L. linguist, educator, linguist, department chairman; b. Somerset, Pa., Dec. 10, 1937; m. Carol Archie; 1 child, David. BA in Philosophy and Religion, Swarthmore Coll., 1959; diploma in lit., U. Paris, Sorbonne, 1961, cert. in French lit., 1962; MA in Linguistics, George Washington U., 1966; PhD in Linguistics, U. Pa., 1969. Sr. fellow King's Coll., Cambridge, England, 1970—74; assoc. prof. U. Mass., Amherst, 1974; vis. prof. U. Amsterdam, Netherlands, 1977, U. Tel Aviv, 1978—79; fellow Max Planck Inst. for Psycholinguistics, Nijmegen, Netherlands, 1984—85; Fulbright scholar U. Antaanarivo, Madagascar, 1995. Co-author: Boolean Semantics for Natural Language, 1985; editor: Universal Grammar: 15 Essays, 1987; mem. adv. editl. bd.: Lang. Rsch., 1985—, consulting editor: Jour. Semantics, 1987—, Jour. Lang. and Computation, 1997—. Grantee, NSF, 2000—01, Binational Sci. Found., 2000, 2002; Acad. Senate grantee, UCLA, 1997. Mem.: AAAS, ACLU, Linguistic Soc. Am., Am. Math. Soc. Green Party. Achievements include discovery of accessiblity hierarchy in syntactic typology; conservativity constraint on natural language quantification. Avocations: poetry, art. Office: UCLA Dept Linguistics 3125 Campbell Hall Box 951543 Los Angeles CA 90095

KEENAN, JAMES FRANCIS, lawyer, insurance executive; b. Portland, Maine, Apr. 6, 1939; s. Michael Francis and Ruth Mary (Niles) K.; m. Sandra Annis, July 2, 1966; children— Tina, Michael, Angela, Paige, James, Jr. B.A., Bates Coll., 1961; J.D., Boston U., 1964, LL.M., 1975. Bar: Maine 1964, U.S. Dist. Ct. Maine 1965. Atty. Unionmutual Life Ins. Co., Portland, 1964-68, assoc. counsel, 1968-75, v.p., 1975— ; dir. Unionmutual Charitable Found., Portland, 1980-84. Author: (with Douglas Thornsjo) The Mutual Company, 1972. Trustee Bates Coll., Center Meml. Hosp., Standish, Maine, Sch. Adminstrv. Dist., Buxton, Maine. Fellow Am. Coll. Investment Counsel; mem. Am. Land Title Assn., Assn. Life Ins. Counsel, ABA, Maine Bar Assn. Home: RR 1 Box 8450 Sebago Lake ME 04075-9801 Office: UNUM Life Ins Co Unionmutual Life Ins Co 2211 Congress St Portland ME 04122-0003

KEENAN, JAMES GEORGE, classics educator; b. NYC, Jan. 19, 1944; s. George F. and Cecilia Anna (Schmidt) K.; m. Laurie Haight; children: James, Kathleen, Kenneth, Mary, Lisa, Brian, Laura. AB, Holy Cross Coll., 1965; MA, Yale U., 1966, PhD, 1968. Asst. prof. Classics U. Calif., Berkeley, 1968-73; assoc. to full prof. Classics Loyola U. of Chgo., 1973—, chmn. classics, 1978-84, acting chmn., 1987-88. Cons. Petra Scrolls Conservation Project, 1995. Co-editor: edition of Greek papyri: The Tebtunis Papyri, vol. IV, 1976. Fellow Nat. Endowment for Humanities, 1973-74; travel grantee Am. Council Learned Socs., 1974, 83, 86; grant-in-aid Am. Philos. Soc., 1987. Mem. Am. Philol. Assn., Am. Soc. Papyrologists (pres. 1989-93), Chgo. Classical Club (pres. 1999-2001), Classical Assn. Midwest and South, Assn. Internat. des Papyrologues (mem. com. 1995—), Egypt Exploration Soc., Internat. Soc. Arabic Papyrology. Roman Catholic. Office: Loyola U Chgo Dept Classical Studies 6525 N Sheridan Rd Chicago IL 60626-5344 E-mail: jkeenan@luc.edu.

KEENAN, JAMES JOSEPH, organizational consultant, communications educator; b. N.Y.C., Oct. 13, 1931; s. James Joseph and Genevieve Agnes (Commerford) K.; m. Elizabeth Leontine Myers, Feb. 7, 1960; children: James Joseph III, Thomas J., Elizabeth M., Patrick J., Michael J.J. BA, Manhattan Coll., 1953; MA, Fordham U., 1955; PhD, Columbia U., 1964. Lic. psychologist, Conn. Sr. rsch. scientist Inst. for Rsch. in Human Devel., Phila., 1956-57; mng. scientist Dunlap and Assocs., Darien, Conn., 1957-70; prin. exec. Keenan Assocs., Wilton, Conn., 1970—. Prof. Grad. Sch. Communications, Bus. Sch., Fairfield (Conn.) U., 1970—; orgn. cons. GE, IBM, Xerox, Mastercard, Peat Marwick Mitchell, GTE, Merrill-Lynch, A&E Networks, Pitney-Bowes, Westinghouse, Douglas Aircraft, 3M, Atari, Apple, 1957—; chmn. bd. sci. advisors Muzak Corp. Author: USAF Handbook for Human Performance Development, 1965, U.S. Navy Handbook for Human Performance Development, 1967, Human Performance and Communication Systems, 1981, The Communications Generalist, 1989, Corporate Catechisms: The Values of America's Largest Companies, 1997, The Intellectual Community, 1997, Managing Information and Communication Across the Enterprise, 1997, Ekistic-Macroergonomics, 1997, Communication Capital in Organizations, 2000. Comdr. USN, 1954-57. Mem. APA (various offices), Internat. Communication Assn., Human Factors and Ergonomics Soc. Am., New Eng. Psychol. Assn. Avocations: antique carousel model making, sports, music. Office: 117 Cavalry Rd Wilton CT 06897-3636

KEENAN, JOHN FONTAINE, judge; b. N.Y.C., Nov. 23, 1929; s. John Joseph and Veronica (Fontaine) K.; m. Diane R. Nicholson, Oct. 6, 1956; 1 child, Marie Patricia BBA, Manhattan Coll., N.Y., 1951; LLD (hon.), Manhattan Coll., 1989; LLB, Fordham U., 1954; LLD (hon.), Mt. St. Vincent Coll., 1989. Bar: N.Y. 1954, U.S. Dist. Ct. (so. dist.) N.Y. 1983. From asst. dist. atty. to chief asst. dist. atty. N.Y. County Dist. Atty.'s Office, 1956-76; spl. prosecutor, dep. atty. gen. City of N.Y., 1976-79; chmn. bd., pres. N.Y.C. Off-Track Betting Corp., 1979-82; criminal justice coord. City of N.Y., 1982-83; judge U.S. Dist. Ct. So. Dist. N.Y., N.Y.C., 1983—; chief asst. dist. atty. Queens County Dist. Atty.'s Office, N.Y., 1973. Adj. prof. John Jay Coll. Criminal Justice, N.Y.C., 1979-83, Fordham U. Sch. Law, N.Y.C., 1992, 93; mem. Fgn. Intelligence Svc. Ct., 1994-2001, Judicial Panel on Multi-Dist. Litigation, 1998—. Contbr. articles to law jours. Chmn. Daytop Village, Inc., N.Y.C., 1981-83. Served with U.S. Army, 1954-56. Recipient Frank S. Hogan award Citizens Com. Control of Crime in N.Y., 1975, Emory R. Buckner award Federal Bar Coun., 1993; cert. of recognition Patrolmen's Benevolent Assn., 1976; 1st Ann. Hogan-Morgenthau Assocs. award N.Y. County Dist. Atty.'s Office, 1976, Medal of Achievement, 1992; Excellence award N.Y. State Bar Assn., 1978, award N.Y. Criminal Bar Assn., 1979, Disting. Faculty award Nat. Coll. Dist. Attys., 1978, Louis J. Lefkowitz award Fordham Urban Law Jour., 1983, Charles Carroll award Guild Cath. Lawyers, 1994, Ellis Island medal of honor, Nat. Ethnic Coalition of Orgns. Found., Inc., 1998. Mem.: Brehon Soc. (award 2002), Skytop Club, Amackassin Club. Republican. Roman Catholic. Office: US Dist Ct US Courthouse 500 Pearl St Rm 1930 New York NY 10007-1312

KEENAN, JOHN PAUL, management educator, consultant, psychologist; b. Boston, Mar. 18, 1944; s. John W. and Claire (Gallagher) K.; m. Kathleen Lennon, Aug. 7, 1976; children: Christopher, Sean Patrick. BA, U. Santa Clara, 1967; MA, San Jose State U., 1969; PhD, U.S. Internat. U., San Diego, 1978. Instr. Chapman Coll., Orange, Calif., 1971-79; asst. prof. mgmt. Coll. of St. Rose, Albany, N.Y., 1979-83; dean C.C. Low County, Beaufort, S.C., 1983-86; assoc. prof. mgmt., dir. leadership devel. programs Mgmt. Inst., U. Wis. Sch. Bus., Madison, 1986-98; acting dean sch. leadership and human devel., assoc. prof. St. Bonaventure U., Buffalo, 1998—2001; exec. dir. leadership programs ACCEL-Medaille Coll., Amherst, NY, 2001—02. Acting dean Sch. of Leadership and Human Devel., exec. dir. Leadership programs ACCEL-Medaille Coll., Amherst, NY; pres., CEO John Keenan & Assocs., Orchard Park, NY, 1986—; exec. v.p. Coun. on Employee Responsibilities and Rights, Norfolk, Va., 1993—; spkr. in field; presenter in field. Co-author: Whistleblowing: Managing Dissent in the Work Place, 1985, Whistleblowing Research, 1985, Foundations of Leadership: New Manager Leadership Guide, 1997, Foundations of Leadership: Facilitator's Guide, 1997, Fastart: An Indepth Seminar for New Managers, 1998; editor-in-chief Employee Responsibilities & Rights Jour., 1999—; contbr. over 120 articles to profl. jours. Mem. APA, ASTD, Acad. Mgmt., Decision Scis. Inst., Inst. Mgmt. Scis., Soc. for Indsl. and Orgnl. Psychology, Assn. on Employment Practices and Principles (pres.1998—, program chmn. 1993, 97, 2000), Assn. Employment Practices and Prins. Avocations: swimming, hiking, all sports. Home: 2 Hillsboro Dr Orchard Park NY 14127-3411 E-mail: jkeenan945@aol.com.

KEENAN, LINDA LEE, paralegal; b. Lackawanna, N.Y., Mar. 12, 1951; d. David Lee and Beverly Ingaborg (Palmberg) Conway; m. Robert Joseph Keenan Jr., Sept. 10, 1983; children: Kristyn Marie, Beau, Bear, Tammy Ann. AS in Legal Studies, Teikyo Post U., 1995, BS in Liberal Arts summa cum laude, 1997; MA in History, Western Conn. State U., 1999. Cert. legal asst.; lic. real estate agt., Conn., real estate appraiser, Conn. Sec. I.B.M., Rye, N.Y., 1968-69; bus. mgr. Redding (Conn.) Country Club, 1973-86; paralegal Koskoff, Koskoff & Bieder, Danbury, Conn., 1986-2001. Adj. prof. Teikyo Post U., 2000—. Vol., court monitor Children in Placement, Danbury, 1993. Mem. NAFE, ATLA, AAUW, Phi Theta Kappa Honor Soc., Alpha Chi Honor Soc. Avocations: astronomy, astrology, writing, metaphysical study, history. Home: 14 Country Ridge Rd Danbury CT 06811-3211

KEENAN, MICHAEL EDGAR, marketing professional; b. Columbus, Ohio, Mar. 15, 1934; s. Edgar Charles and Kathryn Ellen (Dowden) K.; divorced; children: Margaret, Matthew, Emily, Jennifer, Andrew, Martha. AB, Duke U., 1955. Media buyer Compton Advt., N.Y.C., 1957-59; assoc. media dir. Foote, Cone & Belding, N.Y.C., 1959-61; media dir. Lennen & Newell, N.Y.C., 1961-63; sr. v.p., dir., cons. products div. Fuller & Smith & Ross, N.Y.C., 1963-70; chmn. Keenan & McLaughlin Inc., N.Y.C., 1970-82, cons., 1982-85; mng. dir. Western International Media Corp., N.Y.C., 1985-98; pres. Keenan & Co., Inc., N.Y.C., 1998—; CEO TELA Interactive, Inc., New York, N.Y., 1998—. Lectr. mktg. NYU, 1960-64; cons. FTC, Washington. Served with CIC, AUS, 1955-57. Mem. Am. Assn. Advt. Agys. (chmn. N.Y. coun. 1978), Nat. Agri-Mktg. Assn. (past pres. 1979), Rear Guard (treas., pres.), Thursday Club (chmn. 1960-2002). Republican. Roman Catholic. Avocation: sailing. Home: 63 Avenue A New York NY 10009-6539 Office: Keenan & Co Inc 666 5th Ave Ste 281 New York NY 10103-0001

KEENAN, MIKE, professional hockey team coach; m. Nola Keenan; 1 child, Gayla. Student, St. Lawrence U., N.Y. Player Roanoke Valley Rebels, So. Hockey League, Va., 1973-74; coach Met. Toronto Hockey League, Ont., Can., Peterborough Petes, Ont. Hockey League, 1979-80; head coach Can. Nat. Jr. Team, 1980, Rochester Ams., Am. Hockey League, N.Y., 1980-83, Toronto Hockey Team, Can. Collegiate League, Ont., 1983-84, Phila. Flyers, NHL, 1984-88, Chgo. Blackhawks, NHL, 1988-92, gen. mgr., 1990-92; head coach N.Y. Rangers, NHL, 1993-94; head coach, gen. manager St. Louis Blues, 1994-96; head coach Vancouver Canucks, 1998-99, Florida Panthers, 2001—. Named Most Valuable Player, Roanoke Valley Rebels, So. Hockey League, 1974; winning coach World Amateur Hockey Championships, 1980, Calder Cup Championship, 1982-83, Can. Collegiate Championship, U. Toronto, 1983-84, Stanley Cup Championship, 1994, Can. Cup Championship, 1987, 91; recipient Jack Adams award as NHL Coach of Yr., 1985; Coach of Yr. award Sporting News, 1985, Hockey News, 1985; Coach, NHL All-Star team 1985-86,1987-88,1992-93; Coach, Canadian national team, 1993. First season as NHL coach led Phila. Flyers to best record in NHL, 1984-85. Address: 265 S Fed Hwy Ste 308 Deerfield Beach FL 33441 Office: Florida Panthers One Panther Parkway Sunrise FL 33323

KEENAN, RETHA ELLEN VORNHOLT, retired nursing educator; b. Solon, Iowa, Aug. 15, 1934; d. Charles Elias and Helen Maurine (Konicek) Vornholt; m. David James Iverson, June 17, 1956; children: Scott, Craig; m. Roy Vincent Keenan, Jan. 5, 1980. BSN, State U. Iowa, 1955; MSN, Calif. State U., Long Beach, 1978. Cert. nurse practitioner adult and mental health. Pub. health nurse City of Long Beach, 1970-73, 94-96, cons., 1998, 99, 2000, coord. continuing edn., 1999, 2000. Pub. health nurse Hosp. Home Care, Torrance, Calif., 1973-75; patient care coord. Hillhaven, L.A., 1975-76; mental health cons. InterCity Home Health, L.A., 1978-79; instr. C.C. Dist., L.A., 1979-87; instr. nursing El Camino Coll., Torrance, 1981-86; instr. nursing Chapman Coll., Orange, Calif., 1982, Mt. St. Mary's Coll., 1986-87; cons., pvt. practice, Rancho Palos Verdes, Calif., 1987-89, 98, 99. Contbg. author: American Journal of Nursing Question and Answer Book for Nursing Boards Review, 1984, Nursing Care Planning Guides for Psychiatric and Mental Health Care, 1987-88, Nursing Care Planning Guides for Children, 1987, Nursing Care Planning Guides for Adults, 1988, Nursing Care Planning Guides for Critically Ill Adults, 1988. Mem. Assistance League of Temecula Valley, Calif. NIMH grantee, 1977-78. Mem. Sigma Theta Tau, Phi Kappa Phi, Delta Zeta. Republican. Lutheran. Avocations: traveling, writing, reading. Home: PO Box 205 Temecula CA 92593-0205

KEENAN, ROBERT ARTHUR, bank executive, consultant; b. Evergreen Park, Ill., Mar. 27, 1965; s. Robert Arthur and Katherine Joanne (Lyne) K.; m. Theresa Lynn Mendick, Oct. 5, 1991; children: Alexis, Lauren, Nicole, Hannah. BBA in Fin., U. Okla., 1988; MPA, Drake U., 2002. Ops. mgr. Sears Credit, Omaha, 1988-92, group asst mgr. West Des Moines, 1992-94; owner, pres. Movies to Go Video, Des Moines, 1994; asst. v.p. collections Norwest Card Svcs., West Des Moines, 1994-97; mayor/coun. mem. City of West Des Moines, 1994-97; v.p. strategic implementation Chase Manhattan Bank, Matteson, Ill., 1997-2000; mem. The Anlyn Group, 2000—, Protuiti, 2003. Mem. adv. bd. Consumer Credit Coun., Des Moines, 1993-94; Presdl. advance White House, 2000—. Bd. dirs. Visitors Bur., Des Moines, 1996-97, Rep. Mayor's Leaders, Washington, 1995-96; interim chief of staff Sen. Quandahl, Omaha, 1999; lead advance Bush for Pres., 1999-2000; campaign chmn. Burns for House, 2000; appointed Indsl. Comml. Commn. of Tinley Park, 2000. Mem. Am. Assn. Polit. Cons. Midwest (bd. dirs.), Inter Credit Assn. (bd. dirs. 1989-91), West Des Moines Chamber (bd. dirs. 1995-97), Lambda Chi Alpha Alumni (pres. 1997). Republican. Roman Catholic. Avocations: family, politics, golf, volleyball, sailing. Home and Office: Ste 100 7878 Marquette Dr N Tinley Park IL 60477-4564 E-mail: rak2016@aol.com.

KEENAN, ROBERT JOSEPH, trade association executive; b. San Francisco, May 25, 1946; s. Lawrence Alexander and Elma Patricia (Frenor) K.; m. Hildegard I. Gerlitz, Aug. 22, 1969; children: Michael Alexander, Patrick Sean. BS in Pub. Rels., Armstrong Coll., Berkeley, Calif., 1971; cert. in orgnl. mgmt., U. Santa Clara, 1975. Asst. mgr. Redwood City (Calif.) C. of C., 1971-73; exec. v.p. Lancaster (Calif.) C. of C., 1973-76, Montclair (Calif.) C. of C., 1976-79, Calif. Electric Sign Assn., Claremont, 1979-91, Bldg. Industry Assn. Tulare/Kings Counties, Visalia, Calif., 1991—. Chmn. Lancaster Inc. Com., 1974-76; dir., mktg. chair Workforce Coalition, Visalia, 1995-99; mem. select com. unlicensed contractors Calif. State Assembly, 1987-92. Author city incorp. game, 1974 (Congl. record 1975). Author chpt. 2.5 Calif. Bus. and Profl. Code, 1983-88, Calif. Electric Sign Assn., Claremont, 1989-90; author AB2823 Bldg. Industry Assn., Visalia, 1996; creator, coord. Bus., Industry and Govt. Coalition of the South San Joaquin Valley, 2001-03. With U.S. Army, 1966-69. Republican. Roman Catholic. Avocations: reading, sailing, billards, writing. Office: Bldg Industry Assn 315 W Oak Ave Visalia CA 93291-4928 E-mail: biabob@comcast.net.

KEENAN, TERRANCE, foundation executive; b. Phila., Feb. 1, 1924; s. Peter Joseph and Marie (Sloupova) K.; m. Joette Kathryn Lehan, Oct. 20, 1979. AB, Yale U., 1950; JD (hon.), Alderson-Broaddus Coll., Philippi, W.Va., 1973. Asst. headmaster Thomas Jefferson Sch., St. Louis, 1950-55; writer Merrill Lynch, N.Y.C., 1955-56; asst. editor office reports Ford Found., N.Y.C., 1956-65; sr. exec. asso. Commonwealth Fund, N.Y.C., 1965-72; v.p. Robert Wood Johnson Found., Princeton, N.J., 1972—. Bd. dirs. Grantmakers in Health, Washington. With USNR, 1943-46. Mem. Pub. Relations Soc. Am., Phi Beta Kappa. Clubs: Yale (N.Y.C.); Nassau (Princeton). Republican. Roman Catholic. Home: 435 Sterling St Newtown PA 18940-2142

KEENAN-ABILAY, GEORGIA ANN, service representative; b. Denver, Oct. 3, 1936; d. Lawrence Edward and Helen Kathleen (Gray) K.; m. Charles Henry Dupree, May 31, 1958 (div. Nov. 1977); children: Phoenix, Therese, Mark, John; m. Joseph D. Abilay, Nov. 26, 1988. BA, Regis Coll., 1968; MA, St. Thomas U., 1978. With reservations United Airlines, Denver, 1956-57; stewardess Trans World Airlines, Chgo., 1957-58; in elem. edn. Notre Dame Sch., Denver, 1969-72; dir. religious edn. Notre Dame Parish, Denver, 1972-77, Archdiocese Denver, 1977-80; v.p., treas. Kilfinane and Cook, Denver, 1980-82; dir. human resources Cosmopolitan Hotel, Denver, 1982-83, Kaanapali Beach Hotel, Lahaina, Hawaii, 1983-85, Royal Lahaina Resort, Hawaii, 1985-90; corp. dir. human resources Hawaiian Hotels and Resorts, Lahaina, 1988; dir. human resources Rock Resorts Lanai Resorts Ptnrs., Island of Lanai, 1990-94; ptnr. Blue Ginger Cafe, Lanai, 1995—. Trainer Amfac Hotels and Resorts, Hawaii, 1984-86; vice chmn. Maui Hotel Assn., 1987; bd. dirs. Project 714, Lahaina, 1987. Bd. dirs. Archdiocesan Women's Bd., Denver, 1981-83, Passages, Denver, 1980-83, Maui Econ. Devel. Bd., Kahalui, 1984; chairperson Charity Walk, 1984-86. Named Handicapped Employer of Yr., State of Hawaii, 1987. Mem. Council Hawaii Hotels, Am. Soc. Personnel Assn. Clubs: Distributive Edn. of Am. (Hawaii) (bd. dirs. 1984—). Avocations: fishing, boating. Home: PO Box 721 Lanai City HI 96763-0721 Office: Blue Ginger Cafe PO Box 1090 Lanai City HI 96763-1090

KEENE, DONALD, writer, translator, language educator; b. 1922; BA, Columbia U., 1942, AM, 1947, PhD, 1949; DLitt, U. Cambridge, 1978. Lectr. Cambridge U., 1948-53; guest editor Asahi Shimbun, Tokyo, 1982-92; prof. Columbia U., N.Y.C., 1955-92, prof. emeritus, 1992—. Author: The Battles of Coxinga, 1951, The Japanese Discovery of Europe, 1952, 69, Japanese Literature: An Introduction for Western Readers, 1953, Living Japan, 1957, Bunraku, The Puppet Theatre of Japan, 1965, No: The Classical Theatre of Japan, 1966, Landscapes and Portraits, 1971, Some Japanese Portraits, 1978, World Within Walls, 1978, Meeting with Japan, 1978, Travels in Japan, 1981, Dawn to the West, 1984, The Pleasures of Japanese Literature, 1988, Travelers of a Hundred Ages, 1989, Seeds in the Heart, 1993, On Familiar Terms, 1994, Modern Japanese Diaries, 1995, The Blue-Eyed Tarokaja, 1996, Emperor of Japan, 2002, Five Modern Japanese Novelists, 2003, Yoshimasa and the Silver Pavilion, 2003; editor: Anthology of Japanese Literature, 1955, Modern Japanese Literature, 1956, Twenty Plays of the No Theatre, 1970; translator: The Setting Sun, 1956, Five Modern No Plays, 1957, No Longer Human, 1958, Sources of Japanese Tradition, 1958, Major Plays of Chikamatsu, 1961, The Old Woman, the Wife and the Archer, 1961, After the Banquet, 1965, Essays in Idleness, 1967, Madame de Sade, 1967, Friends, 1969, Chushingura, 1971; The Man Who Turned into a Stick, 1972, Three Plays by Kobo Abe, 1993, The Narrow Road to Oku, 1996, The Tale of the Bamboo Cutter, 1998, The Breaking Jewel, 2003. Office: Columbia Univ 407 Kent Hall New York NY 10027

KEENE, JACK DONALD, molecular genetics and microbiology educator; b. Jacksonville, Fla., June 21, 1947; s. Jack Donald and Stella Collene (Ellis) K.; m. Judy May Keene, Sept. 6, 1969; children: Mike, Lisa. AB, U. Calif., Riverside, 1969; PhD, U. Wash., 1974. Staff fellow NINDS/NIH, Bethesda, Md., 1974-78; asst. prof. microbiology and immunology Duke U. Med. Ctr., Durham, NC, 1979-84, assoc. prof., 1984-88, prof., 1988-92, chmn., 1992—2002, James B. Duke disting. prof., 1997—, dir. Ctr. for RNA Biology, dept. molecular genetics and microbiology, 2002—. Exptl. virology study sect. NIH, 1984—88; mem. nat. sel. and adv. bd. PEW Scholars in the Biomed Scis., 1991—96; mem. molecular biology study sect. NIH, 1991—95, chmn., 1993—95; co-chmn. Diversity Biotech. Consortium, Santa Fe, 1994—; dir. basic sci. rsch. Duke U. Comprehensive Cancer Ctr., Program in Genetics, Program in Molecular and Cellular Biology Duke U., 1995—2003; dir. combinatorial scis. ctr. Duke U. Med. Ctr., 1994—2000; biotech. cons. LipoGen, Inc., BioWhittaker, Inc., Med. and Biol. Labs., Inc., Nagoya, Japan; co-founder SARCO, Inc., Combinatorial Sci. Systems, Inc., ChemCodes, LLC; founder Ribonomics, Inc., Research Triangle Park, NC; 00704469. Assoc. editor Virology, 1983—; mem. editl. bd. Jour. of Virology, 1985-95, Molecular and Cellular Biology, 1991—, Alliance Cellular Signaling; editor Microbiology and Molecular Biology Revs., 1992—, editor-in-chief, 2000—; editor Molecular Diversity, 1995—, Jour. Biol. Chemistry, 2003—; primary reviewer Jour. Immunology, 1996—. Mem. fellowship com. Arthritis Found., 1990-92, mem. rsch. com., arthritus found, 1990-92. Recipient Faculty Rsch. award Am. Cancer Soc., Devil's Bag award Arthritis Found.; Nanaline Duke Faculty Scholar, PEW Scholar in the Biomed. Scis. Fellow Am. Acad. Microbiology; mem. Am. Soc. Virology, Am. Soc. Biochemistry and Molecular Biology, Am. Soc. Microbiology (mem. pub. bd. 2000—), Ribonucleic Acid Soc., The Henry Kunkel Soc. Office: Duke Univ Med Ctr Box 3020 Mol Gen and Microbiol Dept Research Dr/414 Jones Bldg Durham NC 27710

KEENE, JOHN CLARK, lawyer, educator; b. Phila., Aug. 17, 1931; s. Floyd Elwood and Marthe (Bussiere) K.; m. Ana Maria Delgado, July 21, 1973; children: Lisa Keene Kerns, John, Suzanna Tonra, Katharine, Peter; stepchildren: Carlos, René, Mario, Raúl, Silvio Navarro, Carmen Peláez. BA, Yale U., 1953; JD, Harvard U., 1959; M in City Planning, U. Pa., 1966. Bar: Pa. 1960. Assoc. Pepper, Hamilton & Scheetz, Phila., 1959-64; prof. city and regional planning U. Pa., Phila., 1968—, chmn., 1989-93, univ. ombudsman, 1978-84, chmn. faculty senate, 1998-99; ptnr. Coughlin, Keene & Assocs., Phila., 1981—2000, Keene and Assoc., Phila., 2001—; chair doctoral program in city and regional planning U. Pa., 2002—. Vis. prof. U. Paris X, 1991. Author: (with Robert E. Coughlin) The Protection of Farmland, 1981, Growth Without Chaos, 1987, (with others) Untaxing Open Space, 1976, (with Samuel Hamill) Growth Mgmt. in NJ, 1989, (with Robert Coughlin and Joanne Denworth) Guiding Growth: Managing Urban Growth in Pa., 1991, 93, (with Julia Freedgood) Saving Am. Farmland: What Works, 1997. Trustee ex officio Phila. Mus. Art, 1978-80; mem. sci. and tech. adv. com. Chesapeake Bay Program. Lt. USN, 1953-56. Fulbright fellow Tunisia, 1985. Mem. Am. Inst. Cert. Planners, Phila. Club, Merion Cricket Club. Home: 1527 Montgomery Ave Bryn Mawr PA 19010-1659 Office: U Pa 127 Meyerson Hall Philadelphia PA 19104 E-mail: keenej@pobox.upenn.edu.

KEENE, KENNETH PAUL, lawyer; b. Torrington, Wyo., Oct. 29, 1940; s. Lyndell Franklin and Marion (Morgan) K.; m. Katherine LaHeist Keith Bell, Sept. 10, 1966 (div. May 1992); children: Elizabeth LaHeist Keene Lusby, Kenneth Paul Jr., Susan Morgan. BS, U. Nebr., 1962, JD cum laude, 1965. Bar: Nebr. 1965, Colo. 1968, Ariz. 1989. Shareholder Hecox, Tolley, Keene & Beltz, PC, Colorado Springs, Colo., 1970-94; ptnr. Rothgerber, Johnson & Lyons LLP, Colorado Springs, 1995—. Bd. dirs. Cheyenne Mountain Zoo, Colorado Springs, 1997—. Capt. JAGC, U.S. Army, 1965-69. Mem. Colo. Bar Assn., Nebr. Bar Assn., Ariz. Bar Assn., El Paso County Bar Assn. (probate sect., past pres.), Colorado Springs Estate Planning Coun. (past pres.), Cheyenne Mountain Country Club, El Paso Club, Kissing Camels Club. Republican. Office: Rothgerber Johnson & Lyons 90 S Cascade Ave Ste 1100 Colorado Springs CO 80903-1677 E-mail: kkeene@rothgerber.com.

KEENE, LONNIE STUART, lawyer; b. Milw., Sept. 13, 1954; s. Harold William and Phyllis K. BS, U.S. Mil. Acad., 1976; MPA, Harvard U., 1984; JD, NYU, 1998. Bar: N.Y. Asst. prof., instr. U.S. Mil. Acad., West Point, N.Y., 1984-87; asst. army attache U.S. Embassy, Beijing, 1988-90; mem. policy planning staff U.S. Dept. State, Washington, 1990-94; sr. policy analyst, office sci. & tech. policy The White House, Washington, 1994-95; assoc. Linklaters, London, 1998-99, Milbank, Tweed, Hadley & McCloy, London, Hong Kong,

1999—2001, Wollmuth Maher & Deutsch, NYC, 2002; v.p., asst. gen. counsel Goldman, Sachs & Co., N.Y.C., 2002—. Lt. col. U.S. Army, 1976—95, ret. U.S. Army. Decorated Legion of Merit; Olmsted scholar George and Carol Olmsted Found., Beijing, 1981-83. Mem. Coun. Fgn. Rels. (Internat. Affairs fellow 1990-91), Harvard Club N.Y.C. Avocations: golf, art, travel, skiing. Office: One New York Plz New York NY 10004 E-mail: Lonnie.Keene@gs.com.

KEENE, MARY ELLEN, federal agency executive; b. Washington, July 30, 1955; d. William Charles and Doris Eva (Springer) Keene; m. Randy Duane Ferryman, Dec. 4, 1982. BS in Edn. with honors, George Mason U., 1977; MPA, Harvard U., 1992. With CIA, Washington, 1974—, imagery analyst specializing mil. assessments, 1979-84, mgr., sr. departmental requirements officer, 1984-86, first-line mgr., later middle mgr. planning/programming unit, 1986-87, first-line mgr. imagery analytic unit, 1987-88, with Intelligence Cmty. Staff, Com. Imagery Requirements and Exploitation, 1988-90, mid. mgr. customer svcs., 1990-93, mid. mgr. imagery analytic element, 1993-95, mgr. comptr. function, 1995-98, mid. mgr. all-source analytic unit, 1998-2000, sr. mgr. resource mgmt. function, cmty. staff, 2000—. Mem. Kappa Delta Pi. Avocations: reading, gardening, collecting hummels, dogs.

KEENE, RICK, state legislator; b. Hayfork, Calif. m. Jancie Keene; children: Erin, Christopher, Rosie, Caitlin, Lucy. BA in Psychology and Religious Studies, Calif. State U., 1982; JD, Calif. No. Sch. Law, 1989. Laywer; businessman; mem. Chico Planning Commn., 1992—94; mem. city coun. Chico City, mayor; mem., dist. 3 Calif. State Assembly, 2002—. Chair Water, Parks and Wildlife; mem. Natural Resources, Budget Com. Republican. Mailing: PO Box 942849 Rm 5160 Sacramento CA 94249 Office: 1550 Humboldt Rd Ste 4 Chico CA 95928*

KEENE, SAMUEL JAMES, JR., reliability engineer researcher, educator; b. Washington, Dec. 28, 1939; s. Samuel James and Althea (Dudley) K. BSc in Physics, U. Md., 1962; MSc in Physics, Drexel U., 1966; PhD in Ops. Rsch., U. Colo., 1986. Reliability engr. Bendix, Towson, Md., 1962-64; rsch. scientist NASA Goddard Space Flight Ctr., Greenbelt, Md., 1964-67; adv. engr. IBM, Boulder, Colo., 1967-93; cons. engr. Performance Tech., Boulder, 1993—; six sigma master black belt Seagate Tech. Corp., 98—. Adj. prof. Prairie View (Tex.) A&M U., 1973-74; instr. U. Colo., Boulder, 1984-85, Nat. Techs. U., Ft. Collins, Colo., 1992-96; mem. Colo. State U. Quality Improvement Inst., Ft. Collins, 1982—. Contbr. chpts. to books and articles to profl. jours. Scoutmaster Boy Scouts Am., Boulder, 1966-80; Sunday sch. tchr. LDS Ch., Boulder, 1968-83; baseball coach Little League Am., Boulder, 1976-82. Recipient Alan Chop award Am. Soc. Quality, 1999. Fellow IEEE; mem. IEEE Reliability Soc. (exec. com. 1976-79, 81-83, 84-87, 88-90, 91-93, 96-99, pres. 1991-92, chmn. software reliability tech. com., chmn. reliability prediction tech. com., video tutorial chmn., award 1996, Reliability Engr. of Yr. award 1996). Achievements include Six Sigma Master Black Belt. Avocations: hiking, fishing, camping, cycling. Home: PO Box 337 Lyons CO 80540 Office: Seagate Storage Products 389 Disc Dr Longmont CO 80503-7664 Fax: 720-684-1128. E-mail: s.keene@ieee.org.

KEENE-BURGESS, RUTH FRANCES, military official; b. South Bend, Ind., Oct. 7, 1948; d. Seymour and Sally (Morris) K.; m. Leslie U. Burgess, Jr., Oct. 1, 1983; children: Michael Leslie, David William, Elizabeth Sue, Rachael Lee. BS, Ariz. State U., 1970; MS, Fairleigh Dickinson U., 1978; grad., U.S. Army Command and Gen. Staff Coll., 1986. Inventory mgmt. specialist U.S. Army Electronics Command, Phila., 1970-74, U.S. Army Communications-Electronics Material Readiness Command, Fort Monmouth, N.J., 1974-79; chief inventory mgmt. div. Crane (Ind.) Army Ammunition Activity, 1979-80; supply systems analyst Hdqrs. 60th Ordnance Group, Zweibruecken, Fed. Republic Germany, 1980-83; chief inventory mgmt. div. Crane (Ind.) Army Ammunition Activity, 1983-85, chief control div., 1985; inventory mgmt. specialist 200th Theater Army Material Mgmt. Ctr., Zweibruecken, 1985-88; analyst supply systems U.S. Armament, Munitions and Chem. Command, Rock Island, Ill., 1988-89; specialist logistics mgt. U.S. Army Signal Command, Ft. Huachuca, Ariz., 1989—. Troop leader Girl Scouts Am. Mem. Federally Employed Women (chpt. pres. 1979-80), NAFE, Soc. Logistics Engrs., Assn. Computing Machinery, Am. Soc. Public Adminstrn., Soc. Profl. and Exec. Women, AAAS. Democrat.

KEENEY, JOHN C. lawyer; b. Wilkes-Barre, Pa., Feb. 19, 1922; s. James M. and Mae M. (Clark) Keeney; widower; children: John C. Jr., Terence, Jean Marie, Joan, Kathleen. BS, U. Scranton, 1947; LLB, Dickinson Sch. of Law, Carlisle, Pa., 1949; LLM, Geo. Washington Law Sch., Washington, 1953. Chief Smith Act Unit, internal security sect. Dept. Justice, Washington, 1957-60, dep. chief organized crime sect. criminal divsn., 1966-69, chief fraud sect. criminal divsn., 1969-73, dep. asst. atty. gen. criminal divsn., 1973—. 1st lt. U.S. Army Air Force, 1943-45 ETO. Recipient Disting. Career award Pres. Reagan, 1983, Disting. Alumnus in Govt. award U. Scranton, 1997, Atty. Gen.'s Disting. Svc. award, 1987, D.C. Bar award for disting. govt. svc., 1996, Life Time Achievement award Dickinson Sch. Law, 2002. Roman Catholic. Home: 11101 Lund Pl Kensington MD 20895-1624 Office: US Dept Justice 10th And Pennsylvania NW Washington DC 20530-0001

KEENEY, JOHN CHRISTOPHER, JR., lawyer; b. Washington, Aug. 29, 1951; s. John Christopher and Eugenia M. (Brislin) Keeney; m. Kathleen V. Gunning; children: Katherine, Jaclyn. AB summa cum laude, U. Notre Dame, 1973; JD cum laude, Harvard U., 1976. Bar: Md. 1976, DC 1977, U.S. Dist. Ct. DC 1978, U.S. Dist. Ct. Md. 1977, U.S. Ct. Appeals (4th cir.) 1977, U.S. Ct. Appeals (DC cir.) 1978, U.S. Supreme Ct. 1980, U.S. Ct. Appeals (7th cir.) 1984, U.S. Ct. Appeals (10th cir.) 1989, U.S. Ct. Appeals (11th cir.) 1990, U.S. Ct. Appeals (9th cir.) 1997, U.S. Ct. Appeals (6th cir.) 1999. Law clk. to presiding judge U.S. Dist. Ct. Md., Balt., 1976-78; assoc. Hogan & Hartson, Washington, 1978-84, ptnr., 1985—, ptnr. in charge pro bono cmty. svcs. dept., 1989—93. Adj. instr. legal ethics Am. U. Las Sch., 2000—02. Co-author: (book) Civil and Criminal Remedies for Racially and Religiously Motivated Violence, 1983, 2d edit., 1999. Dir. Pub. Justice Ctr., Balt., 1990—95, 1997—2000; co-chair Dem. Nat. Lawyers Coun., 1999—; counsel for del. selection Babbitt for U.S. Pres. campaign, 1987—88; counsel Dem. credentials com., 1989—91; hearing officer Dem. Nat. Conv., 1992, 1996; chmn. Berlage for County Coun. campaign, Montgomery County, Md., 1989—94; bd. dirs. Washington Lawyers Com. for Civil Rights and Urban Affairs, 1999—. Mem.: ABA (former co-chair adjudication com., ad. law and regulatory practice sec 1999—2002, ho. dels. 2003—), DC Bar (bd. govs. 2000—, pres.-elect 2003—), Phi Beta Kappa. Roman Catholic. Home: 5516 Lincoln St West Bethesda MD 20817-3724 Office: Hogan & Hartson 555 13th St NW Ste 10W-206 Washington DC 20004-1109 E-mail: jckeeney@hhlaw.com.

KEENEY, RALPH LYONS, decision and risk analyst, educator; b. Lewistown, Mont., Jan. 29, 1944; s. Alonzo Stevens and Anna Murel (Lyons) K.; m. Janet L. Beach, Jan. 21, 1984; 1 child, Gregory. BS, UCLA, 1966; MS, MIT, 1967, profl. degree in elec. engring., 1968, PhD in Ops. Rsch., 1969. Engr. Bell Telephone Labs., Holmdel, N.J., 1966-69; asst. prof. civil engring., staff mem. Ops. Rsch. Ctr. MIT, Cambridge, 1969-72, assoc. prof. mgmt. and ops. rsch., 1972-74; rsch. scholar Internat. Inst. Applied Sys. Analysis, Laxenburg, Austria, 1974-76; head decision analysis Woodward-Cycle Cons., San Francisco, 1976-83, v.p., 1980-83; prof. mgmt. and engring. U. So. Calif., 1983—2002; rsch. prof. Fuqua Sch. Bus., Duke U., 2002—. Pvt. cons., 1969—. Author: Siting Energy Facilities, 1980, Value-Focused Thinking, 1992; co-author: (with Howard Raiffa) Decisions with Multiple Objectives, 1976, (with John S. Hammond and Howard Raiffa) Smart Choices, 1999. Recipient Lanchester prize Ops. Rsch. Soc. Am., 1976, Ramsey medal, 1989, Philip McCord Morse lectureship, 1993. Mem. NAE, Inst. Ops. Rsch. & Mgmt. Sci., Soc. Risk Analysis. Achievements include research in decision analysis, risk analysis; probabalistic models. Home: 101 Lombard St Apt 704W San Francisco CA 94111-1195 E-mail: keeneyr@aol.com.

KEENEY, STEVEN HARRIS, lawyer; b. Phila., Oct. 1, 1949; s. Arthur Hail and Virginia (Tripp) K.; m. Jean Ashburn, May 10, 1974 (div. Oct. 1986); 1 child, Christian Jeffrey. BA with honors, Trinity Coll., Hartford, Conn., 1971; MA, Hartford Sem. Found., 1973; JD, U. Conn., 1980. Bar: Ky. 1980, U.S. Dist. Ct. (we. dist.) Ky. 1981, U.S. Dist. Ct. (ea. dist.) Ky. 1983, U.S. Ct. Appeals (6th cir.) 2001. Staff reporter/edn. editor The Hartford Courant, 1971-74; asst. to supt. Hartford Pub. Schs., 1974-77; assoc. Igor Sikorsky & Assocs., Hartford, 1979-80, Brown, Todd & Heyburn, Louisville, 1980-82; ptnr. Barnett & Alagia, Louisville, 1982-88, Keeney & Willock, Louisville, 1988-90; prin. Amerilaw, Louisville, 1990-93; pres. LawTech Svcs. Co., Louisville, 1993—2002; mng. mem. Trautwein & Keeney PLLC, Louisville, 1993—2002, Keeney Law Office, LLC, Louisville, 2002—; city atty. City of Pineville, Ky., 2003—. Co-author/editor: Death Benefit: A Lawyer Uncovers A 20 Year Pattern of Seduction, 1993, 94, Reader's Digest Today's Best Non-Fiction Vol. 24, 1994; contbr. articles to profl. jours. Bd. dirs. Hospice of Louisville, Inc., 1984-86; exec. dir. Juvenile Justice Pub. Edn. Project, West Hartford, Conn., 1978-80; pres. bd. dirs. Stage One: Louisville Children's Theatre, 1982-83; founding bd. dirs. Ky. Citizens for Arts, Frankfort, 1983; mem. Lebanon (Conn.) Bd. Edn., 1975-80; campaign mgr. Mazzoli 3d C.D. Ky., Jefferson County, 1982, 84; elder 2d Presbyn. Ch., Louisville, 1984-86, ctrl. pres., 1990-, commr. counsel Recipient Disting. Contbn. award Nat. Com. for Prevention of Child Abuse, Ky. chpt., 1982, Disting. Svc. award Conn. Assn. Bds. of Edn., 1976, Profl. Achievement for Gen. Reporting Series award Soc. Profl. Journalists, Sigma Delta Chi, Conn. chpt. 1974. Mem. ABA (editl. com. The Tax Lawyer 1984-89), Assn. Trial Lawyers of Am., Nat. Assn. Criminal Def. Lawyers, Ky. Acad. Trial Atty's., Ky. Bar Assn., Louisville Bar Assn., Million Dollar Advocates Forum, Jefferson Club, Hon. Order of Ky. Cols. Democrat. Presbyterian. Avocations: bibliophile, marksman, golf. Office: Keeney Law Office PO Box 263 Harrods Creek KY 40027

KEENHOLTZ, STEVEN LAURENCE, physician; b. N.Y.C., Oct. 4, 1950; s. Samuel and Adele (Karp) K.; m. Roberta Meck, Jan. 31, 1976; children: Erica, Dana, Ross. BA, Case Western Res., 1972, MD, 1976. Diplomate Am. Bd. Internal Medicine, Am. Bd. Infectious Diseases. Intern, resident Balt. City Hosp., 1976-79; fellow Tufts New England Med. Ctrs., Boston, 1979-81; pvt. practice Danvers, Mass., 1981—. Cons. VNA North Shore, Danvers, Mass. Bd. dirs. Strongest Link AIDS Svc., 1983. Mem. Mass. Med. Soc., Soc. Hosp. Epidemiologists, Infectious Disease Soc., Phi Beta Kappa. Office: 140 Commonwealth Ave Danvers MA 01923-3629 E-mail: keen@mediaone.net.

KEENMON, KENDALL A. geologist, consultant, writer; s. Fred B. Keenmon and Myrtie May Andrews; m. Elizabeth Ann Keenmon. BS, U. Mich., Ann Arbor, 1947, MS, 1948, PhD, 1950. Geologist Shell oil Co., Wichita, Kans., 1950—56, Oklahoma City, 1956—61; rsch. geologist Shell Oil Co., Houston, 1961—71, staff geologist, 1971—85; owner K-Tech, Houston, 1985—. Pilot U.S. Army Air Corps, 1943—45. Home: 5158 Imogene St Houston TX 77096

KEENY, SPURGEON MILTON, JR., association executive; b. N.Y.C., Oct. 24, 1924; s. Spurgeon Milton and Amelia (Smith) K.; m. Sheila Spear, May 3, 1952; children Christopher Spear, Christy Virginia, Spurgeon Milton III. BA, Columbia U., 1944, MA in Physics, 1946; postgrad., Sch. Internat. Affairs and Russian Inst., 1946-47; LLD (hon.), U. Notre Dame, 1991. With Directorate of Intelligence, Hdqrs. USAF, 1950-55; mem. staff Panel on Peaceful Uses Atomic Energy, Joint Congl. Com. Atomic Energy, Washington, 1955-56; chief atomic energy div. Office of Asst. Sec. Def. for Research and Engring., Washington, 1956-57; mem. Gaither security resources panel Exec. Office of Pres., 1957; tech. asst. to President's Sci. Adviser, Washington, 1958-69; sr. staff mem. Nat. Security Council, 1963-69; asst. dir. for sci. and tech. U.S. Arms Control and Disarmament Agy., Washington, 1969-73, dep. dir., 1977-81; scholar-in-residence Nat. Acad. Scis., Washington, 1981-85; pres., exec. dir. Arms Control Assn., Washington, 1985 2001; sr. fellow Nat. Acad. Sci., Washington, 2002—. Dir. policy and program devel. Mitre Corp., McLean, Va., 1973-77; mem. U.S. del. to Geneva Conf. Experts on Nuclear Test Detection, 1958; to Geneva Conf. on Discontinuance of Nuclear Weapons Tests, 1958-60; chief U.S. del. U.S./Soviet Talks on Theater Nuclear Forces, 1980; mem. adv. com. Program Sci. and Internat. Affairs, Harvard, 1973-77; dep. chmn. com. environ. decision making Nat. Acad. Scis., 1974-77; chmn. Nuclear Energy Policy Study Ford Found., 1975-77; mem. com. on internat. security and arms control Nat. Acad. Scis., 1981—; mem. com. on Technical Issues Relating to Ratification of the Comprehensive Test Ban Treaty, Nat. Acad. Scis., 2000—. Co-author: Nuclear Power Issues and Choices, 1977; Nuclear Arms Control Background and Issues, 1985; Management and Disposition of Excess Weapons Plutonium, 1994, The Future of U.S. Nuclear Weapons Policy, 1997, Comprehensive Nuclear Test Ban Treaty, 2002. Served to 1st lt. USAF, 1948-50. Recipient Rockefeller Pub. Service award, 1970; Disting. Honor award U.S. Arms Control and Disarmament Agy., 1981 Fellow Am. Acad. Arts Scis., Am. Phys. Soc. (mem. study group on light-water reactor safety 1974-75, forum award 1986); mem. Council on Fgn. Relations, Phi Beta Kappa. Home: 3600 Albemarle St NW Washington DC 20008-4216 Office: Nat Acad Scis CISAC 500 5th St NW Washington DC 20001 E-mail: sskeeny@aol.com., skeeny@nas.edu.

KEEP, MARCUS FLOYD, neurosurgeon; b. N.Y.C., Mar. 15, 1959; s. Charles Russell Keep Jr. and Nancy Garland Stotz. AB in Religion, Dartmouth Coll., 1980; BS in Chemistry, U. S.C., 1981; MD, Med. U. S.C., 1988; postgrad., Shanxi U., Taiyuan, China, 1981-82, St. George's U., Grenada, W.I., 1984-85. Surgery intern Med. U. S.C., Charleston, 1988-89; neurosurgery resident Montreal Neurol. Inst., McGill U., Que., Can., 1989-94; rsch. fellow Restorative Neurology Unit, Lund (Sweden) U., 1994-96; pres. Restorative Neurosurgery Found., Honolulu, 1996—; CEO, founder Maas BiolAB, LLC, Honolulu, 1997—; assist. prof. div. neurosurgery U. N.Mex., Albuquerque, 2002—. Rsch. fellow INSERM-Neuromorphology Lab.-Salpetriere Hosp., Paris, 1989—90; asst. prof. dept. surgery John A. Burns Sch. Medicine, U. Hawaii, Honolulu, 1997—2002, asst. prof. dept. anatomy, 2000—02; rschr. Lab. Matrix Pathology, Honolulu, 1999—2002, Ctr. for Study of Neurol. Disease, Honolulu, 1997—98. Patentee in field; contbr. chapters to books, sci. articles to profl. jours. V.p. Nova Arts Found., Honolulu, 1997—2002; mem. instnl. rev. bd. St. Francis Med. Ctr., Honolulu, 1999—2001; mem. sci. adv. com. Clin. Rsch. Ctr., Honolulu, 2000—01; union rep. Montreal Neurol. Inst., Assn. Residents of McGill, Montreal, 1992—94; pres. Fellows' Soc. of Montreal Neurosurg. Inst., 1993—94. Rsch. grantee Ingeborg V.F. McKee Fund, 2001, RCMI-NIH, 2001-02, Bradley & Victoria Geist Found., 1998, 99, 2000, Omina-Freundeshilfe Found., 1994; fellow Phadhar Hosp., India, 1988, Burn Unit, Cali, Colombia, Ptnrs. of the Ams., 1987. Fellow: Royal Coll. Surgeons of Can.-Neurosurgery; mem.: Rocky Mountain Neurosurg. Soc., Soc. Stereotactic and Functional Neurosurgery, Congress Neurol. Surgeons, Cell Transplant Soc., Hawaii Assn. Neurol. Surgeons (treas. 1997—2000, v.p. 2000—02), Soc. for Neurosci., Am. Soc. for Neural Transplantation and Repair, Am. Epilepsy Soc., Am. Assn. Neurol. Surgeons., Internat. Brain Rsch. Orgn., Mass. Soc. Mayflower Descs., Outrigger Canoe Club. Home: 1934 Quail Run Loop NE Albuquerque NM 87122 E-mail: mkeep@maasbiolab.com.

KEEPIN, GEORGE ROBERT, JR., physicist; b. Oak Park, Ill., Dec. 5, 1923; s. George Robert and Erlene Marie (Bennett) K.; m. Madge Mary Twomey, June 13, 1948; children: Robert, William, Ardis, Mavis, Denice. PhB, U. Chgo., 1943; BS, MIT, 1946, MS, 1947; PhD in Physics, Northwestern U., 1949. Tchg. fellow dept. physics MIT, Cambridge, 1947; postdoctoral fellow U. Calif., Berkeley, 1950-52; rsch. physicist Los Alamos (N.Mex.) Sci. Lab., 1952-63, group leader nuclear safeguards rsch., 1966-76, dir. nuclear safeguards program, 1976-80; head physics divsn. IAEA, Vienna, Austria, 1963-65, spl. adviser to dep. dir. gen. nuclear safeguards, 1982-85; fellow Los Alamos Nat. Lab., 1985—. Mem. U.S. del. UN Atoms-for-Peace Conf., Geneva, 1955, 71, IAEA tech. adviser, 1964 Author: Progress in Nuclear Energy-Delayed Neutrons, 1956, Physics of Nuclear Kinetics, 1965; Arms Control Verification: The Technologies That Make It Possible, 1986; editor: Nuclear Analysis R and D; patentee in field. Fellow Los Alamos Nat. Lab, Am. Phys. Soc., Am. Nuclear Soc. (exec. com. 1967-69); mem. Inst. Nuclear Materials Mgmt. (nat. chmn. 1978-80, Disting. Service award 1984), N.Y. Acad. Scis., Sigma Xi Home: 600 La Bajada Los Alamos NM 87544-3805

KEEPORTS, DAVID DALE, physical science educator; b. York, Pa., June 15, 1951; s. Dale and Madeline (Mitzel) K. BS in Chemistry, U. Del., 1973; MS in Chemistry, Yale U., 1974; PhD in Phys. Chemistry, U. Wash., 1982. Asst. prof. phys. scis. Mills Coll., Oakland, Calif., 1982-87, assoc. prof., 1987-93, prof., 1993—. Author ednl. software: ; contbr. articles to sci. jours. Mem. Am. Chem. Soc., Am. Assn. Physics Tchrs., Sigma Xi. Home: 154 Oarsman Ct Hercules CA 94547-1500 Office: Mills Coll Dept Chemistry Physics Oakland CA 94613

KEER, LEON MORRIS, engineering educator; b. Los Angeles, Sept. 13, 1934; s. William and Sophia (Bookman) Keer; m. Barbara Sara Davis, Aug. 18, 1956; children: Patricia Renee, Jacqueline Saundra, Harold Neal, Michael Derek. BS, Calif. Inst. Tech., 1956, MS, 1958; PhD, U. Minn., 1962. Registered profl. engr., Calif. Mem. tech. staff Hughes Aircraft Co., Culver City, Calif., 1956-59; research fellow, instr. U. Minn., Mpls., 1959-62; asst. prof. Northwestern U., Evanston, Ill., 1964-66, assoc. prof., 1966-70, prof. engring., 1970—, Walter P. Murphy prof. mech. and civil engring., 1994—, assoc. dean research and grad. studies, 1985-92, chmn. dept. civil engring., 1992-97. Preceptor Columbia U., N.Y.C., 1963—64; co-dir. Ctr. for Surface Entring. and Tribology, 1997—; dept. acad. advisor civil and structural engring. Hong Kong U., 1998—; Chau Wei-Yin meml. lectr. Hong Kong Poly. U., 2000. Co-editor: (monograph) Solid Contact and Lubrication, 1980; contbr. articles to profl. jours. Fellow, NATO, 1962, Guggenheim Found., 1972, Japanese Soc. for the Promotion of Sci., 1986. Fellow: NAE (elected 1997), ASME (life; tech. editor Jour. Applied Mechanics 1988—92, Innovative Rsch. award tribology divsn. 2001, Daniel C. Drucker medal 2003), ASCE (life; chmn. engring. mech. divsn. 1992—93), Acoustical Soc. Am., Am. Acad. Mechanics (sec. 1981—88, pres.-elect 1987—88, pres. 1988—89); mem.: Tau Beta Pi, Sigma Xi. Home: 2601 Marian Ln Wilmette IL 60091-2207 Office: Northwestern U Dept Civil Engring 2145 Sheridan Rd Dept Civil Evanston IL 60208-0834 E-mail: l-keer@northwestern.edu.

KEES, MARY ADELE, school psychologist; b. Rice Lake, Wis., Sept. 9, 1948; d. Lloyd Robert and Irene Margaret (Kies) Bushland; m. Lowell Lee Kees, Mar. 9, 1968; children: Erik, Kealynn, Ian. BS in Elem. Edn., U. Wis., River Falls, 1975, MSE in Sch. Psychology, 1990, MSE in Reading, 1991, MSE in Guidance and Counseling, 1995, Ednl. Specialist degree, 2000. Lic. sch. psychologist, Wis. Admissions coord. St. Croixdale Hosp., Prescott, Wis., 1980-84; edn. coord. River Hills Hosp., Prescott, 1984-89; sch. psychologist Prescott sch. Dist., 1989—. EMT Rivers Falls Ambulance Svc. Mem. Nat. Assn. Sch. Psychologists, Wis. Assn. Sch. Psychologists. Avocation: reading. Home: N8520 1197th St River Falls WI 54022-4716 Office: Prescott Sch Dist 505 Campbell St N Prescott WI 54021-1073 E-mail: keesm@prescott.k12.wi.us.

KEESEE, PATRICIA HARTFORD, volunteer; b. Nashville, Apr. 29, 1928; d. William Donald and Mary Carolyn (Gwyn) Hartford; m. Thomas Woodfin Keesee Jr., June 26, 1953 (dec. Jan. 2000); children: Thomas Woodfin III, Anne Hartford Keesee Niemann; 1 stepson: Allen P.K. Keesee. BA in English, Radcliff Coll., 1950; BA in Environ. Scis., SUNY, Purchase, 1977. Lab. asst. Rockefeller U. (formerly Rockefeller Inst. Med. Rsch.), N.Y.C., 1951-54. Chmn. Byram com. Nature Conservancy, Bedford, N.Y., 1978-81; mem. Conservation Bd. Town of Bedford, 1978-88, Westchester County Environ. Mgmt. Commn., 1979-88, Coun. of N.Y. Bot. Garden, Bronx, N.Y., 1982—, Wetlands Commn., Bedford, 1988-97; trustee Lower Hudson chpt. Nature Conservancy, Katonah, N.Y., 1980-90, 91-99, chmn., 1983-86, vice chmn., 1995-99; pres. Fed. Conservationists of Westchester County, Purchase, 1985-87; trustee N.Y. State Bd. Nature Conservancy, Albany, 1983-91, vice-chmn., 1986-88; bd. dirs. Lady Bird Johnson Wildflower Ctr., 2000—. Mem. N.Y. Acad. Scis., Garden Club Am. (conservation com. 1983-85, 95-97, vice chmn. conservation com. 1985-87, bd. dirs. 1989-91, vice chmn. scholarship com. 1991-94). Episcopalian. Avocations: gardening, hiking, tennis, birding, botanizing. Home: 140 Sarles Rd RD 3 Mount Kisco NY 10549-4733

KEESEY, RICHARD E. retired behavioral neuroscience educator; b. York, Pa., Oct. 14, 1934; s. Richard E. and Josephine Bruner Keesey; 1 child, Ian W. AB, Dartmouth Coll., 1956; ScM, Brown U., 1958, PhD, 1960. Postdoctoral rsch. fellow Brain Rsch. Inst., UCLA, 1960—62; asst. prof. U. Wis., Madison, 1962—65, assoc. prof., 1965—69, prof., 1969—99, prof. emeritus, 1999—. Vis. lectr. Sydney (Australia) U., 1974. Office: Univ Wis 1202 W Johnson St Madison WI 53706

KEES-FOLTS, DEBORAH, pediatrician, educator; b. Annapolis, Md., Aug. 10, 1958; d. James A. Kees and Betty Lou Stull; m. Thomas S. Folts, Jan. 3, 1987; children: Claire Elizabeth Folts, Benjamin Paul Folts. BA, Dartmouth Coll., 1980; MD, Ohio State U., 1984. Cert. pediat. Am. Bd. Pediat., 1989, pediat. nphrology Am. Bd. Pediat., 1993. Assoc. prof. Pa. State Coll. Medicine, Hershey, 1992—, dir., pediat. clerkship, 2002—. Past-pres. Kidney Found. Ctrl. Pa., Harrisburg, 1993—2002. Master: Am. Soc. Pediat. Nephrology; fellow: Am. Acad. Pediat.; mem.: Am. Soc. Nephrology. Office: Pa State Childrens Hosp PO Box 850 Hershey PA 17033-0850

KEESHEN, KATHLEEN KEARNEY, public relations consultant; b. N.Y.C., Dec. 4, 1937; d. James William and Hannah Pauline (Mansfield) Kearney; 1 child (by previous marriage), John Christopher Day; m. Walt Keeshen Jr.; stepchildren: Michael Patrick, Walt John III, Kathleen Marie, William Thomas, Ralph Timothy. BA in English, U. Md., 1959, MA in Journalism, 1973, PhD in Am. Studies, 1983; MLA, Stanford U., 1995. Cert. profl. sec. Congl., legal, med., acad., corp. sec. various orgns., East and Midwest, 1954-63; staff and mgmt. positions IBM, Washington, Md., 1963-73, lab. comm. mgr. Systems Comm. Div. Manassas, Va., 1974-76, comm. staff corp. hdqrs. Armonk, N.Y., 1977-83, comm. and community rels. mgr. Almaden Rsch. Ctr. San Jose, Calif., 1983-92; prin. Keeshen Comm., Coyote (Calif.) Press., 1992—. Lectr. in field. Contbr. articles to profl. jours. Mem. adv. bd. Friends of San Jose Pub. Libr., 1987—, Silicon Valley Info. Ctr., 1986-92, Media Report to Women; mem. corp. task force Stanford U. Inst. for Rsch. on Women and Gender, 1990—, affiliated scholar, 1992-94, assocs. bd., 1994-96; affiliated scholar Beatrice M. Bain Rsch. Group on Gender, U. Calif., Berkeley, 1994-95; libr. commr. City of Morgan Hill, Calif., 1999-2003, commr. chair, 2001-2002 Mem. Am. Journalism Historians Assn., Assn. for Edn. in Journalism and Mass Comm., Women in Comm., San Jose Rotary Club, San. Jose Profl. Womens Literary Assn., Calif. Writers Club, Alpha Xi Delta, Calif. Libr. Assn., Calif. Assn. of Libr. Trustees and Commrs., Santa Clara Art Assn., Los Gatos Art Assn. Office: Keeshen Comm Coyote Press PO Box 13154 Coyote CA 95013-3154

KEESLER, RACHAEL GAY, management professional; b. Wauwatosa, Wis., July 19, 1965; d. Robert Williams and Ruth May Harvey; m. Randall A. Keesler, Dec. 24, 1997; children: Sarah, Jessica, Michael. Svc. mgr. Marcus Corp., Milw., 1982-85, mgr., 1985-88; mgr., sr. mgr. Terration, Milw., 1988-95; mgr., trainer Clark Mktg., Milw., 1995—. Contbr. poetry to profl. publs. Mem. The Am. Poetry Soc., Nat. Authors Registry (Pres. award 1994), Internat. Soc. of Authors and Artists. Roman Catholic. Avocations: writing, reading, camping, drawing. Home: 5863 S Hately Ave Cudahy WI 53110-2713 Office: Clark Mktg 5101 S 108 St Hales Corners WI 53130 E-mail: RedPenInc1@aol.com.

KEESLING, BRIAN, writer; b. Honolulu, Hawaii, May 8, 1956; s. Cecil Sailor and Mabel Eleanor Keesling. BFA, NYU, 1978. Author: (short stories) Numerous titles in variety of lit. and comml. mags. (The Writer's Voice New Voice award, 1990, First Pl. in Cream City Review's Fiction award, 1999). Avocation: dressage rider. Personal E-mail: briankeesling@msn.com.

KEESLING, KAREN RUTH, lawyer; b. Wichita, Kans., July 9, 1946; d. Paul W. and Ruth (Sharp) Keesling. BA, Ariz. State U., 1968, MA, 1970; JD, Georgetown U., 1981. Bar: Va. 1981, Fla. 1981. Asst. dean of women U. Kans., Lawrence, 1970-72; exec. sec., sec.'s adv. com. on rights and responsibilities of women HEW, Washington, 1972-74; dir. White House Office of Women's Programs, Washington, 1974-77; head civil rights and equal opportunity sect., Gov. Div., Congl. Rsch. Svc. Libr. Congress, Washington, 1977-80; legis. aide Sen. Nancy Kassebaum, Washington, 1979-81; mem. pers. office staff Office of Pres.-elect, Washington, Jan. 1981; pvt. practice Falls Church, Va. and Peoria, Ariz., 1981-88, 90—; dept. for equal opportunity dept. Dept. Air Force, Washington, 1981-82, dep. asst. sec. manpower res. affairs and installations, 1982-83, prin. dep. asst. sec. manpower res. affairs, 1983-87, prin. dep. asst. sec. readiness support dept., 1987-88, prin. dep. asst. sec. manpower and res. affairs, 1988, asst. sec. manpower and res. affairs, 1988-89; acting wage and hour adminstr. U.S. Dept. Labor, Washington, 1992-93; pvt. practice Falls Church, Va., Peoria, Ariz. Bd. advisers Outstanding Young Women Am., 1983—90. Mem. Nat. Women's Polit. Caucus, Washington, 1980, Nat. Fedn. Rep. Women's Club, Washington, 1975; chair pers. com. Faith Presbyn. Ch., 2000—. Named One of Ten Outstanding Young Women of Am., 1975; recipient Alumni Achievement award, Ariz. State U., 1976, Elizabeth Boyer award, Women's Equity Action League, 1986, Meritorious Civilian award, USAF, 1987, Woman of Distinction award, Nat. Conf. Coll. Women, Student Leaders and Women of Distinction, 1988, Exceptional Civilian Svc. award, USAF, 1988. Mem.: Va. Bus. and Profl. Women's Found. (trustee 1985—93), The Women's Inst. Inc. (adv. coun. 1985—96), No. Va. Women atty.'s Assn. (steering com. 1990—95),

Va. Fedn. Bus. and Profl. Women's Clubs (2d v.p. 1987—88, 1st v.p. 1988—89, pres.-elect 1989—90, pres. 1990—91), Fla. Bar Assn., Va. Bar Assn., Ariz. Bar Assn., P.E.O., U.S. Com. for UNIFEM (gen. counsel 1983—), Pi Beta Phi. Avocation: Avocation: golf (Kans. Women's Golf Champion 1966, Wichita Women's Champion 1968, 70, Outstanding Woman Golfer in Kans. 1966). Home: 9606 W Lindgren Ave Sun City AZ 85373 E-mail: Keeslingkr@aol.com.

KEESLING, RUTH MORRIS, foundation administrator; b. New Brunswick, N.J., Apr. 4, 1930; d. Mark Loren and Louise Weber Morris; m. Thomas Marion Keesling, June 30, 1956; children: Thomas Mark, James H., Frank M. BS in Journalism, U. Colo., 1953. Advt. dept. Burlingame (Calif.) Advance, 1953—54; news dept. Oakland (Calif.) Tribune, 1954; pub. rels. Mark Morris Assoc., Inc., Topeka, 1955; co-owner Pub. Rels., Inc., Denver, 1955—64; pres. Digit Fund, Denver, 1986—88; founder, sponsor Mountain Gorilla Vet. Project, Denver, 1986—2001; founder, pres. Mountain Gorilla Conservation Fund, Denver, 2001—. Founder Morris Animal Found., Denver, 1955—; pres. Dian Fossey Gorilla Fund, Denver, 1988—91, pres. internat., 1991—93; bd. trustees Dian Fossey Gorilla Fund Europe, London, 1989—; trustee Denver Zool. Found., Denver, 1969—; lectr. mountain gorillas; sponsor, founder Mt. Gorillas in Africa, 1987—; founder Wildlife Animal Medicine Dept. Makerene U., Uganda, 1994; head task force Rwandan Govt., 2000. Author: (brochures) Small Animal Clinical Nutrition, 1959; designer (exhibitions) Mus. Display Diane Fossey items, 1992—94. Recipient Outstanding Alumni award, U. Colo., 1976, award for animal welfare, Collier County Humane Soc., 2002, Lifetime Achievement award, Brit. Airways, 2002, award, Collier County Humane Soc., 2002. Mem.: Port Royal Club, Naples Yacht Club, Denver Country Club, Pi Beta Phi (chmn. adv. bd. 1957—60, mem. house bd. 1958—61, Carolyn Lichtenberg Crest award 2000). Home: 3220 Cherryridge Rd Englewood CO 80110 Office: Mountain Gorilla Conservation Fund PO Box 2211 Englewood CO 80150-2211 Fax: 303-781-0929. E-mail: RuthKee@aol.com.

KEETON, J. E. retired psychiatrist; b. Brilliant, Ala., Oct. 8, 1925; s. James Willie and Mary Etta (Dodd) K.; m. Mary Ann Trantham, May 31, 1953 (dec. Dec. 1989); children: Jonathan Eric, David Wright, Adam Blake. BS, Birmingham So. U., 1951; MD, U. Ala., 1955. Intern U. Chgo. Clinics, 1955-56; resident psychiatry Inst. Living, Hartford, Conn., 1956-59; dir. day hosp. Vets. Hosp., Washington, 1960-61, asst. chief psychiatry, 1961-64, pvt. practice psychiatry Bethesda, Md., 1964-78; staff psychiatrist Vets. Med. Ctr., Tuscaloosa, Ala., 1978-97; ret., 1998. Dir. clozapine rsch. Vets. Hosp., Tuscaloosa, 1991-97. Pharmacist mate USN, 1944-46. Mem. Am. Psychiat. Assn. (life). Home: 4324 Stonehill Ln Tuscaloosa AL 35405-5441

KEETON, MORRIS TEUTON, research scholar; b. Clarksville, Tex., Feb. 1, 1917; s. William Robert and Ernestine (Tuten) K.; m. Ruth Urice, Jan. 9, 1944 (dec. Dec. 1997); children: Gary KaDel, Scot, Gerlinde Joan. BA, So. Meth. U., 1935, MA, 1936, Harvard U., 1937, PhD, 1938; LHD (hon.), Thomas A. Edison Coll., 1982, U. Md., 1983, SUNY, 1983, U. N.H., 1988, DePaul U., 1988, Antioch U., 1989. Ordained to ministry Meth. Ch., 1946. Instr. philosophy and social sci. So. Meth. U., 1938-41; ednl. sec. Brethren Civilian Pub. Svc., 1942-45; faculty Antioch Coll., 1947-77, prof. philosophy and religion, 1956-77, pastor, 1947-60, from dean faculty to provost, v.p., 1963-77; from exec. dir. to pres. Council Advancement Exptl. Learning, Columbia, Md., 1977-89, sr. fellow, 1990; dir. Inst. for Rsch. on adults in Higher Edn. U. Md. Univ. Coll., College Park, 1990-98, sr. scholar, 1997—. Vis. adj. prof. Sch. for New Learning, DePaul U., 1989-90; coll. examiner North Ctrl. Assn. Colls. and Secondary Schs., 1960-77; exec. bd. Commn. Instns. Higher Edn., 1973-77; chmn. commn. on higher edn. and the adult learner Am. Coun. on Edn., 1981-89; bd. edn. Yellow Springs Exempted Village Sch. Dist., 1961-65; head mission in Germany, Am. Friends Svc. Com., 1953-55, chmn. internat. confs. and seminars program com., 1959-63, chmn. diplomats conf., Clarens, Switzerland, 1961, chmn. mission to Germany, 1963; chmn. steering com. Coop. Assessment Exptl. Learning, 1974-77; trustee Fielding Inst., 1982-88, chair bd. trustees, 1986-88; cons. Cambridge Coll., 1991-2000; chmn., adv. panel Goddard Coll., 1999-2000; participant Radcliffe Intellectual Renewal Seminars, 1999-2000; mem. Commn. on the Future, Howard C.C., 1999-2001. Author: The Philosophy of Edmund Montgomery, 1950, Values Men Live By, 1960, Shared Authority on Campus, 1971, Models and Mavericks--A Profile of Liberal Arts Colleges, 1971; co-author: Journey Through a Wall, 1964, Ethics for Today, 4th edit., 1967, 5th edit., 1972, Struggle and Promise: A Future for Colleges, 1969, Experiential Learning, 1976, Learning by Experience-What, Why, How, 1978; editor: (with Harold Titus) The Range of Ethics, 1966; co-editor: (with Pamela Tate) Sourcebooks on New Directions in Experiential Learning, 1978-83; (with Barry Sheckley and Lois Lamdin) Employability in a High Performance Economy, 1993; (with Barry Scheckley) Improving Employee Development, 1997, Effectiveness and Efficiency in Higher Education for Adults, 2002. Pres. Columbia Forum, 1990-93; regent Land Rover U. N.Am., 1996-97. Guggenheim fellow, 1946; named to Internat. Adult and Cont. Edn. Hall of Fame, 1999; recipient Pres. medal U. Md. U. Coll., 2000. Fellow Soc. Religion in Higher Edn.; mem. Am. Philos. Assn. (life, sec.-treas. Western div. 1959-61, chmn. Carus Lectures com. 1965-69), AAUP, Am. Assn. Higher Edn. (exec. com. 1965-66, dir. campus governance program 1966-69, pres. 1972-73). Democrat. Home and Office: 10989 Swansfield Rd Columbia MD 21044-2707

KEETON, ROBERT ERNEST, federal judge; b. Clarksville, Tex., Dec. 16, 1919; s. William Robert and Ernestine (Tuten) K.; m. Elizabeth E. Baker, May 28, 1941; children: Katherine, William Robert. BBA, U. Tex., 1940, LLB, 1941; SJD, Harvard U., 1956; LLD (hon.), William Mitchell Coll., 1983, Lewis and Clark Coll., 1988. Bar: Tex. 1941, Mass. 1955. Assoc. firm Baker, Botts, Andrews & Wharton (and successors), Houston, 1941-42, 45-51; assoc. prof. law So. Meth. U., 1951-54; Thayer teaching fellow Harvard U., 1953-54, asst. prof., 1954-56, prof. law, 1956-73, Langdell prof., 1973-79; assoc. dean Harvard, 1975-79; judge Fed. Dist. Ct., Boston, 1979—. Commr. on Uniform State Laws from Mass., 1971-79; trustee Flaschner Jud. Inst., 1979-86; exec. dir. Nat. Inst. Trial Advocacy, 1973-76; ednl. cons., 1976-79; mem. com. on ct. adminstrn. U.S. Jud. Conf., 1985-87, mem. standing com. on rules, 1987-90, chmn., 1990-93. Author: Trial Tactics and Methods, 1954, 2d edit., 1973, Cases and Materials on the Law of Insurance, 1960, 2d edit., 1977, Legal Cause in the Law of Torts, 1963, Venturing To Do Justice, 1969, (with Jeffrey O'Connell) Basic Protection for the Traffic Victim: A Blueprint for Reforming Automobile Insurance, 1965, After Cars Crash: The Need for Legal and Insurance Reform, 1967, (with Page Keeton) Cases and Materials on the Law of Torts, 1971, 2d edit., 1977, Basic Text on Insurance Law, 1971, (with others) Tort and Accident Law, 1983, 2d edit., 1989, (with others) Prosser & Keeton, Torts, 5th edit., 1984, Pocket Part, 1988, (with Alan Widiss) Insurance Law, 1988, Judging, 1990, Judging the American Legal System, 1999, Guidelines for Drafting, Editing, and Interpreting, 2002; also articles. Served to lt. comdr. USNR, 1942-45, PTO, 1945-56. Recipient Wm. B. Jones award Nat. Inst. Trial Advocacy, 1980; recipient Leon Green award U. Tex. Law Rev., 1981, Francis Rawle award Am. Law Inst.-ABA, 1983, Samuel E. Gates litigation award Am. Coll. Trial Lawyers, 1984 Fellow Am. Bar Found., mem., Am. Acad. Arts and Scis., Am. Bar Assn., Mass. Bar Assn., State Bar Tex., Am. Law Inst., Am. Risk and Ins. Assn., Chancellors, Friars, Order of Coif, Beta Gamma Sigma, Beta Alpha Psi, Phi Delta Phi, Phi Eta Sigma. Office: US Dist Ct 1 Courthouse Way Ste 3130 Boston MA 02210-3005

KEETS, JOHN DAVID, JR., insurance company executive; b. Atlantic City, N.J., Apr. 1, 1948; s. John D. and Doris F. (Fleiss) Keets; m. Julianne Zellers, Nov. 3, 1973; children: J. David, Brian. BA, High Point Coll., 1970. CLU., cert. fin. planner, chartered fin. cons. Account exec. Mgmt. Recruiters, Phila., 1972-75; sales mgr. Cigna Fin. Svc., Miami (Fla.), Balt., 1975-82; agy. mgr. Fidelty Mut., Balt., 1983-85, Provident Mut. Ins. Co., Phila., 1985-88; regional v.p. Equitable Ins. Co., Mpls., 1988-90; prin. Keets & Assocs., Mpls., 1991—; mgr. Prudential Ins. Co., Mpls., 1993-94; v.p. bus. devel. Carlson Mktg. Group, Mpls., 1994-96; gen. mgr. Mut. of Omaha Cos., Mpls., 1998-2000; regional dir. 10F Foresters, 2000—. With U.S. Army, 1970-72, Germany. Mem. Mpls. Assn. Life Underwriters, Gen. Agts. and Mgrs. Assn, Internat. Assn. Fin. Planners, Am. Soc. CLU, Chartered Fin. Cons. Avocations: golf, boating. Home: 2420 Comstock Ln N Minneapolis MN 55447-2303

KEEVEY, RICHARD FRANCIS, government official, educator; b. Phila., June 20, 1942; s. Richard Patrick and Eileen (Wright) K.; m. Elizabeth Regina Dwyer, Aug. 5, 1967; children: Richard, Michael, John. BA, La Salle Coll., Phila., 1964; M of Govt. Adminstrn., U. Pa., 1967. Various positions Commonwealth of Pa., City of Phila., State of N.J., 1967-70; dir. adminstrn., fiscal officer dept. community affairs N.J. Dept., Trenton, 1971-75, asst. to dir. div. budget and acctg. Treasury Dept., 1975-81, supr. Bur. Budget, Office Mgmt. and Budget, 1981-83, dep. budget dir., dep. conptr., 1983-89, dir. Office Mgmt. and Budget, 1989-94; dep. under sec. for fin. mgmt. Dept. Def., Washington, 1994-95, dir. defense fin. and acctg. agy., 1995-97; CFO U.S. Dept. Housing and Urban Renewal, 1997-99; dir. budget and fin. practice Arthur Andersen, Washington, 1999—2002; dir. adminstrv. and fin. programs Unisys corp., McLean, Va., 2002—. Instr. Rutgers U., New Brunswick, N.J., 1971-75; adj. prof. fin. Rider Coll., Lawrenceville, N.J., 1979-82, mem. adv. com. grad. program in pub. mgmt., 1983-87; adj. prof. Seton Hall U., South Orange, N.J., 1990-93; adj. prof. budgeting systems George Mason U., Fairfax, Va., 1999-2001. vis. prof. Princeton U., 2002-03. Contbr. articles to profl. jours.; mem. bd. editors Pub. Adminstrn. Rev., 1979-84. Coach Little League Baseball and Soccer, 1975-82; trustee Police Athletic League Sports, Cinnaminson, N.J., 1978-81; mem. counsle president's adv. bd. La Salle U., 1984-87; bd. dirs. Zurbrugg Meml. Hosp., Willingboro, N.J., 1985-88; mem. Leadership N.J. Class of 1990, 1989—; pres. Cinnaminson Twp. Bd. Edn., 1980-90; mem. N.J. Commn. on Capital Budgeting and Planning, N.J. Bldg. Authority, N.J. Commn. on Health Benefits and Pensions, N.J. Transit Corp., N.J. Capital Joint Mgmt. Commn., N.J. Lease Mgmt.-Planning Bd. Recipient: Ken Howard award Career Achievement in Budget and Finance Am. Soc. Pub. Adminstrn., 2000; decorated DSM, medal for outstanding svc. U.S. Dept. Def., 1996. Mem. Nat. Assn. State Budget Officers, Nat. Assn. Comptrs., Am. Soc. for Pub. Adminstrn. (N.J. Pub. Adminstr. of Yr. award 1992), Assn. Govtl. Accts. (Disting. Leadership award N.J. chpt. 1991), Govt. Fin. Officers Assn. (tech. group to rev. budgets for nat. award certs.). Home: 2808 Roesh Way Vienna VA 22181-6165 Office: Unisys Corporation 8008 Western Drive Mc Lean VA 22101

KEEVIL, NORMAN B. mining executive; b. Cambridge, Mass., Feb. 28, 1938; s. Norman Bell and Verna Ruth (Bond) Keevil; m. Joan E. McDonald, Dec. 1990; children: Scott, Laura, Jill, Norman Bell III. BA in Sci., U. Toronto, Ont., Can., 1959; PhD, U. Calif., Berkeley, 1964; LLD (hon.), U. B.C., 1993. V.p. exploration Teck Corp., Vancouver, B.C., Can., 1962-68, exec. v.p., 1968-81, pres., CEO, 1981-89, chmn., pres., CEO, 1989-94, pres., CEO, 1994-2000, CEO, 2000—; chmn. Teck Cominco Ltd., Vancouver, 2001—. Named Mining Man of Yr., No. Miner, 1979. Mem. Soc. Exploration Geophysicists, Prospectors and Developers Assn. (Disting. Svc. award 1990, Viola R. MacMillan Developer's award 1997), Can. Inst. Mining and Metallurgy (Selwyn G. Blaylock medal 1990, Inco medal 1999), Royal & Ancient Golf Club (St. Andrews, Scotland), Shaughnessy Golf and Country Club, Vancouver Club. Office: Teck Cominco Ltd 200 Burrard St # 700 Vancouver BC Canada V6C 3L9

KEEVIL, PHILIP CLEMENT, investment banker; b. London, Oct. 19, 1946; s. Ambrose Clement Arthur and Olwen Marjorie Enid (Gibbins) K.; m. Augusta Day McGrail, June 10, 1972; children: Adrian Ambrose Clement, Augusta Hall, Peter Larimer. BA, Oxford U., Eng., 1968, MA, 1972; MBA, Harvard U., 1975. Mgr. Unilever plc, Eng., 1968-73; assoc. Morgan Stanley & Co., N.Y.C., 1975-78, Lazard Freres & Co., N.Y.C., 1979-80, v.p., 1981-82, gen. ptnr., 1983-87; mng. dir., head mergers and acquisitions S.G. Warburg and Co. Inc., N.Y.C., 1987-91, head investment banking, 1991-95; mng. dir. head internat. mergers and acquisitions Salomon Brothers Inc., N.Y.C., 1995-97; head European mergers and acquisitions Salomon Smith Barney, London, 1997-2000; mng. dir., head mergers and acquisitions Schroder Salomon Smith Barney, London, 2000—02. Bd. dirs. S.G. Warburg & Co., Ltd., London, 1987-95, Am. for Oxford Inc., 1995-02; mem. devel. bd. Said Bus. Sch., Oxford (Eng.) U., 1999—. Freeman of City of London, 1968; liveryman Worshipful Co. of Poulters, London, 1968—; mem. of the Court, 1992—, renter warden, 1998-99, upper warden, 1999-2000, master, 2000-01; vestryman St. John's Ch., Locust Valley, N.Y., 1986-89; trustee St. Bernard's Sch., N.Y., 1991-97, St. Andrew's Sch., Del., 1993-2001; bd. govs. City of London Sch. for Girls, 2002--. Baker scholar Harvard Bus. Sch., Boston, 1975. Fellow: Royal Soc. Arts; mem.: Brit.-Am. C. of C. (dir. 1993—2000, dep. chmn. 1999—2001), London Rowing Club, Queenwood (Cobham, Eng.), Cavalry and Guards (London), Leander Club (Henley, Eng.), Wyandanch Club, L.I. Club, Knickerbocker Club, Racquet and Tennis Club (N.Y.C.), Brook Club, Piping Rock Club (Locust Valley) (gov. 1986—96). Episcopalian. Avocations: choral music, field sports, racquet sports. Office: Schroder Salomon Smith Barney 33 Canada Sq Canary Wharf London E14 5LB England E-mail: philip.keevil@ssmb.com.

KEEZER, JAMES ROBERT, music educator; b. Bloomington, Ill., Feb. 23, 1947; s. William Stillman and Cynthia Jean Keezer; m. Helen Elizabeth Larrington, Dec. 31, 1973; children: Amy Elizabeth, Nathan Stillman, Natalie Jean, Alisha Anne. MusM, U. of Nev., Reno, Nevada, 1981; BS, U. of Colo., 1969. Music educator Sch. Dist. 25, Pocatello, Idaho, 1997—; music/orch. educator Sch. Dist. 91, Burley, Idaho, 1982—96; music educator Hecla - Houghton Sch., Hecla, SD, 1979—82, Salida sch., Salida, Colo., 1976—76, Peetz Plateau Sch., Peetz, Colo., 1972—74. Profl. banjo player, New Orleans, 1994; profl. guitarist Harrah's Showroom, Reno, 1975—76. Condr. Magic Philharm. Orch., Burley, Idaho, 1984—93. With USN, 1969—71, Guam. Recipient Musician of the Yr., Burley Music Club, 1987. Mem.: Internat. Jazz Educators, Music Educator's Nat. Conf. Avocations: hiking, photography, music. Home: 493 Hyde Avenue Pocatello ID 83201-3267 Personal E-mail: espnat@aol.com.

KEFALIDES, NICHOLAS ALEXANDER, physician, educator; b. Alexandroupolis, Greece, Jan. 17, 1927; came to U.S., 1947, naturalized; s. Athanasios and Alexandra (Aematidou) K.; m. Eugenia Georgia Kutsunis, Nov. 24, 1949; children: Alexandra Jane (dec.), Patricia Ann, Paul Thomas. BA, Augustana Coll., Rock Island, Ill., 1951; BS, U. Ill., Chgo., 1953, MS in Biochemisry, MD, U. Ill., Chgo., 1956, PhD in Biochemistry, 1965; MS (hon.), U. Pa., 1971; doctorate (hon.), U. Reims, France, 1987. Resident in internal medicine U. Ill. Coll. Medicine, Chgo., 1960-62, NIH fellow in infectious disease, 1962-64, asst. prof. medicine, 1964-65, U. Chgo., 1965-69, assoc. prof. medicine, 1969-70; assoc. prof. medicine and biochemistry U. Pa., Phila., 1970-74, prof. medicine, 1974—, prof. biochemistry and biophysics, 1975—; assoc. dean rsch. U. Pa. Sch. Medicine, 1994-95. Vis. prof. Oxford (England) U., 1977—78, 1984—85; mem., chmn. pathobiochemistry study sect. NIH, 1982—86; dir. project on burns NIH, USPHS, Lima, Peru, 1957—60, Connective Tissue Rsch. Inst., Phila., 1977—2002; chmn. Instn. Rev. Bd. U. Pa., 1995—98, exec. chmn., 1998—; initiator, chair Gordon Rsch. Confs. on Basement Membranes, 1982. Contbr. chpts. to books, articles to profl. jours. Served as surgeon USPHS, 1957-60. Recipient Borden Rsch. Found. award, 1956, award for pioneering rsch. on connective tissue Collagen Gordon Confs. and Collagen Corp., 1997; Guggenheim fellow, 1977. Fellow AAAS; mem. Am. Assn. Pathologists, Am. Soc. Clin. Investigation, Am. Soc. Biochemistry and Molecular Biology, Am. Soc. Cell Biology. Achievements include discovery of Collagen type IV in basement membranes and its role in suppressing tumor cell growth. Office: U Pa Univ City Sci Ctr 3701 Market St Rm 468 Philadelphia PA 19104-5502

KEFAUVER, WELDON ADDISON, publishing executive; b. Canal Winchester, Ohio, Apr. 3, 1927; s. Ross Baker and Virginia Marie (Burtner) K. BA, Ohio State U., Columbus, 1950. Mem. faculty Columbus Acad., 1956-58; mng. editor Ohio State U. Press, 1958-64, dir., 1964-84, dir. emeritus, 1984—. Dir. Am. Univ. Press Services, Inc., 1971-72, 76-79; mem. U.S. del. 2d Asian Pacific Conf. Publs., Taiwan, 1978 Author: Scholars and their Publishers, 1977; editorial adv. bd. Scholarly Publishing. Served with AUS, 1945-46. Recipient Centennial Service award Ohio State U., 1970; citation Ohioana Library Assn., 1974; Disting. Service award Ohio State U., 1986; recognized for service to Ohio State U. by Ohio Senate and Ohio Ho. of Reps., 1986. Mem. Assn. Am. Univ. Presses (v.p. 1971-72, dir. 1971-72, 76-79, pres. 1977-78), Soc. Scholarly Pub., Nathaniel Hawthorne Soc., AAUP, Phi Eta Sigma, Phi Kappa Phi Clubs: Torch (Columbus), Crichton (Columbus), Ohio State U. Faculty (Columbus). Home: 675 Eastmoor Blvd Columbus OH 43209-2252 Office: 1050 Carmack Rd Columbus OH 43210-1002

KEFFER, CHARLES JOSEPH, consultant; b. Phila., Aug. 7, 1941; s. Raphael Joseph and Clara Emelia (Fefolt) K.; m. Barbara Franke, Aug. 27, 1966; children— Susan Marie, David Charles, Peter John, Dennis Paul BS, U. Scranton, 1963; AM, Harvard U., 1964, PhD, 1969. From instr. to assoc. prof. physics U. Scranton, Pa., 1967-73; dean coll. U. St. Thomas, St. Paul, 1973-77, v.p. acad. affairs, 1973-84, provost, 1977-98. Cons.-evaluator N. Central Assn., Chgo., 1980-98. Chmn. Midway Tng. Services, St. Paul, 1977-87. Grad. fellow NSF, Harvard U., 1963-65; summer leadership fellow Bush Found., 1977 Mem. Democratic Farm Labor Party. Roman Catholic Avocation: soccer.

KEFFER, MARIA JEAN, environmental auditor; b. Sacramento, Dec. 10, 1951; d. George Edwin and Genevieve Nellie (Babuska) Scott; m. Gerry Craig Keffer, Nov. 6, 1971; children: Annemarie, Gregory, Margaret. AA in Liberal Arts, San Bernardino Valley Coll., Calif., 1973; BS in Natural Scis., U. Alaska, 1988, MS in Environ. Quality, 1995. Cert. environ. auditor Nat. Registry of Environ. Profls., prin. environ. auditor/EARA - U.K.; registered environ. health specialist, Nat. Environ. Health Assn. and State of Calif. Rsch. lab. assoc. VA/Loma Linda (Calif.) Hosp., 1988-90; environ. health specialist San Bernardino County, Calif., 1990-91, S&S Engring., Eagle River, Alaska, 1991-92; regulatory specialist ENSR Consulting and Engring., Anchorage, 1992-94; quality assurance environ. specialist Alyeska Pipeline Svc. Co., Anchorage, 1994-98; ISO 14001 project mgr. Hoefler Consulting Group, Anchorage, 1998—. Mem. Environ. Auditing Roundtable Office: Hoefler Consulting Group 701 Sesame St Ste 200 Anchorage AK 99503-6641

KEFFLER, KARL JOSEPH, investment company executive, lawyer; b. St. Louis, July 1, 1943; s. Karl Leopold and Dorothea Agnes (Lucas) K. Student, U.Notre Dame, 1961-62; BA cum laude, Regis U., 1965; JD, St. Louis U., 1968; postgrad., Northwestern U., Chgo., 1972, Oxford (Eng.) U., 1995. Bar: Mo. 1969, U.S. Dist. Ct. D.C. 1970, Ill. 1987. Spl. agt. FBI, Washington, Mpls., San Francisco, 1968-71; asst. pros. atty. Office Pros. Atty. St. Louis County, Clayton, Mo., 1971-74; pvt. practice, St. Louis, 1974-81; trust officer Merc. Trust Co., NA, St. Louis, 1981-85; trust exec., head trust dept. People's Bank & Trust Co., Waterloo Iowa, 1985-86, Ill. Nat. Bank, Springfield, 1987-88, 1st Comml. Bank, Little Rock, 1988-89; pvt. investor St. Louis, 1989-97; exec. v.p., chief investments officer St. Louis Capital Mgmt., LLC, 1997—. Author investment newsletter Capital Idea, 1998. Bd. dirs. Springfield Symphony, 1987. Mem. Mo. Bar, Soc. Former Spl. Agts. FBI, Am. Mensa, Phi Delta Phi. Avocations: sports, art collecting, music. Home: 155 N Hanley Rd Apt 105 Saint Louis MO 63105-4106 Office: St Louis Capital Mgmt LLC 9845 Northbridge Rd Saint Louis MO 63124-1025 E-mail: KARLJKEFFLER@prodigy.net.

KEGEL, GUNTER HEINRICH REINHARD, physics educator, researcher; b. Herborn, Germany, June 16, 1929; came to U.S., 1964; s. Wilhelm Ottmar and Gertrud Marie Karoline K.; m. Brita Inga Maria Ahlnas, Sept. 7, 1957; children: Thomas Marcus, Ann Christina. BS, Univ. do Brasil, Rio de Janeiro, 1951; PhD, MIT, 1961. Prof. Pontificia Univ. Catolica, Rio de Janeiro, 1961-64, U. Mass. Lowell, Lowell, 1964—. Adj. prof. Univ. do Brasil, Rio de Janeiro, 1952-56; cons. in field. Contbr. articles to profl. jours. Mem. IEEE, Am. Phys. Soc., Am. Nuc. Soc., Electrochem. Soc., Am. Vacuum Soc., Material Rsch. Soc. Office: U Mass Lowell 1 University Ave Lowell MA 01854-5009 Fax: 978-459-6561. E-mail: gunter_kegel@uml.edu.

KEGEL, WILLIAM GEORGE, mining company executive; b. Pitts., Mar. 15, 1922; s. William G. and Gertrude (Holl) K.; m. Jacqueline Treacy, Feb. 17, 1942; children: Kathy, Danyele, Janice, Jacqueline, William, Madeline, Colleen, Lisa, Brian. Student elec. engring. U. Pitts., 1940-43; LLD (hon.), Ind. U. of Pa., 1986. Mgr. mech. and elec. depts. Lee Norse Co., 1941-50; with Jones & Laughlin Steel Corp., Pitts., 1950-76, gen. mgr. raw materials and traffic, 1975-76; pres. Cerro Marmon Coal Group, 1976-79; pres., chief exec. officer Rochester & Pitt. Coal Co., Indiana, Pa., 1979-88, chmn. bd., 1988-98. Dir. emeritus Savs. and Trust Co. Pa., Indiana. Mem. Indiana (Pa.) Airport Authority, 1980-2001; bd. dirs. Brownsville Gen. Hosp., 1964-71; mem. Centerville Borough Council, 1952-60. Mem. AIME, Coal Mining Inst. Am., Am. Mining Congress (dir.), Pitts. Coal Mining Inst., Duquesne Club, Ind. Country Club, Laurel Valley Country Club. Republican. Roman Catholic. Home: 61 Duck Woods Dr Southern Shores NC 27949

KEGELES, LAWRENCE STEVEN, psychiatrist, researcher; b. Madison, Wis., Feb. 9, 1947; s. Gerson and Bertha (Webber) K.; m. Wendy Carol Winer, Aug. 10, 1987; 1 child, Laura Rosalyn. AB, Princeton U., 1969; PhD in Physics, U. Pa., 1974; MD, Mt. Sinai Sch. Medicine, N.Y.C., 1991. Lic. physician, N.Y. Rsch. assoc. U. Pa., Phila., 1974-76, U. Alberta, Edmonton, Can., 1976-78, Stevens Inst. Tech., Hoboken, N.J., 1978-80; mem. tech. staff AT&T Bell Labs., Murray Hill, N.J., 1981-87; postdoctoral resident Columbia Presbyn. Hosp., N.Y.C., 1991-95, rsch. fellow in psychiatry, 1995-99, asst. attending psychiatrist, 1998-99; asst. prof. clin. psychiatry Columbia U., N.Y.C., 1999, asst. prof. clin. psychiatry and radiology, 2000—. Adj. rsch. faculty Mt. Sinai Sch. Medicine, 1991—. Contbr. more than 40 articles to profl. jours. Eli Lilly & Co. fellow, 1995; Nat. Alliance for Rsch. on Schizophrenia and Depression grantee, 1995-99, NIMH grantee, 1999—; Bristol-Myers Squibb fellow, 2000. Mem. AMA, Soc. Nuc. Medicine, Soc. for Neurosci., Internat. Soc. for Magnetic Resonance in Medicine, Sigma Xi. Office: Columbia Presbyn Hosp Dept Psychiatry 1051 Riverside Dr New York NY 10032-1013

KEGERREIS, ROBERT JAMES, management consultant, marketing educator; b. Detroit, Apr. 2, 1921; s. I. G. and A. M. (Merry) K.; m. Katherine L. Falknor, Oct. 30, 1943; children: Merry, Duncan, Melissa. BA, BS, Ohio State U., 1943, MBA, 1946, PhD, 1968, U. Dayton, 1982, EdD (hon.), EdD (hon.), U. Dayton; LLD (hon.), U. Akron, Wilberforce U.; ScD (hon.), Cen. State U., Japan, 1992; EconD (hon.), Okayama U., Japan, 1992. Economist Fed. Res. Bank, Cleve., 1946-49; pres. KV Stores, Inc., Woodsfield, Ohio, 1949-69; v.p., sec. KBK Devel. Co., Inc., 1955-62; assoc. prof. Ohio U., Athens, 1967-69; dean Coll. Bus. and Adminstrn. Wright State U., Dayton, Ohio, 1969-71, v.p. adminstrn., 1971-73, pres., 1973-85; cons. RJK Co., Dayton, 1985—. Bd. dirs. Robbins & Myers, Dayton, Miami Valley Rsch. Found., Tait Found. Exec. dir. Arts Ctr. Found., Dayton. Lt. (j.g.) USN, 1943-46. Mem. Moraine Country Club, Bicycle Club, Pelican Bay Country Club. Methodist. Avocations: flying, golf. Office: Kettering Tower Ste 1480 Dayton OH 45423-1000

KEGLEY, JACQUELYN ANN, philosophy educator; b. Conneaut, Ohio, July 18, 1938; d. Steven Paul and Gertrude Evelyn (Frank) Kovacevic; m. Charles William Kegley, June 12, 1964; children: Jacquelyn Ann, Stephen Lincoln Luther. BA cum laude, Allegheny Coll., 1960; MA summa cum laude, Rice U., 1964; PhD, Columbia U., 1971. Asst. prof. philosophy Calif. State U., Bakersfield, 1973-77, assoc. prof., 1977-81, prof., 1981—. Vis. prof. U. Philippines, Quezon City, 1966-68; grant project dir. Calif. Council Humanities, 1977, project dir. 1980, 82; mem. work group on ethics Am. Colls. of Nursing, Washington, 1984-86; mem. Am. Bd. Forensic Examiners; chair acad. senate Calif. State U., 2000—. Author: Introduction to Logic, 1978, Genuine Individuals and Genuine Communities, 1997; editor: Humanistic Delivery of Services to Families, 1982, Education for the Handicaped, 1982, Genetic Knowledge, 1998; mem. editl. bd. Jour. Philosophy in Lit., 1979-84; contbr. articles to profl. jours. Chair CSU Acad. Senate, 1999—; Bd. dirs. Bakersfield Mental Health Assn., 1982—84, Citizens for Betterment of Community. Recipinet Outstanding Leadership award Calif. State U., 1997-98, Outstanding Prof. award Calif. State U., 1989-90, Golden Roadrunner award Bakersfield Community, 1991, Wang Family Excellence award, 2000. Mem. Philosophy of Sci. Assn., Soc. Advancement Am. Phil. soc. (chmn. Pacific div. 1979-83, nat. exec. com. 1974-79), Philosophy Soc., Soc. Interdisciplinary Study of Mind, Am. Philosophical Assn. (bd. mem. 1999-2003, chair com. on tchg.), Dorian Soc., Phi Beta Kappa. Democrat. Lutheran. Avocations: music, tennis. Home: 7312 Kroll Way Bakersfield CA 93309-2336 Office: Calif State U Dept Philosophy Bakersfield CA 93311

KEHEW, GEORGE MANSIR, artist; b. Harvey, Ill., Aug. 17, 1923; s. George Henry and Blanche Willard (Holt) K.; m. Dolores Smith, Mar. 21, 1947; children: Eric Wayne, Roger Mark, Jai Lynne. Student, Chouinard Art Sch., L.A., Art Ctr. Coll. of Design. Cert. indsl. edn. tchr. Calif., Calif. C.C. tchr. in art, design and photography. Various positions in field to illustrator Northrop Aircraft Corp., Hawthorne, Calif., 1957-59; lead man, tech. illustrators Cannon & Sullivan, San Diego, 1959-61; art dir. Applied Oceanog. Group, Scripps Inst. Oceanography U. Calif., San Diego, 1961-66, illustrator, photographer Office Learning Resources, 1966-67; artist Complete Art Svc., San Diego, Calif., 1966-68; illustrator, tng. visuals Grumman Aerospace, NAS Miramar, Calif., 1972-73; visual info. specialist Naval Edn. and Tng. Support Ctr., San Diego, 1973-85. Alt. mem. Equal Employment Opportunity Com., San Diego, 1983. Artist/author: Mac Goes to the Hospital, Best Friends Animal Coloring and

Activity Book; creator ofcl. Squadron patch (Red Wolf) for VF-1 Mira Mar Naval Air Sta., logo for Scripps Applied Oceanographic Group, Point Loma, Calif., (game) Bushwacker; syndicated cartoon strip Hamalot; exhibiting cartoonist 1968 Terre Des Hommes, Man and His World, Pavilion de L'Humor, Montreal; designer, dir. TV show packaging for Art Around Us, San Diego Area Instrnl. TV Authority, 1965, others; represented in Vincent Price Sears travel show, 1965-67, others; contbr. articles to Desert Mag. Sgt. U.S. Army, PTO, 1942-46. Recipient art awards including Bicentennial First Ann. Best of Show award, 1976, Merit award in publs. San Diego C.C., 1972, award for best painting St. George Art Mus., 1999, Sweepstakes award Washington County Fair Juried Show, 1999-2000, 3d pl. award Springville Juried Art Show, 2000; grantee in field. Democrat. Avocations: mountain biking, cross country skiing, sailing, classic guitar. E-mail: kehewart@infowest.com.

KEHLBECK, JOSEPH H. software developer and consultant; b. Clifton, N.J., Sept. 14, 1926; s. Joseph John and Elizabeth Harriet (Lockhoff) K.; m. Mary Kathryn Russell, Nov. 15, 1957; 1 child, Keith Alan. BS in Engring., State U. Iowa, 1950; MBA in Fin., Rutgers U., Newark, 1954. Registered profl. engr., Calif. Various positions Gen. Electric, 1952-69, mgr. mfg. engring., 1969, mgr. mfg. Trenton, N.J., 1969-72, Louisville, 1972-77, mgr. material resource ops., 1977-85, gen. mgr. internat. purchasing Bridgeport, Conn., 1986; cons., software developer Kehlbeck & Assocs., Prospect, Ky., 1987—. Mem. adv. bd. On Display, San Ramon, Calif., 1998-99; bd. dirs. Philippine Appliance Co., Manila, 1979-85. Author: Production Leveling, 1959. With U.S. Army, 1943-45, lt. Res., 1946-52. Recipient award Order of Engrs., 1977. Fellow Inst. Indsl. Engrs. (pres. 1977), Hunting Creek Country Club (bd. dirs.), Shriners, Tau Beta Pi. Avocations: golf, tennis. Office: Kehlbeck & Assocs 7812 Cedar Ridge Ct Prospect KY 40059-9491 E-mail: kehlbeck@aol.com.

KEHLMANN, ROBERT, artist, critic; b. Bklyn., Mar. 9, 1942; BA, Antioch Coll., 1963; MA, U. Calif., Berkeley, 1966. Instr. glass design Calif. Coll. Arts and Crafts, Oakland, 1978-80, 91, Pilchuck Glass Ctr., Stanwood, Wash., 1978-80; guest curator Mus. Glass, Tacoma, Wash., 2001. One-man shows include Richmond Art Ctr., Calif., 1976, William Sawyer Gallery, San Francisco, 1978, 82, 86, Gallerie M. Kassel, Fed. Republic Germany, 1985, Anne O'Brien Gallery, Washington, 1988, 90, Dorothy Weiss Gallery, San Francisco, 1993, Hearst Art Gallery, Moraga, 1996; group shows include Am. Craft Mus., N.Y.C., 1978, 86, Corning (N.Y.) Mus. Glass, 1979, Tucson Mus. of Art, 1983, Kulturhuset, Stockholm, 1985; represented in permanent collections at Corning Mus. Glass, Leigh Yawkey Woodson Art Mus., Hessesches Landes Mus., Germany, Bank of Am. World Hdqrs., San Francisco, Toledo Mus. Art, Hokkaido Mus. Modern Art, Sapporo, Japan, Huntington Mus. of Art, W.Va., Am. Craft Mus., N.Y.C., Musée des Arts décoratifs, Lausanne, Switzerland, Oakland Mus. Author: Twentieth Century Stained Glass: A New Definition, 1992, The Inner Light: Sculpture By Stanislau Libensky and Jaroslava Brychtova, 2002; contbg. editor: New Glass Work mag., 1988-89; editor: Glass Art soc. Jour., 1981-84. Chmn. Landmarks Preservation Commn., Berkeley, 1979-85. NEA grantee, 1977, 78. Mem. Glass Art Soc. (bd. dirs. 1980-84, 89-92, hon. life).

KEHOE, CHRISTINE T. state official; b. Troy, N.Y., Oct. 3, 1950. BA, SUNY, Albany, 1972. Editor San Diego Enyzette, 1984—86; coord. San Diego AIDS Assistance Fund, 1987—88; exec. dir. Hillcrest Bus. Assn., 1988—89; aide San Diego City Coun., 1989—92; cmty. devel. specialist San Diego, 1992—93; mem. San Diego City Coun., 1993—2000; mem. city mgr.'s office Econ. Devel., 1993; candidate Calif. Dist. 49 U.S. Congress, 1998; state assembly mem. Dist. 76 Calif. State Assembly, 2000—. Mem. arts, entertainment, sports, tourism and Internet media com.; mem. housing and cmty. devel. com.; mem. pub. employees, retirement and social security com.; mem. transp. com.; mem. water, parks, and wildlife com.; mem. VA com.; chair select com. on park and river restoration, 2001—; chair pub. safety and neighborhood svcs. com., 1995—96; legis. aide State of Calif., 1992; coun. rep. City of San Diego, 1989—92; campaign coord. San Diegans for Neil Good, 1987, San Diego Says No on 64, 1986. Mem.: NOW, San Diego Assn. Govt., San Diego Small Bus. Adv. Bd., San Diego Cen. Dem. Com. (mem. San Diego City Coun. 1993—2000, chair subcom. on econ. prosperity 1998), Calif. Women in Edn., Sierra Club, San Diego Dem. Club. Democrat. Mailing: Rm 3152 PO Box 942849 Sacramento CA 95814 Office: Ste C-207 1010 University Ave San Diego CA 92130

KEHOE, DENNIS JOSEPH, lawyer; b. Culver City, Calif., Nov. 12, 1937; s. Ignatius Dennis and Anne Theresa K.; m. Jacqueline Mona, Aug. 25, 1962; children: Theresa, Suzanne, Patrick, Michael, Kevin. BS in Commerce, U. Santa Clara, 1960; LLB, U. Calif. Hastings Coll. Law, 1963. Bar: Calif. 1964, U.S. Dist. Ct. (no. dist.) Calif. 1964, U.S. Ct. Appeals (9th cir.) 1964, U.S. Supreme Ct. 1980. Asst. county counsel Santa Cruz County, Calif., 1964-66; assoc. Adams, Levin, Kehoe, Bosso, Sachs & Bates and predecessor, Santa Cruz, 1966-70, ptnr., 1970-87; sole practice Santa Cruz, 1987—. Mem. Calif. State Bar Assn., Santa Cruz County Bar Assn. Office: 311 Bonita Dr Aptos CA 95003-4891 E-mail: kehoelaw@hotmail.com.

KEHOE, JOHN KIMBALL, management educator, management consultant; b. Chicago, Ill., June 20, 1936; s. John J. and Eleanor M. Kehoe; m. Mary Corleen, Aug. 3, 1974; children: Megan Rose, Nancy Kimball. BA, Northwestern U., Evanston, Ill., 1958; MA, St. Louis U., 1964; Dr. of Bus. Admin., Harvard U., Cambridge, Mass., 1975. Pers. rep. Eli Lilly and Co., Indpls., 1974—75, comp. analyst, 1976, sr. sales recruiter, 1977—78, internat. pers. adv., 1979—80, HR mgr. for rsch., 1981; dir. mgmt. devel. Eli Lilly & Co., Indpls., 1982—84; dir. exec. devel. SCH Healthcare Sys., Houston, 1985—89; dir. Exec. ed. Rice U, Houston, 1989—92; assoc. dean Fuqua Sch., Duke U, Durham, NC, 1992—93; dir. custom prog. Ctr. for Creative Leadership, Greensboro, NC, 1993—95; sr. cons. Pers. Decisions Internat., Mpls., 1995—97, Profit Link, Naperville, Ill., 1997—2002; lectr. in mgmt. Rice U, Houston, 2002—. Tchg. asst. Harvard U., 1970—72; instr. Harvard Bus. Sch., Boston, 1970—74; lectr. Ind. U., Indpls., 1977—83; assoc. dean exec. ed. Duke U, Durham, NC, 1992—93; adj. faculty Rice U, Houston, 1987—92, dir. exec. ed., 1989—92, lectr. in mgmt., 2001—. Mem.: Harvard Bus. Sch. Club of Houston (assoc.). Achievements include Two presentations at Nat. meeting of Academy of Mgt. Avocation: community svc.. Home: 6010 Pin Oak Place Spring TX 77379-8825

KEHOE, JOHN P. investor relations and corporate development consultant; b. NYC, Aug. 5, 1938; s. John M. and Mary K. (Denning) K.; m. Veronica Lally McAuley, Dec. 1, 1984; children: John Michael, Maura Ann, Kevin Denning, Brendan, Allise McAuley Cert. in investment analysis, N.Y. Inst. Fin., 1960; MS in Bus. Policy, Columbia U., 1979; BA in English Lit., Fordham U., 1985. Sr. assoc. Baker Weeks & Co., Inc., N.Y.C., 1957-61; v.p., asst. to pres. McDonnell & Co., Inc., N.Y.C., 1961-65, sr. v.p., chmn. investment policy com., 1965-67; pres. McDonnell Fund, N.Y.C., 1965-67; exec. v.p. Crosby M. Kelly Assocs. Ltd., N.Y.C., 1967-69; pres., founder, chmn. Kehoe, White, Savage & Co. (Kehoe Ptnrs., Inc.), N.Y.C., 1969—98; chmn. Kehoe Ptnrs., Inc., N.Y.C., 1998—; sr. advisor Abernathy MacGregor Group, N.Y.C., 2000—. Lectr. in field Served as sgt. USMCR, 1958-64. Mem.: Nat. Assn. Corp. Dirs., Nat. Investor Rels. Inst. (charter), N.Y. Roadrunners Club, Ea. Yacht Club (Marblehead, Mass.), Racquet and Tennis Club, Princeton Club (N.Y.C., Beta Gamma Sigma, Phi Kappa Phi. Home: 55 E 72nd St New York NY 10021-4149 also: 63 Cleveland Dr Montauk NY 11954-5030 Office: Kehoe Ptnrs Inc 501 Madison Ave Fl 13 New York NY 10022 E-mail: jpk@abmac.com.

KEHOE, L. PAUL, state judge; b. Carthage, N.Y., May 21, 1938; s. Leo A. and Mildred (Piddock) K.; m. Elizabeth M. Weber, 1963; children: L. Paul, John Michael, Patrick Lewis. BA, Syracuse U., 1959, JD, 1962. Bar: N.Y. 1962. Dist. atty., Wayne County, N.Y., 1967-71; mem. N.Y. Assembly, 1979-80, N.Y. State Senate, 1981-92; justice N.Y. Supreme Ct., 1993—; adminstrv. judge 7th Jud. Dist., 1996-2000; assoc. Justice Appellate Divsn., 4th Dept., 2000—. With AUS, 1962-63. Mem. ABA, Wayne County Bar Assn., N.Y. State Bar Assn., Elks. Republican. Office: 50 East Ave Ste 627 Rochester NY 14604-2214 E-mail: lpkehoe@courts.state.ny.us.

KEHOE, TERRENCE EDWARD, lawyer; b. Washington, June 21, 1955; s. Edward Thomas and Dorothy (Dunbar) K.; m. Priscilla Joan O'Brien, Nov. 24, 1984; children: Ryan Edward, Brendan Charles. BA, U. N.C., 1976; JD, Georgetown U., 1981. Bar: Fla. 1981, U.S. Supreme Ct. 1987; bd. cert. criminal appellate lawyer. Assoc. James M. Russ P.A., Orlando, Fla., 1981-85, Haas Boehm Brown Rigdon Seacrest & Fischer P.A., Orlando, 1985-88; pvt. practice Orlando, 1988—. Mem. Nat. Assn. Criminal Def. Lawyers, Fla. Assn. Criminal Def. Lawyers. Home: 1911 Ivanhoe Rd Orlando FL 32804-5938 Office: 18 W Pine St Orlando FL 32801-2612 E-mail: tekehoelaw@aol.com.

KEHOE, THOMAS J. food products executive; b. N.Y.C., N.Y., Apr. 9, 1949; s. Thomas J. and Aileen F. Kehoe; m. Carole M. Cassidy, Oct. 1, 1994; m. Doreen A. Hydell, Sept. 1, 1975 (div. June 1, 1990); children: Yvonne, Thomas, Matthew, Veronica, Rebecca, Marrielle. BA, U. Dayton, 1971. Sales and mktg. exec. Xerox Corp., N.Y.C., 1971—75; owner Bayville (N.Y.) Fish, 1976—78; polit. cons. Kehoe Associs., Strafford, NH, 1978—80; dir. mktg. PG Assco Inc., Syosset, NY, 1980—82; pres., ptnr. Galilee Seafood, N.Y.C., 1982—87; pres. Thomas J. Kehoe Inc., Northport, NY, 1982—96; pres., ptnr. K&B Seafood Inc., East Northport, NY, 1990—. Dir. Mid Atlantic Fishery Devel. Coun., 1985—88. Coach Eaton's Neck Basketball, 1987—92; coach, v.p. Northport Little League, 1987—94. Mem.: Juko Kai Internat., East Northport C. of C., U.S. Fencing Assn., N.Y. Athletic Club. Avocation: martial arts. Home: 51 Mariners Ln Northport NY 11768 Office: K&B Seafood Inc 176 Laurel Rd East Northport NY 11731 Fax: 631-261-0382. E-mail: tkehoe@attglobal.net.

KEHOE, VINCENT JEFFRÉ-ROUX, photographer, author, cosmetic company executive; b. Bklyn., Sept. 12, 1921; s. John James and Bertha Florence (Roux) K.; m. Gena Irene Marino, Nov. 2, 1966. Student, MIT, 1940-41, Lowell Technol. Inst., 1941-42, Boston U., 1942; BFA in Motion Picture and TV Prodn., Columbia U., 1957. Dir. make-up dept. CBS-TV, N.Y.C., 1948-49, NBC Hallmark Hall of Fame series, 1951-53; make-up artist in charge of make-up numerous film, tv and stage prodns., 1942—; dir. make-up Turner Hall Corp., 1959-61, Internat. Beauty Show, 1962-66. Pres., dir. rsch., founder Rsch. Coun. Make-Up Artists, Inc., 1963-; chief press officer Spanish Pavilion N.Y. World's Fair, 1965; free-lance photographer, 1956-; founder 10th Rgt. of Foot, Am. Contingent, 1968, Nat. Assn. Taurino Clubs, 1961, Club Taurino N.Y., 1960. Author: The Technique of Film and Television Make-Up for Color, 1970, The Make-Up Artist in the Beauty Salon, 1969, We Were There: April 19, 1775, 1974, A Military Guide, 1974, 2nd rev. edit., 1993, 3rd rev. edit., 1998-99, The Re-Created Officer's Guide, 5 vols., 1996-98, The Technique of the Professional Make-Up Artist, 1985, 2nd edit., 1995, Special Make-Up Effects, 1991, The British Story of the Battles of Lexington and Concord, 2000; author, photographer: (bullfighting book) Aficionado! (N.Y. Art Dirs. Club award 1960), Wine Women and Toros! (N.Y. Art Dirs. award 1962); prodr.: (documentary color film) Matador de Toros, 1959; contbr. photographs to numerous mags. including Time, Life, Sports Illustrated, Argosy, Popular Photography. Served with U.S. Army, WWII, ETO. Decorated Purple Heart, Bronze Star, CIB; recipient Torch award Coun. of 13 Original States, 1979. Fellow Co. Mil. Historians; mem. Tenth Foot Royal Lincolnshire Regimental Assn. (life; Hon. Col. 1968), Soc. Motion Picture and TV Engrs. (life), Acad. TV Arts and Scis., Soc. Army Hist. Rsch. (Eng., life), Brit. Officers Club New Eng. (life), Army Hist. Found. (life), 10th Mountain Divsn. Assn. (life), NRA (life), 70th Divsn. (life), Am. Chem. Soc., DAV (life), Eagle Scout Assn. (life), Naval Club (London). Home and Office: PO Box 850 Somis CA 93066-0850

KEHOE, WILLIAM FRANCIS, lawyer; b. Stoneham, Mass., Dec. 3, 1933; s. William Andrew and Josephine Agnes (Crowley) K.; m. Dorothy Landry Kehoe; children by previous marriage: John William, Kathleen Emily. AB summa cum laude, Dartmouth Coll., 1955; MA, Yale U., 1956; LLB, Harvard U., 1963. Bar: Mass. 1963, U.S. Dist. Ct. Mass. 1964. Instr. English Middlebury (Vt.) Coll., 1956-57; ptnr. Gaston & Snow, Boston, 1970-91; counsel Hutchins, Wheeler & Dittmar, Boston, 1991-94, Taylor, Ganson & Perrin, Boston, 1995—. Mng. trustee Katharine L.W. and Winthrop Murray Crane, 3d Charitable Found.; mem. standing adv. com. on rules of civil procedure Supreme Jud. Ct.; lectr., panelist Mass. Continuing Legal Edn. Program and Mass. Jud. Inst. Author: Enjoying Ireland, 1966; contbr. articles and revs. to profl. jours. Served with U.S. Army, 1957-59. Fulbright scholar, Trinity Coll., Dublin, Ireland, 1959-60. Fellow Am. Coll. Trust and Estate Counsel; mem. Boston Bar Assn., Phi Beta Kappa. Office: Taylor Ganson & Perrin 160 Federal St Fl 20 Boston MA 02110-1722

KEHOE, WILLIAM JOSEPH, educator, researcher, writer, consultant; b. Cin., Feb. 19, 1941; AB, U. Cin., 1964; MBA, Xavier U., 1969; MA, Marshall U., 1973; D of Bus. Adminstrn., U. Ky., 1976. O'Dell prof. commerce U. Va., Charlottesville, 1975—, assoc. dean, 1982-92, internat. bus. area chair, 1993-99; pres. Albemarle County Police Found., 1993-95; bd. dir. Va. aviation Bd., 2002—; mem. Policy Cmty. VTRANS 2025, 2002—. Bd. dirs. Fcdn. Bus. Honor Socs. Chmn. Charlottesville Airport Authority, 1993, 96, 97, 98, 99, 2000, vice chmn., 1992, 95; bd. dirs. Va. Aviation Bd., 2002—; pres. Jr. Achievement Ctrl. Va., 1985-87; vice chmn. Paramount Theatre and Cultural Ctr., 1990-92; mem. Albermarle County Indsl. Devel. Authority, 1986-94; chmn. Albemarle County Fiscal Resource Com., 1989-91; mem. Regional Econ. Adv. Coun., Commonwealth of Va., 1994-98; chmn. Thomas Jefferson area United Way, 1994. Served with USMC. Recipient Leaders' Leader award, 1988, Disting. Leadership award Nat. Assn. Community Leadership, 1989; Doctoral Consortium fellow, fellow George H. Gallup Internat. Inst. Fellow Am. Soc. Bus. and Behavioral Scis., Soc. Mktg. Advances, Raven Soc. of U. Va.; mem. Am. Acad. Mgmt., Am. Mktg. Assn., Soc. for Bus. Ethics, Acad. Internat. Bus., Charlottesville C. of C. (chmn. 1990), Allied So. Bus. Assn. (pres. 1992), Am. Soc. Bus. and Behavioral Scis., Rotary (Charlottesville), Beta Gamma Sigma (bd. dirs. 1990-2000). Home: PO Box 4454 Charlottesville VA 22905-4454

KEHRES, DAVID GEORGE, microbiologist, researcher; b. Cleveland, Ohio, Feb. 28, 1950; s. Frank Boepple and Jean Drage Kehres; m. Mary Louise Sbrocco, Feb. 8, 1984; 1 child, Philip James. BA, Williams Coll., 1968—72; PhD, Case Western Res. U., 1986—93. Sr. rsch. assoc. Case Western Res. U., Cleve., 1993—. Contbr. articles to profl. jours. Mem.: Am. Soc. for Microbiology. Achievements include research in characterization of manganese transport proteins in bacteria; characterization of role of manganese in bacterial carbon and nitrogen metabolism. Home: 29817 Cresthaven Dr Willowick OH 44095 Office: Case Western Reserve University 10900 Euclid Ave Cleveland OH 44106-4965 Office Fax: 216-368-3395. E-mail: dgk2@po.cwru.edu.

KEHRET, PEG, writer; b. LaCrosse, Wis., Nov. 11, 1936; d. Arthur Robert and Elizabeth (Showers) Schulze; m. Carl Edward Kehret, July 2, 1955; children: Bob. C., Anne M. Kehret Konen. Student, U. Minn., 1954-55. Trustee Pacific Northwest Writers Conf., Seattle, 1983-86. Author: Vows of Love and Marriage, 1979, Refinishing and Restoring Your Piano, 1985, Winning Monologs for Young Actors, 1986, Deadly Stranger, 1987 (Children's Choice award, 1988), The Winner, 1988, ENCORE!-More Winning Monologs for Young Actors, 1988, Nightmare Mountain, 1989 (Young Hoosier Book award, 1992, Golden Sower award Nebr. Libr. Assn., 1993, Iowa Children's Choice award, 1994, Maud Hart Lovelace award, 1995), Wedding Vows, 1989, Sisters, Long Ago, 1990, Cages, 1991 (Maud Hart Lovelace award, 1996), Acting Natural, 1992, Terror at the Zoo, 1992 (Pacific N.W. Young Reader's Choice award, 1995, N.Mex. Land of Enchantment award, 1995, Iowa Children's Choice award, 1996), Horror at the Haunted House, 1992 (Sequoyah Children's Book award, 1995, Young Hoosier award, 1995), Night of Fear, 1994, Richest Kids in Town, 1994, Cat Burglar on the Prowl, 1995, Danger at the Fair, 1995, Bone Breath and the Vandals, 1995, Don't Go Near Mrs. Tallie, 1995, Desert Danger, 1995, The Ghost Followed Us Home, 1996, Earthquake Terror, 1996 (W.Va. Children's Book award, 1998, Children's Crown award Nat. Christian Sch. Assn., 1998, Utah Children's Book award, 1999, Va. Young Readers award, 1999), Race to Disaster, 1996, Screaming Eagles, 1996, Backstage Fright, 1996, Small Steps: The Year I Got Polio, 1996 (Soc. Children's Book Writers and Illustrators Golden Kite award nonfiction, 1997, PEN Ctr. USA West award, 1997, Dorothy Canfield Fisher award, 1998, Mark Twain award, 1999, Young Hoosier award, 2001), Searching for Candlestick Park, 1997, The Volcano Disaster, 1998 (Fla. Sunshine award, 2000), The Blizzard Disaster, 1998, The Flood Disaster, 1999, Shelter Dogs, 1999, I'm Not Who You Think I Am, 1999, The Secret Journey, 1999, My Brother Made Me Do It, 2000, Don't Tell Anyone, 2000, The Hideout, 2001, Saving Lilly, 2001 (Henry Bergh award ASPCA, 2001), The Stranger Next Door, 2002, Five Pages a Day: A Writer's Journey, 2002, Spy Cat, 2003, (plays) Cemeteries are a Grave Matter, 1977, Let Him Sleep 'Till It's Time for His Funeral, 1978, Spirit!, 1979 (Forest Roberts Playwriting award No. Mich. U., 1979, Best New Play award Pioneer Drama Svc., 1980), Dracula, Darling, 1980, Charming Billy, 1981, (musical) Bicycles Built for Two, 1985; contbr. articles to mags., short stories to mags.; author: Escaping the Giant Wave, 2003. Vol. Humane Soc., SPCA, Bellevue, Wash., 1975—. Recipient Achievement award Pacific N.W. Writers, Celebrate Lit. award N.W. Reading Coun. of Internat. Reading Assn., 1993, Lamplighter award, Nat. Christian Sch. Assn., 2003; named Artist of Yr., Redmond, Wash., Arts Commn., 1998. Mem. Author's Guild, Soc. Children's Book Writers. Office: Curtis Brown Ltd Ten Astor Pl New York NY 10003

KEHRT, ALLAN WILLIAM, architectural firm executive; m. Michaele Kehrt; children: Matthew, Emily, Kathleen. BA in Econs., Ohio Wesleyan U., 1967; MArch, Va. Polytechnic Inst. and State U., 1978. Registered architect, N.J., Fla. Asst. prof. design Coll. Architecture and Urban Studies Va. Polytechnic Inst. and State U., Blacksburg, 1977-79; mgr. C.D.P. Assocs., Wilmington, Del.; with Geddes Brecher Qualls Cunningham, Princeton, N.J.; founding and design ptnr. KSS Architects, Princeton, 1983—. Vis. critic, lectr. Va. Polytechnic Inst. and State U., U. Pa.; past treas., bd. dirs. Life Industries Corp.; adj. faculty Coll. Arch., Phila. Univ. Vice chmn. N.J. Planning Bd., Cranbury; active N.J. Environ. Commn., Cranbury; past chmn. N.J. Hist. Preservation Commn., Cranbury. With USN, 1967-71. Recipient awards Interfaith Forum Religion, Art and Architecture, 1993, Franklin award March of Dimes Birth Defect Found., 1999. Fellow AIA; mem. N.J. Soc. Architects (awards 1986, 87, 89, 90, 93, 94, 96, 98, 2000, 01), Phi Kappa Phi, Tau Sigma Delta. Office: KSS Architects 337 Witherspoon St Princeton NJ 08542-3470 E-mail: akehrt@kssarch.com.

KEICHER, WILLIAM EUGENE, electrical engineer; b. Pitts., Dec. 28, 1947; s. William John and Gina Rina (Magrini) K.; m. Barbara Marie Gurgacz, Aug. 12, 1972; children: Lisa Anne, Kathy Marie, William Michael. BSEE, Carnegie-Mellon U., 1969, MSEE, 1970, PhD in Elec. Engring., 1974. Sr. elec. engr. CBS Labs., Stamford, Conn., 1974-75; mem. tech. staff Lincoln Lab., MIT, Lexington, Mass., 1975-83, asst. group leader, 1983-85, group leader, 1985-93, 2000—, assoc. group leader, 1993-2000. Cons. Sci. and Engring. Support Group for Strategic Def. Initiative, Arlington, Va., 1988; co-chair for numerous confs. in field. Editor: Millimeter Wave Technology, 1982, Applied Laser Radar Technology, 1993, Industrial Applications of Laser Radar, 1994; contbr. articles to profl. publs.; patentee spatial filter sys. Capt. U.S. Army, 1974. Mem. IEEE (sr.), Optical Soc. Am., Nat. Rsch. Coun. (Air Force sci. and tech. com. on rev. of Air Force hypersonic tech. program 1997-98), Assn. Old Crows. Roman Catholic. Avocations: astronomy and astrophotography, history, snorkeling, travel, microcomputers. Home: 6 Winn Valley Dr Burlington MA 01803-4727 Office: MIT Lincoln Lab 244 Wood St Lexington MA 02421-6426 E-mail: keicher@ll.mit.edu.

KEIDEL, ROBERT WOOLER, management consultant, writer, educator; b. Phila., Feb. 25, 1943; s. Philip Charles and Phyllis (Wooler) K.; m. Carole Anne Zneimer, Sept. 28, 1974; children: Andrew Lewis, Carly Margaret. BA, Williams Coll., 1964; MBA, U. Pa., 1966, PhD, 1979. Mgmt. analyst Wofac Co. div. Sci. Mgmt. Corp., Moorestown, N.J., 1970-72; corp. project mgr. Walworth Co., Bala-Cynwyd, Pa., 1972-74; mgmt. rsch. analyst Mgmt. and Behavioral Sci. Ctr. Wharton Sch., Phila., 1974-75; orgn. cons. Jamestown (N.Y.) Area Labor Mgmt. Com., 1975-77; program cons. Nat. Ctr. for Productivity and Quality of Working Life, Washington, 1977-78; cons. U.S. Office of Personnel Mgmt., Washington, 1978-79; asst. prof. Temple U., Phila., 1979-83; prin. Robert Keidel Assocs., Wyncote, Pa., 1983—. Bd. dirs. Robert Wooler Co., Dresher, Pa.; lectr. U. Pa., Phila., 1997-99; vis. assoc. prof. Drexel U., Phila., 1999—. Author: Game Plans, 1985, Corporate Players, 1988, Seeing Organizational Patterns, 1995. Lt. USN, 1966-70. Fellow Wharton Sch., U. Pa. (sr.), U.S. Office Personnel Mgmt. (faculty); mem. Acad. Mgmt., Am. Ctr. for Quality of Work Life (sr. field assoc.), Strategic Mgmt. Soc. Avocations: reading, writing, drawing, golf. E-mail: rwkeidel@aol.com.

KEIDERLING, TIMOTHY ALLEN, chemistry educator, researcher; b. Waterloo, Iowa, June 22, 1947; s. Glenn Allen and Ethel V. (Kalainoff) K.; m. Candace Ruth Crawford, Sept. 4, 1976; 1 son, Michael Crawford. B.S., Loras Coll., 1969; M.A., Princeton U., 1971, Ph.D., 1974. NSF fellow Princeton U., 1969-72; research assoc. U. So. Calif., Los Angeles, 1973-76; asst. prof. U. Ill., Chgo., 1976-81, assoc. prof. chemistry, 1981-85, prof., 1985— ; guest prof. Max Planck Inst., Garching, Fed. Republic Germany, 1984; sr. vis. Oxford U., 1994. Contbr. over 220 articles to profl. jours. Fellow Fulbright Found. 1984, Guggenheim Found. 2003; grantee NSF, NIH, Petroleum Research Found., 1976—; sr. rsch. scholar U. Ill., 1991-94. Mem. Am. Chem. Soc., Am. Phys. Soc., Biophys. Soc., Soc. Applied Spectroscopy. Achievements include the development of technique of vibrational circular dichroism, making of first such measurements of polypeptides, proteins and nucleic acids, and first magnetic applications to small molecules. Office: U Ill Dept Chemistry 845 W Taylor St M/C 111 Chicago IL 60607-7056

KEIL, HAROLD H. (BILL KEIL), writer; b. Portland, Oreg., Apr. 11, 1926; s. Harry G. and Elizabeth M. K.; m. Gloria I. Trantanella, Feb. 27, 1959; children: Richard T., Gregory H. BS in Forestry, Oreg. State Coll., 1950. Ski editor The Oregonian newspaper, Portland, 1959-75, KOIN-TV, Portland, 1968-75; city forester Portland Park Bur., 1952-56; assoc. editor, logging & forestry editor The Timberman, The Lumberman, and Forest Industries mags., Portland, 1956-60; editor World Wood mag., Portland, 1960-71; pub. affairs officer U.S. Bur. Land Mgmt., Portland, 1975-88; U.S. corr. Wood-Based Panels Internat. Mag., Sevenoaks, Kent, England, 1988—; freelance writer numerous newspapers and mags., 1950—. Adv. bd. Mt. Hood Nat. Forest, Portland, 1985-87. Author: Trails & Roads of Forest Park, 1973; editor: American Ski Annual, 1956, World Forestry Statistical Yearbook, 1961-71. Tax increment adv. com. Clackamas County, Oreg., 1988-90; com. chmn. U.S. Ski Assn., Denver, 1953-65; mem. Nat. Wildfire Disaster Commn., 1989-91. Staff sgt. U.S. Army, Philippines, 1944-46. Mem. Soc. Am. Foresters (publicity chmn. 1959-60), N.Am. Ski Journalists Assn. Outdoor Writers Assn. Am., Nat. Press Photographers Assn., N.W. Outdoor Writers Assn. Avocations: skiing, hiking, photography.

KEIL, JOHN MULLAN, advertising agency executive, artist; b. Rochester, N.Y., Dec. 30, 1922; s. Alvin Richard and Elizabeth (Mullan) K.; m. Barbara Louise Miller, Sept. 16, 1950; children— Peter Mullan, Nicholas John, Elizabeth Jane. BA, U. Rochester, 1946. Copywriter advt. dept. Armstrong Cork Co., Lancaster, Pa., 1946-48, Wendell P. Colton Advt., N.Y.C., 1948-51, Needham & Grohmann, Inc., N.Y.C., 1951-55, v.p., account exec., 1955-60; v.p., creative dir. Dancer, Fitzgerald, Sample, Inc., N.Y.C., 1960-64, copy group head, 1964-67, v.p., 1967-70, sr. v.p., creative dir., 1970-75, dir., 1971-87, exec. v.p., 1975-87, chmn. creative planning con., 1973; exec. creative dir. Dancer, Fitzgerald, Sample, 1983-86; dir. creative devel. DFS-Dorland Worldwide, 1986-87; creative cons. Saatchi & Saatchi Adv. Worldwide, 1987—. Lectr. Amos Tuck Sch. Dartmouth Coll., Assn. Nat. Advertisers; Phillips Meml. lectr. U. Fla., 1987; painter acrylic on wood Frank J. Miele Gallery, N.Y.C., Toadhall Gallery, N.Y.C., Reed Gallery, Chester, Vt., So. Vt. Art Ctr., Manchester, Vt., Hartnett Gallery/U. Rochester. Author: The Creative Mystique, How To Manage It, Nurture It, Make It Pay, 1985, How to Zig in a Zagging World, 1987; contbr. articles to Jour. Advt., Air and Space, Smithsonian, Time, N.Y. Times. Vice chmn. Zoning Bd. Appeals, Grandview-on-Hudson, N.Y., 1961-71; pres., trustee Rockland Country Day Sch., 1970-75; mem. trustees coun. U. Rochester, 1979-85, trustee, 1986-91 (life trustee, 1991—), U. Rochester Sports Hall of Fame, 2000, N.Y. State Coun. Governing Bds., 1989-94, Nat. Crime Prevention Coun., 1987—; trustee Tappan Zee Preservation Coalition, 1995—; mem. corp. Nyack Hosp., 2001—. Served with USAAF, 1943-45. Decorated D.F.C., Air medal with two oak leaf clusters; recipient Silver Bell award Advt. Coun., 1981, 84, Carl M. Loeb, Jr.-McGruff award Nat. Crime Prevention Coun., 1987. Mem. Alpha Delta Phi. Clubs: Nyack (N.Y.) Field, Upper Nyack Tennis. Home: 251 River Rd Nyack NY 10960-5001 Home (Summer): 7128 Westminster West Rd Putney VT 05346 E-mail: bobo5@optonline.net.

KEIL, KLAUS, geology educator, consultant; b. Hamburg, Germany, Nov. 15, 1934; s. Walter and Elsbeth K.; m. Rosemarie, Mar. 30, 1961; children: Kathrin R., Mark K.; m. Linde, Jan. 28, 1984. MS, Schiller U., Jena, Germany, 1958; PhD, Gutenberg U., Mainz, Fed. Republic Germany, 1961; Doctorate (hon.), Friedrich-Schiller U., Jena, Germany, 2002, U. N.Mex., Albuquerque, 2003. Rsch. assoc. Mineral. Inst., Jena, 1958-60, Max Planck-Inst. Chemistry, Mainz, 1961, U. Calif., San Diego, 1961-63; rsch. scientist Ames Rsch. Ctr. NASA, Moffett Field, Calif., 1963-68; prof. geology, dir. Inst. Meteoritics, U. N.Mex.,

Albuquerque, 1968-90; pres., prof. U. N.Mex., 1985-90, chmn. dept. of geology, 1986-89; prof. geology U. Hawaii, Honolulu, 1990—, rsch. prof., head planetary geoscis. div., 1990-93, dir. Hawaii Inst. Geophysics and Planetology, 1994—; cons. Sandia Labs., others. Contbr. over 600 articles to sci. jours. Recipient Apollo Achievement award, NASA, 1970, George P. Merrill award, NAS, 1970, Exceptional Sci. Achievement medal, U. N.Mex., 1983, Leonard medal, Meteoritical Soc., 1988, Zimmerman award, U. N.Mex., 1988, numerous others, new extraterrestrial mineral Keilite named after him. Fellow Meteoritical Soc., AAAS, Mineral. Soc. Am., Am. Geophys. Union, German Mineral. Soc., Microbeam Analysis Soc. (Pres.'s Sci. award 2002), others. Office: U Hawaii at Manoa Hawaii Inst Geophys & Planetology Honolulu HI 96822

KEIL, M. DAVID, retired international association executive; b. Hinsdale, Ill., Jan. 22, 1931; s. Milton Derby and Lydia Anne (Landwehr) K.; m. Marilyn Jean Martin, May 15, 1976 BSJ, Northwestern U., Evanston, Ill., 1952. Brand mgr. Armour & Co., Chgo., 1953-60; sr. v.p. Young & Rubicam, Chgo., 1960-74, Sandy Corp., Detroit, 1974-75, D'Arcy-MacManus & Masius, Chgo., 1976-80; pres., mng. dir. Audit Bur. Circulations, Schaumburg, Ill., 1980-96; ret., 1996. Named to Medill Sch. Journalism Hall of Fame, 1997. Mem. Internat. Fedn. Audit Burs., Circulation (sec. gen. 1986-88), Hinsdale Golf Club, Chgo. Symphony Orch., U. Club Chgo. Lutheran. Avocations: sports, reading, travel, music.

KEIL, MARILYN MARTIN, artist; b. Balt., Nov. 6, 1932; d. Francis and Mary Blanche (Murphy) Martin; m. Herbert Bruce Keil, Dec. 18, 1954; children: Braden, Mary-Beth, Sue-Ann, Nancy, Bryant. Student, Corcoran Sch. Art, Washington, 1991-94, U. Md., 1995. Active art in embassies program U.S. Dept. State; juried Washington area printmakers calendar Balt. Mus. fine Arts, 1995—. One-woman show Ralls Collection, Washington, 1993; exhibited in group shows at Rockville Art League (watercolor award), 1991, Corcoran Sch. Art, 1994, Nat. Cathedral, Washington, 1994, U. Md. Sch. Arts and Sociology, 1995, West Gallery, 1995, Md. Fedn. Art, 1996; contbr. juried Washington Area Printmakers Calendar, Va. Mus. Fine Art, 1997, Calendar Corcoran Gallery, 1998, Nat. Gallery of Art, 1999; represented in permanent collections at Corcoran Gallery Art, Washington, 1996, Nat. Mus. Women in the Arts, 1996, Libr. of Congress, 1996, juried Washington Printmakers Original Print Calendar, 2000, 01. Bd. dirs. Potomac Glen Civic Assn., Potomac, Md., 1988-94. Mem. AAUW, Rockville Art League, Nat. Mus. Women in the Arts (charter), Washington Area Printmakers, Golden Key, Alpha Lambda. Avocations: etching, lithography. Home: 11540 S Glen Rd Potomac MD 20854-1852

KEIL, MARK, information systems researcher; b. Wilmington, Del., May 8, 1960; s. Charles Kornhauser and Barbara Pearl (Silverman) K.; m. Judith Lisa Fridovich, June 10, 1984; children: David, Sara. BSChemE, Princeton U., 1982; MS in Mgmt. Info. Sys., MIT, 1986; D in Bus. Adminstrn., Harvard U., 1991. Engr. DuPont Co., Wilmington, 1982-84; project mgr. Cambridge (Mass.) Inst. Info. Sys., 1986-87; cons. Cons. for Mgmt. Decisions, 1987; rsch. assoc. Harvard Bus. Sch., Boston, 1987-90; instr. Harvard U. Extension Sch., Cambridge, 1988-91; asst. prof. Ga. State U., Atlanta, 1991-97, assoc. prof., 1997—. Contbr. articles to Sloan Mgmt. Rev., MIS Quar., Jour. Mgmt. Info. Sys., Comm. ACM. Pres. Condominium Assn., Brookline, Mass., 1990-91. Am. Assembly Collegiate Sch. Bus. doctoral fellow, 1987. Mem. IEEE, Acad. Mgmt., Assn. for Computing Machinery, Assn. Info. Sys., Informs. Achievements include research in techniques to identify and avoid project escalation. Office: Ga State U PO Box 4015 Atlanta GA 30302-4015

KEIL, STEPHEN LESLEY, astrophysicist; b. Billings, Mont., Feb. 21, 1947; s. Nolan F. and Billy Lou (Benjamin) K.; m. Alice Ann Orient, June 18, 1972; children: Pamela Lynn, Wesley Forrester. BS in Physics, Univ. Calif., Berkeley, 1969; PhD in Astronomy, Boston U., 1975. Teaching fellow Boston (Mass.) Univ., 1969-74; postdoctoral fellow Univ. Colo., Sunspot, N.Mex., 1975-76; rsch. fellow, applied math. dept. Univ. Sydney, Australia, 1976-78; NRC fellow Sacramento Peak Obs., Sunspot, 1978-80, rsch. scientist, 1980-83; chief, solar rsch. USAF Solar Rsch. Br., Sunspot, 1983-99; dir. Nat. Solar Observatory, Sunspot, 1999—. Mem. Nat. Solar Obs. adv. com., Tucson, 1983-89, NSF Astronomy Survey com., Washington, 1990-91; prin. investigator USAF Solar Mass Ejection Imager, 1996-99; project dir. Advanced Tech. Solar Telescope, 2000—. Editor: (workshop proceedings) Small-Scale Dynamical Processes in Quiet Stellar Atmospheres, 1984; co-editor: (workshop proceedings) Solar Drivers of Interplanetary and Terrestial Disturbances. Mayor Sacramento Peak Community, Sunspot, 1990-91, treas., 1981-87. Maj. USAF, 1980-85. Named Company Grade Officer of Yr., USAF, 1984, Officer of the Yr., Geophysics Lab., Boston, 1983. Mem. Internat. Astron. Union, Am. Astron. Soc., Am. Phys. Soc., Calif. Scholarship Fedn. (life). Achievements include first to make an accurate determination of the height variation of convective penetration in the solar atmosphere. Home: 3015 Corona Loop Sunspot NM 88349 Office: National Solar Observatory 1 Corona Loop Sunspot NM 88349 E-mail: skeil@sunspot.noao.edu.

KEILITZ, GENE MARTIN, retired association administrator; b. Caro, Mich., June 3, 1933; s. Otto Ethlyn and Mildred Ethyl (Horst) K.; m. Marlene Josephine Keihl, Jan. 27, 1968; children: Kelli Ann Hannum Spencer, Kirsten Lynn Keilitz-Schuknecht. D Chiropractic, Nat. Coll. Chiropractic, 1955. Sales rep. Cenco Instruments, Chgo., 1959-66; owner Pewter Bell Restaurant, Traverse City, Mich., 1966-75; exec. v.p. Chateau Grand Traverse, Traverse City, 1975-77; sales mgr. Great Lake Gauge, Bridgeport, Mich., 1977-78; self-employed sales rep. Traverse City, 1978-80; exec. dir. Grand Traverse Area United Way (how N.W. Mich. United Way), Traverse City, 1980-91; v.p. United Way of Mich. (now. Mich. Assn. of United Ways), Lansing, 1991-96; ret., 1996. Bd. dirs. Aspen Inst. Non Profit Sector, Washington, 1994-2000, Camp Roy El, Traverse City, Mich., 1985—, Mich. Restaurant Assn., Detroit, 1968-70; mem. pub. policy com. United Way of Am., Alexandria, Va., 1995-99; chmn., bd. dirs. Munson Healthcare Regional Found., Traverse City, 1997—; pres., bd. dirs. Traverse Bay Regional Planning Com., 1982-85; sec., mem. Midwest Ski Operators, Pontiac, 1969-71; dist. sec. Rotary, 1988-91, bd. dirs. Rotary Camps and Svcs., 1987-91; retiree mentor United Way, 2001. With USAF, 1955-59. Mem. Inland Seas Ednl. Assn. (bd. dirs., 1st v.p. 1996—2001). Republican. Lutheran. Avocations: single-engine flying, cross-country skiing, gardening. Home: 195 Mathison Rd S Traverse City MI 49686-1861 E-mail: gkeilitz@chartermi.net.

KEILL, STUART LANGDON, psychiatrist; b. Binghamton, N.Y., Oct. 5, 1927; s. Kenneth and Dorothy B. (Langdon) K.; m. Joanne Veness, Sept. 2, 1950; children: Elinor Anne Moran, Patricia J., Brian S., Victoria M. Keill Lo Russo. BA, Princeton U., 1947; MA, Cornell U., 1948; MD, Temple U., 1952. Intern Highland Hosp., Rochester, N.Y.; resident in psychiatry N.Y. State Psychiat. Inst., Presbyn. Hosp., Columbia U., N.Y.C., 1955-58; dir. edn., dir. West Side Community Mental Health Ctr., N.Y.C., 1958-71, Roosevelt Hosp., N.Y.C., 1958-71; regional dir. N.Y. State Dept. Mental Health, 1971-75; prof. clin. psychiatry SUNY, Stony Brook, 1975-80; chmn. dept. psychiatry Nassau County Med. Ctr., East Meadow, N.Y., 1975-80; clin. prof. psychiatry SUNY, Buffalo, 1980-86, emeritus prof. psychiatry, 1993—; chief psychiat. service VA Med. Ctr., Buffalo, 1981-86; prof. of psychiatry Sch. of Medicine U. Md., 1986-94, vice chmn. dept. psychiatry, 1986-93, prof. sch. social work, 1993-94, acting chmn., 1991-92; clin. prof. psychiatry Sch. Medicine NYU, 1994—; counselor Advocates Coalition for Psychiat. Patients, 1980-86; med. dir. Inst. for Psychiatry and Human Behavior, 1986-93. Mem. adv. com. mental health laws Md. Atty. Gen. Office, 1987-93 Author: (with others) Textbook on Administrative Psychiatry, 1992; also 52 articles; mem. editl. bd. Social Work and Health Care, 1975—, Social Work in Mental Health Care, 2000—, Hosp. and Community Psychiatry; assoc. editor Gen. Hosp. Psychiatry Jour., 1981-94. Chmn. Nassau coun. Health Systems Agy., 1977-80; mem. adv. com. Dr. Glory's Children's Theatre, N.Y.C., 1980—; mental health laws adv. com. State's Atty. Gen., 1987; warden Christ Ch., Oyster Bay, 2002—. With USN, 1953-55. Recipient Julius T. Marcus award dept. psychiatry SUNY, Stony Brook, 1980 Fellow Am. Coll. Psychiatrists, Am. Psychiat. Assn. (Distinction in adminstrn. award 1990); mem. MEDIPP Psychiatry Council (dist. chmn. 1981-86), Am. Assn. Psychiat. Adminstrs. (pres. 1981-82), Am. Hosp. Assn. (chmn. psychiat. services sect. 1985), Am. Assn. Gen. Hosp. Psychiatrists (pres. 1985-87), N.Y. Soc. Clin. Psychiatry (pres. 1974-75, chmn. pub. psychiatry com.), Md. Psychiatric Soc.

KEILLER, JAMES BRUCE, college dean, clergyman; b. Racine, Wis., Nov. 21, 1938; s. James Allen and Grace (Modder) K.; m. Darsel Lee Bundy, Feb. 8, 1959; 1 dau., Susanne Elizabeth. Diploma, Beulah Heights Bible Coll., 1957; BA, William Carter Coll., 1963, EdD (hon.), 1973; LLB, Blackstone Sch. Law, 1964; MA, Evang. Theol. Sem., 1965, BD, 1966, ThD, 1968; MA in Ednl. Adminstrn., Atlanta U., 1977; degree, Nat. Tax Tng. Sch., Monsey, N.Y., 1986; postgrad., Atlanta Law Sch., Harvard U., 2001—03; Eds, Georgia State U., 1987; DD, Heritage Bible Coll., 2001. Ordained to ministry Internat. Pentecostal Assemblies, 1957. Pastor Maranatha Temple, Boston, 1957-58, Midland (Mich.) Full Gospel Ch., 1958-64; v.p. acad. dean Beulah Heights Bible Coll., Atlanta, 1964—, trustee, 1964-92; nat. dir. youth and Sunday sch. dept. Internat. Pentecostal Assemblies, 1958-64, dir. world missions, 1964-76; missionary editor Bridegroom's Messenger, 1964—; dir. global missions Internat. Pentecostal Ch. of Christ, 1976—, mem. exec. com., 1976—; mem. exec. bd. Mt. Paran Christian Sch., 1980-91. Named Alumnus of Yr. William Carter Coll., 1965. Fellow: Coll. of Preceptors; mem.: Soc. for Bibl. Lit., Am. Acad. Religion, Little Mountain Village Condo Assn. (bd. dirs. 1994—), Intercollegiate Studies Inst., Nat. Fedn. for Decency (bd. dirs.), Evang. Theol. Soc., Am. Bd. Master Educators (cert.), Am. Inst. Parliamentarians, Ind. Order Foresters, So. Accrediting Assn. Bible Colls. (exec. sec. 1970—93), Kiwanis (lt. gov. Ga. dist. 1986—87, chmn. human values state com. Ga. dist. 1989—90). Republican. E-mail: bhbc@beulah.org. Fax: (404)-627-0702. Home: 21A Little Mountain Vlg Ellenwood GA 30294-3150 Office: Beulah Heights Bible Coll 892 Berne St SE Atlanta GA 30316-1873

KEILLOR, GARRISON EDWARD, writer, radio host; b. Anoka, Minn., Aug. 7, 1942; s. John P. and Grace R. (Denham) K.; m. Jenny Lind Nilsson; children: Jason P., Maia Grace. BA, U. Minn., 1966. Author: Happy to be Here, 1982, Lake Wobegon Days, 1985, Leaving Home, 1987, We Are Still Married: Stories and Letters, 1989, WLT: A Radio Romance, 1991, The Book of Guys, 1993, Cat, You Better Come Home, 1995, The Old Man Who Loved Cheese, 1996, (with J. Nilsson) The Sandy Bottom Orchestra, 1996, Wobegon Boy, 1997, Me, by Jimmy (Big Boy) Valente, 1999, Lake Wobegon Summer 1956, 2001, Love Me, 2003; creator, writer and host radio show A Prairie Home Companion; contbr. articles to mags. and newspapers (Harpers, The Atlantic Monthly, The N.Y. Times, others). Recipient Grammy award for best non-mus. recording Lake Wobegon Days, 1987, Ace award, 1988, Best Mus. and Entertainment Host awards, 1988, 89, medal for spoken lang. Am. Acad. and Inst. Arts and Letters, 1990, Nat. Humanities medal, 1999, Pres. Clinton; inducted into Am. Acad. Arts and Scis., 1999. Democrat. Episcopalian. Address: A Prairie Home Companion 45 7th St E Saint Paul MN 55101-2202*

KEILTY, BRYAN T. government agency administrator; BA, St. Bonaventure U. Supervisory budget analyst U.S. Dept. of Labor, Washington, 1971-82, supervisory manpower devel. specialist, 1982-84, budget officer Office Asst. Sec. for Adminstrn. and Mgmt., 1984-86, dep. contr., 1986-91, dep. adminstr. Office Strategic Planning & Policy Devel., 1991-92, adminstr. Office Fin. and Adminstrn. Mgmt., 1992—.

KEIM, BETTY LOU, actress, literary consultant; b. Malden, Mass., Sept. 27, 1938; d. Buster and Dorothy Clair (Tracy) Keim; m. Warren Berlinger, Feb. 18, 1960; children: Lisa, David, Edward, Elizabeth. Grad., Lodge Acad., N.Y.c., 1956. Appeared in films These Wilder Years, 1956, Teenage Rebel, 1956, Wayward Bus, 1957, Some Came Running, 1958; appeared on Broadway in Strange Fruit, Rip Van Winkle, Crime and Punishment, Texas Lil Darlin, The Remarkable Mr. Pennypacker, Roomful of Roses; appeared on TV in Omnibus, Playhouse 90, Alcoa Hour, Philco PlayHouse; appeared in TV series My Son Jeep, The Deputy. Assoc. Aid Project L.A., 1984-97; life mem., vol. Actors Fund of Am. Recipinet Motion Picture award Calif. Women's Club, 1956, Filmdoms Famous Five award Film Daily Critics, 1956, Laurel award, 1956.

KEIM, DONALD BRUCE, finance educator; b. Bethlehem, Pa., Feb. 7, 1953; s. Elwood Benjamin and Doris Mae (Wanamaker) K.; m. Susan Langshaw, July 10, 1976; children: Sarah Elizabeth, Julia Diane. BSBA, Bucknell U., 1975; MBA, U. Chgo., 1980, PhD, 1983; MS (hon.), U. Pa., 1988. Rsch. assoc. Fed. Deposit Ins. Corp., Washington, 1978; lectr. Loyola U. of Chgo., 1981-82; asst. prof., fin. U. Pa., Phila., 1982-88, assoc. prof. fin., 1988-94, prof. fin., 1994—98, John B. Neff prof. fin., 1998—. Vis. prof. INSEAD, Fontainebleau, France, 1994, 96-98; vis. scholar Dimensional Fund Advisors, Santa Monica, Calif., 1990, 1995-96; mem. acad. adv. bd. Brandywine Asset Mgmt., Wilmington, Del., 1993-2000. Assoc. editor Jour. of Fin. and Quant. Analysis, 1993-2001; co-editor European Fin. Rev., 1998—; contbr. articles to profl. jours. Rsch. grantee Inst. for Quantitative Rsch., 1984, 92, 99; recipient Graham and Dodd award Fin. Analysts Fedn., 1987, 99, N.Y. Stock Exch. award, 1996. Mem. Am. Fin. Assn., Western Fin. Assn. (program com. 1992-96, 2000-2003), European Fin. Assn. (program com. 1996-2003). Avocations: music, photography, golf, gardening. Office: Univ Pa The Wharton Sch 2300 Steinberg Hall Philadelphia PA 19104

KEIM, MICHAEL RAY, dentist; b. Sabetha, Kans., June 8, 1951; s. Milton Leroy and Dorothy Juanita (Stover) K.; m. Christine Anne Lorenzen, Nov. 20, 1971; children: Michael Scott, Dawn Marie, Erik Alan. Student, U. Utah, 1969-72; DDS, Creighton U., 1976. Pvt. practice, Casper, Wyo., 1976—. Mem. vertical math. com. Natrona County Sch. Dist., 1997-2000; mem. Coll. Nat. Finals Rodeo Com., 2002—. Mem. organizing bd. dirs. Ctrl. Wyo. Soccer Assn., 1976-77; mem. Casper Mountain Ski Patrol, Nat. Ski Patrol Sys., 1980-2000, Big Horn Ski Patrol, 2001—, avalanche and ski mountaineering advisor No. Divsn. Region III, 1992-96, outdoor emergency care instr. trainer, 1996-99, 1st asst. patrol dir., 1996-98, patrol dir., 1998-99; bd. dirs., dep. commr. for fast pitch Wyo. Amateur Softball Assn., 1980-84; bd. dirs. Ctrl. Wyo. Softball Assn., 1980-84; head coach Big Horn Mountain Ski Team, 2002—; pres. Wyo. Spl. Smiles Found., 1995-96; mem. organizing com. Prevent Abuse & Neglect thru Dental Awareness Coalition, Wyo., 1996; mem. adv. com. Natrona County Headstart, 1985—; mem. City of Casper Leisure Svc. Adv. Com., 2002-. Recipient Purple Merit Star for Saving a Life, 1992, Hixon award, 2002. Fellow Acad. Gen. Dentistry; mem. ADA, Acad. Computerized Dentistry, Fedn. Dentaire Internat., Pierre Fauchard Acad., Wyo. Acad. Gen. Dentistry (sec.-treas. 1980-82, pres. 1982-87), Wyo. Dental Assn. (bd. dirs. 1992-97, chmn. conv. 1999—, ADA alt. del. 1994-95, v.p. 1993-94, pres.-elect 1994-95, pres. 1995-96, editor 1997—), Wyo. Dental Polit. Action Com. (sec.-treas. 1985-97), Ctrl. Wyo. Dental Assn. (sec.-treas. 1981-82, 2002-03, pres. 1982-83, 2003—), Wyo. Dental Hist. Assn. (bd. dirs. 1989-95), Wyo. Donated Dental Svcs. (organizing bd. dirs. 1994, pres. 1995-96), Kiwanis (v.p. Casper club 1988-89, bd. dirs. 1986-96, pres.-elect 1989-90, pres. 1990-91, internat. del. 1989-91, chmn. internat. rels. com. 1992-99, Rocky Mountain dist. lt. gov.-elect divsn. 1 1997-98, lt. gov. divsn. 1 1998-99, Hixon award, 2002), Creighton Club (pres. 1982-84). Methodist. Avocations: hunting, skiing, sports, woodworking, photography. Home: 58 Jonquil St Casper WY 82604-3863 Office: 1749 S Boxelder St Casper WY 82604-3538

KEIM, WAYNE FRANKLIN, retired genetics educator, plant geneticist; b. Ithaca, N.Y., May 14, 1923; s. Franklin David and Alice Mary (Voigt) K.; m. Ellen Joyce Neumann, Sept. 6, 1947; children: Kathryn Louise Keim Logsdon, David Wayne, Julie Anne Keim Hughes. BS with distinction, U. Nebr., 1947; MS, Cornell U., 1949, PhD, 1952. Instr., then asst. prof. Iowa State U., Ames, 1952-56; from asst. prof. to prof. Purdue U., West Lafayette, Ind., 1956-75; vis. prof., NSF sci. faculty fellow U. Lund (Sweden), 1962-63; vis. prof. Colo. State U., Fort Collins, 1971-72, prof. dept. agronomy, 1975-92, chmn. dept., 1975-85. Recipient Best Tchr. award Sch. Agr., Purdue U., 1965, 68 Fellow AAAS, Am. Soc. Agronomy (Agronomic Edn. award 1971, Agronomic Svc. award 1991), Crop Sci. Soc. Am. (pres. 1983-84); mem. Am. Inst. Biol. Sci., Agronomic Sci. Found. (trustee). Home: 1441 Meeker Dr Fort Collins CO 80524-4311 Office: Colo State U Dept Soil Crop Scis Fort Collins CO 80523-0001

KEINER, CHRISTIAN MARK, lawyer; b. Omaha, Mar. 16, 1953; s. John Frederick Keiner and Geraldine Elizabeth (Smith) Eadie; m. Rosemary Monique White, Nov. 21, 1980; 1 child, Colin MacGregor. BA with high honors, U. Calif., Santa Barbara, 1977; JD with distinction, U. of Pacific, 1980. Bar: Calif. 1980, U.S. Ct. Appeals (9th cir.) 1988, U.S. Supreme Ct. 1991. Assoc. Biddle, Walters, Bukey, Sacramento, 1980-82, Biddle and Hamilton, Sacramento, 1982-92; pvt. practice, Sacramento, 1992-98; ptnr. Girard and Vinson, Sacramento, 1998—. Contbr. articles to law jours. Bd. dirs. Calif. Found. for Improvement Employer-Employee Rels., Sacramento, 1994-99, Calif. Coun. Sch. Attys., Sacramento, 1996-98; instr., mem. labor-mgmt. adv. com. U. Calif. Davis Ext., Sacramento, 1986-99. Recipient award for adminstrv. law Am. Jurisprudence, 1979. Mem. ABA (pub. law sect.), Sacramento County Bar, Harry S. Truman Club (pres. 1992), Order of Coif. Democrat. Roman Catholic. Office: Girard and Vinson 1006 4th St 8th Fl Sacramento CA 95814-3326 E-mail: keiner@gandv.com.

KEINER, R(OBERT) BRUCE, JR., lawyer; b. Washington, July 12, 1942; s. R. Bruce and Alice Miriam (Draeger) K.; m. Suellen Terrill, June 15, 1968; children: Scott, Grant, Terrill. BA, Dickinson Coll., 1964; LLB, U. Va., 1967. Bar: D.C. 1968, U.S. Supreme Ct. 1980. Assoc. to ptnr. Jones, Day, Reavis & Pogue, Washington, 1970-79; ptnr. Crowell & Moring, Washington, 1979—; pres. Internat. Aviation Club of Washington, 1995. Pres., bd. trustees Maret Sch., 2000—. Capt. U.S. Army, 1968-69. Mem.: Internat. Aviation Club Washington (pres. 1995). Home: 1730 Crestwood Dr NW Washington DC 20011-5334 Office: Crowell & Moring 1001 Pennsylvania Ave NW Fl 10 Washington DC 20004-2595 E-mail: rbkeiner@crowell.com.

KEINER, SUELLEN TERRILL, lawyer; b. Cin., Sept. 29, 1944; d. William A. and Lois (Hamilton) Terrill; m. R. Bruce Keiner Jr., June 15, 1968; children: Scott, Grant, Terrill. Student, Inst. Polit. Studies, Paris, 1964-65; BA, Bryn Mawr Coll., 1966; JD, Georgetown U., 1971. Bar: D.C. 1971, U.S. Supreme Ct. 1975. Fgn. documents analyst CIA, Washington, 1966-67; rsch. analyst Civil Rights divsn. U.S. Dept. Justice, Washington, 1968, 70; law clk. Weyerhaeuser Co., Tacoma, 1968-69, D.C. Superior Ct., Washington, 1971; atty. Terris & Assocs., Washington, 1972-78; asst. solicitor U.S. Dept. Interior, Washington, 1978-81; cons. for natural resources mgmt. Coun. of State Planning Agys., Washington, 1982-84; dir. litigation project Environ. Policy Inst., Washington, 1984-86; dir. program on environ. governance and mgmt. Environ. Law Inst., Washington, 1988-2000; dir. Ctr. for Economy and Environment Nat. Acad. Pub. Adminstrn., Washington, 2000—. Pres. Crestwood Citizens Assn., Washington, 1982-84. Office: Nat Acad of Pub Adminstrn Ste 1090 E 1100 New York Ave NW Washington DC 20005

KEIPER, JEFFREY LYNN, counselor, therapist, lawyer; b. Johnstown, Pa., May 4, 1965; s. Donald E. and Barbara A. K. BS, U. Pitts., 1988; MA, Duquesne U., 1993, JD, 2001. Bar: Pa. 2001, U.S. Dist. Ct. (we. dist.) Pa. 2001; nat. cert. psychologist, lic. profl. counselor. Youth adv. Cambria Youth Adv. Program, Johnstown, 1988-89; caseworker Cambria County Children and Youth Svc., Ebensburg, Pa., 1989-93; psychol. svcs. assoc. II, psychol. svcs. assoc. supr. Cambria County Mental Health, Mental Retardation, Drug and, Johnstown, 1993—; pvt. practice law, 2001—. Cons. in field. Mem. ABA, Pa. Bar Assn., N.Am. Assn. Masters in Psychology, Pa. Social Svc. Union. Home: 102 Midway Dr Johnstown PA 15905-3827 Office: Lincoln Ctr 416 Main St Johnstown PA 15901

KEIPER, MARILYN MORRISON, elementary education educator; b. South Gate, Calif., June 12, 1930; d. David Cline and Matilda Ruth (Pearce) M.; m. Edward E. Keiper, June 18, 1962; children: Becky S. Swickard, Edward M. BA, Calif. State U., L.A., 1954; postgrad., UCLA, 1968. Elem. tchr. Rosemead (Calif.) Sch. Dist., 1954—. Recreation leader L.A. County, 1951-62, 2d reader 1st Ch. Christ Scientist, Arcadia, Calif., 1991-94; mem. cons. Janson Adv. Group, Rosemead, 1985-95; bd. dirs. Janson PTA, Rosemead, 1985-99; participant Sta. KNBC Spirit of Edn., 1990-92; leadership team Jason Sch.; mem. M.B. Janson Leadership team. Named Tchr. of the Yr., L.A. County, 1983-84; recipient Recognition award for outstanding service to children, Theta Kappa Chpt. Delta Kappa Gamma, 1996; featured in articles in Pasadena Star News, Rosemead C. of C., 2000; Janson Sch. auditorium named Keiper Auditorium in her honor for outstanding svc. to sch., 2001. Fellow Rosemead Tchrs. Assn., Delta Kappa Gamma.

KEIR, GERALD JANES, banker; b. Ludlow, Mass., Aug. 22, 1943; s. Alexander J. and Evelyn M. (Buckley) K.; m. Karen Mary Devine, July 22, 1972; children: Matthew J., Katherine B., Megan E. BA, Mich. State U., 1964, MA, 1966. Reporter Honolulu Advertiser, 1968-74, city editor, 1974-86, mng. editor, 1986-89, editor, 1989-95; exec. v.p. corp. comms. First Hawaiian Bank, Honolulu, 1995—. Co-author: Advanced Reporting: Beyond News Events, 1985, Advanced Reporting: Discovering Patterns in News Events, 1997. Bd. dirs. First Hawaiian Found., Salvation Army Bd. Hawaii, East-West Ctr. Found. Recipient Nat. Reporting award Am. Polit. Sci. Assn., 1971, Benjamin Fine Nat. award Am. Assn. Secondary Sch. Prins., 1981; John Ben Snow fellow, 1983, NEH fellow, 1973. Mem. Social Sci. Assn., Honolulu Cmty.-Media Coun., Fin. Svcs. Roundtable Pub. Affairs Coun. Office: First Hawaiian Bank PO Box 3200 Honolulu HI 96847-0001 E-mail: gerry.keir@fhwn.com.

KEISER, BERNHARD EDWARD, engineering company executive, consulting telecommunications engineer; b. Richmond Heights, Mo., Nov. 14, 1928; s. Bernhard and Helen Barbara Julia (Buerkle) K.; m. Florence Evelyn Keiser, Jan. 22, 1955; children: Sandra, Carol, Nancy, Linda, Paul. BSEE, Washington U., St. Louis, 1950, MSEE, 1951, DScEE, 1953. Registered profl. engr., Va., Md.. Mgr. plans and programs RCA, Cape Canaveral, Fla., 1964-67, adminstr. advanced system planning Moorestown, N.J., 1967-69; v.p., tech. dir. Page Communication Engring., Washington, 1969-70; dir. advanced engring. Atlantic Rsch. Corp., Alexandria, Va., 1971-72; dir. anaylsis Fairchild Space & Electronics Co., Germantown, Md., 1972-75; pres. Keiser Engring., Inc., Vienna, Va., 1975—. Author: EMI Control in Aerospace Systems, 1979, Principles of Electromagnetic Compatibility, 1979, rev. edit. 1987, Broad band Coding, Modulation and Transmission Engineering, 1989, rev. edit. 1994; co-author: Digital Telephony and Network Integration, 1985, rev. edit. 1995. Fellow IEEE (chmn. No. Va. sect. 1980-81), Washington Acad. Scis., Radio Club Am. Republican. Lutheran. Home and Office: 2046 Carrhill Rd Vienna VA 22181-2917 *I am neither the master of my fate nor the captain of my soul. I owe everything to the Lord Jesus Christ, who is my Savior, my Redeemer.*

KEISER, DAVID WHARTON, biotechnology executive; b. East Orange, N.J., July 13, 1951; s. Robert Emil and Jean Gage (Van Buskirk) K.; m. Barbara Ann Blecher, Aug. 28, 1976; children: Stephanie, Amanda, Joseph. BA in Psychology, Gettysburg Coll., 1973; postgrad., Med. Sch. U. Basel, 1975-76. Area mgr. Hoffmann-La Roche, Basel, Switzerland, 1981-83; new bus. opportunities mgr. Mundipharma AG, Basel, 1984-85; mgr. licensing G.D. Searle and Co., Skokie, Ill., 1985-86, dir. licensing, Europe, 1987-89, sr. dir. licensing, 1989-90, sr. dir. Asia/Pacific ops., 1990-92; exec. v.p., chief operating officer Alexion Pharma, New Haven, 1992—2002, pres., COO, bd. dirs., 2002—. Bd. dirs. Conn. United for Rsch Excellence, 1997-99. Bd. dirs. A Better Chance, Madison, Conn., 1997-99. With Swiss Army, 1978-85. Mem. Licensing Execs. Soc. Avocations: travel, languages, golf, hiking, investing. Office: Alexion Pharma Inc 352 Knotter Dr Cheshire CT 06410

KEISER, EDMUND DAVIS, JR., biologist, educator; b. Appalachia, Va., Feb. 18, 1934; s. Edmund Davis and Ora Elizabeth (Wade) K.; m. Alice Sue Tucker, Sept. 10, 1982; children: Mark Edmund, Julie Ann; stepchildren: Louis King III, Jenifer King. BA, So. Ill. U., 1956, MS, 1961; PhD in Zoology, La. State U., 1967. Tchr. sci. Kinmundy High Sch., Ill., 1956-57, Mt. Vernon Twp. Sch. Dist., Ill., 1957-58; dist. sci. coordinator Freeburg Sch. Dist. 70, Freeburg, Ill., 1958-62; instr. biology La Salle-Peru-Oglesby Jr. Coll., La Salle, Ill., 1962-64; teaching asst. La. State U., Baton Rouge, 1964-66; asst. prof. U. Southwestern La., Lafayette, 1966-70, assoc. prof., 1970-75, prof. biology, 1976, mem. coun. grad. coords., 1973-76; prof. biology U. Miss., Lafayette, 1976—, chmn. dept. University, 1976-87. Mem. Atchafalaya River Basin Rsch. Coun., 1972-74; mem. exec. coun., state dir. sci. teaching La. Acad. Scis., 1972-74; rsch. assoc. Gulf South Rsch. Inst., 1972-74; dir. Lafayette Natural History Mus. and Planetarium, 1973, Atchafalaya River Basin herpetofaunal study U.S. Fish and Wildlife Svc., 1973-76; mem. exec. coun. Gopher Tortoise Soc., 1979-81; commr. Miss. Dept. Wildlife Conservation, 1978-79, 80-84, chmn., 1983-84; cons. U.S. Fish and Wildlife Svc., 2000--; rsch. assoc. Miss. Mus. Natural Sci., 2001--. Mem. Miss. Wildlife Heritage Com., 1980-84, Miss. Gov.'s Select Com. on Radioactivity and Radioactive Waste Depository, 1979-80; environ. cons. NASA/Lockheed Sci. and Engring., 1990-91, 94-95, NASA/Sverdrup Engring., 1994-95; cons. on aquatic ecosys. U.S. Army C.E., 1992-95, 98-2002; cons. NASA/GBTech, 1998-2000, Miss. Dept. Wildlife, Fisheries and Parks, 1998—, Tetra Tech., Inc. Atlanta, 2000-01; cons. Nat. Park Svc., 2001-02, U.S. Fish and Wildlife Svc., 2002—. Recipient numerous grants; Disting. Prof. award U.

Southwestern La., 1973; Govs. Meritorious Service award State of Miss., 1979; citation for outstanding sci. teaching Nat. Sci. Tchrs. Assn.-Ill. Supt. Public Instrn., 1962 Fellow Explorers Club; mem. Soc. for Study Amphibians and Reptiles, Herpetologists League, Golden Key Honor Soc., Sigma Xi (chpt. pres. 1976, 79-80), Beta Beta Beta, Phi Eta Sigma, Phi Kappa Phi. Home: 211 Saint Andrews Cir Oxford MS 38655-2518 Office: U Miss Dept Biology University MS 38677 E-mail: bykeiser@olemiss.edu.

KEISER, HARRY ROBERT, physician; b. Chgo., Aug. 9, 1933; s. Harry Rudolph and Anna Mae (Hungerford) Keiser; m. Linda Lee Hallsten, June 11, 1965 (div. 1989); children: Harry Rudolph, Robert Hungerford; m. Phyllis Swain Bentz, May 9, 1992. BA, Northwestern U., 1955, MD, 1958. Diplomate Nat. Bd. Med. Examiners, Am. Bd. Internal Medicine. Intern Phila. Gen. Hosp., 1958-59; resident in internal medicine VA Research Hosp., Chgo., 1959-60; clin. assoc. Nat. Heart Inst., NIH, Bethesda, Md., 1960-63; resident in internal medicine U. Calif. Hosp., San Francisco, 1963-64; sr. investigator, then acting chief exptl. therapeutics br. Nat. Heart Inst., 1964-73; clin. asst. prof. medicine Georgetown U. Med. Sch., 1965-90, clin. prof. medicine, 1990—; dep. chief hypertension-endocrine br. Nat. Heart, Lung and Blood Inst., 1974-85; chief hypertension-endocrine br., 1985-98; clin. dir. inst., 1976-98, commd. officer USPHS, 1960-98, med. dir., 1972-98; scientist emeritus NIH, 1998—. Contbr. articles to profl. jours. Fellow: ACP; mem.: Am. Heart Assn., Am. Soc. Hypertension, Am. Soc. Pharmacology and Exptl. Therapeutics, Am. Fedn. Med. Rsch., Sierra Club. Home: 2573 SW Bridgeview Ter Palm City FL 34990 Office: Nat Heart Lung & Blood Inst 10 Center Dr MSC 1754 Bldg 10 Bethesda MD 20892-1754 E-mail: hkeiser@aol.com.

KEISER, JOHN DOUGHERTY, business educator; b. Bellefonte, Pa., May 7, 1962; s. James Ralph and Josephine Dougherty Keiser; m. Lynn Marie Pelkey, July 1, 2000; 1 child, Alecia Marie Rumpp. BS, Pa. State U., 1984; PhD in Orgnl. Behavior, U. of Ill., Urbana, 1995. Asst. prof. U. of Mass., Amherst, 1995—2001, SUNY, Brockport, NY, 2001—. Recipient Anbar Citation of Excellence, Anbar Electronic Ingelligence, 2000. Mem.: Soc. for Bus. Ethics, Acad. of Mgmt. Achievements include research in changes in the traits of American CEOs between 1960 and 1989, and research in service and nonprofit organizations. Home: 21 Brockway Pl Brockport NY 14420 Office: SUNY 350 New Campus Dr Brockport NY 14420 E-mail: jkeiser@brockport.edu.

KEISER, JOHN HOWARD, academic administrator; b. Mt. Olive, Ill., Mar. 12, 1936; s. Howard H. and Lorraine G. K.; m. Nancy Peterka, June 27, 1959; children: John, Sam, Joe. BS in Edn, Eastern Ill. U., 1958; MA, Northwestern U., 1960, PhD in History, 1964. Prof. history Westminster Coll., Fulton, Mo., 1963—65, Eastern Ill. U., Charleston, 1965—71; v.p. acad. affairs Sangamon State U., Springfield, Ill., 1971—78, acting pres., 1978; pres. Boise (Idaho) State U., 1978—93, S.W. Mo. State U., Springfield, 1993—. Author: Building for the Centuries, Illinois, 1865-1898, 1977, Illinois Vignettes, 1977. Bd. dirs. Abraham Lincoln coun. Boy Scouts Am., Springfield, Ore-Ida Council, Boise, Ozarks Trail coun. Springfield, NPR. Recipient Harry E. Pratt Meml. award Jour. Ill. History, 1970, 72; award of merit Ill. State Hist. Soc., 1980; award of merit Am. Assn. State and Local History, 1980, nat. medal of honor DAR, 1998, CEO Leadership award CASE, 1999. Mem.: Labor History Soc., Ill., Am. Hist. Soc., Orgn. Am. Historians, Spfld. C. of C., Rotary. Roman Catholic. Office: SW Missouri St U Off Pres 901 S National Ave Springfield MO 65804-0027

KEISER, PAUL HAROLD, retired hospital administrator; b. Dalton, Ohio, June 1, 1927; s. Austin R. and Elrena E. (Tschantz) K.; m. Nancy F. Homan, May 27, 1950; children— James William, Martha Ann Lee, Elizabeth Louise Green, Patricia Elrena Bell. BS, Mt. Union Coll., 1948; MS in Hosp. Adminstrn., Northwestern U., 1952. Adminstr. Community Hosp. Evanston, Ill., 1952-54, Burlington Hosp., Iowa, 1954-67; pres. York Hosp., Pa., 1967-88, ret., 1988. Lectr., seminar leader Northwestern U., Chgo., 1952-54, U. Iowa Hosp., Iowa City, 1955-59; lectr. George Washington U., 1969-86. Contbr. articles to profl. jours. Bd. dirs. United Way, York, Pa., 1970-78, York Habitat for Humanity, 1992-98, 99—, York County Parks Charitable Trust Bd., 1989-, vice chmn., 1990-; bd. dirs. York County Farm and Natural Land Trust, 1992-98, mem. adv. bd., 1998—; dir. adv. bd. Pa. State U., York, 1979—; sec. North Codorus Twp. Plan Commn., 1994-96; mem. North Codorus Twp. Bd. Suprs., 1995—, vice chmn., 1997-99, chmn. 2000-2002, S.E. (York County) Regional Police Bd., chmn. 2002-, mem. gov. bd. Byrnes Health Edn. Ctr., 1995—. Fellow Am. Coll. Hosp. Adminstrn. (life, regent 1964-67); mem. Iowa Interprofl. Assn. (pres. 1963-64), Iowa Hosp. Assn. (pres. 1961-62), Am. Hosp. Assn. (del. 1975-86), Hosp. Assn. Pa. (chmn. bd. dirs. 1983, bd. dirs. svcs. corp. 1986-89), Northwestern U. Hosp. Adminstrn. Alumni Assn. (pres. 1957-58), Rotary (bd. dirs. 1979-82), Sigma Alpha Epsilon. Republican. Presbyterian. Avocations: tennis; woodworking; handyman. Home: 3053 Markle Rd York PA 17403-9103

KEISER, TERRY DEAN, biologist, educator; b. Canton, Ohio, Oct. 27, 1942; s. Dean Robert and Neva Juanita K.; m. Patricia D. Peterson, Sept. 1, 1971 (div. Nov. 1976); m. Christine E. Provines, July 14, 1984. BS, Ohio Northern U., 1964; MS, Bowling Green State U., 1966. Instr., prof. Ohio Northern U., Ada, Ohio, 1966—, chair, 1992—, Biggs Endowed Chair in Sci., 2000—. Dir. Nature Ctr., Stone Creek, Ohio, 1990—, Midwest Biodiversity Inst., Columbus, 1998—, Flagship GM Ctr., Kenton, Ohio, 1996—; chair Ohio Biol. Survey, Columbus, Ohio, 1992—; cons. U.S. Geol. Survey/Nat. Water Quality Assessment, Columbus, 1995—. Contbr. articles to profl. jours. Chair Ada/Liberty Ambulance bd., Ohio, 1994-98, Ada Area Doctors com., 1995—; pres. Ada City Coun., 1984-2001, Ada Cmty. Improvement Corp., 1993; trustee Hardin County Humane Soc.; mem. Ohio Bicentennial Commn. Fellow Ohio Acad. Sci.; mem. Ohio Scientific Rsch. Assn. (pres. 2001-2003), Masons, Elks. Avocations: travel, nature study. Home: 220 E High St Ada OH 45810-1556 Office: Ohio Northern Univ Dept Biol Sciences Ada OH 45810 E-mail: t-keiser@onu.edu.

KEISLER, PETER DOUGLAS, federal agency administrator, lawyer; b. Hempstead, N.Y., Oct. 13, 1960; s. William and Sydelle (Prisand) K. BA, Yale U., 1981, JD, 1985. Bar: Pa. 1985, D.C. 1989. Law clk. to hon. judge Robert Bork U.S. Ct. Appeals (D.C. cir.), Washington, 1985-86; assoc. counsel to Pres. of U.S. White House, Washington, 1986-88; law clk. to assoc. justice Anthony Kennedy U.S. Supreme Ct., Washington, 1988-89; assoc. Sidley & Austin, Washington, 1989—93; ptnr., 1993—2002; prin. dep. assoc. atty. gen U.S. Dept. Justice, Washington, 2002; acting assoc. atty. gen, 2002—03; asst. atty. gen., civil division, 2003—. Mem. ABA, Pa. Bar Assn., D.C. Bar Assn. Republican. Jewish. Home: 4964 Allan Rd Bethesda MD 20816-2722 Office: Robert F Kennedy Bldg 10th St & Constitution Ave NW Rm 314 Washington DC 20530*

KEISTER, BEVERLY JANE, accountant; b. Louisville, Sept. 6, 1955; d. Joe Tivis and Leta Fern Keister; 1 child, Sara. BSBA in Food and Lodging Sys. Mgmt., BA in Acctg., M Accountancy, So. Ill. U., 1983. CPA. Acct. Peat, Marwich & Mitchell, St. Louis, 1984-87; asst. contr. Prime Bank, Decatur, Ga., 1987-91; project mgr. Arthur Andersen, Atlanta, 1991-92; mgr. Hazlett, Lewis & Bieter, Atlanta, 1992-96; CFO Cobb C. of C., Marietta, Ga., 1996-97, fin. acct. Watkins Engrs. & Contractors, Tallahassee, Fla., 1997—. Mem. Ga. Soc. CPA, Golden Key Honor Soc. (pres. 1982-83), Nat. Honor Soc., moose, Beta Alpha Psi. Democrat. Methodist. Avocations: flying, boating, swimming, skating, dancing. Office: Watkins Engrs & Constructors 2101 Maryland Cir Tallahassee FL 32303

KEITEL, JOYCE GILLILAN, English educator, director; b. Kearny, N.J., Apr. 8, 1941; d. Dean Hartman Gillilan; children: Laurel A. Rudzik, Laurence Dean Schrader, Michael Eugene Schrader. MA in English, U. of Mo., 1983. English instr. Columbia Coll., Jefferson City, Mo., 1984—, dir., 1986—. Home: 3426 B Knipp Dr Jefferson City MO 65109 Personal E-mail: jgkeitel@mchsi.com. E-mail: jgkeitel@ccis.edu.

KEITER, AARON, lawyer; b. Phila., May 26, 1946; s. Joseph and Lisa (Brahen) K.; B.S., Pa. State U., 1968; M.B.A., Widener Coll., 1973; J.D., U. Houston, 1976; m. Eileen Marsha Brown, Sept. 16, 1972; children— Justin Alan, Ashley Rochelle. Trader investment div. Phila. Nat. Bank, 1972-73; admitted to Tex. bar, 1976; tax specialist Coopers & Lybrand, Houston, 1976-77; gen. counsel Jetero Corp., Houston, 1977-79, Allison/Walker Interests, Inc., Houston, 1979-81; partner firm Goldberg & Keiter, Houston, 1981-83; sr. ptnr. Keiter, Blustein, DuBois & Krocker, Houston, 1983-85; ptnr. Keiter & Blustein, P.C., Houston, 1985-88; of counsel Weiner, Strother and Blustein, 1988-89; ptnr. Neely & Keiter, P.C., 1989-91, pvt. practice, 1991-2001, with Strother, Keiter & Mulder, P.C., 2001—; mem. faculty U. Houston Law Sch., 1975-76. Served with U.S. Army, 1968-72; lt. col. Res. Decorated Bronze Star, Air medal, Joint Service Commendation medal (retired); recipient Am. Jurisprudence award, 1974; Sutherland scholar, 1964-66, ROTC scholar, 1966-68. Mem. Am. Bar Assn., State Bar Tex., Houston Bar Assn., Fed. Bar Assn. Republican. Jewish. Club: Houston City. Office: 4545 Mount Vernon St Houston TX 77006-5815

KEITH, ANDREA L. marketing professional; BS in Chemistry, Bradley U., 1981—85; MBA, Ill. Benedictine U., 1993—95, MS in Orgn. Behavior, 1995—97. Bus. devel. mgr. Loders Croklaan/Unilever, Channahon, Ill., 1985—2003; dir. global mktg. Particle Dynamics, St. Louis, 2003—. Exec. mem. Coun. for Responsible Nutrition, Washington, 1997—2003. Mem.: Food Exec. Women (corr.; treas. 1990—93), Am. Assn. Pharm. Scientists (corr.), Am. Assn. Cereal Chemists (corr.), Am. Oil Chemists Soc. (corr.), America's Registry Outstanding Professionals (corr.). Office: Particle Dynamics 2503 S Hanley Rd Saint Louis MO 63144 Office Fax: 314-968-5208. Personal E-mail: andrea_keith@hotmail.com. E-mail: akeith@particledynamics.com.

KEITH, BARRY HAROLD, environmental scientist; b. Northbridge, Mass., Sept. 16, 1954; s. Harold and Louise Thobia (Hansen) K.; m. Pamela Jean Clemons, May 16, 1981; stepchildren: Shanti, Leif. BS, U. N.H., 1976, MS, 1982. Registered profl. forester, Maine, N.H., profl. Wetland Sci.; cert. wildlife biologist. Wildlife biologist U.S. Army C.E., Franklin, N.H., 1976-77, 78; terrestrial ecologist Wilbur Smith & Assocs., Inc., Concord, N.H., 1977; sr. ecologist BCI Geonetics, Inc., Laconia, N.H., 1977-78; ind. consulting ecologist Laconia, 1978-79; wetlands project mgr. N.H. Extension Svc., Conway, 1979-80; environ. scientist B.H. Keith Assocs., Freedom, N.H., 1980—. Cons., U.S. Am. Internat. Devel., Washington, 1987—. Contbr. articles to environ. publs. Mem. Freedom (N.H.) Conservation Commn., 1988—; selectman Town of Freedom, 1999—. Mem. Wildlife Soc. (bull. editorial referee 1983), Soc. Wetland Scientists, Soc. Ecol. Restoratin and Mgmt., Soc. Am. Foresters, N.H. Assn. Wetland Scientists, Ducks Unlimited (chmn. 1985-92, Disting. Svc. award), Soc. for Protection of N.H. Forests, Freedom Club. Republican. Avocations: fishing, hunting, hiking, antiques, wildlife art. Office: BH Keith Assocs Elm St Freedom NH 03836

KEITH, BRIAN THOMAS, automobile executive; b. Houston, Aug. 2, 1951; s. Thomas Ross and Elsie Ann (Carden) K.; m. Anna Lee Rogers, Nov. 17, 1973; children: Kevin Patrick, Lindsay Rogers. BSBA, Samford U., 1973. Educator installation IBM, Birmingham, Ala., 1971-73; salesman Albeco-Ala. Bus. Equipment Co., Birmingham, 1973-74; pres., owner Walter S. White Auto Parts, Inc., Birmingham, 1974—. Bd. dirs. Ala. Power Co. Vendor Rels. Bd., Birmingham, Automotive Wholesalers Worker Compensation Trust, 2001--; trustee Automotive Wholesalers Ins. Trust, Montgomery, 1985—, treas. investment com., 1992—, chmn. trust, 1996-99; industry spkr. Automotive Market Rsch. Coun., 1995, Automotive Wholesalers Assn. Ala. and Ga., Automotive Aftermarket Industry Assn. Pub. mag. Auto Svc. and Repair, 1988—; contbr. articles to publs. and mags. V.p. Park Bd. Patriot Baseball, Homewood, Ala., 1985-89; celebrity fundraiser Am. Cancer Soc., 1993; mem. canvass com. All Sts. Ch., Homewood, 1986-90, youth com., 1992-99; active St. Andrews Soc. of the Middle South. Named Outstanding Young Men in Am., U.S. Jaycees, 1983; recipient Tech. Tng. award Arvvin Industries, 1983-88. Mem. Automotive Aftermarket Assn. S.E. (bd. dirs. 1985—, chmn. 1986-91, treas. 1992-95, 98—, polit. action com. 1992-99, exec. com. 1991—, Leadership award 1991), Automotive Aftermarket Industry Assn. (bd. dirs. 1992-98, nat. polit. action com. 1993-99, co-chmn. automotive com. 1994-98), Birmingham C. of C., U.S. C. of C., Young Exec. Forum, Assn. Enterprises (pres. 1991-92), Jr. Achievement, Nat. Fedn. Ind. Bus. Episcopalian. Avocations: family, golf, travel.

KEITH, BRUCE EDGAR, political analyst, genealogist; b. Curtis, Nebr., Feb. 17, 1918; s. Edgar L. and Corinne E. (Marsteller) Keith; m. Evelyn E. Johnston, Oct. 29, 1944; children: Mona Louise, Kent Marsteller, Melanie Ann. AB with high distinction, Nebr. Wesleyan U., 1940; MA, Stanford U., 1952; grad. Command and Staff Marine Corps Schs., 1958, sr. resident, Naval War Coll., 1962; PhD, U.Calif., Berkeley, 1982. Commd. 2d lt. U.S. Marine Corps, 1942; advanced through grades to col., 1962; ret., 1971; officer in charge Marine Corps Nat. Media, N.Y.C., 1946—49; support arms coord. 1st Marines, Seoul, Republic of Korea, 1950; cmmdg. officer 3d Bn, 11th Marines, 1958—59; ops. officer Pres. Dwight D. Eisenhower visit to Okinawa, 1960, Fleet Marine Force, Pacific Cuban Missile Crisis, 1962; mem. U.S. del. SEATO Planning Conf., Bangkok, 1964; G-3 Fleet Marine Force, Pacific, 1964—65; head strategic planning study dept. Naval War Coll., 1966—68; genealogist, 1967—; exec. officer Hdqrs. Marine Corps programs, Washington, 1968—71; election analyst inst. govtl. studies U. Calif., Berkeley, 1974—86; polit. analyst, 1986—; tchg. asst. U.Calif., Berkeley, 1973—74. Contbr. Book; author: (Book) A Comparison of the House Armed Services Committees in the 91st and 94th Congresses: How They Differed and Why, 1982, The Johnstons of Morning Sun, 1979, The Marstellers of Arrellton, 1978, The Morris Family of Brookville, 1977, Japan-The Key to America's Future in the Far East, 1962, A United States General Staff" A Must or a Monster?, 1950; co-author: California Votes, 1960—72, 1974, The Myth of the Independent Voter, 1992, Furher Evidence on the Partisan Affinities of Independent Leaners, 1983. Bd. dirs. Bay Area Funeral Soc., 1980—83, v.p., 1981—83. Decorated Bronze Star, Navy Commendation medal, Presdl. Unit Citation with 3 bronze stars.; recipient Phi Kappa Phi Silver medal, Nebr. Weslyan U., 1940, Alumni award, 1964. Mem.: Ret. Officers Assn., Am. Acad. Polit. and Social Sci., Acad. Polit. Sci., Am. Polit. Sci. Assn., No. Calif. Marine Corps Assn., World Affairs Coun., Marines Meml. (San Francisco), Commonwealth of Calif. (San Francisco), Masons, Pi Gamma Mu, Phi Kappa Phi. Republican. Unitarian. Address: PO Box 2368 Walnut Creek CA 94595-0368

KEITH, DAMON JEROME, federal judge; b. Detroit, Mich., July 4, 1922; s. Perry A. and Annie L. (Williams) K.; m. Rachel Boone Keith, Oct. 18, 1953; children: Cecile Keith, Debbie, Gilda. BA, W.Va. State Coll., 1943; JD, Howard U., 1949; LLM, Wayne State U., 1956; PhD (hon.) (hon.), U. Mich., Howard U., Wayne State U., Mich. State U., N.Y. Law Sch., Detroit Coll. Law, W.Va. State Coll., U. Detroit, Atlanta U., Lincoln U., Marygrove Coll., Detroit Inst. Tech., Shaw Coll., Ctrl. State U., Yale U., Loyola Law Sch., L.A., Ea. Mich. U., Va. Union U., Ctrl. Mich. U., Morehouse Coll., Western Mich. U., Tuskegee U., Georgetown U., Hofstra U., DePaul U. Bar: Mich. 1949. Atty. Office Friend of Ct., Detroit, 1951—55; sr. ptnr. firm Keith, Conyers Anderson, Brown & Wahls, Detroit, 1964—67; mem. Wayne County Bd. Suprs., 1958—63; dist. judge U.S. Dist. Ct. (ea. dist.) Mich., 1967—77, chief judge, 1975—77; judge U.S. Ct. Appeals (6th cir.), Detroit, 1977—95, sr. judge, 1995—. Mem. Wayne County (Mich.) Bd. Suprs., 1958—63; chmn. Mich. Civil Rights Commn., 1964—67; pres. Detroit Housing Commn., 1958—67; commr. State Bar Mich., 1960—67; mem. Mich. Com. Manpower Devel. and Vocat. Tng., 1964, Detroit Mayor's Health Adv. Com., 1969; rep. dist. judges 6th Cir. Jud. Conf., 1975—77; adv. com. on codes of conduct Jud. Conf. U.S., 1979—86; subcom. on supporting pers. Jud. Conf. Com. on Ct. Adminstrn., 1983—87; chmn. Com. on the Bicentennial of Constn. of Sixth Cir., 1985—; nat. chmn. Jud. Conf. Com. on the Bicentennial of Constn., 1987—; mem. Commn. on the Bicentennial of U.S. Constn., 1990; lectr. Howard U., 1972, Ohio State U. Law Sch., 1992, N.Y. Law Sch., 1992; guest lectr. Howard U. Law Sch., 1981; Bicentennial of Constn. lectr. W.Va. State Coll., 1987; keynote speaker Black Law Students Assn., Harvard Law Sch., 1987. Contbr. Trustee Med. Corp. Detroit, Interlochen Arts Acad., Cranbrook Sch., U. Detroit, Mich. chpt. Leukemia Soc. Am.; mem. Citizen's Adv. Com. Equal Ednl. Opportunity Detroit Bd. Edn.; gen. co-chmn. United Negro Coll. Fund Detroit; 1st v.p. emeritus Detroit chpt. NAACP; mem. com. mgmt. Detroit YMCA; mem. Detroit coun. Boy Scouts Am., Detroit Arts Commn.; vice chmn. Detroit Symphony Orch.; vis. com. Wayne State U. Law Sch.; adv. coun. U. Notre Dame Law Sch.; chmn. Citizen's Coun. for Mich. Pub. Univs.; deacon Tabernacle Missionary Bapt. Ch.; Deacon Bapt ch.; bd. dirs. Detroit Bd. Table, NCCJ. With AUS, WWII. Named 1 of 100 Most Influential Black Ams., Ebony Mag., 1971—92, Damon J. Keith Elementary Sch. named in his honor, Detroit Bd. Edn., 1974, Damon J. Keith Ann. Civic and Humanitarian award established in his honor, Highland Park YMCA, 1984, 15th Mich. Legal Milestone The Uninvited Ear presented in honor of The Keith Decision, 1991; recipient Mich. Chronicle outstanding Citizen award, 1960, 1964, 1974, Alumni citation, Wayne State U., 1968, Ann. Jud. award, 1971, Citizen award, Mich. State U., Disting. Svc. award, Howard U., 1972, Jud. Independence award, 1973, Spingarn medal, NAACP, 1974, Fed. Judge of Yr. award, Black Law Students Assn., 1974, award for Outstanding Contbns. to Black Community, Nat. Assn. Black Social Workers, 1974, Judge of Yr. award, Nat. Conf. Black Lawyers, 1974, Bill of Rights award, Jewish Community Coun., 1977, A. Philip Randolph award, Detroit Coalition Black Trade Unionists, 1981, Human Rights Day award, B'nai B'rith Women's Coun. Met. Detroit, Robert L. Millender award, So. Christian Leadership Conf. Mich. chpt., 1982, Afro-Asian Inst. award, Histadrut in Israel, 1982, civil rights lectr. award, Creighton U. Ahmanson Law Ctr., 1983, Nat. Human Rels. award, Greater Detroit Roundtable of NCCJ, 1984, Knights of Charity award, Pontifical Inst. for Mission Extension, 1986, Disting. Pub. Svc. award, Mich. Anti-Defamation League of B'nai B'rith, 1987, Nat. Chpt. award, 1988, Black Achievement award, Equitable Fin. Cos., 1987, Menorah award, Afro-Asian Inst. Histadrut of Israel, 1988, Dr. George Derry award, Marygrove Coll. Detroit, One Nation award, The Patriots Found./GM, 1989, 1st Ann. Move Detroit Forward award, City of Detroit, 1990, Gov's. Minuteman award, Rotary Club Lansing, 1991. Mem.: ABA (coun. sect. legal edn. and admission to bar), Am. Judicature Soc., Nat. Lawyers Guild, Detroit Bar Assn. (pres'. award), Mich. Bar Assn. (champion of justice award), Nat. Bar Assn. (William H. Hastie award Jud. Coun., 8th Ann. equal Justice award), Detroit Cotillion Club, Alpha Phi Alpha. Office: US Ct Appeals US Courthouse 231 W Lafayette Blvd Rm 240 Detroit MI 48226-2779 also: Potter Stewart US Courthouse 100 E 5th St Cincinnati OH 45202-3988*

KEITH, DAVID, symphony orchestra conductor; b. Tacoma, Oct. 9, 1930; s. David and Barbara (Ferry) K.; m. Ginni Paynton, July 5, 1972. Student, San Francisco Conservatory of Music, 1948-50; studied choral conducting, Rodney Eichenberger, U. Wash., 1968; studied orchestral conducting, Dr. Stanley Chapple and Vilem Sokol, U. Wash., 1968-72; studied piano with, Ira Schwarz, Can., Louise van Ogle, U.S. Assoc. condr. Bellevue (Wash.) Philharm. Orch., 1968-70; condr., music dir. Seattle Concert Orch., 1970-73; founder, music dir. emeritus, condr. laureate L.A. Mozart Orch., 1974-91, also trustee, 1974-91. Founder, mus. dir. Nightingale, 2003—. Avocations: breeding purebred, all-black German shepherds. Office: LA Mozart Orch 1771 Seaview Trl Los Angeles CA 90046

KEITH, DELORESE PARKER, elementary school educator; b. Lynchburg, Va., July 21, 1931; d. Charles Edward and Odell Routon Parker; m. Charles Elisha Keith, July 5, 1958; children: Edward, Sharon Keith Brem. BA in Edn. and Psychology, Lynchburg Coll., 1952; student in Theatre, SUNY, 1979—81, MS in Edn., 1983. Cert. tchg. permanent Cert. N.Y., Collegiate Profl. Cert. State of Va. Elem. tchr. Fairfax County Schs., Va., 1952—56, USAF, Japan, 1956—57, Oyster Bay & Greene Pub. Schs., NY, 1958—76; humanities instr. Broome Cmty. Coll., Binghamton, NY, 1979—84; resource tchr. for gifted Fluvanna County Schs., Va., 1985—88; historic intpreter Monticello Edn. Dept., Charlottesville, Va., 1989—98. Puppeteer & instr. Kids on the Block and Therapeutic Recreation, Charlottesville, Va., 1990—; bd. mem. Girls Scouts of Am., varrious, 1972—96. Trainer Girl Scouts of Am., various, 1972—96. Recipient Jeannie Special Achievement Award in Childrens Theatre, Broome Cmty. Coll., 1980, Thanks Badge award, Girl Scouts USA, 1984, cert. of Appreciation Award, Charlottesville Parks and Recreation, 1994. Episc. Avocations: hiking, oragami, candle making, painting, travel. Home: 1405 Auburn Dr Charlottesville VA 22902

KEITH, GARNETT LEE, JR., investment executive; b. Atlanta, Nov. 27, 1935; s. Garnett Lee and Agnes (Roark) K.; m. Martha Holmes, Oct. 12, 1957; children: Suzanne, Geoffrey. B.Indsl. Engring., Ga. Inst. Tech., 1957; MBA, Harvard U., 1962. Asst. sec. Irving Trust Co., 1962-64; v.p. Irwin Mgmt. Co., 1964-75; pres. Irwin Union Corp., 1975-76; vice chmn. Prudential Ins. Co., Newark, 1977-96; chmn., CEO Seabridge Investment Advisors, Summit, 1996—. Bd. dirs. Super Valu Stores, Minn. Trustee Drew U., Madison, N.J. Mem. Inst. Chartered Fin. Analysts. Clubs: Harvard (N.Y.C.). Republican. Office: Seabridge Investment Advisors 450 Springfield Ave Ste 301 Summit NJ 07901-2610

KEITH, JENNIE, anthropology educator and administrator, writer; b. Carmel, Calif., Nov. 15, 1942; d. Paul K. and Romayne Louise (Fuller) Hill; m. Marc Howard Ross, Aug. 25, 1968 (div. 1978); 1 child, Aaron Elliot Keith Ross; m. Roy Gerald Fitzgerald, June 21, 1980; 1 child, Kate Romayne Keith-Fitzgerald. BA, Pomona Coll., 1964; MA, Northwestern U., 1966, PhD, 1968; Dr.Letters (hon.), Pomona Coll., 2002. NIMH fellow, Paris, 1968-70; asst. prof. anthropology Swarthmore Coll., 1970-76, assoc. prof., 1976-82, prof., 1982—, Centennial prof. anthropology, 1990—, chmn. sociology and anthropology, 1987-92, provost, 1992-2001; exec. dir. Eugene M. Lang Ctr. for Civic and Social Responsibility, 2002—. Mem. rsch. edn. rev. com. NIMH, Washington, 1979-82; co-dir. workshop on age and anthropology Nat. Inst. Aging, Washington, 1980-81, task group leader nat. rsch. plan on aging, 1981; mem. human devel. rev. bd. NIH, 1985-89; mem. adv. coun. Brookdale Found., 1990-93. Author: Old People, New Lives, 1977, 2d paperback edit., 1982 (Am. Jour. Nursing Book of Yr. 1978), Old People as People, 1982; co-author: The Aging Experience, 1994 (Richard Kalish award Gerontol. Soc. Am. 1994); co-editor: New Methods for Old-Age Research, 1980, 2d edit., 1986, Age in Anthropological Theory, 1984; mem. editorial bd. Gerontologist, 1981-89, Jour. Gerontology, 1987-91, Jour. Aging Studies, 1989-98; assoc. editor Rsch. on Aging, 1981-88. Bd. dirs. Cmty. Svcs., Folsom, Pa., 1980-82, Inst. Outdoor Awareness, Swarthmore, 1980—; bd. dirs. Kendal-Crosslands, 1987-92, chmn., 1989-92, Kendal Corp., 1992-95. Conf. grantee Nat. Inst. Aging, 1980, rsch. grantee, 1982-90. Fellow Am. Anthrop. Assn., Gerontol. Soc. Am. (exec. bd. behavioral and social scis. sect. 1985-87, program chmn. 1989, chair 1989-90, publs. com. 1993-95); mem. Assn. Anthropology and Gerontology (founder, sec. 1980-81). Office: Swarthmore Coll Lang Ctr for Civic and Social Responsibi Swarthmore PA 19081 E-mail: jkeith1@swarthmore.edu.

KEITH, KENT MARSTELLER, YMCA leader, academic administrator, corporate executive, government official, lawyer, author; b. N.Y.C., May 22, 1948; s. Bruce Edgar and Evelyn E. (Johnston) K.; m. Elizabeth Misao Carlson, Aug. 22, 1976. BA in Govt., Harvard U., 1970; BA in Politics and Philosophy, Oxford (Eng.) U., 1972, MA, 1977; JD, U. Hawaii, 1977; EdD, U. So. Calif., 1996. Bar: Hawaii 1977, D.C. 1979. Assoc. Cades, Schutte, Fleming & Wright, Honolulu, 1977-79; coord. Hawaii Dept. Planning and Econ. Devel., Honolulu, 1979-81, dep. dir., 1981-83, dir., 1983-86; energy resources coord. State of Hawaii, Honolulu, 1983-86, chmn. State Policy Coun., 1983-86; chmn. Aloha Tower Devel. Corp., 1983-86; project mgr. Mililani Tech. Park Castle and Cooke Properties, Inc., 1986-89, v.p. pub. rels. and bus. devel., 1988-89; pres. Chaminade U., Honolulu, 1989-95; v.p. devel. and comm. YMCA Honolulu, 1998—2001, sr. v.p., 2001—. Author: Jobs for Hawaii's People: Fundamental Issues in Economic Development, 1985, The Paradoxical Commandments: Finding Personal Meaning in a Crazy World, 2001, Anyway: The Paradoxical Commandments, 2002; contbr. articles on ocean law to law jours. Trustee Hawaii Loa Coll., 1986—89, vice chmn., 1987—89; bd. dirs. St. Louis Sch., 1990—95, Hanahauoli Sch., 1990—98, Cath. Charities, 1997—2003; chmn. Manoa Neighborhood Bd., 1989—91; mem. platform com. Hawaii Dem. Conv., 1982, 1984, 1986; pres. Manoa Valley Ch., Honolulu, 1976—78; mem. Diocesan Bd. Edn., 1990—95, chmn., 1990—93. Rhodes scholar, 1970; named one of 10 Outstanding Young Men of Am., U.S. Jaycees, 1984; recipient Disting. Alumni award U. Hawaii, 1993. Mem. Am. Assn. Rhodes Scholars, Internat. House of Japan, Nature Conservancy, Pla. Club, Pacific Club, Harvard Club Hawaii (Honolulu, bd. dirs. 1974-78, sec. 1974-76), Rotary (Honolulu Sunrise). Home: 2626 Hillside Ave Honolulu HI 96822-1716 E-mail: kentkeith@hotmail.com.

KEITH, PAULINE MARY, artist, illustrator, writer; b. Fairfield, Nebr, July 21, 1924; d. Siebelt Ralph and Pauline Alethia (Garrison) Goldenstein; m. Everett B. Keith, Feb. 14, 1957; 1 child, Nathan Ralph. Student, George Fox Coll., 1947-48, Oreg. State U., 1955. Illustrator Merlin Press, San Jose, Calif., 1980-81; artist, illustrator, watercolorist Corvallis, Oreg., 1980-94. Author 6 chapbooks including Christmas Thoughts, Retelling the Story, 1985, Poems, 1999; editor: Four Generations of Verse, 1979; author numerous poems; contbr. articles to profl. jour; one-woman shows include Roger's Meml. Libr., Forest Grove, Oreg., 1959, Corvallis Art Ctr., 1960, 98-99, Human Resources Bldg., Corvallis, 1959-61, Corvallis Pastoral Counseling Ctr., 1992-94, 96, Hall

Gallery, Sr. Ctr., 1993-2003, Consumer Power, Philomath, Oreg., 1994, 2002, Art, Etc., Newburg, Oreg., 1995-2002; exhibited in group shows at Hewlett-Packard Co., 1984-85, Corvallis Art Ctr., 1992, Chintimini Sr. Ctr., 1992, 1994, 2001-02. Co-elder First Christian Ch. (Disciples of Christ), Corvallis, 1988-89, co-deacon, 1980-83, elder, 1991-93; sec. Hostess Club of Chintimini Sr. Ctr., Corvallis, 1987, pres., 1988-89, v.p., 1992-94; mem. Luth. Ch. Coun., 1998, 99-2000. Recipient Watercolor 1st price Benton County Fair, 1982, 83, 88, 89, 91, 2d prize, 1987, 91, 3d prize, 1984, 90, 92. Mem. Oreg. Assn. Christian Writers, Internat. Assn. Women Mins., Am. Legion Aux. (elected poet post II Covallis chpt. 1989-90, elected sec. 1991-92), ArtVine (Pres.'s Choice, 1999-2002). Republican. Avocations: nature walks, singing in church choir. Office: 304 S College St Newberg OR 97132-3114

KEITH, ROBERT WILLIAM, banker; b. Chgo., July 28, 1926; s. Nathan William Keith and Myrtle A. (Bull) Simons; m. Helen L. Weichel, Sept. 4, 1948; children— Melissa, Matthew, Andrew Student, Wentworth Military Acad., 1944; BS, U. Mo., 1947; MBA, Hofstra U., 1956. Employment mgr. Equitable Life Assurance Soc., N.Y.C., 1947-56; asst. treas. Hanover Bank, N.Y.C., 1956-59; asst. v.p. Mfrs. Hanover Trust Co., N.Y.C., 1959-63, v.p., 1963-77, sr. v.p., 1977-83, exec. v.p., 1983-86. Regent Stonier Grad. Sch., Washington, 1981-84. Fellow Life Office Mgmt. Assn.; mem. CLU (chartered), Am. Inst. Banking (life), Am. Bankers Assn. (chmn. pers. divsn., dir. 1980-81), Beta Gamma Sigma, Beta Theta Pi, North Fork Country Club. Republican. Presbyterian.

KEITH, TAMMY LEAH, geriatrics nurse; b. Roaring Spring, Pa., Apr. 2, 1958; d. Ronald Robert and Doris Marie (Ott) Ferry; m. Phillip W. Keith; 1 child, Jamie Marie. Diploma, Altoona Hosp. Sch. Nursing, 1979. RN, Pa.; cert. in CPR. Charge nurse, staff nurse Nason Hosp., Roaring Spring, 1979-83; nursing supr. Morrison's Cove Home for Aged, Martinsburg, Pa., 1983—. Substitute organist, ch. sch. pianist Trinity United Meth. Ch., Roaring Spring, Pa., 1974-79; asst. troop leader Girl Scouts U.S.A., 1988-92; mem. Friendship Fire Co. 1 Inc., Ctrl. H.S. Alumni Band, Ctrl. H.S. Alumni Chorus. Mem. Altoona Hosp. Sch. Nursing Alumni Assn. Republican. Methodist. Avocations: traveling, baking, reading, walking. Home: 430 Locust St Roaring Spring PA 16673-1734 Office: Morrison's Cove Home for Aged 429 S Market St Martinsburg PA 16662-1098

KEITH, THOMAS WARREN, JR., marketing executive; b. Evanston, Ill., Sept. 27, 1951; s. Thomas and Patricia (Ogden) K. BA, Colgate U., Hamilton, NY, 1973; MBA, Columbia U., N.Y.C., 1975. Acct. exec. Leo Burnett Co., Chgo, 1975-80, Needham Harper & Steers, Chgo, 1980-81; acct. supr. Tatham-Laird & Kudner, Chgo, 1981-85; mktg. dir. Dean Foods Co., Franklin Park, IL, 1986-90; pres. Thomas Keith & Assoc., Mktg. Svcs., Evanston, Ill. Dir. Dairy Nutrition Coun., Ill., 1989-90; dir. Dairy Coun. of Wis., Ill., 1987-90. Home and Office: 1005 Dempster St Evanston IL 60201-4210 E-mail: tom@advertising-marketing.com.

KEITH, TIMOTHY ZOOK, psychology educator; b. Providence, R.I., May 7, 1952; s. Charles Herbert and Julia Mercer (Zook) K.; m. Mary Anne Forbes, Aug. 16, 1975 (dec. Mar. 1989); children: Davis Henry, Scott Forbes, William Howe; m. Patricia Josephine Berg, Sept. 15, 1990. BA, U. N.C., 1974; MA, East Carolina U., 1978; PhD, Duke U., 1982. Licensed psychologist, N.C. Lead psychologist Montgomery County Schs., Troy, N.C., 1978-80; sch. psychologist Durham (N.C.) City Schs., 1981-82; asst. prof. U. Iowa, Iowa City, 1982-85, assoc. prof., 1985-87, Va. Poly. Inst. and State U., Blacksburg, Va., 1987-91, prof., 1991-93, Alfred (N.Y.) U., 1993-97, Powell prof. of psychology and schooling, 1997—2001; prof. of ednl. psychology U Tex., 2001—. Rsch. cons. Iowa Dept. Corrections, 1985-86, Iowa Dept. Edn., Des Moines, 1983-87; nat. adv. com. mem. Buros Inst. Mental Measurements, 1992—95. Contbr. articles to profl. jours.; author: (videotape) Sch. Psychologist's Applications of Computers in Edn., 1984; mem. editl. bd. Sch. Psychology Rev., 1985-, assoc. editor, 1987-90, Jour. Sch. Psychology, 1987-99, Jour. Psychoednl. Assessment, 1994—; assoc. editor Sch. Psychology Quarterly, 1996-2000. Recipient award, N.C. Sch. Psychology Assn., 1981, Disting. Rsch. award, N.C. Assn. Rsch. in Edn., 1981, 1993, Ea. Ednl. Rsch. Assn., 1993, Rsch. Excellence award, Iowa Ednl. Rsch. and Evaluation Assn., 1985, Women's Rsch. award, Iowa Psychol. Assn., 1987, Presdl. award, Iowa Sch. Psychologists Assn., 1987, Outstanding Article award, Sch. Psychology Quar., 1993, Jour. Sch. Psychology, 1999, Articles of Yr. award, Sch. Psychology Rev., 1999, Rsch. Excellence award, Mensa Internat., 2001; fellow sr. rsch. fellow, Office Ednl. Rsch. and Improvement, U.S. Dept. Edn., 1998—2001, Measurement/Learning/Cons., LLC, 2000, Riverside Pub., 2001, Woodcock-Muñoz Found., 2003; grantee, Iowa Measurement Rsch. Found., 1984—85, U. Iowa, 1983—84, 1985—86, Va. Dept. Edn., 1991—93, sr. rsch. fellow, Office Ednl. Rsch. and Improvement, U.S. Dept. Edn., 1987—88. Fellow APA (mem. membership com. sch. psychology divsn. 1985, program co-chmn. 1993-95, Lightner Witmer award 1988); mem. NASP, Am. Ednl. Rsch. Assn., Am. Psychol. Soc., Sigma Xi. Episcopalian. Home: PO Box 160427 Austin TX 78716 Office: Dept of Ednl Psychology U Tex SZB 504 Austin TX 78712 E-mail: tim.keith@mail.utexas.edu.

KEITHLER, JOHN WILLIAM, investment executive; b. Elizabeth, N.J., Mar. 2, 1947; s. George King and Mary Keithler; m. Karen Dorothy Keithler, Apr. 13, 1996; 1 child, Jennifer Lynn Mirande. BS in Commerce, Rider U., 1970. Cert. cash mgr. Corp. banker Chase Manhattan Bank, N.Y.C., 1970-80; fin. planner Am. Brands, Inc., N.Y.C., 1980-85, cash mgr., 1985-86; investment mgr. Group Health Inc., N.Y.C., 1987—. With USN, 1971. Mem. Treasury Mgmt. Assn., Assn. for Fin. Profls. Avocations: foreign travel, stamp collecting, coin collecting. E-mail: kdkeithler@aol.com.

KEITHLEY, BRADFORD GENE, lawyer; b. Nov. 23, 1951; s. Sanderson Irish and Joan G. (Kenneday) K.; m. Ginger W. Wilhelmi, Mar. 26, 1994; children: Paul Michael, Rachel Austin Bernstein. BS, U. Tulsa, 1973; JD, U. Va., 1976. Bar: Va. 1976, Okla. 1978, D.C. 1979. Atty. Office of Gen. Counsel to Sec. USAF, Washington, 1976-78; ptnr. Hall, Estill, Hardwick, Gable, Collingsworth and Nelson, Tulsa, 1978-84; sr. v.p. gen. counsel natural gas divsn. Arkla, Inc. (now CenterPoint Energy, Inc.), Shreveport, La., 1984—90; ptnr. co-head global oil and gas practice team Jones Day, Dallas, 1990—. Mem. ABA, Fed. Energy Bar Assn., Va. State Bar, Okla. Bar Assn., D.C. Bar Assn., Am. Gas Assn. (mem. legal sect.), Dallas Petroleum Club. Home: 12652 Sunlight Dr Dallas TX 75230-1856 Office: Jones Day 2727 N Harwood Dallas TX 75201-1515

KEITHLEY, ROGER LEE, judge; b. Macomb, Ill., July 19, 1946; s. Gilbert Lee and Mary Jane (Torrance) K.; m. Karen Sue Metzger, Apr. 1, 1973; children: Roger Livingston, Terrance Christopher, Kathryn Suzanne. BS, U. Ill., 1968; JD, Harvard U., 1973. Bar: Colo. 1973, U.S. Dist. Ct. Colo. 1973, U.S. Ct. Appeals (10th cir.) 1976. Law clk. to justice Colo. Supreme Ct., Denver, 1973-74; trial atty. SEC, Denver, 1974-76; assoc. Morrato, Gueck & Colantuno, Denver, 1976-80; ptnr. Krys, Boyle, Golz & Keithley, Denver, 1980-86, Law, Knous & Keithley, Denver, 1986-90, Law, Keithley & Tuttle, Denver, 1990-93; pvt. practice Roger L. Keithley, P.C., Denver, 1993-98; presiding disciplinary judge Colo. Supreme Ct., 1998—. Prof. physics U. Asmara, Eritrea, Ethiopia, 1969-70. With U.S. Army, 1968-70. Mem.: ABA, Am. Law Inst., Denver Bar Asn., Colo. Bar Assn. Home: 5239 E 17th Ave Denver CO 80220-1313 E-mail: rlkeithley@aol.com.

KEKATOS, DEPPIE-TINNY Z. microbiologist, researcher, lab technologist; b. Buffalo, Oct. 16, 1960; d. Soter Spyros and Mary Soter (Kassimis) Zarifopoulos; m. Dion Kekatos; 1 child, Mary. BS, CUNY, 1983; MS, St. John's U., Jamaica, N.Y., 1986; grad. pharmacy technician program, ICS, 1999. Lic. lab. technologist, N.Y. Clin. lab. technologist trainee Booth Meml. Hosp., Flushing, N.Y., 1986-87; clin. lab. technologist L.I. Jewish Hosp., New Hyde Park, N.Y., 1988-89, Elmhurst (N.Y.) Hosp., 1990-95; asst. supr. microbiology United Health Labs., Woodside, N.Y., 1995-96; clin. lab. technologist Elmhurst Hosp., N.Y., 1999—. Mem. Am. Pharm. Assn., St. John's U. Alumni Fedn. Office: Elmhurst Hosp Microbiology Lab 79-01 Broadway Elmhurst NY 11373 Home: 38 Whitson St Forest Hills NY 11375 E-mail: deppiet@aol.com.

KEKES, JOHN, philosopher, educator; b. Budapest, Hungary, Nov. 22, 1936; came to U.S., 1965, naturalized, 1977; s. Eugene and Anna (Borsodi) K.; m. Jean Justilliano, May 20, 1968. BA, Queen's U., Kingston, Ont., Can., 1961, MA, 1962; PhD, Australian Nat. U., 1967. Instr. to assoc. prof. philosophy Calif. State U., Northridge, 1965-71; prof. U. Sask., Regina, Can., 1971-74, SUNY, Albany, 1974—, chmn. dept. philosophy, 1974-77, prof. philosophy and pub. policy, 1981—. Sr. rsch. fellow Ctr. for Philosophy of Sci., U. Pitts., 1984-85; vis. prof. U.S. Mil. Acad., West Point, N.Y., 1985-86, Nat. U. Singapore, 1989, Portuguese Cath. U., Lisbon, 2001. Author: A Justification of Rationality, 1976, The Nature of Philosophy, 1980, Dimensions of Ethical Thought, 1987, The Examined Life, 1988, Moral Tradition and Individuality, 1989, Facing Evil, 1990, The Morality of Pluralism, 1993, Moral Wisdom and Good Lives, 1995, Against Liberalism, 1997, A Case for Conservatism, 1998, Pluralism in Philosophy: Changing the Subject, 2000, The Art of Life, 2002; gen. editor: Studies in Moral Philosophy, 1986—91; editor: Pub. Affairs Quar., 1999—2001. Recipient Comdrs. Pub. Svc. award U.S. Army, 1986; Rockefeller Found. humanities fellow, 1980-81, fellow Earhart Found., 1983, 88, 89, 98, 2002; resident scholar Rockefeller Found. Study Ctr., Bellagio, Italy, 1982, 89. Mem. Am. Philos. Assn., Royal Inst. Philosophy Home: 2041 Cook Rd Charlton NY 12019-2909 Office: SUNY Dept Philosophy Albany NY 12222-0001 E-mail: jonkekes@nycap.rr.com.

KELALIS, BARBARA ANNA LISA, interior design company executive; b. San Antonio, Mar. 12, 1940; d. William Lewis and Wilma Ann (McClish) Wilson; m. Daniel Steen Fletcher, June 12, 1965 (div. 1968); m. Panayotis Petro Kelalis, Apr. 8, 1970; 1 child, Steven Michael Fetcher. BA, UCLA, 1964; postgrad., Rochester Community Coll., 1972-74. Interior designer Hilton Hotels Office, Beverly Hills, 1975-78, Rochester-Tour-of-Homes, 1978-86; pres. Camelot Designs, Inc., 1986—. Pres. Cmty. Concerts, Rochester, 1972. Recipient Golden Poet awards, 1989, 90. Avocations: tennis, ballet, horseback riding, painting, writing short stories.

KELALIS, PANAYOTIS, pediatric urologist; b. Nicosia, Cyprus, Jan. 17, 1932; came to U.S., 1960, naturalized, 1969; s. Peter and Julia (Petrides) K.; m. Barbara Wilson, Apr. 8, 1970. Student, U. Edinburgh, 1950-51; MB, BChir, U. Dublin, 1957; MS in Urology, Mayo Grad. Sch. Medicine, 1964. Resident in urology Mayo Grad. Sch. Medicine, Rochester, Minn., 1960-64; asst. to staff Mayo Clinic, 1964, cons. urology, 1965—, head sect. pediatric urology, 1975-91, chmn. dept. urology, 1982-91, 1991-2000, chair internat. activities, 1991—; prof. urology Mayo Med. Sch., 1975—, Anson L. Clark prof. pediatric urology, 1983—. Assoc. dir. surgery and subspecialities Mayo Grad. Sch. Medicine, 1994-2001. Editor: Clinical Pediatric Urology, 2 vols., 1976, 3rd edit., 1992; contbr. numerous sci. articles to profl. jours., chpts. in books. Hon. consul Republic of Cyprus. Recipient Edward J. Noble Found. award, 1964, Pediatric Urology medal, 1996; decorated knight Order of St. Andrew. Fellow ACS; mem. Am. Assn. Genito-Urinary Surgeons, Internat. Soc. Urology, Am. Urol. Assn., Soc. Pediatric Urology (pres.), Am. Acad. Pediatrics (pres., chmn. urology sect., Urology medal 1996), Sociedad Latino Americana de Urologia Infantile (hon.), Assn. Francaise d'Urologie (hon.), Hellenic Urol. Soc. (hon.), Sociedad Argentine de Urologia (corr.), Venezuelan Urol. Soc. (corr.). Office: Mayo Clinic 4500 San Pablo Rd S Jacksonville FL 32224-3899

KELBLE, JACK R. electronics executive; BS, Purdue U., West Lafayette, Ind., 1965; MS, U. Pa., 1969. With Raytheon Co., 1979—, mgr. equipment devel. labs., dir. data acquisitions systems, v.p. integrated systems, v.p., gen. mgr. elec. systems surveillance and reconnaissance, pres. space and airborne systems, 2002—. Bd. dirs. HRL Rsch. Labs., HE Microvae, Software Productivity Consortium. Office: Raytheon Co PO Box 902 2000 E El Segundo Blvd El Segundo CA 90245-0902*

KELBLE, WILLIAM FRANCIS, information services editor; b. Abington, Pa., Dec. 6, 1953; s. J. Richard and Mary Dolores (Bedesem) K.; m. Catharine Louise McGurk, Nov. 18, 1978. BA in Journalism, Pa. State U., 1975; MBA, Rutgers U., 1991. News reporter Montgomery Newspapers, Ft. Washington, Pa., 1976-78, night editor, 1978-79; copy editor Herald-Jour., Syracuse, N.Y., 1979-81, wire editor, 1981-82; editor Dow Jones & Co., Princeton, 1982-84, asst. news editor, 1984-86, news editor, project mgr., 1986-94, assoc. dir., 1994-96, dep. editorial dir., 1996-97, mng. editor, 1997-99; dir. creation content Factiva, 1999—2002, dir. content, 2002—. Recipient Keystone Press award Pa. Newspaper Pubs. Assn., 1979. Mem. Soc. Profl. Journalists. Home: 17 Neshanic Dr Ringoes NJ 08551-1845 Office: Factiva PO Box 300 Princeton NJ 08543-0300 E-mail: bill.kelble@factiva.com., w.kelble@worldnet.att.net.

KELCH, ROBERT PAUL, former dean, pediatric endocrinologist; b. Detroit, Dec. 3, 1942; s. Paul and Iona Bertha (Schmitt) Kelch; m. Jeri Anne Parker, Aug. 17, 1963; children: Randall Paul, Julie Marie. PhB, Wayne State U., Detroit, 1964; MD, U. Mich., Ann Arbor, 1967. Intern then Wyeth pediatric residency fellow U. Mich. Med. Center, 1967—70, research fellow, 1969—70, mem. faculty, 1972—94, prof. pediatrics, 1977—94, acting chmn. dept., 1979—80, chmn. dept., 1981—94; physician-in-chief C.S. Mott Children's Hosp. U. Mich., 1983—94; chief clin. affairs U. Mich. Hosps., 1989—92; NIH trainee pediatric endocrinology U. Calif. Med. Center, San Francisco, 1970—72; prof. pediat., dean U. Iowa Coll. Medicine, Iowa City, 1994—2003, v.p. statewide health svcs., 2001—02; exec. v.p., med. affairs, prof. pediatrics U. Michigan, Ann Arbor, 2003—. Co-author: A Practical Approach to Pediatric Endocrinology, 1975; contbr. articles to med. jours. With USNR. Fellow: Am. Acad. Pediat.; mem.: Midwest Soc. Pediat. Rsch. (pres. 1983—84), Lawson Wilkins Pediat. Endocrine Soc., Ctrl. Soc. Clin. Rsch., Assn. Med. Sch. Pediat. Dept. Chmn. (pres. 1989), Am. Soc. Clin. Investigation, Am. Fedn. Clin. Rsch., Endocrine Soc., Am. Bd. Pediat. (sec.-treas. 1992, chmn. 1995), Soc. Pediat. Rsch. (pres. 1988), Inst. Medicine NAS. Methodist. Office: U Michigan 1301 Catherine St Ann Arbor MI 48019-0626*

KELDMANN, ERIK CHRISTIAN VILHELM, innovation company executive; b. Naestved, Sealand, Denmark, Feb. 7, 1940; s. Charles Johannes and Karen Rigmor (Hansen) K.; m. Annelise Keldmann, Apr. 6, 1963; children: Troels, Linda. BSc in Mech. Engring., Odense Teknikum, 1965. Devel. engr. Motorfabriken Bukh, Kalundborg, Denmark, 1965-67; mgr. R&D Carmen-Clairol, Kalundborg, 1967-71; pres. Ve-va Cons., Jerslev, Denmark, 1971-85, Elpan-Wanpan, Odense, 1974-85; v.p. R&D Superfos Bldg. Components, Vebaek, Denmark, 1985-86; pres. E.K. Innovation, Odense, 1985—. Bd. dirs. Servodan, Direct-Haler A/S, E.K. Innovation A/S; co-founder High Performance Inst. Co-author: The Innovation-Tree; patents include heat embracement, zone impregnation and direct inhaler. Recipient Initiative Diploma for Entrepreneurship Nat. Soc. Danish Work, 1977. Mem. Acad. Using Philosophy, Soc. Exec. Engrs., Rotary (chpt. pres.). Avocation: classic cars. Office: EK Innovation Aaloekken 44 5250 Odense Denmark E-mail: ekinnovation@post.tele.dk.

KELEHEAR, CAROLE MARCHBANKS SPANN, senior legal secretary; b. Morehead City, N.C., Oct. 2, 1945; d. William Blythe and Gladys Ophelia (Wilson) Marchbanks; m. Henry M. Spann, June 5, 1966 (div. 1978); children: Lisa Carole, Elaine Mabry; m. Zachariah Lockwood Kelehear, Sept. 15, 1985. Student, Winthrop Coll., 1963-64; grad., Draughon's Bus. Coll., 1965; cert. in med. terminology, Greenville Tech. Edn. Coll., 1972; grad., Millie Lewis Modeling Sch. Office mgr. S.C. Appalachian Adv. Commn., Greenville, 1965-68, Wood-Bergheer & Co., Newport Beach and Palm Springs, Calif., 1970-72; asst. to Dr. J. Ernest Lathem Lathem & McCoy, P.A., Greenville, 1972-75; asst. to Gov. Robert E. McNair, McNair, Konduros, Corley, Singletary and Dibble Law Firm, Columbia, S.C., 1975-77; office mgr. Dr. James B. Knowles, Greenville, 1977-78, Constangy, Brooks & Smith, Columbia, 1978-83; legal asst. to sr. ptnr. William L. Bethea Jr., Bethea, Jordan & Griffin, P.A., Hilton Head Island, 1983—88; legal asst. Rajko D. Medenica, MD, PhD, 1988—95; adminstr. Dibble Law Offices, Columbia, 1995-96; sr. legal sec. Haynsworth Sinkler Boyd, P.A., Columbia, 1997—. Notary pub.; vol. Ladies aux. Greenville Gen. Hosp., 1966-72, South Coast Hosp., Laguna Beach, Calif., 1973, St. Francis Hosp, Greenville, 1974-76, Hilton Head Hosp., 1983-92. Mem. Hilton Head Hosp. Aux., Profl. Women's Assn. Hilton Head Island, Am. Bus. Women's Assn., Nat. Assn. Female Execs., Am. Soc. Notaries, Beta Sigma Phi.

KELEHER, JAMES P. bishop; b. July 31, 1931; BA, St. Mary of the Lake Sem., Mundelein, Ill., 1954; DST, St. Mary of the Lake Sem., 1961, Licentiate in Sacred Theology, 1968; MA in Ednl. administrn., Loyola U., Chgo., 1967; PhD, Gregorian U., Rome. Ordained priest Roman Cath. Ch., 1958. Rector Quigley Sem. South, Chgo., 1976—78; pres., rector St. Mary of the Lake Sem., Mundelein, Ill., 1978—84; bishop Belleville, Ill., 1984—93, Kansas City, 1993—. Mem. Papal Visitation Com. for Sems.; chmn. bishop's com. on priestly formation; mem. com. migration; mem. com. econ. concerns of the Holy See Nat. Conf. Cath. Bishops. Mem.: Midwest Assn. Theol. Schs., Nat. Cath. Edn. Assn. (sem. dept.). Office: Archdiocese of Kansas City Chancery Office 12615 Parallel Kansas City KS 66109*

KELEHER, MICHAEL CASSAT, cabinet maker; b. Asheville, N.C., June 8, 1955; s. Michael Francis and Barbara Nell (Cassat) K.; m. Jann Bridgett Wright, Sept. 9, 1978 (div. Oct. 1993); 1 child, Michael Francis; m. Jennifer Lou Pataky, Nov. 12, 1999. Student, N.C. State U., 1973-74; cert. in cabinet making, A-B Tech. Inst., Asheville, 1975. Owner Creative Woodcrafters, Inc., Asheville, 1976—. Advisor bldg constrn. and cabinetry course A-B Tech. Coll., 1987—. Co-chmn. South Pack Sq. Adv. Com., Asheville, 1985-86; bd. dirs. 1st Presbyn. Ch. Child Care Ctr., 1992-95, chmn., 1995). Mem. N.C. Soc. Mayflower Descs., Ensign-Rhododendron Royal Brigade of Guards, Highlands Sports Car Club (v.p. 1991-92, pres. 1992-93). Republican. Avocations: teaching high speed on track driving, sports car racing, camping, target shooting, autocrossing (1994 state champion d stock class). Office: Creative Woodcrafters Inc 17 Westside Dr Asheville NC 28806-2846

KELEHER, MICHAEL LAWRENCE, lawyer; b. Albuquerque, Sept. 21, 1934; s. William A. Keleher and Loretta Barrett; m. Margaret Anne Wills, June 10, 1961; children: Anne Barrett, Elizabeth Katherine, Margaret Mary, Mary Ann, Loretta Wills, Michael Wills. BA, U. N. Mex., 1956; MA, NYU, 1958; JD, U. Miss., 1962. Bar: N.Mex. 1962. Atty. Keleher & McLeod PA, Albuquerque, 1962—2001, of counsel, 2001—. Mem. N.Mex. Old Lincoln County Meml. Commn., 1969—76; chmn. N.Mex. Diamond Jubilee/U.S. constl. Bicentennial Commn., 1986—89; bd. dirs. Bernalillo County unit Am. Cancer Soc., 1966—74, pres., 1969—70; mem. Albuquerque Environ. Planning Commn., 1973—75, chair land controls bd., 1974—75; mem. Shared Vision, Inc., 1994—98; trustee U. Albuquerque, 1970—78, sec., 1974—78; chair N.Mex. State U. Rio Grande Hist. Collectors, 1978—79; chmn. Archdiocese Santa Fe Devel. Coun., 1990—93; trustee Archdiocese Santa Fe Cath. Found., 1991—2003, pres., 1997—99; spiritial affiliate Order of Friars Minor; pres. Guadalupe Inst.; bd. dirs. Robert O. Anderson Schs. Mgmt. Found., 1995—99. Lt. (j.g.) USNR, 1956—58. Mem.: ABA, N.Mex. Bar Assn., U. N.Mex. Alumni Lettermen's Assn., Phi Theta Phi, Sigma Chi. Democrat. Roman Catholic. Office: Keleher & McLeod PA 201 3rd St NW Albuquerque NM 87102-3370 E-mail: mlk@keleher-law.com.

KELEMEN, CHARLES F. computer science educator; b. Mt. Vernon, N.Y., Jan. 7, 1943; s. Frank K. and Eleanor E. (Scott) K.; m. Sylvia J. Brown, July 26, 1975; children— Rebecca, Colin, Elizabeth. BA, Valparaiso U., 1964; MA, Pa. State U., 1966, PhD, 1969. Asst. then assoc. prof. Ithaca Coll., N.Y., 1969-80; prof. LeMoyne Coll., Syracuse, N.Y., 1980-84, Swarthmore Coll., Pa., 1984—, chmn. divsn. natural scis. and engring., 2000—03, Edward Hicks Magill prof. math. and natural scis., 2002—. Cons. in field; chair computer sci. dept. Swarthmore Coll., 1984-99, 2001—; vis. assoc. prof. Cornell U., Ithaca, N.Y., 1978, summers 1979-81. Co-author: (with others) Fundamentals of Computing II Abstraction Data Structures, and Large Software Systems, 1995, Fundamentals of Computing II C++ Laboratory Manual, 1995. Grantee NSF, 1977-81 Mem. Assn. Computing Machinery, IEEE, Computer Soc., Math. Assn. Am. Office: Swarthmore Coll Dept Computer Sci Swarthmore PA 19081 E-mail: ckeleme1@swarthmore.edu.

KELEMEN, JOHN, neurologist, educator; b. Nyíregyháza, Hungary, Apr. 28, 1948; s. Ignac and Anna (Hartman) K. BA, SUNY, Binghamton, 1970; MD, Georgetown U., 1974. Cert. Am. Bd. Psychiatry and Neurology-Neurology, Am. Bd. Electrodiagnostic Medicine. Med. intern Nassau County Med. Ctr., East Meadow, N.Y., 1974-75, neurology resident, 1975-78, staff neurologist, 1980-85, dir. MDA clinic, 1980-85, chief neuromuscular program, 1981-85; neuromuscular fellow Tufts U.-New Eng. Med. Ctr., Boston, 1978-80; pntr. Island Neurol. P.C., Plainview, N.Y., 1985—; clin. asst. prof. neurology NYU Sch. of Medicine, 1996—. Clin. asst. prof. neurology Cornell U. Med. Coll., N.Y.C., 1986-95; tchg. residents and med. students Stony Brook U., Cornell U., NYU, Manhasset, East Meadow, 1980—; lectr. in field. Contbr. chpts. to books and articles to profl. jours. Rsch. grantee Muscular Dystrophy Assn., Boston, 1979, Nassau Heart Assn., East Meadow, 1984. Fellow Am. Acad. Neurology. Avocations: tennis, sailing, skiing, computers, cinema. Office: Island Neurol PC 824 Old Country Rd Plainview NY 11803-4935

KELEN, JOYCE ARLENE, social worker; b. N.Y.C., Dec. 5, 1949; d. Samuel and Rebecca (Rochman) Green; m. Leslie George Kelen, Jan. 31, 1971; children: David, Jonathan. BA, Lehman Coll., 1970; MSW, Univ. Utah, 1974, DSW, 1980. Recreation dir. N.Y.C. Housing Authority, Bronx, 1970-72; cottage supr. Kennedy Home, Bronx, 1974; sch. social worker Davis County Sch. Dist., Farmington, Utah, 1976-86; clin. asst. prof. U. Utah., Salt Lake City, 1976—; sch. social worker Salt Lake City Sch. Dist., 1986—. Cons. in field, Salt Lake City, 1981—. Editor: To Whom Are We Beautiful As We Go?, 1979; contbr. articles to profl. jours. Utah Coll. of Nursing grantee, 1985. Mem. Nat. Assn. Social Workers (chairperson Gerontology Council, 1983-84, Utah Sch. Social Worker of Yr., 1977), NEA, Utah Edn. Assn., Davis Edn. Assn. Democrat. Jewish. Avocations: tennis, camping, guitar. Home: 128 M St Salt Lake City UT 84103-3854 Office: Rose Park Elem Sch 1105 W 10th North Salt Lake City UT 84116

KELFER, MARVIN GERALD (JERRY KELFER), lawyer; b. Chgo., Mar. 6, 1930; s. Morris and Goldye (Kahn) K.; m. Roxana Michael, Apr. 9, 1960; children— Dana, Traci, Leslie. B.B.A., U. Tex., 1951; J.D. magna cum laude, St. Mary's U., 1960. Bar: Tex. 1960, U.S. Supreme Ct. 1980. With Morris Kelfer & Son Furniture Mfg., San Antonio, 1960-62; assoc. Waitz, Bretz & Collins Attys.-at-law, San Antonio, 1962-65; house counsel Travis Savs. & Loans Assn., San Antonio, 1965-68, pres., 1976—, chmn. bd., 1978— ; sole practice, San Antonio, 1968-73; ptnr. Kelfer & Coatney, P.C., Attys.-at-law, San Antonio, 1973-76; sr. mem. Brock & Kelfer, San Antonio, 1983— . Bd. dirs. San Antonio Econ. Found., 1978-84; pres. Temple Beth El, San Antonio, 1984-86; active Reagan/Bush campaign Republican Party, San Antonio, 1980, 84; alt. del. Rep. Nat. Conv., Detroit, 1980; mem. Rep. State Fin. Com., San Antonio, 1980; mem. Bd. Fgn. Scholarships, Washington, 1983-86; U.S. Holocaust Meml. Council. Served with USAF, 1951-55; Labrador. Recipient award for Advt., Freedoms Found., Valley Forge, Pa., 1984. Mem. State Bar Tex., ABA, San Antonio Bar Assn., Tex. Savs. and Loan League (chmn. atty. com. 1977-78, 83-84, bd. dirs. 1984-87, chmn. nat. rep. com. 1979-80), U.S. League Savs. Instns. (constn. com. 1981), Phi Delta Phi. Jewish. Office: Travis Savs and Loan Assn 9311 San Pedro Ave San Antonio TX 78216-4458

KELL, LYLE NICHOLAS, retired minister, retired real estate broker; b. Sedro Woolley, Wash., May 8, 1924; s. Tate Maxville and Nancy Arzelia (Howard) Kell; m. Dorothy Jane Rasar; children: Nicholas Raymond, Brenda Jane. Student, U. Wash., Seattle U., 1960—62, Seattle Pacific Coll., 1960—62, Golden Gate Bapt. Theol. Sem., Federal Way, Wash., 60's—70's. Lic. ins. agt. Wash.; ordained minister Bapt. Ch., 1965; lic. real estate broker Wash. Log truck driver Lyman Timber Co., Sound View Pulp Co., Hamilton, Wash. 1947—51; switchman Gt. No. R.R., Seattle, 1953—59; broker, owner Spring Homes Realty/Kell Lynnwood Properties/Kell Realty Inc. Seattle/Lynnwood/Arlington, 1962—85; pastor Northgate Bapt. Ch., Seattle 1965—72, First Bapt. Ch. of Martha Lake, Lynnwood, Wash., 1973—80. Author: Personal Biography of World War II, 1997. Mem. exec. bd., co-chmn. Snohomish County Vets. Assistance Fund Bd., Wash., 1995—; nat. chaplain WWII USN Armed Guard Hdqs., Rolesville, NC, 1995—; chaplain U.S. Senate, Washington, 1997; missionary to vets. Puget Sound Bapt. Assn. of Wash. State, 2002; chaplain Post 1561 VFW, Arlington, Wash., 1995. Served with USN, 1943—46. Decorated 5 Small Bronze Stars USN, China Svc. medal with clasp, Russian medal, World War II Combat Ribbon U.S. Govt.; recipient 2 Spl. Recognition awards, Downtown Seattle Kiwanis Club, 1963. Mem. VFW (nat. chaplain 1995—96), DAV, SAR. Baptist. Home: 2821 180th St NE Arlington WA 98223

KELL, MICHAEL JON, physician, researcher; b. Dhahran, Saudi Arabia, Nov. 1, 1949; arrived in U.S., 1951; s. Edgar Michael Kell and Elvira Therea Hannevig; children: Alexander Niels, Andrew Halvdan. BSChemE, U. Calif. Santa Barbara, 1971; MSChemE, MIT, 1972; MD cum laude, Emory U., 1985 PhD with highest honors, 1985. Diplomate Am. Bd. Anti-Aging Medicine, Am

cad. Pain Mgmt. Rschr. Dow Chem., Wayland, Mass., 1973-74; program mgr. ordis-Dow, Concord, Calif., 1976—79; med. dir. Michael Jon Kell, PhD & ssoc., P.C., Atlanta, 1987-2000; rsch. dir. Urine Drug Testing, Inc., Marco land, 1997—; med. dir. Pvt. Clinic Labs., Inc., Atlanta, 1991—2000; editor, uthor Harrison Publs., Suwanee, Ga., 2000—. Exec. dir. Expert Witness & ons. Group. Author: (book) My Boyhood, 1965, Journey to Planet Earth, 967, Electrostatic Fields and Surface Potentials from Individual, 1985, The ong of Solomon. A 3000 Year Postcript, 1985, The Journey of Self, 1987, etermining Disability and Personal Injury Damage, 4th edit., 2000, Medical ractice for Trial Lawyers, 5th edit., 2001; author: (with others) Noise, npedance and Single Channels, 1983, Charged Membrane Proteins, Vault of depti, 1995; contbr. articles to profl. jours. Fellow, NSF, 1982; scholar, uropean Molecular Biology, 1982; Merit scholar, Brown U., 1967. Pres. ndgrad. Rsch. grantee, U. Calif., 1971, Grass Found. fellow, Marine Biol. ab., 1982. Fellow: Am. Chem. Soc., Am. Soc. Clinic Hypnosis (approved ons.), Nat. Acad. Clin. Biochemistry, Am. Bd. Forensic Medicine, Am. Bd. orensic Examiners, Am. Acad. Pain Mgmt. Achievements include invention ; patents for biotechnology; full foreign fillings. Avocations: writing, lecturg, meditating, philosophy, mathematics. Office: The Labyrinth Inst 4399 Voodland Brook Dr Atlanta GA 30339 E-mail: mjkell@alum.mit.edu.

ELL, SCOTT K. lawyer; b. Lake Worth, Fla., Jan. 11, 1928; s. Scott Kell and rances (Aborn) Jefferson; m. Virginia Kell, Sept. 30, 1990. BA, Ill. Wesleyan ., 1953; student, U. Ill., 1953—54; JD, Lincoln Coll. Law, 1953. Bar: Ill. 953, Ohio 1963, Mo. 1967. Pvt. practice, Montgomery City, Mo., 1967—, ermann and Montgomery City, Mo., 1997—. Mem. Assn. Trial Lawyers Am., Mo. Bar Assn., St. Louis Met. Bar Assn. Office Fax: 573-564-1500. E-mail: ellaw@ktis.net.

ELL, VETTE EUGENE, retired lawyer; b. Marengo, Iowa, Oct. 17, 1915; Eugene S. and Florence (Vette) K.; m. Alice Eaton, Sept. 3, 1938; 1 child, Michael V. JD, U. Iowa, 1940. Bar: Iowa 1940, Ill. 1948. Ptnr. Joslyn, Parker Kell, Woodstock, Ill., 1948-67, Kell, Conerty & Poehlmann, Woodstock, 967-84; sr. ptnr. Kell, Nuelle & Loizzo, Woodstock, 1985-97; ret., 1997. Lectr. . Continuing Edn. Inst. Lt. USN, 1943-45, PTO. Mem. Ill. Bar Assn., Soc. rial Lawyers, Am. Coll. Trial Lawyers, Internat. Coll. Trial Lawyers. Episcoalian.

ELLAIGH, KATHLEEN, conservatory artistic director; b. N.Y.C., June 28, 955; d. Joseph Anderson and Alice Rendell (French) Kelly; m. Joel Wayne obertson, Oct. 1, 1988; children: Christopher, Sarah. BFA summa cum laude, . Ill., 1976. Performer United Stage, Mich., 1977-78, Hartman Stage, Conn., 978-79, Guiding Light-CBS TV, N.Y.C., 1979-81; dir. Center Stage Bravo, 981-82; performer Nassau Rep., N.Y., 1983-84, Sail-Away Prodns., World ruises, 1983-86; producer (transferred from City of London Festival) Narnia, donai Arts Found., N.Y.C., 1986; performer All My Children, N.Y.C., 1987, merica's Most Wanted, Fox TV, N.Y.C., 1988; producer, assoc. producer donai Arts Found., N.Y.C., 1988-90; founder, artistic dir. Action Theatre onservatory, Clifton, N.J., 1990—; dir. Waldwick, N.Y.C., 1992, An Evening Ed Dixon One-Acts, N.Y.C., 1994, The Fourth Chair, N.Y.C., 1995, A hristmas Carol, NJ, 2000, 2001, Our Town, NJ, 2002, Narnia, 2003. Prodr. umors, 2000, Social Security, 2000, The Miracle Worker, 2001, Witness for e Prosecution, 2001, The Conservatory Players, NJ, The Good Doctor, 2002, welve Angry Men, 2002, Comedy Tonight: Durang Style, 2003; make-up artist arah Caldwell's bicentennial prodn., Be Glad Then America, Pa., 1976; ake-up artist, instr. Nat. Acad. Dance, 1974—77; playwright-in-residence ittle Theatre/Genesius Guild, Ill., 1971 72, Ill., 1981—90, 1971—72, NY, 981—90; artistic dir. Art for God's Sake, Montclair, NJ, 1992, Montclair, 94; valuator Rising Star Awards, 1998—; liturgist, N.Y.C., Montclair, 1982—90, .Y.C., Montclair, 1999—. Author: (plays) The Separate World, 1971, Chapter , 1981, Alternatives, 1993, Bridges, 1993, The Music's Not So Beautiful nymore, 1994, Hijinks, 1996; lyricist, gook writer for musical Beauty's Rose, 989. Chmn. Episcopal Peace Fellowship, N.Y.C., 1982-86; mem. Diocesan ask Force on World Peace, N.Y., 1982-88. Phi Kappa Phi Acad. scholar, 975-76. Mem. Am. Fedn. TV and Radio Artists, Screen Actors Guild, Actors quity Assn., Actors Fund, Episcopal Actors Guild, Genesius Guild (sec. 987-88), Phi Kappa Phi. E-mail: atcstudios@aol.com.

ELLAM, BECKY, business educator, consultant, b. Austin, Tex., Sept. 7, 938; d. Carruth Brisco and Madge Lee (Swindell) K.; m. June 20, 1958 (div. 979); m. Thomas G. Dougherty, June 21, 1987. BA, Calif. State U., Hayward, 973; postgrad., U. San Diego, 1978-79, U. So. Calif., L.A., 1979; MBA, Nat. ., 1982. Legal sec. Neil Strain, San Mateo, Calif., 1967-69, Hrusoff & raham, Attys., La Mesa, Calif., 1975-77; owner, mgr. DataText, San Diego, 976-80; paralegal Miller, Boyko and Bell, San Diego, 1976-77; legal adminstr. ade & Hayne, Attys., San Diego, 1977-79, Thacher & Hurst, P.C., San Diego, 979-80; mgmt. cons. Profl. Bus. Svcs., San Diego, 1980-84; instr. Kings River ommunity Coll., Reedley, Calif., 1984-97, pres. senate, 1992-94; instr. Madera Calif.) C.C., 1997—, bus. dept. chair, 1998—. State rep. Calif. Acad. Senate, acramento, 1984-87; cons. post secondary edn. Calif. State Dept. of Edn., acramento, 1985-88; computer cons. Bus. Solutions, Fresno, Calif., 1988—. oord. Faculty Assn. of Community Colls., Sacramento, 1985—; bd. dirs. omen's Polit. Inst., L.A., 1982-84, Children Svcs. Network, Fresno, 1990—. amed Outstanding Leader of the Yr., Las Mujeres of Calif., 1982. Mem. Am. ssn. Women of Cmty. and Jr. Colls., Nat. Fedn. Bus. and Profl. Women, Fresno us. and Profl. Women (pres. 1989-90, Fresno County Woman of the Yr. 1990), ffice Automation Soc. Internat. (edit. bd. dirs. 1989—), Delta Kappa Gamma, lpha Psi (pres. 1992-94). Presbyterian. Avocations: travel, antique collector, ardening, quilting. Office: Clovis Community Coll 390 W Fir Clovis CA 3612-8321

ELLAM, NORMA DAWN, medical, surgical nurse; b. Benton Harbor, lich., June 13, 1938; d. Edgar Arnold and Bernice (Cronk) K. AA, San ernardino Valley Coll., 1958; student, Calif. State Coll., Long Beach, 961-1964, 1965, 1966, 1967; BS, San Diego State Coll., 1961; MS, Calif. State ., Fresno, 1972. Nursing instr. Porterville (Calif.) State Hosp., 1968-69; staff urse Northside Psychiat. Hosp., Fresno, 1969-72; nursing instr. Pasadena Calif.) City Coll., 1972-73; night shift lead Fairview Devel. Ctr., Costa Mesa, alif., 1973-96; freelance writer, 1996—. Contbr. articles to newspapers and ags. Vol. Spanish translator for Interstitial Cystitis Assn. Recipient Cert. of ppreciation for vol. work Interstitial Cystitis Assn. Mem. ANA (Calif. chpt.), m. Translators Assn. (assoc.), Soc. Urologic Nurses and Assocs., Inc., Phi appa Phi. E-mail: nor5kellam@aol.com.

ELLAR, MARIE TERESE, special education educator; b. St. Louis, Oct. , 1934; d. Paul and Frances Marie (O'Hallaron) Robyn; m. John Cullen agerty, Jan. 17, 1959 (dec. 1977); children: John Cullen Jr., Anne Rose; m. ohn W. Kellar, Dec. 26, 1974 (dec.); children: Stephen, Joyce, Robert, Barbara, ichael, Richard. BS in Elem. Edn., Maryville Coll., St. Louis, 1956; MAT, ebster U., 1975; postgrad., Fontbonne Coll., Clayton, Mo., 1981. Cert. elem. n., social studies, English, learning disabilities, emotionally disturbed, ehavior disordered. 1st grade tchr. Kratz Sch., St. Louis County, 1956-63; omebound tchr. Sch. Dist. Webster Groves, Mo., 1964-67, Spl. Sch. Dist. St. ouis County, 1965-67; tchr. Webster U., 1974-75, Miriam Sch., Webster roves, 1980—84; adminstr., 1984-89; pvt. practice, 1989—. Learning cons. . Ambrose Sch., 1989—; presenter and spkr. in field. Contbr. articles to profl. urs. Active St. Gerard Majella Ch.; vol. March of Dimes, ARC, Am. Cancer oc. Mem. Coun. for Exceptional Children, Mo. Assn. for Children with earning Disabilities (Tchr. of Yr. 1984), Nat. Cath. Edn. Assn. (Disting. Tchr. ward 2002), Adults With Learning Disabilities, Delta Epsilon Sigma, Pi ambda Theta Roman Catholic. Avocations: drawing, painting, reading.

ELLAWAY, PETER, neurophysiologist, researcher; b. Johannesburg, Reublic of South Africa, Oct. 20, 1920; s. Cecil John Rhodes and Doreen lizabeth (Joubert) K.; m. Josephine Anne Barbieri, Apr. 1957; children: David, dianne, Kevin, Christina, Jaime. BA, Occidental Coll., 1942, MA, 1943; PhD, cGill U., 1947; MD (hon.), U. Gothenberg, Sweden, 1977. Diplomate Am. d. Clin. Neurophysiology, 1953. Lectr. physiology McGill U., Montreal, Que., n., 1946-47, asst. prof. physiology, 1947-48; assoc. prof. Baylor U. Coll. edicine, Houston, 1948-61, prof., 1958-71, prof. neurology, 1978—2003, of. div. neurosci., 1990—2003, dir. lab. clin. electrophysiology, 1948-65; dir. ept. clin. neurophysiology The Meth. Hosp., Houston, 1948-71, mem. attendg staff, 1948—2003, chief, 1971-1999, sr. attending Neurophysiology, 1971—2003; cons., neurophysiologist Hermann Hosp., Houston, 1949-73, dir. dept. electroencephalography, 1955-73; dir. electroencephalography lab. Ben Taub Gen. Hosp., Houston, 1965-79; mem. cons. staff, chief neurophysiology svc. Dept. Medicine Tex. Children's Hosp., Houston, 1972—2002; mem. cons. staff neurology St. Luke's Episc. Hosp., Houston, 1971-73, mem. cons. staff neurophysiology, chief neurophysiology svc., 1973—2003. Dir. Blue Bird Circle Children's Clinic Neurol. Disorders The Meth. Hosp., 1949-60, dir. Blue Bird Circle Rsch. Labs., 1960-79, chmn. Instnl. Rev. Bd. Human Rsch., 1974-90, dir. Epilepsy Rsch. Ctr., 1975-99; chmn. appointment and promotions com. Baylor U. Coll. Medicine, 1968-71, chief sect. neurophysiology Dept. Neurology, 1977-98; cons., electrophysiologist VA Hosp., Houston, 1949—; cons. electroencephalography So. Pacific Hosp. Assn., Houston, 1949-57; cons., neurophysiologist M.D. Anderson Hosp. and Tumor Inst., Houston, 1953-62; mem. coun. adminstrs. Tex. Med. Ctr., Houston, 1954-60; cons. electroencephalography sect. NIH, 1961-62; hon. pres. Internat. Congress Clin. Neurophysiology, 1993. Author numerous books; editor Electroencephalography and Clin. Neurophysiology, 1968-71, cons. editor, 1972-75, hon. cons. editor, 1989; mem. edit. bd. Jour. Clin. Neurophysiology, 1993; contbr. over 180 articles to profl. jours. Recipient Sir William Osler medal Am. Assn. History of Medicine, 1946; grantee NIH, NASA; named Grass lectr. Am. Soc. EEG Technologists, 1989; Berger lectr., 1982, 92. Fellow Am. Acad. Pediat. (hon.), Am. Electroencephalographic Soc. (hon., coun. 1954, 64-66, treas. 1956-58, pres.-elect 1962-63, pres. 1963-64, Jasper award 1990); mem. APA, Am. Epilepsy Soc. (sec.-treas. 1955-58, pres.-elect 1959, pres. 1960, Lennox lectr. 1981, Disting. Clin. Investigator award 1989, Lennox award 1996), Am. Physiol. Soc., Am. Acad. Neurology, Am. Neurol. Assn., Can. Physiol. Soc., Internat. Fedn. Clin. Neurophysiology (hon. pres. internat. congress), Internat. League Against Epilepsy (Am. br.), So. Electroencephalographic Soc. (coun. 1953, v.p. 1954, pres. 1955), Ea. Assn. Electroencephalographic Soc., Ctrl. Encephalographic Soc., Houston Neurol. Soc. (v.p. 1957, pres. 1967, chmn. bd. trustees 1970-73), Soc. Neurosci., Child Neurology Soc., Epilepsy Assn. Houston/Gulf Coast (profl. adv. bd. 1985-92). Avocations: scuba diving, photography. Home: Houston, Tex. Died June 25, 2003.

KELLAWAY, RICHARD ALLEN, minister, art association administrator, coordinator; b. Newton, Massachusettes, July 27, 1934; s. Arthur Kendall and Bertha Allen (Sturtevant) K.; m. Jean Helen (Dickinson), July 27, 1967; children: Ronald, Andrea. BA, Antioch Coll., 1956; MA, So. Ill. Univ., 1957; BTh, Harvard Univ., 1961. Min., then intern min. First Unitarian Ch., New Bedford, Mass., 1960-68, 80—; min. 4th Universal Soc., N.Y.C., 1968-76; assoc. dir. Unitarian Universal Svc. Com., Boston, 1976-80; min. Unitarian Universal Ch., Sarasota, Fla., 1981-86, First Unitarian Ch., New Bedford, Mass., 1986—99; founding pres. New Bedford Art Mus., Mass., 1995—; coord. N. Am. Internat. Assn. for Religious Freedom, 2001—. Pres. Tryworks Collection, New Bedford, Mass., 1994—; v.p. Friends of Haffenreffer Mus., Bristol, R.I., 1995-2000. Author: The Trying Out, 1968; co-curator Mex. Mask 20 th Century, 1995—; contbg. articles to profl. jour. Avocations: art, travel. Home and Office: Tryworks Collection 5 Dover St New Bedford MA 02740-6258 E-mail: ishmael@empire.net.

KELLEGHAN, KEVIN MICHAEL, writer, trainer; b. Chgo., Sept. 23, 1934; s. James Harold and Angela (Morris) K.; m. Beatriz Monges, Aug. 23, 1956 (dec. 2000); children: Michael Kevin, James Patrick. BA in English, St. Ambrose U., 1956. Gen. mgr. Kelmon S.A., Acapulco, Mex., 1957-61; dir. pub. rels. Televisa S.A., Mexico City, Mex., 1961-65; pres. Comm. Corp., Mexico City, Mex., 1965-72; freelance journalist Mexico City, Mex., 1972-79; founding gen. mgr. Computerworld/Mexico, Mexico City, Mex., 1979-81; chief adminstrv. officer Harper & Row Latin Am., 1982; editor, bus. and oil industry Daily Iberian, Iberia, La., 1984-85; pres. CED Sems. Internat., Rockford, Ill., 1984—. Founding editor-in-chief Rockford mag., 1983; cons. in field. Author: Supervisory Skills for Editors, News Directors and Producers, 2001, Business Journalism, 1998, (ghost) Learn How You Can Invest or Retire in Mexico, 1972; contbr. over 3000 articles to profl. jours. Precinct capt. Rep. Party, Chgo., 1957; former chmn. bd. dirs. Crusader Ctrl. Clinic Assn., Rockford. Mem. ASTD (bd. dirs. 1992-99), Authors Guild, Authors League Am., Rockford Area Soc. Human Resource Mgmt., Rockford Writers League (founder). Roman Catholic. Avocations: woodcarving, public speaking, graphic design, computers, reading. Home and Office: 504 Fairview Blvd Rockford IL 61107-4861

KELLEHER, CATHERINE PATRICIA, nursing educator; b. Jersey City, New Jersey, May 3, 1947; d. Vincent John and Kathryn Helen (Petsu) K. BSN cum laude, Georgetown U., 1969; MS, U. Calif., San Francisco, 1970; MPH, Harvard U., 1979; ScD, Johns Hopkins U., 1985. Staff nurse McAuley Neuropsychiat. Inst. St. Mary's Hosp., San Francisco, 1970-71, 74; postgrad. rsch. nurse/faculty HEW commune health edn. grant San Francisco Med. Ctr. Sch. Nursing U. Calif., 1971-74; mem. faculty San Francisco Med. Ctr. divsn. Continuing Edn. in Nursing U. Calif., 1973-74; dir. video, telemedicine project Thomas A. Dooley Found., N.Y.C., 1975-76; audiovisual supr. Brookdale Hosp. Med. Ctr., Bklyn., 1976, clin. coord., 1976-78; rsch. assoc. Bur. Med. Svcs. USPHS Adminstrn., Hyattsville, Md., 1980; rsch. assoc. Office of Rsch. Balt. USPHS Hosp., 1981, Wyman Park Health Sys., Balt., 1981-83; staff nurse Henry Phipps Psychiat. Clinic Johns Hopkins Med. Instns., Balt., 1979, 84, sr. rsch. assoc. Office Med. Practice Evaluation, 1985; rsch. assoc. Oncology Ctr. Johns Hopkins U. Sch. Medicine, Balt., 1985-91; asst. prof. Sch. Nursing Johns Hopkins U., Balt., 1990—95, asst. prof. Oncology Ctr. Sch. Medicine, 1991-95, asst. prof. dept. health policy and mgmt. Sch. Hygiene and Pub. Health, 1993-95; dir. MSN/MPH joint degree program Schs. Nursing and Hygiene and Pub. Health Johns Hopkins U., 1992-95; faculty assoc. dept. health policy and mgmt. Sch. Hygiene and Pub. Health Johns Hopkins U., 1995-97, faculty assoc. Sch. Nursing, 1995-96; sr. rsch. assoc./program evaluator Vis. Nurse Svc. of N.Y., Ctr. for Home Care Policy Rsch., N.Y.C., 1995-97; assoc. prof., dir. rsch. and project evaluation Lienhard Sch. Nursing Pace U., 1997-99, dir. evaluation Henry Street Settlement Primary Health Care Nursing Svcs. Lienhard Sch. Nursing, 1997-99; assoc. prof. Pace U. leinhard Sch. Nursing, Pleasantville, 1999-2000; special project director NY County Health Svcs. Review Org., NYC, 2000—01; project dir., cons. N.Y.C. Home Care Svcs., 2000—01. Adj. instr. Sch. Nursing Georgetown U. Med. Ctr., Washington, 1985-86, Inst. for Health Policy Analysis Sch. Medicine Georgetown U. Med. Ctr., 1985-89; mem. adv. coun. Johns Hopkins U. Sch. Nursing Rsch., 1990-95; mem. Johns Hopkins U. Interdivisional Curriculum Adv. Group, 1992—; mem. generic data elements working group and severity of illness task force Office Clinical Quality Assessment and Rsch. Initiative Johns Hopkins U., 1992-93; cons. State Md. Dept. Health and Mental Hygiene, 1990-95, Divsn. Nursing Indian Health Svc., 1992, Robert Wood Johnson Found., 1989, Health Svcs. Rsch. and Devel. Svc. VA Adminstrn., 1986-88, Ctr. for Home Care Policy and Rsch. Vis. Nurse Svc. of N.Y., 1995, Johns Hopkins U. Sch. Nursing, 1995-96, Ramathibodi Sch. Mahidol U. Dept. Nursing Faculty of Medicine, Bangkok, Thailand, 1996-97, United Hosp. Fund of N.Y., 1996, Nat. League for Nursing, 1997, N.Y. Acad. Medicine, 1997, NIH Epidemiology and Disease Control Study Sect., Subcom., 1996; mem. interdivisional working group for Ctr. for Am. Indian and Alaskan Native Health, Sch. Hygiene and Pub. Health Johns Hopkins U., 1992-95, mem. Child and Adolescent Mental Health Svcs. Ctr., 1994—; adj. prof. NYU Sch. Edn. Divsn. Nursing, 1995-97; faculty assoc. dept. health policy and mgmt. Johns Hopkins U. Sch. Hygiene and Pub. Health, 1995-97, Johns Hopkins U. Sch. Nursing, 1995-96; mem. adv. bd. Pace U. Leinhard Sch. Nursing, 1996-97, adjunct prof. Dvsn. Nursing Sch. Edu., NYU, 1995-97, cons. SEIU Home Care Ind. Benefit Fund, New York, NY, 1999-2000; assoc. prof. U. Md. Nursing Sch., 2001-; affiliate ctr. for rsch. on aging U. Md., 2002-, interdisciplinary gerontology doctoral program, 2002-. Author: (with others) A Clinical Information System for Oncology, 1989, Graduate Education fro Advanced Practice in Community/Public Health Nursing, 2000; contbr. articles to profl. jours., chpts. in books. Harvard U. scholar, 1978-79, Johns Hopkins U. scholar, 1979-85; grantee NIGH, 1990, USPHS, 1981, NY State Health Dept., 1995-97; recipient Nat. Rsch. Svc. award HHS, Dept. Pub. Health Svcs., HRA, BHP, 1980-84. Mem. ANA, APHA (med. care, gerontology, cmty. health worker, pub. health nursing sects., chair Masters in Nursing-Masters in Pub. Health joint degree program task force pub. health nursing sect. 1994-97, liaison to Assn. Cmty. Health Nursing Educators 1994-97, mem. legis. com. 1994-95), Assn. for Health Svcs. Rsch., Md. Pub. Health Assn. (mem. program com. 1993-94, bd. dirs. 1994-95), Assn. Cmty. Health Nursing Educators (mem. edn. com. 1994-96, chair edn. com., 1996-2000, exec. bd., 1996-97), Nat. League for Nursing (mem. coun. cmty. health svcs. 1993-95), Md. Nurses Assn. (dist. 2, mem. cmty. svc. task force 1993-95, bd. dirs. 2002-, legis. com. 2002--), Delta Omega (Alpha chpt. Pub. Health Honor Soc. 1985), Sigma Theta Tau (Tau chpt. 1969, Nu Beta chpt. 1992), others. Home: 218 N Charles St Apt 2210 Baltimore MD 21201 Office: U Maryland Sch of Nursing 655 W Lombard Rm 475C Baltimore MD 21201 E-mail: kelleher@son.umaryland.edu., CKelleher1@aol.com.

KELLEHER, DANIEL FRANCIS, lawyer; b. Wilmington, Del., May 8, 1935; s. Harry James and Marjorie (Lancaster) K.; children: Hillary, Brendan, Peter; m. Jane Mignanelli, Dec. 27, 1991. AB, St. Marys Sem. and U., 1958; LLB, Georgetown U., 1961. Bar: D.C. 1962, Del. 1962. Ptnr. Theisen, Lank & Kelleher, Wilmington, 1962-72; assoc. judge Del. Family Ct., 1972-78; ptnr. Trzuskowski, Kipp & Kelleher PA, Wilmington, 1978—. Atty. Del. State Senate, 1967-68. Bd. dirs. YMCA, 1974-81; active Del. Alcoholism Coun., 1974-81, pres., 1977-80; bd. dirs. Beechwood Sch., 1973-80, pres., 1975-80; trustee, chmn. Del. Childrens Trust Fund, 1985-02. Mem. ABA, Del. State Bar Assn., Am. Judicature Soc., Nat. Coun. Juvenile Ct. Judges, Greenville Country Club (Wilmington, v.p. 1980-82). Roman Catholic. Address: PO Box 429 Wilmington DE 19899-0429 E-mail: dkelleher@tkkp.com.

KELLEHER, HERBERT DAVID, airline executive, lawyer; b. Camden, N.J., Mar. 12, 1931; s. Harry and Ruth (Moore) K.; m. Joan Negley, Sept. 9, 1955; children: Julie, Michael, Ruth, David. BA cum laude, Wesleyan U., 1953; LLB cum laude, NYU, 1956. Bar: N.J. 1957, Tex. 1962. Clk. N.J. Supreme Ct., 1956-59; pres., CEO Southwest Airlines, Dallas; chmn., 2001—. Assoc. Lum, Biunno & Tompkins, Newark, 1959-61; ptnr. Matthews, Nowlin, Macfarlane & Barrett, San Antonio, 1961-69; sr. ptnr. Oppenheimer, Rosenberg, Kelleher & Wheatley, Inc., San Antonio, 1969-81; founder, gen. counsel, pres., chmn., dir. Southwest Airlines Co., Dallas, 1967—, also CEO. Past chmn. adv. bus. coun. Bus. Sch. U. Tex.; past pres. bd. trustees St. Mary's Hall, San Antonio; past pres. Travelers Aid Soc., San Antonio. Named CEO of Yr., The Fin. World, 1982, 90, Best Chief Exec. Regional Airline Industry Wall St. Transcript, 1982, Gold award, 1992, Bronze award, 1993, Great Entrepreneur 1992 Southwest CEO Coun.; named to Tex. Bus. Hall Fame, 1988; recipient Fin. Mgmt. award Air Transport World, 1982, Airline Industry Svc. award, 1988, Best Managed Airline, Airline Exec. award, 1990, Master Entrepreneur award Inc. Mag., 1991, Disting. Bus. Leadership award Coll. Bus. Adv. Coun. Univ. Tex., 1992, Bus. Statesman award Harvard Bus. Sch. Club Dallas, 1992, Pro Bono Publico award Dallas Advt. League, 1992, Stewardship of Tex. Values award Tex. Lyceum, 1992, Aircraft Operations Excellence award Am. Inst. Aeronautics and Astronautics, 1994; Olin scholar, Root Tilden scholar. Fellow Tex. Bar Found. (life); mem. ABA, San Antonio Bar Assn., Dallas Bar Assn., State Bar Tex. Home: 144 Thelma Dr San Antonio TX 78212-2516 Office: SW Airlines Co PO Box 36611 Dallas TX 75235-1611

KELLEHER, JAMES RAYMOND, health care corporation executive; b. N.Y.C., Sept. 14, 1948; s. James Raymond and Constance (Roche) K.; m. Anne Gilmartin, May 6, 1972; children: Brian James, Michael Patrick. BS, Fairfield U., 1970; MBA, St. John's U., N.Y.C., 1975. Plant controller Gen. Foods, Topeka, 1976-79; owner Rutland Corp., Newport, R.I., 1979-81; asst. controller C.R. Bard-Davol, Cranston, R.I., 1981-83; controller cardiopulmonary div. C.R. Bard, Santa Ana, Calif., 1983-84, v.p., controller cardiosurgery div. Billerica, Mass., 1984-88, asst. corp. controller, 1988-94; v.p., gen. mgr. export divsn. C.R. Bard Inc., Murray Hill, N.J., 1994-96, area v.p. Ams., 1996 98, pres. Internat.-Asia and Ams., 1999—. Served with U.S. Army N.G., 1970-76 Roman Catholic. Home: 71 Linden Dr Basking Ridge NJ 07920-1963 Office: CR Bard Inc 730 Central Ave New Providence NJ 07974-1199

KELLEHER, NEIL L. chemist, educator; b. Clinton, Md., Apr. 28, 1970; s. William J. and Ann C. Kelleher; m. Jennifer Kelleher, Aug. 12, 1992; children: Emily, Lauren. BS in Chemistry, BA in German, Pacific Luth. U., 1992; postgrad., U. Konstanz, Germany, 1992—93; MS in Bioanalytical Chemistry, Cornell U., 1995, PhD in Bioanalytical Chemistry, 1997. Fulbright scholar U. Konstanz, Germany, 1992—93; rsch. asst. Cornell U., Ithaca, NY, 1993—97; postdoctoral asst. Harvard Med. Sch., 1997—99; asst. prof. U. Ill., Urbana-Champaign, 1999—. Contbr. articles. Recipient Burroughs Wellcome award in pharm. scis., 2000—03, NIH, 2000—02, Rsch. Corp. Innovation award, 2001, Career award, NSF, 2002—; grantee, NIH, 1993—96; Searle scholar, 2000—03, Cotrell scholar, 2002, Packard fellow, 2002—. Mem.: AAAS, Am. Soc. Mass Spectrometry (Rsch. award 2001), Am. Chem. Soc. Office: Univ Ill Dept Chemistry 53 Roger Adams Lab 47-5 600 S Mathews Ave Urbana IL 61801

KELLEHER, RICHARD CORNELIUS, marketing and communications executive; b. Buffalo, Nov. 21, 1949; s. Cornelius and Lucile Norma (White) K.; m. Sherri Fae Anderson, Mar. 17, 1981 (div. 1991); children: Erin Marie, Shawn Michael. BA, U. New Mex., 1975; MBA, U. Phoenix, 1984. Reporter, photographer Daily Lobo, Albuquerque, 1973-75; mgn. editor News Bulletin, Belen, New Mex., 1975-77; various corp. mktg. titles AT&T Mountain Bell, Denver, 1978-84; exec. editor Dairy Mag., Denver, 1984-86; communications dir. Am. Heart Assn., Phoenix, 1987-90; cons. Kelleher Communications & Mktg., Phoenix, 1990—. Spl. writer Denver Post, 1977-82, Denver Corr. Billboard Mag., 1977-82. Mem. Gov.'s Roundtable on Employee Productivity, Gov. of Ariz., 1990-91; vol. communications Am. Cancer Soc., 1990-92. Recipient Harvey Communications Study award, 1986. Toastmasters.

KELLEHER, ROBERT JOSEPH, judge; b. N.Y.C., Mar. 5, 1913; s. Frank and Mary (Donovan) K.; m. Gracyn W. Wheeler, Aug. 14, 1940; children: R. Jeffrey, Karen Kathleen Kelleher King. AB, Williams Coll., 1935; LL.B., Harvard U., 1938. Bar: N.Y. 1939, Calif. 1942, U.S. Supreme Ct 1954. Atty. War Dept., 1941-42; asst. U.S. atty. So. Dist. Calif., 1948-50; pvt. practice Beverly Hills, 1951-71; U.S. dist. judge, 1971-83; sr. judge U.S. Dist. Ct. 9th Cir., 1983—. Mem. So. Calif. Com. Olympic Games, 1964; capt. U.S. Davis Cup Team, 1962-63; treas. Youth Tennis Found. So. Calif., 1961-64. Served to lt. USNR, 1942-45. Recipient Bicentennial Medal award Williams Coll., 2001; enshrined in Internat. Tennis Hall of Fame, 2000. Mem. So. Calif. Tennis Assn. (v.p. 1958-64, pres. 1983-85), U.S. Lawn Tennis Assn. (pres. 1967-68), Internat. Lawn Tennis Club U.S.A., Gt. Britain, France, Can., Mex., Australia, India, Israel, Japan, All Eng. Lawn Tennis and Croquet (Wimbledon), Harvard Club (N.Y./So. Calif.), Williams Club (N.Y.), L.A. Country Club, Delta Kappa Epsilon. Home: 2311 Roscomare Rd #5 Los Angeles CA 90077 Office: US Dist Ct 255 E Temple St Ste 830 Los Angeles CA 90012-3334

KELLEHER, TIMOTHY JOHN, publishing company executive; b. Massillon, Ohio, Jan. 4, 1940; s. John Joseph and Catherine Isabelle (Quinlan) K.; m. Mary Gray Thornton, Aug. 27, 1966; children— Catherine, Joseph, Sarah BS in Polit. Sci., Xavier U., Cin., 1962; postgrad., Xavier U., 1965, Morehead State U., Ky., 1975-76. Mgr. labor rels. GM, Norwood, Ohio, 1964-73; pers. mgr. Rockwell Internat., Winchester, Ky., 1973-77, dir. labor rels. Troy, Mich., 1977-82; v.p. human resources Detroit Free Press, 1982-89; sr. v.p. labor rels. Detroit Newspaper Agy., 1989—. Dir. Detroit Macomb Hosp. Corp. Bd. dirs. Greater Detroit Alliance of Bus., annually 1983-89, Winchester/Clark Hist. Soc., Ky., 1975, pres., 1976-77; bd. dirs. New Detroit Inc., annually 1983-89 Served to sgt. U.S. Army, 1962-64 Mem. Coop. Edn. Assn. Ky. (bd. dirs. 1975-77, Employer of Yr. award 1976), Indsl. Rels. Rsch. Assn., Xavier U. Alumni Assn. (pres. Detroit chpt. 1991-93), Forest Lake Country Club (bd. dirs. 1991-94, 2000-02, pres. 2002). Republican. Roman Catholic. Avocations: golf, fishing. Home: 4072 Cranbrook Ct Bloomfield Hills MI 48301-1714 Office: Detroit Newspaper Agy 615 W Lafayette Blvd Detroit MI 48226-3124 E-mail: TKelleher@dnps.com.

KELLER, ALEX JAY, plastic and reconstructive surgeon; b. Nov. 12, 1949; BA, NYU, 1971, MD, 1975. Resident NYU, 1975-78, 80-83, Long Island Jewish Hosp., 1978-80; pvt. practice plastic and reconstructive surgery Great Neck, N.Y., 1983—. Office: 900 Northern Blvd Great Neck NY 11021-5302 E-mail: akplastic@worldnet.att.net.

KELLER, ARMOR, artist, arts advocate; b. Montgomery, Ala., June 16, 1937; d. Alton Mason and Margaret Elizabeth (Bell) ARmor; m. Ronald Thomas Keller, Nov. 28, 1958; 1 child, Kimberlin Marie. Student, Huntingdon Coll., 1955-56, U. Guam, 1972-74; BA, U. Ala., 1982. Mem. planning bd. Nat. Book Makers Conf., Tuscaloosa, Ala., 1995; panelist grant rev. Ala. State Coun. on Arts, Montgomery, 1995, 96, 98; judge high sch. art exhibn. 6th Congl. Dist. Arts Caucus, Birmingham, Ala., 1995, 96; cons. Birmingham Mus. Art, 1996.

Shows include Meridian (Miss.) Mus. Art, 1986, Vanderbilt U., Nashville, 1987, Birmingham Mus. Art, 1989, Birmingham So. Coll., 1990, Kennedy-Douglas Ctr. for the Arts, Florence, Ala., 1992, Wiregrass Mus. Art, Dothan, Ala., 1993, Ctr. Cultural Arts, Gadsden, Ala., 1994, Kentuck Mus., Northport, Ala., 1994, Ch. of the Nativity, Huntsville, Ala., 1996, Huntsville Mus. Art, 1999, Heritage Hall Mus., Talladega, Ala., 2000, Masur Mus. Art, Monroe, La., 2001, Mercedes-Benz Internat., Mus. and Visitor Ctr., Tuscaloosa, Ala., 2003; featured in (film, book, calendar) Wild Wheels, 1992, 93, Smithsonian, Japan Esquire, Spiegel; illustrator: Haiku: The Travelers of Eternity, 2001. Artist del. Sister City Commn., Japan, 1994; mem. Sister City Japan Com., Birmingham, 2002—. Fellow Escape to Create Seaside (Fla.) Inst., 1993, 94. Mem. Nat. League Am. Pen Women, Watercolor Soc. Ala. (pres. 1988-89), Birmingham Art Assn. (pres. 1982-83), Montgomery Art Guild (pres. 1976-78), Space One Eleven (pres. 1991-93), Bluff Park Art Assn. (project dir. 1997), Japan Am. Soc. of Ala. (bd. dirs. 2002-2003). Avocations: tai chi, ikebana, travel, music. Home: 204 Vestavia Cir Birmingham AL 35216-1328

KELLER, ARTHUR MICHAEL, computer science researcher; s. David and Luba Keller. BS summa cum laude with honors, Bklyn. Coll., 1977; MS, Stanford U., 1979, PhD, 1985. Instr. computer sci. Stanford (Calif.) U., 1979-81, rsch. asst., 1977-85, acting asst. chmn. dept. computer sci., 1982, rsch. assoc., 1985, 89-91, vis. asst. prof., 1987-89, rsch. scientist, 1991-92, sr. rsch. scientist, 1992-99, Advanced Decision Systems, Mountain View, Calif., 1989-92; chief tech. advisor Persistence Software, San Mateo, Calif., 1991-99; co-founder, COO, CFO Mergent Sys. Inc., Palo Alto, Calif., 1996-99; chief tech. advisor, co-founder Target Mining Corp., Los Altos, Calif., 1998—2003, also bd. dirs.; co-founder, mng. ptnr. Minerva Cons., Palo Alto, Calif., 1999—. Sys. analyst Bklyn. Coll. Computer Ctr., 1974-77; summer rsch. asst. IBM, Thomas J. Watson Rsch. Ctr., Yorktown Heights, N.Y., 1980; acad. assoc. IBM San Jose Rsch. Lab., 1981; asst. prof. U. Tex., Austin, 1985-88, adj. asst. prof., 1988-89; mem. program com. Internat. Conf. on Data Engring., L.A., 1986, 87, 89, Internat. Conf. on Very Large Data Bases, Amsterdam, The Netherlands, 1989; mem. program com. Internat. Workshop on Advanced Transaction Models & Architectures, Goa, India, 1996, Internat. Conf. on Info. & Knowledge Mgmt., Rockville, Md., 1996; chief tech. advisor Online HR Corp., Mountain View, Calif., 1999—; bd. advisors Propel Software Corp., San Jose, 2000-02; interim CEO, co-founder, bd. dirs. Globalline Network, Mountain View, Calif., 2000—; bd. dirs. Broader Minds Inc., Austin; vis. prof. U. Calif., Santa Cruz, 2001-03; advisor Serus Corp., Mountain View, Calif., 2001—. Author: A First Course in Computer Programming Using Pascal, 1982. Bd. dirs. Congregation Kol Emeth, Palo Alto. Grad. fellow NSF, 1977-80. Mem. IEEE (vice chmn. com. database engring. Computer Soc. 1986-87), Assn. Computing Machinery, TeX Users Group (fin. com. 1983-85, internat. coord. 1985-87), Chai Soc. (communications officer 1987-89, v.p. publicity 1989-90). Avocations: singing, travel. Home: 3881 Corina Way Palo Alto CA 94303-4507 Office: Minerva Cons 3881 Corina Way Palo Alto CA 94303-4507

KELLER, BARRY R. physician; b. N.Y.C., Aug. 13, 1939; m. Holly Rosenblatt Keller, June 23, 1963; children: Corey Elise, Jesse M. AB, U. Pa., Phila., 1960; MD, SUNY Downstate Med. Ctr., Bklyn., 1965. Diplomate Am. Bd. Pediatrics. Intern, resident in pediatrics Jewish Hosp. Bklyn., N.Y.C., 1965-67; resident in pediat. Montefiore Hosp. Med. Ctr., Bronx, 1967-68; capt. USAF Med. Corps, 1968-70; chief pediat. Ft. Wolters, Tex., 1969-70; fellow pediat. endocrinology Bronx Mcpl. Hosp. Ctr., 1970-71; instr. in pediat. Albert Einstein Coll. Medicine, Bronx, 1970-71; pediatrician Martin Luther King Health Ctr., Bronx, 1971-72; mem. group pediatric practice Pediatric Assocs., Danbury, Conn., 1972-78; pvt. practice pediat. Danbury, 1978—; attending physician Danbury Hosp., 1972—. Sch. med. adv. Redding Sch. Sys., 1993—. Mem. adv. bd. Wooster Cmty. Art Ctr., Danbury, 1995—. Fellow Am. Acad. Pediatrics; mem. Conn. State Med. Soc., Fairfield Cty. Med. Soc. Avocations: painting, photography, travel. Office: 16 Hospital Ave Danbury CT 06810-5927

KELLER, BEN ROBERT, JR., gynecologist; b. Big Spring, Tex., July 9, 1936; s. Ben Robert and Rowena Ward (Gibson) Keller; m. Anne Ivey Keller; children: Gwenyth Sue Keller Wood, Jennifer Lynn, Amy Jo Keller McGinnis, Ben Robert III, Destry S. L.(dec.). BA, U. Tex., 1959; MD, U. Tex., Dallas, 1961. Diplomate Am. Bd. Obstetrics and Gynecology. Intern Hermann Hosp., Houston, 1961-62, ob-gyn resident, 1962-65; pvt. practice Arlington, Tex., 1967-79, 87—, Glenwood Springs, Colo., 1979-87, Arlington, 1987—. Clin. instr. U. Tex., Dallas, 1975—79; assoc. clin. prof. U. Colo., Denver, 1983—86; mem. active staff Arlington Meml. Hosp., 1989—; courtesy staff S. Arlington Med. Ctr., 1990—. Author: The Hormone Way to Health and Happiness. Chmn. spkrs. bur. Am. Cancer Soc., Arlington, 1968—73; mem. Arlington Drug Abuse Com., 1969—72, Glenwood Springs Coun. on Drug Abuse, Colo., 1984—87; chmn. Texpac com. Tarrant County, Ft. Worth, 1972—75; chmn. bd. elders 1st Christian Ch., Arlington, 1975—76; bd. dirs. Planned Parenthood N. Tex., 1990—98. Capt. M.C. USAF, 1965—67. Mem.: Tarrant County Med. Soc., Tex. Med. Assn. (del. 1972—79, treas. 1974—79), Sunlight Ski Club (chmn. bd. dirs. 1985—86), Rotary Internat. Republican. Mem. Christian Ch. (Disciples Of Christ). Avocations: creative writing, music, golf, tennis, hunting. E-mail: benjr@sbcglobal.net.

KELLER, BILL, editor; Reporter The Portland Oregonian, 1970—79, The Congressional Quarterly Weekly Report, 1980—82, The Dallas Times Herald, 1982—84; corr. N.Y. Times, Washington, 1984—86, corr. Moscow, 1986—91, bureau chief, 1989—91, Johannesburg, 1992—95, reporter, foreign editor, 1995—97, mng. editor, 1997—2001; op-ed columnist & sr. writer N.Y. Times Magazine, 2001—03; exec. editor N.Y. Times, 2003—. Recipient Pulitzer Prize for coverage of the Soviet Union, 1989. Office: NY Times 229 W 43rd St New York NY 10036-3959*

KELLER, DENNIS JAMES, management educator; b. July 6, 1941; s. Ralph and Dorothy (Barckman) K.; m. Constance Bassett Templeton, May 28, 1966; children: Jeffrey Breckenridge, David McDaniel, John Templeton. AB, Princeton U., 1963; MBA, U. Chgo., 1968. Account exec. Motorola Comm., Chgo., 1964-67; v.p. fin. Bell & Howell Comm., Waltham, Mass., 1968-70; v.p. mktg. Bell & Howell Schs., Chgo., 1970-73; pres. Keller Grad. Sch. Mgmt., Chgo., 1973-81, chmn., CEO, 1981—2002, chmn., co-CEO, 2002—. Chmn. bd., CEO DeVry Inc., 1987-2002, chmn., co-CEO, 2002—; cons., evaluator North Central Assn., Chgo., 1979-84; bd. dirs. Templeton Kenly & Co., Broadview, Ill., Nicor Inc. Trustee Glenwood (Ill.) Sch. for Boys, 1980-2002, Chgo. Zool. Soc., Brookfield, Ill., 1979-, Princeton (N.J.) U., 1994-98, 2000-, Lake Forest Acad.-Ferry Hall, Ill., 1980-87, George M. Pullman Found., Chgo., 1987-2002; bd. trustees U. Chgo., 1998-; bd. dirs. Great Books Found., Chgo., 1986-98; chmn. U. Chgo. Grad. Sch. Bus. Coun., 1994-2002, Princeton U. Sch. Engring. and Applied Scis. Leadership Coun., 1992-; commr. North Cen. Assn.-Commn. on Instns. of Higher Edn., 1985-88. Nat. Merit scholar, 1959-63; U. Chgo. Grad. Sch. Bus. fellow, 1967-68. Mem. Hinsdale Golf Club, Econ. Club, Comml. Club Chgo., Chgo. Club, Nantucket Golf Club, Sankaty Head Golf Club. Republican. Mem. United Ch. of Christ. Office: DeVry Inc 1 Tower Ln Ste 1000 Oakbrook Terrace IL 60181

KELLER, EDWARD LOWELL, electrical engineer, educator; b. Rapid City, S.D., Mar. 6, 1939; s. Earl Lowell and E. Blanche (Oldfield) K.; m. Carole Lynne Craig, Sept. 1, 1963; children: Edward Lowell, Craig, Morgan. BS, U.S. Naval Acad., 1961; PhD, Johns Hopkins U., 1971. Mem. faculty U. Calif., Berkeley, 1971—, assoc. prof. elec. engring., 1977-79, prof., 1979-94, prof. emeritus, 1994—; assoc. dir. Smith Kettlewell Eye Rsch. Inst., San Francisco, 1998—; chmn. bioengring. program U. Calif., Berkeley and San Francisco, 1989; chmn. engring. sci. program Coll. of Engring. U. C., Berkeley, 1991-94. Contbr. articles to sci. jours. Served with USN, 1961-65. Sr. Von Humboldt fellow, 1977-78 Fellow IEEE; mem. AAAS, Assn. for Rsch. in Vision and Ophthalmology, Soc. for Neurosci., Internat. Neural Network Soc. Achievements include rsch. on oculomotor system and math. modelling of nervous system. Office: Smith-Kettlewell Eye Rsch Inst 2318 Fillmore St San Francisco CA 94115-1813 E-mail: elk@ski.org.

KELLER, ELIOT AARON, broadcasting executive; b. Davenport, Iowa, June 11, 1947; s. Norman Edward and Millie (Morris) Keller; m. Sandra Kay McGrew, July 3, 1970; 1 child, Nicole. BA, U. Iowa, 1970; MS, San Diego State U., 1976. Corr. Sta. WHO-AM-FM-TV, Des Moines, 1969-70; newsman Sta. WSUI-AM, Iowa City, 1968-70; newsman, corr. Sta. WHBF-AM-FM-TV, Rock Island, Ill., 1969; newsman Sta. WOC-AM-FM-TV, Davenport, 1970; freelance newsman and photographer Iowa City, 1969-77; pres., dir. KZIA, Inc. (formerly KRNA, Inc. and Communicators, Inc.), Cedar Rapids, Iowa, 1971—98; gen. mgr. Sta. KRNA FM, Iowa City, 1974-98, Sta. KQCR FM, Cedar Rapids, 1994-95, Sta. KXMX FM, Cedar Rapids, 1995-98, Sta. KZIA-FM, Cedar Rapids, 1998—. Adj. instr. dept. comm. studies U. Iowa, Iowa City, 1983, Iowa City, 84, mem. prof. adv. bd. Sch. Journalism and Mass Comm., 2002—; mem. adv. bd. dept. comm. arts Wartburg Coll., Waverly, Iowa, 2001—. Named Broadcaster of Yr., Iowa Broadcasters Assn., 2001. Mem.: Iowa City Area C. of C. (chair transp. com.), Iowa Assn. R.R. Passengers (excursion chair), R.R. Passenger Car Alliance, Mid-Continent Rlwy. Hist. Soc. (bd. dirs.). Jewish. Home: 1244 Devon Dr NE Iowa City IA 52240-9628 Office: Sta KZIA FM 1110 26th Ave SW Cedar Rapids IA 52404-3430 E-mail: eliot@kzia.com. *The chance only comes once.*

KELLER, GEORGE CHARLES, higher education consultant, writer; b. N.J., Mar. 14, 1928; s. Charles and Elizabeth K.; m. Gail Faithfull, 1960 (div. 1973); children: Bayard, Elizabeth; m. Jane Eblen, 1975. AB, Columbia U., 1951, MPhil, 1954. Academic dir. Gt. Books Found., Chgo., 1954-56; instr. polit. sci. Columbia U., N.Y.C., 1957-59, asst. dean, 1959-61, editor, 1962-70; asst. to chancellor SUNY, Albany, 1970-78; asst. to pres. U. Md., College Park, 1979-82; sr. v.p. Barton-Gillett Co., Balt., 1983-88; sr. fellow Grad. Sch. Edn. U. Pa., Phila., 1988-94. Author: Academic Strategy, 1983; co-author: Post-Land Grant University, 1981, The Best of Planning, 1997; editor: Planning for Higher Education, 1990-97; contbr. numerous articles, revs. to ednl. publs. With USN, 1946-48. Recipient Sibley award, Coun. for Advancement and Support of Edn., 1963, 64, 65, U.S. Steel Found. award, 1965; named Best U.S. Edn. Writer, Atlantic mag., 1968; James Fisher Award from CASE,2003. Mem. Assn. Study Higher Edn., Soc. Coll. and Univ. Planning (Founders award 1988). Office: 4900 Wetheredsville Rd Baltimore MD 21207-6625

KELLER, GLEN ELVEN, JR., lawyer; b. Longmont, Colo., Dec. 21, 1938; s. Glenn Elven and Elsie Mildred (Hogsett) K.; m. Elizabeth Ann Kauffman, Aug. 14, 1960; children: Patricia Carol, Michael Ashby. BS in Bus., U. Colo., 1960; JD, U. Denver, 1964. Bar: Colo. 1964, U.S. Dist. Ct. Colo. 1964, U.S. Ct. Appeals (10th cir.) 1982. Assoc. Phelps, Hall & Keller and predecessor, Denver, 1964-67, ptnr., 1967-73; asst. atty. gen. State of Colo., Denver, 1973-74; judge U.S. Bankruptcy Ct., Dist. Colo., 1974-82; ptnr. Davis, Graham & Stubbs LLP, Denver, 1982—. Lectr. law U. Denver, 1977-87; adj. prof., 1987-98, Frank E. Rickston Jr. adj. prof. law, 1998—; ct. adminstrn. com. Jud. Conf. US; fin. com. sch. constrn. Colo. Lawyers' Com., 1997-2000, exec. com., 1999-2000, chmn. task force on sch. discipline, 1999-2000; bd. dirs. Western Stock Show Assoc.; adj. instr. law U. Colo., 2003. Mem. Colo. Bd. Health, 1968-74, pres., 1970-74; pres., dir. The Westernaires, Golden, Colo., Jefferson County R-1 Sch. Bd., 1984-89; dir. Jefferson County Sch. Fin. Corp., 1992—. Named Colo. Horse Person of Yr., Colo. Horse Coun., 1999, Best Lawyers in Am., 1995-. Fellow Am. Coll. Bankruptcy; mem ABA, Colo. Bar Assn., Denver Bar Assn., Nat. Conf. Bankruptcy Judges, Law Club. Republican. Office: Davis Graham & Stubbs LLP 1550 17th St Ste 500 Denver CO 80202-1202

KELLER, JACK, agricultural engineering educator, consultant; b. Roanoke, Va., Jan. 5, 1928; s. Eugene and Clara (Lauber) Keller; m. Sara Altick, June 4, 1954; children: Andrew A., Jeffery S., Judith. BSCE, U. Colo., 1953; MS in Irrigation Engring., Colo. State U., 1955; PhD in Agrl. Engring., Utah State U., 1967. Registered profl. engr., Utah, Calif. Work unit engr. USDA Soil Conservation Svc., Victor, Colo., 1953; sales engr. So. Irrigation Co., Memphis, 1955-56; chief irrigation engr. W.R. Ames Co., San Jose, Calif., 1956-60; prof. Utah State U., Logan, 1960-88, dept. chmn., 1979-85, project mgr., 1978-88; pres., founder Keller-Bliesner Engring. Co., Logan, 1962—, CEO, 1989—. Co-dir. U.S. AID Water Mgmt. Synthesis Project, Logan, 1978—88, team leader tech. assistance teams, worldwide, 1980—98; chmn. Conservation Verification Cons. IID/MWD Conservation Agreement, Imperial, Calif., 1992—; sr. policy advisor to Egyptian Ministry Pub. Works and Water Resources U.S. AID WRSR Activity, 1995—98; sr. rsch. assoc. Internat. Water Mgmt. Inst., 1995—2000; sr. adv. agrl. water use efficiency program CALFED, 1999—; sr. irrigation policy advisor, bd. dirs. Internat. Devel. Enterprises, 2000—; team leader Project Advisor Cons. Navajo Indian Irrigation Project, 2001—. Co-author: Trickle Irrigation Design, 1974, Sprinkle and Trickle Irrigation, 1990; contbr. NRC com. Soil and Water Rsch. Priorities for Devel. Countries, Washington, 1988; chmn. Red River Chloride Control Panel, Tulsa, 1988. With USN, 1945—47, PTO, sgt. USAF, 1951—53. Named Engr. of Yr., Utah Joint Engring. Coun., 1988. Fellow: ASCE, Am. Soc. Agrl. Engrs. (award for advancement of surface irrigation 2002); mem.: NAE, The Irrigation Assn. (Man of Yr. 1972), Internat. Commn. Irrigation and Drainage. Mem. Bahai Ch. Achievements include patents in field. Avocation: Avocations: bicycling, hiking, gardening, fishing. Home: 35 River Park Dr Logan UT 84321-4345 Office: Keller-Bliesner Engring 78 E Center St Logan UT 84321-4619

KELLER, JAMES, state supreme court justice; b. Harlan, 1942; m. Elizabeth Keller; 2 children. Student, Ea. Ky. U.; JD, U. Ky. Pvt. practice; master commr. Fayette Cir. Ct., 1969-76, judge, 1976-99; justice Ky. Supreme Ct., 1999—. Mem. Ky. Bar Assn., Fayette County Bar Assn. Office: Supreme Ct Ky 155 E Main St Ste 200 Lexington KY 40507-1332 E-mail: JamesKeller@mail.aoc.state.ky.us.*

KELLER, JAMES ROBERT, business development director; b. Madison, Wis., Apr. 24, 1960; s. Robert Harold Keller and Jane Elizabeth Garvoille. BA in Polit. Sci., German Lit. cum laude, U. Wis., 1983, MA in German Lit., 1985; PhD in German Lit., CUNY, 1999. Promotion asst. Springer Verlag, N.Y.C., 1989—91; instr., adj. asst. prof. CUNY, 1992—98; vendor relations coord. Berlitz Global Net, N.Y.C., 1999—2001; mgr. Network Omni, Thousand Oaks, Calif., 2001; bus. devel. dir. thebigword, Newbury Park, Calif., 2002—. Author: The Role of Political and Sexual Identity in the Works of Klaus Mann, 2001. Fulbright scholar, 1984, German Acad. Exch. Svc. scholar, 1984. Mem.: MLA, L.A. C. of C., Am. Translators Assn. Avocations: reading, tennis, travel, swimming, translating. Home: Apt 459 1890 W Hillcrest Dr Newbury Park CA 91320 Office: thebigword Ste 104 1000 Bus Ctr Dr Newbury Park CA 91320

KELLER, JAMES WARREN, college administrator; b. San Francisco, June 28, 1950; s. Ralph Waldo and Jane (Kephart) K.; m. Joan Hardie McIlhiney, June 5, 1976; children: Christina Elizabeth, Kathryn Michele. AB in Econs., Stanford U., 1972; MBA, Santa Clara U., 1977. Ops. officer Bank of Am., Mt. View, Calif., 1972-73; bus. mgr. Palo Alto (Calif.) Unified Sch. Dist., 1973-89; asst. vice chancellor West Valley-Mission Coll., Saratoga, Calif., 1989-91; vice chancellor Foothill-De Anza Coll., Los Altos Hills, Calif., 1991—2002; exec. vice chancellor San Mateo County C.C. Dist., San Mateo, Calif., 2002—. Mem. Assn. Calif. C.C. Bus. Ofcls. (dir. 1993-99, pres. 1999—). Avocations: golf, woodworking, guitar. Home: 12412 Titus Ave Saratoga CA 95070-4030 Office: Foothill-De Anza Coll 12345 El Monte Rd Los Altos CA 94022-4504 E-mail: kellerj@smccd.net.

KELLER, J(AMES) WESLEY, credit union executive; b. Jonesboro, Ark., Jan. 6, 1958; s. Norman Grady and Norma Lee (Ridgeway) Patrick; m. Patricia Marie Delavan, July 7, 1979. Student, U. Miss., 1976-78; BS in Bus. and Mgmt., Redlands U., 1991, MBA, 1994. Sr. collector Rodkwell Fed. Credit Union, Downey, Calif., 1978-79; acct. Lucky Fed. Credit Union, Buena Park, Calif., 1979-84; pres., CEO Long Beach (Calif.) State Employees Credit Union, 1984—2000, Ocean Crest Credit Union, 2000—. Mem. Credit Union Exec. Soc., Calif. Credit Union League (bd. govs. Long Beach chpt., treas. 1985-86), So. Calif. Credit Union Mgrs. Assn., U. Redlands Whitehead Leadership Soc., Nat. Assn. State Chartered Credit Unions (chmn. 1995-97), Kiwanis. Republican. Baptist. Avocations: photography, skiing, woodworking, biking. Office: Ocean Crest Credit Union 3840 N Long Beach Blvd Long Beach CA 90807-3312

KELLER, JASON, race car driver; b. Greenville, S.C., Apr. 23, 1970; m. Deborah Keller; children: Joe, Jade. Student, Clemson U. Race car driver Busch Series. Named All Pro Series Rookie of the Yr., 1990. Office: c/o PPC Racing 177 Knob Hill Rd Mooresville NC 28117

KELLER, JOHN FRANCIS, retired wine company executive, mayor; b. Mt. Horeb, Wis., Feb. 5, 1925; s. Frank S. and Elizabeth K. (Meier) K.; m. Barbara D. Mabbott, Feb. 18, 1950; children: Thomas, Patricia, Daniel, David, John. BBA in Acctg., U. Wis., 1949; MBA, U. Chgo., 1963; grad., Stanford Exec. Program, 1978. CPA, Wis., Ill. Acct. Bank of Am., 1949-51; mgr. statis. contro and gen. accounting Miller Brewing Co., Milw., 1951—58; contr. Maremor Corp., 1958-68; with Heublein, Inc., 1968-84; v.p. fin. Hamm's Brewing Co 1968-70; v.p. fin., dir. United Vintners, Inc., San Francisco, 1970-80, chmn. bd CEO, dir., 1980-84; group v.p. Heublein Wines Group, 1980-84; pres. IS Wines of Calif., 1983-85; adminstrv. dir. Winegrowers of Calif. (a Calif. sta mktg. order for wineries and grape growers), 1985-87; mgmt. cons. J.F. Kell & Assocs., 1985—2000. Lectr., assoc. prof. Calif. State U./Hayward Grad. Sc Bus. and Econs., 1978-82; adj. prof. Golden Gate U. Grad. Sch. Bus., 1983-8 lectr., instr. Coll. San Mateo, 1990; bd. dirs. Servicor, Inc., Duckhorn Vineyard Fife and Horn Vineyards. Active Boy Scouts Am., 1952—58; dir. Serra H. Bd., 1979—82; bd. dirs. U. Wis. Found., 1986—92, Seton Health Svcs. Found 1988—2002, chmn., 1994—96; bd. dirs. Seton Med. Ctr., 1989—96; sec.-trea St. Bartholomew Cath. Ch., 1992—94; bd. dirs. Cath. Health Care We 1996—2001, fin. and investment com.; pres. bd. dirs. Alemany Scholarshi Found., 1983—95; bd. dirs. Peace and Justice Task Force Commn., 1986—9 dir. St. Vincent de Paul-San Meteo County, 1997—; bd. dirs. Big Bros., Sa Francisco, 1971—75, Hill High St., St. Paul, 1969—70, Lesley Found 1983—85; vol. Internat. Exec. Svc. Corp., 1995—2000; councilman City Hillsborough, Calif., 1982—91, mayor, 1988—90; mem. parish coun. S Lamberts Cath. Ch., 1966—68; pres. parish coun. St. Bartholomew Cath. Ch 1980; mem. Pastoral Planning Commn., San Francisco, 1994—95; trustee S Patrick's Sem., 1994—, investment advisor, 1990—. 2d lt. 82d Airborne divs AUS, 1944—46, ETO, with USAR, 1946—52. Decorated Knight of Magistr Grace in Obedience, Order of Malta, Knight of Grand Cross, Equestrian Ord of the Holy Sepulchre of Jerusalem; recipient Disting. Bus. Alumnus award, U Wis. Sch. Bus., 1990, St. Louise de Marillas award, Daughters of Charity. Me AICPA, Fin. Execs. Inst., Wis. Soc. CPAs, Calif. Soc. CPAs, Nat. Assn. Accts VFW, American Legion, JUnipero Serra Internat. (pres. 1992-94), Commo wealth Club, World Trade Club, Peninsula Golf and Country Club, Phi Kapp Alpha (past treas., bd. dirs.). Home and Office: 785 Tournament Dr Hillsbo ough CA 94010-7423 Fax: 650-572-0987. E-mail: jf.keller@comcast.net.

KELLER, JOHN WARREN, lawyer; b. Niagara Falls, Aug. 6, 1954; s. Josep and Edith Lilian (Kilvington) K.; m. Sandra D. Hubbard, Dec. 18, 198 children: Sean, Christopher. BA, Rider U., 1976; JD, Coll. William and Mar 1979. Bar: Ky. 1980. Staff atty. Appalachian Rsch. & Def. Fund Ky., Inc Barbourville, 1979-82; assoc. F. Preston Farmer Law Offices, London, Ky 1982-88; ptnr. Farmer, Keller & Kelley, London, 1988-91, Taylor, Kelle Dunaway & Toons, London, 1991—, Lexington, Ky., 1991—. Mem. Fla. Ad Com. on Arson Prevention, 1990—; chmn. bd. dirs. Appalachian Rsch. & De Fund Ky., 1994-96; founder, chmn. bd. dirs. Ky. Lawyers for Legal Svcs. to th Poor. Contbg. editor: ABA Annotations to Homeowner's Policy, 3rd edit., 199 ABA Bad Faith Annotations, 2d edit., 2001. Pres. Access to Justice Found 1996—; bd. dirs. Christian Ch. in Ky., 1994—98; elder First Christian Ch London, 1994—97, 2002—, chmn. bd. elders, 2002—. Recipient Access t Justice award Ky. Legal Svcs. Programs, 1995, Outstanding Svc. award K chpt. Nat. Soc. Profl. Ins. Investigators, 2000. Fellow: Ky. Bar Foun (sec.-treas. 2003—, bd. dirs. 2000—); mem.: ABA (vice chair property ins. la com. 1992—97), Nat. Soc. Profl. Ins. Investigators (bd. govs. 2001—, 2d v. 2002—03, 1st v.p. 2003), Laurel County Bar Assn. (pres. 1992—93), Ky. B Assn. (bd. govs. 1996—2002, Donated Legal Svcs. award 2001), The Hono able Order of Ky. Cols. Office: Taylor Keller & Dunaway 1306 W 5th S London KY 40741-1615 also: Hamburg Place Office Park 1795 Alysheba Wa Ste 2101 Lexington KY 40509 E-mail: wkeller@tkdlaw.com.

KELLER, JOSEPH BISHOP, mathematician, educator; b. Paterson, N.J., Ju 31, 1923; s. Isaac and Sally (Bishop) Keller; m. Evelyn Fox, Aug. 29, 1963 (di Nov. 17, 1976); children: Jeffrey M., Sarah N. BA, NYU, 1943, MS, 1946, PhI 1948. Prof. math. Courant Inst. Math. Scis., NYU, 1948—79; chmn. dept. mat Univ. Coll. Arts and Scis. and Grad. Sch. Engring. and Sci., 1967—73; pro math. and mech. engring. Stanford U., 1979—93, prof. emeritus, 1993—. Ho prof. math. scis. Cambridge U., 1990—; rsch. assoc. Woods Hole Ocean graphic Instn., 1965—; Gibbs lectr. Am. Math. Soc., 1977; von Neumann lec Soc. Indsl. and Applied Math., 1983; Rouse Ball lectr. U. Cambridge, En 1993. Contbr. articles to profl. jours. Recipient von Karman prize, Soc. Ind and Applied Math., 1979, Eringen medal, Soc. Engring. Scis., 1981, Timos enko medal, ASME, 1984, U.S. Nat. medal of Sci., 1988, NAS award Applied Math. and Numerical Analysis, 1995, Frederic Esser Nemmers prize math., Northwestern U., Evanston, Ill., 1996, Wolf prize, Israel, 1997. Mem NAS, Soc. Indsl. and Applied Math., Am. Phys. Soc., Am. Math. Soc., Am Acad. Arts and Scis., Royal Soc. (fgn.). Home: 820 Sonoma Ter Stanford C 94305-1072 Office: Stanford U Dept Math Stanford CA 94305-2125

KELLER, JOYCE, television and radio host, counselor, writer; d. Josep Michael and Grace Marie; m. Jack Keller; children: Elaine, Scott. Ce hypnotherapist, counselor. Host, prodr. Trim & Slim WSNL-TV; host, prod creator Joyce Keller Mag. Show Viacom/Joyce Keller Show WGBB; hos prodr. Joyce Keller's Mag. Show Viacom. Guest on shows Ricky Lake, Reg Geraldo, Donahue, Oprah Winfrey, Joan Rivers, Bob Grant, Joan Hambur Sally Jessy Raphael, Soupy Sales, A Current Affair, CNBC's Real Persona Wake Up America, Entertainment Tonight, America's Talking; regular featu on WOR's Joey Reynolds Show, Lifetime TV Online Romance Connectio Relationships, WOR Radio Network, Lifetime TV. Author: Calling All Angel Complete Book of Numerology, Seven Steps to Heaven, How to Communica with Those You've Loved and Lost, Heart Hunting; columnist: Nightlife Mag 1981—90, Update Mag., 1990—; host (radio show) WG-BB 1240-AM Radi The Joyce Keller Show. Named Best TV Fitness Show, World Body Bld Guild. Mem. ASTARA, Nat. Assn. Talk Show Hosts. Home and Office: 1 Jean Rd West Islip NY 11795-2909 E-mail: joycekeller@mindspring.com.

KELLER, JUAN DANE, lawyer; b. Cape Girardeau, Mo., Jan. 30, 1943; Irvin A. and Mercedes (Crippen) K.; m. Sandra Anne Solomon; children: Mar John, Katharine, Robert, Michael, Cassandra. AB in History, U. Mo., 1965, J 1967; LLM, Georgetown U., 1971. Bar: Mo. Assoc. Bryan, Cave, St. Loui 1971-78, ptnr., 1979—. Contbg. author: Missouri Bar Taxation Handboo 1988-95. Capt. JAGC, U.S. Army, 1967-71. Mem. ABA, Mo. Bar (tax co 1971—), Met. St. Louis Bar Assn., Order of Coif. Methodist. Office: Bry Cave 1 Metropolitan Sq Ste 3600 Saint Louis MO 63102-2750 E-ma jkeller@bryancave.com.

KELLER, KENNETH CHRISTEN, advertising executive; b. Feb. 17, 193 s. Theodore G. and Edna L. (Christen) K.; m. Mary Carolyn Folsom, Sept. 1960; children: Kathryn Elizabeth, David Folsom. Student, Ohio State U 1957-59. Part-time staff announcer WMNI, Columbus, Ohio, 1958-59, WTV and WBNS-TV, Columbus, 1959; staff announcer WRFD, Worthington, Ohi 1959-61; staff announcer, news supr., program dir. WOSU, Columbus, 1961-6 on-air talent Sta. WBNS, Columbus, 1962-65; copywriter Joe Hill & Assoc Columbus, 1965-66; creative dir. Myers, Ault & Assocs., Columbus, 1966-7 co-owner, account exec. Angeletti, Wise & Keller, Columbus, 1970-7 co-owner TRIAD, Columbus, 1972-86, owner, 1986—2001, co-owner, 2002— V.p., dir. creative services, TRIAD, Columbus, 1972-85, pres., 1985-200 chmn., 2002—. Bd. dirs. Friends of WOSU, 1981-88, pres., 1985-87; apptd. Franklin County Commrs. to bd. dirs. Cen. Ohio Mktg. Coun., 1986-89; me congregation coun. All Saints Ch., 1995-2001, v.p., 1999-2001; pronounc Scripps-Howard Regional Spelling Bee, 1984—. Recipient Lyricist Best Rad Comml. award Internat. Assn. Fairs and Expns., Ohio State Fair, 1978, 8 Mem. AFTRA (chpt. pres. 1978), Kiwanis Club Columbus (trustee 1999-200 Columbus Soc. Communicating Arts (life, pres. 1977). Home: 270 Park Bl Worthington OH 43085-3660 E-mail: kkeller5@columbus.rr.com.

KELLER, KENNETH HARRISON, engineering educator, science poli analyst; b. N.Y.C., Oct. 19, 1934; s. Benjamin and Pearl (Pastor) K.; m. Doroth Robinson, June 2, 1957 (div.); children: Andrew Robinson, Paul Victor; Bonita F. Sindelir, June 19, 1981; children: Jesse Daniel, Alexandra Ame AB, Columbia U., 1956, BS, 1957; MS in Engring., Johns Hopkins U., 196 PhD, 1964. Asst. prof. dept. chem. engring. U. Minn., Mpls., 1964-68, asso prof., 1968-71, prof., 1971—, prof. Hubert H. Humphrey Inst. Pub. Affai 1996—, Charles M. Denny Jr. prof., assoc. dean Grad. Sch., 1973-74, 99— acting dean Grad. Sch., 1974-75, head dept. chem. engring. and materials sc 1978-80, v.p. acad. affairs, 1980-85, pres., 1985-88; Philip D. Reed sr. fell for sci. and tech. Coun. on Fgn. Rels., 1990-96, sr. v.p., 1993-95. Cons. in fie mem. cardiology adv. com. NIH, 1982-86; mem. sci. and tech. adv. panel to

CIA, 1995-99; mem. commn. on phys. scis., math. and applications NRC, 1996-2000; bd. dirs. LASPAU: Acad. and Profl. Programs for the Ams., 1996—; trustee Sci. Mus. Minn., 1997—; chmn. Med. Technology Leadership Forum, 1998—. Mem. adv. com. program for Soviet emigré scholars, 1974-82; bd. govs. Argonne Nat. Lab., 1982-85; bd. dirs. Walker Art Ctr., 1982-88, Charles Babbage Found., 1991-99. Served from ensign to lt. USNR, 1957-61. NIH Spl. fellow, 1972-73; vis. fellow Woodrow Wilson Sch. of Pub. and Internat. Affairs, Princeton U., 1988 90. Founding fellow Am. Inst. for Med. and Biol. Engring.; fellow AAAS; mem. Am. Soc. Artificial Internal Organs (pres. 1980-81), AIChE (Food and Bioengring. award 1980), Am. Coun. for Emigrés in the Professions (dir. 1972-80), Nat. Acad. Engring., Mpls. C. of C. (bd. dirs. 1985-88), Coun. Fgn. Rels., Phi Beta Kappa, Sigma Xi (nat. lectr. 1978-80). Office: Hubert H Humphrey Inst U Minn 301 19th Ave S Ste 300 Minneapolis MN 55455-0411

KELLER, MARGARET ANNE EIKREM, pediatrician, educator; b. Boston, May 29, 1947; d. Lynwood Olaf and Margaret Rosemarie (McDonough) Eikrem; m. Robert Alan Keller, Oct. 2, 1971; children: Karen Marie, Lisa Marie. BS, MIT, 1968; postgrad., Sch. of Medicine, Washington U., St. Louis, 1968-70; MD, Albert Einstein Coll. Medicine, 1972. Diplomate Am. Bd. Pediat., Am. Bd. Pediat. Infectious Diseases. Intern, resident, chief resident Univ. Hosp., UCSD Med. Ctr., San Diego, 1972-75, fellow, pediat. infectious disease, 1975-76, Harbor-UCLA Med. Ctr., Torrance, Calif., 1976-78; asst. prof. pediat. UCLA Sch. Medicine, Harbor-UCLA Med. Ctr., Torrance, Calif., 1978-85, assoc. prof. pediat., 1985-2001, prof. pediat., 2001—. Sec., v.p. Faculty Soc., Harbor-UCLA, 1983-85, chmn. bioethics com., Harbor-UCLA Med. Ctr., 1986—, dir. program for pediat. HIV/AIDS, 1991—; mem. vaccine subcom., Pediat. AIDS Clin. Trials Groups, NIH, Washington, 1998-2002; mem. AIDS adv. bd. for Congresswoman Juanita Millender-McDonald, Carson, Calif., 1998—; sec., bd. dirs., Harbor-UCLA Rsch. and Edn. Inst., Torrance, 1999-2002 Contbr. numerous articles to profl. jours. Girl Scout leader, L.A. Girl Scout Coun., 1995-2001. Fellow Am. Acad. Pediat., Infectious Disease Soc. Am.; mem. Am. Pediat. Soc., Soc. Pediat. Rsch., L.A. Acad. Medicine. Democrat. Avocations: swimming, dancing, piano. Office: Harbor-UCLA Med Ctr Dept Pediat 1000 W Carson St Torrance CA 90502-2004

KELLER, MARTHA ROCK, artist, educator; b. Youngstown, Ohio, Sept. 25, 1926; d. Louis Henry Rock and Emma Josephine Benson-Rock; m. Robert Brindle Keller, Oct. 18, 1952; children: Ruth Ann, Paul Robert. BA, Ohio Wesleyan U., 1948; MS, Syracuse U., 1951; MFA, U. Mich., 1969. Lab. technician Brookhaven (L.I.) Nat. Lab., 1948-49; lab. technician zoology dept. Syracuse (N.Y.) U., 1949-50; lab. technician UCLA, Long Beach, 1950-51; instr. art Schoolcraft Coll., Livonia, Mich., 1972-84; instr. art dept. Toledo (Ohio) Mus. Sch., U. Toledo, 1984-85; lectr. art dept. Ea. Mich. U., Ypsilanti, 1987-88. Adj. prof. Sch. Art and Design, U. Mich., Ann Arbor, 1976-82, 94—; exch. artist City of Ann Arbor/Tübingen, Germany, 1989; lectr. Ann Arbor Dist. Libr., 1997. Exhibited works at Mich. Theater, 1999, U. Mich., 1999—, Pfizer Global R&D Pharm. Divsn., 2001; represented in permanent collections Chrysler World Hdqs., Auburn Hills, Mich., Omega Healthcare Investors, Inc., Ann Arbor, Mich.; featured artist TV show Painting the Town, 1997; co-author: Public Art in Ann Arbor and Washtenaw County, 1995; contbr. articles to profl. jours. Active Commn. on Art in Pub. Places, Ann Arbor, 1998—2002; bd. dirs. Ann Arbor Art Ctr., 1975, gallery adv. bd., 2002—. United Presbyterian. Home: 1603 E Stadium Blvd Ann Arbor MI 48104-4452 Office: Martha Keller Studio 213 S Main St Ann Arbor MI 48104-2105 E-mail: mrkeller@umich.edu.

KELLER, MARY BETH, consumer research consultant; b. N.Y.C., Dec. 18, 1960; d. Thomas Francis and Cynthia Ann E. BA in Psychology, U. Rochester, 1982. With Mfrs. Hanover Trust Co., N.Y.C., 1982-88, mgmt. trainee, 1982-85, quality circle facilitator human resources area, 1982-83, fin. planner, 1983-84, account analysis supr. cen. bookkeeping, 1984, communication officer, Communications & Mktg. Ops. div., 1984-86, dir. course adminstrn. corp. profl. devel., 1986-87, tng. analyst, 1987-95; creative rsch. assoc. Saatchi & Saatchi Worldwide Advt., N.Y.C., 1988-95; owner, prin. cons., consumer rsch., new product devel. Creative Waves: Innovations in Qualitative Rsch., Pleasantville, N.Y., 1995—. Editor employee publ., 1985-86, employee devel. course catalog, 1986. Mem. U. Rochester Admissions Network, 1982—. Recipient Productivity awards Ops. div. Mfrs. Hanover Trust, 1983, 84, 85. Mem. Nat. Assn. Bank Women (chmn. edn. and tng. 1987-88, trainer 1987-88, scholarship award 1987), Am. Bus. Women's Assn., Rsch. Cons. Assn., U. Rochester Alumni Assn. (editor newsletter 1983-86, founder, pres. N.Y. chpt. 1982-88), Qualitative Rsch. Cons. Assn. Clubs: Rochester Alumni (pres. 1982-86). Roman Catholic. Avocations: family, church, creative writing, crafts. Home and Office: 20 Wilton Rd Pleasantville NY 10570-2022

KELLER, MICHAEL ALAN, librarian, educator, musicologist; b. Sterling, Colo., Apr. 5, 1945; s. Ephraim Richard and Mary Patricia (Warren) K.; m. Constance A. Kyle, Sept. 3, 1967 (div. Aug. 1979); children: Kristen J., Paul B.; m. Carol Lawrence, Oct. 6, 1979; children: Laura W., Martha M. BA, Hamilton Coll., 1967; MA, SUNY, Buffalo, 1970, postgrad., 1970-91; MLS, SUNY, Geneseo, 1972. Asst. libr. for reference and cataloging SUNY Music Libr., Buffalo, 1970-73; acting undergrad. libr. Cornell U., Ithaca, N.Y., 1976, music libr., sr. lectr., 1973-81; head music libr. U. Calif., Berkeley, 1981-86; assoc. univ. libr. for collection devel. Yale U., 1986-93; director Stanford (Calif.) U. Librs., 1993-94, univ. libr., dir. acad. info. resources, 1994—; pub. HighWire Press, Stanford, 1995—, Stanford U. Press, 2000—. Cons. numerous orgns.; mem. Nat. Digital Libr. Fedn., 1993—, chair exec. com., 2002—; mem. Bibliog Commn., Repertoire Internat. de la Presse Mus. de XIXve Siecle, 1981—84; chmn. music program com. Rsch. Librs. Group, 1982—86; reviewer NEH, 1982—88, panelist, 1979—95; chmn. Assoc. Music Librs. Group, Joint Com. Retrospective Conversion in Music, 1989—93; mem. collection mgmt. devel. com. Rsch. Librs. Group, 1986—91, chmn., 1989—91, mem. program adv. com., 1991—93; dir. Berkeley Italian Renaissance Project, 1985—95, Digital Libr. Fedn., 1994—; mem. bd. overseers Stanford U. Press, 1997—; mem. gov. com. Stanford-Japan Ctr. Rsch.; mem. adv. bd. Ebrary, Inc., 1999—; bd. dirs. Alibris Inc., 1999—; dir. Long Now Fedn., 1999—; trustee Hamilton Coll., 2001—; mem. info. tech. adv. group New Libr. of Alexandria, Egypt, 2001—. Author: MSS on Microfilm in Music Libr. at SUNYAB, 1971, (with Duckles) Music Reference and Rsch. Materials: an annotated bibliography, 1988, 94; contbr. articles to profl. jours. Firefighter, rescue squad mem. Cuyuga Heights Vol. Fire Co., N.Y., 1980-81; bd. dirs. Long Now Found., 1998—; bd. trustees, Hamilton Coll., 2001—. Recipient spl. commendation Nat. Music Clubs, 1978, Berkeley Bronze medal U. Calif.-Berkeley, 1983, Deems Taylor award ASCAP, 1988; NDEA Title IV fellow SUNY-Buffalo, 1967-70, Pierson Coll., Yale U., Stanford U., 1994-95, World Econ. Forum, 2000, 01; Cornell Coll. Arts and Scis. rsch. grantee, 1973-81, U. Calif.-Berkeley humanities rsch. grantee, 1983-84, Coun. on Libr. Resources grantee, 1984, 93-99, Libr. Assn. U. Calif. grantee, 1985-86, NEH grantee, 1986; recipient various grants NSF, 1999—, State Libr. Calif., Mellon Found. Mem. ALA, AAUP, Music Libr. Assn. (bd. dirs. 1975-77, fin. com. 1982-83, editl. com. index and bibliography series 1981-85), Internat. Assn. Music Librs., Am. Musicol. Soc. (com. on automated bibliography 1982-83, coun. 1986-88), Conn. Acad. Arts and Scis. (bd. dirs.), Ctr. Rsch. Librs. (adv. com. 1988-90), Conn. Ctr. for Book (bd. dirs.), Book Club of Calif., Bohemian Club, San Francisco. Home: 809 San Francisco Ter Stanford CA 94305-1070 Office: Stanford U Cecil Green Libr Stanford CA 94305-6004 E-mail: michael.keller@stanford.edu.

KELLER, NADYA CLARK, retired biochemistry educator, researcher; b. St. Francis, Kans., July 28, 1933; d. Albert Vernon and Lois Beatrice (Needles) Clark; m. Karl Ernest Keller, Feb. 13, 1954 (div. Oct. 1965); children: Karen Sue Keller Searight, Kevin Dean. AB, Ft. Hays U., 1965; PhD, U. Okla., 1970. Dir. metabolic lab. Cornell U. Med. Ctr./N.Y. Hosp., N.Y.C., 1970-73; prof. biochemistry Northwestern State U., Natchitoches, La., 1973-2000, Richard Lounsbery prof., 1994-2000; ret., 2000. Contbr. articles to profl. jours. Mem. AAAS, Am. Chem. Soc., La. Acad. Scis. (pres-elect 1992-93, pres 1993-95, editor newsletter 1995-97), Sigma Xi (pres. local chpt. 1974). Office: Northwestern State Univ La Scholars Coll Natchitoches LA 71497-0001 E-mail: kkeller@nsula.edu., keller@cp-tel.net.

KELLER, NANCY JOAN BYERS, retired education educator; b. Tiffin, Ohio; children: Thomas, Victoria, Susan. BA in Elem. Edn., State Univ. Coll., Fredonia, N.Y., 1964, MS in Edn., 1966; EdD in Reading and Lang. Arts, SUNY, Buffalo, 1973. Cert. tchr., N.Y. First grade tchr. Brocton (N.Y.) Ctrl. Schs., 1964-65; grad. asst. reading ctr. State Univ. Coll., Fredonia, 1965-66, third grade instr., supr. student tchrs., 1966-68, instr., 1969-72; third grade tchr. Fredonia Ctrl. Schs., 1968-69; grad. asst., summer faculty mem. SUNY, Buffalo, 1972-73; dir. Boorady Meml. Reading Ctr., Dunkirk, N.Y., 1973-75, Model Comprehensive Svcs., Dunkirk, N.Y., 1975-76; prof. edn. Bemidji (Minn.) State U., 1976-87; prof., dir. reading programs SUNY, Oneonta, 1987-97. Cons. local pub. schs., N.Y., Minn., 1969-95. Editor: Phonics in Proper Perspectives, 7th and 8th edits.; contbr. poems to anthologies, Phonics for Teachers; choreographer interpretive ballet for TV documentary. Adminstrv. bd. mem., mem. outreach team First United Meth. Ch., N.Y., Minn. Mem. Internat. Reading Assn, N.Y. State Tchrs. Assn., Catskill Area Reading Coun., United Univ. Profs., Assn. Federated Tchrs. Avocations: reading, gardening, antiques, the arts, writing poetry.

KELLER, NATASHA MATRINA LEONIDOW, nursing administrator; b. Nyack, N.Y., June 12, 1958; d. Paul and Matrina (Butich) L.; children: Alexandra, Mary, John. AAS, Rockland C.C., 1979; BS in Nursing cum laude, SUNY Coll. Technology, Utica, 1982; MS in Nursing magna cum laude, Syracuse U., 1985. RN, N.Y.; cert. nurse adminstr. Staff nurse Englewood Hosp., N.J., 1979-80; chare nurse Mary Imogene Bassett Hosp., Cooperstown, N.Y., 1980-82, nursing svc. coord., 1983-86, asst. dir. sys. devel., 1986-87; assoc. nursing practice coord. Strong Meml. Hosp.-U. Rochester, N.Y., 1987-88; asst. dir. nursing Bayfront Med. Ctr., St. Petersburg, Fla., 1988—, adminstr. on duty, 1998. Translator: Excellence in Russian Language, 1976 (Otrada award). Served as 1st lt. USAFR, 1990-91, Persian Gulf War, Saudi Arabia. Mem. Fla. Orgn. Nurse Execs., Tampa Bay Orgn. Nurse Execs., Sigma Theta Tau. Office: Bayfront Med Ctr 701 6th St S Saint Petersburg FL 33701-4814 Fax: 727-893-6859. E-mail: natasha.keller@bayfront.org.

KELLER, PAUL, advertising agency executive; b. Mainz, Germany, Sept. 23, 1921; came to U.S., 1937, naturalized, 1942; s. Bernhard and Johanna (Metzger) K.; m. Ruth Ettinghouse, Dec. 25, 1948; children: Steven A., Richard M., Susan F. BA, NYU, 1948; MA, Columbia U., 1949. Research analyst N.W. Ayer, N.Y.C., 1950-55; media research dir. Bryan Houston, N.Y.C., 1955-57; v.p., dir. media and rsch., corp. sec., bd. dirs. Reach McClinton, N.Y.C., 1957-69; v.p., assoc. rsch. dir. Ted Bates Advt., N.Y.C., 1969-80, sr. v.p., rsch. dir., 1980-84; prin. Keller Cons. Co., 1985—. Vol. cons. Nat. Exec. Svc. Corps, 1985—. With U.S. Army, 1942-45, PTO. Decorated Bronze Star, Purple Heart. Mem. Phi Beta Kappa, Pi Mu Epsilon.

KELLER, RANDAL JOSEPH, toxicology educator; b. Salem, Ind., Nov. 22, 1957; s. Frank Joseph and Virginia Francis (Barrett) K.; m. Pamela Marie Stroman, Sept. 17, 1994. BA, Eisenhower Coll., Seneca Falls, N.Y., 1979; MS, Utah State U., 1984, PhD, 1988. Cert. indsl. hygienist; cert. safety profl.; diplomate Am. Bd. Toxicology. Postdoctoral fellow Nat. Ctr. Toxicology Rsch., Jefferson, Ark., 1988-90; instr. U. Ark. for Med. Scis., Little Rock, 1990-91, coord. occupl. and environ. health program, 1991-96; assoc. prof. dept. occupl. safety and health Murray (Ky.) State U., 1996—. Peer reviewer Ctr. for Indoor Air Rsch., 1995—. Contbr. articles to profl. jours. Rsch. grantee U.S. EPA, Washington, 1993-96, NIOSH, Morgantown, W.Va., 1993-95. Fellow Am. Acad. Indsl. Hygiene; mem. Am. Indsl. Hygiene Assn. (pres. elect. Ark. sect. 1993-94, pres. 1994-95), Am. Conf. Govt. Indsl. Hygienists, Am. Soc. Safety Engrs., Am. Soc. Toxicology (1st pl. award metals splty. sect. 1986). Republican. Avocations: racquetball, dog training, running, reading, microbrewing. Home: 411 N 10th St Murray KY 42071-1949 Office: Murray State U Dept Occupl Safety & Health PO Box 9 Murray KY 42071-0009 E-mail: randal.keller@murraystate.edu.

KELLER, RIC, congressman, lawyer; b. Orlando, Sept. 5, 1964; m. Cathy; children: Nick, Christy. BA, East Tenn. State U.; JD, Vanderbilt U. Former ptnr. Rumberger, Kirk and Caldwell; mem. U.S. Congress from 8th Fla. dist., 2001—. Mem. Congressional com. House Edn., Judiciary. Chmn. bd. Orlando/Orange County COMPACT program. Republican. Office: 419 Cannon House bldg Washington DC 20515-0908*

KELLER, ROBERT BOUNDS, marketing professional, consultant, inventor; b. Corpus Christi, Tex., June 18, 1957; s. John Leeman (dec.), (stepfather) Berl Dennis Himes and Lell (Edge) K. Himes; m. Karen Lee Himes, Mar. 26, 1983; children: Crystal Lee, Ashley Brooke, Robert Kyle. BBA in Mktg., Tex. A&M U., 1985. Lic. ins. broker, Tex. Sales rep. General Mills, Inc., Corpus Christi, 1985-86, territory mgr., 1986-87, key acct. mgr. San Antonio, 1987-88, regional sales asst. Houston, 1988-89; tech. sales specialist Vanier Graphics Corp., Houston, 1989-90; mktg. and sales mgr. Dr. Pepper Co., Dallas, 1990-95; dir. mktg. Apollo Group, Inc., Phoenix, 1995-96; v.p. mktg. Winterland Prodns., San Francisco, 1997-98; v.p. mktg. and bus. devel. Latent Image Tech., Ltd., Jerusalem, Israel, 1998—. Mem. Am. Mktg. Assn., Promotion Mktg. Assn., Point-Of-Purchase Advt. Inst., Tex. A&M Alumni Assn., Tex. A&M 12th Man Found., Tex. A&M Lettermans Assn. Avocations: golf, internet (web-surfing), travel, water sports, reading. Home: 11803 Moorcreek Dr Houston TX 77070-2417

KELLER, ROBERT L. sociologist, educator; b. Denver, Aug. 17, 1945; s. Leland W. and Helen M. Keller; m. Sally L. Henderson, July 26, 1947; 1 child, Patrick S. BA, U. Colo., 1968; MS, Colo. State U., 1970; PhD, U. Mont., 1976. Instr. sociology S.W. Mo. State U., Springfield, 1970—71; instr. sociology/anthropology U. Wis., Fond du Lac, 1971—72; prof. criminology Colo. State U., Pueblo, 1974—. Cons. in field; expert witness criminal and civil cases. Co-author (co-editor): Prison Crisis, 1992. Mem. Pueblo Cmty. Corrections Bd., 1976—96. Mem.: Union of Concerned Scientists, ACLU, Greenpeace. Green Party. Roman Catholic. Avocation: fly fishing. Home: 238 W Winterhaven Dr Pueblo West CO 81007 Office: Colorado State Univ 2200 Bonforte Blvd Pueblo CO 81001

KELLER, ROBERT M. real estate broker; b. El Paso, Tex., Sept. 7, 1933; s. Nathan Hale and Dorothy (Feld) K.; m. Janis Melvin, June 21, 1958; children: Robert Jr., Russell, Kenneth. BA, Tex. Western Coll., 1955. Real estate broker Russ Lyon Real Estate, Phoenix, Ariz., 1955-58, James Keller Realtors, El Paso, 1958-97, Keller-Koch Realtors, El Paso, 1997—. Bd. dirs. El Paso Indsl. Devel. Coop., 1983, Keystone Preservation Assn., El Paso, 1999, Human Sys. Rsch. Coop., Las Cruces, N.Mex., 1999—; pres. comml. divsn. El Paso Bd. Realtors, 1973. Mem. Soc. Indsl. and Office Realtors (pres. chpt., v.p. dist., regional v.p., mem. bd. dirs., mem. exec. com.), Mensa, Coronado Country Club. Avocations: golf, pilot, archaeology. Home: 813 Wingfoote Rd El Paso TX 79912-3417 Office: Keller-Koch Realtors 4110 Rio Bravo St Ste 205 El Paso TX 79902-1026

KELLER, ROBERT SCOTT, education educator; s. Robert Ray and Marilynn Ann Keller; m. Sara Lynn Volz, Apr. 15, 1972; children: Danielle Catherine, Robert Kenneth. BA, St. Olaf Coll., 1989—93; PhD, U. of N.C.-Chapel Hill, 1993—99. Asst. prof. of math. Loras Coll., Dubuque, Iowa, 1999—; math. mentor Dubuque Cmty. Sch. Dist., Dubuque, Iowa, 2002—, grad. tchg. cons. Ctr. for Tchg. and Learning, U. of NC at Chapel Hill, Chapel Hill, NC, 1997—98; tchg. asst. U. of NC at Chapel Hill, Chapel Hill, NC, 1993—98. Sec., gen. edn. com. Loras Coll., Dubuque, Iowa, 2000—01, chair, math. com., 2000—; textbook reviewer Key Coll. Pub., United States, 2000—02, McGraw-Hill Publishers, United States, 2001—02; faculty cons. Ednl. Testing Svc., 2001—; developer, algebra i in-service tng. Dubuque Cmty. Sch. Dist., 2002—. Author (none): (jour. article) Lecture Notes in Computer Sci.; author: (article) For Your Consideration. Mem.: Humanistic Math. Network, Math. Assn. of Am., Phi Beta Kappa, Delta Epsilon Sigma. Independent. Mem. Methodist Ch. Avocation: music composition. Office: Loras Coll 1450 Alta Vista Dubuque IA 52004

KELLER, SHIRLEY INEZ, accountant; b. Ferguson, Iowa, Sept. 15, 1930; d. Adelbert Leslie and Inez Marie (Abbey) Hilsabeck; m. Earl Wilson Keller, Feb. 2, 1957 (dec. 1987); children: Earl William, Cynthia Marie, Eric Walter, Kenneth Paul. Student, U. Iowa, 1949-51; AS, Cameron U., 1971, BS, 1973; postgrad., Arapahoe Community Coll., 1986. High speed radio operator U.S. Army Signal Corps, N.Y.C., Japan, 1951-57; auditor U.S. Dept. Justice, Washington, 1973-76, U.S. Dept. Energy, Oklahoma City, 1976-83, U.S. Dept. Interior, Albuquerque, 1983-86, acct. Denver, 1986-95, ret., 1995. Seminar instr. U.S. Dept. Interior, Denver, other cities, 1989-94. Author: Oil and Gas Payor Handbook, 1993. Scorekeeper Boy's Baseball, Lawton, Okla., 1964-72; den mother Boy Scouts Am., Lawton, 1965-66. Sgt. U.S. Army, 1951-57. Decorated Merit Unit Commendation, U.N. Commendation, Korean Svc. medal. Mem. Toastmasters Internat. (sec. Buffalo chpt. 1991, sgt.-at-arms Buffalo chpt. 1992, Competent Toastmaster 1993). Democrat. Roman Catholic. Avocations: family activities, gardening, water aerobics, physical fitness, making chocolate truffles. Home: PO Box 280535 Lakewood CO 80228-0535

KELLER, STANLEY, lawyer; b. N.Y.C., Aug. 16, 1938; s. Irving S. and Ceil (Silverstein) K.; m. Sandra Freshman, Dec. 25, 1960; children: Andrew J., Eric L., Matthew A. AB, Columbia U., 1959; LLB, Harvard U., 1962. Bar: Mass. 1962. Assoc. Palmer & Dodge LLP, Boston, 1962-68, ptnr., 1969—. Lectr. Boston U. Law Sch., 1969-79; treas., trustee Mass. Continuing Legal Edn., Inc., Boston, 1985-91; panelist continuing legal edn. programs for profl. orgns. Chmn. legal sect. United Way of Boston, 1982. Fellow Am. Bar Found., Mass. Bar Found.; mem. ABA (chair fed. regulation of securities com.), Mass. Bar Assn. (chmn. bus. law sect. 1983-85), Boston Bar Assn. (chmn. corp. law com. 1988-89, chmn. bus. law sect. 1989-91, co-chair legal opinions com. 1992-95, co-chair com. to revise Mass. Bus. Corp. Law 1992—), Tri Bar Opinion Com. Jewish. Office: Palmer & Dodge LLP 111 Huntington Ave Boston MA 02199-7613 E-mail: skeller@palmerdodge.com.

KELLER, THEODORE G., JR., investment property owner and manager; b. Toledo, Ohio, July 22, 1933; s. Theodore George and Edna Louise (Christen) K.; m. Carolyn Mary Lord, Aug. 25, 1956 (dec. May 1985); children: Bradford W., Matthew C., Theodore G. III, Lathrop L.; m. Gayla Claire Rampel, Sept. 20, 1986. BS, Miami U., Oxford, Ohio, 1955; MBA, U. Pa., 1959. Advt. mgr. Procter & Gamble, Cin., 1959-73; v.p. Eastern Airlines, Miami, Fla., 1973-76, Sara Lee Corp., Chgo., 1976-78; corp. officer, exec. v.p. Pet Inc., St. Louis, 1978-92; v.p., gen. mgr. Right Assocs., St. Louis, 1992-96; owner, mgr. 22 Cottage St., LLC, South Orange, NJ, 1986—. Pres., bd. govs. Naples Bath and Tennis Club, 2002-. Lt. USNR, 1951-59. Republican. Avocations: tennis, sailing. Home: 3162 SE Torch Lake Dr Bellaire MI 49615-9331 also: 1031 Oriole Cir Naples FL 34105-7425 E-mail: gaylaandted@earthlink.net.

KELLER, THOMAS FRANKLIN, business administration educator; b. Greenwood, S.C., Sept. 22, 1931; s. Cleaveland Alonzo and Helen (Seago) K.; m. Margaret Neel Query, June 15, 1956; children: Thomas Crafton (dec.), Neel McKay, John Caldwell. AB, Duke U., 1953; MBA, U. Mich., 1957, PhD, 1960; HHD (hon.), Clemson U., 1987. CPA, N.C. Mem. faculty Fuqua Sch. Bus. Duke U., Durham, N.C., 1959—, assoc. prof., 1962-67, prof., 1967-74, R.J. Reynolds prof., 1974—, chmn. dept. mgmt. scis., 1974-96, vice provost, 1971-72, dean Fuqua Sch. Bus., 1974-96; dean Fuqua Sch. Bus. Europe, Frankfurt, 1999-2001. Mem. editorial bd. Duke U. Press, 1970-87; vis. assoc. prof. Carnegie Mellon U., 1966-67, U. Wash., Seattle, 1963-64; cons. to govt. and industry; Fulbright-Hays lectr., Australia, 1975; bd. dirs. Hatteras Income Securities Inc., Charlotte, N.C., Nations Funds Inc., Charlotte, Wendy's Internat., Dublin, Ohio, DIMON Inc., Danville, Va., Biogen, Cambridge, Mass. Author: Accounting for Corporate Income Taxes, 1961, Intermediate Accounting, 1963, 68, 74, Advanced Accounting, 1966, Financial Accounting Theory vol. 1, 1964, 73, 84, vol. 2, 1969, Earnings or Cash Flows: An Experiment on Functional Fixation and the Valuation of the Firm, 1979; editor: monographs Financial Information Needs of Security Analysts, 1977, The Impact of Accounting Research on Practice and Disclosure, 1978; contbr. articles to profl. jours. Elder Presbyn. Ch.; trustee Stillman Coll., Tuscaloosa, Ala.; dir. N.C. Zool. Soc., Rsch. Triangle Regional Partnership, Research Triangle Park, N.C. With AUS, 1953-55. Recipient Outstanding Educator award, N.C. Assn. CPA's, 1997, Univ. medal, Duke Univ., 2001; fellow Haskins and Sells Found., U. Mich., 1959, Ford Found., Duke U., 1960, 1961. Mem. AICPA, Am. Acctg. Assn. (v.p. 1967-68, editor jour. 1972-75), N.C. Assn. CPAs, Fin. Execs. Inst., University Club, Phi Beta Kappa, Phi Kappa Sigma, Beta Gamma Sigma, Alpha Kappa Psi. Avocations: hiking, fishing, reading, sailing. Office: Duke U Fuqua Sch Bus Durham NC 27708-0120 E-mail: tfk1@mail.duke.edu.

KELLER, THOMAS MICHAEL, mathematician, educator; b. Wiesbaden, Hessen, Germany, Dec. 2, 1967; arrived in U.S., 1998; s. Willi Heinrich and Ingeborg Rosa Keller; m. Christine Ingrid Urmetzer, Jan. 6, 1998. BSc, Johannes Gutenberg U., Mainz, Germany, 1990, MSc, 1993, PhD summa cum laude, 1995. Rsch. asst. Friedrich-Schiller-U., Jena, Germany, 1995—96; vis. asst. prof. Ohio U., Athens, 1996—96, rsch. fellow, 1996—96; hon. fellow U. Wis., Madison, 1997—97; rsch. fellow U. Leicester, England, 1997—98; asst. prof. Tex. State Univ. - San Marcos, San Marcos, 1998—2001, assoc. prof., 2001—. Referee for various math. jours. Contbr. articles to profl. jours. Pvt. U.S. Army, 1987—88. Scholar Grad. fellow, Rheinland-Pfalz, 1993—95; Rsch. fellow, German Rsch. Coun., 1996—98. Mem.: Math. Assn. Am., Am. Math. Soc. (reviewer for math. reviews 2000—). Roman Catholic. Achievements include research in reducing the well-known Taketa problem in the character theory of finite solvable groups to p-groups in the above-mentioned papers. Avocations: travel, reading. Office: Tex State Univ - San Marcos 601 University Dr San Marcos TX 78666 Office Fax: 512-245-3425. E-mail: keller@swt.edu.

KELLER, TIFFANY LEE, business educator; b. Britt, Iowa, Nov. 9, 1965; d. Lloyd Orville and Dorothy Lee Stimson; 1 child, Pamela. BA Psychology, U. Iowa, 1988; PhD Orgnl. Behavior, SUNY, 1994. Asst. prof. mgmt. Arkansas State U., Jonesboro, Ark., 1994—96; vis. asst. prof. mgmt. Purdue U., West Layfette, Ind., 1996—97; asst. prof. leadership studies U. Richmond, Va., 1997—2001; dir. Brain Leadership Program Baldwin-Wallace Coll., Berea, Ohio, 2001—. Contbr. articles to profl. jours., chapters to books. Grantee scholarship grant, Jepson Sch. Leadership Studies, 1997—98. Mem.: Acad. Mgmt., Soc. Indl. and Orgnl. Psychology, Am. Psychol. Assn. Office: Baldwin-Wallace Coll 275 Eastland Rd Berea OH 44017-2088 Office Fax: 440-826-5932. Business E-Mail: tkeller@bw.edu.

KELLER, WILLIAM FRANCIS, publishing consultant; b. Meyersdale, Pa., May 22, 1922; s. Lloyd Francis and Dorothy Marie (Shultz) K.; m. Frances Jane Core, Mar. 31, 1944. AA, Potomac State Coll. of W.Va. U., 1941; BS, U. Md., 1943, MS, 1945. Ednl. rep. Blakiston Co., 1945-51, assoc. editor, 1951-54; editor coll. div. McGraw Hill Book Co., N.Y.C., 1954-56; editor-in-chief Blakiston divsn. McGraw Hill Book Co., 1956-65, gen. mgr. div., 1965-68; pres. Year Book Med. Publs., Chgo., 1968-81, chmn. bd., 1968-82; pub. cons. Crystal Lake, Ill., 1982-95; adminstrv. sec. Am. Med. Pubs. Assn., 1985-91. Served with U.S. Army, 1945-46. Office: 7916 W Hillside Rd Crystal Lake IL 60012-2939 E-mail: w.f.keller@world.net.att.com.

KELLERMAN, EDWIN, lawyer, physician; b. Phila., Feb. 9, 1932; AB, U. Pa., 1954; MD, Northwestern U., 1959; JD, Temple U., 1984. Bar: Pa. 1984, U.S. Dist. Ct. (ea. dist.) Pa. 1984, U.S. Ct. Appeals (3d cir.) 1985, U.S. Ct. Claims 1995; diplomate Am. Bd. Internal Medicine, Am. Bd. Nephrology. Intern Jersey City Med. Ctr., 1959-60; resident Mt. Sinai Hosp., 1962-63, Jackson Meml. Hosp., 1963-64; NIH fellow Hahnemann Med. Coll., 1964-65; pvt. practice medicine NJ, 1965-72, 1995—, 1972-86; sole practice health care law, 1984—. Cons. in medicine, Social Security Adminstrn., 1979-84. Contbr. to Legal Medicine, 1988, 90, 95. Capt. M.C., U.S. Army, 1960-62. Fellow Am. Coll. Legal Medicine.

KELLERMAN, JONATHAN SETH, writer, pediatric psychologist; b. N.Y.C., Aug. 9, 1949; s. David Kellerman and Sylvia Fiacre; m. Faye Marilyn Marder, July 23, 1972; children: Jesse, Rachel, Ilana, Aliza. BA in Psychology, UCLA, 1972; MA in Psychology, U. So. Calif., 1973, PhD in Clin. Psychology, 1974. Lic. psychologist, Calif. Intern in psychology Children's Hosp. of Los Angeles, 1973-74, postdoctoral fellow, 1974-75, U. Southern Calif. Sch. Medicine, Los Angeles, 1974-75, staff psychologist, 1975-78, asst. clin. prof. pediatrics, 1978—, clin. assoc. prof. pediatrics, 1979-98, clin. prof. pediats., psychology, 1998—. Founding dir. Psychosocial Program Children's Hosp., Los Angeles, 1977-81. Author: Psychological Aspects of Childhood Cancer, 1980, Helping the Fearful Child, 1981, When the Bough Breaks, 1985, Blood Test, 1986, Over the Edge, 1987, The Butcher's Theater, 1988, Silent Partner, 1989, Time Bomb, 1990, Private Eyes, 1992, Devil's Waltz, 1993, Bad Love, 1994, Daddy, Daddy Can You Touch the Sky?, 1994, Self-Defense, 1995, Jonathan Kellerman's ABC of Weird Creatures, 1995, The Web, 1996, The Clinic, 1997, Survival of the Fittest, 1997, Billy Straight, 1998, Savage Spawn, 1999, Monster, 1999, Doctor Death, 2000, Flesh And Blood, 2001, The Murder Book, 2002. Recipient Samuel Goldwyn Creative Writing award UCLA, 1972,

Anthony Boucher award Bouchercon, 1986, Disting. Alumnus award dept. psychology UCLA, 1997. Mem. Am. Psychol. Assn. (Media award 1994, Presdl. award 1998), Mystery Writers of Am. (Edgar Allan Poe award 1985, nominated Shamus award 2001). Jewish. Avocations: painting, guitar playing and collecting, book collecting, art collecting.

KELLERMAN, RICK DEAN, physician, academic administrator; b. Hays, Kans., Jan. 8, 1954; s. James Vernon and Phyllis Eileen Kellerman; m. Janet Louise Grass, Apr. 11, 1980; children: Katherine, James, John. BA, Fort Hays State U., 1975; MD, U. Kans., 1978. Diplomate Am. Bd. Family Practice. Intern Wesley Med. Ctr., Wichita, Kans., 1978, resident in family practice, 1979-81; fellow McLennan County (Tex.) Med. Edn. and Rsch. Found., 1981-82; instr. Med. Sch. U. Kans., Wichita, 1981-82, chair dept. family practice, 1997—; pvt. practice Plainville, 1982-88; dir. Smoky Hill Family Practice Residency, Wichita, 1988-96; primary care fellow Pub. Health Svc., 1997. Chair Primary Care Residency Dirs. Coun., 1995—96. Contbr. . Mem.: AMA, Nat. Rural Health Assn., Kans. Hosp. Assn. (bd. dirs. 2000—), Kans. Med. Soc., Soc. Tchrs. Family Medicine, Kans. Acad. Family Physicians (pres. 1982), Am. Acad. Family Physicians (bd. dirs. 2003—). Home: 521 N Armour St Wichita KS 67206-1513 Office: U Kans Sch Medicine Wichita 1010 N Kansas St Wichita KS 67214-3124

KELLERMAN, SHIRLEY ROSE, artist; b. Comyn, Tex., Jan. 9, 1928; d. William Ellis and Rose Bessie (Touchtone) Pulley; m. Robert Eugene Kellerman, Sept. 3, 1949; children: Scott, Shellie. B in Journalism, U. Tex., 1949; postgrad., Tex. Christian U., Ft. Worth, 1965—. Represented by Evelyn Siegel Gallery, Ft. Worth, 1994—, McMahon Fine Arts, Ruidoso, N.Mex., 2000—. One person shows include Dallas Gallery, Ruidoso, N.Mex., 1991, Trinity Arts Guild, Bedford, Tex., 1993, Gallery 10, Ft. Worth, 1994, Fenton's Art Gallery, Ruidoso, 1994, 97, Evelyn Siegel Gallery, Ft. Worth, 1996, 2001, McMahon Fine Arts, Ruidoso, N.Mex., 2000—; exhibited in group shows at Mus. of the Horse, Ruidoso, 1994-2002, Evelyn Siegel Gallery, 1994-97. Mem. Nat. Mus. Women in Arts (charter). Avocations: piano, poetry, golf, mountain home. Studio: 4833 Lafayette Ave Fort Worth TX 76107-3725 also: 103 Spring Canyon Rd Ruidoso NM 88345-7221

KELLERMANN, ARTHUR L., medical educator; MD, Emory U., 1980; MPH, U. WAsh., 1985. Chief, prof. emergency medicine, chmn., dir. Emory U., 2000—, dir. Ctr. Injury Control, 1996—. Contbr. articles to profl. jours. Mem.: Inst. of Medicine. Office: Ctr Injury Control Rollins Sch Pub Health 1518 Clifton Rd NE Atlanta GA 30322-4201

KELLERMANN, KENNETH IRWIN, astrophysicist, scientist; b. N.Y.C., July 1, 1937; s. Alexander Samuel and Rae (Goodstein) K.; m. Michele Kellermann; children: Sarah, David (dec.). SB, MIT, 1959; PhD, Calif. Inst. Tech., 1963. Rsch. scientist CSIRO, Sydney, Australia, 1963-65; asst. scientist Nat. Radio Astronomy Obs., Green Bank, W.Va., 1965-67, assoc. scientist, 1967-69, scientist, 1978; asst. dir. Max Plank Inst. for Radio Astronomy, Bonn, Fed. Republic of Germany, 1978, dir., 1978-79, outside sci. mem., 1980—; sr. scientist Nat. Radio Astronomy Obs., Charlottesville, W.Va., 1980—, chief scientist, 1996—. Adj. prof. U. Ariz, Tucson, 1970-72; rsch. prof. U. Va., Charlottesville, 1985—. NSF fellow, Washington, 1965-66; recipient Rumford prize Am. Acad. Arts Scis., 1970, Warner prize Am. Astron. Soc., 1971, Gould prize NAS, 1973. Mem. NAS (chair astronomy sect. 1995-98, councilor 1999-2002), Am. Philos. Soc., Internat. Astron. Union (pres. com. 40 1982-85, pres. U.S. nat. com. 1990-92), Am. Astron. Soc., Internat. Radio Sci. Union, Am. Acad. Arts and Scis., Australian Astron. Soc., Russian Acad. Scis. Avocation: amateur radio. Office: Nat Radio Astron Obs Edgemont Rd Charlottesville VA 22903 E-mail: kkellerm@nrao.edu.

KELLETT, JANET, telecommunications industry executive, educator; b. Chicago, Ill., Aug. 19, 1946; d. Ralph Curtis and Shirley (Mills) Baker; m. Gordon Neil Kellett, June 21, 1969; children: Karen Kellett Hufford, Edward Baker. BS, The Coll. of William & Mary, Williamsburg, Va., 1968; PhD bus., Va. Commonwealth U, Richmond, Va., 2002. Auditor/mathematician US Gen. Acctg. office, Norforlk, Va., 1968, Richmond, Va., 1969—71; mgr. Verizon, Richmond, Va., 1971—97; instr. Va. Commonwealth U, Richmond, Va., 2000—01; vis. asst. prof. of bus. The Coll. of William & Mary, Williamsburg, Va., 2003. Recipient Dean's Scholar, Va. Commonwealth U, 2002. Mem.: Ctr. Advancement Rsch. Methods and Analysis (assoc.), Orgnl. Behavior Tchg. Soc. (assoc.), S. Mgmt. Assoc. (assoc.), Acad. of Mgmt. (assoc.), Beta Gamma Sigma (assoc.), Phi Kappa Phi (assoc.). Home: 7628 Piney Branch Rd Richmond VA 23225

KELLEY, A. BENJAMIN, author, consultant; b. N.Y.C., May 15, 1936; s. Hubert Williams and Anna Alberta (Davis) K.; children: Sumako Chongyol, Hubert Chongsu. Student, Def. Lang. Inst., 1955, Naganuma Inst., Tokyo, 1957-58, Sophia U., 1957, Harvard U. Bus. Sch., 1972. News editor Shipping and Trade News, Japan, 1957-60; Washington transp. corr. N.Y. Jour. Commerce, 1960-63; policy adviser ICC, 1963-65; mgr. transp. and communications dept. U.S. C. of C., 1966-67; dir. pub. affairs Fed. Hwy. Adminstrn., 1967-69; sr. v.p. Ins. Inst. Hwy. Safety, Washington, 1969-85; pres. A.B. Kelley Corp., Crofton, Md., 1985-96, Inst. for Injury Reduction, Crofton, 1988-95; pvt. auto safety cons., 1996—. Vis. faculty mem. Tufts U. Med. Sch., 2001-; exec. dir. Pub. Health Advocacy Inst., 2001—; guest lectr. Johns Hopkins Sch. Pub. Hygiene and Pub. Health, 1974-95, U. So. Calif., 1974, U. Fla., 1972, UCLA, 1970, U. Calif., Davis, 1977; bd. dirs. Center Auto Safety, 1975—, Com. on Non-Theatrical Events, 1984—1992 Author: The Pavers and The Paved, 1971; author-narrator: Boobytrap!, 1971, Cars That Crash and Burn, 1973, Crashes That Need Not Kill, 1976, Faces in Crashes, 1984; also articles. Served with AUS, 1954-57. Recipient Golden Eagle award Council Internat. Nontheatrical Events, 1971, 73, 76, 1st prize Zagreb (Yugoslavia) Film Festival, 1973, 75, Bronze Venus Medallion Virgin Islands Internat. Film Festival, 1976 Mem. Internat. Transp. Research Forum (past dir.), Nat. Safety Coun. (past dirs.), Am. Assn. Automotive Medicine, Soc. Automotive Engrs., Ctr. for Auto Safety (bd. dirs.).

KELLEY, ALLEN CHARLES, economist, educator; b. Everett, Wash., Sept. 5, 1937; s. Charles Edward and Velma L. (Allen) K.; m. Patty Ann Cochran, June 20, 1959; children: Brian Allen, Mark Andrew, Michael Charles. Student, Linfield Coll., 1955-57; AB, Stanford U., 1959, PhD, 1964. Vis. research fellow Australian Nat. U., 1962-63; cons. Rand Corp., 1962-67; acting asst. prof. Stanford U., 1963-64; faculty U. Wis., Madison, 1964-72, prof., 1970-72; prof. econs. Duke U., Durham, N.C., 1972-81, James B. Duke prof., 1981—, chmn. dept., 1973-80; asso. dir. Center for Demographic Studies, 1973—. Vis. prof. Monash U., Melbourne, Australia, 1970-71; Esmee Fairbairn research prof. Herriot Watt U., Edinburgh, Scotland, 1978; research scholar Internat. Inst. Applied Systems Analysis, Laxenburg, Austria, 1979 Author: (with J.G. Williamson and R.J. Cheetham) Dualistic Economic Development, 1972, (with B.A. Weisbrod et al.) Disease and Economic Development, (with J.G. Williamson) Lessons from Japanese Development - An Analytical Economic History, 1974, The Professor's Guide to TIPS, 1975, (with R.M. Schmidt) The User's Guide to TIPS, 1975, TIPS Program Manual, 1976, (with J.G. Williamson) Modeling Urbanization and Economic Growth, 1980, (with A. Khalifa and M.E. El-Khorazaty) Population and Development in Rural Egypt, 1982; mem. editorial bd. Jour. Econ. Edn, 1973— ; Contbr. articles, revs. to profl. jours. Scholar, fellow Weyerhaeuser Co., 1955-59; Scholar, fellow Ford Found., 1961-62; Scholar, fellow Earhart Found., 1959-61; Scholar, fellow Social Sci. Research Council, 1962-63; Richard I. Downing fellow econs. U. Melbourne, 1987-88; grantee Carnegie Found., 1964-65; grantee Exxon Edn. Found., 1965-67, 68-70, 71-74; grantee Ford Found., 1973-79; grantee Nat. Inst. Edn., 1974-75; grantee NSF, 1966-68; grantee Rockefeller Found., 1967-69; grantee Sloan Found., 1969-73, 79—; co-recipient Arthur Cole prize Econ. History Assn., 1972. Mem. Am. Econ. Assn. (chmn. com. econ. edn. 1978—), So. Econ. Assn. (v.p. 1981-82), Internat. Union for Sci. Study Population, Population Assn. Am., Joint Council on Econ. Edn. (trustee 1978—, exec. com. 1978—), Phi Beta Kappa. Home: 4607 Chicopee Trl Durham NC 27707-5208 Office: Duke U Econs Dept Durham NC 27708

KELLEY, ALOYSIUS PAUL, university administrator, priest; b. Carlisle, Pa., Oct. 4, 1929; s. Aloysius Paul and Teresa (Barron) K. AB, St. Louis U., 1955, MA, PhL, St. Louis U., 1956; STL, U. Innsbruck, Austria, 1963; PhD, U. Pa., 1968; LLD (hon.), Sacred Heart U., 1985. Joined S.J., 1949; ordained priest Roman Catholic Ch., 1962; chmn. dept. classics Georgetown U., 1969-71, asst. acad. v.p., 1971-72, acting acad. v.p., 1972-74, exec. v.p. for acad. affairs and provost, 1974-79; pres. Fairfield (Conn.) U., 1979—. Trustee Georgetown Prep. Sch., 1969-72, Loyola Coll., Balt., 1971-75, Scranton U., 1974-80, Bridgeport Area C. of C., 1979-82, St. Joseph's U., Phila., 1980-86, Georgetown U., 1982-88, 89-95, Conn. Grand Opera, 1980-82, John Carroll U., 1987-93, LeMoyne Coll., 1993-99, The Gesu Sch., 1993-97, St. Joseph's Prep. Sch., 1997—2002, St. Peter's Coll., 1998—, Nat. Assn. Ind. Colls. and Univs., 1997-2000; mem. D.C. Commn. Postsecondary Edn., 1974-79; vice chmn. Conn. Conf. Ind. Colls., 1980-81, chmn., 1981-83; pres. New Eng. Colls. Fund, 1993-95. Fulbright-Hayes fellow, 1971 Mem. Am. Philol. Assn., Am. Assn. Univ. Adminstrs., Am. Assn. Higher Edn., Patterson Club, Newcomen Soc. Democrat. Home and Office: Fairfield U Office of the Pres 1073 N Benson Rd Fairfield CT 06824-5195

KELLEY, BERNARD J. pharmaceutical executive; BS in Engr., U.S. Naval Acad., 1963. Assoc. engr. facilities engring. Merck and Co., Inc., Whitehouse Station, NJ, 1967—68, indsl. engr. MSD ops., 1968—71, mgr. indsl. and quality control engring., 1971—73, mgr. pharm. indsl. engring., MSD ops., 1973—75, mgr. facilities planning, MSD ops., 1975—76, mgr. ops., MSD Elkton Pharm. Labs., 1976—79, dir. packaging ops., MSD ops., 1979, dir. pharm. mfg., MSD ops., 1979—80, sr. dir. tech. svcs., MSD ops., 1980—83, sr. dir. materials mgmt., MSD ops., 1983—85, exec. dir. mfg. ops., MSDI, 1985; v.p. mfg. ops. Merck Sharp & Dohme Internat., 1985—86; pres. Hubbard Farms, 1986—89; v.p. bus. affairs MSD AgVet, 1989—91; sr. v.p. adminstrn., planning, quality mfg. divsn. Merck & Co., Inc., 1991—93, sr. v.p. ops. mfg. divsn., 1993, pres. mfg. divsn., 1994—. Office: Merck and Co Inc One Merck Dr Whitehouse Station NJ 08889-0100

KELLEY, BRIAN P. transportation executive; b. Cin. BA in Econs., Coll. Holy Cross. With Procter & Gamble; sr. exec. appliance bus. GE, 1983; v.p. Global Consumer Svcs. Ford Motor Co., 2001—02, pres. Lincoln Mercury oper. unit, 2002; CEO SIRVA, Westmont, Ill., 2002—, bd. dirs. Office: SIRVA World Hdqrs 700 Oakmont Ln Westmont IL 60559*

KELLEY, BRUCE DUTTON, pharmacist; b. Hartford, Conn., Jan. 4, 1957; s. Roger Weston and Elizabeth Morrill (Atwood) K.; m. DawnRenee Chiocco, Jan. 19, 1990. Student, U. Hartford, 1975-77; BS in Pharmacy, U. Colo., 1985; diplomas in Russian, Moscow U., Moscow, 1993, 95; BA in Russian, U. Colo., 1995. RPh, Colo. Pharmacist King Soopers, Inc., Boulder, Colo., 1990—; asst. tour leader in Russia U. Tex., El Paso, 1991. Russia asst. guide, U. Ariz., Tucson, 1992 (summer). Vol. Warderburg Student Health Ctr., U. Colo., Boulder, 1981-83, Am. Diabetes Assn. Mem. NRA, Nat. Eagle Scout Assn., Am. Legion, Boulder Cosmopolitan Club, Niwot Optimist Club. Republican. Avocation: hiking. Home: 6152 Willow Ln Boulder CO 80301-5356 Office: King Soopers Inc 6550 Lookout Rd Boulder CO 80301-3303 E-mail: otsapetra3@aol.com.

KELLEY, BRUCE GUNN, insurance company executive, lawyer; b. Phila., Mar. 17, 1954; s. Robb Beardsley and Winifred Elizabeth Gray (Murray) K.; m. Susan Aldrich Barnes, Oct. 1, 1983; children: Dashle Gunn, Barnes Gunn, Onnalee Kinkaid. AB, Dartmouth Coll., 1976; JD, U. Iowa, 1979. Bar: Iowa 1979; CPCU; CLU. Assoc. Bradshaw, Fowler, Proctor & Fairgrave, Des Moines, 1979-84, ptnr., 1984-85; gen. counsel Employers Mut. Casualty Co., Des Moines, 1985-89, exec. v.p., 1989-91, pres., 1991—, also bd. dirs. Trustee Am. Inst. for Chartered Property Casualty Underwiters/Ins. Inst. Am.; bd. dirs. Alliance Am. Insurers; chmn. adv. bd. Iowa Pub. Employees Retirement Sys. Trustee Nat. Com. on Drunk Drivers; chmn. Salisbury House Found. Mem. Iowa Bar Assn., Des Moines Club, Rotary, Masons. Republican. Mem. United Church of Christ. Home: 14 Glenview Dr Des Moines IA 50312-2546 Office: EMC Ins Cos PO Box 712 Des Moines IA 50303-0712

KELLEY, CHRISTOPHER DONALD, lawyer; b. Manhasset, N.Y., Nov. 6, 1957; s. Donald Kelley and Audrey (Wuestman) Raebeck; m. Nancy Nagle, June 27, 1981. BA in History with high honors, Coll. William and Mary, 1978; JD cum laude, N.Y. Law Sch., 1981. Bar: N.Y. 1982, U.S. Dist. Ct. (ea. dist.) N.Y. 1984. Assoc. Twomey Latham & Shea, Riverhead, N.Y., 1981-85; ptnr. Twomey Latham Shea & Kelley, Riverhead, N.Y., 1985-99, mng. ptnr., 1999—. Chmn. East Hampton (N.Y.) Dem. Com., 1982-86, 87-88, 92-2002, East Hampton Town Zoning Bd. Appeals, 1986-87. Mem. N.Y. Bar Assn. (environ. law sect.), Suffolk County Bar Assn., N.Y. County Bar Assn., Am. Trial Lawyers Assn. Episcopalian. Home: 727 Accabonac Rd East Hampton NY 11937-1807 Office: Twomey Latham Shea & Kelley 33 W 2nd St Riverhead NY 11901-2701 E-mail: ckelley@suffolklaw.com.

KELLEY, CLEOPHUS O. city official; b. Birmingham, Ala., Sept. 17, 1932; s. Gladys Turner Kelley; m. Ann E. Kelley, Mar. 26, 1952 (div.); children: Cleophus O. Jr., Michael, Kelvin, Regina. Student, U. Cin., 1997, Ohio State Employment Relation Sch., 1991, Padgett Thompson Bus. Sch., 1991. With Fleet Svcs., 1057-60, Pub. Works Dept., Cin., 1960-99; asst. supt. Pub. Svc. Dept., Cin., 2000—. U. Cincinnati Leadership Development, 1997. Vice pres. Cin. Middle Mgmt. Bd., 1988-90; leader Boy Scouts Am., Cin., 1951-75. Mem. Solid Waste Assn. N.Am, Am. Public Works Assn. Office: City of Cincinnati 3320 Millcreek Rd Cincinnati OH 45223-2419

KELLEY, DANA LYN, social studies educator, consultant; b. Phila., Dec. 17, 1971; d. William Edward and Sandra Joanne Kelley; m. Edward Henry Grieb, June 22, 2002. MA in Edn., Georgian Ct. Coll., Lakewood, N.J., 1995—2002. Internet curriculum & tng. specialist New Forum Publishers/Beyond Books, Conshohocken, Pa., 1999—2001; social studies tchr. Moises Molina H.S., Dallas, 2000—. Social studies cons. Region 10 Edn. Svc. Ctr., Richardson, Tex., 2001—. Personal E-mail: dkelley1776@aol.com.

KELLEY, DANIEL, architectural firm executive; BS in Architecture, Ga. Inst. Tech., 1975; M in Architecture, Harvard Grad. Sch. of Design, 1977. Cert. NCARB, Pa., Ind., S.C. Adj. prof. dept. architecture Drexel U., 1983—; vis. instr. U. of Pa., Grad. Sch. of Fine Arts, 1986; ptnr. MGA Ptnrs., Phila., 1990—. Lead designer Ctr. for Biostats., Info. Tech., The Milton Hershey Ctr., Pa. State U., 1992, Haffnre Hall, Bryn Mawr Coll., 1996, Pembroke and Merion Halls, Bryn Mawr Coll., Pa., 1998, Annenberg Sch. for Commn., U. Pa., 1999, Acad. Masterplan, Bryn Mawr Coll., Pa., 2000, Tyler Sch. Of Art Masterplan, Temple U., 2000, Facilities Svcs. and Children's Ctr., U. of Pa., 2000, Commencement Ceremony, U. Pa., 2001, Theater/Neal Marshall Edn. Ctr., Ind. U., Bloomington, 2002, Internat. House, 2002, Hamilton Coll. House Renovation, U. of Pa., 2003. Recipient Design Competition Winning Entry, Suffolk County Courthouse, Va., 1985, Nat. Fgn. Affairs Tng. Ctr., Va., 1986. Mem.: The Carpenter's Co. of Phila., The Phila. Athenaeum, Pa. Soc. of Architects, Am. Inst. of Architects Phila. Chpt. (Design Excellence 1999, 2000, 2001). Office: MGA Ptnrs Architects 234 Market St Philadelphia PA 19106 Fax: 215-923-4258.*

KELLEY, DAVID BRIAN, community college dean, educator, consultant; b. Somerville, Mass., June 30, 1951; s. John Dennis and Mary Agnes Kelley; m. Jane Aria, Oct. 13, 1974; children: Kathleen, MaryElizabeth. BS, Salem State Coll., 1974; MS, Simmons Coll., 1976; EdD, Boston U., 1985. Libr. Fitchburg (Mass.) State Coll., 1977-79; dean No. Essex C.C., Haverhill, Mass., 1979—; exec. dir. Mass. Colls. Online, 2002—. Ednl. tech. cons. numerous cos. and colls., 1977—; bd. dirs. Tchg. Academic Survival Skills. Author: Analysis of Training and Human Resource Development Programs, 1985. Chair various statewide ednl. policy groups. Recipient Edn. Policy fellowship Inst. Ednl. Leadership, 1984-85. Mem.: Assn. Ednl. Comms. and Tech. Avocations: sailing, skiing, travel, reading. Home: 65 Cochrane St Melrose MA 02176-1504 Office: No Essex CC Elliott Way Haverhill MA 01830-2399 E-mail: dkelley@mca.mass.edu.

KELLEY, DAVID CHRISTOPHER, philosopher; b. Lakewood, Ohio, June 23, 1949; s. Walter Carl and Patricia Kelley; m. Susan McCloskey, Mar 25, 1982. BA, MA, Brown U., 1971; PhD, Princeton U., 1975. Asst. prof. philosophy Vassar Coll., Poughkeepsie, N.Y., 1975-84; freelance writer, lectr., 1984-89; exec. dir. Objectivist Ctr., Poughkeepsie, 1990—. Vis. lectr. in philosophy Brandeis U., Waltham, Mass., 1989-90 Author: The Evidence of the Senses, 1986, The Art of Reasoning, 1990, Unrugged Individualism, 1996, A Life of One's Own, 1998, Contested Legacy of Ayn Rand, 2000; co-author: Laissez Parler, 1985. Mem. Am. Philos. Assn. Office: Objectivist Ctr 11 Raymond Ave Ste 31 Poughkeepsie NY 12603-2344 E-mail: dkelley@objectivistcenter.org.

KELLEY, DAVID E. producer, writer; b. Waterville, Maine, Apr. 4, 1956; m. Michelle Pfeiffer, 1993; 2 children. BA, Princeton U., 1979; JD, Boston U., 1983. CEO David E. Kelley Prodns., Inc., L.A. Writer, story editor, exec. story editor, supervising prodr., exec. prodr. L.A. Law (Emmy award for Outstanding Drama Series 1989, 90, Emmy award for outstanding writing in a drama series 1990); writer, exec. prodr. Picket Fences (Emmy award for outstanding drama series 1993, 94), Chicago Hope, 1994-2000, The Practice, 1997— (Golden Globe award for best tv drama 1998, Emmy award for outstanding drama series, 1998, 99), Ally McBeal, 1997-2002 (Golden Globe winner, Emmy award for best tv series-musical or comedy 1997, 98, Emmy award for outstanding comedy series 1999), Snoops, 1999-2000, Boston Public, 2000—, Girl's Club, 2002, The Brotherhood of Poland, New Hampshire, 2003-. Office: David E Kelly Prodns care 20th Century Fox 10201 W Pico Blvd Bldg 80 Los Angeles CA 90064-2606 also: William Morris Agency One William Morris Pl Beverly Hills CA 90212*

KELLEY, DELORES GOODWIN, state legislator; b. Norfolk, Va., May 1, 1936; d. Stephen Cornelius and Helen Elizabeth (Jefferson) Goodwin; m. Russell Victor Kelley, Jr., Dec. 26, 1956; children: Norma Kelley Johnson, Russell III, Brian. BA, Va. State Coll., 1956; MA, NYU, 1958, Purdue U., 1972; PhD, U. Md., 1977. Dir. religious edn. N.Y.C. Protestant Coun., Bronx, 1959-60; tchr. N.Y.C. Pub. Schs., Bklyn., 1962-64, Ctrl. Sch. Dist., Plainview, N.Y., 1965-66; asst. prof. Morgan State U., Balt., 1966-70; prof. speech comms. and English Coppin State Coll., Balt., 1973—; mem. Md. Ho. of Dels., Annapolis, 1991—98; former chmn. Joint Com. on Fed. Rels./Md. Senate; vice-chmn. exec. nomination com. Md. Senate, 1998—. Joint com. legis. policy, joint com. legis. ethics, co-chair joint com. on fair practices Md. State Senate, 1998—2002, joint com. on health care delivery and fin., 2000—, fin. com.; chair joint com. on Port of Balt., 2003—; senate chair Joint Com. on Adminstrv., Exec. and Legis. Rev., 2001—02; vice-chair sen. com. exec. nomination; vice-chair Balt. County Senate Delegation, 2003—; panelist, reviewer NEH, Washington, 1978—82, Nat. Inst. Justice, 1998—; dean Coppin State Coll., Balt., 1979—82; fellow Am. Coun. on Edn., Washington, 1982—83; vice-chair bd. dirs. Harbor Bank Md., 1982—; mem. Gov.'s Commn. on Adoption, 1995, Atty. Gen's. and Lt. Gov's. task force on family violence, 1996—, Md. Commn. on Criminal Sentencing Policy, 1996—, Md. Commn. on Infant Mortality, 1999—2002; mem. strategic planning com. Balt. County Schs., 1999—2000; adv. com. Md. Medicaid, 1998—. Editor (monograph) Concepts of Race, 1981; moderator (TV series) Teaching Writing: Process Approach, 1982. Sec. Md. Dem. Party, Annapolis, 1986-90; bd. dirs. Balt. Urban League, 1986-89; pres. Black Jewish Forum, Balt., 1990-92; commr. Md. Commn. on Values, Annapolis, 1980-85; bd. dirs. Balt. Mental Health Systems, 1991-95; host Internat. Visitors Ctr., 1976—; commn. mem. Md. Commn. Hereditary and Congenital Disorders, Balt., 1992-95; del. White House conf. on Aging, 1995. Fellow Purdue U., 1970-72; grantee Md. Com. for Humanities, Balt., 1977-78, NEH, Washington, 1988-89; recipient Racial Justice award YWCA of Met. Balt., 1995; named to Md. Top 100 Women, Warfields Bus. Record, 1995, 97. Mem. Nat. Inst. Justice (panelist, rev. 1997). Inst. for Govtl. Svcs. (bd. dirs. 1993-94), Nat. Polit. Congress Black Women (bd. dirs., Balt. chair 1993-95), Women Legislators Md. (1st v.p. 1995-96, pres. 1998-99), 10th Dist. Dem. Club Md. (founder, pres. 1995—). Baptist. Avocations: travel, public speaking, reading. Office: 302 James Senate Office Bldg Annapolis MD 21401-1991 E-mail: delores_kelley@senate.state.md.us.

KELLEY, DONALD REED, historian; b. Elgin, Ill., Feb. 17, 1931; s. Walter Louis and Helen Lenore (Davis) K.; m. Bonnie Gene Smith, June 30, 1979; 1 son, John Reed. BA, Harvard Coll., 1953; MA, Columbia U., 1956, PhD, 1962; postgrad., U. Paris, 1958-59. Instr. Queens Coll., 1960-63; asst. prof. So. Ill. U., 1963-65, SUNY, 1965-68, assoc. prof., 1968-70, prof., 1970-72; vis. prof. Harvard U., 1972-73; prof. U. Rochester, NY, 1973—, Marie Curran Wilson and Joseph Chamberlain Wilson prof. history, 1984-91; James Westfall Thompson prof. Rutgers U., New Brunswick, NJ, 1991—. Author: Foundations of Modern Historical Scholarship, 1970, François Hotman, 1973, The Beginning of Ideology, 1981, Historians and the Law in Postrevolutionary France, 1984, History, Law, and the Human Sciences, 1984, The Human Measure, 1990, The Writing of History and the Study of Law, 1997, Faces of History, 1998, The Descent of Ideas, 2002, Fortunes of History, 2003; editor: The Monarchy of France (Claude de Seyssel), 1981, History of Ideas, 1990, Versions of History, 1991, The Shapes of Knowledge, 1991, What is Property? (P.-J. Proudhon), 1994, History and the Disciplines, 1997; exec. editor Jour. History of Ideas, 1985—. With U.S. Army, 1953—55. Fulbright fellow, 1958-59, Newberry libr. fellow, 1965, Am. Coun. Learned Socs. fellow, 1967-68, Folger Libr. fellow, 1970, 85; mem. Inst. for Advanced Study, 1969-70, 77-78, 96-97; Guggenheim fellow, 1974-75, 81-82, NEH fellow, 1977-78, Nat. Humanities Ctr. fellow, 1984, Shelby Cullom Davis Ctr. fellow, Princeton U., 1987-88, Wilson Ctr. fellow, 1992-93. Fellow Am. Acad. Arts and Scis.; mem. Am. Philos. Soc., Am. Hist. Assn., Renaissance Soc. Am., Medieval Acad., Internat. Soc. Intellectual History (pres.). Home: 45 Jefferson Ave New Brunswick NJ 08901-1737 Office: Rutgers U Dept History New Brunswick NJ 08901

KELLEY, DOUGLAS EATON, military officer; b. Cleve., July 17, 1960; s. Robert Ernest Vinson and Elizabeth Caroline (Kirsheman) K.; m. Mary Josephine Horlacher, May 7, 1983; children: Katherine Elizabeth, Caroline Josephine, Douglas Eaton Jr. BA in Psychology, The Citadel, 1982; MA in Mgmt. and Supervision, Cen. Mich. U., 1986; grad., Squadron Officers Sch., 1987, Air Command and Staff Coll., 1995, Armed Forces Staff Coll., 1996, Air War Coll., 1999. Commd. USAF, 1982, advanced through grades to lt. col., 1986; dep. missile combat crew commdr., dep. flight commdr. 741st Strategic Missile Squadron, Minot AFB, N.D., 1983, missile combat crew commdr., 1985-86; missile combat crew instr. 91st Strategic Missile Wing, Minot AFB, N.D., 1984-85, missile combat crew evaluator, 1986-87; airborne missile ops. officer 4th Airborne Command and Control Squadron, Ellsworth AFB, S.D., 1987, comdr. airborne missile combat crew, 1987-88, airborne launch control system scheduler, and plans officer, 1988-89, asst. chief airborne launch control system plans sect., 1990, chief airborne launch control system targeting, 1991; chief intercontinental ballistic missile emergency actions Hdqrs. Strategic Air Command, Offutt AFB NE, Nebr., 1991, ICBM emergency actions devel. officer Offutt AFB, Nebr., 1991-92; ICBM emergency war order tng. and evaluation officer Hdqrs. Air Combat Command, Langles AFB, Va., 1992-93; ICBM emergency war order policy officer Hdqrs. Air Force Space Command, Peterson AFB, Colo., 1993-94; nat. mil. command sys. command and control officer, dep. chief, command control br. Hdqrs. U.S. Strategic Command Offutt AFB NE, 1994-97; comdr., current ops. flight 91st Ops. Support Squadron Minot AFB ND, 1997-98, ops. officer 741st Missile Squadron, 1998-2000; comdr. 576th Flight Test Squadron Vandenberg AFB, Calif., 2000—01; mission dir. Cheyenne Mountain Ops. Ctr. N. Am. Aerospace Def. Command, 2001—. Republican. Protestant. Avocations: music, record collecting, sports, personal fitness, recreational vehicle travel. Home: 15495 Holbein Dr Colorado Springs CO 80921-2518

KELLEY, EDWARD ALLEN, publisher; b. Clinton, Mass., June 28, 1927; s. Edward Francis Kelley and Lillian Marion (Keigwin) French; m. Margaret Jordan Talbott, Feb. 24, 1962; children: Catherine, Edward, Michael. BA, Trinity Coll., Hartford, Conn., 1950; STM, Gen. Theol. Sem., N.Y.C., 1953. Prodn. asst., customer svc. rep. Colonial Press, Clinton, 1953-57; mgr. bookstore Morehouse-Barlow Co. Inc., N.Y.C., 1957-61, v.p., editorial dir., 1961-74; sr. v.p. Oxford U. Press, N.Y.C., 1974-83; pres. Kelley Assocs., Ridgefield, Conn., 1983-87; pres., pub. Morehouse Pub. Co., Ridgefield, 1988-97; pvt. practice pub. cons. Ridgefield, 1997—. Editor The Episcopal Ch. Ann., 1967-74, 87-97. With USNR, 1945-47, World War II. Democrat. Episcopalian. Avocations: golf, reading.

KELLEY, EDWARD WATSON, JR., former federal agency administrator; b. Eugene, Oreg., Jan. 27, 1932; s. Edward Watson and Allie (Autry) K.; children: Kinsloe K. Queen, James M., Michael; m. Janet H. Kelley. BA, Rice U., 1954; MBA, Harvard U., 1959. Pres., chief exec. officer Kelley Industries, Inc.,

Houston, 1959-81; chmn. bd. Investment Advisors, Inc., Houston, 1981-87; mem. bd. govs. FRS, Washington, 1987—2001. Lt. (j.g.) USNR, 1954-56. Mem. Houston Country Club (bd. dirs. 1984-87), Bayou Club. Methodist.*

KELLEY, EUGENE JOHN, retired business educator; b. N.Y.C., July 8, 1922; s. Eugene Lawrence and Agnes Regina (Meskill) K.; m. Dorothy W. Kane, Aug. 3, 1946; 1 child, Sharon A.; m. Linda S. Phillips, Sept. 30, 1992. BS, U. Conn., 1945; MBA, Boston U., 1949, MEd, 1948; PhD, NYU, 1955. Instr. mktg. Babson Inst., 1947-49; dir. divsn. bus. adminstrn. Clark U., 1949-56, asst. prof., 1949-54, assoc. prof., 1954-56; vis. lectr. Harvard U. Bus. Sch., 1956-57; asst. prof. Mich. State U., East Lansing, 1957-58, assoc. prof., 1958-59; prof. mktg., asst. dean Grad. Sch. Bus. Adminstrn. NYU, N.Y.C., 1959-60, prof., assoc. dean, 1960-64; rsch. prof. bus. adminstrn. Coll. Bus. Adminstrn. Pa. State U., 1963-88, dean, 1973-88; dean and rsch. prof. emeritus Pa. State U., 1988; disting. prof. mktg. Fla. Atlantic U., Boca Raton, 1989—, dir. Ctr. for Svcs. Mktg. and Mgmt., Coll. Bus., 1990—. Regional dir. Mellon Bank Central; mem. nat. adv. Council SBA; mem. Commn. on Edn. for Bus. Professions of Nat. Assn. State Univs. and Land Grant Colls.; cons. GAO, N.J. Bd. Higher Edn. Author: Marketing Planning and Competitive Strategy, 1972, Managerial Marketing: Policies, Strategies and Decisions, 1973, Social Marketing: Perspectives and Viewpoints, 1973; Editor: Jour. Mktg. 1967-73. Served with USAAF, 1942-43. Mem. Am. Mktg. Assn. (pres. 1982-83, dir., mem. disting. mktg. educator com.), Acad. Mgmt., Am. Assembly Collegiate Schs. of Bus. Home: 629 Cricklewood Dr State College PA 16803 Office: Pa State Univ Bus Adminstrn University Park PA 16802

KELLEY, FRANK JOSEPH, lawyer, former state attorney general; b. Detroit, Dec. 31, 1924; s. Frank Edward and Grace Margaret (Spears) Kelley; m. Nancy Courtier; children: Karen Ann, Frank Edward II, Jane Francis. Pre-law cert., U. Detroit, 1948, JD, 1951. Bar: Mich. 1952. Pvt. practice law, Detroit, 1952—54, Alpena, 1954—61; atty. gen. State of Mich., Lansing, 1962—98; pvt. practice Lansing, 1998—. Instr. econs. Alpena CC, 1955—56; instr. pub. adminstrn. Alpena County, 1956; atty. city real estate law U. Mich. Extension, 1957—61. Mem. Alpena County Bd. Suprs., 1958—61; pres. Alpena Cmty. Svcs. Coun., 1956; chmn. Gt. Lakes Commn., 1971; founding dir., 1st sec. Alpena United Fund, 1955; founding dir., 1st pres. Northeastern Mich. Child Guidance Clinic, 1958; pres. bd. dirs. Northeastern Mich. Cath. Family Svc., 1959. Mem.: ABA, Nat. Assn. Attys. Gen. (pres. 1967), State Bar Mich., 26th Jud. Cir. Bar Assn. (pres. 1956), Internat. Movement Atlantic Union, KC (4 deg., past legal adv.), Alpha Kappa Psi. Address: 101 S Washington Sq Fl 9 Lansing MI 48933-1731

KELLEY, GEORGE LAWRENCE, JR., lawyer; b. N.Y.C., July 26, 1937; s. George L. and Gertrude (Berger) K.; m. Dana Ruth Murray, Dec. 19, 1970; children— Jessica Wynne, Todd Sterling. A.B., Dartmouth Coll., 1959; J.D., Harvard U., 1962. Bar: N.Y. 1963, Pa. 1976. Vice pres. Hayden Stone, Inc., N.Y.C., 1966-70; asst. gen. counsel INA Corp., Phila., 1970-80; assoc. Erskine, Wolfson & Kelley, P.C., Phila., 1980-82; of counsel Gratz, Tate, Spiegel, Ervin & Ruthrauff, Phila., 1982-88, Leonard, Tillery & Davison, Phila., 1988—; panel mem. Am. Arbitration Assn., Phila., 1982— . Pres., Wynnewood Civic Assn., Pa., 1984-85; co-chmn., founder Concerned Citizens for Rail Transp., Phila., 1981-83. Mem. ABA, Pa. Bar Assn., Phila. Bar Assn. Republican. Unitarian. Clubs: Union League (Phila.); Merion Cricket (Haverford, Pa.). Home: 207 Almur Ln Wynnewood PA 19096-1712 Office: Leonard Tillery & Davison 1530 Chestnut St Philadelphia PA 19102-2739

KELLEY, GEORGE LORENZE, psychologist, consultant; b. Va., May 7, 1924; s. George Lorenze and Ruby Kishpaugh K.; m.Nancy Katherine Keck, July 6, 1967; 1 child: Karen Marie. Student, U. Florence, Italy, 1945; BS, Auburn U., 1950; MSc, North Tex. State U., 1964; D, U. Tulsa, 1969; MPH post doctorate, Yale U. Sch. Medincine, 1974. CEO Kelley Enterprises, Birmingham, Ala., 1950—64; rsch. fellow Okla. State U., 1964-66; chief psychologist Bur. Indian Affairs, Navajo and Zuni Indian Reservations, 1966; prof. psychology Appalachian State U., Boone, N.C., 1966-68; chief psychologist Model Cities Program, Tulsa, 1968-69; chief psychologist health dept. U.S. Virgin Islands, 1970-73; prof. psychology Coll. U.S. Virgin Islands, 1970-73; chief behavior scientist, helmsman M.S. Yankee Trader-World Circumnavigation Voyage, 1977-78; chm. bd., chief psychologist Internat. Prep. Sch., throughout world, 1978-80; chief psychologist, prof. Parkwood Clinic, Tulsa, Okla., 1981-87; disting. prof. U.S. Internat. U., San Diego, 1988-96; CFO Mentor Assoc., Escondido, Calif., 1995—. Cons. USAF, Bur. Indian Affairs, U. N.Mex., Lyndon Johnson Mental Health Ctr., Pago Pago Am. Samoa; min. edn., New Guinea; commr. Pitcairn Island. Contbr. to articles, radio, TV. Mem. Excellence 2000, Albany, Ga. With USAAC, 1942-46, ETO. Recipient 13 citations and decorations for combat flying, USAAC, 1942-46. Mem. APA (divsn. 22, 25, 28, 32), Nat. Assn. Counselors, Elks, Masons (32 deg.), Scottish Rite, Shriners, Civitan Club, Tau Kappa Alpha, Phi Delta Kappa, Alpha Phi Omega, Psi Chi, Lambda Chi Alpha. Avocations: classic cars, sailing, yoga. Home: 1313 6th Ave Albany GA 31707-4404 Office: 2155 Lemon Ave Escondido CA 92029-4404 Mailing: 1315 6th Ave Albany GA 31707-4404 Office Fax: 760-740-0259. E-mail: george.kelley.eph.74@aya.yale.edu., nk4u@usa.net.

KELLEY, JAMES FRANCIS, lawyer; b. Dec. 30, 1941; s. James O'Connor and Marcella Cecilia (Salb) K.; children: Sarah, Leah, Laurence. AB, Yale U.; JD, U. Chgo. Bars: N.Y. 1967, Tex. 1981. Assoc. Breed, Abbott & Morgan, NYC, 1967-75; dep. gen. counsel United Tech. Corp., Hartford, Conn., 1975-81; sr. v.p., gen. counsel Diamond Shamrock Corp. (name now Maxus Energy Corp.), Dallas, 1981-88; ptnr. Jones, Day, Reavis & Pogue, Dallas and Paris, 1988-93; sr. v.p. law, gen. counsel Georgia-Pacific Corp, 1993-2000; currently holds the position of exec. v.p. & Gen. coun., 2000-pres.; Gov. Dallas Symphony Assn., 1985-89; bd. dir. North Tex. Pub. Broadcasting Found., Dallas, 1983-91, mem. exec. com., 1988-91; bd. dirs. Atlanta Symphony Orch., 1994—, mem. exec. com., 1996—, vice chair fin. com., 1996—; bd. dirs. Ga. Trust Hist. Preservation, 1994—; mem. bd. visitors Emory U., 1999—. Mem. ABA, Assn. Gen. Counsel. Office: Georgia-Pacific Corp 133 Peachtree St NE Ste Bsmt Atlanta GA 30303-1847

KELLEY, JAMES FRANCIS, civil engineer; b. Boston, Mar. 30, 1920; s. James Aloysius and Rose Frances (Berlo) K.; m. Mary Elizabeth Kelly, June 17, 1946; children: Margaret Coronite, James Francis Jr., Rosemary Doran, Kathleen Clancy. Assoc. Civil and Structural Engring., Northeastern U., Boston, 1950. Registered profl. engr., profl. land surveyor. Sr. engring. aide City of Quincy (Mass.) Engring. Dept., 1942-48; planning engr., design engr. Mass. Dept. Pub. Works, Boston, 1948-64, maintenance engr., dep. chief engr., 1964-77; pvt. cons. J.F. Kelley & Assocs., Quincy, 1977-91; chmn. Quincy Planning Bd., 1990—. Contbr. articles to profl. jours. Mem. NAS (transp. rsch. bd. 1968-88), Am. Pub. Works Assn. (life), Nat. Order WW II Battlefield Commns. (life), VFW (life), Am. Legion, KC (life). Roman Catholic. Home: 63 Vershire St North Quincy MA 02171-2528 Office: Quincy Planning Bd 1305 Hancock St Quincy MA 02169-5111

KELLEY, JAMES RUSSELL, lawyer; b. Conneaut, Ohio, Feb. 25, 1948; s. Russell Wynne and Mattie Lou (Robertson) K.; m. Lissa Galloway, Jan. 7, 1984; 1 child, Kathleen Anne. BA, Vanderbilt U., 1970; JD, Emory U., 1975, LLM in Taxation, 1977. Bar: Ga. 1975, U.S. Dist. Ct. (no. dist.) Ga. 1975, U.S. Ct. Appeals (5th cir.) 1975, Tenn. 1977, U.S. Dist. Ct. (mid. dist.) Tenn. 1977, U.S. Ct. Appeals (6th cir.) 1977. Systems analyst Standard Oil of Ohio, Cleve., 1970-72; assoc. Greene, Buckley, DeRieux & Jones, Atlanta, 1975-77, Dearborn & Ewing, Nashville, 1977-80, ptnr., 1980-90, Neal & Harwell, PLC, Nashville, 1990—. Bd. dirs. Mid-South Comml. Law Inst., Nashville. Author: (with others) Corporations-Formation, 1980; contbg. editor: Norton Bankruptcy Law and Practice, 1987—. Fellow: Am. Coll. Bankruptcy; mem.: Order of the Coif, Am. Bankruptcy Inst. (past chmn.). Office: Neal & Harwell PLC 2000 One Nashville Pl Nashville TN 37219 E-mail: jkelley@nealharwell.com.

KELLEY, JEFFREY WENDELL, lawyer; b. Urbana, Ill., June 8, 1949; s. Wendell J. and Evelyn V. (Kimpel) K.; m. Marsha Lynn Adams, Aug. 21, 1971; children: Julie M., Anna E., Adam J., Grant W. BA, Lipscomb Coll., 1971; postgrad., Vanderbilt U., 1971-72; JD, U. Ill., 1975. Bar: Ga. 1975, U.S. Dist. Ct. (mid. and no. dists.) Ga. 1975, U.S. Ct. Appeals (11th cir.) 1982. Assoc. Powell, Goldstein, Frazer & Murphy, Atlanta, 1975-82, ptnr. litigation dept., with bankruptcy splty., 1982—. Speaker in field. Notes and comments editor U. Ill. Law Rev., 1974-75. Mem. ABA (litig. com.), Am. Bankruptcy Inst. (mem. com.), Ga. Bar Assn. (bench and bar com. 1988), Atlanta Bar Assn. (chmn. law day 1980), Lawyers Club Atlanta (rules and judiciary com. 1995). Republican. Avocations: reading, golf, tennis. Office: Powell Goldstein Frazer & Murphy 191 Peachtree St NE Fl 16 Atlanta GA 30303-1740 E-mail: jkelley@pgfm.com.

KELLEY, JOHN F. airline executive, Chmn., pres., CEO Alaska Air Group, Seattle. Office: Alaska Air Group PO Box 68900 Seattle WA 98168-0900

KELLEY, JOHN HENRY, electronics company executive; b. Somerville, Mass., May 6, 1941; s. John Dennis and Mary Agnes (Barry) K.; m. Melanie Ann Groszko, July 12, 1969; children: John Dennis, Dennis Barry. AB, Boston Coll., 1967, MBA, 1969; MS in Mgmt., MIT, 1980; JD, Suffolk U., 1971. Chief fin. officer M/A-COM, Inc., Burlington, Mass., 1979-83; pres., chief executive officer Lawrence Lab. Inc., Chatsworth, Calif., 1983-84; chief exec. officer Azonix Corp., Burlington, Mass., 1984-86; pres., chief exec. officer Cyborg Corp., Newton, Mass., 1986-87, also bd. dirs., 1986—; chmn. bd. Fidelis Group Inc., Newton, Mass., 1983—, pres., chief exec. officer, 1986—. Bd. dirs. VenturCom, Inc., Cambridge, Mass., Cyborg Technology Inc., Newton. Served to capt. USMC, 1960-66, Vietnam. Decorated Silver Star. Mem. Am. Mgmt. Assn., Am. Electronics Assn., Mass. High Tech. Coun. Republican. Roman Catholic. Home: 39 Juniper Ave Wakefield MA 01880-1140 Office: Fidelis Group Inc PO Box 1532 Wakefield MA 01880-5532

KELLEY, JOHN JOSEPH, JR., lawyer; b. Cleve., June 17, 1936; s. John Joseph and Helen (Meier) K.; m. Gloria Hill, June 20, 1959; children: John Joseph III, Scott MacDonald, Christopher Taft, Megan Meredith. BS cum laude in Commerce, Ohio U., 1958; LL.B., Case Western Res. U., 1960. Bar: Ohio bar 1960. Clk. firm Walter & Haverfield, Cleve., 1957-60; assoc. Walter, Haverfield, Buescher & Chockley, Cleve., 1960-66, partner, 1967-72; chief exec. officer Fleischmann Enterprises, Cin., 1972-77; pvt. practice law Cin., 1977-87; ptnr. Kohnen & Patton, Cin., 1988—. Chmn. bd. Basic Packaging Systems, Inc., 1982-87; dir. Orgamac Leasing Ltd; pres. Naples Devel. Inc., 1974-87, Yankee Leasing Co. Mem. Lakewood (Ohio) City Council, 1965-72, pres., 1972; mem. exec. com. Cuyahoga County (Ohio) Republican Central Com., 1965-72; mem. Hamilton County (Ohio) Rep. Policy Com.; Ohio chmn. Robert Taft, Jr. Senate Campaign Com., 1970, 76; bd. govs. Case Western Res. U., 1961, 84-87. Mem. Assn. Ohio Commodores, ABA, Ohio State Bar Assn., Cin. Bar Assn. Clubs: Cin. Country, Queen City (Cin.); Naples Bath and Tennis. Home: 5 Woodcreek Dr Cincinnati OH 45241-3255 Office: PNC Center 261 E Main St ste 800 Cincinnati OH 45202 E-mail: jkelley@kohnenpatton.com.

KELLEY, JOHN PAUL, communications consultant; b. Columbus, Ohio, May 12, 1919; s. John Adrian and Josephine (Nash) K.; m. Dorothy Rose Peters, July 31, 1942; children: John M., Ann P., Daniel O., Peter D. BS in Journalism, Ohio State U., 1941; MBA, Harvard U., 1946. Mgr. sales promotion Seiberling Rubber Co., Akron, Ohio, 1946-48; account supr. Batten, Barton, Durstine & Osborn, Cleve., 1948-51; mgr. consumer advt. Monsanto Chem. Co., St. Louis, 1951-54; pres. Mumm, Mullay & Nichols, Advt. Agy., Columbus, 1954-59; v.p. Goodyear Tire and Rubber Co., Akron, 1959-84; communications consultant, 1984—. Lt. AUS, 1943-46. Mem. Assn. Nat. Advertisers (past chmn.), Advt. Coun. (past chmn. bd. dirs.). Republican. Roman Catholic. Home: 76240 Fairway Dr Indian Wells CA 92210-8822 E-mail: jpk240@msn.com.

KELLEY, JOSEPH E. career officer; BS, USAF Acad., 1974; MD, Rush U., 1977; student, Sch. Aerospace Medicine, Brooks AFB, Tex., 1984, Air Command and Staff Coll., 1986, Air War Coll., 1988, George Washington U., 1992; physician in mgmt. I, ACP Execs., Sheppard AFB, Tex., 1992, physician in mgmt. II, 1994, physician in mgmt. III, 1997. Diplomate Am. Bd. Surgery. Commd. capt. USAF, 1977, advanced through grades to brig. gen., 1997; intern then resident in gen. surgery David Grant Med. Ctr., Travis AFB, Calif., 1977-82; gen. surgeon then chief surgery Nellis USAF Hosp., Nellis AFB, Nev., 1982-84; chief hosp. svcs. Misawa USAF Hosp., Misawa Air Base, Japan, 1984-86; comdr. 90th Strategic Hosp., Francis E. Warren AFB, Wyo., 1986-89, 857th Strategic Hosp., Minot AFB, N.D., 1989-91, Fifth Med. Group, Minot AFB, 1991-92, Ehrling Bergquist Hosp., Offutt AFB, Nebr., 1992-93; chief med. resources, directorate med. programs/resources Office Air Force Surgeon Gen., Bolling AFB, D.C., 1993-95; command surgeon Pacific Air Forces, Hickam AFB, Hawaii, 1995-96; comdr. 74th Med. Group, Wright-Patterson AFB, Ohio, 1996—; lead agt. Dept. Def. Health Svc. Region 5, Wright-Patterson AFB, Ohio, 1996—. Air Force state faculty mem. course ATLS. Decorated Legion of Merit. Mem. ACP Execs., Soc. Med. Cons. Armed Forces. Office: 74 MDG/CC 4881 Sugar Maple Dr Wright Patterson Afb OH 45433-5546

KELLEY, KARL NEAL, psychology educator; b. Richmond, Va., Feb. 25, 1960; s. James Alexander and Margaret (Kirby) K.; m. Jaineen Jackson, May 9, 1986; 1 cchild, Maryemma. BS, Va. Commonwealth U., 1982, MS, 1985, PhD, 1987. Vis. asst. prof. U. Richmond, 1986-87; prof. psychology North Ctrl. Coll., Naperville, Ill., 1987—. Author: Perspectives in Industrial and Organizational Psychology, 2000. Mem. APA, Soc. for Indsl. and Orgnl. Psychology. Home: 517 Wingfoot Dr North Aurora IL 60542 Office: North Central Coll Dept Psycholoyg Naperville IL 60566 E-mail: knk@noctrl.edu.

KELLEY, KEVIN H. insurance company executive; b. Boston, Oct. 12, 1950; s. Hugh and Anne Kelley; m. Maryellen Moran; children: Meghan, Maura, Katherine. BS/BA, Boston U., 1972. CPCU. Trainee Fireman's Fund, Boston, 1973-75; exec. underwriter Lexington Ins. Co. (AIG), Boston, 1975-78, casualty mgr., 1979-83, exec. v.p., 1984-86, pres., 1987-97, chmn., CEO, 1997—. Roman Catholic. Office: Lexington Ins Co 200 State St Boston MA 02109-2677

KELLEY, LARRY DALE, retired army officer; b. Geary, Okla., Sept. 1, 1944; s. Cecil and Myrtle Irene (Burch) K.; m. Ellen Neeley; children: Sara M., Rebecca I., Lynette C., Stacey A. BS, Cameron U.; M in Criminal Justice, Okla. City U.; MBA, U. Okla. Enlisted U.S. Army, 1964, advanced through grades to lt. col., 1990, spl. forces officer, capt., 1964-79; ret., 1992; asst. sales mgr. Pacesetter Corp., Okla., 1980; acctg. mgr. Hertz Corp., Okla., 1981-84; systems mgr. U.S. Army, 1985-92; exec. dir. Sanctuary, Inc., 1994-95. Bd. dirs. Muskogee Fed. Credit Union. V.p. student senate Cameron U., Lawton, pres. student senate; pres. chpt. 32 Spl Forces Assn., chpt. 95 Res. Officers Assn., 1988. Decorated Bronze Star, Vietnamese Cross of Gallantry, Combat Infantryman's badge, Parachutist badge. Mem. VFW (life), DAV (life), Res. Officers Assn. (life), Ret. Officers Assn. (life), Spl. Forces Assn. Avocations: model railroading, geneal. rsch., travel.

KELLEY, MARGARET MARY, music educator, musician; b. Milw., Oct. 16, 1952; d. Thomas Crawford and Josephine (Kenney) K. BM, U. Iowa, 1975; MM, U. Idaho, 1978, MEd, 1979. Pianist, Pullman, Wash., 1980—; mem. piano faculty Lewis-Clark State Coll., Lewiston, Idaho, 1984-87, U. Idaho, 2001—. Performed as soloist, chamber, accompanist, 1971—; author: In Good Time: College, 2000, Getting There, 2001. Spay/neuter chair Humane Soc., Moscow, Idaho, 1996—, bd. dirs. 2000—, pres. bd. dir. 2001-. Mem. ACLU (bd. dirs. Pullman), Music Tchrs. Nat. Assn., Pullman Music Tchrs. (pres. 1982-83, 87-88, v.p. 1983-85, treas. 1990—), Amnesty Internat. Avocations: writing, running, swimming, reading. Home: 860 SW Alcora Dr Pullman WA 99163-2053

KELLEY, MARK ALBERT, physician, educator, health care executive; b. Boston, Oct. 31, 1947; s. Albert Joseph and Virginia Marie Kelley; m. Gail Riggs Kelley, Aug. 4, 1974; children: Christopher Riggs, Amy Morgan. AB, Harvard U., Cambridge, Mass., 1969; MD, Harvard U., Boston, 1973. Diplomate Am. Bd. Internal Medicine, Am. Bd. Pulmonary Disease, Am. Bd. Critical Care. Intern Hosp. U. Pa., Phila., 1973—74, resident, 1974—76, chief med. resident, 1977—78, fellow in pulmonary diseases, 1976—77; dir. pulmonary fellowship U. Pa., Phila., 1979—82, from asst. to assoc. prof. medicine, 1979—92, prof., 1992-2000; dir. pulmonary fellowship tng. program, 1979—82; vice chmn. med. U. Pa. Sch. Medicine, Phila., 1986—90; dir. pulmonary fellowship tng. program, 1979—82; assoc. chmn. clin. svcs., dir. med. residency tng. program, 1982—86; dir. faculty group practice, 1985—90; vice dean clin. affairs U. Pa. Sch. Medicine, Phila., 1990—99; chief of medicine Phla. VA Med. Ctr., 1999—2000; exec. v.p., chief med. officer, CEO Henry Ford Health Sys., Detroit, 2000—; fellow in pulmonary disease Hosp. U. Pa., Phila., 1978—79. Spkr. in field. Mem. editl. bd. Annals Internal Medicine, 1990—93, Critical Care Medicine, 1992—98. Fellow: ACP, Am. Coll. Chest Physicians; mem.: Am. Bd. Med. Specialties, Soc. Critical Care Medicine, Am. Bd. Internal Medicine (critical care medicine test com. 1988—93, chmn. 1990—93, bd. govs. 1990—98, exec. com. 1993—98, sec.-treas. 1994—96, chmn. 1997—98, sec.-treas. found. bd. 1999—2003, chmn. 2003—), Am. Thoracic Soc. (chmn. nat. manpower study 1996—2000, critical care work force project 2001—), Alpha Omega Alpha. Office: 1 Ford Pl Detroit MI 48202-3450

KELLEY, MARY ELIZABETH (MARY LAGRONE), information technology executive; b. Temple, Tex., Feb. 12, 1947; d. Harry John and Mary Erma (Windham) LaGrone; m. Roy Earl Kelley, May 10, 1968; children: Roy John, James Lewis, Joanna Marylu. BS, U. Mary Hardin-Baylor, 1968. Cert. tchr., Tex. Math tchr. Killeen (Tex.) High Sch., 1977-78; clk. typist Readiness Region VIII, Aurora, Colo., 1979; statis. clk. Fitzsimons Army Med. Ctr., Aurora, 1980-81, mgmt. asst., 1981-83; clk. typist Corpus Christi (Tex.) Army Depot, 1984; mgmt. asst. Health Care Studies and Clin. Investigation Act, Fort Sam Houston, Tex., 1984-85; computer programmer/analyst Health Care Systems Support Act, Fort Sam Houston, 1985-88, computer systems analyst, 1988-92, computer specialist, 1992-94, data base adminstr., 1994-96, Lotus Notes sys. adminstr., 1996-98; process integrator, asst. comdr. force integration U.S. Army Med. Dept. Ctr. and Sch., Fort Sam Houston, 1998-99, computer specialist, 1999—2002, info. tech. specialist, 2002—. Tchr. Fitzsimons Army Med. Ctr., 1978-79, cons., 1978-79. Author: (databases) Health Care Management System, 1988-94. Vol. Parents Encouraging Parents, Denver, 1979-83, Friends of Safe House, Denver, 1980-83, Heidi Search Ctr., San Antonio, 1990, Family Assistance Crisis Team, San Antonio Police Dept., 1997-99, Vols. in Policing, San Antonio Police Dept., 1998-99; founder Top of the HIll Residents' Alliance, San Antonio, 1997. Recipient achievement medal for civilian svc., Dept. Army, 1991. Mem. DAR, Daus. of Republic of Tex., United Daus. of Confederacy, Tex. Soc. of Mayflower Descs., Alpha Chi, Delta Psi Theta, Sigma Tau Delta, Alpha Phi. Roman Catholic. Avocations: reading, needlework, genealogy, Special Olympics, writing poetry.

KELLEY, MARYELLEN R. economist, management consultant; b. Boston, Apr. 26, 1951; d. Albert Francis and Agnes Mary (Athy) K.; m. Bennett Harrison, Jan. 25, 1981, (dec. Jan. 17, 1999). BA, Brandeis U., 1971; M in City Planning, Harvard U., 1976; PhD in Mgmt., MIT, 1984. Harman fellow Harvard U., Cambridge, 1982-83; asst. prof. mgmt. U. Mass., Boston, 1984-88; vis. asst. prof. mgmt. and pub. policy Carnegie Mellon U., Pitts., 1988-89, asst. prof. mgmt. and pub. policy, 1989-91, assoc. prof. mgmt. and pub. policy, 1991-97; sr. economist Nat. Inst. Standards and Tech., 1997—2000; prin. Pamet Hill Assocs., 2001—. Vis. scholar MIT Indsl. Performance Ctr., Cambridge, 1994—96; vis. assoc. prof. tech. policy dept. polit. sci. MIT, Cambridge, 1994—95. Contbr. articles to Scientific, Economic and Mgmt. jours. Dissertation fellow AAUW, 1981. Mem. AAAS, Acad. of Mgmt. Office: Pamet Hill Assocs PO Box 636 Truro MA 02666-0636 E-mail: Maryellen.Kelley@direcway.com.

KELLEY, MAURICE LESLIE, JR., gastroenterologist, educator; b. Indpls., June 29, 1924; s. Maurice Leslie and Martha (Daniel) K.; m. Carol J. Povec, Feb. 11, 1967; children: Elizabeth Ann, Mary Sarah. Student, U. Vt., Va. Poly. Inst., Princeton U., 1943-45; MD, U. Rochester, 1949. Intern, resident Strong Meml. Hosp., Rochester, N.Y., 1949-51, Bixby fellow in medicine, 1953-56, fellow in gastroenterology Mayo Clinic, Rochester, Minn., 1957-59; asst. prof. medicine U. Rochester, 1959-64, assoc. prof., 1964-67; practice medicine specializing in gastroenterology Rochester, N.Y., 1959-67; assoc. prof. clin. medicine Dartmouth Med. Sch., 1967-74, prof. clin. medicine, 1974-88; chmn. sect. internal medicine Hitchcock Clinic, 1972-74, chmn. sect. gastroenterology, 1974, 88; prof. medicine emeritus Dartmouth Med. Sch., 1988—; mem. staff Strong Meml. Hosp., Hitchcock Clinic, Mary Hitchcock Meml. Hosp. Cons. Canandaigua VA, Rochester Gen., Genesee hosps., VA. Med. Ctr., White River Junction. Contbr. articles to profl. jours., chpts. to books. Served with AUS, 1942-45; M.C. USAF, 1951-53. Fellow ACP (gov. for N.H. 1974-78, Laureate award 1993), Am. Gastroenterol. Assn.; mem. Am. Soc. Gastrointestinal Endoscopy, AMA (chmn. sect. gastroenterology 1970-71), Am. Physiol. Soc., Alpha Omega Alpha. Avocations: sports cars, cinema. Home: 15 Ledge Rd Hanover NH 03755-1612 Office: Dartmouth-Hitchcock Med Ctr 1 Medical Center Dr Lebanon NH 03756-0002

KELLEY, MICHAEL GARHART ROOSEVELT, historian, educator, writer; b. Cambridge, Mass., July 25, 1943; s. John Joseph Kelley and Elisabeth Ann Garhart. BA in History magna cum laude, Boston U., 1966, MA in History, 1967; PhD in Scottish History, U. Edinburgh, Scotland, 1973. Prof. history, chair history dept. Blackburn Coll., Carlinville, Ill., 1974—85; vis. prof. U. San Francisco, 1983—84, Calif. Poly. State U., San Luis Obispo, Calif., 1987—88; chmn. dept. history Utah State U., Roosevelt/Vernal, 1989—97. Accreditation team mem. North Ctrl. Coll. Assn., Ill., 1978—79; founding assoc. editor The Outlaw Trail Jour., 1991. Contbr. Charter mem. Outlaw Trail Assn., Utah, 1991; bd. dirs. Macoupin County Mental Health, Carlinville, 1980—85; bd. advisors Am. Biog. Inst., Raleigh, 1994—; dir. Am. Bicentennial, Carlinville, 1976; bd. dirs. 150th Hist. Anniversary, Macoupin County, 1979. Fellow Postgrad. fellow, U. Edinburgh, 1970—72, Midwest Faculty fellow, U. Chgo., 1979, Summer fellow, NEH, 1980. Fellow: Dutch Settlers Soc. of Albany (life), Internat. Biog. Assn. (life), The Augustan Soc. (life). Roman Catholic. Avocations: local and regional history, environmentalist, politics. Home: Apt 111 1008 Larkin St San Francisco CA 94109

KELLEY, MICHAEL JAMES, medical services executive, author; m. Linda. BS, Fla. Atlantic U., 1976, MBA, 1980. Advisor to prime minister Turks and Caicos Islands, Brit. West Indies, 1978-79; chief adminstr. Ft. Lauderdale (Fla.) Eye Inst., 1980-87; v.p. Ambassador Real Estate Equities Corp., Tamarac, Fla., 1984-89, also bd. dirs.; exec. v.p. Ambassador Fin. Group Inc., Tamarac, Fla., 1985-89; exec. dir. Retina Consultants Southwest Fla., Ft. Myers, 1990—2000; CEO Vision Rehab. Strategies, Ft. Myers, 1994—2000; CFO, bd.dirs. Lifevision, 1996—2000; exec. dir. Carter Eye Ctr., Dallas, 2000—. Mem.: AAO Network for Adminstrs. (chmn. 1998—2000), Fla. Atlantic U. Alumni Assn. (bd. dirs. 1989—93), Med. Group Mgmt. Assn. (exec. com. 1994—98, OA pres. 1996). Avocations: skiing, boating. Office: Ste 700 7502 Greenville Dallas TX 75231

KELLEY, MICHAEL JOHN, newspaper editor; b. Kansas City, Mo., July 5, 1942; s. Robert Francis and Grace Lauretta (Schofield) K.; 1 child, Anne Schofield BA, Rockhurst Coll., 1964. Reporter, polit. writer Kansas City Star & Times, 1960-69; asst. Sen. Thomas F. Eagleton, Washington, 1969-76; pres. Swensen's Midwest, Inc., Kansas City, 1976-80; exec. asst. Ctrl. States Pension Fund, Chgo., 1981-83, 85-87; asst. mng. editor Kansas City Times, 1984; editor The Daily Southtown, Chgo., 1987-97; mng. editor Las Vegas (Nev.) Sun, 1997—. Office: Las Vegas Sun 2275 Corporate Cir Henderson NV 89074

KELLEY, PATRICIA, marketing representative; b. Carrollton, Ga., Jan. 21, 1953; BA in Journalism, Ga. State U., 1974; BSN, West Ga. Coll., 1990. RN Fla. Pub. rels. asst. Grady Meml. Hosp., Atlanta, 1974-77; editorial asst. Childers & Sullivan, Huntsville, Ala., 1977-78; sales rep. AAA Employment Agy., Huntsville, 1978-80; editor Wright Pub. Co., Atlanta, 1980-82; elect./electronic drafter PRC Cons., Atlanta, 1980-87; researcher Dept. Nursing at West Ga. Coll., Carrollton, 1989-90; med./surg. nurse Tanner Med. Ctr., Carrollton, Ga., 1989-90, Delray Community Hosp., Delray Beach, Fla., 1990-91; sales rep. Innovative Med. Svcs., 1991-94; with staff devel., employee rels. Beverly Oaks Rehab. and Nursing Ctr., 1994-95; sales rep./pub. rels. rep. Columbia HCA, Melbourne, Fla., 1996-99; bus. writer/pub. rels. cons. Cocoa Beach, Fla., 2000—. Vol. Project Response, Brevard County Sexual Assault Victim Svcs. All-Am. scholar U.S. Achievement Acad., 1990, recipient Nat. Coll. Nursing award, 1989. Mem. NOW, Space Coast Bus. Writer's Guild, Omicron Delta Kappa. Democrat. Home: 768 Beacon St Palm Bay FL 32907

KELLEY, PATRICIA LOU, social work educator; b. Mpls., Jan. 11, 1935; d. Oral Robert and Gladys (Alexander) Neal; m. Verne Robert Kelley, Aug. 20, 1960; children: Elizabeth, Carolyn. BA, Carleton Coll., 1956; MSW, U. Minn., 1959; PhD, U. Iowa, 1981. Lic. social worker, Iowa; bd. cert. diplomate in clin. social work. Caseworker Family Service Agy., Milw., 1959-60, Cedar Rapids,

Iowa, 1962-65; clin. social worker Mental Health Ctr., Spencer, Iowa, 1967-70; psychiat. social worker U. Iowa, Iowa City, 1960-62, asst. dir. psychology tng. clinic, 1970-75, asst. prof. social work, 1975-81, assoc. prof., 1981-93, prof., 1993—, dir. Sch. of Social Work, 1994-98; pvt. practice Iowa City, 1975—91. Cons. Mental Health Ctr., Iowa City, 1972-74, VA Hosp., Knoxville, Iowa, 1979-81, St. Lukes Hosp., Cedar Rapids, Iowa, 1988-92, Family Resources, Davenport, Iowa, 1991-93; supr. family therapy tng. program Menniger Found., Des Moines, 1982-85; vis. scholar U. South Australia, 1991; vis. prof. Wilfrid Laurier U., Waterloo, Ont., 1993; named to State Bd. Social Work Examiners, Iowa, 1993; vis. lecr. divsn. continuing edn. City U. Hong Kong, 2003, U. Iceland, 2003; testified U.S. Senate Sub-com. on Family, Children and Alcohol, 1987. Author: Uses of Writing in Psychotherapy, 1990, Developing Health Stop-families, 1995; mem. editl. bd.: Jour. Ind. Social Work, 1985—90, Jour. Personal and Interpersonal Loss, 1995—, cons. editor: Social Devel. Issues, 1996—; editor: Jour. of Brief Therapy, 2001—; contbr. articles to profl. jours. Dem. committeeman, Iowa City, 1980-84; bd. dirs. Johnson County United Way, Iowa City, 1982-88. Vis. scholar Sch. Social Studies U. South Australia, 1991; hon. fellow Flinders U., Adelaide, 1999; Consortium of Internat. Assns. grantee Mid-West U., 1982; Old Gold fellow U. Iowa, 1982; Internat. Travel grantee, 1994, 95, 99, 2003; Lois and Samuel Silberman Fund--N.Y. Cmty. Trust awardee, 1999; U. Iowa Spelman Rockefeller grantee, 2000; Iowa State Dept. Edn. grantee, 2000, 2001, 2002. Mem. Am. Assn. Marriage and Family Therapy (pres Iowa div. 1986-88, Nat. Divisional Svc. award 1992), Nat. Assn. Social Workers (del. Nat. Assembley 1981), Council on Social Work Edn., Nat. Acad. Cert. Social Workers. Democratic. Unitarian. Home: 376 Koser Ave Iowa City IA 52246-3038 Office: U Iowa Sch Social Work Iowa City IA 52242 E-mail: patricia-kelley@uiowa.edu.

KELLEY, PATRICK ALAN, neurologist, educator; b. Hinsdale, Ill., Sept. 24, 1947; s. Joseph John and Carol (Obalil) K.; m. Anne Nancy Trifilo, Feb. 22, 1975 (div. Aug. 1979). BA, Knox Coll., 1969; MD, Loyola U., Maywood, Ill., 1973. Diplomate Am. Bd. Psychiatry and Neurology. Resident in neurology Tufts U., Boston, 1974-77; asst. clin. prof. U. Conn., Farmington, 1977-79, U. Tenn., Chattanooga, 1979-88; staff neurologist Group Health Assn., Washington, 1988-94; chmn. dept. neurology Humana Group Health Plan, Washington, 1991-97; asst. clin. prof. George Washington U., Washington, 1988—; staff neurologist Kaiser Permanente, Kensington, Md., 1997—. Neurol. cons., Washington Hosp. Ctr., 1988—, Meml. Hosp., Chattanooga, 1979-88; clin. instr. neurology, Northeastern U., Boston, 1976-77. Author: Clinical Medicine: Selected Problems with Pathophysiologic Correlations, 1988. Candidate for Ho. of Dels., Gen. Assembly of Commonwealth of Va., 1999; mem. Pres.'s club Rep. Nat. Com., Washington, 1996—. Fellow Am. Acad. Neurology; mem. AMA (Physician Recognition award 1998), Am. Epilepsy Soc., Am. Med. EEG Assn., Med. Soc. Va., Phi Beta Kappa. Republican. Roman Catholic. Avocations: collecting original french impressionist prints, collecting editions of thomas jefferson's work. E-mail: PAKIrishmD@aol.com.

KELLEY, PAUL LEWIS, retired educator; b. Englewood, Tenn., Jan. 13, 1928; s. Lewis Edgar Kelley and Iva Pearl Webb; m. Norma Anne Sawyer, Dec. 21, 1958; children: Michael, John. BS, Tenn. Poly. Inst., 1949; MA, Northwestern U., 1955; EdD, U. Tenn., Knoxville, 1971. Tchr. Christenberry Jr. H.S., Knoxville, 1949-59, Fulton H.S., Knoxville, 1959-65; prin. South H.S., Knoxville, 1965-70, West H.S., Knoxville, 1971-73; asst. supt. Knoxville City Schs., 1973-82; prof. edn. Knoxville Coll., 1983-94; ret. Author: Historic Fort Loudoun, 1958. Pres. Knoxville Tchrs. League, 1958-60, Child and Family Svcs., Knoxville, 1967-68, Ft. Loudoun Assn., Knoxville, 1982-84; mem. Knox County Bd. Edn., Knoxville, 1991—. Cpl. U.S. Army, 1950-52. Recipient Silver Beaver award Boy Scouts Am., 1983. Mem. Tenn. Sch. Bd. Assn., Phi Delta Kappa. Republican. Methodist. Avocations: reading, gardening, hiking. Home: 1009 E Churchwell Ave Knoxville TN 37917-4422 E-mail: kelley1928@aol.com.

KELLEY, REBECCA CROUSE (REBECCA ANN KELLEY), lawyer, academic administrator, not-for-profit fundraiser; b. Balt., June 13, 1971; d. Harry Thomas Crouse and Barbara Jean Young; m. Michael A. Kelley, Apr. 23, 1999. BA in Polit. Sci. with honors, Goucher Coll., 1993; JD, U. Cin., 1997. Bar: Ohio 1997. Tchr. acad. and h.s. God's Bible Sch. and Coll., Cin., 1993-94, dir. instnl. law, 1994-97, dir. devel., 1997-99, Urban League of Greater Cin., 1998-99, v.p. devel. and strategic imperatives, 1999-2000; dir. planned giving and grants YMCA of Greater Cin., 2000—02, dir. fin. devel., 2002—. Adj. prof. God's Bible Sch. and Coll. Cin., 2001—. Author (monthly column) God's Revivalist & Bible Advocate, 1997, 98. Trustee Goucher Coll., Towson, Md., 1993-96; bd. dirs., sec. Burlington (Ky.) Bible Method, 1994-97; vol. Tenant Info. Project, 1994-95, Vol. Income Tax Asst., Cin., 1995; bd. dirs. Neighborhood Health Care, Inc., 2002—; pres. Mt. Auburn Cmty. Coun., Cin., 1996-98; sec., treas. Sustainable Cin. Project; pres. Greater Cin. Grant Seekers Network. Mem. Assn. Fundraising Profls., Ohio State Bar Assn., Cin. Bar Assn., Greater Cin. Planned Giving Coun. (bd. dirs. 2002—), Assn. of Profl. Dirs. of YMCAs, N.Am. YMCA Devel. Assn. Avocations: piano, reading, writing, travel. Home: 830 Sunderland Dr Cincinnati OH 45255-4519 Office: YMCA of Greater Cin 1105 Elm St Cincinnati OH 45202 E-mail: rkelley@cincinnatiymca.org, rkelley4@cinci.rr.com.

KELLEY, RICHARD ALLEN, JR., software engineer; b. San Diego, Calif, Sept. 16, 1954; s. Richard Allen and Hilja Jean (Cooke) K.; m. Laura Jean Carlson, Mar. 20, 1976. BS in Math., U. Wash., 1979. Assoc. tech. fellow The Boeing Co., Seattle, 1980—. Newsletter editor Friends of Snoqualmie Valley, Snoqualmie, Wash., 1987-88. With U.S. Army, 1973-75. Mem. Assn. for Computing Machinery. Lutheran. Avocations: hiking, horseback riding. Home: 22410 Hobson Rd SE Yelm WA 98597-8926

KELLEY, RICHARD ROY, hotel executive; b. Honolulu, Dec. 28, 1933; s. Roy Cecil and Estelle Louise (Foote) K.; m. Jane Zieber, June 2l, l955 (dec. l978); children: Elizabeth, Kathryn, Charles, Linda J., Mary Colleen; m. Linda Van Gilder, June 23, 1979; children: Christopher Van Gilder, Anne Marie. BA, Stanford U., 1955; MD, Harvard U., 1960. Pathologist Queen's Med. Ctr., Honolulu, 1962-70, Kapiolani Maternity Hosp., Honolulu, l96l-70; asst. prof. pathology John A. Burns Med. Sch., U. Hawaii, Honolulu, 1968-70; chmn. bd. Outrigger Enterprises, Honolulu. Bd. dirs. First Hawaiian Bank, Outrigger Internat. Travel, Inc. Former trustee, past chmn. Punahou Sch.; dean's adv. bd. Travel Industry Mgmt. Sch., U. Hawaii; former vice-dean Ednl. Inst. AH & MA Pres.'s Acad. Bd. Regents; former chmn. bd. councilors Hawaii Pacific divsn. Am. Cancer Soc., past chmn. commn. on performance stds. State of Hawaii; trustee Kent-Denver Sch., Craig Hosp., Denver. Named Marketer of Yr., Am. Mktg. Assn., 1985, Communicator of Yr., Internat. Bus. Communicators, 1987, Salesperson of Yr., Sales & Mktg. Execs. Honolulu, 1995; named to Hawaii Bus. Hall of Fame, 1993; recipient Hope award Multiple Sclerosis Soc., 1995, Ihe award Hawwaii Army Mus. Soc., 2000, Lifetime Achievement award Nat. Assn. Indsl. and Office Properties, 2003. Mem.: World Travel and Tourism Coun., World Pres.'s Orgn., Pacific Asia Travel Assn., Japan Hawaii Econ. Coun., Chief Execs. Orgn., Hawaii Visitors Bur. (bd. dirs., chmn. 1991—92). Office: Outrigger Hotels & Resorts 2375 Kuhio Ave Honolulu HI 96815-2992 E-mail: richard.kelley@outrigger.com.

KELLEY, ROBERT OTIS, medical science educator; b. Santa Monica, Calif., Apr. 30, 1944; s. David Otis and Onetia May (Nettles) K.; m. Marcia Jean Bell; children: Jennifer Leigh, Karin Michelle, Matthew Philip, Sarah Ann. BS, Abilene Christian U., 1965; MA, U. Calif., Berkeley, 1966, PhD, 1969. Asst. prof. U. N.Mex. Sch. of Medicine, Albuquerque, 1969-74, assoc. prof., 1974-79, prof., 1979—; chmn. dept. anatomy U. N.Mex. Sch. Medicine, Albuquerque, 1981-97; assoc. vice chancellor rsch., exec. dean grad. coll. U. Ill., Chgo., 1997-99; dean Coll. Health Scis., U. Wyo., 1999—. Vis. scientist Okazaki (Japan) Nat. Labs., 1984-85; mem. study sect. NIH, Bethesda, Md., 1982-86, U.S. Med. Licensing Exam. Step 1, 1995—; anatomy com. Nat. Bd. mex. Examiners, Phila., 1992—. Author: Basic Histology, 1989; editor Cell and Tissue Rsch., 1970—, Anat. Record, 1970-97; contbr. articles to profl. jours. Patroller Nat. Ski Patrol, 1970—. Recipient Rsch. Career Devel. award NIH, 1972-77, Kaiser award U. Calif., Irvine, 1976; Internat. Exch. Scholar NSF; NIH grantee, 1970— Fellow Am. Socs. for Exptl. Biology (pub. affairs exec. com. 1993—), Am. Soc. Cell Biology, Soc. for Devel. Biology, Electron Microscopy Soc. Am. (bd. dirs. 1987—), Am. Assn. Anatomists (exec. com. 1988—), Assn. Am. Med. Colls. (exec. coun. 1995—, chair assembly 1997-99), Nat. Caucus of Basic Biomed. Sci. Chairs, Nat. Bd. Med. Examiners. Democrat. Protestant. Avocations: sailing, skiing, soaring, scuba diving, backpacking. Address: 1162 Granito Dr Laramie WY 82072-5027 Office: U Wyo PO Box 3432 Laramie WY 82071-3432

KELLEY, ROBERT PAUL, JR., management consultation executive; b. Mansfield, Ohio, Mar. 27, 1942; s. Robert Paul and Rachel Marie Kelley; m. Mimi Grant, June 15, 1975; children: Robert, Laura, Elizabeth. BBA, Notre Dame U., 1964; MBA, Harvard U., 1969. Corp. devel. exec. Holly Sugar Corp., 1969-70; mktg. cons., supr. Laventhol & Horwath, L.A., 1972-73; dir. mktg., entertainment and mdsg. Knott's Berry Farm, Buena Park, Calif., 1974-76; sr. v.p. mktg. Am. Warranty Corp., L.A., 1978-80; co-founder Gen. Group of Cos., 1981; CEO Strategy Network Corp., 1976—. CEO So. Calif. Tech. Exec. Network, 1985—; co-founder, CEO ABL Health Care Exec. Network, 1989-91; chmn. bd. Micro Frame Tech., Inc., 1990-95, chmn. emeritus, 1995-2000; chmn. bd. ABL Orgn., 1991—; chmn., CEO Quickstart Tech., 1993-94; chmn, bd. V-Systems, Inc., 1994-99; mem. adv. bd. Westec Security Group, 1996-99; mem. adv. bd. Impac Tech., Inc., 1998-99; chmn. bd. dir. Upstanding Sys., Inc., 1999-2003; chmn. bd. dir. China Mfg. Network, 2003. Author:: The Board of Directors and its Role in Growing Companies, 1984, Break-Through Boards of Directors, 1999; co-author: Better Than Money Resource Capitalism, 1993. Served with USNR, 1964-67. Home: 6004 E West View Dr Orange CA 92869-4314 Office: 930 W Town and Country Rd Orange CA 92868-4714

KELLEY, ROBERT SUMA, network engineer; b. Chgo., July 2, 1961; s. Jerry Dean and Jean (Laine) K.; m. Melissa Ann Beacham, Aug. 15, 1999. BA in Philosophy, Western Md. Coll., 1985; MBA in MIS, Ind. U., 1989. Human resource specialist Marriott Corp., Gaithersburg, Md., 1985-86; mgr. in tng. Courtyard by Marriott, Fairfax, Va., 1986-87; sys. analyst Hewlett-Packard, Palo Alto, Calif., 1989-98, network engr. Sunnyvale, Calif., 1998—. Mem. adv. com. for implementation of Calif. Assembly bill for improving edn. opportunities for learning disabled children, 1991-94. Counselor Camp Allen for the Physically Handicapped, Manchester, N.H., 1977; track coach for disadvantaged youth Rockville (Md.) Recreation, 1980. Avocation: endurance horseback riding. Office: Agilent Techs 5301 Stevens Creek Blvd Santa Clara CA 95051-7201 Mailing: 8 Camellia Ct East Palo Alto CA 94303

KELLEY, ROBIN D. G. education educator, writer; b. New York, NY, Mar. 14, 1962; B, Calif. State Long Beach, 1980—83; D, UCLA, 1983—87. Assoc. prof. U. of Mich., 1991—95; prof. NYU, NYC, 1995—. Chair of history dept. NYU, 2002—. Author: (book) Freedom Dreams: The Black Radical Imagination, Yo' Mama's Disfunktional!: Fighting the Culture Wars in Urban America (best book of 1997 by Village Voice; outstanding book on human rights, Gustavus Myers Ctr. for the Study of human rights in the US, 1997-99, 1997), Race Rebels: Culture, Politics, and the Black Working Class (outstanding book, Nat. Conf. of Black Polit. Scientists, 1995), Hammer and Hoe: Alabama Communists During the Great Depression (Elliot Rudwick prize, orgn. of Am. Historians, 1991; co-winner, Francis Butler Simkins prize, So. Hist. Assn., 1991); editor: To Make Our World Anew: A History of African Americans (history book club; choice outstanding academic title; outstanding book on human rights, Gustavus Myers Ctr., 2001). Adv. bd. mem. North Star Fund, NYC, 1999—2002; bd. mem. Am. Social History Project, NYC, 1997—2002, Davis-Putter Scholarship Fund, Boston, 1995—2002, NY Workers Rights Bd., NYC, 1998—2003; exec. bd. mem. Soc. of Am. Historians, NYC, 2002—03. Recipient ABC Clio award, Orgn. of Am. Historians, 1995; Ctr. for Advanced Study in the Behavioral Sciences, Stanford U., 1997—98, Montgomery fellowship, Dartmouth Coll., 2000, 2002, Schomburg Scholars-in-Residence fellowship, NY Pub. Libr., 2000—01. Office: New York University 53 Washington Square South New York NY 10012 Home Fax: 212-995-4017; Office Fax: 212-995-4017. Personal E-mail: robin.kelley@nyu.edu. E-mail: robin.kelley@nyu.edu.

KELLEY, SHEILA SEYMOUR, public relations consultant; b. Bronxville, N.Y. d. William Joseph and Jane (Seymour) K.; m. Robert Max Kaufman, 1959. BA magna cum laude, Syracuse U., 1949. Reporter Yonkers Herald Statesman, N.Y.C., 1950; reporter, editor Close Up column Herald Tribune, N.Y.C., 1950-53; writer, producer Sta. WNBC-TV, N.Y.C., 1953-54; media cons. to Senator Jacobs K. Javits, N.Y.C., 1956-74, press sec. Washington, 1958-61; account supr., v.p. Harshe Rotman Druck, N.Y.C., 1961-76; founder, pres. VOTES, Inc., N.Y.C., 1973-75; v.p. Doremus Pub. Rels., N.Y.C., 1976-86, sr. v.p., 1987-90, exec. v.p., 1990, Gavin Anderson & Co., N.Y.C., 1990-96, sr. counselor, 1996-97; prin. The Dilenschneider Group, N.Y.C., 1997—. Mem.: Women Execs. in Pub. Rels. (pres. 1987—88, dir. found. 1999—, bd. dirs. 2003), Pub. Rels. Soc. Am. (accredited), Hon. Order Ky. Cols., Phi Beta Kappa. Republican. Avocations: skiing, golf, gardening. E-mail: sbskk@aol.com.

KELLEY, SYLVIA JOHNSON, financial services firm executive; b. Butte, Mont., Dec. 29, 1929; d. John O. and Hilja W. (Koski) J.; m. Dan H. Kelley, June 1, 1950 (div. Jan. 1973); children: David D., Bruce J., Sheila K. Miller, Kathleen Kelley; m. Richard T. Marshall, June 10, 1979. CLU; ChFC; cert. fin. planner; registered fin. cons.; cert. sr. advisor. Legal sec. various law firms, L.A., 1959-69; registered rep. Met. Life, N.Y.C., 1969-75, SMA Equities, Inc., Worcester, Mass., 1975-89, Multi-Fin. Securities Corp., Denver, 1989—2003; pres., CEO Geneos Advance Funding, Inc., El Paso, Tex., 1981—; registered rep. Geneos Wealth Mgmt. Co., 2003—. Contbr. articles to profl. jours. Bd. dirs., chmn. bus. adv. com. Marina Del Rey C. of C., 1974-75; bd. dirs., pub. rels. chmn. Am. Heart Assn., El Paso, 1972-74; charter pres. El Paso Exec. Women's Coun., 1972-73; mem. fin. adv. com. El Paso C.C., 1992-95; bd. dirs., past pres. El Paso Estate Planning Coun., 1993-2001. Mem. Am. Soc. CLUs and ChFC (past pres. El Paso chpt., bd. dirs. 1981-85), Registry of CFP Practitioners (cert. sr. advisor). Avocations: contract bridge, ballroom dancing, international travel, photography. Office: Advance Funding Inc 5959 Gateway Blvd W Ste 250 El Paso TX 79925-3316

KELLEY, VIRGINIA WIARD (JUDY KELLEY), dance educator; b. Washington, Nov. 17, 1937; d. David Kyle and Mary Margaret (Barber) Wiard; m. Leo Gilbert Kelley, July 2, 1960; children: Cheryl, Raymond, John, Brenda. Degree in bus. adminstrn., Miller-Motte Bus. Coll., 1958; dance edn. degree, Kent State U., 1986. Grad. Dance Masters of Am. Performer Tony Grant Stars of Tomorrow, Atlantic City, N.J., 1951-53; performer Cressetts Betty Cress Dance Studio, tour of East Coast, 1958, Jacksonville, N.C., 1958-59; instr., performer, choreographer Cuppett's Performing Arts Ctr., Vienna, Va., 1981-99, Vienna Comty. Ctr., 1982-99. Actress Wilmington (N.C.) Theatrical Soc., 1957; performer Miss Wilmington Pageant, 1958. Helper Dem. Party, Vienna, 1992. Named Ms. Senior N.C., 2000. Mem. Dance Masters of Am. (dance educator 1981—), Cameo Club. Democrat. Roman Catholic. Avocations: tap dancing, weight lifting, line dancing, swimming. Home: 1207 Brougham Dr Wilmington NC 28412-7203 Fax: 910-792-6886. E-mail: traintap@aol.com.

KELLEY, WAYNE PLUMBLEY, JR., retired federal official; b. Rochester, N.Y., May 23, 1933; s. Wayne Plumbley and Elspeth Barbour (Moore) K.; m. Margaret Mary Ruikka, June 22, 1964; children: Wayne Plumbley, Richard Daniel. BA, Vanderbilt U., 1955. City editor, state capitol reporter Chronicle, Augusta, Ga., 1960-65; Washington corr., reporter Atlanta Jour., 1965-69; assoc. editor Congl. Quar. Inc., Washington, 1969-72, mng. editor, 1972-74, exec. editor, 1974-80, pub., 1980-90, exec. v.p., 1984-90; supt. documents Govt. Printing Office, Washington, 1991-97; ret., 1997. Mem. adv. com. Am. U. Sch. Comms., 1985-90. Served with U.S. Army, 1956-57. Recipient James Madison award, Coalition on Govt. Info., 1998; Nieman fellow, Harvard U., 1963—64. Mem. Am. Polit. Sci. Assn. (Congl. fellowship adv. com. 1975-90)

KELLEY, WILLIAM NIMMONS, physician, educator, science administrator, dean; b. Atlanta, June 23, 1939; s. Oscar Lee and Willa Nimmons (Allen) Kelley; m. Lois Faville, Aug. 1, 1959; children: Margaret Paige, Virginia Lynn, Lori Ann, William Mark. MD, Emory U., 1963; MA (hon.), U. Pa., 1989. Diplomate Am. Bd. Internal Medicine (chmn. 1985-1986). Intern in medicine Parkland Meml. Hosp., Dallas, 1963—64, resident, 1964—65; sr. resident medicine Mass. Gen. Hosp., Boston, 1967—68; clin. asso., sect. on human biochem. genetics NIH, 1965—67; teaching fellow medicine Harvard U. Med. Sch., 1967—68; asst. prof. to prof. medicine, asst. prof. to asso. prof. biochemistry, chief div. rheumatic and genetic diseases Duke U. Sch. Medicine, 1968—75; Macy faculty scholar Oxford U., 1974—75; prof., chmn. dept. internal medicine, prof. dept. biol. chemistry U. Mich. Med. Sch., Ann Arbor, 1975—89; Robert G. Dunlop prof. medicine, biochemistry and biophysics U. Pa., Phila., 1989—2000, dean Sch. Medicine, 1989—2000; CEO U. Pa. Med. Ctr. and Health System, Phila., 1989—2000; prof., 2000—. Human gene therapy subcom. NIH, 1986—92, recombinant DNA com., 1988—92, dirs. adv. com., 1992—95; bd. dirs. Merck & Co., Beckman Coulter, Inc., Advanced Biosurfaces, GenVec, Inc. Author (with J.B. Wyngaarden): Gout and Hyperuricemia, 1976; author: (with I.M. Weiner) Uric Acid, 1979; author: (with Harris, Ruddy and Sledge) Textbook of Rheumatology, 1981, 5th edit., 1997, Arthritis Surgery, 1994; author: (with M. Osterweis and E.R. Rubin) Emerging Policies for Bio-Medical Research (Health Policy Annual III), 1993; editor-in-chief: Textbook of Internal Medicine, 1989, Textbook of Internal Medicine, 3rd edit., 1997, Essentials of Internal Medicine, 1994; contbr. articles to profl. jours. Trustee Emory U., 1992—, Emory U., Woodruff Health Scis. Ctr. Recipient C.V. Mosby award, 1963, John D. Lane award, USPHS, 1969, Rsch. Career Devel. award, 1972—75, Geigy Internat. prize rheumatology, 1969, Heinz Karger Meml. Found. prize, 1973, Disting. Med. Achievement award, Emory U., 1985, John Phillips Meml. award and medal, ACP, 1990, Nat. Med. Rsch. award, Nat. Health Coun., 1993, Robert H. Williams award, Assn. Profs. of Medicine, 1995, David E. Rogers award, Assn. Am. Med. Coll., 1999, Emory medal, 2000; scholar, Mead Johnson, 1967, Josiah Macy Found., 1974—75; Clin. scholar, Am. Rheumatism Assn., 1969—72. Master: ACP; fellow: AAAS, Am. Coll. Rheumatology, Am. Philos. Soc., Am. Acad. Arts and Scis.; mem.: Assn. Profs. Medicine (sec.-treas. 1987—89), Am. Soc. Internal Medicine, Am. Soc. Human Genetics, Ctrl. Rheumatism Soc. (pres. 1978—79), Australian Rheumatism Assn. (hon.), Royal Coll. Physicians Ireland (hon.), Am. Coll. Rheumatology (editl. bd. 1972—77, pres. 1986—87, Gold Medal award 1997), Assn. Am. Physicians (sec.-treas. 1987—89), Am. Fedn. Med. Rsch. (pres. 1979—81), Am. Soc. Biochemistry and Molecular Biology (editl. bd. 1976—81), Am. Soc. Clin. Investigation (editl. bd. 1974—79, pres. 1983—84), Inst. Medicine of NAS (chmn. sect. 4 1988—90, chmn. membership com. 1990—94, coun. mem., exec. com. 1996—2001), Ctrl. Soc. for Clin. Rsch. (pres. 1986—87), Alpha Omega Alpha, Sigma Xi. Home: 768 Woodleave Rd Bryn Mawr PA 19010-1709 Office: Univ of Pa Health Sys 757 Biomed Rsch Bldg II/III Philadelphia PA 19104 E-mail: kelleyw@hotmail.com.

KELLEY-HALL, MARYON HOYLE, retired social worker; b. Anderson, Ind., Aug. 5, 1924; d. Arthur Dent and Mildred Madeline (Hall) Hoyle; m. Dean M. Kelley, June 8, 1946; 1 child, Lenore Wadsworth Hervey; m. Richard A. Hall, Oct. 14, 2000. AB, U. Denver, 1945; MSW, Columbia U., 1967. Psychiat. social worker Rockland State Hosp., Orangeburg, N.Y., 1963-67, psychiat. social work supr., 1967-70; dir. social svcs. Rockland Children's Psychiat. Ctr., Orangeburg, 1970—72, chief child care svc., 1972—73; chief children's habilitation svc. Suffolk Devel. Ctr., Melville, NY, 1974—79; med. social worker Suffolk County Health Svcs., Hauppauge, NY, 1983-89; med. social work supr. Brentwood (N.Y.) Family Health Ctr., 1990—93. Home: 800 S 15th St # I-869 Sebring OH 44672

KELLGREN, GEORGE LARS, manufacturing company executive; b. Boras, Sweden, May 23, 1943; came to U.S., 1979; s. Lars Anders and Ann-Marie (Fröberg) Kjellgren; m. Rubi Caridad Godoy, Nov. 6, 1982; children: Adrian Anders, Derek Lars, Viveka Victoria. BS, Umea U., Sweden, 1967. Researcher, developer Husqvarna (Sweden) Arms Factory, Husquarna, 1968; tech. officer Council for Sci. and Industrial Research, Pretoria, Republic of South Africa, 1969-74; mng. dir. Interdynamic Forsknings AB, Stockholm, 1975-79; tech. dir. Intratec U.S.A., Inc., Miami, 1979-83; pres. Grendel, Inc., Cocoa, Fla., 1983-95; CEO Kel-Tec CNC Industries, Inc., Cocoa, 1995—. Contbr. articles to profl. jours.; inventor firearms. Republican. Lutheran.

KELLIHER, RICHARD JAMES, psychologist; b. Evanston, Ill., Jan. 3, 1946; MA, Bradley U., 1975; D of Psychology, Ill. Sch. Prof. Psychology, 1988. Lic. psychologist, Calif. Founder, dir. A Ctr. for Cognitive Therapy, Santa Barbara, Calif., 1990—. With U.S. Army, 1968-75. Mem. Am. Psychol. Assn., Calif. Psychol. Assn., Internat. Assn. Cognitive Therapy, Internat. Assn. Psychoanalytic Psychotherapy. Office: A Ctr for Cognitive Therapy 22 W Mission St Ste C Santa Barbara CA 93101-2450 E-mail: Dr_Richard@compuserve.com.

KELLING, GEORGE HORTON, retired military officer; b. St. Louis, Mo., Dec. 7, 1937; s. Jordan Albert and Ruth Carolyn Kelling; m. Betty Marie Wilson, Dec. 21, 1958; children: George Albert, Mary Ann Jennings. BA, Westminster Coll., 1958; MA, Trinity U., 1980; PhD, U. Tex., 1988. Cert. Spanish linguist. Commd. 2d lt. U.S. Army, 1958, leader med. unit small unit 24th Infantry Divsn., 1959—62; mil. med. adminstr. William Beaumont Gen. Hosp., El Paso, Tex., 1962—65; med. co. exec. officer 1st Cavalry Divsn. U.S. Army, An Khe, Vietnam, 1965—66; adjutant Brooke Army Med. Ctr., Ft. Sam Houston, Tex., 1966—70; mil. pers. dir. Womack Army Hosp., Ft. Bragg, NC, 1970—72; med. advisor to Paraguayan Army U.S. Mil. Group Paraguay, Asuncion, 1972—75; comdr. 1st Med. Group U.S. Army, Ft. Sam Houston, Tex., 1975—77, ret., 1978; inspector gen. Med. Field Svc. Sch., Ft. Sam Houston, Tex., 1977—78; instnl. historian Wilford Hall Air Force Med. Ctr., Lackland AFB, Tex., 1989—2000; ret., 2000. Author: (book) Countdown to Rebellion, 1990; contbr. articles to profl. jours. and encys. Decorated Bronze Star, Legion of Merit, Meritorious Svc. medal. Avocations: military history, history of the British Empire, militaria collecting, dogs. Home: 4223 Dauphine Dr San Antonio TX 78218 E-mail: gih.kelling@worldnet.att.net.

KELLISON, DONNA LOUISE GEORGE, accountant, educator; b. Hugoton, Kans., Oct. 16, 1950; d. Donald Richard and Zepha Louise (Lowry) George. BA in Elem. Edn. with honors, Anderson (Ind.) U., 1972; MS in Elem. Edn., Ind. U., 1981. CPA, Ind.; lic. tchr., Ind.; lic. in ins., Ind.; cert. gen. securities rep.; cert. investment advisor. Tchr. elem. Maconaquah Sch. Corp., Bunker Hill, Ind., 1972-73; office mgr. Eskew & Gresham, CPA's, Louisville, Ky., 1973-78; para-profl. Blue & Co., Indpls., 1979-83, tax compliance specialist, 1983-84, tax sr., 1984-86, tax supr., 1986-87, tax mgr., 1987-90, tax prin., 1990-92, tax sr. mgr., 1992-94, tax dir., 1995—; pres. Blue Benefits Cons., Inc., 1998—, Olympic Fin. Svcs. LLC, 1999—. Vol. Children's Clinic, Indpls., 1985-92; chairperson Most Wanted campaign Am. Cancer Soc., 1995; bd. dirs. Indpls. Estate Planning Coun., 1995—, sec., 1995-96, vice-chair, 1998, chair 1998-99. Mem. AICPA, Ind. CPA Soc. (tax inst. com. 1989-93, govt. rels. com. 1994-95), Ind. Tax Inst. (chair 1993). Presbyterian. Home: 382 Pintail Ct Carmel IN 46032-9125 Office: 12800 N Meridian St Ste 400 Carmel IN 46032

KELLISON, STEPHEN GEORGE, actuarial consultant; b. Ord, Nebr., Mar. 20, 1942; s. Orin Albian and Sarah Viola (Crouch) K.; m. Chery Le Wagner, June 14, 1963 (div. Jan. 1970); m. Erica Elizabeth Bowers, Jan. 27, 1978 (div. June 1985); m. Maureen Antoinette Gage, Nov. 15, 1986. AB, U. Nebr., Lincoln, 1963, MS, 1967. CFP. Actuarial supr. Occidental Life Ins. Co., L.A., 1963-65; actuary Lincoln Liberty Life Ins. Co., Lincoln, Nebr., 1965-66; prof. U. Nebr., 1966-75; consulting actuary G.V. Stennes & Assocs., Dallas, 1975-76; exec. dir. Am. Acad. Actuaries, Washington, 1976-88; chmn. Dept. Risk Mgmt. and Ins. Ga. State U., Atlanta, 1989-93; sr. v.p. instnl. svcs. Am. Gen. Retirement Svcs., Houston, 1994—2001. Mem. tech. panel Social Security Adv. Bd., 2003—; chmn. tech. panel Social Security Adv. Coun., 1989—91; pub. trustee Social Security and Medicare, 1995—2000; mem. task force on interest methods Fin. Acctg. Stds. Bd., 1989—95; sec. Actuarial Edn. and Rsch. Fund, 1989—92. Author: The Theory of Interest, 1970, 2d edit., 1991, Fundamentals of Numerical Analysis, 1975. Fellow Soc. Actuaries (bd. dirs. 1973-75, 90-93, v.p. 1999-2001); mem. Nat. Acad. Social Ins., Am. Acad. Actuaries (bd. dirs. 1975-76), Internat. Actuarial Assn., Phi Beta Kappa. Home and Office: 9301 Wickham Way Orlando FL 32836-5518 E-mail: sgkellison@aol.com.

KELLNER, GEORGE, securities executive; b. Budapest, Hungary, Nov. 28, 1942; came to U.S., 1947; s. Paul J. and Clara Elizabeth Kellner; m. Martha Bicknell, July 22, 1967; children: Peter B., Catherine S. BA, Trinity Coll., 1964; JD, Columbia U., 1967, MBA, 1973. Cert. fin. analyst. Assoc. Carter, Leelyard & Milburn, N.Y.C., 1967-70; v.p. Madison Fund, N.Y.C., 1970-75; ptnr. I. Boesky & Co., N.Y.C., 1975-77; sr. v.p. Donaldson, Lulkins & Jennette, N.Y.C., 1977-81; mng. ptnr. Kellner Dileo & Co., N.Y.C., 1981—. Chmn. bd. dirs. Childtime Children's Ctr., Farmington, Mich., KD Equities. Bd. dirs. Phoenix House, N.Y.C., 1992—; trustee Milton (Mass.) Acad., 1988-, Trinity Coll., Hartford, Conn., 1989—, Bard Coll., Annandale-on-Hudson, 1999—; bd.

overseers Leonard Stern Sch. Bus., N.Y.C., 1995—. Mem. Univ. Club, Union Club, Maidstone Club. Avocations: skiing, tennis, mountain climbing, travel, squash. Office: 900 3d Ave New York NY 10022

KELLNER, JAMIE, broadcasting executive; With CBS, 1969; former v.p. first-run programming, devel., sales Viacom Enterprises; pres. Orion Entertainment Group, 1979—86; pres., CEO Fox Broadcasting Co., L.A., 1986—93; CEO, pres. WBTV Network, Burbank, Calif. Office: WBTV Network 4000 Warner Blvd Bldg 34R Burbank CA 91522-0001

KELLNER, MARK ALLEN, writer; b. N.Y.C., July 17, 1957; s. Jacques and Arlene Kellner; m. Jean Ann Viechec. Student, Boston U., 1975—77. Editl. dir. Kellner Editl. Svcs., Marina del Rey, Calif., 1998—; editor-in-chief PC Portables Mag./LFP, Inc., Beverly Hills, Calif., 1996—98; sr. editor Govt. Computer News, Silver Spring, Md., 1996—96; editor, "Report on AT&T" Capitol Pubs., Alexandria, Va., 1988—93; "On Computers" columnist The Washington Times, Washington, 1991—. Team mem. USIS Y2K Lecture Team, Nairobi, Kenya, 1999; lectr. World Journalism Inst., L.A., 2002—. Author: Y2K: Apocalypse or Opportunity, 1999, God on the Internet, 1996, WordPerfect 3.5 for Macs For Dummies, 1995; contbr. ; editor: Philatelic Communicator, 1995—96. Recipient Cahners Editl. Merit award, Cahners Pub. Inc., 1996, Linn's Lit. award, Linn's Stamp News (Amos Press, Inc.), 1974. Mem.: Am. Philatelic Soc. Avocation: philately. Personal E-mail: mark@kellner.com. Business E-Mail: mark@kellner2000.com.

KELLNER, MILLICENT H. social worker, researcher; b. Mar. 28, 1947; BA, Douglass Coll., New Brunswick, N.J., 1968; MA, Rutgers U., 1970, MSW, 1976, PhD, 1988. Lic. clin. social worker, N.J.; cert. ednl. supr., N.J. Co-adj. instr. Rutgers Grad. Sch. Social Work, New Brunswick, N.J., 1979-84; rsch. and project devel. specialist CPC-High Point Schs., Morganville, N.J., 1986—. Lectr. High Point Sch., Morganville, N.J., 1994—; rschr. in field. Author: In Control, 2001 (Pres. award Asah, 2001); contbr. articles to profl. jours. Mem. Zoning Bd., East Windsor, N.J., 1989-94; bd. dirs. Crohn's and Colitis Found. Am., 1998—. Mem. NASW, APA, Nat. Assn. Pvt. Schs. for Exceptional Children (co-chair outcome com. 1998—), Assn. Schs. and Agys. for the Handicapped (co-chair outcome com. 1998—), Acad. Cert. Social Workers, Sch. Social Work Assn., Assn. Pvt. Spl. Edn. Ctrs. Office: 1 High Point Center Way Morganville NJ 07751-4213

KELLNER, RICHARD GEORGE, mathematician, computer scientist; b. Cleve, July 10, 1943; s. George Ernst and Wanda Julia (Lapinski) K.; m. Charlene Ann Zajc, June 26, 1965; children: Michael Richard, David George. BS, Case Inst. Tech., 1965; MS, Stanford U., 1968, PhD, 1969. Staff mem. Los Alamos Sci. Lab., N.Mex., 1969—79, Los Alamos Nat. Lab., 1983—88; co-owner, dir. software devel. KMP Computer Systems, Inc., Los Alamos, 1979—84; mgr. spl. projects KMP Computer Systems divsn. 1st Data Resources, Inc., Los Alamos, 1986—87, with microcomputer divsn., 1988. Owner CompuSpeed, 1986—; co-owner Computer-Aided Communications, 1982-84; v.p., COO, bd. dir. Applied Computing Systems Inc., 1988-2003; cons., 1979—; owner Sys. Automation Tech., 2003-. Recipient Commendation award for outstanding support of operation Desert Storm. Mem. IEEE, Assn. Computing Machinery, Math. Assn. Am., Soc. Indsl. and Applied Math., Am. Math. Soc. Home: 8 Lookout Ln Santa Fe NM 87506-8258

KELLNER, TATANA, artist, art educator; b. Prague, Nov. 21, 1950; came to U.S., 1969; d. Eugene and Eva (Freund) K. BA, U. Toledo, 1972; MFA, Rochester Inst. Tech., 1974. Artistic dir. Women's Studio Workshop, Inc., 1974—, artist, instr. Art in Edn. Initiative, 1986—, N.Y. State Coun. on the Arts, 1986—, Kingston (N.Y.) Consol. Sch. Dist., 1986—; represented by Goldstrom Gallery, N.Y.C. Artist in residence Visual Studies Workshop, Rochester, N.Y., 1987, Artpark, Lewiston, N.Y., 1987, Yaddo, Saratoga Springs, N.Y., 1988, Va. Ctr. for the Arts, Sweet Briar, 1992, 99, The MacDowell Colony, Peterborough, N.H., 1986, 92, 2001, Banff Ctr. for the Arts, 1995, Ragdale, Evanston, Ill., 1986, others; tech. cons. fine arts dept. SUNY, New Paltz, 1974-75; vis. artist in residence U. So. Maine, Gorham, 1997; lectr. in field. Exhibited in group shows including Everson Mus., Syracuse, N.Y., 1990, Harwick Cll., 1990, Multimedia Arts Ctr., N.Y.C., 1990, Rensselaer County Coun. for Arts, Troy, N.Y., 1992, Hera Gallery, Wakefield, R.I., 1992, Harper Collins Publs., N.Y.C., 1993, SUNY, New Paltz, 1993, Pratt Manhattan Gallery, 1993, Blum Helman Gallery, N.Y.C., Marywood Coll., Slatedale, Pa., 1994, Ohio State U., Columbus, 1994, Ormond (Fla.) Meml. Art Mus., 1995, Warren St. Gallery, Hudson, N.Y., Klutznick Nat. Jewish Mus., Washington, 1995, 494 Gallery, N.Y.C., Photographic Resource Ctr., Boston, 1995, Forman Gallery, Jamestown, N.Y., 1995, Monmouth Mus., Lincroft, N.J., 1996, U. Ariz. Mus. Art, Tucson, 1999-2000, Neuberger Mus., Purchase, N.Y., 1998; numerous others; one-person exhbns. include Kleinert Arts Ctr., Woodstock, N.Y., 1989, The Queens Mus. at Bulova Corp. Ctr., N.Y.C., 1991, CEPA Gallery, Buffalo, 1993, Harwick Coll., Oneonta, N.Y., 1994, SUNY Oswego, 1994, We. Mich. U., Kalamazoo, 1995, Bloomsburg (Pa.) U., 1995, Soc. Contemporary Photography, Kansas City, Mo., 1996, The Floating Gallery Ctr. Photography, Winnipeg, Man., Can., 1996, Ctr. Visual Arts U. Toledo (Ohio), 1997, Mednick Gallery U. Arts, Phila., 1997, Ft. Lewis Coll., Durango, Colo., 1997, Marist Coll., Poughkeepsie, N.Y., 1997, Gallerie Sans Nom, Moncton, Can., 1997, Lake George (N.Y.) Arts Project, 1998, Goldstrom Gallery, N.Y.C., 1998, Sarek Gallery, Bucknell U., Pa., 2001, CEPA Gallery, 2002; represented in permanent collections Mus. Modern Art Libr., U. Toledo, Walker Arts Ctr. Libr., Rochester Inst. Tech., Mobil Corp., Met. Mus. Libr., numerous others; author 12 artists' books. Mentor Empire State Coll., 1978-81, curator art gallery, 1994. Grantee N.Y. State Coun. on Arts, 1980, Empire State Crafts Alliance, 1989, Individual Artist N.Y. Found. for the Arts, 1992, 96, 97; recipient Photographer's Fund award Ctr. for Photography, 1984, 2000, award Ruth Chenven Found., 1985, Arax award Dutchess C.C. 25th Ann. Competition, Purchase award, Toledo (Ohio) Mus. Art, Rochester (N.Y.) Inst. Tech. Home: 552 Binnewater Rd Kingston NY 12401-8458 Office: Women's Studio Workshop PO Box 489 Rosendale NY 12472-0489 E-mail: wsw@ulster.net.

KELLOGG, C. BURTON, II, financial analyst; b. Plainfield, NJ, June 22, 1934; s. Chester M. and Alice L.; m. Dorothy E. Harasty, July 31, 1954; children: Katharine E., Patricia A., Peter B. BA in Econs., Dartmouth Coll., 1956; MBA in Fin., Columbia U., 1958. With A.M. Best Co., N.Y.C., 1958-68, v.p. Oldwick, NJ, 1968—2003, sr. v.p., 1981—, corp. sec. bd. dirs. Editor: Best's Insurance Reports, 1963-94. Sec. Westfield, N.J. YMCA, 1972-76. Mem. Assn. Ins. and Fin. Analysts, Echo Lake Country Club (trustee 1985-90). Office: AM Best Co Ambest Rd Oldwick NJ 08858

KELLOGG, DALE M, editor; b. Princeton, NJ; d. Pettersen B. Marzoni and Suzanne Gifford; 1 child, Lorelei M. BA, Mont. State U., 1984—86. Exec. adminstr. Nat. Ctr. for Atmospheric Rsch., Boulder, Colo., 1991—2002. Mayor Town of Va. City, Mont., 1980—84. Office: RCC WG1 DSRC R/AL8 325 Broadway Boulder CO 80305 Office Fax: 303-497-5628. Personal E-mail: dkellogg@ucar.edu. E-mail: ipcc-wg1@al.noaa.gov.

KELLOGG, DARRELL DEAN, lawyer; b. Plainville, Kans., Oct. 29, 1931; s. Orville M. and Cozetta J. (Gager) K.; m. Shirley D. Hillyer, Sept. 12, 1953; children: Roxanne, Kevin, Brett, AB, U. Kans., 1953; JD, U. Chgo., 1959. Bar: Kans. 1959. Mem. Kahrs, Nelson, Fanning, Hite & Kellogg, 1963—. Mem. Wichita Bd. Edn., 1967-73, chmn. supt. screening com.; bd. dirs. Wichita Legal Aid Soc., Urban Ministry, Quivira Council Boy Scouts Am.; trustee Wichita Hist. Mus., 1977-81; bd. dirs. Hist. Cow Town, Wichita, 1977—, v.p., 1984, pres. 1987. Served with USAF, 1953-56. Recipient Wichita Pub. Schs. Citizen's award, 1975. Mem. ABA, Kans. Bar Assn. (chmn. pub. relations com. 1965-68, chmn. aviation sect. 1973-75, exec. council 1976-82, pres. 1984-85), Wichita Bar Assn. (pres. jr. bar 1961-62, bd. govs. 1976-78), Kans. Assn. Sch. Bds. (pres. 1971, del. nat. assembly 1970-72), Nat. Assn. Sch. Bds. (legis. com. 1971-72), Lambda Chi Alpha. Home: 9820 W 10th St N Wichita KS 67212-4385 Office: 220 W Douglas Ave Wichita KS 67202-3108

KELLOGG, DAVID, publisher; b. N.Y.C., Aug. 26, 1950; s. George Dwight and Wynne (Krementz) K.; m. Sandra Ruffer, Aug. 29, 1976; children: Matthew Dwight, Benjamin William. Student, Groton Sch., Mass., 1968; BA cum laude, Yale U., 1972. Pers. dir. Krementz and Co., Newark, N.J., 1972-74; scriptwriter CBS-TV, N.Y.C., 1974-76; asst. to the pres. Walker and Co., N.Y.C., 1976-79; sr. editor Pergamon Press, Elmsford, N.Y., 1979-83; dir. pubs. Coun. on Fgn. Rels., N.Y.C., 1983—; pub. dir. Fgn. Affairs Mag., N.Y.C., 1987—92, pub., 1992—; v.p. corp. affairs Coun. Fgn. Rels., 1997—2002, sr. v.p. corp. affairs, 2002—. Mem.: Coun. Fgn. Rels.

KELLOGG, DEREN EARL, historian; b. Lansing, Mich., Nov. 17, 1966; s. Earl Duane and Janice Kay Kellogg; m. Melissa Kay Kelly, Dec. 29, 2001; 1 child, Madeleine Louise Kelly-Kellogg. BA, Luther Coll., Decorah, Iowa, 1989; MA, PhD, U. of Ill., 1998. Author: (doctoral dissertation) The Lincoln Administration and the Southwestern Territories (Abraham Lincoln Inst. Hay-Nicolay Scholars prize, 2001); contbr. articles to profl. jours. Mem.: Am. Hist. Assn., Orgn. of Am. Historians. Mennonite. Home: Unit 122 111 Bean Creek Rd Scotts Valley CA 95066 Office: Gale Group 362 Lakeside Dr Foster City CA 94404 Personal E-mail: derenk66@msn.com.

KELLOGG, FREDERIC RICHARD, religious studies educator; b. San Angelo, Tex., Dec. 16, 1939; s. John Franklin III and Naomi Lucille (Cory) K., m. Jeannette Villeret Boykin, June 1, 1963; children: Christopher, Mark. BS summa cum laude, La. Tech. U., 1962; ThM with honors, So. Meth. U., 1965; postgrad., U. Goettingen, 1965-66; PhD, Yale U., 1972. Ordained to ministry Meth. Ch., 1969. Asst. prof. religion Emory & Henry Coll., Emory, Va., 1969-75, assoc. prof., 1975-83, Floyd Bunyan Shelton prof., 1984—, acting dean faculty, 1993-94. Mem. Am. Acad. Religion, Soc. Biblical Lit., Mid. East Studies Assn. Democrat. Home: PO Box 24 Emory VA 24327-0024 Office: Emory & Henry Coll Dept Religion PO Box 947 Emory VA 24327

KELLOGG, FREDERICK, historian; b. Boston, Dec. 9, 1929; s. Frederick Floyd and Stella Harriet (Plummer) K.; m. Patricia Kay Hanbery, Aug. 21, 1954 (dec. 1975); 1 child, Kristine Marie Calvert. AB, Stanford U., 1952; MA, U. So. Calif., 1958; PhD, Ind. U., 1969. Instr. Boise State U., 1962-64, asst. prof., 1964-65, assoc. prof., 1966-67; instr. history U. Ariz., 1967-68, asst. prof., 1969—71, assoc. prof., 1971—. Vis. asst. prof. U. Idaho, 1965. Author: A History of Romanian Historical Writing, 1990, The Road to Romanian Independence, 1995, O istorie a istoriografiei romane, 1996, Drumul Romaniei spre independenta, 2002; mng. editor Southeastern Europe/L'Europe du sud-est, 1974-2002, mem. editl. bd., 2002—; contbr. articles to acad. publs. Founder, chmn. Idaho Hist. Conf., 1964. Recipient cert. recognition Soc. Romanian Studies, 1993, Nicolae Iorga prize Romanian Acad., 1997; named hon. mem. Inst. de istorie "Alexandru D. Xenopol", 1991; rsch. grantee ACLS, 1970-71, sr. rsch. grantee Internat. Rsch. and Exchs. Bd., 1973-74; U.S.-Romania Cultural Exch. Rsch. scholar, 1960-61, Sr. Fulbright-Hays Rsch. scholar, Romania, 1969-70. Mem. Am. Hist. Assn., Am. Assn. for Advancement of Slavic Studies, S.E. European Studies Assn. Office: U Ariz Dept History Tucson AZ 85721-0001 E-mail: kellogg@u.arizona.edu.

KELLOGG, HERBERT HUMPHREY, metallurgist, educator; b. N.Y.C., Feb. 24, 1920; s. Herbert H. and Gladys (Falding) K.; m. Jeanette Halstead, July 20, 1940; children— Thomas Bartlett, Jane Falding, David Humphrey, Elizabeth Ann. BS, Columbia, 1941, MS, 1943. Asst. prof. mineral preparation Pa. State U., State Coll., 1942-46; faculty Columbia U., N.Y.C., 1946—, Stanley-Thompson prof. chem. metallurgy, 1968-90, prof. emeritus, 1990—. Chmn. titanium adv. com. Office Def. Mblzn., 1954-58 Research; contbr. numerous articles to publs. Recipient Best Paper award extractive metals div. Am. Inst. Mining., Metall. and Petroleum Engrs.; James Douglas Gold medal Am. Inst. Mining, Metall. and Petroleum Engrs., 1973 Fellow AIME (chmn. extractive metallurgy div. 1958), Metall. Soc., Instn. Mining and Metallurgy (London); mem. NAE, Sigma Xi, Tau Beta Pi. Home: Closter Rd Palisades NY 10964

KELLOGG, JAMES CRANE, lawyer; b. Summit, N.J., July 2, 1939; s. James Crane and Elizabeth (Irwin) K.; m. Gail Chambers, Aug. 25, 1962; children: James, Katherine, Elizabeth. AB, Princeton U., 1961; JD, Harvard U., 1964. Bar: N.J. 1965, N.Y. 1966, Fla. 1979. Assoc. Shearman & Sterling, N.Y.C., 1965-70; v.p. Walston & Co., N.Y.C., 1970-73; ptnr. Gifford, Woody, Palmer & Serles, N.Y.C. 1973-85, Townley & Updike, N.Y.C., 1986—; dir. Prudential Ins. Co., Newark. Pres. Frost Valley YMCA, Claryville, N.Y., 1983—; past pres. Children's Specialized Hosp., Mountainside, N.J.; trustee Ocean Med. Ctr., Point Pleasant, N.J., 1983, Sky Club, Bay Head Yacht Club (trustee N.J. chpt. 1977-83, 86-89). Democrat. Presbyterian Home: 700 Clayton Ave Bay Head NJ 08742-5305

KELLOGG, JAMES WARNER, aerospace management consultant; b. Selfridge AFB, Mich., Feb. 18, 1941; s. Joseph Warner and Eleanor Elaine (West) K.; m. Martha Sumners, Apr. 14, 1962 (div. Jan. 1988); m. Betty Russell, June 19, 1988; children: James Warner Jr., Robert West, Karen Kellogg Price. BA in Math., U. Tex., 1963; M in Adult Edn., U. South Fla., 1973; MBA, Webster U., 1989. Commd. 2d lt. USAF, 1963, advanced through grades to col., 1993, ret., 1987; br. mgr. Randolph (Tex.)-Brooks Fed. Credit Union, 1987-89; mgr. for customer svc. and consumer lending Security Svc. Fed. Credit Union, San Antonio, 1989-90; fin. cons. Prin. Fin. Group, San Antonio, 1990-91; project mgr. McDonnell Douglas. Specialized undergrad. pilot tng. project mgr. McDonnell Douglas/USAF, Randolph AFB, 1991-94; fin. cons. Windcrest United Meth., San Antonio, 1991-94; fighter tng. integrator, analyst for Royal Saudi AF, 1994-95, dir. Base Ops., Fighter Tng. Base, Boeing, 1995-99; mgr. Integrated Support for F-18 A-F, F-15, Av-8B, T-45 Boeing, 2000-01, mgr. internat. repairs/retrofit svcs., 2001—, program mgr. integrated logistics support. Com. chmn. Boy Scouts Am., San Antonio, 1989-94. Decorated Legion of Merit, Sec. Air Force, Washington, 1987; named Outstanding Grad., Webster Alumni Assn., St. Louis, 1989. Mem. Air Force Assn. (life mem., area v.p. 2000), Order of Daedalians (life mem., flight capt. 1982-83, 86-87), San Antonio Plaza Club, Phi Kappa Phi. Methodist. Avocations: hunting, fishing, jogging. Home: 4525 Old Pond Dr Plano TX 75024 E-mail: jwkellogg501@cs.com.

KELLOGG, JOSEPH K., JR., military career officer; b. Dayton, Ohio, May 12, 1944; BA in Polit. Sci., U. Santa Clara; MA in Polit. Sci., U. Kans.; grad., Command and Gen. Staff Coll., U.S. Army War Coll. Commd. 2nd lt. U.S. Army, 1967, advanced through grades to maj. gen., 1996, various positions, 1967-83, comdr. 1st Bn. (airborne), 504th Inf., 82d Airborne Divsn., 1983-85, ops. officer Office of the Chief of Staff Washington, 1985-86, G-3 (ops.), 7th Inf. Divsn. (light) Ft. Ord, Calif., 1987-88, comdr. 3d Brigade, 7th Inf. Divsn. (light), 1988-90, chief of staff 82d Airborne Divsn., 1990-91, 1991, asst. divsn. comdr. (ops.) 82d Airborne Divsn., 1991-92; commdg. gen. spl. ops. command Europe U.S. European Command, Germany, 1992-94; asst. dep. chief of staff for combat devel. U.S. Army Tng. and Doctrine Command, Ft. Monroe, Va., 1994-96, dep. chief of staff for combat devel., 1994-96; commdg. gen. 82nd Airborne Divsn. U.S. Army, Ft. Bragg, 1996-98, asst. dep. chief of staff for ops. and plans Washington, 1998—. Office: US Army 200 Defense Pentagon Washington DC 20310-0001

KELLOGG, PAUL, general & artistic director opera company; b. Hollywood, Calif. BA, U. Tex.; student, Sorbonne, France, U. Nancy, Columbia U. Head Lower Sch.; prof. then headmaster Allen-Stevenson Sch.; artistic dir. Glimmerglass Opera, Cooperstown, NY, 1979—; gen., artistic dir. N.Y.C. Opera, 1996—. Adjudicator Met. Opera Nat. Coun. Auditions. Mem.: OPERA Am. (bd. dirs.). Office: NYC Opera NY State Theater 20 Lincoln Center Plz New York NY 10023-6913

KELLOGG, ROBERT LELAND, English language educator; b. Ionia County, Mich., Sept. 2, 1928; s. Charles Edwin and Lucille Jeanette (Reasoner) K.; m. Joan Alice Montgomery, Apr. 4, 1951; children: Elizabeth Joan, Jonathan Montgomery, Stephen Robert. BA, U. Mich., 1950; MA, Harvard U., 1952, PhD, 1958. Mem. faculty U. Va., 1957-99, prof. English, 1967-99, chmn. dept., 1974-78, dean Coll. Arts and Scis., 1978-85, prof. emeritus, 1999—; prin. Monroe Hill Coll., 1985-88. Vis. prof. U. Iceland, 1999—2001. Author: (with Robert Scholes) The Nature of Narrative, 1966, A Concordance to Eddic Poetry, 1988; translator of works from Icelandic; contbr. to profl. jours. Served with USAR, 1954-56. Am.-Scandinavian Found. fellow, 1956-57; Guggenheim fellow, 1968-69 Mem. Medieval Acad. Am., Modern Lang. Assn., South Atlantic Modern Lang. Assn. (pres. 1974-75), Raven Soc., Phi Beta Kappa (pres. local chpt. 1981) Clubs: Colonnade. Democrat. Home: 261 E Jefferson St Charlottesville VA 22902-5175 Office: U Va Bryan Hall Charlottesville VA 22904-4121 E-mail: rlk@virginia.edu.

KELLOGG, WILLIAM WELCH, meteorologist, researcher; b. New York Mills, N.Y., Feb. 14, 1917; s. Frederick S. and Elizabeth (Walcott) K.; m. Elizabeth Thorson, Feb. 14, 1942; children: Karl S., Judith K. Liebert, Joseph W., Jane E., Thomas W. BA, Yale U., 1939; MA, UCLA, 1942, PhD, 1949. With Inst. Geophysics UCLA, L.A., 1946-52, asst. prof., 1950-52; scientist Rand Corp., Santa Monica, Calif., 1947-59, head planetary scis. dept., 1959-64; assoc. dir. Nat. Ctr. Atmospheric Research, Boulder, Colo., also dir. lab. atmospheric scis., 1964-73, sr. scientist, 1973-87; sr. rsch. assoc. Nat. Ctr. Atmospheric Rsch., Boulder, Colo., 1994—. Mem. earth satellite panel IGY, 1956-59; mem. space sci. bd. Nat. Acad. Scis., 1959-68, mem. com. meteorol. aspects of effects of atomic radiation, 1956-58, mem. com. atmospheric scis., 1966-72, mem. polar research bd., 1972-77; mem. Rocket and Satellite Research Panel, 1957-62; mem. adv. group supporting tech. for operational meteorol. satellites NASA-NOAA, 1964-72; rapporteur meteorology of high atmosphere, commn. aerology World Meteorol. Orgn., 1965-71; chmn. internat. commn. meteorology upper atmosphere Internat. Union Geodesy and Geophysics, 1960-67, mem., 1967-75; mem. internat. com. climate Internat. Assn. Meteorology and Atmospheric Physics, 1978-87; mem. sci. adv. bd. USAF, 1956 65; chmn. meteorol. satellite com. Advanced Research Projects Agy., 1958-59; mem. panel on environment President's Sci. Adv. Com., 1968-72; mem. space program adv. council NASA, 1976-77; chmn. meteorol. adv. com. EPA, 1970-74, mem. nat. air quality criteria adv. com., 1975-76, air pollution transport and transformation adv. com., 1976-78; mem. council on carbon dioxide environ. assessment Dept. Energy, 1976-78; adv. to sec. gen. on World Climate Program, World Meteorol. Orgn., 1978-79; dir. research Naval Environ. Prediction Research Facility, Monterey, Calif., 1983-84; chmn. adv. com. Div. Polar Programs NSF, 1983-86; researcher on meteorology, dynamics and turbulence of upper atmosphere, prediction radioactive fallout and dispersal, applications of infrared techniques, atmospheres of Mars and Venus, theory of climate and causes of climate change Served as pilot-weather officer USAAF, 1941-46. Co-recipient spl. award pioneering work in planning meteorol. satellite Am. Meteorol. Soc., 1961; recipient Risseca award contbn. human relations in scis. Jewish War Vets. U.S.A., 1962-63, Exceptional Civilian Service award Dept. Air Force, 1966, Spl. award for pioneering meteorol. satellites Dept. Commerce, 1985, Spl. Citation award for atmospheric conservation Garden Club of Am., 1988. Fellow Am. Geophys. Union (pres. meteorol. sect. 1972-74), Am. Meteorol. Soc. (council 1960-63, pres. 1973-74), AAAS (chmn. atmospheric and hydrospheric sect. 1984); mem. Sigma Xi. Home: 445 College Ave Boulder CO 80302-7131 *If there is anything that generally characterizes a gratifying and successful career in science, it is the challenge of diversity. The really important problems of the universe, and especially of society, involve several disciplines, and we are compelled to work at these discipline interfaces. Pigeon holes are for pigeons, not scientists.*

KELLOGG FAIN, KAREN, retired history and geography educator; b. Pueblo, Colo., Oct. 10, 1940; d. Howard Davis and Mary Lucille (Cole) Kellogg; m. Sept. 1, 1961; divorced; 1 child, Kristopher. Student, U. Ariz., 1958-61; BA, U. So. Colo., 1967; MA, U. No. Colo., 1977; postgrad., U. Denver, 1968, 72-93, Colo. State U., 1975, 91, Chadron State Coll., 1975, U. No. Ill., 1977, 83, Ft. Hayes State Coll., 1979, U. Colo., 1979, 86-87, 92, Ind. U., 1988. Cert. secondary tchr. Colo. Tchr. history and geography Denver Pub. Schs., 1967-96; tchr. West H.S., Denver, 1992-96. Area adminstr., tchr. coord. Close Up program, Washington, 1982-84; reviewer, cons. for book Geography, Our Changing World, 1990. Vol., chmn. young profls. Inst. Internat. Edn. and World Affairs Coun., Denver, 1980—; mem. state selection com. U.S. Senate and Japan Scholarship Com., Denver, 1981-89, Youth for Understanding, Denver; mem. Denver Art Mus., 1970—; vol. Denver Mus. Natural History, 1989—, Am. Cancer Soc. "Jail and Bail", 1996, "Climb the Mountain", 1996, Denver Conv. Bur., 1997; bd. overseas Dept. Def. Dependents Sch., Guantanamo Bay, Cuba, 1990-91; screening panelist Tchr. to Japan Program Rocky Mtn. Regional Fulbright Meml. Fund, 1997; vol. tour guide Colo. State Capitol, 1997-2001. Fulbright scholar Chadron State Coll., Pakistan, 1975; Geog. Soc. grantee U. Colo., 1986; recipient award for Project Prince, Colo. U./Denver Pub. Schs./Denver Police Dept., 1992. Mem.: AAUW, Colo. Coun. on Internat. Orgns. (mem. bd. 1999—), Colo. Geographic Alliance (steering com. 1986), Rocky Mountain Regional World History Assn. (steering com. 1984—87), Am. Forum for Global Edn., Fulbright Assn. (bd. dirs. and regional liaison Colo. chpt. 2001—), World History Assn., Nat. Coun. Social Studies (del. 1984), Colo. Coun. Social Studies (sec. 1984—86), Denver Bot. Gardens, Kappa Kappa Iota, Gamma Phi Beta. Episcopalian. Avocations: traveling, hosting international visitors, swimming, reading. Home: 12643 E Bates Cir Aurora CO 80014-3315 E-mail: karenfain@hotmail.com.

KELLOGG-SMITH, PETER, sculptor; b. N.Y.C., Apr. 21, 1920; s. Jewell and Margaret (Shearer) Kellogg-Smith; children by guardianship: Peter von Pein, Lee von Pein Schreitz, Ruth Bueneman, Cynthia Taylor Dax; grad. Putney Sch., Vt., 1939; studied yacht design with Franz Plunder, 1940-43; AB, St. John's Coll., Annapolis, Md., 1943; MA in Philos. Edn., Putney-Antioch Grad. Sch. Tchr. Edn., 1962; postgrad. U. Md., 1968. Tchr. Ojai (Calif.) Valley Sch., 1944-47; founding dir.-tchr. Happy Valley Sch., Ojai, 1948; yacht designer, broker, Chestertown, Md. 1949-57; asst. head, tchr. Gunston Sch., Centerville, Md., 1950-57; tchr. Grapho-English, Abana, Turkey, 1956; founding dir., tchr. Key Sch., Annapolis, Md., 1958-62; founding dir., hands-on tchr. oceanography Bay Country Sch., Arnold, Md., 1963-72; tchr. stone carving Acad. Arts, Easton, Md., 1972-76. Prin. works include marble carving under Etienne Desmet, Carrara, Italy, 1972, under Kenneth Davis, Carrara, 1974, drawing and modeling with Reuben Kramer, modeling and bronze casting with Arthur Benson, 1975-79; patentee new type engine and marine hardward. Bd. dirs. Fairhaven "free" sch.; ind. counselor students and parents on ednl. problems. Westinghouse Sci. fellow MIT, 1952; recipient Best in Show award Chestertown Arts League Show, numerous awards for sculpture. Avocations: traveling, playing music, sailing. Address: 202 Divinity Ln Arnold MD 21012-1301

KELLS, ALBERT JOHN, financial consultant; b. Providence, Jan. 20, 1935; s. John S. and Mary M. (Wise) K.; m. Carole P. Coloura, July 6, 1957; children: Karen A., Kathleen M. BS in Fin., Bryant Coll., Providence, 1960; MBA, U. Conn., 1967. Fin. analyst Rexall Drug & Chem., Stamford, Conn., 1960-63; econ. analyst The Fantus Co., N.Y.C., 1963-64; budget mgr. CBS Inc., Stamford, 1964-67; strategic planning mgr. IBM, East Fishkill, N.Y., 1967-90; mergers and acquisitions cons. The Gottesman Co., N.Y.C., 1991, Kells & Co., Stormville, N.Y., 1991—. Chmn. Kells Found., 1981-92; mem. Rep. Nat. Com., 1979. Capt. U.S. Army, 1954-64. Mem. Inst. of Indsl. Engrs. Avocations: tennis, history, computers. Home and Office: 105 Townview Dr Wappingers Falls NY 12590-7017

KELLS, KARI JOY, indexer, librarian, b. Columbus, Ohio, May 25, 1970; d. Paul Kerry and Myrnella Joy (Barney) McDowell; m. Raymond Lee Bero, Nov. 9, 1992 (div. 1998). BA, U. Ill., 1993, MS, 1994. Owner, indexer Index West (formerly Bero-West Indexing Svcs.), Olympia, Wash., 1994—; libr. U. Wash., Seattle, 1994-95; libr. faculty, internet trainer Pierce Coll., Lakewood, Wash., 1995-97; libr. faculty Highline C.C., Des Moines, Wash., 1997-99, Pierce Coll., Puyallup, Wash., 1999—. Contbr. articles to profl. jours. Mem. Am. Soc. Indexers (Web Site com. 1995-98, Webmaster 1995-97, vice chmn. Pacific N.W. chpt. 1997-98, chmn. Pacific N.W. chpt. 1998-99, Webmaster Pacific N.W. chpt. 1996—). Office: PO Box 615 Olympia WA 98507 E-mail: info@indexw.com.

KELLS, LYMAN F. research scientist; b. Seattle, May 19, 1917; s. Lucas Carlisle and Edith Rosetta (Stefani) Kells; divorced; children: Leila S. Newcomb, Christina V. Cohen. PhD, U. Wash., 1944. Rsch. scientist Manhattan project Kellex Corp., Carbide Carbon, N.Y.C., 1944-46; rsch. chemist Std. Oil Devel., N.J., 1946-48; mem. faculty Hunter Coll., N.Y.C., 1948-49; asst. prof. Iona Coll., New Rochelle, N.Y., 1949-51; rsch. chemist Gen. Chem. Divsn., Allied Chem., Morristown, N.J., 1951-61; spl. lectr. Newark Coll. Engring., 1961; assoc. prof. chemistry East Tenn. State U., Johnson City, 1962-64; prof. chemistry Westmar Coll., LeMars, Iowa, 1964-74; ind. theoretical rschr. Seattle, 1974—. Author: (Collected Works) Physical Chemistry, Physics and Astronomy, 1972, Reaction Mechanisms, Kinetics, Molecular Bonding, 1973, Supplement Number Two: Variable Stars, Velocity of Light, Nature of Theories, 1978, Binary Theory of Variable Stars and the Velocity of Light, 1984, Astrometry, Binary Theory and Observations, 1990, Variable Stars, Relativity, Nature of Sciences, 1992. Fellow: AAAS; mem.: N.Y. Acad. Scis., Astron. Soc. Pacific, Am. Chem. Soc., Am. Astron. Soc. Democrat. Unitarian Universalist. Home: 13716 12th Ave SW Apt 47 Seattle WA 98166-1143

KELLS, MELVIN RICHARD See ROBERTS, MEL

KELLUM, BETSY M. artist, educator; b. Sheffield, Ala., Oct. 20, 1943; d. DeWitt O'Kelly and Emily (Weigel) Myatt; m. Joseph W. Kellum, Apr. 3, 1965; children: Trisha K. Smith, Tracy L. BA, Coll. William and Mary, 1965. Tchr. Pub. Schs., Fairfax, Va., Rockville, Md., Henrico, Va., 1965-74; artist Midlothian, Va., 1993—. Exhibited pastels in show at Cudahy Gallery, Richmond, Va., 2000, Degas Pastel Soc., New Orleans, 2001, Hermitage Found. Mus., Norfolk, Va., 1999, LaFord Galleries, Pitts., 1998, Pastel Soc. West Coast, Calif., 2002, Fort Walton Beach (Fla.) Mus., 2002; pastels published in various publs. Recipient awards for pastels. Mem. Vienna (Va.) Arts Soc. (pres. 1993-94), Assoc. Pastellists On The Web (signature mem.), Pastel Soc. West Coast (Disting. Mem., awards of excellence 1996, 97, 98, 2002), Am. Artist Profl. League, Pastel Soc. Am. (signature mem.), Southea. Pastel Soc. (signature mem.). Avocations: golf, fitness, stained glass. Address: 2808 Sugarberry Ln Midlothian VA 23113-1198

KELLUM, DONALD ARTHUR, military officer; b. Schofield Barracks, Hawaii, Dec. 13, 1935; s. Harry Snow and Edna Lois (Pickels) Kellum; m. Martha Ann Myers, Mar. 10, 1957; children: Kathryn Ann Kellum Comer, Donald Wainright. B in Gen. Edn., U. Nebr., Omaha, 1962; MS in Pub. Adminstrn., George Washington U., 1966. Commd. officer USAF, 1953, advanced through grades to col., fighter, bomber navigator, 1956—75, numbered Air Force vice comdr., 1975—77, numbered Air Force dir., 1977—86, ret., 1986; def. cons. JAYCOR, 1986—88; co-founder, bd. dirs., sr. mil. scientist Simulation Techs., Inc., 1988—. Decorated Legion of Merit with two oak leaf clusters, DFC, Purple Heart, Air medal with eleven oak leaf clusters, Air Force Commendation medal. Home: 904 Sassafras Dr Sumter SC 29150

KELLY, A. DAVID, lawyer; b. St. Paul, June 8, 1948; s. David and Katherine (Tappins) K.; m. Elizabeth Woehrle, Oct. 25, 1978; children: Charles, George. BA, Carleton Coll., 1970; JD, Harvard U., 1973. Bar: Minn. 1973. Ptnr. Faegre & Benson, Mpls., 1973-90, Oppenheimer, Wolff & Donnelly, Mpls., 1990-95, Kelly, Hannaford & Battles, Mpls., 1995—. Trustee Carleton Coll., Northfield, Minn., 1972-76,, Minn. Mus. Am. Art, 2003—; chmn. Voyageurs Nat. Pk. Assn., Mpls., 1984-90; treas. Messiah Episc. Ch., St. Paul, 1988-96; pres. St. Paul Boys' and Girls' Club, 1992-93. Office: Kelly Hannaford & Battles 2000 Campbell Mithun 222 South Ninth St Minneapolis MN 55402-3309

KELLY, ALAN, public relations executive; BA in Pub. Rels., U. So. Calif.; M in Comm. Rsch., Stanford U. V.p. client svcs. Cunningham Comm.; v.p. Jennings & Co. (now GCI/SF); sr. v.p. Hi-Tech Comm. (now Golin/Harris); founder, pres., CEO Applied Comm. Pub. quarterly column MC Magazine. Office: Applied Comm Corp 185 Berry St Ste 6500 San Francisco CA 94107-1728

KELLY, ALAN M. dean; Undergrad. degree, U. Reading, Eng., 1958; vet. degree, U. Bristol, Eng., 1962; PhD in Pathology, U. Pa., 1967. Mem. faculty U. Pa. Sch. Vet. Medicine, Phila., 1967, head lab. pathology, chair grad. group pathology, acting chair and chair dept. pathobiology, prof. pathology, 1979—, U. Pa. Grad. Sch. Arts and Scis. and Grad. Group in Comparative Med. Scis.; dean U. Pa. Sch. Vet. Medicine, Phila., 1994—. Chair Genova oversight com. U. Pa. Co-author: (book) Neuromuscular Development and Disease; contbr. chapts. to books, articles to refereed jours. Mem.: ASPCA, Inst. for Human Gene Therapy Adv. Bd., Zool. Soc. Phila. Achievements include research in skeletal muscle development; muscle disease. Office: U Pa Sch Vet Medicine 110 Rosenthal Philadelphia PA 19104-4192

KELLY, ANASTASIA DONOVAN, lawyer; b. Boston, Oct. 9, 1949; d. Charles A. and Louise V. Donovan; m. Thomas C. Kelly, Aug. 23, 1980; children: Michael, Brian. BA cum laude, Trinity Coll, 1971; JD magna cum laude, George Washington U., 1981. Bar: D.C. 1982, Tex. 1982. Analyst Air Line Pilots Assn., 1971-74; dir. employee benefits Martin Marietta Corp., Bethesda, Md., 1974-81; assoc. Carrington, Coleman, Sloman & Blumenthal, Dallas, 1981-85, Wilmer, Cutler & Pickering, Washington, 1985-90, ptnr., 1990-95; sr. v.p., gen. counsel, sec. Fannie Mae, Washington, 1995-99, Sears, Roebuck & Co., 1999—2003. Named one of Outstanding Young Women of Am., 1980. Mem. Am. Bar Found., Order of Coif. Republican. Roman Catholic.

KELLY, ANTHONY ODRIAN, flooring manufacturing company executive; b. Dublin, June 12, 1935; s. John Peter and Delia Mary (Finnegan) K.; m. Sheila Josephine Clancy, Sept. 4, 1963; children— Barbara Anne, Adrienne Elizabeth, Damian Anthony. Grad., Coll. Commerce, Dublin, 1958; MBA, Columbia U., 1965, doctoral degree, 1971. Adj. asst. prof. Columbia U., N.Y.C., 1968-69; dir. econ. studies Sperry & Hutchinson Co., 1969-71, asst. to pres. furnishings divsn., 1975; dir. mktg. Irish Agrl. Devel. Co., 1971-74; sr. v.p. mktg. Bigelow-Sanford, Inc., Greenville, S.C., 1976-79, exec. v.p., COO, 1979-85, pres., CEO, 1985-86; pres., chief ops. officer Mannington Mills Inc., 1992, pres., CEO, 1993-2000, ret., 2000. Ford Found. fellow; Samuel Bronfman fellow. Mem. Inst. Cost and Mgmt. Accts., Kiawah Island Club, Beta Gamma Sigma.

KELLY, ARTHUR LLOYD, management and investment company executive; b. Chgo., Nov. 15, 1937; s. Thomas Lloyd and Mildred (Wetten) Kelly; m. Diane Rex Cain, Nov. 25, 1978; children: Mary Lucinda, Thomas Lloyd, Alison Williams. BS with honors, Yale U., 1959; MBA, U. Chgo., 1964. With A.T. Kearney, Inc., 1959-75, mng. dir., 1964-70, v.p. for Europe Brussels, 1970-73, internat. v.p. London, 1974-75, ptnr., dir., 1969-75, mem. exec. com., 1972-75; pres., COO, dir. LaSalle Steel Co., Chgo., 1975-81; pres., CEO, dir. Dalta Corp., Chgo., 1982—; mng. ptnr. KEL Enterprises L.P., Chgo., 1983—. Dir. BASF Aktiengesellschaft, Ludwigshafen, Germany, BMW A.G., Munich, DataCard Corp., Minnetonka, Minn., Deere & Co., Moline, Ill., No. Trust Corp., Chgo., Snap-On, Inc., Kenosha, Wis., HSBC Trinkaus & Burkhardt KGaA, Dusseldorf; trustee U. Chgo.; mem. adv. coun. Ditchley Found., Oxford, England; bd. dirs. Chgo. Coun. Fgn. Rels. Fellow: Royal Geog. Soc. London (life); mem.: Coun. Fgn. Rels. N.Y.C., World Pres.' Orgn., Yale Club, Racquet Club, Econ. Club, Comml. Club, Casino Club, Brook Club, Beta Gamma Sigma. Office: 20 S Clark St Ste 2222 Chicago IL 60603-1805

KELLY, ARTHUR PAUL, physician; b. Asheville, N.C., Nov. 23, 1938; s. Joseph Paul and Amanda Lee (Walker) Kelly; m. Beverly Gayle Baker, June 25, 1966; children: Traci Allyce, Kara Gisele. BA, Brown U., 1960; MD, Howard U., 1965. Intern Harper Hosp., Detroit, 1965-66; resident in dermatology Henry Ford Hosp., Detroit, 1968-71; instr. in dermatology Brown U., Providence, 1971-73; asst. prof. internal medicine Charles R. Drew U. Medicine and Sci., Los Angeles, 1973-77, prof. L.A., 1983; chief div. dermatology King.-Drew Med. Ctr., L.A., 1976—, interim chmn. dept. internal medicine, 1985-86, vice chmn., 1987-91, chmn., 1992-95; assoc. prof. medicine U. So. Calif., L.A., 1977-80; prof. UCLA, 1995—. Contbr. articles to profl jours, chapters to books. Served to capt U.S. Army, 1966—68, Vietnam. Recipient Act-So award, NAACP, 1983. Fellow: Am Acad Dermatology; mem.: Am Dermatology Asn (vpres 1997—98, pres 1998—99), Asn Profs Dermatology (pres-elect 1996—98, pres 1998—2000), Nat Med Asn (chmn sect dermatology 1978—80, Outstanding Minority Dermatology Fellow 1972), Metropolitan LA Dermatology Soc (vpres 1986—87, pres 1987—88). Democrat. Avocations: travel, tennis. Office: King/Drew Med Ctr 12021 S Wilmington Ave Los Angeles CA 90059-3019 E-mail: apkelly@cdrewu.edu.

KELLY, BARBARA SUE, psychologist; b. Somers Point, N.J., June 24, 1958; d. Joseph Raymond and Catherine Agnes Kelly. BA, Muhlenberg Coll., 1980; MA, Marywood Coll., 1983; PhD, Walden U., 2001. Lic. psychologist, Pa. Cmty. social worker Ctr. for Human Devel., Millville, N.J., 1984-87; counselor I Cape Counseling Svcs., Cape May Courthouse, N.J., 1987-88; biofeedback therapist Guardian Group, Inc., Plymouth Meeting, Pa., 1992-97; v.p. Psychol. Wellness Assocs., Deptford, N.J., 1996—. Fellow Biofeedback Cert. Inst. Am.; mem. APA, Pa. Soc. Behavioral Medicine and Biofeedback. Avocations: cooking, gardening, music, reading. Office: Psychol Wellness Assocs LLC PO Box 5025 Deptford NJ 08096-0025

KELLY, BRENDAN WILLIAM, retired engineering executive; b. Montreal, Que., Can., July 23, 1934; s. Roger Bernard and Anastasia (Mullan) K.; m. Nancy Ann Keyser, June 27, 1959; children: Janice, Linda, Deborah. Diploma chem. engring., BSc, Royal Mil. Coll., Kingston, Ont., 1955; B of Chem. Engring., McGill U., Montreal, 1956. Prodn. supr. DuPont of Can., North Bay, Ont., 1956-60; sales & svc. engr. Huyck Can. Ltd., Arnprior, Ont., 1960-68; mktg. mgr., pres. Scapa Dryers Can. Ltd., Joliette, Que., 1968-81; pres. KRC Rolls subs. Scapa, Salisbury, N.C., 1981-96; chief exec. engineered rolls divsn., dir. Scapa Group plc, Blackburn, Lancashire, Eng., 1987-96. Bd. dirs. 12 subs. cos. of Scapa Group, U.S., Can., Austria, U.K. Patentee for Reversible Forming Fabric Having Dominating Floats on Each Face. Republican. Roman Catholic. Avocations: tennis, sailing, golf.

KELLY, BRIAN MATTHEW, industrial hygienist; b. Ogdensburg, N.Y., June 16, 1956; s. Lauris F. and Catherine M. (McEvoy) K. BA, SUNY, Oswego, 1978; BS, Clarkson U., 1981; MS in Indsl. Safety, Cen. Mo. State U., 1990. Cert. indsl. hygienist Am. Bd. Indsl. Hygiene; cert. accident investigator U.S. Dept. Energy, NASA and Nuc. Regulatory Commn. Maintenance engr. Kelly Sales Corp., Madrid, N.Y., 1978-80, carpenter, 1981-82; hygienist indsl. hygiene and toxicology prin. mem. tech. staff ES&H, quality assessments dept. Sandia Nat. Labs., Albuquerque, 1983—. Mem. tech. adv. bd. Albuquerque (N.Mex.) Tech. Vocat. Inst., 1989—. Mem. bd. environ. auditing cert. Mem. Am. Indsl. Hygiene Assn. (chmn. mgmt. com. 2002, indsl. hygiene conf. and exposition, mgmt. leadership session chmn.), Am. Conf. Govtl. Indls. Hygienists, Am. Soc. Safety Engrs., Am. Acad. Indsl. Hygiene, Bd. Environ. Auditing Certification (cert. profl. environ. health and safety auditor), Gamma Sigma Epsilon, Phi Kappa Phi. Republican. Roman Catholic. Avocations: cycling, fishing, carpentry. Home: 1455 Beall St Bosque Farms NM 87068 E-mail: bmkelly@sandia.gov.

KELLY, CAROL WHITE, company executive; b. Shreveport, La., Dec. 23, 1946; d. Verlin Ralph and Mary Louise (Humphries) White; m. James Patrick Kelly, June 6, 1968; children: Mary Louise, Christopher John. BA, Centenary Coll. La., Shreveport, 1968. Corp. sec., treas. Kelly Law Firm P.C., Atlanta, 1986—. Mem. NAFE, Ga. Baptist Med. Guild (life), Atlanta Hist. Soc., Atlanta Ballet Guild (life), Internat. Platform Assn., High Mus. Art, Episcopal Ch. Women (sec.-treas. 1976-80), Mil. and Hospitaller Order St. Lazarus of Jerusalem (life), Chi Omega Alumnae Assn. (pres. 1979-80). Avocations: travel, pub. speaking, collecting teapots. Office: Kelly Law Firm PC 200 Galleria Pkwy SE Ste 1510 Atlanta GA 30339-5946

KELLY, CHARLES ARTHUR, lawyer; b. Evanston, Ill., Mar. 2, 1932; s. Charles Scott and Bess (Loftis) K.; m. Frances Kates, Sept. 9, 1961 (div. 1979); children: Timothy, Elizabeth, Mary; m. Patricia Lynn Francis, June 28, 1979. BA with honors, Amherst Coll., 1953; LLB, Harvard U., 1956. Bar: D.C. 1956, Ill. 1956. Assoc. Hubachek & Kelly, Chgo., 1956-64, ptnr., 1964-82, Chapman & Cutler, Chgo., 1982—99, of counsel, 2002—. Sec. Speedfam Internat., Inc., 1992-99, gen. counsel, 1998-99. Bd. dirs. Gads Hill Ctr., Chgo., pres., 1977—82; bd. dirs. Quetico Superior Found., Mpls., v.p., 1964—; bd. dirs. Lakeland Found., Chgo., 1960—96, pres., 1970—85, Ernest C. Oberholtzer Found., Mpls., 1962—2002, v.p., treas., 1998—2002; bd. dirs. Chgo. Hearing Found., 1990—94, Wilderness Rsch. Found., Chgo. Recipient Legion of Merit, USAF, 1982. Fellow Am. Coll. Trust and Estate Counsel; Mem. ABA, Chgo. Bar Assn., Ill. Bar Assn., Fed. Bar Assn., Univ. Club, Mid-Am. Club, Mich. Shores Club (Wilmette, Ill.), Harvard Club (Boston). Republican. Presbyterian. Office: Chapman and Cutler 111 W Monroe St Ste 1800 Chicago IL 60603-4096 E-mail: ckelly@chapman.com.

KELLY, CHARLES J., JR., investment company executive; b. June 10, 1929; s. Charles J. and Margaret (Grimes) K.; m. Marguerite Stehli, Dec. 23, 1962; children: Karen Grimes (Mrs. B.H. Warner IV), Marguerite Grace (Mrs. James J. Walton), Lisa Stehli Kelly-Wolf. BA, Stanford U., 1951; LL.B., Yale U., 1954. Bar: N.Y., U.S. Supreme Ct. Asso. atty. Chadbourne, Parke, Whiteside & Wolff, N.Y.C., 1957-58; spl. counsel CAB, 1959-60; spl. asst. to Sec. Comm., Washington, 1960-61; with Reynolds & Co., 1961-62; partner Kelly, Grimes & Winston, 1962-69; pres., dir. Meridian Investing and Devel. Co., N.Y.C., 1969-72, pres., chief exec. officer, 1972-74; pres. Capital Strategy, Inc. Bd. dirs., mem. exec. com. Balt. Bancorp, Bank of Balt.; trustee The Hotel Investors, 1970-77; dir. Big Sky Montana, 1971-75, Sta. KTCA-TV, Mpls., 1978-85; mng. dir. Weeden and Co.; assoc. mem. NYSE, 1985-88; chmn. Capital Strategy, 1988—; dir. Caribbean Marine Rsch. Found., 1993—. Author: The Sky's The Limit: The History of the Airlines, 1962; repub. with introduction by Charles A. Lindbergh, 1972. Bd. dirs. Charles A. Lindbergh Fund; founder Citizens for Colin Powell, 1996 Presdl. Draft, 1994—. 1st lt. USAF, 1954-56. Mem. Racquet & Tennis Club (N.Y.C.), Yale Club (N.Y.C.), Met. Club (Washington). Office: 3018 N St NW Washington DC 20007-3404

KELLY, CHERYL ANN, healthcare administrator; b. Bay City, Mich., July 28, 1956; d. Frederick Joseph and Julie Frances (Filary) Budzinski; m. Hugh Paul Kelly, Aug. 3, 1979; 1 child, Jenna Ann. BS, U. Mich., 1977; MS, U. Ariz., 1981, MBA, 1988. Cert. rehab. counselor. Tchr. Northview Pub. Schs., Grand Rapids, Mich., 1977-78; rehab. counselor St. Mary's Hosp., Tucson, 1980-81; mgr. Jewish Family Service, Tucson, 1981-82; service coordinator Pima County, Tucson, 1982-86; bus. devel. officer Western Savs. and Loan, Tucson, 1986-88; dir. social services Carondelet Holy Family, Tucson, 1988-89; dir. mktg. Devon Gables Healthcare, 1989-90; asst. adminstr. Desert Life, Valley House, 1990; healthcare adminstr. The Forum, Tucson, 1990-93; adminstr. Manor Care Health & Rehab. Ctr., Tucson, 1993-95; asst. hosp. adminstr. Am. Transitional Hosp., Tucson, 1995-97; adminstr. Vencor Villa Campana, Tucson, 1997-98; exec. dir. Alterra Sterling Ho., Tucson, 1998—. Instr. U. Phoenix, 1991—. Bd. dirs. Tucson Old Pueblo Exchange, 1987; vol., Make a Wish Found. Mem. NAFE. Republican. Roman Catholic.

KELLY, CHRISTINA, editor; BA in english and history, Colgate U. Contbg. editor US; editor Sassy, 1988—94; dep. editor/founding editor Jane Mag., 1997—2000; exec. editor YM Mag., editor-in-chief, 2001—. Publisher: freelance articles include Rolling Stone, Spin, Premiere, The Rolling Stone Book of Women in Rock. Mem.: ASME. Office: YM Magazine 15 East 26th St New York NY 10010

KELLY, CHRISTOPHER A. brigadier general United States air force; m. Kathy Kelly; children: Nick, Matthew. BS in Mgmt., USAF Acad., 1974; grad., Squadron Officer Sch, Maxwell AFB, Ala., 1979; MS in Mgmt., Webster U., 1984; student, Air Command and Staff Coll., Maxwell AFB, Ala., 1986, Indsl. Coll. of Armed Forces, Ft. McNair, Washington, 1991; nat. securities studies, Johns Hopkins U., 1998. Commd 2d lt. USAF, 1974, advanced through grades to brig. gen., 1998; instr., pilot, evaluator pilot 61st airlift squadron 314th airlift wing USAF, Little Rock AFB, Ark., 1975-81; staff officer Air Staff Tng. Program Hdqs., USAF, Washington, 1981-82; programming officer Hdqs. Mil. Airlift Commmand, Scott AFB, Ill., 1982-85; chief pilot 345th tactical airlift squadron USAF, Yokota Air Base, Japan, 1986-88; dep. exec. asst. chmn. Joint Chiefs of Staff, Washington, 1991-93; comdr. 38th ops. group USAF, Plattsburgh AFB, N.Y., 1993-94; chief spl. air missions Office Vice Chief of Staff Hdqrs. USAF, Washington, 1994-95; exec. officer to vice chief of staff Hdqs. USAF, Washington, 1995-96; comdr. 100th air refueling wing USAF, RAF Base Mildenhall, Eng., 1996-97, comdr. 97th air mobility wing Altus AFB, Okla., 1997-99; dep. dir. Strategic Planning & Policy HQ US Pacific Command, Camp H.M. Smith, Hawaii, 1999-2000; vice comdr. 15th Air Force Air Mobility Command, Travis AFB, Calif., 2000—. Decorated Legion of Merit, Defense Superior Svcs. medal, Combat Readiness medal with one oak leaf cluster, Meritorious Svc. medal with three oak leaf clusters, Air Force Commendation medal. Office: Travis AFB 60 AMW/CV 60 Support Group Travis AFB CA 94535-5049

KELLY, CHRISTOPHER PAT, dean, educator; b. Las Vegas, Nev., July 22, 1947; s. James Albert and Patsy Jean Kelly; m. Wendy Leigh Miller, Nov. 24, 1989; children: Brandon Charles Dimick, Heather Dawn Roberts. EdD, U. of Nev., Las Vegas, Las Vegas, Nev., 1999—2002, MS Acctg., 1993—96, Med, 1973—75, BS Bus. Adminstrn., 1966—70. Acct. Sunrise Hosp., Las Vegas, Nev., 1971—72; bus. edn. tchr./coord. Clark County Sch. Dist., Las Vegas, Nev., 1973—78; prof./chair of acctg. C.C. of So. Nev., North Las Vegas, Nev., 1978—98, dean of bus., industry, and pub. services, 1998—. Author: (dissertation) A Comparative Study of Funding Mechanisms for Cmty. Colleges in the State of Nev. and Selected States. Recipient Burlington Outstanding Tchg. Faculty, C.C. of So. Nev., 1993, Who's Who Among America's Teachers, Ednl. Comm. Inc., 1993-1995, NISOD Excellence Award, Nat. Inst. for Staff and Orgn. Devel. U. of Tex. at Austin, 1994, Disting. Men in So. Nev., Disting. Pub. Co., 2000-2002. Mem.: Inst. of Mgmt. Accountants, UNLV Alumni Assn. (bd. dirs.). Avocation: tennis. Office: Cmty Coll of So Nevada 3200 East Cheyenne Avenue - Z2A North Las Vegas NV 89030-4296 Office Fax: 702-651-4486. E-mail: chris_kelly@ccsn.nevada.edu.

KELLY, CHUCK H. singer, writer, trombonist; b. Dallas, Aug. 19, 1930; s. John Richard and Pauline Madrid (Campbell) K.; m. Jaye P. Morgan, Dec. 5, 1959 (div. Dec. 1960); m. Beverly M. Wolfe, July 24, 1961; children: David Gregory, Shawn Charles. BA in Comm. Arts, Sierra U., 1983, MA in Comm., Orgnl. Theory, 1984. Ind. trombonist, singer various big bands, entertainers, nationwide, 1952-80; ind. comml. singer nationwide, 1956-76; ind. motion picture voice-track singer, 1966-70; ind. tech. writer/cons., 1980—. Author: (novelization) High Stakes, (novels) Sammy, 2000, Silent Obsession, 2000, (children's novella series) Legend of Otherland: Evil Does Exist, 2001, Legend of Otherland: Adventure Underground; tech. writer/editor Alchemy of Intelligence, 1984; tech. editor: Pharmacology, Biology and Clinical Applications of Androgens, 1996; converted articles from rsch. scientists for med. ref./text books; trombonist with various big bands including Glenn Miller (dir. Ray McKinley), 1955, Dizzy Gillespie, 1955-56; singer with various entertainers including Betty Hutton, 1958, Paula Kelly and the Modernaires, 1959-64, Jerry Lewis, 1962-63, Bob Newhart, 1963-64, Ronald Reagan, 1963, Bing Crosby, 1966-71, Andy Griffith, 1968, Dick van Dyke, 1968, Jim Nabors, 1968, Danny Thomas; comml. singer for numerous cos. including Oldsmobile, 1961, Sears, 1972; singer in numerous motion pictures including Hello Dolly, 1968, Sweet Charity, 1969, Peter Gunn, 1969; singer, performer various TV shows including Danny Kaye Show, 1965-67, George Gobel Show, 1962-63, Red Skelton Show, 1964-69; tech. writer for various corps. including Hughes Aircraft Co., Northrop Corp; contbr. articles to profl. jours. Served with USN, 1951. Sierra U. scholar, 1983. Mem. AFTRA, ASCAP, SAG, Soc. of Singers (bd. dirs. 1986-92). Democrat. Avocations: hypnotism, psychology, writing, metaphysics. Home and Office: PO Box 30065 Long Beach CA 90803 E-mail: lamplitr@ix.netcom.com.

KELLY, CLEO PARKER, retired bank executive; b. Moreland, Ala., Feb. 25, 1918; d. Lee Reynold and Mittie Revis; m. Albert Francis Parker, Nov. 4, 1933 (dec. Nov. 15, 1983); 1 child, Brenda Faye Floyd; m. Emmett Smith Kelly, Oct. 8, 1985. AS in Banking, Broward C.C., Ft. Lauderdale, Fla., 1980; BA in Psychology, U. Miami, Fla., 1964. Sec., clk. Morgan County Office Dep. Sheriff, Decatur, Ala.; dep. cir. ct. clk. Morgan County Cir. Ct. Clks. Office, Decatur; legal sec. Hare, Wynn & Newell, Birmingham, Nichols, Gaither, Green, Frater & Beckham, Miami; numerous secretarial positions First Nat. Bank Miami; various positions Barnett Bank (now Bank Am.), Hollywood and Miami, Fla., asst. v.p. Vol. Hospice Broward County, Ft. Lauderdale, 1988, Hollywood Hills Meth. Ch., Fla., tchr. Sunday sch. Named Woman of Yr., Hollywood Bus. and Profl. Womens Club, 1977. Democrat. Methodist. Avocations: golf, walking. Home: 3300 Golf St Hollywood FL 33021

KELLY, CURTIS HARTT, retired publishing executive; b. Ft. Atkinson, Wis., May 17, 1935; s. Curtis and Edna (Guenther) K. BA, Yankton Coll., 1957. With fin. divsn. Scott Foresman Co., Glenview, Ill., 1962-86, with info. sys. divsn., 1986-97. Home: 1639 W Touhy Ave Apt G Chicago IL 60626-2561

KELLY, DANIEL GRADY, JR., lawyer; b. Yonkers, N.Y., July 15, 1951; s. Daniel Grady and Helene (Coyne) K.; m. Annette Susan Wheeler, May 8, 1976; children— Elizabeth Anne, Brigid Claire, Cynthia Logan. Grad., Choate Sch., Wallingford, Conn., 1969; BA magna cum laude, Yale U., 1973; JD, Columbia U., 1976. Bar: N.Y. 1977, U.S. Dist. Ct. (so. and ea. dists.) N.Y. 1977, Calif. 1986, U.S. Dist. Ct. (cen. dist.) Calif. 1987. Law clk. to judge U.S. Ct. Appeals (2d cir.), N.Y.C., 1976-77; assoc. Davis Polk & Wardwell, N.Y.C., 1977-83; sr. v.p. Lehman Bros., N.Y.C., 1983-85; sr. v.p., gen. counsel Kaufman & Broad, Inc., L.A., 1985-87; ptnr. Manatt, Phelps, Rothenberg & Phillips, L.A., 1987-90, Sidley & Austin, L.A. and N.Y., 1990-99, Davis Polk & Wardwell, N.Y.C. and Menlo Park, Calif., 1999—. Mem. editl. bd. Columbia Law Rev., 1975-76. Office: Davis Polk & Wardwell 1600 El Camino Real Menlo Park CA 94025-4119 E-mail: dankelly@dpw.com.

KELLY, DANIEL JOHN, physician; b. Binghamton, N.Y., June 23, 1940; s. William James and Mary Elizabeth (Schmitt) K.; m. Lois Ann Lanshe, Aug. 21, 1965; children: Britton James, Jeffrey Daniel, Reid William, Piper Ann. AB in History, Yale U., 1962; MD, Jefferson Med. Coll., 1966. Diplomate in Pathology, Nuclear Medicine, Dermatopathology. Intern Naval Hosp., Boston, 1966-67, resident Oakland, Calif., 1966-71, asst. chief lab. Great Lakes, Ill., 1971-73, chief lab. svcs., 1973-75; co-dir. lab. Highland Park (Ill.) Hosp., 1975-97, dir. lab., 1980-89, 96-97; co-dir. lab. Lake Forest (Ill.) Hosp., 1975-97, dir. lab., 1989-91; with Dean, Hoffman & Clark Pathologists S.C., Lake Forest, 1975-97, Associated Lab. Physician Svcs., Wauwatosa, Wis., 1997-99; chief of staff elect Highland Park (Ill.) Hosp., 1992-94, chief of staff, 1994-96, also bd. dirs.; with Consolidated Pathology Cons., S.C., Lake Bluff, Ill., 1999—. Med. exec. com. Highland Park Hosp., 1992-97, Lake Forest Hosp., 1989-91. Bd. dirs. Lake Forest Hist. Preservation Found., 1979-88; mem. bldg. rev. bd. City Govt., Lake Forest, 1989-93; mem. clin. lab. and blood bank adv. bd. Ill. Dept. Pub. Health, 1990-95; mem. Am. Pathology Found. Comdr. USNR, 1966-75. Fellow Coll. Am. Pathology, Am. Soc. Clin. Pathology, Internat. Acad. Pathologists, Am. Assn. Clin. Scientists; mem. AMA, Ill. Soc. Pathologists, Am. Soc. Microbiology, Am. Soc. Dermatopathology, Internat. Soc. Dermatopathology, Am. Acad. Dermatology, Assn. Military Surgeons. Roman Catholic. Avocations: reading, art, music, fishing. Home: 499 E Illinois Rd Lake Forest IL 60045-2364 Office: Dept Pathology Lake Forest Hosp 660 N Westmoreland Rd Lake Forest IL 60045-1659 Fax: 847-535-6237. E-mail: djdock@webtv.net.

KELLY, DANIEL THOMAS, statistician; b. Phila., Oct. 19, 1976; s. Joseph Andrew and Katherine Theresa Kelly. BS, Loyola Coll., Balt., 1998; M in Stats., N.C. State U., 2000. Sr. project analyst II Fleet Credit Card Svcs., Horsham, Pa., 2000—. Presdl. scholar, Loyola Coll. in Md., 1994—98, Gertrude M. Cox Meml. fellow, N.C. State U., 1998—99, Alumni fellow, 1998—99. Mem.: Am. Statis. Assn., Pi Mu Epsilon, Alpha Sigma Nu, Phi Kappa Phi, Phi Sigma Iota, Mu Sigma Rho, Phi Beta Kappa. Personal E-mail: statdan@yahoo.com.

KELLY, DAVID AUSTIN, investment counselor; b. Mt. Kisco, N.Y., June 24, 1938; s. William Andrew and Katharine Elizabeth (Barrett) K.; m. Judith Boesel, June 18, 1966; children: Carolyn K. Patten, Douglas Austin. BA, Lafayette Coll., 1962; MBA, U. Chgo., 1964. Chartered fin. analyst. Asst. v.p. investment mgmt. group Citibank, N.Y.C., 1964-69; portfolio mgr., v.p. J.M. Hartwell & Co., Inc., N.Y.C., 1969-72; pres., CEO P/H Mgmt. Corp., Pitts., 1972-74; asst. treas. Gulf Oil Corp., Pitts., 1974-80; v.p., treas. Borden, Inc., N.Y.C., 1980-95, treas., prin. fin. officer, dir. BCP Mgmt., Inc., Borden Chemicals and Plastics Ltd. Partnership, 1987-95; pres. Three Lakes Advisors, Inc., 1996—. Past bd. dirs. Ctr. for Redirection through Edn., Inc., Bedford Hills, N.Y. Past councilor N.Y. Soc., Order of Founders and Patriots Am.; mem. fin. policy com. Lafayette Coll., Easton, Pa., 1976-79; treas. bd. dirs. The Greenwich (Conn.) Land Trust Inc. Served with U.S. Army, 1957-59. Mem. NAM (chmn. auditing com. 1983-92), Assn. for Investment Mgmt. and Rsch., N.Y. Soc. Security Analysts, Stanwich Club (Greenwich, Conn.). Home: 303 Overlook Dr Greenwich CT 06830-6716 Office: Three Lakes Advisors Inc 303 Overlook Dr Greenwich CT 06830-6716 E-mail: thrlakeadv@aol.com.

KELLY, DEE J. lawyer; b. Bonham, Tex., Mar. 7, 1929; s. Dee C. and Era L. (Jones) K.; m. Janice LeBlanc, Dec. 30, 1954; children: Cynthia Kelly Barnes, Dee J., Craig LeBlanc. BA, Tex. Christian U., 1950; LL.B., George Washington U., 1954. Bar: Tex. 1954. Pvt. practice law, Ft. Worth, 1956-79; founding, sr. ptnr. Kelly, Hart & Hallman, Ft. Worth, 1979—. Bd. dirs. A.M.R., 1983—2000, Justin Industries, Inc., 1986—2000, The SABRE Group Holdings, Inc., 1996—2000. Trustee Tex. Christian U., 1971—; bd. dirs. Tex. Turnpike Authority, 1967-76, chmn., 1969-76; bd. regents Tex. State U. System, 1969-75; trustee U. Tex. Law Sch. Found., 1983-2002; bd. dirs. Ctr. Am. and Internat. Law; trustee Scott and White Meml. Hosp. and Scott, Sherwood and Bridley Found., 1989-98, U. Tex. Southwestern Moncrief Radiation Ctr., 1985-; bd. visitors U. Tex. Cancer Ctr., 1980-87; mem. Joint Select Com. on Judiciary, 1988, Task Force on Jud. Selection, 1995-96, Fed. Jud. Evaluation Com., 1989—; dir. Southwestern Expn. and Livestock Show, 1986—; mem. bd advisors George Washington U. Law Sch., 2001—. 1st lt. USAF, 1951-53.

Named Disting. Alumni, Tex. Christian U., 1982, George Washington U., 2001, Ft. Worth's Outstanding Bus. Exec., 1993, Ft. Worth's Outstanding Citizen, 2000; recipient Horatio Alger award Horatio Alger Assn. Disting. Ams., 1995, Blackstone award, 1998. Fellow Am. Bar Found.; mem. Tarrant County Bar Assn., Tarrant County Bar Found., Tex. Bar Found. (founding mem.). Avocation: golf. Home: 1315 Hillcrest St Fort Worth TX 76107-1577 E-mail: dee_kelly@khh.com.

KELLY, DENNIS MICHAEL, lawyer; b. Cleve., May 6, 1943; s. Thomas Francis and Margaret (Murphy) K.; m. Marilyn Ann Divoky, Dec. 28, 1967; children: Alison, Meredith. BA, John Carroll U., 1961-65; JD, U. Notre Dame, 1968. Bar: Ohio 1968. Law clk. U.S. Ct. Appeals (8th cir.), Cleve., 1968-69; assoc. Jones, Day, Reavis & Pogue, Cleve., 1969-75, ptnr., 1975—. Mem. Ohio Bar Assn., Bar Assn. Greater Cleve. Office: Jones Day Reavis & Pogue North Point 901 Lakeside Ave E Cleveland OH 44114-1190 E-mail: dmkelly@jonesday.com.

KELLY, DENNIS RAY, sales executive; b. Olympia, Wash., Aug. 20, 1948; s. William E. and Irene (Lewis) K.; m. Pamela Jo Kresevich, Mar. 16, 1974. BA, Cen. Wash. U., 1972; postgrad., U. Wash., 1977-78. Sales rep. Bumble Bee Sea Foods, Seattle, 1972-74; retail sales mgr. Pacific Pearl Sea Foods, Seattle, 1974-76; regional sales mgr. Castle & Cooke Foods, Seattle, Phila., and N.Y.C., 1976-80; v.p. sales mktg. Frances Andrew Ltd., Seattle, 1980-82; regional sales mgr. Tenneco West, Seattle, 1982-85; sales and mktg. mgr. for western U.S. David Oppenheimer, Seattle, 1985-96; sales mgr. Rogge Co., 1997-2000; pvt. cons., 2000—. Alumni advisor Ctrl. Wash. U., Ellensburg, 1979-87, alumni bd. dirs., 1986—, fund drive chmn., 1988—, vendor rels.-mktg. com., 1998—, mem. sch. cmty. group bd.; pres. Ctrl. Washington U. Alumni Assn.; bd. dirs. Bay Vista Tower Assn., v.p., pres., 1998; mem. Statue of Liberty Ellis Island Found.; chmn. ann. fund drive Ctrl. Wash. U., bd. dirs., 1992; pres. Lake Water Dist., 1998; adv. com. United States Senate Seattle; fire commr. Dist. 6, precinct com. officer. Mem. New Zealand-Am. Soc., Mfrs. Reps. Club Wash. (bd. dirs.). Republican. Avocations: hiking, backpacking, skiing, snowmobiling. Home and Office: PO Box 383 Ronald WA 98940-0383

KELLY, SISTER DOROTHY ANN, Ursuline Provincial college chancellor; b. Bronx, NY, July 26, 1929; d. Walter David and Sarah (McCauley) K. BA in History, Coll. New Rochelle, 1951; MA in Am. Ch. History, Cath. U., Washington, 1958; PhD in Am. Intellectual History, U. Notre Dame, 1970; LittD (hon.), Mercy Coll., Dobbs Ferry, N.Y., 1976; LLD (hon.), Nazareth Coll. of Rochester, N.Y., 1979; DHL (hon.), Coll. St. Rose, 1981, Manhattan Coll., 1979, LeMoyne Coll., 1990, St. Thomas Aquinas Coll., 1990, St. Joseph Coll., Conn., 1996, Iona Coll., 1997. Joined Order of St. Ursula, Roman Cath. Ch., 1952. Assoc. prof. history Coll. New Rochelle, N.Y., 1957—, chmn. dept. history, 1965-67, acad. dean, 1967-72, acting pres., 1970-71, pres., 1972-97, chancellor, 1997—. Mem. Interreligious Coun. New Rochelle, 1974—, exec. com., 1974-79, v.p., 1980-84, pres., 1984-88, mem. Commn. Ind. Colls. and Univs. State of N.Y., 1976-78, chmn. bd. trustees, 1978-80, mem. govt. rels. com., 1980-81; chmn. Com. Higher Edn. Opportunity, 1976-78; mem. commr. of edn. Adv. Coun. on Higher Edn. for N.Y. State, 1975-77, subcom. on postsecondary occupational edn., 1975-77; exec. com. Empire State Found. Ind. Liberal Arts Colls., 1975—, vice chmn., 1977-81, chmn., 1981—; trustee, mem. exec. com. Assn. Colls. and Univs. State of N.Y., 1976-80; mem. com. on purpose and identity Assn. Cath. Colls. and Univs., 1975-80; mem. steering com. Neylan Conf., 1978-81, mem. bishops and pres. com., 1979-84; mem. adv. coun. on fin. aid to students Office Edn., HEW, 1978-86; chmn. Women's Coll. Coalition, 1981-83; chmn. govt. rels. adv. com. Nat. Assn. Ind. Colls. and Univs., 1981-82, chair, 1987-88. Chair City-wide Confs., New Rochelle, 1977-79; bd. dirs. United Way Westchester, 1977-84, mem. planning, allocations, evaluation com., 1977-80, nominating and campaign coms., 1990—; bd. dirs. Westchester County Assn., 1980-90, New Rochelle Community Action Program, 1982-83, New Rochelle Cmty. Fund, 1989-91; mem. steering com. Westchester County Women's Hall of Fame, 1984-85; bd. dirs. Vis. Nurse Svcs. in Westchester, Inc., 1983-86, chair nominating com., 1985-86; trustee LeMoyne Coll., 1982-88, vice chairperson, 1984-87; mem. bd. govs. New Rochelle Hosp. Med. Ctr., 1987—; trustee United Student Aid Funds, 1980-90, Ursuline Sch., New Rochelle, 1988—, Cath. U. Am., 1988—, Am. Coun. on Edn., 1990—, Ind. Coll. Fund Am., 1982-85; mem. ofcl. U.S. del. to UN 4th World Conf. on Women in Beijing, 1995; mem. nat. adv. bd. Nat. Mus. Women in the Arts, 1996—. Recipient Medallion award Westchester C.C., 1978, Leadership award Am. Soc. Pub. Adminstrn., 1986, Sch. Svc. award Thornton-Donovan Sch., 1977, Henry D. Paley award, 1994, Father Theodore M. Hesburgh award, 1998, N.Y. State Gov.'s award for excellence, 1997; inducted into Westchester County/Avon Women's Hall of Fame, 1989; Paul Harris fellow, 1997. Mem. AAUP, AAUW, NCCJ (trustee 1989—), Am. Hist. Assn., Nat. Fedn. Bus. and Profl. Women, Am. Assn. Higher Edn., Nat. Assembly Women Religious, Am. Coun. Edn. (bd. dirs. 1990), Assn. Am. Colls. (bd. dirs. 1983-86), Tchrs. Ins. and Annuity Assn. Am. (trustee 1987—, fin. com. 1987-88, exec. com. 1988—, audit com. 1990—, products and svcs. com. 1990-91, nominating and pers. com. 1991), Assn. Colls. Mid-Hudson Area (pres. 1979-81, exec. com. 1982—).

KELLY, DOROTHY ANN, language educator, writer; b. N.Y.C., N.Y., July 5, 1948; BS, SUNY, Buffalo, 1970; MA, Hofstra U, 1974; ArtsD, Adelphi U, 1990. Speech-lang. tchr. pathologist various private and pub. inst., Suffolk County, NY; assoc. prof., dept. chair St. Joseph's Coll., Patchogue, NY, 1991—; editl. cons. Advance for Speech-Lang. Pathologists, King of Prussia, Pa., 1991—. Author: Ctrl. Auditory Processing Disorder: Strategies For Use in Children and Adolecants, 1995, A Winner's Workbook, 1998; author: (asessment pub.) Screening for Ctrl Auditory Processing Difficulties, 2001. Mem.: Am. Psychological Assn. (assoc.), Am. Speech-Lang.-Hearing Assn. (assoc.). Avocations: reading, travel, writing. Office: St Joseph's College 155 W Roe Blvd Patchogue NY 11772 Home: 44 Long Meadow Place S Setauket NY 11720

KELLY, EDMUND FRANCIS, insurance company executive; b. 1946; With Aetna Life & Casualty Co., 1974-92; pres., COO Liberty Mut. Ins. Co., Boston, 1992-98, pres., CEO, 1998—. Office: 175 Berkeley St Boston MA 02116-5066

KELLY, EDMUND JOSEPH, lawyer, investment banker; b. Mount Vernon, N.Y., May 18, 1937; s. Hugh Joseph and Catherine (Rice) K.; m. Joan Anne Fee, Nov. 18, 1961; children: Kathleen Kelly Broomer, Edmund Murphy, Thomas More, Mary Kelly Mehr, Michael McNaboe. AB cum laude, Coll. of Holy Cross, 1959; JD (James Kent scholar), Columbia U., 1962. Bar: N.Y. 1962. Sec. of Air Force Office of Gen.Counsel, Washington, 1962-65; assoc. White & Case, N.Y.C., 1965-70, ptnr., 1971-84; vice chmn. Dominick & Dominick Co., N.Y.C., 1984-91, Eighteen Seventy Corp., Purchase, N.Y., 1991—. Lectr. Practicing Law Inst., Am. Mgmt. Assn.; bd. dirs. Fed. Paper Bd. Co., Inc., Montvale, N.J., 1981-96; bd. dirs., mem. exec. com. Chgo. Pneumatic Tool Co., N.Y.C., 1980-86. Author: The Takeover Dialogues, A Discussion of Hostile Takeovers, 1987; editor Columbia Law Rev., 1961-62; contbr. articles to legal jours. Air Force mem. Armed Services Procurement Regulation Com., 1964-65. Office: Eighteen Seventy Corp Two Manhattanville Rd Purchase NY 10577-2118

KELLY, EDWARD ALOYSIUS, JR., physician; b. Darby, Pa., Mar. 16, 1948; s. Edward A. and Adele R. (Angelucci) K.; m. Sharon C. Quinn Kelly, May 17, 1975 (div. Mar. 6, 1994); children: Kristin Colleen, Daniel Edward, Megan Grace. AB in Biology, St. Joseph's U., Phila., 1969; MD, Thomas Jefferson U., Phila., 1973. Diplomate Am. Bd. Family Practice. Resident Wilmington (Del.) Med. Ctr., 1973-76; pvt. practice Downingtown (Pa.) Family Practice, 1976—. Profl. cons., 1984—; mem. profl. adv. coun. Blue Shield of Pa., Camp Hill, 1985-97; chmn. dept. family practice Brandywine Hosp., Coatesville, Pa., 1989-94. Sch. and team physician Downingtown Area Sch. Dist., 1983—2001; bd. dirs. Downingtown (Pa.) Sr. Ctr., 1985—. Fellow Am. Acad. Family Physicians, Pa. Acad. Family Physicians (treas. 1983-85, v.p. 1985-86, pres.-elect 1986-87, pres. 1987-88, del. 1992-95). Republican. Roman Catholic. Avocations: golf, skiing, music. Office: 99 Manor Ave Downingtown PA 19335-2601

KELLY, EDWARD JOHN, V, counselor; b. Saratoga Springs, N.Y., July 10, 1936; s. Edward John IV and Blanch Marie (O'Connor) K.; children: Edward J. VI, Patrick J., Kevin J., Michael J., Kathleen M. Student, Union Coll., Schenectady, N.Y., 1954-56; MEd in Guidance and Counseling, Campbell U., Buies Creek, N.C., 1990; student, U. Dayton, 1967; BA in History, N.C. Wesleyan Coll., 1982. Commd. USAF, 1956, advanced through grades to lt. col., 1975; instr. navigation Strategic Air Command USAF, various locations, 1958-69; scheduler KC-135 USAF, Castle AFB, Calif., 1970-71, chief bomber ops., 1972-73, chief KC-135 planner Anderson AFB, Guam, 1973-74; 8AF chief of tng. Anderson AFB, Guam, 1974-75; dir. ops. and tng. USAF, Seymour Johnson AFB, N.C., 1977-78, ret., 1979; job developer, counselor Wayne C.C., Goldsboro, N.C., 1979-80, dir. coop. edn., job placement and apprenticeship, 1980-97. Chmn. County Workforce Devel. Coun., Goldsboro, 1980-97; com. chmn. N.C. Internship Coun., 1985-93, N.C. trails com. chmn. 1989-92. Author: Canoeing the Neuse River, 1983, Your Move Into the World of Work, 1988. Chmn. task force Waynesborough State Pk., 1983-86, 90-94, 95-2002; scoutmaster Boy Scouts Am., Merced., Calif. and Guam, Goldsboro, 1971-86, coun. commr., Goldsboro, 1976-81, 84-88, dist. chmn., 1982-84; cand. Rep. Party, Wayne County, 1982, 84, 86; bd. dirs. Sr. Inst., Ctrl. Fla. C.C., 2003—, pres., 2003; v.p. Silver Springs Shores Residents Assn., 2003—. Recipient Silver Beaver award Boy Scouts Am., 1973. Mem. DAV, VFW, Coop. Edn. Assn., N.C. Coop. Edn. Assn. (bd. dirs. 1985-97, pres. 1994, Outstanding Profl. 1994), N.C. Placement Assn. (program co-chmn. 1990, Outstanding Profl. 1991), Neuse Trails Assn., Air Force Assn. (pres. 1980-82, 90-91, Merit medal 1989), County Pers. Assn. (pres. 1992). Avocations: organic gardening, horticulture, recreational vehicles, canoeing, fishing. Home: 2 Emerald Ct Ocala FL 34472-E-mail: edphylkelly@earthlink.net.

KELLY, ERIC DAMIAN, lawyer, educator; b. Pueblo, Colo., Mar. 16, 1947; s. William Bret and Patricia Ruth (Ducy) K.; children: Damian Charles, Eliza Jane, Valissitie Christina Heeren, Douglas Ray Heeren; m. Sandra Walker, 1996. BA, Williams Coll., 1969; JD, M of City Planning, U. Pa., 1975; PhD, Union Inst., 1992. Bar: Colo. 1975, U.S. Dist. Ct. 1976, U.S. Tax Ct. 1976, U.S. Ct. Appeals (10th cir.) 1986. Chief citizens' participation unit Region III EPA, Phila., 1971-72; project planner Beckett New Town, N.J., 1972-73; v.p., project mgr. Rahenkamp Sachs Wells & Assocs., Inc., Denver and Phila., 1973-76; sole practice Pueblo, 1976-83; pres. Kelly & Potter, P.C., Pueblo, Albuquerque and Santa Fe, 1983-90. Adj. prof. U. Colo. Coll. Architecture and Planning, 1976-90; chmn., prof. Dept. cmty. and regional planning Iowa State U., 1990-95; adj. asst. prof. grad. sch. bus. U. So. Colo., 1986-90; dean coll. architecture and planning Ball State U., 1995-98, prof. urban planning, 1999—; mem. city devel. bd. State of Iowa, 1991-95. Gen. editor Zoning and Land Use Controls, 1995—; author: Enforcing Zoning and Land Use Codes, 1988, Managing Community Growth: Policies, Techniques and Impacts, 1993, Selecting and Retaining Consultants, 1993, Planning, Growth and Public Facilities: A Primer for Public Officials, 1994; editor, prin. author: The Roadtripper, 1969; contbr. articles to profl. planning and legal jours. Mem. adv. bd. Mcpl. Legal Studies Ctr., S.W. Legal Found., 1989—; mem. nat. adv. bd. Rocky Mountain Land Use Inst. Coll. Law U. Denver, 1992—; bd. dirs. Broadway Theatre League, Pueblo, 1976-77, Pueblo Beautiful Assn., 1978-82, Better Bus. Bur., 1988-89; trustee Sangre de Cristo Arts and Conf. Ctr., 1981-87, chmn. 1986; trustee Christ Congl. Ch., 1982-83; mem. Ind. Land Resources Coun., 1999—; bd. dirs., mem. adv. bd. Nature Conservacy Ind. With U.S. Army, 1969-71. Named Outstanding Student, Am. Inst. Planners, 1976; recipient Outstanding Faculty award Order of Omega, 1992. Mem. ABA, Am. Inst. Cert. Planners (charter, elected Coll. of Fellows 1999), Am. Planning Assn. (nat. pres., 1997—, chair planning & law divsn. 1996-97, pres. Iowa chpt. 1994-95, amicus curiae com. 1988-94, 95-97, legis. & policy com. 1993-97, Colo. chpt. excellence award 1989), Williams Coll. Alumni Assn. (class sec. 1969-74, regional sec. 1980-82, class agt. 1985-89), Rotary (local dir. 1988-90, dir., pres. Pueblo Rotary Found. 1988-89, v.p. 1988-89, pres. 1989-90, area rep. for dist. gov. 1991-92), Phi Kappa Phi. Democrat. Home: 2312 W Audubon Dr Muncie IN 47304-2003 Office: Ball State U Coll Architecture Planning Muncie IN 47306-0001

KELLY, FRANCIS J., III, global marketing company president and COO; m. Heather Kelly; children: Whitney, Jay (twins). BA, Amherst Coll.; MBA, Harvard. With Young & Rubicam, N.Y.C., 1978-81; from acct. exec. to sr. v.p., group acct. dir. Humphrey Browning MacDougall, 1983-88; prin., dir. client svcs., COO Leonard Monahan, Lubars & Kelly, Providence, 1989-94; chief mktg. officer, dir. planning and client svcs. Volkswagen, Am. Legacy Found., Talbots, Royal Caribbean, Titleist, FootJoy, The Hartford, Citizens Fin. Arnold Comm., 1994—; pres., COO Arnold Worldwide, Boston. Spkr. in field. Author (with Heather Kelly): What They Really Teach You at the Harvard Business School. Mem.: Essex County Club, Harvard Club Boston, Boston Ad Club (past pres.). Avocations: golf, paddle tennis, traveling, reading, coaching youth sports. Office: Arnold Worldwide 101 Huntington Ave Boston MA 02199-7603

KELLY, GEORGE ANTHONY, clergyman, author, educator; b. N.Y.C., Sept. 17, 1916; s. Charles W. and Bridget (Fitzgerald) K. MA in Social Sci., Catholic U Am., 1943, PhD in Social Sci., 1946. Ordained priest Roman Cath. Ch., 1942, elevated to monsignor, 1960. Priest St. Monica's Parish, N.Y.C., 1945-56; dir. Family Life Bur., 1955-65, Family Consultation Service, 1955-65; dir. dept. edn. Archdiocese N.Y.C., 1966-70; pastor St. John's Ch., N.Y.C., 1970-74; dir. Inst. Advanced Studies in Cath. doctrine, St. John's U., Jamaica, N.Y., 1975-81; exec. sec. Fellowship of Cath. Scholars, 1976, pres., 1986-88. Consultor Archdiocese N.Y., Congregation for the Clergy, Rome, 1984; sec. bd. trustees St. Joseph's Sem.; sec. adv. bd. Pastoral Life Conf.; co-chmn. Archdiocesan Parish Councils, 1966-70 Author: The Parish, 1973, Who Should Run the Catholic Church?, 1976, The Battle for the American Church, 1979, The Crisis of Authority: John Paul II and the American Bishops, 1981, The New Biblical Theorists: Raymond E. Brown and Beyond, 1983, Inside My Father's House, 1989, Keeping the Church Catholic with John Paul II, 1990, The Pastor's Challenge, 1994, The Battle for the American Church Revisited, 1995, The Second Spring fo the Church in America, 2001, others. Recipient 1st Cardinal Wright award Friends of Fellowship of Cath. Scholars, 1979, Faith and Family award Women for Faith and Family, 1988, Pres.'s medal St. John's U., 1992, Courage in Faith award Steubenville U., 1997, Rivs XI award Soc. of Cath. Social Scientists, 1999. Mem. AAUP, Am. Sociol. Assn., Am. Cath. Sociol. Soc., Assn. for Sociology of Religion, Am. Cath. Hist. Soc., Am. Cath. Theol. Soc. Roman Catholic. Address: 10710 Shore Front Pkwy Far Rockaway NY 11694-2637

KELLY, GERALD WAYNE, chemical coatings company executive; b. Charleston, W.Va., May 21, 1944; s. Wayne Woodside (dec.) and Sarrah (Myers) K.; m. (div.); children: Scott Wayne, Lauren Melissa (dec.); m. Elizabeth Long, Nov. 18, 1983. BS, W.Va. U., 1966. From sales corr. to regional mgr. duPont Corp., various locations, 1966-83; bus. mgr. Decatur (Ala.) divsn. Whittaker Corp., 1983-85; v.p. Decatur divsn. Morton Internat., 1985-86, pres. Decatur divsn., 1986-93; v.p. Morton Indsl. Coatings, Morton Internat., Chgo., 1993-99; pres./owner IRP Inc., Falkville, Ala., 1992-99; exec. v.p. D & K Group Inc., Elk Grove Village, Ill., 2001—; CEO D & K Laminex, Inc., Charlotte, NC, 2001—; COO GW Resources, Murrells Inlet, SC; pres. TKO Resources, Murrells Inlet, SC. Bd. dirs. Ind. Cystic Fibrosis Found., Indpls., 1971-73. Mem. Nat. Coil Coaters Assn., Nat. Paint and Coatings Assn., Beta Theta Pi. Republican. Methodist. Avocation: automobiles. Home: PO Box 2990 Murrells Inlet SC 29576 Office: GW Resources Inc PO Box 2540 Murrells Inlet SC 29576 Address: TKO Resources Inc PO Box 2990 Surfside Beach SC 29576 E-mail: jkmek@aol.com.

KELLY, GRACE DENTINO, secondary education educator; b. Peoria, Ill., Mar. 30, 1934; d. Michael and Arnita Balagna (Barto) Dentino; m. Robert N. Kelly, Aug. 31, 1957; children: Susan, James, Stephen, Patrick. Cert. med. tech., St. Francis Sch. Med. Tech., 1955; BS, Bradley U., 1971, MS, 1973. Tchr. sci. St. Mark Sch., Peoria, asst. prin., 1980-83; prin., chmn. jr. H.S. curriculum com. for drug edn. St. Thomas Sch., Peoria Heights, Ill., 1983-89; tchr. biology and chemistry Woodruff High Sch., Peoria, 1989-90; prin. Blessed Sacrament Sch., Morton, Ill., 1991-92, St. Mark Sch., Peoria, 1992-98, Trewyn Mid. Sch., Peoria, 1998—2002; lead tchr. Glen Oak Primary Sch., Peoria, 2002—. Presenter Ill. Math Tchr. Conv., Peoria, 1992; tchr. Aurora (Ill.) U. Mem. adv. bd. Peoria Jour. Star Newspaper, 1973—. Bd. dirs. Spl. People Encounter Christ, 1997. Recipient Econs. Educator award Joint Coun. on Econ. Edn., N.Y.C., 1982—, dedication to excellence in edn. and to justice and equality award NOW, 1998, Esmark Found. award Ill. Coun. Econ. Edn., 1984, Those Who Excell award Ill. State Bd., 1989, PARC award, 1989, Today's Cath. Tchr.'s Project: Sharing award, 1992, Adminstr. of Yr. award Today's Cath. Tchr. Mag., 1992, Jean Tucker award Ill. Valley Mental Health Assn., 1994. Mem. AAUW (Outstanding Cmty. Svc. award, Justice Edn. award 1998), Nat. Sci. Tchrs. Assn., Am. Soc. Clin. Pathologists, Ill. Sci. Tchrs. Assn. (dir. region III, presenter paters), Ill. Jr. Acad. Sci. (dir. region I), Phi Delta Kappa. Roman Catholic. Home: 1815 W High St Peoria IL 61606-1635 Office: Glen Oak Primary Sch 809 Frye St Peoria IL 61603

KELLY, HENRY ANSGAR, English language educator; b. Fonda, Iowa, June 6, 1934; s. Harry Francis and Inez Ingeborg (Anderson) K.; m. Marea Tancred, June 18, 1968; children— Sarah Marea, Dominic Tancred. AB, St. Louis U., 1959, A.M., Ph.L., St. Louis U., 1961; PhD, Harvard U., 1965. Asst. prof. English UCLA, 1967-69, assoc. prof. English, 1969-72, prof. English, 1972—, dir. Ctr. for Medieval and Renaissance Studies, 1998—2003. Author: The Devil, Demonology and Witchcraft, 1968, 74, Divine Providence in the England of Shakespeare's Histories, 1970, Love and Marriage in the Age of Chaucer, 1975, The Matrimonial Trials of Henry VIII, 1976, Canon Law and the Archpriest of Hita, 1984, The Devil at Baptism, 1985, Chaucer and the Cult of St. Valentine, 1986, Tragedy and Comedy from Dante to Pseudo-Dante, 1989, Ideas and Forms of Tragedy from Aristotle to the Middle Ages, 1993, Chaucerian Tragedy, 1997, Inquisitions and Other Trial Procedures in the Medieval West, 2001; co-editor Viator 1970-90, editor, 2003—. Fellow Guggenheim fellow, 1971—72, Nat. Endowment Humanities, 1980—81, 1996—97. Fellow Medieval Acad. Am.; mem. Medieval Assn. of Pacific (pres. 1988-90). Roman Catholic. Home: 1123 Kagawa St Pacific Palisades CA 90272-3838 Office: UCLA Dept English 405 Hilgard Ave Los Angeles CA 90095-9000

KELLY, HUGH RICE, retired lawyer, retired energy executive; b. Austin, Tex., Dec. 16, 1942; s. Thomas Philip and Cecilia Elizabeth (Rice) Kelly; m. Marguerite Susan McIntosh, Dec. 27, 1971; children: Susan McIntosh, Cecilia Rice. BA, Rice U., 1965; JD, U. Tex., 1972. Bar: Tex. 1972, U.S. Dist. Ct. (so. dist.) Tex. 1974, U.S. Ct. Appeals (5th cir.) 1975, U.S. Supreme Ct. 1975. Assoc. Baker & Botts, Houston, 1972-78, ptnr., 1979-84; exec. v.p., gen. counsel Reliant Energy (formerly Houston Lighting & Power Co.), Houston, 1984—2003; ret., 2003. 1st lt. U.S. Army, 1966—69. Fellow: Houston Bar Found., Tex. Bar Found.; mem.: ABA, Houston Bar Assn., State Bar Tex., Coronado Club. Republican. Home: 1936 Rice Blvd Houston TX 77005-1635

KELLY, J. MICHAEL, lawyer; b. Hattiesburg, Miss., Dec. 5, 1943; BA, Emory U., 1966; LLB, U. Va., 1969. Bar: Ga. 1969, U.S. Supreme Ct. 1978, D.C. 1980, Utah 1982, Calif. 1988. Law clerk to Judge Griffin B. Bell (5th cir.) U.S. Ct. Appeals, Atlanta, 1969-70; ptnr. Alston & Bird (formerly Alston, Miller & Gaines), Atlanta, 1970-77, 81-82; counselor to atty. gen. U.S. Dept. Justice, Washington, 1977-79; counselor to sec. U.S. Dept. Energy, Washington, 1979-81; ptnr., shareholder, dir. Ray, Quinney & Nebeker, Salt Lake City, 1982-87; ptnr. Cooley Godward LLP, San Francisco, 1987—. Mem. Omicron Delta Kappa, Phi Alpha Delta. Office: Cooley Godward LLP 1 Maritime Plz Fl 20 San Francisco CA 94111-3510

KELLY, J. MICHAEL, petroleum consultant; b. Roswell, N.Mex., Aug. 12, 1950; s. John Martin and Ester Landenburg Kelly; m. Heidi Craig. BS in Petroleum Engring., N.Mex Inst. Mining and Tech., Socorro, 1972, MS in Petroleum Engring., 1996, PhD in Petroleum Engring., 2000. Prodn. engr. Elk Oil Co., Roswell, 1972—78; pres. Roswell Mfg. & Repair, 1984—94; pres., engr. Keltic Svcs., Inc, Roswell, 1981—; petroleum cons. J. Michael Kelly, Roswell. Dir. Elk Oil Co., Roswell, 1972—; bd. regents N.Mex. Inst. Mining and Tech., Socorro, 1992—97. Mem.: AAAS, Roswell Geol. Assn., Ind. Petroleum Assn. of Am., Soc. of Petroleum Engrs. (sect. pres. 1980—81), Am. Assn. of Petroleum Geologists (assoc.), N.Mex Tech Alumni Assn. (life), Rotary Internat. (group study exch.-team leader dist. 5220 1992, Dist. Found. Svc. award Dist. 5220 1998), Pecos Valley Rotary. Office: J Michael Kelly Box 1116 Roswell NM 88202-1116 Business E-Mail: yllek@ruidoso.org.

KELLY, J. PETER, steel company executive; b. 1941; AB, Harvard U., 1963; JD, Duquesne U., 1972. With LTV Steel Co., Inc., Cleveland, Ohio, 1963—, pres., COO, 1991-2000, chmn., pres. & CEO, 2000—.

KELLY, JAMES, deputy managing editor; b. Brooklyn, NY, Dec. 15, 1953; m. Lisa Henricksson; 1 child, Luke. Grad. Internat. affairs, Princeton Univ., 1977. Senatorial campaign Bill Bradley campaign, NJ, 1977; lead editor Visions 21, NY, NY, 1999—2000; mng. editor Time Mag., NY, NY, 2001. Office: Time Life Bldg Rockerfeller Ctr New York NY 10020

KELLY, JAMES ANDREW, policy research executive, former government official; b. Fond du Lac, Wis., Sept. 15, 1936; s. James Daniel and Clarice K.; m. Audrey Pool, July 30, 1960; children— James, Archer BS, U.S. Naval Acad., 1959; MBA, Harvard U., 1968; postgrad., Nat. War Coll., 1977. Commd. ensign U.S. Navy, 1959, advanced through grades to capt.; staff officer Vietnam Office, Dept. Def., Washington, 1974-75; mil. asst. to U.S. def. rep. Dept. Def., Tehran, Iran, 1975-76, Iran desk officer Washington, 1977-79; comptroller U.S. Pacific Fleet, Pearl Harbor, Hawaii, 1979-82; ret. U.S. Navy, 1982; with Pacific Analysis Corp., Honolulu, 1982-83; dep. asst. sec. Dept. Def., Washington, 1983-86; spl. asst. to pres., sr. dir. Asian affairs NSC, 1986-89; pres. EAP Assocs. Inc., Honolulu, 1989-94, Pacific Forum/CSIS, Honolulu, 1994—2001; asst. sec. for E. Asian & Pacific affairs U.S. Dept. State, Washington, 2001—. Decorated Legion of Merit with gold star Mem. Japan-Am. Soc., U.S. Naval Inst., U.S. Nat. Com. for Pacific Cooperation, Asia Soc. Home: Apt 1232 1600 N Oak St Arlington VA 22209-2767 Office: US Dept State East Asian and Pacific Affairs 2201 C St NW Washington DC 20520

KELLY, JAMES ANTHONY, priest; b. Worcester, Mass., Apr. 22, 1949; s. James and Elisabeth (Allen) K. BA in Philosophy and Govt., Harvard Coll., 1971; PhD in Philosophy, CUNY, 1979. ordained priest Roman Cath. Ch., 1982. Dir. Riverside Study Ctr., N.Y.C., 1977-79; procurator Prelature of Opus Dei, Rome, 1984-88, vicar USA region New Rochelle, N.Y., 1988-98; work with vicar of Opus Dei, 1998—2002; work with Del. Vicar of Opus Dei in Calif., 2002—. Avocations: philosophy of sci., ethics, basketball, jazz, English lit. Home and Office: 765 14th Ave San Francisco CA 94118-3558 E-mail: jakelly@prkvw.com.

KELLY, JAMES EVANS, internist; b. Detroit, July 17, 1926; s. Raymond John and Nora Margaret (Evans) K.; m. Lucille Marie Busch, June 16, 1951; children: James Evans Jr., Mary Eileen, Ann, Peter, Brian, Patrick, Kevin, Megan. Student, U.S. Naval Acad., 1944-46; BS in Biology, U. Detroit, 1947; MD, St. Louis U., 1951. Diplomate Am. Bd. Internal Medicine. Intern Henry Ford Hosp., Detroit, 1951-52, internal medicine resident, 1952-55, assoc. physician oncology divsn., 1958-61; vice chief medicine St. Joseph Hosp., Flint, Mich., 1968-73, chmn. dept. medicine, 1982-92; internal med. staff Monroe (Wis.) Clinic, 1994—. Clin. prof. dept. medicine Mich. State U., East Lansing, 1985-93. Comdr. USN, Fellow ACP; mem. Green County Med. Soc. (pres. 1997-98). Home: W4997 Round Grove Rd Monroe WI 53566-8818 Office: Monroe Clinic 515 22nd Ave Monroe WI 53566-1598

KELLY, JAMES FRANCIS, JR., retired radiologist; b. Omaha, July 25, 1919; Student, Creighton U., 1938-40, MD, 1943. Diplomate Am. Bd. Radiology. Intern Creighton Meml.-St. Joseph's Hosp., Omaha, 1944, resident in radiology, 1944-46, resident, 1948-49; radiologist Bergan Mercy Hosp., Omaha; ret., 1984. With Med. Corps, U.S. Army, 1946-48. Fellow Am. Coll. Radiology; mem. AMA, Radiol. Soc. N.Am., ATS. Home: 3030 South 80th Apt 102 Omaha NE 68124-3260

KELLY, JAMES JOSEPH, printing company executive; b. Steubenville, Ohio, Feb. 26, 1941; s. James Geary and Mary Catherine (Maley) K.; m. Judith Ann Miller, June 29, 1963; children: James M., Heather, Sean. BS in Econs., Xavier U., 1963. Acct. exec. Western Pub. Co., Racine, Wis., 1969-79; sales rep. Quebecor World, Chgo., 1979—, All World Sales Team, 1999—2001. 1st lt. U.S. Army, 1963-65. Mem. Direct Mktg. Assn., Mid. Ohi Direct Mktg. Club, St. Louis Direct Mktg., Xavier U. Alumnae Assn. (v.p., then pres. St. Louis chpt.), Elks, Am. Legion. Republican. Roman Catholic. Avocations: golf, tennis, tournament fishing, running. Home: 216 Greenburn Dr Saint Charles MO 63304-0925 Office: Quebecor World 5933 S Hwy 94 Ste 203 Saint Charles MO 63304

KELLY, JAMES MICHAEL, plant and soil scientist; b. Knoxville, Feb. 2, 1944; s. Woodrow Wilson and Thelma Lucille (Miller) K.; m. Susan Kay Morris, Aug. 9, 1969; children: John Kip, Christopher Kenneth. BS, E. Tenn. State U., 1966; MS, U. Tenn., 1968, PhD, 1973. Cert. profl. soil scientist. Assoc. ecologist NUS Corp., Pitts., 1973-74; rsch. assoc. Forestry Dept. Purdue U., West Lafayette, Ind., 1975-76; program mgr. Tenn. Valley Authority, Oak Ridge, 1977-88, sr. rschr., 1990-94; sr. tech. specialist, team leader, 1994-95; prof., chair dept. forestry Iowa State U., Ames, 1995—2001, chair dept. natural resource ecology and mgmt., 2002—. Vis. prof. agronomy Purdue U., 1988-89; adj. prof. U. Tenn., Knoxville, 1980-95, forestry dept. Purdue U., 1985-95. Author: Carbon Forms and Functions in Forest Soils, 1995; assoc. editor Soil Sci. Soc. Am. Jour., 1989-95, Forest Sci., 1998-2001; editl. bd. Forest Ecology and Management, 2001-; contbr. more than 100 articles to profl. jours. Head referee Ayso Youth Soccer, Oak Ridge, 1985-88; troop com. Boy Scouts Am., Oak Ridge, 1989-95. Oak Ridge Assoc. Univ. fellow, 1970-72; Elec. Power Rsch. Inst. grantee, 1978, 82, 89, 91, 95, NSF grantee, 1995; recipient Rsch. Champion award Elec. Power Rsch. Inst., 2002. Fellow Soil Sci. Soc. Am. (chmn. divsn. S7 1986-87, bd. dirs. 1988-89, awards com. 1992-93, fellows com. 1997-99, profl. svc. com. 2000-02); mem. AAAS, Ecol. Soc. Am., Soc. Am. Foresters, Exptl. Aircraft Assn. (chpt. pres. 1991-93), Trees Forever (bd. dirs. 1995—), Sigma Xi, Gamma Sigma Delta, Xi Sigma Pi. Achievements include research and application of environmental science. Office: Iowa State Univ Dept Natural Resource Ecology & Mgmt Ames IA 50011-1021

KELLY, JAMES P. delivery service executive; b. Jersey City, Apr. 18, 1943; BA, Rutgers U., 1973. With United Parcel Svc. of Am., Inc., Atlanta, 1964—2001, regional mgr., 1987, sr. v.p., labor rels. mgr., 1988, sr. v.p., COO, 1992-94, exec. v.p., COO, 1994-96, vice chmn., COO, 1996-97, chmn., CEO, 1997—2001. Office: UPS 55 Glenlake Pkwy NE Atlanta GA 30328-3474

KELLY, JAMES PATRICK, JR., retired engineering and construction executive; b. Bklyn., July 19, 1933; s. James Patrick and Marion Rita (Gleason) K.; children: Kathryn, Mark, Lisa Angelique, Trevor, Lisa, James (dec.). BSEngring., U.S. Naval Acad., 1955; postgrad., U. Houston, 1968-69. Registered profl. engr., Calif. Asst. site mgr. Pathfinder reactor Allis Chalmers Mfg. Co., Sioux Falls, S.D., 1963-67, nuclear project mgr. Brown & Root, Houston, 1967-69; from constrn. project mgr. to asst. v.p. Gibbs & Hill, Omaha and N.Y.C., 1969-75; pres. Dravo Lime Co., Pitts., 1975-77; group v.p. natural resources Dravo Corp., Pitts., 1976-81, sr. v.p. engring. and constrn., domestic and internat., 1982-84; pres., dir. C.F. Braun & Co., Alhambra, Calif., 1984-86; pres., CEO Hadson Power Systems, Inc., Irvine, Calif., 1986-91, ret., 1991. Bd. dirs. Hadson Corp., 1986—91. Bd. dirs. S.D. Mental Health Assn., 1966-67, Western Pa. Sch. Blind Children, 1978-84; mem. Sioux Falls Bd. Edn., 1965-66, Assn. Retarded Citizens Pitts., 1970—; pres. found. bd. Calif. State U., L.A., 1985-95; pres. Santa Ana Com. for Ednl. and Recreational Redevel. Plan, 1992-93, mem. Devel. Disabilities Area Bd., 1995-98; foreman Orange County Grand Jury, 1997-98. Mem. NSPE, Mensa, Sierra Club. Home: 1413 Franzen Ave Santa Ana CA 92705-6926 E-mail: JPK159@webtv.com.

KELLY, JAMES PAUL, neurologist; b. Chgo., Feb. 23, 1952; m. Anna Maria Kelly; children: Michael, Mary Kate, Shannon, Erin. BA, Western Mich. U., 1974, MA, 1977; MD, Northwestern U., Chgo., 1983. Diplomate Am. Bd. Psychiatry and Neurology. Med. dir. Chgo. Neurol. Inst., 2000—; assoc. prof. neurology Northwestern U. Med. Sch., Chgo., 1998—. Cons. neurologist Chgo. Bears Football Orgn., Lake Forest, Ill., 1996—; dir., co-founder Aspen Neurobehaioral Conf., Aspen, Colo., 1995—99; bd. dirs. Brain Injury Assn. of Am., Alexandria, Va., 1996—99; attending physician Northwestern Mem. Hosp., Chgo., 1995—. Contbr. articles. Med. officer Civil Air Patrol, Homewood, Ill., 1999—2001. Recipient Sheldon Berrol Clin. Svcs. award, Brain Injury Assn. of Am., 1995. Fellow: Am. Acad. Neurology. Office: Chgo Neurol Inst 233 E Erie St Ste 704 Chicago IL 60611 Office Fax: 312-863-3040.

KELLY, JANICE HELEN, elementary school educator; b. Akron, Ohio, Nov. 28, 1951; d. Joe Ralph and Barbara Ann (Goins) Long; m. W. Gary Kelly, May 10, 1973; children: Benjamin, Chad. BS in Elem. Edn., Akron U., 1984; M in Edn., Kent (Ohio) State U., 1994. Cert. elem. tchr., Ohio; nat. bd. cert. Mid. Child. Gen., 1999. Tchr. Suffield United C.C. Coop., Suffield, Ohio, 1984-86, Mogadore (Ohio) Local Schs., 1986—. Cadre mem. Summit County Tech. Acad., Cuyahoga Falls, Ohio, 1994; classroom tchr. SBC Ameritech, Kent State, Ohio, 2000, 2002. Mem., tchr. Randolph (Ohio) United Meth. Ch., 1973—. Recipient Outstanding Educator award Somers Elem. PTA, Mogadore, 1989, Crystal Apple award Plain Dealer, 2003; Eisenhower grantee Kent State U., 1990-92, Tech., Industry, Environ. Edn. grantee Gen Corp, 1993. Mem. ASCD, Ohio Edn. Assn., Mogadore Edn. Assn. (sec. 1990-92, v.p. 1995—, co-pres. 2001-03), Sci. Edn. Coun. Ohio. Avocations: doll-making/collecting, computer technology, golf, swimming. Home: 534 Hartville Rd Atwater OH 44201-9785 Office: Somers Elementary School 3600 Herbert St Mogadore OH 44260-1199

KELLY, JANICE R. psychologist, educator; b. Brodus, Mont. AB, U. Ill., 1981, AM, 1984, PhD, 1987. Prof. dept. psychol. scis. Purdue U., West Lafayette, Ind., 1987—. Author: Time and Human Interaction, 1986, On Time and Method, 1988; contbr. articles to profl. jours. Grantee, NSF, 2002—. Mem.: Am. Psychol. Soc., Soc. for Exptl. Social Psychology, Midwestern Psychol. Assn. (life). Office: Purdue Univ Psychol Sci 703 Third St West Lafayette IN 47907 E-mail: kelly@psych.purdue.edu.

KELLY, JIM (JAMES EDWARD KELLY), former professional football player; b. Pitts., Feb. 14, 1960; B in Bus. Mgmt., U. Miami, Fla., 1982. With Houston Gamblers USFL, 1984-85, Buffalo Bills, 1986—97; founder & pres. Kelly Enterprise, Inc. Named Sporting News U.S. Football League Rookie of Yr., 1984, mem. All-Star team, 1985, Pro-Bowl team, 1987, 88, 90, 91, 92; named to Quarterback of NFL All-Pro Team, Sporting News, 1991; played in Super Bowl XXV, 1990, XXVI, 1991, XXVII, 1992, XXVIII, 1993; named to Pro Football Hall of Fame, 2002 Office: Kelly Enterprise 1961 Whirle Dr Ste 5 Buffalo NY 14221*

KELLY, JOHN A. (JACK KELLY), lobbyist; b. N.Y.C. Student, U. Notre Dame, 1970-73; AA, Holy Cross Coll., 1974; BA in Social Sci., Fordham U., 1980. Peace officer N.Y. State Ct. Sys., 1973-75; legis. asst. Hon. Charles B. Rangel U.S. Ho. Rep., Washington, 1975-78; official U.S. Customs Ct., N.Y.C., 1978-80; nat. campaign dir. Reagon/Bush Campaign, Washington, 1980; dir. presdl. liaison and spl. asst. for polit. affairs Rep. Nat. Com., Washington, 1981-82; mem. credentials and contest com. team George Bush for Pres., Washington, 1988; dep. exec. dir. Presdl. Inaugural, 1989; lead advance V.P. Dan Quayle, 1989-90; ptnr. The McPherson Group, LLP. Prin. fed. and state govt. affairs rep. Perdue Farms Inc., AMDEC, BMW Group AG, BMW U.S. Holding Corp., Peachtree Funding Inc.; mem. adv. coun. on grad. studies and rsch. U. Notre Dame. Mem. adv. com. on govt. affairs U. Notre Dame; bd. dirs. Circles Bd., Kennedy Ctr. for Performing Arts, 1995—; adv. bd. The Army Distaff Found., 2003—. Served to major USAR, 1972—2002. Recipient Spl. award of Honor Internat. Narcotic Enforcement Officers Assn., 1988. Mem. Nat. Chicken Coun., Alliance Automobile Mfrs., Am. League Lobbyists. Office: 925 15th St NW Ste 500 Washington DC 20005-2305 E-mail: jkelly@kellylobbyshop.com.

KELLY, JOHN HUBERT, diplomat, business executive; b. Fond du Lac, Wis., July 20, 1939; s. James Daniel and Clarice L. Kelly; m. Helena Marita Ajo; children: David Snowdon, Maria Louise. BA, Emory U., 1961; advanced studies cert., Georgetown U., 1982. Vice consul Am. Consulate, Adana, Turkey, 1965-66; 3rd sec. Am. Embassy, Ankara, Turkey, 1966-67, 2nd sec. Bangkok, 1968-69; consul Am. Consulate, Songkhla, Thailand, 1969-71; 1st sec. Am. Embassy, Paris, 1976-80; fgn. svc. U.S. Dept. of State, Washington, 1972-76, dep. exec. sec., 1980-81, dep. asst. sec. of state, 1982-85, asst. sec. state for Near East and South Asia, 1989-91; U.S. amb. Am. Embassy, Beirut, 1986-88, amb. Helsinki, Finland, 1991-94; pres. John Kelly Cons., Conyers, 1994—; mng. dir. Internat. Equity Ptnrs., Atlanta, 1995-98. Bd. dirs. Am. Internat. Petroleum Corp. Mem. adv. coun. Una Chapman Cox Found., 1982-86; trustee Lebanese Am. U., 1996-2002. Mem. Coun. on Fgn. Rels., Mid. East Inst. Office: John Kelly Cons 2440 Wall St Ste D Conyers GA 30013-6341

KELLY, JOHN JAMES, lawyer; b. Rockville Centre, N.Y., July 4, 1949; s. John James Sr. and Eleanor Grace (Vann) K.; m. Clara Sarah Gussin; 1 child, John James III. AB in Govt., Georgetown U., 1971, JD, 1975. Bar: Pa. 1976, D.C. 1979, U.S. Dist. Ct. D.C. 1980, U.S. Claims Ct. 1982, U.S. Ct. Appeals (D.C. cir.) 1980, U.S. Ct. Appeals (fed. cir.) 1982. Law clk. to judge U.S. Dist. Ct., Washington, 1975-77; assoc. Corcoran, Youngman & Rowe, Washington, 1977-80, Capell, Howard, Knabe & Cobbs, Washington, 1980-83, Loomis, Owen, Fellman & Howe, Washington, 1983-86, ptnr., 1986-90; v.p., sec., gen. coun. Electronic Industries Alliance, Arlington, Va., 1990-96, exec. v.p., gen. counsel, 1997—; pres. JEDEC Solid State Tech. Assn., 2000—; counsel Howe, Anderson & Steyer, Washington, 1990—. Mem. Jud. Conf., D.C. Cir., Washington, 1983, Jud. Conf. Fed. Cir., Washington, 1988—. Contbr. articles to legal and profl. publs. Mem. ABA, D.C. Bar, Pa. Bar Assn., Am. Soc. Assn. Execs. (bd. dirs. legal section 1989-94, chmn. 1992-93), Fed. Bar Assn., Met. Club. Democrat. Roman Catholic. Office: Electronic Industries Alliance 2500 Wilson Blvd Arlington VA 22201-3834

KELLY, JOHN JOSEPH, JR., government executive; b. Paterson, N.J., Dec. 28, 1940; s. John Joseph Sr. and Helen C. (Ebersach) K.; m. Brenda Ruth Miller, July 1, 1966; children: Elizabeth Ann, Kathleen Anne, John J. BS in Chemistry, Seton Hall, 1963; MS, Pa. State U., 1969; MPA, Auburn U., 1976. Commd. 2d lt. USAF, 1963, advanced through grades to brig. gen., 1989, dir. spl. projects, HQ, 1978-80; comdr. 15 WEA Squadron USAF, McGuire AFB, N.J., 1980-81; dep. dir. programs/policy Air Force info. systems USAF, Washington, 1981-84; vice comdr. 7th Weather Wing Scott AFB, 1984-85; comdr. 5th Weather Wing Langley AFB, Va., 1985-88; comdr. Air Weather Svc. Scott AFB, 1988-91; dir. weather AF/XOW Washington, 1991-94; dir. Nat. Weather Svc., 1998—. Cons. Dept. Commerce, 1991. Fellow Am. Meteorol. Soc., Air Force Assn., Nat. Weather Assn. Roman Catholic. Avocations: golf, reading. Office: NWS 1325 E West Hwy Silver Spring MD 20910-3280

KELLY, JOHN LOVE, public relations executive; b. NYC, Jan. 30, 1924; s. Joseph John McDermott and Mary Florence Keenan (Love) K.; m. Helen M. Griffin Hanrahan, June 28, 1952; children: Janet Ann, J. Scott. BS, St. Peter's Coll., 1951; postgrad., N.C. State U., 1966. Buyer exec. tng. program R.H. Macy's, N.Y.C., 1951 53; mktg. exec. Sanforized divsn. Cluett Peabody Co., N.Y.C., 1953-58; advt. account exec. Batton, Barton, Durstine & Osborn, N.Y.C., 1958-59, advt. mgr. Am. Cyanamid Co., N.Y.C., 1959-64; advt. mgr. fiber divsn. FMC Corp., N.Y.C., 1964—67; v.p., dir. pub. rels. and comm. Avtex Fibers, Inc., Valley Forge, Pa., 1976—85; pres. Kelhan Ltd., 1985—96; cons. Brazilian Govt. Trade Bur., 1990-93, Lenzing of Austria, 1992-97. Cath. co-chmn. Peekskill area NCCJ, 1961-64, bd. dirs. Westchester County, 1969-79; trustee Mercy Coll., Dobbs Ferry, NY, 1965-69; councilman Town of Cortlandt (N.Y.), 1962-66; bd. ethics Zoning Bd., 1971-74; mem. Simon Wiesenthal Ctr., Am. Conf. for Irish Studies, 1975-79, Cardinal's Com. of Laity, 1961-71; mem. Greater NY area coun. Boy Scouts Am., 1971-79; bd. dirs. Siesta Key Assn., 1999—, Interfaith Interracial Coun. Sarasota and Manatee Counties, 2001—; pres. parish bd. St. Thomas More, Sarasota, 1996-2001. Mem. Pub. Rels. Club N.Y., Am. Fiber Mfrs. Assn. (chmn. pub. rels. com., edn. and pub. rels. subcoms.), Bd. Trade N.Y., Am. Israel Friendship League, Am. Irish Hist. Soc., Internat. Platform Assn., St. Peter's Coll. Alumni Assn. (bd. dirs. 1959-65), Hudson Valley Gaelic Soc., Interreligious Affairs Com. and chair Cath./Jewish Spkrs. Bur. Diocese Venice, Fla., Knight Comdr. Equestrian Order of the Holy Sepulchre of Jerusalem, Mission Valley Golf and Country Club (Nokomis, Fla., dir.), Univ. Club N.Y.C. Democrat. Roman Catholic. Office: 9000 Midnight Pass Rd Sarasota FL 34242-2927 E-mail: irishkel@worldnet.att.net.

KELLY, JOHN MARTIN, lawyer; b. Oshkosh, Wis., Dec. 13, 1948; s. Martin Paul and Ivy Cecile (James) Kelly; m. Teresa Jean Wendland, July 24, 1982. BA, U. Wis., Madison, 1971; JD, Georgetown U., 1974; postgrad. in bus., Harvard U., 1976-77. Bar: Wis. 1974, D.C. 1975. Atty. office chief counsel IRS, Washington, 1974-76; assoc. Dempsey Law Office, Oshkosh, 1977-82, ptnr., 1983—. Mem. ABA, Wis. Bar Assn., D.C. Bar Assn., Winnebago County Bar Assn. Office: Dempsey Law Office PO Box 886 Oshkosh WI 54903-0886 E-mail: jmkelly@dempseylaw.com.

KELLY, JOHN MICHAEL, lawyer; b. Hartford, Conn., Aug. 5, 1964; s. William Patrick and Angela Marie (Arnone) K. BA in Polit. Sci., BA in History, Fairfield U., 1986; JD, Western New Eng. Coll., 1991. Bar: Conn. 1991, U.S. Dist. Ct. Conn. 1992. Underwriter Travelers Ins. Co., Hartford, 1986-88; legis. aide Gen. Assembly Conn., Hartford, 1988; law clk. Leone, Throwe & Nagle, East Hartford, Conn., 1989-91; assoc. Law Offices of Richard A. Kablik, P.C., Newington, Conn., 1991-94; atty. Law Offices of Marc Needelman, Bloomfield, Conn., 1995—. Sec. West Meadow Cemetery Expansion Com., Newington, Conn., 1987-90, mem. Ins. Com., 1988-90; mem. Newington Town Coun., 1995—, dep. mayor, 1999—; mem. Dem. State Ctr. Com., 2000—. Mem. Conn. Bar Assn., Harford County Bar Assn., Newington Rotary Club, Newington C. of C. (dir. 1994—, sec. 1995-97, v.p. 1997—). Avocations: running, hockey, softball, politics. Home: 293 Maple Hill Ave Newington CT 06111-2726 Office: Law Offices of Marc N Needelman 800 Cottage Grove Rd Ste 313 Bloomfield CT 06002-3097 E-mail: jkelly0@snet.net.

KELLY, JOHN PATRICK, lawyer; b. Boston, May 9, 1952; s. Patrick and Elizabeth (Glennon) K.; m. Eileen Linda Obuchowski, May 28, 1983; children: John Patrick, Laura Beth, Kevin Sean. AB, Coll. Holy Cross, 1974; JD, Vanderbilt U., 1978. Bar: Mass. 1978, Fla. 1979, US Dist. Ct. (so. dist.) Fla. 1980, US Supreme Ct. 1981; cert. trial lawyer, Fla., litigation specialist, Fla. Law clk. to presiding justice Tenn. Supreme Ct., Nashville, 1978-79; assoc. Fleming, O'Bryan & Fleming, Ft. Lauderdale, Fla., 1979-84, ptnr., 1984-96, Gunster, Yoakley, Valdes-Fauli & Stewart, Ft. Lauderdale, 1996-2000, Lorusso Loud & Kelly LLP, Ft. Lauderdale, 2000—. Lectr. Ctr. for Internat. Legal Studies, Kitzbuhel, Austria, 1999. Co-author Florida Business Litigation Manual, 1989-2000. Mem. Fla. Bar Assn. (civil rules com., lectr. Continuing Legal Edn. 1988-2000, prof. edn. seminars 1991-2000), Am. Arbitration Assn. (arbitrator), Nat. Futures Assn. (arbitrator), Tower Club, St. Thomas More Soc., Nat. Bd. Trial Advocacy, Phi Beta Kappa. Roman Catholic. Avocations: skiing, scuba diving, photography. Office: Lorusso, Loud & Kelly 1955 Paddington Drive Pork City UT E-mail: jkelly@businesslitigation.com.

KELLY, JOHN TERENCE, architect; b. Elyria, Ohio, Jan. 27, 1922; s. Thomas Alo and Coletta Margaret (Conrad) K. BArch, Carnegie Mellon U., 1949; MArch, Harvard U., 1951, M of Landscape Architecture, 1952. Prin. architect John Terence Kelly, Cleve., 1954—. Vis. critic, lectr. U. Mich., U. Cin., Case Western Res. U., McGill U. Bd. dirs. Nova. With inf. AUS, 1943-46. Recipient Cleve. Arts prize in Architecture, 1968, hist. Bldg. award Architects Soc. Ohio, 1986; Charles Eliot Norton fellow, 1952, Fulbright fellow, Munich, Germany, 1953. Mem. AIA (nat. com. design). Home: 2646 N Moreland Blvd Cleveland OH 44120-1461 Office: 2646 N Moreland Blvd Cleveland OH 44120-1461

KELLY, JOHN WILLIAM, JR., university administrator; b. Greenville, S.C., Jan. 5, 1955; s. John William and Betty (Kelley) K.; m. Sarah Ellen Moor Kelly, Feb. 8, 1958; children: Christopher, Kimberly. BS, Clemson U., 1977; MS, Ohio State U., 1979, PhD, 1982. Asst. prof. Tex. A&M U., 1982-85, Clemson (S.C.) U., 1985-89, assoc. prof., 1989-91, prof., dept. head, dir. bot. garden, 1991-96, sch. dir., interim v.p. pub. svc. and agr., 1996-97, v.p. pub. svc. and agr., dir. S.C. Bot. Garden, 1997—. Cons., Clemson, 1985—. Contbr. articles to 50 profl. jours. Bd. dirs. Discover Upcountry, Greenville, S.C., Am. Distance Edn. Corp., Pate Found. Recipient Outstanding Contbr. award S.C. Nurseryman's Assn., 1991. Fellow Am. Soc. Hort. Sci. (v.p. 1995-99, pres. 1999, chmn. bd. dirs. 2000, Outstanding Rschr. 1994, Outstanding Adminstr. 1995, So. region Outstanding Educator 1989); mem. S.C. Greenhouse Growers Assn. (life, exec. sec. 1991). Avocations: gardening, nature. Office: Clemson U Pub Svc and Agr 130 Lehotsky Hall Clemson SC 29634-0101

KELLY, KATHLEEN S(UE), communications educator; b. Duluth, Minn., Aug. 6, 1943; d. Russell J. and Idun N. Mehrman; m. George F. Kelly, Apr. 29, 1961; children: Jodie A., Jennifer L. AA, Moorpark (Calif.) Coll., 1971; BS in Journalism, U. Md., College Park, 1973, MA in Pub. Rels., 1979, PhD in Pub. Communication, 1989. Accredited pub. rels.; cert. fundraising exec. Dir. pub. info. Bowie (Md.) State U., 1974-77; asst. to dean, instr. Coll. Journalism U. Md., College Park, 1977-79, assoc. dir. devel., 1979-82; v.p. Mt. Vernon Coll., Washington, 1982-83; dir. devel. U. Md., College Park, 1983-85, assoc. dean, lectr. Coll. Journalism, 1985-88, asst. dean Coll. Bus. and Mgmt., 1988-90; prof. U. La., Lafayette, 1991—2003; prof., chair dept. pub. rels. U. Fla., Gainesville, 2003—. Cons. NASA, NIH, Mt. St. Marys Coll., 1986—; lectr. CASE, Pub. Rels. Soc. Am., 1987—. Author: Fund Raising and Public Relations: A Critical Analysis, 1991, Building Fund-Raising Theory, 1994, Effective Fund-Raising Management, 1998. Named PRIDE Book award winner Speech Comm. Assn., 1991, article award winner 1994, John Grenzebach award winner for rsch. on philanthropy CASE and Am. Assn. Fund-Raising Coun., 1991, 98, PRIG award winner for outstanding dissertation Internat. Comm. Assn., 1990, winner 1995 Pathfinder award Inst. for Pub. Rels. Rsch. and Edn., Staley/Robeson/Ryan/St. Lawarence prize for rsch. on fund raising and philanthropy Nat. Soc. Fundraising Execs., 1998, Jackson, Jackson & Wagner Behavioral Sci. prize, Pub. Relations Soc. Am. Found., 1999. Fellow Pub. Rels. Soc. Am. (chmn. ednl. and cultural orgn. sect. 1989, pres. Md. chpt. 1986-87, Pres.' Cup 1981, nat. bd. dirs. 1994-96, Jackson Jackson and Wagner Behavioral Sci. prize 1999); mem. Nat. Soc. Fund Raising Execs. (mem. rsch. coun.), Coun. Advancement and Support of Edn. (women's forum 1983), Phi Kappa Phi. Democrat. Avocations: travel, reading. Home: 1922 NW 4th Ave Gainesville FL 32603 Office: U Fla Dept Pub Rels PO Box 118400 Gainesville FL 32611-8400

KELLY, KEVIN, editor; b. Penn State, Pa., Apr. 27, 1952; s. Joseph John and Patricia Kelly; m. Gia-Minn Fuh, Jan. 2, 1987; children: Kaileen, Ting, Tywen. Freelance photographer, 1971-80; editor, pub. Walking! Jour., Athens, Ga., 1982-84, Whole Earth Rev., Sausalito, Calif., 1984-90; exec. editor Wired Mag., San Francisco, 1992-98; chmn. All Species Found., 2001—. Editor: Signal, 1988; author: Out of Control, 1994, New Rules for the New Economy, 1998, Asia Grace, 2002. Recipient Gen. Excellence Nat. Mag. Award, 1993, 96. Mem.: Long Bets Found. (pres. 2002—). Avocation: beekeeping. Home and Office: 149 Amapola Ave Pacifica CA 94044-3102 E-mail: kk@kk.org.

KELLY, KEVIN A. mathematician, educator; b. Montclair, NJ, Jan. 31, 1968; s. Barbara D. and Robert P. Kelly; m. Amy E. Lindstedt, Feb. 14, 1969. BA, Rutgers Coll., New Brunswick, NJ, 1990; MS, MIT, Cambridge, MA, 1993; EdM, Harvard U., Cambridge, MA, 1994. Cert. tchr. Nat. Bd. for Profl. Tchg. Stds., 2001. Tchr. math. Lexington H.S., Mass., 1994—; lectr. Harvard Grad. Sch. Edn., Cambridge, Mass., 2001—02. Recipient Sliffe award for disting. H.S. tchg., Math. Assn. Am., 2001. Mem.: Nat. Coun. Tchrs. of Math., Math. Assn. Am., Nat. Honor Soc., Pi Mu Epsilon, Phi Beta Kappa. Office: Lexington HS 251 Waltham St Lexington MA 02421

KELLY, LAWRENCE M. lawyer; b. New Castle, Pa., Sept. 1, 1953; s. Fred E. and Jora J. (Hassan) K.; m. Marisa L. Kelly, May 28, 1983; children: Lauren Michelle, Erica Megan, Gianna Marie, Ariana Marisa. BS in Edn., Slippery Rock U., 1975; JD, U. Akron, 1983. Bar: Pa. 1983; bd. cert. civil trial specialist Nat. Bd. Trial Adv., Boston, 1995. Ptnr. Luxenberg, Garbett, Kelly, & George, P.C., New Castle, Pa., 1984—. Atty. City of New Castle, 1988-94, New Castle Sanitation Authority, 1994—. Pres. Cray Youth and Family Svcs., New Castle, 1984—; dir. Holy Redeemer Sch., Ellwood City, Pa., 2000-02. Mem.: ATLA, Western Pa. Trial Lawyers (bd. govs.), Pa. Trial Lawyers Assn. (bd. govs.). Democrat. Home: 138 Hemlock Way Ellwood City PA 16117 Office: Luxenberg Garbett Kelly et al 315 N Mercer St New Castle PA 16101 E-mail: lmkelly@zoominternet.net.

KELLY, LUCIE STIRM YOUNG, nursing educator; b. Stuttgart, Germany, May 2, 1925; came to U.S., 1929; d. Hugo Karl and Emilie Rosa (Engel) Stirm; m. J. Austin Young, Aug. 30, 1946 (div. Feb. 1971); m. Thomas Martin Kelly, 1972; 1 child by previous marriage, Gay Aleta (Mrs. Donald Meyer). BS, U. Pitts., 1947, MLitt, 1957, PhD (HEW fellow), 1965; D in Nursing Edn. (hon.), U. R.I., 1977; LHD (hon.), Georgetown U., 1983; DSc (hon.), Widener U., 1984, U. Mass., 1989; D of Pub. Svc. (hon.), Am. U., 1985; DHL (hon.), SUNY, 1996. Instr. nursing McKeesport (Pa.) Hosp., 1953-57, asst. adminstr. nursing, 1966-69; asst. prof. nursing U. Pitts., 1957-64, asst. dean, 1965; prof., chmn. nursing dept. Calif. State U., Los Angeles, 1969-72; co-project dir. curriculum research Nat. League for Nursing, 1973-74; project dir. patient edn., office consumer health edn., also adj. asso. prof. community medicine Coll. Medicine and Dentistry N.J.-Rutgers Med. Sch., 1974-75; prof. pub. health and nursing Sch. Pub. Health and Sch. Nursing Columbia U., N.Y.C., 1975-90, prof. emeritus Sch Pub. Health, Sch. Nursing, 1990—, assoc. dean acad. affairs Sch. Pub. Health, 1988-90, hon. prof. nursing edn. Tchrs. Coll., 1977-93, acting head div. health adminstrn. Sch. Pub. Health, 1980-81, 86-88; on leave as exec. dir. Mid-Atlantic Regional Nursing Assn., 1981-82. Cons. U. Nev., Las Vegas, 1970-72, Ball State U., Ind., 1971, Long Beach (Calif.) Naval Hosp., 1971-72, Travis AFB, Calif., 1972, Brentwood VA Hosp., L.A., 1971-72, Ctrl. Nursing Office VA, Washington, 1971-94, N.J. Dept. Higher Edn., 1974-78, John Wiley Pub., 1974-76, Sch. Nursing Am. U. Beirut; mem. spl. med. adv. group VA Dept. Medicine and Surgery, Washington, 1980-84; cons. nursing com. AMA 1971-74, Citizen's Com. for Children, N.Y.C.; v.p. Pa. Health Coun., 1968-69; mem. adv. com. physicians assts. Calif. Bd. Med. Examiners, adv. com. Cancer Soc. L.A., 1970-72, com. nursing VA, Washington, 1971-74, chair 1975-90, regional med. programs, Pa., 1967-69, Calif. 1970-72; mem. spl. adv. com. on med. licensure and profl. conduct N.Y. State Assembly, 1977-79, mem. nat. adv com. Encore (nat. YWCA post-mastectomy group rehab. project), 1977-83; assoc. mem. N.Y. Acad. Medicine, 1988-90; mem. ethics com. Palisades Med Ctr., 1993—, bd. govs., 1995—, mem. profl. and quality rev. com., 1995—, chair, 1998—, exec. com., 1998-99; 2d vice chair N.Y. Presbyn. Healthcare Sys., Palisades Med. Ctr., 1999-2003, 1st vice chair 2003—; lectr., cons., guest Beijing Med. Coll., China, 1982, Aga Khan U., Pakistan, 1990; bd. visitors U Pitts. Sch. Nursing, 1986-93; mem. edtl. adv. bd. Am. Jour. Pub. Health, 1992 chair, 1993-97; nat. and internat. lectr. in field; chair adv. com. grad. program in pub. health U. Medicine and Dentistry of N.J., 1995-2000. Author: (textbooks) Dimensions of Profl. Nursing, 8th edit., 1999, The Nursing Experience: Trends Challenges, Transitions, 4th edit., 2001; contbg. editor: (jour.) Jour. Nursing Adminstrn., 1975—82; columnist: jour. Nursing Outlook, editor-in-chief 1982—91; mem. bd. advisors (jour.) Nurses Almanac, 1978, Nurse Manager's Handbook, 1979, Nursing Administration Handbook, 1992; editor (editl. bd.) (jour.) Am. Health, 1981—91; editl. bd. (jour.) Nursing and Health Care 1991—95, Internat. Nursing Index, 1997—2001. Bd. dirs. ARC, Los Angeles 1971-72; bd. dirs. Vis. Nurse Service N.Y., 1980-2001, mem. exec. com., chmn human resources, 1989-2001; bd. dirs. Concern for Dying, 1983-89; trustee Calif. State Coll. L.A. Found., 1971-72, U. Pitts., 1984-90, mem. exec. com 1988-90; chair bd. visitors U. Pitts. Sch. Pub. Health, 1988-90; bd. visitors U Miami Sch. Nursing, 1986—; mem. health services com. Children's Aid Soc. N.Y., 1978-84; v.p. Am. Nurses Found., 1980-82; mem. nat. adv. council or nurse tng. HRA, 1981-85; mem. nurses leadership coun. Chlorine Chemistry Coun., 1999—; hon. bd. dirs. NOVA Found., 1998—, Health Professions Panel Am. Legacy Found., 2000—. Named Outstanding Alumna U. Pitts. Sch Nursing, 1966, Pa. Nurse of Yr., 1967, Roll of Honor N.J. State Nurses Assn. 1990; named to Tchrs. Coll. Columbia U. Nursing Edn. Alumni Hall of Fame 1999; recipient Disting. Alumna award U. Pitts. Sch. Edn., 1981, Shaw meda Boston Coll., 1985, Bicentennial Medallion of Distinction, U. Pitts., 1987, R Louise McManus Medallion for Disting. Svc. to Nursing, Tchrs. Coll. Columbia U., 1987, Dean's Disting. Svc. award Columbia Sch. Pub. Health, 1995, Second Century award in health care, Columbia U. Sch. Nursing, 1996. Fellow Am Acad. Nursing (named Living Legend 2001); mem. ANA (dir. 1978-82, Hon Recognition award 1992), APHA (Ruth Freeman Pub. Health Nursing award 1993), Pa. Nurses Assn. (pres. 1966-69), Nat. League Nursing (bd. govs 1991-95), Nurses Ednl. Funds Bd., U . Pitts. Sch. Nursing Alumni (pres. 1959) Vis. Nurse Assn. Ctrl. Jersey (bd. dirs. 1999-2001, mem. bd. trustees), Am Hosp. Assn. (com. chmn. 1967-68), Assn. Grad. Faculty Cmty. Health/Pub Health Nursing (v.p. 1980-81), Sigma Theta Tau (sr. editor Image 1978-81 pres.-elect 1981-83, pres. 1983-85, nat. campaign chair Ctr. for Nursing Scholarship 1987-89, chair devel. com. 1989-95, spl. advisor 1995-97, planned giving task force 1998-2001, Mentor award 1985, 93, 97, Spirit of Philanthropy award 1997), Pi Lambda Theta, Alpha Tau Delta (Cert. of Merit 1968) Achievements include collection of papers in Mugar Library, Boston U. Home 6040 Boulevard E Apt 11G West New York NJ 07093-3827

KELLY, MARGUERITE STEHLI, fashion executive, consultant; b. N.Y.C., June 9, 1931; d. Henry E. and Grace (Hays) Stehli; m. Charles J. Kelly, Jr., Dec 23, 1962; children: Marguerite Grace Kelly Walton, Lisa Stehli Kelly-Wolf BA, Bryn Mawr Coll., 1953. Exec. trainee Macy's, N.Y.C., 1953-54, asst buyer, 1954-57; buyer Bloomingdale's, N.Y.C., 1957-63; pres. Maggie, Inc.

Wayzata, Minn., 1964-86, also brs. Georgetown, D.C., 1964-70, Locust Valley, N.Y., 1970-75; ret., 1986. Founder Workshop for Learning, 1987—. Mem. com. for spl. fund Foxcroft Sch., Middleburg, Va., 1974-76, trustee, 1978-87; mem. alumnae coun. Brearley Sch., N.Y.C., 1973-75; trustee Abbott Northwestern Hosp., Mpls., 1984-86; co-founder Citizens for Colin Powell Presdl. Draft Movement, 1994—. Episcopalian. Home: 3018 N St NW Washington DC 20007-3404

KELLY, MARK E. astronaut; b. Orange, N.J., Feb. 21, 1964; s. Richard and Patricia Kelly; m. Amelia Victoria Babis; 2 children. BS in Marine Engring., Nautical Sci., U.S. Merchant Marine Acad., 1986; MS in Aeronautical Engring., U.S. Naval Postgrad. Sch., 1994. Commd. ensign USN, 1986, advanced through grades to lt. comdr.; with Attack Squadron 128, Naval Air Sta., Whidbey Island, Wash., Attack Squadron 115, Atsugi, Japan; combat pilot Persian Gulf, Operation Desert Storm; project test pilot Carrier Suitability Dept., Strike Aircraft Test Squadron, Naval Air Warfe Ctr., Patuxent River, Md.; instr. pilot U.S. Naval Test Pilot Sch.; astronaut NASA, Houston, with Astronaut Office Computer Support Br. Decorated 4 Air medals with Combat "V", Navy Commendation medal with "V", Navy Achievement medal, Navy Expeditionary medal. Achievements include logged over 3,000 flight hours in over 40 different aircraft; over 375 carrier landings; logged 12 days in space; crew STS-108 Endeavour (2001). Office: Astronaut Office/CB NASA Johnson Space Ctr Houston TX 77058

KELLY, MARY JOAN, librarian; b. Baton Rouge, Nov. 25, 1947; d. Theodore McKowen Sr. and Patricia Marilyn (Faul) Wilkes; m. Karl Joseph Nix; 1 child, Patricia Lynn Woodworth. BS, La. State U., 1970, MEd, 1973, EdD, 1980. Cert. English and social studies tchr., city/parish materials and/or media ctr. dir., sch. libr., La. Instr. conversation class La. State U., Baton Rouge, 1979-80; writer, prodr. The Video Co., Baton Rouge, 1983-90; freelance writer, pre and post video prodn., storyteller DBA-The BookDoctor, Baton Rouge; tchr. East Baton Rouge Parish Sch. Bd., ret., 1991; prin. St. Isidore Mid. Sch., 1991-95; libr. Holy Family Sch., Port Allen, La., 1995—2001, East Baton Rouge Parish Sch. Bd., 2001—. Presenter in field. Contbr. numerous articles to profl. jours.; sponsor yearbook and lit. mags.; storyteller and spkr. Mem. Non-Pub. Sch. Commn., La. Bd. Elem. and Secondary Edn., 1992-97; mem. adminstrn. commn. St. Aloysius Cath. Ch., 1989—, mem. comms. com., 1987—, chmn., 1989—. Mem. NEA, ASCD, La. Assn. Educators (mem. com. 1978-91), East Baton Rouge Parish Assn. Educators (v.p.), La. Assn. Classroom Tchrs. (mem. com. 1972-81), East Baton Rouge Parish Assn. Classroom Tchrs. (pres.), Assn. Ednl. Comm. and Tech., La. Assn. Ednl. Comm. and Tech., Internat. Platform Assn., La. Libr. Assn., Capital Area Reading Coun., Cath. Diocese of Baton Rouge Librs. Assn. (sec. 1996-97, pres. 99-01), East Baton Rouge Parish Librs. Assn., Gamma Beta Phi, Phi Lambda Pi, Phi Delta Kappa. Home: 2005 Lee Dr Baton Rouge LA 70808-3932 Office: Park Forest Elem 10717 Elain St Baton Rouge LA 70814 Business E-Mail: mkelly@ebrpsb.k12.la.us. E-mail: marykelly14@prodigy.net.

KELLY, MARY KATHLEEN, lawyer, researcher; b. Copiague, N.Y., Apr. 30, 1952; d. John Joseph and Catherine Rita Kelly. BA, SUNY, Brockport, 1974; MBA, Rochester Inst. Tech., 1982; JD, U. Buffalo, 1996. Bar: N.Y. 1998. Mgr., counselor Greater Opportunity in Nursing, Rochester, 1974-76; program dir. United Cerebral Palsy, Rochester, N.Y., 1976-78; br. mgr. Quality Care Nursing Svc., Rochester, N.Y., 1978-80; account rep. IBM, Rochester, N.Y., 1980-91; case reviewer Ctr. for Helath Dispute Resolution, Pittsford, N.Y., 1996-97; legal rsch. specialist West Group, Rochester, 1997—; pvt. practice Rochester, 1998—. Mem. N.Y. State Bar Assn., Monroe County Bar Assn., Greater Rochester Assn. Women Attys., 19th Ward Commn. Assn. Avocations: painting, piano, theatre, outdoor activities, gardening. Office: Law Offices of Mary K Kelly PO Box 24366 Rochester NY 14624-0366

KELLY, MARY SUSAN, psychologist, educator; b. N.Y.C., July 15, 1954; d. James J. and Veronica (Jacob) Kelly; m. James Houlihan, July 18, 1992. BA, Boston Coll., 1976; MA, Columbia U., 1980, PhD, 1987. Tchr. Kennedy Meml. Hosp., Brighton, Mass., 1976—79; adj. asst. prof. Teachers Coll., Columbia U., N.Y.C., 1987—93; assoc. prof. Western Conn. State U., Danbury, 1993—94; assoc. prof. clin. pediatrics Albert Einstein Coll. of Medicine, Bronx, 1994—. Dir. Fisher Landau Ctr. for Treatment of Learning Disabilities, Albert Einstein Coll. Medicine. Contbr. articles to profl. jours., including Jour. Sch. Psychology, Brain & Cognition, Jour. Learning Disabilities, Jour. Am. Bd. Family Practice, Contemporary Pediats. Grantee: U.S. Dept. Edn., 1987-89, Fisher-Landau Found., N.Y.C., 1987-91, Bd. Edn. Yonkers, N.Y., 1991-93, LD Access Found., 2001-03. Mem. APA, Am. Psychol. Soc. (charter), Am. Ednl. Rsch. Assn., Internat. Reading Assn., Internat. Dyslexia Assn. Office: Fisher Landau Ctr for Treatment of Learning Disabilities Albert Einstein Coll Med 1165 Morris Park Ave Bronx NY 10461-1915 E-mail: mskelly@aecom.yu.edu.

KELLY, MATTHEW EDWARD, association executive, retired; b. Parkersburg, W.Va., Apr. 15, 1928; s. Matthew Glenn and Lillian (Schottler) K.; m. Mildred Joan Flasch, June 6, 1953. BA, Marietta Coll., 1952. Asst. mgr. Twin Cities Area C. of C., Benton Harbor, Mich., 1955-62; exec. v.p. Oshkosh (Wis.) C. of C., 1962-69, Springfield (Mo.) Area C. of C., 1969-76, Elgin (Ill.) C. of C., 1977-95. Trustee Northwest Suburban Mass Transit Dist., 1979—, City of Elgin Metra Task Force; mem. project mgmt. team Elgin Riverfront Devel. Project, 2000—. Mem. Am. C. of C. Execs. (past dir.), Inst. for Orgnl. Mgmt. (past dir., mem. nat. bd. regents), Rotary (past pres.) Home: Elgin, Ill. Died Aug. 5, 2002.

KELLY, MAURA ANNE, reporter; b. Bridgeport, Conn., Apr. 2, 1971; d. Richard Francis and Margaret Mary Kelly. BA, Boston Coll., 1993; MS in Journalism, Northwestern U., 1994. Intern The Patriot Ledger, Quincy, Mass., 1993; corr. Conn. Post, Bridgeport, 1993; reporter Naugatuck bur. Waterbury (Conn.) Rep.-Am., 1994—95, edn. reporter, 1995, city hall reporter, 1995—96, state capitol reporter, 1996-99; reporter Chgo. Tribune, 2000—01, Associated Press, 2001—. Mem. reporters' roundtable discussion Conn. Jour. on Conn. Pub. TV, Hartford, 1998-99 and WFSB's CT '97, CT '98, Ct '99 in Hartford. Co-recipient Explanatory Reporting-Team Coverage, Pulitzer Prize, 2001. Mem. Soc. Profl. Journalists (Reporting awards Conn. chpt. 1998, 99, 2000), Investigative Reporters and Editors, Boston Coll. Alumni Assn., Northwestern U. Alumni Club Conn. Roman Catholic. Avocations: photography, travel, skiing, tennis, swimming. Home: 2464 N Geneva Terr Apt 2D Chicago IL 60614 Office: Associated Press Ste 2500 10 S Wacker Dr Chicago IL 60606 E-mail: makelly42@hotmail.com.

KELLY, MAXINE ANN, retired property developer; b. Ft. Wayne, Ind., Aug. 14, 1931; d. Victor J. and Marguerite E. (Biebesheimer) Cramer; m. James Herbert Kelly, Oct. 4, 1968 (dec. Apr. 74). BA, Northwestern U., 1956. Sec., Parry & Barns Law Offices, Ft. Wayne, 1951-52; trust sec. Lincoln Nat. Bank & Trust Co., 1956-58; sr. clk. stenographer div. Mental Health, Alaska Dept. Health, Anchorage, 1958-60; office mgr. Langdon Psychiat. Clinic, 1960-70; propr. A-1 Bookkeeping Svc., 1974-75; ptnr. Gonder Kelly Enterprises & A-is-A Constrn., Wasilla, Alaska, 1965-92; sales assoc. Yukon Realty/Gallery of Homes, Wasilla, 1989; sec. Rogers Realty, Inc., Wasilla, 1989, MMC Constrn., Inc., 1992-96. Dir. Alaska Mental Health Assn., Anchorage, 1960-61; pres., treas. Libertarian Party Anchorage, 1968-69, Alaska Libertarian Party, 1969-70. Mem. AAUW (life), Anchorage C. of C., Whittier Boat Owners Assn. (treas. 1980-84). Home: 8653 Augusta Cir Anchorage AK 99504-4202

KELLY, MICHAEL EVANS, public information officer; b. Flint, Mich. s. Raymond John and Katherine (LeVasseur) K.; m. Kay Sampson; children: Johanna Marie, James MIchael. BA in Govt., U. Notre Dame, 1970; MA in Comm., Wayne State U., 1997. Writer, prodr. WFBE Pub. Radio, Flint, 1977-87; exec. dir. Mich. Chiropractic Soc., Lansing, 1986-90; sr. dir. edn. and info. Mich. Credit Union League, Southfield, 1990-97; exec. dir. pub. info. Mott C.C., Flint, 1997—. Numerous appearances on Mich. radio and TV news outlets; author more than 500 articles; prodr. more than 300 radio and 20 TV programs; responsible for numerous videos; presented seminars. Mem. exec. com. Better Bus. Bur. Detroit; mem Selective Svc. Bd. # 25; pub. mem. Mich. Bd. Pharmacy, 1992-99, bd. dirs Flint Bluegrass Festival, 1979-87, Flint Urban Walls, 1977-80; chmn. 5th Congl. Dist. Mich. Rep. Party, 2003—. Recipient Herb Wegner award Credit Union Found., 1998, Philip A. Hart award MIch. Consumer Edn. Conf., 1997, numerous other awards. Mem. Pub. Rels. Soc. Am. (accredited), Consumer Educators of Mich. (pres. 1997-2000), S.E. Mich. Assn. Execs. (pres. 1996-97), Mich. Soc. Assn. Execs. (bd. dirs. 1997-97), Downtown Flint Rotary. Address: 1901 Montclair Ave Flint MI 48503-5334 E-mail: mkelly@mcc.edu.

KELLY, MICHAEL JOSEPH, academic administrator, consultant; b. NYC, July 2, 1931; s. Hugh and Mary Agnes (Harrison) K.; m. Helen Janet Nee, Oct. 4, 1969; children: Joan T., Jean M. BA, Marist Coll., 1955; BEE, Cath. U., 1960, MEE, 1961; DEng, U. Detroit, 1968. Tchr. U. Detroit, 3 yrs., dir. Computer Ctr.; tchr., adminstr. Marist Coll., 4 yrs.; assoc. prof. electrical and mech. engring., dir. engring. case program Stanford U.; mgr. CAD, litho sys. IBM, East Fishkill, NY, 1969-79, mgr. Mfg. Tech. Ctr. Boca Raton, Fla., 1979-84, dir. Quality Inst., 1984, mgr. quality improvement and profl. devel. programs systems tech. divsn., 1986-87; dir. computer integrated mfg. and tech. transfer NJ Inst. Tech., NJ, 1987-89; dir. def. mfg. office Def. Advanced Rsch. Projects Agy., 1989-91; exec. dir. Nat. Adv. Com. on Semiconductors, 1989-91; dir. Mfg. Rsch. Ctr. Ga. Inst. Tech., Ga., 1991-96, prof. technology mgmt., 1995-96; Northrop-Grumman endowed chair mfg. and design Calif. State U., LA, 1996 99; ind. mgmt. and ednl. cons., 1999—. Home: 31 Lieper St South Huntington NY 11746

KELLY, MICHAEL JOSEPH, lawyer; b. Bklyn., Apr. 24, 1947; s. Patrick and Bridget Kelly; m. Sharon Ann Erwin, Aug. 8, 1970; children: Tara Bridget, Liam Patrick, Caitlin Jane, Devon Michael. BA, Syracuse U., 1969; JD, SUNY, Buffalo, 1972. Bar: N.Y. 1972. Assoc. Sam Greene, Syracuse, N.Y., 1972-73; ptnr. Bayer, Dupee & Smith, Rochester, N.Y., 1973-79, Gates & Kelly, Perry, N.Y., 1979-81; pvt. practice, Perry, 1981—. Judge Town and Village of Warsaw, N.Y., 1990-91; asst. dist. atty. Wyoming County, Perry, 1991-97. Pres. Arts Coun. Wyoming County, 1983-84. Mem. ABA, N.Y. State Bar Assn. (bd. dirs. grievance com. 1986-92, svc. recognition award 1986, 92), Wyoming County Bar Assn. (pres. 1985-86), Rotary (bd. dirs., pres. Perry 1995-96), Retrouvaille Buffalo (coord. 2002-). Avocations: tennis, biking, music, reading, gardening. Office: 24 Lake St Perry NY 14530-1516

KELLY, MICHAEL JOSEPH, JR., publishing executive; b. Chgo., May 17, 1957; s. Michael Joseph and Mariann Julia (Williams) K.; m. Martha Joann Hall, Oct. 16, 1982; children: Katherine Rose, Mary Elizabeth, Michael Joseph III. Student, U. Wis., 1975-77; BA, U. Ill., 1979; exec. cert., Columbia U., 1995. Sales rep. Chgo. Tribune, 1980-83, Fortune Mag./Time Inc., Chgo., 1983-84, S.E. mgr. N.Y.C., 1984-87, N.Y. mgr., 1987-89; ea. sales dir. Entertainment Weekly/Time Inc., N.Y.C., 1989-91, v.p. advt. sales, 1991-93, v.p. advt. sales and mktg., 1993-96, pub., 1996—. Bd. mem. Cabin Life Inc., Piermont, N.Y. Bd. mem., com. chair Youth Literacy Vols., Chgo., 1981-85. Mem. Sleepy Hollow Club, Univ. Club N.Y., Alpha Delta Phi (v.p. 1975-79). Avocations: golf, history, yoga.*

KELLY, MICHAEL LEWIS, sales executive; b. San Francisco, June 23, 1952; s. June Sylvia Baird; m. Susan Ann Becker, Nov. 19, 1977; children: Meghan Faye, Courtney Ann. BA, Trinity Coll., Deerfield, Ill., 1976. Dir. of sales Alliance Semiconductor, San Jose, Calif., 1996—98; dir. of sales-Ams. SiRF Tech., San Jose, 1998—. Bd. planning commn. spl. project Hillside Devel. Plan, Milpitas, Calif., 1986—89; bd. of elders NVCC, Milpitas, 1984—89; organizer Young Life Fundraiser, Milpitas, 1984—86; mem. Jr. Golf No. Calif., Santa Cruz, Calif., 1989—90. Republican. Avocations: golf, photography, travel. Home: 79 Castlewood Dr Pleasanton CA 94566 Office: SiRF Tech 148 E Brokaw Rd San Jose CA 95121 E-mail: mkelly@sirf.com.

KELLY, NANCY FOLDEN, arts administrator; b. Fredericksburg, Va., Oct. 28, 1951; d. Virgil Alvis Jr. and Frances Virginia (DeShazo) Folden; m. Frank R. Kelly, Aug. 11, 1973; 1 child, Katherine Elizabeth Kelly. BA in Theatre Arts, Va. Poly. Inst. and State U., 1973; MFA in Theatre Directing, So. Meth. U., 1975. Coord. student programs Lincoln Ctr. Inst., N.Y.C., 1976-79; dir. N.Y.C. Opera Nat. Co. and edn. dept. Lincoln Ctr., 1979-93, mem. coun. on ednl. programs, 1979-93; mng. dir. Broadway Arts Theatre for Young Audiences, N.Y.C., 1994-96; dir. family and cmty. programs Ctrl. Park Conservancy, N.Y.C., 1996-98; fin. mgr. and assoc. dir. devel. Film Soc. Lincoln Ctr., N.Y.C., 1999—. E-mail: nkelly@filmlinc.com.

KELLY, PATRICK JOSEPH, neurosurgeon, educator; b. Lackawanna, N.Y., Sept. 19, 1941; s. Joseph P. and Mary D. (Connor) K.; m. Carol Huey; children: Patrick J., Michael, Caitlin. BS, U. Mich., 1962; MD, SUNY, Buffalo, 1966. Intern U.S. Naval Hosp., Phila., 1966-67; resident in internal medicine Northwestern U., Chgo., 1970-72; from asst. prof. to assoc. prof. U. Tex. Med. Sch., Galveston, 1972-79; assoc. prof. SUNY, Buffalo, 1979-84; prof., cons. Mayo Med. Sch./Mayo Clinic, Rochester, Minn., 1984-93; prof., chmn. neurosurg. dept. NYU Med. Ctr., 1993—. Cons., adv. bd. mem. Jet Propulsion Lab NASA, Pasadena, Calif., 1994—. Author: Tumor Stereotaxis, 1991; co-editor: Computers in Stereotactic Neurosurgery, 1992; mem. editl. bd. Neurosurgery, 1991—, Surg. Neurology, 1990—, Jour. Stereotactic and Functional Neurosurgery, 1986—; contbr. chpts. in books and articles to profl. jours.; profiled Am.'s Top Drs. and Top Drs.: New York Metro Area 2000-2002 of Castle Connolly Guide. Lt. comdr. USN, 1968-70. Recipient Scoville award World Fedn. Neurol. Surgery, 1997; named Citizen of Yr. Buffalo Evening News, 1982, Best Doctors in Am. Good Housekeeping, 1993, Town & Country, 1992, Am. Health, 1996, Top 100, Irish Am. mag., 1996, 99, Best Drs. N.Y., New York Mag., 1999, 2000, 01, 02, Woodward/White, Inc., 1998, 2000, 01, 02; inducted Boys and Girls Clubs Am. Hall of Fame, 2001. Fellow ACS; mem. Am. Soc. Stereotactic Neurosurgery (past pres., bd. dirs.), Am. Assn. Neurol. Surgeons (Van Wagenen fellow 1977, com. chmn.), Acad. Neurol. Surgery, Soc. Neurol. Surgeons (com.), Soc. Neurochurgie de Lange Francaise. Roman Catholic. Avocations: sailing, watercolor painting. Home: 7 Gracie Sq New York NY 10028-8001 Office: NYU Med Ctr 530 1st Ave New York NY 10016-6402 E-mail: kelly@brainscans.com.

KELLY, PAUL JOHN, priest; b. Buffalo, N.Y., Sept. 1, 1943; s. John H. and Gertrude A. (Considine) K. Diploma, Syracuse U., 1965; BA, Wadhams Hall, 1970; STM, St. Mary's Sem. and U., Balt., 1974; MA, Fordham U., 1980. Ordained Roman Cath. priest, 1974. Clergy Diocese of Ogdensburg, N.Y., 1974—. Dir. Pastoral Inst., Wadhams Hall, Ogdensburg, 1972-75, instr., 1978-81; bd. visitors St. Lawrence Psychiat. Ctr., Ogdensburg, 1979-89, chaplain, 1989-94; mem. alcohol and substance abuse subcom. Cmty. Svc. Bd., Hamilton County, N.Y.; mem. adj. faculty St. Bernard's Inst., Albany, 2000—. Author: Trapezus, Trebizond, Trabzon, 1968, A Teilhard Corrigenda, 1975, A Bibliography for Philosophy, 1980; contbr. articles to profl. jours. Avocations: birding, hiking, prisoner rights, rights of the mentally handicapped. Home: PO Box 214 Route 8 Speculator NY 12164

KELLY, PAUL JOSEPH, JR., judge; b. Freeport, N.Y., Dec. 6, 1940; s. Paul J. and Jacqueline M. (Nolan) Kelly; m. Ruth Ellen Dowling, June 27, 1964; children: Johanna, Paul Edwin, Thomas Martin, Christopher Mark, Heather Marie. BBA, U. Notre Dame, 1963; JD, Fordham U., 1967. Bar: N.Mex. 1967. Law clk. Cravath, Swaine & Moore, N.Y.C., 1964—67; assoc. firm Hinkle, Cox, Eaton, Coffield & Hensley, Roswell, N.Mex., 1967—71, ptnr., 1971—92; judge U.S. Ct. Appeals (10th cir.), Santa Fe, 1992—. Mem. N.Mex. Bd. Bar Examiners, 1982—85, N.Mex. Ho. of Reps., 1976—81, chmn. consumer and pub. affairs com., mem. judiciary com.; mem. N.Mex. Pub. Defender Bd., U.S. Jud. Conf. Com. on the Jud. Br., 1994—99, U.S. Jud. Conf. Civil Rules Adv. Com., 2002—; chair 10th Cir. Rules com., 10th Cir. Uniform Criminal Jury Instrn. Com. Bd. visitors Fordham U. Sch. Law, 1992—; pres. Oliver Seth Inn of Ct., 1993—, Roswell Drug Abuse Com. 1970—71; mem. Appellate Judges Nominating Commn., 1989—92, Eastern N.Mex. State Fair Bd., 1978—83; pres. Chaves County Young Reps., 1971—72; vice chmn. N.Mex. Young Reps., 1969—71, treas., 1968—69; pres. parish coun. Roman Cath. Ch., 1971—76; bd. dirs. Zia coun. Girl Scouts Am., Roswell Girls Club; bd. dirs., Chaves County Mental Health Assn., 1974—77; bd. dirs. Santa Fe Orch., 1992—93, Roswell Symphony Orch. Soc., 1969—82, treas., 1970—73, pres., 1973—75. Mem.: State Bar N.Mex. (v.p. young lawyers sect. 1969, mem. continuing legal edn. com. 1970—73, co-chmn. ins. sub-com. 1972—73, mem. Bench-Bar com. 1994—), Fed. Bar Assn. Office: US Court Appeals 10th Circuit Federal Courthouse PO Box 10113 Santa Fe NM 87504-6113

KELLY, PAUL KNOX, investment banker; b. Boston, Feb. 18, 1940; s. Thomas Joseph and Rita Patricia Kelly; m. Nancy Lee Belden, July 17, 1978; 1 child, 3 stepchildren. AB in English, U. Pa., 1962; MBA in Fin., Wharton Sch., 1964. Investment analyst bond dept. Prudential Ins. Co. Am., 1964-65; asst. treas. Comml. Credit Co., 1965-68; v.p. First Boston Corp., N.Y.C., 1968-75; ptnr., mem. mgmt. com., dir. Prescott, Ball & Turben, Cleve., 1975-77; sr. v.p., dir. Butcher & Singer, Inc., 1977-78; exec. v.p., mem. exec. com., dir. Blyth Eastman Dillon & Co., N.Y.C., 1978-80; mng. dir. Merrill Lynch White Weld Capital Markets Group, N.Y.C., 1980-82; exec. v.p., dir. Dean Witter Reynolds, Inc., 1982-84; pres., dir. Quadrex Securities Corp., 1984-85, Peers & Co., N.Y.C., 1985-90, PH II, Inc., Westport, Conn., 1988—, Knox & Co., N.Y.C., 1992—. Trustee U. Pa.; bd. dirs. Knox Enterprises, Inc. Mem. Union Club (Cleve.), Chagrin Valley Hunt Club, Penn Club N.Y., The LInks, Union League (Phila.), The No. Club (Auckland, New Zealand). Office: Knox & Co 33 Riverside Ave Westport CT 06880-4223

KELLY, PAUL V. federal agency administrator; BA in Econ., Merimack Coll.; MS in Mgmt. Sci., U. Lowell; diploma in nat. security studies, Indsl. Coll. of Armed Forces. Commd. ensign USMC, 1979, advanced through ranks to Col., various inf. and fin. mgmt. positions, sr. officer Dept. of Navy liaison to House and Senate appropriations com.; sr. officer legis. asst. to chmn. of Jt. Chiefs of Staff U.S. Dept. of State, dir. Marine Corps War Coll.; ret. USMC, 1999; asst. sec. of state for legis. affairs U.S. Dept. of State, Washington, 2001—. Office: US Dept of State Legis Affairs 2201 C St NW Washington DC 20520 Office Fax: 202-647-2762.

KELLY, PETER, CEO, president; m. Lorraine Kelly; 2 children. Pres., CEO Continuum Health Ptnrs., Inc., 2000—, exec. v.p., COO. Office: Continuum Health Ptnrs 555 W 57 St New York NY 10019

KELLY, QUENTIN PATRICK, lawyer; b. New Orleans, Jan. 3, 1959; s. George F. Kelly and Joan (Maxwell) Florez; m. Elizabeth Price Duffy, Jan. 23, 1988 (div.). BSBA, U. New Orleans, 1981; JD, Loyola U., New Orleans, 1987. Bar: La. 1987, U.S. Dist. Ct. (mid., ea. and we. dists.) La. 1987, U.S. Ct. Appeals (5th cir.) 1987, Calif., 1995. Petroleum landman Ken Savage & Assocs., New Orleans, 1981-83; assoc. Chaffe, McCall, Phillips, Toled & Sarpy, New Orleans, 1986, Capitelli & Wicker, New Orleans, 1987-91; asst. dist. atty. Jefferson Parish, 1991-2001; dep. dist. atty. Santa Barbara County, Calif., 2001—. Contbr. to profl. publs. Mem. ABA, Fed. Bar Assn., La. State Bar Assn., Calif. Bar Assn., Phi Delta Phi. Republican. Roman Catholic. Avocations: tennis, fishing, water skiing, skiing. Home: 915 W Morrison Apt 101 Santa Maria CA 93458

KELLY, QUENTIN THORN, water company executive, inventor, writer; b. New Orleans, La., July 14, 1934; s. Edgar Joseph and Leola (Pilcher) Kelly; m. Peggy R. Richey; children: Lisa Scott Curtis, Carolyn Fields, Quentin T. Jr. Student, Kenyon Coll., Gambier, Ohio. Asst. to pres. Westinghouse Electric Corp., New York City, NY, 1965—72; chmn. and CEO WorldWater Corp., Pennington, NJ, 1984—. Writer MGM Studios, Hollywood (Culver City), Calif. Named to N.J. Inventors Hall of Fame, 1998. Mem.: Williams Club (N.Y.C.). Achievements include invention of Solar Water Pumps, 1992. Office: World-Water Corp 55 Route 31 South Pennington NJ 08534

KELLY, RAYMOND BOONE, III, lawyer; b. Ft. Worth, Oct. 12, 1947; s. Raymond Boone Jr. and Martha (Morehead) K.; m. Ellen McCarthy; children: Alice Katherine, Anne Rowan. BA, Tulane U., 1970; JD, So. Meth. U., 1974. Bar: Tex. 1974. Ptnr. Decker, McMackin & McClane, Ft. Worth, 1974—. V.p., trustee William E. Scott Found., Ft. Worth, 1978—. Bd. dirs., past pres. Goodwill Industries Ft. Worth, 1975-94; bd. dirs. Arts Coun. Ft. Worth and Tarrant County, 1980-91, 95-97, Conf. of S.W. Founds., Dallas, 1986-89, 97-2000, Davey O'Brien Found., 2001—, Big Bros./Bis Sisters, Ft. Worth, 1987-94, Intercultura, Inc., Ft. Worth, 1989-96, chmn., 1992-94, Funding Info. Ctr., 1993-97, Ft. Worth Dallas Ballet, 1996-97, Cmty. Found. North Tex., 1996-2002, All Saints Health Sys., 1997—; trustee Modern Art Mus. Ft. Worth, 1981—, Fort Worth Country Day Sch., 1996—; chmn. All Saints Health Found., 1987—, chmn., 1991-2002, Goodwill Industries Ft. Worth Found., 1997—, Ft. Worth Club, 1999-2002. Mem. ABA, State Bar Tex., Tarrant County Bar Assn., Tarrant County Young Lawyers Assn. (v.p., sec. 1976-77), Ft. Worth Club, Exchange Club, Rivercrest Country Club, Steeplechase Club, Ind. Petroleum Assn. Am., Tex. Oil and Gas Assn. Republican. Episcopalian. Home: 301 Virginia Pl Fort Worth TX 76107-1611 Office: Decker, McMackin & McClane 801 Cherry St Fort Worth TX 76102-3812

KELLY, REGIS BAKER, biochemistry educator, biophysics educator; b. Edinburgh, Scotland, May 26, 1940; m. Rae L. Burke, 1992; children: Gordon, Alison, Colin. BSc, U. Edinburgh, 1961; PhD, Calif. Inst. Tech., 1967. Instr. neurobiology Harvard Med. Sch., Boston, 1969-71; from asst. prof. to prof. biochem. and biophysics U. Calif., San Francisco, 1971—, chair dept. biochemistry and biophysics, 1995—. Dir. cell biology program U. Calif., 1988-95, dir. Hormone Rsch. Inst., 1992—; adv. panelist Nat. Engring. Inst.; mem. study sect. NIH; vis. prof. MIT, Cambridge, 1986—. Helen Hay Whitney Found. fellow, 1967-70, Multiple Sclerosis Soc. fellow, 1970-71. Mem. Soc. Neurosci., Am. Soc. Biol. Chem., Am. Soc. Cell Biology. Office: Univ Calif Dept Biochem & Biophysics PO Box 534 San Francisco CA 94143-0001

KELLY, RITA MAE, academic administrator, researcher; b. Waseca, Minn., Dec. 10, 1939; d. John Francis and Agnes Mary (Lorentz) Cawley; m. Vincent Peter Kelly, June 2, 1962; children: Patrick, Kathleen. BA, U. Minn., 1961; MA, Ind. U., 1964, PhD, 1967; doctorate (hon.), U. Umeå, Sweden, 1998. Rsch. scientist Ctr. for Rsch. in Social Systems, 1968-70; sr. rsch. scientist Am. Inst. for Rsch., Inc., Kensington, Md., 1970-72; cons. OEO, 1972-73; pres. Rita Mae Kelly & Assocs., 1973-75; tenured prof. Rutgers U., 1977-79, prof., 1979-82; from tenured to full prof. Sch. Justice Studies Ariz. State U., Tempe, 1982-87, tenured prof. justice studies, pub. affairs, polit. sci. and women's study, 1987-96, chair, dir. Sch. Justice Studies, 1990-95; dean social scis. U. Tex., Dallas, 1996—. Mem. credentials com. U.S. Dem. Party, Atlanta, 1988; mem. state com. Ariz. Dem. party, Phoenix, 1988; dist. committeeman Tempe Dist. 27 Dem. Party, 1988; charter mem., hon. bd. dirs. Ariz. Women's Inst., 1988; founding mem. Inst. for Women's Policy Rsch., Washington, 1988, Ariz. Found. for Women, Inc., 1995—; bd. dirs. Ariz. Leadership 2000 Alumni Assn., 1993—; co-dir. Ariz. Leadership 2000 and Beyond, 1993—; co-chair Arizonians for a Healthy Future, 1994-95. Author: (with others) The Making of Political Women: A Study of Socialization and Role Conflict, 1978, Promoting Productivity in the Public Sector: Problems, Strategies, Prospects, 1988, Comparable Worth, Pay Equity, and Public Policy, 1988, (with Mary M. Hale) Gender, Bureaucracy, and Democracy: Careers and Equal Opportunity in the Public Sector, 1989, The Gendered Economy, 1991, Advances in Policy Studies Since 1950, 1992, Gender Power, Leadership and Governance, 1995, Gender, Globalization and Democratization, 2000; editor book series Women in Politics Series, 1981-88; editor: (with Dennis J. Palumbo) Type Series in Public Policy, 1989-94; co-editor: Gender, Globalization and Democratization, 2001; editor Women & Politics Jour. Dep. gov. Am. Biog. Inst., 1995—; co-chair Airz. Women's Vote Project, 1996—; coord. scientific rsch. com. engendering globalization democratization internat. Social Sci. Coun., 1998—. Internat. Soroptomists of Phoenix, Inc. grantee, 1987, GTE Found. Rsch. grantee, 1988, Ind. U. Rsch. grantee, 1964-65; Ford Found. fellow, 1962-63; recipient Rutgers U. Outstanding Faculty merit award, 1979, All-Am. Women's award, 1985, YWCA Camden County award, 1980; Fulbright award to Brazil, 1991; recipient Aaron Wildovsky award for best book pub. policy, 1992, 93, Outstanding Mentor award Women's Caucus for Polit. Sci., 1991, 97, Miriam Mills award, 1995; U.S. Dept. Labor Step Out grantee, 1993-95. Mem. Am. Polit. Sci. Assn. (chair roundtable 1985, chair B. William Anderson award com. 1983-84, reviewer 1977-78, 83-84, head policy sect. 1989), APA Soc. for Psychol. Study of Social Issues (chair nat. task force on productivity in the pub. sector 1975-80), Am. Soc. for Pub. Adminstrn. (exec. coun. sect. on mgmt. sci. and policy analysis 1986-89, vice chair planning and evaluation com. 1985-86, Achievement award 1981, Disting. Rsch. award for rsch. on women 1991), Internat. Polit. Sci. Assn. (chair com. on status of women 1986-88), Western Polit. Sci. Assn. (pres. 1988-89), Policy Studies Orgn. (pres. 1988-89, Merriam Mills award 1995, Thomas R. Dye Svc. award 1997). Office: U Tex PO Box 830688 Richardson TX 75083-0688

KELLY, ROBERT A. music educator; s. James J. and Anne W. Kelly. Bachelor, Hartt Coll. of Music, West Hartford, 1969—73; M, Ctrl. Conn. State U., 1978. Music tchr. Catherine M. McGee Mid. Sch., Berlin, Conn., 1973—83; choral dir.. music tchr. Berlin H.S., Berlin, Conn., 1973—. Recipient Tchr. of Yr., Berlin Bd. Edn., 1995. Mem.: NEA, Conn. Edn. Assn., Nat. Band Assn., Am. Choral Dirs. Assn., Music Educators Nat. Conf. Office: Berlin High School 139 Patterson Way Berlin CT 06037 Office Fax: 860-829-0832. E-mail: rkelly@berlinwall.org.

KELLY, ROBERT CORBY, energy executive, writer; b. Detroit, July 15, 1940; s. Robert Corby Kelly and Margaret Elizabeth Murphy; m. Helen Marie Randazzo, Aug. 28, 1970; children: Robert Corby III, Cristy Mary Margaret. BS, U.S. Mil. Acad., West Point, N.Y., 1968; MPA, Harvard U., 1970, PhD in Econs., 1981. Sr. v.p. Houston Nat., Houston, 1985; exec. v.p. Enron Power Corp., Houston, 1985—90; chmn., CEO Enron Europe, London, 1990—93; exec. v.p. Enron Corp., Houston, 1993—95; chmn., CEO Enron Renewable Energy, Houston, 1995—97; ptnr. DKR Devel., LLC, Houston, 2001—; chmn., CEO Country Watch, Inc., Houston, 1997—. Mgr. strategy GE Cogan Protein Group, Schenectady, NY, 1983—84; mgr. planning Continental Resources, Orlando, Fla. and Houston, 1981—83. Author: (book) Carbon Conundrum, 2002, Economics of National Security, 1981. Bd. dirs. Houston World Affairs Coun. Maj. U.S. Army, 1964—81. Decorated Legion of Merit. Roman Catholic. Office: Country Watch Inc 2 Riverway Ste 1770 Houston TX 77056

KELLY, ROBERT EDWARD, JR., lawyer; b. Pitts., Nov. 28, 1950; s. Robert E. Sr. and Adelaide Cecelia (Harris) K.; m. Noreen Theresa Quinn, Oct. 23, 1976; children: Robert E. III, Christopher Patrick, Andrew Clifford. BA, Siena Coll., 1972; JD, Georgetown U., 1975. Bar: Pa. 1975, U.S. Dist. Ct. (we. dist.) Pa. 1975, U.S. Dist. Ct. (ea. and mid. dist.) Pa. 1978, U.S. Ct. Appeals (3d cir.) 1979, U.S. Supreme Ct. 1980, U.S. Dist. Ct. (no. dist.) N.Y. 1992, U.S. Dist. Ct. (no. dist.) Calif. 1994. Assoc. Houston, Harbaugh, Cohen & Lippard, Pitts., 1975-77; assoc., dep. atty. gen. Commonwealth of Pa., Harrisburg, 1977-80; assoc. Duane, Morris & Heckscher, Harrisburg, 1980-86, ptnr., 1986—2002, Kelly, Hoffman & Goduto, LLP, 2002—. Mem. ABA, FBA, Pa. Bar Assn., Pa. Def. Inst., Dauphin County Bar Assn., Pa. Soc., Am. Inns of Ct., St. Thomas More Soc., West Shore Country Club (Camp Hill, Pa.). Republican. Roman Catholic. Home: 3610 Horsham Dr Mechanicsburg PA 17050-2204 Office: Kelly Hoffman & Goduto LLP Commerce Towers 10th Fl 300 N 2d St Harrisburg PA 17101 E-mail: rkelly@khgllp.com.

KELLY, ROBERT EDWARD, engineer, educator; b. Abington, Pa., Oct. 20, 1934; s. Bernard Joseph and Rose Monica (Lautenschlager) K.; m. Karin Elizabeth Lampert, Aug. 15, 1964; children: Nicholas, Jennifer. BA, Franklin & Marshall Coll., 1957; BS, Rensselaer Poly. Inst., 1957; MS in Aero. Engring., MIT, 1959, ScD, 1964. Asst. prof. UCLA, 1967-70, assoc. prof., 1970-75, prof. dept. mech. and aerospace engring., 1975—93, vice chair grad. affairs, 1976, 1994—99; ret. Sr. vis. fellow Imperial Coll. Sci. and Tech., London, 1974; vis. prof. Northwestern U., Evanston, Ill., 1985, U. Manchester, Eng., 1994; vis. scientist Japan Atomic Energy Rsch. Inst., Tokai-mura, 1991; cons. Hughes Aircraft Co., El Segundo, Calif., 1976-83. Assoc. editor Physics of Fluids, 1981-83, 92-97; mem. editl. bd. Phys. Rev. E, 1990-96; contbr. over 70 articles to profl. jours. Fellow Am. Phys. Soc. (chmn. divsn. fluid dynamics 1980-81), ASME. Avocation: gardening. Office: MAE Dept UCLA Los Angeles CA 90095-1597

KELLY, ROBERT EMMETT, telecommunications company administrator; b. Cambridge, Mass., Feb. 6, 1952; s. Charles Patrick and Patricia Anne (McCormack) K.; m. Ann Marie McDonough, June 1, 1991. Student, St. Michael's Coll., Winooski, Vt., 1969—71. Owner, operator REKording, Everett, Mass., 1976—; asst. staff mgr. New Eng. Telephone Co., Boston, 1985-88, ops. mgr. digital provisioning, 1991-93, staff dir. planning systems support, 1993-95; mem. tech. staff Bell Comm. Rsch., Piscataway, N.J., 1988-91; project mgr. Telcordia Techs. (formerly Bell Com. Rsch.), Piscataway, N.J., 1995—. Vol. Cambridge coun. Boy Scouts Am., 1972—. Mem. Audio Engring. Soc. Roman Catholic. Avocations: hiking, golf, song writing, reading. Home: 335 Old New Ipswich Rd Rindge NH 03461-4016 Office: Telcordia Techs ZZZ NH 444 Hoes Ln Piscataway NJ 08854-4120 E-mail: rkelly@telcordia.com.

KELLY, ROBERT F. federal judge; b. 1935; BS, Villanova U., 1957; LLB, Temple U., 1960. Pvt. practice law, Media, Pa., 1961-62, 64-76, Chester, Pa., 1962-64; law clk. to Hon. Francis J. Catania Ct. Common Pleas, Delaware County, Pa., 1964-72; prothonotary Delaware County, 1972-76; former judge Ct. Common Pleas 32d Jud. Dist. Pa.; judge U.S. Dist. Ct. (ea. dist.) Pa., Phila., 1987—, sr. judge, 2001—. Lectr. law Villanova U. Law Sch. Voluntary defender Delaware County, 1962; chmn. Delaware County Rep. Exec. Com., 1972-76, Subcom. on Libr. Programs; mem. Judicial Coun. com. on Automation and Tech., 1989—. Mem. ABA, Am. Judicature Soc., Pa. Bar Assn., Pa. Trial Judges Assn., Delaware County Bar Assn. (judicial counsel's com. automation and tech., 1989—, chmn. subcom. libr. programs). Office: US Dist Ct 11613 US Courthouse 601 Market St Philadelphia PA 19106-1713

KELLY, ROBERT LYNN, advertising agency executive; b. Chgo., Oct. 25, 1939; s. Carl Robert and Annabel Pauline (Lindsay) K.; m. Maria Graciela Gonzalez, Oct. 26, 1963; children: Albert E., Elizabeth A. BA, Gettysburg Coll., 1961. Dir. pub. info. Oxnard AFB, Calif., 1961-64; with Armstrong World Industries, Lancaster, Pa., 1964-67; owner Bob Kelly Advt., Quito, Ecuador, 1967-70; ptnr., writer, acct. exec., mgr. Ibold & Kelly Advt., Lancaster, 1970-72; founder, pres. Kelly Advt., Inc., Lancaster, 1972-84; pres. Kelly Michener, Inc., Lancaster, 1984—. Guest lectr. F & M Coll., and Millersville U., 1971—; lectr. Lancaster Community Gallery, 1977. Contbr. articles to profl. jours. Active various civic orgns.; bd. dirs. Lancaster Cmty. Gallery, 1978-89, v.p., 1983-89; mem. campaign coms. Lancaster County Rep. orgns., 1973-75; bd. dirs. Rockford Plantation, 1979-89, v.p., 1988-89; v.p. Let's Lifebelt Lancaster, 1984-85. With USAF, 1961-64. Mem. Nat. Advt. Agy. Network (nat. chmn. 1984), Am. Assn. Advt. Agys. (chmn. regional bd. govs. 1989-90, mem. regional bd. govs. 1998—), Lancaster Advt. Agy Coun. (sec. 1987-61, pres. 1992—), N.G. Assn. U.S., Sales and Mktg. Exec., Hamilton Club, Lancaster Tennis and Yacht Club (bd. dirs., v.p. 1986-87, commodore 1988-89), Port Herman Beach Assn. (pres. bd. dirs. 1998-99). Episcopalian. Office: Kelly Michener Inc PO Box 959 Lancaster PA 17608-0959

KELLY, ROBERT P. banking executive; b. Mar. 17, 1954; B of Commerce, St. Mary's U., Halifax, N.S.; MBA, City U., London, England. cert. CPA. Sr. mgmt. Toronto Dominion Bank, Canada; exec. v.p., CFO First Union Corp., Charolette, NC, 2000—01; CFO Wachovia Corp., Winston Salem, NC, 2001—. Bd. dirs. Art Gallery Ontario; former chmn. Metro. Toronto YMCA capital campaign. Office: Wachovia Corp 100 North Main St Winston Salem NC 27150

KELLY, ROBERT VINCENT, JR., metal company executive; b. Phila., Sept. 29, 1938; s. Robert Vincent and Catherine Mary (Hanley) K.; m. Margaret Cecilia Taylor, Feb. 11, 1961; children: Robert V. III, Christopher T., Michael J., Tasha Marie. BS in Indsl. Mgmt., St. Joseph's U., Phila., 1960; postgrad., Roosevelt U., 1965-66. Gen. foreman prodn. Republic Steel Corp., Chgo., 1963-68; supt. prodn. Phoenix Steel Corp., Phoenixville, Pa., 1969-73; gen. supt. ops. Continental Steel Corp., Kokomo, Ind., 1973-77; gen. mgr. MACSTEEL div. Quanex Corp., Jackson, Mich., 1977-81; corp. v.p. Quanex Corp., Houston, 1979—, pres. MACSTEEL group Jackson, 1982—. Pres. La Salle Steel Co., Hammond, Ind., 1985-87, Arbuckle Corp., Jackson, 1984-88. Leader, com. mem. Boy Scouts Am., Jackson. Lt. USN, 1960-63. Mem. Am. Mgmt. Assn. (pres.), Inst. Indsl. Engrs., Assn. Iron and Steel Engrs., Am. Soc. for Metals, USN Inst., Jackson C. of C. Clubs: Jackson Country. Avocations: hiking, camping, sailing, scouting. Home: 1734 Metzmont Dr Jackson MI 49203-5379 Office: Macsteel, Quanex Corp 1 Jackson Sq Ste 500 Jackson MI 49201-1446

KELLY, ROBERT WILLIAM, economist; b. Washington, June 11, 1939; s. Robert Joseph and Emily Thersa (Markiewicz) K.; BA, U. Wyo., 1963; MA, U. Pitts., 1965; m. Lily Hsui, Dec. 28, 1966. Econ. adviser to undersec. of state Dept. State, Vietnam, Thailand, Cambodia, 1965-72; dir. policy food controls Cost of Living Council, Exec. Office of Pres., 1973-74; policy adviser to dep. adminstr. Fed. Energy Adminstrn., 1974-75; dir. planning and analysis, Office Commercialization ERDA, 1975-76, dir. commercialization studies, 1976-77; dir. policy analysis Office Energy Rsch., Dept. of Energy, 1977-79, adviser to undersec. energy, 1980-81, dir. U.S. /Korea Coop. Energy Assessment, 1979-80; sr. economist Gas Research Inst., 1981-90; dep. asst. adminstr. Dept. of State/AID Mid. East and North Africa, 1990-93; chief economist Internat. Econ. and Energy Analysis SAIC, 1993-99; fgn. policy advisor Dole for Pres. campaign, 1994-96, pvt. cons., 2000_. Served with USMCR, 1958-60. Ford fellow, 1963-64; recipient cert. of achievement Fed. Energy Adminstrn., 1974; cert. of appreciation Energy R & D Adminstrn., 1976; Cash award Dept. Energy, 1979; Letter of Commendation Republic of Korea, 1980. Mem. Am. Econs. Assn., Rep. Nat. Com. Nat. Policy Forum, Internat. Trade Com. (chmn. 1994-97), foreign policy trade adv. to GOP pres. nom. Sen. Robert Dole, 1994-96, Omicron Delta Epsilon. Roman Catholic. Author articles, papers. Home: PO Box 725 Mc Henry MD 21541-0725 Personal E-mail: rwkelly@mindspring.com.

KELLY, ROBERTO CONRADO (BOBBY KELLY), professional baseball player; b. Panama City, Panama, Oct. 1, 1964; Student, Jose Dolores Moscote Coll., Panama. With N.Y. Yankees, 1982—92, Cin. Reds, 1992—94, Atlanta Braves, 1994, Montreal Expos, 1994—95, L.A. Dodgers, 1995—97, Minn. Twins, 1997—98, Tex. Rangers, 1998—99, N.Y. Yankees, 1999—. Named to All-Star Team, Am. League, 1992, Nat. League, 1993. Office: New York Yankees E 161st & River Ave Bronx NY 10451

KELLY, ROBIN L. state representative; b. New York, NY, Apr. 30, 1956; children: Kelly, Ryan. BA, Bradley Univ., 1977, MA, 1982; PhD (pending), No. Ill., 2002. State Rep. House of Rep., Dist. 38, 2002—; dir. Crisis Nursery, 1984—87; assoc. dir. The Youth Shelters, 1987—90; svc. Bradley Univ., 1990—92; dir. Multicultural Student; dir. of comm. affairs Village of Matteson, 1992—. Commr. Cook County Commn. on Human Rights, 1998—; bd. mem. Rich Twp. Food Pantry Bd., 1995—, Ill. Theatre Ctr., 1993—, Bradley Univ. Coun., 1998—. Democrat. Office: Capitol 252-W Stratton Office Bldg Springfield IL 62706 also: District 3649 West 183rd St, Suite 110 Hazel Crest IL 60429*

KELLY, RODNEY P. career officer; BS in Agr., So. Ill. U., 1966, MBA, 1968; grad., Squadron Officer Sch., 1975, Air Command and Staff Coll., 1978, Air War Coll., 1988. Commd. 2d lt. USAF, 1967, advanced through grades to maj. gen., 1997; standardization and evaluation mem. 12th Flying Tng. Wing, Randolph AFB, Tex., 1975; resource mgr. rated officer assignments Air Force Mil. Pers. Ctr., Randolph AFB, 1975-79; F-15 pilot, A Flight comdr. 525th Tactical Fighter Squadron, Bitburg Air Base, West Germany, 1979-82; chief F-15 standardization and evaluation divsn. 36th Tactical Fighter Wing, Bitburg Air Base, 1982-83; comdr. 527th Aggressor Squadron U.S. Air Forces in Europe, RAF, Alconbury, Eng., 1985-86; dep. comdr. ops. 10th Tactical Reconnaissance Wing, RAF, Alconbury, 1986-87; asst. for air def. NATO policy Office of Sec. of Def., internat. security policy, Washington, 1988-90; vice comdr. 21st Tactical Fighter Wing, Elmendorf AFB, Alaska, 1990-91; comdr. 3d Wing, Elmendorf AFB, 1991-93; Pacific Air Forces asst. dir. ops. Hdqs. Pacific Air Forces, Hickam AFB, Hawaii, 1993-95, dir. plans, 1995-96, Hdqs. N.Am. Aerospace Def. Command, Peterson AFB, Colo., 1996-97; dir. ops. Hdqs. U.S. Space Command, Peterson AFB, 1997-99; asst. dep. chief of staff plays and programs Hdqs. USAF, Washington, 1999—. Decorated Def. Superior Svc. medal, Legion of Merit with oak leaf cluster, Meritorious Svc. medal with 3 oak leaf clusters. Office: HQ USAF/XP Asst Dep Chief Staff Plans 1070 Air Force Pentagon Washington DC 20330-1070 E-mail: rodney.kelly@pentagon.af.mil.

KELLY, RUTH, state agency administrator; b. Mt. Vernon, N.Y. d. John Edwin and Ruth Elizabeth (Brady) Dowling; m. Paul Joseph Kelly Jr., June 27, 1964; children: Johanna, Paul Edwin, Thomas Martin, Christopher Mark, Heather Marie. BA, Seton Hall Coll., 1962; MA, Duke U., 1964. Assoc. tech. staff Bell Labs., N.Y., 1964-65; office mgr. Santa Fe Mountain Ctr., N.M., 1989-91, A.G. Edwards & Sons, Santa Fe, N.M., 1992-94; dir. Bds. and Commns. Office Gov., Santa Fe, 1995—. Chmn. Roswell Pub. Libr., N.M., 1975-76. Mem. bd. of Zia, Girl Scout Coun., Artesia, N.M., 1980; treas. Republican Party Santa Fe Co., 1993-94. Recipient Trustee of Yr. award, N.M. Libr. Assn., 1977. Mem. Federated Republican Women of Santa Fe. Avocations: reading, aerobics, golf, skiing, pub. affairs. Office: Office of Gov State Capitol Bldg 400 Santa Fe NM 87503-0001

KELLY, STEPHEN EULESS, ophthalmologist; b. Oklahoma City, July 2, 1944; s. Harold Shaw and Mart Will (Euless) K. BS with honors, U. Okla., 1966; MD, Washngton U., St. Louis, 1970. Diplomate Am. Bd. Ophthalmology. Intern Lenox Hill Hosp., N.Y.C., 1970-71; resident in ophthalmology N.Y. Eye and Ear Infirmary, N.Y.C., 1972-75, attending surgeon, 1999—; corneal fellow Manhattan Eye, Ear and Throat Hosp., N.Y.C., 1975-76, attending surgeon, 1976—; pvt. practice Cataract & Corneal Assocs., N.Y.C., 1976—. Investigator Excimer Laser-FDA, 1991—96; lectr. Coll. Physicians and Surgeons Columbia U., N.Y.C., 1997—2000. Sec., dir. Microsurg. Rsch. Found., 1976—. Maj. USAR, 1970-76. Fellow ACS, Am. Acad. Ophthalmology (Honor award 1985); mem. AMA (Physician's Recognition award 2002), Am. Soc. of Cataract and Refractive Surgery, Internat. Soc. Refractive Surgery. Office: Cataract & Corneal Assocs 154 E 71st St New York NY 10021-5125

KELLY, SUE W. congresswoman; b. Lima, Ohio, Sept. 26, 1936; m. Edward; 4 children. BA, Denison U., 1958; MA in Health Advocacy, Sarah Lawrence Coll., 1985. Rschr. New England Inst. Med. Rsch., 1958; tchr. John Jay Jr. H.S., 1962-63, Harvey Sch.; real estate rehabilitator, 1963—; campaign coord. Rep. Hamilton Fish, N.Y., 1971-72; intern Ruth Taylor Home, 1973-74; florist, owner Somerstown Flower Shop, 1978-79; patient advocate St. Luke's Hosp., 1984-87; adj. prof. of health advocacy Sarah Lawrence Coll., 1987-92; mem. 105th to 108th Congress from 19th N.Y. dist. U.S. Ho. of Reps., 1995—. Mem. fin. svcs. subcom. on fin. instns. and consumer credit opportunity SBA; mem. regulatory reform and paperwork reduction Transp. and Infrastructure subcoms. on aviation, hwys. and transit, water resources and environ. Republican. Office: US House Reps 1127 Longworth Bldg Washington DC 20515-3219*

KELLY, SUSAN CROCE, corporate affairs professional; b. Berkeley, Calif., Feb. 6, 1947; d. D. Fred and Helen June (Morris) Croce; m. James Michael Kelly, Jan. 30, 1970 (div. 1976); 1 child, Brendan Croce Kelly; m. Joel L. Kirkpatrick, March 16, 1991. BS, Purdue U., 1969; MA, St. Louis U., 1973. Reporter St. Louis Globe Democrat, 1969-72; reporter, photographer Springfield (Mo.) Newspapers Inc., 1973-76; pub. rels. specialist Monsanto Co., St. Louis, 1976-78, pub. rels. mgr. Monsanto Europe SA Brussels and London, 1978, mgr. editorial svcs., then mgr. sci. communications St. Louis, 1979-83, pub. rels. dir., then dir. corp. communications, 1984-85; freelance writer St. Louis, 1986; dir. corp. affairs Sandoz Agro Inc., Des Plaines, Ill., 1987-90; v.p. corp. affairs Sandoz Agro, Inc., Des Plaines, Ill., 1990-94; exec. v.p. The Cresta Group, 1994—; pres. Kirkpatrick Internat., Inc., Houston, 1997—. Pub. affairs oversight coun. Nat. Agr. Chem. Assn., Washington, 1989-94; pub. rels. com. Western Agr. Chem. Assn. Author: Route 66, 1988; contbr. articles to mags. and newspapers. Bd. dirs. Theatre Project Co., St. Louis, 1984-86, Tex. Artists Mus., 1996-98; comm. com. Met. Planning Coun., Chgo., 1992-97; pub. rels. com. Churchill Meml., Fulton, Mo., 1983-88; v.p. Hadley Twp. Dem. Club, Clayton, Mo., 1984. Mem. Pub. Rels. Soc. Am. (chpt. pres. 1986), Arthur Page Soc. Roman Catholic. Avocations: aviation, italian cooking. E-mail: kirkpatrickintl@aol.com.

KELLY, THADDEUS ELLIOTT, medical geneticist; b. N.Y.C., 1937; MD, Med. Coll. S.C.; PhD, Johns Hopkins U. Diplomate Am. Bd. Genetics (pres. 1993-94), Am. Bd. Pediat. Prof. pediat. U. Va., Charlottesville, dir. med. genetics. Office: U Va Hosp Div Med Genetics PO Box 800386 Charlottesville VA 22908-0386

KELLY, THOMAS, advertising executive; V.p. media svcs. Hawthorne Direct, Fairfield, Iowa, pres., CEO. Office: Hawthorne Direct Inc PO Box 1366 300 N 16th St Fairfield IA 52556-2604

KELLY, THOMAS CAJETAN, archbishop; b. Rochester, N.Y., July 14, 1931; s. Thomas A. Kelly and Katherine Eleanor (Fisher) Conley. AB, Providence Coll., 1953; STL, Dominican House of Studies, Washington, 1959; D in Canon Law, U. St. Thomas, Rome, 1962; STD (hon.), Providence Coll, 1979; DHL (hon.), Spalding Coll., 1983. Ordained priest Roman Cath. Ch. 58, aux. bishop 77. Sec. Dominican Province, N.Y.C., 1962—65; sec. Apostolic Del., Washington, 1965—71; assoc. gen. sec. Nat. Conf. Cath. Bishops-U.S. Cath. Conf., Washington, 1971—77; gen. sec. U.S. Cath. Bishops Conf., Washington, 1977—82; archbishop Archdiocese of Louisville, 1982—. Chmn. Cath. Conf. Ky., Louisville, 1982—. Chancellor Bellarmine Coll.; bd. dirs. St. Luke Inst. Recipient Veritas medal, St. Catharine Coll., 1984. Mem.: Nat. Cath. Edn. Assn. (chmn. bd. dirs. 1991—94), Canon Law Soc. Am. Roman Catholic. Home and Office: 212 E College St Louisville KY 40203-2334

KELLY, THOMAS JESSE, JR., molecular biologist; b. Birmingham, Ala., Nov. 21, 1941; s. Thomas Jesse and Agnes (Allen) K.; m. Mary Lucinda Schwartz, June 25, 1969; children: Mark Thomas, Andrew Samuel. BA with honors, Johns Hopkins U., 1962, PhD in Biophysics, 1968, MD, 1969. Served with USPHS, 1970-72. Postdoctoral fellow Harvard Med. Sch., Boston, 1968, Johns Hopkins U. Sch. Medicine, Balt., 1969-70; staff assoc. Nat. Inst. Health, Bethesda, Md., 1970-72; asst. prof. microbiology Johns Hopkins U. Sch. Medicine, Balt., 1972-75, assoc. prof., 1976-79, Boury Prof. molecular biology and genetics, 1980—2002, dir. dept., 1982—2002; dir. Sloan-Kettering Inst., 2002—. Chmn. study sect. virology NIH, 1988-90. Mem. editorial bd. Jour. Biol. Chemistry, 1982-94, Jour. Virology, 1980-90, Virus Rsch., 1983-93, Oncogene Rsch., 1989-94, Seminars in Virology, 1989-95, Am. Soc. Biochem. Molecular Biology, 1989-94. Awards assembly Gen. Motors Cancer Prize; bd. dirs. Passano Found. Recipient Career Devel. award NIH, 1972-77. Fellow Am. Acad. Arts and Sci.; mem. NAS, Am. Soc. Biological Chemists, Am. Soc. Microbiology, Am. Soc. Virology, Phi Beta Kappa, Alpha Omega Alpha, Inst. Medicine. Office: Sloan-Kettering Inst 1275 York Ave New York NY 10021

KELLY, THOMAS MICHAEL, lawyer; b. Atlanta, Oct. 5, 1958; s. Edward (dec.) and Marie K. AB cum laude, Columbia U., 1979; JD cum laude, Harvard U., 1983. Bar: N.Y. 1985. Law clk. to Hon. Eugene Nickerson U.S. Dist. Ct. (ea. dist.) N.Y., Bklyn., 1983-84; assoc. Debevoise & Plimpton, N.Y.C., 1984-93, ptnr., 1993—. Mem. Assn. of Bar of City of N.Y. Democrat. Office: Debevoise & Plimpton 919 3rd Ave 42d Fl New York NY 10022-6225

KELLY, THOMAS PAINE, JR., lawyer; b. Tampa, Fla., Aug. 29, 1912; s. Thomas Paine and Beatrice (Gent) K.; m. Jean Baughman, July 25, 1940; children: Carla (Mrs. Henry Dee), Thomas Paine III, Margaret Jo (Mrs. Jeffrey Holmes). AB, U. Fla., 1935, JD, 1936. Bar: Fla. 1936, U.S. Dist. Ct. (no. dist.) Fla. 1936, U.S. Ct. Appeals (5th cir.) 1936, U.S. Dist. Ct. (mid. dist.) Fla. 1940, U.S. Dist. Ct. (so. dist.) Fla. 1939, U.S. Ct. Appeals (11th cir.) 1983, U.S. Supreme Ct. 1990. Since practiced in, Tampa; assoc. McKay, Macfarlane, Jackson & Ferguson, 1939-40; ptnr. McKay, MacFarlane, Jackson & Ferguson, 1940-48, Macfarlane, Ferguson, Allison & Kelly, 1948-83, sr. ptnr., 1983-91; of counsel Shear, Newman, Hahn & Rosenkranz, 1992-95; shareholder MacFarlane Ferguson & McMullen, P.A., Tampa, Fla., 1996—. Chmn. Tampa Com. 100, 1960-61; pres. Tampa Citizens' Safety Coun., 1961-62; Bd. dirs. Tampa chpt. ARC, 1955-62, pres., 1958-59; bd. dirs. Boys Clubs Tampa, 1956-67, pres., 1966-67. Col. F.A. AUS, 1940-45. Decorated Silver Star. Fellow Am. Coll. Trial Lawyers, Internat. Acad. Trial Lawyers; mem. Am. Bar Assn., Bar Assn. Hillsborough County, Fla. Bar (chmn. com. profl. ethics 1953-58, chmn. com. ins. and negligence law 1962-63, chmn. fed. rules com. 1969-70). Republican. Home: 5426 Lykes Ln Tampa FL 33611-4747 Office: McFarlane Ferguson & McMullen PO Box 1531 Tampa FL 33601-1531 E-mail: tpk@mac.com.

KELLY, TIMOTHY MICHAEL, newspaper publisher; b. Ashland, Ky., Nov. 28, 1947; s. Robert John and Pauline Elizabeth (Henneman) K.; m. Carol Ann Knight, Aug. 2, 1969; children: Kimberly, Kevin. BA, U. Miami, Fla., 1970. Sports copy editor, writer The Courier-Jour., Louisville, 1970-71; exec. sports editor The Phila. Inquirer, 1971-75; dep. mng. editor Dallas Times Herald, 1975-81; mng. editor The Denver Post, 1981-84; exec. editor Dallas Times Herald, 1984; editor Daily News, Los Angeles, 1984-87; mng. editor The Orange County Register, Santa Ana, Calif., 1987-89; editor, sr. v.p. Lexington Herald-Leader, Lexington, Ky., 1989-96, pub., 1996—. Juror Pulitzer Prize, 1987-88. Recipient Knight-Ridder Excellence award for Cmty. Svc., 1995, Ida B. Wells award, 1999, Ky. Journalism Hall of Fame award, 2000. Roman Catholic. Office: Lexington Herald Leader 100 Midland Ave Lexington KY 40508-1999 E-mail: tkelly@herald-leader.com.

KELLY, TIMOTHY WILLIAM, lawyer; b. Apr. 27, 1953; s. George Raymond and Mary Therese (Kelly) K.; m. Mary Teresa Harms, May 24, 1980; children: Ryan Timothy, Colin Patrick, Kaitlynn Elizabeth. BS in Bus. Adminstrn., U. Dayton, 1975, JD, 1978. Bar: Ill. 1978, U.S. Dist. Ct. (cen. and no. dists.) Ill. 1979. Staff counsel Praire State Legal Aid, Bloomington, Ill., 1978-81; felony asst. McLean County Pub. Defenders, Bloomington, 1981-83; assoc. Jerome Mirza & Assocs., Bloomington, 1983-88; asst. prof. polit. sci. Ill. State U., Normal, 1980-83; faculty mem. Ill. Inst. Continuing Legal Edn. Lectr. in field. Contbr. articles to profl. jours. Bd. dirs. Bloomington/Normal Day Care Assn., 1982-83; civil actions arbitrator and mediator McLean County, 1996—. Named one of Top Three Attys. in McLean, Bus. to Bus. Mag., 1997. Fellow Ill. Bar Found.; mem. ATLA, Ill. State Bar Assn. (mem. civil practice and procedure sect. coun. 1992—, chmn. 1998, Allerton house steering com. 1994, 96, 98, tort law sect. coun. 1995—, assembly mem. 1995—), Ill. Trial Lawyers Assn. (mem. bd. mgrs. 1992—, continuing legal edn. com. 1995-96, exec. com. 1996, chmn. ins. law com. 1996-98), Chgo. Bar Assn., McLean County Bar Assn. (sec. 1984-85), McLean County Inns of Ct., IICLE (bd. dirs. 2000—). Democrat. Roman Catholic. Office: 205 N Williamsburg Dr Ste A Bloomington IL 61704-7721 E-mail: twkelly271@aol.com.

KELLY, TOM (JAY THOMAS KELLY), retired professional sports team manager; b. Graceville, Minn., Aug. 15, 1950; s. Joseph Thomas and Anna Grace (Heisenbottle) K.; children: Sharon Clare, Thomas John. Student, Mesa (Ariz.) Jr. Coll., 1968-69. Profl. baseball player Minn. Twins, Mpls., 1968-77, coach, 1982-86, mgr., 1987—2001, mgr. minor league team Toledo, 1978-82. Managed Minn. Twins team to World Series Championship, 1987, 91; named Am. League Mgr. of Yr. Sporting News, 1991. Mem. Assn. Profl. Baseball Players, U.S. Trotting Assn., Nat. Greyhound Assn. Avocation: harness racing. Office: Minn Twins Hubert H Humphrey Metrodome 34 Kirby Puckett Pl Minneapolis MN 55415-1596

KELLY, WILLIAM CHARLES, JR., lawyer; b. Mpls., June 9, 1946; s. William Charles and Marian Eileen (Moritz) K.; m. Cynthia Ann Churchill, June 28, 1969; children: Patrick, Brian. AB, Harvard U., 1968; JD, Yale U., 1971. Bar: Maine 1972, D.C. 1973, U.S. Supreme Ct. 1973. Law clk. to Judge Coffin U.S. Ct. Appeals (1st cir.), Portland, Maine, 1971-72; law clk. to Justice Powell U.S. Supreme Ct., Washington, 1972-73; exec. asst. to sec. HUD, Washington, 1975-77; ptnr. Latham & Watkins, Washington, 1978—. Bd. dirs. Nat. Low Income Housing Coalition, Washington, 1983-94, The Governance Inst., 1986—, Washington Legal Clinic for the Homeless, 1999—; trustee Sheridan Sch., 1992-98; mem. Ashoka World Coun., 1997—; dir. Ashoka Innovators for the Public, 1999—. Lt. USNR, 1973-75. Mem. ABA, D.C. Bar Assn. Office: Latham & Watkins Ste 1000 555 11th St NW Washington DC 20004-1304

KELLY, WILLIAM GARRETT, judge; b. Grand Rapids, Mich., Nov. 30, 1947; s. Joseph Francis and Gertrude Frances (Downes) K.; m. Sharon Ann Diroff, Aug. 11, 1979; children: Colleen, Joseph, Caitlin, Meaghan and Patricia. BA, U. Detroit, 1970, JD, 1975. Bar: Mich. 1975, U.S. Dist. Ct. (we. dist.) Mich. 1975. Tchr. Peace Corps, Ghana, Republic of West Africa, 1970-72; asst. prosecutor Kalamazoo (Mich.) Prosecutor's Office, 1975-77; atty. Office of Defender, Grand Rapids, 1977-78; judge 62d B Dist. Ct., Kentwood, 1979—. Faculty Mich. Jud. Inst., Lansing, 1985—, 2d Nat. Conf. on Ct. Tech., Denver, 1988, Nat. Jud. Coll., 2001—; chmn.-elect Jud. Conf. State Bar Mich., 1990-91, chmn., 1991-92. Bd. dirs. Nat. Ctr. for State Cts., 1994-2000; pres. Kentwood Jaycees, 1979-80. Named one of Five Outstanding Young Men of Mich., Mich. Jaycees, 1982. Mem. ABA (chmn. nat. conf. spl. ct. judges 1992-93, chmn. traffic ct. program 2002-), State Bar Mich., Grand Rapids Bar Assn., Cath. Lawyers Assn. Western Mich. (pres. 1987), Mich. Dist. Judges Assn. (pres. 1989). Roman Catholic. Office: 62d B Dist Ct 4740 Walma SE Kentwood MI 49512

KELLY, WILLIAM HENRY, computer company executive, mayor; b. Kingston, N.Y., June 27, 1940; s. William Aloyishus Kelly and Jeanette Wilhelm; m. Ann Kelly, Nov. 9, 1996; children: Morgan Sarah, Kevin John. BSE, Villanova U., 1962; MA in Econ., Georgetown U., 1970. Sales engr. Allis-Chalmers, Milw., 1962-64; regional mgr. Electronic Assocs., West Long Branch, N.J., 1964-69, Honeywell Inc., Mpls., 1969-70; v.p. Leasco Computer, Great Neck, N.Y., 1971-76; pres. WHK Leasing, Northport, N.Y., 1976—. Dir. N.Y. Conf. Mayors, Albany, 1985—; outside dir. N.Y. Partnership Cultural Flagship, Troy, 1998—. Contbg. editor: Empire State Report, 1994-98. Mayor, Village of Asharoken, 1982—; pres. N.Y. Conf. of Mayors, 1988-89, Tri-County Village Ofcls., 1989, Suffolk County Village Ofcls., 1988-90; trustee Phila. Soc., 2001—. Mem. Phila. Soc. (v.p. 1994, 2003), Kiwanis (pres. Norport chpt. 1982). Roman Catholic. Avocations: currency collecting, flying, real estate, reading, writing. Home: 220 Asharoken Ave Northport NY 11768-1160 Office: WHK Leasing 816 Woodbury Rd Woodbury NY 11797-1411

KELLY, WILLIAM MICHAEL, investment executive; b. Pittsfield, Mass., Feb. 3, 1944; children: Alyssa A., Eileen J.; m. Christina E. Houlihan, 2003. BA in Polit. Sci., St. Anselm Coll., 1966; MA in Polit. Sci., Duquesne U., 1968; MBA in Fin., NYU, 1972. Portfolio mngr., v.p. Chase Manhattan Bank, N.Y.C., 1968-77; v.p. Nat. Aviation and Tech., N.Y.C., 1977-80; mng. assoc. Lingold Assocs., N.Y.C., 1980—. Trustee 1st Eagle Internat. Fund, N.Y.C., 1994—; trustee 1st Eagle Fund Am., N.Y.C., 1998—, 1st Eagle Sogen Funds, 2000—; mng. gen. ptnr. ML Venture Ptnrs. II, N.Y.C., 1991-2001; dir., treas., Black Forest Consortium, Inc., Black Forest Preserve, N.Y., 1989—; trustee N.Y. Found., 1985—, chmn., 1992-95; asst. treas. Neuroscis. Rsch. Found., Calif, 1982-99; v.p., treas. Sergei Zlinkoff Fund Med. Edn., 1992—; trustee St. Anselm Coll., N.H., 1998—. Bd. govs. Eugene Lang Coll, 1994-02; trustee Pathways for Youth, 1976—, pres. 1981-84. Mem. AAAS, (investment and fin. com. 1985-99), N.Y. Acad. Scis., 1987— (fin. affairs com.), Sleepy Hollow Country Club, The Union League Club. Office: 500 5th Ave Fl 50 New York NY 10110-5099

KELLY, WILLIAM STATES, data network engineer; b. Frederick, Md., Oct. 15, 1956; s. William Tolson III and Jane Randall (States) K. BS, Union Coll., Schenectady, 1978; MS, U. Ariz., 1983. City planner Bur. Planning, Schenectady, 1978 79; grad. teaching asst. systems engring. dept. U. Ariz., Tucson, 1981-83; systems engr. Gen. Dynamics, San Diego, 1983-85; staff engr. Martin Marietta, Littleton, Colo., 1985-88; data network engr. Apollo Travel Svcs./United Airlines, Englewood, Colo., 1988-97, ICG Comms., Englewood, 1997-98, Quest Comms., Englewood, 1998—. Mem. user adv. coun. Gen. Rsch. Corp., Inc., San Diego, 1991-96; mem. user group AT&T-Accunet, Bridgewater, N.J., 1991; presenter C.A.C.I. Simulation Conf., 1988. Contbr. articles to profl. publs. Mem. Orchard Creek Park Assn., Greenwood Village, Colo., 1990-2000. Office: ICG Comms 931 15th St Denver CO 80202 Home: 760 S Garfield Denver CO 80209

KELLY, WILLIAM WATKINS, educational association executive; b. Asheville, N.C., Sept. 21, 1928; s. John Jackson and Trula (Watkins) K.; m. Laura Jane Kelly, Feb. 14, 1953 (div. Jan. 14, 1983); children: William Watkins, Robert Jackson, Blair Massey, Gregory Clark.; m. Catherine Messer Penney, Jan. 22, 1983. BA, Va. Mil. Inst., 1950; A.M., Duke U., 1955, PhD, 1957. Commandant cadets, tchr. English John Marshall High Sch., Richmond, Va., 1950-52, instr. English Va. Mil. Inst., 1952-55, English Air Force Acad., 1957-58, asst. prof., 1958-60, English Va. Mil. Inst., 1960-62; asst. prof. Am. Thought and language Mich. State U., 1962-65, assoc. prof., 1965-69; assoc. dir. The Honors Coll., 1965-68, dir., 1968-69; pres. Mary Baldwin Coll., 1969-76, Transylvania U., Lexington, Ky., 1976-81; sr. assoc. Univ. Assos., 1981-82; exec. v.p. L.Q.C. Lamar Soc., 1981-82; pres. Ala. Assn. Ind. Colls. and Univs., 1982-88, Ga. Found. for Ind. Colls. Inc., Atlanta, 1988-96; pres. emeritus, 1996—; pres. Assn. Pvt. Colls. and Univs. in Ga., Atlanta, 1990-96; sr. v.p. Jon McRae & Assocs. Inc., Atlanta, 1996—2001; dir. coll. and unv. rels. Connexxia, 2001—. Mem. Va. Commn. on Status of Women, 1973-76, Ky. Commn. on Status of Women, 1977-81; chmn. Ky. Rhodes Scholar Selection Com., 1978-79; pres. Coun. Ind. Ky. Colls. and Univs., 1978-80; bd. dirs. Ala. Humanities Found., 1983-88, chmn. bd. dirs., 1985-87; bd. dirs., exec. com. Ga. Humanities Coun., 1989-96, vice chair, 1991-93, chair, 1994-96. Author: Ellen Glasow: A Bibliography, 1964. Bd. dirs. ODK Found., 2002—, Ky. State C. of C., 1980—82; trustee Greensboro Coll., 1993—2000, 2002—, Ellis L. Phillips Found. intern Rutgers U., 1964-65; Ala. recipient IBM Disting. Performance award Ind. Coll. Funds Am., 1986, Outstanding Ala. Fund Raising Exec. award Nat. Soc. Fund Raising Execs., 1986, Leadership award Brunswick Pub. Charitable Found., 1993; Danforth fellow, 1953-57; Duke scholar, 1954-55; William Watkins Kelly Endowed Scholarship in the Humanities established Ga. Found. Ind. Colls., 1996. Fellow Found. Ind. Higher Edn. (nat. presiding officer 1992-94, Disting. Performance award 1996); mem. MLA, Am. Studies Assn., Soc. Values in Higher Edn., Am. Assn. Higher Edn., Ellen Glasgow Soc. (pres. 1973-75), Newcomen Soc. N.Am., Rotary (Paul Harris fellow), Phi Beta Kappa, The Fellows of Phi Beta Kappa (bd. dirs. 2000—), Omicron Delta Kappa (Found. bd. dirs. 2002—), Rotary. Home: 4015 Brockton Close Marietta GA 30068-4931 Office: Connexia 4000 Interstate Noth Pkwy Ste 820 Atlanta GA 30339 Fax: 770-690-8581. E-mail: Bill.Kelly@connexia.com.

KELLY-JONES, DENISE MARIE, critical care nurse; b. Staten Island, N.Y., Nov. 16, 1966; d. Edward Augustine and Dorothy Catherine (Ferrante) K. AAS, Coll. of S.I., 1987, BSN, 1989; MS in Adult N.P., SUNY, Stony Brook. Cert. adult/acute care cardiothoracic surg. nurse practitioner ANCC; CCRN; cert. Nat. Field Archery Assn./Nat. Archery Assn. archery instr., 1997—. From staff nurse to critical care nurse, 1989-94; nurse practitioner Univ. Hosp. at Stony Brook, 1994-96; nurse practitioner cardiac surgery Union Meml. Hosp., 1996-2000, Englewood Hosp. and Med. Ctr., 2000—. Mem. AACN (Greater Washington area chpt.).

KELM, BONNIE G. art museum director, educator; b. Bklyn., Mar. 29, 1947; d. Julius and Anita (Baron) Steiman; m. William G. Malis; 1 child, Michael Darren. BS in Art Edn., Buffalo State U., 1968; MA in Art History, Bowling Green (Ohio) State U., 1975; PhD in Arts Adminstrn., Ohio State U., 1987. Art tchr. Toledo Pub. Schs., 1968—71; ednl. cons. Columbus (Ohio) Mus. Art, 1976—81; prof. art Franklin U., Columbus, 1976—88; legis. coord. Ohio Ho. of Reps., Columbus, 1977; pres. bd. trustees Columbus Inst. for Contemporary Art, 1977—81; tech. asst. cons. Ohio Arts Coun., Columbus, 1984—88; dir. Sunte Gallery Franklin U., Columbus, 1978—88; dir. art mus. Miami U., Oxford, Ohio, 1988—96, assoc. prof., 1988—96; dir. Muscarelle Mus. of Art Coll. William and Mary, Williamsburg, Va., 1996—2002, assoc. prof. art and art history, 1996—2002; dir. Univ. Art Mus. U. Calif., Santa Barbara, 2002—. Adj. prof. dept. art history U. Art Mus. U. Calif., Santa Barbara; grant panelist Ohio Arts Coun., Columbus, 1985-87, 91-95; art book reviewer William C. Brown Pub., Madison, Wis., 1985-92; mem. acquisitions adv. bd. Martin Luther King Ctr., Columbus, 1987-88; field reviewer Inst. Mus. Svcs., Washington, 1990—; chairperson grant panel Art in Pub. Places, 1992-95; trustee Ohio Mus. Assn., 1993-96; state apptd. mem. adv. com. Ohio Percent for Art, 1994-96; bd. dirs. U.S. Nat. Com. Internat. Coun. Museums, 1998—; bd. dirs., southeast rep. Assn. Univ. & Coll. Mus. Galleries, 1998—. Author, editor (mus. catalogues) Connections, 1985, Into the Mainstream: Contemporary Folk Art, 1991, Testimony of Images: PreColumbian Art, 1992, Collecting by Design: The Allen Collection, 1994, Photographs by Barbara Hershey: A Retrospective, 1995, Georgia O'Keeffe in Williamsburg, 2001; contbr. chpt. to book Modernism Gender & Culture, 1997, articles to profl. jours. Founding mem., mem. adv. coun. Columbus Cultural Arts Ctr., 1977-81; coord., curator Cultural Exch. Program, Honolulu-Columbus, 1980; mem. acad. women achievers YWCA, 1991—; guest spkr. 1991 Scholastic Arts Award, Cin., 1991; keynote spkr. Ohio Mus. Assn., ann. meeting, 1992; spkr. Internat. Coun. Mus. Triennial Conf., Quebec City, 1992, Internat. Coun. Mus. Triennial Congress, Barcelona, Spain, 2001, session chair; session chair Midwest Mus. Assn. ann. meeting, St. Louis, 1993; session chair Am. Assn. Mus. ann. meeting, Balt., 2000; presenter East-West Ctr. Internat. Conf., Honolulu, 2000. Recipient Marantz Disting. Scholar award Ohio State U., 1995, Gelpe award YWCA, 1987, Cultural Advancement of City of Columbus award, The Columbus Dispatch, 1984, Disting. Svc. award, Columbus Art League, 1984, Critic's Choice award Found. for Cmty. of Artists, N.Y., 1981; Fulbright scholar USIA, 1988 (The Netherlands); NEH fellow East-West Ctr., Honolulu, 1991. Mem. Am. Assn. Mus. (advocacy task force, surveyor mus. assessment program 1996—, nat. program com. 2001), Assn. of Coll. and Univ. Mus. and Galleries, Western Mus. Assn., Assn., Fulbright Assn., Coll. Arts Assn. (session chair, spkr. ann. meeting 2003), Internat. Coun. Mus., Calif. Assn. Mus. Office: Univ Art Mus U Calif Santa Barbara 1626 Arts Bldg Santa Barbara CA 93106 E-mail: bgkelm@uam.ucsb.edu. *Pay attention to all of the potentials and resources that others overlook in your every day environment. Never let any one convince you that something you're committed to is impossible. Make an art of putting people and possibilities together.*

KELMACHTER, LESLIE DEBRA, lawyer; b. Bklyn. d. Meyer and Jean Muraskin (Metcalf) K. BA magna cum laude, SUNY, New Paltz; JD, Albany Law Sch. Bar: N.Y. 1978, U.S. Dist. Ct. (no. dist.) N.Y., U.S. Dist. Ct. (ea. dist.) N.Y. 1989, U.S. Dist. Ct. (so. dist.) N.Y. 1995. Atty. Legal Aid Soc., Schenectady, 1977—79, atty., juvenile rights divsn. N.Y.C., 1979—86; atty., asst. corp. counsel Law Dept., City of N.Y., 1986—90; ptnr. Schneider, Kleinick, Weitz, Damashek & Shoot, N.Y.C., 1990—99, Meyers, Meyers and Kelmachter, N.Y.C., 1999—2000, The Jacob D. Fuchsberg Law Firm, LLP, N.Y.C., 2000—. Dean N.Y. State Trial Lawyers Inst.; co-chair Decisions, Mealey's Nat. Lead Litigation Conf., 1999. Participant, fund raiser Race for the Cure, N.Y.C., 1995—98; competitor N.Y.C. Ctrl. Park Triathalon, 1999. Mem.: NYS Trial Lawyer Inst. (Dean, chair of Decisions annual semiar), N.Y. State Trial Lawyers Assn. (bd. dirs.), Bar Assn. City of N.Y. (chair tort litigation com. 2001—). Office: 500 Fifth Ave 45th Flr New York NY 10010

KELMAN, ARTHUR, plant pathologist, educator; b. Providence, Dec. 11, 1918; s. Philip and Minnie (Kollin) K.; m. Helen Moore Parker, June 22, 1949; 1 child, Philip Joseph. BS, U. R.I., 1941, DSc (hon.), 1977; MS, N.C. State U., 1946; PhD, 1949. Faculty N.C. State U., Raleigh, 1948-65, prof., 1957-65, W.N. Reynolds distinguished prof. plant pathology, 1961-65, univ. dist. scholar, 1990—; chmn. dept. plant pathology U. Wis., Madison, 1965-75, L.R. Jones Disting. prof., 1975-89, prof. bacteriology, 1977-89, WARF Sr. Disting. Rsch. prof., 1984-89; chief scientist Competitive Grants Program Nat. Rsch. Initiative, Coop. State Rsch. Svc., USDA, 1991-93. Vis. investigator Rockefeller Inst., 1953-54; chmn. div. biol. sci. Assembly Life Sci. NRC, 1980-82, chmn. bd. basic biology, Commn. Life Scis., 1984-85 Author: The Bacterial Wilt Caused by Pseudomonas solanacearum, 1953. Served with AUS, 1942-45. NSF sr. postdoctoral fellow Cambridge (Eng.) U., 1971-72; recipient E.C. Stakman award, 1987. Fellow AAAS, Am. Acad. Arts and Scis., Am. Phytopath. Soc. (chmn. sourcebook com., councilor-at-large, v.p. 1965-66, pres. 1966-67, award of distinction 1983), Am. Acad. Microbiology; mem. NAS (coun. 1986-89, chmn. sect. applied biology 1981-83, chmn. class VI Applied biology and agrl. scis., 1988-91), Internat. Soc. Plant Pathology (v.p. 1968-73, pres. 1973-78), Soc. Gen. Microbiology, Am. Soc. Microbiology, Am. Inst. Biol. Sci., Phytopathol. Soc Japan (hon.), Sigma Xi, Alpha Zeta, Gamma Sigma Delta, Phi Kappa Phi, Phi Sigma, Xi Sigma Pi. Home: 1406 Springmoor Cir Raleigh NC 27615-5703 Office: NC State Univ Dept Plant Pathology PO Box 7616 Raleigh NC 27695-0001 E-mail: arthur_kelman@ncsu.edu.

KELMAN, BRUCE JERRY, toxicologist, consultant; b. Chgo., July 1, 1947; s. LeRoy Rayfield and Louise (Rosen) K.; m. Jacqueline Anne Clark, Feb. 5, 1972; children: Aaron Wayne, Diantha Renee, Coreyanne Louise. BS, U. Ill., 1969, MS, 1971, PhD, 1975. Diplomate Am. Bd. Toxicology. Rsch. assoc. U. Tenn., Oak Ridge, 1974-76, asst. prof., leader prenatal toxicology group, 1976-79; mgr. devel. toxicology sect. Battelle NW, Richland, Wash., 1980-84, assoc. mgr. biology and chemistry dept., 1984-85, mgr., 1985-89, mgr. new products devel. Life Scis. Ctr., 1989-90; mgr. Internat. Toxicology Office Battelle Meml. Inst., Richland, 1986-89, mng. scientist, mgr. toxicology dept. Failure Analysis Assocs., Inc., Menlo Park, Calif., 1990-93; mgr. toxicology and risk assessment Golder Assocs. Inc., Redmond, Wash., 1993, nat. dir. health and environ. scis., 1994-98; pres. GlobalTox, Inc., 1998—. Mem. Nation Rsch. Coun. com. on possible effects of electromagnetic fields on biologic sys., 1993-96; adj. prof. N.Mex. State U., Las Cruces, 1983- . Mem. editorial bd. Trophoblast Rsch., 1983-93, Biological Effects of Heavy Metals, 1990. Adv. coun. Seattle Fire Dept., 1988-90; mem. Wash. Gov.'s Biotech. Targeted Sector Adv. Com., 1989-90. Fellow Am. Acad. Vet. and Comparative Toxicology; mem. Am. Coll. Occupl. and Environ. Medicine, Soc. Toxicology (founding pres. molecular biology splty. sect. 1988-89, pres. metals splty. sect. 1985-86, cert. of recognition 1989), Am. Soc. for Exptl. Pharmacology and Therapeutics, Soc. for Exptl. Biology and Medicine (award of merit 1980), Teratology Soc., Wash. State Biotech. Assn. (bd. dirs. 1989-90). Office: GlobalTox Inc 18372 Redmond-Fall City Rd Redmond WA 98052 E-mail: bkelman@globaltox.com.

KELMAN, EDWARD MICHAEL, lawyer; b. N.Y., Aug. 29, 1943; s. Jack H. and Evelyn (Karp) K.; children: Matthews S., Joshua K. AB, Cornell U., 1965; JD, NYU, 1968. Bar: N.Y. 1969, Conn. 1972. Asst dist. atty. N.Y. County Dist. Atty.'s Office, 1968-71; assoc. Glazer & Wechsler, Stamford, Conn., 1971-72, Squadron, Gartenberg, Elenoff & Plesent, N.Y., 1972-73; sr. atty. CBS Records, CBS, Inc., N.Y., 1973-76; asst. gen. atty. CBS Pub., CBS, Inc., N.Y., 1976-77; v.p. law Chappell Music Co., N.Y., 1977-80; of counsel Law Offices of Michael Sukin, N.Y., 1980-82; v.p. bus. affairs and acquisitions Thorn EMI Video & TV, N.Y., 1982-83; pvt. practice entertainment and media law N.Y., 1983—. Vice chmn. Mayor's TV & Film Commn., Stamford, 1986—; cons. First Night Entertainment Com., Stamford, 1990. Recipient Spl. award Rec. Ind. Assn. Am., 1975. Mem. NARAS, Assn. Bar City N.Y., Conn. Bar Assn., Nat. Acad. Popular Music, Cornell Club of N.Y. Avocations: sports, movies, theatre. Office: 521 Fifth Ave 26th Fl New York NY 10175 Fax: 212-750-1356. E-mail: Emknyc@aol.com.

KELMAN, GARY F. environmental engineer; b. Phila., May 1, 1953; s. Gabriel Morton and Minnie (Meckler) K.; m. Wendy Joan Davidov, May 2, 1982; children: Graham Bennett, Ariel Megan. BS in Life Scis., Phila. U., 1974; MS in Civil Engring., U. Md., 1977. Environ. engr. JTC Environ. Cons., Bethesda, Md., 1977-79; water resources engr. State of Md. Dept. Natural Resources, Annapolis, 1979-80; pub. health engr. State of Md. Dept. Environ., Balt., 1980-86, head pretreatment sect., 1986—. Contbg. editor, photographer: Environmental Practice, 1999—2002. Recipient Cert. of Appreciation, Gov. Md., 1993. Mem. ASCE (assoc.), Nat. Assn. Environ. Profls. (co-editor conf. procs. 1991, 93, pres. 1993-94), Am. Chem. Soc., Water Environ. Fedn., Sigma Xi (assoc.). Avocations: piano, computers, antique map collecting. Home: 8398 Windtree Ct Millersville MD 21108-2558 Office: State of Md Dept Environ 1800 Washington Blvd Baltimore MD 21230-1708

KELMAN, HERBERT CHANOCH, psychology educator; b. Vienna, Mar. 18, 1927; came to U.S., 1940, naturalized, 1950; s. Leo and Lea (Pomeranz) K.; m. Rose Brousman, Aug. 23, 1953. BA, Bklyn. Coll., 1947, L.H.D. (hon.), 1981; B.H.L., Sem. Coll. Jewish Studies, N.Y.C., 1947; MS, Yale U., 1949, PhD, 1951; A.M. (hon.), Harvard U., 1968; diploma (hon.), U. San Martin de Porres, Peru, 1979; L.H.D. (hon.), Hofstra U., 1983; D in Polit. Sci. and Sociology honoris causa, U. Complutense de Madrid, 1995. Rsch. asst. Yale U., 1947-51; rsch. fellow Johns Hopkins U., 1951-54; fellow Center Advanced Study Behavioral Scis., 1954-55, 67; rsch. psychologist NIMH, 1955-57; lectr. social psychology Harvard U., 1957-62; fellow Inst. Social Rsch., Oslo, 1960-61; prof. psychology U. Mich., 1962-69, chmn. doctoral program social psychology, 1966-67; rsch. psychologist Ctr. for Rsch. on Conflict Resolution, 1962-69; Richard Clarke Cabot prof. social ethics Harvard U., 1968-99, Richard Clarke Cabot rsch. prof. social ethics, 1999—, chair doctoral program in social psychology, 1994-97; exec. com. Weatherhead Ctr. for Internat. Affairs, 1976—, dir. Program on Internat. Conflict Analysis and Resolution, 1993—2003, chair Middle East Seminar, 1977—. Vis. fellow Battelle Seattle Rsch. Ctr., 1972-73; disting. vis. prof. Am. U., Cairo, 1977; resident scholar Bellagio Study and Conf. Ctr., 1977, 85; fellow Woodrow Wilson Internat. Ctr. for Scholars, 1980-81; vis. scholar Truman and Davis Insts., Hebrew U. of Jerusalem, 1985; resident scholar Tantur Ecumenical Ctr. for Theol. Rsch., Jerusalem, 1985; Sterling McMurrin disting. vis. prof. U. Utah, 1985; vis. prof. Wirtschaftsuniversität, Vienna, 1994; chmn. internat. conf. social-psychol. rsch. in developing countries U. Ibadan, Nigeria, 1966; vis. scholar Austrian Inst. Internat. Affairs, Vienna, 2000; vis. prof. Austrian Inst. for Internat. Affairs, 2002. Author: A Time to Speak: On Human Values and Social Research, 1968; co-author: Cross-National Encounters, 1970, Crimes of Obedience: Toward a Social Psychology of Authority and Responsibility, 1989; editor, co-author: International Behavior: A Social-Psychological Analysis, 1965; co-editor, co-author: The Ethics of Social Intervention, 1978; contbr. articles to profl. jours. Mem. adv. com. govt. programs behavioral sci. NRC-Nat. Acad. Sci., 1966-68; nat. field rep. CORE, 1954-60; mem. nat. adv. council War Resisters League, 1952-71; mem. exec. com. Fellowship in Israel for Arab-Jewish Youth, 1977-96 (Disting. Svc. award 1995), Jewish Peace Fellowship, 1986-98; mem. exec. coun. Nat. Peace Acad. Campaign, 1977-85; trustee Internat. Ctr. for Peace in Middle East, 1982—2001; mem. adv. coun. Nat. Peace Inst. Found., 1984-92, Jewish Alliance for Justice and Peace, 2002—; bd. dirs. Nat. Peace Found., 1992-95, adv. bd., 1995—; mem. psychology tng. rev. com. NIMH, 1969-73; mem. acad. coun. Ctr. for Psychol. Studies in the Nuclear Age, 1985-96 (Recognition award 1990); mem. adv. bd. New Outlook, 1987-93, Ctr. Internat. Understanding, 1994-2001, Carmel Inst. Social Studies, Israel, 1996—, Workable Peace Project, Consensus Bldg. Inst., 1997—, Conflict Mediation Ctr., Ecuador, 1998—, Peace Village, Cyprus, 1999—, Friends of Open House, 2002--, Faculty for Israeli-Palestinian Peace, 2002--; mem. adv. com. Sadat Lecture for Peace, U. Md., 1998—; assoc. internat. mem. Jewish Theater of Austria, 1999—; bd. advisors Ctr. for Peace Studies, U. Okla., U. Haifa, Horizon Studies and Rsch. Ctr. of Amman, Bethlehem U., 2001—. Recipient Socio-Psychol. prize AAAS, 1956, N.Y. Acad. Sci. award, 1983, Mass. Psychol. Assn. award, 1983, Grawemeyer award for Ideas Improving World Order, 1997, Austrian medal of honor for Sci. and Art, First Class, 1998, Ben-Gurion medal, Ben Gurion U. of Negev, 2001, Alumni Achievement award Bklyn. Coll., 2002; Western Behavioral Scis. Inst. fellow, 1964, Guggenheim fellow, 1980-81, Jennings Randolph Disting. fellow U.S. Inst. Peace, 1989-90. Fellow Soc. Psychol. Study Social Issues (pres. 1964-65, Kurt Lewin Meml. award 1973, Disting. Svc. award 1998), APA (life mem., com. on sci. and profl. ethics and conduct 1968-71, coun. 1968-71, dir. 1971-75, pres. divsn. on personality and social psychology 1970-71, bd. social and ethical responsibility 1972-74, com. on internat. rels. in psychology 1987-90, award for disting. contbn. to psychology in pub. interest 1981, disting. group psychologist award divsn. group psychology and group psychotherapy 1995, lifetime contbn. award divsn. peace psychology 1997, James McKeen Lattell award 2000), Inst. Soc. Ethics and Life Scis. (dir. 1969-72); mem. Soc. Exptl. Social Psychology, Am. Sociol. Assn. (chmn. social psychology sect. 1977-78, disting. career award peace and war sect. 1995), Internat. Studies Assn. (pres. 1977-78), Internat. Peace Rsch. Assn., Internat. Assn. Cross-Cultural Psychology, Internat. Assn. Applied Psychology (pres. div. polit. psychology 1990-94), Interam. Soc. Psychology (gov. 1972-73, pres. 1976-79, Interam. Psychology award 1983), Internat. Soc. Polit. Psychology (Sanford award 1983, pres. 1985-86), Peace Sci. Soc. (pres. 1975-76), Internat. Soc. Ednl. Cultural Sci. Interchanges (4th Ann. award 1976), Internat. Assn. Conflict Mgmt. (lifetime achievement award 1998), Psychologists for Social Responsibility (pres. 1990-92, award for best theoretical rsch. article in peace psychology 1989, disting. contbn. award 1992), Coun. Fgn. Rels. Home: 984 Memorial Dr Cambridge MA 02138-5741 E-mail: hck@wjh.harvard.edu.

KELMAN, MARYBETH, health care consultant, health policy analyst; b. Aug. 16, 1944; AS in Nursing, Rutgers U., 1964; BA, Douglas Coll., 1977; MA, Rutgers U., 1988. Program dir. health promotion N.J. Hosp. Assn., Princeton, 1983-87; policy analyst N.J. Dept. Human Svcs., Trenton, 1988-89; exec. dir. Eye Screening Coord. Coun. N.J., Inc., Monmouth Junction, 1989 91; health care cons. N.J. Divsn. Pensions and Benefits, Trenton, 1992—. Chmn. bd. trustees Forums Inst. for Pub. Policy, Princeton, 1998—. Office: 50 W State St PO Box 295 Trenton NJ 08625-0295 E-mail: mbkelman@att.net.

KELMAN, STEVEN JAY, management educator; b. N.Y.C., May 1, 1948; s. Kurt and Sylvia (Etman) K.; m. Shelley Metzenbaum, July 5, 1980, children: Jody, Leora. AB summa cum laude, Harvard Coll., 1970; PhD, Harvard U., 1978. Asst. prof. pub. policy Harvard U., 1978-80; with Federal Trade Commn., Washington, 1980-81; assoc. prof. and prof. pub. mgmt. Harvard U., 1982-93, 97—; adminstr. Office of Fed. Procurement Policy, Washington, 1993-97. Democrat. Jewish. Office: Harvard Univ JFK Sch of Government Cambridge MA 02138 E-mail: steve_kelman@harvard.edu.

KELMENSON, LEO-ARTHUR, advertising executive; b. N.Y.C., Jan. 3, 1927; s. Joseph A. and Ruth (Rothberg) K.; m. Gayle Frances Abrams, Sept. 1989; children from previous marriage: Todd-Arthur, Joel Adam. BS, Columbia U., 1951; postgrad., Grad. Sch. Bus., 1952. From TV prodn. to sr. v.p., asst. to pres. Lennen & Newell, 1951-65; exec. v.p., mem. exec. com. Norman Craig & Kummel, 1965-66; sr. v.p., dir., mem. exec. com. Kenyon & Eckhardt, 1967-68, chmn., chief exec. officer, 1968-86; chmn. Bozell, Jacobs, Kenyon & Eckhardt, 1986-93, chmn. exec. com.; chmn. Bozell Worldwide; chmn. bd. advisors, chmn. devel. com. Tisch Sch of Arts NYU, 1988—; chmn. Bozell de Mexico, 1992-99, FCB Worldwide, N.Y.C., 1999—. Pres. Kelmenson Funds Ltd.; dir. Lorimar, Locations Unltd., On-Line Software Internat.; bd. trustees Am. Cinematheque; lectr. New Sch. Social Rsch.; Adviser communications office U.S. Atty. Gen., 1960-63; spl. project officer Dept. State, 1952-64; co-founder, v.p., dir. African Med. and Rsch. Found., 1957—. Author: (poetry) Epilogue, 1964; also short stories. Mem. pub. rels. com. Nat. Cancer Found., 1958—; adv. com. Nat. Cultural Center, 1962; pres. Shoes for Little Souls, 1960, Remsenburg Assn., 1968; bd. dirs. ASPCA, Stop Cancer Found., 1990, 91; mem. pres.'s adv. coun. Am. Diabetes Assn., 1977-78. Served with USMCR, World War II. Recipient Theodore Roosevelt Man of Year award, 1955; Silver Quill Poetry award, 1955; Res. Officers Assn. award, 1965; Guggenheim World Peace award, 1951; Am. Jewish Com. Humanitarian award; Humanitarian award St. Frances Cabrini. Mem. U.S. Olympic Com., N.Y. Advt. Club, Soc. Am. Businessmen Club, Sigma Phi Epsilon. Clubs: Sands Point, Ocean Reef, Key Largo, Sands Point Yacht, L.I. Polo, U.S. Yacht Racing Assn. (N.Y.). Office: NYU Tisch Sch Arts New York NY 10003 Fax: 212-885-3399. E-mail: lkelmenson@fcb.com.

KELSAY, DANIELLE MARIE RUBINO, audiologist; b. Chgo., Jan. 25, 1962; d. Donald Philip and Barbara Ann (Neubaum) Rubino; m. Troy Allan Kelsay, Sept. 6, 1987; children: Quintin Daniel, Bailey Troi. BS in Biology, U. Iowa, 1984, MA in Audiology, 1987. Tchg. asst. dept. speech pathology and audiology U. Iowa, Iowa City, 1985-87, clin. audiologist, fellow dept. otolaryngology, 1987-88, clin. audiologist I, 1988-91, rsch. audiologist dept. otolaryngology, 1990—, aural rehab. supr. dept. speech pathology and audiology, 1991-92, clin. audiologist II dept. otolaryngology, 1991—2002, clin. assoc. prof. dept. speech pathology and audiology, 2002—. Author (chpt. in book) Hearing Care for Children, 1995, (manuals) Five Steps to Improving Your Child's Use of a Cochlear Implant, 1993, Stepping Out Specific Activiies to do at Home, 1993; contbr. articles to profl. jours. Master gardener Iowa State U. ext. svc., Iowa City, 1995—. Mem. Am. Speech Lang. Hearing Assn., Omnicron Delta Kappa. Avocations: gardening, camping, golf, raquetball, biking. Office: Dept Otolaryngology U Iowa 200 Hawkins Dr Iowa City IA 52242-1009

KELSAY, DAVID ROLAND, chemist; b. Clinton, Mo., July 25, 1955; s. Ralph Waldo and Mary Fern K.; m. Joyce Elaine Hopkins, Oct. 22, 1983; children: Rebecca Sue, Rachael Anne. BA in Chemistry, William Jewell Coll., 1977. Lab. tech. Upsher Labs., Kansas City, 1978-80; process attendant Kansas City Power & Light, Clinton, Mo., 1980-86, plant chemist, 1986 . State committeeman Mo. Rep. Party, 1992-2002, congrl. dist. chmn., 1994-98, 2000—, county com. chmn., 1988-98, 2000—, county com. sec., 1998-2000; mem. apportionment com. Mo. Ho. of Reps. Baptist. Avocations: sports, reading, geneology, civil war studies. Home: 901 Willow St Clinton MO 64735-3057 Office: Kansas City Power & Light 400 SW Hwy P Clinton MO 64735-9093 E-mail: jkelsay@iland.net.

KELSCH, JOAN MARY, elementary education educator; b. Allentown, Pa., Jan. 19, 1953; d. Paul Thomas and Dorothy Mildred (Grim) Reichart; m. William Joseph Kelsch, July 27, 1974; children: Daniel, Dorothy. BS, West Chester (Pa.) State Coll., 1974. Cert. tchr., Pa. Elem. tchr. St. Francis Acad., Bally, Pa., 1974-79, 86—, substitute tchr., 1979-82, establisher, tchr. kindergarten, 1982-86, coord. reading, 1976-79, coord. religion, 1986—; head tchr. St. Francis Academy, Bally, Pa., 2000—; mentor tchr. St. Francis Acad., Bally, Pa., 1986-87; coord. Rainbows Peer Support Program, 1993-95. Mem., chairperson Mid. States Evaluation Coms., 1986-87, 98-99; playground supr. Bally Recreation Com., summer 1990, pool mgr., summer 1991; trained mem. IST, 1995; instr. homebound, 1999. Mem. Internat. Reading Assn., Home and Sch. Assn. (faculty rep.), Tri-County Reading Assn., Keystone State Reading Assn., Allentown Diocese Assn. Lay Tchrs. Avocations: reading, sewing, travel, collecting, crafts. Home: 331 Main St Bally PA 19503 Office: Saint Francis Acad 7th And Pine Sts Bally PA 19503

KELSEY, ANN LEE, library administrator; b. Kokomo, Ind., June 20, 1946; d. Harry Willard and JoAnn Kelsey. BA in Anthropology and English cum laude, U. Calif., Riverside, 1968; MLS, UCLA, 1969. Adminstrv. libr. U.S. Army Spl. Svcs., Cam Ranh Bay, Vietnam, 1969-70; children's libr. Elmont (N.Y.) Meml. Libr., 1970-71; libr. Queensborough Pub. Libr., Jamaica, N.Y., 1971-73; children's libr. Upper Saddle River (N.J.) Pub. Libr., 1973-75; prin. libr. Morris County Libr., Whippany, N.J., 1975-83; assoc. dir. Learning Resource Ctr., County Coll. Morris, Randolph, N.J., 1983—. Networked assoc. fellow 60s workgroup Inst. for Advanced Tech. in Humanities, U. Va., 1994—; ptnr., cons. libr. automation and planning DocuMentors, Rockaway, N.J., 1985—; ind. cons. infosys., Whippany, 1978—. Co-author: Planning for Automation: A How-To-Do-It Manual for Librarians, 1993, 2d edit., 1997, Writing and Updating Technology Plans: A Guidebook with Sample plans in CD-ROM, 1999, Planning for Integrated Systems and Technologies, 2001; contbr. chpt. to: Insider's Guide to Library Automation, 1993; editor: Resources for Teaching the Vietnam War: An Annotated Guide, rev. edit., 1996; also articles. V.p. Project: Hearts and Minds, Inc., Greenwich, Conn., 1995; bd. dirs. N.J. Vietnam Vets. Oral History Project, Kean U., 1998; mem. edn. adv. com. N.J. Vietnam Vets. Meml. Found., Vietnam Era Ednl. Ctr., 1998; mem. Morris County Dem. com., 1992; bd. dirs. N.J. Vietnam Vets. Meml. Found., 2001. Named to honor roll Vietnam Women's Meml. Project, Washington, 1993; recipient award African Am. Cultural Coun. Virginia Beach, 1999. Mem. ALA (travel grantee 1988), Am. Soc. Info. Sci., Spl. Librs. Assn. (pres. N.J. chpt. 1989-90, chairperson cataloging com. 1992-93), N.J. Libr. Assn. (chairperson automated libr. svcs. sect. 1992-93, mem. pers. adminstrn. com. 1986-87, mem. pay equity task force 1985-86), Women's Overseas Svc. League (scholarship com. chair 2003-), Phi Beta Kappa. Avocations: bicycling, internet, gardening. Office: DocuMentors 7 Valley View Dr Rockaway NJ 07866-1506 E-mail: aKelsey@ccm.edu.

KELSEY, CLYDE EASTMAN, JR., philosophy and psychology educator; b. Wadena, Minn., Mar. 30, 1924; s. Clyde Eastman and Lorraine (Lamb) Bagley) K.; m. Betty Jean Williams, Apr. 1, 1949 (dec.); children: Becky Kelsey Marcin, Nancy Kelsey Eargle; m. Jamie Lee Reagan, 1987. BA, U. Tex., El Paso, 1948; MA, U. Tulsa, 1951; PhD, U. Denver, 1960; hon. degree, U. de Oriente, Venezuela, 1969. Dir. counseling bur. U. Tex., El Paso, 1951-61, prof., head dept. philosophy, psychology, 1961-62, vice chmn. dept. philosophy and psychology, 1951-61; dean students, dir. Inter-Am. Inst., 1962-66; program adv. Venezuela, Ford Found., 1966-69; vice chancellor public affairs U. Denver, 1969-72; v.p. devel. and univ. relations Tex. Tech U., Lubbock, 1972-81, prof. edn., 1981-88, prof. emeritus, 1988—; sr. rsch. fellow Nat. Center Higher Edn. Mgmt., 1983-87. Lectr. 4th Army U.S., 1961-65; cons. U.S. Dept. State, Peace Corps, 1961-66; mem. adv. bd. Kans. Wesleyan Coll., 1960-71; vis. scientist NSF, 1962-66; v.p. Colo. Ptnrs. of Alliance, 1971-73; examiner, cons. Tex. State Bd. of Examiners of Psychologists, 1992-98; cons. Agy. for Internat. Devel., Coll. Bd., Civil Svc. Commn., World Bank to India, Saudi Arabia, Turkey, Republic of Mauritius, InterAm. Bank to Guyana, S.A. Contbr. articles to profl. jours. Bd. dirs. El Paso Mental Health Assn., 1951-58, pres. 1953-55; bd. dirs. El Paso Sch. Retarded Children, 1952-57, pres., 1953-55; bd. dirs. Lubbock Goodwill Industries, 1972-85, v.p., 1973-77, pres., 1978-80; bd. dirs. St. Mary's Hosp. Found., 1986-2000, chmn., 1994-96. With USNR, 1942-45. Decorated Order San Carlos Republic Colombia, 1964; recipient Disting. Alumni Service award U. Denver, 1972; Fulbright scholar Colombia, 1960-61 Fellow Tex. Acad. Sci.; mem. APA, Tex. Psychol. Assn., Phi Beta Delta. Home: 13413 North Shore Dr Montgomery TX 77356

KELSEY, DONALD ROSS, chemist; s. H. Ross and Lois Kelsey. Ph. D., Calif. Inst. of Tech., Pasadena, CA, 1968—72; B. S., Ctrl. Mo. State U., Warrensburg, MO, 1964—68. Postdoctoral fellow Yale U., New Haven, Conn., 1972—74; sr. rsch. scientist Union Carbide Corp., Bound Brook, NJ, 1974—86, Amoco Performance Products, Bound Brook, NJ, 1986—87; staff rsch. chemist Shell Chem. Co., Houston, Tex., 1987—. Recipient R&D 100 award R&D Mag., 1998, Disting. Alumni award Ctrl. Mo. State U., 1996, Tex. Inventor of Yr. award State Bar Tex., 2003. Mem. Am. Chem. Soc. (Nat. Merit award 1968, Team Innovation award 2000), Am. Inst. Chemists. Achievements include 54 U.S. patents on engineering thermoplastics, polymerization catalysts, metathesis polymers and polymer processes; research on Ni-catalyzed coupling, molecular modeling and polyesters; co-development of Corterra(R) poly(trimethylene terephthalate) polyester.

KELSEY, FRANCES OLDHAM (MRS. FREMONT ELLIS KELSEY), government official; b. Cobble Hill, Vancouver Island, Can., July 24, 1914; came to U.S., 1936, naturalized, 1956; d. Frank Trevor and Katherine (Stuart) Oldham; m. Fremont Ellis Kelsey, Dec. 6, 1943; children— Susan Elizabeth, Christine Ann. B.Sc., McGill U., 1934, M.Sc., 1935; PhD, U. Chgo., 1938, MD, 1950. Instr., asst. prof. pharmacology U. Chgo., 1938-50; editorial assoc. AMA, Chgo., 1950-52; assoc. prof. pharmacology U. S.D., 1954-57; med. officer FDA, Washington, 1960-63, chief investigational drug br., 1963-66, dir. divsn. oncology and radiopharm. drug products, 1966-67; dir. divsn. sci. investigations Office of Compliance, FDA, Rockville, Md., 1967-95, dep. for sci. and medicine Office of Compliance, 1995—. Author: (with F.E. Kelsey, E.M.K. Geiling) Essentials of Pharmacology, 1960. Recipient Pres.'s award for Distinguished Fed. Civilian Service (refusal to approve coml. distbn. thalidomide in U.S.), 1962. National Women's Hall of Fame, 2000. Mem. Am. Soc. Pharmacology and Exptl. Therapeutics, Am. Med. Writers Assn., Teratology Soc., Sigma Xi, Sigma Delta Epsilon. Office: FDA Office of Compliance 7520 Standish Pl Rockville MD 20855-2730

KELSEY, GEORGE E. language educator; b. Woodbury, N.J., Dec. 14, 1929; s. William Albright and Clara Mabel Kelsey; m. Martha Marie Nystedt Kelsey, Aug. 18, 1951; children: William, Paul, Linda, Lois. Diploma, Providence Bible Inst., 1950; BA, Wheaton Coll., 1952, MA, 1955; D of Divinity, Denver Sem., 1984. Pastor Bible Ch., Chgo., 1951—53; mem. staff archaeol. expedition Wheaton (Ill.) Coll., 1953, 1954; missionary Conservative Bapt., Amman, Jordan, 1955—2000; founder, dir. Kelsey Arabic Lang. Sch., Amman, 1965—2000; lectr., spkr. on Islam and Mid. East, 2000—. Author: Speaking Arabic, 2 vols., 1995, Mechanics of Pronunciation, 1995, Dictionary, Arabic/English Theological, 1996. Treas. Evang. Relief Soc., Amman; pastor Evang. Ch., Amman, 1956—2000. Named Alumnus of Yr., Wheaton Coll. Alumni Assn., 1995; recipient A.J. Gordon Missionary Svc. award, Gordon Coll., Mass., 2000. Republican. Avocations: Arabic literature, Greek, ancient coins, hiking. Home: 9A Pembroke Ln Whiting NJ 08759 E-mail: abubilly@cs.com.

KELSEY, MICHAEL LOYAL, geography educator; b. Greeley, Colo., Dec. 15, 1953; s. Loyal Lee and Luwanda Marie (Steffens) K. BS, Salisbury State U., 1976; MA in Geography, U. Northern Colo., 1988; PhD in Geography, Kent State U., 1993. Founder, mgr. Salisbury (Md.) State U. Book Co-op., 1975-76; mgmt. trainee J.C. Penney Co., Inc., Salisbury, 1976-77; cost acctg. and time study mgr. W.D. Byron & Sons, Inc., Williamsport, Md., 1978-83; corp. inventory controller Stuart McGuire Co., Inc., Salem, Va., 1983-84; owner, mgr. New Century Ribbon Co., Greeley, Colo., 1984-88; instr., doctoral teaching fellow Kent (Ohio) State U., 1988-91; instr. Montgomery Coll., Rockville, Md., 1991-93; prof., chmn. geography and econs. dept. Aims Coll., Greeley, 1993—. Officer, bd. dirs. Seagulf Concepts, Inc., Salisbury, Md., 1975-76; cons. Laserhead Graphics, Greeley, 1993—. Dir. Internat. Ctr. Recipient top bus. student award Rotary Internat., Salisbury, 1975, grad. fellowship U. No. Colo., Greeley, 1986-87, award for tchg. excellence, 1996, Sam W. Walton Free Enterprise fellow and Free Enterprise Educator award, 1996; grantee IBM Corp., Rockville, Md., 1992, NSF Geographic Info. Sys., 1998. Mem. Assn. Am. Geographers, Nat. Coun. for Geographic Edn., Gamma Theta Upsilon (pres. U. No. Colo. 1987-89), Phi Kappa Phi, Omicron Delta Kappa. Home: 4040 W 12th St Apt 6 Greeley CO 80634-2508 Office: Aims CC 5401 20th St Greeley CO 80634-3002

KELSEY, PENELOPE MYRTLE, education educator; d. Charles and Vicki Kelsey; m. David Chinander, Jan. 23, 1968. PhD, U. Minn., 2002. Sr. intern Native Am. Women's Health Edn. Resource Ctr., Lake Andes, SD, 1995; fellow Office of Equal Opportunity, U. Minn., Mpls., 1996—97; tchg. asst. Eng. U. Minn., Mpls., 1997—2001, Ruth Miller fellow, 2002; asst. prof. Rochester Inst. Tech., NY, 2002—03. MacArthur fellow, U. Minn., 2000—01. Mem.: MLA. Office: Rochester Inst Tech 1 Lomb Memorial Dr Rochester NY 14623 Office Fax: 585-475-7120. E-mail: pmkgsl@rit.edu.

KELSEY, RONALD GRANT, environmental engineer; b. Town of Orleans, N.Y., July 22, 1944; s. Lynwood Jerome and Dorothy Mable (Simpkins) K.; m. Brunhilde Mariana Bethea, Sept. 25, 1967 (div. Sept. 1980); children: Anna Marie, Robert Phillip; m. Linda Loraine York, Mar. 24, 1987; 1 child, Grant Alexander. BS in Civil Engring., Norwich U., 1965; MS in Sanitary Engring., Va. Poly. Inst. & State U., 1974; MA in Bus. Mgmt., Ctrl. Mich. U., 1981. Commd. 2d lt. U.S. Army Corps of Engrs., 1965, advanced through grades to col., 1988, ret., 1992; sr. environ. engr. Meta, Inc., Gaithersburg, Md., 1992-95; dir. govt. environ. svcs. AWK Cons. Engrs., Turtle Creek, Pa., 1995—, Envirohealth Mktg.-An Ind. Rep. of Equinox Internat., Frederick, Md., 1995-96; sr. environ. engr. TRW, FAASpt, Leesburg, Va., 1997-98; sr. environ. planner URS Greiner Woodward Clyde, Hunt Valley, Md., 1999; sr. environ. engr. Northrop Grumman FAASpt, Leesburg, 1999—. Decorated Bronze star Dept. of the Army, Vietnam, 1968, Meritorious Svc. medal with two oak leaf clusters Dept. of the ARmy, Washington, 1977, 83, 85, Legion of Merit with two oak leaf clusters Dept. of the Army, 1985, 89, 92. Mem. ASCE, Soc. Am. Mil. Engrs. (pres. 1991-92, Gavel award 1992), Water Environment Fedn., Hiram Lodge (master mason). Republican. Lutheran. Avocations: jogging, reading, traveling, enviromental issues. Home: 525 Sage Hen Ct Frederick MD 21703-1302 Office: FAA Chesapeake Bay SMO-82AC Leesburg VA 20176 E-mail: ronald.ctr.kelsey@faa.gov.

KELSEY, STERETT-GITTINGS, sculptor; b. Greenwich, Conn., Dec. 16, 1941; 2 children. BFA in Sculpture, RISD, 1964. Represented in permanent collections Hirschhorn Mus., Nat. Art Mus. of Sport, Royal Porcelain Mus., Hakone Open-air Mus., Stamford Ctr., Westchester Capital Corp., McDonald Corp., Doral Corp, Pegasus Venture Capital, Pepsi Cola Co., Georgetown U. Intercultural Ctr., Choate Rosemary Hall Sch., Garrison Forest Sch., McGhee Libr., Stamford Ctr. Performing Arts, Anne Norton Mus., Landegger Collection, Conn., Goergen Collection, Conn., Bankson Collection, Schaffer Collection, New Rochelle, N.Y., Parsons & Whittemore Internat., Rye Brook, N.Y., others. Mailing: Kelsey Sculpture Roxbury CT 06783 E-mail: kelsey@kelseysculpture.com.

KELSO, DAVID WILLIAM, artist, fine arts publishing executive; b. Van Nuys, Calif., Jan. 29, 1948; s. William Joseph and Elsa Estra (Scipione) K.; m. Christine Durone Mehling, June 10, 1983. BA, U. Calif., Riverside, 1969; postgrad., U. Calif., Berkeley, 1970. Printer El Dorado Press, Berkeley, 1972-78, Crown Point Press, Oakland, Calif., 1978-79; dir., printer Made in California Editions, Oakland, Calif., 1980—. Author: (catalog) Small Wonders, 1997. Recipient purchase award N.W. Internat. Small Format Print Exhbn., Seattle, 1978, juror's award Berkeley (Calif.) Art Ctr., 1991; purchase award L.A. Printmaking Soc., juror's award, 1999; purchase award Portland (Oreg.) Art Mus., 1997, Best of Show award Hand-Pulled Prints VII, Tex., 1999, James D. Phelan award in printmaking San Francisco Found., 2001. Mem. Rutgers Archives for Printmaking Studios, Vicente Dance Club. Avocations: social dancing, backpacking, biking. Office: Made in Calif Intaglio Edits 3246 Ettie St Ste 16 Oakland CA 94608-4016 E-mail: madeinca2d@earthlink.net.

KELSO, GWENDOLYN LEE, silver appraiser, consultant; b. Washington, Jan. 5, 1935; d. Leon Hugh and Katherine Estelle (Henderson) K. Mgr. Shaw & Brown Co., Washington, 1967-71, Chas. Schwartz & Son, Washington, 1972-76; silver appraiser Washington, 1976—; ptnr. The Silver Lion, Washington, 1983-85; owner, mgr. The Rampant Lion, Washington, 1985—. Cons. FBI and law enforcement agys. and ctrs., 1982—; cataloguer, conservator his. silver belonging to USN and U.S. Naval Acad., 1987—; appraiser presentation silver aboard U.S. Naval vessels and at installations, 1986—; cataloguer, conservator silver Forbes mag. collection, N.Y.C., 1989; mem. USS Alexandria Commissioning Com., 1990, USS Maryland Commissioning Com., 1993; conservator State of Md. for preservation battleship USS Maryland presentation silver, 1990—; instr. USN pers. for care and maintenance preservation silver; guest curator Washington Nat. Cathedral, 1997-98; cons. in field. Author: God's Treasures At Risk?, 1999, United States Navy Presentation Silver-A History and a Manual for its Care and Preservation, 1989, Silver Reflections an American Naval History, 1991 (exhbn. catalogue) Silver for Sacred Spaces—Four centuries of Ecclesiastical Silver from the Judeo-Christian Tradition, Washington Nat. Cathedral, 1998. Mem. NAFE, Internat. Soc. Appraisers (scholar 1989), Am. Soc. Appraisers (sr.), Appraisers Assn. Am., N.Y. Silver Soc., Silver Soc. (London), U.S. Naval Inst., Navy League U.S., Newcomen Soc. U.S. Republican. Episcopalian. Avocations: writing, travel, sewing, volunteering. Home and Office: 3731 39th St NW Washington DC 20016-5522

KELSO, JOHN HODGSON, former government official; b. Iowa City, June 16, 1925; s. Edward Lewis and Eliza (Hodgson) K.; m. Marian Louise Towers, Aug. 22, 1948; 1 child, John T. BA, State U. Iowa, 1949, MA, 1950. Occupational research analyst Bur. Naval Personnel, Dept. Navy, Washington, 1951-55; orgn. and methods examiner Agr. Research Services, Dept. Agr., Washington, 1955-57; mgmt. analyst mgmt. adv. br. Bur. State Services, USPHS, HEW, Washington, 1957-58, chief survey group, 1958-60, chief mgmt. adv. br., 1960-62, asst. exec. officer, 1962-66; exec. officer USPHS, Bethesda, Md., 1966-68; asso. adminstr. mgmt. Health Services and Mental Health Adminstrn., 1968-73; dir. office regional operations USPHS, Office Asst. Sec. for Health, HEW, 1973-76; dep. adminstr. Health Services Adminstrn., 1976-81, acting adminstr., 1981-82; dep. adminstr. Health Resources and Services Adminstrn., 1982-94, acting adminstr., 1985-86, 88-89. Cons. United Network for Organ Sharing, Richmond, Va., 1994—. Served with AUS, 1943-46. Recipient Superior Svc. award USPHS, 1969, Disting. Svc. award HEW, 1972, Presdl. Meritorious Rank award 1983, Disting. Presdl. Rank award 1989, Surgeon Gen.'s medallion, 1989. Mem. Sigma Alpha Epsilon. Methodist.

KELSO, LINDA YAYOI, lawyer; b. Boulder, Colo., 1946; d. Nobutaka and Tai Ike; m. William Alton Kelso, 1968. BA, Stanford U., 1968; MA, U. Wis., 1973; JD, U. Fla., 1979. Bar: Fla. 1980. Assoc. Mahoney, Hadlow & Adams, Jacksonville, Fla., 1979-82, Commander, Legler, Werber, Dawes, Sadler & Howell, Jacksonville, 1982-86, ptnr., 1986-91, Foley & Lardner, Jacksonville, 1992—. Mem. ABA (bus. law sect.), Jacksonville Bar Assn., Phi Beta Kappa, Order of Coif. Avocations: music, gardening, cooking. Office: Foley & Lardner 200 N Laura St Jacksonville FL 32202-3510 E-mail: lkelso@foleylaw.com.

KELSO, LYNN A. acute care nurse practitioner; b. Pitts., July 11, 1961; d. Harry Gladden and Colette Louise (Franz) K. BSN, W.Va. U., 1984; MSN, Case Western Res. U., 1991; CRNP, U. Pitts., 1993; postgrad., U. Ky., 2002—. RN, Pa., Ky.; cert. ACLS; Acute Care Nurse Practitioner, APRN, BC. Acute care nurse practitioner liver transplant ICU U. Pitts. Med. Ctr., Pitts., 1993-95; asst. prof. ACNP program U. Ky., 1996—; acute care nurse practitioner with Pulmnary/Crit Care Chandler Med.Ctr., 1996—2002; acute care nurse practitioner St. Joseph's Med. Ctr., 2003—. Mem.: AACN, Nat. Orgn. Nurse Practitioner Faculty, So. Nurses Rsch. Soc., Soc. Critical Care Medicine, Am. Acad. Nurse Practitioners, Sigma Theta Tau. Home: 1725 Fox Head Ct Lexington KY 40515-1318

KELSO, MARY JEAN, author; b. Eugene, Oreg., Nov. 27, 1938; d. Thomas Jasper and Eula Ethel (Warren) Williams; m. Byron Eugene Kelso Sr., June 30, 1956; children: Byron Jr., Bryon, Wendy Lynne Whiteman, Byron III. Editorial asst. Aster Pub., Springfield, Oreg., 1983-84; customer svcs. rep. El Jay divsn. Cedarapids Inc., Eugene, Oreg., 1984-95. Author, illustrator: Mystery of Virginia City, 1984, Abducted, 1986, Sierra Summer, 1992, A Virginia City Mystery, 1992; pub. Goodbye, Bodie, 1988. Avocations: travel, photography, painting. Address: PO Box 855 Marcola OR 97454 E-mail: mjkel@aol.com.

KELSO, R. RANDALL, law educator; b. Indpls., Nov. 12, 1955; s. Charles Davidson and Margaret Jane (Tandy) K. B.A., U. Chgo., 1976; J.D., U. Wis., 1979. Instr., U. Miami (Fla.) Sch. Law, 1979-80; assoc. in law Columbia U., N.Y.C., 1980-82; prof. Law South Tex. Coll. Law, Houston, 1983— . Co-author coursebook: Studying Law: An Introduction, 1984. Contbr. articles to profl. publs. Office: South Tex Coll Law 1303 San Jacinto St Houston TX 77002-7013

KELTER, RICHARD JOHN, physician; b. N.Y.C., Apr. 6, 1946; s. Joseph John and Viola Giorgia (Ades) K.; m. Louise Carolyn Kohlberg, Sept. 7, 1974; children: Michael Jacob, Stephanie Jill. BA, U. Pa., 1967; MD, U. Louis Pasteur, Strasbourg, France, 1974. Diplomate in internal medicine and geriatrics Am. Bd. Internal Medicine. Intern Brookdale Hosp. Med. Ctr., 1974-75; resident Bklyn. Hosp. Med. Ctr., 1975-77; mem. staff Tuxedo (N.Y.) Meml Hosp., 1977-78, Good Samaritan Hosp., Spring Vally, N.Y., 1978; physicia emergency rm. Old Bridge (N.J.) Regional Hosp., 1979-80, mem. staff 1980-81, Centrastate Med. Ctr., Freehold, N.J., 1979—; pvt. practice Manala pan, N.J., 1979—; mem. staff Raritan Bay Med. Ctr., 1996—2002. Mem. Am Gertiatric Soc., Am. Soc. Internal Medicine, Med. Soc. N.J., Monmouth Count Med. Soc. Avocations: baking, wines, opera, singing. Office: 368 Union Hill R Manalapan NJ 07726-1850 E-mail: rkelter@pol.net.

KELTNER, ROBERT EARL, lawyer, researcher, business executive; b Parkersburg, W.Va., Apr. 11, 1940; s. Earl L. and Chloe H. (Hendershot) K.; child, David B. BA, Marietta Coll., 1959; JD, W.Va. U., 1962; PhD, Thoma Edison Coll., 1965. Bar: W.Va. 1962, U.S. Supreme Ct. 1968. Assoc. Redmond Campbell & Keltner, Parkersburg, 1962-64; sr. ptnr. Keltner & Yankiss Parkersburg, 1964-80; pres. Americar Inc., 1986—90, Big K Co., 1990—, Paln Tree Tel. Co., 1990—97. Psychotherapist Palm Beach Health Clinic, 1965; U.S Appeals agt., Parkersburg, 1966-75; cons. Pacific Test Labs., L.A., 1970— pres. United Innkeepers Am., Fla., 1973—, Americar Inc., Palm Tree Motel Inc. Mem. ABA, W.Va. State Bar Assn., Wood County Bar Assn., Am Arbitration Assn., Lawyer Pilots Assn., Internat. Platform Assn., Kiwanis (pres 1968). Methodist. Address: 4415 N Tamiami Trl Sarasota FL 34234-386 Office: Keltner & Yankiss 2404 7th Ave Parkersburg WV 26101-5824 Address 2660 17th St Sarasota FL 34234

KELTON, ARTHUR MARVIN, JR., real estate developer; b. Bennington Vt., Sept. 12, 1939; s. Arthur Marvin and Lorraine (Millington) K.; m. Elain White, Nov. 1, 1986; 1 child, Ashley. BA, Dartmouth Coll., 1961; postgrad., U Vt., 1963. Ptnr. Kelton and Assocs., Vail, Colo., 1966-77; pres. Kelton, Garto and Assocs. Inc., Vail, 1977-84, Kelton, Garton, Kendall, Vail, 1984-93 Christopher, Denton, Kelton, Kendall, Vail, 1993—2001, Kelton & Kendall Vail, 2001—. Head agt. Dartmouth Alumni Fund, Hanover, N.H., 1985-90 class pres., 1990-96; Dartmouth Alumni Coun., 1996—; pres. Vail Valley Med Ctr. Found., 1991—; bd. overseers Hanover Inn, 2002—, Dartmouth Rea Estate Coun., 2003—. Republican. Congregationalist. Avocations: skiing, golf wingshooting. Home: 1034 Homestake Cir Vail CO 81657-5111 Office: Kelto & Kendall 225 Wall St Ste 200 Vail CO 81657-3615 Fax: 970-476-7994 E-mail: akjr@vail.net.

KELTS, DAVID WILLIAM, elementary education educator; b. Loma Linda Calif., Nov. 21, 1948; s. Donald Romayne and Beverly Oneida (Brandt) K. BA Claremont McKenna Coll., 1970, cert., 1972. Tchr. grade 4 Carnelian Elem Sch., Alta Loma, Calif., 1970-73; tchr. elem. grades Dept. Def. Dependent Schs., Sollars Sch., Misawa AFB, Japan, 1973-78, 88-95; tchr. grade 3 Dept Def. Dependents Schs., Lajes Elem. Sch., Lajes AFB, Azores, 1978-79, Dept Def. Dependents Schs., M. C. Perry Sch., Iwakuni, Japan, 1979-80, tchr. grad 5, 1980-88; tchr. Illesheim Elem. Sch., 2002—. Coach little league, Alta Loma 1973; scoutmaster Cub Pack 941 Boy Scouts Am., Alta Loma, 1973; active bas chapel coun., Iwakuni, 1981-88; lay leader base chapel, Misawa AFB, 1989-95 life mem. Carnelian Elem. Sch. PTA, Alta Loma. Recipient Human Goal award, Misawa AFB, 1976. Mem. Fed. Edn. Assn. (Pacific area dir. 1995-2001) N.E. Asia Tchrs. Assn. (officer 1981-85, 89-95, rep. 1993-94), Pacific Sci. Tchrs Assn., Lajes Tchrs. Assn. Republican. Presbyterian. Avocations: travel, reading cooking, computers, biking.

KELTY, PAUL DAVID, physician, educator; b. Louisville, Oct. 2, 1947; s William Theadore and Mary Frances (Hinton) K. BEE, U. Louisville, 1970 MD, 1978; MS, Ohio State U., 1971. Mem. tech. staff Bell Labs., Whippany N.J., 1970-72; design engr. Gen. Electric Co., Louisville, 1972-74; intern S Mary's Med. Ctr., Evansville, Ind., 1978-79, resident in ob-gyn., 1979-82 practice medicine, specializing in ob-gyn. Corydon, Ind., 1982—. Clin. inst Dept. Ob-Gyn U. Louisville (Ky.) Sch. Medicine, 1987—. Mem. AMA, Am Soc. Reproductive Medicine, Am. Inst. Ultrasound in Medicine, N.Y. Acad Scis., Sigma Xi, Phi Kappa Phi, Tau Beta Pi, Sigma Tau, Sigma Pi Sigma, Et Kappa Nu, Gamma Beta Phi, Omicron Delta Kappa. Roman Catholic. Hom and Office: 2000 Edsel Ln NW Corydon IN 47112

KELZ, ROCHELLE SHELLE K. academic administrator; d. Samuel an Florence W. Kanter; m. Theodore Kelz, Dec. 19, 1965 (div.); children: Meliss B. children: Max B.; m. Arnold Abrams, July 28, 1988. BS, Northwestern U Evanston, IL, 1966, MA, 1968, PhC, 1969, PhD, 1971; I.E.M. Cert., Harvar U., Cambridge, MA, 1998. Cert. K-12 Tchr. Spanish & French Ill., 1966 Bilingual Tchr. Ill., 1982. Tchg. asst., Northwestern U., Evanston, Ill 1967—69; prof. of Spanish, French & Fnglish as a second lang. North Pk. U Chgo., 1969—80; vis. prof. of med. Spanish U. of Ill. at Chgo., 1980—84, U of Ill. at Chgo. Med. Ctr., 1980—87; dir. of ext. programs & evening coll. Nort Pk. U., Chgo., 1982—90; dir. of ext. programs Roosevelt U., Chgo., 1990—94 dean of liberal arts & sciences C. S. Mott CC, Flint, Mich., 1994—98; dean c arts & sciences Ind. U., Kokomo, 1998—2001; v.p. of academic affairs Cir State Tech CC, Ohio, 2001—. Cons. mem. Leadership Coun. for Fg Languages and Internat. Studies, Ill. State Bd. of Edn., 1986—93; expert Il State Bd. of Edn., Springfield, 1986—93, fgn. lang. cons., 1986—94; alumr adv. bd. of directors Coll. of Arts & Sciences, Northwestern U., Evanston, Ill 1992—94; fgn. lang. adv. bd. Truman Coll., Chicago, Ill., 1994—95; alumr admission coun. Northwestern U., Evanston, Ill., 1995—; bd. mem., sch improvement Mott Mid. Coll. H.S., Flint, Mich., 1995—98; dir. Spanis Speaking Info. Ctr., Flint, Mich., 1995—98; adv. bd. TEAMS, Flint, Mich 1995—98; chair Riegle Dinner for Russian Resettlement, Flint, Mich 1997—98; co-chair, gen. programs Rotary Club of Flint, Flint, Mich 1997—99; pres. Liberal Arts Network for Devel., Mich., 1999; progra planning com. Cin. Pub. Schools, 2001—, program implementation com 2002—; steering com. Greater Cin. Tech Prep Consortium, 2001—. Autho (book) Diego Sanchez de Badajoz and the Old Testiment, 1971, Conversationa Spanish for Medical Personnel, 1978 (Nominee for AMWA Med. Book Awar 1978), Conversational Spanish for Medical Personnel, 2nd ed, revised & great expanded, 1982, (books, dictionary) Delmar's English/Spanish Pocket Dictio nary for Health Professionals, 1997 (Outstanding U. Prof. of Spanish in the US 1987), (book) Conversational Spanish for Health Professionals, 1999, translat american dental assoc.-spanish & french; editor: (bilingual newsletter) Chicag Area AATSP Chapter Newsletters, 1977-, 1991 (1st Place-Award of Ge Excellence, 1991). Chair membership com. Network for Youth Svcs 1990—93; mem. Kokomo/Howard County C.of C., Kokomo, Ind 1999—2001, Met. Growth Alliance, Cin., 2001; panelist Flint (Mich.) Jou Citizens' Adv. Panel, 1998; mem. Flint Women's Forum, 1995—98, Urba League of Flint, 1996—98, Chicago-Area Hispanic C. of C., 1982—94 Mexican Mus. & Fine Arts Ctr., Chgo/, Ala., 1985—94, Ctr. for Quality Mgmt Cin., 2001; local planning team mem. Wellhead Protection Mgmt., Kokom Ind., 1999—2000; mem. Mi Raza Fine Arts Coun., Chgo., 1980—90, Altrus Kokomo, Ind., 2000—01, Women's Bus. Coun., Kokomo, Ind., 1999—200 Nat. Alliance for Hispanic Health, National Organization, 1984. Nomine Athena Award, Flint, MI's Women's Organizations, 1997; recipient Outstandin U. Prof. of Spanish in the US, Am. Assn. of Teachers of Spanish & Portugues 1987, Pan Hellenic Scholarship Award, Northwestern U., 1966. Mem.: TESO (hospitality co-chair, nat. conv. 1991), Am. Assn. of Higher Edn., Am. Assn. Cmty. Colleges, Alumni Assn., Northwestern U. (class rep. 1986—87), Interna Trade Club of Chgo. (chair, academic liaison com. 1988), Profl. Standar Com., IL State Bd. of Edn. (chair 1986—94), Ill. Fgn. Lang. Leadership Cou (treas. 1992—94), Network for Youth Services, Am. Coun. on the Tchg. of Fg Languages (pub. rels. chair 1990—94), Nat. Coun. of Instrnl. Administrator Ind. Campus Compact, Chgo. Met. Bd. for Higher Edn. (bd. mem. 1982—94 Coun. of Colleges of Arts & Sciences, Greater Ill. ESL Program Director Network (bd. mem. 1985—91), Coalition for Lang. and Internat. Studies (pre 1990—91), Chgo. Area Chpt. of Am. Assn. of Teachers of Spanish Portuguese (editor & editor in chief, greater chgo. area newsletter 1978—94 Ill. Coun. on the Tchg. of Fgn. Languages (editor state newsletter 1987—90 Ill. Fgn. Lang. Teachers' Assn. (newsletter -spanish editor 1983—85), Nat. So for Experiential Edn., Nat. Assn. for Bilingual Edn., MLA, Ctrl. States Conf. c the Tchg. of Fgn. Languages (adv. coun. 1988), Ctr. for Quality Mgm Academic Quality Improvement Project, Ill. Coun. on the Tchg. of Fg Languages (pres. 1990—91). Jewish. Avocations: reading, music. Offic Cincinnati State Tech& CC 3520 Central Plwy Cincinnati OH 45223-26 E-mail: shelle.kelz@cincinnatistate.edu.

KEM, RICHARD SAMUEL, retired army officer; b. Richmond, Ind., Aug. 9, 934; s. Charles Edward and Janice Allene (Beard) K.; m. Ann Callahan, May , 1960; children: Michelle, John Samuel, Steven Edward. BS, U.S. Mil. Acad., 956; MS in Civil Engring., U. Ill., 1962; MS in Internat. Affairs, George Washington U., 1972; postgrad., Naval War Coll., 1972, Northwestern U., 1979, Harvard U., 1983. Commd. 2d lt. U.S. Army, 1956, advanced through grades to naj. gen., 1984; comdg. officer 577th Engr. Bn. Vietnam, 1968-69; staff, faculty J.S. Mil. Acad., West Point, N.Y., 1969-71; staff officer Mil. Personnel Center, 972-74, Office Army Chief Staff, 1974-75; chief public affairs Office Chief Engrs., 1975-76; comdg. officer 7th Engr. Brigade, Germany, 1976-78; chief nstallations and constrn. U.S. Army Europe, 1978-79; dep. asst. chief engrs., 979-80; dep. dir. civil works Office Chief Engrs., 1980; comdr., div. engr. Ohio River div., 1981-84; bd. engrs. Rivers and Harbors, 1982-84, Mississippi River Commn., 1982-84; comdg. gen. U.S. Army Engr. Sch. and Fort Belvoir, Va., 984-87; dep. chief of staff, engr. U.S. Army, Europe, 1987-88, chief of staff, 988-89; dep. chief of engrs. Washington, Washington, 1989-90; ret., 1990; dir. pub. works Arlington (Va.) County, 1990—. Decorated DSM with oak leaf cluster, Legion of Merit with oak leaf cluster, Bronze Star. Mem. ASCE, Soc. Am. Mil. Engrs., Am. Def. Preparedness Assn., Army Engr. Assn. (bd. dirs. 992—), Am. Pub. Works Assn. (bd. dirs. 1989-90). Episcopalian. Office: Arlington County 2100 Clarendon Blvd Arlington VA 22201-5445

KEMBLE, JAMES RICHARD, retired engineering services executive; b. Mishawaka, Ind., Sept. 28, 1935; s. Richard Ralph and Lucille Marie (Wickey) K.; m. Dorothy Faye Millican, Oct. 1960 (div. 1961); m. Anne Duval, Oct. 6, 962; children: Dawn Marie, Joseph James, Lisa Marie, Theresa Marie. Student, Notre Dame U., 1953-54, Purdue U., 1954-59; B in Gen. Studies, U. Nebr., Omaha, 1969. Clk. stock rm. Powell Tool Supply, Inc., South Bend, Ind., 952-54; truck driver South Bend Supply Co., 1959; commd. 2d lt. U.S. Army, 959, advanced through grades to maj., 1967, ret., 1979; tech. writer VSE Corp., Alexandria, Va., 1979-80, sr. logistic engr., 1980-82, div. mgr. plans and programs, 1982-84, mgr. air launched missile group, 1984-86; asst. v.p., mgr. Systems Engring. Group, Washington, 1986-94; v.p., mgr. air systems ops. divsn. Value Sys. Svcs., Arlington, Va., 1994-95; ret., 1995. Decorated Bronze Star, Meritorious Svc. medal with 3 oak leaf clusters, Joint Svc. Commendation medal, Army Commendation medal with 1 oak leaf cluster. Mem. KC. Roman Catholic. Avocations: reading, personal computing, writing, volksmarching. Home: Unit 415 5300 Holmes Run Pkwy Alexandria VA 22304-2834

KEMBLE, PENN, government official; m. Marie-Louise Caravatti. BA, U. Colo., 1962. Program dir. League for Indsl. Democracy, 1963-69; chmn. Frontlash, Inc., 1969-72; spl. asst., speech writer Senator Patrick Moynahan of N.Y., 1978-79; producer, writer WETA-TV, Washington, 1979-81; pres. Prodemca, 1981-88; mem. bd. for Internat. Broadcasting, 1991-93; dep. dir. USIA, 993-99, acting dir., 1999-2000; spl. rep. U.S. Dept. State SOS Office, 2000—02; sr. scholar at Freedom House, dir. project on democracy and the global edn., 2002—. Bd. dirs. Dem. Inst. for Internat. Affairs; mem. radio programs adv. coun. USIA, sr. scholar, Freedom House, dir. Project on Democracy and global edn. Contbr. articles to Commentary, The New Republic, N.Y. Times, Washington Post.

KEMENY, M. MARGARET, oncologist, hospital administrator, surgeon; b. Elizabeth, NJ, May 7, 1946; d. George Kemeny and Ellen Sagi. BS, Harvard U., 964—68; MD, Columbia U. Coll. of Physicians and Surgeons, 1972. Dir., cancer ctr. Queens Cancer Ctr., 2001—; divsn. chief, surg. oncology SUNY Stony Brook. Pres. Assn. of Women Surgeons. Editor: Journal of Clinical Oncology. Bd. of governors ACS, Chicago. Recipient Vis. Prof. for AWS, Assn. of Women Surgeons, 2002. Fellow: ACS. Home: 36 Perry St New York NY 0014 Office: Queens Cancer Center at Queens Hospital 82-68 164th St Jamaica NY 11432 Office Fax: 718-883-6295. E-mail: kemenym@nychhc.org.

KEMERER, CHRIS F. information scientist, educator; s. Raymond Louis and Elizabeth B. Kemerer; m. Anne Goodale Kemerer, June 16, 1984. BS, U. Pa., 979; PhD, Carnegie Mellon U., 1987. Prin. Am. Mgmt. Sys., Arlington, 979—83; career devel. assoc. prof. MIT, 1987—95; prof. info. sys. U. Pitts., 995—. Program chair ICIS-16, Netherlands, 1995; dept. editor Mgmt. Sci., 997—2002; editor in chief Info. Sys. Rsch., 2002—. Editor: (book) Software Project Management, 1997, Information Technology and Industrial Competitiveness, 1998, author over 50 rsch. papers. Rsch. Grant, Nat. Sci. Found., 000—02. Office: Univ Pitts 278A Mervis Hall Pittsburgh PA 15260

KEMERY, WILLIAM ELSWORTH, psychotherapist, hypnotherapist; b. Portland, Oreg., Apr. 16, 1929; s. William Elsworth Jr. and Charlotte Francis (Leydic) K.; m. Norma Mae Ishmael, Nov. 22, 1963 (div. May 1972); children: William M., Robert Z.; m. Marlene Agnes Kwiatkowski, Dec. 15, 1983; children: William E., William M., Robert Z., Bradley E. DD, Episcopal Sem., Balt., 1953; BA, Fresno State U., 1954; PhD (hon.), Hamilton State, 1973; Masters, Newport Internat. U., 1976, PhD, 1979. Cert. psychotherapist, hypnotherapist, sex therapist. Psychotherapist, Chula Vista, Calif., 1967—; founding dir. Calif. Hypnotists Examining Coun., L.A., 1974; pres., fellow Acad. Sci. Hypnotherapy, San Diego, 1974—; bishop Holy Episcopal Ch., Chula Vista, 978—. Dir. Assn. of Spiritual Psychology, San Diego, 1968—. Contbr. articles to profl. jours. Named Hon. Mayor, Chula Vist C. of C., 1967, Knight of Grace, Order of St. John of Jerusalem, 1981. Fellow Nutrition and Preventive Medicine Assn.; mem. Internat. Assn. Clin. Hypnotherapy (life), Acad. Orthomolecular Psychiatry, Assn. Humanistic Psychology, Internat. New Thought Alliance, Am. Guild Hypnotherapists, Am. Mental Health Counselors Assn., Am. Assn. Sex Educators, Counselors and Therapists. Republican. Avocations: swimming, hiking, jazz, photography. Home and Office: 379 G St Chula Vista CA 1910-4513 E-mail: docbill1@mindspring.com.

KEMMERER, LISA ANN, humanities educator; d. Walter Lloyd Kemmerer and Ruthli Frieda Amsler-Kemmerer. AA, Skagit Valley C.C., Mt. Vernon, Wash.; BA, Reed Coll., 1988; MTS, Harvard U., 1993; PhD in Philosophy, Glasgow, Scotland, 2000. Horse trainer, Mt. Vernon, Wash., 1975—79; forest fire fighter DNR, Sedro Woolley, Wash., 1979—83; instr. Outward Bound, Mazama, Wash., 1980—82; salesperson Mcht., Sydney, Australia, 1981; tchr. U. of Alaska, Anchorage, Western Wash. U. - Fairhaven, Bellingham, 1997, North Idaho Coll., Cour deAlene, Idaho, 2001; lectr. Mont. State U., Billings, 2002—. Rschr., writer in field; spkr. Alaska Humanities Forum, 1994—97. Contbr. scholarly articles to profl. publs. Mem. various city choirs, Anchorage, Glasgow, Billings, 1994—2003; mem. Peace Seekers, Billings; presenter slide shows of travels for local cmty. and schools Mt. Vernon; polit. activist Anchorage, 1994—97; writer, presenter Sunday sermon, preparer Sunday svcs. Unitarian Universalists, Anchorage; artist Social Activism, Hoquiam, Wash., 2000—02. Recipient Watson fellowship, Watson Found., 1988, rsch. grant, Culture and Animals Found., 1997; grantee, Harvard Pluralism Project, 2002, U. of Alaska, 1996, Harvard Pluralism Project, 1993, Alaska Humanities Forum Grant, 1996. Avocations: kayaking, cycling, music, travel, gardening.

KEMMERER, PETER REAM, financial executive; b. N.Y.C., Dec. 20, 1942; s. Mahlon Sistie and Colette Noel (Fitch) K.; m. Lillian Reilly, Sept. 15, 1990. BS, Georgetown U., 1966; MBA, Am. U., 1970; MA, New Sch., 1975. Analyst Corp. planning Otis Elevator Co., N.Y.C., 1971-74; mgr. fin. and adminstrn. bus. equipment div. SCM Corp., N.Y.C., 1975-80; pres. Mesa Verde, Inc., Cranbury, N.J., 1980—, also bd. dirs. Mng. ptnr. Jezel-Bezel Ptnrs., Cranbury, 1980—. Mem.: Princeton (N.Y.C.). Roman Catholic. Avocations: sailing, reading, sports. Office: 37 N Main St Cranbury NJ 08512-3203

KEMMERER, SHARON JEAN, computer systems analyst; b. Sellersville, Pa., Apr. 11, 1956; d. John Musselman and Esther Jone (Landis) K. BS, Shippensburg U., 1978; MBA, Marymount U., 1982. Mgmt. analyst Navy Internat. Logistics, Phila., 1978-81; computer systems analyst Navy Supply Sys. Commn., Crystal City, Va., 1981-86, Nat. Inst. Stds. and Tech., Gaithersburg, Md., 1986—. Bd. dirs. ComSci, Derwood Sta., 1994-97; adult tutor, 1991-95; mem. diversity bd. Nat. Inst. Stds. and Tech., 1997—. Contbr. articles, poetry to newspapers; author publs. Moderator Lung Assn., Fairfax, Va., 1986; vol. Project Heart, Washington, 1986—87, Montgomery County Health Buddy, 1988—99, Stepping Stones Shelter for Homeless, 1989—91, Pets on Wheels, 1994—96, Avon 3 Day Breast Cancer 60 mile walk, 2000, Habitat for Humanity, Montgomery County, 2001—, Burgundy Crest Vols., 2002—; dir. Global Village Mission trips Habitat For Humanity Internat., 2000—; mem. Global Village Mission Trips; deacon Alexandria (Va.) Ch., 1985—86, v.p. coun., 1985, ch. coun., 1995—2001; mem. adv. bd. to dean of edn. and human resources Shippensburg U., 2002—. Lutheran. Avocations: renovation, tennis, antiques, volleyball, power walking. Office: Nat Inst Stds and Tech Mfg Engring Lab Gaithersburg MD 20899-0001

KEMMERLY, JACK DALE, retired state official, aviation consultant; b. El Dorado, Kans., Sept. 17, 1936; s. Arthur Allen and Eythel Louise (Throckmorton) K.; m. Frances Cecile Gregorio, June 22, 1958; children: Jack Dale Jr., Kathleen Frances, Grant Lee. BA, San Jose State U., 1962; cert. in real estate, UCLA, 1970; MPA, Golden Gate U., 1973; cert. labor-mgmt. rels., U. Calif., Davis, 1978; cert. orgnl. change, Stanford U., 1985. Right of way agt. Calif. Div. Hwys., Marysville, 1962-71; adminstrv. officer Calif. Dept. Transp., Sacramento, 1971-82, dist. dir. Redding, 1982-83, chief aeros. Sacramento, 1984-94; mgmt. cons. U.S. Dept. Transp., Riyadh, Saudi Arabia, 1983-84. Chmn. tech. adv. com. on aeronautics Calif. Transp. Commn. Bd. dirs. Yuba-Sutter Campfire Girls, 1972-73. With USN, 1954-57. Recipient superior accomplishment award Calif. Dept. Transp., 1981. Mem. Nat. Assn. State Aviation Ofcls. (nat. pres. 1989—), Am. Assn. State Hwy. and Transp. Ofcls. (aviation com. 1985-94), Calif. Assn. Aerospace Educators (adv. bd. 1984—), Calif. Assn. Airport Execs., Calif. Aviation Coun., Aircraft Owners and Pilots Assn. (dir. regional reps.), Elks (exalted ruler Marysville, Calif. 1974-75). Republican. Roman Catholic. Avocations: non-partisan political activities, reading, flying. Office: 1285 Charlotte Ave Yuba City CA 95991-2803 E-mail: jackkemmerly@sysmatrix.net.

KEMMETT, WILLIAM JOSEPH, poet, educator; b. Boston, Nov. 19, 1936; s. William J. Kemmett and Mildred Bouvé; m. Jacqueline B. Tompkins, Aug. 2, 1956; children: William III, Kimberley Ann, Christopher, John, Gerald. Student, Harvard U., 1979—81; MFA, Norwich U., 1986. Adj. prof. English and writing Massasoit Coll., Brockton, Mass., 1991—. Author: Flesh of a New Moon, 1991, The Bradford Poems, 1996, Hole in the Heart, 2001. Recipient Mass. Artists Found. award, 1979, 1st prize Yankee Mag. 1986, 96, 2d prize, 1995, 3d prize, 1986, 95. Mem. Poetry Soc. Am., New Eng. Poetry Club (contest dir. 1978-82).

KEMMIS, DANIEL ORRA, cultural organization administrator, author; b. Fairview, Mont., Dec. 5, 1945; s. Orra Raymond and Lilly Samantha (Shidler) K.; m. Jean Larson; children: Abraham, Samuel, Deva, John. BA, Harvard U., 1968; JD, U. Mont., 1978. Bar: Mont. 1978. State rep. Mont. Ho. of Reps., Helena, 1975-84, minority leader, 1981-82, Speaker of House, 1983-84; ptnr. Morrison, Jonkel, Kemmis & Rossbach, Missoula, 1978-80, Jonkel & Kemmis, 1981-84; mayor City of Missoula, Mont., 1990-96; dir. Ctr. Rocky Mountain West Univ. Mont., Missoula, 1996—. Cons. No. Lights Inst., Missoula, Mont., 1985-89; Kennedy fellow Inst. Politics Harvard U., 1998. Author: Community and the Politics of Place, 1990, The Good City and the Good life, 1995, This Sovereign Land, 2001; contbr. articles to profl. jours. Candidate for chief justice Mont. Supreme Ct.; mem. Am. Planning Assn. Growing Smart Initiative; former mem. adv. bd. and bd. dirs. Nat. Civic League, 1990-93; mem. adv. bd. Pew Partnership for Civic Change, 1991-97, Brookings Instn. Ctr. Urban and Met. Policy; chmn. leadership tng. coun. Nat. League Cities, 1992-94; bd. dirs. Redefining Progress, Charles F. Kettering Found., N.W. Area Found., Inst. for Environ. and Natural Resources U. Wyo., Bolle Ctr. for People and Forests, U. Mont., Missoula Redevelopment Agency; fellow Dallas Inst.for Humanities and Culture 1991-98; presdl. appt. Am. Heritage Rivers Commn., 1998. Inst. Politics fellow Kennedy Sch. Govt., Harvard LU., 1998; named Disting. Young Alumnus U. Mont., 1981, 100 Visionaries, Utne Reader, 1995; recipient Charles Frankel prize NEH, 1997, Disting. Achievement award, Soc. for Conservation Biology, 1997, Wallace Stegner award, Ctr. Am. West, 1998. Democrat. Home: 521 Hartman St Apt 10 Missoula MT 59802-4771 Office: U Mont Milw Sta 2nd Fl Ctr Rocky Mountain W Missoula MT 59812-3096

KEMNITZ, JOSEPH WILLIAM, physiologist, researcher; b. Balt., Mar. 15, 1947; s. Harold Clarence Kemnitz and Alice Mae (Ziebarth) Delwiche; m. Amanda Marye Tuttle, Jan. 5, 1991; children: Julia Ellen, Joseph Andrew. BA, U. Wis., 1969, PhD, 1976. Rsch. assoc. Wis. Nat. Primate Rsch. Ctr., Madison, 1976-79, asst. scientist, 1979-84, assoc. scientist, 1984-94, sr. scientist and assoc. dir., 1995-96, dir., 1996—; assoc. scientist dept. medicine U. Wis., Madison, 1991-94, sr. scientist dept. medicine, 1995-97, prof. dept. physiology. Cons. NIH, Bethesda, Md., 1981—; mem. Children's Diabetes Ctr., Madison, Wis., 1990—; steering com. Inst. on Aging, Madison, 1989—. Assoc. editor Hormones and Behavior, 1986-96; contbr. articles to profl. jours. Grantee (various) NIH, 1977—. Mem. Am. Physiol. Soc., Am. Inst. Nutrition, Am. Diabetes Assn., Am. Soc. Primatologists, Gerontol. Soc. Am., N.Am. Assn. Study of Obesity, Internat. Primatol. Soc. Office: Primate Rsch Ctr UW 1220 Capitol Ct Madison WI 53715-1237

KEMNITZ, THOMAS MILTON, publisher; b. Washington; s. Milton Neumann and Esther L. K.; m. Myrna Kaye Glick, Dec. 10, 1982; 1 son, Thomas Milton Jr. BA, U. Mich., 1964; PhD, U. Sussex, Eng., 1969. Prof. U. N.H., Durham, 1969-75; pres. Kemnitz Audio Video, Boston, 1976-78, Trillium Press Inc., Unionville, N.Y., 1978—. Chmn. bd. Royal Fireworks Printing Co., 1989—; pres. KAV Books Inc., 1980—. Author: Kids Working with Computers (12 vol. series), 1983-85, Brain Booster, 1985, Computer Ethics, 1985, Buck Fang's Logo Challenge, 1985, other books and pieces of software; pub. Our Gifted Children mag. Office: Royal Fireworks Printing Co #1 1st Ave Unionville NY 10988-0399

KEMP, ANN, retired librarian; b. Providence, Ky., Aug. 2, 1941; d. Charlie and Rubye (Sigler) Kemp Page. BA, Belmont U., 1964; MLS, Vanderbilt U., 1965, postgrad., 1968-79. Cert. tchr. Ky. Libr. Nashville Pub. Libr., 1965, U. Louisville Libr., 1965-67, Dawson Springs (Ky.) Ind. Schs., 1967-93; instr. Murray (Ky.) State U., 1973-78. Instr. Murray (Ky.) State U., 1973-78. Author: Poem, The ABC's of Parthenon. Mem.: Ky. Libr. Assoc., Ky. Edn. Assoc., Nat. Edn. Assoc., The Parthenon Patrons. Baptist. Avocations: studying architecture and folklore, writing poetry. Home: 113 Woodlawn Dr Madisonville KY 42431-3254

KEMP, BARRETT GEORGE, lawyer; b. Dayton, Ohio, Feb. 22, 1932; s. Barrett M. and Gladys M. (Linkhart) K.; children: Becky A., Barrett George II; m. Shirley, 1997. BSC, Ohio U., 1954; JD, Ohio No. U., 1959. Bar: Ohio 1959. With FBI, 1959-61; mem. B.G. Kemp Law Firm, St. Marys, Ohio, 1961—. Law dir. City of St. Marys, 1964-80. Sec., treas. Cmty. Improvement Corp., 1967-79; founder St. Marys Sister City, Inc.; founder, organizer sister city with Ho Kudan-cho, Japan, 1985. With U.S. Army, 1954—56. Recipient Outstanding Citizen award City of St. Marys, 1973, Builder of Bridges award St. Mary's C. of C., 1995. Mem. Ohio Bar Assn., Auglaize County Bar Assn., Rotary (v.p. 1968, pres. 1969, Lifetime achievement 1997, Four Aves. of Cvs. citation 1999), Masons, Shriners, Scottish Rite. Office: Ste 203 Cmty First Bank & Trust Bldg Saint Marys OH 45885

KEMP, DANIEL WARREN, lawyer; b. Ironton, Ohio, Oct. 7, 1945; s. Warren Daniel and Evelyn Mary (Ball) K.; m. Judith Elizabeth Renz, Aug. 28, 1965; children: Brian Daniel, Nicole Elizabeth. BA, Ohio U., 1967; JD, U. Cin., 1970. Bar: Ohio 1970. Counsel Cin. Gas & Elec. Co., 1970-81; asst. counsel Armco Inc., Middletown, Ohio, 1981-84, assoc. counsel, 1985-89, corp. counsel, corp. dir., 1989-91; asst. gen. counsel Am. Elec. Power Svc. Corp., Columbus, Ohio, 1991—2002. Contbr. articles to profl. jours. Mem. ABA, Ohio Bar Assn., Cin. Bar Assn. (com. chmn. 1976-78), Columbus Bar Assn., Butler County Bar Assn., Masons. Republican. Presbyterian. Home: 830 Gatehouse Ln Columbus OH 43235-1734

KEMP, DEBORAH K. secondary school educator; b. Fitchburg, Mass., Dec. 16, 1953; d. Albert and Joan Page; m. Donald G. Kemp, Aug. 16, 1975; 1 child, Justin S. BS in Psychology, Fitchburg State Coll., 1975, MEd, 1995. Travel agt. Crimson Travel Svc., Cambridge, Mass., 1979—89; tchr. Fitchburg Pub. Schs., 1995—. Author: Kiss of the Geisha, 2002, Kyoto Connection, 2001, Captive in Kyoto, 2002. Mem.: Mensa. Democrat. Roman Catholic. Avocations: reading, writing, walking, photography. Home: 58 Mount Globe St Fitchburg MA 01420-7555

KEMP, EMORY LELAND, civil engineering educator; b. Chgo., Oct. 1, 1931; s. Emory Leland and Anita (Hucker) K.; m. Janet Karen Dodd, July 26, 1958; children— Mark, Alison, Geoffrey. BSc(hon.), U. Ill., 1952, PhD, 1962; MSc in Engring, U. London, 1958; Diploma (Fulbright fellow), Imperial Coll. Sci. and Tech., London, 1955. Registered profl. engr., W. Va.; chartered civil and structural engr., U.K. Asst. engr. Ill. State Water Survey, Urbana, 1952; asst. engr. rsch. and devel. lab. US Army, Ft. Belvoir, Va., 1952-54; structural engr. Sir Bruce White Wolfe Barry & Ptnr. and Ove Arup & Ptnr., London, 1956-59; fellow and instr. dept. theoretical and applied mechanics U. Ill., Urbana, 1959-62; assoc. prof. dept. civil engring. W.Va. U., Morgantown, 1962-66, prof., 1966—, chmn. dept., 1967-74, dir. program for history sci. and tech., 1975-88, dir. Inst. for History of Tech. and Indsl. Archaeology, 1989—. Served with U.S. Army, 1952-54. Fellow Inst. Civil Engrs., ASCE, Am. Concrete Inst.; mem. Inst. Structural Engrs., Soc. Indsl. Archeology, Soc. for History of Tech., Newcomen Soc., Pub. Works Hist. Soc., Phi Kappa Phi, Tau Beta Pi, Chi Epsilon. Methodist. Home: 429 Riley Ave Morgantown WV 26505-3726 E-mail: elkemp31@aol.com.

KEMP, EUGENE THOMAS, retired veterinarian; b. McDonough, N.Y., Mar. 22, 1930; s. Oswald Milton and Almira Dorothy (Allen) K.; m. Ruth Emer Stoll, Sept. 29, 1951 (dec. Sept. 1977); 1 child, William Allen; m. Margaret Atenna Rowland, Dec. 27, 1980. BS, Cornell U., 1951, DVM, 1957. Sr. ptnr. Day Hollow Animal Clinic, Owego, N.Y., 1957-2000. Author: Surfs on a Flet, 2002; contbr. Bd. dirs. First Ch. of Nazarene, Owego, 1991-98; v.p. Tioga County Bd. Health, 1988-96, pres., 1996—; mem. Owego-Apalachin Bd. Edn., 1961-71; mem. Broome-Tioga Bd. Coop. Edn. Svcs., Binghamton, 1969-83, pres., 1971-76; founding pres. Broome-Tioga Coun. Sch. Bd. Pres., 1973. Mem. So. Tier Vet. Med. Assn. (pres. 1992). Republican. Avocations: jazz piano, creative writing. Home: 478 Hiawatha Rd Owego NY 13827-5307

KEMP, FLO, artist; b. N.Y.C., Oct. 21, 1941; M. Edward John Kemp; children: Christopher, Karen. BA, Montclair State Coll., 1963; MA, Hofstra U., 1975. Spanish tchr. Huntington (N.Y.) Sch. Dist. 3, 1963-66; artist, 1979—. V.p. Northport Galleries, Huntington, 1986-88; mem. Artist in Embassy Program, Taipei, 2003. Exhibited at invitational shows Gallery North, Setauket, N.Y., 1996, 98, 2000, 01, 02, 03, C.W. Post Coll. N.Y., 1997, 2000, Heckscher Mus., N.Y., 2000, Atelier 14, Chelsea, N.Y., 2000, Catharine Lankard Waffle Club. Recipient awards Terrance Gallery, N.Y., Parrish Mus., Southampton, N.Y., Firehouse Gallery, Nassau C.C., N.Y., Best of Show award Ann Arbor Arts Festival, 2000. Mem. Nat. Assn. Women Artists (chmn. traveling print exhbn. 1990-92, 94-97, speaker L.I. Art Symposium Museums at Stony Brook, 1993, J. Childs Willis award, 1994, John Henry Stukey award 1995, 97). Avocations: walking, swimming.

KEMP, GEOFFREY THOMAS HOWARD, international affairs specialist; b. U.K., May 20, 1939; came to U.S., 1967, naturalized, 1974; s. Thomas Howard and Gwendoline (Reeves) K.; m. Vivian Reubens, Sept. 1968 (div. 1979); m. Tamara Levin Weisberg, Nov., 1998. BA, Oxford U., 1963, MA, 1967; PhD, MIT, 1971. Research assoc. Internat. Inst. Strategic Studies, London, 1965-67; research assoc. Ctr. Internat. Studies, MIT, Cambridge, 1967-71; assoc. prof. internat. politics Fletcher Sch. Law and Diplomacy, Tufts U., 1971-80; spl. asst. to Pres. for nat. security affairs White House, Washington, 1981-85; sr. fellow Ctr. for Strategic and Internat. Studies, Georgetown U., Washington, 1985-86; sr. assoc. Carnegie Endowment for Internat. Peace, 1986-95; dir. regional strategic programs Nixon Ctr., Washington, 1995—. Author: The Control of the Middle East Arms Race, 1991, Forever Enemies? American Policy and the Islamic Republic of Iran, 1994; co-author: Strategic Geography and the Changing Middle East, 1997. Served to lt. Army U.K., 1958-60 Mem. Council on Fgn. Relations (internat. affairs fellow 1976), Internat. Inst. Strategic Studies, Oxford Union Soc. Avocations: tennis, evelyn waugh literature, movies, english watercolor paintings. Office: Nixon Ctr 1615 L St NW Washington DC 20036-5610 E-mail: gkemp@nixoncenter.org.

KEMP, JAMES WILLIAM, graphic artist; b. Alliance, Ohio, Aug. 7, 1950; s. Albert William and Ethel Jean (Bricker) K.; m. Anita Karl, design ptnr., Aug. 20, 1999 BA, U. Pa., Phila., 1972; MLS, CUNY, 2001. Project editor Random House, Inc., N.Y.C., 1972-78; prin. designer, ptnr. Compass Projections Design Studio, Bklyn., 1978—; head libr. Poly Prep. CDS, Bklyn., 1999—. Map, lettering designer Random House, NYC, 1978—, Harcourt Brace, San Diego, 1982—, Franklin Libr., NYC, 1978-85, Doubleday, NYC, 1985—, Simon and Schuster, NYC, 1992—, Rolling Stone Mag., NYC, 1980-81, 89-93, NY Times, 1988—, Kirshenbaum & Bond, NYC, 1997, 98, Romann Group, NYC, 1998, Pub. Affairs Books, 1998—. Exhibited in group shows at Art Dir. Club, NYC, 1981, 90, 91, 95, Master Eagle Gallery, NYC, 1981, 83-84, 87, 90, Donnell Libr., NYC, 1987, ITC Gallery, NYC, 1987, 90-93, Berthold Type Ctr., Toronto, Ont., Can., 1988, 90, Cooper-Hewitt Mus., NYC, 1996, AIGA Gallery, NYC, 1999; contbr. articles to profl. jour.; artwork appearing in books and anns. Co-founder Summer Mus. Theater for Young Adults, Bennington, Vt., 1985-96. Recipient cert. of excellence Am. Inst. Graphic Arts, NYC, 1987, Type Dir. Club, NYC, 1989-94, merit award Art Dir. Club, NYC, 1991, 94; inducted, Bata Phi Mu, libr. hon. soc., 2003 Mem.: Beta Phi Mu. Avocations: writing, drawing. Home and Office: 20 Henry St Apt 5E Brooklyn NY 11201-1348

KEMP, JOHN RANDOLPH, journalist, author; b. New Orleans, Feb. 6, 1945; s. Frank LaGrange and Eileen Moira (O'Brien) K.; m. Elizabeth Ruth Earhart, June 15, 1968; 1 child, Virginia Elizabeth Cabell. BA, Loyola U., New Orleans, 1968; MA, U. So. Miss., 1973; postgrad., La. State U., 1975-77. Chief curator La. State Mus., New Orleans, 1972-78; journalist The Times-Picayune, New Orleans, 1978-83, contbg. art critic, 1984-97; freelance writer Covington, La., 1983—; dir. univ. rels. Southeastern La. U., Hammond, 1983-97; assoc. commr. for comm. La. Bd. Regents, 1997—2002; assoc. dir. La. Endowment for the Humanities, 2002—. Art critic Sta. WYES-TV, New Orleans, 1987—; co-founder New Orleans Writers Conf., 1989. Author: Martin Behrman of New Orleans: Memoirs of a City Boss, 1977, New Orleans: An Illustrated History, 1981, rev. edit., 1997, Lewis Hine: Photographs of Child Labor in the New South, 1986, Manchac Swamp: Louisiana's Undiscovered Wilderness, 1996; co-editor: Louisiana Images, 1880-1920: A Photographic Essay by George Francois Mugnier, 1975, Louisiana's Black Heritage, 1978, Alan Flattmann's French Quarter Impressions, 2002; contbr. articles to numerous nat. and regional mags. and publs., 1983—, articles to ann. Fodor guidebooks, 1984—, Time Out Guides, London, 1998—. Pres. Northlake Mus. and Nature Ctr., Covington, La., 1984-85; bd. dirs. Christ Episcopal Sch., Covington, 1986-89; mem. adv. bd. New Orleans Tennessee Williams Literary Festival, 1992—. Fellow Nat. Trust and Williamsburg Foundn.'s Summer Inst. for Hist. Adminstrn.; grantee NEH and Nat. Endowment for the Arts. Mem.: New Orleans Big Easy Entertainment (awards nominating com.), La. Higher Edn. Pub. Rels. Assn. (pres. 1991—93), Am. Coun. on Edn.'s Commn. on Govt. and Pub. Affairs, Am. Assn. State Colls. and Univs. (com. mem. Washington 1990—), Coun. Advancement and Support Edn. (trustee 2001—04, chmn. nat. commn. on comm. 2001—04, bd. dirs. dist. IV 1989—90, 1993—95, nat. commn. on comm. 1997—2000, numerous awards 1984—), Baton Rouge Press Club, New Orleans Press Club. Avocations: photography, travel. Home: 401 W 24th Ave Covington LA 70433-2513 Office: La Endowment for Humanities 938 Lafayette St Ste 300 New Orleans LA 70113-

KEMP, KARL THOMAS, insurance company executive; b. Petoskey, Mich., Dec. 16, 1940; s. Vernon L. and Dorothy Jean (Olson) K.; m. Mary Ormston Graham, July 21, 1973; children: Karl Thomas Jr., John Walter, James Edward. BA, Harvard U., 1964. V.p. corp. fin. GEICO Corp., Washington, 1966-81; sr. v.p., pres. Resolute Reins. Co., N.Y.C., 1981-90; pres., CEO White Mountains Ins. Group, Ltd., Hanover, N.H., 1997—. Bd. dirs. Folksamerica Holdings, Inc., N.Y.C., chair Human Resources Com., 1996—; bd. dirs. FSA Holdings, N.Y.C., chair human resources com., 1994—; bd. dirs. Eldorado Bancshares, Inc., Calif., chair human resources com., 1996—; bd. dirs. Main St. Am. Holdings, Keane, N.Y., exec. com., 1994—; pres., CEO White Mountain Holdings, Inc., Hanover, 1994—; bd. dirs. Amlin, plc., London. Mem. Am. Bonanza Soc., Aircraft Owners and Pilots Assn., Harvard Club (N.Y.C., Vt., N.H.). Avocation: flying. Home: 6 Goodfellow Rd Hanover NH 03755-4800 Office: White Mountains Ins Group Ltd 28 Gates St White River Junction VT 05001

KEMP, KATHLEEN NAGY, lawyer; b. McKeesport, Pa., Mar. 29, 1949; d. Homer Edward and Jeanne Eileen (Wunder) Nagy; m. K. Lawrence Kemp, May 30, 1970 (div.); children: Paul Gregory, Carolyn Elaine. BS, U. Pitts., 1971, JD, 1981. Bar: Pa. 1981, U.S. Dist. Ct. (we. dist.) Pa. 1981, U.S. Ct. Appeals (3rd cir.) 1986, U.S. Tax Ct. 1986, U.S. Supreme Ct. 1986. Ptnr. Kemp & Kemp, New Kensington, Pa., 1982-95; pvt. practice Murrysville, Pa., 1995—2002, Laurel Legal Svcs., Inc., Greensburg, Pa., 2002—. Bd. dirs. Westmoreland

Casemgmt. and Svcs. Inc., treas., 2002. Pres. New Kensington chpt. NOW, 1973; bd. dirs. Easter Seal Soc., New Kensington, 1982; bd. dirs., chmn. Alle-Kiski Symphony, New Kensington, 1989; chmn. Citizen Adv. Bd. Mental Health/Mental Retardation Ctr., New Kensington, 1983; chmn. Official Com. YMCA swim team parents group, 1990; mem. adv. com. Municipality Murrysville Cable Access Channel, 1997-2002; bd. dirs. Mental Health Assn. Westmoreland County, 2001—; sec. bd. dirs. Associated Lutheran Missions, Inc, 2002-03. Mem. Westmoreland Bar Assn. (membership com.), Mental Health Assn. Westmoreland County (bd. dirs. 2001—), Allegheny Mountain YMCA Master's Swimming Assn. (sec. 1997-99, YMCA Master's Swimming Nat. Champion 1995), New Kensington Area C. of C. (bd. dirs. 1990-95), East Suburban C. of C. (bd. dirs. 1996-98). Avocations: reading, swimming, needle-work. Home: 1946 Pennsylvania Ave West Mifflin PA 15122 E-mail: kkemp@wpalaw.org.

KEMP, KENNETH OMER, writer, lawyer; b. San Diego, May 9, 1955; s. Omer Carroll and Virginia (Tensmeyer) Kemp. AA, Grossmont Jr. Coll., 1974; BA, Brigham Young U., 1980, JD, 1984. Bar: Calif. 85, Utah 92. Writer, San Diego, 1987—. Writer, dir. : (films) Wildest Dreams; Fedora, 1995 (Golden Eagle award, Coun. on Internat. Non-Theatrical Events, 95, Best of Fest award Breckenridge Film Festival, 95, Silver Apple award, Nat. Ednl. Media Network, 96, Movies on a Shoestring award Rochester Film Festival, 96, Togetherness award Family Film Festival, 99, Children's Choice award ALA, 00); co-author (with David Scheerer): (screenplays) Full Circle, 1998; co-author: (with Robert Rees) Crucifixion of Innocents, 1990, Past Perfect, 1991; author, pub.: I Hated Heaven, 1998, Dad Was A Carpenter, 1999 (Grand prize Nat. Self-Published Book Awards, 99, Best Non-Fiction Audiobook award Ind. Pub.'s Assn., 99); author: (screenplays) Download, 1988, I Hated Heaven, 2001, American Scarlet, City on a Hill, 2004. E-mail: kk@kennykemp.com.

KEMP, LORETTA CHRISTINE, human services administrator; d. John Elmer and Valarie Lydia Bruce; m. Jesse Bernard Kemp, Aug. 15, 1970; 1 child, Joel Bernard. BA cum laude, U. Pitts., 1969, MA in Tchg., 1970. Tchr. Pitts. Pub. Schs., 1970—74; tchr., counselor, supr., divsn. dir., dir. ops. Pitts. Opportunities Industrialization Ctr., Inc., 1974—83; rsch. asst. U. Pitts., 1994—97; lead paint edn. coord. Tri-City Cmty. Action Program, Inc., Malden, Mass., 1990—99, dep. dir., 1999—. Mem. Malden-Everett (Mass.) Family Network Coun.; facilitator Tri-City Workforce Devel. Task Force, Malden, 2000—, Cmty. Tech. Access Coalition, Malden, 2000—; mem. Everett Cmty. Partnerships for Children, 2000—; exec. and needs assemssment com. Medford Health Matters, 2000—; needs assessment and strategic planning com. Cmty. Planning Com. Adult Basic Edn. Svcs., 2001—; mem. Malden Asian Disability Advocacy Coalition, 2002—; Asian new yr. com. Malden Asian Pacific Am. Coalition, 2003—. Chairperson region II consortium Healthy Start, Inc., Pitts., 1993—97; founder landscape arch. project Hill Dist. Consensus Group, Pitts., 1995—97; co-founder African Am. Ctr. Advanced Studies' Coun., Pitts., 1990; chairperson Youth Fair Chance, Pitts., 1994—97. Avocations: reading, music. Office: Tri-City Cmty Action Program Inc 110 Pleasant St Malden MA 02148 Personal E-mail: lkemp@tri-cap.org. E-mail: lkemp@tri-cap.org.

KEMP, ROBERT GRANT, biochemist, educator; b. Massillon, Ohio, Feb. 12, 1937; s. Arthur H. Kemp, Evelyn A. Kemp; m. Judith W. Shimberg; children: Suzanne Mynard, Kathryn Guylay, Joanna Shimberg, Jessica Shimberg; m. Marilyn Baranowski (div. Apr. 1, 1983). BA, Coll. Wooster, 1959; PhD, Yale U., 1964. Prof. Med. Coll. Wis., Milw., 1966—76, Chgo. Med. Sch., North Chicago, Ill., 1976—, dept. chmn., 1976—89. Mem. rsch. com. Leukemia Rsch. Found., Chgo., 1982—86; mem. NIH Study Sect., Bethesda, Md.; bd. dirs. Schweppe Found., Chgo.; mem. USMLE Step I Test Com., Phila., 2000—. Author: Biochemical Problems and Calculations, 1975; contbr. articles to scientific jours.; mem. editl. bd.: Jour. Cyclic Nucleotide Rsch., 1971—78, Jour. Biol. Chem., 1990—2000. Fellow, NIH, 1961—63, U. Wash., Seattle, 1964—66, Wash. State Heart Assn., 1965—66, Fulbright Found., 1971. Mem.: AHA (investigator 1968—73), ASBMB (mem. com. 1986—88), AAAS, Am. Soc. Biochemistry and Molecular Biology. Office: The Chgo Med Sch 3333 Green Bay Rd North Chicago IL 60064 Office Fax: 847-578-3240. Business E-Mail: kempr@finchcms.edu.

KEMP, ROGER LARK, city manager, writer; b. St. Paul, Minn., Aug. 1, 1946; s. Charles Woodrow and Eva Audrey Kemp; life ptnr. Jill Kemp, Nov. 16, 1974; 1 child, Jonathan David. BS, San Diego State Univ., 1972, MPA, 1974; PhD, Golden Gate Univ., San Francisco, 1979, MBA, 1984. City mgr. Seaside, Seaside, Calif., 1979—83, City of Placentia, Calif., 1983—88, City of Clifton, NJ, 1988—93, City of Meriden, Conn., 1993—. Editl. adv. bd. MacMillan Pub. Co., New York, NY, 1996, ABC-CLIO, Santa Barbara, Calif., 1997, Internat. City Mgr. Assn., Washington, 1998. Author: (book) Coping with Proposition 13, Managing America's Cities, Inner City Renewal. Mem. Meriden Econ. Devel. Corp., Meriden, Conn., 1993, Wallingford Recycling Project, Wallingford, Conn., 1994, Regional Coun. of Governments, North Haven, Conn., 2002; mem., site visit team Nat. Assn. of Schools of Pub. Affairs & Admin., Washington, 1996. Yn2, 1966—70. Mem.: City Mgmt. Assn., Conn. chapt. (v.p. 2001—02), Am. Soc. for Pub. Admin., Conn. Chapt. (pres. 1999—2002). Achievements include patents for Cutback Management Process/Flow Chart, 1980. Avocations: walking, biking, hiking, editing. Home: 421 Brownstone Ridge Meriden CT 06451-3627 Office: City Hall 142 East Main Street Meriden CT 06450-560 Personal E-mail: rlkbsr@snet.net.

KEMP, ROLAND CONNOR, lawyer; b. Dallas, May 29, 1943; s. William Thomas and Martha Belle (Arney) K.; m. Carol Ann DeRosa, Dec. 12, 1966 (div. Oct. 13, 1989); children: Thomas Roland, Patrick Michael. BA, Baylor U., 1965, postgrad., 1966; JD, U. Tex., 1972. Bar: Tex. 1972, U.S. Dist. Ct. (so. dist.) Tex. 1973, U.S. Dist. Ct. (we. dist.) Tex. 1973, U.S. Ct. Appeals (5th cir.) 1973, U.S. Supreme Ct. 1977. Law clk. U.S. Dist Ct. So. Dist. Tex., Houston, 1972-74; assoc. Schlanger, Cook, Cohn & Mills, Houston, 1974-76, Fred Parks & Assocs., Houston, 1977-80; sole practice Houston, 1980-87; ptnr. Henderson & Kemp, Houston, 1988—. Chmn. bd. dirs. Timberlane Mcpl. Utility Dist., Harris County, Tex., 1973. Served to capt. USAF, 1966-70. Mem. State Bar Tex., Houston Bar Assn., Phi Delta Phi. Office: PO Box 90775 Houston TX 77290-0775

KEMP, SARAH (SALLY LEECH), developmental psychologist, neuropsychologist; b. Bryn Mawr, Pa., Sept. 13, 1940; d. Thomas Bailey and Mary Elizabeth (Veasey) Leech; m. G. Philip Fritz, June 18, 1960 (dec. May 1968); 1 child, Mary Elizabeth Fritz Fitch; m. Garry Colquhoun Kemp, July 25, 1970; children: Sarah K., Hannah Middlebrook. BA, Calif. State U., Sacramento, 1963; MA, U. Tulsa, 1970; EdM, Columbia U., 1989, PhD, 1991. Tchr., counselor, psychometrist, various cities, 1968-85; program asst. for neuroscience and edn. program Tchrs. Coll., Columbia U., 1985-88; neurodevelopmental specialist Tulsa Devel. Pediatrics and Ctr. for Family Psychology, 1988—, ptnr., 1991; developmental psychologist Tulsa, 1990—. Instr. ednl. and devel. neuroscience Tchrs. Coll., Columbia U., fall 1987, summer 1988; adj. asst. prof. pediatrics U. Okla. Med. Sch., Tulsa, 1991—; pres. Neuropsychoednl. Svc. PC; presenter in field. Author (with Ursula Kirk and Marit Korkman): NEPSY, a Developmental Neuropsychological Assessment, 1998, The Essentials of NEPSY, 2000. Lector Trinity Episc. Ch., 1990—; bd. dirs. Magic Empire coun. Girl Scouts U.S.A., 1993—2000. Mem. Internat. Neuropsychological Soc., Assn. for Children and Adults With Learning Difficulties, Rodin Remediation Soc. Episcopalian. Achievements include neuropsychological test development and research on attention deficit disorder, autism, and school-related problems. Office: Tulsa Devel Pediatrics 4520 S Harvard Ave Ste 200B Tulsa OK 74135-2919

KEMP, SHAWN T. professional basketball player; b. Elkhart, Ind., Nov. 26, 1969; Student, U. Ky., Trinity Valley C.C., 1988—89. Basketball player Seattle Supersonics, 1989—97; forward Cleve. Cavaliers, 1997. Mem. Dream Team II, 1994. Named to NBA All-Star team, 1993, All-NBA 2d team, 1994. Office: Portland Trailblazers Rose Quarter One Center Court Portland OR 97227

KEMP, STEPHEN FRANK, pediatric endocrinologist, educator, composer; b. Newport, Oreg., Mar. 21, 1947; s. Frank Shirley and Charla Mae (Wait) Kemp. BA, U. Oreg., 1969; PhD in Biochemistry, U. Chgo., 1974, MD, 1976. Diplomate Am. Bd. Pediat. Intern Stanford U., 1976-77, resident in pediat., 1977-78, fellow in pediat. endocrinology, 1978-80; asst. prof. pediat., chief pediat. endocrinology U. South Ala., Mobile, 1980-84; ast. prof. pediat. U. Ark. for Med. Sci., 1984-86, asst. prof. biochemistry, 1985-95, assoc. prof. pediat., 1986-95, chief pediat. endocrinology, 1987—2001, prof. pediat., 1995—. Composer (various choir, organ and orchestral works) ; contbr. V.p. Ala. affiliate Am. Diabetes Assn., 1982—84, pres., 1986—88, chmn. youth com. Ark. affiliate, mem. camp com.; bd. dirs. Human Growth Found., v.p., 1999—2000, pres., 2000—. Recipient Postdoctoral Nat. Rsch. Svc. award, NIH, 1978—80. Fellow: Am. Coll. Endocrinology; mem.: Med. Assn. State Ala., So. soc. Pediat. Soc., Endocrine Soc., Am. Fedn. Clin. Rsch., Am. Pediat. Soc. Democrat. Episcopalian. Home: 8 Victoria Cir Maumelle AR 72113-6423 Office: U Ark for Med Sci Dept Pediatrics 800 Marshall St Little Rock AR 72202-3510 E-mail: kempstephenf@uams.edu.

KEMP, STEPHEN FREDERICK, physician; b. Richmond, Va., Dec. 30, 1960; BA, Duke U., 1983; BS, Va. Commonwealth U., 1986; MD, Med. Coll. Va., 1990. Diplomate in allergy and immunology and in clin. and lab. immunology Am. Bd. Allergy and Immunology; diplomate Am. Bd. Internal Medicine, Nat. Bd. Med. Examiners. Aide Fairfield Br. County of Henrico Pub. Libr., Richmond, Va., 1979; clk. emergency dept. Richmond Meml. Hosp., 1984-88; clk. hosp. learning resource ctr. Med. Coll. of Va. Hosps., 1987-88; resident physician dept. internal medicine U. Tenn. Coll. Medicine, Memphis, 1990-93; advanced subsplty. resident divsn. allergy immunology dept. internal medicine U. South Fla., Tampa, 1993-95, advanced subsplty. resident clin. lab. immunology divsn., 1995-96; asst. prof. medicine and pediats. divsn. divsn. allergy and immunology, depts. internal medicine and pediats. U. South Ala., Mobile, 1996-97; asst. prof. pediat. U. Miss. Med. Ctr., 1998—, asst. prof. medicine, 1998—2003, assoc. prof. medicine, 2003—, med. co-dir. adult asthma svcs. Pharm. Care Clinic, 1998—; chmn. performance improvement com. Dept. Medicine, 2001—; chief allergy and immunology sect. VA Med. Ctr., Jackson, 1998-99, cons., 1999—. Physician participant Am. Acad. Immunology Health Policy Edn. Network, 1993—96; fee-basis physician allergic and immunologic evaluations Vets. Compensation and Pension Clinic, James A. Haley Vet. Hosp., Tampa, 1994—96, fee-basis physician gen. med. evaluations, 1994—96; asst. collection and analysis of air pollen samples Hillsborough County, 1993—94, chief analyst collection and microscopic analysis of air pollen sample, 1994—96; facilitator, educator U. Ill. Coll. Medicine, Rockford, 1999. Editor allergy and immunology sect., CME, So. Med. Assn., 1997-99; contbg. editor Jour. Investigational Allergology and Clin. Immunology, 2000—; editor, co-editor 2 allergy-immunology books, author, co-author, editor, co editor more than 50 rsch. papers, editls., book chpts., Internet CME articles, audiotapes, and abstracts; rsch. co-investigator in more than 40 pharm. and clin. trials. Physician vol. asthma and allergy sect. Judeo-Christian (Free) Health Clinic, Tampa, 1994—96; influenza vaccine adminstrn. for men's and women's basketball teams U. South Fla., Tampa, 1993; cardiac emergency med. tech. Henrico Vol. Rescue Squad, Richmond, 1982—88, Tuckahoe Vol. Rescue Squad, Richmond, 1988. Fellow: Am. Coll. Allergy, Asthma and Immunology (editl. bd. 1997—2002, anaphylaxis com. 2003—, insect hypersensitivity com. 2000—), Am. Acad. Allergy, Asthma and Immunology (aerobiology com. 1995—98, anaphylaxis com. 1995—, chmn. anaphylaxis com. 2003—, vice chmn. anaphylaxis com. 2001—03, immunotherapy com. 2002—, adverse reactions to foods com. 1995—2002, urticaria and angioedema com. 1995), ACP-Am. Soc. Internal Medicine; mem.: AMA, So. Soc. Clin. Investigation, Ctrl. Med. Soc., Am. Lung Assn., European Acad. Allergology and Clin. Immunology (affiliate), Joint Coun. Allergy, Asthma and Immunology, Miss. State Med. Assn., Am. Fedn. Med. Rsch. (councilor So. sect. 2001—02), Phi Sigma, Phi Kappa Phi, Omicron Delta Kappa (charter). Avocations: golf, bowling, soccer, hiking, painting miniature figures. Office: U Miss Med Ctr Dept Medicine Divsn Allergy & Immunology 2500 N State St Jackson MS 39216-4500

KEMP, SUZANNE LEPPART, elementary education educator, clubwoman; b. N.Y.C., Dec. 28, 1929; d. John Culver and Eleanor (Buxton) Leppart; m. Ralph Clinton Kemp, Apr. 4, 1953; children— Valerie Gale, Sandra Lynn, John Maynard, Renee Alison. Grad. Ogontz Jr. Coll., 1949; B.S., U. Md., 1952. Elem. sch. tchr. Mem. Nat. Soc. Women Descs. of Ancient and Hon. Arty. Co., Nat. Soc. Daus. of Founders and Patriots of Am. (corr. sec.), Nat. Soc. Sons and Daus. of Pilgrims, Nat. Soc. U.S. Daus. of 1812 (chpt. organizing Md. state pres. 1977-79, chpt. v.p 1979—), Nat. Soc. New Eng. Women (colony pres. 1978-80, Nat. Soc. Colonial Dames XVII Century (state chmn. heraldry and coats of arms 1977-79), Nat. Soc. D.A.R. (chpt. regent 1970-73, chpt. v.p., Md. soc. chmn. transp. 1976-79), Md. State Officers Club, Md. Hist. Soc., Friends of Animals, Defenders of Animal Rights Inc., U. Md. Alumni, English Speaking Union, Star Spangled Banner Flag House Assn., Potter-Balt. Clayworks, Balt. Mus. Art, Walters Art Gallery, Dames of the Court of Honor, Kappa Delta Alumni. Clubs: Baltimore Country; Lago Mar (Ft. Lauderdale, Fla.); Roland Park Women's; Woodbrook-Murray Hill Garden Club, Federation Garden Clubs. Editor; The Spinning Wheel, 1973-76. Home: 7 Ruxton Green Ct Baltimore MD 21204-3548

KEMP, THOMAS JOSEPH, retired electronics company executive; b. Holy Cross, Iowa, Aug. 17, 1943; s. Joseph Peter and Margaret Gertrude (Wilgenbusch) K.; m. Ruth Anne Pfohl, Aug. 22, 1964; children: Geoffrey Joseph, Jennifer Anne, Julie Marie, Jack Thomas. BA in Bus. Acctg., Loras Coll., 1964; MS in Sys. Mgmt., St. Mary's U., San Antonio, 1978. Commd. 2d lt. USAF, 1964, advanced through grades to lt. col., 1980, pilot, mgr., 1964-85; ret., 1985; Instructional systems design mgr., dep. program mgr. United Airlines Svcs. Corp., Irving, Tex., 1985-87; divsn. mgr., project mgr. Flight Safety Svcs. Corp., Irving, 1987-90; program mgr. ElectroCom Automation, Arlington, Tex., 1990—2002; mgr. Integrated Logistics Support Siemens Dematic, Arlington, 1997—2002. Congl. advisor Vets. and Budget Com., Ft. Worth, 1994—; pres. Tarrant County Vets. Coun., Ft. Worth, 1995-96. Mem. VFW (life), Mil. Officers Assn. Am. (life), Air Force Assn. (life, state pres. Tex. 1995-97, nat. v.p. 1998-99, nat. dir. 2000—, exec. com. 2000—, Texoma region pres. 1999-2000, Exceptional Svc. award 1990, 91, 94, Presdl. citation 2000, Mem. of Yr. 2002), Am. Legion, KC (Grand Knight 2003—, Knight of Month and Family of Month awards). Republican. Roman Catholic. Avocations: fishing, golf, gardening. Home: 3608 Kimberly Ln Fort Worth TX 76133-2147 E-mail: tjkafatx@flash.net.

KEMPA, GERALD, manufacturing company executive; b. Chgo., Sept. 24, 1934; s. Stanley John and Mary (Michalek) Kempa; m. Annette Marie Valentino, Sept. 3, 1960; children: Gerald, Amanda, Leslie Anne. BS, No. Ill. U., 1958, MS, 1960. Sales rep. Adams Corp. divsn. Beatrice Foods, N.Y.C., 1960-63, regional sales mgr., 1963-65, v.p. mktg. Beloit, Wis., 1965-70; pres. Treat Potato Chip Co. divsn. Beatrice Foods, Riverhead, N.Y., 1970-74, Beatrice Frosted Foods divsn. Beatrice Foods, L.I. City, N.Y., 1974-80; v.p. sales and mktg. Carey-McFall Corp., Montgomery, Pa., 1981-86, sr. v.p., 1986—, also bd. dirs.; pres. GK Assocs., 1993. Pres GK Assocs, Manhasset, NY, 1993. Mem.: Am Window Coverings Mfrs Asn (trustee 1986—88). Roman Catholic. Home: Apt 202 400 E 70th St New York NY 10021 Office: Carey McFall Corp 104 W 40th St New York NY 10018-3617

KEMPE, FREDERICK SCHUMANN, newspaper editor, columnist, author; b. Salt Lake City, Sept. 5, 1954; s. Fritz Gustav and Johanna Irmgardt (Schumann) K. BA in Comm. magna cum laude, U. Utah, 1976; MA in journalism, Columbia U., 1977; LLD (hon.), U. Md., 1995; HD (hon.), Queen Coll., 1999; LHD (hon.), Queens Coll., 1999. Frankfurt corr. AP-Dow Jones, Germany, 1978-79; Bonn corr. Newsweek, Germany, 1979-81; London corr. The Wall St. Jour. (USA), 1981-84, Vienna bureau chief, 1984-86, chief diplomatic corr., 1986-89; founder, mng. editor Cen. European Econ. Rev., 1993-94, editor, 1995-96; mng. editor Wall St. Jour. Europe, Brussels, 1992-96, editor, assoc. publ., 1998—. Author: Divorcing the Dictator: America's Bungled Affair with Noriega, 1990, Siberian Odyssey: A Voyage Into the Russian Soul, 1992, Father/Land: A Personal Search for the New Germany, 1999. Bd. dirs. Aspen Inst. Berlin, Am. Inst. for Contemporary German Studies, Washington, Economia, Prague, Czech Republic. Recipient Quentus Wilson award U. Utah, 1987, Alumni Achievement award Columbia U. Grad. Sch. Journalism, 2002; named Top Young Alumnus of Yr. U. Utah, 1987. Mem. Coun. Fgn. Rels. Office: Wall Street Jour Europe Blvd Brand Whitlock 87 1200 Brussels Belgium E-mail: fred.kempe@wsj.com.

KEMPE, LUDWIG GEORGE, neurological surgeon; b. Prenzlau, Germany, Oct. 16, 1915; came to U.S., 1946; s. George Joseph and Maria Theresa (Koustantin) K.; m. Czenta Groll, Dec. 23, 1955 (dec. March 20, 1996); m. Louise Goin. MA, Konigsberg Coll., Fed. Republic of Germany, 1936; MD, U. Berne, Switzerland, 1942. Diplomate Am. Bd. Neurol. Surgery. Commd. 2d lt. U.S. Army, 1951, advanced through grades to col., 1965, ret., 1974; instr. Neuroanatomy U. Berne, Switzerland, 1940-41; chief surgeon U.S. Air Command, Arctic, 1951-52; asst. surgeon US Army, Ft. Dix, N.J., 1952-64; chief neurosurgery Walter Reed Meml. Hosp., Washington, 1964-73; ret. U.S. Army, 1974; prof. Neurosurgery U. S. C. Med. Sch., Charleston, S.C., 1974-84; Georgetown U., Washington, 1980-84. Assoc. prof. George Washington U., Washington, 1964-73; rsch. prof. Anatomy U.S.C., Charleston, 1974-84; cons. Neurosurgery Sugeon Gen. U.S. Army, Washington, 1965-73, chmn., dir. tng. program Neurosurgery, Neurolog. Rsch., Walter Reed Hosp., 1963-73. Author Operative Neurosurgery, 1970, 75, 81, 86; editor 3 neurology jours.; contbr. numerous articles to profl. jours. Col. U.S. Army, 1951-74. Decorated with Legion of Merit (2 oak leaf clusters) U.S. Army, Washington, 1965, '69, 74, Order of Dumas, Govt. of Brazil, 1969, Great Cross of Merit, Fed. Republic of Germany, 1975. Fellow Am. Coll. Surgery; mem. (sr.) Am. Assn. of Neurol. Surgeons, Congress of Neurol. Surgeons, Soc. of Neurol. Surgeons, Military Surgeons U.S.A.; (hon.) German Soc. Neurol. Surgeons, Yugoslav Soc. Neurol. Surgeons; Am. Anatomic Soc. Avocations: med. illustrations, computer graphics, history, ornithology. Home: 12 Valley View Dr Pisgah Forest NC 28768-9509

KEMPE, ROBERT ARON, venture management executive; b. Mpls., Mar. 6, 1922; s. Walter A. and Madge (Stoker) K.; m. Virginia Lou Wiseman, June 21, 1946; children: Mark A., Katherine A. BS in Chem. Engring., U. Minn., 1943; postgrad. metallurgy, bus. adminstrn., Case Western Res. U., 1946-49. Various positions TRW, Inc., Cleve., 1946-49, div. sales mgr., 1953; v.p. Metalphoto Corp., Cleve., 1954-63, pres., 1963-71, Allied Decals, Inc., affil., Cleve., 1963-68; v.p., treas. Horizons Rsch. Inc., 1970-71; pres. Reuter-Stokes, Inc. (now subs. of GE Co.), 1971-87, Kempe Everest Ltd., Hudson, Ohio, 1987—; assoc. Paul Williams & Assocs., Medina, Ohio, 1987—. Bd. dirs. Bicron Corp., 1987-90, TGM Detectors, Inc., 1988-92, Chagrin Valley Enterprises. Contbr. articles to profl. jours. Lt. (j.g.) USNR, 1944-46, PTO. Mem. Am. Nuclear Soc. (exec. officer, past chmn. No. Ohio sect.), Am. Soc. Metals, Am. Chem. Soc., OHIO Citizens Adv. Coun. on Radiological Safety, Chemists Club (N.Y.C.), Country Club of Hudson, Sigma Chi. Achievements include patents in Method of and Apparatus for Making Poppet Valves, Method of making Hollow Valves, Method of Making Hollow Castings, Method of Coating of Molybdenum Articles; vitreous coated refractory metals, method for producing the same and vitreous enamel composition, coated refractory body, aluminum plate with plural images and method of making same, process for developing photosensitized anodized aluminum plates. Home: 244 E Streetsboro St Hudson OH 44236-3474 Office: Kempe Everest Ltd 10 W Streetsboro St Hudson OH 44236-2850 Fax: 1-877-471-6005. E-mail: kempe@alltel.net.

KEMPER, CHRISTINA, small business owner, respiratory therapist, elementary educator; b. St. Louis, Feb. 16, 1952; d. Edward James and Norma Helen (Renner) K.; m. Don Eichholz, Dec. 23, 1972 (div. Apr. 1994); children: Cheri L., Derek V. BS in Edn., U. Mo., St. Louis, 1976, MA in Polit. Sci., 1980; AA in Respiratory Therapy, Maryville U., 1983. Registered respiratory therapist. Staff therapist respiratory care various hosps., St. Louis, 1974—. Tchr. Parish Sch. Religion, St. Joseph's Ch., Manchester, Mo.; leader Girl Scouts Am., St. Louis. Mem. NOW (treas.), Am. Assn. for Respiratory Care, Nat. Bd. for Respiratory Care, Kappa Delta Pi. Avocations: floral designing, reading, interior decorating. Home: 12930 Twin Meadow Ct Creve Coeur MO 63146-180[illegible] E-mail: christiekemper@yahoo.com.

KEMPER, DAVID WOODS, II, banker; b. Kansas City, Mo., Nov. 20, 1950; s. James Madison and Mildred (Lane) K.; m. Dorothy Ann Jannarone, Sept. 6, 1975; children: John W., Elizabeth C., Catherine B., William L. BA cum laude Harvard U., 1972; MA in English Lit., Oxford, Worcester Coll., 1974; MBA Stanford U., 1976. With Morgan Guaranty Trust Co., N.Y.C., 1975-78; v.p. Commerce Bank of Kansas City, Mo., 1978-79, sr. v.p., 1980-81; pres. Commerce Bancshares, Inc., 1982-86, pres., ceo, 1986-91, chmn., pres., ceo 1991—; also dir. Commerce Bancshares, Inc; chmn. Commerce Bank N.A., St. Louis, 1985—. Bd. dirs. Kansas City, Tower Properties, Kansas City, Ralcorp Holdings, Inc. Contbr. articles on banking to profl. jours. Trustee Mo. Bot. Garden, Washington U., Donald Danforth Plant Sci. Ctr. Mem. Acad. Arts and Scis., Fin. Svcs. Roundtable, Kansas City Country Club, River Club (Kansas City), St. Louis Club, St. Louis Country Club, Racquet Club, Old Warson Country Club (St. Louis). Office: Commerce Bancshares Inc 8000 Forsyth Blvd Clayton MO 63105

KEMPER, DONNA MAE, artist, illustrator; b. Almont, Mich., Aug. 1, 1954; d. Orville Henry and Josephine (Kramer) Williams; m. John Michael Kemper, June 14, 1986. BS in Fine Art & Psychology, Grand Valley State U., 1982; apprenticeship Larry Blovits PSA, Grand Rapids, Mich., 1984-87. Artist Kemper Art Studio, Grand Rapids, 1983—. Finalist landscape comp. Artist's Mag., 1991, 98; Pastel Soc. Am. scholar. Mem.: Am. Artist Profl. League. Avocations: martial arts, tai chi, Kung Fu, gardening. Office: Kemper Studio PO Box 2045 Grand Rapids MI 49501-2045 E-mail: dmkemperstudio@i2k.com.

KEMPER, DORLA DEAN EATON (DORLA DEAN EATON), real estate broker; b. Calhoun, Mo., Sept. 10, 1929; d. Paul McVay and Jesse Le[illegible] (McCombs) Eaton; m. Charles K. Kemper, Mar. 1, 1951; children: Kevin Kei[illegible], Kara Lee. BS in Edn., Ctrl. Mo. State U., 1952. Tchr. pub. schs., Twin Falls, Idaho, 1950-51, Mission, Kans., 1952-53, Burbank, Calif., 1953-57; real estate sales, 1967-68, 1971-73, Deanie Kemper, Inc. Real Estate Brokerage, Loomis, Calif., 1974-76, pres., 1976-91; sr. couns. Capital holdong Corp., Louisville, 1991-93. Pres. Battle Creek Park Elem. Sch. PTA, St. Paul, 1966-67; mem. Placer County (Calif.) Bicentennial Commn., 1976; mem. Sierra Coll. Adv. Com., 1981—; active Placer County Hist. Soc. Named to Million Dollar Club (lifetime) Sacramento and Placer County bds. Realtors, 1978-94; designate Grad. Realtors Inst., Cert. Residential Specialist. Mem. Nat. Assn. Realtors, Calif. Assn. Realtors, Nat. Assn. Real Estate Appraisers, Placer County (mem. profl. stds. com.), Bds. Realtors, DAR (chpt. regent 1971-73, organizing chpt. regent 1977—, dist. dir. 1978-80, state registrar Calif. 1980-82, state vice regent 1982-84, state regent 1984-86, nat. resolutions com., nat. rec. sec. gen. 1986-89, nat. chmn. units overseas 1983-86, nat. pres. gen. 1995-98, hon. nat. pres. gen. 1998—, nat. chmn. WWII Meml. Campaign 1998-2001), Nat. Gavel Soc., Dau. Am. Colonists, Colonial Dames Am., Internat. Platform Assn., Hidden Valley Women's (pres. Loomis club 1970-71), Auburn Travel Study (pres. 1979). Republican. Home: 8165 Morningside Dr Granite Bay CA 95746-8163

KEMPER, JAMES DEE, lawyer; b. Olney, Ill., Feb. 23, 1947; s. Jack O. and Vivian L. Kemper; m. Diana J. Deig, June 1, 1968; children: Judd, Jason. BS, Ind. U., 1969, JD summa cum laude, 1971. Bar: Ind. 1971. Law clk. U.S. Ct. Appeals (7th cir.), Chgo., 1971-72; mng. ptnr. Ice Miller, Indpls., 1972—. Note editor Ind. U. Law Rev., 1970-71; contbr. articles to profl. jours. Past officer, bd. dirs. Marion County Assn. for Retarded Citizens, Inc., Indpls.; past bd. dir. Cen. Ind. Easter Seal Soc., Indpls., Crossroads Rehab. Ctr., Inc, Indpls.; pres. bd. govs. Orchard Country Day Sch., Indpls.; mem. bd. Eiteljorg Mus. Native Americans, Butler U. Fellow Ind. Bar Found.; mem. ABA (employee benefit com.), Ind. Bar Assn., The Group, Inc., Midwest Pension Conf., U.S. C. of C. (employee benefit com.), Stanley K. Lacy Leadership Alumni. Office: Ice Miller 1 American Sq Indianapolis IN 46282-0020

KEMPER, JOHN DUSTIN, mechanical engineering educator; b. Portland, Oreg., May 29, 1924; s. Clay Wallace and Leona Bell (Landis) K.; m. Barbara Jeanne Lane, June 28, 1947; 1 dau., Kathleen Lynne. BS, UCLA, 1949, MS, 1959; PhD, U. Colo., 1969. Chief mech. engr. Telecomputing Corp., North Hollywood, Calif., 1949-55, H.A. Wagner Co., Van Nuys, Calif., 1955-56; v.p. engring. Marchant div. SCM Corp., Oakland, Calif., 1956-62; faculty U. Calif. Davis, 1962-91, prof. engring., 1967-91, dean coll. Engring., 1969-83, ret. 1991. Panel chmn. Engring. Grad. Edn. and Research, NRC, 1985. Author Engineers and Their Profession, 1967, 5th edit., 2001, Introduction to the Engineering Profession, 1985, 2d edit., 1993, (with G.C. Andrews) Canadian Professional Engineering Practice and Ethics, 1992, Birding Northern California, 1999, Southern Oregon's Bird Life, 2002. Served with USAF, 1944-4[illegible] Fellow ASME (chmn. San Francisco sect. 1962-63), AAAS; mem. Am. Soc. Engring. Edn. Achievements include having engineering building on University of California-Davis campus named after him.

:MPER, JONATHAN MCBRIDE, banker; b. Kansas City, Mo., July 23, 53; s. James Madison Jr. and Mildred (Lane) K.; m. Nancy Lee Smith, Nov. 1983; children: Charlotte Lee, Nicolas Thornton, David Benjamin Royce. , Harvard U., 1975, MBA, 1979. Asst. bank examiner Fed. Res. Bank, Y.C., 1975-76; asst. treas. Second Dist. Securities, N.Y.C., 1976-77; account icer Citicorp, Chgo., 1981-83; v.p. Commerce Bank of Kansas City, Mo., 33-84, sr. v.p., 1984-85, pres., 1985—, chief exec. officer, 1988—, also bd. s. Bd. dirs. Tower Properties, Greater Kansas City Community Found.; e-chmn. Commerce Bancshares, 1988—. Treas., bd. dirs. Truman Libr. Inst.; dirs. Civic Coun. Kansas City. Office: Commerce Bank of Kansas City 1000 ılnut St PO Box 419248 Kansas City MO 64141-6248

:MPER, KIRBY WAYNE, physics educator; b. N.Y.C., Apr. 13, 1940; s. 'red Andrew and Anna (Bobetsky) K.; m. Margaret Ray Thurman, Aug. 24, 54; children: Margaret, Andrew, Ann. BS, Va. Tech. U., 1962; PhD, Ind. U., 58. Assoc. prof. Fla. State U., Tallahassee, 1975-79, prof., 1979-94, disting. h. prof., 1994—, dir. grad. physics program, 1982-88, assoc. chmn., 1985-88, accelerator lab., 1990-97, chairperson dept. physics, 1997—2003, v.p. rsch., 03—. Vis. fellow Australian Nat. U., Canberra, 1977, 81; trustee SURA, ashington, 1984-88. Recipient Rsch. Support award NSF, 1974—, Coll. Tchg. ard Fla. State U., 1990. Fellow Am. Phys. Soc. (Jesse W. Beams award, 00). Democrat. Roman Catholic. Home: 550 Litchfield Rd Tallahassee FL 312-1857 Office: Fla State U Dept Physics Tallahassee FL 32306

:MPER, ROBERT VAN, anthropologist, educator, minister; b. San Diego, v. 21, 1945; s. Ivan L. and Roberta (King) K.; m. Sandra L. Kraft, Sept. 9, 57; 1 child, John Kraft. BA, U. Calif., Riverside, 1966; MA, U. Calif., rkeley, 1969, PhD, 1971; MDiv, So. Meth. U., 1999. Ordained to ministry esbyn. Ch., 1999. Postdoctoral fellow U. Calif., Berkeley, 1971-72; asst. prof. Meth. U., Dallas, 1972-77, assoc. prof., 1977-83, prof., 1983—, chmn., 32-94. Visiting rsch. scholar U. Iberoamericana, Mexico City, 1970, 79-80, : U.S.-Mex. Studies, LaJolla, Calif., 1983, U. Nat. Autónoma Mex., Mexico y, 1990-91, El Colegio de Michoacán, Zamora, Mex., 1991; sec. Inst. Study Earth and Man, Dallas, 1989-92; Coun. Preservation Anthrop. Records; anding chair Commn. Anthropology Tourism, Internat. Union Anthrop. and hnol. Scis., 1993-96. Author: Migration and Adaptation, 1977; co author: story of Anthropology, 1977; co-editor: Anthropologists in Cities, 1974, gration Across Frontiers, 1979, (series) Contemporary Urban Studies, 90—, Chronicling Cultures, 2002; editor Socio Cultural Anthropology, Am. thropologist, 1985-90, Human Orgn., 1995-98; mem. editl. bd. Ency. World ltures, 1990-96, Ency. Urban Cultures, 1999—2002. Elder North Pk. esbyn. Ch., Dallas, 1987-89, 95-97; parish assoc. Trinity Presbyn. Ch., 99-2002; mem. Mcpl. Libr. Adv. Bd., Dallas, 1975-79; bd. dir. Oasis Housing rp., 2000—, Presbyn. Assn. Cmty. Transformation, 2003—. Fulbright fellow, 79-80, 91-92, Wenner-Gren fellow, 1974-76, 79-83, Woodrow Wilson fellow, 56-67. Fellow AAAS, Am. Anthrop. Assn. (bd. dirs. 1990-92), Soc. Applied thropology (chmn. Malinowski award com. 1979-80, bd. dirs. 1995-98); m. Latin Am. Studies Assn. (co-chmn. XI Internat. Congress 1983), Soc. an Anthropology (pres. 1988-90), Soc. Latin Am. Anthropology (pres. 81-82), Phi Beta Kappa (pres. chpt. 1987-88). Home: 10617 Cromwell Dr llas TX 75229-5110 Office: So Meth Univ Dept Anthropology 3225 Daniel e Dallas TX 75205-1437

:MPF, DONALD G., JR., lawyer; b. Chgo., July 4, 1937; s. Donald G. and rginia (Jahnke) K.; m. Nancy Kempf, June 12, 1965; children: Donald G. III, arles P., Stephen R. AB, Villanova U., 1959; LLB, Harvard U., 1965; MBA, Chgo., 1989. Bar: Ill. 1965, U.S. Supreme Ct. 1972, N.Y. 1986, Colo. 1992. soc. Kirkland & Ellis, Chgo., 1965-70, ptnr., 1971-2000; exec. v.p., chief al officer, sec. Morgan Stanley, N.Y.C., 2000—. Trustee Chgo. Symphony ch., 1995—, N.Y.C. Opera, 2002, Am. Inns of Ct., 1997-, v.p., 2002—; bd. ws. Chgo. Zool. Soc., 1975—, Art Inst. Chgo., 1984—; bd. dirs. United arities Chgo., 1985—, chmn. bd., 1991-93. Capt. USMC, 1959-62. Fellow a. Coll. Trial Lawyers; mem. Am. Econ. Assn., ABA, Chgo. Club, Econ. ıb, Univ. Club, Mid-Am. Club, Saddle and Cycle Club (Chgo.), Snowmass ıb) Club, Quail Ridge (Fla.) Club, Westmoreland Club. Roman Catholic. dress: Morgan Stanley 1585 Broadway Fl 39 New York NY 10036-8200 nail: donald.kempf@morganstanley.com.

:MPF, JANE ELMIRA, marketing executive; b. Phila., Sept. 28, 1927; d. pert Thomas and Alice (Gaston) Mullen; m. Peter Kempf, Sept. 4, 1948 (dec. ır. 1985); children: Peter Albert, Jan Michael, Richard Allen, Jeffery Val. ad. high sch., Yeadon, Pa. News dir. Sta. WIFF, Auburn, Ind., 1968-69; city tor The Evening Star, Auburn, 1969-76, columnist, 1969—2001; paralegal arren Sunday Atty., Auburn, 1977-85; mktg. mgr. City Nat. Bank, Auburn, 36-89; with communications mktg. Lincoln Fin. Corp., Ft. Wayne, Ind., 39-90; prin. JK Communications Bus. Svcs., Auburn, Ind., 1990—, Auburn b. Co., 1997—. Prin. Auburn (Ind.) Pub. Author: Jane's Friends and Family okbook, vol. 1, 1997, vol. 2, 1999. Mem. Auburn Network Enterprising omen, Ladies Literary Club, PEO Sisterhood (past pres., treas.), Auburn C. of (past sec., bd. dirs.). Presbyterian. Home: 1117 Packard Pl Auburn IN 706-1340 Office: Auburn Pub Co 1117 Packard Pl Auburn IN 46706-1340

:MPF, MARTINE, voice control device manufacturing company executive; Strasbourg, France, Dec. 9, 1958; came to U.S., 1985; d. Jean-Pierre and gitte Marguerite (Klockenbring) K. Student in Astronomy, Friedrich Wilm U., Bonn, Fed. Republic of Germany, 1981-83. Owner, mgr. Kempf, nnyvale, Calif., 1985—. Inventor Comeldir Multiplex Handicapped Driving stems (Goldenes Lenkrad Axel Springer Verlag 1981), Katalavox speech ognition control system (Oscar, World Almanac Inventions 1984, Prix Grand cle, Comite Couronne Francaise 1985). Recipient Medal for Service to manity Spinal Cord Soc., 1986; street named in honor in Dossenheimchersberg, Alsace, France, 1987; named Citizen of Honor City of ssenheim-Kochersberg, 1985, Outstanding Businessperson of Yr. City of nnyvale, 1990. Avocations: flying, piano, violin, bassoon, studying foreign guages. Office: PO Box 61103 Sunnyvale CA 94088-1103

:MPFF, JUERGEN, language educator; s. Hermann Kempff and Marianne msdorf; m. Lois May Chambers, Sept. 15, 1980; children: Daniel H., arcus J., Nicole B. BA in Spanish Lit., BA in German Lit., U. Calif., San ego, 1983; MA in Hispanic Linguistics, U. Calif., Santa Barbara, 1986, PhD Hispanic Linguistics, 1989. Asst. prof. U. of Wis., Oshkosh, Wis., 1989—93; tr. security of employment U. Calif., Irvine, 1993—. Spanish lang. curricun dir. U. of Calif., Irvine, Calif., 1993—. Editor: (guide) Research on US dents Abroad, 1989; contbr. articles to profl. jours. Regional referee ninstr. Am. Youth Soccer Orgn., Irvine, Calif., 1999—2001. Mem.: Am. nfedn. Tchrs. Fgn. Lits., MLA, Am. Assn. Tchrs. Spanish and Portuguese, ma Delta Pi (faculty advisor 1996—2003, cert. merit 2001—02). Avocans: golf, travel, instructional technology. Office: U Calif 322-H Humanities ll Irvine CA 92697-5275 Office Fax: 949-824-2803. E-mail: mpff@uci.edu.

:MPIN, FREDERICK GUSTAV, JR., lawyer, educator; b. Phila., Apr. 19, 22; s. Frederick Gustav and Lydia Edith (Anton) K.; m. Jean Lucille Robb, . 13, 1945 (dec.); children— Frederick Gustav III, Karen Ann Hauckes. C, Temple U., Phila., 1942; JD, U. Pa., 1944. Sole practice law, Phila., 45-49; prof. law U. Pa. Wharton Sch., Phila., 1949-87, vice dean, 1964-72, ertus prof. law, 1987—; ret., 1987. Author: Historical Introduction to glo-American Law in a Nutshell, 3d edit., 1990; co-author: Legal Aspects of Management Process, 4th edit., 1990, Introduction to Law and the Legal ocess, 3d edit., 1980, The Legal Environment of Insurance, 4th edit., 1993. cipient Lindback award for Disting. Teaching, U. Pa., 1963 Mem. Am. Bus. w Assn., Am. Soc. for Legal History. Republican. Lutheran. Avocations: otography, swimming. Home: 515 Harriet Ln Havertown PA 19083-1817 ice: U Pa Wharton Sch Steinberg Hall-Dietrich Hall Philadelphia PA 19104

:MPLEY, RITA A. film critic, editor; b. Frankfort, Ky., Sept. 12, 1945; d. ah and Musaetta (Lathrem) Abrams; m. Edward Ronald Schneider, Aug. 11, 36 BJ, U. Mo., 1967. Reporter Copley News Svc., La Jolla, Calif., 1967-68; oc. editor John F. Holman & Co., Washington, 1968-71; reporter Graphic s Mag., Washington, 1972-75; freelance editor-writer Washington, 1975-76; g. editor Washington Dossier, 1977-79; editor/critic Washington Post, 1979—. Commentator Sta. WETA, 1989-96, Sta. WBIG, 1997—. Host Washington Post Live on Line. Grantee Alicia Patterson Found. fellow, 2002. Mem. Kappa Tau Alpha. Office: The Washington Post 1150 15th St NW Washington DC 20071-0002

KEMPNER, JOSEPH, aerospace engineering educator; b. Bklyn., Apr. 25, 1923; s. Arthur and Anna (Richman) K.; m. Carol F. Brown, Jan. 12, 1947; children: Robert M., Marien A. Barker. B.Aero. Engring. summa cum laude, Poly. Inst. Bklyn., 1943, M.Aero. Engring., 1947, PhD in Applied Mechanics, 1950. Registered profl. engr., N.Y. Research fellow Poly. Inst. Bklyn., 1944, mem. faculty, 1947-90, prof. applied mechanics and aerospace engring., 1957-90, prof. emeritus, 1990—, chmn. undergrad. aerospace studies, asst. dir. research, 1962-63, dir. applied mechanics, 1964-76, head dept., 1966-76; aero. engr. NASA, 1944-47. Cons. indsl. and govt. research labs; former mem. adv. group II, ship structural design procedure and analysis, ship research com. Maritime Transp. Research Bd., Nat. Acad. Scis.-NRC; also former mem. com. basic research, adv. to Army Research Office, 1973-76, 81-85; prin. investigator research contracts Office Naval Research and Air Force Office Sci. Research. Contbr. articles to profl. jours. Recipient citation disting. research Poly. chpt. Sigma Xi, 1973; named Outstanding Educator Am., 1973, 74-75 Fellow N.Y. Acad. Scis. (I.B. Laskowitz Gold medal 1973), Am. Acad. Mechanics; assoc. fellow AIAA; mem. Am. Soc. Engring. Edn., Sigma Xi, Tau Beta Pi, Sigma Gamma Tau. Home: 82 Murray Hill Ter Marlboro NJ 07746-1751 Office: 333 Jay St Brooklyn NY 11201-2907

KEMPNER, MARVIN A. broadcasting corporation executive; b. Albany, N.Y., July 7, 1921; s. Marvin William and Anna K.; m. Aileen Juvelier, Aug. 20, 1950 (div. 1974); children: Candice Ann, Daniel Henry; m. Jeanne Kay Cantor, Aug. 26, 1976 (dec. 1990). Student, U. Buffalo, 1941. Acct. exec. Louis G. Cowan Inc., N.Y.C., 1946-48; v.p. Richard H. Ullman Inc., Buffalo, N.Y., 1949-60, pres. N.Y.C., 1960-62, Mark Century Corp., N.Y.C., 1962-68; pres. broadcasting divsn. Music Makers Inc., N.Y.C., 1968-71; v.p. Music Makers Pub. Co., N.Y.C., 1968-71; prin., owner M.A. Kempner Inc., N.Y.C., 1971—. Bd. dirs. So. Fla. RR Mus., Deerfield Beach. Author: Can't Wait Till Monday Morning, 1998. Treas. Scleroderma Found., Watsonville, Calif., 1992-98. Corp. USAF, 1943-46. Mem. Friars Club (Book Warming award 1999). Republican. Avocations: golf, photography, modeling and building railroad diaramas, public speaking. Home: 11820 Fountainside Cir Boynton Beach FL 33437-4921 E-mail: mksand@earthlink.net.

KEMPNER, MAXIMILIAN WALTER, law school dean, lawyer; b. Berlin, Feb. 27, 1929; came to U.S., 1939; s. Paul H. and Marga Marie (von Mendelssohn) K.; m. Barbara Paige Mooney, 1952; children: Paul, Daphne, Emily Mayne. BA, Harvard U., 1951, LLB, 1954; LLM, Columbia U., 1957; LLD, Vt. Law Sch., 1997. Bar: N.Y. bar 1954. With Webster & Sheffield, N.Y.C., 1957-91; dean Vt. Law Sch., South Royalton, 1991-96. Chmn. Vt. Legis. Apportionment Bd.; dir. Lawyers Com. for Civil Rights under Law. Trustee Marlboro Sch. Music, Inc., Conservation Law Found.; former dir. Legal Aid Soc., Am. Coun. on Germany, Albert Schweitzer Fellowship, Coun. on Libr. Resources; active Coun. Fgn. Rels., Inc. With U.S. Army, 1954-56. Fellow Am. Bar Found. (life); mem. ABA (past chmn. legal edn. and admissions to bar sect.), Am. Law Inst. (life), Assn. Bar City N.Y., N.Y. State Bar Assn., Harvard Law Sch. Assn. N.Y.C. (past pres.).

KEMPNER, MICHAEL W. public relations executive; b. Chgo., Jan. 31, 1958; s. Lester T. and Lois Kempner; m. Jacqueline Steinberg, Oct. 24, 1987; children: Zachary, Melissa. BS, Am. U., 1981. Spl. asst. to Gov. of N.J., Trenton, 1977-79; state campaign dir. Pres. Jimmy Carter, Washington, 1979-80; dep. fin. chair Dem. Nat. Comm., 1980-82; legis. dir. Congressman Torricelli, Hackensack, N.J., 1983-84; pres. Winter's Chocolates, Emerson, N.J., 1984-86, The MWW Group, East Rutherford, N.J., 1986—. Bd. dirs. N.J. Drug Abuse Resistance Edn. Contbr. articles to popular mags. Former fin. vice chair Dem. Nat. Com.; regional chmn. fin. Dem. senatorial campaign, Washington, 1990, chmn. fin. com. Congressman Torriceli, Hackensack, 1984—, committeeman Bergen County Dem. Com., 1991, bd. advisors Ctr. Food Action, Englewood, N.J., 1990-91. Named Entrepreneur of Yr. finalist, 1991, 92, 93, 94. Mem. Pub. Rels. Soc. Am., Young Pres. Orgns., mem. 1992 U.S Olympic Com., regl fin. chmn., mem. Am. Bankruptcy Inst., and Turnaround mgmt. Assn. Office: The MWW Group 1 Meadowlands Plz Fl 6 East Rutherford NJ 07073-2100

KEMPSKI, RALPH ALOISIUS, bishop; b. Milw., July 16, 1934; s. Sigmund Joseph and Cecilia Josephine (Chojnacki) K.; m. Mary Jane Roth, July 30, 1955; children— Richard, Joan, John BA, Augsburg Coll., 1960; M.Div., Northwestern Luth. Theol. Sem., 1963; D.Div., Wittenberg U., Springfield, Ohio, 1980. Pastor Epiphany Luth. Ch., Mpls., 1963-68, St. Stephen Luth. Ch., Louisville, 1968-71, Our Saviour Luth. Ch., West Lafayette, Ind., 1971-79; bishop Ind.-Ky. Synod Luth. Ch. Am., Indpls., 1979-87, Ind.-Ky. Synod Evang. Luth. Ch. Am., 1987-98. Bd. dirs. Ind. Coun. Chs., 1979-96, v.p., 1991-94, pres., 1994-96 ; bd. dirs. Ky. Coun. Chs., Luth. Sch. Theology, Chgo., Luth. Sch., Columbia, S.C., Wittenberg U., Springfield, Ohio, Suomi Coll.; governing bd. Nat. Coun. Chs. Christ U.S.A., N.Y.C., 1981-88, Luth. Theol. So. Sem., 1988-96, Trinity Sem., 1996-98. Mem. governing bd. Suomi Coll., Hancock, Mich., 1998-2001; bd. dirs. Spencer County Mental Health Assn., 2003—. Lutheran. Avocations: gardening, reading, travel, flying.

KEMPSKIE, JEFFREY T. music educator; b. Worcester, Mass., July 20, 1979; MusB, U. of Mass., 1997—2001. Mass. Tchg. Cert. Mass. Dept. of Edn., 2001. Music dir. The Newman Ctr., Amherst, Mass., 1998—2001; choral dir. Quabbin Regional Mid./High Sch., Barre, Mass., 2001—. Music dir. Calliope Productions, Boylston, Mass., 1997—2001. Mem.: Mass. Music Educator's Assn., Am. Choral Director's Assn.

KEMPSTER, NORMAN ROY, journalist; b. Sacramento, Jan. 4, 1936; s. Roy Dixon and Viola Alice (Cox) K.; m. Jane Leon, June 30, 1957; children: Jill Suzanne Zemke, David Norman. BA, Calif. State U., 1957. Reporter U.P.I., 1957-73, Washington Star-News, 1973-76; reporter Washington bur. L.A. Times, 1976—80, reporter Jerusalem bur., 1981—84, reporter Washington bur., 1984—2001. Joe Alex Morris meml. lectr. Harvard U., 1983, adj. prof. Lenoir-Rhyne Coll., Hickory, NC, 2003—. Served with AUS, 1959-61. Profl. Journalism fellow, 1967; recipient Gerald Loeb award, 1980 Mem. Fgn. Press Assn. in Israel (v.p. 1982-83), White House Corrs. Assn. (dir. 1974-75), State Dept. Corrs. Assn. (treas. 1986, v.p. 1987, pres. 1988), Overseas Writers of Washington (pres. 1989-91). Episcopalian. Home and Office: 321 N Cedar St Lincolnton NC 28092 E-mail: nrkempster@aol.com.

KEMPSTER, WILLIAM GEOFFREY, conductor, music educator; s. Geoffrey Thomas and Barbara Gretel Kempster. MusD, U. of Alta., 1999. Dir. of choral activities U. of N.H., Durham, NH, 1999—. Dir. Ensemble de la Rue, Edmonton, Canada, 1998—. Director and producer (albums) One, The Cry; composer: (songs) The Busy Box, Collisions. Scholar, U. of Alta., 1998—99. Mem.: Am. Choral Dirs. Assn. Home: 1 Longmarsh Road Barrington NH 03825 Office: University of New Hampshire Music Dept PCAC 30 College Road Durham NH 03824 Office Fax: 603-862-3155. E-mail: william.kempster@unh.edu.

KEMPTHORNE, DIRK ARTHUR, governor; b. San Diego, Oct. 29, 1951; s. James Henry and Maxine Jesse (Gustason) K.; m. Patricia Jean Merrill, Sept. 18, 1977; children: Heather Patricia, Jeffrey Dirk. BS in Polit. Sci., U. Idaho, 1975. Exec. asst. to dir. Idaho Dept. Lands, Boise, 1975-78; exec. v.p. Idaho Home Builders Assn., Boise, 1978-81; campaign mgr. Batt for Gov., Boise, 1981-82; lic. securities rep. Swanson Investments, Boise, 1983; Idaho pub. affairs mgr. FMC Corp., Boise, 1983-86; mayor Boise, 1984—91; U.S. Senator from Idaho, 1993-98; gov. State of Idaho, 1999—. 1st v.p. Assn. of Idaho Cities, 1990-93; chmn. U.S. Conf. of Mayors Standing Com. on Energy and Environment, 1991-93, mem. adv. bd., 1991-93 ; sec. Nat. Conf. of Rep. Mayors and Mcpl. Elected Officials, 1991-93; mem. Senate Armed Svcs. Com., 1993-98, Senate Small Bus. Com., 1993-98, Senate Environ. and Pub. Works Com., 1993-98, Nat. Rep. Senatorial Com., 1993-98; chmn. Senate Drinking Water, Fisheries and Wildlife Subcommittee, 1995-98, mem. advisory commn. on Intergovernmental Rels., 1995-96; chmn. Armed Svcs Personnel Subcommittee, 1996-98. Pres. Associated Students U. Idaho, Moscow, 1975; chmn. bd. dirs. Wesleyan Presch., Boise, 1982-85; mem. magistrate commn. 4th Jud. Dist., Boise, 1986-93; mem. task force Nat. League of Cities Election, 1988; bd. dirs. Parents and Youth Against Drug Abuse, 1987—; mem. bd. vis. USAF Acad., 1994—; chmn. Idaho Working Ptnrs. Ltd., 1993—; hon. chmn. Idaho Congressional Award, 1994—. Named Idaho Citizen of Yr. The Idaho Statesman, 1988, Legislator of the Year Nat. Assn. Counties, 1995, State Legislator of the Year Nat. Assn. of Towns and Townships, 1995; recipient U.S. Conference of Mayor's Nat. Legis. Leadership award, 1994, Disting. Svc. award Nat. Conf. State Legislatures, 1995, Disting. Congressional award Nat. League of Cities, 1995, Guardian of Freedom award Council of State Governments, 1995. Republican. Methodist. Office: Office of Governor PO Box 83720 Boise ID 83720-0034 also: Office of the Governor 700 West Jefferson, 2nd Floor Boise ID 83702 Fax: 208-334-2175.*

KENAGY, CHERI LYNN, nurse; b. Houston, Tex., Nov. 12, 1958; d. Kenneth Leigh and Mary Louise Kenagy; m. William L Balan, July 30, 1982 (dec. Jan. 15, 1991); children: Rhett Kenagy-Balan, Natasha Kenagy-Balan. Attended, San Jacinto Coll., 1980. Cert. LVN. Hosp. staff relief Advantage Nursing, Houston, 1998—; staff nurse Beacon Health, Ltd., Houston, 2000—. C.p.r. instr. AHA, Houston, 1998—. Conservative. Presbyterian. Avocations: travel, scuba diving. Home: 5226 Kent Dr Pasadena TX 77505

KENAGY, ROBERT COFFMAN, planning consulting company executive; b. Hartford, Conn., July 10, 1931; s. Herbert Glenn and Mary Emily (Hardesty) K.; m. Karen Miriam Emanuelson, June 8, 1957; children: Neil S., Lynn S., Gretchen P. BA, Princeton U., 1953; postgrad., U. Pa., 1953-54. Various mktg. mgmt. positions IBM, N.Y.C., White Plains, Armonk, N.Y., 1957-69; v.p. mktg. Data Dimensions, Inc., Greenwich, Conn., 1969-73; fin. prin. Sidney A. Staunton, Inc., New Canaan, Conn., 1973-78; pres. RCK Mgmt. Co., Ltd., New Canaan, Litchfield, Conn., 1978—. Mem. Larchmont-Mamroneck (N.Y.) Bd. Edn., 1968-72; bd. dirs. YMCA, New Canaan, 1975-81, pres., 1980-81, trustee The Aloha Found., Fairlee, Vt., 1976-91, pres., 1983-84, trustee emeritus, 1991—; trustee First Congl. Ch., Litchfield, 2002—; bd. dirs. United Way, New Canaan, 1979-82, campaign chmn., 1979-80. 1st lt. U.S. Army, 1954—56. Mem. Princeton Club N.Y. Avocations: singing, travel. Home and Office: RCK Mgmt Co Ltd 24 Fox Crossing Ln Litchfield CT 06759-2305

KENAS-HELLER, JANE HAMILTON, musician; b. Fond du Lac, Wis., June 17, 1951; d. Vern Aaron and Marilyn Jane (Bluemke) Kenas; m. Irwin L. Heller. MusB, U. Wis., Stevens Point, 1975; MA, Northeastern Ill. U., 1987. Staff accompanist dept. music Northeastern Ill. U., Chgo., 1982—. Music dir. USO Tour to Europe, Germany, 1973; music dir., composer Harlequin Players Theatre Co., Palatine, Ill.; accompanist Park Ridge (Ill.) Chorale; condr. Temple Beth El High Holiday Choir, Northbrook, Ill. Composer: (mus. play) The Adventures of Goldilocks, 1990; (one-act opera) Romance Novel, 1993. Organist Edgewater Presbyn. Ch., Chgo. Office: Northeastern Ill U 5500 N Saint Louis Ave Chicago IL 60625-4679

KENAT, THOMAS ARTHUR, chemical engineer, consultant; b. Cleve., Aug. 6, 1942; s. Arthur Brian and Frances Lillian (Kuenzli) K.; m. Wynne Irene Kalvesmaki, June 13, 1964; children: Steven Thomas, Lisa Marie. BSChemE, Carnegie Inst. Tech., 1964, MSChemE, 1965; PhD in Chem. Engring., Carnegie-Mellon U., 1968. Registered profl. engr., Ohio. Rsch. engr. Chemstrand Rsch. Ctr., Durham, N.C., 1968-69, B. F. Goodrich Co., Brecksville, Ohio, 1969-74, sr. rsch. engr., 1974-80, sr. engring. scientist, 1981-83, sr. R & D assoc., 1983-88, Camet Co., Hiram, Ohio, 1988-89; sr. project mgr. Quantum Techs., Inc., Twinsburg, Ohio, 1989-92; prin. cons. KenaTech Process Engring., Medina, Ohio, 1992—. Contbr. articles to profl. jours. Elder Prince of Peace Luth. Ch., Medina, Ohio, 1975-90; mem. Medina Community Band, 1983—. Mem. AIChE, Am. Chem. Soc., Am. Guild Organists, Kiwanis. Republican. Lutheran. Avocations: music, sailing, pipe organ restoration. Office: KenaTech Process Engring PO Box 1842 Medina OH 44258-1842 E-mail: tak@kenatech.com.

KENDALL, BURTON NATHANIEL, software designer; b. San Francisco, Dec. 15, 1940; s. Nathaniel James and Helen Louise (Born) K.; m. Margaret Elizabeth Maninger, Aug. 14, 1963 (div. July 1978); 1 child, Anne; m. Sally Joan Towse, Feb. 24, 1979; children: James, Samuel. BSc in Physics, Stanford (Calif.) U., 1962; PhD in Physics, Brown U., 1969. Asst. prof. U. Calif., Santa Barbara, 1969-73; dir. info. systems Systems Control, Inc., Palo Alto, Calif., 1973-78; sr. prin. scientist Measurex Corp., Cupertino, Calif., 1978-89; dir. tech. Octel Communications Corp., Milpitas, Calif., 1989-96; chief tech. officer Life Masters, Inc., South San Francisco, Calif., 1996—2000; prin. engr./mgr. Qualcomm, Campbell, Calif., 2000—. Mem. adv. panel NASA, Mt. View, Calif., 1987-89; cons. Towse-Kendall Assocs., Saratoga, Calif., 1978—. Contbr. 30 articles to profl. jours. Mem. AAAS, Am. Phys. Soc. (life), Sigma Xi. Achievements include patents on real-time distributed data-base mgmt. systems, system and process for processing info., and two patents on clustered voice processing systems. Office: Qualcomm 675 Campbell Tech Pky Campbell CA 95008

KENDALL, CHARLES TERRY, librarian; b. Chambersburg, Pa., Aug. 13, 1949; s. Guy William and Virginia Mae (Naugle) K.; m. Alice Marie Bienz, Aug. 21, 1971; children: Terri, Anita, Kendra. BA, Huntington (Ind.) Coll., 1971; MLS, George Peabody Coll., 1972; postgrad., Asbury Theol. Sem., 1982-83; MA in Religion, Anderson (Ind.) U., 1990. Dir. Byrd Meml. Libr. Anderson Sch. Theology, Anderson U., 1983-89; theol. studies libr. Anderson U. Libr., 1989-98, archivist, 1992-98; dir. Mabee Libr. Sterling (Kans.) Coll., 1998—. Mem. ALA, Kans. Libr. Assn. Office: Mabee Library Sterling Coll Sterling KS 67579

KENDALL, FRANK RUSSELL, SR., lawyer; b. Houston, June 14, 1920; s. William E. and Theodora Dudley (Kuker) K.; m. Anne Benson, Sept. 9, 1942; children: Theodora, Bernard, Frank, John, Thomas. Student, Gregorian U., Rome, 1937-40, U. Houston, 1940-42; LLB, South Tex. Coll. Law, 1949. Bar: Tex. 1949, U.S. Dist. Ct. (so. dist.) Tex. 1949, U.S. Ct. Appeals (5th cir.) 1949, U.S. Supreme Ct. 1969, U.S. Ct. Claims 1974. Asst. dist. atty. Harris County State of Tex., Houston, 1948-52; ptnr. Vinson & Elkins, Houston, 1953—. Vice gov. Gen. Equestrian Order of the Holy Sepulchre of Jerusalem, Protection of Holy See. Lt. (s.g.) USNR, 1942-45, PTO. Mem. ABA, Am. Coll. Trial Lawyers, Tex. Bar Assn., Tex. Bar Found., Houston Bar Assn. Roman Catholic. Office: Vinson & Elkins 1001 Fannin St Ste 3300 Houston TX 77002-6706

KENDALL, GREGORY R. art educator; b. Akron, Ohio, Aug. 11, 1950; s. Harles R. Kendall and Clara B. Oborne; m. Joanne K. Kendall, Mar. 4, 1973; children: Sarah Anderson, Elizabeth Gleason, Joel, Mary. BFA in Studio Arts, U. Minn., 1982; MATS in Theology, Zoe U., 1995; MA in Painting, U. Wis., Superior, 1996; MFA in Painting, Western Mich. U., 1998. Cert. journeyman cabinetmaker St. Paul Tech. Inst. Tchg. asst. Western Mich. U., Kalamazoo, 1997—98; substitute tchr. Ironwood (Mich.) Schs., 1998—2000, Bessemer (Mich.) City Sch. Dist., 1998—99; adj. prof. painting Gogebic C.C., Ironwood, 1999—. Editor-in-chief: Artedland; Represented in permanent collections U. Wis.-Superior, Western Mich. U., 1998, exhibitions include Lizzards Gallery, Duluth, Minn., 1999, Mich. Tech. U., Houghton, 1999, Arts in Harmony, 2001, Franklin Sq. Gallery, Southport, NC, 2001, Floors N'Mor, Bessemer, 2002, Pine Tree Gallery, Ironwood, 2002, U. Wis.-Superior, 2002—03. With Mich. NG, 2000—. Recipient Robert and Eleanor DeVies award, 1998, Merit award, Elk River Arts Coun., 2001. Mem.: Chronicle of Higher Edn., Coll. Art Assn., ArtServe Mich. Home: 360 Korpela Rd Wakefield MI 49968 E-mail: gkendall2002@yahoo.com.

KENDALL, HARRY OVID, internist; b. Eugene, Oreg., Nov. 29, 1929; s. Edward Lee and Jessie Avis (Giem) K.; m. Katherine Alexander, June 20, 1951 (div. 1957); 1 child, Jessica Gail Gress; m. Barbara Ann Matt, Jan. 21, 1961 (div. June 1, 1977); children: David Lee, Brian Padraic; m. Wanda Eve Helmer, July 2, 1993. AB, U. Redlands, 1952; MD, Yale U., 1955. Diplomate Am. Bd. Internal Medicine, Am. Bd. Pulmonary Disease. Intern in internal medicine UCLA Med. Ctr., 1955-57; resident in internal medicine West L.A. VA Med. Ctr., 1957-59; staff physician U.S. Naval Regional Med. Ctr., San Diego, 1959-62, Tulare-Kings Counties Hosp., Springville, Calif., 1962-63; staff physician, ptnr. So. Calif. Permanente Med. Group, Fontana, Calif., 1963-67, Kaiser Hosp. and So. Calif. Permanente Med. Group, San Diego, 1967—95; dir.

respiratory care Kaiser Hosp., San Diego, 1967—95. Attending physician San Bernardino County Hosp., 1964—67; asst. clin. prof. medicine U. Calif. San Diego Med. Ctr., 1976—95; com. mem. numerous hosps. and med. clinics. Mem. NAACP, Amnesty Internat., ACLU. Lt. USNR, 1954-56, lt. comdr. 1961, comdr. 1973. Mem. Am. Thoracic Soc., cAlif. Thoracic Soc., San Diego Pulmonary Soc. Avocations: western history, paleontology, geneology, book collecting.

KENDALL, JACQUELINE A. social worker; b. Detroit, May 13, 1956; d. Arnold W. and Gertrude L. Kendall. BS in Edn., Weber State Coll., 1985; MSW, U. S.C., 1988; BS in Social Work, Weber State Coll., 1985. Lic. master social worker. Family support counselor. Recipient Elizabeth Poat award of excellence, ARC, 1997, Clara Barton award for vol. leadership, 1999, 6th man award, Leukemia and Lymphoma Soc., 2000. Mem.: Nat. Assn. Nonthetic Counselors, Am. Acad. Bereavement Facilitators.

KENDALL, JOHN WALKER, JR., medical educator, researcher, university dean; b. Bellingham, Wash., Mar. 19, 1929; s. John Walker and Mathilda (Hansen) K.; m. Elizabeth Helen Meece, Mar. 19, 1954; children: John, Katherine, Victoria. BA, Yale Coll., 1952; MD, U. Wash., 1956. Intern, resident in internal medicine Vanderbilt U. Hosp., Nashville, 1956-59, fellow in endocrinology, 1959-60, U. Oreg. Med. Sch., Portland, 1960-62; asst. prof. medicine Oreg. Health Scis. U., Portland, 1962-66, assoc. prof. medicine, 1966-71, prof. medicine, 1971—, head divsn. metabolism, 1971-80; dean Oreg. Health Scis. U. Sch. Medicine, Portland, 1983—92; assoc. chief staff-rsch. VA Med. Ctr., Portland, 1971-83, dep. chief of staff, 1993, VA disting. physician, 1993-96, acad. affiliates officer, 1997—, grad. med. edn. adv. com., 2001—. Cons. Med. Rsch. Found. Oreg., Portland, 1975-83; sec. Oreg. Found. Med. Excellence, Portland, 1984-89, pres., 1989-91; grad. med. edn. adv. com. Dept. Vets. Affairs, 2001—; commn. mem. VA Cares, 2003--. Lt. comdr. M.C., USN, 1962-64 Recipient Outstanding Physician award Found. Med. Excellence, 1995. Mem. AMA (governing coun. med. sch. sect. 1989-93, chair 1991-92, alt. del. 1992-93, Oreg. del. 1994-98, rep. Coun. Grad. Med. Edn. 1993-94), Assn. Am. Physicians, Am. Soc. Clin. Investigation, Am. Fedn. Clin. Rsch., We. Soc. Clin. Rsch. (councillor 1972-75), Endocrine Soc., Multnomah County Med. Soc. (treas. 1989, pres. 1991), Med. Rsch. Found. (Mentor award 1992), Royal Soc. Medicine (endocrinology sect. coun. 1999—). Presbyterian. Home: 2121 SW Evergreen Ln Portland OR 97201-1816 Office: Oreg Health Scis U Sch Medicine L-607 3181 SW Sam Jackson Park Rd Portland OR 97239

KENDALL, JULIUS, consulting engineer; b. Boston, May 14, 1919; m. Edythe Tobias; children: Jane, Richard Tobias. BS in Aero. Engring., Northeastern U., 1941; MS, MIT, 1941. Registered Profl. Engr., N.Y., N.J., Mass., Conn., Maine; cert. fluid power engr. V.p. Greer Hydraulics, N.Y.C., 1945-56, Arkwin Industries, Inc., Westbury, N.Y., 1956-58; pres. Kenett Corp., Westboro, Mass., 1958-91; cons. engr. Kendall Cons. Group, Weston, Mass., 1991—; v.p. Kenett Hydraulic Distbn. divsn. Entwistle Co., Hudson, Mass., 1993—. Cons. in field. Patentee in field. Contbr. many articles to profl. jours. With USN, 1941-46. Mem. Am. Soc. Naval Engrs., ASME, Soc. Automotive Engrs., Fluid Power Soc., Aleppo Yacht Club, Shriners, Masons. Avocations: fishing, boating, golf. Home and Office: 57 Colchester Rd Weston MA 02493-1601 E-mail: jkendall@entwistleco.com.

KENDALL, KAY LYNN, interior designer, consultant; b. Cadillac, Mich., Aug. 20, 1950; d. Robert Llewellyn and Betty Louise (Powers) K.; 1 child, Anna Renee Easter. BFA, U. Mich., 1973. Draftsman, interior designer store planning dept. Jacobson Stores, Inc., Jackson, Mich., 1974-79, sr. interior designer store planning dept., 1981-98; prin., pres. Kay Kendall Designs LLC (Kendall Interior Design and Devel.), Jackson, 1979—; sr. interior designer Maddalena's Inc., Jackson, 1998—2002; realtor Edward Surovell Realtors, Chelsea, Mich., 2000—. Cons. in field. Big sister Big Bros./Big Sisters Jackon County. Mem. Am. Soc. Interior Designers (profl. mem., assoc. Ctrl. Mich. chpt.), Nat. Assn. Realtors, Ann Arbor Area Assn. Realtors, Mich. Assn. Realtors. Avocations: tennis, golf, gardening, skiing. Home: 701 Church St Grass Lake MI 49240-9206 Office: Edward Surovell Realtors 323 S Main St Chelsea MI 48118 E-mail: kkendall@acd.net.

KENDALL, LAUREL ANN, geotechnical engineer; b. Detroit, Dec. 4, 1956; d. James McNair and Dorothy Mildred (Frost) K. BSE in Environ. Sci., U. Mich., 1979, MSCE, 1983. Registered profl. engr., Mich., Ill., Ohio. With Bechtel Assocs. P.C., 1979-84; project mgr. NTH Cons., 1984-90; gen. mgr. solid waste ops. Wayne Disposal, Inc. (purchased by Allied Waste Industries), 1990-97, dist. landfill gen. mgr., 1997-99, dist. environ. mgr., 1999-2000; dir. landfill ops. The Environtl. Quality Co., 2000—01; mgr. geoenviron. svcs. The Mannik & Smith Group, Inc., 2002—. Instr. Lawrence Inst. Tech., Southfield, Mich., 1985-91, Wayne State U., 1991—. Mem. ASCE (past pres. Mich. sect.), Mich. Soc. Profl. Engrs. (past pres. Oakland chpt.), Engring. Soc. Detroit (landfill design conf. organizing com. 1995—). Congregationalist. Avocations: gardening, jogging, mountain biking, cross-country skiing. Office: Mannik & Smith Group 15300 Rotunda Dr Dearborn MI 48120

KENDALL, LAUREL MARGARITE, curator, anthropologist, educator; b. San Francisco, Dec. 24, 1947; d. Henry George Kendall and Ramona Melawia Pezzini; m. Homer Farrand Williams, Aug. 15, 1981; 1 child, Henry Sheldon Namsop Williams. BA, U. Calif., Berkeley, 1969; MA, Columbia U., 1975, MPhil, 1976, PhD, 1979. Postdoctoral rsch. fellow U. Hawaii, Honolulu, 1979—81; vis. asst. prof. U. Kans., Lawrence, 1981—82; asst. curator Am. Mus. Natural History, N.Y.C., 1983—88, assoc. curator, 1988—93, curator, 1993—. Adj. assoc. prof. Columbia U., N.Y.C., 1990—94, adj. prof., 1994—. Author: Shamans, Housewives and Other Restless Spirits, 1985, The Life and Hard Times of a Korean Shaman, Getting Married in Korea, 1996. Mem.: N.Y. Acad. Sci. (adv. coun. mem. sect. for anthropology 1998—), Assn. for Asian Studies, Am. Anthropology Assn., Soc. for Anthropology Religion (mem. adv. bd. 1998—2002). Office: Am Mus Natural History Dept Anthropology Central Park West @ 79th St New York NY 10024

KENDALL, LEIGH WAKEFIELD, surgeon; b. Brattleboro, Vt., Mar. 8, 1937; s. Irwin Samuel and Laura Eliza (Walbridge) K.; m. Grace Eleanor Fullarton, July 1, 1961; children: William Leigh, Bradley Edward. AB, U. Pa., Phila., 1959; D of Medicine, U. Vt., 1963; MS, U. Ill., Chgo., 1965. Diplomate Nat. Bd. Med. Examiners, Am. Bd. Surgery; cert. ACLS. Intern then resident surgery U. Ill. Hosp., Chgo., 1963-69; rsch. fellow Am. Cancer Soc., Chgo., 1964-65, clin. fellow, 1968-69; staff surgeon USN Hosp., Great Lakes, Ill., 1969; surgeon USN Hosp. Ships, Vietnam, 1969-70; pvt. practice Lancaster, Pa., 1971-93; med. dir. Alliance Health Plan, Lancaster, 1995—; assoc. med. dir. St. Joseph Regional Health Network, Lancaster and Reading, 1999—; med. dir. St. Joseph Hosp., Lancaster, 2000—, Lancaster Regional Med. Ctr., 2000—. Instr. surgery U. Ill. Hosp., Chgo., 1968-69; active staff St. Joseph Hosp., Lancaster, 1971—, sect. chief gen. surgery, 1981-88, chmn. dept. surgery, 1989-93; mem. courtesy staff Lancaster Gen. Hosp., 1971—; cons. surgery Franklin & Marshall Coll., Lancaster, Masonic Homes, Elizabethtown, Pa., staff physician, Millersville, U., 1993—; staff physician cardiac rehab., Lancaster Gen. Hosp. Health Campus, 1995-98. Lt. comdr. USNR M.C., 1959-71, Vietnam. Decorated 1st Class Mil. Honor medal Republic of Vietnam. Fellow ACS, Internat. Soc. Surgeons; mem. AMA, Pa. Med. Soc., Warren H. Cole Soc. (pres. 1994-95), Royal Soc. Medicine (Eng.), Am. Coll. Physician Execs., Intrepids Club, Sigma Nu. Republican. Episcopalian. Avocations: photography, travel. Home: 1314 Quarry Ln Lancaster PA 17603-2424 Office: Med Affairs Office Lancaster Regional Med Ctr Lancaster PA 17604-3434

KENDALL, LEON THOMAS, finance and real estate educator, retired insurance company executive; b. Elizabeth, N.J., May 20, 1928; m. Nancy O'Donnell; 6 children. BS in Acctg. magna cum laude, St. Vincent Coll., 1949; MBA in Mktg., Ind. U., 1950, DBA in Econs., 1956; LLD (hon.), Cardinal Stritch Coll., 1988. Teaching asso. Ind. U. Sch. Bus., 1950-53; economist Fed. Res. Bd., Atlanta, 1956-58, U.S. Savs. and Loan League, Chgo., 1958-64; v.p., economist N.Y. Stock Exchange, 1964-67; pres. Assn. Stock Exchange Firms, 1967-72, Securities Industry Assn., 1972-74; chmn., dir. Mortgage Guaranty Ins. Corp., Milw., 1974-89; vice chmn. MGIC Investment Corp., 1980-89; Norman Strunk prof. fin. instns. Kellogg Sch. of Mgmt., Northwestern U., Evanston, Ill., 1988—. Bd. dirs. Anthracite Capital, Inc., CoreCar, Inc., CBOE; commr. N.J. Mortgage Study, 1971-72; mem. Wis. Expenditures Study Commn., 1985-86. Author: (with Miles Colean) Who Buys the Houses, 1958, The Savings and Loan Business: Its Purposes, Functions and Economic Justification, 1962, Anatomy of the Residential Mortgage, 1964, Readings in Financial Institutions, 1965, The Exchange Community in 1975, 1965; editor: Thrift and Home Ownership: Writings of Fred T. Greene, 1962; contbr.: chpt. to American Enterprise: The Next Ten Years, 1961, The World Capital Shortage, 1977, Securitization Primer, 1996. Mem. deans adv. council Ind. U. Sch. Bus.; mem. adv. bd. Fed. Home Loan Mortgage Corp; vis. com. divsn. social scis. U. Chgo. Served with USAF, 1954-56. Grad. fellow Ind. U., 1950-53; Found. for Econ. Edn. fellow Pitts. Plate Glass Co., 1952 Mem. Acad. Alumni Fellows Ind. U. Sch. Bus., Lambda Alpha, Delta Epsilon Sigma, Beta Gamma Sigma. Office: MGIC Investment Corp MGIC Pla Milwaukee WI 53201

KENDALL, PHILLIP ALAN, lawyer; b. Lamar, Colo., July 20, 1942; s. Charles Stuart and Katherine (Wilson) K.; m. Margaret Roe Greenfield, May 2, 1970; children: Anne, Timothy. BS in Engring., Stanford U., 1964; JD, U. Colo., Boulder, 1969; postgrad., U. Freiburg (Germany), 1965-66. Engr. Siemens Halske, Munich, 1965; of counsel Kraemer, Kendall & Benson LLC, Colorado Springs, Colo., 1969—. Gen. counsel Peak Health Care, Inc., Colorado Springs, 1979-87; bd. dirs. Wells Fargo Banks Colorado Springs. Pres. bd. Colorado Springs Symphony Orch. Assn., 1977-80; bd. dirs. Penrose Hosps., Colorado Springs, 1982-88; pres. bd. Citizen's Goals, Colorado, 1984-86; bd. dirs. Legal Aid Found., Denver, 1988-94, chmn., 1991-93; bd. dirs. Colo. chpt. Nature Conservancy, 1996—, chair 2001—. Recipient Medal of Distinction-Fine Arts, Colorado Springs C. of C., 1983. Mem. ABA, Am. Bar Found., Colo. Bar Found., Colo. Bar Assn. (bd. govs. 1985-88, outstanding young lawyer 1977), El Paso County Bar Assn. (bd. trustees 1983-85), Colorado Springs Estate Planning Coun.(lectr charitable estate planning). Avocations: triathlons, helicopter skiing, marathon swimming, windsurfing, sailing. Home: 1915 Wood Ave Colorado Springs CO 80907-6714 Office: Kraemer Kendall & Benson LLC Ste 300 430 N Tejon St Colorado Springs CO 80903-1167 E-mail: pkendall@k2blaw.com.

KENDALL, REBECCA O. lawyer, pharmaceutical company executive; BS, Ind. U., 1970, JD, 1975. Bar: Ind. 1975. Lectr. Ind. U. Sch. Bus., 1979-80; counsel Nat. Ins. Assn., 1980-81; atty. Eli Lilly and Co., Indpls., 1981-83, sec., gen. counsel Elanco Products co. divsn., 1983-88, sec., gen. counsel Pharm. divsn., 1988-93, dep. gen. counsel, asst. sec., 1993-95, v.p., gen. counsel, 1995-98, sr. v.p., gen. counsel, 1998—. Office: Eli Lilly and Co Lilly Corp Ctr Indianapolis IN 46285-0001

KENDALL, ROBERT DANIEL, priest, theology educator; b. Miami, Ariz., Jan. 11, 1939; s. Robert Daniel and Loretto Agnes (Jakle) K. BA, Gonzaga U., 1963, MA, 1964; ThM, Santa Clara U., 1971; SSL, Pontifical Bibl. Inst., Rome, 1973; STD, Gregorian U., Rome, 1975. Tchr. Brophy Coll. Prep., Phoenix, 1964-67; asst. prof. Gonzaga U., Spokane, Wash., 1975-79; from asst. prof. to assoc. prof. U. San Francisco, 1979-90, prof., 1990—. Author: Focus on Jesus, 1996, The Resurrection, 1997, The Bible for Theology, 1997, The Trinity, 1999, The Incarnation, 2001, The Convergence of Theology: A Festschrift in Honor of Gerald O'Collins, S.J., 2001.. Mem. Soc. Jesus, Cath. Bibl. Assn. Avocations: swimming, family genealogy. Home: 2600 Turk Blvd San Francisco CA 94118-4347

KENDALL, SUSAN GARDES, librarian; b. Hagerstown, Md., Aug. 24, 1948; d. George Austin and Jeanne Faust (Smith) Gardes; m. Steven Walter Kendall, May 25, 1974; children: Kimberly Ann, Kristen Jeanne. BA, William Woods Coll., Fulton, Mo., 1970; MA, Ohio State U., 1971; MLS, Simmons Coll., 1974. Reference libr. Simmons Coll., Boston, 1973-74, Harper Coll., Palatine, Ill., 1976-81, Marquette U., Milw., 1982; head adult svcs. Brookfield (Wis.) Pub. Libr., 1982-87, Batavia (Ill.) Pub. Libr., 1988-90; reference libr. Cobb County Pub. Libr., Marietta, Ga., 1990-93, br. mgr., 1993—. Treas. Mgmt. Recruiters, Lithia Springs, Ga., 1990—; bd. dirs. Gardes Investments Ltd., Columbus, Ohio, 1972—. Contbr. articles to profl. jours. Vol. Olympic Games, Atlanta, 1996; leader Girl Scouts, 1982-94. Mem. S.E. Librs. Assn. (award com. 1993-95, 98—), Ga. Libr. Assn. (pub. librs. 1993-95, award com. 1996-97, v.p. 1997-98, scholarship chair 2000—). Methodist. Office: Cobb County Libr Sys 266 Roswell St NE Marietta GA 30060-2005

KENDALL, SUSAN HAINES, library director; b. Greenville, Ohio, Nov. 5, 1952; d. Kenneth Edward and Zelda Lucille (Delk) Haines; m. John Leroy Sweigart, May 25, 1974 (div. 1986); m. Patrick William Kendall, Nov. 28, 1986. BS in Edn., Wright State U., 1977; MLS, Ball State U., 1981. Cert. tchr., Ohio; cert. libr., Ohio. Libr. clk. Greenville (Ohio) Pub. Libr., 1971-77; libr. asst. Flesh Pub. Libr., Piqua, Ohio, 1977-78, Amos Meml. Pub. Libr., Sidney, Ohio, 1978-81; libr. dir. Preble County Dist. Libr., Eaton, Ohio, 1981—. Tech. task force Ohio Pub. Libr. Info. Network, Columbus, 1993-95, bd. dirs. 1995-2003. Editor Preble's Pride quar., 1986—; contbr. to Ohio Librs., 2000. Bd. dirs. Preble County Hist. Soc., 2000—. Mem. ALA, Ohio Libr. Assn. (mem. coun. S.W. chpt. 1984-86, asst. coord. 1986-87, coord. 1988-89), Miami Valley Librs. (coun. 1981—, v.p. 2002—), Commodore-Preble DAR, Preble County Genealogy Soc. (v.p. 2003), Eaton/Preble County C. of C. Republican. Methodist. Avocations: genealogy, motorcycling. Office: Preble County Dist Libr 450 S Barron St Eaton OH 45320-2402 E-mail: skendall@infinet.com.

KENDALL LEVINE, JUDY, real estate broker, interior designer, writer; d. Allen Harvern Emerman and Serena Roth; m. Ira Bradley Levine, Jan. 10, 1975; children: Jonathan Alexander Levine, Ross Stewart Levine. BA, Finch Coll., 1972. Sales broker Gumley Haft Kleier, N.Y.C., 1997—; interior designer Kendall Assocs., Inc, N.Y.C., 1980—; v.p. Douglas Elliman, N.Y.C., 2003—. Poetry studies N.Y. Pub. Libr., N.Y.C., 2000—02; advisor emergency housing for victims of Sept.11th, N.Y.C., 2001. Author: (poetry) A Childs' Prayer, 2001. Pediatric dir. donor affairs N.Y. Presbyn. Hosp., N.Y. Weil Cornell Med. Ctr., N.Y.C., 1989—93. Mem.: Soc. Libr., Real Estate Bd. of N.Y., Soc. of Journalists & Authors. Avocations: cultural activities, charitable affilations, crafts, golf. Home: 23 East 74th St New York NY 10021 Office: Douglas Elliman 575 Madison Ave New York NY 10022 Office Fax: 212-891-7239.

KENDALL-TACKETT, KATHLEEN ANN, researcher, health psychologist; b. Ogden, Utah, Nov. 21, 1959; d. Leland Dale and Josephine Patricia (Jones) Kendall; m. Douglas Tackett, Aug. 1, 1981; children: Kenneth, Christopher. BA, Calif. State U., Chico, 1982, MA, 1984; PhD, Brandeis U., 1990. Rsch. fellow Family Rsch. Lab., U. N.H., Durham, 1990-92; rsch. scientist Stone Ctr., Wellesley (Mass.) Coll., 1992-94; dir., cons. psychologist Perinatal Edn. Group, Henniker, N.H., 1994-96; rsch. assoc. Family Rsch. Lab., U. N.H., 1995—; rsch. assoc. prof. psychology U. N.H., 2001—. Author: Postpartum Depression, 1993, Hidden Feelings of Motherhood, 2001, Treating the Long-Term Health Effects of Childhood Abuse, 2003, The Well-Ordered Home, 2003; editor: The Health Consequences of Abuse in the Family, 2003; mem. editl. bd. Jour. Child Sexual Abuse, 1995—, Internat. Jour. Child Abuse and Neglect, 1995—; author rsch. studies. Trustee Ctr. for Perinatal Rsch. N.J., 1992—97; mem. Breastfeeding Promotion Task Force N.H., 1996—2000, chair, 2001—; leader LaLeche League Maine/N.H., 1994—, assoc. area profl. liaison, 2001—02, area profl. liaison, 2002—. Recipient Presdl. Visiting Scholar award Calif. State U., Chico, 1999; dept. Justice grantee, 1990, Outstanding alumni award, Calif. State U., Chico, 2003. Fellow: APA (divsn. health psychology); mem.: Internat. Soc. for Prevention of Child Abuse and Neglect (Outstanding Rsch. Study award 1994), Am. Profl. Soc. on Abuse of Children (book rev. editor 1991—95, v.p. 1992—94). Republican. Evangelical. Avocations: music, needlework, reading. Office: Family Rsch Lab U NH 126 HSSC Durham NH 03824 E-mail: kkendallt@aol.com.

KENDE, ANDREW STEVEN, chemist, educator; b. Budapest, Hungary, July 17, 1932; arrived in U.S., 1941, naturalized, 1951; s. George and Elizabeth Kende; m. Frances Boothe, Sept. 14, 1954; 1 child, Mark. AB, U. Chgo., 1951; MS, Harvard, 1954, PhD, 1957. Sr. rsch. scientist Lederle Labs., Am. Cyanamid Co., Pearl River, NY, 1957-63, rsch. assoc., 1963-66, rsch. fellow, 1966-68, cons., 1968-94; prof. chemistry U. Rochester, NY, 1968—, Charles Frederick Houghton prof. chemistry, 1981-2000, prof. oncology, 1982-2000, chmn., 1979-83, assoc. chmn., 1989-90. Vis. prof. SUNY, Buffalo, 1967, Mich. State U., East Lansing, 1968, U. Genéve, 1974, U. Amsterdam, 1989; cons. study sect. NIH, 1972—76, chmn., 1974—76; vis. scholar Stanford U., 1975; cons. Dow Chem. Co., 1975—2001, Bausch and Lomb Co., 1985—90, Eastman Kodak Co., 1987—94, Procter and Gamble Pharms., 1988—, Dow Agrosciences, 1994—2002; Bicentenary lectr. Royal Australian Chem. Inst., 1988; pres. Organic Syntheses Inc., 1992—2002. Mem. bd. editors Organic Reactio 1968—83; editor-in-chief: Organic Reactions, 1983—88; mem. bd. edit Chem. Revs., 1973—76, Organic Syntheses, 1978—87, Synthetic Com 1981—96; assoc. editor: Jour. Organic Chemistry, 1997—2002. Am. Can Soc. fellow, Glasgow (Scotland) U., 1956—57, Guggenheim fellow, 1978— Fellow: Japan Soc. Promotion Sci.; mem.: Am. Chem. Soc. (mem. exec. Rochester sect. 1970—72, chmn. organic chem. divsn. 1978—79, mem. ed bd. Jour. Am. Chem. Soc. 1995—2000, Arthur C. Cope Sr. scholar 200 Home: 19 Larchwood Dr Pittsford NY 14534-2432 Office: U Rochester Ri Campus Dept Chemistry Rochester NY 14627-0216 E-m kende@chem.rochester.edu.

KENDE, CHRISTOPHER BURGESS, lawyer; b. NYC, Apr. 28, 1948; Herbert Alexander and Helga Henrietta (Wieselthier) K.; m. Barbara Gonzal May 22, 1976. BA, MA, Brown U., 1970; JD, NYU, 1973. Bar: NY 19 Mass. 1975, DC 1988, Calif. 1996, US Dist. Ct. (So. and Ea. dists.) NY 19 US Ct. Appeals (2nd cir.) 1976, US Ct. Appeals (9th cir.) 1996, US Supreme 1978. Staff atty. Legal Aid Soc., NYC, 1973-76; assoc. Dewey, Ballantine et NYC, 1976-78, Hill Betts & Nash, NYC, 1978-82, ptnr., 1982-89, Holtzma Wise & Shepard, NYC, 1989-96, Cozen O'Connor, NYC, 1996—. Cont articles to profl. jours. Recipient Silver medal Caisse des Depots, 1984. Me ABA, NY County Lawyers Assn. (past chmn. com. on admiralty and mariti law 1998-99), Maritime Law Assn. (marine ecology com., com. on the CM French Maritime Law Assn., Union Internat. des Avocats (pres. ins. l commn.), India House, Edgartown Yacht Club, Univ. Club NY, The Travell (Paris), Yacht Club de France, Order of Coif, Phi Beta Kappa. Democr Presbyterian. Avocations: sailing, motorcycling, tennis, fitness, gardeni Home: 545 W End Ave Apt 2B New York NY 10024-2723 Office: Cozen O'Connor 45 Broadway New York NY 10006-3007 E-m ckende@cozen.com.

KENDE, HANS JANOS, plant physiology educator; b. Szekesfeherv Hungary, Jan. 18, 1937; came to U.S., 1965, naturalized, 1970; s. Istvan a Katalin (Grosz) K.; m. Gabriele F. Guggenheim, May 15, 1960; childr Benjamin R., Michael, Judith N. Nat. PhD, U. Zurich, Switzerland, 1960; D (hon.), U. Fribourg, Switzerland, 1995 Research Council fellow, Ottawa, Ca 1960-61; research fellow Calif. Inst. Tech., Pasadena, 1961-63; plant physio gist Negev Inst. of Arid Zone Research, Beersheva, Israel, 1963-65; assoc. pr Mich. State U.-Dept. Energy Plant Research Lab., East Lansing, 1965-69, pr 1969—; dir. Dept. Energy Plant Research Lab. Mich. State U., 1985- program mgr. for plant growth and devel. USDA, Washington, 1992. Vis. pr Swiss Fed. Inst. Tech., Zurich, 1972-73, 79-80; vis. scientist Friedrich Miesc Institut, Basel, Switzerland, 1991. Mem. editorial bd. Plant Physiology, 19 84, Biochemie und Physiologie der Pflanzen, 1975-93, Plant Molecular Bi ogy, 1981-83, Planta, 1982-97; (editorial bd.) Jour. Plant Growth Regulati 1982-84, Sci., 1997-2000, Plant Jour., 1998—; contbr. articles to profl. jou Mem. adv. panel for devel. biology NSF, 1974-77. Guggenheim fellow, 1972- Fellow AAAS; mem. NAS, Am. Soc. Plant Biologists (Stephen Hales pr 1998), Leopoldina German Acad. Natural Scis. Home: 805 Virginia Ave E Lansing MI 48823-2835 Office: Mich State U Plant Rsch Lab East Lansing 48824

KENDE, STEPHEN JAMES, insurance sales executive; b. N.Y.C., May 1947; s. Stephen and Helene (Donahue) K.; m. Sally McMahon, June 12, 19 children: Stephen, Alexander. BA, Norwich U., Northfield, Vt., 1970. CL 1981. Ins. salesman, Moscow, Vt., 1977—. Capt. U.S. Army, 1970-77. Me Million Dollar Round Table, Assn. for Advanced Life Underwriters, Am. S CLUs, Internat. Forum, Internat. Assn. Fin. Planning, Burlington Assn. L Underwriters, Norwich U. Alumni Assn. (bd. dirs. 1977-80). Home and Offi PO Box 175 Moscow VT 05662-0175

KENDER, WALTER JOHN, horticulturist, educator; b. Camden, N.J., D 20, 1935; s. Walter and Martha K.; m. Carole Holm, May 26, 1957; children David, Lily BS, Del. Valley Coll., 1957, DSc (hon.), 1993; MS, Rutgers 1959, PhD, 1962. From asst. prof. to assoc. prof. horticulture U. Maine, Oro 1962-69; mem. faculty Cornell U., N.Y. State Agrl. Expt. Sta., Gene 1969-82, prof. pomology, 1975-82, head dept. pomology and viticultu 1972-82; chmn. dept. pomology Cornell U., Ithaca, N.Y., 1975-82; dir. cit research and edn. ctr. U. Fla., Lake Alfred, 1982-96, prof., 1982-2001, pr emeritus, 2001—. Co-chmn. task force fruit rsch. N.E. USDA State Exptl. St 1973-75; sec. Internat. Working Group Juvenility Woody Plants, 1974-82; co Winrock Internat. (USAID) Pakistan, 1989, Indonesia, 1992, P.R. Dept. A 1996; disting. scientist Agrl. U., Wageningen, Netherlands, 1974; mem. adv. Archbold Biol. Sta., 1991-2001. Contbg. author: Blueberry Culture, 19 contbr. profl. jours. Fellow AAAS, Am. Soc. Hort. Sci. (dir. 1975-85, trus endowment fund 1982-87); mem. N.Y. State Hort. Soc., Internat. Soc. H Sci., Internat. Citriculture Soc. (corr.), Am. Pomological Soc. (mem. adv. co Inst. Food Tech. (Fla.), Coun. Agrl. Sci. and Tech., Fla. State Hort. Soc. (h mem. 2000, pres. 1996, chmn. of bd. 1997), N.Y. State Fruit Testing As (sec.-treas. 1972-82), Farm Bur. Adv. Com., Haines City Citrus Growers As (bd. dirs. 1991-96), Fla. Citrus Showcase (bd. dirs. 1996-2000), Sigma Xi (p chpt. pres.). Office: Citrus Rsch & Edn Ctr 700 Experiment Station Rd La Alfred FL 33850-2243 E-mail: kender@lal.ufl.edu.

KENDIG, CALVIN FRIDY, JR., financial consultant, electrical engine consultant; b. Phila., June 18, 1953; s. Calvin Fridy and Margurette Erb Kend BSEE, Pa. State U., 1976. Registered investment advisor, fin. cons.; profl. en Tex., Pa. Constrn. engr. Bechtel Power Corp., San Francisco, 1976—86; proj mgr. Weston Engring., West Chester, Pa., 1986—89, Barton Malow Engrin Sarasota, Fla., 1989—90; owner Kendig Corp., Sarasota, 1990—94; br. m owner SunAmerica Securities, Sarasota, 1994—. Sr. cons. U.S. EPA, Saras 1992—93; sr. adv. mem. John Nuveen and Co., Sarasota, 1997—2001; a mem. Nat. Capts. Assn., Sarasota, 2000—02. Author: My Pile of Pennies, 19 contbr. articles to profl. jours. Pres. Civilian Law Enforcement Assn., Saras 2002, Sarasota Expansion Bd., Sarasota, 1998; v.p. Ctr. for Positive Livi Sarasota, 1995; hon. bd. dirs. AIDS Soc. Fla., Bradenton, Fla., 1992, A Cancer Soc., Sarasota, 1990; hon. mem. cabinet Gov. Dick Thornbur Harrisburg, Pa., 1984. Capt. USCG. Mem.: Citizen Emergency Response Te Assn. (pres. Sarasota chpt.), Assn. Profl. Engrs., Assn. Registered Investm Advisors, Assn. Registered Fin. Cons. (cert. estate advisor). Achieveme include patents for specialty tools to be worn on fingers to hold objects in pla carburetor body designed to pre-cool airflow by utilizing uniform fuel fl research in hypolon cable problems used in nuclear power plants. Offi SunAmerica Securities Inc 4322 Marcott Cir Sarasota FL 34233

KENDIG, WILLIAM LAMAR, retired government official, accountant; York, Pa., Apr. 11, 1938; m. Esther Delores Mostoller, Oct. 14, 1961; 1 ch Marc Daniel. BS, Elizabethtown Coll., 1960; MBA, Am. U., 1965, PhD, 19 Spl. agt. U.S. Treasury Dept., Washington, 1961-65; staff asst. Procter & Gam Co., Cin., 1965-66; mgr., cons. Price Waterhouse & Co., Washington, 1968- asst. vice chancellor U. Md., College Park, 1971-74, acting vice chancel 1974-75; dir., mgmt. cons. U.S. Dept. Interior, Washington, 1975-76, dep. audit and investigations, 1977-78, acting insp. gen., 1978-79, dep. asst. s 1979-81, dir. fin. mgmt. and dep. chief fin. officer, 1981-94, acting prin. dep. a sec., 1988. Mem. Fed. Acctg. Stds. Adv. Bd., 1991-94; ind. cons., 1996 Contbr. articles to profl. jours. Chmn. ops. com., chmn., mem. steering com. Corridor Concerned Citizens, 2001—02; mem. Mayor's Compensation Co Prescott, Ariz., 1999. Named Meritorious Exec., Pres. of U.S., 1986, Disti Exec., 1988; recipient Donald Scantlebury award Joint Fin. Mgmt. Impro ment Program, 1990. Mem. Fed. Fin. Mgrs. Coun. (chmn. 1982-85, chair mg control coord. com. 1987-92), Assn. Govt. Accts. (nat. exec. com. 1984- Chpt. Outstanding Achievement award 1983, 86, Frank Greathouse Disti Leadership award 1992, Cornelius E. Tierney/Ernst & Young Lifetime Rs Achiever award 1996), Pub. Employees Roundtable (bd. dirs. 1987-89, Di award 1988), Sr. Execs. Assn. (bd. dirs. 1985-91, Ted Kern award 198 Worldwide Assurance for Employees Pub. Agys. (bd. dirs. 1993-96), Nat. As Ret. Fed. Employees (1st v.p. Prescott chpt. 2001-02, pres. 2003). Avocatio reading, exercising. E-mail: kendig@commspeed.net.

KENDLER, BERNHARD, editor; b. Cin., Jan. 28, 1934; s. Harry Harlan Mildred (Black) K.; m. Jill Ferguson, Dec. 12, 1975. BA in English, NY 1955; MA in Comparative Lit, U. Mich., 1956. Research asst. Calif. Tc Assn., 1958-60; editor A.S. Barnes & Co., Inc., N.Y.C., 1960-62; copy ed

J.B. Lippincott Co., Phila., 1962-63; mng. editor, editor, exec. editor Cornell U. Press, Ithaca, N.Y., 1963—. Mem. Am. Studies Assn., Phi Beta Kappa. Home: 47 Sheraton Dr Ithaca NY 14850-1680 Office: Cornell U Press PO Box 250 Sage House 512 E State St Ithaca NY 14850-4412 E-mail: bk32@cornell.edu.

KENDLER, HOWARD H(ARVARD), psychologist, educator; b. NYC, June 9, 1919; s. Harry H. and Sylvia (Rosenberg) K.; m. Tracy Seedman, Sept. 20, 1941 (dec. July 2001); children: Joel Harlan, Kenneth Seedman. AB, Bklyn. Coll., 1940; MA, U. Iowa, 1941, PhD, 1943. Instr. U. Iowa, 1943; research psychologist OSRD, 1944; asst. prof. U. Colo., 1946-48; assoc. prof. NYU, 1948-51, prof., 1951-63; chmn. dept. Univ. Coll., 1951-61; prof. U. Calif., Santa Barbara, 1963-89, prof. emeritus, 1989—, chmn. dept. psychology, 1965-66. Project dir. Office Naval Rsch., 1950-68; prin. investigator NSF, 1953-65, USAAF, 1951-53; mem. adv. panel psychobiology NSF, 1960-62; tng. com. Nat. Inst. Child Health and Human Devel., 1963-66; cons. Dept. Def., Smithsonian Instn., 1959-60, Human Resources Rsch. Office, George Washington U., 1960; vis. prof. U. Calif., Berkeley, 1960-61, Hebrew U., Jerusalem, 1974-75, Tel Aviv U., 1990; chief clin. psychologist Walter Reed Gen. Hosp., 1945-46. Author: Basic Psychology, 1963, 3d edit., 1974, Basic Psychology: Brief Version, 1977, Psychology: A Science in Conflict, 1981, Historical Foundations of Modern Psychology, 1987, Amoral Thoughts About Morality: The Intersection of Science, Psychology, and Ethics, 2000; co-author: Basic Psychology: Brief Edition, 1970; co-editor: Essays in Neobehaviorism: A Memorial Volume to Kenneth W. Spence; assoc. editor: Jour. Exptl. Psychology, 1963-65; contbr. to profl. jours., chpts. to books. Served as 1st lt. AUS. Fellow Center for Advanced Studies in Behaviorial Scis., Stanford, Calif., 1969-70; NSF grantee, 1954-76 Mem. Am. Psychol. Assn. (pres. div. exptl. psychology 1964-65, pres. div. gen. psychology 1967-68), Western Psychol. Assn. (pres. 1970-71), Soc. Exptl. Psychologists (exec. com. 1971-73), Psychonomic Soc. (governing bd. 1963-69, chmn. 1968-69), Sigma Xi. Home and Office: 300 Hot Springs Rd Santa Barbara CA 93108 E-mail: kendler@psych.ucsb.edu.

KENDRICK, BUDD LEROY, psychologist; b. Pocatello, Idaho, Apr. 19, 1944; s. Oscar Fredrick Kendrick and Miriam Stuart (Thorn) Stewart; m. Sue Lorraine Allen, Nov. 11, 1966; children: Aaron Matthew and Edgar Seth; m. Beverly Ann Dockter, Dec. 26, 1978; children: Cassandra Rachelle, Angela Priscilla. BA, Idaho State U., 1967, MEd, 1969, EdD, 1974. Lic. psychologist, lic. counselor, Idaho; lic. clin. profl. counselor Mont.; cert. health svc. provider in psychology, nat. cert. counselor; cert. clin. mental health counselor; nat. bd. cert. fellow hypnotherapist; cert. profl. qualification in psychology, critical incident stress mgmt. provider, Red Cross disaster mental health svc. provider. Tchr. psychology Pocatello High Sch., 1967-69; dir. counseling services Midwestern Coll., Denison, Iowa, 1969-70; rehab. counselor Idaho Div. of Vocat. Rehab., Pocatello, 1970-73; counselor (doctoral internship) Counseling Ctr., Idaho State U., Pocatello, 1973-74; rehab. counselor Idaho Div. of Vocat. Rehab., Pocatello, 1974-75; chief of psychology Mental Health Devel. to Disabilites Program, Boise, 1975—; pvt. practice psychology Boise, Idaho, 1977—. Vice-chmn. Idaho State Counselor Licensing Bd., 1982-84, chmn. 1984-85, sec. 1985-86; bd. dirs. Nat. Bd. Cert. Counselors Inc., Alexandria, Va., 1986-93, sec., treas., 1987-89; licensure com. Idaho Personnel and Guidance Assn., 1975-78, chmn. 1977-78, rep. Am. Personnel and Guidance Assn. Licensure Network, 1977-78; allied clin. staff Intermountain Hosp., Boise, 1983-93, Northwest Passages Adolescent Hosp., Boise, 1986-93, Saint Alphonsus Regional Med. Ctr., Boise, 1986-93; designated examiner and dispositioner involuntary commitments and guardianships State of Idaho, 1981—; cons. Idaho Personnel Commn., 1982—; grad. sch. lectr. Idaho State U., 1975; grad. sch. faculty affiliate, Coll. of Idaho, Caldwell, 1981-86; presenter concerning counselor credentialing issues, 1981-86; treas. Idaho Mental Health Assn., 1980-81; mem. Idaho Psychology, Social Work reclassification task force, 1990-91; mem. Idaho Assn. Counseling and Devel. Legis. Task Force for Third Party Benefits for Lic. Profl. Counselors, 1990. Editor: Directory of the Idaho Psychol. Assn., 1983; author numerous articles on hypnosis, counseling and profl. credentialing. Mem. adv. bd. Trio (Upward Bound, Talent Search, Head Start), Idaho State U., 1975-76; mem. Human Rights Com., Idaho State Sch. and Hosp., 1977. Recipient Disting. Svc. award Idaho Pers. & Guidance Assn., 1978, Profl. Achievement award Idaho State U., 1987, Spl. Recognition award Idaho Assn. for Counseling and Devel., 1989, Lawrence Schumacher Meml. Employee of Yr. award State of Idaho, 1995, Friend of Rsch. and Assessment for Counseling, Inc., Disting. Grad. award Idaho State U., 2001. Fellow Am. Coll. Advanced Practice Psychologists (founding mem. Idaho chpt.), Idaho Psychol. Assn. (sec. 1982-84); mem. Idaho Mental Health Counselors Assn. (charter), Idaho Counseling Assn. (leadership coun. 1977-78), Am. Counseling Assn. (pub. policy and legis. com., mem.-at-large 1992-94, chairperson nat. licensure subcom. 1992-94), Am. Mental Health Counselors Assn., Am. Psychol. Assn. (divsn. 17 counseling psychology, div. 30 psychol. hypnosis), Sons of Confederate Vets., Chi Sigma Iota Internat. Profl. Counseling and Acad. Honor Soc., Idaho Hist. Soc. (cert. Idaho pioneer descendant), Stuart-Mosby Hist. Soc. Avocations: sword collecting, genealogy, collecting limited edits. Civil War pewter sculptures, War Between the States history, collecting autographed celebrity photographs.

KENDRICK, DAVID ANDREW, economist, educator; b. Gatesville, Tex., Nov. 14, 1937; s. Andrew Green and Nina Alice (Murray) K.; m. Gail Tidd, July 1, 1964; children— Ann, Colin. BA, U. Tex., 1960; PhD (Woodrow Willson fellow 1961-62), MIT, 1965. Asst. prof. Harvard U., Cambridge, Mass., 1966-70; vis. scholar Stanford U., Calif., 1969-70; vis. prof. MIT, Cambridge, 1978-79; prof. econs. U. Tex., Austin, 1970—. Author: (with A. Stoutiesdijk) The Planning of Industrial Investment Programs, 1978, (with P. Dixon and S. Bowles) Notes and Problems in Microeconomic Theory, 1980, Stochastic Control for Economic Models, 1981, Feedback: A New Framework for Macroeconomic Policy, 1988, Models for Analyzing Comparative Advantage, 1990. Served with U.S. Army, 1960-61. Ford faculty fellow, 1969-70 Fellow AAAS; mem. Econometric Soc., Am. Econs. Assn., Soc. Econ. Dynamics and Control. (pres. 1980), Soc. Computational Econs. (pres. 1998). Home: 7209 Lamplight Ln Austin TX 78731-2119 Office: U Tex Dept Econs ECB 3-134E Austin TX 78712

KENDRICK, JAMES EARL, business consultant; b. Indpls., Sept. 12, 1940; s. John William and Mab.e E. (Coleman) K.; m. Carrie L. Fair, July 19, 1969; children: Carrie F., Leslie F., John F. BA, Butler U., 1963; postgrad., Ind. U., 1963-65. Exec. dir. Knox County Econ. Opportunity Coun., Barbourville, Ky., 1965-66; rsch. scientist NYU, 1967-68; mgr. Volt Info. Scis., Washington, 1968-71, Nat. Urban Coalition, 1972-74; pres. Kendrick & Co., Washington, 1974-91, sr. v.p., 1992-93; pres. P2C2 Group, Silver Spring, Md., 1994—. Devel. cons. Coppin State Coll., Balt., 1995-99, Exec. Office of the Pres. of The U.S., 1999-2000. Author: Community Energy Workbook, 1974; National Urban Agenda Survey, 1974; (video) Americans on the Move, 1984; (software) Help for PC DDS, 1985, Children of 2010, 1999; contbr. articles to profl. jours. and newsletters. Recipient Rural Svc. award OEO, 1968; citation Washington chpt. Am. Soc. Tng. and Devel., 1971; named one of Outstanding Young Men of Am., 1974, Ranked Among the Best 100 Mgmt. Firms in N.Am. by Consulting News, 1993. Mem. Inst. Mgmt. Consultants. E-mail: p2c2@erols.com.

KENDRICK, JOHN WHITEFIELD, economist, educator, consultant; b. N.Y.C., July 27, 1917; s. Benjamin Burks and Elizabeth W.W. (Shields) K.; m. Maxine Fillyaw; children: Bonnie Elizabeth, Karen Johanna, John Burks. AB, U. N.C., 1937, MA, 1939; PhD, George Washington U., 1955. Economist Nat. Resources Planning Bd., Washington, 1941-43, U.S. Dept. Commerce, Washington, 1946-53, chief economist, 1976-77; sr. staff mem. Nat. Bur. Econ. Rsch., N.Y.C., 1953-56, part-time, 56-78; prof. econs. George Washington U., Washington, 1956-88, prof. emeritus, 1988—. Univ. prof. U. Conn., Storrs, 1964-66; vis. prof. Georgetown U., UCLA, Stanford U., U. Hawaii, Simon Fraser U., v.p. for econ. rsch. The Conf. Bd., N.Y.C., 1972-73, part-time, 1973-76; dir., trustee Pioneer Mut. Funds, Boston, 1961—; bd. dirs. Am. Productivity and Quality Ctr., Houston, 1977—; cons. AT&T, 1964-83, Office Mgmt. and Budget, NSF, GAO, other cos. and govt. agys.; mem. Conf. on Rsch. in Income and Wealth, chmn. 1963-64; adj. scholar Am. Enterprise Inst., 1980-86. Author: Productivity Trends in the United States, 1961 (Pres. Kennedy Libr. award 1962), (with Daniel Creamer) Measuring Company Productivity: Handbook with Case Studies, 1961, rev. edit., 1965, Economic Accounts and Their Uses, 1972, The Formation and Stocks of Total Capital, 1976 (also Russian trans.), Improving Company Productivity, 1977, (with E. Grossman) Productivity in the United States: Trends and Cycles, 1980, (with John B. Kendrick) Personal Productivity, 1988 (trans. in Korean and Japanese), other books; editor 6 conf. vols.; mem. editorial bds. Rev. of Income and Wealth, Bus. Econs.; contbr. over 150 articles to profl. jours. 1st lt. A.C., U.S. Army, 1943-45; served with U.S. Strategic Bombing Survey, 1945-46, ETO. Recipient Graham Dodd award for article Fin. Analysts Jour., 1962, Abramson award for article in Bus. Econs. jour., 1987. Fellow Am. Statis. Assn., Nat. Assn. Bus. Economists; mem. Am. Econ. Assn., So. Econ. Assn. (pres. 1982-83), Nat. Economists Club (pres. 1975-76, chmn. bd. 1976-77), World Acad. Productivity Sci., Atlantic Econ. Soc. (disting. assoc., pres. 1992-93), George Washington U. Club, Phi Beta Kappa. Unitarian-Universalist. Avocations: swimming, walking, reading, tv talk shows. Office: George Washington U Dept Econ Washington DC 20052-0001 Home: Apt 1228 3440 S Jefferson St Falls Church VA 22041-3131

KENDRICK, KERRY, military officer; b. Southside, Tenn. Degree in polit. sci., Austin Peay State U., 1977; MPA, Jacksonville State U. Commd. 2d. lt. US Army, advanced through grades to col., dept. provost marshal, platoon leader 501st mil. police co., chief enlisted evaluations army mil. polic sch., co. comdr., recorder promotion bd., assignment officer mil. police br., personnel policy joint staff, force protection officer dept. army, served in Ops. Desert Shield and Desert Storm, exec. officer Protection Officer and Law Enforcement Divsn., staff leader combined arms & svc. staff sch., commdr. 728th mil. police battalion Taegu, Republic of Korea, comdr. 89th mil. police brigade; chief staff Army Rsch. Lab., Adelphi, Md. Recipient Bronze Star medal, U.S. Army, Meritorious Svc. medal with five oak-leaf clusters, Joint Svc. Commendation medal, Army Commendation medal, Army Achievement medal. Office: US Army Rsch Lab Attn AMSRL-CS-EA-PA 2800 Powder Mill Rd Adelphi MD 20783-1197

KENDRICK, MARK CLEVELAND, real estate executive; b. Augsburg, Germany, Dec. 30, 1957; (parents Am. citizens); s. Chester Delmon and Eva Anna (Mittendorfer) Kendrick; m. Sharon K. Greenland, 1993. AA in Law Enforcement, Fayetteville (N.C.) C.C., 1982; BA in Social Work, Meth. Coll., Fayetteville, 1983; M in Guidance, Campbell U., Ft. Bragg, N.C., 1986. Cert. internat. employee assistance profl., nat. employee assistance profl., N.C.; lic. employee assistance profl., N.C. Emergency response team Moore Meml. Hosp., Pinehurst, N.C., 1974-76; mgr. Fleishman's, Fayetteville, 1977-78; mgr. furnishings Nowells, Fayetteville, 1978-79; deputy Cumberland Co. Sheriff's Dept., Fayetteville, 1982-83; ptnr. Kendrick Real Estate, Fayetteville, 1983—, KD Graphics, Fayetteville, 1999—; pres., CEO KV Cons., Inc./Today's EAP, 1995—. Vol. N.C. Dept. of Corrections, 1981-82, intern, 1980; dep. Cumberland County Sheriff's Dept., 1982—, dep. search and recovery team, 1991-97; comptr. Cape Fear Regional Fair Assn., 1985-88; v.p. Cumberland County Heart Assn., 1984-85; sub-sgt. Cumberland County Rescue Squad, 1979-82; adv. commn. Fayetteville Parks and Recreation, 1982-86; bd. dirs. Fayetteville Sr. Citizens Svc. Ctr., 1983-86, Fayetteville Parks and Recreation Five Yr. Study Commn., 1984-86, Cumberland Interfaith Hospitality Network, Inc., 1995-97; pres. Cumberland County Smart Start, 1995-97; Fayetteville City Councilman, 1986—; mem. Fayetteville Revitalization Commn., 1986-89, Fayetteville-Cumberland County Liaison Com., 1986-89, City-County Fire Liaison Com., 1986-89, ARC Disaster Team, 1984-86, Young Dem. Club, N.C. Transp. Adv. Com., 1989—; chmn. City Streets-Sidewalks and Transp. Com., 1989—, City County Liaison, 1986-87, PWC Deregulation com., 1998—; mem. travic, comm. and pub. policy com. N.C. League Municipalities, 1999—; mem. pub. safety and crime prevention com. Nat. League Cities, 1999—; sec. Myrover-Reese Fellowship Homes, Inc., 1992—, chmn., 2001-; exec. com. Fayetteville Hospitality House, 1992-96; chmn. N.C. Partnership for Children, 1995-97, mem. state strategic planning com., 1996-97; active Fayetteville Once and for All com., 1995—; Sunday Sch. dir. Grace Bapt. Ch., 1996—, deacon, 1996-2002; bd. dirs. Homeless Coalition, 1997-99; mem. City-County Joint Planning Study Com., 1999—; vice chmn. Metro Planning Orgn., NC, 1998—; mem. alumni bd. dirs. Meth. Coll., 2000—. Named 1st 10th Degree Jaycee in Nation U.S. Jaycees, 1985, one of Five Outstanding Young Men in N.C. Farm Bur., 1985, Outstanding Young Person in Govt., 1986; recipient Disting. Svc. award, 1985, Charles Kulp Jr. Meml. award U.S. Jaycees, 1985, Thomas Jefferson award State of N.C. and Sta. WTVD-TV, 1986. Mem. Fayetteville Jaycees (pres. 1984-85, treas. 1985-87), N.C. Jaycees (regional dir. 1985-86, awards chmn. 1986-87, Freedom Guard award 1984, Linn D. Garibaldi award 1985-86, Larry Bowers Meml. award 1986), Meth. Coll. Alumni Assn. (bd. dirs. 1985-95, v.p. 1993-95), KP, Toastmasters (N.C. state speaker 1984), Lions (v.p., Fayetteville host 1996-97, pres. 1997-98), Lambda Chi Alpha. Democrat. Baptist. Avocations: gun collecting, golf, scuba diving, travel, drums. Office: 2927 Rosecroft Dr Fayetteville NC 28304

KENDRICK, PETER MURRAY, communications executive, investor; b. Winchester, Mass., Oct. 8, 1936; s. Wallace Dolloff and Esther (Burke) K.; m. Grace Terry, June 17, 1967; children: Caroline, Timothy. BSBA, Babson Coll., 1962. Office mgr. Am. Hosp. Supply Corp., Chgo. and Charlotte, N.C., 1962-65; registered rep. Hayden, Stone & Co., 1966-69; gen. mgr. Continental Cablevision, Concord, N.H. and Jackson, Mich., 1969-74; pres. New Eng. Cablevision, Portland, Maine, 1974-79, chmn. bd., 1980; pres. Home Theater Network, Portland and N.Y.C., 1977-87; chmn. bd. Envirologic Data Corp., Portland, 1984-86; sr. v.p. Watson Techs., Portland, 1994-96; pres., CEO, chmn. Internet Maine, Internet N.E., Inc. (merger Harvard Net, Inc.), Portland, 1997; interim CEO Compass Cablesys., Portland and Marblehead, Mass., 1998—99. Founder, pres. The Travel Channel, 1981-86; founder The Disney Channel, 1981; vice chmn. bd. dirs., pres., treas. Internat. Cablevision, Inc., Bronxville, N.Y., 1987-93; chmn. bd. Kendrick Corp., Portland, Maine, 1986—, Kendrick Tech. Corp., 1992—, Legal Document Systems, Inc., Washington, 1993-94, The Film Channel, Inc., Portland, 1987-90, Yankee Books, Camden, Maine, 1989-91. Trustee North Yarmouth Acad., Yarmouth, Maine, chmn. ann. giving campaign, 1986-87. With USAF, 1956-59. Recipient Highest Programming award Cable TV Nat. Assn., 1973, 86. Mem. New Eng. Cable TV Assn. (v.p. 1972, pres. 1975), Mich. Cable TV Assn. (v.p. 1973), Portland Country Club, Portland Yacht Club, Cable TV Pioneers. Office: 4 Landing Woods Ln Falmouth ME 04105-1948 E-mail: kendrick@maine.rr.com.

KENDRICK, ROBERT WARREN, county official; b. Houston, July 9, 1946; s. Alford Manuel and Alpha Mae (Carter) K.; m. Margaret Walker, June 9, 1973. BA, U. Houston, 1969, JD, 1977; mgmt. cert., Harvard U., 1989. Cert. security cons., law enforcement and security instr.; tech. mgmt. cert. Tex. A&M U., 1996. Dist. exec. Boy Scouts Am., Monroe, La., 1974; corp. security coord. Foley's Dept. Stores, Houston, 1975-77, staff legal asst., 1978-81; exec. dir. Crimestoppers of Houston, Inc., 1982; coord. criminal justice ct. U. Houston-Downtown, 1983-85, assoc. dir. criminal justice ct., 1985-87, dir. criminal justice ct., 1987-89, exec. dir. divsn. continuing edn., dean's coun., 1989-96, spl. asst., provost, 1996-97; adminstrv. supt. precinct 3 Harris County, 1997—; chair e-govt. policy com., Dept. Justice Houston Project, 1998—. Bd. dirs. Am. Soc. Indsl. Security Found., Washington, 1988—, Internat. Found. Protection Officers, Cochrane, Can., 1988-89, U. Tex. Health Sci. Ctr. Cmty. Adv. Bd., Houston, 1987-89. Mem. edit. adv. bd. Security Jour., 1989-98. Councilman, City of Bellaire, Tex., 1984-86, planning and zoning commr., 1982-84; bd. dirs. Learning Resource Network, 1993-97; mem. regional criminal justice planning com. Houston-Galveston Area Coun. Govts., 1984—; founding bd. dirs. Crime Stoppers Houston, 1981; grand juror Harris County Grand Jury, Houston, 1989; mem. Mayor's Tex. City Action Plan Task Force, 1993; mem. Mayor's Imagine Houston Project, 1994-96; criminal justice com. Leadership Houston, 1989—; chmn. profl. devel. Press Club of Houston, 1996-97; commr. Joint City/County Commn. on Children, 1997—; chair Harris County Internet com., 1998—. Capt. U.S. Army, 1971-73. Recipient Corp. Security award Security World Mag., 1977. Mem. Am. Soc. Indsl. Security (chpt. chmn. 1980, Security Svc. award 1994), Risk and Ins. Mgmt. Soc. (local bd. mem. 1979-81), Tex. Pub. Rels. Assn., Harris County Area Chiefs of Police, Buffalo Bayou Partnership (security com. advisor 1988—), Houston C. of C. (chmn. crime control com. 1988—), Leadership Houston (grad., bd. dirs. 1987—). Avocations: mil. history, Titantic Hist. Soc., swimming. Office: Harris County Precinct 3 16635 Clay Rd Houston TX 77084-4007 E-mail: bob_kendrick@co.harris.tx.us.

KENDRICK, WILLIAM BRYCE, biology educator, writer, publisher, consultant; b. Liverpool, Lancashire, Eng., Dec. 3, 1933; arrived in Can., 1958; s. William and Lillian Maud (Latham) K.; m. Laureen Anne Carscadden, Dec. 14, 1978; children: Clinton, Kelly. BSc with honors, U. Liverpool, 1955, PhD, 1958, DSc, 1980. Postdoctoral fellow NRC, Ottawa, Ont., Can., 1958-59; rsch. scientist Agr. Can., Ottawa, 1959-65; asst. prof. U. Waterloo, Ont., 1965-66, assoc. prof., 1966-71, prof., 1971-94, disting. prof. emeritus, 1994—, assoc. dean, 1985-93. Adj. prof. U. Victoria, B.C., 1994—; propr. Mycologue Pub. and Cons. Author: The Fifth Kingdom, 1985, 2d rev. and enlarged edit., 1991, 3rd edit., 2001, CD Rom version 3.5, 2003, A Young Person's Guide To The Fungi, 1986; co-author: Genera of Hyphomycetes, 1980, An Evolutionary Survey of Fungi, Algae and Plants, 1992; editor: Taxonomy of Fungi Imperfecti, The Whole Fungus, Biology of Conidial Fungi; contbr. articles to profl. jours. Guggenheim fellow, 1979-80. Fellow Royal Soc. Can.; mem. Acad. Sci. (hon. sec. 1984-91), Mycological Soc. Am. (Disting. Mycologist award 1995), Br. Mycol. Soc. (centenary fellow 1996), Can. Botan. Assn. (Lawson medal 2001). Mem. Green Party. Avocations: reading, music, walking, photography, rowing. Home and Office: 8727 Lochside Dr Sidney BC Canada V8L 1M8 E-mail: bryce@mycolog.com. *Curiosity is the key to a full life. Keep on asking questions-and keep on trying to answer them-until the day you die.*

KENDZIOR, ROBERT JOSEPH, marketing executive; b. Mar. 24, 1952; s. Joseph W. and Josephine R. Kendzior. BArch, Ill. Inst. Tech., 1975. Account supr. Burger King Corp. Rogers Merchandising, Inc., Chgo., 1975-77; account exec. Walgreen Corp. Eisaman, Johns & Laws Advt., Inc., Chgo., 1977-78, v.p. mktg. Dunkin Donuts Am., Inc., Randolph, Mass., 1978-95; v.p., chief mktg. officer Factory Card Outlet Am., Inc., Chgo., 1995-98; v.p. internat. mktg. Allied Domecq Retailing, 1999—; v.p. Internat. Mktg. and Retail Concepts, Randolph. Acting dir., bd. dirs. Baskin-Robbins Japan. Recipient Most Valuable Promotion award PepsiCo, 1984. Mem. Triangle Fraternity.

KENEALLY, KATHRYN MARIE, lawyer; b. Dayton, Ohio, Apr. 30, 1958; d. William Henry and Joanna Gertrude K.; m. Thomas Marshall, Oct. 16, 1992. BA, Cornell U., 1979; JD, Fordham U., 1982; LLM in Taxation, NYU, 1993. Bar: N.Y., 1983, U.S. Dist. Ct. (so., ea. dists.) N.Y., 1983, U.S. Ct. Appeal (2d, 3d, 11th cirs.), U.S. Tax Ct. Law clk. to Hon. E. R. Neaher U.S. Dist. Ct. (ea. dist.) N.Y., Bklyn., 1982-83; assoc. Skadden Arps Slate Meagher & Flom, N.Y.C., 1983-85, Kostelanetz Ritholz Tigue & Fink, N.Y.C., 1985-90, ptnr., 1990-93, Kostelanetz & Fink, LLP, N.Y.C., 1993-99; mem. Owen & Davis, PC, N.Y.C., 2000—02; ptnr. Fulbright & Jaworski, L.L.P., N.Y.C., 2002—. Columnist The Champion, 1996—, Jour. Tax Practice and Prodecure, 1999—; co-author: Practice Under Federal Sentencing Guidelines, 1998; contbr. articles to profl. jours. Mem. practitioners adv. group U.S. Sentencing Commn., 1993—. Mem. ABA (chmn. taxation sect., civil and criminal tax penalties com. 200-02), Nat. Assn. Criminal Def. Lawyers (life). Home: 48 Charlotte Pl Hartsdale NY 10530-2602 Office: Fulbright & Jaworski LLP 660 Fifth Ave New York NY 10103 E-mail: kkeneally@fulbright.com.

KENEALLY, THOMAS MICHAEL, author; b. Australia, Oct. 7, 1935; s. Edmund Thomas and Elsie Margaret (Coyle) K.; m. Judith Mary Martin, Aug. 21, 1965; children: Margaret Ann, Jane Rebecca. Ed., St. Patrick's Coll., Strathfield, N.S.W. Writings include (fiction) The Place at Whitton, 1965, The Fear, 1965, Bring Larks and Heroes, 1967, Three Cheers for the Paraclete, 1968, The Survivor, 1969, A Dutiful Daughter, 1971, The Chant of Jimmie Blacksmith, 1972 (Heinemann award for lit. Royal Soc. Lit. 1973), Blood Red, Sister Rose, 1974, Gossip From the Forest, 1975, Moses the Lawgiver, 1975, Season in Purgatory, 1977, A Victim of the Aurora, 1977, (children's book) Ned Kelly and the City of Bees, 1978, Passenger, 1979, Confederates, 1979, The Cut-Rate Kingdom, 1980, Schindler's List, 1982 (Booker McConnell prize for fiction 1982, Fiction prize L.A. Times 1983), Outback, 1983, (play) Bullie's House, 1985, A Family Madness, 1985, The Playmaker, 1987, To Asmara, 1989, Flying Hero Class, 1991, (non-fiction) The Place Where Souls Are Born, 1992, (non-fiction) Now and in Time to Be, 1992, Woman of the Inner Sea, 1992, Jacko: The Great Intruder, 1994, A River Town, 1995, Homebush Boy-A Memoir, 1995; (plays) Halloran's Little Boat, 1966, Childermass, 1968, An Awful Rose, 1972; (non-fiction) The Great Shame, 1999, (fiction) Bettany's Book, 2000, (non-fiction) An American Scoundrel, The Life of the Notorious Civil War General Dan Sickles, 2002, An Angel in Australia, 2002, (non-fiction) Lincoln, 2003. Inaugural mem. Australia-China Coun., 1978-83; mem. adv. panel Australian Constn. Commn., 1985-88; mem. Literary Arts Bd. Australia, 1985-88; chmn. Australian Rep. Movement, 1991-93, dir., 1994—. Decorated Officer Order of Australia; recipient Miles Franklin award, 1967, 68, Captain Cook Bi-Centerary prize, 1970. Fellow Royal Soc. Lit. (London), Am. Acad. Arts and Scis.; mem. PEN, Australian Soc. Authors (chmn. 1987-90), Nat. Book Coun. Australia (pres. 1985-90. Office: Curtis Brown (Australia) P/L PO Box 19 Paddington NSW 2021 Australia

KENEALY, PATRICK, publishing company executive; b. Boston, Oct. 31, 1959; s. William Patrick and M. Carol Kenealy. BA in Econs., Harvard U., 1980. Tech. editor GML Corp., Lexington, Mass., 1977-81; sr. editor Cahners Pub. Co., Boston, 1981-83; assoc. pub. Ziff-Davis Pub. Co., N.Y.C., 1983-86; pres., pub. Digital News Pub. subs. IDG Communications, Boston, 1986—; CEO, pres., publ. IDG's PC World Mag., 1990—96; mng. gen. ptnr. IDG Ventures, 1996—2002; CEO IDG, Framingham, Mass., 2002—. Sr. editor Mini-Micro Systems mag.; editor Digital Rev. mag. Mem. Assn. for Computing Machinery, Bus. and Profl. Advt. Assn., Am. Bus. Pubs., Soc. Am. Magicians. Republican. Home: 7 Hancock Ave Lexington MA 02420-3412 Office: IDG 2d Fl 492 Old Connecticut Path Framingham MA 01701

KENEN, PETER BAIN, economist, educator; b. Cleve., Nov. 30, 1932; s. Isaiah Leo and Beatrice (Bain) K.; m. Regina Horowitz, Aug. 21, 1955; children: Joanne Lisa, Marc David, Stephanie Hope, Judith Rebecca. AB, Columbia U., 1954; MA, Harvard U., 1956, PhD, 1958. Mem. faculty Columbia U., 1957-71, prof. econs., 1964-71, chmn. dept., 1967-69, provost univ., 1969-70; prof. econs. and internat. fin. Princeton (N.J.) U., 1971—, dir. internat. fin. sect., 1971-99; Ford rsch. prof. U. Calif., Berkeley, 1979-80. Rschr. on internat. monetary theory and policy; cons. Coun. Econ. Advisors, 1961, U.S. Treasury, 1962-68, 77-80, 95-98, Bur. Budget, 1964-68, IMF, 1990, 92. Author: British Monetary Policy and the Balance of Payments (1951-1957), 1960, Giant Among Nations, 1960; author: (with A.G. Hart and A. Entine) Money, Debt and Economic Activity, 4th edit., 1969; author: (with R. Lubitz) International Economics, 3d edit., 1971; author: A Model of the U.S. Balance of Payments, 1978; author: (with P.R. Allen) Asset Markets, Exchange Rates and Economic Integration, 1980; author: Essays in International Economics, 1980, Managing Exchange Rates, 1988, Exchange Rates and Policy Coordination, 1989, Exchange Rates and the Monetary System, 1994, Economic and Monetary Union in Europe, 1995, International Economy, 4th edit., 2000, The International Financial Architecture: What's New? What's Missing?, 2001; editor: International Trade and Finance, Frontiers for Research, 1975; editor: (with others) The International Monetary System Under Flexible Exchange Rates, 1982; editor: (with R.W. Jones) Handbook of International Economics, 1984; editor: Managing the World Economy, 1994, Understanding Interdependence, 1995; editor: (with A.K. Swoboda) Reforming the International Monetary and Financial System, 2000; contbr. articles to profl. jours. Recipient David A. Wells prize Harvard U., 1958-59, Univ. medal Columbia U., 1977; Ctr. Advanced Study Behavioral Scis. fellow, 1971-72, John Simon Guggenheim Found. fellow, 1975-76, Res. Bank Australia fellow, 1983-84, Royal Inst. Internat. Affairs fellow, 1987-88, German Marshall Fund fellow, 1987-88, Houblon-Norman fellow Bank of Eng., 1991-92, fellow Res. Bank New Zealand, 2002. Mem. Am. Econ. Assn., Coun. Fgn. Rels., Royal Econ. Soc., Group of Thirty. Home: 176 Western Way Princeton NJ 08540-7208 Office: Princeton U Dept of Econs Fisher Hall Princeton NJ 08544-1021

KENIGSBERG, MARTIN IRA, psychologist; b. N.Y.C., Apr. 27, 1952; s. Samuel and Phyllis (Gordon) K.; m. Sharon Rene Finkelstein, June 26, 1977; children: Adam, Phyllis, Max. AB, AM, Stanford U., 1974; PhD, Pa. State U., 1978. Lic. psychologist Calif; Diplomate Am. Bd. Profl. Psychology. Intern VA Med. Ctr., Palo Alto, Calif., 1977-78; NIH fellow Stanford (Calif.) U. Med. Ctr., 1978-80; coord. psychol. svcs. UCLA Ctr. Health Enhancement, 1980; staff psychologist VA Med. Ctr., Long Beach, Calif., 1981—. Fellow Acad. Clin. Psychology (v.p.); mem. APA. Avocations: paleontology, volleyball. Office: VA Med Ctr Psychology 06/116B 5901 E 7th St Long Beach CA 90822-5201 E-mail: martin.kenigsberg@med.va.gov.

KENISON, LYNN T. chemist; b. Provo, Utah, Feb. 20, 1943; s. John Silves and Grace (Thacker) Kenison; m. Daralyn Wold, June 10, 1969; children: Marlene, Mark, Evan, Guy, Amy, Suzanne. BS in Chemistry, Brigham Young U., 1968, MS in Chemistry, 1971. Tchr. Weber County Sch. Dist., Ogden, Utah, 1968-69; bench chemist Salt Lake City/County Health Dept., 1971-74; chemist

U.S. Dept. Labor, OSHA Salt Lake Tech. Ctr., 1974—, bench chemist, 1974-77, supr., br. chief, 1977-84, sr. chemist, 1984—. Tech. writer OSHA; safety officer OSHA Tech. Ctr., 2002—. Editor: Review Methods and Analytical Papers Before Publication, 1984—; tech. writer:. Scouting coord. Boy Scouts Am., cubmaster local pk., 1990—94, unit commr. scouting, 1995—97; vol. spkr. in local pub. schs., 1988—2003; councilman City of West Bountiful, Utah, 1980—83, 1985—89; missionary LDS Ch., 1962—64. Mem.: Fed. Exec. Assn. (Disting. Svc. award, Jr. award for Outstanding Fed. and Cmty. Svc. 1980), Am. Indsl. Hygiene Assn., Toastmasters Internat. (treas. Salt Lake City chpt. 1987—91). Avocations: woodworking, boy scout activities. Home: 1745 N 600 W West Bountiful UT 84087-1150 Office: US Dept of Labor OSHA Salt Lake Tech Ctr 1781 S 300 W Salt Lake City UT 84115-1802

KENISON, RAYMOND ROBERT, fraternal organization administrator, director; b. Mo., Sept. 23, 1932; s. Raymond Roy and Emma Oleta (Holder) K.; m. Marjorie White, Feb. 1, 1955; children: Debra Kenison Brown, Peggy Kenison Crim, Raymond Roger, Robert B. AA, Hannibal LaGrange Coll., 1953; BA, U. Mo., 1961; postgrad., Cen. Bapt. Sem., Kansas City, 1957, Midwestern Bapt. Sem., 1965; cert. fin. planner, Coll. Fin. Planning, Denver; DivD, Hannibal LaGrange Coll., 1994. Cert. instr. Pastor First Bapt.Ch., Bates City, Mo., 1954-56, Friendship Bapt. Ch., Mexico, Mo., 1956-62, Immanuel Bapt. Ch., Hannibal, Mo., 1962-77; dir. devel. Mo. Bapt. Children's Home, Bridgeton, 1977-80, exec. dir., 1980—; pres., 1992—. Pres. bd. trustees Hannibal-Lagrange Coll.; co-founder, pres. Viability R & D Group. Mem. Child Welfare League of Am. Inc.; Nat. Soc. of Fund Raising Execs.; pres. Hannibal Coun. Alcohol and Drug Abuse; bd. dirs. Hannibal Cmty. Chest, 1974-79, pres. Hannibal Ministerial Alliance; bd. dirs. Alliance for Children and Families, Mo. Alliance for Children and Families. Kenison Complex named in his honor. Mem. Nat. Foster Parents Assn., So. Bapt. Child Care Execs. (pres.), Nat. Assn. of Homes for Children (sec.), Mo. Child Care Assn. (bd. dirs., pres. 1994—), S.W. Assn. of Child Care Execs., Inst. CFPs, Hannibal Investment Club (pres. 1976-78, 82-83), Viability R&D Group (co-founder, pres.). Home: 4 River Hills Hannibal MO 63401-6218 Office: Mo Bapt Children's Home 11300 Saint Charles Rock Rd Bridgeton MO 63044-2793

KENISTON, KENNETH, psychologist, educator; b. Chgo., Jan. 6, 1930; s. Hayward and Roberta (Cammell) K.; m. Ellen Wyllar, June 20, 1960 (div. Aug. 1975); children: Ann Rogers, Sarah Hayward; m. Suzanne Berger, Jan. 10, 1976; 1 child, Daniel Eben. BA, Harvard Coll., 1951; DPhil, Oxford U., 1956; LLD (hon.), Notre Dame U., 1971; DSc (hon.), Colgate U., 1972. From rsch. asst. to rsch. assoc. dept. social rels. Harvard U., Cambridge, Mass., 1955-62; from asst. prof. to assoc. prof. psych. Yale Med. Sch., New Haven, 1962-68, prof. psych., 1968-75; Andrew W. Mellon prof. human devel. Mass. Inst. Tech., Cambridge, 1975—. Lectr. on clin. psychology Harvard U., 1958-62, resident fellow, asst. sr. tutor Eliot House, 1953-59; assoc. dir., acting dir., then dir. Behavior Scis. Study Ctr., Yale Med. Sch., 1965-72; fellow Davenport Coll., Yale U., 1962-75; chmn., exec. dir. Carnegie Coun. on Children, New Haven, 1972-78; dir. program in sci., tech. and soc. Mass. Inst. Tech., 1987-92, dir. grad. studies, 1993-96, dir. projects, 1996—; dir. MIT India Program, 1998—; mem. Carnegie Commn. on Higher Edn., 1968-73, bd. dirs. Overseers Harvard Coll., 1969-75,MacArthur Prize Fellows selection com., 1979-85; com. on selection Guggenheim Found., 1992-94; vis. scholar Ecole de Mines, Paris, 1980-81; vis. prof. U. Paris Sorbonne, 1986-87, Centro de Estudios Avanzados de Ciencias Sociales, Madrid, 1990, Nat. Inst. Advanced Studies, Indian Inst. Sci., Bangalore, 1999, 2001. Author: The Uncommitted, 1966, Young Radicals, 1968, All Our Children, 1977, The Fragile Contract, 1994, Earth, Air, Fire, Water, 1999; contbr. articles to profl. jours., chpts. to books. Rhodes scholar Balliol Coll., Oxford U., 1951-53; jr. fellow Harvard U., 1953-56; Guggenheim fellow, 1980-81. Fellow AAAS; mem. Coun. Fgn. Rels., Phi Beta Kappa, Sigma Xi. Office: Mass Inst Tech E51-163 77 Massachusetts Ave Cambridge MA 02139 E-mail: kken@mit.edu.

KENKEL, JAMES LAWRENCE, economics educator; b. Cin., Mar. 25, 1944; s. Lawrence J. and Mildred (Schmidt) K.; children: Julie, Tim. BA, Xavier U., Cin., 1966; MA, Purdue U., 1968, PhD, 1969. Prof. econs. U. Pitts., 1969—; cons. Fed. Home Loan Bank Bd, Washington, 1971-72, Jones & Laughlin Steel, Pitts., U.S. Steel, Pitts., Sony Corp., Nat. Steel, EPA, Mellon Bank, Westinghouse. Author: Risk in Mortgage Lending, 1973, Linear Dynamic Economic Models, 1974; Statistics for Management, 1996. Mem. Am. Econ. Assn., Am. Statis. Assn., Econometric Soc. Avocations: tennis, skiing, baseball. Home: 807 Academy Pl Pittsburgh PA 15243-2000 Office: U Pitts Forbes Quad Pittsburgh PA 15260

KENLEY, LUKE, state legislator; m. Sarah Butler; 3 children. Student, Miami U., 1967; JD, Harvard U., 1972. With law firm Cadick, Burns, Duck &@ Neighbours, 1972-74; pres. Kenley's Supermarkets Inc., 1974-98; mem. Ind. State Senate, 1992—, mem. pub. policy com., edn. com., budget subcom., chair pub. affairs subcom., mem. judiciary com., mem. probate code and trusts subcom., chmn. adminstrv. rules oversight com. Bd. dirs. Noblesville Boys and Girls Club; active First United Meth. Ch.; judge Noblesville City Ct., 1974-89. Office: 200 W Washington St Indianapolis IN 46204

KENLY, GRANGER FARWELL, marketing consultant, college official; b. Portland, Oreg., Feb. 15, 1919; s. F. Corning and Ruth (Farwell) K.; m. Suzanne Warner, Feb. 7, 1948 (div. Nov., 1977); children: Margaret F., Kenly Granger Farwell Jr.; m. Stella S. Angevin, Oct. 8, 1978. AB cum laude, Harvard U., 1941. Adminstrv. asst. to v.p. Poole Bros., Inc., Chgo., 1941-42; asst. advt. mgr. Sunset Mag., San Francisco, 1946-47; pub. relations, sales promotion mgr. Pabco Products, Inc., San Francisco, 1947-51; v.p. mgmt., supr. Needham, Louis & Brorby, Inc., Chgo., 1951-60; mgr. mktg. plans dept. Pure Oil Co., Palatine, Ill., 1961-62, v.p. pub. relations, personnel, 1962-66; v.p. pub. affairs Abbott Labs., North Chicago, Ill., 1966-71; v.p. corporate and investor relations IC Industries, Inc., Chgo., 1972-83; career devel. officer Lake Forest Coll., Ill., 1984—; chmn., exec. bd. Keystone-Garrett Properties, Houston, 1984—. Mem. 22d Ann. Global Strategy Conf. U.S. Naval War Coll., 1970; mem. pub. affairs council Am. Productivity Ctr., 1980-85. Bd. dirs. Evanston Hosp., 1963-82; trustee Ill. Soc. Prevention Blindness, 1958-64, Lawson YMCA, Chgo., 1972-83, Off the Street Boys Club, Chgo., 1978—; mem. Exec. Service Corps Chgo., 1984—. Served to maj. USAAF, 1942-46, ETO. Mem. Chgo. Club, Univ. Club (Chgo.), Onwentsia Club (Lake Forest, Ill.), Edgartown (Mass.) Yacht Club, The Reading Room (Edgartown), Hole-in-the-Wall Golf Club (Naples, Fla.), Naples Yacht Club. Republican. Episcopalian. Office: Lake Forest Coll Career Placement Officer Sheridan and College Rd Lake Forest IL 60045

KENNAN, ELIZABETH TOPHAM, former university president and history educator; b. Phila., Feb. 25, 1938; AB summa cum laude, Mt. Holyoke Coll., 1960; MA, Oxford (Eng.) U., 1962; PhD, U. Wash., 1966; LHD (hon.), Trinity Coll., 1978, Amherst Coll., 1980, St. Mary's Coll., 1982, Oberlin Coll., 1983; LLD (hon.), Smith Coll., 1984; LittD (hon.), Cath. U. of Am., 1985, U. Mass., Amherst, 1988. Asst. prof. history Cath. U., Washington, 1966-70, assoc. prof. history, dir. medieval and Byzantine studies, 1970-78, dir. program in early Christian humanism, 1970-78; pres. Five Colls. Inc., 1985-94; pres., prof. history Mt. Holyoke Coll., South Hadley, Mass., 1978-95, pres. emeritus, 1996. Bd. dirs. Coun. on Libr. Resources, 1980-95; mem. com. Folger Shakespeare Libr., 1994-2001; lead dir. N.E. Utilities, Hartford, Conn.; bd. dirs. The Putnam Funds, Boston, Talbots, Hingham, Mass. Co-author: (under pseudonym Clare Munnings) Overnight Float, 2000; contbr. articles to profl. jours. including Georgetown Univ. Press, Univ. of Wash. Press, Cath. Univ. of Am., Cath. Univ. Press, Cistercian Publs., Mem. Coun. on Econ. Devel., 1991-95; mem. bd. selectors Jefferson awards Am. Inst. for Pub. Svc., 1991-96; trustee U. Notre Dame, 1985-94, Miss Porter's Sch., 1980-85; mem. higher edn. program com. Dana Found., 1986-90; mem. Indo-U.S. Subcommn. on Edn. and Culture, 1986-91; vice chmn. 1000 Friends of Mass., 1989-91; mem. Mass Gov.'s Nominating Coun., 1990-91; trustee Trustees for the Reservations, 1999—, Centre Coll., Danville, Ky., 2001—, Midway Coll., Midway, Ky. Marshall scholar, 1960; Woodrow Wilson fellow (hon.), 1960. Mem. Coun. Fgn. Rels. Home and Office: Cambus-Kenneth Farm PO Box 1989 Danville KY 40423

KENNAN, KENT WHEELER, composer, educator; b. Milw., Apr. 18, 1913; s. Kossuth Kent and Sara Louise (Wheeler) K. Student, U. Mich., 1930-32; B.Mus. in Composition and Theory, Eastman Sch. of Music U. Rochester, 1934, M.Mus. in Composition, 1936; student, Royal Acad. of Santa Cecilia, Rome, 1938. Mem. faculty Kent (Ohio) State U., 1939-40; tchr. composition, orchestration, counterpoint and theory U. Tex., Austin, 1940-42, 45-46, 49-83, prof. emeritus; tchr. theory Ohio State U., 1947-49; tchr. composition, orchestration Eastman Sch. of Music, summers 1954, 56. Composer music performed under Toscanini, Ormandy, Hanson, Stokowski, others, by N.Y. Philharm. Symphony, Phila. Orch., Chgo., Houston, Detroit, San Antonio, Boston Symphonies, others; composer: Night Soliloquy, other orch. works, 5 Preludes for Piano, Retrospectives (12 pieces for piano), Sonata for Trumpet and Piano, also vocal, choral and chamber music; author: Counterpoint, 4th edit., 1999; (with D. Grantham) Technique of Orchestration, 6th edit., 2002. Served with USAAF, 1942-46. Recipient Prix de Rome in Music, 1936 Mem.: ASCAP, Pi Kappa Lambda, Phi Mu Alpha, Delta Tau Delta. Address: 1034 Liberty Park Dr Apt 248 Austin TX 78746-6852 E-mail: kwhe@earthlink.net.

KENNAN, STEPHANIE ANN, policy advisor; b. Frankfurt am Main, Germany, Oct. 25, 1958; d. Ralph Hyde and Loretta (Pumphrey) K. BA in Am. Govt. and Fgn. Affairs, U. Va., Charlottesville, 1980; MA in Creative Writing, Johns Hopkins U., Balt., 1997. Legis. asst. Rep. Larry Smith, Washington, 1983-85; asst. dir. edn. Group Health Assn. Am., Washington, 1985-86; legis. rep. Am. Assn. Ret. Persons, Washington, 1986-89, Am. Coll. Emergency Physicians, Washington, 1989-94; dir. fed. rels. Md. Dept. Health, Balt., 1995-97; sr. policy advisor U.S. Senator Ron Wyden, Washington, 1998—. Mem. Montgomery Couty (Md.) Commn. on Aging, 1983-86. Co-author: Health Care Playbook, 1994; contbr.: Public Health Administration, 2000; contbr. articles to profl. jours., books. Mem. Nat. Press Club. Episcopalian. Office: 516 Hart Senate Office Bldg Washington DC 20510-0001

KENNARD, JOYCE L. judge; b. Bandung, West Java, Indonesia, May 6, 1941; AA, Pasadena City Coll., 1970; BA, U. So. Calif., 1971, MPA, JD, U. So. Calif., 1974. Former judge L.A. Mcpl. Ct., Superior Ct., Ct. Appeal, Calif.; assoc. justice Calif. Supreme Ct., San Francisco, 1989—. Office: Calif Supreme Ct 350 Mcallister St San Francisco CA 94102-4783

KENNARD, LYDIA H. airport terminal executive; BA, Stanford U.; MS, MIT; JD, Harvard U. Former pres./prin.-in-charge KDG Devel. Constrn. Consulting, L.A.; former mem. L.A. Planning Commn.; dep. exec. dir. design and constrn. L.A. World Airports, 1994-99, interim exec. dir., 1999-2000, exec. dir., 2000—. Lawyer in real estate and constrn. law. Active UniHealth Found. Bd.; past mem. Calif. Med. Ctr. Found. Bd., Equal Opportunity Adv. Coun. So. Calif. Edison. Named Woman of Yr. L.A. chpt. Women's Trans. Seminar, 1995, Civic Leader of Yr. Nat. Assn. Women Bus. Owners-L.A., 2000. Office: LA World Airports PO Box 92216 Los Angeles CA 90009-2216*

KENNARD, MARY ELIZABETH, lawyer; b. Phila., Dec. 1, 1954; d. Rodman Ramos and Mary Elizabeth Kennard. BAS, Boston U., 1976; JD, Temple U., 1980; LLM, George Washington U., 1982. Bar: Pa. 1980, R.I. 1988, D.C. 1988, U.S. Dist. Ct. (we. dist.) Pa. 1985, U.S. Ct. Appeals (3d cir.) 1985, U.S. Dist. Ct. R.I. 1988, U.S. Ct. Appeals (1st cir.) 1899, U.S. Dist. Ct. D.C. 1996, U.S. Supreme Ct. 1985. Assoc. Obermayer, Rebmannn, Maxwell & Hippel, Phila., 1979-80; asst. exec. dir. Nat. Assn. Coll. and Univ. Attys., Washington, 1981-83; asst. univ. counsel U. Pitts., 1984-85; asst. to v.p. for legal affairs Howard U., Washington, 1985-87; legal counsel U. R.I., R.I. Coll. and C.C. of R.I., Kingston, 1987-94; v.p., gen. counsel Am. U., Washington, 1995—. Bd. dirs. Washington Trust Bank, Washington metro area Am. Corp. Counsels Assn. Mem. Nat. Assns. Coll. and Univ. Attys., R.I. Black Lawyers Assn. Democrat. Avocation: golf. Office: American Univ 4400 Massachusetts Ave NW Washington DC 20016-8165

KENNARD, RAEBURN GLEASON, lawyer; b. Salt Lake City, May 19, 1946; s. Frankland James and Gladys (Bischoff) K.; m. Nancy Valleau, Aug. 20, 1970 (dec. 1999); children: Elisse, Nathan R., Ashley, Dawn M., Aaron T., Emily; m. Suzanne Southam, Jun 25, 1999. BA in Econs., Brigham Young U., 1970; JD, Duke U., 1973. Bar: Utah 1973. Law clk. U.S. Dist. Ct., Salt Lake City, 1973-74; ptnr. Kirton and McConkie, Salt Lake City, 1974—; sec., gen. counsel Deseret Trust Co., Salt Lake City, 1976—. Mem. ABA (tax sect., exempt orgns. com., religious orgns. sub-com.). Mem. Ch. of Jesus Christ of Latter-day Saints. Home: 12082 Joey Park Cir Draper UT 84020-8442 Office: 60 E South Temple Ste 1800 Salt Lake City UT 84111-1004

KENNARD, WILLIAM EARL, former lawyer; b. L.A., Jan. 19, 1957; s. Robert A. and Helen Z. (King) K.; m. Deborah D. Kennedy, Apr. 9, 1984. BA, Stanford U., 1978; JD, Yale U., 1981. Bar: Calif. 1981, D.C. Ct. Appeals 1985, U.S. Ct. Appeals (D.C. cir.) 1994, U.S. Supreme Ct. 1994. Fellow Nat. Assn. Broadcasters, Washington, 1981-82, asst. gen. counsel, 1983-84; assoc. Verner, Liipfert, Bernhard, McPherson & Hand, Washington, 1984-89, ptnr., 1990-93; gen. counsel FCC, Washington, 1993-97, chmn., 1997—2001; sr. fellow Aspen Commn. and Soc. Program, Washington, 2001—. Office: Aspen Inst 1333 New Hampshire Ave NW Washington DC 20036

KENNE, LESLIE F. military officer; B in Aero. Engring., Auburn U., 1970; grad., Squadron Officer Sch., 1975; M in Procurement Mgmt., Webster Coll., 1979; grad., Armed Forces Staff Coll., 1981, Nat. War Coll., 1986, Def. Sys. Mgmt. Coll., 1988; advanced mgmt. program, U. N.H., 1993; nat. and internat. security mgmt., Harvard U., 1995. Cert. level III program mgmt., level III test and evaluation. Commd. 2d lt. USAF, 1971, advanced through grades to maj. gen., 1998; maintenance supr. 474th Orgnl. Maintenance Squadron, Takhli Royal Thai AFB, Thailand, 1973-74; project mgr., dep. test dir. range measurement sys. jt. test Tactical Fighter Weapons Ctr., Nellis AFB, Nev., 1975-78; program mgr. Office of Sec. of Def.-directed joint tests Air Force Test and Evaluation Ctr., Kirtland AFB, N.Mex., 1978-81; chief airborne sys. test br., chief elec. sys. test divsn. 324th Test Wing, Eglin AFB, Fla., 1982-85; dir. ops. and support Airborne Warning and Control Sys. Program Officer, Hanscom AFB, Mass., 1986-88; chief spl. projects divsn. directorate spl. programs Office of Asst. Sec. of Air Force for Acquisitions, Washington, 1988-90; dir. LANTIRN Sys. Program Office Aero. Sys. Divsn., Wright-Patterson AFB, Ohio, 1993-94; dep. dir. fighters and C2 and weapons programs Office of Asst. Sec. of Air Force for Acquisition, Washington, 1992-93; dir. F-16 Sys. Program Office Aero. Sys. Ctr., Wright-Patterson AFB, 1993-94, vice comdr., 1994-95, Sacramento Air Logistics Ctr., McClellan AFB, Calif., 1995-96; dep. dir. Joint Strike Fighter Program, Arlington, Va., 1996-97, dir., 1997-99; comdr. Electronics Sys. Ctr., Hanscom AFB, Mass., 1999—. Decorated Legion of Merit, Bronze Star, Meritorious Svc. medal with 2 oak leaf clusters. Office: Hanscom AFB ESC / CC Hanscom AFB MA 01731-5000

KENNEDY, ADRIENNE LITA, playwright; b. Pitts., Sept. 13, 1931; d. Cornell Wallace and Etta (Haugabook) Hawkins; m. Joseph C. Kennedy, May 15, 1953 (div. 1966); children: Joseph C., Adam. BS, Ohio State U., 1953; student creative writing, Columbia U., 1954-56; student playwrighting, New Sch. Social Research, Am. Theatre Wing, Circle in the Sq. Theatre Sch., 1957-58, 62. Mem. playwriting unit Actors Studio, N.Y.C., 1962-65; lectr. Yale U., New Haven, 1972-74; CBS fellow Sch. Drama, N.Y.C., 1973; lectr. Princeton (N.J.) U., 1977; vis. assoc. prof. Brown U., 1979-80. Rep. to conf. Internat. Theatre Inst., Budapest, 1978; vis. lectr. Harvard U., 1990, 91, vis. prof., 1997—. Author: (plays) Funnyhouse of a Negro, 1964, Cities in Bezique, 1965, A Rat's Mass, 1966, A Lesson in Dead Language, 1966, The Lennon Plays, 1968, Sun, Cities of Bezique, 1969; A Movie Star Has To Star in Black and White, 1976, Ohio State Murders, She Talks to Beethoven, 1990, (with Adam Kennedy) Sleep Deprivation Chamber, 1995; (memoirs) People Who Led to My Plays, 1987 (Manhattan Borough Pres.'s award 1988), Letter to My Students, Lancashire Lad; commd. by Empire State Youth Inst., 1979, Onestes, Electra, Juilliard Sch. Music, 1980, Black Children's Day, Rites and Reason, Brown U., 1980; represented in numerous anthologies Norton Anthology of Am. Lit. Recipient Obie award, 1964, 96, Pierre Lecomte du Novy award Lincoln Ctr., 1994, award Am. Acad. Arts and Letters, 1994; fellow Guggenheim Found., 1968, Rockefeller Found., 1967-68, NEA, 1993, Lila Wallace Readers Digest, 1994, Yale U., 1974-75; grantee Nat. Endowment Arts, 1973, Rockefeller Found., 1974, Creative Artists Pub. Svc., 1974; Disting. lectr. U. Calif., Berkeley, 1980, 86. Mem. PEN (bd. dirs. 1976-77). Address: 325 W 89th St New York NY 10024 *I believe in listening to one's inner voices.*

KENNEDY, ANTHONY MCLEOD, United States supreme court justice; b Sacramento, July 23, 1936; AB, Stanford U., 1958; student, London Sch Econs.; LLB, Harvard U., 1961; JD (hon.), U. Pacific, 1988, U. Santa Clara 1988. Bar: Calif. 1962, U.S. Tax Ct. 1971. Former ptnr. Evans, Jackson & Kennedy; prof. constl. law McGeorge Sch. Law, U. of Pacific, 1965-88; judge U.S. Ct. Appeals (9th cir.), Sacramento, 1976-88; assoc. justice U.S. Supreme Ct., Washington, 1988—. Mem. bd. student advisors Harvard Faculty, 1960-61 Fellow Am. Bar Found. (hon.), Am. Coll. Trial Lawyers (hon.); mem Sacramento County Bar Assn., State Bar Calif., Phi Beta Kappa. Office: US Supreme Ct Supreme Ct Bldg 1 1st St NE Washington DC 20543-0001*

KENNEDY, BARBARA ELLEN PERRY, art therapist; b. Columbus, Ohio Apr. 22, 1937; d. Donald Earl Perry and Elsie Irene (Strait) Perry Modglin; m Marvin Roosevelt Kennedy, July 1, 1955 (div. Sept. 1969); children: Sherry Lynn Kennedy Anderson, Michelle Reneé Kennedy Byrd. AS in Mental Health Technology cum laude, Purdue U., 1975, BA in Psychology, 1976; MA in Ar Therapy, Wright State U., 1990. Registered art therapist; cert. social worker cert. marriage and family therapist. Probation officer intern Allen County Juvenile Probation Dept., Ind., 1975; prodn. supr. asst. Allen County Assn. fo Retarded, Ft. Wayne, Ind., 1975, relief supr. semi-ind. living, 1975-76; occup therapist asst. Logansport State Hosp., Ind., 1977; rehab. therapist Richmond State Hosp., Ind., 1977—, recreation therapy dir. acute intensive treatment unit 1983-85, dir. art therapy dept., 1986—, art tchr., art therapist with MIDD adolescent and geriatric, 1995—. Pvt. counselor, 1986—; counselor Menta Health Assn., Richmond, 1986; art therapy counselor Battered Women' Shelter, Richmond, 1986; counselor Dayton (Ohio) Pub. Sch., Family Svc Assn., 1989-90, expressive therapy counselor with Mentally Ill Chemically Addicted population, 1993—; lectr. in field of mental health and art therapy Author, editor: Mental Stimulation Activities, 1992. Mem. com. LWV, Rich mond, 1977-80; publicity officer USCG Aux., Richmond, 1985; chairperso legis. group AAUW, Richmond, 1982-84; bd. dir. Community Coun. o Disabilities Awareness, Richmond, 1985-86; vol. ARC, Muncie, Ind. and F Wayne, 1969-73; vol. tutor Adult Literacy Resource Ctr., 1991—; pres Richmond Art Club, 1996-97; active Fountain City Wesleyan Ch. Recipien Merit scholarship Purdue U., 1971-76, Gov.'s Showcase award State of Ind 1990. Mem. Am. Art Therapy Assn., Buckeye Art Therapy Assn., Ind. Ar Therapy Assn. (v.p. 1992-95), Mensa. Mem. Wesleyan Ch. Avocations: sailing hiking, piano, reading, art. Office: Richmond State Hosp 498 NW 18th S Richmond IN 47374-2898 Personal E-mail: barbiecutie47374@cs.com.

KENNEDY, BEVERLY (KLEBAN) BURRIS, financial advisor, tv and radi talk show host; b. Pitts., Sept. 23, 1943; d. Jack and Ida (Davis) Kleban; m Thomas E. Burris, Dec. 31, 1967 (div.); 1 child, Laura Danielle Burris; m. E A. Kennedy, Jan 14, 1984; stepchildren: Kathleen, Patricia, Thomas. BS, Pa State U., 1964; postgrad., Va. Commonwealth U., 1967. Founder, exec. di Broward Art Colony, Inc., Broward County, Fla., 1978-80; dir. sales Holiday Inn, Plantation, Fla., 1980-81; agent, registered rep. Equitable Life Assuranc Soc., Ft. Lauderdale, Fla., 1982—; pres. Fin. Planning Svcs. Assn., Inc., Ft Lauderdale, Fla., 1984-86; owner, fin. cons. Beverly B. Kennedy & Assocs., Ft Lauderdale, Fla., 1982—; republican nominee for U.S. Congress 19th Dist Fla., 1996; dir. of rsch. tech. & grants adminstrn. Diversity Planning Instit 2002—. Adv. bd. Transflorida Bank, 1983-88; bd. arbitration Nat. Assn Securities Dealers, Inc., 1992-97. Talk show host Sta. WWNN, 1992-93. Bd dirs. Community Appearance Bd., 1988-89, Riverwalk, Ft. Lauderdale, 1988 89, First Charter Sch. of Excellence, Ft. Lauderdale, 1997-2003; trustee Police and Fireman Fund of Fort Lauderdale, 1990-91; appointed by gov. to Fla. State Bd. Profl. Engrs., 1988-91; cons. Com. on Fin. for Nat. Coun. examiners fo Engring and Surveying, 1990-91; Rep. nominee for U.S. Congress 20th dist Fla., 1992, 94, 19th dist., 1996; appointed to silver haired legis. of Fla 1999-2003, exec. bd. coalition of condominiums and home owners assoc 2001-2003. Named Woman of the Year (Bus. for Profit), Women in Commu nications, Broward County, 1986, Bus. & Profl. Women, 1988-89, Oustandin Alumni, Pa. State Univ. Coll . Edn., 1988-89, A Woman of History, Nova S U., 2001. Mem. Internat. Assn. Fin. Planning, Nat. Assn. Life Underwriters East Broward Fed. Women's Rep. Club (pres. 1992-93). Home and Office: 324 Seaward Dr Lauderdale By The Sea FL 33062 Fax: 954-783-0583. E-mail ekenn@bellsouth.net.

KENNEDY, BRENDA S. performing arts center executive, theatrical ligh designer; b. Las Vegas, Nev., Jan. 17, 1955; d. Wanda Marie and Milton Re Linn; m. Donald P. Kennedy, June 7, 1975 (div. Nov. 19, 2001); children: Rya Rex, Krista Marie, Dawnie Rose, Breanna (Annie) Linn. AA in Gen. Studies C.C. So. Nev., 1989; BA in Bus. Mgmt., St. Regis U., 2002. Ho. mgr. C.C. So Nev. Performing Arts Ctr., 1996—2000; performing arts ctr. asst. dir. C.C. So Nev., 2000—02, performing arts ctr. dir., 2002—. Mem. C.C. So. Nev. Lectur Com., 2000—; chmn. C.C. So. Nev. Honors Com., 2000—02, Campu Environment Coun., North Las Vegas, 2000—02; mem. Nev. C.C. Conf 2001—02. V.p. Tule Springs Preservation Com., Las Vegas, 1998—2003; vic chair Congress of States Nat. Parent Tchr. Assn., Chgo., 1999—2001; pres. Nev Parent Teachers Assn., Las Vegas, 1999—2001. Recipient Hon. Life Member ship, Nat. PTA, 1994, Nev. PTA, 1996, Parent Hall of Fame, Clark County Sch Dist., 1996, High Honors, Phi Theta Kappa, 1989. Mem.: AAUP (assoc.), Nev Faculty Alliance (assoc.). Democrat. Latter Day Saint. Avocations: theatre rapelling, hiking, camping, music. Office: Community College Southern Ne vada 3200 East Cheyenne Ave North Las Vegas NV 89030

KENNEDY, B(YRL) J(AMES), medicine and oncology educator; b. Plain view, Minn., June 24, 1921; s. Arthur Sylvester and Anna Margaret (Fass bender) K.; m. Margaret Bradford Hood, Oct. 21, 1950; children: Sharon Lynn James Bradford, Scott Douglas, Grant Preston. BA, BS, U. Minn., 1943, MB 1945, MD, 1946; MS in Exptl. Medicine, McGill U., Montreal, Que., Can 1951. Diplomate Am. Bd. Internal Medicine, Am. Bd. Med. Oncology. Intern i medicine Mass. Gen. Hosp., Boston, 1945-46, resident in medicine, 194 51-52; fellow in medicine Harvard Med. Sch.-Mass. Gen. Hosp., 1947-49; rsch fellow in medicine McGill U. Med. Sch., 1949-50; fellow in medicine Corne U. Med. Sch., N.Y.C., 1950-51; asst. prof. medicine U. Minn. Med. Sch., Mpls 1952-57, assoc. prof., 1957-67, prof., 1967-91, Masonic prof. oncology 1970-91, prof. emeritus, 1991—, Regents prof. medicine, 1988-91, Regent prof. emeritus, 1991—, B.J. Kennedy chair in clin. med. oncology, 200 Contbr. articles to profl. jours. Past chmn. bd. Presbyn. Homes of Minn., S Paul, bd. dirs., 1964-93. Recipient Nat. Divsn. award Am. Cancer Soc., 197 Recognition award Assn. Comty. Cancer Ctrs., 1985, Spl. Recognition awar Am. Soc. Internal Medicine, 1989, Charles Bolles Bolles-Roger award Henne pin Med. Soc., 1996; B.J. Kennedy Lectureship in Oncology named in his hono Minn. Med. Found., 1990, B.J. Kennedy Oncology Scholarship named in hi honor Minn. Med. Found., 1998, B.J. Kennedy Chair in Med. Oncology name in his honor Minn. Med. Found., 1999. Fellow ACP (master 1996, Laurea award Minn. 1992); mem. AMA (Sci. Achievement award 1992), Am. Canc Soc. (Disting. Svc. award 1991, Medal of Honor-Clin. Rsch. award 1996), Am Soc. Clin. Oncology (pres. 1987-88), Am. Assn. Cancer Rsch., Am. Ass Cancer Edn. (pres. 1982-83, Margaret Hay Edwards Achievement medal 1990 Minn. Med. Alumni (Harold S. Diehl award 1999), Town and Country Club (S Paul). Avocation: photography. Home: 1949 E River Pky Minneapolis M 55414-3675 Office: U Minn Med Sch and Hosp MMC 286 Mayo 420 Delawa St SE Minneapolis MN 55455-0374 E-mail: kenne018@tc.umn.edu.

KENNEDY, CHARLES, retired neuroscientist, retired medical educator; Buffalo, Aug. 27, 1920; m. Eulsum Kennedy, Aug. 27, 1968; 3 children fro previous marriage. BA in Chemistry cum laude, Princeton U., 1942; MD, U Rochester, 1945. Diplomate Am. Bd. Pediats., Am. Bd. Psychiatry an Neurology, lic. N.Y., Pa., DC, Maine, Md. Intern in pathology New Have Hosp., 1945-46; instr. pathology Sch. Medicine Yale U., New Haven, 1945-4 fellow in child psychiatry Children's Hosp., Buffalo, 1948-49, resident pedi trician, 1949-51; fellow in physiology Grad. Sch. Medicine U. Pa., Phila 1951-53, assoc. pediats. Sch. Medicine, 1952-55, assoc. in neurology, 1955-5 asst. prof. neurology in pediats., 1958-61, assoc. prof., 1961-67; chief divs neurology, dir. child neurology Children's Hosp., Phila., 1959-67; prof. pediats neurology Sch. Medicine Georgetown U., Washington, 1971-90, prof. emeritu 1990—. Vis. fellow in neurology Neurol. Inst. Columbia Presbyn. Med. Ct 1957—58; mem. Lab. Clin. Sci. Nat. Inst. Mental Health, 1967—68, La Cerebral Metabolism, 1968—95; cons. Pa. Hosp., Phila., 1960—69, Hosp. U Pa., Phila., 1961—67, Bd. Edn. Cty of Phila., 1962—64; lectr. U.S. Nav Hosp., Phila., 1962—68; mem. adv. com. dyslexia State of Tex., 1965; gue

ectr. Nat. Naval Med. Ctr. Uniformed Svcs. U. Health Scis., 1977—87. Mem. editl. bd. Pediat. Rsch., 1978—84, Brain Rsch., 1980—96, Jour. Cerebral Blood Flow and Metabolism, 1981—88. Lt. (j.g.) USNR, 1946—48. Fellow, Life Ins. Med. Rsch. Fund, 1951—53. Fellow: Coll. Physicians Phila.; mem.: Profs. Child Neurology, Child Neurology Soc., Soc. Neuroscience, Assn. Rsch. Nervous and Mental Disease, Phila. Neurol. Soc. (v.p. 1967), Phila. Pediat. Soc. (pres. 1964), Internat. Soc. Cerebral Blood Flow and Metabolism (dir. 1989—93, chmn. fin. com. 1992—96), Internat. Soc. Neurochemistry, Nat. Bd. Med. Examiners (mem. pediat. com. 1960—64), Am. Soc. Neurochemistry, Am. Acad. Neurology (chmn. sect. child neurology 1964—66, mem. com. problems mental reatardation 1965—67), Am. Neurol. Assn., Am. Acad. Pediats., Am. Pediat. Soc. E-mail: chasken@attglobal.net.

KENNEDY, CHARLES ALLEN, lawyer; b. Maysville, Ky., Dec. 11, 1940; s. Elmer Earl and Mary Frances Kennedy; m. Patricia Ann Louderback, Dec. 9, 1961; 1 child, Mimi Mignon. AB, Morehead State Coll., 1965, MA in Edn., 1968; JD, U. Akron, 1969; LLM, George Washington U., 1974. Bar: Ohio 1969. Asst. cashier Citizens Bank, Felicity, Ohio, 1961-63; tchr Triway Local Sch. Dist., Wooster, Ohio, 1965-67; with office of gen. counsel Fgn. Agr. and Spl. Programs Divsn. USDA, Washington, 1969-71; ptnr. Kauffman, Eberhart, Cicconetti & Kennedy Co., Wooster, 1972-86, Kennedy, Cicconetti, Knowlton & BuyTendyk, LPA, Wooster, 1986—. Mem. ABA, FBA, ATLA, Am. Coll. Barristers, Ohio State Bar Assn., Ohio Acad. Trial Lawyers, Wayne County Bar Assn., Exch. Club, Lions, Elks, Phi Alpha Delta, Phi Delta Kappa. Republican. Home: 275 W Henrietta Wooster OH 44691 Office: Kennedy Cicconetti & Know Ken 558 N Market St Wooster OH 44691-3406 E-mail: Knndy558@netscape.net.

KENNEDY, CHERYL LYNN, museum director; b. Pekin, Ill., Nov. 25, 1946; d. Paul Louis and Ann Marie (Bingham) Wieburg; children: Kurt Alan, Kimberly Ann. Grad. high sch., Pekin, Ill.; BA, Eastern Ill. U. Prin., and profl. quilter, Mahomet, Ill., 1976-81; program coord. Early Am. Mus., Mahomet, 1981-85; dir. Early Am. Mus. Champaign County Forest Preserve, Mahomet, 1986—. Chmn. Ill. Quilt Rsch. Project Early Am. Mus. and Land of Lincoln Quilt Assn., 1986—, Ill. Historic Sites Adv. Coun., 2000—03 mem. adv. com. AAM Mus. Assessment Program, 2002--. Historian Meth. Local History Com., Mahomet, 1984-86. Mem. Assn. Midwest Mus., Am. Assn. Mus. (assessment adv. com.), Am. Assn. State and Local History, Ill. Assn. Mus. (past pres., advocacy chair), Ill. Heritage Assn., Ill. State Hist. Soc., Champaign County Hist. Soc., Nat. Quilt Assn., Am. Quilt Soc., Antique Quilt Study Group, Quilt Conservancy. Avocations: quilting, women's history, walking, gardening. Office: Early Am Mus PO Box 1040 Mahomet IL 61853-1040 E-mail: ckennedy@prairienet.org.

KENNEDY, CHESTER RALPH, JR., former state official, art director; b. Middleboro, Mass., Apr. 22, 1926; s. Chester Ralph and Mary Carmen (Mello) K.; m. Barbara Ann Partridge, June 27, 1953; children: Karen Brooke, Scott Douglas. BFA, Mass. Coll. Art, 1951; postgrad., New Eng. Adult Edn. Inst., 1959, Boston U., 1966, Brandies U., 1985. Supt. pub. health edn. Mass. Dept. Pub. Health, Boston, 1953-56, coordinator health edn., 1956-74, asst. dir. health edn., 1974-81, dir. health edn., 1981-84, dist. health officer, 1984-89; ret., 1989. Asst. art dir. Barchét Studios, Middleboro, 1949-59, art dir., co-owner, Sherborn, Mass., 1959—; cons. USPHS, Assn. State and Territorial Health Officers; lectr., instr. Harvard, Boston U., Mass. Coll.; mem. Acad. Master Plan Adv. Commn., Mass. State Coll. System; exhibit chmn. 22nd World Health Assembly. Editor: Commonwealth of Mass. Secretarial Reference Manual, 1969; designer blue ribbon exhibit New Eng. Hosp. Assembly, 1969; designer five pvt. homes. Pres. Pub. Health Museum in Mass., 1991-93, mem. exec. bd., 1993-, exec. dir., 2002-; pres. Reach Out, Inc., 1970-74, bd. dirs., 1974-; bd. dirs. Greater Framingham Mental Health Assn., 1974-76; elected to Sherborn Bd. Health, 1974-86; mem. Solid Waste Recovery Tech. Com., 1975-84; co-chair Coalition Organized for Health Edn. in Schs., 1982-89. Served with USN, 1944-46. Recipient Boy Scouts Am. Organizer award, 1941, Commonwealth Mass. Disting. Svc. citation, 1971, Health Edn. citation New Eng. Consortium Health Edn. Assn., 1975, Coalition Organized for Health Edn. in Schs. citation, 1989, hon. award, 2002, Reach Out award, 1977, Southeastern Assn. Health Bds. award, 1989, Michael Dukakis Gov.'s award, 1989, Mass. Dept. Pub. Health award, 1989, Pub. Health Museum Organizer award Mass. Ho. of Reps., 1993, Gov. William Weld Museum Founder award, 1993. Mem. New Eng. Health Edn. Assn. (pres. 1971-72), Mass. Health Coun., New Eng. Health Promotion Coun., Soc. Pub. Health Edn., Mass. Audubon Soc., Mass. Archeol. Soc., Mass. Coll. Art Alumni (pres. 1968-72), Assn. Mass. State Colls. Alumni (pres. 1973-75), Mass. Pub. Health Assn. (health edn. chmn. 1974-76, 25 yr. award 1986, Paul Revere award 1990), Mass. Health Officers Assn. emeritus, Curtis M. Hillard award 1989, exec. sec. 1992-98), Mass. Assn. Health Bds. (hon., exec. bd. 1990-94), New Eng. Pub. Health Assn. (pres. 1984-85, Ira Hiscock award 1980, 25 yr. award 1989, pres.'s award, 2001). Office: Barchét Studios 178 Washington St Sherborn MA 01770-1022 E-mail: chet.kennedy@att.net.

KENNEDY, CHRISTOPHER ROBIN, ceramic engineer, director; b. Ottawa, Ont., Can., June 25, 1948; s. Robert Alvin and Ruth Christina (Downie) K.; m. Christine Willa Wayman, Jan. 28, 1978; children: Scott Wayman, Stuart James. BS, Rutgers U., 1969; MS, Pa. State U., 1971, PhD, 1974. Asst. ceramist Argonne Nat. Lab., Ill., 1974-79; ceramist Argonne (Ill.) Nat. Lab., 1979-82; staff engr. Exxon Rsch. and Engring. Co., Florham Park, N.J., 1982-83, group leader materials devel. group, 1984; mgr. materials rsch. sect. Lanxide Corp., Newark, 1984-87, mgr. def. products devel. sect., 1987-92; mgr. composite devel. and engring. sect., 1992-93; v.p. tech. Lanxide Corp., Newark, 1993-98; dir. R & D Ceramco, Burlington, N.J., 1998—. Contbr. numerous articles to profl. jours. Patentee in field. Mem. Am. Ceramic Soc., Nat. Inst. Ceramic Engrs., Keramos. Office: 6 Terri Ln Burlington NJ 08016-4905

KENNEDY, COLLEEN GERALYN, nurse, social worker; b. S.I., NY, Feb. 2, 1955; d. James Martin and Eleanor S. (Dehlinger) K.; m. Edward Francis Humphries, July21, 1990; children: Michael J. Carlucci, Stephen Edward Humphries. AAS in Nursing, Coll. S.I., 1976; BSW, Adelphi U., 1982, MSW, 1984. RN, N.Y.; cert. social worker, N.Y. Staff nurse S.I. Hosp., 1976—80, social work asst., 1980—84, clin. social worker, 1984—85; asst. dir. social work Eger Health Care Ctr., S.I., 1985—87; systems analyst program devel. and evaluation St. Vincent's Med. Ctr., S.I., 1987—89; asst. dir. Ctr. Chem. Dependency, Bayley Seton Hosp., S.I., 1989—93; med. coord., managed care, utilization mgmt., quality assurance Bayley Seton Hosp., S.I., 1993—95; dir. health and mem. svcs. Health Plus Prepaid Health Svcs. Plan, Inc., Bklyn., 1995—99; pres. Kennedy Cons., NY, 1999—. V.p. Olde Towne Cons./Compliance Gateway Inc., NY, 1999—2002; pres., CEO Aptus Compliance Tech., Inc., 2002—; v.p. parents league S.I. Acad., devel. com. bd. Named to Outstanding Young Women of Am., 1984. Mem. NASW, ACSW, NAFE. Democrat. Roman Catholic. Avocations: calligraphy, gourmet cooking. Office: 51 Manor Rd Staten Island NY 10314 E-mail: ckennedy@si.rr.com.

KENNEDY, COLLEEN MARY, lawyer; b. Milw., May 26, 1955; d. William Frederick Kennedy and Mary Patricia (Boyle) Radford; m. Thomas J. Kelly, Jr., Apr. 30, 1983; children: Caitlin, Patrick BA, U. Colo., 1977; JD, Antioch Sch. Law, Washington, 1980. Bar: D.C. 1981, U.S. Dist. Ct. D.C. 1981, U.S. Ct. Appeals (D.C. cir.) 1981. Law clk. to Judge William S. Thompson and Henry Greene, D.C. Superior Ct., Washington, 1980-81; asst. U.S. atty. U.S. Atty.'s Office, Washington, 1981—. Bd. dirs. Montgomery County (Md.) Assn. Retarded Citizens, 1991-96, KEEN (Kids Enjoy Exercise Now), 1995-98. Democrat. Roman Catholic. Avocations: swimming, reading, hiking, skiing, golfing. Office: US Atty's Office 555 4th St NW Ste 10842 Washington DC 20530-2733

KENNEDY, CORNELIA GROEFSEMA, federal judge; b. Detroit, Mich., Aug. 4, 1923; d. Elmer H. and Mary Blanche (Gibbons) Groefsema; m. Charles S. Kennedy, Jr. (dec.); 1 son, Charles S. III. BA, U. Mich., 1945, JD with distinction, 1947; LL.D. (hon.), No. Mich. U., 1971, Eastern Mich. U., 1971, Western Mich. U., 1973, Detroit Coll. Law, 1980, U. Detroit, 1987. Bar: Mich. 1947. Law clk. to Chief Judge Harold M. Stephens, U.S. Ct. of Appeals, Washington, 1947-48; assoc. Elmer H. Groefsema, Detroit, 1948-52, partner Markle & Markle, Detroit, 1952-66; judge 3d Judicial Circuit Mich., 1967-70; dist. judge U.S. Dist. Ct., Eastern Dist. Mich., Detroit, 1970-79, chief judge, 1977-79; circuit judge U.S. Ct. Appeals, (6th cir.), 1979-99, sr. judge, 1999—. Mem. Commn. on the Bicentennial of the U.S. Constitution (presdl. appointment). Recipient Sesquicentennial award U. Mich. Fellow Am. Bar Found.; mem. ABA, Mich. Bar Assn. (past chmn. negligence law sect.), Detroit Bar Assn. (past dir.), Fed. Bar Assn., Am. Judicature Soc., Nat. Assn. Women Lawyers, Am. Trial Lawyers Assn., Nat. Conf. Fed. Trial Judges (past chmn.), Fed. Jud. Fellows Commn. (bd. dirs.), Fed. Jud. Ctr. (bd. dirs.), Phi Beta Kappa. Office: US Ct of Appeals 6th Circuit 532 Potter Stewart US Courthouse 100 E Fifth St Cincinnati OH 45202

KENNEDY, CORNELIUS BRYANT, retired lawyer; b. Evanston, Ill., Apr. 13, 1921; s. Millard Bryant and Myrna Estelle (Anderson) K.; m. Anne Martha Reynolds, June 20, 1959; children: Anne Talbot, Lauren K. Mayle. AB, Yale U., 1943; JD, Harvard U., 1948. Bar: Ill. 1949, D.C. 1965. Assoc. Mayer Meyer Austrian & Platt, Chgo., 1949-54, 55-59; asst. to U.S. atty. Dept. Justice, Chgo., 1954-55; counsel to minority leader U.S. Senate, 1959-65; sr. ptnr. Kennedy & Webster, Washington, 1965-82; of counsel Armstrong, Teasdale, Schlafly & Davis, Washington, 1983-88; public mem. Adminstrv. Conf. U.S., 1972-82, sr. conf. fellow, 1982-90, chmn. rulemaking com., 1973-82; ret., 1988. Contbr. articles to law jours. Fin. chmn. Lyric Opera Co., Chgo., 1954; chmn. young adults group Chgo. Coun. Fgn. Rels., 1958-59; pres. English Speaking Union Jrs., Chgo., 1957-59; trustee St. John's Child Devel. Ctr., Washington, 1965-67, 75-87, pres., 1983-85 ; exec. dir. Supreme Ct. Hist. Soc., 1984-87. 1st lt., AC U.S. Army, 1942-46. Fellow Am. Bar Found.; mem. Am. Law Inst., ABA (coun. sect. adminstrv. law 1967-70, chmn. sect. 1976-77), Fed. Bar Assn. (chmn. com. adminstrv. law 1963-64), Legal Club Chgo., Explorers Club, N.Y.C. Club, Capitol Hill Club, Chevy Chase Club, Sailing Club of Chesapeake, Adventurer's Club. Home: 8462 Brook Rd Mc Lean VA 22102-1703

KENNEDY, DALLAS CLARENCE, II, physicist, educator, writer; b. Washington, Nov. 1, 1962; s. Edwin Dallas and Dora (Funari) K. BS, U. Md., 1984; MS, Stanford U., 1986, PhD, 1989. Asst. engr. Nat. Security Agy., Fort G.G. Meade, Md., 1983-84; grad. tchg. and rsch. asst. Stanford U., Calif., 1984-89; postdoctoral fellow U. Pa., Phila., 1989-91; rsch. assoc. Fermi Nat. Accelerator Ctr., Batavia, Ill., 1991-93; asst. prof. U. Fla., Gainesville, 1993-00. Sr. tech. writer The MathWorks; contbr. articles to profl. jour, Am. Red Cross, Hyattsville, 1976-1984 Advisor First Amendment Coalition, Gainesville, 1994-96. Mem. Am. Phys. Soc. (particles and fields and astrophysics divsn.), George C. Marshall Inst. Sci. and Pub. Policy, U. Fla. Hillel Found. (faculty advisor 1994-2000), Sigma Pi Sigma, Phi Beta Kappa. Office: The Mathworks Inc 3 Apple Hill Dr Natick MA 01760 E-mail: helioplex@earthlink.net

KENNEDY, DANE KEITH, history educator; b. Bonne Terre, Mo., May 30, 1951; s. William Joseph Kennedy and Helen Marie Mueller; m. Martha Hoeprich, June 16, 1974; 1 child, Alene Elizabeth. BA, U. Calif., Berkeley, 1973, MA, 1975, PhD, 1981. Asst. prof. U. Nebr., Lincoln, 1981—87, assoc. prof., 1987—94, prof., 1994—2000, chair dept. history, 1997—2000; Elmer L. Kayser prof. George Washington U., Washington, 2000—. Vis. fellow Davis Humanities Ctr. U .Calif., Davis, 1989—90. Author: Islands of White, 1987, The Magic Mountains, 1996, Britain and Empire, 1880-1945, 2002. Bd. dirs. German Hist. Inst., Washington, 2000—; chair internat. com. Am. Hist. Assn., Washington, 2000—. Crossing Borders grantee, Ford Found., 1997—2002, Indo-Am. fellow, Coun. for Internat. Exch. of Scholars, 1991, Guggenheim fellow, 2003—. Fellow: Royal Hist. Soc. Home: 9741 Water Oak Dr Fairfax VA 22031 Office: George Washington U Dept History Washington DC 20052 Office Fax: 202-994-6231.

KENNEDY, DANIEL, mathematics educator; b. Rochester, N.Y., July 19, 1946; s. Edwin Gerald and Nancy Helen (Colgan) K. AB in Math., Coll. Holy Cross, Worcester, Mass., 1968; MS in Math., U. N.C., 1971, PhD in Math., 1973. Camp dir. Camp Pathfinder, Algonquin Park, Ont., Can., 1976-91, program dir., 1976-95; dormitory parent/advisor The Baylor Sch., Chattanooga, 1980—, Cartter Lupton disting. prof., 1981—, chmn. math., 1976-94. Mem. Advanced Placement Calculus Test Devel. Com. The Coll. Bd., N.Y.C., 1986-94, chair, 1990-94, math. scis. adv. bd. mem., 1991-95; exam leader Advanced Placement Calculus Ednl. Testing Svc., Princeton, N.J., 1994-97; advanced placement cons. Coll. Bd., Atlanta, 1980-2003. Recipient Presdl. award for Excellence in Sci. and Math. Tchg. NSF Presdl. Awards Com., 1995; Tandy tech. scholar Tandy Corp., 1992, Siemens Advanced Placement scholar, 1998. Mem. Math. Assn. Am., Nat. Coun. Tchrs. Math. (program chmn. regional meeting 1990, referee and reviewer 1982—), Tenn. Math. Tchrs. Assn. (v.p. 1987-89), Chattanooga Area Math. Tchrs. Assn. (v.p. 1979-81, pres. 1983-89, editor 1981-86). Democrat. Roman Catholic. Avocations: cooking, cryptic crosswords, 45 rpm record collecting, art. Home and Office: Baylor Sch PO Box 1337 Chattanooga TN 37401-1337 E-mail: dkennedy@chattanooga.net.

KENNEDY, DANIEL JOHN, national and international public relations consultant, communications executive; BA in Comm., U. Wis.; MEd in Media/Comm., U. Mass. Pub. rels. and mktg. comm. exec. Kurt Salmon Assocs., 1973-78; sr. comm. mgr. J.C. Penney Co., 1978-88; v.p. mktg. comm. Ruder Finn Pub. Rels., N.Y.C., 1988-90; internat. dir. media rels. Simon & Schuster, 1990-92; mng. dir. Daniel Kennedy Communications Svcs., 1992—. Adj. prof. Baruch Coll., CUNY, 1996-97, Fashion Inst. Tech., SUNY, 1996-97, Marymount Manhattan Coll., 1996-2001; guest spkr. various colls. and univs.; juror news and pub. affairs categories TV Acad. Emmy awards; cons. in field. Recipient Mercury award for internat. pub. rels. accomplishments, 1997, Gold, Silver and Bronze Bulldog awards for excellence in media rels. and publicity, 1998, Meritorius award Women Execs. Pub. Rels., 1998, ACE award Internat. Assn. Bus. Communicators, 1998. Address: 157 W 79th St New York NY 10024-6400

KENNEDY, DAVID BOYD, foundation executive, lawyer; b. Ann Arbor, Mich., Sept. 2, 1933; s. James Alexander and Elizabeth (Earhart) K.; m. Sally Martin Pyne, 1964; children: Jane Elizabeth Mack, Douglas Earhart. Student, McGill U., 1951-52, U. Mich., 1952-54; AB, Ind. U., 1958; LLB, U. Mich., 1963. Bar: Mich. 1964, Wyo. 1965. Pvt. practive law, Sheridan, Wyo., 1964-84; pres. Earhart Found., Ann Arbor, Mich., 1985—2003, trustee, 1979—. Trustee Citizens Rsch. Coun. of Mich.; chmn., bd. dirs. Inst. for Justice, Washington; mem. bd. overseers Hoover Instn./Stanford U. Mem. Wyo. Ho. Reps., 1967-72; chmn. Wyo. Rep. State Ctrl. Com., 1971-73; Rep. nat. committeeman, 1976-80, vice chmn., 1978-80; atty. gen. State of Wyo., 1974-75; mem. Mont Pelerin Soc.; apptd. mem. Pres.'s Com. on Arts and Humanities, Washington, 1990-93; bd. dirs. Philanthropy Roundtable, Washington, 1993-2000; bd. dirs. Univ. Music Soc., 1986-90, pres., 1990; trustee World of Learning, Inc., Brattleboro, Vt., 1993-98. With U.S. Army, 1954-57. Mem. Wyo. Bar Assn., Mich. Bar Assn. Republican. Office: Earhart Found 2200 Green Rd Ste H Ann Arbor MI 48105-1569

KENNEDY, DAVID J. lawyer; b. N.Y.C., July 11, 1971; s. James Joseph and Anne Veronica (Hearne) K.; m. Aldina Maria Vazao, Apr. 11, 1997; 1 child, Dylan Jeronimo. BA, Harvard U., 1993; JD, Yale U., 1997. Bar: Conn. 1997, N.Y. 1998, U.S. Ct. Appeals (2d cir.) 1998, U.S. Dist. Ct. (so. dist.) N.Y. 1999. Pub. Interest Law fellow Alliance for Justice, Washington, 1997-98; law clk. to Hon. Kimba M. Wood U.S. Dist. Ct. (so. dist.) N.Y., N.Y.C., 1998-99; law clk. to hon. Wilfred Feinberg U.S. Ct. Appeals (2d cir.), 1999-2000; asst. U.S. Atty., So. Dist. N.Y., 2000—. Mem. grad. rev. bd. Harvard Lampoon, 1993—; contbr. articles to law rev. Contbg. mem. Dem. Nat. Com., Washington, 1995—. Harry S Truman scholar, 1992, Henry Luce scholar, 1993. Roman Catholic. Avocations: cooking, reading, bears. Home: 3235 Cambridge Ave Bronx NY 10463-3622

KENNEDY, DAVID L. social worker, military officer; b. L.A., Sept. 3, 1946; BS, Calif. State U., L.A., 1974; MSW, U. Calif., Berkeley, 1976. ACSW, DCSW. Enlisted USN, 1980—, advanced through grades 0-6; various to head social work dept. Nat. Naval Med. Ctr., Bethesda, Md.; chief of aux. svcs. Naval Hosp., Rota, Spain; sr. health analyst Bur. of Medicine and Surgery, Washington; dir. of opers. Navy Region Southwest, San Diego; exec. officer Naval Med. Clinic, Patuxent River, Md. Mem.: Fed. Social Workers Consortium, NASW. Office: Naval Med Clin 47149 Buse Rd Patuxent River MD 20670

KENNEDY, DAVID MICHAEL, historian, educator; b. Seattle, July 22, 1941; s. Albert John and Mary Ellen (Caufield) Kennedy; m. Judith Ann Osborne, Mar. 14, 1970; children: Ben Caufield, Elizabeth Margaret, Thomas Osborne. BA, Stanford U., 1963; MA, Yale U., 1964, PhD, 1968; MA, Oxford U., 1995; D (hon.), LaTrobe U., 2001. From asst. prof. history to prof. Stanford U., Calif., 1967—80, prof., 1980—, chmn. program in internat. relations, 1977—80, assoc. dean Sch. Humanities and Scis., 1981—85, William Robertson Coe prof. history and Am. studies, 1987—93, Donald J. McLachlan prof. history, 1993—, chair, history dept., 1990—94. Vis. prof. U. Florence, Florence, Italy, 1976—77; lectr. Internat. Comms. Agy., 1976—77, Ireland, 1980; vis. prof. Am. history Oxford U., 1995—96, Tanner lectr., 2003. Author: Birth Control in America: The Career of Margaret Sanger, 1970, Over Here: The First World War and American Society, 1980; author: (with Thomas A. Bailey and Lizabeth Cohen) The American Pageant: A History of the Republic, 12th edit., 2002; co-editor: Power and Responsibility: Case Studies in American Leadership, 1986; author: Freedom from Fear: The American People in Depression and War, 1929-1945, 1999; mem. adv. bd. (TV program) The American Experience, Sta. WGBH, 1986—. Mem. planning group Am. Issues Forum, 1974—75; bd. dirs. CORO Found., 1981—87, Environ. Traveling Companions, 1986—, Stanford U. Bookstore, 1994—, The Pulitzer Prizes, 2002—. Recipient Bancroft prize, 1971, John Gilmary Shea prize, 1970, Richard W. Lyman award, Stanford U. Alumni Assn., 1989, Pulitzer prize, 2000, 2002, Frances Parkman prize, 2000, Ambs. Book prize, 2000, Calif. Book award, 2000; fellow, Am. Coun. Learned Socs., 1971—72, John Simon Guggenheim Meml. Found., 1975—76, Ctr. for Advanced Study in Behavioral Scis., 1986—87, Stanford Humanities Ctr., 1989—90. Fellow: Am. Philos. Soc., Am. Acad. arts and Scis.; mem.: Soc. Am. Historians, Orgn. Am. Historians, Am. Hist. Assn. Democrat. Roman Catholic. Office: Stanford U Dept History Stanford CA 94305 E-mail: dmk@stanford.edu.

KENNEDY, DAVID TINSLEY, retired lawyer, labor arbitrator; b. Richmond, Va., Mar. 6, 1919; s. David Tinsley and Lilian Brady (Butcher) K.; m. Jean Elizabeth Stephenson, Nov. 26, 1949 (dec.); children: David T. III, Thomas D., Michael F. JD, U. Va., 1948. Bar: Va. 1948, W.Va. 1949, U.S. Dist. Ct. (so. dist.) W.Va. 1949, U.S. Ct. Appeals (4th cir.) 1963. Atty. Dist. 29 United Mine Workers Am., Beckley, W.Va., 1949-61; ptnr. Kennedy & Vaughan, Beckley, 1962-98; ret., 1999. Arbitrator Coal Arbitration Svc., Washington, 1970-98; emeritus dir. Raleigh County Nat. Bank, Beckley. Mem. Raleigh County Dem. exec. com., 1980-86, chmn., 1986-90. Lt. col. U.S. Army, 1942-46, PTO. Mem. ABA, W.Va. State Bar, Va. State Bar, Assn. Trial Lawyers Am. Roman Catholic. Home: 102 Mollohan Dr Beckley WV 25801-2135 E-mail: kennedy25801@aol.com.

KENNEDY, DAVID WILLIAM, otolaryngologist, educator; b. York, Eng., June 27, 1948; s. Michael Leo and Winifred Pearl (Shepherd) K.; m. Edna Mae Schirmer, Apr. 20, 1978; children: Garrett David, Kirin Suzanne. Ed. pre-med. program, Ampleforth Coll., York, 1962-66; MD, Royal Coll. Surgeons, Ireland, 1972. Diplomate Am. Bd. Otolaryngology, Am. Bd. Head and Neck Surgery; lic. physician Pa., Md. Intern St. Laurence's Hosp., Dublin, 1972-73; asst. resident in surgery Johns Hopkins U., Balt., 1973-74, asst. resident in otolaryngology, 1974-77, mem. staff, 1977-91, chief resident in otolaryngology, asst. prof. otolaryngology, 1977-78, asst. prof., 1978-86, assoc. prof. otolaryngology-head and neck surgery, 1986-91, assoc. prof. neurosurgery, 1987-91; mem. staff Loch Raven VA Hosp., Balt., 1980-87, cons. physician, 1987-91; mem. staff Sinai Hosp. Balt., 1981-88; chmn. U. Pa. Med. Ctr., Phila., 1991—; mem. staff VA Hosp., Phila., 1991—; vice dean profl. svcs. U. of Pa. Sch. of Medicine, 2002—; sr. v.p. U. of Pa. Health Sys., 2002—. Invited spkr. Nasal Endoscopy Surgery Workshop, Beijing, 2000, Croucher Advanced Study Inst. Course, Hong Kong, 2000, 50th Course of Microendoscopic Sinus Surgery, São Paulo, 2000, 1st Congress of Internat. Fedn. of Facial Plastic Surgery Socs. and Internat. Symposium of Rhinology and Paranasal Sinus, 2000, XVIII Congress of European Rhinologic Soc., Barcelona, 2000, Congress of Polish Soc. Otolaryngologists, 2000, Hosp. of Trelleborg FESS Course, Malmo, Sweden, 2000, Pan Am. Congress Otorhinolaryngology, Lima, Peru, 2000, 7th Ann. Conf. on Diseases of the Nose and Paranasal Sinuses, Cairo, 2001, XX Internat. Symposium Infection and Allergy of the Nose and IV Congress of Russian Rhinology Soc., Yaroslav, Russia, 2001; guest lectr. ACP-Am. Soc. Internat. Medicine, 2000, guest spkr., 01. Contbr. or co-contbr. 13 chpts. to books, including: Rhinitis, 2nd edit., 1991, Diseases of the Nose, Throat, Ear, Head and Neck, 1991, Otolaryngology, 3rd edit., 1991, Surgery for Skull Base Tumors, 1991, Diseases of the Sinuses: Diagnosis and Management; contbr. numerous articles to profl. jours.; mem. editl. bd. Ear, Nose and Throat Jour., 1983—, Am. Jour. Rhinology, 1986—, Laryngoscope, 1988—, Auris Nasus Larynx, 1996—, ACTA Oto-Rhino-Laryngologica Belgica, 1995—; editor-in-chief (otolaryngology) Am. Jour. Rhinology, 1984—, Current Opinion in Otolaryngology and Head and Neck Surgery, 1992—, Jour. Otolaryngology, 1993—; editor Auris Nasus Larynx, 1996—, ACTA Oto-Rhino-Larynngologica Belgica, 1995—. Recipient Leonard Abrahamson Meml. Gold medal, 1971, Lyons Meml. medal, 1971, gold medal Coombe Lying-In Hosp., 1971, Reuben-Harvey prize, 1972, Coun.'s prize and gold medal, 1972, Sr. William Wilde medal, 1995, Predl. Citation AAO-HWS, 2002; rsch. grantee Schering Corp., 1981, HHS, 1983-88, Norwich-Eaton Corp., 1984-86, Minn. Mining and Mfg. Co., 1984, Healthtek, 1990-91. Fellow Am. Acad. Otolaryngology-Head and Neck Surgery (mem. hearing subcom. 1985-91, mem. rhinology-paranasal sinus com. 1986-93, 97—, mem. CPT com. 1992-97, legis. alt. bd. govs. 1991—, mem. adv. coun. on continuing edn. with TV subcom. 1994, instr. endoscopic sinus surgery 1985, mem. internat. otolaryngology com. 2000)), Royal Coll. Surgeons (anatomy demonstrator/lectr. 1972-73, vis. prof. 1980-81, Sir William Wheeler Meml. medal 1972, Fitzsimmons Gold medal for surgery 1972, Bronze medal), Royal Coll. Surgeons (Ireland); mem. ACS (com. on emerging surg. tech. and edn. 1999), AMA (hon.), NAS-Inst. Medicine, Am. Rhinologic Soc. (bd. dirs. 1988-96, v.p. 1989-90, pres. 1992-93, cons. to bd. dirs. 1987-88), Internat. Symposium on Infection of the Nose (bd. dirs., pres. 1989, 97), Internat. Symposium on Infection and Allergy of the Nose (pres. 1997), Internat. Rhinologic Soc. (bd. dirs. 1995—), Phila. Laryngol. Soc., Assn. Acad. Depts. of Otorhinolaryngology (pres. 1996-98), Soc. Univ. Otolaryngologists (mem. nominating com. 1985-86), Nat. Acad. of Scis., Inst. of Medicine, Pa. Acad. Otolaryngology, John Morgan Soc., Johns Hopkins Med. and Surg. Assn., Danish Otolaryngology Soc. (hon.), Johns Hopkins Soc. Scholars. Achievements include introduction of endoscopic sinus surgery to U.S.; development of extended applications of endoscopic surgical techniques; clinical development of surgical localizers. Office: Univ Pa Med Ctr 5 Ravdin 3400 Spruce St Philadelphia PA 19104-4206

KENNEDY, DEBBIE A. plastic surgeon; b. Plattsburg, N.Y., Apr. 3, 1958; d. Paul F. and Kathleen A. (Bell) K.; m. Martin F. Moriarty, June 26, 1993. BA in Biology and Chemistry, Coll. of St. Rose, 1980; MD, U. Vt., 1984. Diplomate Am. Bd. Plastic Surgeons, Am. Bd. Surgeons. Intern in gen. surgery St. Elizabeth's Hosp. of Boston, 1984-85, resident in gen. surgery, 1985-89; resident in plastic surgery Albany (N.Y.) Med. Ctr. Hosp., 1989-91, clin. instr. divsn. plastic surgery, 1991-98, clin. assoc. prof. surgery, 1998—. Clin. instr. surgery Tufts U., Boston, 1988-89; mem. ad hoc com. on plastic laser surgery Child's Hosp., Albany, 1997, mem. performance improvement com., 1996—, mem. med. records com., 1993—; lectr., spkr., cons. in field. Contbr. articles to profl. jours. Cosmetic fellow, Miami, Fla., 1992. Fellow ACS; mem. Assn. Women Surgeons, Am. Soc. Plastic and Reconstructive Surgeons (mem. women's plastic surgeon's com. 1996-99), Soc. Plastic Surgeons Upstate N.Y., Am. Med. Women's Assn., N.Y. State Med. Soc., Nat. Coalition Physicians Against Family Violence, Delta Epsilon Sigma, Kappa Gamma Pi, Alpha Omega Alpha. Office: Albany Plastic and Reconstructive Surgery Ctr 4 Executive Park Albany NY 12203-3717

KENNEDY, DEBORA A. lawyer; b. Oct. 4, 1942; BA, U. Wash., 1964; JD, U. Wis., 1979. Mng. atty. Wis. Legis. Ref. Bur., Madison, 1998—. Rschr. (book) The Rights of the Critically Ill, 1983. V.p. Vilas Neighborhood Assn., Madison, 1998. Mem. Phi Beta Kappa. Office: Legis Ref Bur 100 N Hamilton St Madison WI 53703-4118

KENNEDY, DEBRA JOYCE, marketing professional, b. July 9, 1955; d. John Nathan and Drea Hannah (Lancaster) Ward; m. John William Kennedy, Sept. 3, 1977 (div.); children: Drea, Noelle. BS in Comm., Calif. State Poly. U., 1977; MA in Orgnl. Mgmt., U. Phoenix, 2003. Pub. rels. coord. Whittier (Calif.) Hosp., 1978—79, pub. rels. mgr., 1980; pub. rels. dir. San Clemente (Calif.)

Hosp., 1979—80; dir. pub. rels. Garfield Med. Ctr., Monterey Park, Calif., 1980—82; dir. mktg. and cmty. rels. Charter Oak Hosp., Covina, 1983—85; mktg. dir. CPC Horizon Hosp., Pomona, 1985—89; dir. mktg. Sierra Royale Hosp., Azusa, 1989—90; mktg. rep. PacifiCare, Cypress, 1990—92; regional medicare mgr. Health Net, Woodland Hills, Calif., 1992—95; dist. sales mgr. Kaiser Permanente Health Plan, Pasadena, Calif., 1995—. Contbr. articles to profl. jours. Mem.: Healthcare Pub. Rels. and Mktg. Assn., Healthcare Mktg. Assn., Am. Soc. Hosp. Pub. Rels., Covina and Covina West C. of C., Soroptimists, West Covina Jaycees. Republican. Methodist.

KENNEDY, DONALD, editor, environmental scientist, educator; b. NYC, Aug. 18, 1931; s. William Dorsey and Barbara (Bean) Kennedy; children: Laura Page, Julia Halestepchildren: Cameron Rachel, Jamie Christopher. AB, Harvard U., 1952, AM, 1954, PhD, 1956; DSc (hon.), Columbia U., Williams Coll., U. Mich., U. Ariz., U. Rochester, Reed Coll., Whitman Coll., Coll. William & Mary. Mem. faculty Stanford (Calif.) U., 1960-77, prof. biol. scis., 1965-77, chmn. dept., 1965-72, sr. cons. sci. and tech. policy Exec. Office of Pres., 1976, commr. FDA, 1977-79, provost, 1979-80, pres., 1980-92, prof. emeritus, Bing prof. environ. sci., 1992—. Bd. overseers Harvard U., 1970—76; bd. dirs. Health Effects Inst., Nat. Commn. Pub. Svc., Carnegie Commn. Sci., Tech. and Govt. Author: Academic Duty, 1997; mem. editl. bd. Jour. Neurophysiology, 1969—75, Sci., 1973—77; editor-in-chief: Sci., 2000—; contbr. articles to profl. jours. Bd. dirs. Carnegie Endowment Internat. Peace. Fellow: AAAS, Am. Acad. Arts and Scis.; mem.: NAS, Am. Philos. Soc. Office: Stanford U Inst for Internat Studies Encina Hall 401 Stanford CA 94305-6055 Business E-Mail: kennedyd@stanford.edu.

KENNEDY, EDWARD MOORE, senator; b. Boston, Feb. 22, 1932; s. Joseph Patrick and Rose (Fitzgerald) K.; m. Joan Kennedy (div.); children: Kara Anne, Edward Moore, Patrick Joseph; m. Victoria Anne Reggie, 1992. AB, Harvard U., 1956; postgrad., Internat. Law Sch., The Hague, Netherlands, 1958; LL.B., U. Va., 1959. Bar: Mass. 1959, U.S. Supreme Ct. 1963. Asst. dist. atty., Suffolk County, Mass., 1961-62; U.S. senator from Mass., 1962—; chmn. judiciary com., 1979-81; ranking Dem. mem. labor and human resources com., 1981—; also mem. armed service, joint econ., labor and human resources (chmn. full com., chmn. subcom. on health 1971-80) and judiciary coms.; also mem. Dem. steering & coordination com., chmn. health, edn., labor and pensions com. Author: Decisions for a Decade, 1968, In Critical Condition: The Crisis in America's Health Care, 1972, Our Day and Generation, 1979, (with Mark O. Hatfield) Freeze: How You Can Help Prevent Nuclear War, 1979. Pres. Joseph P. Kennedy, Jr. Found., from 1961; trustee Children's Hosp. Med. Ctr., Boston, John F. Kennedy Library, Boston Symphony (emeritus), John F. Kennedy Ctr. for Performing Arts, Robert F. Kennedy Meml. Found., Boston Coll., Mass. Gen. Hosp. Served with AUS, 1951-53. Decorated knight comdr. Order of Phoenix (Greece), grande croce Al Merito della Republica Italiana (Italy), Order el Sol (Peru); named One of 10 Outstanding Young Men, U.S. Jaycees, 1967; recipient meritorious svc. citation U.S. Com. for Refugees and Am. Immigration and Citizenship Coun., Solidarity award Nat. Conf. on Soviet Jewry, award Nat. Mil. Family Assn., 1985, Homeric award Chian Fedn., Scopus award Am. Friends Hebrew U., Hubert H. Humphrey award Leadership Conf. on Civil Rights, others. Mem. Tech. Assessment Bd., Congl. Friends of Ireland, Biomed. Ethics Bd., Arms Control Observer Group, Commn. on the Bicentennial of the U.S. Constitution, Martin Luther King Jr. Fed. Holiday Commn., NAACP. Democrat. Office: US Senate 317 Russell Senate Bldg Washington DC 20510-0001*

KENNEDY, ELIZABETH, health facility administrator; b. Binghamton, N.Y., Mar. 19, 1944; d. Robert D. and Doris Beverly (Bryde) Courtright; m. Leon C. Kennedy, Aug. 29, 1964; children: Andrew, Tracey, Brian, Kristie. AAS, Ind.-Purdue U., 1986; BSN, Ind. Wesleyan U., 1996. RN, Ind.; lifetime ARC nurse. DON Summit House, Ft. Wayne, Ind., 1986-87; staff nurse Mark Souder, M.D., Auburn, Ind., 1988; DON Kendallville (Ind.) Nursing Home, 1988-89, Lifecare Ctr., Lagrange, Ind., 1989-91; asst. DON Arbors at Ft. Wayne, Ind., 1991-92; nursing supr. Allen Home, Health Care & Hospice, 1993-95; DON Courtland Health and Rehab. Ctr., Ft. Wayne, 1996—; staff nurse Interim Health Care, Ft. Wayne, Ind., 1996-97; agy. nurse The Arc of N.E. Ind., 1997-98; DON The Cedars, Leo, Ind., 1998-99; RN cons. Prof. Nursing Svc., 1989-99; clin. educator Parkview Health Sys., Ft. Wayne, Ind., 1999-2000; case mgr. mr/dd In Case Mgmt., Indpls., 1999-2000; mgr. extended care unit Don Adams County Meml. Hosp, Decatur, Ind., 2000; dir. nursing Englewood Health and Rehab. Ctr., Ft. Wayne, Ind., 2001—02; nursing mgr. Wash. House Treatment Ctr., 2001—; dir. nursing Riverbend H.C., Ft. Wayne, 2001; RN coord. Ft. Wayne State Devel. Ctr., 2002—; asst. dir. nursing Univ. Park Nursing Ctr., Ft. Wayne, 2002—03; with Don Kendallville Manor, Kendallville, Ind. Instr. ARC., 1986, AHA CPR, 1998; assoc. faculty dept. nursing Purdue U., Ft. Wayne, 2000. Recipient Scottish Rite Nursing scholarship. Home: 8233 Red Shank Ln Fort Wayne IN 46825 E-mail: tishrn@comcast.net.

KENNEDY, ELIZABETH MAE, musician; b. Medford, Mass., Oct. 16, 1949; d. Thomas Power and Anne Cecelia (Coyne) Sullivan; m. William David Kennedy, Oct. 12, 1970 (div. 1984); children: Mary Elizabeth, Jonathan Martin. AS, N.S. C.C., 1969; student, Aquinas Coll., 1991-92. Cert. liturgical musician music and liturgy. Retail sales mgmt. Jordan Marsh Co., Peabody, Mass., 1966-69; retail mgmt. Sears, Roebuck and Co., Lynn, Mass., 1969-70; asst. bookkeeper Henry Leather Co., Peabody, Mass., 1970-76; office mgr. Bartlett and Steadman Co. Inc., Marblehead, Mass., 1981-90. Bandleader, performer New England Area, 1983—; music dir., contract organist St. John The Evangelist Ch., Swampscott, Mass., 1985-98; co-founder New Sch. of Music and Performing Arts, Marblehead, Mass., 1994; dir. music St. Charles Borromeo Ch., Waltham, Mass., 1998-99, Incarnation Parish, Melrose, Mass., 1999—. Organizer Devereux Neighborhood Assn.; active North Shore Piano Tchrs. Guild, 1988—, v.p., 1998-2000, co-pres., 2000-02; chairperson Marblehead Festival of the Arts, 1998-99. Democrat. Roman Catholic. Avocations: reading, swimming, midi, computers. Home: 46 Ocean Ave Marblehead MA 01945-3616 Fax: 781-631-1519. E-mail: elizmkenn@aol.com.

KENNEDY, EUGENE CULLEN, psychology educator, writer; b. Syracuse, N.Y., Aug. 28, 1928; s. James Donald and Gertrude Veronica (Cullen) K.; m. Sara Connor Charles, Sept. 3, 1977. AB, Maryknoll Coll., 1950; STB, Maryknoll Sem., 1953, MRE, 1954; MA, Cath. U. Am., 1958, PhD, 1962; LHD (hon.), Barat Coll., 1990. Instr. psychology Maryknoll Sem., Clarks Summit, Pa., 1955-56, Cath. U., Washington, 1959-60; prof. psychology Maryknoll Coll., Glen Ellyn, Ill., 1960-69, Loyola U., Chgo., 1969-95, prof. emeritus, 1995—. Cons. Menninger Found., 1965-67; mem. profl. adv. bd. Chgo. Dept. Mental Health; bd. dirs., cons. King Kullen Grocery Co., 1985—, mem. exec. com., 1994—; ptnr. Associated Growth Investors, 1992—; bd. dirs. Crown Mktg. Group, Inc. Author 40 books, including Himself! The Life and Times of Richard J. Daley, 1978 (Carl Sandburg award 1978), Father's Day, 1981 (Soc. of Midland Authors fiction award 1981, Friends of Lit. award 1981, Carl Sandburg award 1981), Queen Bee, 1982, The Now and Future Church, 1984, (with Sara Charles) Defendant, 1985, Tomorrow's Catholics, Yesterday's Church, 1988, Fixes, 1989, Cardinal Bernardin, 1989, (with Sara Charles) On Becoming a Counselor, 1990, (with Sara Charles) Authority, 1996, This Man Bernadin, 1996, My Brother Joseph, 1997, The Unhealed Wound, 2001, Thou Art That, 2001, Meditations at the Center of the World, 2002, Cardinal Bernardin's Stations of the Cross, 2003; author TV play: I Would Be Called John, PBS, 1987; also articles, book revs.; columnist Religion News Svc., 1991-92, 97—, Chgo. Tribune, 1992-93. Trustee U. Dayton, 1977—86. Recipient Thomas More medal, 1972, 78, Wilbur award Religious Pub. Relations Council. Fellow Am. Psychol. Assn. (div. pres. 1975-76); mem. Authors Guild. Democrat. Roman Catholic. Home: 1300 N Lake Shore Dr Chicago IL 60610-2169 *My principal goal in all my work is to try to understand and to try to help others understand what is so human about all of us.*

KENNEDY, EUGENE PATRICK, biochemist, educator; b. Chgo., Sept. 4, 1919; s. Michael and Catherine (Frawley) K.; m. Adelaide Majewski, Oct. 27, 1943; children: Lisa Kennedy Helprin, Sheila Kennedy Violich, Katherine Kennedy Diller. BSc, DePaul U., 1941; PhD (Nutrition Found. fellow), U. Chgo., 1949, ScD (hon.), 1977; AM (hon.), Harvard U., 1960. Rsch. chemist chem. rsch. dept. Armour & Co., 1941-47; postdoctoral fellow Am. Cancer Soc., U. Calif., Berkeley, 1949-50; with Ben May Lab. Cancer Rsch., dept. biochemistry U. Chgo., 1950-56, prof. biochemistry, 1956-60; sr. postdoctoral fellow NSF, Oxford U., England, 1959-60; Hamilton Kuhn prof. biol. chemistry Harvard Med. Sch., 1960—, head dept., 1960-65; Macy scholar Cambridge U., 1976. Recipient Glycerine rsch. award, 1955; Am. Oil Chemist Soc. Lipid Rsch. award, 1970; Gairdner Found. award, 1976; Ledlie prize, 1976, Alexander von Humboldt prize, 1984; Passano Found. award, 1986, Heinrich Wieland Prize, 1986, William C. Rose Award in biochemistry. Am. Soc. Biochem. and Molecular Biology, 1992. Mem. NAS, Am. Chem. Soc. (Paul Lewis award 1958), Am. Soc. Biol. Chemists (pres. 1970-71), Am. Acad. Arts and Scis., Am. Philos. Soc. Home: 221 Mount Auburn St Cambridge MA 02138-4874 Office: Harvard Med Sch Dept Biol Chemistry Boston MA 02115

KENNEDY, EUGENE RICHARD, microbiologist, university dean; b. Scranton, Pa., July 3, 1919; s. Thomas A. and Margaret (Culkin) K.; m. Marjorie Giblin, July 24, 1945; children— Anne, Michael, Christine. BS, U. Scranton, 1941; MS, Cath. U., 1943; PhD, Brown U., 1949. Diplomate Am. Bd. Microbiology. Serologist Walter Reed Army Med. Center, Washington, 1942; instr. bacteriology and immunology R.I. Hosp. Sch. of Nursing, Providence, 1946-48, Brown U., Providence, 1946-48; instr. Cath. U. Am., Washington, 1949-51, asst. prof., 1951-55, assoc. prof., 1956-66, prof. microbiology, 1966-85, prof. emeritus, 1985—, dean Sch. Arts and Scis., 1973-85. Contbr. articles to profl. jours. Served to capt. Med. Service Corps U.S. Army, 1943-46. Mem. Am. Soc. for Microbiology, AAAS, Sigma Xi, Phi Beta Kappa. Home: 15100 Interlachen Dr Apt 912 Silver Spring MD 20906-5608 Office: Cath U McCort-Ward Bldg Washington DC 20064

KENNEDY, EVELYN SIEFERT, foundation executive, textile specialist; b. Pitts., Nov. 11, 1927; d. Carmine and Assunta (Iacobucci) Rocci; m. George J. Siefert, May 30, 1953 (dec. 2000); children: Paul Kenneth, Carl Joseph, Ann Marie; m. Lyle H. Kennedy II, Oct. 12, 1974 (dec. 1990); m. Frederick J. Commentucci, Feb. 24, 2001. BS magna cum laude, U. R.I., 1969, MS in Textiles and Clothing, 1970. accredited appraiser of personal property, Internat. Soc. Appraisers. With Pitts. Pub. Schs., 1945-50, Goodyear Aircraft Corp., Akron, Ohio, 1950-54; clothing instr. Groton (Conn.) Dept. Adult Edn., 1958-68; pres. Sewtique, Groton, 1970—, Sewtique II, New London, Conn., 1986; v.p. Kennedy Capital Advisors, Groton, 1973-85, Kennedy Mgmt. Corp., Groton, 1974-85, Kennedy Intervest, Inc., Groton, 1975-85; pres., exec. dir. PRIDE Found., Inc., Groton, 1978—. Clothing cons. Coop. Ext. Svc., Dept. Agr.; internat. lectr. on clothing for disabled and elderly; adj. faculty U. Conn., Ea. Conn. State Coll., St. Joseph Coll.; hon. prof. U. R.I., assoc. prof., 1987—, fed. expert witness Care Label Law, FTC, 1976; mem. Major Appliance Consumer Action Panel, 1983-89. Author: Dressing With Pride, 1980, Clothing Accessibility: A Lesson Plan to Aid the Disabled and Elderly, 1983, Textiles Speak, 1996. Regional adv. coun. SBA Active corps Execs., Hartford, 1985—; bd. dirs. Sml. Bus. Devel. Ctr., 1989—, Easter Seal Rehab. Ctr. Southeastern Conn., Southeastern Conn. Women's Ctr., 1997—, Women's Ctr. New London County, 1997—; bus. adv. coun. U. R.I., 1979—, trustee, 1985—; active LWV; mem. Groton Vocat. Edn. Adv. Coun. Recipient award of distinction U. R.I., 1969, Adv. of Yr. SBA, 1984, Outstanding Svc. in Cmty., 1991; named Woman of Yr. Bus. and Profl. Women's Club, 1977, Conn. Home Economist of Yr., 1987. Mem. Internat. Sleep Coun. (consumer affairs rep., Sml. Bus. Adminstrn. award 1991), Internat. Soc. Appraisers (accredited appraiser personal property, panelist FMHA roster, farmer's credit mediator 1989—), Nat. Assn. Bedding Mfrs., Conn. Home Economists in Bus. (founder 1977, Women of Yr. 1987), Nat. Home Economists in Bus. (chmn. internat. rels., nat. fin. chmn. 1986), Am. Home Econs. Assn., Coll. and Univ. Bus. Instrs. of Conn., Am. Occupl. Therapy Assn. (resource cons. 1986—), Web-Re-Stor Assn. (wedding restoration specialist 1993-2000), Southeastern Women's Network, Fashion Group, Costume Soc. Am., New London Zonta Club, Bus. and Profl. Women's Club (Outstanding Women of Yr. 1977), Omicron Nu, Phi Kappa Phi. Office: 391 Long Hill Rd Groton CT 06340-3812 E-mail: textileappraisal@aol.com.

KENNEDY, FAYE, retired social worker, author; b. Kansas City, Mo., Apr. 3, 1931; d. Wiley Choice and Zella Rae (Jackman) K.; m. Patrick Joseph Daly, Jan. 7, 1961. AA, Pasadena City Coll., 1951; BA, Hunter Coll., 1955; cert., Alliance Francaise, Paris, 1956. Vocat. counselor N.Y. State Divsn. Employment, N.Y.C., 1957-65; social worker N.Y. State Div. Parole, N.Y.C., 1965-77. Author: Good-bye, Diane, 1976; assoc. editor Afro-Hawaii News, 1990-92. Hawaii adv. com. U.S. Civil Rights Commn., Honolulu, 1990—; active Hawaii State Commn. on Status of Women, Honolulu, 1993-95, Hawaii Civil Rights Commn., Honolulu, 1995-2003, Martin Luther King Jr. Commn., Honolulu, 1989-93; del. Hawaii Dem. Party State Cen. Com., 1994—, Dem. Nat. Conv., 1996, 2000; bd. dirs. Hawaii Literacy, Inc., 1987-97, Hawaii Youth at Risk, 1991-94, ACLU of Hawaii, 1999-2002. Recipient Gov.'s Cert. of Appreciation, State of Hawaii, 1989-93, Making of the King Holiday award Martin Luther King Jr. Commn., 1991, Outstanding Achievement award Hawaii Literacy, Inc., 1988, 92, Outstanding African Ams. citation Mahogany, 1996, Afro-Hawaii News, 1992, Hawaii Personalities Recognition citation RSVP mag., 1989, Lifetime Dedication to Pub. Svc. cert. Honolulu City Coun., 1996. Mem. Hawaii Women's Polit. Caucus (v.p. programs 1990—, bd. dirs.), Hawaii Yacht Club. Democrat. Avocations: reading, writing, movies, gardening. Home: 3071 Felix St Honolulu HI 96816-1911

KENNEDY, FREDERICK MORGAN, retired secondary school educator; b. Oklahoma City, May 5, 1943; s. Fredrick Theodor and Ruthy Marie Kennedy; m. Claudette Alberta Carter, Aug. 14, 1966; children: Kimberly Michelle, Cheryl Ann. BS, Langston U., 1965; MA, Kent State U., 1979. Cert. tchr., Ohio; ordained local elder African Meth. Episcopal Ch.; lic. life health ins., Securities. Tchr. math., occupational work adjustment Cleve. City Schs., 1965-96. Curriculum writing com. Cleve. City Schs., 1987, 89, 92. Treas. Quinn Chapel AME Ch., Cleve., 1985-97, 2001—, ch. adminstr., 1989-97, 2002—. Mem. Ohio Vocat. Assn. (life), Indsl. Arts Club (membership com. 1992), Occupational Work Adjustment (instrs. div.), Langston U. Nat. Alumni Assn. (life, pres. Cleve. chpt.), Phi Beta Sigma (life). Democrat. Home: 17201 Dynes Ave Cleveland OH 44128-3320 E-mail: fckck@core.com.

KENNEDY, GARY J. psychiatrist; b. Dallas, Nov. 1, 1948; m. Jenny McCord, Sept. 1, 1969. BA, U. Tex., 1970, MD, 1975. Diplomate Am. Bd. Psychiatry and Neurology with added qualifications in geriatrics. Resident U. Tex., San Antonio, 1975-79; instr. psychiatry Albert Einstein Coll. Medicine, Bronx, N.Y., 1979-84, rsch. fellow, 1982-84, assoc. prof. psychiatry, 1989-95, prof. psychiatry and behavioral sci., 1996—; fellow Montefiore Med. Ctr., Bronx, 1979-81, psychobiology rsch. fellow, 1980-82; dir. divsn. geriatric psychiatry AECOM/Montefiore Med. Ctr., Bronx, 1987—. Author: Geriatric Mental Health Care; contbr. articles to profl. jours. Recipient Extraordinary Psychiatrist award Nat. Alliance for Mentally Ill, 2003; WHO travel study fellow, Israel, U.K., 1983, Brookdale Ctr. on Aging Hunter Coll. fellow, 1989; recipient New Investigator Rsch. award Nat. Heart, Lung & Blood Inst., NIH, 1984, Community Svc. award Bronx Geriatric Mental Health Com., 1990; rsch. grantee Nat. Inst. Aging, 1986-90. Mem. APHA (Archstone Found. award), Am. Psychiat. Assn., Am. Assn. Geriatric Psychiatry (pres.), Gerontol. Soc. Am., Am. Geriatrics Soc. Office: Montefiore Med Ctr 111 E 210th St Bronx NY 10467-2401 Fax: 917-432-1712. E-mail: gkennedy@aecom.yu.edu.

KENNEDY, GEORGE DANNER, chemical company executive; b. Pitts., May 30, 1926; s. Thomas Reed and Lois (Smith) K.; m. Valerie Putis; children: Charles Reed, Jamey Kathleen, Susan Patton, Timothy Christian. BA, Williams Coll., 1948. With Scott Paper Co., 1947-52, Champion Paper Co., 1952-65; pres. Brown Co., 1965-71; exec. v.p. Internat. Minerals & Chem. Corp., Northbrook, Ill., 1971-78, pres., 1978-86; chmn. Mallinckrodt Group (formerly IMCERA), St. Louis, 1986—, CEO, 1983-91; also bd. dirs., chmn. exec. com. IMCERA (formerly Internat. Minerals & Chem. Corp.), Northbrook, Ill. Former chmn. nominting com. Kemper Nat.; former chmn. compensation com., bd. dirs. exec. com. Am. Nat. Can Co.; dir. Health Share, Acton, Mass; mng. ptnr. Berkshires Capital Investors, Willistown, Mass. Bd. dirs. Children's Meml. Hosp. and Children's Meml. Med. Ctr., Inst. Internat. Edn., Sand County Found.; trustee Chgo. Symphony; gov. mem. Chgo. Orch. Assn.; dir. Lyric Opera Chgo., Ctr. for Workforce Preparation and Quality Edn.; regional trustee Boys and Girls Club of Am.; trustee Nat. Com. Against Drunk Driving. Mem. Indian Hill Club, Chgo. Club, Sleepy Hollow Country Club, Taconic Golf Club. Office: PO Box 559 Winnetka IL 60093-0559

KENNEDY, GEORGE FRANCIS, publishing executive; b. Providence, Sept. 23, 1936; s. Amos Huntington Kennedy and Theresa Catherine Glancy; m. Sonya R. K., Dec. 13, 1963 (div. 1969). BA, Brown U., 1958; MA, U. Mich., 1959, candidates cert. (PhD), 1963. Instr. U. Mich., Ann Arbor, 1960-63; editor mng. editor Willow Run Labs, U. Mich., Ann Arbor, 1963-68; sr. editor, pub info. officer Inst. Sci. and Tech., U. Mich., Ann Arbor, 1969-70; trainer curriculum developer, dir. pub. info. High/Scope Ednl. Rsch. Found., Ypsilanti Mich., 1970-72; part-time instr. Washtenaw C.C., Ann Arbor, 1989—; bus mgr., pub. Prakken Publs., Inc., Ann Arbor, 1972—, part owner, 1990—, pres. 1990-92, v.p., 1995—. Chmn. bus. edn. com., Ann Arbor Pub. Schs., 1983-90 chmn. bus. edn. adv. com., Washtenaw C.C., 1989-91; mem. Washtenaw Edn.-Work Consortium, Ann Arbor, 1991-96. Contbr. articles to profl. publs Chmn. printing and pub. divsn., Washtenaw United Way, 1985-86. Mem. Am Soc. Tng. & Devel. (program coord. 1994), Ann Arbor Area Pers. Assn. (human resources chmn. 1985-90), Ann Arbor Area C. of C. (human resources com 1990-95), Phi Beta Kappa, Phi Kappa Phi. Democrat. Roman Catholic Avocations: softball, basketball, filmmaking, local theater. Home: 921 Raymond St Ann Arbor MI 48103-4533 Office: Prakken Publs Inc 3970 Varsity Dr Ann Arbor MI 48108-2226

KENNEDY, GEORGE WENDELL, prosecutor; b. Altadena, Calif., Aug. 5 1945; s. Ernest Campbell Kennedy and Mildred (Onstott) Stuckey; m. Jane Lynn Stites, Aug. 3, 1978; children: Campbell, Britton. BA, Claremont Men's Coll., 1968; postgrad., Monterey Inst. Fgn. Studies, 1968; JD, U. So. Calif. 1971; postgrad., Nat. Coll. Dist. Attys., 1974, F.B.I. Nat. Law Inst., 1989. Bar Calif. 1972, U.S. Dist. Ct. (no. dist.) Calif. 1972, U.S. Ct. Appeals (9th cir.) 1972. Dep. dist. atty. Santa Clara County, San Jose, Calif., 1972-87, asst. dist atty., 1987-88, chief asst. dist. atty., 1988-90, dist. atty., 1990—. Author California Criminal Law Practice and Procedure, 1986. Active NAACP 1989—, police chiefs' assn. Santa Clara County, San Jose, 1990—; chair domestic violence coun. Santa Clara County, San Jose, 1990-92; bd. dirs Salvation Army, 1993. Recipient commendation Child Advocates of Santa Clara & San Mateo Counties, 1991, Santa Clara County Bd. Suprs., 1992, Valley Med. Ctr. Found., 1992, 93; elected Ofcl. of Yr. award Am. Electronics Assn. 1998. Mem. Nat. Dist. Attys. Assn., Calif. Dist. Attys. Assn. (bd. dirs. 1988-90 officer 1993-97, pres. 1997-98), Santa Clara County Bar Assn., Rotary Club Avocation: sailing. Office: 70 W Hedding St 5th Flr West Wing San Jose CA 95110

KENNEDY, GREGORY DUSTIN, journalist; b. Ft. Worth, Tex., Sept. 15 1975; s. Michael Lee and Patricia Lynn Kennedy; m. Kathleen Lynn Washburn BA in Journalism, U. Okla., 1998. Sports writer The Shawnee (Okla.) News-Star, 1995—99; staff writer The Daily Oklahoman. Beat reporter Norman City Hall, Cleveland County Dist. Ct., 1999—2002. Mem.: Nat. Sportswriters and Sportscasters Assn., Soc. Profl. Journalists. Avocations: sports, movies baseball card collecting. Home: 2821 Creekview Terrace Norman OK 73071 Office: The Daily Oklahoman 219 34th Ave SW Norman OK 73072 Home Fax 405-292-6121. Personal E-mail: gregandkatiek@aol.com.

KENNEDY, GWENDOLYN DEBRA, artist, scriptwriter, playwright; b. Daly City, Calif., Nov. 18, 1960; d. Adolphus Brooks and Ella (Robinson) K. children: Gwendolyn Fincher, Edward James, Jr. AA in Theater Prodn., City Coll. San Francisco, 1992. Artist Walt Disney Animation Art, 1991; artist animation and fine art www.blackpantherpartypress.tv, 1994—; owner Black Panther Party Press and Pub., 1993—. Owner mail order co. La Chateau D'Gwendolyn Kennedy Co., 1991—. Author: Billie Holliday Collection Book 1993, Kane Kut Murder Trial, 1993, Poetic Justice, 1994, No Struggle No Progress, 1995, Nyami the Sky God, 1996. Recipient Journalist of Yr. award City News Svc., Mo., 1995. Lutheran. Avocations: guitar, ballet, art, track piano, computers. Home: 285 Bellevue Ave Daly City CA 94014-1305 Office PO Box 135 Daly City CA 94016-1305

KENNEDY, HAROLD EDWARD, lawyer; b. Pottstown, Pa., Oct. 18, 1927 s. Freeman S. and Alice (Brehm) K.; m. Eleanor Henry, Jan. 9, 1960; children Kathleen, Nancy, Harold, Robert, Ellen, Anne, Susan. Student, Colgate U. 1945-47; LLB, Syracuse U., 1952. Bar: N.Y. 1952, U.S. Dist. Ct. (no. dist.) N.Y 1954, U.S. Supreme Ct. 1956, U.S. Dist. Ct. (so. dist.) N.Y. 1962. Ptnr. Taylor & Kennedy, Amsterdam, N.Y., 1952-59; sr. assoc. Kissam & Halpin, N.Y.C. 1959-60; vice chmn., gen. counsel, dir. mergers and acquisitions Foster Wheeler Corp., Clinton, N.J., 1960-94, legal advisor, 1994-97, also bd. dirs. Bd. dirs W.I. Refining Ltd. Trustee First Presbyn. Ch., Orange, N.J., 1973-76, St Barnabas Corp., 1996—; sec., 1996—, St. Barnabas Med. Ctr., 1986—, Kessler Inst. for Rehab., 1987-97, vice chmn., 1992-97, Union Hosp., 1994—, Beth Israel Hosp., 1996—; bd. visitors Syracuse U. Coll. of Law, 1987—. Served with USAF, 1945-47. Mem. Order of Coif, Baltusrol Golf Club, Sea Pine Country Club.

KENNEDY, J. JACK, JR., court administrator, lawyer; b. Abingdon, Va., June 11, 1956; s. J. Jack Sr. and Bobbie Lee (Porter) K.; m. Susan Maura Muir, June 30, 1979; children: J. Jack III, Jillian Susanne. BS, U. Va., Wise, 1978; cert. in internat. study, U. London, 1977; MA in Polit. Sci., East Tenn. State U., 1982 JD equivalent, Va. State Bar, 1982; BA in Orgnl. Mgmt., Va. Intermont Coll. 1994. Bar: Va. 1982, U.S. Dist. Ct. (we. dist.) Va. 1982, U.S. Ct. Appeals (4th cir.) 1982, U.S. Tax Ct. 1982, U.S. Ct. Claims 1982, Supreme Ct. Va. 1982, U.S. Internat. Ct. Trade 1992. Mem. Va. Ho. of Dels., Richmond, 1988-91, Va. State Senate, Richmond, 1991-92; clk. Cir. Ct. for Wise County and City of Norton Va., 1995—. Dir. Coalition for Open Govt., 2000—; bd. dirs. Kennedy & Kennedy Investment Corp., Turkey Gap Coal Co., Inc., MyWiseCounty.com FNB, S.E. Bank Adv. Bd.; pres. Southwestern Va. Tech. Coun. 2002; bd. mem U. Va. Coll. at Wise 2002—; mem. bd. Va. Geographic Info. Network, 2002— State pres. Young Dems. Va., 1984-85; nat. sec. Young Dems. Am., 1985; chmn Norton (Va.) Dem. Com., 1982-92, 95-99, 9th Congl. Dist. Dem. Com 1985-89; del. Dem. Nat. Conv., 1976, 84, 88, 92, 2000; state chmn. Va. Assn Local Dem. Chairmen, 1986-87; vice chair Dem. Party Va., 2001-02; bd. dirs chmn. Va. Land Records Mgmt. Task Force, 1997-2000; chair Wise County Dem. Com., 2003. Named Outstanding Young Dem. Va., 1985; recipient Tech Innovation award Va. Supreme Ct., 1997; fellow Nat. Ctr. for State Cts., 1999 Fellow Inst. for Ct. Mgmt.; mem. ABA, Nat. Assn. for Ct. Mgmt., Va. State Bar Va. Bar Assn., Wise County and City of Norton Bar Assn. (pres. 1997), Wise County C. of C. (v.p.), Va. Cir. Ct. Clks. Assn., Kiwanis, Phi Sigma Kappa Baptist. Avocations: international travel, reading, internet technology, space exploration. also: Court House PO Box 1248 Wise VA 24293-1248 Home and Office: PO Box 3444 Wise VA 24293-3444 E-mail: jack@jackkennedy.net.

KENNEDY, JACK, secondary education journalism educator; b. Iowa City Iowa, July 12, 1950; s. John William and Barbara Fern (Guffey) K.; m. Kathleen Ann Gowey, Sept. 25, 1971; children: Lesley Kathleen, Sara Ann, Philip John BA in English, U. Iowa, 1976, MA in Edn., 1981. Tchr., journalism adviser Regina High Sch., Iowa City, 1976-80, City H.S., Iowa City, 1980-99, vice prin., 1999—2001; tchr. Heritage H.S., Littleton, Colo., 2002—. Journalism adv. Heritage H.S., 2002—. With USAF, 1971-74. Nat. HS Journalism Teacher of the Yr., Dow Jones Newspaper Fund, 1993. Mem.: NEA, Journalism Edn. Assn. Democrat. Avocations: reading, singing, coaching youth sports. Office Hertiage High Sch 1401 W Geddes Ave Littleton CO 80120 Home: 2268 W Ashwood Ln Highlands Ranch CO 80129

KENNEDY, JACK LELAND, lawyer; b. Portland, Oreg., Jan. 30, 1924; s. Ernest E. and Lera M. (Talley) K.; m. Clara C. Hagans, June 5, 1948; children James M., John C. Student, U.S. Maritime Commn. Acad., Southwestern U. L.A.; JD, Lewis and Clark Coll., 1951. Bar: Oreg. 1951. Pvt. practice, Portland ptnr. Kennedy & King, Portland, 1971-77, Kennedy, King & McClurg Portland, 1977-82, Kennedy, King & Zimmer, Portland, 1982-98, Kennedy Watts, Arellano & Ricks L.L.P., Portland, 1998—. Trustee Northwestern Coll. Law, Portland; dir. Profl. Liability Fund, 1979-82. Contbr. articles to legal jours. Mem. bd. visitors Lewis and Clark Coll. With USNR, 1942-46. Recipient Disting. Grad. award Lewis and Clark Coll., 1983. Fellow Am. Coll. Trial Lawyers, Am. Bar Found. (life), Oreg. Bar Found. (charter); mem. ABA (ho. of dels. 1984-88), Oreg. State Bar (bd. govs. 1976-79, pres. 1978-79), Multnomah Bar Assn., City Club, Columbia River Yacht Club. Republican. Office: Kennedy Watts Arellano & Ricks LLP 2850 Pacwest Ctr 1211 SW 5th Ave Portland OR 97204-3713

KENNEDY, JACK STANNERS, lawyer; b. Terre Haute, Ind., Apr. 14, 1945; BA magna cum laude, Harvard U., 1967; JD, U. Va., 1972. Bar: Conn. 1972. With Robinson & Cole LLP, Hartford, mng. ptnr., 1994-2000. Mem. editorial bd. Va. Law Review, 1970-72. Mem. ABA (sect. bus. law), Conn. Bar Assn. (past chair sect. bus. law), Order of Coif. Office: Robinson & Cole LLP 280 Trumbull St Hartford CT 06103-3597

KENNEDY, JAMES ANDREW, chemical company executive; b. Millburn, N.J., Dec. 15, 1937; s. James Andrew and Dorothy Frances (Van Cleve) K.; m. Judith Lynne Tunstall, Jan. 26, 1974; children— Brian James, Karen Jeanne, Kevin Van Cleve. BA in Econs., Holy Cross Coll., Worcester, Mass., 1959; MBA in Fin. and Mktg., Columbia U., N.Y.C., 1962. With Nat. Starch and Chem. Co., 1967-77, from v.p. internat. divsn. to exec. v.p., dir., COO, 1977-90; pres., CEO Nat. Starch and Chem. Corp., Bridgewater, N.J., 1990-99, chmn., 1996-97; bus. group pres. Unilever, 1996-97; exec. v.p., dir. Imperial Chem. Industries, Eng., 1997; chmn. Nat. Starch and Chem. Co., Bridgewater, N.J., 1997-99; ret., 1999. Lectr. Notre Dame U., NYU, Pace U., Am. Mgmt. Assn., Babcock Sch. Mgmt. Wake Forest U.; dir. Guardian Life Ins. Co. Am., 2000—; bd. dirs. Unilever U.S., Inc., Guardian Lif Ins. Co. Am., Freedom House Found. Trustee, chmn. bd. trustees N.J. Inst. Tech., 2000—. Served to lt. (j.g.) USN, 1959-61. Mem. NAM (bd. dirs.), Chem. Mfrs. Assn. (bd. dirs.). Home: 11 Crest Dr Bernardsville NJ 07924-1707 Office: Nat Starch & Chem Co 10 Finderne Ave Bridgewater NJ 08807-3355

KENNEDY, JAMES C. publishing and media executive; b. Honolulu, 1947; married. BBA, U. Denver, 1970. With Atlanta Newspapers, 1972-79, prodn. asst., 1972-76, exec. v.p., gen. mgr., 1976-79; pres. Grand Junction Newspapers, 1979-80; pub. Grand Junction Daily Sentinel, 1980-85; v.p. Cox newspapers div. Cox Enterprises Inc., Atlanta, 1985-86, exec. v.p., 1986-87, pres., chief oper. officer, exec. v.p., 1986-87, also chmn., 1987—88, now chmn., chief exec. officer, 1988—. Office: Cox Enterprises Inc PO Box 105357 Atlanta GA 30348-5357 also: 1601 W Peachtree St NE Atlanta GA 30309-2641*

KENNEDY, JAMES H. biologist, educator; b. Garrett, Ind., May 20, 1947; s. Guy E. and Mildred H. Kennedy; m. Virginia J. Tummon, Aug. 28, 1970; 1 child, Amanda Tara. PhD, Va. Tech, 1975. Tchr. Centennial Sch. Dist., Warminster, Pa., 1969—71; fishery biologist Pa. Fish Commn., Tionesta, Pa., 1972—73; sr. ecologist Ichthyological Assocs., Ithaca, NY, 1973—75, NUS Corp., Pitts., 1981—82; owner Water Sci. Assocs. Inc, Coraopolis, Pa., 1982—87; prof. biol. scis. U. of North Tex., Denton, Tex., 1987—, dir. of water rsch. field sta., 1987—. Adj. prof. Sch. of Pub. Health U. of North Tex. Health Sci. Ctr., Fort Worth, Tex. Contbr. over 75 articles to profl. jours. Grantee BioComplexity grant, NSF, 2002—, Bayer, 1989—98, Ciba-Giegy, 1989—98, Hoechst Roussel Agri-Vet, 1989—98, Charn Uswachode Found., 1999—2000. Mem.: N.Am. Benthological Soc., Soc. of Environ. Toxicology and Chemistry (bd. of editors 1994—97), Am. Entomol. Soc. (life). Home: 2010 Williamsburg Row Denton TX 76201 Office: University of North Texas PO Box 310559 Biological Sciences Denton TX 76203-0559 Office Fax: 940-565-4297. Personal E-mail: kennedy@unt.edu. E-mail: kennedy@unt.edu.

KENNEDY, JAMES WILLIAM, JR., (SARGE KENNEDY), special education administrator, consultant; b. Santa Rosa, Calif., Oct. 6, 1940; s. James William and Kay Jean (Eaton) Kennedy; m. Lorene Adele Dunaway, May 12, 1962 (div. Sept. 1971), children: Sean, Erin, Mark; m. Patricia Carter Critchlow, Nov. 5, 1988; stepchildren: Jennifer, Dayna, Joy; m. Carolyn Judith Nighsonger, Mar. 30, 1972 (div. Dec. 1979). BA, San Francisco State U., 1964, MA, 1970. Tchr., prin., coord. spl. edn., dir. Spl. Edn. Local Plan Area Napa County (Calif.) Schs., 1968-83; spl. edn. compliance cons. overseas dependent schs. Mediterranean region Dept. Def., 1983-84; adminstr. Spl. Edn. Local Plan Area and dir. spl. programs Tehama County Dept. Edn., Red Bluff, Calif., 1985-99, asst. supt. student programs/ Spl. Edn. Local Plan Area Ops., 1999—. Editor: (profl. jour.) Calif. Fed. Coun. Exceptional Children Jour., 1971—77, 1981—83. Mem. Wilson Riles Spl. Edn. Task Force, Calif., 1981—82, Spl. Edn. Fiscal Task Force, Calif., 1987—89. Named Outstanding Spl. Edn. Adminstr. Calif., Spl. Edn. Adminstrs. in County Offices of Edn. in Calif., Spl. Edn. Local Plan Area Adminstrs.. Calif., and Calif. Fedn. Coun. Exceptional Children, 1998. Mem.: Spl. Edn. Adminstrs. in County Offices of Edn. in Calif., Spl. Edn. Local Plan Area Adminstrs. Assn. Calif. (co-chair fin. com. 1993—), Coun. for Adminstrs. Spl. Edn., Calif. Fedn. Coun. Exceptional Children (treas. 1992—), Internat. Coun. for Exceptional Children (sgt. at arms 1980—95), Profl. Football rschers. Assn., San Francisco State Alumni Assn. Democrat. Avocations: sports history, pop music history, Spanish and Portuguese cultures. Office: Tehama County Dept Edn PO Box 689 Red Bluff CA 96080-0689 E-mail: skennedy@tcde.tehama.k12.ca.us.

KENNEDY, JERRIE ANN PRESTON, public relations executive; b. Quanah, Tex. Student, Sunset Sch. Preaching, Lubbock, Tex., 1975-78, Jo-Susan Modeling Sch., Nashville, 1984, Film Actors Lab., 1986. Co-prodr. Vincent Cirrincione & Assocs., NY, 1986; paralegal Arlington Career Inst., 1998—; freelance internat. mktg. and pub. rels. exec. Military del. NATO Allies for The French Liaison, Ft. Hood, Tex., 1992, Vietnam War (Diplomatic immunity) 1972-1975. Author screenplay, fed. and cmty. pub. spl. events prodn. US Activist Women's Rights in the State of Tex., 2003. Recipient 1st and 3d pl. awards Modeling Assn. Am., NYC, 1985.

KENNEDY, JOE DAVID, JR., (JOEY KENNEDY), editor; b. Dayton, Tex., Mar. 28, 1956; s. Joe David Sr. and Patricia Ann (Harper) K.; m. Veronica Elaine Pike, Feb. 2, 1980. BA, U. Ala., Birmingham, 1988, postgrad. Reporter gen. assignments Houma (La.) Daily Courier, 1974-76; dir. news, sports Sta. KJIN-AM/KCIL-FM, Houma, 1976-77; reporter gen. assignments Cullman (Ala.) Times, 1977-78; asst. sports editor Anniston (Ala.) Star, 1978-81; sports copy editor Birmingham News, 1981-83, asst. editor lifestyle, 1983-85, editor photography, 1985-86, Sunday editor, 1986-89, editor book revs., 1986-95, editl. writer, columnist, 1989—. Book reviewer Sta. WVTM-TV, Birmingham, 1990-91. Contbr. Redbook mag., 1997, 98. Mem. Houma-Terrebonne Bicentennial Commn., 1975-76; press sec. rep. gubernatorial candidate Guy Hunt, Ala., 1978; tutor literacy Birmingham Pub. Schs. Adult Learning Ctr., 1990-91; judge J.C. Penney Golden Rule Awards for Vols., 1992; lectr. Lee Coll. Springs Art Festival, Baytown, Tex., 1992; mem. adv. bd. Sch. Journalism, U. Miss., 1992-98; bd. dirs. So. Mus. Flight, 1992-93; mem. Leadership Birmingham Class, 1994-95, AIDS Care Team, 1994-2000; bd. dirs. A Baby's Place, 1996-97; mem. Ct. Appointed Spl. Advocates for Children, 1996—; bd. dirs. PATH Orgn. for Homeless, 1997-99; deacon Southside Bapt. Ch.; reading tutor 4th graders Birmingham Pub. Schs., 1999. Nominee for Pulitzer prize, 1994; named Comm. Alumnus of Yr., U. Ala., Birmingham, 1991, One of the Top 20 Grads., 1994; recipient various awards, La. Press Assn., 1974—77, Ala. Press Assn., 1989—2001, Best Commentary award, 1992, 2000, Ala. Sportswriters Assn., 1978—81, Hector award, Troy State U., 1991, 1992, 1994, 1995, Pulitzer prize for edtl. writing, 1991, Nat. Edn. Writers Assn., 1994, Ed. Press Award, John S. Coley award as Outstanding Graduate Student, U. Ala.-Birmingham, 2003; scholar Howton Scholarship in Creative Writing, 2002—03. Mem. U. Ala. Birmingham Nat. Alumni Soc. (bd. dirs. 1999—, v.p. 2002—, Outstanding Grad. Student Sch. Arts & Humanities 2003). Avocations: civil war history, reading, writing. Home: 1635 11th Pl S Birmingham AL 35205-5907 Office: Birmingham News 2200 4th Ave N Birmingham AL 35203-3840 E-mail: joeyjoey@bellsouth.net., jkennedy@bhamnews.com.

KENNEDY, JOHN BAPTIST, civil engineer; BSc with honors, U. Cardiff, Wales, 1955; PhD, U. Toronto, 1961; DSc, U. Wales, 1984. Engr. bridge design, 1955-61; asst. prof. U. Windsor, Ont., Can., 1961-63, assoc. prof., 1963-66, prof., head dept. civil engring., 1966-97, prof. emeritus, disting. prof., 1997—. Recipient Galbraith prize Engring. Inst. Can., 1966, Gzowski meda., 1966, Duggan medal, 1978, T.Y. Lin award ASCE, 1982, Arthur Wellington prize, 1995, 99, Prix P.L. Pratley award Can. Soc. Civil Engring., 1995, 97. Office: U Windsor Civil Engring 8109 Lambton Tower Windsor ON Canada N9B 3P4 E-mail: cjk@uwindsor.ca.

KENNEDY, JOHN EDWARD, lawyer; b. Mpls., Feb. 18, 1947; s. John Edward and Margaret (Greathouse) K.; m. Linda Bagwell, June 22, 1968; children: John Harlan, Linda Elizabeth. AB cum laude, Harvard U., 1968, JD magna cum laude, 1971. Bar: Tex. 1971, U.S. Dist. Ct. (so. dist.) Tex. 1972, U.S. Ct. Appeals (5th cir.) 1972, U.S. Supreme Ct. 1975, U.S. Ct. Appeals (D.C. cir.) 1984. Assoc. Vinson & Elkins, Houston, 1971-80, ptnr., 1980—. Served to 2d lt. USAR, 1972. Mem. ABA, Houston Bar Assn., Fed. Energy Bar Assn. Clubs: Houston Ctr. Presbyterian. Home: 2617 Pemberton Dr Houston TX 77005-3441 Office: Vinson & Elkins LLP 2500 First City Tower Houston TX 77002-6760

KENNEDY, JOHN FORAN, retired lawyer; b. Toronto, Ont., Can., July 25, 1924; came to U.S., 1926, naturalized, 1944; s. Francis Regis and Ellen Susanna (Lunney) K.; m. Carmelita Margaret Stanka, June 20, 1964 (dec. 1997); 1 son, John Regis Joseph. A.B., Dartmouth Coll., 1949; LL.B., Cornell U., 1952; postgrad. U. Chgo., 1958-60. Bar: Ill. 1954. Mem. trust dept. First Nat. Bank, Chgo., 1952-58; trust officer First Nat. Bank, Lake Forest, Ill., 1959-65; ptnr. Snyder, Clarke, Dalziel, Holmquist & Johnson, Waukegan, Ill., 1966-75; ptnr. Kennedy & Clark, Lake Forest, 1976-82; ptnr. Holmstrom & Kennedy, P.C., 1983-92; cons. various attys. Past pres. Family Service of South Lake County, Ill.; bd. dirs. Lake Forest/Lake Bluff United Way. Served with U.S. Army, 1943-46. Mem. Lake County Bar Assn., Lake Forest C. of C. (past pres.), Deer Path Art League, Phi Alpha Delta. Roman Catholic. Home: 435 Park Ln Lake Bluff IL 60044-2322

KENNEDY, JOHN HARVEY, chemistry educator; b. Oak Park, Ill., Apr. 24, 1933; s. John Harvey and Margaret Helen (Drenthe) K.; m. Joan Corinne Hipsky, June 9, 1956 (div. Mar. 1969); children: Bruce Laurence, Bryan Donald, Brent Peter, Jill Amy.; m. Victoria Jane Matthew, July 2, 1970; 1 child, Karen Anne. BS, UCLA, 1954; AM, Harvard U., 1956, PhD, 1957. Sr. research chemist E.I. du Pont de Nemours, Wilmington, Del., 1957-61; asst. prof. chemistry U. Calif., Santa Barbara, 1961-63, 67-69, assoc. prof., 1969-76, prof., 1976-93, prof. emeritus, 1993—, chmn. dept., 1982-85; assoc. prof. Boston Coll., Chestnut Hill, 1963-64; head inorganic chemistry Gen. Motors, Santa Barbara, 1964-67. Cons. Eveready Battery Co., Cleve., 1983-2000; vis. prof. U. N.C., Chapel Hill, 1980-81, Japan Soc. Promotion of Sci., Nagoya, 1974-75, Leningrad State U., 1989, China Acad. Scis., 1990. Author: Analytical Chemistry, Principles, 1990, Analytical Chemistry, Practice, 1990; contbr. articles to profl. jours.; patentee in field. Mus. dir. Christ the King Episcopal Ch., Santa Barbara, 1982-98. Mem. Am. Chem. Soc., Electrochem. Soc. Democrat. Avocation: music. Home: 5357 Agana Dr Santa Barbara CA 93111-1601 Office: U Calif Dept Chemistry Santa Barbara CA 93106 E-mail: jvkennedy@aol.com.

KENNEDY, JOHN JOSEPH, bank financial officer; b. Bklyn., Jan. 28, 1948; s. John J. and Doris M. (Maguire) K.; m. Linda Graham, Sept. 27, 1969; children: John, Richard, Graham. BS, Fordham U., 1969. CPA, N.Y. Acct. Peat, Marwick, Mitchell & Co., N.Y.C., 1971-83; sr. v.p., controller Generale Bank, N.Y.C., 1984-93; sr. v.p., COO First Bank of the Americas, N.Y.C., 1994-97; gen. mgr. Banco de Bogota, N.Y.C., 1997—. Served to 1st lt. U.S. Army, 1969-71. Mem. AICPA, N.Y. State Soc. CPA's. Roman Catholic. Home: 29 Rockwell Cir Marlboro NJ 07746-1156 Office: Banco de Bogota 375 Park Ave Fl 33 New York NY 10152-0002

KENNEDY, JOHN W. health products executive; b. Montreal, Can. BS in Molecular Biology, U. New Brunswick, Fredericton, Can., 1979; M in Molecular Biology, McMaster U., Hamilton, Ont., 1984. Mgr. Syntex Can., 1979—84; with Am. Cyanamid, 1984—92; dir. global oncology divsn. Lederle Pharm., Wayne, NJ, 1992—94; gen. mgr. to v.p. mktg. endocrinology Serono Can., Inc., Norwell, Mass., 1994—98; pres., CEO Hemosol Inc., Mississauga, Canada, 1998—. Office: Hemosol Inc 2585 Meadowpine Blvd Mississauga ON L5N 8H9 Canada Office Fax: 905-286-6300. E mail: sheagelman@hemosol.com.

KENNEDY, JOHN WILLIAM, lawyer; b. Toronto, Ont., Can., Apr. 26, 1926; s. John and Mary (Strong) K.; m. Mary Alice Millar, Aug. 12, 1952; children: Sandra Kennedy Forster, William L., Mary Lee Kennedy de Vales, Elizabeth. BA, U. Alta., Can., 1950, LLB, 1951. Bar: Alta. 1952, Queen's counsel 1969. Assoc. Smith Clement Partee & Whittaker, Edmonton, Alta., 1951-53; ptnr. Cornie Kennedy, Edmonton, 1953-87; agt.-gen. for China, S.E. Asia, Australia and New Zealand Province of Alta., Hong Kong, 1985—. Chmn. bd. Churchill Devel. Corp., Edmonton, 1980-84. Bd. govs. U. Alta., 1981-85; treas. Edmonton South Progressive Conservative Assn., 1965-84; mem. fin. com. Alta. Progressive Conservative Assn., 1972-84. Served to lt. Royal Can. Navy, 1948-53. Mem. Internat. Bar Assn. (treas. 1982-86, council 1980—), Edmonton Bar Assn., Law Soc. Alta., Can. Bar Assn. (past chmn. comparative law com.), Edmonton Club, Mayfair Golf and Country Club (Edmonton), Centre Club. Office: 1900 Scotia Pl 10060 Jasper Ave Edmonton AB Canada T5J 3V4

KENNEDY, JOHN WILLIAM, engineering company executive; b. Summit, N.J., May 20, 1956; s. William John and Jean Mary (Krutisia) Kennedy; m. Cecelia Marie Hamrock, Dec. 26, 1981; 1 child, Sean Michael. BS with honors, North Adams State Coll., 1978; MBA with honors, Columbia Pacific U., 1987, BS in Indsl. Engring., 1988; PhD in Bus. Mgmt., LaSalle U. Cert. tchr. N.J. Tchr. Mountainside (N.J.) Sch. Dist., 1979-82, Chatham (N.J.) Boro Sch. Dist., 1982-83; plant mgr. The Chatham Club Recreation Ctr., 1982-85; ops. mgr. Coleman Equipment, Inc., Irvington, N.J., 1985-91; project mgr., acct. mgr. automated sorting systems div. Sandvik Process Systems, Totowa, N.J., 1991-95; gen. mgr. sales and engring. Barnett Industries, Irvington, N.J., 1995-96; pres., owner The Multitech Group Inc., South Plainfield, N.J., 1996—. Plant mgr., ops. mgr., cons. Madison Cmty. Pool, NJ, 1971—87. Contbr. tech. articles to tech. publs. Active Denville area Boy Scouts Am., NJ, 1984—, chmn. dist. advancement com., 1990—95, exec. bd., 1995—, dist. oper. com. chmn., 1998—; area com. Spl. Olympics, Flanders, NJ, 1987—, event dir. Morris, Sussex and Warren counties, 1998—; exec. bd. Morris-Sussex Boy Scouts Am., 1996—; active Madison Environ. Commn., Madison Planning Bd. Named Eagle Scout, Boy Scouts Am., 1970; named to Eagle Scout Hall of Fame, 1999; recipient Lifetime Achievement award, Boy Scouts Am. Patriots' Path Coun., 2001. Mem.: Am. Soc. for Quality Control, Inst. Indsl. Engring., Am. Mgmt. Assn. Republican. Roman Catholic. Achievements include co-pantentee vacuum lifter, air logic weightless circuit. Avocations: camping, biking, racquetball, softball, coins. Home: 198 Kings Rd Madison NJ 07940-2238 Office: Multitech Group Inc 165A Ryan St South Plainfield NJ 07080-4206

KENNEDY, JOSEPH PATRICK, II, utilities executive, former congressman; b. Brighton, Mass., Sept. 24, 1952; s. Robert F. and Ethel (Skakel) K.; m. Sheila Rauch, 1979 (div.); 2 children: Joseph P. III, Matthew; m. Beth Kelly, Oct. 1993. BA, U. Mass., Boston, 1976. Chmn., pres. Citizens' Energy Corp., 1979-87, 98—; mem. 100th-105th Congress from 8th Mass. dist., 1987—99; ranking minority mem. banking & fin. svcs. subcom. on housing & cmty. devel., mem. com. on vets.' affairs. Active Can. Robert F. Kennedy Meml. Democrat. Office: Citizens Energy Corp 530 Atlantic Ave Boston MA 02210-2218

KENNEDY, JOSEPH PAUL, chemist, researcher; b. Budapest, Hungary, May 18, 1928; arrived in U.S., 1956; s. Laszlo and Rosa (Farkas) Kennedy; m. Ingeborg G. Hausen, Feb. 10, 1956; children: Katherine, Cynthia, Julie. PhD, U. Vienna, Austria, 1954; MBA, Rutgers U., 1961; D (hon.), Kossuth U., Hungary, 1989. Rsch. fellow Sorbonne, U. Paris, 1955; rsch. assoc. McGill U., Montreal, Canada, 1956; rsch. chemist Celanese Corp., Summit, NJ, 1957-59, sr. rsch. assoc. Esso Rsch. Engring. Co., Linden, NJ, 1959-70; prof. polymer sci. U. Akron, Ohio, 1970-80, disting. prof. polymer sci. and chemistry, 1980—. Cons. Akron Cationic Polymer Devel. Co., 1983—. Author: (book) Cationic Polymerization, 1975, Carbocationic Polymerization, 1982, Designed Polymers by Carbocationic Macromolecular Engineering: Theory and Practice, 1992. Named Outstanding Rschr., Alumni Assn. U. Akron, 1979; recipient Morley award and medal, Cleve. Am. Chem. Soc., 1982, award Disting. Svc. in Sci., Soc. Polymer Sci., Japan, 2000. Mem.: Am. Chem. Soc. (Polymer Chemistry award 1985, 1995, Applied Polymer Sci. award 1995, George Stafford Whitby award 1996), Hungarian Acad. Scis. Avocation: Japanese art of the Meiji. Home: 510 Saint Andrews Dr Akron OH 44303-1228 Office: U Akron Inst Polymer Sci Akron OH 44325-0001 E-mail: kennedy@polymer.uakron.edu.

KENNEDY, JOSEPH WINSTON, lawyer; b. Marshalltown, Iowa, June 5, 1932; s. Roy Wesley and Julia Harriet (Plum) K.; m. Barbara B. Bowman, July 11, 1954 (div. June 1982); children: Kimberle Ann, Kamella Lucille; m. Paula Terry Smith, Nov. 24, 1984. BS cum laude, McPherson (Kans.) Coll., 1954; JD with honors, George Washington U., 1958. Bar: Kans. 1958, U.S. Dist Ct. Kans. 1958, U.S. Ct. Appeals (10th cir.) 1976, U.S. Supreme Ct. 1970. Spl. agt. Office of Naval Intelligence, Washington, 1954-58; assoc. Morris, Laing, Evans & Brock, Wichita, Kans., 1958-62; ptnr. Morris, Laing, Evans, Brock & Kennedy, Wichita, 1962—. Chmn. profl. divsn., atty. United Way of the Plains, Wichita, 1990-93. Recipient Best Lawyers in Am. award, 1987, 89-90, 91-92, 93-94, 95-96. Mem. ABA, Kans. Bar Assn. (bd. law examiners 1993-2002), Wichita Bar Assn. (bd. govs. 1964-66). Office: Morris Laing Evans Brock & Kennedy 200 W Douglas Ave Fl 4 Wichita KS 67202-3013 E-mail: jkennedy@morrislaing.com.

KENNEDY, KAREN SYENCE, advertising agency executive; b. Bklyn., May 7, 1943; d. Bruno Weinschel and Pearl Heyman; first marriage: Michael Syence; children: Sherry, Scott; m. Peter Kennedy, Aug. 25, 1979. BS, Boston U., 1963. Advt. mgr. Weinschel Engring., Gaithersburg, Md., 1965-68; mktg. svcs. mgr. Rixon Electronics, Silver Spring, Md., 1968-70; pres. Comm. Unltd., Chevy Chase, Ltd., 1970-74; v.p. Ehrlich Manes & Assocs., Bethesda, Md., 1974-77; pres. Rainbow Tree, St. Croix, V.I., 1978-80; advt. programs dir. GE, McLean, Va., 1980-81; pres. Karen Syence Kennedy Assocs., Fairfax, Va., 1981-83, pres., CEO, KSK Comm., LLC, Vienna, Va., 1983—2002; ptnr. EPB Comms., N.Y.C., 1999—2002; pres. Karen Syence Kennedy Assocs., Great Falls, Va., 2002—. Mem. exec. bd. NextGen Fund; pres. Treasure Beach Found., 2003—. E-mail: ksk001@earthlink.net.

KENNEDY, KATHLEEN, film producer; m. Frank Marshall. Student, San Diego State U. With KCST, San Diego; pres. Amblin Entertainment, Universal City, Calif. Assoc. prodr.: (films) Poltergeist, 1982, Twilight Zone-The Movie, 1983, Indiana Jones and the Temple of Doom, 1984, Reform School Girls, 1986; prodr.: (films) E.T. The Extra-Terrestrial, 1982 (Academy award nomination for best picture 1982); (with Quincy Jones, Frank Marshall, and Spielberg) The Color Purple, 1985 (Academy award nomination for best picture 1985); (with Marshall and Art Levinson) The Money Pit, 1986; (with Marshall and Spielberg) Empire of the Sun, 1987, Always, 1989; (with Richard Vane) Arachnophobia, 1990; (with Marshall and Gerald R. Molen) Hook, 1991; (with Robert Watts) Alive, 1993; (with Molen) Jurassic Park, 1993, (with Marshall) Milk Money, 1994; (with Clint Eastwood) The Bridges of Madison County, 1995, Twister, 1996; (with Steven Spielberg), The Six Sense, 1999, Snow Falling on Cedars, 1999, A Map of the World, 1999, Artifical Intelligence: AI, 2001, Jurassic Park III, 2001, Seabiscuit, 2003; exec. prodr.: (films)Roller Coaster Rabbit, 1990, A Dangerous Woman, 1993, Schindler's List, 1993 (Academy award for best picture 1993), Trail Mix-Up, 1993, A Far Off Place, 1993, Balto, 1995, Congo, 1995, The Indian in the Cupboard, 1995; (with Marshall and Spielberg) Gremlins, 1984, The Goonies, 1985, Back to the Future, 1985, Young Sherlock Holmes, 1985, *batteries not included, 1987, Jurassic Park: The Lost World, 1997, Dad, 1989, Back to the Future Part II, 1990, Gremlins 2: The New Batch, 1990, Back to the Future Part III, 1990, Joe Versus the Volcano, 1990, Cape Fear, 1991, We're Back! A Dinosaur's Story, 1993, (with Marshall) Fandango, 1985; (with Marshall, Spielberg, and David Kirschner) An American Tail, 1986; (with Marshall, Spielberg, Peter Guber, and Jon Peters) Innerspace, 1987; (with Spielberg) Who Framed Roger Rabbit, 1988; (with Marshall, Spielberg, and George Lucas) The Land Before Time, 1988; (with Marshall and Lucas) Indiana Jones and the Last Crusade, 1989; (with Marshall and Kirschner) An American Tail: Fievel Goes West, 1991; (with Peter Bogdanovich) Noises Off, 1992; (with Marshall and Molen); (with Molen, Kirschner, William Hanna, and Joseph Barbera) The Flintstones, 1994, Olympic Glory, 1999, Signs, 2002; exec. prodr. TV Tummy Trouble, 1989, The Sports Pages, 2001

KENNEDY, KATHY KAY, library director; b. New Kensington, Pa., Oct. 21, 1942; d. Lawrence Michael Kennedy and Vivian Mae Smeltzer. BA in English, Thiel Coll., 1964; MSLS, Drexel Inst. Tech., 1967. Bibliographer Union Libr. Catalog, Phila., 1964-67; sci./tech. librarian Carnegie Libr. of Pitts., 1967-73, adult svcs. specialist, 1973-74; libr. dir. Peoples Libr., New Kensington, pa., 1974-87; adult svcs. librarian Monroeville (Pa.) Pub. Libr., 1987-89, asst. dir., 1989-93, dir., 1993—. Editor: Review of Iron and Steel Literature, 1972. Bd. dirs. Pa. Citizens for Better Librs., Greensburg, 1996—, Monroeville Arts Coun., 1989-91; mem. bd. assocs. Thiel Coll., 2002--. Mem. Pa. Libr. Assn. (pres. 1995, editor jour. 1976-78, Cert. of Merit 1982), Bus. and Profl. Women of Pitts. (pres. 1975-77), McKeesport Bus. and Profl. Women (Woman of Yr. 1999), Pa. Fedn. Bus. and Profl. Women (dist. dir. 1984-85), Allegheny County Libr. Assn. (bd. dirs. 1999-2001). Lutheran. Avocations: music, theater, reading, travel. Office: Monroeville Pub Libr 4000 Gateway Campus Blvd Monroeville PA 15146-3381

KENNEDY, KENNETH ADRIAN RAINE, biological anthropologist, forensic anthropologist; b. Oakland, Calif., June 26, 1930; s. Walter Burkhart and Margaret Miriam (Madge) K.; m. Mary Caroline Marino, Aug. 5, 1961 (div.); m. Margaret Carrick Fairlie, Aug. 10, 1969. BA, U. Calif., Berkeley, 1953, MA, 1954, PhD, 1962. Diplomate Am. Bd. Forensic Anthropology; lic. lay reader. Instr. U. Calif., 1962-63; asst. prof. anthropology Cornell U., Ithaca, NY, 1964-68, assoc. prof., 1968—81, prof. ecology, anthropology and Asian studies, 1981—. Sec. Am. Bd. Forensic Anthropology, 1999—2002; cons. forensic anthropology N.Y. State, 1964—; field rsch. in India, Pakistan, Sri Lanka, 1963—. Author 12 books; mem. editl. bd. Am. Jour. Phys. Anthropology, 1998-2001, acting editor-in-chief, 1985; field editor Am. Anthropologist, 1982-85; contbr. numerous articles to sci. jours. Guest White House state dinner reception for Pres. Sri Lanka, 1984. Sgt. U.S. Army, 1954-57. Grantee NSF, Smithsonian Instn., Howard Found., NEA, Am. Inst. Indian Studies, numerous others. Fellow AAAS, Am. Acad. Forensic Scis. (sec.-treas. forensic anthropology sect. 1993-94, chmn. 1994-95, chmn. phys. anthropology sect. 1994-95, T. Dale Stewart award in forensic anthropology 1987); mem. Am. Anthrop. Assn. (chmn. biol. anthropology sect. 1986-88, mem. long-range planning com. 2002—, William W. Howells Book award 2002), Am. Assn. Phys. Anthropologists (exec. bd. 1990-96, v.p. 1994-96), Cornell Rsch. Club (pres. 1978-80, 89-90), Sigma Xi (pres. 1984-85). Episcopalian. Avocations: violin, playing in chamber music groups. Office: Cornell U Ecology & Evolutionary Bio Corson Hall Ithaca NY 14853-2701 E-mail: kak10@cornell.edu.

KENNEDY, LAWRENCE ALLAN, mechanical engineering educator; b. Detroit, May 31, 1937; s. Clifford Earl and Emma Josephine (Muller) K.; m. Valaree J. Lockhart, Aug. 3, 1958; children: Joanne E., Julie A., Janet A., Raymond L., Jill M., Brian G. BS, U. Detroit, 1960; MS, Northwestern U., 1962, PhD, 1964. Registered profl. engr., N.Y. Chmn. dept., prof. mech. and aero. engring. SUNY-Buffalo, 1964-83; chmn. dept. mech. engring., prof. Ohio State U., Columbus, 1983-93, Ralph W. Kurtz disting. prof., 1992-95; dean coll. engring. U. Ill., Chgo., 1995—, prof. mech. engring. and chem. engring., 1995—, Standley Kaplan prof., 2002—. Vis. assoc. prof. mech. and aero. engring. U. Calif.-San Diego, 1968-69, VonKarman Inst., Rhode-St. Genese, Belgium, 1971-72; Goebel vis. prof. mech. and aero. engring. U. Mich., Ann Arbor, 1980-81; vis. prof. mech. & aerospace engring. Princeton U., 1993-94; cons. Cornell Aero. Lab., Buffalo, 1968-72, Tech. Adv. Service, Fort Washington, Pa., 1969—, Ashland Chem. Corp., Dublin, Ohio, 1983-90, Mech. Engring. Sci. and Application, Buffalo, 1972-83, Columbia Gas, 1987-92; vis. faculty fellow mech. and aerospace engring. Princeton U., 1994. Contbr. numerous articles on engring. to profl. jours.; editor: Progress in Astronautics and Aeros., Vol. 58, 1978, Exptl. Thermal and Fluid Scis., 1987-95; editor in chief Jour. Thermal & Fluid Scis., 1997—; assoc. editor Applied Mechanics Revs., 1985-88, Jour. Propulsion & Power, 1992-98. Recipient Ralph R. Teetor award 1984, AT&T Found. award, 1987, Ralph Coats Roe award, 1993; NATO fellow, 1971-72, NSF fellow, 1968-69, W.P. Murphy fellow, 1960-63; Agard lectr., 1971-72. Fellow AIAA, ASME, AAAS, Am. Phys. Soc.; mem. Combustion Inst., Am. Soc. Engring. Edn., Soc. Automotive Engrs. Roman Catholic. Avocations: skiing, squash, hiking, music. Home: 24306 Turnberry Ct Naperville IL 60564-8127 Office: Coll Engring M/C 159 851 S Morgan St Chicago IL 60607-7042

KENNEDY, LAWRENCE WILLIAM, historian; b. Riverside, Calif., Aug. 4, 1952; s. Paul James and Eileen Lawlor K.; m. Judith Ann McCarthy, May 18, 1974; children: Patrick Lawrence, Paul Robert. AB, Boston Coll., 1975, AM, 1978, PhD, 1987. Tchr. history St. Sebastian's Country Day Sch., Newton, Mass., 1975-76, Boston Coll. H.S., Dorchester, Mass., 1976-85, chair history dept., 1983-85; lectr. in history Boston Coll., Chestnut Hill, Mass., 1987-92; consulting historian Boston Redevel. Auth., Boston, 1987-92; asst. prof. history U. Scranton, Pa., 1992-98, assoc. prof. history, 1998—. Lectr. Tufts U., Medford, Mass., 1987, U. Mass., Boston, 1992. Author: Planning the City upon a Hill; Boston since 1630, 1994, (with Walter Muir Whitehill) Boston: A

Topographical History, 2000. Trustee Lackawanna Hist. Soc., 1995-99; bd. dirs. SCOLA Vols. for Literacy, 2001—, pres., 2003—; treas., com. mem. Troop 201 Boy Scouts Am., Clark's Summit, Pa., 1993-97; mem. Friends of the Abington Cmty. Libr., Clark's Summit, 1993—. Mem. Urban History Assn., Mass. Hist. Soc., New Eng. Hist. Assn. Democrat. Home: 903 Poplar St Clarks Summit PA 18411-1747 Office: U Scranton Dept History 800 Linden St Scranton PA 18510-2429 E-mail: lawrence.kennedy@scranton.edu.

KENNEDY, LEILA, accounting educator; b. Murray City, Ohio, June 19, 1941; d. Carl Eugene and Jesse Marie (Mentzer) Wynegar; m. Gary Nelson Retterer, Sept. 28, 1958 (div. Jan. 1962); children: April Anne, William Eugene; m. Junior Everett Kennedy, May 31, 1963. BS in Acctg., Bluefield State Coll., 1989; MS in Acctg., Marshall U., 1992. Faculty Nat. Bus. Coll., Bluefield, Va., 1992; adj. faculty Bluefield State Coll., W. Va., 1991-92, instr. bus., 1992-93, asst. prof., 1993-98, assoc. prof., 1998—. Cons. in field. Avocations: crochet, knitting, reading. Office: Greenbrier Cmty Coll 101 Church St Lewisburg WV 24901-1303 E-mail: lkennedy@bluefieldstate.edu.

KENNEDY, LEO RAYMOND, engineering executive; b. Cleve., Dec. 29, 1942; s. Leo Raymond and Jane (Brady) K.; m. Doris Elaine Jurgens, Feb. 18, 1967; children: James Raymond, Brian Robert, Kristin Lee. BS, U.S. Mil. Acad., 1965; EdM, U. Ill., 1972; MBA, L.I. U., Greenvale, N.Y., 1975; grad., Army War Coll., Carlisle, Pa., 1986. Commd. 2d. lt. U.S. Army, 1965, advanced through grades to col., 1987, adc, 1970; assoc. dir. admissions U.S. Mil. Acad., West Point, N.Y., 1972-75; dir. pers. mgmt. armored divsn. U.S. Army, Killeen, Tex., 1976-78, chief staff divsn. Clay Kaserne, Germany, 1980-82, comdr. battalion Colorado Springs, Colo., 1982-85, inspector gen. inf. divsn., 1985-86, dir. resource mgmt. Pentagon Washington, 1986-92; pres., CEO Kennedy & Assocs., Fairfax, Va., 1993-96; divsn. mgr. Sci. Applications Internat. Corp., McLean, Va., 1996-2000, v.p., 2000—. Acquisition budget com. Army program, Washington, 1987-92; guest spkr. fed. budgeting process, Washington, 1988-92. Decorated Legion of Merit, Bronze Star medal. Mem. AUSA, TROA (life), USAWC (life), Soc. Mil. Comptrs., Non-Commd. Officers Assn. (hon. life), N.Y. Acad. Sci., Kappa Delta Pi. Republican. Roman Catholic. Avocations: squash, racquetball, basketball, railroading.

KENNEDY, LINDA DALE, music educator, pianist, organist; d. William Lawrence and Jessie Merle Dale; m. Kurt Kennedy, June 7, 1969; children: Jennifer Tish, Terra Lee. MusB, Southeastern La. U., Hammond, 1968, MusM, 1975. Cert. profl. music tchr. Music Tchrs. Nat. Assn., Ark. State Music Tchrs. Assn. Instr. Yamaha Music Program, New Orleans, 1968—69; pvt. practice Piano Studio of Linda Kennedy, Maumelle, Ark., 1975—; organist - accompanist F.E. Warren Air Force Base, Cheyenne, Wyo., 1969—71, Woodland Pk. Bapt. Ch., Hammond, La., 1972—75, Goodwood Bapt. Ch., Baton Rouge, 1976—79, Ct. St. United Meth. Ch., Hattiesburg, Miss., 1981—85, Winfield United Meth. Ch., Little Rock, 1987—2001, First United Meth. Ch., North Little Rock, 2001—. Contbr. articles to profl. jours. Adv. com. Maumelle Performing Arts Coun., Ark., 2002—. Mem.: Nat. Guild Piano Tchrs., Ark. Fedn. Music Clubs (state composition chairperson 2003—), Music Tchrs. Assn. Ctrl. Ark. (pres. 1997—2001, v.p., sec.), Ark. State Music Tchrs. Assn. (sec.), Music Tchrs. Nat. Assn., Nat. Guild of Piano Tchrs., Little Rock Musical Coterie (assoc.). Methodist. Home Fax: 501-851-4989. E-mail: pianolk@aol.com.

KENNEDY, LINDA MANN, neuroscience educator, researcher; b. Malden, Mass, July 29, 1939; d. Alfred William Mann and Etta May (Maglue) Stenquist; m. Richard Dearman Kennedy, Apr. 15, 1961; children: Pamela Lee, Ruth Alexander. Diploma in nursing, New England Deaconess Hosp., 1959; AB, Simmons Coll., 1975; PhD, Harvard U., 1980. RN, Mass. Staff nurse Lahey Clinic, Boston, 1959-61, various hosps., Mass., Ga., 1962-72; tchg. asst. Simmons Coll., Boston, 1972-75; vis. rsch. fellow Cornell U., Ithaca, NY, 1978-81; rsch. assoc. Worcester (Mass.) Found. Exptl. Biology, 1980-83; rsch. asst. prof. Clark U., Worcester, 1983-84, asst. prof., 1984-91, assoc. prof., 1991—, U. Mass. Med. Sch., 1995—2000. Co-founder, co-dir., dir. interdisciplinary neurosci. program Clark U., Worcester, 1984—91; mem. AREA grant study sects. NIH, Washington, 1988—89; mem. Area grant study sects. Nat. Inst. Neurol. and Comm. Disorders and Stroke, 1988—89, Nat. Inst. Deafness and Other Comm. Disorders, 1988—89; vis. scientist Weizmann Inst. Sci., Rehovot, Israel, 1991—92; mem. adv. panel Sensory Sys. Program, ILI program and ADVANCE Instnl. Transformation Program, NSF, Washington, 1993—; co-founder, co-dir., dir. interdisciplinary neurosci. program Clark U., 1994—98; vis. program dir. Sensory Sys. program NSF, 2000—02. Mem. editl. com. Univ. Press New England, 1989-91; contbr. articles to profl. jour. Mem. conservation com. Town of Framingham, Mass., 1973-74. Recipient Grad. fellowship for women Danforth Found., 1975-79, Rsch. Svc. award NIH, 1980-83, multiple Rsch. grants NSF, NIH, 1978—. Mem. New Eng. Psychol. Assn. (hon.), Assn. Chemoreception Sci. (exec. bd. councilor 1986-88), Soc. for Neurosci., Soc. for Values in Higher Edn., European Chemoreception Orgn., Internat. Brain Rsch. Orgn., Assn. for Women in Sci., Assn. Univ. Prof. Unitarian Universalist. Avocations: scuba diving, classical and jazz concerts, travel, reading mysteries. Home: 98 Waterford Dr Worcester MA 01602-3512 Office: Clark Univ Dept Biology Worcester MA 01610

KENNEDY, MARC J. lawyer; b. Newburgh, N.Y., Mar. 2, 1945; s. Warren G. K. and Frances F. (Levinson) K.; m. Karen Karatsu; children: Michael L., Kayla R., Shawna D. BA cum laude, Syracuse U., 1967; JD, U. Mich., 1970. Bar: N.Y. 1971. Assoc. Davies, Hardy, Ives & Lawther, N.Y.C., 1971-72, London, Buttenweiser & Chalif, N.Y.C., 1972-73, Silberfeld, Danziger & Bangser, N.Y.C., 1973; counsel Occidental Crude Sales, Inc., N.Y.C., 1974-75; v.p., gen. counsel Internat. Ore & Fertilizer Corp., N.Y.C., 1975-82; asst. gen. counsel Occidental Chem. Corp., Houston, 1982; v.p., gen. counsel Occidental Chem. Agrl. Products Inc., Tampa, Fla., 1982-87; v.p., gen counsel agrl. products group Occidental Chem. Corp., Tampa, 1987-91, assoc. gen. counsel Dallas, 1991—. Faculty mentor Columbia Pacific U., Mill Valley, Calif., 1981—88. Contbr. articles to profl. jours. Mem. governing bd. Ctr. for Brain Health U. Tex. Dallas, 2001—; trustee Bar Harbor Festival Corp., N.Y.C., 1974-87; bd. dirs. Am. Opera Repertory Co., 1982-85; mem. com. planned giving N.Y. Foundling Hosp., 1977-88; Explorer post advisor Boy Scouts Am., 1976-78. Mem. ABA (vice-chmn. com. internat. law liaison young lawyers sect. 1974-75, chmn. sub-com. proposed trade barriers to the importation of products into U.S. 1985-88, vice chmn. corp. counsel com. 1992-93, co-chmn. corp. counsel com. 1993-98), N.Y. State Bar Assn., Am. Corp. Counsel Assn., Tex. Bar Assn. Office: Occidental Chem Corp PO Box 809050 Dallas TX 75380-9050

KENNEDY, MARJORIE ELLEN, librarian; b. Dauphin, Man., Can., Sept. 14, 1946; d. Stanley Harrison and Ivy Marietta (Stevens) May; m. Michael P.J. Kennedy, Apr. 3, 1980. BA, U. Sask., Regina, 1972; BLS, U. Alta., Edmonton, 1974; BEd, U. Regina, 1981. Profl. A cert. edn., Sask. Elem. sch. tchr. Indian Head (Sask) Pub. Sch., 1965-66, Elgin Sch., Weyburn, Sask., 1967-68; tchr., libr. Ctrl. Sch., Prince Albert, Sask., 1970-71; elem. sch. tchr. Vincent Massey Sch., Prince Albert, 1969-70, 72-73; children's libr. J.S. Wood br. Saskatoon (Sask.) Pub. Libr., 1974-77, asst. coord. children's svcs., 1977-79; programme head, instr. libr. tech. Kelsey Inst., Saskatoon, 1979—; head libr. and info. tech. SIAST-Kelsey Campus, Saskatoon. Presenter workshops on reference materials for elem. sch. librs., storytelling and libr. programming for children, 1980—; vol. dir. Children's Lit. Workshops, Sask. Libr. Assn., 1979-80; mem. organizing com. Sask. Libr. Week, Saskatoon, 1988. Mem. Vanscoy (Sask.) and Dist. Agr. Soc., 1983-95. Named to Libr. Edn. Honor Roll ALA, 1987. Mem. Can. Libr. Assn. (instl. rep. 1984—), Sask. Libr. Assn. (insl. rep. 1984—, mem. children's sect. 1982-83), Sask. Assn. Libr. Techs. (instl. rep. 1984—), Can. Club (bd. mem. 1981-84). Mem. United Ch. Can. Avocations: antique doll restoration, porcelain doll making, antiques, pottery, gardening. Office: Kelsey Inst Box 1520 Libr Info Tech Program Saskatoon SK Canada S7K 3R5 E-mail: Kennedy@siast.sk.ca.

KENNEDY, MARK ALAN, secondary school educator; b. Oklahoma City, Okla., July 20, 1951; s. Millford Gordon and Lyn (Cheaney) Kennedy. BA with honors, Calif. State U., 1978; postgrad., Western Sem., 1978-79, Fuller Sem., 1980-83; MEd, U. LaVerne, 1997. Cert. tchr., Calif. Sales mgr. Kennedy Investments, Ontario, Calif., 1980-83; regional v.p. A.L. Williams, Rancho Cucamonga, Calif., 1983-89; loan officer Funder's Mortgage Corp., Covina, Calif., 1989-90; math., social sci. tchr., lang. devel. specialist Ontario-Montclair Sch. Dist., 1990-96, San Bernardino County Cmty. Sch., 1996—, lead tchr., 1998—2000, acting prin., 1998-99. Tchg. asst. Western Sem., Portland, Oreg., 1978-79; instr. Cmty. Inst., 1979; adj. prof. tchr. edn. Chapman U., 2001—; soccer coach DeAnza Mid. Sch., Ontario, 1990-93, core team leader, coop tchr., 1992-95, student coun. advisor, 1992-93, bilingual adv. coun., 1992-96, dist. lang. arts/social sci. trainer, 1993-94; advisor U. Calif. Riverside Honors Students' Inner City Literacy Program, 1993-95; mentor tchr. Ontario-Montclair Sch. Dist., 1994-95; cons. Inst. in Local Self Govt., Sacramento, 1994-96, Assn. Calif. Sh. Adminstrs., 1994-2002; learning styles cons., 1994—; mem. sch. attendance rev. bd., 1996-99. Author: Lessons from the Hawk, 2001, Dance of the Dolphin, 2003; contbr. some 20 articles to profl. jours. With USN, 1971-75. Named Tchr. of Yr., Inland Coun. for Social Studies, 2000, San Bernardino County Alternative Educators, 2003. Mem. ASCD, Assn. Calif. Sch. Adminstrs., Calif. Tchrs. Assn. (mem. joint program quality rev. bd.), Nat. Dropout Prevention Network, Phi Alpha Theta (mem. chair 1976-78). Episcopalian. Avocations: German and Latin philosophy and literature, exegesis of koine Greek, conversational Spanish, Shaolin Kempo, Kung Fu San Soo. Office: West End Cmty 1135 W 4th St Ontario CA 91762-1796

KENNEDY, MARK R. congressman; b. Benson, Minn., Apr. 11, 1957; m. Debbie; 4 children. BA, St. John's U., Minn.; MBA, U. Mich. CPA. Mem. U.S. Congress from 6th Minn. dist. (formerly 2nd), 2001—. Mem. agriculture com., transportation and infrastructure com.; subcom. gen. farm commodities, risk mngmt., conservation, credit, rural devel. and rsch., aviation, highways and transit (vice ch.). Republican. Office: 1415 Longworth House Office bldg Washington DC 20515-2302*

KENNEDY, MARLA CATHERINE, psychologist; b. Milw., June 28, 1935; d. Raymond G. and Catherine (Wimmer) Mueller; m. William Robert Kennedy, Mar. 2, 1957; children: Joseph, Timothy, Kristin, William, Daniel. BS, Alverno, Milw., 1956; MA, U. Minn., 1983, postgrad., 1983-1989. Lic. psychologist, lic. marriage and family therapist. Intern with mentally ill and mentally retarded Met. Clin., Mpls., 1984—85; pvt. practice psychology, marriage and family therapy Mpls., 1985—. Spkr. in field; part-time at Family Svc. Greater St. Paul, 1989-98; dir., co-counselor Adlerian Family Edn. Ctr., 1983-85. Contbr. articles to profl. jours. Bd. dirs. Books for Africa, 1997 2002; co founder Community Line (now First Call for Help); pres. Legions of PTAs; active YWCA Shelter for Women, St. Paul; vol. Rams Juvenile Justice, 1983-2003. Mem. Am. Acad. Neurology Aux. (bd. dirs.), Minn. Assn. Marriage and Family Therapists, Minn. Assn. Group Psychotherapists (pres. 1998-00), Alfred Adler Assn. (bd. dirs. 1965-80), AAUW (bd. dirs.), New Century (bd. dirs.), Women's Investment Club (treas.), Mensa, Phi Lambda Theta. Unitarian Universalist. Avocations: swimming, tennis, reading.

KENNEDY, MARY SUSSOCK, artist; b. Liverpool, Eng., Oct. 29, 1926; came to U.S., 1951; d. Charles Archibald and Maria (Mullin) Sussock; m. Rogers Jack Kennedy, May 18, 1946 (dec. Jan. 1987); children: Jacollyn Fenny-Maria, Beverley Gillian, Kimberley Tara. AAS with highest honors, Fashion Inst. Tech., N.Y., 1975; BA summa cum laude, Montclair State Coll., 1977; postgrad., Montclair State Univ., 1977-78. Portrait, stage and wedding photographer Wilkinson and Kennedy, Liverpool, 1943-47; freelance artist Montville, Barnegat Light, NJ, 1956-73; freelance artist Key Largo, Fla., 1984—; grad. asst. in sculpture Montclair State Univ., Upper Montclair, NJ, 1977-78; diamond stylii maker Rogers Kennedy Inc., Saddle Brook, N.J., 1978-84. One woman show at Fashion Inst. Tech., N.Y., 1974; exhibited in group shows at Smithsonian Instn., Washington, 1963, Montclair Art Mus., 1964, U.S. Custom House, N.Y.C., 1979, also exhibit opened by Princess Grace in Monaco, 1960; sculpture exhibited in two person show at Montclair State Univ., 1977. Mem. Phi Kappa Phi. Democrat. Episcopalian. Avocations: anthropology, reading, travel, gardening. Home: PO Box 2560 Key Largo FL 33037-7560

KENNEDY, MARY VIRGINIA, diplomat; b. Pocatello, Idaho, Sept. 5, 1946; d. Charles Millard and Martha Lorissa (Evans) K. BA, U. Denver, 1968, MA, 1969; MAT, U. Idaho, 1971, JD, 2001. Tchr. cert. Idaho. Recreation aide ARC, South Vietnam, 1969-70; ops. officer State Dept. Ops. Ctr., Washington, 1977-78; spl. asst. amb. Philip Habib, Washington, 1979-80, Sec. State, Washington, 1980-81; econ. officer U.S. Embassy, Cairo, 1981-84; consul Am. Consulate, Adana, Turkey, 1985-88; Pearson fellow Office Cong. Bereuter Ho. Reps., 1988-89; exec. asst. Dept. Sec. State, Washington, 1989-91; dep. chief mission Dept. State U.S. Embassy, Kuwait, 1991-93; consul gen. Am. Consulate, Karachi, Pakistan, 1994-96; dean Sch. Profl. Area Studies, Fgn. Svc. Inst., 1996-98; student Coll. Law U. Idaho, 1998—2001. Bd. trustees Idaho State Hist. Soc., 1999—2002. Mem. Am. Fgn. Svc. Protective Assn. (bd. dirs. 1988-91), Phi Beta Kappa, Mortar Bd. Home: 5137 Admiral Way SW Seattle WA 98116 Address: PO Box 16634 Seattle WA 98116-0634 E-mail: niact@aol.com.

KENNEDY, MATTHEW LAWRY, film historian, anthropologist; b. Redding, Calif., Mar. 14, 1957; s. Laurence Joseph and Carolyn (Cook) K. BA in Theater Arts, UCLA, 1979; MA in Anthropology, U. Calif., Davis, 1993. Exec. asst. to dir. Calif. Arts Council, Sacramento, 1986-91. Cons. Nat. Endowment for Arts, 1988, Calif. Arts Coun., 1994; tchr. City Coll. San Francisco, San Francisco Conservatory of Music. Author: Marie Dressler, 1999; contbr. articles to mags. and newspapers. Scholar U. Calif., 1975, Merce Cunningham Dance Found., 1983-84; Fulbright fellow, 1992. Avocations: travel, swimming, yoga. Office: City Coll San Francisco Box L213 50 Phelan Ave San Francisco CA 94112-1821

KENNEDY, MICHAEL JOHN, lawyer; b. Spokane, Wash., Mar. 23, 1937; s. Thomas Dennis Kennedy and Evelyn Elizabeth (Forbes) Gordon; m. Pamalee Hamilton, June 14, 1959 (div. July 1968); children: Lisa Marie, Scott Hamilton; m. Eleanore Renee Baratelli, July 14, 1968; 1 child, Anna Rosario. AB in Econs., U. Calif., Berkeley, 1959; JD, U. Calif., San Francisco, 1962. Bar: Calif. 1963, N.Y. 1976, U.S. Ct. Appeals (9th cir. 1963), U.S. Supreme Ct. 1967, U.S. Ct. Appeals (5th cir.) 1975, U.S. Ct. Appeals 2d cir.) 1977, U.S. Ct. Appeals (1st 3d and 4th cirs.) 1979, U.S. Ct. Appeals (3d and D.C. cirs.) 1982. Assoc. Hoberg & Finger, San Francisco, 1962-67; staff counsel Emergency Civil Liberties, N.Y.C., 1967-69; ptnr. Kennedy & Rhine, San Francisco, 1969-76; sole practice N.Y.C., 1976—. Served to 1st lt. U.S. Army, 1963-65. Mem. ABA, N.Y. Criminal Bar Assn., Nat. Assn. Criminal Defenders. Clubs: N.Y. Athletic. Democrat. Roman Catholic. Office: 425 Park Ave New York NY 10022-3506 Home: 150 Central Park S New York NY 10019

KENNEDY, MURIEL, psychologist, consultant, educator; b. Bamberg, S.C., Mar. 29, 1965; d. Harold Lee Kennedy (dec.) and Virginia Morgan Kennedy Marion. BS, U. S.C., 1987; MS, Howard U., 1993, PhD, 1995. Lic. psychologist, Va., Md., D.C. Nuc. engr. Charleston Naval Shipyard, Charleston, S.C., 1987-90; psychology assoc. Child Advocacy Network, Balt., 1996-97; clin. psychologist Child and Family Therapy Ctr., Washington, 1997—. Clin. cons. Inst. for Life Enrichment, Washington, 1997—, Baraka Pastoral Counseling Ctr., Largo, Md., 1997—; adj. prof. Howard U., Washington, 1997—; exec. dir. Perico Inst. for Youth Devel. Entrepreneurship, Inc.; co-founder New Life Enrichment Ctr., Inc. Mem. Assn. Black Psychologists (treas. 1996-97, pres.-elect 1998-99, pres. 1999-2000, immediate past pres. 2000-2001), Psi Chi. Democrat. Baptist. Avocations: inspirational writing, listening to music, poetry, the arts, sports. Home: 116 Adams St NW Washington DC 20001-1611 E-mail: murielkenn@yahoo.com.

KENNEDY, PATRICK F. federal official; b. Chgo., June 22, 1949; m. M. Elizabeth Swope. BA, Georgetown U.; diploma Sr. Seminar in Fgn. Policy. Mem. Fgn. Svc., 1973, regional adminstrv. officer, 1973-74; pers. officer Bur. African Affairs, 1975-76; spl. asst. to under sec. for mgmt. Dept. of State, 1977-81, supervisory gen. svcs. officer, 1981—85, exec. dir., then dep. exec. sec., 1985-90, adminstrv. counselor Cairo, 1991-93, asst. sec. adminstrn. Washington, 1993—2001; amb./dep. U.S. rep. for mgmt. and reform United Nations. Office: US Mission to the UN 799 UN Plz New York NY 10017

KENNEDY, PATRICK J. congressman; b. Brighton, Mass., July 14, 1967; s. Edward M. and Joan (Bennett) K. Degree in Social Science, Providence Coll., 1991. Mem. R.I. Ho. Repr., 1989—95, U.S. Congress from 1st R.I. dist., 1995—; mem. appropriations com. Chmn. House Rules Com., 1992; del. 1988 Dem. Nat. Conv.; co-founder, co-chmn. Congressional Portuguese-Am. Caucus; mem. New Eng. Caucus, Congressional Caucus on Armenian Issues, Older Americans Caucus, Democratic Task Force on Tax Policy, AIDS PAC Congressional adv. bd., Italian-Am. Congressional Delegation; co-sponsoramendment in Older Americans Act, Higher Edn. Accumulation Program. Bd. dirs. R.I. Spl. Olympics, R.I. March of Dimes, Nat. Com. for Prevention of Child Abuse (R.I. chpt.), Big Brother R.I. Mem. R.I. Lung Assn. (bd. dirs.), R.I. Mental Health Assn. (bd. dirs.), Friends of Ireland. Democrat. Address: 249 Roosevelt Ave Pawtucket RI 02860-2908 Office: US House Reps 407 Cannon Ho Office Bldg Washington DC 20515-3901 E-mail: patrick.kennedy@mail.house.gov.*

KENNEDY, PAUL MICHAEL, history educator; b. Wallsend, U.K., June 17, 1945; came to U.S., 1983; s. John Patrick and Margaret (Hennessy) K.; m. Catherine Urwin, Sept. 2, 1967 (dec. June 1998); children: James, John, Matthew; m. Cynthia Farrar, Aug. 18, 2001. BA, Newcastle (Eng.) U., 1966; PhD, Oxford (Eng.) U., 1970; MA, Yale U., 1983; hon. doctorate, U. Ohio, 1989, U. New Haven, 1989, U. Newcastle, 1991, L.I. U., 1993, Union Coll., 1994, Alfred U., 1994, U. East Anglia, 1994, Conn. Coll., Quinnipiac Coll., 1999, U. Leuven, 2001. Lectr. history U. East Anglia, U.K., 1970-74, reader, 1974-82, prof., 1982-83; Dilworth prof. history Yale U., New Haven, 1983—; dir. Internat. Security Studies, 1990—. DeVane lectr., 1992-93; Lewis lectr. Princeton U., 1990; Ford's lectr. Oxford U., 1984; Gabriel Silver lectr. Columbia U., 1988; Brodie lectr. UCLA, 1993; 1st ann. Nobel Peace lectr. Oslo, 1992; Bruno Keisky lectr., Vienna, 1994; Roskill Meml. lectr., Cambridge, 1997; rsch. asst. Sr. Basil Liddell Hart, 1966-70; vis. fellow Ins. for Advanced Study, Princeton, N.J., 1978-79; co-dir. of Secretariat to report on UN in Its Second-Half Century, 1993-96. Author, editor 13 books including Preparing for the Twenty-First Century, The Rise and Fall of Great Powers, Strategy and Diplomacy, The War Plans of the Great Powers. Recipient Wolfson prize Wolfson Found., U.K., 1989, Acqui Storia prize, Italy, 1990; fellow Alexander von Humboldt Found., 1968, 72; named Comdr. of the British Empire, 2000. Fellow Royal Hist. Soc., Am. Acad. Arts and Scis., Am. Philos. Soc., Brit. Acad.; mem. Assn. Am. Historians. Roman Catholic. Home: 409 Humphrey St New Haven CT 06511-3710 Office: Yale U Internat Security Studies 31 Hillhouse Ave New Haven CT 06511-3704

KENNEDY, RAYMOND ARTHUR, writer; b. North Wilbraham, Mass., Mar 3, 1934; s. James Patrick and Orise Marie (Belanger) Kennedy; 1 child Branwynne. BA, U. Mass., 1960. Editl. asst. G&C Merriam Co., Springfield Mass., 1961; writer Collier's Ency., N.Y.C., 1961—66; anthropology editor Ency. Americana, N.Y.C., 1966—70; editor USIA, Washington, 1970—80 lectr., fiction workshops Columbia U., N.Y.C., 1981—. Lectr. grad. level fiction workshops Boston U., NYU; lectr. aesthetics, Orchard Hill Residence Coll. U Mass., 1980; USIA-sponsored spkr., Germany, 92, Germany, 94. Author: My Father's Orchard, 1963, Good Night, Jupiter, 1970, Columbine, 1981, The Flower of the Republic, 1983, Lulu Incognito, 1988, Ride a Cockhorse, 1991 The Bitterest Age, 1994, The Romance of Eleanor Gray, 2003; contbr. Pfc U.S Army, 1954—56. Fellow Fiction, N.Y. State Found. Arts, 1986.

KENNEDY, RENEAU CHARLENE UFFORD, forensic psychologist, consultant; b. Weiser, Idaho, June 18, 1954; d. Eldon Luther and Iris Jean (Hetrick) Ufford; m. Allen Ken Kennedy (div. Apr. 1999). BS in Psychology and Speech Willamette U., 1975; MS in Psychology, U. Oreg., 1981; EdD in Psychology Boston U., 1994; postgrad., Harvard U., 1994-98. Lic. psychologist. Tchr. counselor Victorian Dept. Edn., Melbourne, Australia, 1975-78, 80; fellow in clin. and forensic psychology The McLean Hosp., Harvard Med. Sch., Belmont 1986-87, fellow in neuropsychology dept. neurology, 1987-89; clin. fellow in forensic psychology Harvard Med. Sch./Mass. Gen. Hosp., Boston, 1992-98 cons. Mass. Dept. Youth Svcs., Boston, 1994-95, Ky. Justice Cabinet, Frankfort 1995; pvt. practice Weston, Mass., 1996—, Honolulu, 1997—. Affiliate clin tng. supr., course instr. Am. Sch. Profl. Psychology, Honolulu; dir. tng. Forensic and Behavioral Scis. Inst., Honolulu, 1998-2000, Honolulu Family Therapy Ctr., 2000—; clin. fellow MGH Law and Psychiatry Svc., 1992-98; cons., spkr in field. Mem. Ky. Justice Cabinet Juvenile Task Force, Frankfort, 1994-96 Mass. Child Death Rev. Team, Boston, 1995-97, Mass. Ct. Subcom. on Risk Assessment, Dedham, 1995—; col., aide de camp Commr. of Ky. State Police Frankfort, 1994, 95, 96. Predoctoral fellow Harvard Med. Sch., Boston 1992-94; named to Hon. Order of Ky. Cols. Mem. APA, Soc. for Personality Assessment, Hawaii Psychol. Assn., Homicide Rsch. Working Group, Psi Chi Phi Delta Kappa, Pi Lambda Theta. Avocations: scuba diving, triathlon events exotic travel. Home and Office: 3001 Diamond Head Rd Honolulu H 96815-4716 Fax: 808-923-2299. E-mail: rkennedy@lava.net.

KENNEDY, RICHARD MCKINNE, III, anesthesiologist; b. Birmingham Ala., May 29, 1951; s. Richard McKinne Jr. and Jane Huggin K.; m. Catherine Hood, Aug. 21, 1976; children: Clayton Hughes, Jane Fleming, Andrew McDaniel. AB, U. N.C., 1973; JD, U. S.C., 1976, MD, 1991. Diplomate Am Bd. Anthesiology. Jud. law clk. Hon. Robert F. Chapman, Columbia, SC 1976-78; ptnr. Kennedy & Price Attys., Columbia, SC, 1978-87; intern in internal medicine Richland Meml. Hosp., 1991—92; asst. county atty. Richland County, Columbia, SC, 1985-87; anesthesia resident Richland Meml. Hosp. Columbia, SC, 1992—95; ptnr. M.D. Anesthesia LLC, Orangeburg, SC 1995-98; staff anesthesiologist Vets. Hosp., Columbia, SC, 1998—. Contbr articles to profl. jour. State committeeman SC Rep. Com., Columbia, 1981-82 asst. prof. of Clinical Surgery, Univ. of SC Sch. of Medicine, bd. gov. SC Patient Compensation Fund. Mem. Am. Soc. Anesthesiologists, SC Soc. Anesthesiologists (pres. elect) SC Med. Assn., Columbia Med. Soc. (exec. com.). Presbyterian. Avocations: skiing, golf, boy scouts volunteer. Home: 15 Point Comfort Columbia SC 29209 Office: Dorn VA Hosp Garners Ferry Rd Columbia SC 29209

KENNEDY, ROBERT, international affairs educator; b. Newark, Sept. 20 1939; s. Cecil L. (stepfather) and Marie E. (Rega) Smith; m. Vevonna M. Clark Nov. 4, 1966; children: Shaun C., Teague C. BS, USAF Acad., Colorado Springs, Colo., 1963; MA, Georgetown U., 1964, PhD, 1978; D (honoris causa) Bulgarian Nat. Def. Acad., 2002. With USAF, 1963-71; fgn. affairs officer U.S Arms Control and Disarmament Agy., Washington, 1974; sr. researcher strategic studies inst. U.S. Army War Coll., Carlisle, Pa., 1974-83, Dwight D. Eisenhower prof. nat. security studies, 1983-85; dep. comdt. NATO Def. Coll., Rome 1985-88; prof. dept. nat. security studies U.S. Army War Coll., 1988-89; prof sch. internat. affairs Ga. Inst. Tech., Atlanta, 1989-97. Dep. dir., co. dir. Ctr. for Internat. Strategy, Tech. and Policy, Atlanta, 1990-97; dir. Marshall European Ctr. for Security Studies, Garmisch, Germany, 1997-2002, prof. Sam Nunn Sch Internat. Affairs, Ga. Inst. Tech., Atlanta, 2002—; cons. Inst. for Pub. Policy Devel., Washington, 1977-78. Author, editor: The Defense of the West Strategic and European Security Issues, 1984, U.S. Policy Towards the Soviet Union: A Long Term Western Prospective 1987-2000, 1988, Alternative Conventional Defense Postures for the European Theater, Vol. I, 1990, Vol. 2 1992, Vol. 3, 1993; mem. various adv. and editl. bds., U.S., Europe; contbr articles to profl. publs.; founding ed. editor The Atlanta Papers, 1996—. Mem exec. com., chmn. joint chiefs of staff Process for Accreditation of Joint Edn Washington, 1991-97; acad. assoc. Atlantic Coun. U.S., 1989—. With USAFR 1971-86. Recipient Superior Civilian Svc. award, U.S. Army, 1989, Joint Disting. Civilian Svc. award, 2002; named Oustanding Young Men of Am., U.S Jaycees, 1972; Fulbright scholar, 1965-66, Comdr. by Pres. Romania, 2002 Georgetown U. fellow, 1974, Atlantic Coun. U.S. non-resident sr. fellow 1983-84. Mem. Internat. Inst. for Strategic Studies, Internat. Studies Assn (chmn. sect. on mil. studies 1985-87), Acad. Security, Def., and Law Enforcement, Russian Fedn. Avocations: water and snow skiing, surf boarding woodworking, furniture making. Home: 6975 Hunters Knoll Atlanta GA 3002

KENNEDY, ROBERT ALAN, educational administrator; b. Benson, Minn Sept. 29, 1946; s. William Henry and Mary Rose (Pothen) K.; m. Mary Elle Rumpho, June 9, 1984; children: Caleb, Alex, Bryce, Curran. BS, U. Minn 1968; PhD, U. Calif., Berkeley, 1974. Asst. prof. U. Iowa, Iowa City, 1974-7 assoc. prof. to prof. Wash. State U., Pullman, 1979-85; prof., chmn. Ohio Stat U., Columbus, 1987; program dir. NSF, Washington, 1987-89; v.p. res. U. Md College Park, 1989-92; v.p. rsch., assoc. provost grad. studies Tex. A&M U College Station, 1992-2000; exec. v.p., provost U. Maine, 2000—. Contb articles to profl. jours. Home: 25 Jackson Dr Veazie ME 04401-7073

KENNEDY, ROBERT EDWIN, university administrator; b. Portland, Oreg. s. Edwin Ruthvin and Hazel Claire (Powell) K.; m. Mary Elizabeth Paxton children: Robert Jr., Maridel, Stephen, Susan. BA in English, San Diego Stat

U., 1938; MA in Journalism, Stanford U., 1950; PhD in Ednl. Adminstrn., Claremont U., 1966; M in Pub. Svc., Calif. Poly. State U., 1979. Reporter San Diego Sun, 1937; exec. sec. Civic Affairs Conf., San Diego, 1938; advt. mgr. Hamilton's Ltd. Fine Foods, San Diego, 1939; with Calif. Poly. State U., San Luis Obispo, 1940—79, dept. head journalism, 1940-50, asst. to pres., 1951-56, dean Arts & Scis., 1957-58, v.p., 1959-66, pres., 1967-79, pres. emeritus, 1980—. Reporter San Diego Daily Jour., San Luis Obispo Telegram-Tribune, Palo Alto Times, summers 1940-50; chair chancellor's coun. pres., Calif. State Univ. Sys., 1973-75, chair adv. com., trustee career edn.; bd. dirs. Am. Assn. State Colls. and Univs., 1970-75, Am. Coll. Pub. Rels. Assn., 1953-60. Author: Learn by doing: Memoir of University President, 2001; contbr. articles to newspapers, profl. jours. New libr. named in his honor, Robert E. Kennedy Libr., Calif. Poly. State U., 1978; named Outstanding Citizen, San Luis Obispo C. of C., 1978. Mem. Phi Beta Kappa, Sigma Delta Chi. Democrat. United Methodist. Avocation: photography. Home: 1385 Cazadero St San Luis Obispo CA 93401

KENNEDY, ROBERT EMMET, JR., history educator; b. N.Y.C., Dec. 19, 1941; s. Robert Emmet and Jean (MacLeod) K.; m. Jane Marie McMahon, June 23, 1968; children: Mara, Gaëlle Marie, Daniel Patrick, Robert Emmet III. BA, Johns Hopkins U., 1963; MA, Boston Coll., 1965; PhD, Brandeis U., 1973. Instr. history Merrimack Coll., 1964-66; instr. history Kent State U., Ohio, 1968-69; asst.-associé U. Toulouse, France, 1969-73; asst. prof. European history George Washington U., Washington, 1973-77, assoc. prof., 1977-82, prof., 1982—. Co-editor: The Shaping of Modern France: Writings on French History since 1715, 1969; author: A Philosopher in the Age of Revolution: Destutt de Tracy and the Origins of "Ideology," 1978, A Cultural History of the French Revolution, 1989; co-author: Theatre, Opera and Audiences in Revolutionary Paris: Analysis and Repertory, 1996. Fellow Am. Council Learned Socs., 1977-78, Woodrow Wilson Internat. Ctr. for Scholars, 1983-84 Mem. Soc. French Hist. Studies, Nat. Assn. Scholars, The Hist. Soc. (editl. bd.). Roman Catholic. Office: George Washington Univ Dept History Washington DC 20052-0001 E-mail: ekennedy@gwu.edu.

KENNEDY, R(OBERT) EVAN, engineering executive, consultant, retired structural engineer; b. Worland, Wyo., Mar. 31, 1916; s. Robert Eaker and Addie Miranda (Pritchard) K.; m. Betty Lou Kaser, Feb. 3, 1945; children: Anne Louise, Carter Evan, Robert Gordon. Student, Jamestown (N.D.) Coll., 1934-35; BS in Civil Engrng., U. Colo., 1938. Recorder U. S. Geol. Survey, Denver, 1938-39; jr. hydraulic engr. Colo. Water Consv. Bd., Denver, 1939-41; structural draftsman, jr. designer Am. Bridge Co., Trenton, N.J., 1941-42; stress analyst Goodyear Aircraft Corp., Akron, Ohio, 1942-44, liaison engr., group leader, sect. head Phoenix, 1944-46; sales rep. Luby-Sonnen Co., Madison, Wis., 1946; project engr. Rentenbach Engrng. Co., Knoxville, Tenn., 1946-47; field mgr. Kaser Constrn. Co., West Des Moines, Iowa, 1947; design engr. Moffatt, Nichol & Taylor, Portland, Oreg., 1947-49, Cooper & Rose, Portland, 1949-51; chief structural engr. Barrett & Logan Architects, Portland, 1951-52, Edmundson, Kochendoerfer & Kennedy A/E, Portland, 1952-53, chief engr., 1954-55, ptnr., 1955-68; mng. ptnr. Edmundson, Kochendoerfer, Kennedy-Daniel, Mann, Johnson, Mendenhall, Portland, 1968-74; v.p. Daniel, Mann, Johnson and Mendenhall, Baltimore, 1974-79; assoc. Tibbets, Abbott, McCarthy and Stratton, Washington, 1980-84; pres. Kennedy Assocs., Inc., Portland, 1984—. Bd. dirs., treas. Terwilliger Plaza; chmn. Seismic Design Com., Portland, 1948-50, bd. dirs., treas. Portland Bldg. Code Revisions Com., 1950-53; observer, cons. Effects Nuclear Test U.S. Dept. Commerce, Yucca Flats, Nev., 1955; instr. Oreg. Bd. Higher Edn. Architects Registration Exams., Portland, 1954-58, Engrs. Registration Exams., 1960-63; lectr. Oreg. Dental Sch. Disaster Planning, Portland, 1960-64; mem. A/E Selection Bd. U.S. Gen. Svcs. Adminstrn. NW Divsn., Auburn, Wash., 1973, Nat. Def. Exec. res. U. S. Bur. Pub. Rds., Washington, 1964-71; bd. mem. Portland Chess & Success, 1998—. Contbr. articles to profl. jours. Vice chmn. Fernwood Grade Sch. PTA, Portland, 1952-53, Portland Traffic Safety Commn., 1964-74; chmn. scholarship Grant H.S. Dad's Club, Portland, 1964-67; chmn. engrs. divsn. Portland United Good Neighbors, 1965, chmn. profl. divsn., 1967, 68; pres. Portland City Club, 1968; chmn. Interfaith Housing Com., Portland, 1969-73, Dulaney Towers Condo Bd., Towson, Md., 1975-78, Dulaney Towers Maintenance Bd., 1976-78, Balt. Energy Coun., 1978, Waterford Condo. Bd., Kensington, Md., 1985-88, Am. Plz. Condo. Bd., 1999; pres. Portland Housing Devel. Corp., Portland, 1970-74, Metrohousing, Inc., Portland, 1971-74; mem. Portland Symphonic Choir, 1958-64, Multnomah County Bldg. Code Appeals Bd., Portland, 1964, Nat. Mcpl. League, 1968-79, nat. conv. sect. convenor, 1976, 77, Mayor's Adv. Com., Portland, 1968-69, Congressman Wendell Wyatt Re-election Com., Portland, 1968; treas. Am. Plaza Condo Assn. Bd., Portland, 1991-96; mem., elder Towson Presbyn. Ch., 1974-79. Recipient Meritorious Svc. award City Portland, 1952, Nat. Design Honor award HUD, Washington, 1976, Grand Design award Am. Consulting Engrs. Coun., Washington, 1996, Outstanding Vol. award Am. Plz. Condo, 2001. Mem. ASCE (bd. dirs. Oreg. sect. 1953-55, Capital sect. 1980-90, sect. 1983, mem. Md. sect. 1974-90, Oreg. sect. 1990—), ASTM (chmn. NW dist. 1970), Am. Concrete Inst., Soc. Am. Mil. Engrs. (Merit award Portland Post 1973), Structural Engrs. Assn. Oreg. (life; founder, pres. 1949), Profl. Engrs. Oreg. (bd. dirs. 1948-74, chmn. Conv. 100 Yrs. Engrng., founder Engr. Yr. award 1952), Prestressed Concrete Inst., Engrng. Coun. Rsch. Inst., Consulting Engrs. Coun. Oreg. (treas. 1960, Engrng. Excellence Project award 1996), Toastmasters. Republican. Home and Office: 2545 SW Terwilliger Plz #1121 Portland OR 97201-6312 Address: 2545 SW Terwilliger Blvd No 1121 Portland OR 97201-6312 E-mail: revank@msn.com.

KENNEDY, ROBERT PHILIP, civil engineer; b. Glendale, Calif., Apr. 2, 1939; BS, MS, Stanford U., 1961, PhD of Structural Engring., 1967. Rsch. engr. Northrop Corp., 1963—64; dir. engrng. mechs. Holmes & Narver, 1966—76; v.p. engrng. decision Analysis Corp., 1976—80; pres. Structural Mechanics Assn., 1980—86, RPK Structrual Mechanics Consulting, Escondido, Calif., 1986—. Mem. ASCE (Stephen Bechtel Energy Engr. award 1992), Nat. Acad. Engrs., Am. Concrete Inst., Earthquake Engrng. Rsch. Inst. Home and Office: RPK Structural Mechanics Cons 28625 Mountain Meadow Rd Escondido CA 92026-6912 Office Fax: 760-751-3537.

KENNEDY, ROBERT SPAYDE, electrical engineering educator; b. Augusta, Kans., Dec. 9, 1933; s. Kirk Randel and Marene Lucile (Spayde) K.; m. Eleanor Emma Stagliola, June 27, 1981; children: Carole Lesley, Nancy Allison, Nina Margret. BSEE, U. Kans., 1955; MSEE, MIT, 1957, DSc in EE, 1963. Instr. engrng. MIT, Cambridge, 1958-63, asst. prof., 1963-67, assoc. prof., 1967-74, prof., 1974-94; prof. emeritus, 1994—. Dir. MIT Communication Forum, 1986-88; housemaster MacGregor House, MIT, 1985-91; pres. Eastport Healthcare, Inc. Author: Fading Dispersive Communication Channels, 1968; contbr. numerous articles to jours. in field. Pres., chief pilot Quoddy Air. Fellow IEEE (pres. info. theory group 1976-77). Avocations: flight instructor, pilot. Home: 3 Green St Eastport ME 04631-1315 Office: PO Box 311 Eastport ME 04631-0311 E-mail: alias@ptc-me.net.

KENNEDY, ROBINETTE, anthropologist, researcher; b. Reidsville, Ga, May 22, 1948; d. James Clifford and Dana Kate (Williams) Kennedy. BA in Journalism, U. Ga., Athens, 1970; MA in Humanistic Psychology, W.Ga. State U., Carrollton, 1973; PhD in Psychology, Saybrook Grad. Sch., San Francisco, 1981. Social worker Grady Hosp. Emory U. Dept. Medicine, Atlanta, 1970—71; rsch. asst. Dept. Family Rsch. Emory U., Atlanta, 1971—72; anthropology field work Ind. scholar, Crete, Greece, 1975—77; sr. rsch. assoc. Dept. Clin. Rsch. Ga. Mental Health Inst., Atlanta, 1978—80; clin. anthropologist Pvt. Practice, Crete, Greece, 1981—. Contbr. chapters to books. Achievements include first to document the structural role of women's friendships in a traditional culture. Home: PO Box W Mountain City GA 30562

KENNEDY, ROGER GEORGE, museum director, park service executive; b. St. Paul, Aug. 3, 1926; s. Walter J. and Elisabeth (Dean) K.; m. Frances Hefren, Aug. 23, 1958; 1 dau., Ruth. Grad., St. Paul Acad., 1944; BA, Yale, 1949; LL.B., U. Minn., 1952. Bar: Minn. 1952, D.C. 1953. Atty. Justice Dept., 1953; corr. NBC, 1954-57; dir. Dallas Council World Affairs, 1958; spl. asst. to sec. Dept. Labor, 1959; successively asst. v.p., v.p., chmn. exec. com., dir. Northwestern Nat. Bank St. Paul, 1959-69; v.p. finance, exec. dir. Univ. Found., Minn., 1969-70; v.p. financial affairs Ford Found., N.Y.C., 1970-78, v.p. arts, 1978-79; dir. Nat. Mus. Am. History Smithsonian Instn., Washington, 1979-92, dir. emeritus, 1993—; dir. Nat. Park Svc., Washington, 1993-97. Spl. asst. to sec. HEW, 1957, cons. to sec., 1969 Author: Minnesota Houses, 1967, Men on a Moving Frontier, 1969, American Churches, 1982, Architecture, Men, Women and Money, 1985, Orders from France, 1989, Greek Revival America, 1989; editl. dir.: Smithsonian Guide to Historic America, 12 vols., 1989-90, Rediscovering America, 1990, Mission 1993, Hidden Cities, 1993, Burr, Jefferson, and Hamilton, 1999, Mr. Jefferson's Last Cause, 2003; appearances on NBC radio and TV Today, also others, 1954-57; contbr. articles to mags. and profl. jours. Served with USNR, 1944-46. Office: 855 El Caminito Santa Fe NM 87505-2842

KENNEDY, RONALD CRAIG, anesthesiologist; b. Paris, Tex., July 31, 1943; s. Alexander Craig and Florence Wilkison Kennedy; m. Elaine Stamberg, Dec. 28, 1966; children: Kimberly L., Christopher R. BA, DePauw U., 1965; postgrad., U. Cin., 1966; MD, St. Louis U., 1970. Diplomate Am. Bd. Anesthesiology. Intern St. John's Mercy Hosp., St. Louis, 1970-71; family practice Grand Junction, Colo., 1974-75; resident in anesthesia U. Vt. Med. Ctr., Burlington, 1975-77; pvt. practice anesthesiology Elliot Hosp., Manchester, NH, 1977—99, chief of anesthesiology, 1988-90; anesthesiologist Waldo County Gen. Hosp., Belfast, Maine. Mem. choir Brookside Ch., Manchester, 1977-98. Comdr. USN, 1971-74. Congregationalist. Avocations: running, hiking, biking, photography, skiing. Home: 70 Kaler Rd Belfast ME 04915

KENNEDY, RUSSELL EDWARD, academic administrator; s. Russell Eugene and Alice Louise Kennedy; m. Karen Sue Janowiak, Mar. 26, 1977 (div. Oct. 18, 1988); children: Colleen June Kennedy Frazer, Matthew David, Brian Daniel, Curtis Russell. BS in Edn., Ind. U., 1973; MS in Adminstrn., U. Notre Dame, 1986. Cert. Am. Soc. for Hosp. Pub. Rels. and Mktg., 1984. News anchor, prodr., reporter Marion (Ind.) Cable TV, Inc., 1973; news reporter, announcer WGOM-AM/WMRI-FM, Marion, 1973—74; news anchor, prodr., reporter WNDU AM-FM-TV, South Bend, Ind., 1974—77, asst. news dir., 1977—80; cmty. rels. mgr. St. Joseph's Med. Ctr., South Bend, 1980—84, dir. cmty. rels., 1984—85, dir. mktg., 1985—86; dir. market comm. St. Joseph's Care Group, South Bend, 1986—89; adj. faculty mem., pub. speaking and radio news Ind. U., South Bend, 1989—91; dir. edn. Oaklawn Cmty. Mental Health Ctr. and Hosp., Elkhart/Goshen, Ind., 1989—93; mktg. dir. CPC Valle Vista Hosp., Greenwood, Ind., 1993—94; pvt. practice mktg. cons. Indpls., 1994—95; dir. edn. and pub. affairs Mental Health Assn. in Marion County, Indpls., 1995—98; media specialist Media Wisc, Indpls., 1998—2000, gen. edn. instr. ITT Tech. Inst., Indpls., 2000—01, assoc. dean, 2001—. Chair nat. membership com. Soc. Profl. Journalists, 1979—80; pres. Michiana Chpt., Soc. Profl. Journalists, South Bend, 1979—80, South Bend Press Club, 1982—83, Ind. Soc. for Healthcare Pub. Rels. and Mktg., 1988—89; mem. coun. on pub. rels. Ind. Hosp. Assn., 1988. Contbr. articles to profl. jours. Chair of one of six pilot sites nationally for anxiety disorders edn. program NIMH, Washington, 1996—98; mem., subcommittee on outreach, edn., and communication Ind. Governor's Adv. Panel on Children's Health Ins., 1998; mem., cmty. adv. com., Marion County cmty. health assessment project Marion County Dept. of Pub. Health, Indpls., 1996; selected by u. adminstrn. to serve on 14-mem. student bd. Ind. U. Meml. Union, Bloomington, Ind., 1971—72. Recipient CASPER Award for Campaign on Clin. Depression, United Way Ctrl. Ind., 1998; Hoosier Scholar, State Ind., 1969. Mem.: AAUP, Computer Profls. for Social Responsibility, Alpha Epsilon Rho, Phi Delta Kappa Internat. Office: ITT Tech Inst 9511 Angola Ct Indianapolis IN 46268

KENNEDY, SAMUEL VAN DYKE, III, journalist, educator; b. Auburn, NY, July 18, 1936; s. Samuel V., Jr. and Marion Huse (Blanchard) Kennedy; m. Bourke Larkin, Oct. 10, 1969 (div. 1994); children: Mary Morgan, Larkin Ellen, Lesley Chandler. BA, Cornell U., 1959; MA, Syracuse U., 1976, PhD, 1993. Reporter/editor Citizen-Advertiser, Auburn, 1960-75; asst. prof. Syracuse U., 1976-80, assoc. prof., 1980-2001. Cons. in field, Syracuse, 1985—. Author: (book) Samuel Hopkins Adams and the Business of Writing, 1999. Bd. dirs. Auburn Players Cmty. Theater, 1961—; trustee Osborne Meml. Assn., Auburn, 1973—. Mem.: Orgn. Am. Historians, Am. Journalism Historians Assn., Assn. Edn. Journalism & Mass Comm. Avocation: community theater. Home: 3692 Ensenore Rd Moravia NY 13118 E-mail: samkennedy@baldcom.net.

KENNEDY, SANDRA ELAINE, small business owner; b. Jacksonville, Fla., Apr. 27, 1948; d. Amos Edward and Janette Majorie Cordell; m. Charles Stephen Phillips, Oct. 19, 1967 (div. July 8, 1991); children: Amber Mechelle Geiger, Laurie Beth Johns; m. James Hilliard Kennedy, Jr.; children: Andrew Jordon, Justin Franklin Hilliard, Nicole. Student, No. Va. Coll., U. S.C. Learning disability asst. Dept. Def., Keflavick, Iceland, dir. spl. svcs. Exmouth, Australia, spl. edn. asst. Quantico, Va.; specialist FBI, Washington; dir., owner Tiny Junction, Inc., Columbia, SC. Cons. Mil. Base, Exmouth, Australia, 1980—82, FBI, Washington, 1984—90, Parkway Acad., Columbia, 1999—2000. Author: Drax Stone, 1999, Rainbow Collection, 2000, The Bartwell Tradegy, 2001. Grantee, Dept. Health and Human Svcs., 1992. Mem.: S.C. Autism Soc. Avocations: painting, writing. Home: 305 St Thomas Ch Rd Chapin SC 29036 Office: Tiny Junction Inc 1106 Old Two Notch Rd Lexington SC 29073

KENNEDY, STEPHEN DANDRIDGE, economist, researcher; b. N.Y.C., Feb. 25, 1942; s. Joseph Conrad and Frances (Midlam) K.; m. Joanna Court Bartlett, Nov. 27, 1965; children: Julia Paca, Benjamin Bartlett. AB, Harvard U., 1963; PhD, MIT, 1972. Mem. staff com. on banking and currency U.S. Ho. of Reps., Washington, 1964-66; adminstrv. asst. The Fed. Home Loan Bank Bd., Washington, 1966-67; analyst Abt Assocs., Inc., Cambridge, Mass., 1970, v.p., 1975, chief scientist, 1988—. Adj. lectr. John F. Kennedy Sch. Govt., Harvard U., 1995. Bd. trustees The Commonwealth Sch., 1997—2002. Episcopalian. Avocations: gardening, sailing. Office: ABT Assocs Inc 55 Wheeler St Cambridge MA 02138-1192

KENNEDY, STEPHEN SMITH, hematologist, oncologist, educator; b. Byrn Mawr, Pa., June 9, 1947; s. J. Howard and Katharine (Smith) K.; m. Marion Sue Painter, Mar. 24, 1973; children: Janis Louise, Emily Katharine. BA in English Lit., Princeton U., 1969; MD, U. Va., 1973. Diplomate Am. Bd. Internal Medicine, Am. Bd. Hematology, Am. Bd. Oncology. Intern U. Iowa, 1973-74, resident internal medicine, 1974-75, Dartmouth-Hitchcock Med. Ctr., 1977-78, fellow hematology, oncology, 1978-80; career hematology registrar U. Cape Town (South Africa), 1980-81; oncologist, hematologist Oncology Hematology Assoc. S.W. Va., Inc., Roanoke, 1981—. Instr. clin. medicine Dartmouth-Hitchcock Med. Ctr., 1978-80; clin. asst. prof. internal medicine, U. Va., Roanoke, 1982-92, clin. assoc. prof., 1992—; chief dept. med. specialties Roanoke Meml. Hosp.; staff Cmty. Hosp. Roanoke Valley, Lewis-Gale Hosp., Alleghany Regional Hosp., Radford Cmty. Hosp., Wythe County Cmty. Hosp., Montgomery Regional Hosp., Stonewall Jackson Hosp. Contbr. articles to profl. jours. Surgeon USPHS, 1975-77. Am. Cancer Soc. fellow, 1979-80, Leukemia Rsch. Ctr. fellow U. Cape Town, South Africa, 1980-81. Fellow ACP, AMA, Am. Soc. Hematology, Am. Soc. Clin. Oncology, Roanoke Valley Acad. medicine, Med. Soc. Va. Office: Oncology Hematology Assoc SW Va Inc 2013 S Jefferson St Roanoke VA 24014-2419

KENNEDY, THOMAS J. lawyer; b. Milw., July 29, 1947; s. Frank Philip and June Marian (Smith) K.; m. Cathy Ann Cohen, Nov. 24, 1978; children: Abby, Sarah. BA, U. Wisc., 1969, JD cum laude, 1972. Bar: Wis. 1972, U.S. Dist. Ct. (ea. and we. dists.) Wis. 1972, Ariz. 1981, U.S. Dist. Ct. Ariz. 1981, U.S. Ct. Appeals (7th cir.) 1980, U.S. Ct. Appeals (9th cir.) 1981, U.S. Ct. Appeals (D.C. cir.) 1983, U.S. Supreme Ct. 1984, U.S. Ct. Appeals (11th cir.) 1986. Assoc. Goldberg, Previant, Milw., 1972-79, Brynelson, Herrick, Madison, Wisc., 1979-81; ptnr. Snell & Wilmer, Phoenix, 1981-93, Lewis and Roca, Phoenix, 1993-96, Ryley, Carlock and Applewhite, Phoenix, 1996-99, Gallagher & Kennedy, 1999—2000, Sherman & Howard, 2000—. Contbg. editor The Developing Labor Laws, 2d, 3d edits., The Fair Labor Standards Act. Mem. ABA, Ariz. State Bar, State Bar Wisc., Maricopa County Bar Assn. Avocations: tennis, reading, hiking.

KENNEDY, THOMAS PATRICK, financial executive; b. N.Y.C., Oct. 13, 1932; s. Andrew Francis and Marie P. (Scullen) K.; m. Mary P. Drennan, Jan. 14, 1956 (dec.); children: Thomas Patrick, Kevin M. (dec.), Michael J., Mary P. Kennedy Handsman, Deborah A. Kennedy Carter. BS, St. Peter's Coll., 1958; postgrad., Seton Hall U., 1959. Accountant Haskins & Sells CPAs, N.Y.C., 1953-54; staff Emerson Radio & TV, N.Y.C., 1957-58; various exec. positions CBS, N.Y.C., 1958-67; with Ford Found., N.Y.C., 1967; dir. fin. Pub. Broadcasting Lab., N.Y.C., 1967-69; with Children's TV Workshop (Sesame St.), N.Y.C., 1969-80, v.p. fin. and adminstrn., 1969-78, treas., 1969-78, sr. v.p., 1978-80; exec. dir. Ctr. Non-Broadcast TV, 1980-85; pres. Tomken Mgmt., Ltd., 1980—, chmn. bd., 1983—; chmn. bd., chief exec. officer Effie Techs., Inc., 1984—. V.p., corp. fin. Jersey Capital Mkts Group, Inc., 1987-88; chief exec. officer, chmn. bd. Corp. Strategies Group, Inc., 1988-89; v.p. Vantage Securities, Inc. (co-venture with Whitehall Fin. Group), 1991-94; cons. in field; bd. advisers Franciscan Comm. Ctr.; bd. dirs., exec. dir. Ctr. for Non-Broadcast TV, 1980-85. With C.E., U.S. Army, 1954-55, Korea. Mem. Fin. Execs. Inst., Internat. Radio and TV Soc., Inst. Broadcast Fin. Mgmt., Nat. Assn. Accts., Internat. Broadcast Inst., Internat. Inst. Comm., Internat. Assn. Fin. Execs., Am. Assn. Individual Investors, Am. Legion, Korean War Vets., Brevard Vets. Council, Vets. Fgn. Wars, N.Y. Athletic Club, Knights of Columbus. Republican. Roman Catholic. Home and Office: 3400 Ocean Beach Blvd Apt 713 Cocoa Beach FL 32931-4180 E-mail: tkennedy@cfl.rr.com.

KENNEDY, WILBERT KEITH, SR., agronomy educator, retired university official; b. Vancouver, Wash., Jan. 4, 1919; s. Wilbert Parsons and Gracie Evelyn (Woolf) K.; m. Barbara Josephine Barber, Dec. 9, 1941 (dec. Nov. 1999); children: Wilbert Keith, James Clayton. BS, Wash. State U., 1940; MS in Agr., Cornell U., 1941, PhD, 1947. Asst. prof., asst. agronomist Wash. State Coll., 1947-48, assoc. prof., assoc. agronomist, 1948-49; prof. agronomy Cornell U., Ithaca, N.Y., 1949—; assoc. dir. research N.Y. State Coll. Agr., Cornell U.; also assoc. dir. Cornell U. Agr. Exptl. Sta., 1959, dir. research and dir. expt. sta., 1959-65; assoc. dean N.Y. State Coll. Agr., 1965-67, vice provost univ., 1967-72, dean, 1972-78, provost univ., 1978-84, provost emeritus, 1984—; with Atlantic Philantropic Svc. Co., Ithaca, 1988—. Cons. Rockefeller Found., Kasetsart U., Thailand, 1968, Ford Found., Malaysia, 1970 Contbr. articles to profl. jours. Mem. sch. bd., Dryden, N.Y., 1953-55; exec. com. Louis Agassiz council Boy Scouts Am., 1955-70; active local Community Chest; bd. dirs. Tompkins Community Hosp., 1984-94, pres., 1986-88. Served to maj. AUS, 1942-46. Guggenheim fellow; Fulbright scholar, 1956-57; recipient N.Y. Farmers award, 1958, Merit Cert. award Am. Grassland Council, 1964 Fellow Am. Soc. Agronomy, AAAS; mem. Sigma Xi, Phi Kappa Phi, Alpha Zeta. Lodges: Rotary. Home: 410 Savage Farm Dr Ithaca NY 14850-6506 E-mail: wkk4@msn.com.

KENNEDY, WILLIAM F. army reserve technician; b. N.Y.C., Mar. 12, 1940; m. Janet Kennedy. BA, U. Mass., 1973; cert., Bentley Coll. Inst. Paralegal Studies. Enlisted U.S. Army, 1977, advanced through grades to chief warrant officer, 1997; ret., 1997. Author: (poems and short stories) Life and Eternity, 1958, (poems) Korea in My Eyes, 1960, (self-pub. anthology) A Corkscrew, Please, 2002. Mem.: DAV (comdr. chpt. 45 2000—02), VFW (post 1628). Avocations: chess, swimming, travel. E-mail: wfkenn@hotmail.com.

KENNEDY, WILLIAM JOSEPH, novelist, educator; b. Albany, N.Y., Jan. 16, 1928; s. William Joseph and Mary Elizabeth (McDonald) K.; m. Ana Daisy Dana Segarra, Jan. 31, 1957; children: Dana Elizabeth, Katherine Anne, Brendan Christopher. BA, Siena Coll., 1949; LHD (hon.), Russell Sage Coll., 1980; LittD (hon.), Siena Coll., 1984, Coll. St. Rose, 1985; ArtsD (hon.), LHD (hon.), Rensselaer Poly. Inst., 1987; LHD (hon.), L.I. U., 1989, Fordham U., 1992, Trinity Coll., 1992, Notre Dame, 2001, DePaul U., 2002. Asst. sports editor, columnist Glens Falls Post Star, N.Y., 1949-50; reporter Albany Times-Union, N.Y., 1952-56, spl. writer, 1963-70; asst. mng. editor, columnist P.R. World Jour., San Juan, 1956; reporter Miami Herald, Fla., 1957; corr. Time-Life Publs. in P.R., 1957-59; founding mng. editor San Juan Star, 1959-61; lectr. SUNY, Albany, 1974-82, prof. English, 1983—. Vis. prof. Cornell U., Ithaca, N.Y., 1982-83; founder N.Y. State Writers Inst., 1983. Author: (book) The Ink Truck, 1969, Legs, 1975, Billy Phelan's Greatest Game, 1978, O Albany, 1983, Ironweed, 1983 (Pulitzer prize, 1984, Nat. Book Critics Circle award, 1984, film script, 1987), Quinn's Book, 1988, Very Old Bones, 1992, Riding the Yellow Trolley Car, 1993, The Flaming Corsage, 1996, Roscoe, 2002, (film script with Francis Ford Coppola) The Cotton Club, 1984, (children's books with Brendan Christopher Kennedy) Charlie Malarkey and the Belly Button Machine, 1986, Charlie Malarkey and the Singing Moose, 1994, (play) Grand View, 1996; contbr. short stories and articles to profl. jours. and mags. Served U.S. Army, 1950-52. Recipient Creative Arts award Brandeis U., 1986, Gov. N.Y. Arts award, 1984, Comdr. Order of Arts and Letters, France, 1993; MacArthur Found. fellow, 1983, Nat. Endowment of the Arts fellow, 1981. Mem.: Am. Acad. Arts and Scis., Acad. Motion Picture Arts and Scis., Am. Acad. Arts and Letters. Office: NYS Writers Inst U Albany 1400 Washington Ave Albany NY 12222-0100

KENNEDY, X. J. (JOSEPH KENNEDY), writer; b. Dover, N.J., Aug. 21, 1929; s. Joseph Francis and Agnes (Rauter) K.; m. Dorothy Mintzlaff, 1962; children: Kathleen, David, Matthew, Daniel, Joshua. BSc, Seton Hall U., 1950; MA, Columbia U., 1951; cert., U. Paris, France, 1956; LHD (hon.), Lawrence U., 1988; DFA (hon.), Adelphi U., 1998; DLitt, Westfield State Coll., 2002. Teaching fellow U. Mich., Ann Arbor, 1956-60, instr. English, 1960-62; lectr. English Woman's Coll., U. N.C., Greensboro, 1962-63; asst. prof. English Tufts U., Medford, Mass., 1963-67, assoc. prof., 1967-73, prof., 1973-79. Vis. lectr. Wellesley Coll., 1964, U. Calif., Irvine, 1966—67. Author: Nude Descending a Staircase, 1961, 2d edit., 1994, Introduction To Poetry, 1966, 10th edit., (with Dana Gioia) 2002, Growing into Love, 1969, Breaking and Entering, 1971, Emily Dickinson in Southern California, 1974, Celebrations After the Death of John Brennan, 1974, (with J.E. Camp, Keith Waldrop) Three Tenors, One Vehicle, 1975, One Winter Night in August, 1975, Introduction to Fiction, 1976, (with Dana Gioia) 8th edit., 2002, Literature, 1976, (with Dana Gioia) 8th edit., 2002, The Phantom Ice Cream Man, 1979, (with Dorothy M. Kennedy) The Bedford Reader, 1982, (with Dorothy M. Kennedy and Jane Aaron) 8th edit., 2003, Did Adam Name the Vinegarroon?, 1982, French Leave: Translations, 1983, Hangover Mass, 1984, (with Dorothy M. Kennedy) Knock at a Star: a Child's Introduction to Poetry, 1982, revised edit., 1999, The Owlstone Crown, 1983, The Forgetful Wishing-Well, 1985, Cross Ties: Selected Poems, 1985, Brats, 1986; (with Dorothy M. Kennedy) The Bedford Guide for College Writers, 1987, 6th edit., (with Dorothy M. Kennedy and Sylvia A. Holladay) 2002, Ghastlies, Goops and Pincushions, 1989, Fresh Brats, 1990, Winter Thunder, 1990, The Kite That Braved Old Orchard Beach., 1991, (with Dorothy M. Kennedy) Talking Like the Rain, 1992, The Beasts of Bethlehem, 1992, Dark Horses: New Poems, 1992, Drat These Brats!, 1993, The Minimus Poems, 1996, Uncle Switch, 1997, The Eagle as Wide as the World, 1997, Elympics, 1999, Elefantina's Dream, 2002, Exploding Gravy, 2002, The Lords of Misrule: Poems, 1992-2001, 2002; translator: Lysistrata in Penn Greek Drama Series, 1999; poetry editor: Paris Rev., 1961-64; editor: (with J.E. Camp) Mark Twain's Frontier, 1963, (with J.E. Camp, Keith Waldrop) Pegasus Descending, 1971, 2nd edit. 2003, Messages, 1973, Tygers of Wrath: poems of hate, anger and invective, 1981; editor, pub. (with Dorothy M. Kennedy) Counter/Measures mag, 1971-74. Judge Nat. Coun. on Arts poetry book selections, 1969, 70, T.S. Eliot prize Thomas Jefferson Univ. Press, 1998, X.J. Kennedy poetry award Tex. Rev., 1998, 90, 2000. With USN, 1951-55. Recipient Lamont Poetry award Acad. Am. Poets, Bess Hokin prize Poetry mag., 1961; Golden Rose award New Eng. Poetry Club, 1974; Los Angeles Times book award for poetry, 1985, Michael Braude award for light verse Am. Acad. and Inst. Arts and Letters, 1989, Aiken-Taylor award U. of the South, 1999, Excellence of Poetry for Children award, Nat. Coun. Tchrs. of English, 2000; grant Nat. Council Arts and Humanities, 1967-68; Shelley Meml. award, 1970; Bread Loaf fellow in poetry Middlebury Coll., 1960; Guggenheim fellow, 1973-74; Bruern fellow in Am. civilization U. Leeds, 1974-75. Mem. Assn. Lit. Scholars and Critics, John Barton Wolgamot Soc., PEN (mem. coun. New Eng. 1996—), MLA, Poetry Soc. Am., Nat. Coun. Tchrs. English, Authors Guild, Phi Beta Kappa, Sigma Tau Delta (hon.). Home: 22 Revere St Lexington MA 02420-4424

KENNEDY-MINOTT, RODNEY, international relations educator, former ambassador; b. Portland, Oreg. s. Joseph Albert and Gainor (Baird) Minott; children: Katharine Pardow, Rodney Glisan, Polly Berry AB, Stanford U., 1953, MA, 1956, PhD, 1960. Instr. history Stanford U., 1960-61, asst. prof., asst. dir. history of western civilization program, 1961-62, asst. dir. summer session, 1962-63, dir. summer session, 1963-65; mem. staff Congresswoman Edith Green of 1st Dist. Oreg., 1965; assoc. prof. Portland State U., 1965-66; assoc. prof., assoc. dean instrn. Calif. State U., Hayward, 1966-67, prof., 1967-77, head div. humanities, 1967-69; ambassador to Sweden and chmn. Swedish Fulbright Com., 1977-80; adj. prof. Monterey Inst. Internat. Studies, Calif., 1981; exec. v.p. Direction Internat., Washington, 1982-83; sr. rsch. fellow Hoover Instn., 1981—85, emeritus, 1985—; chmn. Alpha Internat., Washing-

ton, 1983-85. Sr. fellow Ctr. Internat. Rels., UCLA, 1986-90; sr. rsch. fellow Hoover Instn., 1985-93; sr. lectr. Naval Postgrad. Sch., 1990-2002; prof. nat. security affairs tng., U.S. Naval Postgrad. Sch., Monterey, Calif., 1990-2002, acad. assoc. for area studies, 1995-97; dir. environ. security program U.S. Naval Postgrad. Sch., 1999-2002, Homeland Def. Program, U.S. Naval Postgrad. Sch., 2002, emeritus Stanford U., 1993. Author: Peerless Patriots: The Organized Veterans and the Spirit of Americanism, 1962, The Fortress That Never Was: The Myth of Hitler's Bavarian Stronghold, 1964, The Sinking of the Lollipop: Shirley Temple v. Pete McCloskey, 1968, Regional Force Application: The Maritime Strategy and Its Affect on Nordic Stability, 1988, Tension in the North: Sweden and Nordic Security, 1989, Lonely Path to Follow: Non-aligned Sweden, United States/NATO, and the U.S.S.R., 1990, (with Ciro E. Zoppo) Nordic Security at the Turn of the 21st Century, 1992. Mem. adv. bd. Ctr. for the Pacific Rim U. San Francisco, 1988-93. With U.S. Army, 1946-48, USAR, 1948-52. Mem.: VFW, Navy League, U.S. Naval Inst., Marines Meml. Assn., Amnesty Internat., World Affairs Coun., Am. Fgn. Svc. Assn. (assoc.), Am. Legion, Officer Clubs Mil. Dist. Washington D.C., Stanford U. Faculty Club.

KENNEDY-NOLLE, SHARON DIANE, educator; b. Rockville Centre, N.Y., Oct. 20, 1962; d. Don Guida and Ann Linden; m. Christopher Nolle, June 21, 1990; children: Patrick, Warren. BA, Vassar Coll., 1984; MFA, U. Iowa, 1987, PhD, 2002; MA, N.Y. U., 1989, Johns Hopkins U., 1990. Tchr. asst. U. Iowa, Iowa City, N.Y. U., N.Y.C., 1987—89, Johns Hopkins U., Balt., 1989—90; instr. Mt. Hood C.C., Kurashiki, Japan, 1991; tchg. asst. U. Iowa, Iowa City, 1998—98. Adj. asst. prof. Iona Coll., 2003. Editor: (book introduction) Belle Boyd in Camp & Prison, 1998. Fulbright grant, N.Y. U., 1988, Carl Seashore fellow, U. Iowa, 1998—99. Mem.: MLA, Constance Fenimore Woolson Soc. (pres. 2002—), Civil War Preservation Trust, Ctr. Study of So. Culture. Avocations: travel, writing, reading, civil war history.

KENNEFICK, CHRISTINE MARIE, materials scientist; b. Washington, July 4, 1962; d. Albert Richard and Margaret Elizabeth (Hesselbirg) K. BS with distinction, Stanford U., 1984, MS, 1986; PhD, Cornell U., 1991. Rsch. assoc. NASA Lewis Rsch. Ctr., Cleve., 1991-93; scientist Max-Planck Inst., Stuttgart, Germany, 1994-96; Am. Soc. Engring Edn. postdoctoral fellow U.S. Army Rsch. Lab., Aberdeen, Md., 1997-98; rsch. assoc. Air Force Rsch. lab., Dayton, Ohio, 1998-2000; vis. prof. Shippensburg (Pa.) U., 2001—02. Mem. Am. Ceramic Soc., Am. Phys. Soc., Materials Rsch. Soc., N.Y. Acad. Scis.

KENNELL, RICHARD WAYNE, recording artist, business manager; b. Ft. Wayne, Ind., Aug. 11, 1952; s. John Charles and Betty June (Miller) K.; m. Leah Marie Waybright, Aug. 1, 1976. Student, Ind. U., Ft. Wayne, 1970-71, James Madison U., 1974. Rec. artist (bassist) Arista Records/Happy the Man, Reston, Va., 1974-79; rec. studio owner, producer, bus. mgr. The Inner Circle, White Plains, N.Y., 1984-96; bus. mgr. Inner Workings, Briarcliff Manor, N.Y., 1996—. Albums include Happy the Man, 1977, reissued, 1999, Crafty Hands, 1978, reissued, 1999, Better Late, 1983, Retrospective, 1989, Beginnings, 1990, Past, Present, Future, 1991, Happy the Man Live, 1994, Death's Crown, 1999, Beauty Gone Wild, 2001. Served with U.S. Army, 1971-73. Mem. ASCAP, Audio Engring. Soc., Am. Fedn. Musicians, Nat. Acad. Rec. Arts and Scis. Avocations: travel, computers, reading. Home: PO Box 122 Millwood NY 10546-0122 Office: 522 N State Rd Ste 102 Briarcliff Manor NY 10510-1540

KENNELLY, BARBARA B. former congresswoman, federal agency administrator; b. Hartford, Conn., July 10, 1936; d. John Moran and Barbara (Leary) Bailey; m. James J. Kennelly, Sept. 26, 1959 (dec. 1995); children: Eleanor Bride, Barbara Leary, Louise Moran, John Bailey. BA in Econs, Trinity Coll., Washington, 1958; grad., Harvard-Radcliffe Sch. Bus. Adminstrn., 1959; MA in Govt, Trinity Coll., Hartford, 1971. Mem. Hartford Ct. of Common Council, 1975-79; sec. of state State of Conn., Hartford, 1979-83; mem. 98th-105th Congresses from 1st Dist. Conn., Hartford, 1982-98; mem. ways and means com.; counselor, assoc. commr. Social Security Adminstrn., 1999-2000; sr. adv. Baker & Hostetler, Washington; currently pres. & CEO Nat. Com. to Preserve Social Sec. & Medicare. Trustee Trinity Coll., Hartford, Conn.; active in numerous polit., civic, and goft. orgns. Greater Hartford, Conn.; co-chair Ctr. for Democracy, Washington. Democrat. Roman Catholic. Office: Natl Com Preserve Social Security & Medicare 10 G St NE Ste 600 Washington DC 20002*

KENNELLY, JOY A. public relations specialist; d. Leo Patrick and Dianne Kennelly; 1 child, Elijah. Cert. in Bible, Mont. Wilderness Bible Coll., Augusta, Mont., 1983; AA, El Camino Coll., 1987; BA, Seattle Pacific U., 1991. Founder, artistic dir. Short Pictures Internat. Film Festival, Hollywood, Calif., 1996—2000; project mgr. Rubin Postaer and Assocs., Santa Monica, Calif., 2000; event prodr. Penton Media, Darien, Conn., 2000—01; freelance writer L.A. Conv. and Visitors Bur., 2002. Adoption activist Rose Vista Maternity Home, Mar Vista, Calif., 2000—; dir. Hungarian Orphan Toy Dr.; pub. advocate for adoption. Recipient Outstanding Svc. award. Avocations: swimming, travel, public speaking, racquetball. Personal E-mail: joykennelly@yahoo.com.

KENNELLY, SISTER KAREN MARGARET, retired academic administrator, church administrator, nun; b. Graceville, Minn., Aug. 4, 1933; d. Walter John Kennelly and Clara Stella Eastman. BA, Coll. St. Catherine, St. Paul, 1956; MA, Cath. U. Am., 1958; PhD, U. Calif., Berkeley, 1962. Joined Sisters of St. Joseph of Carondelet, Roman Cath. Ch., 1954. Prof. history Coll. St. Catherine, 1962-71, acad. dean, 1971-79; exec. dir. Nat. Fedn. Carondelet Colls., 1979-82; province dir. Sisters of St. Joseph of Carondelet, St. Paul, 1982-88; pres. Mt. St. Mary's Coll., L.A., 1989-2000, pres. emerita, 2000—; congl. dir. Sisters of St. Joseph of Carondelet, St. Louis, 2002—. Cons. N. Ctrl. Accreditation Assn., Chgo., 1974—84, Ohio Bd. Regents, Columbus, 1983—89; trustee colls., hosps., Minn., Mo., Wis., Calif., 1972—; chmn. Sisters St. Joseph Coll. Consortium, 1979—82. Editor, co-author: Am. Cath. Women, 1989; author (with others): Women of Minnesota, 1977; author: Women Religious and the Intellectual Life: The North American Achievement, 1996; co-editor: Gender Identities in American Catholicism, 2001; : Cath. Coll. Women in Am., 2002. Bd. dirs. Am. Coun. on Edn., 1997—99, Nat. Assn. Ind. Colls. and Univs., 1997—2000, Assn. Cath. Colls. and Univs., 1996—2000, Western Region Nat. Holocaust Mus., 1997—2000. Fellow Fulbright, 1964. Mem.: Western Assn. Schs. and Colls. (sr. commn. 1997—2000), Assn. Cath. Colls. and Univs. (exec. bd. 1996—2000), Am. Coun. Edn. (bd. dirs. 1997—99), Nat. Assn. Ind. Colls. and Univs. (bd. dirs. 1997—99), Am. Assn. Rsch. Historians Medieval Spain, Medieval Acad., Am. Cath. Hist. Assn. Avocations: skiing, cuisine. Office: Congl Ctr 2311 Lindbergh Blvd Saint Louis MO 63131 E-mail: kkennelly33@hotmail.com.

KENNELLY, LAURA BALLARD, writer, educator; b. Denton, Tex., July 28, 1941; d. E. Garrett and Laura L. (Hutchins) Ballard; m. Kevin J. Kennelly, Aug. 26, 1961 (div. 1996); children: Kathryn, Kevin G., Patrick J., Daniel T., Brendan C.; m. Robert Mayerovitch, Sept. 6, 1996. BA, U. North Tex., 1961, MA, 1969, PhD, 1975. Vis. prof. English U. North Tex., Denton, 1975—95, prodn. assoc. Studies in the Novel, 1987—92; bibliographic editor Restoration: Studies in English Literary Culture, 1980—2000. Asst. editor Bach: Jour. Riemenschneider Bach Inst., Baldwin-Wallace Coll., 2000—. Author: The Passage of Mrs. Jung: Poems, 1990; editor Grasslands Rev., 1987—, A Certain Attitude: Poems, 1995; contbr. scholarly articles to profl. jours., poetry, essays, and fiction to various publs. Dir. Birth Right of Denton, 1983-85. Grantee South Ctrl. MLA, 1990, Michael Kraus rsch. Am. Hist. Assn., 1992; Am. Antiquarian Soc. rsch. assoc., 1990, fellow, 1994-95. Mem. Am. Soc. for 18th Century Studies (affil. socs. coord. 1991-1998), Am. Hist. Assn., South Ctrl. Soc. for 18th Century Studies, East Ctrl. Soc. for 18th Century Studies, Tex. Assn. Creative Writing Tchrs. (pres. 1993-95). Roman Catholic. Avocations: running, biking. Office: Bach Inst Baldwin-Wallace Coll 275 Eastland Rd Berea OH 44017

KENNER, BRIDGET AGATHA, mental health services professional; b. Kitty Village, Demerara, Brit. Guiana; arrived in U.S., 1968; d. Harry and Maudlin Imelda Bakker; m. Malcolm Vinsent Kenner; 1 child, Marvin. State enrolled nurse, Royal Victoria Hosp., Kent, Eng., 1964; state registered nurse, Harefield Hosp., Middlesex, Eng., 1967; BS, Washington Saturday Coll., 1995, MS, 1996. Cert. diplomate in psychotherapy Am. Psychotherapy Assn., addictions counselor/nat. addictions counselor level II, nat. cert. addictions counselor level II, lic. profl. counselor. Staff nurse Washington Hosp. Ctr., 1969—74; counselor PSI Svcs., Washington, 1986—, program dir., 1991—92, activities coord., 1992—2000, mental health therapist, 2000—. Mem. exec. bd. dirs. D.C. Mental Health Counselors Assn.; bd. dirs. Profl. Alcoholism and Drug Abuse Counselors Assn., Washington. Mem.: Nat. Assn. Substance Abuse Counselors, Profl. Assn. Substance Abuse Counselors (bd. mem.), Am. Psychotherapy Assn., Consumer and Regulatory Affairs. Avocations: gardening, reading, cooking, exercising, shopping. Home: 5821 Colorado Ave Washington DC 20011

KENNER, CAROL J. federal bankruptcy judge; b. 1950; BA, Syracuse U., 1972; JD magna cum laude, New Eng. Sch. Law, 1977; postgrad., NYU Sch. Law, 1976-78. Bar: Mass. 1977. With Weil, Gotshal & Manges, N.Y.C., 1977-78, Widett, Slater & Goldman, Boston, 1978-81; pvt. practice Herrick & Smith, Boston, 1981-86; judge U.S. Bankruptcy Ct., 1986—; chief judge U.S. Bankruptcy Ct., Dist. Mass., Boston, 1994-98. Adj. faculty mem. Suffolk U. Sch. Law, 1998—; mem. Jud. Nominating Com., 1982-86 Mem. Mass. Bar Assn. (bd. dirs. 1982-84), Womens Bar Assn. (founding mem., v.p., bd. dirs. 1979-81). Office: US Bankruptcy Ct Thomas P O'Neill Fed Bldg 10 Causeway St Rm 1101 Boston MA 02222-1009

KENNER, MARILYN SFERRA, civil engineer; b. Youngstown, Ohio, Oct. 16, 1959; d. Joseph James and Mary (Conti) Sferra; m. Walter Sherden Kenner, July 7, 1984. B in Engring., Youngstown State U., 1982. Registered profl. engr., Ohio. Design and constrn. engr. Mahoning County Engr.'s Office, Youngstown, 1982-89, chief dep. engr., 1989—. Mem. engring. dean search com. Youngstown State U. Mem. Mahoning Valley Soc. Profl. Engrs. (pres., v.p. 1990-93, treas. 1987-90). Democrat. Roman Catholic. Home: 6941 Lockwood Blvd Youngstown OH 44512-4014 Office: Mahoning County Engr Office 940 Bears Den Rd Youngstown OH 44511-1218

KENNER, MARY ELLEN, marketing and communications executive; b. Darlington, Wis., Jan. 7, 1941; d. Horace James and Adean Elizabeth Smith; m. John Miller Kenner, Sept. 27, 1975. BS, Marquette U., 1963; MBA, U. West Fla., 1988. Fashion dir. spl. events Federated Store, Milw., 1962-63; mktg. odcl. Ohio Bell and Wis. Telephone Cos., 1963-66; coll. mktg. instr. Milw. Inst. Tech., 1966-67; advt. positions AT&T and Wis. Telephone Co., 1967-78; advtsg. dir. No. States Power Co., Mpls., 1978-83; pres. Kenner Enterprises, 1983—. Adj. prof. U. West Fla., 1988-89; dir. mktg. and communications Printing Industries Am., Alexandria, Va., 1989-91; dir. mktg. and pub. rels. Am. Production & Inventory Control Soc., 1992-97; dir. mktg. Grad. Sch. U. Md. U. Coll., 1997—; adj. assoc. prof. U. Md.; mem. steering com. 1st Conf. Consumerism. Mem. Am. Mktg. Assn., Am. Soc. Assn. Execs. (cert. assn. exec.), Direct Mktg. Assn. Wash. (cert. online prof.), Milw. Advtsg. Club (dir. 1969-72, sec. 1973-76), U. West Fla. Alumni Assn., Marquette U. Alumni Assn., Belleek Collectors Club. Roman Catholic. Home: 12908 Tourmaline Ter Silver Spring MD 20904-5349

KENNETT, LEE BOONE, JR., historian, educator; b. Greensboro, N.C., Aug. 11, 1931; s. Lee Boone and Dorothy Mary Kennett; m. Julianne Smythe Hudgens, June 24, 1961 (div. July 1977); children: Caroline Allison, John Calvin; m. Anne Marie Lucille Durand, Feb. 17, 1987. Student, Guilford Coll., N.C., 1948—50; BA, U. N.C., 1952; MA, U. Miss., 1956; PhD, U. Va., 1958. Asst. prof. Converse Coll., Spartanburg, SC, 1958—60; lectr. So. Ill. U., Carbondale, 1960—61; asst. prof. U. Ga., Athens, 1962—66, assoc. prof., 1966—78, prof. history, 1978—87, rsch. prof., 1987—93, prof. emeritus, 1993—; assoc. prof. Guilford Coll., NC, 1967—68. Founder, dir. Consortium on Revolutionary Europe, 1969—74; mem. fellowship selection bd. Inst. of Internat. Edn., 1978, 80; organizer Internat. Conf. on Aviation, Nat. Air and Space Mus., Washington, 1990; directeur d'études associé Ecole Pratique des Hautes Etudes, 4th sect., U. Paris, 1978; Lindbergh prof. Nat. Air and Space Mus., Smithsonian Instn., 1989—90; guest lectr. aero. sect. Inst. Phys. Sci. and Tech., Russian Acad. Sci., 1991. Author: (book) The French Armies in the Seven Years' War, 1968, The French Forces in America, 1780-1783, 1977, A History of Strategic Bombing, 1982, G.I.: The American Soldier in WW II, 1987, The First Air War, 1914-1918, 1990, Marching Through Georgia, 1995, Gettysburg: le tournant de la guerre de Sécession, 1997, Sherman: A Soldier's Life, 2001; co-author: The Gun in America, 1975; co-editor: French Military Aviation: A Bibliographical Guide, 1989; translator (editor): The Russian Campaign, 1812, 1970, Clement Ader's Aviation Militaire, 2003; contbr. Decorated Chevalier, Ordre des Palmes Académiques France; recipient Claiborne History prize, U. Miss., 1956, Fulbright Lectureship to France, 1966—67, Bicentennial Lectureship to France, Fulbright Found., 1974—75, Gilbert Chinard prize, Soc. for French Hist. Studies, 1978, Nat. Book prize, Phi Alpha Theta, 1979, Excellence in Rsch. award, U. Ga., 1980, Disting. Svc. award, Inst. Internat. Edn., 1981; fellow James Wilford Garner fellow, U. Miss., 1955—56, Virginia Mason Davidge fellow, U. Va., 1956—57; grantee Advanced Rsch. grantee, U.S. Army Mil. History Inst., 1979, Rsch. grantee, USAF Hist. Rsch. Ctr., 1988; Fulbright fellow, France, 1960—61. Mem.: So. Hist. Assn., Soc. for Mil. History, Orgn. Am. Historians, N.C. Civil War Roundtable, Greensboro Hist. Mus., Centre d'etudes d'histoire de la Défense, Am. Hist. Assn., Phi Beta Kappa. Home: 1840 Neelley Rd Pleasant Garden NC 27313 E-mail: amd2ba@aol.com.

KENNEVAN, WALTER JAMES, computer science educator; b. N.Y.C., Aug. 29, 1912; s. David A. and Ellen Kathleen (Grogan) K.; m. Marguerite Roberta Stevens, Oct. 12, 1940; children: JoEllen Kennevan Berlin, Steven David. BS in Commerce, Columbus U. Am., 1938; MS in Commerce, Cath. U. Am., 1940, M Fiscal Adminstrn., 1943. Mgmt. supr. Nat. Capital Housing Authority, Washington, 1942-48; asst. comptroller Bur. Ordnance U.S. Dept. Navy, Washington, 1948-57; dir. computer systems Office of Navy Comptroller Washington, 1957-69; prof. info. sci. Am. U., Washington, 1969-77, prof. emeritus, 1977—. Cons. NIH, Washington, 1964-65, U.S. Dept. State, Washington, 1964-65, U.S. Civil Svc. Commn., Washington, 1964-65. Author: Management and Computer Systems, 1973; contbr. articles to numerous publs. Mem. Cen. Suffrage Com. D.C., 1946-47, Vets. of the Battle of the Bulge. Staff sgt. U.S. Army, 1943-46, ETO. Mem. Am. Legion, Soc. Info. Mgmt. (nat. sec. 1975), Acad. Mgmt., Assn. Systems Mgmt., Ancient Order of Hibernians, Kenwood Country Club. Democrat. Roman Catholic. Avocation: golf. Home: 3356 S Lambert St Eugene OR 97405

KENNEY, ALAN ADAMS, lawyer, accountant; b. Richfield, Utah, Nov. 2, 1939; s. Don Earl and Armenia (Adams) K.; m. Margaret Compton, Apr. 30, 1976; children— Matthew, Travis. B.S., Brigham Young U., 1964; J.D., U. Colo., 1969. Bar: Colo. 1969, U.S. Dist. Ct. Colo. 1969; C.P.A., Colo. Mem. tax staff Arthur Andersen & Co., Denver, 1969-70; tax atty. Samsonite Corp., Denver, 1970-72; gen. counsel Storage Tech. Corp., Louisville, Colo., 1972— . Served to sgt. USAF, 1962-66. Mem. Am. Corp. Counsel Assn. (dir. Colo. chpt.), ABA, Colo. Bar Assn., Denver Bar Assn., Computer Law Assn., Am. Soc. Corp. Secs., Beta Alpha Psi. Home: 10150 Arapahoe Rd Lafayette CO 80026-9312 Office: Storage Tech Corp PO Box 98 Louisville CO 80027-0098

KENNEY, BELINDA JILL FORSEMAN, technology company executive; b. Oak Ridge, Tenn., Dec. 18, 1955; d. Jack Woodrow and Betty Jean Forseman; m. Ronald Gene Kenney, Feb. 23, 1985; 1 child, Brandon. BS, U. Tenn., 1977, postgrad., 1977-78; MBA, Emory U., 2000. Sales rep. Xerox Corp., Nashville, 1978—82, maj. account sales mgr., 1982—83, region sales ops. mgr. St. Louis, 1984—86, dist. sales mgr. Overland Park, Kans., 1987—89, dist. mgr. San Antonio, 1989—95, v.p. Houston, 1995—97, v.p., region gen. mgr. Bus. Svcs. Atlanta, 1998—99, sr. v.p. region mgr. NASG, 2000—01; corp. v.p. worldwide mktg. and corp. strategy Storage Tech. Corp., Superior, Colo., 2001—. Exec. in residence Leeds Sch. Bus. U. Colo. Patron M.D. Anderson Cancer Ctr.; bd. dirs. Wise Women's Coun.; exec.-in-residence Leeds Sch., U. Colo.; bd. dirs. Women's Vision Found., Denver, United Way Boulder County. Mem. Rocky Mountain MENSA, StorageTek Women's Alliance. Lutheran. Avocations: jogging, reading, tennis, health and fitness. Office: 1 Storagetek Dr Louisville CO 80028-0001

KENNEY, CHARLES DENNISON, political science educator; b. Lexington, Ky., Oct. 11, 1957; s. Vincent Paul (m) and Margaret Dennison Kenney; m. María Caridad Marchand, Dec. 28, 1985; children: Pablo Damián, María Margarita, Tomás Carlos, Andrés Arturo. BA, U. Notre Dame, 1980, MA, 1997, PhD, 1998. Parish and cmty. organizer Cath. Charities, Oakland, Calif., 1980-83; lay missionary Congregation of Holy Cross, Lima, Peru, 1984-88; rschr. Instituto Bartolomé de las Casas, Lima, 1985-91; asst. prof. U. Okla., Norman, 1997—. Mem. editl. bd. Elecciones. Fulbright Fgn. scholar, 2000; Jr. faculty rsch. grantee U. Okla., 1999, 2000. Mem. Latin Am. Studies Assn. (past chair Peru sect.), Am. Polit. Sci. Assn. Democrat. Roman Catholic. Office: U Okla 455 W Lindsey Rm 205 Norman OK 73019

KENNEY, DION PATRICK, business strategist, entrepreneur; b. Middletown, N.Y., Apr. 26, 1962; s. John Michel Kenney and Joan Elizabeth (Bennett) Klein. BS in Physics, Fla. State U., 1984; MS in Physics, Tex. A&M U., 1989; MBA, U. Pa., 1995. Engr. Navair-Dept. of Navy, Lakehurst, N.J., 1985-86, Stratford, Conn., 1986-87; software engr. Unisys, Houston, 1990-93; mktg. and bus. planning profl. Health Care Devel. Internat., Tarrytown, N.Y., 1993-95; founder, pres. Cybernet Info. Systems, Yorktown Heights, N.Y., 1994—. Dir. bus. planning AHSC Group, LLC, Tarrytown, N.Y., 1995-2002; prin. cons. Y2 Mktg., N.Y.C., 2002—. Home: 8 Parkway Dr Yorktown Heights NY 10598-6407 Office: 777 Old Sawmill River Rd Tarrytown NY 10591

KENNEY, DONNA DENISE, accountant; b. Bklyn., Oct. 4, 1960; d. Donald and Sherry Sheila (Nedol) Yules; m. Eugene L. Kenney, Jr., May 31, 1981; children: Kyle Asher, Graham Stewart. BBA in Bus. Mgmt., Adelphi U., 1981, MBA with distinction, 1989. CPA, N.Y. Grad. asst. dept. acctg. and law Adelphi U., Garden City, N.Y., 1984-89; mgr. David Berdon & Co., LLP, Jericho, N.Y., 1994-99; tax mgr. Bertelsmann, Inc., N.Y.C., 1999—. Mem. N.Y. State Soc. CPAs (com. mem. acctg. and auditing Suffolk chpt. 1991-92, award of honor 1989), Delta Mu Delta, Eta Chi Alpha. Office: Bertlesmann Inc 1540 Broadway New York NY 10036-4039

KENNEY, ESTELLE KOVAL, artist; b. Chgo., Feb. 15, 1928; d. Hyman English and Florence (Browman) Koval; B.F.A., Art Inst. Chgo., 1976, M.F.A., 1978; postgrad. Yale U., 1980; m. Herbert Kenney, Feb. 6, 1948; children— Carla, Robert. Art therapist Grove Sch., Lake Forest, Ill., 1973-78, New Trier High Sch. and Central High Sch., Winnetka, Ill., 1978-79, Mosely Sch., Chgo., 1979, Cove Sch., Evanston, Ill., 1979-82; dir. art therapy concentration, instr. painting and drawing Loyola U., Chgo., 1981— ; pres., art dir. Nuts on Clark Inc., Chgo.; one woman shows: Evanston (Ill.) Library, 1971, Zaks Gallery, Chgo., 1977, 79, 82, Renaissance Soc.-Bergman Gallery, U. Chgo., 1980; group shows include; Ill. State Mus., 1975, Women Artists, Here and Now, 1976, Chgo. Connections travelling exhbn., 1976-77, Nat. Women's Caucus for Art, 1977, Nancy Lurie Gallery, 1978, Marycrest Coll. Gallery, Davenport, Iowa, 1982, Chgo. Internat. Art Expo, 1981, 82, 83, Notre Dame U. Gallery, South Bend, Ind., 1982; represented in permanent collections: Ill. State Mus., Springfield, Union League Club of Chgo. Mem. Am. Art Therapy Assn., Ill. Art Therapy Assn. (pres. 1979—), Coll. Art Assn. Home: 3830 N Clark St Chicago IL 60613-2812 Office: Loyola University of Chicago Dept Fine Arts 6525 N She Ridan Rd Chicago IL 60626 E-mail: estellekenneynutsonclark@nutsonclark.com.

KENNEY, FRANK DEMING, lawyer; b. Chgo., Feb. 20, 1921; s. Joseph Aloysius and Mary Edith (Deming) K.; m. Virginia Stuart Banning, Feb. 12, 1944; children: Claudia Kenney Carpenter, Pamela Kenney Voetberg, Sarah Kenney Swanson, Stuart Deming Kenney AB, U. Chgo., 1948, JD, 1949. Bar: Ill. 1948, U.S. Dist. Ct. (no. dist.) Ill. 1949. Assoc. J.O. Brown, Chgo., 1948-49; assoc., ptnr. Winston & Strawn, and predecessors, Chgo., 1949-92, ret., 1992. 1st lt. AUS, 1942-46, CBI, PTO. Mem. ABA, Ill. Bar Assn., Chgo. Bar Assn. (chmn. real property law com. 1982-83), Lawyers Club Chgo., Fox River Valley Hunt Club, Quadrangle Club, Nat. Beagle Club Am. (bd. dirs. 1981-92), Spring Creek Basset Hunt Club (master 1977-93, chmn. bd., 1993-98, hon. chmn. bd. 1998-2002, hon. master 2002-), Kappa Sigma (nat. housing fin. commr. for U.S. and Can., 1959-91). Republican. Roman Catholic. Home: PO Box 581 333 Old Sutton Rd Barrington IL 60010-9368 Office: Winston & Strawn 35 W Wacker Dr Ste 3800 Chicago IL 60601-1695

KENNEY, H(ARRY) WESLEY, JR., producer, director; b. Dayton, Ohio, Jan. 3, 1926; s. Harry Wesley and Minnie Ruth (Keeton) K.; m. Kay Ann Snure (div. 1964); children: Nina, Harry Wesley III, Kara; m. Heather North, May 22, 1971; 1 child, Kevin. BFA, Carnegie Inst. Tech., 1950. Dir. Fights at St. Nicks, Rocky King Detective, Night Beat Dumont Network, N.Y.C., 1950-57; producer, dir. TV shows True Story, Modern Romances NBC, N.Y.C., 1957-61; freelance dir. Omnibus, N.Y.C., 1958; dir. theater prodn. My Three Angels Totem Pole Playhouse, 1955; dir. theater prodn. The King and I Melody Fair Summer Theatre, Niagra Falls, 1959; dir. theater prodn. Twelfth Night Antioch, Yellow Springs, Ohio, 1962; dir. TV series The Doctors NBC, N.Y.C., 1964-66, exec. producer, dir. TV series Days of Our Lives Los Angeles, 1967-77; dir. TV series All in the Family CBS, Los Angeles, 1974, dir. pilots The Jeffersons, Filthy Rich, Ladies Man, Rosenthal & Jones, Side By Side, exec. producer, dir. TV series The Young and the Restless, 1981-86; producer, dir. (spl.) Miss Kline, We Love You ABC, 1974, exec. producer, dir. TV series General Hospital, 1987-90; freelance dir., 1990—. Cons. Televisa-Mexico City UCLA Ext. Sch., 1990, guest instr. TV directing, 1975, guest instr. multiple camera directing, 1991, 93; instr. profl. seminar in TV for Televisa, 1990; guest lectr. profl. seminar dor srs. and students in drama Carnegie Mellon U., Pitts., 1990; assoc. prof. TV prodn. UCLA Sch. Theatre, Film and TV, 1993, 94, 95, 96, 97, 98, 99, 2001, 02, 03; assoc. prof. TV prodn. Sch. Cinema and TV U. So. Calif., 1998, 99—. Dir. closed cir. med. shows including Dr. Salk Polio Vaccine Report from U. Mich., Ann Arbor, 1956; dir. (theater prodns.) Ten Little Indians, Advent Theatre, L.A., 1991, The Best Christmas Pageant Ever, 1993, Love Letters, W.Va. Pub. Theatre, Morgantown, 1994, Shadowlands, Tracy Roberts Theater, 1995 (Dramalogue award for Directing), Scrooge, W.Va. Pub. Theatre, 1995; dir. Sebiyophrenin: The Relapse, 3-part series; dir. (infomercials) Elements of Beauty-The Merle Norman Experience, 1993, Therapy Without Tears-The EMLA Study, 1993; dir. (series spls.) Soap Break, CBS, 1994-95 (Emmy nomination). Served with USN, 1943-46. Recipient 7 Emmy awards Acad. TV Arts and Scis. 1973, 78, 79, 82, 83, 84, 86, 13 Emmy award nominations Acad. TV Arts and Scis., 1972-88, 95 Mem. Dirs. Guild Am., Producers Guild Am., Actors Equity, Omega Delta Kappa. Avocations: athletics, tennis, traveling, bungy jumping. Home: 12996 Galewood St Studio City CA 91604-4045 E-mail: marle333@aol.com. *I recognize myself as an "average guy" with an average intelligence and talent and more than average patience and luck. An awareness of this fact has allowed me to accept the success I have had, always working for something better, but recognizing those shortcomings that have at times made me fail. Also because of this, thank God, I have had more than my share of happiness.*

KENNEY, JOHN PATRICK, dentist; b. Joliet, Ill., July 8, 1946; s. John Edward and Nellie Kenney; m. Catherine McGehee, June 1, 1968 (div.); 1 child, David J. BS in Mktg., Christian Bros. Coll., 1968; DDS, Loyola U., Maywood, Ill., 1977, Cert. in Pedit. Dentistry, 1979; MS in Oral Biology, Loyola U., Chgo., 1979. Diplomate Am. Bd. Forensic Odontology. Supr. passenger services Am. Airlines, Chgo., 1968-72; pvt. practice in pediatric dentistry Park Ridge, Ill., 1980—; asst. prof. pediat. dentistry Northwestern U., Chgo., 1983-97, clin. assoc. prof. pediat. dentistry, 1997-2000; chief forensic odontologist Cook County Med. Examiner, 1991-97; assoc. prof. clin. surgery Northwestern U. Med. Sch., 2000—. Forensic odontologist Cook County Med. Examiner, Chgo., 1984-97, Kane County (Ill.) Coroner, Geneva, 1984-97; cons. forensic odontologist Am. Airlines, Chgo., 1979, Midwest Express Airlines, Milw., 1985, Am. Eagle Airlines, Ind., 1995, United Express Airlines, Quincy, Ill., 1996, Comair Airlines, Mich., 1997, U.S. Army Central ID Lab., Honolulu, 1997—, Amtrak, Ill., 1999, NYCME, 2001; mem. Nat. Disaster Med. Sys. D-Mort team USPHS, forensic oversight com., 2001—; dir. Identification Svcs. Dupage County Ill. Coroners Office, 1997—. Mem. editl. bd. Jour. Forensic Scis., 1997—; contbr. articles to profl. jours. Dep. coroner DuPage County, 2001—. Fellow Am. Acad. Pediatric Dentistry, Am. Acad. Forensic Scis., Peirre Fauchard Soc., Royal Soc. Medicine; mem. ADA, Internat. Orgn. for Forensic Odonto-stomatology (v.p. 1984-87), Internat. Assn. for Identification (cert. sr. crime scene analyst 1991—), Am. Acad. Pediatric Dentists, Am. Bd. Forensic Odontology (bd. dirs., 1990-96, 2000—, treas. 1991-93, v.p. 1994, pres. 1995-96), Ill. State Dental Soc., Ill. Soc. Pediatric Dentists (bd. dirs. 1987-90), Chgo. Dental Soc., Kiwanis (pres. 1983-84, Disting. Pres. 1984). Office: 101 S Washington Ave Park Ridge IL 60068-4200

KENNEY, JOHN JOSEPH, lawyer; b. N.Y.C., July 13, 1943; s. Joseph Charles and Regina Elizabeth (Hulbert) K.; m. Charlotte O'Brien, May 23, 1971; 1 child, Alexander Hulbert. BA, St. Michael's Coll., 1966; JD, Fordham U., 1969. Bar: N.Y. 1970, U.S. Dist. Ct. (so. dist.) N.Y. 1973, U.S. Ct. Appeals (2d cir.) 1973, U.S. Dist. Ct. (ea. dist.) N.Y. 1980, U.S. Supreme Ct. 1991.

Assoc. Dunnington, Bartholow & Miller, N.Y.C., 1969-71; asst. U.S. atty. U.S. Dist. Ct. (so. dist.) N.Y., N.Y.C., 1971-80; assoc. Simpson, Thacher & Bartlett, N.Y.C., 1980-81, ptnr., 1981—. Mem. deptl. disciplinary com. Appellate Divsn. 1st Dept., 2002—. Counsel, Village of Bronxville, 1983-86; mem. Planning Bd. of Bronxville, 1992-98, counsel, 1981-83; trustee Hist. Deerfield Inc., 1992-98, Bennington Coll., 1999—, Bronxville Pub. Libr., 2003-; bd. dirs. Citizens Crime Commn., 1998—, Am. Assn. for Internat. Commn. Jurists, 2000—. Recipient John Marshall award U.S. Dept. Justice, 1980. Fellow Am. Coll. Trial Lawyers; mem. ABA, Fed. Bar Coun. (pres. 1994-96), Assn. Bar City N.Y. (chmn. criminal law com. 1992-95), New York County Lawyers Assn. (pres. 1996-97), N.Y. State Bar Assn. (exec. com. 1997-2000). Republican. Roman Catholic. Home: 8 The Byway Bronxville NY 10708-4934 Office: Simpson Thacher & Bartlett 425 Lexington Ave 15th Fl New York NY 10017-3954 E-mail: jkenney@stblaw.com.

KENNEY, JOHN MICHEL, architect; b. N.Y.C., Oct. 22, 1938; s. John Peter and Madeline Loretta (Fuller) K.; children: John Michel, James Brian, Dion Patrick. AAS, Orange County Community Coll., 1966; student, Columbia U., 1969. Registered arch., N.Y., N.J., Conn., Ill., Pa., Del., Ill., S.C., N.C., Ga. V.p., ptnr., dir. health facilities Perkins & Will Architects, White Plains, N.Y., 1968-81; mng. mem. AHSC Archs. P.C., Tarrytown, N.Y., 1981—, AHSC/Melellan, Copenhagen. Mng. mem. AHSC Group LLC; co-chmn. AHSC/Destefano and Ptnrs., Chgo.; pres. ArquInter-AHSE Europe, Madrid. Vice chmn. Orange County Dem. Coms., N.Y., 1968; chmn. Dem. Com., Middletown, N.Y., 1966-68; co-chmn. Robert Kennedy Presdl. Election Primary, Orange/Sullivan County, 1968; mem. United Hosp. Fund; bd. mem. Aging in Am. Found. Mem. AIA, Nat. Coun. Archtl. Registration Bds., N.Y. Soc. Hosp. Planning, Am. Assn. Hosp. Planners, N.Y. Acad. Scis. Democrat. Avocations: skiing, sailing, travelling. Office: AHSC Architects 777 Old Saw Mill River Rd Tarrytown NY 10591-6717

KENNEY, JOHN PETER, dean, educator; b. Lawrence, Mass., May 1, 1952; s. John Peter and Catherine Mary Kenney; m. Ann Jason Kenney, Aug. 24, 1974; children: Madeline E., J. Edward. AB in Classics and Philosophy, Bowdoin Coll., 1974; PhD in Religious Studies, Brown U., 1982. From asst. to full prof. Reed Coll., Portland, Oreg., 1980—95; vis. scholar Harvard U., Cambridge, Mass., 1984—85; dean coll., prof. religious studies St. Michael's Coll., Colchester, Vt., 1995—. Author: Mystical Monotheism, 1991; editor: The School of Moses, 1995; contbr. articles. Fellow, Nat. Endowment for Humanities, 1984—85, 1991—92. Mem.: N.Am. Patristic Soc., Am. Acad. Religion, Phi Beta Kappa. Republican. Roman Catholic. Avocations: walking, gardening. Office: St Michaels Coll 1 Winooski Pk Colchester VT 05439

KENNEY, MARY R. software engineer; b. Richmond, Va., 1945; d. Thomas W. and Clara G. K.; m. Jeremy M. (div.). BS and MS in Math., Howard U., 1967; MS in Computer Sci., Steven's Inst., 1984. Sr. math. aide Ctr. Naval Analysis, Rosslyn, Va., 1967-77; sr. programmer analyst Control Data Corp., Rockville, Md., 1977-81; software quality engr. AT&T Bell Labs., Piscataway, N.J., 1981-84, Bellcore, Piscataway, 1984-99, Telcordia Techs., Piscataway, 1999—. Chair fundraising Youth in Sports Found., Piscataway, 1995-97; mem. fundraising com. Cmty. League Active Youth, New Brunswick, N.J., 1994, N.J. Rams, Newark, 1992-93. Mem. AAUW, NAFE, ACM, Am. Mgmt. Assn. Avocations: reading, crochet, bowling. Office: Telcordia Techs Inc 3 Corp Pl Piscataway NJ 08854

KENNEY, RAYMOND JOSEPH, JR., lawyer; b. Boston, Aug. 3, 1932; m. Claire L. Ducey; children: Marianne Lordi, Raymond Joseph III, Stephen V., John M. AB cum laude, Boston Coll., 1953, JD, 1958. Bar: Mass. 1958, U.S. Dist. Ct. 1960, U.S. Ct. Appeals (1st cir.) 1969, U.S. Supreme Ct. 1985, U.S. Ct. Appeals (11th cir.) 1995. Mem. firm Martin, Magnuson, McCarthy & Kenney (and predecessor firms), Boston, 1958—. Instr. law Mass. Dept. Edn., U. Ext., 1958-60, Boston U., 1961-66; corporator Winchester Savs. Bank, 1973—, Winchester Hosp., 1980—; lectr. continuing legal edn.; mem. Winchester Fin. Com., 1967-70, chmn., 1970-71; moderator Town of Winchester, 1972-77; chmn. Mass. Jud. Nominating Commn., 1975-77; mem. standing com. on civil rules Supreme Jud. Ct., 1977—; mem. time standards com. Mass. Superior Ct., 1990—; chmn. Mass. Clients Security Bd., 1984-87; dir. Mt. Vernon House, Winchester, 1990—. Author: Mass. Practice series (West), 1998—, Mass. Law Rev.; editor-in-chief, 1973-76; contbr. articles to legal jour. Bd. dirs. Winchester chpt. ARC, 1968-71; pres. Mass. Continuing Legal Edn., 1980-83. Fellow Am. Coll. Trial Lawyers (state committeeman 1982-86), Am. Bar Found., Mass. Bar Found. (pres. 1984-88, trustee 1994-96); mem. ABA (del. 1976-78), Am. Judicature Soc. (dir. 1978-81), New Eng. Bar Assn. (pres. 1980-81), Mass. Bar Assn. (pres. 1977-78, founding chmn. sr. lawyers sect. 1999-2001), Middlesex Bar Assn., Mass. Def. Lawyers Assn. (Def. Lawyer of Yr. 1995), Internat. Assn. Def. Counsel, Boston Coll. Alumni Assn. (pres. 1983-84, 50th Ann. Disting. Law Alumnus award). Home: 8 Vinebrook Way Woburn MA 01801 Office: Martin Magnuson McCarthy Kenney 101 Merrimac St Boston MA 02114-4716 *The continued well-being of society is dependent upon maintaining vitality in the law. The law must, and does, contain within itself the means to attain its own advancement, thereby preserving and enhancing that vitality. One of life's great privileges is to have been afforded the opportunity to labor in a profession which so reaches the very essence of human relationships.*

KENNEY, THOMAS FREDERICK, broadcasting executive; b. Dearborn, Mich., Sept. 25, 1941; s. Charles B. and Grace M. (Wilson) K.; m. Beth H. Rockwood, Aug. 22, 1964; children: Sean, Blair. BS, Mich. State U., 1964. Program mgr. Sta. WMBD-TV, Peoria, Ill., 1969-71; exec. producer Sta. WJZ-TV, Balt., 1971-73; program mgr. Sta. KFMB-TV, San Diego, 1973-75; program mgr., then dir. broadcasting ops. Sta. KHOU-TV, Houston, 1975-79; v.p., gen. mgr. KHOU-TV, 1979-84, Sta. WROC-TV, Rochester, N.Y., 1984-90; owner Santa Fe Wireless, Inc., Gainesville, Fla., 1990—99; dist. mgr. Trader Pub. Co., Phoenix, 1999—. Freelance TV cons., Houston, 1984. Home and Office: 1858 E Campbell Ave Gilbert AZ 85234-8228

KENNEY, WILLIAM FITZGERALD, lawyer; b. San Francisco, Nov. 4, 1935; s. Lionel Fitzgerald and Ethel Constance (Brennan) K.; m. Susan Elizabeth Langfitt, May 5, 1962; children: Anne, Carol, James. BA, U. Calif.-Berkeley, 1957, JD, 1960. Bar: Calif. 1961. Assoc. Miller, Osborne Miller & Bartlett, San Mateo, Calif., 1962-64; ptnr. Tormey, Kenney & Cotchett, San Mateo, 1965-67; pres. William F. Kenney, Inc., San Mateo, 1968—; gen. ptnr. All Am. Self Storage, 1985—, Second St. Self Storage, 1990-96, Cochrane Rd. Self Storage, 1996—, Marine Bus. Ctr., 1998—; pres. The Positive Edge, 2000—. Trustee San Mateo City Sch. Dist., 1971-79, pres., 1972-74; pres. March of Dimes, 1972-73; bd. dirs. Boys Club San Mateo, 1972-90, Samaritan House, 1989—, Lesley Found., 1992—. With U.S. Army, 1960-62. Mem. State Bar of Calif. (taxation com. 1973-76), San Mateo County Bar Assn. (bd. dirs. 1973-75), Calif. Assn. Realtors (legal affairs com. 1978—), San Mateo C. of C. (bd. dirs. 1987-93), Self Storage Assn. (we. region, pres. 1989-90, nat. bd. dirs. 1990-97, nat. v.p 1994-95, pres. 1996), Rotary (pres. 1978-79), Elks (exalted ruler 1974-75). Republican. Roman Catholic. Home: 221 Clark Dr San Mateo CA 94402-1004 Office: 120 N El Camino Real San Mateo CA 94401-2705 E-mail: bill1135@rcn.com.

KENNEY, WILLIAM JOHN, JR., real estate development executive; b. Huntington Park, Calif., Mar. 9, 1949; s. William John Sr. and Dorothy Marie (Smith) K.; m. Susan Louise Wattson, Sept. 26, 1987. BS in Econs., Calif. State U., Fullerton, 1970, BBA, 1971. Lic. real estate broker, Calif., Ariz.; cert. leasing specialist. Leasing agt. John S. Griffith, Irvine, Calif., 1972-78, dir. leasing, 1978-84; v.p. leasing John S. Griffith (now Donahue Schriber), Newport Beach, Calif., 1984-85, sr. v.p., 1986-91, sr. v.p. devel., 1991-95; founder The Kenney Co., 1995—. Speaker numerous orgns. Bd. dirs. Riverside YMCA, 1989-92. Recipient Certs. Appreciation Hemet C. of C., Riverside (Calif.) Bd. Realtors, Hemet Valley Kiwanis, Riverside Kiwanis. Mem. Calif. Bus. Properties Assn. (chmn. 1988-89, dir. 1976-96), Internat. Coun. Shopping Ctrs. (assoc., chair govt. affairs com. 1994-98), Newport Harbor Bd. Realtors (cert. appreciation), Frank Miller Club (life), Balboa Yacht Club (sec. 2003). Avocations: surfing, fishing, skiing. Office: The Kenney Co 824 Harbor Island Dr Newport Beach CA 92660-7228

KENNICUTT, ROBERT CHARLES, JR., astronomer; b. Balt., Sept. 4, 1951; s. Robert Charles and Joyce Ann K.; m. Norma Graceila Crosa Kennicutt, Feb. 17, 1976 (div. Jan. 18, 1996); 1 child, Laura. BS in Physics, Rensselaer Polytech. Inst., Troy, N.Y., 1973; MS in Astronomy, PhD in Astronomy, U. Wash., Seattle, 1978. Carnegie fellow Hale Observatories, Pasadena, Calif., 1978-80; asst. prof. astronomy U. Minn., Mpls., 1980-85, assoc. prof. astronomy, 1985-88; assoc. prof., astronomer U. Ariz., Tucson, 1988-92, prof., astronomer, 1992—; Beatrice Tinsley Centennial prof. U. Tex., Austin, 1994. V.p. AAS, Washington, 1998-01; com. on Astronomy and Astrophysics Nat. Rsch. Coun., Washington, 1998-2001; Space Telescope Sci. Inst. coun., AURA, Washington, 2000--; next generation space telescope interim sci. working group, NASA, Washington, 2000-01, adv. com., chmn. 1996-99; vis. com. chmn. NOAO Observatories, AURA, Washington, 1996-2000; vis. com. European Southern Observatory, Garching bei Munich, Germany, 1997-2003, Gemini Obs., AURA, 2003—. Author: Galaxies: Interactions and Induced Star Formation, 1998; editor-in-chief The Astrophys. Jour., 1999—. Named Alfred P. Aloan fellowship 1983-87, Beatrice M. Tinsley Centennial professorship, U. Tex. at Austin, 1994, Carnegie fellowship Carnegie Instn. Washington, 1978-80, Blaauw Prof. U. Groningen, 2001. Fellow Am. Acad. Arts & Scis.; mem. AAS (v.p. 1998-01), Internat. Astron. Union, Astron. Soc. pf the Pacific. Office: Steward Observatory U Arizona Tucson AZ 85721 Fax: 520-621-1532. E-mail: rkennicutt@as.arizona.edu.

KENNISH, ARTHUR, internist, cardiologist; b. N.Y.C., Feb. 28, 1950; s. Howard L. and Betty I. (Friedman) K.; m. Fran Ptazynska, Mar. 11, 1972; children: Brian, Lauren, Lisa. BS, Cooper U., 1971; MD, PhD, Albert Einstein Med. Ctr., 1977. Resident in internal medicine Mt. Sinai Hosp., 1977-80, fellow in cariology, 1980-82; attending physician Mt. Sinai Med. Ctr., N.Y.C., 1982—. Office: 108 E 96th St New York NY 10128-6217 E-mail: akennish@hotmail.com.

KENNON, ROZMOND HERRON, retired physical therapist; b. Birmingham, Ala., Dec. 12, 1935; m. Gloria Oliver; children: Shawn, Rozmond Jr. BA, Talldega Coll., 1956; cert., U. Colo., 1957. Asst. chief phys. therapist St. John's Hosp., St. Paul, 1957-58, Creigthon Meml. St. Joseph's Hosp., Omaha, 1958-61; asst. chief, phys. therapist Sister Kenny Inst., Mpls., 1962, chief phys. therapy, 1962-64; cons. in phys. therapy Mt. Sinai Hosp., Mpls., 1963-70; pvt. practice, 1964-98. Contbr. articles to profl. jours. Bd. dirs. Southdale YMCA, Edina Human Rights, Southside Med. Ctr., Mpls., Boy Scouts Am.; trustee Talladega (Ala.) Coll.; pres., CEO Daniel Kennon and Verna Herron Kennon Family Found.; pres. Talladega Bd. Trustees; exec. bd. dirs. Greater Ala. Coun. Boy Scouts Am. Mem. Am. Phys. Therapy Assn., Am. Registry Phys. Therapists, Ala. Phys. Therapy Assn. (mem. social-econ. com., past chmn. profl. practice com., bd. dirs., past sec.). Home: 5120 Lake Crest Cir Hoover AL 35226-5027

KENNY, BERNARD F. state legislator, lawyer; b. Jersey City, Nov. 17, 1946; m. Roberta Riccio, 1981; children: Alessandra, Bernard F. III, Francis. BA, U. Pa., 1968; JD, Fordham Law Sch., 1976. Of counsel Sarkisan & Florio, Hoboken, N.J.; mem. N.J. Gen. Assembly, Trenton, 1987-93, N.J. Senate, Trenton, 1993—. Mem. Supreme Ct. com. N.J. Gen. Assembly, 1985—, mem. dist. 6 ethics com., 1985—, mem. mcpl. govt. com., select com. on drug abuse, Supreme Ct. task force on drugs and the courts, 1990; mem. budget, revenue and fin. com. N.J. Senate; counselor Pvt. Industry Coun., Hudson County, N.J., 1983—. Counselor Am. Cancer Soc., 1984-87. Address: 235 Hudson St Ste 1 Hoboken NJ 07030-5829*

KENNY, CHARLES JAMES, economist, researcher; b. Oxford, United Kingdom, Oct. 12, 1970; s. Anthony and Nancy Kenny. BA in history, Cambridge U., 1991; MA in devel. studies, London U., 1992; MA in internat. econ., Johns Hopkins SAIS, 1993. Sr. economist The World Bank, Washington, 1995—. Contbr. articles to profl. jours. Office: The World Bank 1818 H St NW Washington DC 20433

KENNY, DAVID, internet professional services executive; BS, Gen. Motors Inst.; MBA, Harvard Bus. Sch. Ptnr. Bain & Co., 1996; vice-chmn. Bronner, Slosberg, Humphrey, Inc., 1996—97, ptnr., CEO, 1997—99; chmn., CEO Digitas, Boston, 1999—. Office: Digitas Prudential Tower 800 Boylston St Boston MA 02199-8001 E-mail: dkenny@digitas.com.

KENNY, GEORGE JAMES, lawyer; b. Jersey City, Feb. 18, 1935; s. George W. and Alice M. Kenny; m. Sandra B. Kenny, Oct. 10, 1959; children: Erin, Michael, Thomas, Patricia, Brendan, Mary, Timothy. BS in Econs., Seton Hall U., 1956; LLB, Rutgers U., 1959. Bar: N.J. 1961, U.S. Dist. Ct. N.J. 1961, U.S. Dist. Ct. (so. and ea. dists.) N.Y., 1991, U.S. Supreme Ct. 1966, N.Y. 1983, U.S. Ct. Appeals (3d cir.) 1987, U.S. Ct. Appeals (4th cir.) 1988; cert. Civil Trial Atty. N.J. Supreme Ct. 1982. Jud. clerkship to Hon. Theodore J. Labrecque N.J. Superior Ct., 1960-61; assoc. Connell & Foley, LLP, Roseland and Newark, 1961-68; ptnr. Connell, Foley & Geiser, 1968—. Adj. faculty Rutgers U. Sch. Law Mem. editl. bd. N.J. Law Jour., 1984—; author: New Jersey Insurance Law, 2d edit, 2001; contbr. articles to profl. jours. Trustee Essex County Coll. 1971-78 (chmn. 1973-74), Legal Svcs. Found. Essex County, 1989-2001. Fellow Am. Coll. of Trial Lawyers, Am. Bar Found.; mem. ABA (sec. of litigation, coun. mem. 1991-94, chmn. ins. coverage litigation com. 1988-91, fed. judiciary com. 1999-2002), N.J. State Bar Assn. (trustee 1968-69, 89-93), Essex County Bar Assn. (trustee, officer 1974-81, pres. 1981-82), Practicing Law Inst. N.J. Supreme Ct. coms.; Inst. Continuing Legal Edn., Adv. Am. Bd. Trial Advs., Internat. Assn. Def. Counsel. Democrat. Roman Catholic. Avocation: reading. Office: Connell Foley LLP 85 Livingston Ave Roseland NJ 07068-3702 E-mail: gkenny@connellfoley.com.

KENNY, H. SHARIE, music educator; b. Ft. Worth, Tex., Feb. 19, 1950; d. Newman and Ruth Woodson Van Tassel; m. Jack C. Kenny, Mar. 31, 1972; children: Allyson Kenny Kellner, Rosalyn Ruth. MusB, Tex. Christian U., 1972; RN, Meth. Hosp. Sch. of Nursing, Lubbock, TX, 1975. Cert. activity dir. Tarrant County Coll., Ft. Worth. Office and surg. nurse George Atkinson, MD, Dallas, 1975—78; piano instr. Arlington, Tex., 1978—; nurse and activity asst. Stonegate Nursing Ctr., Ft. Worth, 1998—2000; entertainer for nursing facilities Nursing Ctrs., Arlington and Ft. Worth, 2000—01; asst. activities dir. Arlington Villa Retirement & Nursing Ctr., 2001—03. Festival coord. Arlington Music Teachers Assn., 1986—88. Stephen min. St. Alban's Episcopal Ch., Arlington, 1991—93, acolyte, 1988—96. Mem.: Activity Dirs. Assn., Nat. Guild Piano Tchrs., Suzuki Assn. of the Ams., Nat. Music Tchrs. Assn. Avocations: reading, swimming, gardening, clogging, crafts.

KENNY, JANE MARIE, government agency administrator; b. Jersey City; m. Greg Myer; 3 children. B, Trinity Coll., Washington, 1974; M in English and Am. Lit., Rutgers U., 1982. Chief policy and planning Gov. Whitman, 1994—96; v.p. corp. cmty. affairs Beneficial Mgmt. Corp., Peapack, NJ, 1990—94; cabinet sec. Gov. Tom Kean, 1986—90; commr. NJ Dept. Cmty. Affairs, 1996—2001; regional adminstr. region 2 US EPA, 2001—. Recipient Nat. Pub. Svc. award, Women in Govt. award, Good Housekeeping. Fellow: Nat. Acad. Pub. Adminstrs. Office: US EPA Region 2 290 Broadway New York NY 10007-1866

KENNY, JOHN EDWARD, computer analyst; b. Buffalo, Oct. 28, 1945; s. Thomas Edmund and Dorothy Elizabeth (Krull) K. AAS, Erie C.C., 1972. Systems analyst Nat. Fuel Gas, Buffalo, 1969-70; programmer Svc. Systems Corp., Clarence, N.Y., 1974-77, Carborundum, Niagra Falls, N.Y., 1973-74; analyst, programmer A. Marine Midland Bank N.A., Buffalo, 1977-83; sr. analyst, programmer, project leader Empire of Am., FSA, Buffalo, 1983-85, applications project supr., 1985-89, asst. v.p. software devel., 1989-91; pres. Can.-Am. Bus. Svcs., 1991—, GPS Sys., 1995—; sr. analyst, programmer Cardinal Health Corp., Amherst, N.Y., 1995—. Data processing cons. First Union Nat. Bank NC, Elec. Data Sys. Plano, Tex., 1996—, Ernst & Young LLP-Med. Mutual of Ohio, 1997-2000; computer analyst Citicorp Student Loan Corp., Pittsford, N.Y., 1996-97; tchr. programming langs. Advanced Tng. Ctr., Buffalo; cons. M&T Bank Corp., Buffalo, 2000-01, Tyco Electronics, Harrisburg, Pa., 2001-02, Antares Mgmt. Solutions, Cleve., 2002—; instr. computer tech. Acad. Med. Arts and Bus., Harrisburg, 2001-02. Mem. Rep. Presdl. Task Force; mem. Town of Tonawanda Conservative Com., 1980-2002, chmn., 1993-96; state committeeman 29th U.S. Congl. Dist., 1996-1999; mem. Erie County Conservative Com., 1980-2002, mem. exec. bd., 1994-97; 911 asst. Erie County Ctrl. Police Svcs., 1995-1997. Mem. Am. Inst. Banking, Assn. Sys. Mgmt., Kenton C. of C., Greater Fort Erie C. of C. Can., US Golf Assn. (patron), Judges and Police Conf. Erie County (NY), Tonawanda Chmn. Men's Club, KC, Lions, Internat. Order Alhambra, World Future Soc. (profl.). Republican (nat. com.). Roman Catholic. Home and Office: 212 McKinley Ave Kenmore NY 14217-2438 E-mail: jktg2@aol.com.

KENNY, MARY ALICE, lawyer, law librarian; b. Evergreen Park, Ill., July 5, 1961; d. Ronald Stanley and Kathleen Regina (Fawcett) Adams; m. James Michael Kenny, Sept. 3, 1988; children: Daniel Patrick, Eileen Anne. BS, Ill. State U., 1984; JD, DePaul U., 1988; M of Libr. and Info. Sci., Rosary Coll., River Forest, Ill., 1997. Bar: Ill. 1988, U.S. Dist. Ct. (no. dist.) Ill. 1988, U.S. Cir. Ct. (7th cir.) Ill. 1988; cert. instr. h.s. grades 6-12, Ill. Br. law libr., dir. Cook County Law Libr., Bridgeview, Ill., 1989-97; paralegal educator Am. Inst. Paralegal Studies, Oakbrook Terrace, Ill., 1990-97; pvt. practice Oak Lawn, Ill., 1992—; adj. prof. law, ref. libr. Sch. Law Libr. Loyola U., Chgo., 1998—. Adv. bd. Am. Inst. Paralegal Studies, Oakbrook Terrace, 1994—96, Inst. Paralegal Studies Loyola U., Chgo. Contbg. author: Bar None: 125 Years of Women Lawyers in Illinois, (booklet) Union List of Holdings of the Branch Libraries of the Cook County Law Library, 1995, 96; contbr.: (book) Legal Research and Writing Exercises for Paralegals, 1992. Bd. dirs. Queen of Peace H.S. Alumnae Assn., Burbank, Ill., 1996—. Mem.: ABA, Chgo. Assn. Law Librs., Am. Assn. Law Librs. (Chgo. chpt.), Am. Assn. Law Schs. Democrat. Roman Catholic. Office: 16335 Harlem Ave Ste 400 Tinley Park IL 60477-2594 E-mail: mkenny@luc.edu.

KENNY, PHILIP WILLIAM, lawyer; b. Mt. Vernon, N.Y., Nov. 9, 1946; s. Paul James and Ethel Roma (Dooley) K.; m. Ellen Goldberg, Feb. 16, 1974 (div. Nov. 1980); m. Christine Madge Dockum, Nov. 29, 1980; children: Merideth, Jason, Matthew. BA, Fordham U., 1968; JD, N.Y. Law Sch., 1973. Bar: N.Y. 1974. Sole practice, Star Lake, N.Y., 1975-80; atty. Nationwide Ins. Co., Syracuse, N.Y., 1980-83; assoc. Meiselman, Farber, Poughkeepsie, N.Y., 1983-84, Grogan & Botti, P.C., Goshen, N.Y., 1984-86; atty. Office of Ct. Adminstrn., Poughkeepsie, NY, 1986—92; pvt. practice Poughkeepsie, 1992—. Served with U.S. Army, 1968-70. Roman Catholic. Home: 505 Stanton Ter Poughkeepsie NY 12603-1165 Office: Dutchess County Ct 99 Cannon Street Poughkeepsie NY 12601

KENNY, ROGER MICHAEL, executive search consultant, writer; b. N.Y.C., Oct. 3, 1938; s. Michael F. and Mary T. (Glynn) K.; m. Carole Ann Smith, Oct. 3, 1959; children: Glynn Scott, Lynn Marie. BBA, Manhattan Coll., 1959; MBA, N.Y. U., 1961. With Port Authority of N.Y. and N.J., 1959-67, mgr. bus. ops., 1965-67; assoc. Spencer Stuart & Assos., N.Y.C., 1967-70, v.p. West Coast ops., 1970-77; sr. v.p., ptnr. Spencer Stuart & Assocs., 1977-82, Boardroom Cons., N.Y.C., 1982—. Mng. dir. Boardroom Cons. Co-author: E-Board Strategies: How To Survive and Win, 2000; contbr. articles to profl. jours. Bd. overseers Conrad N. Hilton Coll. Hotel and Restaurant Mgmt. U. Houston. Mem.: Assn. Exec. Search Cons. (bd. dirs., Gardner Heidrick award 2001), Am. Soc. Public Adminstrs., Nat. Assn. Corp. and Profl. Recruiters, Westchester Country Club, Econ. Club, Sky Club, Imperial Russian Order of St. John of Jerusalem (Knights of Malta). Home: 33 Mount Holly Dr Rye NY 10580 1858 Office: Boardroom Cons 530 5th Ave New York NY 10036-5101 E-mail: rkenny@boardroomconsultants.com. *People who are willing to experiment seem to be the most successful, at least in terms of their achievements. A completely empirical approach to life is impossible. First of all, the necessary facts aren't always available and too frequently the wrong conclusions are derived from too much empiricism.*

KENNY, SHIRLEY STRUM, academic administrator; b. Tyler, Tex., Aug. 28, 1934; d. Marcus Leon and Florence (Golenternek) Strum; m. Robert Wayne Kenny, July 22, 1956; children: David Jack, Joel Strum, Daniel Clark, Jonathan Matthew, Sarah Elizabeth. BA, BJ, U. Tex., 1955; MA, U. Minn., 1957; PhD, U. Chgo., 1964; LHD (hon.), U. Rochester, 1988, Chonnam U., 1996, Donguk U., 2000. Chair English dept. U. Md., College Park, 1973-79, provost Arts and Humanities, 1979-85; pres. CUNY Queens Coll., Flushing, 1985-94, SUNY, Stony Brook, 1994—; chair Brookhaven Sci. Assocs. Mem. regional adv. bd. Chase Manhattan Corp. Author: The Conscious Lovers, 1968, The Plays of Richard Steele, 1971, The Performers and Their Plays, 1982, The Works of George Farquhar, 2 vols., 1988, British Theatre and the Other Arts, 1984; contbr. articles to profl. jours. Bd. dirs. Goodwill Greater N.Y., L.I. Assn. Named Outstanding Woman, U. Md., 1983, Outstanding Alumnus, U. Tex. Coll. Comm., 1989, Disting. Alumna, U. Tex., 1999; recipient Disting. Alumnus award, U. Chgo. Club Washington, 1980, Svc. and Leadership award, N.Y. Urban League, 1988. Mem.: Boyer Comm. Educating Undergrads, Assn. Am. Colls. and Univs. (bd. dirs. 1988—96). Office: SUNY 310 Adminstrn Bldg Stony Brook NY 11790-0701

KENOFER, DORIS DILLON See DILLON, DORIS

KENOFF, JAY STEWART, lawyer; b. L.A., Apr. 29, 1946; s. Charles Kapp and Martha (Minchenberg) K.; m. Pamela Fran Benyas, Sept. 1, 1979 (div. Dec. 1981); m. Luz Elena Chavira, June 9, 1991. AB, UCLA, 1967; MS, U. So. Calif., L.A., 1972; JD, Harvard U., 1970. Bar: Washington 1970, Calif. 1971, U.S. Ct. Appeals (9th cir.) 1974, U.S. Dist. Ct. (so., cen. dists. Calif.) 1974, U.S. Ct. Mil. Appeals 1974. Assoc. Wyman, Bautzer, Rothman & Kuchel, Beverly Hills, Calif., 1974-76, Epport & Delevie, Beverly Hills, 1977-78; ptnr. Bushkin, Gaims, Gaines & Jonas, L.A., 1978-86; prof. Sch. of Law Northrup U., Inglewood, Calif., 1981-85; ptnr. Kenoff & Machtinger LLP, L.A., 1986—. Judge pro tem L.A. Mcpl. Ct., 1985—; arbitrator, mediator Ctr. for Comml. Mediation, L.A., 1986—; mediator L.A. Superior Ct., 1987—, mem. settlement panel, 1987—. Author: Entertainment Industry Contracts, 1986; contbg. editor Entertainment Law & Finance. Commdr. USN Navy Judge Adv. Corps, USNR, 1968-91. Mem. Beverly Hills Bar Assn., Harvard-Radcliffe Club. Democrat. Jewish. Avocations: tennis, skiing, movies. Office: Kenoff & Machtinger LLP 1901 Ave of Stars Ste 1050 Los Angeles CA 90067-6022 E-mail: jskentlaw@earthlink.net.

KENOTE, MARIE HERSETH, music educator; b. Seattle, Oct. 2, 1956; d. John Andrew and Betty Jane Herseth; m. Peter D. Kenote, Dec. 26, 1981; children: Anne Kristine, Rebekah Rae, Ruth Ellen. MusB, New Eng. Conservatory Music, 1977; MusM, Juilliard Sch. Music, 1980; D of Musical Arts, Rutgers U., 2000. Instr. Music Luther Coll., Decorah, Iowa, 1981—83; asst. prof. Music Nyack Coll., NY, 2001—. Prin. flute Britt Music Festival, Medford, Oreg., 1979—98, Rochester Symphony Orch., Minn., 1981—83; substitute flutist N.Y. Philharm., N.Y.C., 1984—, N.J. Symphony, Newark, 1999—; instr. Music Drew U., Madison, NJ, 1998—; program annotator N.Y. Philharm. Chamber Music Series, 1998—2003. Performer (rec.): N.Y. Philharm., 1984—99, Rutgers U. Glee Club, 2000, Manhattan Chamber Orch., 2001. Mem., supporter Fulbright Alumni Assn., Washington, 1998—2003. Fellow, Tanglewood Festival, 1977; grantee, Fulbright Assn., 1977—78. Mem.: Nat. Alliance for Excellence (mem. adv. bd. 1996—), Am. Bach Soc., Nat. Flute Assn., Fulbright Alumni Assn. Republican. Avocations: golf, reading, hiking, skiing, tennis. Office: Nyack College 1 South Blvd Nyack NY 10960*

KENRICH, JOHN LEWIS, retired lawyer; b. Lima, Ohio, Oct. 17, 1929; s. Clarence E. and Rowena (Stroh) Katterheinrich; m. Betty Jane Roehll, May 26, 1951; children: John David, Mary Jane, Kathryn Ann, Thomas Roehll, Walter Clarence. BS, Miami U., Oxford, Ohio, 1951; LLB, U. Cin., 1953. Bar: Ohio 1953, Mass. 1969. Asst. counsel B.F. Goodrich Co., Akron, Ohio, 1956-65; asst. sec., counsel W.R. Grace & Co., Cin., 1965-68, v.p. Splty. Products Group divsn., 1970-71; corp. counsel, sec. Standex Internat. Corp., Andover, Mass., 1969-70; v.p., sec. Chemed Corp., Cin., 1971-82, sr. v.p., gen. counsel, 1982-86, exec. v.p., chief adminstrv. officer, 1986-91, ret., 1991. Trustee Better Bus. Bur., Cin., 1981-90; mem. bus. adv. coun. Miami U., 1986-88; mem. City Planning Commn., Akron, 1961-62; mem. bd. visitors Coll. Law U. Cin., 1988-92; mem. area coun. trustees Franciscan Sisters of Poor Found., Cin., 1989-93; bd. govs. Ohio River Valley chpt. Arthritis Found., 1992-95, 2000—; mem. Com. on Reinvestment City of Cin., 1991-93. 1st lt. JAGC U.S. Army, 1954-56. Mem. Cin. Bar Assn., Beta Theta Pi, Omicron Delta Kappa, Delta Sigma Pi, Phi Eta Sigma. Republican. Presbyterian. Home and Office: 1350 Indian Mound Trail Vero Beach FL E-mail: JKenrich@msn.com.

KENRICK, CHARLES WILLIAM, lawyer; b. Chgo., June 16, 1946; s. Ralph Schwarting and Angela Augusta (Shostrom) K.; m. Patricia June Ogilvie, Dec. 27, 1969; children: Hugh, Alex, Graham, Charlotte, Blair. AB cum laude, Kenyon Coll., 1968; JD, Duquesne U., 1972. Bar: Pa. 1972, U.S. Dist. Ct. (we. dist.) Pa. 1972, U.S. Ct. Appeals (3rd cir.) 1977, U.S. Supreme Ct. 1984, U.S. Ct. Appeals (6th, 7th and 10th cirs.), 1988. From assoc. to ptnr. Dickie, McCamey & Chilcote, Pitts., 1972—98, mng. ptnr., 1993-97; ptnr. Gorr Moser Dell & Loughney, Pitts., 1999-2000, Grogan & Graffam, Pitts., 2000—. Articles editor Duquesne U. Law Rev., 1971; editor Pitts. Legal Jour., 1980-84. Fellow: ABA, Allegheny Bar Found. (ho. of dels. 1980—2000), Pa. Bar Found.; mem.: Pa. Bar Assn., Allegheny County Bar Assn. (bd. govs. 1984—, adminstrv. v.p. 1986—, pres.-elect 1990, pres. 1991), Duquesne U. Law Alumni Assn. (pres. 1985—86), Kenyon Coll. Alumni Assn. Pitts. (pres. 1983—84), Duquesne Club, Valley Brook Club, Rivers Club. Democrat. Office: Grogan & Graffam 4 Gateway Ctr 12th Fl Pittsburgh PA 15222-1000

KENT, AIMEE BERNICE PETERSEN, interior designer, artist, landscape designer; b. North Vancouver, B.C., Can., Apr. 13, 1939; d. Samuel Nathaniel and Aimee Selena (Topping) Hadley; m. Gary Andrew Petersen, May 1, 1959; children: Todd William, Troy Andrew; m. Michael Douglas Kent, Aug. 1, 1998. Student, U. Wash., 1957—59, Edmonds (Wash.) C.C., 1967—74. Owner, designer The Designing Woman, Edmonds, 1979—. Pres. Ballinger Elem. PTA, 1969-71, Madrona Jr. H.S., 1973, 74; deaconess United Presbyn. Ch., Edmonds, 1967-75. Recipient Golden Acorn award Ballinger Sch. PTA, 1972; named Woman of Yr., Jr. Women Federated Women's, 1967. Mem. Nat. Fedn. Ind. Bus. People, Better Bus. Bur., Bus. and Profl. Women, Women Investing Now (founder 1991, pres. 1997-2000), Edmonds C. of C., Sons of Norway (Lodge 130 social chmn. 1987-93). Presbyterian. Avocation: artist. Home: 23807 113th Pl W Woodway WA 98020-5204 Office: 23807 113th Pl W Woodway WA 98020-5204

KENT, ALLEN, library and information sciences educator; b. N.Y.C., Oct. 24, 1921; s. Samuel and Anna (Begun) K.; m. Rosalind Kossoff, Jan. 24, 1943; children: Merryl Frances Kent Samuels, Emily Beth Kent Yeager, Jacqueline Diane Kent Maryak, Carolyn May Kent Hall. BS in Chemistry, CCNY, 1942. Sci. editor Intersci. Pubs., 1946-51; research assoc. Ctr. Internat. Studies, MIT, 1951-53; prin. documentation engr. Battelle Meml. Inst., Columbus, Ohio 1953-55; asso. dir. Ctr. for Documentation and Communication Research; prof. library sci. Western Res. U., Cleve., 1955-63; dir. office communications programs, chmn. interdisciplinary doctoral program info. sci., prof. info. sci., edn. and computer sci. U. Pitts., 1963-76; Univ. Disting. Service prof. library and info. sci. and assoc. dean U. Pitts. Sch. Library and Info. Sci., 1976-91, interim dean, 1985-86, prof. emeritus, 1992. Mem. mgmt. info. com. Health and Welfare Assn. Allegheny County, Pa., 1972-80; dir. Marcel Dekker, Inc., N.Y., 1978-93. Author (with others): Machine Literature Searching, 1956; author: (with J.W. Perry) Documentation and Information Retrieval, 1957; author: Tools for Machine Literature Searching, 1958, Centralized Information Services, 1958, Mechanized Information Retrieval, 1962, 2d edit., 1966, also fgn. transls. Specialized Information Centers, 1965, Information Analysis and Retrieval, 1971, Resource Sharing in Libraries, 1977, On-Line Revolution in Libraries, 1978, Structure and Governance of Library Networks, 1979, Use of Library Materials, 1979, Information Technology, 1982; editor, co-editor numerous books in field, exec. editor Ency. Libr. and Info. Sci., 1968—2003, Ency. Computer Sci. and Tech., 1972—2002, Ency. Microcomputers, 1984—2001, Ency. of Telecomm., 1988—98. Chmn. bd. Interuniv. Comms. Coun. Inc., 1971-74. Served with USAAF, 1942-46. Recipient Info. Tech. Merit award Eastman Kodak Co., 1968 Fellow AAAS; mem. ALA, Assn. Computing Machinery, Am. Soc. Info. Sci. (award of merit 1977, award for Best Info. Sci. Book of Yr. 1980, Pioneer in Info. Sci. 1987), Acad. Sr. Profls. Eckerd Coll. Home: 5108 Brittany Dr S Apt 601 Saint Petersburg FL 33715-1525 *My goal has been to be useful. This entails service, dedication to my profession and to the institution which supports my work, and absolute standards of honesty.*

KENT, BARTIS MILTON, retired physician; b. Terrell, Tex., June 23, 1925; s. Bartis William and Annie (Smalley) K.; m. Ann L. Kiel, July 6, 1954; children: Susan Ruth, Martha Lucille, Bartis Michael. Student, So. Meth. U., 1942-44; MD, Baylor U., 1948. Diplomate Am. Bd. Internal Medicine. Intern Jefferson Davis Hosp., Houston, 1948-49; resident pathology Mass. Meml. Hosps., Boston, 1951; resident in internal medicine Baylor U., 1953-56; indsl. physician Humble Oil Co., Houston, 1949-51; instr. dept. medicine U. Iowa, 1956-58; staff physician Iowa City VA Hosp., 1956-58; practice medicine specializing in internal medicine Muskogee, Okla., 1958—2002. Cons. Muskogee VA Hosp.; clin. asst. prof. medicine U. Okla. Sch. Medicine, 1975—. Chmn. Muskogee County chpt. Am. Nat. Red Cross, 1963-65. Served with USAF, 1951-53. Decorated Air medal. Fellow A.C.P.; mem. Indsl. Med. Assn., Soc. Nuclear Medicine, Am. Fedn. Clin. Research, Am. Heart Assn., Aerospace Medicine Assn., Am., Okla. socs. internal medicine, Muskogee C. of C. Methodist. Mason (Shriner). Home: 800 N 45th St Muskogee OK 74401-1505

KENT, BRUCE JONATHAN, pharmaceutical executive; b. Johnstown, Pa., Sept. 25, 1962; s. Reg and Barbara Lee (Petz) K.; m. Nan Ellen Chapple Kent, Sept. 3, 1988; children: Alexandra Nika-Chapple, Connor Stewart-Chapple, Grace Corina-Chapple. BS in Fin., Pa. State U., 1985. Mktg. rep. Mobil Oil Corp., Phila., 1986-87; med. sales rep. Abbott Labs., Johnstown, 1987-88; med. rep. Ciba Pharms., Johnstown, 1988-90, dist. bus. mgr. Balt., 1990-95, head managed healthcare ops. Summit, N.J., 1995-97; dir. corp. account ops. Novartis Pharms., East Hanover, 1997-99, exec. dir., field analysis and incentives, 1999-2000, exec. dir. e-sales, 2000—. Republican. Baptist. Avocations: football, golf, family activities, coaching basketball. Home: 1115 Croton Rd Flemington NJ 08822-5608 Office: Novartis Pharms 59 Rt 10 East Hanover NJ 07936 E-mail: bruce.kent@pharma.novartis.com., kcatfam@patmedia.net.

KENT, CALVIN ALBERT, university administrator; b. Kansas City, Kans., Sept. 8, 1941; m. Nita Sue Davis, Aug. 23, 1963; children: Nita Christine, Anna Elaine. BA, Baylor U., 1963; MA, U. Mo., 1965, PhD, 1967; postgrad., U. Va., 1967, Wichita State U., 1972, U. Chgo., 1975, Rice U., 1987. Instr. econs. U. Mo., Columbia, 1963-64; instr. social scis. Stevens Coll., Columbia, 1964-67; faculty U. S.D., Vermillion, 1967-78, prof. econs., 1973-78, dir. public fin. studies, 1971-78; Herman W. Lay prof. pvt. enterprise, dir. Center Pvt. Enterprise Baylor U., Waco, Tex., 1978-90; adminstr. Energy Info. Adminstrn., Washington, 1990-93; dean, Lewis Disting. chair bus. Coll. Bus. Marshall U., Huntington, W. Va., 1993—. Exec. dir. S.D. Council on Econ. Edn., 1969-78; chief economist taxation coms. S.D. Legislature; cons. S.D. Dept. Rev. Alderman, Vermillion, 1969-78; mem. Pres.'s Adv. Com. Entrepreneurship Edn., 1983-85. Author: Indian Poverty, 1969, Taxation of Cooperative Enterprise, 1970, Death Taxes in the American States, 1974, Municipal Regulation and Franchising, 1975, Encyclopedia of Entrepreneurship, 1981, The Environment for Entrepreneurship, 1984, Entrepreneurship and the Privatization of Government, 1987, The Texas Economy, 1989, Entrepreneurship Education: Present Practices Future Direction, 1990, The Public Utilities Holding Company Act: 1935-92, 1993, Agenda for Fair Taxation, 1998; contbr. articles to profl. jours. Pres. City Coun., Vermillion, 1974-78; vice chmn. S.D. Mcpl. League, Dist. 2, 1972-74; councilman City of Huntington, W.Va., 1997—, City of Woodway, Tex., 1985-90, mayor, 1986-90; co-chair Gov.'s Commn. on Tax Fairness, 1997-2000; mem. Tri-State Airport Authority, v.p., 2001—. Outstanding Tchr., U. S.D., 1970-72, Outstanding Prof., Baylor U., 1983; Outstanding Young Religious Leader, 1976, Disting. Prof. Baylor Sch. Bus., 1981, Piper Prof. Piper Found., 1988; recipient Freedoms Found. at Valley Forge award for excellence in pvt. enterprise edn., 1980, Sargent Americanism award, 1986, John Schramm Leadership award Nat. Assn. Econ. Edn. and Joint Coun. on Econ. Edn., NSF award, 1974, Gov.'s citation for disting. achievement, 1996. Mem. Nat. Assn. Econ. Educators (pres. 1978-80), Assn. Pvt. Enterprise Edn. (sec.-treas. 1982-90, Disting. Svc. award 1988, Outstanding Scholar award 1992, bd. dirs. 1994), Soc. Econ. Educators (sec.-treas. 1987-90, v.p. 1993, pres. 1994), Rotary (pres. 1999-2000, Paul Harris fellow), Masons. Republican. Presbyterian. Home: 133 Woodland Dr Huntington WV 25705-1349

KENT, CHARLES IMBRIE, III, artist, former university official; BS, West Chester (Pa.) U., 1936; MS, Case Western U., 1940; postgrad., Pa. State U., 1946. Dir. of guidance Hershey (Pa.) Pub. Sch. Dist., 1940-46; pers. dir. Hershey Chocolate Corp., 1946-52; dean of students Franklin and Marshall Coll., 1953-55; dir. student pers. and guidance Millersville U., 1955-68, organizer, 1st dir. Master's Program Guidance and Counseling, 1962-77, assoc. v.p. acad. affairs, 1965-77; portrait and landscape artist, 1958—. Mem. Pa. State Com. for Certification for Guidance Dirs., Counselors, and Tchrs., 1960-65. Pres. Lancaster (Pa.) Hearing Conservation Ctr., 1959-70, 76-84; pres. YMCA, Lancaster, 1977-81, bd. dirs., 1960-83, 94—, chmn. pers. com. bd. dirs., 1994—; founder Lancaster YMCA Found., 1979—; chmn. state com. YMCA Profl. Recruitment, 1960-70. With USN, WW2, 1943-46, Korea, 51-52. Recipient Disting. Alumnus award West Chester U., 1984, Michael Engel award Lancaster County Art Assn., 1990. Mem. Lancaster County Art Assn. (Hershey, Pa., life, pres. 1980-84), Hershey, PA, Am. Legion (svc. officer Post 384 1946-55), Masons (worshipful master Lodge 666, master of lodge 1955-56, builder and temple master Hershey 1956, 50 yr. pin 1996), Hamilton Club. Republican. Avocations: portrait art, handball, golf, gardening, orchid growing. Home: PO Box 3227 Village Homestead Lancaster PA 17604-3227

KENT, CHRISTOPHER R. communications executive; b. Flint, Mich., Sept. 26, 1971; BA, Kalamazoo Coll., 1993; MALD, Tufts U. Fletcher Sch.of Law and Diplomacy, 1996. Tech. specialist internet mktg. MCI, Arlington, VA, 1996-97, mgr. wireless mktg. and pricing Washington, 1997-2000; sr. project mgr. Tech. Prodigy Comms., SBC, Austin, Tex., 2000—02.

KENT, DAVID CHARLES, lawyer; b. Shreveport, La., July 23, 1953; s. Keith C. and Louise (Goode) K.; m. Carol Elizabeth Hittson, July 3, 1976; children: John, Meredith, Robert. BA, Baylor U., 1975, JD, 1978. Bar: Tex. 1978, U.S. Dist. Ct. (no. dist.) Tex. 1980, U.S. Ct. Appeals (5th cir.) 1980, U.S. Dist. Ct. (so. and we. dists.) Tex. 1981, U.S. Ct. Appeals (11th cir.) 1981, U.S. Dist. Ct. (ea. dist.) Tex. 1981; bd. cert. civil trial law, personal injury trial law. Briefing atty. Supreme Ct. Tex., Austin, 1978-79; ptnr. Hughes & Luce L.L.P., Dallas, 1979-2000, Diamond McCarthy Taylor Finley Bryant & Lee, LLP, 2000—. Bd. dirs. Law Focused Edn., Inc., 1997-2003. Editor: Managing Scarce World Resources, 1975, Crime and Justice in America, 1976, Medical Care and Health in America, 1977, Meeting America's Energy Needs, 1978; contbr. articles to profl. jours. Coord. employee campaign United Way Dallas, 1981-90, teamwalk March of Dimes, Dallas, 1981-87; nat. exploring com. Boy Scouts Am., Irving, Tex., 1982-92; mem. HOBY Tex. North, bd. dirs., 1999-2003, sec., 2000-03; mem. Baylor Parents League, pres. North Dallas Area chpt., 1999-2001; pres. Twin Bridge Homeowners Assn., 2000-02; bd. dirs. High Adventure Treks for Dads & Daus., Inc. Named Outstanding Young Lawyer Dallas, Dallas Assn. Young Lawyers, 1989; recipient Cert. Recognition United Way, 1983. Fellow: Tex. Bar Found., Dallas Bar Found.; mem.: ATLA, ABA, Coll. of State Bar of Tex., Dallas Bar Assn. (chair Tex. h.s. mock trial program 1994—99, chair Law Day com. 2000—01, chair Speakers Com. 2002, Outstanding Com. Chair award 1998), Baylor U. Alumni Assn. (scholarship com. 1980—81). Republican. Methodist. Office: Diamond McCarthy Taylor Finley Bryant Lee 1201 Elm St 34th Flr Dallas TX 75270 E-mail: dkent@diamondmccarthy.com.

KENT, DEBORAH WARREN, hypnotherapist, consultant, lecturer; b. N.Y.C., May 6, 1947; d. Fred Warren and Margo (Lefebre) North. BS in Spl. Edn., U. Cin., 1969; MS in Counseling, CUNY, Hunter Coll., 1973; cert. master level hypnotherapist, Am. Hypnosis Tng. Acad., Silver Spring, Md., 1987; MSW, Columbia U., 1997. Cert. clin. mental health counselor, social worker; nat. cert. counselor; nat. cert. clin. hypnotherapist. Remediation specialist, counselor, psychometrist N.Y.C. Bd. Edn., 1973-79; cons. on assessment and remediation, N.Y.C., 1979-81; prodn. mgr. The Singing Experience, N.Y.C., 1981-83; hypnotherapist Inst. for Hypnotherapy, N.Y.C., 1983-85; pvt. practice hypnotherapy and counseling, N.Y.C., 1985—. Conducted workshops and seminars in clin. hypnosis, comm. skills and tng., stress mgmt.; lectr. to bus. and univs.; vocat. specialist Alternatives for Growth, N.J.; cons. vocat. case mgmt. assessment Ams. with Disabilities Act, 1994-96; social work cons. personal svc. unit Nat. Maritime Union, N.Y.C., chem. dependency coord., 1997-99, clin. svcs. utilization rev. coord., USCG liaison. Author, columnist Ofcl. Map and Guide mag., 1990-91. Action writer Nat. Abortion Rights Action League, Washington, 1987—; co-developer Counselors Legis. Action Support System, 1989; v.p. Joint Coun. for Mental health Svcs., 1989-97. Recipient Profl. Svc. award Am. Mental Health Counselors Assn., 1992. Fellow Am. Acad. Pain Mgmt., Am. Assn. Profl. Hypnotherapists (cert.); mem. ACA, ASCD (N.Y.C. br.), NASW (N.Y.C. chpt., chem. dependency com.), Nat. Certified Counselors, Am. Mental Health Counselors Assn., Nat. Bd. Cert. Clin. Hypnotherapists (diplomate, examining bd., chairperson ethics com. 1993-97), Acad. Clin. Mental Health Counselors, Cert. Clin. Mental Health Counselors (approved clin. supr.), Nat. Soc. Neurolinguistic Programming (cert.), Am. Assn. for Assessment in Counseling (bd. dirs.), Am. Acad. Experts in Traumatic Stress (diplomate), N.Y. Mental Health Counselors Assn. (legis. rep. 1989-95, v.p. 1989-91), N.Y. Counselors Assn. (Legis. Svc. award 1991). Avocations: acting, singing, performing. Home and Office: 245 E 19th St #18K New York NY 10003 E-mail: dk4hypnos@aol.com.

KENT, DENISE ANN, nurse, educator, nursing administrator; b. San Francisco, Mar. 28, 1959; d. Herbert James and Joan Frances (Galvin) K. BSN, U. San Francisco, 1981, MPA/HSA, 1985; DPA, U. So. Calif., 1997. RN, Calif.; cert. case mgr.; cert. in healthcare quality; cert. pub. health nurse, Calif. Staff nurse St. Luke's Hosp., San Francisco, 1981-85; nurse, dir. Seton Coastside, Moss Beach, Calif., 1985-94; nurse, case mgr. RSK Co. CNA Ins., San Bruno, Calif., 1995—, v.p. cost mgmt., 1997-2000; prof. U. Phoenix, 1995—; dir. case mgmt. EK Health Svcs., San Jose, Calif., 2000—01; dir. quality assurance and edn. Thap!, Emeryville, Calif., 2001—02, Med. Mgmt. DHP Group, Mill Valley, Calif., 2002—. Bd. regents Sacred Heart Cathedral Prep. Sch., 1994—. Mem. Soroptimist Internat. of San Francisco (bd. dirs. 1998—), Bethany Sr. Housing. E-mail: drdeniseann@aol.com.

KENT, EDGAR ROBERT, JR., investment banker; b. Balt., May 28, 1941; s. E. Robert and Marian (Mueller) K.; children: E. Robert, Josephine Townsend, Louise Daniel. BS, Princeton U., 1963; MBA, Columbia U., 1966; JD, U. Md., 1975. CFA. Mng. dir. DeutscheBancAlex.Brown, Balt., 1968-2001; dir. Alex-.Brown Realty, Balt., 2001—. Trustee Calvert Sch., Balt., Ctr. Stage, Balt., Endowment Fund of U. Md., Balt. Cmty. Found. Home: 103 Castlewood Rd Baltimore MD 21210-1360 Office: Alex Brown Realty 225 Redwood St Baltimore MD 21202-3298

KENT, E(VERETT) ALLEN, performing arts administrator, theatrical producer; b. Ronan, Mont., Oct. 16, 1938; s. George Douglas Kent and Fern Louise Hickman-Reed; m. Janice Gay Gustafson-Kent, June 2, 1962 (dec. June 1962); 1 child, Kyla Kolleen; m. Gloria Madeline Sontag-Kent, Mar. 21, 1969 (div. Apr. 6, 1990); 1 child, Patrick. BA, U. Wash., 1965, MA, 1967; PhD (abd), Wayne State U., 1974. Actor Aqua Theater, 1958, Bellevue Playbarn, 1959; actor-technician Erie Playhouse, 1960; floor mgr. KING-TV, 1965; prodn. stage mgr. sch. drama U. Wash., 1965-66; stage mgr. A Contemporary Theater, 1966; tech. dir., lighting designer Pitts. Playhouse, 1966-67; tech. dir. Lorretto Hilton Rep. Co., 1967, St. Louis Mcpl. Opera; dir., designer, tech. dir., instr. Florissant Valley C.C., St. Louis, 1967-69; tech. dir. Mo. Repertory Theatre, Kansas City, 1969-70; dir., designer Eastern Wash. U., Cheney, 1969-73; arts and crafts specialist Dept. Commerce State of Alaska, 1974—75; dir. Performing Arts Ctr. U. Alaska, Anchorage, 1975-80, assoc. prof., chair dept. theater and dance, 1975-80; CEO Alaska Theatrical Svcs., Inc., Eagle River, 1974-87, KAE Enterprises, Ltd., Eagle River, 1987-90, Kent Artist Svcs., N.Y.C., 1990-96; mng. dir. Denishawn Repertory Dance Co., N.Y., N.J., 1991-93; exec. dir. Jennifer Muller/The Works Dance Co., 1990-91, Williams Ctr. for Arts, Rutherford, N.J., 1992-93; producing artistic dir. Music Theatre North, Potsdam, N.Y., 1993-94; gen. mgr. Garth Fagan Dance, Rochester, N.Y., 1995-96; mng. dir. Ballet: The Daring Project, 1996-97; CEO Am. Theatrical Svcs., 1996—; dir. devel. Repertorio Espanol, 1992. CEO Am. Classic Theater, 1999—; artistic dir. Spokane Civic Theater, 1971, Sky Hook Prodn. Co., 1999—; exec. dir. Magic Cir. Ctr. for the Arts, 2000; founder dept. theatre U. Alaska, Anchorage, 1976; lighting designer Alaska Repertory Theatre, Anchorage, 1977; lobbyist Anchorage Faculty Assn. U. Alaska, 1978—80; arts cons. Actors Studio, Town Hall, N.Y.C., 1991; dance panelist N.J. State Coun. on Arts, 1991—93; exec. dir. Greater Palmer C. of C., Palmer, Alaska, 2002—. With U.S. Army, 1961—67. Recipient Artist award Alaska State Coun. Arts, 1980. Mem. Soc. Stage Dirs. and Choreographers, Actors' Equity Assn. Roman Catholic. Avocations: hunting, fishing. Address: 305 N Valley Way #D4 Palmer AK 99645 E-mail: ev@palmerchamber.org.

KENT, GARY WARNER, film director, writer; b. Walla Walla, Wash., June 7, 1933; s. Arthur Everett and Iola Pearl (Nixdorff) K.; m. Joyce Peacock, 1954; children: Greg, Colleen, Andy; m. Rosemary Gallegly, 1960; children: Chris, Alex, Mike; m. Shirley Willeford, July 3, 1977. Student, U. Wash., 1951-52, San Diego State U., 1952-53, Del Mar Coll., 1956. Broadcaster Sta. KSIX, Corpus Christi, Tex., 1955, Sta. KTHT, Houston, 1956; actor Alley and Playhouse Theatres, Houston, 1956-59; actor motion pictures, 1959-73; gen. ptnr. PMK Prodns., Dallas, 1973-80, Signature Prodns., Austin, Tex., 1982-85; v.p. Power Dance Corp., Austin, L.A., Tex., 1985—. Produced stunts and spl. effects (film) Targets, Paramount, Phantom of the Paradise, 20th Century Fox, Hell's Angels on Wheels, Fanfare, Psychout, Am. Internat., Satan's Sadists, Dracula vs. Frankenstein, Lost, Independent Internat., Man Called Dagger, MGM, The Forest, Wide World Entertainment, Return of County Yorga, Vampire, Killers Three, Savage Seven, Dick Clark Prodns., The Shootings, Ride the Whirlwind, New Pacific Films, Flight of Black Angel, 1991 Warbirds, 1991, Lethal Pursuit, Guns of Dragon, Colof of Night, 1994; (TV) Daniel Boone, 20th Century TV, Man From U.N.C.L.E., MGM, New Adam Twelve, Warner Bros.; stunt cons. Mon Frere Prodns., 1995; stunt coord. Bubba-Hotep, 2002. Writer, dir.: Rainy Day Friends, 1987, The Pyramid, 1987; (movie) L.A. Bad, 1990; author: Where's Bassett's Body?, 1992, Streetcorner Justus, 1994, Streetcorner II The Frontier, 1997, Orphan Train, 1997, Groom Lake, 2001, Legend of fu John, 2001, The Fabulous Blues, 2003, The Texas Writer's Project, 2003. Active Spl. Olympics, Austin, 1990. With USN, 1953-55. Recipient Best Spl. Stunt award in motion pictures Stuntman awards, Hollywood, Calif., 1987, 1st place Lone Star Screenplay Competition, Dallas, 1997. Mem. SAG, AFTRA, Amnesty Internat., Greenpeace, Austin Film Soc., The Hope Found., Austin Writer's League, Ind. Feature Project West. Democrat.

KENT, HARRY ROSS, construction executive, lay worker; b. Upland, Pa., Oct. 17, 1921; s. Bernard Cleveland and Edith Mary (Johnson) K.; m. Aurelia Naomi Canady, Jan. 15, 1945; children: Jennifer Gayle, Edith Marie. BS in Physics and Chemistry, Coll. William and Mary. Instr. physics Citadel, 1947-51; with Canady Constrn. Co., 1951-78, sec.-treas., 1960-74, pres., 1974-78; v.p. K.C. Stier & Co., Inc., 1974-78; v.p., sec. Stier, Kent and Canady, Inc., 1978—. Mem. exec. coun. World Meth. Coun., 1991-96. Mem. commn. on stewardship and fin., Asbury Meml. Meth. Ch., Charleston, 1949-2000, treas. 1951-58, 68-99, lay mem. ann. conf. 1955 70, 80—, trustee, 1963-74, chmn. long-range planning com., 1957-70, former tchr. ch. sch.; mem. bd. bldg. and ch. location Charleston Dist. United Meth. Ch., 1950 01, pres. bd. missions and ch. extension, 1958—, dist. trustees, 1960-2001, chmn. bd. dist. trustees, 1984-2001, chmn. bd. missions, 1975—, chmn. dist. com. on devel., 2002—; mem. bd. lay activities S.C. ann. conf. United Meth. Ch., 1957-96, mem. coordinating coun., 1960-68, vice-chmn. continuing com. on merger, conf. lay leader, 1970-80, chmn. equitable salary commn., 1984-88, mem. coun. on fin. and adminstrn., 1988-96, vice chair 1992-95, chair 1995-96, del. Southea. jurisdiction conf., 1960, 64, 72, 76, 80, 84, 88, 92, 96, 2000, gen. conf. 1966, 68, 70, 72, 76, 80, 84, 88, 92, gen. coun. on ministries, 1980-88, chmn. Africa sect. of advance com., mem. gen. bd. discipleship, 1988-96; conf. pres. United Meth. Men, 1984-92; mem. exec. bd. Coastal Carolina coun. Boy Scouts Am., 1960-, chmn. Charleston dist. bd., 1967; various exec. positions St. Andrew's schs. PTA, 1963-68; bd. dirs. Piedmont Nursing Ctr., 1967-82, treas. 1970-82; vice chmn. civil engring. adv. bd. Trident Tech. Coll., Charleston, 1969-71, chmn. 1971-80; pres. Charleston Boys Coun., 1982-86, 91-94, v.p. 1987-91; mem. S.C. State Licensing Bd. for Contractors, 1980-2000, vice chair 1989-91, chair 1992-2000. Lt. cmmdr. USNR, WWII. Recipient God and Country award, Scouters award, Scoutmasters Key 65 Yr. Vet. award, Silver Beaver award Boy Scouts Am., God and Svc. award United Meth. Ch./Boy Scouts Am. Mem. ASTM, Associated Gen. Contractors, Am. Phys. Soc., Am. Assn. Physics, Tchrs., Charleston Trident C. of C. Home: PO Box 9005 Orangeburg SC 29116-9005

KENT, JEANNE YVONNE, artist, poet; b. Lawrence, Mass., Feb. 6, 1947; d. Gerard George and Cecile Fecteau Galarneau; m. Martin Joseph Kent, Dec. 4, 1971; children: Nicole Michelle, Sarah. Student, Lowell State Tchr.'s Coll., 1966-68, Northea. U., 1970-73; BFA, Mass. Coll. Art, 1989; BA in English, U. Mass., 2003. Resident asst., slide lectr. Elderhostel Mass. Coll. Art, Boston, 1988; slide lectr. Weymouth North H.S., East Weymouth, Mass., 1990, 93; instr. art Lee Wards Arts and Crafts Store, Quincy, Mass., 1990, Roslindale Comm. Ctr., Roslindale, Mass., 1996. One-woman shows include Rubin O'Barry's Coffee Shop, Jamaica Plain, Mass., 1989, Brookline Pub. Libr., 1995, Brookline Art Soc., West Roxbury (Mass.) Pub. Libr., 1995, Boston Pub. Libr. Jamaica Plain Branch, 1998, Jamo's Restaurant, Roslindale, Mass, 1998, exhibited in group shows at Mass. Coll. Art, Boston, 1988—89, 1995, Arts in the Pks., Boston, 1989, Brookline (Mass.) Art Soc., 1989—97, Boston Visual Artist's Union, 1990, Arnold Arboretum of Harvard U., Jamaica Plain, 1992, West Roxbury Pub. Libr., 1996, Picture This Gallery, West Roxbury, 1996, West Roxbury Pub. Libr., 1996—97, Greater Rosindale Art Assn., 1997, Boston City Hall, 1997, State House, Boston, Jamaica Plain Art Assn., 1998, Lowell St. Gallery, Cambridge Art Assn., 1998, Eliot Sch. Fine and Applied Arts, Jamaica Plain, 1998; author: (poems) Watermark, 2003, Hypergraphia, 2003, Concrete Wolf, 2003; contbr. poems to various publs. Recipient Intergenerational Poetry hon. mention award, West Roxbury Pub. Libr., 1989, 4th Pl. painting award, Dedham (Mass.) Arts and Crafts Fair, 1990, Calendar Illustration painting award, 1st ann. Dedham Cmty. Art Competition, Dedham Cmty. Ho. Gallery, 1993, Juror's Choice award, Cambridge Art Assn. image and verse show, 1998, Harold Taylor prize, Acad. Am. poets, 2001, John Holmes prize, New Eng. Poetry Club, 2002. Mem. Cambridge Art Assn., Greater Roslindale Arts Assn. Jehovah'S Witness. Avocations: reading, poetry, tennis, walking, diary-keeping. Home: 5 Eastland Rd Jamaica Plain MA 02130-4616

KENT, JEFFREY FRANKLIN, professional baseball player; b. Bellflower, Calif., Mar. 7, 1968; Grad., Edison H.S., Calif. Played 2d base Toronto Blue Jays, 1992; 2d baseman N.Y. Mets, 1992-96, San Francisco Giants, 1997—2002, Houston Astros, 2003—. Office: Houston Astros PO Box 288 Houston TX 77001-0288

KENT, JILL ELSPETH, entrepreneur, art dealer, lawyer; b. Detroit, June 1, 1948; d. Seymour and Grace (Edelman) K.; m. Mark Elliott Solomons, Aug. 20, 1978. BA, U. Mich., 1970; JD, George Washington U., 1975, LLM, 1979. Bar: D.C. 1975. Mgmt. intern U.S. Dept. Transp., Washington, 1971-73; staff analyst Office Mgmt. and Budget, Exec. Office of Pres., Washington, 1974-76; legis. counsel U.S. Treasury Dept., Washington, 1976-78, dir. legis. reference divsn. Healthcare Financing Adminstrn., 1978-80; sr. budget examiner Office Mgmt. and Budget, Exec. Office Pres., Washington, 1980-84; chief Treasury, Gen. Svcs. Office of Mgmt. and budget, Washington, 1984-85; dep. asst. sec. for deptl. fin. and planning U.S. Dept. Treasury, Washington, 1985-86, dep. asst. sec. for dept. fin. and mgmt., 1986-88, asst. sec. of treasury, 1988-89; CFO U.S. Dept. State, Washington, 1989-93, acting under sec. of state for mgmt., 1991; exec. devel. program Office of Mgmt. and Budget, Washington, 1984; CFO George Washington U. Med. Ctr., Washington, 1993-97; v.p. IPAC, 1997-98, The Columbus Group. Pres., CEO Atlantic Threadworks Inc.; gen. mgr. The Frogeye Co., 1995—; adj. prof. pub. policy, U. Md., 1993—. Bd. dirs. Mobile Med. Care INc., 1987-91; Trustee Newport Sch., 1988-91, Washington Civic Symphony, 1994-95; bd. dirs. China Found., 1997—; sr. counselor Atlantic Coun. U.S., 1997—. Recipient Adminstrs. award Healthcare Financing Adminstrn., 1980; named on of Top 40 Performers, Mgmt. mag., 1987, Disting. Svc. award Dept. Treasury, 1989, Am. Assn. Govt. Accts. award, 1992, Disting. Svc. award Dept. State, 1993. Mem. ABA, D.C. Bar Assn., Pres's. Coun. on Mgmt. Improvement, CFO Roundtable Healthcare Forum, Fin. Execs. Inst., Exec. Women in Govt. (treas. 1991-92, pres. 1992-93), Va. Assn. of Female Execs. (adv. coun. 1990), Coun. Excellence in Govt. (prin. 1993—). Republican. Home: 2419 California St NW Washington DC 20008-1615 E-mail: jkent@atlanticthreadworks.com.

KENT, JOHN BRADFORD, lawyer; b. Jacksonville, Fla., Sept. 5, 1939; s. Frederick Heber and Norma Cleveland (Futch) Kent; m. Monett Powers, Dec. 18, 1969; children: Monett, Susan, Sally, Katherine. AB, Yale U., 1961; JD, U. Fla., 1964; LLM in Taxation, NYU, 1965. Bar: Fla. 1964, U.S. Dist. Ct. (mid. dist.) Fla. 1965, U.S. Tax Ct. 1965, U.S. Ct. Appeals (11th cir.) 1973, U.S. Supreme Ct. 1973, U.S. Dist. (so. dist.) Fla. 1981, Nebr. 1995. Assoc. Ulmer, Murchison, Kent, Ashby & Ball, Jacksonville, 1965-67; ptnr., shareholder Kent, Watts & Durden, P.A. and predecessor firms, Jacksonville, 1967-85; shareholder Carlton, Field, Ward, Emmanuel, Smith, Cutler & Kent, Jacksonville, 1985-88,

Kent, Crawford, P.A., Jacksonville, 1988—2003, Marks Gray, P.A., Jacksonville, 2003—. Past pres., trustee Fla. Cmty. Coll. Found.; past. pres., bd. dirs. N.E. divsn. Children's Home Soc. Fla.; past bd. dirs. Jacksonville Legal Aid Soc. Mem.: Nat. Assn. Theatre Owners Fla. (bd. dirs., officer 1969—2000), Rotary (past officer, Paul Harris fellow). Office: Marks Gray PA 1200 Riverplace Blvd Ste 800 Jacksonville FL 32207

KENT, JULIE, ballet dancer, actress, model; b. Bethesda, Md., July 11, 1969; d. Charles Lindbergh and Jennifer Elsie Cox; m. Victor Barbee, 1996. Grad. high sch., Potomac, Md. Apprentice Am. Ballet Theatre, N.Y.C., 1985-86, mem. corps de ballet, 1986-1990, soloist, 1990-93, prin. dancer, 1993—. Starring role (films) Dancers, 1986, Center Stage, 2000; performed as a guest artist nationally and internationally. Recipient Prix de Lausanne Internat. Ballet competition, 1986, 1st prize at Erik Bruhn Competition in Toronto, 1993, Prix Benois de la Danse, Stuttgart, Germany, 2000; named one of 50 Most Beautiful People, People Mag., 1993. Office: Am Ballet Theatre 890 Broadway Fl 3 New York NY 10003

KENT, LINDA GAIL, dancer; b. Buffalo, Sept. 21, 1946; d. Jerol Edward and Dorismae (Kohler) K.; m. Nicholas Wolff Lyndon, June 9, 1996. BS, Juilliard Sch., 1968. Dancer Alvin Ailey Am. Dance Theater, 1968-74, then prin. dancer, 1970-74; prin. dancer Paul Taylor Dance Co., N.Y.C., 1975-89; dir. dance Perry-Mansfield Performing Arts Sch. and Camp, Steamboat Springs, Colo., 2001—. Faculty Juilliard Sch., 1984—; artist-in-residence Union Theological Seminary, N.Y. Mem. Am. Guild Mus. Artists, Actors Equity. Democrat. Unitarian Universalist. Home: 91 Payson Ave New York NY 10034-2722 Office: The Juilliard Sch Dance Divsn 60 Lincoln Center Plz New York NY 10023-6588

KENT, M. ELIZABETH, lawyer; b. N.Y.C., Nov. 17, 1943; d. Francis J. and Hannah (Bergman) K. AB, Vassar Coll. magna cum laude, 1964; AM, Harvard U., 1965, PhD, 1974; JD, Georgetown U., 1978. Bar: D.C. 1978, U.S. Dist. Ct. D.C. 1978, U.S. Ct. Appeals (D.C. cir.) 1978, U.S. Supreme Ct. 1983, U.S. Dist. Ct. Md. 1985. From lectr. to asst. prof. history U. Ala., Birmingham, 1972-74; assoc. Santarelli and Gimer, Washington, 1978; sole practice Washington, 1978—. Mem. Ripon Soc., Cambridge and Washington, 1968-93; rsch. dir. Howard M. Miller for Congress, Boston, 1972; vol. campaigns John V. Lindsay for Mayor, 1969, John V. Lindsay for Pres., 1972, John B. Anderson for Pres., 1980. Woodrow Wilson fellow 1964-65; Harvard U. fellow 1968-69. Mem.: ACLU, ABA, Superior Ct. Trial Lawyers Assn., DC Assn. Criminal Def. Lawyers (bd. dirs. 2001—), Women's Bar Assn., DC Bar Assn., Phi Beta Kappa. Republican. Avocations: history, politics. Home: 35 E St NW Apt 810 Washington DC 20001-1520 Office: 601 Indiana Ave NW Ste 500 Washington DC 20004-2918 E-mail: kentlaw@earthlink.net.

KENT, PAULA, public relations, marketing and management consultant, lecturer; b. N.Y.C.; d. John and Estelle (Frye) Smith; BS, State Tchrs. Coll., Worcester, Mass., 1939; MS, Boston U., 1941; m. Stanley J. Lloyd, Jan. 23, 1943; children: Diane Adrienne Noel, Robin Michele Cheri, Kevin Christopher Kent, Gisele Nicolette Jolie. Methods engr. Internat. Bus. Machines, 1941-42; personnel dir., fashion editor Daily Jour., San Diego, also radio sta. KSDJ, 1946-48; fashion and beauty editor, columnist The San Diego Union, 1949-64; promotion dir. The San Diego Union and the Evening Tribune, 1948-71, also UCLA Extension Div. Faculty, 1961 63; pub. relations, mktg. and mgmt. cons., 1970—; v.p. La Jolla Clin. Labs., Inc., 1970-81. Lectr. mktg. workshop tour, speaker at seminars, Brussels, London, Paris, Madrid, 1972; speaker nat. and regional confs. in maj. U.S. cities; del. Nat. Fedn. Press. Women Touring Russia, 1973. Formerly active ARC, Am. Cancer Soc., Med. Aux. San Diego. Officer USN; lt. (sr.g.) USCG, 1942-45. Recipient over 158 awards 1950—, including: 39 nat., 18 western states, over 100 Calif. state awards, 13 Lulus L.A. Advt. Women's Assn., 1 local award, resulting from ann. competitions sponsored by Los Angeles Advt. Women's Club, Nat. Newspaper Publs. Assn., Calif. Press Women, Los Angeles Sales Promotion Execs. Assn., Nat. Fedn. Press Women, Editor and Pub. Mag.; recipient Outstanding Service award Boy Scouts Am., 1962, 65; civic awards City of San Diego, Distinguished Service award Investment Edn. Inst., Detroit, 1969, Golden Spear award Twin Cities Sales Promotion Execs. Assn., Mpls., 1965; Outstanding Service thru Annual Investment Clinics N.Y. Stock Exchange, 1964, L.A. Theta Sigma Phi Walter O'Malley Unique Coverage award, 1968; named Woman of Achievement San Diego, 1958, 59, 64, Woman of Valor, 1958, Woman of Year, San Diego, 1965, Woman of Achievement, Nat. Fedn. Bus. and Profl. Women's Clubs, 1966; Advt. Man of Distinction, San Diego, 1970, Don award, Legion of Portola, 1968.; fellow Boston U. 1940-41. Mem. Advt. and Sales Club San Diego (dir. 1951-71), Sales and Marketing Execs. Club San Diego (pres. 1970-71), Personnel Mgmt. Assn. (hon. mem., plaque 1963), Sales and Mktg. Execs. Internat. (dir. at large 1971-73), Sales Promotion Execs. Assn. Los Angeles (Man of Year 1965), Am. Advt. Fedn. (western region chmn. edn. com., mem. nat. edn. com. 1971-72) Nat. Newspaper Promotion Assn. (pres. Western region 1964, dir. 1968-70, chmn. western regional conv. 1964), Calif. Assn. Press Women, Nat. Fedn. Press Women, Internat. Newspaper Promotion Assn. (bd. dirs. 1971-73), Am. Mgmt. Assn. (San Diego pres's coun. bus., profl. womens' clubs outstanding svc. plaque 1969). Roman Catholic. Editor: Monthly Bull., Personnel Mgmt. Assn., 1955-59, monthly bull., Sales Execs. Club. Chmn. San Diego's Ann. Giant Sales Rally, 1953-55, 70-71, co-chmn., 1964, 65; chmn. Advt. Recognition Week Campaign, 1953-54, Nat. Unltd. Hydroplane Races, San Diego, 1953-54, sponsor rep. Evening Tribune; pub. relations advisor Nat. Mrs. Am. Pageant, honored by London Press Club Members Luncheon, 1970, San Diego 200th Anniversary celebration; producer, emcee ann. Holiday for Housewives, San Diego, 1955-60; producer, co-ordinator U. Calif., Today's World, San Diego, 1962; exec. dir., producer, dir. San Diego Ann. Golden Gloves Boxing Tournament, 1961-68; producer San Diego Ann. Metrotennis Championships, 1952-70; dir. Ann Power Boat Regatta, 1950-62; exec. dir. Ann Jr. Golf Championships; dir. Ann. Hole-in-One Tournament, 1951-70; master ceremonies, producer, emcee Gentlemen of Distinction Awards, 1967, 68, 69; producer/dir. San Diego Advt. Salesrama, 1971; producer, dir. master ceremonies San Diego Ann. Woman of Yr. Awards, 1967, 68, 69; producer/designer 34 exhibits for convs. and fairs; developed and produced A Day in San Diego for European Travel Commn., 1964; produced and emceed Ann. Boy Scout Jamboree Stage Show, 1967. Del. Nat. Fedn Press Women touring Russia. Commd. ensign, Women's Reserve, USNR, 1942, transferred USCG, served from ensign to lt. (sr.g.), 1943-46. Avocation: world travel. Office: PO Box 2243 La Jolla CA 92038-2243

KENT, ROBERT BRYDON, law educator; b. Lowell, Mass., Dec. 2, 1921; s. Silas Stanley and Madeleine (Brydon) K.; m. Barbara Tuttle, Mar. 31, 1951; children: Robert Brydon, Dorothy Clarke, Elizabeth Montgomery, Hugh Clarke. AB, Harvard Coll., 1943; LLB, Boston U., 1949; LLD (hon.), Roger Williams U., 2001. Bar: Mass. 1948. Pvt. practice, Ware, Mass., 1948-50; instr. Boston U. Sch. Law, Mass., 1950-52, asst. prof., 1952-54, prof., 1954-81; prof. law, dean U. Zambia Sch. Law, Zambia, 1970-72; dir. Law Practice Inst., Zambia, 1970-71; Ford fellow in law tchng. Harvard U. Law Sch., 1960-61, part-time vis. prof., 1973-74; vis. prof. Cornell Law Sch., 1980-81, prof., 1981-92, prof. emeritus, 1992—, assoc. dean, 1982-86. Hon. vis. fellow Trinity Coll., Oxford U., 1976; reporter com. on civil rules Supreme Ct. RI, Superior Ct. RI, Dist. Ct. RI; cons. criminal procedure; disting. vis. prof. Roger Williams U. Sch. Law, 1997-2003; vis. prof. Boston U. Sch. Law, 2000-01. Author: (with Austin W. Scott) Cases and Other Materials on Civil Procedure, 1967, Rhode Island Practice: Civil Rules with Commentaries, 1969. Moderator Town of Lexington, Mass., 1965-70, selectman, 1977-81; vice chmn. Civil Liberties Union of Mass., 1966-69; exec. com. Law Assn. of Zambia, 1970-72; trustee Kimball Union Acad., pres., 1973-76. Served with US Army, 1943-46. Fulbright prof. sch. law U. Zambia, 1988. Mem. Am. Law Inst. Democrat. Unitarian Universalist. Home: 1 Doran Farm Ln Lexington MA 02420-2128 Office: Roger Williams Sch Law Ten Metacom Ave Bristol RI 02809 E-mail: rkent@earthlink.net.

KENT, ROBERT JOHN, marine biologist; b. N.Y.C., May 20, 1948; s. Stanley Paul and Mary Katherine (Ladany) K. BA, SUNY, Buffalo, 1970; MA in Environ. Studies, SUNY, Stony Brook, 1984. Instr. Butler County Community Coll., Butler, Pa., 1975-78; coop. extension agt., 4 H natural resources specialist Cornell Coop. Extension, Riverhead, N.Y., 1978-89; sea grant program coord. N.Y. Sea Grant, Riverhead, 1989—, interim assoc. dir., 1995. Adj. lectr. Marine Scis. Rsch. Ctr., SUNY, Stony Brook, 1994—. Contbr. articles to profl. publs. Recipient Spl. Svc. award Coop. Extension 4-H Agts., 1981, Epsilon Sigma Phi Outstanding Team Achievement award, 1992, Outstanding Marine Edn. Program award Coastal Extension Profls., Ithaca, 1984, 86, Outstanding Program Achievement award Cornell U., 1986, State Early Career award Epsilon Sigma Phi, 1988, Northeast Coop. Extension Dirs. award, 1996. Mem. Assn. Natural Resources Ext. Profls. (pres. N.Y. chpt.), Nat. Marine Educators Assn. Episcopalian. Avocation: cultural activities. Office: New York Sea Grant 3059 Sound Ave Riverhead NY 11901-1098 Office Fax: 631-369-5944. E-mail: rjk13@cornell.edu.

KENT, SHERIE LYNN, music educator; d. David Jenner and Delcena Robson Hatch; m. Lloyd E. Kent, May 21, 1983; children: Brandon Horace, Sean Lloyd, Adam Charles. BA in Edn.(hon.), Ariz. State U., 1983. Piano tchr., Mesa, Ariz., 1981—; tchr. Mesa Pub. Schs., Mesa, Ariz., 1983—98. Contbr. Mem. SIAC Sch. Com., Mesa, 1993—96, Sch. Improvement Bd., Mesa, 2001—03. Mem.: Desert Valley Music Tchrs. Assn., East Valley Music Tchrs. Assn., Ariz. Music Tchrs. Assn., Music Tchrs. Nat. Assn. Mem. Lds Ch. Avocations: gardening, reading, music. Home: 1710 E Evergreen St Mesa AZ 85203

KENT, SUSAN, library director, consultant; b. N.Y.C., Mar. 18, 1944; d. Elias and Minnie (Barnett) Solomon; m. Eric Goldberg, Mar. 27, 1966 (div. Mar. 1991); children: Evan Goldberg, Jessica Goldberg; m. Rolly Kent, Dec. 20, 1991. BA in English Lit. with honors, SUNY, 1965; MS, Columbia U., 1966. Libr., sr. libr. N.Y. Pub. Libr., 1965-67, br. mgr. Donnell Art Libr., 1967-68; reference libr. Paedergaat br. Bklyn. Pub. Libr., 1971-72; reference libr. Finkelstein Meml. Libr., Spring Valley, N.Y., 1974-76; coord. adult and young adult svcs. Tucson Pub. Libr., 1977-80, acting libr. dir., 1982, dep. libr. dir., 1980-87; mng. dir. Ariz. Theatre Co., Tucson, Phoenix, 1987-89; dir. Mpls. Pub. Libr. and Info. Ctr., 1990-95; city libr. L.A. Pub. Libr., 1995—. Tchr. Pima CC, Tucson, 1978; grad. libr. sch. U. Ariz., Tucson, 1995—; panelist Ariz. Commn. Arts., 1981—85; mem. bd. devel. and fundraising Child's Play, Phoenix, 1983; reviewer pub. programs NEH, 1985, panelist challenge grants, 1986—89, panelist state programs, 1988; cons., presenter workshops Young Adult Svcs. divsn. ALA, 1986—88; bd. dirs., mem. organizing devel. and fundraising com. Flagstaff (Ariz.) Symphony Orch., 1988; cons. to librs. and nonprofit instns., 1989—90, 1992—; bd. advisors UCLA Grad. Sch. Edn. and Info. Scis., 1998—2001; presenter in field. Contbr. articles to profl. jours. Chair arts and culture com. Tucson Tomorrow, 1981—85; commr. Ariz. Commn. Arts, 1983—87; bd. dirs., v.p. Ariz. Dance Theatre, 1984—86; bd. dirs. Arizonans Cultural Devel., Ariz., 1987—89, YWCA Mpls., 1991—92; bd. dirs. women's studies adv. coun. U. Ariz., 1985—90; participant Leadership Mpls., 1990—91. Recipient Libr. of the Yr., Libr. Jour., 2002, Info. Assocs. Exec. Leadership award, UCLA Anderson Sch., 2001; fellow, Sch. Libr. Sci., Columbia U., 1965—66. Mem.: ALA (mem. membership com. S.W. regional chair 1983—86, mem. com. appts. 1986—87, gov. coun. 1990—98, planning and budget assembly del. 1991—93, chair conf. com. 1996—97, Joseph Lippincott award 2003), Coun. Libr. and Info. Resources (bd. dirs. 2000—, Libr. of the Yr. award 2002), Libr. Adminstrn. and Mgmt. Assn. (mem. John Cotton Dana Award com. 1994—95), Urban Librs. Coun. (mem. exec. bd. 1994—2001, treas. 1996—98, vice chair/chair elect 1998, 1999, chair 1999—2000), Calif. Libr. Assn., Pub. Libr. Assn. (mem. nominating com. 1980—82, v.p. 1986—87, pres. 1987—88, chair publs. assmebly 1988—89, chair nat. conf. 1994, chair legis. com. 1994—95). Office: LA Pub Libr 630 W 5th St Los Angeles CA 90071-2002 E-mail: skent@lapl.org.

KENT, SUSAN, anthropologist, educator, anthropologist, researcher; b. Oakland, Calif., June 26, 1952; d. Ted and Shirley Rich Kent. MA, Wash. State U., 1975, PhD, 1980. Vis. asst. prof. Iowa State U., Ames, Iowa, 1982—83, U. Ky., Lexington, 1985—86; asst. prof. Old Dominion U., Norfolk, Va., 1986—90, assoc. prof., 1990—96, full prof., 1996—2000, eminent prof., 2000—. Asst. field and labatory dir. Lind Coulee PaleoIndian Archaeological Excavations, Rural Central Washington, Wash., 1974—75; archaeologist I Navajo Indian Irrigation Excavations, Navajo Indian Reservation, N.Mex., 1977—78; dissertation field work Participant Observation Fieldwork Among Rural Navajo Indians, Navajo Mountain, Utah, 1978—79; rschr. Ethnographic Study of the Tulalip Indian Religious Practices and Ideology Pertaining to the Forest, Tulalip Indian Reservation, Wash., 1980—81; project p.i. excavation of Mesa Verde Pueblo II Pueblo archaeological site Excavation and Analysis of Anasazi Archaeological Site, Colo., 1982—83; project p.i. Kalahari Kutse Basarwa (Bushmen) Hunter-Gatherer Participant Observation Rsch., Kutse, Kalahari Desert, Botswana, 1987—97, Caledon (South Africa) River Archaeological Project, 1999—. Author: (book) Analyzing Activity Areas: An Ethnoarchaeological Study of the Use of Space; editor: Ethnicity, Hunter-gatherers, and the Other: Association Or Assimilation?, Gender in African Archaeology, Cultural Diversity Among Twentieth Century Foragers: An African Perspective, Diet, Demography, and Disease: Changing Views of Anemia, Domestic Architecture and the Use of Space: An Interdisciplinary Cross-Cultural Study, Farmers As Hunters-The Implications of Sedentism, Method and Theory for Activity Area Research-An Ethnoarchaeological Approach; contbr. articles to profl. jours. Book rev. editor for am. antiquity Soc. for Am. Archaeology, Washington, 2000. Recipient Disting. Scholar Award in Anthropology, Va. Social Scis. Soc., 2001; grantee, Fulbright Found., 1989, Wenner Gren Found. for Anthrop. Rsch., 1990, 1998, Wenner-Gren Found. for Anthrop. Rsch., 2002, Smithsonian Instn., 1992, Swan Fund, Pitt Rivers Mus., 1993—95, NSF, 1999. Fellow: Royal Anthrop. Inst. Gt. Britain (assoc.); mem.: Current Anthropology (assoc.), Soc. for Africanist Archaeology (assoc.), South African Archaeological Soc. (assoc.), Soc. for Paleoanthropology (assoc.), Soc. for Am. Archaeology (assoc.), Am. Anthrop. Assn. (assoc.; mem. com. on the status of women in anthropology 2001—, sec. archaeol. divsn. 1992—94, editor archaeology divsn. column 1992—94, mem. spl. reorganization com. 1997). Achievements include research in Middle Stone Age Archaeological Research, South Africa; Fieldwork with Kutse Basarwa (Bushmen) hunter-gatherers, Kalahari Desert, Botswana; Mesa Verde Anasazi Archaeological Investigations; Navajo Indian Ethnographic Fieldwork; PaleoIndian Archaeological Research. Avocations: travel, photography, writing, reading. Office: Old Dominion Univ Anthropology BAL 723 Hampton ODU Norfolk VA 23529 Home Fax: 757-683-5634; Office Fax: 757-683-5634.

KENT, JR. THOMAS JEFFERSON, JR., corporate financial executive; b. Guyton, Ga., Oct. 8, 1976; s. Thomas Jefferson Kent, Sr. and Ophlia Anna Kent. BS in Polit. Sci., Wilberforce U., Ohio, 1996—2001; MBA, U. of Leicester, Eng., 2002—. CEO Kent Internat. Holding Co., N.Y.C., 2001—, T.K. Devel. Corp., N.Y.C., 2001—. Head/bd. of directors James & Kent Found., N.Y.C., 2002—. Mem. Met Rep. Club, N.Y.C., 2001; bd. mem. World Federalist, N.Y.C., 2002. Mem.: The Churchhill Soc. (assoc.), Am. Soc. (assoc.), The Free Masons of the State of NY (life). Republican. Episcopalian. Avocations: golf, polo, tennis. Home: PO Box 1095 New York, NY 10185 Office: Kent Internat Holding Co PO Box 1095 New York NY 10185 E-mail: tkent50@hotmail.com.

KENTRIS, GEORGE LAWRENCE, lawyer; b. Detroit, Mich., Nov. 3, 1949; s. Michael Nicholas and Mary (Cassimatis) K.; m. Susan Jo Van Dorn, Nov. 18, 1972; children: Emily Joya, Vanessa, Ann Alexia. BA, Ohio State U., 1971; JD, U. Toledo Coll. Law, 1976. Bar: Ohio 1976, U.S. Dist. Ct. (no. dist.) Ohio 1977, U.S. Supreme Ct. 1980, U.S. Ct. Appeals (6th cir.) 1989. Asst. pros. atty. Hancock County Ohio Prosecutors Office, Findlay, Ohio, 1977-85; assoc. Noble, Bryant & Needles, Findlay, Ohio, 1977-81; pvt. practice Findlay, Ohio, 1981-87, 99—; sr. ptnr. Kentris & Wolph, Findlay, Ohio, 1987-92; sr. atty. Kentris & Assocs., Findlay, Ohio, 1992-96; sr. ptnr. Kentris, Brown & Powell, Findlay, Ohio, 1996-97; pres. Kentris, Brown, Powell & Balega Co., LPA, Findlay, Ohio, 1997-98. Franchisee Taco Bell Corp., Ohio, 1982—; licensee Pizza Hut Inc., 1999—; officer, dir. Findlay TV Corp., 1991-97. Bd. trustees Am. Cancer Soc. Hancock County, Findlay, 1980-94, pres., 1985-86; mem. Hancock County Rep. Exec. Com., 1982-98, treas., 1984-86; bd. dirs. Jr. Achievement of Hancock Co., Inc., 1991-98, Franchisee Choice Hotels, 1998—; dir. Unified Foodservice Purchasing Coop, LLC, 1999-2003; rep. Franmac, 2001—, mem. agreement revision com., 2002—; chmn. Franchise Rels., Integrated Expansion and Devel. Com., 2001—; mem. Yum Brands Five Concepts Coun., 2002—. Mem. Findlay/Hancock County Bar Assn. (cert. grievance com. 1987-98, chmn. 1995, sec. 1993, treas. 1980-81). Mem. Greek Orthodox. Avocations: golf, sports cars. Office: George L Kentris Atty at Law 431 E Main Cross St Findlay OH 45840-4822 E-mail: gkentris@aol.com.

KENVIN, ROGER LEE, writer, retired English educator; b. N.Y.C., May 26, 1926; s. James Marion and Gladys Irene (Macdonald) K.; m. Verna Rudd Trimble, Apr. 5, 1952; children: Brooke Trimble Kenvin Goldstein, Heather Trimble Kenvin Hietala. BA, Bowdoin Coll., 1949; MA, Harvard U., 1956; MFA, Yale U., 1959, DFA, 1961. Copywriter Crowell-Collier Pub., N.Y.C., 1950-53; tchr. Le Rosey, Rolle, Switzerland, 1953-55; prof. English and drama Mary Washington Coll., Fredericksburg, Va., 1959-68, chmn. dept. drama, 1972-82; prof., chmn. dept. speech and drama U. Notre Dame and St. Mary's Coll., South Bend, Ind., 1969-72; prof., chmn. dept. theatre and dance Calif. Poly. State U., San Luis Obispo, 1983-88. Vis. lectr. Isabella Thoburn Coll., Lucknow, India, 1965-66. Author: (plays) Krishnalight, 1976, (short stories) The Gaffer and Seven Fables, 1987, Harpo's Garden, 1997, The Cantabrigian Rowing Society's Saturday Night Bash, 1998, After the Silver Age, 1998, Trylons and Perispheres, 1999, (memoir) Long Run and Teatro Ruggiero, 2003; co-author: (travel essays) Necessary Ports, 2000, Magellan Moon, 2002. With USN, 1944-46. Mem. Phi Beta Kappa. Home: 575 Fairview Ave Arcadia CA 91007-6736

KENWOOD, JOEL DAVID, lawyer; b. Paterson, N.J., June 17, 1951. BA, Stanford U., 1973; JD, Am. U., 1977. Bar: Fla. 1978, D.C. 1985, Colo. 1989; cert. civil trial law and bus. litigation law, civil trial advocacy. Assoc. Jeffer, Walter, Tierney, Dekorte, Hopkinson & Vogel, Palm Beach, Fla., 1978-79, Baskin & Sears, Palm Beach, Fla., 1979-82; ptnr. Heeg, Kenwood & Stone PA, Boca Raton, Fla., 1982-86, Woods, Oviatt, Gilman, Sturmant & Clarke, Boca Raton, Fla., 1987-93; pvt. practice Boca Raton, Fla., 1993—. Mem. Fla. Bar Assn. (comml. litigation com. 1984—, copr., banking and bus. law com., jud. nominating procedures com. 1986), Palm Beach County Bar Assn. (chmn. jud. rels. com. 1984-85, chmn. appellate practice com. 1983-84, chmn. legis. liaison com. 1985-86), South Palm Beach County Bar Assn. (bd. dirs. 1983—, sec. 1984-85, treas. 1985-86, v.p. 1986-87, pres. 1988-89). Office: 6100 Glades Rd Ste 204 Boca Raton FL 33434-4370

KENWORTHY, HARRY WILLIAM, company executive; b. Utica, N.Y., Nov. 15, 1947; s. Robert Wild and Marcina Agnes (Suraske) K.; m. Elaine Fedor, July 17, 1971; children: Rebekah, Amanda. BS in Materials Engring., Rensselaer Poly. Inst., 1969; MBA in Fin., Syracuse U., 1973. Registered profl. engr., Conn.; cer. quality engr. Process engr. Revere Copper & Brass, Rome, N.Y., 1969-70, supr., 1970-72; ops. mgr. BZ industries, Little Falls, N.Y., 1973-74; asst. plant mgr. Die Molding Corp., Canastota, N.Y., 1974-75, plant mgr., 1975-78; ops. mgr. Rogers Corp., Willimantic div., South Windham, Conn., 1978-83, div. mgr., 1983-93; v.p. Willimantic divsn. Rogers Corp., South Windham, Conn., 1993-95, v.p. High Performance Elastomers divsn., 1995—2001, v.p. mfg., 2001—. Examiner Malcolm Baldrige Nat. Quality Awards, 1989, 90, 91; chmn. Conn. Mfg. Coun.; bd. dirs. Miller Co., Rogers Inoac Corp., Nagoya, Japan. With USNG, 1969-75. Mem. Am. Soc. Quality Control (sr. mem.), Assn. Mfg. Excellence. Republican. Roman Catholic. Avocations: tennis, golf, coin collecting. Office: 1 Technology Dr PO Box 188 Rogers CT 06263-0188

KENWORTHY, WILLIAM EUGENE, judge; b. Las Animas, Colo., Apr. 27, 1933; s. William Sydner and Joyce Lovelle (Thedford) K.; m. Lucille Nicoletta Capozzola, July 20, 1963; children: William D., Kathryn J., Randal A. BS, U. Denver, 1955, LLB, 1956. Bar: Colo. 1957, U.S. Dist. Ct. Colo. 1957, U.S. Ct. Appeals (10th cir.) 1962, U.S. Supreme Ct. 1972. Assoc. Fugate & Mitchem, Denver, 1960-63, ptnr., 1964-67; counsel Navajo Freight Lines, Denver, 1967 69; gen. counsel Rocky Mountain Motor Tariff Bur., Denver, 1970-87; ptnr. Rea, Cross & Auchincloss, Washington, 1988-97; adminstrv. law judge Office of Hearings and Appeals Social Security Adminstrn., Pitts., 1997—. Instr. Coll. Law, U. Denver, 1965-66. Author: Transportation of Hazardous Materials, 2d edit., 1992, Corporate Counsel's Guide to Occupational Safety and Health Law, 1993, with supplements, Transportation Safety and Insurance Law, 2 vols., 1998, with ann. supplements, Killer Roads, 1999; writer columns Electric Light and Power, 1966-84, Heavy Duty Trucking, 1993—; also articles. Served with USNR, 1957-60; comdr. Res. ret. Mem. Assn. Transp. Practitioners (pres. 1985-86), Denver Bar Assn., Colo. Bar Assn., Transp. Lawyers Assn., Fed. Bar Assn., Mil. Officers Assn., Exch. Club, Kiwanis (pres. local club 1965-66). Republican. Roman Catholic.

KENYHERCZ, THOMAS MICHAEL, pharmaceutical company executive; b. Jan. 6, 1950; s. William Stephen and Goldie Elizabeth (Matica) K.; m. Linda Jane Kostyshak, Mar. 20, 1973; 1 child, Craig Thomas. BS, Youngstown State U., 1971; MS, U. Cin., 1973, PhD in Analytical Chemistry, 1975. Cert. regulatory affairs profl. Postdoctoral fellow in bioanalytical chemistry Purdue U., 1975-77; scientist, sr. scientist, mgr. prodn. support labs. Ortho Pharm. Corp., Raritan, N.J., 1977-80; dir. product devel., quality assurance & regulatory affairs Janssen Pharmaceutica Inc., Piscataway, N.J., 1980-85; pres. KROSS, Inc., Hillsborough, N.J., 1985—. Founder KROSS Coatings, Inc., 1987—, Telluride Pharm. Corp., 1994—; founder, pres. Telluride Analytical Svcs. Corp., 1997—; founder KROSS Devel. Corp., 2001-; participant FDA-approved Orphan Drug Devel. program, IND Treatment of Cachexic AIDS Patients, 1996. Mem. editl. bd.: Jour. Automated Chemistry, 1975—. Coach basketball St. Mary's Sr. H.S., 1979-83; active Ctr. for Creative Living, Religious Sci. Ch. Princeton. Recipient SBIR Rsch. award EPA Phase I and II for studies of marine contamination, 1987, 88, FDA Orphan Drug designation, 1994; Lowenstein Schubert Twitchell fellow U. Cin., 1975, Kissinger fellow Purdue U., 1975-77. Mem. Am. Mgmt. Assn., Am. Assn. Clin. Chemists, Am. Assn. Anti Aging Med., Am. Chem. Soc., Am. Assn. Pharm. Scientists, Am. Soc. for Quality Control, U.S.-N.I.S. C. of C., Electrochem. Soc., Parenteral Drug Assn., Pharm. Mfrs. Assn., Drug Info. Assn., Regulatory Affairs Profl. Soc., Am. Soc. Pharmacognosy, Western Electroanalytical Theoretical Soc., Licensing Execs. Soc., Aquinas Inst., Controlled Release Soc., Soc. for Biomaterials. Byzantine Catholic. Office: Telluride Compound 300 Valley Rd Bldg 278 Hillsborough NJ 08844 E-mail: krossinc@ix.netcom.com.

KENYON, CARLETON WELLER, librarian; b. Lafayette, N.Y., Oct. 7, 1923; s. Herbert Abram and Esther Elizabeth (Weller) K.; m. Dora Marie Kallander, May 21, 1948; children: Garnet Eileen, Harmon Clark, Kay Adelle. AB, Yankton Coll., 1947; MA, JD, U. S.D., 1950; A.M. in L.S, U. Mich., 1951. Bar: S.D. 1950. Asst. law librarian, head catalog librarian U. Nebr., 1951-52; asst. reference librarian Los Angeles County Law Library, 1952-54, head catalog librarian, 1954-60; law librarian State of Calif., Sacramento, 1960-69; became cons. Library of Congress, Washington, 1963, asso. law librarian, 1969-71, law librarian, 1971-89. Cons. county law libraries; lectr. legal bibliography and research. Author: California County Law Library Basic List Handbook and Information of New Materials, 1967; compiler: Calif. Library Laws; assisted in compiling checklists of basic: Am. publs. and subject headings; contbr. articles and book revs. to law revs., library jours. Served with USAAC, 1943-46. Mem. ABA, State Bar S.D., Am. Assn. Law Librarians (chmn. com. on cataloging and classification 1969-71, mem. staff Law Library Inst. 1969, 71), Law Librarians Soc. Washington. Home: 4239 44th Ct NE Salem OR 97305-2117

KENYON, CYNTHIA, medical researcher; BS in Chemistry and Biochemistry, U. Ga., 1976; PhD, MIT, 1981. Post-doctoral fellow Med. Rsch. Coun. Lab. Molecular Biology, Cambridge, England; prof. U. Calif., San Francisco, 1986—, Herbert Boyer Disting. prof. biochemistry and biophysics. Contbr. articles to profl. jours. Mem.: AAAS, NAS. Office: Dept Biochemistry and Biophysics U Calif Box 2200 Genentech Hall S312D San Francisco CA 94143*

KENYON, DAPHNE ANNE, economics educator; b. Augusta, Ga., Aug. 14, 1952; d. Lawrence Austin and Shirley (Knaus) Kenyon; m. Peter George Kachavos, Oct. 22, 1988. BA, Mich. State U., 1974; MA in Econs., U. Mich., 1976, PhD in Econs., 1980. Asst. prof. Dartmouth Coll., Hanover, N.H., 1979-83; sr. analyst U.S. Adv. Commn. on Intergovt. Relations, Washington, 1983-85; fin. economist U.S. Treasury Dept., Washington, 1985-87; sr. research assoc. Urban Inst., Washington, 1987-88; Lincoln fellow Lincoln Inst. of Land Policy, Cambridge, Mass., 1988-89; asst. prof. econs. Simmons Coll., Boston, 1989-90, assoc. prof. econs., 1991-98, chair dept. econs., 1996-99, prof. econs., 1998-2000; pres. The Josiah Bartlett Ctr. for Pub. Policy, 1999—2002; prin. D.A. Kenyon & Assocs., 2002—. Cons. U.S. IRS Adv. Panel, Washington, 1987-99; appt. to Mass. Dept. of Revenue Adv. Group, 1991; bd. dirs. New Eng. Econ. Project, v.p., 1997-98, pres., 1999. Assoc. editor Urban Studies, 1988-93, mem. U.S. editl. adv. com., 1993—; co-editor: Coping with Mandates, 1990,

Competition Among States and Local Governments, 1991; N.H. corr. State Tax Notes, 1990-93; mem. editl. bd. Mass. Benchmarks, 1997-99; columnist: State Tax Notes, 2003—; contbr. articles to profl. jours. Active NH Gov.'s Revenue Adv. Com., Concord, 1982, 98, N.H. State Consensus Revenue Estimating Panel, 2000-03, Windham NH Sch. bd., 2000-03, vice chmn. 2002-03. Fellow Grad. fellow, NSF, 1974. Mem. Am. Econ. Assn. (com. on the status of women in econs. profession 1995-98), Nat. Tax Assn. (bd. dirs. 1996-99, chair intergovernmental fiscal rels. com. 1996-98, program chair 1999), Nat. Tax Jour. (referee Ea. Econ. Jour.). Episcopalian.

KENYON, EDWARD TIPTON, lawyer; b. Summit, N.J., Jan. 27, 1929; s. Theodore S. and Martha (Tipton) K.; m. Dolores Cetrule, July 11, 1953; children: David S., James N., Jonathan W., Theodore H. AB, Harvard U., 1950; LL.B., Columbia U., 1953. Bar: N.Y. 1956, N.J. 1957. Assoc. Thacher, Proffitt, Prizer, Crawley & Wood, N.Y.C., 1955-56; law clk. to presiding judge U.S. Dist. Ct. N.J., Newark, 1956-57; assoc. Jeffers, Mountain & Franklin, Morristown, N.J., 1957-59, Bourne, Noll and Kenyon and predecessor firm, Summit, 1959-62, ptnr., 1962-97, of counsel, 1997—. Bd. dirs. Atlantic Mgmt. Corp., 1990-98. Trustee Summit Art Ctr., 1960—72, Trinity-Pawling Sch., Pawling, NY, 1977—2003, Pingry Sch., Martinsville, NJ, 1970—97, Martha's Vineyard Preservation Trust, 1999—, Overlook Hosp., Summit, 1967—75, pres., 1973—75; trustee Overlook Hosp. Found., 1975—84, sec., 1977—80, v.p., 1980—81, pres., 1981—84; trustee Winston Sch., Summit, 1986—93, v.p., 1987—90, pres., 1990—92; mem. planning bd. Town of Chilmark, 1998—, chmn., 2000—; deacon Ctrl. Presbyn. Ch., Summit, 1960—65, trustee, 1965—72, 1987—93, pres., 1970—72, 1988—91; deacon First Congl. Ch., West Tisbury, Mass., 2000—; bd. dirs. Overlook Mgmt. Corp., 1988—97. With M.C. U.S. Army, 1953—55. Mem. ABA, N.Y. State Bar Assn., N.J. Bar Assn., Summit Bar Assn. (pres. 1983-84), Union County Bar Assn., Am. Coll. Trust and Estate Counsel, Am. Law Inst. Clubs: Beacon Hill (trustee 1977-81, pres. 1979-81), Edgartown Yacht Club, Harvard of N.Y.C, Harvard of N.J. (trustee 1958-69, pres. 1968-69). Home: 49 N Abels Hill Rd Chilmark MA 02535-2026 Office: 382 Springfield Ave Summit NJ 07901-2707

KENYON, GARY MICHAEL, gerontology educator, researcher; b. Montreal, Que., Can., June 12, 1949; s. Raymond George and Frances Evelyn (Duhault) K. B in Commerce cum laude, Loyola U., Montreal, 1970; BA, Concordia U., Montreal, 1977, MA, 1981; PhD, U. B.C., 1985. Postdoctoral fellow Andrew Norman Inst. U. So. Calif., L.A., 1985-86; postdoctoral fellow Swedish Inst. Linkoping U., Sweden, 1986-87; prof., chmn. dept. gerontology St. Thomas U., Fredericton, N.B., Can., 1987—. Adj. prof. McGill U. Ctr. for Studies in Aging, Montreal; hon. rsch. assoc. U. N.B., 1996—. Author: Emergent Theories of Aging, 1988, Metaphors of Aging, 1991, Aging and Biography, 1996, Restorying Our Lives, 1997, Ordinary Wisdom, 2001, Narrative Gerontology, 2001; editor: jour. Gnosis, 1979—81; rev. editor: Can. Jour. on Aging, 1989—90; contbr. articles to profl. jours. Can. Govt. Social Scis. and Humanities fellow, 1983-85. Mem. Gerontology Soc. Am., Can. Assn. Gerontology, N.B. Assn. Gerontology (bd. dirs.). Avocations: skiing, cooking, wines, Tai Chi (instr.), language study. Office: St Thomas U Dept Gerontology Fredericton NB Canada E3B 5G3 E-mail: kenyon@stthomasu.ca.

KENYON, GEORGE LOMMEL, pharmaceutical educator, dean; b. Wilmington, Del., Aug. 29, 1939; s. Westcott Clarke and Harriet Lommel K.; m. Dorothy Christine Naumann, June 20, 1964 (div. June 1979); m. Lucy Ann Waskell, Jan. 1, 1981; 1 child, Karen Elisabeth. BS in Chemistry, Bucknell U., 1961; AM in Chemistry, Harvard U., 1963, PhD in Chemistry, 1965. Postdoctoral fellow in biochemistry MIT-NIH, Cambridge, Mass., 1965-66; asst. prof. chemistry U. Calif., Berkeley, 1966-72, from asst. to assoc. prof. pharm. chemistry San Francisco, 1972-77, prof., 1977-98, dean Sch. Pharmacy, 1993-98; prof. Coll. Pharmacy, U. Mich., Ann Arbor, 1998—, dean, 1998—. Editor-in-chief Bioorganic Chemistry, 1997—; contbr. over 200 articles to sci. publs.; patentee in field. Recipient T.O. Soine Meml. award U. Minn., 1992, Alumni award for Outstanding Achievement, Bucknell U., 1996. Fellow AAAS, N.Y. Acad. Scis.; mem. Am. Chem. Soc. (chmn. biol. chemistry divsn. 1992-94), Am. Soc. Biochemistry and Molecular Biology. Avocation: birdwatching. Office: U Mich Coll Pharmacy 428 Church St Ann Arbor MI 48109-1065

KENYON, KAREN BETH SMITH, literature educator, writer; b. Oklahoma City, Sept. 4, 1938; d. Claude Emory and Evelyn Grace (Brown) Smith; m. Richard Bertram Kenyon, Feb. 14, 1963 (dec. Nov. 1978); 1 child, Richard Laurence. BA with honors, San Diego State U., 1977, MA in English, 1987. Instr. Mira Costa Coll., Cardiff, Calif., 1981—; instr. extended studies U. Calif., San Diego, 1982—; instr. San Diego State U., 1985—. Author: Sunshower, 1981, The Bronte Family, 2003; contbr. over 800 articles to profl. jours. Recipient Creativity award, San Diego Ctr. for Creativity, 1973, Poetry award, Atlantic Monthly, 1975. Mem.: Soc. Children's Book Writers and Illustrators, PEN. Democrat. Mailing: PO Box 12604 La Jolla CA 92039

KENYON, REGAN CLAIR, educational research executive; b. St. Louis, Jan. 31, 1949; s. Robert Clair and Nina Naomi (Giesler) K.; m. Mary Margaret Quinlan, June 2, 1979; children: Regan Clair Jr., Moriah Quinlan. BA, U. Mo., 1969, MEd, 1973; EdD, Harvard U., 1983. Tchr., Ferguson, Mo., 1971-74; prin. Manor Sch., St. Croix, 1974-77, Country Day Sch., St. Croix, Virgin Islands, 1977-78; exec. asst. U.S. Dept. Edn., Washington, 1978-80; adminstrv. asst. Harvard U., Cambridge, Mass., 1980-81; cons. to pres. MA Higher Edn. Assistance Corp., Boston, 1981-83; pres. Secondary Sch. Admission Test Bd., Princeton, N.J., 1983—. Cons. fed. and state govt. founds., Washington, 1979—; founder, pres. Princeton Inst. Ednl. Rsch., 1987—. Contbr. articles to profl. jours.; inventor, editor in field. Mem. N.J. State Bd. Edn., Trenton, N.J., 1987-91, Nat. State Bds. Edn., Washington, 1987-91. Fellow Edn. Policy for George Washington U. Inst. for Ednl. Leadership, Washington, 1978-79; Gustav Harris scholar Harvard U., 1980-83; recipient Horace Mann Prof. Contbr. citation U.S. Dept. Edn., 1980; named Disting Alumni Mo. U., 1996. Mem. Am. Ednl. Rsch. Assn., Inst. for Ednl. Leadership, Harvard Club, Nassau Club, Phi Delta Kappa. Roman Catholic. Avocations: tennis, golf, ski, fishing, hiking. Home: 5 Cedar Brook Ter Princeton NJ 08540-7407 Office: Secondary Sch Admission Test Bd CN5339 Princeton NJ 08543

KENYON, ROBERT WAYNE, career officer; b. Charlottesville, Va., Dec. 31, 1954; s. Robert Sharples and Beryl Louise (Snell) K.; m. Ha Le Kenyon, July 18, 1982; children: Jennifer, Meghan. BA cum laude, U. South Ala., 1978; grad. with honors, U.S. Army Mil. Police Sch., 1984; MS cum laude, Jacksonville State U., 1985; MBA Bus., Tulane U., 1995; grad., USAF Air War Coll., 2000, U.S. Army War Coll., 2002. With U.S. Army, 1978, advanced through grades to col., 2002, mil. police officer, 1978—83; ordnance officer USAR, New Orleans, 1995—98, civil affairs officer, 1998—99, bn. comdr., 1999—2001, dep. provost marshal, 2001—02; adminstrv. contracting officer USN, 1993—, group comdr., 2003—. Mem. awards bd. Supr. Shipbuilding, New Orleans, 1999—. Mem. Assn. U.S. Army, Res. Officers Assn. Avocations: golf, exercise. Home: 2109 Tezcuco Ln Marrero LA 70072

KEOGH, HEIDI HELEN DAKE, advocate; b. Saratoga, N.Y., July 12, 1950; d. Charles Starks and Phyllis Sylvia (Edmunds) Dake; m. Randall Frank Keogh, Nov. 3, 1973; children: Tyler Cameron, Kelly Dake. Student, U. Colo., 1972. Reception, promotions Sta. KLAK, KJAE, Lakewood, Colo., 1972-73; acct. exec. Mixed Media Advt. Agy., Denver, 1973-75; writer, mktg. Jr. League Cookbook Devel., Denver, 1986-88; chmn., coord. Colorado Cache & Creme de Colorado Cookbooks, 1988-90. Speakers bur. Mile High Transplant Bank, Denver, 1983-84, Writer's Inst., U. Denver, 1988; bd. dirs. Stewart's Ice Cream Co., Inc., Jr. League, Denver. Contbr. articles to profl. jours. Fiscal officer, bd. dirs. Mile High Transplant Bank; blockworker Heart Fund and Am. Cancer Soc., Littleton, Colo., 1978—, Littleton Rep. Com., 1980-84; fundraising vol. Littleton Pub. Schs., 1980-98; vol. Gathering Place Assn., bd. dirs., 1996—, pres., 2003—, chmn. Brown Bag benefit, 1996; vol. Hearts for Life, 1991—, Oneday, 1992, Denver Ballet Guild, 1992—, Denver Ctr. Alliance, 1993—, Newborn Hope, 1980—, Girls, Inc., 1995—, Girls Hope, VOA Guild, 1996—, Le Bal de Ballet, 1998—, The Denver Social Register and Record, 1999—. Mem. Jr. League Denver (pub. rels. bd., v.p. ways and means 1989-90, planning coun./ad hoc 1990-92, sustainer spl. events 1993-94, found. 2002—), Community Emergency Fund (chair 1991-92), Jon D. Williams Cotillion at Columbine (chmn. 1991-93), Columbine Country Club, Gamma Alpha Chi, Pi Beta Phi Alumnae Club (pres. Denver chpt. 1984-85, 93-94, nat. conv. chmn. Denver 2001), Pi Beta Phi Found. (grantee 2000-05). Episcopalian. Avocations: traveling, skiing, golf, family activities. Home: 63 Fairway Ln Littleton CO 80123-6648

KEOGH, JAMES, journalist; b. Platte County, Nebr., Oct. 29, 1916; s. David James and Edith (Dwyer) K.; m. Verna Pedersen, May 17, 1940; children—Kevin, Katherine Ann Ph.B., Creighton U., 1938. Reporter Omaha World-Herald, 1938-48, city editor, 1948-51; contbg. editor Time mag., 1951-52, assoc. editor, 1952-56, sr. editor, 1956-61, asst. mng. editor, 1961-68, exec. editor, 1968; spl. asst. Pres. U.S., 1969-70; freelance writer, 1971-72; dir. USIA, 1973-77; exec. dir. The Business Roundtable, 1977-86. Author: This is Nixon, 1956, President Nixon and the Press, 1972, Centennial in Belle Haven, 1989, One of a Kind, 1995, Living By Our Wicks, 1999; editor: Corporate Ethics: A Prime Business Asset, 1988. Bd. dirs. The Phila. Fund, 1987-2003. Recipient Distinguished Nebraskan award, 1972 Mem.: Belle Haven (Greenwich, Conn.) (pres.-commodore 1967-68, 84). Home: 202 W Lyon Farm Dr Greenwich CT 06831-4353

KEOGH, KEVIN, lawyer; b. Omaha, Dec. 24, 1941; s. James Charles and Verna Marion (Pedersen) K.; m. Susan Elizabeth Mary Griffiths, Apr. 26, 1975; children: James, Caroline, Colin, Brendan. AB with honors, Holy Cross Coll., 1963; JD, Harvard U., 1966. Bar: N.Y. 1969, Conn. 1977, U.S. Ct. Appeals (2nd cir.) 1975. Assoc. Breed, Abbott & Morgan, N.Y.C., 1969-75, ptnr., 1975-88, White & Case, N.Y.C., 1988—, exec. ptnr., 1992—. Dir. United Hosp. Fund of N.Y., 1984-88; vol. U.S. Peace Corps., Nicoya, Costa Rica, 1966-68. Mem. Am. Yacht Club (commodore 1985-86, Disting. Svc. award 1989), Yacht Racing Assn. L.I. Sound (Pres. 1983-84, Disting. Svc. award 1985), N.Y. Yacht Club (competitions com. 1990-92). Republican. Episcopalian.. Home: 18 Sherwood Farm Ln Greenwich CT 06831-4410 Office: White & Case 1155 Avenue Of The Americas New York NY 10036-2787 E-mail: kkeogh@whitecase.com.

KEOGH, MARTIN JAY, dancer, educator; b. Oshawa, Canada, Jan. 11, 1958; s. John Neville and Linda Esther Keogh; m. Lisa Anne Hunscher; 1 child, Dylan Ambrose. Studied, Stanford U., Palo Alto, Calif., 1976—77; BA, U. Calif., Berkeley, 1992—94. Cert. Dharma tchr. Chogye Sch. of Zen Buddhism, 1979. Founder The Dancing Ground, Berkeley, Calif., 1982—, Spring/Fall Dance Studio, Berkeley, Calif., 1984—95; prin. aerial trapeze dancer The Motivity Co., Berkeley, Calif., 1984—86; master tchr., adj. faculty Stanford U., Palo Alto, Calif., 1992; instr. Instituto Nacional de Bellas Artes, San Miguel de Allende, Mexico, 1997—2000; prin. tchr. Seattle Festival of Alternative Dance and Improvisation, 1997—. Dir. Empty Gate Zen Ctr., Berkeley, Calif., 1978—79; curator CI25, Oberlin College, Ohio, 1998. Author: (book) As Much Time as it Takes, 2000, The Art of Waiting, 2003; writer, choreographer, performer (one-man shows) Out on a Limb, co-creator and co-star (two man show) Cat's Pause and Bare Feat. Cons. Touchdown Dance for the Visually Impaired, San Francisco, 1994—97; theater dir. Alliance for Radical Change, Stanford U., Palo Alto, Calif., 1976—77; bd. mem., lectr. San Francisco Sex Info., San Francisco, 1996—97. Mem.: Mensa, Phi Beta Kappa. Office: The Dancing Ground 24 Holmes St North Easton MA 02356 Office Fax: 510-405-2050. E-mail: contactintensive@aol.com.

KEOGH, MARY CUDAHY, artist; b. Milw., Nov. 11, 1920; d. John and Katherine (Reed) Cudahy; m. Frank Stephen Keogh, Jan. 17, 1947 (dec. 1980); children: Mary K., Anne C., Patricia, Margaret E.; m. Warren Stringer, July 5, 1985. Student, Smith Coll., 1939-42; BFA, Milw. Downer Coll., 1944; post grad., Parsons Sch. of Design, 1945. Artist, 1969—. Lectr. Woman's Club of Wis., 1977, workshops, Omaha, 1978-80, demo. Cape Coral (Fla.) Art League, 1991. One and two person shows include Lee County Alliance for the Arts, 1988, 90, 96, Barbara Mann Hall, Ft. Myers, 1992, Phillips Gallery, Sanibel, Fla., 1993, Uihlein-Peters Gallery, Milw., 1994, Alliance for the Arts, 1996, Phillips Gallery Sanibel, 1997, Syzygy Gallery, 2000; exhibited in group shows at Sarasota Visual Arts Ctr., 1995, Fla. Artists' Group, Winter Haven, 1996, Lee County Alliance for the Arts, 1996, Women's Caucus for Art, Longboat Key, Fla., 1997, Fla. Artists Group, Venice, 1997, Venice Biennial, 1997, Phillips Gallery, 1998; represented in permanent collections U. Utah, Cedar City, Northwestern Bell, Omaha, Health Park, Ft. Myers, others; retrospective Art House, 2003. Named Best of Show, Nebr. Wesleyan Coll., Lincoln, 1988; recipient 3d place, Sarasota Visual Arts Ctr., 1995, Big Arts, Sanibel, 1995, honorable mention award, Venice (Fla.) Biennial, 1997, Fla. Artist Group award, Jacksonville Mus. Contemporary Art, 1998, Best of Show, Big Arts Sanibel, 2000, 2d award, Big Arts, 2000, award, Flag Ann. Exhbn., 2001, Flag Invitational, 2002. Mem. Women Contemporary Artists (Best of Show spring show), Nat. Mus. Women in the Arts (charter), Fla. Artists Group. Roman Catholic. Avocations: cooking, traveling. Home: 9439 Coventry Ct Sanibel FL 33957-4231 E-mail: mkeoghstringer@aol.com.

KEOGH, RICHARD JOHN, firearms and explosives consultant; b. Woonsocket, R.I., Sept. 23, 1932; s. Michael Joseph and Dora Marie (Rumgay) K. BBA, U. Mass., 1958; MA, Pepperdine U., 1974. Lic. explosive disposal technician, Mass.; expert witness explosives and firearms, Hawaii, Mass. Commd. 2d lt. U.S. Army, 1958, advanced through grades to maj., 1967; stationed at various locations including Korea and Vietnam, 1958-73; ret. USAR, 1979; disposal specialist USN, Lualualei, Hawaii, 1973-76; mgmt. analyst Marine Corps Air Sta., Kaneohe Bay, Hawaii, 1976-93. Contbr. articles to profl. jours. Pres. Assn. of Owners Palms Condominium, Honolulu, 1978-80. With USAR, 1973-79. Decorated 3 Bronze Stars, 2 Purple Hearts, 2 Air medals, Cross of Gallantry, Commendation medal; recipient Founders award Order of the Arrow Boy Scouts Am., 1989, FBI Cert. of Appreciation, 1991, Silver Beaver award Boy Scouts Am., 1993. Mem. VFW (life), DAV (life), Internat. Assn. Bomb Technicians and Investigators (life, Hawaii chpt. dir. 2000—), Nat. Auto Pistol Collectors Assn., Ohio Gun Collectors Assn., Bay Colony Weapons Collectors, Hawaii Rifle Assn. (pres. 1994-96, 2000-02), Gun Owners Action League, Am. Legion (life), Mil. Order Purple Heart (life). Avocations: rifle shooting, ammo reloading, photography. Home: 431 Nahua St Apt 203 Honolulu HI 96815-2915

KEOHANE, NANNERL OVERHOLSER, university president, political scientist; b. Blytheville, Ark., Sept. 18, 1940; d. James Arthur and Grace (McSpadden) Overholser; m. Patrick Henry III, Sept. 16, 1962 (div. May 1969); 1 child, Stephan Henry; m. Robert Owen Keohane, Dec. 18, 1970; children: Sarah, Jonathan, Nathaniel. BA, Wellesley Coll., 1961, Oxford U., Eng., 1963; PhD, Yale U., 1967. Faculty Swarthmore Coll., Pa., 1967—73, Stanford U., Calif., 1973—81, fellow Ctr. for Advanced Study in the Behavioral Scis., 1978—79, 1987—88; pres., prof. polit. sci. Wellesley (Mass.) Coll., 1981—93, Duke U., Durham, NC, 1993—. Bd. dirs. IBM. Author: Philosophy and the State in France: The Renaissance to the Enlightenment, 1980; co-editor: Feminist Theory: A Critique of Ideology, 1982. Trustee Colonial Williamsburg Found., 1988—2001, Nat. Humanities Ctr., 1993—, Doris Duke Charitable Found., 1996—. Named to National Women's Hall of Fame, 1995; fellow Dissertation fellow, AAUW; scholar Marshall scholar, 1961—63. Fellow: Am. Philos. Soc., Am. Acad. Arts and Scis.; mem.: Coun. on Fgn. Rels., Watauga Club, Saturday Club, Phi Beta Kappa. Democrat. Episcopalian. Office: Duke Univ Box 90001 207 Allen Bldg Durham NC 27708-0001

KEOHANE, ROBERT OWEN, political scientist, educator; b. Chgo., Oct. 3, 1941; s. Robert Emmet and Mary Irene (Pieters) K.; m. Nannerl Overholser, Dec. 18, 1970; children: Jonathan, Sarah, Stephan, Nathaniel BA, Shimer Coll., 1961; MA, Harvard U., 1964, PhD, 1966; D (hon.), U. Aarhus, Denmark, 1998. From instr. to assoc. prof. Swarthmore Coll., Pa., 1965-73; from assoc. prof. to prof. Stanford U., Calif., 1973-81, chmn. dept. polit. sci., 1980-81; prof. politics Brandeis U., Waltham, Mass., 1981-85; prof. govt. Harvard U., Cambridge, Mass., 1985-96, chmn., 1988-92, Stanfield prof. internat. peace, 1989-96; James B. Duke prof. polit. sci. Duke U., Durham, N.C., 1996—. Author: After Hegemony, 1984, International Institutions and State Power, 1989, Power and Governance in a Partially Globalized World, 2002; co-author: Power and Interdependence, 1977, Designing Social Inquiry, 1994; co-editor: Transnational Relations and World Politics, 1972, The New European Community, 1991, Institutions for the Earth, 1993, After the Cold War, 1993, Ideas and Foreign Policy, 1993, Global Interdependence and Local Communitities, 1994, Internationalization and Domestic Politics, 1996, International Environmental Aid, 1996, Imperfect Unions, 1999, Exploration and Contestation in World Politics, 1999, Legalization and World Politics, 2001, Humanitarian Intervention, 2003; editor: Neorealism and Its Critics, 1986; editor Internat. Orgn., 1974-80; contbr. articles to profl. jours. Chmn. New Democratic Coalition Delaware County, Pa., 1969-71; pres. Triangle Land Conservancy, 2000-02. Recipient Sumner prize Harvard U., 1966, Grawemeyer award, 1989; fellow Ctr. Advanced Study in Behavior Scis., 1977-78 87-88; Guggenheim fellow, 1992, Frank Kenan fellow Nat. Humanities Ctr., 1995-96. Mem. Am. Acad. Arts and Scis., Am. Polit. Sci. Assn. (pres. 1999-2000), Am. Econ. Assn., Coun. Fgn. Rels. (Internat. Affairs fellow 1968-69), Internat. Studies Assn. (pres. 1988-89). Home: 1508 Pinecrest Rd Durham NC 27705-5817

KEOUGH, DONALD RAYMOND, investment company executive, director; b. Maurice, Iowa, Sept. 4, 1926; s. Leo H. and Veronica (Henkels) K.; m. Marilyn Mulhall, Sept. 10, 1949; children: Kathleen Anne, Mary Shayla, Michael Leo, Patrick John, Eileen Tracey, Clarke Robert. BS, Creighton U., 1949, LLD (hon.), 1982, U. Notre Dame, 1985, Emory U., 1993, Trinity U., Dublin, Ireland, 1993, Clarke U., 1994. With Butter-Nut Foods Co., Omaha, 1950-61; with Duncan Foods Co., Houston, 1961-67; v.p., dir. mktg. foods div. Coca-Cola Co., Atlanta, 1967-71, pres. div., 1971-73; exec. v.p. Coca-Cola USA, Atlanta, 1973-74, pres., 1974-76; exec. v.p. Coca-Cola Co., Atlanta, 1976-79, sr. exec. v.p., 1980-81, pres., COO, dir., 1981-93; chmn. bd. dirs. Coca-Cola Enterprises, 1986-93; advisor to bd. Coca-Cola Co., Atlanta, 1993-98. Bd. dirs. Convera Corp., McDonald's Corp., USA Networks, Inc., YankeeNets LLC; chmn. bd. Allen & Co., Inc., Atlanta, 1993—. Mem. president's coun. Creighton U.; trustee emeritus U. Notre Dame and Lovett Sch. With USNR, 1944-46. Mem. Capital City Club, Piedmont Driving Club, Commerce Club, Peachtree Golf Club. Office: 200 Galleria Pky NW Ste 970 Atlanta GA 30339-5945

KEOUGH, JAMES GILLMAN, JR., minister; b. Reading, Pa., June 2, 1947; s. James Gillman Sr. and Nora (Deturck) K.; m. Dawn Eileen Wiest, Sept. 17, 1976; children: Cynthia Ann, James Michael, Wendy Sue, Danielle Lynn, Erin Mae, Bevin Leigh. BA in History Edn., Messiah Coll., Grantham, Pa., 1970; MDiv, Lancaster (Pa.) Theol. Sem., 1973; D of Ministry, Ashland (Ohio) Theol. Sem., 1980. Ordained to ministry United Ch. Christ, 1973. Minister St. Luke's United Ch. Christ, Kenhorst, Pa., 1972-75, Congl. Ch., Winchester, Va., 1975-78, 1st Congl. Ch., Newton Falls, Ohio, 1978-82, Cen. Congl. Ch., Middleboro, Mass., 1982-85; sr. minister 1st Congl. Ch., Pontiac, Mich., 1985—. Founder Prayer Unlimited, Waterford, Mich., 1997—. Author: Teaching Prayer in the Local Parish, 1980, Prayer Unlimited, 1997. Mem. Oakland County Rep. Club, Mich. Rep. 500 Club; bd. dirs. Clinton Valley coun. Boy Scouts Am.; bd. dirs. Boys Clubs Am., Pontiac; pres. Somebodycares, Pontiac, 1983—. Mem. Nat. Assn. Congl. Christian Chs., S.E. Mich. Congl. Ministerium, Independence Twp. Pastors Assn., Kiwanis. Avocations: reading, hiking, fishing. Home: 3062 St Jude Dr Waterford MI 48329-4359 Office: 1st Congl Church Clarkston Rd at Pine Knob Rd PO Box 221 Clarkston MI 48347-0221

KEOUGH, JOSEPH ALOYSIOS, judge; b. Providence, Apr. 8, 1941; s. s. Joseph A. and Mary (Crane) K.; m. Joanne Lee, Oct. 9, 1965; children: Joseph, Maureen, Kathleen, Colleen. BA, Providence Coll., 1962; JD, Suffolk U., 1970. Bar: R.I. 1970, U.S. Dist. Ct. R.I. 1971. Assoc. McGee, Fifford, Farrelly & Keough, Providence, 1970-75; ptnr. Keough, Parker, Gearon & Viner, Pawtucket, R.I., 1975-97; mcpl. ct. judge City of Pawtucket, 1974-97. Dir., sec. First Bank & Trust, Providence; dir. East Greenwich Dairy; pres. Ross Brooks Ent., Pawtucket, 1979—. Exec. sec. R.I. Dem. Com., 1976; del. Dem. Nat. Conv., R.I., 1972; chmn. appeals City of Pawtucket, 1968-74. Burke scholar R.I. Golf Assn., 1958. Mem. Am. Arbitration Assn., Pawtucket County Club (v.p., sec., pres.), Elks, Irish Kings. Roman Catholic. Home: 72 Anawan Rd Pawtucket RI 02861-3327 Office: RI Superior Ct 250 Benefit St Providence RI 02903

KEPHART, LARRY ROBERT, architect; b. Clearfield, Pa., Sept. 1, 1949; s. Robert Joseph and Nora Elizabeth (Livergood) K. Student, Pa. State U., 1967-69. Drafter RCP Architects, Johnstown, Pa., 1970-72; office mgr. R. William Clayton Jr., Ft. Lauderdale, Fla., 1972-80; project architect C.F. McKirihan, Ft. Lauderdale, 1980-81, A. Nicholas Hosking, Ft. Lauderdale, 1981-82, Randall F. Keller, Ft. Lauderdale, 1982-83; architect, mgr. info. systems Vander Ploeg & Assocs., Boca Raton, Fla., 1983—; propr. Laroke Microcomputer Cons., 1993—. Vis. lectr. Ft. Lauderdale Art Inst., 1983—. Mem. Rotary (bd. dirs. 1981), Masons. Avocations: computer programming, reading, wargames, automobile restoration. Home: 772 Tivoli Cir Apt 204 Deerfield Beach FL 33441-8137 Office: Vander Ploeg & Assocs 155 E Boca Raton Rd Boca Raton FL 33432-3911 E-mail: webmaster@laroke.com.

KEPLEY, STEPHEN RICHARD, optometrist; b. Jan. 28, 1955; s. Joseph Charles and Diane Boehms Kepley, Aug. 18, 1984; children: Jason, Kate, Rachel. BA, Catawba Coll., 1977; OD, So. Coll. Optometry, 1983. Assoc. Drs. Tedeson & Kepley, Vero Beach, Fla., 1985-86; physician, owner Visual Concepts Family Eye Care, Vero Beach, 1986—. Examiner Fla. Bd. Optometry; pres. Fla. Optometric Consortium, 1993-95 (bd. dirs.); mem. peer rev. and quality assurance com. Vision Svc. Plan Fla Vision screening adv. bd. Indian River County Sch. Dist., 1994—. Mem. Optometric Assn., Fla. Optometric Assn. (past chmn. continuing edn. com.), So. Coun. of Optometrists, Treasure Coast Optometric Soc. (past pres.), Rotary, Beta Sigma Kappa. Republican. Avocation: antique autos. Office: Ste B 1960 25th Ave Vero Beach FL 32960

KEPLINGER, BRUCE (DONALD KEPLINGER), lawyer; b. Kansas City, Kans., Feb. 4, 1952; s. Donald Lee and Janet Adelheit (Viets) K.; children: Mark William, Lisbeth Marie, Kristen Michelle, Kailyn Emily, Courtney Nicole; m. Carol Ann Heinz, Apr. 12, 1991. BA with highest distinction, U. Kans., 1974; JD cum laude, So. Meth. U., 1977. Bar: Kans. 1977, U.S. Dist. Ct. Kans. 1977, Mo. 1980, U.S. Dist. Ct. Mo. 1980, U.S. Ct. Appeals (10th cir.) 1985, U.S. Supreme Ct. 1989. Assoc. Clark, Mize & Linville, Salina, Kans., 1977-79, Blackwell, Sanders et al, Kansas City, Mo., 1979-82; ptnr. Payne & Jones, Overland Park, Kans., 1982-94, Norris, Keplinger & Hillman, LLC, Overland Park, 1994—. Master Kansas Inns of Ct.; chmn. Kansas Lawyer Svcs Corp., 1992-01. Contbr. articles to profl. jours. V.p. Friends of Libr., Johnson County, Kans., 1980-85; deacon Village Presbyn. Ch., 1982-86; trustee United Meth. Ch. of Resurrection, trustee, 2002—. Mem.: ABA, Fedn. Def. and Corp. Counsel, Def. Rsch. Inst., Kans. Assn. Def. Counsel (pres.-elect 1992—93, pres. 1993—94), Mo. Bar Assn., Kans. Bar Assn. (chmn. kans. lawyer svc. corp. 1992—2001), Assn. Def. Trial Attys. (state chmn. 1996—, exec. coun. 1999—2002), Internat. Assn. Def. Counsel, Hallbrook Country Club. Republican. Avocations: reading, golf. Office: Norris Keplinger & Hillman LLC 6800 College Blvd Ste 630 Overland Park KS 66211-1556 E-mail: bkeplinger@k-c-lawyers.com.

KEPLINGER, MICHAEL SCOTT, lawyer; b. Martinsburg, W.Va., Mar. 26, 1940; s. Raymond Lester and Bertha Louise (Kidwiler) K.; m. Helen Bunten, Dec. 27, 1963; children: Michael Scott, Gregory Thomas. BS in Chemistry, W.Va. U., 1963; JD, Georgetown U., 1971. Bar: Md. 1972. Computer scientist Nat. Bur. Stds., Washington, 1967-76; asst. exec. dir. Nat. Commn. on New Technol. Uses of Copyrighted Works, Washington, 1976-78; spl. legal asst. to register U.S. Copyright Office, Washington, 1978-80, chief info. and rev. divsn., 1980-83, policy planning advisor, 1983-84; sr. counselor Office Legis. and Internat. Affairs U.S. Patent and Trademark Office, Washington, 1984—. Cons. World Intellectual Property Orgn.; dep. head Del. to Diplomatic Conf. on Certain Copyright and Neighboring Rights Matters, 1996; chief copyright negotiator for Agreement on Trade Related Aspects of Intellectual Property (TRIPS) for the U.S., 1990-95; negotiator for Diplomatic Conf. on Protection of Audiovisual Performers, Dec. 2000. Home: 5001 Nahant St Bethesda MD 20816-2462 E-mail: michael.keplinger@uspto.gov.

KEPNER, ANNE JONES, lawyer; b. Norwalk, Conn., Jan. 15, 1969; d. Thomas David Jr. and Elizabeth Call Jones; m. Thomas James Kepner, June 12, 1999. BS in Health Sci., San Jose (Calif.) State U., 1991; JD, U. Calif., San Francisco, 1995. Assoc. Licardo, Rossi, et al, San Jose, 1996-97, Hoge, Fenton, Jones & Appel, San Jose, 1997—. Mem. Santa Clara Bar Assn. (bd. dirs. 1996-98, pres. barristers sect. 1998-99), Rotary Internat., Valle Monte League. Office: Hoge Fenton Jones and Appel 60 S Market St Ste 1400 San Jose CA 95113-2396

KEPPEL, JOHN H. minister; b. Bellaire, Ohio, Jan. 02; s. John Henry Keppel and Doris Thurber; m. Mildred Elizabeth Winterhalter; children: John Daniel, Mark Warren, Joel Kristan. BA, Bethany Coll., 1943; MA, Yale Div. Sch., 1946. Ordained min. Christian Ch. (Disciples of Christ). Min. Christian Ch. (Disciples of Christ), Republic, Pa., 1946—51, Havre de Grace, 1951—55, Indpls., 1958—67, Columbus, Ohio, 1967—76, Fairview Heights, Ill., 1975—79, Wheeling, W.Va., 1979—88, Ch. of Christ, Falkirk, Scotland, 1955—58. Recipient Outstanding Achievement award, Bethany Alumni Assn., 1999. Mem.: Kiwanis (com. chmn. 1980—88). Democrat. Home: 33 Biltmore Ave Wheeling WV 26003-1415

KEPPEL, TIMOTHY ANDERSON, humanities educator, writer; b. Alamogordo, N.Mex., Oct. 21, 1955; s. Robert Alvin and Nancy (Peeler) K. BA, U. N.C., 1978; MFA, U. Calif., Irvine, 1981; PhD, Fla. State U., 1996. Social worker City of Phila., 1989-92; instr. C.C. of Phila., 1991-92, Fla. State U., Tallahassee, 1992-95; prof. lit. U. del Valle, Cali, Colombia, 1995—. Cons. Consejo Nacional de Acreditación, Bogota, 1992—. Contbr. articles, over 30 short stories to jours. in Can., U.S. and S.Am. Vol. Witness for Peace, Nicaragua, 1985. U. Calif.-Irvine Regents fellow, 1979. Mem. MLA, Coll. Lang. Assn., Phi Beta Kappa, Phi Kappa Phi. Home: 4404 Woodbridge Ct Raleigh NC 27612-3916 Office: Univ del Valle AA25360 Cali Colombia

KEPPEL, WILLIAM JAMES, lawyer, educator, writer; b. Sheboygan, Wis., Sept. 25, 1941; s. William Frederick and Anne Elizabeth (Cinealis) K.; m. Polly Holmberg, June 26, 1965; children: Anne Rusert, Timothy, Matthew. BA, Marquette U., 1963; JD, U. Wis., Madison, 1970. Bar: Minn. 1970, U.S. Dist. Minn. 1970, U.S. Ct. Appeals (8th cir.) 1973, U.S. Dist. Ct. (we. dist.) Wis. 1979, U.S. Supreme Ct. 1979, U.S. Ct. Claims 1982. Assoc. Dorsey & Whitney, Mpls., 1970-76, ptnr., 1979-96; assoc. prof. Hamline U. Sch. Law, 1976-79, disting. practitioner in residence, 1996-2000. Instr. U. Minn. Law Sch.; adj. prof. William Mitchell Coll. Law, St. Paul; state adminstrv. law judge, 1977-79, 98—; chmn., dir. Legal Advice Clinics, Ltd.; dir. Legal Assistance of Minn., Inc.; head Hennepin County Pub. Defender's Office for Misdemeanors. Author: (with Mc Farland) Minnesota Civil Practice (4 vols.), 1979, 3d edit., 1999, Administrative Practice and Procedure, 1999; co-author, editor: Minnesota Environmental Law Handbook, 2nd edit., 1995; contbr. articles and monographs to legal jours. Lt. USN, 1963-67, Vietnam. Mem. ABA, Minn. Bar Assn. Roman Catholic. Home: 10 Luverne Ave Minneapolis MN 55419-2612

KEPPELMAN, NANCY, lawyer; b. Abington, Pa., June 28, 1950; d. H. Thomas and Helene A. (Harrow) Keppelman; m. Michael E. Smerza, Sept. 9, 1978. Student, Oberlin (Ohio) Coll., 1968-70; BA, U. Mich., 1972, JD, 1978; Cert., Inst. for Paralegal Tng., Phila., 1972. Bar: Mich. 1978, U.S. Dist. Ct. (ea. dist.) Mich. 1978, U.S. Tax Ct. 1986. Legal asst. Dykema, Gossett et al, Detroit, 1972-75; assoc. Butzel, Keidan et al, Detroit, 1978-80, Law Offices of Brook McCray Smith, Ann Arbor, Mich., 1980-82, Miller, Canfield et al, Detroit, 1982-89, Stevenson Assocs., Ann Arbor, 1989-90; shareholder/lawyer Stevenson Keppelman Assocs., Ann Arbor, 1991—. Condr. seminars in field. Co-author, editor QDROs, EDROs and Division of Employee Benefits in Divorce, A Guide for Michigan Practitioners, 2002; contbr. articles to profl. jours. James B. Angell scholar, U. Mich., 1972. Fellow Mich. State Bar Found., Am. Coll. Benefits Counsel; mem. ABA, State Bar Mich. (mem. taxation coun. 1991-94), Washtenaw County Bar Assn., Women Lawyers Assn. Mich. (bd. dirs., pres. Washtenaw region 1990-93). Avocations: birdwatching, music, hiking. Office: 444 S Main St Ann Arbor MI 48104-2304 E-mail: kep@skalaw.com.

KEPPLE, THOMAS RAY, JR., college administrator; b. Pitts., Mar. 19, 1948; s. Thomas Ray and Virginia Grace (Hudson) K.; m. Jane Donaldson, Aug. 22, 1971 (dec. 1977); m. Patricia Witcher, May 24, 1994. BA, Westminster Coll., 1970; MBA, Syracuse U., 1973, EdD, 1984. Dir. tech. tng. Morse divsn. Borg-Warner Corp., Ithaca, N.Y., 1970-73; dir. adminstrv. svcs. Rhodes Coll., Memphis, 1975-81, dean adminstrv. svcs., 1981-86, provost, 1986-89; v.p. Univ. South, Sewanee, Tenn., 1989-98; pres. Juniata Coll., Huntingdon, Pa., 1998—. Founding chair bd. dirs. Prepaid Tuition Consortium, The Ind. 529 Plan; chmn. Brethren Coll. Abroad Consortium. Author: Incentive Early Retirement Programs for Faculty. Bd. dirs. Sewanee Housing Inc., 1993-98; mem. exec. com. Vollintine Evergreen Cmty. Assn., Memphis, 1976-85, pres., 1981; mem. Biomed. Rsch. Zone Bd., 1986; sec.-treas. Health and Ednl. Facilities Bd. of Franklin County; bd. dirs. Liberty Bowl Classic, co-chair Gov.' Rendell's higher edn. transition com. Mem. Internat. Soc. Planning and Strategic Mgmt. (v.p. coms. 1984-85, pres. 1985-87), Assn. Ind. Colls. and Univs. Pa. (bd. dirs.), Nat. Assn. Coll. and Univ. Bus. Officers, Am. Assn. Higher Assn., Memphis Acad. Forum (pres. 1985-86), Coll. and Univ. Personnel Assn., Assn. Physical Plant Adminstrs., Univ. Club (N.Y.), Omicron Delta Kappa. Mem. Brethren Ch. Avocations: swimming, oil painting. Home: 2201 Washington St Huntingdon PA 16652-9762 Office: Juniata Coll Office of the Pres 1700 Moore St Huntingdon PA 16652-2119 E-mail: kepplet@juniata.edu.

KEPPLER, HERBERT, publishing company executive; b. N.Y.C., Apr. 21, 1925; s. Victor and Josephine T. (Windmann) K.; m. Louise M. Lyman, July 7, 1956; children— Kathryn Louise, Thomas Victor. BA, Harvard, 1945. Reporter N.Y. Sun, 1948-49; with Modern Photography, N.Y.C., 1950-87, editorial dir., pub., 1967-87; v.p. photog. pub. div. ABC Leisure Mags. Inc. div. ABC, N.Y.C., 1974-78, sr. v.p. photog. pub. div., 1978-87; v.p., pub. dir. photography CBS Mags. Am. Photo and Popular Photography, 1987-88, Diamandis Communications Inc., 1988-90, Hachette Mags. Inc., 1990-93, Hachette Filipacchi Media U.S., Inc., 1993—. Author: Official 35mm Camera Rating Guide, 1957, Keppler on the Eye-Level Reflex, 1960, How to Make Better Pictures in Your Home, 1962, 124 Ways to Test Cameras, Lenses and Equipment, 1962, The Pentax Way, 1966, The Nikon-Nikkormat Way, 1976. Served to ensign USNR, 1945-46. Mem. Rolls-Royce Owners Club. Home: 119 N Highland Pl Croton on Hudson NY 10520-2113 Office: Hachette Filipacchi Media US Inc 1633 Broadway New York NY 10019-6708 E-mail: hkeppler@hfmus.com.

KEPPLER, WILLIAM EDMUND, multinational company executive; b. N.Y.C., June 12, 1922; s. Louis and Amelia (Koszut) K.; m. Natalie E. Lang, July 15, 1944 (dec. 1990); children: Gail, William Edmund, Jean; m. Margaret Delaney, June 20, 1992. BSChemE, Pratt Inst., 1942; MSChemE, NYU, 1944. Vice pres. Merck Sharp & Dohme, West Point, Pa., 1965-71; Vice pres. Squibb Corp., Holmdel, N.J., 1971-73; pres. Bell Mgmt., Blue Bell, Pa., 1973-74, Engel Industries, St. Louis, 1974-75; corp. sr. v.p. tech. ops./mgmt. systems Schering-Plough Corp., 1975-87; pres. Bell Mgmt., Inc., 1987—. Tchr. chem. engring. Cooper Union, NYU, Bucknell U. Bd. dirs. Phila. chpt. Am. Cancer Soc., 1979; pres. Montour County (Pa.) Cerebral Palsy, 1953-57. Fellow AIChE; mem. Whitemarsh Valley Country Club (Lafayette Hill, Pa.), PGA Nat. Golf Club (Palm Beach Gardens, Fla.). Episcopalian. Home and Office: 407 Eagleton Cove Way Palm Beach Gardens FL 33418-8464

KEPROS, JOHN PAUL, trauma surgeon; b. Cresco, Iowa, Apr. 19, 1964; s. Stanley George and Rita Wilma Kepros; m. Michele Rene Hurrell, Sept. 27, 1997; children: Ethan, Brandon, Madison. BSE in Biomed. Engring., U. Iowa, 1987, MD, 1991; MS, Mich. State U., 1996. Diplomate Am. Bd. Surgery with subspecialty in critical care. Intern LDS Hosp., Salt Lake City, 1991—92; resident Mich. State U., East Lansing, 1992—98; fellow Yale U., New Haven, 1998—99; trauma surgeon Swedish Med. Ctr., Englewood, Colo., 1999—, co-med. dir. ICU, 2002—, prin. investigator, 2000—; pvt. practice trauma surgery Mile High Surg. Specialists, Englewood, 1999—. Contbr. Recipient Resident Tchg. award, Mich. State U., 1994, 1996. Mem.: AMA, Soc. Critical Care Medicine, Western Trauma Assn. Roman Catholic. Achievements include development of evidence based medical practices in the ICU. Avocations: reading, travel. Home: 8861 S Chestnut Hill Ln Highlands Ranch CO 80130 Office: Mile High Surgical Specialists 601 E Hampden #340 Englewood CO 80110

KER, IAN TURNBULL, priest, scholar; b. Naini Tal, India, Aug. 30, 1942; s. Charles Murray and Joan May (Knox) K. BA, Balliol Coll., Oxford, 1964; PhD, Trinity Coll., Cambridge, 1969. Lectr. in English lit. U. York, 1969-74; endowed chair in theology and philosphy U. St. Thomas, Minn., 1987-89; tutor in theology Campion Hall, Oxford, 1996—. Vis. prof. humanities Franciscan U., Steubenville, Ohio, 1993; Cath. chaplain Southampton U., 1982-87; sr. Cath. chaplain Oxford U., 1989-90; dean grad. rsch. Maryvale Inst., Birmingham, 1991-96. Author, editor 18 books, including: The Achievement of John Henry Newman, 1990, (biography) John Henry Newman: A Biography, 1988; editor: Newman: Idea of a University, 1976, The Catholic Revival in English Literature, 1845-1961, 2003. Mem. Cath. Theol. Assn. Avocations: walking, listening to music. Home: 171 The Hill Burford OX18 4RE England Office: Campion Hall Brewer St Oxford OX1 1QS England

KERAMATI, SHAHIN, cardiologist; b. Teheran, Iran, Sept. 9, 1967; arrived in U.S., 1982; s. Mohammad Ali and Zahra Keramati; married; 1 child, Nikki Rachel. BS in Biology, BA in History, Tufts U., 1989; MD, U. Calif., San Diego, 1993. Diplomate Am. Bd. Interventional Cardiology, Am. Bd. Internal Medicine, Am. Bd. Cardiology. Chief of cardiology Coast Cardiology, Encinitas, Calif., 2001—; clin. prof. medicine U. Calif. San Diego Sch. Medicine, 2001—; ptnr. San Diego Heart and Vascular Assocs., 2002—. Cardiologist Scripps La Jolla Hosp., San Diego, 2001—, Scripps Mercy Hosp., San Diego, 2001—, U. Calif. San Diego Med. Ctr., 2001—. Contbr. articles to profl. jours. Mem.: AMA, Am. Coll. Cardiology. Republican. Office: San Diego Heart & Vascular Assocs 4060 4th Ave Ste 240 San Diego CA 92103

KERBER, FRANK JOHN, diplomat; b. Indpls., June 13, 1947; s. Charles John and Romilda Ida (Molengraft) K.; m. Melanie Alice Niewoehner, July 29, 1989; 1 child, Brandon Eric Kerber. BA in Philosophy cum laude, Athenaeum of Ohio, 1969; MS, Georgetown U., 1976. Faculty coll. prep. sch., Cin., 1970-74; mgmt. cons. USAID, various locations, 1976-80; program officer USAID Mission, Tunis, Tunisia, 1980-84, Dept. of State, 1984; vice consul U.S. Consulate Gen., Winnipeg, Can., 1985-86; econ./comml. affairs officer Jordan, Lebanon and Syria, 1986-88; officer for East-West Affairs European Bur. Office of Regional Polit. and Econ. Affairs, 1988-90; A.I.D. liaison officer Bangui, Ctrl. African Republic, 1991-93; econ. officer Kingston, Jamaica, 1993-96; internat. economist Bur. Internat. Orgn. Affairs, Washington, 1996-98; spl. asst. to Amb. Schifter, 1998-2000, Ireland desk officer, 2000—02; with U.S. Mission to European Union, Brussels, 2002—. Mem. Am. Fgn. Svc. Assn. Home: USEU/NAS PSC 82 Box 002 APO AE 09710 Office: USEU Brussels Belgium E-mail: kerberf@state.gov.

KERBER, LINDA KAUFMAN, historian, educator; b. N.Y.C., Jan. 23, 1940; d. Harry Hagman and Dorothy (Haber) Kaufman; m. Richard Kerber, June 5, 1960; children: Ross Jeremy, Justin Seth. AB cum laude, Barnard Coll., 1960; MA, NYU, 1961; PhD, Columbia U., 1968; DHL, Grinnell Coll., 1992. Instr., asst. prof. history Stern Coll., Yeshiva U., N.Y.C., 1963-68; asst. prof. history San Jose State Coll., (Calif.), 1969-70; vis. asst. prof. history Stanford U., (Calif.), 1970-71; asst. prof. history U. Iowa, Iowa City, 1971-75, prof., 1975-85, May Brodbeck prof., 1985—. Vis. prof. U. Chgo., 1991-92. Author: Federalists in Dissent: Imagery and Ideology in Jeffersonian America, 1970, paperback edit., 1980, 97, Women of the Republic: Intellect and Ideology in Revolutionary America, 1980, paperback edit., 1986, Toward an Intellectual History of Women, 1997, No Constitutional Right to Be Ladies: Women and the Obligations of Citizenship, 1998, paperback edit., 1999 (Littleton-Griswold prize in legal history Am. Hist. Assn., Joan Kelley prize in womens history Am. Hist. Assn.); co-editor: Women's America: Refocusing the Past, 1982, 5th edit., 2000, U.S. History As Women's History, 1995; mem. editl. bd. Signs: Jour. Women in Culture and Society, Jour. Women's History; contbr. articles and book revs. to profl. jours. Fellow Danforth Found., NEH, 1976, 83-84, 94, Am Coun. Learned Socs., 1975, Nat. Humanities Ctr., 1990-91, Guggenheim Found., 1990-91, Radcliffe Inst. for Advanced Study, 2003. Mem. Orgn. Am. Historians (pres. 1996-97), Am. Hist. Assn., Am. Studies Assn. (pres. 1988), Am. Soc. for Legal History, Berkshire Conf. Women Historians, Soc. Am. Historians, Japan U.S. Friendship Commn., PEN/Am. Ctr., Am. Acad. Arts and Scis. Jewish. Office: U Iowa Dept History Iowa City IA 52242

KERBER, RICHARD E. cardiologist; b. N.Y.C., May 10, 1939; s. Max and Pauline Kerber; m. Linda K. Kaufman; children: Ross, Justin. AB in Anthropology, Columbia U., 1960; MD, NYU, 1964. Diplomate Am. Bd. Internal Medicine, Am. Bd. Cardiology. Med. intern/resident Bellevue Hosp., N.Y.C., 1964—66; med. resident Stanford (Calif.) U. Hosp., 1968—69, cardiology fellow, 1969—71; asst. prof. internal medicine U. Iowa, Iowa City, 1971—74, assoc. prof. internal medicine, 1974—78, prof. medicine, 1978—. Editor: Echocardiography in Coronary Artery Disease, 1988. Capt. U.S. Army, 1966—68. Grantee RO1 grant, NHLBI, 1995—. Fellow: Am. Coll. Cardiology, Am. Heart Assn., Am. Heart Assn. (mem. coun. on cardiopulmonary and critical care 1997—99, 1997—99, award of Meritorious Achievement 1996, Scientific Coun. Dist. Achievement award 2001), Am. Coll. Cardiology (gov. for Iowa 1976—79, 1976—79); mem.: Assn. Am. Physicians, Assn. Univ. Cardiologists, Am. Soc. for Clin. Investigation, Am. Soc. Echocardiology (sec. 1978—80, treas. 1993—95, v.p. 1995—97, pres. 1997—99, sec. 1978—80, treas. 1993—95, v.p. 1995—97, pres. 1997—99). Office: U Iowa Dept Medicine 200 Hawkins Dr Iowa City IA 52242-1009

KERBIS, GERTRUDE LEMPP, architect; m. Walter Peterhans (dec.); m. Donald Kerbis (div. 1972); children: Julian, Lisa, Kim. BS, U. Ill.; MA, Ill. Inst. Tech.; postgrad., Grad. Sch. Design, Harvard U., 1949-50. Archtl. designer Skidmore, Owings & Merrill, Chgo., 1954-59, C.F. Murphy Assocs., Chgo., 1959-62, 65-67; pvt. practice architecture Lempp Kerbis Assocs., Chgo., 1967—; lectr. U. Ill., 1969; prof. William Rainey Harper Coll., 1970—95, Washington U., St. Louis, 1977, 82, Ill. Inst. Tech., 1989-91. Archtl. cons. Dept. Urban Renewal, City of Chgo.; mem. Northeastern Ill. Planning Commn., Open Land Project, Mid-North Community Orgn., Chgo. Met. Housing and Planning Council, Chgo. Mayor's Commn. for Preservation Chgo.'s Hist. Architecture; bd. dirs. Chgo. Sch. Architecture Found., 1972-76; trustee Chgo. Archtl. Assistance Ctr., Glessner House Found., Inland Architect Mag.; lectr. Art Inst. Chgo., U. N.Mex., Ill. Inst. Tech., Washington U., St. Louis, Ball State U., Muncie, Ind., U. Utah, Salt Lake City. Prin. archtl. works include U.S. Air Force Acad. dining hall, Colo., 1957, Skokie (Ill.) Pub. Library, 1959, Meadows Club, Lake Meadows, Chgo., 1959, O'Hare Internat. Airport 7 Continents Bldg, 1963; prin. developer and architect: Tennis Club, Highland Park, Ill., 1968, Watervliet, Mich. Tennis Ranch, 1970, Greenhouse Condominium, Chgo., 1976, Webster-Clark Townhouses, Chgo., 1986, Chappell Sch., 1993; exhibited at Chgo. Hist. Soc., 1984, Chgo. Mus. Sci. and Industry, 1985, Paris Exhbn. Chgo. Architects, 1985, Spertus Mus.; represented in permanent archtl. drawings collection Art Inst. Chgo. Active Art Inst. Chgo.. Recipient award for outstanding achievement in professions YWCA Met. Chgo., 1984 Fellow AIA (bd. dirs. Chgo. chpt. 1971-75, chpt. pres. 1980, nat. com. architecture, arts and recreation 1972-75, com. on design 1975-80, head subcom. inst. honors nomination); mem. Chgo. Women in Architecture (founder), Chgo. Network, Internat. Women's Forum, Arts Club Chgo., Cliff Dwellers (bd. dirs. 1987-88, pres. 1988, 89), Lambda Alpha. Office: Lempp Kerbis Assocs 172 W Burton Pl Chicago IL 60610-1310

KERBY, ROBERT BROWNING, media consultant; b. Waynesboro, Va., Oct. 21, 1938; s. Guy Albert and Josephine (Carpenter) Kerby. BSBA, Va. Poly. Inst., 1960; postgrad., U. Richmond, 1964, Va. Commonwealth U., 1965, U. Va., 1968. Rep. mfrs. Josten Co., Owatonna, Minn., 1960-67; gen. sales mgr. Sta. WANV, Waynesboro, 1967; tech. editor GE, Waynesboro, 1967-72; v.p., CEO Fishburne Hudgins Ednl. Found., Inc., Waynesboro, 1972-86, 1986—. Advisor Sovran Bank, Waynesboro, 1982—89; comm. cons. RF Comm. Cons., Waynesboro, 1986—; chmn. Target-2000 com. City of Waynesboro, 1988—; mem. adv. bd. Augusta med. Ctr. Lifetime Fitness Opn., 2002. Designer, author: catalogue Fishburne Mil. Sch., 1981 (1st pl. award Printers Assn. Va., 1982). Chair funding dir. Shenandoah Valley Art Ctr., Waynesboro; chamn. fund raising and adv. bd. Salvation Army, 1967—68; mem. libr. adv. bd. City of Waynesboro, 1995, vice-chair, 2000; chmn. prof. adv. bd. Waynesboro First Aid Crew; mem. adv. bd. Lifetime Fitness Ctr. Augusta Med. Ctr., 2002; chmn. publicity Robinson for Congress, 1970; bd. dirs., chmn. Waynesboro Redevel. Housing Authority, 1970—72; trustee Waynesboro Pub. Libr., 1995, vice-chmn., 2000, chmn., 2001; trustee Fishburne-Hudgins Ednl. Found., Inc., 1997; pres. Alumni Assn. Offices, 1960—71. Named Outstanding Vol. of the Yr., City of Waynesboro, 1990. Mem.: SAR, Am. Radio Relay League, Quarter Century Wireless Assn. Republican. Methodist. Office: RF Comm Cons PO Box 991 Waynesboro VA 22980-0723 E-mail: rbkerby@intelos.com.

KERCHER, DAVID MAX, mechanical engineer; b. Goshen, Ind., Nov. 18, 1931; s. Maxwell Mease and Rosemary (Harper) K.; m. Betty Noreen Raycroft, June 7, 1958; children: Kimberly S., Matthew R., Andrew D.R., Steven R., Elizabeth J., Jason R., Amy N. BSME, Purdue U., 1958; MS in Aerospace Engring., U. Cin., 1967. Engr. large jet engine divsn. GE, Cin., 1958-71, sr. engr., 1966-71, unit mgr., 1968, engr. missile and space div. Burlington, Vt., 1959-60, unit mgr. gas turbine dept. Schenectady, 1972-81, sr. engr., 1982, sub-sect. mgr. aircraft engine group Lynn, Mass., 1983-84; sr. engr. GE Aircraft Engines, Lynn, 1985-89, prin. engr., 1989—2001; ret., 2002. V.p. Sunrise Orchards, Inc., Goshen, Ind., 1996—2002, also bd. dirs. Contbr. articles to profl. jours.; 15 patents on gas turbine cooling. Sgt. USAF, 1950-54, USAFR, 1955-58. Fellow ASME (gas turbine heat transfer com. 1980—, vice chmn. com. 1992-94, chmn. 1994-96); mem. AIAA (sr.), ASME Internat. Gas Turbine Inst., Am. Legion (life), Air Force Assn. (life), Tau Beta Pi, Pi Tau Sigma. E-mail: dave@Kercher.org.

KERCKHOFF, SYLVIA STANSBURY, mayor; b. Toledo, June 7, 1928; d. Paul William Stansbury and Lass Elizabeth Hackney; m. Alan Chester Kerckhoff, June 11, 1949; children: Steven, Sharon. BS, U. Wis., 1950; MAT, Duke U., 1960. Kindergarten tchr. Madison (Wis.) Schs., 1950-52; rsch. asst. Vanderbilt U., Nashville, 1957-58; jr. and sr. h.s. tchr. City Schs., Durham, N.C., 1959-60, 69-81; city coun. mem. City of Durham, 1981-93, mayor, 1993-99. Co-chair Violence Prevention Commn., Durham, 1993-97; mem. Chamber Commerce Bd., Durham, 1993-97; founder Mayor's Univ. Adv. Coun., Durham, 1993-97; co-chair City-County Com., Durham, 1993-97. Chair N.C. League Municipalities, Transp., Comm. and Pub. Safety, 1996-97; mem. Gov.'s Transit 2000 Commn., N.C., 1996; v.p. N.C. League Women Voters, 1966-69, fin. chair, Durham League Women Voters, 1960-70; co-chair Youth Coordinating Bd., 1998—; v.p. pres. bd. dirs. Durham United Way, 1999. Recipient Leadership award Duke U. med. Ctr., Durham, 1995, Durham County Women's Commn. Svc. award, 1993, Community Leadership in Arts award Durham Arts Coun., 1991; inductee DeVilbiss H.S. Hall of Fame, Toledo, 1998. Democrat. Presbyterian. Avocations: reading, tennis, music, hiking, travel. Home: 1511 Pinecrest Rd Durham NC 27705-5816

KEREIAKES, DEAN JAMES, cardiologist; b. Louisville, Jan. 8, 1953; s. James G. and Helen (Christy) K.; m. Anne Sugar, June 20, 1981; children: Jennifer, David, Andrew, Nicholas. BS, U. Cin., 1974, MD, 1978. Diplomate Am. Bd. Internal Medicine, Am. Bd. Cardiology. Intern, resident U. Calif., San Francisco, 1978-80; sr. resident Mass. Gen. Hosp., Boston, 1980-81; chief med. resident H.C. Moffitt Hosp., San Francisco, 1981-82; adult cardiology fellow U. Calif., San Francisco, 1982-84; coronary angioplasty fellow San Francisco Heart Inst., 1984, Sequoia Hosp., Redwood City, Calif., 1984; attending cardiologist The Christ Hosp., Cin., 1985—; CEO, dir. rsch. Ohio Heart Health Ctr., 2000—. Med. dir. The Christ Hosp., 1986-95, Carl & Edythe Lindner Ctr. Clin. Cardiovasc. Rsch., Cin., 1995—; prof. clin. medicine Ohio State U., 1995—; mem. ACC/AHA task force com on angioplasty and unstable angina guidelines AHA/ACC, 1987—. Mem. editl. bd. Circulation, sect. editor, mem. editl. bd. Jour. Invasive Cardiology, Am. Heart Jour., Am. Jour. Cardiology. Fellow Am. Coll. Cardiology; mem. AMA, Am. Heart Assn., Alpha Omega Alpha, Phi Beta Kappa. Republican. Avocation: wine collecting. Office: The Ohio Heart Health Ctr 2123 Auburn Ave Ste 136 Cincinnati OH 45219-2906

KERENS, STEVEN ROBERT, real estate executive; b. St. Louis, July 30, 1947; s. Robert Joseph and Mildred Minnie Kerens; children: Scott Steven, Sara Ann. BA, So. Ill. U., 1969; R.E. cert., U. Wis., 2002. Tchr. Dept. Edn., Gunnedah, Australia, 1971—73; housing adminstr. So. Ill. U., Edwardsville, 1974—79; v.p. property mgmt. Lieberman Corp., St. Louis, 1979—84; v.p. real estate investments Mason Realty, St. Louis, 1984—85; dir. property mgmt. Lipton Realty, St. Louis, 1985; pres. Dover Realty, St. Louis and Kansas City, 1986—99; dir. real estate svcs. Paramount Fin. Corp., Granville, Ohio, 1999—. Mem. faculty Inst. Real Estate Mgmt., Chgo., 1982—. Vol. Habitat for Humanity, St. Louis, 1992; bd. dirs., bd. pres. Combinations, St. Louis, 1992-93. Mem. Inst. Real Estate Mgmt. (cert. property mgr.). Democrat. Avocations: reading, photography, writing. Home: PO Box 501 Granville OH 43023 Office: Paramount Fin Corp 4009 Columbus Rd Granville OH 43023 E-mail: stevkerens@aol.com.

KERES, KAREN LYNNE, English language educator; b. Evanston, Ill., Oct. 22, 1945; d. Frank and Bette (Pascoe) K.; m. Walter Wilson Berg. BA, St. Marys Coll., 1967; postgrad., U. Notre Dame, 1967-68; MA, U. Iowa, 1969. Assoc. prof. English, humanities and fine arts William Rainey Harper Coll., Palatine, Ill., 1969-95, prof., 1995—, Palomar Coll., San Marcos, Calif., 1990-93. Cons. in field. Mem. MLA, Ill. Assn. Tchrs. English, Am. Fedn. Tchrs., Nature Conservancy, Mensa. Home: 222 Fairfield Dr Island Lake IL 60042-9622 Office: William Rainey Harper Coll Dept Liberal Arts Palatine IL 60067 *Experienced consultant in professional organizations: negotiating, multicultural and diversity issues. Develop and structure work force team goals for diverse employees. Written and inter-personal communication consultant.*

KERIN, NICHOLAS ZEEV, cardiologist, researcher; b. Bacau, Romania, Mar. 11, 1938; arrived in U.S., 1970; s. Leon Cristian and Lili Gutman; m. Jeny Unterman, Sept. 21, 1965; children: Dolly, Iris, Daniel. MD, Tel-Aviv U., 1967. Rotating intern Edith Wolfson Hosp., Asaf-Harofeh, Israel, 1967—68; internal medicine resident Donolo's Hosp., Tel-Aviv, 1968—70; cardiology fellow Univ. Hosps., Cleve., 1970—71; cardiology fellow, catheterization lab. VA Hosp., Cleve., 1971—73; asst. in medicine, dept. cardiology Mt. Sinai Hosp., Cleve., 1973—76; dir. Noninvasive Lab. Sinai Hosp. Detroit, 1976—84, assoc. staff, sect. cardiovasc. medicine, 1976—86, dir. arrhythmia clinic, 1980—94, dir. cardiology fellowship program, 1984—89, acting chief cardiovasc. medicine sect., 1985—86, acting staff, 1986—, assoc. chief sect. cardiovasc. diseases, 1987—91, co-chief, 1991—93, dir. Lipid Clinic, 1991—96, dir. cardiac rehab., 1991—93; attending Grace Hosp., Detroit, 1993—, Botsford Gen. Hosp., Farmington Hills, Mich., 1996—, dir., Lipid Clinic, 1997—99. Instr. to asst. prof. medicine Case Western Res. U., Cleve., 1973—76; asst. to assoc. prof. medicine Wayne State U., Detroit, 1977—95, prof. medicine (clinician-educator), 1995—; dir. Atrial Fibrillation Clinic Wayne State Med. Sch., 2002—; editl. cons. Catheterization and Cardiovasc. Diagnosis, Am. Heart Jour., Am. Jour. Cardiology, Am. Jour. Clin. Pharmacology, Archives Internal Medicine; editl. bd. Jour. Clin. Pharmacology, 1991—94, Am. Jour. Therapeutics, 1994; presenter in field. Contbr. articles to profl. jours. Fellow: ACP, Clin. Coun. Am. Heart Assn., Am. Coll. Clin. Pharmacology, Am. Coll. Chest Physicians, Am. Coll. Cardiology; mem.: N.Am. Soc. Pacing and Electrophysiology, Inc., Wayne County Med. Soc., Detroit Heart Club (sec-treas. 1985, pres.-elect 1986, pres. 1987), Mich. State Med. Soc., Mich. Heart Assn., Am. Soc. Echocardiography, Am. Heart Assn. Office: Harper U Hosp 3990 John R Detroit MI 48201

KERKER, MILTON, chemistry educator; b. Utica, N.Y., Sept. 25, 1920; s. Samuel and Sarah (Cohen) K.; m. Reva Stemerman, June 16, 1946; children: Ruth Ann, Martin Joseph, Susan Lee, Joel Leon. AB, Columbia U., 1941, MA, 1947, PhD, 1949; D.Sc., Lehigh U., 1975, Clarkson U., 1985. Mem. faculty Clarkson U., Potsdam, N.Y., 1949—, prof. chemistry, 1956-91, Thomas S. Clarkson prof., 1974-91, prof. emeritus, 1991—, Centennial prof., 1996—, also chmn. dept., 1960-64, dean Sch. Arts and Sci., 1964-74, dean Sch. Sci., 1981-85. Unilever vis. prof. U. Bristol, Eng., 1967-68; vis prof. Hebrew U., 1974-75; Welch Found. lectr., 1965; Langmuir lectr. Am. Chem. Soc., 1980; lectr. Friday Evening Discourse, Royal Instn. London, 1988. Author: Electromagnetic Scattering, 1963, The Scattering of Light and Other Electromagnetic Radiation, 1969; editor-in-chief Jour. Colloid and Interface Sci., 1965-92; contbr. articles to profl. jours. Served with U.S. Army, 1942-45. Decorated Bronze Star; Ford Found. fellow, 1952-53. Fellow Optical Soc. Am.; mem. Am. Chem. Soc. (chmn. div. colloid and surface chemistry 1965-66, Kendall award 1971), Internat. Union Pure and Applied Chemistry (sec. Commn. on Colloids 1977-83), History Sci. Soc., AAAS Home: Unit 104 7405 W Country Club Dr N Sarasota FL 34243-4512

KERLIN, GILBERT, lawyer; b. Camden, NJ, Oct. 10, 1909; s. Ward Dix Sr. and Jenny (Gilbert) K.; m. Sarah Morrison, Aug. 23, 1941; children: Sarah Gund, Gilbert Nye, Jonathan Otis. BA, Harvard U., 1933, LLB, 1936. Bar: U.S. Ct. Appeals (2d cir.) 1937, U.S. Supreme Ct. 1945. Of counsel Shearman & Sterling, NYC, 1936—. Chmn. bd. dirs. Wave Hill Inc. Served to lt. col. USAF, 1942-46. Democrat. Unitarian. Home: Dodgewood Rd Bronx NY 10471 Office: Shearman & Sterling 153 E 53rd St New York NY 10022

KERLIN, KARLA DIANE, prosecutor; b. Erie, Pa., July 12, 1964; BS in Psychology, U. Pitts., 1986; JD, Southwestern U., 1990. Bar: Calif. 1990, NC 1998. Dep. dist. atty. L.A. County Dist. Atty.'s Office, L.A., 1990—. Bd. dirs.

Gramercy Housing Group, L.A., 1994—, pres., 1995-2000. Mem.: Women Lawyers Assn. L.A. (pres. 2002—03). Democrat. Office: LA County Dist Attys Office 210 W Temple St Los Angeles CA 90012-3210

KERLIN, MAX L. academic administrator; b. New Castle, Ind., Mar. 22, 1952; s. Edmund L. and Joyce L. Kerlin. BS, Ind. U., 1977; MS, Purdue U., 1981. Budget officer Miami U., Oxford, Ohio, 1988—92; dir. resource mgmt. U. N.Mex., Albuquerque, 1992—. Mem.: Ind. U. Alumni Assn., Phi Kappa Phi. Avocations: watch collecting, travel, investing. Home: Apt D401 3901 Indian School Rd Albuquerque NM 87110 Office: Univ of New Mexico Scholes Hall 235 Albuquerque NM 87131

KERMAN, ARTHUR KENT, physicist, educator; b. Montreal, May 3, 1929; s. Samuel and Ida (Birn) K.; m. Enid Ehrlich, Dec. 21, 1952; children: Ben, Daniel, Elizabeth, Melissa, James. B.Sc., McGill U., 1950; PhD, MIT, 1953. Mem. faculty dept. physics MIT, Cambridge, 1956, prof., 1964—, dir. Ctr. Theoretical Physics, 1976-83, dir. lab. nuclear scis., 1983-92. Vis. prof. SUNY-Stony Brook, 1970-71; adj. prof. Bklyn. Coll., 1971-75; cons. Argonne Nat. Lab., 1961-83, mem. sci. and tech. adv. com., 1984-90; cons. Brookhaven Nat. Lab., 1965-81, mem. relativistic heavy ion collider policy com., 1985-95, vis. com. 1973-78, chmn. 1977; cons. Lawrence Berkeley Lab., 1975-80, mem. vis. com., 1980-83, chmn. 1981; cons. Lawrence Livermore Lab., 1964—, chmn. phys. sci. advi. com. 1992-96; cons. Nat. Ignition Facility, 1997-99; cons. Los Almos Sci. Lab, 1961—, mem. physics div. adv. com., 1984-96, mem. theol. div. adv. com. 1972, LANSCE divsn. adv. com., 1998-2003; cons. Nat. Bur. Stds., 1980-81, Oak Ridge Nat. Lab., 1979-85, Sandia Nat. Lab., 1998-99; mem. U. Calif. Pres.'s Sci. and Academic Adv. Com. 1981-92; mem. White House Sci. Coun., 1982-85, panel on sci. and tech. in govt., 1985, fed. lab. rev. panel, 1982-83; mem. adv. com. Woods Hole Sub-panel of U.S. Dept. Energy, 1982, com. on sci., engring. and pub. policy rsch. briefing panel on sci. frontiers and superconducting super collider NRC, 1985, nuclear sci. adv. com. Dept. Energy and NSF, 1982-85; mem. U.S. Dept. Energy Fusion Policy Adv. Com., 1990, mem. U.S. Dept. Energy Inertial Confinement Fusion Adv. Com. 1992-96; mem. vis. com. Stanford U. Physics Dept., 1984, Yale U. Physics Dept., 1984, FONDS F.C.A.C. Comite des centres de Recherches pour le Laboratoire de Physique Nucleaire U. Montreal, 1982; mem. NIF Coun., 1997-99, NIF Programs Rev. Com., 2000-02; mem. Physics and Advanced Tech. Adv. Com., 1996—; Nat. Acad. Scis. panel on Inertial Confinement Fusion and Sci. Based Stockpile Stewardship, 1996-97, dirs. adv. com. Lawrence Livermore Nat. Lab., 1994-96; Ligo oversight bd. for MIT and Caltech, 1998-2002; cons. ORNL, 2002—, U. Rochester Lab. for Laser Energetics, 2002—; sci. advisor to asst. dep. adminstr. rsch., devel. and simulation DOE/NNSA, 2000—. Assoc. editor: Rev. Modern Physics, 1968-71. NRC fellow Calif. Inst. Tech., 1953-54, Niels Bohr Inst., Copenhagen, 1954-56; Guggenheim fellow U. Paris, 1961-62. Fellow Am. Phys. Soc. (program com. 1978-79, exec. com. div. nuclear physics 1970-72, pub. com. div. nuclear physics, Tom W. Bonner prize com. 1982-83), Am. Acad. Arts and Scis.; mem. N.Y. Acad. Scis. Office: MIT Dept Physics Rm 6-302A 77 Massachusetts Ave Cambridge MA 02139-4307

KERMAN, BARRY MARTIN, ophthalmologist, educator; b. Chgo., Mar. 31, 1945; BS, U. Ill., 1967, MD with high honors, 1970. Diplomate Am. Bd. Ophthalmology. Intern Harbor Gen. Hosp., Torrance, Calif., 1970-71; resident in ophthalmology Wadsworth VA Hosp., L.A., 1971-74; fellow in diseases of the retina, vitreous and choroid Jules Stein Eye Inst., UCLA, 1974-75; fellow in ophthalmic ultrasonography Edward S. Harkness Eye Inst., Columbia U., N.Y.C., 1975, U. Iowa Hosps., Iowa City, 1975; asst. prof. ophthalmology UCLA/Harbor Gen. Hosp., 1976-78; asst. clin. prof ophthalmology UCLA, 1978-83, assoc. clin. prof., 1983-95, clin. prof., 1995—, dir. ophthalmic ultrasonography lab., 1976—2003; cons. ophthalmologist L.A., 1976—2002, San Francisco, 2002—. Chief ophthalmology Century City Hosp., 1995-98; mem. exec. bd. Am. Registry Diagnostic Med. Sonographers, 1981-87; jour. reviewer in field. Contbr. articles to profl. jours. With USAFR, 1971-77. Fellow Am. Acad. Ophthalmology; mem. Am. Soc. Cataract and Refractive Surgery, L.A. Soc. Ophthalmology (emeritus), Am. Assn. Ophthalmic Standardized Echography, Societas Internat. Pro Diagnostica Ultrasonica in Ophthalmic in Ophthalmology, Western Retina Study Club. Office: 490 Post St Ste 640 San Francisco CA 94102

KERMAN, JOSEPH WILFRED, musicologist, critic; b. London, Apr. 3, 1924; U.S. citizen; married, 1946; 3 children. PhD in Music, Princeton U., 1951. Instr. music Princeton U., 1948-49; dir. grad. studies Westminster Choir Coll., 1949-51, from asst. prof. to assoc. prof., 1951-60, chmn. dept., 1961-64, 91-93; prof. music U. Calif., Berkeley, 1960-94, Jerry and Evelyn Hemmings Chambers prof. music, 1985-87, prof. emeritus, 1994—; C.E. Norton prof. poetry Harvard U., 1997. Heather prof. music Oxford U., 1972-74. Author: Opera as Drama, 1956, rev. edit., 1989, The Elizabethan Madrigal, 1962, The Beethoven, Quartets, 1967, The Masses and Motets of William Byrd, 1981, Contemplating Music, 1985, Write All These Down, 1994, Concerto Conversations, 1999; (with others) History of Art and Music, 1968, Listen, 1972, 8th edit., 2003, The New Grove Beethoven, 1983; editor: Beethoven: Autograph Miscellany, 1970, Music at the Turn of the Century, 1970; co-editor Jour. 19th Century Music U. Calif., 1977-88; contbr. essays and revs. to Hudson Rev., N.Y. Rev. Recipient Nat. Inst. Arts and Letters award, 1956, Kinkeldey award Am. Musicol. Soc., 1970, 81, Deems Taylor award ASCAP, 1981, 95; Guggenheim fellow, 1960, Fulbright fellow, 1967, NEH fellow, 1982. Fellow Am. Philosophical Soc., Am. Acad. Arts and Scis., Brit. Acad. (corr.), Royal Musical Assn. (hon. fgn.), Am. Musicol. Soc. (hon.). Office: U Calif Berkeley Dept Music Berkeley CA 94720-1200 E-mail: josephkerman@comcast.net.

KERMES, CONSTANTINE JOHN, artist, industrial designer; b. Pitts., Dec. 6, 1923; s. John Demetrios and Katina (Katerinis) K.; m. Bessie Saratopoulos, Sept. 14, 1952; children: Harriet Kermes Shuman, Kathy Kermes Dixon. BFA, Carnegie Mellon U. Designer Am.-Std. Co., Pitts., 1952-55; indsl. design cons. New Holland N.A. subs. Fiat, Modena, Italy, 1955-82, cons. designer, 1982—. One man shows include Grimaldis Gallery, Balt., 1979, 80, Reading (Pa.) Mus., 1980, Jacques Seligmann Gallery, N.Y.C., 1951, 52, 54, 56, 59, 61, 64, 65, 70, 75, 78, 79, Hancock Shaker Mus., Pittsfield, Mass., 1989, Demuth Found., Lancaster, Pa., 1987, Millport Mus., Lancaster, 1989, William Pa. Mus., Harrisburg, 2000, Balt. Watercolor Soc., 2001, Lancaster Mus. of Art, Pa. 2002; exhibited in group shows at Butler Inst. Am. Art, Youngstown, Ohio, 1964, Pa. Watercolor Soc., 1979, 80, 91, Art 81, Washington, 1985, 91, Mus. Art, Lancaster, 1996, Ctrl. Mkt. Art Gallery, Lancaster, 2002, Westmoreland Mus. Art., Greensburg, Pa., 2003; juried exhibitor Okla. Watercolor Soc., 2001, 2002, Millersville (Pa.) U., Elizabethtown (Pa.) Coll., Lancaster (Pa.) Mus. Art; represented in permanent collections Storm King Art Ctr., Mountain View, N.Y., Pa. State U., Hershey (Pa.) Med. Ctr., Ford Motor Co., Pa. Hist. Mus., Hancock Shaker Mus., Mus. Art, Lancaster; illustrator Shaker Architecture, 1970; author, illustrator: American Icons, 1975; 24 patents for farm equipment designs. Recipient Am. Design Rev. award Indsl. Design mag., 1962, 64, 68, 72, Design award Am. Iron and Steel Inst., 1963, 69, 73, 75, award York (Pa.) Art Assn., award Berks Art Alliance, 2000, Hazleton Art League, 2000, York Art Alliance, 2000, Lancaster County Art Mus., Potomac Soc. award, 2001, prize Mid-Atlantic States Waer Color, 2001, award Balt. Watercolor Soc., Art of State award William Penn Mus., Harrisburg, York, Pa. Art Assn. 200o, 01, 02/ Mem. AHEPA (Lancaster), Pa. Watercolor Soc., Hamilton Club (Lancaster). Greek Orthodox. Home and Office: 981 Landis Valley Rd Lancaster PA 17601-4816

KERMODE, FRANK (JOHN KERMODE), literary critic, educator; b. Douglas, Isle of Man, Nov. 29, 1919; s. John Pritchard and Doris (Kennedy) K. BA, Liverpool U., 1940, MA, 1947; DHL (hon.), U. Chgo., 1975; DLitt (hon.), Liverpool U., 1981; PhD (hon.), Amsterdam U., 1988, Newcastle U., 1993, Yale, 1995, U. Wesleyan, 1997, U. London, 1997, U. Sewanee, 1999, Columbia U., 2003. J.E. Taylor prof. English Manchester U., Eng., 1958-65; Winterstoke prof. English Bristol U., Eng., 1965-67; Lord Northcliffe prof. English U. Coll. London, 1967-74; King Edward VII prof. English Cambridge U., 1974-82; vis. prof. humanities Columbia U., N.Y.C., 1983, 85. Charles E. Norton prof. Harvard U., 1977-78; Henry Luce prof. Yale Y., 1994. Author: Romantic Image, 1957, Wallace Stevens, 1960, The Sense of an Ending, 1967, D.H. Lawrence, 1973, The Classic, 1975, The Genesis of Secrecy, 1979, The Art of Telling, 1983, Forms of Attention, 1985, History and Value, 1988, An Appetite for Poetry, 1989, The Uses of Error, 1991, Not Entitled, 1995, others; (with Anita Kermode) The Oxford Book of Letters, 1995, Shakespeare's Language, 2000, Pleasing Myself, 2001, Pieces of My Mind, 2003; co-editor Encounter, 1965-67; (with Robert Alter) The Literary Guide to the Bible, 1987; editor Modern Masters Series, 1969—, Oxford Authors, 1984—. Served to lt. Royal Navy, 1940-46. Decorated officier Ordre des Arts et Sciences (France), 1973; named Knight Bachelor granted by the Queen of Eng., 1991; King's Coll. hon. fellow, 1987—. Fellow Brit. Acad., Royal Soc. Lit.; mem. Am. Acad. Arts and Scis. (hon.), Am. Acad. Arts and Letters (hon.), Accademia dei Lincei. Home: 9 The Oast House Pinehurst Grange Rd Cambridge CB3 9AP England E-mail: frankkermode@lineone.net.

KERMODE, JOHN COTTERILL, pharmacology educator, researcher; b. Changi, Singapore, June 10, 1949; arrived in U.S. 1983; s. Alfred Cotterill and Rose Price (Roberts) K.; m. Jaehwa Choi, June 27, 2000. BA with honors, Cambridge (Eng.) U., 1970, MA, 1974; PhD, London U., 1983. Rsch. scientist U. Coll. Hosp. Med. Sch., London, 1970-74; rsch. biochemist U. Coll. Hosp., London, 1975-83; postdoctoral fellow U. Conn. Health Ctr., Farmington, Conn., 1983-87; postdoctoral assoc. U. Vt., Burlington, 1987-90; rsch. chemist McGuire VA Med. Ctr., Richmond, Va., 1990-93; rsch. asst. prof. Med. Coll. Va., Richmond, 1990-93; asst. prof., dept. pharmacology and toxicology U. Miss. Med. Ctr., Jackson, Miss., 1993-98, assoc. prof., 1998—. Mem. editl. bd. Jour. Receptor & Signal Transduction Rsch., 1991-2002; contbr. articles to profl. jours. Recipient Earnest G. Spivey Meml. Rschr. award, 1994; Cambridge (Eng.) U. scholar, 1967, Basic Sci. All Star Prof. award Carl G. Evers, M.D., Soc., 2000, 2001, 2002, 2003; Am. Heart Assn. grantee, Va., 1991, Miss., 1994, 97, Southeast, 1999, 2003, Nat. Heart Found. grantee, 1997, 98, Am. Lung Assn. grantee, 1997. Mem. Internat. Soc. Thrombosis and Haemostasis, Am. Soc. Pharmacology & Exptl. Therapeutics (councilor divsn. Cardiovasc. Pharmacology 2002—). Avocations: photography, travel, tennis, contract bridge, downhill skiing. Home: 57 Redbud Ln Madison MS 39110-9260 Office: U Miss Med Ctr 2500 N State St Jackson MS 39216-4500

KERN, ARTHUR STEPHEN, physician; b. Newark, N.J., Dec. 19, 1930; s. Meyer and Fannie (Greenberg) K.; m. Ruth E. Feingold; children: Melissa, Laurence, Deborah. BA, Harvard U., 1952; MD, Tulane U., 1955. Diplomate Am. Bd. Ophthalmology. Intern U.S. Naval Hosp., Portsmouth, Va., 1955-56, resident, 1956-59. Ltd. comdr. USN, 1955-62. Avocations: running, tennis, bridge. Office: 90 Millburn Ave Millburn NJ 07041-1933

KERN, BERNARD DONALD, retired educator, physicist; b. New Castle, Ind., Oct. 31, 1919; s. William Bernard and Cecile McDonald (Hudson) K.; m. Nedda Wisler Burdsall, Aug. 20, 1946; children: Richard B., Jonathan K., Arthur R. BS, Ind. U., 1942, MS, 1947, PhD, 1949. Physicist Signal Corps and Manhattan Project, Chgo., 1942-43; sr. physicist Oak Ridge Nat. Lab., 1949-50; faculty U. Ky., 1950-85, prof. physics, 1958-85, chmn. dept. physics and astronomy, 1967-69, prof. emeritus, 1985—. Physicist U.S. Naval Radiol. Def. Lab., San Francisco, 1957-58, cons., 1957-69; prof. Inst. Teknologi Bandung (Indonesia), U Ky., State Dept. Ednl. Assistance Program, 1961- 62 Author articles on nuclear physics. Served to lt.(jg) USNR, 1943-46. Fellow Am. Phys. Soc.; mem. Am. Inst. Physics, Am. Assn. Physics Tchrs. Home: 681 Providence Rd Lexington KY 40502-2214

KERN, CHARLES WILLIAM, retired university official, chemistry educator; b. Middletown, Ohio, July 13, 1935; s. Charles Albert and Charme (Bowman) K.; m. Regine Bouchard. BS, Carnegie Inst. Tech., 1957; PhD, U. Minn., 1961; postgrad., Columbia U., 1961-63. Postdoctoral fellow in chem. physics Columbia U., N.Y.C., 1961-63; asst. prof. chemistry SUNY, Stony Brook, 1964-66; adj. assoc. prof. chemistry Ohio State U., Columbus, 1966-71, adj. prof. chemistry, 1971-76, acad. vice chmn., dept. chemistry, 1972-73, prof. chemistry, 1976-80; rsch. scientist Battelle Meml. Inst., Columbus, Ohio, 1966-72, mgr. chem. physics sect., 1972-76, dir. phys. scis. program, 1973-76, inst. scientist, 1973-76, dir. Battelle Inst. program, 1976-84, cons., 1976-84; program dir. theoretical chem. physics, div. chemistry NSF, Washington, 1978-80, sr. staff assoc., computer sci. rsch. network project dir., div. math. and computer scis., 1980-83, program dir. structural chemistry and thermodynamics, acting sect. head phys. chemistry and chem. dynamics, div. chem., 1983-84, acting dir. div. chemistry, 1984-85, dep. dir. div. chemistry, 1985-86; asst. dir. gen. sci., Office of Sci. and Tech. Policy Office of the Pres., Washington, 1986; dean Ohio State U., Columbus, 1986-92; prof. chemistry Coll. Math. and Phys. Scis. Ohio State U., Columbus, 1986-92; v.p. rsch., dean Grad. Sch., Northwestern U., Evanston, Ill., 1992-93, v.p. rsch. and grad. studies, 1993-98, prof. chemistry, 1992-98, prof. emeritus, 1998—. Chmn,. Sch. Many-Body Techniques in Chemistry, Seattle, 1969, Carnegie-Mellon U. Admissions Coun., 1970-72, Summer Rsch. Conf. on Theoretical Chemistry, Boulder, Colo., 1975; co-chmn. Current Biol. Problems, A Sch. for Phys. Scientists, 1977; exec. sec. NSF Dir.'s Task Force on Advanced Sci. Computing Resources, 1983-84. Assoc. editor Chem. Physics Letter, 1967-81; contbr. numerous articles to profl. jours. Mem. AAAS, Am. Chem. Soc., Am. Phys. Soc.

KERN, CLIFFORD HAROLD, JR., retired lawyer; b. New Orleans, Dec. 2, 1915; s. Clifford Harold and Sadie Judith (Schwartz) K.; m. Nettie Cahn Hirsch, June 14, 1947; children— Clifford Harold III, Jay H. LL.B., Tulane U., 1938, J.D., 1969. Bar: La. 1939, U.S. Dist. Ct. (ea. dist.) La. Ptnr. Kuhner & Kern, New Orleans, 1939-46; asst. to pres., treas., sec., v.p. Imperial Shoe Store Inc., New Orleans, 1946-77; assoc. Dresner & Dresner, New Orleans, 1977-92, ret., 2001. Pres. Sugar Bowl Football Classic, 1974-75, chmn. bd., 1983-84. Served as lt. comdr., submarine service USN, 1941-46. Elected to New Orleans Football Hall of Fame, 1977. Mem. ABA, La. State Bar Assn., New Orleans Bar Assn., New Orleans C. of C., Mil. Order World Wars, Navy League U.S., Retired Officers Assn. Home: 2100 St Charles Ave Apt 7L New Orleans LA 70130

KERN, DONALD MICHAEL, internist; b. Belleville, Ill., Nov. 21, 1951; s. Donald Milton and Dolores Olivia (Rust) K. BS in Biology, Tulane U., 1973; MD magna cum laude, U. Brussels, 1983. ECFMG cert.; lic. Calif. Intern in surgery Berkshire Med. Ctr., Pittsfield, Mass., 1983-84; intern in psychiatry Tufts New England Med. Ctr., Boston, 1984-85; resident in internal medicine Kaiser Found. Hosp., San Francisco, 1985-87; with assoc. staff internal medicine Kaiser Permanente Med. Group, Inc., San Francisco, 1987-89; assoc. investigator AIDS Clin. Trial Unit Kaiser Permanente Med. Ctr., Stanford U., Nat. Inst. Allergy & Infectious Disease, San Francisco, 1988-90; mem. staff internal medicine Kaiser Permanente Med. Group, South San Francisco, 1989-96; mem. staff Desert Med. Group, Palm Springs, Calif., 1996—, assoc. med. dir., 2002—. Democrat. Roman Catholic. Avocations: theatre, ballet, traveling, 17th and 18th century french antiques. Office: Desert Medical Group 275 N El Cielo Rd Palm Springs CA 92262

KERN, EDNA RUTH, insurance executive; b. Rochester, N.Y., Dec. 31, 1945; d. Carl H. and Mildred B. (Fronk) McRorie; m. Charles E. Kern, Nov. 1, 1968 (div. July 1975); 1 child, Barbara Renee. BBA summa cum laude, Tex. Wesleyan Coll., 1978. CLU, ChFC. Pvt. detective Statewide Detective Agy., Orlando, Fla., 1968-78; agt. Pacific Mut. Ins., Ft. Worth, 1978-79, Conn. Mut. Ins., Ft. Worth, 1979-83; gen. agt. Gen. Am. Life Ins., Ft. Worth, 1983-85; ins. owner Kern and Assocs. (now Edna Kern, P.C.), Ft. Worth, 1985—. Life underwriters tng. fellow Nat. Assn. Life Underwriters. Pres. All Sts. Hosp. Execs. Forum, Ft. Worth, 1986-87, Women's Health Forum, 1994-96. Mem. Nat. Assn. Health Underwriters (registered, sec.-treas. 1990-91, Disting. Svc. award), Tex. Assn. Health Underwriters (state sec., bd. dirs. 1987-88, pres. 1988-90, Outstanding Texan of Yr. award, Hollis Roberson award), Ft. Worth Assn. Life Underwriters (bd. dirs. 1986-91, moderator 1984-86, chmn. health com. and edn. com. 1986-88), Tarrant County Assn. Health Underwriters (pres. 1986-87), Sales and Mktg. Execs. (bd. dirs. Ft. Worth chpt. 1985-87, v.p. 1986-87, sec. 1994-95, pres. 1995-96), Mensa. Republican. Avocations: travel, community involvement. Office: Edna Kern PC PO Box 100356 Fort Worth TX 76185-0356 E-mail: ekern@charter.net.

KERN, GEORGE CALVIN, JR., lawyer; b. Balt., Apr. 19, 1926; s. George Calvin and Alice (Gaskins) K.; m. Joan Shorell, Dec. 22, 1962; 1 child, Heath. BA, Princeton U., 1947; LLB, Yale U., 1952. Bar: N.Y. 1952. Chief U.S. Info. Ctr., Mannheim, W.Ger., 1947-48; dep. dir. pub. info. Office U.S. Mil. Govt. for Germany, Berlin and Nurnberg, 1948-49; assoc. Sullivan & Cromwell, N.Y.C., 1952-60, ptnr., 1960—. Publ. Cub newspaper, Tehachapi, Calif., 1974—; bd. dirs. McJunkin Corp., Charleston, W.Va. Lt. USN, 1944-46. Home: 830 Park Ave New York NY 10021-2757 Office: Sullivan & Cromwell 125 Broad St Fl 28 New York NY 10004-2489

KERN, HEATH THAYER, producer; b. N.Y.C., Sept. 19, 1964; s. George C. and Joan Kern. BA, Denison U., 1986; MPA, Harvard U., 2002. Segment prodr. COUR-TV, N.Y.C., 1996-99; assoc. prodr. Fox News Channel, N.Y.C., 1999—. Mem. Colony Club. Office: Fox New Channel 1211 Ave of Americas New York NY 10036 E-mail: heath.kern@foxnews.com.

KERN, IRVING J. lawyer; b. Bridgeport, Conn., Sept. 8, 1946; BS with high honors, U. Conn., 1968; JD, U. Va., 1971. Bar: Conn. 1971, U.S. Dist. Ct. Conn. 1971, U.S. Ct. Appeals (2nd cir.) 1971. Mem. Cohen & Wolf P.C., Bridgeport. Mem. ABA, Conn. Bar Assn., Bridgeport Bar Assn., Beta Gamma Sigma, Phi Kappa Phi. Office: Cohen & Wolf PC PO Box 1821 1115 Broad St Bridgeport CT 06604-4247

KERN, IRVING JOHN, retired food company executive; b. N.Y.C., Feb. 10, 1914; s. John and Min (Weitzner) Kleinberger; m. Beatrice Rubenfeld, June 22, 1941; children— John A., Arthur H., Robert M. BS, NYU, 1934, student Grad. Sch. Art and Sci., 1960-65; DHL, Mercy Coll., Dobbs Ferry, N.Y., 1980. Asst. buyer Bloomingdale's Dept. Store, N.Y.C., 1934-40; with Dellwood Foods, Inc., Yonkers, N.Y., 1945-82, pres., 1966-77, chmn. and chief exec. officer, 1977-82. Dir. Scarsdale Nat. Bank; adj. prof. polit. sci., San Diego State U., 1989-95. Mem. County Mental Health Svcs. Bd. of Westchester County, 1954-59; mem. bd. dirs., sec. Westchester County Assn., 1950-57, 76-80; exec. bd. Westchester County Better Bus. Bur., 1970-73; bd. dirs. Westchester Coalition, 1972-80, Westchester Minority Bus. Assistance Orgn., 1973-75, Milk Industry Found., 1976-82, Nat. Dairy Coun., 1979-81; bd. dirs., vice chmn. Westchester Pvt. Industry Coun., 1979-82; mil. adv. coun. Ctr. for Def. Info., 1986-97. Lt. col. AUS, 1940-45. Decorated Bronze Star. Mem. N.Y. Milk Bottlers Fedn. (pres., dir.), Met. Dairy Inst. (exec. v.p., dir.), Phi Beta Kappa, Tau Epsilon Phi.

KERN, JEFFREY D, writer; b. Aurora, Ill., Dec. 31, 1965; married. BS Mktg./Advt., U. of Nev., Las Vegas, 1989. Freelance writer Jeffrey D. Kern, Las Vegas, Nev., 2000—. Author: (magazine and web writer/author) various (Strathmore's Who's Who In Bus. Listing, 2002). Office: Jeffrey D Kern Writer 7500 West Lake Mead Blvd Ste 9-488 Las Vegas NV 89128 Office Fax: 702-838-5779. E-mail: kerncom@cox.net.

KERN, JEROME H. lawyer; b. N.Y.C., June 1, 1937; s. Michael and Rebecca (Saltzman) K.; m. Mary Rossick; children: Jonathan Sterry, Peter M. AB, Columbia U., 1957; LLB, NYU, 1960. Law clk. to justice U.S. Ct. Appeals (2d cir.), N.Y.C., 1960-61; assoc. Simpson Thacher & Bartlett, N.Y.C., 1961-63; ptnr. Wachtell, Lipton, Rosen, Katz & Kern, N.Y.C., 1963-68; sr. and mng. ptnr. (investment banking) J.H. Kern & Co., N.Y.C., 1971-76; ptnr. Greenbaum, Wolff & Ernst, N.Y.C., 1977-82, Olwine, Connelly, Chase, O'Donnell & Weyher, N.Y.C., 1982-86; sr. ptnr., mem. exec. com. Shea & Gould, N.Y.C., 1986-91; pvt. practice Law Offices of Jerome H. Kern, N.Y.C., 1992; Baker and Botts, N.Y.C., 1992-98; vice chmn. TeleCommunications, Inc., Denver, 1998-99; chmn., CEO On Command Corp., Denver, 2000—01. Adj. asst. prof. law NYU, 1964-71. Mng. editor NYU Law Rev., 1959-60. Bd. trustees NYU Law Ctr. Found.; chmn. bd. dirs. VOA Colo., Inst. for Children's Mental Disorders, City Meals-On-Wheels, N.Y.C.; co-chmn. Colo. Symphony Found. Root-Tilden scholar NYU, 1957-60. Mem. ABA, N.Y. State Bar Assn., Assn. Bar City N.Y.

KERN, JOHN MCDOUGALL, lawyer; b. Omaha, Nov. 28, 1946; m. Susan McDougall Kern, Oct. 15, 1977. BA, Creighton U., 1970; JD cum laude, George Washington U., 1973. Bar: D.C. 1973, Calif. 1980, U.S. Dist. Ct. D.C. 1974, U.S. Dist Ct. (no. dist.) Calif. 1980, U.S. Dist. Ct. (ctrl. dist.) Calif. 1996, U.S. Ct. Appeals (D.C. cir.) 1974, U.S. Ct. Appeals (9th cir.) 1978; bd. cert. specialist in civil trial advocacy, Nat. Bd. Trial Advocacy. Asst. U.S. atty. criminal divsn. Office of U.S. Atty. D.C., Washington, 1973-78; asst. U.S. atty. civil divsn. Office U.S. Atty. No. Dist. Calif., San Francisco, 1978-82; v.p., dir. Crosby, Heafey, Roach & May P.C., San Francisco, Oakland, L.A., 1981—2003; with Carlson, Calladine & Peterson, LLC, San Francisco, 2003—. Faculty Nat. Inst. Trial Advocacy, 1987—; spkr. numerous programs, confs.; lectr. in field. Contbr. abstracts, book chpt., articles to profl. jours. Mem. Am. Bd. Trial Advocates (advocate), Am. Inn of Ct., Assn. Bus. Trial Lawyers, Nat. Inst. Trial Advocacy. Address: 18th Fl Two Embarcadero Ctr San Francisco CA 94111 Business E-Mail: jkeru@ccp.law.com. E-mail: jmckern@sbcglobal.net.

KERN, JOHN WORTH, III, judge; b. Indpls., May 25, 1928; s. John Worth and Bernice (Winn) K.; children: John, Stephen. BA, Princeton U., 1949; LLB, Harvard U., 1952. Bar: D.C. 1953, U.S. Ct. Appeals (D.C. cir.) 1955. With CIA, 1952-54; law clk. to chief judge U.S. Ct. Appeals D.C. Cir. Ct., 1954-55; asst. U.S. atty. D.C. Dist. Dept. Justice, Washington, 1955-59; assoc. Kilpatrick, Ballard & Beasley, Washington, 1959-65; with Dept. of Justice, Washington, 1965-68; judge D.C. Ct. Appeals, Washington, 1968-84, sr. judge, 1987—. Dean Nat. Jud. Coll., Reno, 1984-87. Mem. D.C. Bar. Presbyterian. Office: DC Ct Appeals 500 Indiana Ave NW Washington DC 20001-2138

KERN, PAUL JOHN, army officer; b. Orange, N.J., June 16, 1945; s. Bruno Michael and Marjorie (Bolan) K.; m. Dolores I. Mercaldo, Aug. 28, 1971; children: Paul John Jr., Alexander Matthew. BS, U.S. Mil. Acad., 1967; MS in Mech. and Civil Engring., U. Mich., 1973; fellow nat. security, Harvard U., 1986-87. Registered profl. engr., Va. Commd. 2d lt. U.S. Army, 1967, advanced through grades to lt. gen., 1997, platoon leader, staff mem., 1967-69; troop comdr. 11th Armored Cavalry Regiment, Republic Vietnam, 1969-70; asst. prof., course dir. dept. engring. U.S. Mil. Acad., West Point, N.Y., 1973-76; ops. officer 2d bn., 33d Armor, 3d Armor Div., Kirch Goens, Fed. Republic Germany, 1976-78; br. chief Bradley Program Mgmt. Office, Warren, Mich., 1979-82; team chief reseach and devel. U.S. Army Staff, Pentagon, Washington, 1982-84; bn. comdr. 5th bn., 32d Armor, 24th Infantry Div., Ft. Stewart, Ga., 1984-86; mil. asst. Dep. under Sec. Def., Pentagon, Washington, 1987-89; comdr. 2d brigade, 24th Infantry Divsn. Saudi Arabia/Iraq, 1989-91; dir. requirements Army staff, 1991-92; asst. divsn. comdr.-maneuver, 24 Infantry Divsn., 1992-93; mil. asst. to Sec. of Def., 1993-96; comdg. gen. 4th Inf. Divsn., Ft. Hood, Tex., 1996-97; dir. acquisition corps Pentagon, Washington, 1997—. Co-author: Acquisition Managers - Role and Reality, 1987. Decorated Bronze Star with 3 oak leaf clusters, Silver Star, Purple Heart with 2 oak leaf clusters, Legion of Merit. Mem. Soc. Automotive Engrs. (Teetor award 1975), Armor Assn., Assn. U.S. Army, Coun. Fgn. Rels., U.S. Naval Inst., Chi Epsilon. Roman Catholic. Avocations: sailing, woodworking, computers. E-mail: kernp@sarda.army.mil.

KERN, TERRY C. judge; b. Clinton, Okla., Sept. 25, 1944; s. Elgin L. Kern and Lora Lee (Miller) Renegar; m. Charlene Heinen, Dec. 26, 1970; children: Lauren, Suzanne, Justin Hunter. BS, Okla. State U., Stillwater, 1966; JD, U. Okla., 1969. Bar: Okla. 1969, U.S. Dist. Ct. (ea. dist.) Okla. 1974, U.S. Dist. Ct. (we. dist.) Okla. 1979, U.S. Dist. Ct. (no. dist.) Okla. 1993, U. S. Ct. Appeals (10th cir.) 1979. Gen. atty. FTC, Washington, 1969—70; ptnr. Fischl, Culp, McMillin, Kern and Chaffin, Ardmore, Okla., 1971—86; founding ptnr., pres. Kern, Mordy and Sperry, Ardmore, 1986—94; dist. judge U.S. Dist. Ct. (no. dist.) Okla., Tulsa, 1994—, chief judge, 1996—. Mem. Jud. Conf. Com. on Security and Facilities, 10th Cir. Jud. coun. Chmn. bd. dirs. Southern Okla. Meml. Hosp., Ardmore, 1982—92, chmn., 1989—91. Served with USAR, 1970—75. Named to, Beta Theta Pi Hall of Fame, 2000; recipient Leadership Legacy award, Okla. State U., 2000, Disting. Alumnus award, 2001. Fellow: Okla. Bar Found. (pres. 1991, Disting. Svc. award 1992), Am. Bar Found.; mem.: ABA, Tulsa City Bar Assn. (bd. dirs.), Fed. Judges Assn., U. Okla. Coll. Law Assn., Okla. Bar Assn., Am. Bd. Trial Advocates (Okla. chpt.), W. Lee Johnson Inn of Ct. (master of bench). Democrat. Episcopalian. Office: US Dist Courthouse 333 W 4th St Tulsa OK 74103-3839

KERNAN, BARBARA DESIND, senior government executive; b. N.Y.C., Jan. 11, 1939; d. Philip and Anne (Feuer) Desind; m. Joseph E. Kernan, Feb. 14, 1973. BA cum laude, Smith Coll., 1960; postgrad. Oxford U., 1963; MA, Harvard U., 1963; postgrad. in edn. policy George Washington U., 1980. Editor Harvard Law Sch., 1960-62; tchr. English, Newton High Sch. (Mass.), 1962-63;

editor Allyn & Bacon Pubs., Boston, 1963-64; edn. assoc. Upward Bound, Edn. Assocs., Inc., Washington, 1965-68; edn. program specialist Title I, Elem. and Secondary Edn. Act, U.S. Office Edn., 1969-73; fellow Am. Polit. Sci. Assn., Senator William Proxmire and Congressman Alphonzo Bell, 1973-74; spl. asst. to dep. commr. for elem. and secondary edn. and dir. dissemination, sch. finance and analysis, U.S. Office Edn., 1975-77, chief program analysis br. div. edn. for disadvantaged, 1977-79; chief grant program coordination staff Office Dep. Commr. for Ednl. Resources, 1979-80; chief priority concerns staff Office Asst. Sec. Mgmt., U.S. Dept. Edn., Washington, 1980-81; dir. div. orgnl. devel. and analysis Office of Dep. Undersec. for Mgmt., 1981-86; Sr. Exec. Svc. candidate on spl. project to improve status of women Sec. Transp., Washington, 1983-84; inducted Sr. Exec. Svc., 1986; assoc. adminstr. for adminstrn. Nat. Hwy. Traffic Safety Adminstrn., U.S. Dept. Transp., 1986-94, career devel. leader to presdl. mgmt. interns, 1989-91; trustee Capricorn Galleries, Bethesda, Md., 1996-97; owner Philip Desind Collection, Am. Realism Fine Arts, 1997—; pres. Capricorn Galleries, Potomac, Md., 1997—. Recipient awards U.S. Office Edn., 1969, 71, 77, U.S. Dept. Edn., 1981 86, U.S. Dept. Transp., 1991, 94, Small Agy. Coun., 1990; scholarships U. Mich., 1956-58, Smith Coll., 1958-60, Harvard U., 1962 63; Am. Polit. Sci. Assn. fellow, 1973-74; Sr. Exec. fellow John F. Kennedy Sch. Govt. Harvard U., 1983. Office: Capricorn Galleries 10236 River Rd Potomac MD 20854-4905

KERNAN, JEROME BERNARD, retired marketing educator, researcher; b. Cin., Nov. 22, 1932; s. E. B. and Alice (Gerver) Kernan; children: Kathleen Kernan Bedree, Brian Michael. BA, U. Cin., 1957; MS, U. Ill., 1959, PhD, 1962; post-doctoral studies in computer simulation, Carnegie Mellon U., Pitts., 1962; post-doctoral studies in math., U.Kans., 1963. Prof. emeritus George Mason U. Consumer rsch. cons., 1965—. Co-author: 6 books on consumer behavior and mktg., 1968—71; contbr. of more than 120 articles to profl. jours. Pres. Sacred Heart Sch. Bd., Austin, Tex., 1964—67; cons. Several not-for-profit agys., 1970—88. With USAF, 1951—53. Co-recipient Ferber award, Jour. Consumer Rsch., 1992, Best Article award, Am. Acad. Advt., 1993. Mem.: Soc. for Consumer Psychology, Assn. for Consumer Rsch. (pres. 1978), Am. Mktg. Assn. Avocations: motorsport, golf. Home: 879 Pine Valley Ln Cincinnati OH 45245

KERNAN, JOSEPH E. governor; m. Maggie Kernan, 1974. BS, U. Notre Dame, 1968. Product mfg. mgr. Proctor & Gamble Co., 1976; sales exec. Schwarz Paper Co., 1976-80; city contr. South Bend, Ind., 1980-84; mayor, 1988; v.p., treas. MacWilliams Corp., 1984-88; lt. gov. State of Ind., Indpls., 1996—2003, gov., 2003—. Bd. trustees St. Joseph Med. Ctr. Bd. dirs. St. Joseph County Spl. Olympics, Notre Dame Club, Jr. Baseball Assn., Northside L.L.; campaign cabinet United Way, 1979-82; treas. Studebaker Music Inc. Comdr. USN, 1969-75. Recipient two Purple Heart medals, two Air medals, award for Individual Excellence. Democrat.*

KERNAN, WALTER NEWBERRY, physician; b. Boston, Mar. 27, 1956; s. Walter Newberry and Sarah (Wigglesworth) K.; m. Mary Elizabeth Murray, Aug. 23, 1986; children: Julia, Brian, Sarah. BA, Harvard, 1978; MD, Dartmouth, 1984. Diplomate Am. Bd. Internal Medicine, Diplomate Nat. Bd. Medical Examiners. Intern in medicine Johns Hopkins Hosp., 1984-85, resident in medicine, 1985-87; fellow in medicine Yale Sch. Medicine, New Haven, 1987 89; instr. in medicine Yale U., 1989-90, asst. prof., 1990, assoc. prof., 1995—. Attending physician Yale-New Haven Hosp., West Haven VA Hosp.; course dir. Ambulatory component of the Internal Medicine clerkship; reviewer numerous jours. Contbr. articles to profl. jours. Recipient The Dean's Med. Edn. Farr award Yale U. Sch. Medicine, 1997, The Med. Educator award Soc. Gen. Internal Medicine New Eng. Region, 1996. Mem. Am. Coll. Physicians, Soc. General Internal Medicine, Sydenham Soc., Alpha Omega Alpha. Office: Yale U Sch Medicine Dept Internal Medicine PO Box 208025 New Haven CT 06520-8025 Home: 140 Northrop Rd Woodbridge CT 06525-1744

KERNAN, WILLIAM FRANK, career officer; BA in History, Our Lady of Lake U., 1973; MA in Pers. Adminstrn., Ctrl. Mich. U.; student, Infantry Advanced Course, 1973-74, U.S. Army Command, Gen. Staff, Coll., 1978-79, U.S. Army War Coll., 1986-87. Commd. 2d lt. U.S. Army, 1968, advanced through grades to gen., 2000, platoon leader Co. D. 1-327 Inf. Bn., 101st Airborne Divsn., 1969; reconnaisance platoon leader Tiger Force, liason officer 101st Airborne Divsn. U.S. Army, Vietnam, 1969-70; co. comdr. 2-325 Airborne Inf., 82d Airborne Divsn. Fort Bragg, N.C., 1970-71; comdr. San Antonio Dist. Recruiting Command U.S. Army, Austin, Tex., 1974-76; co.comdr. HHC 2d Bn. (Rangers), 75th Infantry, Fort Lewis, Wash., 1976-77; co. comdr. Co. A., 2d Bn. (Rangers), 75th Infantry, Fort Lewis, 1977-78; recorder secretariat for dept. of army selection bds., later pers. mgmt. officer, Combat Arms Divsn., U.S. Army Pers. Ctr, Alexandria, Va., 1979-81; exchange officer, rifle company comdr. 3d bn. Brit. Parachute Regiment, UK, 1981-83; exec. officer 2d bn. 508th inf. (airborne) to bn. comdr. 2-508th Inf. (Airborne), 82d Airborne Divsn., Fort Bragg, N.C., 1983-85; comdr. 3d bn. 504th inf. (airborne) 82d Airborne Divsn., Fort Bragg, 1985-86; battalion comdr. 1-75th Rangers, 1987-88; from dep. comdr. to comdr. 75th Ranger Regiment, Fort Benning, Ga., 1988-91; asst. divsn. comdr. 7th Infantry Divsn., Ft. Ord, Calif., 1991-93; dir. strategic plans, policies, assessments J-5 U.S. Spl. Ops Command, McDill AFB, Fla., 1993-96; commanding gen. 101st Airborne Divsn. and Fort Campbell, Fort Campbell, Ky., 1996-98, XVIII Airborne Corps & Fort Bragg, 1998-2000; commdr. in chief U.S. joint Forces Commd./Supreme Allied Commdr. Atlantic, 2000—. Decorated Defense Disting. Svc. medal, Disting. Svc. medal with oak leaf cluster, Legion of Merit with 3 oak leaf clusters, Bronze Star medal with V device, Bronze Star medal with oak leaf cluster, Purple heart, Meritorious Svc. medal with 3 oak leaf clusters, Air medals, Army Commednation medal with 4 oak leaf clusters, Army Achievment medal. Office: Supreme Allied Commdr Atlantic and Cinc Joint Forces Command Norfolk VA 28307

KERNEN, WILL, lawyer; b. Boston, July 4, 1951; s. Judson and Olive (Bardsley) K.; m. Cindy M. Krueger, June 21, 1970; children: Kerry, Kurt, Kyle, Kasey, Kathy. BA, Bridgewater State Coll., 1974; JD, Ohio State U., 1976. Bar: Ohio, U.S. Dist. Ct. (so. dist.) Ohio 1978. Assoc. Lappen & Lilley, Logan, Ohio, 1977-78; ptnr. Lappen, Lilley, Kernen & Co., L.P.A., Logan, 1978 96. Law dir. City of Logan, 1978-79; law librarian Hocking County Law Library, 1980-83; acting judge Hocking County Mcpl. Ct., Logan, 1983-87. Bd. dirs. Logan-Hocking City Sch. Dist., 1979-83; counsel Hocking County Rep. Party, 1979. Served with U.S. Army, 1968-71, Germany. Mem. ABA, Ohio Bar Assn., Hocking County Bar Assn. (v.p. 1978-79, pres. 1989—), Jaycees (pres. Logan 1983-84 dist. dir. Ohio 1984-85). Home: 26816 Darl Rd Rockbridge OH 43149-9601 Office: PO Box 388 Logan OH 43138-0388 E-mail: kernenlaw@hocking.net.

KERNER, FRED, book publisher, writer; b. Montreal, Can., Feb. 15, 1921; s. Sam and Vera (Goldman) K.; m. Jean Elizabeth Somerville, July 17, 1945 (div. Apr. 1951); 1 son, Jon Fredrik; m. Sally Dee Stouten, May 18, 1959; children: David, Diane. BA, Sir George Williams U. (now Concordia U.), Montreal, 1942. Mem. editl. staff Saskatoon (Can.) StarPhoenix, 1942; Asst. sports editor Montreal Gazette, 1942-44; news editor Can. Press, Montreal, Toronto, N.Y.C., 1944-50; asst. night city editor A.P., N.Y.C., 1950-57; editor Hawthorn Books, Inc., N.Y.C., 1957-58, pres., 1964-68; exec. editor Crest-Premier Books, Hall House, Fawcett World Libr., N.Y.C., 1958-63; editor-in-chief Crest-Premier Books, Fawcett World Libr., N.Y.C., 1963-64; pres. Centaur House, Inc. (pubs.), 1964-80, Paramount Securities Corp., 1965-67, Veritas Internat. Pubs., 1976—91, Publishing Projects, Inc., 1967—, Communications Unltd., 1968—; editorial dir. book and edni. divs. Reader's Digest, Can., 1968-75; v.p., pub. dir. Harlequin Enterprises Ltd., 1975-83, sr. cons. editor, 1984-96, editor emeritus, 1983—; v.p. Publitex Internat. Corp. (pubs.), 1968-75; pres. Athabaska House, 1975-77. Dir. Nat. Mint, Inc., others; panelist various profl. confs.; chmn. Internat. Affairs Conf. Coll. Editors, 1965; drama festival adjudicator, 1940-48; Broadway theatrical script cons., 1948-56; speechwriter Adlai Stevenson, 1952, 56; ghostwriter Dr. Joyce Brothers, Anita Colby, Enid Haupt, and others; mem. nat. negotiating com. Am. Newspaper Guild, 1949-54, Wire Svc. Guild, 1954-57, chmn. grievance com., 1955-57; instr. Insider's Guide to Writing and Pub., U. Toronto, 1999—. Author: (with Leonid Kotkin) Eat, Think and Be Slender, 1954, 2d edit., 2000, (with Walter M. Germain) The Magic Power of Your Mind, 1956, (with Joyce Brothers) Ten Days to a Successful Memory, 1957, Stress and Your Heart, 1961, 2d edit., 2000; pseudonym Frederick Kerr: Don't Count Calories!, 1962, 2d edit. (as Fred Kerner), 2000, (with Walter M. Germain) Secrets of Your Supraconscious, 1965, (with David Goodman) What's Best for Your Child and You, 1966, (with Jesse Reid) Buy High, Sell Higher, 1966; (pseudonym M.N. Thaler) It's Fun to Fondue, 1968, (with Ion Grumeza) Nadia, 1977, Careers in Writing, 1985, Mad About Fondue, 1986, (with Andrew Willman) Prospering Through the Coming Depression, 1986, Home Emergency Handbook and First-Aid Guide, 1990, Fabulous Fondues, 2000; contbg. author; Successful Writers and How They Work, 1958, Words on Paper, 1960, Overseas Press Club Cookbook, 1964, The Senior's Guide to Life in the Slow Lane, 1986, The Writer's Essential Desk Reference, 1991, 96, Lifetime: A Treasury of Uncommon Wisdoms, 1992, Chambers's Ency.; books transl. into French, German, Japanese, Portuguese, Spanish and Italian; editor: Love is a Man's Affair, 1958, 2d edit., 2000, Treasury of Lincoln Quotations, 1965, new edit. 1996, The Canadian Writer's Guide, 9th edit., 1985, 10th edit., 1988, 11th edit., 1992, Selling Your Short Fiction, 1992. Mem. local sch. bd., N.Y.C., 1967-68; chmn. sch. com. Westmount High Sch., 1970-72; mem. sch. com. Roslyn Sch., 1973; chmn. publs. com. Edward R. Murrow Meml. Fund; judge Dr. William Henry Drummond Nat. Poetry Contest; trustee Gibson Lit. Awards, C.A.A. Lit. Awards, Benson & Hedges Lit. Awards, CA&B Student Creative Writing Awards, Random House Can. Short Story Competition, 2002; bd. govs. Concordia U., 1975-79, hon. life mem. Can. Pubs. Coun., founding mem. exec. com. Pub. Lending Rights Commn., 1986-89, vice chmn., 1988-89; founding dir. Toronto Book and Mag. Fair, bd. dirs., 1990-94. Recipient Queen's Silver Jubilee medal, 1977, Allan Sangster award, 1982, Internat. Pub. award Air Can., 1982, 2 internat. awards for advertorial writing, 1990, Apex award for newsletter editing, 1992. Fellow Can. Copyright Inst. (vice chmn. 1995, chmn. 2000-02), World Intellectual Property Orgn. (del.), Acad. Can. Writers (vice chmn., bd. govs. 1986—); mem. European Acad. Arts, Scis. and Humanities, Orgn. Can. Authors and Pubs. (founding dir.), Can. Authors Assn. (v.p. 1972-80, founding dir. Lit. Luncheons, pres. Montreal br. 1974-75, nat. pres. 1982-83, founding editor Nat. Newsline 1982, pub. Can. Author 1982-95, hon. life, chmn. editl. adv. com. Can. Authors Assn. 1978-94, chmn. grievance com. 1983-93, pub. com. 1986-92), Periodical Writers' Assn. Can. (chmn. grievance com. 1990, contracts com.), Can. Writers' Found. (bd. govs. 1982—), Assn. Am. Pubs. (hon. life), Mystery Writers Am. (editor Third Degree, co-chmn. awards com.), Writers' Union Can. (hon. life, chmn. grievance com. 1990-99, contracts com. 1990-2002), Soc. Profl. Journalists' Pres.'s Club, Book and Periodical Coun. (bd. govs. 1983-94), Authors Guild, Authors League Am., Internat. P.E.N., Nat. Spkrs. Assn., Am. Acad. Polit. and Social Sci., Can. Assn. Restoration of Lost Positives (pres.), Can. Soc. for Preservation of the Natural Bowtie (pres.), Sir George Williams U. Alumni Assn. (founding pres. N.Y.C. br., exec. com. 1970-75, pres. 1971-73), GeorgiAntiques (founding dir.), Avodah Honor Soc., Advt. Club, Deadline Club, Overseas Press Club, Dutch Treat Club (N.Y.C.), Toronto Press Club, Author's Club (London), Sigma Delta Chi. Home: 1405-1555 Finch Ave E Willowdale ON Canada M2J 4X9

KERNER, JOSEPH FRANK, JR., management consultant, educator; b, Cleve., Dec. 29, 1938; s. Joseph Frank Sr. and Magarat Ann (Majoris) K.; m. Marilyn Joy Long, June 14, 1964; children: Joseph, Mark, Michael, Erin. BA, Miami U., Oxford, Ohio, 1961; postgrad., Case Western Res. U., 1963-68. Dir. bus. tech. Marion (Ohio) Tech. Coll., 1969-75; mgr. benefits Cen. Net Bank, Cleve., 1975-78; mgr. compensation L.B. Foster, Pitts., 1978-80; mgr. compensation and benefits Rubbermaid, Wooster, Ohio, 1980-82; dir. compensation and benefits ChemLawn, Columbus, Ohio, 1982-84; v.p. First Nat. Bank of Commerce, New Orleans, 1984-85; instr. Bliss Coll., Columbus, 1985-88; regional v.p. Primerica Fin. Svcs., Columbus, 1985-95; pres. JFK Consultancy & Kerner Connection, Columbus, 1988—; mktg. dir. WMA Securities, 1995-97; v.p. mktg. Environ. Energy Alt. Fuel, 1995-97; mktg. advisor TAASI, 1995-98. Adj. prof. Coll. Fin. Planning, 1988—; co. advisor Ohio Bus. Week, 1994—. Author: National Underwriter: Agent Exposes Himself, 1987, Pension Actuary: My Vision, 1994. Bd. dirs. Environ. Energy, Inc.; mem. Nat. Rep. Glee Club. Mem. Am. Soc. Pension Actuaries (bd. dirs. 1966-69, edn. coord. 1990—, joint bd. enrolled actuary exam. rev. com., editor Pension Actuary 1994, govtl. affairs com. 1993—, cert. fed. tax., cert. data educator), Kiwanis (immediate past pres., club builder New Albany, Ohio), Data Processing Mgmt. Assn. (faculty student chpt. of yr. 1970). Republican. Lutheran. Avocations: snow and water skiing, fishing. Home: 1118 Elizabeth Ave Columbus OH 43227-1853 E-mail: JFKequal@aol.com.

KERNER, MICHAEL BERNARD, gastroenterologist; b. Newark, May 13, 1945; s. Irving and Betty Kerner; m. Cynthia Iris Spitzer, Mar. 24, 1974; children: Jessica, Caroline, David. BA, Rutgers U., 1967; MD, Bowman Gray Sch. Medicine, 1971. Diplomate Am. Bd. Internal Medicine and Gastroenterology. Intern NYU/Manhattan VA Med. Ctr., Manhattan, 1971-72; resident NYU Med. Ctr., Manhattan, 1972-74, gastroenterology fellow, 1974-76; physician, ptnr. Assocs. in Digestive Diseases, Springfield, N.J., 1976—. Asst. clin. prof. medicine Columbia U., N.Y.C., 1989-2002, UMDNJ Med. Sch., 1989—. Named in Top Gastroenterologists in N.J. N.J. Monthly Mag., 1996, named One of Top Doctors in N.Y. Met. Area Castle Connolly Guide, 2001, 02, 03. Fellow ACP, Am. Coll. Gastroenterology; mem. Am. Soc. Gastrointestinal Endoscopy, Am. Gastroenterology Assn., N.J. Soc. for Gastrointestinal Endoscopy (pres. 1985). Home: 21 Hemlock Rd Livingston NJ 07039-1423 Office: 25 Morris Ave Springfield NJ 07081-1404 E-mail: associates.dd@verizon.net.

KERNER, MICHAEL PHILIP, lawyer; b. N.Y.C., July 21, 1953; s. Arthur and Rosalind (Mehr) K. BA, Antioch Coll., 1976; JD, Lewis & Clark U., 1979; LLM in Taxation with honors, Golden Gate U., 1995. Bar: Calif. 1980 (cert. specialist probate, trusts & estate planning), U.S. Dist. Ct. (no. and ea. dists.) Calif. 1983, U.S. Ct. Appeals (9th cir.) 1983, U.S. Tax Ct., 1996. Staff atty. U.S. EPA, Washington, 1979-80, asst. regional counsel region 9 San Francisco, 1980-83; ptnr. Kerner, Weppner & Rosenbaum, San Francisco, 1983-95; prin. Kerner & Assocs., San Francisco, 1996-2000; ptnr. Janin, Morgan & Brenner, San Francisco, 2000—. Bd. dirs. Solano County Legal Assistance, Vallejo, Calif., 1983-86; arbitrator San Francisco Superior Ct., 1991-94. Editor law rev. and law jours. Mem. ABA, Solano County Bar Assn., Bar Assn. of San Francisco, Nat. Assn. of Trust & Estate Profls. Democrat. Jewish. Avocations: windsurfing, snowboarding, road and mountain biking. E-mail: mpk@jmblaw.com.

KERNEY, YOLONDA V. music historian; d. James Bell Kerney, Jr. and Nancy McKinney Kerney. MusB, Howard U., 1996, MMus, 2003. Music libr. U.S. Libr. Congress, Washington, 1995—. Chair Daniel Murray African Am. Culture Assn. of the Libr. of Congress, Washington, 1999—. Vol. tutor Met. Delta Adult Literacy Coun., Washington, 1996—2002. Recipient Outstanding Svc. citation, Met. Delta Adult Literacy Coun., 1999; fellow Jr. fellow, Libr. Congress, 1995. Mem.: Black Caucus of the ALA, ALA, Libr. Congress Pa., Music Libr. Assn., TransAfrica Forum. Republican. Episcopalian. Avocation: research of the negro spiritual and historical documents related to slavery in America. E-mail: yker@loc.gov.

KERNOCHAN, JOHN MARSHALL, lawyer, educator; b. New York, Aug. 3, 1919; s. Marshall Rutgers and Caroline (Hatch) K. BA, Harvard U., 1942; JD, Columbia U., 1948. Bar: N.Y. 1949. Asst. dir. Legis. Drafting Research Fund Columbia U., N.Y.C., 1950-51, acting dir., 1951-52, dir., 1952-69, lectr. law, 1951-52, assoc. prof., 1952-55, prof., 1955-77, Nash prof. law, 1977-89, Nash prof. law emeritus, 1990—; spl. lectr., 1991—2000; co-dir. Ctr. for Law and Arts (now Kernochan Ctr. Law, Media & Arts), 1999—. Cons. Temporary State Commn. to Study Orgnl. Structure of Govt. N.Y.C., 1953; exec. dir. Coun. for Atomic Age Studies, 1956—59, co-chmn., 1960—62; chmn. bd. Galaxy Music Corp., 1956—89; bd. dir. E.C. Schirmer Music Co., Inc.; pres. Gaudia Music & Arts, Inc., 1987—. Author: The Legislative Process, 1980; co-author: Legal Method Cases and Materials, 1980; contbr. articles to profl. jour. Mem. civil and polit. rights com. President's Commn. on Status of Women, 1962-63; dir. emeritus Vol. Lawyers for the Arts; mem. legal and legis. com. Internat. Confedn. Soc. Authors and Composers. Mem. Assn. Bar City of N.Y. Internat. Lit. and Artistic Assn. (mem. d'honneur, internat. exec. com., mem. U.S.A. group), Copyright Soc. U.S.A. (exec. com. 1986-89), Assn. Tchrs. and Rschr. in Intellectual Property. Office: Columbia Univ Sch Law 435 W 116th St New York NY 10027-7297

KERNOCHAN, SARAH M. film director, scriptwriter, composer; b. N.Y.C., Dec. 30, 1947; m. James Lapine; 1 child, Phoebe. Student, Sarah Lawrence Coll., 1966—69. Writer Village Voice, N.Y.C. Co-prodr. and dir. : (films) Marjoe, 1972 (Acad. award best documentary); co-writer 9 1/2 Weeks, 1986; writer Dancers, 1987; writer, with James Lapine, Impromptu, 1991; writer Sommersby, 1993; dir.: The Hairy Bird (aka Strike, All I Wanna Do), 2000, Thoth, 2002 (Acad. award best documentary); story : What Lies Beneath, 2000; author: Dry Hustle, 1997; recording artist: House of Pain, 1973, Beat Around the Bush, 1974; score composer : Sleeparound Town, 1983.*

KERNODLE, LUCY HENDRICK, school system nurse; b. Rutherfordton, N.C., Oct. 7, 1947; d. Harry Vance and Elizabeth Bruce (Beavers) Hendrick; m. Harold Barker Kernodle Jr., June 8, 1968; children: Carey Elizabeth, Katherine Suzanne. BSN, Duke U., 1969. RN, N.C.; cert. sch. nurse. Generalized pub. health nurse Met. Health Dept., Nashville, 1969-71, 73-74; pediatric orientation coord. Alamance County Hosp., Burlington, N.C., 1985-90; sch. system nurse Burlington City Schs., 1990-96; lead nurse Alamance-Burlington Schs., 1996—. Mem. woman's health steering com. Alamance Regional Med. Ctr., 1994—2001; mem. Healthy Alamance Substance Abuse Task Force, 1996—; mem. Health Alamance Asthma Coalition, 1996—. Deacon, elder, tchr. Sunday sch., youth advisor, mem. Christian edn. com. 1st Presbyn. Ch., 1977—; mem. Alamance County Svc. League, 1978-84, svc. chmn., 1983-84; mem. Alamance Caswell Med. Aux., Burlington, 1976—, pres., 1981. Named Outstanding Vol., Substance Abuse Task Force, 2001. Mem. ANA, Profl. Educators in N.C. (bd. dirs. 1993-94), Sch. Nurse Assn. of N.C. (exec. com. 1992-2001, pres. 1999-2000, named Sch. Nurse of Yr. 2003), Nat. Sch. Nurses Assn. Republican. Presbyterian. Avocations: sailing, reading. Home: 639 Still Run Ln Graham NC 27253-7702 Office: Alamance-Burlington Schs 1712 Vaughn Rd Burlington NC 27217-2916

KERNODLE, ROBERT GARY, dance and exercise ecucator; b. Greensboro, N.C., Sept. 30, 1953; s. Robert G. and Madge C. (Carter) K. Student, U. N.C., 1972-74, U. N.C., Greensboro, 1977-82, N.C. State U., 1975-76, N.C. Sch. of the Arts, Winston Salem, 1977. Tchr. Greensboro (N.C.) Coll., 1987-89; substitute tchr. Ctr. for Creative Leadership, 1990—. Advisor, choreographer Sports Ventures, Inc., Charlotte, N.C., 1990s; mem. exec. bd., editor N.C. Dance Alliance, 1985-88. Contbr. articles to profl. jours. Avocations: poetry, abstract painting, dance, any physical activity.

KERNS, ALLEN FRANKLIN, education educator; s. Cylde Allen and Mabel Della Kerns; m. Jean Lillian Ruby, Aug. 12, 1944; children: Mark Allen, Timothy Allen. BA, Eastern Nazarene Coll., Wollaston, Ma., 1949; MDiv., Boston U., Boston, Mass., 1952; MS, Fla. State U., 1971; EdD, Nova U., Ft. Lauderdale, Fla., 1979. Cert. ordained Meth. minister Mass., Ohio, and Mich.; rehabilitation counselor. Min. Meth. Ch., Mass.; rehab. counselor Calif. Dept. of Rehab., Downey, Calif., 1961—67, Fla. Dept. of Vocat. Rehab., 1967—71; dir. Pinellas County Vocat. Evaluation Ctr., Clearwater, Fla., 1971—74; adj. prof. U. of So. Fla., 1974—87. Cons. Medical Rehab. Ctr., 1974—91, edn. centers, 1974—91, London Sch. of Econ. and Polit. Sci., U. of London. Author: (book) Career Based Assessment, 1990; co-author: Vocat. Evaluation in Spl. Edn., 1987, Dictionary of Worker Traits (Vol. I and II), 1987; author: Improving Occupl. Programs for the Handicapped, 1975. Conducted workshops, Conf., and seminars for Vocat. Rehab. Counselors. Recipient directing an exemplary pilot program of Vocat. Evaluation in the Edn. Instn., U.S. Dept. of Health, Edn., and Welfare, Bur. of the Handicapped, 1970, Wm. M. Rabucha Award for Outstanding Svc. and Leadership, Fla. Vocat. Evaluation, 1978. Who's Who in the So. and S.W., 17th Edit., 1980, 1981, The Internat. Who's Who of Intellectuals, Internat. Biog. Ctr., Cambridge, Eng., 1981, 1982, Two Ann. Awards"Allen F. Kerns Award" Outstanding Employer and Prof., Fla. Job Placement Div., 1984, Svc. to Fla. Spl. Needs Educators and Vocat. Evaluators, Fla. Fedn. Div. of Career Devel., 1987. Mem.: Nat. Rehab. Assn. (job placement div., pres. S.E. div., founder Fla. Chpt.). Democrat. Methodist. Avocations: genealogy, reading Bible in different lang., organ, piano. Home: 4251 Kendale Rd Columbus OH 43220-4139

KERNS, BRIAN D. former congressman; b. Ind., May 22, 1957; s. Noel and Rosalie K.; m. Lori Myers. BA in polit. sci., MPA, Ind. State U. Dir. publs. and pub. rels. St. Joseph's Coll., Rensselaer, Ind.; pub. info. specialist State Ind. Dept. Natural Resources; reporter, photographer WTWO TV, Terre Haute, Ind.; former Chief of Staff, Deputy Chief of Staff, Spokesman Capitol Hill; mem. U.S. Congress from 7th Ind. dist., 2001—03. Mem. Congressional com. Transportation and Infrastructure, Internat. Rels., Policy; subcom. Highways and Transit, Water Resources and Environ., East Asia and Pacific, Nat. Security, Foreign Affairs, Retirement Security, Captial Markets, Tax Policy, Americas; Reg. Rep. for Ind., Ill. and Mich. Recipient Best Feature Story Yr., United Press Internat., Zorah Shrine Childrens Adv. award. Mem.: Eagles, Elks, Masons. Republican. Episcopalian.*

KERNS, DAVID VINCENT, lawyer; b. Jan. 29, 1917; s. Clinton Bowen and Ella Mae (Young) K.; m. Dorothea Boyd, Sept. 5, 1942; children: David V., Clinton Boyd. *Father Clinton Bowen Kerns, U. Minn. 1915, was a mechanical engineer specializing in copper mining and a citrus grower. Mother Ella was a pianist and artist. Son David, Jr., PhD. FSU 1970, is an electronics engineer and Provost of Olin College of Engineering, Needham, Mass. His wife Sherra is vice-president, innovation and research, Olin College. Son Clinton Boyd Kerns and his wife Virginia Ann live in New Iberia, LA. and have four children. He is district manager for the veterinary division of Butler Pharmaceutical Company. Granddaughter Melissa works for Time-Life magazines in New York City and grandson David III is creative director for Metropol Online, Copenhagen, Denmark.* BPh, Emory U., 1937; JD, U. Fla., 1939. Bar: Fla. 1939, U.S. Dist. Ct. (mid. dist.) Fla. 1939, (so. dist.) Fla. 1978, (no. dist.) Fla. 1981, U.S. Ct. Appeals (11th cir.) 1981, U.S. Supreme Ct. 1988. Assoc. Sutton & Reeves, Tampa, Fla., 1939-41, Fowler & White, Tampa, 1945-47; ptnr. Moran & Kerns, Tampa, 1948-49; resident atty. Fla. Road Dept., 1949-53; rsch. asst. Supreme Ct. Fla., 1953-58; dir. Fla. Legis. Reference Bur., 1958-68, Fla. Legis. Svc. Bur., 1968-71, Fla. Legis. Libr. Svcs., 1971-73; gen. counsel Fla. Dept. Adminstrn., 1973-82; mem. Fla. Career Svc. Commn., 1983-86; spl. master Fla. Senate, 1987-96; legal cons. chief inspector gen. Fla. Gov. Office, 1995-98. *David V. Kerns is a member: Lambda Chi Alpha: Alpha Kappa Psi; Phi Alpha Delta; U.S. Sup. Ct, Hist, Soci; International Christian Leadership Assn.; Tallahassee Amateur Radio Society (KD4CAF); Big Bend Model Railroad Assn.; National Model Railroad Assn.; Train Collectors Assn.; National Railway Historical Society; Friends of Gulf Coast Limited.* Contbr. articles to profl. jours. Served with U.S. Army, 1941-45. Mem. Fla. Govt. Bar Assn. (pres. 1966, J. Ernest Webb Meml. award 1982), Fla. Bar (bd. govs. 1978-84), Tallahassee Bar Assn. (spl. dir. 1993-95). Democrat. Methodist. Home: 418 Vinnedge Ride Tallahassee FL 32303-5140

KERNS, GERTRUDE YVONNE, psychologist; b. Flint, Mich., July 25, 1931; d. Lloyd D. and Mildred C. (Ter Achter) B.; BA, Olivet Coll., 1953; MA, Wayne State U., 1958; PhD, U. Mich., 1979. Sch. psychologist Roseville (Mich.) Pub. Schs., 1958-68, Grosse Pointe (Mich.) Pub. Schs., 1968-86; pvt. practice psychology, Grosse Pointe, 1980—; instr. psychology Macomb C.C., 1959-69. Author: A Second Heartbeat, 1979. Mem. Am. Psychol. Assn., Mich. Psychol. Assn., Lakeshore Psychol. Assn. (pres. 1988-89), Psi Chi. Home: 28820 Grant St Saint Clair Shores MI 48081-3207 Office: 131 Kercheval Ave Ste 140 Grosse Pointe Farms MI 48236-3630

KERNS, WILMER LEE, social science researcher; b. Dayton, Va., May 17, 1932; s. Lee Doil and Madeline A. (Grim) K.; m. Marian Iris May, Mar. 21, 1957 (div. 1963); children: Mark Wayne, Susan Kaye Kerns Mitchell; m. Shirley Mitchell Walton, June 19, 1965; children: Robert Todd, Lynelle Madeline, Jacob Scott Walton. AB, Trevecca Nazarene Coll., 1957; AM, U. Mich., 1960; PhD, Ohio State U., 1971. Cert. tchr., counselor, Va. Math. tchr. Norfolk (Va.) Pub. Schs., 1957-59; counselor Washington-Lee High Sch., Arlington, Va., 1960-65; social worker Arlington (Va.) County Pub. Schs., 1965-67; civil rights specialist U.S. Office Edn., Washington, 1967-69; rsch. assoc. Ohio State U., Columbus, 1969-71; assoc. regional commr. Social and Rehab. Svc., Chgo., 1971-74, planning officer Washington, 1974-75, divsn. chief, 1975-77; sr. rsch. analyst Social Security Adminstrn., Washington, 1977-97; ret., 1997. Author: Shanholtzer History and Allied Family Roots, 1980, Historical Records of Old Frederick and Hampshire Counties, Va., 1992; Frederick County, Virginia: Settlement and First Families, 1730-1830, 1995; columnist The W.Va. Advocate, 1982-92 (Excellence in Journalism award 1992). Lay minister Truro Episcopal Ch., Fairfax, Va., 1988-91. With USN, 1950-53. Decorated Air medal; named Disting. West Virginian, Gov. of W.Va.,

1989. Mem. Morgan County Hist. Soc., Winchester-Frederick County Hist. Assn. Republican. Avocations: mountain music, historical and genealogical research. Home: 4715 38th Pl N Arlington VA 22207-2914

KERNSTOCK, ELWYN NICHOLAS, political science educator, author; b. Bronx, N.Y., Dec. 24, 1917; s. Charles Henry and Irene (Paollilo) K.; m. Peggy Giles, Dec. 20, 1947; children: Stephan Giles, Nicholas Charles, Christopher John, Wendy Kernstock Robinson. BS in Edn., Ctrl. Conn. State Coll., 1963, MS, 1965; PhD, U. Conn., 1972. Commd. 2d lt. U.S. Army, 1943, advanced through grades to maj., 1962, ret., 1962; instr., chmn. social studies various secondary schs., Conn., 1962-70; faculty St. Michael's Coll., Winooski, Vt., 1971-88, prof. emeritus, 1988—; prof. Acad. Sr. Profls. U. West Fla., 2000—. Pres. New Britain Edn. Assn., 1964; del. Conn. Dem. Conv., 1970, Vt. Dem. Conv., 1972, 1974, 1976, 1980, 1984, 1992, 1994; adv. to chmn. Vt. Dem. Com., 1974—76; Dem. candidate for Congress Vt., 1978; Fla. state legis., 2000; elected committeeman Santa Rosa County, Fla., 1996, Esambia County, Fla., 2001; Dem. candidate for state legis. Fla., 2000; pres. New Britain Unitarian Universalist Soc., 1962. Co-recipient 9th Ann. Freedom of Choice award Pro Choice Vt., 1994. Mem. Am. Polit. Sci. Assn., New Eng. Polit. Sci. Assn., Americans United for Separation Ch. and State (mem. adv. bd. 1987-93, 98—, 99-, pres. N.W. Fla. chpt.), Ret. Officers Assn. Home: 10100 Hillview Rd # 2105 Pensacola FL 32514-5436 E-mail: ekernstock@yahoo.com.

KERPPOLA, TOM KLAUS WILLIAM, research scientist, educator; b. Helsinki, Finland, Oct. 21, 1962; came to U.S., 1981; s. Klaus William Mikael Kerppola and Mariitta Anna Aulikki (Meurman) Tuomala; m. Raili Emilia Kulmala, Sept. 19, 1982; 1 child, Marianna Eeva Aulikki. BS in Biochemistry and Biophysics, BS in Biology, MS in Biochemistry and Biophysics, Wash. State U., 1985; PhD of Biochemistry, U. Calif., Berkeley, 1989. Undergrad. rsch. asst., grad. rsch. asst. Wash. State U., Pullman, 1982-85; grad. rsch. asst., postdoctoral fellow U. Calif., Berkeley, 1985-90; postdoctoral fellow Roche Inst. Molecular Biology, Nutley, N.J., 1990-92, rsch. fellow, 1992-94; assoc. investigator Howard Hughes Med. Inst., 1994—; assoc. prof. dept. biol. chemistry U. Mich., 1994—. Contbr. articles to profl. jours. Deacon First Congl. Ch., Montclair, N.J., 1991-94. Mem. Phi Beta Kappa, Phi Kappa Phi. Lutheran. Avocations: bicycling, hiking, camping, watersports. Office: Howard Hughes Med Inst U Mich Med Sch 4570 MSRB II 1150 W Med Ctr Dr Ann Arbor MI 48109

KERR, ALEXANDER DUNCAN, JR., lawyer; b. Pitts., May 6, 1943; s. Alexander Duncan Sr. and Nancy Greenleaf (Martin) K.; m. Judith Kathleen Mottl, May 25, 1969; children: Matthew Jonathan, Joshua Brandon. BS in Bus., Northwestern U., 1965, JD, 1968. Bar: Ill. 1968, Pa. 1969, U.S. Dist. Ct. (ea. dist.) Pa. 1969, U.S. Dist. Ct. (no. dist.) Ill. 1969, U.S. Ct. Appeals (3rd and 7th cirs.) 1969, U.S. Supreme Ct. 1969. Assoc. Clark, Ladner, Fontenbaugh & Young, Phila., 1968-69, 73-74; asst. U.S. atty. U.S. Dept. Justice, Chgo., 1974-79; assoc., ptnr. Keck, Mahin & Cate, Chgo., Oak Brook, Ill., 1979-90; shareholder Tishler & Wald, Ltd., Chgo., 1990—. Staff atty. Park Dist. La Grange, Ill., 1985-2001; active Ill. St. Andrew Soc., North Riverside, 1982—, pres., 1995-97; vestryman, lay reader, chancellor, chalice bearer Emmanuel Episcopal Ch., 1980-99; mem. Pack 177, Troop 19, Order of the Arrow, Boy Scouts Am., La Grange, 1980-2000. With USN, 1969-75. Mem. Am. Legion, DuPage Club, Atlantis Divers. Home: 709 S Stone Ave La Grange IL 60525-2725 Fax: 708-354-1208. E-mail: akerr@tishlerandwald.com.

KERR, ALLEN STEWART, retired psychologist; b. Evanston, Ill., Nov. 13, 1928; s. Charles Allen and Mildred (Latham) Kerr; m. Charlyn Floyd, July 19, 1952; children: Betsy Kerr Hedding, Chet, Peggy Kerr Ihinger, Cindy Kerr Levesque. BA, Brown U., 1950; D of Psychology, Forest Inst. Profl. Psychology, 1988. Lic. psychologist Ga. Salesman Sleepeck Printing Co., Bellwood, Ill., 1953—68, v.p. sales, 1968—83; staff psychologist The Bradley Ctr., Columbus, Ga., 1988—94; sr. psychologist The Pastoral Inst., Columbus, Ga., 1994—99; ret., 1999. Lt. j.g. USN, 1950—53. Recipient Bell Ringer award, Mental Health Assn., Columbus, Ga., 1995. Mem.: APA, Ga. Psychol. Assn., Rotary (Muscogee charter mem., pres. 1997—98). Methodist. Avocations: golf, photography, writing, travel. Home: 887 Oakwood Dr Columbus GA 31904-2483 E-mail: askchar@earthlink.net.

KERR, ANTHONY ROBERT, scientist; b. Farnborough, Hants, England, Aug. 30, 1941; s. Cecil Edwin and Stella Mary (Williams) K.; m. Tanya Ross, Jan. 24, 1974; 1 child, Tristan Duncan Ross. B of Engring. with honors, U. Melbourne, Australia, 1963, M of Engring. Sci. with honors, 1967, PhD, 1969. Rsch. scientist Commonwealth Sci. & Indsl. Rsch. Orgn., Sydney, Australia, 1969-71; engr. Nat. Radio Astronomy Obs., Charlottesville, Va., 1971-74; scientist NASA Goddard Inst. Space Studies, NYC, 1974-84, Nat. Radio Astronomy Obs., 1984—. Vis. prof. elec. engring. U. Va., 1984—, vis. prof. astronomy, 1986—; cons. M/A-Com Microwave Assoc., Burlington, Mass., 1980-83, NASA Goddard Space Flight Ctr., Greenbelt, Md., 1987-88. Author over 80 sci. and tech. papers. Recipient Exceptional Engring. Achievement medal NASA, 1983. Fellow IEEE (mem. editorial bd. Transactions on Microwave Theory and Techniques, 1980—, Microwave prize 1978); mem. Am. Inst. Physics, Internat. Union Radio Sci. Office: Nat Radio Astronomy Obs 2015 Ivy Rd Charlottesville VA 22903-1733

KERR, BAINE PERKINS, JR., lawyer, writer; b. Houston, June 23, 1946; s. Baine Perkins and Mildred Pickett (Caldwell) Kerr; m. Cynthia Anne Carlisle; children: Dara, Baine. BA, Stanford U., 1968; MA, U. Denver, 1976, JD, 1979. Bar: Colo. 1979, U.S. Dist. Ct. (Colo.) 1979, U.S. Ct. Appeals 1979. Editor-in-chief Place Mag., Palo Alto, Calif., 1971—74; ptnr. Hutchinson, Black, Hill & Cook, Boulder, Colo., 1979—. Elections supr., Bosnia-Herzegovina, 1997; fiction writer. Author: Jumping Off Place, 1981, Harmful Intent, 1999, Wrongful Death, 2002. Recipient Editor's prize, Mo. Rev., 1992; fellow, Nat. Endowment for the Arts, 1983. Mem.: ABA, Boulder County Bar Assn., Colo. Bar Assn. Democrat. Office: 921 Walnut St Ste 200 Boulder CO 80306

KERR, BAINE PERKINS, oil company executive; b. Rusk, Tex., Aug. 24, 1919; s. James Herman and Myrta Blake (Perkins) K.; m. Mildred Pickett Caldwell, June 13, 1942; children: Baine Perkins, John Caldwell, James Robinson, Mary Blake Kerr Winters. BA, LL.B., U. Tex. at Austin, 1942. Bar: Tex. 1942. Practiced in, Houston, 1945-77; partner firm Baker & Botts, 1955-77; dir. Pennzoil Co., Houston, 1964-94, chmn. exec. com., 1972-94, pres., 1977-85, dir. emeritus, 1994—. Served with USMCR, 1942-55. Mem. Chancellors, Order of Coif, Phi Beta Kappa. Office: Esperson Bldg 808 Travis St Ste 2200 Houston TX 77002-5704

KERR, BARBARA PROSSER, research scientist, educator; b. Asheville, N.C., Dec. 28, 1925; d. George Holcomb and Gertrude Berenice (Parker) Prosser; m. William Albert Kerr, June 18, 1950 (div. May 1959); 1 child, Diana. BA, U. Chgo., 1951; MSW, Ariz. State U., 1971. Cert. clin. social worker, psychiatry and mental health nursing. Exec. sec. Union Theol. Sem., N.Y.C., 1961-67; case worker Dept. Pub. Welfare, Wilmington, Del., 1967-69; psychiatric nurse St. Luke's Hosp. and Med. Ctr., Phoenix, 1969-70; emergency rm. social worker Maricopa Med. Ctr., Phoenix, 1971-82; dir. Kerr-Cole Sustainable Living Ctr., Taylor, Ariz., 1983—. Adv. Solar Cookers Internat., Sacramento, 1993—. Author: The Expanding World of Solar Box Cookers, 1991; inventor Solar Box Cooker, 1976, Solar Wall Oven, 1986. Home: PO Box 576 Taylor AZ 85939 E-mail: kerrcole@skyboot.com.

KERR, CLARK, academic administrator emeritus; b. Stony Creek, Pa., May 17, 1911; s. Samuel William and Caroline (Clark) K.; m. Catherine Spaulding, Dec. 25, 1934; children: Clark E., Alexander W., Caroline M. BA, Swarthmore Coll., 1932, LLD, 1952; MA, Stanford U., 1933; postgrad., London Sch. Econs., 1936, 39; PhD, U. Calif., 1939; LLD, Harvard U., 1958, Princeton U., 1959, others. Traveling fellow Am. Friends Svc. Com., 1935-36; instr. econs. Antioch Coll., 1936-37; tchg. fellow U. Calif., 1937-38; Newton Booth fellow, 1938-39; acting asst. prof. labor econs. Stanford, 1939-40; asst., later assoc. prof. U. Wash., 1940-45; assoc. prof., prof., prof. emeritus, dir. Inst. Indsl. Rels., U. Calif., Berkeley, 1945-52, chancellor, 1952-58, pres., 1958-67, pres. emeritus, 1974—. Chmn. Carnegie Commn. on Higher Edn., 1967-73, Carnegie Coun. Policy Studies in Higher Edn., 1974-79; vice chmn. divsns. War Labor Bd., 1943-45; nat. arbitrator Armour Co. and United Packing House Workers, 1945-52; impartial chmn. Waterfront Employers, Pacific Coast and Internat. Longshoremen's and Warehousemen's Union, 1946-47; pub. mem. Nat. WSB, 1950-51; various arbitrations in pub. utilities, newspaper, aircraft, canning, oil, local transport and other industries, 1942— ; mem. adv. panel Soc. Sci. Rsch., NSF, 1953-57; chmn. Armour Automation Com., 1959-79; chmn. bd. arbitrators U.S. Postal Svc. and Nat. Assn. Letter Carriers (AFL-CIO) and Am. Postal Workers Union (AFL-CIO), 1984 Author: (with E. Wight Bakke) Unions, Management and the Public, rev. edit., 1960, 67, (with Dunlop, Harbison, Myers) Industrialism and Industrial Man, rev. edit., 1964, 73, The Uses of the University, rev. edit., 1972, 82, 95, 2001, Labor and Management in Industrial Society, 1964, Marshall, Marx and Modern Times, 1969, Labor Markets and Wage Determination: The Balkanization of Labor Markets and Other Essays, 1977, Education and National Development: Reflections from an American Perspective during a Period of Global Reassessment, 1979, The Future of Industrial Societies, 1983, (with Marian L. Gade) The Many Lives of Academic Presidents, 1986; editor: (with Paul D. Staudohar) Industrial Relations in a New Age, 1986, Economics of Labor in Industrial Society, 1986, (with Dunlop, Lester, Reynolds; editor Bruce E. Kaufman) How Labor Markets Work: Reflections on Theory and Practice, 1988, (with Marian L. Gade) The Guardians: Boards of Trustees of American Colleges and Universities, 1989, The Great Transformation in Higher Education, 1960-80, 1991, Troubled Times for American Higher Education: The 1990s and Beyond, 1994, Higher Education Cannot Escape History: Issues for the Twenty-First Century, 1994, (with Paul D. Staudohar) Labor Economics and Industrial Relations: Markets and Institutions, 1994, The Gold and the Blue, Vol. 1: Academic Triumphs, 2001. Vol. II Pol. Turmoil, 2003. Trustee Rockefeller Found., 1960-76; mem. bd. mgrs. Swarthmore Coll., 1969-80, life mem., 1981. Recipient Harold W. McGraw Jr. prize in Edn., 1990; named Hon. fellow London Sch. Econs. Mem. Am. Econ. Assn., Royal Econ. Assn., Am. Acad. Arts and Scis., Indsl. Rels. Rsch. Assn., Nat. Acad. Arbitrators, Phi Beta Kappa, Kappa Sigma. Mem. Soc. Of Friends. Home: 8300 Buckingham Dr El Cerrito CA 94530-2530 Office: U Calif Inst Indsl Rels 2521 Channing Way # 5555 Berkeley CA 94720-5556

KERR, DAVE, state official, marketing professional; m. Patty Kerr; children: Ryan, Dan. Degree in Biol. Sci., Psychology, Kans. State U., 1968; MBA, U. Kans., 1970. Leader com. on Econ. Devel., Edn.; candidate Kans. Senate, 1984; senator State of Kans., 1984—; served Kans. Senate, 1988, 1992, 1996, 2000; pres. Kans. State Senate Dist. 34, 2000—. Mem. bd. dirs. Hutchinson Hosp. Corp.; mem. bd. dirs. Reno County Mental Health Adv. Com.; with Hutchinson Hosp. Bd. Dirs., Bds. Leadership Hutchinson, Hutchinson C.of C., Healthy Families, Nickerson and Hutchinson HS booster clubs. Mem.: Kans. Tech. Enterprise Corp. (mem. bd. dirs. 1987—98), Republican Ctrl. Com. (sec. 1981—84), Kans. C. of C. and Industry, Kans. Farm Bur., Legis. Post Audit, Joint Pensions, Investments and Benefits (vice chmn.), Legis. Coordinating Coun. (chmn.), Interstate Coop. (chmn.), Ways and Means Com., Commerce Com., Calendar and Rules Com. (chmn.). Republican. Office: State Capitol PO Box 2620 Hutchinson KS 67504 Business E-Mail: kerr@senate.state.ks.us.*

KERR, DAVID WYLIE, natural resource company executive; b. Montreal, Que., Can., Dec. 14, 1943; s. Dudley Holden and Cecilia (Maguire) K.; m. Sheryl Lee Drysdale, Nov. 1, 1969; children: Ross, Tamara. BSc, McGill U., Can., 1965, chartered acct., 1969. Chartered acct. Touche Ross & Co., Montreal, 1965-70, 1970-72; CFO Edper Investments Ltd., Toronto, Ont., Can., 1972-78; COO Hees Internat. Corp., Toronto, 1978-85; exec. v.p. Brascan Ltd., Toronto, 1985-86; sr. v.p. strategic planning Noranda Inc., Toronto, 1986-87, pres., 1987-90, pres., CEO, 1990—2002, chmn., 2002—, also bd. dirs. Bd. dirs. Brascan Corp., Falconbridge Ltd., Shell Can. Ltd., Sustainable Devel. Tech. Can. Found. Mem. Granite Club, Rosedale Golf Club. Mem. United Ch. Can. Avocations: bicycling, fitness, farming, golf. Office: Noranda Inc/BCE PL 181 Bay St Ste 200 Toronto ON Canada M5J 2T3

KERR, DONALD MACLEAN, JR., physicist; b. Phila., Apr. 8, 1939; s. Donald MacLean and Harriet (Fell) K.; m. Alison Richards Kyle, June 10, 1961; 1 dau., Margot Kyle. B.E.E. (Nat. Merit scholar), Cornell U., 1963, MS, 1964, PhD (Ford Found. fellow, 1964-65, James Clerk Maxwell fellow 1965-66), 1966. Staff Los Alamos Nat. Lab., 1966-76, group leader, 1971-72, asst. div. leader, 1972-73, asst. dir., 1973-75, alt. energy divsn. leader, 1975-76; dep. mgr. Nev. ops. office Dept. Energy, Las Vegas, 1976-77; acting asst. sec. def. programs Dept. Energy, Washington, 1978, dep. asst. sec. def. programs, 1977-79, dep. asst. sec. energy tech., 1979; dir Los Alamos Nat. Lab., 1979-85; sr. v.p. EG&G, Inc., Wellesley, Mass., 1985-88, exec. v.p., 1988-89, pres., bd. dirs., 1989-92; exec. v.p., bd. dirs. Sci. Applications Internat. Corps., San Diego, 1993-96, Info. Sys. Labs., San Diego, 1996-97; asst. dir. FBI, Washington, 1997—2001; dep. dir. sci. and tech. CIA, Washington, 2001—. Mem. Navajo Sci. Com., 1974-77, Def. Sci. Bd., 1993-98; mem. sci. adv. panel U.S. Army, 1975-78; mem. engring. adv. bd. U. Nev., Las Vegas, 1976-78, Cornell U., 1985—; chmn. com. R&D Internat. Energy Agy., 1979-85; mem. nat. security adv. coun. SRI Internat., 1980-89; mem. adv. bd. U. Alaska Geophys. Inst., 1980-85; mem. sci. adv. group Joint Strategic Planning Staff, 1981-91; mem. adv. bd. Georgetown U. Ctr. Strategic Internat. Studies, 1981-87; mem. adv. com. Naval Rsch., 1982-85; mem. corp. Draper Lab., 1982-97; mem. DCI Nonproliferation Adv. Panel, 1993-98; mem. bd. San Diego Tech. Coun., 1994-97; bd. dirs. Resources for the Future, Washington. Published research on plasma physics, microwave electronics, ionospheric physics, energy and nat. security. Trustee New Eng. Aquarium, 1989-93. Fellow AAAS, Am. Phys. Soc.; mem. Am. Geophys. Union, Nat. Assn. Mfrs. (bd. dirs. 1986-92), Southwestern Assn. Indian Affairs, World Affairs Coun. Boston (bd. dirs. 1988-92), Atlantic Coun. (bd. dirs. 1991-97), Cosmos Club (Washington), Sigma Xi, Tau Beta Pi, Eta Kappa Nu.

KERR, DOROTHY MARIE BURMEISTER, marketing executive, consultant; b. Chgo., Oct. 1, 1935; d. Edwin Charles and Dorothy Gladys (Braithwaite) Burmeister; m. James Robert Kerr, Aug. 27, 1955 (div. Jan. 1970); 1 child, Kathryn Elizabeth; m. James Mullinix, Apr. 20, 1978; 1 son, Mark Edwin Mullinix. BA, Cornell U., 1956. Publicity dir. United chpts. Phi Beta Kappa, Washington, 1957-62; dir. circulation and promotion The Am. Scholar, Washington, 1957-62; pres., creative dir. Dorothy Kerr & Assocs., Inc., Washington, 1962-79, 89-93, Milw., 1995—, sec.-treas., 1979-89; circulation mktg. mgr. U.S. News and World Report, 1979-84, assoc. circulation dir., 1985; circulation dir. Atlantic, 1985; v.p., dir. mktg. Walter Karl Cos., 1986-89; v.p. mktg. GEICO Life Ins. Co., Washington, 1989-90, Equifax Consumer Direct, Washington, 1990-92; v.p. bus. devel. DCI Mktg., Milw., 1993-95; dir. database mktg. and strategic info. Strong Capital Mgmt., Milw., 1995-96; exec. dir. Ctr. for Deaf and Hard of Hearing, Brookfield, Wis., 1999—. Cons. Annenberg Sch. Communication, U. Pa., Phila., 1973-75; lectr. George Washington U., 1974-76, adv. bd. editing and pub. program. Bd. dirs. Florence Crittenton Home, Washington, 1968-71; bd. dirs. Better Bus. Bur. Met. Washington, mem. exec. com., 1978-93; bd. dirs. Wis. BBB, 1997—, mem. exec. com., 1998—, sec., 1998-99, vice chmn., 1999-2002, chmn., 2001—; bus. adv. com. Washington Tech. Inst., 1976; Washington adv. council SBA, 1976-78. Recipient Man of Year award Mail Advt. Club, 1971; named Woman of Yr. Women's Direct Response Group, 1992. Mem. Am. Mktg. Assn., Direct Mktg. Assn. (chmn. ethics oper. com. 1988-89, judging chmn. Echo awards com. 1994-95), Nat. Soc. Arts and Letters (treas. 1979-83), Assn. Direct Mktg. Agys. (dir., exec. v.p. 1978-79), Wis. Direct Mktg. Assn. (bd. dirs., program chair 1994-95, pres. 1995-96, steering com. 1998-99, Direct Mktg. Profl. of the Yr. 1998), Milw. Advt. Club (v.p. pub. svc. 1995-96, v.p. programs 1996-98), Washington Advt. Club (dir., pres. 1979-80), Capital Spkrs. Club (Washington, v.p. 1971), Direct Mktg. Club (Washington, pres. 1965), Rotary Club Milw., Inc., Kappa Delta. Home and Office: 1509 E Standish Pl Milwaukee WI 53217-1960 E-mail: dkerr@dorothykerrassociates.com. *Much of what must be done in life is neither exciting nor glamorous, but one should be willing to do whatever is needed; any task worth doing is worth doing well.*

KERR, FORREST DAVID, actor, writer, producer; b. Burnet, Tex., Jan. 25, 1949; s. Forrest and Dorothy Web (Dennis) K.; m. Kathleen Mable Keller, Dec. 6, 1969 (div. Mar. 1975). Student, C.C. Balt., 1970-71; AS in Bus. Adminstrn., Austin C.C., 1980; postgrad., St. Edwards U., Austin, 1980-81, Am. Acad. Dramatic Arts, Pasadena, Calif., 1990, UCLA, 1992. Control clk. Social Security Adminstrn., Balt., 1970-71; assoc. br. mgr. Fin. Am., Smyrna, Del., 1971-75; br. mgr. Investors Loan Corp., Alexandria, Va., 1865-77; mgr.-in-tng. Gt. Western Fin., Austin, 1977-78; leasing agt. Safty Kleen Corp., Austin, 1979-80; tech. staff asst. Austin C.C., 1982; mgr. main br. Jim Walter Homes Corp., Corpus Christi, Tex., 1983-84; dir. sales Royal T Homes Corp., Houston, 1985-87; gen. mgr. Conner Home Sales Corp., Houston, 1987-88, Times Manufactured Housing and Tomball (Tex.) Mobile Homes, 1988-89; asst. mgr. Florsheim Thayer McNiel, Northridge, Calif., 1990-91; apprentice editor Concorde/New Horizon Films, Venice, Calif., 1991-92; freelance writer and prodr., Thorne Pictures, Palos Verdes, Calif., 1993—; ptnr., CEO Pacific Coast Pictures, 2002—. Cons. Am. Cons. League, Houston, 1988-90; copy editor Fieldings Worldwide Travel Guides, Redondo Beach, Calif., 1994 Author: (screen plays) Unlikely Angel, 1990, Thunderbirds, 1992; appeared in (plays) Mousetrap, My Sister Eileen, (films) Sudden Death, Melrose Place, Man of Her Dreams, Sheriff Garrett, 1992, Graveyard Man, 1992, Chauffer, 1993, Featured Detective, 1994, Ken Osborn, 1996; assoc. prodr. (films) Thornes of Fate, 1993; (videos) Elinor Rigby, 1991, Hard Luck Woman, 1992; writer, prodr., dir. (play) The Way It Wasn't, 1989. Mem. ind. feature project, Santa Monica, Calif., 1993—; vol. Book Pals, SAG Found., L.A., 1995; founding mem. Secret Rose Theater, 1999—, Interweave, 1999; mem. Stolen Memories, 1999, Arrest and Trial, 2001, Unsolved Mysteries, 2001, Mandalay Media Repertory Co., 2001—. Mem. SAG (Screen Actors Guild awards, nominating com. L.A. 1996, 2000, conservatory 1995—, casting com. 1997—), Phi Theta Kappa. Avocations: hiking, bicycling, frisbee, billiards and pool, reading.

KERR, FREDERICK HOHMANN, retired health care company executive; b. Pitts., July 11, 1936; s. Nathan Frederick and Laura Marie (Hohmann) K.; m. Ethyl Nylene Bashline, 1960 (div. 1969); m. Phyllis Jensen, Aug. 21, 1970, 1 child, Linda Jean. BA, Pa. State U., 1958; MPA, U. Pitts., 1961; LLD (hon.), Luth. Coll. Health Professions, Ft. Wayne, Ind., 1996. Exec. sec. Pa. Economy League Fayette County Br., Uniontown, Pa., 1959, Armstrong County Br., Kittanning, Pa., 1959-62; exec. sec. Woodbury Tax Rsch. Conf., Sioux City, Iowa, 1962-65; pub. svc. dir. City of Sioux City, 1965-66; from asst. administr. to assoc. administr. St. Luke's Regional Med. Ctr., Sioux City, 1966-71; administr., CEO, Meml. Hosp. of Michigan City, Inc., Ind., 1971-75; pres., CEO, St. Luke's Hosp., Maumee, Ohio, 1975-86, Luth. Hosp. Ind., Luth. Coll. Health Professions, Ft. Wayne, 1986-95; v.p. for devel. Quorum Health Resources, Inc., Brentwood, Tenn., 1995-2001. Dir. Ohio Hosp. Ins. Co., Columbus, treas. 1981-84. Trustee Ohio Hosp. Assn., Columbus, 1983—85; dir. Siouxland United Way, 1960—71, Ft. Wayne Pub. TV, 1990—91, United Way Allen County, Ft. Wayne, 1990—94; mem. Iowa Intergovtl. Rels. Com., Des Moines, 1964—67; mem. Rancho Vistoso Adv. Bd. N.W. Med. Ctr., Tucson, 2002—. Mem.: ASPA (life; nat. coun. 1966—69), Am. Protestant Health Assn. (vice chmn. 1988—90). Avocations: wine appreciation, writing. *Being a servant is the most distinguished career of all.*

KERR, GARY ENRICO, lawyer, educator; b. Kewanee, Ill., Feb. 8, 1948; s. Roy Harrison and Marietta (Dani) K.; m. Eileen Elizabeth Straeter, Aug. 18, 1978; 1 child, Victoria Elizabeth. BA, No. Ill. U., 1970; JD, Northwestern U., Chgo., 1973. Bar: Ill. 1974, U.S. Dist. Ct. (cen. dist.) Ill. 1982, U.S. Ct. Appeals (7th cir.) 1983, U.S. Supreme Ct. 1983. Adminstrv. asst. Office Supt. Pub. Instrn. State Ill., Chgo., Springfield, 1971-74; asst. legal advisor Ill. State Bd. Edn., Springfield, 1974-78; spl. counsel Ill. State Comptroller, Springfield, 1978-79; pvt. practice Springfield, 1979—. Adj. faculty Sangamon State U. (now Ill. State U.), Springfield, Ill., 1994; pres., dir. counsel Kerr Products, Inc., Kewanee, Ill., 1980—; instr. paralegal program Robert Morris Coll., Springfield, 1992. Atty. South County Democrats, Sangamon County, Ill.; founder, mgr., Springfield (Ill.) Area Youth Jazz Band. Fellow Ednl. Policy program Inst. Ednl. Leadership, George Washington U., 1976-77. Mem. Ill. State Bar Assn. (chmn. sch. law sect. coun. 1983-84), Sangamon County Bar Assn., Automotive Parts and Accessories Assn. (mem. govtl. affairs and internat. trade com. 1997). Avocations: snow skiing, tennis, fishing. Office: Gary Kerr Ltd 1020 S 7th St Springfield IL 62703-2417 E-mail: kerrltd@aol.com.

KERR, GIB, financial planner; b. Ottawa, Ont., Can., Apr. 21, 1927; came to U.S., 1966; s. Francis and Gladys (Larmondra) K.; m. Shirley Cochrane, June 15, 1952 (div. Apr. 1971); chldren: Judith Ann, Brian Jeffrey (dec.), Barry Philip, Sandra Gail, Randolph James. Grad. high sch., Ottawa. CLU; CFP; ChFC; registered investment advisor. Lab asst. E.B. Eddy Pulp and Paper Co., Hull, Canada, 1946—47; spl. svcs. mgr. Bell Telephone Co. of Can., Ottawa, 1947—57; owner, operator Spotlight Studios, Ottawa, 1957—57; corp. pres., career mgr. G.K.E. Inc., Ottawa, L.A., 1957—70; entertainer L.A., 1970—77; fin. planner, 1977—. Personal mgr. for Rich Little, 1958-69. Author: Budget for the Lazy Person, 1988; (tng. manuel) Who's The Boss, 1989, Talk, 1986, Gib Kerr Guitar Method, 1993. Bd. dirs. Beverlywood Mental Health Ctr., L.A., 1989-91. Mem. Inst. CFPs (v.p. L.A. soc. 1991—, pres.-elect 1993-94, pres. 1994-96), West L.A. Le Tip (pres. 1988-90), Concerned Planners Group (founder, chmn. 2001-03), Internat. Assn. Qualified Fin. Planners (media chmn. 2003—).. Avocations: music, philosophy. Home and Office: 5307 Sepulveda Blvd Apt 120 Sherman Oaks CA 91411-3450 E-mail: gibkerr@gibkerr.com.

KERR, HARRY DAVIDSON, emergency physician; b. Greensburg, Pa., June 17, 1942; MD, N.Y. Med. Coll., 1975. Diplomate Am. Bd. Emergency Medicine, Am. Bd. Internal Medicine. Intern McGaw Med. Ctr.-Northwestern U., 1975-76, resident, 1976-78; mem. staff Columbia Hosp., 1987—. Mem.: APHA, ACP, Milw. Acad. Medcine, Milwaukee County Med. Soc., Wis. Med. Soc., Soc. Acad. Emergency Medicine, Am. Coll. Emergency Physicians.

KERR, JAMES WILSON, engineer; b. Balt., May 21, 1921; s. James W. and Laura Virginia (Wright) K.; m. Mary Thomas Montgomery, Feb. 25, 1945 (div., dec.); children: April Kerr Miller, Catherine Kerr Wood (dec.), Wilson, Andrew; m. June Walker, Dec. 27, 1977 (div.); m. Janice White Bain, Jan. 19, 1985. BS with honors, Davidson Coll., 1942; MS, NYU, 1948; postgrad., Freiburg U., 1957-60, Brookings Inst., 1970, 758; PhD, Kennedy Western U., 1989. Registered profl. engr., Calif. Commd. 2d lt. U.S. Army, 1942, advanced through grades to lt. col., 1964, with inf., World War II, Korea, electronics staff, 1948-51, weapons rsch., 1953-57, adviser French Army, 1957-60, staff electronics, 1960-62, rsch. mgr., divsn. dir. CD Pentagon, 1962-64, as civilian, 1964-81; asst. assoc. dir. Fed. Emergency Mgmt. Agy. for Rsch., 1981-85; sr. staff Michael Rogers, Inc., Winter Park, Fla., 1986—. Dr. Mt. St. Helen's Tech. Office, 1980; v.p. Latherow & Co., Arlington, Va., 1965-86; radiol. officer Talbot County, Md., 1997—. Author: Korean-English Phrase Book, 1951, 19th Century Korea Postal Handbook, 1965, 2d edit., 1990; editor Korean Philately mag., 1971-80, 85-95; contbr. articles to profl. jours. Advanced English instr. French Army, 1957-60; cons. Am. Nat. Red Cross Mus., 1968-85, Smithsonian Instn. Dept. Postal History, 1966-85, NSF, 1976-85; vol. fireman N.Y. State, 1946-48, Fairfax County, Va., 1969—; fire commr. Fairfax County, 1975-81, chmn., 1977-81, Orange County, Fla., 1986—; pres., 1987-90, Pike County, Ala., 1994-98, Talbot County, Md., 1997—; active Boy Scouts Am., in U.S., Asia, Europe, 1933—; chmn. libr. bd. Orangeburg, N.Y., 1946-48. Decorated bronze star with three oak leaf clusters, Purple Heart; recipient silver beaver award Boy Scouts Am., 1956, James E. West award, 1994; Fulbright selectee, Japan, 1986. Fellow AAAS (life), Explorers Club (emeritus); mem. NAS (various coms. 1962-87), IEEE (life, sr.), NSPE, Internat. Assn. Fire Chiefs (chmn. rsch. com. 1969-88, chief sci. adviser 1982-86), Fed. Fire Coun., Nat. Fire Protection Assn. (chmn. hosp. disaster com. 1973-86), Presdl. Nat. Def. Execs., SAR (fire safety medal 1995), Black Forest Mardi Gras (Germany), Nat. Comms. Club, Pentagon Officers Athletic Club, Univ. Club Fla., Marshyhope Rod & Gun, Korean War Vets. Assn. (nat. bd. dirs. 1999), Elks, Phi Beta Kappa, Gamma Sigma Epsilon, Delta Phi Alpha. Presbyn. (elder 1963—). Home: PO Box 1537 Easton MD 21601-8929 Office: MR Inc 199 E Welbourne Ave Winter Park FL 32789-4365

KERR, JANET SPENCE, physiologist, pharmacologist; b. New Haven, May 30, 1942; d. Alexander Pyott and Janet Blake (Conley) Spence; m. Thomas Albert Kerr Jr., July 24, 1965; children: Sarah Patterson, Matthew Spence, Timothy Marden. BA, Beaver Coll., 1964; MS, Rutgers U., 1969, PhD, 1973. Asst. prof. Rutgers U., Camden, N.J., 1973-76; rsch. assoc. U. Pa. Sch. Medicine, Phila., 1976-79; asst. prof. U. Medicine and Dentistry N.J.-Rutgers Med. Sch., New Brunswick, 1979-84; prin. rsch. scientist DuPont Pharms. Co., Wilmington, Del., 1985—2001; sr. investigator ENANTA Pharms., 2002, Merck Pharms. Co., Inc., 2003—. Sec. Biochem. Pharmacology Discussion Group, 1997—; vis. scientist Med. Sch. Harvard U., 2002—03; sr. investigator Merck & Co., Inc., 2003—. Contbr. articles to profl. jours. Busch fellow

Rutgers U. Mem. AAAS, Am. Heart Assn., Am. Fedn. Clin. Rsch., Am. Physiol. Soc., Am. Thoracic Soc., Am. Assn. Cancer Rsch., Inflammation Rsch. Assn. (bd. dirs. 1996-98), N.Y. Acad. Scis., Sigma Xi. E-mail: janetskerr@hotmail.com.

KERR, KIRKLYN M. university administrator, veterinary pathologist, researcher; b. Green Bank, W.Va., May 1, 1936; married, 1957; 3 children. BS, U. W.Va., 1961, MS, 1966; DVM, Ohio State U., 1961; PhD in Vet. Pathology, Tex. A&M U., 1970. Diplomate Am. Coll. Vet. Pathology. Vet. practitioner North Side Vet. Clinic, Carlisle, Pa., 1961-62; rsch. assoc. vet. microbiology & pathology W.Va. U., Morgantown, 1962-65; form instr. to assoc. prof. vet. pathology Tex. A&M U. Coll. Vet. Medicine, 1965-72; assoc. prof. vet. pathobiology, dir. divsn. applied pathology Ohio State U. Coll. Vet. Medicine, 1972-78, dir. Ohio Agrl. Rsch. & Devel. Ctr., prof. poultry sci., 1987-91, prof. vet. preventive medicine, mem. faculty dept. preventive medicine, 1991-93; asst. dean rsch. and advanced studies, head vet. sci. La. State U. Sch. Vet. Medicine, La. State U. Agrl. Ctr., 1978-87; dean, dir. Coll. Agr. and Natural Resources U. Conn., Storrs Mansfield, 1993—. Mem. AVMA, Am. Assn. Avian Pathologists, Am. Coll. Vet. Pathologists, Farm Bur., Conn. Vet. Medicine Assn. Achievements include research in veterinary pathology, mycoplasmatacea, cancer research in animals. Office: U Conn Coll Agriculture & Natural Rsch 1376 Storrs Rd U-66 Storrs Mansfield CT 06269-4066

KERR, KLEON HARDING, former state senator, educator; b. Plain City, Utah, Apr. 26, 1911; s. William A. and Rosemond (Harding) K.; m. Katherine Abbott, Mar. 15, 1941; children: Kathleen, William A., Rebecca Rae. AS, Weber Coll., 1936; BA, George Washington U., 1939; MS, Utah State U., Logan, 1946. Tchr. Bear River H.S., Tremonton, Utah, 1940-56, prin. jr. high sch., 1956-60, prin., 1960-71. City justice Tremonton, 1941-46; sec. to Senator Arthur V. Watkins, 1947. Author: (poetry) Open My Eyes, 1983, We Remember, 1983, Trouble in the Amen Corner, 1985, Past Imperfect, 1988, A Helping Hand, 1990, Sound of Silence, 1991, Power Behind the Throne, 1992, Unreachable Goal?, 1993, The Only Difference, 1994, Please Boss, 1995, Beach Comber, 1995, Under the Hood, 1999; (history) Those Who Served Box Elder County, 1984, Those Who Served Tremonton City, 1985, Diamond in the Rough, 1987, Facts of Life, 1987, Gettin' and Givin', 1989, Wells Without Water, 1998, Hand in Pocket, 1998, I Want to Come Home, 1997, No Days Off, 1999. Mayor Tremonton City, 1948-53; mem. Utah Local Govt. Survey Commn., 1954-55; mem. Utah Ho. of Reps., 1953-56; mem. Utah State Senate, 1957-64, chmn. appropriation com., 1959—, majority leader, 1963; mem. Utah Legis. Coun.; dist. dir. vocat. edn. Box Elder Sch. Dist. Recipient Alpha Delta Kappa award for outstanding contbn. to edn., 1982, award for outstanding contbrs. to edn. and govt. Theta Chpt. Alpha Beta Kappa, 1982, Excellence Achieved in Promotion of Tourism award, Allied Category award Utah Travel Coun., 1988, Merti award, 1993, Andy Rytting Cmty. Svc. award, 1991; named Tourism Ambassador of Month, 1986. Mem. NEA, Utah Box Elder edn. assns., Utah Sheriff's Assn. (hon.), Bear River Valley C. of C. (sec., mgr. 1955-58), Lions, Kiwanis, Phi Delta Kappa. Mem. Ch. of Jesus Christ of Latter-day Saints. Home: PO Box 246 Tremonton UT 84337-0246

KERR, LOU C. foundation administrator; b. Oklahoma City, Jan. 24, 1937; d. Lem C. and M. Mae (Beck) Coker; m. Robert S. Kerr, Jr., July 21, 1972; children: Steven S., Laura Kerr Ogle. BS in Edn. and Health, DHL (hon.), Oklahoma City U. V.p. The Kerr Found., Inc., Oklahoma City, 1985-99, pres., 1999—. Dir. UMB Bank, Oklahoma City; founder, dir. Red Earth, Inc., Oklahoma City; adv. com. Breast Cancer Prevention and Treatment, 1994—; mem. Commn. on the Status of Women, 1994-99, 2000—; mem. Gov.'s State White House Conf. on Aging; mem. selection com. for Truman Found. Scholars, 1991—; mem. Social Security Disability Task Force; chair State Capitol Preservation Commn., 1990—; adv. coun. for gov. Okla. Environ. Concerns Coun., vice chair for gov., others. Vice pres. fundraising campaign Allied Arts, 1985, v.p. exec. com., 1988-89, sec. exec. com., 1990—; bd. advisors ANSER-Ctr. for Internat. Aerospace Coop., 1995-98; mem., founder Atty. Gen.'s Consumer Adv. Com.; founder Bizzell Libr. Soc., U. Okla.; exec. com., v.p. Ctr. of the Am. Indian/Red Earth, 1983—; bd. dirs., exec. com. Ctrl. Okla. Coun. of World Affairs; bd. dirs. Am. Cancer Soc., Oklahoma County unit, 1995-97, Internat. Women's Forum, Washington, 1992—; founder, chair Okla. Internat. Women's Forum, 1990—; nat. trustee Nat. Symphony Orch., Washington, 1999—; trustee NPR Found., Washington, 2001—; chair State Capitol Preservation Commn., Oklahoma City, 1990—; mem. Women's Leadership Bd., Kennedy Sch. of Govt.-Harvard U., Cambridge, 1999—; mem. nat. bd. Fund for Am., 1989—; 3d v.p. Red Lands coun. Girl Scouts U.S., 1993-97; v.p. Global Family Found.; adv. bd. Hazel K. Goddess Fund for Stroke Rsch. in Women, Internat. Gymnastics Hall of Fame, 1997—; exec. com. Lyric Theatre of Okla., Inc., 1992—; adv. bd. dirs. Okla. Brest Inst., 1992-97; adv. trustee Oklahoma City U., exec. bd. Norick Art Mus. and chair and exec. bd. Dulaney-Browne Libr. Soc.; bd. govs. Okla. Ctr. of Sci. and Arts, Inc., 1987-97; bd. dirs., co-chair Okla. Ind. Colls. Found., 1994—; v.p. Sister Cities, Inc., 1989—, mem. exec. bd.; bd. trustees Totts Gap, 2000—; bd. visitors Okla. U. health Sci. Ctr.; trustee Okla. Sch. Sci. and Math Found.; adv. dir. Tulsa Ballet Theatre; trustee United Meth. Found. for Christian Higher Edn., 1996—, numerous others. Named to Okla. Commerce and Industry Hall of Honor, Oklahoma City U., 2000; knighted into The Byzantine Order of the Holy Sepulchre; recipient Vis A Tergo award Women's Bus. Ctr., 1997, Women Who Make a Difference award Internat. Women's Forum, 1994, Cert. of Merit Vol. Action Com. of Cmty. Coun., Okla. Tourism and Recreation Indsl. Gov.'s award, Nat. Others award Salvation Army, Kirkpatrick Petree award for outstanding cmty. svc. Oklahoma City U. Music Theatre Soc., 1988, Gov.'s Arts award Okla. State Arts Coun., 1988, Woman of Distinction award, Girl SCouts Red Lands Coun., 2002; named to Wall of Fame Okla. City Pub. Sch. Found., 2001. Democrat. Methodist. Office: The Kerr Foundation Inc 12501 N May Ave Oklahoma City OK 73120 Fax: (405) 749-2877. E-mail: lkerr@thekerrfoundation.org.

KERR, MARGARET ANN, elementary education educator; b. Ashland, Ohio, Jan. 8, 1951; d. Wallace Amander and Beulah Elizabeth (Westerfeld) Canfield; m. Roger William Kerr Jr., June 12, 1970; children: Robert, Thomas. BS in Edn., Ashland U., 1973; MA in Edn., LaVerne Coll., 1975. Cert. elem. tchr., reading specialist, nat. bd. cert. tchr. Tchr. Ruggles-Troy Sch., Ohio, 1973-76, Nankin (Ohio) Sch., 1977-79, Mapleton Sch. Dist., 1981-82; kindergarten tchr. Mapleton Sch., 1982-92; tchr. chpt. 1 extended day kindergarten Mapleton Schs., 1992-94, reading recovery tchr., 1994—2001, tchr. 1st grade, 2001—. Organizer, tchr. pre-sch., 1981; coord. for active parenting Mapleton Schs., 1992-94. Treas. PTA; co-chmn. Mapleton New Bldg. Campaign; mem. Nankin Fedn. Ch., Mapleton Acad. Booster, Mapleton Sports Booster. Mem. NEA, Ohio Edn. Assn., Mapleton Edn. Assn. Avocations: reading, walking, computers, working with young people. Home: 705 State Route 302 Ashland OH 44805-9529 E-mail: mkerr@bright.net.

KERR, NANCY KAROLYN, pastor, mental health consultant; b. July 10, 1934; d. Owen W. and Iris Irene (Israel) K.; m. Richard Clayton Williams, June 28, 1953 (div.); children: Richard Charles, Donna Louise. Student, Boston U., 1953; AA, U. Bridgeport, 1966; BA, Hofstra U., 1967; postgrad. in clin. psychology, Adelphi U. Inst. Advanced Psychol. Studies, 1968-73; MDiv, Associated Mennonite Bibl. Sems., 1986. Ordained pastor Mennonite Ch., 1987; apptd. pastor Kamloops Presbytery Ch., Can., 1992. Pastoral counselor Nat. Coun. Chs., Jackson, Miss., 1964; dir. teen program Waterbury (Conn.) YWCA, 1966-67; intern in psychology N.Y. Med. Coll., 1971-72, rsch. cons., 1972-73; coord. home svcs., psychologist City and County of Denver, 1972-75; cons. Mennonite Mental Health Svcs., Denver, 1975-78; asst. prof. psychology Messiah Coll., 1978-79; mental health cons., 1979-81; called to ministry Mennonite Ch., 1981; pastor Cin. Mennonite Fellowship, 1981-83, mem. Gen. Conf. Peace and Justice Reference Coun., 1983-85; instr. Associated Mennonite Bibl. Sems., 1985; tchg. elder Assembly Mennonite Ch., 1985-86; pastor Pulaski Mennonite Ch., 1986-89; exec. dir., pastoral counselor Bethesda Counseling Svcs., Prince George B.C., 1989-99; pvt. practice, 1999—. Spl. ch. curriculum Nat. Coun. Chs., 1981; mem. Cen. Dist. Conf. Peace and Justice Com., 1981-89; mem. exec. bd. People for Peace, 1981-83. Active Prince George Ministerial Assn., chmn. edn. and airport chapel coms., 1990—92; elder St. Giles Presbyn. Ch., 1996—2000; bd. dirs. Tri-County Counselling Clinic, Memphis, Mo., 1980—81, Boulder (Colo.) ARC, 1977—78, PLURA, B.C. Synod, 1995—98, Prince George Neighbor Link, 1995—99, Davis County Mins. Assn., v.p., 1988—89; mem. Waterbury Planned Parenthood Bd., 1964—67, MW Children's Home Bd., 1974—75; mem. crisis bd. ARC, 2000—, 2000—; mem. Mennonite Disabilities Respite Care Bd., 1981—86, Prince George Children's Svcs. com., 1992—94; adv. com. Prince George Planning Coun., 1997—98; mem. housing Prince George adv. bd. Mennonite Cen. Com., 1998—99. Mem. APA (assoc.), Can. Psychol. Assn., Soc. Psychologists for Study of Social Issues, Christian Assn. Psychol. Studies, Soc. Bibl. Lit. & Exegesis. Office: Nancy Kerr Counselling Svcs 110-154 Quebec St Prince George BC Canada V2L 1W2

KERR, STANLEY MUNGER, investigator, lawyer, educator; b. Des Moines, Sept. 30, 1949; s. Richard Dixon and Arlene Mae (Munger) K.; m. Myrna Anita Hill, May 22, 1971; children: Mila Anee, Tamara Eve. Student, Christian Coll. of the S.W., 1967-69, U. Tex., 1970-71; BA, Huston-Tillotson Coll., 1975; JD, U. Tex., 1977. Bar: Tex. 1977. Instr. govt. Huston-Tillotson Coll., Austin, 1978-81; investigator City of Austin, Tex., 1981-87; pvt. practice Austin, 1977-88; mental health atty. Travis County Probate Ct., 1988—. Mcpl. ct. judge City of Austin, 2000—. Gen. counsel, bd. dirs. Operation PUSH, Austin, 1979-81; chmn. Cmty.-Police Rels. Adv. Coun., Austin, 1981-84; precinct chmn. Travis County Dem. Party, Austin, 1978-82; state del. Dem. Party State Conv., Tex., 1976, 78, 80, 82, 84, 86; sr. warden, mem. Bishop Com., St. James Episcopal Ch., Austin, 1972-79, 85—; cons. interracial marriage and children; min. Ch. Christ. Mem. State Bar Tex., Austin Black Lawyers Assn., Am. Fedn. State, County and Mcpl. Employees. Home: 1412 Springdale Rd Austin TX 78721-1353 Office: Probate Ct PO Box 1748 Austin TX 78767-1748

KERR, STEPHEN PAUL, music educator; b. Painsville, Ohio, Oct. 24, 1958; s. Robert George and Sharlie Lou Kerr; m. Martha Lynn Hansen, Oct. 12, 1985; children: Michael Robert, Stephanie Lynn. BS in Music Edn., Liberty U., 1982; EdM Va. Tech., 1992; PhD in Music Edn., U. N.C., Greensboro, 2002. Band dir. Fla. Christian Sch., Miami, 1982—88, Lynchburg (Va.) Christian Acad., 1988—90; brass/band dir. Liberty U., Lynchburg, 1990—. Orch. dir. Thomas Rd. Bapt. Ch., Lynchburg, 1996—. Mem.: Music Educators Nat. Conf., Coll. Band Dirs. Nat. Assn. Office: Liberty Univ 1971 University Blvd Lynchburg VA 24502

KERR, STERLING, III, social and advocacy administrator; b. Groveton, N.H., Aug. 26, 1939; s. William S. and Hope L. (Durow) Kerr; m. Maria J. Kerr, Aug. 22, 1959 (div. Sept. 1992); children: William, Mark, Scott. BED, Plymouth State Coll., 1964; Cert., San Diego State U., 1966; MA, U. Okla., 1967, PhD, 1970. Cert. fin. planner. Prof. geography U. West Fla., Pensacola, 1970-74; mgr. Travelers Ins., Pensacola, 1974-79; fin. planner E.F. Hutton Fin., Pensacola, 1979-82; investment advisor Granada Corp., Houston, 1982-85, Sterling Kerr & Assocs., Sarasota and Largo, Fla., 1985-96, investment banker Largo, 1996-99; dir. gift planning SUNY, Potsdam, 1999-2001; nat. dir. gift planning AARP Found., Washington, 2001—. Advisor Summer Bay, Inc., Kissammee, Fla., 1997-98; cons. internat. fin. Provence, LLC, Ft. Myers, Fla., 1998; prof. SUNY, 2000-01. Author: (booklets) The Potsdam Story, 1999, International Investing, 2000, also brochures. Exec. com. Leave A Legacy, St. Lawrence County, N.Y., 1999-2000. With USN, 1957-60. Recipient U. Okla. Sponsor's award, 1968, Scholarship award, 1969. Mem. CASE, Am. Coun. on Gift Annuities. Avocation: racewalking. Office: AARP Andrus Found 601 E St NW Washington DC 20049

KERR, THOMAS HENDERSON, III, electrical engineer, researcher; b. Washington, Nov. 9, 1945; s. Thomas Henderson Jr. and Norma Elaine (McAllister) K.; m. Aniece Ragland, July 5, 1975; children: Thomas Henderson IV, Stephen McAllister Pearson. BSEE magna cum laude, Howard U., 1967; MSEE, U. Iowa, 1969, PhD, 1971. Rsch. asst., 1967, 69; teaching asst., 1968; control engr. R & D Ctr. GE, Schenectady, NY, 1971-73; tech. staff The Analytic Sci. Corp., Reading, Mass., 1973-79; sr. analyst systems engr. Intermetrics Inc., Cambridge, Mass., 1979-86; with tech. staff Lincoln Lab. MIT, Lexington, Mass., 1986-92; CEO, prin. investigator TeK Assoc., Lexington, Mass., 1992—. Cons. Nat. Security Indsl. Assn., Boston, 1979-86; instr. Northeastern U., Boston, 1990-95. Contbr. more than 150 articles to profl. jours. Math. tutor Civic Ctr., Schenectady, 1971, Union Coll., Schenectady, 1972-73, Union Meth. Ch., Boston, 1973-74. Recipient NSF traineeship, 1968-70, Award for Sci./Math. Proficiency, 1963, Music Educator's award, 1963, Writing Contest award Fed. Power Commn., 1967, Western Electric award, 1965, McDonnell-Douglas award, 1966. Mem.: IEEE Aerospace and Electronics Sys. (M. Barry Carlton award 1987), AIAA (sr.), IEEE (sr.; chmn. control sys. sect. Boston 1990—92, 2001—, chmn. steering com. 1992—94, vice chmn. 1995—96, 1998—2000), Assn. Computing Machinery, Soc. Photogametry and Instrumentation Engrs., Math. Assn. Am., Am. Statis. Assn., Inst. of Nav., Am. Def. Preparedness Assn. (life), Eta Kappa Nu, Sigma Pi Sigma, Pi Mu Epsilon, Tau Beta Pi, Sigma Xi. Methodist. Achievements include development of automated fault detection algorithms for submarine and aircraft navigation systems; performed early GPS validation testing aboard submarine; development of decentralized Kalman filter algorithms for navigation:INS/JTIDS/GPS; simplified implementation of extended Kalman filters for target tracking; development of associated statistical tests for real time fault detection, closed-form test cases for software validation of linear systems and Kalman filters, inexpensive, commercially available Kalman filter software TK-MIP for the PC that includes on-line tutorials to lead and prompt the novice user, Cramer-Rao lower bounds for strategic radar tracking; applied decentralized 2-D Kalman filters to image restoration and multisensor fusion; performed a critical evaluation of current GPS limitations as well as its benefits; subcontracting to MITRE, XonTech and Raytheon national missile defense radar tracking evaluations and to Arete Assocs. for some navigation analysis and MatLab coding. Home: 11 Paul Revere Rd Lexington MA 02421-6632 E-mail: thomas_h_kerr@msn.com.

KERR, THOMAS JEFFERSON, IV, academic official; b. Columbus, Ohio, Oct. 8, 1933; s. Thomas Jefferson and Ruth Glenora (Powell) K.; m. Donna Jean Lawton, June 11, 1955; children: Thomas Jefferson V, Cheryl Lee, Kathleen Anne. BS, Cornell U., 1956; MA, U. Buffalo, 1959; PhD (univ. fellow), Syracuse U., 1965; LHD (hon.), Otterbein Coll., 1984; LLD (hon.), Kendall Coll., 1996. Asst. prof., then prof. history Otterbein Coll., Westerville, Ohio, 1963-71, acting acad. dean, 1969-70, pres., 1971-84, Grant Med. Ctr. Found., Columbus, 1984-89, Kendall Coll., Evanston, Ill., 1990-96, pres. emeritus, 1996—. Chmn. Assn. Ind. Colls. and Univs., Ohio, 1976-78, Ohio Found. Ind. Colls., 1978-80 Mem. Greater Columbus Arts Coun., 1975-78; trustee Nationwide (now Gartmore) Funds, 1971—, Blue Cross Ctrl. Ohio, 1978-84, Grant Hosp., 1975-84, Ill. Restaurant Assn. Ednl. Found., 1991-96; mem. exec. com. Ill. Ind. Colls. and Univs., 1993-95; mem. Franklin County Draft Bd., 1969-71. Recipient Cokesbury Grad. Coll. Teaching award, 1963 Mem. Masons, Rotary, Phi Kappa Phi, Kappa Phi Kappa, Omicron Chi Epsilon, Phi Eta Sigma. Republican. Methodist. Home: 4890 Smoketalk Ln Westerville OH 43081-4431

KERR, THOMAS ROBERT, lawyer; b. Covington, Ky., July 25, 1950; s. Thomas Hoover and Joann (Moffett) K.; m. Janice Duncan, May 26, 1973; children: Julie Ann, Jennifer Suzanne, Jill Mackenzie. BBA, U. Ky., 1972; JD, Chase Coll. Law, 1977. Bar: Ky. 1977, U.S. Dist. Ct. (ea. dist.) Ky. 1977. Sole practice, Covington, 1977—. Mem. pro-bono panel, Covington, 1980—; pub. defender Kenton County Pub. Defender's Office, Covington, 1977—. State rep. Ky. Gen. Assembly, Frankfort, 1985—; dir. Community Coun. on Religious Edn., Covington, 1985—; dir. Victims Assistance Network, Frankfort, 1985—, Calvary Christian Sch., Covington, 1981-87; deacon Calvary Bapt. Ch., Latonia, Ky., 1982; bd. dirs. No. Ky. Area Devel. Dist., 1988-93, Good Will, 1993—. With Air NG, 1971-77. Named One of Outstanding Young Men of Am., 1980, 83. Mem. Ky. Bar Assn., No. Ky. Bar Assn., Am. Trial Lawyers Assn., Ky. Acad. Trial Attys., Covington Christian Businessmans Assn. Clubs: Taylor Mill (Ky.) Swim (bd. dirs. 1983-87). Democrat. Baptist. Avocations: tennis, reading, various sports. Home: 5415 Old Taylor Mill Rd Covington KY 41015-2239 Office: 732 Scott St Covington KY 41011-2418

KERR, WALTER BELNAP, retired missile instrumentation engineer, English language researcher, consultant; b. Salt Lake City, Oct. 14, 1926; s. Walter Affleck and Marion Adeline (Belnap) K.; m. Raida Nebeker, May 2, 1952 (dec. Mar. 1992); children: Valerie Jean Kerr Lynch, Grant Mercer, Janice Arlene Kerr Hahn, Marilyn, m. Lillian Hamilton Nelson Ettinger, Oct. 1, 1992; children: Edgar Nelson Jr., James Nelson, Patricia Nelson Hardwick, Douglas Nelson. BA in French, U. Utah, 1951, BSEE, 1955; MBA in Internat. Bus., U. So. Calif., 1972. Electrical engr. Hughes Aircraft Co., L.A., 1955-61, 67-69; missile instrumentation engr. Hercules Inc., Salt Lake City, 1961-66, 84-89, Rockwell Internat., Anaheim, Calif., 1969-70; investment broker Titan Capital Corp., L.A., Ogden, Utah, 1970-79; electrical engr. White Motor Corp., Ogden, 1979-84; tax examiner IRS, Ogden, 1990-91, ret., 1991. Cons. Soc. for the Advancement of Good English, Pittsford, N.Y., 1985-86. Author: Instrumentation Methods, 1963, Stewart Lives, 2003, (card) Pocket Guide to Good English, 1984; columnist Correct Corner, Cherokee Scout newspaper, 1996-99; inventor Juggler St. Benedict's Hosp., and various nursing homes, grade schs., h.s., univs., shopping ctrs. and chs., 1947—. With USN, 1945-46, 1st lt. U.S. Army, 1951-53. Mem. IEEE, The Planetary Soc., World Wildlife Fund, Soc. for the Preservation of English Lang. and Lit., Soc. for Alphanumeric Improvement, Sierra Club. Republican. Mem. Lds Ch. Avocations: tennis, juggling, planetoid research, kite flying, computing, astronomical model building. Home: 395 Messer Rd Murphy NC 28906-9197

KERR, WILLIAM ANDREW, lawyer, educator; b. Harding, W.Va., Nov. 17, 1934; s. William James and Tocie Nyle (Morris) K.; m. Elizabeth Ann McMillin, Aug. 3, 1968 AB, W.Va. U., 1955, JD, 1957; LLM, Harvard U., 1958; BD, Duke U., 1968. Bar: W.Va. 1957, Pa. 1962, Ind. 1980. Assoc. McClintic, James, Wise and Robinson, Charleston, W.Va., 1958; assoc. Schnader, Harrison, Segal and Lewis, Phila., 1961-64; asst. prof. law Cleve. State U., 1966-67, assoc. prof. law, 1967-68; assoc. prof. Ind. U., Indpls., 1968-69, 72-74, prof., 1974-98, prof. emeritus, 1998—; contract atty. Indpls. Pub. Defender Agy., 1998—. Asst. U.S. atty. So. Dist. Ind., Indpls., 1969-72; exec. dir. Ind. Jud. Ctr., 1974-86; dir. research Ind. Pros. Attys. Council, 1972-74; mem. Ind. Criminal Law Study Commn., 1973-89, sec., 1973-83; reporter speedy trial com. U.S. Dist. Ct. (so. dist.) Ind., 1975-84; trustee Ind. Criminal Justice Inst., 1983-86; bd. dirs. Indpls. Lawyers Commn., 1975-77, Ind. Lawyers Commn., 1980-83; mem. records mgmt. com. Ind. Supreme Ct., 1983-86. Author: Indiana Criminal Procedure: Pretrial, 1991, Indiana Criminal Procedure: Trial, 2 vols., 1998. Bd. dirs. Ch. Fedn. Greater Indpls., 1979-87. Served to capt. JAGC, USAF, 1958-61. Decorated Air Force Commendation medal; Ford Found. fellow Harvard Law Sch., 1957-58; recipient Outstanding Prof. award Students Ind. U. Sch. Law, 1974, Disting. Service award Ind. Council Juvenile Ct. Judges, 1979, Outstanding Jud. Edn. Program award Nat. Council Juvenile and Family Ct. Judges, 1985. Mem. Ind. State Bar Assn., Indpls. Bar Assn., Phila. Bar Assn., W.Va. Bar Assn., Nat. Dist. Attys. Assn., Am. Judicature Soc., Fed. Bar Assn. (Outstanding Service award Indpls. chpt. 1975), Order of Coif, Phi Beta Kappa. Office: 55 Monument Cir Ste 1017 Indianapolis IN 46204-5901

KERR, WILLIAM REVILL, housing association executive; b. Glasgow, Scotland, Apr. 26, 1948; s. William McFadzean and Helen (Bloomer) K.; m. Maria Donnelly, Sept. 22, 1980. MBA, Glasgow U., 1996; MSc in Corp. Adminstrn., Glasgow Caledonian U., 1998; PhD, Strathclyde U., 2001. Gen. mgr. Marine Highland, Troon, Scotland, 1985-86, Ellersley House, Edinburgh, Scotland, 1986-88; sec. Malin Housing Assn., Turnberry, Scotland, 1988—2003; gen. mgr. Glasgow Acad., 2003—. Ambassador The Prince's Scottish Youth Bus. Trust; chmn. Ayrshire Econ. Forum. Author: Tourism Policy and the Strategic Management of Failure, 2003. Fellow Chartered Inst. Secs. (assoc.), Inst. Sales and Mktg. Mgmt.; mem. Chartered Inst. Mktg. (registered marketer), Hotel Catering and Instnl. Mgmt. Assn. Mem. Ch. of Scotland. Avocations: hiking, collecting books, sports, politics. Home: 20 Burness Ave KA74QB Ayr Scotland Office: Malin Housing Assn Malin Ct KA269PB Turnberry Scotland

KERR, WILLIAM ROBERT, economist, consultant; b. Birmingham, Ala., Sept. 10, 1974; s. Joseph Richard and Carole Stevenson Kerr. BS Sys. Engring. and Econs., U. Va., 1996; postgrad., MIT. White House intern Exec. Office of the Pres., Washington, 1995—96; comms. cons. Deloitte Cons., Washington, 1996—98, Hong Kong, 1998—2000. Recipient All ACC Scholar Athlete award, Atlantic Coast Conf., 1996; fellow Grad. Student fellowship, NSF, 2000—. Avocations: piano, fitness instruction, international travel, religion, philosophy. Home: 166 Boston St # 2 Boston MA 02125-1142 E-mail: wkerr@mit.edu.

KERR, WILLIAM T. publishing and broadcasting executive; b. Seattle, Apr. 17, 1941; m. Mary Lang, Oct. 15, 1966; 1 child, Susannah Gaskill Kerr Adler. BA, U. Wash., 1963, Oxford U., Eng., 1965; MA, Harvard U., 1967, MBA, 1969. V.p. Dillon Read & Co., N.Y.C. and London, 1969-73; cons. McKinsey & Co., N.Y.C., 1973-79; v.p. New York Times Co., N.Y.C., 1979-91; pres. New York Times Mag. Group, N.Y.C., 1985-91; exec. v.p., pres. mag. group Meredith Corp., Des Moines, 1991-94, pres., chief oper. officer, bd. dirs., exec. com., 1994-96, pres., CEO, 1997-98, chmn., 1998—. Bd. dirs. Storage Tek Corp., Prin. Fin. Group, Maytag Corp., Oxford U. Press. Mem.: Internat. Fedn. Periodical Press (chmn.), Mag. Pubs. Am., Reform Club (London), Des Moines Club, Wakonda Club, Quogue Field Club, The Brook Club (N.Y.C.), Union Club (N.Y.C), Century Assn. (N.Y.C.). Roman Catholic. Home: 11409 Golfview Ln North Palm Beach FL 33408 Office: Meredith Corp 1716 Locust St Des Moines IA 50309-3023

KERREBROCK, JACK LEO, aeronautics and astronautics engineering educator; b. Los Angeles, Feb. 6, 1928; s. Oscar A. and Florence (Hoy) K.; m. Bernice Veverka, Apr. 11, 1953; children: Christopher, Nancy, Peter. Student, U. Oreg., 1946-47; BS, Oreg. State Coll., 1950; MS, Yale, 1951; PhD, Calif. Inst. Tech., 1956. Aero. research scientist Lewis Lab., NASA, Cleve., 1951-53; research fellow Calif. Inst. Tech., 1955-56; engring. leader Oak Ridge Nat. Lab., 1956-58; sr. research fellow Calif. Inst. Tech., 1958-60; mem. faculty M.I.T., 1960-2001, Richard C. Maclaurin prof. aeros. and astronautics, 1975-96, dir. Gas Turbine and Plasma Dynamics Lab., 1969-78, head div. energy conversion and propulsion, 1970-81, head dept. aeros. and astronautics, 1978-81, 83-85, assoc. dean engring., 1985-89, acting dean, 1989; assoc. adminstr. Office Aeros. and Space Tech., NASA, Washington, 1981-83. Mem. Air Force Sci. Adv. Bd., 1972-88; mem. NASA Rsch. and Tech. Adv. Com., 1975-77; mem. Aeronautics and Space Engring. Bd. NRC, 1976-81, 92-95; mem. aero adv. com. NASA, 1978-81, Nat. Commn. on Space, 1984-86; mem. Air Force Studies Bd. NRC, 1990-92, com. on Earth-Orbit Propulsion, 1991-92; mem. adv. com. Space Sta. NASA, 1987-92; chmn. com. Space Sta. NRC, 1992-95; trustee Inst. for Def. Analysis, 1984-2000, Aerospace Corp., 1986-88; bd. dirs. Orbital Scis. Corp., Aerodyne Rsch. Inc. Recipient Gas Turbine Power award ASME, 1971, John Leland Atwood award ASEE and AIAA, 1992; Fairchild Disting. scholar Calif. Inst. Tech., 1990. Fellow AIAA (hon.); mem. Nat. Acad. Engring., Am. Acad. Arts and Scis. Home: 108 Tower Rd Lincoln MA 01773-4403

KERREY, BOB (J. ROBERT KERREY), academic administrator, former senator; b. Lincoln, Nebr., Aug. 27, 1943; s. James and Elinor Kerrey; m. Sarah Paley; children: Benjamin, Lindsey, Henry. BS in Pharmacy, U. Nebr., 1965. Owner, founder, developer Grandmother's Restaurants, Omaha, 1972—75; owner, founder Prairie Life Ctr., Lincoln and Omaha, Nebr.; gov. State of Nebr., Lincoln, 1983—87; ptnr. Printon, Kane & Co., Lincoln, Nebr., 1987—89; U.S. Sen. from Nebraska, 1989—2001; pres. New Sch. U., N.Y.C., 2001—. Mem. Agrl., Nutrition & Forestry Com.; ranking minority mem. appropriations subcom. Treasury, Postal Svc. & Gen. Govt.; select com. Intelligence, Fin., Prodn. & Price Competitiveness Com. Bd. dirs. Lincoln Ctr. Assn., Nebr. Easter Seal Soc. With USN, 1966—69, Vietnam. Decorated medal of Honor, Bronze Star, Purple Heart. Mem.: Lincoln C. of C., DAV, VFW, Am. Legion, Sertoma, Lions, Phi Gamma Delta. Congregationalist. Office: New Sch U Johnson and Kaplan Bldg Rm 800 66 W 12th St New York NY 10011

KERRI, KENNETH DONALD, civil engineering educator; b. Napa, Calif., Apr. 25, 1934; s. Kenneth R. and Eunice E. (Beck) K.; m. Judith Reeves, Aug. 22, 1958; children: Christopher, Kathleen. BSCE, Oreg. State U., 1956, PhDCE, 1965, MS in Sanitary Engring., U. Calif., Berkeley, 1959. Registered profl. engr., Calif.; diplomate Am. Acad. Environ. Engring. Asst. sanitary engr. USPHS, San Francisco, 1956-58; asst. prof. Sacramento State U., 1959-63; assoc. prof. Calif. State U., Sacramento, 1963-68, project dir., 1965—99, prof., 1968—99. Cons. in field, Sacramento, 1960—. Author: Operation of Waste Water Treatment Plants, 1980, Water Treatment Plant Operation, 1983, Small Water System O&M, 1993. Fellow ASCE; mem. Nat. Environ. Tng. Assn. (pres. 1979-80, Trainer of Yr. 1982), Assn. Bds. Cert. (pres. 1983), Calif. Water Pollution Control Assn. (pres. 1983-84), Water Environment Fedn. (hon.). Office: Calif State U 6000 J St Sacramento CA 95819-6025

KERRICK, DAVID ELLSWORTH, lawyer; b. Caldwell, Idaho, Jan. 15, 1951; s. Charles Ellsworth and Patria (Olesen) K.; m. Juneal Casper, May 24, 1980; children: Peter Ellsworth, Beth Anne, George Ellis, Katherine Leigh. Student, Coll. of Idaho, 1969-71; BA, U. Wash., 1972; JD, U. Idaho, 1980. Bar: Idaho 1980, U.S. Dist. Ct. Idaho 1980, U.S. Ct. Appeals (9th cir.) 1981. Mem. Idaho Senate, 1990-96, majority caucus chmn., 1992-94, majority leader, 1994-96. Mem. S.W. Idaho Estate Planning Coun. Mem. ABA, Assn. Trial Lawyers Am., Idaho Bar Assn. (3d dist. pres. 1985-86), Idaho Trial Lawyers Assn., Canyon County Lawyers Assn. (pres. 1985). Lodges: Elks. Republican. Presbyterian. Avocations: skiing, photography. Office: PO Box 44 Caldwell ID 83606-0044

KERRICK, DONALD L. career officer; b. Apr. 27, 1949; Maj. gen., dep. asst. to pres. for nat. security affairs White House Staff, The White House, Washington, 1997-99; asst. to chmn. Jt. Chiefs of Staff, Washington, 1999—.

KERRIDGE, RONALD DAVID, lawyer; b. Houston, Mar. 23, 1962; s. Isaac Curtis and Ruth Stewart Kerridge; m. Elisabeth Michele Crook, June 20, 1987 (div. Aug. 1997); children: Merritt Cottrell, Wynne Banning. AB summa cum laude, Princeton U., 1984; JD magna cum laude, Harvard U., 1987. Bar: Tex. 1987, U.S. Tax Ct. 1991. Assoc. Carrington, Coleman, Sloman & Blumenthal, Dallas, 1987-93; ptnr. Sayles & Lidji, Dallas, 1994-96, Hughes & Luce, LLP, Dallas, 1996—. Episcopalian. Office: Hughes & Luce LLP 1717 Main St Ste 2800 Dallas TX 75201-4605 E-mail: rkerridge@hughesluce.com.

KERRIGAN, D. CASEY, physiatrist, educator; d. Edna Kerrigan; m. Robert Kusyk; children: Jayme Kusyk, Kellyn Kusyk. BA in Biology, U. Chgo., 1983; MD, Harvard U., 1987; MS in Kinesiology, UCLA, 1992. Diplomate Nat. Bd. Med. Examiners, cert. Am. Bd. Phys. Medicine and Rehab. Instr. physiatry dept. neurology Harvard Med. Sch., Boston, 1992—94, asst. prof. dept. neurology, 1995, asst. prof. dept. phys. medicine and rehab., 1996—97, assoc. prof., 1998—2002; attending physiatrist Spaulding Rehab. Hosp., Boston, 1991—95; asst. in neurology dept. neurology Mass. Gen. Hosp., Boston, 1994—95, cons. neurology, 1996—97, attending physiatrist dept. phys. medicine and rehab., 1998—2002; prof. dept. phys. medicine and rehab. U. Va., Charlottesville, 2002—, attending physiatrist dept. phys. medicine and rehab., 2000—. Dir. clin. gait lab. analysis svc., Boston, 1993—2002; dir. specialized outpatient gait clinic Spaulding Rehab. Hosp., Boston, 1994—2002, founder and dir. gait lab., 1992—2002; assoc. dir. phys. medicine and rehab. residency program Harvard Med. Sch., Boston, 1993—2002, dir. rsch., 1996—2002; founder, dir. Ctr. for Rehab. Sci. Spaulding Rehab. Hosp. and Harvard Med. Sch., Boston, 1998—2002; chair dept. phys. medicine and rehab. U. Va., Charlottesville, 2002—; mem. Am. Gait Lab. Accreditation Bd.; mem. study com. for proposals for Jahnigen Career Devel. Scholars award Am. Geriatric Soc./Hartford Project. Recipient Scholar-Athlete award, U. Chgo., 1982, Leo G. Rigler award, Cedars-Sinai Med. Ctr., 1991, Clin. Investigator award, Nat. Ctr. for Med. Rehab. and Rsch., NIH, 1995, Outstanding Svc. award, Helping Hounds Ltd., 1995, Ptnrs. in Excellence award, Ptnrs. HealthCare Sys., 1996, Excellence in Rsch. Writing award, Am. Jour. Phys. Medicine and Rehab., 1998, The Ralph Goldman Intern of the Yr. award, 1998, Elizabeth and Sidney Licht award, Archives of Phys. Medicine and Rehab., 1998, Midcareer Investigator award, NIH, 2000; grantee Feasible Quantitative Analysis, Bioengineering Tech. Sys., 1992, Gait Lab. Devel., Ellison Found., 1992—94, Earle P. Charlton Found., 1993—94, Vets. Adminstrv. Cons., 1994—97, NIH Nat. Ctr. for Med. Rehab. Rsch., 1995—2000, John W. Alden Trust, 1997—99, Dept. Def., 1998—99, Retirement Rsch. Found., 2000—01, NIH Nat. Inst. of Aging; scholar, Harvard Med. Sch., 1983, UCLA, 1990. Mem.: AMA, New Eng. Soc. Phys. Medicine and Rehab. (chair sci. program. com. 1993—96), Assn. Acad. Physiatrists (nomination com., legis. affairs com., governance com., Young Academician award 1996, Hon. Mention award 1997, 1999), Calif. Soc. Phys. Medicine and Rehab. (mem. resident coun., pres. 1990—91, Robert Taylor award 1991), Am. Congress Rehab. (mem. info. techs. task force), Am. Acad. Phys. Medicine and Rehab. (pres. 1989—90, chair membership com. 1994—97, resident physician coun., ex-officio bd. dirs., rsch. adv. and advocacy com., Outstanding Svc. award 1992), North Am. Soc. Gait and Clin. Movement Analysis (ad hoc formation com., charter mem., sci. planning com.). Office: U Va Dept Phys Medicine and Rehab 545 Ray C Hunt Dr Ste 240 Charlottesville VA 22908 Office Fax: 434-243-5639.

KERRIGAN, JOHN E. academic administrator; Chancellor emeritus U. Wis., Oshkosh. Office: Gruenhagen Hall 208 Osceola St Oshkosh WI 54901 E-mail: kerrigan@uwosh-edu.

KERRIGAN, NANCY, professional figure skater, former Olympic athlete; b. Woburn, Mass., Oct. 13, 1969; d. Daniel and Brenda Kerrigan; m. Jerry Solomon, 1995; 1 child, Matthew Eric Solomon. Bronze medalist World Championships, 1991, 92, Olympic Games, Albertville, France, 1992; U.S. nat. champion, 1993; silver medalist Olympic Games, Lillehammer, Norway, 1994. Numerous commercials and product endorsements including Walt Disney Co., Reebok, Northwest Airlines, Frosted Cheerios, Ray Ban, Revlon, Aetna U.S. Healthcare, Salvino Bammers, AquaTrend, Tostitos, sportsinstruction.com; author: In My Own Words, 1996, (with Mary Spencer) Artistry on Ice, 2002; choreographer Halloween on Ice, (video) Fairy Tales on Ice; performer: Champions on Ice Tour, 1992-02; host Lifetime TV, 2002-03; TV spls. incl. Dreams on Ice, Breaking the Ice, Nancy Kerrigan and Friends, Holiday Celebration on Ice, One Enchanted Evening, Divas on Ice; TV host Nancy Kerrigan's World of Figure Skating (host), 2002, Grand Prix of Figure Skating, ISU Grand Prix Lifetime TV, 2003; released Shining Through as part of Reflections Off the Ice CD, 1999; starred as Sandy in Grease on Ice, 1998-99, Broadway on Ice, Branson, Mo., 2000, Footloose on Ice, 2001; appeared in TV movies and shows including Boy Meets World, 1995, The Journey of Allen Strange, 1998, Ice Angel, Hollywood Squares, 2003, Family Feud, 2003. Spokesperson Lions Club, 1994, Children's Trust Fund, 1997, Spalding Rehab. Hosp., MADD, Fight for Sight; founder, benefactor Nancy Kerrigan Found.; hon. chair Nancy Kerrigan Golf Classic, 2000—; bd. dirs. Ice Castle Theatre, Myrtle Beach, S.C. Recipient Bronze medal World Figure Skating Championships, 1991, Silver medal, 1992, Bronze medal U.S. Pro Championships, 1997, Bronze medal Goodwill Games, 2000, Outstanding Mother award Mother's Day Found., 2001, Henry Iba Outstanding Citizen-Athlete award Rotary Club, Tulsa, Okla., 2002. Office: care of StarGames Bldg 1 40 Salem St Lynnfield MA 01940

KERRY, JOHN FORBES, senator; b. Denver, Dec. 11, 1943; s. Richard John and Rosemary (Forbes) K.; m. Teresa Heinz, May 25, 1995; children from previous marriage: Alexandra, Vanessa. BA, Yale U., 1966; MA, JD, Boston Coll., 1976. Bar: Mass. 1976. Nat. coordinator Vietnam Vets. Against The War, 1969-71; asst. dist. atty. Middlesex (Mass.) County, 1976-79; ptnr. firm Kerry & Sragow, Boston, 1979-82; lt. gov. State of Mass., 1982-84; U.S. senator from Mass., 1985—; chmn. Dem. Senatorial campaign com., 1986-88. Mem. Fgn. Rels. Com., Fgn. Rels. subcom. Internat. Ops., Sen. Dem. Steering & Coordination Com.; mem. Com. Banking, Housing & Urban Affairs, ranking minority mem. Com. Small Bus., Select Com. on Intelligence; ranking minority mem. Commerce, Sci. & Transp. subcom. on Oceans & Fisheries. Author: The New Soldier, 1971, The New War, 1997. Democratic candidate for Congress from 5th Mass. Dist., 1972; bd. vistors Walsh Sch. Fgn. Service, Georgetown U. Served to lt. (j.g.) USNR, 1966-69. Decorated Silver Star; decorated Bronze Star with oak leaf cluster, Purple Hearts (3) Mem. Vietnam Veterans Am. (founder). Democrat. Roman Catholic. Office: US Senate 304 Russell Senate Bldg Washington DC 20510-0001*

KERSCHNER, LEE R(ONALD), academic administrator, political science educator; b. May 31, 1931; m. Helga Koller, June 22, 1958; children: David, Gabriel, Riza. BA in Polit. Sci. (Univ. fellow), Rutgers U., 1953; MA in Internat. Relations (Univ. fellow), Johns Hopkins U., 1958; PhD in Polit. Sci. (Univ. fellow), Georgetown U., 1964. From instr. to prof. polit. sci. Calif. State U., Fullerton, 1961-69, prof., 1988—; state univ. dean Calif. State Univs. and Colls. Hdqrs., Long Beach, 1969-71, asst. exec. vice chancellor, 1971-76, vice chancellor for adminstrv. affairs, 1976-77, vice chancellor acad. affairs, 1987-92; exec. dir. Colo. Commn. on Higher Edn., Denver, 1977-83, Nat. Assn. Trade and Tech. Schs., 1983-85, Calif. Commn. on Master Plan for Higher Edn., 1985-87; interim pres. Calif. State U., Stanislaus, 1992-94, spl. asst. to the chancellor, 1994-97; exec. vice chancellor Minn. State Colls. and Univs., St. Paul, 1996-97; vice chancellor emeritus Calif. State U., 1997—. Mem. Calif. Student Aid Commn., 1993-96; cons. in field. Mem. exec. com. Am. Jewish Com., Denver, 1978-83; internat. bd. dirs. Amigos de las Americas, 1982-88 (chmn. 1985-87). Served with USAF, 1954-58; col. Res., ret. Home: PO Box 748 Weimar CA 95736-0748

KERSELS, MARTIN, artist; BA in Art, UCLA, 1984, MFA in Art, 1995. One-man shows include A/B Gallery, L.A., 1993, Dan Bernier Gallery, Santa Monica, Calif., 1995, 1998, Jay Gorney Modern Art, N.Y.C., 1996, Madison (Wis.) Art Ctr., 1997, Theoretical Events, Naples, Italy, 1998, Georges-Phillippe and Nathalie Vallois, Paris, 1999, exhibited in group shows at Kohn Turner Gallery, L.A., 1994, Otis Parsons Gallery, 1994, Mus. d'Art Moderne Ville de Paris, 1995, David Zwirner Gallery, N.Y.C., 1995, Ten in One Gallery, Chgo., 1996, Mus. Contemporary Art, Miami, 1996, Stephen Wirtz Gallery, San Francisco, 1997, Whitney Mus. Am. Art, N.Y.C., 1997, Mcpl. Art Gallery, L.A., 1997, Soledad Lorenzo Gallery, Madrid, 1997, Saatchi Gallery, London, 1998, Cahors Festival, France, 1999, others; performer: Sweaters, 1985, Shape of Pools Today, 1987, Kay Sir Ra Sir Ra, 1989, Weight, 1992; mem. SHRIMPS performace collaborative. Office: care Deitch Projects 76 Grand St New York NY 10013-2220

KERSEY, TALANA S. mental health counselor; b. Joliet, Ill., May 5, 1947; d. Elgin L. and Virgil D. McMahon; m. Joel Allen Kersey, Dec. 7, 1991; children: Michelle Talana, Eric Charles, Kelly Brooke. BA in Edn., Ariz. State U., 1970; MS in Mental Health Counseling, Nova Southeastern U., 1996. Lic. mental health counselor, real estate salesman, Fla.; cert. tchr., Fla. Secondry tchr. Orange County Schs., Orlando, Fla.; acad. instr. Brevard Start Ctr., Titusville, Fla.; eligibility specialist Ill. Aid to Families and Dependent Children, Apopka; tchr. C.H. Price Mid. Sch., Interlachen, Fla.; instr., job developer displaced homemaker program Santa Fe C.C., Gainesville, Fla.; therapist, mental health counselor Meridian Behavioral Healthcare, Inc., Gainesville, 1996—, Nick Ungson MD, P.A., Leesburg, Fla. Pvt. tutor, Gainesville, 1991-93. Vol. tchr. Head Start, Phoenix, 1970, Sparc, shelter for abused women, Gainesville, 1989; mem. planning bd. Gainesville Area Women's Network, 1990. Mem. ACA, NEA, Real Estate Edn. Assn. Avocations: piano, decorating, sewing. Office: Meridian Behavioral Healthcare 4300 SW 13th St Gainesville FL 32608

KERSH, DEWITTE TALMADGE, JR., lawyer; b. Balt., June 1, 1930; s. DeWitte Talmadge and Marianna (Snyder) K.; m. Sharon R. Doherty, Aug. 2, 1986; children: DeWitte III, Sarah Anne. BS, Cornell U., 1952, LLB, 1957. Bar: R.I. 1958, N.H. 1991, U.S. Dist. Ct. R.I. 1959, U.S. Dist. Ct. N.H. 1991. Ptnr. Tillinghast, Collins & Graham, Providence, 1965-93; counsel Tillinghast, Licht, Perkins Smith & Cohen, Providence, 1993—. Adj. instr. Law Sch. Roger Williams U. Planning bd., selectman Town of Waterville Valley, NH; co-chair, sec. Waterville Valley Found. Fellow Am. Acad. Matrimonial Lawyers; mem. R.I. and N.H. Bar Assns. (pro bono svc. 1987-94), R.I. Family Ct. Bench and Bar (past. pres.), Rotary (pres. 1989-90). Republican. Unitarian Universalist. Home: PO Box 346 Waterville Valley NH 03215-0346 Office: Tillinghast Licht et al 10 Weybosset St Providence RI 02903

KERSHNER, ROBERT M. ophthalmologist, educator, research scientist; Ophthalmic physician and surgeon Eye Laser Ctr, Tucson, 2003—. Prof., rsch. scientist in field. Office: Eye Laser Ctr 1925 W Orange Grove Rd #303 Tucson AZ 85704-1152

KERSHNER, RODGER A. corporate lawyer; BS, Wayne State U., 1971; JD, Detroit Coll. of Law, 1976. Bar: Mich. 1976. Assoc. gen. counsel ANR Pipeline Co., 1978-88; v.p., gen. counsel CMS Energy Corp., 1988-95, sr. v.p., gen. counsel, 1995—. Pres. Bay Harbor Co. Mem. bd. control Mich. Technol. U. Mem.: Bay Harbor Yacht Club (founding). Office: CMS Energy Corp 330 Town Center Dr Dearborn MI 48126-2738 E-mail: rkershner@cmsenergy.com.

KERSLAKE, KENNETH ALVIN, artist, printmaker, art educator; b. Mt. Vernon, N.Y., Mar. 8, 1930; s. Archibald and Cecilia Fox (Gotterson) K.; m. Sarah Jane Allen, Aug. 25, 1956; children: Scott Paul, Katherine Rachel. Student, Pratt Inst., 1950-53; BFA, U. Ill., 1955, MFA, 1957. Grad. asst. U. Ill.-Champaign, 1955-57; interim instr. U. Ill., Champaign, 1957-58; instr. U. Fla., Gainesville, 1958-60, asst. prof. art, 1961-68, assoc. prof., 1969-74, prof., 1974-91, Disting. Svc. prof., 1991-96, Disting. svc. prof. emeritus, 1996—. Workshop lectr. U. Alaska-Fairbanks, 1982, Frogman's Print & Paper Workshop, Vermillion, S.D., 2000, Penland (N.C.) Sch. Crafts, 2000; artist-in-residence U. Mo.-Columbia, 1980, Frans Masereel Print Ctr., Kasterlee, Belgium, 1986, U. Tex., Austin; invited faculty U. Ga. Studies Abroad Program, Cortona, Italy, 1982; juror Fla. Printmakers 3rd Ann. Exhbn., 1989, Honolulu Printmakers 62nd Ann. Exhbn., 1990, Pacific States Nat. Print Exhbn., U. Hawaii, Hilo, 1992, Nat. Print Exhbn., U. Tex., Tyler, 1999, Regional Print Exhbn., Alma (Mich.) Coll., 2000, 1st Internat. Print Exhbn., Art & Culture Ctr., Hollywood, Fla., 2000, Juried Traveling Show, So. Graphics Coun., 2000—; exch. prof. Coll. of Art, Edinburgh, Scotland, 1995. Exhibitions include Impressions of Forty Years: The Prints of Kenneth A. Kerslake, Samuel P. HArn Mus. Art, U. Fla., Fla. Ctr. Arts, Gainesville and Vero Beach, Fla., 1997, LeMoyne Art Found., Tallahassee, Fla., 1998, U. Hawaii, Hilo, 1999, Webster U., Ga. Coll. and State U., St. Louis and Atlanta, Pacific Rim Internat. Exhbn., 2001 (Purchase award, 2001), 28th Bradley Nat. Print and Drawing Exhbn., Bradley U., Peoria, Ill. (Dean's Purchase award), The Boston Printmasters, 2001 (N.Am. Print prize, 2001), Herron Sch. Art, Indpls., 2003, featured in publs. including, Forty American Contemporary Printmakers. Recipient Joseph Pennell award Library of Congress, 1975, Assoc. Am. Artist award Associated Am. Artist Gallery, 1979, Disting. Faculty award Fla. Blue Key-U. Fla., 1979, Tchr. Improvement Program award, 1993, Purchase award Pacific Rim Internat. Print Exhbn. U. Hawaii, Hilo, 2001, Purchase award 28th Bradley Nat. Print and Drawing Exhbn. Bradley U., Peoria, Ill., Exhbn. award Boston Printmakers North Am. Print Exhbn., 2001; named Tchr. of Yr., Coll. Fine Arts, U. Fla., 1987; grantee Tamarind Found. Inc., 1964. Mem. Soc. Am. Graphic Artists, Fla. Printmakers Soc., Samuel P. Harn Mus. Art Alliance, Boston Printmakers, Print Club Phila., So. Graphics Coun. (organized 15th ann. conf., pres. 1990-92, newsletter editor), Am. Print Alliance (exec. bd., exec. com. 1992-93). Democrat. Episcopalian. Home: 1114 NW 36th Dr Gainesville FL 32605-4945 Office: U Fla Coll Fine Arts Sch Art and Art History Gainesville FL 32611 E-mail: kerslake@ufl.edu.

KERSTETTER, WAYNE ARTHUR, law educator, lawyer; b. Chgo., Dec. 1, 1939; s. Arthur Edward and Lillian (Asplund) K. BA, U. Chgo., 1964, JD, 1967. Bar: Ill. 1968. Gen. counsel Ill. Drug Abuse Treatement Program, 1968—70; admin. and rsch. assoc. Ctr. for Studies in Crimincal Justice, U. Chgo. Law Sch., 1970—72; asst. commr. N.Y. Police Dept., N.Y.C., 1972-73; supt. Ill. Bur. Investigation, Chgo., 1973-76; assoc. dir. Ctr. for Studies in Criminal Justice, U. Chgo., 1976-78; assoc. prof. criminal justice, dept. criminal justice U. Ill., Chgo., 1978-2000. Sr. rsch. fellow Am. Bar Found., Chgo., 1982-93, fellow, 1993—; cons. U.S. Civil Rights Commn., U. Chgo., ABT Assocs., Univ. Research Assocs., Police Found. Mem. transition team Mayor Washington, Chgo., 1983, Criminal Justice Project of Cook County, 1987. Served with USNR, 1962-64. Rsch. grantee Nat. Inst. Justice, 1976, Chgo. Bar Found., 1979-80, Am. Bar Found., 1983; fellow Ctr. for Studies in Criminal Justice, U. Chgo. Law Sch., 1978-82.

KERSTIENS, GENE J. mathemagenician, consultant; b. Phoenix, Nov. 7, 1926; s. Joseph Henry and Evangeline Kerstiens; m. Dorothy Louise Bishop, Jan. 27, 1951; children: Rita, Theresa, Mark, Frank, Helen, John, Christopher, Fredryc. BA, U. Portland, 1951; MA, U. Ariz., 1952; EdD, Nova U., Ft. Lauderdale, Fla., 1978. Prof. English El Camino Coll., Torrance, Calif., 1956—71; vis. prof. edn. Western Wash. State U., Bellingham, 1971—72; dean learning assistance El Camino Coll., Torrance, 1972—86; acting dir. Nat. Ctr. for Developmental Edn., Boone, NC, 1987—88; dir. learning assistance Scottsdale C.C., Ariz., 1988—92; dir. Andragogy Assocs., Torrance, 1992—. Cons. adult learning programs Pub. Broadcasting Svc., N.Y.C., 1970—73; developer, pub. English Modular Minicourses, 1972, Academic Skills series, 1977; pub. Study Behavior Inventory, 1994. Author: Study-Reading for College Courses, 1968 (Merit award, 1970); compiler (monograph) Junior-Community College Reading/Study Skills: An Annotated Bibliography, 1970; editor: Educulture, 1971—85; mem. editl. bd. Jour. Developmental Edn., 1980—. Mem. ACLU. With U.S. Army, 1945—47. Fellow: Am. Coun. of Developmental Edn. Assns.; mem.: Coll. Reading and Learning Assn. (pres. 1971, Lifetime Achievement award 1981). Avocations: sailing, travel, hiking, parachuting, motorcycling. Home and Office: Andragogy Associates 3434 W 227 Pl Torrance CA 90505-2632

KERSTING, EDWIN JOSEPH, retired university dean, veterinarian; b. Ottawa, Ohio, Nov. 4, 1919; s. Alphonse A. and Mary (Frey) K.; m. Billy Kate Walker, Mar. 23, 1946; children: Karl W., Ann L. D.V.M., Ohio State U., 1952, MS, U. Conn., 1964. Pvt. practice vet. medicine, Charleston, W.Va. and Columbus, Ohio, 1952-62; research asst. U. Conn., Storrs, 1961-62, assoc. prof. clin. vet. medicine, state extension veterinarian, 1962-65, asst. dean resident instrn. Coll. Agr., dir. Ratcliffe Hicks Sch. Agr., 1965-66, dir. internat. programs in agr., 1965-83, dean Coll. Agr. and Natural Resources, 1966-83, dir. Storrs Agrl. Expt. Sta., dir. Conn. Coop. Extension Service, 1966-83, prof. clin. vet. medicine dept. pathobiology, 1966-85, acting dean designate proposed Sch. Vet. Medicine, 1975-81, ret., 1985; research coordinator Hartford Hosp., Conn. 1985-90, chmn. sci. rev. com., 1986-88. Mem. adv. bd. to U.S. Sec. Agr. Animal Health Scis. Rsch. Program, 1978-84; bd. overseers Sch. Vet. Medicine, U. Pa.; assoc. mem. univ. bd. trustees, 1978-91, mem. adv. coun. Coll. Vet. Medicine Cornell U., 1978-83; cons. dept. surg. rsch, 1964-85; mem. rsch. com. Hartford (Conn.) Hosp., 1985-90; cons. Hartford Hosp., 1990-96, adv. com. Northeastern Rsch. Ctr. for Wildlife Diseases, 1971-83; cons. Ministry Agr., Belize, 1968-83, adv. com. Conn. Soil Conservation Svc.; ex-officio bd. overseers Bartlett Arboretum, 1967-83. Contbr. articles to profl. publs. Pres. Conn. Lung Assn., 1977-79; exec. com. Eastern States Expn., 1968-91, emeritus mem. Conn. trustees, 1992. Served with U.S. Army, Am. Field Svc. and USCG, 1942-44. Mem. AAAS, AVMA, Royal Soc. Health, Sigma Xi, Alpha Zeta, Epsilon Sigma Phi, Gamma Sigma Delta, Phi Zeta, Phi Kappa Phi.

KERTH, LEROY T. physics educator; b. Visalia, Calif., Nov. 23, 1928; s. Lewis John and Frances (Niccolls) K.; m. Ruth Lorraine Littlefield, Nov. 19, 1950; children: Norman Lewis, Randall Thomas, Christine Jane, Bradley Niccolls. AB in Physics, U. Calif., Berkeley, 1950, PhD, 1957. Mem. staff Lawrence Berkeley Lab, U. Calif., Berkeley, 1950-59, sr. scientist, 1959-61, assoc. prof. physics U. Calif., Berkeley, 1961-65, prof., 1965-93, prof. emeritus 1993—, assoc. dean Coll. Letters and Scis., 1966-70, spl. asst. to chancellor 1970-71, assoc. dir. for info. and computing scis. div., 1983-87, assoc. lab. dir. for gen. scis., Lawrence Berkeley Lab., 1987-89, assoc. lab. dir. sci. and tech. resources, Lawrence Berkeley Lab., 1990-92. Fellow Am. Phys. Soc. Home: 5 Los Conejos Orinda CA 94563-2214 Office: U Calif Lawrence Berkeley Lab Berkeley CA 94720-0001 E-mail: ltkerth@lbl.gov.

KERTZ, MARSHA HELENE, accountant, educator; b. Palo Alto, Calif., May 29, 1946; d. Joe and Ruth (Lazear) K. BSBA in Acctg., San Jose State U., 1976, MBA, 1977. CPA, Calif., cert. tax profl. Staff acct. Steven Kroff & Co., CPA's, Palo Alto, 1968-71, 73-74; contr. Rand Teleprocessing Corp., San Francisco, 1972; auditor, sr. acct. Ben F. Priest Accountancy Corp., Mountain View, Calif., 1974-83; tchr. San Jose Unified Regional Occupation Program, San Jose, 1977; pvt. practice accounting San Jose, 1977-2000; lectr. San Jose State U., 1977—. Bd. dirs. San Jose State U. Coll. of Bus. Alumni Assn. Mem. AICPA, Nat. Soc. of Tax Profls., Am. Inst. Tax Studies, Am. Acctg. Assn., Calif. Soc. CPAs, San Jose State U. Coll. Bus. Alumni Assn. (bd. dirs.), Beta Alpha Psi, Beta Gamma Sigma. Democrat. Jewish. Avocations: piano, travel, art history. Home: 4544 Strawberry Park Dr San Jose CA 95129-2213 Office: San Jose State U Acctg & Fin Dept San Jose CA 95192-0066 E-mail: kertz_m@cob.sjsu.edu, MarshaHK@aol.com.

KERWIN, LARKIN, retired physics educator; b. June 22, 1924; m. Maria Guadalupe Turcot, 1950; 8 children. Cert. engring. studies, St. Francis Xavier U., 1943, BSc summa cum laude, 1944; MSc magna cum laude, MIT, 1946; DSc magna cum laude, U. Laval, 1949; LLD (hon.), St. Francis Xavier U., 1970, U. Toronto, 1973, Concordia U., Montreal, 1976, U. Alta., 1983, U. Dalhousie, 1983, U. Moncton, 1985; DSc (hon.), U. B.C., 1973, McGill U., 1974, Meml. U. Newfoundland, 1978, U. Ottawa, 1981, Royal Mil. Coll. Can., 1982, U. Winnipeg, 1983, U. Windsor, 1984, U. Montreal, 1991; DCivil Law (hon.), Bishop's U., 1978. Tchg. asst. St. Francis Xavier U., 1944; lab. demonstrator U. Toronto, 1945; rsch. physicist Geotech. Corp., Cambridge, Mass., 1945; lab. asst. physics dept. U. Laval, Que., 1946-48, from asst. prof. to assoc. prof., 1948-56, prof., chair atomic physics, 1956, dir. Mass Spectrometry Lab., 1955-66, chmn. dept. physics, 1961-67; dir. Van de Graaf Accelerator Lab., 1961-72, vice-dean faculty of scis., 1967-68, acad. vice-rector, 1969-72, rector, 1972-77, prof. emeritus, 1991. Pres. Assn. Univ. and Coll. Can., 1975-75, Nat. Rsch. Coun. Can., 1980-89, Can. Space Agy., 1989-92, Can. Acad. Engring., 1989-90. Author: Atomic Physics, An Introduction, 1963; mem. editl. bd. Interdisciplinary Sci. Revs. Mag., 1981—; contbr. numerous articles to profl. jours. Trustee Nat. Museums of Can., 1980-89; adv. coun. Ottawa chpt. Can. Soc. Weizmann Inst. Sci., 1981; Can. rep. Versailles conf. on tech. and employment, 1982; bd. govs. Carleton U., 1983-86. Named knight, Equestrian Order of Holy Sepulchre of Jerusalem, 1970, knight comdr., 1972, comdr. with star, 1974, officer, Order of Can., 1978, knight grand cross, Equestrian Order of Holy Sepulchre of Jerusalem, 1980, companion, Order of Can., 1980, Officer, Order of Que., 1987, officier, Legion Honor, France, 1989; named to Ordre du Merite, Soc. Saint-Jean Baptiste de Que., 1979; recipient Centenary medal, 1967, Jubilee medal, 1977, Centenary medal of Roumania, 1977, medal of Laval Alumni, 1978, Gold medal, Can. Coun. Profl. Engrs., 1982, Outstanding Achievement award, Govt. Can., 1987, Centenary medal, 2002, Jubilee medal, 2002. Fellow AAAS, Royal Soc. Can. (pres. 1977-78), Royal Soc. Arts, Am. Inst. Physics; mem. Internat. Union Pure and Applied Physics (pres. 1987-91), Assn. Canadienne Française pour l'Avancement des Sc. (Pariseau medal 1965, Jacques Rousseau medal 1983), Am. Phys. Soc., Corp. Profl. Engr. Que., Sociedad Mexicana Fisica, Can. Assn. Physicists (pres. 1954, Gold medal 1969), Acadèmie des Grands Québecois.

KERWIN, MARY ANN COLLINS, lawyer; b. Oconomowoc, Wis., Oct. 16, 1931; d. Thomas Patrick and Florence Mary (Morris) Collins; m. Thomas Joseph Kerwin, Dec. 27, 1954; children: Thomas, Edward, Gregory, Mary, Anne, Katherine, John, Michael. BA, Barat Coll., 1953; JD, U. Denver, 1986. Bar: Colo. 1987. Tchr. Country Grade Sch., Wheaton, Ill., 1953-54; travel agt. Chgo. Athletic Club, 1954-55; legal intern City Atty.'s Office, Denver, 1985, Dist. Atty.'s Office, Denver, 1985; atty. Kerwin and Assocs., Denver, 1987-92, Decker, DeVoss & O'Malley, P.C., Denver, 1992-93, King Peterson Brown, LLC, Englewood, Colo., 1993-95; assoc. Daniel F. Lynch, P.C., Denver, 1995-99. Legal compliance dept. editor United Banks Colo., Inc., Denver, 1988-93. Author: (with others) The Womanly Art of Breastfeeding, 1958, also revised edits., 1963, 81, 87, 91, 97; contbr. articles to profl. jours. Mem. Colo. Breastfeeding Task Force, 1990-93, 96—; adv. bd. St. Luke's Woman's Hosp., Denver, 1986—, Colo. Sudden Infant Death Syndrome Program, 1992-94; sch. bd. Christ the King Sch., Denver, 1970-73; great books leader Jr. and Collegiate Great Books, Denver, 1963-82; marriage spkr. Cath. Archdiocese, Denver, 1965-75; co-founder, bd. dirs. La Leche League Internat., Franklin Park, Ill., 1956—, founder state orgn., 1960—, chmn. bd. 1980-83, sec. 1988-91. Recipient Margaret Burke Disting. Svc. Alumni award Barat Coll., 1999; named One of Ten Outstanding Alumnus Barat Coll., 1988. Mem. Colo. Bar Assn., Colo. Women's Bar Assn., Denver Bar Assn., Colo. Alumnae Assn. (pres. 1968-70), Theresians (pres. 1974-76). Avocations: reading, biking, swimming, tennis, singing. Home: 5130 Nassau Cir W Cherry Hills Village CO 80110 E-mail: makerwin@aol.com.

KERWIN, WALTER THOMAS, JR., career officer, consultant; b. West Chester, Pa., June 14, 1917; s. Walter Thomas and Mary Joseph (Farra) K.; m. Barbara Walker Connell, July 10, 1940 (dec. 1980); children: Bruce Richard, Ann Walker; m. Marion Thompson McCutcheon, Oct. 27, 1984. BS, U.S. Mil. Acad., 1939; postgrad., Command and Gen. Staff Coll., 1948, Armed Forces Staff Coll., 1953, U.S. Army War Coll., 1957, Nat. War Coll., 1960; LLD (hon.), U. Akron, 1976; M in Mil. Art and Sci. (hon.), Command and Gen. Staff Coll., 1978. Commd. 2nd lt. U.S. Army, 1939, advanced through grades to gen., 1973, commdg. gen. 3d armored divsn. arty., 1961-63, chief nuclear activities SHAPE NATO Paris, 1963-65, commdg. gen. 3d armored divsn. Frankfurt, Germany, 1965-66, asst. dep. chief staff ops. gen. staff Washington, 1966-67, chief staff mil. asst. command Saigon, Vietnam, 1967-68, commdg. gen. II field force Vietnam Bien Hoa, 1968-69, dep. chief staff pers. gen. staff Washington, 1969-72, commdg. gen. continental army command Norfolk, Va., 1973, commdg. gen. forces command Atlanta, 1973-74, vice chief staff Washington,

1974-78. Cons. Martin Marietta Corp., Bethesda, Md., 1978-94, Lockheed-Martin, 1994-97; assoc. dir. ops. Los Alamos (N.Mex.) Sci. Lab., 1953-56; bd. dirs. Gen. Employment Enterprises, Oakbrook, Ill., 1984-2001; mem. bd. mgrs. Army Emergency Relief, 1982—; mem. sci. adv. group Def. Nuc. Agy., 1980-86; mem. tactical tech. adv. group Land Warfare Def. Advance Rsch. Projects, 1983-88; Dept. Def. proxy dir. DKI Electronics-Electro. Tec Corp., Precision Products, Inc., Martin Electronics Fri Corp., Triangle Microwave Inc., 1986-89. Chmn. Army Air Force Mut. Aid Assn., Arlington, Va., 1982-97, chmn. emeritus 1997—; bd. advisors Army Hist. Found., 1995-97, bd. dirs., 1997—; mem. coun. trustees Assn. U.S. Army, 1979-82; bd. visitors Nat. Def. U., 1982-90. Recipient Disting. Svc. medal Commonwealth of Pa., 1975, Outstanding Alumnus award U.S. Army War Coll., 1997, Disting Grad award Assn. Grads. U.S. Mil. Acad., 2003, numerous mil. awards and decorations; named to Henderson Hall of Fame, West Chester, Pa., 1991, Res. Officers Assn. of U.S. Minute Man Hall of Fame, 1978; honored with Papal Benemerenti medal Pope Paul VI, 1977. Fellow: Nat. Def. U. Capstone Program (emeritus); mem.: U.S. Field Arty. Assn. (pres. 1980—97), West Point Soc. (Castle Duty Hon. Country award 1993, Artillery Ctr. Auditorium, Ft. Sill, Okla., dedicated Kerwin Hall 2001), Am. Def. Preparedness Assn. (comdr. Chief award 1984). Avocations: fishing, wilderness hiking.

KERWIN, WILLIAM JAMES, electrical engineering educator, consultant; b. Portage, Wis., Sept. 27, 1922; s. James William and Nina Elizabeth Kerwin; m. Madolyn Lee Lyons, Aug. 31, 1947; children: Dorothy E., Deborah K., David W. BS, U Redlands, 1948; MS, Stanford U., 1954, PhD, 1967. Aero. research scientist NACA, Moffett Field, Calif., 1948-59; chief measurements research br. NASA, Moffett Field, Calif., 1959-62, chief space tech. br., 1962-64, chief electronics research br., 1964-70; head electronics dept. Stanford Linear Accelerator Ctr., 1962; prof. elec. engring. U. Ariz., Tucson, 1969-85, prof. emeritus, 1986—. Cons. Power Electronics, 1980—. Author: (with others) Active Filters, 1970, Handbook Measurement Science, 1982, Instrumentation and Control, 1990, Handbook of Electrical Engineering, 1993, 97; contbr. articles to profl. jours.; patentee in field. Served to capt. USAAF, 1942-46. Recipient Invention NASA, 1969, 70; recipient fellow NASA, 1966-67 Fellow IEEE (Centennial medal 1984) Home: 1981 W Shalimar Way Tucson AZ 85704-1250 Office: U Ariz Dept Elec And Computer Engri Tucson AZ 85721-0001

KERXTON, ALAN SMITH, lawyer; b. Balt., Mar. 19, 1938; s. Benjamin and Eva (Smith) K.; m. Leslie Lurie, Aug. 2, 1961; children: Amy Lynn, Susan Deborah, Katherine Diane. BA, Ohio State U., 1960, JD, 1962. Bar: DC 1963, Md. 1965. Atty. corp. reorganization br. SEC, Washington, 1963-66; pvt. practice Washington, Potomac, Md., 1966—; prin. Ezrin, West and Kerxton, Chartered, 1976-84, Dunnells and Duval, Washington, 1990-93, Holland and Knight, Washington, 1994-97; of counsel Stein, Sperling, Rockville, Md., 1998—. Lectr. Cath. U. Am. Law Sch., fall 1973. With U.S. Army, 1962-63. Mem. ABA, D.C. Bar Assn., Montgomery County Bar Assn. Home: 11815 Beekman Pl Potomac MD 20854-2177 Office: 25 W Middle Ln Rockville MD 20850-2214 E-mail: akerxton@steinsperling.com.

KERYCZYNSKYJ, LEO IHOR, county official, educator, lawyer; b. Chgo., Aug. 8, 1948; s. William and Eva (Chicz) K.; m. Alexandra Irene Okruch, July 19, 1980; 1 child, Christina Alexandra. BA, BS, DePaul U., 1970, MS in Pub. Svc., 1975; JD, No. Ill. U., 1979; postgrad., U. Ill., Chgo., 1980-82. Bar: Ill. 1981, U.S. Dist. Ct. (no. dist.) Ill. 1981, U.S. Ct. Appeals (7th cir.) 1981, U.S. Tax Ct. 1981, U.S. Ct. Claims 1982, U.S. Ct. Mil. Appeals 1982, U.S. Ct. Appeals (fed. cir.) 1983, U.S. Supreme Ct. 1984. Condemnation awards officer Cook County Treas.'s Office, Chgo., 1972-75, adminstrv. asst., 1975-77, dep. treas., 1977-87, chief legal counsel, 1987-96, dir. fin. svcs., 1988-96; pvt. practice, 1996-98; adv. Office of Profl. Stds. Chgo. Police Dept., 1998—. Adj. prof. DePaul U., Chgo., 1979-95; elected chmn. bd. dirs., 1st Security Fed. Savs. Bank Chgo., 1992-93. Capt. Ukrainian Am. Dem. Orgn., Chgo., 1971. Recipient Outstanding Alumni award Phi Kappa Theta, 1971. Mem. ABA, Ill. State Bar Assn., Ill. Trial Law Assn., Ukrainian Am. Bar Assn., Chgo. Bar Assn., Ill. Assn. County Ofcls., Internat. Assn. Clerks, Recorders, Election Ofcls. and Treas., Shore Line Interurban Hist. Soc. (bd. dirs., legal counsel 1987-2001, pres. and chmn., 1993-98), Theta Delta Phi. Ukrainian Catholic. Home: 2324 W Iowa St Apt 3R Chicago IL 60622-4720 Office: Office Profl Stds 10 W 35th St Chicago IL 60616

KERZ, LOUISE, historian; b. N.Y.C., Sept. 16, 1936; d. Louis and Catharine Sohn; m. Leo Kerz, Apr., 1965 (dec. 1976); children: Jonathan, Antony; m. Al Hirschfeld, Oct. 1996 (dec. 2003). Student, Queens Coll., 1954-56, Marymount Coll., 1972-74. Theatre producer Leo Kerz Prodns., N.Y.C., 1960-74; theatrical curator N.Y. Cultural Ctr., N.Y.C., 1974, Theatre of Max Reinhardt, 1974, N.Y. Pub. Libr. Lincoln Ctr., N.Y.C., 1984, Calif. Mus. Sci. and Industry, L.A., 1985, The Demille Dynasty, 1984; rsch. cons. CBS: On the Air, 1978, Smith-Hemion TV Prodns., L.A., 1987—, The Phantom of the Opera, 1995. Dir. rsch. Greengage Prodns., Julie Andrews/Greengage Prodns., LA, 1988, Tony Awards Telecast 50th Anniversary Show, 1947—96; rsch. cons. TV Acad. Hall of Fame and Tony Awards telecasts, 1993—96; dir. rights and permissions The Line King (The Al Hirschfeld Story-nominated for Oscar 1996) NY Times, TV documentary; rsch. historian "Broadway", six-part TV series, 1997; spl. cons. The Demille Family-Documentary Am. Movie Channel, 1997; exec. cons., liaison Hirschfeld Exhbns., catalogs, books and events Mus. of City of NY, cons. Hirschfeld's NY exhibit, 2001; cons. Hirschfeld's Hollywood exhibit Acad. Motion Picture Arts & Scis., Beverly Hills, Calif., 2001; cons. catalogues to exhibits Pub. Harry N. Abrams, 2001. Assoc. prodr. on Broadway : Rhinoceros, 1961; contbg. editor: N.Y.C. Access, 1983; picture editor The DeMilles: An American Family, 1988, curator, dir. Exhibit Broadway, 1995, picture editor Al Hirschfeld: On Line, 1998, curator, photographer (exhibitions) Hirschfeld Celebration at Leica Gallery, N.Y.C., 2002; one-woman shows include The Leica Gallery, N.Y.C., 2002. Vol. Persian Gulf war Am. Jewish Congress, Israel, 1991; elected mem. Tony Awards nominating com. Am. Theatre Wing, 2000-2003; co-chair Al Hirschfeld Centennial, assoc. prodr. Al Hirschfeld 100th Birthday Salute, 2003. Mem. Theatre Libr. Assn. Democrat. Address: c/o Al Hirschfeld 122 E 95th St New York NY 10128-1705

KES, VICKI PAULETTE, museum director; b. Bessemer, Ala., June 2, 1952; d. Gerald Vance and Marjorie Jean (Bush) George; m. Pieter A. Kes, Sr., Nov., 2002; children: Alissa Hubbard, Rebecca Hubbard. Office worker Mining Corp. of the South, Vance, Ala., 1978-79; artist, sign painter Bob's Sign Shop, Midfield, Ala., 1980—; dir. Iron & Steel Mus. of Ala., McCalla, 1980—. Program completion Office of Mus Programs, Smithsonian, Washington, 1987. Artist (book) Tannehill Crafts, 1982. Events Planner Ala. Reunion State of Ala., Montgomery, 1989. Recipient Top 20 Events in the South East award SE Tourism Soc., Atlanta, 1986-87, 88, 91, Head Start Vol. award, 1994. Mem. Ala. Preservation Alliance, Soc. Indsl. Archaeology, Nat. Trust for Hist. Preservation, Birmingham Area Mus. Assn., Am. Assn. State and Local History (program completion 1980), Am. Assn. Mus., Ala. Mus. Assn. (sec.-treas. 1983-85, chair com. Southeastern Museums Conf. 1999, co-chair com. 2000, Meritorious Svc. award 1983), Ala. State Employees Assn. (pres. Tannehill chpt. 1993-99). Democrat. Baptist. Avocations: pen, ink drawings, painting. Home: 16920 Brooke Dr Mc Calla AL 35111-2251 Office: Tannehill Historical State Park 12632 Confederate Pkwy Mc Calla AL 35111-2620 E-mail: tannehillmuseum@att.net.

KESARIS, PAUL, publishing executive; Sr. v.p. Congl. Info. Svc., Bethesda, Md., 2000—. Office: Congrl Info Svc 4520 E West Hwy Bethesda MD 20814-3319

KESHAVARZIAN, ALI, gastroenterologist, educator; b. Teheran, Iran, Jan. 24, 1951; married; 2 children. MD, Teheran U., 1976. Diplomate Am. Bd. Internal Medicine, Am. Bd. Gastroenterology, lic. physician Md., Ill., U.K. Intern Teheran U. (Pahlavi) Hosp., 1975—76; sr. ho. officer in medicine Western Teheran Nat. Ins. Health Hosp., 1976—77; sr. ho. officer in gastroenterology Guy's Hosp. Med. Sch., London, 1977—79, lectr. in medicine, 1979; registrar in gen./renal/gastroenterology medicine Hillingdon Hosp., Uxbridge, England, 1980—95; registrar in gen. and chest medicine Royal Postgrad. Med. Sch., Ealing Hosp., Southall Middlesex, England, 1982; registrar in gastroenterology Royal Postgrad. Med. Sch., Hammersmith Hosp., 1983, rsch. fellow, sr. registrar in gastroenterology, 1984; fellow in gastroenterology U. Md. Sch. Medicine, 1984—86, instr. medicine, 1985—86; attending physician Balt. VA Hosp., 1986; asst. prof. medicine Loyola U. Med. Sch., 1986—89, assoc. prof. medicine, 1989—93, assoc. prof. pharmacology, 1990—94, prof. pharmacology, prof. medicine, 1993—99, dir. divsn. digestive diseases and nutrition, 1995—98; attending physician Loyola U. Med. Ctr., 1986—99, Hines VA Hosp., 1986—99, chief sect. gastroenterology, 1992—98; attending physician Rush Presbyn. St. Luke's Med. Ctr., Chgo., 1999—, prof. molecular biophysics and physiology, dir. sect. gastroenterology and nutrition, 2000—; prof. medicine, prof. pharmacology Rush U., Chgo., 1999—, Josephine Dyrenforth chair gastroenterology, 2001—. Contbr. numerous articles to profl. jours.; reviewer jours. in field, mem. editl. bd. Am. Jour. Gastroenterology, Jour. Clin. Gastroenterology and Hepatology. Grantee, NIH, 1987—91, 1990—93, 1991—93, 1992—95, 1994—95, 1998—99, 2002—, Wyeth/Genetics Inst., 2000—01, Otsuka Am. Pharm., 1997—99, 2000—01, Ross Labs., 1988—89, 1989—90, 1992—94, Abbott Lab., 1990—91, 1991—93, 1992—93, 1992—94, Serono Labs., 1994—95, Marion Merrell Dow, 1994—95, Procter and Gamble, 1993—95, 1995—97, CATO, 1998, Quaker Oats, 1997—99, Oxis Internat., 1997—99, Pfizer, 1997—98, AEOLUS Pharm., 1998—99, Inst. Neurosci. and Aging, 1986—87, VA Rehab. R&D, 1994—95. Fellow: ACP, Am. Coll. Gastroenterology (rsch. com. 1997—99, ednl. affairs com. 1999—, grantee), Royal Coll. Physicians; mem.: Rsch. Soc. on Alcoholism, Internat. Soc. Biomed. Rsch. on Alcoholism, Am. Fedn. Clin. Rsch., Midwest Gut Club, Chgo. Soc. Gastroenterology (bd. dirs. 1994—2003, pres. 2001—02), Am. Motility Soc., Am. Gastroenterol. Assn. (pub. com. 1999—2002), Brit. Soc. Gastroenterology (basic sci. group), Am. Soc. Gastrointestinal Endoscopy, Am. Assn. Study of Liver Diseases, Ctrl. Soc. Clin. Rsch., Royal Coll. Physicians. Home: 2300 Lincolnwood Dr Evanston IL 60201 Office: Rush Presbyn St Luke's Med Ctr 1725 W Harrison Ste 206 Chicago IL 60612 Office Fax: 312-563-3883. Business E-Mail: ali_keshavarzian@rush.edu.

KESHGEGIAN, ALBERT ARAKEL, pathologist; b. Bklyn., Jan. 22, 1949; s. Charles and Asdghig (Hovsepian) Keshgegian; m. Patrice Anne Sookiasian, Dec. 22, 1974; children: Gregory Arakel, Mark Garabed, James Albert Armenag. BA summa cum laude in Biochemistry, U. Pa., 1969, PhD in Biochemistry, 1974, MD, 1975. Diplomate Am. Bd. Pathology in anatomic and clin. pathology; lic. physician, Pa. Resident pathology Hosp. U. Pa., 1975-78, chief resident pathology, 1978-79; asst. instr. pathology U. Pa. Sch. Medicine, 1975-79, asst. prof., 1979-81; adj. asst. prof. pathology and lab. medicine, 1981-85, adj. assoc. prof. pathology and lab. medicine, 1985-94; adj. asst. prof. microbiology and cell biology Pa. State U., 1982-87; assoc. prof. pathology Thomas Jefferson U., 1985-99, clin. prof. pathology, anatomy and cell biology, 1999—; assoc. dir. dept. pathology, chief clin. pathology Bryn Mawr (Pa.) Hosp., 1988-97; med. dir. Main Line Clin. Labs., Wynnewood, Pa., 1997—; sys. chmn. dept. pathology Main Line Hosps., 1998—. Acting assoc. dir. protein chemistry divsn. William Pepper Lab., Hosp. U. Pa., 1978-79, dir. protein chemistry divsn., 1979-81; asst. pathologist The Lankenau Hosp., Phila., 1981-82, assoc. pathologist, 1982-87, dir. immunopathology, co-dir. clin. chemistry sects., 1981-87, dir. hematology sect., 1984-87; chmn. instnl. rev. bd. Bryn Mawr Hosp., 1989-97, Main Line Hosps., 2001—; med. scientist trainee NIH, 1969-75. Contbr. articles to profl. jours. Fellow: Am. Soc. Clin. Pathologists, Coll. Am. Pathologists; mem.: Am. Assn. Clin. Chemistry, Alpha Epsilon Delta, Phi Beta Kappa. Home: 45 Sugar Maple Dr Newtown Square PA 19073-2020 Office: Lankenau Hosp Dept Path 100 E Lancaster Ave Ste 1 Wynnewood PA 19096 3498

KESKINOCAK, PINAR, adult education educator; d. Huseyin and Fikret Keskinocak; m. Bulent Basaran, Sept. 2, 1999; 1 child, Evren Basaran. BS, Bilkent U., Ankara, Turkey, 1987—91; MS, Bilkent U., 1991—92; MSIA, Carnegie Mellon U., 1992—94, PhD, 1992—97. Post-doctoral fellow IBM T.J. Watson Rsch. Ctr., Yorktown Heights, NY, 1997—99; asst. prof. Ga. Inst. of Tech., 1999—. Cons. Ciscorp, Pitts., 1995—96, United Airlines (Avolar), Chgo., 2001—01. Recipient The Daniel H. Wagner Prize for Excellence in Ops. Rsch. Practice, 1998, Best Workshop Paper Award, Workshop on Agents in E-commerce, Hong Kong, 1999, NSF Career Award, NSF, 2001. Mem.: INFORMS (v.p. meetings, INFORMS forum for women in or/ms 2002, INFORMS forum on edn. 2002—). Achievements include patents for Optimization prediction for indsl. processes.

KESLER, JAMES L. ophthalmologist; b. Vincennes, Ind., July 8, 1949; s. Richard Kesler and Bonnie L. (Perrott) Treece; m. Jana L. Blake, Aug. 29, 1970; children: Jason, Jessica. BS Biochemistry with distinction, U. Ill., 1971; MD, Washington U., 1975. Diplomate Am. Bd. Ophthalmology, Nat. Bd. Med. Examiners. Resident U. Va., Charlottesville, 1975-76, Barnes Hosp./Washington U., St. Louis, 1976-79; ophthalmologist Coastal Carolina Eye Clinic, Wilmington, N.C., 1979—. Cons. in ophthalmology Duke U., 1998—. James scholar U. Ill., 1967-71. Fellow ACS (bd. dirs. N.C. chpt. 1997-2002), Am. Acad. Ophthalmology (councillor 1996-2000); mem. AMA, N.C. Med. Soc., N.C. Soc. Ophthalmology (pres. 1988), New Hanover-Pender County Med. Soc. (pres. 1991), Excellence in Primary Eye Care (founding mem.), Nat. Parliamentarian Soc., Cmty. Eyecare (bd. dirs. 1999—), Phi Beta Kappa, Alpha Omega Alpha. Avocations: biking, tennis, baseball, basketball, reading. Office: Coastal Carolina Eye Clinic 1120 Med Ctr Dr Wilmington NC 28401

KESLER, JAY LEWIS, academic administrator; b. Barnes, Wis., Sept. 15, 1935; s. Elsie M. Campbell Kesler; m. H. Jane Smith; children: Laura, Bruce, Terri. Student, Ball State U., 1953-54; BA, Taylor U., 1958, LHD (hon.), 1982; Dr. Divinity (hon.), Barrington Coll., 1977; DD (hon.), Asbury Theol. Sem., 1984, Anderson U., 1999; HHD (hon.), Huntington Coll., 1983; LHD, John Brown U., 1987; LLD (honoris causa), Gordon Coll., 1992; DD (hon.), Union U., 2000, Trinity Internat. U., 2001; LHD (honoris causa), So. Wesleyan U., 2002. Dir. Marion (Ind.) Youth for Christ, 1955-58, crusade staff evangelist, 1959-60, dir. Ill.-Ind. region, 1960-62, dir. coll. recruitment, 1962-63, v.p. personnel, 1963-68, v.p. field coordination, 1968-73, pres., 1973-85, also bd. dirs.; pres. Taylor U., Upland, Ind., 1985-2000, chancellor, 2000—03, pres. emeritus, 2003—; tchg. pastor Upland Cmty. Ch., 2002—. Bd. dirs. Star Fin. Group, Christianity Today, Brotherhood Mut. Ins. Co., Nat. Ass. Evangs., Youth for Christ Internat., Youth for Christ U.S.A.; mem. bd. reference Christian Camps Inc.; mem. Council for Christian Colls. and Univs., bd. mem., 2001; chmn. United Christian Coll. Fund; mem. adv. bd. Christian Bible Soc.; co-pastor 1st Bapt. Ch., Geneva, 1972—85; mem. faculty Billy Graham Schs. Evangelism; lectr. Staley Disting. Christian Sch. Lecture Program; past gov.'s appointee Ind. Commn. on Youth. Spkr. on Family Forum (daily radio show and radio program), 1973-98; mem. adv. com. Campus Life mag.; author: Let's Succeed With Our Teenagers, 1973, I Never Promised You a Disneyland, 1975, The Strong Weak People, 1976, Outside Disneyland, 1977, I Want a Home with No Problems, 1977, Growing Places, 1978, Too Big to Spank, 1978, Breakthrough, 1981, Parents & Teenagers, 1984 (Gold Medallion award), Family Forum, 1984, Making Life Make Sense, 1986, Parents and Children, 1986, Being Holy, Being Human, 1988, Ten Mistakes Parents Make With Teenagers (And How to Avoid Them), 1988, Is Your Marriage Really Worth Fighting For?, 1989, Energizing Your Teenagers' Faith, 1990, Raising Responsible Kids, 1991, Grandparenting: The Agony and the Ecstasy, 1993, Challenges for the College Bound, 1994, Emotionally Healthy Teenagers, 1998; contbr. articles to profl. jours. Bd. advisors Prison Fellowship Internat., Christian Camps Inc., Christian Educators Assn. Internat., Evangelicals for Social Action, Love and Action, Venture Middle East, Internat. Com. of Reference for New Life 2000. Named sr. fellow, Coun. Christian Coll., 2000, Sagamore of the Wabash, 2000; recipient Angel award, Religion in Media, 1985, Outstanding Youth Leadership award, Religious Heritage Am., 1989. Office: Taylor U Office Pres 236 W Reade Ave Upland IN 46989-1002

KESLER, JOHN A. lawyer, land developer; b. Clark County, Ill., Apr. 25, 1923; s. Hal H. and Clara (Hurst) K.; m. Maxine Ruth Weaver, May 13, 1948; children: Nicki Kesler Cotsworth, Bradley Weaver, John A. II. AB, Ind. State U., 1948; JD, Ind. U., 1951. Bar: Ind. 1951, Ill. 1951. Chief dep. prosecutor County Vigo, Terre Haute, Ind., 1954-58; probate commr. Cir. Ct., 1971-74; mem. ho. reps. Ind. Legis., 1969-73; asst. state atty. County Madison, Edwardsville, Ill., 1985-88; pvt. practice law Terre Haute, 1951—. Pres. Wabash Valley Land Developers, Inc., Terre Haute, 1979—. Staff sgt. U.S. Army, 1943-46. Recipient Legion of Honor; recipient Good Govt. award West Vigo Jaycees, 1971, Civic Svc. award U.S. Jaycees, 1957; named Outstanding Pub. Offcl. Terre Haute Jaycees. Mem. ABA, Nat. Assn. Criminal Def. Lawyers, Ill. State Bar Assn., Ind. Bar Assn., VFW, Am. Legion, United War Vets. Coun. Vigo County (past commdr.), SAR (state pres.), Exchange Club (pres.), Ind. U. Emeritus Club, Shriners, Grand Soc. Sycamores, Honorable Order of Ky. Cols., Grotto, I.U. Emeritus Club. Democrat. Methodist. Avocations: bowling, genealogy, reading. Home: 76 S Thorpe Pl West Terre Haute IN 47885 Office: 219 Ohio St Terre Haute IN 47807-3420

KESLER, STEPHEN EDWARD, economic geology educator; BS with honors, U. N.C., 1962; PhD, Stanford U., 1966. Asst. prof. econ. geology La. State U., Baton Rouge, 1966-70; assoc. prof. U. Toronto, Ont., Can., 1970-77; prof. U. Mich., Ann Arbor, 1977—, assoc. chair, 1998—. Vis. scientist Nat. Inst. Geography, Guatemala, 1966-69, Consejo Recursos Minerales, Mexico City, 1974-75; with Dirección General Minas, Santo Domingo, 1983-84; cons. exploration for metallic and non-metallic mineral deposits. Author: Our Finite Mineral Resources, 1975; (with others) Economic Geology of Central Dominican Republic, 1984, Mineral Resources: Economics and the Environment, 1994; assoc. editor Econ. Geology, 1981-91, Ore Geology Revs., 1999—; mem. editl. bd. Jour. Geochem. Exploration, 1984-98. Pres. bd. trustees Lord of Light Luth. Ch., 1989-91. Fellow Geol. Soc. Am., Soc. Econ. Geologists (councillor 1983-86, internat. lectr. 1989-90, v.p. 1990-91, Thayer Lindsley lectr. 1994-95, pres. 1998-99); mem. Assn. Exploration Geochemists (councillor 1981-84), Soc. Mining Engrs. of AIME (program chmn. 1977). Lutheran. Office: U Mich Dept Geol Scis Ann Arbor MI 48109

KESSEL, BRINA, ornithologist, educator, researcher; b. Ithaca, N.Y., Nov. 20, 1925; d. Marcel and Quinta (Cattell) K.; m. Raymond B. Roof, June 19, 1957 (dec. 1968). BS (Albert R. Brand Bird Song Found. scholar), Cornell U., 1947, PhD, 1951; MS (Wis. Alumni Research Found. fellow), U. Wis.-Madison, 1949. Student asst. Patuxent Research Refuge, 1946; student teaching asst. Cornell U., 1945-47, grad. asst., 1947-48, 49-51; instr. biol. sci. U. Alaska, summer 1951, asst. prof. biol. sci., 1951-54, assoc. prof. zoology, 1954-59, prof. zoology, 1959-96, head dept. biol. scis., 1957-66; dean U. Alaska (Coll. Biol. Scis. and Renewable Resources), 1961-72, curator terrestrial vertebrate mus. collections, 1972-90, curator ornithology collection, 1990-95, adminstrv. assoc. for acad. programs, grad. and undergrad., dir. acad. advising, office of chancellor, 1973-80; sr. scientist U. Alaska, 1996-99, prof. emeritus, dean emeritus, curator emeritus, 1999—. Project dir. U. Alaska ecol. investigations for AEC Project Chariot, 1959—63; ornithol. investigations N.W. Alaska pipeline, 1976—81, Susitna Hydroelectric Project, 1980—83. Author books; contbr. articles to profl. jours. Honored by U. Alaska with ann. award, "Brina Kessel Medal for Excellence in Science." Fellow AAAS, Am. Ornithologists' Union (v.p. 1977, pres.-elect 1990-92, pres. 1992-94), Arctic Inst. N.Am.; mem. Wilson, Cooper ornith. socs., Soc. for Northwestern Vertebrate Biology, Pacific Seabird Group, Assn. Field Ornithologists, Sigma Xi (pres. U. Alaska 1957), Phi Kappa Phi, Sigma Delta Epsilon. Achievements include research in European Starling in North America; biogeography, seasonality, and the biology of birds in Alaska. Office: U Alaska Mus PO Box 80211 Fairbanks AK 99708-0211 E-mail: ffbxk@uaf.edu.

KESSEL, JOHN HOWARD, political scientist, educator; b. Dayton, Ohio, Oct. 13, 1928; s. Arthur V. and Helen (Hopkins) K.; m. Margaret Sarah Wagner, Aug. 22, 1954; children— Robert Arthur, Thomas John. Student, Purdue U., 1946 48; BA, Ohio State U., 1950; PhD, Columbia U., 1958. Instr. Amherst and Mt. Holyoke colls., 1957-58; instr., asst. prof. Amherst Coll., 1958-61; asst. prof. U. Wash., 1961-65; Arthur E. Braun prof. polit. sci. Allegheny Coll., Meadville, Pa., 1965-70; prof. polit. sci. Ohio State U., Columbus, 1970-94, prof. emeritus, 1994—. Vis. prof. U. Calif., San Diego, 1977, U. Wash., 1980, Am. U., 1980. Author: The Goldwater Coalition: Republican Strategies in 1964, 1968, The Domestic Presidency, 1975, Presidential Campaign Politics: Coalition Strategies and Citizen Response, 1980, 4th edit., 1992, Presidential Parties, 1984, Presidents, the Presidency, and the Political Environment, 2001; co-editor: Micropolitics-Individual and Group Level Concepts, 1970, Theory Building and Data Analysis in the Social Sciences, 1984, Researching the Presidency: Vital Questions, New Approaches, 1993; editor Am. Jour. Polit. Sci, 1974-76; contbr. articles to profl. jours. Mem. exec. council Inter-Univ. Consortium for Polit. Research, 1964-65, 67-68; Exec. dir. Nixon-Lodge Vols. Mass., 1960; dir. arts, scis. div. Republican Nat. Com., 1963-64. Served with USN, 1950-53. Guest scholar, Brookings Inst., 1972, vis. scholar, Am. Enterprise Inst., 1980—82. Mem. Am. Polit. Sci. Assn. (exec. council 1969-71), Midwest Polit. Sci. Assn. (pres. 1978-79) Home: 516 E Schreyer Pl Columbus OH 43214-2273 E-mail: kessel.1@osu.edu.

KESSEL, JOHN PHILIP, lawyer; b. Richmond, Ind., Nov. 19, 1947; s. John Jeffrey and Virginia Starr K.; m. Elizabeth M. Costello, Sept. 18, 1982; children: Jeffrey L. BA in Econs., U. Mich., 1969; JD, Cath. U., 1975. Bar: D.C. 1975, Va. 1980, Md. 1983; bd. cert. in civil trial advocacy. Staff mem. Congresswoman Martha W. Griffiths, Washington, 1969-71; clk. Williams, Connolly & Califano, Washington, 1971-75; law clk. Judge Catherine B. Kelly, Washington, 1975-76; ptnr. Kessel & Tierney, Washington, 1976-78; assoc. Milton Heller & Assocs., Washington, 1978-90, Chaikin & Karp, Washington, 1990-96; ptnr. Karp, Frosh, Lapidus, Rockville, Md., 1996—. Mem. Trial Lawyers Assn. D.C. (treas. 1996-97, sec. 1997-98, v.p. 1998-99, pres.-elect 1999-2000, pres. 2000-01, Lawyer of Yr. 1989). Office: Karp Frosh Lapidus 1370 Piccard Dr #290 Rockville MD 20850 E-mail: philk@karpfrosh.com.

KESSEL, LLOYD R. nursing administrator, educator; b. Dickinson, N.D., Oct. 24, 1952; s. Wendell Kasper and Tomasita (Martinez) Kessel; m. Kathleen Kessel, Nov. 24, 1988; children: Taylor Steven, Danielle Rose. BSN, Mary Coll., Bismarck, N.D., 1975; MSN summa cum laude, U. of Mary, Bismarck, 1989. Dir. nursing svcs. Richardton (N.D.) Community Hosp.; sr. staff nurse oper. room Whittaker Life Scis., Khamis Mushayt, Saudi Arabia; health care officer S.W. Milti-County Correction Ctr., Dickinson; instr. nursing Dickinson State U.; supr. oper. room, anesthesia, day surgery St. Joseph's Hosp., Dickinson, dir. respiratory care svcs., dir. acute care nursing; coord. therapeutic svcs. Dakota Juvenile Corrections Facility, 2000—. Prodr.(poet): ; contbr. Mem.: ANA, N.D. Nursing Assn. (ethics com., psychiat./mental health nursing com.), S.W. Mental Health Assn., N.D. Psychiat. Nursing Edn. Coun., Assn. Oper. Rm. Nurses, Sigma Theta Tau. Home: 1140 Alder Ave Dickinson ND 58601-4189

KESSEL, MARK, lawyer; b. Krasnik, Poland, June 14, 1941; arrived in U.S., 1948; s. Leo and Erna (Friedman) Kessel; m. Elaine Keit, Aug. 29, 1966; children: Greer Kessel Hendricks, Robert W. BA with honors in Econs., CUNY, 1963; JD magna cum laude, Syracuse U., 1966. Bar: N.Y. Assoc. Shearman & Sterling, N.Y.C., 1971-77, ptnr., 1997—2001, mng. ptnr., 1990-94; mng. dir. Symphony Capital LLC, N.Y.C., 2002—. Bd. dirs. Harrods Ltd., Antigenics, Inc., 1993—2003. Bd. visitors Syracuse U. Coll. Law; bd. dirs. San Francisco Psychoanalytic Inst., 1988—90, Mus. City of N.Y., 1993—2003, W.M. Keck Found., L.A., 1985—86; dir. Heller Fin., Inc., 1992—2001. Capt. JAGC U.S. Army, 1963—71. Avocations: reading, running. Office: Symphony Capital LLC 875 3d Ave New York NY 10022

KESSEL, RICHARD GLEN, zoology educator; b. Fairfield, Iowa, July 19, 1931; BS in Chemistry summa cum laude, Parsons Coll., 1953; MS in Zoology and Physiology, U. Iowa, 1956, PhD in Zoology and Cytology, 1959; postgrad., Marine Biol. Lab., 1957. Trainee dept. anatomy Bowman Gray Sch. Medicine, Wake Forest U., 1959-60; Nat. Inst. Gen. Med. Sci. postdoctoral rsch. fellow Bowman Gray Sch. Medicine, Wake Forest U., Winston-Salem, N.C., 1960-61, instr. anatomy, 1959-61, asst. prof., 1961; asst. prof. zoology U. Iowa, Iowa City, 1961-64, assoc. prof., 1964-68, prof., 1968—. Vis. investigator Hopkins Marine Sta., Pacific Grove, Calif., 1966; ind. investigator Marine Biol. Lab., Woods Hole, Mass., summers 1960, 62, 64 Author: (with C.Y. Shih) Scanning Electron Microscopy in Biology: A Students' Text-Atlas of Biological Organization, 1974, (with R.H. Kardon) Tissues and Organs: A Text-Atlas of Scanning Electron Microscopy, 1979, (with C.Y. Shih) Living Images, 1982, (with R. Roberts and H. Tung) Freeze Fracture Images of Cells and Tissues, 1991, Basic Medical Histology, 1998; assoc. editor Jour. Exptl. Zoology, 1978-82; mem. editorial bd. Jour. Submicroscopic Cytology, 1980—; mem. internat. bd. editors Scanning Electron Microscopy in Biology and Medicine; contbr. articles to profl. jours., chpts. to books Grantee USPHS, 1961-78, NSF, 1969-71, Whitehall Found., 1982-84; Bodine fellow; George Lincoln Seeley scholar; Nat Inst. Gen. Med. Sci.-USPHS, 1964-69. Mem. AAAS, Am. Soc. Cell Biology, Am. Assn. Anatomists, Electron Micros. Soc. Am., Am. Physiol. Soc., Soc. for Study

of Reprodn., Am. Soc. Zoologists, Am. Inst. Biol. Sci., Soc. Devel. Biology, Sigma Xi, Phi Kappa Phi, Beta Beta Beta. Office: Univ Iowa Dept Biol Scis Iowa City IA 52242 E-mail: richard-kessel@uiowa.edu.

KESSELL, CHARLES ARTHUR, music educator, musician; b. Chicago, Ill., Aug. 9, 1955; s. William Arthur and Jane Catherine (Buddemeyer) Kessell; m. Diana Lee Castellanos, Sept. 10, 1983; 1 child, Benjamin. BA in Music Edn., DePaul U., Chgo., 1979. Music dir. St. Sebastian Parish, Chgo., 1974—83, Our Lady of Perpetual Help Parish, Glenview, Ill., 1983—88; mem., archdiocesan music com. Archdiocese of Chgo., Office for Divine Worship, 1985—89; liturgist, music dir. St. Ita Parish, Chgo., 1988—98, St. Isaac Jogues Parish, Chgo., 1998—; music dir., instr. Edgebrook Music Acad., Chgo., 1998—; music dir. One World Choirs, Chgo., Irish Heritage Singers, Chgo., 2000—. Freelance musician, Chgo., 1974—; chgo. area Indiana sales rep. Levsen Organ Co., Buffalo. Composer (arranger): (irish folk music) Tir Na Ceol, 2002. Den leader, asst. cubmaster, cubmaster, asst. scoutmaster, scoutmaster, dist. tng. chair, roundtable commr. dist. commr. BSA., Chgo., 1987—99. Recipient Order of the Arrow, BSA, 1996. Mem.: Pueri Cantores, Percussive Arts Soc., Am. Guild English Handbell Ringers, Nat. Assn. Pastoral Musicians, Irish Am. Heritage Ctr., Am. Guild of Organists. Roman Catholic. Avocations: camping, canoeing, fishing, kayaking. Home: 6042 W Grace Chicago IL 60634 Office: St Isaac Jogues Parish 8149 Golf Road Niles IL 60714 Home Fax: 847-967-1091. Personal E-mail: perc55@juno.com.

KESSELMAN, JONATHAN RHYS, economics educator, public policy researcher; b. Columbus, Ohio, Mar. 17, 1946; s. Louis C. and Jennie K.; m. Sheila Kaplan, Mar. 12, 1973; 1 child, Maresa. BA with honors, Oberlin Coll., 1968; PhD in Econs., MIT, 1972. Asst. prof. econs. U. B.C., Vancouver, Can., 1972-76, assoc. prof., 1976-81, prof., 1981—, dir. Ctr. for Rsch. on Econ. and Social Policy, 1992—. Rsch. assoc. Inst. for Rsch. on Poverty, Madison, Wis., 1974-75; vis. scholar Delhi Sch. Econs., New Delhi, 1978-79; cons. econs., 1973—; prin. investigator Equality, Security and Community Rsch. Project, 1998-. Author: Financing Canadian Unemployment Insurance, 1983, Rate Structure and Personal Taxation, 1990, General Payroll Taxes, 1997; editorial bd.: Can. Pub. Policy, 1997—, Can. Tax Jour., 1999—; contbr. numerous articles on taxation, income security, employment policy to profl. jours. Bd. dirs. Tibetan Refugee Aid Soc., Vancouver, 1980-82; mem. adv. panel Can. Ministry Employment and Immigration, Ottawa, Ont., 1982-83; mem. B.C. Econ. Policy Inst., 1983-86; trustee pension plan U. B.C., 1988-90; chmn. Musqueam Indian Band Taxation Adv. Coun., 1992-96, mem., 1996-98; mem. B.C. Premier's Forum on New Opportunities for Working and Living, 1994-95; mem. compliance adv. com. Revenue Can. Taxation, 1997-99. Sr. scholar Oberlin Coll., 1967-68; NSF fellow, 1968-70; grantee U.S. Dept. Labor, 1971-72; leave fellow Can. Coun., (locat.) New Delhi, 1978-79; grantee Social Sci. and Humanities Rsch. Coun. Can., 1983-84, 90—; vis. fellow Australian Nat. U., Canberra, 1985; professorial fellow in econ. policy Res. Bank of Australia, 1985; recipient Doug Purvis award, Can. Econ. Assn., 1998. Mem. Am. Econ. Assn., Can. Econs. Assn., Can. Tax Found. (Douglas Sherbaniuk award 2002). Home: 4273 Musqueam Dr Vancouver BC Canada V6N 3R8 Office: U BC Dept Econs 997-1873 E Mall Vancouver BC Canada V6T 1Z1

KESSELRING, LINDA J. medical editor, writer; b. Waynesboro, Pa., Dec. 23, 1953; BA in Chemistry, Shippensburg U., 1975; MS in Profl. Writing, Towson U., 1994. Med. copy editor Harper & Row Pubs., Hagerstown, Md., 1975—81; editor Frederick Cancer Rsch. Facility Nat. Cancer Inst., Frederick, Md., 1981—84; tech. editor, writer Md. Inst. for Emergency Med. Svcs. Sys., Balt., 1984—94; tech. editor, writer emergency medicine U. Md. Sch. Medicine, Balt., 1994—. Mng. editor, TraumaCare Internat. Trauma Anesthesia and Critical Care Soc., Balt., 1988—. Mem.: Am. Med. Writers Assn. (mid-Atlantic chpt. pres. 1996—97), Coun. Sci. Editors, Bd. Editors in Life Scis. Office: Emergency Medicine U Md Sch Medicine 419 W Redwood St Ste 280 Baltimore MD 21201 Personal E-mail: lkessel112@aol.com.

KESSINGER, MARGARET ANNE, medical educator; b. Beckley, W.Va., June 4, 1941; d. Clisby Theodore and Margaret Anne (Ellison) K.; m. Loyd Ernst Wegner, Nov. 27, 1971. MA, W.Va. U., 1963, MD, 1967. Diplomate Am. Bd. Internal Medicine and Med. Oncology. Internal medicine house officer U. Nebr. Med. Ctr., Omaha, 1967-70, fellow med. oncology, 1970-72, asst. prof. internal medicine, 1972-77, assoc. prof., 1977-90, prof., 1990—, assoc. chief oncology hematology sect., 1988-91, chief oncology hematology sect., 1991-99; assoc. dir. clin. rsch. U. Nebr. Med. Ctr./Eppley Cancer Ctr., Omaha, 1999—. Contbr. articles to profl. publs. Fellow ACP, Am. Assn. Cancer Edn.; mem. Am. Soc. Clin. Oncology, Am. Assn. Cancer Rsch., Internat. Soc. Exptl. Hematology, Am. Soc. Hematology, Sigma Xi, Alpha Omega Alpha. Republican. Methodist. Avocations: aviation, gardening, canning, skiing. Office: U Nebr Med Ctr 987680 Nebraska Med Ctr Omaha NE 68198-0001 E-mail: makessin@unmc.edu.

KESSLER, A. D. business, financial, investment and real estate advisor, consultant, educator, lecturer, author, broadcaster, producer; b. N.Y.C., May 1, 1923; s. Morris William and Belle Miriam (Pastor) K.; m. Ruth Schwartz, Nov. 20, 1944 (div. 1974); children: Brian Lloyd, Judd Stuart, Earl Vaughn; m. Jaclyn Jeanne Sprague. Student U. Newark, 1940-41, Rutgers U., 1941-42, 46, Albright Coll., 1942, Newark Coll. Engring., 1946; PhD in Pub. Adminstrn. U. Fla., 1972; MBA, Kensington U., 1976, PhD in Mgmt. and Behavioral Psychology, 1977. Sr. cert. rev. appraiser; cert. bus. counselor; cert. exchanger; registered mortgage underwriter; registered investment advisor. Pvt. practice real estate, ins. and bus. brokerage, N.J., Pa., Fla., N.Y., Nev., Calif., Hong Kong, 1946—; pres. Armor Corp., 1947-68; pres. Folding Carton Corp., Am., N.Y.C., 1958-68; exec. v.p. Henry Schindall Assocs., N.Y.C., 1966-67; tax rep. Calif. State Bd. Equalization, 1968-69; aviation cons. transp. div. Calif., Dept. Aeros., also pub. info. officer; 1969-71; FAA Gen. Aviation Safety Counselor; broker, mgr. La Costa (Calif.) Sales Corp., 1971-75; chmn. bd. Profl. Ednl. Found., 1975—, Timeshare Resorts Internat., 1975—, Interex, Leucadia, Calif., 1975-82, The Kessler Orgn., Rancho Santa Fe, Calif., 1975—, The Kessler Fin. Group, Fin. Ind. Inst., 1977—; pres. Ednl. Video Inst., 1978—, Fin. Planning Inst., 1975—, Rancho Santa Fe Real Estate & Land, Inc., 1975—; treas., exec. bd. dirs. Nat. Challenge Com. on Disability, 1983-90; dir. Practice Mgmt. Cons. Abacus Data Systems, 1984—; broker mgr. Rancho Sante Fe Acreage & Homes, Inc., 1987-89; mktg. dir. Commercial Real Estate Services, Rancho Santa Fe, 1987—; cons. broker Glenct. Properties Ptnrs., 1989-90; dir. U.S. Advisors, 1989—; founder Creative Real Estate Movement, 1946—; pub., editor in chief Creative Real Estate Mag., 1975—; pub. Creative Real Estate Mag. of Australia and New Zealand; founder, editor Moderator of Tape of the Month Club; founder, producer, chmn. Internat. Real Estate Expo; chmn. bd. The Brain Trust, Rancho Santa Fe, Calif., 1977—; fin. lectr. for Internat. Cruise Ships, Cunard Line, Norwegian Am. Cruises, P&O, Princess, others; lectr. life enrichment and stress mgmt. Internat. Cruise Ships; Calif. adj. faculty, prof. fin. Clayton U., St. Louis; developer, operator Barnegat Baywood Seaplane Base, Barnegat Bay, N.J.; owner, operator Skyline Airport, Hunterdon County, N.J. Scoutmaster Orange Mountain coun. Boy Scouts Am., 1955-62; harbor master N.J. Marine Patrol, 1958-67; dep. sheriff, Essex County, N.J., 1951-65; mem. pres.' adv. bd. Seton Hall U., 1961-64; chmn. Stop Smoking, 1990, Quick Study, 1990; feature broadcaster/producer Kalaidascope Radio Mag., Am. Radio Network, 1990—. Served with USAF, 1942-45. Decorated D.F.C., Air medal, Purple Heart; named to French Legion of Honor, Order of Lafayette; named a flying col, a.d.c., Gov. of Ga., 1957. Mem. Am. Soc. Editors and Pubs., Author's Guild, Internat. Platform Assn., Nat. Speakers Assn., Nat. Press Photographers Assn., Guild Assn. Airport Execs., Aviation and Space Writers Assn., Nat. Assn. of Real Estate Editors, Internat. Exchangors Assn. (founder), Air Force Assn. (dep. comdr. N.J. chpt. 1955-57). Clubs: Nat. Press, Overseas Press, La Costa Country, Cuyamaca, Rancho Santa Fe Country, Passport. Lodges: Masons, Shriners. Author: A Fortune At Your Feet, 1981, How You Can Get Rich, Stay Rich and Enjoy Being Rich, 1981, Financial Independence, 1987, The Profit, 1987, A Fortune at Your Feet in the '90s, 1994, The Midas Touch, Turning Paper Into Gold, 1994; author, instr. Your Key to Success seminar, 1988, Your Key to Creative Real Estate Success tng. program, 1996; The A to Z of Lease Purchase and 11 Other Options Training Prog.; editor: The Real Estate News Observer, 1975—; fin. editor API, 1978—; fin. columnist Money Matters, 1986—; syndicated columnist, radio and TV host of "Money Making Ideas," 1977—; songwriter: Only You, 1939, If I'm Not HomeFor Christmas, 1940, Franny, 1940, Flajaloppa, 1940, They've Nothing More Dear Only They've Got It Here, 1941, The Summer of Life, 1956; producer (movies) The Flight of the Cobra, Rena, We Have Your Daughters, Music Row; speaker for radio and TV as The Real Estate Answerman, 1975—; host (radio and TV show) Ask Mr. Money; conceptualist, exec. prodr. (TV show) The Trading Game, 1994; exec. prodr., moderator (TV show) A.D. Kessler's Real Estate Roundtable, 1993—. Inventor swivel seat, siptop, inflatumbrella. Home: PO Box 1144 Rancho Santa Fe CA 92067-1144

KESSLER, ALAN CRAIG, lawyer; b. Washington, Sept. 16, 1950; s. Alfred Milton and Josephine (Taub) K.; m. Gail Elaine Strauss, June 16, 1974; children: Stacy Ilana, Mark Jay, Daniel Jordan. BA with honors, U. Del., 1972; JD with honors, U. Md., 1975. Bar: Pa. 1975, U.S. Dist. Ct. (ea. dist.) Pa. 1975, U.S. Ct. Appeals (3d and 6th cirs.) 1975. Assoc. Dilworth, Paxson, Kalish, Levy & Kauffman, Phila., 1975-77, Berger & Montague, P.C., Phila., 1977-81; ptnr. Mesirov, Gelman, Jaffe, Cramer & Jamieson, Phila., 1981-91, Buchanan Ingersoll, P.C., Phila., 1991-99, Wolf, Block, Schorr & Solis-Cohen, 1999—. Instr. Inst. for Paralegal Tng., Phila., 1977-96. Fin. com. Dem. City Com. Phila., 1981-84, dep. counsel, 1980-84; chmn. bd. Bldg. Stds. City of Phila., 1983-84, bd. licenses and inspections rev., 1984-91; mem. City Planning Commn., Phila., 1992-97, Presdl. Transition Team, 1992-93; commr. Lower Merion (Pa.) Twp., 1988-2000, Mayors Commn. Homelessness, 1990—, Mayors Com. on Spl. Svcs. Dist., 1989—; vice-chmn. Pres. Commn. on Risk Assessment and Risk Mgmt., 1993-97; bd. dirs., pres. Randolph Ct. Assn., Phila., 1980-85; bd. dirs., v.p. South St. Neighbors Assn., Phila., 1983-87, Park Towne Pl. Tenants Assn., 1977-79; bd. dirs. Support Ctr. for Child Advs., 1983-94, Phila. Indsl. Devel. Corp.; exec. com. Ctrl. Phila. Devel. Corp., 1989—, Jewish Employment Vocat. Svcs., 1989—, Phila. 2000.; chair Supreme Ct. of Pa. Commn. on CLE, 1999—; mng. trustee Dem. Nat. Com., 1992—, fin. vice-chair, 2000—; bd. govs. U.S. Postal Svc., 2000—. Mem. ABA, Pa. Bar Assn., Phila. Bar Assn. (exec. bd. dirs. young lawyers sect., legis. liaison com., officer various coms.), Racquet Club, Radnor Valley Country Club. Democrat. Jewish. Home: 204 Daisy Ln Wynnewood PA 19096-1654 Office: Wolf Block Schorr & Solis-Cohen 1650 Arch St Fl 22 Philadelphia PA 19103-2097 E-mail: akessler@wolfblack.com.

KESSLER, AVRAHAM ALBERT, economist, researcher; b. N.Y.C., Sept. 11, 1924; s. William Meyer Zeev and Gussie Golda (Laskin) K.; m. Naomi Lynfield, June 3, 1954; children: Shueli,Timnah. BS in Social Sci., CCNY, 1946; MA, U. Wis., 1948, PhD, 1968. Cons. Prime Ministers Office and Fin. Ministry, Jerusalem, Israel, 1950-53; external lectr. Hebrew U., Jerusalem, 1951-54; economist Econ. Adv. Staff Prime Ministers Office, Jerusalem, 1953-55; rsch. economist Falk Project for Econ. Rsch., Jerusalem, 1956-58; freelance econ. cons. Jerusalem, 1958-62; external lectr. Bar-Ilan U., Ramat, Gan, 1960-63; exec. dir. Assn. for Housing of the Aged, Jerusalem, 1977-83; exec. dir., chmn. Econ. Rsch. Corp., Ltd., Jerusalem, 1962—. Mem. various govt. commns. and adv. coms. Author: Israel's Cross-Section Terms of Trade, 1958, monograph Fundraising in European Jewish Communities, 1967, Research and Development Manpower in the 1990's, 1987; contbr. articles to profl. jours. With U.S. Army, 1943-46, ETO. Social Sci. Rsch. Coun. rsch. fellow, 1949-50; Nat. Coun. for Rsch. and Devel. grantee, 1987, 89-95. Mem. Am. Econ. Assn., Israel Econ. Assn., Soc. for Jewish Demography and Stats., Israel Gerontol. Assn., Israel Mgmt. Assn., Assn. Ams. and Cans. in Israel (nat. pres. 1965-67), Phi Beta Kappa. Avocations: talmud, bible study. Office: ECORES-Econ Rsch Corp Ltd PO Box 981 Jerusalem 91009 Israel

KESSLER, BERNARD MILTON, organizational and human resources development specialist; b. N.Y.C., Apr. 20, 1927; s. Irving and Yolanda (Michalovich) K.; m. Bernice Lubowsky, Dec. 26, 1948; children: Susan Beth, Mark David. BBA, CCNY, 1950; MA, NYU, 1966; PD, Fordham U., 1980; PhD, Columbia Pacific U., 1981. Cert. tchr., sch. adminstr. and supt. schs., N.Y. V.p. Al Paul Lefton Co., N.Y.C., 1950-65; elem. tchr. Greenburgh Dist. 8, Hartsdale, N.Y., 1965-67; mgr. edn. systems and services Olivetti Corp. Am., Hartsdale, 1967-71; dir. project redesign Mamaroneck (N.Y.) Pub. Schs., 1971-73; prin. Chatsworth Ave. Sch., Larchmont, N.Y., 1973-75; pres. Bernard M. Kessler Assocs., N.Y.C., 1971—; pres. exec. devel., counseling, tng. Beam Pines; exec. v.p., human resource counseling KLG Productivity Assn., Inc., N.Y.C. Cons. Xerox Corp., Stamford, Conn., 1972-73, HEW, 1970—, Citicorp, Inc., Comvestrix, Inc., 1980—, N.Y. Stock Exchange, Am. Stock Exchange, Beneficial Fin., Cigna, 1986—, ADP, Inc., 1986—, Linotype Corp., 1986—. Designer and producer packaged learning program Active Listening for Results, 1974, Stress Analysis and Control, 1983; contbr. articles to profl. jours. Chmn. bd. Artists for Environment Found., 1969-78, pres., 1978-81; past v.p. Lincoln State Acad. Store Front Sch. Served with USCGR, 1944-46. Mem. Am. Soc. Tng. and Devel. (Torch award 1979), N.Y. Acad. Scis., Orgn. Devel. Network, N.Y. Orgn. Devel. Network, Met. N.Y. Assn. Applied Psychology, Internat. Registry of Orgn. Devel. Profls., Phi Delta Kappa. Home and Office: 2213 Mohansic Ave Yorktown Heights NY 10598-3625 E-mail: bernie88@optonline.net.

KESSLER, DAVID A. dean, medical educator; b. N.Y.C., May 31, 1951; married; 2 children. BA, Amherst Coll., 1973; JD, U. Chgo., 1978; MD, Harvard U., 1979; APC, NYU Sch. Bus. Food and drug law Columbia U. Sch. of Law; med. dir. Einstein-Montefiore Hosp., N.Y.C.; commr. FDA Dept. Health and Human Svcs., Rockville, Md., 1990—97; dean Yale U. Med. Sch., 1997—. Prof. pediat. and pub. health Sch. Pub. Health, Yale U. Recipient Medal of Honor, ACS, 1996. Mem.: Inst. Medicine. Office: Deans Office 333 Cedar St New Haven CT 06510-3206

KESSLER, DIANE COOKSEY, religious organization administrator, minister; b. Jan. 8, 1947; BA in Religion, Oberlin Coll., 1969; MA in Religion and Soc., Andover Newton Theol. Sch., 1971, postgrad., 1979—; DD (hon.), Episcopal Divinity Sch., 2001. Ordained to ministry United Ch. of Christ, 1983. Assoc. dir. for strategy and action Mass. Coun. Chs., Boston, 1975-88, exec. dir., 1988—. Ind. preacher; speaker in field. Author: Parents and the Experts, 1974, God's Simple Gift: Meditations on Friendship and Spirituality, 1988; co-author Councils of Churches and the Ecumenical Vision, 2000; editor Together on the Way, 1999; co-editor Encounters for Unity, 1995; also articles; mem. editl. adv. bd. Theology and Pub. Policy, 1989, 98, Mid-Stream, 1995-98. Former mem. adv. bd. Mass. Dept. Revenue; active Wellesley Congl. Ch.; mem. coun. for ecumenism United Ch. of Christ, 1984-94, chairperson coun. 1988-89, 90-91; mem. Atty Gen.'s Adv. Com. on Pub. Charities, 1988—, World Coun. of Churches, Joint Working Group, 1998-2005; trustee Hancock Variable Series Trust I; bd. dirs. Howard Benevolent Soc., 1989-96, New Eng. Holocaust Meml. Com., 1st Ch. Legacy Fund. Recipient Outstanding Woman award Coll. Club, 1990, Focolare award, 1994, Social Action Ministries award, 1995, Patron of Christian Unity award, 1998. Mem. Valiant Woman award 1991), Boston Min.'s Club. Office: Mass Coun Chs 14 Beacon St Ste 416 Boston MA 02108-3704 E-mail: council@masscouncilofchurches.org.

KESSLER, DONALD JOE, research scientist, physicist, consultant; b. Houston, Jan. 30, 1940; s. Joseph Valentine and Mazie Irene (Doegen) Kessler; m. Mary Sue Cain, Dec. 31, 1969 (div. May 1978); m. Lynn Ellen Eddy, Jan. 24, 1990. BS in Physics, U. Houston, 1965. Meteroid scientist NASA, Houston, 1965-70, flight contr., 1970-74, atmospheric scientist, 1974-78, orbital debris rsch. developer, 1978-90, sr. scientist orbital debris, 1990-96; ret., 1996. Orbital debris and meteoroid cons., 1996—. Co-editor: Space Debris Jour., 1998—2002; founding editor:, 2002—, contbg. author: Orbital Debris: A Technical Assessment, 1995, Interagency Report on Orbital Debris, 1995; contbr. articles to profl. jours. With U.S. Army, 1958—61. Recipient NASA Medal for exceptional Sci. Achievement, 1989. Mem.: AIAA (Losey Atmospheric Sci. award 2000). Avocations: skiing, scuba diving. Home and Office: 25 Gardenwood Ln Asheville NC 28803

KESSLER, EDWIN, meteorology educator, consultant; b. Bklyn., Dec. 2, 1928; s. Edwin and Marie Rosa (Weil) K.; m. Lottie Catherine Menger; children: Austin Rainier, Thomas Russell. AB, Columbia Coll., 1950; MS in Meteorology, MIT, 1952, ScD in Meteorology, 1957. Chief synoptic meteorology sect. Weather Radar br. Air Force Cambridge Rsch. Lab., Bedford, Mass., 1954-61; sr. rsch. scientist Travelers Rsch. Ctr., Hartford, Conn., 1961-62, dir. atmospheric physics div., 1962-64; dir. Nat. Severe Storms Lab., Norman, Okla., 1964-86; adj. prof. U. Okla., 1964—. Vis. prof. MIT, 1975-76, McGill U., Can., 1980; bd. dirs. LINK, Norman, N.Am. Transp. Inst., Norman Area Land Conservancy, Inc., Norman chpt. LWV. Editor: Thunderstorms, A Social Scientific and Technological Documentary, 3 vols., 1982, 2d edits., 1983-88, paperback edits., vol. 1, 1988, vol. 2, 1992; contbr. over 250 reports, and about 100 peer-reviewed articles to profl. jours. State chair Common Cause, Okla., 1993-99, vice chair, 1999-. With U.S. Army, 1946-47. Recipient award for outstanding authorship NOAA, 1971 Fellow AAAS, Am. Meteorol. Soc. (nat. councilor 1966-69, past mem. coms. on hurricanes, atmospheric electricity, agr. and forestry, cloud and precipitation physics, severe local storms, past chmn. com. on weather radar, cert. cons. meteorologist, Cleveland Abbe award for disting. svc. 1988); mem. AIAA (sr. mem.), LWV, Royal Meteorol. Soc. (fgn.), Am. Geophys. Union, Sigma Xi. Achievements include research in agriculture and energy; manager of 350 acres of pasture, streams and wilderness in central Oklahoma. Office: U Okla 100 E Boyd St Rm 684 Norman OK 73019-1028 Fax: 405-360-3246. E-mail: kess3@swbell.net.

KESSLER, GLADYS, federal judge; b. 1938; BA, Cornell U., 1959; LLB, Harvard U., 1962. Staff atty. enforcement divsn. Nat. Labor Rels. Bd., 1962-64; legis. asst. Sen. Harrison A. Willians, N.J., 1964-66, Rep. Jonathan B. Bingham, 1966-68; staff atty. office labor rels N.Y.C. Bd. Edn., 1968-69; ptnr. Berlin, Roisman and Kessler (and successor firms), 1969-77; assoc. judge D.C. Superior Ct., 1977-94; judge U.S. Dist. Ct. D.C., Washington, 1994—. Asst. lectr. law sch. George Washington U., 1971-73; del. to judicial adminstrn. divsn. D.C. Superior Ct., 1985-90; mem. adv. bd. Ctr. for Dispute Settlement Inst. for Judicial Adminstrn., State Justice Inst., mem. adv. com. nat. judicial edn. project on domestic violence; mem BNA adv. bd. Alternative Dispute Resolution Report, 1987-90; mem. family law cirriculum planning com. Georgetown U.; lead judge permanency planning project Nat. Coun. Juvenile and Family Ct. Judges; chair Nat. Conf. on Bioethics, Family and the Law, D.C., 1991; mem. faculty Nat. Inst. Trial Advocacy; exec. com. Nat. ABA Jud. Divsn./Conf. of Federal Trial Judges, 1997-2000; with U.S. Jud. Conf. Com. on Ct. Adminstrn. and Mgmt., 1999. Contbr. articles to legal jours. Recipient Women Lawyer of Yr. award Women's Bar Assn., 1983, Svc. award D.C. Coalition Against Domestic Violence, 1987, Judicial Excellence award Trial Lawyers Assn. Washington, 1987. Fellow Am. Bar Found.; mem. ABA (judicial adminstrn. divsn., com. on bioethics and AIDS, adv. com. on youth, alcohol and drug problems, nat. adv. bd. on child support and criminal justice, individual rights and responsibilities sect.), Am. Judicature Soc. (bd. dirs. 1985-89), Nat. Assn. Women Judges (v.p. 1979-81, pres. 1981-82), Nat. Ctr. for State Cts. (bd. dirs. 1984-87), Women's Legal Def. Fund (founding pres. 1971), Women Judges' Fund. for Justice (bd. dirs. 1980—), Found. for Women Judges (pres. 1980-82). Office: US Courthouse 333 Constitution Ave NW Washington DC 20001-2802

KESSLER, HAROLD ALLAN, epidemiologist, hospital administrator; b. Chgo., Ill., June 11, 1949; s. Morton Paul and Shirley Rose Kessler; m. Andrea Ellen Rivkin, June 17, 1972; children: Jori Lyn Greenberg, Erin Michele, Adam Ross, Todd Jared. MD, Rush Med. Coll., 1974. Diplomate infectious disease Am. Bd. of Internal Medicine. Assoc. dir., sect. of infectious diseases Rush-Presbn.-St. Luke's Med. Ctr., Chgo., 1993—; assoc. dean, postgrad. med. edn. Rush Med. Coll., Chgo., 2000—. Fellow: ACP, Infectious Diseases Soc. Am. Office: Rush Med Coll Ste 143 AAF 600 S Paulina Northbrook IL 60062

KESSLER, HERBERT LEON, art historian, educator, university administrator; b. Chgo., July 20, 1941; s. Ben and Bertha K.; m. Johanna Zacharias, Apr. 24, 1976; 1 dau., Morisa. AB, U. Chgo., 1961; MFA, Princeton U., 1963, PhD, 1965. Asst. prof. U. Chgo., 1965-68; assoc. prof., 1968-73; prof., 1973-76; chmn. dept. art, univ. dir. fine arts, 1973-76; prof. Johns Hopkins U., Balt., 1976—, chair dept. art, 1976-89, 95-98. Guest prof. Bibliotheca Hertziana, Rome, 1996-97, dean Sch. Arts and Scis., 1998-99; vis. prof. Harvard U., 2000, Ecole des Hautes Etudes, 2000. Author: French and Flemish Illuminated Manuscripts, 1969, The Illustrated Bibles from Tours, 1977, The Cotton Genesis, 1986, The Dura Synagogue Frescoes and Christian Art, 1990, Studies in Pictorial Narrative, 1994, The Poetry and Paintings in the First Bible of Charles the Bald, 1997, The Holy Face and the paradox of Representation, 1998, Rome 1300: On the Path of the Pilgrim, 2000, Spiritual Seeing: Picturing God's Invisibility in the Middle Ages, 2000. Old St. Peter's and Ch. Decoration in medieval Italy, 2002. Sr. fellow Dumbarton Oaks, Washington, 1980-86; Woodrow Wilson fellow; Inst. Advanced Study fellow; Am. Council Learned Socs. fellow; Am. Philos. Soc. fellow; Guggenheim fellow; fellow Am. Acad. in Rome Fellow Medieval Acad. Am., Am. Acad. Arts and Scis.; mem. Coll. Art Assn., Phi Beta Kappa. Home: 3601 Greenway Apt 809 Baltimore MD 21218 Office: Johns Hopkins U Baltimore MD 21218 E-mail: hlk@jhu.edu.

KESSLER, IRVING ISAR, epidemiologist, consultant; AB in Math., NYU, 1952; MA in Endocrinology, Harvard U., 1955, PhD in Epidemiology, 1969; MD, Stanford U., 1960; MPH, Columbia U., 1962. Diplomate Nat. Bd. Med. Examiners, Am. Bd. Preventive Medicine; lic. physician Md. Prof. epidemiology Johns Hopkins U., 1972-84; chmn. dept. epidemiology and preventive medicine U. Md. Sch. Medicine, Balt., 1978-88; prof. oncology U. Md. Sch. Medicine Cancer Ctr., Balt., 1984—; prof. medicine U. Md. Sch. Medicine, Balt., 1985—, prof. dermatology, 1995—. Prof. dept. epidemiology & preventive medicine U. Md. Sch. Medicine, 1988-2001; emeritus, 2002-, exec. com. U. Md. Med. Sys., 1984-88; bd. dirs. Md. Med. Rsch. Inst.; v.p. for health scis., bd. dirs. ECRI, Plymouth Meeting, Pa., 1992-93; sci. advisory bd. Ctr. for Indoor Air Rsch., 1988—; mem. hazardous and toxic substances study commn., State of Md., 1983-84; cons. and lectr. in field. Bd. dirs. Israel Cancer Rsch. Found.; chmn. advisory panel on toxic shock syndrome AMA, 1984-85. Capt. USPHS res. Recipient Faculty Rsch. award Am. Cancer Soc. Fellow Am. Pub. Health Assn., Am. Coll. Preventive Medicine; mem. AAAS, Am. Epidemiol. Soc., Am. Assn. for Cancer Rsch., Am. Coll. Occupl. Medicine, N.Y. Acad. Sci., Md. Gerontological Assn. (founder, bd. dirs., chmn., program com., pres. 1984-85, Gerontology Recognition award 1989), D.A. Boyes Soc. Gynaecologic Oncology (hon.), Phi Beta Kappa, Soc. Sigma Xi. Office: 9-34 MSTP 10 S Pine St Baltimore MD 21201-1596 E-mail: ikessler@erols.com., ikessler@epi.umaryland.edu. *Epidemiology is the scientific discipline underlying preventive medicine which bridges the gap between medical science and human health. In an era of escalating health costs and diminishing faith in the medical care system, my professional career has been dedicated to the development of preventive medicine as an academic discipline and an instrument of public health policy. Of equal concern to me has the enhancement of preventive medicine as a rewarding career for the finest of our nation's young physicians. Unfortunately in recent years, epidemiologists have increasingly emphasized the statistical rather than biomedical significance of research findings, thereby rendering the field much less attractive to well-trained physicians concerned with the entiology and control of disease.*

KESSLER, JEFFREY L. lawyer; b. N.Y.C., Feb. 19, 1954; s. Milton M. and Edith H. Kessler; m. Regina T. Dessoff, May 21, 1977; children: Andrew Zalman, Leora Miriam. BA, JD summa cum laude, Columbia U., 1977. Bar: N.Y. 1978, U.S. Dist. Ct. (so. dist.) N.Y. 1978, U.S. Supreme Ct. 1985. Assoc. Weil, Gotshal & Manges, N.Y.C., 1977-85, ptnr., 1985—. Adj. assoc. prof. Fordham Law Sch., 1988—; founder, bd. advisors study pvt. antitrust litig. Georgetown U., 1983-85. Mem. editl. bd.: Columbia U. Law Rev., 1976—77, Competition Laws Outside the U.S., 2001—03, editor-in-chief: State Antitrust Practice Statutes, 1999; co-author: International Trade and U.S. Antitrust Law; contbr. articles to profl. jours. Kent scholar, 1975-76, Stone scholar, 1976-77. Mem. ABA (antitrust law sect., vice-chmn. Sherman Act Sect. 2 com. 1989-90, chmn. internat. law com. 1990-94, co-chmn. pub. com. 1994-96, coun. mem. 1996-99, internat. task force 2001-03), Columbia Coll. Alumni Assn. (bd. dirs. 1996-99), Phi Beta Kappa. Democrat. Jewish. Office: Dewey Ballantine LLP 1301 Avenue of the Americas New York NY 10019-6092 E-mail: JKessler@DeweyBallantine.com.

KESSLER, JOAN BLUMENSTEIN, lawyer; AB in English, U. Mich., 1967, PhD in Speech Communication, 1973; MA in Speech Communication, UCLA, 1969; JD, Loyola U., L.A., 1986. Bar: Calif 1987. Tchr., debate coach various pub. high schs., 1967-70; instr. dept. speech Monroe C.C., Rochester, N.Y., 1970-71; instr. communication and law Loyola U., Chgo., 1976, asst. prof., 1973-76; assoc. prof. dept. speech communication Calif. State U., Northridge, 1977-83; extern Calif. Ct. Appeal, 1985-86; assoc. Frandzel and Share, L.A., Calif., 1986-90, Gold, Marks, Ring and Pepper, 1990-93; shareholder Kessler & Kessler, A Law Corp., Century City, Calif., 1994—. Contbr. articles to profl jours. Mem advancement comt Univ Mich Grad Sch, 1992—; bd govs City of Hope, 1996—2000; bd dirs San Fernando Valley unit Am Cancer Soc, 1982—83; bd dirs, chair long-range planning comt St Vincent's Hosp Fund, 1990—. Office: Kessler & Kessler A Law Corp 2029 Century Park E Ste 1520 Los Angeles CA 90067-3002 Business E-mail: jkessler@kesslerandkessler.com.

KESSLER, JOAN F. lawyer; b. June 25, 1943; m. Frederick P. Kessler, Sept. 1967; 2 children. BA, U. Kans., 1961-65; postgrad., U. Wis., 1965-66; JD cum laude, Marquette U., 1968. Law clk. Hon. John W. Reynolds U.S. Dist. Ct. (ea. dist.) Wis., Milw., 1968-69; assoc. Warschafsky, Rotter & Tarnoff, Milw., 1969-71; pvt. practice Milw., 1971-74; assoc. Cook & Franke, S.C., Milw., 1974-78; U.S. atty. Eastern Dist. Wis., Milw., 1978-81; ptnr. Foley & Lardner, Milw., 1981—. Lectr. profl. responsibility U. Wis. Law Sch., Marquette U. Law Sch., Milw., 1994-96; mem. bd. govs. State Bar of Wis., 1985-89, 90-92, 93-95, chair, 1993, bd. dirs. family law sect., 1991-94; mem. Jud. Coun. Wis., Madison, 1989-92; mem. Milw. Bd. Attys. Profl. Responsibility, 1979-85. Bd. dirs. Legal Aid Soc., 1974-78, v.p., 1978, Urban League, 1980-82, Women's Bus. Initiative Corp., 1989-91, Girl Scouts U.S., Milw., 1994-96; bd. dirs., pres. Voters for Choice in Wis., 1989-93. Fellow Am. Matrimonial Lawyers (bd. govs. 1990-96, v.p. 1996-99), Am. Law Inst., Am. Bar Found.; mem. ACLU (Best Lawyers in Am. 1993-98). Office: Foley & Lardner 777 E Wisconsin Ave Ste 3800 Milwaukee WI 53202-5367

KESSLER, JOHN ALLEN, physician, biomedical researcher; b. Phila., Dec. 5, 1946; s. Irving Kenneth and Bettina (Chertcoff) K.; m. Marilyn Jean Cozzens, Apr. 14, 1972; children: Eric, Justin, Timothy, Allison. AB, Princeton U., 1967; MD, Cornell U., 1971. Med. intern and resident Mt. Sinai Hosp., N.Y.C., 1971-73; rsch. fellow NIH, Bethesda, Md., 1973-75; resident in neurology N.Y. Hosp./Cornell Med. Ctr., N.Y.C., 1975-78; from asst. prof. to assoc. prof. Cornell U. Med. Coll., N.Y.C., 1978-83; assoc. prof. neurology Albert Einstein Coll. Medicine, Bronx, N.Y., 1983-86, prof. neurology, 1986—, Alper chair neurology, 1993, dir. Rose Kennedy Ctr., 1993-98. Boshes Prof. and chmn. neurology dept. Nortwestern U. Med. Sch., 2000—; dir. Feinberg Neurosci. Inst., 2000—; chmn. dept. neurology Jacobi/North Bronx Network, 1997-2000; mem. NIH Study Sect., 1993-96; chmn. adv. com. March of Dimes, 1999—; mem. numerous adv. panels, 2000—. Contbr. more than 150 articles to profl. jours.; patentee in field. Past pres. Stamford (Conn.) Little League. Lt. comdr. USCG/USN, 1973-75. Recipient Polk Rsch. prize Cornell U. Med. Coll., Cotzius award Cerebral Palsy Assn. Office: Northwestern Univ Med Sch 303 E Chicago Ave Chicago IL 60611 E-mail: JAKessler@Northwestern.edu.

KESSLER, JOHN PAUL, JR., financial planner; b. Bronxville, N.Y., Sept. 4, 1946; s. John Paul and Helen Claire (Hopper) K. BBA in Fin., Tex. Tech. U., 1965-71. CFP; registered investment advisor. Agt. Met. Life Ins. Co., Lubbock, Tex., 1970-73; pension trust adminstr. Rep. Nat. Life, Dallas, 1973-78, Am. Founders Life, Austin, 1979-81; acct. for state appropriations Tex. State Comptr., Austin, 1981-84; fin. planner J. Paul Kessler & Assocs., Dallas, 1984-95, Kessler Fin. Assocs., Dallas, 1995—. Pension cons. Kessler Fin. Group, Dallas, 1984—. Mem. Am. Mgmt. Assn., Dallas Estate Planning Coun., Dallas Benefit Soc., Nat. Assn. Securities Dealers (registered rep.), Tex. Tech Alumni Assn., McKinney C. of C. Republican. Presbyterian. Avocations: golf, travel. Office: Kessler Fin Assocs PO Box 2382 Mc Kinney TX 75070-1860

KESSLER, JUDD LEWIS, lawyer; b. Newark, Apr. 10, 1938; s. Samuel W. and Ethel S. (Shapiro) K.; m. Marian Osterweis, Jan. 7, 1979 (div. 1986); m. Carol Ann Farris, Oct. 19, 1987; 1 child, Samuel Farris. AB, Oberlin Coll., 1960; LLB, Harvard U., 1963. Bar: N.J. 1963, D.C. 1972, Md. 1989, U.S. Dist. Ct. N.J., U.S. Dist. Ct. D.C., U.S. Dist. Ct. Md., U.S. Ct. Appeals (4th cir.), U.S. Supreme Ct. 1968. Assoc. Toner, Crowley, Woelper and Vanderbilt, Newark, 1963-66; asst. gen. counsel U.S. Agy. for Internat. Devel., Washington, 1966-82; ptnr., chmn. internat. bus. practice group Porter, Wright, Morris & Arthur, Washington, 1982—. Author: (with others) Legal Aspects of Exporting, 1986; contbr. articles to profl. jours. Bd. dirs. Congregation Har Shalom, Potomac, Md., 1998-2001. Recipient Outstanding Career Achievement award U.S. Agy for Internat. Devel. 1982; named Presdl. Appointment to Sr. Fgn. Svc., 1982. Master: London Court Internat. Arbitration; mem.: ABA, Fed. Bar Assn. (chmn. internat. sect. 1983—87, nat. coord. Export Legal Assistance Network 1985—, Pres.'s E Excellence Export Svc. award 1997), Am. Soc. Internat. Law, Internat. C. of C. (mem. U.S. arbitration com. 2000), Inter-Am. Bar Found. (pres. 1994—), Inter-Am. Bar Assn., Am. Arbitration Assn. (mem. internat. panel arbitrators 1997—), Cosmos Club. Office: Porter Wright Morris & Arthur 1919 Penn Ave NW Washington DC 20006-3434

KESSLER, KEITH LEON, lawyer; b. Seattle, July 18, 1947; s. Robert Lawrence and Priscilla Ellen (Allbee) K.; m. Lynn Elizabeth Eisen, Dec. 24, 1980; children: William Moore, Christopher Moore, Bradley Moore, Jamie Kessler. BA in Philosophy, U. Wash., 1969, JD, 1972. Bar: Wash. 1972, U.S. Dist. Ct. (we. dist.) Wash. 1973, U.S. Dist. Ct. (ea. dist. 1992); U.S. Ct. Appeals (9th cir.) 1973, U.S. Supreme Ct. 1975. Law clk. to Hon. Robert Finley Wash. Supreme Ct., Olympia, Wash., 1972-73; ptnr. Kessler, Tegland & Urmston, Seattle, 1973-75, Kessler & Urmston, Seattle, 1975-76, Kessler, Urmston & Sever, Seattle, 1976-77, Kessler & Sever, Seattle, 1977-79; assoc. Stritmatter & Stritmatter, Hoquiam, Wash., 1980-83; ptnr. Stritmatter, Kessler & McCauley, Hoquiam, Wash., 1983-93, Stritmatter Kessler, Hoquiam, Wash., 1993-97, Stritmatter, Kessler, Whelan, Withey, Hoquiam, 1997—. Chmn. LAW PAC, Seattle, 1991-93; mem. pattern jury instrns. com. Wash. Supreme Ct., 2000—. Editor: Trial Evidence, 1996, author: (with others) Motor Vehicle Accident Litigation Desk Book, 1988, 1995, 97; contbr. chpt. to book. Pres. Kairos Ctr., Aberdeen, Wash., 1984-86; co-founder Grays Harbor Support Group; bd. dir. Wash. State Head Injury Found., Bellevue, Wash., 1993-96. Recipient Founders award Wash. State Head Injury Found., 1990, Silver award United Way, 1992 Mem. Am. Bd. Trial Advocates, (pres. Wash. chpt. 1997), Wash. State Trial Lawyers Assn. (pres. 1990-91, named trial lawyer of yr., 1994), Damage Attys. Round Table (pres. 2002-03), Wash. Trial Attys. Political Forum (chmn. 1993-95), Wash. Def. Trial Lawyers (named Outstanding Plaintiff Trial Lawyer 2002), Trial Lawyers for Public Justice (state exec. com. 1994—). Office: Stritmatter Kessler Whelan Withey 413 8th St Hoquiam WA 98550-3607 E-mail: keith@skww.com.

KESSLER, KENDALL SEAY FERIOZI, artist; b. Washington, Nov. 4, 1954; d. Dan John and Anne Fletcher (Trotter) Feriozi; m. Clyde Thomas Kessler, June 25, 1977; 1 child, Alan. BA in Art Edn., Va. Poly. Inst. and State U., 1976; MFA in Painting and Printmaking, Radford U., 1983. Tchr. art, Spanish Cherrydale Christian Sch., Arlington, Va., 1976-77; tchr. community arts sch. Radford (Va.) U., 1980-82, adminstr., 1982-83; tchr. art Fine Arts Ctr., Pulaski, Va., 1984; instr. art Radford U., 1985-87, 88-93, interim gallery dir., 1987-88, asst. prof. art, 2000—; freelance profl. artist, tchr. Radford, 1993—. Illustrator (poetry books) Shooting Creek, 1982, Dancing at Big Vein, 1987, Preservations, 1989; book jacket illustrator: The Rosewood Casket by Sharon McCrumb, 1996; exhibited in group shows Agora Gallery, Soho, N.Y., 1994, 95; exhibited and represented by Studios on the Sq., Roanoke, Va., Fine Art Ctr. for the New River Valley, Pulaski, Va., Somerhill, Chapel Hill, N.C., Art Pannonia, Blacksburg, Va., New River Valley Mall, Christiansburg, Va. Officer PEO Sisterhood, Radford, 1992-94, mem., 1989—; mem. Lamplighters, Radford Pub. Libr., 1991—. Recipient Am. Artist award Pastel Soc. West Coast 4th Nat. Exhibit, Sacramento, Daniel Greene 1st place award for oils Paris (Tex.) Art Fair, 1991, Best in Show award Fincastle (Va.) Arts Festival, 1997. Mem. Nat. Mus. Women in Arts, Blacksburg Regional Art Assn., Lynwood Artists, Piedmont Arts Assn. Avocations: theatre, literature, music, skating. Home: PO Box 3612 Radford VA 24143-3612 Business E-Mail: kkessler@radford.edu.

KESSLER, LAWRENCE W. law educator, lawyer; b. N.Y.C., Sept. 28, 1942; s. Leo and Agatha (Welsch) K.; m. Bonnie B. Blankfeld, June 25, 1968; children— Brett, Nicholas. B.A., Columbia Coll., 1964, J.D., 1967. Bar: N.Y. 1967, Ohio 1974, U.S. Ct. Appeals (2d cir.) 1968, U.S. Dist. Ct. (so. and ea. dists.) N.Y., 1968. Law clk. U.S. Dist. Ct., N.Y.C., 1967-68; trial counsel Fed. Defender div. N.Y. Legal Aid Soc., N.Y.C., 1968-71; assoc. prof. law U. Cin. Coll. Law, 1971-74; assoc. prof. Hofstra Law Sch., Hempstead, N.Y., 1974-80, prof. law, 1980— ; dir. Hofstra Trial Techniques Program; asst. team leader Northwest Regional Intensive Program in Trial Advocacy, Ithaca, N.Y., 1977-78, team leader, Hempstead, 1979, 80, 81, co-dir., team leader, 1982, 83, 84, 85, team mem., Gainsville, Fla., 1980, Cambridge, Mass., 1985. Contbr. articles to profl. jours. Bd. dirs. Ednl. Assistance Ctr. of Long Island, Nassau, N.Y., 1982—, Long Island Advocacy Ctr., 1984— ; chmn. Tri-State Air Com., Cin., 1974; vice chmn. Cin. Environ. Task Force, 1972-73. Home: 100 Country Club Dr Port Washington NY 11050-4551 Office: Hofstra Law Sch 1000 Hempstead Tpke Uniondale NY 11553-1113

KESSLER, LEONA HANOVER, interior designer; b. Phila., Sept. 15, 1925; d. Herman and Ida (Gleaner) Hanover; m. Sydney Kessler, Aug. 28, 1948; children: Andrew Louis, Todd Hanover. BS in Textile Engring., Phila. U., 1948. Pvt. practice interior design and cons. Lee Kessler Interiors, Phila., 1957—. Textile designer, stylist, color cons.; mem. faculty Moore Coll. Art, 1970-72, Art Inst. Phila., 1973-78, Phila. Coll. Textiles and Sci., 1978-81; juror textile design and interior design; works exhibited designer showcases, local house tours, faculty shows. Author: That Which Was Once a Warp, 1971; contbr. articles and photographs to mags. and newspapers. Recipient Graham W. Littlewood III Outstanding Alumna award Phila. Coll. Textiles Sci., 1998, Sara Tyler Wister scholar; named Alumnus of Month, Textile Engr., 1971. Mem. Am. Soc. Interior Designers (dir. Pa. East chpt. 1967-78, chpt. recognition awards 1974, 80, Nat. Medalist award 1988). Address: 101 Hawthorne Ct Wyomissing PA 19610-1028

KESSLER, LINDA JOAN, artist, educator; b. Bklyn., Aug. 20, 1954; d. Irving and Irene Kessler. BA, Bklyn. Coll., 1975; student, Art Students League, N.Y.C., 1980-88; MFA, Pratt Inst., N.Y.C., 1997. Owner, photographer Focus Pocus Children's Photography, Bklyn. Heights, 1997—; art tchr. Bklyn. Coll. Acad., 2000—. Artist in residence Niangua Art Colony, Stoutland, Mo., 1986; presenter in field. Exhbns. include Lever House, 1965, Union League Club, N.Y.C., 1988, Salmagundi Club, 1989, 90, Belanthi Gallery, Bklyn., 1989, 90, 91, Helio Gallery, N.Y.C., 1989, Recipient Best in Show award Micro/Macro Exhbn., Helio Gallery, N.Y.C., 1989. Mem.: Nat. Assn. Woman Artists (Ada Cecere Meml. award 1994, Hazel Witte Meml. award 1995), N.Y. Artists Equity, Am. Soc. Media Photographers. Avocations: travel, yoga, bicycle riding, dancing, camping. Home: 54 Orange St Brooklyn NY 11201 E-mail: lkessler@focuspocusphoto.com.

KESSLER, LYNN ELIZABETH, state legislator; b. Seattle, Feb. 26, 1941; d. John Mathew and Kathryn Eisen; m. Keith L. Kessler, Dec. 24, 1980; children: William John Moore, Christopher Scott Moore, Bradley Jerome Moore, Jamie. Attended, Seattle U., 1958-59. Mem. Wash. Ho. of Reps., 1993—. Majority leader, mem. rules com., mem. appropriations com. Exec. dir. United Way Grays Harbor, 1984-92; mem. adv. coun. Head Start, 1986-89, Cervical Cancer Awareness Task Force, 1990-91, vocat. adv. coun. Hoquiam High Sch., 1991—, strategic planning com. Grays Harbor Community Hosp., 1991-92, Grays Harbor Food Bank Com., 1991-92, Grays Harbor Dem. Ctrl. Com.; vice-chair Grays Harbor County Shorelines Mgmt. Bd., 1988-90; chair Disability Awareness Com., 1988-90, Youth 2000 Com., 1990-91; pres. Teenage Pregnancy, Parenting and Prevention Adv. Coun., 1989-91; v.p. Grays Harbor Econ. Devel. Coun., 1990-92; trustee Grays Harbor Coll., 1991-2001, Aberdeen YMCA, 1991—. Mem. Aberdeen Rotary (pres. 1993-94). Home: 62 Kessler Ln Hoquiam WA 98550-9742 Office: Wash Ho of Reps Legislative Bldg 3rd Fl Olympia WA 98504-0001

KESSLER, LYNNE MARIE, secondary education educator; b. Chippewa Falls, Wis., July 19, 1946; d. Elza Eugene and Rosemarie Joslyn Grove; m. Gerald William Kessler, Nov. 25, 1966; children: Scott, Kathy, Eric. BS in Edn., Ea. Ill. U., 1969. Cert. secondary edn. tchr. Tchr. Effingham H.S., 1970-84, Effingham (Ill.) Jr. H.S., 1984—. Coach Scholar Bowl, Effingham, 1997—. Methodist. Avocations: cross stitching, flower gardening, sewing. Office: Effingham Jr HS 600 S Henrietta Effingham IL 62401-4440

KESSLER, MARK ALLEN, political scientist, educator; b. McKeesport, Pa., Jan. 3, 1955; s. Robert and Rae (Alpern) K.; m. Stephanie Weko, Aug. 14, 1983. BA, U. Pitts., 1977; MA, Pa. State U., 1979, PhD, 1985. Prof. politi. sci. Bates Coll., Lewiston, Maine, 1983—, chair polit. sci., 1993-97, chair divsn. social sci., 2000—. Author: Legal Services for the Poor, 1987; co-author: The Play of Power, 1996; contbr. articles to profl. jours. NSF grantee, 1981. Mem.: Law and Soc. Assn., Am. Judicature Soc., Am. Polit. Sci. Assn. Democrat. Jewish. Home: 241 5th St Providence RI 02906-3763 Office: Bates Coll 174 Pettingill St Lewiston ME 04240-5324 E-mail: mkessler@bates.edu.

KESSLER, MICHAEL GEORGE, forensic accountant; b. Bklyn., Dec. 31, 1951; s. Anthony and Mildred Kessler; children: Jonathan, Timothy. AA, St. Johns U., Jamaica, N.Y., 1971, BS, 1973, MBA, 1978; cert. advanced grad. study, Pace U., 1980. Diplomate Am. Bd. Forensic Accts.; cert. tchr., N.Y., fraud examiner, internat. investigator, forensic acct. Cash control officer R.H. Macy's, N.Y.C., 1969-73; sr. auditor Blue Cross-Blue Shield Greater N.Y., N.Y.C., 1973-78; prin. spl. audit investigator N.Y. State Atty. Gen., N.Y.C., 1978-81, regional chief auditor investigator, 1981-83, asst. chief auditor investigator, statewide tng. officer, 1983-87; chief investigations N.Y. State Tax and Fin., 1987-88; dep. insp. gen. Met. Transp. Authority, 1988; pres. Kessler Internat., N.Y.C. Contbg. author HEW audit manual; author: Kessler Report; contbr. articles to profl. jours. Recipient Spl. Recognition award for unique achievement and svc., N.Y.C. Mem. Am. Soc. Indsl. Security, Nat. Law Enforcement Assocs., Am. Coll. Forensic Examiners, Assn. Cert. Fraud Examiners. Office: Kessler Internat 45 Rockefeller Plz Ste 2000 New York NY 10111-2000 E-mail: mkessler@investigation.com.

KESSLER, RICHARD J. psychiatrist; b. Bklyn., Feb. 3, 1948; s. Nathan and Harriet (Fleischman) K.; m. Luba Nowik; children: Rachel A., Lena S. BA, Alfred U., 1968; DO, U. Osteo. Med. & Health Scis., Des Moines, 1972. Diplomate Am. Bd. Psychiatry & Neurology. Staff psychiatrist, fellowship dir. L.I. Jewish Med. Ctr., Glen Oaks, N.Y., 1976-94; dir. psychiat. svcs., med. dir. Adults and Children with Learning and Devel. Disabilities, Bethpage, N.Y., 1994—. Med. dir. Oceanside (N.Y.) Counseling Ctr., 1983-94; pvt. practice, Roslyn, N.Y., 1975—; asst. clin. prof. Albert Einstein Coll. Medicine. Fellow Am. Psychiat. Assn.; mem. Am. Psychoanalytic Assn., Nassau Psychiat. Soc. (pres. 1990). Avocations: sports, theater, reading, food and wine. Office: ACLD 807 S Oyster Bay Rd Bethpage NY 11714-1000

KESSLER, RICHARD PAUL, JR., lawyer; b. Latrobe, Pa., July 11, 1945; s. Richard Paul Sr. and Dorothy Henrietta (Comp) K.; m. Kathleen Jane Parker, June 17, 1973 (dec. May 11, 1996); 1 child, Grace Elizabeth; m. Susan Kessler, Oct. 2000. BA, Fairfield (Conn.) U., 1968; JD, Emory U., 1971. Bar: Ga. 1971, U.S. Dist. Ct. (no. dist.) Ga. 1973, U.S. Ct. Appeals (5th cir.) 1974, U.S. Ct. Appeals (11th cir.) 1981, U.S. Supreme Ct. 1995. Law clk. to presiding justice U.S. Dist. Ct. (no. dist.) Ga., 1971-73; ptnr. Macey, Wilensky, Cohen, Wittner & Kessler, LLP, Atlanta, 1973—. Lectr. Practising Law Inst., 1981, 83, Fin. Svc. Corp. Career Conf., Atlanta, 1986, Ga. and Ala. Insts. of Continuing Legal Edn., 1993-95; panelist Credit Union Nat. Assn., Inc. League Attys. Conf., 1980-82, 87, 88-93, ABA, 1990-91; participant Nat. Conf. Commrs. on Uniform State Laws Drafting Com. on U.C.C. Articles, 3, 4, 4A, 1985-90; chair corp. and banking law sect. State Bar Ga., 1995-96. Author: What You Should Know About the New Bankruptcy Code, 1979, Guide to the Bankruptcy Laws: The Bankruptcy Reform Act of 1978, 79, Guide to the Bankruptcy Laws: The Bankruptcy Reform Act of 1978 (Bankruptcy Code) as Amended by the Bankruptcy Amendments and Federal Judgeship Act of 1984, The Bankruptcy Judges, U.S. Trustees and Family Farmer Bankruptcy Act of 1986; contbr. articles to profl. jours. Mem.: East Lake Golf Club. Office: Ste 600 285 Peachtree Center Ave NE Atlanta GA 30303-1229 E-mail: rkessler@maceywilensky.com.

KESSLER, ROBERT ALLEN, data processing executive; b. N.Y.C., Feb. 2, 1940; s. Henry and Caroline Catherine (Axinger) K.; m. Marie Therese Anton, Mar. 17, 1967; children: Susanne, Mark. BA in Math., CUNY, 1961; postgrad., UCLA, 1963-64. EDP analyst Boeing Aircraft, Seattle, 1961-62; computer specialist System Devel. Corp., Santa Monica, Calif., 1962-66; mem. tech. staff Computer Scis. Corp., El Segundo, Calif., 1966-67, sr. mem. tech. staff, 1971-72, computer scientist, 1974-81; systems mgr. Xerox Data Systems, L.A., 1967-71; prin. scientist Digital Resources, Algiers, Algeria, 1972-74; sr. systems cons. Atlantic Richfield, L.A., 1981-94; computer cons., 1994—. Mem. Big. Bros. L.A., 1962-66; precinct capt. Goldwater for Pres., Santa Monica, 1964; mem. L.A. Conservancy, 1987. Mem. Assn. Computing Machinery. Avocations: racquetball, theatre, gourmet dining. Home: 6138 W 75th Pl Los Angeles CA 90045-1634 Office: Pfizer Health Solutions 2400 Broadway Santa Monica CA 90404-3030 E-mail: kesslb1@pfizer.com.

KESSLER, RONALD, author; b. N.Y.C., Dec. 31, 1943; s. Ernest Borek and Minuetta K.; m. Pamela Johnson Whitehead; children: Greg, Rachel Kessler. Student, Clark U., Worcester, Mass., 1962-64. Reporter Worcester Telegram, 1964; reporter, editorial writer Boston Herald, 1964-68; N.Y. bur. reporter Wall Street Jour., 1968-70; investigative reporter Washington Post, 1970-85; journalist/author, 1985—. Author: The Life Insurance Game, 1985, The Richest Man in the World: The Story of Adnan Khashoggi, 1986, Spy vs. Spy: Stalking Soviet Spies in America, 1988, Moscow Station: How the KGB Penetrated the American Embassy, 1989, The Spy in the Russian Club: How Glenn Souther Stole America's Nuclear War Plans and Escaped to Moscow, 1990, Escape from the CIA: How the CIA Won and Lost the Most Important KGB Spy Ever to Defect to the U.S., 1991, Inside the CIA: Revealing the Secrets of the World's Most Powerful Spy Agency, 1992, The FBI: Inside the World's Most Powerful Law Enforcement Agency, 1993, Inside the White House: The Hidden Lives of the Presidents and the Secrets of the World's Most Powerful Institution, 1995, The Sins of the Father: Joseph P. Kennedy and the Dynasty He Founded, 1996, Inside Congress: The Shocking Scandals, Corruption, and Abuse of Power Behind the Scenes on Capitol Hill, 1997, The Season: Inside Palm Beach and America's Richest Society, 1999 (basis for A&E TV prodn.), The Bureau: The Secret History of the FBI, 2002, The CIA at War: Inside the Secret Campaign Against Terror, 2003; contbr.: Microsoft Encarta Encyclopedia. Recipient public affairs reporting award Am. Polit. Sci. Assn., 1965; citation Freedoms Found., 1966; 1st prize in newswriting UPI, 1967; Sevellon Brown Meml. award AP, 1967; sci. writers award ADA, 1968; 1st place in public service award Md.-Del.-D.C. Press Assn., 1972; outstanding series award AAUW, 1972; Bill Pryor Meml. Reporting award, 1973; Front Page award Washington-Balt. Newspaper Guild, 1973; George H. Polk Meml. award for community service, 1973; for nat. reporting, 1979; Washington Dateline award for bus. reporting Sigma Delta Chi-Soc. Profl. Journalists, 1987; 1st pl. in investigative reporting Assn. Area Bus. Publs., 1987; named Washingtonian of Yr. Washington Mag., 1972; Dow Jones Inc Newspaper Fund intern, 1964. Home and Office: 2516 Stratton Dr Potomac MD 20854-6231 E-mail: KesslerRonald@cs.com.

KESSLER, ROSLYN MARIE, financial analyst; b. Bloomington, Ind., Dec. 5, 1953; d. Ivan Gordon and Carmen Karina (Babbensingh) Samuels; m. Terrance Jude Kessler, Mar. 19, 1982 (div. Mar. 19, 1993); 1 child, Jude. BS in Acctg., SUNY, Albany, 1990; MBA in Fin., U. Rochester, 1994. CPA, N.Y.; cert. mgmt. acct., internal auditor, fin. mgr.; accredited purchasing practitioner. Staff tax acct., auditor Arthur Andersen & Co., Rochester, N.Y., 1990-92; pvt. practice Rochester, N.Y., 1992; fin. analyst Xerox Corp., Rochester, N.Y., 1993-2000; tech. mgr. Am. Inst. Cert. Pub. Accts., N.Y.C., 2000—03, Hubbell Corp., Orange, Conn., 2003—. Grad. tchg. asst. acctg., 1992-94; William E. Simon Grad. Sch. Bus. Adminstrn. scholar, 1992-94, Glenbrook Neighborhood Assn., 2001-. Legis. chair PTA, Winslow Elem. Sch., 1991-92, PTA Brighton H.S., 1996-2000; com. mem. Boy Scouts Am., Rochester, 1991-92; vol. Wesley-on-East Nursing Home, Rochester, 1992-95. Mem. AICPA, Am. Fin. Assn., Inst. Cert. Mgmt. Accts., N.Y. Assn. CPA Candidates (dir. 1991-92, pres. 1992-93), Conn. Soc. CPAs., Inst. Internal Auditors. Avocations: bicycling, statistics, futures/options.

KESSLER, SEYMOUR, clinical psychologist, consultant; b. N.Y.C., Sept. 3, 1928; s. William and Gussie Kessler; m. Hilda Kessler, Oct. 17, 1953; children: Chanan Elliot, Zev Arturo. BS, CCNY, 1960; PhD, Columbia U., 1965, The Wright Inst., Berkeley, Calif., 1977. Lic. clin. psychologist, Calif.; diplomate Am. Bd. Med. Genetics. Rsch. assoc. dept. psychiatry Stanford (Calif.) U. Sch. Medicine, 1965-67, sr. scientist, adj. prof. dept. psychiatry, 1967-75; dir. genetic counseling program Health and Med. Scis., U. Calif., Berkeley, 1975-85, assoc. clin. prof. dept. pediats., 1986—. Author: Heart Bypass, 1995; author, editor: Genetic Counseling: Psychological Dimensions, 1979; co-author: Psyche and Helix, 2000. Mem. Alameda County Grand Jury, 1998-99. Mem. Huntington's Soc. Am. (bd. dirs. No. Calif. chpt. 1980-90). Avocations: music, playing the cello. Home: 770 Hilldale Ave Berkeley CA 94708-1318 Office: PO Box 7702 Berkeley CA 94707-0702

KESSLER, STEPHEN JAMES, writer, editor; b. L.A., Jan. 12, 1947; s. Jack and Nina (Ifland) K.; 1 child, Claire Kessler-Bradner. BA, Bard Coll., 1968; MA, U. Calif., Santa Cruz, 1969. Editor Green Horse Press, Santa Cruz, 1973-79; editor, pub. Alcatraz Edits., Santa Cruz, 1979-85, The Sun, Santa Cruz, 1986-89; editor The Redwood Coast Rev., Gualala, Calif., 1999—; freelance poet, translator, essayist, journalist, 1972—. Author: (translation) Save Twilight, 1997, (poems) After Modigliani, 2000, (poems) Tell It to the Rabbis, 2001; editor mag./anthology Alcatraz, 1979-85; contbr. essays to Poetry Flash, 1985-98.

KESSLER, STEVEN FISHER, lawyer; b. McKeesport, Pa., June 29, 1951; s. Robert and Rae (Alpern) K.; children: Matthew, Katie. BA, U. Pitts., 1973, JD, 1976. Bar: Pa. 1976, U.S. Dist. Ct. (we. dist.) Pa. 1976. Staff atty. Neighborhood Legal Services, McKeesport, Pa., 1976-79; solicitor City of McKeesport, 1980-82; sole practice, McKeesport, 1982—; solicitor McKeesport Housing Corp., 1985—; chmn. bd. dirs. McKeesport Devel. Corp., 1984—. Mem. Am. Arbitration Assn. (panel arbitrators 1981—). Democrat. Home: 1337 Foxwood Dr Monroeville PA 15146-4436 Office: 332 5th Ave Mc Keesport PA 15132-2616

KESSLER, WALLACE FRANK, school director, tour developer; b. Mar. 22, 1938; m. Susan Carol Morse, June 20, 1969 (div. Nov. 1972). BA, U. Vt., Burlington, 1959, postgrad., 1963. Cert. secondary tchr., Vt. Founder, cultural program tchr. Cutler Acad., Craftsbury, Vt., 1959-63; founder outdoor program, English dept. The Stowe (Vt.) Sch., 1963-66; asst. to headmaster, tchr. Pine Ridge Sch., Williston, Vt., 1967-71; dean of students Middlesex Coll., Stowe, 1966; founder, operator Introspect Sch., Stowe, 1972-85; headmaster Vt. Land and Sea Sch., Springfield, 1985-86; mgr. Tauck Tours, Westport, Conn., 1987—; founder, Walrus Tours Youth World Camps, Balt., 1986—; founder St. Stephen's Sch., Austin, Tex., 1996—. Mem. scis. selection com. Vt. Acad. Arts, Montpelier, 1966-68. Avocations: bicycling, hiking, basketball, literature, conservation. Office: Youth World Camps 222 Milford Mill Rd Baltimore MD 21208 Home: 1201 Robert E Lee R Austin TX 78704

KESSLER, WILLIAM EUGENE, health care executive; b. St. Louis, Dec. 15, 1944; s. Joseph John and Margaret Mary (Burns) K.; m. Patricia Christine Wilson, Nov. 9, 1968; children: Christina, William, John, Timothy, Jennifer, Catherine, Joseph, Daniel. BS in Commerce, St. Louis U., 1966, MHA, 1968. Various positions St. John's Hosp., St. Louis, 1963-67; adminstrv. resident St. Mary's Hosp., Grand Rapids, Mich., 1967-68; pres. St. Anthony's Health Ctr., Alton, Ill., 1971—. Chmn., prof. and tech. adv. com. Joint Commn. on Accreditation Healthcare Orgn., 1990-94; speaker profl. and community settings, 1972—; preceptor St. Louis U., 1980—, U. Mo., Columbia, 1991; bd. dir. Hosp. Assn. Met. St. Louis, 1975-85. Contbr. articles to profl. jour., 1972—. Admissions advisor US Mil. Acad., 1973-83; treas., bd. dir. Cath. Childrens' Home Alton, 1981-89; v.p. diocesan bd. edn. Diocese of Springfield, Ill., 1981-82, pres. 1982-84, mem. bd. edn. 1986-92; mem. diocesan fin. coun., 1987—; chmn. ARC, Alton, 1983-85; bd. dir. Am. Cancer Soc., Alton, 1984-90; pres. St. Louis Metropolitan Hosp. Coun., 1996. Served to capt. US Army, 1968-71. Decorated Army Commendation medal; recipient Alton Jaycees Disting. Svc. award, Alumni Merit award St. Louis U., 1994, Knight of the Equestrian Order of the holy Sepulchre, 1997, Received "Proecclesia it Pontifice", Cross Granted by Pope John Paul II, 2002; Mealy HS, Alumni Merit Award, 2002. Fellow: Am. Coll. Healthcare Execs. (regent's adv. coun. 1987—93, nominating com. 1991—94, regent 2002, chair ethics com., Regent's award, Sr. Healthcare Exec. of the Yr. award 1993); mem.: Southwestern Ill. Indsl. Assn. (exec. com. 1983—88, bd. dirs. 1989—, chmn. 1997), St. Louis U. Hosp. Adminstrn. Alumni Assn. (pres. 1978), Cath. Health Assn. U.S.A. (bd. dirs. 1987—, exec. com. 1989—92, chmn.-elect 1990—, chair 1991), Ill. Hosp. Assn. (exec. com. 1981—86, chmn. 1984—85), Am. Hosp. Assn. (Ho. of Dels. 1984—88), Stadium (St. Louis), Stadium Club (St. Louis), Rotary (pres. Alton chpt. 1981-82, Paul Harris fellow 1985), Rotary (pres. Alton chpt. 1981—82, Paul Harris fellow 1979, 1985). Avocations: photography, sports, family travel. Home: 1216 N Hanser Ln Godfrey IL 62035-1840 Office: St Anthony's Health Ctr St Anthony's Way PO Box 340 Alton IL 62002-0340 also: St Clare's Hosp 915 E 5th St Alton IL 62002-6434

KESSLER, WILLIAM HENRY, architect; b. Reading, Pa., Dec. 15, 1924; s. Frederick H. and Lucia W. (Kline) K.; m. Margot Walbrecker, May 11, 1946; children: Tamara Kessler Checkley, Chevonne Kessler Patten. BA in Architecture, Inst. Design, Chgo., 1948; M.Arch., Harvard U., 1951. Chief designer Yamasaki, Leinweber & Hellmuth, Detroit, 1951-55; prin. Kessler, Francis & Cardoza (formerly William Kessler and Assocs., Inc.), Detroit, 1955—. Adj. prof. U. Mich. Coll. Architecture Prin. works include Center Creative Studies, Detroit, Harvard U. Sch. Pub. Health, Boston, Indsl. Tech. Inst., Ann Arbor, Mich., State of Mich. Library Museum and Archives, Detroit Sci. Center, New Detroit Gen. Hosp.-Wayne State U. Health Care Inst, Detroit. Councilman, Grosse Pointe Park, Mich., 1966-67. Served with USAAF, 1943-46. Recipient over 130 archtl. design awards Fellow AIA (Gold medal Detroit chpt. 1974), Mich. Soc. Architects (Gold medal 1976) Home: Grosse Pointe, Mich. Died Nov. 16, 2002.

KESSLER, WOODROW BERTRAM, family practice physician, geriatrician, educator; b. N.Y.C., Sept. 27, 1926; s. Robert Theodore and Bess Doris (Oumansky) K.; m. Anita Andar, Dec. 21, 1950; children: Rex Keith, Ginger Dale. BS, Case Western Reserve U., 1947; PhD, Rutgers U., 1951; MD, Temple U., 1962. Diplomate Am. Bd. Family Practice, Am. Bd. Geriat. Instr. U. Tex., Houston, 1951-52; rsch. assoc. Vanderbilt U., Nashville, 1952-54, E.R. Squibb, New Brunswick, N.J., 1954-58; rsch. assoc. prof. U. Miami, 1958-60, Temple U., Phila., 1960-62; med. intern Temple U. Hosp., Phila., 1962-63, med. resident, 1963; rsch. physician E.I. DuPont, Wilmington, Del., 1964-65; pvt. med. practice, 1965—; clin. assoc. prof. internal medicine Temple U. Health Scis. Ctr., 1967—; attending staff Temple U. Hosp., 1967—; dir. clin. pharmacology/investigation dept. endocrinology Temple U. Health Scis. Ctr., 1980-91; physician chief grade U.S. Dept. Vet.'s Affairs Ambulatory Care, Phila., 1994-96. Penn fellow Children's Hosp. Phila., 1977; hosp. appointments include Crozer-Chester Med. Ctr., Riddle Meml. Hosp., Coatesville VA Med. Ctr.; cons. endocrinologist Haverford (Pa.) State Hosp., 1967-69, Haverford Gen. Hosp.; cons. Hoechst Internat., A.H. Robins, Abbott Pharms., Revlon/Armour, Ciba/Geigy, Ortho Pharms., Farmitalia Urba, Milan, Merck, Sharp & Dohme, Ayerst Labs., Adria Labs., Syntex Labs., Serono Labs., Oxford Rsch. Internat., Lederle Labs., Harris Labs., AT&T, Bell Atlantic; pres., CEO Providence Med. Assocs.; pres., exec. mng. officer Providence Med. Ctr.; chmn. bd. Pa. Physicians Plan, Inc.; dir. Pa. Adminstrv. Med. Svcs.; dir. Triage Med. Svcs., Inc.; mng. dir. Wallingford Med. Ctr.; chmn. bd. Am. Health & Accident Ins. Co.; dir. Tele-Diagnostics, Inc.; med. dir. dept. mil. affairs Southeastern Pa. Vets. Ctr. Contbr. articles to profl. jours.; patentee in field of disease-tracking sys. Fellow Coll. Physicians of Phila.; mem. AMA, AAUP, Endocrine Soc., Am. Bd. Family Practice (charter), Am. Soc. Contemporary Medicine and Surgery, Drug Info. Assn., Am. Soc. Internal Medicine, Am. Acad. Family Practice, Pa. Med. Soc., N.Y. Acad. Scis., Delaware County Med. Soc., Endocrine Soc. Phila., Sigma Xi. Avocations: chess, travel. Office: TDx 415 S Providence Rd Media PA 19063-3839

KESSLER-HARRIS, ALICE, historian, educator; b. June 2, 1941; AB cum laude, Goucher Coll., 1961; MA, Rutgers U., 1963, PhD, 1968; LLD (hon.), Goucher Coll., 1991; PhD (hon.), Uppsala U., 1995. Vis. faculty Sarah Lawrence Coll., 1974-76; vis. sr. lectr. U. Warwick, 1979-80; prof. history Hofstra U., Hempstead, N.Y., 1981-88, Temple U., 1988-90, Rutgers U., New Brunswick, N.J., 1990-99, Columbia U., N.Y.C., 1999—, R. Gordon Hoxie Prof. Am. History, 2001—, chair, history dept., 2003—. Author: Women Have Always Worked: An Historical Overview, 1981, Out to Work: A History of Wage-Earning Women in the United States, 1982, A Woman's Wage: Historical Meanings and Social Consequences, 1990, In Pursuit of Equity: Women, Men and the Quest for Economic Citizenship in Twentieth Century America, 2001; co-editor: Past Imperfect: Alternative Essays in American History, 1973, Women in Culture and Politics: A Century of Change, 1986, Faith of a Woman Writer: Essays in Twentieth Century Literature, 1988, Perspectives on American Labor History: The Problem of Synthesis, 1990, U.S. History as Women's History, 1995, Protecting Women: Labor Legislation in Europe, Australia and the United States, 1880-1920, 1995; contbr. articles to profl. jours. NEH fellow, 1976-77, 85-86, Rockefeller Found. fellow, 1988-89, Guggenheim fellow, 1989-90, Radcliffe Inst. Advanced Studies fellow, 2001—. Mem.: ACLU, Labor and Working Class History Assn., Berkshire Conf. Women Historians, Am. Studies Assn., Orgn. Am. Historians, Am. Hist. Assn. E-mail: AK571@columbia.edu.

KESSLER-HODGSON, LEE GWENDOLYN, actress, corporate executive; b. Wellsville, NY, Jan. 16, 1947; d. James Hewitt and Reba Gwendolyn (Adsit) Kessler; m. Bruce Gridley, June 22, 1969 (div. Dec. 1979); m. Jeffrey Craig Hodgson, Oct. 31, 1987. BA, Grove City Coll., 1968; MA, U. Wis., 1969. Prof. Sangamon State U., Springfield, Ill., 1969-70; pers. exec. Bullock's, L.A., 1971-74; owner Brunnen Enterprises, L.A., 1982—. Author: A Child of Arthur, 1981; producer, writer play including Anais Nin: The Paris Years, 1986; appeared in TV movies, mini-series including Roots, 1978, Backstairs at The White House, 1979, Blind Ambition, 1980, Hill Street Blues, 1984-87, Murder By Reason of Insanity, 1985, Hoover, 1986, Creator, 1987, Our House, 1988, Favorite Son, 1988, Lou Grant 1983-84, Barney Miller, 1979, L.A. Law, 1990, Hunter, 1991, (screenplay) Settlers Way, 1988; (TV series) Matlock, L.A. Law others. Knapp Prize fellow U. Wis., 1969. Mem. AFTRA, SAG, Actors Equity Assn. Republican. Mem. Ch. Scientology. Avocations: singer, directing, motivational speaking. Home: 2856 Country Woods Ln Palm Harbor FL 34683 E-mail: kesslerl@bww.com.

KESSNER, DOLLY EUGENIO, music educator, musician; b. Hanapepe, Kauai, Hawaii, Nov. 7, 1946; d. Hermogenes Narcissus and Librada Manuel Eugenio; m. Daniel Aaron Kessner, June 29, 1968; children: Darren Eugene, Demian Edward. BA in Music Edn., U. of Calif., L.A., 1968, MA in Composition, 1971; PhD in Music Theory, U. of So. Calif., L.A., 1992; studied piano with, Aube Tzerko; studied composition with, Henri Lazarof, Leon Kirchner, Robert Linn; studied speculative theory with, Robert Moore, William Thomsen. Music prof. Moorpark (Calif.) Coll., 1990—, chair music and dance dept., 2000—. Asst. prof. U. of So. Calif., L.A., Calif. State U., Northridge; tchg. assoc. UCLA; premieres of works by Max Lifchitz, Anthony Vazzana, William Toutant, Frank Campo, Morten Lauridsen, Paul Pisk, Leonard Berkowitz, John Vincent; soloist Orquesta Sinfonica de El Salvador, San Salvador, 1997, Filarmonica Marea Neagra, Constanta, Romania, 1994, Constanta, 94, Constanta, 98. Composer: Five Piano Pieces, Toccata for piano; rec. artist, solo pianist: CD Lyric Piece for piano and orchestra, record Equali II for piano/celeste and 3 percussionists, CD In the Center. Recipient Grad. Merit fellowship in music, U. of So. Calif., 1987—89; grantee Fund for U.S. Artists at Internat. Festivals and Exhbns., NEA, US Info. Agy., Rockefeller Found., Pew Charitable Trusts, Arts Internat., 1996. Mem.: Assn. for Tech. in Music, Coll. Music Soc. Office: Moorpark Coll 7075 Campus Rd Moorpark CA 93021 Personal E-mail: dkessner@vcccd.net.

KESSNER, MICHEAL J. elementary school educator; b. Dallas, Apr. 21, 1975; s. Michael H. and Jayne S. Kessner. AAS, Eastfield Coll., Mesquite, Tex., 1995; BA, So. Meth. U., 1997; M in Elem. Edn., Tex. A&M U., 2002. Cert. tchr., Tex. Educator The Sci. Place, Dallas, 1991—99; tchr. Garland (Tex.) Ind. Sch. Dist., 1997-98, Mesquite (Tex.) Ind. Sch. Dist., 1998—. Mem. Assn. of Tex. Educators, Girl Scouts Am. (asst. leader 1992-95). Office: Mary Moss Elem Sch 1208 New Market Rd Mesquite TX 75149-5710

KESTEL, FRANCES MARY, nursing educator; b. Phila., Oct. 4, 1954; d. Walter Karl and Martha Viola (Adolf) K. ADN, Bucks County C.C., 1974; BSN, Gwynedd Mercy Coll., 1989. Cert. diabetes educator. Staff nurse Holy Redeemer Hosp. & Med. Ctr., Meadowbrook, Pa., 1974-87, diabetes nurse educator, 1987-93; staff nurse home care Kimberly Quality Care, Conshohocken, Pa., 1991-92; staff nurse IV team Holy Redeemer Hosp. & Med. Ctr., Meadowbrook, 1991-92; clin. instr. Germantown Hosp. & Med. Ctr., Phila., 1992-93, diabetes nurse educator, 1993-98; staff devel. instr. Albert Einstein Healthcare Network, Willowcrest, 1998—. Contbr. articles to med. jours. Bd. dirs. Am. Diabetes Assn., Montgomery County, Pa., 1989-93, chmn. patient edn. com. Recipient Lois Ryan Allen Publ. award Nurses Assn. for Tchr. Edn., 1993. Mem. Am. Assn. Diabetes Educators, Triade (sec. 1989-90), Sigma Theta Tau. Avocations: reading, crafts.

KESTENBAUM, HAROLD LEE, lawyer; b. Bronx, N.Y., Sept. 27, 1949; s. Murray Louis and Yetta (Weiner) K.; m. Felice Gail Kravit, Aug. 11, 1973; children: Michelle, Benjamin. BA, Queens Coll., 1971; JD, U. Richmond, 1975. Bar: N.Y. 1976, N.J. 1977, U.S. Dist. Ct. (so. and ea. dist.) N.Y. Assoc. Wayne and Reiss, N.Y.C., 1975-76, Natanson, Reich and Barrison, N.Y.C., 1976-77, Goldstein and Axelrod, N.Y.C., 1977-81; pvt. practice N.Y.C. and L.I., 1981—2002; counsel Farrell Fritz, P.C., 2003—; chmn. of the bd. Franchise It Corp., Bohemia, N.Y., 1984-89; pres., chief exec. officer Mr. Sign Franchising Corp., 1987-89. Bd. dirs. Sbarro Inc., RezConnect Techs., Inc. GarageTek, Inc., Ultimate Francluse Sys., Inc., Wall St. Deli Sys., Inc.; cons. in field. Mem. ABA, N.Y. Bar Assn., N.J. Bar Assn., Nassau County Bar Assn. Republican. Jewish. Avocations: softball, weight training. Office: 14th Fl EAB Plz West Tower Uniondale NY 11556-0120

KESTER, CHARLES MELVIN, lawyer; b. Batesville, Ark., Jan. 19, 1968; s. Monty Charles and Phyllis Smith Kester; m. Cheryl Goodwin, June 1, 1991. BA in Philosophy summa cum laude, Liberty U., 1991; JD magna cum laude, Georgetown U., 1994. Bar: Ark. 1994, U.S. Dist. Ct. (ea. and we. dists.) Ark. 1995, U.S. Ct. Appeals (8th cir.) 1995, U.S. Ct. Fed. Claims, 2002, U.S. Supreme Ct. 1998. Law clk. U.S. Ct. Appeals 8th Cir., Fargo, N.D., 1994-95; atty. Lingle Law Firm, Rogers, Ark., 1995-96; pvt. practice law Fayetteville, Ark., 1996—. Assoc. editor Georgetown Law Jour., 1993-94; contbr. articles to profl. jours. Mem. Ark. Bar Assn. (appellate practice com. 1997-2000, young lawyers sect. adv. coun. 1998-99, sec. labor and employment law sect. 2002, treas. 2001), Ark. Trial Lawyers Assn. (amicus curiae com. 1997-2003), Phi Alpha Delta. Avocations: camping, rock climbing, spelunking. Home: 13602 White Oak Ln Fayetteville AR 72704-8312 Office: 1160 N College Ave Ste 1 Fayetteville AR 72703-1907

KESTER, DALE EMMERT, pomologist, educator; b. Audubon, Iowa, July 28, 1922; s. Raymond and Fannie (Ditzenberger) K.; m. Daphne Dougherty; children: William Raymond, Nancy Inman. BS in Horticulture, Iowa State Coll., 1947; MS in Horticulture, U. Calif., Davis, 1949, PhD in Plant Physiology, 1951. Rsch. asst. dept pomology U. Calif., Davis, Calif., 1947-51, lectr., jr. pomologist, 1951-53, asst. prof., asst. pomologist, 1953-60, assoc. prof., assoc. pomologist, 1960-69, prof., pomologist, 1969-91, prof. emeritus, 1991—. Vis. scholar dept. genetics U. Wis., Madison, 1962-63, Volcanic Rsch. Inst., Bet Dagan, Israel, 1975. Co-author: Plant Propagation: Principles and Practices, 1959, 7th revised edit., 2002; contbr. numerous articles to profl. and popular publ. 1st lt. USAF, 1943-45, ETO. Fellow Am. Soc. Hort. Sci. (Stark award 1980); mem. Internat. Plant Propagators Soc. (sec. 1961, 1st v.p. 1996, pres. 1997), Alpha Zeta, Gamma Sigma Delta, Phi Beta Kappa, Pi Alpha Xi. Republican. Presbyterian. Achievements include introduction of 7 almond cultivars and 3 almond rootstocks. Home: 1515 Shasta Dr Apt 2327 Davis CA 95616-6684 Office: U Calif Dept Pomology Davis CA 95616

KESTER, RANDALL BLAIR, lawyer; b. Vale, Oreg., Oct. 20, 1916; s. Bruce R. and Mabel M. (Judd) K.; m. Rachael L. Woodhouse, Oct. 20, 1940; children: Laura, Sylvia, Lynne. AB, Willamette U., 1937; JD, Columbia U., 1940. Bar: Oreg. 1940, U.S. Dist. Ct. Oreg. 1940, U.S. Ct. Appeals (9th cir.) 1941, U.S. Supreme Ct. 1960. Assoc., then partner firm Maguire, Shields, Morrison & Bailey, Portland, 1940-57; justice Oreg. Supreme Ct., Salem, 1957-58; partner Maguire, Shields, Morrison, Bailey & Kester, 1958-66, Maguire, Kester & Cosgrave, 1966-71, Cosgrave & Kester, Portland, 1972-78, Cosgrave, Kester, Crowe, Gidley & Lagesen, Portland, 1978-89, Cosgrave, Vergeer & Kester, Portland, 1989—. Instr. Northwestern Coll. Law, 1947-56; gen. solicitor northwestern dist. U.P. R.R., 1958-79; sr. counsel UPRR Co., 1979-81 Co-author: The First Duty: History of the U.S. District Court of Oregon, 1993; contbr. articles to profl. jours. Past v.p. Portland area council Boy Scouts of Am.; past pres. Mountain Rescue and Safety Council Oreg.; past trustee Willamette U.; past bd. dirs. Oreg. Symphony Soc., Oreg. Mus. Sci. and Industry. Recipient Silver Beaver award Boy Scouts Am., 1956, alumni citation Willamette U., 1987. Fellow Am. Acad. Appellate Lawyers; mem. ABA, Am. Bar Found. (life), Multnomah Bar Assn. (past pres. 1956, Professionalism award 1991), Oreg. State Bar (treas. 1965-66, Disting. Svc. award pub. utility sect. 1991), Am. Law Inst. (life), Nat. Ski Patrol, Mt. Hood Ski Patrol (past pres.), Mazamas (past pres., climbing chmn.), Wy'east Climbers, Portland C. of C. (pres. 1973, chmn. bd. 1974), U.S. Dist. Ct. Oreg. Hist. Soc. (past pres, bd. dirs.) Oreg. Ethics Commons (co-founder, sec.), Phi Delta Phi, Beta Theta Pi, Tau Kappa Alpha. Clubs: Arlington (Portland), City (Portland) (v.p. 1978-80, pres. 1986-87), University (Portland), Multnomah Athletic (Portland). Republican. Unitarian Universalist. Office: Cosgrave Vergeer & Kester LLP 805 SW Broadway 8th Fl Portland OR 97205 E-mail: rkester@cvk-law.com.

KESTER, STEWART RANDOLPH, banker; b. Bronxville, N.Y., July 30, 1927; s. Robert Livingston, Jr. and Mae Anna (Jones) K.; m. Marion Fay Syrett, Sept. 23, 1950; children: Cheryl, Stewart Randolph, Valerie, Marcia. BA, Colgate U., 1949. Sales rep. Procter & Gamble Co., N.Y.C., 1949-55; mng. ptnr. Kester Bros., Pompano Beach, Fla., 1955-86, R&S Properties, Pompano Beach, 1956-90, Fla. Coast Banks, Inc., Pompano Beach, 1973-75, vice chmn. bd., 1975-84, chmn. bd., 1984-85, chmn. exec. com., dir.; dir. Barnett Bank So. Fla. N.A., 1985-89, also bd. dirs.; with Kester Bros. Realty Inc., 1991—; pres. Crail Creek Assocs. LC, 1997—. Bd. dirs. Big Sky Western Bank, Mont., chmn. of bd., 2000—; pres. Jefferson Valley Ranch, Whitehall, Mont.; sec.-treas. Westfork Devel. Co. Inc., Big Sky, 1991—2000; ptnr. Big Sky Ranch, Inc. LLC. Vice mayor, commr., Pompano Beach, 1964-66, mayor, 1966-67; mem. Broward County Charter Commn., 1974-75; pres. United Way of Broward County, 1978-79; chmn. bd. trustees Pompano Police Edn. Fund, Inc., 1975-86; mem. exec. com. Broward chpt. NCCJ, 1983-86; bd. dirs. Ft. Lauderdale Symphony, Broward Workshop, Inc., 1981-85; founding dir., pres. Pompano Beach Bd. Trade, 1978-86; founding dir., v.p. Broward Community Found., 1985-89; bd. dirs. Big Sky Assn. for Arts, 1989-95, Vigilante Theatre Corp., 1992-94. With AUS, 1946-47. Named Outstanding Young Man Pompano Beach Jaycees, 1962; recipient Service award Ft. Lauderdale C. of C., 1975, Silver Medallion award NCCJ, 1984, Community Svc. award Pompano Beach C. of C., 1983, 85. Mem. Pompano Beach Hist. Soc., Greater Pompano Beach C. of C. (past dir.), Pompano Beach Exch. Club (past pres., charter mem., Book of Golden Deeds award 1976), Montana Hist. Soc., Custer Battlefield Mus. and Hist. Commn., Custer Battlefield Preservation Commn., Mus. of the Rockies, Buffalo Bill Hist. Ctr., Mus. of Art (Ft. Lauderdale), Sons of the Revolution (N.Y.). Republican. Presbyterian. Office: Kester Bros Realty Inc 619 E Atlantic Blvd PO Box 91 Pompano Beach FL 33061-0091

KESTERMAN, FRANK RAYMOND, investment banker; b. N.Y.C., May 5, 1937; s. Francis Anthony and Marion Catherine (Curth) K.; m. Iris Joan Jacobs, Mar. 21, 1964; children: Leslie Ann, Noel John-Francis, Amanda Hope. BS, U.S. Mcht. Marine Acad., King's Point, N.Y., 1959; MBA, Am. U., 1968; postgrad. advanced internat. studies, Johns Hopkins U., 1974-75; cert. advanced comml. banking, U. Va., 1982; postgrad., George Washington U., 2001—. CPA, Md. Ensign USN, 1959, advanced through grades to lt. (j.g.), 1961, nuclear power engr., 1961-66; asst. to dir. research U.S. Maritime Adminstrn., Washington, 1967-72; pres. Internat. Services Corp., Washington, 1972-76; v.p. Shipbuilders Council Am., Washington, 1976-80, R.I. Hosp. Trust Nat. Bank, Providence, 1981-86; sr. v.p. 1st Oxford Corp., Washington, 1987-90; dir. risk assessment divsn. Fin. Mgmt. Svc. U.S. Dept. Treasury, Washington, 1991-99; sr. fin. mgmt. Exec. Office of the Pres., Washington, 2000—01; sr. advisor credit and cash mgmt. OMB, Washington, 2000—01; sr. advisor, CFO Fed. Student Aid Dept. Edn., 2001—. Adj. prof. Sch. Fgn. Svc. and Sch. Bus., Georgetown U., 1996-98, Nat. Def. U., 2003-; advisor acquisitions P.R. Maritime Shipping Authority, San Juan, 1972-75; dep. dir. UN Port Project, Muscat, Oman, 1973-75; cons. on ship fin. World Bank, The Philippines, 1974, on port projects, Mex. and Panama, 1980; U.S. Dept. Treasury guest lectr. All Russia Acad. Fgn. Trade, Moscow, 1993, Ctrl. Bank Kazahkstan, Almati, 1993; Russian fin. mgr. intern program, Washington, 1994; advisor to Ukraine on small bus. loans, Kiev, 1994, Armenia, Yervan, 1995; v.p. Gore-Chernomyrdin Mission to Moscow, 1997. Adv. editor: Jour. Maritime Law and Commerce, 1972-87; contbr. articles to profl. jours. Bd. dirs. USMMA Found., 1990-92; adv. com. Pres.'s Nat. Security Telecomm., 1997. Recipient V.P. Gore's Hammer award for reinventing govt., 1995, 96; sec. treasury award Fin. Innovations, 1996. Mem. AICPA, Md. Assn. CPAs, D.C. Inst. CPAs, Assn. Govt. Accts. Avocation: community theatre. Home: 4 Winterberry Ct Bethesda MD 20817-4846 Office: 830 1st St NE Washington DC 20202

KESTERSON, DAVID BERT, English language educator; b. Springfield, Mo., Feb. 19, 1938; s. Homer Russell and Dorothy (Mace) K.; m. Cheryl Renee Monk; children: A. Todd, Chad Russell. BSE, S.W. Mo. State U., 1959; MA, U. Ark., 1961, PhD, 1965. NDEA fellow, 1959-62; grad. teaching asst. U. Ark., Fayetteville, 1962-64; asst. prof. English N.C. State U., Raleigh, 1964-68; from asst. prof. to prof. English North Tex. State U. (name now U. North Tex.), Denton, 1968—, disting. Alumni prof., 1979, chmn. dept. English, 1981-86, assoc. dean Coll. Arts and Scis., 1986-92; sr. Fulbright lectr. U. Würzburg (Germany), 1985; interim dean Coll. Arts and Scis. U. North Tex., Denton, 1992-93, vice provost, 1993-98, v.p. for acad. affairs, 1998-2000, provost, v.p. acad. affairs, 2000—03. Cons. presses on manuscripts in Am. lit Author: Josh Billings, 1973, Bill Nye, 1980; monograph Bill Nye: The Western Writings, 1976; editor: Studies in the Marble Faun, 1971, Critics on Poe, 1973, Critics on Mark Twain, 1973, Critical Essays on Hawthorne's The Scarlet Letter, 1988; founding editor: Hawthorne Soc. Newsletter (now Nathaniel Hawthorne Rev.), 1974-82; assoc. editor: Studies in the Novel, 1970—, Nathaniel Hawthorne Jour., 1980-82. With USAR, 1956-60. Recipient Mortar Bd. Outstanding Educator award, 1980; Outstanding Alumnus award S.W. Mo. State U., 1986, Disting. Grad. Alumnus award Dept. English U. Ark., 1988. Mem. Nathaniel Hawthorne Soc. (co-founder, 1st pres. 1974-76), Am. Humor Studies Assn. (pres. 1980-81), South Ctrl. MLA (exec. com. 1976-77), MLA (del. assembly 1977-80, 84-87), Melville Soc., Soc. Study So. Lit. (pres. 1999-01), Mark Twain Circle, Thoreau Soc., Thomas Wolfe Soc., Fulbright Assn., POE Studies Assn., Phi Kappa Phi, Phi Beta Delta, Golden Key. Office: U North Tex Office PO Box 311307 Denton TX 76203-1190 E-mail: kesterson@unt.edu.

KESTERSON, RAY BRENT, college dean, retired air force officer; b. St. Louis, June 10, 1941; s. Ellis O. and Gladys M. Kesterson; m. Betty J. Wagoner, June 8, 1963; children: Michelyne, Jeff. BA in Edn., Okla. Bapt. U., 1963; MRE, So. Sem., Louisville, 1966. Cert. tchr., Ky. Asst. prin. Parkland Elem. Sch., Louisville, 1965-66; tchr. Parkland Jr. H.S., Louisville, 1966-67; commd. 2d lt. USAF, 1967; assigned to Lowry AFB, Colo., 1967—69; advanced through grades to lt. col. USAF, 1983; assigned to Can. Forces Sta., Val d'Or, Que., 1969-71; Air Force ROTC prof. Grove City (Pa.) Coll., 1971-74; advisor Air Force Assistance Team, Tehran, Iran, 1974-76; asst. tng. dir. Def. Fgn. Lang. Inst., Monterey, Calif., 1976-79; exec. officer Air Tng. Command, San Antonio, 1979—83; tng. liaison officer Hdqs. Pacific Air Forces, Honolulu, 1983-86; chief standardization and evaluation Keesler Tech. Tng. Ctr., Biloxi, Miss., 1986-90; ret., 1990; dean tech. edn. Richland Coll., Dallas, 1991—. Author: Performance Criteria Analysis Manual, 1995 (Tex. Skill Stds. Leadership award 1996). Mem. Tex. Assn. Coll. Tech. Educators (bd. dirs. 2001-), Richardson C. of C. (edn. com. 1997-2001). Avocation: desktop publishing. Home: 6012 Charleston Dr Frisco TX 75035 Office: Richland Coll 12800 Abrams Rd Dallas TX 75243 E-mail: bkesterson@dcccd.edu., brentkes@aol.com.

KESTIN, HOWARD H. judge; b. Passaic, N.J., July 24, 1937; s. Oscar and Annette K.; m. Joan H. Bard, Aug. 22, 1970: children: Bette Lynn, Anita Louise. BS, St. Louis U., 1959; JD, Rutgers U., 1962; LLM, U. Va., 1995. Bar: N.J. 1962, U.S. Supreme Ct. 1965. Law sec. to assoc. justice N.J. Supreme Ct., 1962—63; dep. atty. gen. N.J., 1963—65; asst. dir. Inst. Continuing Legal Edn., Newark, 1965—66, 1969—70, exec. dir., 1970—78; dir. State N.J. Legal Svcs. to Poor Program, Trenton, 1966—68; pvt. practice law Wayne, NJ, 1968—69; prof. Rutgers U., 1969—78; chief adminstrv. law judge, dir. Office Administrv. Law State N.J., 1978—83; judge family and civil law divsns. Superior Ct. N.J., Paterson, 1983—91, judge Appellate Divsn., 1992—2002, presiding judge, 2002—. Adj. prof. law Seton Hall U. Sch. Law, Newark, 1972-84. Moderator-host The Blessings of Liberty, Sta. WNBC-TV, 1971, The Right of the People, Sta. WNBC-TV, 1975. Recipient Media awards for TV series on Bill of Rights, N.J. Bar Assn./ABA, 1971. Mem. Am. Law Inst. (life), N.J. Bar Assn. (chmn. adminstrv. law sect. 1972-74, chmn. young lawyers sect. 1968-69, trustee 1969-70), N.J. Supreme Ct. (chmn. com. on legal edn. and admissions to bar 1976-79, chmn. standing com. on paralegal edn. and regulation 1993-2000), Passaic County Bar Assn., Assn. CLE Adminstrs. (chmn. stds. and accreditation com. 1972-78, v.p. 1978). Jewish. Office: Superior Ct of NJ Appellate Divsn Ct Plz N 25 Main St Hackensack NJ 07601-7015

KESTLE, JOHN R.W. pediatric neurosurgeon, epidemiologist; b. Toronto, Ont., Can., May 8, 1959; came to U.S., 1998; s. John R.W. and Marion G. Kestle; m. Lynn K.M. Harlow, May 25, 1984; children: Rebecca, Mathew, Brian. BSc in Biology, U. Western Ont., London, Can., 1980, MD, 1984; MSc in Clin. Epidemiology, McMaster U., Hamilton, Ont., 1989. Intern St. Michael's Hosp., Toronto, 1984-85; resident in neurosurgery U. Toronto, 1985-91; fellow in pediatric neurosurgery Hosp. for Sick Children, Toronto, 1991-92; pediat. neurosurgeon B.C.'s Children's Hosp., Vancouver, Can., 1992-98; asst. prof. U. B.C., Vancouver, 1992-98; pediat. neurosurgeon Primary Children's Med. Ctr., Salt Lake City, 1998—; assoc. prof. U. Utah, Salt Lake City, 1998—. Dir. Neurosurg. Trials Methodology Ctr., Vancouver, 1992-98, Salt Lake City, 1998—; prin. investigator in field; mem. sci. adv. bd. Clin. Outcome Studies in Neurosurgery, 1994-96. Fellow Royal Coll. Surgeons (Can.); mem. Hydrocephalus Rsch. Found. (dir. clin. studies 1999—, sci. rev. panel 1995—), Am. Soc. Pediat. Neurosurgeons, Am. Assn. Neurol. Surgeons, Can. Neurosurg. Soc. Avocations: hockey, skiing, biking. Office: Primary Children's Med Ctr 100 N Medical Dr Salt Lake City UT 84113-1103 E-mail: john.kestle@hsc.utah.edu.

KESTNBAUM, ALBERT S. advertising executive; b. N.Y.C., 1939; s. Nathan and Marian (Lanxner) K.; m. Roberta Anne; children: Ellen, Suzanne, Amy, David. BA, NYU, 1959; MBA studies, CCNY, 1961. Sr. v.p. advt. J.B. Williams Co., N.Y.C., 1968-72; pres., chmn. bd. Parkson Advt. Agy., N.Y.C., 1972-80; pres. Chestnut Communications, Greenwich, Conn., 1980—. Mem. Dirs. Guild Am., Acad. TV Arts and Scis., Friars Club, Milbrook Club. Office: 15 E Putman Ave Greenwich CT 06830 *The best opportunities for success come from thorough, audacious and determined effort, in areas where your skills are most substantial, and where the potential reward is great. Often, the key ingredient to success is giving yourself permission to fail.*

KETCHAM, BEVERLY LYNN, biologist, educator; b. Norwalk, Conn., Nov. 6, 1949; d. William and Mercedes Mary Ketcham. AA, C.C. Balt., 1969; BS, Frostburg State Coll., 1971; MS, W.Va. U., 1973; EdD, Ball State U., 1978. Instr. biology Ball State U., Muncie, Ind., 1976—78; sales assoc. Ball Stores Collegiene Shop, Muncie, 1978—80; buyer Ball Stores, Inc., Muncie, 1980—81; asst. prof. biology Del Mar Coll., Corpus Christi, Tex., 1982—87; computer sales assoc. CompuSolve, Corpus Christi, 1987—88; sales assoc. J.C. Penney, Corpus Christi, 1988—92; adj. prof. biology Hillsborough C.C., Tampa, Fla., 1992—93, assoc. prof. biology, 1993—98, prof. biology, 1998—. Author: Biological Science I Laboratory Manual, 1996, Microbiology and Human Disease Laboratory Manual, 2003. Mem.: Higher Edn. Consortium for Math. and Sci., Am. Assn. Women in C.C., Fla. Assn. C.C., Am. Inst. Biol. Scis., Nat. Assn. Biology Tchrs. Republican. Roman Catholic. Avocations: horseback riding, reading, movies. Office: Hillsborough CC 2112 N 15th St Tampa FL 33605 Fax: 813-253-7775. E-mail: bketcham@hccfl.edu.

KETCHAM, GALE GIROUX, medical group administrator; b. Ithaca, N.Y., July 10, 1949; d. Jack C. Giroux and Myrtle Giroux Barber; m. William V. Ketcham, Aug. 19, 1972; children: Jack W., Brian J. BA, SUNY, Cortland, 1971; MBA, Marist Coll., Poughkeepsie, N.Y., 1985. Cert. tchr. K-9 French, N.Y. Computer programmer Lansing Rsch., Ithaca, 1971-72; substitute tchr. Wappingers Sch. Dist., Wappingers Falls, N.Y., 1973; data processing mgr. Mid-Hudson Med. Group, Fishkill, N.Y., 1974-80, adminstr., 1981—. Mem. Southern Duchess County C. of C., Med. Group Mgmt. Assn., 1981—. Avocations: tennis, soccer, water skiing, sailing, swimming. Office: Mid-Hudson Med Group PC 64 Jackson St Fishkill NY 12524-1120

KETCHAM, ORMAN WESTON, lawyer, former judge; b. Bklyn., Oct. 1, 1918; s. Walter Seymour and Arline May (Weston) K.; m. Anne Phelps Stokes, Dec. 22, 1947; children: Anne Weston Ketcham Felder, Helen Phelps Ketcham Ryan, Elizabeth Miner Ketcham Mercogliano, Susan Stokes Ketcham. BA, Princeton U., 1940; postgrad., Yale U., 1940-41, LLB, 1947, JD, 1971. Bar: D.C. 1948. With Covington & Burling, Washington, 1947-53; asst. gen. counsel Fgn. Ops. Adminstrn., Washington, 1953-55; trial atty. antitrust div. Justice Dept., 1955-57; judge Juvenile Ct. D.C., 1957-71, Superior Ct. D.C., 1971-77; sr. staff atty. Nat. Center State Cts., 1977-81; sr. fellow Washington Coll. Law Inst., 1981-83. Adj. prof. law Georgetown U., 1963-67, U. Va., 1971-77, William and Mary Coll., 1978-80, Am. U., 1981-92; mem. U.S. Edn. Appeal

Bd., 1982-90. acting chmn., 1984-85; mem. coun. of judges Nat. Coun. on Crime and Delinquency, 1959-83, bd. dirs., 1974-83; mem. U.S. del. UN Congress on Crime, Stockholm, 1965, Geneva, 1975; mem. Nat. Com. on Secondary Edn., 1970-74; chmn. adv. coun. to Select Com. on Crime, Ho. of Reps., 1969-70 Author: (with others) Justice for the Child, 1961, Changing Faces of Juvenile Justice, 1978, (with Monrad G. Paulsen) Cases and Materials Relating to Juvenile Courts, 1967. Washington rep. Fund for the Republic, 1953; mem. vis. com. Brookings Instn., 1971-76; bd. dirs. Children's Nat. Med. Ctr., 1987-90. Mem. ABA, Bar Assn. D.C., Am. Law Inst., Nat. Coun. Juvenile and Family Ct. Judges (pres. 1965-66), Internat. Assn. Youth Magistrates (v.p. 1966-74) Clubs: Cosmos, Princeton (Washington), Chevy Chase. Congregationalist. Home: 2 E Melrose St Chevy Chase MD 20815-4204

KETCHAM, RICHARD SCOTT, lawyer; b. Columbus, Ohio, Jan. 8, 1948; s. Victor Alvin and Dorothy Eloise (Becher) K.; m. Kim Michelle Halliburton, Apr. 7, 1984 (div. 1989); 1 child, Kate Erin; m. Christy M. Canaday, Sept. 9, 1990 (div. 1994). BS, Bowling Green (Ohio) State U., 1970; JD cum laude, Capital U., Columbus, 1974. Bar: Ohio 1974, U.S. Dist. Ct. (so. dist.) Ohio 1979. Asst. pros. atty. Franklin County (Ohio) Pros., Columbus, 1974-79, sr. asst. pros. atty., 1979-84; ptnr. Ketcham & Ketcham, Columbus, 1984—. Mem. task force Legal Aid Referral Project, Columbus Bar Assn. Homeless Project, 1989—. Mem. Gov.'s Task Force on Family Violence, 1984-86. Mem. Nat. Assn. Criminal Def. Lawyers, Ohio Assn. Criminal Def. Lawyers (bd. dirs. 1989—, v.p. CLE, sec.), Ctrl. Ohio Assn. Criminal Def. Lawyers (pres. 1994-95, bd. dirs. 2001—), Ohio State Bar Assn., Columbus Bar Assn. (chmn. criminal law com. 1994-95, 95-96), Franklin County Trial Lawyers. Avocations: fishing, basketball, model railroads, gardening. Home: 1937 Elmwood Ave Columbus OH 43212-1112 Office: Ketcham & Ketcham 755 S High St Columbus OH 43206-1908 E-mail: rsketch@msn.com.

KETCHAM, SALLY ANN, historic site staff member, consultant; b. Norfolk, Nebr., Mar. 11, 1928; d. William Ralph and Sallie Gertrude (Marshall) Johnson; m. Richard W. Ketcham, Jan. 24, 1962; children: Sallie Jane, William Marshall. Student, Colo. Woman's Coll., 1946—47; BA, U. Nebr., 1950, MA, 1956. Curator of history Nebr. State Hist. Soc., Lincoln, 1951—60; furnishing curator U.S. Nat. Pk. Svc., Omaha, 1960—62, rsch. specialist San Francisco, 1962—64, Washington, 1962—67; contractor U.S. Nat. Pk. Svc. and others, 1968—96, U.S. Fish and Wildlife, Omaha, 1979. Restoration chmn. Gen. Crook House, Omaha, 1980—86, Avery House, Ft. Collins, 1985—; steering com. Amigos de la Romero House, Ft. Collins, 2001—02. Co-author: (book) Sautterhouse Five, 1983; contbr. articles. Mem. Landmark Preservation Com., Ft. Collins, 1984—90, Poudre Landmarks Fedn., Ft. Collins, 1986—2000, Colo. Hist. Soc.; v.p. Douglas County Hist. Soc., Omaha, 1980—86; pres. Ft. Collins Hist. Soc. Recipient Disting. Svc. award, Douglas County Hist. Soc., 1984, Award of Excellence, City of Ft. Collins, 1990, Superior Svc. award, Nat. Park Svc., Outstanding Cmty. Svc. award, PLF, 2003. Mem.: Ft. Laramie Assn. (hon.). Home: 1132 Lindenwood Dr Fort Collins CO 80524

KETCHAM, WARREN ANDREW, psychologist, educator; b. Manistee, Mich., June 28, 1909; s. Perry Warren and Anna Ella (Ulrich) K.; m. Edna May Wearne, Nov. 23, 1962 (dec. Mar. 1991). BM, U. Mich., 1932, MA, 1947, PhD, 1951. Lic. psychologist Mich., Tex. Tchr. Reed City (Mich.) Pub. Schs., 1934-36, Melvindale (Mich.) Pub. Schs., 1936-38; supr. Dearborn (Mich.) Pub. Schs., 1938-43; sch. psychologist Ferndale (Mich.) Pub. Schs., 1950-53; prof., sch. psychologist U. Mich., Ann Arbor, 1953-77, prof. emeritus, 1978—; pvt. practice clin., indsl., orgnl. psychology Mich. and Tex., 1964—. Cons. Am. Sch., Guatemala City, Guatemala, 1958-80. Sgt. U.S. Army, 1943-45, PTO. Fulbright scholar Leeds U., 1959, Hinsdale scholar U. Mich., 1951. Fellow Am. Psychol. Assn.; mem. Am. Soc. Clin. Hypnotists, Mich. Soc. Clin. Psychologists, Mich. Psychol. Assn., Nat. Registered Health Svc. Providers in Psychology. Home and Office: 608 E Lake Rd Harbor Springs MI 49740-1220

KETCHAND, ROBERT LEE, lawyer; b. Shreveport, La., Jan. 30, 1948; s. Woodrow Wilson and Attie Harriet (Chandler) K.; m. Alice Sue Adams, May 31, 1969; children: Peter Leland, Marjory Attie. BA, Baylor U., 1970; JD, Harvard U., 1973. Bar: Tex. 1973, Mass. 1973, D.C. 1981. Assoc., ptnr. Butler & Binion, Houston, 1976-85, Washington, 1981-82; shareholder Brodsky & Ketchand, Houston, 1985-88; ptnr. Webster & Sheffield, Houston, 1988-90; atty. pvt. practice, Houston, 1990-92; ptnr. Short & Ketchand, Houston, 1992-2001; dir. Boyer & Ketchand, P.C., Houston, 2001—. Founder, chmn. bd. dirs. Rolling Waters, d/b/a Houston Legal Clinic. Pres. Prisoner Svcs. Com. Houston, 1986; deacon South Houston Bapt. Ch., 1976—; gen. counsel, dir. Houston Met. Ministries, 1986-88; dir. Interfaith Ministries Greater Houston, 1996-98; gen. counsel Houston Bus. Roundtable, 1988—. Lt. USNR, 1973-76. Mem. ABA, Tex. Bar Assn., Houston Bar Assn. (chmn. dispute com. 1989-90). Avocations: reading, family. Home: 2707 Carolina Way Houston TX 77005-3423 Office: Boyer & Ketchand PC 9 Greenway Plz Ste 3100 Houston TX 77046 Fax: 713-871-2024. E-mail: rketchand@boyerketchand.com.

KETCHERSID, WAYNE LESTER, JR., medical technologist; b. Seattle, Oct. 16, 1946; s. Wayne Lester and Hazel May (Greene) K.; m. Wilette LaVerne Mautz, Oct. 6, 1972; 1 son, William Les. BS in Biology, Pacific Luth. U., 1976, BS in Med. Tech., 1978; MS in Adminstrn., Ctrl. Mich. U., 1990; postgrad., Kennedy Western U., 1996—. Cert. med. technologist; cert. clin. lab. dir. Nat. Cert. Agy. for Med. Lab. Pers. Staff technologist Tacoma Gen. Hosp., 1978-79, chemistry supr., 1979-81, head chemistry, 1981-83, Multicare Med. Ctr., 1984-86, mgr., 1986-93, clin. lab. scientist, 1993—. Contbr. articles to profl. jours. Mem. Nat. Rep. Com. With U.S. Army, 1966-68. William E. Slaughter Found. scholar, 1975-76. Mem. Am. Soc. Clin. Lab. Sci. (cert., chmn. region IX adminstrn. 1984-94, nat. del. 1984—, vice chmn. govt. affairs com. 1991-92, chmn. 1992-93, vice chair 1993-94, bd. trustees polit. action com. 1991-97, treas. 1994-97, nat. licensure coord. 1996—, sec./treas. bd. dirs. 1996-2001, jud. com. 2001—, nominee Mem. of Yr. 1992, Bd. Dirs. award 1994, Mendelson award 1994, Pres. award 1996), Wash. State Soc. Clin. Lab. Sci. (chmn. biochemistry sect. 1983-86, dist. pres. 1986-99, co-chair ann. meeting 1996, cert. merit 1983, 84, 86, 88, pres. 1988-89, 89-90, mem. of yr. 1990, chmn. govt. affairs com. 1991-92, chmn. 1992—, Pres.'s award 1996, 97), Am. Soc. Clin. Pathologists (med. technologist), N.w. Med. Lab. Symposium (chmn. 1986-88, 90, 92), Alpha Mu Tau. Lutheran. Office: 2906 S 274th Pl Auburn WA 98001-1803 E-mail: wayketch@aol.com.

KETCHUM, DAVID STOREY, retired fundraising executive; b. Pitts., Sept. 28, 1920; s. Carlton G. and Mildred (Storey) K.; m. Sally Louise Doerschuk, Jan. 14, 1950; children: Louise Anne, Laura Jean. AB, Cornell U., 1941. Sales rep. IBM Corp., 1941-42; with Ketchum, Inc., Pitts., 1945-82, pres., CEO, 1965-78, chmn. bd., 1978-82. Past pres. Hist. Soc. Western Pa., Children's Home Pitts.; former trustee Shadyside Presbyn. Ch., Pitcairn-Crabbe Found., Winchester-Thurston Sch., Presbyn.-Univ. Hosp., Animal Rescue League Western Pa.; past v.p. Coun. Chs. Pitts.; past pres. Am. Assn. Fund Raising Counsel; mem. coun. Cornell U.; former mem. Rep. Fin. Com. of Allegheny County. Capt. USAAF, 1942-45. Decorated Soldier's Medal, Bronze Star. Mem. Duquesne Club, Fox Chapel Racquet Club, Sigma Alpha Epsilon. Home: 131 Yorkshire Dr Pittsburgh PA 15208-2640

KETCHUM, IRENE FRANCES, library foundation board; b. Hammond, Ind., Jan. 19, 1914; d. Peter H. and Theresa C. (Weis) Young; m. Alden W. Ketchum, Sept. 17, 1936 (dec. 1973); 1 child, William H. Grad. high sch., Hammond, 1932. Cert. mcpl. clk. Mng. editor Herald Newspapers, Gary, Ind., 1950-55; clk.-treas. Town of Highland, Ind., 1956-79; trustee, bd. sec. Lake County Pub. Libr., Merrillville, Ind., 1980-95; past trustee, 1995—; pres., 1995. Active Ind. State Libr. Adv. Com., Indpls., 1988—90; treas. Highland Cmty. Events Coun., 1975—; mem. Friends of Ind. Librs., Friends of Lake County Pub. Libr., Lake County Pub. Libr. Found.; pres. Highland Women's Dem. Club, 1978; auditor Highland Dem. Club, 1980—89. Named Sagamore of the Wabash, 1996, Fraternalist of Yr., Fraternal Congress, 2002. Mem. Internat. Inst. Mcpl. Clks., Ind. League Mcpl. Clks. and Treas. (assoc., treas., sec., v.p., pres. 1967-68), Girl Scouts USA (life). Roman Catholic. Avocations: community service volunteer, reading, travel.

KETCHUM, JAMES ROE, curator; b. Rochester, N.Y., Mar. 15, 1939; s. George Roe and Mary Louise (Frantz) K.; m. Barbara M. Van Ness, Aug. 18, 1962; children: John Van Ness, Sarah Graham, Timothy Roe, Chester Arthur. AB, Colgate U., 1960; postgrad., Georgetown U., 1960-61, George Washington U., 1961-62. Staff historian Dept. Interior, Washington, 1960-62; registrar The White House, Washington, 1962-63, curator, 1963-70, U.S. Senate, Washington, 1970-95, curator emeritus, 1995—. Editor: The White House: An Historic Guide, 1962-70; contbr. numerous articles to profl. jours. and encys. Mem. Com. Preservation of White House, 1964-70; trustee U.S. Capitol Hist. Soc., 1971-79; alt. mem. Fed. Coun. Arts and Humanities, 1974-95; trustee Woodrow Wilson Birthplace Found., 1980—. Member Am. Assn. Museums, City Mus. Washington, Nat. Trust Historic Preservation, Theta Chi. Office: US Senate Commn Art Us Capital Bldg Rm S-411 Washington DC 20510-0001

KETCHUM, PATRICIA SUGRUE, lawyer; b. N.Y.C., Jan. 14, 1938; d. Thomas Joseph and Mary Margaret (Ganey) Sugrue; m. A. Bertrand Channon, Apr. 15, 1961 (div. 1982); children: Thomas Sugrue Channon, Aengus Brian Channon; m. Robert H. Ketchum, Sept. 11, 1999. AB, Bryn Mawr Coll., 1958; JD, William and Mary Coll., 1980. Bar: Va. 1980, U.S. Ct. Appeals (4th cir.) 1980, D.C. 1981, U.S. Dist. Ct. (ea. dist.) Va. 1983, U.S. Dist. Ct. (D.C. dist.) 1983. Atty. benefits rev. bd. U.S. Dept. of Labor, Washington, 1980-81; law clk. to presiding justice U.S. Bankruptcy Ct., Alexandria, Va., 1981-83; assoc. Docter, Docter & Salus, P.C., Washington, 1983-85; atty. Adminstrv. Office of The U.S. Cts., Washington, 1985—. Mem. ABA (bus. bankruptcy com. bus. law sect.), Va. State Bar Assn., D.C. Bar Assn. Home: 1607 22nd St NW Washington DC 20008-1921 Office: Adminstrv Office US Courts Washington DC 20544

KETCHUM, WILLIAM CLARENCE, author, educator; b. Columbia, Mo., Mar. 29, 1931; s. William C. and Mildred Ann (Roberts) K.; m. Erica Stoller; children: Aaron, Alison, Ian. BA, Union Coll., 1953; JD, Columbia U., 1956. Bar: N.Y. 1960. Atty. Kriendler & Kriendler, N.Y.C., 1956, Martin, Clearwater & Bell, N.Y.C., 1960-65, R.S. Lane, N.Y.C., 1965-69; law sec. to Judge Lane of Civil Court, New York County N.Y.C., 1969-76; instr. course on Am. antiques New Sch., N.Y.C., 1970-87; instr. antiques course CUNY-Hunter Coll., 1978-79; mem. faculty NYU, 1984—, Folk Art Inst., 1987—, Marymount Coll., Tarrytown, N.Y., 1987-92. Guest curator Mus. Am. Folk Art, N.Y.C., 1974—, curator spl. projects, 1985-90, mem. nat. adv. com., 1992—; guest curator Nassau County Fine Arts Mus., 1980, Boscobel Restoration, 1995; curator Female Folk Artists U.S., Japan, 1988-89, Am. Bd. Games Katonah (N.Y.) Mus. Art, 1992, Scarsdale (N.Y.) Hist. Soc., 1993-94; guest spkr. Seminar on Early Am. Life, Pa. Farm Mus., Lancaster, 1974, Smithsonian Instn., 1976, Mercer Mus., Hancock Shaker Mus., 1977; guest lectr. Flemington Hist. Soc., 1975-76, antiques seminar NYU, 1973-75, 78-79, 81-84, New Haven Hist. Soc., 1975, Shelburne (Vt.) Mus., 1976, 78, St. Mary's of the Woods Coll., Terre Haute, Ind., 1976-78, Cooper-Hewitt Mus., 1978, Nassau County Fine Arts Mus., 1980, Mus. Am. Folk Art, 1978-84, Peale Mus., Balt., 1984, Del. Art Mus., 1985, N.Y. State Mus., 1985, 2000, Seattle Art Mus., 1986-87, Jacksonville (Fla.) Mus. Art, 1987, Marymount Coll., 1987-92, Hiram (Ohio) Coll., 1988, Triton Mus., Santa Clara, Calif., 1988, Chautauqua (N.Y.) Inst., 1989, Art and Culture Ctr. Hollywood, Fla., 1990, Philbrook Mus. Art, Tulsa, 1991, Katonah (N.Y.) Mus. Art, 1993, 99, Scarsdale (N.Y.) Hist. Soc., 1993, Claremont State (N.Y.) Hist. Site, 1994, Edinboro (Pa.) Coll., 1994-2000, Bruce Mus., 1995, 2002, Mus. of City of N.Y., 1995, Canterbury (N.H.) Shaker Village, 1997, N.Y. State Archaeol. Assn., 1997, 2000, N.Y. Hist. Assn., 1999-2001, Conn. Ceramic Cir., 1997, 2002, Am. Soc. Appraisers, 2000, 03; cons. antique series Time-Life, Inc., 1976-78; series cons. Knopf Collectors' Guides to Am. Antiques, 1982-84; spokesperson QVC, 1993; cons. material culture, archaeol. excavations Ft. Edward and Ft. William Henry, N.Y., 1994—, N.Y. State Hist. Assn., 1996—. Author: Early Potters and Potteries of New York, 1970, second ed. 1987; The Pottery and Porcelain Collectors Handbook, 1971; American Basketry and Woodenware, 1974; American Bottles, 1975; American Hooked Rugs, 1976; A Catalog of American Antiques, 1977, rev., 1990; The Family Treasury of Antiques, 1978; Catalog of American Collectibles, 1979, rev., 1990; Western Memorabilia, 1980; Auction, 1980; Collecting American Craft Antiques, 1980; Toys; Furniture 2, 1981; The Catalog of World Antiques, 1981; The Book of Boxes, 1982; Chests, Cupboards, Desks and Other Pieces, 1982, A Guide to Bottle Collecting, 1985; Am. Folk Art of the Twentieth Century, 1983; Pottery and Porcelain, 1983; Collecting Toys for Fun & Profit, 1985; Collecting 40's and 50's Collectibles for Fun and Profit, 1985; Sports Collectibles for Fun and Profit, 1985; All American, Folk Arts and Crafts, 1986; American Country Pottery, 1987, Making a Living in Antiques, 1990, Holiday Collectables, 1990, American Redware, 1990, Am. Stoneware, 1991, Country Wreaths and Baskets, 1991, Collecting the West, 1992, Western Memorabilia Identification and Price Guide, 1993, American Pottery & Porcelain, Identification and Price Guide, 1994, American Cabinetmakers, 1995, American Folk Art, 1995, The Art of Grandma Moses, 1996, Simple Beauty: The Shakers in America, 1996, The Art of the Golden West, 1996, Remington and Russell, 1997, Native American Art, 1997; contbg. author: The American Sporting Collectibles Handbook, 1982, Is It Genuine, 1986, The Dictionary of Art, 1994, The Encyclopedia of New York, 2000, American Folk Articles: Les Primitife Americains, 2001, The Encyclopedia of Fork Art, 2003; also articles to profl. jours. Lt., USNR, 1956-60. Recipient Amb. of Honor award English Speaking Union, 1984. Mem. Assn. of Bar of City of N.Y. (mem. com. uniform state laws 1972-76, mem. art com. 1976-78), N.Y. State Hist. Soc., N.E. Archeol. Assn. Home: 241 Grace Church St Rye NY 10580-4217 E-mail: esto2@esto.com.

KETELS, GERHARD H. lawyer; b. Hackensack, N.J., June 1, 1958; BA, Yale U., 1980; JD, U. Pa., 1983. Bar: N.Y. 1984. Trainee Allianz Ins. Co., Munich, 1983—85; mgr. Munich Re, Germany, 1986—99; sr. v.p. Hannover Re, Germany, 1999—2001; sec., gen. counsel Clarendon Ins. Group, N.Y.C., 2001—. Bd. dirs. Atlantic Capital, Corp., Redland Ins., Co., Clarendon Am. Co., Harbor Splty. Ins. Co. Office: Clarendon Ins Group 1177 6th Ave New York NY 10036

KETHA, VENKATA KRISHNA MOHAN, microbiologist, researcher; b. Madras, Tamilnadu, India, Apr. 6, 1967; PhD, U. of Madras, 1992—98. FDA Reviewer Training U.S. FDA, 2002, Case Seminar Series U.S. FDA, 2002, Lab animal care NIH, 2000. Post doctoral fellow Cber, Fda, Bethesda, Md., 1999—2002, vis. assoc., 2002—. Rsch. assoc. U. of Madras, India, 1998—99; post doctoral fellowship Oak Ridge Inst. for Sci. and Edn., 1999—2002; jr. and sr. rsch. fellowship Coun. for Sci. and Indsl. Rsch., India, 1992—97. Contbr. articles to profl. jours. Reviewer Infectious Diseases Soc. of Am., Boston, Mass., 2001. Recipient Travel Grand award, Am. Soc. for Virology, 2000, Oak Ridge Inst. for Sci. and Edn., 2002, Reward and Recognition award, U.S. FDA, 2002, Jr. Best Paper award, Indian Assn. of Med. Microbiologists, 1996. Mem.: Am. Soc. for Microbiology, European Soc. for Clin. Virology (assoc.), Am. Assn. for the Advancement of Sciences (assoc.), Soc. for Exptl. Biology and Medicine (assoc.), Am. Soc. for Virology (assoc.), Sigma Xi, the Sci. Rsch. Soc. Achievements include research in virus-host interactions/ molecular virology. Home: 1001 Rockville Pike #321 Rockville MD 20852 Office: US Food and Drug Administrn 9000 Rockville Pike Bldg 29A Rm 2C-15 Bethesda MD 20892 Personal E-mail: kctham@hotmail.com.

KETNER, KENNETH LAINE, philosopher, educator; b. Mountain Home, Okla., Mar. 24, 1939; s. Louis Elaine and Johnnie Lucille (Hannah) K.; m. Berti Gabriella Zehetmeier, Aug. 24, 1964 (dec. Oct. 1996); 1 child, Kenneth Laine Jr. BA in Philosophy, Okla. State U., 1961, MA, 1967; MA in Folklore, UCLA, 1968; PhD in Philosophy, U. Calif., Santa Barbara, 1972. Part-time instr. Okla. State U., 1964-67; tchg. asst. U. Calif., Santa Barbara, 1969-70; mem. faculty Tex. Tech U., Lubbock, 1971—, prof. philosophy, 1977-98, chmn. dept., 1979-81; founder, dir. Inst. Studies in Pragmaticism, 1972—, Charles Sanders Peirce prof. philosophy, 1981-98, Charles Sanders Peirce interdisciplinary prof., 1998—, Paul Whitfield Horn prof., 1999—. Asst. prof. philosophy and folklore UCLA, summers, 1972, 74; co-organizer C.S. Peirce Bicentennial Internat. Congress, Amsterdam, Netherlands 1976; Peirce Sesquicentennial Internat. Congress, Harvard U., 1989. Author: A Critical Study of Stephen C. Pepper's Approach to Metaphysics, 1967, An Essay on the Nature of World Views, 1972, An Emendation of R.G. Collingwood's Doctrine of Absolute Presuppositions, 1973; editor, compiler: Charles Sanders Peirce: Contributions to the Nation, 4 parts, 1975, 78, 79, 87, Comprehensive Bibliography of Works of C.S. Peirce, 1977, rev. edit., 1986, Reasoning and the Logic of Things, 1993, A Thief of Peirce, 1995, His Glassy Essence: an Autobiography of C.S. Peirce, 1998; founder, gen. editor Peirce Studies, 1979—, Philosophical Inquiries, 1989—, more. Capt. USAR, 1962-64. Grantee NSF, Nat. Endowment Humanities, Am. Coun. Learned Socs. Fellow Charles S. Peirce Soc. (pres. 1983); mem. Am. Philos. Assn., Freemason, Tau Kappa Epsilon. Democrat. Home: PO Box 65135 Lubbock TX 79464-5135 Office: Texas Tech Univ Library 305 Lubbock TX 79409-0002

KETRON, CARRIE SUE, secondary school educator; b. Clifton, Tex. d. Randolph Allen and Mary (Waggoner) Ogden; m. N.M. Ketron, Aug. 4, 1984; children: John, Robert. B of Applied Arts and Scis., U. North Tex., 1990, MEd, 1993. Tchr. Duncanville (Tex.) High Sch., 1982--. Named Tchr. of Yr., Tex. Vocat. Tech. Assn., 1990, Outstanding Nat. Career & Tech. Tchr. of Yr., 1997. Mem. Golden Key Honor Soc., Am. Vocat. Assn., Cosmetology Instructors' of Pub. Schs. (parliamentarian 1989-90), Vocat. Indsl. Clubs Am. (advisor 1986-93), Iota Lambda Sigma Sigma (pres. 1995-96), Phi Theta Kappa, Alpha Chi. Baptist.

KETT, JOSEPH FRANCIS, historian, educator; b. N.Y.C., Mar. 11, 1938; s. Joseph Francis and Anne (Barry) K.; m. Eleanor Hess, June 26, 1965; children: Jennifer, John. BA magna cum laude, Coll. Holy Cross, 1959; MA, Harvard U., 1960, PhD, 1964. Instr. in history Harvard U., Cambridge, Mass., 1964-65; asst. prof. U. Va., Charlottesville, 1966-69, assoc. prof., 1970-76, prof., 1976—, chmn. dept. history, 1985-90. Author: The Formation of the American Medical Profession, 1780-1860: The role of Institutions, 1968, Rites of Passage: Adolescence in America, 1790—, 1977, The Pursuit of Knowledge Under Difficulties, 1994; co-author: The Enduring Vision, 1989, (with E. Donald Hirsch and James Trefil) Dictionary of Cultural Literacy, 1988, 2d edit., 1993, 3d edit. 2002; contbg. author: Cultural Literacy: What Every American Needs to Know (Hirsch), 1986; also articles. Fellow Charles Warren Ctr. Harvard U., 1969-70. Office: U Va Dept History Randall Hall Charlottesville VA 22903-3284

KETTANEH, ANTHONY C. small business owner, consultant; b. Beirut, Lebanon, June 24, 1937; s. Francis Anthony and Mary Shoucair Kettaneh; m. Nouna Mragel Kettaneh; 1 child, Leigh; m. Ruth Sullivan Polley, May 27, 2000. BS, Fordham U., 1960; JD, Boston U., 1963. Job acct. Gilbane Bldg. Co., Providence, 1963—65; rsch. analyst Mass. Inst. of Tech., Cambridge, 1967—69; pres./CEO Social Tech. Sys., Newton, Mass., 1969—72; with Kettaneh Group, Beirut, 1972—, chmn., 1984. Author (editor): (book) Project Romulus, 1968; co-author: (article) Harvard Bus. Rev., 1968. Lectr. US Info. Agy., Africa/Nr. East, 1976—82. Mem.: NY Acad. of Sci. Achievements include patents for deep infrared laser used for fracturing rock or concrete (1970). Home: 2263 Edsall Ave Bronx NY 10463 Office: E Distributor & Forwarders 1775 Broadway Ste 527 New York NY 10019-1903

KETTEL, EDWARD JOSEPH, oil company executive, retired; b. N.Y.C., Sept. 13, 1925; s. Harold J. and Evelyn M. (Melbourne) K.; m. Janet M. Johnson, Nov. 27, 1952; children: Dorothy A., David A. Student, St. John's U., 1943; BA, St. Francis Coll., 1949; MA, Columbia U., 1953. Ins. mgr. Arabian Am. Oil Co., 1950-56, Ethyl Corp., 1956—63, Sinclair Oil, 1963—65; asst. treas. Atlantic Richfield Co., L.A., 1965-85, Chevron Corp., San Francisco, 1985-94; expert witness, 1994—. Chmn. bd. Oil Ins., Ltd.; pres. Greater Pacific, Ltd.; dir. Am. S.S. Owners Mut. Protection and Indemnity Assn., Inc., Internat. Tanker Indemnity Assn., Ltd. With inf. AUS, 1943-46. Decorated Purple Heart with oak leaf cluster. Mem. Am. Petroleum Inst., Mfrs. Chem. Assn., Nat. Fire Protection Assn., Risk and Ins. Mgmt. Soc., N.Y. Athletic Club, L.A. Athletic Club, Palos Verdes Country Club, Ocean Colony Golf Club, Westhampton Beach Yacht Squadron Ltd.

KETTELKAMP, DONALD BENJAMIN, retired surgeon; b. Anamosa, Iowa, Jan. 21, 1930; s. Enoch George and Elsie (Norden) K.; m. Alice June Mencke, Dec. 30, 1954; children: Karen June, Lisa Marie, Suzanne D., Jonathan B.; m. Clemencia Oliveros Brandon, Apr. 28, 1989. BA, Cornell U., Mt. Vernon, Iowa, 1952; MD, U. Iowa, 1955, MS, 1960. Diplomate Am. Bd. Orthop. Surgery. Intern Thomas D. Dee Meml. Hosp., Ogden, Utah, 1955—56; resident orthopedic surgery U. Iowa, Iowa City, 1958—61; practice medicine specializing in orthopaedic surgery Anchorage, 1961—64; asst. prof. Albany (N.Y.) Med. Coll., 1964—66, assoc. prof., 1966—68, U. Iowa, Iowa City, 1968—71, prof., 1971; prof., chmn. dept. orthopaedic surgery U. Ark., Little Rock, 1971—74, Ind. U., Indpls., 1974—84; assoc. dean Tex. Tech. U., El Paso, 1984—87; exec. dir. Am. Bd. Orthop. Surgery, Chgo., 1986—94. Trustee: Jour. Bone and Joint Surgery, 1991—96. Mem.: ACS, Knee Soc., Assn. Orthopaedic Chairmen (pres. 1981), Am. Orthopaedic Assn. (pres. 1989—90), Am. Soc. Surgery of Hand, Continental Orthopaedic Soc., Russell Hibbs Soc., Am. Acad. Orthopaedic Surgeons.

KETTEMBOROUGH, CLIFFORD RUSSELL, computer scientist, consultant, manager; b. Romania, June 8, 1953; came to U.S., 1983; s. Peter and Connie I. MS in Math., U. Bucharest, Romania, 1976; MS in Computer Sci., West Coast U., L.A., 1985; MS in Mgmt. Info. System, West Coast U., Los Angeles, 1986; PhD in Computer and Info. Sci., Pacific We. U., 1988; MBA, U. LaVerne, 1992; PhD in Bus. Adminstrn., U. Santa Barbara, 1996; EdD in Computer Tech. in Edn., Nova Southeastern U., 1998. Lic. mathematician. Mathematician, programmer Nat. Dept. Chemistry, Bucharest, 1976-80; sr. programmer, analyst Nat. Dept. Metallurgy, Bucharest, 1980-82; sr. software engr. Xerox Corp., El Segundo, Calif., 1983-88; task mgr. Rockwell Internat., Canoga Park, Calif., 1989-91, cons., 1991-93; mgr. micro devel. Transam. Corp., L.A., 1993-95; MIS dir. Maxicare Health Plans, L.A., 1995-96; computer and info. scientist Jet Propulsion Lab.-NASA, Pasadena, Calif., 1988-89, project mgr., 1996—. Adj., asst. prof. W. Coast U., Chapman U., U. Redlands, Nat. U., U. Phoenix, Union Inst., Pepperdine U., UCLA Ext., Keller Grad. Sch., 1991—. Contbr. articles to profl. jours. Sec. Romanian Nat. Body Bldg. Com., Bucharest, 1980-82; pres., chmn. Bucharest Mcpl. Body Bldg. Com., 1978-82. Served to lt. Romanian Army, 1978. Mem. IEEE, Assn. for Computing Machinery. Republican. Avocations: soccer, body building, traveling. Home: 6004 N Walnut Grove Ave San Gabriel CA 91775-2530

KETTENHOFEN, GRETCHEN MARIA, development executive; b. Canaan, Conn., Nov. 7, 1940; d. Leo J. and Alice G. (Stere) K.; m. Gunther Mittendorf, Apr. 19, 1986. BA cum laude, Barnard Coll., 1957; postgrad., New Sch., 1971-73. Cert. fund raising exec. Mgr. field survey Audits and Svcs., N.Y.C., 1965-70; exec. v.p. Lee Slurzberg Rsch., N.Y.C., 1970-87; dir. devel. Coun. Econ. Priorities, N.Y.C., 1988-94; office mgr. Christ Ch., Canaan, 1996—, dir. Treasure Shop, 2001—; dir. devel. Coun. Creative Projects, Lee, Mass., 1995-97; exec. dir. North Canaan Housing Authority Wangam Village, Canaan, Conn., 1997-99; dir. devel. Douglas Libr., Canaan, Conn., 1998—2002. Com. mem. govt. affairs Nat. Soc. Fund Raising Execs., N.Y.C. Contbr. article to profl. jour. Active Coun. on Govt. Housing Com., Conn. Chair stewardship com. Holy Apostles Ch., N.Y.C., 1988-93, mem. vestry, 1990-93; chair Interparish Coun., N.Y.C., 1993; chair stewardship com., mem. vestry Christ Ch., Canaan, 1997-1999. Episcopalian. Home: PO Box 1266 Canaan CT 06018-1266

KETTER, DAVID LEE, lawyer; b. Portsmouth, Ohio, Jan. 7, 1929; s. William Leslie and Dorothy Aileen (Weidner) K.; m. Beverly Jane Kinker, June 10, 1951; children— Michael David, Sandra Lee, Beth Ann, Richard Douglass AB, Ohio U., 1953; JD, U. Cin., 1955. Bar: Ohio 1955, Pa. 1964. Trial lawyer Dept. Justice, Washington, 1955-56; trial lawyer Chief Counsel's Office, IRS, Pitts., 1956-62; assoc. Kirkpatrick, Pomeroy, Lockhart & Johnson, Pitts., 1962-65; ptnr. Kirkpatrick & Lockhart, LLP, Pitts., 1965-94, of counsel, 1995—. Served as sgt. USMC, 1946-47, 50-52 Mem. ABA (tax sect.), Pa. Bar Assn. (tax sect.), Allegheny County Bar Assn. (chmn. tax sect. 1964-66), Estate Planning Coun. (bd. dirs. 1975-77), Pitts. Tax Club (pres. 1985-86), Order of Coif, Duquesne Club, Rivers Club, Valley Brook Country Club (sec. 1977-78). Clubs: Duquesne, Rivers, Valley Brook Country (McMurray, Pa., sec. 1977-78). Republican. Methodist. Avocations: golf, tennis, shooting. Home: 160 Canterbury Rd Mc Murray PA 15317-2802 Office: Kirkpatrick & Lockhart LLP Henry W Oliver Bldg 535 Smithfield St Pittsburgh PA 15222-2312 E-mail: dketter@kl.com.

KETTERER, ANDREW, state commissioner, former state attorney general; b. Trenton, N.J., Jan. 17, 1949; s. Frederic and Loretta (Mehan) Ketterer; m. Susanne Powell, 1978; 1 child, Andrew Powell. BA magna cum laude, Conn. Coll., 1971; JD, Northeastern U., 1974. Former mem. Maine Ho. of Reps.; atty.

gen. State of Maine, 1995—2001; commr. State of Maine's Comm. on Govtl. Ethics and Election Practices, Augusta, Maine, 2002—. Dir., vice chmn. Norridgewock Indsl. Com., 1982; dir. Ctrl. Maine Airport Authority, 1982—; sec., treas. Youth and Family Svcs., Skowhegan, Maine, 1980; chmn. Madison Dem. Town Com., Maine, 1980—; del. Somerset County Dem. Com., 1980—, Dem. State Conv., 1980—82. Mem.: ATLA, ABA, Somerset County Bar Assn., Maine Bar Assn., Norridgecock C. of C. (pres. 1982—83), Elks. Democrat. Home: 10 Laney Rd Skowhegan ME 04976-9400 Office: 135 State House Station Augusta ME 04333-0135

KETTERER, MARK WILLIAM, psychologist, research scientist; b. Philadelphia, Pa., Oct. 8, 1951; PhD, U Md., 1981. Cert. Psychologist Mich., 1993. Sr. bioscientific staff Henry Ford Hosp., Detroit, 1989—. Author (scientist): (studies of psychosocial stress in heart) Multiple Sci. Articles (Dlin/Fisher Clin. Rsch. Award, 1991). Fellow: Acad. of Psychosomatic Medicine, APA; mem.: Am. Psychosomatic Soc. Democrat. Office: Henry Ford Hosp/CFP6 2799 West Grand Blvd Detroit MI 48202 Office Fax: 313-916-8846. E-mail: markwketterer@cs.com.

KETTERLE, WOLFGANG, physics educator; b. Heidelberg, Germany, Oct. 21, 1957; came to the U.S., 1990; divorced; three children. Physics pre-diploma, U. Heidelberg, 1978; physics diploma, Tech. U., Munich, 1982; PhD in Physics, Ludwig-Maximilians U. Munich, 1986. Rsch. asst. Max-Planck Inst. for Quantum Optics, Garching, Germany, 1982-85, staff scientist, 1985-88; rsch. scientist dept. phys. chemistry U. Heidelberg, 1989-90; rsch. assoc. MIT, Cambridge, Mass., 1990-93, asst. prof. physics, 1993-97, prof., 1997—. Recipient Technology Innovation award Discover Magazine, 1998, Fritz London prize in low temperature physics, 1999, Dannie-Heineman prize Acad. Scis., Göttingen, Germany, 1999, Benjamin Franklin medal in physics, 2000, NATO/DAAD Postdoctoral fellow, 1990—91, David and Lucile Packard fellow, 1996, The Nobel Prize in Physics, 2001. Fellow Am. Phys. Soc. (Disting. Traveling lectr. 1998, Rabi prize 1997), Am. Acad. Arts and Scis., Inst. of Physics; mem. German Phys. Soc. (Gustav-Hertz prize 1997), Am. Optical Soc., European Acad. Scis. and Arts, Acad. of Scis. in Heidelberg, Nat. Acad. Scis. Office: MIT 77 Massachusetts Ave Cambridge MA 02139-4307 E-mail: ketterle@mit.edu.

KETTINGER, DAVID JOHN, broadcast executive; b. Abington, Pa., Feb. 21, 1954; s. Ralph Joseph and Mary Elizabeth (Reilly) K. Student, Villanova U., 1973-75. Disc jockey Radio Sta. WBUX, Doylestown, Pa., 1975-77; disc jockey, rschr. Radio Sta. WPST, Trenton, N.J., 1977-80; disc jockey, pub. rels. dir. Radio Sta. WKHI-FM, Ocean City, Md., 1980-81, ops. dir., program dir., 1981-82; advt. cons. sales dept., producer Agy. Voice Overs, Ocean City, 1983-89, asst. sales mgr., 1989-90; sales mgr. Stas. WWTR and WETT, Ocean City, 1990-91; sales mgr., disk jockey Radio Stas. WWTR and WETT, Ocean City, 1991-94; disc jockey Radio Sta. WQHQ-FM, Salisbury, Md., 1990-91; part-time air announcer, comml. producer, copywriter United Artist Cable TV of Ea. Shore, 1991-92; sta. mgr., with sales dept. Radio Sta. WLVW-FM and WLBW-FM, Salisbury, Md., 1994-2000, Cumulus Broadcasting, Inc.; sales staff Radio Sta. WRXS-FM, Atlantic Radio Braodcasting, LLC, Ocean City, Md., 2000; comm. dir., custome rels. mgr. Millsboro Ford, Millsboro, Del., 2000—. Vol. fireman Weldon Fire Co. (mem. fire prevention and publicity coms.), 1972-81; active Muscular Dystrophy Assn., Ocean City Power Squadron. Republican. Roman Catholic. Avocations: boating, sketching, autograph collecting, impersonations, golf. Home: 788 Ocean Pkwy Ocean Pines MD 21811-1726 Office: Millsboro Ford Rt 113 PO Box 369 Millsboro DE 19966 E-mail: davek@millsboroford.com.

KETTL, DONALD FRANCIS, political science educator; b. Phila., Feb. 9, 1952; s. Raymond Paul and Mary Louise Kettl; m. Susan Carmela Amato, July 25, 1950. BA, Yale U., 1974, PhD, 1978. Asst. prof. polit. sci. Columbia U., N.Y.C., 1978-79, U. Va., Charlottesville, 1979-85, assoc. prof., 1985-89, Vanderbilt U., Nashville, 1989-90; prof. U. Wis., Madison, 1990—. Author: Leadership at the Fed, 1986, Sharing Power: Public Governance and Private Markets, 1993, Improving Government Performance: An Owner's Manual, 1993, The Global Public Management Revolution: A Report on the Transformation of Governance, 2000, The Transformation of Governance, 2002, Deficit Politics, 2002, Team Bush: Leadership Lessons from the Bush White House, 2003. Chair, Gov.'s Blue-Ribbon Commn. on State-Local Partnerships for the 21st Century, Wis., 2000-2001, chair Blue-Ribbon Comm. on Campaign Fin. Reform, 1996-97. Office: U Wis-Madison 1225 Observatory Dr Madison WI 53706 Fax: (608) 265-3233.

KETTLE, SALLY ANNE, consulting company executive, educator; b. Omaha, Feb. 2, 1938; d. H. Eugene and Elaine Josephine (Winston) Smiley; m. William Frederick Kettle, July 20, 1968 (div. 1973); children: Christopher, Winston. BEd, U. Nebr., 1960, postgrad. Cert. tchr., S.C., Nebr. Tchr. Dist. 66 Pub. Schs., Omaha, 1966-72; owner, mgr. The Rick Rack, Ltd., Lakewood, Colo., 1974-75; coord. merchandising communications 3M, St. Paul, 1978-80, sr. coord. internat. corp. comm., 1981-83; corp. dir. communications Intran Corp., St. Paul, 1984; pres. Sally Kettle & Co., Bloomington, Minn., 1985-95, Apple Valley, Minn., 1994—. Mem. cmty. faculty Met. State U., Mpls., 1983-90, 97—, St. Olaf Coll., Northfield, Minn., 1992-94, asst. prof. econs., 2000-01; mem. adj. faculty U. Minn. Sch. Journalism and Mass Comm., Mpls., St. Thomas U., 1994-95, Northwestern Coll., 1998-2000. TV hostess City of Bloomington Cable TV, 1984-86. Co-founder Women's Resource Ctr., bd. dirs., mem. adv. bd., 1978-88; chair 13th Precinct, Bloomington, 1978-83; bd. dirs. 41st Sen. Dist., Bloomington, 1982-83; cable TV commr. Bloomington City Coun., 1984-85; pub. rels. com. U.S. Olympic Festival, 1989-90; bd. dirs. Minn. Prayer Breakfast Bd., 1984—; mem. Better Bus. Bur.; founder Ad Rev. Coun.; v.p. Christian Mgmt. Assn., Minn.; internat. com. bd. Carlson Grad. Sch. Mgmt., U. Minn.; mem. state ctrl. com. and platform commn. DFL, 1988-90; bd. dirs. Fellowship of Christian Athletes, 1988-89; pub. rels. com., vice chair bd. comms. '96 Billy Graham Minn. Crusade, 1996; bd. commrs. Shoreland Zoning Commn. Dakota County, Minn., 1996—, vice chair, 1998—. Named one of Outstanding Young Women of Am., 1965. Mem. Am. Advt. Fedn. (conf. com. 1985-87, pub. svc. com. 1986-88), Pub. Rels. Soc. Am., Advt. Fedn. Minn. (bd. dirs. 1982-86), Minn. Women's Econ. Roundtable, Internat. Platform Assn., Nat. Grad. Women's Honor Soc., Minn. Press Club (co-chair newsmaker com., bd. dirs. 1989-92), Phi Delta Gamma, Kappa Alpha Theta. Avocations: reading, sewing, entertaining, volunteering. Home: 13390 Gunflint Path Apple Valley MN 55124-7376

KETTLER, CARL FREDERICK, airline executive; b. N.Y.C., Dec. 19, 1936; s. William Henry and Martha Maria (Allmendinger) K.; m. Marianne Louis Slagboom, Dec. 19, 1970; 1 child, Patricia Heidi. BS in Aeronautics, St. Louis U., 1965; MBA, U. Calif., Berkeley, 1966. Project mgr. corp. planning Trans World Airlines, 1968-69; dir. internat. market planning Flying Tiger Ln., 1969-71; spl. asst. to U.S. Senator Henry Bellmon, 1971-74; dir. fed. affairs Air Transport Assn. Am., Washington, 1974-78; co-organizer Midway Airlines, Inc., 1974-79; asst. to pres. Airbus Industries No.Am., N.Y.C., 1978-80; vice chmn. bd. govs. Flight Safety Found., 1979-81; prtnr. Sunburst Energy Inc., Enid, Okla., 1980-82; co-founder, exec. v.p., COO Trans-Cen. Airlines, Oklahoma City, 1980—; founder T.H.E. Airline Inc., 1981; chmn., pres. Kettler Korp, Inc., 1981—; founder Kettler Komputer Svcs. Inc., 1987—, Kettler Employee Leasing Inc., 1981—; co-founder Kettler & Kettler Employment Svcs., Inc., Flemington, N.J., 1981; founder, pres. Kettler Airline Planning Svcs., Inc. Advisor to Reagan White House on Nat. Security, 1980-84; lectr. St. Louis U., 1968—; cons. aviation and internat. trade. Founder, pres. Oak Summit Sch. Hist. Soc., Citizens Against Ruining the Environ (CARE), 1985—; del. Rep. Nat. Conv., 1992. With USAF, 1955—61. Recipient Outstanding Svc. award Smithsonian Astrophys. Obs., 1959, Alumni Merit award St. Louis U., 1991. Mem. Nat. Def. Transp. Assn., Am. Inst. Aeronautics and Astronautics (air transport tech. com.), Okla. Heritage Assn., Okla. State Soc., Internat. House (Berkeley), Calif. Alumni Assn., U. Calif. at Berkeley, Ducks Unltd., Grand Nat. Quail Club (exec. com.), Capitol Hill Club, Nat. Aviation Club, Internat. Aviation Club, Wings Club, Aero Club, Alpha Eta Rho, Alpha Sigma Chi, Alpha Sigma Nu (Nat. Jesuit Scholastic Honors award, 1965), Gamma Phi Epsilon. Roman Catholic. Avocations: politics, piloting, boating, travel, writing. Home: 59 Everitts Hill Rd Flemington NJ 08822-4005 E-mail: kettler@blast.net.

KETTLESON, DAVID NOEL, retired orthopaedic surgeon, timber manager; b. St. Paul, Dec. 20, 1938; s. John Benton and Dorothy S. (Elkins) K.; m. Karen Nordstrom, Aug. 25, 1961; children: Maria, Daniel, Laura. BA, U. Minn., 1960, BS, MD, 1964. Diplomate Am. Bd. Orthopaedic Surgery. Intern St. Mary's Hosp., Duluth, Minn., 1964-65; resident in orthopaedic surgery U. Minn. Hosp., Mpls., 1965-69; v.p., sec., treas. Orthopaedic Surgery, Inc., Omaha, 1971-92; pres. Nebr. Spine Surgeons, Omaha, 1992-94; ret., 1994; owner Eagleview Farms, Crosslake, Minn., 1994—. Chmn. dept. orthopaedics Immanuel Med. Ctr., Omaha, 1978-82. Served to maj. USAF, 1969-71. Named Minn. Outstanding Tree Farmer of Yr., Am. Forest Found., 2001. Fellow N.Am. Spine Soc.; mem. AMA, Mid Cen. States Orthopaedic Soc. (sec. 1974-85), Nebr. Orthopaedic Soc. (sec. 1974-85), Scoliosis Rsch. Soc., Am. Tree Farm System. Republican. Avocations: hunting, springer spaniels, collecting decoys.

KETTLEWELL, GAIL BIERY, academic administrator; b. Dresden, Ohio, Apr. 5, 1939; d. Graydon Adams and Mildred K. (Cox) Biery; m. Charles G. Kettlewell, Sept. 9, 1960; children: Christian, Abigail, Nathaniel. BA, Muskingum Coll., 1961; MA, Old Dominion U., 1973; EdD, Va. Poly. Inst. and State U., Blacksburg, Va., 1985. Librarian Knox County Library, Mt. Vernon, Ohio, 1961-62; tchr. Fairfax County Pub. Schs., Alexandria, Va., 1968-70, Portsmouth (Va.) Pub. Schs., 1962-68, 70-72; assoc. prof. Tidewater C.C., Portsmouth, 1974-83; vice chancellor So. Ark. U. Tech., Camden, 1984-90; provost No. Va. C.C., Manassas, 1990—2002; dir. D.A. program George Mason U., 2002—. Chmn. Internat. Applied Arts and Scis. Inst., 1999—2001. Author: Guide for Peer Tutors, 1981; co-author: (with Alice Hedrick) An Approach to Language, 1978, (with Betty J. Perkinson) Reading/Thinking/Writing, 1983, 2d edit., 1989, 3d edit., 1994; mem. editl. bd. Workforce, 1994. Bd. dirs. Ark. Literacy Coun., Little Rock, 1988, Prince William County chpt. ARC, 1991-94, 96-01, Prince William Litter Control Coun., 1991, Manassas Mus. Assocs., 1991-94, Manassas Ctr. for Arts, 1994-99, Prince William/I66 Partnership, 1994-2002, Prince William/Manassas Conv. and Visitors Bur., 2001; pres. Prince William Habitat for Humanity, 2001—; mem. Ark. Tech. Com., Little Rock, 1989-90, Am. Coun. Edn. Commn. on Women, 1994-97, Manassas Tourism Coun., 1994-96, Manassas Bus. Coun., 1994-96; coord., organizer Ouachita-Calhoun Literacy Coun., Camden, Ark., 1987-89; active Cmty. Theatre, 1983—. Fellow Western Carolina U., 1976, Old Dominion U., 1967; recipient Community Svc. award, Portsmouth, Va. Mem. AAUW, ASTD, NAFE, Am. Coun. Edn. (com. on women 1994-97), Va. Assn. Female Execs., Manassas Bus. Coun., DAR, North Ctrl. Assn. Schs. and Colls. (rev. com. 1987—), Ark. Assn. for Devel. Edn. (pres. 1988-89), Children Am. Revolution (orgn. sr. pres. 1989-90), Fedn. Civic Clubs (v.p 1980, pres. 1981—), Prince William/Greater Manassas C. of C. (bd. dirs. 1994-2002), Rotary (bd. dirs. 1992-94), Delta Kappa Gamma (internat. fellowship 1982, v.p. 1980-81, pres. 1988-89, 1st v.p. 1992-93), Phi Theta Kappa (hon.), Phi Delta Kappa. Episcopalian. Office: George Mason U Coll of Arts and Scis Fairfax VA 22030-4444 Home: 13456 Victory Gallop Ln Gainesville VA 20155 E-mail: gkettlew@gmu.edu.

KETTLING, VIRGINIA, health facility administrator; b. Toldeo, Aug. 9, 1932; d. Charles Albert and Elizabeth (Knapp) Reuthe; m. George Kettling, June 16, 1962; children: Elys, Kandys, Gynevra, Geoff. BSN, Capital U., 1955; MA, Ohio State U., 1962. Cert. nursing admin. advanced. Asst. prof., dir. baccalaureate program U. Cin., 1965-71; asst. v.p., nursing dir. Bethesda Hosp. Sch. Nursing, Cin., 1971-77; clin. asst. prof. U. Wis., Milw., 1981-88; chief nurse exec. Mt. Sinai Med. Ctr., Milw., 1977-88; v.p. patient care United Samaritans Med. Ctr., Danville, Ill., 1988-97; cert. parish nurse Bethel Luth. Ch., Danville, 1997—; now ret. Cons. D.A.C.C. assoc. degree program, 1998—; interim pres. Lakeview Coll. of Nursing, Danville, Ill., 1999-2000, planning devel. fiscal officer, 2000. Named nominee Wisc. Nurse Exec. Yr. Mem. Am. Orgn. Nurse Execs., Ill. Orgn. Nurse Execs., Am. Hosp. Pub. (reviewer of books), Am. Coll. Healthcare Execs., Midwest Alliance Nursing, Exec. Club Danville. Home: 958 Algoma Dr Port Washington WI 53074

KETTNER-POLLEY, RICHARD BRIAN, director; b. Kalamazoo, Mich., May 11, 1953; s. Robert Lloyd Polley, Barbara Jean Polley; life ptnr. William Anthony Kettner-Polley. BS, Mich. State U., 1975; MA, Harvard U., 1977, PhD, 1979. Asst. prof. U. Ariz., Tucson, 1981—88; assoc. prof. Lewis & Clark Coll., Portland, Oreg., 1988—92; prof. George Fox Coll., Newberg, Oreg., 1993—95; prof., MBA chair ISIM U., Denver, 1998—99; acad. chair MBA programs Jones Internat. U., Englewood, Colo., 1999—2000; sr. acad. dir. U. Denver, 2000—03; prof., dir. edn. Colo. Tech. U., Colorado Springs, 2003—. Editor small group rsch. Sage Pub., Thousand Oaks, 1984—; sr. rsch. prof. NSF, 1986—87, Fulbright Found., 1986—87. Author: (book) The SYMLOG Practitioner, 1988, (Article) Academy of Management Selected Proceedings, 1984; contbr. articles. Mem.: Acad, Mgmt. (local arrangements chair 2001—02, WIlliam Jerome Arnold award 1984). Home: 133 Illini Dr Woodland Park CO 80863 Office: Colo Tech U 4435 N Chestnut St Colorado Springs CO 80907 E-mail: rkpolley@coloradotech.edu.

KETTUNEN ZEGART, MAR(GARET) JEAN, artist, art educator; b. Lansing, Mich., Aug. 19, 1926; d. Arne Gerald and Ruth M. (Cresswell) Kettunen; m. Harold Jerome Zegart, Aug. 3, 1954 (div. Dec. 1964); children: Benjamin Arne, Kathleen Anne (dec.), Johnathan Morris, Jamin Andrew. Student, Cranbrook Art Acad., Bloomfield Hills, Mich., 1946; BA cum laude, Mich. State U., 1947; MA in Painting, U. Calif., Berkeley, 1954; studied and worked in printmaking studios, 1948—53, studied with major artists, 1944—54. Cert. in gen. secondary edn., art and English; cert. in arts adminstrn. Asst. to art editor Glamor, Conde Nast Publs., N.Y.C., 1947-53; designer, sec. Smith, Tepper Sundberg, San Francisco, 1953-54; instr. painting Coll. of Marin, Kentfield, Calif., summer 1961; educator, adult educator La Serna H.S., East Whittier (Calif.) Sch. Dist., 1961-62; Fulbright exch. tchr. Testwood Hampshire Schs., Totten, Hants, Eng., 1979-80; art educator, arts cons. Tamalpais (Calif.) H.S., 1961, 62-91. One-woman shows include Wittenborne Schultz, Inc., N.Y.C., Marin County Civic Ctr., Mus. of Modern Art, San Francisco, Kings Gallery, others, exhibited in group shows at San Francisco Mus. Modern Art Rental Galleries, Kings' Gallery/UU Ctr., San Francisco, Bklyn. Mus., Phila. Print Club, Palace of the Legion of Honor, Met. Mus. Art, N.Y., others, Represented in permanent collections Suomi Coll., Mich. State U., Guggenheim Mus., Mus. Modern Art, N.Y.C., Pub. Libr., Whitney Mus., Musea de Arte Moderna, Sao Paulo, Brazil, Brit. Mus., London, others. Mem.: NEA (life), Marin Ret. Tchrs. Assn. (bd. dirs., newsletter editor, pub. rels.), San Francisco Mus. Modern Art, San Francisco Mus. Soc., Graphic Art Coun., Calif. Tchrs. Assn. (life), Friend of Del Norte, Mill Valley Outdoor Art Club (bd. dirs., civics and conservation chair, 2d v.p.). Avocations: reading, attending theatre, opera and ballet, family genealogy. Home: 118 Highland Ln Mill Valley CA 94941-3564 E-mail: kettz@aol.com.

KEULEGAN, EMMA PAULINE, special education educator; b. Washington, Jan. 21, 1930; d. Garbis H. and Nellie Virginia (Moore) K. BA, Dumbarton Coll. of Holy Cross, 1954. Cert. tchr. elem. and spl. edn. Tchr. St. Dominic's Elem. Sch., Washington, 1954-56, Sacred Heart Acad., Washington, 1956-59, Our Lady of Victory, Washington, 1959-63, St. Francis Acad., Vicksburg, Miss., 1963-78, Culkin Acad., Vicksburg, 1978-91, substitute tchr. spl. edn., 1991—. Treas. PTA, Vicksburg, 1980; pres. Vicksburg Genealogical Soc., 1999. Mem.: DAR (chpt. regent 1967—69, sec. 1994, chpt. chaplain 1996, chpt. libr. 2002, chpt. membership chmn.), Daus. of United Confederacy (chpt. chaplain), Soc. Descs. of Knights of Most Noble Order of the Garter, Sovereign Colonial Soc. Am. Royal Descent, Soc. Magna Charta Dames and Barons (state chaplain 2001), Daus. of the War of 1812 (state chaplain 1998, hon. state pres. 2002, state pres. 2002—, hon. state pres. 2003), Daus. Am. Colonists (chaplain 1985—89, state pres. 1992—94, hon. state pres. 1994—), Colonial Dames 17th Century (state v.p. 1987—89, state pres. 1989, hon. state pres. 1991—), Internat. Reading Assn. (pres. Warren County chpt.), Vicksburg Geneal. Soc. (pres. 2003). Republican. Roman Catholic. Avocations: stamp and coin collecting, needlework, reading. Home: 215 Buena Vista Dr Vicksburg MS 39180-5612 Office: Cedars Elem School 235 Cedars School Circle Vicksburg MS 39180-2571

KEUNE, RUSSELL VICTOR, retired architect; b. Chgo., 1938; m. Ingrid Christina Friberg, 1968; 1 child, Eric Richard. BArch, U. Ill., Urbana, 1961, MArch, 1965. Registered arch., Va. Restoration arch. Nat. Park Svc., U.S. Dept. Interior, Washington, 1961-63, from staff arch. of Hist. Am. Bldgs. Survey to asst. keeper of Nat. Register Hist. Places, 1965-68; rsch. and tchg. asst. U. Ill., Urbana, 1963-65; from dir. dept. field svcs. to sr. v.p. preservation programs Nat. Trust for Hist. Preservation, Washington, 1969-83; pvt. practice, 1983-84; sr. project mgr. Geler Brown Renfrow Archs., Washington, 1984-86; v.p. for programs U.S. Com., Internat. Coun. on Monuments and Sites, Washington, 1986-93; dir. internat. rels. AIA, Washington, 1993-99. Mem. U.S. delegation 7th Gen. Assembly Internat. Ctr. for Study of Preservation and Restoration of Cultural Property, Rome, 1973, UNESCO Conv. Conf. on Preservation of Hist. Quars., Towns and Sites, Warsaw, Poland, 1975; mem. U.S. exch. delegation Preservation Hist. and Cultural Property, USSR, 1974; mem. task force on tourism and preservation Pacific Area Travel Assn., Macau and The Philippines, 1980, mem. task force on preservation of Chinatown, Singapore, 1985; acad. specialist on hist. preservation to Yemen Arab Republic USIA, 1989; guest lectr., spkr. numerous colls., univs., pub. agys., profl. and preservation orgns. Fellow AIA (mem. hist. resources com. 1968—, chmn. 1988-89), Internat. Coun. Monuments and Sites (bd. dirs. 1977-80, 83-86); mem. Assn. Preservation Tech. (v.p. 1974-77), Ea. Park and Monument Assn., Hist. Am. Bldgs. Survey Found. (vice chmn. 1983-93), Hist. Preservation Roundtable, Cosmos Club, Lamda Alpha. E-mail: rkeune@earthlink.net.

KEUP, LINDA C. management educator; d. James A. and Margaret T. Rodacker; m. David G. Keup, June 7, 1970; children: Sarah Margaret, Benjamin Ward, Christine Marie. BS, Minot State U., 1969; MBA, U. of ND, Grand Forks, 1987; PhD, U. of Man., Winnipeg, Can., 2000. Asst. prof. mgmt. Minot State U., Minot, ND, 1988—2000, Concordia Coll., Moorhead, Minn., 2000—. Commr. Minot Housing Authority, Minot, ND, 1991—93; mem. Taube Mus. Art, Minot, ND, 1992—93, 2000—02. Leadership fellow, Bush Found., 1993. Mem.: Adminstrv. Scis. Assn. Can., Acad. Mgmt. Republican. United Methodist. Avocations: reading, canoeing. Office: Concordia Coll 901 8th St S Moorhead MN 56562

KEUSCH, GERALD T. health services administrator; b. N.Y.C., Apr. 30, 1938; m. Kathleen Baden, Mar. 23, 1985; 3 children. AB, Columbia Coll., 1958; MD, Harvard U., 1963. Diplomate Am. Bd. of Internal Medicine, Am. Bd. Infectious Diseases. Asst. to prof. Mount Sinai Sch. of Medicine, N.Y., 1970-78; prof. medicine Tufts U. Sch. of Medicine; chief divsn. of georgraphic medicine and infectious disease New England Med. Ctr., Boston; dir. Fogarty Internat. Ctr. NIH, Dept. Health and Human Svcs., Bethesda, Md., 1998—. Contbr. articles to profl. jours. Recipient Career Scientist award Health Rsch. Coun. of City of N.Y., Inc., 1973-76, Rsch. Career Devel. award Nat. Inst. of Allergy and Infectious Diseases, 1974-79; Heath-Clark award U. London Sch. of Hygiene and Tropical Medicine, 1991. Mem. AAAS, Am. Fedn. for Clin. Rsch., N.Y. Acad. of Sci., Infectious Disease Soc. of Am. (councillor 1999—, Maxwell Finland lecture award 1997, Squibb award 1981), Am. Soc. for Microbiology, Harvard Soc., Am. Soc. for Clin. Investigation, MA Infectious Disease Soc. (treas. 1987-91, pres. 1992-95), Assn. of Am. Physicians. Avocation: music. Office: 31 Center Dr MSC 2220, Room B2C29 Bethesda MD 20892-2220

KEVESS-COHEN, RUTH M. internist, geriatrician; b. Bklyn., June 24, 1957; d. Arthur Shepard and Hilde (Weingarten) Kevess; m. David Jonathan Cohen, June 17, 1979; children: Alison, Susanna, Benjamin, Jeremy. AB summa cum laude, Harvard-Radcliffe, 1979; MD, Johns Hopkins U., Balt., 1983. Diplomate Am. Bd. Internal Medicine with subspecialty in geriatrics; cert. med. dir. Intern, then resident in internal medicine George Washington U. Hosp., 1983-86; ptnr. Cameron Med. Group, Silver Spring, Md., 1986—; med. dir. transitional care ctr. Holy Cross Hosp., Silver Spring, 1996—; med. dir. Care Matrix of Silver Spring, 1996-99; physician advisor Kensington (Md.) Pk. Assisted Living, 1999-2000. Cons. quality assurance Birch & Davis, Silver Spring, 1993-96. Adv. bd. Iona Sr. Svcs., Washington, 1996. Fellow ACP; mem. Montgomery County Med. Soc., Am Med. Dirs. Assn., Phi Beta Kappa, Alpha Omega Alpha. Democrat. Jewish. Avocation: crafts. Office: Cameron Medical Group 8700 Georgia Ave Ste 400 Silver Spring MD 20910-3605

KEVLES, DANIEL JEROME, history educator, writer; b. Phila., Mar. 2, 1939; s. David and Anne (Rothstein) K.; m. Bettyann Holtzmann, May 18, 1961; children: Beth Carolyn, Jonathan David. BA in Physics, Princeton U., 1960; postgrad., Oxford U., 1960-61; PhD in History, Princeton U., 1964. From asst. to prof. history Calif. Inst. Tech., Pasadena, 1964-86, Koepfli prof. humanities, 1986-2001, head program in sci., ethics, and pub. policy, 1987-2001; vis. prof. Yale U., New Haven, 2000-01, Stanley Woodward prof. history, 2001—. Vis. rsch. fellow U. Sussex, Brighton, Eng., 1976; vis. prof. U. Pa., Phila., 1979, Princeton U., 1999; dir. studies Ecole des Hautes Etudes en Sciences Sociales, Paris, 1991; chmn. faculty Calif. Inst. Tech., 1995-97. Author: The Physicists, 1978 (Nat. Hist. Soc. prize 1979), In the Name of Eugenics, 1985; (mag. series) Annals of Eugenics (Page One award 1985), The Baltimore Case, 1998 (Watson Davis prize); co-author: Inventing America, 2002; co-editor: The Code of Codes, 1992; contbr. articles to N.Y. Rev. Books, other mags. Charles Warren fellow Harvard U., 1981-82, Ctr. for Advanced Study Behavioral Scis. fellow, 1986-87, Nat. Endowment for Humanities sr. fellow, 1981-82, Guggenheim fellow, 1983. Fellow: AAAS (chmn. sect. L 1983—85), Soc. Am. Historians; mem.: PEN, Am. Philos. Soc., History Sci. Soc. (coun. 1980—82, com. publ. 1984—88, Sarton lectr. 1985, George Sarton medal 2001), Am. Hist. Assn., Orgn. Am. Historians, Am. Acad. Arts and Scis., Author's Guild, Century Assn., Yale Club (N.Y.C.), Phi Beta Kappa. Democrat. Office: Yale U Dept History PO Box 208324 New Haven CT 06520-8324 E-mail: daniel.kevles@yale.edu.

KEVORKIAN, RICHARD, artist; b. Dearborn, Mich., Aug. 24, 1937; s. Kay and Stana (Bedeian) K.; m. Salpy Bouroujian; children: Anna, Raffi, Soseh and Ellina (twins). Serar. BFA, Richmond Profl. Inst., 1961; MFA in Painting, Calif. Coll. Arts and Crafts, 1962. Instr. drawing and painting Richard Bland Coll., Petersburg, Va., 1961-64; instr. dept. fine arts Va. Commonwealth U., Richmond, 1962-66, asst. prof. dept. painting and printmaking, 1967-69, assoc. prof., 1969-77, prof., 1967-93, prof. emeritus, 1993, chmn. dept., 1969-81. One-man exhbns. include Aaron Gallery, Washington, Marita Gilliam Gallery, Raleigh, N.C.; exhbns. include Birmingham Mus. Art, Ala., 1977, Greenville County Mus. Art, S.C., 1977, Southeastern Ctr. Contemporary Art, Winston-Salem, N.C., 1977, 78, Hunter Mus. Art, Chattanooga, 1978, Va. Mus. Fine Art, 1983, U. Tenn., Knoxville, 1983. Mem. selection bd. for visual arts Va. Ctr. for Creative Arts, Sweet Briar. Served with N.G., 1955-63 NEA individual sr. artists grantee, 1972, Va. Commonwealth U. Sch. Arts faculty creative research grantee, 1974, Nat. Endowment for Arts, Southeastern Ctr. Contemporary Arts grantee, 1976; Guggenheim fellow, 1978 Home: 7909 Rock Creek Rd Richmond VA 23229-6643 E-mail: rekev@attbi.com.

KEWALRAMANI, LAXMAN SUNDERDAS, surgeon, consultant; b. Jaipur, India, Mar. 10, 1943; came to U.S., 1970, U.S. citizen; s. Sunderdas K. and Sugnidevi Kewalramani; m. Dropadi Chellani, May 29, 1970; children: Anupama, Mukul. MB, BS, U. Rajasthn, Jaipur, 1965, M of Surgery, 1969. Diplomate Am. Bd. Phys. Medicine & Rehab., Am. Bd. Electrodiagnostic Medicine (fellow). Fellow neurol. surgery U. Calif. Davis-Sacramento Med. Ctr., 1970-71, resident in phys. medicine and rehab., 1971-73; asst. prof. dept. phys. medicine and rehab. U. Calif., Davis, 1973-76; asst. prof. depts. phys. medicine and rehab. Baylor Coll. Medicine, Houston, 1976-79; assoc. prof. sect. rheumatology and rehab. dept. medicine sch. medicine La. State U., New Orleans, 1979-82; dir. rehab. rsch., coord. patient care La. Rehab. Inst. and Charity Hosp., New Orleans, 1979-82; pvt. practice in phys. medicine and rehab., orthopedic medicine, electrodiagnostic medicine and thermography, 1982—; med. dir. Health South Rehab. Ctr., Harahan, La., 1989-91; med. dir. rehab. unit Chalmette (La.) Med. Ctrs., 1991-92; med. dir. spine and orthopedic inst. Elmwood Med. Ctr., Jefferson, La., 1993-95. Sr. disability analyst Am. bd. Disability Analysts, 2001; cons. rehab. medicine svc. crippled children svcs. sect. VA Hosp., 1975-76; mem. quality assurance com. Charity Hosp. and La. Rehab. Inst., New Orleans, 1979-82; presenter in field. Reviewer manuscripts, cons. editorial bd. Archives Phys. Medicine and Rehab., 1977-80; contbr. 2 chpts. to books and 96 articles to profl. jours. Cons. Cluster Living and Shared Providers, 1978; trustee New Orleans Pharmacy Mus., 1993—. Fellow: Am. Acad. Pain Mgmt., Am. Acad. Phys. Medicine and Rehab. (assessment diagnostic and therapeutic modalities and devices, subcom. med. practice 1985—86); mem.: Am. Assn. Indian Profls. (pres. New Orleans chpt. 2003), Internat. Med. Soc. Paraplegia, Orleans Parish Med. Soc., La. Phys. Medicine and Rehab. Soc., La. State Med. Soc., Am. Assn. Electromyography and Electrodiagnosis (liaison rep. to profl. stds. com. 1984—), Am. Assn. Electrodiagnostic Medicine, Am. Assn. Physicians India (ethics and grievance com.

1992—), Am. Spinal Injury Assn. Republican. Hindu. Avocations: reading, music, collecting time pieces and writing instruments, abstract painting. Home: 738 English Turn Ln New Orleans LA 70131-3349 Office: 3301 Saint Charles Ave New Orleans LA 70115-4533

KEWLEY, SHARON LYNN, systems analyst, consultant; b. Geneseo, Ill., Sept. 23, 1958; d. James Leslie and Geraldine (Myers) K. BBA with honors, U. Miami (Fla.), 1988. Gen. agt. Varvaris & Assocs., Cedar Rapids, Iowa, 1981-84; programmer, analyst U. Miami, Coral Gables, Fla., 1984-88; systems analyst Metro Dade County, Miami, Fla., 1988-91; sys. analyst Nat. Coun. on Compensation Ins., Boca Raton, Fla., 1991-93; owner Boca Byte, Boca Raton, 1993—. Mem. NAFE, Kendall Jaycees, Nat. Gold Key Honor Soc., PADI Divemaster. Republican. Lutheran. Avocations: cruising, world travel, scuba diving. Office: Boca Byte PO Box 7072 Boca Raton FL 33431-0072 E-mail: kewstan@aol.com.

KEY, HELEN ELAINE, accountant, consulting company executive, educator; b. Cleve., Jan. 16, 1946; d. Maud and Helen (Key) Vance. BS, W.Va. State Coll., 1968; MEd, Cleve. State U., 1977, PhD, 2003. Prin. Cleve. Bd. Edn., 1968—. Instr. Cuyahoga Community Coll., Cleve., part-time, 1969—, Dyke Coll., Cleve., part-time, 1979-85; pres. H.E. Key & Assos., Cleve., 1983—; treas. BK4W Inc., Cleve., 1981; sec. Progressive Pioneers, Inc. Mem. AAUW, NAACP, NEA, Am. Assn. Notary Pubs., Women Bus. Owners Assn., Cleve. Area Bus. Tchrs., Toastmistress Club (sec. 1978), Pi Lambda Theta, Alpha Kappa Alpha. Democrat. Baptist. Home: 564 Wilkes Ln Cleveland OH 44143-2622 E-mail: hekey-clev@worldnet.att.net.

KEY, JACK DAYTON, librarian; b. Enid, Okla., Feb. 24, 1934; s. Ernest Dayton and Janie (Haldeman) K.; m. Virgie Ruth Richardson, Aug. 12, 1956; children— Toni, Scot, Todd. BA, Phillips U., Enid, Okla., 1958; MA, U. N.Mex., 1960; MS, U. Ill., 1962. Staff supr. Grad. Library U. Ill., 1960-62; pharmacy librarian U. Iowa, 1962-64; med. librarian Lovelace Found. for Med. Edn. and Research, Albuquerque, 1965-70; dir. Mayo Med. Ctr. Librs., Rochester, Minn., 1970-94, dir. emeritus, 1994—; prof. emeritus biomed. comm. Mayo Med. Sch. Cons. in field; participant Naval War Coll. Conf., 1979; Alberta A. Brown lectr. Western Mich. U., 1979 Author: The Origin of the Vaccine Inoculation by Edward Jenner, 1977, William Alexander Hammond (1828-1900), 1979; editor: Library Automation: The Orient and South Pacific, 1975, Automated Activities in Health Sciences Libraries, 1975-78, Classics and Other Selected Readings in Medical Librarianship, 1980, Journal of a Quest for the Elusive Doctor Arthur Conan Doyle, 1982, Medical Vanities, 1982, William A. Hammond, M.D., 1828-1900: The Publications of an American Neurologist, 1983, Classics in Cardiology, Vol. 3, 1983, Vol. 4, 1989, Medical Casebook of Dr. Arthur Conan Doyle from Practitioner to Sherlock Holmes and Beyond, 1984, Medicine, Literature and Eponyms: An Encyclopedia of Medical Eponyms Derived from Literary Characters, 1989, Conan Doyle's Tales of Medical Humanism and Values, 1992; contbr. articles to profl. jours. Served with USN, 1952-55. U. N.Mex. fellow, 1958-59, N.Mex. Library Assn. Marion Dorroh Meml. scholar, 1960, Rotary Paul Harris fellow, 1979; recipient Outstanding Hist. Writing award Minn. Medicine, 1980, Spl. Svc. award Am. Acad. Dermatology, 1992, Farthing award Baker St. Jour., 1993; decorated knight Icelandic Order of Falcon, 1980; named to Phillips U. Hall Fame, 1988. Mem. Med. Library Assn., Am. Inst. History Pharmacy, Am. Assn. History Medicine, Am. Med. Writers Assn., Am. Osler Soc. (pres. 1990-91), Mystery Writers of Am., Alcuin Soc., Baker St. Irregulars, Ampersand Club, Sigma Xi (cert. of recognition 1982) Mem. Christian Ch. (Disciples Of Christ). Home: PO Box 231 54 Skyline Dr Sandia Park NM 87047-0231 Office: Mayo Clinic Rochester MN 55905-0001

KEY, JAMES EVERETT, ophthalmologist; b. Freeport, Tex., July 19, 1944; s. James Everett and Margaret Ann (Parker) K.; m. Betty Wilson, Dec. 22, 1967; children: Peter Wilson and Courtney Brooke (twins). BA, U. Tex., 1966; MD, Baylor U., 1970. Diplomate Am. Bd. Ophthalmology. Mem. staff Coll. Medicine Baylor U., Houston, 1976-89, clin. assoc. prof. ophthalmology, 1989-93, clin. prof. ophthalmology, 1994—. Chief ophthalmology St. Luke's Episcopal Hosp., Houston, 1987—. Contbr. articles to jours., chpts. to books, editor medical textbooks. Trustee U. of South, Sewanee, Tenn., 1991-96, 98-2000. Lt. USN, 1972-73. Recipient Honor award Am. Acad. of Ophthalmology, 1990. Fellow Am. Acad. Ophthalmology (Hon. award); mem. AMA, Contact Lens Assn. Ophthalmologists (past pres.), Harris County Med. Assn., Tex. Ophthal. Assn. (past bd. dirs.), Houston Ophthal. Soc. (past pres.), Phi Beta Kappa. Episcopalian. Office: 6624 Fannin St Ste 2100 Houston TX 77030-2333 E-mail: eyemed1@swbell.net.

KEY, JANICE DIXON, physician, medical educator; b. Hickory, N.C., Aug. 14, 1954; d. Charles Dennis and Mary Louise (Edgerton) Dixon; m. L. Lyndon Key Jr., May 27, 1973; children: Rebecca Louise, Emily Edgerton. BS, U. N.C., 1976, MD, 1980. Clin. instr. Harvard Med. Sch., Boston, 1984-85; clin. assoc. prof. Sch. of Medicine, U. N.C., Greensboro, N.C., 1985-91; asst. prof. Med. U. of S.C., Charleston, S.C., 1991-98, assoc. prof. pediat., 1998—. Author: Ambulatory Pediatric Care, 1992, Sleepwell Series, vol. 3, 2003; contbr. articles to profl. jours. Pres. Charleston County Med. Soc., 2002—; com. mem. S.C. Adolescent Task Force, Charleston, 1993, S.C. Dept. Edn., Columbia, 1992, S.C. Sch. Health Advisory, Columbia, 1992; co-chair Sch. Health Com., Charleston, 1992—; cmty. adv. bd. Jr. League, Charleston, 1994 Recipient Faculty Rsch. award U. N.C., 1978. Fellow Am. Acad. Pediat.; mem. Am. Soc. Human Genetics, Soc. Adolescent Medicine (chpt. pres. 1991-98), Am. Med. Women's Assn., S.C. Med. Assn. (del., com. chairperson 1996—), S.C. Pediat. Med. Soc. (CME com. 1994-96), Alpha Omega Alpha, Phi Beta Kappa, Phi Eta Sigma. Democrat. Presbyterian. Office: 135 Rutledge Ave Charleston SC 29425-0001

KEY, KAREN LETISHA, pharmaceutical executive; b. Sanford, N.C., Jan. 17, 1957; d. Kermit Lee and Ruth (Whitaker) K. BS in Phys. Edn., Appalachian State U., 1978; MBA, U. N.C., 1993. Profl. sales rep. Burroughs Wellcome Co., Florence, S.C., 1982-84, field trainer Kernersville, N.C., 1984-87; field mgmt. trainee then asst. product mgr. Cardiovasculars/Antivirals/Psychotropics, Research Triangle Park, N.C., 1987-90, dist. sales mgr. psychiatry, 1990-91, asst. to sr. v.p. prodn. and engring., 1991-92, mgr. mktg. tng. and devel., 1991-92, product mgr. neuromuscular blockers, 1993-94; product mgr. Zovirax/Valtrex, 1994-95; project mgr. care mgmt. divsn. Glaxo Wellcome, Raleigh, N.C., 1995, dir. bus. ops., 1996-98, dir. U.S. bus. devel., 1998-2000; dir. worldwide bus. devel. GlaxoSmithKline, 2001—. Mem. Lakewood Bapt. Ch. Republican. Baptist. Avocations: golf, windsurfing, water sports. Office: GlaxoSmithKline Bldg 50 2235 Five Moore Dr Research Triangle Park NC 27709

KEY, MARY RITCHIE (MRS. AUDLEY E. PATTON), linguist, writer, educator; b. San Diego, Mar. 19, 1924; d. George Lawrence and Iris (Lyons) Ritchie; children: Mary Helen Key Ellis, Harold Hayden Key (dec.), Thomas George Key. Student, U. Chgo., summer 1954, U. Mich., 1959; MA, U. Tex., 1960, PhD, 1963; postgrad., UCLA, 1966. Asst. prof. linguistics Chapman Coll., Orange, Calif., 1963-66, asst. prof. linguistics U. Calif., Irvine, 1966-71, assoc. prof., 1971-78, prof., 1978—, chmn. program linguistics, 1969-71, 75-77, 87—. Cons. Am. Indian langs., Spanish, in Mexico, 1946-55, S.Am., 1955-62, English dialects, 1968-74, Easter Island, 1975, Calif. Dept. Edn., 1966, 70-75, Center Applied Linguistics, Washington, 1967, 69; lectr. in field. Author: Comparative Tacanan Phonology, 1968, Male/Female Language, 1975, 2d edit., 1996, Paralanguage and Kinesics, 1975, Nonverbal Communication, 1977, The Grouping of South American Indian Languages, 1979, The Relationship of Verbal and Nonverbal Communication, 1980, Catherine the Great's Linguistic Contribution, 1980, Polynesian and American Linguistic Connections, 1984, Comparative Linguistics of South American Indian Languages, 1987, General and Amerindian Ethnolinguistics, 1989, Language Change in South American Indian Languages, 1991; founder, editor: newsletter Nonverbal Components of Communication, 1972-76; mem. editoral bd. Forum Linguisticum, 1976—, Lang. Scis., 1978—, La Linguistique, 1979—, Multilingua, 1987—; contbr. articles to profl. jours. Recipient Friends of Libr. Book award, 1976, hon. mention, Rolex awards for Enterprise, project Computerizing the Languages of the World, 1990; U. Calif. Regent's grantee, 1974, Fulbright-Hays grantee, 1975; faculty rsch. fellow, 1984-85. Mem. Linguistic Soc. Am., Am. Dialect Soc. (exec. council; regional sec. 1974-83), Internat. Reading Assn. (dir. 1968-72), Delta Kappa Gamma (local pres. 1974-76). Office: U Calif-Irvine Dept Linguistics Irvine CA 92697-5100

KEY, RANDALL DON, band director, musician; b. Decatur, Ala., Aug. 21, 1971; s. Donald E. and Annie Jo Key. AA, Wallace State Coll., Hanceville, Ala., 1991; MusB in Edn., U. Montevallo, 1994; MA in Edn., U. North Ala., 1998. Band dir. Cullman (Ala.) H.S. and Cullman Mid. Sch., 1994—. Clinician; studio musician; mem. band Chosen Few Horns, Soul Soc.; performed with Dickie Betts, Danny Glover, Percy Sledge, The Drifters, Big Sandy and the Flyrite Boys, Jeff Cook and the Chosen Few, Alabama. Bd. dirs. Cullman City Schools Found., 1999—2000, Ala. Sch. of Gospel Music, Boaz. Mem.: NEA, Ala. Bandmasters's Assn., Ala. Edn. Assn., Internat. Assn. of Jazz Educators, Music Educators Nat. Conf. Avocations: kayaking, running, hiking. Home: 301 Simpson St SE Hartselle AL 35640 Office: Cullman H S 510 13th St Cullman AL 35055 Office Fax: 256-734-9570. Personal E-mail: randallk@hiwaay.net. E-mail: randallk@hiwaay.net.

KEY, TARA ANN, clinical social worker; b. Southfield, Mich., June 19, 1966; d. Bruce Stewart and Doris Ann (Diehl) Baldwin; m. Denman Arlan Key, Oct. 17, 1989. BSW, East Tex. State U., 1988; MS in Social Work, U. Tex., Arlington, 1992. Lic. master social worker, Tex.; advanced clin. practitioner, Tex. Intern in social work, cons. Terrell (Tex.) State Hosp., 1988-89, clin. social worker, 1989-91; dir. social svcs. Terrell Care Ctr., 1991-92; clin. social worker VA Med. Ctr., Dallas, 1992—. Clin. instr. psychiatry U. Tex. Southwestern Med. Sch., Dallas, 1994-97; field instr. masters level social work U. Tex. at Arlington, 1998—. Vol. Spl. Olympics, Commerce, Tex., 1988. Recipient Mental Health and Behavioral Scis. Svc. Dirs. award Dept. Vets. Affairs, 1994. Mem.: Alpha Delta Mu. Avocations: archaeology, travel, gardening, mountain biking, camping. Home: 541 Oxbow St Mesquite TX 75149-4851 Office: VA Med Ctr 4500 S Lancaster Rd Dallas TX 75216-7256

KEY, TED, cartoonist; b. Fresno, Calif., Aug. 25, 1912; s. Simon Leon and Fanny (Kahn) K.; m. Anne Elizabeth Wilkinson, Sept. 30, 1937 (dec. July 5, 1984); children: Stephen Lewis, David Edward, Peter Lawrence; m. Bonnie Williams-Cohen, Nov. 17, 1987. BA, U. Calif., Berkeley, 1933. Assoc. editor Judge mag., N.Y.C., 1937-39; radio staff writer J. Walter Thompson Advt. Agy., N.Y.C., 1939-43; cartoonist Hazel Saturday Evening Post, Phila., 1943-70, King Features Syndicate, 1969—. Cartoonist, writer The Econs. Press, Inc., Fairfield, N.J., 1957—; screenwriter Walt Disney Prodns., Burbank, Calif., 1970-77. Writer, cartoonist for CBS, NBC, mags., books, newspapers; playwright (NBC radio prodn.) The Clinic (pub. in anthology Best Broadcasts Of 1939-40); creator (cartoon features) Diz and Liz for Jack and Jill mag., 1961-71, (TV series) Hazel, Peabody and Sherman for Bullwinkle and Rocky Show (TV series), 1959; writer: Hazel, NBC-TV (4 yrs.), CBS-TV (1 yr.), 1946, Here's Hazel, 1949, Many Happy Returns, 1950, If You Like Hazel, 1952, So'm I, 1953, Hazel Rides Again, 1955, Fasten Your Seat Belts, 1956, Phyllis, 1957, All Hazel, 1958, The Hazel Jubilee, 1959, The Biggest Dog in the World, 1960, Hazel Time, 1962, Life With Hazel, 1965, Diz and Liz, 1965, Squirrels in the Feeding Station, 1967, Hazel Power, 1971, Right On Hazel, 1972, Ms. Hazel, 1972, Hazel's Feline Funnies, 1982; story/screenwriter: Million Dollar Duck, The Cat From Outer Space (also wrote novel), Gus; writer: Positive Attitude Posters, 1965-2003, Sales Bullets, 1960-2003; cartoons included in New Yorker, Esquire, Look, Life, Ladies Home Jour., McCall's, Good Housekeeping, Better Homes and Gardens, People, Mademoiselle. Master sgt. Signal Corps AUS, 1943-46. Mem. Nat. Cartoonists Soc. (Best Syndicated Panel award 1977), Writers Guild Am. West.

KEY, THOMAS MARSHALL, music educator; b. Union City, Tenn., Dec. 20, 1971; s. Thomas Marshall Sr. and Suzanne Wright Key; m. Jennifer Lynne Lillard-Key, June 10, 1995; children: Vivian Suzanne, Thomas Marshall Key III. BS in Music Edn., Austin Peay State U., 1994, MusM, 1996. Cert. tchr. Tenn. Dir. bands Halls (Tenn.) H.S., 1994—95, N.E. Mid. Sch., Clarksville, Tenn., 1998—2001, N.E. H.S., Clarksville, 2001—02; choir and youth dir. Excell Bapt. Ch., Clarksville, 1998—99; music tchr. Sango Elem. Sch., Clarksville, 1996—98; dir. bands Crestview Mid. Sch., Covington, Tenn., 2002—. Mem.: Tenn. Music Educators Assn., Mid. Tenn. Sch. Band and Orch. Assn., Music Tchrs. Nat. Conf. Avocation: raising orchids. Home: 515 Cherry St Dyersburg TN 38024 Office: Crestview Mid Sch 201 Mark Walker Blvd Covington TN 38019

KEYES, ALAN L. radio and talk show host, former federal government official; b. N.Y.C., Aug. 7, 1950; m. Jocelyn Marcel; children: Francis, Maya & Andrew BA, Harvard U., 1972, PhD, 1979. Commd. fgn. service officer Dept. State, 1978, consular officer, 1979-80, desk officer, 1980-81, policy planning staff, 1981-83, asst. sec. for internat. orgn. affairs, 1985—88; U.S. rep. to econ. and social council UN, 1983-85; pres. Citizens Against Govt. Waste, 1988—92; interim pres. Ala. A&M Univ., 1991; cand. U.S. Senate Md., 1988, 1992; cand. U.S. Pres., 1996, 2000; natl. talk radio show host The Alan Keyes Show: America's Wake Up Call; founder & pres. The Declaration Foundation. Author: Masters of the Dream: The Strength and Betrayal of Black America, 1995, Our Character, Our Future: Reclaiming America's Moral Destiny, 1996. Office: Declaration Foundation 721-R Second St NE Washington DC 20002

KEYES, ALLEN E. retired judge; b. Marlette, Mich., Feb. 22, 1926; s. Elmer James and Myra Blanche Keyes; m. Roma Janice Turner, Feb. 23, 1952; children: Janice, Barbara, Cheryl, David. AB, Wayne State U., 1951, JD, 1956. Bar: Mich. 1956. Claims adjuster Mich. Mut. Liability Co., Detroit, 1953-55, State Farm Ins., Detroit, 1955-57; sole practitioner gen. law practice, Marlette, 1957-58, 68-75; pros. atty. Sanilac County, Sandusky, Mich., 1958-68; cir. ct. judge State of Mich., Sandusky, 1975-90. Mediator St. Clair County, 1990—. Bd. dirs. United Way, Sandusky, 1961-63, Marlette Comty. Hosp., 1968-75. 1st lt. USAF, 1951-53. Recipient Silver Anniversary award Wayne State U., 1981. Avocations: golf, bowling. Home: 3920 Jack Pine Ln Port Huron MI 48060-1578

KEYES, ARTHUR HAWKINS, JR., architect; b. Rutland, Vt., May 26, 1917; s. Arthur Hawkins and Blanche (Emery) K.; m. Lucile Sheppard, Mar. 29, 1941; children: Arthur S., Spencer S., Janet S. AB cum laude, Princeton U., 1939; M.Arch., Harvard U., 1942. Partner Keyes, Lethbridge and Condon, Washington, 1956-75; partner Keyes Condon Florance (Architects), Washington, 1975-80, pres., 1980-85; chmn. Keyes Condon Florance Eich Baum Esocoff King, 1985-92; chmn. emeritus, 1992—; pres. Sea Ridge Devel. Corp., Washington Bldg. Congress, 1964-65; chmn. alumni adv. council Sch. Architecture, Princeton U., 1965-73. Trustee Hist. Soc. Washington D.C. Served with USNR, 1942-46. Fellow AIA (spl. presdl. citation 1982); mem. Nat. Trust Hist. Preservation, Com. of 100 on the Fed. City. Clubs: Cosmos, Chevy Chase. Republican. Home: 2605 31st St NW Washington DC 20008-3519 Office: Internat Square 1825 Eye St NW Ste 250 Washington DC 20006-5428 E-mail: akeyes@dc.smithgroup.com.

KEYES, DANIEL, author; BA in Psychology, Bklyn. Coll., 1950, MA in English, 1961. Assoc. fiction editor Magazine Mgmt. Co., N.Y.C., 1950-52; v.p. Fenko and Keyes Photography, Inc., 1952-53; tchr. English N.Y.C. Bd. Edn., 1955-62; instr. English Wayne State U., Detroit, 1962-66; mem. faculty Ohio U., Athens, 1966—, prof. English and creative writing, 1972-97, prof. emeritus, 2000—; agt. William Morris Agy., N.Y.C., Calif. Author: (novels) Flowers for Algernon (Hugo award 1959, Nebula award 1966, movie version: Charly, 1968), The Touch, 1968, The Fifth Sally, 1980, (nonfiction) The Minds of Billy Milligan, 1981 (Spl. award Mystery Writers Am., Kurd Lasswitz award, 1st prize Best Fgn. Book award 1986), Unveiling Claudia, 1986, Daniel Keyes Collected Stories, 1993 (Japan), The Milligan Wars, 1994 (Japan), Daniel Keyes Reader, 1995 (Japan), Until Death Do Us Part: The Sleeping Princess, 1998 (Japan), (TV movie) Flowers for Algernon, 2000, (non-fiction) Algernon, Charlie and I: A Writer's Journey, 2000; (13 episode TV series) flowers for Algernon (Japan), 2002, The Touch, revised 2003; supervising prodr. (TV movie) The Mad Housers, 1990. With U.S. Maritime Svc., 1945—47. Ohio Arts Council Individual Artist fellow, 1986-87; recipient Baker Fund award 1986-87, Disting. Alumnus Honor award Bklyn. Coll. CUNY, 1988. Mem. PEN, Dramatists' Guild, Mystery Writers of Am., Sci. Fiction Writers Am. (Author Emeritus award 2000). Office: 7491 N Federal Hwy C5-110 Boca Raton FL 33487-1625 E-mail: dankeyes@usa.com.

KEYES, DAVID TAYLOR, telecommunications company administrator; b. Providence, Feb. 18, 1947; s. Leonard Taylor and Alice (Whitwam) K.; m. Martha Ann Bearden, Dec. 22, 1973; children: Joshua Ryan, Caroline Louise. BBA, Fla. Internat. U., 1977; MS in Mgmt. Sci., U. Miami, 1982. Cert. quality engr., quality auditor. Communications technician Network Ops. AT&T, Miami, Fla., 1973-81, sales supr. Nat. Accounts, 1981-84, staff supr. Network Engring. Atlanta, 1984-87, quality cons. Network Svc. div. Conyers, Ga., 1987—. With USN, 1967-73, Vietnam. Mem. Am. Soc. Quality Control. Home: 4158 Azalea Ct Snellville GA 30039 E-mail: davidkeyes@att.net.

KEYES, GWENDOLYN REBECCA, lawyer, educator; b. Livingston, N.J., Nov. 2, 1968; d. Andrew J. and Ursula Y. Keyes. BS in Fin., Rutgers U., 1990; JD, Emory U., 1993. Bar: Ga. 1993. Asst. solicitor-gen. Dekalb County Solicitor-Gen.'s Office, Decatur, Ga., 1993-94; asst. dist. atty. Fulton County Dist. Atty.'s Office, Atlanta, 1994-97; contract atty. Atlanta, 1997-98; solicitor-gen. Dekalb County Solicitor-Gen.'s Office, Decatur, 1999—. Mem. Supreme Ct.'s Commn. on Equality, Atlanta, 1999—; mem. Leadership DeKalb Ga., 2000; elder First African Presbyn. Ch. Recipient Trail Blazer award Cmtys. Am., Inc., 1998, Justice Robert Benham Cmty. Svc. award. Mem. Nat. Coun. Negro Women, Ga. Assn. Black Women Lawyers, Hispanic Bar Assn., Dekalb Lawyers Assn. (past pres. 1998), Dekalb Bar Assn., Rotary. Democrat. Avocations: reading, tennis. Office: Dekalb County Solicitor-Gen Office 556 N Mcdonough St Decatur GA 30030-3308

KEYES, JAMES HENRY, manufacturing company executive; b. LaCrosse, Wis., Sept. 2, 1940; s. Donald M. and Mary M. (Nodolf) K.; m. Judith Ann Carney, Nov. 21, 1964; children: James Patrick, Kevin, Timothy. BS, Marquette U., 1962; MBA, Northwestern U., 1963. Instr. Marquette U., Milw., 1963-65; CPA Peat. Marwick & Mitchell, Milw., 1965-66; with Johnson Controls, Inc., Milw., 1967—, mgr. sys. dept., 1967-71, divsn. contr., 1971-73, corp. contr., treas., 1973-77, v.p., CFO, 1977-85, exec. v.p., 1985-86, pres., 1986-99, chief operating officer, 1986-88, chief exec. officer, 1988—2002, chmn. bd. dirs., 1993—. Bd. dirs. Baird Capital Devel. Fund. 1st Wis. Trust Co., LSI Logic, Inc., Universal Foods Corp. Active Milw. Symphony Orch., 1980—. Mem. Fin. Execs. Inst., Am. Inst. CPA's, Wis. Inst. CPA's., Machinery and Allied Products Inst. Office: Johnson Controls Inc 5757 N Green Bay Ave Milwaukee WI 53209-4408

KEYES, JEFFREY J. lawyer; BA magna cum laude, U. Notre Dame, 1968; JD cum laude, U. Mich., 1972. Bar: Minn. 1972. Sharcholder Briggs and Morgan, P.A., Mpls.; fellow Am. Coll. Trial Lawyers, Mpls. Mem. Gov.'s Task Force on Tort Reform, 1986; chmn. fed. practice com. U.S. Dist. Ct. Minn., 1990-93, 2002—, chmn. adv. group on civil justice reform act, 1991-93; trainer U.S. Magistrate Judges Tng. Conf. on Settlement, Mpls., 1992; lectr. in field. Contbr. articles to law jours. Mem. ABA (chmn. antitrust sect. franchise com. 1989-90, contbg. editor Antitrust Monograph 1987, co-editor Antitrust Sect. State Antitrust Law Handbook, Minn. chpt. 1990), Minn. State Bar Assn. (co-chair Women in the Legal Profn. task force 1996-97, chmn. civil litigation sect. 1985-86), Hennepin County Bar Assn. Office: Briggs and Morgan 2400 Ids Ctr Minneapolis MN 55402

KEYES, JOAN ROSS RAFTER, education educator, author; b. Bklyn., Aug. 12, 1924; d. Joseph W. and Hermia (Ross) Rafter; m. William Ambrose, Apr. 26, 1947 (dec.); children: William, Peter, Dion, Kenzie. BA, Adelphi U., Garden City, N.Y., 1945; MS, Long Island U., Greenvale, N.Y., 1973. Prodn. asst. CBS Radio, N.Y., 1943-44; cub news reporter Bklyn. Daily Eagle, 1945-46; advt. copywriter Gimbel's Dept. Store, N.Y., 1946-47; adj. prof. L.I. U., Greenvale, N.Y., 1984—; tchr. Port Wash. Pub. Schs., N.Y., 1970-94. Lectr., cons. pub. sch. dists. nationwide, 1978—; workshop leader Tchrs. English to Speakers Other Langs. convs., 1981—. Author: Beats, Conversations in Rhythm, 1983, (video program) Now You're Talking, 1987, (computer program) Quick Talk, 1990, Oxford Picture Dictionary for Kids Program, 1998; contbr. articles to ednl. mags. Lectr., catechist Our Lady of Fatima Ch., Port Washington, 1987—; vol. Earthwatch, Mallorca, 1988. Australia/New Zealand ednl. grantee Port Washington Pub. Schs., 1992. Mem. Tchrs. of English to Speakers of Other Languages, Am. Fedn. of Tchrs., N.Y. State United Tchrs., Port Wash. Tchrs. Assn. Republican. Roman Catholic. Avocations: music, painting, travel, tennis, golf. E-mail: joanrosskeyes@aol.com.

KEYES, MARGARET NAUMANN, home economics educator; b. Mt. Vernon, Iowa, Mar. 4, 1918; d. Charles Reuben and Sarah (Naumann) K. BA, Cornell Coll., Mt. Vernon, 1939, L.H.D., 1976; MS, U. Wis., 1951; PhD (Ellen H. Richards grad. fellow), Fla. State U., 1965; H.H.D., Coe Coll., 1977. Tchr. home econs. Stanley (Iowa) High Sch., 1939-42, Washington Jr. High Sch., Clinton, Iowa, 1942-44, Clinton High Sch., 1944-50; instr. related art U. Iowa, Iowa City, 1951-57, asst. prof. related art dept. home econs., 1957-68, assoc. prof., 1968-75, prof., 1975-88; research prof. U. Iowa Found., 1971-74. Author: Nineteenth Century Home Architecture Iowa City, 1967, expanded edit., 1993, Old Capitol: Portrait of an Iowa Landmark, 1988; mem. editorial bd., Home Econs. Research Jour; contbr. articles to periodicals. Mem. Terr. Hill Planning Commn. for Iowa, Terr. Hill Authority for Iowa; mem. design rev. bd. Iowa City Urban Renewal Commn.; dir. research Old Capitol Restoration Com., 1971-75; dir. Old Capitol, 1975-88; mem. Iowa State Hist. Bd., vice chmn. 1986-90, chmn., 1990-92. Recipient Peterson/Harlan award State Hist. Soc. of Iowa, 1994, Nat. History Award medal DAR, 1996; named Dist. Friend of U. Iowa Alumni Assn., 1989. Mem. Am. Home Econ. Assn. (exec. bd., chmn. art sect.), Iowa Home Econs. Assn., AAUP, Soc. Archtl. Historians, Am. Soc. Interior Designers, Interior Design Educators Council, Iowa Soc. Preservation Hist. Landmarks (dir. 1970-75), Cornell Coll. Alumni Assn. (dir. 1970-73), Nat. Trust Hist. Preservation (bd. advs. 1974-77), Internat. Fedn. Home Econs. (individual), Victorian Soc. Am. (v.p., dir. 1974-80), Iowa Centennial Meml. Found., Altrusa Club (pres. 1969-70), Phi Beta Kappa, Omicron Nu, Omicron Delta Kappa. Democrat. Presbyterian.

KEYES, MARION ALVAH, IV, manufacturing company executive; b. Bellingham, Wash., May 11, 1938; s. Marion Alvah and Winnefred Agnes (Nolte) K.; m. Loretta Jean Mattson, Nov. 17, 1962; children: Marion A., Zachary Leigh (dec.), Richard. BS in Chem. Engring., Stanford U., 1960; MSEE, U. Ill., 1968; MBA, Baldwin Wallace Coll., 1981. Registered rofl. engr., Calif., Wis., N.Y., Ill., Ohio. Tchg. asst. dept. math. Stanford U., 1958-59; tech. Stanford Aerosol Labs., 1957-59; chem. engr. Ketchikan (Alaska) Pulp Co., 1960-63; dir engring. Control Sys. divsn. Beloit (Wis.) Corp., 1963-70; gen. mgr. digital sys. divsn. Taylor Instrument Co., Rochester, N.Y., 1970-75; v.p. engring. Bailey Controls Co., 1975-80; sr. v.p., group exec. Indsl. Products and Svcs. Group; pres. Bailey COntrols, Ohio, 1980-85; mem. exec. operating bd. McDermott Internat. Inc., 1985-89; pres., CEO Bailey Controls Co., Wickliffe, Ohio, 1989-90; chmn. Dcom Corp., Eastlake, Ohio, 1990-93; sr. v.p. tech. and bus. devel. process group, pres. Rosemount Analytical Inc. divsn. Emerson, St. Louis, 1993—. Bd. dirs. Fibermark Corp. Author: Offshore Platform Automation, 1990; editor: A Glossary of Automatic Control Terminology, 1970; contbr. articles to profl. jours.; holder 54 U.S. and more than 100 fgn. patents. Past bd. advisors Fenn Coll. Engring., Cleve. State U.; bd. dirs. Baldwin Coll., United Cerebral Palsy, Cleve.; past prs., mem. exec. bd. N.E. Ohio coun. Boy Scouts Am.; past pres. Area 5 Boy Scouts Am. Named to, Measurement and Control Hall of Fame. Fellow ISA (hon. life), TAPPI (Pioneer award), IEEE, Am. inst. Chemists, Instrument Soc. Am. (life hon.), Ohio acad. Scis. (life, bd. dirs., Centennial honoree 1991); mem. AIChE, Cleve. Engring. Soc. (bd. dirs.), Soc. Am. Mil. Engrs. (life), Am. Assn. Artificial Intelligence (charter), Am. Mgmt. Assn., U.S. Automation Rsch. Coun., Am. Automatic Control Coun. (past. sec. and bd. dirs., Am. Chem. Soc., Wis. Acad. Arts, Scis. and Letters, Cleve. World Trade Assn. (Man of Yr. 1984), Canterbury Golf Club, Mo. Athletic Club. Republican. Roman Catholic. Home: 8 Washington Terr Saint Louis MO 63112-1914 Office: 8100 W Florissant Ave K-Annex Saint Louis MO 63136 E-mail: bud@keyes.org.

KEYES, RALPH JEFFREY, writer; b. Cin., Jan. 12, 1945; s. Scott Sherman and Charlotte Esther (Shachmann) K.; m. Muriel Lee Gordon, Feb. 13, 1965; children: David, Scott. BA in History, Antioch Coll., 1967. Asst. to pub. Newsday, Garden City, N.Y., 1968-70; fellow Ctr. Studies Person, La Jolla, Calif., 1970-80; writer Phila., 1980-90. Bd. trustees Antioch Writer's Workshop, Yellow Springs, 1992—. Author: We, The Lonely People: Searching for Community, 1973, Is There Life After High School?, 1976, The Height of Your Life, 1980, Chancing It: Why We Take Risks, 1985, TimeLock: How Life Got So Hectic and What You Can Do About It, 1991, Sons on Fathers: A Book of Men's Writings, 1992, "Nice Guys Finish Seventh": False Phrases, Spurious Sayings, and Familiar Misquotations, 1992, The Courage to Write: How Writers Trascend Fear, 1995, The Wit and Wisdom of Harry Truman, 1995, The Wit and

Wisdom of Oscar Wilde, 1996, The Writer's Book of Hope: Getting From Frustration to Publication, 2003; co-author: The Innovation Paradox: The Success of Failure, The Failure of Success, 2003; contbr. articles to mags. and newspapers. Recipient Headliner of Yr. in lit. San Diego Press Club, 1976, Citation for Nonfiction, The Athenaeum, 1985; Individual Artist's fellow Ohio Arts Coun., 1998. Fellow: Western Behavioral Sci. Inst.; mem.: Author's Guild. Avocations: travel, running, watching soccer games. Home: 690 Omar Cir Yellow Springs OH 45387-1420 E-mail: ralph@ralphkeyes.com.

KEYES, ROBERT W. physicist, researcher; b. Chgo., Dec. 2, 1921; s. Lee P. and Katherine K.; m. Sophie Skadorwa, June 4, 1966; children— Andrew, Claire. BS, U. Chgo., 1942, MS, 1949, PhD, 1953. With Argonne Nat. Lab., 1946-50; staff mem. Westinghouse Research Lab., Pitts., 1953-60; mem. research staff IBM Research Lab., Yorktown Heights, N.Y., 1960—. Vis. physicist Am. Phys. Soc. Vis. Indsl. Physicists Program, 1974-75, 77; vice chmn. Gordon Conf. on High Pressure Physics, 1970; chmn. Gordon Conf. on Chemistry and Physics of Microstructure Fabrication, 1976, Nat. Materials Adv. Bd. (ad hoc com. on ion implantation as a new surface treatment tech.), 1978, Internat. Conf. Heavily Doped Semiconductors, 1984; mem. Nat. Acad. Scis.-NAE-NRC evaluation panel Nat. Bur. Standards, 1970-73; cons. physics survey com., mem. statis. data panel Nat. Acad. Sci.-NRC Council Physics Survey Com., 1972; mem. data and info. panel Nat. Acad. Sci.-NRC Com. on Survey of Materials Sci. and Engring., 1974; Girling Watson vis. prof. elec. engring. U. Sydney, Fall 1996. Author: Physics of VLSI Systems, 1987; assoc. editor Revs. Modern Physics, 1976-95; corr.: Comments on Solid State Physics, 1970-85. Served with USN, 1944-46. Recipient Outstanding Contbn. award IBM, 1963 Fellow Am. Phys. Soc. (chmn. com. applications of physics 1976-78), IEEE (chmn. subcom. cultural and sci. relations 1976, mem. del. to USSR 1975, W.R.G. Baker prize 1976, awards bd. 1984-85); mem. Nat. Acad. Engring., Nat. Audubon Soc., Conn. Orinthological Assn. Office: IBM PO Box 218 Yorktown Heights NY 10598-0218

KEYFITZ, NATHAN, sociologist, demographer, educator; b. Montreal, Que., Can., June 29, 1913; s. Arthur and Anna (Gerstein) K.; m. Beatrice Orkin, Oct. 8, 1939; children: Barbara Lee, Robert Norman. BS, McGill U., Montreal, 1934; PhD, U. Chgo., 1952; MA (hon.), Harvard U., 1972; LLD (hon.), U. Western Ont., 1973, U. de Montréal, 1981, McGill U., 1984, U. Alta, 1985, U. Siena, Italy, 1991, Carleton U., 1993, U. de Québec, 1993. Census clk., statistician, sr. research statistician Dominion Bur. Statistics, Govt. Can., 1936-59; dir. Colombo Plan Bur., Sri Lanka, 1956-57; prof. sociology U. Toronto, Ont., Can., 1959-63, U. Montreal, 1962-63; prof. U. Chgo., 1963-68, chmn. sociology dept., 1965-68; prof. demography U. Calif., Berkeley, 1968-72; Andelot prof. sociology and demography Harvard U., 1972-82, chmn. dept. sociology, 1978-80, emeritus, 1982—; Robert Lazarus prof. social demography Ohio State U., Columbus, 1980-84, prof. emeritus, 1984—; with Internat. Inst. Applied Systems Analysis, 1984-93; researcher Initiatives on Children, Am. Acad. Arts and Scis., Cambridge, Mass., 1994—. Tech. assistance assignments, Burma, 1951, Indonesia, 1952-53, 64, 79, 85-89, Argentina, 1960, Santiago, Chile, 1963, Moscow, 1977, 85, People's Republic China, 1981; vis. fellow Stanford U., 1986. Author: Introduction to the Mathematics of Population, 1968, 2d edit., 1977, Applied Mathematical Demography, 1977, Population Change and Social Policy, 1982, (with Wilhelm Flieger) World Population Growth and Aging, 1990; contbr. articles to profl. jours. Trustee Nat. Opinion Research Ctr., 1966—. Recipient Lazarsfeld award Am. Sociol. Assn., 1990, Common Wealth award, 1991; decorated Cross of Honor for Sci., Austria, 1993; named Laureate, Internat. Union Sci. Study Population, 1997, Norberg award Population Coun. of N.Y. Fellow Royal Soc. Can., Am. Statis. Assn. (chmn. social stats. sect. 1961), Royal Statis. Soc. (hon.), Statis. Soc. of Can. (hon.); mem. NAS, Am. Acad. Arts and Scis., Can. Polit. Sci. Assn. (chmn. sociology and anthropology sect. 1961), Inter-Am. Statis. Inst., Internat. Statis. Inst., Population Assn. Am. (pres. 1969-70), Phi Beta Kappa. Home: 1580 Massachusetts Ave Apt 7C Cambridge MA 02138-2928 E-mail: keyfitz@netscape.net.

KEYKO, GEORGE JOHN, electronics company executive; b. New Britain, Conn., May 6, 1924; s. John Simonovich and Nellie Ivanovna (Gretcha) K.; m. Anne Romanchuk, Jan. 31, 1948; children: David, Mark. BS, Yale U., 1949. Spl. rep. Lederle Labs., Conn., N.Y, 1949-52; pres. Tchr. Toys, Inc., Conn., 1952-56; sales mgr. Washington Forge, N.J., 1956-60; sales mgr. shaver divsn. Ronson Corp, Woodbridge, N.J., 1960-63; sales mgr. Caravelle and BEP divsn. Bulova Watch Co., N.Y.C., 1963-66; v.p. mktg. Technipower divsn. Benrus Watch Co., Ridgefield, Conn., 1966-68; exec. v.p. Heuer Time & Electronics Corp., Springfield, N.J., 1969, pres., 1970-75; now pres. ARK, Inc. Bd. dirs. New Products Devel. Assocs., Pasta 101 Co. Inc., Santa Barbara, Calif., ARK, Inc., Westfield, N.J., BAAG, Inc, Plainfield, Sark Investors Inc., Linden, N.J. Home: 30 Blue Ridge Cir Plainfield NJ 07060-3319

KEYLER, ROBERT GORDON, material handling company executive; b. Elgin, Ill., May 9, 1958; s. Robert Dean and Lois Jean (Hobbs) K.; m. Linda Jane Mendez, Sept. 21, 1988 (div. Jan. 1993). Grad., Morris County Vo-Tech., 1980. Mgr. Gardentown Ctr., Rockaway, N.J., 1976-80, Genuine Parts-NAPA, Albuquerque, 1980-88; owner G&B Enterprises, Albuquerque, 1988-91; sales rep. Parts Plus of Albuquerque, 1989-91; v.p. sales and purchasing Material Handling Specialists, Albuquerque, 1991-98; prin., owner Hawkwind Enterprises, Tijeras, N. Mex., 1999—. Cons. in field. Sponsor Youth of Unity, Albuquerque, 1980-2001; bd. dirs. Unity Ch., Albuquerque, 1986—, pres., 1987; founder Christ Unity at The Edge of the Woods, Edgewood, N.Mex., co-min., 1998-2000, min., 2002--. Avocations: youthwork, backpacking, ballooning. Home and Office: 11 Constellation Dr Tijeras NM 87059-8108 E-mail: bob0558@earthlink.net.

KEYS, ANTHONY C. management information systems educator; arrived in U.S., 1988; s. Stanley and Dorothy Keys; m. Catherine M. Murtagh, Apr. 12, 1986; children: James, Alastair, Owen, Kevin. BSc, Reading U., Reading, England, 1978; MBA, Shenandoah U., 1991; PhD, Va. Poly. Inst. and State U., 1995. Tchr. of physics Furze Platt Comprehensive Sch., Maidenhead, England, 1981—85, Langley Grammar Sch., Slough, England, 1985—88; vis. asst. prof. Wichita (Kans.) State U., 1995—96; asst. prof. of mgmt. info. sys. Marshall U., Huntington, W.Va., 1996—2000; asst. prof. mgmt. info. sys. U. of Wis., Eau Claire, 2000—. Mem.: Am. Assn. for Artificial Intelligence, Inst. for Ops. Rsch. and Mgmt. Sci., Decision Sciences Inst. Office: U Wis-Eau Claire 105 Garfield Ave Eau Claire WI 54702-4004 Office Fax: 715-836-4959. E-mail: keysac@uwec.edu.

KEYS, ARLANDER, federal judge; b. 1943; BA, DePaul U., 1972, JD, 1975. Trial atty. Nat. Labor Rels. Bd., 1975-80; regional atty. Fed. Labor Rels. Authority, Chgo., 1980-86; adminstrv. law judge SSA, Dept. of HHS, 1986-88, chief adminstrv. law judge, 1988-95; magistrate judge U.S. Dist. Ct. (no. dist.) Ill., 1995-98, presiding magistrate judge, 1998—. With USMC, 1963—67. Mem. ABA, Fed. Bar Assn. (pres. Chgo. chpt.), Ill. Jud. Coun., Chgo. Bar Assn., Cook County Bar Assn., 7th Cir. Bar Assn., Just the Beginning Found. Office: US Dist Ct 219 S Dearborn St Ste 2240 Chicago IL 60604-1802 Fax: 312-554-8546.

KEYS, JOHN W., III, federal agency administrator; b. Sheffield, Ala. m. Dell Keys. BCE, Ga. Inst. Tech., 1964; Masters Degree, Brigham Young U., 1971. Registered engr., Colo., Wyo., Mont., N.D. Civil and hydraulic engr. Bur. Reclamation, 1964—79, N.W. regional dir.; commr. Bur. Reclamation, Dept. Interior, Washington, 2001—. Coll. football referee, 1970—; H.S. football referee, 1962—. Office: US Dept Interior Bur Reclamation 1849 C St NW Washington DC 20240

KEYS, LESLEE FRANCES, historic preservation planner; b. Anderson, Ind, Oct. 31, 1955; d. George Lyle and Donna Faye (Oldham) K.; m. John Albert Machnic, 1976 (div. 1997); children: Evan Benjamin, Ethan Andrew. BS, Ball State U., 1976; MA in History, Va. Tech., 1977, M in Urban and Regional Planning, 1979. Survey and inventory technician Regional Preservation Office, Dayton, Ohio, 1979, Ohio Hist. Preservation Office, Columbus, Ohio, 1980; planner Dept. Planning, Dayton, 1980-83; exec. dir. Riverside Avondale Preservation, Jacksonville, Fla., 1984-86; dir., hist. preservation analyst Jefferson County Hist. Preservation, 1986-93; mgr. Hist. Fla. Keys Preservation Bd., Key West, 1993-97; hist. resources adminstr. Regional Preservation Office, St. Augustine, Fla., 1997—2002; exec. dir. Ximenez-fatioHouse Mus., 2002. Instr. Fla. Jr. Coll., Jacksonville, 1985-86; adj. faculty U. Louisville, 1990, Barry U., 1996-97; adjunct faculty, Flagler Coll., 2002-; bd. dir. Leadership Monroe County, Fla., 1996-97; bd. dir. Nat. Alliance Pres. Commn., 1996-2004; Fla. Trust for Hist. Preservation, Bd. of Trustees, 2002-. Author: Blueprint for Rehabilitation, 1982; editor: Historic Jefferson County, 1992. Ky. col. Hon. Order of Ky. Cols., 1989. Recipient Preservation award Dayton Coun. Neighborhoods, Dayton, 1983, Preservation award Jacksonville Hist. Landmarks Commn., Jacksonville, 1986, Svc. to Preservation award Ida Lee Willis Meml. Found., Commonwealth of Ky., 1991, award for excellence Hist. Fla. Keys Found., Key West, 1997. Mem. Am. Inst. Cert. Planners, Am. Planning Assn., Nat. Alliance Preservation Commns. (bd. dir. 1996—), Nat. Trust for Hist. Preservation, Fla. Trust for Hist. Preservation. Methodist. Avocations: renovating houses, distance running, reading. Office: Ximenez-Fatio House 28 Cadiz St Saint Augustine FL 32084

KEYS, MARTHA MCDOUGLE, educational administrator; b. Erie, Pa., May 20, 1938; d. Marshall and Helen (Siegel) McD. BA in English, Grove City Coll.; MEd in Counseling, U. Rochester, N.Y.; EdD, Calif. Coast U. Field supr. Calif. Sch. Profl. Psychology, 1969-75, Sonoma (Calif.) State U., 1969-75, U. Santa Clara, Calif., 1969-75; counselor, instr. Stanford (Calif.) U., 1969-75; counselor The Door, N.Y., 1975-76; lang. arts coord. Learning Skills Ctr., Coll. of New Rochelle (N.Y.), 1980-87; assoc. dir. Coun. for Internat. Understanding of Myrin Inst., 1987-89; exec. dir. Moorhead Kennedy Inst., N.Y.C., 1990-96. V.p.Moorhead Kennedy Assocs.; exec. prodr. 360 Degree Prodns., Inc.; pres. Something In Common, Inc., 1996—. Author simulations (with Moorhead Kennedy) Hostage Crisis, 1987, Death of a Dissident, 1989, Sacrilege in Talbotsville, 1990, Fire in the Forest, 1990, Hinomaru, 1992, Metalfabriken, 1993, Grocery Store, 1993, Toxic International, 1993, Atomic, 1994; (films) Cultural Baggage, 1995, Read My Lips, 1996, Sign of the Times, 1998. Home: 15915 84th Dr Jamaica NY 11432-2528

KEYS, PAUL ROSS, university provost/academic affairs official; b. St. Louis, Mar. 21, 1940; s. Charles and Josie (Jones) K.; m. Donnielesky Harrington, May 23, 1998; children from a previous marriage, Pamela, Roderick. BS, St. Louis U., 1963, MSW, 1971; PhD, U. Wis., Milw., 1983. Exec. dir. Champaign (Ill.) Urban League, 1969; dep. dir. Concentrated Employment Program, St. Louis, 1971; asst. dir. legis. NASW, Washington, 1971-74; exec. dir. Cmty. Svcs. Coun., Columbia, Mo., 1974-76; dir. Broward County (Fla.) Dept. Human Svcs., 1976-78; dep. adminstr. Comty. Svcs. divsn. State of Wis., 1978-81; prof. Hunter Coll., CUNY, 1983-94; faculty doctoral program CUNY, 1987-94; dean Coll. Health and Human Svcs., S.E. Mo. State U., Cape Girardeau, 1994-2000, also assoc. provost. Fellow Ctr. Social Adminstrn., Hunter Coll., 1985-94. Author: New Management in Human Services, 1988, 2d edit., 1995; founding editor Jour. Multicultural Social Work, 1989—; contbr. articles to profl. jours. Capt. USAF, 1963-69. Recipient Martin Luther King/Woodrow Wilson fellowship, 1970, Commendation Resolution, Mo. Gen. Assembly, 1976, GARIOA/Fulbright Rsch. fellowship, Tokyo, 1990-91, Disting. Alumni Svc. award St. Louis U. Sch. Social Svcs., 1996, Exemplar Mgmt. Excellence award Nat. Network for Social Work Mgrs., 1999; named to Sumner H.S. Hall of Fame, 2001. Mem. Am. Pub. Welfare Assn. (exec. com. 1988), Omega Psi Phi (Cmty. Svc. award 1977). Avocations: travel, computer software, jazz. Office: Provost's Office Governors State Univ 1 University Pkwy University Park IL 60466 E-mail: p-keys@govst.edu.

KEYSAR, KRISTA LYNN, music educator; b. Clinton, Md., Feb. 23, 1979; d. Robert Wayne Gardiner and Suzanne (Gardiner) Coons; m. Gregory Thomas Keysar, Aug. 4, 2001. MusB, Cleve. (Ohio) Inst. Music, 2001. Pvt. piano instr., Waldorf, Md., 2001—. Mem.: Md. State Music Tchrs. Assn., Nat. Piano Tchrs. Guild, Music Tchrs. Nat. Assn. Republican. Evang. Avocation: photography. E-mail: klkeysar@hotmail.com.

KEYSER, FRANK RAY, JR., lawyer, former governor; b. Chelsea, Vt., Aug. 17, 1927; s. Frank Ray and Ellen L. (Larkin) K.; m. Joan Friedgen, July 15, 1950; children: Christopher Scott, Carol Ellen, Frank Ray III. Student, Tufts Coll., 1946-49, LLD, 1961; LLB, Boston U., 1952; LLD, Norwich U., 1962. Bar: Vt. 1952. Practiced in, Chelsea, 1952-65; mem. Vt. Ho. of Reps., 1955-59, speaker, 1959-60; gov. Vt., 1961-63; mem. Wilson & Keyser, 1952-65; v.p., pres., chmn. Vt. Marble Co., 1965-79. Of counsel Keyser, Crowley P.C.; chmn. bd. dirs. Hitchcock Clin. Ctrl. Dir. Green Mt. Coun. BSA. With USNR, WWII. Named Outstanding Young Vermonter Vt. Jr. C. of C., 1959; One of 10 Outstanding Young Men in in Nation, Jr. C. of C., 1961 Mem. ABA, Vt. Bar Assn., Vt. Golf Assn. (past pres.), Am. Legion, Masons. Republican. Address: 64 Warner Ave Proctor VT 05765-1322 E-mail: frkeyser@adelphin.net.

KEYSER, JANET MARIE, pharmaceutical industry executive; b. Phila. BS in Biology, Ursinus Coll., Collegeville, Pa., 1980. Vet. asst. Center Square (Pa.) Vet. Clinic, 1980-81; from toxicology biologist to sr. dir. clin. quality assurance Merck & Co., Inc., West Point, Pa., 1981—2001, sr. dir. clin. quality assurance, 2001—. Mem. choir, mem. revision com. St. John's Luth. Ch., Sumneytown, Pa., 1992—. Mem. Bus. and Profl. Women's Club (sec.-treas. 1983-88), PEO. Republican. Avocations: children's sporting events, horseback riding, hiking, tennis, running. Office: Merck & Co Inc BLA-32 West Point Pike West Point PA 19486

KEYSER, LESLIE D. writer; b. Mainville, Pa., June 15, 1923; s. Leslie William and Mabel Bird (Breisch) K.; m. Evelyn Margaret Schramm, Mar. 4, 1955. Student, Bloomsburg Coll., 1946-48, U. Ctr. of Nice, France, 1952-53, Sorbonne U., Paris, 1953-54. Designer Magee Carpet Co., Bloomsburg, Pa., 1955-76; dir. Suncom Industries, Bloomsburg, 1976-86; designer Bloomsburg Carpet, 1986-92; freelance writer Bloomsburg, 1992—. Author: Wild Oats, 1999, The Returning, 1999, (novella) The Golden Tether, 1999, JCT, 2001. With U.S. Coast Guard, 1942-46. Mem. Am. Legion. Avocations: classical music, reading. Home: 105 Knights Dr Bloomsburg PA 17815 E-mail: lkeyser@ptd.net.

KEYSER, RANDALL E. exercise physiologist; b. Logan, W.Va., Sept. 24, 1950; s. Avery Eugene (Gene) and Weltha Jewell Keyser; children: Rachael, Jordan, Rebekah. PhD, U. of Toledo, 1986. Diplomate Am. Coll. Sports Medicine 1989. Chief, cardiovasc. physiology and rehab. sect. Butterwoeth Hosp., Grand Rapids, Mich., 1987—94; asst. prof. dept. phys. therapy U. of Md. Sch. Medicine, Balt., 1994—2002, assoc. prof., 2003—. Adj. assoc. prof. Mich. State U., East Lansing, 1989—94. Contbr. Grantee, NIH. Fellow: Am. Coll. Sports Medicine (treas. Midwest chpt. 1989—92, sec. 1992—93); mem.: Am. Heart Assn. (chair exercise and cardiac rehab. com. 1992—94), Am. Heart Assn. of Mich. (bd. dirs. 1988—94, treas. 1992—93, sec. 1993—94, v.p.-elect 1994—95, vice chair comm. com. 1991—94). Achievements include research in areas of cardiovascular rehabilitation and impairment of the oxidative metabolic pathway in people with disabilities. Office: University of Maryland Baltimore 100 Penn St Baltimore MD 01082 Office Fax: 410-706-6387. E-mail: rkeyser@som.umaryland.edu.

KEYSER, RICHARD LEE, distribution company executive; b. Harrisburg, Pa., Oct. 28, 1942; s. Harold L. and Mary J. K.; m. Mary Ellen Carter, June 20, l964; children: Jeffrey, Jennifer. BS, U.S. Naval Acad., 1964; MBA, Harvard U., l97l. Commd. ensign USN, 1964, advanced through grades to lt., 1966; resigned, 1969; mktg.-analysis mgr. Fleetguard, Inc., Dallas, 1971-72, dir. logistics Cookeville, Tenn., 1973-77; gen. mgr. parts ops. Cummins Engine Co., Inc., Columbus, Ind., 1977-83, exec. dir. mktg. ops., 1983-84; pres. NL-Hycalog, Houston, 1984-86; v.p. ops. W.W. Grainger, Inc., Chgo., 1986-87, exec. v.p., 1988-90, pres., 1991—, CEO, now chmn., 1995—. Bd. dirs. Morton Internat. County chmn. blood program ARC, Cookeville, 1976-77; bd. dirs. Preserve To Enjoy, Inc., Columbus, 1983-84, Irene Josselyn Clinic, Northfield, Ill., 1989-92, Lake Forest Grad. Sch. Mgmt., 1992—, Evanston Hosp. Corp., 1996—. Former lt. comdr. USNR. Fellow Am. Prodn. and Inventory Control Soc. (cert.); mem. Chgo. Club, Harvard Bus. Sch. Club Chgo. (v.p. 1988-89, pres. 1989-90), Comml. Club Chgo. Office: WW Grainger Inc 100 Grainger Pkwy Lake Forest IL 60045-5201

KEYSER, SAMUEL JAY, linguistics educator, university official; b. July 7, 1935; s. Abraham L. and Sabina (Shaplen) K.; children: Rachel Suzanne, Beth Rebecca, Benjamin Jay Kendall; m. Nancy Kelly, 2001. BA, George Washington U., 1956; BA with honors, Oxford (Eng.) U., 1958, MA, 1962, Yale U., 1960, PhD, 1962. Mem. staff Rsch. Lab. Electronics MIT, Cambridge, 1961-62; mem. faculty Brandeis U., Waltham, Mass., 1965-71, Univ. Coll. London, 1971-72; head dept. linguistics U. Mass., Amherst, 1972-77; head dept. linguistics and philosophy MIT, Cambridge, 1977—84, assoc. provost for inst. life, 1985—94, spl. asst. to the provost, 1994-98, spl. asst. to Chancellor, 1998—, emeritus, 1998—, interim alcohol coord., 1999-2000. Co-author: English Stress: Its Form, Its Growth and Its Role in Verse, 1971, Beginning English Grammar, 1973, CV Phonology, 1983, Rule Generalization and Optionality in Language Change, 1985, Prolegomenon to a Theory of Lexical Argument Structure, 2002; author: (poems) Raising the Dead, 1993, (children's stories) The Pond God and other stories, 2003; editor (with K. Hale): The View From Building 20, 1993; editor: Linguistic Inquiry, 1970—, Current Studies in Linguistics, 1972—, Linguistic Inquiry Monograph Series, 1976—. Peter de Florez chair MIT, 1989. With USAF, 1962-65. Fulbright scholar, 1956-58, sr. Fulbright scholar, 1971-72; recipient Disting. Alumnus award George Washington U., 1992. Mem. Linguistic Soc. Am., MIT Alumni Assn. (hon. mem.), Phi Beta Kappa. Home: 7 Frost St Cambridge MA 02140-1502 Office: Dept Linguistics & Philosophy Rm E39-353 MIT Cambridge MA 02139-4307 E-mail: keyser@mit.edu. *People, like organizations, are very good at starting things and very bad at stopping them. This goes for projects, marriages, and careers. I have found that the best way to stop something is to start something. It makes the stopping much, much easier, at least until the last stop.*

KEYSER-FANICK, CHRISTINE LYNN, banking executive, marketing, strategic planning, investments and insurance professional; b. Ft. Dodge, Iowa, Nov. 16, 1956; d. Archie Harlan and LaVonne Janette (Larsen) Keyser. AA, Iowa Cen. C.C., Ft. Dodge, 1976; BA, U. No. Iowa, 1979; MA, Drake U., 1985; grad. with honors, Sch. Bank Mktg., Boulder, Colo., 1990, Stonier Grad. Sch. Banking, U. Del., 1996. Lic. group I ins. Educator Marshalltown (Iowa) Cmty. Schs., 1979-84; v.p. LaGrave Klipfel Clarkson, Inc., Des Moines, 1985-87; pub. rels. and mktg. cons. Des Moines, 1987-88; asst. prof. Drake U., Des Moines, 1988; dir. mktg. 1st Interstate Bank, Des Moines, 1988-89; v.p. Am. Trust & Savings Bank, Dubuque, Iowa, 1989-94; sr. v.p. San Antonio Fed. Credit Union, 1994—. Exec. v.p. SACU Fin. Solutions, Ltd.; spkr. in field; v.p. Women in Mgmt., 1991, pres.-elect, 1992—93, pres., 1993. Contbr. articles to Iowa Commerce Mag., 1988-93. Bd. dirs. Iowa Soc. to Prevent Blindness, Des Moines, 1987—91, Dubuque Main St. Ltd., 1990—93, v.p., 1993, bd. dirs. Dubuque Symphony Orch., 1990—93, Dubuque Coun. for Diversity, 1992—94; bd. dirs., bus. devel. chair Dubuque Main St., 1991—94; pub. rels. com., devel. com. Girl Scouts of the San Antonio Area, 1994—, fund devel. com., 1996—, bd. dirs., 1999—, bd. sec., 2002—; mem. pub. rels. com., memls. com. San Antonio chpt. Am. Heart Assn., 1998—; mem. Leadership San Antonio Class XXV. Named New Bd. Mem. of Yr., Iowa Soc. to Prevent Blindness, 1988, Vol. of Yr., Iowa Main St., 1993; recipient Nat. Charlotte Danstrom Women of Achievement award, 1992, Outstanding Vol. award Am. Heart Assn., 1999; selected to Class of Leadership Program, San Antonio, 1999-00. Mem. Pub. Rels. Soc. Am. (pres. Greater Dubuque chpt. 1993, v.p. 1991-92, pres. San Antonio chpt. 1997, bd. dirs. 1995—, assembly del. 1995-97, accredited), Bank Mktg. Assn. (adv. coun. 1989-93, speaker conv. 1998), Am. Mktg. Assn., ITS Inc. Mktg. Com. Advertisers of Dubuque (legis. chair 1990-93, bd. dirs. 1991-93), Dubuque Area C. of C. (membership adv. coun. 1993-94, media coord. Iowa Trade Symposium 1990, All Am. City com. 1994-95), Raddon Fin. Group (speaker 1998). Avocations: writing, volleyball, walking. Home: 8642 Wrexham Heights San Antonio TX 78254-2257 Office: San Antonio Fd Credit Union PO Box 1356 San Antonio TX 78295-1356

KEYSSAR, ALEXANDER, historian, educator; s. Alexander and Grace (Atkinson) Keyssar. BA, Harvard U., 1965, PhD, 1970. Boyd prof. history Duke U., Durham, NC, 1986—2001; Stirling prof. history and social policy Harvard U., Cambridge, Mass., 2001—. Author: Out of Work: The First Century of Unemployment in Massachusetts, 1987 (Frederick Jackson Turner award, Taft prize, New Eng. Hist. Assn. Book prize, 1987), The Right to Vote, 2001 (Beveridge Award, Am. Hist. Assn.; finalist, Pulitzer prize in History; finalist, L.A. Times Book award, Genovese prize, 2001); author: (with Daniel Kevles, Pauline Maier, and Merritt Roe Smith) Inventing America: A History of the United States, 2002. Office: JFK Sch Govt Harvard U 79 JFK St Cambridge MA 02138 Office Fax: 617-496-9053.

KEYT, DAVID, philosophy and classics educator; b. Indianapolis, Feb. 22, 1930; s. Herbert Coe and Hazel Marguerite (Sissman) K.; m. Christine Harwood (Mullikin) June 25, 1975; children by previous marriage: Sarah, Aaron. AB, Kenyon Coll., 1951; MA, Cornell U., 1953, PhD, 1955. AB Kenyon Coll., 1951; instr. dept. philosophy U. Wash., Seattle, 1957-60, asst. prof., 1960-64, assoc. prof., 1964-69, acting chmn. dept. philosophy, 1967-68, 70, 86, prof., 1969—, chmn. dept. philosophy, 1971-78, adj. prof. classics, 1977-79, winter and spring of, 94. Vis. asst. prof. dept. philosophy UCLA, 1962-63; vis. assoc. prof. Cornell U., 1968-69; vis. prof. U. Hong Kong, autumn 1987, Princeton U., autumn 1988, U. Calif., Irvine, autumn 1990; vis. scholar Social Philosophy and Policy Ctr., Bowling Green State U.,autumn, 2001. Co-editor: (with Fred D. Miller Jr.) A Companion to Aristotle's Politics, 1991; Author: Aristotle Politics, Books V, VI, 1999; contbr. articles in field to profl. jour. Served with U.S. Army, 1955-57. Inst. for Rsch. in the Humanities fellow U. Wis., 1966-67; Ctr. for Hellenic Studies fellow, 1974-75; mem. Inst. for Advanced Study, 1983-84. Mem., Am. Philos. Assn., Soc. Ancient Greek Philosophy. Home: 12032 36th Ave NE Seattle WA 98125-5637 Office: U Wash Box 353350 Dept Philosophy Seattle WA 98195-3350 E-mail: keyt@u.washington.edu.

KEYVAN, SHAHLA, nuclear engineer, educator; arrived in U.S., 1971; d. Mahmood Keyvan and Forough Mortazavi. BS in Engring., U. Wash., 1974; MS in Nuc. Engring., Nuclear Engr. in Nuc. Engring., MIT, 1978; PhD in Nuc. Engring., U. Calif., Berkeley, 1983. Reactor operating license Nuc. Regulatory Commn., Wash., D.C., 1979, U.S. Nuc. Regulatory Commn., Wash., D.C., 1993. Cons. Argonne Nat. Lab., Idaho Falls, 1989; assoc. prof. nuc. engring. dept. U. Mo., Columbia, 1990—2001, rsch. prof., dir. ctr. artificial intelligence engring. and edn., 2001—. Panelist grad. fellowship program NSF, Arlington, Va., 1993—96. Author: (electronic books) Fundamentals Of Nuclear Technology, Introduction to Nuclear Reactor Physics, A Demo Module on Radiation Energy Deposition, A Demo Module on Fundamentals of Radiation Measurement, A Demo Module on Radiation Decay, A Demo Module on Binding Energy; contbr. articles to profl. jours. Grantee, Dept. of Energy Small Bus. Innovation Rsch. Program, 1984—87, Dept. of Energy, 1998—2003, NSF, 1991—93, 1994—97, 1998—2001, Mo. Inst. Instrnl. Devel., 1997—98, Mo. Dept. Econ., 1998—2001. Mem.: Am. Soc. Engring. Edn., Am. Nuc. Soc. (faculty advisor 1990—93, sec. Mo. sect. 1991—94), Phi Kappa Phi, Sigma Xi, Tau Beta Pi. Achievements include patents pending for automated inspection system for nuclear fuel pellet; automated nuclear fuel size measurement; flame image features and their analysis. Office: U Mo E2403D MAE Dept Columbia MO 65211 Office Fax: 573-884-5090. E-mail: keyvan@missouri.edu.

KEZER, PAULINE RYDER, state government executive, management consultant; b. Boston, Feb. 4, 1942; d. Paul Washington and Madeline (Farmer) Ryder; m. Kenneth Ronald Kezer, Sept. 23, 1962; children: Anne Elizabeth, Pamela Lynne, Cynthia Karen. B in Psychology, Colby Coll., 1963; postgrad., Ctrl. Conn. State Coll., 1978, 83. Tutor sci. and humanities New Britain (Conn.) Schs. Teenage Parent Program, 1964-78; mem. Conn. Ho. of Reps., Hartford, 1979-85, asst. minority leader, 1981-84, asst. majority leader, 1985-86; sec. of state State of Conn., Hartford, 1991-94, asst. treas. intergovtl. affairs, 1998-99. Bd. dirs. New Eng. Caucus Women Legislators, 1983-84, chmn., 1985-86; CEO, Kezer Cons., 2000—; pres. Conn. Order Women Legislators, Hartford, 1981-82; mem. adv. com. Ctrl. Conn. State U. Polit. Inst., New Britain, 1983-84; mem. adv. bd. Colonial Bank, Plainville, Conn., 1980-85; CEO Hartford Ballet, 1995-97; asst. treas., dir. unclaimed property divsn. State of Conn., 1998-99. Camp dir. Girl Scout Coun., 1972-81, assoc. chair, 1975-78, v.p., 1979-85, nat. bd. dirs., 1984-93; pres., v.p., treas., bd. dirs. YWCA, New Britain, 1971-79; chmn., sec. Inland Wetlands Com., 1972-79; chmn. State Employees Campaign for Charitable Giving, 1992; active Rep. Town Com., Plainville, 1977-84; exec. bd. Ea. region Coun. State Govts., Cmty. Health Charities of Conn., 1993—; vol. New Britain Cancer Soc., 1980-85; bd. dirs. Collaboration for Conn.'s Children, 1985—, Conn. Spl. Olympics, 1993-94, Am. Leadership Forum, 2001-; adv. bd. Tunxic C.C., 1984—; nat. rev. team Projects Hometown Am., 1986; hon. chair Conn. Citizen Bee, 1992; vice-chair Conn. Rep. Party, 1987-89; gov. chair, Greater Hartford United Way, 1993-94; co-chair, founder, bd. dirs. Conn. Race for the Cure, Susan G. Komen Found. for Breast Cancer Rsch., 1993-99; chmn. Conn. Sports Mus. Hall of Fame

Dinner, 1994; Rep. candidate for Gov. of Conn., 1994; bd. nominating chair Conn. Combined Health Appeal, 1995-98; exec. bd. Cmty. Health Charities Conn., 1998-2001, nat. bd., 1999—; bd. dirs. Bishops Fund for Children, 1998—, trustee 1999-2002, pres. 2002-; bd. dirs., v.p. Women's Campaign Sch. at Yale, 1993-99; co-chair, bd. dirs. Conn. Komen Race for the Cure, 1994-99; nat. bd. dirs., vice-chair, 1999—; choir mem. St. Mark's Episcopal Ch., 1998-2002, chair planned giving com., 2000-. Harvard U. fellow Inst. Politics, 1990, Am. Leadership Forum fellow, 1991-92; recipient Thanks Badge and Conn. Yankee award Conn. Yankee Girl Scout coun., Farmington, 1982, 79, Women Helping Women award Soroptimists, 1984—, Women of Mert award, Conn. Valley Girl Scouts, 1993, DKG award, 1994; named Outstanding Citizen, Jaycees, Plainville, Conn., 1980, Outstanding Vol., New Britain YWCA, 1978, Legislator of Yr., Conn. Valley Girl Scout Coun., Hartford, 1984. Mem. Nat. Order Women Legislators (legis. chair 1986), Nat. Assn. Sec. State Regional V.P., Women Execs. in State Govt., Conn. Fedn. Rep. Women (2d v.p. 1992—), Ea. Region Coun. State Govts. (exec. bd. 1991-92), Nat. Assn. Secs. of State (exec. bd. 1991-92, Alpha Delta Pi. Republican. E-mail: pauline@kezerconsulting.com.

KEZLARIAN, NANCY KAY, marriage and family therapist; b. Royal Oak, Mich., Aug. 26, 1948; d. Barkev A. and Nancy (Israelian) K.; m. Robert S. Vinetz, M.D., Aug. 1995. Student, U. Vienna, Austria, 1969; BA, Albion Coll., 1970; MA in Theatre and TV, U. Mich., 1971; MA in Clin. Psychology, Pepperdine U., 1992. Cert. secondary tchr., Mich., Calif.; lic. marriage family therapist. Tchr. West Bloomfield Hills (Mich.) High Sch., 1971-76; tchr. ESL, L.A. Pub. Schs., 1976-80; personnel dir. Samuel Goldwyn Co., L.A., 1985-86; dir. adminstrn. and human resources (Norman Lear) Act III Communications, L.A., 1986-90; dir. programs Salvation Army Booth Meml. Ctr., L.A., 1993-94; asst. exec. dir. Florence Crittenton Ctr., L.A., 1994-96, exec. dir., 1996-2000; pvt. practice marriage and family therapy, 2000—. Owner, mgr. KAZ, hand painted clothing co., L.A., 1980-85; mem. Screen Actors Guild. Actress My Seventeenth Summer, The Big Blue Marble, 1979 (Emmy award for childen's TV programming). Bd. dirs. Calif. Assn. Children's Homes. Named Tchr. of Yr., West Bloomfield Hills High Sch., 1976. Mem. SAG, Pers. and Indsl. Rels. Assn. (legis. rep. dist. 5 1989, 90), Calif. Assn. of Marriage and Family Therapists, L.A. Group psychtherapy Soc., Rotary Internat., Psi Chi. Avocations: writing, world mythologies, theatre, abstract artist, vegetarian chef.

KEZSBOM, ALLEN, lawyer; b. N.Y.C., July 5, 1941; BA cum laude, Bklyn. Coll., 1962; LLB magna cum laude, Harvard U., 1965. Bar: N.Y. 1966, U.S. Dist. Ct. (so. dist.) N.Y. 1968, U.S. Dist. Ct. (ea. dist.) N.Y. 1972, U.S. Ct. Appeals (1st cir.) 1982, U.S. Ct. Appeals (2d cir.) 1971, U.S. Ct. Appeals (6th cir.) 1986, U.S. Ct. Appeals (8th cir.) 1981, U.S. Ct. Appeals (11th cir.) 1983, U.S. Supreme Ct. 1978. Assoc. Kaye, Scholor, Fierman, Hays & Handler, N.Y.C., 1966-71, ptnr., 1972-86, Fried, Frank, Harris, Shriver & Jacobson, N.Y.C., 1986—. Vis. lectr. Yale Law Sch., New Haven, Conn., 1992-93. Mem. Harvard Law Rev., 1963-65; contbr. articles to profl. jours. Knox fellow Harvard Law Sch., 1965-66. Mem. ABA (antitrust sect., litigation sect., nat. resources, energy & environ. law), N.Y. State Bar Assn. (antitrust sect., litigation, environ.), Assn. Bar City N.Y. Office: Fried Frank Harris Shriver & Jacobson 1 New York Plz Fl 22 New York NY 10004-1980

KHABAROVSKY, BARON See DRUTCHAS, GERRICK GILBERT

KHABASHESKU, VALERY N. chemist, educator; b. Odessa, Ukraine, Aug. 14, 1950; s. Nikolai F. and Tatyana F. Khabashesku; m. Olga K. Sokolikova, May 30, 1981; 1 child, Dmitry V. MS in Chemistry Cum Laude, Lomonosov Moscow State U., 1973; PhD in Organic Chemistry, Zelinsky Inst. Organic Chemistry, USSR Acad. Scis., 1979; DS in Chemistry, Zelinsky Inst. Organic Chemistry, Russian Acad. Scis., 1998. Prin. scientist Zelinsky Inst. Organic Chemistry, Russian Acad. Scis., Moscow, 1998—. Faculty fellow Rice U., Houston, 2001—. Recipient First prize, Coun. Mendeleev Chem. Soc. USSR, 1976, Zelinsky Inst. Organic Chemistry, 1976, award and medal, Pres. USSR Acad. Scis., 1983, First prize, Zelinsky Inst. Organic Chemistry, 1987, Laureate, State Prize of Russia, Russian Govt., 2001. Achievements include patents for solid state synthesis of amorphous carbon nitride, a-C3N4; first direct spectroscopic characterization of silicon-carbon double bond; first preparation of sphere-shaped nanoscale carbon nitride of C3N4 stoichiometry; research in direct spectroscopic characterization and theoretical modelling of short-lived molecules with silicon-oxygen, germanium-oxygen and germanium-carbon double bonds; neutralized nitrogen beam assisted cryogenic synthesis of carbon nitride thin films; chemical functionalization and applications of carbon nanotubes, fullirenes and nanodiamonds. Home: 2421B Dorrington St Houston TX 77030 Office: Rice U Dept Chemistry Ctr Nanoscale Sci & Tech 6100 Main St Houston TX 77005 Personal E-mail: khval@rice.edu. E-mail: khval@rice.edu.

KHABIBULIN, NIKOLAI, professional hockey player; b. Sverdlovsk, Russia, Jan. 13, 1973; Goaltender Phoenix Suns. Office: Tampa Bay Lightning Hockey Club 401 Channelside Dr Tampa FL 33602

KHACHADURIAN, AVEDIS, physician; b. Aleppo, Syria, Jan. 6, 1926; s. Khachadur and Aznive (Demirjian) K.; m. Laura Hadidian, July 27, 1961; children: Cynthia, Linda. BA, Am. U. of Beirut, 1949, MD, 1953. Resident internal medicine Am. U. of Beirut, 1953-56; fellow Postgrad. Sch. Medicine, London, 1956-57, Harvard Med. Sch., 1957-59; asst. prof. biochemistry and medicine Am. U. of Beirut, 1959-64, assoc. prof., 1964-71, prof., 1971; prof. pediatrics, dir. Clin. Research Center, Northwestern U. Med. Sch., 1971-73; prof. medicine, head div. endocrinology metabolism and nutrition U. Medicine and Dentistry N.J.-R.W. Johnson Med. Sch., Piscataway, N.J., 1973; mem. staff pediatrics Children's Meml. Hosp., Chgo. Cons. U. Chgo. Sch. Medicine. Mem. Am. Diabetes Assn., N.Y. Acad. Sci., Am. Fedn. Cin. Rsch., Am. Heart Assn., Am. Inst. Nutrition, Endocrine Soc., N.Y. Lipid Rsch. Club, Sigma Xi, Alpha Omega Alpha. Achievements include rsch. in genetics; natural history, pathogenesis and treatment of hereditary hyperlipidemias; diabetes; studies on various inborn errors of metabolism; osteoporosis.

KHACHATOURIANS, GEORGE (GHARADAGHI), microbiologist, educator; b. Nov. 21, 1940; s. Sumbat and Mariam (Ghazarian) Khachatourians; m. Lorraine M. McGarth, Oct. 14, 1974; 1 child, Ariane K. BA, Calif. State U., San Francisco, 1966, MA, 1969; PhD, U. B.C., Vancouver, Can., 1971. Postdoctoral fellow Biol. Div. Oak Ridge (Tenn.) Nat. Lab., 1971-73; rsch. assoc. U. Mass. Med. Sch., Worcester, 1973-74; from asst. prof. to assoc. prof. microbiology dept. U. Sask., Saskatoon, Canada, 1974—80, prof., 1980-81, prof. applied microbiology and food sci., 1981—, coord. ag-biotech. human resources tng. and rsch., 1998—, head dept., 2001—, dir. agrl. biotechnology initiative. Mem. task force biotechnology Govt. of Can., Ottawa, Ont., 1980—81; mem. oper. grants panel Can. Agr., 1981—84; mem. biomedical grants panel Sask. Health Rsch., 1988—91; pres. Khachatourians Enterprises Inc.; vis. prof. U. B.C., Vancouver, 1992; advisor Food Biotechnology Commn. Network, Ottawa, 1996—98, Biotechnology Human Resources Coun. Task Force, Ottawa, 1997—99; bd. dirs. Nutracenticals Network Sask. Sci. Adv., Cell Cultivation Pilot Plant Facility, PhilomBios Inc., Biolin Rsch. Inc., Dumas Enterprises Inc., Mycogen Corp.; founding dir. BioInsecticide Rsch. Labs., Ctr. Molecular Agr. Applied Biotechnology. Co-editor: (book series) Food Biotechnology-Microorganisms, 1995, Applied Mycology and Biotechnology, 2001—; assoc. editor: Can. Jour. Microbiology and Food Biotech.; assoc. editor Agr. and Food Prodn., vol. 1, 2001; assoc. editor: Applied Mycology and Biotech., The Biotechnology Revolution in Global Agriculture, 2001; assoc. editor Agr. and Food Prodn., vol. 1, 2002; sr. editor: Transgenic Plants and Crops, 2002, sr.editor: Fungal Geromics, 2003; contbr. Bd. dirs. Can. Coll. Microbiologists, Biotechnology Human Resources Coun. Can., Coll. Univ. Program Task Force. Recipient Golden Wheel award, Rotary Internat., 1996; grantee, Nat. Sci. Engring. Rsch. Coun., Ottawa, 1974—92, 2001—, Sask. Agr. Rsch. Found., 1981—85, NRC, 1977—78, Agrl. Devel. Found., Regina, 1985—, AgriFood Innovation Fund, 1998—. Mem.: AAAS, Sask. Adv. Technol. Assn. (bd. dirs.), Am. Assn. Integrative Studies, Soc. Invertabrate Pathology, Am. Entomol. Soc., Can. Soc. Microbiology, Am. Soc. Microbiology, Am. Chem. Soc. Achievements include patents for anucleated live E. coli vaccines. Home: 1125 13th St E Saskatoon SK Canada S7H 0C1 Office: U Sask Applied Micro-Food Sci Dept Saskatoon SK Canada S7N 5A8 Fax: 306-966-8898. E-mail: khachatouria@sask.usask.ca.

KHACHATURIAN, ZAVEN SETRAK, neuroscientist; b. Aleppo, Syria, Apr. 15, 1937; s. Setrak N/A and Rahel N/A Khachaturian; m. Alidz Thelma Asadourian; 1 child, Ara. BA, Yale U., New Haven, 1961; PhD, Case Western Res. U., Cleve., 1967; postgrad., Columbia U., N.Y.C., 1967—69. Chief, physiology of aging br. Nat. Inst. on Aging/NIH, Bethesda, Md., 1981—86; interim sci. dir. Pitts. Biotech. Ctr., Pitts., 1986—87; prof. heath svcs. adminstrn. Grad. Sch. of Pub. Health, U. of Pitts., 1986—87; v.p. for rsch. U. of Pitts. Heath Ctr., 1986—87; assoc. dir. neurosci. and neuropsychology of aging Nat. Inst. on Aging/NIH, Bethesda, Md., 1987—95, dir., office of Alzheimer's rsch., 1985—95; dir. Ronald & Nancy Reagan Rsch. Inst. of the Alzheimer's Assn., Chgo., 1995—99; pres. KRA, Inc. Internat. Cons. on Alzheimer's & Aging, Potmac, Md., 1995—. Sci. - rsch. adminstrn. NIH/Pub. Health Svc./DHHS, Bethesda, Md., 1977—95; brain rschr. - memory & learning U. of Pitts. Med. Sch., 1969—77. Editor: (book) Annals N.Y. Acad. Science, Alzheimer's Disease: A Compendium of Current Theories, 2000, Alzheimer's Disease: Cause(s), Diagnosis, Treatment, & Care, 1996; author: (article - diagnosis of alzheimer's disea) Archives of Neurology, 1985; editor: (book) Alzheimer's Disease. New Treatment Strategies, 1992, Calcium, Membranes, Aging & Alzheimer's Disease - NY Acad. Sci, 1989; contbr. Founder & pres. Armenian-Am. Club of Pitts., 1973—77. Named Scientist of the Yr., Maturity News Svc., 1992, Co Honoree, with Mrs. Nancy Reagan (Pub. Svc. for Alzheim's Disease), NYC Rita Hayworth Gala Com., 1996; recipient Dir.'s Award, NIH, 1983, Sr. Exec. Svc. award, Dept. HHS, 1988, President's award, Nat. Alzheheimer's Assn., 1993. Mem.: IEEE, AAAS, Soc. for Neurosci., Dana Alliance for Brain Initiatives. Independent. Presbyterian (Armenian). Avocation: woodworking. Office: Khachaturian Radebaugh & Associates Inc 8912 Copenhaver Dr Potomac MD 20854 Office Fax: 301-294-7203. E-mail: zaven_khachaturian@kra.net.

KHACHEMOUNE, AMOR, physician; s. Louiza Khoualed and Mahfoud Khechmoune; m. Faiza Kada, Jan. 3, 1997; 1 child, Nour Leila. MD, Nat. Inst. for Med. Scis., Constantantine, Algeria, 1989. Specialization in Dermatology Universite de Lille II, France, 1993, cert. Advanced Studies of Cosmetic Dermatology Univeriste de Lille II, France, 1993, Wound Specialist Am. Acad. of Wound Mgmt., 2000. Primary care physician pvt. practice, Ain Kechera, Algeria, 1989; cons. dermatologist and primary care team coord. ID formation, Lille, France, 1993—96; sr. rsch. fellow Cardiology Rsch. Found., Washington, 1996—98; med. intern Boston Med. Ctr., Brockton Hosp., 1998—99; wound healing fellow Boston U. Sch. of Medicine, 1999—2001; prodn. mgr., rsch. assoc. Harvard Med. Sch., Brigham and Women's Hosp., Divsn. of Interventional Cardiology, Boston, 2001; sr. dermatology resident Georgetown U. Med. Ctr., Washington, 2001—. Guest spkr. Nat. and Internat. Dermatology and Wound Healing meetings. Editor: (editorial board) The Internet Journal of Dermatology; presenter (peristomal pyoderma gangrenosum successf) Peristomal Pyoderma Gangrenosum Successfully Treated with Graftskin. Kupiec A, Grekin DA, Kauffman CL, Khachemoune A. Wound healing symposium. Baltimore April 27-30, 2002, (world congress of dermatology 2002) Newborn derived skin substitues and their use in chronic wounds. Khachemoune A. 20th World Congress of Dermatology. Paris, France. July 1st- 5th 2002., Factor Leiden mutation associated with leg ulceration. American Academy of Dermatology meeting. Khachemoune A. Oral presentation. AAD meeting, New Orleans, LA (Feb 2002), White sponge nevus successfully treated with minocycline. Khachemoune A, Bouadjar B. (Poster presentation AAD meeting Feb 2002), Heck's disease. Khachemoune A, Bouadjar B. (Poster presentation AAD meeting Feb 20002), Factors that influence healing in chronic venous ulcers treated with Cryopreserved Cultured Human Epidermal Allografts. Khachemoune A, Bello YM. Phillips TJ. (poster presentation wound healing symposium Las Vegas 2001), Cryofibrinogenemia presenting as leg ulceration. Khachemoune A, Bello YM, Phillips TJ. Oral presentation at the American Academy of Dermatology meeting, Washington DC 03/02/2001, The use of cryopreserved cultured human epidermal allografts in a large recalcitrant venous leg ulcer: A case study. Bello YM, Manzoor J, Rojas AI, Khachemoune A, Green H, Phillips TJ. 2000 symposium on advanced Wound care & medi, Lansky AJ, Mehran R, Popma JJ, Abizaid AS, Saucedo J, Khachemoune A, Ho K, Kuntz RE, Bonan R. Favourable coronary remodelling in patients with non flow limiting dissections after coronary intervention: results from the Internation, Saucedo JF, Abizaid A S, Kennard ED, Curran MJ, Khachemoune A, Kada F, Brahimi A, Baim D. Vessel Size in an independent Predictor of 1 Year Clinical Events After New Device Angioplasty: A NACI Registry Report. Circulation. 1997., Diagnosis and Management of Chronic leg ulcers: A wound specialist approach. Khachemoune A. 20th World Congress of Dermatology. Paris, France. July 1st- 5th 2002., Atypical chronic lower extremity ulcers: Clinical vignette and discussion. Khachemoune A. 20th World Congress of Dermatology. Paris, France. July 1st- 5th 2002., reviewer Jour. of Am. Acad. of Dermatology, (profl. med. jours.) Am. Family Physician; author: (70 scientific papers) Publications in medical journals; contbr. editor (profl. jour.) Skin and Aging. Fellow: Am. Acad. of Wound Mgmt. (licentiate). Achievements include research in Use of skin substitutes in wound healing. Avocation: karate doshototakan. Office: Georgetown U Med Ctr Divsn Dermatology 3800 Reservoir Rd NW 5 PHC Washington DC 20007

KHACHIAN, ELISA ARPENIA, artist, educator; b. Worcester, Mass., May 6, 1935; d. Mihran and Hrag (Sohigian) Tufenkjian; m. Richard Khachian, June 16, 1957; children: Carol Garinther, Nancy Quinn, Gary, Sue Hendricks. BS, R.I. Sch. Design, 1957. Art tchr. elem. schs., Concord, Mass., 1958-59; art vol. tchr. Fairfield (Conn.) Sch. Sys., 1972-79; art instr. Darien (Conn.) Arts Coun., 1990-94. Pvt. tchr. and cons., Fairfield, 1989—. Represented in permanent collections Nat. Assn. Women Artists, Zimmerli Mus., Rutgers U., New Haven Paint & Clay Club; group shows include Inheritance Project, Beacon St. Gallery, Chgo., 2002, NAWA Millenium Collection, UN, N.Y., 2002, Silvermine Guild Galleries, 2002; contbr. articles to profl. mags. Vol. Fairfield Sch. Sys., 1972-87. Recipient Charlie Fischer Prize Brush, Palette Club, 1988, Best drawing/painting award Discovery Mus. Barnum Festival, Best Featured Artist, Conn. Women Artists, 2000, Conn. Watercolor Soc. award, 2000; Conn. Commn. for Arts grantee, 2002. Mem.: Conn. Watercolor Soc. (award 1989, 1994, Woman Artist of Yr. 1996, award 2000, 2001, numerous other awards), Silvermine Arts Ctr. (bd. dirs. 1995), Art. Pl. Gallery (sec. 1990—95), Conn. Women Artists (award 2000, 2001, numerous other awards), Am. Assn. Women Artists (numerous awards), Internat. Arts Soc. (assoc. mem., Hon. Menetion 1998), New Haven Paint and Clay Club (merit award 2001). Avocations: grandchildren, gardening, writing, travel, walking, teaching. Home and Office: 213 Hollydale Rd Fairfield CT 06430-2231

KHAJAWALL, ALI MOHAMAD, psychiatrist; b. Srinagar, Kashmir, Mar. 28, 1944; s. Gulam Rasool and Sitara (Begum) K.; m. Farida Rajab, Apr. 24, 1979; 1 child, Farhad Ali. FAC, S.P. Coll., Srinagar, 1961; MBBS, Srinagar Med. Coll., 1966. Intern Cook County Hosp., Chgo., 1973-74, resident Mo. Inst. Psychiatry, 1974-78; asst. prof. U. So. Calif., L.A., 1983-84, U. Calif., Irvine, 1984-86; cons. Med. Bd. Calif., Sacramento, 1986-87; cons. surveyor HCFA, Washington, 1987-91; cons. psychiatrist forensic out-patient L.A. County, 1991; cons. reviewer CMRI, San Francisco, 1992; sr. psychiatrist MSH, Norwalk, Calif., 1978—. Spokesman, founder Kashmiri Am. Coun., Washington, 1990; 1st sec. Kashmir Am. Mission; del. Rep. Presdl. Campaign, Washington, 1992, mem. Rep. Presdl. Task Force, 1993, Coun.; Rep. Senatorial Inner Circle. Col. USAR. Decorated Congl. award of merit, Army commendation medal.; recipient Meritious Svc. Medal. Mem. AMA, AMSUS, USAA, IMA. Avocation: international politics and conflict resolution. Home: 1538 Sunbluff Dr Diamond Bar CA 91765-3906 also: PO Box 4040 Diamond Bar CA 91765-0040 Office: Met State Hosp 11401 Bloomfield Ave Norwalk CA 90650-2084

KHALADJAN, MIKHAIL NIKOLAEVICH, educator, song writer; b. Krasnodar, Russia, Mar. 21, 1961; came to U.S., 1992; s. Nikolai N. and Tamara M. (Doroshenko) K.; 1 child, Gerard. BA in Design, City U. Indsl. Design, Krasnodar, Russia, 1978; M in Pedagogy, Moscow External U. Humanities, 1993, D in Pedagogy, 1994. Sr. designer Voskhod, Moscow, 1989-90; dir. Intermezzo Firm, Moscow, 1990-91; v.p. Moscow External U. Humanities, 1991-92; pres. Internat. Ctr. Authorized Edn., Inc., Beverly Hills, Calif., 1992—. Bd. dirs. Moscow External U. of the Humanities, Zentrum für Internat. Freundschaft und Kultur (Germany). Author: (textbook) Commercial Advertising, 1993; co-author: (with others) Manifesto of the Authorized Revival of Secondary Education, 1996, A Young Man's Book: The Ethical Code of the Authorized Personality, 1997; composer: Seasons, 1994, 95; mem. editl. bd. The MEUH Gerald, Russia. Recipient cert. of acknowledgement World Peace Prayer Soc., 1995, cert. of achievement Hollywood Song Jubilee, 1996. Mem. AAAS, Internat. Acad. Authorized Edn. (academician diploma, Acad. World Star), Am. Assn. Univ. Adminstrs., N.Y. Acad. Scis., Internat. Coun. on Edn. for Tchg. Avocations: music, design, history of edn., cooking. Office: Internat Ctr Autorized Edn PO Box 17211 Beverly Hills CA 90209-3211 E-mail: icae@earthlink.net.

KHALADJAN, NIKOLAI NIKOLAEVICH, academic administrator; b. Sevastopol, USSR, Feb. 23, 1931; s. Tigran Avanesovich and Anna Karlovna (Vaivads) K.; m. Tamara Mihkailovna Doroshenko, Sept. 22, 1954; children: Dubrova Ludmilla Nikolaevna, Mikhail Nikolaevich. M of Culture, Leningrad Inst. Culture, 1960; Cand Philosophy, Moscow State U., 1971; D of Pedagogy, Moscow External U. Humanities, 1992. Sr. lectr. Inst. Structural Engring. and Architecture, Dnepropetrovsk, Ukraine, 1976-79, Moscow State U., 1980s, Inst. Civil Aviation, Moscow, 1984; dean of faculty Moscow Vet. Acad., 1984, Moscow State Acad. Pub. and Design, 1984-91; pres. Moscow External U. Humanities, 1991—. Bd. dirs. Horizont Zentrum der Internationalen Freundschaft und Cultur, Cologne, Germany, 1996—; co-chair I.C.A.E., Inc., Beverly Hills, Calif., 1992—. Author: Manifesto of Authorized Education, 1993, Manifesto of the Authorized Revival of Secondary Education, 1996, The Autoengineering, 1995, Legenda-Kovalenda Art of Ironworks, History of Krasnodar Region, 1992; editl. dir. Megu Herald, Moscow, 1994—; pub. The Intellectual newspaper, Moscow, 1991—. Dir. Dept. Aesthetical Devel. of Children and Youth, Krasnodar Region, 1960s; founder Inst. of Design in No. Caucasus, Krasnodar, 1975; organizer mass movement in higher edn. for rsch. and study of Slavonic langs., USSR, 1980s; founder Inst. Civil Edn. of the Armed Forces, Moscow, 1995. Recipient medal USSR Nat. Achievement Exhbn., 1979, Eileen Tosney award for excellence in prractice of higher edn., 1996; The Nikolai N. Khaladjan Internat. award established in his name Am. Asn. Univ. Adminstrs., 1997. Mem. AAAS, Internat. Coun. on Edn. for Tchg. (life), N.Y. Acad. Scis., Am. Assn. Univ. Adminstrs. Avocations: music, singing and songwriting, history of philosophy and education. Office: Pres/Moscow External U Hum 37 Perovskaya Str 111141 Moscow Russia also: PO Box 17211 Beverly Hills CA 90209-3211

KHALEDI, MORTEZA G, chemistry educator; b. Shiraz, Fars, Iran, Mar. 15, 1956; s. Enayat Ollah and Hadjieh Khaledi; m. Shahrzad Afshinpour, July 24, 1958; 1 child, Arras Darius. PhD, U. of Fla., 1985. Assoc. prof. N.C. State U., Raleigh, 1991—97, prof. of chemistry, 1997—. Tchr, rschr. N.C. State U., Raleigh, 1988—2003. Recipient award, NIH, 1988—2003. Mem.: Am. Chem. Soc. Achievements include discovery of chemical analysis. Office: N C State U Dept of Chemistry Raleigh NC 27695-8204 Office Fax: 919-515-2545. E-mail: morteza_khaledi@ncsu.edu.

KHALESSI, MOHAMMAD R. structural engineer, researcher; b. Yazd, Iran, Nov. 18, 1952; came to U.S., 1976; s. Mohammad-Ali and Farangis (Bahadorani) K.; m. Fariba Touhidi, Aug. 14, 1977 (div. 1984); 1 child, Ahoo; m. Mercedeh Rusty, Oct. 25, 1986; 1 child, Bobak. BS, Arya Mehr U., Tehran, Iran, 1976; MS, UCLA, 1978, PhD, 1983. Engr. C.F. Braun, Alhambra, Calif., 1980-81; rsch. engr. UCLA, 1981-83; sr. engr. Allied Signal, Torrance, Calif., 1983-87; sr. engring. splst. Boeing N.Am., Downey, Calif., 1987 97; chief technologist Mitratech Probabilistic, Fountain Valley, Calif., 1997-99; chief product devel. officer Unipass Techs., Inc., Irvine, Calif., 1999—, also bd. dirs. Bd. dirs. Advanced Probabilistic Rsch., Inc.; adv. Unicorp, VanNuys, Calif., 1995—. Contbr. articles to profl. jours. Recipient Outstanding Engring. Merit award Orange County (Calif.) Engring. Coun., 1994. Fellow Inst. Advancement Engring.; mem. AIAA, SAE (chair subcom. probabilistic method, comm. 1994—, tech. adv. leadership coun. for probabilistic methods 1995—, Disting. Probabilistic Methods Implementations award 1996). Republican. Moslem. Achievements include pioneering work in practical application of probabilistic methods, integration of probabilistic methods with finite element technique, identification of most-probable-failure point in original space. Office: Unipass Techs 18008 Sky Park Cir Ste 125 Irvine CA 92614-6470

KHALFIN, IGOR B. research scientist; b. Kiev, Ukraine, Dec. 19, 1957; came to U.S., 1995; s. Boris and Alla Khalfin; m. Marina Falkenhof; 1 child, Alexandra. MSc in Physics, Kazan State U., Russia, 1979; PhD in Physics, Bar-Ilan U., Ramat-Gan, Israel, 1994. Chmn. Electronics Engr. Firm, Kiev, 1987-91; rsch. scientist Bar-Ilan U., 1991-95; cons. Baff B.V., Rotterdam, The Netherlands, 1995; vis. prof. U. N.C., Charlotte, 1996-97; rsch. scientist Health Sci. Ctr., SUNY, Brooklyn, 1997-98; chief staff scientist/rsch. and devel. mgr. Pohlemus Inc., Colchester, Vt., 1998—2002. Sr. cons. Glace, N.Y.C., 1996-98, 2002-; staff scientist Rockwell Collins, San Jose, Calif., 2003-. Contbr. over 40 articles to profl. jours.; 3 patents in field. Recipient award for excellence in tech. comms. Pen Well Pub. Co., 1998. Mem. N.Y. Acad. Scis. Home: 4149 Garibaldi Pl Pleasanton CA 94566 Office: 2701 Orchard Pkwy MS69 San Jose CA 95134

KHALID, HUMAYUN, computer scientist, consultant; b. Karachi, Sind, Pakistan, July 9, 1968; s. Khalid Yousuf and Maimoona Khalid; m. Nuzhat Sultana, July 4, 1997; children: Nimra, Nabihah. BE in Elec. Engring. magna cum laude, CCNY, 1992; ME in Elec. Engring., 1993; PhD, CUNY, 1996. Rsch. assoc. U.S. Dept. Def., N.Y.C., 1996; staff electronic engr., scientist Motorola, Inc., Austin, 1996-98; sr. staff scientist, 1998-2000; sr. cons. Dell Computer Corp., Austin, 2000—. Mem. program com. Symposium on Performance Evaluation of Computer and Telecomm. Sys. (SPECTS), 2000. Contbr., editor numerous articles to profl. jours. Contbr. North Austin Muslim Cmty. Ctr., 1996-2000. Univ. fellow CUNY, 1995; univ. tuition scholarCUNY, 1995. Mem. IEEE (editor papers and proceedings), Soc. Computer Simulation Internat., Inst. Elec. and Electronics Engrs. Pakistan (life). Moslem. Home: 100 Cassat Cove Austin TX 78753 Office: Dell Computer Corp One Dell Way Round Rock TX 78682

KHALIL, MOHAMMAD ASLAM KHAN, environmental science and engineering educator, physics educator; b. Jhansi, India, Jan. 7, 1950; came to U.S., 1963; s. M. Ahsan Khan and Aleem-Un-Nisa K.; m. Giti Ara Eshraghi, June 1973; children: Kathayoon Azra, Kaviyaan Aslam. BPhys, BA in Math. and Psychology, U. Minn., 1970; MS in Physics, Va. Polytechnic Inst., 1972; PhD in Physics, U. Tex., 1976; MS in Environ. Sci., Oreg. Grad. Ctr., Beaverton, 1979; PhD in Eviron. Sci., Oreg. Grad. Ctr., 1979. Tchg. asst. dept. physics Va. Polytechnic Inst. and State U., 1970-71; grad. asst. dept. math. and physics U. Tex., Austin, 1971-72, tchg. asst. dept. physics, 1972-73, 76, rsch. scientist asst. Ctr. for Particle Theory, 1972-76; instr. dept. physics Pacific U., Forest Grove, Oreg., 1978; rsch. asst. dept. environ. sci. Oreg. Grad. Ctr., Beaverton, 1977-79, asst. prof. dept. environ. sci., 1980-82, assoc. prof. dept. environ. sci., 1982-84, prof. dept. chem., biol. and environ. sci., 1984-86, prof. Inst. Atmospheric Sci., 1986-90, prof. dept. environ. sci. and engring., dir. Global Change Rsch. Ctr., 1990-95; prof. dept. physics Portland State U., Oreg., 1995—. Owner Andarz Co., Portland, 1981—. Editor: Chemosphere: Global Change Science; mem. editl. bd. Handbook of Environ. Chemistry, Environ. Sci. and Pollution Rsch. Internat., Atmospheric Environment; contbr. some 200 articles to profl. jours. Grantee NSF, EPA, Dept. Energy, NASA. Mem. Am. Phys. Soc., Am. Chem. Soc., Am. Geophys. Union, Sigma Xi. Office: Portland State U Dept Physics PO Box 751 Portland OR 97207 0751 also: Andarz Co 9961 NW Kaiser Rd Portland OR 97231-2701 E-mail: aslam@global.phy.pdx.edu.

KHALIL, MOUNIR A. librarian, educator; b. Ashiwai, Fayuum, Egypt, Nov. 14, 1936; arrived in U.S., 1969; s. Amin Khalil and Mounirah A. Kerolos; m. Sawsan G. Aziz, May 31, 1951; 1 child, Richard. BA in Geography, Cairo U., 1958, BA in Libr. Sci., 1962; MLS in Libr. and Info. Scis., Pratt Inst., 1971, MS in Computer Sci., 1977; adv. cert. in Grad. Sch. Libr. and Info. Scis., U. Pitts., 1977. Cert. med. libr. Med. Libr. Assn. Head libr. Higher Inst. Petroleum, Suez, Egypt, 1962—66, Higher Inst. Social Work, Cairo, 1966—69; reference libr. Queensborough Pub. Libr., Jamaica, NY, 1969—73; br. libr. Bklyn. Pub. Libr., 1974—86; tech. libr. Health Ins. Plan, N.Y.C., 1986—89; chief access series City Coll. CUNY, N.Y.C., 1989—92, reference libr., 1993—; dir. tech. svcs. N.J. Inst., Newark, 1993. Part-time instr. Katharine Gibbs Sch., N.Y.C., 1986—92; adj. asst. prof. GSLIS Queens Coll., 1990; spkr. in field. Contbr. articles to profl. jours. Mem. Coptic Orthodox Ch. Bd., Bklyn., 1995. Bailey scholar, Queens Borough Pub. Libr., 1972, ALA Libr. Automation fellow, Al-Bayyt U., Jordon, 1997, Rsch. award, CUNY Rsch. Found., 2003—. Mem.: ALA, Internat. Fedn. Libr. Assn.s and Instns. (roundtable on bookmobiles

1999—), Spl. Librs. Assn. (moderator conf.). Achievements include development of electronic ILL and document delivery services. Avocations: chess, gardening, soccer, reading, travel. Office: City Coll CUNY West 138th St & Convent Ave Manhattan NY 10031

KHALIMSKY, EFIM, mathematics and computer science educator; b. Odessa, USSR, June 23, 1938; came to U.S., 1978; s. David Khalimsky and Olga Weizman; m. Elena Merems, May 19, 1962; 1 child, Olga. MS in Math. with honors, Pedagogical Inst., Odessa, 1960; PhD in Math., Pedagogical Inst., Moscow, 1969. Tchr. high sch., Odessa, 1960-66; assoc. prof. Pedagogical Inst., Magnitogorsk, USSR, 1969-72; sr. research scientist Research and Prodn. Inst. for Food Industry, Odessa, 1972-73, Econs. Inst. Acad. Sciences, Odessa, 1973-77; asst. prof. Manhattan Coll., Riverdale, N.Y., 1980-85; assoc. prof. CUNY, 1979-80, Coll. of Staten Island (N.Y.), 1985-89; prof. Cen. State U., Wilberforce, Ohio, 1989—. Author: Ordered Topological Spaces, 1977, (with others) The Planning of Economical and Ecological Research at Sea Basins, 1976, (with others) Economical and Ecological Management of Water Resources, 1976, (with others) Methodological Foundations on Developing MIS System for Water Resources, 1976; area editor Jour. Applied Math. and Simulation, 1987—; contbr. numerous articles to profl. jours. Named Best Scientist USSR Acad. Sciences, 1986. Mem. IEEE, Am. Math. Soc., Assn. Computing Machinery, Soc. Indsl. and Applied Math., Ops. Research Soc. Am. Home: 1260 Brentwood Dr Dayton OH 45406-5713

KHALSA, SHAKTI PARWHA KAUR, not for profit foundation executive; b. Mpls., June 19, 1929; d. Jacob Garon and Fay Weinberg. Student, UCLA, 1947-48. V.p., dir. 3HO Found., L.A., 1969—; v.p. Sikh Dharma, L.A., 1971—. Tchr. yoga, 1969—. Author: Kundalini Yoga: The Flow of Eternal Power, 1996, Kundalini Postures and Poetry, 2003; editor: Golden Temple Conscious Cookbook; sr. editor: mag. Beads of Truth, 1971—92, founder, editor: newsletter Sci. of Keeping Up, 1980—2001, cons. editor: Prosperity Paths, 1989—, Kundalini Rising, 1993—, contbg. editor: Aquarian Times, 2001—; performer: (albums) Lord of Miracles, 2003. Minister Sikh Dharma religion, 1975—; v.p. Sikh Dharma, bd. dirs; exec. com. Khalsa Coun., 1975—. Office: 3HO Foundation PO Box 351149 Los Angeles CA 90035-9549

KHAMOUNA, MO, communications associate, consultant; b. Casablanca, Morocco, Jan. 6, 1959; came to U.S., 1988; s. Ahmed and Malika (Katim) K.; m. Lori McNutt, July 20, 1990; children: Jasmine, Zackary. Diploma d'Etudes U. Gen./ Am. Studies, U. Paris, France, 1988; BS in Tourism & Recreation, U. Nebr., Kearney, 1993; MS in Tourism & Recreation, Black Hills State U., 1996. Proficiency cert. travel & tourism McCook C.C. Dir. recreation Spearfi Parks & Recreation Dept., Spearfish, S.D., 1995; comm. assoc. Nebr. Coll. Tech. Agr., Curtis, 1996—. V.p., cons. U.S. Hwy 83 Trade & Tourism Assn., Nebr., 1997—; pres. Prairie Lakes Country Travel Coun., McCook, Nebr., 1999—. Active Nebraskans for Peace. Named Hon. Citizen of Tanyang Municipality Magistrate, South Korea, 1998. Mem. Internat. Peace Acad., Nat. Recreation and Park Assn. (nat. certification bd. 1994-95), Rotary (pres.-elect). Avocations: book collecting, wilderness vision quest, travelling, low impact camping. Home: Badger St # 26 Stockville NE 69042 Office: Nebr Coll of Tech Agr RR 3 RR 3 Box 23A Curtis NE 69025-9525 Fax: 308-367-5209. E-mail: mkhamouna1@unl.edu.

KHAN, AHMED MOHIUDDIN, finance, insurance executive; b. Hyderabad, Andhra Pradesh, India, Nov. 14, 1955; s. Mohammad Mominuddin and Mehar-Unnisa Begum Hyderabad; m. Marjorie L. Klein-Khan, Mar. 31, 1983; 1 child, Yosef F. MBA, U. Palm Beach, 1975; PhD in Bus. Adminstrn., Northwestern U., 2000. Inventory auditor RGIS, Inc., Chgo., 1975-78; staff acct. Sommerset, Inc., Chgo., 1978-85; fin. cons. Provident Mutual Fin. Svc., Inc., Phoenix, 1985-92; pres. Khan and Assocs., Fin./Ins. Svcs., Phoenix, 1992—. Author: Financial-Insurance Services in the New Millenium, 2000. Named Hon. Mem. Exec. Hall of Fame, 2000, named one of Outstanding Scholars of 20th Century; recipient Nat. Sales Achievement award, 2000, Nat. Quality award, 2000. Mem. Assn. MBA Execs., Nat. Assn. Ins. Fin. Advisors, Millon Dollar Round Table. Democrat. Moslem. Avocations: golf, traveling, classical music. Home and Office: 4643 E Grandview Rd Phoenix AZ 85032-3416 E-mail: amkhan_2001@yahoo.com.

KHAN, AMANULLAH, physician; b. Jullundhar, India, Mar. 2, 1940; came to U.S., 1964; s. Ahmad Ali and Qamar (Nisa) K.; m. Fran Elise Austin, Dec. 9, 1972; children: Roxanna, Sabrina, Amanda. Licentiate state med. faculty, West Pakistan Med. Sch., 1959; MBBS, King Edward Med. Coll., Lahore, 1963; PhD, Baylor U., 1968. Diplomate: Am. Bd. Allergy and Immunology, Am. Bd. Lab. Immunology. Rotating intern Samaritan Hosp., Troy, N.Y., 1965-66; fellow in hematology and oncology Wadley Insts. of Molecular Medicine, Dallas, 1966-69, chief research fellow, 1969-70, chmn. dept. immunotherapy, 1970-91; mem. staffs HCA Plano Med. Ctr., Doctor's Hosp., Dallas, Richardson Med. Ctr., St. Paul Med. Ctr., North Central Med. Ctr., McKinney. Author: Immune Regulators in Transfer Factor, 1979, Inteferon: Properties and Clinical Uses, 1980, Experimental Hematology Today, 1980, Human Lymphokines, 1982; editor: Jour. Clin. Hematology and Oncology, 1971-87; mem. editorial bd.: Exptl. Hematology, 1973-75; patentee in field; contbr. articles to sci. jours. Bd. dirs. St. Vincent Med. Found.; mem. Homeland Security Task Force of Tex., 2001-02; mem. Pres.'s Adv. Commn. on Asian Ams. and Pacific Islanders. Recipient Pres. of Pakistan Gold medal Pakistan Acad. of Med. Scis., 1992. Fellow ACP, Am. Coll. Allergists; mem. Am. Assn. Immunologists, Am. Soc. Clin. Oncology, Am. Soc. Hematology, AMA, Dallas County Med. Soc., Tex. Med. Assn., King Edward Med. Coll. Alumni Assn. (pres. 1974-75, 78-79), Assn. Pakistani Physicians N. Am. (pres. 1983-84) Office: Cancer Ctr Assocs 5959 Harry Hines Blvd Ste 620 Dallas TX 75235-5328 E-mail: aukhanmd@aol.com.

KHAN, AMIR U. agricultural engineering consultant; b. Kathgodam, Uttar Pradesh, India, June 15, 1927; came to U.S., 1948; s. Abdul Rehman and Shah Khan; m. Shaheda A. Samad, Mar. 24, 1960; children: Aida, Ayesha, Mona, Omar. BS, Aligarh (India) U., 1947; MS in Gen. Agr., Mich. State U., 1949, MS in Agrl. Engring., 1952, PhD in Agrl. Engring., 1968. Mng. ptnr. Agrimac Industries, Rampur, Uttar Pradesh, 1953-58; dep. dir. Ministry of Industries, Govt. India, New Delhi, 1958-59; head agrl. machinery div. Voltas Ltd., Bombay, 1959-63; rsch. assoc. Mich. State U., East Lansing, 1964-66; head agrl. engring. dept. Internat. Rice Rsch. Inst./Ford Found., Manila, 1968-76; resident rep. Internat. Rice Rsch. Inst., Islamabad, Pakistan, 1976-82, head agrl. engring. dept. Manila, 1982-87; agrl. mechanization advisor, Nat. Agrl. Rsch. Project Winrock Internat., Giza, Egypt, 1987-94. Bd. dirs. Phillipine Soc. Agrl. Engrs., 1984-86; cons. in field. Co-author: Rural Small Scale Industry in China, 1974, Agriculture of Egypt, 1993; contbr. over 100 articles to various publs.; holder 25 patents in agrl. machinery. Mem. Toledo Islamic Ctr., 1965—. Recipient LDC Innovation award Am. Assn. Engring. Socs., 1985, Internat. Inventors award King Gustav of Sweden, 1986 Fellow Am. Soc. Agrl. Engrs. (Kishida INternat. award 1988), Indian Soc. Agrl. Engrs. (hon. life, Commendation medal 1987), Pakistan Soc. Agrl. Engrs. (hon. life, sec.-treas. 1979, Adamjee Gold medal award 1982). Avocations: collecting antique watches, art nouveau antiques. Home: 300 Coventry Ct Perrysburg OH 43551-1269 E-mail: auk27@hotmail.com.

KHAN, ARFA, radiologist, educator; b. Srinagar, Kashmir, India, Dec. 4, 1943; came to U.S., 1966; d. Ghulam Rasool and Ruqia Hayat; m. Faroque A. Khan, Apr. 16, 1966; children: Arif O., Shireen. B of Medicine, B of Surgery, Govt. Med. Coll., Kashmir, 1964. Diplomate Am. Bd. Radiology. Intern Barberton (Ohio) Citizen Hosp., 1966-67; resident in radiology L.I. Jewish Med. Ctr., New Hyde Park, N.Y., 1967-70, from instr. to assoc. prof. radiology, 1970-93, prof., 1993—, assoc. chmn. radiology, 1994-2000; program dir., 1995. Contbr. 50 articles to radiology jours. Fellow Am. Coll. Radiology; mem. Am. Coll. Radiology, Am. Soc. Neuroradiology, Am. Soc. Head & Neck Radiology, Am. Soc. Thoracic Radiology, Radiol. Soc. N.Am. Democrat. Moslem. Avocations: cooking, tennis, aerobics, gardening, skiing. Fax: 718-343-7463. E-mail: khan@lij.edu.

KHAN, DANYAL MUSHTAQ, pediatric cardiologist; b. Rawalpindi, Punjab, Pakistan, Feb. 26, 1971; s. Mushtaq and Naheed Khan; m. Mehreen Rizwan; children: Arham Mushtaq, Raahym Mushtaq. MBBS, Aga Khan U. Med. Coll., Karachi, Pakistan, 1993. Diplomate Am. Bd. of Pediat. Pediatric resident Pa. State U. Hershey Med. Ctr., Hershey, 1995—98; pediatric cardiology fellow U. Miami (Fla.), Jackson Meml. Hosp., 1998—2001; pediatric interventional cardiology fellow Miami Children's Hosp., 2001—02, pediatric cardiologist, 2002—. Mem.: AMA, Soc. Cardiac Angiography and Intervention, Am. Acad. Pediat., Am. Coll. Cardiology. Achievements include research in use of helex atrial septal defect occluder's use in non-centrally located and complex defects. Home: 4460 NW 107 Ave Apt 202 Miami FL 33178 Office: Miami Children's Hosp 3200 SW 60 court Suite # 104 Miami FL 33155 Office Fax: 305-662-8304. Personal E-mail: danyakhan@hotmail.com. E-mail: danyal.khan@mch.com.

KHAN, EAKALAK, civil engineering educator; b. Chiang Mai, Thailand, Aug. 20, 1968; came to U.S., 1991; s. Zafar and Ploenchit Khan. B in Engring., Chiang Mai U., 1990; MS in Agrl. Engring., U. Hawaii, 1993; MS in Civil Engring., UCLA, 1994, PhD in Civil Engring., 1997. Registered profl. engr., N.J., Thailand. Engr. Envirtech Cons. Co. Ltd., Bangkok, 1990; jr. expert U. Hawaii, Honolulu, 1993; postdoctoral rsch. assoc. UCLA, 1998; asst. prof. civil engring. Bklyn. Poly. U., 1999—2002, N.D. Stat U., Fargo, 2002—. Inventor in field. Rsch. grantee Ahmanson Found., 1994, 95, Santa Monica Bay Restoration Project, 1995, 96, EarthShell Corp., Inc., 1997, State of Calif., 1998, State of N.Y., 2002. Mem. ASCE, Am. Water Work Assn., Assn. Environ. Engring. and Sci. Profs., Internat. Assn. Water Quality, Water Environment Fedn. E-mail: Eakalak.Khan@ndsu.nodak.edu.

KHAN, HABIB URREHMAN, neurologist; b. Karachi, Sindh, Pakistan, July 6, 1964; came to U.S., 1993; s. Abdul Rehman Khan and Hamida Rehman; m. Marium Habib, Apr. 8, 1992; children: Musaab Bin Habib, Fatimah Habib. MBBS, Dow Med. Coll., Karachi, 1988; MD, Edn. Commn. Fgn. Med. Grads., 1993. Ho. officer surgery Civil Hosp., Karachi, 1988-89, ho. officer medicine, 1989; sr. med. officer Alrahman Med. Ctr., Karachi, 1989-93; intern in neuromedicine U. Medicine Dentistry, Newark, 1994-95, resident in neurology, 1995—98; fellow SUNY, 1998—99; dir. sleep lab., dir. neurophysiology lab., chief neurology Casa Grande (Ariz.) Regional Med. Ctr., 2000—. Scholar, Wyeth Pharm., 1999. Fellow Mini Epilepsy Fellowship Network; mem. AMA, Am. Acad. Neurology, Am. Assn. Sleep Medicine, Pakistan Med. Dental Coun. Avocations: cricket, reading, swimming. Office: Casa Grande Regional Med Ctr 1820 E Florence Blvd Ste D Casa Grande AZ 85222 E-mail: khanhabib@hotmail.com.

KHAN, HALIMUR R. language educator; b. Dhaka, Bangladesh, Dec. 14, 1956; s. Hafizullah Khan and Anjuma Khatoon; m. Nazmun Khan, Jan. 21, 1993; children: Kingshok, Priyana. PhD, U. Mich., 1990. Asst. prof. Wayne State U., Detroit, 1993—98; vis. asst. prof. U. Mich., Ann Arbor, 1998—99; asst. prof. Colgate U., Hamilton, NY, 1999—. Contbr. Mem.: AAASS, AATSEEL. Avocations: chess, tennis, fishing. Home: 32 College St Hamilton NY 13346 Office: Colgate Univ 219C Lawrence Hall Hamilton NY 13346

KHAN, JAMIL AKBER, chemical company executive; b. Karachi, Pakistan, Mar. 17, 1952; came to U.S., 1976; s. Mehboob and Shamim Akhter Khan; m. Susan Mandelin, Feb. 27, 1981; children: Farooq J., Omar J. PhD, U. London, 1976; MBA, U. New Haven, 1987. Rsch. fellow Uniroyal, Inc., Middlebury, Conn., 1978-84, mktg. specialist, 1978-85; mktg. dir., v.p. Tech. & Mktg. Internat., Middlebury, 1985-87; mktg. mgr. Montedison/Ausimont, N.Y.C., 1987-88; sales and mktg. mgr. Ausimont, Morristown, N.J., 1988-90, Enimont/Enichem, N.Y.C., 1990-94; dir. sales Enichem Americas, Houston, 1994—. Editor: Physical Chemistry, 1974; numerous patents in field. Mem. edn. com. UNICEF; mem. Mt. Arlington (N.J.) Bd. Edn., 1998. Fellow Royal Soc. Chemistry U.K., Am. Inst. Chemistry; mem. AMA (hon. lectr. 1990-98), Am. Chem. Soc., Soc. Automotive Engrs. Avocations: tennis, reading, lecturing, writing.

KHAN, MASRUR ALI, nuclear and chemical engineer, physicist; b. Faridpur, Bangladesh, Sept. 24, 1949; arrived in U.S. 1971; s. Yakub Ali Khan and Mahbuba (Karim) Begum; m. Cynthia Louise Reilly, Aug. 8, 1975; children: Tarik, Alia. BS in Physics with honors, U. Dhaka, 1971; BSChemE, U. Wis., 1974, BS in Nuclear Engring., 1976. Group leader for environ. group Commonwealth Edison Co.; project mgr. Carolina Power and Light Co., Brunswick Steam Electric Plant, 1981-88; cons. H.B. Robinson, 1988-89, Pub. Svc. Electric and Gas Co., 1989-94, Pa. Power and Light Co., 1990-92; pres. KCS Consulting, LLC, Cary, NC, 2002—; ind. safety reviewer ComEd Nuclear Sites, 1996-97; mentor Ont. Power Generation, Toronto, Can., 1998—. Mgmt. cons., ind. safety reviewer N.Y. Power Authority's Design Basis Documents. Contbr. articles to profl. jours. Mem. ASME, AIChE, Am. Mgmt. Assn., Project Mgmt. Inst., Am. Nuc. Soc. Home: 217 Brendan Choice Cary NC 27511-5508

KHAN, MOHAMMAD ASAD, geophysicist, educator, former energy minister and senator of Pakistan; b. Aima, Lahore, Pakistan, Aug. 13, 1940; came to U.S., 1964; s. Ghulam Qadir and Hajira (Karim) K.; m. Tahera Pathan, Jan. 4, 1974; 1 dau., Shehzi Samira. BS, U. Punjab, Lahore, Pakistan, 1957, MS, 1963; postgrad., Harvard U., 1964-65; PhD (East West Center scholar), U. Hawaii, 1967. Lectr. in geophysics U. Punjab, 1963-64; asst. prof. geophysics and geodesy U. Hawaii, 1967-71, assoc. prof., 1971-74, prof., 1974-96, prof. emeritus, 1996—; minister of petroleum and natural resources Govt. Pakistan, 1983-86, senator, 1984-86; cabinet mem. Eonc. Coordination Commn. of the Cabinet, Govt. of Pakistan, 1983-86; chmn. internat. advisors, 1987—. Chmn. Hydrocarbon Devel. Inst., Pakistan, 1984-86, Attock Oil Refinery, Pakistan, 1984-86; cabinet mem. Nat. Econ. Council, Govt. Pakistan, 1984-86; NSF and NASA fellow Summer Inst. Dynamical Astronomy at MIT, 1968-69; cabinet mem. Econ. Coord. Com. Cabinet Govt. Pakistan, 1983-86; sr. vis. scientist geodynamics Goddard Space Flight Ctr., NASA, Greenbelt, Md., 1972-74; sr. scientist Computer Scis. Corp., Silver Spring, Md., 1974-76, sr. cons., 1976-77; diplomatic minister/adviser Resource Survey and Devel. Pakistan, 1974-76; sr. resident assoc. Nat. Acad. Scis., 1972-74; leader Am. Asian Studies and Contemporary Social Problems Seminar Series, Honolulu, 1968-69 Contbr. articles to profl. publs. Chmn. East and West: A Perspective for the 80's; mem. Hawaii Environ. Council, 1979-83, chmn. exec. com., 1979-83, vice chmn., 1981-83; chmn. Pakistan Relief Fund, Honolulu, 1971. Recipient Gold medal Rawalpindi Union of Journalists, 1985, Pakistan Engring. Coun., 1985, Pakistan Assn. of Minorities, 1984, 85, Disting. Alumnus award for pofl. excellence and leadership U. Hawaii, 1995. Fellow Explorers Club; mem. Geol. Soc. U. Punjab (pres. 1962-63), Am. Geophys. Union, Pakistan Assn. Advancement Sci., Am. Geol. Inst., Am. Geophys. Union, East West Ctr. Alumni Assn. (dir. 1976-80), Internat. Alumni of East West Ctr. (exec. com., chmn. 1977-80, Disting. Alumnus award for Outstanding Career Achievements and Leadership 1984). Achievements include research in geophysics, geodetic and oceanographic applications of satellites, geodynamics, planetary interiors, global tectonics, global correlations, core-mantle boundary problems, equilibrium figures, gravity, isostasy, satellite altimetry, geodesy, earth models, geophysical exploration, ocean dynamics. Office: U Hawaii-Hawaii Inst Geophysics Planetology Post 602 Honolulu HI 96822-2219 *Most men stand the test of adversity quite well, but if you really want to test the character of a man, give him power.*

KHAN, NAVEED I. school librarian; s. Abdul Hamid Khan and Aziz Akhtar. Master in Info. Sci., NC Ctrl. U., 1997; MLS, U. Punjab, Lahore, Pakistan, 1988. Project libr. Lahore U. Mgmt. Sci., 1990—93; reference libr. US Info. Svc., Lahore, Pakistan, 1993—96; systems libr. NC Ctrl. U., Durham, 1997—. Mem.: Libr. Congress. Personal E-mail: nkhan@nccu.edu. E-mail: nkhan@nccu.edu.

KHAN, RASHID HUSSAIN, physician, researcher; b. Meerut, India, Mar. 28, 1939; came to U.S., 1992; s. Hamid Hussain and Maimoona Begum (Khan) K.; m. Sabiha Perveen Khan, Mar. 7, 1969. MSc, U. Karachi, 1965; PhD, U. Western Ont., 1972; MD, U. Tecnologia de Santiago, Dominican Republic, 1983. Diplomate Am. Bd. Internal Medicine, 2001; Lic. physician, N.C. Rsch. assoc. McMaster U. Med. Ctr., Hamilton, Ont., Can., 1979-80, Toronto Western Hosp., 1983-87, 90-92, U. Toronto, 1985-87, Queen's U. and Kingston (Ont.) Gen. Hosp., 1987-90; resident in medicine Mercy Cath. Med. Ctr., Darby, Pa., 1992-96, chief resident in medicine, 1996-97; physician MMC-PC, Murphy, N.C., 1997—, vice chief med. staff., 2000-2001. Contbr. articles to profl. jours.; patentee in field. Sci. fellow Am. Coll. Allergy and Immunology. Mem. AMA, So. Med. Assn. Avocations: fishing, gardening, hunting, reading, computers. Home: 4270 Highway 64 W Murphy NC 28906-8122 Office: 536 Hwy 64 W Murphy NC 28906 E-mail: sabrashk@webworkz.com.

KHAN, SAEED AHMAD, internist, cardiologist; b. Lahore, Pakistan, Sept. 1, 1938; came to U.S., 1982; s. Abdur Rehman and Khurshid Begum Khan; children: Imtiaz A., Soheel A., Tariq A., Yasmin. MBBS, Panjab U., 1960. Diplomate Am. Bd. Internal Medicine; cert. in advanced achievement in internal medicine. House physician in internal medicine St. Luke's Hosp., Bradford, Eng., 1967; thoracic med. registrar Milford (Eng.) Chest Hosp., 1967-69, med. registrar internal medicine, 1971-72, Southend (Eng.) Gen. Hosp., 1969-70; chief med. resident Norwalk (Conn.) Hosp., 1972-73, cardiology resident, 1973-74; internist, dir. ICU and CCU VA Hosp., Martinsburg, W.Va., 1974-75; internist, cardiologist Benton Med. Ctr., Franklin Hosp., 1975—. Chief of medicine The Franklin Hosp., Benton, 1988—, chief of staff 1996—. Fellow ACP, AMA, Am. Coll. Chest Physicians (assoc.); mem. Am. Soc. Internists, Am. Coll. Cardiology. Avocation: ping-pong. Office: Benton Med Ctr 205 Bailey Ln Benton IL 62812-1921

KHAN, SOHAIB AHMED, cancer researcher, molecular cell biology educator; b. Azamgarh, U.P., India, June 12, 1946; came to U.S., 1975; s. Aqueel Ahmed and Siddiqa (Khanam) K.; m. Huma Khan, Apr. 16, 1980; children: Sofia, Nadia. BS, Aligarh (India) U., 1966, MS, 1969, PhD, 1974. Vis. scientist Tata Inst. Fundamental Rsch., Bombay, 1974-75; cancer rsch. scientist Roswell Park Meml. Inst., Buffalo, 1975-79; sr. rsch. assoc. Case Western Res. U., Cleve., 1979-80; asst. prof. cell biology U. Cin., 1981-87—, assoc. prof., 1987-2000, prof., 2000—. Cons. Govt. of India, Washington, 1987; v.p. Biotech. Forum Inc., Cin., 1988—; cons. Marion Merrill Dow Co., Cin., 1995, Lifesensors, Inc., Phila., 1999—. Editor: Protooncogenes/Growth Factor, 1995; mem. editl. bd. Endocrinology, 1998—. Bd. mem. Internat. Acad. Cin., 1999—. Recipient young investigator award NIH, Bethesda, Md., 1978, Star award Ohio Cancer Rsch. Assocs., Columbus, Ohio, 1996. Mem. AAAS, Endocrine Soc., Am. Soc. Cell Biology, Am. Soc. Biochemistry and Molecular Biology. Avocations: tennis, gardening, stamps. Home: 8767 Weller Rd Cincinnati OH 45249-2711 Office: U Cin Med Ctr Vontz Ctr Molecular Studies 3125 Eden Ave Cincinnati OH 45267-0001 E-mail: Sohaib.Khan@uc.edu.

KHAN, ZILLUR RAHMAN, foundation executive; b. Hoogly, India, Nov. 21, 1938; came to U.S., 1964; s. Abdur Rahman and Khadija Khatun Khan; m. Tanjina Khan, Jan. 23, 1992; children: Riaz, Tamiz, Kabir, Mary Khadija, Wasima. BA with honors, Dhaka (Bangladesh) U., 1957, MA, 1958, Claremont (Calif.) Grad. Sch., 1963, PhD, 1967. Coord. Asian studies U. Wis., 1966-90, chmn. dept. polit. sci., 1987-99; pres. Am. Muslim Alliance, Wis., 1996-98, Bangladesh Found., Chgo., 1982—. Pres. polit. sci. group N.Am. Assn. Muslim Natural and Social Scientists, 1976-80; cons. UN Devel. Program, N.Y.C., 1988-90; vis. lectr. Carleton U., Can., 1971-72; vis. prof. U. Man., Can., 1988-89. Author: Leadership in the Least Developed Nation, 1983, From Martial Law to Martial Law, 1984, The Third World Charismat, 1996; editor: SAARC and the Super Powers, 1992; co-editor: Bengal Studies: A Collection of Essays, 2003. Founder trustee Am. Inst. Bangladesh Studies, Phila., 1986-98; bd. advisors Bangladesh Assn., Chgo., 1996—, Am. Muslim Alliance, Wis., 1998—. Mem. Am. Polit. Sci. Assn. (Outstanding Tchg. award 1994), Internat. Polit. Sci. Assn., India Assn. (pres. 1980-81), Candlelight Club (pres. 1982-83), Optimists (pres. 1983-85, Man of Yr. 1985). Democrat. Moslem. Avocations: music, photography, travel. Home: 1840 Cliffview St Oshkosh WI 54901 Office: U Wis Oshkosh WI 54901 E-mail: khan@uwosh@edu.

KHANDEKAR, JANARDAN DINKAR, oncologist, educator; b. Indore, India, Feb. 1, 1944; came to U.S., 1971; s. Dinker and Sulaochan (Dawlae) K.; m. Amita Oomen, Aug. 28, 1971; children: Manoj, Melin. MD, MBBS, U. Indore, 1969; sabbatical, Northwestern U., Baylor U., 1992. Diplomate Am. Bd. Internal Medicine, Am. Bd. Med. Oncology. Intern M.Y. Hosp., Indore, 1967-70; resident in medicine Allegheny Gen. Hosp., Pitts., 1972-73; head divsn. med. oncology Evanston (Ill.) Hosp., 1975-98, from asst. attending physician to assoc. attending physician, 1975-79, sr. attending physician, 1979—; fellow Med. Rsch. Coun., Montréal, Que., Can., 1970-71, Tufts U., Boston, 1973-75; asst. prof. medicine Northwestern U., Chgo., 1975-80, assoc. prof., 1980-86, prof. medicine, 1986—, Kellogg/Scanlon chair in oncology, 1991-98; dir. cancer control Northwestern U. Cancer Ctr., Chgo., 1991—; assoc. dir. Kellogg Cancer Care Ctr. Evanston Hosp., 1979-87, dir., 1987—; Louise Coon chmn. dept. medicine Evanston Northwestern Healthcare, 1998—. Active NIH Ad Hoc Com. on Nat. Prostate Cancer Program, NIH Team for Audit Clin. Trials at Yale U., Roswell Park Meml. Inst., Mayo Clinic, etc.; chmn. rsch. com. and adv. com. Searle Clin. Pharmacology Unit; sr. investigator Eastern Coop. Oncology Group, 1976-83, Community Clin. Oncology Program, 1983—; lectr. in field. Author: (with others) Radiation-Associated Thyroid Carcinoma, 1977, Adjuvant Therapy of Cancer, 1977; contbr. over 135 articles to profl. jours. Recipient cert. of merit Nat. Cancer Inst. Humanitarian award Cancer Wellness Ctr., 2003; grantee Ill. Cancer Coun., 1983-98, Duke U., 1983-90, Nat. Cancer Inst., 1983—, Women's Health Inst., 1993, Evanston Hosp., 1993—, NIH, 1988-91, 93—. Fellow ACP (laureate); mem. AAAS, Am. Soc. Clin. Oncology, Am. Fedn. Clin. Rsch., Am. Assn. Cancer Rsch., Inst. Medicine (Chgo.). Office: Evanston Hosp 2650 Ridge Ave Evanston IL 60201-1781

KHANG, CHULSOON, economics educator; b. Kaesong City, South Korea, May 10, 1935; s. Woon-sung and Ji-chung (Lim) K.; m. Yee Yu Lau, Sept. 15, 1959; children— Kenneth, Maurice BA in Econs., Mich. State U., 1959; MA in Econs., U. Minn.-Mpls., 1962, PhD in Econs., 1965. Asst. prof. econs. San Diego State U., 1963-66; asst. prof. econs. U. Oreg., Eugene, 1966-69, assoc. prof., 1969-73, prof., 1973-97, prof. emeritus, 1997. Vis. prof., research grantee U. New South Wales, Australia, 1972-73; vis. prof., Fulbright fellow Hanguk U. Fgn. Studies, Seoul, Korea, 1979; vis. prof. U. Hawaii, Honolulu, 1989. Referee, Am. Econ. Rev., Jour. Internat. Econs., Rev. Econ. Studies, Jour. Fin., Jour. Polit. Econs., Jour. Banking and Fin., Jour. Econs. and Bus., Internat. Econ. Rev. Contbr. articles to profl. jours. Mem. Eugene Area Korean Assn. (past pres.), Am. Econ. Assn. Republican. Home: 224 Edgewood Dr Port Ludlow WA 98365-9225 Office: U Oreg Dept Econs Eugene OR 97403

KHANNA, ASHISH, pharmacist; b. Bombay, Maharashtra, India, Mar. 24, 1971; s. Siri Ram and Shobha Khanna; m. Priti Hegde, Apr. 14, 2000. PhD, SUNY, Buffalo, 1999. Registered pharmacist 1993. Grad. rsch. asst. SUNY, Buffalo, 1994—99; rsch. investigator Bristol-Myers Squibb, Princeton, NJ, 1999—. Contbr. Vol. Network of Indian Profls., Phila. chpt., Phila., 2000. Recipient Outstanding Svc. award, Hindu Cultural Soc. of Western N.Y., 1997; grantee, Mark Diamond Rsch. Found., 1997—98; scholar Grad. scholar award, Buffalo Pharmaceutics, 1998. Mem.: Am. Assn. of Pharm. Scientists, Mensa. Home: 835 Meetinghouse Rd Ambler PA 19002 Office: Bristol-Myers Squibb PO Box 5400 Princeton NJ 08543 Office Fax: 609-818-3675. E-mail: ashish.khanna@bms.com.

KHANNA, KANWAL, rheumatologist; b. Larned, Kans., Aug. 25, 1958; s. Jaswant Lal and Prabha Khanna; m. Marcia Gabriel Nino, Dec. 17, 1988; children: Deven Neal, Jacqueline. BS in Biol. Scis. with honors, Stanford U., 1980; MD, U. Calif., San Francisco, 1984. Diplomate Am. Bd. Internal Medicine, Am. Bd. Rheumatology. Resident in internal medicine Cedars-Sinai Med. Ctr., L.A., 1984-87; fellow in rheumatology Harbor-UCLA Med. Ctr., Torrance, Calif., 1987-90; pvt. practice rheumatology Modesto, Calif., 1991—. Contbr. articles to profl. jours.; author abstracts in field. Relevance reviewer Am. Bd. Internal Medicine, 1995; mem. expert witness panel Med. Bd. Calif., 1996. Fellow ACP, Am. Coll. Rheumatology; mem. Calif. Med. Assn., Stanislaus Med. Soc., Mensa Soc., Phi Beta Kappa. Avocations: tennis, fitness, cooking, travel. Office: 1429 College Ave # M Modesto CA 95350-4046

KHANNA, KISHANLAL K. lawyer, educator; b. Lahore, Punjab, India, Feb. 18, 1939; s. Kharatiram and Prakashvati Khanna; m. Arun Prabha Bhalla, Apr. 23, 1966; children: Namita, Karunesh. BE, U. Bombay, Bombay, India, 1959; MPA, Kent State U., Kent, OH, 1971, PhD Pub. Admin., 1974; LLB, U. Bombay, Bombay, India, 1994, LLM, 1996; PhD, 2001. Lic.: Bar Assn., New Delhi, India 1995; Grad. Brit. Instn. of Radio Engineers, 1960. Sr. class 1 gazetted officer Govt. of India, Various, India, 1961—86; math & sci. tchr. Canton, Ohio Pub. Schools, Canton, Ohio, 1972—73; vis. asst. prof. No. Ill. U., Dekalb, Ill., 1973—74, Kans. State U., Kansas, Kans., 1974—75; sr. prof. & phd guide U. Bombay, Bombay, 1978—95; mng. dir. Unique Integrated Transp. & Mgmt. Consultancies, Bombay, 1986—95; atty. Supreme Ct. India, Bombay, 1995—, Colo. Dir. fin. Mudra Dance Studio. Author: (book) Behavioral Approach to Bureaucratic Development, Bureaucratic Blunder-world, Proactive

Bureaucracy, Executive Psychosis, Executive Decision Making, Management of State Enterprises in India, Logistics Management, Judicial Systems of the Third World: The Case of India. Maj. Corps of Engineers, 1963—78, India. Recipient scholarship, U. Bombay, 1954—59, scholarships, Kent State U., 1971—73, Merit Award for top ranking LLM, U. Bombay, 1996. Mem.: Indian Inst. of Public Admin., Inst. of Rail Transp. (life), Indian Soc. Tng. and Devel. (life), Bombay Mgmt. Assn. (life). Avocations: Hindi stage, Hindi music. Home: 16835 E Navarro Drive Aurora CO 80013 Home Fax: 303-824-8803. Personal E-mail: kishanaruna@aol.com.

KHANNA, YASH KUMAR, family practice physician, pediatrician; b. Lahore, India, Dec. 28, 1941; came to U.S., 1970; s. Sohan Lal and Savitri (Mehra) K.; m. Christine Anne Warren, Sept. 22, 1972; children: Rajan Yash, Nisha, Dev Yash. MBBS, King George Michael Coll., Lucknow, India, 1964. Diplomate Am. Bd. Pediat., Am. Bd. Forensic Examiners, Child Health Royal Coll. Physicians and Surgeons, London. Sr. house officer Monsall Hosp., Bouth Hall Children's Hosp., Manchester, Eng., 1966-68, Joyce Green Hosp., Dastford, Eng., 1969-70; house officer, emergency physician St. Mary's Hosp., Orange, N.J., 1971-87, resident in pediat., 1971-73; pvt. practice physician Orange, N.J., 1973—; med. dir. Quick Med.-West Essex Med. Group, West Caldwell, N.J., 1983—, pres.-elect, 1997-2000, pres. med. staff, 2001. Asst. surgeon Ctrl. Health Svcs., New Delhi, 1965-66; house physician and surgeon Irwin Hosp., New Delhi, 1964-65; mem. med. staff Hosp. Ctrs. at Orange, N.J., 1973—, pres. med. staff, 1986-87, pres.-elect med. staff, 1997—, pres. med. staff Hosp. Ctrs. at Orange 2001—; bd. govs. Cathedral Healthcare Sys. N.J., 2001—. Mem. adv. com. to the handicapped Twp. of Livingston, N.J.; trustee Hosp. Ctr. at Orange, 1986-96, mem. Cath. Healthcare Bd. of Gov., 2001—. Recipient Med. Outreach award Grace Reformed Bapt. Ch., Newark, 1997, Hind Ratann award NRI Soc. India, 2002. Mem. AMA, Am. Assn. Physicians from India, N.J. Med. Soc., Essex County Med. Soc., Orange Mountain Med. Soc., Indian Physicians Assn. N.J., Asian Music Acad. (founder, pres. 1999—). Democrat. Hindu. Avocations: music, antiques. Home: 112 Shrewsbury Dr Livingston NJ 07039-3404 Office: Family Medicine/Pediat 280 Henry St Orange NJ 07050-3422 also: Quick Med-West Essex Med Group 526 Bloomfield Ave West Caldwell NJ 07006-7504 E-mail: yashk@aol.com.

KHANZADIAN, VAHAN, tenor; b. Syracuse, N.Y., Jan. 23, 1939; s. Avedis Sarkis and Araxey (Youghian) K. BS, SUNY, Buffalo, 1962; post grad., Curtis Inst. Music, Phila., 1961-63. Debut as Ruggero in La Rondine, San Francisco Spring Opera, 1968; leading roles in Wozzeck, Fra Diavolo, Les Troyens, Madama Butterfly, Lucia Di Lammermoor, Tosca; appeared throughout U.S., Can.; appeared in title role in Don Carlo, Basel, Switzerland, 1992; debut as Calaf in Puccini's Turandot with Bavarian State Opera, Munich, Germany, 1995; appeared with all major opera cos., and opera festivals, including San Antonio, Ravinia, Tanglewood, Saratoga, Opera de Colombia; numerous solo recitals throughout N.Am.; appeared with symphony orchs., including Chgo., Boston, Phila., Cleve., Minn., Indpls., St. Louis, Milw., Pitts.; TV appearances include Gherman in Tchaikovsky's Queen of Spades; soloist in world premier of Menotti's Landscapes and Remembrances, PBS, 1976; leading tenor Met. Opera, 1991-99, debut as Gustavo in Un Ballo in Maschera, Met. Opera, 1993, Lyric Opera Chgo., 1993. Appeared in Sondheim's "Follies" at Paperhill Playhouse, 1998, which is recorded on a new CD. Served with U.S. Army, 1964-65. Sullivan Found. grantee, 1971-74; Rockefeller Found. grantee, 1971-73 Address: PO Box 741 Hunter NY 12442-0741 *My ethnic background, Armenian, with its strong Christian influence was instrumental in projecting the importance of family, religion, education, and culture. The strength and knowledge attained in this environment guided me in the arts, where I was fortunate to have had the discipline and the opportunity to pursue my goal of making a contribution in serving music.*

KHANZHINA, HELEN P. English educator, translator; b. Perm, Russia, Aug. 28, 1954; came to U.S., 1995; d. Pavel L. and Dina B. Wexler; m. Yevgenii A. Khanzhin, Dec. 4, 1975 (div. Jan. 1984); 1 child, Dmitri. MA in English Lit., U. Perm, 1976; PhD in World Lit., U. St. Petersburg, 1985; assoc. prof. diploma, USSR State Com. Nat. Edn., Moscow, 1991. Asst. then assoc. prof. dept. world lit. U. Perm, 1976-95; lectr. dept. English div. continuing edn. U. Va., Charlottesville, 1996-98. Interpreter Lang. Learning Enterprises, Washington, 1996—; libr. joint state govt. commn. gen. assembly Commonwealth Pa., Harrisburg, 1998—; lectr. divsn. comm., arts and social sciences Harrisburg C.C., 1998—; lectr. Sch. of Humanities Pa. State U., Harrisburg, 1999—2000. Author: The Making of the National Tradition in American Romantic Poetry and William Cullen Bryant's Creative Work, 1987, Genre, Mode and Style in American Romantic Poetry, 1998; editor: Problems of Method and Poetics in World Literature of the Nineteenth and Twentieth Centuries, 1995, 97; contbr. articles to profl. jours. Vis. scholar grantee USIA, 1993-94, Brit. Coun. Beatrice Ward Found., 1990. Mem. MLA, Am. Assn. Tchrs. Slavic and E. European Langs., Pa. Libr. Assn., Spl. Librs. Assn. Avocations: classical music, jazz, ballet, painting, sculpture. Office: Joint State Govt Commn 108 Fin Bldg Harrisburg PA 17120 E-mail: ykhanzhina@legis.state.pa.us.

KHARADIA, VIRABHAI CHELABHAI, economist, educator, researcher; b. Laxmipura, Gujarat, India, Jan. 21, 1939; came to U.S., 1969; s. Chelabhai Manabhai and Joitiben Chelabhai K.; m. Kokila Virabhai, Apr. 26, 1961; children: Shanta, Geeta, Bharat. B in Commerce, Maharaja Sayajirao U. Baroda, Gujarat, 1964, M in Commerce, 1966; MS, U. Ill., 1971, PhD in Econ. and Fin., 1973. Lectr. banking and fin. Maharaja Sayajirao U. of Baroda, Gujarat, 1966-69; from asst. to assoc. prof. N.W. Mo. State U., Maryville, 1973-77, prof., 1977—, chmn. dept. econ., 1979-93. Vis. prof. Internat. U. Bus. and Econ., Beijing, 1985; tchr. internat. enrichment program Imperial Coll., London, 2001. Contbr. articles to profl. jours. Recipient Acctg. prize H.L. Coll. of Commerce, 1960; fellow U. Ill., 1969-70, 71, 72-73. Avocations: racquetball, biking, jogging, gardening, traveling. Office: NW Mo State U Dept Econ Maryville MO 64468 E-mail: vkharad@mail.nwmissouri.edu.

KHARE, MOHAN, chemist, researcher; b. Varanasi, India, May 15, 1942; came to U.S., 1967, naturalized, 1971; s. Dwarka Nath and Rampyari Devi Khare Srivastava; m. Meena K., Nov. 20, 1973; 1 child, Rohit. BSc, Banaras Hindu U., 1961, MSc, 1963, PhD, 1967. Rsch. assoc. U. Md., College Park, 1967-69, Oreg. State U., Corvallis, 1969-70; sr. rsch. assoc. Cornell U., Ithaca, N.Y., 1970-78; analytical specialist Hydroscience Inc., (subsidiary of Dow Chem. Co.), Knoxville, Tenn., 1978-80; tech. specialist IT Envirosciences subs. IT Corp., Knoxville, 1980-82; rsch. prof. chemistry U. Nev., Las Vegas, 1982-84, mgr. organic div. quality assurance lab. under coop. agreement with EPA, 1982-84; mgr. organic analysis lab. Environ. Monitoring Svcs. Rockwell Internat., Thousand Oaks, Calif., 1984-85; dir. environ. analytical lab. EA Engring, Sci., and Tech., Inc., Sparks, Md., 1985-87; sr. v.p. Recra Environ., Inc., Columbia, Md., 1987-89; pres., chief exec. officer Envirosystems, Inc., Columbia, 1989—. Cons. to toxic and hazardous waste analytical labs.; mem. panel peer rev. Toxic Organics Lab. Contbr. articles to profl. jours. including protocols and standard oper. procedures for hazardous waste analytical programs. Mem. Am. Chem. Soc., Internat. Union Pure and Applied Chemistry, Internat. Assn. of Environ. Testing Lab. Home: 10189 Maxine St Ellicott City MD 21042-6351 Office: Envirosystems Inc 9200 Rumsey Rd Ste 102B Columbia MD 21045-1934 E-mail: info@envsystems.com.

KHASDAY, ALYCE FIELD, literary and film agent, psychic consultant, business owner, investment coach; b. Bklyn., May 2, 1943; children: Jamie, Cortnie. Student, NYU, 1961-63; grad., La Varenne Culinary Inst. Sales mgr. Malom Lingerie, N.Y.C., 1962-66; sales coord. Sherman Underwear, N.Y.C., 1966-71; pub. rels. cons. Espon, Can., Can., 1977; organizer press confs. preventive medicine, 1977—; pres., fin. planner Greenbelt Equities, Inc., N.Y.C., 1982-84; archtl. planner, developer, pres. Kasday Design, N.Y.C., 1977-87; pres., syndicator, developer real estate, mgr. M & M Mgmt. Corp., Fla., 1984—; pres., CEO, Kombucha Magic Mushroom Farms, Inc., health beverage co., N.Y.C., N.Y.; prin. Khasday Konsulting LLC, 2003—. Asst. chef to Isabelle Marique, N.Y.C., Albert Jorant, Paris; founder Psychic Life Counselling, Fla., 1990—; psychic cons. various orgns. including Am. Women in Radio and T.V. Avocations: swimming, biking, skiing, french cooking. Office: 500 E 77th St Apt 520 New York NY 10162-0002 also: Kombucha Magic Mushroom Farms Inc PO Box 20717 New York NY 10021-0074

KHATAMEE, MASOOD AHMAD, obstetrician, gynecologist; b. Mashhad, Iran, Feb. 12, 1936; s. Ahmad and Cobra (Tadbir Kashani) K.; married, Mar. 11, 1966; children: Pira, Neda, Yalda. MD, Shiraz U., Iran, 1961. Diplomate Am. Bd. Ob-Gyn. Intern Nemazee Hosp., 1960-61; resident in ob-gyn. Bellevue Hosp. Ctr., N.Y.C., 1962-66, fellow in infertility, 1966-67; exec. dir. Fertility Rsch. Found., N.Y.C.; mem. staff Lenox Hill Hosp., N.Y.C., Beth Israel-North Divsn., N.Y.C., NYU Med. Ctr., N.Y.C. Clin. prof. NYU Sch. Medicine; pres. Iranian Am. Med. Assn., 1998-2000; founder Soc. Prevention Human Infertility; founder, pres. Shiraz U. Sch. Medicine Alumni Assn. USA, Inc., 1988-89. Pres. Iranian Am. Rep. Party, N.Y.c., 1994—. Fellow ACOG; mem. Am. Fertility Soc., Fertility Rsch. Found. Home: 23 Church St Alpine NJ 07620 Office: Fertility Rsch Found 877 Park Ave New York NY 10021-0341 E-mail: frfbaby@msn.com.

KHATIB, RUSTOM ATFAT, gynecologist, researcher, endocrinologist, consultant, economist; b. Beirut, Sept. 3, 1962; s. Atfat Rustom and Samia Ibrahim (Jannoun) K.; m. Mona Adnan Tabbara, Feb. 11, 1993; children: Samia Karla, Ryan Atfat. BS with honors, Am. U. Beirut, 1984, MD, 1988; MBA, Hamilton U., Wyoming, 1995; postgrad diploma in econs., U. London, 2000; PhD Business Admin., Hamilton U., Wyoming, 2001. Resident in ob-gyn. Am. U. Beirut, 1992-94; fellow in reproductive endocrinology Mich. State U., Saginaw, 1994, clin. instr., 1992-94; clin. cons. Rizk Hosp., Beirut, 1994—. Clin. cons. European Heart Ctr., Saida, 1994-96; chmn. ob-gyn. United Med. Group, Beirut, 1996—; sci. cons. Beirut Fertility Ctr., 1994-99; dir. fertility unit European Heart Ctr., Saida, 1994-96, United Med. Group, Beirut, 1997--; dir. fertility svc. Jubeily Hosp., Saida, 1996-99; cons. Fertility Unit Kasab Hosp., Saida, 2000—; mem. acad. coun. London Diplomatic Acad.; mem. sci. faculty Internat. Biog. Ctr., Cambridge, England. Contbr. articles to profl. jours. including Gynecologic Oncology, Fertility and Sterility, European Jour. Obstets., Clin. Consultation in Ob-Gyn. Advisor Lebanese Environmentalist Group, Beirut, Lebanon, 1996; sec. gen. United Cultural Conv., Raleigh, NC, 2000—. Recipient Physician's Recognition award AMA, 1994, Ob-Gyn. Rsch. award Saginaw Coop. Hosps., 1994. Fellow Am. Coll. Surgeons; mem. Am. Soc. for Reproductive Medicine, N.Y. Acad. Scis., European Soc. for Human Reproduction and Embryology, Am. Soc. for Reproductive Medicine, Greenpeace. Office: United Med Group Abdul Aziz St Al Mabani Ctr 14-5354 Beirut Lebanon Fax: 9611749695. E-mail: 362812@cyberia.net.lb.

KHATON, SABRINA ROSLYN, librarian, accountant; b. New Orleans, Mar. 29, 1955; d. Harold Ralph and Edna Eunice (Carstarphen) K; m. Reginald Sanders, Nov. 24, 1979 (div.); children: Adam James, Evan Alan; m. Darryl A. Derbegry, Aug. 26, 1993. BS in Acctg., Xavier U., New Orleans, 1977. Acct. Sub Sea Internat. Inc., New Orleans, 1976-81; grants and projects acct. Xavier U., New Orleans, 1981-85; fiscal officer for office of employment tng. & devel. City of New Orleans, 1986-88; librarian Fisk-Howard Elem. Sch., New Orleans, 1989—90; accountant Christopher Homes Inc., 1990—. Cons. JTPA Grant Proposals, New Orleans, 1988—; tax preparer, cons. Law Office of Darryl A. Derbigny, New Orleans, 1985—. Recording sec. minority task force Xavier U., New Orleans, 1983-85; mem. Mayor of New Orleans' Women Support Group, 1986-88. Recipient Supervisory award Dunn & Brad Street, 1987. Mem. Delta Sigma Theta (amenities chairperson 1973-74). Democrat. Lutheran. Avocations: bicycling, cooking, tennis. Home: 7451 Restgate Rd New Orleans LA 70127-1841 Office: Law Office Darryl Derbigny 2136 N Galvez St New Orleans LA 70119-1631

KHATSENKO, OLEG GENNADY, research scientist; b. Kamishin, Russia, May 26, 1963; arrived in U.S., 1994; s. Gennady Gregory and Valentina Peter Khatsenko; m. Anna Anatoly Kondratiev, Mar. 1, 1989; children: Katherine, Maxim. MS, Novosibirsk State U., Russia, 1985; PhD, Oxford Brookes U., London, 1994. Jr. rschr. Inst. Clin. and Exptl. Medicine, Novosibirsk, 1985—90; postdoctoral scientist U. Calif., Irvine, 1994—97, ISIS Pharms., Carlsbad, Calif., 1997—2000; scientist II Celgene Corp., San Diego, 2000—. Contbr. Brit. Coun. grantee, 1990. Mem.: Am. Assn. Pharm. Scientists, Internat. Soc. Study of Xenobiotics. Russian Orthodox Ch. Achievements include research in effect of nitric oxide on cytochome P450 in vitro and in vivo; inhibition of cytochrome P450 activity in vitro and during endotoxin schock in vivo. Avocations: butterfly collecting, skiing, hiking.

KHATTER, PRITHIPAL SINGH, radiologist; b. Ferozepore Cant, Punjab, India, Feb. 1, 1936; came to U.S., 1976; s. Harnam Singh and Jagjit Kaur; m. Kamal Jit Kaur Chahal; children: Avinash, Boldy. MB BChir, Med. Coll., Amritsar, Punjab, 1959; diploma in radiology, GSVM Med. Coll., Kanpur, 1961, diploma in clin. pathology, 1962, MD in Radiology, 1965. Diplomate Am. Bd. Radiology. Resident in diagnostic radiology VA Med. Ctr., Dallas, 1976-78; radiologist, clin. pathologist Jit & Pal X-Rays (P) Ltd., Moradabad, India, 1965-76; radiologist, chief VA Med. Ctr., Huntington, W.Va., 1978-90; clin. faculty radiology, from instr. to assoc. prof. Marshall U. Sch. Medicine, Huntington, 1978-90; radiologist Radiology, Inc., Huntington, 1980-90, Davis Meml. Hosp., Elkins, W.Va., 1990-96, Radiol. Cons. Assn., Fairmont, W.Va., 1996-98, Radiology Physicians Assocs., 1998—. Named Hometown Hero, Town of Elkin, 2002. Fellow Indian Med. Assn.; mem. Indian Radiology Assn. Avocations: reading, music, tennis, badminton. Home: 50 Eastridge Dr Elkins WV 26241-9585 Office: Davis Meml Hosp Gorman & Reed Elkins WV 26241-1484

KHAVARI, KHALIL AKHTAR, psychology educator; b. Tehran, Iran, Nov. 10, 1932; s. Ardeshir Akhtar and Rouhanghiz Khalili K.; m. Sue Williston, June 6, 1959; children: Paul, Katherine. BS, Bradley U., 1960, MS, 1963; PhD, Ind. U., 1967. Asst., assoc. then prof. psychology U. Wis., Milw., 1967-95, founder, dir. Midwest Inst. on Drug Use, 1974-77, co-founder, coord. peace studies program, 1987-89. Referee, cons. in field. Author: Creating a Successful Family, 1989, Together Forever: A Practical Guide to Successful Marriage, 1993, Introduction to the Baha'i Faith, 1997, Spiritual Intelligence, 2000. Mem. aux. bd. Baha'i Faith, Milw., 1981-86, founding mem. Baha'i Internat. Health Assn., Ft. Lauderdale, Fla., 1984-90; life mem. Tlinget Indian Tribe, Alaska. Avocations: reading, travel, tennis, hiking, gardening. E-mail: Kk1844@aol.com.

KHAWAJA, IRFAN AHMAD, columnist, philosopher, educator; b. Jersey City, Apr. 26, 1969; s. Aftab Alam and Asia Bano Khawaja; life ptnr. Hilary Ruth Persky. AB, Princeton U., 1991; MA, U. Notre Dame, 1994. Adj. prof. philosophy Coll. N.J., NJ, 1997—. Columnist Pakistan Today, Fontana, Calif. Contbr. book revs. to profl. publs. Mem. Nat. Assn. of Scholars, Princeton, NJ. Jaquelyn Hume fellow, Inst. for Humane Studies, George Mason U., 1994. Mem.: Coun. on Democracy and Tolerance, NJ Assn. Biomed. Rsch.

KHAWAJA, XAVIER, biochemical pharmacologist; b. La Ferte sous Jouarre, Seine et Marne, France, Mar. 6, 1960; came to U.S., 1995; s. Ishtiaque and Anne Marie (Bourgeois) K. BSc. with honors, Chelsea Coll., London, 1982, MSc, 1984; PhD, U. Sussex., Brighton, Eng., 1987. Post doctoral rsch. fellow Med. Rsch. Coun., Brighton, Sussex, Eng., 1987-88, Wellcome Trust, Brighton, Sussex, Eng., 1988-91; sr. rsch. scientist Wyeth Ayerst Rsch. Labs., Taplow, Berkshire, Eng., 1991-95, prin. rsch. scientist Princeton, N.J., 1995—. Contbr. articles to profl. jours. including Diabetes, Jour. Neurochemistry, Brain Rsch., Peptides, Jour. Neurosci. Rsch. Achievements include contributions to the knowledge of opioids and opioid receptors involvement in the regulation of food intake, glucose homeostasis and their central and peripheral effects related to obesity and type 2 diabetes; contributions to the knowledge of G-protein coupled receptor characterization and signal transduction events in the central nervous system; contributions to the field of proteomics, functional genomics, neuroscience and psychiatric and neurodegenerative disorders. Office: Wyeth-Ayerst Rsch CN 8000 Princeton NJ 08543 E-mail: khawajx@wyeth.com.

KHAWLI, LESLIE ALBERT, research scientist, educator; s. Albert Antoine and Corinne Khawli; m. Carole Chammas, July 2, 1995; children: Michelle Leila, Joelle Corinne. PhD, U. So. Calif., L.A., 1986. Postdoctoral fellow Harvard Med. Sch., Boston, 1986—88; asst. prof. U. So. Calif., L.A., 1988—94, assoc. prof., 1994—2001, prof., 2001—. Tchg. grad. and med. students U. So. Calif., L.A., 1988—; cons. Peregrine Pharms., Tustin, Calif., 1989—, Cancer Therapeutics, Inc, L.A., Calif., 1995—, NeoTherapeutics, Inc., Irvine, Calif., 1997—2002. Scientist (cancer research) Interface between immunochemistry and nuclear medicine, primarily on the generation of new approaches for the successful immunodiagnosis and therapy of human cancer using genetically engineered monoclonal antibodies. Recipient Rsch. Travel award, NSF, 1983, Rsch. Svc. award, NIH, 1986-1988, Rsch. award, Nat. Cancer Inst., 1992-1995, Contbn. and Excellence in Cancer Rsch. award, Found. for Better Medicine, 2000; Rsch. fellowship, Harvard Med. Sch., 1986-1988, Pilot Rsch. Project grant, Am. Cancer Soc., 1992-1993, Rsch. grant, Nat. Cancer Inst., 1992-1995, Tobacco-Related Disease Rsch. Program, 1994-1996, Cancer Therapeutics, 1994-2003, Perigrine Pharms., 1995-2003, NIH, 2000-2003, Calif. Cancer Rsch. Program, 2000-2003. Mem.: Am. Assn. of Pharm. Scientists, Am. Chem. Soc., Am. Assn. for Cancer Rsch., Soc. of Nuc. Medicine. Achievements include patents for Use Of Promising Immunoregulatory Antibody/Cytokine Fusion Proteins For The Immunotherapy Of Solid Tumors; M-aminophenyltrialkylstannane; Radiohalogenated Half-Antibodies and Maleimide Intermediate Therefor; Modified Antibodies with Controlled Clearance Time; Antibodies Modified at Two Separate Sites; Antibodies with Reduced Net Positive Charge; Vasopermeability Enhancing Peptide of Human Interleukin-2 and; Published many articles and chapters in the fields of cancer research. Office: Univ So Calif 2011 Zonal Ave HMR 304A Los Angeles CA 90033 Office Fax: 323-442-3049. E-mail: lkhawli@usc.edu.

KHAYAT, ROBERT CONRAD, academic administrator; b. Moss Point, Miss., Apr. 18, 1938; m. Margaret Denton; children: Margaret D. Khayat Bratt, Robert C. Jr. BA in Edn., U. Miss., 1961, JD, 1966; LLM, Yale U., 1981. Bar: Miss. 1966. With Wash. Redskins, 1960—64; pvt. practice in law, mcpl. judge City of Moss Point, Pascagoula, Miss., 1967-69; mcpl. judge City of Oxford, Miss.; pvt. practice in law Oxford, 1975-77; mem. faculty Sch. Law U. Miss., University, 1969—, vice-chancellor for univ. affairs, 1984-89; pres. NCAA Found., 1989—92; prof. law, interim dir. athletics U. Miss., University, 1994, chancellor, 1995—. Contbr. articles to profl. jours. Pres. C. of C., Oxford Lafayette County, Fellowship of Christian Athletes. Recipient Disting. Am. award, Nat. Football Found., 1987, 1989, 2003, Outstanding Law Prof. of the Yr.; scholarship established in his name, 1995, Oxford Lafayette County Citizen of the Yr., 1989, Career Achievement award, NFL Alumni Assn., 1998; fellow, Yale U., 1981; scholar, Miss Law Jour., 1994. Mem.: ATLA, ABA, Miss. Bar Found. (trustee 1988—89), Miss. State Bar Assn., Phi Kappa Phi, Phi Delta Phi, Omicron Delta Kappa, Lamar Order. Office: U Miss Chancellor's Office 331 Martindale University MS 38677*

KHAZEN, ALEKSANDR MOISEYEVICH, physicist; b. Russia, Feb. 28, 1933; s. Moisey M. and Isida A. (Neimark) K.; m. Rimma B. Zil'ber, Dec. 17, 1963; children: Igor, Anatoly, Irina. MSc in Thermodynamics and Electronics, Power U., 1957; MS in Math. and Mechanics, Lomonosov State U., 1962, PhD in Physics and Math., 1965. Supr. of studies of scientific rsch. lab. Inst. of Mechanics, Lomonosov State U., 1960-93. Author: The Laws of Evolution of Life and "Just Society,", 1997, 2nd edit., 1998, Introduction of the Measure of Information into the Axiomatic Basis of Mechanics, 1996, 2d edit., 1998, What is Possible and Impossible in Science or Where the Limits to Artificial Intelligence, 1988 (diploma in contest 1989), Field, Waves, Particles and their Models, 1979 (medal 1980), Interference, Lasers and Superfast-acting Computers, 1972, Modern Electronics, 1972 (medal 1980), Magnetic Elements in Electronics, 1968, Introduction into Electronics, 1968, Nature's Intelligence and Intelligence of Man, 2000, The First Principles of the Brain Work Which Guarantee the Possibility of Knowing the Nature, 2001; contbr. over 100 articles to profl. jours. Mem. N.Y. Acad. Sci. Achievements include 26 patents from US, Eng., Russia, Denmark and France. Home: 7 Village Green Apt J Budd Lake NJ 07828-1307 E-mail: akhazen@yahoo.com.

KHE, SRIRAM, planning educator; b. Sengottai, India, Feb. 24, 1964; s. Ramaswamy and Pravathy K.; m. Sonya Christian, Feb. 13, 1993; 1 child, Eisha. B of Engring., U. Madras, Coimbatore, India, 1985; M, U. So. Calif., 1990, PhD, 1993. Temp. planner So. Calif. Assn. Govts., L.A., 1993, Met. Transp. Authority, L.A., 1993-94; assoc. prof. Kern Coun. Govts., Bakersfield, Calif., 1994-2000; lectr. Calif. State U., Bakersfield, 2000—02; assoc. prof. Western Oreg. U., Monmouth, 2002—. Adj. prof. Calif. State U., Bakersfield, 1998—. Contbr. articles to profl. jours. Mem. Assn. Am. Geographers, Am. Planning Assn. Office: Western Oreg U HSS 219 345 Monmouth Ave Monmouth OR 97361 E-mail: khes@wou.edu.

KHEDOORI, TOBA, artist; b. Sydney, Australia; BFA, San Francisco Art Inst., 1988; MFA, UCLA, 1994. Represented by David Zwirner Gallery, NYC. One-woman shows include Hirshhorn Mus., Mus. Contemporary Art LA, Walker Art Ctr., Whitechapel Art Gallery, London, Mus. Gegenawartskunst, Basel, exhibited in group shows at Mus. Moder Art, NYC, Mus. Contemporary Art, Chgo., Mus. Modern Art, Copenhagen. Fellow MacArthur Found. fellow, 2002. Address: David Zwirner Gallery 43 Greene St New York NY 10013*

KHEEL, ANN SUNSTEIN, civic worker; b. Pitts., Nov. 5, 1915; m. Theodore Woodrow Kheel, July 1, 1937; children: Ellen Margaret Kheel Jacobs, Robert Jeffrey, Constance Elizabeth, Martha Louise, Jane Kheel Stanley, Katherine Emily. AB with honors, Cornell U., 1936. Columnist Ithaca (N.Y.) Jour., 1936-37; assoc. editor Cornell Alumni News, 1936-37, Tide Mag., N.Y.C., 1937-39; info. specialist, editor Land Policy Rev., USDA, Washington, 1939-43. Bd. dirs. Riverdale Neighborhood Assn., Riverdale/Bronx, N.Y., 1953-65, v.p., 1958-60; del. to President's Com. on Equal Employment Opportunity, Washington, 1963, 64; spl. corr. N.Y. Herald Tribune, 1957; bd. dirs. N.Y. Urban League, 1965—, founder, chmn. ann. Frederick Douglass Awards Dinners, 1966-91; corp. mem., trustee Schomburg Center for Research in Black Culture, 1971-86; mem. Mayor's Screening Panel for Bd. of Higher Edn. of N.Y.C., 1964-66; trustee Rand Inst. of N.Y.C., 1973-76; mem. Coop. Edn. Commn., N.Y.C. Bd. Edn., 1968-80; chmn. State Parks and Recreation Commn. for N.Y.C., 1977-86. Bd. dirs. Rainforest Alliance, 1996—2003. Home: 407 W 246th St Bronx NY 10471-3302

KHEEL, THEODORE WOODROW, lawyer, arbitrator and mediator; b. N.Y.C., May 9, 1914; s. Samuel and Kate (Herzenstein) K.; m. Ann Sunstein, July 1, 1937; children: Ellen Jacobs, Robert J., Constance, Martha, Jane Kheel Stanley, Katherine Fleischman. AB, Cornell U., 1935, LLB, 1937. Bar: N.Y. 1937. Ptnr. Battle Fowler, 1949-82; of counsel Battle Fowler (now Paul Hastings Janowsky & Walker), 1982—. Pres. Earth Pledge Found., 1991—; pres. Found. for Prevention & Early Resolution of Conflict, 1994—; mem. presdl. bds. various labor disputes, 1962-66; spl. cons. Pres.'s Com. on EEO, 1962-63. Author: Transit and Arbitration, 1960, Pros and Cons of Compulsory Arbitration, 1961, How Race Relations Affect Your Business, 1963, Guide to Fair Employment Practices, 1964, Kheel on Labor Law, 1974—, Keys to Conflict Resolution, 1999. Pres. Nat. Urban League, 1956-60; mem. Pres.'s Nat. Citizens Com. for Cmty. Rels., 1964-68. Mem. Am. Arbitration Assn. (bd. dirs.). Home: 407 W 246th St Bronx NY 10471-3302 Office: 75 E 55th St Fl 5 New York NY 10022-3205

KHERA, RAJ PAL, civil and environmental engineering educator; b. Jhang, Punjab, India, Mar. 27, 1935; came to U.S., 1961; s. Dharampal and Dharamwati (Verma) K.; m. Astrid Karin Szallies; children: Kamni, Navin. Student, Tech. U., Berlin, 1960-61; MSCE, Ohio State U., 1962; PhD, Northwestern U., 1967. Registered profl. engr., N.J., N.Y. Engr. Salzgitter (Fed. Republic of Germany) Stahlbau, 1959-60, Steffen and Noele, Berlin, 1960-61; prof. civil and environ. engring. N.J. Inst. Tech., Newark, 1966—. Cons. Raamot Assocs., N.Y.C., 1968-72, Converse Cons. East, West Caldwel, N.J., 1980—. Author: Geotechnology of Waste Management, 1990, 2nd edit., 1998; contbr. numerous articles to profl. jours. Fulbright fellow, 1979; named rsch. scientist German Acad. Exch., Bonn, 1980; recipient several grants including NSF, N.J. State. Fellow ASCE (mem. several coms., editor procs. 1986), Am. Soc. Engring. Edn. (mem. several coms.), Assn. Indians in Am. (v.p. 1988-90). Office: NJ Inst Tech 323 Martin Luther King Jr Blvd Newark NJ 07102-1824

KHERDIAN, DAVID, writer; b. Racine, Wis., Dec. 17, 1931; s. Melkon and Veron (Dumehjian) K.; m. Kato Rozeboom, 1968 (div. 1970); m. Nonny Hogrogian, Mar. 17, 1971. BS in Philosophy, U. Wis., 1960. Lit. cons. Northwestern U., 1965; founder/editor Giligia Press, 1966-72; rarebook cons. Fresno State Coll., Calif., 1968-69, lectr., 1969-70; ofcl. poet-in-the-schs. State of N.H., 1971; editor Ararat mag., 1971-72; dir. Two Rivers Press, Aurora, Oreg., 1978-86. Poetry judge, lectr., reader of own poetry; founder, editor (with Nonny Hogrogian) The Press at Butternut Creek, 1987-88. Author: On The Death of My Father and Other Poems, 1970, Homage to Adana, 1970, Looking Over Hills, 1972, The Nonny Poems, 1974, Any Day of Your Life, 1975,

Country, Cat: City, Cat, 1978, I Remember Root River, 1978, The Road From Home: The Story of an Armenian Girl (Lewis Carroll Shelf award, Boston Globe/Horn Book award, Newbery Honor Book award, Jane Addams Peace award, Banta award), 1979, The Farm, 1979, It Started With Old Man Bean, 1980, Finding Home, 1981, Taking the Soundings on Third Avenue, 1981, The Farm: Book Two, 1981, Beyond Two Rivers, 1981 (Friends of Am. Writers award), The Song in the Walnut Grove, 1982, Place of Birth, 1983, Right Now, 1983, The Mystery of the Diamond in the Wood, 1983, Root River Run, 1984, The Animal, 1984, Threads of Light: The Farm Poems Books III and IV, 1985, Bridger: The Story of a Mountain Man, 1987, Poems to an Essence Friend, 1987, A Song for Uncle Harry, 1989, the Cat's Midsummer Jamboree, 1990, The Dividing River/The Meeting Shore, 1990, On a Spaceship with Beelzebub: By a Grandson of Gurdjieff, 1990, The Great Fishing Contest, 1991, Friends: A Memoir, 1993, Juna's Journey, 1993, Asking the River, 1993, By Myself, 1993, My Racine, 1994, Lullaby for Emily, 1995, Seven Poems for Mikey, 1997, The Rose's Smile, 1997, I Called It Home, 1997, The Golden Bracelet, 1998, Chippecotton: Root River Tales of Racine, 1998, The Neighborhood Years, 2000, The Revelations of alvin Tolliver 2001, Seeds of Light: Poems From a Gurdjieff Community, 2002; also bibliographies.; editor: Visions of America by the Poets of Our Time, 1973, Settling America: The Ethnic Expression of 14 Contemporary Poets, 1974, Poems Here and Now, 1976, Traveling America with Today's Poets, 1976, The Dog Writes on the Window with His Nose and Other Poems, 1977, If Dragon Flies Made Honey, 1977, I Sing the Song of Myself, 1978, Beat Voices: An Anthology of Beat Poetry, 1995; co-editor: Down at the Santa Fe Depot: 20 Fresno Poets, 1970; translator: The Pearl: Hymn of the Robe of Glory, 1979, Pigs Never See the Stars: Armenian Proverbs, 1982, Monkey: A Journey to the West, 1992, Feathers and Tails: Animal Fables From Around the World; editor: A Journ. of Ethnic-Am. Lit., 1995-97, Stopinder: A Grudjieff Jour. For Our Time, 2000-2003. Served with AUS, 1952-54. Office: 600 W 12th St Mcminnville OR 97128 E-mail: tavit@attbi.com. *The poet understands that everything is connected and all is one. This is all he really knows. But knowing this he is permitted to speak, quietly, disturbing nothing, removing nothing, revealing only the new-old relationships he has been given to see.*

KHETTRY, URMILA, pathologist; m. Jayant K. Khettry. MB, BChir, Delhi U., 1972. Dir. surg. pathology Deaconess Hosp., Boston, 1990—96, liver and liver transplant pathologist Lahey Clinic Med. Ctr., Burlington, Mass., 1999. Contbr. scientific papers. Mem.: AASLD. Hindu. Avocations: travel, reading. Office: Lahey Clinic Medical Center 41 Mall Rd Burlington MA 01805 Office Fax: 781-744-5263. E-mail: urmila_khettry@lahey.org.

KHILNANI, PRAVEEN G.R. education professional; b. Karachi, Pakistan; came to the U.S., 1986; BSc, U. Calif., Berkeley, 1994; MSc, Yale U., 1997. Founder, CEO All Diesel Sys., Karachi, 1983-93; lectr. U. Calif., Berkeley, 1994; rsch. supr. SRC, Berkeley, 1995; rsch. fellow PCI-U.N. NGO, N.Y.C., 1996; tchg. fellow Yale U., New Haven, 1996-97; pres. Calif. Ednl. Svcs., Mountain View, 1997—, Khilnani & Assocs., 2001—. Mem. adv. com. Fremont (Calif.) Adult Sch., 1998-99, pres. 2001—; dir. Independent Way, Hayward. Horace Albright scholar U. Calif., Berkeley, 1993; Gilman Ordmay fellow Yale U., New Haven, 1996. Mem. Toastmasters Internat. (v.p. 2000-01), Yale U. Alumni (class agt. 1997—). Avocations: golf, reading, biking, films, rollerblading.

KHILNANI, VINOD M. manufacturing executive; m. Gita Khilnani; 2 children. MS, Delhi U.; MBA, SUNY, Albany. CPA, CMA. With Cummins Engine, 1978-96; CFO Dayton (Ohio) Superior Corp., 1996-97.

KHIM, JAY WOOK, high technology systems integration executive; b. Taegu, Korea, Oct. 22, 1940; came to U.S., 1965; s. Joon Mook and Soon E. (Lee) K. BS in Agrl. Econs., Kyung Pook U., Korea, 1963, MA in Agrl. Econs., 1966; postgrad. PhD program in Econs., U. Md., 1965-69; LLD (hon.), Randolph-Macon Coll., 1988; PhD (hon.), Kyungpook Nat. U., Republic of Korea, 1990. Mem. rsch. staff Brookings Instn., Washington, 1967-69; sr. economist NAB, Dept. of Labor, Washington, 1969-72; sr. assoc. Planning Rsch. Corp., Washington, 1972-74; chmn., CEO JWK Internat. Corp., Washington, 1974—, Internat. Trade and Investment Corp., Washington, 1977—. Bd. dirs. Millennium Bank. Author: The Third Eye, 1998; author, editor more than 100 research reports, articles for fed. govt. in fields of health, energy, def., transp., housing and internat. affairs Bd. dirs. Fulbright Found., 1999—, Asia Soc., Washington, 1999—, George Mason Inst., George Mason U., Fairfax, Va., 1983—, United Bank, 1997—, No. Va. Cmty. Found., 1998—, Worf Trap Found. for Performing Arts, 1998—; mem. World Presidents Orgn., 1992—, chmn. Washington Met. chpt., 1994-2000; bd. govs. U. Md. Alumni Assn.; bd. trustees Fairfax Hosp. Assn., 1986-2001; candidate for U.S. Congress from 11th Va. dist., 1992; chmn. fin. com. Rep. Party, Va.; commr. Small and Minority Bus. Commn., Fairfax County, 1992. Fulbright scholar, 1965, 66; recipient Sam Ill Found. award Korea, 1962, 63 Mem. Young Pres.'s Orgn., Pres. Club of Am. Mgmt. Assn., Nat. Security Assn., Am. Def. Preparedness Assn., Am. Econ. Assn., Fairfax C. of C. (bd. dirs. 1984-87), World Pres.'s Orgn. (chmn. Washington Met. chtp. 1994-95), City Club, Tower Club, Robert Trent Jones Club, Tournament of Players Club, Internat. Club (D.C.), River Bend Country Club, Fairbanks Golf and Country Club (San Diego). Office: JWK Internat Corp Ste 800 7617 Little River Tpke Annandale VA 22003-2689 also: 10900 Tara Rd Potomac MD 20854-1342

KHISMATULLIN, DAMIR BORISOVICH, physicist, mathematician; b. Ufa, Bashkortostan, Russia, Aug. 20, 1972; arrived in U.S., 2000; s. Boris Nikolaevich Egorov and Flyura Shaikhinurovna Khismatullina; m. Liudmila Irekovna Bikbulatova, Aug. 9, 1996; 1 child, Emma Damirovna Khismatullina. MSc with hons. in Theoretical Physics, Bashkir State U., Ufa, Russia, 1994, PhD in Physics & Math., 1998. Rsch. asst. Inst. of Mechanics Ufa (Russia) Br. of Russian Acad. of Sciences, 1994—97, rsch. assoc. Inst. of Mechanics, 1997—2000; asst. prof. of applied math. Bashkir State U., 1999—2000; rsch. asst. prof. of aerospace and mech. engring. Boston (Mass.) U., 2000—01; rsch. asst. prof. of math. Va. Poly. Inst. and State U., Blacksburg, Va., 2001—03; sr. rsch. scientist, dept. biomed. engring. Duke U., Durham, NC, 2003—. Fellow, NSF-NATO, 2000—01. Mem.: AIChE, Russian Acoustical Soc., Soc. for Indsl. and Applied Math., Soc. of Rheology, Am. Phys. Soc., Acoustical Soc. of Am., Biomedical Engring. Soc. (assoc.). Russian Orthodox. Achievements include development of computational models for leukocyte-endothelial adhesion and theoretical models for interaction of nonlinear waves in bubbly liquids; research in radial oscillations of a sonoluminescing bubble; shape oscillations of a viscoelastic drop; radial oscillations of ultrasound contrast agents in blood; effect of inertia on breakup of very viscous drops in shear flow. Avocation: bicycling. Office: Duke U Dept Biomed Engring 136 Hudson Hall Box 90281 Durham NC 27708 Office Fax: 919-684-4488. E-mail: damir@duke.edu.

KHLABYSTOVA, MILENA, web programmer, educator; b. Saratov, Russia, Dec. 6, 1972; arrived in U.S., 1997; d. Alexander Khlabystov and Valeria Zadorozhnaya; life ptnr. Baird. MSc in Computational Physics, St.Petersburg (Russia) State U., 1997; PhD in math., Inst. of Tech., 2003. Cert. programmer for the Java 2 Platform Sun Microsystems, 2001, web components developer Sun Microsystems, 2003. Grad. tchg. asst. St. Petersburg State U., 1994—95, Ga. Inst. Tech., Atlanta, 1997—2001, tchg. instr., 1999—2000, grad. rsch. asst., 2001—03. Java/web application developer Ga. Inst. Tech., Atlanta, 2001—03. Contbr. articles to profl. jours. Recipient Soros Student award, G. Soros Found., 1995—97. Mem.: Am. Math. Soc., Pi Mu Epsilon. Achievements include research in nonlinear equations, solitons, Lorentz gaes, Lattice gases and cellular automata.

KHO, EUSEBIO, surgeon; b. The Philippines, Dec. 16, 1933; came to U.S., 1964; s. Joaquin and Francisca (Chua) K.; m. Grace Casas Lim, May 24, 1964; children: Michelle Mae, April Tiffany, Bradley Jude, Jaclyn Ashley, Matthew Ryan. AA, Silliman U., The Philippines, 1955; MD, State U. Philippines, 1960. Diplomate Am. Bd. Surgery. Rotating intern Philippine Gen. Hosp., U. Philippines, 1959-60; resident gen. practice Silliman U. Med. Ctr., 1960-63; virology rschr. Van Howelling Lab. Silliman U., 1963-64; intern in surgery Francis Scott Key Med. Ctr., 1964-65, resident in gen. surgery, 1965-67; fellow in surgery Johns Hopkins, 1965-67; rsch. assoc. pediat. surgery U. Chgo. Hosps., 1967-68; resident in gen. surgery then chief resident U. Tex. Hosp., San Antonio, 1968-70; hosp. surgeon St. Anthony Hosp., Louisville, 1970-72; practice medicine specializing in surgery Scottsburg, Ind., 1972—. Chmn. dept. surgery Scott County Meml. Hosp., 1973—; cons. surgeon Washington County Meml. Hosp., Salem, Ind., also Clark County Meml. Hosp., Jeffersonville, Ind., 1973—; courtesy surgeon Suburban Hosp., Louisville, 1973—; gen. surgeon 5010 U.S. Army Hosp., Louisville, 1980—. Bd. dirs. Make-A-Wish Found., Ind., 1992—. Col. M.C., USAR, 1980—, Operation Desert Storm, 1990-91. Named to Chgo. Filipino Am. Hall of Fame in medicine, 1998; recipient Outstanding Svc. Overseas award U. Philippines Med. Alumni Soc., 2002. Fellow ACS, Am. Soc. Abdominal Surgeons, Am. Coll. Emergency Physicians; mem. AMA (Physician's Recognition award 1969, 72), Am. Coll. Internat. Physicians (founding mem., trustee 1974—), Ind. State Med. Assn., Soc. of The Philippines, Ky. Med. Assn. Philippines Med. Assn. of Ind. Ky. (disting. svc. award 2000), Surgeons in Am. (life), Assn. Philippine Practicing Physicians in Am. (life), Assn. Mil. Surgeons U.S. (life), Res. Officers Assn. U.S. (life), Mark Ravitch Surg. Assn., Bradley Aust. Surg. Soc., N.Y. Acad. Scis., Hon. Order Ky. Cols., Masons, Optimists Club. Presbyterian. Home: 14 Carla Ln Scottsburg IN 47170-9707 Office: 137 E Mcclain Ave Scottsburg IN 47170-1846

KHO, JAMES WANG, computer scientist; b. Manila, Philippines, Sept. 6, 1944; came to U.S., 1966, naturalized, 1973; s. Eng-Too Lao and Lour-Chii Lim (Wang) K.; m. Joanne Jane Chan, June 22, 1976. MS, U. Wis., 1968, PhD, 1972, MBA, 1976; IEM cert., Harvard U., 1998. Project and research specialist U. Wis., Madison, 1966-71; prof. computer sci. Wayne State U., Detroit, 1971-73, Calif. State U., Sacramento, 1973—2000, chmn. dept., 1977—87, assoc. dean engring., 1995—98, assoc. v.p. adminstrn., 1998—2000; coll. pres. DeVry U., 2000—; v.p. DeVry, Inc., 2001—. Computer sci. cons., State of Calif., 1975—90, lectr. in field for univs.; owner, operator import bus. Contbr. articles to profl. jours. Vis. scholar Am. Coun. on Edn. fellow, 1997—98; Calif. State U. Exec. fellow, 1997—99. Mem. Assn. Computing Machinery, Am. Inst. Decision Scis., Soc. Computer Simulation, Soc. Gen. Systems Research, Ops. Research Soc. Am., Data Processing Mgmt. Assn., Beta Gamma Sigma, Phi Kappa Phi, Pi Gamma Mu. Office: 6000 J St Sacramento CA 95819-2605

KHOJASTEH, ALI, medical oncologist, hematologist; b. Shiraz, Pars, Persia, Nov. 10, 1947; came to U.S., 1974; s. Mostafa and Pari Jan (Azimi) K.; children: Artemis, Amitis. Degree, Pahlavi U., Shiraz, 1968, MD, 1974. Vice dean Sch. Medicine Shiraz U., 1980-82, chmn. med. dept. Sch. Medicine, 1982-83; chief med. oncology Ellis Fischel Cancer Ctr., Columbia, Mo., 1983-87, chmn. med. dept., 1987-90, chief of staff, 1988-89; med. dir. St. Mary Cancer Ctr., Jefferson City, Mo., 1993—; pres. Columbia Comprehensive Cancer Care Clinic and Rsch. Inst., 1990—. Assoc. prof. U. Mo., Columbia, 1989—; prin. investigator Ellis Fischel CCOP, Columbia, 1988-90; chmn. Mo. Acad. Sci. Oncology, 1988-89, Mo. Cancer Pain Initiative, 1991-96; investigator Nat. Cancer Inst., 1990—; liaison Am. Coll. Surgeons, 1992—, Am.'s Top Physicians Consumers Rsch. Coun., 2003. Contbr. articles to New Eng. Jour. Medicine, Cancer, Am. Jour. Medicine, Am. Jour. Hematology, Jour. Clin. Oncol. Cancer Bull., Jour. Pain Sys. Mgmt., Can. Jour. Medicine; author: (with others) Pulmonary Medicine, Cancer and Heart, Chemotherapy Resource Book, Small Intestinal Disease; named in Guide to America's Top Physicians, 2003. Grantee, Purdue Fredrick Co., Conn., 1994—, Adria Lab., Columbus, 1988—, Glaxo Rsch. Lab., Research Triangle Park, N.C., 1988—91, Ciba-Geigy Co., 1990—91, Merrill Dow Co., 1991—95, Pfizer, 1995—, Matrix Pharm., 1996, Ross Lab., 1996, Aronex Pharm., 1997, Merck Rsch. Lab., 1997, Ligand Lab., 1997, Maxim-Pharm., 1998, Nat. Cancer Inst. (Can.), 1998, Glaxo-Wellcome, 1998, Bayer Lab., 1999, Amgen, 1999, Arugon Lab., 1999, Pharmacia & Upjohn Lab., 2000, Hoffman-Roche Lab., 2000, Sanofi-Synthelabo Lab. (France), 2000, PI of prospective study of hemalologic and neoplastic disorders, UN Project, 2001, UN, 2001, Pro-Neuron Lab., 2002, Johnson and Johnson Lab, 2003, Aventis Lab., 2003, Bristol Meyers Squib Lab., 2003. Fellow ACP, Royal Soc. Medicine (Eng.); mem. Am. Soc. Clin. Oncology, Am. Soc. Internat. Medicine, Smithsonian Soc., N.Y. Acad. Sci., Mo. Acad. Scis. (chmn. oncology sect. 1988-89), So. Med. Assn., Am. Soc. Hematology. Zoroastrian. Home: 2801 Greenbriar Dr Columbia MO 65203-3663 Office: Columbia Comprehensive Cancer Care Clinic 500 Keene St Ste 202 Columbia MO 65201-8104 E-mail: drkhojasteh@hotmail.com.

KHOKHLOV, VLADIMIR ABRAMOVICH, pianist, educator; b. St. Petersburg, Fla, May 25, 1943; s. Abram Mendelevich and Nina Dmitrievna Khokhlov; m. Aina Jana M. Kalnciema, July 14, 1974 (div. Sept. 1989); m. Irisa Voldemara M. Levica Kaupman, Nov. 4, 1989; children: Mark, Maya. BFA, St. Petersburg State Conserv., Russia, 1961, MFA, 1968; postgrad., Fla. State U., 2000—02. Tchr. Leningrad Cmty. Coll., Russia, 1965-68; soloist, accompanist Karelian Philharm., Petrozavodsk, Russia, 1968-70, Lenconcert Philharm. Dept., Leningrad, 1970-74, Latvian State Philharm., Riga, 1974-91; tchr. Latvian Music Acad., Riga, 1985-91; piano performer, tchr. Tampa, 1991—, Faculty of Livine, Sch. of Music, Washington, 2002—03. Mem. artistic bd. Latvian Philharmonic, Riga, 1986-90; music dir., bd. dir. Russian Heritage, St. Petersburg, Fla., 1997—; choir condr. Latvian Cmty. Choir, St. Petersburg, 1991—; coach, accompanist singers winning numerous awards in vocal competitions, Greece, 1983, Latvia, 1975, 79, Lithuania, 1977, Italy, 1984, 85, Japan, 1990. Composer: Piano Ensembles (Latvian folk songs), 1981, Compositions for Kokle, Xilophono, Voice, 1974-91, Music Book for Kokle, 1982, record, CD Jewish IImpressions, Jewish Folk Songs, 1989, 95. Mem., organizer People's Front, Latvian Philharmonic Group, Riga, 1988-91. Recipient honor award for best accompaniment Jury of E. Darzins Vocal Competition, Riga, 1975, honor diplomas for best asscompaniment Jury of USSR Vocal Competition, Vilnius, Lithuania, 1977, Latvian State award, 1977, Jury of A. Kalnins Vocal Competition, Riga, 1979, honorable mention Jury of Internat. Pinaut Soc. Competition, NYC, 1996, winner of Willa Chapman Award Competition for Grad. Students of Fla. State Univ., 2000. Mem. Nat. Music Tchr. Assn., Fla. State Music Tchrs. Assn., Tampa Music Tchr. Assn., Russian Heritage. Democrat. Avocations: gardening, travel, basketball. Home and Office: 14941 Old Pointe Rd Tampa FL 33613-1618

KHOLODNYI, VALERY ALEXANDROVICH, energy executive, researcher; MS, Moscow Inst. of Electronics and Math., 1987, PhD, 1990. Dir. of quantitative analysis Reliant Resources, Houston, 2002—. Invited spkr. Energy and Power Risk Mgmt. Congress, 2002, Enterprise Wide Risk Mgmt. Conf., 2001, Energy Fin. Conf., U. Tex. at Austin, 2001, Second World Congress of Nonlinear Analysts, 1996, Ann. Meeting of the Am. Math. Soc., 2002. Author: (book) Foreign Exchange Option Symmetry, 1998, Foundations of Foreign Exchange Option Symmetry, 1998, Beliefs-Preferences Gauge Symmetry Group and Replication of Contingent Claims in a General Market Environment, 1998. Mem.: Internat. Fedn. of Nonlinear Analysts, Am. Math. Soc. Avocations: swimming, camping, golf. Personal E-mail: valery_kholodnyi@hotmail.com.

KHONSARI, MICHAEL M. mechanical engineering educator; b. Aug. 17, 1957; m. Karen Sue Troy, Sept. 1, 1990. BS in Mech. Engring. with honors, U. Tex., 1978, MS in Mech. Engring., 1979, PhD in Mech. Engring., 1983. Rsch. and teaching asst. U. Tex., Austin, 1978-83; asst. prof. Ohio State U., Columbus, 1984-87, U. Pitts., 1988-90, assoc. prof., 1990-96; prof. So. Ill. U., Carbondale, 1996-99, prof., chmn. dept. mech. engring. and energy processes, 1996-99; Dow Chem. endowed chair, prof. mech. engring. La. State U., Baton Rouge, 1999—, Dow Chem. endowed chair in rotating machinery, 1999—. Apptd. project dir. and assoc. commr. Sponsored R&D at La. Bd. Regents La., Exptl. Program Stimulate Competitive Rsch., 2003—; mem. mech. engring. grad. com. U. Pitts., 1988-90, design interest group, 1988-96; mem. faculty ctr. motion control U. Pitts.; reviewer NSF, NASA, Am. Chem. Soc. Books, McGraw Hill Books, Addison Wesley Books, Prentice-Hall Books, Holt Rinehart and Winston Books; lectr. in field. Assoc. editor ASME Jour. Tribology, 1997—, STLE Tribology Transactions, 1990—; mem. editl. bd. Tribological Acta, 1994—; mem. editl. bd., reviewer Jour. Engring. Design Graphics, 1987—; contbr., reviewer, mem. editl. bd. adv. com. CRC Handbook of Lubrication, vol. III, 1991-93; reviewer Lubrication Engring. Jour., Wear Jour., Rheology Jour., Heat Transfer Jour., Tribology Jour., Applied Mechanics Jour.; co-author: Applied Triology, 2001; pub. abstracts and reports; referee various jours.; contbr. articles to profl. jours. Recipient Found. award ALCOA, 1990, 91. Fellow Soc. Tribology Lubrication Engrs. (bearings com. 1985—, chmn. 1988-91, assoc. editor, rev. Tribology Transactions 1990—, assoc. editor Jour. Tribology 1997—, Presdl. Rsch. Coun. award 1993), ASME (conf. planning com. 1989-96, reviewer Jour. Tribology and conf. papers, chmn. ASME/Soc. Tribology and Lubrication Engrs. Internat. Conf. in Tribology 1996, Burt L. Newkirk award 1990); mem. Sigma Xi. Achievements include research in thermal effects in hydrodynamic bearings, thermal effects in wet clutches, hot spot prediction in mechanical components, Thermoclastic instability, powder lubrication, multi-phase flows in bearings, friction associated with instrument pointing mechanisms operating under ultra low speeds. Office: La State U Dept Mech Engring 2508 Ceba Baton Rouge LA 70803-0001 E-mail: Khonsari@me.lsu.edu.

KHOO-ZENG, MAY-SZE (MACY KHOO-ZENG), music educator; b. Kuala Lumpur, Malaysia, Jan. 25, 1970; came to U.S., 1988; d. Kay-Hock and Monica (Wee) Khoo; m. Sibo (Bob) Zeng, Dec. 29, 1990. BA in Music, Seattle Pacific U., 1991; Advanced Cert., Royal Sch. Music, London, 1993. Pvt. music educator, Arcadia, Calif., 1991—. Piano instr. various piano competition winners, disting. students from Royal Sch. Exams, London, honor and award winners of Calif. Cert. of Merit evaluation; piano competition cons. 1993 Am. Chinese Cultural Assn. Competition. Recipient Piano Hall of Fame award, Piano Guild U.S.A., 1998. Mem. Music Tchrs. Nat. Assn., Nat. Guild Piano Tchrs., Nat. Guild Audition (chairperson Acadia Ctr. 1999—), Calif. Music Tchrs. Assn. Home: 1901 Watson Dr Arcadia CA 91006-4669

KHORANA, HAR GOBIND, professor, chemist; b. Raipur, India, Jan. 9, 1922; s. Shri Ganpat Rai Khorana and Shrimati Krishna (Devi) Knorana; m. Esther Sibler, 1952; children: Julia, Emilie;1 child, Dave Roy. BS, Punjab U., 1943, MS, 1945; PhD, Liverpool (Eng.) U., 1948; DSc (hon.), U. Chgo., 1967, Simon Fraser U., Vancouver, Can., 1969, U. Liverpool, Eng., 1971, U. Punjab, India, 1971, U. Miami, 1994; degree (hon.), U. Bergen, Norway, 1996; others (hon.). Head organic chemistry group B.C. Rsch. Coun., 1952—60; vis. prof. Rockefeller Inst., N.Y.C., 1958—; prof., co-dir. Inst. Enzyme Rsch. U. Wis., Madison, 1960—70, prof. dept. biochemistry, 1962—70, Conrad A. Elvehjem prof. life scis., 1964—70; Alfred P. Sloan prof. biology and chemistry MIT, Cambridge, 1970—97, A.P. Sloan prof. emeritus, sr. lectr., 1997—. Vis. prof. Stanford U., 1964; mem. adv. bd. Biopolymers; rschr. chem. methods for synthesis of nuccleotides, coenzymes and nucleic acids, elucidation on the genetic code, lab. synthesis of genes, biol. membrane and light-transducing pigments. Author: Some Recent Developments in the Chemistry of Phosphate Esters of Biological Interests, 1961; editl. bd. Jour. Am. Chem. Soc., 1963—, contbr. numerous articles to profl. jours., —. Recipient Merck award, Chem. Inst. Can., 1958, Gold medal, Profl. Inst. Pub. Svc. Can., 1960, Dannie-Heinneman Preiz, Göttingen, Germany, 1967, Remsen award, Johns Hopkins U., 1968, Am. Chem. Soc. award for creative work in synthetic organic chemistry, 1968, Louisa Gross Horwitz prize, 1968, Lasker Found. award for basic med. rsch., 1968, Nobel prize in Medicine, 1968, elected to Deutsche Akademie der Naturforscher Leopoldina, HalleSaale, Germany, 1968; fellow Overseas, Churchill Coll., Cambridge, Eng., 1967. Fellow: AAAS, Am. Acad. Arts and Scis., Chem. Inst. Can.; mem.: NAS, others, Japanese Biochem. Soc. (fgn. hon.), Royal Soc. Edinburgh, Pharm. Soc. Japan (hon.), Royal Soc. (London), Pontifical Acad. Scis. (Rome), Indian Acad. Scis. (fgn. mem.), Am. Philos. Soc. Office: MIT 77 Massachusetts Ave Rm 68-680A Cambridge MA 02139-4307*

KHOREY, DAVID EUGENE, lawyer; b. Pitts., Oct. 5, 1959; s. Eugene George and Margaret (Yanyo) K.; m. Jennifer Ann Robinson, Dec. 29, 1983; children: Christopher David, Katherine Ann, Joanna Dale. BA with honors, U. Notre Dame, 1981; JD, Vanderbilt U., 1984. Bar: Mich. 1984, U.S. Dist. Ct. (we. dist.) Mich. 1984, U.S. Ct. Appeals 1989, U.S. Dist. Ct. (ea. dist.) Mich. 1990, U.S. Supreme Ct. 1999. Assoc. Varnum, Riddering, Schmidt & Howlett, Grand Rapids, Mich., 1984-89, ptnr., 1989—, chair labor practice group, 2000—. Instr. seminars Mich. Inst. of Continuing Legal Edn., Nat. Bus. Inst., Stetson Coll., NACUA Conf. Co-author: Developing Labor Law; mem. editl. bd. State Bar Mich. Mem. ABA (labor sect., com. devels. law under the nat. labor rels. act), State Bar Assn. Mich. (vice chair labor and employment sect.). Office: Varnum Riddering Schmidt & Howlett PO Box 352 Bridgewater Pl Grand Rapids MI 49501-0352

KHORRAM, K. DAVID, ophthalmologist; b. Shiraz, Iran, Jan. 12, 1963; arrived in U.S., 1965; s. Houshang and Tabandeh (Fereydoon-Nejad) Khorram; m. Mara Blonigen, Nov. 19, 1994. BA with honors, Northwestern U., Evanston, Ill., 1984; MD with distinction, U. Ky., 1988. Diplomate Am. Bd. Ophthalmology. Intern U. Chgo., 1988-89; resident in ophthalmology Northwestern U., Chgo., 1989-92; dir. divsn. ophthalmology LBJ Tropical Med. Ctr., Pago Pago, American Samoa, 1992-93; cons. eye surgeon, physician Commonwealth Health Ctr., Saipan, Mariana Islands, 1993-94, med. dir. ctr. for eye disease, 1994-98; ophthalmologist Marianas Eye Inst., Saipan, Mariana Islands, 1998—. Contbr. Mem.: Am. Acad. Ophthalmology, Alpha Omega Alpha. Baha'I. Office: PO Box 503900 Saipan MP 96950-3900

KHORRAM, OMID ALEXANDER, obstetrics-gynecology educator; b. Shiraz, Iran, Feb. 23, 1958; came to U.S., 1973; s. Nosrat and Azam (Azari) K.; m. Avid Hojjaty, Sept. 18, 1985; children: Nima David, Naseem Melissa, Nadia Rose. BA, U. Calif., 1979; PhD, U. Tex. Health Sci. Ctr., 1984; MD, Tex. Tech., 1989. Diplomate in ob-gyn. and in reproductive endocrinology/infertility Am. Bd. Ob-Gyn. Resident in ob/gyn U. Calif., San Francisco, 1989-93, fellow in reproductive endocrinology San Diego, 1993-95, clin. instr., 1993-95; assoc. prof. ob-gyn. U. Wis., Madison, 1995—, UCLA, 2000—. Berlex Found. scholar, 1995. Fellow Am. Coll. Ob-gyn.; mem. Am. Soc. Reproductive Medicine, N.Am. Menopause Soc., Alpha Omega Alpha. Avocations: jogging, camping, racquetball. Home: 2638 Colt Rd Rancho Palos Verdes CA 90275-7105 Office: Harbor-UCLA MC Box 489 1000 W Carson St Torrance CA 90502

KHOSLA, VED MITTER, oral and maxillofacial surgeon, educator; b. Nairobi, Kenya, Jan. 13, 1926; s. Jagdish Rai and Tara V. K.; m. Santosh Ved Chabra, Oct. 11, 1952; children: Ashok M., Siddarth M. Student, U. Cambridge, 1945; L.D.S., Edinburgh Dental Hosp. and Sch., 1950, Coll. Dental Surgeons, Sask., Can., 1962. Prof. emeritus, dir. postdoctoral studies in oral surgery Sch. Dentistry U. Calif., San Francisco, 1968—; chief oral surgery San Francisco Gen. Hosp. Lectr. oral surgery U. of Pacific, VA Hosp.; vis. cons. Fresno County Hosp. Dental Clinic.; Mem. planning com., exec. med. com. San Francisco Gen. Hosp. Contbr. articles to profl. jours. Examiner in photography and gardening Boy Scouts Am., 1971-73, Guatemala Clinic, 1972. Granted personal coat of arms by H.M. Queen Elizabeth II, 1959 Fellow Royal Coll. Surgeons (Edinburgh), Internat. Assn. Oral Surgeons, Internat. Coll. Applied Nutrition, Internat. Coll. Dentists, Royal Soc. Health, AAAS, Am. Coll. Dentists; mem. Brit. Assn. Oral Surgeons, Am. Soc. Oral Surgeons, Am. Dental Soc. Anesthesiology, Am. Acad. Dental Radiology, Omicron Kappa Upsilon. Clubs: Masons. Home: 1525 Lakeview Dr Hillsborough CA 94010-7330 Office: U Calif Sch Dentistry Oral Surgery Div 3D Parnassus Ave San Francisco CA 94117-4342 *It is part of the cure to wish to be cured. With God all things are possible.*

KHOURI, GEORGE GEORGE, ophthalmologist; b. Beirut, May 24, 1957; came to U.S., 1976; BA summa cum laude, Rollins Coll., 1978; MD, Am. U. of Beirut, 1983. Diplomate Am. Bd. Ophthalmology. Intern in internal medicine Am. U. Hosp. and Med. Ctr., Beirut, 1982-83; rsch. fellow in ocular pharmacology and physiology Wilmer Inst., Johns Hopkins Hosp., Balt., 1983-84; resident in ophthalmology U. Chgo. Hosps. and Clinics, 1984-87; clin. fellow Retina Assocs. & Schepens Eye Rsch. Inst. Mass. Eye and Ear Infirmary/Harvard Med. Sch., Boston, 1987-88; asst. prof. Tufts U. Sch. Medicine, Boston, 1988-92; staff ophthalmologist Dept. Vets. Affairs Med. Ctr., Boston, 1988-92, Malden (Mass.) Hosp., 1992-93, Melrose (Mass.)-Wakefield Hosp., 1992-93; pvt. practice West Palm Beach, Fla., 1994—. Presenter in field. Contbr. articles to profl. pubs. Vol. eye surgeon Aravind Eye Hosp., India, 1993, Lumbini (Nepal) Eye Hosp., 1993, Nepal Eye Hosp., Kathmandu, 1993, Lighthouse for Christ Eye Ctr., Mombasa, Kenya, 1993. Eye rsch. grantee Mass. Lions, 1992-93, VA, 1990-92. Fellow Am. Acad. Ophthalmology; mem. Am. Soc. Cataract and Refractive Surgery, Internat. Soc. Refractive Surgery. Avocations: swimming, travel, horseback riding. Office: Palm Beach Eye Ctr Ste 8100 1411 N Flagler Dr West Palm Beach FL 33401-3411

KHOURY, GEORGE GILBERT, printing company executive, baseball association executive; b. St. Louis, July 30, 1923; s. George Michael and Dorothy (Smith) K.; m. Colleen E. Khoury Czerny, Apr. 3, 1948; children: Colleen Ann, George Gilbert. Grad., St. Louis U., 1946. V.p. Khoury Bros. Printing, St. Louis, 1946—; exec. dir. George Khoury Assn. Baseball Leagues, Inc., St. Louis, 1967—. Author: (novels) Brothers, Bombshells, Baseball, 2003.

Served with U.S. Army, 1943-45, NATOUSA, MTO. Decorated Purple Heart with oak leaf cluster. Roman Catholic. Office: George Khoury Assn Baseball Leagues 5400 Meramec Bottom Rd Saint Louis MO 63128-4624 E-mail: czernyce@msn.com.

KHOURY, HANI, surgeon, educator; b. Damascus, Syria, Oct. 15, 1949; MD, Damascus U., 1973. Diplomate Am. Bd. Surgery, Am. Bd. Colon and Rectal Surgery. Intern St. Francis Med. Ctr., Trenton, N.J., 1974-75; resident St. Joseph's Hosp. Med. Ctr., Paterson, N.J., 1975-79; fellow in colon and rectal surgery U. Tex. Health Sci. Ctr., Houston, 1979-80; mem. staff St. Joseph's Hosp., Paterson, 1981—, Wayne (N.J.) Gen. Hosp., 1981—, Mountainside Hosp., Montclair, N.J., 1995—, Christ Hosp., Jersey City, 1997—. Clin. asst. prof. Seton Hall U. Grad. Sch., 1988—. Fellow ACS, Am. Soc. Colon and Rectal Surgery. Office: 502 Hamburg Tpke Ste 107 Wayne NJ 07470-8446

KHOURY, MATTHEW W. academic administrator; s. E. George and Cynthia Khoury; m. Dianna Marie Cassin, Nov. 7, 1999; children: Daniel Edward, David William. BA in English, Plymouth State Coll., 1997; MS in Adminstrv. Sci., U. Wis., Green Bay, 2001. Dir. residence hall St. Norbert Coll., De Pere, Wis., 1998—2002; complex dir. Ea. Ill. U., Charleston, 2002—. Scholar All-Am. scholar, USSA, 1997. Mem.: Gt. Lakes Assn. Coll. U. Housing Officers, Nat. Assn. Student Pers. Adminstrs., Phi Kappa Phi, Sigma Nu Chi (hon.).

KHOURY, NIDAL Y. physician; b. Damascus, Syria, June 6, 1944; came to U.S., 1972; s. Joseph and Nadima (Elkhoury) K.; m. Christine Chahla, Mar. 10, 1990; children: Kristy Lauren, Joe Kevin, Neil Christian. MD, Damascus U., 1969. Diplomate Am. Bd. Internal Medicine, Am. Bd. Gastroenterology. Intern, resident in surgery and pathology St. Clare's Hosp., N.Y.C., 1972-75; resident in internal medicine L.I. Coll., 1975-77, fellow in gastroenterology, 1977-79; pvt. practice Bklyn., 1979—; attending physician L.I. Coll. Health, Bklyn., Luth. Med. Ctr., Bklyn., N.Y. Meth. Hosp., L.I. Coll. Hosp.; instr. SUNY. Mem. ACP, Amer. Med. Dirs. Assn., Am. Geriatric Soc., Bayridge Med. Soc. (pres. 1998-99). Office: 336 78th St Brooklyn NY 11209-3013

KHOURY, PHILIP S. academic administrator; b. Washington, D.C., Oct. 15, 1949; s. Shukry E. and Angela Mansur (Jurdak) K.; m. Mary Christina Wilson, Aug. 28, 1980. BA with hons., Trinity Coll., 1971; PhD, Harvard U., 1980. Asst. prof. MIT, Cambridge, Mass., 1981-84; assoc. prof. Mass. Inst. Tech., Cambridge, Mass., 1984-90, prof., 1990—, assoc. dean Sch. Humanities, Arts, and Social Sci., 1987-90, acting dean, 1990-91, dean, 1991—, Kenan Sahin dean, 2002—, 2002—. Mem. editl. bd. Jour. Interdisciplinary History, 1987—, Hist. Abstracts, 1990—, The Beirut Rev., 1991-93. Author: Urban Notables and Arab Nationalism, 1983, Syria and the French Mandate, 1987; co-editor Tribes and State Formation in the Middle East, 1990, The Modern Middle East: A Reader, 1993, 2nd ed. 2003, Recovering Beirut: Urban Design and Post-war Reconstruction, 1993. Trustee Am. U. Beirut, 1997—, Toynbee Prize Found., 1998—, World Peace Found., 1999—, Trinity Coll., 2000—; dir. Harvard Coop. Soc., 1998—. Fellow Am. Acad. of Arts Scis., 2002-. Thomas J. Watson fellow Watson Found., 1971-72; Fulbright scholar, 1976-77; Post-Doctoral Social Sci. Rsch. Coun., 1983-84; Mellon fellow Aspen Inst., 1984-85; Class of 1922 Career Devel. Professorship, MIT, 1984-86. Mem. AAAS, Am. Hist. Assn. (George Louis Beer Prize 1987), Middle East Studies Assn. (pres. 1998, dir. 1990 92, 97 2000), Brit. Soc. for Middle East Studies; Pi Gamma Mu. Avocation: tennis. Office: MIT Office Dean Sch Hum/Arts/Social Scis 77 Massachusetts Ave Cambridge MA 02139-4307 E-mail: khoury@mit.edu.

KHOUZAM, HANI RAOUL, psychiatrist, physician, educator; b. Heliopolis, Egypt, June 5, 1950; came to U.S., 1980; s. Raoul Aniss Khouzam and Jeannette (Guindi) Roufael; m. Lynda Margaret Dickerson, Nov. 20, 1982; children: Andrea Adahlia, Andrew Amaris, Adam Yurie Alexander. MB BCh, Faculty Medicine Cairo, Egypt, 1977; MPH, Tulane U., 1981. Diplomate Am. Bd. Psychiatry and Neurology with spl. certification in Geriatric Psychiatry; cert. ednl. commn. fgn. med. grads. Med. house officer Cairo U. Teaching Hosps., 1978-79; psychiatrist Shaalan M.D., Inc., Cairo, 1979-80; rsch. scholar Okla. Med. Rsch. Found., Oklahoma City, 1982-83; resident in psychiatry U. Okla. Health Scis. Ctr., Oklahoma City, 1983-87; staff psychiatrist Okla. County Crisis Intervention Ctr., Oklahoma City, 1987-90; med. dir., inpatient psychiatry unit VA Med. Ctr., Oklahoma City, 1990-92, dir. consultation liaison psychiatry Manchester, NH, 1992—95; asst. prof. psychiatry dept. psychiatry and behavioral scis. Coll. Medicine U. Okla., Oklahoma City, 1990—92; staff psychiatrist VA Med. Ctr., N.H., 1992-2000, VA Ctrl. Calif. Health Care Sys., Fresno, Calif., 2000—, med, dir. chem. dependency treatment program, 2000—. Adj. asst. prof. psychiatry Dartmouth Med. Sch., Lebanon, NH, 1992—95, adj. assoc. prof. psychiatry, 1995—2000; clin. instr. in medicine Harvard Med. Sch., Boston, 1994—; assoc. clin. prof. psychiatry U. Calif. San Francisco Med. Edn. Program, Fresno, 2001—. Author: Emergency Psychiatric Interventions, 1988; contbr. to profl. jours. Hubert H. Humphrey fellow in pub. health, USIA, New Orleans, 1980-81. Fellow Egyptian Sci. Soc., Am. Psychiatric Assn.; mem. Egyptian Med. Assn., N.H. Psychiatric Soc. Coptic Catholic Christian. Avocations: reading, writing, bible study, music, stamp collecting. Home: 7377 N Carruth Ave Fresno CA 93711-0513 Office: VA Ctrl Calif Health Care Sys Dept Psychiatry 2615 E Clinton Ave Fresno CA 93703

KHOUZAM, RAMI NADIM, physician; b. Cairo, Oct. 6, 1970; s. Nadim Nassif Khouzam and Nora Zaki Bestawros; m. Samia Fouad Attallah, Oct. 3, 1975. MD, Ain Shams U. Coll. Of Medicine, Egypt, 1994. Cert. Am. Bd. of Internal Medicine, 2002. Internal medicine resident Tucson Med. Ctr., 1999—2002, chief resident internal medicine, 2002—. Author: (med. jour. article) Heart And Lung Jour., Angiology Med. Jour., The Jour. of Vascular Diseases. Recipient Acp Vignette First prize Winner, Tucson Hospitals Med. Edn. Program, 2001. Mem.: Jesuit HS Alumni Assn., Assn. Of French Speaking Drs., Residents' Com., ACP (assoc.). Home: 2345 N Craycroft Rd Apt# 206 Tucson AZ 85712 Office: Tucson Med Ctr 5301 E Grant Rd Tucson AZ 85733 Home Fax: 509-691-6970. Personal E-mail: ramithmep@yahoo.com. E-mail: khouzamrami@yahoo.com.

KHOZEIMEH, ISSA, electrical engineer, educator; b. Tehran, Iran, Dec. 25, 1939; came to U.S., 1959; s. Ismail and Zohreh (Alam) K.; m. Nahid Khozeimeh; children: Lili, Nini. BSEE, George Washington U., Washington, 1966; MSEE, 1973, D in Engring., 1984, DSc in Engring. Mgmt., 1993. Registered profl. engr. Jr. engr. Potomac Electric Power Co., Washington, 1967-68; substation engr., 1968-73; design standrads engr., 1973-79; sr. engr. substation design, 1979-80; dept. head, chief elec. engr. David Volkert and Assocs., Bethesda, Md., 1980-88; mgr. Util. Svcs. Metro. Washington Airports Auth. Dulles Internat. Airport, 1988—; prof. engring. and mgmt. U. Md., Balt., 1998—; prof. mgmt. U. Balt., 1999—. Pres. Internat. Mktg. and Consulting Corp., Washington, 1980-82; v.p. Horizon Internat., Washington, 1982-88; pres. Forum Internat. Glen Echo, Md., 1988—; prof. U. Md., Balt., 1998—, U. Balt., 1999—. Author: An Automated Maintenance Management System for International Airports, 1993; contbr. articles to profl. jours. Recipient Sch. of Engring Svcs. award, 1976, Gen. Alumni Assn. Svc. award, 1971, George Washington U., 1976, Engr. Coun. Cert. of Appreciation, 1984, 85, Disting. Svc. award 1986, Disting. Alumni Svc. award George Washington U. Alumni Assn., 1998, Tech. Forum Leadership award, 1999, Outstanding Profl Efforts award Met. Washington Airport Authority, 2000. Mem.: NSPE, IEEE (sr.), Washington Soc. Engrs., Md. Soc. Profl. Engrs. (pres. 1992—96, 2002—, Disting. Sr. Engr. award 1997), Instrument Soc. Am. Republican. Moslem. Avocations: water skiing, snow skiing, hiking, reading, publishing, lecturing, travel. Home: PO Box 557 Glen Echo MD 20812-0557 Office: Metro Washington Airports Authority Dulles Internat Airport PO Box 17045 Washington DC 20041-7045 E-mail: khozeimeh@hotmail.com., issa.khozeimeh@mwaa.com.

KHRAPUNOV, SERGEI, biophysicist; b. Novosibirsk, Russia, Apr. 20, 1942; s. Nikolai Khrapunov and Nina Khrapunova; m. Eleonora Vyadro, July 12, 1941; children: Tim, Yuriy, Inna Khrapunova. BS, Sevastopol Poly. Inst., Ukraine, 1960—65; MS, Kiev Nat. U., 1971—76; PhD in Biochemistry, Nat. Acad. Sci., Kiev, 1977, DSc in Molecular Biology, 1985. Chief, prof. Dept. of Gen. & Molecular Genetics, Kiev Nat. U., Kiev, Ukraine, 1985—97; prin. assoc. Albert Einstein Coll. of Medicine, Bronx, NY, 1997—. Mem.: Ukranian Genetical Soc., Ukranian Biophysical Soc., Am. Biophysical Soc. Achievements include research in Histone and nucleosome structure; Two-quantum mode of DNA cleavage by laser radiation; Dependence of DNA bendability on DNA sequence; Structure of TATA binding protein (TBP). Office: Albert Einstein Coll Medicine 1300 Morris Park Ave Bronx NY 10461 E-mail: khraps@aecom.yu.edu.

KHRISTICH, DIMITRI, hockey player; b. Kiev, Ukraine, July 23, 1969; arrived in U.S., 1990; m. Erin Khristich. Left wing Washington Capitals, 1988—92, L.A. Kings, 1996—97, Boston Bruins, 1997—99, Toronto Maple Leafs, 1999—. Mem. NHL All-Star Game, 1997, U.S. Olympic Hockey Team, 1998. Avocation: golf. Office: Toronto Maple Leafs Air Canada Ctr 40 Bay St Ste 300 Toronto ON Canada M5J 2X2

KHRUSHCHEV, SERGEI NIKITICH, engineering educator, educator; b. Moscow, July 2, 1935; came to U.S., 1991; s. Nikita Sergeevich and Nina Petrovna K.; m. Galina Mikhailovna Shumova, June 1, 1957 (div. Jan. 1978); children: Nikita, Sergei, m. Valentina Nikolaevna Golenko, Oct. 15, 1985. MEE, Moscow Electric Power Inst., 1958; PhD, Min. Higher Specialized Edn., USSR, 1962; D of Tech. Scis., Coun. Ministers, USSR, 1988. From engr. to dep. sect. head Mashinostroenie, Moscow, 1958-68; from sect. head to dep. dir. Control Computer Inst., Moscow, 1968-87; 1st dep. gen. dir., v.p. rsch. Electronmash, Moscow, 1987-90; sr. vis. scholar ctr. fgn. policy devel. Thomas J. Watson Jr. Inst. for Internat. Studies, 1991-96, sr. fellow, 1996—. Lectr. in field. Columnist Asia, Inc., 1992-97; author: Khrushchev on Khrushchev, 1990, Nikita Khrushchev and the Creation of a Super Power, 2000; editor: Nikita Khrushchev Memoirs, 1970, 74, 90, 99; contbr. articles to profl. jours. Served with Russian mil. Harvard U. fellow, 1990; recipient Gold, Silver and Bronze medals Soviet Union Engring. Soc., 1971, 78, 80, 82, Lenin prize, 1960, prize Coun. Ministers, 1985. Mem. Russian Space Acad. (hon.), Internat. Acad. Informatization, Russian Soc. Informatics, Russian Engring. Soc., Acad. Vladimir Chelomey Scientists and Engring. Soc. Avocations: nature, collecting butterflies. Home: 3 Laurelhurst Rd Cranston RI 02920-8106 Office: Tomas J Watson Jr Inst for Internat Studies 111 Thayer St Providence RI 02912-9042 Fax: 401-863-7440.. E-mail: sergei_Khrushchev@brown.edu.

KHUBCHANDANI, INDRU TEKCHAND, colon and rectal surgeon; b. Karachi, India; s. Tekchand and Sarsati Khubchandani; m. Lynne Adderley, July 11, 1965; children: Joya, Mona, Sonya. MD, Grant Med. Coll., Bombay, India, 1956; postgrad., Royal Coll. of Surgeons, Eng., 1960; MS, Temple U., 1964. Diplomate Am. Bd. Colon and Rectal Surgeons. Fellowship. in gen. surg. New Eng. Hosp., Boston, 1961-62; res. Temple Univ. Med. Sch., Phila., 1962-64; chief divsn. colon and rectal surg. Healtheast Teaching Hosps., Allentown, PA, 1979-93; prog. dir. colon and rectal residency bd. dirs., 1983-93; prof. surgery Pa. State U., Hershey, 1995—, Hanneman U., Phila.; assoc. U. Pa. Bd. dirs. Healtheast, 1983—90, Slate Belt Med. Ctr. Mem. editl bd. Jour ColoProctology, 1980, Phila. Jour. Diseases of Colon and Rectum, 1980-96, Revista Brasileira de ColoProctologia, Italian Jour. of ColoProctology, 1997—. Pres. Harry E. Bacon Found., 1985; fund raiser Rep. Party. Recipient medal of honor, Assn. Latin Am. de Coloproctologia, Tchr. of Yr. award, Lehigh Valley Hosp., 2000, 2001, 2002. Fellow Royal Coll. Surgs. (Edinburgh); mem. Am. Soc. Colon and Rectal Surgs. (chmn. sci. and comml. exhibits 1979-94, Best Paper awds. 1970, 81, Rowell awd. 1985), Am. Gastroenterological Soc., Cuban Soc. Coloproctology (hon.), Assn. Surgeons India, Assn. Colon and Rectal Surgeons India (pres. 1990), Royal Soc. Med., N.E. Soc. Colon and Rectal Surgeons (pres. 1988), Pa. Soc. Colon and Rectal Surgeons (dir. gen. 1980—), Chilean Soc. Coloproctology (hon.), Venezuelan Soc. Colon and Rectal Surgeons (hon.), Sociedad Gallegade De Patologia Digestiva, La Coruna, Spain (hon.), Yugoslovia Soc. Coloproctology, Brazilian Soc. Colon and Rectal Surgeons (hon.), Assn. of Colon and Rectal Surgeons of India (hon.), Union League (Phila.), Hindu Club, Lehigh Country Club, Contemporary Club, Pa. Soc. Club, Rotary, Masons. Office: 1275 S Cedar Crest Blvd Allentown PA 18103-6207 E-mail: indruk@aol.com.

KHUONG, LOC HUU, corporate financial executive; arrived in U.S., 1975; s. Ba Huu and Le Ngoc Tran Khuong. BBA, Loyola U., Chgo., 1984; MBA, U. Phoenix, 1994; DBA, Nova Southeastern U., 2002. Pub. acct. Ernest Frieir & Assocs., CPA's, Chgo., 1980—82; internal auditor AB Dick Co., Chgo., 1983—84; audit mgr. Cenco, Inc., Oak Brook, Ill., 1984—86; v.p., fin. Indsl. Wastes/ChemLime, Elizabeth, NJ, 1986—89; v.p. fin. Chemstar Lime Corp., Phoenix, 1990—94; dir. bus. analysis Chem. Lime, Ft. Worth, 1995—98; asst. to the CEO Chem. Lime Inc., Ft. Worth, 1998—. Adj. prof. DeVry U., Irving, Tex., 1997—2001; cons. Irvine Biomed., Telcom Netriz, Calif., 1998—99; dir., cons. Chambers Interests, Tex., 2000. Mem.: Nat. Lime Assn., Acad. Mgmt., Am. Mgmt. Assn., Sigma Beta Delta Internat. Avocations: writing, golf, astronomy.

KHURANA, POONAM, neonatologist; d. Charanjit and Shanta Khurana; 1 child, Nishant Khurana Dhawan. MBBS, Govt. Med. Coll., Patiala, Punjab, India, 1978—82; Diploma in Child Health, Punjabi U., Patiala, Punjab, India, 1990—91. Diplomate Am. Bd. of Pediat., 1999. Fellowship in neonatal-perinatal medicine St. Christopher's Hosp. for Children, Phil., Pa., 1999—2002; clin. instr. of pediat. MCP Hahnemann U., Phil., Pa., 2000—02; neonatologist Robert Wood Johnson U Hosp., Hamilton, NJ, 2002—, CentraState Hosp., Freehold, NJ, 2002—, Lourdes Med. Ctr. of Burlington County, Willingboro, NJ, 2002—. Presenter in field. Contbr. articles to profl. jours. Finalist Thomas Boggs award, Pa. Med. Soc. Mem.: Am. Acad. of Pediat. Achievements include research in Hypoxic Brain injury in the Newborn Piglet and Guinea Pig models. Home: 150E Wynnewood Rd #28B Wynnewood PA 19096 Personal E-mail: poonam.khurana@drexel.edu.

KHURANA, RAMESH CHANDER, physician, nutritionist, educator; b. Bhalwal, Punjab, India, June 1, 1942; came to U.S., 1966; s. Ram L. and Sumitra B. Khurana; m. Saroj B. Khurana, Feb. 14, 1967; children: Anju, Ajay. MD, All India Inst. Med. Scis., New Delhi, 1964. Diplomate in internal medicine and endocrinology Am. Bd. Nutrition, Am. Bd. Physicians Nutrition Specialists. Chief of endocrinology St. Clair Hosp., Pitts., 1973-89; clin. asst. prof. medicine U. Pitts. Sch. Medicine, 1973—. Author: Diabetes Mellitus: Current Concepts, Diabetes: Answers to 100 Questions, You & Your Hormone Glands, Weight Control with Emotional Nourishment, Khurana Clinic Recipe Book, The Treatment of Premenstrual Tension Syndrome; contbr. more than 80 articles to profl. jours. Fellow ACP, Am. Coll. Endocrinology, Am. Coll. Nutrition; mem. AMA, Am. Diabetes Assn., Pa. Med. Soc. Avocations: golf, music. Office: Khurana Clinic 700 Washington Rd Pittsburgh PA 15228-2002

KHURANA, RAMESH KUMAR, neurologist; b. Amritsar, India, Jan. 7, 1946; MBBS, Med. Coll., 1968. Asst. prof. Johns Hopkins Sch. Medicine, Balt.; clin. assoc. prof. U. Md., Sch. Medicine, Balt.; chief divsn. neurology Union Meml. Hosp., Balt. Contbr. articles to profl. jours. Fellow Am. Acad. Neurology, Am. Headache Soc., Assn. Indian Neurologists Am. (pres. 1997-99). Office: 10780 Hickory Ridge Rd Columbia MD 21044

KHURI, FADLO RAJA, oncologist, educator; b. Boston, Sept. 13, 1963; s. Raja Najib and Soumaya Makdisi Khuri; m. Lamya Raja Tannous, June 15, 1991; children: Raja, Layla, Rayya. Student, Am. U. of Beirut, 1982; BS, Yale U., 1985; MD, Columbia U., 1989. Cert. bd. cert. diplomate. Intern in internal medicine Boston City Hosp., Boston U., 1989—90; resident Boston City Hosp., 1990—92; fellow in hematology and med. oncology Tufts-New Eng. Med. Ctr., Boston, 1992—95; instr. medicine U. Tex. M.D. Anderson Cancer Ctr., Houston, 1995—96, asst. prof., 1996—2001, assoc. prof., 2001—02; assoc. dir. clin. and translational rsch. Winship Cancer Inst., Emory U., Atlanta, 2002—; Blomeyer prof. hematology, oncology, medicine, pharmacology and otolaryngology. 1st author: clin. investigation Nature Medicine, 2000, Journal of the National Cancer Institute, 1997, Journal of Clinical Oncology, 2000. Recipient Cancer Devel. award, Am. Cancer Soc., 1996; scholar R.G. Haddad scholar, 1985—89; funding, NIH/Dept. of Def., 1996—. Mem.: Radiation Therapy Oncology Group (chmn. chemoprevention com. 1998—2002), Am. Soc. for Clin. Oncology, Am. Assn. for Cancer Rsch. Office: Emory U Winship Cancer Inst Hematology and Oncology Ste B4100 1365 Clifton Rd Atlanta GA 30322 Office Fax: 404-778-5016. E-mail: fadlo_khuri@emoryhealthcare.org.

KHURI, NICOLA NAJIB, physicist, educator; b. Beirut, May 27, 1933; came to U.S., 1959, naturalized, 1970; s. Najib N. and Odette (Joujou) K.; m. Elizabeth Anne Tyson, Dec. 9, 1955; children: Suzanne Odette, Najib Nicholas. B.A with high distinction, Am. U. Beirut, 1952; PhD, Princeton U., 1957. Asst. prof. Am. U. Beirut, 1957-58, 60-61, assoc. prof., 1961-62; mem. Inst. Advanced Study, Princeton U., 1959-60, 62-63; vis. assoc. prof. Columbia, 1963-64; assoc. prof. Rockefeller U., 1964-68, prof., 1968—. Cons. Brookhaven Nat. Lab., 1963-73; mem. Carnegie Panel on U.S. Security and Arms Control, 1981-83; vis. scientist European Ctr. for Nuclear Research, Geneva, Centre d'Etudes Nucléaires, Saclay, France, Max Planck Inst. für Physik, Munich, Fed. Republic Germany. Contbr. articles to profl. jours. Trustee Am. U. Beirut. Fellow Am. Phys. Soc.; mem. Council on Fgn. Relations. Clubs: Century (N.Y.C.). Office: Rockefeller U New York NY 10021 Home: # 6B 433 E 51st St New York NY 10022-6472

KHUSHF, GEORGE PETER, bioethicist; b. Flushing, N.Y., July 13, 1961; s. Mikhail Georges and Rosa Marie (Acksteiner) K.; m. Cheryl Renee Elam, May 31, 1986; children: Abigail Christine, Michael Joseph. BS summa cum laude, Tex. A&M Univ., 1983; MA, Rice Univ., 1990, PhD with distinction, 1993. Grad. teaching fellow Rice Univ., Houston, 1986-88; Fulbright fellow The Univ. Tubingen, Tubingen, Germany, 1988 89; rsch. assoc. Ctr. for Ethics, Medicine & Pub. Issues, Houston, 1989-93; mng. editor The Journal of Medicine & Phil., Houston, 1993-95; humanities dir. Ctr. for Bioethics, Univ. S.C., Columbia, 1995—; asst. prof. phil. Univ. S.C., Columbia, 1995—2001, assoc. prof. philosophy, 2001—. Asst. editor: Jour. Medicine & Phil., 1995—, Christian Bioethics, 1995—; editor section on orgnl. ethics HEC Forum; contbr. articles to profl. jours. Mem. ethics com. S.C. Medical Assn. Rockwell vis. scholar U. Houston, 1995. Mem. Am. Phil. Assn., Am. Soc. for Bioethics and Humanities, Am. Acad. Religion, Hegel Soc. Am., N.A. Kant Soc., Phi Kappa Phi, Tau Beta Phi, Phi Eta Sigma. Office: Univ S C Dept Phil & Ctr For Bioethics Columbia SC 29208-0001

KHUTORYANSKY, NAUM M. mathematician, educator; b. Kiev, Ukraine, Apr. 9, 1946; s. Mark Naumovich Khutoryansky and Genya Davidovna Tsipenyuk; m. Dina G. Baskin, July 19, 1968; 1 child, Natalie. BS, MS in applied math., Gorky State U., Nizhny Novgorod, Russia, 1964—70, PhD in applied math., 1971—74; DSc, Supreme Attestation Commn. of the USSR, Moscow, 1989—89. Jr. scientist Gorky State U., Nizhny Novgorod, Russia, 1975—76, sr. scientist, 1976—84, sci. dir., rsch. dept., 1984—93; rsch. assoc. prof. Drexel U., Phila., 1994—2000; sr. statistician Novo Nordisk Pharmaceuticals, Inc., Princeton, NJ, 2000—01, prin. statistician, 2001—. Adj. prof. Gorky State U., Nizhny Novgorod, Russia, 1976—92; vis. scientist Linkoping U., Sweden, 1991; adj. assoc. prof. Drexel U., Phila., 1995—2000. Author: (book) Boundary Element Method in Solid Mechanics. Recipient Silver Medal, Exhbn. of Nation's Achievements of the USSR, 1989; grantee, Russian Found. for Basic Rsch., 1992. Mem.: Soc. of Indsl. and Applied Math., Am. Statis. Assn. Achievements include research in new representation formulas and fundamental solutions of piezoelectricity and viscoelasticity; development of new approaches in boundary integral equations of solid and fluid mechanics; nw statistical imputation methods for incomplete longitudinal datan; research in fracture mechanics for piezoelectric bodies. Office: Novo Nordisk Pharmaceuticals Inc 100 College West Rd Princeton NJ 08540 E-mail: nakh@nnpi.com.

KIAMIE, DON ALBERT NAJEEB, accountant; b. Bronx, N.Y., Jan. 23, 1944; s. Samie and Carmen (Torres) K.; m. Olive F. Howell, Sept. 9, 1972; children: Matthew, Marie, Melinda. BS, Fordham U., 1965; MBA, NYU, 1967. CPA, N.Y. Sr. acct. Peat, Marwick, Mitchell & Co., N.Y.C., 1967-70; asst. mgr. stds. acctg. Gen. Foods Corp., N.Y.C., 1970-77; mgr. fin. reporting/planning Qwip Sys. divsn. Exxon Corp., N.Y.C., 1977-79; asst. controller NBC, N.Y.C., 1980-83; exec. v.p., CFO Windsor Mgmt. Corp. and Kiamie Related Properties, 1983—; also bd. dirs.; prof. NYU Grad. Sch., 1998—. Adj. prof. NYU Grad. Sch. Cont. Profl. Studies. Mgr. Lions Babe Ruth Club, 1967-71; soccer and baseball coach Shrub Oak Athletic Club, 1983-87; pres. Pelham Babe RuthLeague,d 1970-71, Pelham Young Rep. Club, 1970-71, v.p. Holy Spirit Parish Coun., 1977-78, chmn. teen group, 1977-78, chmn. fin. com., 1977-78; eucharistic min., dir. youth music group Holy Roary Ch., 1988—; soccer coach AYSO, 1988—; leader GOP 35th Dist. Town of Mt. Pleasant, N.Y., 1991—. Mem. AICPA, N.Y. Soc. CPAs (real estate com. chair 2001—, dir., officer, com. chair Westchester chpt. 1998—). Roman Catholic. Home: 21 Main St Hawthorne NY 10532-2017 E-mail: donalbert@mindspring.com.

KIANG, ASSUMPTA (AMY KIANG), brokerage house executive; b. Beijing, Aug. 15, 1939; came to U.S., 1962; d. Pei-yu and Yu-Jean (Liu) Chao; m. Wan-lin Kiang, Aug. 14, 1965; 1 child, Eliot Y. BA, Nat. Taiwan U., 1960; MS, Marywood Coll., Scranton, Pa., 1964; MBA, Calif. State U., Long Beach, 1977. Cert. fin. mgr. Data programmer IBM World Trade, N.Y.C., 1963; libr. East Cleve. Pub. Libr., 1964-68; lectr. Nat. Taiwan U., Taipei, 1971-73; reference libr. U.S. Info. Svc., Taipei, 1971-74; v.p., sr. fin. advisor Merrill Lynch, Santa Ana, Calif., 1977—, v.p., sr. fin. cons. Costa Mesa, Calif., 1996—. Author numerous rsch. reports in field. Founder Pan Pacific Performing Arts Inc., Orange County, Calif., 1987; pres. women league Calif. State. U., Long Beach, 1980-82. Mem. AAUW (treas. Newport-Costa Mesa br. 1996—), Chinese Bus. Assn. Soc. Calif. (chmn. 1987—, v.p. 1986-87), Chinese Am. Profl. Women's League (treas. 1993, pres. 1997—), Pacific Rim Investment and trade Assn. (vice-chair 1994-96), U.C.I. Chancellor's Club, Old Ranch Country Club, Ctr. Club (bd. dirs. exec. women's coun. Orange County 1998—). Democrat. Roman Catholic. Office: Merrill Lynch 650 Town Center Dr Ste 500 Costa Mesa CA 92626-1905 E-mail: AKiang@pclient.ml.com.

KIANG, BARBARA NORRIS, scientific research assistant; b. Tacoma, Wash., Apr. 21, 1942; d. William Foster Norris and Sarah Louise (Ryder) Craig; m. Nelson Yuan-Sheng Kiang, Dec. 18, 1976. BA, Carleton Coll., 1963; MA, Mount Holyoke Coll., 1965. Rsch. asst. Eaton Peabody Lab., Boston, 1965-80; sr. rsch. asst. Mass. Eye & Ear Infirmary, Boston, 1980-90, lab. mgr., 1990-95, part-time rsch. asst., 1996—, MIT, Cambridge, 1995-96, Mass. Gen. Hosp., Boston, 1996—, Mass. Eye & Ear Infirmary, Boston, 1997—. Contbr. articles to profl. jours. E-mail: bnk@epl.meei.harvard.edu.

KIANG, WALTER T. environmentalist, state official; b. Suzhou, Jiangsu, China, Jan. 6, 1934; came to U.S., 1963; s. Chester T. and Maria (Chen) K.; m. Sunny Sun, Sept. 6, 1964. BL, Nat. Taiwan U., Taipei, 1956, MA, 1959; M URPL, Va. Tech. U., 1966; MS, U. Pa., 1971; MPA, SUNY, Albany, 1977. Instr. Nat. Taiwan U. Coll. Law, 1962—63; sect. chief W.Va. Dept. Commerce, Charlestwon, 1966-68; outdoor recreation planner U.S. Dept. Interior, Washington, 1976-77; assoc. planner Office of Planning Coordination and Office of Parks Recreation and Historic Preservation State of N.Y., Albany, 1968-75, project rev. coord. Office f Parks Recreation and Historic Preservation, 1977-88, enciron. coord. Office of Alcoholism and Substance Abuse Svcs., 1988—2002. Hon. prof. Soochow U., Suzhou, Jiangsu, 1996—. Former exec. sec. Nat. Assn. Youth Orgns., Taipei; leading mem. steering com. Citizens for County Exec., Albany, 1972; pres. Chinese Cmty. Ctr., Albany, 1980, Chinese Am. Alliance, Albany, 1988, Cheng-Hua Edn. Found., Inc. USA, 2000—. Named hon. pres. Quanghan (Sl'Chan, China) 2d H.S., 2000; scholar Govt. of Taiwan, 1956-59. Mem. ASAP, Am. Inst. Cert. Planners (life), Internat. Assn. Conflict Mgmt., Phi Tau Phi. Republican. Avocations: bridge, tennis. Home: 38 Briarwood Rd Albany NY 12211

KIBBE, JAMES WILLIAM, real estate broker; b. Bound Brook, N.J., Oct. 5, 1926; s. Orlando A. and Anna Rose (Tomb) K.; m. Bettie Brooks Dailey, June 11, 1949; children: James William Jr., Linda Jean. BS, U. Md., 1951. Salesman real estate Eig & Mc Keever, Silver Spring, Md., 1955-57, Weaver Bros., Inc., Chevy Chase, Md., 1957-70, asst. v.p. sales, leasing dept., 1970-72, mgr. sales, 1972-89, v.p., 1973-82, sr. v.p., 1983-89; sr. v.p., dir. sales The Michael Co., Lanham, Md., 1989-95; sr. v.p., dir. indsl. Barrueta, Washington, 1995-96; sr. v.p. Carey Winston/Barrueta, Bethesda, Md., 1996-98, Transwestern Carey Winston, Bethesda, 1998—. Lectr. in field; chmn. Brokers and Salesmen's council, 1968-69. With USNR, 1944-46. Mem. Soc. Indsl. Office Realtors (pres. Md. and Washington chpt. 1985-86, nat. bd. dirs. 1988-90), Nat. Assn. Indsl. Office Pks. (bd. dirs. 1987), Nat. Inst. Real Estate Brokers (state chmn. 1968-70), Nat. Assn. Realtors, New Am. Network (adv. bd. dirs. 1986-99, chmn. adv. bd. 1991-93), Md. Assn. Realtors, Washington Bd. Trade, Washington Builders Assn., D.C. Assn. Realtors, Montgomery County Bd. Realtors, Lions (started health fairs chmn. 25 yrs.). Republican. Methodist. Home: 1000 Ashland Dr Ashton MD 20861-9718 Office: Transwestern Carey Winston Ste 400A 7600 Rockledge Dr Bethesda MD 20817

KIBBEY, HAL STEPHEN, science writer; b. West Point, N.Y., Oct. 29, 1943; s. Donald Eugene and Mary Elizabeth (Lichliter) K.; m. Martha Ann Harsanyi, Dec. 12, 1970; children: Carolyn Ann, Laura Ann. BA, Cornell U., 1965; MA, Ind. U., 1969. Rsch. asst., rsch. assoc. Ind. U., Bloomington, 1970-75, publ. editor, 1975-79, sci. writer, 1979—. Free lance writer and editor, Bloomington, 1985—. Editor: Science Development: The Building of Science in Less Developed Countries, 1975. Pres. Rogers-Binford Elem. Sch. PTO, 1991-93; bd. dirs. Monroe County Civic Theater, 1995-96. Mem. ACLU, Nat. Assn. Sci. Writers, U.S. Chess Fedn. (life). Democrat. Methodist. Avocations: chess, singing, acting, writing and directing plays. Home: 1109 E Hunter Ave Bloomington IN 47401-5035 Office: Ind U Office Comm & Mktg 530 E Kirkwood Ave Bloomington IN 47408-4062 E-mail: hkibbey@indiana.edu.

KIBEL, HOWARD DAVID, psychiatrist; b. N.Y.C., May 6, 1937; s. Israel and Celia (Weinman) K.; m. Renee Marilyn Chernoble, Dec. 24, 1960; children: Darrin Scott, Gary Alan, Seth Martin. BA, Columbia U., 1958; MD, SUNY, Bklyn., 1962. Diplomate Am. Bd. Psychiatry and Neurology. Intern So. Pacific Gen. Hosp., San Francisco, 1962-63; resident in psychiatry Menninger Sch. Psychiatry, Topeka, 1963-66; pvt. practice Mt. Kisco, N.Y., 1967-78; dir. group psychotherapy West County Med. Ctr., Valhalla, N.Y., 1972-76; assoc. dir. psychiatry No. Westchester Hosp., Mt. Kisco, N.Y., 1976-78; coord. group psychotherapy N.Y. Hosp.-Cornell Med. Ctr., White Plains, N.Y., 1978-94; assoc. prof. clin. psychiatry Cornell U. Med. Coll., White Plains, N.Y., 1984-94; prof. psychiatry N.Y. Med. Coll., Valhalla, 1994—98, clin. prof. psychiatry, 1998—; dir. group therapy Westchester County Med. Ctr., Psychiat. Inst., Valhalla, 1994—99. Adj. clin. prof. psychiatry Weil Med. Coll., Cornell U. Contbr. chpts. to books, articles to profl. jours.; editor: The Difficult Patient in Group, 1990. Vice pres. Physicians for Automotive Safety, N.Y., Conn., 1977-88. Fellow Am. Psychiatric Assn. (disting. life fellow), Am. Group Psychotherapy Assn. (disting. fellow, program chmn. 1974-78, pres. 1986-88), Internat. Assn. Group Psychotherapy (bd. mem. 1998-2003, co-chmn. sci. program com., sec. 2003—). Democrat. Jewish. Office: 503 Grasslands Rd Ste 104 Valhalla NY 10595-1503

KIBLER, WILLIAM WESTCOTT, French language and literature educator; b. Rochester, N.Y., Jan. 22, 1942; s. Charles L. and Ruth Isabel (Westcott) K.; m. Nancy Irene Schwan, June 29, 1968; children: Mary Alis, Charlotte. AB, Notre Dame U., 1963; MA, U. N.C., 1966, PhD, 1968. Asst. prof. French U. Ark., Fayetteville, 1967-69, U. Tex., Austin, 1969-73, assoc. prof., 1973-81, prof., 1981-83, Superior Oil-Linward Shivers Centennial prof. medieval studies, 1983—. Author: An Introduction to Old French, 1984; author, editor: Chrétien de Troyes' Lancelot, 1981, Chrétien de Troyes' Yvain, 1985; co-author: Lion de Bourges, 1980, Guillaume de Machaut, Judgement du roy de Behaigne and Remede de Fortune, 1988; editor: Eleanor of Aquitaine: Patron and Politician, 1976. Mem. South Cen. MLA (pres. 1986-87), Medieval Acad. Am. (councillor 1993-96), Société Rencesvals (pres. 1978-82, editor-in-chief Am.-Can. br. jour. Olifant 1986-91). Episcopalian. Avocations: squash, philately, gardening. Office: The Univ of Tex at Austin Dept of French & Italian Austin TX 78712

KIBRICK, ANNE, retired nursing educator and university dean; b. Palmer, Mass., June 1, 1919; d. Martin and Christine (Grigas) Karlon; m. Sidney Kibrick, June 16, 1949; children: Joan, John. RN, Worcester (Mass.) Hahnemann Hosp., 1941; BS, Boston U., 1945; MA, Columbia Tchrs. Coll., 1948; EdD, Harvard U., 1958; LHD (hon.), St. Joseph's Coll., Windham, Maine, 1973. Asst. edn. dir. Cushing VA Hosp., Framingham, Mass., 1948—49; asst. prof. nursing Simmons Coll., Boston, 1949—55; dir. grad. div. Boston U. Sch. Nursing, 1958—63, dean, 1963—68, prof., 1968—70; chmn. dept. nursing Boston Coll. Grad. Sch. Arts and Sci., 1970—74; founding chmn. Sch. Nursing Boston State Coll., 1974—82; founding dean Sch. Nursing U. Mass., Boston, 1974—88, prof., 1988—93, prof. emeritus, 1993—. Mem. editl. bd. Mass. Jour. Cmty. Health. Mem. Brookline Town Meeting, 1995—2000; mem. nat. adv. bd. Hadassah Nurses Coun., 1996—; bd. dirs. Brookline Mental Health Assn., Met. chpt. ARC, Children's Ctr. Brookline and Greater Boston, Inc., 1984—89, Boston Health Care for Homeless, 1988—90, Landy-Kaplan Nurses Coun., 1992—, treas., 1994—96. Named to, Nursing Edn. Alumni Assn. Tchr.'s Coll., Columbia U. Hall of Fame, 1999. Fellow: Am. Acad. Nursing; mem.: Inst. of Medicine of NAS, Mass. Blueprint 2000, Mass. Orgn. Elder Ams. (bd. dirs. 1988—2000), Mass. Med. Soc. (postgrad. med. inst. 1983—96, bd. dirs. 1983—96, exec. com. 1989—96), Nat. Acads. of Practice, Mass. Nurses Found. (v.p. 1983—86), AIDS Internat. Info. Found. (founding mem. 1985), Mass. Nurses Assn. (dir. 1982—86, charter inductee to Hall of Fame 2000), Nat. Mass. League Nursing (pres. 1971—73), ANA, Pi Lambda Theta, Sigma Theta Tau. Home: # 312 130 Seminary Ave Auburndale MA 02466

KICE, JOHN EDWARD, engineer, consultant, engineer, educator; b. Wichita, Kans., Sept. 11, 1949; s. Jack and Ruth (Jones) Kice; m. Susan Pappas; children: Adam, Jason. BS in Flour Milling Sci. and Bus. Adminstrn., Kans. State U., 1972; BS in Engring., Wichita State U., 1980; grad. diploma, Glasgow Caladonian U., 2000. Registered profl. engr., Kans. Design engr. Kice Industries, Wichita, 1973-84, v.p. engring., 1984—2003; lectr. Kans. State U., 2003—. Lectr. Wichita State U., 1980-86. Recipient Disting. Svc. award Assn. Operative Millers, 1988, 90, 92, 94, 96. Achievements include patents for Positive Displacement Air Pump, Reciprocating Airlock Valve, Rotary Mixing Damper, Blade Type Mixing Damper, Conveying Air Velocity Control, Pneumatic Conveying Injector, Machinery Access. Office: Kice Industries Inc 5500 Mill Heights Dr Wichita KS 67219

KICH, ROLF, communications scientist, consultant; b. Panambi, Rio Grande do Sul, Brazil, Sept. 25, 1956; s. Elio and Margarethe K.; m. Catherine Nguyen, May 3, 2003. BSEE, Calif. State U., Fresno, 1981. Sr. scientist (level 7) Boeing Satellite Systems, El Segundo, Calif., 1999—; sr. scientist (level 6) Hughes Space Comm., El Segundo, Calif., 1994—99, scientist, 1989—94, sr. tech. staff, 1987—89; supr. Hughes Aircraft, Space and Comm., El Segundo, Calif., 1984—87. Cons. microwave component design Kich Industries, Redondo Beach, Calif., 2002—. Scoutmaster Boy Scouts Am., Clovis, Calif., 1978—79, leader Irvine, Calif., 2001—03. Republican. Achievements include patents for communication satellite aluminum high power filter, one of the enabling technologies used on Direct TV home broadcast satellite transmission; 22 issued patents in the microwave component field; patents pending for electronically switchable ferrite power divider. Avocations: photography, hiking, backpacking, woodworking. Home: 1624 Harper Ave Redondo Beach CA 90278 Personal E-mail: rolf@kichindustries.com.

KICKERT, JULIANA ARLENE, investor; b. Blue Island, Ill., Sept. 1, 1943; d. Robert J. and Delia (Vander Giessen) K.; m. Durwood Perry Long, July 14, 1973 (div. Oct. 1974). AA, U. Fla., 1963, BS, 1965; MS, Ind. U., 1971. Registered real estate sales, Ill., Chgo. Instr. Chgo. Bd. Edn., 1965-71; dir. legal office program Sauk Area Career Ctr., Crestwood, Ill., 1973-76; real estate sales Kahn Kaplan Realty, Inc., Chgo., 1977-86; pvt. investor Sedona, Ariz. Apptd. Yavapai County Mounted Posse Search and Rescue Team, 1994—. Recipient Life Time Coop. Sales award North Side Real Estate Bd., Chgo., 1984, Top 20 Residential Salesperson award Condex Info. Svcs., 1984, 86; named Ariz. Horsewoman of Yr. Bridle & Bit Newspaper, 1990. Mem. Verde Valley Horsemen's Coun., Sedona Saddle Club (founding mem., pres. 1990-92, bd. dirs. 1993-94), Mensa, Delta Pi Epsilon. Republican. Avocations: international travel, skiing, sailing, horseback riding, photography. Home and Office: PO Box 459 Placerville CO 81430-0459

KICKISH, MARGARET ELIZABETH, elementary school educator; b. Atlantic City, N.J., Nov. 30, 1949; d. James Bernard and Margaret Elizabeth (Egan) Parlett; m. Robert Anthony Kickish, June 30, 1973; children: Eileen, Kathleen, Robert Jr. BS, Franciscan U., 1971; MEd, Coll. N.J., 1977. Cert. elem. tchr., learning disabilities tchr. cons. Tchr. Our Lady Star of the Sea Sch., Atlantic City, 1971-75, Weymouth Twp. Elem. Sch., Dorothy, NJ, 1975-89; curriculum coord. Port Republic (N.J.) Sch., 1990-91; tchr. Brigantine (N.J.) Bd. Edn., 1991-94, supr. curriculum and instrn., 1995—. Cognetics coach St. Joseph Sch., Somers Point, NJ, 1989—. Treas. PTA, Somers Point, 1987—89, pres., 1989—90; asst. coach Somers Point Softball Assn., 1991—; rec. sec. Parents Orgn. Mainland Regional HS, 2001—; mem. choir St. Joseph Ch., Somers Point, 1985—. Mem.: ASCD, NEA, AAUW, Assn. Learning Cons., Coun. Exceptional Children, Prins. and Suprs. Assn., N.J. Edn. Assn., S. Jersey Irish Cultural Soc., Seashore Mother of Twins Club, Phi Delta Kappa, Delta Zeta, Kappa Delta Pi. Democrat. Roman Catholic. Avocations: swimming, bicycling, reading, travel, crafts. Home: 526 9th St Somers Point NJ 08244-1458 Office: Brigantine Bd of Edn 301 E Evans Blvd Brigantine NJ 08203-3424 E-mail: mskick@aol.com.

KICKLIGHTER, CLAUDE MILTON, federal agency administrator, retired army officer; b. Glennville, Ga., Aug. 22, 1933; s. Claude Wilton and Ruby Dell (Drake) K.; m. Elizabeth Exley, Apr. 24, 1954; children: Elizabeth Jane, Claude M., Richard Van. AB, Mercer U.; MA, George Washington U.; grad. Nat. and Internat. Security Program, Harvard U., 1981, grad. Sr. Mgrs. in Govt. Program, 1982. Commd. officer U.S. Army, 1955, advanced through grades to lt. gen.; staff Dept. Army, 1968-70; with 101st Airborne Div., Vietnam, 1970-71; comdr. 1st Bn. 21st Field Arty., Ft. Carson, Colo., 1972-73; staff Office Joint Chief of Staff, 1974-75, Office Def. Rep-Iran, Teheran, 1975-76; comdr. 24th Inf. Div. Arty., Ft. Stewart, Ga., 1977-78; asst. div. comdr., 1978-79; asst. chief staff logistics Allied Forces Central Europe, The Netherlands, 1979-81; comdg. gen. Security Assistance Center, Alexandria, Va., 1981-83; chief of staff U.S. Army Materiel Devel. and Readiness Command, Alexandria, 1983-84; comdg. gen. 25th Inf. Div., Schofield Barracks, Hawaii, 1984-86; asst. dep. chief of staff of logistics Washington, 1986-87; dir. of army staff Office of Chief of Staff, Washington, 1987-89; comdg. gen. U.S. Army Western Command, Ft. Shafter, Hawaii, 1989-90; comdr. U.S. Army Pacific, Hawaii, 1989—91; dep. under sec. of army int. affairs U.S. Army, 1995—99; asst. sec. for policy and planning U.S Dept. Veterans Affairs, Washington, 2001—03, asst. sec. for policy, planning and preparedness, 2003—. Contbr. article to mil. jours. Decorated D.S.C. with bronze oak leaf cluster, Def. Superior Svc. medal, Legion of Merit with three bronze oak leaf clusters, Bronze Star, Meritorious Svc. medal with bronze oak leaf cluster, Air medal with bronze oak leaf cluster, Army Comendation medal with four bronze oak leaf clusters, Argentina Order of May, others. Episcopalian. Office: US Dept Veterans Affairs Policy Planning and Preparedness 810 Vermont Ave NW Washington DC 20420 Office Fax: 202-273-5993.

KICZA, MARY E. federal agency administrator; Lead sys. engr. Centaur Engring. Support Group Kennedy Space Ctr., Fla., 1982; assoc. ctr. dir. space sci. programs Goddard Space Flight Ctr., Greenbelt, Md., assoc. ctr. dir.; dep. divsn. dir. Office of Space Sci. Solar Sys. Exploration Divsn., program mgr. Discovery program NASA, Washington, 1992—94, asst. assoc. adminstr. tech. Office Space Sci., 1994—96, assoc. adminstr. biol. and phys. rsch., 2002—. Office: NASA Mail Code U 300 E St SW Washington DC 20546

KIDD, DEBRA JEAN, communications executive; b. Chgo., May 13, 1956; d. Fred A. and Jean (Pezzopane) Winchar: m. Kim Joseph Kidd, July 22, 1978; children: Jennifer Marie, Michele Jean. AA in Bus. with high honors, Wright Jr. Coll., 1977. Legal sec. Sidley & Austin, Chgo., 1977-80; investment adminstr. Golder, Thoma & Co., Chgo., 1980-81, exec. asst., 1981-84; sales rep. Dataspeed, Inc., Chgo., 1984, midwestern regional mgr., 1985; comm. cons. Chgo. Comm., Inc., Chgo., 1986-88; owner, founder Captain Kidd's Video, Niles, 1981-84. Editor: Lion's Roar, 1993-95. Vol. Am. Lung Assn., Chgo., 1979; vol. tchr. religious edn. Our Lady Mother of Ch., Norridge, Ill., 1981-83, St. Raymonds, Mt. Prospect, 1993-94, 2000—; vol. Parents Who Care, 1988-94, pres., 1991-93; vol. PTA Lion's Park Sch., 1993-95, bd. dirs., 1993-94; founder Young Journalist Club, 1994-95; leader Girl Scouts, 1992—, cons., 1994—, del., 1995—, registrar, 1996-97, organizer, 1996—, svc. unit mgr., 2000—; referee assignor Green White Soccer, 2001--; vol. Hearts Across Am., 2001--. Mem. NAFE, Nat. Assn. Bus. Women, Nat. Assn. Profl. Saleswomen, Phi Theta Kappa. Roman Catholic. Avocations: camping, skiing, snorkeling, sailing, reading. E-mail: dkidd739@aol.com.

KIDD, JAMES MARION, III, allergist, immunologist, naturalist, educator; b. Baton Rouge, Dec. 15, 1950; s. James Marion Jr. and Germaine Elizabeth (Hunt) K.; children: Mackenzie Elizabeth, Katherine Anne. MD, La. State U., 1976. Diplomate Am. Bd. Internal Medicine, Am. Bd. Allergy and Immunology; lic. physician, La., Fla., Wis. Resident physician La. State U. Sch. Medicine, New Orleans, 1977—79; rsch. fellow Med. Coll. Wis., Milw., 1980-82; pvt. practice in allergy and immunology Allergy, Asthma, and Immunology Clinic, Baton Rouge, 1982—; clin. asst., prof. medicine La. Sch. Medicine, New Orleans, 1982—; clin. asst., prof. community medicine and pub. health Tulane U. Sch. Medicine, New Orleans, 1992—2003. Dir. Baton Rouge Pollen Counting Sta., Nat. Allergy Bur. Fellow Am. Coll. Physicians, Am. Acad. Pediat., Am. Acad. Allergy and Immunology, Royal Soc. of Medicine (U.K.), La. Allergy Soc. (pres. 1989-90, exec. sec.-treas. 1992-96), Baton Rouge Allergy Soc. (pres. 1990-95), Rotary (Paul Harris fellow). Office: James M Kidd III MD 8017 Picardy Ave Baton Rouge LA 70809-3538 Fax: 225-768-7642. E-mail: drjmkidd3@aol.com.

KIDD, JASON, professional basketball player; b. San Francisco, Mar. 23, 1973; Guard Dallas Mavericks, 1994—96, Phoenix Suns, 1996—2001; player NJ Nets, 2002—. Active West Dallas Cmty. Ch.; founder Jason Kidd Found., Jason Kidd Basketball Scholarship Fund. Named Pac-10 Player of Yr., 1993—94, Nat. Freshman of Yr., The Sporting News and USA Today, 1993—94, Schick Rookie of the Yr. (with Grant Hill), 1994—95. Achievements include being tied for fourth on all-time NBA rookie impact list, 1994-95. Avocations: R&B music, movies, baseball. Office: New Jersey Nets 390 Murray Hill Parkway East Rutherford NJ 07073

KIDD, JOHN EDWARD, lawyer, corporate executive; b. Jan. 17, 1936; s. Edward F. and Mary (Feczko) K.; m. Elaine Mitchell, Feb. 23, 1963; children: John Mitchell, David Alan, Cynthia Lorraine. BS in Physics, LeMoyne Coll., 1957; LLB, Georgetown U., 1961. Bar: Va. 1961, U.S. Supreme Ct. 1966, U.S. Tax Ct. 1966, N.Y. 1968, U.S. Ct. Appeals (2d cir.) 1968, U.S. Ct. Appeals (4th cir.) 1968, U.S. Dist. Ct. (so. and ea. dists.) N.Y. 1969, U.S. Dist. Ct. (no. dist.) Calif. 1980, U.S. Ct. Appeals (3d, 5th, 9th, and 11th cirs.) 1981, U.S. Dist. Ct. (ea. dist.), Va. 1993. Patent examiner U.S. Patent Office, Washington, 1957-60; patent advisor USN, Washington, 1960-62; trial atty. Dept. Justice, Washington, 1963-67; counsel to Copyright Office, Washington, 1966-67; spl. counsel Dept. Justice, 1967; assoc. Kenyon & Kenyon, N.Y.C., 1967-70; assoc., ptnr. Pennie & Edmonds, N.Y.C., 1971-85; mng. ptnr. intellectual property group Anderson, Kill, Olick & Oshinsky, P.C., 1986-91; mng. ptnr. group and exec. com. Shea & Gould, 1991-94; ptnr. Rogers & Wells, 1994—2000, exec. com., mng. ptnr. intellectual property and tech. group, 1994—2000; counsel Baseball Hall of Fame, 1995-2001; sr. ptnr., global leader intellectual property Clifford, Chance, Rogers & Wells, 2000—; patent examiner U.S. Patent Office, Washington, 1957-60; sr. ptnr. Clifford Chance US, LLP, 2002—. Referee 9th Jud. Dept. N.Y. Supreme Ct., 1968-69; exec., chmn. bd. E.M. Kidd, Ltd.; chmn. Symposium on Presdl. Patent Reform Commn., 1966; lectr., mem. faculty Practicing Law Inst., 1967, 84-96, 99-2003; mem. Bicentennial Commn. U.S. Claims Ct., 1987-89; guest lectr. Inventor Hall of Fame, 1996-2000; patent litigation lectr. Practicing Law Inst., 2001, Am. Intellectual Property Law Assn., 2001. Contbr. over 40 articles to profl. jours. Active United Fund of Westchester, Comty. Fund of Bronxville, Westchester coun. Boy Scouts Am.; trustee LeMoyne Coll. Alumni. Mem. ABA (lectr. 1984-94), ATLA, Am. Intellectual Property Assn., U.S. Trademark Assn., Copyright Soc. Am., N.Y. State Bar Assn. (chmn. spl. com. on patents and trademarks 1982-86), Fed. Cir. Bar Assn., N.Y. Intellectual Property Assn. (bd. dirs. 1998-91, chmn. arbitration com., 1999-2002), Licensing Exec. Soc. (co-chmn. N.Y.C. sect. 2002-03), Assn. of Bar of City of N.Y., The Law Soc., London, Eng., The Oaks Country Club (Sarasota, Fla.), Yale Club, Sky Club, Rockefeller Club, Delta Theta Phi. Office: Clifford Chance US LLP 200 Park Ave New York NY 10166-0899 Home (Winter): 538 Dove Pointe, The Oaks Osprey FL 34229 E-mail: john.kidd@cliffordchance.com.

KIDD, ROBERT HUGH, financial executive, accountant; b. Toronto, Ont., Can., June 1, 1944; B in Commerce, U. Toronto, 1966; MBA, York U., Toronto, 1972. Chartered acct. Acct. KPMG, Toronto, 1966-72, ptnr., 1973-81; CFO, sr. v.p. George Weston Ltd., Toronto, 1981-95; chmn. Canadian Ranpart Oil & Gas Ltd., Calgary, Alberta, 1981-86; pres. Location Rsch. Co. Can. Ltd., Mississauga, Ont., 1982; CFO InContext Syss. Inc., 1995-96, Lions Gate Entertainment Corp., 1997-98, Tech. Convergence, 2000—01. Bd. dirs. Genesis Microchip, Inc., Canclean Svcs. Ltd., Hostopia.com Inc., Macgregor Meat and Seafood, Inc. Author: Earnings Forecast, 1976; co-author: Terminology for Accountants, 1976. Vice chmn. Appleby Coll. Found. Recipient Victoria Coll. Gold medal U. Toronto, 1966, Gov. Gen.'s Gold medal Can. Inst. Chartered Accts., 1968. Fellow Inst. Chartered Accts. Ont. Avocations: skiing, swimming, boating, golf. E-mail: bobkidd2@earthlink.net.

KIDDER, C. ROBERT, food products executive; b. 1943; BSIE, U. Mich., 1966; MS, Iowa State U., 1968. With Ford Motor Co., Detroit, 1968-69, McKinsey & Co., N.Y.C., 1972-78, Dart Industries, 1978-80, Duracell Europe, 1980-81, Duracell Internat. Inc., 1981-95, pres., CEO, 1988-95, past chmn., CEO; chmn., CEO Borden, Inc., Columbus, Ohio, 1995—. Bd. trustees Ohio U., 2003—. With USN, 1969—72. Office: Borden Inc 180 E Broad St Columbus OH 43215-0003

KIDDER, CRAIG STEPHEN, artist, digital photographer; b. Riverside, Calif., Aug. 9, 1963; s. Charles Edward and Donna Faye Kidder; life ptnr. Richard Carrasco Valle. Owner csk Designs & Visuals, Belmont Shore/Long Beach, Calif., 1985—; designer/creative cons. Tustin Florist, Tustin, Calif., 1991—98. Floral deisgn, Spring, 1990 (FTD Area 10A/B 2nd Pl., 1990). Personal E-mail: C.Kidder@verizon.net. Business E-Mail: CSKDesign@yahoo.com.

KIDDER, FRED DOCKSTATER, lawyer; b. Cleve., May 22, 1922; s. Howard Lorin and Virgina (Milligan) K.; m. Eleanor (Hap) Kidder; children—Fred D. III, Barbara Anne Donelson, Jeanne Louise Haffeman. BS with distinction, U. Akron, 1948; JD, Case Western Res. U., 1950. Bar: Ohio 1950, Tex. 1985, U.S. Dist. Ct. (no. dist.) Ohio 1950, U.S. Dist. Ct. (no. dist.) Tex. 1985. Assoc. Arter & Hadden and predecessors, Cleve., 1950-79, ptnr., 1960-79, Jones, Day, Reavis and Pogue, Cleve., 1980-89, regional mng. ptnr. Tex., 1985-86; gen. counsel Lubrizol Corp., Cleve., 1989-92, spl. counsel, 1993—. Contbr. articles to profl. jours. Mem. Cleve. Growth Assn., Shaker Heights Citizens Com., Citizens League Cleve.; former pres. Estate Planning Coun.; former co-chmn. bd. trustees Lake Erie Coll.; former bd. trustees, v.p., Alzheimer's Assn., Cleve.; mem., bd. trustees Cleve. Sight Ctr.; past mem. alumni coun. U. Akron; past. corp. coun. Dallas Mus. Art; past pres. Case Western Reserve U. Law Sch. Alumni Assn.; past chmn. Shaker Heights Recreation Bd. Mem. ABA, Am. Soc. Corp. Secs., Tex. Bar Assn., Ohio State Bar Assn., Estate Planning Coun. (past pres.), Blue Coats, Soc. Benchers (past chmn.), Union Club, Pepper Pike Club (past sec.), The Country Club, Cleve. Skating Club, Order of Coif, Ct. of Nisi Prius (former judge), Phi Eta Sigma, Beta Delta Psi, Phi Sigma Alpha, Phi Delta Theta, Phi Delta Phi. Office: The Lubrizol Corp 29400 Lakeland Blvd Wickliffe OH 44092-2298

KIDDER, GEORGE HOWELL, lawyer; b. Boston, June 14, 1925; s. Henry Purkitt and Julia Edwards (Howell) K.; m. Ellen Windom Warren, Aug. 17, 1946 (dec. May 1956); children: Susan Warren, George Howell, Stephen Wells; m. Priscilla Peele Hunnewell, Sept. 3, 1958 (dec. Nov. 1993); children: Priscilla Hunnewell, Timothy Hurd, Peter Arnold; m. Nancy D. Kidder, June 3, 1995. Grad., St. Mark's Sch., Southborough, Mass., 1943; student Navy V-12 program, Williams Coll., 1943-44; B in Naval Sci., Tufts Coll., 1945; LLB, Harvard, 1950; DD (hon.), Episcopal Div. Sch., 1987. Bar: Mass. 1951. With Office Gen. Counsel CIA, 1952-54, 1950-52; assoc. Hemenway & Barnes, 1950—52, 1954—55, ptnr., 1956-97, of counsel, 1997—. Mem. panel neutral mediators and arbitrators Jud. Arbitration and Mediation Svc./Endispute, 1997—. Trustee Episcopal Ch. Found., Episcopal Divinity Sch., Cambridge, Mass., 1967—86, 1998—, pres. bd. trustees, 1977—86, hon. trustee, 1986—98; chancellor Episcopal Diocese of Mass., 1988—, dir., Trustees of Donations; trustee St. Mark's Sch., 1959—84, pres. bd. trustees, 1974—84; trustee Fenn Sch., Concord, 1956—77, pres. bd. trustees, 1960—73; trustee Concord Acad., 1963—78, pres. bd. trustees, 1971—78; trustee Boston Symphony Orch., 1977—94, pres. bd. trustees, 1987—94, life trustee, 1994—; trustee Children's Med. Ctr. and Children's Hosp. Corp., 1982—97, chmn. bd. dirs., 1992—97; trustee Wellesley Coll., 1962—80, trustee emeritus, 1980—; bd. dirs. Greater Boston Legal Svcs., 1961—87; dir. Controlled Risk Ins. Co., Ltd., 1988—99, chmn. bd. dirs., 1991—98; dir. Risk Mgmt. Found. Harvard Med. Instns., Inc., 1988—98, chmn. bd. dirs., 1991—98; trustee Harvard Med. Ctr. Inc., 1989—; trustee, mem. exec. com. WGBH Ednl. Found., 1987—, vice chmn., 1998—2003. Fellow Am. Coll. Probate Counsel; mem. Am. Law Inst., Internat. Acad. Estate and Trust Law; Mem. Tau Beta Pi. Home: 110 Spencer Brook Rd Concord MA 01742-5206 Office: 60 State St Boston MA 02109-1800 E-mail: gkidder@hembar.com.

KIDDER, J. PENELOPE, consultant, mental health services administrator; b. Canton, Ohio, Apr. 19, 1949; d. Robert Price and Virginia Mae (Coburn) K. BA, Hiram (Ohio) Coll., 1971; MA, U. Iowa, 1976; postgrad., U. So. Miss., 1977-80. Lic. profl. clin. counselor. Instr. U. So. Miss., Long Beach, 1984-89; dir. extended care svcs. Gulf Coast Mental Health, Gulfport, Miss., 1980-89; assoc. dir. Stow Clinic Portage Path Mental Health, Akron, Ohio, 1989-91; exec. dir. Residential Support Svcs., Wooster, Ohio, 1991-95; dir. adult client svcs. Columbiana County Mental Health, Lisbon, Ohio, 1995-96; exec. dir. Island Crisis Help, Kailua-Kona, Hawaii, 1996-97; prin. cons. Kidder Mgmt. Svcs., Kailua-Kona, 1997—; clin. dir. Transitional Living, Hamilton, Ohio, 2000—02; exec. dir. Outreach Cmty. Living Svcs., Wooster, Ohio, 2003—. Instr. Mt. Union Coll., Alliance, Ohio, 2003—. Contbr. articles to profl. jours. Bd. dirs. United Way of North Columbiana, Salem, Ohio, 1996, Big Island Substance Abuse Coun., Hilo, Hawaii, 1997-98, Kona Krafts, Kealakekua, Hawaii, 1998-2000. Mem.: APA (assoc.). Office: Kidder Mgmt Svcs 3470 Wales Rd NW Ste A-6302 Massillon OH 44646 E-mail: jpenny@aol.com.

KIDDER, RAY EDWARD, physicist, consultant; b. N.Y.C., Nov. 12, 1923; s. Harry Alvin and Laura Augusta (Wagner) K.; m. Marcia Loring Sprague, June 12, 1947 (div. Aug. 1975); children: Sandra Laura, David Ray, Matthew Sprague. BS, Ohio State U., 1947, MS, 1948, PhD, 1950. Physicist Calif. Rsch. Corp., La Habra, 1950-56, Lawrence Livermore Nat. Lab., Livermore, Calif., 1956—. Mem. adv. bd. Inst. for Quantum Optics, Garching, Germany, 1976-90; bd. editors Nuc. Fusion IAEA, Vienna, 1979-84; cons. Sci. Applications Internat. Corp., San Diego, 1991-94; mem. hon. adv. bd. Inst. for Advanced Physics Studies, La Jolla, Calif., 1991—. Contbr. chpts. to books. With USN, 1944-46. Recipient Humboldt award Alexander von Humboldt Found., 1988. Fellow Am. Phys. Soc. (Szilard award 1993); mem. AAAS, Sigma Xi. Achievements include research in physics of nuclear weapons, inertial confinement fusion, megagauss magnetic fields, laser isotope enrichment, containment of low-yield nuclear explosions. Home: 637 E Angela St Pleasanton CA 94566-7413 Office: Lawrence Livermore Nat Lab PO Box 808 Livermore CA 94551-0808

KIDDER, THOMAS MICHAEL, otolaryngologist; b. Los Angeles, Oct. 2, 1942; s. Edwin Ralph and Margaret Irene (Collins) K.; m. Eileen Elizabeth, June 26, 1965; children: Terese Marie, Steven Mark. BS in Biology, Marquette U., 1964, MD, 1968. Diplomate Am. Bd. Otolaryngology. Intern Columbia Hosp., Milw., 1968-69; residency in otolaryngology Med. Coll. Wis., Milw., 1969-73, assoc. prof. clin. surgery, 1984—90, assoc. prof. otolaryngology, 1990—; practice medicine specializing in otolaryngology Milw., 1975—90. Chief of staff St. Luke's Hosp., Milw, 1984-86. Lt. comdr. USN, 1973—75, lt. col. USAR, 1990—92. Fellow: ACS, Am. Acad. Otolaryngology (instr.); mem.: AMA, Milw. Acad. Medicine, Am. Cancer Soc. (bd. dirs. Milw. 1986—), Am. Head and Neck Soc. Roman Catholic. Avocations: kayaking, cycling, woodcarving, photography. Home: 4019 E Allerton Ave Cudahy WI 53110-1204 Office: Med Coll Wisc Clinics CHW MS 782A PO Box 1997 Milwaukee WI 53201 E-mail: tkidder@mcw.edu.

KIDDER, TRACY (JOHN TRACY KIDDER), writer; b. N.Y.C., Nov. 12, 1945; s. Henry Maynard and Reine Marie (Tracy) K.; m. Frances Toland, Jan. 1971. AB, Harvard U., Cambridge, Mass., 1967; MFA, U. Iowa, Iowa City, 1974. Contbg. editor Atlantic Monthly, Boston, 1982—. Author: The Road to Yuba City, 1974, The Soul of a New Machine, 1981 (Pulitzer prize 1982, Am. Book award 1982), House, 1985, Among Schoolchildren, 1989 (Robert F. Kennedy book award), Old Friends, 1993, Home Town, 1999, Mountains Beyond Mountains, 2003; author numerous articles, short stories and book revs. Served to 1st lt. U.S. Army, 1967-69, Vietnam.

KIDD HILL, LEONICE THOMPSON, musician, writer; b. South Hanson, Mass., Apr. 20, 1914; d. Ray Forest and Lula Alice (Stockwell) Thompson; m. G. Philip Kidd, Feb. 14, 1948 (dec. Mar. 1997); m. Dudley A. Hill, 2001. BMusic with honors, New Eng. Conservatory, Boston, 1936. Nat. cert. music tchr. Organist, choir dir. Ch. of the Ascension, East Cambridge, Mass., 1939-44; pvt. tchr. organ and piano Hanson, Mass., 1936-47; pbt tchr. theory and piano Buffalo, 1961-65, Prospect Heights, Ill., 1965-69; pvt. tchr. piano St. Paul, 1970-76; organist, choir dir. Ch.of Our Saviour, Seabrook Island, S.C., 1978-83;

pvt. tchr. piano and harpsichord, organist King's Grant Retirement Comty., Martinsville, Va., 1995—98. Author: They All Sat Down, Pianists in Profile, 1986, 95; author 12 ednl. coloring books Composer Highlights series, 1991, 94; editor The Insider, 1998—; contbr. articles to profl. jours. Recipient 1st Honorable Mention award Nat. League Am. Pen Women, 1992. Mem. Piedmont Music Tchrs. Assn. (v.p. 1997-98), Music Tchrs. Nat. Assn. (nat. cert.), Nat. Fedn. Music Clubs (life). Episcopalian. Home: 117 Mill Trace Rd Martinsville VA 24112-6654

KIDDIE, THOMAS JAMES, application developer, educator; b. Newark, May 16, 1955; s. Thomas James and Ann Irene Kiddie; life ptnr. Arno Schuechen, Sept. 20, 1961. BA, Rutgers Coll., 1973—77; MA, Rutgers U., 1977—83, PhD, 1977—87. Sr. software programmer Bell Laboratories, Piscataway, NJ, 1980—84; mem. of tech. staff Bell Comm. Rsch., Piscataway, NJ, 1984—90, software engr. Naples, Italy, 1990—95; adj. prof. of comparative lit. U. of Md., Naples, Italy, 1991—95; telecom. bus. mgr. Telcordia Technologies, Cologne, Germany, 1995—2002, wireless telecom. bus. mgmt. Piscataway, NJ, 2002—. Author: (monograph) Eros and Ataraxy. Mem.: MLA. Home: 124 Demott Ln Somerset NJ 08873 Office: Telcordia Technologies 444 Hoes Ln Piscataway NJ 08854 Personal E-mail: tkiddie@patmedia.net.

KIDDOO, ROBERT JAMES, engineering service company executive; b. Kansas City, Mo., July 8, 1936; s. Robert Leroy and Margaret Ella (Wolford) K.; m. Patricia Anne Wakefield, Apr. 17, 1957; children: Robert Michael, Stacey Margaret Kiddoo-Lee. BSBA, UCLA, 1960; MSBA, Calif. State U., Northridge, 1969; MBA, U. So. Calif., 1972, D of Bus. Adminstrn., 1978. Cert. mgmt. acct. Asst. v.p., nat. divsn. loan officer Crocker-Citizen's Nat. Bank, L.A., 1958—69; v.p., CFO, dir. corp. sec. Kirk-Mayer, Inc., L.A., 1969—87; prof. emeritus acctg. and info. sys. Calif. State U., Northridge, 1970—; region adminstr. mgr. CDI Corp.-West, Chatsworth, Calif., 1990; exec. v.p. Kirk-Mayer, Inc., L.A., 1990—92; pres. Creative Software Designs, Inc., Northridge, Calif., 1995—2002. Asst. v.p. financial affairs, univ. contr. Calif. State U., Northridge, 1997-2000. With U.S. Army, 1955-56. Mem. Mensa, Ltd., Beta Gamma Sigma, Beta Alpha Psi. Office: Calif State Univ Acctg And Is Northridge CA 91330-8372

KIDMAN, NICOLE, actress; b. Honolulu, Hawaii, June 20, 1967; m. Tom Cruise, 1990 (div. 2001); children: Isabella Jane Kidman, Connor Antony Kidman. Film appearences include BMX Bandits, 1983, Bush Christmas, 1983, Wills & Burke, 1985, Archer's Adventure, 1985, Windrider, 1986, Watch the Shadows Dance (aka Nightmaster), 1986, Bit Part, 1987, Emerald City, 1989, Dead Calm, 1989, Days of Thunder, 1990, Flirting, 1991, Billy Bathgate, 1991 (Golden Globe Award nomination 1992), Far and Away, 1992, Malice, 1993, My Life, 1993, Batman Forever, 1995, Portrait of a Lady, 1996, To Die For, 1995 (Golden Globe award), The Peacemaker, 1997, Practical Magic, 1998, Eyes Wide Shut, 1999, The Others, 2001 (nominee Best Performance by Actress in Motion Picture-Drama Golden Globe award 2002, Best Actress KCFCC award 2001), Moulin Rouge, 2001 (Best Actress in Motion Picture Musical/Comedy Golden Globe award 2001, nominee Best Actress in Leading Role Acad. award 2002, Best Actress London Film Critics Cir. award 2001), The Hours, 2002 (Best Actress British Academy of Film and Television Arts award 2003, Best Actress Academy award, 2003, Best Actress in Leading Role, British Acad. Film Award (BAFTA), 2003, Best Actress Golden Globe, 2003), Birthday Girl, 2002; TV appearances include Five Mile Creek, 1983, Chase Through the Night, 1983, Matthew and Son, 1984, Bangkok Hilton, 1989 (Australian Film Inst. Best Actress in Miniseries), Vietnam, 1985 (Australian Film Inst. Best Actress in Miniseries); theatrical prodns. include The Blue Room, London, 1997-98, Broadway, 1998-99. Recipient ShoWest Dist. Decade Achievement award, 2002. Address: Creative Artists Agy 9830 Wilshire Blvd Beverly Hills CA 90212*

KIDONAKIS, NIKOLAOS, physicist; b. Thessaloniki, Greece, Jan. 7, 1969; came to US, 1986; s. Ioannis and Dimitra (Tseliou) K.; m. Natalia Miasnikova, Dec. 20, 1995; children: Dorian Euphorion, Dimitrios Apollon. BS with honors, Calif. Inst. Tech., 1990; cert. advanced study in math., U. Cambridge, Eng., 1991; PhD, SUNY, Stony Brook, 1996. Rsch. fellow U. Edinburgh (Scotland), 1996-98; rsch. assoc. Fla. State U., Tallahassee, 1998—2001; vis. asst. prof. So. Meth. U., Dallas, 2001—02; vis. scientist U. Rochester, NY, 2002; Marie Curie rsch. fellow U. Cambridge, England, 2002—. Vis. scientist Brookhaven Nat. Lab., Upton, N.Y., 1996, Fermi Nat. Accelerator Lab., Batavia, Ill., 1999; scientific assoc. CERN/European Lab. Particle Physics, Geneva, 1997. Ref. The Phys. Rev., 1997—; contbr. articles to profl. jours. Office: Cavendish Lab Univ Cambridge Madingley Rd Cambridge CB3 0HE England E-mail: kidonaki@hep.phy.cam.ac.uk.

KIDWELL, CLARA SUE, education educator; b. Tahlequah, Okla., July 8, 1941; d. Hardin Milton and Martha Evelyn Kidwell. BA, U. of Okla., 1962, MA, 1963, PhD, 1970. Instr. of history Kans. City Art Inst., 1968—70; coord. of publications Exptl. Edn. Unit, U. of Wash., Seattle, 1969—70; instr. of social sci. Haskell Indian Jr. Coll., Lawrence, Kans., 1970—72; asst. prof. Am. Indian Studies Dept., U. of Minn., 1972—74; assoc. prof. to full prof. Native Am. Studies, program, U. of Calif., 1974—93; vis. assoc. prof. Native Am. Studies Program, Dartmouth Coll., NH, 1980; asst. dir. for cultural resources Nat. Mus. of the Am. Indian, Washington, 1993—95; dir., native am. studies program U. of Okla., 1995—. Chair, bd. of trustees The jacobson Found., Norman, Okla., 1998—. NDEA fellowship, U.S. Dept. of Edn., 1963—66, Rockefeller Found. Humanities fellowship, Rockefeller Found., 1976—77, grant to direct summer institutes for coll. teachers, Nat. Endowment for the Humanities, 1987, 1990. Mem.: Western History Assn., Am. Soc. for Ethnohistory, Orgn. of Am. Historians. Avocation: baking. Office: University of Oklahoma 633 Elm St Rm 216 Norman OK 73019

KIDWELL JR. ROLAND E. finance educator, writer, researcher; b. Washington D.C., June 26, 1957; s. Roland E. and Jane H. Kidwell; m. Linda Katherine Elizabeth Achey, Dec. 28, 1991; children: Kelly Virginia Kidwell, Tracy Jane Kidwell, Rosalind Louise Kidwell. PhD in Bus. Adminstrn., La. State U., Baton Rouge, 1994; M of Bus. Adminstrn., Radford U., Va., 1987; B of Sci. in Journalism, U. of Md., 1978. Reporter Roanoke Times & World-News, Va., 1978—83, city editor, 1983—89; asst. prof. LSU in Shreveport, La., 1993—96, Niagara U., Lewiston, NY, 1996—2002, assoc. prof., 2002—; acad. rsch. fellow La. State U., Baton Rouge, 1989—93. Consulting Ind., Youngstown, NY, 1996—. Author: (textbook) HRM From A to Z, (book chapters and cases) Articles and/or cases published in Nonprofit Management Education, Research on Ethical Issues in Organizations, Cases, Incidents and Experiential Exercises in HRM, newspaper articles, (newspaper articles college) University of Maryland Student Newspaper (Two Sigma Delta Chi writing awards, 1977). Pres. and bd. mem. Niagara Area Habitat for Humanity, Niagara Falls, NY, 1999—2003. Grantee Rsch. Grants, LSU in Shreveport, 1994, 1995, Niagara U., 1997, 2001. Mem.: Acad. of Mgmt., Soc. for Human Resource Mgmt. Independent. Protestant. Achievements include Outstanding Senior in the College of Journalism, University of Maryland 1978; Niagara University Excellence in Teaching Award, 2000-2001. Avocations: reading, travel, writing, sports. Office: Niagara Univ Dept of Commerce Perboyre Hall Niagara University NY 14109 Office Fax: 716-286-8206. Personal E-mail: rek@niagara.edu. E-mail: rek@niagara.edu.

KIECHEL, BARBARA BERNADETTE, vocational school educator; b. Allentown, Pa., Oct. 18, 1949; d. F. Joseph and Josephine Marie (Johnson) Mucellin; m. Gary Lee Kiechel, May 17, 1975; children: Angela, Jonathan, Marie. AA, Lehigh Carbon C.C., Schnecksville, Pa., 1969; BS, Temple U., 1978, MA, 1981. Cert. supr. comprehensive vocat. edn. tchr., Pa. Tchr. Lehigh Career & Tech. Inst., Schnecksville, 1974-81; curriculum devel. specialist Lehigh County Vocat.-Tech. Sch., Schnecksville, 1981-97, supr. curriculum and instrn., 1997-99, supr. vocat. programs, 1999—. Resident leadership resource person, Temple U., Phila., 1982-83, grad. leadership devel. program, 1983-84, others. Coord. United Way Campaign, Schnecksville, 1989—, strategic planning internat. facilitator, 1994-96; asst. leader Great Valley Girl Scout Coun., Emmaus, Pa., 1989-95; ch. organist St. Francis of Assisi Ch., Allentown, Pa., 1964-75. Recipient Cert. Achievement Dept. Edn., 1990, Cert. Vol. Achievement award United Way, 1992, 94. Mem. NEA, Pa. Sch. Edn. Assn. Democrat. Avocations: gardening, hiking. Home: 5064 Jasper Rd Emmaus PA 18049-5217 Office: Lehigh Career and Tech Inst 4500 Education Park Dr Schnecksville PA 18078-2501 E-mail: kiechlb@LCTI.org.

KIECHEL, WALTER, III, editor; b. Tecumseh, Nebr. BA, Harvard Coll., 1968, MBA, JD, 1977. Reporter, researcher Fortune Mag., 1977-78, assoc. editor, 1978-82, mem. bd. editors, 1982-88, asst. mng. editor, 1988-92, exec. editor, 1992-94, mng. editor, 1994-95; editor for bus. devel. Time, Inc., N.Y.C., 1995; editor Mgmt. Update newsletter Harvard Bus. Sch. Pub. Co. Cons. Bain & Co., 1996; pub. Harvard Bus. Rev., 1997; editl. dir., sr. v.p. H.B.S.P. Co., 1998. With USN. Office: 509 Madison Ave 15th Fl New York NY 10022 Home: 929 Washington St Hoboken NJ 07030 E-mail: wkiechel@hbsp.harvard.edu., wkhelios@aol.com.

KIECOLT-GLASER, JANICE KAY, psychologist; b. Oklahoma City, June 30, 1951; d. Edward Harold and Vergie Mae (Lively) Kiecolt; m. Ronald Glaser, Jan. 18, 1980. BA in Psychology with honors, U. Okla., 1972; PhD in Clin. Psychology, U. Miami, 1976. Lic. psychologist, Ohio. Clin. psychology intern Baylor U. Coll. Medicine, Houston, 1974-75; postdoctoral fellow in adult clin. psychology U. Rochester, N.Y., 1976-78; asst. prof. psychiatry Ohio State U. Coll. Medicine, Columbus, 1978-84, assoc. prof. psychiatry and psychology, 1984-89, prof. psychiatry and psychology, 1989—, dir. divsn. health psychology, 1994—, active various coms. Mem. AIDS study sect. NIMH, 1988-91. Editl. bd. Brain, Behavior and Immunity jour., 1986—, Health Psychology jour., 1989—, Brit. Jour. Health Psychology, 1996—, Jour. Behavioral Medicine, 1994—, Psychosomatic Medicine, 1990—, Jour. Cons. and Clin. Psychology, 1992—, Jour. Gerontology, 1992—; reviewer Jour. Personality and Social Psychology, Psychiatry Rsch. jour.; contbr. articles to profl. jours., chpts. to books. NIMH grantee, 1985—; recipient Merit award NIMH, 1993; Ohio State Disting. scholar, 1994. Fellow Am. Psychol. Assn. (Outstanding Contbns. award 1988), Acad. Behavioral Medicine Rsch.; mem. Phi Beta Kappa, Inst. Medicine. Avocations: jogging, fiction writing. Office: Ohio State U Coll Medicine Dept Psychiatry 1670 Upham Dr Columbus OH 43210

KIEF, PAUL ALLAN, lawyer; b. Montevideo, Minn., Mar. 22, 1934; s. Paul G. and Minna S. K. BA, LLB, U. Minn., 1957. Bar: Minn. 1957, U.S. Dist. Ct. Minn. 1964, U.S. Tax Ct. 1968, U.S. Supreme Ct. 1981; cert. criminal trial law specialist Nat. Bd. Trial Advocacy. Gen. practice, Bemidji, Minn., 1959—; ptnr. Kief, Fuller, Baer & Wallner, Ltd., Bemidji, Minn., 1973-97; owner Paul A. Kief Law Firm, Bemidji, Minn., 1998—; pub. defender 9th Jud. Dist. Minn., Bemidji, Minn., 1966-98; panel atty. Fed. Pub. Defender Dist. Minn., 1999—. Chief pub, defender, Benudji, Minn., 1968—94; vol. atty. Minn. Civil Liberties Union; mem. adv. bd. Innocence Project of Minn.; panel atty Legal Svcs., Northwest, Minn. Vice chmn. Beltrami County Planning Commn., 1964-68; chmn. adv. com. Gov.'s Crime Commn., 1971-77; mem. Minn. Task Force on Standards and Goals in Criminal Justice, 1975-76, Crime Victims Task Force, 1985, Jud. Selection Com., 1987, Com. on Criminal Jury Instrn. Guides, 1988-90; bd. dirs. Legal Svcs. Northwest Minn., 1990-96; capt. CAP, 1969—. Served with USAR, USNG, 1958-64. Mem. ABA, ATLA, NACDL, MACDL, Nat. Bd. Trial Advocacy (cert. crim. law trial specialist 1998), Minn. Bar Assn., Minn. Trial Lawyers Assn., 15th Dist. Bar Assn. (past sec.), Beltrami County Bar Assn. (past pres.), Lawyer-Pilots Bar Assn., Minn. Criminal Def. Lawyers Assn. Clubs: Toastmasters. Democrat. Congregationalist. Home: PO Box 212 Bemidji MN 56619-0212 Office: 514 America Ave NW PO Box 212 Bemidji MN 56619-0212 E-mail: paky@paulbunyan.net.

KIEFE, CATARINA ISABEL, medical educator; m. Robert Michael Farmer. PhD, SUNY, 1973; MD, U. Calif., San Francisco, 1983. Diplomate Am. Bd. Internal Medicine. Lectr. math. U. Calif., Berkeley, 1973—75; asst. prof. math. U. Porto, 1973—76; asst. prof. math. and stats. U. N.Mex, Albuquerque, 1976—79; from asst. to assoc. prof. medicine Baylor Coll. Medicine, Houston, 1986—92; assoc. prof. medicine U. Ala., Birmingham, 1993—98, prof. medicine, 1998—. Dir. ctr. for outcomes and effectiveness rsch. and edn. U. Ala., Birmingham, 1998—, dir, divsn. preventive medicine, 2001—, sr. scholar Lister Hill Ctr. for Health Policy, 1994—; sr. quality scholar Birmingham Vets. Affairs Med. Ctr., 1998—. Contbr. over 100 articles to profl. jours. Grantee, multiple fed. agencies and pvt. founds. Fellow: ACP. Office: U Ala at Birmingham MT 621 1530 3rd Ave S Birmingham AL 35294-4410 Fax: 205-975-5153. Personal E-mail: ckiefe@uab.edu.

KIEFER, ANNA JACQUELYNN, music educator; b. Davenport, Iowa, Mar. 30, 1978; d. Dale Robert and Colleen Janice Kiefer. MusB, Trinity U., San Antonio, TX, 2000. Tchr. Elssy Martin Piano Studio, San Antonio, 1997; founder, tchr. True Studio Piano Camp, Musical Arts Ctr. Piano Camp, San Antonio, 1997—2001; tchr. Anna Kiefer Piano and Music Theory Studio, San Antonio, 1998—. Tutor music theory Trinity U., San Antonio, 1997; accompanist Tezel Oaks Ch. of Nazerene, San Antonio, 2000, Palo Alto Coll., San Antonio, 2001—02; theory chair San Antonio Music Teachers Assn., San Antonio, 2003—. Composer: (orchestral music) Leonardo and Janet, 2000. Recipient Carolyn Calvert scholar, Trinity U., 1997. Mem.: San Antonio Music Tchrs. Assn. (chair theory 2003—), Tex. Music Tchrs. Assn., Music Tchrs. Nat. Assn., Alpha Lambda Delta, Mu Phi Epsilon, Phi Kappa Lambda. Roman Catholic. Personal E-mail: annakiefer@yahoo.com.

KIEFER, DON RUSSELL, writer, researcher; b. New Knoxville, Ohio, Apr. 3, 1941; s. Wilbur Frederick and Matilda Alvina (Kuck) Kiefer; m. Bonnie Katharyn Voison, Feb. 15, 1964 (div. 1977); 1 child, Monte Alan. At, North American Sch. of Conservation, Scranton, Pa., 1988. Lic. pvt. pilot F.A.A., 1985. Mgr. body shop Katterheinrich Motors, New Knoxville, Ohio, 1959—71; mgr. owner Muntzinger/Kiefer Body, Celina, Ohio, 1971—78; mgr. sales Isley's Recreation, Mesa, Ariz., 1978—86; columnist Mesa (Ariz.) Tribune, 1986—89; pub. affairs officer Colossal Cave Pk., Vail, Ariz., 1988—93; writer Golden West Pub., Phoenix, 1991—98; mgr. sales Quality Decision, Mesa, 1993—2001; owner Shadow Pub., Mesa, 2000—. Mem. adv. bd. U.S. Forest Svc., Nat. Park Svc. Author: (books) Hiking Ariz., 1991, Hiking Ariz. II, 1993, Hiking No. Ariz., 1995, Hiking Ctrl. Ariz., 1995, Hiking So. Ariz., 1995, Haunts of Ariz., 2000. Recipient pres. sports award, Pres. George Bush, 1991, participation award, B. Dalton Booksellers, 1992, letter of commendation, Senator John McCain, 1993, rsch. certificates, various ranger districts and pk. svcs., 1987—91, vol. certificates, Nat. Pk. Svc., 1989—96. Democrat. Avocations: hiking, travel, genealogy, writing, research. Office: Shadow Publishing 108 North Greenfield #2256 Mesa AZ 85205 Home: 108 North Greenfield #2256 Mesa AZ 85205

KIEFER, HELEN CHILTON, emergency and trauma physician, neurologist; b. Washington; d. Frank McGlowing and Sue (Stanford) Chilton; m. John Harold Kiefer, Feb. 4, 1961 (div. July 1971); 1 child, Steven Chilton. AB in Chemistry magna cum laude, Cornell U., 1961; PhD in Biochemistry, U. Chgo., 1971; MD with honors, Northwestern U., 1981. Lic. physician, Ill., N.Mex.; diplomate Am. Bd. Emergency Medicine. Resident neurology U. Ill. Med. Sch., Chgo., 1983-85; physicist, computer programmer physics div. Los Alamos (N.Mex.) Sci. Labs., 1965—67; asst. prof. dept. biochemistry Northwestern U. Med. Sch., Chgo., 1972-78; editor Marcus Acad. Media, Chgo., 1978-81; clin. assoc. prof. dept. biochemistry Loyola Med. and Dental Sch., Chgo., 1978-81; pvt. practice emergency/trauma medicine Chgo., 1983—; dir. med. rsch. for biotech., assoc. med. dir. high tech. Abbott Labs., Abbott Park, Ill., 1986-89; assoc. ctr. for biotechnology Northwestern U., 1992. Adj. assoc. prof. dept. biomed. engring. and grad. multidisciplinary program in neurosci. Northwestern U., Evanston, Ill., 1989-90; affiliate Internat. Human Genome Mapping Project, 1991—; vis. prof. dept. bioengring. U. Wash., Seattle, 1982-83; mem. presdl. adv. com. NIH, 1976-80; CEO, pres. Childstone Prodns. and Pub., 2000; co-owner Caremore Emergency Svcs., 2001; program project rev. bds. NIH, 1978-80. Woodrow Wilson fellow, NSF fellow, Danforth Found. fellow, NIH postdoctoral fellow. Mem. N.Y. Acad. Scis., Phi Beta Kappa, Alpha Omega Alpha. Home and Office: 86 A Sunlit Dr W Santa Fe NM 87508

KIEFER, J. RICHARD, JR., retired corporate executive; b. Phila., Mar. 3, 1928; m. Gwendolen Clara Watkins, June 20, 1953; children: David Richard, Linda Lauretta, Nancy Ellen, Carol Gwen. BSChemE, Drexel U., 1950; postgrad., Temple U. With McCloskey Corp., Phila., 1947-89, Valspar Corp., 1989-90; with rsch. and devel. McCloskey Corp., Phila., with customer product evaluation dept., v.p. community, industry and regulatory affairs. Mem. Friends of Acad. Vocal Arts, Olney Symphony Assn., Pa. Ballet Assn., Zool. Soc. Phila., Franklin Inst., Friends of Pennypack Park; ; mem., vol. twilight walking tours guide Friends of Independence Nat. Hist. Park; mem. Funeral Consumers Alliance Greater Phila., past pres., treas., bd. dirs.; vol. tour guide Phila. Soc. Preservation Landmarks, Hist. Power House, Phila. Cultural Coun. Recipient Sr. Statesman award Phila. Paint Industry. Mem. Phila. Paint and Coatings Assn. (past pres., past bd. dirs.), Phila. Soc. Coatings Tech. (past pres., bd. dirs., by-laws com., Liberty Bell, Tech Comm. and Benjamin Franklin awards), Fed. Soc. Coatings Tech. (hon. mem., past coun., bd. dirs., exec. com., Trigg award), Soc. Gallows Birds, N.E. H.S. Alumni Assn. (class reunion treas.), Masons (32d degree, former chmn. Trustees Charity Funds of Lodge, advisor to trustees, mem. com. masonic edn., Columbia chpt. Joppa coun., high 12 past pres), Pa. Lodge Rsch., Philalethes Soc., Alpha Phi Omega, Zeta Theta (co-founder). Avocations: travel, classical music, attending ballet performances, opera, theater. Home: 1027 Loney St Philadelphia PA 19111-2624 E-mail: welshamer@juno.com.

KIEFER, JOHN HAROLD, chemical engineering educator; b. New Ulm, Minn., Aug. 27, 1932; s. Harold Lyle and Margaret Olivia (Bentdahl) K.; m. Helen Murelle Chilton (div.); 1 child, Steven; m. Barbara June Berg, Dec. 30, 1971; children: Amy, Andrew. BS, U. Minn., 1954; PhD, Cornell U., 1961. Postdoctoral fellow Cornell U., Ithaca, N.Y., 1959-61; staff mem. Los Alamos (N.Mex.) Sci. Lab., 1961-66; assoc. prof. chem. engring. U. Ill., Chgo., 1966-72, prof. chem. engring., 1972—, acting head, 1989-90, 95, head, 1996—2001, emeritus, 2002—. Joint appointee Argonne (Ill.) Nat. Lab., 1985-91. Grantee Dept. of Energy, 1978—, NSF, 1983, U.S. Israel Binat. Sci. Found., 1988. Office: U Ill 810 S Clinton St Chicago IL 60607-4408

KIEFER, KAREN LAVERNE, lawyer; b. Lancaster, Ohio, Nov. 8, 1952; d. Ray E. and Marilyn L. (Keister) K. BA in Econs., Chatham Coll., 1974; MBA in Fin., George Washington U., 1977; JD in Internat. Law, U. Balt., 1982. Bar: Md. 1987, D.C. 1988, Pa. 1998. Counsel Europe, Israel and Am. Westinghouse Elec. Corp., Balt., 1974-84; mgr. Internat. Ops. Gould Inc., Washington, 1985-87; pvt. practice law Annapolis, Md., 1987—, Scottdale, Pa., 1987—. Founder, owner Mainsail of Annapolis Yacht Chartering, 1979—; incorporator, legal counsel Scottdale Cmty. Pool. Pub.: The Cormany Diaries, A Northern Family in the Civil War, 1982. Sponsor U.S. Naval Acad. Midshipmen, Annapolis 1981-97; coach Naval Acad. Sailing Squadron, 1991-97. Mem. ABA, D.C. Bar Assn., Md. Bar Assn., Pa. Bar Assn., Am. Soc. Internat. Law, Am. Mgmt. Assn., Westmoreland County Bar Assn. Avocations: swimming, sailing, music, arts.

KIEFER, MATTHEW J. lawyer; b. Detroit, Sept. 15, 1954; s. John B. and Madeline Kiefer; m. Nancy E. Porter, June 8, 1985; children: Emma Rose, Madeline. BA magna cum laude, Boston U., 1976; JD, U. Mich., 1982. Assoc. Fine & Ambrogne, Boston, 1982—86, DiCara, Selig, Sawyer & Holt, Boston, 1986—88, ptnr., 1988—90, Peabody & Brown, Boston, 1990—98, Goulston & Storrs, P.C., Boston, 1998—. Lectr. Harvard Grad. Sch. Design, Cambridge, 1999—; bd. dirs. Emerald Necklance Conservancy; pres., bd. dirs. Hist. Boston. Contbr. articles to profl. jours. Commr., vice chair Boston Landmarks Commn., 1991—98; commr. Truro (Mass.) Hist. Commn., 2001—; pres. Arboretum Pk. Conservancy, Boston, 1994—. Recipient Loeb fellowship in advanced environ. studies, Harvard U. Grad. Sch. Design, 1995—96. Mem.: Loeb Fellowship Assn., Boston Bar Assn. Office: Goulston & Storrs 400 Atlantic Ave Boston MA 02110

KIEFER, WILLIAM NATHANIEL, school system administrator, career army officer; b. Lancaster, Pa., Nov. 6, 1943; s. Paul Edward and Frances Adell Kiefer; m. Karen O'Brien, July 31, 1971; children: Ingrid, Olivia. BA, Millersville U., 1972, MS, 1974; EdD, Walden U., 1980. Tchr. Penn Manor Sch. Dist., Millersville, Pa., 1974-75; sch. psychologist Sch. Dist. Lancaster, Pa., 1975-76, dept. head, 1976-87, alt. sch. prin., 1987-92, elem. prin., 1992-96, dir. planning and quality sys., 1996—2003; supt. Hamburg (Pa.) Area Sch. Dist., 2003—. Co-author: I Like It When You Help Me Learn To Read, 1986, Shape Up Your Local School, 2002. Mem. svc. acad. bd. 16th Congl. Dist., Lancaster, 1997-2000. Capt. U.S. Army, 1966—69, to maj. gen. USAR, 1969—98. Republican. Roman Catholic. Avocations: fishing, sailing, woodworking.

KIEFF, ELLIOTT DAN, medical educator; b. Phila., Feb. 2, 1943; s. Irving N. and Florence (Prussel) K.; m. Jacqueline Louise Silverman, June 11, 1944; children: David, Scott, Elizabeth. AB, U. Pa., 1963; MD, Johns Hopkins U., 1966; PhD, U. Chgo., 1971. Intern medicine U. Chgo., 1966-67, resident medicine, 1967-70, asst. prof. medicine, 1971-77, assoc. prof. medicine and molecular genetics, 1977-80, prof. medicine and molecular genetics, 1980-85, L. Block prof. biol. scis., 1985-87, chief infectious disease, 1971-87; Harriet Ryan Albee prof. medicine, microbiology and molecular genetics Harvard U., Boston, 1987—, chief infectious disease Brigham Hosp., 1987, chair virology, 1991—; Meyer hon. vis. prof. U. Calif., San Francisco, 1991—. Assoc. editor Virology, 1980—, Jour. of Virology, 1982—, reviewing editor, Science, 1996—. Recipient Langer award Langer Cancer Rsch., 1983, Finland award, 1987, Ricketts award, 1996. Mem. Nat. Acad. Scis., Am. Soc. Clin. Ivestigation, Assn. Am. Physicians, Inst. Medicine, Inter Urban Club. Clubs: Quadrangle (Chgo.); Harvard (Boston, N.Y.C.). Avocation: tennis. Home: 269 Lee St Brookline MA 02445-5914 Office: Havard Univ Med Sch 181 Longwood Ave Boston MA 02115-5804

KIEFFER, ANDREW VAN ATTA, artist; b. Rochester, N.Y., Oct. 23, 1954; s. James Milton Kieffer and Eleanor Jane Van Atta. BA with honors, Ithaca Coll., 1976; studied with Ctrl. Tibetan Lama Pema Dorjé, Boudhanath, Nepal, 1980—81; postgrad., U. Wis., 1981. Elem. edn. tchr. Broward County Schs., Ft. Lauderdale, Fla., 1982—83; art tchr. Broward C.C., Hallendale, Fla., 1983—84; assembly line packer Nalge Corp., Penfield, NY, 1984—85; nutrition advisor Gen. Nutrition Ctr., Victor, NY, 1985—. Mural, Manpower, 1978; author: Look To Your Own Feet, 1992. Roman Catholic. Avocations: swimming, treadmill jogging, music. Home and Office: U-ME-1 Art Studio Apt 5 2048 Monroe Ave Rochester NY 14618

KIEFFER, JAROLD ALAN, publications company executive, writer; b. Mpls., May 5, 1923; s. Charles O. and Edith Ida (Feinberg) K.; m. Frances Clarfield, Aug. 13, 1949; children: Edith Charlotte, Charles Edward, Philip William. BA, U. Minn., 1947, PhD, 1950. Teaching asst. polit. sci. dept. U. Minn., 1949, tchg. asst. social sci. program, 1950-51; rsch. asst., world affairs program Mpls. Star, 1949-50; exec. sec. def. moblzn. manpower coms., staff asst. to exec. sec. Office Def. Moblzn., Exec. Office of Pres., 1951-52, staff sec., 1952, asst. to exec. officer, exec. sec. borrowing authority review bd., 1953, spl. asst. to dir., 1955-56, acting dep. asst. dir. nat. security affairs, 1956-57, cons., 1958; exec. asst. to dir. orgn. and personnel, exec. sec. personnel adv. com. AEC, 1952-53; asst. to Arthur S. Flemming, mem. 2d Hoover Commn., 1953-55; chmn. Herbert Hoover's liaison to Task Force on Pers. and Civil Svc., 1953-55; asst. to Arthur S. Flemming, mem. and asst. to chmn. Pres.'s Adv. Com. on Govt. Orgn., 1953-61, cons., 1958; asst. to Meyer Kestenbaum, spl. asst. to Pres. for Hoover Commn. and intergovtl. relations commn. matters, The White House, 1955-56; adviser to Meyer Kestnbaum, 1956-57; asst. to Nelson Rockefeller for policy and issues studies, NY Gubernatorial Campaign, 1957-58. Cons. to sec. HEW, Washington, 1958, asst. to sec., 1958-59, asst. to sec. for program analysis, 1959-61; sec. bd. trustees Nat. Cultural Center, 1959-63, exec. dir., 1961-63; renamed John F. Kennedy Center for Performing Arts; asso. prof. polit. sci. U., Oreg., 1963-67, acting chmn. polit. sci. dept., 1964, asst. to pres., 1963-67; chmn. public affairs and adminstrn. programs, prof. public policy and adminstrn. Lila Acheson Wallace Sch. Community Service and Pub. Affairs, 1967-69; U. Oreg. chmn. Interdisciplinary Masters Program on Pub. Affairs, 1965-69; dir. Macalester Found. for Higher Edn., 1969-70; exec. officer bd. trustees Macalester Coll., 1970-71, also adj. prof. polit. sci., 1969-71; dir. Office Internat. Tng., AID, State Dept., 1971-72, asst. adminstr. for population and humanitarian assistance, 1972-75; adj. prof. internat. rels. Am. U., Washington, 1975, staff dir. pres.' panel on biomed. rsch., 1975-76. Dep. commr. social security U.S. Dept. HHS, 1976-77; staff dir. Task Force on House Adminstrv. Sys., Commn. on Adminstrv. Rev., U.S. Ho. Reps., 1977; dir. Nat. Com. on Careers for Older Ams., Acad. Edn. Devel., Inc., 1978-80, staff dir., 1981 White Ho. Conf. on Aging, 1980-82; vice chmn. Gov. Planning Coun. Arts and Humanities, State of Oreg., 1965-67; chmn. Project 70's Task Force on State Govt. Reorgn., Oreg. Gov.'s Office, 1968-69; chmn. task force on Strategic Perspectives on Aging, Fairfax, Va., 1986; cons. Office High Speed Ground Transp., U.S. Office Edn., 1971; officer, mem. exec. com. Lane County Auditorium Assn., Oreg., 1963-69; exec. coun. United Way, Fairfax, 1985-88; bd. dirs. World Population Soc., 1983-2002 pres., 1990-92; bd. dirs. Fairfax Vol. Action Ctr., 1967-91, hon. bd. mem., 1991-93; mem. Gov.'s Job Tng. Coordination Coun., Commonwealth Va., 1987-94, chmn. older worker and

youth com., 1989-94, mem. exec. com., 1990-94; mem., chmn. transp. com. Fairfax Area Commn. on Aging, 1991-95, exec. com., 1993-95; bd. dirs., sec. No. Va. Coalition of Vol. Interfaith Caregivers, Inc., 1991-94; bd. dirs. Fairfax Alliance for Human Svcs., 1996—, chmn., 2001—. With AUS, 1942-46. Mem. ASPA (life), Am. Polit. Sci. Assn., Advanced Transit Assn. (dir. 1976—, chmn. 1983-84, sec.-treas. 1985-95, chmn. 1995-2000), Sr. Employment Resources Inc. (chmn. 1985—, editor SER Publs., 1989-97), Kieffer Publs. (pres., editor 1998—). Home: 9019 Hamilton Dr Fairfax VA 22031-3075

KIEFFER, SUSAN WERNER, geologist, educator, real estate developer, consultant; b. Warren, Pa., Nov. 17, 1942; BS in Physics and Math., Allegheny Coll., 1964; MS in Geol. Scis., Calif. Inst. Tech., 1967, PhD in Planetary Scis., 1971; DSc (hon.), Allegheny Coll., 1987. Rsch. geochemist UCLA, 1971-73, asst. prof. geology, 1973-79; geologist U.S. Geol. Survey, Flagstaff, Ariz., 1979-90; prof. geology Ariz. State U., Tempe, 1988—, Regents prof., 1991-93; prof., head dept. geol. sci. U. B.C., Vancouver, Canada, 1993-95; co-founder Kieffer & Woo, Inc., Palgrave, Ont., Can., 1996-2000; founder Kieffer Inst. for Devel. of Sci. Based Edn., 1997-99; Walgreen prof. geology U. Ill., Urbana, 2001—. W.H. Mendnhall lectr. U.S. Geol. Survey, 1980. Editor (with A. Navrotsky): Microscopic to Macroscopic: Atomic Environments to Mineral Thermodynamics, 1985. Recipient Disting. Alumnus award, Calif. Inst. Tech., 1982, Meritorious Svc. award, Dept. Interior, 1986, Spendiarov award, Soviet Acad. Scis., 1990; fellow Alfred P. Sloan Found. fellow, 1977—79, MacArthur fellow, 1995—. Fellow: Mineral Soc. Am. (award 1980), Meteoritical Soc., Geol. Soc. Am. (Arthur L. Day medal 1992), Am. Geophys. Union, Am. Acad. Arts and Scis.; mem.: NAS. Avocations: athletics, music. Office: U Ill Dept Geology MC 102 1301 W Green St Urbana IL 61901 Office Fax: 217-244-8725. E-mail: skieffer@uiuc.edu.

KIEFNER, JOHN ROBERT, JR., lawyer, educator; b. Peoria, Ill., May 31, 1946; s. John Robert and Luna Merle (Froment) K.; m. B.C. Clayton, Feb. 14, 1989; 1 child, John William. BA, Johns Hopkins U., 1968; JD, Stetson U., 1971. Bar: Fla. 1971, U.S. Ct. Appeals (D.C. cir.) 1971, U.S. Ct. Appeals (11th cir.) 1981, U.S. Dist. Ct. (no. dist.) Fla. 1971, U.S. Dist. Ct. (mid. dist.) Fla. 1981, U.S. Ct. Mil. Appeals 1971, U.S. Tax Ct. 1979, U.S. Supreme Ct. 1979. Staff atty. SEC, Washington, 1971-74, br. chief, 1974-77, regional trial counsel, 1977-82; mem. Robbins, Gaynor, Burton, Hampp, Burns, Bronstein & Shasteen, St. Petersburg, Fla., 1982-86; ptnr. Riden, Earle & Kiefner, P.A., St. Petersburg, 1986-99, Harris, Barrett, Mann & Dew, L.L.P., St. Petersburg, 1999—2001, Kiefner & Renaldo, P.A., St. Petersburg, 2001—. Adj. prof. law Stetson U., St. Petersburg, 1982—. Past chmnn. Combined Fed. Campaign, 1976-77. Capt. U.S. Army, 1968-76. Recipient Cert. of Merit, SEC, 1982; Charles A. Dana scholar, 1970-71. Mem. ABA, ATLA, Fla. Bar Assn., St. Petersburg Bar Assn., Fla. Acad. Trial Lawyers, Pinellas County Trial Lawyers Assn., Fed. Bar Assn., Nat. Assn. Colls. and Univs. (recruitment com.), St. Petersburg Area C. of C., Johns Hopkins U. Alumni Assn., Masons, Shriners. Lutheran. Home: 227 126th Ave E Treasure Island FL 33706 Office: Kiefner & Renaldo PA Ste 300 146 2nd St N Saint Petersburg FL 33701 E-mail: JKiefner@Kiefnerrenaldolaw.com.

KIEFT, GERALD NELSON, mechanical engineer; b. Chgo., Dec. 29, 1946; s. Ralph and Alice (Nelson) K.; m. Linda Louise Fank, Oct. 28, 1967; children: Gerald Nelson II, Dawn Michelle. BSME, Midwest Coll. Engring., Lombard, Ill., 1971. Sr. designer Clark Equipment Co., Aurora, Ill., 1971-73; project engr. Elgin (Ill.) Sweeper Co., 1974-86, GPI Industries, W. Chgo., Ill., 1986—. Inventor in field. Company chmn. United Way Campaign, Elgin, 1977. Presbyterian. Home: 42w192 Silver Glen Rd Saint Charles IL 60175-8339 Office: GPI Industries Ste 700 800 E Northwest Hwy Palatine IL 60074-6513

KIEHL, E. ROBERT, manufacturing executive, consultant; b. Phila., Apr. 28, 1920; s. Eugene Phillip and Ida Jean Kiehl; m. Margaret Eleanor Swigart, Oct. 7, 1944; children: Robert Edward, John Marsh, Christine Margaret. BS in chem. engring., Drexel U., 1943; at, Princeton (NJ) U., 1960—65. Chemist, engr. Allied Chem. Corp., Phila., 1940—43, project engr., 1943—44, plant mgr. Bethlahem, Pa., 1944—47, plant and works mgr. Edgewater, NJ, 1947—65; dir. oper. Allied Chem. Corp. Barrett Divsn., NYC, 1965—67; mgr. Gypsum Divsn. Celotex Corp., Tampa, Fla., 1967—84; cons. Internat. Exec. Svc. Corps, Stamford, Conn., 1987—. Chmn. materials handling com. Gypsum Assn., 1971—76; spkr. All Soviet Conf. on Gypsum, Moscow, 1979; chmn. mfg. and mining com. Gypsum Assn., 1979—83; spkr. Bur. of Standards, Washington, 1981; vol. exec. internat. projects Internat. Exec. Svc. Corps, Stamford, Conn., 1987—. Mem. bd. of edn. N. Highland Regional High Sch., Allendale - Saddle River, NJ, 1960—67; com. chmn. Boy Scouts of Am., New Milford, NJ, 1957—59; mem. adv. bd. Comprehensive Zoning Plan, Clearwater, Fla., 1995—96. With U.S. Army, 1938—43. Mem.: Pi Kappa Phi. Republican. Episcopalian. Achievements include expert in fields of prodn. of coal for chemicals and distallation polyurethane foam, microwave cured fiberboard, pvc panels and gypsum products. Avocations: antique car restoration, gardening, bridge, philately. Home: 3241 San Mateo St Clearwater FL 33759

KIEHN, MOGENS HANS, aviation engineer, consultant; b. Copenhagen, July 30, 1918; came to U.S., 1957; s. Hans-Christian and Lydia-Thea-Constans (Theill) K.; children: Marianne, Hans. BS, ME, PE, Tech. Engring., Copenhagen, 1940; MS, Copenhagen, 1942; degree in Army Intelligence, Def. Indsl. Security Inst., 1972. Registered profl. engr., Ariz., also chemical engineer. Pres. Hamo Engring., Copenhagen, 1939-47, Evanston, Ill., 1958—70; engr. Sundstrand, Rockford, Ill., 1957-58; pres., owner Kiehn Internat. Engring. Co., Phoenix, 1970—; chmn., pres. ETO Internat. Engring., Phoenix, 1970—. Tech. engring. cons. Scandinavian Airlines, Sundstrand Engring., McDonnell Douglas, Ford, GM, Chrysler, Honeywell, Motorola, Gen. Electric, Hughes Aircraft; chmn. bd. Internat. Tech. Engring. Recipient 32 patents including rehab. hosp. lighting for highmast, drafting machine, tooling machinery, parts for aircraft, garbage and pollution machine, optical coupler, also others. With Finnish Army, 1939, Danish Underground, 1940-45, Morocco French Fgn. Legion, 1948-54, Vietnam. Mem. AIII, NSPE, Soc. Illuminating Engrs., Nat. Geog. Soc., Am. Fedn. Police, East Africa Wildlife Soc., Interpol Intelligence and Organized Crime Orgn., Adventures Club Denmarkk, Honors Club, Am. Inst. of Aeronautics and Astronautics., St. Joseph's Legacy Club., St. Joseph's Indian Sch. Office: Kiehn Internat Tech Engring PO Box 1561 Scottsdale AZ 85252-1561

KIEHNE, FRANK CHARLES, JR., foreign affairs adviser; b. Burlington, Iowa, Feb. 2, 1925; s. Frank Charles Kiehne and Grace May (Archer) Keihne; m. Dolores Yulon Gutman, June 17, 1945; children: John Charles, James Wesley, Thomas Matt, Jeffrey Scott. AA, Bowling Green State U., 1944; BS, George Williams Coll., Chgo., 1947, MS, 1951. Community and student dir. southtown dept. YMCA of Chgo., 1947-50; exec. dir. country club br. YMCA, Kans. City, Mo., 1950-55; asst. gen. dir. YMCA of Met. St. Louis, 1955-61; CEO, YMCA of Reading and Berks County, Pa., 1961-70, YMCA of Met. Washington, 1970-73; exec. dir. internat. com. YMCA of USA, N.Y.C., 1973-80; refugee dir. ch. world svc. Nat. Coun. Chs., N.Y.C., 1981-82; exec. dir. Pvt. Agys. in Internat. Devel. (now Am. Coun. Vol. Internat. Action), Washington, 1982-84; sec. for refugees World Alliance of YMCAs, Geneva, 1986-90; fgn. affairs advisor to Congressman Donald M. Payne, Washington, 1990—96. Coord. fgn. affairs task force Congl. Black Caucus, 1992—95, fellow, 1996—. Editor: Palestinian Situation, 1989; author: (with others) Fair Play in Sports, 1979; contbr. articles to profl. jours. Pres. Reading Libr. Co., 2003—; mem. nat. adv. bd. Peace Acad., Washington, 1976—80; co-founder World Affairs Coun., Reading and Berks County, Pa., 1970; Human Rels. Coun., 1967; mem. Greater Reading Coun. of Chs., 1962—64; Mem. subcom. Mayor's Commn. on Human Rels., Chgo. and Kansas City, Mo, 1951—55; co-founder Econ. Opportunity Coun. Reading and Berks County, 1964; mem. Planned Parenthood Coun. Bd., 1964—68; planning divsn. United Cmty. Svcs. of Reading and Berks County, v.p. coordination in devel.; trustee Reading Pub. Libr., 2000—02, YMCA of Reading and Berks Counties, 2000—; mem. Christ Epsic. Ch., Reading, Pa. Officer USMCR, 1943—45. Named Disting. Alumnus George Williams Coll., 1970; recipient Cert. of Merit Am. Cancer Soc. Mem.: Latin Am. Paper Money Soc., Soc. Paper Money Collectors, Hist. Soc. Berks County, Internat. Bank Note Soc., Nat. YMCA of the U.S. Archives com., YMCA Assn. Profl. Dirs., Am. Acad. Polit. Sci., Africare (life). Avocations: collecting international bank notes, swimming. Home: 512 Elm St Reading PA 19601-3306 Fax: 610-376-5663. E-mail: kiehnef@aol.com.

KIEKHOFER, WILLIAM HENRY, lawyer; b. Madison, Wis., June 19, 1952; s. William and Emily (Graham) K.; m. Leslie A. Cohen., Jan. 27, 1956; children: Allison Laura, Phoebe Leigh, Rachel Elizabeth. BA, U. Wis., 1976; JD, U. So. Calif., 1980. Assoc. Sidley & Austin, L.A., 1980-82, Fried & King, L.A., 1982-83, McKenna Conner & Cuneo, L.A., 1983-90; ptnr. Kelley Drye & Warren LLP, L.A., 1990—. Office: Kelley Drye & Warren 777 S Figueroa St Ste 2700 Los Angeles CA 90017-5825

KIEL, BRENDA KAY, medical/surgical nurse; b. Osage, Iowa, Nov. 9, 1965; d. Leslie A. and Margaret L. (Troge) M.; m. Chad Kiel, Aug. 29, 1998. AS, N.E. Iowa Tech. Inst., 1986. Cert. ACLS, med.-surg. nurse, emergency rm. nurse, neonatal ruscitation. Staff nurse med./surg. wing St. Joseph Community Hosp., New Hampton, Iowa, 1986-98; clinic nurse Mercy Family Care Buffalo Ctr. (Iowa) Clinic, 1998—.

KIEL, FREDERICK ORIN, lawyer; b. Columbus, Feb. 22, 1942; s. Fred and Helen Kiel; m. Vivian Lee Naff, June 2, 1963; 1 child, Aileen Vivian. AB magna cum laude, Wilmington Coll., 1963; JD, Harvard U., 1966. Bar: Ohio 1966, U.S. Supreme Ct. 1972. Assoc. Peck, Shaffer & Williams, Cin., 1966-71, ptnr., 1971-80, Taft, Stettinius & Hollister, Cin., 1980-89; pvt. practice law Cin., 1990—. Lectr. and expert witness in field; co-founder Bond Attys.' Workshop, 1976. Editor: Bond Lawyers and Bond Law: An Oral History, 1993, Bondletter, 1991—, Anderson Insights, 1992—; contbr. articles on mcpl. bond fin. to profl. jours. Arbitrator Mcpl. Securities Rulemaking Bd., 1985-92; mem. Anderson Twp. Govtl. Task Force, 1986—; sec. Anderson Twp. Greenspace Adv. Com., 1990—; rep. precinct exec. Precinct H Anderson Twp., 1991-92, 94-2001, Precinct X Anderson Twp., 2001—; twp. atty. Anderson Twp., 1997—; sec. Anderson Twp. Rep. Screening Com., 1999 Mem. Ohio State Bar Assn., Cin. Bar Assn., Nat. Assn. Bond Lawyers (co-founder, dir. 1979-84, pres. 1982-83, hon. dir. 1984—, editor The Quar. Newsletter and The Bond Lawyer 1982—, Bond Atty.'s Workshop steering com. 1976, 83, 85, scrivener com. stds. of practice 1987-89), Queen City Club. Office: 1095 Nimitzview Dr Ste 103 Cincinnati OH 45230-4392

KIEL, PAUL EDWARD, lawyer; b. Jersey City, Mar. 14, 1957; s. Frank Thomas and Theresa Barbara (Miros) K.; m. Audrey Ann Szotak, Oct. 12, 1985. BA, Rutgers U., 1979; JD, Dickinson Sch. Law, 1982. Bart: N.J. 1983, Pa. 1983, U.S. Dist. Ct. N.J. 1983, U.S. Dist. Ct. (ea. dist.) Pa. 1983. Law clk. to judge Superior Ct. N.J., Elizabeth, 1982-83; assoc. MacDonald, Ryan & Jackel, Ridgewood, N.J., 1983-84, Harwood Lloyd, Hackensack, N.J., 1984—. Advisor Explorer Law Post, Hackensack, 1985-98 Mem. ABA, N.J. Bar Assn., Pa. Bar Assn., Bergen County Bar Asn., Phi Beta Kappa, Phi Alpha Theta. Republican. Roman Catholic. Office: Harwood Lloyd 130 Main St Hackensack NJ 07601-7152

KIELAROWSKI, HENRY EDWARD, marketing executive; b. Pitts., Dec. 29, 1946; s. Henry Andrew Kielarowski and Evelyn Marie Kline Boileau; m. Lynda Blair Powell, Aug. 1971 (div. 1976); children: Amorette, Blair. BA, Duquesne U., Pitts., 1969; MA, PhD, Duquesne U., 1974. Pres. Communicators, Inc., Pitts., 1974-76; mktg. specialist McGraw-Hill, Inc., N.Y.C., 1976-81; mktg. dir. Fidelity S.A., Allison Park, Pa., 1981-86; exec. v.p. ARC Systems, Inc., Pitts., 1986-88; v.p. mktg. Providian Financial Corp., San Francisco, 1988-98; pres. La Playa Cons., Inc., San Francisco, 1999—; founder Moksha Tribe EDM Collective. Author: Microcomputer Consulting in the CPA Environment, 1987; contbr. articles to profl. jours. Mem. Am. Mktg. Assn. (mktg. excellence award 1988), Direct Mktg. Assn. Democrat. Avocations: writing, mobile DJ, film making, DJ and producing of house music. Home: 1496 La Playa St San Francisco CA 94122-2813 E-mail: bonerinc@aol.com.

KIELHORN, RICHARD WERNER, chemist; b. Berlin, June 17, 1931; s. Richard H. and Auguste (Lammek) K.; m. Anneliese Heinrich, Aug. 9, 1952; children: Anita, Margit. BS, Chem. Tech. Sch., Berlin, 1953. Lab. tech. Zoellner Werke, Berlin, 1950-57, Montrose Chem. Corp., Henderson, Nev., 1957-78; chief chemist Stauffer Chem. Corp., Henderson, 1978-88, Pioneer Chlor Alkali Co., Henderson, 1988-92. Tax. cons. H&R Block, Las Vegas, Nev., 1972-96, Exec. Tax Svc., instr., 1978-95. Mem. ASTM, Am. Chem. Soc., Am. Statistical Assn., Nat. Soc. Tax Profls., Nat. Assn. Tax Profls. Home: 1047 Westminster Ave Las Vegas NV 89119-1825 E-mail: rkielhorn@aol.com.

KIELMEYER, WILLIAM HENRY, ceramic engineer, researcher; b. Columbus, Ohio, Jan. 6, 1943; s. Petr Henry and Dorothy Ruth (Potts) K.; m. Marjorie E. Kaufman, Oct. 5, 1968; children: Cheryl A., Thomas W. BS in Ceramic Engring., Ohio State U., 1966, MS, 1973. Project engr. Owens-Corning Fiberglas Corp., Granville, Ohio, 1968-72; rsch. engr. Johns-Manville Sales Corp., Littleton, Colo., 1973-78, sr. rsch. engr., 1978-86, rsch. assoc., 1987—. Mem. Am. Ceramic Soc. Republican. Lutheran. Achievements include 17 patents, including co-patentee process for making high-purity silica fiber for use in space shuttle reusable surface insulation; loose-fill residential insulation, commercial insulation materials and systems, manufacturing processes for dual glass and cladglass fibers. Home: 3374 W Chenango Ave Englewood CO 80110-6312 Office: 10100 W Ute Ave Littleton CO 80127-5002

KIELSMEIER, CATHERINE JANE, school system administrator; b. San Jose, Calif. d. Frank Delos MacGowan and Catherine Doris McGowan; m. Milton Kielsmeier; children: Catherine Louise, Barry Delos. MS, U. So. Calif., 1964, PhD, 1971. Tchr. pub. schs., Maricopa, Calif.; sch. psychologist Campbell Union Sch. Dist., Calif., 1961-66; asst. prof. edn. and psychology Western Oreg. State Coll., Monmouth, 1966-67, 70; asst. rsch. prof. Oreg. Sys. Higher Edn., Monmouth, 1967-70; dir. spl. svc. Pub. Sch., Santa Rosa, Calif., 1971-91; cons., 1991—. Author: Tibetan Lang. Pre-Primer, 1999, Tibetan Sadhana Vocabulary, 2003. Bd. dir. Sonoma County Coun. Cmty. Svc., 1976-82, Sonoma County Orgn. for Retarded/Becoming Ind., 1976-84, bd. dir., 1978-82; bd. dir. Gold Ridge Sangha, 1994-97, Hosp. Chaplaincy Svc., 1996—. Office: 7495 Poplar Dr Forestville CA 95436-9671

KIELY, DAN RAY, telecommunications and banking consultant; b. Ft. Sill, Okla., Jan. 2, 1944; s. William Robert and Leona Maxine (Ross) K. BA in Psychology, U. Colo., 1966; JD, Stanford U., 1969. Bar: Colo. 1969, D.C.1970, Va. 1973; cert. property mgr. Assoc. Holme, Roberts and Owen, Denver, 1969—70; pres. DeRand Equity Group, Arlington, Va., 1973-89; pres., chmn. bd. Bankwest Corp and related banks, Denver; pres., dir. United Gibralter Corp. Del., Inc., 1987—92; ptnr. Starlin & Kiely, P.C., 1989-94; trustee DeRand Real Estate Investment Trust, 1974—. Chmn. Pace Holdings, Inc., Washington, 1988—93, Washington Capital Corp., 1989—; spkr., lectr. in field. Deacon, McLean (Va.) Bapt. Ch., 1977-80. Officer USAR, 1969-73. Decorated Legion of Merit. Mem. ABA, Nat. Bd. Realtors, Inst. Real Estate Mgmt., Nat. Assn. Rev. Appraisers, Internat. Coun. Shopping Ctrs., Nat. Assn. Real Estate Investment Trusts, Internat. Inst. (cert. valuer), Colo. Indsl. Bankers Assn. (bd. dirs. 1985-87). Home: 67 Norwich C West Palm Beach FL 33417-7939 E-mail: dankiely@aol.com.

KIELY, GARRETT PAUL, publishing executive; b. Orange, N.J., Oct. 10, 1961; s. Garrett Paul Jr. and Margaret Ann (Hollywood) K.; m. Catherine Anne Mahoney, Oct. 20, 1990; children, Thomas Garrett, Julia Catherine, Daniel Michael. BA, Georgetown U., Washington, 1983. Product mgr. Springer-Verlag N.Y., N.Y.C., 1984-87; advt. and promotion mgr. Palgrave Macmillan/St. Martin's Press, N.Y.C., 1987-88, mktg. dir., 1988-91, dir., v.p., 1991-99, pres., pub., 1999—. Office: Palgrave Macmillan/St Martins Press 175 5th Ave Rm 200 New York NY 10010-7703

KIENBAUM, THOMAS GERD, lawyer; b. Berlin, Nov. 16, 1942; came to U.S., 1957; s. Gerd Wilhelm Kienbaum and Albertine Brigitte (Kramm) Kettler; m. Karen Smith, June 24, 1966 (div.); 1 child, Ursula; m. Elizabeth Hardy, Jan. 22, 1992. AB, U. Mich., 1965; JD magna cum laude, Wayne State U., 1968. Bar: Mich. 1968, Ill. 1991, U.S. Supreme Ct. 1983. Assoc. Dickinson, Wright, Moon, Van Dusen & Freeman, Detroit, 1968-76, ptnr., 1976-97; ptnr., founder Kienbaum Opperwall Hardy & Pelton, Detroit and Birmingham, 1997—. Contbr. legal articles to profl. publs. Bd. dirs. Wayne County Neighborhood Legal Svc., 1972-76, 87-88. Fellow ABA, State Bar of Mich. Found.; mem. Am. Judicature Soc., Coll. Labor and Employment Lawyers, State Bar Mich. (pres. 1995-96), Detroit Bar Assn. (pres. 1985-86), Barristers Assn. (pres. 1978-79), Oakland County Bar Assn., Order of the Coif. Avocations: reading, skiing, squash, sailing. Office: Kienbaum Opperwall Hardy & Pelton 325 S Old Woodward Ave Birmingham MI 48009-6202

KIENER, JOHN LESLIE, judge; b. Ft. Madison, Iowa, June 21, 1940; s. Cyril Joseph and Lucille Olive (Golden) K.; m. Carol Lynn Winston, June 4, 1966; children: Susan, Gretchen. BA cum laude, Loras Coll., 1962; JD, Drake U., 1965. Bar: Iowa 1965, Tenn. 1972, U.S. Supreme Ct. 1974. Practice law, Decorah, Iowa, 1965-68; asst. atty. gen. State of Iowa, 1968-72; ptnr. Cantor & Kiener, 1972-80; city judge City of Johnson City, Tenn., 1975-80, gen. sessions judge, 1980—. Continuing edn. tchr., bus. law East Tenn. State U., 1975—. Contbr. and articles editor in Jonesborough Herald and Tribune. Mem. ABA, Tenn. Bar Assn., Washington County Bar Assn., Rotary, Elks. Republican. Avocations: stamp collecting, genealogy. Home: 2403 Camelot Cir Johnson City TN 37604-2938 Office: Gen Sessions Ct Downtown Ctr Courthouse 101 E Market St Ste 7 Johnson City TN 37604-5722 E-mail: ckiener@preferred.com.

KIENITZ, LADONNA TRAPP, librarian, municipal official, lawyer; b. Bay City, Mich. d. Orlin D. and Mary (Stanford) Trapp; m. John Kienitz, Feb. 9, 1951 (div. Dec. 1974); children: John, Jim, Rebecca, Mary, Timothy, David. BA, Westmar Coll., 1951; MA in Libr. Sci., Dominican U., River Forest, Ill., 1970; M Mgmt., Northwestern U., 1984; JD, Western State U., Fullerton, Calif., 1995. Head libr. Woodlands Acad., Lake Forest, Ill., 1973-77; project officer North Suburban Libr. Sys., Wheeling, Ill., 1977-78; libr. dir. Lincolnwood (Ill.) Pub. Libr. Dist., 1978-86; city libr. City of Newport Beach, Calif., 1987—, dir. cmty. svcs., 1994—2002. Mem. ALA, ABA, Pub. Libr. Assn. (pres. 1995-96), Calif. Bar Assn., Calif. Libr. Assn., Calif. Bar Assn., Orange County Bar Assn.

KIENOW, BARRY SCOTT, construction executive, architect; b. Creighton, Nebr., Sept. 29, 1961; s. Ronald Willis and Lorraine Loy Kienow; m. Vanessa Lynn Kienow; children: Drew J. Throsh, Barry S. Kienow Jr. Student, U. Nebr., 1980-84. USDA inspector Plantation Foods, Waco, Tex., 1988-90; asst. prodn. mgr. Fleetwood Homes of Tex., Belton, 1990—.

KIENZLE, JOHN FRED, history educator; b. Allentown, Pa., Apr. 1, 1945; s. Fred John and Florence Mary K.; m. Patricia Catharine Evertsen, Aug. 22, 1970. BA in history, Albany State U., 1967; MA in History, NYU, 1969; PhD in History, Princeton U., 1972. Retail sales clk. Floyd Bennett Stores, Patchogue, N.Y., 1960-63; cafeteria worker Albany State Dorms, 1963-67; libr. aide NYU, N.Y.C., 1967-69, Firestone Libr.,Princeton (N.J.) U., 1969-70; tchr. history Maple Hill H.S., Castleton, N.Y., 1970—. Mem. Met. Mus. Art, 1987—, Lake Chaplain Maritime Mus., 1994—, N.C. Maritime Mus., 1999—, Schodack Faculty Assn., 1970—; trustee Maple Hill H.S. Amateur Radio Club, 1975—; radio officer Rensselaer County (N.Y.) Civil Emergency Svcs., 1980—. Mem. Archaeol. Inst. Am. Republican. Roman Catholic. Avocations: sailing, flying, amateur radio, astronomy, photography. Office: Maple Hill H S 1216 Maple Hill Rd Castleton On Hudson NY 12033-1604 E-mail: jkienzle@albany.net.

KIER, ANN BURNETTE, pathologist; b. Littlefield, Tex., June 29, 1949; m. Friedhelm Schroeder, Dec. 9, 1978; 1 child, Hilary. BA, U. Tex., 1971; BS, Tex. A&M U., 1973, DVM, 1974; PhD, U. Mo., 1979. Diplomate Am. Coll. Lab. Animal Medicine. From asst. to assoc. prof. dept. pathology U. Mo., Columbia, 1979-87; from assoc. prof. to prof. U. Cin., 1987-93; prof., dept. head Tex. A&M U., College Station, 1994—. Contbr. articles to profl. jours. and chpts. to books. Avocations: scuba diving, piano, reading. Home: PO Box 500 Wellborn TX 77881-0500 Office: Tex A&M U Dept Pathobiology College Station TX 74467

KIER, CARLOS M. rheumatologist; b. Ft. Worth, Tex., Apr. 28, 1945; s. James M. and Martha A. Kier; children: Catherine A., Kenneth M., Alexandra M. BS in Biology (pre-med.), U. Tex., Arlington, 1966; MD with honors, U. Tex., Galveston, 1970. Diplomate Am. Bd. Rheumatology, Am. Bd. Internal Medicine. Intern medicine, 1966—70; resident, 1971—73; fellow rheumatology, 1973—74, 1976—77; pvt. practice, 1978—; rheumatologist, 1980—. Exec. com. and pres. Big Bros.-Big Sisters, Arlington, Tex., 1983—92. Maj. USMC, 1974—76, Ft. Hood, Tex., served in U.S. Army, 1974—76. Named Top Dr., Guide to Top Doctors, 2003. Fellow: ACP, Am. Coll. Rheumatology; mem.: Alpha Omega Alpha. Office: Carlos M Kier MD PA 909-B Medical Centre Drive Arlington TX 76012-4757 Office Fax: 817-274-9254. E-mail: ckier@attglobal.net.

KIEREN, THOMAS HENRY, management consultant; b. Milw., July 23, 1941; s. Henry Lawrence and Hildegard (Luketell) K. BS, Holy Cross Coll., 1963; MBA, U. Chgo., 1968; postgrad., Harvard U., 1963. Mgr. Touche, Ross & Co., 1968-69; asst. v.p. Sunbeam Corp., Chgo., 1969-75; dir. bus. strategy ACF Industries, Inc., N.Y.C., 1975-78; dir. bus. and fin. planning GAF Corp., N.Y.C., 1978-82; dir. bus. planning Engelhard Corp., Edison, N.J., 1982-83; founder, pres., mng. dir. Manhattan Cons. Group, Inc., N.Y.C., 1983—. Bd. dirs. Mothers Stores, Inc.; chmn. mergers and acquisitions, seminar program Exec. Enterprises, Inc., N.Y.C., 1984-87; founder, chmn. Ducks Unltd., Inc., Passaic County; bd. dirs., chmn. Custom Corporate Photography, Inc., 2002--. Author, editor, lectr.: for AMA in corp. strategy, acquisitions and turnaround mgmt., 1980—; contbr. articles. Del. to White House conf. on small bus., Washington, 1986; pres. Bus. Execs. for Bush, 1998; area coord., mem. fin. com. Courter for Gov. of N.J., 1989; mem. fin. com. Whitman for Gov. of N.J. Campaign, 1993, 1997, mem. Inaugural Ball com., 1998; mem. Task Force on Tech. Policy Nat. Assn. Mfrs., Commn. Regulatory Reform and Govt. Waste; bd. dirs. Boy Scouts of Am.; mem. coun. N.Y. Philharm., 1980—; founder Chgo. Symphony Soc., Ctr. for Industry and Corp. Performance, Oak Ridge, NJ; founder, chmn. Greater Wayne Area Young Reps., Inc., 1992—2002; bd. dirs. N.J.-Straight and Narrow, Inc. Mem.: Product Devel. and Mgmt. Assn. (nat. v.p., bd. dirs., founder N.Y. chpt., Leadership award 1993), U. Chgo. Bus. Sch. Alumni Assn. (bd. dirs. 1983—85), Baruch Sch. of Bus. (adj. prof. of bus. strategy), Fordham Grad. Sch. of Bus., Amateur Comedy Club, U. Chgo. Bus. Sch. Club of N.Y. (founder, bd. dirs.), U. Club Chgo., Holy Cross Coll. Club of N.Y., Trout Unltd., Inc. (bd. dirs. N.Y. chpt.). Republican. Roman Catholic. Avocations: fly fishing, tennis, sports car racing, skiing, portrait and interior photography. Office: The Manhattan Cons Group Inc 226 E 54th St Ste 800 New York NY 10022-6207

KIERNAN, EDWIN A., JR., lawyer, corporation executive; b. N.Y.C., Aug. 2, 1926; s. Edwin A. and Helen M. (Clarke) K.; m. Ellen Mary Irving, Feb. 18, 1952; children: Robert Clarke, Katherine Waters. AB, Columbia, 1947, JD, 1950; LL.M., NYU, 1957. Bar: N.Y. 1950. Assoc. Simpson Thacher & Bartlett, N.Y.C., 1950-52, 54-55, Wickes, Riddell, Bloomer, Jacobi & McGuire, N.Y.C., 1956-59; atty. Western Electric Co., Inc., 1959-60, Interpublic Group of Cos., Inc., N.Y.C., 1960-64, mng. atty., 1964-68, asst. sec., asst. gen. counsel, 1968-79, sec. and gen. counsel, 1980-88, v.p., 1973-81, sr. v.p., 1981-88. Sec. McCann-Erickson, Inc., N.Y.C., 1962-79 Lt. (j.g.) USNR, 1944-46, 52-54. Mem. ABA, Phi Beta Kappa. Home: Apt 328 10100 Cypress Cove Dr Fort Myers FL 33908-7662 E-mail: EnEkiernan@aol.com.

KIERNAN, OWEN BURNS, educational consultant; b. Randolph, Mass., Mar. 9, 1914; s. Thomas Francis and Elizabeth (Burns) K.; m. Esther Harriet Thorley, July 13, 1940; children: Joan Ann, Nancy Elizabeth, John Albert. BS, Bridgewater (Mass.) State Coll., 1935; M.Ed., Boston U., 1940, Sc.D. (hon.), 1968; Ed.D., Harvard U., 1950; L.H.D. (hon.), Lesley Coll., 1956; LL.D., Northeastern U., 1961; Litt.D. (hon.), Stonehill Coll., 1965; Ped.D. (hon.), R.I. Coll., 1966. Prin. Henry T. Wing High Sch., Sandwich, Mass., 1938-44; supt. schs. Wayland and Sudbury, Mass., 1944-51, Milton, 1951-57; commr. edn., 1957-68; exec. dir. Nat. Assn. Secondary Sch. Prins., 1969-79; dir. sch. div. McManis Assos., Inc., 1980-82; cons. Washington, 1983—. Past chmn. Mass. Bd. Edn., Mass. Bd. Vocat. Edn.; corp. mem. MIT Trustee U. Mass.; trustee Lowell Tech. Inst., Mus. Fine Arts, Mus. Sci. Boston, Boston U.; bd. dirs. Atlantic Council U.S.; chmn. edn. com. Atlantic Treaty Assn., 1968-72; gov. bd. Atlantic Info. Centre for Tchrs., London, 1968-76; exec. com. U.S. People-to-People Program. Mem. Am. Assn. Sch. Adminstrs., New Eng., Mass. supts. assns., Council Chief State Sch. Officers (pres. 1967), Phi Delta Kappa. Home: 36 Fernbrook Ln Centerville MA 02632-2908

KIERNAN, RICHARD FRANCIS, publisher; b. N.Y.C., Apr. 17, 1935; s. James J. and Grace (Nolan) K.; m. Jane V. Eickmeyer, Dec. 29, 1962; children: Christopher R., Peter T., Kathy Lynn. BS, U. Conn., 1957. Salesman Med.

Econs. Co., Oradell, N.J., 1963-65, sales mgr., 1965-67, gen. mgr. Chgo., 1967-68; pub. Med. Econs. mag., Oradell, 1970-72, sr. v.p., pub., 1990-95; sr. v.p., pub., Redbook, Annual, Med. Econs. mag., Bus. and Health mag., Drug Topics mag., Montvale, N.J., 1991—; pres. Medical Econs. Profl. Info. Svc. Group, 1995—; pub. RN Mag., Oradell, 1968-70; pres. Cliggott Pub. Co., Greenwich, Conn., 1972-75; exec. v.p. Biomed. Info. Inc., N.Y.C., 1975-79; pres. Hosp. Pubs., Inc., Secaucus, N.J., 1979-89; chmn. R.F. Kiernan Assocs., Ridgewood, N.J., 1989-90; pres., COO PISG, Med. Econs., 1994—. Bd. dirs. Argus Press Holdings, USA; treas. Pharm. Adv. Council, 1979-81, pres., 1981; v.p. Devel. Med. Econs. Co. With U.S. Army, 1957-63. Mem. Pharm. Advt. Coun. (pres.), Assn. Clin. Pubs. (pres.), N.Y. Athletic Club, Ridgewood Country Club, Leland (Mich.) Country Club. Home and Office: 153 Hamilton Rd Ridgewood NJ 07450-1102

KIERNAN, THOMAS EDWARD, lawyer; b. Buffalo, Minn., Apr. 6, 1962; s. Daniel Patrick and Ardis Jane Kiernan; m. Julie R. Nilson, June 25, 1988. BA in Polit. Sci., U. Wis., Eau Claire, 1986; JD, William Mitchell Coll. Law, St. Paul, 1990. Bar: Minn. 1990. Assoc. Rinke-Noonan, St. Cloud, Minn., 1990-94; ptnr. Roes, Larsen & Kiernan, Annandale, Minn., 1994-99; pvt. practice Kiernan Personal Injury Atty. P.A., Buffalo, Minn., 1999—. Named Super Lawyer, Law and Politics mag., 1999, named Rising Star, 2002. Mem. Minn. Bar Assn. (cert. civil trial specialist 1997). Democrat. Roman Catholic. Avocations: reading, golf, movies, boating. Office: PO Box 433 Buffalo MN 55313-0433

KIERSCH, GEORGE ALFRED, geological consultant, retired educator; b. Lodi, Calif., Apr. 15, 1918; s. Adolph Theodore and Viola Elizabeth (Bahmeier) K.; m. Jane J. Keith, Nov. 29, 1942; children: Dana Elizabeth Kiersch Haycock, Mary Annan, George Keith, Nancy McCandless Kiersch Bohnett Student, Modesto Jr. Coll., 1936-37; BS and Geol. Engr., Colo. Sch. Mines, 1942; PhD in Geology, U. Ariz., 1947. Geologist 79 Mining Co., Ariz., 1946-47; geologist underground explosion tests and Folsom Dam-Reservoir Project U.S. C.E., Calif., 1948-50; supervising geologist Internat. Boundary and Water Commn., U.S.-Mex., 1950-51; asst. prof. geology U. Ariz., Tucson, 1951-55, dir. Mineral Resources Survey Navajo-Hopi Indian Reservation, 1952-55; exploration mgr. resources survey So. Pacific Co., San Francisco, 1955-60; assoc. prof. geol. sci. Cornell U., Ithaca, N.Y., 1960-63, prof., 1963-79, prof. emeritus, 1979—, chmn. dept. geol. scis., 1979—. Geol. cons., Ithaca, 1960-78, Tucson, 1978—; chmn. coordinating com. on environment and natural hazards, Internat. Lithosphere Program, 1986-1991. Author: Engineering Geology, 1955, Mineral Resources of Navajo-Hopi Indian Reservations, 3 vols., 1955, Geothermal Steam-A World Wide Assessment, 1964; author: (with others) Advanced Dam Engineering, 1988; editor/author: Heritage of Engineering Geology--First Hundred Years 1888-1988 (vol. of Geol. Soc. Am.), 1991; editor: Case Histories in Engineering Geology, 4 vols., 1963-69, Engineering GeoSciences and Military Operations, 1998; mem. editorial bd. Engrng. Geology/Amsterdam, 1965—. Mem. adv. coun. to bd. trustees Colo. Sch. Mines, 1962-71, pres. coms., 1990-2000; mem. nine coms. NAE/NAS, 1966-90; reporter coordinating com. 1-CC1 Nat. Hazards U.S. GeoDynamics Com., 1985-90. Capt. C.E., U.S. Army, 1942-45. NSF sr. postdoctoral fellow Tech. U. Vienna, 1963-64; recipient award for best article Indsl. Mktg. Mag., 1964, Palmes Academiques award French Govt., 1999. Fellow ASCE, Geol. Soc. Am. (chmn. div. engrng. geology 1960-61, mem. U.S. nat. com. on rock mechanics 1980-86, Disting. Practice award 1986, Burwell award 1992); mem. Soc. Econ. Geologists, U.S. Com. on Large Dams, Internat. Soc. Rock Mechanics, Internat. Assn. Engrng. Geologists (U.S. com. 1980-86, chmn. com. 1983-87, v.p. N.Am. 1986-90), Assn. Engrng. Geologists (1st receipient Claire P. Holdredge award 1965, 93, hon. mem. 1985), Cornell Club (N.Y.C.), Statler Club, Tower Club (Ithaca), Mining Club of Southwest (Tucson). Republican. Episcopalian. Home and Office: 42927 Cherbourg Ln Lancaster CA 93536-4826

KIERSCHT, MARCIA SELLAND, academic administrator, psychologist; b. Rugby, N.D. d. Osmund Harold and Cynthia (Thoresen) Selland; m. Charles M. Kierscht, Aug. 19, 1961 (div. 1972); children: Cynthia Ann, Matthew Mason. BA, U. Iowa, 1960, MA, 1962; PhD, Vanderbilt U., 1975. Lic. psychologist, Ill., Minn. Sch. psychologist South Suburban Cook County, Homewood, Ill., 1962-64, Dist. 108, Highland Park, Ill., 1964-65, Spl. Edn. Dist. Lake County Ill., Gurnee, 1966-72; psychol. examiner John F. Kennedy Ctr., George Peabody Coll., 1972-73; instr. in pediatrics Med. Sch. Vanderbilt U., Nashville, 1975-76; assoc. prof. Moorhead (Minn.) State U., 1976-80, asst. to pres., 1980-86; provost, chief exec. officer Tri-Coll. U., Fargo, N.D., 1986-90; dean grad. and profl. sch. Hood Coll., Frederick, Md., 1990-93; v.p. Consortium of Univs. of the Washington Met. Area, 1993-94; pres. Stephens Coll., Columbia, Mo., 1994—. Contbr. articles to profl. jours. V.p. Plains Art Mus., Moorhead, 1986-88; chmn. bd. govs. Fargo-Moorhead Area Found., Fargo, 1983-90; bd. dirs. United Way, Columbia, 1994-2001; mem. mgmt. coun. div. III, NAAA, 2001--. Recipient Pembina Trail award Minn. Hist. Soc., 1994. Mem. Am. Coun. on Edn., Coun. of Fellows, Fargo C. of C., Columbia C. of C. (bd. dirs.), Montgomery County High Tech. Coun., Rotary Club (Moorhead, Columbia, Fredericktowne), Cosmos Club, Washington. Office: Office of Pres 1200 E Broadway Columbia MO 65201-4978

KIERULFF, STEPHEN CHARLES, psychologist; b. L.A., 1942; s. Charles and Barbara K.; m. Carol Winter, 1970 (div. 1983); 1 child, Benjamin. BA, U. Calif., Berkeley, 1963; MA, William Paterson Coll., 1975; PhD, U.S. Internat. U., 1980. Lectr. Calif. State U., Long Beach, 1983-84; outreach profl. Orange County Drug Abuse Svcs., Anaheim, Calif., 1985-86; assoc. prof. Cleveland Coll., L.A., 1985; psychotherapist pvt. practice, Inglewood, Calif., 1989—, Santa Monica, Calif., 1995—. Adj. prof. U.S. Internat. U., San Diego, 1984-91, U. Profl. Studies, San Diego, 1993. Contbr. articles to profl. jours. Mem. Zero Population Growth, L.A., 1990-95, Peace Rsch. Group, L.A., 1985-90. Mem. APA, Calif. Psychol. Assn., Assn. Humanistic Psychology, Psi Chi. Avocations: walking, reading, writing. Office: 111 N La Brea #609 Inglewood CA 90301 E-mail: doctorkierulff@aol.com.

KIES, DAVID M. lawyer; b. N.Y.C., Jan. 25, 1944; s. Saul and Lillian (Schultz) K.; m. Emily Bardack, July 6, 1966 (div. 1985); children: Laura, Adam, Abigail; m. Anne Monteith, Oct. 7, 1990 (div. 1998); 1 child, Samuel; m. Kathryn L. Danes, Mar. 11, 2001. AB, Haverford Coll., 1965; JD, NYU, 1968. Bar: N.Y. 1968, U.S. Dist. Ct. (so. dist.) N.Y. 1969, U.S. Ct. Appeals (2d cir.) 1969. Assoc. Sullivan & Cromwell, N.Y.C., 1968-76, ptnr., 1976—, dir. London office, 1992-95; dir. Imclone Systems, Inc. Former trustee Haverford Coll. Root Tilden fellow, NYU Law Sch., 1965. Mem. ABA, N.Y. State Bar Assn., Assn. Bar City of N.Y. Democrat. Jewish. Office: Sullivan & Cromwell 125 Broad St Fl 28 New York NY 10004-2489

KIES, KENNETH J. lawyer; b. Ft. Benning, Ga., Jan. 4, 1952; s. Robert Herman K.; m. Kathleen Barbara Clark, Oct. 11, 1986. BA, Ohio U., 1974; JD, Ohio State U., 1977; LLM in Taxation, Georgetown U., 1986. Bar: Ohio 1977, U.S. Tax Ct. 1978, D.C. 1987, U.S. Supreme Ct. 1992. Assoc. Baker & Hostetler, Cleve., 1977-81; asst. minority tax counsel Com. on Ways & Means U.S. Ho. of Reps., Washington, 1981-82, chief minority tax counsel, 1982-87; ptnr. Baker & Hostetler, Washington, 1987-95; chief of staff joint com. on taxation U.S. Congress, Washington, 1995-98; mng. ptnr. Price Waterhouse Coopers, Washington, 1998—2002; mng. dir. Fed. Policy Group, Clark Cons., Washington, 2002—. Contbr. articles to profl. jours. Mem. Capitol Hill Club, Washington Golf and Country Club, Robert Trent Jones Golf Club. Republican. Office: Fed Policy Group 101 Constitution Ave NW 701E Washington DC 20001-2133

KIESBYE, STEFAN, writer, educator; b. Eckernförde, Holstein, Germany, Feb. 20, 1966; arrived in U.S., 1996; s. Hans Uwe and Ruth Helene (Mattern) Kiesbye; m. Sanaz Samimy Kiesbye, Nov. 26, 1999. BA, Free U., Berlin, 1996; MA in Am. Studies, SUNY, Buffalo, 1998; MFA in Creative Writing, U. Mich., 2001. Actor Modernes Theater, Berlin, 1991—93; lectr. U. Mich., Ann Arbor, 2001—02; lectr. creative and argumentative writing Ea. Mich. U., Ypsilanti, 2002—. Author: (story collection) Queen City, 2001 (Chamberlain award, 2001), (chapbook) The End of Some Things, 2003 (Flash Point award, 2002). Scholar, German Acad. Exch. Svc., 1996—97; Colby fellow, U. Mich., 1999—2001. Office: Ea Mich Univ 612 Pray Harrold Ypsilanti MI 48197

KIESEL, ILMAR OTTO, retired radiologist; b. Tiflis, Caucasus, Russia, Oct. 14, 1912; came to U.S., 1949; MD, U. Tartu, Estonia, 1938. Cert. in radiology. Intern U. Tartu, 1937-38, resident in roentgenology, 1938-42; resident U. Minn. Hosp., 1957-60, Mpls. VA Hosp., 1957-60; prof. emeritus Oreg. Health Scis. U. Mem. AMA, Am. Coll. Radiology, Radiol. Soc. N.Am.

KIESLER, CHARLES ADOLPHUS, psychologist, academic administrator; b. St. Louis, Aug. 14, 1934; m. Teru Morton, Feb. 28, 1987; 1 child, Hugo; children from previous marriage: Tina, Thomas, Eric, Kevin. BA, Mich. State U., 1958, MA, 1960; PhD (NIMH fellow), Stanford U., 1963; D (hon.), Lucian Blaga U., Romania, 1995. Asst. prof. psychology Ohio State U., Columbus, 1963-64, Yale U., New Haven, 1964-66, assoc. prof., 1966-70; prof., chmn. psychology U. Kans., Lawrence, 1970-75; exec. officer Am. Psychol. Assn., Washington, 1975-79; Walter Van Dyke Bingham prof. psychology Carnegie Mellon U., Pitts., 1979-85, head psychology, 1980-83, acting dean, 1981-82, dean Coll. Humanities and Social Scis., 1983-85; provost Vanderbilt U., 1985-92; chancellor U. Mo., Columbia, 1992-96, Weil Disting. prof. health svcs. mgmt., 1996-98; prof., sr. advisor San Diego State U., 1998-99. Pres., CEO, Virtual Univ. Internat., 1996-97. Author: (with B.E. Collins and N. Miller) Attitude Change: A Critical Analysis of Theoretical Approaches, 1969, (with S.B. Kiesler) Conformity, 1969, The Psychology of Commitment: Experiments Linking Behavior to Belief, 1971, (with N. Cummings and G. VandenBos) Psychology and National Health Insurance: A Sourcebook, 1979, (with A.E. Sibulkin) Mental Hospitalization: Myths and Facts About a National Crisis, 1987, (with C. Simpkins) The Unnoticed Majority: Psychiatric inpatient care in general hospitals, 1993. Served with Security Service USAF, 1952-56. Recipient Disting. Alumnus award Mich. State U., 1987, Gunnar Myrdal award for Evaluation Practice Am. Evaluation Assn., 1989. Fellow AAAS, APA (Distng. Contbr. to Rsch. in Pub. Policy award 1989), Am. Psychol. Soc. (founding past pres. 1988-90); mem. AAUP, Inst. of Medicine of Nat. Acad. Scis., Sigma Xi, Psi Chi, Phi Kappa Phi. Home and Office: 3427 Mount Laurence Dr San Diego CA 92117-5649 E-mail: ckiesler@san.rr.com.

KIESLING, ERNST WILLIE, civil engineering educator; b. Eola, Tex., Apr. 8, 1934; s. Alfred William and Louise (Kern) K.; m. Juanita Haseloff, Aug. 25, 1956; children: Carol, Chris, Max. BS in Mech. Engrng, Tex. Tech. Coll., 1955; MS in Applied Mechanics, Mich. State U., 1959, PhD, 1966. Registered profl. engr. Asst. prof. Tex. Tech. Coll., 1959-63; sr. research engr. S.W. Research Inst., San Antonio, 1966-69; prof. civil engrng. Tex. Tech U., Lubbock, 1969—, chmn. dept. civil engrng., 1969-88, assoc. dean engrng., 1988-93; prof. civil engrng. Tex. Tech. U., Lubbock, 1993—. NSF faculty fellow, 1963-64 Fellow ASCE; mem. NSPE (life), Am. Soc. Engrng. Edn., Nat. Storm Shelter Assn. (exec. dir. 2001—), Sigma Xi, Chi Epsilon, Tau Beta Pi. Achievements include pioneering work in storm shelter research and utilization. Home: 5111 97th St Lubbock TX 79424-4867 Office: Tex Tech U Dept Civil Engrng Lubbock TX 79409

KIESLING, SCOTT FABIUS, linguist, educator; b. Bloomington, Indiana, May 30, 1967; s. Herbert John and Iris F. Kiesling; m. Julie Wallace Vanneman, July 1, 1995; children: Charles children: Emma. PhD, Georgetown U., Washington, 1996, MS, 1992; BA, U. of Pennsylvania, Philadelphia, Pa., 1989. Lectr. linguistics U. of Sydney, Australia, 1996—99; post doctoral rschr. linguistics Ohio State U., Columbus, 1999—2000; asst. prof. linguistics U. Pitts., 2000—. Office: Univ Pitts Dept Linguistics 2816 Cath of Learning Pittsburgh PA 15260 Office Fax: 412-624-6130. Business E-Mail: sfkiesling@yahoo.com.

KIESSLING, LAURA LEE, chemist, researcher; b. Milw, Wis, Sept. 21, 1960; d. William E. and LaVonne V. (Korth) K. SB, MIT, 1983; PhD, Yale U., 1989. Teaching asst. MIT, Cambridge, Mass., 1982-83, Yale U., New Haven, 1983-84, rsch. asst., 1984-89; rsch. fellow Calif. Tech. U., Pasadena, Calif., 1989-91; asst. prof. chemistry U. Wis., Madison, Wis., 1991-97, assoc. prof., 1997-99, prof. chemistry, prof. biochemistry, 1999—. Cons. Ophidian, Inc., 1997-99, Alfred P. Sloan Found. Fellowships, 1997—; mem. bioorganic and natural products study sect. NIH, 1997-2000; Fellow, Am. Assoc. for the Advancement of Sci., 2003; elected Acad. of Arts and Sci., 2003; sci. adv. bd. Promega Corp., 1999—; selection com. for editor Jour. Organic Chemistry, 1999. Mem. editl. bd. Chemistry and Biology, 1997—, Organic Reactions, 2000—; contbr. articles to profl. jour. Recipient Dow Chems. New Faculty award, 1992, Shaw Scientist award, 1992-97, Nat. Young Investigator award NSF, 1993-98, Beckman Young Investigator award, 1994-96, Zeneca Excellence in Chemistry award, 1996, Dreyfus Tchr.-Scholar award Dreyfus Found., 1996; Postdoctoral fellow Am. Cancer Soc., 1989-91, MacArthur fellow John D. and Catherine MacArthur Found., 1999, Alfred P. Sloan Found. fellow, 1997. Mem. AAAS, Am. Chem. Soc. (Cope scholar 1999, Isbell award 2000), Soc. Glycobiology, Am. Soc. for Biochemistry and Molecular Biology, Sigma Xi, Phi Lambda Upsilon. Avocations: canoeing, rowing, running. Office: U Wis Dept Chemistry 1101 University Ave Madison WI 53706-1322 Fax: 608-265-0764.

KIEST, ALAN SCOTT, social services administrator; b. Portland, Oreg., May 14, 1949; s. Roger M. and Ellen Kiest; m. Heather L. Griffin; 1 child, Jennifer S. BA in Polit. Sci., U. Puget Sound, Tacoma, 1970; MPA, U. Wash., 1979. Welfare eligibility examiner Wash. Dept. Social and Health Services, Seattle, 1970-72, caseworker, 1972-76, service delivery coordinator, 1976-82; community svcs. office adminstr. Wash. Dept. Social and Health Svcs., Seattle, 1982—. Planning commr. City of Lake Forest Park, 1987, mem. city coun., 1988—, chair city fin. com., 1992-97, vice chmn. city budget com., 1998—; mem. King County Mangaged Health Care Oversight Com., 1993-95; mem. King County Human Svcs. Roundtable, 1995-2000, vice chair, 1998-2000. Mem. Eastside Cmty. coun. United Way of King County, 1998--, chair, 2001-02; mem. exec. com. bd. dirs. United Way of King County, 2001-02, cmty. devel. com. Mem. Suburban Cities Assn. Avocations: travel, music. Home: 18810 26th Ave NE Lk Forest Park WA 98155-4146 Office: Wash Dept Social & Health Svcs 14360 SE Eastgate Way Bellevue WA 98007-6462 E-mail: akiest@excite.com.

KIETZMAN, KRIS, music educator; m. Brian Kietzman; 5 children. MusB in Edn., Valparaiso U., 1985. Lic. Tchr. N.D. Instr. music Edgeley Pub. Sch., Edgeley, ND, 1998—. Dir.: (director of a musical) Tom Sawyer and Various others. Mem. Zion Luth. Ch., Edgeley, 1998—2002. Mem.: NEA, Music Educators Nat. Conf., Am. Choral Dirs. Assn. Avocations: singing, sewing, spending time with my family.

KIEVAL, JOSHUA, cardiologist, educator; b. Atlanta, May 9, 1948; MD, U. Rochester, 1974. Diplomate Am. Bd. Internal Medicine, Am. Bd. Cardiovascular Diseases, Am. Bd. Interventional Cardiology. Intern U. S. Fla. Affiliated Hosps., 1974-75; resident in medicine Boston City Hosp., 1975-77; fellow in cardiology U. Miami (Fla.) Hosps., 1977-79; co-dir. cardiovascular lab. JFK Med. Ctr., West Palm Beach, Fla., 1987—; ptnr. Palm Beach Heart Assocs., West Palm Beach, Fla. Clin. assoc. prof. medicine U. Miami Sch. Medicine, 1987—. Fellow: CCP, ACP (coun. clin. cardiology), Soc. Cardiac Angio and Intervention, Am. Heart Assn., ACSA&I, Am. Coll. Cardiology. Office: Palm Beach Heart Assocs 5511 S Congress Ave Ste 125 Lake Worth FL 33462-1140 E-mail: palmbeachheart@pol.net.

KIEWRA, GUSTAVE PAUL, psychologist, educator; b. Garden City Park, N.Y., July 25, 1943; s. Gustave Francis and Alice (Kozyrski) K.; m. Donna Elaine Womack, Nov. 29, 1969; children: Amy Marie, Christopher Paul, Jessica Lauren. BA, Franklin Coll., 1967; MA, Ball State U., 1968, EdD, 1972. Instr. psychology Fla. Jr. Coll., Jacksonville, 1968-70; counselor, asst. prof. counselor edn. Western Ky. U., Bowling Green, 1972-76; prof. psychology Piedmont Va. C.C., Charlottesville, 1976—. Mem. psychology peer group planning com. Va. C.C. Sys., 1996; mem. bldg. com. Piedmont Va. C.C., 1993-98, planning coun., 1996—, mem. info. techs. com., 1996-2000, phys. facilities com., 1999—, coll. diversit com., 1999-2002, exterior signage & way finding com., 1999-2000, safety com., 2002—. Bd. dirs. Western Albemarle Rescue Squad, Crozet, Va., 1987, 88, Am. Lung Assn., Charlottesville, 1986-88; coord. Neighborhood Watch, Crozet, 1985-98; mem. sch. improvement com. Crozet Elem. Sch., 1990-91; mem. Piedmont (Va.) Cmty. Coll. Planning Coun., 1995-96. Recipient svc. award Piedmont Va. C.C., 1981, 86, 91, 96, 2001. Mem. APA, Va. Psychol. Assn., Am. Assn. Marriage and Family Counselors, Va. C.C. Assn. (rep. faculty affairs com. 1990-92), Faculty Profl. Assn., Internat. Platform Assn., Lions (pres. Crozet, Va. 1989-92, Key award 1991, Advancement Key award 1991, Master Key award 1992, 100% Pres. award 1990-92, Dist. Gov. Membership Growth award 1990-92, Va. Multiple Dist. 24 Achievement award 1990-92, Pres. Svc. Appreciation award 1992, Achievement award medal 1992, Melvin Jones fellow Internat. Found.), Phi Delta Kappa, Phi Theta Kappa (hon., faculty advisor 1980-88), Phi Delta Theta. Avocations: volleyball, hiking, gardening, physical conditioning, community service. Home: 1440 Birchwood Dr Crozet VA 22932-9441 Office: Piedmont Va CC 501 College Dr Charlottesville VA 22902-7589 E-mail: gkiewra@pvcc.vccs.edu.

KIFFMEYER, MARY, state official; b. Balta, N.D., Dec. 29, 1946; m. Ralph Kiffmeyer; children: Christina, Patrick, James, John. RN, St. Gabriel's Sch. Nursing, Little Falls, Minn.; student, Anoka Ramsey C.C. RN, Minn.; cert. election judge. Co-owner RK Anesthesia, Big Lake, Minn.; sec. of state State of Minn., St. Paul, 1999—. Republican. Office: 180 State Office Bldg 100 Dr Martin Luther King Jr Blvd Saint Paul MN 55155-1210

KIGER, JOSEPH CHARLES, history educator; b. Kenton County, Ky., Aug. 19, 1920; s. Carl C. and Genevieve (Hoelscher) K.; m. Jean Myrick Moore, Mar. 27, 1947; children: Carl A., John J. AB, Birmingham-So. Coll., 1943; MA, U. Ala., 1947; PhD, Vanderbilt U., 1950. Teaching fellow Vanderbilt U., 1948-50; instr. history U. Ala., summer 1950, Washington U., St. Louis, 1950-51; dir. research select com. to investigate founds. U.S. Ho. of Reps., 1952; staff asso. Am. Council Edn., Washington, 1953-55; asst. dir. So. Fellowships Fund, Chapel Hill, N.C., 1955-58; asso. prof. history U. Ala., 1958-61; prof. history U. Miss., 1961—, chmn. dept. history, 1969-74, emeritus, 1990—, dir. program on founds. and Comparable orgs., 1993—2002, sr. rsch. assoc. Croft Inst. for Internat. Studies, 2002—. Cons. non-profit orgns., also govt., 1954— Author: Operating Principles of the Larger Foundations, 1954, (with others) Sponsored Research Policy of Colleges and Universities, 1954, American Learned Societies, 1963, (with others) A History of Mississippi, 1973; editor: Research Institutions and Learned Societies, 1982, International Encyclopedia of Foundations, 1990, Internat. Encyclopaedia of Learned Societies and Academies, 1993; co-editor: Foundations, 1984, Historiographic Review of Foundation Literature, Motivations and Perceptions, 1987, Philahthropic Foundations in the Twentieth Century, 2000. Served to capt. USMCR, 1942-46. Guggenheim fellow, 1960; grantee Russell Sage Found., 1953; grantee Rockefeller Found., 1961; grantee Am. Philos. Soc., 1964; grantee Am. Council of Learned Socs., Nat. Acad. Scis., 1980 Mem. Am. Hist. Assn., So. Hist. Assn. (life). Office: U Miss 215 Crost Inst for Internat Studies University MS 38677

KIGER, ROBERT WILLIAM, botanist, science historian, educator; b. Washington, Oct. 4, 1940; s. William Joseph and Marian (Calvert) K.; m. Suellen Montgomery, June 11, 1968; children: David M., James R. AA with honors, Montgomery Jr. Coll., 1964; BA in Spanish with Social Scis. minor, Tulane U., 1966; MA in History, U. Md., 1971, PhD in Botany, 1972. Tchr. Poolesville Elem. Sch., Md., 1966-67; grad. teaching asst. dept. history U. Md., College Park, 1968-69, grad. teaching asst. dept. botany, 1969-70, grad. rsch. asst. dept. botany, 1969-70; assoc. editor, rsch. botanist Flora N.Am. Program dept. botany Smithsonian Inst., Washington, 1972-73; asst. dir., sr. rsch. scientist Hunt Inst. Bot. Documentation, Carnegie Mellon U., 1974-77, dir., prin. rsch. scientist, 1977—; rsch. assoc. sect. botany Carnegie Mus. Natural History, Pitts., 1978—. Adj. scientist Pitts. Poison Ctr., Children's Hosp., 1990—; adj. prof. biol. scis. dept. biol. scis. Carnegie Mellon U., 1984-99, history of sci. dept. history, 1979—, disting. svc. prof. botany dept. biol. scis., 1999—; mem. internat. com. Internat. Congress Systematic and Evolutionary Biology, 1980-90, asst. treas., 1980-90, sec.-gen., 1990-96; mem. adv. com., editorial com. Flora of N.Am. Project, 1983—; cons. Chgo. Botanic Garden, Glencoe, Ill., 1980-83, 87-88, 89, Carnegie Mus. Natural History, Pitts., 1984, European Sci. Found., Stasbourg, France, 1987, Commn. Preservation and Access, Wye, Md., 1991, FBI, Martinsburg, W.Va., 1997. Editor: Memoirs of the Torrey Botanical Club, 1975-88, Huntia, 1978-92, bibliographic editor (all vols.) and taxonomic editor (various families), Flora of North America, 1987—; exec. editor Hunt Inst. publs., 1977—; contbr. articles to profl. jours. Chmn. Lawrence Meml. Award Com., 1979—; steering group Com. Organize a Flora of N.Am. Project, 1982-83; sec. for N.Am. Commn. Taxonomic Database Plant Sci. IUBS, 1986-89, working parties for devel. various standards, 1986—, program com., 1987-90, global plant species info. group, 1990—; mem. adv. com. computer databasing Mo. Botanical Garden, St. Louis, 1988-89, Rocky Mountain Flora Project, 1993—; botanical info. adv. workshop BIOSIS, Washington, 1990; chmn. judges for botany Internat. Sci. and Engring. Fair, Pitts., 1989. With USMC, 1960-61, USMCR, 1960-66. Grantee NSF, 1971-73, 78-80, 90; recipient Full Merit scholarship Montgomery Jr. Coll., 1963-64, Partial Merit scholarship Tulane U., 1964-66, NSF Grad. traineeship U. Md., 1970, Carroll E. Cox award U. Md., 1972-73. Fellow Linnean Soc. London; mem. AAAS, Botanical Soc. Am. (sec./treas. hist. sect. 1979-92, chmn. archives and history com. 1985-86), Am. Assn. Botanical Gardens and Arboreta, Am. Inst. Biol. Scis., Am. Soc. Plant Taxonomists, Internat. Assn. Plant Taxonomy, Internat. Soc. for History and Philosophy Sci., Assn. Tropical Biology, Coun. Botanical and Horticultural Librs., History Sci. Soc., Soc. Econ. Botany, Soc. Study Evolution, Soc. Systematic Biology, Torrey Botanical Club (assoc. editor 1975—), New Eng. Botanical Club. Avocations: music, model aviation, bicycling, motorcycling, photography. Home: 1183 Bucknell Dr Monroeville PA 15146-4319 Office: Carnegie Mellon U Hunt Inst Bot Documentation 5000 Forbes Ave Pittsburgh PA 15213-3890 E-mail: rkiger@andrew.cmu.edu.

KIGER, RONALD LEE, contract negotiator; b. Pasadena, Calif., Dec. 30, 1940; s. Wallace Lee and Ilo Marie (Smith) K.; m. Carole Ann Bates, Apr. 10, 1965 (div. Dec. 1978); children: Darren Lee, Lorene Elizabeth. Student, U. Calif., Berkeley, 1958-62; BBA, Armstrong Coll., 1964. Auditor GAO, San Francisco, 1964-66; sr. auditor Def. Contract Audit Agy., San Francisco, 1966-84; material price analyst Lockheed Missiles and Space Co., Sunnyvale, Calif., 1984-91, Lockheed Martin Aeronautical Systems, Marietta, Ga., 1991—. State dir. U.S. Jaycees, Castro Valley, Calif., 1968, pres., 1969, dist. lt. gov., Alameda County, Calif., 1970, state credentials chmn., Calif., 1970. Mem. Assn. Govt. Accts. (sec. 1968, spl. activities dir. 1982-83, pres. 1983-84, newsletter editor 1984-85, nat. chpt. recognition com. 1985-87, regional v.p. western region, 1988-89, nat. awards com. 1989-91, nat. nominating com. 1990). Democrat. Mem. Christian Ch. Avocations: golf, reading, crossword puzzles. Home: 4523 Savage Dr Marietta GA 30066-1425

KIHLE, DONALD ARTHUR, lawyer; b. Noonan, N.D., Apr. 4, 1934; s. J. Arthur and Linnie W. (Ljunngren) K.; m. Judith Anne, July 18, 1964; children: Kevin, Kirsten, Kathryn, Kurte. BS in Indsl. Engring., U. N.D., 1957; JD, U. Okla., 1967. Bar: Okla. 1967, U.S. Dist. Cts. (we. and no. dists) Okla. 1967, U.S. Ct. Appeals (10th cir.) 1967, U.S. Supreme Ct. 1971. Assoc. Huffman, Arrington, Scheurich & Kincaid, Tulsa, 1967-71, ptnr., 1971-78; shareholder, dir., officer Arrington Kihle Gaberino & Dunn, Tulsa, 1978-97, pres., 1994-97; shareholder, dir. Gable & Gotwals, Tulsa, 1997-99, advisor, dir., 1999-2001. Dist. chmn. Boy Scouts Am., 1983-85, cubmaster, 1986-88, coun. coms., 1988-96, campiree chmn., 1990; mem. Statewide Law Day Com., 1982-86, chmn., 1983-85; trustee Brandon Hall Sch., Atlanta, 1991—, chmn., 1995-99. Lt. U.S. Army, 1957-59. Recipient Silver Beaver award Boy Scouts Am. Mem.: ABA, Tulsa County Bar Assn., Okla. Bar Assn. (chmn. constl. bicentennial com. 1986—89), Tulsa Club (bd. govs. 1987—94, pres. 1992), So. Hills Country Club, Q Club (scribe 1991—), Rotary, Order of Arrow (vigil), Order of Coif, Sigma Chi (Tulsa alumni pres. 1995—97), Phi Delta Phi, Sigma Tau. Republican. Home: 4717 S Lewis Ct Tulsa OK 74105-5135 Office: 1100 ONEOK Plz 100 W 5th St Tulsa OK 74103-4240 E-mail: dkihle@gablelaw.com.

KIKEL, RUDY JOHN, editor, writer; b. Bklyn., Feb. 23, 1942; s. Rudolph and Pauline (Staudacher) K. BA, St. John's U., 1963; MA, Pa. State U., 1965; PhD, Harvard U., 1975. Tchr. Suffolk U., Boston, 1970—75; arts editor Bay Windows Newspaper, Boston, 1983—. Author: Lasting Relations, 1982, Long Division, 1993, Period Pieces, 1997; editor: Gents, Bad Boys and Barbarians, 1995. Address: 154 W Newton St Boston MA 02118-1203 E-mail: rudyk@aol.com.

KIKEN, MICHAEL STEPHEN, obstetrician, gynecologist; b. Jersey City, N.J., July 4, 1943; m. Barbara Kiken, Aug. 11, 2002; children: Elizabeth, Laura. BS, St. Peter's Coll., 1965; MD, U. Pitts., 1969. Diplomate Am. Bd. Obstetricians and Gynecologists. Intern U. Pitts., Magee Womens' Hosp., 1969-70, resident, 1970-73, Mass. Gen. Hosp., Brigham Hosp., Boston, 1971; attending

staff Kaiser Found. Hosp., Walnut Creek, Calif., 1973-74, John Muir Meml. Hosp., Walnut Creek, 1974-81; ob/gyn. Alamo (Calif.) Med. Group, 1974-81; attending staff Canton-Potsdam (N.Y.) Hosp., 1981-98, Kaiser Permanente Med. Group, Springfield, Va., 1998-2001, Fairfax (Va.) Hosp., 1998-2001, Southside Comty. Hosp., 2001—02, Shenandoah Valley Med. Sys., Inc., City Hosp., Martinsburg, W.Va., 2002—. Cons. gynecologist St. Lawrence U., Canton, N.Y., 1982-94. Lt. col. U.S. Army N.G., 1969-81. Fellow ACOG. Avocations: running, weight training.

KIKER, BILLY FRAZIER, economics educator; b. Elkin, N.C., Apr. 21, 1936; s. William James and Ruby Lucille K.; m. Martha Jane Parker, Aug. 4, 1962; children: Todd, Jonathan, David. AB, Lenoir-Rhyne Coll., 1961; PhD, Tulane U., 1965. From asst. prof. to prof. Econs. U. S.C., Columbia, 1965—; Univ. Chr. prof. Dept. Econs., Columbia, 1973—; chmn. dept. U. S.C., Columbia, 1973-87, dir. Ctr. for Studies in Human Capital, 1972-75. Vis. prof. U. Edinburgh, Scotland, 1973, U. Minho, Portugal, 1995, 96, Wirtschafts U., Vienna, Austria, 1997; pvt. practice cons. economist, Columbia, 1972. Author: Human Capital in Retrospect, 1968, Macroeconomic Analysis, 1974; editor: Investment in Human Capital, 1971; contbr. numerous articles to profl. jours. Fulbright scholar U. Porto, Portugal, 1988. Mem. Am. Econ. Assn., Nat. Assn. Forensic Econs. Methodist. Avocations: sailing, tennis. Home: 637 Woodland Hills Rd W Columbia SC 29210-5640 Office: U of SC Coll Of Bus Admin Columbia SC 29208-0001

KIKO, PHILIP GEORGE, lawyer; b. Massillon, Ohio, July 16, 1951; s. Willard LeRoy and Stella Jane (Schroeder) K.; m. Colleen Duffy; children: Jamie Lynn, Sarah Elizabeth, Philip George Jr., Michael Ryan. BA, Mount Union Coll., 1973; JD, George Mason Sch. Law, 1977. Bar: Va. 1977, D.C 1978, U.S. Ct. Appeals (D.C. cir.) 1978. Assoc. legal counsel, broadcast asst. Nat. Rep. Congl. Com., Washington, 1973-79; exec. asst., legis. counsel Congressman Sensenbrenner, Washington, 1979-83; assoc. counsel judiciary com. U.S. Ho. Reps., Washington, 1983-86; acting dir. policy and enforcement Office for Civil Rights U.S. Dept. Edn., Washington, 1986-87; officer, bd. dirs. Kiko Heating & Air Conditioning, Canton, Ohio, 1973-89; legis. counsel Dept. Interior, Washington, 1987-89, dir. budget and program resource mgmt., 1989-92, dep. dir. office hearings and appeals, 1992-94; assoc. adminstr. procurement and purchasing U.S. Ho. of Reps., Washington, 1995-96, dep. chief of staff, counsel sci. com., 1997—98; chief of staff, counsel Congressman James Sensenbrenner, 1999-2000; chief of staff, gen. counsel House Com. on the Judiciary, 2001—. Active Arlington Rep. Com., 1978-86, 1995-2001, Fair Housing Bd., Arlington, 1980, St. Charles Parish Coun., 1997—; v.p. Arlington Hts. Citizen Assn., 1991-96, 2002-; pres. St. Charles Sch. PTO, 1994-99, 2001--; scoutmaster Boy Scouts Am., 2000—. Recipient Exceptional Svc. award Sec. Interior, 1988, Presidl. Meritorious Svc. award, 1992. Mem. Va. State Bar Assn., D.C. Bar Assn. Roman Catholic. Avocations: running, hunting, fishing. Home: 3500 Arlington Blvd Arlington VA 22204-1721 Office: US Ho of Reps House Judiciary Com 2138 Rayburn House Office Bldg Washington DC 20515-4909

KIKOLER, STEPHEN PHILIP, lawyer; b. N.Y.C., Apr. 24, 1945; s. Sigmund and Dorothy (Javna) K.; m. Ethel Lerner, June 18, 1967; children: Jeffrey Stuart, Shari Elaine. AB, U. Mich., 1966, JD cum laude, 1969. Bar: Ill. 1969, U.S. Dist. Ct. (no. dist.) Ill. 1969, U.S. Ct. Appeals (7th cir.) 1988, U.S. Ct. Appeals (11th cir.) 1994, U.S. Ct. Appeals for the Armed Forces 1970, U.S. Supreme Ct. 1994. Capt. Judge Advocate Gen.'s Corps U.S. Army, 1970-73; with Much, Shelist, Freed, Denenberg, Ament & Rubenstein PC, Chgo. Mem. ABA, Ill. State Bar Assn., Chgo. Bar. Assn. (real property law com., mechanics' liens subcom.). Home: 2746 Norma Ct Glenview IL 60025-4661 Office: Much Shelist Freed Denenberg Ament & Rubenstein PC 191 N Wacker Dr Chicago IL 60606-1615 E-mail: skikoler@muchshelist.com.

KIKUKAWA, RANDALL HIROYUKI, university administrator; b. Milw., Oct. 23, 1957; s. Herbert Hiroyuki and Ayako Sally Kikukawa; life ptnr., Gregory Kent Fisher, 1990. AB, Harvard U., 1979; MA, U. Calif., Berkeley, 1981, postgrad., 1981-84. Sr. adminstrv. analyst U. Calif., San Francisco, 1986—. Mem. adv. bd. Arcadia Health Care, San Francisco, 1995—2001. Mus. dir., Gay Asian Pacific Alliance Men's Chorus, San Francisco, 1991—; bd. mem., Golden Gate Men's Chorus, San Francisco, 1985—, Lesbian/Gay Chorus of San Francisco, 1989-92. Mem. Gay and Lesbian Assn. Choruses, Bay Area Harvard Gay and Lesbian Caucus. Democrat. Roman Catholic. Avocations: foreign travel, choral music. Home: 116 Eureka St San Francisco CA 94114-2435

KILANOWSKI, DANA MARCOTTE, historian, writer, filmmaker, archaeologist; b. Grand Forks, N.D., Aug. 30, 1946; d. Virgil Wallace and Lucille Hogan (Weidel) Marcotte; m. Samuel Joseph Kilanowski, Aug. 30, 1975; children: Kristen Marcotte, Samantha Marcotte. BA, U. N.D., 1975. Acting dir. non-acad. employment U. N.D., Grand Forks, 1968-71; historian, archaeologist Computer Scis. Corp., Edwards AFB, Calif., 1987-94; pres. Dana Marcotte Kilanowski Prodns., Palmdale, Calif., 1994—. Guest historian The History Channel, N.Y.C., 1997; oral historian 100th anniversary of flight Soc. of Exptl. Test Pilots, 2003. Co-author: The Quest for Mach One, 1997 (Best Book award Am. Libr. Assn. 1998, 99); contbr.: Our American Century: A Century of Flight, 1999; exec. co-prodr. (TV show and video) Mach One, 1997; prodr. (video documentary) The Happy Bottom Riding Club, 1994; contbr. articles to profl. jours. Pres. Officers Wives Club, Edwards AFB, 1985-86, PTA, Edwards AFB, 1986; dir. Flight Test Hist. Found., Lancaster Calif., 1991—; guest lectr. Antelope Valley (Calif.) Schs., 1987—. Recipient Commendation, Air Force Flight Test Ctr., 1989, Commendation, Jet Pioneers of Am., 1991, Key Rsch. Historian award Dept. of Def. and Ctr. Environ. Excellence, 1997. Mem. AAUW, Nat. Coun. Pub. History, Nat. Trust Hist. Preservation, South West Oral History Assn., Oral History Assn., Am. Film Inst. Republican. Roman Catholic. Avocations: reading, hiking, swimming, water skiing. Home and Office: Dana Marcotte Kilanowski Prodns 41445 Almond Ave Palmdale CA 93551-2843 E-mail: skilano@prodigy.net.

KILBANE, ANNE L. judge; b. Cleve., Sept. 22, 1941; d. Thomas Bryan and Nora (Coyle) K. BA in Chemistry, Seton Hill Coll., Greensburg, Pa., 1963; JD, Cleve. Marshall Coll. Law, 1976. Bar: Ohio 1977, U.S. Dist. Ct. (so. dist.) Ohio 1977, U.S. Dist. Ct. (no. dist.) Ohio 1978), U.S. Ct. Appeals (6th cir.) 1978, U.S. Supreme Ct. 1985. Sr. chemist Dept. of Health City of Cleve., 1963-66; chief brewing chemist, asst. quality control mgr. Carling Brewing Co., Cleve., 1966-71; chemist, plant mgr. Phillips Syrup Corp., Parma, Ohio, 1971-75; asst. to dir. law City of Cleve., 1975-77; assoc. Kilbane & Kilbane, Columbus, Ohio, 1977-78, Nurenberg, Plevin, Heller, Cleve., 1978-86, ptnr., 1986-99; judge Ohio Ct. of Appeals (8th dist.), Cuyahoga County, Ohio, 1999—. Lectr. in field. Mem. Ohio State Bar Assn. (negligence subcom.), Ohio Women's Bar Assn. (founding), Ohio Jud. Conf., Ohio Ct. Appeal Judge's Assn., Cuyahoga County Bar Assn. (appellate sect.), Cleve. Bar Assn. (appellate sect., commn. on women in the law), Nat. Lawyers Assn., 6th Cir. Jud. Conf. (life), Cleve. Marshall Alumnae Assn. (life), Am. Chem. Soc., Delta Theta Phi. Office: Cuyahoga County Ct House 1 W Lakeside Ave Cleveland OH 44113-1023

KILBANE, THOMAS M. lawyer; b. Cleve., Mar. 1, 1953; s. Thomas M. and Kathleen K.; m. Helen Crowley, June 26, 1976; children: Catherine Ann, Patrick Thomas, Michael Crowley. BA magna cum laude, Xavier U., 1974; postgrad., Miami U., Ohio, 1975; JD with highest distinction, John Marshall Law Sch., 1978. Bar: Ill. 1978, Wash. 1980, U.S. Dist. Ct. (no. dist.) Ill. 1978, U.S. Dist. Ct. (we. dist.) Wash. 1980, U.S. Ct. Appeals (5th and 9th cirs.) 1981, U.S. Dist. Ct. (ea. dist.) Wash. 1992. Jud. extern U.S. Dist. Ct. Ill., Chgo., 1977; jud. clk. to presiding justice Ill. Appellate Ct., Chgo., 1978-80; assoc., shareholder Garvey, Schubert & Barer, P.C., Seattle, 1980-85, 86-89; shareholder Ater Wynne LLP, Seattle, 1990—. Editor-in-Chief John Marshall Law Rev., 1977-78. Trustee Queen Anne Cmty. Coun., Seattle, 1983-85; mem. Queen Anne Land Use Rev. Com., 1983-85; mem. branch bd. Sammamish Family YMCA, 1993-95. Chgo. Bar Found. grantee, 1978. Mem. ABA (bus., environment and energy, sects.), Wash. State Bar Assn. (bus., environment and land use sects.), King County Bar Assn., Alpha Sigma Nu. Home: 7551 Madrona Dr NE Bainbridge Island WA 98110-2901 Office: Ater Wynne LLP 601 Union St Ste 5450 Seattle WA 98101-2327 E-mail: tmk@aterwynne.com.

KILBANE, THOMAS STANTON, lawyer; b. Cleve., Mar. 7, 1941; s. Thomas Joseph and Helen (Stanton) K.; m. Sally Conway Kilbane, June 4, 1966; children: Sarah, Thomas, Eamon, James, Carlin. BA magna cum laude, John Carroll U., 1963; JD, Northwestern U., 1966. Bar: Ohio 1966, U.S. Dist. Ct. (no. dist.) Ohio 1969, U.S. Supreme Ct. 1975, U.S. Ct. Claims 1981, U.S. Ct. Appeals (6th cir.) 1982, U.S. Ct. Appeals (3d cir.) 1990, U.S. Ct. Appeals (5th cir.) 1998, U.S. Ct. Appeals (2d, 7th and 9th cirs.) 2002, U.S. Ct. Appeals (4th cir.) 2003. Assoc. Squire, Sanders & Dempsey, Cleve., 1966-76, ptnr., 1976—, adminstrv. com., 1979-80, mgmt. com., 1981-83, 87-90, mng. ptnr. litigation practice area, 1991—. Fed. ct. panelist U.S. Dist. Ct. (no. dist.) Ohio. Mem. editl. bd. Northwestern U. Law Rev., 1965-66. Active Rep. Presdl. Task Force; bd. dirs. United Way Svcs. Capt. U.S. Army, 1967-69, Vietnam. Decorated Bronze Star; named Greater Cleve. Cath. Man of Yr., 1996. Fellow ABA, Am. Coll. Trial Lawyers, Internat. Acad. Trial Lawyers, Master Bencher of Anthony J. Celebrezze Inns of Ct.; mem. Fed. Bar Assn., Am. Coll. Barristers, Ohio Bar Assn. (AAA corp. counsel com., ctr. for pub. resources constrn. com.), Greater Cleve. Bar Assn., Def. Rsch. Inst., Jud. Conf. 8th Jud. Dist. Ohio (life), Union Club, The 50 Club, The Club, Alpha Sigma Nu. Republican. Roman Catholic. Office: Squire Sanders & Dempsey 4900 Key Tower 127 Public Sq Cleveland OH 44114-1304 E-mail: tkilbane@ssd.com.

KILBORN, PETER THURSTON, journalist; b. Providence, Apr. 7, 1939; s. John Wiggins and Eleanor Artemesia (McIntire) K.; m. Susan Holly Woodward, Jan. 29, 1966; children: David Thompson, Elizabeth Artemesia Wilhelm. BA, Trinity Coll., 1961; MSJ, Columbia U., 1962. Reporter Providence Jour.-Bulletin, 1963-64; Paris corr. McGraw-Hill World News, N.Y.C., 1966-68; reporter, writer Bus. Week Mag., N.Y.C., 1969-71, L.A. bur. chief, 1971-73; cos. editor Bus. Week, N.Y.C., 1973-74; reporter N.Y. Times, N.Y.C., 1974-75, London corr., 1975-77, editor Sunday bus. sect., 1979-82, econs. editor Washington bur., 1982-83, sr. econs. corr. Washington bur., 1983-89, nat. corr. Washington bur., 1989—; bus. editor Newsweek Mag., N.Y.C., 1977-78. Trustee Trinity Coll., Hartford, Conn., 1990-96. Profl. journalism fellow Stanford U., 1968-69. Mem. U. Club (N.Y.C.). Office: The NY Times 1627 I St NW Washington DC 20006-4007

KILBOURN, JOSEPH A. lawyer; b. Providence, R.I., June 16, 1926; s. Jonathan Francis Kilbourn and Clara Vivell Kent; m. Elaine Mary Deran, Aug. 1, 1959; children: Mary, Pamela, Kent, Connor, Andrew. BA, Yale U., 1948; LLB, Columbia U., 1952. Bar: N.Y. 1953. Assoc. Bigham, Englar, Jones & Houston, N.Y.C., 1953-63, ptnr., 1963-98, of counsel, 1998—. Chmn. excess, surplus lines, reins. com. tort and ins. practice sect. ABA, 1991-92. Pres. Rowayton (Conn.) Hose Co. vol. fire co., 1975-80, 83-84. Staff sgt. U.S. Army, 1944-46. Mem. Comml. Bar Assn. (London, hon.), Order of Founders and Patriots Am. (atty. gen. 1994-96, sec. gen. 1996-98, gov. gen. 1998-2000, Disting. Svc. award 2000), Soc. Colonial Wars in State of Conn. (mem. coun. 1977—), Norwalk Yacht Club. Avocation: sailing. Home: Apt 206 114 Strawberry Hill Ave Stamford CT 06902 Office: Bigham Englar Jones & Houston 40 Wall St New York NY 10005 E-mail: jkilbourn@bejh.com.

KILBOURN, WILLIAM DOUGLAS, JR., law educator; b. Colorado Springs, Colo., Dec. 9, 1924; s. William Douglas and Clara Howe (Lee) K.; m. Barbara Ruth Neff, Sept. 16, 1950; children: Jonathan VI, Katharine Ann. BA, Yale U., 1949; postgrad., Columbia U., 1949-50, LLB, 1953. Bar: Mass. 1962, Oreg. 1953, Minn. 1974. Acct. Arthur Andersen & Co., 1949-50; assoc. Davies, Biggs, Strayer, Stoel & Boley, Portland, Oreg., 1953-56; asst. prof. law U. Mont., 1956-57; assoc. prof. law U. Mo., 1957-59; prof. law, founding dir. grad. tax program Boston U., 1959-71; prof. law U. Minn., 1971-98, prof. emeritus, 1998—. Dir. U. Mont. Tax Inst., 1956; of counsel Palmer & Dodge, Boston, 1964-75, Oppenheimer, Wolff & Donnelly, St. Paul and Mpls., 1980-94; mem. exec. com. Fed. Tax Inst. New Eng., 1966-72; mem. adv. com. Western New Eng. Coll. Tax Inst; vis. prof. law Duke U., 1974-75, U. Tex., 1977, Washington U., St. Louis, 1977; past ednl. advisor Tax Execs. Inst.; lectr. in 31 states, Mex., The Caribbean, D.C.; expert witness in field. Editor: Estate Planning and Income Taxation, 1957; contbr. articles to profl. jours. Dist. dir. United Fund, Belmont, Mass., chair fair practices com. Recipient numerous tchg. awards; Kent scholar, Stone scholar Columbia U. Law Sch. Mem. ABA (tax sect., corp. stockholder rels. com. 1962-76, chair subcom. inc. 1968-73), Boston Bar Assn. (chair tax sect. 1967-70), Boston Tax Forum, Boston Tax Coun. Avocations: tennis, botany, landscape gardening. Home: 2681 E Lake Of The Isles Pkwy Minneapolis MN 55408-1051

KILBOURNE, BARBARA JEAN, health and housing executive; b. Milw., Mar. 21, 1941; d. Burton Conwell and Marjorie Janet (Tufts) K.; m. Kenneth Keith Kauffman, Feb. 10, 1962 (div. 1983). BA, U. Minn., 1972; MBA, Coll. St. Thomas, St. Paul, 1980. Adminstr. Ebenezer Soc., Mpls., 1974-85; v.p., dir. housing Walker Residence and Health Svcs., Inc., Mpls., 1985-88; exec. v.p. Oblate Ministries Health and Aging, West St. Paul, Minn., 1988-94; cons., 1995—; pres. Barbara J. Kilbourne, Ltd., 1996—2002; exec. dir. Cath. Health Assn. Minn., 1997—2002; v.p. mem. svcs. and internal ops. Minn. Health and Housing Alliance, 2001—. Bd. dirs. CommonBond Communities, St. Paul, Villa Guadalupe, Chgo., Minn. Am. Red Cross Mpls. chpt., 1997-2002; chair Villa Guadalupe, 1999—, Minn. State Operated Svcs., 2000-02. Author: Family Councils in Nursing Homes, 1981. Chmn. bd. dirs. LifeWorks, Eagan, Minn., 1985-96, Minn. Assn. Homes for Aging, 1991-92, Sem. Plaza, Red Wing, 1995-97; project chair Dialog 2000, Dakota County, Minn., 1988-91; bd. dirs. ARC, Mpls., 1997-2002, Common Bond Cmtys., 1999-2002, Villa Guadalupe, Chgo, chair 1999—. Mem. Minn. Rural Health Assn. (bd. dirs. 1998-2001). Episcopalian. Avocations: piano, golf, hiking. Home: 1021 Sibley Memorial Hwy Saint Paul MN 55118-6100 Office: 2550 University Ave Ste 350 S Saint Paul MN 55114

KILBOURNE, EDWIN DENNIS, virologist, educator; b. Buffalo, July 10, 1920; s. Edwin I. and Elizabeth (Alward) K.; m. Joy Schmid, Dec. 20, 1952; children: Edwin Michael, Richard Schmid, Christopher Norton, Paul Alward. AB, Cornell U., 1942, MD, 1944; DSc honoris causa, Rockefeller U., 1986. Asst. Rockefeller Inst., 1948-51; mem. faculty Tulane U., 1951-55, Cornell U. Med. Coll., N.Y.C., 1955-68, prof. pub. health, dir. div. virus research, 1961-68; prof., chmn. dept. microbiology Mt. Sinai Sch. Medicine, City U. New York, 1968-86, disting. service prof., 1986—; rsch. prof. N.Y. Med. Coll., 1999—2002, emeritus, 2002—. Chmn., bd. dirs. Aaron Diamond AIDS Rsch. Ctr. for the City N.Y., 1989-94. Author: (with Wilson G. Smillie) Human Ecology and Public Health, 4th edit, 1968, Influenza, 1987; Editor: The Influenza Viruses and Influenza, 1975. Mem. Health Research Council N.Y.C., 1968-75. Recipient R.E. Dyer Lectureship award NIH, 1973, Borden award Assn. Am. Med. Colls., 1974, Dowling Lectureship award, 1976, Thomas Francis Lectureship award, 1976, Nat. Acad. Scis. 1977, Harvey Lectureship award, 1978, award of distinction Cornell U. Med. Alumni Assn., 1979, acad. medal N.Y. Acad. Medicine, 1982, Jacobi Medallion award Mt. Sinai Alumni Assn., 1991, Fogarty scholar award NIH, 1992. Fellow N.Y. Acad. Scis., Am. Philos. Soc.; mem. Harvey Soc., So. Soc. Clin. Rsch., Ctrl. Soc. Clin. Rsch (emeritus), AAAS, Am. Assn. Immunologists, Am. Acad. Microbiology, Soc. Exptl. Biology and Medicine, Am. Soc. Clin. Investigation (emeritus), N.Y. Acad. Medicine, Am. Pub. Health Assn., Assn. Am. Physicians, Am. Soc. Microbiology, Infectious Diseases Soc. Am. Avocation: rsch. and publs. on hormonal influences, genetic studies and exptl. transmission of viruses, recombinant virus vaccines especially influenza. Home: 23 Willard Ave Madison CT 06443-3202 E-mail: ekilbourne@snet.net.

KILBOURNE, KRYSTAL HEWETT, retired rail transportation executive; b. Sandersville, Ga., Apr. 7, 1940; d. John Ray and Kathleen (Perkins) Hewett; m. Alan Arden Kilbourne, July 1, 1961 (div. May 1972); children: Arden Alan, Keith Ray. A, U. Ga., 1960. Tchr. Massey Bus. Coll., Jacksonville, Fla., 1968-72, editor, reporter, photographer, 1968-72; asst. to pres. Luter Advt. Agy., Jacksonville, Fla., 1973-74; asst. to dir. Leukemia Soc., Jacksonville, Fla., 1975-76; asst. to pres. TeleCheck Corp., Jacksonville, Fla., 1979; mgr. customer svc. railroad ops. CSX Transp., Jacksonville, Fla., 1980—2002; ret., 2002. Chair CSX Equal Employment Opportunity Coun., 1992-94. Tuition scholar U. Ga., 1958; recipient Transp. Workers Leadership award, 1995. Mem. Nat. Assn. Railway Bus. Women, Am. Coun. Railroad Women. Democrat. Presbyterian. Avocations: oil painting, poetry, snorkeling, traveling, reading. Home: 4856 Deermoss Way S Jacksonville FL 32217-9306

KILBRIDE, THOMAS L. judge; m. Mary Kilbride; 3 children. BA magna cum laude, St. Mary's Coll., 1978; JD, Antioch Sch. Law, 1981. Practicioner U.S. Dist. Ct., Ill., U.S. Seventh Cir. Ct. Appeals; Supreme Ct. justice Ill. State Supreme Ct., 2000—. Former mem. bd. dirs., former v.p., former pres. Ill. Twp. Attys. Assn. Vol. legal adv. Cmty. Caring Conf., Quad City Harvest Inc.; charter chmn. Quad Cities Interfaith Sponsoring Com.; former mem. Rock Island Human Rels. Com.; former vol. lawyer, charter mem. Ill. Pro Bono Ctr. Mem.: Rock Island County Bar Assn., Ill. State Bar Assn.

KILBURN, KAYE HATCH, medical educator; b. Logan, Utah, Sept. 20, 1931; d. H. Parley and Winona (Hatch) K.; m. Gerrie Griffin, June 7, 1954; children: Ann Louise, Scott Kaye, Jean Marie. BS, U. Utah, 1951, MD, 1954. Diplomate Am. Bd. Internal Medicine, Am. Bd. Preventive Medicine. Asst. prof. Med. Sch. Washington U., St. Louis, 1960-62; assoc. prof., chief of medicine Durham (N.C.) VA Hosp., 1962-69; prof., dir. environ. medicine Duke Med. Ctr., Durham, 1969-73; prof. medicine and environ. medicine U. Mo., Columbia, 1973-77; prof. medicine and cmty. medicine CUNY Mt. Sinai Med. Sch., 1977-80; Ralph Edgington prof. medicine U. So. Calif. Sch. Medicine, L.A., 1980—. Pres. Neurotest Inc., 1988—; pres. Workers Disease Detection Svc. Inc., 1986-95. Author: Chemical Brain Injury, 1998, Endangered Brains, 2003; editor-in-chief Archives of Environ. Health, 1986—; editor Jour. Applied Physiology, 1970-80, Environ. Rsch., 1975—, Am. Jour. Indsl. Medicine, 1980—; contbr. more than 250 articles to profl. jours. Capt. M.C., U.S. Army, 1958-60. Avocations: travel, oil painting, swimming, hunting. Home: 3250 Mesaloa Ln Pasadena CA 91107-1129 Office: 1000 S Fremont St Bldg 7/401 Alhambra CA 91803 E-mail: kilburn@usc.edu.

KILBURN, PENELOPE WHITE, retired data processing executive; b. Freeport, N.Y., June 25, 1940; d. William Prescott and Marian (Churchill) White; m. Edwin Allen Kilburn, Feb. 7, 1964; children: Penelope Allen, Nancy Kitchen. BA, Barnard Coll., 1962. Elem. sch. tchr. Holmdel (N.J.) Bd. Edn., 1975-78; tech. writer Continental Data Ctr., Neptune, N.J., 1983-86; with Johnson & Higgins, N.Y.C., 1986-89; asst. v.p., 1989-91; v.p. Johnson & Higgins, N.Y.C., 1991-95, ret., 1995. Sustaining mem. Jr. League, Phoenix, 1995; chmn. St. Georges refugee com., Rumson, NJ, 1981—83; mem. vestry St. Lukes, Branchport, NY, 1995—2000, warden, 2000—; trustee Keuka Coll., Keuka Park, NY, 1997—. Episcopalian. Avocation: gardening. Home: 513 E Bluff Dr Penn Yan NY 14527-8926

KILBY, JACK ST. CLAIR, electrical engineer; b. Jefferson City, Mo., Nov. 8, 1923; s. Hubert St. Clair and Vina (Freitag) Kilby; m. Barbara Annegers, June 27, 1948; children: Ann, Janet Lee. BEE, U. Ill., 1947; MS, U. Wis., 1950; DEng (hon.), U. Miami, 1982; DSc (hon.), U. Wis., 1990; DEng (hon.), Rochester Inst. Tech., 1986; DSc (hon.), U. Ill., 1988; DSc, Rensselaer Poly. Inst., 1990; DSc (hon.), Yale U., 1996. Program mgr. Globe-Union, Inc., Milw., 1948—58; asst. v.p. Tex. Instruments, Inc., Dallas, 1958—70; self-employed inventor Dallas, 1970—; disting. prof. elec. engring. Tex. A&M U., 1978—85; inventor monolithic integrated circuit, others. Cons. to govt. and industry. With U.S. Army, 1943—45. Named to Nat. Inventors Hall of Fame, U.S. Patent Office, 1981; recipient Nat. Medal of Sci., 1969, 1990, Ballentine medal, Franklin Inst., 1967, Alumni Achievement award, U. Ill., 1974, Holley medal, ASME, 1982, 1989, Nobel prize in physics, 2000. Fellow: IEEE (Sarnoff medal 1966, Brunetti award 1978, Medal of honor 1986); mem.: NAE (Zworykin medal 1975, co-recipient Charles Stark Draper prize 1989, Kyoto prize for tech. achievement 1993). Home: 7723 Midbury Dr Dallas TX 75230-3211 Office: Ste 155 6600 Lyndon B Johnson Fwy Dallas TX 75240-6531

KILCHER, JEWEL See JEWEL

KILCULLEN, MAUREEN, librarian, educator; b. Canton, Ohio, Oct. 29, 1954; d. Thomas Vincent and Betty Jane (Rawley) Kilcullen. BA in History, Kent State U., 1981, MLS, 1984. Libr. reference/audiovisual Barberton Pub. Libr., Barberton, Ohio, 1985—90; assoc. prof., reference libr. Stark Campus Kent State U., Canton, Ohio, 1990—. Contbr. chapters to books, articles to profl. jours. Vol. Dublin Irish Festival, Dublin, Ohio, 1995—. Recipient Regional Campus Vice Provost award Outstanding Service, Kent State U. Regional Campuses, 1997. Mem.: ALA, Acad. Libr. Assn. Ohio, Assn. Coll. and Rsch. Librs. Democrat. Roman Catholic. Avocations: reading, gardening, genealogy, photography. Office: Kent State Univ Stark Campus 6000 Frank Ave Canton OH 44720 Office Fax: 330-494-6212. Personal E-mail: mkilcullen@stark.kent.edu. Business E-mail: mkilcullen@stark.kent.edu.

KILDE, SANDRA JEAN, nurse anesthetist, educator, consultant; b. Eau Claire, Wis., June 25, 1938; d. Harry Milan and Beverly June (Johnson) K. Diploma, Luther Hosp. Sch. Nursing, Eau Claire, 1959; grad. anesthesia course, Mpls. Sch. Anesthesia, 1962; BA, Met. State U., St. Paul, 1976; MA, U. St. Thomas, 1981; EdD, Nova Southeastern U., 1987. RN, Wis., Minn. Oper. rm. nurse Luther Hosp., Eau Claire, 1959-61, head nurse oper. rm., 1961-63; supr. oper. rm. Midway Hosp., St. Paul, 1963-66; staff anesthetist North Meml. Med. Ctr., Robbinsdale, Minn., 1967-68, St. Joseph's Hosp., St. Paul, 1992-99, R.C. Shefland Anesthesia, Ltd., Bemidji, Minn., 2003—. Program dir. Mpls. Sch. Anesthesia, St. Louis Park, Minn., 1968-96; adj. assoc. prof. St. Mary's U., Winona, Minn., 1982-96, adj. prof., 1996—, program dir. Masters Degree Program, 1984-96, staff anesthetist, R.C. Shefland Anesthesia, Ltd., 2003-; nurse anesthesia cons., 1996—; ednl. cons. accreditation visitor Coun. on Accreditation of Nurse Anesthesia Ednl. Programs, Park Ridge, Ill., 1983-92, 99—, elected to coun., 1992-99, vice chmn., 1994-97, chmn., 1997-99; corp. mem. Aitkin Cmty. Hosp., Inc. dba Riverwood HealthCare Ctr., 2000—, also bd. dirs.; presenter in field. Choir dir. Grace Luth. Ch., McGregor, Minn., 1988—, mem. ch. coun., 1992—97, 1998—2001, pres. ch. coun., 1992—97. Recipient Good Neighbor award Sta. WCCO, Mpls., 1980, Disting. Alumni Achievement award Nova Southeastern U., 1993, Lifetime Achievement for Excellence in Edn. award Mpls. Sch. Anesthesia Class of 1999, 1999, Cert. of Appreciation Aitkin County Bd. Commrs. and Aitkin County Health and Human Svc. Adv. Com., 2001. Mem. Am. Assn. Nurse Anesthetists (pres. 1981-82, pres. and bd. dirs. Edn. and Rsch. Found., 1981-83, cert. profl. excellence 1976, Program Dir. of Yr. award 1992), Minn. Assn. Nurse Anesthetists (pres. 1975-76). Lutheran. Avocations: gardening, fishing, photography, choir directing, playing guitar and piano. Home and Office: PO Box 80 Palisade MN 56469-0080

KILDEE, DALE EDWARD, congressman; b. Flint, Mich., Sept. 16, 1929; s. Timothy Leo and Norma Alicia (Ullmer) K.; m. Gayle Heyn, Feb. 27, 1965; children: David, Laura, Paul. BA, Sacred Heart Sem., 1952; tchr.'s cert., U. Detroit, 1954; MA, U. Mich., 1961; postgrad. (Rotary Found. fellow), U. Peshawar, Pakistan, 1958-59. Tchr. U. Detroit H.S., 1954-56, Flint Central H.S., 1956-64; mem. Mich. Ho. of Reps., 1964-74, Mich. Senate, 1975-76, U.S. Congress from 7th Mich. dist., 1977-93, U.S. Congress from 5th Mich. dist. (formerly 9th), 1993—; sr. mem. edn. and the workforce com., ranking minority mem. subcom. on early childhood, youth, & families; chair Congl. Auto Caucus, 1993—; co-chair Native Am. Caucus, 1997; mem. resources com.; mem. edn. and the workforce com. Mem. NAACP (life), Am. Fedn. Tchrs., Urban League, K.C., Optimists, Phi Delta Kappa. Lodges: K.C; Optimists. Democrat. Office: US Ho of Reps 2107 Rayburn House Bldg Washington DC 20515-2209 also: 432 N Saginaw St Ste 410 Flint MI 48502-2018*

KILE, MARCIA ANN, education consultant; b. York, Pa., Mar. 2, 1947; d. Earl Henry and Catherine Edith (Ernst) Bose; m. Bruce Walter Kile, Aut. 9, 1969; 1 child, Hayley Ayne. AA, York Jr. Coll., 1967; BS, Millersville U., 1969. Cert. tchr. Pa. Tchr. Shippensburg U. Migrant Child Devel. Program, 1979-85; program cons. migrant edn., ESL coord. Lincoln Intermediate Unit #12, Gettysburg, Pa., 1986—. Mem. adv. bd. Gettysburg Adolescent Parenting Program, 1992; mem. Rep. William Goodling's Edn. adv. bd., Pa., 1993. Testifier U.S. Ho. of Reps. Edn. Com., Washington, 1993. Mem.: ASCD, Nat. Assn. Bilingual Edn., Tchrs. English to Spkrs. Other Langs. Avocations: historical restoration, herb gardening. Home: 960 Flohrs Church Rd Biglerville PA 17307-9559 Office: Lincoln Intermediate Unit 12 Migrant and ESL Program 57 North 5th St Gettysburg PA 17325-1870 E-mail: mkile@blazenet.net.

KILEY, DANIEL URBAN, landscape architect, planner; b. Boston, Sept. 2, 1912; s. Louis James and Louise (Baxter) Kiley; m. Anne Lothrop Sturges, June 11, 1942; children: Kathleen, Kor, Christopher, Antonia, Timothy, Christina,

Aaron Alcott, Caleb. Student, Harvard Grad. Sch. Design, 1936—38; LHD (hon.), Green Mountain Coll., 1993. From apprentice to assoc. Warren Manning (landscape design and regional planning), Cambridge, Mass., 1932—38; planning technician Concord (N.H.) City Plan Bd., 1938; arch. Nat. Pk. Svc., 1939, U.S. Housing Authority, 1940; assoc. Town Planning, Washington, 1940; pvt. practice as landscape architect, site planner, architect, 1940—. Lectr., critic Balt. Mus., 1949, Worcester (Mass.) Mus., 1950, La. State U., 1950, Cornell U., 1957, Met. Mus., 1959, N.C. State Coll., 1958, Rensselaer Poly. Inst., 1960, Harvard U., 1962—63, Clemson Coll., 1963, also univs. Ill., Minn., Pa. Syracuse, Va., Wash., Tokyo, Kyoto, Hiroshima, Fukuoka, Yale U., U. Calif. Berkeley, U. Utah, Salt Lake City, Harvard U., Archtl. Assn. London, Dallas Inst. Forum, Beijing, China, Nanking (Shanghai, Hangchow, also Osaka U. Japan), Lawrence Tech. U., Detroit, Royal Inst. Architects, London; landscape arch. in residence Am. Acad. in Rome, 1975—76, mem. jury, 1990; Graham Found. lectr., Chgo., 76; mem. design rev. panel Redevel. Land Agy., Washington; participant Symposium on Dan Kiley, 1980; keynote spkr. Am. Soc. Landscape Archs. Fla. chpt.; lectr. U. Va., 1985, NAD, 1990, U. Fla., 1991, symposium N.Y. Botanical Garden, 1991. Author: The Early Gardens, 1999, articles; prin. works include Collier Residence, Falls Church, Va., 1940, Nuremburg Courtroom, Nuremburg, Germany, 1945, Jefferson Meml. Arch, St. Louis, 1947, Kitimat, B.C., Can. new city, 1951, USAF Acad., Colorado Springs, Colo., 1955, The Miller House, Columbus, Ind., 1955, Rockefeller Inst., N.Y., 1956, Irwin Miller residence, Columbus, Ind., 1956, Union Carbide and Carbon, Westchester, N.Y., 1957, Reynolds Metals Co., Richmond, Va., 1958, Independence Mall, 3d block, Phila, 1959—60, U. Minn., Mpls., 1960, Lincoln Ctr., N.Y.C., 1960, Yale U., 1961, Dulles Internat Airport, Washington, 1961—63, Nat. Acad. Sci., 1961, Cummins Engine Plant, Columbus, Ind., 1962, Chrysler-Cummins Plant, Darlington, Eng., Burr-McManus Plz., Hartford, Conn., 1962, Rochester Inst. Tech., 1962, Oakland (Calif.) Mus., 1962, The Chgo. Filtration Plant, 1962, Nat. Ctr. Atmospheric Rsch., Boulder, Colo., 1963, Fredonia (N.Y.) State Coll., 1963, Potsdam (N.Y.) State Coll., U. Lagos, Nigeria, Ctrl. Filtration Plant, Chgo., Chgo. Art Inst., 1963, Independence Mall, 3d block, Phila., 1963, Dulles Internat. Airport, Chantilly, Va., 1963, Ford Found. Bldg., N.Y.C., 1964, The North Christian Ch., 1964, Irwin Union Bank and Trust Co., 1968, Washington Mall and Tidal Basin, 1968, The Oakland Mus., 1969, Ford Found. Office Bldg., N.Y.C., 1969, 10th St. Overlook, Washington, 1970, Ft. Lawton Pk., Seattle, 1972, La. Defense, Paris, 1972, Victorian Garden, Smithsonian Instn., 1976, N.Y. Bot. Garden master plan, 1973, Ind. Bell Tel., 1974, East Wing Nat. Gallery Art, Washington, 1976, interior ct., Yale Ctr. Brit. Art, 1977, Coca-Cola World Hdqs. master plan, Atlanta, 1977, Woodruff Pk., 1977, Cary Arbotetum, Millbrook, N.Y., 1977, N.Y. Bot. Gardens, Bronx, 1978, campus plan, Gallaudet Coll. for Deaf, Washington, J.F. Kennedy Libr., Boston, 1978, Cummins Brussels, Belgium, 1978, Belle Isle Pk., Detroit, 1978, Detroit Art Inst., 1979, Dallas Art Mus., 1980, London Std. Chartered Bank, 1980, San Antonio Art Mus., 1981, Brit. Rys., London, 1981, Bank of Korea, Seoul, 1981, Silicon Valley Fin. Ctr., 1984, N.C. Nat. Bank, Tampa, Fla., 1987, Joslyn Art Mus., Omaha, 1985, U.S. Embassy, Amman, Jordan, 1985, Vanderbilt U. Campus, 1985, Lake Shore Pk., Chgo., 1985—86, St. John's Coll., 1986, Fountain Pl., Dallas, 1986—87, Carnegie Ctr. Charlotte, N.C., 1987, Nelson-Atkins Mus., 1987, Henry Moore Sculpture Pk., 1988, Nat. Sculpture Garden on the Mall, Washington, 1989, A G Group Hdqs., Brussels, 1989, Buck Ctr. for Rsch. on Aging, Novato, Calif., 1989, UMB-Warner, LA, 1989, Washington Internat. U., Va., 1989, Getty Mus., LA, 1989, St. Louis Art Mus., 1989—, Guam Legis. Bldgs., Agana, 1990—, Norman Lear, Brentwood, Calif., 1990, Bailey Plz., Cornell U., 1990, Riverside Pk., Corning, N.Y., 1990, Superblock Master Plan, LA, 1990, Westmount Pub. Libr., Montreal, 1991, Navy Pier, Chgo., 1991—, Twin Farms Inn, Barnard, Vt., 1991—, Pierpont Morgan Libr., N.Y.C., 1992—, U. Ottawa, Can., 1992—, Ct. of Human Rights, Strasbourg, France, 1992, Lehr Res., Miami, 1993, Mashantucket Pequot Mus., Conn., 1993, Kimmel Res., Salisbury, Conn., 1993, Buck Ctr., Novato, Calif., 1993, Lloyd's Register of Shipping Hdqs., Sussex, Eng., 1993—, West Palm Beach Pks., Fla., 1993—, London Archtl. Edn. Econ. Galleries, 1994, Kusko Res., Williamstown, Mass., 1995, numerous others, joint exhbn., USA/USSR, 1990. Mem. BiState Planning Commn. Lake Champlain Basin Region, 1959—63; mem. Pres.'s Adv. Coun. Planning Pennsylvania Ave., Washington, 1962—65, Vt. Bd. Archs. Registration, 1963; jury S.W. Redevel. Area, Washington, Boston Redevel. Authority, 1963, Nat. Honor Awards, Urban Redevel. Authority, also FHA, Washington, 1964; design adv. group Cambridge (Mass.) Redevel. Bd., 1978; mem. tech. rev. com. on state use plan State of Vt., 1975. Capt. U.S. Army, World War II. Decorated Legion of Merit; co-recipient 1st prize Jefferson Nat. Expansion Meml. Competition, 1947; named Thomas Jefferson prof. landscape architecture, U. Va., 1988, Daniel Urban Kiley lectr., Harvard U. Grad. Sch. Design, 1983; recipient 1st prize, U. N.H. Student Union Bldg. Competition, 1951, AIA honor award, Concordia State Coll., Ft. Wayne, Ind., 1960, Stiles and Morse Colls., Yale U., 1963, Dulles Airport, Washington, 1963, Ind. Bell Tel. Co., Columbus, hon. mention, Chgo. Tribune Better Homes for Family Living, 1947, award of merit, House and Home mag., 1957, 1st prize, Progressive Architecture mag., 1961, award of merit, Am. Soc. Landscape Archs., 1962, Gold medal, Phila. chpt. AIA, Gov.'s Design award, State of Calif., 1966, Bard award, N.Y.C. Lincoln Ctr. North Ct., 1967, N.Y.C. Ford Found. Ct., 1968, Allied Profession medal, AIA, 1971, Archs. Collaborative award, 1972, Thomas Jefferson medal, 1988, Creative Arts Citation, Brandeis U., 1990, Urban Design award, Dallas, 1989, Dallas Urban Design award, Fountain Pl., 1990, Chgo Archtl. award, Ill. AIA, 1991, Gov.'s award for Excellence in the Arts, Vt. Coun. on the Arts, 1991, Kansas City Urban Design award Excellence, Nelson-Atkins Mus. Art., Henry Moore Sculpture Garden, 1991, Merit award, ASLA, 1991, Excellence on the Waterfront award, NCNB Plz., 1992, Outstanding Lifetime Achievement award, Alumni Coun. Harvard Grad. Sch. Design, 1992, 25 Yr. award Ford Found. Bldg., Am. Inst. Archs., 1995, Arnold W. Brunner prize in Architecture, Am. Acad. Arts and Letters, 1995, Celebration of Yr. of the Landscape, Am. Acad. Rome, 1990; fellow Disting. Designer, NEA, 1988. Mem.: NAD. Address: 250 Garen Rd Charlotte VT 05445-9186*

KILEY, LEO AUSTIN, retired military officer, nuclear energy industry executive; b. Boston, May 22, 1918; s. Leo Austin and Pauline Marie Kiley; m. Luna Delia Hamilton; children: Michael John, Karen Lee. SB in Chem. Engring., MIT, 1939; PhD in Chemistry, Ohio State U., 1952; LLD (hon.), NM State U., 1967. Commd. USAF, 1940, advanced through grades to brig. gen., ret., 1969; gen. mgr. GE Co., Largo, Fla., 1969—78; v.p. Los Alamos (N.Mex.) Tech. Assoc. Inc., 1979—92, cons., 1992—98; ret., 1998. Trustee Coll. of Santa Fe, Santa Fe, 1981—90. Decorated Legion of Merit,, DSM. Mem.: MIT Alumni Assn., Alpha Chi Sigma. Roman Catholic. Mailing: 780 Camino Pinones Santa Fe NM 87505

KILEY, THOMAS, rehabilitation counselor; b. Mpls., Aug. 28, 1937; s. Gerald Sidney and Veronica (Roberts) K.; m. Jane Virginia Butler, Aug. 25, 1989; children: Martin, Truman, Tami, Brian. BA in English, UCLA, 1959; MS in Rehab. Counseling, San Francisco State U., 1989. Cert. rehab counselor, nat. and Hawaii. Former rsch. profl., businessman various S.E. Asian cos., U.S. Army; sr. social worker Episcopal Sanctuary, San Francisco, 1986-88; dir. social svcs. Hamilton Family Ctr., San Francisco, 1988-89, rehab. specialist Intracorp, Honolulu, 1989-91; v.p. Heritage Counselling Svc., Honolulu, 1991—. Pres. Hunter Employment Svcs., Yuma, Ariz., El Centro, Salinas, Calif., 1995—, Algo Enterprises, Yuma, 1998—. With U.S. Army. Mem. Am. Counseling Assn., Nat. Assn. Rehab. Profls. in Pvt. Sector, Am. Rehab. Counselors Assn. (profl.), Nat. Rehab. Assn., Rehab. Assn. Hawaii, Rotary, Phi Delta Kappa. Office: Heritage Counselling Svcs PO Box 4699 Yuma AZ 85366-4699

KILEY, THOMAS FRANCIS, civil engineer, lawyer; b. Lynn, Mass., July 21, 1925; s. John J. and Katherine L. Hayes K.; m. Constance Mary Carroll, May 30, 1949; children: Stephen, Shelagh, Mary, Katherine, Thomas F. Jr. BSCE, Cornell U., 1948; JD, Boston Coll. Law Sch., 1951. Bar: Mass. 1951, Fed. 1952; registered profl. engr., Mass. 1959. Structural designer Jackson & Moreland, Boston, 1948-50; structure designer B&M R.R., Boston, 1950-51; chief engr. A. Cefalo & Sons, Lynn, Mass., 1952-55; chief engr., owner Cefalo & Kiley, Lynn, 1955-60; owner T.F. Kiley Constrn. Co., Lynn, 1960-77, T.F. Kiley Engring. Co., adrLynn, 1977—; sole practice T.F. Kiley Atty., Lynn, 1951—. Mem. Mass. Conv. Ctr. Authority Designer Selection Panel, 1983—. Mem. planning bd. City of Lynn, Mass., 1956-65; spl. town counsel Swampscott, Mass., 1972-76; chmn., designer selection panel, Swampscott, 1975-85. Mem. ASCE, Mass. Bar Assn., Cornell Soc. Engrs., Swampscott Hist. Soc. (pres. 1985-89, 94-96). Home: 17 Priscilla Rd Swampscott MA 01907-2815 Office: TF Kiley Engring Inc TF Kiley Atty 583 Chestnut St Ste 8 Lynn MA 00194-2600

KILGORE, DONALD GIBSON, JR., pathologist; b. Dallas, Nov. 21, 1927; s. Donald Gibson and Gladys (Watson) K.; m. Jean Upchurch Augur, Aug. 23, 1952; children: Michael Augur, Stephen Bassett, Phillip Arthur, Geoffrey Scott, Sharon Louise. Student, So. Meth. U., 1943-45; MD Southwestern Med. Coll., U. Tex., Dallas, 1949. Diplomate Am. Bd. Pathology, Am. Bd. Dermatopathology, Am. Bd. Blood Banking. Notary Pub. Intern Parkland Meml. Hosp., Dallas, 1949—50; resident in pathology Charity Hosp. La., New Orleans, 1950—54, asst. pathologist, 1952—54; pathologist Greenville (S.C.) Hosp. Sys., 1956—, dir. labs., 1985—96, Greenville Meml. Hosp., 1972—96. Cons. pathologist St. Francis Hosp., 1963—, Shriners Hosp., Greenville, 1963—, Easley Baptist Hosp.; vis. lectr. Clemson U., 1963—; asst. prof. pathology Med. U. S.C., 1968—; pres. Pathology Assocs. of Greenville, 1983—96. Deacon Westminster Presbyn. Ch., 1961, ruling elder, 1969, trustee, 2001—; mem. bd. govs. S.C. Patient Compensation Fund, 1977—2001; bd. govs. Roper Mountain Sci. Ctr., 2001—. Capt. M.C. USAFR, 1954—56. Recipient Disting. Svc. award S.C. Hosp. Assn., 1976; awarded Order of The Palmetto by S.C. Gov. David M. Beasley, 1996. Fellow: Am. Soc. Dermatopathology, Am. Soc. Clin. Pathologists (councilor S.C. 1959—62), Coll. Am. Pathologists (life; assemblyman S.C. 1968—71); mem.: AMA (life; ho. of dels. 1978—94), Greater Greenville C. of C. (pres. ednl. task force 1965—70, elected trustee sch. dist. of Greenville County 1970—90), S.C. Soc. Pathologists (pres. 1969—72), S.C. Inst. Med. Edn. and Rsch. (pres. 1974—80), Nat. Assn. Med. Examiners, Greenville County Dental Soc. (life), Am. Assn. Blood Banks (life; adv. coun. 1962—67, insp. committeeman Southeast dist. 1965—2001), Clan Douglas Soc. N.Am. (life), Am. Coll. Nuc. Medicine, Am. Soc. Cytology, S.C. Med. Assn. (exec. coun. 1969—76, pres. 1974—75, exec. coun. 1978—94, A.H. Robins award for Outstanding Cmty. Svc. 1985), So. Med. Assn., Soc. Med. Friends of Wine, Epicurean Assn. of Am. (selection com.), Confrerie de la Chaine des Rotisseurs (bailli and echanson de l'ordre mondial, Greenville chpt.), Richard III Soc. (co-chmn. Am. 1966—75), Hist. Greenville Found. (exec. com. 1994—2001, pres. 1998—2000), S.W. R.R. Hist. Soc., S.C. Gov.'s Task Force on Hist. Preservation and Heritage Tourism, Roper Mountain Science Ctr. Assn. (bd. dirs. 2001—), Brit. Museum Soc., U.S. Power Squadron, Confrerie des Chevaliers du Tastevin (chevalier Atlanta chpt.), Soc. Wine Educators, Greenville County Hist. Soc. (life), Preservation Soc. of Charleston (life), S.C. Hist. Soc. (life), Tex. State Hist. Assn. (life), Thomas Wolfe Soc. (life), Medieval Acad. of Am. (life), Archeol. Inst. Am. (life), Brookgreen Gardens Found. (life), Friends of Tewkesbury Abbey (life), Am. Numis. Soc. (life), Soc. Ancient Numismatics (life), Royal Numis. Soc. (life), S.C. Numis. Assn. (life), Mensa (life), S.C. Congress Parents and Tchrs. (life), Canterbury Cathedral Trust in Am. (life), Assn. Friends of Lincoln Cathedral (life), Wine Acad. Am. (life), Clan MacDuff Soc. Am. (life; exec. coun. 1980—2000), So. Meth. U. Alumni Assn. (life), Highland Park H.S. Alumni Assn. (life), Am. Wine Soc. (life), Blue Ridge Numismatic Assn. (life), Confrerie de Les Grapilleurs du Beaujolais (chevalier), Acad. Gastronomique Brillat-Savarin, L'Academie de Gastronomie Brillat-Savarin des Etats-Unis, Soc. Wine Educators, St. Andrews Soc. Upper S.C. (bd. govs. 1991—93), Soc. Med. Friends of Wine, Chandon Club, Commerce Club (life), Poinsett Club (life), Thirty-Nine Club (pres. 1981—82), Torch Club (pres. 1964—65), Greenville Country Club (life), Rotary (Paul Harris fellow 1988), Phi Chi, Phi Eta Sigma. Democrat. Home: 105 Wren Way Greenville SC 29605-5321 Office: 8 Memorial Medical Ct Greenville SC 29605-4400

KILGORE, EDWIN CARROLL, retired government official, consultant; b. Coeburn, Va., Jan. 24, 1923; s. Cecil Abram and Elizabeth Delle (Horne) K.; m. Ann Hitch, Dec. 30, 1944; children: Ashby Caroline, Elizabeth Cato. BS in Mech. Engring, Va. Inst. Poly., 1944; grad., Fed. Exec. Inst., 1969. With NASA (and predecessor), 1944-81; dep. assoc. adminstr. ops. Langley (Va.) Rsch. Ctr., 1975-76, dir. mgmt. ops., 1976-79, assoc. adminstr. mgmt. ops., 1979-81; cons. to NASA Washington, 1981—. Pres. Old Dominion U. Rsch. Found., Va. Air and Space Ctr. Recipient Outstanding Leadership award NASA, Disting. Svc. medal, Apollo Spl. Achievement award, Solid Propellant Spl. Achievement award, Roger Jones award Am. U. Va., State Sr. Tennis Champion, 1993, 94, 99. Mem. AIAA, Pi Tau Sigma, Omicron Delta Kappa. Clubs: Hampton Kiwanis (pres. 1969). Methodist. Office: Acad Pub Admin Washington DC 20005

KILGORE, EUGENE STERLING, JR., former surgeon; b. San Francisco, Feb. 3, 1920; s. Eugene Sterling and Mary (Kirkpatrick) K.; m. Marilynn Wines; children: Eugene Sterling, Marilynn Ann. BS, U. Calif., Berkeley, 1941; MD, U. Calif., San Francisco, 1949. Intern in medicine Harvard service Boston City Hosp., 1949-50; intern in surgery Roosevelt Hosp., N.Y.C., 1950-51, resident gen. surgery, reconstructive hand surgery, 1951-55; practice medicine specializing in reconstructive hand surgery San Francisco, 1955—; assoc. clin. prof. surgery U. Calif.-San Francisco, 1955-75, clin. prof., 1975-91, prof. emeritus, from 1991; chief hand surgery dept. surgery U. Calif. Hosp., also San Francisco Gen. Hosp., 1965-91; chief hand service Ft. Miley Vets. Hosp., San Francisco, 1965-91, Martinez (Calif.) Vets. Hosp., 1970-91, Livermore (Calif.) Vets. Hosp., 1965-70; chief hand service plastic surgery tng. service St. Francis Meml. Hosp., 1965-91, chief of surgery, 1979—, chief surgery emeritus, 1984-99; ret., 1999. Cons. hand surgery numerous pvt. hosps., San Francisco, 1955— Author numerous publs. in field. Served to lt. col., inf. AUS, 1941-45. Decorated Bronze Star; recipient Gold Headed Cane, AOA medal; Kaiser award for excellence in teaching U. Calif.-San Francisco Sch. Medicine, 1976, Charlotte Baer Meml. Clin. Faculty award U. Calif., 1993, Alumnus of Yr. award U. Calif. Med. Sch., 1998. Mem. AMA, ACS, Am. Assn. Surgery of Trauma, Am. Trauma Soc., Am. Soc. Surgery of Hand, Carribean Hand Soc., San Francisco Surg. Soc. (pres. 1979-80), Pacific Coast Surg. Assn., City Club. Clubs: Rotary; Bohemian (San Francisco). Home: Belvedere Tiburon, Calif. *The road to success lies in meeting responsibility with an open, inquisitive mind and hard work, tempered with humility, kindness, time for family, for play, for the arts as well as a good laugh. The lasting measure of success is how much remains after you have gone that continues to be of value to others.* Died Apr. 6, 2003.

KILGORE, JEFFREY HARPER, lawyer; b. Prescott, Ariz., Feb. 17, 1948; s. Richard B. Kilgore and Margaret (Poling) Keller; m. Janice Raley, June 7, 1969 (div. June 1980); children: Christopher A., Adam Harper; m. Mary Russell, Jan. 8, 1983; 1 child, Kelsey Love. BA in Banking and Fin., N. Tex. State U., 1970; JD, U. Houston, 1973. Bar: Tex. 1973, U.S. Ct. Appeals (5th cir.) 1975, U.S. Supreme Ct. 1976, U.S. Dist. Ct. (no. dist.) Tex. 1974, U.S. Dist. Ct. (so. dists.) Tex. 1983. Pvt. practice, Dallas, Irving and Galveston, Tex., 1973—. Cons. toxic tort-benzene leukemia cases, 1983—; mediation/arbitration Kilgore Mediation Ctr., 1997—; chmn. Mediation Svcs. Bd. Galveston, 1999-2001. Mem. vestry St. Mark Episcopal Ch., Irving, Tex., 1975-78, Trinity Episcopal Ch., Galveston, 1985-88, 98-2000; bd. dirs., trustee Trinity Episcopal Sch., 1998—. Mem. Assn. Trial Lawyers Am., Tex. State Bar Assn. (mem. litigation and alternate dispute resolution sect.), Galveston County Bar Assn., Lions (bd. dirs. Irving chpt. 1975-83, bd. dirs. Galveston chpt. 1983-87, named Irving chpt. Outstanding Lion 1983), Mediation Assn. of Galceston County (pres. 1998-2000), NASD Regulation Mediator, NASD Regulation Arbitration Bd. Democrat. Avocations: sailing, scuba diving, photography. Office: 2020 Broadway St Galveston TX 77550-4636

KILGORE, JERRY, state attorney general; m. Marty Kilgore; children: Klarke, Kelsey. JD, Coll. William & Mary, 1986; grad., U. Va. Prin. Richmond law firm Sands Anderson Marks & Miller; asst. Commonwealth atty. Scott County; asst. U.S. atty. gen. Western Dist. Va.; state, fed. prosecutor State of Va.; sec. pub. safety former Gov. George Allen's Cabinet, 1994—97; atty. gen. State of Va., 2002—. Republican. Office: 900 E Main St Richmond VA 23219*

KILGORE, JOHN EDWARD, JR., former petroleum company executive; b. Wichita Falls, Tex., Jan. 12, 1921; s. John Edward and Lillian (Amery) K.; m. Constance M. Brewer, May 1947; m. Emilie Smith Gilbreath, Nov. 1965; children: John Edward III, Constance Pritchett, Ralph Amery, Robert Monell, Alexander Gray; m. Annie deMontel Rassman, Oct. 25, 1986. AB, Amherst Coll., 1941; LLB, Harvard U., 1944; D in Bus, Adminstrn. (hon.), Husson Coll., 1995. Bar: Tex. 1948. Ptnr. Kilgore & Kilgore, Dallas, 1948-57, J.H. Whitney & Co., N.Y.C., 1957-68, John E. Kilgore & Co., 1968-83; founder, chmn. Cambridge Royalty Co., Petroleum Royalties Ireland Ltd., 1970-86; founder, mng. dir. Cambridge Petroleum Royalties Ltd., 1972-80. Bd. dirs. TATEX. Trustee German Marshall Fund of U.S., 1978-89, Husson Coll., 1997—. With USNR, 1942-45. Mem. Union Club (N.Y.C.), Phi Beta Kappa. Office: PO Box 127 Surry ME 04684-0127

KILGORE, L(EROY) WILSON, minister; b. Elmira, N.Y., Feb. 25, 1917; s. Roy Dunning and Bertha Pearl (Bush) K.; m. Ursula Dunbar, June 27, 1940 (wid. 1960); children: Keith, Sharon, Paul, Debra; m. Lois Morse Bell, Feb. 14, 1961; children: Kristie, Richard III, Nancy, Douglas, Cynthia. BA, Colgate U., 1939; MDiv, Colgate-Rochester Div. Sch., 1942; DD (hon.), Colgate U., 1964. Ordained to ministry Presbyn. Ch., 1942. Pastor 1st Presbyn. Ch., Hartford, Conn., 1943-53; sr. pastor Lakewood Presbyn. Ch., Cleve., 1953-64, Cherry Hill Presbyn. Ch., Dearborn, Mich., 1964-72, Valley Presbyn. Ch., Scottsdale, Ariz., 1972-86; interim minister 3d Presbyn. Ch., Rochester, N.Y., 1987-88, 1st Presbyn. Ch., Tulsa, 1990-91, Kirk in the Hills Presbyn. Ch., Bloomfield Hills, Mich., 1995-96. Trustee San Francisco Theol. Seminary, San Anselmo, Calif., 1978-90; mem. support agy, Presbyn. Ch. USA, 1978-86; chmn. com. on communication Presbyn. Ch. USA, 1980-82; moderator Grand Canyon Presbytery, 1986-87. Author: What a Way to Live, 1977, When the River Runs Backward 1983, 2d edit. 1989. Active Acad. of Parish Clergy, 1976—; trustee, pres. Westminster Village Retirement Ctr., Scottsdale, 1990-95. Mem. Rotary. Home and Office: # 112 7501 E Thompson Peak Pkwy Scottsdale AZ 85255-4525 E-mail: lkresort@aol.com.

KILGORE, MARCHON JUNE, transportation company executive, genealogist; b. Owosso, Mich., 1946; d. Cameron Blaine Miller and C. June Kibby; m. Gerald Lee Kilgore, Jan. 20, 1969; children: Stefan Allen, Julie Theresa. Owner, mgr., farmer, Eagle, Mich., 1978-2000; owner trucking co. MJK Ltd Inc., 2000—. Mem. East Ky. Geneal. Soc., Lewis County Geneal. Soc., Ky. Geneal. Soc., Shiawassee County Hist. Soc., Shiawassee County Genal. Soc., Thomas Minor Soc. Republican. Baptist. Avocations: sewing, reading, investing. Home: 4157 U Dr S Athens MI 49011-9329

KILGORE, TERRY LEE, lawyer; b. Mansfield, Ohio, May 5, 1948; s. Kenneth Burr and Velma (Gatton) K.; m. Renee Mary Bassak, Sept. 16, 1972; children: Todd Lee, Michelle Renee. BA in Polit. Sci. cum laude, Wittenberg U., 1970; JD cum laude, Ohio State U., 1973. Bar: Ohio 1973, U.S. Dist. Ct. (no. dist.) Ohio 1974, U.S. Ct. Appeals (6th cir.) 1975. Ptnr. Weldon, Huston & Keyser, Mansfield, 1973-94; pvt. practice Columbus, 1994—. Mem. Interprofl. Edn. and Practice Commn., Ohio State U., Columbus, 1978—; chmn/ Mansfield CSC, 1976-85. Mem.: ATLA, ABA, Ohio Bar Assn., Liederkranz Club (Mansfield). Republican. Lutheran. Avocations: sailing, biking. Home and Office: 3031 Birch Hollow Way Columbus OH 43231-7674 Fax: 614-794-6993. E-mail: tkilgore13@ameritech.net.

KILGORE, TULASI, artist, art educator; b. Columbus, Ohio, Nov. 16, 1953; d. Richard Nathaniel Kilgore and Ruth Eudora Sharp; life ptnr. Rj Zimmer. BFA, Ohio State U., 1977; MFA, Miami U., Oxford, Ohio, 1979. Asst. prof. art W.Va. State Coll., Institute, 1989—93; v.p. edn. Dupage Art League & Gallery, Wheaton, Ill., 1993—94; multimedia prodr. Compudoc Interactive Media, Warren, NJ, 1994—96; asst. v.p, client tech. Merrill Lynch, Pennington, NJ, 1996—2002; pres. The Joy of Handspinning, Helena, Mont., 1999—. Lectr. Lewis & Clark Pub. Libr., Helena, 2002—; instr. The Fiber Whorl, Helena, 2002—. Interactive multimedia cd rom, Handspinning Basics and Techniques For Beginners; author, editor, photographer: handbook How to Handpaint Fiber and Yarn; exhibitions include Agora Gallery, N.Y.C. Recipient Golden Web award, The Internet Assn. of Webmasters and Designers, 2000—01, Website Award of Excellence, Maestro Awards, 2000—01, Alpaca - Spl. Divsn., First Prize/Spl. award, Md. Wool and Sheep Festival, 2000. Mem.: The Chronicle of Higher Edn., Helena Weavers and Spinners Guild (pres. 2003—), Mont. Assn. Weavers and Spinners, The Handweavers Guild Am. Avocations: hiking, camping, guitar, yoga, reading. Office: The Joy of Handspinning PO Box 1572 Helena MT 59624 Home Fax: 406-457-9159; Office Fax: 406-457-9159. Personal E-mail: handspinning@hotmail.com. E-mail: info@joyofhandspinning.com.

KILGOUR, DAVID, Canadian member of parliament; b. Winnipeg, Man., Can., Feb. 18, 1941; s. David Eckford and Mary Sophia (Russell) K.; m. Laura Mae Scott, June 22, 1974; children: Margot, Eileen, David, Hilary. Bar: B.C., 1967, Man. 1970, Alta. 1972. Mem. House of Commons, 1979—; apptd. parliament sec. to govt. house leader, 1979; opposition critic for crime prevention, 1981-83; dep. critic external affairs, 1983-84; apptd. parliament sec. to min. external rels., 1984; parliament sec. to min. Indian affairs and no. devel., 1985; parliament sec. to min. transport, 1986; asst. city prosecutor, 1967-68; adv. counsel Dept. Justice, Ottawa, 1968-69; chief crown atty. Dauphin Judicial Dist., Man., 1971-72; a sr. agt. Alta. Gen. and Constl. Adv., 1972-79; dep. speaker, chmn. coms. whole house House of Commons, Ottawa, Ont., Can., 1994-97; sec. state Latin America & Africa, 1997—2002, Asia-Pacific, 2002—. Author: Uneasy Patriots: Western Canadians in Confederation, 1988, Inside Outer Canada, 1990, Betrayal: The Spy Canada Abandoned, 1994. Mem. Can. Bar Assn. Office: House of Commons Rm 163 East Block Ottawa ON Canada K1A 0A6 also: Wellington St Ontario Ot K1A 0A6 Canada

KILGOUR, FREDERICK GRIDLEY, librarian, educator; b. Springfield, Mass., Jan. 6, 1914; s. Edward Francis and Lillian Bess (Piper) K.; m. Eleanor Margaret Beach, Sept. 3, 1940; children: Martha, Alison, Meredith. AB, Harvard U., 1935; student, Columbia Sch. Library Service, summers 1939-41; LLD (hon.), Marietta Coll., 1980, Coll. of Wooster, 1981; DHL (hon.), Ohio State U., 1980, Denison U., 1983, U. Mo., Kansas City, 1989. Staff Harvard Coll. Library, 1935-42, OSS, 1942-45; dep. dir. office of intelligence collection and dissemination U.S. Dept. State, 1946-48; librarian Yale Med. Library, 1948-65; asso. librarian for research and devel. Yale U. Library, 1965-67; mng. editor Yale Jour. Biology and Medicine, 1949-65; lectr. in history of sci. Yale U., 1950-59, lectr. history of tech., 1961-67; fellow Davenport Coll., 1950-67; pres., exec. dir. Online Computer Library Ctr., OCLC, Inc., 1967-80, vice chmn. bd. trustees Online Computer Library Ctr., 1981-83; founder trustee Online Computer Libr. Ctr., 1984—; Disting. rsch. prof. U. N.C., Chapel Hill, 1990—. Author: Library of the Medical Institution of Yale College and Its Catalogue of 1865, 1960, The Library and Information Science CumIndex, 1975, The Evolution of the Book, 1998; co-author: Engineering in History, 1956, 90; author: Collected Papers, 2 vols., 1984; editor: Book of Bodily Exercises, 1960, Jour. Library Automation, 1968-71; contbr. articles to profl. jours. Served as lt. (j.g.) USNR, 1943-45, overseas duty. Decorated Legion of Merit; recipient Margaret Mann citation in cataloging and classification, 1974, Melvil Dewey medal, 1978; Acad./Research Librarian of Year, 1979; Library Info. Tech. award, 1979, numerous others Mem. ALA, Am. Soc. Info. Sci. (Merit award 1979), Cosmos Club. Home: 207 Carolina Meadows Villa Chapel Hill NC 27517-8500 Office: Sch Info & Libr Sci U NC 100 Manning Hall CBH3360 Chapel Hill NC 37599-3360 E-mail: kilgour@ils.unc.edu.

KILGUSS, ELSIE SCHAICH, artist, gallery owner; b. Manhattan, NY, Aug. 04; BS in Advt., Mktg., Bryant Coll.; studied with Charles Sovek, studied with Betty Cappelli, 1968, studied with Henry Hensche, Lois Griffel; grad., RISD; student, Cape Sch. Art. With Horton, Church & Goff, Advt. Agy., Providence; represented by Gallery at Chatham, Mass., 1990-99; owner, instr. Studio Zwei, Wickford, R.I., 1991—. Art instr. Wickford Art Assn., 1990-98, Warwick Art Mus., 1998-2000, Attleboro Mus., 2000—, South County Art Assn., 2000-02. One-woman shows include Wickford Art Festival, 1988—, Gallery at Chatham, 1990—99, Studio Zwei Gallery, Wickford, 1991—, Alfred Butler & Co., North Kingstown, 1992—, Fleet Bank, 1992—, R.I. State House, Providence, 1993—, Art in the Garden, 1995, 1997, 1999, Aszzo, 1998—99, Music on the Hill Anniversary Art Show, 1998, Cafe Gallery, 1998—99, Dodge House Gallery, Providence, 1999, 2001, Providence, 2001, 2003, Warwick Mus. Art, 2000; two-woman shows B&H Framing, 1987, Artists Gallery, Wickford, R.I., 1990, Maxwell Mays Gallery-Providence Art Club, 1991, 1997, Providence Art Club, 1993, 1995, 1997—98; Exhibited in group shows at Warwick (R.I.) Art Mus., 1987, 1989, 1991, 1997—99, Helme House, Kingston, R.I., 1990, 1993, 1995, 1997, 2000, 2002, Woods-Gerry Gallery, Providence, 1991, Wickford Art Assn. Gallery, North Kingstown, 1991, 1993, 1995, 1997, 1999, R.I. Sch. Design Mus., Providence, 1992, Spring Bull Gallery, Newport, R.I., 1993, 1999, Newport, RI, 2001—02, Newport ArtMus., 1990, 1993, 1995, 1997, 1999—2001, 2003, R.I. Watercolor Soc., Pawtucket, 1993, 1995, 1997, 2000,

2003, South County Helme House, 2001—02, Spring Bull Gallery, 2002—03, Represented in permanent collections Alfred Butler & Co., Carribean Villas, others; catalog covers Providence Mag., R.I. Sch. Design, Cape Cod Mag., North Kingstown Villager. Mem.: Am. Soc. Marine Artists, Am. Watercolor Soc., Nat. Mus. Women in Arts, Warwick Mus., Boston Mus. Fine Arts, RISD Mus., Attleboro Mus., Newport Mus., Copley Soc. (Boston), Creative Arts Ctr., Newport Artist's Guild, South County Art Assn., Wickford Art Assn. (art instr. 1990—91, 1998—99, past pres. 1991), R.I. Watercolor Soc., Oil Painters Am. (assoc.), Providence Art Club. Studio: Studio Zwei Gallery 2 Main St North Kingstown RI 02852-5016 E-mail: ekilguss@aol.com., studiozwei.2main@aol.com.

KILIAN, MICHAEL DAVID, journalist, columnist, writer; b. Toledo, July 16, 1939; s. D. Frederick and Laura Casmere (Dulski) K.; m. Pamela H. Reeves, Oct. 17, 1970; children: Eric, Colin. Student, New Sch. for Social Rsch., N.Y.C., 1957-58, U. Md., 1964. Writer Sta. KNTV, San Jose, Calif., 1960-63; reporter City News Bur., Chgo., 1965-66; reporter, asst. polit. editor Chgo. Tribune, 1966-71, editl. writer, 1971-86, editl. page columnist, 1971-86, Washington columnist, corr., cultural commentator, 1986—. Commentator Sta. WBBM, CBS, 1973-82, Sta. WTTW-TV, 1975-78, Nat. Pub. Radio, 1978-79; host. "DC Jour.: CLTV News, 1995-2000; correspondent Roy Leonard Show, WGN, 1996-99. Author: Who Runs Chicago?, 1979, The Valkyrie Project, 1981, Who Runs Washington?, 1982, Northern Exposure, 1983, Blood of the Czars, 1984, Heavy Losses, 1985, By Order of the President, 1986, Dance on a Sinking Ship, 1988, Looker, 1991, The Last Virginia Gentleman, 1992, The Big Score, 1993, Bad Girl Blues, 1994, Postcard from Hell, 1995, Major Washington, 1998, Murder at Manassas, 1999, A Killing at Ball's Bluff, 2000, The Weeping Woman, 2001, The Ironclad Alibi, 2002, The Uninvited Countess, 2002, A Grave at Glorieta, 2003, A Sinful Safari, 2003, (comic strip) Dick Tracy, 1993—. Capt., CAP, 1976—; staff officer USCG Aux., 2002—. With U.S. Army, 1963-65. Recipient Humor Writing award UPI, 1971 Mem. White House Corrs. Assn., English Speaking Union (life), The Woods Club. Presbyterian. Office: Chgo Tribune 1325 G St NW Washington DC 20005-3104

KILIAN, THOMAS RANDOLPH, rural economic developer, consultant; b. Vilas, S.D., Mar. 23, 1924; s. Ward Van and Mabel Amanda (Peterson) K.; m. Lorna Jean Pearson, Aug. 27, 1949; children: James, Peter, Mary, Susan. BA, Augustana Coll., 1949; MS, Boston U., 1950; PhD, Mich. State U., 1968; student, Harvard U., 1971, 79. Dir. pub. rels. Waldorf Coll., Forest City, Iowa, 1950-52, Augustana Coll., Sioux Falls, S.D., 1952-61, v.p. development, 1961-73, exec. v.p., 1975-82; sec. S.D. Dept. Edn./Cultural Affairs, Pierre, S.D., 1973-75; pres. N. Ctrl. Univ. Ctr., Sioux Falls, S.D., 1975-85, N. Ctrl. Univ. Ctr. C.C., Sioux Falls, S.D., 1977-85; prin. EOS Futures Group, Sioux Falls, S.D., 1985-87; dir. Rural Initiative Ctr., Sioux Falls, S.D., 1987—. Author: (book) Power Constructs, 1969, Your Way, 1996; contbr. articles to profl. jours. Pres. S.D. Heritage Fund, Pierre, 1983-95, S.D. State Hist. Soc., Pierre, 1987-97, Minnehaha Century Fund, Sioux Falls, 1990—; chmn. S.D. Rev. Bd. Hist. Preservation Bd., Sioux Falls, 1992-95, Ctr. for Western Studies, Sioux Falls, 1970-95, 96—; past chmn. S.D. Pub. TV Bd., Pierre; convenor Sioux Falls Beautiful, 1997—. Mem. S.D. Future Soc. (S.D. coord.). Democrat. Lutheran. Avocations: natural history, local history, archaeology, future studies. Home: 2700 S Jefferson Ave Sioux Falls SD 57105-4416 Office: Rural Initiative Ctr 1320 S Minnesota Ave Ste 204 Sioux Falls SD 57105-0657

KILIANSKI, STEPHEN, psychologist, educator; b. Passaic, N.J., Nov. 29, 1951; s. Ernest and Patricia Kilianski; m. Suzanne Hagert, July 22, 1983; children: Mark, Scott. BA in Psychology, Rutgers U., 1974; MA in Psychology, Montclair State U., 1997; PhD in Psychology, Rutgers U., 2001. Regional mgr. client rels. Harrington Inc., Columbus, Ohio, 1981—85; programmer/analyst Chubb & Son, Inc., Warren, NJ, 1985—97; instr. psychology Montclair State U., Upper Montclair, NJ, 1996—, Rutgers U., Madison, NJ, 1998—, Drew U., Madison, 2003—. Contbr. Mem.: APA, Soc. for Psychol. Study of Social Issues, Am. Psychol. Soc. Home: 22 Hawthorne Ave Nutley NJ 07110 Office: Rutgers Univ 53 Ave E Piscataway NJ 08854-8040

KILKELLY, MARJORIE LEE, state legislator, community development official; b. Hartford, Conn., Dec. 1, 1954; d. Bruce Hamilton and Corlys Lucille (Lux) Brewer; children: Jeffrey Jr. (dec.), Robert, Sarah A.E. BS in Human Svcs., MS in Cmty. Econ. Devel., N.H. Coll., 1986; postgrad., Harvard U., 1997. Asst. to dir. Lincoln County Summer Youth Employment Program, Wiscasset, Maine, 1978; coordinator Community Food & Nutrition Program Coastal Enterprises, Inc., Wiscasset, 1978-79, Coastal Econ. Devel. Corp., Wiscasset, 1979-80, dir. Head Start Program Bath, Maine, 1980-84; asst. instr. N.H. Coll., Manchester, 1985-86; dir. Jr. Tots Wiscasset Recreation Program, 1985-88; dir. food services Boothbay Sch. Dept., Boothbay Harbor, Maine, 1985-88; owner Hurricane Hill Catering Co., Wiscasset, 1989—; mem. Maine Ho. of Reps., Augusta, 1986-96; house chair com. on agr., forestry and conservation, 1995-96; co-chmn. coastal caucus Maine Ho. of Reps., Augusta, spkr. pro tem, 1996—, candidate for speaker of house, 1992, candidate for house majority whip, 1994, chmn. agr., forestry and conservation com., 1995—; candidate Maine Senate, 1996; state senator, chmn. agriculture conservation and forestry com., island fish and wildlife com. State of Maine, 1996-98, chmn. Nat. Conf. State Legislators agr. com., 1997—; mem. Harvard state and local govt. ofcls. program Kennedy Sch. Govt., 1997—; cmty. devel. dir. Island Inst., Rockland, Maine, 1997—, community devel. dir., 1997—. Treas. Coastal Enterprises, Inc., Rundlet Block, Wis., 1981-90; rep. to Internat. Conf. on Econ. Devel., New Delhi, 1983—; 3d Selectman Town of Wiscasset, 1993-97; dir. devel. Maine Hospice Coun., 2000; owner Hurrican Hill Cons.; dir. N.E. States Assn. for Agrl. Stewardship, 1996-02. Mem. planning com. Blaine House Conf. on Families, 1979-80; active Maine Human Svcs. Coun. Sta. 23, Augusta, 1980-88; Sunday sch. tchr., lectr. St. Philips Episcopal Ch., Wiscasset, 1984-85, chmn. coord. com. food bank, 1986-88, sr. warden, 1995-98; chmn. Wis. Dem. Com., 1986; nat. chmn. Schs. S.O.S. Nat. Hunger Awareness Program, Denver, 1986; mem. exec. com. Maine Rural Devel. Coun., 1995—; spkr. pro tempere 118th Legislature, 1996; candidate Main State Senate Dist. 16, 1996; chair comm. adv. panel on decommissioning Maine Yankee Nuclear Plant, 1997, mem. legis. select com.; bd. dirs. Miles Health Care, Damanscotta, Mass., 1996—, Mid Coast United Way; chmn. Citizens Adv. Panel on Decommissioning Maine Yankee Atomic Power Plant, 1997—; lay dep. Nat. Episc. Ch. Conv., 1996—. Recipient Good Governance award, Maine Merchants Assn., 2000; fellow New Eng. Rural, Coun. State Govts. Toll, Flemming fellow, Ctr. Policy Alternatives, 1999, Eisenhower Exch., 1999; grantee Maine Welfare Edn. Employment Tng. Program, 1983. Mem. Bus. and Profl. Women (Maine Young Career Woman award 1989), Huntoon Hill Grange Club, Lincoln County Pomona Grange Club, Sportsmans Alliance Club of Maine, Am. Coun. Young Polit. Leaders, United Way of Mid Coast Maine (bd. mem.), Miles Hlth. Care Bd., U. Maine Bd. of Agr., Northeast States Assn. for Agrl. Stewardship (chair). Clubs: Maine Farm Bur., Maine State Grange. Democrat. Episcopalian. Avocations: horseback riding, gourmet cooking, fishing. Home: PO Box 180 W Alna Rd Wiscasset ME 04578-0180 Office: Maine State Senate State Capitol Augusta ME 04333-0001 E-mail: kilkelly@wiscasset.net.

KILL, LAWRENCE, lawyer; b. N.Y.C., Apr. 11, 1935; s. Bernard and Dora (Laskin) K.; m. Karyl Klein, Oct. 21, 1962; children: Debra, Andrea, Brenda. BBA, CCNY, 1957; LLB cum laude, Fordham U., 1960. Bar: N.Y. 1961. Trial atty. antitrust div. U.S. Dept. Justice, Washington, 1961-66; assoc. Chadbourne & Parke, N.Y.C., 1966-72; ptnr. Anderson Kill & Olick PC, N.Y.C., 1972—. Editor-in-chief: Fordham Law Rev, 1959-60. Served with U.S. Army, 1960-61. Mem. Assn. Bar City N.Y., ABA, N.Y. State Bar assn. Home: 29 Queens Ln New Hyde Park NY 11040-1213 Office: Anderson Kill & Olick PC Ste 383 1251 Avenue Of The Americas Fl C31 New York NY 10020-1182 E-mail: lkill@andersonkill.com.

KILL, SISTER MARIETTA, nun, music educator; b. Landeck, Ohio, Jan. 28, 1932; d. Eugene Rosalia Barbara Kill. EdB, Mary Manse Coll., 1966; MusB, St. Joseph's Coll., Rensselaer,Ind., 1968; MusM, De Paul U, 1973. Elem. tchr. Sisters of St. Francis of Tiffin (Ohio), 1954—68, pvt. music tchr., 1970—2003. Organist Cath. Ch., Toledo Diocese, Ohio, 1954—, mem. Diocesan Ligurgical Comm.; chair Motherhouse Liturgical Comm., 1970—87; chairperson OMTA Music Festival, Tiffin, 1981—. Mem.: Ohio Music Tchr. Assn. (assoc.; chair music Festival of North Ctrl. District 1972—). Avocations: gardening, stamp collecting. Home and Office: 200 St Francis Ave Tiffin OH 44883

KILLACKEY, DOROTHY HELEN, real estate professional, former educator; b. Pitts., Mar. 29, 1927; d. Edward G. and Dorothy Marie (Krauss) Buschow; m. Feb. 5, 1949 (div. Sept. 1985); children: Thomas, Maureen, Nancy, Edward. BA, Columbia U., 1948; MS, Western Conn. State U., Danbury, 1971; 6th Yr. Profl. Deg., Western Conn. State U., 1980. Elem. tchr. Brewster (N.Y.) Pub. Schs., 1965-89; tchr. title I summer sch. Govt. Title I, Brewster, 1973-80; from real estate salesman to broker Prudential Spectra Realty, Brewster, 1983—2002. Ch. parochial bd. dirs. St. Lawrence O'Toole Ch., Brewster, 1974-76; pres. J.F. Kennedy Sch. Union, Brewster, 1975-77. Editor J.F. Kennedy Sch. Writing Anthology, 1982-89. Mem. choir, soloist St. Lawrence O'Toole Ch., Brewster, 1970-90; mem. Historic Preservation Com., Brewster, 1991-93; vol. RSVP Program Putnam County, 1997—; biographer Putnam County Sr. Citizens; mem. Putnam City Children's Com., 1999—; coord. SeniorNet Srs. Teach Sr. Computer, 2002—. Nancy Barrelle scholar Western Conn. State U., 1979; named Putnam County Sr. Citizen of 1999, Putnam County Execs., Humanitarian award, Ret. Sr. Vols., 2003. Mem. Phi Delta Kappa, Delta Kappa Gamma (Alpha Omicron chpt. pres. 1999—). Avocations: reading, piano, gardening. Home: 401 Stonewall Ln Brewster NY 10509-6010

KILLAM, DAVID E. retired music educator; b. Boxford, Mass., Sept. 16, 1934; s. Paul L. and Edith C. Killam; m. Barbara T. Taylor, Jan. 25, 1969. BS in Ed., U. Lowell, 1956; MDiv, Tufts U., 1960; MusM, U. Mich., 1968. Cert. Medicare counselor Health Ins. Edn. Assistance Counseling Svc. Dir. of music Colebrook (N.H.) Sch. Dist., 1960—94. Poet, spkr. Poetry Soc. N.H., Bethlehem Poetry Coun.; mem. N.E. Kingdom Internat. Wind Symphony, North Country Band, Whitefield and Lancaster Summer Bands. Contbr. articles to profl. jours., poetry and short stories to anthologies. Former sch. bd. mem. Columbia Sch. Dist. Named N.H. Tchr. of Yr., N.H. State of Edn., 1974; named to Hall of Fame, N.H. Music Educators Assn., 1999; recipient Goodhue-Elkins award, N.H. Audubon, 2000. Home: 1845 US Rt 3 Colebrook NH 03576

KILLAM, JILL MINERVINI, oil and gas company executive; b. Pitts., Sept. 6, 1954; d. Virginio Lucien and Helen Elizabeth (Safgren) Minervini; m. Clayton Henry Killam, June 4, 1973. AAS with high honors, Eastfield Jr. Coll., Mesquite, Tex., 1974; BBA with high honors, U. Tex., Arlington, 1985. CPA, Tex. Asst. to treas. CKB & Assocs., Dallas, 1985—89, v.p., chief acctg. officer, 1989—92; v.p., CFO Box Energy Corp. (formerly OKC Ltd. Partnership), Dallas, 1992—96; v.p. fin. and adminstrn. Fremont Energy L.P., Dallas, 1997—2001; CFO Box Exploration LLC, Richardson, Tex., 2001. Mem. AICPA (Elijah Watt Sells award 1985), Tex. State Bd. Pub. Accts. (lic., Spl. award for Outstanding Achievement 1986), Tex. Soc. CPAs (state and Dallas chpt.), Petroleum Accts. Soc. Dallas. Republican. Roman Catholic. Avocation: water skiing. Office: Box Exploration LLC 1177 Rockingham Ln Ste 200 Richardson TX 75080 E-mail: jkillamcpa@yahoo.com.

KILLE, JOHN WILLIAM, JR., toxicology and biomedical product consultant; b. Tampa, Fla., June 17, 1943; s. John William and Myrtle Kille; m. Elaine Anderson; children: Amy, Lindsey, Thomas; m. Camille Ragazzo, Sept. 22, 1991; 1 stepchild, Richard. AB, Lafayette Coll., 1965; MS, Villanova U., 1968; PhD, U. Va., 1972. Diplomate Am. Bd. Toxicology. NIH rsch. trainee Worcester Found. for Exptl. Biology, 1970-72; rsch. fellow Cambridge (Eng.) U., 1972-73; lectr., rschr. Northwestern U., Evanston, Ill., 1974-78; group leader for drug safety Ortho Pharm. Co. divsn. Johnson & Johnson, Raritan, N.J., 1978-88; assoc. dir. product safety and regulatory affairs McNeil Splty. Products Co. divsn. Johnson & Johnson, New Brunswick, N.J., 1988-93; sr. toxicologist Cantox, Inc., Bridgewater, N.J., 1994-96; prin. J.W. Kille Assocs., Stanton, N.J., 1996—. Cons. to various pharm., food and biotech. cos. and legal firms, 1994—96; cons. Johnson & Johnson, Emisphere Techs., Hydro Med. Scis., Helicon Therapeutics, Norgine Internat. Ltd. (U.K.), various other domestic and internat. projects, Canada, Mexico, Australia, 1996—, England, 1996—; advisor Office Tech. Assessment, U.S. Congress, 1984. Contbr. articles to sci. jours. Chmn. Family Life Edn. Com., Bloomsbury, N.J., 1985-86. Rsch. fellow Lalor Found., 1972-73, WHO, 1972-73. Mem. Am. Coll. Toxicology, Genetic Toxicology Assn., Inst. Food Technologists, Regulatory Affairs Profls. Soc., Soc. Toxicology (program com. Mid-Atlantic chpt. 1996—, chmn. edn. and pub. comms. com. 1999—), Teratology Soc., Mid-Atlantic Reprodn. and Teratology Assn. (pres. 1986-87). Avocations: listening to music and singing in choral groups, camping, hunting, fishing, stained glass creations. Office: PO Box 69 Stanton NJ 08885-0069 Fax: 908-236-0921. E-mail: jwkille@blast.net.

KILLEBREW, ELLEN JANE (MRS. EDWARD S. GRAVES), cardiologist, educator; b. Tiffin, Ohio, Oct. 8, 1937; d. Joseph Arthur and Stephanie (Beriont) K.; m. Edward S. Graves, Sept. 12, 1970. BS in Biology, Bucknell U., 1959; MD, N.J. Coll. Medicine, 1965. Diplomate in cardiovasc. disease Am. Bd. Internal Medicine. Intern U. Colo., 1965-66, resident, 1966-68; cardiology fellow Pacific Med. Ctr., San Francisco, 1968-70; dir. coronary care Permanent Med. Group, Richmond, Calif., 1970-83; asst. prof. U. Calif. Med. Ctr., San Francisco, 1970-83, assoc. prof., 1983-93; clin. prof. medicine U. Calif., San Francisco, 1992—, mem. admissions panel, 1998—. Admissions panel joint med. program U. Calif. San Francisco/U. Calif. Berkeley, 1998—; expert med. reviewer Calif. Med. Br., 1999; expert med. reviewer Bd. of Med. Examiners Calif., 1999—. Contbr. chpt. to book. Recipient Physician's Recognition award continuing med. edn., Lowell Beal award excellence in tchg., Permante Med. Group/House Staff Assn., 1992; Robert C. Kirkwood Meml. scholar in cardiology, 1970. Fellow ACP, Am. Coll. Cardiology; mem. Fedn. Clin. Rsch., Am. Heart Assn. (rsch. chmn. Contra Costa chpt. 1975—, v.p. 1980, pres. chpt. 1981-82, chmn. CPR com. Alameda chpt. 1984, pres. Oakland Piedmont br. 1995—, bd. dirs. western affiliate). Home: 30 Redding Ct Belvedere Tiburon CA 94920-1318 Office: 280 W Macarthur Blvd Oakland CA 94611-5642 also: 901 Nevin Ave Richmond CA 94801-3143 E-mail: Ellen.Killebrew@k.p.org.

KILLEBREW, JAMES ROBERT, architectural engineering firm executive; b. Okmulgee, Okla., Dec. 10, 1918; s. Robert Herman and Edith (Tyler) K.; m. Emma Herrington, Feb. 24, 1989; 1 child by previous marriage, Laura Janice. BS in Archtl. Engring., U. Tex., 1948. Registered architect, Tex. registered profl. engr., Tex. Prin. James R. Killebrew, FAIA, PE, architect, cons. engr., Granbury, Tex.; sr. structural engr. DFW Internat. Airport, 1991—. Sr. cons. architect engr. Yandell-Hiller, 1989-90, Dallas-Ft. Worth Airport/Am. Airlines; sr. structural engr. Dallas-Ft. Worth Internat. Airport Bd. Prin. archtl. works include Gen. Hosp. Plainview, Tex., Vernon (Tex.) Hosp., Vernon Geriatrics Psychiat. Hosp., Wichita Gen. Hosp., Gen. Hosp. Nocona (Tex.), Sci. Bldg., Phys. Edn. Bldg., Midwestern State U., Teenage Drug Addiction Center, Vernon, Fine Arts Bldg. at Midwestern State U., AC Spark Plug Ceramics Complex-Gen. Motors Corp., Parker Sq. Savs. and Loan, Union Sq., Four Story Savs. & Loan Bldg., Wichita Falls, Sprague Electric Co., Howmet Turbine, Wichita Clutch Corp., G.H. Foster Plant, Family YMCA, SW Nat. Bank Tower; coord. measuring machine for Gen. Motors-CPC plant, Arlington, Tex. Elder Christian Ch., 1979-81. Lt. comdr. USN, 1940-45, PTO; capt. Res. (ret.). Fellow AIA (pres. Wichita Falls chpt. 1966-67, 81); mem. Nat. Soc. Profl. Engrs., Tex. Soc. Profl. Engrs. (pres. N. Tex. chpt. 1960-61), Am. Soc. Archtl. Engrs. (charter mem.), ASHRAE, Wichita Falls C. of C. (chmn. various coms.), Navy League (pres. 1967-68), Fine Art Soc. Tex. (pres. 1970, chmn. bd. 1973). Mem. Christian Ch. Club: Rotary (pres. 1983-84). Achievements include inspection for expansion of terminals, multi-story parking facilities, aircraft rescue fire fighting training facility, hangar addition, FAA technical facility and five story parking garage, DFW runway 16/34 East UPS Hdqs., Terminal 3E-B code inspection, American Airlines new 3-EA terminal 5 story parking garage, new consol. rent-a-car parking facility, airport expansion, others. Home: 6 Windy Knoll Ct Grapevine TX 76051-3843 E-mail: jkillebrew@dfwairport.com. *The practice of architecture requires the efforts of many talented professionals and personnel aspiring to be professionals. No longer does one man act as master builder (or designer). If I have attained a notable degree of success, it is due to the combined efforts through many years, of all the excellent associates with which I have been fortunate to know.*

KILLEEN, EDWARD JOSEPH, actor, designer; b. New Orleans, Sept. 20, 1954; s. D. Miller and Viviana Mae Conner; adopted s. Joseph Henry and Teresa Mary (Gordon) K. BA in English, St. Joseph Sem. Coll., St. Benedict, La., 1976. Conv. registrar & city guide New Orleans Met. Conv. & Visitors' Bureau (NOMCVB), 2003; geophys. info. coord. Western Geco., 1997-2001; stage mgr. Rivertown Repertory Theater, 1995—; designer designs and ideas, New Orleans, 1982—; state pub. rels. coord. Easter Seal Soc. La., Metairie, 1982-84; West Tex. and N.Mex. sales rep. Wang's Internat., Inc., Memphis, 1986-87; set contractor Kenner Community Theater, Metairie, La., 1987, Le Petit Theatre de Vieux Carre, New Orleans, 1987; design asst. Jeff. Performing Arts Soc., Metairie, 1989-92. Bd. dirs. NestEGG Prodns., sec., 1998—. Graphic designer Wildlife Conclave, Tex. A&M U., 1984. Community rep. March of Dimes Birth Defects Found., New Orleans, 1980-82. Recipient Big Easy award, Best Supporting Actor award, New Orleans, 1995, Storer Boone Stage award, 1993. Avocation: carpentry. Mailing: PO Box 1915 Metairie LA 70004-1915

KILLEEN, MICHAEL JOHN, lawyer; b. Washington, Oct. 5, 1949; s. James Robert and Georgia Winston (Hartwell) K.; m. Therese Ann Goeden, Oct. 6, 1984; children: John Patrick, Katherine Therese, Mary Clare, James Philip. BA, Gonzaga U., 1971, JD magna cum laude, 1977. Bar: Wash. 1977, U.S. Dist. Ct. (we. dist.) Wash. 1979, U.S. Ct. Appeals (9th cir.) 1984, U.S. Supreme Ct. 1990. Jud. clk. Wash. State Ct. Appeals, Tacoma, 1977-79; assoc. Davis Wright Tremaine, Seattle, 1979-85, ptnr., 1985—. Bd. dirs. Seattle Goodwill, 1987—, sec., 1998-02. Author: Guide to Strike Planning, 1985, Newsroom Legal Guidebook, 1996, Employment in Washington, 1984—. Active Gonzaga Law Bd. Advisors, Spokane, Wash., pres., 1992-96. Recipient Freedom's Light award Washington Newspaper Pub. Assn., 1999, Disting. Alumni award Gonzaga U., 2002. Mem. ABA, Wash. State Bar Assn., King County Bar Assn. (treas. 1987-89, pres. award 1989). Democrat. Roman Catholic. E-mail: mikekilleen@dwt.com.

KILLEEN, THERESE, therapist; b. New Orleans, Oct. 3, 1953; d. Thomas B. Killeen and Mary Elizabeth Patterson; m. Timothy D. Brewerton, June 16, 1990. BSN, Med. U. S.C., 1989, MSN, 1990; PhD in Nursing, U. S.C., 1998. Coord. substance abuse svcs. Med. U. SC, Charleston, SC, 1990-94, coord. evening program, therapist, rsch. coord., 1992—99; tng. dir. NIDA Clin. Trials Network, 2000—. Asst. prof. dept. psychiatry and behavioral sci. MUSC Coll. Nursing, 1998—. Named nursing rsch. fellow of yr. 1996 ANA; Nat. Inst. Nursing fellow, 1997. Mem. Sigma Theta Tau. Democrat. Roman Catholic. Avocations: running, diving, biking. Home: 306 Carolina Blvd Isle Of Palms SC 29451-2111 Office: Med U SC 67 President St Charleston SC 29403-5712

KILLEN, CARROLL GORDEN, electronics company executive; b. Provencal, La., Mar. 22, 1919; s. Carroll Graves and Ella (Crowder) K.; m. Clara Donald Butler, Aug. 15, 1941; children: Carroll Gorden III, Margaret Karen, Lloyd Butler, Sara Elizabeth Grad., La. State U.; BS, La. Northwestern State Coll. Electronics engr. Magnolia Petroleum Co., Dallas, 1940-42; electronics engr. Watson Labs., Red Bank, N.J., 1942-45; chief application engr. Sprague Electric Co., North Adams, Mass., 1947-55, mgr. field engring., 1955-60, v.p. mktg. and sales, 1960-73, sr. v.p. mktg. and sales, 1973-85; v.p., gen. mgr. Tansitor Electronics, Inc., Bennington, Vt., 1985-92, dir., 1992—2001, ret., 2001. Dir. Cera-Mite Corp., Grafton, Wis., 1992-2001; cons. U.S. Dept. Def., Washington, 1949-73, U.S. Dept. Commerce, 1984-95; dir. Tantalum Internat. Study Ctr., Brussels, Belgium, 1983-85, mem. exec. com., 1983-95; pres. T.I.C., 1984-85. Author: Factors Influencing Capacitor Reliability, 1955 Chmn. Bennington Town Rep. Com., 1997—. Served to 1st lt. USAF, 1945-47, PTO Mem. IEEE (chmn. conf. bd. 1971-74, chmn. electron conf. 1976-79, life members com., tech. activities bd., pub. rels. com.), Electronic Industries Assn. (gov. 1976-2001), Am. Ordinance Assn., Newcomer Soc., Nat. Security Indsl. Assn. (trustee 1980-85), Am. Mgmt. Assn., Masons, Sales Execs. Club, Bennington Town Rep. Com. (chmn. 1997—). Republican. Baptist. Avocations: gardening, woodworking, photography. Home and Office: 511 Gage St Bennington VT 05201-1922 E-mail: cgkillen@ieee.org.

KILLENBERG, GEORGE ANDREW, newspaper consultant, former newspaper editor; b. St. Clair County, Ill., Mar. 30, 1917; s. George W. and Lavina (Ruhl) K.; m. Therese Murphy, June 3, 1943; children: George M., Mary K. Riley, John A., Terry M. Hatcher, Susan M. McGinn. BS, St. Louis U., 1954, MA, 1958. Engaged in pub. rels., 1935-41; mem. staff St. Louis Globe-Democrat, 1941—; city editor St. Louis Globe-Dem., 1956-66, mng. editor, 1966-79, exec. editor, 1979-84. Past chmn. Mid-Am. Press Inst. Bd. dirs. Boys Town Mo., 1960-88. With AUS, 1942-46. Mem. Press Club (St. Louis, pres. 1964), Sigma Delta Chi. Roman Catholic. Home: 3042 Hatherly Dr Saint Louis MO 63121-4534 E-mail: gkillenber@aol.com.

KILLGORE, ANDREW IVY, former ambassador; b. Greensboro, Ala., Nov. 7, 1919; s. Robert Morris and Mary Elmae (Wimberly) K.; m. Marjorie Davis Nicholls; children: Elizabeth Nicholls Krieger, Andrew Nicholls, Jane G., Roberta K. McInerney. BS, Livingston U., 1943; JD, U. Ala., 1949. Bar: Ala. bar. Selector-analyst U.S. Displaced Persons Commn., 1949-50, displaced populations officer, 1950-51; visa officer Am. Embassy, London, 1951-53; evaluator Dept. State, 1953-55, internat. relations officer, 1961-62; polit. officer Beirut, 1956-57; consul Jerusalem, 1957-59; polit. officer Amman, Jordan, 1959-61; officer-in-charge Iraq-Jordan affairs, 1962-65; pub. affairs officer USIS, Baghdad, Iraq, 1965-67; polit. officer Dacca, East Pakistan (now Bangladesh), 1967-70; polit.-econ. officer Arab Region North Directorate, 1970-72; counselor polit. affairs Tehran, Iran, 1972-74; charge d'affaires Manama, Bahrain, 1974; dep. chief mission Wellington, N.Z., 1974-77; amb. to Qatar Doha, 1977-80; ret., 1980. Pub. Washington Report on Middle East Affairs. Former pres. Am. sect. Musa Al-Alami of Jericho Found.; pres. Am. Ednl. Trust. Lt. (j.g.) USN, 1943-46. Recipient Fgn. Svc. Cup, 1996. Mem.: Army and Navy, Cosmos. Office: 1904 18th St NW Washington DC 20009-7738

KILLGORE, LE, journalist, political columnist; b. Poughkeepsie, N.Y., Mar. 16, 1926; m. James A. Killgore, July 24, 1948; children: Lynne, Robert, Andrew. BA in Romance Langs., Skidmore Coll., 1948; postgrad., Auburn U., 1961-62. Classroom tchr. music Stare Baldwin Sch., Dallas, 1949-50, The Little Sch., Dallas, 1950-51; substitute tchr. DOD Sch., Clark AB, Philippines, 1964-65, Dayton Ohio Schs., 1966-67, Jeb Stuart High Sch., Fairfax County, Va., 1967-68; staff writer Standard-Times, San Angelo, Tex., 1972-79, sr. staff writer, 1979-83, polit. affairs editor, 1983-92; host radio pub. affairs show, polit. cons. San Angelo, 1992—. Co-host radio/TV pub. affairs show; host radio pub. affairs show; writer quar. newsletter for state rep. Staff writer, editor Officers Wives Club mags., Clark AB, Philippines, 1964, McClellan AFB, Calif., 1966, Panama Canal Zone, 1969-71. Bd. dirs. Adult Literacy Coun. of Concho Valley, Sr. Svcs. Adv. Bd.; chair Outreach Ministry, Diaconate, 1st Presbyn. Ch. San Angelo, Recipient Overall Excellence in News Gathering award Headliners Club, 1973, Outstanding Continuous Coverage of Edn. award Tex. State Tchrs. Assn., 1977, Excellence in Health-related Reporting Tex. Med. Assn., 1977. Mem. Soc. Profl. Journalists (pres. San Angelo chpt. 1984, bd. dirs. 1986, 87, 89). Avocations: cooking, sewing, needlework, music. E-mail: leeo@airmail.net.

KILLGORE, MARK WILLIAM, civil engineer; b. Vancouver, Wash., Jan. 1, 1956; s. Charles Roy and Barbara May (Coullahan) K.; m. Maria Teresa Preciado Lopez, Aug. 13, 1993; children: Shannon Rose, Jason Philip, David William. BCE, BA in Spanish, Seattle U., 1978; MS in Civil Engring., U. Wash., 1984. Am. Asns. Engring. Socs. rep. to NAFTA Forum. Asst. engr. CRS Group, Seattle, 1978-81; assoc. engr. Ebasco Svcs. Inc., Bellevue, Wash., 1981-82, sr. assoc. engr., 1982-84, engr., 1985-88, sr. engr., 1988-91, prin. engr., 1991-93, Raytheon Infrastructure Svcs., Inc., 1993-95, Foster Wheeler Environ. Corp., 1995—98, Louis Berger Group, Bellevue, 1998—. AAES rep. to NAFTA Forum. Author: Applying GIS to PMF Analysis in Microcomputer Environment, 1990, NAFTA Handbook for Water Resources Managers and Engineers, 1995. Cubmaster Boy Scouts Am., Bellevue, 1988-91. Mem. ASCE (pres. Seattle sect. 1992-93, vice chair internat. activities com. 1999, Outstanding Young Men Zine IV), Am. Geophys. Union, Tau Beta Pi. Achievements include research on the hydraulic jump in a small rectangular channel. Home: 10824 158th Ct NE Redmond WA 98052-2656 Office: Louis Berger Group 12011 Bel-Red Rd Ste 200 Bellevue WA 98005

KILLGORE, WILLIAM DALE (SCOTT), JR., neuropsychologist; b. Anchorage, Sept. 2, 1965; s. William Dale and Judith Janine Killgore; m. Desiree Baisden Conrad; children: Siobhan Conrad, Turner Conrad. AA in Liberal Arts, AAS in Radio-TV-Film, San Antonio Coll., 1986; BA summa cum laude, U. N.Mex., 1990; MA in Clin. Psychology, Tex. Tech. U., 1992, PhD in Clin. Psychology, 1996. Lic. clin. psychologist N.H. Predoctoral fellow psychology Yale Sch. Medicine, New Haven, 1995—96; postdoctoral fellow clin. neuropsychology U. Okla. Health Scis. Ctr., Oklahoma City, 1996—97, U. Pa. Med.

Ctr., Phila., 1997—99; postdoctoral fellow functional neuroimaging Harvard Med. Sch./McLean Hosp., Belmont, Mass., 1999—2000; instr. psychology Harvard Med. Sch., Belmont, 2000—; asst. rsch. psychologist McLean Hosp./Harvard Med. Sch., Belmont, Mass., 2000—; rsch. psychologist Walter Reed Army Inst. Rsch., Silver Spring, Md., 2002—. Prin. investigator, NICHD Small Grant McLean Hosp./Harvard Med. Sch., Belmont, 2002—; presenter in field. Contbr. articles to profl. jours. Capt. U.S. Army, 2002—03. Grantee, Nat. Inst. Child Health and Human Devel./NIH, 2002—; scholar Maxey Scholarship in Psychology, Tex. Tech. U., 1990—96. Avocations: martial arts, running, reading. Office: Harvard Med Sch/McLean Hosp 115 Mill St Belmont MA 02478 Home: 208 Park Ave Apt 609 Gaithersburg MD 20877 Business E-Mail: william.d.killgore@us.army.mil.

KILLHOUR, WILLIAM GHERKY, paper company executive; b. Phila., June 2, 1925; s. William Brelsford and Jean (Gherky) K.; m. Josephine Quarrier Greenwood, July 12, 1947; children: Daphne S. (Mrs. John David Polys), William Brelsford II, Jean Gherky (Mrs. David Akers), Gilson Engel. AB in Econs., U. Pa., 1947. Salesman Quaker City Paper Co., York, Pa., 1947-50; co-founder W.B. Killhour & Sons, Inc., Phila., 1950, salesman, treas., mgr. printing paper divsn., 1950-61, pres., 1961-84; v.p. sales Killhour Comml. Paper Co., Hilton Head Island, S.C., 1984—. Mem. Paper Distbn. Coun. of U.S., 1977-81; past mem. mcht. adv. com. Sorg Paper Co., Scott Paper Co., Howard Paper Mills, Kimberly Clark. Pres. Stafford Sch. PTA, 1959; advisor Savannah Coll. Arts and Designs; head coach, founder Hilton Head H.S. crew, 1989-99; active Land Bank Commn., Town of Hilton Head Island, 1994—. Lt. (j.g.) USNR, 1944-46; PTO. Mem. U.S. Rowing Assn. (cert., past chmn. Masters com., coach 1991, rep. S.E. U.S.A. region 1994—), Paper Trade Assn. Phila. (pres. 1966), Nat. Paper Trade Assn. (regional dir. 1974—, indsl. paper com. 1972-73, nat. treas. 1977-78, nat. v.p. 1978-80, pres. 1980-81), Susquehanna Litho Club (pres. 1970), Jr. Execs. Club Graphic Arts Phila. (dir. 1955-60), St. Andrews Soc. Phila., York Club Printing House Craftsmen, Fearing Family Orgn., Mayflower Soc., Merion Cricket Club, Palmetto Rowing Club (founder, pres., head coach Hilton Head), Phila. Racquet Club (chmn. squash racquets com. 1972-82), Country of York, Undine Barge Club, Spanish Wells Golf Club (Hilton Head), Masons, S.C. Yacht Club (Hilton Head, Nat. age group champion double sculls 1982, 85, 91, nat. single sculls champion 1985, world single sculls champion 1990, Can. Henley single sculls champion 1985, world 8-oar crew champion Toronto 1985, world 4-oar crew champion 1985, 87, 90-95, world double sculls bronze 1985, world double sculls champion 1990-92, nat. 8-oar crew age group champion, 1986, 88-90, 92-93, nat. 4-oar crew age group champion 1987-91, Nat. Quad champion 1991, World Quad 1993-94, world 8 champion 1985, 87-90, 92-93, 95, single scull winner Head of Chattahoochie Regatta, Atlanta 88, others), Pa. Soc. Sons Revolution.

KILLIAN, EDWARD JAMES, pediatrician; b. Bklyn., Nov. 14, 1927; s. Edward James and Helen Marie K.; m. Henriette Marian Killian, 1957; children: Christopher Edward, Bryan Alfred, Paul Matthew. BS, St. John's Coll., 1950; MD, SUNY, 1954. Diplomat Am. Bd. Pediatrics, Nat. Bd. Med. Examiners; lic. physician, N.Y. Intern Bklyn. Hosp., 1954-55, resident, 1955-57, attending pediatrician, 1959-61, Southside Hosp., Bayshore, N.Y., 1961-93, Good Samaritan Hosp., West Islip, N.Y., 1961-93, ret., 1994. Capt. USAF Med. Corps, 1957-59. Fellow Am. Acad. Pediatrics; mem. AMA, Med. Soc. State N.Y. (life), Suffolk County Med. Soc. (life), Suffolk Pediatric Soc. (emeritus). Avocations: swimming, hiking, gardening. Home: PO Box 432 English Mills Way Woodstock VT 05091

KILLIAN, GEORGE ERNEST, educational association administrator; b. Valley Stream, N.Y., Apr. 6, 1924; s. George and Reina (Moeller) K.; m. Janice E. Bachert, May 26, 1951 (dec.); children: Susan E., Sandra J.; m. Marilyn R. Killian, Sept. 1, 1984 BS in Edn., Ohio No. U., 1949; EdM, U. Buffalo, 1954; PhD in Phys. Scis., Ohio Northern U., 1989; PhD (hon.), U.S. Sports Acad., 1998. Tchr.-coach Wharton (Ohio) High Sch., 1949-51; insp. USN, Buffalo, 1951-54; dir. athletics Erie County (N.Y.) Tech. Inst., Buffalo, 1954-69, asst. prof. health, phys. edn., recreation, 1954-60, asso. prof., 1960-62, prof., 1962-69; exec. dir. Nat. Jr. Coll. Athletic Assn., Colorado Springs, Colo., 1969—. Editor: Juco Rev., 1960— . Served with AUS, 1943-45. Recipient Bd. Trustees award Hudson Valley C. of C., 1969, Erie County Tech. Inst., 1969, Service award Ohio No. U. Alumni, 1972, Service award Lysle Rishel Post, Am. Legion, 1982; named to Ohio No. U. Hall of Fame, 1979, Olympic Order, IOC, 1996, Women's Basketball Hall of Fame, 2000. Mem. U.S. Olympic Com. (dir.), Internat. Olympic Com., Am. Legion, Internat. Basketball Fedn. (pres. 1990-98), Internat. U. Sports Fedn. (1st v.p. 1995, pres. 2000), Phi Delta Kappa, Delta Sigma Phi. Clubs: Masons, Rotary. Home: 325 Rangely Dr Colorado Springs CO 80921-2655 Office: Nat Jr Coll Athletic Assn PO Box 7305 Colorado Springs CO 80933-7305 E-mail: gkillian@njcaa.org.

KILLIAN, JANE CAROLYN CRAWLEY, computer consultant; b. Campbellsville, Ky., Nov. 17, 1950; d. J.B. and Elizabeth (Perkins) C. BS, Ea. Ky. U., 1972, MA, 1974. Bus. educator Ky. Bus. Coll., Lexington, 1972-74, LaBelle High Sch., Fla., 1974-76, Cyesis Ctr., Ft. Lauderdale, Fla., 1979, Ft. Lauderdale Coll., 1979, Fla. Coll. Bus., Pompano Beach, 1979-83, Broward County Sch. Bd., Fla., 1983-84, instr. visually handicapped, 1976-78; bus. and computer educator Businessland, Ft. Lauderdale, 1984-90; computer cons., 1990—; IDX computer trainer U. Miami, Fla., 2001—. Dir. edn. Fla. Coll., 1981-83; ednl. cons. Hammel Coll., 1983. Recipient cert. of Recognition for outstanding service aiding in finding missing children Broward County Sheriff's Dept., 1985; commd. Ky. Col. Gov. of Ky., 1988. Mem. Am. Council of Blind, Visually Handicapped Transcribers Assn. Republican. Baptist. Avocations: reading, interior designing.

KILLIAN, JANICE KAY NELSON, music educator, researcher; b. Mitchell, S.D., Jan. 31, 1946; d. Selmer J. and V. Nadine (Barriger) Nelson; m. Larry H. Killian II, June 18, 1981; children: Larry H. III, Michael R. Student, Augustana Coll., Sioux Falls, S.D., 1964-66; BME, U. Kans., 1968; MA, U. Conn., 1973; PhD, U. Tex., 1980. Cert. tchr., Tex., Minn., Conn., Kans. Music tchr. East Hartford (Conn.) Sch. Dist., 1969-74; choral dir. Edina (Minn.) Sch. Dist., 1974-77; asst. instr. U. Tex., Austin, 1977-80; asst. prof. SUNY, Buffalo, 1980-83; choral dir. Austin (Tex.) Sch. Dist., 1983-85, Carrollton (Tex.)-Farmer's Br. Sch. Dist., Carrollton, Tex., 1985-90; prof. Tex. Woman's U., Denton, 1990—2002, dir. music programs, 1999—2002; prof. Tex. Tech U., Lubbock, 2002—, chair music edn., 2002—. Adj. prof. U. Tex., Austin, 1983-84; cons. Hal Leonard Pub. Corp., Milw., 1994—. Author: Teacher Resource Kit for Choir, 1999, (textbook series) Essential Elements for Grades 7-12 Choir, 1996; mem. editl. rev. bd. Jour. Rsch. in Music Edn.; contbr. articles to profl. jours. Recipient Mary Mason Lyons award Tex. Woman's U., 1995, PTA Lifetime award Carrollton PTA, 1989, Supt.'s award Carrollton Pub. Schs., 1988, East Hartford Pub. Schs., 1973. Mem. Am. Choral Dirs. assn. (collegiate advisor 1980—), Nat. Assn. for Music Therapy, Tex. Music Educators Assn. (collegiate chair, head coll. divsn., v.p. 2000-02), Tex. Music Educators Conf., Tex. Music Adjudicators Assn., Music Educators Nat. Conf. (state collegiate chair), Rotary. Office: Tex Tech U Sch of Music Lubbock TX 79409-2033

KILLIAN, LAWRENCE HARDING, II, (LARRY H. KILLIAN), sculptor; b. San Antonio, May 6, 1943; s. Lawrence Harding and Dorothy Louise (Wright) K.; m. Beverly Gayle Schlueder, Dec. 21, 1963 (div. 1979); children: Lawrence Harding III, Michael Ray; m. Janice Kay Nelson, June 18, 1981. Student, Tex. A&M, 1961; BS in Indsl. Arts, Southwest Tex. State, 1971, postgrad., 1971-72, RIT Coll., 1981. Instr., job corps. and trade schs., Tex., 1971-75; owner of metal fabrication and welding bus., 1975-81; salesperson Hart Graphics, Austin (Tex.) Times Printing, Random Lake, Wis., 1982-93; freelance metal sculptor Gainesville, Tex., 1991—2002, Lubbock area, 2002—. Exhibitions include World Trade Ctr., Dallas. Active Leadership Gainesville, 1999. Southwest Tex. State U. scholar, 1970. Mem.: Rotary, Lions (pres. 1993). Avocations: antiques, real estate, travel, online trading. Home and Office: 355 CR 160 Garza Co Rt 2 Box 147A Post TX 79356-9731 E-mail: killian@direcway.com.

KILLIAN, LEWIS MARTIN, sociology educator; b. Darien, Ga., Feb. 15, 1919; s. Lewis Martin and Edith (Robinson) K.; m. Katharine Newbold Goold, Apr. 11, 1942; children: Katharine Newbold, Lewis Martin, John Calhoun. AB, U. Ga., 1940, MA, 1941; PhD, U. Chgo., 1949. Asst. prof. sociology U. Okla., 1949-52; asso. prof. sociology Fla. State U., 1952-57, prof., 1957-68, chmn. dept. sociology, 1966-68; prof., head dept. sociology U. Conn., 1968-69; prof. U. Mass., Amherst, 1969-84, prof. emeritus, 1984—. Vis. prof. UCLA, 1965-66, U. Hawaii, 1972; vis. lectr. Thames Poly., London, 1980-81; adj. prof. U. W. Fla., 1986—; Disting. vis. prof. U. Del., 1986. Author: (with Ralph H. Turner) Collective Behavior, 1957, 3d rev. edit., 1987, (with Charles M. Grigg) Racial Crisis in America, 1963, The Impossible Revolution, 1968, White Southerners, 1970, rev. edit., 1985, The Impossible Revolution: Phase II, 1974, Black and White: Reflections of a White Southern Sociologist, 1994. Cons. com. disaster studies NRC, 1952-57, cons. to atty. gen. of Fla., 1954-55; chmn. human rights advocacy com., dist. 1, State of Fla., 1991-93, 2000-; mem. Fla. Statewide Human Rights Advocacy Com., 1994-2000; mem. Fla. Local Advocy Coun., 2002—. Col. USAR, ret. Decorated Legion of Merit; Guggenheim fellow, 1975-76 Mem. Am. Sociol. Assn., So. Sociol. Soc. (pres. 1989-90), Phi Beta Kappa, Omicron Delta Kappa, Kappa Alpha, Phi Kappa Phi. Home: 10100 Hillview Rd Apt 1108 Pensacola FL 32514-5446

KILLIAN, ROBERT KENNETH, former lieutenant governor; b. Hartford, Conn., Sept. 15, 1919; s. Edward F. and Annie (Nemser) K.; m. Evelyn Farnan, Dec. 7, 1942; children— Robert Kenneth, Cynthia Elaine. BA, Union Coll., 1942; LL.B., U. Conn., 1948; LL.D., Sacred Heart U., Bridgeport, Conn., 1976, Union Coll., Schenectady, 1978. Bar: Conn. bar 1948. Since practiced in, Hartford; partner firm Gould, Killian & Wynne, asst. corp. counsel, 1951-54; atty. gen. State of Conn., 1967-75, lt. gov., 1975-79; chmn. Hartford Dem. Town Com., 1963-67, Hartford Civic Center and Coliseum Commn., 1980—. Trustee Nat. Jewish Hosp. and Research Center, Denver. Served with inf. AUS, 1942-46. Decorated Purple Heart; recipient numerous citations by civic and pub. service orgns. Mem. Am., Conn., Hartford County bar assns. Clubs: K.C, Elks. Democrat. Roman Catholic. Home: 234 Terry Rd Hartford CT 06105-1113 Office: One Commercial Plaza Hartford CT 06103

KILLIAN, ROBERT KENNETH, JR., judge, lawyer; b. Hartford, Conn., Jan. 29, 1947; s. Robert Kenneth Sr. and Evelyn (Farnan) K.; m. Candace Korper, Oct. 6, 1979; children: Virginia, Carolyn. BA, Union U., 1969; JD, Georgetown U., 1972. Bar: Conn. 1972, U.S. Ct. Appeals (2nd cir.) 1973, D.C. 1974, U.S. Ct. Appeals (D.C. cir.) 1974. Bur. chief Sta. WTIC-AM-FM-TV, Washington, 1969-72; spl. asst. Senator Abe Ribicoff, Washington, 1972-73; ptnr. Gould, Killian, Wynne et al, Hartford, 1972-84; judge Conn. Probate Ct., Hartford, 1984—; ptnr. Killian & Donohue, Hartford, 1985—98, Killian Donohue & Shipman LLC, Hartford, 1998—2001, Killian Donohue & Jaff LLC, 2001—. Spl. counsel Lt. Gov. Conn., Hartford, 1974-78; mem. exec. com. Conn. Probate Assembly, 1987—, pres.-judge, 1997-99; mem. investment adv. coun. State of Conn., 1995-99; mem. Jud. Commn. on Attys.' Ethics, 1990—. Author: Basic Probate in Connecticut, 1990, 8th edit., 2002. Regent, U. Hartford; trustee Hartt Sch. Music; chmn. Conn. chpt. March of Dimes, 1986—; bd. dirs. Yeats Drama Found., 1989—; incorporator St. Francis Hosp. and Med. Ctr. Recipient 1st Pl. award New England Conv. Magicians, 1965; named Conn.'s Outstanding Probate Judge, Conn. Probate Assembly, 1990. Mem. ABA, ATLA, Nat. Coll. Juvenile and Family Ct. Judges, Nat. Conf. Probate Judges, Conn. Bar Assn., Conn. Trial Lawyers Assn., Psychic Entertainer's Assn., Internat. Brotherhood Magicians, Soc. Am. Magicians (chmn. nat. conv. 1977). Democrat. Roman Catholic. Home: 83 Bloomfield Ave Hartford CT 06105-1007 Office: Killian Donohue & Jaff LLC 363 Main St Hartford CT 06106-1885 E-mail: bob@kdjlaw.com.

KILLIAN, WILLIAM PAUL, industrial corporate executive; b. Sidney, Ohio, Apr. 26, 1935; s. Ray and Eric K.; m. Beverly Ann Buchanan, Sept.7, 1957; children: William, Katherine, Michael. B in Chem. Engring. with honors, Ga. Inst. Tech., 1957; M in Engring. Adminstrn. with honors, U. Utah, 1968. Chem. engr. Esso, Baton Rouge, 1957—58; mgr. research and devel. mfg. engring., then plant mgr. Thiokol Corp., Brigham City, Utah, 1958—68; mgr. corp. project mgmt. Masonite Corp., Chgo., 1968—70, mgr. new bus. ventures, 1970—73; mgr. strategic planning, chem. and metall. group Gen. Electric Co., Pittsfield, Mass. and Columbus, Ohio, 1973—77; v.p. corp. planning and devel. Hoover Universal Inc., Ann Arbor, Mich., 1977—85; v.p. corp. devel. Johnson Controls Inc., Milw., 1985—87, v.p. corp. devel. and strategy, 1987—2000. Bd. dirs., vice chmn. Aqua-Chem. Inc., Milw.; bd. dirs. RBC Bearing Corp., Fairfield, Conn., Premix Inc., North Kingsville, Ohio; chmn., bd. advisors iNUX, Inc., Tampa. Bd. advisors Salvation Army, Sarasota; bd. dirs. All Faiths Food Bank, Sarasota, Fla. Mem.: Coun. Strategy Planning & Devel., Strategic Leadership Forum, Mfrs. Alliance (past chmn.), Coun. Strategic Planning Execs. of Conf. Bd. (past chmn.), Assn. for Corp. Growth Internat. (bd. dirs. Tampa Bay chpt., past nat. pres., past pres. Wis. chpt.), Mensa Soc, Koseme Soc., Tau Beta Pi, Phi Eta Sigma, Pi Delta Epsilon, Phi Kappa Phi, Omicron Delta Kappa. E-mail: wkillian@comcast.net.

KILLINGBECK, JANICE LYNELLE (MRS. VICTOR LEE KILLINGBECK), journalist; b. Flint, Mich., Nov. 11, 1948; d. Leonard Paul and Ina Marie (Harris) Johnson; m. Victor Lee Killingbeck, Sept. 26, 1970; children: Deeanna Dawn, Victor Scott. BA, Mich. State U., 1970; postgrad., Delta Coll., 1971-72; MA in Humanities, Ctrl. Mich. U., 2002. Tourist counselor Mich. Dept. State Hwys., Clare, 1969; copy editor Mich. State News, East Lansing, 1969-70; gen. reporter Midland (Mich.) Daily News, 1970; substitute tchr. Saginaw (Mich.) Pub. Schs., 1971; pub. rels. teller 1st State Bank of Saginaw, 1971-75; crew leader spl. census in Buena Vista Twp. Detroit Regional Office, U.S. Bur. Census, 1976, interviewer ann. housing survey-std. met. statis. areas, 1977-78, interviewer on-going health surveys, 1979-85, Nat. Crime Survey, 1985-86; editor AMEN newsletter United Meth. Women, Saginaw, 1984-87, Bridgeport-Birch Run Weekly News, 1986-93; owner Have Camera Will Travel, 1993—. Accelerated reader para-profl. A.A. Claytor Elem. Sch. Buena Vista Sch. Dist., Saginaw, Mich., 1997, libr., 1998—. Mem. Women in Comm., Sigma Delta Chi. Methodist. Home: 4946 Hess Rd Saginaw MI 48601-6809 Office: 3200 Perkins St Saginaw MI 48601-6563 E-mail: killingbeckj@email.bvsd.k12.mi.us.

KILLINGER, KERRY KENT, bank executive; b. Des Moines, June 6, 1949; m. Debbie Roush. BBA, U. Iowa, 1970, MBA, 1971. Exec. v.p. Murphey Favre, Inc., Spokane, 1976-82; exec. v.p. fin. mgmt., investor rels., corp. mktg. Wash. Mutual, Seattle, 1983-86; sr. exec. v.p., 1986-88; pres., dir. Wash. Mutual Savs. Bank, Seattle, 1988—, CEO, 1990—, chmn. bd., 1991—. Bd. dirs. Wash. Savs. League; mem. Thrift Inst. Adv. Coun. to Fed. Res. Bd., 1992-94; speaker in field. Bd. dirs. Fed. Home Loan Bank of Seattle, 1995—, Seattle Repertory Theatre, 1990—, Washington Roundtable, 1990—, Downtown Seattle Assn., 1991, Leadership Tomorrow, Seattle Found., 1992—; mem. Alliance for Edn., 1992—, chair, 1994-96, co-chmn. AIDS Walk-a-thon, Seattle, 1990; chair Partnership for Learning, 1997. Fellow Life Mgmt. Inst.; mem. Soc. Fin. Analysts, Greater Seattle C. of C. (bd. dirs. 1992—), Rotary. Office: Wash Mutual Bank 1201 3rd Ave Seattle WA 98101

KILLINGSWORTH, MARK R. economics educator, consultant; b. Balt., Dec. 8, 1946; s. Charles C. and Beverly H. (Kritzman) Killingsworth; m. Vivienne Lynch, June 21, 1969 (dec. Mar. 1994); children: Siân, Katherine; m. Cheryl G. Levine, May 25, 1997 (div. Apr. 2001); m. Wendy Young, July 28, 2002. BA in Econs., U. Mich., 1967; MPhil in Econs., Oxford U., 1969, DPhil in Econs., 1977. Asst. prof. econs. Fisk U., Nashville, 1969-76; asst. prof. econs. Barnard Coll. Columbia U., N.Y.C., 1976-78; from asst. prof. to prof. econs. Rutgers U., New Brunswick, N.J., 1978—, chair dept. econs., 2000—03. Cons. econs. U.S. Dept. Justice, U.S. Dept. Labor, U.S.E.E.O.C., 1974—. Author: Labor Supply, 1983, Economics of Comparable Worth, 1990; co-editor: Comparable Worth: Analyses and Evidence, 1989; contbr. article to profl. jour. Mem. Gov.'s Commn. Pinelands Agr., N.J., 1984-85; sec. N.J. Com. Selection for Rhodes Scholarships, 1998-2002. Rhodes Scholar, 1967. Mem. Am. Econ. Assn. (mem. editl. bd. Jour. Econ. Lit. 1987-89), Econometric Soc., Phi Beta Kappa. Avocations: opera, 20th century history. Office: Rutgers U Dept Econs New Jersey Hall New Brunswick NJ 08901

KILLINGSWORTH, VERNON SCOTT, technology lawyer; b. Cuthbert, Ga., Sept. 22, 1950; s. Lewis Manry Killingsworth and Margery Phillips Dews; m. Patricia M. Killingsworth, Oct. 27, 1979; children: Elizabeth Anne, Laura Catherine. BA, Yale U., 1972, JD, 1975. Bar: Ga. Assoc. Powell, Goldstein, Frazer & Murphy, Atlanta, 1975-82, ptnr., 1982—, co-chair tech. and intellectual property practice, 1997—. Moderator Legal Writing Forum Counsel Connect, 1997-99, High Tech and WWW Forum, Law News Network, 1999. Editl. bd. Internat. Jour. of e-Bus. Strategy Mgmt., 1999—; bd. editors E-Commerce Law Report, Internat. Property Counselor, 1998—; contbr. articles to profl. jours. Bd. govs. Assn. of Yale Alumni, New Haven, 1989-92, assembly del., 1986-89; alumni fellow Davenport Coll., Yale U., New Haven, 1989—. Mem. ABA (com. on cyberspace law), Computer Law Assn., Licensing Execs. Soc., Tech. Assn. of Ga., Yale Club of Ga. (v.p. programs, dir. 1992-93), Druid Hills Golf Club. Democrat. Avocation: writing. Office: Powell Goldstein Frazer & Murphy 191 Peachtree St NE Fl 16 Atlanta GA 30303-1740

KILLIP, THOMAS, cardiologist; AB, Swarthmore Coll., 1948; MD, Cornell U., 1952. Diplomate in internal medicine and cardiovasc. disease Am. Bd. Internal Medicine. Med. intern Strong Meml. Hosp., 1952—53; resident medicine N.Y. Hosp., 1953-58, resident medicine and cardiology, 1954-55; rsch. fellow Karolinska Inst., Stockholm, 1960-61; chmn., dept. medicine Henry Ford Hosp., Detroit, 1979—84; Harriman Prof. Medicine Cornell U., 1968—74; chief divsn. cardiology N.Y. Hosp., N.Y.C., 1961—74; attending physician Beth Israel Med. Ctr., N.Y.C., 1984—86, exec. v.p. medical affairs, 1984—86; dir. Heart Inst. Continuum Health Ptnrs., Inc., 1998—2002; interim pres. and CEO Beth Israel Med. Ctr., N.Y.C., 2002—. Prof. medicine Albert Einstein Coll. Medicine. Office: Beth Israel Med Ctr First Ave at 16th St New York NY 10003 Fax: 212-420-4222. E-mail: tkillip@bethisraelny.org.

KILLORIN, ROBERT WARE, lawyer; b. Atlanta, Nov. 12, 1959; s. Edward W. and Virgina (Ware) K. AB cum laude, Duke U., 1980; JD, U. Ga., 1983. Bar: Ga. 1984, U.S. Dist. Ct. (no. dist.) Ga. 1984, U.S. Ct. Appeals (11th cir.) 1984. Ptnr. Killorin & Killorin, Atlanta, 1984—. Mem. Atlanta Bar Assn., Ga. Def. Lawyers Assn., State Bar Ga. (chair SCOPE com. 1986, young lawyers sect. legis. affairs com. 1989-91, instr. mock trial program 1989—), Ga. C. of C. (govtl. affairs com.), Internat. Assn. Def. Counsel, 11th Cir. Hist. Soc., Assn. Trial Lawyers Am., Nat. Assn. Underwater Instrs., Nat. Speliological Soc., Mil. Order of Carabao, U. Ga. Pres.'s Club, Explorer's Club. Avocations: forestry, scuba diving, basketball, tennis. Office: Killorin & Killorin 5587 Benton Woods Dr NE Atlanta GA 30342-1308

KILLOUGH, STEPHEN PINCKNEY, financial executive, lawyer; b. Terrell, Tex., Nov. 4, 1935; s. Isaac Franklin and Grace Lillian (Yarbrough) K.; m. Deborah Marie Spitler, Mar. 16, 1963; children— Elizabeth Victoria, Richard Carter. B.A. in English and History, Baylor U., 1957; LL.B., J.D., Cumberland Sch. Law of Samford U., 1960. Bar: Tex., 1960, U.S. Ct. Mil. Appeals, 1961, U.S. Ct. Claims, 1962, U.S. Supreme Ct., 1963. City atty. City of Amarillo (Tex.), 1964-66; sole practice Lumpkin, Watson & Smith, Amarillo, 1966-70; assoc. counsel asst. sec. Fin. Am. Corp., Allentown, Pa., 1970-78; sr. v.p., gen. counsel Mfrs. Hanover Financial Services, Huntingdon Valley, Pa., 1978— ; dir. Ritter Life Ins. Co., Pa., 1978—, Tempco Life Ins. Co., Ariz., 1981—, Mfrs. Hanover Indsl. Banks, Colo., 1982—, Oil and Gas Research, St. Joseph, Mo., 1960. Served to capt. U.S. Army, 1960-64. Baylor U. Scholar, 1953, Mem. Tex. Bar Assn., ABA, Nat. Consumer Fin. Assn. (chmn. real estate subcommittee), Am. Fin. Services Assn. (dir., chmn. real estate adv. group, 1984, vice chmn. law forums 1987, 88). Republican. Episcopalian. Office: 1 Oxford Valley Ste 609 2300 E Lincoln Hwy Langhorne PA 19047

KILMAN, JAMES WILLIAM, surgeon, educator; b. Terre Haute, Ind., Jan. 22, 1931; s. Arthur and Irene (Piker) K.; m. Priscilla Margaret Jackson, June 20, 1968; children: James William, Julia Anne, Jennifer Irene. BS, Ind. State U., 1956; MD, Ind. U., 1960. Intern Ind.U. Med. Ctr., Indpls., 1960-61; resident surgery Ind.U. Med. Center, 1961-66, asst. prof., 1966-69, assoc. prof., 1969-73; prof. surgery Ohio State U. Coll. Medicine, 1973-91, prof. surgery emeritus, 1991—; chmn. dept. thoracic surgery Children's Hosp., 1975-91; attending surgeon Univ. Hosp., Columbus, Ohio; attending staff Children's Hosp., Columbus, pres. staff, 1978; attending staff Grant Hosp., Riverside Hosp. Cons. surgeon VA Hosp., Dayton; pres. Columbus Acad. Medicine, 1977 Trustee Central Ohio Heart Assn., Acad. Medicine Edn. Found., Children's Hosp., 1978— . Served with USNR, 1951-55. USPHS Cardiovascular fellow, 1963-64; recipient Alumni Achievement award, Ind. State U., 1989. Fellow ACS, Am. Coll. Cardiology, Am. Acad. Pediats., Coll. Chest Physicians; mem. Columbus Surg. Soc. (pres. 1974, hon. mem. 1993), Columbus Acad. Medicine (coun. 1971-73), Am. Surg. Assn., Soc. Univ. Surgeons, Am. Assn. Thoracic Surgery, Cen. Surg. Assn., Western Surg. Assn., Soc. Vascular Surgery, Internat. Cardiovasc. Soc., Internat. Soc. Surgeons, Chest Club, Cardiovasc. Surgery Club, City Club, Palm Aire Country Club, Faculty Club, Capital Club, Columbus Athletic Club, Pickaway County Country Club, Am. Boxer Club (bd. dirs. 2000-2003, pres. 2001-2003, AKC del. 2002—), Sigma Xi, Alpha Omega Alpha. Achievements include rsch., articles on infant cardiopulmonary bypass and surgery for congenital heart lesions. Home and Office: 4231 Jackson Pike Grove City OH 43123-9198 Home: 7517 Fairlinks Ct Sarasota FL 34243-3846 E-mail: B16doc@aol.com.

KILMANN, RALPH HERMAN, business educator; b. N.Y.C., Oct. 5, 1946; s. Martin Herbert and Lilli (Leob) Kilmann; children: Catherine Mary, Christopher Martin, Arlette Martin. BS, Carnegie Mellon U., 1970; MS, Carnegie-Mellon U., 1970; PhD, UCLA, 1972. Instr. U. Pitts. Katz Grad. Sch. Bus., 1972, asst. prof., 1972-75, assoc. prof., 1975-79, prof., 1979—, George H. Love prof. orgn. and mgmt., 1991—2001, coord. orgnl. studies group, 1981-84, 86-89, dir. program in corp. culture, 1983—; pres. Organizational Design Cons., Pitts., 1975—; vis. scholar Calif. State U. Long Beach Coll. Bus. Adminstrn., 2002—03. Author: Social Systems Design: Normative Theory and the MAPS Design Technology, 1977, Beyond the Quick Fix: Managing Five Tracks to Organizational Success, 1984, Managing Beyond the Quick Fix: A Completely Integrated Program for Creating and Maintaining Organizational Success, 1989, Escaping the Quick Fix Trap: How to Make Organizational Improvements That Really Last, 1989, Workbook for Implementing the Five Tracks: Vols. I and II, 1991, Logistics Manual for Implementing the Five Tracks: Planning and Organizing Workshop Sessions, 1992, Workbook for Continuous Improvement: Holographic Quality Management, 1993, Quantum Organizations: A New Paradigm for Achieving Organizational Success and Personal Meaning, 2001 ; co-author: Methodological Approaches to Social Science: Integrating Divergent Concepts and Theories, 1978, Corporate Tragedies: Product Tampering, Sabotage and Other Catastrophes, 1984, The Management of Organization Design: Vols. I and II, 1976, Producing Useful Knowledge for Organizations, 1983, Gaining Control of the Corporate Culture, 1985, Corporate Transformation: Revitalizing Organizations for a Competitive World, 1988, Making Organizations Competitive: Enhancing Networks and Relationships Across Traditional Boundaries, 1991, Managing Ego Energy: The Transformation of Personal Meaning into Organizational Success, 1994; mem. editorial bd. Jour. Mgmt., 1983-86, Acad. Mgmt. Exec., 1987-90, Jour. Organizational Change Mgmt., 1988—; developed Kilmann Insight Test, Learning Climate Questionnaire, Thomas-Kilmann Conflict-Mode Instrument in Ednl. Testing Svc., MAPS Design Tech. for Social Systems Design, Kilmann-Saxton Culture-Gap Survey, Kilmann's Organizational Belief Survey; contbr. chpts. to books, articles to profl. jours. Mem. Eastern Acad. Mgmt. (treas. 1975-76, dir. 1983-86), Am. Psychol. Assn., Inst. Mgmt. Scis. (1st prize Nat. Coll. Planning competition 1976), Beta Gamma Sigma, Sigma Xi. *Some live only for themselves, some sacrifice their lives for others. The space between is enjoying one's life while contributing to society. No one should have the full responsibility for saving the world, nor the complete freedom to ignore the future.*

KILMARTIN, JOSEPH FRANCIS, JR., business executive, consultant; b. Mar. 11, 1924; s. Joseph Francis and Lauretta M. (Collins) K.; m. Gloria M. Schaffer, June 26, 1954; children: Joanne, Diane. Student, St. Thomas Sem., 1944; BA, Holy Cross Coll., 1947. Prodn. mgr. A.C. Gilbert Co., New Haven, 1947-49; prodr. NBC-TV, N.Y.C., 1950-53; v.p. sales Cellomatic Corp., N.Y.C., 1953-59; sr. v.p. Transfilm Inc., N.Y.C., 1959-62, MPO Videotronics, N.Y.C., 1962-66; pres. Bus. Programs Inc., Larchmont, N.Y., 1966-75, Greenwich, Conn., 1975—. Pres. Kilarnold Corp.; lectr. in field, cons. Mexican Dept. Agrarian Affairs and Colonization, 1974—. Profl. performer: (Broadway show) Small Wonder, (TV shows) Your Hit Parade, Philco Playhouse, Armstrong Circle Theatre, 1949-50. Active fund-raising Cmty. Chest, 1947-49, ARC, 1947-49, Boy Scouts Am., 1958-66, United Fund, 1970-73; mem. Congl. Adv. Bd., Presdl. Task Force, Atlantic Coun., Conn. Venture Group, Mil. Affairs Coun., Fayetteville, N.C., Harnett County Strategic Planning Commn.; bd. dirs. Lee County Arts Coun.; mem. exec. com., chmn. Lee County Rep. Party Coun.; chmn. Carolina Trace Cmty. Action Com. Recipient medal of excellence Mex. Agrarian Affairs and Colonization Dept., 1976, Golden Medallion award in bus. comm. Miami Internat. Film Festival, 1978, Cmty. Developer of Yr. award Nat. Mfg. Housing Inst., 1998, Cmty. Betterment award N.C. House of Reps.,

1998-99, Sovereign Mil. Order of the Temple of Jerusalem, 1998. Mem. Am. Mgmt. Assn., TV Execs. Soc., Pres.'s Assn., Larchmont Club (N.Y.), Yacht Club, Westchester Country Club, Univ. Club (N.Y.C.), Carolina Trace Country Club, Lambs Club. Home: 241 Lakeview Dr Sanford NC 27332-8397 E-mail: jkilma5437@aol.com.

KILMER, EVE ANN, psychologist; b. Paris, Mar. 1, 1957; came to U.S., 1957; d. Jay Erwin and Barbara (Natali) Silverman; m. Mark Eugene Kilmer, July 11, 1993; children: Thomas, Lisa. BA summa cum laude, Calif. State U., Northridge, 1988; MA, Calif. Sch. Profl. Psychology, L.A., 1990, PhD, 1992. Lic. psychologist. Therapist Wright Inst., Century City, Calif., 1990-92; registered psychologist Didi Hirsch Cmty. Mental Health Ctr., Culver City, Calif., 1992-94; psychologist in pvt. practice, Boulder, Colo., 1989—. Cons. Psychology Advanced Study Systems, L.A., 1994—; mem. faculty Calif. Sch. Profl. Psychology, L.A., 1997—, Loyola Marymount U., L.A., 1995—, Pepperdine U., Malibu, Calif., 1997—. Mem. APA. Office: 100 Arapahoe Ave Ste 7 Boulder CO 80302 Home: 2785 Lafayette Dr Boulder CO 80305

KILMER, MAURICE DOUGLAS, marketing executive; b. Flint, Mich., Sept. 14, 1928; s. John Jennings and Eleanor Minnie (Gerholz) K.; m. Vera May Passino, Mar. 30, 1950; children: Brad Douglas, Mark David, Brian John, David Scott, Karen Sue. B of Indsl. Engring., Gen. Motors Inst., 1951; MBA, U. Minn., 1969. Quality svcs. mgr. ordnance div. Honeywell, Hopkins, Minn., 1964-69, product assurance dir. peripheral ops. San Diego, 1969-71; pres. Convenience Systems, Inc., San Diego, 1972-75; salesman real estate Forest E. Olson Coldwell Banker, La Mesa, Calif., 1976-77, resident mgr. Huntington Beach, Calif., 1977-78; mgmt. cons. Century 21 of the Pacific, Santa Ana, Calif., 1978-83, dir. broker svcs. Anaheim, Calif., 1983-85; exec. dir. Century 21 of S.W., Phoenix, 1985-86; sales assoc. Century 21 Rattan Realtors, San Diego, 1986-88; mgr. Rattan Realtors, San Diego, 1988-92, relocation dir., 1993-98; retired, 1998; cons. Underwater Camera Co. Am., 2002. With U.S. Army, 1951-53. Mem. Am. Soc. for Quality Control, San Diego Bd. Realtors. Republican. Avocations: music, watercolor painting. Home: 6783-2 Alvarado Rd San Diego CA 92120-5213 E-mail: mkilmer@cox.net.

KILMER, NEAL HAROLD, software engineer; b. Orange, Tex., Apr. 24, 1943; s. Harold Norval and Luella Alice (Sharp) K.; m. Jody Geary, Oct. 24, 1998. BS in Chemistry and Math., Northwestern Okla. State U., 1964; MS in Chemistry, Okla. State U., 1971; PhD in Chemistry, Mich. State U., 1979. Rsch. assoc. N.Mex. Petroleum Recovery Rsch. Ctr., N.Mex. Inst. Mining & Tech., Socorro, 1979-81, rsch. chemist, 1981-85, lectr. geol. engring., 1984, asst. prof. mining engring., 1985-86; phys. scientist Phys. Sci. Lab., N.Mex. State U., Las Cruces, N.Mex., 1986-96; software engr. Honeywell (formerly AlliedSignal), Las Cruces, 1996—. Contbr. articles to profl. jours. Mem. Am. Chem. Soc., Am. Inst. Physics, Optical Soc. Am., Sigma Xi, Pi Mu Epsilon, Phi Lambda Upsilon. Presbyterian. Avocation: square and round dancing. Home: 398 No Problem Dr Las Cruces NM 88005-3951 Office: Software Maintenance & Tng Facility PO Box 9000 Las Cruces NM 88004-9000

KILMER, VAL, actor; b. Los Angeles, Dec. 31, 1959; m. Joanne Whalley, 1988 (div. 1996); 1 child, Mercedes. Educ., Hollywood's Professional Sch., Juillard. Appeared in plays Electra and Orestes, Henry IV, Part One, 1981, As You Like It, 1982, Slab Boys (Broadway Debut), 1983, Hamlet, 1988, 'Tis Pity She's A Whore, 1992; motion pictures include Top Secret!, 1984, Real Genius, 1985, Top Gun, 1986, Willow, 1988, Kill Me Again, 1989, The Doors, 1991, Thunderheart, 1991, True Romance, 1993, The Real McCoy, 1993, Tombstone, 1993, Wings of Courage, 1995, Batman Forever, 1995, Heat, 1995, The Island of Dr. Moreau, 1996, The Ghost and the Darkness, 1996, Dead Girl, 1996, The Saint, 1997, The Prince of Egypt (voice) 1998, Joe the King, 1999, At First Sight, 1999, Pollock, 2000, Red Planet, 2000, Hard Cash (aka Run for the Money), 2002, The Salton Sea, 2002, Masked and Anonymous, 2003, Wonderland, 2003; TV appearances include The Murders in the Rue Morgue, 1986, The Man Who Broke 1,000 Chains, 1987, Gore Vidal's Billy the Kid, 1989. Office: William Morris Agy One William Morris Pl Beverly Hills CA 90212

KILNER, URSULA BLANCHE, genealogist, writer; b. Chgo., Feb. 2, 1925; d. Frederic Russell and Blanche (Miller) Gamble; m. Glen Kilner, May 12, 1950 (dec. Feb. 1998). BA cum laude, Mt. Holyoke Coll., 1946; MA, Columbia U., 1947, postgrad., to 1951. Asst. to editor Grolier Pub., N.Y.C., 1947; mgr. Magnamusic Inc., Garrison, N.Y., 1954-55; publicity and fundraising Little Guild of St. Francis Inc., Cornwall, Conn., 1957-68; lectr. U. Conn., Torrington, 1964-66; genealogist Bird Bottom Genealogy, Salisbury, Conn., 1979—. Owner, mgr. The Tenth Muse, phonograph and stereo co., 1958-60; reporter The Comml. Record, 1960-61. Author, editor: A Revolutionary Cook Book, 1985, A Cook Book for All Seasons, 1994; columnist The Voice, 1993-2003; book reviewer Heritage Books; contbr. articles to profl. jours. Mem. Planning and Zoning Commn., Salisbury, Conn., 1981-82, N.Y. State Hist. Assn. Mem.: DAR (chpt. registrar Salisbury Arsenal), N.Y. State Hist. Assn., Ill. Geneal. Soc., N.Y. Hist. Assn., Essex (Mass.) Soc. Genealogists, Nat. Geneal. Soc., Soc. Genealogists, Conn. Gravestone Studies, Assn. Gravestone Studies, Vt. Genealogists Soc., Suffolk County Hist. Soc., Conn. Soc. Genealogists, Am. Coll. Genealogists (asst. nat. registrar 1990—91, cert. genealogist), N.H. Genealogy Soc. (life), Nat. Soc. Huguenots (life; adv. bd. 1993—2001, Conn. registrar 1998—2001), N.H. Soc. Genealogists (life), N.Y. Geneal./Biog. Soc. (life), New Eng. Hist./Geneal. Soc. (life), Salisbury Assn., Sons and Daus. First Settlers Newbury, Van Voorhees Family Soc., Greyhound Friends West, Inc., Nat. Soc. Colonial Dames XVII Century (organizing pres. Winthrop Fleet chpt. 1990, Conn. state registrar 1995—99, chpt. pres. 1999—2001, ret.), Sheffield Hist. Soc. (life), Morse Family Soc. (life), Piscataqua Pioneers N.H. (life), Kewanee (Ill.) Hist. Soc. (life), Andover (Mass.) Hist. Soc. (life), Nat. Soc. Daus. Am. Colonists (ret. Conn. registrar), Seeley Family Soc., Whitlock Family Soc., Ea. Star. Avocations: knitting, lecturing, saving greyhounds, greenhouse plants. Home and Office: Bird Bottom Farm RR 1 Salisbury CT 06068-9802

KILPATRICK, CAROLYN CHEEKS, congresswoman; b. Detroit, June 25, 1945; d. Marvell and Willa Mae (Henry) Cheeks; divorced; children: Kwame, Ayanna. AS, Ferris State Coll., Big Rapids, Mich., 1965; BS, Western Mich. U., 1972; MS in Edn., U. Mich., 1977. Tchr. Murray Wright High Sch., Detroit, 1972-78; mem. Mich. Ho. of Reps., Lansing, 1978-96, U.S. Congress from 13th Mich. dist. (formerly 15th), Washington, 1997—; mem. appropriations com. Del. Dem. Convs., 1980, 84, 88. Participant Mich. African Trade Mission, 1984, UN Internat. Women's Conf., 1986; del. participant Mich. Dept. Agr. to Nairobi (Kenya) Internat. Agr. Show, 1986. Recipient Anthony Wayne award Wayne State U., Disting. Legislator award U. Mich., Disting. Alumni award Ferris State U., Woman of Yr. award Gentlemen of Wall St., Inc., Burton-Abercrombie award 15th Dem. Congrl. dist. Mem. Nat. Orgn. 100 Black Women. Democrat. Office: House of Reps 1610 Longworth House Office Bldg Washington DC 20515-2215*

KILPATRICK, HENRY EDWARD, economist, educator; b. Sanford, Fla., Aug. 12, 1948; s. Henry Edward and Niki G. Kilpatrick; m. Nancy Jane Story, Apr. 24, 1982 (div. Oct. 15, 2002). BS, Valdosta State U., Ga., 1971; MA, Pa. State U., 1974; PhD, George Mason U., Fairfax, Va., 1998. CEO Econpolicy, Arlington, Va., 1995—; assoc. Brown, Williams, Moorhead & Quinn, Washington, 2000—. Economist FERC, Washington, 1977—93; rsch. fellow The Inst. of Pub. Policy, George Mason U., 1993—99; adj. faculty George Mason U., Fairfax, Va., 1997—; sr. fellow and assoc. asst. prof. George Mason U. Sch. of Pub. Policy, 2000—; v.p. of econs. ACI Aviation, Inc, Warrenton, Va., 2002—; adj. asst. prof. U. of Md., Univ. Coll., Coll. Pk., 2002—. Contbr. Adv. commn. Arlington County Parks and Recreation Commn., Arlington, Va., 1990—97; mem. of the bd. and chmn. of the investment com. Resources Fed. Credit Union, Washington, 1985—92. Fellow Grad. Rsch. fellow, George Mason U., 1994—96. Mem.: Policy Studies Orgn., So. Econ. Assn., Am. Econ. Assn., Mycol. Assn. of Wash., DC (pres. 2002—03). Achievements include research in that contributed to the understanding of complex phenomena and dynamic increasing returns through doctoral dissertation, papers, talks and publications. Office: Brown Williams Moorhead & Quinn 1155 15th St NW Washington DC 20005 Personal E-mail: hkilpatr@juno.com. E-mail: hkilpat@bwmq.com.

KILPATRICK, JAMES JACKSON, JR., columnist, writer; b. Oklahoma City, Nov. 1, 1920; s. James Jackson and Alma Mia (Hawley) K.; m. Marie Louise Pietri, Sept. 21, 1942 (dec. May 1997); children: Michael Sean, Christopher Hawley, Kevin Pietri; m. Marianne Means, June 19, 1998. BJ, U. Mo., 1941. Reporter Richmond (Va.) News Leader, 1941-49, chief editorial writer, 1949-51, editor, 1951-67; writer nat. syndicated columns, TV commentator. Author: The Sovereign States, 1957, The Smut Peddlers, 1960, The Southern Case for School Segregation, 1962, The Foxes' Union, 1977, (with Eugene J. McCarthy) A Political Bestiary, 1978, (with William Bake) The American South: Four Seasons of the Land, 1980, The American South: Towns and Cities, 1982, The Writer's Art, 1984, The Ear is Human, 1985, A Bestiary of Bridge, 1986, Fine Print - Reflections on the Writing Art, 1993; editor: We the States, 1964; co-editor: The Lasting South, 1957. Vice chmn. Va. Com. on Constl. Govt., 1962-68; chmn. Va. Magna Carta Com., 1965; trustee Thomas Jefferson Ctr. for Protection of Free Expression, 1990—, Supreme Ct. Hist. Soc., 1987—. Recipient medal of honor for distinguished service in journalism U. Mo., 1953; ann. award for editorial writing Sigma Delta Chi, 1954; William Allen White award U. Kans., 1979; Carr Van Anda award Ohio U., 1987; named to Okla. Hall of Fame, 1978 Fellow Soc. Profl. Journalists; mem. Nat. Conf. Editorial Writers (chmn. 1955-56), Black-Eyed Pea Soc. Am. (No. 1 Pea pro tem 1965—), Gridiron Club. Whig. Episcopalian.

KILPATRICK, KWAME, mayor; Doctorate, Detroit Coll. Law; BS in political sci., Fla. A&M Univ. Mayor City of Detroit, 2002—. Designer Clean Mich. Initiative, 1998. Democrat. Office: 1600 W Lafayette Blvd Detroit MI 48216*

KILRAIN, SUSAN, astronaut; b. Augusta, Ga., Oct. 24, 1961; d. Joe and Sue Still; m. Colin James Kilrain. MS in Aerospace Engring., GA. Inst. Tech., 1985; grad., Test Pilot Sch. Wind tunnel project officer Lockheed Corp., Marietta, Ga.; commd. ensign USN, 1985, advanced through grades to lt. comdr., flight instr. TA-4J Skyhawk; naval aviator EA-6A Electric Intruders for Tactical Electronic Warfare Sq. 33, Key West, Fla.; with NASA Johnson Space Ctr., Houston, 1995—, with Vehicle Sys. and Ops. Br. Astronaut Office, pilot STS-83, 1997, pilot STS-94, 1997, spacecraft communicator in mission control. Decorated Def. Superior Svc. medal, Navy Meritorious Svc. medal, Navy Commendation medal, Navy Achievement medal, (2) NASA Space Flight medals, Nat. Def. Svc. medal; recipient 10 Outstanding Young Ams. award U.S. Jr. C. of C., Good Scout award, 1997. Mem. Assn. Naval Aviation, Assn. Space Explorers, Ga. Tech. Found. Avocations: triathlons, martial arts, playing piano. Office: NASA Lyndon B Johnson Space Ctr Houston TX 77058

KILROY, JAMES FRANCIS, educator; b. Chgo., Sept. 7, 1935; s. John Patrick and Nora (Joyce) K.; m. Mary Elizabeth Carroll, July 1, 1961; children— Maurya, James Dennis, Mark Justin. BA, DePaul U., 1957; MA, U. Iowa, 1961; PhD, U. Wis., 1965. Tchr. Pub. High Schs., Chgo., 1957-61; asst. prof. Vanderbilt U., 1965-69, assoc. prof., 1969-77, prof., 1977-84, chmn. dept. English, 1979-83, assoc. dean Grad. Sch., 1973-76; dean Coll. Arts and Scis. Tulane U., 1984-88, dean Faculty of Liberal Arts and Scis., 1988-90, provost, 1991-96, prof., 1996—. Author: James Clarence Mangan, 1970, The Playboy Riots, 1971, The Modern Irish Drama (3 vols.), 1975, 76, 78, The Playboy as Poet, 1969, The Chiastic Structure of Tennyson's In Memoriam, 1977, The Irish Short Story, 1984; co-editor: Lost Plays of the Irish Renaissance, 1970 Am. Council Learned Socs. fellow, 1967-68; Nat. Endowment Humanities fellow, 1968 Mem. MLA, Am. Com. for Irish Studies Roman Catholic. Office: Tulane Univ Dept English 210 Norman Mayer Hall New Orleans LA 70118-5698

KILROY, JOHN MUIR, lawyer; b. Kansas City, Mo., Apr. 12, 1918; s. James L. and Jane Alice (Scurry) K.; m. Lorraine K. Butler, Jan. 26, 1946; children: John Muir, William Terence. Student, Kansas City Jr. Coll., 1935-37; AB, U. Kansas City, 1940; JD, U. Mo., 1942. Bar: Mo. 1942. Practice in, Kansas City, 1946—; ptnr. Shughart, Thomson & Kilroy, 1948—, pres., 1977-86, chmn. bd. dirs., 1980-88, chmn. emeritus, 1988—. Instr. med. jurisprudence U. Health Scis., 1973-93; panelist numerous med.-legal groups ACS, Mo. Med. Assn., Kans. U. Med. Sch., S.W. Clin. Soc. Contbr. articles to profl. jours. Chmn. bd. dirs. Kansas City Heart Assn.; mem. adv. bd. Midwest Christian Counseling Svc.; bd. dirs., pres. Della Lamb Cmty. Svc., 1991, chmn. bd. dirs., 1993; bd. dirs. Laubach Literacy Coun., 1998-2001, Kingswood Manor, 1992-94, Mo. Meth. Found., 1993-2002. Named Man of Yr., Sigma Chi, 1989. Fellow Am. Coll. Trial Lawyers; mem. ABA, Mo. Bar Assn. (chmn. med. legal com.), Kansas City Bar Assn. (Litigator Emeritus award 1990), Internat. Assn. Barristers, Internat. Assn. Def. Counsel, Am. Coll. Legal Medicine, Am. Bd. Profl. Liability Attys., Fedn. Ins. Counsel, Law Soc. U. Mo., Order Barristers U. Mo., Lawyers Assn., Kansas City (pres. 1968), Kansas City C. of C., Univ. Club (v.p. 1984, pres. 1985), Indian Hills Country Club, Kansas City Club. Home: 6860 Tomahawk Rd Shawnee Mission KS 66208-2176 Office: Shughart Thomson & Kilroy 120 W 12th St Ste 1800 Kansas City MO 64105-1922

KILROY, WILLIAM TERRENCE, lawyer; b. Kansas City, Mo., May 24, 1950; s. John Muir and Katherine Lorraine (Butler) K.; m. Marianne Michelle Maurin, Sept. 8, 1984; children: Kyle E., Katherine A. BS, U. Kans., 1972, MA, 1974; JD, Washburn U., 1977. Bar: Mo. 1977. Assoc. Shughart, Thomson & Kilroy, Kansas City, Mo., 1977-81, mem., dir., 1981—. Contbr. articles to profl. publs. Mem. Kans. City Citizens Assn., 1980—; pres., bd. govs. Sch. Law Washburn, 1992-94; with Civic Coun. of Greater Kansas City, 1999—; legal coun. Heart of Am. Coun. Boy Scouts Am., 1988-92, mem. exec. com., 1988-95, Cmty. adv. Greater Kans. City Cmty. Found. and Affiliated Trusts, 1993-2000; bd. dirs. Kansas City Neighborhood Alliance, 1998—, Greater Kansas City Crime Commn. Mem. Lawyers Assn. Kansas City, Kansas City Bar Assn. (chmn. civil rights com. 1984), Mo. Bar Assn., ABA (subcom. on arbitration, labor law sect. 1977—), Greater Kansas City C. of C., Kansas City Club, Kansas City Country Club. Office: Shughart Thomson & Kilroy 12 Wyandotte Plz 120 W 12th St Ste 1500 Kansas City MO 64105-1929

KILSCH, GUNTHER H. lawyer; b. N.Y.C., Jan. 8, 1930; s. Frederick and Toni (Becher) K.; m. Kathryn A. Severance, Mar. 28, 1959; children: Nancy, Peter, Ann, Sarah. AB, Queens Coll./CUNY, 1957; LLB, NYU, 1963. Bar: N.Y. 1964, U.S. Dist. Ct. (so. and ea. dists.) 1966, U.S. Ct. Appeals (2d cir.) 1993; diplomate Am. Bd. Profl. Liability Attys. Assoc. Schaffner D'Onofrio, N.Y.C., 1964-68, John J. Tullman, N.Y.C., 1968-71, Kroll, Edelman & Lanzone, N.Y.C., 1971-73, Martin, Clearwater & Bell, N.Y.C., 1973-75, Montfort, Healy, McGuire & Salley, Mineola, N.Y., 1975-77; mem. firm McAloon & Friedman, P.C., N.Y.C., 1977-99, of counsel, 2000—; sole practice, 1999—. Warden, mem. vestry Christ Ch. Riverdale, Bronx, N.Y. Cpl. AUS, 1953-55. Fellow Am. Bar Found. (life), N.Y. Bar Found. (life); mem. N.Y. State Bar Assn. (mem.-at-large exec. com. 2001—, mem. Ho. of Dels. 1979-80, 93-94, 98--, chair tort reparations com. 1992-97, sec. trial lawyers sect. 1976-77, vice chair 1977-78, chair 1978-79, life mem. exec. com. 1968—), Am. Bd. Trial Advs. (pres. N.Y.C. chpt. 1998, 99, del. nat. bd. dirs. 2001—), N.Y. County Lawyers Assn. Episcopalian. Avocations: photography, boating, hiking, choir. Home: 46 Sunnyside Dr Yonkers NY 10705-1731 Office: McAloon & Friedman PC 116 John St Fl 29 New York NY 10038-3498 E-mail: guntherkilsch@mcf-esq.com, g.kilschp.c@worldnet.att.net.

KILSON, MARION, college dean; b. New Haven, May 8, 1936; d. J.G. and Emily L. (Greene) Dusser de Barenne; m. Martin L. Kilson, Aug. 8, 1959; children: Jennifer Kilson-Page, Peter, Hannah Kilson Kuchtic. BA, Radcliffe Coll., 1958; MA, Stanford U., 1959; PhD, Harvard U., 1967. Instr., asst. prof. U. Mass., Boston, 1966-68; fellow Radcliffe Inst., 1968-70; assoc. prof. Simmons Coll., Boston, 1969-73; prof. sociology Newton (Mass.) Coll., 1973-75; dir. rsch., and dir. Bunting Inst., Cambridge, Mass., 1975-80; dean Emmanuel Coll., Boston, 1980-86; rsch. fellow Harvard Div. Sch., Cambridge, 1986; assoc. editor Simon & Schuster, Newton, Mass., 1987-89; dean Arts and Scis. and Grad Sch., Salem (Mass.) State Coll., 1989—2001; ret., 2001. Mem. adv. bd. Bunting Inst., 1992-98; chair New Eng. Bapt. Hosp. Sch. Nursing, Boston, 1992-97. Author: Kpele LaLa, 1971, African Urban Kinsmen, 1974, Royal Antelope & Spider, 1976, Mother of the Japan Mission, 1991, Claiming Place, 2001. Bd. dirs. AAUW Edn. Found., 1993-99, program v.p., 1996-99. Fellow Am. Anthropol. Soc., Anthropology Assn.; grantee NIMH, 1965—66, NEH, 1968, 1972, 1974. Fellow Am. Anthropol. Assn.; mem. AAUW (Mary Lyon award 1994, pres. Mass. chpt. 2000—), Mass. Women in Pub. Higher Edn. (pres. 1995-96). Home: 4 Eliot Rd Lexington MA 02421-5610 E-mail: marionkilson@worldnet.att.net.

KILTS, JAMES M. consumer products company executive; b. 1948; BA, Knox Coll., 1970; MBA in Mktg., U. Chgo., 1974. Exec. Philip Morris Cos., from 1970, exec. v.p. in-charge Kraft Foods Worldwide, 1994-97; pres. Kraft USA, 1989-94; pres., CEO Nabisco Holdings Corp., Parsippany, NJ, 1998-2000; CEO, chmn. Gillette Co., Boston, 2001—. Exec.-in-residence U. Chgo. Grad. Sch. Bus., also mem. adv. com. Trustee Knox Coll. Office: Gillette Co Prudential Tower Building Boston MA 02199

KILTY, JEROME TIMOTHY, playwright, stage director, actor; b. Balt., June 24, 1922; s. Harold Joseph and Irene (Zellinger) K.; m. Cavada Humphrey, May 11, 1956. BA, Harvard U., 1949. Prof. drama U. Okla., Norman, 1971, U. Tex., Austin, 1972, U. Kans., Lawrence, 1973; appointed to O'Conner Chair of Lit., Colgate U., Hamilton, N.Y., 1974-75, 91-92; instr. in drama Harvard U., Cambridge, Mass., 1983-85, 89. Co-founder, dir., actor Brattle Theatre Co., Cambridge, Mass., 1948-52; actor N.Y.C. stage and TV, 1952-57, including Relapse, 1951, Quadrille, 1952, Misalliance, 1953; played: Falstaff, Iago, City Centre, 1954; writer, actor Dear Liar, Chgo. and London, 1957 (Berlin Festival Critics award 1961, Baton Du Brigadier 1962-63, Palma D'Oro 1962-63, Stanislavsky Centenary medal 1963), dir. revival, Paris, 1974, 80, Rome, 1975, 85, for TV, Hallmark Hall of Fame, 1981, dir. Australian Premiere, 1993, Melbourne; writer, dir. for TV Ides of March, London, 1963, Long Live Life, San Francisco, 1967; dir. Marie Bell, Elisabeth Bergner, Maria Casares, Pierre Brasseur in various French, German, Italian prodns., 1962-65; assoc. dir., Am. Conservatory Theatre, San Francisco, 1966-68, Am. Shakespeare Co., Stratford, Conn., 1965-68; dir. Possibilities, N.Y.C., 1968, Sarah Ferrati in Mrs. Warren's Profession (in Italian), Rome, 1976; writer, dir. Don't Shoot Mable, It's Your Husband, 1968; writer, actor Dear Love, Boston, 1969, London, 1973, The Laffing Man, 1975; dir., actor Androcles and the Lion, 1985, Love's Labor's Lost, 1985; writer: The Little Black Book, N.Y.C., 1972, Look Away, N.Y.C.; musicals What the Devil, 1977, Barnum, 1978; play Hey Marie!, 1979; dir. Julius Caesar, San Diego Nat. Shakespeare Festival, 1979, Love's Labor's Lost, 1980, Misalliance, Denver, 1980, I, James McNeill Whistler, Hartford Stage Co., Peter Pan, Kansas City, Mo., 1985; appeared in play A Month in the Country, N.Y.C., 1979 80, Enter a Free Man, N.Y.C., 1984, Foxfire, Kansas City, Mo., 1985; mem., Hartman Theatre Co., 1981-82, 86-87, played the Doctor in Three Sisters and Ernest in Bedroom Farce, dir. Tammy Grimes in The Millionairess; star The Magistrate; mem., Am. Repertory Theatre Co., Cambridge, Mass., 1983-2000, created role: The King in Big River, 1983, directed, played Armado in Love's Labor's Lost, 1985, played Abel Bishop in Right You Are (If You Think So), 1988, played Don Antonio in Saturday, Sunday, Monday, 1988; played title role in King Lear, Col. Treletsky in Platonov, played James Tyrone with Claire Bloom in Long Day's Journey into Night, 1996, played Old Ekdal in Wild Duck, 1997; created role Chairman Bowman in Mastergate by Larry Gelbart, 1989, repeated role on Broadway, Criterion Theater, 1989; co-star: A Moon for the Misbegotten, Cort Theatre, N.Y.C., 1984; repeated role of Phil Hogan, Am. Repertory Theatre (Best Actor award Boston Theatre Critics 1984); mem. Hartford Stage Co., 1985-86, played in The Tempest, Twelfth Night, directed and acted in Androcles and the Lion; played Boss Mangan in Heartbreak House, Yale Repertory Theatre, 1986; dir. The Seagull, Am. Conservatory Theatre, San Francisco, 1987, The Man Who Was Peter Pan, Am. Repertory Theater, Cambridge, 1990, Arms and the Man, Alley Theater, Houston, 1995; co-star The Doctor's Dilemma, N.Y.C., 1990, played Harry Hope in The Iceman Cometh, Chgo., 1990 (Joseph Jefferson award 1991); author plays About to Begin, 1988, Margaret Sanger/Unfinished Business, 1989, The Hermit of Yalta, 1993; starred with Opera Co. of Boston in world premiere of The Balcony, 1990, Bolshoi Theatre, Moscow, 1991, starred in Gigli Concert, Court Theatre, Chgo., Spoleto Festival U.S.A., 1992, The Substance of Fire, Asolo Theatre, Sarasota, Fla., 1992, Stages Repertory Theatre, Houston, 1994, Love Letters, Asolo Theatre, 1993, King Lear, Asolo Theatre, 1993; played Horace Vandergelder in The Matchmaker, McCarter Theater, Princeton, N.J., 1994, Gov. Danforth in The Crucible, Alley Theater, Houston, 1994, King Lear, Nebr. Shakespeare Festival, 1995, Tobias in A Delicate Balance, Stages Repertory Theater, Houston, 1996. Athol Fugard's Valley Song, Arizona Theatre Co., 1997, Michael James in Playboy of the Western World, Steppenwolf Theatre, Chicago, 1998, Long Wharf Theatre, New Haven; guest starred as King Lear, Arizona State Univ., 1998; played Leo Tolstoy in world premiere of The Last Station, Vt. State Co., Burlington, 1999, Scrooge, Va. Stage Co., Norfolk, 1999, 2000, Drummond in Inherit the Wind, Mo. Repertory Co., Kansas City, Ford's Theatre, Washington, 2000; played Sean O'Casey in I Knock at the Door, Westport, Conn., 2001; co-starred in world premiere The Astronaut, Westport, Conn., 2002. Served to capt. USAAF, 1942-46, ETO. Decorated D.F.C., Air Medal with seven clusters. Mem. Signet Soc. Clubs: Players (N.Y.C.). Home: PO Box 1074 Weston CT 06883-0074

KIM, CALEB CHUL-SOO, theology studies educator, minister; b. Seoul, Republic of Korea, Nov. 25, 1958; arrived in U.S., 1994; m. Manok Kim, Dec. 7, 1961; children: Da Eun, Eunice Da-Hyeh. BA, Kon-Kuk U., Seoul, 1985; MDiv, Chong-Shin Theol. Sem., Seoul, 1988; ThM, Fuller Theol. Sem., 1995, PhD, 2001. Adj. instr. Sch. of World Mission of Chong-Shin Grad. Sch., Seoul, Republic of Korea, 1998—2001; adj. faculty mem. Fuller Theol. Sem., Pasadena, Calif., 2001—. Sgt. Korean Army, 1979—81, South Korea. Recipient Folk Religious Studies award, Fuller Theol. Sem., 2002. Office: Negst PO Box 24686 Nairobi 00502 Karen Kenya Personal E-mail: kimwithnegst@yahoo.com.

KIM, CHANGWOOK, computer science educator; b. Taegu, Korea, Jan. 18, 1953; came to U.S., 1980; s. Jeonghan and Yungeum (Park) K.; m. Hae Reung Park, Aug. 14, 1980; children: Andrew Eugene, David Yuson. BS, Seoul Nat. U., 1975; MS, Pa. State U., 1982; PhD, Northwestern U., 1986. Systems programmer Korea Telecommunications Co., Seoul, 1978-80; teaching asst. Northwestern U., Evanston, Ill., 1984-85, U. Tex., Richardson, 1985-86; asst. prof. U. Okla., Norman, 1986-92, assoc. prof., 1992—. Contbr. articles to profl. jours. Lt. Korean Navy, 1975-78. Mem. IEEE, European Assn. Theoretical Computer Sci., Assn. Computing Machinery. Avocations: fishing, tennis, Go. Office: U Okla Sch Computer Sci Norman OK 73019-0001

KIM, CHARLES CHANGYOUNG, trade association executive, lawyer; b. Seoul, South Korea, Apr. 16, 1962; came to U.S., 1964; s. Jinak and Kero Lee K. BA, Columbia U., 1987; JD, Cath. U., Washington, 1996. Bar: Md. 1997. Instr. English Hyundai Engring. & Constrn. Co., Seoul, 1987-88; from asst. to chmn. to v.p. internat. Olympic Cultural Ctr., Seoul, 1988-91; dep. nat. dir. Asian Pacific Am. coalition Bush/Quayle Presdl. Campaign, Washington, 1992; from asst. dir. to dir. state legis. programs Am. Cons. Engrs. Coun., Washington, 1998-99, dir. state legis. programs, asst. gen. counsel, 1999-2000, dir. state legis. programs, gen. counsel, 2000—01, gen. counsel, 2001—. Law rev. staff mem., law sch. commencement class spkr. Vol. fl. mgr. Rep. Nat. Conv., San Diego, 1996; vol. asst. to the deputy spl. asst. to pres. for pub. liaison, The White House, Washington, 1992. Mem.: Md. Bar Assn., Am. Soc. Assn. Execs., Capital Toastmasters (v.p. edn. 1999—2000, pres. 2000—01), Univ. Club Washington. Republican. Avocations: history, heraldry, fencing. Office: Am Coun Engring Cos 1015 15th St NW 8th Fl Washington DC 20005-2605 E-mail: ckim@acec.org.

KIM, CHARLES WESLEY, microbiology educator; b. Nashville, Mar. 20, 1926; s. Herbert Hyungsik and Kyung Sook (Lee) K.; m. Soo Johung, June 9, 1956; 1 child, Charles W. Jr. BA, U. Calif., Berkeley, 1949; MS in Pub. Health, U. N.C., 1952, PhD in Parasitology and Microbiology, 1956. Instr., asst. prof. N.Y. Med. Coll., N.Y.C., 1956-59, 59-64; assoc. scientist, scientist Brookhaven Nat. Lab., Upton, NY, 1965-68, 68-70; assoc. dean basic health sci. SUNY, Stony Brook, 1972-74, assoc. vice provost, 1974-83, assoc. prof., 1970-87, prof. microbiology and medicine, 1987—, prof. emeritus, 1996—. Author: Microbiology Review, 1962, 11th edit., 1995; editor: Trichinellosis, 1974, 4th edit., 1985; editl. bd. Exptl. Parasitology, 1984—; reviewer Am. Jour. Tropical Medicine and Hygiene, 1990-93. Moderator N.E. Synod Presbyn. Ch., 1997—98; bd. dirs. Mountain Retreat Assn., 2000—; mem. gen. assembly coun. Presbyn. Ch. (USA), 2000—, mem. exec. com. gen. assembly coun., 2003—; bd. govs. Friends of Sunwood, Stony Brook, 1973—85, Suffolk Symphonic Soc., Suffolk County, NY, 1975—77; mem. devel. com. Mus. Stony Brook, 1983—85; bd. govs. Long Is. Coun. of Chs., 1999—; mem. gov. bd. Three Village Hist. Soc., 2000—01; liaison Med. Benevolence Found., 2000—. Tropical medicine fellow La. State U. Sch. Medicine, 1958, USPHS fellow Argonne Nat. Lab., U. Chgo., 1964-65, Royal Soc. Tropical Medicine and Hygiene fellow, London, 1975. Mem. Internat. Commn. Trichinellosis (pres.

1988-93), Am. Soc. Parasitologists (chmn. nominating com. 1987), Am. Soc. Tropical Medicine and Hygiene, N.Y. Soc. Tropical Medicine (pres. 1985-86), Sigma Xi (chpt. pres. 1993-94), Delta Omega. Fax: 631-751-3010.

KIM, CHIN-WOO, linguist, educator; b. Chungju, Korea, Mar. 22, 1936; came to U.S., 1961, naturalized, 1983; s. Hyong-gi and Kyong ok K.; m. Beverly Jean Kircher, June 14, 1964 (div. June 1982); children: Joseph H., Daniel H; m. Kui-Soon Choe, Oct. 29, 1988. BA in English, Yonsei U., Seoul, Korea, 1958, Wash. State U., 1962; MA, UCLA, 1964, PhD in Linguistics, 1966. Asst. prof. linguistics U. Ill., Urbana, 1967-69, assoc. prof. linguistics, East Asian langs., speech, and English as an internat. language, 1969-72, prof., 1972—, chmn. dept. linguistics, 1979-86, dir. Ill.-Tehran Rsch. Ctr., 1974-76, assoc. dir. Linguistic Inst., 1977, dir. Program in East Asian Studies, 1990-91; assoc. dir. Konan Internat. Exchange Ctr. Konan U., Kobe, Japan, 1993-94; head linguistics U. Ill., 1999. Vis. prof. linguistics U. Hawaii, 1972-73, 86-87, Korea U., Seoul, 1995-96; vis. prof. English Yonsei U., Korea, 1983-84, Konan U., Kobe, Japan, 1993-94; adj. prof. U. Tehran, Irean, 1974-76. Author works in field. Bd. dirs. East Asian Language Inst. Ind. U., 1984—; pres., bd. trustees Korean Language Sch., Urbana, Ill., 1988-92. Served with Korean Air Force, 1958-61. Am. Council Learned Socs. fellow, 1965-66; postdoctoral fellow MIT, 1966-67; Ctr. Advanced Study Fellow, U. Ill., 1984-85, Overseas Korean of the Year Award, Korean Broadcasting Soc., 2001. Mem. Linguistic Soc. Am., Linguistic Soc. Korea, Internat. Cir. Korean Linguistics (pres. 1978-80), Assn. for Asian Studies, Internat. Soc. for Korean Studies (chair lang. and linguistics com. 1990—), Internat. Assn. Humanistic Studies of Language (pres. 2000-). Home: 1401 N Rain Tree Woods Urbana IL 61802-7749 Office: U Ill Dept Linguistics 707 S Mathews Ave Urbana IL 61801-3625 *I grew up in an economically poor and politically oppressive and unstable environment (Japanese colonial rule, World War II, Korean War). The educational system mirrored such a society (books were scarce, pencils were used down to the one-inch length, and classes were often cancelled), but I was determined to learn, as I did not want to let the poor environment be an excuse for ignorance. Now in the States, it saddens me to see many people not realize and make use of excellent opportunities they have, for I believe that in the presence of excellence, mediocrity is a sin.*

KIM, CHONG LIM, political science educator; b. Seoul, Korea, July 17, 1937; came to U.S., 1962; s. Soo Myung and Chung Hwa (Moon) K.; m. Eun Hwa Park, Aug. 21, 1963; children: Bohm S., Lahn S., Lynn S. BA, Seoul Nat. U., 1960; MA, U. Oreg., 1964, PhD, 1968. Instr. U. Oreg., Eugene, 1965-67; asst. prof. U. Iowa, Iowa City, 1968-70, assoc. prof., 1970-75, prof., 1975—. Author: Legislative Connection, 1984, Legislative Process in Korea, 1981, Patterns of Recruitment, 1974; editor: Legislative Systems, 1975, Political Participation in Korea, 1980; contbr. numerous articles to profl. jours. Mem. Am. Polit. Sci. Assn., Midwest Polit. Sci. Assn. Avocations: reading, travel. Office: U Iowa Dept Polit Sci Iowa City IA 52242 E-mail: chongkim@uiowa.edu.

KIM, CHONG SOONG, aerosol science and inhalation technology researcher; b. Inchon, Korea, Dec. 1, 1945; came to U.S., 1971; m. Insook Park, June 10, 1972; children: Jeffrey Hosuk, Audrey Wonkyung, Monica Sookyung. BSME, Seoul Nat. U., 1968; MSME, U. Wis., 1973; PhD, U. Minn., 1978. Rsch. engr. Atomic Energy Rsch. Inst., Seoul, 1970-71; aerosol specialist Mt. Sinai Med. Ctr., Miami Beach, Fla., 1978-80, dir. Aerosol Rsch. Lab., 1980-90; chief human dosimetry sect. U.S. EPA Health Effects Rsch. Lab., Chapel Hill, NC, 1993—95; sr. rsch. scientist U.S. EPA Nat. Health and Environ. Effects Rsch. Lab., Research Triangle Park, N.C., 1990—. Vis. scientist GSF Inst. Biophys. and Radiation Rsch., Germany, 1980; vis. scientist divsn. mech. engring. Korea Inst. Sci. and Tech., Seoul, 1985, U. Pisa (Italy) Sch. Medicine, 1987; adj. asst. prof. U. Miami (Fla.) Sch. Medicine, 1983-86, adj. assoc. prof., 1987-90; adj. assoc. prof. U. N.C. Sch. Medicine, Chapel Hill, 1990-2000, adj. prof., 2000—; adj. assoc. prof. dept. mech. engring. N.C. State U., Raleigh, 1997-2000, adj. prof., 2001—; adj. prof. dept. environ. sci. engring. U. N.C. Sch. Pub. Health, Chapel Hill, 2001—i; nvited spkr. U.S.-Germany Environ. Workshop, 1987, Internat. Conf. for Aerosols in Medicine, 1988, Korean Internat. Workshop in Sci. and Engring., 1989, Respiratory Drug Delivery Symposium, 1990, Internat. Symposium on Clean Room Tech. and Contaminations Control, 1990, FDA Sci. Adv. Bd. Mtg., 1993, Assn. Ofcl. Analytic Chemists Internat. Symposium, Fine Particle Soc. ann. meeting, 1994, Am. Respiratory Care Found., 1999, The Royal Soc., London, 2000, European Sci. Found.-NSF Nanoparticle Symposium, Dublin, Ireland, 2000, Am. Assn. Aerosol Rsch. ann. conf., 2000, Asian Aerosol Conf., Busan, Korea, 2001, Internat. Aerosol Conf., Taipei, China, 2002; ad hoc referee NIH, 1988, 91, 99, VA, 1989,.99, 2003, NSF, 1990. Mem. editl. bd. Jour. Aerosol Medicine, 1988—, Aerosol Sci. Tech., 1998—; contbr. articles to profl. jours.; inventor aerosol rebreathing system. Mem. ASME, Am. Assn. Aerosol Rsch., European Aerosol Assn., Internat. Soc. Aerosols in Medicine. Presbyterian. Home: 109 Brighton Ct Chapel Hill NC 27516-9005 E-mail: kim.chong@epa.gov.

KIM, CHOONG-MAN JOSEPH, radiologist; b. Seoul, Republic of Korea, Sept. 19, 1939; came to U.S., Dec. 1969; s. Chang-Wu Austin and Bok-Nam (Chang) K.; m. Charlyn Young-Hee Oh, Dec. 28, 1969; children: Ronald, Herbert, Daniel, Peter, Timothy. MD, Korea U., Seoul, 1985. Diplomate Am. Bd. Nuclear Medicine. Dir. dept. radiology and nuc. medicine Oteen VA Hosp., Asheville, N.C., 1976-77; staff radiologist S.W. Mich. Radiol. Svcs., Niles, 1977-85, Pawating Hosp., Niles, 1985-92; pres. Michiana Radiology, P.C., Niles, 1992-94, Niles Imaging Physicians, P.C., 1994—. Mem. AMA, Am. Coll. Radiology, Soc. Nuc. Medicine, Coll. Nuc. Physicians. Office: Niles Imaging Physicians PC PO Box 454 31 N Saint Joseph Ave Niles MI 49120-2207

KIM, DAE RYONG, management information systems educator; b. June 18, 1959; m. Jung Hwa Lee, Apr. 24, 1988; children: Jennifer, Harrison. MS, Iowa State U., 1992; PhD, U. of Miss., 1996. Instr. U. of Miss., Oxford, Miss., 1993—95, U. of Ulsan, Ulsan, Republic of Korea, 1996—98, asst. prof., 1998—2001; assoc. prof. Del. State U., Dover, Del., 2001—. Dept. chmn. U. of Ulsan, 1998—2001; cons. Electronic Commerce Resource Ctr., Ulsan, 2000—; web mgr. U. of Ulsan, 1997—2001, computer lab supr., 1997—2001; lab supr. Del. State U., 2001—. Editor: The Complete Success II: The Christians Who Succeed at Their Home, 2000; author: Unemployment, Setting Out a New Life, 2000; translator: Computers, Communications, and Information, 2001; editor: Yeungsang Acad. Jour., 2000—; contbr. articles to profl. jours. Grantee Munsu Rsch. grant, U. of Ulsan, 1998, Distance Learning Rsch. grant, Korea Rsch. Found., 2000, Rsch. grant, Del. State U., 2002. Mem.: Korean Internet & Electronic Commerce Assn. (dir. 2000—), Korean Assn. Indsl. Bus. Adminstrn. (mng. dir. 2000—), Korea Soc. of Mgmt., Korea Soc. of MIS, Korea Assn. Info. Sys., Decision Sci. Inst., Inst. Operating Rsch. and Mgmt. Scis., Assn. for Info. Sys. Avocations: tennis, golf, running, travel, reading. Office: Del State U Sch Mgmt Dept Mgmt 1200 N DuPont Hwy Dover DE 19901 Office Fax: 302-857-6908. Personal E-mail: drkim23@hotmail.com. E-mail: dkim@dsc.edu.

KIM, DAVID SANG CHUL, publisher, evangelist, retired seminary president; b. Seoul, Republic of Korea, Nov. 9, 1915; arrived in U.S., 1959; m. Eui Hong Kang, Jan. 6, 1942; children: Sook Hee, Sung Soo, Hyun Soo, Young Soo, Joon Soo. BA in English Lit., Chosen Christian Coll., Seoul, 1939; postgrad., U. Wales, 1954-55, Western Conservative Bapt. Sem., 1959-61, U. Oreg., 1962-63, MA, 1965; post grad., Pacific Sch. Religion, Berkeley, Calif., 1965-66; PhD, Pacific Columbia U., 1988. Staff Chosen Rubber Industry Assn., Seoul, 1939-45; fin asst. US Mil. Govt., Kunsan City, Republic of Korea, 1945-48; govt. ofcl. Ministry of Fin., Ministry of Social Affairs and Health, Ministry of Fgn. Affairs Govt. of Republic of Korea, Seoul, 1948-59; charter mem. Unification Ch., Seoul, 1954—, 1st missionary to Eng., 1954-55, missionary, evangelist, 1959-70; counseling supr. Clearfield Job Corps Ctr., Utah, 1966-70; founder, pres., owner The Cornerstone Press (now Rose of Sharon Press), 1978-85; charter mem., trustee World Relief Friendship Found., Inc. (now Internat. Relief Friendship Found., Inc.), 1974—; pres. Internat. One World Crusade Inc., 1975—. Founder, United Faith, Inc., Portland, Oreg., 1970—, Global Edn. R & D Fund, Inc., 1981-96; pres. Unification Theol. Sem., 1974-94; charter mem., trustee Nat. Coun. Ch. and Social Action, 1976-96; adv. fin. supporter Global Congress of World Religions, Inc., 1978-96; charter mem. Internat. Religious Found., Inc., 1982—; v.p. Unification Thought Inst., 1989-97; founder, pres. Marriage and Family Inst. Am., 1994—; chmn. inauguration The Family Fedn. for Unification and World Peace, The Netherlands, 1996—; pres. emeritus Unification Theol. Sem., 2000—. Author: Individual Preparation for His Coming Kingdom: Interpretation of the Principle, 1964, Victory Over Communism and the Role of Religion, 1972; editor: (book series) Day of Hope in Review, Part 1-1972-1974, 1974, Part 2-1974-1975, 1975; exec. prodr.: (radio) The Unification Hour, 1975—2001; editor: (book series) Part 3-1976-1981, 1981; exec. prodr.: (radio) True Love Journey, 1993—2001; contbr. articles to profl. jour. Recipient Byzantine Golden medal Am. Inst. Patristic Byzantine Studies, Inc., 1992, Spl. Award for disting. Svc. Unification Ch., Internat., 1996. Address: PO Box 1755 South Rd Sta Poughkeepsie NY 12601-0755

KIM, DONNA MERCADO, state senator; b. Honolulu, July 31, 1952; BA, Wash. State U., 1974. Recreation dir.; small bus. exec. dir.; comm. sales rep.; hotel catering sales rep.; pub. rels. dir. KUMU Radio; Dem. senator dist. 15 Hawaii State Senate. Past mem. Pres.'s Nat. Com. on Transp.; past mem. steering com. Nat. League Cities, Econ. Devel.; bd. dirs. Bank of Am. Hawaii; trained facilitator The Pacific Inst. Active Aliamanu unit Boys and Girls Club Honolulu, Hawaii's Jr. Miss, Inc., Planned Parenthood, YMCA Century Club; mem. Hawaii Korean Millenium Commn.; bd. trustees Palama Settlement. Named one of Three Outstanding Young Persons, Hawaii Jaycees, 1988; recipient Outstanding Alumni award Farrington H.S., 1997. Mem. ASPA (Outstanding City and County Adminstr. award 1997), Asian Pacific Am. Mcpl. Ofcls., Kaliki Bus. Assn., Hawaii Korean C. of C. (hon.), Filipino C. of C. Office: Hawaii State Senate State Capitol Rm 218 415 S Beretania St Honolulu HI 96813 Fax: 808 587-7205. E-mail: senkim@Capitol.hawaii.gov.*

KIM, DOOHIE, retired public health educator; b. Taegu, Korea, Sept. 17, 1935; s. Dong-Hoon and Hong-Dahl (Chae) K.; m. Keun-Ok Ahn, Mar. 24, 1959; children: Ji-Eoun, Ji-Kwan, Nah-Youn. BA, Kyungpook Nat. U., Daegu, Republic of Korea, 1961, MA, 1963, PhD, 1970. Instr. Sch. Medicine Kyungpook Nat. U., 1968—70, asst. prof., 1970—75, assoc. prof., 1975—78, prof., 1978—95, dir. med. libr., 1978—80, dean Sch. Pub. Health, 1990-92, 94-95, emeritus prof., 1996—; prof. and dean Sch. Medicine Dongguk U., Kyung-ju, Republic of Korea, 1995—2001; ret., 2001. Com. mem. Provincial Com. for Environ. Contamination, Taegu, Korea, 1975-79; adv. mem. Taegu Supervising Corp. for Korean Indsl. Safety, 1985-95.. Author: Environmental Sanitation, 1975, Introduction of Health Science, 1989, Practice of School Health, 1979, Making Health for Prolonging Life, 1994. Adv. mem. Provincial Policy Com. of Kyungpook-do Korea, Taegu, 1979-81, Policy Com. Taegu City, 1981-83. Maj. Korean mil., 1964-67. Recipient Letters of Commendation, Prime Ministry Korea, 1963, Minister of Helath and Social Affairs of Korea, Seoul, 1985, Pres. of Kyungpook Nat. U., Taegu, 1987. Mem. APHA, Am. Coll. Preventive Medicine (internat. mem.), Korean Soc. Preventive Medicine (pres. 1987-89, Plaque 1990), Korean Indsl. Health Assn. (leader Kyungpook br. 1974-80), Internat. Commn. Occupl. Health, Korean Soc. Agrl. Medicine and Rural Health (pres. 1994-96). Home: Lombard Mantion 2-101 1-3 Sooseong 2ka Taegu 706-776 Republic of Korea E-mail: doohi@hanmail.net.

KIM, DUCKSOO, radiologist, inventor and educator; b. Seoul, Korea, Aug. 16, 1948; came to U.S., 1977; s. Changkun and Sunchom (Cho) K.; m. Eunjoo Lee, May 22, 1978; children: LeeAnn, SueAnn, Andrew. BS, Cath. U., Seoul, 1969, MD, 1973; postgrad., Stanford (Calif.) U., 1981-83. Diplomate Am. Bd. Radiology; lic. physician, Mass., N.Y., Calif. Intern St. Mary's Hosp., Seoul, 1976-77, McKeesport (Pa.) Hosp., 1977-78; resident in diagnostic radiology Beth Israel Hosp., Newark, 1978-81; NIH fellow in cardiovascular and interventional radiology Stanford (Calif.) U. Med. Ctr., 1981-83; instr. radiology Harvard Med. Sch., Boston, 1983-86, asst. prof. radiology, 1986-92, assoc. prof. radiology, 1992-98; dir. Divsn. Cardiovascular and Interventl. Radiology Beth Israel Hosp., Boston, 1983-96; co-dir. divsn. cardiovascular and interventional radiology Beth Israel Deaconess Med. Ctr., Boston, 1996-98; prof. radiology and surgery U. Mass. Med. Sch., Worcester, 1999—; dir. divsn. cardiovascular/interventional radiology U. Mass. Med. Ctr., Worcester, 1999—. Vis. prof. radiology U. Zurich, 1987, Nat. Rsch. Ctr. of Surgery, Ministry of Health, Russia, 1992; lectr. in field; rschr. in field. Author: Peripheral Vascular Imaging and Intervention, 1992; reviewer Catheterization and Cardiovascular Diagnosis, 1992-94, Hepatology, 1993; contbr. articles to profl. jours., chpts. in books. Sec. Korean Cath. Community, Boston, 1988-89, v.p., 1989-91, pres., 1991-92. Capt. Korean Army, 1973-76. Cath. U. Med. Coll. scholar, 1969-73; NIH grantee, 1981-83. Fellow Am. Coll. Angiology, Internat. Coll. Angiology, Am. Heart Assn., Soc. of Cardiovascular and Interventional Radiology; mem. AMA, Radiol. Soc. N.Am., Am. Coll. Radiology, New Eng. Soc. for Cardiovascular and Interventional Radiology (pres. 1992-93), New Eng. Korean Med. Soc., Norfolk Dist. Med. Soc., Mass. Med. Soc., Soc. of Magnetic Resonance in Medicine, Soc. of Magnetic Resonance Imaging, New Eng. Alumni Assn. of Cath. U. Med. Coll. (pres. 1991-92). Roman Catholic. Avocations: tennis, golf. Home: 9 Cedar Hill Rd Dover MA 02030-1631 Office: U Mass Med Ctr 9 Cedar Hill Rd Dover MA 02030-1631

KIM, E. HAN, finance and business administration educator; b. Seoul, Korea, May 27, 1946; came to U.S., 1966; s. Chang Yoon and Young Ja (Chung) K.; m. Tack Han, June 14, 1969; children— Juliane H., Elaine H., Deborah H. BS, U. Rochester, 1969; MBA, Cornell U., 1971; PhD, SUNY-Buffalo, 1975. Asst. prof. Ohio State U., Columbus, 1975-77, assoc. prof., 1979-80; assoc. prof., then prof. fin. and bus. adminstrn. U. Mich., Ann Arbor, 1980-84, Fred M. Taylor Disting. prof., 1984—, chmn. dept. fin., 1988-91; dir. Mitsui Life Fin. Rsch. Ctr., 1990—. Vis. assoc. prof. U. Chgo., 1978-79; vis. rsch. fellow Korea Devel. Inst., 1986-87; econ. cons. Govt. of Korea, 1985-87, 98; Cycle and Carriage vis. prof. Nat. U. Singapore, 1989; Yamaichi prof. econs. U. Tokyo, 1990-91; cons. Bank of Korea, 1985, U.S. Dept. Treasury, IRS, 1988-94, World Bank, 1989-91, 93, Posco, 1995-98, Korea Stock Exch., 1997-98; co-chair Citizens for Econ. Freedom, 1997-99; bd. dirs. Posco, Hana Bank, Posco. Assoc. editor Jour. Fin., 1979-83, 88-92, Fin. Rev., 1982—, Internat. Jour. Fin., 1990—, Internat. Rev. Fin. Analysis, 1990-92, Rev. No. Am. Jour. of Econs. and Fin., 1990—, Rev. Quantitative Fin. and Acctg., 1990—, Pacific Basin Fin. Jour., 1991-96; edit. bd. Jour. Bus. Rsch., 1977—; adv. bd. Asia-Pacific Jour. Mgmt., 1990-96, Jour. Asian Bus., 1996—; contbr. articles to profl. jours. Mem. Korea-Am. Econ. Assn. (sec. gen. 1985, v.p. 1986, pres. 1996), Am. Econ. Assn., Am. Fin. Assn., Western Fin. Assn. Avocations: tennis, golf. Office: U Mich Sch Bus Adminstrn Ann Arbor MI 48109

KIM, EARNEST JAE-HYUN, import and export company executive; b. Seoul, Korea, Dec. 9, 1938; s. Chang-Nyun and Gui-Nim (Yun) K.; m. Jung-Ki Eun, Mar. 25, 1967; children: Yoo-Kyoung, Ja-Hong, Yung-Ju, Do-Hyung. Degree, Hanyang U., 1961; postgrad., Sung Kyun Kwan U., 1975. Reporter Daily Econ. News, Seoul, 1966-74; exec. dir. STAF Corp., Seoul, 1975-82; dir. Korea Fedn. Handicrafts Coops., Seoul, 1979-82; pres. Buenos Amigos, Inc., Laredo, Tex., 1982-95, Buenos Hermanos L.L., 1992—, Nueva Moda Mundo, Mexico City, Mex., 1990—, Buenos Amigos de Mex. S.A., 1994—, Amiguitas S.A. de C.V., Mexico City, 1995—. Inventor, patentee Method of Casting, Method of Jewelry Making. Mem. Adv. Coun. on Democratic and Peaceful Unification of Korea, 1999—. Recipient Spl. Congl. Recognition, Congressman Albert Bustamante, 1988, Cert. of Excellence, Senator Judith Zaffirini, 1983, Cert. of Appreciation, Mayor of Laredo, 1988, Cert. of Appreciation, Am. Legion, 1988, recognition award of achievement and contbn. Ministry Commerce, Industry and Energy Korea, 1999. Mem. Laredo C. of C., Korean Assn. Mex. (pres. 1998-99), Korean C. of C. (v.p. nat. chpt. 1999-01), Overseas Korean Trade Assn. (bd. dirs. 1999-01, v.p. 2001-2004), Lions (v.p. Laredo 1991—, pres. award 1989), Laredo Country Club, Coral Golf Resort (Mex.). Buddhist. Avocation: golf. Address: PO Box 6566 Laredo TX 78042-6566 Office: Casa Beauty SA de CV Carmen 58 Col Centro Mexico City 06020 Mexico Home: Apt 201 1555 Vista Club Cir Santa Clara CA 95054-3723 E-mail: happy88@prodigy.net.mx.

KIM, EDWARD, medical association administrator; AB, Harvard U., 1980—84; MD, Jefferson Med. Coll., 1984—88. Psychiatry Am. Bd. of Psychiatry and Neurology, 1993, Geriatric Psychiatry Am. Bd. of Psychiatry and Neurology, 1995. Med. dir., geriatric services St. Barnabas Behavioral Health, Livingston, NJ, 1996—98; med. dir., acute adult services UMDNJ, U. Behavioral Healthcare, Piscataway, NJ, 1998—2001; med. dir., adult services UMDNJ-U. Behavioral Healthcare, Piscataway, NJ, 2001—. Bd. of trustees Brain Injury Assn. of NJ, 2000—02. Mem.: Am. Neuropsychiatric Assn., Am. Coll. of Physician Executives, Am. Psychiat. Assn. Office: UMDNJ-U Behavioral Healthcare 671 Hoes Lane Piscataway NJ 08855-1392 E-mail: kimed@umdnj.edu.

KIM, EDWARD WILLIAM, ophthalmic surgeon; b. Seoul, Korea, Nov. 25, 1949; came to U.S., 1957; s. Shoon Kul and Pok Chu (Kim) K.; m. Carole Sachi Takemoto, July 24, 1976; children: Brian, Ashley. BA, Occidental Coll., Los Angeles, 1971; postgrad., Calif. Inst. Tech., 1971; MD, U. Calif., San Francisco, 1975; MPH, U. Calif., Berkeley, 1975. Diplomate Nat. Bd. Med. Examiners, Am. Bd. Ophthalmology. Resident in ophthalmology Harvard U.-Mass. Eye and Ear Infirmary, Boston, 1977-79; clin. fellow in ophthalmology Harvard U., 1977-79, clin. fellow in retina, 1980; practice medicine in ophthalmic surgery Laguna Hills, San Clemente, Calif., 1980—. Vol. ophthalmologist Eye Care Inc., Ecole St. Vincent's, Haiti, 1980, Liga, Mex., 1989, Tonga, 1997; chief staff, South Coast Med. Ctr., 1988-89; assoc. clin. prof. dept. ophthalmology, U. Calif., Irvine. Founding mem. Orange County Ctr. for Performing Arts, Calif., 1982, dir. at large, 1991; pres. Laguna Beach Summer Music Festival, Calif., 1984. Reinhart scholar U. Calif.-San Francisco, 1972-73; R. Taussig scholar, 1974-75. Fellow ACS, Am. Acad. Ophthalmology, Internat. Coll. Surgeons; mem. Calif. Med. Assn., Keratorefractive Soc., Orange County Med. Assn., Mensa, Expts. in Art and Tech. Office: Harvard Eye Assocs 665 Camino De Los Mares Ste 102 San Clemente CA 92673-2840

KIM, GEUN-EUN, surgeon, educator; b. Seoul, Korea, 1941; came to U.S., 1965; s. Doo-Man and Ki-Ok; m. Eun-Kyung Choi; children: Catherine, Judy. MD, Seoul Nat. U., 1965. Cert. in surgery. Intern Einstein Med. Ctr., Phila., 1965-66, resident, 1966-70; fellow in vascular surgery NYU Med. Ctr., 1970; with Beth Israel Hosp., N.Y.C., Downtown Hosp. Clin. prof. surgery N.Y. Med. Coll.; prof. surgery Coll. Medicine, Ulsan U., Seoul; dir. Ctr. for Vascular Disease, Asan Med. Ctr. Fellow ACS; mem. Assn. for Acad. Surgery, Internat. Cardiovasc. Soc., Soc. Vascular Surgery, N.Y. Soc. Surgery, Ea. Vascular Soc., Korean Surg. Soc. (hon.). Office: Ctr Vascular Disease Asan Med Ctr Song Pa Ku Seoul Republic of Korea E-mail: gebkim7@yahoo.com.

KIM, HAN PYONG, dentist, researcher; b. Seoul, Korea, May 2, 1945; s. Koe Jin and Jung Bok (Park) K.; m. Young Sook Yoon, Apr. 27, 1974; 1 child, Sung Mo. MA, DDS, Seoul Nat. U., 1975; PhD, Yonsei U., Seoul, 1982; MA, Monterey Inst. Internat. Study, 1996. Prof. Yonsei U., Seoul, 1977-84; vis. scholar UCLA, 1982; project rschr. for health care sys. Korea Dental Assn., Seoul, 1988-92. Mem. bd. health ins. Nat. HIC, Seoul, 1990-92. Mem. Pres.'s Leadership Circle, Washington, 1995. Avocations: golf, fishing, photography. Home: 57 Burlingame Irvine CA 92602

KIM, HAN-SEOB, pathologist; b. Seoul, South Korea, Sept. 5, 1934; came to U.S., 1969; s. Y.S. and S.Y. (Ahn) K. MD, Seoul Nat. U., 1959, PhD, 1968. Resident Baylor Affiliated Residency Program, Houston, 1965-66, 69-72; from instr. to assoc. prof. Baylor Coll. Medicine, Houston, 1972-93, prof. dept. pathology, 1993—. Office: Baylor Coll Medicine Dept Pathology Houston TX 77030

KIM, HO GILL, poet; b. Sachon, South Korea, June 22, 1943; s. Jong Soo and Ul Soon (Lee) K.; m. Sherrie Chul Ja Park, Mar. 19, 1970; children: Brian Ki-Man, Eugene Yoo-Jin. BA, Gyeng Sang Univ., Jin-Joo, Korea, 1970; MS in Econs., Kun Kook Univ., Seoul, 1975. Airline pilot Korean Airlines, Seoul, 1972-81; columnist Korean Central Daily News, L.A., 1981-83; pres. Everglobe Enterprises Inc. dba Sunflower Farms, L.A., 1984—. Editor: Literary realm, 1987-95, Korean American Literature, 1982-86, SiJo World, 1999—; author poetry. Capt. Korean Army, 1965-71, Vietnam. Decorated Military Merit Vietnam War Korean Army, 1971; recipient Anti-Communist Poetry award Korea Def. Ministry, 1969, Overseas Korean Literary award Chu Kang Literary Soc., 1997, Modern Si Jo Poetry award Modern SiJo Publ. Co., 1998. Mem. SiJo Soc. Am. (pres. 1995), Korean Literary Soc. Am. (pres. 1982—, adv.), Internat. Pen Club, Acad. Am. Poets, World Korean Writers Network (pres. 2000—). Office: 1937 E VErnon Ave Vernon CA 90058

KIM, HONG NACK, political science educator; b. Youngchun, Korea, Aug. 20, 1933; came to U.S., 1956, naturalized, 1973; s. Sang Do and Nam Jo (Sung) K.; m. Boohi Suh, Mar. 26, 1967; children: Michael, Jeffrey, Brian Kim. BA, Seoul Nat. U., Korea, 1956; MA, Georgetown U., 1960, PhD, 1965. Lectr. Georgetown U., Washington, 1965-66; asst. prof. North Tex. State U., Denton, 1966-67, 1967-72, assoc. prof., 1972-77; prof. polit. sci. W.Va. U., Morgantown, 1977—. Author: Scholars Guide to Washington, D.C. for East Asian Studies, 1979; editor-in-chief: Internat. Jour. of Korean Studies, 2000—; editor: Asian Forum, 1972-74, Polit. Studies Rev., 1984-87; co-editor: Essays in Political Science, 1972, Korean Reunification: New Perspectives and Approaches, 1984; contbr. articles to various publs. Pres. Korean Assn. W.V., 1981-82, Assn. Korean Polit. Scientists N.Am.83-85. Fulbright-Hays Faculty Rsch. Abroad grantee U.S. Dept. Edn., 1979, 82; Fulbright Lecturing/Rsch. grantee U.S. Info. Agy., 1990; recipient Outstanding Rsch. award W.Va. U., 1985. Mem. Am. Polit. Sci. Assn., Assn. Asian Studies. Democrat. Presbyterian. Home: 1270 Braewick Dr Morgantown WV 26505-3339 Office: W Va U Dept Polit Sci Morgantown WV 26505 E-mail: Hongkim@wvu.edu.

KIM, HONG KOOK, electrical engineer, researcher; s. Sun Duk Kim and Young Ja Son; m. Byung Sook Min, May 5, 1991; 1 child, Peter Chang Yup. BS, Seoul Nat. U., 1988; MS, Korea Advanced Inst. of Sci. and Tech., Seoul, 1990; PhD, Korea Advanced Inst. of Sci. and Tech., Taejon, 1994. Sr. rschr. Samsung Advanced Inst. of Tech., Suwon, Republic of Korea, 1990—98; sr. engr. MMC Tech., Inc., Seoul, 1998; rsch. scientist Korea Advanced Inst. of Sci. and Tech., Taejon, 1998; cons. AT&T Labs-Rsch., Florham Park, NJ, 1998—2000, sr. tech. staff mem., 2000—. Dir., publ. chair conf. procs. Procs. of 2001 N.E. Regional Conf. Editor: (newsletter) Ksea Echoes; contbr. articles to profl. jours. Recipient Excellent Student Award, Seoul Nat. U., 1986, Cum Laude, 1988, Best Patent Award, Samsung Advanced Inst. of Tech., 1996; scholar U. Scholarship, Seoul Nat. U., 1984-1987, Govt. Scholarship, Korea Advanced Inst. of Sci. and Tech., 1988-1989, Indsl. Scholarship, Samsung Electronics, 1990-1994. Mem.: IEEE, Inc. (IEEE) (piscataway, nj.), Korean-American Scientists and Engineers (KSEA) (vienna, verginia), Internat. Speech Communication Assn. (ISCA). Achievements include patents for method for generating random code book of code-excited linear prediction coding; research in cepstrum-domain acoustic feature and model compensation for automatic speech recognition in noise; development of speech recognition algorithms in noisy environment; design of front-end algorithm for wireless speech recognition; patents for voice coding and decoding method and device; apparatus for quantizing spectral envelope including error selector for selecting a codebook index of a quantized LSF having a smaller error value and method therefor; bitstream-based feature extraction method for a front-end speech recognizer; frame erasure concealment technique for a bitstream-based feature extractor; development of voice recognition dialing system; speaker-dependent voice dialer for CDMA cellular phones; voice dialer for Samsung digital keyphone; contributed to inention of internat. telcomms. union standardization. Avocations: skiing, golf, jogging, Web surfing. Office: AT&T Labs-Rsch Rm D107 180 Park Ave Florham Park NJ 07932

KIM, HOON, statistician, educator; s. Kijeon Kim and Eun Eom; m. Moonah Yoon, July 23, 1995; 1 child, Lani Iris Jeeyoun. PhD in Stats., U. Mo., Columbia, 1999. Asst. prof. stats. S.W. Mo. State U., Springfield, 1999—2002, Calif. Poly. U., Pomona, 2002—. Contbr. articles to profl. jours. Grantee R & D, Mo. Dept. Agr., 2001. Mem.: Calif. Faculty Assn., Am. Statis. Assn. Office: Cal Poly Pomona Dept Math and Stats 3801 W Temple Ave Pomona CA 91768

KIM, HWA-JIN, music educator; b. Daegu, South Korea, Oct. 10, 1966; d. Hyn-Chul Choi and Sook-Ja Kim; m. Paul Sung Kim, Sept. 13, 1994; children: Grace, Christie. MusB, Seoul Nat. U., 1989; MusM, Manhattan Sch. of Music, 1991, MusD, 2000. Faculty mem. N.Y. Bethesda Theol. Sem., Queens, NY, 1992—93; music faculty Ref. Presbyn. Sem. of the East N.Y., 1993—94; assoc. tchr. Manhattan Sch. of Music, NYC, 1993—94; music faculty The Music Sch., Providence, 1998—2000; music instr. Blue Ridge Cmty. Coll., 2000—; adj. asst. prof. U. N.C. in Asheville, NC, 2003—. Co-prodr.(and performer): (album) The Lords Prayer, 2002. Mem.: Music Teachers Nat. Assn., Coll. Mus. Soc. Avocations: reading, walking, swimming. E-mail: hwajinkim@ad.com.

KIM, HYO SOOK, anesthesiologist; b. Republic of Korea, 1940; d. Kyu T. and Ki Won (Shin) Kim; m. Chong H. Kim, Nov. 23, 1968; children: Jeanne I. Kim, Katherine M. Kim, Riena Y. Kim. MD, Korea U. Med. Coll., Seoul, 1964. Diplomate Am. Bd. Anesthesiology. Intern St. Joseph's Hosp., 1965; resident U. Chgo. Hosp., 1966-67, Children's Meml. Hosp., Chgo., 1968, fellow, 1969-70; chief anesthesiologist Seaway Hosp., Trenton, Mich.; instr. Dept. Anesthesiology U. Chgo., 197-72; clin. asst. prof. Surgery Mich. State U., 1976-82. Fellow Am. Coll. Anesthesiologists; mem. AMA, Am. Soc. Anesthesiologists, Am. Soc. for Regional Anesthesia, Internat. Anesthesia Rsch. Soc., Am. Acad. Med. Acupuncture. Office: 18445 Vanhorn Woodhaven MI 48183

KIM, HYUNJOONG, education educator; m. Hyosook Lee, Jan. 8, 1994; children: Seo-Yeon Joanne, Nicole Hee-Yeon. BS, Yonsei U., 1991, MS; PhD, U. Wis., 1998. Prof. stats. Worcester Poly. Inst., Mass., 1998—2001, U. Tenn., Knoxville, 2001—. Office: U Tenn 328 Stokely Mgmt Ctr Knoxville TN 37996 Office Fax: 865-974-2490.

KIM, IH CHIN, pediatrician; b. Aug. 6, 1925; came to U.S., 1953, naturalized, 1965; s. Young Whan and Young Ho (Cho) K.; m. Helen Fern Wagner, Mar. 15, 1957 (dec.); children: Catherine Joy Kim Smith, Stephen Thomas. Student, Yon Sei U., 1944-46; postgrad., U. Pa., 1954-55. Diplomate Am. Bd. Pediatrics. Intern Transp. Hosps., Seoul and Pusan, Korea, 1950-51; resident in pediatrics Pusan Children's Charity Hosp., 1951-53, Children's Hosp. Phila., 1953-55; fellow in pediatric gastroenterology, 1955-58; rsch. assoc., 1958-67; med. staff, 1963-67; pvt. practice in pediatrics, 1965—, Phillipsburg, N.J., 1971—. Staff dept. pediatrics Hahnemann Med. Coll. and osp., Phila., 1967-96, Easton H osp., 1965—, Warren Hosp., Phillipsburg, N.J., 1966—, chief dept. pediatrics, 1978-90; clin. asst. prof. pediatrics Hahnemann Med. Coll., Phila., 1971-96. Contbr. articles to med. jours. Fellow Am. Acad. Pediatrics; mem. AMA, Country Club Northampton County. Presbyterian. Address: 6 Ivy Ct Easton PA 18045-5816 Office: 545 Heckman St Phillipsburg NJ 08865

KIM, ILKI, physicist; b. Seoul, Republic of Korea, Nov. 6, 1967; arrived in U.S., 2001; s. Jinho and Inja (Heo) Kim; m. Sung-Eun (Yoo), Dec. 7, 2002. B of Engring, Seoul Nat. U., 1991; diploma of physics, U. Hamburg, Germany, 1994; PhD, U. Stuttgart, Germany, 2000. Postdoctoral acad. staff Inst. for Theoretical Physics 1 U. Stuttgart, 2000; postdoctoral rsch. assoc. U. Notre Dame, Ind., 2001, N.C. State U., 2001—. Contbr. articles to profl. jours. With Korean Mil., 1995—97. Mem.: NY Acad. Scis. Home: 3129E Aileen Dr Raleigh NC 27606 Office: NC State U Dept of ECE EGRC 334B Campus Box 8617 Raleigh NC 27695-8617 Address: c/o Jinho Kim Apkujong-dong Hyundai Apt 125-506 Seoul 135-110 Republic of Korea E-mail: ikim4@eos.ncsu.edu.

KIM, JAEGWON, philosophy educator; b. Taegu, Korea, Sept. 12, 1934; came to U.S., 1955, naturalized, 1966; m. Sylvia Hughes, June 18, 1961; 1 child, Justin Lee. AB, Dartmouth Coll., 1958; PhD, Princeton U., 1962. Instr. philosophy Swarthmore Coll., 1961-63; asst. prof. philosophy Brown U., 1963-67, vis. prof., 1975, William Perry Faunce prof. philosophy, 1987—; chair dept. Borwn U., 1990-99; assoc. prof. philosophy U. Mich., 1967-70, prof., 1971-87, chmn. dept., 1979-87, Roy Wood Sellars prof. philosophy, 1986-87. Assoc. prof. Cornell U., 1970-71; prof. Johns Hopkins U., 1977-78; vis. prof. Stanford U., 1967; Fulbright lectr., Republic of Korea, 1984, Seoul Nat. U., 2000; vis. McMahon-Hank prof. U. Notre Dame, 1999, 2001—. Author: Supervenience and Mind, 1993, Philosophy of Mind, 1996, Mind in a Physical World, 1998; editor: (with Alvin I. Goldman) Values and Morals, 1978, (with A. Beckermann and H. Flohr) Emergence or Reduction?, 1992; (with E. Sosa) A Companion to Metaphysics, 1995, Metaphysics: An Anthology, 1999, Epistemology: An Anthology, 2000, Supervenience, 2002; co-editor: Nous; contbr. numerous articles to profl. publs. Fellow Am. Coun. Learned Soc., 1980-81, NEH, 1985; NSF grantee, 1977-79. Mem. Am. Philos. Assn. (chmn. com. on status and future of profession 1976-81, mem. bd. officers 1976-81, 88-90, v.p. ctrl. divsn. 1987-88, pres. 1988-89), Philosophy of Sci. Assn. (mem. governing bd. 1979-81), Am. Acad. Arts and Scis., Coun. Philos. Studies. Office: Brown U Dept Philosophy Providence RI 02912-0001

KIM, JAI BIN, civil engineering educator; b. Seoul, Korea, May 17, 1934; came to U.S., 1955; s. M.Y. and Y.W. Kim; m. Yung Ja Hong, June 17, 1960; children: Clara A., Vivian T., Robert H., Patricia A. BSCE, Oreg. State U., 1959, MSCE, 1960; PhD in Civil Engring., U. Md., 1965. Registered profl. engr., Pa., Md., N.J., Va., Conn. Chief rsch. engr. D.C. Govt. Dept. Hwys. and Traffic, Washington, 1964-66; asst. prof. Bucknell U., Lewisburg, Pa., 1966-72, assoc. prof., 1972-76, prof., chmn. civil and environ. engring., 1976—. Pres. structural cons. co. BKLB, Inc., Lewisburg, 1982—. Patentee in field. Mem. ASCE (mem. bridge inspection com. 1990—, mem. wood com. 1990—), Transp. Rsch. Bd. (com. on bridge constrn. 1988—). Republican. Office: Bucknell U Dept Civil/Environ Engring Moore Ave Lewisburg PA 17837 E-mail: jaikim@bucknell.edu.

KIM, JAI SOO, physics educator; b. Taegu, Korea, Nov. 1, 1925; came to U.S., 1958, naturalized, 1963; s. Wan Sup and Chanam (Whang) K.; m. Hai Kyou Kim, Nov. 2, 1952; children: Kami, Tomi, Kihyun, Himi. BSc in Physics, Seoul Nat. U., Korea, 1949; MS in Physics, U. Sask., Can., 1957, PhD, 1958. Asst. prof. physics Clarkson U., Potsdam, N.Y., 1958-59, U. Idaho, Moscow, 1959-62, assoc. prof., 1962-65, prof., 1965-67; prof. atmospheric sci. and physics SUNY, Albany, 1967-95, chmn. dept. atmospheric sci., 1969-76; emeritus prof., 1995—; rep. Univ. Corp. for Atmospheric Research SUNY, Albany, 1970-76, cons. Korean Studies Program Stony Brook, 1983-85. Vis. prof. Advanced Inst. Sci. and Tech., Seoul, Korea, 1983; cons. U.S. Army Research Office, 1978-79, Battelle Meml. Inst., 1978-81, Environ. One Corp., 1978-84, N.Y. State Environ. Conservation Dept., 1976-82, Norlite Corp., 1982-84, Korean Antarctic Program, 1988—. Contbr. articles to profl. jours. Mem. Am. Inst. Physics, Am. Geophys. Union, Sigma Xi. Home: 22 Westover Rd Slingerlands NY 12159-3646 Office: 1400 Washington Ave Albany NY 12222-0100 E-mail: kim9664@msn.com.

KIM, JAY, former congressman; b. Korea, 1939; m. Jennifer Kim, June, 1961; children: Richard, Kathy, Eugene. BS, MCE, U. So. Calif.; MPA, Calif. State U. Coun. mem. City of Diamond Bar, Calif., 1990, mayor, 1991; mem. 103rd Congress from 41st dist. Calif., 1993-98. Pres., founder Jaykim Engrs. Inc. Recipient Outstanding Achievement in Bus. and Community Devel. award, Engr. of Yr. award, Caballero de Distinction award, Engr. Bus. of the Yr. award, others. Republican. Methodist. Address: Image Media Svc 7927 Jones Branch Dr Ste 100N Mc Lean VA 22102-3328

KIM, JEONGBIN JOHN, mechanical engineering educator; b. Seoul, Korea, Oct. 20, 1947; came to U.S., 1972; s. Wanson Kim and Ilyun Wu; m. Mee-Joo Julie Kim, June 18, 1977; 1 child, June M. BS, Seoul Nat. U., 1970; MS, Brown U., 1974; PhD, Stanford (Calif.) U., 1978. Nat. rsch. coun. fellow NASA Ames Rsch. Ctr., Moffett Field, Calif., 1978-80; asst. prof. Stanford U., 1980-82; rsch. scientist NASA Ames Rsch. Ctr., Moffett Field, 1982-87, sect. head., 1987-93, branch chief, 1992-93; prof. U. Calif., L.A., 1993—. Fellow Am. Phys. Soc. Democrat. Presbyterian. Office: U Calif Dept Mech/Aerospace Engring 420 Westwood Plz Los Angeles CA 90095-1597

KIM, JEONG-KYUN, metallurgist, researcher; b. Kwang-Ju, Korea, Aug. 29, 1960; came to U.S., 1992; s. Jae-Hoo Kim and Soon-Ja Jung; m. Eun-Young Jang, Jan. 9, 1988; children: Tae-Eum, Tae-Lim, Grace. BS, Chon-Nam U., Kwang-Ju, 1987; MS, Korea Advanced Inst. Sci. & Tech., Seoul, 1990; PhD, U. Wis., Milw., 1997. Rschr. Korea Atomic Energy Rsch. Inst., Tae-Jon, Korea, 1990-92; rsch. asst. U. Wis., Milw., 1992-97, postdoctoral fellow, 1997-98, rsch. assoc., 1998-2000; sr. scientist MER Corp., Tucson, 2000—. Contbr. articles to profl. jours. Mem. Am. Foundrymen's Soc., Minerals, Metals and Materials Soc. Office: 7960 S Kolb Rd Tucson AZ 85706

KIM, JIN GYO, management educator; b. Susan, Korea, June 3, 1966; s. Yong Jik Kim and Jang Ja Song; m. Young Hee Shin, June 23, 1996. MA, Sogang U., Seoul, Korea, 1993; PhD, U. Toronto, Can., 2002. Prof. MIT-Sloan Sch. Mgmt., Cambridge, Mass. Recipient Best Paper award, Korean Mktg. Assn., 1994. Mem.: Informs, Am. Mktg. Assn. Office: MIT Sloan Sch Mgmt E56-323 38 Memorial Dr Cambridge MA 02142

KIM, JOHN CHAN KYU, electrical engineer; b. Tokyo, June 15, 1935; came to U.S., 1958; s. Ke Jun and Young Sok Kim; m. Tong-Rahn Chu, Sept. 11, 1965; children: Janet M., William H., Douglas S. Student, Seoul Nat. U., 1954-57; BSEE, Tri-State U., 1959; MSEE, Mich. State U., 1960, PhD in Elec. Engring., 1962. Instr. Tri-State U., Angola, Ind., 1961-62; sr. rsch. engr. Systems Rsch. Labs., Inc., Dayton, Ohio, 1962-64, Honeywell, Inc., Mpls., 1964-65; sr. staff engr. E-System Inc., Falls Church, Va., 1965-69; head analysis sect., C3 dept. TRW, Inc., Fairfax, Va., 1969-74, sr. staff engr., systems engring. lab., 1974-79, mgr. undersea surveillance dept., 1979-81, asst. project mgr. WWM-CCS Support Project, 1981-85, dep. project mgr., Navy Comms. Project, 1985-88, advanced systems mgr., Navy Systems Ops., 1988-92, sr. staff engr., Air Traffic Control Systems Project, 1992-95, tech. fellow, 1995-2001; program officer navigation tech. Office Naval Rsch. Dept. Def., Arlington, Va., 2001—. Author: Naval Shipboard Communications Systems, 1994. Bd. dirs. Vol. Ctr. of Fairfax (Va.) County, 1992—; scoutmaster Boy Scouts Am., McLean, 1983-84; nat. judge Mathcounts, Alexandria, Va., 1996—; engring. and devel. com. Air Traffic Control Assn. Mem. IEEE, Armed Forces Comms. and Electronics Assn., Nat. Security Industry Assn., Air Traffic Control Assn., Inst. Navigation. Methodist. Avocations: cycling, swimming, carpentry. Home: 8006 Snowpine Way Mc Lean VA 22102-2420 Office: Office of Naval Rsch Dept of Defense North 800 N Quincy St Arlington VA 22217 E-mail: johnckim@starpower.net.

KIM, KI HANG, mathematician; b. Moon Duck, Pyongnam, Korea, Aug. 5, 1936; arrived in U.S., 1953; s. Jin Gyong Kim and Mee Lan Hong; m. Myong Ja Kim, Aug. 1, 1963; children: John Churl, Linda Youngmee. BS in Math., U. So. Miss., 1960, MS in Math., 1961; PhD in Math., George Washington U., 1971. Instr. math. U. Hartford, 1961—66; lectr. math. George Washington U., Washington, 1970—72; assoc. prof. math. St. Mary's Coll. Md., St. Mary's City, Md., 1970—72, U. N.C., Pembroke, 1972—74; prof. math. Ala. State U., Montgomery, 1974—83, disting. prof. math., 1983—. Vis. prof. U. Lisbon, 1974, Stuttgart (Germany) U., 1978, Chinese Acad. Scis., Beijing, 1983. Editor-in-chief: jour. Math. Social Scis., 1981—94; editor: Jour. Pure and Applied Math., 1987—, (jour.) Future Generations Computer Sys., 1983—; author: 7 advanced math. books. Specialist U.S. Army, 1955—57. Grantee, NSF, 1971—. Home: 416 Arrowhead Dr Montgomery AL 36117 Office: Ala State U 915 S Jackson St Montgomery AL 36101 E-mail: kkim@asu.alasu.edu.

KIM, KUN-KIL, emergency medicine physician; b. Taegu, Korea, 1944; came to U.S., 1975; MD, Nat. U., Taegu, 1969. Cert. in emergency medicine. Rotating intern U. Alta. Hosp., Edmonton, Canada, 1972—74; resident in gen. surgery Jewish Meml. Hosp., N.Y.C., 1975—76; resident in gen. practice Jackson Park Hosp., Chgo., 1976—78; emergency rm. physician Palisades Gen. Hosp., Bergen, NJ. Mem. AMA, Am. Coll. Emergency Physicians, Med. Soc. N.J. Office: Palisades Gen Hosp Emergency Room 7600 River Rd North Bergen NJ 07047

KIM, KWAHNG SOO, finance educator; b. Kim Chun, KyungSang BukDo, Korea (South), Dec. 5, 1956; s. Jong Dae and HeeSoon Kim; m. EunHee Kim, Jan. 3, 1985; 1 child, Jin Young. BS in Polit. Sci., U Bridgeport; MBA, U. Bridgeport, 1992, MS in Indsl. Rels., 1994; PhD in Mgmt. Sys., U. New Haven, 2000. Adj. prof. U. New Haven, West Haven, 1997—2000, U. Hartford, Conn., 1999—2000; asst. prof. Fitchburg (Mass.) State Coll., 2000—. Dir. Jinhung Optical Mfg. Inc., Daegu, Daegu City, Korea (South), 1985—92. Assoc. editor: North Ctrl. Jour.; contbr. articles to profl. jours. Mem.: Acad. Mgmt., Alpha Beta Gamma. Republican. Office: Fitchburg State College 160 Peral Street Department of Business Fitchburg MA 01420 Personal E-mail: kw_kim@msn.com.

KIM, KWAN EUN, nephrologist, educator; b. Wejoo, Republic of Korea, Dec. 2, 1933; arrived in U.S., 1961, naturalized, 1973; s. Chul Ryun Kim and Kap Wna Lee; m. Jung Sun Kim, Feb. 23, 1963 (dec. Dec. 27, 1999); children: Kenneth Samuel, John Hyunsnik. MD, Yonsei U., Seoul, Republic of Korea, 1959. Diplomate Am. Bd. Internal Medicine, 1968, Am. Bd. Nephrology, 1972. Intern Kings County Hosp., Bklyn.; resident in internal med., 1963—67; resident in nephrology and hypertension, 1963—67; from sr. instr. in medicine to prof. Hahnemann Med. Coll., Phila., 1969—76, prof. medicine, 1976—, dir. Renal-Hypertension Lab., 1970—. Mem. adv. bd. Coun. High Blood Pressure Am. Heart Assn., 1978—84. Co-editor: Hypertension: Mechanisms and Management, 1973, Blood Pressure Regulation by Central Nervous System, 1976, Hypertension in the Young and Old, 1981; reviewer: profl. jours.; contbr. more than 140 articles to profl. jours. Recipient Academic Achievement award, Yonse U., 1999, Dr. Charles D. Schwartz Excellence in Tchng. award, Drexel U. Sch. of Med., 2003; grantee, NIH; scholar, Searle Co., 1975, Merck Co., 1994. Fellow: ACP, Am. Coll. Cardiology, Am. Heart Assn. (mem. coun. for high blood pressure rsch. 1984—); mem.: Internat. Soc. Nephrology, Am. Soc. Nephrology, Internat. Soc. Hypertension, Am. Soc. Hypertension (specialist in clin. hypertension 1999—), Chapel of Four Chaplains (legion of honor 1980). Home: 8 Pikes Way Cheltenham PA 19012 Office: Hahnemann Univ Hospital MS 245 245 North 15th Street Philadelphia PA 19102

KIM, KYOU YUNG, economist, educator; b. Jinahn, South Korea, June 6, 1951; s. Chong Keun Kim and Sun Keum Lee; m. Joo Yung Yoon, July 7, 1951; children: Jung Hoon, Tai Ho. BA, Seoul Nat. U., 1975, MBA, 1981; PhD, U. Pa., 1986. Fin. officer Naval Corps, Kimhai, South Korea, 1975-78; fellow Korea Internat. Econ. Inst., Seoul, 1978-81; vis. asst. prof. Ariz. State U., Tempe, 1986-87; sr. fellow Korea Econ. Rsch. Inst., Seoul, 1987-89; exec. dir. Ssangyong Investment Corp., Seoul, 1989-91; vis. scholar Hoover Inst., Palo Alto, Calif., 1996-97; prof. fin. Chosun U., Kwangju, South Korea, 1991—. Author: Understanding Modern Investment Theory, 1998; contbr. articles to profl. jours. Mem. Korea Securities Assn., Korean Fin. Assn., Assn. Korean Fin. Mgmt. Office: Coll Bus Chosun U 375 Seosukdong Dongku Kwangju 501-759 Republic of Korea

KIM, KYUNG-SUN, library and information scientist, educator; b. Seoul, South Korea, 1964; came to U.S., 1994; d. Jin-Guil and Ha-Woon (Ahn) K. BA, Duksung U., Seoul, 1987; MA, U. Montreal, 1994; PhD, U. Tex., Austin, 1998. Asst. prof. U. Mo., Columbia, 1998-2001, U. Wis., Madison, 2001—. Reviewer Interactive Learning and Info. Sys., 1999—, Jour. Libr. and Info. Sci. Edn., 2000—, Libr. Resources and Tech. Svcs., 2000—; contbr. articles to profl. jours. Mem. ALA, Assn. Computing Machinery, Assn. Libr. and Info. Sci. Edn., Am. Soc. Info. Sci. and Tech. Office: U Wis 4217 HC White Hall 600 North Park St Madison WI 53706

KIM, LILLIAN G. LEE, retired administrative assistant; b. Toishan, Canton, China, June 17, 1919; came to the U.S., 1921; d. Yick You and Lucy Yu Oy (Louie) Lee; m. Herman Hom Kim, Oct. 12, 1941. Cert., Ea. U., 1941. Stenographer, sec. Peabody Book Shop, Balt., 1937-38; sec. Prisoners Aid Assn., Balt., 1938-41; sec. Civilian Def. Exec. Office Balt. Mcpl. Govt., 1942-44, sec. to safety dir., 1944-48; sec.-stenographer, asst. supr. stenography divsn. Ctrl. Payroll Bur., 1948-64, adminstrv. sec., supr. adminstrv. and stenographic sect., 1946-63, supr. adminstrv. sect., 1964-77; ret., 1977. Ctrl. payroll councilwoman Classified Mcpl. Employee Assn., Balt., 1949-77, columnist Hall Light, 1950-77; chair ret. employee group CHICA-Combined Health/Industry Comb. Appeal and United Way, Balt., 1970-77; bd. dirs. Women's Civic League; pres., bd. dirs. AARP (Rodgers Forge Chpt. 2360), 1996-, publicity and pub. rels. officer, corr. sec., 1997-99; lectr. in field. Author: (with Lee Yick You and Louie Yu Oy) Early Baltimore Chinese Families, 1976, Chinese Americans-A Part of America, 1977; Letters to the Editor: (tribute to Marhsall Sisters) History of Grace & St. Peter's Chinese Ch. Sch., 1975, Tien Nien Poems, Lectures, and Speeches, Gnin-Gnin's China: Our Heritage, 1980, Grace and St. Peter's Chinese Church School (founders Frances L. and Florence M. "Daisy" Marshall), Chinese Traditions, Customs, and Festivals; author short stories, essays, 1960-70; edit. publ. Wah Kue Sim Mon (bilingual news bull.), 1998, Tien Nien Chatter; cmty. news columnist Towson Times, 1978—; freelance writer Senior Digest, 1990—; Gone But Not Forgotten: Nostalgic Maryland Memories, 1993, editor-pub. Tien Nien Chatter, 1946-60; contbg. writer Hall Light, 1950-77. Founder Chinese Young People's Fellowship, sec., mem. pub. rels. sect. 1946-60, pres., 1960-65; mem. Senator Charles Mc-Mathias Jr.s' Select. Immigration Com., 1960s; founder, exec. sec. Grace and St. Peter's Bilingual Chinese Lang. Sch., Balt., 1954-73, supr., 1964-85, dir., prin., 1974—, compiler evening prayer svc. and hymn book; vestrywoman Grace and St. Peter's Ch., Balt., mem. parish activity planning, 1969—, compiler bilingual evening prayer svc.; sec. bd. trustees Grace and St. Peter's Sch., Balt., 1980-86, trustee, 1987-90; exec. bd. Boy Scouts Am., 1978-95; bd. dirs. Women's Civic League, 1979-82, exec. bd., 1999; mem. Bishop's Guild, Diocese of Md., 1960-99; mem. Holly Tour Com., Inc. of Balt., 1975-85, sec., 1978-82; sec., pub. rels. Chinese Women's Assn. Balt., 1937-46; Chinese interpreter of Am. laws, social security taxes, federal and state taxes to Chinese; represented Chinese immigrants in cts. as a vol.; advocate Family Reunionifications, Canton, Balt., 1964; participant Testimonial Dinner Tribute to Councilman Leon A. Rubenstein, Senator Charles McMathias Retirement Dinner; spkr. Tribute to Senator Barbara A. Mikulski; del. to Md. Diocesan Conv., selected lay reader Diocesan Conv. Holy Eucharist Svc., St. Anne's Ch., Annapolis, numerous other diocesan activities; cmty. advocate Dept Justice, Immigration and Naturalization Svc., 1997—; initator, coord. Grace and St. Peter's Chinese Lunar New Yr., Balt.; compiler bilingual citizenship study guide; mem. exec. bd. Boy Scouts Am., 1978-1995; organizer Tiger Club program; apptd. to serve on Senator Charles McMathias Jr.'s select immigration com., 1960s. Recipient awards, including Spl. Baltimorean award, 1976, Balt.'s Best Blue and Silver awards, numerous times, award for outstanding svc. in promoting internat. rels., Carnation Volunteerism award, Balt. City Outstanding Woman of Yr. award, Baltimore County Exec. Proclamation, 1985, Balt. County Woman of Yr., 1986, GERI award, 1990, Baltimore County Execs.'s Baltimore County Exec. citation-Humanitarian award honoree, 1993, Gold 13 medal WJZ-TV, Exec. Citation Humanitarian award Baltimore County, Golden Rule award JC Penney's, Best of Towson, 1998, First Place Best Vol. award Readers of Towson Times, 1998; Congratulatory Honors award Club 88 Tchrs. of Lyndhurst Elem. Sch. No. 88), 1999, award for outstanding svc. tchg. and promoting lang., culture, tradition, and history Coordination Coun. for N.Am. Affairs, Dist. Svc. to Balt. Chinese Cmty. award Balt. chpt. Orgn. Chinese Ams., Outstanding Achievement award Dorothy G. Reddick, 1999, Feast of the Dedication cert. of appreciation Grace and St. Peter's Parish, 1999, My Most Significant Memory of 20th Century award Dept. Aging, 2000. Mem. AARP (pub. rels. dir., bd. dirs.), Episcopal Asiamerica Ministry (parish rep. 1975-93, diocesan rep. 1994—), DAR (medal of honr.), Walters Art Mus., Balt. Mus. Art, Md. Hist. Soc., Stars Spangled Banner Assn., Johns Hopkins Alumni Assn., UCLA Alumni Assn., Washington Nat. Episcopal Cathedral Assn., Ellis Island Found.-Statue of Liberty, Chinese Hist. Soc. Am. (life), Chinese Hist. Soc. So. Calif. (life), Assn. Chinese Schs., Chinese Lang. Tchrs. Assn., Crozier Soc. Md. Assn. of Deaf, Historic Towson, Inc., Balto Coun. Fgn. Affairs, Reagan Ranch, W Y P R Radio News Sta., Friends of Nat. Parks at Gettysburg, U.S. Capitol Hist. Soc., Nat. Trust for Historic Presevation, Chesapeake Bay Found. Democrat. Episcopalian. Avocations: community service, gardening, bowling, reading. Home: 524 Anneslie Rd Baltimore MD 21212-2009 Office: Grace & St Peters Chinese Lang Sch 707 Park Ave Baltimore MD 21201-4703

KIM, MARIANNE WEISS, humanities educator; b. Herrenberg, Württemberg, Germany, June 24, 1938; arrived in U.S., 1962; d. Karl Bernhard Weiss and Helene Dengler; m. Norman Won Kim, Jan. 24, 1963; children: Christine V. Levy, Bernard C. BA in Speech Pathology, U. Houston, 1985, BA in German Lit., 1986, MA in German Lit., 1989. Instr. U. Houston, 1986—88; lectr. Dillard U., New Orleans, 1990—92. Adj. assoc. prof. Tulane U., New Orleans. Mem. Trinity Ch. Episcopal, New Orleans, 1993—2003. Mem.: AAUP, Tulane Univ. Women's Assn. (treas. 2002—03), Am. Recorder Tchrs. Assn. (bd. dirs. 2001—), Am. Assn. Tchrs. German (bd. dirs. 2001—), Delta Phi Alpha, Golden Key. Avocations: music, gardening, art.

KIM, MI JA, dean, academic administrator; b. Seoul, Republic of Korea, Jan. 23, 1940; came to U.S., 1966; d. Si Hyung and Jung Kwon (Ahn) Lee; m. Heung Soo Kim, Jan. 14, 1964; children: Yoon Hi and Joseph. BS in Nursing, Yon Sei U., Seoul, 1962; PhD in Physiology, U. Ill., Chgo., 1975; JD (hon.), North Park Coll., 1995. Staff nurse Severance Hosp., Seoul, 1962-63; health nurse Am. Embassy, Seoul, 1963-66; asst. prof. Coll. Nursing/Univ. Ill., Chgo., 1975-79, assoc. prof., 1979-84, prof., 1984—, assoc. dean for rsch. dir. of grad. studies and assoc. dean acad. affairs, 1984-88, acting dean, 1988-89, dean, 1989-95, vice chancellor for rsch. and dean of grad. coll., 1995-99, dir. Acad. of Internat. Leadership Devel., 2001—. Cons. Nat. Ctr. Nursing Rsch., Bethesda, Md., 1987-91, Bd. Regents Higher Edn., Boston, 1989, WHO, Geneva, 2000, Nat. Inst. Gen. Med. Scis., NIH, 2000; mem. nat. adv. coun. Nat. Ins Mem. adv. bd. Health of the Pub., PEW Charitable Trust, Robert Wood Johnson found., 1992-96; adv. coun. Ctr. Bioethics and Human Dignity, 1994—. Named 100 Most Influential Women in Chgo., Chgo. Tribune, 1991, Univ. Scholar, U. Ill., 1985-88, Outstanding Nurse Educator, Korean Nurses Assn., Seoul, 1983; recipient Disting. Health and Edn. award Midwest Cmty. Coun. Chgo., 1994, Book of Yr. award Am. Jour. Nursing, 1984, Golden Apple award, students of Coll. Nursing, U. Ill., 1976, 78; Fulbright scholar Yon Sei U., Seoul, 2001. Fellow Am. Acad. Nursing; mem. North Am. Nursing Diagnosis (bd. dirs. 1985-92), Am. Thoracic Soc., Chgo. Lung Assn. (bd. dirs. 1977-97, Leadership Recognition award 1996), Chgo. Heart Assn. (bd. govs. 1980-88), Am. Physiol. Soc., Internat. Leadership Inst. (adv. coun. 1998-99), Sigma Theta Tau (Disting. lectr. 1987, Mary Tolle Wright award for Excellence in Leadership, 1997). Avocation: golf. Office: U Ill Chgo Rm 1156 Coll of Nursing Chicago IL 60612-7350 E-mail: mjkuic@uic.edu.

KIM, MICHAEL CHARLES, lawyer; b. Honolulu, Mar. 9, 1950; s. Harold Dai You and Maria Adrienne K. Student, Gonzaga U., 1967-70; BA, U. Hawaii, 1971; JD, Northwestern U., 1976. Bar: Ill. 1977, U.S. Dist. Ct. (no. dist.) Ill. 1977, U.S. Ct. Appeals (7th cir.) 1981, U.S. Supreme Ct. 1986. Assoc. counsel Nat. Assn. Realtors, Chgo., 1977-78; assoc. Rudnick & Wolfe, Chgo., 1978-83, Rudd & Assocs., Hoffman Estates, Ill., 1983-85; ptnr. Rudd & Kim, Hoffman Estates and Chgo., 1985-87; prin. Michael C. Kim & Assocs., Chgo. and Schaumburg, Ill., 1987-88; ptnr. Martin, Craig, Chester & Sonnenschein, Chgo. and Schaumburg, 1988-91, Arnstein & Lehr, Chgo., 1991—. Gen. counsel Assn. Sheridan Condo-Coop Owners, Chgo., 1988—; adj. prof. John Marshall Law Sch., Chgo. Author column Apt. and Condo News, 1984-87; co-author Historical and Practice Notes; contbr. articles to profl. jours. Bd. dirs. Astor Villa Condo Assn., Chgo., 1987-91, 2002—, treas. 1987-89, 2002—, sec., 2002. Mem. ABA, Chgo. Bar Assn. (chmn condominium law subcom. 1990-92, chmn. real property legis. subcom. 1995-97, vice chmn. real property law com., 1998-99, chmn. real proprty law com. 1999-2000), Ill. State Bar Assn. (real estate law sect. coun. 1990-94, corp. and securities law sect. coun. 1990-92), Asian Am. Bar Assn. Greater Chgo. Area (bd. dirs. 1987-88, 90-91), Cmty. Assns. Inst. Ill. (bd. dirs. 1990-92, pres. 1992), Coll. Cmty. Assn. Lawyers (bd. govs. 1994-98), Univ. Club (Chgo.). Avocations: squash, photography, travel. Office: Arnstein & Lehr 120 S Riverside Plz Ste 1200 Chicago IL 60606-3910

KIM, MOON HYUN, endocrinologist, educator; b. Seoul, Korea, Nov. 30, 1934; s. Jae Hang and Kum Chu (Choi) K.; m. Yong Cha Pak, June 20, 1964; children: Peter, Edward. MD, Yonsei U., 1960. Diplomate: Am. Bd. Ob-Gyn. (examiner 1979-98). Sr. instr. Ob-Gyn Yonsei U., Seoul, 1967-68; intern Md. Gen. Hosp., Balt., 1961-62; resident in Ob-Gyn Cleve. Met. Gen. Hosp., 1962-66; fellow in reproductive endocrinology U. Wash., Seattle, 1966-67, U. Toronto, Ont., Can., 1968-70; asst. prof. Ob-Gyn, also chief endocrinology and infertility U. Chgo., 1970-74; asso. prof. Ob-Gyn Ohio State U., Columbus, 1974-78, prof., 1978-92, chief div. reproductive endocrinology, 1974-92, vice chmn. dept. ob-gyn, 1982-96. Richard L. Meiling chair in ob-gyn., Ohio State U., 1987-98; prof. U. Calif., Irvine, 1998—. Editor: Am. Jour. Ob-Gyn., 1990-2002, editor-in-chief, 2003--; contbg. author books; contbr. articles to profl. jours. Recipient McClintock award U. Chgo., 1975; named Prof. of Yr. Ohio State U., 1976; recipient Clin. Teaching award, 1980 Fellow Am. Coll. Ob-Gyn; mem. Am. Gynecol. and Obstetric Soc., Am. Fertility Soc., Chgo. Gynecol. Soc., Endocrine Soc., Soc. Study Reprodn., Soc. Gynecol. Investigation. Home: 24 Whistler Ct Irvine CA 92612-4069 Office: Univ Calif Irvine Med Ctr 101 The City Dr S Bldg 22A Orange CA 92868-3201

KIM, NAM-DEUK, electrical engineer, researcher; b. Munkyung, South Korea, Mar. 7, 1971; came to U.S., 1993; s. Joong-Ki Kim and Oksoon Pan; m. Jungyun Lee, May 25, 1996; children: Hyunrae, Wonrae. BS, Kwangwoon U., Seoul, South Korea, 1992; MS, Iowa State U., 1995, PhD, 2000. Rsch. asst. Ctr. Nondestructive Evaluation, Ames, Iowa, 1994-2000, Coll. Vet. Medicine, Ames, 1996-97, Iowa State U., Ames, 2000—; sr. R&D engr. Digimarc, Burlington, Mass., 2003—. Scholar Iowa State U., 1998-99; fellowship NAFSA. Mem. IEEE, SPIE. Avocations: basketball, singing. Home: 26 Lucerne Dr Andover MA 01810 Office: 63 Third Ave Burlington MA 01803 E-mail: namdeuk@yahoo.com.

KIM, NICOLE Y. music educator, pianist; b. Daegu, Republic of Korea, Dec. 23, 1958; arrived in U.S., 1982; d. Kirin Choi and Ock Ryun Um; 1 child from previous marriage, Lowell. MusB, Seoul Nat. U., Korea, 1980; MusM, San Francisco Conservatory of Music, 1984; MusD, U. So. Cal., LA, 1993. Cert. NCTM, Music Tchrs Nat. Assn., 2003. Ch. pianist Korean Meth. Ch. in LA, 1986—87; instr. LA Conservatory, 1987—89; prof. Cerritos Coll., Norwalk, Calif., 1996—98, Suwon Women's Coll., Republic of Korea, 1999—2000; owner and head tchr. Dr. Kim's Piano Studio, Bellevue, Wash., 2000—. Adjudicator Young Musicians Competition, LA, 1991; soloist Music of City of Bellflower, Bellflower, Calif., 1998. Performer concerts and recitals. Named award winner, Joanna Hodge Internat. Piano Competition, 1985. Mem.: Wash. State Music Tchrs. Assn. Avocations: painting, carpentry, reading.

KIM, PAUL DONGUK, academic administrator, religious organization administrator, minister; s. SuHak and Jung Kim; m. Haekyong Lydia Kim, Apr. 22, 1983; children: Moses Hee, Hanna Hee. Ordained minister, cert. Christian counselor. Pres. World Evang. Mission, Ambler, Pa., 1992—; chmn. bd. of trustees Henderson Christian U., Cramerton, NC, 1999—. Named Hon. Citizen, City of Little Rock, 1992; named to Order of the Long Leaf Pine, State of N.C., 1993; recipient cert. of appreciation, City of Charlotte, N.C., 1997. Republican. Office: Henderson Christian U 288 8th Ave Cramerton NC 28032 Fax: 704-823-7749. E-mail: hendersonunivorg@aol.com.

KIM, PETER SUNGBAI, pharmaceutical executive, educator; b. Atlanta, Apr. 27, 1958; s. Mi Heh (Ryu) K.; m. Kathryn H. Spitzer; children: Michael, Jeremy, Alexander. AB magna cum laude with distinction, Cornell U., 1979; PhD, Stanford U., 1985. Whitehead fellow Whitehead Inst., Cambridge, 1985-88, assoc. mem., 1988-92; asst. prof. biology MIT, Cambridge, 1988-92, assoc. prof., 1992-95; asst investigator Howard Hughes Med. Inst., Cambridge, 1990—93, assoc. investigator, 1993—97, investigator, 1997—2001; mem. Whitehead Inst., Cambridge, 1992-2001; prof. MIT, Cambridge, 1995-2001; exec. v.p. R&D Merck Rsch. Labs., West Point, Pa., 2001—02, pres., 2003—. Recipient Excellence in Chemistry award ICI Pharms., 1989, Walter J. Johnson prize Jour. Molecular Biology, 1989, Nat. Acad. Sci. Molecular Biology award, 1993, Eli Lilly Biol. Chemistry award Am. Chem. Soc., 1994, DuPont Merck Young Investigator award Protein Soc., 1994, Ho-Am. prize for basic sci. Samsung Found., 1998, Hans Neurath award The Protein Soc., 1999. Fellow AAAS, Biophys. Soc., Am. Acad. Microbiology; mem. NAS, Inst. Medicine. Office: Merck Rsch Labs WP14-3500 770 Sumneytown Pike West Point PA 19486

KIM, PYUNG-SOO, martial arts educator; b. Seoul, Korea, Dec. 4, 1939; came to U.S., 1968; s. Chong Won and Duk In (Lee) Kim; m. Sonnya Park Kim; children: Sean Kim, Tasha Kim. BA in Russian Lang. and Lit., Han Kuk U. Fgn. Studies, Seoul, 1963. 10th degree Black Belt, 1994. Founder Kong Soo Do Club, Joong Ang H.S., Seoul, 1954, Kwon Bop Martial Arts Club, Han Kuk U. Fgn. Studies, Seoul, 1957-63; tchr. Spl. Police Detachment Korean Pres., 1958; tchr. hand-to-hand combat tng. Republic of Korea Army, 8th Divsn., 1961-63; founder Korean Tae Kwon/Karate Acad., Seoul, 1963; chief instr. Kang Duk Won Martial Arts Assn., Seoul, 1964, 8th U.S. Army and HQ I Corps, 1964-67, founder Kim Soo Coll. Tae Kwon-Karate, Houston, 1968, ChaYon-Ryu, Houston, 1970—; founding pres. Byung in Martial Arts Friendship Assn., Houston, 1994-97. Lectr. in field; faculty martial arts instr. U. Houston and Rice U., 1970—; Tae Kwon Do coord. U.S. Olympic Festival '86, Houston; fight choreographer Houston Grand Opera, 1986; presdl. appt. to Com. on Unification of Korea, 1986-93; advisor World Martial Arts Coun., 1990; mem. adv. bd. Asia Houston Network. Editor, corr. Black Belt Mag., 1964-67; author: Palgue 1,2,3, 1973, Palgue 4,5,6, 1974, Palgue 7 & 8: Black Belt Requirements, 1976, History of ChaYon-Ryu, 1990, Chayon-Ryu, Taekwondo, 2000 (in Russian). Advisor Asia Houston Network. Recipient citation for contbn. to elevating Korean nat. image in world Korean Govt., 1970, Leadership commendation Mayor Kathy Whitmire, 1987, commendation U.S. Pres. Bill Clinton, 1993, 98, Ednl. Leadership citation Gov. Ann Richards, 1993, Gov. G.W. Bush, 1998, Leadership commendation Mayor Bob Lanier, 1993, Lifetime Achievement award of honor World karate Union Hall of Fame, 1997, Leadership Commendation, Mayor Lee Brown, 2003, Leadership citation, Gov. Rick Perry, 2003; named Best Karate Instr. in Houston, Houston Press, 1990, Grandmaster of the Yr., Tex. Martial Arts Hall of Fame, Man of Yr. Am. All-Open Hall of Fame, 1991, World Karate Union Hall of Fame, Internat. Martial Arts Hall of Fame, 1997. Avocation: golf. Office: ChaYon-Ryu Internat Martial Arts Assn 1740 Jacquelyn Dr Houston TX 77055-3604 E-mail: kimsookarate@ev1.net., kimsoo@ev1.net.

KIM, SAN-KY, vocalist; BA, Australian Nat. U., Australia, 1985; MusB, Australian Nat. U. Inst. of Arts Music, 1988; MusM, Curtis Inst. of Music, 1991. Soloist Czech Nat. Theater, Prague, Czech Republic, 1991—93, Bieler Stadts Theater, Biel, Switzerland, 1993—94, Theater Vorpommern, Stralsund, Germany, 1995—97, Coburger Stadts Theater, Coburg, Germany, 1997—2000; fellow Temple U., Phila., 2000—. Recipient New Zealand Found. award, Australia, 1988. Home: 4519 Regent St Philadelphia PA 19143 Office: Esther Boyer Coll of Music Temple U 2001 N 13th St Philadelphia PA 19122

KIM, SEOCK-HO, educator; b. Pusan, South Korea, Feb. 20, 1961; came to U.S., 1984; s. Duk-Joon Kim and Myung-Hwa Yoon; m. Mi-Ran Cho, Aug. 16, 1987; children: Naanhee Kristin, Yoonhee Kathleen. BA, Korea U., Seoul, 1983; MS, U. Wis., 1986, PhD, 1991. Asst. scientist U. Wis., Madison, 1991-95; asst. prof. U. Ga., Athens, 1995-2001, assoc. prof., 2001—. Contbr. articles to profl. jours. 2d lt. Korean Army, 1997-98. Fellow Ctr. for Future Human Resource Studies, Seoul, 1996—. Mem. APA, Am. Ednl. Rsch. Assn., Am. Statis. Assn., Inst. Math. Stats., Nat. Coun. Measurement in Edn., Psychometric Soc. Home: 1180 Chaddwyck Dr Athens GA 30606-7004 Office: U Ga 325 Aderhold Hall Athens GA 30602 E-mail: skim@coe.uga.edu.

KIM, SEUNG-LAE, accounting educator, researcher; b. Seoul, Republic of Korea, May 4, 1949; arrived in U.S., 1984; s. Kyu-Ha Lee; m. Lois Kye-Sook Kim, Oct. 20, 1979; children: Eunice Yun-Kyung, Jane Elizabeth. BA, Korea U., Seoul, 1972, MBA, 1975; PhD, Pa. State U., 1989. Asst. prof. Kang Won Nat. U., Chun-chon, Republic of Korea, 1980—84; instr. Pa. State U., State College, 1984—88; asst. prof. Drexel U., Phila., 1989—96, assoc. prof., 1996—. Contbr. articles to profl. jours. Ch. elder, Bible tchr. Emmanuel Ch. (PCA), Phila., 2001—03. Presbyterian. Avocations: fishing, table tennis, tennis. Office: LeBow Coll Bus Drexel Univ Decision Sciences 33rd & Arch St Philadelphia PA 19104

KIM, SOOK CHA, artist; b. Choong-Joo, Korea, Mar. 30, 1940; arrived in U.S., 1973; d. Kyung Nam Chai and Choon Yi Lim; m. Myung Hak Kim, Dec. 5, 1967; 1 child, Young Kyoon. BFA, Hong-Ik U., 1965, MFA, 1967. Owner Morning Star Art Gallery, Washington, 1995—2003. Featured artist New Art Internat. 1997 Edit.; group exhibits Gallery Close. Recipient Gold medal--Art Addiction Internat. prize Most Talented Artists Competition, Sweden, 1997, Cert. of Merit 6th Internat. Female Artist Art Exhbn. on Internet Art Mus., 1999. Home: 6540 Braddock Rd Alexandria VA 22312-2206

KIM, STEVE, music educator, musician; b. Tacoma, Jan. 6, 1955; m. Deirdre Marie Curle, May 17, 1999; 1 child, Angela West. Pvt. studies with Gary Peacock, 1975—77, pvt. studies with Ray Brown, 1985—85, pvt. studies with Charles Banacos, 1985—2003. Composer Bill Evans Dance Co., 1980—88; bassist Scott Cossu, 1985—90; assoc. prof. Pacific Luthern U., Tacoma, 1991—92, Shoreline (Wash.) C.C., 1997—; bassist Larry Coryell, 1998—98, Alphonse Mouzon, 1998—98. Cultural amb. City of Seattle, 1987—87; centennial artist Wash. State Centennial Commn., 1989—89. Composer: Three Themes from Josephine (Individual Artist Grant, 1985); musician (composer/producer): (recording) Apologies To The Great White Hope; composer: (film score) The Man From Wakpala. Scholar, Ford Found., 1974. Mem.: Am. Fedn. Musicians. Home: 4952 Thirteenth Ave South Seattle WA 98108 Office: Shoreline Community College 16101 Greenwood Ave Shoreline WA 98133-5667 Personal E-mail: kimspeak@qwest.net.

KIM, SUNG WAN, educator; b. Pusan, South Korea, Aug. 21, 1940; came to U.S., 1966; BS, MS, Seoul U.; PhD, U. Utah. Asst. rsch. prof. U. Utah, Salt Lake City, 1971-73, asst. prof., 1974-76, assoc. prof., 1977-79, prof., 1980—, dir. Ctr. Controlled Chemical Delivery, 1986—. Mem. study section SGYB, NIH, Bethesda, Md., 1985-89, 95—. Editor numerous books; patentee in field; contbr. articles to profl. jours. Recipient Founders award CRS, 1995, Clemson Basic Rsch. award Biomaterials Soc., 1987, Gov.'s medal for sci., State of Utah, 1989, Inst. Soc. Blood Purification award, 1995. Fellow Am. Assn. Pharm. Sci., Am. Inst. Med. Bioengring, Biomaterials Soc. Home: 1711 Devonshire Dr Salt Lake City UT 84108-2362 Office: U Utah Ctr Controlled Chem Delivery 30 52000 E BPRB Rm 201 Salt Lake City UT 84112

KIM, TAESOO, language educator; s. Seok Bong and Ki Hang Kim; m. Myong J. Kim, Oct. 4, 1986; children: Alice, Aron, Ana. BA in Edn. of 2d Lang., Jeon Ju U., Republic of Korea, 1983; BS in Polit. Sci., Han Kuk U. of Fgn. Studies, Seoul, 1987. Instr., Korean U. Anchorage, 1990—; tchr. Korean Lang. Sch., Anchorage, 1990—99; owner Radio Korea Alaska, Anchorage, 1993—99. Master Champ Tae Kwon Do Sch., Anchorage, 1989—; pres. Tae Kwon Do Alaska, Anchorage, 2002—. Editor: The Korea Post, 1999—2000. Exec. dir. Korean Cmty. of Anchorage, 1990—94. Office: Super Com LLC 700 W 6th Ave #113-A Anchorage AK 99501 Office Fax: 907-349-4762. E-mail: tae soo kim@hotmail.com.

KIM, WAN HEE, electrical engineering educator, business executive; b. Osan, Korea, May 24, 1926; came to U.S., 1953, naturalized, 1962; s. Sang Chul and Duck Hyung (Chong) K.; m. Chung Sook Noh, Jan. 23, 1960; children: Millie, Richard K. B.E., Seoul Nat. U., 1950; MS in Elec. Engring, U. Utah, 1954, PhD, 1956. Research asst. U. Ill., Urbana, 1955-56; research staff IBM Research Ctr., Poughkeepsie, N.Y., 1956-57; asst. prof. Columbia U., N.Y.C., 1957-59, assoc. prof., 1959-63, prof. elec. engring., 1963-78; chmn., CEO Tech. Assessment Corp. Internat., 1991—. Chmn. Tech. Cons., Inc., N.Y.C., 1962-69; chmn. KOMKOR Am., Inc., N.Y.C., 1970-72; spl. advisor for the pres. and govt. Republic of Korea, 1967-79; advisor Korea Advanced Inst. Sci., Seoul, 1971-73; chmn. Korea Inst. Electronics Tech., 1977-81; mem. bd. Korea Telecommunication Electric Rsch. Inst., 1977-81; pres. WHK Engring. Corp. Am., 1982-84, WHK Electronics Inc., 1982-84; chmn., chief exec. officer Industries Assn. Electronic Korea, 1978-81; chmn. WHK Industries Inc., 1984-88, AEA Corp., WHK-FJF&M Assocs., 1988-89; pres. Asian Electronics Union, 1979-83; pub. Electronic Times of Korea, 1982-83, Dr. Kim Report on Korea, 1988-2001; cons. The World Bank, Washington, other indsl. orgns.; chmn., CEO Tech. Assessment Corp. Internat. (TACI), 1991—; bd. dirs., chmn. exec. com. Xentex Techs., Inc., 2000—. Author (with R.T. Chien): Topological Analysis and Synthesis of Communication Networks, 1962; author: (with H.E. Meadows) Modern Network Analysis, 1970; author: (Auto Biography) Embracing Two Suns, 1999, numerous articles, —. U.S. rep. on U.S.-Japan Scientists Coop. Program.; trustee U.S.-Asia Inst., Washington, 1984-88. Served with Korean Army, 1950-53. Decorated Bronze Star; recipient Achievement medal U.S.-Asia Inst., Industry medal Republic of Korea, 1989; Guggenheim grantee, 1964, NSF rsch. grantee, 1958-78. Fellow IEEE, Union Radio Scientifique Internat. (mem. U.S. nat. com. Commn. Band C 1963-78), Sigma Xi, Tau Beta Pi. Achievements include being honorarily named the father of Korean electronics industry for his contbrn. to promotion of industry. Home: PO Box 778 Palo Alto CA 94302-0778 E-mail: whkim@msn.com. *Be prepared five minutes earlier than others.*

KIM, YEONG K. polymer composite process specialist, researcher; b. Incheon, Korea, Feb. 21, 1958; s. Young H. and Sook K. (Park) K.; m. Hyewood Jung, Apr. 5, 1964; children: Brian, David. BS, Inha U., 1984, MS, 1986; PhD, U. Ill., 1996. Sr. rsch. engr. Korean Inst. Aerospace Tech., Seoul, 1986-98; rsch. assoc. Northwestern U., Evanston, Ill., 1998—2001; vis. scholar Ga. Inst. Tech., Atlanta, 2001—02; sr. scientist Samsung Co. Ltd., Seoul, Republic of Korea, 2002—. Reviewer Jour. Composite Materials, 1998—; contbr. articles to profl. jours. Mem. ASME, Am. Soc. Composites, Soc. for Advancement of Material and Process Engring. Avocations: travel, movies, music. Fax: 847-491-5227. E-mail: yeong.kim@ece.gatech.edu.

KIM, YONG CHOON, philosopher, theologian, educator; b. Kyongju, Korea, Jan. 1, 1935; came to U.S., 1958, naturalized, 1972; s. Chang Ho and Chung Ja (Choe) K.; m. Joyce Chungja Whang, Dec. 18, 1965; 1 dau., Grace. BA, Belhaven Coll., Jackson, Miss., 1960; Th.M., Westminster Theol. Sem., Phila., 1964; PhD, Temple U., 1969. Asst. prof. Asian studies York Coll., Pa., 1969-70; asst. prof. philosophy and religion Cleve. State U., 1970-71; asst. prof. philosophy U. R.I., Kingston, 1971-74, assoc. prof., 1974-79, prof., 1979—. Founder, dir. Korean-Am. Christian Studies Inst., 1981— Author: Oriental Thought, 1973, The Ch'ondogyo Concept of Man: An Essence of Korean Thought, 1978; cons. editor Dictionary World Philosophy, 2001; author, cons. editor Ency. of Asian Philosophy, 2001. Korean Culture and Arts Found. grantee, 1977; Korea Found. fellow, 1992. Mem. Assn. Asian Studies, Am. Acad. Religion, Soc. for Asian and Comparative Philosophy, AAUP, Korean-Am. Univ. Profs. Assn. (dir. Eastern region 1986-90, 97—, chair law and ethics com. 1990-96). Home: 134 Parkwood Dr Kingston RI 02881-1600 Office: Univ RI Dept Philosophy Kingston RI 02881 E-mail: yongkim@uri.edu.

KIM, YOON BERM, immunologist, educator; b. Pyongnam, Korea, Apr. 25, 1929; came to U.S., 1959, naturalized, 1975; s. Sang Sun and Yang Rang (Lee) K.; m. Soon Cha Kim, Feb. 23, 1959; children: John, Jean, Paul. MD, Seoul Nat. U., 1958; PhD, U. Minn., 1965. Intern Univ. Hosp. Seoul Nat. U., 1958-59; asst. prof. microbiology U. Minn., Mpls., 1965-70, assoc. prof., 1970-73; mem., head lab. ontogeny of immune system Sloan Kettering Inst. Cancer Research, Rye, N.Y., 1973-83; prof. immunology Cornell U. Grad. Sch. Med. Scis., N.Y.C., 1973-83, chmn. immunology unit, 1980-82; prof. microbiology, immunology and medicine, chmn. dept. micorbiology and immunology Finch U. Health Scis., Chgo. Med. Sch., 1983—, acting dean Sch. Grad. and Postdoctoral Studies, 1994-95. Mem. Lobund adv. bd. U. Notre Dame, 1977-88. Contbr. numerous articles on immunology to profl. jours. Recipient rsch. career devel. award USPHS, 1968-73, Morris Parker Meritorius Rsch. award U. Health Scis., Chgo. Med. Sch., 1984, Ham Choon Disinction in Med. Rsch. Grand prize Seoul Nat. U. Coll. Medicine Alumni Assn., 2003. Fellow Am. Acad. Microbiology; mem. AAAS, Korean Acad. Sci. and Tech., Assn. Gnotobiotics (pres.), Internat. Assn. for Gnotobiology (founding), Am. Assn. Immunologists, Am. Soc. Microbiology, Am. Assn. Pathologists, Korean-Am. Med. Assn., N.Y. Acad. Scis., Soc. for Leucocyte Biology, Internat. Soc. Devel. Comparative Immunology, Harvey Soc., Internat. Soc. Interferon and Cytokine Rsch., Korean Acad. Sci. and Tech., Chgo. Assn. Immunologists (pres.), Assn. Med. Sch. Microbiology and Immunology Chairs, Internat. Endotoxin Soc. (charter), Soc. Natural Immunity (charter), Sigma Xi, Alpha Omega Alpha. Achievements include discovery of the unique germfree dolostrum-deprived immunologically "virgin" piglet model used to investigate ontogenic development and regulation of the immune system including T/B lymphocytes, natural killer/killer cells, and macrophages; research on ontogeny and regulation of immune system, immunochemistry and biology of bacterial toxins, host-parasite relationships and gnotobiology. Home: 313 Weatherford Ct Lake Bluff IL 60044-1905 Office: Finch U Health Scis Chgo Med Sch 3333 Green Bay Rd North Chicago IL 60064-3037 E-mail: kimy@finchcms.edu.

KIM, YOUNG HO, orthodontist; b. Seoul, Korea, Oct. 17, 1927; came to U.S., 1952, naturalized, 1962; s. Woo Hyun and Doo Keum (Park) K.; m. Mazie Ann Lim, May 19, 1956; children: Stuart K., Jonathan C. D.D.S., Seoul Nat. U., 1949; M.S., U. Rochester, 1958; D.M.D., Tufts U., 1960. Diplomate Am. Bd. Orthodontists. Specialist in orthodontics, Weston, Mass., 1964— ; instr. Harvard Dental Sch., 1960-65; assoc. prof. Boston U. Grad. Sch. Dentistry, 1967-70; vis. clin. prof. Yonsei U. Coll. Dentistry, 1972; cons. VA Hosp., West Roxbury, Mass., 1974-83; assoc. clin. prof. Tufts U. Sch. Dental Medicine, 1981-92. Chmn. bd. trustees Myung Hwee Won Found., 1976-86; pres. North Atlantic Component of The Angle Soc. Orthodontists, 1989-90; pres. Multiloop Edgewise Arch-Wire Technic and Rsch. Found., 1991—. Mem. ADA, Am. Assn. Orthodontists, Mass. Dental Soc., Angle Soc. Orthodontists, Omicron Kappa Upsilon. Home: 396 Glen Rd Weston MA 02493-1403 Office: 30 Colpitts Rd Weston MA 02493-1534

KIM, YOUNG KIL, aerospace engineer; b. Pusan, Korea, June 18, 1956; came to U.S., 1984; naturalized, 1988; s. Tae Hyun and Myong Ok (Shin) K.; m. Susan Katherine Hong, July 16, 1981; children: Steven Charles, Christina Kay. BS, Seoul Nat. U., Rep. of Korea, 1979; MS, Ga. Inst. Tech., 1985, PhD in Aerospace Engring., 1991. Rsch. engr. Korean Inst. Aero. Tech. Korean Air Lines, Seoul, 1978-84; vis. rsch. engr. Agy. for Def. Devel., Daedog, Republic of Korea, 1981-82; rsch. assoc. Univs. Space Rsch. Assn., Huntsville, Ala., 1991-93; rsch. engr. U. Ala. Rsch. Inst., Huntsville, 1993-96; sr. rsch. engr. U. Ala. in Huntsville Rsch. Inst., 1996-2000; aerospace engr. NASA Marshall Space Flight Ctr., Ala., 2000—. Adj. prof. dept. mech. and aerospace engring. U. Ala., Huntsville, 2001 Mem. AIAA. Roman Catholic. Avocations: tennis, golf. Home: 9010 Cannstatt Dr SE Huntsville AL 35802-3716 Office: TD55 NASA/MSFC Huntsville AL 35812 E-mail: young.k.kim@nasa.gov.

KIM, YOUN-SUK ERNEST, economist, educator; b. Kwangju, Korea, Sept. 15, 1934; arrived in U.S., 1959, naturalized, 1977; m. Y. Hannar, Apr. 24, 1966; children: Y. Herb, Nancy Y., John Y. BA, Seoul Nat. U., 1958; MA, New Sch., 1967, PhD, 1973. Statistician Am. Photog. Corp., 1963—67; econometrician Candeub, Fleissig & Assocs., planning cons., 1968—70; adj. prof. Fairleigh Dickinson U., Teaneck, NJ, 1971—73; mem. faculty, asst. prof. Kean U., Union, NJ, 1974—78, assoc. prof. econs., 1979—84, prof., 1985—. Vis. prof. Seoul (Republic of Korea) Nat. U., 1987—88; vis. prof. grad. sch. Hankuk U., 1999; pres. Korean-Am. U. Profs. Assn., 1996—98. Author: Political Economics of U.S. Trade, 1988, Postwar Japan's Foreign Trade, 1991, Japanese Foreign Trade, 1992, U.S.-Korea Economic Partnership, 1995, Vision of Korea's Economy in the 21st Century, 1996, Economics of the Triad: Conflicts and Congruence of the U.S.A., Japan and Korea, 1997, New Economics, 1998, The IMF Program and Korean Economy, 2001, The Role of Government in Competitive Economies; mem. editl. bd. Human Sys. Mgmt.; editor: Internat. Jour. Korean Studies, 2001—; contbr. articles to profl. jours., also books. Nat. screening com. mem. (E. Asia) Inst. Internat. Edn. Fellow, Gateway Inst. for Regional Devel., 2001—; grantee, N.E. Asia Coun., Kean U., Korea Econ. Rsch. Inst., 1987. Mem.: Assn. Asian Studies, Korea-Am. Econ. Assn. (pres. 1993—), Japan Econ. Seminar, Atlantic Econ. Soc., Eastern Econ. Assn., Western Econ. Assn., Am. Econ. Assn. Democrat. Office: Kean Univ Morris Ave Union NJ 07083-7117 Home: Apt 24 1720 E Newport Ave Milwaukee WI 53211-2851 E-mail: ykim@kean.edu., younkim@aol.com.

KIM, ZAEZEUNG, allergist, immunologist, educator; b. Hamhung, Korea, Feb. 21, 1929; came to U.S., 1967; s. Suh and Suyeo (Hahn) K.; m. Youngju Kim, June 2, 1961; children: Keungsuk, Maria. Student, Hamhung Med. Coll., Korea, 1946-50; MD, Seoul U., Korea, 1960; PhD in Immunology, U. Cologne, Fed. Republic of Germany, 1968. Diplomate Am. Bd. Allergy and Immunology. Intern Seoul Nat. U. Hosp., 1960-61, resident in medicine, 1961-63, Heidelberg U. Hosp., Fed. Republic of Germany, 1963-64; research fellow Max-Planck Inst., Cologne, 1965-67; fellow in hematology U. Tex., Houston, 1967-68; resident in allergy and immunology Temple U. Hosp., Phila., 1968-69; fellow in medicine Ohio State U., Columbus, 1969-71; instr. medicine Med. Coll. Wis., Milw., 1972-75, asst. prof., 1975-78, assoc. clin. prof., 1978—; practice medicine specializing in allergy and immunology Racine, Wis. Contbr. articles to profl. jours. Fellow Am. Acad. Allergy and Immunology, Am. Coll. Allergists; mem. AMA. Home: 461 W Sunnyview Dr Apt 13 Oak Creek WI 53154-3893 Office: 461 W Sunnyview Dr Apt 13 Oak Creek WI 53154-3893

KIMANI, GRACE ALEXANDRA, internist; b. Peterborough, England, May 16, 1963; d. Astley and Salome (Taylor) Brown; m. Anthony Philip Kimani, July 23, 1988; children: Destiny, Daniel. BS, Oral Roberts U., 1988; MD, Morehouse Sch. Medicine, Atlanta, 1994. Diplomate Am. Bd. Internal Medicine. Intern Ga. Bapt. Med. Ctr., Atlanta, 1995-96, resident, 1996-98; pvt. practice Crawford Long Hosp. Mem. ethics com. Ga. Bapt. Med. Ctr.; presenter in field. Mem. AMA, Am. Coll. Physicians. Avocations: playing piano, tennis, novels, traveling, languages. Home: PO Box 54712 Atlanta GA 30308-0712

KIMBALL, BRUCE ARNOLD, soil scientist; b. Aitkin, Minn., Sept. 27, 1941; s. Robert Clinton and Rica (Barneveld) K.; m. Laurel Sue Hanway, Aug. 20, 1966; children: Britt, Rica, Megan. BS, U. Minn., 1963; MS, Iowa State U., 1965; PhD, Cornell U., 1970. Soil scientist USDA-Agrl. Rsch. Svc. U.S. Water Conservation Lab., Phoenix, 1969—, rsch. leader Environ. and Plant Dynamics Rsch. Group, 1990—. Editor: Impact of Carbon Dioxide, Trace Gases and Climate Change on Global Agriculture, 1990; co-editor: Carbon Dioxide Enrichment of Greenhouse Crops, 1986; assoc. editor Global Change Biology; contbr. articles to profl. jours. Named Highly Cited Rschr. in agr., Ins. for Sci. Info. Fellow: Am. Soc. Agronomy (chmn. program divsn. A3 1988, assoc. editor 1977—83, bd. dirs. 1994—97), Soil Sci. Soc. Am.; mem.: AAAS. Avocations: computers, biking. Office: US Water Conservation Lab 4331 E Broadway Rd Phoenix AZ 85040-8832

KIMBALL, CATHERINE D. state supreme court justice; b. Alexandria, La., Feb. 7, 1945; m. Clyde W. Kimball; 3 children. JD, La. State U., 1970. Law clerk US Dist. Court, Western Dist. La., 1970; spec. coun. La. Attorney Gen. Office, 1971—73; gen coun. La. Commn. Law Enforcement & Admin. Crim. Just., 1973—81; priv. law prac., 1975—82; judge La. Dist. Ct. (18th dist.), 1982—92; assoc. justice Supreme Ct. of La., 1992—. Office: Supreme Ct of La 301 Loyola Ave New Orleans LA 70112-1814

KIMBALL, CLYDE WILLIAM, physicist, educator; b. Laurium, Mich., Apr. 20, 1928; s. Clyde D. and Gertrude M. (O'Neil) K. BS in Engring. Physics, Mich. Coll. Mining and Tech., 1950, MS, 1952; PhD in Physics, St. Louis U., 1959. Staff scientist aeronutronic div. Ford Co., 1960-62; assoc. physicist Argonne Nat. Lab., Ill., 1962-64; prof. physics No. Ill. U., De Kalb, 1964—, Presdl. rsch. chair, 1982-86, rsch. prof., 1986-88, disting. prof., 1988—, advisor to pres. sci. and tech., 1982-88, dir. lab. for nanosci., engring. and tech., 2002—. Program dir. low temperature physics Materials Research Div., NSF, Washington, 1978-79; chair, bd. govs. Consortium for Advanced Radiation Sources, 1994—; exec. com. Basic Energy Sci. Synchrotron Rsch. Ctr., 1994—. Contbr. articles to profl. jours. Served with U.S. Army, 1952-54 Fellow Am. Phys. Soc.; mem. AAAS, Am. Assn. Physics Tchrs., Sigma Xi. Home: PO Box 842 Dekalb IL 60115-0842 Office: No Ill U Dept Physics Faraday West 217 Dekalb IL 60115

KIMBALL, CURTIS ROLLIN, financial analyst; b. Grand Rapids, Mich., Dec. 21, 1950; s. Rollin Hibbard and Jane Ann (Walterman) K.; m. Marilyn M. Quaderer; 1 child, Neil Curtis. BA, Duke U., 1972; MBA, Emory U., 1984. Comml. lending and trust portfolio mgr. Wachovia Bank and Trust Co. N.A., Winston-Salem, N.C., 1972-81; v.p., trust mgr. bus. owner svcs. group Citizens and So. Bank, Atlanta, 1981-88; prin., nat. dir. Willamette Mgmt. Assocs., Inc., Portland, Oreg., 1988—, mng. prin. Atlanta office Atlanta, 1995—. Chair activities coun. Portland Art Mus., 1993-94; bd. dirs. Cmty. Action Ctr.; founding mem. Ga. Shakespeare Festival, 1986; mem. AIMR-CFA. Fellow Inst. CFAs (coun. of examiners 1997, mem. disciplinary rev. com. 2000); mem. Am. Soc. Appraisers (sr. mem., pres. Atlanta chpt. 1985-86, treas. 1996-98, treas. Portland chpt. 1993-94, bus. valuation com., 2001-), Nat. Assn. Bus. Economists (pres. Portland chpt. 1992-93), Family Firm Inst., Inst. Mgmt. Accts., Employee Stock Ownership Plan Assn., Indian Hills Country Club. Republican. Episcopalian. Avocations: running, tennis. Office: Willamette Mgmt Assocs Inc 1355 Peachtree St NE Ste 1470 Atlanta GA 30309-3274

KIMBALL, DONALD ROBERT, retired food company executive; b. Anderson, Ind., Mar. 4, 1938; s. Robert Martin and Mary Lucille (Gibson) K.; m. Mari-Anne Talbot, Apr. 6, 1985; children: Randy, Rick, Sharon-Lee, Douglas, David. BS in Agr., Purdue U., 1960. Registered profl. sanitarian, Ind. Pub. health sanitarian Div. Dairy Products, Ind. Bd. Health, LaPorte, 1962-66, milk sanitation rating officer Indpls., 1966-75, chief milk sanitation rating officer, 1973-75, dir., 1975-87; dir. regulatory affairs Dean Foods Co., Rockford, Ill., 1987-2000, dir. farm rels., 1990-98, ret., 2000. Contbr. articles to profl. jours. Capt. U.S. Army, 1960-68. Recipient Disting. Svc. award, Midwest Dairy Products Assn., 1988. Mem. Internat. Assn. for Food Protection, Nat. Conf. Interstate Milk Shipments (single svc. containers com., drug residue program rev. com., methods for making ratings com., coun. III), Assn. Food and Drug Ofcls., Dairy Practices Coun., Conf. Food Protection (coun. I), Ill. Food Safety Task Force, Dairy Shrine. Methodist. Avocations: golf, hiking.

KIMBALL, DOROTHY JEAN, foundation executive; b. Riceville, Miss., Dec. 27, 1927; d. Hiram William and Norma Lucille (Wilson) Cutrer; m. Peter Nolan Kimball, Nov. 30, 1946; children: Donna Jean, Brenda Gail. Student, La. State U., 1947-48. With E.B. Badger & Sons Constrn. Co., Baton Rouge, 1944-45; sec. State of La. Dept. Edn., Baton Rouge, 1945-49; sec., bkpr. Better Bus. Bur. of Baton Rouge, Inc., 1950-52; pvt. sec., nat. comdt., mgr. nat. hdqtrs. Marine Corps League, Baton Rouge, 1952-54; sec., bookkeeper Louis B.

Rogers Constrn. Co., Baton Rouge, 1954; sec. to pres. Crawford Corp., Baton Rouge, 1955-64; sec-v.p. Crofton (Md.) Corp., 1964-74; sec.-treas. W.H. Crawford, Baton Rouge, 1975-89; found. exec. Crawford Found., Baton Rouge, 1990-96. Notary pub. State of Md., 1964-74. Named Baton Rouge High Magnet Sch. Hall of Fame, 1999. Mem. City Club, Country Club of La., Rolls Royce Club (entertainment com. 1985-87). Republican. Baptist. Avocations: fishing, reading, dancing. Home and Office: 1418 Applewood Rd Baton Rouge LA 70808-5905

KIMBALL, GEORGE EDWARD, III, sports columnist; b. Grass Valley, Calif., Dec. 20, 1943; s. George Edward and Rita Sue (Leslie) K.; children: Darcy Maeve, George E. IV. Student, Mass. Bay C.C., U. Kans., U. Iowa. Sports editor Boston Phoenix, 1970-79; sports columnist Boston Herald, 1980—. Columnist for Irish Times; featured sports columnist N.Y. Post, 1993; boxing commentator Fox SportsNet, 2002-03. Author: Only Skin Deep, Sunday's Fools; co-host SportsCall, Sta. WRKO, 1986-87, Old Colony Sports Network, 1996-97; appeared numerous TV programs; contbr. articles to mags., author numerous poems. Dem. candidate for sheriff, Douglas County, Kans., 1970. Recipient Best Sports Column award UPI, 1984, 86, Nat Fleischer award Boxing Writers Assn., 1985, First pl., 2002, Best Golf Column award Golf Writers Assn., 1992; named Boston's Best Sports Columnist Boston Mag., 1987. Mem. South Shore Country Club, Higham (bd. dirs.), European Club (senate) Brittas Bay, Ireland), Royal Dublin Golf Club, St. Andrews Golf Club (Scotland). Office: News Group Boston Inc PO Box 2096 One Herald Sq Boston MA 02106

KIMBALL, HARRY RAYMOND, medical association executive, educator; b. L.A. MD, Wash. U., 1962. Intern King County Hosp., Seattle, 1962—63; resident in internal medicine U. Wash. Hosps., Seattle, 1963—64, 1967—68; fellow infectious diseases NIH Hosps., Bethesda, Md., 1964—67; pres. Am. Bd. Internal Medicine, Phila., 1991—. Office: Am Bd Internal Medicine 510 Walnut St Ste 1700 Philadelphia PA 19106-3699 Fax: 215-446-3473.

KIMBALL, JUDITH GIENCKE, occupational therapist, educator; b. Tacoma, July 28, 1946; d. Edgar John and Carlyn Ann (Brendemuehl) Giencke; m. Charles Henry Kimball, June 8, 1968; children: Amy Lynn, Heather Suzanne, Emily Sarah. BS, Boston U., 1968; MS, Syracuse U., 1972, PhD, 1980. Registered occupl. therapist, Am. Occupl. Therapy Certification Bd.; lic. school psychologist, N.Y. Dir. occupl. therapy Upstate Med. Ctr., Syracuse, N.Y., 1968-73; dir. occupl. therapy edn. V.A. Hosp., Syracuse, 1973-75; owner Kimball Assocs., Minoa, N.Y., 1972-81; prof., founding chmn. dept. occupational therapy U. New. Eng., Biddeford, Maine, 1981—. Cons. Portland Schs. (Maine), 1994—; pvt. practice, Biddeford, Maine, 1981—. Contbr. chpts. to books, articles to profl. jours. Bd. dirs., chmn. Maine State Ballet, 1988—. Fellow Am. Occupl. Therapy Assn. (chair and founder edn. spl. interest sect. 1990-95), World Fedn. Occupl. Therapy, Maine Occupl. Therapy Assn. (cert. of merit for execellence in edn.). Avocations: choral singing, skiing, ballet, tap dancing. Home: 10 Lily Pond Ave Biddeford ME 04005-9566 Office: Univ New England 11 Hills Beach Rd Biddeford ME 04005-9599 E-mail: JKimball@mailbox.une.edu.

KIMBALL, JUSTIN, photographer, educator; BFA, R.I. Sch. Design; MFA in Photography, Yale U. Photographer. Vis. asst. prof. art and photography Amherst Coll., 2001—. Recipient Guggenheim fellowship, 2003. Office: Amherst Coll Dept Fine Arts Campus Box 2249 107 Fayerweather Hall Amherst MA 01002-5000*

KIMBALL, LYNN JEROME, historian; b. La Junta, Colo., Sept. 21, 1943; s. Stanley Jerome and Ruth Estelle (Wilson) K.; m. Kathleen May Seker Mitchell, Nov. 13, 1965 (div. Mar. 1974); children: Scott, Lori, Todd; m. Dorothy Jean Bumar, Dec. 15, 1984; children: Donald, Wendy. BS, U.S. Naval Acad., Annapolis, Md., 1965; MS, U.S. Naval Postgrad. Sch., Monterey, Calif., 1971. Commd. USMC, 1965, advanced through grades to lt. col., dir. plans & policies Joint Spl. Ops. Command, 1980-83, ops. officer 3d Marine Divsn. Okinawa, Japan, 1983-84, battalion comdr. Marine Corps Base Camp Lejeune, N.C., 1984-87; def. attache Am. Embassy, Santo Domingo, Dominican Republic, 1988-90; dir. ops. and tng. Marine Corps Base USMC, Camp Lejeune, 1990-91, dir. environ. tng. Marine Corps Base, 1991-92, ret., 1991; writer, historian, 1992—. Vis. lectr. Profl. Mil. Edn., Camp Lejeune, 1990-2001. Columnist Jacksonville Daily News, 1996—, Tideland News, 1996—, Richlands Advertiser, 1996—; author: Battle of New River, 1996, Diary of J.Q.A. Morris, 1997, Camp Lejeune Oral History Project, 2002, Semper Fidelis: A Brief History of Onslow County and MCB Camp Lejeune, 2002; contbr. articles to profl. jours. Adv. bd. Onslow County Bd. Tourism, Jacksonville, N.C., 1995-2002, Onslow County Mus., 1995—. Mem. Marine Corps Assn., U.S. Naval Inst., Sons Confederate Vets., Marine Corps Historical Found., Onslow Hist. Soc., Civil War Roundtable Eastern N.C. Republican. Baptist. Avocations: weight training, bicycling, walking, Civil War histo. Home: 227 Creedmoor Rd Jacksonville NC 28546-6028

KIMBALL, ROBERT ERIC, author; b. N.Y.C., Aug. 23, 1939; s. Morris Harold and Eve (Schulman) K.; m. Abigail Leon Kuflik, May 23, 1972; children: Philip Zachary, Miranda Erica. BA, Yale U., 1961, LL.B., 1967. Carnegie teaching fellow Am. history Yale U., New Haven, 1961-62; legis. asst. to Rep. John V. Lindsay, 17th Congl. Dist. N.Y., 1962-63; dir. Republican Legis. Research Assn., 1963-64; curator Yale Collection of Lit. Am. Mus. Theatre, 1967-71; lectr. Am. studies Yale, 1970, 74; music, dance reviewer N.Y. Post, 1973-87, chief classical music critic, 1987-88; pres. Roxbury Recs., 1988-90; music, dance reviewer Nat. Broadcasting Co., 1975-77; sr. research fellow, vis. prof. music Inst. for Studies in Am. Music, Bklyn. Coll., City U. N.Y., 1974-75; lectr. drama NYU, 1979-80; lectr. music Yale U., 1980-81; cons. Goodspeed Opera House, 1974-75, 82-83. Artistic advisor to estate of Ira Gershwin, Irving Berlin; cons. to Cole Porter Mus. and Lit. Property Trusts, music divsn. Libr. Congress. Co-producer: Black Broadway, N.Y.C., 1979, 80; Author: Cole, 1971, (with William Bolcom) Reminiscing With Sissle and Blake, 1973, (with Alfred Simon) The Gershwins, 1973, The Unpublished Cole Porter, 1975, The Complete Lyrics of Cole Porter, 1983; (with Dorothy Hart) The Complete Lyrics of Lorenz Hart, 1986, (with Tommy Krasker) Catalog of the American Musical, 1988, The Complete Lyrics of Ira Gershwin, 1993; contbr. articles and revs. to periodicals and profl. jours.; liner notes for recs. Grove's Dictionary of Music. Prin. asst. to Republicans in U.S. Congress during passage of Civil Rights Act, 1964; v.p. Alwyn Ct. Tenants Assn.; corr. sec. Yale '61. Recipient Drama Desk award for rediscovering lost mus. theater manuscripts, 1987. Mem. Theatre Library Assn., Folio Soc., Trollope Soc., Dutch Treat Club, Elihu Club (v.p. 1979-80, pres. 1980-82), Elizabethan Club of Yale, Freighter Travel Club Am. Address: 180 W 58th St New York NY 10019-2145 *In striving to survive as a generalist in our increasingly specialized world, I have been guided and encouraged by these words from the Roman playwright Terence: "Homo sum; humani nil a me alienum puto"—I am a man, and consider nothing human alien to me.*

KIMBALL, ROGER, editor, writer; m. Alexandra Elizabeth Mullen, Jan. 16, 1993; 1 child, James Hilton. BA, Bennington Coll., 1975; MA, MPhil, Yale U., 1983. Mng. editor The New Criterion, N.Y.C., 1989—. Bd. dirs. Nat. Ctr. Study Civic Literacy. Author: (book) Tenured Radicals, Art's Prospect, Experiments Against Reality, The Long March, Lives of the Mind, The Survival Of Culture, Physics And Politics; editor: Against the Grain, The Future Of The European Past, The Betrayal Of Liberalism, Against The Idols Of The Age. Bd. dirs. St. John's Coll., Annapolis, Md., 2002, Gilder Lehrman Inst., N.Y.C., 1999. Mem.: Yale Club, Century Club. R-Conservative. Roman Catholic. Office: The New Criterion 850 7th Ave New York NY 10019 Home Fax: 212-247-3127; Office Fax: 212-247-3127.

KIMBALL, SPENCER D. music educator, small business owner; MusB, U. Utah, 1987. Cert. Secondary Music Tchr. 1987, lic. Real Estate Broker 1998, cert. Endorsed to teach music at all grade levels, K-12. Tchr. music Seboyeta/Cubero Elementaries, Grants/Cibola County, N.Mex., 1999—2001; dir. band/chorus Zuni Mid. Sch., Zuni, N.Mex., 1998—99; dir. band Whitehorse H.S., Montezuma Creek, Utah, 1994—98; tchr. music Red Mesa Sch. Dist., Teec Nos Pos, Ariz., 1989—94; dir. band/chorus k-12 music Challis Sch. Dist., Challis, Idaho, 1988—89; ind. bus. owner Kimball Enterprises, Salt Lake City, 2002—; tchr. Jordan Sch. Dist., 2002—03. Coach basketball Whitehorse H.S., Montezuma Creek, 1994—95, Red Mesa Jr. H.S., Red Mesa, 1990—92, Challis Jr. H.S., Challis, 1988—89. Author (poetry collection): Cry From the Dust Collection, 2001; editor (own several websites promoting Am. values and patriotism): americahistory.net, 2002. Proponent Salt Lake County Safe Drinking Water Act, Salt Lake City, 2002. Mem.: World Wide Dream Builders. Mem. Lds Ch. Office Fax: 888-255-7642.

KIMBALL, SPENCER LEVAN, lawyer, educator; b. Thatcher, Ariz., Aug. 26, 1918; s. Spencer Woolley and Camilla (Eyring) K.; m. Kathryn Ann Murphy, June 12, 1939; children: Barbara Jean (Mrs. Thomas Sherman), Judith Ann (Mrs. William Stillion), Kathleen Louise, Spencer David, Kent Douglas, Timothy Jay; m. Virginia Barrus Johnson, June 4, 1994. BS, U. Ariz., 1940; postgrad., U. Utah, 1946-47; BCL, Oxford (Eng.) U., 1949; SJD, U. Wis., 1958. Bar: Utah 1950, Mich. 1965, Wis. 1968, U.S. Dist. Ct. (we. dist.) Wis. 1968, U.S. Supreme Ct. 1982, U.S. Ct. Appeals (9th cir.) 1986. Assoc. prof. U. Utah Coll. Law, Salt Lake City, 1949-50, dean, 1950-54, prof., 1954-57, rsch. prof. emeritus, 1993—; prof. U. Mich., 1957-68, dir. legal rsch. Law Sch., 1962-67; staff dir. Wis. Ins. Law Revision Project, 1966-79; prof. law, dean U. Wis. Law Sch., 1968-72; exec. dir. Am. Bar Found., Chgo., 1972-82; prof. law U. Chgo., 1972-88, Seymour Logan prof., 1978-88, Seymour Logan prof. emeritus, 1988—. Author: Insurance and Public Policy (Elizur Wright award), 1960, Introduction to the Legal System, 1966, Essays in Insurance Regulation, 1966, Cases and Materials on Insurance Law, 1992; (with Werner Pfenningstorf) The Regulation of Insurance Companies in the United States and the European Communities: A Comparative Study, 1981; editor: (with Herbert Denenberg) Insurance, Government and Social Policy, 1969, (with Werner Pfenningstorf) Legal Service Plans, 1977; bd. editors: Jour. Ins. Regulation, Internat. Jour. Ins. Law, Assicurazioni; contbr. articles to profl. jours. Lt. USNR, 1943-46. Recipient Rsch. award Am. Bar Found.; award Outstanding Rsch. in Law and Gov't, 1984, Am. Bar Assn. Sect. of Torts and Ins. Practice, Robert B. McKay award Lifetime contbns. to Ins. and Tort Law, 1991. Fellow Am. Bar Found., Wis. Bar Found.; mem. ABA, Mich. State Bar, Utah State Bar, Wis. State Bar, Internat. Assn. Ins. Law (hon. pres., past pres. U.S. chpt., mem. presdl. coun.) Phi Beta Kappa, Phi Kappa Phi. Home: 241 N Vine Apt 1001W Salt Lake City UT 84103-1936

KIMBELL, DAVID LAWRENCE, music educator; b. Lakeland, Fla., Aug. 19, 1952; s. John Philip Kimbell and Carol Milyko; m. Georgina Louise Smith, Nov. 23, 1989; children: Douglas Daniel Lammy, Michael Burton Lammy, Jeffrey Lee Lammy. Grad., E.L. Vandermeulen HS, Port Jefferson, N.Y., 1970; studied piano with Lillian Milyko, studied cello with Carment Rasmussen, David Vanderkooi, studied guitar with Nicholas Zaninovic, John Johns, studied violin with Dorothy Mauney. Pvt. music tchr. Kimbell Studio, Hilton Head Island, SC, 1986—, freelance musician, 1991—2001; orch. dir. Hilton Head HS, Hilton Head Island, 1996—. Chmn., grants rev. panel Self Family Arts Ctr., Hilton Head Island, 1995—97; music show dir. Arts Ctr. Coastal Carolina, Hilton Head Island, 1991—2001; gen. mgr., asst. condr. Hilton Head Youth Orch., 1996—. Composer: (modern dance) Days; prodr.: (CD) Jaime Michaels: A Quiet Heart; musician: Hilton Head Orch., 1986—, Hilton Head Philharm., 1986—. V.p., treas. Hilton Head Island Inst. Arts, 1994—97; music dir. fund raising concerts, 1995—96; staff musician St. Luke's Episcopal Ch., Hilton Head Island, 1991—99, 2003—, asst. music dir., 2000—01; music dir. Providence Presbyn. Ch., Hilton Head Island, 2000—02. Mem.: Music Tchrs. Nat. Assn. Achievements include development of original method for guitar instruction. Home and Office: 47 Queens Way Hilton Head Island SC 29928 Home Fax: 843-785-5493.

KIMBELL, MARION JOEL, retired engineer; b. McDonough, Ga., Sept. 7, 1923; s. Charles Marvin and Mary (McMillian) K.; m. Judy Weidner, Dec. 18, 1946; children: Nancy, Susan, Candice. BS in Civil Engring., U. Houston, 1949, MChE, 1953. Registered profl. engr., Calif. Civil engr. U.S. Dept. Interior, Lemmon, S.D., 1954; chief piping engr. M.W. Kellog Co., Paducah, Ky., 1955; nuclear engr. Westinghouse Atomic Power Divsn., Pitts., 1956-59; control systems prin. engr. Kaiser Engrs., Oakland, Calif., 1959-80; control systems supervising engr. Bechtel Inc., San Francisco, 1980-86, ret., 1986. Control systems tchr. Laney Coll. cons. engr. NASA, Gen. Atomic Co.; mem. adv. bd. on radiation tech. Chabot Coll. Contbr. articles to profl. jours. Served as sgt. U.S. Army, 1943-46. Mem. Instrument Soc. Am. (sr. mem. exec. com.), Moose. Home: 22324 Ralston Ct Hayward CA 94541-3336 E-mail: joekm@netscape.net.

KIMBERLIN, SAM OWEN, JR., financial institutions consultant; b. Wichita Falls, Tex., Feb. 4, 1928; s. Sam Owen and Mary Ruth (Crowell) K.; m. Alison Gray, Dec. 20, 1955; children: S. Scott, David Winston. BBA, U. Tex., Austin, 1951, LLB, 1953; grad. in banking, Rutgers U., 1972. Bar: Tex. 1953. First asst. Office Dist. Atty., Austin, 1953-54; asst. atty. gen. Office Atty. Gen. State Tex., Austin, 1955; gen. counsel Tex. Dept. Banking, Austin, 1956-62; exec. dir. Assn. State Chartered Banks in Tex., Austin, 1962-64; exec. v.p. Tex. Bankers Assn., Austin, 1964-88; mng. dir. TBA Svcs. Co., Inc., Austin, 1988-90; cons. Austin Trust Co., 1990—, Thornhill Securities, Inc., Austin, 1990—. Chmn. devel. bd. Austin Trust Co., 1991—. Author: Banking in Texas, 1972 (honors award 1972); co-author: Fight Your Texas Tax Appraisal and Win, 1997. Adv. coun. on property tax cons. Tex. Dept. Licensing and Regulation, 1996—; chmn. appraisal rev. bd. Travis Ctrl. Appraisal Dist., 1995-96; trustee S.F. Austin High Continuing Edn. Found. With USMC, 1946-48. Mem. Am. Soc. Assn. Execs., Tex. Assn. Bank Counsel, Adms. Club, Headliners Club, Tarry House Lodge. Methodist. Avocations: tennis, skiing. Home: 3503 Scenic Hills Dr Austin TX 78703-1044 Office: PO Box 5930 Austin TX 78763-5930 E-mail: samkim@austin.rr.com.

KIMBERLING, CLARK HERSHALL, mathematics educator, small business owner; b. Hinsdale, Ill., Nov. 7, 1942; s. Delmer Hershall and Jocelyn Leigh (Babel) K.; m. Margaret Penelope Mitchell, May 30, 1966; children: Amy, David, Brian. BA, North Tex. State U., 1964; MA, La. State U., 1966; PhD, Ill. Inst. Tech., 1970. Instr. N.W. Mo. State Coll., Maryville, 1967-69, Ill. Inst. Tech., Chgo., 1969-70; asst. prof. U. Evansville, Ind., 1970-75, assoc. prof., 1975-81, prof., 1982—; pres. Math. Software Co., Evansville, 1987—. Author: (with others) Emmy Noether: A Tribute to Her Life and Work, 1982; author: (book and software) Triangle Centers and Central Triangles, 1998, Geometry in Action, 2003; author: (online Book) Encyclopedia of Triangle Centers; author numerous computer software programs including The Geometric Constructor, 1985-90; editor divsn. music U. Evansville Press, 1976-88; editor computer corner Ind. Math. Tchr., Ball State U., 1986-91; contbr. articles to profl. jours.; composer for ch. choirs: This Easter Morn, 1997, The King of Love My Shepherd Is, 1997, Ring Out the Glad Tidings, 2000, O God, Beneath Your Hand, 2002, O God, Who at the Dawn of Time, 2002, The Hills are Hushed This Night of Nights, 2002, Four Anthems for Mixed Voices and Handbells, 2003, others. Choir dir. St. Paul's Episcopal Ch., Henderson, Ky, 1978-84; bd. dirs. Fibonacci Assn., Santa Clara, Calif., 1999—; adv. bd. Forum Geometricorum, Boca Raton, Fla., 2000—. Mem. Nat. Coun. Tchrs. Math., Am. Math. Soc. (spl. session organizer 1999), Math. Assn. Am., Fibonacci Assn. (assoc. editor 1990—, bd. dirs. 2000--), U. Evansville Alumni Assn. (Outstanding Faculty Rsch. and Scholarly Activity award 1987). Achievements include introductions of new notable points in the plane of a triangle: isoperimetric point, Exeter point, other points on the Euler line); interspersions, dispersions and generalized Wythoff arrays. Home: 2316 E Gum St Evansville IN 47714-2338 Office: U Evansville 1800 Lincoln Ave Evansville IN 47714-1506

KIMBERLY, JOHN ROBERT, management educator, consultant; b. New Haven, Sept. 16, 1942; s. John T. and Beatrice (Branch) K.; m. Barbara Lenox Christy, June 27, 1970; children: Laura Lenox, John Fowler, Nina-Charlotte Marie. BA, Yale U., 1964; MS, Cornell U., 1967, PhD, 1970. Asst. prof. sociology U. Ill., Champaign/Urbana, 1970-74; vis. fellow Ecole Polytechnique, Paris, 1975-76; from asst. to assoc. prof. Sch. Mgmt. Yale U., New Haven, 1977-82; from assoc. to full prof. Wharton Sch., U. Pa., Phila., 1983—, Henry Bower prof., 1989—. Rsch. prof. Ecole Polytechnique, Paris, 1989-91; cons. OECD, 1975—, Office Tech. Assessment U.S. Congress, 1982-84, Robert Wood Johnson Found., Princeton, N.J., 1984-85; mem. health care tech. study sect. HHS, Washington, 1986-89; Novartis prof. in healthcare mgmt. INSEAD, 1999-2002. Author: The End of an Illusion, 1984, Cases in Health Policy and Management, 1985, The Migration of Managerial Innovation, 1993; editor: The Organization Life Cycle, 1980, Managing Organizational Transitions, 1984; contbr. articles to profl. jours. Bd. dirs. Wissahickon Hospice, Phila., 1985—, Chestnut Hill Hosp. Health Care, 1992—, Bach Festival Phila., 1992—, Community Fin. Bancorp, 1993—. Grantee HCA Found., Nashville, 1984-86, HHS, Washington, 1986—, Commonwealth Found., N.Y.C., 1986-87, Robert Wood Johnson Found., Princeton, 1986-87, Kaiser Family Found., 1994-96; Salmon and Rameau fellow INSEAD, Fountainbleau, France, 1996-99, 2002—. Mem. Am. Sociol. Assn., Acad. of Mgmt., Am. Pub. Health Assn. Avocations: restoration of antique cars and boats, tennis, skiing. Office: U Pa Wharton Sch Philadelphia PA 19104

KIMBLE, MELINDA LOUISE, environmental administrator; m. James R. Phippard; 4 stepchildren. B in Econs., M in Econs., U. Denver; MPA in Econs., Kennedy Sch. Fgn. svc. officer Dept. of State, Washington, 1971-89, sr. fgn. svc. officer, 1989-93, min. counselor, 1993-97, dep. asst. sec. Bur. Internat. Orgn. Affairs, 1993-97, prin. dep. asst. sec. Oceans and Internat. Environ. and Sci. Affairs, 1997-99; v.p. programs UN Found., Washington, 2000—03, sr. v.p. programs, 2003—. Recipient award Global Alliance for Women's Health, Internat. Honor award USDA, Disting. Honor award Dept. State, 2000. Office: 1225 Connecticut Ave NW 4th Fl Washington DC 20036-1815

KIMBLE, WILLIAM EARL, lawyer; b. Denver, May 4, 1926; s. George Wilbur and Grace (Fick) K.; m. Jean M. Cayia, Dec. 27, 1950; children: Mark, Cary, Timothy, Stephen, Philip, Peter, Michael. LL.B., U. Ariz., 1951. Bar: Ariz. 1951. Spl. agt. FBI, 1951-52; pvt. practice Bisbee, 1952-60, Tucson, 1962—; judge Superior Ct. Ariz., 1960—62; ptnr. Kimble, Nelson, Audilett & McDonough, 1962—. Commr. Ariz. Oil and Gas Commn., 1958-60; adj. prof. law U. Ariz. Coll. Law, 1962-86. Author: The Consumer Product Safety Act, 1973, Products Liability, 1977; sr. editor Consumer Products Alert newsletter, 1980-81; editor, pub. In Def. of Elec. Accidents newsletter, 1993—. Founder Naval War Coll. Found.; Rep. nominee Ariz. atty. gen., 1956; Rep. nominee Ariz. U.S. Congress, 1964. Served with USNR, 1944-46. Fellow Am. Coll. Trial Lawyers; mem. Sigma Chi, Phi Alpha Delta. Home: 3544 E Placita de Pipo Tucson AZ 85718 Office: Kimble Nelson Audilett & McDonough 335 N Wilmot Rd Ste 500 Tucson AZ 85711-2636

KIMBLER, LARRY BERNARD, real estate executive, accountant; b. Lucasville, Ohio, Sept. 6, 1938; s. Benjamin F. and Elizabeth L. (Kerr) K.; m. Susanna Hayes, June 20, 1964; children: Beth Ann, Carolyn Sue. BBA, U. Cin., 1964. CPA, Ohio; lic. real estate broker, Tex. Acct. Peat, Marwick, Mitchell & Co., Cin., 1964-68; mgr. acctg. and taxes Andrew Jergens & Co., Cin., 1968-70; exec. v.p. Am. Lakes & Land Co., Houston, 1970-74; from group controller real estate and minerals to gen. mgr. land utilization Internat. Paper Co., 1974-81; pres. Internat. Paper Realty Co., N.Y.C., 1977-81; v.p. corp. real estate GTE, Stamford, Conn.; also pres. GTE Realty Corp., 1981-89; prin. Kimbler Assocs., Inc., Stamford, 1989-91; exec. v.p. The Staubach Co., Dallas, 1991—2002, also bd. dirs.; chmn. Washington Staubach Addison Airport Venture, 2002—. Bd. dirs. Stamford Econ. Assistance Corp.; past pres. Westchester So. Conn. chpt., NACORE; trustee, treas. Low-Heywood Thomas Sch., Stamford; lectr., speaker in field; mem. adv. bd. Homer Hoyt Inst.; officer, bd. dirs. Indsl. Devel. Rsch. Coun.; editl. adv. bd. Bldg. Econs. Contbr. articles to profl. jours. With AUS, 1956-59. Mem. Am. Inst. Corp. Asset Mgmt. (bd. govs.), Nat. Assn. Corp. Real Estate Execs. (master corp. real estate designation, chpt. pres.), Am. Inst. CPAs, Indsl. Devel. Research Council (bd. dirs., Officer Disting. Svc. award 1983, 87, Master Profl. designation), Am. Found. for Blind (chmn. bd. dirs. SW Region, nat. trustee), Bent Tree Country Club (bd. dirs., exec. com. 1999-2002). Presbyterian. Republican. Home: 5403 Bent Trail Dallas TX 75248-2034 Office: 15601 Dallas Pkwy Ste 400 Addison TX 75001-6055

KIMBRELL, GRADY NED, writer, educator; b. Tallant, Okla., Apr. 6, 1933; s. Virgil Leroy Kimbrell and La Veria Dee Underwood; m. Marilyn Louise King, May 30, 1953 (div.); m. Mary Ellen Cunningham, Apr. 11, 1973; children: Mark Leroy, Lisa Christine, Joni Lynne. BA, Southwestern Coll., Winfield, Kans., 1956; MA, Colo. State Coll., 1958. Cert. tchr. (life), Calif., Colo.; cert. adminstr., Calif. Bus. tchr. Peabody (Kans.) High Sch., 1956-58, Santa Barbara (Calif.) High Sch., 1958-65, coordinator work edn., 1965-75, dir. research and evaluation, 1975-88. Author: Introduction to Business and Office Careers, 1974, The World of Work Career Interest Survey, 1986; co-author: Succeeding in the World of Work, 1970, 7th rev. edit., 2003, Entering the World of Work, 1974, 3rd rev. edit., 1988, The Savvy Consumer, 1984, Personal and Family Economics, 1996, Marketing Essentials, 1991, 2nd edit., 1997, 3d edit., 2003, Office Skills, 1998, 3d edit., 2003, Advancing in the World of Work, 1992, Exploring Business and Computer Careers, 1998, Employment Skills for Office Careers, 1998. With U.S. Army, 1953-55. Mem. NEA, Calif. Assn. Work Experience Educators, Nat. Work Experience Edn. Assn., Calif. Tchrs. Assn., Coop. Work Experience Assn. Republican. Avocations: breeding and racing quarter horses, photography. E-mail: gradykim@cox.net.

KIMBRELL, ODELL CULP, JR., internist; b. Spartanburg, S.C., May 2, 1927; s. Odell Culp and Leona (Nicholas) K.; m. Etta Lou; children from former marriage: Odell Culp III, Cynthia Anne. AB, Duke U., 1947; MD, U. Pa., 1951. Diplomate: Am. Bd. Internal Medicine, Am. Bd. Life Ins. Medicine. Intern Med. Coll. Va., Richmond, 1951-52, resident in internal medicine, 1954-56; sr. resident in internal medicine VA Hosp., Phila., 1956-57; practice medicine specializing in internal medicine and endocrinology Gallipolis, Ohio, 1957-60, Raleigh, N.C., 1960-93; practice ins. medicine, 1967—; mem. hon. staff Wake Med. Ctr.; clin. prof. medicine U.N.C. Med. Sch., 1970-90. Med. dir., cons. Pa. Life Ins. Co. Contbr. articles to med. jours. Bd. dirs. Wake County Hosp. System Inc., Raleigh, 1971-81, sec., 1973-74, chmn., 1974-76; bd. dirs. Wake Health Facilities and Service Inc., 1975-81, pres., 1975-76; chmn. Wake County Heart Fund, 1961; deacon Hudson Meml. Presbyn. Ch., Raleigh, 1971-73. Served with USAF, 1952-54. Fellow ACP; mem. AMA, N.C. Med. Soc., Wake County Med Soc., Am. Soc. Internal Medicine, N.C. Soc. Internal Medicine, Am. Acad. Ins. Med., Mid-Atlantic Med. Dirs. Club (pres. 1979-80, 92). Home: 1905 Hunting Ridge Rd Raleigh NC 27615-5515 Office: 201 Shannon Oaks Ste 200 Cary NC 27511 *Serving through devoted application of mind, body and spirit.*

KIMBRELL, WILLARD DUKE, textile company executive; b. Gaston County, N.C., Dec. 28, 1924; s. Curtis C. and Carolyn (Carter) K.; m. Dorothy Rhyne, Feb. 9, 1932; 3 children. BS in Textiles, N.C. State Coll., 1949; PhD, U. N.C., Charlotte. Various positions Parkdale Mills, Inc., Gastonia, N.C., 1938—, CEO, 1961—. Bd. dirs. Am. Textile Mfg., Inman Mills; pres. Gaston Cmty. Found. Trustee Bowman Gray Sch. Medicine, U. N.C.; dir. YMCA, Gastonia. With USAF. Mem. Am. Yarn Spinners Assn. (pres.), N.C. Textile Mfrs. Assn. (pres.). Republican. Office: 531 Cotton Blossom Cir Gastonia NC 28054 E-mail: dkimbrell@parkdalemills.com.

KIMBRIEL-EGUIA, SUSAN, design planner; b. San Francisco, July 22, 1949; d. Scott Slaughter and Kathleen (Edens) Smith; m. Floyd Thomas Kimbriel; children: John Thomas, Tammy Lee Petersen; m. Candelario Eguia, Feb. 14, 1991; 1 child, Daniel. Accredited Nat. Assn. Family Child Care. Engring. planner, sys. adminstr. various mainframe and PC based sys. Northrop Aircraft, Hawthorne, Calif., 1982-91; owner, operator Susie's Day Care/PreSchool, Palmdale, Calif., 1995—. Mem.: Antelope Valley Child Care Assn., Nat. Assn. for Family Child Care. Avocations: handcrafts, gardening, computer graphics.

KIMBROUGH, LORELEI, elementary education educator; b. Chgo. d. Paul and Lina (Higgs) Bobbett; m. James Kimbrough; children: Denise, Devi, Paul, Jeri Lynn, Sandra, Diane, James III. BS in Edn., Ill. State U., 1947; postgrad., DePaul U., Chgo. U. Cert. tchr., Ill. Tchr. of Latin and English, Greensboro (N.C.) Pub. Schs.; spl. edn. tchr. Chgo. State Hosp./Reed Zone Ctr., Chgo., Jewish Children's Bur., Chgo.; elem. tchr. Chgo. Bd. of Edn., Pasadena (Calif.) H.S.; English tchr. Malala H.S., Madang, 1993-94; tchr. jr. H.S. Cathedral Chapel Cath. Sch., 1995-96, Holy Trinity Sch., L.A., 1998-2000. Tutor to fgn. students. Missionary worker L.A. Archdiocese, Papua New Guinea; vol. ARC, Solheim Luth. Home, Glendale Meml. Hosp. 4-year scholar State of Ill., Chgo. Musical Coll. award. Mem. Nat. Coun. Tchrs. of English, Ill. Coun. of Social Studies, Nat. Coun. Social Studies. Home: 86 S Daisy Ave Pasadena CA 91117

KIMBROUGH, ROBERT AVERYT, lawyer; b. Sarasota, Fla., Nov. 2, 1933; s. Verman T. and Edith (Averyt) K.; m. Emilie Hudson, Aug. 24, 1957; children: James E., Robert A. Jr. BS, Davidson Coll., 1955; LLB to JD, U. Fla., 1960. Bar: Fla. 1960, U.S. Dist. Ct. Fla. 1962. Pvt. practice, Sarasota, 1960—. Chmn.,

bd. trustees, Ringling Sch. Art & Design, Sarasota, 1983-85; chmn. Sarasota Welfare Home Inc., 1986-89; pres. Fla. West Coast Symphony, Sarasota, 1986-90. Recipient Champion Higher Edn. in Fla., Ind. Coll. and Univs. of Fla., 1984-85, Alumnus of Yr. award Phi Delta Theta, 1997. Mem. ABA, Fla. Bar, Sarasota County Bar Assn., Sarasota Yacht Club, Kiwanis. Republican. Presbyterian. Avocations: flying, fishing, boating. Home: 7100 S Gator Creek Blvd Sarasota FL 34241-9729 Office: 1530 Cross St Sarasota FL 34236-7015 E-mail: rak@KimbroughKoach.com.

KIMES, BEVERLY RAE, editor, writer; b. Aug. 17, 1939; d. Raymond Lionel and Grace Florence (Perrin) K.; m. James H. Cox, July 6, 1984. BS, U. Ill., 1961; MA in Journalism, Pa. State U., 1963. Dir. publicity Mateer Playhouse, Neff's Mill, Pa., 1962, Pavillion Theatre, University Park, Pa., 1963; asst. editor Automobile Quar. Publs., N.Y.C., Princeton, N.J., 1963-64, assoc. editor, 1965-66, mng. editor, 1967-74, editor, 1975-81, The Classic Car, 1981—. Mem. bd. corporators Mus. of Transp., Brookline, Mass.; trustee Nat. Automotive History Collection, Detroit Pub. Libr., Saratoga (N.Y.) Automobile Mus., Rolls-Royce Found. Author: The Classic Tradition of the Lincoln Motor Car, 1968, (with R.M. Langworth) Oldsmobile: The First Seventy-Five Years, 1972, The Cars That Henry Ford Built, 1978, (with Rene Dreyfus) My Two Lives, 1983, (with Robert C. Ackerson) Chevrolet: A History from 1911, 1984, The Standard Catalog of American Cars 1805-1942, 1985, The Star and the Laurel: The Centennial History of Daimler, Mercedes and Benz, 1986, The Classic Era, 2001; editor: Great Cars and Grand Marques, 1976, Packard: History of the Motor Car and the Company, 1979, Automobile Quarterly's Handbook of Automotive Hobbies, 1981, The Classic Car: The Ultimate Book About the World's Grandest Automobiles, 1990. Recipient Thomas McKean trophy, 1983, 85, 86, 2001, Moto award Nat. Assn. Automotive Journalists, 1984, 85, 86, 97, Disting. Svc. citation Automotive Hall of Fame, 1993, Best Mag. Article and Best of the Best, Internat. Automotive Media Assn., 2002. Mem.: Soc. Automotive Historians (pres. 1987—89, Cugnot award 1978—79, 1983, Friend of Automotive History award 1985, Cugnot award 1985—86, Benz award 1994, 1998, Cugnot award 2001, 2002), Internat. Motor Press Assn.

KIMETHU, SUSAN WANJA, computer specialist, database manager; b. Nairobi, Kenya, Mar. 13, 1956; d. Samuel Kimama Ngaii and Mary Nyambura Kimama; m. Daniel Mburu Kimethu; children: Hosea Kimethu Mburu, Samuel Kimama Mburu, Esther Njeri Mburu. Diploma, Kenya Tech. Coll., 1983; MBA, Baldwin Wallace Coll., 1992; PhD in Bus. Adminstrn., Kennedy Western U., 2002. Cert. Oracle database adminstr.; h.s. tchr. Sr. acct. Ameritrust Bank, Cleve., 1993—94; sr. fin. analyst Key Bank, Cleve., 1994—98; instr. Sawyer Bus. Coll., Cleve., 1994—98; database mgr. Telesis Of Ohio, Cleve., 1997—99; sr. bus. analyst Emerald Health, Cleve., 1998—99; database mgr. Orbital Computers, Cleve., 2000—01; computer specialist United Labor Agy., Cleve., 2001—. Tchr. Lifest High Sch. Ctr., Grove City, 2003. Author: Following & Obeying God in Your Youth, 2001, Kids, Let's Follow Christ, 2002, Kids, Let's Follow Christ Workbook, 2002. Mem.: Network Administrs., Oracle User Group. Office: Dansu Pubs LLC PO Box 957 Grove City OH 43123-0957 Fax: 831-603-3550. E-mail: skimethu@hotmail.com.

KIMM, MICHAEL S. lawyer; b. Scoul, July 12, 1963; came to U.S., 1974; s. Chun Teak and Chong Sim K. BA, Fordham U., 1987; JD, Boston U., 1991. Bar: N.J. 1991, N.Y. 1992, U.S. Dist. Ct. N.J. 1991, U.S. Dist. Ct. (so. and ea. dists.) N.Y. 1993, U.S. Ct. Appeals (2nd, 3rd and Fed cirs.) 1994, U.S. Supreme Ct. 1995. Pvt. practice, Hackensack, NJ. Mng. editor: Boston U. Internat. Law Jour., 1990-91; contbr. articles to profl. jours. Gen. counsel Korean-Am. Assn. for Rehab. of Disabled, Queens, N.Y., 1992-94. Mem. ABA, N.J. State Bar Assn., N.Y. State Bar Assn. Office: 185 Great Neck Rd Great Neck NY 11021 Address: 190 Moore St # 272 Hackensack NJ 07601

KIMM, SUE YOUNG SOOK, academic medical researcher; b. Seoul, Republic of Korea, Feb. 11, 1938; came to U.S., 1956. d. Lloyd C. and Diana Duk-Sil (Cha) K.; m. Seymour Grufferman, Dec. 23, 1967. AB, Bryn Mawr (Pa.) Coll., 1960; MD, Yale U., 1964; MPH, Harvard U., 1968, MS, 1974. Diplomate Nat. Bd. Med. Examiners, Am. Bd. Pediatrics, Am. Coll. Epidemiology. Intern, then resident in pediatrics Children's Hosp. Med. Ctr., Boston, 1964-66; resident in pediatrics Case-Western Res. U. Hosp., Cleve., 1966-67; cons. pediatrician Tokyo Sanitarium Hosp., 1969-71; chief of pediatrics, asst. prof. Gondar Pub. Health Coll. Haile Sellassie I. U., Gondar, Ethiopia, 1971-73; fellow Ctr. for Community Health & Med. Care Harvard U., Boston, 1974-75; asst. prof. pediatrics Sch. of Medicine Duke U., Durham, N.C., 1976-87; acting chief nutrition rsch. sect. Nat. Heart, Lung & Blood Inst. NIH, Bethesda, Md., 1985-87; asst. v.p. for health promotion Health Scis. Ctr. U. Pitts., 1987-91; assoc. prof. dept. clin. epidemiology/preventive medicine Sch. Medicine, U. Pitts., 1987-97; prof. dept. family medicine/clin. epidemiology U. Pitt., 1997—. Cons. Nat. Heart, Lung & Blood Inst. NIH, Bethesda, 1987—; grant reviewer NIH, Bethesda, 1987—; mem. Nat. Cancer Inst. Rev. Subcom., Bethesda, 1997-2000, Nutrition Study Sect., NIH, Bethesda, Md., 2000—. Mem. editl. bd. Jour. Epidemiology and Biostatistics, 1996—; contbr. articles to med. jours. Vol. physician AMA, South Vietnam, 1968; cons. family health project Pitts. Urban League, 1989. Harvard U. fellow, 1974-75; Bryn Mawr Coll., Yale U. scholar, 1956-60; recipient Cert. of Appreciation, NIH, 1987. Fellow Am. Heart Assn. (epidemiology coun.); mem. Am. Coll. Epidemiology, Preventive Cardiology Soc., No. Am. Assn. for Study of Obesity, Pitts. Athletic Assn., Dandie Dinmont Terrier Club. Avocations: decorative arts, horticulture. Home: 432 Morewood Ave Pittsburgh PA 15213-1814 Office: U Pitts Sch Medicine 3518 5th Ave Pittsburgh PA 15261-0001

KIMMEL, ELLEN BISHOP, psychologist, educator; b. Knoxville, Tenn., Sept. 16, 1939; d. Archer W. and Mary Ellen (Baker) Bishop; divorced; children: Elinor, Ann, Jean, Tracy. BA summa cum laude, U. Tenn., 1961; MA, U. Fla., 1962, PhD, 1965. Asst. prof., rsch. assoc. Ohio U., 1965-68; asst. prof. U. South Fla., Tampa, 1968-72, assoc. prof., dean Univ. Studies Coll., 1972-73, prof. psychology and ednl. psychology, 1975-95, chair, 1992-94, Disting. prof., 1996—. Disting. vis. prof. psychology Simon Fraser U., Vancouver, B.C., Can., 1980-81; cons. numerous sch. systems, bus. and govt. Author books; contbr. articles to profl. jours., chpts. to books. Mem. Fla. Blue Ribbon Task Force on Juvenile Delinquency, 1976-77; mem. Fla. Gov.'s Commn. on Women, 1979-83; mem. adv. bd. Stop Rape, Good Govt., Inc.; bd. dirs. NCCJ. Recipient Outstanding Svc. award State of Fla., 1975, Outstanding Tchg. award U. South Fla., 1978, Career Achievement award U. Tenn., 1983, Professorial Excellence award Fla. State U. Sys., 1997, Disting. Sr. Scholar Spl. Commendation of Honor, AAUW, 2001; 17 rsch. grants. Fellow: APA (governing coun. 1982—85, pres. divsn. 1986—88, Disting. Leadership award 1993), Am. Assn. Applied and Preventive Psychology (bd. dirs. 1994—97, charter fellow, program chair 1991, Disting. Edn. award 1994), Am. Psychol. Soc. (charter fellow, conf. chair 1990); mem.: Southeastern Psychol. Assn. (pres. 1977—79), Assn. Women in Psychology (Disting. Publ. award 2000), Athena Soc., Omicron Delta Kappa, Delta Kappa Gamma, Sigma Xi. Democrat. Office: U South Fla EDU 162 Tampa FL 33620

KIMMEL, HERBERT DAVID, psychology educator; b. N.Y.C., May 22, 1927; s. Max and Lillian (Neuwirth) K.; m. Barbara B. Ellis; children: Elinor, Ann Kimmel Ritter, Jean, Tracy. BS, U. Fla., 1948; MA, NYU, 1951; PhD, U. So. Calif., 1958. Lic. psychologist, Fla. Sch. psychometrist William S. Hart Union High Sch., Newhall, Calif., 1950-52; rsch. asst., rsch. assoc., project dir. Mgmt. and Mktg. Rsch. Corp., Human Factors Rsch., 1953-58; asst. prof., then assoc. prof. psychology U. Fla., Gainesville, 1958-65; prof. psychology Ohio U., Athens, 1965-68, U. So. Fla., Tampa, 1968-86, chmn. dept. psychology, 1968-72, disting. rsch. prof., 1986-93, disting. rsch. prof. emeritus, 1993—. Disting. vis. prof. U. Tulsa, fall 1976; vis. prof. psychology U. P.R., summer 1963, Duke U., spring 1961; vis. scientist Human Factors Rsch., Inc., summer 1964; gastprof. U. Giessen, summer, 1982; prof. U. Trier, 1987-94, mem. sci. adv. bd. Ctr. Rsch. in Psychobiology and Psychosomatics, 1994-98; mem. clin. ethics com. M.D. Anderson Cancer Ctr., 1999-2002; mem. pain mgmt. task force, M.D. Anderson Cancer Ctr., 2001-02. Author: Experimental Principles and Design in Psychology, 1970, Experimental Psychopathology, 1971, Biofeedback and Self-Regulation, 1979, The Orienting Reflex in Humans, 1979; author chpts. to books; masthead cons. editor Jour. Exptl. Psychology, 1960-74; mem. editorial bd. Behavior Therapy and Exptl. Psychiatry, 1976—, Jour. Behavioral Assessment, 1979—, Jour. Clin. and Cons. Psychology, 1981-88; mem. editorial bd. Pavlovian Jour. of Biol. Scis., 1976-78, mng. editor, 1978-83; ad hoc editor for various publs. in field; contbr. articles for profl. jours. Recipient A. von Humboldt Sr. Scientist award U. Tuebingen, 1980-81; grantee NIMH, 1959-72, Office Naval Rsch., 1960-61, U.S. Office Edn., 1969-70, Nat. Libr. Medicine, 1973-76, U.S. Army Med. Rsch. and Devel. Command, 1974-83, NSF, 1976-78, German Rsch. Soc., 1983. Fellow APA; mem. N.Y. Acad. Scis., Southeastern Psychol. Assn., Psychonomic Soc., Psychometric Soc., So. Soc. for Philosophy and Psychology (pres. 1977-78), Pavlovian Soc. (2d v.p. 1980, 1st v.p. 1981, pres. 1982, exec. com. 1983—). Home: 20 Menotti St Charleston SC 29401

KIMMEL, MARK, author, venture capital company executive; b. Denver, Feb. 15, 1940; s. Earl Henry and Gerry Claire Kimmel; m. Gloria J. Danielewicz, Jan. 29, 1966 (div.); children: Kenton, Kristopher; m. Heidi J. Moller, Sept. 5, 1999. BSEE, BS in Mktg., U. Colo., 1963; MBA in Fin., U. So. Calif., 1966; MA in Psychology, Regis U., 2000. Sales engr., market rsch. analyst 3M Co., Calif. and Minn., 1963-70; mktg. mgr. Am. Computer and Comms., Calif., 1970-71; mgr. new bus. devel. Motorola, Inc., Schaumburg, Ill., 1971-76; v.p. corp. devel. Nat. City Lines, Denver, 1976-77; pres. Enervest, Inc., Denver, 1977-84; gen. ptnr. Columbine Venture Fund Ltd., 1983-91, Columbine Venture Fund II, 1983-91, Columbine Venture Mgmt. I, 1983-91, Columbine Venture Mgmt. II, 1983-91; pres. Columbine Venture Mgmt. Inc., 1983-91, Paradigm Ptnrs., Inc., 1992-96; writer, 1996—. Author: Trillion, 2002. Mem. Nat. Assn. Small Bus. Invesetment Cos. (past bd. govs.), Venture Capital Assn. Colo. (past chmn.). E-mail: markkimmel@ridgwayco.net.

KIMMEL, MORTON RICHARD, lawyer; b. N.Y.C., Nov. 10, 1940; s. Benjamin Bert and Sylvia (Alabaster) K.; m. Marcia Harriet LaPotin, Sept. 10, 1967; children: Wayne Douglas, Michelle Wendy, Karen Paige, Larry Keith. BA, Temple U., 1962; JD, George Washington U., 1965. Bar: Del. 1965, D.C. 1966. Law clk. Del. Superior Ct., Wilmington, 1965-66; ptnr. Kimmel, Carter, Roman & Peltz P.A., Wilmington, 1970—. Supr. Del. Justices of the Peace, 1970-72; rep. State Farm Ins. Co., 1968-90, trustee lawyers' fund for client protection, 1985-97; arbitrator and mediator; lectr. in fields of criminal law, ins. law, personal injury law, law office mgmt., trial practice, ethics, professionalism, mediation and arbitration, 1970—. Author: You Can Do It, 1973, Emergency Medicine, 1982, Delaware Arbitration Manual, 1984, The Delaware Bar in the 20th Century, 1994. Mem. ATLA, Am. Bd. Trial Advs., Del. Trial Lawyers Assn., Fedn. Ins. Counsel, Def. Rsch. Inst. (chmn. Del. 1976-77). Democrat. Jewish. Avocations: sports, reading. Office: Kimmel Carter Roman & Peltz PA 913 N Market St Wilmington DE 19801-3019 E-mail: mrkimmel@kcrlaw.com.

KIMMEL, RICHARD E. music educator; b. Somerset, Pa., Mar. 15, 1966; s. Ellis Franklin and Donna Lee Kimmel. MusB Edn., Shenandoah U., Winchester, VA, 1988; Masters of Edn., Ind. U. of Pa, Indiana, PA, 1994. Music education K-12 Pa, 1989. Organist / handbell choir dir. First Presbyn. Ch., Johnstown, Pa., 1989—; music educator No. Cambria Sch., Northern Cambria, Pa., 1989—. Mem.: Music Educators Nat. Conf. R-Consevative. Avocations: travel, bike riding, music. Home: 302 Pennview Street Ebensburg PA 15931 Office: Northern Cambria School 601 Joseph Street Northern Cambria PA 15714 E-mail: RKi15530@wmconnect.com.

KIMMEL, ROBERT MICHAEL, education educator, consultant; m. Dee-Anne M. Kimmel, June 27, 1965; children: Richard L., Brian C., David I., Jeffrey S., Johanna L. BS, Mass. Inst. of Tech., 1964, MS, 1965, Materials Engr., 1967; DSc, Mass. Insitutute of Tech., 1968. Rsch. scientist Celanese Rsch. Co., Summit, NJ, 1968—70, sr. rsch. scientist, 1970—73; group leader Celanese Plastics Co., Greer, SC, 1973—75, project mgr., 1975—77, market specialist, 1977—79; industry manager-packaging and specialties Am. Hoechst Corp., Greer, SC, 1979—85, process rsch. mgr., 1985—88; bus. manager-packaging and specialties Hoechst Celanese Corp., Greer, SC, 1987—91; rsch. manager-new films Hoechst AG, Wiesbaden, Germany, 1991—94; new bus. devel. mgr. Hoechst R&D Corp., Greer, SC, 1994—98; pres. Reedy River Assocs., Simpsonville, SC, 1999—; assoc. prof. packaging sci. Clemson U., SC, 1999—. Lectr. The Fiber Soc., Princeton, NJ, 1975—76. Grad. Leadership Greenville, SC, 1988—89; chmn. Suzuki Acad. of Talent Edn., Greenville, SC, 1984—89. Fellow, Mass. Inst. of Tech., 1966; scholar, Nat. Merit Scholoarship Corp., 1960—64; Rohm & Haas Fellow, Mass. Inst. of Tech., 1967. Mem.: Soc. of Plastics Engrs. Achievements include patents for Seven patents in films And fibers. Office: Dept of Packaging Sci Clemson Univ Box 340370 Clemson SC 29634-0370 E-mail: kimmel@clemson.edu.

KIMMEL, SANFORD RICHARD, family physician, pediatrician, educator; b. Dennison, Ohio, July 25, 1949; s. Morris Henry and Elaine K.; m. Sharon Lynn Posey, June 15, 1980; children: Isaac David, Katherine Marie. BS, Ohio State U., 1971, MD, 1974. Diplomate Am. Bd. Family Practice, Am. Bd. Pediatrics. Resident in family medicine St. Elizabeth Med. Ctr., Dayton, 1974-77; assoc. residency dir. Grant-Livingston Family Practice Ctr., Columbus, Ohio, 1977-78; resident in pediat. Columbus Children's Hosp., 1978-80; gen. pediatrician Pediat. Assocs. Findlay, Ohio, 1980-82; asst. prof. family medicine Med. Coll. Ohio, Toledo, 1982-90, assoc. prof., 1990—2001, prof., 2001—. Postdoctoral fellow faculty devel. Mich. State U., East Lansing, 1983-84; panel mem., infant expert Bright Futures, Nat. Ctr. for Edn. in Maternal and Child Health, 1992-96; mem. vaccine risk/benefit comm. adv. bd., 1998-2000. Editor: Well Child Care, 1995; guest editor: Pediat./Adolescent Medicine in Primary Care, 1999, Pediatric Medicine in Primary Care, 2000, 2001; contbr. ; assoc. guest editor: Vaccines Across the Life Span, 2001, 2003, editor. Mem. Toledo chpt. Safe Kids Coalition, Toledo, 1994—, Ptnrs. for Health Kids, Toledo, 1996; bd. dirs. Maumee Valley dhpt. Am. Diabetes Assn., 1989-99, pres. chpt., 1993-94. Recipient Excellence in Tchg. award Med. Coll. Ohio Family Practice Residents, Toledo, 1996. Fellow Am. Acad. Pediat., Am. Acad. Family Physicians; mem. Soc. Tchrs. of Family Medicine (chair steering com. group on immunization edn. 1998-2002), Ohio Acad. Pediat., Ohio Acad. Family Physicians, Phi Beta Kappa. Avocations: collecting die-cast model cars, bicycling. Office: Med Coll Ohio Family Practice Ctr 1015 Garden Lake Pkwy Toledo OH 43614-2798 E-mail: skimmel@mco.edu.

KIMMEL, SIDNEY, apparel company executive; b. 1930; Founder, pres. Jones Apparel Group (Divsn. W.R. Grace & Co.), Bristol, Pa., 1970-75, chmn., CEO, 1975—, pres., 1994-96. Office: Jones Apparel Group 250 Rittenhouse Cir Bristol PA 19007-1616 Fax: 215-785-1795.

KIMMEL, TROY MAX, JR., meteorologist; b. Kilgore, Tex., Aug. 2, 1957; s. Troy Max and Diane King (Lipscomb) K. BS in Geography, Tex. A&M U., 1983. News editor, weathercaster Sta. KCNY, San Marcos, Tex., 1975-77, Sta. WKCU-AM-FM, Corinth, Miss., 1977-78; weathercaster Sta. KBTX-TV, Bryan, Tex., 1979-84; meteorologist Sta. KVUE-TV, Austin, Tex., 1984-89; chief meteorologist, 1989-93, Lower Colo. River Authority, Austin, 1993-94, Sta. KTBC-TV, Austin, 1994-97, Sta. KVET/KASE/KFMK, 1997—; weekend meteorologist KEYE 42 TV, 1998-99; chief meteorologist Sta. KEYE-TV, Austin, Tex., 2000—. Lectr. dept. geography U. Tex., Austin, 1988—, mgr. weather and climate resource ctr.; mgr. KimCo Meteorol. Svcs., Austin, 1981—; faculty advisor Kappa Sigma, U. Tex., 1991-98, Pi Kappa Alpha, U. Tex., 1998—; mem. housing corp. Pi Kappa Alpha, Southwestern U., 1989-92. Bd. dirs. Brazos Valley chpt. March of Dimes, Bryan, Tex., 1981-84, Ctrl. Tex. chpt., 1984-86, Capital Area United Cerebral Palsy, 1988-90, 93-95; co-host, host Muscular Dystrophy Telethon, Sta. KBTX-TV, Bryan, 1982-83, Sta. KVUE-TV, Austin, 1987; co-host United Cerebral Palsy Telethon, Sta. KVUE-TV, 1986-87, Children's Miracle Network Telethon, 1988-89, 91, 92, 93; mem. cmty. adv. coun. AIDS Svcs. Austin, 1998-2000; vol. civilian instr. weather safety/recognition Austin Police Dept. Tng. Acad., 1993—; mem. CD battalion aviation divsn. Austin Police Dept., 2002—. Recipient Outstanding Achievement awards UPI, 1983, 85, Best TV Weathercast in Tex. award UPI, 1984-87, Best Weathercast in Austin, Austin Chronicle, 1990, 91, 95, 98, Best Weathercast in Tex. award AP, 1990, 92, 2d pl., 1991. Mem. Am. Meteorol. Soc. (TV and radio seals of approval, sec.-treas. Cen. Tex. chpt. 1985-86, v.p. 1986-87, pres. 1987-90, nat. bd. on women and minorities 1991-94, nat. bd. Broadcast Meteorology 1992-94, nat. bd. on continuing edn., Outstanding Broadcaster Svc. award 1998), Nat. Weather Assn. (TV Seal of Approval, Broadcaster of Yr. 1988), Tex. Alliance for Geog. Edn. Methodist. Avocation: aircraft models and airline timetables. Home: 6512 Sans Souci Cove Austin TX 78759-5163 Office: KVET/KASE/KFMK Radio 706 N Lamar Blvd Austin TX 78703-5416 also: KEYE 42 TV 10700 Metric Blvd Austin TX 78758 E-mail: tkimmel@mail.utexas.edu., tmkimmel@keyetv.com.

KIMMELMAN, BURT JOSEPH, English language and literature educator; b. Bklyn., May 6, 1947; s. David Brown and Sylvia Kimmelman; m. LaVonne Mack, June 6, 1970 (div. Sept. 1, 1974); m. Diane Maureen Ellis Simmons, Dec. 28, 1989; 1 child, Jane Zvi Kimmelman. BA, SUNY, Cortland, 1983; MA, CUNY, 1986, PhD, cert. in medieval studies, 1991. Adj. lectr. Hunter Coll. CUNY, 1984-87, adj. lectr. Queens Coll., 1987-88, adj. lectr. Bklyn. Coll., 1987-89; adj. lectr. N.J. Inst. Tech., Newark, 1988-90, spl. lectr., 1990-93, asst. prof., 1993-98, assoc. prof., 1998—. Author: Musaics, 1992, The Poetics of Authorship in the Later Middle Ages, 1996, The Winter Mind, 1998, First Life, 2000, The Pond at Cape May Poiint, 2002; co-author: Environmental Protection, 1997; sr. editor: Poetry New York: A Journal of Poetry and Translation, 1985-00. Office: NJ Inst Tech Newark NJ 07102 E-mail: kimmelman@njit.edu.

KIMMEY, JAMES RICHARD, JR., foundation administrator; b. Boscobel, Wis., Jan. 26, 1935; s. James Richard and Frances Dale (Parnell) Kimmey; m. Sarah Webster Eastman, June 21, 1958; children: Elisabeth Webster, James Richard III. BS, U. Wis., 1957, MS, 1959, MD, 1961; MPH, U. Calif. at Berkeley, 1967. Diplomate Am. Bd. Preventive Medicine. Intern Univ. Hosps., Cleve., 1961-62; med. resident Univ. Hosp., Madison, 1962-63; served from surgeon to med. dir. USPHS, 1963-68, chief kidney disease br., 1964-66, regional health dir., 1967-68; exec. dir. Cmty. Health Inc., N.Y.C., 1968-70, Am. Pub. Health Assn., 1970-73; sec. Health Policy Coun. Wis., 1973-75; pres. James R. Kimmey Assos., Inc., 1975-85; dir. Midwest Ctr. Health Planning, 1976-79; exec. dir. Inst. Health Planning, 1979-87; prof. pub. health, dir. Ctr. for Health Svcs. Edn. Rsch. St. Louis U. Med. Ctr., 1987-91; dean sch. pub. health St. Louis U., 1991-93, v.p. health scis., 1993-98, exec. v.p., 1998-2000; dir. Inst. Urban Health Policy, 2000-2001; pres. Mo. Found. for Health, 2001—. Adj. prof. NYU, N.Y.C., 1968—70; lectr. Johns Hopkins, 1971—73; clin. instr. U. Wis., 1974—87; pres. Inst. Health Planning, 1979—86; chair Task Force Accreditation Health Professions, 1997—99, St. Louis ConnectCare, 1998—2001; dir. Ctr. Engring. Tech., 1998—2001; vice chair St. Louis Access Health, 1999—2001. Editor: (book) The Nation's Health, 1972—73; mng. editor: Am. Jour. Pub. Health, 1970—73, mem. editl. adv. bd.: Health Cost Mgmt., 1983—87; contbr. articles to profl. jours. Pres. World Fedn. Pub. Health Assns., 1972—73; mem. sci. adv. bd. Gorgas Inst., 1970—73; bd. dirs. Internat. Union Health Edn., 1970—73. Decorated USPHS Commendation medal. Fellow: APHA (governing coun. 1978—81, chmn. cmty. health planning sect. 1979—80, governing coun. 1983—87, 1989—92), Am. Coll. Preventive Medicine; mem.: Prospective Payment Assessment Commn. (commr. 1991—97), Mo. Pub. Health Assn. (Mo. Communicator of the Yr. award 1994), Am. Coll. Health Adminstrs., Am. Health Planning Assn. (dir. 1974—75, 1977—78, corp. sec. 1977—78, pres. 1980—81, Richard H. Schlesinger award 1978, James R. Kimmey award 1994), Alpha Sigma Nu, Delta Omega, Alpha Omega Alpha, Phi Eta Sigma. Democrat. Episcopalian. Home: 1614 S 18th St Saint Louis MO 63104-2504 Office: Grand Ctrl Bldg Ste 400 1000 St Louis Union Sta Saint Louis MO 63103 E-mail: jkimmey@mffh.org.

KIMMICH, CHRISTOPH MARTIN, academic administrator, educator; b. Dresden, Jan. 16, 1939; s. Emil and Dora (Dreher) K.; m. Flora Graham Horne, July 10, 1965. BA, Haverford Coll., 1961; DPhil, U. Oxford, Eng., 1964. Asst. then assoc. prof. Columbia U., N.Y.C., 1965-73; assoc. then full prof. Bklyn. Coll., CUNY, 1973—, assoc. provost, 1984-88, provost, v.p. acad. affairs, 1988-97; interim chancellor CUNY, N.Y.C., 1997-99; pres. Bklyn. Coll., 2000—. V.p. bd. dirs. rsch. and devel. fedn. Bklyn. Coll., 1989—; chmn. bd. dirs. rsch. found. of CUNY, 1997-1999, mem., 2000—; bd. dirs. Bklyn. Philharm., 2003—. Author: The Free City, 1968, Germany and the League of Nations, 1976, German Foreign Policy: 1918-1945, 1981, 2d edit., 1991. Trustee St. Antony's Coll. Trust, N.Y.C., 1978-2000; bd. dirs. Northeastern Sci. Found., Troy, 1987-98, Coll. Cmty. Svcs., Inc., Bklyn., 1988-95, chmn., 2000—; bd. trustees Cranbury Pub. Libr., 1997-2000. Fulbright scholar, 1961; Internat. Affairs fellow, 1974; Guggenheim fellow, 1983. Mem. Phi Beta Kappa. Home: 183 Plainsboro Rd Cranbury NJ 08512-2603 Office: Bklyn Coll Office of the Pres 2900 Bedford Ave Brooklyn NY 11210-2889

KIMMICH, HAYDEE JAVIER, orthopedist, consultant; b. Cabo Rojo, P.R., Apr. 25, 1927; d. Bartolome Javier Petrovich and Herminia Deprez Boscio; m. Homer Kimmich (dec. Oct. 7, 1985); children: John Kimmich, Denise Dijkstal. BA, Adelphi U., 1947; MD, Med. Coll. Pa., 1951. Diplomate Am. Bd. Surgery. Med. dir. State Ins. Fund, San Juan, P.R., 1953-57; resident Temple U., Phila., 1958-60; pvt. practive Springfield, Ill., 1961-74; med. dir. Rotary Rehab. Ctr., Mobile, Ala., 1974-76; commd. col. USAF, 1977, chief orthopedic Eglin Air Force Hosp., 1977-80; commd. capt. USN, 1984, chief orthopedic Bethesda Naval Hosp., 1984-95, sr. cons. Naval Hosp., 1995-2001. Asst. prof. Uniformed Sensice U. for Health Scis., Bethesda, Md., 1984-2001. Contbr. articles to profl. jours. Vol. physician U.S. AID, Vietnam, 1967, 97, orthopedic overseas, Riua, Peru, 1984. Named Woman of Yr. in Medicine and Military EL-DIA, 1998. Mem. Smithonian Assn., Audubon Soc., Academic Orthopedic Soc., Sierra Club, Ruth Jackson Found. Democrat. Avocations: sailing, traveling, cooking. Office: US Navy Naval Hosp Jacksonville FL 32210

KIMMICH, JON BRADFORD, computer science program executive; b. Lancaster, Pa., Aug. 8, 1964; s. John Howard and Alice (Ingram) K. BS in Computer Sci., Ind. U. Pa., 1986; MS in Computer Sci., Ohio State U., 1988; MBA, Seattle U., 1993. Developer Microsoft, Redmond, Wash., 1988-93, lead program mgr., sr. producer, 1993-97, lead product planner, 1997—. Dir. PKT Found. Contbr. articles to profl. jours. Trustee PKT Found. Mem. IEEE (Computer Soc.), Assn. for Computing Machinery, Acad. Interactive Arts and Scis., Internat. Interactive Comms. Soc., Am. Film Inst. Achievements include 7 patents pending. Home: 1442 W Lake Sammamish Pkwy SE Bellevue WA 98008-5218 Office: Microsoft Corp 1 Microsoft Way Redmond WA 98052-8300

KIMMINAU, JOAN A. marketing professional; b. Concordia, Kans., Apr. 17, 1947; d. John Leo Sheahan and Katherine Elizabeth Menges; m. Kenneth A. Kimminau, June 24, 1967 (div. June 24, 1997); 1 child, Angela Kimminau Schulte. Author: (poetry) The Miraculous Medal Mag., 1990, Verses Mag.; Iliad Press, 1995—97, 1999, Aspirations of Pen & Thought, 1997, (book) Unleash the Power. Mem.: Nebr. State Poetry Soc., Cath. Daughters of the Ams. (regent 1985—87), Nebr. Mothers Assn. Roman Catholic. Avocations: hiking, gardening, travel. Business E-Mail: joanpoet@yahoo.com.

KIMMITT, JOSEPH STANLEY, political consultant; b. Lewistown, Mont., Apr. 5, 1918; s. Joseph Henry Kimmitt and Margaret Bowe; m. Eunice Leona Wegener, Mar. 20, 1947; children: Robert, Jay, Tom, Mark, Mary, Judy. Student, U. Mont., 1940-41; BS, Utah State U., 1960; LLD (hon.), Mont. Tech., 1977. Commd. 2d lt. U.S. Army, 1942, advanced through grades to col., ret., 1966; adminstrv. asst. to majority leader U.S. Senate, Washington, 1966, sec. for majority, 1966-77, sec. of the senate, 1977-81; v.p. govt. affairs Hughes Helicopter Co., Washington, 1981-84; asst. to pres. for govt. affairs McDonnell Douglas Helicopter Co., Washington, 1984-97; ptnr. Kimmitt, Coates & McCarthy, Washington, 1997-2003, Kimmitt, Senter, Coates & Weinfurter, Washington, 2003—. Bd. dirs. Mont. Energy, Butte, Mont., U. Mont. Found., Missoula. Local pres., state v.p. Jaycees, Logan, Utah, 1948; bd. mem. March of Dimes, Arlington, Va.; bd. advisors Dem. Leadership Coun., Washington. Recipient various mil. awards U.S. Army, 1941-66. Mem. KC, Assn. U.S. Army (bd. dirs.), Nat. Def. Indsl. Assn. (bd. dirs.). Democrat. Roman Catholic. Home: 6004 Copely Ln Mc Lean VA 22101-2507 Office: Kimmitt Senter Coates & Weinfurter 1730 M St NW Ste 911 Washington DC 20036-4512

KIMMITT, ROBERT MICHAEL, executive, banker, diplomat, lawyer; b. Logan, Utah, Dec. 19, 1947; s. Joseph Stanley and Eunice L. (Wegener) K.; m. Holly Sutherland, May 19, 1979; children: Kathleen, Robert, William, Thomas, Margaret. BS, U.S. Mil. Acad., 1969; JD, Georgetown U., 1977. Bar: D.C. 1977. Commd. 2d lt. U.S. Army, 1969, advanced through grades to maj., 1982, served in Vietnam, 1970-71; maj. gen. USAR, 1999—; law clk. U.S. Ct. Appeals, Washington, 1977-78; sr. staff mem. NSC, Washington, 1978-83, dep. asst. to Pres. for nat. security affairs and exec. sec. and gen. counsel, 1983-85; gen. counsel U.S. Dept. Treasury, Washington, 1985-87; ptnr. Sidley & Austin, Washington, 1987-89; undersec. for polit. affairs Dept. State, Washington, 1989-91, ambassador to Germany, 1991-93; mng. dir. Lehman Bros., Washington, N.Y.C., 1993-97; sr. ptnr. Wilmer, Cutler & Pickering, Washington, 1997-00; vice-chmn., pres. Commerce One, Pleasanton, Calif., 2000-01; exec. v.p. AOL Time Warner, Washington, 2001—. U.S. mem. panel of arbitrators Ctr.

Settlement of Investment Internat. Disputes, 1988—89; bd. dirs. Allianz Life Ins. Co. N.Am., Xign Corp. Bd. dirs. German Marshall Fund, Atlantic Coun., Mike Mansfield Found., Am. Inst. Contemporary German Studies, Georgetown U. Decorated Bronze star (3), Purple Heart, Air medal, Vietnamese Cross of Gallantry, German Svc. Cross, German Army Cross in Gold; recipient Arthur Flemming award Downtown Jaycees, 1987, Alexander Hamilton award U.S. Dept. Treasury, 1987, Presdl. Citizens medal, 1991, Def. Disting. Civilian Svc. medal, 1993. Mem. Am. Acad. Diplomacy, Assn. Grads. U.S. Mil. Acad. (trustee 1976-82), Coun. Fgn. Rels. Roman Catholic. Office: AOL Time Warner 800 Connecticut Ave NW Washington DC 20006

KIMNACH, MYRON WILLIAM, botanist, horticulturist; b. Los Angeles, Dec. 26, 1922; s. Elmer Edward and Ida (Johnson) K.; m. Maria Jaeger, Nov. 17, 1961. Grad. h.s. Asst. mgr. U. Calif. Botanic Garden, Berkeley, 1951-62; curator Huntington Bot. Gardens, San Marino, 1962-88; book-dealer Monrovia, Calif. Contbr. articles profl. jours. Pres., bd. dirs. Palm Soc., 1976-78. With USCG, 1943-46. Fellow Cactus and Succulent Soc. Am. (pres. 1970-71, bd. dirs. 1968-74, editor jour. 1993-2003). Home and Office: 509 Bradbury Rd Monrovia CA 91016-3704 E-mail: mkimnach@aol.com.

KIMPORT, DAVID LLOYD, lawyer; b. Hot Springs, S.D., Nov. 28, 1945; s. Ralph E. and Ruth N. (Hutchinson) K.; m. Barbara H. Buggert, Apr. 2, 1976; children: Katrina Elizabeth, Rebecca Helen, Susanna Ruth. AB summa cum laude, Bowdoin Coll., 1968; postgrad., Imperial Coll., U. London, 1970-71; JD, Stanford U., 1975. Bar: Calif. 1975, U.S. Supreme Ct. 1978. Assoc. Baker & McKenzie, San Francisco, 1975-82, ptnr., 1982-90, Nossaman, Guthner, Knox & Elliot, 1990—. Active San Francisco Planning and Urban Rsch., 1978—, The Family, 1987—. Served with U.S. Army, 1968-70. Mem. ABA, San Francisco Bar Assn., Commonwealth Club of Calif., Phi Beta Kappa. Democrat. Episcopalian. Office: Nossaman Guthner Knox & Elliott 50 California St Fl 34 San Francisco CA 94111-4624

KIMURA, DOREEN, psychology educator, researcher; b. Winnipeg, Man., Can. 1 child, Charlotte Vanderwolf. BA, McGill U., Montreal, Que., Can., 1956, MA, 1957, PhD, 1961; LLD (hon.), Simon Fraser U., 1993, Queen's U., 1999. Lectr. Sir George Williams U. (now Concordia U.), Montreal, 1960-61; rsch. assoc. otol. rsch. lab. UCLA Med. Ctr., 1962-63; rsch. assoc. Coll. Medicine, McMaster U., Hamilton, Ont., 1964-67; assoc. prof. psychology U. Western Ont., London, 1967-74, prof., 1974-98, coord. clin. neuropsychology program, 1983-97. Supr. clin. neuropsychology Univ. Hosp., London, 1975-83; vis. prof. psychology Simon Fraser U., 1998—. Author: Neuromotor Mechanisms in Human Communication, 1993, Sex and Cognition, 1999, French, Japanese, Swedish, Spanish edit.; contbr. numerous articles to profl. jours. Recipient Outstanding Sci. Achievement award Can. Assn. Women in Sci., 1986, John Dewan award Ont. Mental Health Found., 1992; fellow Montreal Neurol. Inst., 1960-61. Geigy fellow Kantonsspital, Zürich, Switzerland, 1963-64. Fellow Royal Soc. Can., Can. Psychol. Assn. (Disting. Contbns. to Sci. award 1985); mem. Soc. Acad. Freedom & Scholarships (founding pres. 1992-93, 98-2000). Office: Simon Fraser U Dept Psychology Burnaby BC Canada V5A 1S6 E-mail: dkimura@sfu.ca.

KIM-YI, SUNGSOOK, music educator, pianist; b. Seoul City, Republic of Korea, Feb. 12, 1972; arrived in U.S., 1993; d. So Am Kim and Kyung Ja Jung; m. Ki Song Yi, Aug. 15, 1998. BA, Sungkyul U., An Yang, Republic of Korea, 1994; M in Ch. Music with honors, So. Bapt. Theol. Sem., 1998. Piano tchr., 1988—; children's choir dir. Kings Bapt. Ch., Taylorsville, Ky., 1996—97, ch. pianist, 1996—99; profs. asst. So. Bapt. Theol. Sem., Louisville, 1997—98; instr. The Studio of Wendy Kitts, Louisville, 1998—99; ch. pianist First Bapt. Ch. Springfield, Va., 2000—. Piano instr. Jr. Music Camp, Bedford, Ind., 1996, Bedford, 97, Bedford, 98; lectr. in field; judge various music competitions. Mem.: No. Va. Music Tchrs. Assn., Music Tchrs. Nat. Assn. Baptist. Avocations: yoga, ballet, cello, art museums, interior decorating. Home: 13134 Quail Creek Ln Fairfax VA 22033

KINAKA, WILLIAM TATSUO, lawyer; b. Lahaina, Hawaii, Apr. 4, 1940; s. Toshio and Natsumi (Hirouji) K.; m. Jeanette Louisa Ramos, Nov. 23, 1968; children: Kimberly H., Kristine N.Y. BA in Polit. Sci., Whittier Coll., 1962; MA in Internat. Rels., Am. U., 1964, JD, 1973. Bar: D.C. 1975, U.S. Ct. Appeals (D.C. cir.) 1975, U.S. Dist. Ct. D.C. 1975, U.S. Tax Ct. 1975, U.S. Ct. Mil. Appeals 1975, Hawaii 1976, U.S. Dist. Ct. Hawaii 1976, U.S. Ct. Appeals (9th cir.) 1976. Career trainee CIA, Langley, Va., 1966; legis. asst. Sen. Hiram L. Fong, Washington, 1966-76; assoc. Ueoka & Luna, Wailuku, Hawaii, 1977-85; pvt. practice law Wailuku, Hawaii, 1985—; grand jury counsel 2d Cir. Ct., 1985-86. Ct. arbitrator, 1989—; legal cons. Hale Mahaolu Elderly Housing, Kahului, 1976—. Active Dem. Party of Hawaii, Wailuku, 1988-89; pres. Nat. Eagle Scout Assn. of Boy Scouts Am., Wailuku, 1983-91; bd. dirs. Wailuku Main St. Assn., 1988-94, Maui Adult Day Care Ctr., Puunene, pres. 2000—; bd. dirs. Kahului; Maui Coun., Boy Scouts of Am.; bd. dirs. Maui Youth Intervention Program, Inc., pres. 1993—; bd. dirs. Iao Intermediate Sch. Renaissance Ednl. Found., pres. 1999—. Mem. Hawaii Bar Assn., Maui Bar Assn., Maui Japanese C. of C., Maui C. of C., Nat. Eagle Scout Assn. (pres. Wailuku 1983-91). United Ch. of Christ. Avocations: scouting, gardening, swimming, poetry writing. Home: 639 Pio Dr Wailuku HI 96793-2622 Office: 24 N Church St Ste 201 Wailuku HI 96793-1606

KINASEWITZ, GARY THEODORE, medical educator; b. N.Y.C., Aug. 17, 1946; m. Kathlee Anne O'Sullivan, Aug. 16, 1969; children: Amanda, Judith, Gregory. BS, Boston Coll., 1968, MEd, 1969; MD, Wayne State U., 1973. Diplomate Am. Bd. Internal Medicine. Rsch. assoc. U. Pa., Phila., 1978-79, asst. prof. medicine, 1979-80, La. State U. Med. Ctr., Shreveport, 1980-83, assoc. prof. medicine and physiology, 1983-88; coord., cardiovascular rsch. N.W. La. Biomed. Rsch. Ctr., Shreveport, 1987-88; prof. medicine and physiology La. State U. Med. Ctr., Shreveport, 1988, Okla. U. Health Scis. Ctr., Oklahoma City, 1988—, chief pulmonary and crit. care medicine, 1988—; mem. cardiovascular biology Okla. Med. Rsch. Found., Oklahoma City, 1994—. Mem. rsch. adv. com. N.W. La. Biomed. Rsch. Found., 1985-88; univ. rep. Am. Fedn. Clin. Rsch., 1984-87. Author: (book) Pulmonary Function Testing: Principles and Practice, 1984. Bd. dirs. Am. Heart Assn., La., 1983-87, Am. Lung Assn., Okla., 1991—. Recipient Albert Hyman award Am. Heart Assn., La., 1981. Fellow ACP, Am. Coll. Chest Physicians (pathophysiology adv. com. 1983-86, bd. govs. 1997-2002, bd. regents 1999-2002); mem. Am. Thoracic Soc. (coun. of chpt. reps. 1992-95), So. Soc. for Clin. Investigation, Ctrl.. Soc. Clin. Rsch., Am. Physiol. Soc., Alpha Omega Alpha. Office: Univ Okla Health Scis Ctr 920 Stanton L Young Blvd Rm 3sp Oklahoma City OK 73104-5020 E-mail: gary-kinasewitz@ouhsc.edu.

KINBERG, JUDY, television producer, director; b. Freeport, N.Y., Sept. 15, 1948; d. Jack H. and Rose M. (Schwartz) K. BA, Hofstra U., 1970. Prodn. asst. various programs including Camera Three CBS TV, N.Y.C., 1970-75; assoc. producer PBS-WNET/Dance in America, N.Y.C., 1975-76, producer, 1977—. NBC co-producer: He Makes Me Feel Like Dancin', 1984 (Acad. award, Emmy award, Chgo. Internat. Film Festival Silver Hugo, CINE Golden Eagle award, Christopher awards); prodr., dir. Who's Dancin' Now? (AFI L.A. Internat. Film Fest. Audience award, Best Documentary, Cine Golden Eagle award, Parents' Choice award), 1999; producer: PBS Dance in America: The Feld Ballet, 1979, The Green Table (with Joffrey Ballet), 1982, The Magic Flute (with N.Y.C. Ballet), 1983, San Francisco Ballet: A Song for Dead Warriors, 1984, A Choreographer's Notebook: Stravinsky Piano Ballets by Peter Martins, 1984, Balanchine, Parts I and II, 1984 (27th Ann. Internat. Film and TV awards of N.Y., gold medal Chgo. Internat. Film Festival Silver Plaque Monitor award, Emmy nomination), San Francisco Ballet in Cinderella, 1985 (Internat. Film and TV Festival of N.Y. gold medal, CINE Golden Eagle award, Parent's Choice award), Mark Morris, 1986 (CINE Golden Eagle award, Am. Film & Video Festival Red Ribbon award), Choreography by Jerome Robbins, 1986 (Chgo. Internat. Film Festival Silver Hugo, CINE Golden Eagle award), Dance Theatre of Harlem in A Streetcar Named Desire, 1986 (Chgo. Internat. Film Festival Silver Hugo), In Memory of...A Ballet by Jerome Robbins, 1987 (Chgo. Internat. Film Festival Silver Hugo, CINE Golden Eagle award), Agnes, the Indomitable de Mille, 1987 (Emmy award, Chgo. Internat. Film Festival Silver Hugo, CINE Golden Eagle award, Emmy nomination), Paul Taylor: Roses and Last Look, 1988, Balanchine and Cunningham: An Evening at Am. Ballet Theatre, 1988, La Sylphide (with the Pa./Milw. Ballet), 1989, A Night at The Joffrey, 1989, (Emmy nomination, Gold medal Internat. Film and TV Festival of N.Y., Best Video Creation IMZ Video Danse Awards, Gold Hugo award Chgo. Internat. Film Festival), The Search for Nijinsky's Rite of Spring, 1989 (producer/dir., Best Documentary IMZ Video Danse Awards, Internat. Film & TV Festival N.Y. Bronze medal), Baryshnikov Dances Balanchine, 1989 (Emmy nomination, finalist Internat. Film and TV Festival of N.Y.), Paul Taylor's Speaking in Tongues (Gold medal Internat. Film and TV Festival N.Y. Gold Plaque award Chgo. Internat. Film Festival), 1991, The Hard Nut with Mark Morris Dance Group, 1992 (Gold medal Internat. Film and TV Festival of N.Y., Emmy nomination), Balanchine Celebration, 1993 (with N.Y.C. City Ballet, Emmy nomination), The Wrecker's Ball, Three Dances by Paul Taylor, 1996 (Rose d'or de Montreaux Festival finalist); producer, dir. Bob Fosse/Steam Heat, 1990 (Emmy award, Ohio State award, Chgo. Film Festival Silver Plaque, Festival Internat. du Film Sur L'Art, Festival Rose d'Or, Montreux), A Tudor Evening with Am. Ballet Theatre, 1990, Balanchine in Am. with the N.Y.C. Ballet, 1990, Ballerinas: Dances by Peter Martins, 1991, A Renaissance Revisited, 1996 (N.Y. Festivals finalist award), (documentary) Variety and Virtuosity/American Ballet Theatre Now, 1998 (Chris award Columbus Internat. Film & Video Festival), Am. Ballet Theatre in Le Corsaire, (Emmy award 2000)From Broadway: Fosse, 2001 (CINE Golden Eagle award); producer PBS Great Performances: Out of Our Fathers' House, 1978; co-producer PBS Dance in America: Pilobolus Dance Theatre, 1977, Trailblazers of Modern Dance, 1977 (1st pl. 9th Ann. Dance Film and Video Festival), San Francisco Ballet: Romeo and Juliet, 1978, Choreography by Balanchine, Part III, 1978 (Chgo. Internat. Film Festival Silver Plaque, Emmy nomination), Choreography by Balanchine, Part IV, 1979 (Emmy award), The Martha Graham Dance Company: Clytemnestra, 1979 (Chgo. Internat. Film Festival Golden Hugo), Two Duets with Choreography by Jerome Robbins and Peter Martins, 1980, Nureyev and the Joffrey Ballet: In Tribute to Nijinsky, 1981 (Peabody award 1981, Emmy nomination), The Tempest: Live with the San Francisco Ballet, 1981, L'Enfant et Les Sortileges, 1981, Paul Taylor: Three Modern Classics, 1982, Paul Taylor: Two Landmark Dances, 1982, Bournonville Dances (with mems. ofN.Y.C. Ballet), 1982; co-producer PBS Theater in America: When Hell Freezes Over I'll Skate, 1979; prodr., dir. PBS Great Performances: The World of Jim Henson, 1994 (Parents Choice honor, 1995, Emmy award), Born to Be Wild: The Leading Men of American Ballet Theatre, 2002 (Festival Rose d'Or Montreux); prodr. PBS Stage on Screen: The Man Who Came to Dinner, 2000, The Women, 2002. Mem. Dirs.' Guild Am., Acad. TV Arts and Scis. Office: Thirteen/WNET/Dance In America 450 W 33rd St Fl 6 New York NY 10001-2603

KINCAID, JAMES LEWIS, lawyer; b. Carthage, Mo., Oct. 3, 1936; s. Joseph Lewis and Kathryn Lucille (Stein) K.; m. Aloah Ann Burke, Aug. 24, 1958; children: Kathryn, James Lewis Jr., Robert, Michael. AB, Harvard U., 1958, LLB, 1961. Bar: Okla. 1961. Assoc. then ptnr. Huffman, Arrington, Scheurich & Kincaid, Tulsa, 1961-70; ptnr. Conner & Winters, Tulsa, 1971-89; dir. Crowe & Dunlevy, Tulsa, 1989—. Mem. Okla. Bar Assn. Office: Crowe & Dunlevy 500 Kennedy Bldg Tulsa OK 74103 E-mail: kincaidj@crowedunlevy.com.

KINCAID, JOHN, political science educator, editor; b. Phila., May 5, 1946; s. John and Louise M. (Berger) K.; children: Karen Louise, Sarah Jeanenne. BA, Temple U., 1967, PhD, 1981; MA, U. Wis., 1968. Instr. St. Peter's Coll., Jersey City, 1969-70; dir. Phoenix Peace Ctr., 1970-72; v.p., treas. Pentagon Papers Fund for Civil Liberties, L.A., 1972-73; instr. Temple U., Phila., 1975-79; asst. prof. North Tex. State U., Denton, 1979-84; assoc. prof. U. North Tex., Denton, 1984-86; dir. rsch. U.S. Adv. Commn. on Intergovtl. Rels., Washington, 1986-87, exec. dir., 1987-94; Robert B. and Helen S. Meyner prof. govt. and pub. svcs. Lafayette Coll., Easton, Pa., 1994—, dir. Meyner Ctr. for Study State and Local Govt., 1994—. Rsch. fellow Ctr. for Study Federalism, Phila., 1982-85. Editor, contbr.: Political Culture, Public Policy and the American States, 1982, Covenant, Polity, and Constitutionalism, 1983, The Covenant Connection: Federal Theology and the Origins of Modern Politics, 2000, Competition among States and Local Governments, 1991; editor The Covenant Letter, 1979-92, Publius: Jour. Federalism, 1981—, (book series) State Government and Politics, 1983—; contbr. articles to profl. jours. Numerous grants NEH, Earhart Found., Ford Found., Fund for Improvement Postsecondary Edn., North Tex. State U., Nat. Inst. Edn., USIA. Mem. Am. Polit. Sci. Assn., Nat. Acad. Pub. Adminstrn., Acad. Polit. Sci., Southwestern Polit. Sci. Assn. (v.p., program chmn. 1984-86, pres. 1993-94). Episcopalian. Avocation: stamp collecting. Office: Lafayette Coll Meyner Ctr Easton PA 18042-1785 E-mail: meynerc@lafayette.edu.

KINCAID, JUDITH WELLS, electronics company executive; b. Tampa, Fla., July 1, 1944; d. George Redfield and Louise Wells (Brodt) K.; one child: Jennifer Wells Maben. A, Stanford U., 1966, MS in Indsl. Engring., 1978. Sci. programmer med. rsch. Stanford (Calif.) U., 1972-77; info. systems mgr. Hewlett Packard Co., Palo Alto, Calif., 1978-2001, mgr. strategic systems, 1985-91; direct mktg. mgr. Hewlett Packard Corp., Palo Alto, Calif., 1991-95, dir. customer relationship mgmt., 1995-2001; pres. JK Assocs., Palo Alto, Calif., 2001—. Author: (book) Customer Relationship Management: Getting It Right, 2003. Mem. Inst. Indsl. Engrs., Dir. Mktg. Assn. (privacy program chair 1998—, bus. to bus. ops. coun. 1998—). Office: JK Assocs LLC 445 Sherman Ste W Palo Alto CA 94306 E-mail: jkincaid@jk-associates.com.

KINCAID, PAUL KENT, public relations professional; b. Topeka, Kans., Oct. 13, 1952; s. E. Leon and Darlene A. (Schrader) K.; m. Janet Lynn Wilenzick, Nov. 8, 1975; children: Jennifer Elizabeth, Brian Christopher. BS in Mass Communications, Phillips U. Asst. news bur. dir. Phillips U., Enid, Okla., 1975-76; news bur. dir. Emporia (Kans.) State U., 1976-77, dir. univ. rels., 1977-86, S.W. Mo. State U., Springfield, 1986-94, assoc. v.p. for univ. advancement, dir. univ. rels., 1994—, also coord. govtl. rels., 1993—. Bd. dirs. Visually Impaired Presch., Springfield, 1989-93, pres. bd. dirs., 1990-92; active Springfield Area C. of C., 1986—. Mem. Pub. Rels. Soc. Am. (accredited), Soc. Profl. Journalists, Coun. for Advancement and Support Edn. (recipient several awards 1976—), Pub. Rels. of the Ozarks, Springfield Advt. Assn., Leadership Springfield Alumni Assn. Avocations: family, tennis, golf, management and leadership theory and practice. Home: 3154 W Tracy Ct Springfield MO 65807-3184 Office: SW Mo State U 901 S National Ave Springfield MO 65804-0088 E-mail: PKK130T@aol.com., PaulKincaid@smsu.edu.

KINCAID, RICHARD D. bank executive; B, Wichita State U.; MBA, U. Tex. With First Nat. Bank Chgo., Barclays Bank PLC; sr. v.p. finance Equity Group Investments, Inc., 1990—95; exec. v.p., CFO Equity Office Properties Trust, exec. v.p., COO, 1997—2001, pres., CEO, 2001—. Mem.: Real Estate Capitol Adv. Com. Office: Equity Office Properties Trust Two N Riverside Plaza Chicago IL 60606

KINCAID, RODNEY LYLE, construction company executive; b. Orlando, Fla., Feb. 9, 1933; s. Marion Troy and Thelma (Sellers) K.; m. Sue Sims, Dec. 16, 1961; 1 child, James Clay. B of Bldg. Constrn., U. Fla., 1958. Estimator H.J. High Constrn. Co., Orlando, 1958-59; office mgr. Innanen Bros. Constrn. Co., Orlando, 1959-60; estimator R.C. Stevens Constrn. Co., Orlando, 1960-62, Sorensen-Fletcher Constrn. Co., Winter Park, Fla., 1962-63; pres. Kincaid Constrn. Co., Winter Park, 1963—. Pres. Cen. Fla. Builder's Exchange, Orlando, 1978-79. Chmn. City of Orlando Bldg. Code Bd., 1973-76, City of Winter Park Code Bd., 1987—; mem. hist. bldg. com. City of Orlando, 1976; mem. econ. devel. task force Greater Orlando Aviation Authority, 1981; 2d v.p. Cen. Fla. Fair, Orlando, 1987, pres., 1990-91; bd. dirs. Better Bus. Bur. Cen. Fla., Inc., 1989-92, chmn. bd., 1993; pres., founder Oldsmobile Club Fla., 1995-97. With U.S. Army, 1953-55. Mem. Greater Orlando C. of C. (v.p. 1981), Pi Kappa Alpha. Clubs: Country of Orlando (bd. dirs. 1983-86), Econs. of Orlando (pres. 1983-84). Republican. Presbyterian. Avocations: tennis, swimming, collecting classic automobiles. Office: Kincaid Constrn Co PO Box 80 400 W Fairbanks Ave Winter Park FL 32790 E-mail: kincaid@kincaidconstruction.com., rodney@kincaidconstruction.com.

KINCAID, STEVEN RANDALL, marketing professional; b. Oklahoma City, July 19, 1953; s. William Calvin Hoover and Mary Elizabeth (Cochran) K. BA, Okla. State U., 1975; MA, U. Ill., 1977, PhD, 1980. Rsch. analyst Gen. Foods Corp., White Plains, N.Y., 1980-82; rsch. assoc. Opinion Rsch. Corp., Princeton, N.J., 1982-85, rsch. dir., 1985-86, rsch. exec., 1986-87, account exec., 1989-91; cons. John Hancock Life Ins. Co., Boston, 1987-88, dir. rsch., 1988-89, Prudential Ins. Co., Newark, 1991-93; sr. assoc. Abt Assocs., Cambridge, Mass., 1993-95; pres. Kincaid Assocs., Boxford, Mass., 1995-98; v.p. Fidelity Investments, Boston, 1998—2003, Bank of Am., 2003—. Named Eagle Scout Boy Scouts Am., 1968. Mem. Am. Assn. Pub. Opinion Research, Am. Polit. Sci. Assn., Applied Polit. Sci. Study Group. (charter), Mktg. Sci. Inst. (trustee), Phi Kappa Phi. Democrat. Methodist. Office: Bank of Am 201 N Tryon St Charlotte NC 28255

KINCANNON, LOUIS, federal agency administrator; b. Waco, Tex., Dec. 1940; m. Lois Claire Green; 2 children. Grad., U. Tex., 1963; postgrad., George Washington U., 1963—65, U. Md., 1966, Georgetown U., 1967. Statistician U.S. Census Bur., Washington, 1963—74, dep. dir., COO, 1982—92, acting dir., 1983—84, 1989; dir. US Census Bur. Dept. Commerce, Washington, 2002—; chief of program rev. staff Social and Econ. Statis. Adminstrn., Dept. Commerce, Washington, 1974; mem. staff Office Mgmt. and Budget, Washington, 1975—77, br. chief, 1978—82; first chief statistician Orgn. for Econ. Cooperation and Devel., Paris, 1992—2000. Spkr. and presenter in field. Mem.: Washington Statis. Soc., Nat. Assn. for Bus. Econs., Am. Statis. Assn., Inter-Am. Statis. Inst., Internat. Statis. Inst. Home: PO Box 66 Paeonian Springs VA 20129 Office: Dept Commerce US Census Bur Federal Center Bldg 3 Washington DC 20233

KINCH, E. L. LEE, lawyer; b. Topeka, May 15, 1939; s. Homer L. and Ellen F. (Shaner) K.; m. Linda K. Gard, Aug. 1964 (div. Apr. 1977); children: Kimberlee Ann, Wade Wesley; m. Mary Elizabeth Peters, Nov. 30, 1987. BA, U. Wichita, 1963; JD, U. Kans., 1966. Assoc. Schultz & Kirby, Wichita, Kans., 1966-67; ptnr. Ratner, Mattox, Ratner, Kinch & Brimer, Wichita, 1967-90, Post, Syrios & Kinch, Wichita, 1990-93; Law Offices E.L. Lee Kinch, 1993—. Author: Kansas Workers' Compensation Manual, 1978. Chmn. Sedgwick County Dem. Party, Wichita, 1986-92, 98—. Mem. ABA, Kans. Trial Lawyers Assn. (bd. govs. 1975—), Kans. Bar Assn., Wichita Bar Assn., ATLA. Avocations: politics, weight lifting, jogging, reading. Office: Pla 300 N Main St PO Box 47192 Wichita KS 67201-7192 E-mail: kinchl@aol.com.

KINCH, MICHAEL S. cancer researcher; b. Hamilton, Ohio, Dec. 10, 1966; m. Kelly Carles, Mar. 20, 1996; 1 child, Grant Kinch Sarah Kinch. PhD - Immunology, Duke U. Med. Ctr., 1993; BS in Molecular Genetics, The Ohio State U., 1989. Postdoctoral fellow U. N.C. - Lineberger Comprehensive Cancer Ctr., Chapel Hill, NC, 1993—96; asst. prof. Purdue U., West Lafayette, Ind., 1996—99, assoc. prof., 1999—2001; assoc. dir. of rsch. and devel. MedImmune, Inc., Gaithersburg, Md., 2001—. Author. Achievements include patents pending for 6+ Patents Pending. Office: MedImmune Inc 35 West Watkins Mill Rd Gaithersburg MD 20878

KINCHEN, THOMAS ALEXANDER, college president; b. Thomasville, Ga., Dec. 28, 1946; s. George H. and Annie L. (Castleberry) K.; m. Ruth Ann Hunter, Aug. 27, 1967; children: Alex, Lisa Ann. AB summa cum laude, Ga. So. Coll., 1969; MEd, U. Ga., 1975; MDiv, New Orleans Bapt. Theol. Sem., 1979, PhD, 1982. Pastor several chs., 1972-76; v.p. New Orleans Bapt. Theol. Sem., 1982-86; exec. dir., treas. W.Va. Conv. So. Bapt., Scott Depot, 1986-90; pres. The Bapt. Coll. of Fla., Graceville, 1990—. Editor Laos: All the People of God, 1984; contbr. articles to profl. jours. Bd. dirs. Area Devel. Coun., Graceville, 1991; mem. edn. commn. So. Bapt. Conv., 1992—; pres. bd. dirs. Jackson County Devel. Coun., 1996. Mem. So. Bapt. Adult Edn. Assn. (pres. 1996-98, v.p. 1994-96), Graceville C. of C. (pres. 1993), Kiwanis, NOBTS (Outstanding Alumnus 2000), ASBCS (bd. dirs. 2000-2003), Phi Kappa Phi, Alpha Psi Omega. Avocations: golfing, fishing, woodworking. Office: The Bapt Coll Fla 5400 College Dr Graceville FL 32440-1831 E-mail: takinchen@baptistcollege.edu.

KIND, KENNETH WAYNE, lawyer, real estate broker; b. Missoula, Mont., Apr. 1, 1948; s. Joseph Bruce and Elinor Joy (Smith) K.; m. Diane Lucille Jozaitis, Aug. 28, 1971; children: Kirstin Amber, Kenneth Warner. BA, Calif. State U., Northridge, 1973; JD, Calif. Western U., 1976. Bar: Calif. 1976, U.S. Dist. Ct. (ea., so., no. dists.) Calif., 1976, U.S. Cir. Ct. Appeals (9th cir.), U.S. Supreme Ct.; lic. NASCAR driver, 1987. Mem. celebrity security staff Brownstone Am., Beverly Hills, Calif., 1970-76; tchr. Army and Navy Acad., Carlsbad, Calif., 1975-76; real estate broker Bakersfield, Calif., 1978—; sole practice, 1976—. Lectr. mechanic's lien laws, Calif., 1983—. Staff writer Calif. Western Law Jour., 1975. Sgt. U.S. Army, 1967-70. Mem. ABA, VFW, Nat. Order Barristers, Rancheros Visitadores. Libertarian. Office: 4042 Patton Way Bakersfield CA 93308-5030

KIND, PHYLLIS, art gallery owner; BS in Chemistry, U. Pa., 1954, PhD in Phys. Chemistry, 1956; MA in English, U. Chgo., 1965. Mem. staff mdse. control Macy's, New York, N.Y., 1948-53; social worker N.Y.C. Dept. Welfare, 1954; 3d grade tchr. N.Y.C. Bd. Edn., 1956-59; various positions Chgo. Bd. Edn., 1960-67; owner Phyllis Kind Gallery, Chgo., 1967, N.Y.C., 1975—. Office: Phyllis Kind Gallery 136 Greene St New York NY 10012-3202

KIND, RONALD JAMES, congressman; b. La Crosse, Wis., Mar. 16, 1963; s. Elroy and Greta Kind; m. Tawni Zappa; 1 child, Johnny. BA with honors, Harvard U., 1985; MA, London Sch. Econs., 1986; JD, U. Minn., 1990. Atty. Quarles and Brady, Milw., 1990—92; district atty. La Crosse County, 1992—96; mem. U.S. Congress from 3d Wis. dist., 1997—; mem. house edn. and workforce com., resources com., agr. com. Active Freshman Bipartisan Campaign Fin. Reform Task Force; co-founder Upper Miss. River Congl. Caucus. Active Boys' and Girls' Club, La Crosse YMCA; bd. dirs. Coulee Coun. Alcohol or Other Drug Abuse. Mem. New Dem. Network, La Crosse Optimists Club. Democrat. Lutheran. Office: 1406 Longworth Bldg Washington DC 20515-4903*

KINDBERG, SHIRLEY JANE, pediatrician; b. Newark, Feb. 4, 1936; d. John Bertil and Mabel Jacoba (deJonge) Kindberg; m. Charles Dale Coln, May 12, 1962; children: Sara Goldstein, Eric Coln, Lois Thompson, Ruth Coln, Mary Kohn. BS, Wheaton Coll., 1957; MD, Baylor U., 1961. Intern Tex. Children's Hosp., Houston, 1961-62; resident Children's Med. Ctr., Dallas, 1962-63; fellow in pediat. pulmonary disease U. Tex. S.W. Med. Sch., Dallas, 1963-64, fellow in pediat. infectious disease, 1965-67; pvt. practice gen. pediat. Dallas, 1969-81; pvt. practice newborns, 1981—. Active N.W. Bible Ch., 1972—; mem. Dallas Symphony Assn. Fellow: Am. Acad. Pediat. (mem. sect. perinatal pediat.); mem.: Tex. Pediat. Soc. (com. fetus and newborn, com. on injury and environ. hazards). Republican. Avocations: cooking, travel, music, fitness. Office: 3600 Gaston Ave Ste 406 Dallas TX 75246-1804 E-mail: colnoma@cs.com.

KINDEL, JAMES HORACE, JR., lawyer; b. L.A., Nov. 8, 1913; s. James Horace and Philipina (Butte) K.; children: William, Mary, Robert, John. AB, UCLA, 1934; LLB, Loyola U., Los Angeles, 1940. Bar: Calif. 1941; CPA, Calif., 1942. Pvt. practice Kindel & Anderson, L.A., 1945—96; of counsel McKenna, Long & Ald, L.A., 1997—. Former ptnr. Coopers-Lybrand; co-owner gravel and poultry bus. Trustee UCLA Found. Mem. ABA, L.A. Bar Assn., Orange County Bar Assn., State Bar Calif., AICPA, Chancery Club, Calif. Club, Phi Delta Phi, Theta Xi. Home: 800 W 1st St Apt 2405 Los Angeles CA 90012-2432 Office: 444 S Flower St Fl 7 Los Angeles CA 90071-2901

KINDER, EUGENE J(OSEPH), psychiatrist, psychoanalyst; b. Chgo., Mar. 5, 1926; s. Joseph Casimer and Helen (Lincoln) K.; m. Patricia N. Chambers, Sept., 1953; children: Jean Marie Kinder Zukowski, Thomas E. MD, Loyola U., Chgo., 1952. Diplomate Am. Bd. Psychiatry and Neurology. Intern St. Anne's Hosp., Chgo., 1952-53; resident psychiatry Georgetown U., Washington, 1957-60; assoc. clin. prof. psychiatry U. Chgo., 1960-62; assoc. clin. prof. Rush Med. Sch., Chgo., 1960-70; clin. dir. Riveredge Hosp., Chgo., 1963-65; assoc. clin. prof. U. Wis., Madison, 1975-79; med. staff Maricopa Med. Ctr., Phoenix, 1979—; pres. Ariz. Psychoanalytic Study Group, Phoenix, 1984—. Mem. staff Camelback Hosp., Scottsdale, Ariz., Meml. hosp., Phoenix Bapt. Hosp., Good Samaritan Hosp., Phoenix, 1979—. Lt. comdr. USNR, 1954-56. Mem. Fellow Am. Psychiat. Assn.; mem. AMA, Am. Psychoanalytic Assn., Colo. Psychiat. Soc., Ariz. Psychiat. Soc. (v.p.), Ariz. Med. Assn., Chgo. Psychoanalytic Soc., Denver Psychoanalytic Soc. Office: 832 Lincoln Pl Boulder CO 80302-7555 E-mail: ekinder@comcast.net.

KINDER, PETER D. state legislator; b. Cape Girardeau, Mo., May 12, 1954; s. James A. and Mary Frances (Hunter) K. JD, St. Mary U., 1979; postgrad., U. Mo. Columbia, SE Mo. State U. Spl. asst. Rep. Bill Emerson, 1981-82; mem. Mo. Senate from 27th dist., Jefferson City, 1992—, pres. pro. tem. Staff counsel, real estate rep., 1983-87; assoc. publ., 1987—; campaign mgr., 1980, 82. Mem. Mo. Bar Assn., Am. Cancer Soc., Mo. Farm Bur., Area Wide United Way, Lions Club. Office: State Capital Bldg Rm 326 Jefferson City MO 65101*

KINDER, SUZANNE FONAY WEMPLE, historian, educator; b. Veszprem, Hungary, Aug. 1, 1927; arrived in U.S., 1948; d. Ernest Fonay and Magda Mihalyfy (Fonay) Szechenyi; m. George Barr Wemple, June 17, 1957 (dec. Apr. 1988); children: Peter Holland Wemple, Stephen Barr Wemple, Carolyn Wemple Steffey; m. Gordon T. Kinder, May 26, 1990. B, English Sisters, Budapest, Hungary, 1945, U. Calif., Berkeley, 1953; MLS, Columbia U., 1955, PhD, 1967. Instr. Stern Coll. Women, N.Y.C., 1962-63; asst. prof. Tchrs. Coll., Columbia U., N.Y.C., 1964-66; from asst. prof. to prof. Barnard Coll., Columbia U., N.Y.C., 1966-92, ret., 1992. Author: Atto of Vercelli: Church, State and Christian Society, 1979, Women in Frankish Society, 1981, 83 (Berkshire prize 1981); co-editor: Women in Medieval Society, 1985; contbr. articles to profl. jours. Recipient grant NEH, 1975, 80, 81-85, Spivack summer grant Barnard Coll., 1970, 81, Fulbright grant, 1982. Mem.: NOW, AAUP. Home: 1285 Gulf Shore Blvd N Naples FL 34102-4911

KINDIG, EVERETT WILLIAM, history educator; b. Kansas City, Kans., Oct. 5, 1936; s. Everett Kenneth and Zella Muriel (Mueller) K.; m. Judith Ann Iler, Nov. 5, 1966; children: Everett William Jr., Aimee Elizabeth. BA, Stanford U., 1958, MA, 1963, PhD, 1975. Tchg. asst. Stanford U., Palo Alto, Calif., 1959-61, grad. asst., 1964-65; instr. San Jose (Calif.) State U., 1967-70; acting asst. prof. Santa Clara (Calif.) U., 1970-71; instr. Midwestern State U., Wichita Falls, Tex., 1971-72, asst. prof., 1972-84, assoc. prof. dept. history, 1984—. Mem. faculty libr. com. Midwestern State U., 1973-92, chmn., 1975-81, mem. rank and tenure com., 1992-95, faculty senate, 1998-2000. Author: Midwestern State University: The Better Part of a Century, 2001; contbr. articles and book revs. to profl. jours. Election judge Wichita County, Tex., 1984-91; lay reader Episc. Ch., Diocese of Ft. Worth, Good Shepherd, Wichita Falls, 1980-93; dir. Episc. Elem. Sch., Wichita Falls, 1980-84; pres. Quail Creek Homeowners Assn., Wichita Falls, 1987-93; cubmaster N.W. Tex. coun. Boy Scouts Am., 1984-85; chmn. Midwestern State U. com. Constl. Bicentennial, 1987-93. Rsch. grantee Hardin Found., Wichita Falls, 1977, Midwestern State U., Wichita Falls, 1977, 88. Mem. Soc. Historians of Early Am. Republic, Mo. Hist. Soc., Stanford Alumni Assn., Phi Alpha Theta (faculty advisor Midwestern State U., 1972—), Coll. Republicans (faculty advisor Midwestern State U. 1980—), Phi Alpha Theta (mem. nat. coun. 2001—). Methodist. Avocations: travel, reading. Home: 4115 Seabury Dr Wichita Falls TX 76308-3107 Office: Midwestern State U 3410 Taft Blvd Wichita Falls TX 76308-2096 E-mail: kindigs@wf.quik.net.

KINDIG, FRED EUGENE EUGENE, statistics educator, arbitrator; b. York, Pa, Sept. 5, 1920; s. Fred E. and Hattie (Keller) K.; m. Marie M. Doyle (dec. 1971); children: Pamela M., Bonita K., Gretchen A., Suzanne J.; m. Grace L. Mathison, Aug. 19, 1972 (dec. 1979); m. Susan S. Friend, Mar. 16, 1980. BS, Pa. State U., 1942; MS, U. Pitts., 1947, PhD, 1951. Indsl. engr., supr. Westinghouse Electric Corp., Pitts., 1942-51; asst. to exec. v. p. Phoenix Glass, Monaca, Pa., 1951-53; asst. and assoc. prof. U. Pitts., 1953-62; prof., coordinator quantitative methods Ohio State U., Columbus, 1962-81, prof. emeritus, 1981—; labor mgmt. arbitrator, 1953—. Author: Fundamentals of Statistical Controls and Fundamentals of Linear Programming, 1956; Contbr. articles to profl. jours. Pres. PTA, various times; mem. Franklin County 648 Bd., 1979-82; trustee, chmn. bd. trustees Columbus State Cmty. Coll., 1982-92; trustee emeritus, 1992—. Mem. Am. Inst. Decision Sci. (v.p. 1969-71), Am. Arbitration Assn., Nat. Acad. Arbitrators, Am. Soc. Quality Control, Inst. Math. Stats., Am. Statis. Assn., Indsl. Relations Research Assn., Ops. Research Soc. Am., Soc. Profls. In Dispute Resolution, Alpha Sigma Phi, Tau Beta Pi, Beta Gamma Sigma. Clubs: Brookside Country, Univ. Home: 213 Saint Antoine St Columbus OH 43085-2242 *Although fate plays an important role, perseverance, absolute honesty, basic integrity, and the highest of moral standards make for an unbeatable combination.*

KINDLER, JEFFREY B. lawyer; b. May 13, 1955; JD, Harvard Law Sch., 1980; BA, Tufts Univ., 1977. Bar: D.C. 1980. V.p. and sr. counsel, litig. and legal policy Gen. Electric; ptnr. Williams and Connolly, Wash., DC; law clk. US Supreme Ct. Justice, william J. Brennan, Jr.; pres. ptnr. brands McDonald's Corp., 1996-97, exec. v.p., gen. counsel, 1997—2002; chmn., CEO Boston Market, Oak Brook, Ill., 2000-2001; pres., ptnr. Brands McDonalds Corp., 2001—02; chmn., CEO Boston Market, 2001—02; sr. v.p. & Gen. Coun. Pfizer, Inc., NYC, 2002. Mem.: Nat. Ctr. for State Cts., Corp. Coun. Adv. Bd., Council of Chief Legal Officers, Civil Justice Reform Group, Am. Bar Assoc., Assoc. of Gen. Coun., City Bar Fund., US Chamber, Atlantic Legal Found., Citizens Crime Comm., Jane Addams Juvenile Ct. Found., Am. Arbitration Assoc. Office: Pfizer Office of Gen Coun 235 E 42nd St New York NY 10017 E-mail: jeff.kindler@mcd.com.

KINDLUND, NEWTON CARLTON, retail executive; b. Detroit, Mich., June 25, 1940; s. Newton K. and Virginia M. Kindlund; children: Anne Kirsten, Erika Page; m. Joanne Weber Kindlund, May 29, 1974; 1 child, Darien F. BA, Mich. State U., 1963; postgrad., Boston Coll., 1969; student, U. Pa., 1977. Nat. sales mgr. Vesely Co., Inc., Lapeer, Mich., 1963-68; v.p. sales and mktg. Midas Internat. Corp., Chgo., 1968-70; pres. Recreation Enterprise Corp., Gainesville, Fla., 1970-73, N.C. Kindlund & Assoc., Glenville, N.C., 1974-75; regional v.p. Recreational Vehicle Industry Assn., Washington, 1976-77; founder, pres. Holiday of Orlando (Fla.), Inc., 1977-85, Holiday RV Rental/Leasing, Orlando, 1985-90; bd. chmn., founder, pres. Holiday RV Superstores, Inc., Orlando, 1987—. Pres. Holiday RV Superstores of N.Mex., Inc., Holiday RV Assurance Svcs., Inc. of Ariz., Holiday RV Superstores of S.C., Inc., Holiday RV Superstores West, Inc.; bd. dirs. Recreational Vehicle Industry Assn., Chgo., 1970-72, Cen. Fla. World Trade Coun., Orlando, 1985-87; adv. bd. Trailer Life Publs., 1985-90. Contbr. articles to profl. jours. Founding bd. mem. Fla. Recreational Vehicle Trade Assn., Tampa, 1978; bd. dirs. Ctrl. Fla. Better Bus.Bur., Winter Park, 1994-95; adv. bd. Crummer Sch. of Bus., Rollins Coll., Winter Park, Fla., 1998, 99; judge Students in Free Enterprise, Clearwater, Fla., 1998, 99; bd. mem. Orlando Festival of Orchestras, 1999, Recreational Vehicle Found. Bd., 1999. Recipient Small Bus. Person of Yr. award Small Bus. Adminstrn., State of Fla., 1982, Entrepreneur of Yr. award Ernst & Young, Inc., Tampa, 1990, 100 award Miami Herald, 1992, 93, semi-finalist Jim Moran Entreprenurial Excellance award Fla. State U., 1996; named one of 500 fastest growing pvt. cos. Inc. Mag., 1983, one of top 150 Fla. pub. corps. Fla. Travel mag., 1993, one of Fla. top 100 cos. Orlando Metro 100, 1993, Industry Exec. of Yr., RV News Mag., 1995. Mem. Fla. RV Trade Assn. (founding mem., bd. dirs. 1987-90), Family Motor Coach Assn. (adv. bd. 1990—), Nat. RV Bus. Assn. (adv. bd. 1989-90), Recreational Vehicle Rental Assn. (nat. chmn. 1992, 93), Recreational Vehicle Dealers Assn. (exec. bd. 1992, 93), Orlando C. of C. (bd. dirs., exec. com. 1984-88, Silver 100 award 1992). Republican. Episcopalian. Avocations: skiing, golf, sailing. kindlund.com. Home: Kindlund Investments Inc Winter Park FL 32789-5747 Address: 280 Stirling Ave Winter Park FL 32789 E-mail: jmkindlund@cfl.rr.com.

KINDREGAN, CHARLES PETER, law educator; b. Phila., June 18, 1935; s. Charles Peter and Catherine (Delaney) K.; m. Patricia Ann. Patterson, Aug. 18, 1962 (dec. 1998); children: Chad, Helen, Tricia, Brian. BA, LaSalle U., 1957, MA, 1958; JD, Chgo.-Kent Coll. Law, 1966; LLM, Northwestern U., 1967. Bar: Ill. 1966, Mass. 1968, U.S. Dist. Ct. Mass. 1970. Instr. Va. Mil. Inst., 1960-62, Loyola U., Chgo., 1964-67; prof. law Suffolk U., Boston, 1967—, assco. dean, 1990-94. Author: The Quality of Life, 1969, Malpractice and the Lawyer, 1981, professional Responsibility of the Lawyer, 1995; co-author: Massachusetts Family Law and Practice, 3d edit., 2003, (with M. Inker) Mass. Domestic Relations Rules Annotated, 2003; contbr. articles to profl. jours. Mem. Hull Bd. Zoning Appeals, Mass., 1969; pres. Beacon Hill PTA, Boston, 1974-75. Mem. ABA (academic rep. to publications bd. family law sect.), Mass. Bar Assn. (task force on model rules of profl. conduct 1982-84, co-chair com. on crisis in probate and family ct. 1994-97), Suffolk Ctr. for Advanced Legal Studies (dir. 1982-87). Democrat. Roman Catholic. Home: 150 Stanford St Apt 710 Boston MA 02114-2597 Office: Suffolk U Law Sch 120 Tremont St Boston MA 02108-4977

KINDRICK, ROBERT LEROY, academic administrator, dean, English educator; b. Kansas City, Mo., Aug. 17, 1942; s. Robert William and Waneta LeVeta (Lobdell) K.; m. Carolyn Jean Reed, Aug. 20 1965. BA, Park Coll., 1964; MA, U. Mo., Kansas City, 1967; PhD, U. Tex., 1971. Instr. Ctrl. Mo. State U., Warrenburg, 1967-69, asst. prof. to assoc. prof., 1969-78, prof., 1978-80, head dept. English, 1975-80; dean Coll. Arts and Scis.; prof. English Western Ill. U., Macomb, 1980-84; v.p. acad. affairs, prof. English Emporia State U., Kans., 1984-87; provost, v.p. acad. affairs, prof. English Eastern Ill. U., Charleston, 1987-91; provost, v.p. acad. affairs, dean grad. studies, dean grad. sch., prof. English, U. Mont., 1991-2000; v.p. for acad. affairs and rsch. Wichita State U. Author: Robert Henryson, 1979, A New Classical Rhetoric, 1980, Henryson and the Medieval Arts of Rhetoric, 1993, William Matthews on Caxton and Malory, 1997, The Poems of Robert Henryson, 1997; editor: Teaching the Middle Ages, 1981—, (jour.) Studies in Medieval and Renaissance Teaching, 1975-80; co-editor: The Malory Debate, 2000; contbr. articles to profl. jours. Chmn. bd. dirs. Mo. Com. for Humanities, 1979-80, Ill. Humanities Coun., 1991; pres. Park Coll. Young Dems., 1963; v.p. Mo. Young Dems., Jefferson City, 1964, campus coord. United Way, Macomb, Ill., 1983; mem. study com. Emporia Arts Coun., 1985-88; mem. NFL Edn. Adv. Ed., 1995—. U. Tex. fellow, 1965-66, Am. Coun. Learned Socs. travel grantee, 1975; Nat. Endowment for Humanities summer fellow, 1977; Medieval Acad. Am. grantee, 1976; Mo. Com. Humanities grantee, 1975-84; Assn. Scottish Lit. Studies grantee, 1979. Mem. Mo. Assn. Depts. English (pres. 1978-80), Mo. Philol. Assn. (founding pres. 1975-77), Medieval Assn. Midwest (councillor 1977—, ex officio bd. 1980—, v.p. 1987-88, exec. sec. 1988—), Ill. Medieval Assn. (founding exec. sec. 1983-93), Mid-Am. Medieval Assn., Rocky Mtn. MLA, Assn. Scottish Lt. Studies, Early English Text. Soc., Societe Rencesvals, Medieval Acad. N.Am. (exec. sec. com. on ctrs. and regional assns.), Internat. Arthurian Soc., Sigma Tau Delta, Phi Kappa Phi, Rotary (editor Warrensburg club). Home: PO Box 20110 Wichita KS 67208-1110 Office: Wichita State U 109 Morrison Hall Wichita KS 67208 E-mail: Robert.Kindrick@Wichita.edu.

KINDSCHUH, JEFFERY ALAN, civil engineer; b. Waupun, Wis., Feb. 24, 1956; s. Calvin Chester and Joyce Nellie (Tornow) K.; m. Billie L. Pearson, Oct. 26, 1985; children: William, Victoria Jeffries. BSCE with honors, USAF Acad., 1978; MS in Constrn. Engring. and Mgmt., U. Mich., 1981. Registered profl. engr.; diplomate environmental engr. (Am. Acad. of Environmental Engrs.). Commd. 2d lt. USAF, 1978, advanced through grades to capt., 1985, resigned, 1985; project mgr. Butt Constrn. Co., Dayton, Ohio, 1985; chief engr. civil engring. dept. Northrop Worldwide Aircraft Svcs., Inc., Enid, Okla., 1985-90; br./regional mgr. G & E Engring., Inc., Oklahoma City, 1990-92, v.p., regional mgr., 1992-96; construction mgr. Enercon Svcs., Inc., Oklahoma City, 1996; pres. Wolverine Constrn. Mgmt., Inc., 1996—98; mgr. constrn. svcs. Std. Testing and Engring. Co., Oklahoma City, 1998—. Active Big Bros./Big Sisters of Greater Dayton, 1982-85. Named Young Engr. of Yr Okla. Soc. Profl. Engrs., 1992. Mem. NSPE (Okla. chpt. sec.-treas. 1986-87, pres. 1987-88, Okla. state v.p. 2002-03), Okla. Soc. of Environ. Profls. (state pres.-elect 1995-96, state pres. 1996-97). United Methodist. Avocation: travel. Home: 5404 NW 115th St Oklahoma City OK 73162-3747 Office: Standard Testing and Engring Co 3400 N Lincoln Blvd Oklahoma City OK 73105

KINDSTEDT, PAUL STEPHEN, food science educator; s. Edward Arvid and Amelia Maria Kindstedt; m. Christina Chunua Ge, May 28, 1994; children: Ingalise Guofan, Annalise Guochang. BS, U. Vt., 1979, MS, 1981; PhD, Cornell U., 1986. Asst. prof. U. Vt., Burlington, 1986—91, assoc. prof., 1991—96, prof., 1996—2003. Assoc. dir. N.E. Dairy Foods Rsch. Ctr., Burlington, 1999—2003. Contbr. articles to peer-reviewed and tech. publs.; author 11 book chpts., book in field; contbr. abstracts to profl. publs. Recipient R.L. Bickford scholarship, U. Vt., 1999, sr. fellowship, CSIRO Food Sci., Australia, 1996. Mem.: Am. Dairy Sci. Assn. (exec. coun. mem.-at-large dairy foods divsn. 1997—2000, Pfizer award 1993). Evangelical Christian. Avocations: hiking, camping, cross country skiing. Office: U Vt 212 Carrigan Hall 536 Main St Burlington VT 05405-0044 Office Fax: 802-656-0001. E-mail: paul.kindstedt@uvm.edu.

KINDT, JOHN WARREN, lawyer, educator, consultant; b. Oak Park, Ill., May 24, 1950; s. Warren Frederick and Lois Jeannette (Woelffer) K.; m. Anne Marie Johnson, Apr. 17, 1982; children: John Warren Jr., James Roy Frederick. AB, Coll. William and Mary, 1972; JD, U. Ga., 1976, MBA, 1977; LLM, U. Va., 1978, SJD, 1981. Bar: D.C. 1976, Ga. 1976, Va. 1977. Advisor to gov. State of Va., Richmond, 1971-72; asst. to Congressman M. Caldwell Butler, U.S. Ho. of Reps., Washington, 1972-73; staff cons. White House, Washington, 1976-77; asst. prof. U. Ill., Champaign, 1978-81, assoc. prof., 1981-85, prof., 1985—. Cons. 3d UN Conf. on Law of Sea; lectr. exec. MBA program U. Ill. Author: Marine Pollution and the Law of the Sea, 4 vols., 1981, 2 vols., 1988, 92, Economic Impacts of Legalized Gambling, 1994; contbr. articles to profl. jours. Caucus chmn., del. White House Conf. on Youth, 1970; co-chmn. Va. Gov.'s Adv. Coun. on Youth, 1971; mem. Athens (Ga.) Legal Aid Soc., 1975-76. Rotary fellow, 1979-80; Smithsonian ABA/ELI scholar, 1981; sr. fellow London Sch. Econs., 1985-86. Mem. Am. Soc. Internat. Law, D.C. Bar Assn., Va. Bar Assn., Ga. Bar Assn. Home: 801 Brookside Ln Mahomet IL 61853-9545 Office: U Ill 350 Commerce W Champaign IL 61820

KINES, JOAN ELAINE, human services administrator, consultant; b. Rome, Ga., Jan. 12, 1949; d. James Benjamin Satterfield and Janie Lee (Potts) Smith. BSBA with honors, Shorter Coll., 2001. Reimbursement specialist Grady Hosp., Atlanta, 1968-73; quality assurance coord. Redmond Park Hosp., Rome, 1974-77; mktg. dir. Zachiarias & Assocs., Columbus, Ga., 1977-79; office mgr. Interstate Health Mgmt., Atlanta, 1980-81; adminstr. Regional Radiation Oncology, Rome, 1982—2000, Regional Radiation Oncology Ctr., Rome, 2000—. Cons. in field. Mem. adv. com. N.W. Ga. Regional Cancer Coalition, 2002—. Mem.: Global Rsch. Sys. (bd. dirs. 1993—2001), Assn. Cancer Execs., Amublatory Care Adminstrs., Am. Coll. Med. Group Adminstrs., Soc. Radiation Oncology Adminstrs. (bd. dirs. 1996—, treas. 1998—2002), Rome C. of C. (polit. action com. 1986—90, bd. dirs. 2003—), Optimist (charter pres. Rome club 1989, membership chmn. 1990, bd. dirs. 1991—95). Avocations: fishing, swimming, reading, travel, hiking. Office: Regional Radiation Oncology Ctr@Rome 321 W 5th St Rome GA 30165-2818

KING, ALFRED MEEHAN, financial executive; b. Boston, Mass, Oct. 31, 1933; s. Lester S. and Marjorie C. (Meehan) K.; m. Mary Jane Oliver, Dec. 19, 1976; 1 child, Thomas A.; stepchildren: Tina Marie Oliver, Katherine Mary Lefebre. AB magna cum laude, Harvard Coll., 1954, MBA, 1959. Acctg. supr. Gen. Motors Co., LaGrange, Ill., 1959-64; asst. contr. J.I. Case Co., Racine, Wis., 1964-69; v.p. fin. Valuation Rsch. Corp., Milw., Minn., 1978-81, 91—, chmn. bd. dir., 1996—. Dir. Valuation Rsch. Corp., Milw., 1980—; mng. dir. Nat. Assn. Accts., Montvale, NJ, 1981-91; adj. asst. prof. U. Wis.-Parkside, Kenosha, 1978-81; adj. instr. Fordham U., NYC, 1989-96; vis. com. Fordham Grad. Sch. of Bus. Adminstrn. Author: Increasing the Productivity of Company Cash, 1969, Total Cash Management, 1994; Valuation, 2002; mem. editl. adv. bd. Jour. Cost Mgmt. and Strategic Fin. Treas. Village of North Bay, Wis., 1972-76, Racine Symphony Orch., 1979-81; mem. Saddle River (NJ) Sch. Bd., 1992-95. Mem. Inst. Mgmt. Acctg. (regent 1978-81, bd. dir. 1995-98), Fin. Exec. Inst., Valley Club (pres. 1983-84). Republican. Presbyterian. Home: 11102 Fawn Lake Pkwy Spotsylvania VA 22553-4667 Office: Valuation Rsch Corp 100 Nassau Park Blvd Princeton NJ 08540-5932 E-mail: alfredking@erols.com.

KING, ALGIN BRADDY, retired marketing educator; b. Latta, S.C., Jan. 19, 1927; s. Dewey Algin and Elizabeth (Braddy) K.; m. Barbara I. Kelley, Nov. 29, 1997: children: Drucilla Ratcliff, Martha Louise. BA in Retailing and Polit Sci. cum laude, U. S.C., 1947; MS, NYU, 1953; PhD, Ohio State U., 1966. Exec. trainee Sears, Roebuck & Co., 1948-48; instr. retailing U. S.C., 1948-51; chief econ. analysis br. dist. OPS, 1951-53; exec. dir. Columbia (S.C.) Mchts. Assn., 1953-54; asst. prof. Tex. A&M U., 1954-55; mem. faculty Coll. William and Mary, 1955-72, prof. bus. adminstrn., 1959-72, dir. Bur. Bus. Research, 1959-63, assoc. dean Sch. Bus. Adminstrn., 1968-72; prof., dean Ctrl. Conn. State U. Sch. Bus., Avon, 1972-73; prof., head dept. bus. and econs. James Madison U., 1973-74; prof., dean Western Carolina U. Sch. Bus., Cullowhee, N.C., 1974-76; prof. mktg. and mgmt. Christopher Newport U., Newport News, Va., 1976-87, dean Sch. Bus. Adminstrn. and Econs., 1977-87; prof. mgmt. and mktg. Towson (Md.) State U. Sch. Bus. and Econs., 1987-96; ret., 2003. Pres. Bus. and Adminstrv. Cons. Ltd. (mgmt. and mktg. cons.); teaching asst. Ohio State U., 1963-64; professorial lectr. George Washington U.; mgmt. cons. CSC, U.S. Army. Author: (with others) Hampton Waterfront Economic Study, 1967, The Source Book of Economics, 1973, Management Perceptions, 1976, International Marketing by Dabringer & Muellach Instrn. Manual, 1991; contbr. chpts. to books and articles to profl. jours. Mem. finance resource group Conn. Council Higher Edn., 1972-73; mem. U.S. Senatorial Bus. Adv. Bd. W.T. Grant Retailing scholar, 1947. Mem. Am. Mktg. Assn., Acad. Mgmt., Am. Inst. Decision Scis., Phi Beta Kappa. Episcopalian. E-mail: aking@towson.edu.

KING, ALMA JEAN, former health and physical education educator; b. Hamilton, Ohio, Feb. 28, 1939; d. William Lawrence and Esther Mary (Smith) K. BS in Edn., Miami U., Oxford, Ohio, 1961; MEd, Bowling Green State U., 1963; postgrad., Fla. Atlantic U., 1969, '92, Nova U., Ft. Lauderdale, Fla., 1979. Cert. elem. and secondry tchr., Ohio, all levels incl. coll., Fla. Tchr. health, physical edn. Rogers Middle Sch., Broward County Bd. Pub. Instrn., 1963-64; assoc. prof. health, phys edn., recreation, dance Broward C.C., Fort Lauderdale, Fla., 1964-94; ret., 1994. Dir. Intramurals and Extramurals Broward C.C., Fort Lauderdale, Fla., 1964-67, chair person Women's Affairs, 1978, health and safety com., 1975, faculty evaluation com. 1980-85, mem. faculty ins. benefits com. 1993-94. Sponsor Broward County Fire Fighters, Police; active mem. Police Benevolent Assn.; Historical Soc. Grantee Broward C.C. Staff Devel. Fund, 1988. Mem. AAHPERD, NEA, Fla. Edn. Assn., Fla. Assn for Health, Physical Edn., Recreation and Dance, Am. Assn. for Advancement of Health Edn., United Faculty of Fla., Fla. Assn. of C.C., Order of the Eastern Star (past Worthy Matron), Order of Shrine. Avocations: concerts, theater, art, historic museums, recreational activities. Home: 4310 Buchanan St Hollywood FL 33021-5917

KING, ALONZO, artistic director, choreographer; Student, Sch. Am. Ballet, Am. ballet theatre Sch., Harkness House Ballet Arts. Art dir. Lines Ballet, San Francisco, 1982—. Master tchr. working with Les Ballets de Monte-Carlo, London's Ballet Rambert, Nat. Ballet of Can., N.C. Sch. of Arts, San Francisco Ballet; inaugurator San Francisco Inst. Choreography, 1982; performer Bella Lewitzky Dance Co., DTH. Commd. to create and stage ballets for The Joffrey Ballet, Dance Theatre of Harlem; ballets in repertoires of Frankfurt Ballet, Dresden Ballet, BalletMet, Washington Ballet, Hong Kong Ballet; choreographer for Les Ballets de Monte-Carlo; choreogrpaher for prima ballerine Natalia Makarova, Patrick Swazye; original works choreographed include Who Dressed You Like a Foreigner, 1998 (2 Isadora Duncan awards for best costumes and mus. composition), Ocean (3 Isadora Duncan Dance award 1994 for outstanding achievement in choreography, original score and co. performance)), Rock, 1995, others. Mem. panels Nat. Endowment for Arts, Calif. Arts Coun., City of Columbus Arts Coun., Lila Wallace-Reader's Digest Arts Ptnrs. Program; former art commr. City and County of San Francisco. Nat. Endowment for Arts Chroeographer's fellow. Office: Lines Ballet Fl 5 26 7th St San Francisco CA 94103-1508

KING, AMY CATHRYNE PATTERSON, retired, mathematics educator, researcher; b. Douglas, Wyo., Dec. 30, 1928; d. John Francis and Mabel Eloise (Wear) Patterson; m. Don R. King, Aug. 8, 1949 (dec. 1985). BS, U. Mo., 1949; MA, U. Wichita, 1960; PhD, U. Ky., 1970. Tchr. Goddard (Kans.) Pub. Schs., 1956-58, U. Wichita, 1960-62; asst. instr. U. Kans., Lawrence, 1962-65; instr. Washburn U., Topeka, 1966-67; teaching asst. U. Ky., Lexington, 1967-70; prof. math. Ea. Ky. U., Richmond, 1970-98; Found. prof. emeritus, 1998—. Presenter in field. Author: instr.'s manual for College Algebra, 1981; (with Cecil B. Read) Pathways to Probability, 1963; contbr. (with others) articles to profl. jours. Departmental rep. for United Way, 1983; pres. Cokesbury Sunday Sch., Centenary United Meth. Ch., 1995-96, tchr. 3-yr.-olds. Recipient Award in Teaching, Ea. Ky. U., Richmond, 1982, Ea. Ky. U. Found. Professorship, 1993. Mem. Am. Math. Soc., Math. Assn. Am. (mem. various coms., 1st award for Disting. Coll. or Univ. Teaching 1992), Nat. Coun. Tchrs. Math., Assn. for Women of Math., Ky. Coun. Tchrs. Math. (Maths. Edn. Svc. and Achievement award 1998), Women in Math. Edn., Ky. Acad. Computer Users' Group, AAUP (treas. local chpt. 1984-86), Pi Mu Epsilon, Kappa Mu Epsilon, Pi Lambda Theta, Sigma Delta Pi, Delta Kappa Gamma (pres. Omicron chpt., 1994-96), Sigma Xi. Phi Kappa Phi. Methodist. Office: Ea Ky Univ Wallace Bldg # 114 Richmond KY 40475-3102

KING, ANDRE RICHARDSON, architectural graphic designer; b. Chgo., July 30, 1931; s. Earl James and Margie Verdetta (Doyle) K.; children: Jandra Maria, Andre Etienne; m. Sally M. Ryan, Sept. 19, 1980. Student, Chgo. Tech. Coll., 1956-57, U. Chgo., 1956-59; BAE., Art Inst. Chgo., 1959; grad., Gemological Inst. Am., 1992. ARK, Archtl. & Environ. Graphic Design Firm est., 1982—; With Skidmore, Owings & Merrill, Chgo., 1956-82; ind. designer, cons., 1982—. Mem. alumni bd. Chgo. Art Inst. Served with USAF, 1951-55. Recipient Design award Art Inst. Chgo., 1959, DESI award, 1982; Hon. consul of Barbados, W.I., 1971— Mem. AIA (assoc.), Am. Inst. Graphic Designers, Soc. Environ. Graphic Designers, Soc. Topographic Arts, Chgo. Soc. Communicating Arts, Art Dirs. Club of Chgo. (pres. 1979-80, 80-82), Art Inst. Chgo. Alumni (bd. dirs.), Arts Club of Chgo., Consular Corps of Chgo., Tavern Club of Chgo., Sigma Pi Phi, Beta Boule. Home: 6700 S Oglesby Ave Chicago IL 60649-1301 Office: 6700 S Oglesby Ave Apt 2406 Chicago IL 60649-1387 *To provide creative excellence for the future through my works.*

KING, ANGUS S., JR., former governor; b. Mar. 31, 1944; m. Mary J. Herman; children: Angus III, Duncan, James, Benjamin, Molly. BA, Dartmouth Coll., 1966; JD, U. Pa., 1969. Bar: Maine 1969. Staff atty. Pine Tree Legal Assistance, Showhegan, Maine, 1969-72; chief counsel Office Senator William D. Hathaway U.S. Senate Subcom. on Alcoholism and Narcotics, Washington, 1972-75; former ptnr. Smith, Lloyd & King, Brunswick, Maine, 1975—83; gov. State of Maine, Augusta, 1995—2003. TV host Maine Watch, Maine Pub. Broadcasting Network, 20 yrs.; v.p., gen. counsel Swift River/Hafslund Co., 1983; founder, pres. N.E. Energy Mgmt. Inc., Brunswick, Maine, 1989-94. Independent. Mailing: PO Box 457 Brunswick ME 04011-0457*

KING, ANN STOCKMAN, librarian, educator; b. N.Y.C., Nov. 6, 1931; d. Frank J. and Natalie A. Stockman; m. Albert M. King; 3 children. BS in Edn., So. Conn. State Coll., New Haven, 1959; MLS, So. Conn. U., 1974; postgrad., St. Joseph's U., Hartford, Conn., 1988. Cert. elem. tchr., media specialist, Conn. Libr. Fairfield (Conn.) Pub. Schs., 1974—98. Mem. Mill River Wetlands Com., Fairfield, 1965—; v.p. AAUW, 1975-77, sec., 1982-84. Claire Fulcher Internat. scholar AAUW, 1988. Mem. Conn. Ednl. Media, Fairfield County Sch. Librs., Southwestern Libr. Coun. Office: Fairfield Woods Middle Sch 1115 Fairfield Woods Rd Fairfield CT 06432-3228

KING, ANTHONY GABRIEL, museum administrator; b. Needham, Mass., June 13, 1953; s. Henry Brazell and Ottilie Rosena (Sandrock) K.; m. Debra Harte, Oct. 3, 1981; children: Courtney, Michael, Shannon, Megan. BS, Springfield (Mass.) Coll., 1976; MA, NYU, 1978. Curatorial asst. Mus. of Am. Indian, N.Y.C., 1975-76; asst. dir. Bronx County Hist. Soc., N.Y.C., 1976-79; exec. dir. Berkshire County Hist. Soc., Pittsfield, Mass., 1979-83, dir. Wash. Hist. Soc., Tacoma, 1983-86, Onondaga Hist. Assn., Syracuse, N.Y., 1986-89; dep. dir. Worcester (Mass.) Art Mus., 1989-98; treas. N.E. Mus. Assn., 1990-94, pres., 1994-96; dep. dir. Clark Art Inst., Williamstown, Mass., 1998—. Adj. faculty museum adminstrn. Harvard U., 1997—, adj. faculty art history and we. civilization Emmanuel Coll., Boston, 1992-98; guest lectr. Tufts U. Grad. Sch. Mem. preservation adv. bd. State of Wash., Olympia, 1984-86, mem. hist. records adv. bd., 1984-86; pres. Tacoma Centennial Com., 1983-84; chmn. Pittsfield Hist. Commn., 1981-83, Pittsfield Civic Ctr. Commn., 1982-83; mem. Steering com. Mass. Arts Advocacy Com., Boston, 1979-83. Mem. Am. Assn. Mus. (bd. dirs. 1994-95, trustee 1994-95), Wash. Mus. Assn., New Eng. Mus. Assn. (trustee 1992-98). Democrat. Roman Catholic. Office: Clark Art Inst 225 South St Williamstown MA 01267-2891

KING, ARTHUR R., JR., education educator, researcher; b. Portland, Oreg., Dec. 17, 1921; BA, U. Wash., 1943; MA, Stanford U., 1951, EdD, 1955. Tchr., counselor Punahou Sch., Honolulu, 1946-49; rsch. assoc. Stanford (Calif.) U., 1949-51; dir. curricular svcs. Sonoma County Schs., Calif., 1951-55; assoc. prof. edn. Claremont Grad. Sch., Claremont, Calif., 1955-65; prof. edn. U. Hawaii, Honolulu, 1965—, dir. Curriculum Rsch. & Devel. Group, 1966—2002, rschr. Edn. Rsch. and Devel. Ctr., 1966-74. Prin. investigator, editor courses Hawaii State Dept. Edn.; head Ocean Project, 1979-90; co-founder Pacific Cir. Consortium. Author: (with John A. Brownell) The Curricu-

lum and the Disciplines of Knowledge: A Theory of Curriculum Practice, 1966; contbr. articles to profl. jours. Served USN, WWII; capt., USNR, ret. Office: U Hawaii at Manoa Curriculum Rsch & Devel Group 1776 University Ave Honolulu HI 96822-2463 E-mail: aking@hawaii.edu., kinga002@hawaii.rr.com.

KING, ARTHUR THOMAS, economics educator, retired air force officer; b. Greensboro, Ala., Feb. 10, 1938; s. Harvey James and Elizabeth (Williams) K.; m. Rosa Marie Bryant, June 24, 1962; children: Donald, Kevin. BS in Biology, Tuskegee U., 1962; MS in Econs., S.D. State U., 1971; PhD in Econs., U. Colo., 1977. Comd. 2d lt. U.S. Air Force, 1962, advanced through grades to lt. col., 1979; asst. prof. econs. U.S. Air Force Acad., 1970-74; ops. planner Davis-Monthan AFB, Tuscon, 1975-76; strategic planner, energy economist Wright-Patterson AFB, Ohio, 1977-79; assoc. prof. econs. Air Force Inst. Tech., 1979-82; prof. econs. Baylor U., Waco, Tex., 1982-95; dean bus., econs. Winston-Salem (N.C.) State U., 1995—. Bd. dirs. Goodwill Industries Am. Inc.; bd. regents Wartburg Coll. Contbr. articles to profl. jours. Mem. Am. Econ. Assn., Nat. Econ. Assn. (bd. dirs., pres.), Nat. Assn. Bus. Econs. Baptist. Home: 1120 Chester Rd Winston Salem NC 27104-1310 Office: Winston Salem State Univ Sch Bus and Econ PO Box 19308 Winston Salem NC 27110

KING, B. B. (RILEY B. KING), singer, guitarist; b. Itta Bene, Miss., Sept. 16, 1925; LHD (hon.), Tougaloo (Miss.) Coll., 1973; MusD (hon.), Yale U., 1977, Berklee Coll. of Music, 1982; D of Fine Arts, Rhodes Coll. of Memphis, 1990. Began teaching self guitar, 1945, later studied Schillinger System, past disc jockey and singer Memphis radio stas., internat. appearances throughout world, recs. RPM, Crown, Bullet, Kent, ABC Records, ABC/Dunhill Records, toured Russia, 1979, albums Back in the Alley, B.B. King in London, Do the Boogie!, Completely Well, Electric B.B.-His Best, The Fabulous B.B. King, Guess Who, Heart and Soul, Live at Cook County Jail, Six Silver Strings, 1985, King of the Blues, Indianola Mississippi Seeds, 1989, Live at San Quentin, 1990 (Grammy award), Blues is King, 1990, Live at the Apollo, 1991 (Grammy award), Live at the Regal, 1991, Spotlight on Lucille, There is Always One More Time, 1992, Singin' the Blues, 1993, On the Road with B.B. King: An Interactive Autobiography, 1996, (guest appearance) Six Pack, 1993, Blues on the Bayou, Let the Good Time roll, 1998, guest artist with U2's Rattle and Hum, 1988, Deuces Wild, 1997, subject, collaborator B.B. King, B.B. King Blues Guitar, 1970, B.B. King Songbook, 1971, B.B. King, The World's Greatest Living Blues Artist, Blues Guitar, A Method by B.B. King, 1973, Riding with the King, 2000, Auld Lang Syne, 2002 (Grammy award, 2003), A Christmas Celebration of Hope, 2002 (Grammy award, 2003), Reflections, 2003; performer: at closing ceremonies Summer Olympics, 1996; author (autobiography, with David Ritz): Blues All Around Me, 1996 (2d prize 8th Ann. Ralph J. Gleason Music Book awards); appeared (films) When We Were Kings, 1996, Blues Brothers, 1998, 2000. Co-founder Found. Advancement Inmate Rehab. and Recreation, 1972—; founding mem. Kennedy Performing Arts Ctr., 1971. Co-recipient Grammy award for Best Rock Instrumental Performance, 1996; named Best Blues Singer Nat. Assn. TV and Radio Announcers, 1974, Blues Act of Yr., Performance Award Polls, 1985, 1987, 1988, Best Blues Instrumentalist, Ebony Mag., 1974—75, Best Male Blues Singer, 1974—75, Blues Guitarist of Yr., Guitar Player Mag., 1970—74, Most Outstanding Blues Singer, Living Blues Mag., 1993—94, 1996—97, Blues Artist of Yr., 1994; named to Hall of Fame and Best Blues Vocalist and Guitarist, Ebony mag., 1974, Blues Found. Hall of Fame, 1980, Rock and Roll Hall of Fame, 1987, Rock Walk, 1989, Amsterdam Walk of Fame, 1989, Hollywood Walk of Fame, 1989; recipient Humanitarian award, Fed. Bur. Prisons, 1972, B'nai B'rith Music and Performance Lodge, N.Y.C., 1973, Gallery of Greats and Best Blues Guitarist, 1974, Artist of the Decade and Humanitarian award, Record World mag., 1974, Grammy award Best Traditional Blues Rec., 1986, Grammy Lifetime Achievement award, 1987, Grammy award Best Rhythm & Blues Vocal Performance, Male, 1970, Grammy award Best Ethnic of Traditional Recording, 1981, Grammy award Best Traditional Blues Recording1993, 1983, 1985, Grammy award Best Traditional Blues Album for Blues Summit, 1993, Grammy award, 1999, Hall of Fame award Nat. Assn. for Campus Activities, 1986, Presdl. medal of the Arts, 1990, Songwriter's Hall of Fame Lifetime Achievement award, 1991, Orville H. Gibson Lifetime Achievement award, Gibson Guitar Co., Nat. award of distinction, U. Miss., 1992, Kennedy Ctr. Honors, 1995, W.C. Handy award Blues Found., 1983, 1985, 1987, 1988, 1991, Lifetime Achievement award, 1997, MTV Video Music award for Best Video from a Film, 1988—89, Image awards, NAACP, 1975, 1981, 1993, Pioneer in Music award, Nat. Assn. Black Owned Broadcasters, 1997, Living Legend award Trumpet Awards, 1997, Golden Mike award, NATRA, 1969, 1974; Nat. Heritage fellow Nat. Endowment of the Arts, 1991. Office: care Sidney A SeidenbergInc 1414 Avenue Of The Americas New York NY 10019-2514 *I would say to all people, but maybe to young people especially— black and white or whatever color— follow your own feelings and trust them; find out what you want to do and do it, and then practice it and practice it every day of your life and keep becoming what you are, despite any hardships and obstacles you meet.**

KING, BARBARA SUE, librarian; b. Okarche, Okla., July 16, 1955; d. Jack C. and Wilma (Smith) Boling; m. Glen M. King, Dec. 31, 1977 (div. June 1992). Assoc., El Reno Jr. Coll., 1975; BS in Libr. Sci., Southwestern Okla. State U., 1977; MLS, U. Okla., 1979. Pub. svcs. libr. Met. Libr. Sys., Oklahoma City, 1979-81, br. head Capital Hill br., 1980-81; reference libr. Oklahoma City C.C., 1981-87, coord. tech. svcs. and collection devel., 1987-89, dir. libr. svcs., 1989—. Mem. Assn. Libr. and Learning Ctr. Dirs. (pres. 1994-95), Okla. Coun. Acad. Libr. Dirs. (sec. 2001-03). Avocations: aerobics, weight lifting, dancing. Office: Oklahoma City CC 7777 S May Ave Oklahoma City OK 73159-4419

KING, BERNARD T. lawyer; b. Gouverneur, N.Y., Feb. 28, 1935; BS, Le Moyne Coll., 1956; JD cum laude, Syracuse U., 1959. Bar: N.Y. 1959. Ptnr. Blitman and King, Syracuse, N.Y. Assoc. editor Syracuse Law Rev., 1958-59; Syracuse Law Sch., bd. of visitors, 1980-; lectr. Labor Studies Program, N.Y. State Sch. Indsl. and Labor Rels., Cornell U., 1974; sec. Onondaga County Indsl. Devel. Agy., 1978-81. Mem., bd. dirs. Syracuse Model Neighborhood Corp., 1972-75, Regents, 1973—, sec., 1983—1984, bd. trustees, 1984-90. vice chmn., bd. trustees, 1988, LeMoyne Coll., 1974-80, v.p. 1977-79, pres., 1979-80; bd. trustees Manlius Pebble Hill Sch. Corp.; mem. United Way Cen. N.Y., 1971-75, bd. dirs., 1981-87; com. mem. 33rd Congl. Dist. Naval Academise Selection Bd., 1980-83. With USAF, 1961-62, Air NG, 1959-65, Salvation Army, mem. bd. 1995. Recipient Disting. Alumni award LeMoyne Coll., 1979, Whitney M. Seymour award Am. Arbitration Assn., 1986. Fellow Am. Bar Found.; mem. ABA (labor law and employment law com. 1963-, chmn. labor and employment sect. 1987-88, sect. del. to ho. of dels., mem. joint com. on employee benefits), Soc. Profls. in Dispute Resolution, Panel of Arbitrators, Am. Arbitration Assn. (bd. dirs. 1988), Onondaga County Bar Assn., N.Y. State Bar Assn. (exec. com., labor law sect. 1976—, chmn. 1980-81), Am. Judicature Soc., ABA Standing comm. on substance abuse; fel. ABA Coll. Labor and Employment Lawyers, ABA Am. Coll. Employment Benefits. Office: Franklin Ctr Ste 300 443 N Franklin St Syracuse NY 13204

KING, BETSY, professional golfer; b. Reading, Pa., Aug. 13, 1955; Winner U.S. Open-Women, 1989, 1990, LPGA, 1992; 3d ranked woman LPGA Tour, 1992. LPGA tour victories include: Orlando Classic, 1984, Columbia Savings Classic, 1984, Henredon Classic, 1986, Rail Charity Classic, 1986, 88, Tucson Open, 1987, Dinah Shore Invitational, 1987, McDonald's Classic, 1987, Atlantic City Classic, 1987, Kemper Open, 1988, Cellular One-Ping Championship, 1988, Jamaica Classic, 1989, Nabisco Dinah Shore, 1990, U.S. Women's Open, 1989, 1990, Corning Classic, 1991, Mazda Championship, 1992, ShopRite Classic, 1995, Corestates Betsy King Classic, 1997, Solheim Cup, 1998. Inductee LPGA Hall of Fame, 1995. Achievements include LPGA leading money winner, 1984, 89, 93. Office: LPGA 100 International Golf Dr Daytona Beach FL 32124-1092

KING, BEVERLY RAE, developmental psychologist; b. Banner Elk, NC, Apr. 27, 1957; d. Alfred Eugene and Margaret Hazel King; children: Jared Alex Deskins, Walter Ryan Deskins. MA, East Tenn. State U., 1990; PhD, Purdue U., 1996. Instr. Ball State U., Muncie, Ind., 1995—97; assoc. prof. SD State U., 1997—2003, U. NC, Pembroke, NC, 2003—. Contbr. chapters to books, articles to jours. Recipient Award for Excellence in E-Learning, SD Bd. of Regents, 2002, award for innovative excellence in tchg., learning and tech., Ctr. for Advancement of Tchg. and Learning, 2003. Mem.: Am. Psychol. Soc. Office: UNC Pembroke Dept Psychology and Counseling 310 Edn Bldg PO Box 1510 Pembroke NC 28372 Office Fax: 605-688-6754. E-mail: beverly_king@sdstate.edu.

KING, BILL JAMES, education educator; b. West Point, NY, Sept. 29, 1961; s. William Elmer King and Anne Marie Murphy, Raymond Louis Topper (Stepfather); m. Jeanette Lee Shrum, Mar. 14, 1987. AS in math and phys. sci., Am. River Coll., 1985—88; BA cum laude, Calif. State U. Sacramento, 1989—93; MA in philosophy, San Francisco State U., 1993—98; MA in theology, The Dominican Sch. of Philosophy and Theology, 1998—2001. Cert. of Ordination World Christianship Ministries, CA, 2000. Petty officer USN, San Diego, 1979—83; muy thai kickboxer World Kickboxing Assn., Imperial Beach, Calif., 1980—83; med. adminstrv. supr. USAFR, Sacramento, 1984—91; platoon seargent Calif. Army N.G., Sacramento, 2000—01; pastor Logos Ministries, Sacramento, 2000—; prof. of philosophy Sierra Coll., Rocklin, Calif., 2002—. Contbr. exhibition, articles to jours. Chaplain USAR, 2001—; Calif. nat. guardsman Calif. Army N.G., 2000—01; organizer/contbr. San Juan Sch. Dist. Night Out At the Sacramento Zoo, Sacramento, 2000; pastor Logos Ministries, Sacramento, 2000; vol. Presston Sch. of Industry Calif. Youth Authority Juvenile Hall, 1988—89, San Quentin Prison Chapel Choir, Calif., 1987—90. 2nd class petty officer USN, 1979—83, San Diego, CA. Decorated Navy Expeditionary Medal USN, Navy Meretorious Unit Commendation, Sea Svc. Deployment Ribbon, Air Force Oustanding Unit Medal USAF, Air Res. Force Meretorious Svc. medal, Air Force Longevity medal; recipient Comdr. Naval Surface Force US Pacific Fleet Letter of Appreciation, USN, 1983. Mem.: Associated Gospel Churches (licentiate), Internat. Soc. for Complexity, Info., and Design (licentiate), The Am. Sci. Affiliation (licentiate), Evang. Philos. Soc. (licentiate), Am. Philos. Assn. (licentiate), Mil. Chaplain Assn. (life), ACLU (life). Non-Partisan. Protestant. Avocations: chess, jogging, reading, billiards, weightlifting.

KING, BILLIE JEAN MOFFITT, former professional tennis player; b. Long Beach, Calif., Nov. 22, 1943; d. Willard J. Moffitt; m. Larry King, Sept. 17, 1965. Student, Calif. State U. at Los Angeles, 1961-64. Amateur tennis player, 1958-67; prof., 1968—; mem. Tennis Challenge Series, 1977, 78; dir., ofcl. spokesperson World TeamTennis, Chgo., 1985—; commentator, analyst Wimbeldon and other tennis events HBO, N.Y.C. Singles champion tournaments Wimbledon, 1966-68, 72, 73, 75, U.S. Open, 1967, 71, 72, 74, U.S. Hardcourt, 1966, Italian Open, 1970, West German Open, 1971, Australian Open, 1968, South African Open, 1966, 67, 69, U.S. Indoor, 1966-68, 71, U.S. Clay Court, 1971, French Open, 1972, Avon, 1980; doubles champion Wimbledon, 1961, 62, 65, 67, 68, 70-73, U.S. Open, 1965, 67, 74, 80, French, 1972, Italian, 1970, South African, 1967-70, Bridgestone, 1976, Virginia Slims, 1974, 76; mixed doubles champion Wimbledon, 1967, 71, 73, U.S. Open, 1967, 71, 73, French, 1967, 70, South African, 1967, Australian, 1968; winner 29 Virginia Slims singles titles, 1970-77, 4 Colgate titles, 1977, Fedn. Cup, 1963-67, 76-79, Wightman Cup, 1961-67, 70, 77, 78; World Tennis Team All-Star, 3 times; host Colgate women's sports TV spl. The Lady is a Champ, 1975; co-founder, dir. Kingdom, Inc., San Mateo, Calif.; sports commentator ABC-TV, 1975-78; co-founder, pub. WomenSports mag., 1974—; founder Women's Tennis Assn., 1973; first woman commr. (Team Tennis League) profl. sports history, 1984; TV commentator HBO-Sports Wimbledon coverage; capt. Fed. Cup for USA, 1995; cons. Virginia Slims World Championship Series; bd. dirs. Challenger Ctr.; amb. Adventures in Movement Charity; coach Fed. Cup Women's Tennis Team, 1995-96, USA Olympic Women's Tennis Team, 1996; nat. spokesperson Literary Vols. Am.; tennis tchr. to profls. Author: Tennis to Win, 1970, (with Kim Chapin) Billie Jean, 1974, (with Cynthia Starr) We Have Come a Long Way, The Story of Women's Tennis, 1988. Named Sportsperson of Yr., Sports Illustrated, 1972; Woman Athlete of Yr., A.P., 1967, 73, Top Woman Athlete of Yr., 1972; Woman of Yr., Time mag., 1976, One of 10 Most Powerful Women in Am., Harper's Bazaar, 1977, One of 25 Most Influential Women in Am., World Almanac, 1977, One of 100 Most Important Ams. of 20th Century, Life mag., 1990; named to Internat. Tennis Hall of Fame, 1987, Nat. Women's Hall of Fame, 1990; Lifetime Achievement award, March of Dimes, 1994. Office: Billie Jean King Ste 983 960 Harlem Ave Glenview IL 60025

KING, C. JUDSON, academic administrator; BChemE, Yale U., 1956; SM, ScDChemE, MIT. Asst. prof. U. Calif., Berkeley, 1963—66, assoc. prof., 1966—69, prof. chem. engring., 1969—, chmn. dept. chem. engring., 1972-81, dean Coll. Chemistry, 1981-87, provost profl. schs. and colls., 1987-94, sr. v.p. academic affairs, provost, 1996—, vice provost rsch. systemwide, 1994—95. Bd. assessment Nat. Bur. Stds. Programs; dir. chem. engring. program divsn. nuclear chemistry Lawrence Berkeley Lab.; chair coun. chem. rsch. Gov.'s Task Force Toxics, Waste and Tech. Recipient Mac Pruitt award, Gov's. Task Force Toxics, Waste and Tech., award for excellence in drying rsch., Internat. Drying Symposium. Fellow: AIChE (William H. Walker award, Clarence G. Gerhold award, Warren K. Lewis award); mem.: NAE (chair com. alternatives to fluorocarbons), NSF, AAAS, Nat. Rsch. Coun. (com. separation sci. and tech.), Am. Chem. Soc. (internat. com. solvent extraction, Rohm & Haas award in Separation Sci. and Tech.), Am. Soc. Engring. Edn. (George Westinghouse award, Centennial medallion). Office: U Calif Office Pres & Regents 1111 Franklin St Oakland CA 96460-0520

KING, CARL EDWARD, employee screening executive; b. Pine Bluff, Ark., June 19, 1940; s. Carl B. King and Claudia Marie (Fulbright) Ingham; m. Jonna Sue DeWeese, Mar., 1964 (div. Nov. 1974); 1 child, Grant Edward; m. Paula Honor Finnell, Mar. 6, 1975. LLB, La Salle Extension U., 1971; BS in Criminal Justice, U. Nebr., Omaha, 1978; M in Bus. Mgmt., Cen. Mich. U., 1979. Enlisted USMC, 1957, commd. 2d lt., 1969, advanced through grades to maj., 1981; ops. officer, co. commdr. Mil. Police Co., Okinawa, Japan, 1973-74; asst. provost marshal USMC, Barstow, Calif., 1975, provost marshal Beaufort, S.C., 1975-77, Kaneohe Bay, Hawaii, 1978-81, ret., 1981; salesman Smith Protective Services, Houston, 1981-82, mgr. investigations div., sales mgr., 1982-83, v.p. mktg., 1983-84; co-founder, CEO Team Bldg. Systems, Houston, 1984—; pres., CEO, founder WNCK, Inc., Houston, 1992—; founder Insights-Corp. Selection Systems, Inc., Houston, 1992—. CEO Insights-Corp. Selection Systems, WNCK, Inc. Mem. loss prevention adv. bd. U. Houston, 1986—. Decorated Bronze Star, Purple Heart with oak leaf cluster. Mem. FBI Nat. Acad., Internat. Assn. Chiefs of Police, Am. Soc. Indsl. Security, Nat. Order Battlefield Commns., Marine Mustang Assn. Republican. Methodist. Avocations: reading, snow skiing, jogging. Home: 15 Palmer Green Pl The Woodlands TX 77381-2820 Office: Insights Corp Selections Sys Ste A4 2408 Temberloch Pl The Woodlands TX 77380 E-mail: carl@insights-inc.com.

KING, CAROL BRENNAN, dean; b. Towanda, Pa., Mar. 14, 1947; d. Robert Edward Brennan, Elizabeth Amanda Hay; m. James Bradley King, June 23, 1965; children: Beth Ann Williams, Amy Gale Logsdon, James R. BA in Comm., SUNY, Binghamton, 1988; MA in English, Binghamton U., 1992. Missionary Bapt. Missions, Chad; dean of women Practical Bible Coll., Bible School Park, NY, 1983—89; faculty Bapt. Bible Coll., Clarks Summit, Pa., 1989—92, assoc. dean, 1993—. Mem.: Assn. Christians in Student Devel., Nat. Coun. Tchrs. English. Office: Baptist Bible College 538 Venard Rd Clarks Summit PA 18411

KING, CAROLYN DINEEN, federal judge; b. Syracuse, N.Y., Jan. 30, 1938; d. Robert E. and Carolyn E. (Bareham) Dineen; children: James Randall, Philip Randall, Stephen Randall. AB summa cum laude, Smith Coll., 1959; LLB, Yale U., 1962. Bar: D.C. 1962, Tex. 1963. Assoc. Fulbright & Jaworski, Houston, 1962—72; ptnr. Childs, Fortenbach, Beck & Guyton, Houston, 1972—78, Sullivan, Bailey, King, Randall & Sabom, Houston, 1978—79; judge U.S. Ct. Appeals (5th cir.), Houston, 1979—99, chief judge, 1999—; with U.S. Jud. Conf., 1999—, exec. com., 2000—, chmn. exec. com., 2002—. Trustee, exec. com., treas. Houston Ballet Found., 1967—70; Houston dist. adv. coun. SBA, 1972—76; Dallas regional panel Pres.'s Commn. White House Fellowships, 1972—76, mem. commn., 1977; bd. dirs. Houston chpt. Am. Heart Assn., 1978—79; nat. trustee Palmer Drug Abuse Program, 1978—79; trustee, sec., treas., chmn. audit com., fin. com., mgmt. com. United Way Tex. Gulf Coast, 1979—85; trustee, exec. com., chmn. bd. trustees U. St. Thomas, 1988—98. Recipient Smith Coll. medal, 1997, Outstanding Alumnus award, Phi Beta Kappa Alumni of Greater Houston, 1998; rsch. fellow, Ctr. for Am. and Internat. Law, 1989—. Mem.: ABA, Philos. Soc. Tex., Houston Bar Assn., State Bar Tex., Am. Law Inst. (coun. 1991—, chmn. membership com. 1997—99), Fed. Bar Assn. Roman Catholic. Office: US Ct Appeals 11020 US Courthouse 515 Rusk Avenue Houston TX 77002-2694

KING, CAROLYN MARIE, mathematics educator; b. Carlisle, Pa., May 11, 1943; d. Charles C. and Ethel M. (Woods) Carothers; m. James E. King, June 6, 1964; children: J. Edward, Scott D. BS magna cum laude, Elizabethtown Coll., 1965; postgrad., Millersville U., 1966-68. Tchr. math. Middletown (Pa.) High Sch., 1965-71, substitute tchr., 1978-84; tchr. math. Derry Twp. Sch. Dist., Hershey, Pa., 1984—. Author: This is St. Peter: A History of St. Peter Lutheran Church, 1993; editor Scroll, 1985—. Mem. NEA, Nat. Coun. Tchrs. Math., Pa. State Edn. Assn., Pa. Coun. Math. Tchrs., Hershey Edn. Assn. Republican. Lutheran. Avocation: crafts. Home: 409 Spring Run Dr Mechanicsburg PA 17055-5574 Office: Derry Twp Sch Dist PO Box 898 Hershey PA 17033-0898 E-mail: cking@hershey.k12.pa.us.

KING, CARY JUDSON, III, chemical engineer, educator, university official; b. Ft. Monmouth, N.J., Sept. 27, 1934; s. Cary Judson and Mary Margaret (Forbes) K., Jr.; m. Jeanne Antoinette Yorke, June 22, 1957; children: Mary Elizabeth, Cary Judson IV, Catherine Jeanne. B. Engring., Yale, 1956; S.M., Mass. Inst. Tech., 1958, Sc.D., 1960. Asst. prof. chem. engring. MIT, Cambridge, 1959-63; dir. Bayway Sta. Sch. Chem. Engring. Practice, Linden, N.J., 1959-61; asst. prof. chem. engring. U. Calif., Berkeley, 1963-66, assoc. prof., 1966-69, prof., 1969—, vice chmn. dept. chem. engring., 1967-72, chmn., 1972-81, dean Coll. Chemistry, 1981-87, provost profl. schs. and colls., 1987-94; vice provost for rsch. U. Calif. Sys., Oakland, 1994-96, interim provost, sr. v.p. acad. affairs, 1995-96, provost, sr. v.p. acad. affairs, 1996—. Cons. Procter & Gamble Co., 1969-87; bd. dirs. Coun. for Chem. Rsch., chmn., 1989, Am. U. of Armenia Corp., chmn., 1995—, Calif. Assn. for Rsch. in Astronomy, 2001—. Author: Separation Processes, 1971, 80, Freeze Drying of Foods, 1971; contbr. numerous articles to profl. jours.; patentee in field. Active Boy Scouts Am., 1947-86; pres. Kensington Community Council, 1972-73, dir., 1970-73. Recipient Malcolm E. Pruitt award Coun. for Chem. Rsch., 1990. Mem. AIChE (Inst. lectr. 1973, Food, Pharm. and Bioengring Divsn. award 1975, William H. Walker award 1976, Warren K. Lewis award 1990, bd. dirs. 1987-89, Clarence G. Gerhold award 1992); mem. AAAS, Nat. Acad. Engring., Am. Soc. Engring. Edn. (George Westinghouse award 1978), Am. Chem. Soc. (Separations Sci. and Tech. award 1997). Home: 7 Kensington Ct Kensington CA 94707-1009 Office: U Calif Office of Pres 1111 Franklin St Fl 12 Oakland CA 94607-5201

KING, CHAD LAVERE, music educator; b. Preston, Idaho, May 16, 1967; s. John Grant and Golda Darlene King; m. Kathleen Mauerman, Aug. 18, 1989; children: Courtney, Kayla, Connor children: Anthony Scott, Andrew James. B in Music Edn., Brigham Young U., Provo, Utah, 1991; MEd, Utah State U., 1997. Music educator Millcreek Jr. High, Bountiful, Utah, 1991—; instrumental edn. instr. Davis Country Sch. Dist., Farmington, Utah, 1991—2002. Student body advisor Millcreek Jr. High, tchr. teen leadership skills. With U.S. Army, 1984—99, with Utah N.G. Achievements include Teacher Of The Year 2001 for Millcreek Junior High And District Horizion Award Winner; over 1/3 of student body involved in band program at Millcreek Jr. High. Home: 2 East Sunrise Way Farmington UT 84025 Office: Millcreek JrHigh 245 East 1000 South Bountiful UT 84010 E-mail: cking@dsdmail.net.

KING, CHARLES MARK, dentist, educator; b. Ft. Benning, Ga., Mar. 15, 1952; s. Charles Ray and Marilyn Anita (Alexander) K.; children: Kelley Michelle, Kevin Marcus, Mark Alexander. BS, U. Ala., 1973, MS, 1977, DMD, 1981; JD, Birmingham Sch. Law, 1997. Lab technician Med. Lab. Assn., Birmingham, Ala., 1973-74; rsch. asst. dept. surgery Univ. Hosp., Birmingham, 1974-76, dept. anesthesiology, 1976-78; gen. practice dentistry Birmingham, 1981—. Clin. instr. U. Ala. Sch. Dentistry, Birmingham, 1982-89; mem. bd. advisors Dist. Dental Assts. Soc., 1984-90. Contbr. articles to profl. jours. Mem. Am. Legion Boys State. Lt. col. USAR. Named Best Clin. Instr., Student Body U. Ala. Sch. Dentistry 1985. Mem.: Assn. Mil. Surgeons U.S., Am. Legion, Masons, Scottish Rite, Shriners, Delta Sigma Delta. Republican. Baptist. Avocations: archery, martial arts, hunting, water sports, flying. Office: PO Box 94805 Birmingham AL 35220-4805

KING, CHARLES ROSS, physician; b. Nevada, Iowa, Aug. 22, 1925; s. Carl Russell and Dorothy Sarah (Mills) K.; m. Frances Pamela Carter, Jan. 8, 1949; children— Deborah Diane, Carter Ross, Charles Conrad, Corbin Kent Student, Butler U., 1943; BS in Bus., Ind. U., 1948, MD, 1964. Diplomate Am. Bd. Family Practice. Dep. dir. Ind. Pub. Works and Supply, 1949-52; salesman Knox Coal Corp., 1952-59; rotating intern Marion County Gen. Hosp., Indpls., 1964-65; family practice medicine Anderson, Ind., 1965—. Sec.-treas. staff Cmty. Hosp., 1969-72, pres.-elect, dir., chief medicine, 1973—, bd. dirs., 1973-75; sec.-treas. St. John's Hosp., 1968-69, chief medicine, 1972-73, chief pediatrics, 1977—; bd. dirs. Rolling Hills Convalescnet Ctr., 1968-73; pres. Profl. Ctr. Lab., 1965—; vice chmn. Madison County Bd. Health, 1966-69, chmn., 1986—; chmn. bd. dirs. Star Fin. Bank, Anderson. Bd. dirs. Family Svc. Madison County, 1968-69, Madison County Assn. Mentally Retarded, 1972-76, Anderson Fine Arts Ctr., 1996—; trustee St. Johns Health System., 1898—; chmn. bd. dirs. Anderson Downtown Devel. Corp., 1980—; mem. Paramont Restoration Steering Com., 1994—; trustee, sec.-tread. St. John's Med. Ctr., 1989—; mem. exec. com. Madison United Way Fund, vice-chmn., 1995, chmn., 1996; mem. exec. com. Stop Teen Pregnancy Program, 1995—; exec. commr. Health Search Madison County, 1995—. With U.S. Army, 1944-46. Recipient Dr. James Macholtz award, Spl. Olympics, 1986, Sagamore of Wabash award, State of Ind. Gov., 2002. Fellow Royal Soc. Health, Am. Acad. Family Practice (charter); mem. AMA (numerous Physicians Recognition awards), Ind. Med. Assn., Pan Am. Med. Assn., Am. Acad. Gen. Practice, Madison County Med. Soc. (pres. 1970), 9th Dist. Med. Soc. (sec.-treas. 1968), Anderson C. of C. (bd. dirs. 1979-82), Indpls. Mus. Art (corp. mem.), Anderson Country Club (bd. dirs. 1976-79), Phi Delta Theta (pres. Alumni Assn. 1952), Phi Chi. Clubs: Anderson Country (bd. dirs. 1976-79). Methodist. Home: 920 N Madison Ave Anderson IN 46011-1208 Office: 2015 Jackson St Anderson IN 46016-4337

KING, CHAROLETTE ELAINE, retired administrative officer; b. Baker, Oreg., Apr. 10, 1945; d. Melvin Howard and Rella Maxine (Gwilliam) Wright; m. Craig Seldon King, April 14, 1965; children: Andrea Karen, Diana Susan. Clerical positions various firms, Idaho, Va., Conn., 1964-71; nursing sec. VA, San Diego, 1974-77; sec. USN, Agana, Guam, 1972-73, procurement clk. Bremerton, Wash., 1977-80, San Diego, 1980, support svcs. supr., 1980-83, div. dir., 1983-87, program analyst, 1987-93, adminstrv. officer, 1993-96, mgmt. analyst, 1996. Recipient Model Agy. cup USN, San Diego, 1986. Republican. Avocations: reading, camping, sewing, writing, quilting.

KING, CHI-YU, research scientist; b. Nanking, Jian-Su, China, Aug. 14, 1934; came to the U.S., 1958; s. Cheng-Wei and Chan-Ron (Chu) K.; m. Bi-Shia Wang, Sept. 8, 1962; children: Tsu-Jae, Hans Tsi-han, Henry Tsi-heng. BSEE, Nat. Taiwan U., Taipei, 1956; MS, Duke U., 1961; PhD, Cornell U., 1965. Rsch. fellow Calif. Inst. Tech., Pasadena, 1965-66; asst. rsch. geophysicist U. Calif., L.A., 1966-68; geophysicist U.S. Geol. Survey, Menlo Park, Calif., 1968-70, 73-95, Nat. Oceanic and Atmospheric Adminstrn., San Francisco, 1970-73; PNC Internat. fellow, guest rschr. U. Tokyo, 1997-99. Vis. prof. Nat. Ctrl. U., Chung-Li, Taiwan, 1973-74; geophysicist, chmn. Earthquake Prediction Rsch. Inc., Los Altos, Calif., 1995—. Editor: Earthquake Hydrology and Chemistry, 1985, (with R. Scarpa) Modeling of Volcanic Processes, 1988; editor or co-editor (spl. publs.) Jour. Geophys. Rsch., 1980, 86, Geophys. Rsch. Letters, 1981, Pure and Applied Geophysics, 2003; mem. edit. bd. Jour. Geodesy and Geodynamics, 2003—; contbr. articles to profl. jours. Preacher, Bible tchr. various Christian chs. Calif., Taiwan, Hong Kong, China, Japan, Saipan, Persian Gulf, Europe, 1972—; chmn. bd. Ch. in Palo Alto, 1972-81, House of Christians, Los Altos, 1981-97. Mem. Am. Geophys. Union (assoc. editor Jour. Geophys. Rsch. 1995-97). Home and Office: 381 Hawthorne Ave Los Altos CA 94022-3845 E-mail: chiyuking@aol.com.

KING, CHRIS ALLEN, military officer; b. Brunswick, Maine, Feb. 7, 1960; BS, U.S. Mil. Acad., 1983; MPA, Princeton U., 1992; MBA, Georgetown U., 2001; student, Nat. War Coll., Wash., D.C., 2003—. Commd. 2d lt. U.S. Army, 1983, advanced through grades to lt. col., 1999, from platoon leader to squadron adj., 1984-87, troop comdr. Bindlach, Germany, 1987-90, from battalion ops.

officer to battalion exec. officer Ft. Riley, Kans., 1996-98, spl. asst. to chief legis. liaison Pentagon, 1998-99, Army congrl. fellow Office Sen. Lieberman, 1999, chief legis. strategy, Army legis. liaison, 2000—02, legis. asst. to chief of staff, 2002—03; asst. prof. dept. social scis. U.S. Mil. Acad., West Point, 1992-95. Deacon Bush Hill Presbyn. Ch., 2001-03. Mem. U.S. Army Armor Assn. (order of St. George award 1995), Beta Gamma Sigma, Phi Kappa Phi. Avocations: backpacking, golf.

KING, CLAUDIA LOUAN, film producer, lecturer; b. Merced, Calif., May 1, 1940; d. Alvin Cecil and Thelma May (Matthew) K.; m. Douglas McLean, July 10, 1965 (div. 1975); children: Kia Gabrielle, Kendra Sue. BA, U. Calif., 1963; MA, Ind. U., 1969. Lectr. U. Fla., Gainesville, 1969-70; asst. prof. U. Nev., Las Vegas, 1973-79; producer Source 17 Prodns., Santa Monica, Calif., 1979-85; freelance producer Chico, Calif., 1985—. Author: Life Mastery: A Self-Esteem Handbook for Adults and Children, 1994, (screenplays) The Garden of Eden, 1983, My Sister's Keeper, 1986, (documentary) The Evolution of Women, 1988, 92 (short stories) In the Realm of the Invisible, 1991; prodr.: Rape is Everybody's Concern, 1978, Los Angeles Personally Yours, 1986; pub. Light Paths Communications, 1994—; artist "Mandalas and Altar Pieces" Steam and Bean, Chico, Calif.; contbr. articles to art mags. Mem. Chico Annie's Com. for Dramatic Arts, 1996; v.p. Chico Dharma Study, 1998; mem. Chico Buddhist Coun.; bd. dirs Chico Dharma Study. Carnegie grantee, 1969; Nev. Endowment for Humanities grantee, 1978. Mem.: Women in Film. Democrat. Avocations: camping, opera. Home: PO Box 3576 Chico CA 95927-3576 E-mail: litpaths@shocking.com.

KING, COLBERT ISAIAH, editor; b. Washington, Sept. 20, 1939; s. Isaiah and Amelia (Colbert) K.; m. Gwendolyn Ann Stewart, July 3, 1961; children: Robert, Stephen, Allison. BA, Howard U., 1961, postgrad., 1969. Attache Dept. State, Washington, 1964—80; dir. govt. rels. Potomac Elec. Power Co., Washington, 1976-77; legis. asst. to Md. Senator Charles McMathias Jr. Washington, 1972-76; spl. asst. to under sec. HEW, Washington, 1970-71; dep. asst. sec. of treasury Dept. Treasury, Washington, 1977-79; U.S. exec. dir. World Bank, 1979-81; exec. v.p., bd. dirs. Riggs Nat. Bank, Washington, 1984—89; mem. editl. bd. Washington Post, 1990—, dep. editor, 2000—. Mem. Coun. for Excellence in Govt. With U.S. Army, 1961-63. Named one of Outstanding Young Men of Am., U.S. Jaycees, 1974; recipient spl. citation Nat. Rehab. Assn., 1975, Svc. award Ctr. for Sickle Cell Disease, Howard U., 1975, Disting. Svc. award U.S. Treasury, 1979, Outstanding Alumnus award, Howard U., 1984, Pulitzer Prize, 2003. Mem. Kappa Alpha Psi. Democrat. Episcopalian. Office: The Washington Post 1150 15th St Washington DC 20071

KING, CORETTA SCOTT (MRS. MARTIN LUTHER KING JR.), educational association administrator, lecturer, writer, concert singer; b. Marion, Ala., Apr. 27, 1927; d. Obidiah and Bernice (McMurray) Scott; m. Martin Luther King, Jr., June 18, 1953 (dec. Apr. 1968); children: Yolanda Denise, Martin Luther III, Dexter Scott, Bernice Albertine. AB, Antioch Coll., 1951; Mus.B., New Eng. Conservatory Music, 1954, Mus.D., 1971; L.H.D., Boston U., 1969, Marymount-Manhattan Coll., 1969, Morehouse Coll., 1970; H.H.D., Brandeis U., 1969, Wilberforce U., 1970, Bethune-Cookman Coll., 1970, Princeton U., 1970; LL.D., Bates Coll., 1971. Voice instr. Morris Brown Coll., Atlanta, 1962; commentator CNN, Atlanta, 1980—, lectr., writer; founding pres., chief exec. officer Martin Luther King Jr. Ctr. for Nonviolent Social Change Inc. Author: My Life With Martin Luther King, Jr., 1969; contbr. articles to mags.; syndicated newspaper columnist N.Y. Times Syndication Sales Corp., 1986-90, United Features Syndicate, 1990-94; concert debut, Springfield, Ohio, 1948; numerous concerts throughout U.S., concerts, India, 1959, performances, Freedom Concert. Del. to White House Conf. Children and Youth, 1960; sponsor Com. for Sane Nuclear Policy, Com. on Responsibility, Moblzn. to End War in Viet Nam, 1966, 67, Margaret Sanger Meml. Found.; mem. So. Rural Action Project, Inc.; pres. Martin Luther King, Jr. Found.; chmn. Commn. on Econ. Justice for Women; mem. exec. com. Nat. Com. Inquiry; co-chmn. Clergy and Laymen Concerned about Vietnam, Nat. Com. for Full Employment, 1974; pres. Martin Luther King Jr. Center for Nonviolent Social Change; co-chairperson Nat. Com. Full Employment; mem. exec. bd. Nat. Health Ins. Com.; active YWCA; bd. dirs. So. Christian Leadership Conf., Martin Luther King, Jr. Found. Gt. Britain; trustee Robert F. Kennedy Meml. Found., Ebenezer Bapt. Ch. Recipient Outstanding Citizenship award Montgomery (Ala.) Improvement Assn., 1959, Merit award St. Louis Argus, 1960, Distinguished Achievement award Nat. Orgn. Colored Women's Clubs, 1962, Louise Waterman Wise award Am. Jewish Congress Women's Aux., 1963, Myrtle Wreath award Cleve. Hadassah, 1965, award for excellence in field human relations Soc. Family of May, 1968, Universal Love award Premio San Valentine Com., 1968, Wateler Peace prize, 1968, Dag Hammarskjold award, 1969, Pacem in Terris award Internat. Overseas Service Found., 1969, Leadership for Freedom award Roosevelt U., 1971, Martin Luther King Meml. medal Coll. City N.Y., 1971, Internat. Viareggio award, 1971, numerous others; named Woman of Year Utility Club N.Y.C., 1962, Woman of Year Nat. Assn. Radio and TV Announcers, 1968, UAW Social Justice award, 1980. Mem. Nat. Council Negro Women (Ann. Brotherhood award 1957), Women Strike for Peace (del. disarmament conf. Geneva, Switzerland 1962, citation for work in peace and freedom 1963), Women's Internat. League for Peace and Freedom, NAACP, United Ch. Women (bd. mgrs.), Alpha Kappa Alpha (hon.) Baptist (mem. choir, guild adviser). Club: Links (Human Dignity and Human Rights award Norfolk chpt. 1964). Address: Martin Luther King Jr Ctr 449 Auburn Ave NE Atlanta GA 30312-1503

KING, DAVE, former professional hockey coach; Formerly with Can. Nat. Hockey Program; head coach Calgary Flames, 1992-95; asst. coach, dir. European scouting Mont. Canadiens, 1996-99; head coach Columbus (Ohio) Blue Jackets, 2000—03. Coached Calgary Flames to 2 straight division titles, 1993-94, 94-95.

KING, DEBORAH SIMPKIN, music, choral, vocal educator; b. Manchester, Tenn., July 9, 1954; d. William Edward and Peggy Lou (Little) Simpkin; children: Patrick King, Michael King. Studied with Carapetyan, others, 1971-91; MusB with honors, Tex. Christian U., 1976; MusM, North Tex. State U., 1981; Mus D, U. North Tex., 1990. Tchg. fellow North Tex. State U., Denton, 1980-85; elem. gifted prog. music instr. All Saints' Cathedral Day Sch., Ft. Worth, 1987-88; music hist. lectr. U. North Tex., Denton, 1988-91; interim prof. Tarrant County Jr. Coll., 1990; asst. prof., coord. choral & vocal studies and grad. studies Jersey City State Coll., 1991-95; founder/artistic dir. Schola Cantorum on Hudson, Jersey City, 1992—; asst. prof. choral, vocal music Kutztown (Pa.) U., 1996-97. Owner voice studios, Jersey City, East Orange, NJ, 1995—. Editor: A Blow Anthology, 1996; alto soloist All Saints' Episcopal Cathedral, Ft. Worth, 1973-88; mezzo soloist in oratorios, concerts, recitals and stage prodns.; choral/vocal workshops, clinics, adjudications, 1980—. Music dir. St. John's Episcopal Ch., Montclair, N.J., 1994—. Mem. Nat. Assn. for Tchrs. of Singing, N.J. Chpt. Am. Choral Dir.'s Assn. (bd. dirs., coord. annual H.S. choral festival), Choral Am., Conductors' Guild, Coll. Music Soc., Alpha Lambda Delta, Pi Kappa Lambda. Democrat. Episcopalian. Avocations: hiking, gardening, low fat cooking.

KING, DEXTER SCOTT, foundation administrator; b. Atlanta, Jan. 30, 1961; Pres. Visionary Devel. Corp., Atlanta; dir. office spl. events and entertainment Martin Luther King, Jr. Ctr. Nonviolent Social Change, Inc. (The King Ctr.), Atlanta, chmn., pres., CEO, also bd. dirs., 1984—. Spkr. in field. Exec. prodr. (record and video project) King Holiday. Named one of 50 Most Beautiful People, People Mag., 1995. Office: King Ctr Nonviolent Social Change 449 Auburn Ave NE Atlanta GA 30312-1503

KING, DIANE AVERBACH, teacher educator; b. Phila., Mar. 28, 1925; d. Louis and Mollie (Chaplick) Averbach; m. Leon King, Nov. 30, 1946; childen: Cheryl, Elliot, Louis. BA, U. Pa., 1945; MA, Dropsie Coll., 1970, PhD, 1979; D Pedagogy (hon.), Jewish Theol. Sem., N.Y.C., 1987. Tchr. Germantown Jewish Ctr., Phila., 1950-67; ednl. cons. Gratz Coll., Phila., 1963-87; acting dir. Ctrl. Agy. for Jewish Edn., Melrose Park, Pa., 1987-88, assoc. dir., 1988-89; assoc. prof. edn. Gratz Coll., Melrose Park, 1979—. Bd. dirs. Averbach Ctrl. Agy. for Jewish Edn., Melrose Park, 1990—, Phila. Jewish Archives, 1992—2001; writer curriculum materials for Jewish schs. Contbg. author: Jewish Life in Philadelphia (1830-1940), 1983, Philadelphia Jewish Life (1940-1985), 1986; contbr. to ency. Recipient humanitarian award Fedn. Jewish Agys., 1983, lifetime achievement award Jewish Educators Assembly-Behrman House Pubs., 1998. Mem. Phi Beta Kappa. Home: 4030 Woodruff Rd Lafayette Hill PA 19444-1618

KING, DON, boxing promoter; b. Cleve., Aug. 20, 1931; s. Clarence and Hattie K.; m. Henrietta King; children: Deborah, Carl, Eric. Boxing promoter, 1972—; owner Don King Prodns., Inc., Fla., 1974—. Promoter various fighters including Muhammud Ali, Sugar Ray Leonard, Mike Tyson, Ken Norton, Joe Frazier, Larry Holmes, Roberto Duran, George Foreman. Office: care Don King Prodns Inc 501 Fairway Dr Deerfield Beach FL 33441-1865

KING, DONALD CHARLES, fire rescue battalion chief; b. Montgomery, Ala., Dec. 6, 1951; s. John Frank and Frances (McGowin) King; m. Charlene Elizabeth Cody, May 23, 1976; 1 child, Kevin Charles. AS in Emergency Med. Tech., Ga. Perimeter Coll., 1973—75; B in pub. mgmt., Fla. Atlantic U., 2001. Cert. Firefighter #90209 Fla., Paramedic #JA0001231 Fla., Fire Officer I # 104776 Fla., NBFSPQ Fire Officer II, Am. Ambulance Assoc. Ambulance Svc. Mgmt., Nat. Fire Academy Exec. Fire Officer. Emergency med. technician Grady Meml. Hosp., Atlanta, 1972—75; paramedic Broward County Fire Rescue, Fla., 1975—80, ops. dist. supr., 1980—91, batallion chief, 1991—2002. Author several rsch. papers in field. Coun. mem. Pompano Beach Ch. of God, Pompano Beach, FLA., 1995—2002. Mem.: Internat. City County Mgmt. Assn., ASPA, Assn. of Pub. Safety Comm. Officers, Nat. Flight Paramedics Assn., Nat. Assn. of Emergency Med. Technicians, Nat. Fire Protection Assn., Fla. Fire Chiefs Assn., Internat. Assn. of Fire Chiefs, Internat. Assn. of Firefighters, NDMS South Fla. Regional DMAT FL-5, State of Fla. Region X CISD Team, Nat. Fire Acad. Alumni Assn. Home: 6723 Skipper Terrace Margate FL 33063 Office: Broward County Fire Rescue 2601 West Broward Blvd Fort Lauderdale FL 33312 Office Fax: 954-831-8265. Personal E-mail: dking33063@aol.com. Business E-Mail: dking@broward.org.

KING, EDWARD LOUIS, retired chemistry educator; b. Grand Forks, N.D., Mar. 15, 1920; s. Edward Louis and Beatrice (Nicholson) K.; m. Joy Kerler, Dec. 20, 1952; children: Paul, Marcia (dec.). Student, Long Beach (Calif.) Jr. Coll., 1938-41; BS, U. Calif., Berkeley, 1942, PhD, 1945. Research chemist Manhattan Project, U. Cal., Berkeley, 1942-46; mem. chemistry faculty Harvard, 1946-48, U. Wis., 1948-62, U. Colo., Boulder, 1963-90, chmn. dept. chemistry, 1970-72. Author: How Chemical Reactions Occur, 1963, Chemistry, 1979; Editor: Inorganic Chemistry, 1964-68. Guggenheim fellow, 1957-58 Mem. Am. Chem. Soc., Phi Beta Kappa, Sigma Xi. Office: U Colo Dept Chemistry PO Box 215 Boulder CO 80309-0215

KING, EDWARD WILLIAM, retired transportation executive; b. North Fork, W.Va., Jan. 29, 1923; s. Edward Ward and Myrtle (Charlton) K.; m. Mary Elizabeth Preston, Oct. 31, 1947 (dec. 1976); children: Edward William Jr., Elizabeth King Brown, Mary King Sullivan; m. Martha Lee Corns Mather, Apr. 7, 1977. Edn., Va. Poly. Inst., Washington and Lee U., U. Tenn.-Knoxville. Pres., treas. Mason & Dixon Lines, Inc., Kingsport, Tenn., until 1974, chmn. bd., treas., 1974—; pres., treas. Crown Enterprises, Inc.; treas. Mason & Dixon Tank Lines, Inc. Chmn. Regular Common Carrier Conf., 1966-67; dir. Kingsport Nat. Bank, Kingsport Fed. Savs. & Loan Seal sale chmn. Sullivan County TB Assn.; mem. Kingsport Bd. Edn.; dir., sec. treas. Holston Valley Hosp., 1956-79; trustee East Tenn. State U. Found. Named Young Man of Yr. Kingsport Jaycees, 1958 Mem. Am. Trucking Assn. (Tenn. v.p., trustee ATA Found.), Trucking Employers, Tenn. Motor Transport Assn. (pres. 1957-58), Kingsport C. of C. (v.p.) Clubs: Ridgefields Country (Kingsport); Kingsport Civitan (pres.). Presbyterian.

KING, ELAINE A. curator, art historian, critic; b. Oak Park, Ill., Apr. 12, 1947; d. Casimir Stanley and Catherine Mary (Chmel) Czerwien. BS, No. Ill. U., 1968, MA, 1974; PhD, Northwestern U., 1986. Cert. Fine Arts Appraisal, 2002. Intern George Eastman House, Rochester, N.Y., 1977; lectr. history of photography Northwestern U., Evanston, Ill., 1977-81; curator Dittmar Meml. Gallery, Evanston, 1978-81; dir. Artemesia Gallery, Chgo., 1976-77; exec. dir., chief curator Carnegie-Mellon Art Gallery, Pitts., 1985—91; prof. critical theory and history of art Carnegie Mellon U., Pitts., 1981—. Bd. dirs. Mountain Lake Criticism Conf., Blacksburg, Va., 1982-91; ind. curator, 1991—; exhbn. rev. panel Pa. Coun. on Arts, 1991; exec. dir., chief curator Contemporary Art Ctr., Cin., 1993-95; guest curator Pitts. Cultural Trust, 1992, 93, 95, 96; 10 year Retrospective of Diane Samuels, Mus. of Art, Györ, Hungary, Györ, 1999, bd. dirs. Mid-Am. Coll. Art Assn.; panel chair Midwest CAA Conf., 1997, 2003; co-coord. Wats:ON Festival, 1996—; adj. prof. U. Cin., 1994; art critic-in-residence U. Ariz., Tucson; Am. guest curator Hungarian Bienale Exhbn. II, Györ, 1993, Master Graphic Arts Internat. Biennial, 1995, 97, 99, 2001, 03; panelist NEA Visual Arts, 1993; grant reviewer Inst. Mus. Sci., Washington, 1994, Ohio Arts Coun. fellowship and grant evaluator, 1994-95; Internat. Rev. panel, AAUW internat. fellowships, Washington, D.C., 2000-03; mem. organizing com. Midwest Mus. Con., 1994-95; Am. rep. Inter Arts Spring 1996 Budapest (Hungary) Crossroads, Am. critic rep. AICA Conf. The Edge, Zagreb, Croatia, Chair Coll. Arts Assoc. Com. disting. exhbn. award, 1995-98, AICA XXXIV Congress Internat. Art Critics, Zagreb, AICA conf. ctrl. European cross-roads, 1996, 97, AICA Congress 2000, London, speaker XXXIII Congress Internat. Art Critics, Warsaw, Poland, 1999, XXXIV Congress Internat. AICA, London, 2000, XXXVII Congress Internat. AICA, Barbados, 2003; plenary spkr. Prague Triennial Symposium, Prague, Czech Republic, 2001; juror exhbn. 3rd Prague Internat; spkr. in field. Curator, author: Crossing Borders: USA/Europe, Alleghany Coll. Art Galleries, 2000, Marking, 1999, The Figure As Fiction, 1993, Alfred DeCredico: Drawings, 1985-93, Emily Cheng: Monoprints, 1994, (exhbn. catalogues) Barry LeVa: 1966-88, Mel Bochner: 1973-85, Elizabeth Murray: Drawings: 1980-86, Michael Gitlin: Sculpture & Drawings, 1990, New Generations: Chgo., 1990, New Generations: N.Y., 1991, Magdalena Jetalová, 1991, Martin Puryear: Sculpture & Drawings, 1987, Abstraction/Abstraction, Tishan Hsu, Paintings, Drawings & Sculpture, 1987, N.Y. Painting Today, Michel Gerand: Drawings and Site Works, 1989, Drawings and Sculpture, 1990, Art in the Age of Information, 1993, Five Artists at the Airport: Insights into Public Art, 1992, Martha Rosler: In Place of the Public, 1994, Shari Zolla, 1997, Lyzabeth Sallan: 2 Installations, Light Into Art: From Video to Virtual Reality (also booklet), David Humphrey: Paintings and Drawings 1987-95 (also catalogue), others; author: The Misunderstood Patron, The National Endowment for the Arts; critic-in-residence Sch. Art, San Juan, PR; free lance art critic, Washington Post, Grapheion, Tema Celeste, & Sculpture, Cin. Enquirer; Grapheion; Art on Paper, Pitt. Post-Gazette, art critic in residence Delaware Contemporary Ctr. for the Arts, 1992, Mid-Atlantic Arts Fellow, 1991, No. Ill. U., 1997; corr. critic, regional editor Diaglogue, Columbus, Ohio, 1984-89; corr. critic Sculpture; contbr. articles to profl. jours. Active Dem. Party, Evanston, Ill., ward judge, 1977-78, precinct capt., 1977. Recipient Hunt Art award, 1977; Art Critics fellow Pa. Coun. on Arts, 1985, 89, 95, 99, 2000; rsch. fellow Smithsonian Inst., 1998, sr. rsch. fellow, 2000—; faculty rsch. grantee, 1985, 87, 89-90, 96-99, 2002, Grant Trust for Mutual Understanding, Rockefeller Found., 1994, Thendora Found., 1995; mem. tech. com., cmty. program scholar Pa. Humanities Coun., 1997; Nat. Mus. Am. Art, 2000, sr. rsch. fellow, short-term rsch. fellow Smithsonian Instn., Nat. Portrait Gallery, 2001; spl. initiatives grantee Pa. Coun. on Arts, 2000; grantee, IREX, 2000; rsch. fellow Inst. for Art History, Acad. Scis., Budapest, Hungary, 2002; fellow Ctrl. European Cultural Inst., 2002. Mem. Coll. Art Assn., Am. Assn. Mus., Assn. Historians Am. Art, Internat. Assn. Art Critics (Am. sect.), Art Table, Midwest Coll. Art Assn. Avocations: cooking, gardening, tennis, swimming, sailing. Office: Carnegie Mellon U CFA Fine Arts Pittsburgh PA 15213 Fax: 412-268-7817. E-mail: eaking13@yahoo.com.

KING, ELIZABETH A. primary school educator; b. Sweetwater, Tex., Dec. 17, 1951; d. Kenneth and Elizabeth H. Allen; m. William S. King, Nov. 5, 1977; children: Rachel E., Megan O. AS, Navarro Jr. Coll., Corsicana, Tex., 1972; BS, Hardin-Simmons U., Abilene, Tex., 1974; MS, Abilene Christian U., Tex., 1988. Kindegarten tchr. Albany I.S.D., Tex., 1974—77, 2nd grade tchr., 1977—. Named Tchr. of Yr., Albany C. of C., 2001. Mem.: NEA, Delta Kappa Gamma. Avocations: crafts, reading, gardening.

KING, FRANCES, education educator; b. Dallas, Nov. 14, 1929; d. Grover W. and Clara (Blailock) Beckham; m. Erwin C. King, Jr., Jan. 27, 1951; children: Carol, Melody. BA, Austin Coll., 1951; Writer's Cert., Children's Inst. of Lit., Redding Ridge, Conn., 1987. Cert. tchr. of mentally retarded, early childhood, learning disabilities, Tex. Tchr., fourth grade O'Brien (Tex.) Consolidated Ind. Sch. Dist., 1958-62; tchr., first grade, early childhood/spl. edn. tchr. Knox City (Tex.) Consolidated Ind. Sch. dist., 1961-71; spl. edn. tchr. mid. sch. Knox City-O'Brien Consolidated Ind. Sch. Dist., 1971-76, 76-89; spl. edn./adult edn. tchr. Knox City-O'Brien and Sweetwater Dist., Knox City, 1995—98; subs. tchr. Knox City-O'Brien Dist., 1989—95. Spl. edn. spelling coach Knox City H.S. Co-author: Guide Program for Special Education. Health chmn. Local R.T.A., 1999—. Named Tchr. of the Yr. in Spl. Edn., Region IVX. Mem.: Retired Tchrs. Assn. (health chmn. local 2002—), ATPE (local pres.), Tex. State Tchrs. Assn. (local pres.).

KING, FREDERIC, health services management executive, educator; b. N.Y.C., May 9, 1937; s. Benjamin and Jeanne (Fritz) K.; m. Linda Ann Udell, Mar. 17, 1976; children from previous marriage: Coby Allen, Allison Beth, Lisa Robyn, Daniel Seth (Yehuda). BBA cum laude, CUNY, 1958. Dir. adminstrn. Albert Einstein Coll. Medicine, Bronx, 1970-72; assoc. v.p. health affairs Tulane Med. Ctr., New Orleans, 1972-77; dir. fin. Mt. Sinai Med. Ctr., N.Y.C., 1977-78; v.p. fin. Cedars-Sinai Med. Ctr., L.A., 1978-82; pres. Vascular Diagnostic Svcs., Inc., Woodland Hills, Calif., 1982-84; exec. dir. South Day Ind. Physician's Med. Group, Inc., Torrance, Calif., 1984-98; ret., 1999. Assoc. adj. prof. Tulane U. Sch. Pub. Health; asst. prof. Mt. Sinai Med. Ctr.; instr. Pierce Coll., L.A. Bd. dirs. Ohr Eliyahu Acad., chmn.; bd. dirs. AMHO Pacific Region, Congregation Beth Jehudah; pres. Torah Learning Ctr. Young Israel Venice. With U.S. Army, 1959-62. Mem. Healthcare Forum, Am. Hosp. Assn., Pres.'s Assn., Calif. Assn. Hosps. and Health Systems. Republican. Home: 8332 N Indian Creek Pkwy Fox Point WI 53217-2612 E-mail: king4444@netvision.net.il.

KING, G. ROGER, lawyer; b. Ashland, Ohio, Sept. 16, 1946; BS, Miami U., 1968; JD, Cornell U., 1971. Bar: Ohio 1971, D.C. 1972. Legis. asst. U.S. Senator Robert Taft Jr., Washington, 1971-73; profl. staff counsel Labor and Human Resources Com., U.S. Senate, Washington, 1973-74; ptnr. Jones Day, Columbus, Ohio. Office: Jones Day 41 S High St Columbus OH 43215-6103 E-mail: gking@jonesday.com.

KING, GARR MICHAEL, federal judge; b. Pocatello, Idaho, Jan. 28, 1936; s. Warren I. King and Geraldine E. (Hanlon) Appleby; m. Mary Jo Rieber, Feb. 2, 1957; children: Mary, Michael, Matthew, James, Margaret, John, David. Student, U. Utah, 1957-59; LLB, Lewis and Clark Coll., 1963. Bar: Oreg. 1963, U.S. Dist. Ct. Oreg. 1965, U.S. Ct. Appeals (9th cir.) 1975, U.S. Supreme Ct. 1971. Dep. dist. atty. Multnomah County Dist. Atty.'s Office, Portland, Oreg., 1963-66; assoc. Morrison, Bailey, Dunn, Carney & Miller, Portland, 1966-71; ptnr. Kennedy & King, Portland, 1971-77, Kennedy, King & McClurg, Portland, 1977-82, Kennedy, King & Zimmer, Portland, 1982-98; judge U.S. Dist. Ct. Oreg., Portland, 1998—. Active various pvt. sch. and ch. bds. Served as sgt. USMC, 1954-57. Fellow Am. Coll. Trial Lawyers (recent 1995-98), Am. Bar Found.; mem. ABA, Oreg. Bar Assn., Multnomah County Bar Assn. (pres. 1975), Jud. Conf. 9th Cir. (del.), Northwestern Coll. Law Alumni Assn. (pres.), Multnomah Athletic Club. Democrat. Roman Catholic. Avocations: tennis, reading, gardening. Office: 907 US Courthouse 1000 SW 3rd Ave Portland OR 97204-2930 E-mail: garr-king@ord.uscourts.gov.

KING, GEORGE RALEIGH, retired manufacturing executive; b. Benton Harbor, Mich., May 13, 1931; s. Maurice Peter and Opal Ruth (Hart) King; m. Phyllis Stratton, July 30, 1950; children: Paula King Zang, Angela King Young, Philip. Student, Adrian Coll., 1950-51. Cert. purchasing profl. exec. status. With Kirsch Co., Sturgis, Mich., 1951—, data processing trainee, 1951-53, data processing mgr., 1953-59, asst. purchasing agt., 1959-62, purchasing agt., 1962-68, dir. purchasing, 1968-91, ret., 1991; corp. cons., 1991—. Author: Rods & Rings, 1972. Elder 1st Presbyn. Ch., Sturgis, 1970; pres. Sturgis Civic Players, 1972. Recipient citation Boy Scouts Am., 1966, Jr. Achievement, 1967; nominated candidate for adminstrn. Fed. Procurement Policy, Reagan Adminstrn., Washington, 1980. Mem. Am. Purchasing Soc. (pres. 1979-81), Nat. Assn. Purchasing Mgmt., southwestern Purchasing Assn., Exchange (pres. Sturgis 1959, dis. gov. dist. and nat. clubs 1961), Berrien Hills Country Club, Rotary (Lakeshore), Masons, Elks. Home: 1804 Lakeshore Dr Apt 16 Saint Joseph MI 49085-1616

KING, GLEN (LENARD GLEN KING), broadcasting educator, composer; b. N.Y.C., Oct. 13, 1935; s. Lawrence Herbert and Marcia Helen (Berger) K.; m. Margaret Elizabeth Gabler, Aug. 26, 1989. BA, Calif. State U., L.A., 1960, MFA, 1964. Prodn. asst. Sta. KABC-TV, L.A., 1963-64; news asst. Sta. KTLA-TV, L.A., 1964-65; disc jockey Sta. KUTE, L.A., 1965-66, Sta. KFOX, L.A., 1966; instr. theater arts Elizabeth Seton Coll., Yonkers, N.Y., 1966-67; assoc. prof. broadcasting West L.A. Coll., Culver City, Calif., 1977-84; prof. broadcasting Los Angeles Valley Coll., Van Nuys, Calif., 1985—; founder Silver Kat Music BMI, 1985—. Supr. student cable internships West L.A. Coll., Culver City, Calif., 1980-85; designer broadcasting and TV aesthetics and documentary curriculums area colls.; owner, mgr. Silver Kat Music Pub. affiliate Broadcast Music Inc.; broadcast cons. CBS News, 1991, KMNY, 1992; prodr., dir. Pub. Access TV Adelphia Cable Co., Charlottesville, 1996-2000, dir. M.S. Telethon, 1996-98. Composer popular, country and gospel songs, 1976—. With USN, 1953-56, Republic of Korea. Winner internat. competition Song Writers Hall of Fame and N.Y. Music Pubs. Group, 1985; recipient 1st prize Am. Song Festival, L.A., 1976, Grand prize, 1979. Mem. BMI (affiliate), Nat. Music Pubs. Assn., Songwriters Guild Am. Avocations: music, antiques, automobiles. E-mail: qualitysongs@yahoo.com.

KING, GUNDAR JULIAN, retired university dean; b. Riga, Latvia, Apr. 19, 1926; came to U.S., 1950, naturalized, 1954; s. Attis K. and Austra (Dale) Kenins: m. Valda K. Andersons, Sept. 18, 1954; children: John T., Marita A. Student, J.W. Goethe U., Frankfurt, Germany, 1946-48; BBA, U. Oreg., 1956; MBA, Stanford U., 1958, PhD, 1964; DSc (hon.), Riga Tech. U., 1991; D Habil. Oecon., Latvian Sci. Coun., 1992. Asst. field supr. Internat. Refugee Orgn., Frankfurt, 1948-50; br. office mfr. Williams Form Engring. Corp., Portland, Oreg., 1952-54; project mgr. Market Rsch. Assocs., Palo Alto, Calif., 1958-60; asst. prof., assoc. prof. Pacific Luth. U., 1960-66, prof., 1966—, dean Sch. Bus. Adminstrn., 1970-90. Vis. prof. mgmt. U.S. Naval Postgrad. Sch., 1971-72, San Francisco State U., 1980, 1987-88; internat. econ. mem. Latvian Acad. Scis., 1990—; regent Estonian Bus. Sch., 1991-99; vis. prof. Riga Tech. U., 1993-97; dir. Baltic Studies fund, 1995—. Author: Economic Policies in Occupied Latvia, 1965, additional books on business, last four in Latvian, 1999—2002; contbr. articles to profl. publs. Mem. Gov.'s Com. Wash. State Govt., 1965-88; mem. study group on pricing U.S. Commn. Govt. Procurement, 1971-72; pres. N.W. Univs. Bus. Adminstrn. Conf., 1965-66. With AUS, 1950-52. Spidola prize Latvian Culture Found., 1999; Fulbright-Hayes scholar, Thailand, 1988, Fulbright scholar, Latvia, 1993-94. Mem. AAUP (past chpt. pres.), Am. Mktg. Assn. (past chpt. pres.), Assn. Advancement Baltic Studies (pres. 1970), Western Assn. Collegiate Schs. Bus. (pres. 1971), Latvian Acad. Scis., Alpha Kappa Psi, Beta Gamma Sigma. Home: PO Box 44401 Tacoma WA 98444-0401 Office: Pacific Lutheran U Tacoma WA 98447-0003 E-mail: Kingga@plu.edu.

KING, GWENDOLYN BAIR, former government staff member, public speaker; b. Hartsville, S.C., Oct. 27, 1915; d. William Parlor and Mary Margaret (Scurry) Bair; m. LaBruce Ward King, Dec. 26, 1937; children: John LaBruce King, Margaret Gwendolyn King Farrow. AB, Coker Coll., 1936. With asst. pers. office Libr. Congress, Washington, 1937-39; sec., dir. Libr. Congress, Union Catalog, Washington, 1939-43; asst. to appointments sec. for the President The White House, Washington, 1953-69, dir. correspondence for Pat Nixon, 1969-74; pub. speaker on White House career Calif., 1977—. Contbr. to Presidential Records, The Nat. Archives, Washington, 1988. Dir. Speakers' Bur., Home Hospice, Santa Rosa, Calif., 1985, cert. caregiver, 1982-84; mem. Oakmont Archtl. Com., Santa Rosa Symphony League. Named Paul Harris Fellow, Rotary Internat., 1983, Citizen of the Day, KABL, San Francisco, 1983. Mem. AAUW, Newcomers Club (pres. Santa Rosa chpt. 1977-78), Oakmont Book Club (chmn. 1981-82), Oakmont Golf Club (sec. 1986), Saturday Afternoon Club, Oakmont Classical Music Soc., PEO. Republican. Avocations: golf, bridge, gardening, travel. Home: 431 Pythian Rd Santa Rosa CA 95409-6346

KING, HARRY RICHARD, heart surgeon; b. Benton Harbor, Mich., Sept. 5, 1935; s. Richard Harry and Ruby Jeanette (Hansen) K.; m. Marianne Werner, Jan. 26, 1963 (div. Oct., 1989); chldren: Anne Marie, Harry Hansen. BA,

Northwestern U., 1957, MD, 1961. Diplomate Am. Bd. Surgery, Am. Bd. Thoracic Surgery. Intern gen. rotating Cook County Hosp., Chgo., 1961-62, resident rotating intern, 1962-66; resident thoracic surgery Chgo. Mcpl. Tuberculosis Sanitarium, 1966; fellow gen. surgery Lahey Clin., Boston, 1967; resident cardiovasc.-thoracic surgery U. Oreg. Med. Sch. Hosp., Portland, 1967-69; pvt. practice cardiovasc. and thoracic surgery Houston, 1990—. Clin. instr. U. Wash. Med. Sch., Seattle, 1971-89. Republican. Avocation: individual sports. Home and Office: 2828 Bammel Ln Apt 811 Houston TX 77098-1131

KING, HENRY LAWRENCE, lawyer; b. N.Y.C., Apr. 29, 1928; s. H. Abraham and Henrietta (Prentky) K.; m. Barbara Hope, 1949 (dec. May 1962); children: Elizabeth King Robertson, Patricia King Cantlay (dec.), Matthew Harrison.; m. Alice Mary Sturges, Aug. 1, 1963 (div. 1978); children: Katherine Masury King Baccile, Andrew Lawrence, Eleanor Sturges; m. Margaret Gram, Feb. 14, 1981 AB, Columbia U., 1948; LLB, Yale U., 1951. Bar: N.Y. 1952, U.S. Supreme Ct., other fed. cts. 1952. With Davis Polk & Wardwell, N.Y.C., 1951—, ptnr., 1961—, mng. ptnr., chmn., 1982-96. Mng. editor Yale Law Jour., 1951. Trustee, chmn. bd. Columbia U., 1983-95, chmn. emeritus, 1995—; chmn. bd. Columiba Presbyn. adv. coun.; pres. Assn. Alumni Columbia Coll., 1966-68, Alumni Fedn. Columbia U., 1973-75; chmn. Coll. Fund, 1972-73; pres. Yale Law Sch. Assn., 1984-86, chmn., 1986-88; pres. Cathedral of St. John the Divine, N.Y.C.; bd. dirs. N.Y. Acad. of Medicine, Citizen's Com. for N.Y.C., Inc., Am. Skin Assn., Fishers Island Devel. Co., Episcopal Charities; vestryman Trinity Ch., N.Y.C., 1991-98; trustee Chapin Sch., 1977-89, Columbia U. Press, 1978-92. Recipient Columbia Alumni medal for conspicuous service, 1968, John Jay award, 1992. Fellow Am. Coll. Trial Lawyers; mem. ABA, Coun. on Fgn. Rels., Am. Law Inst., N.Y. State Bar Assn. (pres. 1988-89), Assn. Bar City N.Y., Am. Judicature Soc., Fishers Island Club, Century Assn., Union Club (N.Y.C.), Jupiter Island Club, Blind Brook Club, Fishers Island Yacht Club, Pilgrims, Church Club (N.Y.C.), Links Club. Home: 115 E 67th St New York NY 10021-5951 also: East End Rd Fishers Island NY 06390 Office: Davis Polk & Wardwell 450 Lexington Ave 27th Fl New York NY 10017-3982 also: 61 Links Rd Hobe Sound FL 33455 E-mail: hking@dpw.com.

KING, HUESTON CLARK, retired otolaryngologist, educator; b. Bklyn., Feb. 3, 1929; s. William Clark and Alice Packard (Hueston) K.; m. Wilma Marguerite Grove, June 13, 1953; children: Brian G., Melinda K. AB in Biology, Princeton U., 1950; MD, Columbia U., 1954. Diplomate Am. Bd. Otolaryngology; lic. physician, Fla.; cert. Nat. Bd. Med. Examiners. Intern Jackson Meml. Hosp., U. Miami (Fla.) Sch. Medicine, 1954-55; resident in otolaryngology Walter Reed Army Med. Ctr., Washington, 1956-58; staff Coral Gables (Fla.) Hosp., 1962-82, Bapt. Hosp., 1962-82, Mercy Hosp., 1962-82, South Miami Hosp., Fla., 1962-82, Cedars of Lebanon Hosp., 1962-82, Jackson Meml. Hosp., 1962-82; with Venice (Fla.) Hosp., 1983-94. From clin. faculty to assoc. prof. dept. otolaryngology U. Miami Med. Sch., 1962-82; clin. prof. dept. otolaryngology U. Tex. Southwestern Med. Ctr., Dallas, U. Fla.; lectr. in field. Author: (textbook) An Otolaryngologist's Guide to Allergy, 1991; sr. author: (textbook) A Practical Guide to Management of Nasal and Sinus Disorders, 1993, Allergy in ENT Practice: A Basic Guide, 1998; editor: Otolaryngologic Allergy, 1981; editor Allergy Digest, food allergy sect. Current Sci., allergy sect. Current Opinion, 1999-01; contbr. chpts. to books, articles to profl. jours. Bd. dirs. Woodmere at Jacaranda, Venice, 1997-99; committeeman Venice Found., 1995-97. Fellow ACS (emeritus), Am. Acad. Facial Plastic and Reconstructive Surgery (emeritus), Am. Acad. Otolaryngic Allergy (past pres. 1979-80, dir. med. edn. 1983-88), Am. Coll. Allergy, Asthma and Immunology; mem. Fla. Med. Assn., Sarasota Couty Med. Assn., Venice Yacht Club. E-mail: drhking@juno.com.

KING, INDLE GIFFORD, industrial designer, educator; b. Seattle, Oct. 23, 1934; s. Indle Frank and Phyllis (Kenney) K.; m. Rosalie Rosso, Sept. 10, 1960; children: Indle Gifford Jr., Paige Phyllis. BA, U. Wash., 1960, MA, 1968. Indsl. designer Hewlett-Packard, Palo Alto, Calif., 1961-63; mgr. indsl. design Sanborn Co., Boston, 1963-65; mgr. corp. design Fluke Corp., Everett, Wash., 1965-97; prof. indsl. design Western Wash. U., Bellingham, 1985—; pres., CEO Teaque Inc., 1998—. Judge nat. and. internat. competitions; cons. in field. Contbr. articles to profl. jours.; designer patents in field. Coach Mercer Island (Wash.) Boys' Soccer Assn., 1972-77; pres. Mercer Island PTA, 1973; advisor Jr. Achievement, Seattle, 1975-78. Recognized as leading one of Am.'s Top 40 Design Driven Cos., ID Jour., 1999. Mem. Idsl. Design Soc. Am. (Alcoa award 1965, v.p. Seattle chpt. 1986-88), Mercer Island Country Club. Office: 2727 Western Ave # 200 Seattle WA 98121

KING, IVAN ROBERT, astronomy educator; b. Far Rockaway, N.Y., June 25, 1927; s. Myram and Anne (Franzblau) K.; m. Alice Greene, Nov. 21, 1952 (div. 1982); children: David, Lucy, Adam, Jane; m. Judith Schultz, Apr. 20, 2002. AB, Hamilton Coll., 1946; AM, Harvard U., 1947, PhD, 1952; Laurea Honoris Causa (hon.), U. Padua (Italy), 2002. Instr. astronomy Harvard U., 1951—52; mathematician Perkin-Elmer Corp., Norwalk, Conn., 1951—52; methods analyst U.S. Dept. Def., Washington, 1954—56; with U. Ill., 1956—64; assoc. prof. astronomy U. Calif., Berkeley, 1964—66, prof., 1966—93, chmn. astronomy dept., 1967—70, prof. emeritus, 1993—; rsch. prof. U. Wash., Seattle, 2002—. Mem. faint object camera team Hubble Space Telescope. Contbr. numerous articles to sci. jours. Served with USNR, 1952-54. Fellow AAAS (chmn. astronomy sect. 1974), NAS, Am. Acad. Arts & Scis., Am. Astron. Soc. (councillor 1963-66, chmn. div. dynamical astronomy 1972-73, pres. 1978-80), Internat. Astron. Union. Achievements include rsch. study of stellar systems. Office: U Wash Dept Astronomy Seattle WA 98195-1580

KING, J. BRADLEY, lawyer; b. Noblesville, Ind., Sept. 2, 1957; s. Charles Joseph and Marina (Davis) K. BA in History & Polit. Sci. with honors, Ind. U., 1978; JD, Coll. of William and Mary, 1981. Bar: Calif. 1981, Ind. 1985. Pvt. practice cons. to local govts., Indpls., 1982-85; staff atty. Legislative Svcs. Agy., State of Ind., Indpls., 1985-90; asst. corp. counsel, chief lobbyist at gen. assembly City of Indpls., 1990-92; gen. counsel State of Ind. Election Commn., Indpls., 1992-99; dir. of elections State of Minn., 1999—2002; co-dir. of elections State of Ind., 2002—. Del. Ind. State Conv., 1998. Sr. warden, vestryman Episcopal Ch. of All Saints, Indpls., 1989-91, 93-96; vestry mem. St. Paul's-on-the-Hill Episcopal Ch., 2001-02; asst. state party rules Ind. Rep. State Com., Indpls., 1997, 2003, chair Ind. presdl. electors meeting, 1996; del. Indpls. conv. Episcopal Diocese, 1995, 2003. Decorated Order of Ky. Cols.; named Election Adminstr. of Yr., Ballot Access News, 1997, Hon. Sec. State of Ind., 1999. Phi Beta Kappa, 1977. Avocations: walking, genealogy, philately, music, travel. Office: 302 W Washington St # E204 Indianapolis IN 46204-2743 E-mail: bking@iec.state.in.us.

KING, JACK A. lawyer; b. Lafayette, Ind., July 29, 1936; s. Noah C. and Mabel E. (Pierce) K.; m. Mary S. King, Dec. 10, 1960; children: Jeffrey A., Janice D., Julie D. BS in Fin., Ind. U., 1958, JD, 1961. Bar: Ind. 1961. Ptnr. Ball, Eggleston, King & Bumbleburg, Lafayette, 1961-70; judge Superior Ct. 2 of Tippecanoe County, Ind., 1970—78; v.p., assoc. gen. counsel Dairyland Ins. Co., 1978—79, v.p., gen. counsel, asst. sec., 1980—85; asst. gen. counsel Sentry Corp., 1979—85; v.p., gen. counsel, asst. sec. Gt. S.W. Fire Ins. Co., 1980-85; v.p., gen. counsel Dairyland County Mut. Ins. Co. Tex., 1980-85; v.p., counsel Sentry Ctr. West, 1981-85; v.p., gen. counsel, asst. sec. Gt. S.W. Surplus Lines Ins. Co., 1981-85; v.p. legal, asst. sec. Scottsdale Ins. Co., 1985-95; asst. sec. Nat. Casualty Co., 1985-95; v.p. Ariz. Ins. Info. Assn., 1988-96; v.p. legal, asst. sec. Scottsdale Indemnity Co., 1992-95; sr. v.p., gen. coun. TIG Excess & Surplus Lines, Inc., 1995-96; exec. dir. Ariz. Ins. Guaranty Funds, 1998-2001. Cons., mediator and arbitrator, 1996-97, 2001—; exec. com. Ariz. Joint Underwriting Plan, 1980-81; mem. Ariz. Property & Casualty Ins. Commn., 1985-86, vice-chmn., 1986; mem. Ariz. Study Commn. on Ins., 1986-87, Ariz. Task Force on Ct. Orgn. and Adminstrn., 1988-89; adv. com. Ariz. Ho. Rep. Majority Leaders, 1989, Ariz. Dept. Ins. Fraud Unit, 1997-97; mem. Ariz. Dept. Ins. Comml. Lines Ins. Market Task Force, 2002. Contbr. to The Law of Competitive Business Practices, 2d edit. Bd. dirs. Scottsdale Art Ctr. Assn., 1981-84. Mem. ABA, Ind. Bar Assn., Maricopa County Bar Assn.

KING, JACQUELINE ELIZABETH, policy analyst, researcher; b. San Francisco, Oct. 10, 1965; d. James Anthony and Joan Arlene K.; m. Dion Frank Vinik, Sept. 7, 2003. BA in French Lit., U. Calif., Berkeley, 1987; MA in Higher Edn., Columbia U., N.Y.C., 1988; PhD in Higher Edn., U. Md., College Park, 1996. Assoc. dir., policy analysis The Coll. Bd., Washington, 1993—96; dir. Ctr. Policy Analysis Am. Coun. on Edn., Washington, 1996—. Author (editor): Financing a College Education: How It Works, How It's Changing, 1999; author: (monograph) Money Matters: The Impact of Race/Ethnicity and Gender on How Students Pay for College, 1999, Gender Equity in Higher Education: Are Male Students at a Disadvantage?, 2000, Crucial Choices: How Students' Financial Decisions Affect their Academic Success, 2002; editor: (journal) Changing Student Attendance Patterns: Implications for Policy and Practice, 2003; contbr. chapters to books, articles. Bd. dirs. Nat. Postsecondary Edn. Data Coop., Washington, 2001—. Recipient Young Leader of the Acad., Change Mag., 1998; grantee, Lumina Found. for Edn., 2003—05. Mem.: Assn. Study Higher Edn. (assoc.). Office: Am Coun Edn One Dupont Circle NW Ste 800 Washington DC 20036

KING, JAMES CECIL, Medievalist, educator; b. Uniontown, Pa., Sept. 14, 1924; s. Joseph Herbert and Eliza Ann (Kelley) K.; m. Diana Hanbury, Sept. 5, 1952 (div. Apr. 1958); children— Christopher Hanbury, Sheila Anne. BA, George Washington U., 1949, MA, 1950, PhD, 1954. Master for French, German and Latin St. Albans Sch. for Boys, Washington, 1952-55; asst. prof. German George Washington U., 1955-60, asso. prof., 1960-65, prof., 1965-90, prof. emeritus, 1990—. Rschr. Langs.-of-the-World Archives, 1960-61. Editor (with Petrus W. Tax) of series Die Werke Notkers des Deutschen, 1972—. Served with U.S. Army, 1943—46. German Acad. Exch. Svc. grantee, 1963. Mem. Linguistic Soc. Am., Medieval Acad. Am., Am. Assn. Tchrs. German, MLA, Am. Goethe Soc., Soc. Germanic Linguistics, AAUP, Phi Beta Kappa. Home: 9296 Bailey Ln Fairfax VA 22031-1930

KING, JAMES E. "JIM", JR., state legislator, personnel executive, consultant; b. Bklyn., Oct. 30, 1939; AA, St. Petersburg Jr. Coll., 1959; BS, BA, Fla. State U., 1961, MBA, 1962. Owner King Temporary Staffing Inc., Southeastern Resources Inc., King Leasing Corp., The Jim King Cos.; mem. Fla. Ho. of Reps., Tallahassee, 1986—99, mem. Rep. legislature leadersip com., Rep. leadership team, 1986-94, minority floor whip, 1988-90; mem. Fla. Sen., Tallahassee, 1999—, pres., 2002—. Chmn. House Rep. Policy Com., 1992-94; chmn. Duval Delegation, 1992; vice chmn. Rep. Reapportionment Com. Vice chmn. Fla. Task Force on Govt.-Financed Health Care; mem. Jacksonville Sports and Entertainment Commn., vice chmn., 1986; mem. exec. com. Fla. Rep. Party, Gtr. Jacksonville Charities Inc.; bd. dirs. Fla. Hospice. With USCG, 1962-60. Recipient Outstanding Leadership award Fraternal Order of Police D.I. Rainey Legis. award Fla. Chiropractic Assn., Hospice Hall of Fame award, Legis. of Yr. award Jacksonville Assn. Realtors, Guardian of Small Bus. award Nat. Fedn. Ind. Bus., Outstanding Bus. and Industry Legislator award; named Outstanding Small Bus. Owner, Outstanding Charitable Corp., Most Outstanding Duval Legislator Jacksonville Jewish Fedn. Mem. Am. Assn. Retired People, Fla. State U. Boosters, Inc. (bd. dirs.), Jacksonville Seminole Boosters Inc. (pres. 1982), Fla. Conservation Assn., Multiple Sclerosis Soc. (mem. nat. adv. bd.), Meninak Club Jacksonville, Mazda Gator Bowl Assn. (mem. exec. bd. 1990), Ducks Unltd. Episcopalian. Home: # 108 9485 Regency Square Blvd Jacksonville FL 32225-8111 Office: Fla State Capitol 402 S Monroe St Rm 222 Tallahassee FL 32399-6526 E-mail: king.james@leg.state.fl.us.*

KING, JAMES EDWARD, retired museum director, consultant; b. Escanaba, Mich., July 23, 1940; s. G. Willard and Grace (Magee) K.; m. Frances Bartos, Jan. 15, 1973; 1 child, Scott E. BS, Alma Coll., 1962; MS, U. N.Mex., 1964; PhD, U. Ariz., 1972. Lab asst. in biology Alma Coll., Mich., 1960-62; rsch. asst. dept. biology U. N.Mex., Albuquerque, 1962-64; teaching asst. dept. botany and plant pathology Mich. State U., East Lansing, 1964-66; plant industry inspector Mich. Dept. Agriculture, Lansing, 1966-68; rsch. asst. dept. geochronology U. Ariz., Tucson, 1968-71, rsch. assoc. dept. geoscis., 1971-72; assoc. curator paleobotany Ill. State Mus., Springfield, 1972-78, head sci. sects. and full curator, 1978-85, asst. dir. for sci., 1985-87; adj. assoc. prof. dept. geology U. Ill., Urbana, 1979-88; dir. Carnegie Mus. Natural History, Pitts., 1987-96, Cleve. Mus. Natural History, 1996—2001; mus. cons., 2001—. Adj. prof. biology Sangamon State U., Springfield, Ill., 1983-87; adj. rsch. scientist Hunt Inst. Bot. Documentation, Carnegie Mellon U., Pitts., 1988—; adj. prof. dept. geology and planetary sci., U. Pitts., 1988-96; vis. scientist in residence Alma (Mich.) Coll., 1985. Author sci. papers on topics related to geology and paleobotany; mem. editorial bd. Jour. Archaeol. Sci., 1980-87. Bd. dirs. Western Pa. Conservancy, 1996-97, Allegheny Land Trust, 1995-96; trustee Chagrin River Watershed Ptnrs., 1997—; mem. exec. com. Univ. Cir., Inc., 1996—. Fellow Ill. State Acad. Sci. (pres. 1981-82); mem. Am. Assn. Mus. (bd. dirs. 1994-97), Am. Quaternary Assn., (treas., exec. com. 1976-84), Am. Assn. Stratigraphic Palynologists, Assn. Sci. Mus. Dirs. (v.p. 1992-93, pres. 1993-96), Assn. Systematics Collections (v.p. 1989-91, pres. 1991-93), Sigma Xi (pres. Springfield chpt. 1985-86). Home and Office: Ste 326 6336 N Oracle Rd Tucson AZ 85704

KING, JAMES FORREST, JR., lawyer; b. Salina, Kans., Jan. 9, 1949; s. James Forrest Sr. and Carolyn (Prout) K.; m. Mary Lou A. Goodwin, May 18, 1985; 1 child, James Forrest King III. BA, U. Md., 1970; JD with honors, George Washington U., 1974. Bar: D.C. 1975, U.S. Dist. Ct. D.C. 1976, U.S. Ct. Appeals (D.C. cir.) 1977, U.S. Supreme Ct. 1979, Md. 1982, U.S. Ct. Appeals (4th cir.) 1985. Atty. Law Offices of Washington, 1975-76; ptnr. Reuss, McConville & King, Washington, 1976-80, Reuss, Herndon, McConville & King, Washington, 1980-85; of counsel Herndon, McConville, Brown, Teller & Hessler, Washington, 1986-87; ptnr. Law Offices of James Forrest King, Washington, 1987—. Mem., bd. dirs. Family Ct. Trial Lawyers Assn., Dist. Col. Superior Ct., 2001—. Commr. D.C. Commn. Human Rights, 1984-90. Mem. Am. Arbitration Assn. (panel mem.), ABA (econs. law practice sect.), Superior Ct. Trial Lawyers Assn. (bd. dirs. 1997—), DC Bar Assn. (co-chmn. divsn. 6, 1981-84, arbitration bd. 1981-83, employment discrimination panel, 1977-80).

KING, JAMES LAWRENCE, federal judge; b. Miami, Fla., Dec. 20, 1927; s. James Lawrence and Viola (Clodfelter) K.; m. Mary Frances Kapa, June 1, 1961; children— Lawrence Daniel, Kathryn Ann, Karen Ann, Mary Virginia BA in Edn., U. Fla., 1949, JD, 1953; LHD (hon.), St. Thomas U., 1992. Bar: Fla. 1953. Assoc. Sibley & Davis, Miami, Fla., 1953-57; ptnr. Sibley Giblin King & Levenson, Miami, 1957-64; judge 11th Jud. Cir. Dade County, Miami, 1964-70; temp. assoc. justice Supreme Ct. Fla., 1965; temp. assoc. judge Fla. Ct. Appeals (2d, 3d and 4th dist.), 1965-68; judge U.S. Dist. Ct. (so. dist.) Fla., Miami, 1970-84, chief judge, 1984-91, sr. judge, 1991—. Temp. judge U.S. Ct. Appeals 5th cir., 1977-78; mem. Jud. Conf. U.S., 1984-87, mem. adv. commn. jud. activities, 1973-76, mem. joint commn. code jud. conduct, 1974-76, mem. commn. to consider stds. for admission to practice in fed. cts., 1976-79, chmn. implementation com. for admission attys. to fed. practice, 1979-85, mem. com. bankruptcy legis., 1977-78; mem. Jud. Conf. U.S., 1984-87; mem. Jud. Coun. 11th Cir., 1989-92; pres. 5th cir. U.S. Dist. Judges Assn., 1977-78; chief judge U.S. Dist. Ct. C.Z., 1977-78; long range planning commn. Fed. Judiciary, 1991-95. Mem. state exec. council U. Fla., 1956-59; mem. Bd. Control Fla. Governing State Univs. and Colls., 1964. Served to 1st lt. USAF, 1953-55 Recipient Outstanding Alumnus award U. Fla. Law Rev., 1980, Lifetime Achievement award Greater Miami Jewish Fedn. Commerce and Professions Attys. Divsn., 1992, 18th Annual Edward J. Devitt Disting. Svc. to Justice award, 2000; The James Lawrence King Fed. Justice Bldg. named in his honor, 1996. Mem. Fla. Bar Assn. (pres. jr. bar 1963-64, bd. govs. 1958-63, Merit award young lawyer sect. 1967), ABA, Am. Law Inst., Inst. Jud. Adminstrn., Fla. Blue Key, Pi Kappa Tau, Phi Delta Phi Democrat. Home: 11950 SW 67th Ct Miami FL 33156-4756 Office: US Dist Ct James King Fed Justice Bldg 99 NE 4th St Rm 1127 Miami FL 33132-2139

KING, JAMES R. lawyer; b. Geneva, Ill., Oct. 24, 1946; BA, Miami U., 1968; JD, Ohio State U., 1974. Bar: Ohio 1974. Ptnr. Jones Day Reavis & Pogue, Columbus. Office: Jones Day Reavis & Pogue 1900 Huntington Ctr Columbus OH 43215-6103

KING, JANE CUDLIP COBLENTZ, volunteer educator; b. Iron Mountain, Mich., May 4, 1922; d. William Stacey and Mary Elva (Martin) Cudlip; m. George Samuel Coblentz, June 8, 1942 (dec. June 1989); children: Bruce Harper, Keith George, Nancy Allison Coblentz Patch; m. James E. King, August 23, 1991 (dec. Jan. 1994). BA, Mills Coll., 1942. Mem. Sch. Resource and Career Guidance Vols., Inc., Atherton, Calif., 1965-69, pres., CEO, 1969—. Part-time exec. asst. to dean of admissions Mills Coll., 1994-99. Proofreader, contbr. Mills Coll. Quarterly mag. Life gov. Royal Children's Hosp., Melbourne, Australia, 1963—; pres. United Menlo Park (Calif.) Homeowner's Assn., 1994—; nat. pres. Mills Coll. Alumnae Assn., 1969-73, bd. trustees, 1975-83; bd. govs. Mills Coll. Alumnae Assn., 1966-73, 75-83, 98-2000, v.p., 2001—. Named Vol. of Yr., Sequoia Union H.S. Dist., 1988, Disting. Woman Mid-Peninsula (forerunner San Mateo County Women's Hall of Fame), 1975; recipient Golden Acorn award for Outstanding Cmty. Svc., Menlo Park C. of C., 1991. Mem. AAUW (Menlo-Atherton br. pres. 1994-96, v.p. programs 1996-97, editor Directory and Acorn, 1994—), Atherlons, Palo Alto (Calif.) Area Mills Coll. Club (pres. 1986), Phi Beta Kappa. Episcopalian. Avocations: reading, gardening.

KING, JANE LOUISE, artist; b. South Bend, Ind., Aug. 9, 1951; d. Bill and Anne Luciel (Hopkins) Berta; m. Gerald William King Jr., July 7, 1973; children: Kelly Anne, Dinah Jolene. Student, Ind. U., South Bend, 1969-70, Ind. U., 1970-71; BFA, Ohio State U., 1973. Ind. artist, Colo., 1974—. Instr. Sangre de Cristo Art Ctr., Pueblo, Colo., 1982, Art Studio, Longmont, Colo., 1989. Exhibited oil and pastel paintings in numerous group shows including 5th Ann. Internat. Exhibit Kans. Pastel Soc., 10th and 22nd Ann. Pastel Soc. Am., N.Y., Colo. State Fairs, Poudre Valley Art League; prin. works represented in numerous pvt. collections; contbr. poems to At Days End, 1994. Leader 4-H Club, Longmont, 1986—; sec. Longmont Artists Guild Gallery, 1988-89, bd. dirs., 1989; supt. 1st Bapt. Ch., Longmont, 1990-91. Mem. Pastel Soc. Am. (assoc.), Colo. Artists Assn. (area 1 rep. 1994), Longmont Artists Guild (Grumbacher award 1992), Longmont Arts Coun., Knickerbocker Artists N.Y., Audubon Artists N.Y. Republican. Avocations: gardening, skiing, horseback riding, music, reading. Home: 1508 Kempton Ct Longmont CO 80501-6716

KING, JANET CARLSON, nutrition educator, researcher; b. Red Oak, Iowa, Oct. 3, 1941; d. Paul Emil and Norma Carolina (Anderson) Carlson; m. Charles Talmadge King, Dec. 25, 1967; children: Matthew, Samuel. BS, Iowa State U., 1963; PhD, U. Calif., Berkeley, 1972. Dietitian Fitzsimmons Gen. Hosp., Denver, 1964-67; NIH postdoctoral fellow dept. nutrition sci. U. Calif., Berkeley, 1972-73, asst. prof. nutrition dept. nutrition sci., 1973-78, assoc. prof. nutrition dept. nutrition sci., 1978-83, prof. nutrition dept. nutrition sci., 1983—, chair dept. nutrition sci., 1988-94; dir. USDA Western Human Nutrition Rsch.Ctr., Davis, Calif., 1995—2002; sr. scientist Children's Hosp. Oakland Rsch. Inst., 2003—; prof. internal medicine U. Calif., Davis, 2003—. Frances E. Fischer Meml. nutrition lectr. Am. Dietetic Assn. Found., 1985, Lotte Arnrich Nutrition lectr. Iowa State U., 1985; Massee lectr. N.D., 1991, Lydia J. Roberts lectr. U. Chgo., 1995, Virginia A. Beal lectr. U. Mass., 1998; vis. prof. U. Calif., Davis, 1998—. Contbr. articles to Jour. Am. Diet. Assn., Am. Jour. Clin. Nutrition, Jour. Nutrition, Nutrition Rsch., Obstetrics and Gynecology, Brit. Jour. Obstetrics and Gynaecology. Recipient Lederle Labs. award in human nutrition Am. Inst. Nutrition, 1989, Internat. award in human nutrition, 1996. Mem. AAAS, Nat. Acad. Scis. Inst. Medicine, Am. Dietetic Assn., Am. Inst. Nutrition, Am. Soc. Clin. Nutrition. Office: Childrens Hosp Oakland Rsch Inst 5700 MKL Jr Way Oakland CA 94609 E-mail: jking@chori.org.

KING, JANET FELLAND, family nurse practitioner; b. Ann Arbor, Mich., May 5, 1947; d. Robert Marcy and Marjorie Marie (Sherman) Felland; m. William Curtis Runyon, May 20, 1967 (div. May 8, 1972); m. Robert Allen King, Oct. 26, 1974; 1 child, Stephen Tremain King. Student, U. Mich., 1965-67, Earlham Coll., 1968-69; BSN, Ball State U., 1971; MNSc, U. Ark., 1976. RN, Idaho. Med. surg. nurse McCullough-Hyde Meml. Hosp., Oxford, Ohio, 1971-72; migrant health nurse Colo. Dept. Health, Lamar, 1972-74; pub. health nurse City Health Dept., Little Rock, 1974-75; family nurse practitioner Idaho Migrant Coun., Burley, 1976-81; pub. health nurse South Ctrl. Dist. Health, Burley, 1981-82; family nurse practitioner Family Health Svcs., Burley, 1982—. Treas. Mini Cassia Child Protection Team, Burley, 1982—; mem. Idaho Health Profl. Loan Repayment Bd., Pocatello, 1992-2000. Vol., nurse and deacon Diocese of Honduras, Roatan, 1990; archdeacon Diocese of Idaho, 1990—, mem. standing com., 1997-2000; trustee Episcopal Camp & Conf. Bd., 1991-99, Alta Retreat Ctr., 2001—; hospice vol., 1994—. Named Woman of Progress, Bus. and Profl. Women, 1981-82; recipient Outstanding Clinician Achievement award N.W. Primary Care Assn., 1992. Mem. Idaho Nurses Assn. (regional rep. 1982-84), Sigma Theta Tau. Episcopalian. Avocations: cross country skiing, hiking. Home: 678 E 400 N Rupert ID 83350-9460 Office: Family Health Svcs 1308 Bennett Burley ID 83318-2170 E-mail: robking@pmt.org.

KING, JENN L. civil engineer; b. Hollywood, Florida, Nov. 8, 1972; d. Thomas Warren and Cydney Dee (Blinn) G. BSCE, Worcester Poly. Inst., 1994. Cert. professional engring. Project engr. Pitman-Hartenstein & Assocs., Jacksonville, Fla., 1995-99, Tinter Assoc., Ft. Lauderdale, Fla., 1999—2001; sr. transp. engr. URS Consultants, Ft. Lauderdale, 2001—. Mem. NSPE, ASCE, Inst. Transportaion Engrs., Florida Engring. Soc., Soc. Women Engrs. Avocations: horseback riding, travel, raising seahorses, camping, reading. Office: URS Consultants 5100 NW 33d Ave Ste 150 Fort Lauderdale FL 33309-6375

KING, JERRY WAYNE, research chemist; b. Indpls., Feb. 19, 1942; s. Ernest E. and Miriam (Sanders) K.; m. Bettie Maria Dunbar, Aug. 8, 1965; children: Ronald Sean, Valerie Raquel, Diana Lynn. BS, Butler U., 1965; PhD, Northeastern U., 1973; fellow, Georgetown U., 1973-74. Rsch. chemist Union Carbide Corp., Bound Brook, N.J., 1968-70; asst. prof. dept. chemistry Va. Commonwealth U., Richmond, 1974-76; rsch. scientist Arthur D. Little, Inc., Cambridge, Mass., 1976-77; rsch. assoc. Am. Can Co., Barrington, Ill., 1977-79; rsch. scientist CPC Internat., Summit-Argo, Ill., 1979-86; lead scientist NCAUR-ARS divsn. USDA, Peoria, Ill., 1986—2002; program mgr. chem. divsn. Los Alamos Lab., 2002—. Guest lectr. in field; v.p. Supercritical Confs. Mem. editl. bd. Jour. Am. Oil Chemists' Soc., Italian Jour. Food Sci., Jour. Supercritical Fluids, Supercritical Fluid Sci. and Tech. Series; contbr. articles to profl. jours. Recipient Scientist of Yr. award Nat. Ctr. Agrl. Utilization Rsch., Agrl. Rsch. Svc., USDA, 1993, Chgo. Chromatography Discussion Group Merit award, 1995, 8th Internat. Symposium on Supercritical Fluid Chromatography and Extraction excellence award, 1998, Merit award Midwest & Tri-State Supercritical Fluid Discussion Group, 1998, Rsch. award for supercritical fluids commercialization Thar Designs, 1998, Underwood Fund award Biotech. and Biol. Scis. Rsch. Coun., U.K., 1998, 1st Pl. award for consumer products Fed. Lab. Consortium for Tech. Transfer-Midwest Area, 2001, honorable mention award for health and medicine, 2001; named v.p. Supercritical Confs. Mem. Assn. Ofcl. Analytical Chemists (Harvey W. Wiley award 1997, Keene P. Dimick award Pitts. conf. 2000), Inst. Food Technologists, Am. Oil Chemists Soc. (Herbert J. Dutton award 2003), Am. Chem. Soc., Assn. Advancement of Indsl. Crops, Acad. Georgofili (Italy, corr.), Internat. Soc. for Advancement of Supercritial Fluids, Soc. Chem. Industry (Eng.), Am. Assn. Cereal Chemists. Home: 1820 W Sunnyview Dr Peoria IL 61614-4662 Office: Los Alamos Nat Lab Chemistry Div C-Act Group PO Box 1663 Mail Stop E 537 Los Alamos NM 87545 E-mail: kingjw@lanl.gov.

KING, JOHN ARTHUR, zoologist, educator; b. Detroit, June 22, 1921; s. Royal Ernest and Matie Neupert King; m. Joan McGinty King, June 25, 1949; children: Christopher, Andrea. BA, U. Mich., 1943, MS, 1948, PhD, 1951. Staff scientist The Jackson Lab., Bar Harbor, Maine, 1951—61; prof. zoology Mich. State U., East Lansing, 1961—86, prof. emeritus zoology, 1986—. Editor: (book) Biology of Peromyscus, 1968. Mem. town council Town of Bar Harbor, Maine, 1958. 2d lt. USAF, 1943—45. Recipient Career Devel. award, NIH, 1963—71; grantee Rsch. grantee, 1955—81. Fellow: Animal Behavior Soc. (sec. 1964—70, pres. 1970); mem.: Am. Soc. Mammalogists (life). Democrat. Achievements include research in in area of social behavior of prairie dogs; effect of early experience on adult behavior. Avocations: nature study, gardening, opera. Home: 4451 Comanche Okemos MI 48864

KING, JOHN CHARLES PETER, newspaper editor; b. Vancouver, B.C., Can., Dec. 13, 1949; s. Charles and Pauline K.; m. Jennifer; children: Sheila, James. BA, York U., 1973. Mem. staff The Globe and Mail Ltd., Toronto, Can., 1970—, night city editor, 1973-75; bur. chief Ottawa, Can., 1975-78; nat. editor Toronto, 1978-81; bur. chief Washington, 1981-84; assoc. editor Report on Bus., Toronto, 1984-87, exec. editor, 1987-93; dep. mng. editor The Globe and Mail, 1993-99, dir. editl. prodn., 1999—2003, dir. editl. tech., 2003—. Dir. Can. Mng. Editors Conf., 1997-98, v.p., 1998-99. Spanish lang. fellow Nat. Press Found., 1987; Thomson scholar, 1987. Mem. Can. Assn. Newspapers Editors (pres. 1999-00).

KING, JOHN ETHELBERT, JR., academic administrator; b. Oklahoma City, r, July 29, 1913; s. John Ethelbert and Iosa (Koontz) K.; m. Glennie Beanland, Dec. 25, 1936; children: Wynetka Ann King Reynolds, Rebecca Ferriss King Stevens. BA, N. Tex. U., 1932; MS, U. Ark., 1937; PhD, Cornell U., 1941; LLD (hon.), Coll. of Ozarks, 1965; LHD (hon.), No. Mich. U., 1966, U. S.C., 1989. Latin tchr., coach Frisco (Tex.) Pub. High Sch., 1933-35; missionary to Native Ams. Presbyn. Ch. U.S.A., Okla., Ariz., 1938-43; asst. prof. N.Y. State Coll. Agr., Cornell U., Ithaca, 1945-47; acad. dean, provost, prof. U. Minn., Duluth, 1947-53; pres., prof. Emporia (Kans.) U., 1953-66; prof., pres. U. Wyo., Laramie, 1966-67; prof., chmn. dept. So. Ill. U., Carbondale, 1967-83; Disting. vis. prof., interim dean U. S.C., Columbia, 1984-90. Ednl. adviser Civilian Conservation Corps, U.S. Forest Svc., Ozone, Ark., 1935-37; mentor Assn. Governing Bds. Univs. and Coll., Washington, 1977-90. Editor: Work and the College Student, 1967, Money, Marbles and Chalk, 1978. Life trustee U. Ozarks, Clarksville, Ark., 1965—. Officer USN, 1943-45, PTO. Recipient Disting. Alumnus award N. Tex. U., Denton, 1965, U. Ark., Fayetteville, 1983. Mem. NEA (life), Am. Assn. Colls. Tchr. Edn. (pres. 1966-67), Rotary, Blue Key, Omicron Delta Kappa, Lambda Chi Alpha, Sphinx Club, Phi Delta Kappa. Avocations: native Am. studies, western U.S. history. E-mail: texasglennie@aol.com.

KING, JOHN JOSEPH, manufacturing company executive; b. Toledo, Jan. 12, 1924; s. Walter and Frances (Gwozd) Kawecka; m. Joy G. Mohler, Jan. 28, 1950; children: Catherine M., Carolyn S., David J., Michael R., Mark A.R. BSME magna cum laude, U. Toledo, 1957, MS in Indsl. Engring., 1961. Registered profl. engr., Ohio. Draftsman, Tecumseh Products Co., 1941-42; die designer Bingham Stamping Co., 1942-46; tool designer Spicer Mfg. Co., 1946-47; product designer Am. Floor Surfacing Co., 1947-50; founder, mgr. engr. Kent Industries, 1950-52; mech. engr. Owens Ill. Inc., Toledo, 1953-63; mgr. rsch. and devel. Permaglass Inc., Genoa, Ohio, 1963-69; founder, pres. Ashur Inc., Rossford, Ohio, 1969—, also chmn. bd. dirs. Patentee in field. Mem. Am. Ceramic Soc., Soc. Mfg. Engrs., Phi Kappa Phi, Tau Beta Pi. Republican. Roman Catholic. Clubs: Devils Lake Yacht. Lodges: KC, Eagles. Home: 1111 W Elm Tree Rd Rossford OH 43460-1338 Office: Ashur Inc 28663 Glenwood Rd Perrysburg OH 43551-3011

KING, JOHN RICHARD, dentist, dentistry educator; b. Bridgeport, Conn., July 17, 1927; s. Louis Robert King and Sadie Schertz; m. Patricia Susan Wolf, June 10, 1951; 1 child, Pamela Joan King Palitz. BA in Biology, Harvard U., 1948; DDS, U. Pa., 1953. Cert. DDS, Conn. Pvt. practice, Bridgeport, Conn., 1953-92; ret., 1992; instr. Tufts Sch. Dental Medicine, Boston, 1954-57; adj. assoc. prof. U. Bridgeport, Fones Sch. Dental Hygiene, Conn., 1962-80; bd. assocs. U. Bridgeport, 1980—. Office holder Bridgeport Dental Assn., 1971-76, del. Conn. State Dental Assn. (chmn. rules and order 1972-80), chmn. Fairfield County (Conn.) Fluoridation com. Mem. Coun. on Continuing Edn., 1977-79, ann. meeting Coun. on Dental Care Programs, Bridgeport Assn. for UN, pres., 1961-62; chmn. UN Day, Bridgeport, 1961-62, United Fund, 1959, ARC, 1960; active Social Svcs. Commn.; mem. human resources comm. Town of Fairfield, Conn., liaison to Fairfield Sr. Housing Authority. With USN, 1945-47. Decorated French-Moroccan Legion of Honor; named Dentist of the Yr., Greater Bridgeport Dental Assn., 1993; recipient Disting. Svc. award Conn. State Health Dept., 1962, Outstanding Svc. award Conn. State Dental Assn., 1997. Mem. Inst. Ret. Profls. (Fairfield U.), Harvard Club of So. Conn., Harvard Varsity Club, Harvard Hasty Pudding Club, Fairfield County Gourmet Club (founding mem.). Republican. Avocations: travel, photography, hiking, golf, reading.

KING, JOSEPH, finance educator, consultant; b. Miami, Fla., Sept. 28, 1954; s. Joseph T. and Clara B. King. BA, St. Thomas U., 1975; MBA, Barry U., 1979; postgrad., Nova U., 1980, Trinity U., 1987. Cert. champion black belt master in 6-sigma quality control Fla. Internat. U. Analyst Equifax, Atlanta, 1972—76; prof. bus. Barry U., Miami, 1979—82, Fla. Internat. U., Miami, 1985—2001, asst. vice provost, 1985—2001; prof. tech. Trinity U., Miami, 1988—. Futurist Kappa Group Internat., Newark, 1980—85; tech. futurist ATT, Basking Ridge, NJ, 1981—86; cons. project mgmt. Am. Tactical Mgmt., Miami, 1981—2003, quality control analyst Hilton Hotels, 1985—87; quality control project mgr. Dept. of Def., Washington, 1987—90. Author: (book) Information Management, 1985 (ATT award, 1986), Artificial Data Stars, 2002 (Internat. Soc. Intercommunicaiton New Ideas award, 2002), The Mark of the Beast 666, 2003 (Flame award, 2003). Chmn. Econ. Task Force, Miami, 1985, South Fla. Devel. Bd., Miami, 1995. Named Outstanding Citizen, City of North Miami, Fla., 1980; recipient Futurist award, Intel Corp., Ft. Lauderdale, 1998. Fellow: Internat. Soc. for New Ideas (chmn. 6th congress 2001, Futurist award 2001), Alpha Phi Sigma; mem.: Phi Beta Kappa. Baptist. Achievements include research in stopping light and light speed minipulation; human chip implant biotechnology identification and tracking; distinguished expert techno-theologist, theology and technology intergration. Avocations: concert pianist, body building. Home: 330 NW 126 St North Miami FL 33168 Office: Trinity Univ 111 NW 183rd St Miami FL 33169

KING, JOSEPH BERTRAM, architect; b. Greenville, S.C., Sept. 14, 1924; s. Joseph A. and Bertram (Kerns) K.; m. Julia Nelson Hipps, Aug. 2, 1945; children: Allen, David, Thomas. Student, Memphis State Coll., 1943; B in Arch. Engring., N.C. State U., 1949. Prin. J. Bertram King, Asheville, N.C., 1952-94. Chmn. Planning and Zoning Commn., Asheville, 1966— ; vice chmn. Met. Planning Bd., 1966-74 Prin. works include Humanities, Social Sci., Art and Mgmt. bldgs., residence hall, student center, U. N.C.-Asheville, occupational edn. bldg, Asheville High Sch., Bank of Asheville, Madison County High Sch, City-County Central Library Bldg, Reynolds High Sch, Sealtest Dairies. Bd. dirs. United Fund; bd. dirs. N.C. Design Found., mem., 1983-87. Served as pilot USAAF, 1942-45, ETO. Decorated Air medal with 2 oak leaf clusters.; Recipient various archtl. honor awards. Fellow A.I.A. (pres. N.C. chpt. 1973); mem. N.C. Bd. Architecture (past pres.), Asheville C. of C. (past pres. 1972), Tau Beta Pi, Sigma Pi Alpha, Phi Kappa Phi. Home: 222 Country Club Rd Asheville NC 28804-2608

KING, JOSEPH WILLET, child psychiatrist; b. Springfield, Mo., Aug. 26, 1934; m. Doris Ann Toby; children: Pamela Renee, Timothy Wells, Michael Brian, Bradley Christopher. BA, So. Meth. U., 1956; MD, U. Tex. Southwestern, 1962. Diplomate Am. Bd. Psychiatry and Neurology; ordained vocational deacon Episcopal Ch., 96. Intern Baylor U. Med. Ctr., Dallas, 1962-63; resident in gen. psychiatry Timberlawn Psychiat. Hosp., 1963-64, Lisbon VA Hosp., 1965; fellow in child psychiatry U. Tex. Southwestern Med. Sch., 1965-67, Hillside Hosp., Glen Oaks, N.Y., 1967; staff child psychiatrist, dir. child and adolescent svcs. Timberlawn Psychiat. Ctr., Inc., Dallas, 1967-78; assoc. attending child psychiatrist dept. psychiatry Baylor U. Med. Ctr., Dallas, 1967-78; active attending child psychiatrist Children's Med. Ctr., Dallas, 1967-78; attending staff Dallas County Hosp. Dist./Parkland Meml. Hosp., 1967-78; cons. child psychiatry Girls Day Care Rehab. Ctr. Dallas County, Dallas, 1970-73; cons. child psychiatry and adminstrn. Meridell Achievement Ctr., Austin, Tex., 1971-73; dir. adolescent svcs. Portsmouth (Va.) Psychiat. Ctr., 1978-79; active attending child psychiatrist Maryview Hosp., Portsmouth, 1978-80; med. dir., chief exec. officer Psychiat. Inst. Richmond, Va., 1980-86; chief exec. officer, psychiatrist-in-chief Shadow Mountain Inst., Tulsa, 1987-90; v.p. Century Healthcare, Tulsa, 1987-90; med. dir. adolescent svcs. Meml. Pavilion, Lanton, Okla., 1997-98; pres., CEO, med. dir. Desert Hills Ctr. for Youth and Families, Tucson, 1998-99; staff psychiatrist Sierra Tucson, Tucson, 1999—. Assoc. clin. prof. Med. Coll. Va., Va. Commonwealth U., 1980-90, Med. Sch. U. Okla., Tulsa, 1987-96; clin. prof. U. Okla., Oklahoma City. Contbr. articles to profl. jours. Fellow: Am. Coll. Psychiatrists, Am. Orthopsychiat. Assn., Am. Soc. Adolescent Psychiatry (life; nat. pres. 1975—76), Am. Psychiat. Assn. (life; Okla. dist. br.); mem.: AMA, Tucson Psychiat. Soc., Ariz. Psychiat. Assn., Tulsa Psychiat. Assn. (bd. dir.), Tulsa County Med. Soc., Okla. Med. Soc., Nat. Assn. Pvt. Psychiat. Hosps. (chmn. adolescent care com. 1971—81, pres. ind. for profit sect. 1991—92, trustee 1992—95, multiple com./task force functions), Am. Acad. Child and Adolescent Psychiatry (ins. com. 1981—86, pres. Okla. coun. 1991—92, state del. to nat. coun.), Dallas County Med. Soc. (various coms.), Alumni Assn. U. Tex. SW Med. Sch. (pres. 1982—85), Blue Key, Beta Theta Pi. Office: Sierra Tucson 39580 S Lago Del Oro Pkwy Tucson AZ 85739-1091 Fax: 520-792-5809.

KING, JOY RAINEY, poet, retired medical secretary; b. Memphis, Aug. 5, 1939; d. Roy Henry and Margaret (Irvin) Rainey; m. Guy Robert King, Dec. 24, 1956; children: William Lonnie, Cheryl King Ramsey. Grad., Whitehaven H.S., Memphis, 1957. Sec. Gen. Telephone Co., Sumter, S.C., 1957-59; med. sec. L.H. Brisco, MD, Tupelo, Miss., 1963-69, James Ballard, MD, Tupelo, 1969-73; with First Nat. Bank of Southaven, Miss., 1973-79. Staff writer Majestic Records and Countrywine Pub. Co. Author: From the Gazebo, 9 poetry books; poem featured: in Baseball Hall of Fame, lyrics: songs America's New Hero, lyrics: songs; author: numerous poems. Recipient Editor's Choice award, 1993, 94, Nat. Libr. Poetry award, 1995-96, Pres.'s recognition lit. excellence Nat. Authors Registry, 1999-2000, Poet of Month award; named Author of Yr., Edizoni U., Trento, Italy, 1999; poem included in Best Poems and Poets of the 20th Century, Internat. Peace Prize, United Cultural Conv., 2002, Internat. Book of Gold prize Wonder of Words, 2003 Mem. Internat. Soc. Poets, Poets Guild, Internat. Poetry Hall of Fame, So. Ill. Writers Guild (sec. 1996-98), Top Recorders Songwriters Assn., Famous Poets Soc., Metverse Muse in India. Baptist.

KING, KANDI J. secondary school educator, consultant; b. Montgomery, Ala., Aug. 8, 1949; d. Jacob J. and Alice J. Melish; m. Don A. King, July 5, 1969 (div.); children: Melissa, Jay S. Student, S.W. Tex. State U., 1967—69; BA, U. Incarnate Word, 1972; student, U. Tex., 1979—80. Tchr. Hambrick Mid. Sch., Houston, 1980—81; dir. forensics Cypress Creek HS, Houston, 1981—83, Jaes Madison HS, San Antonio, 1983—85, Tom C. Clark HS, San Antonio, 1985—98, Winston Churchill HS, San Antonio, 1998—. Named Outstanding Speech Educator, Nat. Fedn. State HS Assn., 1993. Mem.: Am. Fedn. Tchrs., Tex. Forensic Assn. (mem. exec. coun. 1984—), Nat. Forensics League (mem. exec. coun. 1998—), Tex. Speech Comm. Assn. (named Tex. Speech Tchr. of Yr. 1992), Nat. Debate Coaches Assn., Univ. Interscholastic League (regional academic dir. 1997—). Avocations: current events, reading, art. Office: Winston Churchill HS 12049 Blanco Road San Antonio TX 78216

KING, KATHLEEN BERNADETTE, nursing educator; b. N.Y.C., Dec. 12, 1950; d. Thomas Francis and Sarah Ann (McKeon) King; m. John Robert Laing, Nov. 19, 1983; children: James Robert Laing, Genevieve Rebecca Laing. AS in Math. and Sci., Auburn CC, 1970; BSN, SUNY, Brockport, 1973; MS, U. Rochester, 1976, PhD, 1984. Clin. specialist surg. nursing U. Rochester (N.Y.) Med. Ctr., 1976; instr. dept. nursing Hartwick Coll., Oneonta, NY, 1976-79, asst. prof., 1979-80; rsch. asst., predoctoral fellow U. Rochester Sch. Nursing, 1980-84, Robert Wood Johnson clin. nurse scholar, 1984-86, asst. prof., clinician II surg. nursing, 1986-92, assoc. prof., 1992—2000, prof., 2000—. Editor: (book) Cardiovascular Nursing, 1992—96; mem. editl. bd. Heart and Lung, 1987—, Am. Jour. Critical Care, 1991—2000, Heart Disease and Stroke, 1991—94, mem. rev. bd. Nursing Rsch., 1987—, Jour. Personality and Social Psychology, 1987—92, Scandinavian Jour. Caring Scis., 1990—, Jour. Women's Health, 1999—; contbr. articles to profl. jours. Bd. dirs. Am. Heart Assn., Genesse Valley Region. Grantee, U. Rochester Sch. Nursing Alumni Seed Fund, 1974, USPHS, Nat. Heart, Lung and Blood Inst., 1987—92, Am. Heart Assn. N.Y. State Affiliate, 1990—93, USPHS Nat. Inst. Nursing Rsch., 2002—. Mem.: ANA, APA (health psychology divsn.), N.Y. State Nurses Assn. (sec. dist. 15 1977—79, bd. dirs. 1979—81), Eastern Nursing Rsch. Soc., Genessee Valley Nurses Assn., Sigma Xi, Sigma Theta Tau (editor newsletter 1987—90, pres. chpt. 1986—87). Home: 124 Trafalgar St Rochester NY 14619-1224 Office: U Rochester Sch Nursing 601 Elmwood Ave Rochester NY 14642-0001

KING, KATHLEEN PALOMBO, adult education educator, consultant; b. Providence, June 8, 1958; d. Joseph Christopher and Catherine Ann (Walsh) Palombo; m. James Perry King, Jr., Sept. 3, 1983 (div. 1996); children: James Joseph, William Everett. BA in Biochemistry, Brown U., 1981; MA in Missions, Columbia (S.C.) Internat. U., 1983; MEd in Adult Edn., Widener U., 1994, EdD in Higher Edn., 1997. Oper. room technician Kent County Meml. Hosp., Warwick, R.I., 1978; rsch. asst. in biochemistry Brown U., Providence, 1979; rehab. counselor Talbot House, Providence, 1981; owner, cons., educator KP King Computer Svcs., N.J., 1991-98; mem. faculty Pa. Inst. Tech., Media, Pa., 1991-97, coord. continuing edn., 1995; asst. prof. grad. sch. edn. Lincoln Ctr. Fordham U., N.Y.C., 1997-2001, assoc. prof., 2001—03, dir. Regional Ednl. Tech. Ctr., 2003—, prof., 2003—; dir., prin. investigator FIPSE (Fund for the Improvement of Postsecondary Edn.) Learning Anytime Anyway Partnerships, 2000—. Adv. bd. Glencoe Publs., 1994-2001, WNET TV, N.Y.C.; reviewer Jour. Women and Minorities in Sci. and Engring., 1994-98; spkr. at tech. and edn. confs.; organizing advisor Pa. Inst. Tech. Soc. of Women Engrs.; adj. faculty Holy Family Coll. Grad. Sch., Phila., 1996-97, Widener U., Chester, Pa., 1997; presenter in field. Author: A Guide to Perspective Transformation and Learning Activities, 1998, Keeping Pace with Technology: Educational Technology that Transforms, Vol. 1, 2002, Vol. 2, 2003; co-author: (with Lawler) Planning for Effective Faculty Development, 2000; editor Conf. Procs., 1998-2000; tech. editor Jour. Afro-L.Am. Studies and Lit., 1993-97; mem. editl. bd. New Horizons in Adult Edn., 1998—, PAACE Jour. Lifelong Learning, 2001--; mem. rev. bd. Adult Basic Edn., Jour., 1999—; founding editor: Perspectives Jour., 2001-; contbr. articles to profl. jours., reference and text books. Tchr. religious edn., 1985-90. Recipient Adminstr. of Yr., Fordham chpt. Phi Delta Kappa, 2002, Creative Use of Tech. award, Assn. Continuing Higher Edn., 2003. Mem. AAUW, Internat. Soc. for Tech. in Edn., Am. Assn. for Adult Continuing Edn., Commn. Profs. of Adult Edn. (sec.-treas. 2001-02), Am. Assn. Adult and Continuing Edn., N.Y. Assn. Continuing Cmty. Edn. (bd. dirs. 1999-2001, v.p. 2001-03), Pa. Assn. Adult Continuing Edn., Am. Ednl. Rsch. Assn., Internat. Conf. of Univ. Adult Edn., Phi Kappa Phi, Kappa Delta Pi. Avocations: computers, biking. Office: Fordham U Lincoln Ctr 113 W 60th St Rm 1102 New York NY 10023-7484 E-mail: kpking@fordham.edu.

KING, KAY SUE, investment company executive; b. Indpls., Sept. 14, 1948; d. George W. and Nadine M. K.; 1 child, Christopher G. Student, U. Ariz., 1966-70; BS in Edn., Ind. U., 1971; MA in Speech Communication, U. Hawaii, 1974. Tchr. Indpls. High Schs., 1971-1973; sec., treas. G. W. King Co., Indpls., 1974—; domestic sales mgr. Regal Travel, Indpls., 1975-90; pres., bd. dirs. K.S. King, Inc., Indpls., 1977—; mng. ptnr. K.S. King Co., Indpls., 1982—. Mem. pub. rels. com. Indpls. Zoolog. Xoc., 1976-85; vol. Indpls Humane Soc., 1966—, Indpls. Aid to Zoo Horse Show, 1974-78, Save the Ducks campaign, Indpls., 1978, Pan Am. Games Olympic Sports Com., Indpls., 1981-82; tchr. Sunday sch. Meridian St. Methodist Ch., Indpls., 1988-90. Elected Festival Princess 500 Festival Assn., Indpls., 1968. Mem. Internat. Assn. Bus. Communicators, Internat. Wildlife Fedn., Indpls. Zool. Soc. (charter), Indpls. Pub. Libr., Indpls. Children's Mus., Indpls. Ski Club, U. Ariz. Alumni Assn., Ind. Univ. Alumni Assn., Channel 20, Riviera Club, Lilly Pool, Meridian Hills Country Club, Delta Delta Delta. Avocations: swimming, reading, skiing, horseback riding, animals, children. Office: King Co 5665 N Meridian St Indianapolis IN 46208-1502 Home: PO Box 702 Indianapolis IN 46260-0582

KING, KENNETH PAUL, science educator; b. Omaha, Oct. 28, 1960; s. Richard Carlyle King and Karen (Cushman) Cheyney; m. Tina Anne, July 6, 1990; children: Marshall, Harrison. BS, Iowa State U., 1986; MS in Edn., No. Ill. U., 1990, EdD, 1998. Cert. secondary edn., Iowa, adminstrv., Ill. Writer, editor Quaransan Group, Northbrook, Ill., 1991; tchr. physics Sch. Dist. #46, Elgin, Ill., 1986-95; grad. asst. No. Ill. U., DeKalb, 1995-98, instr. sci. tchg. methods, 1996-98, assoc. prof. tchg. and learning, 1998—. Mem. editl. bd. Contemporary Issues in Tech. and Edn., Electronic Jour. Sci. Edn., Assn. History and Computing; mem. publs. bd. Sch. Sci. and Math. Camp dir. Boys Scouts Am., St. Charles, Ill., 1992, 96, sect. dir. nat. camping sch., Naperville, Ill., 1983-92, 96, 2001, 03. Recipient U. Chgo. Teaching Commendation award, 1993. Mem. ASCD, Nat. Assn. Rsch. Sci. Tchg., Ill. Assn. for Supervision and Curriculum Devel., Assn. for the Edn. of Tchrs. of Sci., Sch. Sci. and Math. Achievements include development of telecommunications applications for elementary education, development of technology applications to develop science process skills. Home: 128 Delcy Dr Dekalb IL 60115-1902 Office: No Ill U Gabel Hall Dekalb IL 60115 E-mail: kking1@niu.edu.

KING, KENNETH VERNON, JR., pharmacist; b. Lexington, Miss., Dec. 17, 1950; s. Kenneth Vernon King Sr. and Louise (Jordan) King; m. Oonagh L. Ryan, Nov. 3, 2002; children: Kenneth V. III, Marie Nanette, Jason Guynes. AA, Holmes Jr. Coll., 1971; BS in Pharmacy, U. Miss., 1973; cert. sterile compounding dossage units, Profl. Compounding Ctrs. Am., Houston, 1993; CTS, Ch. Div. Sch. of Pacific, Berkeley, Calif., 2000; MDiv, 2003. Registered pharmacist, Miss., Pa.; registered pharm. tech., Calif.; cert. in sterile aseptic compounding medicinal units, vaccination adminstrn. Am. Pharm. Assn., Ctrs. Disease Control; aspirant, Diocese of Calif. Pharmacist Barretts Drug Store, Greenwood, Miss., 1973-74, Eckerd Drugs, Greenwood, 1974-76, 77-88, Medi-Save Drugs Ellis Isle, Jackson, Miss., 1976, Eckerd Drugs, Pearl, Miss., 1988-90, Jackson, 1990-92; compounding pharmacist Marty's Discount Drugs, Flowood, Miss., 1992-96, co-owner, 1996-99; cons. Sta-Home Hospice care of Miss., Grace House of Jackson, 1992-99, Hospice Care Found., Vicksburg, Miss., 1993-94, So. Care In-Patient Hospice, Brookhaven, Miss., 1998-99, Family Care Hospice, Brandon, Miss., 1998-99; CEO, pres. King Med. Cons. Svcs., 1999—; dir. mktg. Abbott's Counpounding Pharmacy, 2002—; chaplain UCSF Med. Ctr., San Francisco, 2003—. Cons. Whispering Pines Hospice (inpatient), 1992-99, Hospice of Ctrl. Miss. (outpatient), 1993-99, So. Care In-Patient Hospice, Brookhaven, Miss. 1998-99, Family Care Hospice, Brandon, Miss., 1998-99, Abbotts Compounding Pharmacy, 2002--; owner, contractor, rschr., cons. Profl. Pharm. Svcs. in Miss., Jackson; owner Pharmakan Inc., Pharmakeus Inc., King Med. Cons. Svcs., Oakland; clin. pharmacy instr. U. Miss. Sch. Pharmacy, Oxford, 1985-92, 93-99, external residency instr., 1996-99; tchr. environ. illness VA Hosp.; hospice pharmacist, cons., 1992-99; mem. Profl. Compounding Corp. Am., Houston, P2C2 Profl. Care, Inc., Houston; co-writer compounding criteria Miss. State Bd. Pharmacy, Pharmacy Practice Act, 1993, co-investigator prescribing protocols, 1994; participant AIDS Update '96 for Delta Region (Miss., Ark. and La.), Jackson, 1996; opening spkr. PCCA Nat. Conv. on Hospice Practice, 1996; presenter in field; co-panelist, author HCFA waiver for reimbursement pharmacy cons. svcs. by Medicaid; chmn. Miss. HIV/AID Assembly Health Care Provider Network, 1997-98; tech. cons. Profl. Pharmacy Compounding Ctrs. Am., 1998—; facilitator Pace e Bene Franciscan Non Violence Ctr., Berkeley; cons. credentialing Astha specialty practice Am. Pharm. Assn. 1998; tchr. bio-med. ethics. Advisor Leflore County 4-H, Greenwood, 1974-76; aux. patrolman Greenwood Police Dept., 1982-86; drug identification specialist Greenwood Aux. Police Dept., 1984-85; pres., founder Human Ecology Action League Miss., Inc., 1988-99, bd. dirs. 1991—, advt. coord., Atlanta, 1989%, sec., 1984—; coord. Environ. Assocs. Jack Eckerd, Inc., 1990-92; mem. Rainbow Whole Food Coop., 1989—; coord. regional support svcs. HEAL Inc., 1989—; mem. IACP Ethics Com.; mem. Episcopal Discity of Calif. Trinity Parish, San Francisco; mgr. Altar Guild Lay Com., 1999-2002, vestry, 2000-02; mem. clergy staff St. Aidan's Episc. Ch., San Francisco, Calif., 2002—; mem. med. missions to Panama, 2002. Recipient Innovative Pharmacist of Yr. award Miss. Pharm. Assn., 1997; grantee Lilly Internat., 2001—, St. Aidan's Episc. Ch., San Francisco. Aem. Internat. Assn. Compounding Pharmacist, Environ. Coalition of Miss. (co founder), Environ. Assocs. of Jack Eckerd Inc. (coord.), Miss. Soc. Cons. Pharmacists. Achievements include research in experimental, investigational dosage forms for hospice patients.

KING, K(IMBERLY) N(ELSON), computer science educator; b. Apr. 28, 1953; s. Paul Ellsworth and Marcelia Jeannette King; m. Clara Ann Stormes, Sept. 5, 1981 (div. Nov. 1991); m. Susan Ann Cole, Aug. 9, 1996. BS with highest honors, Case Western Res. U., 1975; MS, Yale U., 1976; PhD, U. Calif., Berkeley, 1980. Asst. prof. info. and computer sci. Ga. Inst. Tech., Atlanta, 1980-86, rsch. scientist, 1986-87; assoc. prof. computer sci. Ga. State U., Atlanta, 1987—. Cons. Norfolk So. Rwy., 1991. Author: Modula-2: A Complete Guide, 1988, C Programming: A Modern Approach, 1996, Java Programming: From The Beginning, 2000; columnist Jour. Pascal, Ada, and Modula 2, 1989-90; contbr. articles to profl. jours. Vol. Ga. Radio Reading Svc., Atlanta, 1989—. Grad. fellow NSF, 1975-78; NSF grantee, 1981-84. Mem. AAUP, IEEE Computer Soc., Assn. for Computing Machinery (chmn. program com. 36th annual southeast conf. 1998), Tau Beta Pi. Office: Ga State U Computer Sci Atlanta GA 30303 E-mail: knking@gsu.edu.

KING, L. ELLIS, civil engineer, educator, consultant; b. Jamestown, N.C., Aug. 21, 1939; s. Lee Bolen and Juanita Ethel (Hodgin) K.; m. Rachel Sale Garrett, Oct. 1, 1960. BSCE, N.C. State U., 1961; DEng, U. Calif., Berkeley, 1967. Registered profl. engr., N.C.; ACTAR cert. traffic accident reconstructionist. Asst. prof. W.Va. U., Morgantown, 1967-72, assoc. prof., 1972-73, U. Colo., Denver, 1973-75; prof. Wayne State U., Detroit, 1975-76; prof., chmn. dept. civil engring. U. N.C., Charlotte, 1976-95, prof. civil engring., 1995—2002, prof. emeritus, 2002—. Forensic engring. expert to numerous attys. and corps., 1967—. Contbr. chpts. to books, articles to profl. jours. NSF trainee, 1965-67. Fellow ASCE (Walter L. Huber prize 1973), Inst. Transp. Engrs.; mem. Nat. Soc. Profl. Engrs., Nat. Acad. Forensic Engrs., Transp. Rsch. Bd., Human Factors and Ergonomics Soc. Home: 100 Wrenwood Ln Charlotte NC 28211-1833

KING, LARRY (LARRY ZEIGER), broadcaster, radio personality; b. Bklyn., Nov. 19, 1933; s. Eddie and Jennie Zeiger; m. Alene Akins, 1961 (div. 1963), remarried 1967 (div. 1971); 1 child, Chaia; m. Sharon Lepore, 1976 (div. 1982); m. Julia Alexander, Oct. 7, 1989; 1 child, Andy. Disc jockey various radio stas., Miami, Fla., 1957-71; freelance writer, broadcaster, 1972-75; radio personality Sta. WIOD, Miami, 1975-78; writer entertainment sects. Miami Herald, 7 yrs.; radio talk show host The Larry King Show, 1978—; host 1990 Goodwill Games. Columnist USA Today, Sporting News; host sta. WLA-TV Let's Talk, Washington. Appeared in films Ghostbusters, 1984, Lost in America, 1985; author: Larry King, Tell It To The King, (with B. D. Colen) Mr. King, You're Having a Heart Attack, 1989, Larry King: Tell Me More, When You're From Brooklyn, Everything Else Is Toyko, 1992, (with Mark Stencel) On the Line: The New Road to the White House, 1993. Chmn. Larry King Cardiac Found; hon. trustee Am. Women in Radio and TV Com.; mem. Washington Ctr. for Politics and Journalism, The Read-Am. Adv. Bd., Hart Assist Found. Bd. Recipient Radio award Nat. Assn. Broadcasters, 1985, Jack Anderson Investigative Reporting award, 1985, Peabody award for Larry King Show U. Ga. Sch. Journalism, 1987, award for Larry King Live shows Awards for Cablecasting, 1987, 88, 89, also for excellence in cable TV, 1990, Marconi award Nat. Assn. Broadcasters, 1990; named Best Radio Talk Show Host Washington Jour. Rev., 1986, Broadcaster of Yr. Internat. Radio and TV Soc., 1989; named to Emerson Hall of Fame, Broadcasters Hall of Fame, 1992, Man Of Yr. Am. Heart Assn., 1992. Mem. Friars Club. Office: CNN Larry King Live 820 1st St NE Washington DC 20002-4243*

KING, LARRY, editor; b. Fonda, Iowa; Degree, U. Nebr. From reporter to exec. editor Omaha World-Herald, 1975—98, exec. editor, 1998—. Office: Omaha World-Herald World-Herald Sq 1334 Dodge St Omaha NE 68102-1138*

KING, LARRY L. playwright, actor; b. Putnam, Tex., Jan. 1, 1929; s. Clyde Clayton and Cora Lee (Clark) K.; m. Jeanne Casey, Nov. 25, 1950 (div. Nov. 1964); children: Alexandria, Kerri Lee, Bradley Clayton; m. Rosemarie Courmaris, Feb. 20, 1965 (dec.); m. Barbara Sue Blaine, May 6, 1978; children: Lindsay Allison, Blaine Carlton. Student, Tex. Tech U., 1949-50. Oil field worker El Paso Natural Gas Co., Jal, N.Mex. and Midland, Tex., 1943-45; reporter Hobbs (N.Mex.) Daily Flare, 1949, Midland Reporter-Telegram, 1950 52, Odessa (Tex.) Am., 1952-54; adminstrv. asst. U.S. Congress, Washington, 1954-64; freelance writer Washington, 1964—; pres. Texhouse Corp., Washington, 1979—. Ferris prof. journalism and polit. sci. Princeton (N.J.) U., 1973-75; Disting. Lyndon B. Johnson lectr. Southwest Tex. State University, 1991. Author: (books) The One-Eyed Man, 1966, . . . And Other Dirty Stories, 1968, Confessions of a White Racist, 1971, The Old Man and Lesser Mortals, 1974, Wheeling and Dealing, 1978, Of Outlaws, Con Men, Whores, Politicians and Other Artists, 1980, The Whorehouse Papers, 1981, That Terrible Night Santa Got Lost in the Woods, 1981, None But a Blockhead: On Being a Writer, 1986, Warning: Writer At Work, 1986, Because of Lozo Brown, 1988, True Facts, Tall Tales, and Pure Fiction, 1997, Reflections In A Bloodshot Eye: A Writer's Life in Letters, 1999, (plays) The Best Little Whorehouse in Texas, 1978, The Kingfish, 1979, The Night Hank Williams Died, 1986, The Golden Shadows Old West Museum, 1987, Christmas: 1933, 1987, The Best Little Whorehouse Goes Public, 1994, The Dead Presidents' Club, 1995; also numerous articles; starred in: The Best Little Whorehouse in Texas (on Broadway), 1979, The Night Hank Williams Died (off-Broadway), 1989; contbg. editor Harper's, 1967-71, New Times, 1974-77, Tex. Monthly, 1973-78, Tex. Observer, 1964-74. Sgt. AUS, 1946-49. Recipient Stanley Walker Journalism award Tex. Inst. of Letters, 1972, Tony award League of N.Y. Theatres and Producers, 1978-79, Mary Goldwater award Theatre Lobby, 1988, Helen Hayes award, 1989; elected to Tex. Walk of Stars, 1988, Best Non-Fiction Article of Yr. award Tex. Inst. of Letters 2002; Nieman fellow Harvard U.,

1969-70, Duke U. fellow, 1975-76. Mem. Authors Guild, PEN, Writers Guild Am. East, Actors Equity Assn., Nat. Acad. TV Arts and Scis. (Emmy award 1981), Nat. Writers Union, Screenwriters Guild East, Dramatists Guild, Sandhills Club (Monahans, Tex.), Pelican Club (Odessa), Mystic Knights of the Sea. Democrat. Avocations: breeding show dogs, singing opera, ballet dancing. *I have always avoided strong drink and evil companions.*

KING, LAURA JANE, librarian, genealogist; b. Pemberville, Ohio, Jan. 19, 1947; d. richard D. and Jessie Florence (Brown) Zepernick; m. Bruce William King, June 17, 1972; 1 child, Christian Andrew.. BA, Bowling Green (Ohio) State U., 1969, MEd, 1976; MLS, Kent State U., 1995. Cert. pub. libr. Cert. geneal. lectr. County extension agt. home econs. Ohio Coop. Extension Svcs., Paulding County, 1970-77; asst. dir., historian Pemberville Pub. Libr., asst. dir., br. coord.; mem. PRICE com., vocat. home econs. dept. Paulding Exempted Village, 1975—. Instr. genealogy Continuing Edn. Bowling Green State U., Eastwood Sch. Dist. Cmty. Edn. Mem. Paulding County Bicentennial Commn., 1975—77; state chmn. Friends of Libr., 1992—95; advisor 4-H; mem. Wood County Citizens Com. fo Bicentennial of U.S. Constn. and N.W. Ordinance; chmn. Pemberville Com. for Ohio Bicentennial; mem. Wood County Literacy Bd., Pemberville Sch. Adv. Com.; past sr. state historian Children of Am. Revolution; past pres. Eastwood Local Schs. Band Boosters; corr. docent DAR Mus., Washington; sr. state rec. sec. Children of Am. Revolution; organist First Presbyn. Ch., Pemberville, ch. historian. Recipient Tenure award Coop. Extension Svc., 1975. Mem. ALA, Mary Sherman Hayes Soc. (past sr. v.p.), Flag of the U.S. of Am. (sr. state chmn., sr. state registrar 1994—, sr. state chmn. govt. studies 1998—, sr. state organizing sec. 2000—), Libr. Adminstrn. and Mgmt. Assn., Children of the Am. Revolution (sr. state orgn. sec.), Ohio Geneal. Soc. (pres. Wood County chpt. 1978-80, chmn. pub. rels. chmn. 1982-83, chmn. First Families of Wood County com., state program chmn. ann. conf. 1991, 95, state chmn. History Writing Contest 1993, trustee 1995—), Berks County Geneal. Soc., Palatines to Am., DAR (vice regent chpt. 1975-77, regent chpt. 1979-83, registrar chpt. 1985—, state vice chmn. pages 1978-80, state chmn. lineage rsch. 1980-87, state and divsn. outstanding jr. mem. 1980, state chmn. membership commn. 1983-87, state rec. sec. 1987-89, state corr. sec. 1989-92, area spkr.'s staff, state chmn. Friends of the Libr. 1992-95, chpt. libr. 1998—), U.S. Daus. of 1812 (chmn. state insignia), First Families Ohio, Daus. Union Vets., Nat. Soc. Magna Charta Dames, Colonial Dames 17th Century, Desc. Am. Colonists (chpt. regent 1986—, state chmn. pub. rels. 1987, chmn. mideast region pub. rels.), Bus. and Profl. Women's club (pres. Paulding 1975-76, v.p. 1974-75), Ohio Libr. Assn., Coun. Ohio Genealogists (v.p. 1992), Colonial Order Crown of Charlemagne, SAR (medal of appreciation, Order Eastern Star. Home: 14553 N River Rd Pemberville OH 43450-9797 E-mail: lking@wcnet.org.

KING, LELAND W. architect; b. Battle Creek, Mich., Dec. 17, 1907; s. Leland Wiggins and Elizabeth Gale (Arnold) K.; m. Hametia Fielder, Nov. 29, 1934; children: Sheryl Letia, Louisa Sands. Student, Ga. Sch. Tech., 1927, Armour Inst. Tech. (Chgo. Art Inst., Beaux Arts Design), 1928-29. Registered architect, Colo., Ariz., N.Y., Calif., Nat. Council Archtl. Registration Bds. Archtl. draftsman, designer indsl., sch., hosp. and residential projects, Ga., Ill., Mich., Wis., 1925-32; supr. architect's office U.S. Treasury, 1935-37; field insp. diplomatic and consular bldgs. Dept. State, 1937-40, asso. chief Fgn. Bldg. Ops., 1941-51; dir. and supervising architect, 1952-54; in charge U.S. diplomatic and consular bldg. design and constrn., worldwide; cons. Bd. Edn. White Fish Bay, Milw., 1931-32; tech. adviser to U.S. del. UNESCO Hdqrs. Bldg., Paris, 1952-53; exec. sec. Fgn. Service Bldgs. Com., U.S. Congress, 1952-54; gen. archtl. and indsl. design as asso. Norman Bel Geddes, 1954-55; asso. with James Gordon Carr (Architect), 1956; v.p., dir. architecture Pereira and Luckman, 1956-59; supervising archt. Ampex Corp., 1959-62; pvt. archtl. practice as Leland King, FAIA, 1961—; sr. partner King/Reif & Assos. (architecture and planning), Menlo Park, Calif. Chmn. archtl. and constrn. engring. panel research, adv. council to postmaster gen., 1967, 68; dir., supervising architect U.S. Embassy projects, 1937-54, honor awards Stockholm, Paris, 1953, Memorex project, Santa Clara, Calif., 1972, Mission Control Air Force, 1982; chmn. Bodega Harbour Design Rev. Com. Works exhibited U.S. State Dept., Mus. Modern Art, N.Y.C., 1953, Octagon, 1954, San Jose Mus., 1980. Recipient McGraw-Hill Top Ten Plants award, 1971 Fellow AIA (honor award 1955, chpt. award 1974), Cosmos Club (Washington). Home: 21218 Heron Dr Bodega Harbour Bodega Bay CA 94923

KING, LEO, journalist; b. Cranston, R.I., June 7, 1938; s. Leo C. and Gladys G. (Hall) K.; divorced; children: Scott, Terri Jo. BA in English, R.I. Coll., 1979. Transp. journalist, Middleburg, Fla. Editor Destination Freedom. Avocation: photography. Office: 1723 Farm Way Middleburg FL 32068 E-mail: train181@bellsouth.net.

KING, LEON, financial services executive; b. Phila., 1921; s. Abraham and Ethel (Walton) K.; m. Diane Averbach, Nov. 30, 1946; children: Cheryl, Elliot, Louis. BS in Econs, Wharton Sch., U. Pa., 1945; grad. with honors, Bank Adminstrn. Inst., 1970. CPA, Pa. Pub. acct., 1946-52; contr. hotel divsn. Bankers Securities Corp., 1952-57; contr. Sun-Ray Drug Co., 1957-60, Bellevue Stratford Hotel, 1960-64; with Indsl. Valley Bank and Trust Co., Phila., 1964-83, exec. v.p., 1973-83; with Indsl. Valley Title Ins. Co., Phila., 1964-86, chmn. bd., 1983-86; pres. Bancshares Inc., 1987-97; gen. ptnr. King Assocs. LP, 1996—; pvt. practice, 1987—. Mem. AICPA, Pa. Inst. CPAs, Beta Gamma Sigma. Home: 4030 Woodruff Rd Lafayette Hill PA 19444-1618 *Always be polite and courteous. Treat all people the same regardless of rank, station, or position. We are all human beings and each deserves civility and respect. From a small child to a chief of state, from a beggar to a captain of industry, all should be treated in the same friendly and courteous way.*

KING, LINDA ORR, museum director, consultant; b. Washington, June 21, 1948; d. William Baxter and Jayne (Reiser) Orr; m. James McClain King (dec. Aug. 1997); children: David, Adam, Lindsay. BA, La. State U., 1970, MA in Fine Arts, 1971. Fine arts history asst. La. State U., Baton Rouge, 1967-70, grad. asst., 1970-71; assoc. curator La. State Mus., New Orleans, 1971-74; curator Coastal Ga. Hist. Soc./St. Simons Island Lighthouse Mus., St. Simons Island, 1984-87; dir. Coastal Ga. Hist. Soc., St. Simons Island, 1987-2000; dir. exhibitions and collections Atlanta Hist. Ctr., 2000-01; ind. mus. profl., 2001—. Romanian Mus. advisor U.S. State Dept., 2002. Co-editor: (photograph essay) George Francois Mugnier, 1975. Pres. Glynn County Soc. of St. Vincent de Paul, 1990-94; mem. Glynn County Courthouse Renovation Com., 1989-2000; Ga. state dir. S.E. Mus. Conf., 1990-94, also membership chair; mem. adv. coun. Brunswick Downtown Devel. Authority; mem. Leadership Glynn, 1992; mem. Commn. on Preservation of Ga. State Capitol; chmn. adv. coun. on hist. preservation Coastal Regional Devel. Ctr., 1987-98, chmn., 1996-98. Recipient Kellogg Career Enhancement award, Kellogg Found., 1989, Leadership award, Southeastern Mus. Conf., 1995, Nat. Mus. award, 1999, Ga. History Mus. Exhibit of 2002 award, 2002; fellow Internat. Partnership Among Mus. fellow to Sierra Leone, 1992. Mem. Ga. Assn. Mus. and Galleries (treas. 1987-89, Mus. Profl. of Yr. 1993), Coastal Mus. Assn. (treas. 1987-89), Am. Assn. Mus., Low Country Mus. Network (treas. 1993-99). Roman Catholic. Home: 3514 Paces Pl Atlanta GA 30327 : E-mail: lindaorrking@msn.com.

KING, LIS SONDER, writer; b. Roskilde, Denmark; came to U.S., 1956, naturalized, 1961; d. Carl Otto and Gerda Vohnsen (Sonder) Petersen; m. Robert King, (div. 1972); 1 dau., Dorte; m. Theodore Allin Pace, 1972. Arts degree, Roskilde Katedralskole. Reporter, editor Moreau Pub. Co., Bloomfield, N.J., 1957-59, St. Thomas (V.I.) Daily News, Island Times, San Juan, P.R., 1962-63; editor The Advance, Dover, N.J., 1961-63; dir. pub. rels. Keyes, Martin & Co., Springfield, N.J., 1964-69; pres. Lis King Pub. Rels., Mahwah, N.J., 1969—. Freelance writer, 1977—. Author, editor: St. Thomas Directory, 1962; author: Furniture: Make-Do, Make-Over, Make Your Own, 1977; contbr. articles in major consumer mags., trade publs. and newspapers. Mem. Taxpayers Assn. Mahwah. Avocations: traveling, gardening, reading, breeding great danes. Home and Office: 30 Dundee Ct Mahwah NJ 07430-0725

KING, LLEWELLYN WILLINGS, publisher, lecturer, journalist, commentator; b. Bulawayo, Zimbabwe, Oct. 6, 1939; came to U.S., 1963; s. Herbert Willings and Dorothy Ann (Hooper) K. Student, Churchill Coll., 1951-55; DSc in Engring. (hon.), Stevens Inst. of Tech., 1995, PhD (hon.). City editor The Citizen, Harare, Zimbabwe, 1958-60; sub-editor Ind. TV News, London, 1960-61, Sunday Mirror, London, 1961-63; copy editor N.Y. Herald Tribune, N.Y.C., 1963-64; pres. Sovereign Assocs., N.Y.C., 1964-66; editor wire desk Washington Daily News, 1966-69; asst. editor Washington Post, 1969-70; reporter McGraw Hill, Washington, 1970-73; chmn. King Pub. Group, Washington, 1973—. Founder Women NOW mag., N.Y.C., 1965; pres. Washington-Balt. Newspaper Guild, 1967-70; host cable TV program The Bull and the Bear; host TV program "White House Chronicle". Colunist: Syndicated by King Pub. Group. Mem. Aircraft Owners and Pilots Assn., Nat. Prss, St. James's Club, London Press Club. Avocations: flying, horseback riding, boating. Office: King Pub Group 1325 G St NW Washington DC 20005

KING, LLOYD JOANN, music educator, volunteer; b. L.A., Dec. 24, 1929; d. Ray and Dorothy (Lloyd) Kerst; m. Lawrence Gilbert King, Sept. 15, 1950; children: Kathy Lynn King Scott, Kevin Paul King. AA, L.A. City Coll., 1949; BA, Calif. State U., L.A., 1951; MA in Edn., Eastern Mich. U., 1959. Tchr. 2d grade Long Beach (Calif.) Sch. Dist., 1951-52; tchr 1st grade Am. Sch., Pasay City, Philippines, 1953-54; tchr. 1st and 2d grade L.A. Sch. Dist., 1954; tchr. 2d grade, instrumental music, gen. music Willow Run (Mich.) Sch. Dist., 1954-59; dir. Christian Edn. Meth. Ch., Camarillo, Calif., 1963, 64; co-owner King's Magnavox Music Store, Thousand Oaks, Calif., 1969-74; pvt. music tchr. L.A., Ypsilanti, Mich., Thousand Oaks, Roseburg, Oreg., 1946—. Author: (History of Oreg. PEO) Yesterdays, Today and Tomorrows, 1994, also mag. articles. Elder, Presbyn. Ch., Roseburg, 1991—, treas. women's assn., clerk of session; co-mem. sec.; bd. dirs. Umpqua Symphony Assn. Named Woman of Yr., Thousand Oaks/Conejo Valley C. of C., 1968; recipient scholarships and grants. Mem. AAUW (past state officer), PEO, Oreg. Music Tchrs. Assn., Nat. Music Tchrs. Assn. Republican. Avocations: travel, music, theosophy, genealogy. Home: 1779 NW Riverview Dr Roseburg OR 97470-6104

KING, LONNIE J. dean; m. Sylvia King; 2 children. BS, DVM, Ohio State U.; MS in Epidemiology, U. Minn., 1980; MPA, Am. U., 1991. Pvt. practice as vet., Dayton and Atlanta; dir. govtl. rels. divsn. Am. Vet. Med. Assn., Washington; various staff assignments as vet. med. officer, sta. epidemiologist, dir. devel. Nat. Animal Health Monitoring Sys. USDA Animal and Plant Health Inspection Svc.; dep. adminstr. USDA Animal and Plant Health Inspection Svc. Vet. Svcs., 1988—91; adminstr. USDA Animal and Plant Health Inspection Svc., 1995—; dean Mich. State U. Coll. Vet. Medicine, 1996. Sr. exec. fellowship program Harvard U. Mem.: Am. Coll. Vet. Preventive Medicine (bd. cert. mem.). Office: Mich State U Coll Vet Medicine G100 Vet Med Center East Lansing MI 48824-1316*

KING, LORI SUZANNE, entrepreneur; b. Seattle, Aug. 12, 1954; d. Albert and Margaret E. (Keim) Wolf; m. William R. King, July 5, 1980 (div. 1986); 1 child, Tanzanica S. CPA, Cert. Data Processing, Cert. Bus. Counselor, Wash. Systems analyst Allied Stores, Inc., Seattle, 1974-78; sr. tech. analyst GTE Data Svcs., Everett, Wash., 1978-82; fin. systems mgr. Allied Stores, Inc., Seattle, 1987-88; assoc. broker The Fortune Co., Inc., Seattle, 1988-92; CEO Bus. Exch. Ctr., Inc., Bellevue, Wash., 1990, NSVT.com, Inc., Bellevue, Wash., 1995—2000, King Capital, LLC, 2000—. Dir. TVW Corp., Bellevue, 1990-92. Author tech. articles. Mem. AICPA, Cert. Bus. Counselors, Wash. Soc. CPAs. Avocation: running. Home and Office: 8306 Wilshire Blvd Beverly Hills CA 90211

KING, LOWELL RESTELL, pediatric urologist; b. Salem, Ohio, Feb. 28, 1932; s. Lowell Waldo and Vesta Ethylwin (Snyder) K.; m. Mary Elizabeth Hill, July 9, 1960; children: Andrew Restell, Erika Lillie. BA, Johns Hopkins U., 1953, MD, 1956. Intern Johns Hopkins Hosp., Balt., 1956-57, resident in urology, 1957-62; asst. prof. urology Johns Hopkins U., 1962-63, Northwestern U., 1963-67, assoc. prof., 1967-70, prof., 1970-81, prof. urology and surgery, 1974-81; prof. urology and pediatrics Duke U., Durham, N.C., 1981-97, prof. emeritus, 1997; prof. surgery/urology U. N.Mex., Albuquerque, 1997—. Prof., chmn. dept. urology Presbyn.-St. Luke's Hosp., 1968-70; surgeon-in-chief Children's Meml. Hosp., Chgo., 1974-80 Author: (with P.P. Kelalis) Clinical Pediatric Urology, 1976, 3d edit., 1992; (with A.B. Belman) 4th edit., 2001, Bladder Replacement and Continent Urology Diversion, 1986, 2d edit., 1991, Urologic Surgery in the Neonate and Young Infant, 1992, Reconstructive Urology, 1992, Urologic Surgery in Infants and Children, 1997, Office Guide to Pediatric Urology, 2002; cons. editor Urology; editor profl. jours.; contbr. articles to profl. jours. Vestryman, sr. warden Ch. of Our Savior, 1974-80; bd. dirs. Gads Hill Settlement House, 1969-73. Recipient Gold medal All India Urologic Congress, 1996, Gold medal Mex. Coll. Urology, 1991, Valentine medal N.Y. Acad. Medicine, 2002. Mem. AMA, Am. Urol. Assn. (career achievement award 1996), Am. Acad. Pediats. (chmn. sect. urology 1969-72, sec. 1972-76, pres. 1977-78, Urology medal 1992), Soc. Pediat. Urology (pres. 1983), Soc. U. Urologists, Am. Assn. Genitourinary Surgeons, Clin. Soc. Genitourinary Surgeons (pres. 1996). Republican. Episcopalian. Home: 2012 Dietz Pl NW Albuquerque NM 87107-3220 Office: U NMex Health Scis Ctr Sch Medicine Dept Surgery Divsn Urology 2211 Lomas Blvd NE Albuquerque NM 87106-2745

KING, LYNDEL IRENE SAUNDERS, art museum director; b. Enid, Okla., June 10, 1943; d. Leslie Jay and Jennie Irene (Duggan) Saunders; m. Blaine Larman King, June 12, 1965. BA, U. Kans., Lawrence, 1965; MA, U. Minn.-Mpls., 1971, PhD, 1982. Dir. Univ. Art Mus., U. Minn.-Mpls., 1979—; dir. exhbns. and mus. programs Control Data Corp., 1979, 80-81; exhbn. coordinator Nat. Gallery of Art, Washington, 1980. Recipient Cultural Contbn. of Yr. award Mpls. C. of C., 1978; Honor award Minn. Soc. Architects, 1979. Mem. Assn. Art Mus. Dirs. (chair art issues com. 1998-2000, chair tech. comm. com. 2000, bd. trustees 1998—), Art Mus. Assn. Am. (v.p. bd. dirs. 1984-89), Assn. Coll. and Univ. Mus. and Galleries (v.p. 1989-92), Am. Assn. Mus., Internat. Coun. Mus., Upper Midwest Conservation Assn. (pres. bd. dirs. 1980—), Minn. Assn. Mus. (steering com. 1982), Am. Fedn. Arts Bd. Home: 326 W 50th St Minneapolis MN 55419-1247 Office: Weisman Art Mus 333 E River Rd Minneapolis MN 55455-0367

KING, M. JEAN, association executive; b. Cleve., May 5, 1930; BS in Med. Tech., MS in Microbiology, U. Del., 1960. Med. technologist Del. Hosp., Wilmington, 1950-60; staff microbiologist Wilmington Gen. Hosp., 1960-61, Episcopal Hosp., Phila., 1961-68; mem. faculty dept. microbiology Temple. U. Med. Sch., 1966-68; staff microbiologist Crozier Chester (Pa.) Med. Ctr., 1969-71; pres., founder Ind. Dogs, Inc., Chadds Ford, 1984—; designer Parkinson's Walker Dog Pilot Program, U. Pa. Hosp., Phila., 1997. Pres. Akbash Dogs Internat., 1987; speaker rehab. hosps., svc. orgns., self help groups, radio and TV. Theater pipe organ concert artist Longwood Gardens, Kennett Square, Pa., Dickenson Theater Organ Soc., Wilmington, Del., Sunnybrook Ballroom, Pottsdown, Pa., Marietta (Pa.) Theater, Phoenixville (Pa.) Theater. Founder Parkinsons Walker Dog Pilot Program, U. Pa. Hosp. Recipient award Delta Soc., Am. Animal Hosp. Assn., Gaines Dog Food, 1987-88, Work with Handicapped Population citation Pres. George Bush, 1990, Poor Richard Pro Bono award, 1994; named to Hall of Fame, U. Del., 1988. Mem. Am. Akbash Dog Assn. (pres. emeritus), Delta Soc., Del. County C. of C., Beta Beta Beta. Home: 14 Maple Ln Chadds Ford PA 19317-9201 Office: Independence Knoll 146 Stateline Rd Chadds Ford PA 19317-9047 E-mail: RDR@independencedogs.org.

KING, MARCIA, library director; b. Lewiston, Maine, Aug. 4, 1940; d. Daniel Alden and Clarice Evelyn (Curtis) Barrell; m. Howard P. Lowell, Feb. 15, 1969 (div. 1980); m. Richard G. King Jr., Aug., 1980. BS, U. Maine, 1965; MSLS, Simmons Coll., 1967. Reference, field advisory and bookmobile libr. Maine State Libr., Augusta, 1965-69; dir. Lithgow Pub. Libr., Augusta, 1969-72; exec. sec. Maine Libr. Adv. Com., Maine State Libr., 1972-73; dir. Wayland (Mass.) Free Pub. Libr., 1973-76; state libr. State of Oreg., Salem, 1976-82; dir. Tucson Pub. Libr., 1982-91; mgmt. cons. King Assocs., Tucson, 1991-2000; dir. Gary Pub. Libr., Ind., 2000—. Past chmn. bd. dirs. Tucson United Way; past chmn. adv. bd. com. Sta. KUAT (PBS-TV and Radio); mem. adv. bd. Resources for Women, Inc.; bd. dirs., past chmn. Salvation Army. Mem. ALA, Nat. Ctr. for Non-Profit Bds. Unitarian Universalist. Office: Gary Pub Libr 220 W 6th Ave Gary IN 46402 E-mail: kingmc@garypubliclibrary.org.

KING, MARCIA GYGLI, artist; b. Cleve., June 4, 1931; d. Robert Prescott and Ruth (Farr) Gygli; m. Rollin White King, May 10, 1956 (div. 1974); children: Rollin White King Jr., Edward Prescott King. BA, Smith Coll., 1953; MFA, U. Tex., San Antonio, 1981. Docent Nat. Gallery Art, Washington, 1956-60; organizer, dir. docent program McNay Art Mus., San Antonio, 1964-76; art critic Express news, San Antonio, 1976-77; artist N.Y.C., 1979—. Lectr. Nat. Gallery Art, Washington, 1956-60, div. continuing edn. U. Tex., 1976, So. Meth. U., Dallas, 1984, McNay Art Mus., San Antonio, 1984, Washington Project for the Arts, 1985, Monserrat Coll. Art, Beverly, Mass., 1987, Whitney Mus., Phillip Morris, N.Y.C., 1988, Lehman Coll. CUNY, 1988, MTA Pub. Art Commn. for Creative Stations, N.Y., 1995; panelist Panel on Women in the Arts, Alexandria, Va., 1978, Washington Project for the Arts, 1985, Corpus Christi (Tex.) State U., 1986, Dallas Mus., 1991, New Mus., N.Y., 1993, Mus. Mod. Art, N.Y., 1995. One woman shows include McNamara O'Connor Mus., Victoria, Tex., 1975, Charleton Gallery, San Antonio, 1980, Douglas Coll. Rutgers U., New Brunswick, N.J., 1981, McNay Art Mus., San Antonio, 1984, Mattingly Baker Gallery, Dallas, 1984, White Columns, N.Y., 1985, Parker Smalley Gallery, N.Y., Manhattan Marymount, N.Y., 1986, Ferver Gallery, N.Y., 1987, Katzen Brown Gallery, N.Y.C., 1988, 90, Haines Gallery, San Francisco, 1988, Wallace Wentworth Gallery, Washington, 1988, U. N.C., 1989, Valerie Miller Gallery, Palm Desert, Calif., 1989, Cleve. Ctr. for Contemporary Art, 1989-90, Hal Katzen, N.Y., 1992, 94, Guild Hall Mus., N.Y., 1995, Renee Fotouhi Fine Art, N.Y., 1995, Arts Acad., Md., 1996, Kouros Gallery, N.Y., 1999, Parchman Stremmel Gallery, San Antonio, 2000, San Antonio Art League Mus., 2000, Bklyn. Botanic Garden, 2001, Gallery Camino, Real, Fla., 2002, Gallery 668, N.Y., 2003; represented in collections Bklyn. Mus., Cleve. Mus., Guggenheim Mus., Johnson Mus., Cornell U., Nat. Mus. Women in Arts, Newark Mus., Robert Coll., Istanbul, Ark. Art Ctr., Guild Hall, L.I., McNay Art Mus., San Antonio Art League. Recipient Internat. Women's Yr. Panel award, Tex., 1977, Artist of Yr., San Antonio, 2000, James Kirkeby Nat. Meml. award Tex. Watercolor Soc., 1976, Brewer's Digest award Lone Star Brewery Day, 1963, Annual Z.T. Scott award & cir. Tex. Fine Arts Assn., 1970, Ethel T. Drought Meml. award San Antonio Art League Exhbn., 1971, Best of Show award Tex. Watercolor Show, 1971, First Purchase Prize, Tex. Watercolor Show, 1972, First Purchase Prize, 17th Delta Annual, Ark. Art. Ctr., 1974; named Outstanding Woman in San Antonio, Women's Polit. Caucus, 1979. Avocations: swimming, bicycling. Office: 477 Broome St Apt 63 New York NY 10013-5311

KING, MARCIA JONES, potter, physicist, photographer; b. Oak Park, Ill., May 17, 1934; d. Walter Leland Jones and Florence W. (Dull) Anderson; m. James Craig King, Nov. 1953 (div. 1966); 1 child, James Craig King, Jr. BS, Johns Hopkins U., 1960, PhD, 1969. Elec. engr. Electronic Comm., Inc., Timonium, Md., 1959-63; rsch. assoc. theoretical particle physics Syracuse (N.Y.) U., 1969-72; asst. editor Phys. Rev. Brookhaven Nat. Lab., Upton, N.Y., 1972-74; physicist Argonne (Ill.) Nat. Lab., 1974-78; pvt. practice potter and physicist Syracuse, N.Y., 1978—. Contbr. articles to profl. jours.; exhibitor pots throughout Ctrl. N.Y.; one-woman photography shows in Ctrl. N.Y. and So. Calif.; author: Nature's Telling: Anza-Borrego Desert, 1996. Mem. AAAS, Am. Phys. Soc., Syracuse Ceramic Guild (pres. 1982-84), Phi Beta Kappa, Sigma Xi. Democrat. Home and Office: 228 Buckingham Ave Syracuse NY 13210-3024 E-mail: mking52701@aol.com.

KING, MARGARET ANN, communications educator; b. Marion, Ind., Feb. 27, 1936; d. Paul Milton and Janet Mary (Broderick) Burke; m. Charles Claude King, Aug. 25, 1956; children: C. Kevin, Elizabeth Ann, Paul S., Margaret C. Student, Ohio Dominican, 1953-56, U. Kans., 1980-81; BA in Communication, Purdue U., 1986, MA in Pub. Communication, 1990. Regional rep. Indpls. Juv. Justice Task Force, 1984-85; vis. instr. dept. communication Purdue U., West Lafayette, Ind., 1992-96; v.p. King Mktg. Cons., Inc., 1996—2002; adj. lectr. U. Cin., 2002—. Bd. dirs. Vis. Nurse Home Health Svcs.; adj. instr. U. Cin., 2002—. Contbr. chpt. to book. Grad. mem. Leadership Lafayette, 1983. Purdue U. fellow, 1986-87. Mem. AAUW, Ctrl. States Comm. Assn. (conf. presenter 1989), Golden Key, Phi Kappa Phi. Republican. Roman Catholic. Avocations: poetry writing, vocal and piano music. Home: 7938 Wild Orchard Ln Cincinnati OH 45242-4309 *Personal philosophy: Ignorance is its own reward.*

KING, MARGARET LEAH, history educator; b. N.Y.C., Oct. 16, 1947; d. Reno C. and Marie (Ackerman) King; m. Robert E. Kessler, Nov. 12, 1976; children: David King Kessler, Jeremy King Kessler. BA, Sarah Lawrence Coll., 1967; MA, Stanford U., 1968, PhD, 1972. Asst. prof. dept. history Calif. State Coll., Fullerton, 1969-70; asst. prof. Bklyn. Coll., CUNY, 1972-76, assoc. prof., 1976-86; prof. Bklyn. Coll. and Grad. Ctr., CUNY, 1987—, Claire and Leonard Tow disting. prof., 2000-02. Disting. guest prof. Centre for Reformation and Renaissance Studies, U. Toronto, 1995. Author: (textbook) Western Civilization: A Social and Cultural History, 2d edit., 2002; Venetian Humanism in an Age of Patrician Dominance, 1986, Women of the Renaissance, 1991, The Death of the Child Valerio Marcello, 1994; contbr. articles to profl. jours.; mem. editorial bds. Recipient Howard R. Marraro prize, Am. Cath. Hist. Assn., 1986, Tow award for distinction in scholarship, Bklyn. Coll., 1994—95; fellow, Danforth Found., 1967—72, Woodrow Wilson Found., 1967—68, Am. Coun. Learned Socs., 1977—78, NEH, 1986—87, Leonard and Claire Tow Disting. fellow, 2000—; grantee, Am. Coun. Learned Socs., 1976, Gladys Krieble Delmas Found., 1977—78, 1980—81, 1990, Am. Philos. Soc., 1979, 1990, NEH, 1984. Mem. Am. Hist. Assn. (Howard and Helen Mararro prize 1996), Hist. Soc., Renaissance Soc. Am. (exec. dir. 1988-95, editor Renaissance Quar. 1984-88, 97-2002). Home: 324 Beverly Rd Little Neck NY 11363-1125 Office: CUNY Bklyn Coll Dept History 2900 Bedford Ave Brooklyn NY 11210-2814 E-mail: mking@nyc.rr.com.

KING, MARILYN SODOWSKY, music educator; b. Oklahoma City, Feb. 14, 1938; d. Robert P. and MaryEllen (Graves) Benson; m. Roland Sodowsky, Feb. 7, 1958 (div. June 1972); children: Christi, Robert; m. Kendall Dale King, Dec. 26, 1974 (dec.). BS in Elem. Edn., Okla. State U., 1958, MS in Secondary Edn., 1964. Tchr. music Pub. Sch., Perkins, Okla., 1958-63, Yale, Okla., 1963-65, Cushing, Okla., 1965-68, Stillwater, Okla., 1968-92; pvt. music instr. Stillwater, 1992—. Advisor Alpha Delta Pi, 1993—, named Outstanding Alumnae Advisor award, 1996. Bd. dirs. Pleasant Valley Sch. Found., Stillwater; deacon First Presbyn. Ch., Stillwater; vol. music programs accompanist, Stillwater. Named Okla. Tchr. of Yr., 1990-91, Okla Music Educators Hall of Fame, 1993. Mem. Okla. State U. Alumni Bd. (edn. rep. 1995-97), Okla. State U. Edn. Alumnae Assn. (pres. 1995-96), Stillwater Med. Ctr. Aux. (pres. 1996-97), Stillwater Med. Ctr. Found. (bd. dirs.). Democrat. Avocations: reading, crafts, sewing, travel. Home and Office: 1807 W 5th Ave Stillwater OK 74074-2922

KING, MARY ELIZABETH, writer, educator; b. N.Y.C., July 30, 1940; d. Luther Waddington and Alba Iregui King; m. Peter Gregory Bourne. AB, Ohio Wesleyan U., 1962; PhD, U. Wales, Aberystwyth, 1999. Comm. officer Student Nonviolent Coord. Com., Atlanta, 1963—65; program officer U.S. Office of Econ. Opportunity, Washington, 1968—72; dep. dir. ACTION - a sub-Cabinet fed. agy., Washington, 1977—81; freelance cons., 1981—92; spl. advisor to former Pres. Jimmy Carter, 1984—; prof., internat. politics St. George's U., Grenada, 1999—2001; prof., peace and conflict studies U. for Peace, Costa Rica, 2001—. Mem. Internat. Commn. on Peace and Food, Madras, India, 1989—94; bd. dirs. AMIDEAST Ednl. and Testing Svc., Washington, 1989—. Author: (book) Freedom Song: A Personal Story of the 1960s Civil Rights Movement, 1987, Mahatma Ghandi and Martin Luther King, Jr.: The Power of Nonviolent Action, 1999; contbr. articles to profl. jours. Pres., co-founder Nat. Assn. Women Bus. Owners, Washington, 1976; bd. dirs. Save the Children Fedn., Westport, Conn., 1980—91, Arca Found., Washington, 1980—; bd. selectors The Jefferson Awards, Wilmington, Del., 1993—. Named to Nat. Women's Hall of Fame, Seneca Falls, N.Y., 1992; recipient Disting. Achievement award, Ohio Wesleyan U., 1989, Women's Equity Action League, 1977; fellow, Albert Einstein Instn., 1996—98; disting. scholar, Am. U. Ctr. for Global Peace, Washington, DC, 1997—. Mem.: The Author's Guild, Middle East Studies Assn., Women's Fgn. Policy Group, Women in Internat. Security. Avocations: British antiques and architecture, farming. Home: 2119 Leroy Pl NW Washington DC 20008-1848

KING, MARY LOU, artist, medical technologist; b. Vernon, Tex., Apr. 11, 1927; d. H. Raymond and Alma Vivian (Davenport) Hudson; m. Jack E. King, June 3, 1948; children: Paul Hudson, Karen Anne, Julie Louise. BS in Biology and Med. Tech., N. Tex. State U., 1948; AS in Art, Midland (Tex.) Coll., 1987. Bd. cert. med. technologist Am. Soc. Clin. Pathologists. Dept. head Santa Rosa Hosp., San Antonio, Tex., 1948-49; lab. dir. Drs. Offices, San Antonio, 1949-50; artist pvt. practice, Midland, 1986—. Painter landscapes in water colors; shown in 88 nat. and regional exhbns., with 3 gallery representations; one-person shows include Silvers Gallery, Midland, Tex. State Capital Bldg., Austin,

Gallery of the Woman's Club, Midland, Gallery Theatre Ctr., Midland; invitational shows in China, Norway and Japan; 20 commns.; featured in publs. including Artists of Texas, vol. II & IV, American Artists, Illustrated Survey of Leading Contemporary Watercolorists, Splash IV, The Splendor of Light, Contemporary Watercolorists, Keys to Painting Light and Shadow, 1999, Texas Watercolor Society: Fifty Years of Excellence, 1999, Watercolor (mag.), 1999, The Artist Sketch Book, 2001, Capturing Texture in Watercolors. Bd. dirs. First United Meth. Ch., Midland, 1963-85, adult class leader and lay speaker, 1970—; Troop leader Girl Scouts U.S.A., Midland, 1958-75, officer, dir. coun., trainer, coord., 1968-80. Recipient Thanks award Girl Scouts Am., 1975, Life Membership award, 1990, Woman of Distinction award, 2000. Mem. Tex. Water Color Soc. (signature mem. 1987, regional del. 1988-89, mem. Purple Sage Soc. 1995), West Tex. Watercolor Soc. (signature mem. 1995), So. Watercolor Soc. (signature mem. 1993, regional del. 1995—), Midland Arts Assn. (bd. dirs., officer 1983—), Arts Assembly of Midland (chmn. visual arts, mem. planning coun. 1983-86, Outstanding Svc. award 1985), Watercolor USA Hon. Soc. Avocations: travel with husband in motorhome, dancing, poetry. Home: 4513 Cardinal Ln Midland TX 79707-2203 E-mail: MLJKINGART@aol.com.

KING, MAXWELL CLARK, former academic administrator; b. Ft. Pierce, Fla., Jan. 1, 1928; s. Hiram and Ida (Chandler) K.; m. Doris Warren, Jan. 29, 1953; children: Maxwell Clark II, Pamela King Jones, Carol, Russell E., Dori King Knodel. BS, Auburn (Ala.) U., 1950; MS in Edn., U. Fla., 1954, EdD, 1956; postgrad., U. Tex., 1958-59. Tchr. St. Lucie County High Sch., Ft. Pierce, 1950-51; prin. Dan McCarty High Sch., Ft. Pierce, 1956-60; pres. Indian River Community Coll., Ft. Pierce, 1960-68, Brevard Community Coll., Cocoa, Fla., 1968-99; ret. Cons. overseas liaison com. Am. Coun. on Edn., India, 1978; chmn. C.C.'s for Internat. Devel., Cocoa, 1976—, Fla. Gov.'s Summer Colls. Coun., Tallahassee, 1988-90; mem. exec. com. S. Regional Edn. Bd., Atlanta, 1987-91; bd. dirs. Am. Bank South, Merritt Island, Fla., First Nat. Bank of Merritt Island, Am. Bank, First United Bank, Cmty. Bank of South. Contbr. articles to profl. jours. Bd. dirs. United Way Brevard County, Cocoa, 1969—, Eugene Wuesthoff Meml. Hosp., Rockledge, Fla., 1970—; chmn. bd. dirs. Wuesthoff Health Svcs., Rockledge, 1986—. 1st lt. U.S. Army, 1951-53. Recipient Norm Keller Disting. Svc. award Melbourne Jaycees, 1986, Patrick Henry medal Mil. Order World Wars, 1986, Thomas J. Peters Nat. Leadership award U. Tex., 1989, DeBus award Nat. Space Club, 1997; Eileen Tosney Outstanding Am. Community-Univ. Adminstr., Am. Assn. Univ. Adminstrs., 1989; named laureate Brevard Bus. Leadership Hall of Fame, Jr. Achievement, Cocoa, 1988; Fulbright scholar, India, 1979-81, Republic of China, 1987. Mem. Cmty. Coll. Internat. Devel. (founder, chmn. 1976-98), Assn. Community Coll. Trustees (Nation's Outstanding Community Coll. Pres. award 1976), Am. Assn. Community and Jr. Colls. (bd. dirs. 1978-81), Fla. Assn. Colls. and Univs. (pres. 1971-72), Fla. Assn. Community Colls. (pres. 1965-66), Nat. Pres. Acad. (chmn. 1975-76), Cocoa Beach Area C. of C. (bd. dirs. 1988-91), Kappa Delta Pi, Phi Delta Kappa. Avocations: golf, reading. E-mail: Kingm@worldnet.att.net.

KING, MERVYN ALLISTER, economist, educator; b. Chesham Bois, Eng., Mar. 30, 1948; s. Eric Frank and Kathleen Alice (Passingham) K. BA with first class honors, King's Coll., Cambridge U., Eng., 1969; postgrad., Harvard U., 1971-72; Degree (hon.), Birmingham U., 2001, City U. London, 2002, U. Wolverhampton, 2003. Jr. rsch. officer, dept. allied econs. Cambridge U., 1969-73, rsch. officer, 1973-76, lectr. faculty econs., 1976-77; Esmee Fairbairn prof. investment U. Birmingham, Eng., 1977-84; prof. econs. London Sch. Econs., 1984-95; exec. dir., chief economist Bank of Eng., 1990-97, dep. gov., 1998—2003, gov., 2003—. Vis. prof. econs. Harvard U., 1982, MIT, 1983-84, LSE, 1996; vis. fellow Nuffield Coll., Oxford U., 2002-03; rsch. assoc. Nat. Bur. Econ. Rsch., 1978—; rsch. fellow Centre for Econ. Policy Rsch., 1984—; mem. Econs. Policy Panel, 1985-86; mem. CLARE Group of Economists, 1976-85; bd. dirs. LSE Fin. Markets Group; cons. to N.Z. Treasury, 1979, to OECD, 1982; sr. v.p. Aston Villa F.C., 1995-99; pres. Inst. for Fiscal Studies, 1999-2003; founding mem. Monetary Policy Com., 1997; mem. Grout of Thirty, 1997; pres. Inst. for Fiscal Studies, 1999-2003. Author: Public Policy and the Corporation, 1977; (with J.A. Kay) The British Tax System, 1978, 5th edit., 1990, (with D. Fullerton et al) The Taxation of Income from Capital, 1984, 93; editor: (with T. Liesner) Indexing for Inflation, 1975; mng. editor Rev. Econ. Studies, 1978-83; assoc. editor Jour. Pub. Econs., 1982-99; asst. editor Econ. Jour., 1974-75; editl. bd. Am. Econ. Rev., 1985-88, Jour. Indsl. Econs., 1977-83; contbr. numerous articles to profl. jours. Trustee Kennedy Meml. Trust, 1990-2000; mem. adv. coun. London Symphony Orch. Hon. fellow St. John's Coll., Cambridge, 1997, rsch. fellow Centre for Econ. Policy Rsch., 1984—; hon. sr. scholar King's Coll., 1969, Wrenbury scholar U. Cambridge, 1969, Kennedy scholar Harkness fellow, 1971; hon. rsch. fellow Univ. Coll. London, 1977-79; hon. fellow London Sch. Econs., 003recipient Richards prize King's Coll., 1969, Stevenson prize U. Cambridge, 1970, medal U. Helsinki, Finland, 1982. Fellow Econometric Soc. (mem. Congress program com. 1974, 79, 85), Brit. Acad.; mem. Soc. Econ. Analysis (chmn. 1984-86), Royal Econ. Soc. (mem. coun. and exec. com. 1981-86), Nat. Inst. Econ. and Social Rsch. (gov. 1985—), The Securities Assn. (bd. dirs. 1987-89), European Econs. Assn. (pres. 1993), Am. Acad. Arts and Scis. (fgn. hon.). Office: Bank of England Threadneedle St London EC2R 8AH England

KING, NORAH MCCANN, federal judge; b. Steubenville, Ohio, Aug. 13, 1949; d. Charles Bernard and Frances Marcella (Krumm) McCann; married; 4 children. BA cum laude, Rosary Coll. (now Dominican U.), 1971; JD summa cum laude, Ohio State U., 1975. Bar: Ohio 1975, So. Dist. of Ohio 1980. Law clerk U.S. Dist. Ct., Columbus, Ohio, 1975-79; counsel Frost, King, Freytag & Carpenter, Columbus, Ohio, 1979-82; asst. prof. Ohio State U., Columbus, Ohio, 1980-82; U.S. magistrate judge U.S. Dist. Ct., Columbus, Ohio, 1982—, chief magistrate judge, 2000—. Recipient award of merit Columbus Bar Assn., 1990. Mem.: Columbus Bar Assn., Fed. Bar Assn., Coun. U.S. Magistrate Judges. Office: US Dist Ct 85 Marconi Blvd Rm 235 Columbus OH 43215-2837

KING, ORDIE HERBERT, JR., oral pathologist; b. Memphis, Aug. 11, 1933; s. Ordie Herbert and Hazel (Eaton) K.; m. Violette Papagianis, Mar. 21, 1974; children: Catherine Ann, Alexander Carlos; children by previous marriage: Anna LaVelle, Ordie Herbert III. BS, Memphis State U., 1957; DDS, U. Tenn., 1959, PhD, 1965. Diplomate Am. Bd. Oral Pathology. USPHS postdoctoral fellow U. Tenn., 1960-62, rsch. assoc. dept. pathology, 1963-65, asst. prof. pathology, 1965; resident oral pathology U. Tenn., City of Memphis Hosps., 1962-63; asst. prof. pathology Northwestern U., 1966; assoc. prof. oral pathology St. Louis U., 1967-69, prof., 1969-70, chmn. dept., 1967-70, chmn. dept. dentistry univ. hosps., 1967-70; acting chmn., vis. assoc. prof. oral pathology Washington U., St. Louis, 1969-70; prof. oral pathology, assoc. prof. pathology W.Va. U., Morgantown, 1970-74, prof. pathology, 1974, dir. Cytopathology Lab., Med. Ctr., 1971-74; prof. pathology So. Ill. U. Sch. Dental Medicine, Alton, 1974-97; chmn. dept. diagnostic specialties So. Ill. U., Edwardsville, 1979-92; clin. prof. pathology Washington U. Sch. Dental Medicine, St. Louis, 1979-80. Dir. So. Ill. Pathology Lab., Ltd., Godfrey, Ill., 1977—; dental cons. to chief med. examiner State of Tenn., 1963-65; mem. exec. com. St. Louis U. Hosps., 1967-70; mem. med. staff West Tenn. Cancer Clinic, 1962-65, W.Va. U. Hosp., 1970-74; mem. med./dental staff dept pathology Alton (Ill.) Meml. Hosp., 1986—; cons. VA Hosp., Clarksville, W.Va., 1973-74; dental cons. St. Louis County Med. Examiner, 1968-70; cons. cancer control program Nat. Ctr. for Chronic Disease Control, USPHS, 1967-70; mem. Mo. Bd. Dental Splty. Examiners, 1982-84. Fellow Am. Acad. Oral Pathology; mem. Am. Soc. Cytology, ADA, Am. Cancer Soc. (bd. dirs. W.Va. div. 1972-74), Tenn. Walking Horse Breeders and Exhibitors Assn., Spotted Saddle Horse Breeders and Exhibitors Assn. (pres. 2002-03), Delta Sigma Delta, Kappa Alpha, Phi Rho Sigma, Omicron Kappa Upsilon. Home: 6111 Vollmer Ln Godfrey IL 62035-1062 Office: So Ill Path Lab Ltd Godfrey IL 62035

KING, PAUL MARTIN, lawyer; b. Pitts., Dec. 18, 1946; s. Thomas E. and Alice C. (Myers) K.; m. Mary J. Sargus, Mar. 6, 1976; children— Anne C., M. Elizabeth. B.S. in Bus. Adminstrn., Duquesne U., 1968; J.D., U. Pitts., 1971. Bar: Pa. 1971, U.S. Dist. Ct. (we. dist.) Pa. 1971, U.S. Ct. Appeals (D.C. cir.) 1979. Law clk. Allegheny County Common Pleas Ct., Pitts., 1971-72; atty., sr. atty. PPG Industries, Inc., Pitts., 1972-80, sr. counsel, 1980-82, dir. environ. affairs, 1982— ; adj. prof. law U. Pitts. Contbr. chpts. to books, articles to profl. jours. Mem. ABA (chmn. environ. law com. 1987—), Allegheny County Bar Assn., Chem. Mfrs. Assn. (environ. mgmt. com. 1983-87, chmn. air toxic control policy task group 1986-87). Home: 220 N Bellefield Ave Apt 601 Pittsburgh PA 15213-1467 Office: PPG Industries Inc 1 Ppg Pl # 1P Pittsburgh PA 15272-0001

KING, PETER COTTERILL, former utilities executive; b. White Plains, N.Y., Aug. 23, 1930; s. Robert Cotterill and Ruth (McKeown) K.; m. Nancy English, June 28, 1958; children: Margot E., Philip M., Sabrina P. BS, U.S. Mil. Acad., 1952; MBA, U. Pa., 1958; seminar cert., Harvard, 1968. Commd. 2d lt. U.S. Army, 1952, advanced through grades to 1st lt., 1956; resigned, 1956; col. (Res.); systems engr. IBM Research Ctr., Yorktown Heights, N.Y., 1958-62; v.p. Security Bank & Trust Co., Lawton, Okla., 1962-69; pres. Security Broadcasting Corp., Lawton, 1964-69; adminstr. Southwestern Power Adminstrn., Dept. Interior, 1969-77; pres. EDG Energy Mgmt., Inc., Tulsa, 1977-80; assoc. The Dorchester Cos., Tulsa, 1980-82; dir. First State Financial, Inc., 1982-98. Chmn. United Way campaign, Lawton, 1968; chmn. Okla. Arts and Humanities Council, 1970-72; mem. Lawton City Council, 1968-69; bd. dirs. Tulsa Arts and Humanities Council; trustee Nat. Electric Reliability Council, 1975-77. Republican. Episcopalian. Home and Office: 1123 E 18th St Tulsa OK 74120-7408

KING, PETER JOSEPH, JR., retired gas company executive; b. Concord, N.H., Aug. 5, 1921; s. Peter Joseph and Helen (Hallinan) K.; m. Louise Lynch, Sept. 11, 1948; children: Anne, Peter BS, Georgetown U., 1942; LL.B., Harvard U., 1948, postgrad. Advanced Mgmt. Program, 1966. Bar: N.H. 1949, Mass. 1950, Colo. 1973. Practice law, N.H., 1948-51; with AEC, 1952-53, Colo. Interstate Gas Co., Colorado Springs, 1953-86, pres., chief operating officer, dir., 1977-85, vice chmn., 1985-86, also bd. dirs. Bd. dirs. Myron Stratton Home, Colorado Springs, 1974-93; mem. Colo. Transp. Commn., 1987-95, chmn., 1991-92. 1st lt. AUS, 1942-45, 51-52. Mem. Garden of the Gods Club, El Paso Club. Roman Catholic. Home: 7 Chase Ln Colorado Springs CO 80906-4205

KING, PETER THOMAS, congressman, lawyer; b. N.Y., Apr. 5, 1944; m. Rosemary King; children: Sean, Erin. Grad., St. Francis Coll., 1965; JD, U. Notre Dame, 1968. Atty.; town councilman Town of Hempstead, N.Y., 1977-81; comptr. Nassau County, N.Y., 1981-93; mem. U.S. Congress from 3rd N.Y. dist., Washington, 1993—; mem. fin. svcs. and internat. rels. coms., homeland sec. com. Spl. asst. to Chief Dep. Nassau County Exec.; gen counsel to Nassau Regional Off-Track Betting Corp.; chief dep. Nassau County Atty.; Acting County Atty. Chmn. Town Bd. Com. on Conservation and Waterways. Recipient cert. of achievement for excellence in fin. reporting (7 yrs) Gov. Fin. Officers Assn., cert. of honor Long Island Com. for Soviet Jewry, Alumni Achievement award St. Francis Coll., Huey award Vets. of Viet Nam War. Mem. Am. Legion, Vets. Corps of 69th Infantry, Knights of Columbus (named Citizen of the Yr.), Sons of Italy. Republican. Roman Catholic. Office: US Ho of Reps 436 Cannon Ho Office Bldg Washington DC 20515-3203*

KING, PHILIP GORDON, public relations counselor; b. Ely, Minn., Apr. 11, 1922; s. Herbert Sidney and Ruth Marie (Trimble) K.; m. Onriette Lebron, Feb. 23, 1957; children: Gordon Rivard, Philip David, Bernardine Victoria. A in Bus., Ely Jr. Coll., 1942; BS, Northwestern U., 1948, MA, 1950; postgrad., Columbia U., 1950-51. Tech. dir. Columbia U. Theater, 1950-51, Houston (Tex.) Playhouse, 1951-52, Civic Light Opera, Grand Rapids, Mich., 1952-54, editor/publicist CBS/TV Network, L.A., 1954-60; v.p. Pat McDermott Co., N.Y.C., 1960-62; pub. info. dir. Sta. WCBS-TV, N.Y.C., 1962-65; pub. rels. cons. NEA, N.Y.C., 1965-68; dir. press, radio and TV rels. Washington, 1968-72; pub. info. mgr., 1972-83; pres. King Comms., Washington, 1983-88, Warren, Vt., 1988—; grad. lectr. CCNY, 1962-64. Civilian pers. dir. USO Camp Shows, Paris, Badschualbach, Germany, 1945-46; pub. rels. cons. NEA, Washington, 1983-88, Prentice Hall Inc., Englewood, Cliffs, N.J., 1984, Assn. Supervision and Curriculum Devel., 1984-88, Phi Delta Kappa Internat., 1984-89, Green Mountain Cultural Ctr., 1988—, Internat. TV and Film Festival N.Y., 1988—, League of Vt. Writers, 1989—, The Valley Reporter, 1994—. Capt. U.S. Army, 1942-46, ETO. Mem. NEA, Am. Assn. Pub. Rels. Execs., Edn. Writers Assn. Democrat. Presbyterian. E-mail: news@valleyreporter.com.

KING, RAY JOHN, electrical engineer, educator, business executive; b. Montrose, Colo., Jan. 1, 1933; s. John Frank and Grace (Rankin) K.; m. Diane M. Henney, June 20, 1964; children: Karl V., Kristin J. BS in Electronic Engring., Ind. Inst. Tech., 1956, BS in Elec. Engring., 1957; MS, U. Colo., 1960, PhD, 1965. Instr. Ind. Inst. Tech., 1956-58, asst. prof., 1960-62, acting chmn. dept. electronics, 1960-62; research asso. U. Colo., 1962-65; research assoc. U. Ill., 1965; assoc. prof. elec. engring. U. Wis., Madison, 1965-69, prof., 1969-82, assoc. dept. chmn. for research and grad. affairs, 1977-79; staff rsch. engr. Lawrence Livermore Nat. Lab. (Calif.), 1982-90, sr. scientist high power microwaves program, 1989-90; co-founder KDC Tech. Corp., 1983, v.p., 1990—, cons. Vis. Erskine fellow U. Canterbury, N.Z., 1977; guest prof., Fulbright scholar Tech. U. Denmark, 1973-74 Author: Microwave Homodyne Systems, 1978; contbr. articles to profl. jours.; patentee in field; guest editor spl. issue Subsurface Sensing Techs. and Applications jour., 2000. NSF Faculty fellow, 1962-65. Fellow IEEE (life); mem. IEEE Soc. on Antennas and Propagation (adminstrv. com. 1989-91, chmn. wave propagation stds. com. 1986-89, gen. chmn. symposium 1989), IEEE Soc. Microwave Theory and Techniques, IEEE Soc. Instrumentation and Measurements, Forest Products Soc., Electromagnetics Acad., Internat. Sci. Radio Union (commns. A, B, F), Sigma Xi, Iota Tau Kappa, Sigma Phi Delta. Home: 2595 Raven Rd Pleasanton CA 94566-4605 Office: KDC Tech Corp 2011 Research Dr Livermore CA 94550-3803 E-mail: kdc@ant-s.com., rayking@ieee.com.

KING, RICHARD ALLEN, lawyer; b. St. Joseph, Mo., July 4, 1944; s. Allen Welden and Lola (Donelson) K.; m. Deedee Gershenson, Apr. 19, 1986; children from previous marriage: Mary, Suzanne, Allen. BA, U. Mo., Columbia, 1966, JD cum laude, 1968. Bar: Mo. 1968. Law clk. Office of Chief Counsel, IRS, 1967; assoc. Reese, Constance, Slayton, Stewart & Stewart, Independence, Mo., 1968-73; ptnr. Constance, Slayton, Stewart & King, Independence, 1973-80, Cochran, Kramer, Kapke, Willerth & King, Independence, 1980-81; exec. asst. to gov. State of Mo., Jefferson City, 1981-82, dir. revenue, 1982-85; ptnr. Smith, Gill, Fisher and Butts, Inc., Kansas City, Mo., 1985-87, Wirken & King, Kansas City, 1988-93; chmn., CEO King Hershey, Kansas City, Mo., 1993—. Asst. city counselor City of Independence, 1968—69, mayor, 1974—78; vice chmn. Nat. Conf. Rep. Mayors, 1975—77; chmn. Mo. Gov.'s Task Force on Cmty. Crime Prevention, 1975—76, Kansas City Pub. Improvements Adv. Com., 1991—96, KC Team Effort, 1991—95; pres. Good Govt. League, Independence, 1972—73; mem. Mo. Commn. Human Rights, 1973—74; bd. dirs. Multistate Tax Commn., 1983—85, Chrisman Sawyer Bank, 1989—95. Contbr. articles to profl. jours. Bd. dirs. Am. Cancer Soc., Independence, 1973-79, chmn. crusade, 1973; bd. dirs. Independence Boys Club, 1972-79, Independence Cmty. Assn. Arts, 1973-76, Independence Sanitarium and Hosp., 1974-78, Jefferson City Meml. Hosp., 1981-85, NE Jackson County Mental Health Ctr., 1978-80, Greater Kansas City Nat. Coun. on Alcoholism, 1978-81, Am. Legion Boys State Mo., 1975—, Jefferson City United Way, 1982-85, Multi-State Tax Commn., 1982-85, Jackson County Hist. Soc., 1999—; pres. Friends U. Mo. Truman Campus, 1979-80, Kansas City Consensus, 1989-90; trustee Harry S. Truman Scholarship Found., 1975-78, Kansas City U., 1979-80, Andrew Drumm Inst., 1990—, pres. bd. trustees, 1992-94. Capt. U.S. Army, 1969-72. Recipient Outstanding Young Man of Mo. award Mo. Jaycees, 1975, award Mo. Inst. Pub. Adminstrn., 1983 Mem.: ABA, Independence C. of C. (pres. 1980—81), Mo. Econ. Devel. Fin. Assn. (pres. 1999—2001), Kansas City Bar Assn., Internat. Assn. Gaming Attys., Nat. Assn. Bond Lawyers, Kansas City Bar Assn. (chmn. real estate law com. 1988—89), Ea. Jackson County Bar Assn., Mo. Bar Assn., Order of Coif, Beta Theta Pi, Phi Delta Phi. Unitarian Universalist. Home: 206 E 30th St Kansas City MO 64108-3213 Office: King Hershey Ste 2100 2345 Grand Blvd Kansas City MO 64108-2619 E-mail: rking@kinghershey.com. *There is nothing in life as important as living. "Success" is an objective which all too often deprives its pursuer of the satisfaction he or she seeks. That satisfaction lies in meaningful personal relationships, spiritual communion with a Higher Power, and appreciation for the meaning and purpose of life.*

KING, RICHARD EUGENE, soil scientist, educator; b. Norfolk, Va., Dec. 27, 1948; s. Richard Allen and Dorothy Marietta (Brinkley) K.; m. Carol Janet Maiden, Oct. 7, 1972 (div. 1993); 1 child, Andrew Lee; m. Elizabeth Ann Ellis, June 20, 1997 (separated). BS in Agrl. Econs., Pa. State U., 1971. Cert. profl. soil scientist; cert. profl. in erosion and sediment control. Soil conservationist USDA Soil Conservation Service, West Chester, Pa., 1971-73; specialist soil and water mgmt. Yerkes Assocs. Inc., Bryn Mawr, Pa., 1973-82; ptnr. Momenee-King Assocs., Ardmore, Pa., 1982-86, Bryn Mawr, 1986-89; owner King Environ., Strafford, Pa., 1989-90, ptnr. King of Prussia, Pa., 1990-93, Scranton, Pa., 1993-96; resource specialist Ga. Soil & Water Conservation Commn., Rome, 1996—. With USAR, 1972-78. Mem. Am. Registry Cert. Profl. Agronomy, Crops and Soils (cert.), CPESC Inc. (chmn. 2002—), Soil Sci. Soc. Am., Am. Soc. Agronomy, Am. Planning Assn. (environ. adv. bd. 1983-90), Soil and Water Conservation Soc. Am. (pres.-elect Ga. chpt. 1998, pres. 1999, membership chmn. 2000—). Republican. Avocations: stamp collecting, tennis.

KING, RICHARD HOOD, newspaper executive; b. Boston, Mass, Jan. 24, 1934; s. Gilbert and Frances (Hood) K.; m. Reta Schoonmaker, July 25, 1959; children: D. Whitney, Richard H. Jr., Nanci A. AB, Harvard U., 1955, MBA, 1961. Mgr. acctg. Hitchiner Mfg. Co., Inc., Milford, NH, 1963-68, div. contr. Wallingford, Conn., 1968-71; sec., treas. Smyth Mfg. Co., Inc., Bloomfield, Conn., 1971-72; v.p. fin. Progressive Trade Corp., Glastonbury, Conn., 1972-73; v.p., treas. Hartford Courant Co., Conn., 1973-83, v.p., asst. to gen. mgr., 1986 90, v.p. adminstrn., 1990-96, ret., 1996. Treas. Hartford Courant Found., 1974—96, trustee, 1993—98; v.p., sec., bd. dirs. Better Bus. Bur., Hartford, 1978; bd. dir. Camp Courant, Inc., 1980—96, treas., 1980—96; bd. dirs. Conn. Prison Assn., 1984—91, treas., 1985, chmn. bd. dir., 1986—89; bd. dir. Hartford Symphony Orch., 1990—98; bd. dir., regional v.p. Conn. Audubon Soc., 1991—92, chmn., 1993—95, chmn. emeritus, 1995—98, bd. overseers, 1988—; bd. dir. Penikese Is. Sch., 1998—, treas., 2001—. Lt. j.g. USNR, 1955—57. Mem.: Conn. Daily Newspapers Assn. (treas. 1992, 1st v.p. 1993—95, pres. 1995, exec. dir. 1996—), Fin. Exec. Inst. (treas. Hartford chpt. 1980—81, sec. 1981—82, v.p. 1982—83, pres. 1983—84), Glastonbury C. of C. (treas., exec. bd. dirs. 1991—94), Chapoquoit Yacht Club (West Falmouth, Mass., treas. 1973—74, vice commodore 2001—02), Harvard-Radcliffe Club No. Conn. (v.p. 1989—90, pres. 1990—92). Home: 11 Snug Harbor Ln PO Box 456 West Falmouth MA 02574-0456

KING, RICHARD MAURICE, JR., consultant; b. Wilmington, N.C., Jan. 15, 1935; s. Richard Maurice Sr. and Eleanor (Watson) K.; m. Edith Page Stevenson, Dec. 26, 1960 (dec. Dec. 1979); 1 child, Eleanor King Bohanon. BS in Math., U. N.C., 1956. Statis. engr. E.I. duPont de Nemours, Parlin, N.J., 1956-59; statis. cons., computer group mgr. Am. Cyanamid, Stamford, Conn., 1959-71; various positions in computer mktg. and product mgmt. Xerox Corp., various locations, 1971-87; nat. account mgr. Delphax Sys., Randolph, Mass., 1988-90; product market mgr. Bull Printing Sys., Wellesley, Mass., 1990-91; pres. Logical Imaging Solutions, Santa Ana, Calif., 1993-95; cons. Ptnrs. Cons. Svcs., Laguna Niguel, Calif., 1991—93, 1996—2002; prin. analyst Pacificare Health Sys., Cypress, Calif., 2002—. Home: 30902 Clubhouse Dr Apt 4D Laguna Niguel CA 92677-2381 E-mail: mauriceking@worldnet.att.net.

KING, ROBERT BAINTON, neurosurgeon, educator; b. Pitts., Aug. 26, 1922; s. Charles Glenn and Hilda (Bainton) K.; m. Molly Gibbs, Aug. 26, 1951; children: Nancy, Susan, Kimberly. Student, U. Mich., 1942-43, U. Pitts., 1940-43, MD cum laude, U. Rochester, 1946. Diplomate Nat. Bd. Med. Examiners, Am. Bd. Neurol. Surgery (chmn. 1978-80). Intern and resident Barnes Hosp., St. Louis, 1946 49; instr. anatomy Washington U., St. Louis, 1948-49, instr. neurosurgery, 1951-52, assoc. prof. neurosurgery., 1952-57; prof. neurosurgery Health Sci. Ctr. Upstate Med. Ctr., Syracuse, 1957-88; Disting. svc. prof. neurol. surgery Upstate Med. Univ., Syracuse, 1988—; dir., chmn. neurol. surgery programs SUNY, Syracuse, 1957-88; assoc. dean grad. edn. SUNY Upstate Med. U., Syracuse, 1988—; med. dir. Univ. Hosp., Syracuse, 1988—95. Mem. editorial bd. Archives of Neurology; contbr. over 120 articles to profl. jours. on anatomy, physiology, mgmt. of pain, and med. edn. and econ. Active physician Project Hope, Brazil, 1972-73; cons. Pres. Commn. Study of Ethical Problems in Medicine, 1981, Nat. Adv. Coun. on Health Professions Edn., 1989-92. 1st lt. U.S. Army, 1949-51. Recipient Lifetime Achievement award, U. Tex. MD Anderson Cancer Ctr., 2001, Pres. Disting. Svc. Prof. award, 2002; grantee NINDS Neorology A Study Sec. in Neurology/Surgical Tng. Program investigator Rsch. Grant., 1950—70, tng. grant neurosurgery prin. investigator, 1968—78. Mem. Am. Acad. Neurol. Surgeons (pres. 1977-78, Neurosurgeon of Yr. award 1979), Am. Assn. Neurol. Surgeons (pres. 1980-81, Disting. Svc. award 1981, Cushing medal 1990), Am. Bd. Med. Specialties (pres. 1988-90), Am. Neurol. Assn., Soc. Neurol. Surgeons (pres.1977-78), Disting. Svc. award 1988), Neurol. Soc. Am. Office: Upstate Med U 750 E Adams St Syracuse NY 13066-9729

KING, ROBERT BRUCE, federal judge; b. White Sulphur Springs, W.Va., Jan. 29, 1940; m. Julia Kay Doak, Apr. 16, 1965. BA, W.Va. U., 1961; JD, W.Va. Coll. of Law, 1968. Bar: W.Va. 1968, U.S. Dist. Ct. (so. dist.) W.Va. 1968, U.S. Ct. Appeals W.Va. 1968, U.S. Ct. Appeals (4th cir.) 1970, U.S. Dist. Ct. (no. dist.) W.Va. 1972, U.S. Supreme Ct. 1974, U.S. Dist. Ct. (ea. dist.) Ky. 1975, U.S. Claims Ct. 1985, U.S. Tax Ct. 1991. Asst. mgr. Sam Snead All-Am. Golf Course, Sharpes, Fla., 1965; rsch. asst. State and Cmty. Planning Office, Office of R&D, W.Va. U., Morgantown, W.Va., 1966—68; law clk. Chief Judge John A. Field, Jr. U.S. Dist. Ct. (so. dist.) W.Va., Charleston, 1968—69; assoc. Haynes and Ford, Lewisburg, W.Va., 1969—70; asst. U.S. atty. So. Dist. of W.Va., Charleston, 1970—74; assoc. Spilman, Thomas, Battle and Klostermeyer, Charleston, 1975, ptnr., 1976—77, 1981; U.S. atty. So. Dist. of W.Va., Charleston, 1977—81; ptnr. King Allen Guthrie & McHugh, 1981—98; judge U.S. Ct. Appeals (4th cir.), Richmond, Va., 1998—. Mem. Jud. Investigation Commn. of W.Va., 1990—94; vis. com. Coll. of Law of W.Va. U., 1997—. Scholar Patrick Duffy Koontz. Fellow: Am. Bar Found., Am. Coll. Trial Lawyers; mem.: ABA, Am. Bd. Trial Advocates (W.Va. chpt. pres. 1986—90), Jud. Conf. of 4th Cir. Ct. Appeals, W.Va. Law Sch. Assn., W.Va. U. Alumni Assn., Greenbrier County Bar Assn., Kanawha County Bar Assn., W.Va. Bar Assn., W.Va. Golf Assn., U.S. Golf Assn., Order of the Coif, Phi Alpha Delta, Pi Sigma Alpha. Presbyterian. Office: Ste 7602 300 Virginia St Charleston WV 25301*

KING, ROBERT CHARLES, biologist, educator; b. N.Y.C., June 3, 1928; s. Charles James and Amanda (McCutchen) King. BS, Yale U., 1948, PhD, 1952. Scientist biology dept. Brookhaven Nat. Lab., 1951-55; mem. faculty Northwestern U., 1956—, prof. biology, 1964-99, prof. emeritus, 2000—. Chmn. 8th Brookhaven Symposium in Biology, 1955; vis. investigator, fellow Rockefeller U., 1959; NSF sr. postdoctoral fellow U. Edinburgh, Scotland, 1958, Commonwealth Sci. and Indsl. Research Orgn. Div. Entomology, Canberra, Australia, 1963, Sericultural Expt. Sta., Tokyo, Japan, 1970 Author: Genetics, 2d edit., 1965, A Dictionary of Genetics, 6th edit., 2002, (with W.D. Stansfield) Ovarian Development in Drosophila melanogaster, 1970, also numerous papers; editor: Handbook of Genetics Series, 5 vols., (with H. Akai) Insect Ultrastructure, 2 vols., 1982. Fellow AAAS; mem. Am. Soc. Zoologists, Histochem. Soc., Am. Soc. Cell Biology (treas. 1972-75), Electron Microscopy Soc. Am., Genetics Soc. Am., Am. Soc. Naturalists, Soc. Devel. Biology, Entomol. Soc. Am., Genetics Soc. Can., Genetics Soc. Korea, Sigma Xi (pres. Northwestern U. chpt. 1966-67) Home: 2890 Fredric Ct Northbrook IL 60062-7504

KING, ROBERT EDWARD, retired pharmacy educator; b. Zanesville, Ohio, Dec. 27, 1923; s. Ray Harrison and Edna Elizabeth (Bowman) K.; m. Jane Wanner Klein, Aug. 12, 1950; children: Susan J., Timothy P., Peter R., Christina A., Jonathan D. BS in Pharmacy, Ohio State U., 1944; PhD in Pharmaceutical Chemistry, U. Minn., 1948. Rsch. assoc. Merck Sharp & Dohme, West Point, Pa., 1948-61; prof. pharmacy Phila. Coll. Pharmacy and Sci., 1961-86, prof. emeritus, 1986—. Author: Remington's Pharmaceutical Sciences, 1965-85; editor: (jour.) Parenteral Drug Assn., 1966-78. Republican. Episcopalian. Avocations: reading, gardening. Home: 3475 Aquetong Rd Doylestown PA 18901-9233

KING, ROBERT HENRY, minister, church denomination executive, former educator; b. Sunny South, Ala., Apr. 1, 1922; s. Henry C. and Della S. (Bettis) K.; m. Edna Jean McCord, June 1, 1949; children: Jocelyn, Jann, Roger. BD, Immanuel Luth. Sem., Greensboro, N.C., 1949; MEd, U. Pitts., 1956; MA, Ind. U., 1968, PhD, 1969. Ordained to ministry Luth. Ch.—Mo. Synod, 1949. Pastor Victory Luth. Ch., Youngstown, Ohio, 1949-57, St. Philip Luth. Ch., Chgo., 1957-65; asst. prof. Concordia Tchrs. Coll., River Forest, Ill., 1968-70; prof. edn. Lincoln U., Jefferson City, Mo., 1970-87; v.p. Luth. Ch.—Mo. Synod, St. Louis, 1986—. Pastor Pilgrim Luth. Ch., Freedom, Mo., 1977-97; dir. lay

ministry Concordia Coll., Selma, Ala., 1987-90; vis. instr. Concordia Sem., St. Louis, 1989—; dir. workshop Obot Idim Sem., Nigeria, 1990. Contbr. articles to religious jours. Mem. Jefferson City Sch. Bd., 1973-76. Lilly Found. fellow, 1965. Mem. Am. Assn. Adult Continuing Edn., Mo. Assn. Adult Continuing Edn., Phi Delta Kappa. Lutheran. Office: 901 Roland Ct Jefferson City MO 65101-3576

KING, ROBERT HOWARD, marketing professional; b. Excelsior Springs, Mo., June 28, 1921; s. Howard Churchill King and Nancy (Henry) King Eaton; m. Nancy Brown (dec.); children: John Mcfelley (dec.), Mary Nan King Murphy, Sarah Ann King Robinson; m. Marjorie Kerr, Feb. 26, 1966 (dec.). Student, Kenyon Coll., 1938-40. V.p. sales Ency. Britannica, Inc., Chgo., 1946-61; pres. Spencer Internat., Inc., Chgo., 1961-66; v.p. Dill-Clitherow & Co., Chgo., 1966-68; pres. Time-Life Librs., Inc., Chgo., 1968-79; chmn., pres., CEO World Book, Inc., Chgo., 1979-83; pres. Consumer Mktg. Internat., Inc., Christiansted, St. Croix, 1983—. Bd. dirs. Good Will, Inc., Charlotte, N.C. Capt. U.S. Army, 1942-46, World War II. Mem. Direct Selling Assn. (chmn., Hall of Fame 1980), World Fedn. Direct Selling Assns. (founder, chmn. 1978-81), Direct Selling Edn. Found. (chmn. Circle of Honor 1992), Direct Mkgt. Assn., Chgo. Club, Lighthouse Point Yacht & Racquet Club. Office: 5064 Tipperary Saint Croix VI 00820 also: 9 Estate Parara Saint Croix VI 00820 Office Fax: 340-719-4512. E-mail: doorknocker@viaccess.net.

KING, ROBERT LEE, lawyer; b. Vincennes, Ind., June 19, 1946; s. George W. and Nadine E. K.; children: Jeffrey, Kevin, Allison. Student, U. Denver, 1964-66; BS, Ind. U., 1968; JD, Harvard U., 1972. Bar: Ind. 1973, U.S. Dist. Ct. (no. dist.) Ind. 1973, Fla. 1973. Assoc. English, McCaughan and O'Bryan, Ft. Lauderdale, Fla., 1973-76; ptnr. Andrews, Voorheis, Lehrer & Baggett, Ft. Lauderdale, 1976-86, Birr & King, P.A., Ft. Lauderdale, 1986-96; pvt. practice Ft. Lauderdale, 1997—. Bd. dirs. Playa del Sol Assn., Inc., Ft. Lauderdale, 1978-2002, sec., 1987-96, treas., 1996-97, v.p., 1997-2000. Mem. Ind. Soc. CPAs, Ind. U. Alumni Assn. (pres. Ft. Lauderdale chpt. 1976-85, treas. 1986-90), Mensa, Tower Club, Sigma Chi Alumni Assn. (pres. Ft. Lauderdale chpt. 1981, treas. 1987—). Democrat. Methodist. Avocations: basketball, theater. Office: 2780 E Oakland Park Blvd Fort Lauderdale FL 33306

KING, ROBERT LEROY, business administration educator; b. Decatur, Ga., Jan. 22, 1931; s. John Todd and Charlotte (Stringer) K.; m. Helen Butler Leaptrott, Mar. 25, 1956; children: Robert Todd, Keith Alan, John Christopher. BBA, U. Ga., 1952; MA, Mich. State U., 1953, PhD, 1960; Dr honoris causa, Oskar Lange Acad. Econs., Wroclaw, Poland, 1992. Asst. prof. mktg. U. S.C., Columbia, 1957-61, assoc. prof., 1961-65; prof. mktg. Va. Poly. Inst. and State U., Blacksburg, 1965-82, head dept., 1969-76; prof. bus. adminstrn., head dept. The Citadel, Charleston, S.C., 1982-85, Robert A. Jolley chair bus. adminstrn., 1985-90; dir. internat. bus. studies, prof. mktg. U. Richmond, 1990-96, prof. emeritus, 1996—. Cons. in field; vis. rsch. Warsaw Tech. U., Acad. Econs. in Wroclaw; overseas tchr. in field. Author: An Annotated Index to the Procs. of the Am. Mktg. Assn. Educators Confs., 1973, 90, Procs.: So. Mktg. Assn. 1973 Conf., 1974, Marketing and the New Science of Planning, 1969, Retailing: Theory and Practice for the 21st Century, 1985, Marketing in an Environment of change, 1986, Minority Marketing: Issues and Prospects, 1987, Retailing: Its Present and Future, 1988, Procs. of the 1988 Conf. of the Acad. of Internat. Bus. S.E. U.S. Region, Mktg.: Positioning for the 1990s, 1989, Marketing: Toward the 21st Century, 1991, Retailing: Reflections, Insights and Forecasts, 1991, Developments in Marketing Science, Vol. XIV, 1991, Marketing: Perspectives for the 1990s, 1992, Minority Marketing: Research Perspectives for the 1990s, 1993, Retailing: Theories and Practices for Today and Tomorrow, 1994, Retailing: End of a Century and a Look to the Future, 1997, Internat. Conf. Procs. of Am. Acad. Advt.: 2001 Asia-Pacific Conf., 2001, Internat. Conf. Procs. of Am. Acad. Advt., 2203, Asia-Pacific Conf., 2003; contbr. numerous articles to profl. jours. With AUS, 1953-55, maj. Res., 1955-76. Grantee Ford Found., 1964-65, Va. Poly. Inst. and State U., 1979-82, Citadel Devel. Foun., 1982-90. Mem. Am. Acad. Advt. (exec. sec. 1986-2002, dir. conf. svcs. 2002—, book rev. editor Jour. Advt. 1983-94), Am. Mktg. Assn., Acad. Mktg. Sci. (bd. govs. 1988-94, chmn. bd. govs. 1988-90, v.p. fin., treas. 1986-88), Assn. for Consumer Rsch., Acad. Internat. Bus., Am. Ass. for Advancement of Slavic Studies, Decision Scis. Inst., So. Conf. Slavic Studies, So. Mktg. Assn. (pres. 1972-73), Delta Sigma Pi, Omicron Delta Epsilon, Omicron Delta Kappa, Beta Gamma Sigma. Baptist. Avocations: protography, classical music, history, travel. Home: 2440 Edgeview Ln Midlothian VA 23113-9618 Office: U Richmond Sch Bus Am Acad Advertising Richmond VA 23173 E-mail: rking@richmond.edu.

KING, ROBERT LEWIS, lawyer; b. Johnson City, Tenn., June 20, 1950; s. Herbert and Ruth Marie K. BA, Earlham Coll., 1973; MS, Columbia U., 1974; JD, U. Tenn., 1985; SJD, Widener U., 2003. Bar: Tenn. 1986, D.C. 1989. Fgn. corr. AP, Paris, 1971-72; reporter The Miami (Fla.) Herald, 1974-75; polit. editor The Courier-Post, Cherry Hill, N.J., 1975-78; prof. communications East Tenn. State U., Johnson City, 1978-88; mem. Tenn. Legislature, Nashville, 1978-84; sole practice Johnson City, 1986—. Chmn. law revision subcom. Tenn. Ho. Reps., 1978—84. Recipient Scripps-Howard Pub. Svc. citation, 1977, citation 1990 Dist. Judges for Pro Bono Svcs. to Poor. Mem. ABA (Silver Gavel award 1976), Assn. Trial Lawyers Am., Tenn. Trial Lawyers Assn., N.J. Soc. Profl. Journalists (Investigative Reporting award 1976), Am. Health Lawyers Assn. Home: 1302 Sunset Dr Johnson City TN 37604-3620 Office: PO Box 4055 CRS Johnson City TN 37602-4055 E-mail: KingLaw@chartertn.net.

KING, ROBERT LUCIEN, lawyer; b. Petaluma, Calif., Aug. 9, 1936; s. John Joseph and Ramona Margaret (Thorson) K.; m. Suzanne Nanette Parre, May 18, 1956 (div. 1973); children: Renee Michelle, Candyce Lynn, Danielle Louise, Benjamin Robert; m. Linda Diane Carey, Mar. 15, 1974 (div. 1981); 1 child, Debra; m. J'an See, Oct. 27, 1984 (div. 1989); 1 child, Jonathan F.; m. Marilyn Collins, June 15, 1991. AB in Philosophy, Stanford U., 1958, JD, 1960. Bar: Calif., N.Y. 1961. Asst. U.S. atty. U.S. Atty's. Office (so. dist.), N.Y.C., 1964-67; assoc. Debevoise & Plimpton, N.Y.C., 1960-64, 67-70, ptnr. NYC, 1970—2003, mng. ptnr. LA, 1989—95. Lectr. Practicing Law Inst., N.Y.C., ABA, Asia/Pacific Ctr. for Resolution of Internat. Bus. Disputes, CPR Inst. for Dispute Resolution. Fellow: Am. Coll. Trial Lawyers; mem.: Calif. Bar Assn., Assn. Bar City NY. Democrat. Avocation: poetry. Home: 16 Lockwood Rd Scarsdale NY 10583-5302

KING, ROBERT THOMAS, editor, freelance writer; b. Hillside, N.J., Oct. 29, 1930; s. Philip Arthur and Lucy (Davis) K.; m. Fredericka Bredow, 1978 Ed., Emmanuel Coll., Cambridge, Eng., 1948-50; BA, Birmingham (Eng.) U., 1955; postgrad., Shakespeare Inst., Stratford-Upon-Avon, Eng., 1955-56. Trainee Oxford U. Press, N.Y.C., 1957-59; chief copy editor NYU Press, 1959-61, editor, 1961-63, mng. editor, 1963-66; dir. U. S.C. Press, Columbia, 1966-84. Contbr. articles to profl. jours., mags., newspapers. Recipient Lucy Hampton Bostick award, 1978. Mem. Am. Assn. Univ. Presses (bd. dirs. 1972-74, chmn. goals and long-range problems com.), Andiron Club, Grolier Club, Torch Club (Columbia). Episcopalian (dir. The Episcopalian, vestry, lic. lay reader). Home: 3994 Old Douglass Rd Blackstock SC 29014-8539

KING, ROBERTA See CINCA, SILVIA

KING, RONALD AMOS, federal official, communications professional, retired; b. Livingston, Mont., July 1, 1942; s. Amos Jefferson and Annie Margaret King; m. Lucinda Ann McIntire, Feb. 20, 1959; 1 child, Kerrilee Boggio. AS, Southwestern Coll., 1973; BA, NYU, 1980; MPA, Golden Gate U., 1983. Enlisted USN, 1960, advanced through grades to sr. chief petty officer, adminstr. USN Comdr. Cruiser-Destroyer Flotilla II, 1966-67, instr. USN Combined Svc. Support Program Sch. Alameda, Calif., 1967-70, chief adminstrn. Naval Investigative Svc. Taipei, Taiwan, 1970-71, chief adminstrn. Comdr. Task Force 157 Fleet Post Office N.Y.C., 1974-75, adminstrv. officer USS Milwaukee Norfolk, Va., 1975-78, ret. active duty, 1979; mgmt. analyst USN Manpower and Materials Analysis Ctr., Norfolk, 1978-83, U.S. Dept. Energy, Idaho Falls, Idaho, 1983-87, fed. mgr. Butte, Mont., 1987-92, comm. dir. Idaho Falls, 1993—2003; owner King Consulting LLC, Idaho Falls, Idaho, 2003—. Editor (quar. jour.) Survival Today, 1973. Decorated Vietnam Svc. medal USN, 1965, Nat. Def. Svc. medal USN, 1965, Joint Svcs. Commendation medal USN, 1970, Chinese Meritorious Rememberance medal USN, 1971. Mem. Greater Idaho Falls C. of C. (bd. dirs. 1993-2002), Eagle Rock Masonic Lodge, AEC Sportsmens Club. Methodist. Avocations: traveling, hiking, photography. Home and Office: 2670 Ridgecrest Dr Idaho Falls ID 83404-8312 E-mail: rking235@msn.com.

KING, RONALD BAKER, federal judge; b. San Antonio, Aug. 16, 1953; s. Donald Dick and Elaine (Baker) K.; m. Cynthia Sauer, June 7, 1975; children: Karen Elizabeth, Ronald Baker Jr., Kelsey Ann. BA with high honors, So. Meth. U., 1974; JD with high honors, U. Tex., 1977. Bar: Tex. 1977, U.S. Dist. Ct. (we. dist.) Tex. 1980, U.S. Ct. Appeals (5th cir.) 1981, U.S. Tax Ct. 1985. Briefing atty. Supreme Ct. Tex., Austin, 1977-78; assoc. Foster, Lewis, Langley, Gardner & Banack Inc., San Antonio, 1978-82, ptnr., 1982-88; judge U.S. Bankruptcy Ct. (we. dist.) Tex., San Antonio, 1988—. Mem. Tex. Bar Assn., Nat. Conf. Bankruptcy Judges. Presbyterian. Avocation: basketball. Office: US Bankruptcy Ct PO Box 1439 San Antonio TX 78295-1439

KING, RONALD LEE, accountant, government agency official; b. Scottsbluff, Nebr., Aug. 23, 1941; s. Fred and Dorothy Eldean (Lang) K.; m. Bouala Phannavong Oudomvilay Phasiboribounbane, Dec. 7, 1974; children: Donald, Naransra, Terry. Student, Oceanside-Carlsbad Coll., 1961-62; BS in Acctg., Golden Gate U., 1966. CPA, Calif. Office mgr. Nat. Auto Supply, San Francisco, 1963-66; acct. GAO, San Francisco, 1966-68, supervisory auditor Saigon, Vietnam, 1969-72, Bangkok, 1973-75, Washington, 1975-80, GAO evaluator, 1980-83, group dir., 1983-89, asst. dir. RTC issues, 1989-95, asst. dir. facility mgmt. issues, 1996—. Agy. rep. constrn. sector Nat. Metric Council, Washington 1979-89, Fed. Constrn. Council, 1983-94; mem. conf. planning com. Adv. Bd. on Built Environment, Nat. Acad. Sci., Washington, 1981-83; vol. on assignment in Indonesia, Fin. Svc. Vol. Corps, N.Y., 2002. Cpl. USMC, 1959—63. A.P. Giannini Found. scholar, 1965. Mem. AICPA, Assn. Govt. Accts. Democrat. Lutheran.

KING, RONOLD WYETH PERCIVAL, physics educator; b. Williamstown, Mass., Sept. 19, 1905; s. James Percival and Edith Marianne Beate (Seyerlen) K.; m. Justine Merrell, June 22, 1937 (dec. Aug. 1990); 1 son, Christopher Merrell; m. Mary M. Govoni, June 1, 1991. AB, U. Rochester, 1927, S.M., 1929; PhD, U. Wis., 1932; student, U. Munich, Germany, 1928-29, Cornell U., 1929-30. Asst. in physics U. Rochester, 1927-28; Am.-German exchange student, 1929-30; White fellow in physics Cornell U., 1929-30; U. fellow in elec. engring. U. Wis., 1930-32, research asst., 1932-34; instr. physics Lafayette Coll., 1934-36, asst. prof., 1936-37; Guggenheim fellow Berlin, Germany, 1937-38; with Harvard U., 1938—, successively instr., asst. prof., assoc. prof., 1938-46, prof. applied physics, 1946-72, prof. emeritus, 1972—. Cons. electromagnetics and antennas, 1972— Author: Electromagnetic Engineering, Vol. 1, 1945, 2d edit, Fundamental Electromagnetic Theory, 1963, Transmission Lines, Antennas and Wave Guides, (with A.H. Wing and H.R. Mimmo), 1945, 2d edit., 1965, Transmission-Line Theory, 1955, 2d edit., 1965, Theory of Linear Antennas, 1956, (with T.T. Wu) Scattering and Diffraction of Waves, 1959, (with R.B. Mack and S.S. Sandler) Arrays of Cylindrical Dipoles, 1968, (with C.W. Harrison, Jr.) Antennas and Waves: A Modern Approach, 1969, Tables of Antenna Characteristics, 1971, (with G.S. Smith et al) Antennas in Matter, 1981 (with S. Prasad) Fundamental Electromagnetic Theory and Applications, 1986, (with M. Owens and T.T. Wu) Lateral Electromagnetic Waves Theory and Applications to Communications, Geophysical Exploration and Remote Sensing, 1992 (with G. Fikioris and R.B. Mack) Cylindrical Depole Arrays, 2002; also articles in field. Guggenheim fellow Europe, 1937, 58, IBM scholar Northeastern U., 1985; recipient Disting. Service citation U. Wis., 1973, Pender award U. Pa., 1986. Fellow IEEE (Centennial medal 1984, Grad. Edn. award 1997, Disting. Educator award 2001), AAAS, Am. Acad. Arts and Scis., Am. Phys. Soc.; mem. IEEE Antennas and Propagation Soc. (Disting. Achievement award 1991, Chento Tai Disting. Educator award 2001), AAUP, Internat. Sci. Radio Union, Bavarian Acad. Sci. (contbg. mem.), Phi Beta Kappa, Sigma Xi. Home: 92 Hillcrest Pky Winchester MA 01890-1440 Office: Gordon McKay Lab 9 Oxford St Cambridge MA 02138-2901

KING, ROSALYN MERCITA, social science researcher; b. Jacksonville, Fla., Aug. 16, 1948; d. Morris Charles and Marie (Coleman) K. BS, Howard U., 1970, MA, 1972; EdD, Harvard U., 1979. Dir. police youth project NCCJ, Washington, 1970-73; placement coord. U. North Fla., Jacksonville, 1973-74, instr., student support counselor, 1973-75; career edn. program coord. Roxbury/Harvard Sch. Program, Cambridge, Mass., 1976; rsch. analyst Spl. Commn. on Unequal Ednl. Opportunity Mass. Ho. of Reps., Boston, 1977; program coord. Freedom House, Inc., Roxbury, Mass., 1977-78; sr. program assoc. Expand Assocs., Inc., Silver Spring, Md., 1979; sr. assoc., dir. rsch. Mark Battle Assocs., Inc., Washington, 1980; dir. planning, program devel. and tech. assistance PUSH-Excel Inst. Research and Tng., Washington, 1981; rsch. assoc. So. Ctr. Studies in Pub. Policy Clark Coll., Atlanta, 1981-84; pres. Info. Rsch. Network Svc., Alexandria, Va., 1984—, Bathshua's Greetings, Alexandria, 1988—. Chief racial stats. U.S. Bur. Census, Washington, 1988; vis. prof. psychology Coppin State Coll., Balt., 1989-90; faculty rsch. assoc. U. Md., College Park, 1990-91; adj. lectr. dept. psychology George Mason U., Fairfax, Va., 1991—; adj. prof. psychology Prince George's C.C., Andrews AFB, 1991-94, Mary Washington Coll., Fredericksburg, Va., 1992-93, Catonsville (Md.) C.C., 1991-96, lectr., 1994-96; sr. pub. health analyst Agy. for HIV/AIDS Comm. Pub. Health, Washington, 1992-94; from assoc. prof. to prof. psychology and chair Ctr. for Tchg. Excellence No. Va. Region, No. Va. C.C., Loudoun campus, Sterling, Va., 1996—. Contbr. articles to profl. jours. Mem. Am. Psychol. Soc., Am. Psychol. Assn., Soc. for the Tchg. of Psychology, Psi Chi, Phi Delta Kappa. E-mail: rosalynmercita.king@worldnet.att.net., roking@nvcc.edu.

KING, ROSEMARY M. protective services official, poet; b. Phila., Oct. 22, 1951; d. Thomas and Kathaleen Roslyn Dukes; m. Freddie Lee King, Sr., Mar. 18, 1972 (div.); 1 child, Freddie Lee Jr. B in Humans Svcs., Antioch U., Phila., 1984, MA, 1985. With Hosp. U. Pa., Phila., 1980—85, Palmer, Biezup & Henderson, Phila., 1985—86, Temple U. Hosp., Phila., 1986—87; police officer City of Phila., 1987—. Pub., poet calander of monthly poems, 1999—. Trainer Drug Abuse Resistance Edn. Program, Phila., 1990—, Gang Resistance Edn. Program., Phila., 1993—; mem. Big Sisters Phila., Phila., 2000—. Sgt. USAF Res., 1979—84. Mem.: Fraternal Order Police, Guardian Civic League. Democrat. Roman Catholic. Avocations: reading, writing, travel.

KING, ROY MICHAEL, music educator; b. New Orleans, Nov. 7, 1959; s. Julian L. and Ruth V. King; m. Monya L. King, July 7, 1984; 1 child, Olivia L. B.Mus.Edn., La. State U., 1984, M. Music and Conducting, 1998. Asst. dir. bands East Coweta H.S., Senoia, Ga., 1984—86; dir. bands Fairdale H.S., Louisville, 1986—87; asst. dir. bands Pine Forest H.S., Pensacola, Fla., 1988—93, dir. bands, 1993—96; grad. asst. La. State U., Baton Rouge, 1996—98, asst. dir. bands, 1998—. Mem.: Nat. Band Assn., Coll. Band Dirs. Nat. Assn., La. Music Educators Assn. (bd. dirs. 2002—), Phi Kappa Lambda, Kappa Kappa Psi, Phi Beta Mu. Republican. Episcopalian. Avocation: fishing. Home: 950 S Foster #31 Baton Rouge LA 70806 Office: Louisiana State Univ 292 Band Hall Baton Rouge LA 70803

KING, RUTH MARIE, artist, educator; b. Petaluma, Calif., Oct. 20, 1922; d. Harry Emmett Magill and Mabel Estelle Ristau; m. George W. King Jr. (dec. June 1991); 1 child, Fred R. Grad., Santa Rosa (Calif.) Jr. Coll., 1942. Pres. S.R. Art Guild, Santa Rosa; co-owner Retail and Landscape Nursery, Santa Rosa, 1952-71, King's Nursery, 1971—. Art show judge, juror Calif. State Fair; chair ann. show Workshop of Sonoma County, Sebastopol, Calif., 1998—2000, pres. Exhibitions include Apple Blossom Show. Recipient Best in Show award Sonoma-Marin Fair, 1991, 93, 95, Apple Blossom Show, 1993, 96, Meml. award, 2003, Bodega Bay Fisherman Festival, 1997. Mem. Artists Round Table. Republican. Avocations: gardening, knitting, politics. Home: 2416 Sycamore Ct Santa Rosa CA 95404-2239

KING, SANDRA L. writer; b. Catskill, N.Y., June 13, 1944; s. Galen Millard Swazey and Bernice Ethel Engle; m. Michael J. Lewis (div. Jan. 1975); 1 child, Todd Michael; m. Charles F. King, Feb. 17, 1980. Grad., LaSalle Sr. H.S., Niagara Falls, N.Y., 1961. Adminstrv. asst. Senate Majority Leader, Albany, NY, 1967—72; adminstrv. asst. for press sec. N.Y. Senate, Albany, 1973—77; exec. dir. Suffolk County Bar Assn., 1977—81. Author: Jesus, The Two Become One in Him, 1998, Exodus, God's Portrait of Jesus, 1999, Jesus, the Beginning and the End, 2002. Vol. Meals on Wheels, Port Jefferson, NY, 1982—84. Avocations: bowling, walking, singing, reading, scriptures.

KING, SHARON LOUISE, lawyer; b. Ft. Wayne, Ind., Jan. 12, 1932; AB, Mt. Holyoke Coll., 1954; JD with distinction, Valparaiso U., 1957; LLM in Taxation, Georgetown U., 1961. Bar: Ind. 1957, D.C. 1958, Ill. 1962. Trial atty. tax divsn. U.S. Dept. Justice, 1958-62; sr. counsel Sidley & Austin, Chgo. Bd. dirs. Lawyer's Com. for Better Housing, Inc. Fellow Am. Coll. Tax Counsel; mem. ABA (chmn. com. closely-held corps. taxation sect. 1979-81, regulated pub. utilities com. taxation sect. 1982-83, coun. dir. taxation sect. 1983-86), Chgo. Bar Assn. (bd. mgrs. 1973-75, chmn. fed. tax com. 1983-84), Ill. State Bar Assn. (counsel dir. sect. fed. taxation 1989-91), Women's Bar Assn. Ill. Found. (bd. dirs., v.p., dir. scholarship). Office: Sidley & Austin Bank One Plz 425 W Surf St Apt 605 Chicago IL 60657-6139

KING, SHELDON SELIG, medical center administrator, educator; b. N.Y.C., Aug. 28, 1931; s. Benjamin and Jeanne (Fritz) King; m. Ruth Arden Zeller, June 26, 1955 (div. 1987); children: Tracy Elizabeth, Meredith Ellen, Adam Bradley; m. Xenia Tonesk, 1987. AB, NYU, 1952; MS, Yale U., 1957. Adminstrv. intern Montefiore Hosp., N.Y.C., 1952; adminstrv. asst. Mt. Sinai Hosp., N.Y.C., 1957—60, asst. dir., 1960—66, dir. planning, 1966—68; exec. dir. Albert Einstein Coll. Medicine-Bronx Mcpl. Hosp. Ctr., Bronx, NY, 1968—72; asst. prof. Albert Einstein Coll. Medicine, N.Y.C., 1968—72; dir. hosps. and clinics Univ. Hosp., assoc. clin. prof. U. Calif., San Diego, 1972—81; acting head div. health care scis., dept. cmty. medicine U. Calif. Sch. Medicine, 1978—81; assoc. v.p. Stanford U., 1981—85, clin. assoc. prof. cmty., family and preventive medicine; exec. v.p. Stanford U. Hosp., 1981—85, pres., 1986—89, Cedars-Sinai Med. Ctr., L.A., 1989—94, CEO, 1989—94; exec. v.p. Salick Health Care, Inc., L.A., 1994—99, pres. eastern region, 1996—98; interim dir. UCLA Med. Ctr., 1995; interim COO INFOHEALTH Mgmt. Cons. Corp., 1999—2000, bd. dirs., 2000—; prin. Creative Intellectual Commerce, 2001—; adminstrv. intern Montefiore Hosp., N.Y.C., 1955. Mem. adminstrv. bd. Coun. of Tchg. Hosps., 1981—86, chmn. adminstrv. bd., 1985; preceptor George Washington U., Ithaca Coll., Yale U., U. Mo., CUNY; chmn. health care com. San Diego County Immigration Coun., 1974—77, adv. coun. Calif. Health Facilities Commn., 1977—82; chmn. ad hoc bd. advisors Am. Bd. Internal Medicine, 1985—91; mem. exec. com. St. Joseph Health Sys., 1990—94; acting chmn. Am. Health Properties, 1996—; nat. adv. com. Robert Wood Johnson Exec. Nurse Fellows Program, 1998—. Mem. editl. adv. bd. (book) Who's Who in Health Care, 1977, mem. editl. bd., 1979—84. Bd. dirs. hosp. coun. San Diego and Imperial Counties, 1974—77, treas., 1976, pres., 1977; bd. dirs. United Way San Diego, 1975—80, Vol. Hosps. Am., 1990—94; mem. Accreditation Coun. for Grad. Med. Edn., 1987—90, Prospective Payment Assessment Commn., 1987—90, Inst. of Medicine, 1988—; bd. dirs. Hosp. Fund, 1987—2000. With U.S. Army, 1952—55. Fellow: APHA, Am. Hosp. Assn. (governing coun. Met. sect. 1983—86, coun. on fin. 1987, ho. of dels. 1987—89), Am. Coll. Health Care Execs.; mem.: Am. Podiatric Med. Assn. (project coun. 2000 1985—86), Calif. Hosp. Assn. (trustee 1978—81). E-mail: xenshel@theriver.com.

KING, STEPHEN EDWIN, novelist, screenwriter, director; b. Portland, Maine, Sept. 21, 1947; s. Donald and Nellie Ruth (Pillsbury) K.; m. Tabitha Jane Spruce, Jan. 2, 1971; children: Naomi Rachel, Joseph Hillstrom, Owen Phillip. BS, U. Maine, 1970. Tchr. English, Hampden (Maine) Acad., 1971-73; writer in residence U. Maine at Orono, 1978-79. Novels include Carrie, 1974, 'Salem's Lot, 1975, The Shining, 1976, The Stand, 1978, The Dead Zone, 1979, Firestarter, 1980, Danse Macabre, 1981, Cujo, 1981, Different Seasons, 1982, The Dark Tower: The Gunslinger, 1982, Christine, 1983, Pet Sematary, 1983, The Talisman, 1984, Cycle of the Werewolf, 1985, Skeleton Crew, 1986, It, 1986, The Eyes of the Dragon, 1987, Misery, 1987, The Dark Tower: The Drawing of the Three, 1987, The Tommyknockers, 1987, The Dark Half, 1989, The Stand (uncut), 1990, Four Past Midnight, 1990, The Dark Tower III: The Waste Lands, 1991, Needful Things, 1991, Gerald's Game, 1992, Dolores Claiborne, 1992, Insomnia, 1994, Rose Madder, 1995, Desperation, 1996, The Green Mile (serial), 1996, Bag of Bones, 1997, Wizard & Glass, 1997, The Girl Who Loved Tom Gordon, 1999, Storm of the Century, 1999; short story Night Shift (collection), 1978, Nightmares and Dreamscapes, 1993, Creepshow (comic), 1982, The Plant (self pub.), 1983, 1984, My Pretty Pony, 1988, Dolan's Cadillac, 1989, Six Stories, 1997, On Writing, 2000, Dreamcatcher, 2001, Black House, 2001, Everything's Eventual, 2002, From a buick 8, 2002, Wolves of the Calla, 2003; author numerous other short stories; (as Richard Bachman) Rage, 1977, The Long Walk, 1979, Roadwork, 1981, The Running Man, 1982, Thinner, 1984, Insomnia, 1993, The Regulators, 1996; author numerous short story screenplays; writer, creator TV program "Stephen King's Golden Years", 1991; film director: Maximum Overdrive, 1986; original screenplay: Sleepwalkers, 1991; actor: Knightriders, 1981, Creepshow, 1982, Maximum Overdrive, 1986, Creepshow II, 1988, The Shawshank Redemption, 1995 (USC Scriptor Awd. 1995); creator, writer (TV mini-series) The Stand, 1994, Storm of the Century, 1999 (mini-series). Recipient Medal for Disting. Contbn. to Am. Letters, The Nat. Book Found., 2003. Mem. Author's Guild Am., Screen Artists Guild, Screen Writers of Am., Writer's Guild. Democrat. Office: 49 Florida Ave Bangor ME 04401-3005*

KING, STEPHEN EMMETT, educational administrator; b. Hopkinsville, Ky., June 1, 1942; s. Emmett Southall and Ruth Virginia (Burchfield) K.; m. Linda Johnston, Nov. 11, 1967. MusB, West Ky. U., 1964; MS, Radford U., 1975; EdD, Va. Poly. Inst. and State U., 1991. Dir. bands Coeburn (Va.) H.S., 1964-68, William Byrd H.S., Vinton, Va., 1968-86; supr. fine arts Roanoke County Schs., Roanoke, Va., 1986-97; vis. asst. prof. music edn. Va. Poly. Inst. and State U., Blacksburg, 1997—. Contbr. articles to profl. jours. Active Roanoke Symphony Soc. Bd., 1994-2000—, chair edn. com. 1997-2000—; legis. com Art Coun. Blue Ridge, 1998-2002. Mem. Music Educators Nat. Conf., Va. Edn. Assn., Va. Band and Orch. Dirs. Assn. (sec. 1984-86, pres.-elect 1986-88, pres. 1988-90, Philip Fuller Svc. award 2000), Am. Sch. Band Dirs. Assn. (state chmn. 1986-88), Va. Alliance for Arts Edn. (bd. dirs. 1991-96, sec. 1993-96), Va. Music Edn. Assn. (exec. bd. dirs., pres.-elect 1990-92, pres. 1992-94, v.p. 1994-96, chair editl. bd. 1996-98), Phi Delta Kappa, Phi Beta Mu, Phi Mu Alpha Sinfonia. Home: 5250 Keffer Rd Catawba VA 24070-2122 Office: Va Poly Inst and State U Dept Musc 241 Squires (0240) Blacksburg VA 24061 E-mail: sking@infionline.net.

KING, STEVE, congressman; b. Storm Lake, Iowa, May 28, 1949; m. Marilyn King; 3 children. Student, N.W. Mo. State U., 1967-70. Mem. Iowa Senate from 6th dist., Des Moines, 1996—2002; vice chair natural resources and environ. com.; mem. appropriations com., mem. bus. and labor rels. com.; mem. commerce com., mem. state govt. com.; mem. U.S. Ho. of Reps from 5th Iowa dist., 2003—. Mem. St. Martin's Cath. Ch.; bd. dirs. Odebolt Cmty. Housing. Mem. Iowa Cattleman's Assn., Land Improvement Contractors Am., U.S. C. of C., Odebolt C. of C., SAC County Farm Bur. Republican. Office: 1432 Longworth House Office Bldg Washington DC 20515-1505 E-mail: steve_king@legis.state.ia.us.*

KING, STEVEN C. real estate agent, retired research scientist; b. Plainfield, NH, Dec. 12, 1921; s. Clarence Wheeler King and Flora Belle Rogers; m. Teresa Mary Walker, Dec. 9, 1978 (dec. May 25, 2002); m. Ellena Sanborn Foss (dec. Nov. 10, 1963); children: Gordon, Nancy Petersen; m. Peggy J. Powell. BS, U. N.H., 1947; MS, Cornell U., 1951, PhD, 1953. Cert. Comml. Pilot, single & multi-engine 1969. Assoc. prof. Cornell U., Ithaca, NY, 1953—56; regional coord. Animal Sci. Divsn. USDA, West Lafayette, Ind., 1956—59; geneticist Arbor Acres, Glastonbury, Conn., 1959—60; poultry br. chief Animal Sci. Divsn. USDA, Beltsville, Md., 1960—63, assoc. dir. Animal Sci. Divsn., 1964—67, assoc. dir. Rsch. Program Devel. Staff Washington, 1967—70, dep. adminstr. Agrl. Rsch. Svc. Beltsville, 1970—72, regional adminstr. Agrl. Rsch. Svc., 1972—83; pres. Solar King Supply, Inc., Silver Spring, Md., 1983—86; real estate sales Weichert Realtors, North Potomac, Md., 1986—2000. Author: (book) Changing Times, 2002. Dir. Villages of Wesley Chapel Home Owners Assoc., 2000—02. First lt. AC U.S. Army, 1943—46, China-Burma-India. Fellow: AAAS (none). Liberal. Roman Catholic. Avocation: photography, fishing, swimming, gardening. Home: 162 River Chase Dr Bainbridge GA 39819 Personal E-mail: kingsc@earthlink.net.

KING, STEVEN HAROLD, health physicist; b. Stamford, Conn., June 27, 1959; s. Richard H. and Joan W. (Weaver) K.; m. Kim Yvonne Bulmer, June 18, 1983; children: Christopher K., Brandon S., Arielle L. BA, SUNY, Buffalo, 1981, MA, 1983. Diplomate Am. Bd. Med. Physics, Am. Bd. Health Physics. Asst. health physicist Milton S. Hershey Med. Ctr. Pa. State U., Hershey, 1983—86, assoc. health physicist, 1986 , laser safety officer, 1989—, sr. instr., assoc. dir. divsn. health physics, 2003. Grad. program com. mem. Pa. State U., Harrisburg, Pa., 1989—. Author: (with others) Handbook of Management of Radiation Protection Programs, 1991; contbr. articles to profl. jours. Mem. Am. Assn. Physicists in Medicine, Am. Nuclear Soc., Health Physics Soc. (chair admissions com. 1989-91, pres. Susquehanna Valley chpt. 1989-90, 2001-02). Office: Milton S Hershey Med Ctr 500 University Dr Hershey PA 17033-2391 E-mail: sking@psu.edu.

KING, SUSAN BENNETT, retired glass company executive; b. Sioux City, Iowa, Apr. 29, 1940; d. Francis Moffatt Bennett and Marjorie (Rittenhouse) Sillin; m. Stephen P. Glantz. AB, Duke U., 1962. Legis. asst. U.S. Senate, Washington, 1963-66; dir. Nat. Com. for Effective Congress, Washington, 1967-71, Ctr. Pub. Financing of Elections, Washington, 1972-75; exec. asst. to chmn. Fed. Election Commn., Washington, 1975-77; chmn. U.S. Consumer Product Safety Commn., Washington, 1978-81; dir. consumer affairs Corning (N.Y.) Glass Works, 1982, v.p. corp. communications, 1983-86; pres. Steuben Glass, N.Y.C., 1987-92; sr. v.p. corp. affairs Corning Inc., 1992-94. Trustee Duke U., Durham, NC, 1987—2001, Eurasia Found., Washington, Nat. Pub. Radio Found.; chmn. bd. MDC, Inc., 1995—, Triangle Cmty. Found., 2002—; trustee Triangle Cmty. Found., T; bd. dirs. MPC, Inc., 1995—. Fellow Inst. Politics, Harvard U., 1981.

KING, TALMADGE E. physician; b. Feb. 24, 1948; BA, Gustavus Adolphus Coll., 1970; MD, Harvard U., 1974. Vice chair dept. medicine U. Colo., Denver, 1992-97; exec. v.p. Nat. Jewish Med. and Rsch. Ctr., Denver, 1992-95; vice chmn. medicine U. Calif., San Francisco, 1997—; chief med. svc. San Francisco Gen. Hosp., 2003. Co-author: Nonneoplastic Disorders of the Lower Respiratory Tract, 2002; editor: Interstitial Lung Disease, 2003; sect. editor: Kelley's Textbook of Medicine, 1998. Trustee Gustavus Adolphus Coll., St. Peter, Minn., 1993-2002. Mem. Am. Thoracic Soc. (pres. 1997-98). Office: San Francisco Gen Hosp Med Svcs 1001 Potrero Ave Rm 5h22 San Francisco CA 94110-3594

KING, THOMAS, physician, physiology educator; b. Shanghai, June 1, 1934; came to U.S., 1965; s. Tung Ming and Yen Vee (Sung) K.; m. Amy Penn, July 15, 1959; children: Susan, Caroline. MB, Ch.B., U. Edinburgh, Scotland, 1959, MD, 1963. Asst. prof. medicine Cornell U. Med. Ctr., N.Y.C., 1970-73, assoc. prof. medicine, 1973—, acting chief div. pulmonary and critical care medicine, 1982-85, 91-93, assoc. prof. physiology and biophysics, 1975—. Recipient Pulmonary Acad. award Nat. Heart & Lung Inst., 1972-77. Fellow Royal Coll. Physicians London, Am. Coll. Chest Physicians; mem. N.Y. Trudeau Soc. (pres. 1978-79), Chinese-Am. Med. Soc. (pres. 1984-85), Am. Thoracic Soc., Med. Rsch. Soc. of U.K., Am. Fedn. Clin. Rsch., Am. Physiology Soc. Office: Cornell U Med Ctr 520 E 70th St # 505 New York NY 10021-9800

KING, TIM, orchestra executive; b. Mt. Sterling, Ky. divorced; 1 child, Sara. B Music Edn., Ea. Ky. U.; MusM, U. Louisville. Dir. edn. Louisville Orch., 1985-88, dir. ops., 1987-92, exec. dir., 2000—; gen. mgr. Louisville Gardens, 1992-95; v.p. Ky. Ctr. for Arts, 1995 2000. Soloist Louisville Bach Soc., also local ensembles. Office: Louisville Orch 300 W Main St Ste 100 Louisville KY 40202-2930

KING, VIRGINIA, librarian; b. Akron, Ohio, May 12, 1917; d. Wilson Reed and Eunice Mina (White) K. B.S. in Music Edn., Greenville Coll. (Ill.), 1939, B.A., 1941; M.Music, U. So. Calif., 1954, M.S.L.S., 1967. Music tchr. L.A. Pacific Coll., 1943-45, 46-65, Greenville Coll. (Ill.), 1945-46; music prof. and libr. Azusa Pacific U. (Calif.), 1965-82, music and periodicals libr., 1982-89, ret., 1989. Named Outstanding Tchr., Associated Student Body Azusa Pacific U., 1975.

KING, W. DAVID, magistrate judge; BS, Murray State U., 1967; JD, U. Ky., 1972. Bar: Ky. 1972, U.S. Dist. Ct. (we. dist.) Ky. Pvt. practice, Paducah, Ky., 1972—79; magistrate judge U.S. Dist. Ct. (we. dist.) Ky., Paducah, 1979—. With U.S. Army, 1968-70. Office: US Dist Ct We Dist Ky Fed Bldg Rm 330 501 Broadway St Paducah KY 42001-6856 Fax: 270-415-6480.

KING, WARREN R. judge; Grad., Rensselaer Polytech. Inst.; JD, Am. U.; LLM, Yale U. Atty. U.S. Dist. Ct. D.C.; chief grand jury/intake divsn., dep. and acting chief divsn. Superior Ct. Washington; with Office of Improvements in Adminstrn. of Justice U.S. Dept. Justice; assoc. judge Superior Ct. D.C., Washington, 1981—91, U.S. Ct. Appeals (D.C. cir.), Washington, 1991—, D.C. Ct. Appeals, Washington. Mem. faculty Antioch Sch. Law, 1975—; mem. staff Atty. Gen.'s task force on violent crime; mem. hearing com. Bd. Profl. Responsibility. With USN. Office: Dist of Columbia Court of Appeals 500 Indiana Ave NW Rm 6000 Washington DC 20001-2131

KING, WAYNE EDGAR, journalist, educator; b. McDowell County, N.C., Mar. 31, 1939; s. Weldon Edgar and Mary King; m. Nina Davis, (div. June 1978); m. Paula Theodore Carroll, July 16, 1984. BA in Journalism, U. N.C., 1964. Reporter, editor The Detroit Free Press, 1964-69; editor, bur. chief, corr. The N.Y. Times, N.Y.C., 1969-93; dir. journalism program Wake Forest U., Winston-Salem, N.C., 1993—. Working group on disability in U.S. Pres. The White House, 1996. Mem. editl. bd. Acad. Mag., Washington, 1996-2002. Recipient Pulitzer prize, 1968. Mem. AAUP, Torch Club. Home: 1901 Waycross Dr Winston Salem NC 27106-3416 E-mail: kingwe@wfu.edu.

KING, WILLARD FAHRENKAMP (MRS. EDMUND LUDWIG KING), Spanish language educator; b. Roswell, N.Mex., July 13, 1924; d. W.F. and Willard (Pickerill) Fahrenkamp; m. Edmund Ludwig King, Jan. 29, 1951. Student, Tex. Christian U., 1940-41; BA, U. Tex., 1943, MA, 1946; PhD, Brown U., 1957. Instr. Spanish U. Tex., 1946-47, 49-50; instr. Spanish Brown U., 1950-51, Bryn Mawr (Pa.) Coll., 1958-60, asst. prof., 1960-64, assoc. prof., 1964-70, prof. Spanish, 1970—, Dorothy Nepper Marshall prof. Hispanic studies, 1976—, chmn. dept. Spanish, 1964-89, dir. Hispanic studies program, 1971-92. Corporator Internat. Inst. in Spain, resident dir., 1991-93. Author: Prosa novelística y academias literarias en el siglo XVII, 1963, Juan Ruiz de Alarcón, letrado y dramaturgo, 1989; also articles; editor, translator: Lope de Vega, El Caballero de Olmedo, 1972; translator: Américo Castro, The Spaniards, 1971; editor, commentator Agustín Moreto, El desdén, con el desdén, 1996. Guggenheim fellow, 1965-66 Mem. MLA, Renaissance Soc. Am., Phi Beta Kappa. Home: 171 Western Way Princeton NJ 08540-7207 Office: Thomas Libr Bryn Mawr Coll Bryn Mawr PA 19010

KING, WILLIAM BRUCE, retired lawyer; b. Boston, June 3, 1932, s. Gilbert and Frances (Hood) K.; m. Sheila Malone, July 9, 1955; children: Stephen Bruce, Rachel Creath, Christopher Bruce. AB, Harvard U., 1954, LL.B., 1959. Bar: Mass. 1959. Assoc. firm Goodwin Procter, Boston, 1959-67, ptnr., 1968-99, of counsel, 2000—; prin. William B. King P.C., 1981-99. Mem. bd. investment Cambridge Savs. Bank, 1973—, trustee, 1969—, corporator, 1965—; sec. Bradley Real Estate, Inc., 1963-99; trustee Cambridge Heritage Trust, 1984—; dir. mem. exec. com. Cambridge Fin. Group, Inc., 1998—, Cambridge Appleton Trust, N.A., 1999—. Author: (with others) Real Estate Investment Trusts: Structures, Analysis, and Strategy, 1997. Trustee Buckingham Browne and Nichols Sch., 1970-76, sec., 1970-73, vice chmn., 1974-76; mem. Cambridge (Mass.) Hist. Commn., 1973—, vice chmn., 1973-86, chmn., 1986—; pres Cambridge Civic Assn., 1963-65; bd. govs. Nat. Assn. Real Estate Investment Trusts, 1982-88, chmn. state regulation subcom. of govt. rels. com., 1989-91. Served with USN, 1954-56. Recipient 4th Ann. Industry Leadership award Nat. Assn. Real Estate Investment Trusts, 1995. Mem. ABA, Mass. Bar Assn., Boston Bar Assn., Cambridge-Arlington-Belmont Bar Assn. (pres. 1974-75) Home: 25 Hurlbut St Cambridge MA 02138-1603 Office: Exchange Pl Boston MA 02109-2803 E-mail: basking@comcast.net.

KING, WILLIAM COLLINS, oil company executive; b. Pitts., Aug. 11, 1921; s. William Raffington and Anne Blatchford (Collins) K.; m. Carolyn Ottilie Thorne, Sept. 1, 1951; children: William R., John Thorne, Louise R., Andrew C. BSChemE, Carnegie-Mellon U., 1943; MSChemE, MIT, 1948. With Gulf Rsch. & Devel. Co. div. Gulf Oil Corp., Pitts., 1948-55, with chems. dept., 1955-57, dir. market rsch. and econ. planning chems. dept., 1957-63, world wide coord. chem. ops., 1963-67, v.p. chem. ops. in Europe and Middle East, 1967-72, dir. corp. policy analysis, 1972-80, v.p. corp. planning, 1980-85. Bd. dirs. Fertiberia, S.A., Spain, Rio Gulf Petrolquimica, S.A., Spain, Kuwait Chem. Fertilizer Co., Kuwait; spkr., 1975—, participant nat. and local programs, participant local radio programs. Contbr. articles to profl. publs. Bd. dirs. Hist. Soc. We. Pa., 1977-99, pres., 1986-90, chmn., 1990-98, vice-chmn., 1998-99, trustee emeritus, 1999 (honored with William Collins King Atrium of Senator John Heinz Pitts. Regional History Ctr., 1996); v.p., bd. dirs. Civic Light Opera Co., Pitts., 1978-86 (Golden Hall of Fame, 1996); councillor of the Atlantic Coun. of the U.S., 1985-93. Served with C.E., U.S. Army, 1943-46, CBI. Recipient Alumni Merit award Carnegie Mellon U., 1998. Fellow Am. Chem. Soc.; mem. N.Am. Soc. Corp. Planning (bd. dir. chpt. 1982-85), Strategic Mgmt. Soc., Coun. Planning Execs (conf. bd.), Am. Inst. Chem. Engrs. Clubs: Duquesne; Fox Chapel Racquet, Fox Chapel Golf (Pitts.). *Do all that you do in that way most likely to enhance the self esteem of others.*

KING, WILLIAM H., JR., lawyer; b. Richmond, Va., Nov. 4, 1940; AB, Dartmouth Coll., 1963; LLB, U. Va., 1967; MA (hon.), Dartmouth Coll., 1992. Bar: Va. 1967, Tex. 1993. Mem. McGuireWoods LLP, Richmond. Fellow Am. Bar Found., Am. Coll. Trial Lawyers; mem. ABA. Office: McGuireWoods One James Ctr Richmond VA 23219-4030 E-mail: wking@mcguirewoods.com.

KING, WILLIAM RICHARD, business educator, consultant; b. McKeesport, Pa., Dec. 24, 1938; s. Dewey Clark and Cambria Edith (Jones) K.; m. Fay Eileen Bickerton, June 20, 1958; children: James David, Suzan Lorain, Cambria H.L. BS with honors, Pa. State U., 1960; MS Case Inst. Tech, 1962, PhD, 1964. Indsl. engr. Pitts. Steel Co., 1960; instr., research fellow, research asst. Case Inst. Tech., 1960-64; asst. prof. ops. research, 1964-65; asst. prof. stats. and ops. research Air Force Inst. Tech., 1965-67; assoc. prof. bus. adminstrn. U. Pitts., 1967-69, prof., 1969-85, univ. prof., 1986—, dir. doctoral program, 1971-74, dir. Strategic Mgmt. Inst., 1980-85. On leave as profl. staff mem. U.S. Senate Budget Com., 1976-77; v.p., dir. Cleland-King, Inc., 1969-85; mgmt. cons.; chmn. Internat. Conf. on Info. Systems Profl. Corp., 1987-88; vis. prof. U. Auckland, New Zealand, 1994, Nat. U. of Singapore, 1997, City U. of Hong Kong, 1997, 98. Author: Quantitative Analysis for Marketing Management, 1967, Probability for Management Decisions, 1968, (with David Cleland) Systems Analysis and Project Management, 1968 (McKinsey Found. award 1969), 3d edit., 1983, Management: a Systems Approach, 1972, Marketing Management Information Systems, 1977, (with David Cleland) Strategic Planning and Policy, 1978, (with John Grant) The Logic of Strategic Planning, 1982; also 300 articles in profl. jours.; editor: (with David Cleland) Systems, Organizations, Analysis, Management, 1969, Project Management Handbook, 1983, 2d edit., 1989 (Inst. Indsl. Engrs. Book of Yr. award 1984); (with Gerald Zaltman) Marketing Scientific and Technical Information, 1979, (with D. I. Cleland) Strategic Planning and Management Handbook, 1987, (with P. Gray, E. McLean and H. Watson) Management of Information Systems, 1989, 2nd edit., 1994, (with V Sethi) Organizational Transformation Through Business Process Reengineering, 1998; assoc. editor: Strategic Mgmt. Jour., 1985-89, Mgmt. Sci., 1971-89, MIS Quar., 1980-82, editor-in-chief, 1983-85; area editor: Internat. Jour. Info. and Mgmt. Scis.; cons. editor Prentice Hall Info. Mgmt. Series, 1989-99; mem. editorial adv. bd. Omega: the Internat. Jour. of Mgmt. Sci., Info. Systems Rsch., Jour. Global Info. Mgmt., Jour. Mgmt. Info. Sys., Jour. Global Info. Tech. Mgmt., Jour. Market-Focused Mgmt., Info. Sys. Mgmt., IEEE Transactions on Engring. Mgmt., Encyclopedia Info. Sys. Active YMCA, YMHA; v.p., dir. Pitts. Commerce Inst., 1971-80; bd. dirs. Western Pa. Montessori Sch., 1968-71, pres., 1968-69. Served to 1st lt. USAF, 1965-67. Ford Found. Systems research fellow, 1960-62; Travelers Ins. Co. research fellow, 1963-64, External Examiner City U. of Hong Kong, 1996-99; Alumni Meml. scholar Pa. State U., 1956-60. Fellow AAAS, Decision Sci. Inst., Assn. Info. Sys.; mem. Planning Forum, Ops. Rsch. Soc. Am., Acad. Mgmt., Strategic Mgmt. Soc., Inst. Mgmt. Scis. (v.p. 1986-89, pres. 1989-90), Assn. Info. Sys. (pres. 1995), Assn. Computing Machinery, Am. Mktg. Assn., Soc. Info. Mgmt., World Future Soc., Tau Beta Pi, Beta Gamma Sigma, Alpha Pi Mu, Sigma Tau. Office: Katz Grad Sch Bus U Pitts Pittsburgh PA 15260 E-mail: billking@katz.pitt.edu.

KING, WILLIAM TERRY, retired manufacturing company executive; b. Cleve., Dec. 3, 1943; s. William T. and Marion (Rothweiler) K.; m. Judith Ann Cervantes, Oct. 22, 1943; children: Kimberly, Kelly. BSC, St. Louis U., 1968. Contr. for Can. and Latin Am., Monsanto Co., St. Louis, 1977-82, mgr. internat. fin., 1982-84, dir. ops. analysis, 1984-86, asst. contr., 1986-88, asst. controller, 1993-97; ret., 1997; v.p., contr. Fisher Controls Internat. Inc., Clayton, Mo., 1988-92. Mem. Com. to Elect A.J. Cervantes, St. Louis, 1964-65; v.p. adv. bd. dirs., exec. com., chmn. fin. and planning com. St. Mary's Health Ctr. Mem. Inst. Mgmt. Acctg. (cert.). Republican. Roman Catholic. Avocations: golf, fishing, gardening. Home: 16643 Sterling Pointe Ct Chesterfield MO 63005-4509

KING CALKINS, CAROL COLEMAN, health sciences administrator; b. L.A., May 31, 1949; d. Harold S. and Gladys (Blumenthal) Coleman; 1 child, Katrina Elizabeth King; m. Michael Steven Calkins, Oct. 10, 1987. BA in Psychology, U. Colo., 1972, PhD in Pub. Affairs, 2000; MBA, U. No.Colo., 1982. Dir. group living Nat. Jewish Med. Ctr., Denver, 1980-82, dir. clin. support svcs., 1982-83, dir. spl. projects, 1983-84, asst. dir. adminstrv. svcs., 1984, dir. adminstrv. svcs., 1984-95; dir. facilities ops. U. Colo. Health Scis. Ctr., Denver, 1995—. Asst. adj. prof. U. Colo., Denver; chair purchasing and contract subcom. Denver Health and Hosps. New Authority, 1994—96; spkr. in field. Recorder improvement process coun. Jefferson County (Colo.) Schs., 1989. Mem.: Rocky Mountain Assn. Higher Edn. Facilities Officers, Assn. Commuter Transp. (v.p. Rocky Mountain chpt. 1992), Am. Coll. Healthcare Execs., Colo. Hosp. Assn. Risk Mgrs., Pi Alpha Alpha (chpt. pres.). Avocations: weight training, horseback riding, hiking, snowboarding. Office: Fitzsimons Bldg 500 Mail Stop F410 PO Box 6508 Aurora CO 80045-0508

KINGDON, HENRY SHANNON, retired physician, biochemist, educator, executive; b. Puunene, Maui, Hawaii, July 2, 1934; s. Robert Wells and Anna Catherine (McCune) K.; m. Mary Lee Colman, June 22, 1957 (dec. Aug. 28, 1983); children: Holly, Catherine, Henry Colman; m. Jodi Kremiller, Jan. 26, 1985 AB in Chemistry, Oberlin Coll., 1956; MD, PhD in Biochemistry, Western Res. U., 1963; postgrad., U. Wash., 1962-63. Intern Univ. Hosp., Seattle, 1963-64; resident U. Wash. Affiliated Hosps., Seattle, 1964-65; practice medicine specializing in internal medicine Chgo., 1967-72, Chapel Hill, N.C., 1973-81; asst. prof. medicine and biochemistry U. Chgo., 1967-71, asso. prof., 1971-73, acting chmn. dept. medicine, summer 1971, dir. med. internship program, 1971-72; prof. medicine and biochemistry U. N.C., Chapel Hill, 1973-81; med. dir. Hyland Therapeutics div. Travenol Labs., Glendale, Calif., 1981-84; v.p., med. dir. Hyland div. Baxter Healthcare Corp., Glendale, Calif., 1984-90, v.p., gen. mgr., 1990-91; v.p. sci. affairs, chief med. officer Blood Therapy Group Baxter Healthcare Corp., Deerfield, Ill., 1991-93; v.p., med. dir. Gene Therapy Unit Baxter Biotech., Deerfield, 1993-95; v.p. tech. affairs Baxter Biotech., Deerfield, 1996-99; ret., 1999. Contbr. articles on mechanisms of blood coagulation, primary structure of proteins, and on regulation of anabolic nitrogen metabolism to profl. jours. Served with USPHS, 1965-67. Guggenheim Meml. Found. fellow, 1972-73; NIH grantee, 1957-59, 69-81 Mem. Am. Soc. Biol. Chemists, Am. Soc. Hematology, Internat. Soc. Thrombosis and Haemostasis, Central Soc. Clin. Research, So. Soc. Clin. Research, Phi Beta Kappa, Sigma Xi. Achievements include methods developed regarding eliminating AIDS and hepatitis infectivity from blood products; patentee in field. Home: 46360 Trilakes Rd Drummond WI 54832-9731 E-mail: hskingdon@aol.com. *Look it up; write it down; be on time; do a little extra.*

KINGDON, JOHN WELLS, political science educator; b. Wisconsin Rapids, Wis., Oct. 28, 1940; s. Robert Wells and Catherine (McCune) K.; m. Kirsten Berg, June 16, 1965; children: James, Tor. BA, Oberlin Coll., 1962; MA, U. Wis., 1963, PhD, 1965. Asst. prof. polit. sci. U. Mich., Ann Arbor, 1965-70, assoc. prof., 1970-75, prof., 1975-98, prof. emeritus, 1998—, chmn. dept. polit. sci., 1982-87. Author: Candidates for Office, 1968, Congressmen's Voting Decisions, 1973, 3d rev. edit., 1989, Agendas, Alternatives and Public Policies, 1984, 2d edit., 1995, America the Unusual, 1998. NSF grantee, 1978-82, Soc. Sci. Research Council grantee, 1969-70; Guggenheim fellow, 1979-80, Ctr. for Advanced Study in Behaviorial Scis. fellow, 1987-88. Fellow Am. Acad. Arts and Scis.; mem. Midwest Polit. Sci. Assn. (pres. 1987-88). Office: U Mich Dept Polit Sci Ann Arbor MI 48109

KINGHORN, CAROL ANN, school psychologist; BA in English, Libr. Sci., SUNY, Albany, 1957, MA in English, Secondary Edn., 1958; MA in Sch. Psychology, Hofstra U., 1969, PhD in Psychology, 1973. Various positions, 1953-71; assoc. prof. dept. behavioral scis. N.Y. Inst. Tech., 1971-72, 74; instr. dept. social scis. SUNY, Farmingdale, 1972-73; sch. psychologist Kings Point Sch., Great Neck, N.Y., 1972-74; lectr. grad. dept. psychology Hofstra U., 1973-74; assoc. prof. grad. dept. counselor edn. C.W. Post Coll., 1974-77; psychologist Hofstra U. Counseling Ctr., 1973-77; pvt. practice psychotherapy Hempstead and Roslyn, N.Y., 1974—; psychologist South Shore Ctr. for Psychotherapy, 1974-83; sch. psychologist Garden City (N.Y.) Pub. Schs., 1978—. Mem. Am. Psychol. Assn., Nassau County Psychol. Assn., Nassau County Psychol. Svcs. Inst. (bd. dirs. 1989—). Home: 14 St James Pl Hempstead NY 11550-1118 Office: 1405 Old Northern Blvd Roslyn NY 11576-2146 Also: 131 Fulton Ave Hempstead NY 11550-3711

KINGI, HENRY MASAO, actor, stuntman; b. L.A., Dec. 2, 1943; s. Masao D. Kingi and Henriella (Dunn) Wilkins-Washington; m. Eilene Davis; children: Deanne E., Henry Masao Jr.; m. Lindsay Wagner; children: Dorian H., Alex. Grad. high sch., L.A. Recipient Eagle Spirit award, Am. Indian Film Festival, 1999, Lifetime Achievement award, 1st Ams. in the Arts, 2001. Mem. SAG. Office: PO Box 8861 Universal City CA 91618-8861

KINGMAN, ELIZABETH YELM, anthropologist; b. Lafayette, Ind., Oct. 15, 1911; d. Charles Walter and Mary Irene (Weakley) Yelm; m. Eugene Kingman, June 10, 1939; children: Mixie Kingman Eddy, Elizabeth Anne. BA, U. Denver, 1933; MA, 1935. Asst. in anthropology U. Denver, 1932-34; mus. asst. Ranger Naturalist Staff Mesa Verde Nat. Park, Colo., 1934-38; asst. to husband in curatorial work Indian art exhibits Philbrook Art Ctr., Tulsa, 1939-42, Joslyn Art Mus., Omaha, 1947-69; tutor humnaities dept. U. Omaha, 1947-50; cjhn. bd. govs. Pi Beta Phi Settlement Sch., Gatlinburg, Tenn., 1969-72, Joslyn Art Mus., Omaha, 1947-50; tutor humanities dept. U. Omaha, 1947-50; chmn. bd. govs. Pi Beta Phi Settlement Sch., Gatlinburg, Tenn., 1969-72; asst. to husband in exhibit design mus. Tex. Tech. U., 1970-75; bibliographer Internat. Ctr. ARid and Semi-Arid Land Studies, 1974-75; libr. Sch. Am. Rsch., Santa Fe, N.Mex., 1978-86; rsch. assoc., 1986-98. V.p. Santa Fe Corral of the Westerners, 1985-86. Mem. AAUW, LWV, Archeol. Inst. Am. (v.p. Santa Fe chpt. 1981-83), Santa Fe Hist. Soc. (sec. 1981-83). Home: 604 Sunset St Santa Fe NM 87501-1118

KINGORE, EDITH LOUISE, retired geriatrics and rehabilitation nurse; b. Parsons, Kans., Nov. 18, 1922; d. George Richard and Josephine (Martin) K. Diploma, Mo. Meth. Hosp., St. Joseph, 1955. RN. Staff nurse El Cerrito Hosp., Long Beach, Calif., 1966-69; nurse Alamitos-Belmont Convalescent Hosp., Long Beach, 1973-75; staff nurse Freeman Hosp., Joplin, Mo., 1975-76, Oak Hill Osteo. Hosp., Joplin, 1976-77; surg. care and rehab. nurse St. Francis Med. Ctr., Cape Guiardo, Mo., 1977-78; psychiat. nurse Western Mo. Mental Health Ctr., Kansas City, Mo., 1978; pvt. duty nurse, 1978-83. Historian South Coast Ecumenical Coun., 1993-94. Home: 3333 Pacific Pl Apt 108 Long Beach CA 90806-1287

KINGSBERY, WALTON WAITS, JR., retired accounting firm executive; b. Evergreen, Ala., 1928; s. Walton Waits and Alpha Lee Kingsbery; m. Helen Elizabeth Clayton, 1953; children: Walton Waits, III, J. Clayton, Peter C. Student Washington and Lee U., 1945—47; BS with honors, U. Ala., 1950. CPA, N.J., N.Y., Calif., Ohio. With Price Waterhouse & Co., 1950-88, mng. pntr., 1977—82, mng. ptnr. Western area LA, 1982—87. Mem. bus. adv. bd. Bateman Eichler, Hill Richards, L.A., 1988-90, Employee Office of Atty. Gen. N.J., 1988-95; mem. adv. bd. N.J. Bur. Securities, 1993-98, N.J. Supreme Ct. Com. on Unauthorized Practice of Law, 1990—; commr. N.J. Commn. to Deter Criminal Activity, 1998-01; dir. N.J. Citizens Against Crime, Inc., 1998-01. Author booklets, papers in field. Mem. Shrewsbury (N.J.) Planning Bd., 1972—75; trustee Beech Brook, 1979, Cleve. Playhouse, 1980; clk. Village of Hunting Valley, Ohio; mem. Planning Bd., Spring Lake, NJ, 1997—; trustee Jersey Shore Med. Ctr. Found., 1999—; mem. audit com. Meridian Health Sys., 1999—; bd dirs. Greater Cleve. Growth Assn., 1978—82. With U.S. Army, 1950—53. Mem. AICPA, SAR, Nat. Assn. Accts., Ohio Soc. CPAs, N.J. Soc. CPAs, N.Y. Soc. CPAs, Calif. Soc. CPAs, Bluecoats, Newcomen Soc. N.Am., Cleve. Country Club, Union Club, Cleve. Racquet Club, Duquesne Club (Pitts.), Fifty Club, Calif. Club, Jonathan Club, Lincoln Club (L.A.), Univ. Club (N.Y.C.), Spring Lake Golf Club (trustee, exec. com., com. chmn., treas.), 200 Club, Beverly Hills Country Club (bd. govs.). *From a small town in Alabama to partner of Price Waterhouse in New York, then board member, management committee, head of the Cleveland office, then the west coast practice was a long, interesting road made easier by professional mentors, a loving wife and an understanding family. Service to the government and charitable organizations has enriched career and retirement.*

KINGSBURY, JOHN MERRIAM, botanist, educator; b. Boston, July 4, 1928; s. Willis Albert and Constance Elizabeth (Merriam) K.; m. Louise Arnold Gerken, June 6, 1956; 1 dau., Joanna Merriam. BS, U. Mass., 1950; A.M., Harvard U., 1952, PhD, 1954; Sc.D. (hon.), Dickinson Coll., 1985. Instr. Brandeis U., Waltham, Mass., 1953-54; mem. faculty N.Y. State Coll. Agr. and Life Scis., Cornell U., Ithaca, NY, 1954—83, prof. botany emeritus, 1983—; prof. clin. scis. Coll. Vet. Medicine, Cornell U., 1978-83, dir. arboretum and bot. garden, 1982-83. Instr. Marine Biol. Lab., Woods Hole, Mass., summers 1958-61; founding dir. Shoals Marine Lab., 1972-79; adj. prof. U. N.H., 1976-78; cons. Upstate Med. Ctr., Syracuse, N.Y., 1977-86; instr. Aquavet course Cornell U. - U. Pa., 1978-01; lectr. Cornell U. Adult U., 1978-2001; proprietor Bullbrier Press, 1983—; lectr. Columbus project Sta. WGBH/Pub. Broadcasting Svc., Boston, 1990; mem. endowment com. Shoals Marine Lab., 1992-96, chmn., 1992-94; vis. faculty U. Tasmania, Australia, 1980; dir. Shoals Marine Lab. Cornell U., 2001. Author: Poisonous Plants of the United States and Canada, 1964, Deadly Harvest— A Guide to Common Poisonous Plants, 1965, Seaweeds of Cape Cod and the Islands, 1969, rev. edit., 1997, The Rocky Shore, 1970, Oil and Water: The New Hampshire Story, 1975, 200 Conspicuous, Unusual, or Economically Important Tropical Plants of the Caribbean, 1988, Here's How We'll Do It—An Informal History of the Construction of the Shoals Marine Laboratory, 1991, Recollections and Reminiscences, 2000; mem. editl. bd. Cornell U. Press, 1985-86; compiler: Catalog of the Library at the Bullard Colonial Farm, 1999. NSF faculty fellow, 1958; Fulbright sr. scholar, 1980; recipient Profile Svc. award U. N.H., 1998; named in his honor: Rsch. Vessel John M. Kingsbury, 1984, John M. Kingsbury Dir., Shoals Marine Lab., Cornell U., 2001, John M. & Louise G. Kingsbury Scholarships, Cornell U., 2001, Kingsbury House, Appledore Island, 2001. Fellow Am. Acad. Vet. and Comparative Toxicology (hon.); mem. Bullard Meml. Farm Assn. (clk. 1978—, pres. 1990-94), Sea Edn. Assn. (trustee 1977-92, emeritus, 2002—, pres. 1982-87), Marine Biol. Lab. (life), Nature Conservancy (trustee N.Y. state bd. 1983-90), Audubon Soc. (lectr. Mass. chpt. 1987-89), Mass. Soc. Cin., Sigma Xi, Phi Zeta. Office: Cornell U 135A Guterman Lab Ithaca NY 14853-5903 E-mail: JMK11@cornell.edu.

KINGSBURY, KATHERINE DUFFIELD, social worker; b. N.Y.C., Oct. 13, 1938; d. Marcus McCampbell and Margaret (Doty) Duffield; m. Laurence Kingsbury, June 23, 1962 (div. July 1989); children: Jennifer Katherine, Suzanne Duffield; m. Edwin E. Benton, June 27, 1992. BA, Mt. Holyoke Coll., 1960; MSW, Washington U., St. Louis, 1964. Caseworker Dept. Pub. Welfare, Mt. Vernon, N.Y., 1960-61, Family Counseling Svc., Bound Brook, N.J., 1964-65, Balt., 1968-69; med. social worker Johns Hopkins Hosp., Balt., 1965-68, Yale-New Haven Hosp., 1970-71; dir. Homemaker Home Health Aide Agy., Guilford, Conn., 1977-84; sch. social worker Clinton (Conn.) Bd. Edn., 1986—. Mem. NASW, Acad. Cert. Social Workers. Episcopalian. Avocations: calligraphy, knitting, baking, walking. Home: PO Box 170 39 North St Guilford CT 06437 Office: Board of Edn Glenwood Rd Clinton CT 06412

KINGSBURY, LISA R. instructional design consultant; b. McKeesport, Pa., Mar. 14, 1968; d. Frank A. and Frances V. Rendulic; m. Jeff N. Kingsbury, Aug. 9, 2003. BA in Comm., Calif. U. of Pa., 1990, MA in Comm., 1993. Sr. instructional designer Mellon Fin., Pitts., 1995—2001; instructional design cons. The Abreon Group, Pitts., 2002—. Grant writer Rostraver Libr., Pa.,

1993—97; forensic judge Belle Vernon Area H.S., Pa., 1990—2001. Vol. Rostraver Pub. Libr., Pa., 1991—2000. Mem.: Toastmasters (Divsn. Gov. of Yr. - Dist. 13 2001). Avocations: reading, bicycling, interior decorating. Office: The Abreon Group Foster Plaza 10 Ste 500 680 Andersen Dr Pittsburgh PA 15220

KINGSBURY, MICHAEL BRYANT, organist, retired elementary and secondary education educator; b. Wilmington, N.C., Dec. 25, 1933; s. Walter Russell and Olga Loretta (Lewis) K. BA, Emory U., 1957; MA, Atlanta U., 1978. Cert. mid. sch. sci. tchr., sci. tchr. K-12, social studies tchr., Ga. Tchr. Bouldercrest Elem. Sch., Atlanta, 1958-62; sci. tchr. Northcutt Elem. Sch., College Park, Ga., 1962-66, G.P. Babb Jr. H.S., Forest Park, Ga., 1966-84, Pointe South Mid. Sch., Jonesboro, Ga., 1984-94; organist, choir master Episcopal and Cath. Chs., Atlanta and Decatur, Ga., 1955—; organist, dir. Cath. music Ft. McPherson/U.S. Army, Atlanta, 1994—. Author, editor: Laboratory Manual for Earth Science, 1970. Bd. dirs. Camelot Homeowners Assn., Jonesboro, 1978-84; patron Atlanta Symphony Orch., 1992—; lector St. Luke's Episcopal Ch. Recipient Ritter Music award Atlanta Pub. Schs., 1951, Cmty. Svc. award Clayton County Ret. Tchrs., 1998, Service Playing cert. Am. Guild Organists, Cert. of Appreciation, Clayton County Educators Assn., 1999, others; NSF grant, 1970. Mem. Clayton County Ret. Tchrs. Assn. (pres. 1996—, dirs. dir. 2000-02, Cert. of Appreciation, Plaque 2002), Clayton County Ret. Educators Assn. (pres. 1996-98, dir. 10th dist.), Ga. Ret. Tchrs. Assn. (10th dist. dir. 2000-02), Am. Guild of Organists (membership com. 1958—), Atlanta Music Club. Democrat. Episcopalian. Avocations: walking, bicycle riding, collecting southern writings and gone with the wind memorabilia. Home: 2669 Lake Jodeco Dr Jonesboro GA 30236-5355 Office: Ft McPherson US Army Lee St Atlanta GA 30330

KINGSBURY, ROBERT COBURN, physician, consultant; b. Balt., Nov. 5, 1926; s. Arthur Mack and Emma Shelley Kingsbury; m. Mildred R. Thomas, June 14, 1948; children: Robert Jr., William T., Barry Lee, Joanne L., Jeffrey. BS, U. Md., 1951, MD, 1953. Diplomate Am. Bd. Family Practice. Intern U.S. Naval Hosp., Phila., 1953-54; pvt. practice Federalsburg, Md., 1954-57; partnership practice Seaford, Del., 1957-79; staff phys. Merck & Co., West Point, Pa., 1986-95, dir. health srvs., 1995-96, ret., 1996. With USN, 1944-46, capt., 1979-86. Master Am. Coll. Occupl. and Environ. Medicine; fellow Am. Acad. Family Physicians. Avocations: woodworking, gardening. Home: 226 Lakeside Dr Millington MD 21651

KINGSBURY, SUZANNE NELSON, judge, educator; b. Dayton, Ohio, July 17, 1956; d. Harry Allen and Kae (Williams) N.; m. James Harold Ammons, Dec. 17, 1984. BA in Criminal Justice, Calif. State U., 1981; JD, U. of the Pacific, Sacramento, 1982. Bar: Calif. 1982, U.S. Dist. Ct. (ea. dist.) Calif. 1983. Lawyer Anderson & Goff, Sacramento, 1982-84, Brodovsky, Brodovsky & Grossfeld, Sacramento, 1984-85; dep. dist. atty. III El Dorado County Dist. Atty., South Lake Tahoe, Calif., 1985-90; dep. pub. defender III El Dorado County Pub. Defender, 1990-96; instr. in law and adminstrn. of justice Lake Tahoe Community Coll., 1988—; judge Superior Ct. El Dorado County, South Lake Tahoe, Calif., 1997—, presiding judge, 1999—. Mem. Jud. Coun. Task Force of Self Represented Litigants; mem. Jud. Coun. Task Force on Jud. Ethics Issues; cons. South Lake Tahoe Sexual Assault Response Team, 1985-90; com. mem. Adminstrn. of Justice Adv. Com., Lake Tahoe Community Coll., South Lake Tahoe, 1988—; mem. Lake Tahoe Arson Task Force, 1989-90, South Lake Tahoe Narcotics Enforcement Team, 1988-90; mem. Trial Ct. Presiding Judges Com., mem. exec. com.; mem. planning com. Calif. Jud. Adminstrn. Conf. and Rural Cts. Conf.; vice chair Trial Ct. Presiding Judges Com.; chmn. Trial Ct. Presiding Judges Issues Conf. Bd. dirs. South Lake Tahoe Womens Ctr., sec., 1990-91, v.p., 1992-93, pres., 1993-95, co-v.p., 1997; bd. dirs. Lake Tahoe Edn1. Found. Recipient Disting. Svc. award, Calif. State U. Alumni Assn./Calif. State U., Sacramento, 2002. Mem. Calif. Judges Assn. (criminal law and procedure com.), Am. Judges Assn., Rural Judges Assn., Am. Judicature Soc. Office: Superior Ct State Calif El Dorado County 1354 Johnson Blvd Ste 2 South Lake Tahoe CA 96150-8216

KINGSLAKE, RUDOLF, retired optical designer; b. London, Aug. 28, 1903; came to U.S., 1929; s. Martin and Margaret (Higham) K.; m. Hilda G. Conrady, Sept. 14, 1929; children: David C., Alan H. (dec.). BSc, Imperial Coll., London, 1924, MSc, 1926, DSc, 1950; DSc (hon.), U. Rochester, 1986. Prof. U. Rochester, N.Y., 1929-37, 68-83; optical designer Eastman Kodak Co., Rochester, 1937-68. Author: Lenses in Photography, 1951, 2d edit., 1963, Lens Design Fundamentals, 1978, Optical Systems Design, 1983, A History of the Photographic Lens, 1989, Optics in Photography, 1992; also numerous articles. Named Engr. of Yr., Rochester Engring. Soc., 1978. Fellow Soc. Motion Picture and TV Engrs. (Progress medal 1964), Soc. Photographic Scientists and Engrs.; mem. Optical Soc. Am. (hon., pres. 1947-49, Ives medal 1973), Soc. Photog. Instrumentation Engrs. (life). Home: The Episcopal Ch Home 505 Mount Hope Ave Rochester NY 14620

KINGSLEY, JAMES GORDON, college administrator; b. Houston, Nov. 22, 1933; s. James Gordon and Blanche Sybil (Payne) K.; m. Martha Elizabeth Sasser, Aug. 24, 1956 (div. 1992); children: Gordon Alan, Craig Emerson; m. Suzanne H. Patterson, Oct. 30, 1993; 1 child, Aaron T. AB, Miss. Coll., 1955; MA, U. Mo., 1956; BD, ThD, New Orleans Bapt. Theol. Sem., 1960, 65; HHD (hon.), Mercer U., 1980; LittD (hon.), Seinan Gakuin U., Japan, 1989; postgrad., U. Louisville, 1968-69, Nat. U. Ireland, 1970, Harvard U., 1976. Asst. prof. Miss. Coll., 1956-58; instr. Tulane U., 1958-60; asst. prof. William Jewell Coll., Liberty, Mo., 1960-62; assoc. prof. Ky. So. Coll., Louisville, 1964-67, prof., 1967-69; prof. lit. and religion William Jewell Coll., 1969-93, dean, 1976-80, pres., 1980-93; v.p. Health Midwest, Kansas City, Mo., 1994—2002; dep. dir. Nelson-Atkins Mus. of Art, 1995-96; prin. Halaxton Coll., Grantham, England, 2003—. Vis. fellow Cambridge (Eng.) U., 1988. Author: A Time for Openness, 1973, Frontiers, 1983, Conversations with Leaders for a New Millenium, 1991, A Place Called Grace, 1993, Kansas City Sesquicentennial: A Celebration of the Heart, 2001; contbr. articles to profl. jours. Bd. dirs. Mo. Repertory Theatre, Episcopal Sem. S.W. LaRue fellow, 1976. Mem. English Speaking Union, Burren Conservancy, Cambridge Soc. Episcopalian. Home: Lakewood 402 NE Point Dr Lees Summit MO 64064-1561 Office: Harlaxton College Grantham LINCS NG32 1AG England

KINGSLEY, JEAN-PIERRE, government official; b. Ottawa, Ont., Can., July 12, 1943; s. Oscar and Françoise (Charette-Bertrand) K.; m. Suzanne Potvin, Aug. 19, 1967; children: Marie-France, Justin, Michèle. B. Comm., U. Ottawa, 1965, MA in Hosp. Adminstrn., 1969. Programmer IBM, Ottawa-Hull, 1965-66; field supr. Travelers Ins., Ottawa-Hull, 1966-67; chief hosps. Dept. Vets.' Affairs Govt. Can., Ottawa-Hull, 1969-71, profl. officer Can. Mortgage & Housing Corp., 1971; assoc. exec. dir. and exec. dir. Charles Camsell Hosp., Edmonton, Alta., Can., 1971-73; prin. exec. officer Office of Dep. Min. Health and Welfare, Dept. Nat. Health and Welfare Govt. of Can., Ottawa-Hull, 1973-74, group chief, Treasury Bd. Secretariat, 1974-76; dir. gen. audit br. Pub. Svc. Commn., Ottawa-Hull, 1976-77; pres., CEO Ottawa Gen. Hosp., 1977-81; dep. sec., Ministry of State for Social Devel. Govt. of Canada, Ottawa-Hull, 1981-84, dep. sec. pers. policy, Treasury Bd. Secretariat, 1984-87, asst. dep. registrar gen. Dept. Consumer and Corp. Affairs, 1987-90; chief electoral officer Parliament of Can., Ottawa, 1990—. Chmn. Monfort Hosp., 1981-90; bd. dirs. International Found. for Election Sys., Inst. for Democracy and Electoral Assistance. Avocations: music, community activities, windsurfing, carpentry, swimming. Home: 604-131 Wurtenburg St Ottawa ON Canada K1K 8L9 Office: Elections Canada 257 Slater St Ottawa ON Canada K1A OM6

KINGSLEY, JOHN MCCALL, JR., manufacturing company executive; b. Berlin, Dec. 1, 1931; s. John McCall and Elizabeth (Curry) K.; m. Ines Hinckeldeyn, 1967; children— John M. III, Kate Lund. BA, Yale, 1953; MBA, Harvard, 1955. CPA, N.Y. Sr. staff acct. Price Waterhouse & Co. (C.P.A.'s), N.Y.C., 1957-62; assoc. Dillon, Read & Co., Inc., N.Y.C., 1962-65; v.p. fin. Gen. Host Corp., N.Y.C., 1966-69; v.p. corp. fin. F.S. Smithers & Co., Inc., 1970-71; exec. v.p. Sturm, Ruger & Co., Inc., Southport, Conn., 1971-96; pres. Kingsley Cons., LLC, 1997—. Bd. dirs. Sturm, Ruger & Co., Inc., Stamford, Conn., Neuro Inst. N.J., Newark. With AUS, 1955-57. Mem. Econ. Club N.Y., Round Hill Club, Maidstone Club ((East Hampton, N.Y.). Republican. Episcopalian. Home: 16 Will Merry Ln Greenwich CT 06831-3338 Office: 111 Prospect St Stamford CT 06901-1208 E-mail: johnkingsley@worldnet.att.net.

KINGSLEY, JUDITH, artist; b. N.Y.C. d. Fred and Minna Evelyn (Weisman) Gladstone; m. Theodore Kingsley, Oct. 26, 1950 (dec. May 1964); children: Ellen Kingsley Hirschfeld, Melinda Kingsley Nester; m. John Fitting Jr., Apr. 9, 1976 (dec. Dec. 1997). Student, Syracuse U., 1948-49, Adelphi U., 1949-50, Pratt Inst., Art Students League, N.Y.C., Nat. Acad. Fine Arts, Positano Art Inst., Italy, 1972, China Inst., N.Y.C., 1977. One-woman shows include Galerie Internat., N.Y.C., 1969, Weiner Gallery, N.Y.C., 1970, Palm Beach Gallery, 1971, Lobster Pot Gallery, Nantucket, Mass., 1972, Crystal House Gallery, Miami Beach, Fla., 1973, Springfield (Ill.) Art Assn., 1975, East River Savs. Bank Gallery, Rockefeller Ctr., N.Y., 1976, Bergdorf Goodman Art Gallery, N.Y.C., 1977, Adelphi U. Art Gallery, Garden City, N.Y., 1978, Multiple Images Gallery, Palm Beach, Fla., 1982, Valand Gallery, Naples, Fla., 1983, La Galeria De Santa Fe, 1984, Reece Gallery, N.Y.C., 1979-80, Nelson Rockefeller Collection, N.Y.C., 1981-82, L'Atelier Gallery, Piermont, N.Y., 1991-92, Jain Marunouchi Gallery, N.Y.C., 1995-96, G.G. Rein Gallery, Houston, 1995-96, The Darvish Collection, Naples, 1995-98, Hofburg Palace Exhibit, Vienna, Austria, 1993, No. Trust Bank, Naples, 1998, Naples Art Gallery, The Gallery Botero, Marco Island, Fla., 1998-99, Artsforum Gallery, N.Y.C., 1998-2000, The Gallery at the Registry Resort, Naples, 1999-2000, Alpers Fine Art, Andover, Mass., Charles Hecht Gallery, Palm Desert, Calif., 2001, Marco Polo Galleries, Carmel, Calif., 2001, Cofer Gallerie, Carmel, 2001, Julie Baker Fine Art, Grass Valley, Calif., 2002, The Monkey Tree Gallery, Santa Fe, 2002, Johnson's of Madrid (N.Mex.), 2003. Sec. bd. dirs. N.Y. Artists Equity, 1984-93. Recipient Morilla Oil award, New Rochelle Art Assn., 1973. Mem.: Sierra Club (Santa Fe), Quail Run Club (Santa Fe), Nat. Arts Club NY. Avocations: golf, tennis, swimming, yachting. Home and Office: Quail Run 3101 Old Pecos Trail Santa Fe NM 87505 Studio: The Lofts 3100 Cerrillos Rd Santa Fe NM 87505 E-mail: princesskingsley@aol.com.

KINGSLEY, MARY LEE, marketing professional; d. Thomas Drowne Kingsley and Martha Bush Clark; m. William Charles Johnson, Apr. 23, 1980 (div.); children: Lee Hart Johnson, William Kingsley Johnson. BA in English, Am. U., 1975; MS in Mktg., Johns Hopkins U., 2001. Mem.: BMW Riders Orgn. (contbg. author and editl. cons. jour. 2001). Episcopalian. Avocations: writing, motorcycling, cooking, gardening, needlepoint. Home: 8204 Old Georgetown Rd Bethesda MD 20814-1452 Office: Bank-Fund Staff Federal Credit Union PO Box 27755 Washington DC 20038-7755 E-mail: mlkingsley@bfsfcu.org.

KINGSLEY, NATHAN, journalist, consultant, educator; b. N.Y.C., Nov. 20, 1926; m. Cynthia Jean Kirkpatrick, June 20, 1950; 1 child, Alexandra Marjorie Jane. BS, CCNY, 1948; MA in Polit. Sci., Columbia U., 1977. Reporter, corr. N.Y. Herald Tribune, N.Y.C., 1946-55, assoc. mng. editor, 1963-65; mng. editor news svc. Herald Tribune News Svc., N.Y.C., 1955-59; mng. editor Internat. Herald Tribune, Paris, 1959-63; dir. news Radio Free Europe and Radio Liberty, Munich, 1965-72; spl. corr. radio and TV CBS News, Germany, 1966-72; dep. dir. for programming Voice of Am., 1972-74; v.p., sec. Radio Free Europe and Radio Liberty, Munich and Wash., 1976-80; spl. asst. to asst. sec. state U.S. Dept. State, Washington, 1974-76, pub. and congl. affairs dir., 1986-91; sr. editor spl. project U.S. News and World Report, Washington, 1980-84; chief of corrs. Washington Times, 1984-86; cons., writer Total Comm. Internat., Washington, 1991—; prof. Manship chair, Sch. Mass Comms. La. State U., Baton Rouge, 1996-97. Chmn. bd. dirs. Parkway Comms., Inc., Washington, 1980-84; adj. assoc. prof. media and govt. George Washington U., 1990-93; prof. global media, Inst. Experiential Learning, Washington, 1998-2002. Author: (with others) The Future of Journalism, 1993. Co-chmn. Music for the World Found., Washington, 1993-95. With USN, 1944-46. Poynter fellow Yale U., 1979. Mem. Lansdowne Club, Nat. Press Club, Overseas Press Club (Spot Coverage award 1972), Fed. City Club. Avocations: amateur radio broadcaster, antique book collector. Home and Office: 4217 Leland St Chevy Chase MD 20815-6048

KINGSLEY, PETER BERNARD, physics researcher; b. Boston, Mar. 26, 1952; s. Darwin P. III and Jane (Cotton) K.; m. Lila Jeannette Hickman, July 3, 1982 (div. May 1991); 2 stepchildren; m. Barbara Jo Kingsley, May 10, 1997. BA, Dartmouth Coll., Hanover, N.H., 1974; PhD, Cornell U., 1980. Postdoctoral fellow U. Minn., St. Paul, Navarre & Mpls., 1981-89; instr. Northwestern Coll. Chiropractic, Bloomington, Minn., 1984-89; rsch. assoc. U. Minn., Navarre, 1989-91; asst. mem. St. Jude Children's Rsch. Hosp, Memphis, 1991-96; MRI rsch. physicist North Shore U. Hosp., Manhasset, N.Y., 1996—. Mem. editl. bd. Concepts in Magnetic Resonance, 1997—; patentee in field; contbr. articles to profl. jours. Mem. Internat. Soc. Magnetic Resonance in Medicine. Avocations: bicycling, hiking. Home: 14 Koster Ct Huntington Station NY 11746-1115 Office: North Shore U Hosp 300 Community Dr Manhasset NY 11030-3801 E-mail: Kingsley@nshs.edu.

KINGSOLVER, BARBARA ELLEN, writer; b. Annapolis, Md., Apr. 8, 1955; d. Wendell and Virginia (Henry) K.; m. Steven Hopp, 1985; 2 children. BA, DePauw U., 1977; MS, U. Ariz., 1981; LittD (hon.), DePauw U., 1994. Sci. writer U. Ariz., Tucson, 1981-85; free-lance journalist Tucson, 1985-87; novelist, 1987—. Book reviewer N.Y. Times, 1988—, L.A. Times, 1989—. Author: The Bean Trees, 1988 (ALA award 1988), Homeland and Other Stories, 1969 (ALA award 1990), Holding the Line: Women in the Great Arizona Mine Strike of 1983, 89, Animal Dreams, 1990 (PEN West Fiction award 1991, Edward Abbey Ecofiction award 1991), Another America, 1992, Pigs in Heaven, 1993 (L.A. Times Fiction prize 1993, Mountains and Plains Fiction award 1993, Western Heritage award 1993, ABBY Honor Book 1994), Essays, High Tide in Tucson, 1995, The Poisonwood Bible, 1998 (ABBY Honor Book 2000, PEN/Faulkner honoree 1999, Pulitzer runner-up 1999, Orange Prize short list 1999), Prodigal Summer, 2001 (Bellwether Prize, 2001), Small Wonder, 2002; co-author (with Annie Belt) Last Stand: America's Virgin Lands. Recipient Feature-writing award Ariz. Press Club, 1986; citation of accomplishment UN Nat. Coun. of Women, 1989; Woodrow Wilson Found./Lila Wallace fellow, 1992-93. Mem. PEN Ctr. USA West, Nat. Writers Union, Phi Beta Kappa. Avocations: human rights, environmental conservation, gardening, natural history. Office: PO Box 31870 Tucson AZ 85751-1870 also: care Harper Collins 10 E 53rd St New York NY 10022-5244*

KINGSTON, ALEX(ANDRA), actress; b. London, Mar. 11, 1963; m. Ralph Fiennes, 1993 (div. 1997); m. Florian Haertel, 1998; 1 child. Student, Royal Acad. Dramatic Arts. T.V. and movie actress. Appeared in T.V. films Foreign Affairs, 1993, The Infiltrator, 1995, Weapons of Mass Distraction, 1997; films include The Cook, The Thief, His Wife & Her Lover, 1989, Carrington, 1995, Virtual Encounters 2, 1998, Croupier, 1998, This Space Between Us, 2000, Moll Flanders, 1999, Essex Boys, 2000, Warrior Queen, 2003; T.V. series include The Knock, 1994, ER, 1997—. Recipient SAG award for Outstanding Performance by Ensemble in a Drama Series, 1994. Office: c/o The Gersh Agy 232 N Canon Dr Beverly Hills CA 90210-5302

KINGSTON, DAVID L. retired physicist; b. Lansing, Mich., June 26, 1930; s. Charles L. and Rosaline C. Kingston; m. Janice M. Ebright; children: Charlene, Michelle;1 child, David Jr. BS, Mich. State U., 1953, MS, 1955. Rsch. solid state physicist Air Force Rsch. Lab., Wright-Patterson AFB, Ohio, 1955—93. Councilman City of Fairborn, 1979—81. Capt. USAF, 1955—58. Home: 10 E Routzong Dr Fairborn OH 45324 Personal E-mail: kingpin@donet.com.

KINGSTON, GEORGE WILLIS, retired naval officer, small business owner; b. Omaha, Feb. 26, 1916; s. George Clarence and Minnie Ella (Smead) K.; m. Gertrude Margaret Stoffel, Feb. 14, 1941 (div. 1947); 1 child, Frank Martin; m. Marion Regina MacLachlan Devlieg, Aug. 21, 1947. Student, U. Nebr., 1947-49, U. Md., Washington, 1960-61, George Washington U., 1960; grad., U.S. Naval War Coll, Newport, R.I., 1961. Enlisted man USN, 1934, advanced through grades to comdr., 1958; ret., 1966; product devel. engr. Timber Engring. Co., Washington, 1968-81; owner, mgr. Custom Designs & Plans, Gulf Shores, Ala., 1966-68, Foley, Ala., 1981—2002. Cons. Svc. Corps Ret. Execs., Foley, 1982-96; cons., 1997-2001. Inventor structural wood fasteners. Past mem. bd. dirs. Nat. Safety Coun., Chgo.; chief bldg. advisor ARC, 1969-81, lectr. on disasters and first aid, 1969-85, chmn. Gulf Coast terr, 1985-87, dist. chmn., 1985; bd. dirs. Baldwin Heritage Mus., Elberta, Ala., 1982-94, Lillian (Ala.) Cmty. Club, 1986-88, Care House, Bay Minette, Ala., 1990—, Woodbridge Property Owners Assn., 1998—; mem. exec. com. Baldwin County Rep. Party, 1984—, parliamentarian, 1984-2002; mem. bd. adjustments and appeals City of Foley, Ala., 1996—. Mem.: NRA (life; lectr. 1988), VFW (life; post comdr. 1984—85), Assn. ARC Retirees, People to People Internat. (amb. 1987—97), Nat. Assn. Fleet Tug Sailors (life; chmn. bd. dirs. 1990—2000), Optimists (life; pres. Foley 1991—92, parliamentarian Ala.-Miss. dist. 1992—96, 1997—2001, lt. gov. 1992—93, 1994—95), South Baldwin C. of C. (amb. 1984—), Am. Legion (life). Roman Catholic. Avocations: drawing, writing, shooting. Home and Office: 1611 Woodbridge Foley AL 36535-2267

KINGSTON, JACK, congressman; b. Bryan, Tex., Apr. 24, 1955; m. Libby Kingston; children: Betsy, John, Ann, Jim. BA in Economics, U. Ga. Salesman, v.p. Palmer & Cay Carswell Ins. Co., 1979-92; mem. Ga. State Ho. Reps., 1985-93, 103rd - 108th Congresses from 1st Ga. Dist., 1993—. Mem. Ways and Means Com., 1985-93, Appropriations Com., Congl. Rural Caucus Exec. Bd., 1993—, chmn. Theme Team (house Rep. comm. team). Vol. Hospice, United Way; mem. Atlantic Coast Conservation Assn., Isle of Hope Community Assn. Recipient Guardian of Small Bus. award Nat. Fed. of Ind. Bus. 103, 104, 105, 106, 1992, Sound Dollar award Free Cong. Found., 1994, Golden Bulldog award mems. 103rd, 104th, 105th, 106th cong., 1994, 96, Golden Eagle award Nat. Security Caucus, 1994, cert. recognition inspector. gen. Criminal Investigator Acad., 1994, plaque of appreciation Camden county bd. realtors, 1995, disting. cit. award Armstrong state coll., 1996, merit award the Seniors Coalition, 1996, comm. police award city of Statesboro, 1997, numerous others. Mem. Am. Legislative Exchange Coun., Soc. Chartered Property and Casualty Underwriters, Solomon's Lodge F&AM, Rotary (Paul Harris fellow). Republican. Episcopalian. Office: US Ho Reps 2242 Rayburn HOB Washington DC 20515-1001*

KINGSTON, MAXINE HONG, writer, educator; b. Stockton, Calif., Oct. 27, 1940; d. Tom and Ying Lan (Chew) Hong; m. Earll Kingston, Nov. 23, 1962; 1 child, Joseph Lawrence. BA, U. Calif., Berkeley, 1962; D degree (hon.), Ea. Mich. U., 1988, Colby Coll., 1990, Brandeis U., 1991, U. Mass., 1991. Tchr. English, Sunset High Sch., Hayward, Calif., 1965-66, Kahuku (Hawaii) High Sch., 1967, Kahaluu (Hawaii) Drop-In Sch., 1968, Kailua (Hawaii) High Sch., 1969, Honolulu Bus. Coll., 1969, Mid-Pacific Inst., Honolulu, 1970-77; prof. English, vis. writer U. Hawaii, Honolulu, 1977; Thelma McCandless Disting. Prof. Eastern Mich. U., Ypsilanti, 1986, Chancellor's Disting. Prof. U. Calif., Berkeley, 1990—. Author: The Woman Warrior: Memoirs of a Girlhood Among Ghosts, 1976 (Nat. Book Critics Cir. award for non-fiction, cited by Time mag., N.Y. Times Book Rev. and Asian Mail as one of best books of yr. and decade), China Men, 1981 (Nat. Book award; runner-up for Pulitzer prize, Nat. Book Critics Cir. award nominee 1988), Hawai' One Summer, 1987 (Western Books Exhbn. Book award, Book Builders West Book award), Tripmaster Monkey-His Fake Book, 1989 (PEN USA West award in Fiction), Through the Black Curtain, 1988, To Be The Poet, 2002, The Fifth Book of Peace, 2003; editor: The Literature of California, 2001, (Commonwealth Club Book award 2001); To Be the Poet, 2002; contbr. short stories, articles and poems to mags. and jours., including Iowa Rev., The New Yorker, Am. Heritage, Redbook, Mother Jones, Caliban, Mich. Quarterly, Ms., The Hungry Mind Rev., N.Y. Times, L.A. Times, Zyzzyva; prodr. The Woman Warrior, Berkeley Repertory Co., 1994, The Huntington Theater, Boston, 1994, The Mark Taper Forum, L.A., 1995; host: (TV series) Journey to the West, 1994; subject of documentaries Talking Story, Stories My Country Told Me, Writers and Places; interviews on Dick Cavett, Bill Moyers, Ken Burns' The West, The News Hour with Jim Lehrer. Guggenheim fellow, 1981; recipient Nat. Endowment for the Arts Writers award, 1980, 82, Mademoiselle mag. award, 1977, Anisfield Wolf Book award, 1978, Calif. Arts Commn. award, 1981, Hawaii award for lit., 1982, Calif. Gov.'s award art, 1989, Major Book Collection award Brandeis U. Nat. Women's Com., 1990, award lit. Am. Acad. & Inst. Arts & Letters, 1990, Lila Wallace Reader's Digest Writing award, 1992, Spl. Achievement Oakland Bus. Arts award, 1994; named Living Treasure Hawaii, 1980, Woman of Yr. Asian Pacific Women's Network, 1981, Cyril Magnin award for Outstanding Achievement in the Arts, 1996, Disting. Artists award The Music Ctr. of L.A. County, 1996, Nat. Humanities medal NEH, 1997, Fred Cody Lifetime Achievement award, 1998, John Dos Passos prize for lit., 1998, Ka Palapola Po'okela award 1999, Profiles of Courage honor Swords to Plowshares, 1999, Alumna of Yr. award U. Calif.-Berkeley, 2000, Gold medal Calif. State Libr., 2002. Mem. Am. Acad. Arts and Scis.

KINGSTON, REBECCA EDITH DAWSON, political science educator; b. Windsor, Ont., Can., Dec. 21, 1963; came to U.S., 1994; d. Frederick Temple Kingston and Pauline Boyd Smith. BA, U. Toronto, 1985; MA, U. Paris IV, 1987; PhD, McGill U., Montreal, Can., 1994. Sessional lectr. McGill U., 1993, Ottawa (Ont.) U., 1993-94; assoc. prof. polit. sci. St. Francis U., Loretto, Pa., 1994-2001; asst. prof. polit. sci. U. Toronto, 2001—. Author: Montesquieu and the Parlement of Bordeaux, 1996 (Montesquieu prize 1997). Mem. Am. Polit. Sci. Assn., Can. Polit. Sci. Assn., Am. Soc. 18th Century Studies, Montesquieu Soc. Avocation: tennis. Office: U Toronto Dept Polit Sci 100 St George St Toronto ON Canada M5S 3G3 E-mail: rkingsto@chass.utoronto.ca.

KINGTON, BARRY CLARK, investor, consultant; b. Sept. 2, 1942; s. William Hayes and Margret Elisabeth (Clark) K.; 1 child, Barry Clark. BS, Murray State U., 1969, MSAE, 1990. Owner coal and oil rights; investor stocks and commodities; bus. cons., pres. Point One Adv. Group, Inc., Am. Soc. Farm Mgrs. and Rural Appraisers. Fellow Internat. Soc. Philos. Enquiry (sr.); mem. AAAS, N.Y. Acad. Scis., Triple Nine Soc. (past regent), Appoloosa Horse Club, Archaeol. Inst. Am., Rotary, Mensa (pres. Evansville area 1986-88), Am. Angus Assn., Prometheus Soc (past treas.)., Am. Soc. Agr. Cons., Internat. Soc. Agr. Cons., Aircraft Owners and Pilots Assn., Exptl. Aircraft Assn., Petroleum Club, Masons, Shriners, KT. Home: Kilmarnock Ln Madisonville KY 42431 Office: PO Box 1111 Madisonville KY 42431-0022 E-mail: bckington@netscape.net.

KINGTON, RAYNARD S. federal agency administrator; BS, MD, U. Mich.; MBA, PhD in health policy and economics, U. Pa., The Wharton Sch. Cert. in internal medicine, geriatric medicine and public health and preventive medicine. Resident in internal medicine Michael Reese Med. Ctr., Chgo.; sr. scientist RAND Corp.; dir. divsn. health examination statistics CDC, Nat. Ctr. Health Statistics; assoc. dir. for behavioral and social scis. rsch. NIH, 2000—, dir. office of behavioral and social scis. rsch., 2000—; acting dir. Nat. Inst. on Alcohol Abuse and Alcoholism, 2002. Office: Office of Behav and Soc Sci Nat Inst of Health Bldg 1 Rm 256 1 Ctr Dr Bethesda MD 20892-0183

KINIGAKIS, PANAGIOTIS, research scientist, engineer, inventor, author; b. Chanea, Greece, July 11, 1949; s. John and Evangelia (Vozinakis) K.; m. Kalliopi Paleologos, July 31, 1977 (div. Sept. 2000); children: Evangelia, Maria Anna; m. Tracey Dawn Quart, Jan. 3, 2003. BS, Superior Agrl. Sch., Athens, Greece, 1971, MS, 1973; MS in Food Sci., Rutgers U., 1979. Packaging devel. specialist Am. Cyanamid Co., Clifton, N.J., 1979-81; sr. packaging engr. Warner Lambert Co., Morris Plains, N.J., 1981-83; tech. svcs. supr. M&M Mars Inc., Hackettstown, N.J., 1983-87; sr. tech. prin. Kraft Foods Inc., Glenview, Ill., 1987—, Kraft Food fellow, 2001—. Agrl. engr. Food Agrl. Orgn. div. of UN, Chanea, 1975-77. Patentee pkg. equipment and mfg. systems; contbr. articles to profl. jours. Advisor Greek Orthodox Youth Assn., Randolph, N.J., 1986, Hamilton, N.J., 1990. Mem. ASM, TAPPI, Internat. Materials Info. soc., Inst. Food Tech., Inst. Packaging Profls. (cert.), Soc. Plastics Engrs., N.Y. Acad. Scis. Greek Orthodox. Avocations: golf, volleyball, soccer, tennis, scuba diving. Office: Kraft Foods Inc 801 Waukegan Rd Glenview IL 60025-4391 E-mail: pkinigakis@kraft.com.

KINKLEY, JEFFREY C. historian; b. Urbana, Ill., July 13, 1948; s. Harold Vernon and Emily Jane (Robinson) K.; m. Chuchu Kang, May 16, 1981; 1 child, Matthew. BA, U. Chgo., 1969; MA, Harvard U., 1971, PhD, 1977. Lectr. Harvard U., Cambridge, Mass., 1977-79; asst. prof. St. John's U., N.Y.C., 1979-86, assoc. prof., 1986-93, prof., 1993—. Vis. prof. Columbia U., 1997, chmn. modern China seminar, N.Y., 1987-88, mem. editl. bd. Twentieth-Century, China, 1988—, C.L.E.A.R., 1989—, Modern China, 2000—, Jour. of Asian Pacific Comm., 2000—, Persimmon, 2001—; asst. editor The Jour. of Asian Studies, 1991-94. Author: The Odyssey of Shen Congwen, 1987, Chinese Justice, the Fiction: Law and Literature in Modern China, 2000; editor: After Mao: Chinese Literature and Society, 1985, Surviving the Storm, 1990, Imperfect Paradise, 1995; co-editor: Modern Chinese Writers, 1992; contbr. articles to profl. jours.; translator: Traveller Without a Map. Mem. Assn. for Asian Studies, Am. Hist. Assn. Home: 8 Laurel Ln Bernardsville NJ 07924-2217 Office: St Johns U History Dept Jamaica NY 11439-0001 E-mail: kinkleyj@stjohns.edu.

KINKOPF, NEIL JOESPH, law educator; b. Los Altos, Calif., Sept. 9, 1965; s. Earl William and Marianne Patricia Kinkopf; m. Emily Pelton, Feb. 10, 1996. AB summa cum laude, Boston Coll., 1987; JD magna cum laude, Case Western Res. U., 1991. Law clk. U.S. Ct. Appeals, Lansing, Mich., 1991-92; atty. advisor to U.S. atty. gen. Dept. Justice, Washington, 1993, spl. asst. office legal counsel, 1993-97; assoc. prof. Ga. State U., Atlanta, 1999—. Vis. prof. Case Western Res. U., Cleve., 1997-98; commentator on law and politics for TV, radio and print media. Editor-in-chief Case Western Res. Law Rev., 1990-91; contbr. articles to profl. jours. Domestic policy specialist Clinton/Gore '92, Little Rock, 1992; spl. asst. Presdl. Transition, Washington, 1992-93; spl. coun. White House Counsel's Office, Washington, 1996-97; counselor U.S. Senate, Washington, 1998-99. Sr. fellow Duke U., Durham, N.C., 1998-99. Mem. Order of Coif, Phi Beta Kappa. Home: 1027 Euclid Ave Atlanta GA 30307 Office: 140 Decatur St SE Atlanta GA 30303-3202 E-mail: nkinkopf@gsu.edu.

KINLAW, DENNIS FRANKLIN, clergyman, society executive; b. Lumberton, N.C., June 26, 1922; s. Wade Hampton and Sally (Burney) K.; m. Elsie Blake, Dec. 31, 1943; children: Elizabeth Kinlaw Coppedge, Dennis Franklin Jr., Katherine Kinlaw Key, Susan Kinlaw Masters, Sally Kinlaw Babcock. BA, Asbury Coll., 1943, LHD (hon.), 1980; MDiv, Asbury Theol. Sem., 1946; MA, Brandeis U., 1961, PhD, 1967; LLD (hon.), Houghton Coll., 1971; DD (hon.), Asbury Coll., 1990. Ordained deacon N.C. Conf. United Meth. Ch., 1949, ordained elder, 1951; transferred to Ky. Conf., 1969, ret., 1984. Pastor Meth. Ch., Faison, 1949-53, Loudenville (N.Y.) Community Ch., 1955-61; assoc. prof., prof. Old Testament langs. and lit. Asbury Theol. Sem., Wilmore, Ky., 1963-68, prof. bibl. theology, 1982-83; pres. Asbury Coll., Wilmore, 1968-81, 86-92; founder, pres. Francis Asbury soc., Wilmore, 1982—, Pres. Francis Asbury Soc., Wilmore, 1982—; vis. prof. Seoul (Republic of Korea) Theol. Coll.; bd. dirs. Christianity Today, Carol Stream, Ill., Ludhiana Christian Med. Bd., N.Y.C.; mem. Lausanne Commn. on World Evangelism, Theol. Commn. of World Evang. Fellowship; chmn. bd. OMS Internat., Greenwood, Ind. Author: Preaching in the Spirit, 1985; contbr. commentaries in bibl. publs. Recipient Alumnus award Asbury Theol. Sem., 1961. Mem. Soc. Bibl. Lit. and Exegesis, Wesley Theol. Soc., Evang. Theol. Soc. Home: 140 Lowry Ln Wilmore KY 40390-1219 Office: Francis Asbury Soc PO Box 7 Wilmore KY 40390-0007 E-mail: kinlawdennis@hotmail.com.

KINLEY, CHRISTINE T. certified physician assistant; b. Carter County, Tenn. d. Lon Samuel and Mary (Johnson) Turbyfill; children: Amy Nikol, Michael Lon. Diploma, Johnson City Vocat. Tech. Sch., 1977; BSN, East Tenn. State U., 1988; Physician Asst., Trevecca Nazarene U., Nashville, 1997; postgrad., U. Health Scis., St. John's U., St. Lucia Sch. Medicine. LPN, RN, Tenn.; cert. physician asst. Charge nurse Four Oaks Health Care Ctr., Jonesborough, Tenn.; staff nurse VA Med. Ctr., Johnson, Tenn., nurse recruiter; physician asst. Johnson City Emergency Physicians, 1997-1999, emergency care coverage, 2000—; emergency care coverage Olde Towne Gen. Medicine, 2000—. E-mail: CKinley333@aol.com.

KINLEY, DAVID, physical therapist, acupuncturist; b. Newark, Dec. 16, 1935; m. Helen Sandra Wehrle, Mar. 14, 1958; children: Sandra, Deborah, Denise. D Mechanotherapy, Easton Coll., 1970; postgrad in trad. Chinese acupuncture, Tri State Inst., 1979-82. Lic. in acupuncture, phys. therapy and massage; cert. in hypnosis, biofeedback, touch for health. Pvt. massage practice, Newark, 1957-60; pvt. phys. therapy practice Cranford, N.J., 1960-63; founder, massage instr., phys. therapist, acupuncturist, hypnotherapist Kinley Comprehensive Ctr. for Acupuncture and Phys. Therapy, Clark, N.J., 1963—. Cons. in phys. therapy Vis. Nurse Assn., 1970; practice in biofeedback, 1972; established ctr. for phys. therapy and rehab., Elizabeth, N.J.; clin. affiliate N.Y. State Phys. Therapy Coll., 1982; cons. in acupuncture and phys. therapy Sunny Isles Med. Ctr., Miami Beach, Fla., 1982, pain mgmt. No. Miami Inst. Fla.; founder Kinley Comprehensive Ctr. for Acupuncture/Phys. Therapy, Fla.; asst. in preparation of licensing legis. for N.J. Acupuncture; mem. acupuncture examining bd. N.J. Bd. Med. Examiners. Recipient Lydia Hayes achievement award, 1957. Mem. N.J. State Phys. Therapy Assn. (officer 1959—, pres. 1993, exec. dir., bd.dirs., sr. advisor), Am. Acupuncture Assn. and Oriental Medicine (pres. Acupuncture and Moxibustion Assn. 1973-87), Assn. Applied Psycho Physiology and Biofeedback, Internat. Soc. Profl. Hypnotist, Internat. Soc. Myomassethics, Fla. State Massage Assn., Fla. State Acupuncture Assn., Am. Acad. Environ. Medicine, N.J. Acupuncture Assn. (pres. 1991-93). Avocations: outdoors, swimming, boating, travel, reading. Home and Office: Kinley Inst 668 Raritan Rd Clark NJ 07066-2232

KINLIN, DONALD JAMES, lawyer; b. Boston, Nov. 29, 1938; s. Joseph Edward and Ruth Claire (Byrne) K.; m. Donna C. (McGrath), Nov. 29, 1959; children: Karen J., Donald J., Joseph P., and Kevin S. BS in acctg., Syracuse U., 1968, MBA, 1970; JD, U. Nebr., 1975. Bar: Nebr., 1976, Ohio, 1982, U.S. Supreme Ct., 1979, U.S. Claims Ct., 1982, U.S. Tax Ct., 1982, U.S. Ct. Appeals (5th and fed. cir.), 1982. Atty. USAF, Mather AFB, Calif., 1976-78; sr. trial atty. Air Force Contract Law Ctr., Wright Patterson AFB, Ohio, 1978-86, dep. dir., 1986-87; ptnr. Smith and Schnacke, Dayton, Ohio, 1987-89, Thompson and Hine LLP, Dayton, Ohio, 1989—. Mem. adv. bd. Fed. Publ. Inc., Govt. Contract Costs, Pricing & Acctg. Report. Contbr. articles to legal jours. Pres. Forest Ridge Assn., Dayton,Ohio, 1984-96; sec., gen. counsel U.S. Air and Trade Show, 1994-98, chmn., 1998—; bd. dir. Nat. Aviation Hall of Fame, 1998—. Mem. ABA (chmn. sect. pub. contract law 1993-94), sec., budget and fin. officer sect., coun. mem., chmn. fed. procurement divsn., vice chmn. acctg., cost and pricing com., truth in negotiations com., chmn. cost acctg. stas. sub com.), Fed. Bar Assn., Ohio Bar Assn., Nebr. Bar Assn., Contracts Appeals Bar Assn. (bd. govs. 1998-2001). Avocation: travel. Office: Thompson and Hine LLP 10 W 2nd St Dayton OH 45402-1758

KINMAN, GARY, company executive; Owner, CEO Kinman Assocs., Inc. Office: Kinman Assocs Inc 7300 Industrial Pkwy Plain City OH 43064-8788 E-mail: kinman1@aol.com.

KINNAIRD, SUSAN MARIE, special education educator; b. Grosse Pointe, Mich., May 3, 1954; d. William Burl and Ida Mae (Diehl) Cunningham; m. Henry Wayne Kinnaird Jr., Nov. 30, 1985. BA in Edn., Wayne State U., 1978; MA in Ednl. Adminstrn., U. Houston at Clear Lake, 1990. Cert. elem. tchr., spl. edn. tchr., spl. edn. supr., instrnl. supr., ESL tchr., Tex. Parent trainer Dept. Mental Health, Warren, Mich., 1977-78; spl. edn. tchr. Houston Ind. Sch. Dist., 1978-95, spl. edn. coord., 1995—. Asst. coach Spl. Olympics, Houston, 1982, 84, 88-91; bell choir mem. Cen. Presbyn. Ch., Houston, 1979—. Grantee Houston Bus. Com. for Ednl. Excellence 1991, 92. Mem. Coun. for Exceptional Children (chpt. 100 newsletter editor 1990-92, sec. 1992-93, pres.-elect 1993-94, pres. 1994-95). Roman Catholic. Avocations: sewing, handcrafts, music, reading, travel. Home: 4111 Mona Lee Ln Houston TX 77080-1768 Office: Houston Ind Sch Dist Office of Spl Edn 3830 Richmond Houston TX 77027-

KINNANE, ADRIAN, historian; b. Liverpool, Eng., Sept. 28, 1948; s. John F. Kinnane and Jano Aerona Evans; m. Jo Brooks, July 6, 1991; 1 child, Claire. BA, Boston Coll., 1970; PhD, Cath. U. Am., 1976, U. Md., 2000. Police officer Balt. City Police Dept., 1973—74; clin. psychologist Georgetown U., Washington, 1978—79; clin. asst. prof., dept. child health and devel. Med. Sch. George Wash. U., Washington, 1979—82; clin. psychologist Children's Hosp. Nat. Med. Ctr., Washington, 1979—82; clin. asst. prof. dept. psychiatry Wright State U. Med. Sch., Dayton, 1984—85; clin. psychologist Eugene Meyer III Treatment Ctr. Washington Sch. Psychiatry, 1986—95, dir. fellowship tng. program, 1993—95; sr. historian History Associates Inc., Rockville, Md., 2000—; postdoctoral fellow pediatric psychology U. Md. Med. Sch., Balt. Pvt. clin. psychology cons., Silver Spring, Md., 1977—95. Author: (non-fiction) Policing, DuPont: From the Banks of the Brandywine to Miracles of Science. Capt. USAF, 1982—86. Decorated Air Force Commendation medal USAF. Mem.: Orgn. Am. Historians, Am. Hist. Assn., Surfrider Found. Home: 5309 Massachusetts Ave Bethesda MD 20816-1654 Office: History Associates Inc 300 N Stonestreet Ave Rockville MD 20850 E-mail: akinnane@historyassociates.com.

KINNE, FRANCES BARTLETT, chancellor emeritus; b. Story City, Iowa; d. Charles Morton and Bertha (Olson) Bartlett; m. Harry L. Kinne, Jr. (dec.); m. M. Worthington Bordley, Jr. (dec.). Student, U. No. Iowa; B of Music Edn., M. of Music Edn., Drake U., DFA (hon.), 1981, hon. degree; PhD cum laude, U. Frankfurt, Fed. Republic of Germany, 1957; LHD (hon.), Wagner Coll., N.Y.; LLD (hon.), Lenoir Rhyne Coll.; DHL (hon.), Jacksonville U., 1995; LLD (hon.), Flagler Coll. Tchr. music Kelley (Iowa) Consol. Sch.; supr. music Boxholm (Iowa) Consol. Sch., Des Moines pub. schs.; sr. hostess Camp Crowder, Mo.; dir. recreation VA, Wadsworth, Kans.; lectr. music, English and Western culture Tsuda Coll., Tokyo; cons. music U.S. Army Gen. Hdqrs., Tokyo; mem. faculty Jacksonville (Fla.) U., 1958—, Disting. Univ. prof., 1961-62, prof. music and humanities, 1963—, dean, founder Coll. Fine Arts, interim pres., 1979, pres., 1979-89, chancellor, 1989-94; chancellor emeritus, 1995—. Past chmn. Ind. Colls. and Univs. Fla.; mem. adv. coun. Nat. Soc. Arts and Letters; hon. mem. staff Mayo Clinic, Jacksonville; corporator Charles Schepens Eye Rsch. Inst. of Harvard U., Cambridge, Mass.; mem. adv. bd. Women's Eye Task Force. Author: A Comparative Study of British Traditional and American Indigenous Ballads, 1958, Iowa Girl: The President Wears a Skirt, 2000; contbr. chpt. to book and articles to profl. jours. Bd. govs. Drake U.; bd. dirs. (hon.) Jacksonville Symphony Assn., Bert Thomas Scholarship Found., Doug Milne Found., Jacksonville U.; bd. dirs., exec. com. Eye Rsch. Found.; mem., then chmn. adv. bd. Ronald McDonald House; past mem. bd. govs. Jacksonville C. of C., past v.p.; mem. pres.'s adv. coun. Flagler Coll. Recipient hon. awards Bus. and Profl. Women's Clubs, 1962, Disting. Svc. award Drake U., 1966, 1st Fla. Gov.'s award for achievement in arts, 1972, EVE award in edn., 1973, Arts Assembly Individual award, 1978-79, Roast award Soc. for Prevention of Blindness, 1980, Brotherhood award NCCJ, 1981, Top Mgmt. award Jacksonville Sales and Mktg. Execs., 1981, Alumni Achievement award U. No. Iowa, Ann. Burton C. Bryan award, Pub. Svc. award Physicians Edn. Network, Freedom Found. Valley Forge, Brotherhood of NCCJ award, Disting. Svc. award Fla. Soc. Ophthalmology, Women of Achievement award 1st Coast Bus. and Profl. Women's Club Jacksonville, Disting. Educator award Internat. Longshoremen's Assn., Hope award Nat. Multiple Sclerosis Soc., Disting. Am. award Nat. Football Fedn., Fla. State Mus. Tchrs. award, Outstanding Civic Leader award Civic Roundtable of Jacksonville, Vol. Jacksonville 2d Ann. Bernard Gregory Servant Leader award; named Eve of Decade, Elaine Gordon Lifetime Achievement award Fla. Fedn. Bus. and Profl. Women, 1996, Orderof the South award So. Acad. Letters, Arts and Scis.; inducted into Fla. Women's Hall of Fame, Outstanding Svc. to Theatre Edn. Fla. Assn. for Theatre Edn.; hon. mem. 3d Armored Divsn., U.S. Army; day named in her honor Women's Club of Jacksonville and other orgns.; one of six women featured on History Week posters apptd. by Mayor Jacksonville; bldgs. named in honor: Frances Bartlett Kinne Univ. Ctr. Jacksonville U., Frances Bartlett Kinne Alumni and Devel. Ctr. Drake U., Frances Bartlett Kinne Auditorium at Mayo Clinic, Jacksonville. Mem. AAUW, Nat. Music Tchrs. Assn., Fla. Music Tchr. Assn., Music Educators Nat. Conf., Fla. Music Edn. Assn. (past bd. dirs.), Assn. Am. Colls. (past bd. govs., exec. com.), Friday Musicale (life), Fla. Coll. Music Edn. Assn. (past pres., v.p.), Delius Assn. of Fla. (life), Nat. Assn. Schs. Music (past chmn. region 7), Fine Arts Forum (hon.), Ind. Colls. and Univs. of Fla. (past chmn., 1st woman chmn.), So. Acad. Letters, Arts and Scis., Internat. Coun. Fine Arts Deans (past chmn., 1st woman chmn.), Fla. Women's Hall of Fame (Gov.'s First award), Jacksonville Women's Network Inner Wheel, Nat. Soc. Arts and Letters (adv. coun.), P.E.O., Green Key (hon.), Ret. Officers Assn. (hon. mem. Mayport chpt.), St. John's Dinner Club (past pres.), Exch. Club (Golden Deeds award), River Club (1st woman mem.), Rotary (pres. 2000, one of 1st two women elected bd. dirs. Jacksonville chpt., Paul Harris fellow, 1st woman pres. Rotary Club Jacksonville, 2000—), Alpha Xi Delta, Mu Phi Epsilon (Elizabeth Mathias award, judge internat. music edn. award), Alpha Psi Omega (hon.), Alpha Kappa Pi (hon.), Alpha Kappa Psi (hon.), Beta Gamma Sigma, Omicron Delta Kappa (hon.), Alpha Xi Delta (Woman of Distinction award). Home: 4032 Mission Hills Cir W Jacksonville FL 32225-4635 Fax: 904-646-4904. E-mail: Faltak@aol.com. *It has been a delightful challenge to amalgamate my career with happy experience as a U.S. Army wife - as a young bride assigned to China and evacuated to Occupied Japan - in pursuit of my Ph.D. at the University of Frankfurt in Occupied Germany (the lone American student) as a professor, dean, president, chancellor and now Chan. Emer. of Jacksonville University.*

KINNEAR, JOHN KENYON, JR., architect; b. Bklyn., Aug. 9, 1948; s. John Kenyon and Helen (Knowlton) K.; m. Alice Taylor, Jan. 30, 1971 (div. July 1982); m. Donna Manheim, Nov. 27, 1982. BArch, Pratt Inst., 1972. Registered arch., N.Y., Conn.; cert. Nat. Coun. Archtl. Registration Bds. Prin. Janko Rasic Assocs. Architects, N.Y.C., 1972—2003; pvt. practice N.Y.C., 2003—. Chmn. archtl. adv. com. Town of Ridgefield, Conn. Prin. works include Brit. Meml. Garden, Hanover Sq., N.Y. Recipient Monsanto DOC Nat. Design award, 1993. Mem. AIA, Nat. Trust for Hist. Preservation, Nelson Soc., Soc. for Nautical Rsch., Am. Friends of the Georgian Group (v.p.), Sandanona Hare Hounds, Mashomack Preserve Club. Avocations: horseback riding, historic ship modeling. Home: 90 Cains Hill Rd Ridgefield CT 06877-4209 Office: 317 Madison Ave Ste 1200 New York NY 10017 E-mail: johnkinnearaiae@aol.com.

KINNEBREW, JACKSON METCALFE, lawyer; b. Oklahoma City, June 29, 1941; s. Jackson A. and Mary Lucille (Metcalfe) K.; m. Carole A. Vadner, Sept. 23, 1967; children: Scott, Sarah. BBA in Acctg., U. Okla., 1963; JD, So. Meth. U., 1967, LLM in Taxation, 1973. Bar: Tex. 1968, U.S. Dist. Ct. (no. dist.) Tex. 1968, U.S. Tax Ct. 1970, U.S. Ct. Appeals (5th cir.) 1971, U.S. Supreme Ct. 1971; CPA, Tex. Assoc. Strasburger & Price, Dallas, 1968-74, ptnr., 1975—. Lectr. Wills and Probate Inst., 1980, 81, 83, 89, Practicing Law Inst., 1983; bd. trustees Ctr. Am. and Internat. Law (formerly Southwestern Legal Found.), 1987-. Contbr. legal articles to profl. jours. Gen. counsel Cmtys. Found. of Tex., Dallas, 1987—; fund raising chmn. Boy Scouts Am., Dallas, 1984—86; chmn. legacy com. Am. Cancer Soc., Dallas, 1978—82; interim exec. dir. Cmtys. Found. Tex., Dallas, 2001—. Lt. U.S. Army, 1963—65. Recipient Disting. Alumni award Pub. Interest, So. Meth. U. Sch Law, 2002. Fellow Am. Coll. Trust and Estate Counsel (state chmn. 1984-89, bd. regents 1988-94, membership selection com. 1993-99), Internat. Acad. Estate and Trust Law (academician 1990—); mem. ABA (subcom. chmn. 1979), State Tex. Bar Assn. (lectr. 1981, 82), Dallas Bar Assn. (chmn. probate sect. 1985), Tex. Soc. CPAs, Dallas Estate Planning Coun. (pres. 1985, program v.p. 1984, treas. 1982, sec. 1981), Tex. Bd. Legal Specialization (cert.). Avocations: golf, sports, bridge. Office: Strasburger & Price LLP Bank Am Plz 901 Main St Ste 4300 Dallas TX 75202-3724

KINNELL, GALWAY, poet, translator; b. Providence, Feb. 1, 1927; s. James Scott and Elizabeth (Mills) K.; children: Maud, Fergus. AB summa cum laude, Princeton U., 1948; MA, U. Rochester, 1949. Instr. English Alfred U., N.Y., 1949-51; dir. liberal arts program U. Chgo., 1951-55; Am. lectr. U. Grenoble, France, 1956-57; Fulbright lectr. U. Iran, Teheran, 1959-60; adj. assoc. prof. Columbia U., N.Y.C., 1972, adj. prof., 1974, 76; Citizens' prof. U. Hawaii at Manoa, Honolulu, 1979-81; dir. writing program NYU, N.Y.C., 1981-84, Samuel F.B. Morse prof. arts and scis., 1985-92, Erich Maria Remarque prof. creative writing, 1992—. Lectr. summer session U. Nice, France, 1957; vis. prof. Queens Coll. of CUNY, 1971, Pitts. Poetry Forum, 1971, Brandeis U., 1974, Skidmore Coll., 1975, U. Del., 1978; poet-in-residence Juniata Coll., 1964, Reed Coll., 1966-67, Colo. State U., 1968, U. Wash., 1968, U. Calif., Irvine, 1968 69, U. Iowa, 1970, Holy Cross Coll., 1977; vis. poet Sarah Lawrence Coll., 1972-78, Princeton U., 1976; resident writer Deya Inst., Mallorca, Spain, 1969-70; vis. writer Macquarie U., Sydney, Australia, 1979; poetry dir. Squaw Valley Cmty. of Writers, 1979—. Author: (poetry) What a Kingdom It Was, 1960, Flower Herding on Mount Monadnock, 1964, Body Rags, 1968, Poems of Night, 1968, The Hen Flower, 1969, First Poems: 1946-1954, 1970, The Shoes of Wandering, 1971, The Book of Nightmares, 1971, The Avenue Bearing the Initial of Christ into the New World; Poems 1946-1964, 1974, Mortal Acts, Mortal Words, 1980, Selected Poems, 1982 (Nat. Book award for poetry 1983, Pulitzer Prize for poetry 1983), The Fundamental Project of Technology, 1983, The Past, 1985, When One Has Lived a Long Time Alone, 1990, Imperfect Thirst, 1994, A New Selected Poems, 2000; (novels) Black Light, 1966; (children's) How the Alligator Missed Breakfast, 1982; (non-fiction) The Poetics of the Physical World, 1969, Walking Down the Stairs: Selections from Interviews, 1978, Thoughts Occasioned by the Most Insignificant of All Human Events, 1982, Remarks on Accepting the American Book Award, 1984; translator: Rene Hardy's Bitter Victory, 1956, Henri Lehmann's Pre-Columbian Ceramics, 1962, The Poems of Francois Villon, 1963, Yves Bonnefoy's On The Motion and Immobility of Douve, 1968 (Cecil Hemley Poetry prize Ohio U. Pr. 1968), Yvan Goll's The Lackawanna Elegy, 1970, Yves Bonnefoy's Early Poems, 1947-1959, 1990, The Essential Rilke, 1999; editor: The Essential Whitman, 1987. Fulbright scholar, 1955-56; Guggenheim fellow, 1961-62, 74-75; grantee Ford Found., 1955, Nat. Inst. Arts and Letters, 1962, Rockefeller Found., 1962-63, 68; Amy Lowell travelling fellow, 1969-70, MacArthur fellow, 1984; recipient Longview Found. award, 1962, Bess Hokin prize Poetry Mag., 1965, Eunice Tietjens prize Poetry Mag., 1966, Ingram Merrill Found. award, 1969, Brandeis U. Creative Arts award, 1969, Shelley prize Poetry Soc. Am., 1974, Medal of Merit Nat. Inst. Arts and Letters, 1975, Landon Translation prize, 1979, Hutchinson medal U. Rochester, 2001, Frost medal Poetry Soc. Am., 2002; named Vt. State Poet, 1989-93. Mem. Nat. Acad. and Inst. Arts and Letters, Am. Acad. Arts and Sci., Acad. Am. Poets (chancellor). Office: New York Univ Creative Writing program New York NY 10003-6607

KINNEY, ANNE, federal agency administrator; BA with honors, U. Wis., 1975; PhD in Astrophysics, NYU, 1984. Instrument scientist Space Telescope Sci. Inst., Balt.; head edn. dept. Office of Pub. Outreach; dir. astronomy and physics divsn. Office Space Sci. NASA, Washington. Mem. editl. bd. Astronomy Mag. Contbr. numerous articles to profl. jours. Mem.: Am. Astron. Soc. (mem. coun.). Office: NASA Mail Code S 300 E St SW Washington DC 20546

KINNEY, ARTHUR FREDERICK, literary history educator, writer, editor; b. Cortland, N.Y., Sept. 5, 1933; s. Arthur F. and Gladys (Mudge) K. BA magna cum laude, Syracuse U., 1955; MS, Columbia U., 1956; PhD, U. Mich., 1963. Instr. Yale U., New Haven, Conn., 1963-66; asst. prof. U. Mass., Amherst, 1966-69, assoc. prof., 1969-73, prof., 1973-85, Copeland Prof., 1985—. Adj. prof. Clark U., 1973—, NYU, 1990—; dir. Mass. Ctr. for Renaissance Studies, Amherst; spkr. in field. Author: Faulkner's Narrative Poetics, 1978, Resources of Being: Flannery O'Connor's Library, 1984, Humanist Poetics, 1986, John Skelton: Priest as Poet, 1987, Continental Humanist Poetics, 1989, Dorothy Parker Revisited, 1997, Renaissance Drama, 1999, 2nd edit., 2001, Cambridge Companion to English Literature 1500-1600, 2000, Blackwell Companion to Renaissance Drama, 2001, Lies Like Truth: Shakespeare, Macbeth and the Cultural Moment, 2001, New Essays on Hamlet, 2001, Shakespeare by Stages, 2003; editor: Rogues, Vagabonds, and Sturdy Beggars, 1973, 2nd edit., 1990, Elizabethan Backgrounds, 1974, revised edit., 1990, Renaissance Historicism, 1987, English Literary Renaissance jour., (book series) Twayne English Authors Series-Renaissance, Massachusetts Studies in Early Modern Culture; mem. editl. bd. several jours.; editl. cons. in field:. With AUS, 1956-58. Recipient Disting. Tchg. award U. Mass., 1990, Chancellor's medal, 1985, Univ. Rsch. fellowship, 1976; named Fulbright fellow, Christ Ch., Oxford U., 1977-78, Sr. Huntington Libr. fellow, 1973-74, 78, 83, Sr. NEH fellow, 1973-74, 87-88, Sr. Folger Shakespeare Libr. fellow, 1974, 90, 92. Mem. MLA (pres. coun. of editors of learned jours. 1971-73, 81-83), Shakespeare Assn. Am. (trustee 1995—), Renaissance Soc. Am. (coun. mem.), Renaissance English Text Soc. (pres. 1985—), Sixteenth-Century Studies Conf. Assn, Internat. Sidney Soc. (pres.). Avocations: published photographer, jazz. Home: 25 Hunters Hill Cir Amherst MA 01002-3116 Office: English Dept U Mass Amherst Amherst MA 01003 also: Ctr Renaissance Studies PO Box 2300 Amherst MA 01004-2300

KINNEY, CAROL NAUS ROBERTS, real estate broker; b. Mpls., May 7, 1923; d. Edward Paul and Esther (Colwell) Naus; m. Thomas R. Roberts, May 2, 1942 (dec. Feb. 1968); children: Thomas Naus Roberts, Margaret Elizabeth Roberts, Shelley Roberts; m. Harry E. Kinney, Aug. 30, 1970 (div. Aug. 1988); life ptnr. Allan L. Levine, Feb. 1998. Student, Mt. Holyoke Coll., 1940-42; BA in Bacteriology magna cum laude, U. Minn., 1946. Mem. staff Los Alamos Scientific Lab., 1964-70; co-owner Harry E. Kinney Gen. Contractor, Albuquerque, 1977-81, 86; real estate broker Christopher Webster, Albuquerque, 1992-94, Kate Southard Real Estate, Albuquerque, 1994-98, Carol Kinney Real Estate, Albuquerque, 1998—. City Councillor Los Alamos, N.Mex., 1968-70; chair 100 Yr. Cmty. Outreach U. N.Mex., Albuquerque, 1986-89; chair bd. of ethics and campaign practices City of Albuquerque, 1990-94; bd. N.Mex. Gov.'s Mansion Found., 1988-92, 96—. Honored as Albuquerque Vol. Jr. League of Albuquerque, 1985; entered into Albuquerque Sr. Hall of Fame, 1989—; Albuquerque's First Lady, 1974-78, 81-85. Mem.: Rio Grande Nature Ctr. (trustee 1984—86, 1988—), N.Mex. Symphony (trustee 1992—2001, exec. com. 1998—2001, emeritus trustee 2001—), The Nature Conservancy (trustee 1976—90, 1992—2000, Disting. trustee 2001—), Phi Beta Kappa, Beta Sigma Phi. Republican. Unitarian Universalist. Avocations: skiing, camping, contractor/foreman for building own home. Home and Office: 2917 Calle Del Rio NW Albuquerque NM 87104-3143 Fax: 505-343-9554. E-mail: ckinney@albuquerquehomes.com.

KINNEY, CAROLYN, executive secretary; b. Philipsburg, Pa., Feb. 18, 1957; MD, Boston U., 1981. Sec. Am. Bd. Phys. Medicine & Rehab.; staff Good Samaritan Regional Hosp. Med. Ctr., Phoenix, 1995—; phys. Health South Meridian Point Rehab., Scottsdale, Ariz., 1996—; resident Thomas Jefferson U. Hosp., Phila., 1982—84; intern Thomas Jefferson U. Hosp., Phila., 1981. Office: Am Bd Phys Medicine & Rehab 21 First St Ste 674 Rochester MN 55902-3092

KINNEY, CATHERINE R. stock exchange executive; BS magna cum laude, Iona Coll.; cert. advanced mgmt., Harvard Sch. Bus. Various positions N.Y. Stock Exch., 1974—86, mgr. trading-floor opers. and tech., 1986—95, group exec. v.p., 1995—2002, exec. vice chmn., pres. & co-COO, 2002—. Mem. office of chmn. N.Y. Stock Exch., co-chair mgmt. and oper. coms., bd. mem., MetLife Inc., Depository Trust & Clearing Corp., NYU Downtown Hosp., Securities Industry Automation Corp., 1988—97, mem. exec. com., 1994—97. Bd. regents Georgetown U.; trustee Iona Coll. Office: attn Ray Pellecchia NY Stock Exch 11 Wall St New York NY 10005*

KINNEY, EARL ROBERT, mutual funds company executive; b. Burnham, Maine, Apr. 12, 1917; s. Harry E. and Ethel (Vose) K.; m. Margaret Velie Thatcher, Apr. 23, 1977; children: Jeanie Elizabeth, Earl Robert, Isabella Alice. AB, Bates Coll., 1939; postgrad., Harvard U. Grad. Sch., 1940. Founder, North Atlantic Pack Co., Bar Harbor, Maine, 1941, pres., 1941-42, treas., dir., 1941-64; with Gorton Corp. (became subs. Gen. Mills, Inc. 1968), 1954-68, pres., 1958-68; v.p. Gen. Mills, Inc., 1968-69, exec. v.p., 1969-73, chief fin. officer, 1970-73, pres., chief operating officer, 1973-77, chmn. bd., 1977-81; pres., chief exec. officer IDS Mut. Fund Group, Mpls., 1982-87. Bd. dirs. Idexx Labs., Inc. Trustee Bates Coll., also chmn. alumni drives, 1960-64. Office: 4900 IDS Ctr Minneapolis MN 55402

KINNEY, GREGORY HOPPES, lawyer; b. Anderson, Ind., July 15, 1947; s. Dalton Roth and Effie Eleanor (Hoppes) K. BA, Mich. State U., 1969, M in Labor Rels., 1971; JD, U. Detroit, 1974. Bar: Mich. 1975, U.S. Dist. Ct. (ea. dist.) Mich. 1975, U.S. Dist. Ct. (we. dist.) Mich. 2000, U.S. Ct. Appeals (D.C. cir.) 1975, U.S. Ct. Appeals (6th cir.) 1987. Labor law editor Bur. Nat. Affairs, Washington, 1974; pension cons. Edward H. Friend & Co., Washington, 1975, Wyatt Co., Detroit, 1976-84; pvt. practice Detroit, 1984-86, Troy, Mich., 1986-99, Decatur, Mich., 1999—. Office: PO Box 243 Decatur MI 49045-0243

KINNEY, JAMES HOWARD, lawyer; b. Oklahoma City, Mar. 2, 1937; s. William Edgar and Chrissie (Ballingall) K.; m. June Lassick, Mar. 26, 1961; children: Karen Jill, Scott James. BS in Bus. Mgmt., Calif. State U., Long Beach, 1963; JD, UCLA, 1966. Bar: Calif. 1966, U.S. Dist. Ct. (so. dist.) Calif. 1966. Dep. dist. atty. Ventura (Calif.) County, 1966-68; ptnr. Collins, Gleason & Kinney, Torrance, Calif., 1968-85, O'Melveny & Myers, Los Angeles, 1985—2000; sr. v.p. The Macerich Co., Santa Monica, Calif., 2000—. Lectr. Harbor Coll., L.A., 1971-72. Councilman City of Palos Verdes Estates, Calif., 1983-1990, Mayor, 1985-86, 88-89. With USMC, 1955-58. Mem. Los Angeles County Bar Assn., Internat. Council Shopping Ctrs., Sigma Alpha Epsilon. Republican. also: O'Melveny & Myers 400 S Hope St Los Angeles CA 90071-2801 Office: Ste 700 401 Wilshire Blvd Santa Monica CA 90401-1452

KINNEY, JANIS MARIE, librarian, consultant, storyteller; b. Cresson, Pa., Dec. 26, 1935; d. Cecil and Ruth Ellen (Moyer) Powell; m. James Leroy Kinney; 1 child, Janis Cecilia. BS in Libr. Sci., Clarion U., 1957; MEd in Curriculum and Instrn., Pa. State U., 1987. Librarian N. Huntingdon Sch. Dist., Irwin, Pa., 1957-58, Greater Gallitzin (Pa.) Schs., 1959-61, Hollidaysburg (Pa.) Area Sch. Dist., 1961-90; storyteller Altoona, Pa., 1990—. Chair Allegheny Storytellers of Pa., 1991—; rostered artist Pa. Coun. on the Arts in Edn. Program; cons. various sch. dists.; cons. Old Bedford Village Storytelling Festival, Bedford, Pa., West Overton Village Tellabration; cofounder interdisciplinary arts group Stories in Motion. Author/producer audio cassettes;

featured teller Corn Island Storytelling Festivals, Louisville; contbr. articles to profl. jours. Active Blair County Arts Found., Altoona, 1991—, Blair County Tourist & Conv. Bur., 1992—, Blair County Hist. Soc., 1994—; Pa. Rural Arts Alliance, 1992—. Recipient Disting. Educator award Hollidaysburg Alumni, 1996. Mem. Internat. Order E.A.R.S. (Disting. Svc. award 2001), Nat. Storytelling Assn., Allegheny Storytellers Pa. (founder). Avocations: reading, bicycling, hiking, music, travel. Home and Office: 1900 16th Ave Altoona PA 16601-2502 E-mail: jankin@nb.net.

KINNEY, JEANNE KAWELOLANI, English studies educator, writer; b. Bayville, N.Y., Nov. 22, 1964; d. Robert Warren Stewart and Genevieve Lehuanani (Okilauea) Kinney. BA, Linfield Coll., 1986; MFA, Bowling Green State U., 1988. Tchr. Hawaii Bus. Coll., Honolulu, 1993-95; ESL tchr. GEOs Lang. Corp., Osaka and Kobe, Japan, 1996-97; English tchr. St. Joseph's H.S., Hilo, Hawaii, 2000. Poet-in-the-schs. Dept. Edn., Honolulu, fall 1994; sub. English tchr. St. Andrew's Priory, Honolulu, 1993; adj. English tchr. Chaminade U., Honolulu, spring 1993, 94; basic skills instr. Kamehameha Schs., Honolulu, 1991-92; English tchr., speech coach Punahou Sch., Honolulu, 1989-91. Contbr. to profl. publs. including Hawaii Rev., Kaimana, Ascent, Seattle Rev., Bamboo Ridge Press. Precinct ops. cood. Office Lt. Gov., Hawaii Elections Divsn., 1991-93, precinct worker trainer, 1989-91; v.p. Hawaii Lit. Arts Coun., Honolulu, 1990; pub. rels. officer Hawaii Speech League, Honolulu, 1991. Avocations: dance, swimming, writing, travel, foreign languages. Home: 10 Ululani St # 10 Hilo HI 96720-2979

KINNEY, KATHY, actress; b. Stevens Point, Wis., Nov. 3, 1954; d. Harold and Marian Kinney. Student, U. Wis. Actress playing Mimi Bobeck on The Drew Carey Show ABC-TV, 1995—. Appearances include (films) Parting Glances, 1986, Scrooged, 1988, Arachnophobia, 1990, Stanley and Iris, 1990, The Linguini Incident, 1991, Mr. Jones, 1993, This Boy's Life, 1993, (TV series) Newhart, 1989-90, Grand, 1990, (TV episodes) The Larry Sanders Show, 1992, Seinfeld, 1992, Lois and Clark: The New Adventures of Superman, 1996, (TV movies) Inherit the Wind, 1988, Promised a Miracle, 1988, (TV spls.) Tag Team, 1991, presenter The Eighteenth Ann. Cable Ace Awards, 1996; also various stage appearances. Avocations: restoring old lamps, reading. Office: care The Drew Carey Show Warner Bros TV 4000 Warner Blvd Burbank CA 91522-0001*

KINNEY, KENNETH PARRISH, retired banker; b. Kansas City, Mo., Aug. 5, 1921; s. Wayne William and Dorothy Fay (Parrish) K.; m. Madeline Shriver Brennan, Aug. 2, 1947 (dec. Sept. 1983); children— Ann, Frank, Catherine, William, Madeline, Ellen, Robert; m. Terese Ann Bargen-Cagney, May 25, 1985. AB, Princeton U., 1943; postgrad., Grad. Sch. Bus. Adminstrn., NYU, 1949-51. Sub-acct. Nat. City Bank N.Y., N.Y.C., 1946-50; asst. mgr. Chem. Bank, N.Y.C., 1950-55; sr. v.p. No. Trust Co., Chgo., 1955-86. Bd. dirs. Hinsdale (Ill.) Libr. Bd., 1985—91, Great Books Found., Chgo., 1997—2002. 1st lt. A.C. U.S. Army, 1943—46, ETO. Mem. Bankers Assn. Fgn. Trade (pres. 1969-70), Chgo. Council Fgn. Rels. (treas. 1967-70), Chgo. Com., Union League Club (Chgo.), Hinsdale Golf Club. Home: 633 S County Line Rd Hinsdale IL 60521-4726

KINNEY, LINFORD NELSON, retired army officer; b. Newton, N.J., Sept. 11, 1937; s. Sidney Ayers and Edna Louella (Winfield) K.; m. Joyce Arlene Souder, May 1, 1987. BSBA, Pa. Mil. Coll., 1959; postgrad., Golden Gate Coll., 1967. Commd. 2d lt. U.S. Army, 1959, advanced through grades to col., 1981; pers. officer Mil. Pers. Ctr., Washington, 1974—75; mem. staff Dept. Army, Pentagon, Washington, 1976-77; comdr. U.S. Army Port, Pusan, Korea, 1977-78; dir. hdwrs. MTMC, Washington, 1979-83; dir. New Cumberland (Pa.) Army Depot, 1983-87; comdr. MTMC Terminal Command Far East, Seoul, South Korea, 1987-89; ret., 1989; pres. Beaumont Sq. Homeowners Assn., Mechanicsburg, Pa., 1990—. Mem. Cen. Pa. Coun., Cmty. Assns. Inst., 1999—. Vol. Internat. Exec. Svc. Corps., Stamford, Conn., 1990—; mem. comp plan com. Hampden Twp., 1991, sr. logistics analyst, 1992—98; vice chmn. Hampden Twp. Planning Commn., 1995—. Decorated Def. Superior Svc. medal, Bronze Star, Legion of Merit, Meritorious Svc. medal (3). Mem.: Vietnam Vets. of Am., Army Transp. Assn. Vietnam, Army Transp. Regtl. Assn., Bur. Issues Assn., Mil. Officers Assn. Am. (bd. dirs. Keystone chpt. 1999—), Assn. U.S. Army, Nat. Def. Transp. Assn., Capital City Philatelic Soc., Am. Philatelic Soc., Army Transp. Mus. Found., Mil. Order Fgn. Wars, Am. Legion, Mil. Order World Wars, Theta Chi. Republican. Methodist. Avocations: reading, philately. Home: 1050 Turnberry Ct Mechanicsburg PA 17050-9100

KINNEY, LISA FRANCES, lawyer; b. Laramie, Wyo., Mar. 13, 1951; d. Irvin Wayne and Phyllis (Poe) Kinney; m. Rodney Philip Lang, Feb. 5, 1971; children: Cambria Helen, Shelby Robert, Eli Wayne. BA, U. Wyo., 1973, JD, 1986; MLS, U. Oreg., 1975. Reference libr. U. Wyo. Sci. Libr., Laramie, 1975-76; outreach dir. Albany County Libr., Laramie, 1975-76, dir., 1977-83; mem. Wyo. State Senate, Laramie, 1984-94, minority leader, 1992-94; with documentation office Am. Heritage Ctr. U. Wyo., 1991-94; assoc. Corthell & King, 1994-96, shareholder, 1996-99; owner Summit Bar Rev., 1987—; fin. planner VALIC, 2001—. Author: (with Rodney Lang) Civil Rights of the Developmentally Disabled, 1986; (with Rodney Lang and Phyllis Kinney) Manual For Families with Emotionally Disturbed and Mentally Ill Relatives, 1988, rev. 1991, 99, 2003, Lobby For Your Library, Know What Works, 1992; contbr. articles to profl. jours.; editor, compiler pub. rels. directory of ALA, 1982. Bd. dirs. Big Bros./Big Sisters, Laramie, 1980-83, Children's Mus., 1993-97; bd. dirs. Am. Heritage Ctr., 1993-97, Citizen of the Century, 1997-99, govt. chmn. 1997-99. Recipient Beginning Young Profl. award Mt. Plains Libr. Assn., 1980; named Outstanding Wyo. Libr. Assn., 1977, Outstanding Young Woman State of Wyo., 1980, Arts and Scis. Disting. Alumni award U. Wyo., 1997, Making Democracy Work award Wyo. LWV, 2000. Mem.: ABA, Nat. Conf. State Legislatures (various coms. 1985—90), Laramie Area C. of C. (bd. dirs. 1996—2000, mem. 1999, Top Hand award 1997), Zonta, Kiwanis. Democrat. Avocations: photography, dance, reading, travel, languages. Home: 1415 E Baker St Laramie WY 82072 Office: PO Box 1710 Laramie WY 82073-1710 Fax: 307-742-6644. E-mail: lfk1@aol.com.

KINNEY, MARCELLE ANNE, economist, consultant; b. Wauwatosa, Wis., Oct. 7, 1959; d. Thomas W. and Enid E. (Fish) K. BA in Econs., BS in Chemistry, U. Fla., 1985, MA in Econs., 1987, PhD in Econs., 1992. Economist Tax and Budget Reform Com., Tallahassee, Fla., 1990-91, Fla. Dept. Labor, Tallahassee, 1991-92; pres. Kinney Econ. Consulting, Vakaria and Tallahassee, Fla., 1993—. Bd. dirs. 21st Century Coun., Tallahassee, Fla., exec. dir., 1996; adj. prof. Fla. State U., Tallahassee, 1990, 94. Mem. Jr. League Tallahassee (Fla.), 1994-96, Leadership Tallahassee, 1995-97, Econ. Devel. Commn. of Fla.'s Space Coast, 1998—. Doct. fellow Pub. Policy Ctr., 1989. Mem. Tallahassee Gator Club (v.p. academics 1992-96), South Brevard Panhellenic, South Brevard Zeta Tau Alpha Alumnae (v.p. 1998-2002, pres. 2002—). Republican. Presbyterian. Avocations: reading, gardening, exercising, praying, meditating. Home and Office: 2055 Valkaria Rd Valkaria FL 32950-4328

KINNEY, MARK BALDWIN, educator; b. Bangor, Maine, Dec. 27, 1944; s. Gerald Lewis and Virginia (Baldwin) K.; m. Nancy Pearson Kinney, June 6, 1964; children: Kathryn Louise Hahn, William Kinney. BA, U. Maine, Orono, 1962-66; MA, George Peabody Coll. for Tchrs, Nashville, 1970-71; PhD, George Peabody Coll. for Tchrs, 1971-76. Tchr. math. Hermon (Maine) Sch. Dist., 1967-70; rsch. assoc. Inst. of Gerontology U. Mich., 1974-76; asst. prof. U. Toledo, 1976-80, dir. off-campus edn., 1985-86, dir. student svcs., 1986-87, assoc. prof., 1980-99, dir. Ctr. for Internat. Studies and Programs, 1995-96, Lisle fellow (fellowship pres.), 1984-89; exec. dir. Lisle, Temperance, Mich., 1989—. Vis. lectr. Ea. Mich. U., Ypsilanti, 1973-75; cons. GM Corp., Toledo, Saginaw, 1990-94, U. Toledo Corp, 1993-94; vis. prof. Juhasz Tchr. Tng. Coll., Szeged, Hungary, 2003, U. Szeged, 2003. Author: Staff Training in Geriatric Institutions, 1975, Skills in Interpersonal Comm., 1983, Exercises for the Older Adult, 1988, Empower Ourselves and Others, 1994. George Peabody Coll. Tchg. doctoral fellow U.S. Office of Edn., 1971-72. Mem. Phi Beta Delta, Phi Delta Kappa. Avocations: sailing, swimming, skiing, singing, boat building. Office: Lisle PO Box 87 Presque Isle MI 49777 E-mail: mkinney@utnet.utoledo.edu.

KINNEY, PAUL WILLIAM, investment company executive; b. Denver, Nov. 3, 1952; s. Thomas Grayson and Margaret Jane Kinney; children: Lauren Michele, Hope Elizabeth. AB, Occidental Coll., L.A., 1975; MPA, U. Colo., Denver, 1978. 1st v.p. investments Dean Witter Reynolds Inc., Glendale, Calif., 1978-99; sr. v.p. Morgan Stanley Dean Witter, Glendale, Calif., 1999—. Pres. bd. dirs. Glendale (Calif.) Symphony Orch. Assn., 1995—; bd. dirs. Glendale Cmty. Found., 1995—, cfo. Recipient CIMA (Cert. Investment Management Analyst), Investment Management Con. Assn., Denver, Colo., 2002. Mem. Investment Mgmt. Cons. Assn., Pi Alpha Alpha. Office: Morgan Stanley 801 N Brand Blvd Ste 908 Glendale CA 91203-1243

KINNEY, STEPHEN HOYT, JR., lawyer; b. Albuquerque, Feb. 27, 1948; s. Stephen Hoyt and Harriet May (Gadsden) K.; m. Leslie vanLiew, June 10, 1972; 1 child, Erin. BS, MIT, 1970; JD, Harvard U., 1973. Bar: N.Y. 1974, U.S. Dist. Ct. (so. dist.) N.Y. 1974, U.S. Dist. Ct. (ea. dist.) N.Y. 1974, U.S. Dist. Ct. (no. dist.) N.Y. 1978, U.S. Ct. Appeals (2d cir.) 1975, U.S. Supreme Ct. 1982. Programmer, analyst MIT, 1968-70; law clk. N.J. Organized Crime Unit, Trenton, 1972; assoc. Reid & Priest, N.Y.C., 1973-85, sr. atty., 1985-86, ptnr., 1986-98, Thelen Reid & Priest LLP, N.Y.C., 1998—. Author, editor: Outline of Arbitration, 1984; contbr. articles to profl. jours.; creator software. Mem. ABA, MB Yacht Club (Port Washington, N.Y.). Office: Thelen Reid & Priest 875 Third Ave New York NY 10022-6225 E-mail: skinney@thelenreid.com.

KINNEY, THOMAS J. adult education educator; BA in Psychology, Syracuse U., 1968; MSW in Mgmt., SUNY, Albany, 1974. Dir. profl. development program, Nelson A. Rockefeller coll. pub. affairs and policy U. Albany, SUNY, 1976-99, spl. asst. to provost, 1997-99; chief learning officer, v.p. edn. Premier Health Alliance, Chgo., 1999—; CEO Kinney and Assoc., 2000—; faculty Keller Grad. Sch. Mgmt., 2002—, U. Phoenix Sch. Bus., 2001—. Bd. dirs. Synquest Technologies, Inc.; mem. Task Force N.Y. State Work Force 21st Century; mem. SUNY 2000 Task Group Social Svcs.; dir. Ctr. Profl. Devel. and Continuing Edn. Rsch., chmn. quality forum Rockefeller Coll. Press; prof. Russian Acad. Edn.; co-founder Russian-Am. Ctr. Adult and Continuing Edn., Moscow; mem. task force employee assistance programs N.Y. State Assembly; mem. implementation adv. com. WorkKeys project Am. Coll. Testing; presenter in field. Editor Jour. Continuing Social Work Edn. Named Continuing Educator of Yr., Continuing Edn. Assn. N.Y., 1988; named to Internat. Adult and Continuing Hall of Fame, 1996 Fellow N.Y. State Acad. Pub. Adminstrn.; mem. Am. Assn. Adult and Continuing Edn. (treas., past chair commn. continuing profl. edn., Outstanding Svc. medallion 1994, pres. 1999—), Nat. Univ. Continuing Edn. Assn. (chair divsn. continuing edn. professions, mem. fin. com., mem. task force displaced profls.). Office: PO Box 770536 Ocala FL 34477 E-mail: thomaskinney@msn.com.

KINNEY, VIRGINIA LEE, librarian, educator; b. Barnesville, Ohio, Oct. 21, 1934; d. James Jeffrey and Mary Virginia Groves; m. Royce Bentley Kinney, Mar. 11, 1956; children: Charlotte, William, Robert, Margaret, Mary Elizabeth. BS in Home Econ., Ohio State U., 1956; student, Muskingum Coll., 1963, Ohio U., 1965, U. Dayton, 1988, student, 1991, Urbana U., 1968, student, 1970, student, 1975, student, 1997, student, 1998. Instr. County Ext. Agt. Ohio State U., Columbus, Ohio, 1959—60; tchr. Union Local Head Start, Bethesda, Ohio, 1961—62, Barnesville Elem. Sch., Barnesville, Ohio, 1962—62; libr. Miami County Pub. Libr., Troy, Ohio, 1978—. Instr. Newton Local Chpt. I, Pleasant Hill, Ohio, 1979—88; libr. Newton Local, Pleasant Hill, 1984—2002; instr. Adult Basic & Lit. Edn., Piqua, Ohio, 1988—. State pres. Ohio CowBelles, Ohio, 1984—85; historian Epworth Pk., Bethesda, 1997—; mem. Astrobuds Garden Club, 1973—; bd. dirs. Oakes Beitman Mus., 1985—2000. Mem.: Miami County Assn. Family Consumer Sci., Ohio Assn. Adult & Continuing Edn., Miami County Rep. Women, Human Ecology Alumni Soc., Johnny Appleseed Soc., Alpha Delta Pi Alumnae (state pres. 1992—94). Republican. Home: 8055 W State Rt 718 Pleasant Hill OH 45359

KINNEY, WILLIAM LIGHT, JR., newspaper editor, publisher; b. Bennettsville, SC, Oct. 26, 1933; s. William Light and Annie Laurie (Mayer) K.; m. Margaret Rene Pegues, Mar. 21, 1964; children: Elisabeth Mayer Kinney McNiel, William Light III (dec.). BS, Wofford Coll., 1954, LHD, 1999; BA in Journalism, U. S.C., 1977. Copy editor The State, Columbia, S.C., 1955-58; reporter Marlboro Herald-Advocate, Bennettsville, 1958-59, advt. mgr., 1959-60, bus. mgr., 1960-65, mng. editor, 1965-70, editor, pub., 1970—; pres. Marlboro Pub. Co. Inc., 1970—. Sec. Marlboro Savs. & Loan Assn., Bennettsville, 1970-82, First Nat. Bank of S.C., Bennettsville, 1973-84; mem. adv. bd. S.C. Nat. Bank, Bennettsville, 1984-94, Wachovia Bank, 1994-2000; sec., mem. adv. bd. Security Fed. Savs. & Loan, 1982-90, bd. dirs., 1984-89; pres. Greater Pee Dee Press Inc., 1972-82, Bennettsville Parking and Devel. Co., 1964; v.p. Hamlet (N.C.) News Inc., 1973-82. Editor, pub.: Three Who Dared, 1960, Sherman's March—A Review, 1961, 2002, The Story of the Sculpture Light, 2001. Pres. United Fund, Bennettsville, 1963-64; chmn. Marlboro County com. S.C. Tricentennial, 1970, U.S. Bicentennial, 1974—; councilman, mayor pro tem City of Bennettsville, 1967-69; mem. Marlboro County Devel. Bd., 1958-81; bd. dirs. Kinney Found., 1971-99, chmn. bd. dirs., 1975-99; bd. dirs. Indian Mus. of Carolinas, 1972—; trustee Whipple Found., 1979—, chmn., 1981—; trustee S.C. Press Found., 1978-93, 2000--, vice-chmn., 1985-92, chmn., 1992-93; trustee Neil Monroe Trust Fund, 1965-91, chmn., 1977-91; adv. bd. SBA, 1962-64; chmn. fin. com. 1st Meth. Ch., 1985-87, staff parish com. chmn., 1990-92; active Chancel Choir, 1951—; trustee S.C. Meth. Adv., 1968-78, S.C. Hall of Fame, 1980-88, v.p., 1980-82; dir. S.C. Confedn. Local Hist. Socs., 1974-75, treas., 1975-78, v.p., 1979, pres., 1980-82; warden St. David's Soc., 1978-80, pres., 1980-81; chmn. Jennings-Brown House Restoration, 1974-76, Bennettsville Downtown Commn., 1977-82; v.p. Bennettsville Downtown Devel. Assn., 1993—; trustee Am. Folklife Ctr., Washington, 1982—, chmn. 1987, 92-93, 98-2000, vice-chmn., 1990-92; mem. S.C. Archives and History Commn., 1987—, vice-chmn., 1988-90, 98—, chmn., 1990-93; SC rev. bd. Nat. Register of Hist. Places, 1988—, chmn., 1990—, S.C. State Devel. Bd., 1993; bd. dirs. Friends Brookgreen Gardens, 1991-97, 2001--, pres., 1993-96, trustee, 1993-96; bd. visitors Coker Coll., 1986-89; bd. dirs. S.C. Com. for Humanities, 1981-85, Pawleys Island Civic Assn., 1979—, Palmetto Trails, 1993-97; trustee Scotia Village Retirement Cmty., 1995—; v.p. Marlboro Civic Ctr. Found., 1994—. Named Bennettsville and S.C. Young Man of Yr., 1961, S.C. Amb. for Econ. Devel., 1990, Knight of Justice of the Order of St. John, Knights of Malta, Sovereign Order of St. John of Jerusalem, 1995—. Mem. SAR, Nat. Trust for Historic Preservation (bd. advisors So. Region 1997—, chmn., 2000-02, nat. exec. com. 1999-2002) S.C. Press Assn. (pres. 1972-73), Palmetto Conservation Found. (dir. 1997-2001), Palmetto Trust Hist. Preservation (trustee 2002—), Marlboro County Hist. Preservation Com. (chmn. 1986-96), S.C. C. of C. (bd. dirs. 1964-68, 75-78), Bennettsville C. of C. (bd. dirs. 1964-67, 75-78), Bennettsville Jaycees (pres. 1962), S.C. Jaycees (v.p. 1963, nat. dir. 1964), Marlboro Hist. Soc. (bd. dirs. 1967-79, 2000—, pres. 1975-79, Govs. award 1996, Elizabeth O'Neill Verner Gov.'s award for the arts 2002), U. S.C. Soc. (bd. dirs. 1972-82, vice chmn. 1977-82, S.C. Jean Laney Harris Folk Heritage award 2003), Wofford Coll. Alumni Assn. (bd. dirs. 1968-72), Marlboro Country Club, Marlboro Cotillion (pres. 1984-86), Nat. Debutante Cotillion (sponsor 1987-95), Sans Souci Club (pres. 1980-82), Rotary (bd. dirs. 1968-70, 99-2001, pres. 1970-72), McLeod Med. Ctr. Found. (trustee 1997—), Phi Beta Kappa, Sigma Alpha Epsilon, Sigma Delta Chi. Home: Magnolia PO Box 656 Bennettsville SC 29512-0656 Office: Marlboro Herald-Adv Shiness 100 Fayetteville Ave Bennettsville SC 29512-4022 *"Service to humanity is the best work of life" is a tenet of the Jaycee Creed that still drives me to work through my avocations as well as my vocation to help make my community, state and nation better than I found. These efforts have broadened my horizons, enriched my life and heightened my spirit. I recommend active service to one's home community, state and nation to all.*

KINNINGHAM, ALAN GOODRUM, music educator, composer/arranger; b. Huntingdon, Tenn., Apr. 18, 1956; s. Troy Edward and Evelyn Clara (Goodrum) K.; m. Jennifer Lynn Bennett, May 30, 1977; children: William Andrew, Thomas Bennett. BS in Music Edn., U. Tenn., Martin, 1977; MusM in Music Composition, Tex. A&M Commerce, 1978; DMA in Music Composition, U. Memphis, 1990. Cert. tchr., Tenn. Dir. bands Martin (Tenn.)-Westview High Sch., 1978-85, Covington (Tenn.) High Sch., 1985-87; tchg. asst. band dept. U. Memphis, 1987-89; assoc. dir. bands Munford (Tenn.) High Sch., 1990, Haywood County High Sch., Brownsville, Tenn., 1990-97; dir. music Covington (Tenn.) Crestview Mid. Sch., 1997-2000, Covington H.S., 2000—. Nat. adv. bd. U.S. Achievement Acad., 1985; founder Kinningham Music Svcs., Covington, 1978—. Composer: Freedom's Cries: 1989, 1990, String Quartet #1, 1988, Sonaire #2, 1992, Echoes Past of Future Dreams, 1993, Prospect Variations, 2001, Nettleton Variants, 2002, Overlord, 2003, Sing To Me A Painting, 2003. Music dir. Brighton (Tenn.) Ch. of Christ, 1989-95, treas., 1989-95; deacon Covington (Tenn.) Ch. Christ, 1999—2003, elder, 2003—. Recipient Rafferty award for young composers Evanston (Ill.) Twp. High Sch., 1984, Key to City of Martin, 1985, Haimsohn Composition award U. Memphis, 1988, All-Am. Scholar award U.S. Achievement Acad., 1990. Mem. NEA, Music Educators Nat. Conf., Soc. of Composers, Inc., Am. Soc. Composers and Publishers, Southeastern Composers League, Phi Delta Kappa, Phi Kappa Phi. Avocations: photography, camping. Home: 1834 Kimbrough Dr Covington TN 38019-3612 Office: Covington HS 803 S College Covington TN 38019 E-mail: akinningha@aol.com.

KINNISON, ROBERT WHEELOCK, retired accountant; b. Des Moines, Sept. 17, 1914; s. Virgil R. and Sopha J. (Jackson) K.; m. Randi Hjelle, Oct. 28, 1971; children: Paul F., Hazel Jo Lewis. BS in Acctg., U. Wyo., 1940. CPA, Wyo., Colo. Ptnr. 24 hour auto service, Laramie, Wyo., 1945-59; pvt. practice acctg. Laramie, Wyo., 1963-71, Las Vegas, Nev., 1972-74, Westminster, Colo., 1974-76, Ft. Collins, Colo., 1976-97; ret., 1997. Served with U.S. Army, 1941-45, PTO. Mem. Wyo. Soc. CPAs, Am. Legion (past comdr.), Laramie Soc. CPAs (pres. 1966), VFW, Laramie Optimist Club (pres. 1950), Sertoma Club. Home: PO Box 168 Fort Collins CO 80522-0168

KINNISON, WILLIAM ANDREW, retired university president; b. Springfield, Ohio, Feb. 10, 1932; s. Errett Lowell and Audrey Muriel (Smith) K.; m. Lenore Belle Morris, June 11, 1960; children— William Errett, Linda Elise, Amy Elisabeth. AB, Wittenberg U., 1954, BS in Edn., 1955; MA, U. Wis., 1963; PhD (1st Flesher fellow), Ohio State U., 1967; postgrad., Harvard U. Inst. Ednl. Mgmt., 1970; LL.D., Calif. Luth. Coll., 1983; Th.D., John Carroll U., 1983; LLD, Lenoir-Rhyne Coll., 1987; LHD, Capital U., 1995. Asst. dean admissions Wittenberg U., Springfield, 1958-65, asst. to pres., 1967-70, v.p. for univ. affairs, 1970-73, v.p. adminstrn., 1973, pres., 1974-95, pres. emeritus, 1995—; pres., CEO Heritage Ctr. of Clark County, 1997—2002. Author: Samuel Shellabarger: Lawyer, Jurist, Legislator, 1969, Building Sullivant's Pyramid: An Administrative History of the Ohio State University, 1970, Concise History of Wittenberg University, 1976, An American Seminary, 1980, Springfield and Clark County: an Illustrated History, 1985, also articles. Asst. to dir. Sch. Edn. Ohio State U., Columbus, 1965-67; past chmn. Assn. Ind. Colls. and Univs. Ohio; trustee Ohio Found. Ind. Colls., 1974-95, chair bd. trustees, 1995; chmn. standing com. Luth. World Ministries, 1976-82; mem. exec. coun. Luth. Ch. in Am., 1978-86; mem., chmn. Commn. for a New Luth. Ch., 1982-86; bd. dirs. Am. Assn. Colls., 1982-84. With U.S. Army, 1956-58. Mem. Clark County Hist. Soc. (trustee 1963—), Orgn. Am. Historians, Blue Key, Phi Beta Kappa, Phi Delta Kappa, Kappa Phi Kappa, Pi Sigma Alpha, Tau Kappa Alpha, Delta Sigma Phi, Omicron Delta Kappa. Clubs: Cosmos, Rotary. Home: 1820 Timberline Dr Springfield OH 45504-1236

KINNUNE, WILLIAM P. forest products executive; b. 1939; Grad., U. Wash., 1961. With Willamette Industries, Inc., Portland, Oreg., 1961—, various sales and mgmt. positions, 1961-75, v.p., 1975-77, sr. v.p., from 1977, now exec. v.p. Office: Willamette Industries Inc Wells Fargo Ctr Portland OR 97201

KINO, GORDON STANLEY, electrical engineering educator; b. Melbourne, Australia, June 15, 1928; came to U.S., 1951, naturalized, 1967; s. William Hector and Sybil (Cohen) K.; m. Dorothy Beryl Lovelace, Oct. 30, 1955; 1 child, Carol Ann. B.Sc. with 1st class honours in Math, London (Eng.) U., 1948, M.Sc. in Math, 1950; PhD in Elec. Engring, Stanford U., 1955. Jr. scientist Mullard Research Lab., Salford, Surrey, Eng., 1947-51; research asst., then research assoc. Stanford U., 1951-55, research assoc., 1957-61, mem. faculty, 1961—, prof. elec. engring., 1965—, assoc. dean facilities and planning Sch. Engring., 1986-92, assoc. chmn. elec. engring., 1984-88, W.M. Keck Found. chair engring., 1992-97, W.M. Keck Found. chair engring. emeritus, 1997—; dir. Ginzton Lab., 1994-96. Mem. tech. staff Bell Telephone Labs., 1955-57; cons. to industry, 1957— Author: (with Kirstein, Waters) Space Charge Flow, 1968, Acoustic Devices, 1987, (with Corle) Confocal Scanning Optical Microscopy and Related Imaging Systems, 1996; also numerous papers on microwave tubes; electron optics, plasma physics, bulk effects in semiconductors, acoustic surface waves, acoustic imaging, optical microscopy, fiber optics, nondestructive testing, optical storage. Guggenheim fellow, 1967-68; recipient Applied Research Achievement award Am. Soc. Non-destructive Testing, 1986. Fellow IEEE (Centennial medal, Sonics and Ultrasonics Group Achievement award 1984), Am. Phys. Soc., AAAS; mem. Nat. Acad. Engring. Inventor Kino electron gun, 1959; co-inventor real-time scanning optical microscope, 1987, solid immersion lens, 1989, microfabricated miniature microscope, 1995. Home: 867 Cedro Way Stanford CA 94305-1002 E-mail: kino@stanford.edu.

KINOSHITA, TOICHIRO, physicist; b. Tokyo, Jan. 23, 1925; came to U.S., 1952; s. Tsutomu and Fumi (Ueda) K.; m. Masako Matsuoka, Oct. 14, 1951; children: Kay, June, Ray. BS, Tokyo U., 1947, PhD, 1952. Mem. Inst. for Advanced Study, Princeton, N.J., 1952-54; postdoctoral fellow Columbia U., N.Y.C., 1954-55; rsch. assoc. Cornell U., Ithaca, N.Y., 1955-58, asst. prof., 1958-60, assoc. prof., 1960-63, prof., 1963-92, Goldwin Smith prof., 1992-95, Goldwin Smith prof. emeritus, 1995—. Mem. tech. adv. panel U.S. Dept. Energy, Washington, 1982-83; com. fundamental constants Nat. Rsch. Coun., Washington, 1984-86. Author: Quantum Electrodynamics, 1990; contbr. over 100 articles to profl. jours. Guggenheim fellow, 1973-74; recipient Sun-Amco medal Internat. Union Phys. & Applied Sci., 1998. Fellow NAS, AAAS, Am. Physical Soc. (Recipient J.J. Sakurai prize 1990). Democrat. Home: 5 Winthrop Pl Ithaca NY 14850-1740 Office: Cornell U Newman Lab Ithaca NY 14853 E-mail: tk@hepth.cornell.edu.

KINOSIAN, JANET MARIE, journalist; b. Los Angeles, June 20, 1957; d. Kasper John and Carol Grace (Boghosian) K. BA in Psychology, UCLA, 1980; MA in Psychology, Loyola Marymount, 1987. Intern L.A. Mag., 1980-81; staff writer Orange County Media Group, Costa Mesa, Calif., 1982-84; contbg. editor Orange Coast Mag., Costa Mesa, Calif., 1984-91, Palm Springs Life mag., 1984-95; pres. JMK & Co., Brentwood, Calif., 1991—. Contbr. numerous articles to regional and nat. mags. and newspapers; extensive reporting, writing L.A. Times; internationally syndicated by Times of London, N.Y. Times Syndicate, L.A. Times Syndicate. Co-founder Campus Coalition for Peace, 1978, Internat. Women's Coalition, 1979; mem. Amnesty Internat., 1980-94, Child Help USA, 1985-94, Free Arts for Abused Children, 1991-94; poetry tchr. L.A. Ctrl. Juvenile Hall, East Lake, Violent Offenders. Mem. APA, L.A. Press Club, Hollywood Women's Press Club, Calif. Assn. Ind. Writers, Am. Soc. Journalists, Pi Beta Phi.. Democrat. Presbyterian. Avocations: art, travel, literature, film, poetry. Home and Office: 18001 Leafwood Ln Santa Ana CA 92705-2005

KINOSZ, DONALD LEE, business process consultant; b. Pitts., Dec. 7, 1940; s. Michael and Pearl (Buckner) K.; m. Deborah Michele Reed, June 2, 1978; children: Brigitte, Brenda, Wayne Casey. BS, U. Pitts., 1966, MBA, 1995. Process engr. Alcoa Tech. Ctr., Alcoa Center, Pa., 1966-76, Alcoa, Tenn., 1976-79, mgr. Alcoa Center, Pa., 1979-81, pers. mgr., 1981-83, chem. mgr., 1983-85, ceramics mgr., 1985-88, mgr. quality, 1988-94; cons. Quality Assoc. Inc., 1994—. Prodn. mgr. Anderson County Works, Palestine, Tex., 1978-79; mem. adv. bd. U. Pitts., 1988-94. City councilman City of Lower Burrell, Pa., 1980-88, mayor, 2000—. Fellow Am. Inst. Chemists; mem. Am. Soc. Quality Control, Indsl. Rsch. Inst. (chmn. quality dirs. network), Quality Dirs. Network (founder, past chair), Strongland C. of C. (bd. dirs. 1985—, chmn. bd. 2000), Pa. Quality Leadership Found. (sr. examiner 1994), Sigma Xi, Beta Gamma Sigma. Achievements include patents in anti-pollution method, electrolytic production of magnesium, production of magnesium chloride, regeneration of activated carbon having materials adsorbed thereon, flow control baffles for molton salt electrolysis, metal production, disposal of waste gasses from production of aluminum chloride, electrolytic furnace lining, method of preparing an electrolytic cell for operation, situ cleaning of electrolytic cells, treatment of offgas from aluminum chloride production. Home: 491 Dakota Dr Lower Burrell PA 15068-3305 Office: Quality Assocs Inc 3401 Windy Hill Dr Lower Burrell PA 15068-2201

KINS, JURIS, lawyer; b. Jelgava, Latvia, Apr. 24, 1942; came to U.S., 1949; s. Arnolds and Zenta (Dunis) K.; m. Olita Gita Kakis, Oct. 11, 1969; children: Aleksis A., Mikus N. BSChemE, U. Wis., 1964; MSChemE, U. Mich., 1965; JD, U. Wis., 1969. Bar: Wis. 1969, Ill. 1969. Assoc. ptnr. Chadwell & Kayser, Ltd., Chgo., 1969-90; ptnr. Vedder, Price, Kaufman & Kammholz, Chgo.,

1990-93; Abramson & Fox, Chgo., 1993—. Pres. Latvian Peoples Support Group, Chgo., 1991—. Mem. ABA, Chgo. Bar Assn., Ill. Bar Assn., Wis. Bar Assn., Latvian Bar Assn. Avocations: tennis, skiing. Office: Abramson & Fox One E Wacker Dr Ste 3800 Chicago IL 60601 E-mail: juriskins@aol.com.

KINSEL, JANE F. health science association administrator; b. Havre de Grace, Md., Aug. 10, 1955; d. Harry George and Anna Louise Kinsel; m. Michail V. Sitkovsky, Sept. 17, 1980. BS in Chemistry, U. Del., Newark, 1977; PhD in Pharm. Chemistry, U. Kans., 1981; MBA, U. Pa., 2000. Sr. scientist drug devel. Richardson Vicks Pharm. Co., Shelton, Conn., 1981—85; pharmacologist reviewer divsn. bioequivalence Office of Generic Drugs FDA, Rockville, Md., 1985—89; chief pharm. affairs sect. Pharm. and Regulatory Affairs Br., divsn. of AIDS Nat. Inst. Allergy and Infectious Diseases, NIH, Bethesda, Md., 1989—90, asst. dir. divsn. microbiology and infectious diseases, 1990—98, dir. Office Policy Analysis, 1998—2001; assoc. dir. sci. policy and ops. Nat. Ctr. for Complementary and Alternative Medicine, NIH, 2001—. Bd. dirs. Duska Sci. Co., Bala Cynwyd, Pa. Contbr. ; author: spl. reports. Achievements include patents for on antidiarrheal compositions and use thereof. Office: NIH 6707 Democracy Blvd #407 Bethesda MD 20892

KINSELL, JEFFREY CLIFT, investment banker; b. Santa Barbara, Calif., Sept. 13, 1951; s. Clift Seybert and Shirlee Grace (Burwash) K.; m. Sondra A. Kinsell, May 21, 1987 (div.); children: Amy Elizabeth, Pamela Suzanne. BS in Biology, Tulane U., 1973; MBA in Fin., Acctg., UCLA, 1976. Assoc. mcpl. sales and trading First Boston Corp., N.Y.C., 1976-78, v.p. San Francisco, 1978-88; v.p., western regional mgr. Paine Webber Capital Markets, Inc., San Francisco, 1988-94; v.p. instl. sales A.G. Edwards & Sons, Inc., San Francisco, 1994-96; mng. dir., mgr. tax exempt securities Banc of Am. Securities, LLC, San Francisco, 1996—. Mem. San Francisco Mcpl. Bond Club, Beta Beta Beta, Sigma Alpha Epsilon. Republican. Episcopalian. Avocations: sailing, skiing, travel, photography. Home: 37 Oak Rd Orinda CA 94563-3322 Office: Banc of Am Securities LLC CA5-801-07-33 Transam Bldg 600 Montgomery St 7th Fl San Francisco CA 94111-2702 E-mail: jkinsell@hotmail.com., jeffrey.c.kinsell@bankofamerica.com.

KINSELLA, DAVID, education educator; b. Detroit, Mich., Dec. 9, 1961; m. Linda Angst, Mar. 13, 1993; 1 child, Madeleine. BA, U. of Calif., 1982—85; MPhil, Yale U., 1985—88, PhD, 1988—93. Asst. prof. U. of Mo., 1992—97, Am. U., Washington, 1997—2002; assoc. prof. Portland State U., 2002—. Author: (textbook) World Politics: The Menu for Choice. Fellow Mershon Post-doctoral Fellowship, Ohio State U., 1994-1995. Mem.: Peace Sci. Soc., Am. Polit. Sci. Assn., Internat. Studies Assn. (pres., midwest region 1996—97). Office: Hatfield Sch Portland State U PO Box 751 Portland OR 97207-0751 E-mail: kinsella@pdx.edu.

KINSELLA, RALPH ALOYSIUS, JR., physician; b. St. Louis, June 4, 1919; s. Ralph A. and Mabel Lamb (Downey) K.; m. Margaret Neville Boyle, Aug. 9, 1947; children: Ralph Aloysius, III, Mary, John, Eileen, Michael, Margaret, Matthew, Charles. AB, St. Louis U., 1939, MD, 1943. Diplomate: Am. Bd. Internal Medicine. Intern Presbyn. Hosp., N.Y.C., 1943; postgrad. St. Louis U., 1946-47, mem. faculty, 1948-95, prof. medicine, 1972-95, emeritus prof., 1995—; chief unit II St. Louis U. Med. Service, St. Louis City Hosp., 1958-80, med. dir., 1980-85, St. Louis Univ. Hosp., 1985-95. Pres. Inst. Med. Edn. and Rsch., St. Louis, 1972-95. Served with U.S. Army, 1944-46. Charles H. Nielson fellow, 1947-48; John and Mary Markle scholar, 1948-53. Fellow ACP, AAAS; mem. St. Louis Soc. Internal Medicine, St. Louis Med. Soc., Mo. Med. Soc., Endocrine Soc., Central Soc. Clin. Rsch., AMA, N.Y. Acad. Scis., Univ. Club, Sigma Xi. Roman Catholic. Achievements include rsch. in steroid hormonal biochemistry. Home: 53 Hanley Downs Saint Louis MO 63117-1366

KINSELLA, THOMAS, poet; b. Dublin, May 4, 1928; s. John Paul and Agnes (Casserly) K.; m. Eleanor Walsh, 1955, 3 children. With Irish Civil Service, 1946-65, asst. prin. officer Dept. Fin., 1960-65. Artist in residence So. Ill. U., 1965-67, prof. English, 1967-70; prof. Temple U., Phila., 1970-90; dir. Dolmen Press Ltd., Cuala Press Ltd, Dublin; founder Peppercanister, Dublin, 1972. Author: Poems, 1956, Another September, 1958, Downstream, 1962, Nightwalker and Other Poems, 1968, Notes from the Land of the Dead, 1972, Butcher's Dozen, 1972, Finistere, 1972, New Poems, 1973, Selected Poems 1956-68, 1973, Song of the Night and Other Poems, 1978, The Messenger, 1978, Fifteen Dead, 1979, One and Other Poems, 1979; Songs of the Psyche, 1984; Her Vertical Smile, 1984; St. Catherine's Clock, 1987; Out of Ireland, 1987, Blood and Family, 1988, Poems From Center City, 1990, Personal Places, 1990, Madonna and Other Poems, 1991, Open Court, 1991, From Centre City, 1994, The Dual Tradition: an Essay on Poetry and Politics in Ireland, 1995, Collected Poems, 1996, The Pen Shop, 1997, The Familiar, 1999, Godhead, 1999, Citizen of the World, 2000, Littlebody, 2000, Collected Poems 1956-2001, 2001; editor: Selected Poems of Austin Clarke, 1976; (with Sean O'Tuama) Poems of the Dispossessed 1600-1900 with translations, 1980; The New Oxford Book of Irish Verse (with translations), 1986; transl. (from Old Irish) The Tain, 1970. Recipient Guinness Poetry award, 1958, Triennial Book award, Irish Arts Coun., 1960, Denis Devlin Meml. award, 1966, 1969, 1988, 1994, Field Day/Keough-Notre Dame Centre/Commons Tundish award, 2001; fellow Guggenheim, 1968—69, 1971—72. Mem. Am. Acad. Arts and Scis., Irish Acad. Letters. Home: 639 Addison St Philadelphia PA 19147

KINSER, CYNTHIA D. state supreme court justice; b. Pennington Gap, Dec. 20, 1951; d. Morris and Velda (Myers) Fannon; m. H. Allen Kinser, Jr., March 17, 1974; children: Charles Adam, Terah Diane. Student, Univ. of Ga., 1970-71; BA, Univ. of Tenn., 1974; JD, Univ. of Va., 1977. Bar: Va. 1977, U.S. Dist. Ct. (we. dist.) Va. 1977, U.S. Ct. Appeals (4th cir.) 1977, U.S. Supreme Ct. 1988. Law clk. to Judge Glen M. Williams U.S. Dist. Ct., 1977-78; pvt. law practice, 1978-90; commonwealth's atty. Lee County, Va., 1980-83; magistrate judge U.S. Dist. Ct. (we. dist.) Va., Abingdon, 1990-98; justice Va. Supreme Ct., Richmond, 1998—. Trustee Chapter 7 Panel, U.S. Bankruptcy Ct., 1979-90. Mem. Va. Bar Assn., Va. Trial Lawyers Assn., Am. Bar Assn. Methodist. Office: Supreme Court 100 North 9th Street, 5th Floor Richmond VA 23219*

KINSER, RICHARD EDWARD, management consultant; b. L.A., May 14, 1936; s. Edward Lee and M. Yvonne (Withers) K.; m. Suzanne Carol Logan, Mar. 22, 1958. BA in Econs., Stanford U., 1958. Mgr. U.S. Steel Corp., San Francisco, 1958-65; v.p. Booz-Allen & Hamilton, Inc., 1965-78; sr. v.p., bd. dirs. William H. Clark Assocs., Inc., San Francisco, 1979-81; dep. dir. presdl. personnel The White House, Washington, 1981-83; mng. ptnr. Gould & McCoy, Inc., 1983-86; pres. Kinser & Baillou LLC, N.Y.C., 1986—. Exec. dir. Turn Around Mgmt. program European Bank for Reconstruction and Devel. Bd. dirs. San Francisco Bicentennial Com., 1976; vice chancellor's advisor Oxford U. Fellow Aspen Inst.; mem. White House Fellows Commn., Stanford Alumni Assn., Econ. Club, Capitol Hill Club. Republican. Home: 18 Fairchild Rd PO Box 577 Sharon CT 06069 Office: Fl 36 515 Madison Ave Fl 36 New York NY 10022-5403

KINSEY, CHARLES JOHN, industrial auctioneer, consultant, cattle breeder, farmer; b. Regina, Saskatchew, Can., Aug. 4, 1922; came to U.S., 1929; s. Alfred Richardson and Lola Mae (Lagergren) K.; m. Shirley Elaine Grady, June 25, 1950; children: Rebecca Diane, David Allan, Jane Elizabeth, Thomas Charles. BS, U. Ill., 1951. Fieldman Am. Hampshire Swine Registry, Am. Hampshire Herdsman, Peoria, Ill., 1946-48; exec. sec. Park Ridge (Ill.) C. of C., 1953; indsl. auctioneer S.L. Winternitz & Co., Inc., Chgo., 1954-57; ptnr. Kinsey-Koploy Co., Detroit, 1957-65; pres., prin. Charles Kinsey & Co., Inc., Detroit, 1965—; pres. Mich. Auctioneers Assn., 1960-61; v.p. Mich. Angus Assn., 1963. Cons. A-Line Mfg. Co., Centralia, Ill., 1982—. Author: The Lives and The Times of The Kinsey Brothers, Ernest and Alfred, 1997. Mem. First Presbyn. Ch. Choir, Farmington Hills, Mich., 1959—. Served U.S. Army, 1944-46, Persian Gulf Command, ETO. Recipient Am. Farmer Degree FFA Vocat. Agrl., Urbana, 1940, State PRes. Ill. Assn. Future Farmers Am., 1940-41, Thomas E. Wilson award Ill. 4H Club, Chgo., 1943, State Ill. 4H Livestock Champion, Nat. Hampshire Pig Club contest winner, 1939. Mem. U. Ill. Alumni Assn. (life), Sigma Phi Epsilon (life). Independent. Avocations: baritone soloist, creative writing, voice concerts. Home and Office: Charles Kinsey & Co Inc 40011 Jefferson Novi MI 48375-2026

KINSEY, DONNA LEE, music educator; b. Punxsutawney, Pa., Dec. 18, 1947; d. Donald Joseph White and Sarah Leona Gromley; m. William Robert Kinsey, Mar. 30, 1970; stepchildren: Sheryl Ann Mock, Merrilee Kay Saccol. BS in Music Edn., Ind. U. Pa., 1969; MusM, W.Va. Univ., 1979. Cert. tchr. W.Va. Organist/choir dir. St. John's Luth. Ch., Kittanning, Pa., 1969—71; music tchr. Latrobe Jr. High, Pa., 1971—72; pastoral musician St. Theresa's Roman Cath. Parish, Morgantown, W.Va., 1972—; music tchr. Armstrong Sch. Dist., Kittanning, 1969—71, Monongalia County Schs., Morgantown, 1993—. Asst. organist, choir dir. 1st Presbyn. Ch., Greensburg, Pa., 1971—72; music tchr. St. Francis Ctrl. Sch., Morgantown, 1973—92; chair Music Commn. Diocese, Wheeling/Charleston, W.Va., 1973—99; program chair Nat. Pastoral Musicians Music Edn. Bd., 1992—2002. Mem. bd. W.Va. Children's Chorus Bd., 1992—95. Mem.: Choristers Guild, Am. Guild Organists, Am. Guild English Handbell Ringers (mem. spl. events com., chair 2002—), Music Edn. Assn., Nat. Pastoral Musicians (Nat. Cath. Music Educator of the Yr. 2001—02), Am. Choral Dirs. Assn. Republican. Methodist. Home: 2594 Grafton Rd Morgantown WV 26508 Office: Westwood Mid Sch 670 River Rd Morgantown WV 26501

KINSEY, GARY W. education educator; b. Delano, Calif., June 9, 1952; s. Arthur W. and Betty L. Kinsey; m. Gwynne A. Dennis, June 24, 1974 (div. June 1, 1993); children: John P., Jenna M., Tyler W.; m. Tina M. Pierce, Aug. 29, 1997; children: Brandon Pierce, Rob Pierce, Bryan Pierce, Lindsay Pierce. BS in Social Scis., Calif. State U., Fresno, 1975, MA in History, 1990; MA in Ednl. Adminstrn., U. San Francisco, 1990; EdD in Edn. Policy and Adminstrn., U. So. Calif., 2003. Cert. Ryal profl. clear tchr. in social sci, clear adminstrv. credential, C.C. history tchr., supr. Ranch mgr., ptnr. Dennis and Kinsey Ranch, Firebaugh, Calif., 1975—86; H.S. tchr., activities dir. Firebaugh H.S., 1986—89; jr. H.S. prin. Firebaugh Jr. H.S., 1989—93; H.S. prin. Selma (Calif.) H.S., Calif., 1993—96; dep. prin. Clovis (Calif.) H.S., 1996—2001; assoc. prof., coord. tchr. intern program Calif. State U., Pomona, 2001—. Cons. Paradigm Ednl. Cons., Fresno, 1994—; bd. dirs. Calif. League H.S., Irvine, 1992—99; instnl. reviewer Calif. Commn. on Tchr. Credentialing, Sacramento, 2001—. Author: Eighteenth Century Travelers in the Americas, 1990, Alternative Scheduling in America's High Schools, 2003. Pres. bd. trustees Firebaugh-Las Deltas Unified Sch. Dist., Firebaugh, 1978—83; commr. City of Selma Recreation Dept., 1992—96; pres. Firebaugh-Mendota Rotary, 1978—79; creator, coord. Ctrl. Calif. H.S. Partnership Network. Named Fresno County Adminstr. of Yr., 1992. Mem.: East L.A. Tchr. Intern Consortium (bd. dirs. 2001—), Woodward Park Rotary Club (Interact advisor 1997—2002), Phi Delta Kappa. Republican. Baptist. Avocations: music, guitar, historical research, travel. Office: Calif State Poly U Dept Edn 3801 W Temple Ave Bldg 5-256 Pomona CA 91768 Fax: 559-449-9050. E-mail: gwkinswy@csupomona.edu.

KINSEY, HELEN JOAN, physician; b. Winchester, Tenn., Feb. 10, 1958; BA, Goshen Coll., 1981; MD, Ind. U. Sch. Medicine, 1985. Intern So. Ill. U., 1985-86, resident, 1986-89; physician pvt. practice, Columbus, Ind., 1989—. Office: 411 Plaza Dr # H Columbus IN 47201-2903

KINSEY, JAMES LLOYD, chemist, educator; b. Paris, Tex., Oct. 15, 1934; s. Lloyd King and Elaine Mills K.; m. Berma McDowell, July 28, 1962; children: Victoria, Samuel, Adam. BA, Rice U., 1956, PhD, 1959; NSF fellow, U. Uppsala, Sweden, 1959-60, postdoctoral fellow, U. Calif., Berkeley, 1960-62. Asst. prof. dept. chemistry M.I.T., 1962-67, asso. prof., 1967-74, prof., 1974-88, chmn. dept., 1977-82; D.R. Bullard-Welch Found. prof. sci. Rice U., Houston, 1988—; dean natural scis., 1988-98; interim provost Rice U., Houston, 1993-94. Cons. Los Alamos Nat. Labs., external rev. com. chemistry and laser sci. divsn., 1983—89; Miller rsch. fellow, 1960—62; mem. NAS-NRC Bd. Chem. Scis., 1980—83, co-chmn., 1981—83; mem. steering com. U.S. Army Basic Sci. Rsch.-NRC, 1981—86; mem. oversight rev. com. chemistry divsn. NSF, 1989; mem. vis. com. for divsn. chemistry and chem. engring. Calif. Inst. Tech., 1999—; mem. com. of chemistry facilities and infrastructure U. Calif.-Berkeley, 1992—93; mem. corp. vis. com. for dept. chemistry MIT, 1994—; vis. com. for chemistry Stanford U., 1993—96; mem. external rev. com. for chemistry U. Pa., 2000; mem. adv. com. on rsch. projects State of Tex. Higher Edn. Coordinating Bd., 2000—02; mem. adv. bd. for engring. and scis. Internat. U. Bremen, Germany, 2000—. Assoc. editor Jour. Chem. Physics, 1981-84; mem. editorial adv. bd. Jour. Phys. Chemistry, 1984-88, Ann. Rev. Phys. Chemistry, 1985-89; mem. adv. editorial bd. Chem. Physics Letters, 1992-97; mem. Coun. of Am. Acad. of Arts and Scis., 1997-2001; contbr. articles to profl. jours. Recipient E.O. Lawrence award U.S. Dept. Energy, 1987; Alfred P. Sloan fellow, 1964-68, Guggenheim fellow, 1969-70. Fellow AAAS, Am. Phys. Soc. (exec. com. divsn. chem. physics 1985-88, Earle K. Plyler prize 1995), Am. Acad. Arts and Scis.; mem. NAS, Am. Chem. Soc. (chmn. divsn. phys. chemistry 1985, Nobel Laureate Signature award for grad. edn. 1990), Sigma Xi. Office: Rice U MS-600 PO Box 1892 Houston TX 77251-1892 E-mail: jlkinsey@rice.edu.

KINSEY, JOHN ALLEN, systems engineer, director; b. Salem, N.J., Jan. 24, 1933; s. Charles Allen Kinsey and Margaret Elizabeth Summerlin; m. Becky Lou Schergens, Jan. 1, 1994; children from previous marriage: Steven A., John D., Robert G. BSME, Rutgers U., 1954; postgrad., N.Mex. A&M U., 1955—56, U. Calif., Santa Barbara, 1972—73, U. Houston, Clear Lake, 1989—90, George Mason U., 1991. Test engr. Texaco, Inc., Beacon, NY, 1954—55; sr. design engr. Gen. Dynamics/Convair, Edwards Rocket Base, Calif., 1957—61; mgr. The Aerospace Corp., Vandenberg AFB, Calif., 1961—75, systems engring. dir. El Segundo, Calif., 1975—79, prin. dir. Johnson Space Ctr., Tex., 1979—91, prin. dir., prin. engring. officer Arlington, Va., 1991—. Rules com. Homeowners Assn., Arlington, Va., 1998—99, landscape com., 2002—03, cmty. rep., 2002—03. 1st lt., test engr. U.S. Army, 1955—57, White Sands Proving Ground. Fellow: AIAA (assoc.); mem.: Women in Aerospace, Am. Rocket Soc. Avocations: bridge, boating, reading. Home: 2424 13th Court N Arlington VA 22201 Office: The Aerospace Corp 1500 Wilson Blvd Ste 515 Arlington VA 22209

KINSEY, JONI LOUISE, art history educator; b. Grand Forks, N.D., Nov. 19, 1958; d. Barry Allan and Carmen Louise Kinsey. BFA, U. Tulsa, 1981; MA, Washington U., 1984, PhD, 1989. Vis. asst. prof. Washington U., St. Louis, 1989-91; asst. prof. U. Iowa, Iowa City, 1991-97, assoc. prof., 1997—. Author: Thomas Moran and the Surveying of the American West, 1992, Plain Pictures: Images of the American Prairie, 1996 (Kayden Nat. Book award 1997), The Majesty of the Grand Canyon: 150 Years in Art, 1998; contbr. articles to profl. jours. Bd. dirs. Friends of Hist. Preservation, Iowa City, 1992-2002, pres., 1996-99. Smithsonian Predoctoral fellow Smithsonian Instn., Nat. Mus. Am. Art, Washington, 1987-88; travel to collections grantee Nat. Endowment for the Humanities, 1992, Exhbn. Planning grantee Nat. Endowment for the Humanities, 1995. Fellow Ctr. for Great Plains Studies-U. Nebr. (assoc.); mem. Am. Studies Assn., Coll. Art Assn., Assn. Historians Am. Art, Western Hist. Assn., Midwest Art History Assn. Democrat. Unitarian Universalist. Avocations: old house restoration, travel, sailing, reading. Office: U Iowa Sch Art/Art History 120 N Riverside Dr Side Iowa City IA 52246-3536

KINSEY, RONALD C., JR., lawyer; b. Washington, June 28, 1942; s. Ronald C. Kinsey; m. Maria Emma Pikon, July 20, 2002; children: Kyle, Cara. AB, Dartmouth Coll., 1964; JD, U. Wash., 1967. Bar: Wash. 1970, U.S. Dist. Ct. (we. dist.) Wash. 1973. Dep. pros. atty. King County, Seattle, 1970-71; mcpl. legal cons. Assn. of Wash. Cities, Seattle, 1971-81; mcpl. atty. Holt Law Offices, Issaquah, Wash., 1981-83; pvt. practice law Seattle, 1983-89; marine investigator USCG, Seattle, 1989—; chief Coast Guard Casualty Investigations, Seattle, 1996—. Capt. U.S. Army, 1968-70. Mem. Rotary of Univ. Dist., Seattle Yacht Club, Dartmouth Club of Western Wash. Home: 4346 NE 58th St Seattle WA 98105-2250 E-mail: rkinsey@pacnorwest.uscg.mil.

KINSINGER, JACK BURL, chemist, educator; b. Akron, Ohio, June 23, 1925; s. William Franklin and Idelle (Althaus) K.; m. Addie Jean Parker, Sept. 2, 1946 (div. 1987); children: Paul Craig, Amy Jo; m. Gladys Styles Johnston, 1997. BA, Hiram Coll., 1948; MS, Cornell U., 1951; PhD, U. Pa., 1958. Group leader rsch. Rohm & Haas Co., Phila., 1951-56; from asst. prof. to prof. chemistry Mich. State U., East Lansing, 1957-82, assoc. chmn. dept. chemistry, 1965-69, chmn. dept., 1969-75, asst. v.p. rsch. and devel., 1977, assoc. provost, 1977-82; prof. chemistry Ariz. State U., Tempe, 1982-87, v.p. acad. affairs, 1982-87; pres., CEO, Chgo. Osteo. Health Systems and Midwestern U., 1987-96; ret. Cons. Union Carbide Co., 1958-80, vice chmn. div. polymer chemistry, 1966-68, chmn., 1969; dir. chemistry div. NSF, 1975-77; trustee Kirksville Osteo. Med. Coll., 1984-87, Ariz. State U. Res. Park; exec. com. Fed. Independent Ill. Colls. and Univs., 1993-95. Editor computer symposium Jour. Polymer Sci., 1968. 2nd lt. USAAF, 1943-45. Recipient Disting. Alumnus award Hiram Coll., 1984. Fellow AAAS; mem. Am. Chem. Soc., Coun. Chem. Rsch. (vice chair exec. com. 1980-81). Home: 24548 N 121st Pl Scottsdale AZ 85255 E-mail: jbkgsj623@msn.com.

KINSINGER, ROBERT EARL, property company executive, educational consultant; b. Chgo., Aug. 5, 1923; s. Elmer John and Frances Louise (Ballenger) K.; m. Sylvia Kading, May 20, 1950; children: William, Candace, Lisa. AB, Stanford U., 1948, MA, 1951; Ed.D., Columbia U., 1958; LL.D., Simpson Coll., 1977; L.H.D., Hahnemann U.; Litt.D., Thomas Jefferson U., 1986. Staff mem. U.S. del. 3d Gen. Assembly UN, Paris, France, 1948; regional field rep., mgr. chpt. and regional blood center ARC, Boise, Ida., 1949-56; lectr. Columbia U., 1956, Queens Coll., 1957; ednl. cons. Nat. League Nursing, 1957-60; dir. health careers project SUNY, 1960-66; program dir. W.K. Kellogg Found., Battle Creek, Mich., 1966-70, v.p., 1970-83; chmn. Ednl. Services for the Professions, Inc., 1983-87; pres. Kinland Properties. Cons. in field; vice-chmn., adv. coun. Mich. Comprehensive Health Planning Bd.; chmn. Commn. on Physicians Assts.; dir. Jossey-Bass Inc., Publs., 1982-89; dir., chmn., trustee, exec. com. Fielding Inst., 1985-92, 95—; adv. com. Corp. Cmty. Coll. TV; trustee Aviation Safety Inst. Author: Education for Health Technicians-An Overview, 1965; co-author: Clinical Nursing Instruction by Television, 1965; Editor: Career Opportunities for Health Technicians, 1971. Chmn. bd. overseers U. of State of N.Y. Regents Coll.; mem. exec. com. Commn. for a Nation of Lifelong Learners; dir. Sierra Repetory Theatre; trustee Excelsior Coll.; chmn., trustee Sierra Nonprofit Support Ctr. Lt. USNR, World War II. Recipient commn. of honor SUNY, Farmingdale, 1970; Man of Yr. award Nat. Council Community Services, 1971; Honors of Soc. award Am. Soc. Allied Health Professions. Fellow Am. Soc. Allied Health Profls.; mem. Village West Yacht Club. Avocation: hot-air balloons (piloted first balloon flight over the magnetic north pole 1994). Home and Office: 21901 Confidence Rd Twain Harte CA 95383-9688 E-mail: rkinsinger@compuserve.com. *While the "Golden Rule" should always guide one's relationships, of equal importance is steadfast delivery of what you promise to yourself and to others, and a constant effort to exceed the original promise.*

KINSLER, BRUCE WHITNEY, air traffic controller, aerospace engineer; b. Ukiah, Calif., Jan. 11, 1947; s. John Arthur and Mary Helen (Hudson) Kinsler; m. Mickey Kinsler, Apr. 1, 1969 (div. Nov. 1976); 1 child, Arthur Todd; m. Segundina L. Pangilinan, May 27, 1978; 1 stepchild, Stephanie Lizarraga. AA, El Camino Coll., 1979; BA, Calif. State U., Long Beach, 1984. Air traffic contr. FAA, various locations, 1971-81, air traffic contr. SOCAL TRACON San Diego, 1997—99, automation specialist, 1998—99; cen. sta. mgr. Times Mirror Security Communications, Irvine, Calif., 1982-84; supr. office svcs. Law Offices Paul, Hastings, Janofsky & Walker, L.A., 1984-85; air traffic control cons. Hughes Aircraft Co., Fullerton, Calif., 1985-88, ATC/ADGE sr. sys. engr., 1990-97; engr., scientist space sta. divsn. McDonnell Douglas, Huntington Beach, Calif., 1989-90; mgr. requirements FAAHQ, Washington, 1999—, gr. plans and procedures, 2003—. Author: air traffic control tng. manuals, air def. manuals. Mem. citizens adv. com. Calif. Dept. of Transp., Sacramento, 1982—99, res. detective sheriff Orange County, 1991—99; res. dep. sheriff Prince William County, Va., 2000—. Recipient Plankholder, USN Meml. Mem.: Air Traffic Control Assn. (air traffic control com.), Nat. Corvette Mus. (founding mem.), BMW Car Club Am. Independent. Avocations: sports cars, physical fitness. Home: 13299 Robling Ct Manassas VA 20112-3681 also: DOT FAA ATB 460 800 Independence Ave SW Washington DC 20591-0001 E-mail: bruce.kinsler@faa.gov.

KINSLEY, MICHAEL E. magazine editor; b. Detroit, Mar. 9, 1951; s. George and Lillian (Margolis) K.; m. Patty Stonesifer, 2002. AB, Harvard U., 1972, JD, 1977; postgrad., Magdalen Coll., Oxford U., Eng., 1972-74. Bar: D.C. Mng. editor The Washington Monthly, 1975, The New Republic, Washington, 1976-79, editor, 1979-81, 85-89, sr. editor, 1989-95; editor Harper's Mag., N.Y.C., 1981-83; Am. Survey editor The Economist, London, Eng., 1988-89; contbg. writer Time mag., 1987—. Co-host CNN Crossfire, 1989-95. Editor Slate Mag., 1996-2002, contbg. editor, 2002—. Office: Slate Magazine One Microsoft Way Redmond WA 98052

KINSLEY, WILLIAM BENTON, literature educator, retired; b. Montpelier, Vt., Sept. 11, 1934; emigrated to Can., 1965; s. Benton Rufus and Ann Magadline (Finnegan) K.; m. Therese Huang, Dec. 30, 1964 (dec. Mar. 1996); children: Anne-Marie, Claire, Eliane. Student, Wesleyan U., 1952—55; BA, U. Toronto, 1958; postgrad., U. Lyon, France, 1959; PhD, Yale U., 1965. Instr. St. Michael's Coll., Winooski, Vt., 1958-59, U. Rochester, N.Y., 1963-64; asst. prof. English lit. U. Montreal, Que., Can., 1965-71, assoc. prof., 1971-81, prof., 1981-2001, chmn. dept. etudes anglaises, 1970-71, 75-79, 90-91, 98-99; ret., 2001. Editor: Contexts 2: The Rape of the Lock, 1979. Warden St. Pascal-Baylon Catholic Ch., Montreal, 1981-84, 2003. Can. council fellow, 1972-73 Mem. MLA, Am. Soc. Eighteenth Century Studies (pres. English 1974-75), Can. Soc. Eighteenth Century Studies, Assn. Can. Coll. and Univ. Tchrs. English, Can. Comparative Lit. Assn. Home: 3782 Kent Ave Montreal QC Canada H3S 1N3 Office: U Montreal Etudes Anglaises Case Postale 6128 Sta A Montreal QC Canada H3C 3J7 E-mail: wb.kinsley@umontreal.ca.

KINSLOW, MONICA M. forensic scientist; b. Chgo., Feb. 19, 1956; d. Chris C. and Martha Stratton; m. Keith Kinslow, Mar. 8, 1975; children: Aisha Ebony, Naomi Alice, Miles Keith. BS in Chemistry, Chgo. State U., 1981. Criminalist Chgo. Police Dept., 1988-96; forensic scientist Ill. State Police, Chgo., 1996—. Mem. Midwestern Assn. Forensic Scientists, Am. Chem. Soc. Avocations: church activities, reading. Office: Ill State Police Forensic Sci Ctr 1941 W Roosevelt Rd Chicago IL 60608-1246

KINSMAN, FRANK ELLWOOD, engineering executive; b. Westfield, Pa., Oct. 2, 1932; s. Ellwood L. and Josephine I. (Champney) K. m. Ednamae J. Reuter, June 12, 1954; children: Patricia Bunn, Beverly Armstrong, Cheryl Gray, Lora Algee. BSEE, John Brown U., 1958. Cert. energy mgr. Tech. staff Cornell Aero. Lab., Buffalo, 1958-61; sr. engr. Tex. Instruments, Dallas, 1961-79; v.p. Bywaters & Assocs., Cons. Engrs., 1980-86; pres. Kinsman & Assocs., Cons. Engrs., 1986—2002, v.p., 2003—. Ops. rsch. Cornell Aero. Lab., Buffalo, 1958-61; energy resources mgr. Tex. Instruments, Dallas, 1974-79; energy sys. analysis and design Bywaters & Assocs., also Kinsman & Assocs., Dallas, 1980—; mem. engring. adv. bd. John Brown U., Siloam Springs, Ark., 1970-72, 94-2003; vis. lectr. So. Meth. U., Dallas, 1984-85; energy cons. to univs., schs., hosps. and fed. and state agencies, 1987—. Contbr. articles to profl. jours. Bd. chmn. Grace Bible Ch., Dallas, 1990. With USN, 1950-53. Selected Alumnus of the Yr., John Brown U., 1994. Mem.: ASHRAE, Assn. Energy Engrs. (sr.). Achievements include devel. of material signatures at long infrared wavelengths; rsch. include airborne and satellite data interpretations.

KINSMAN, ROBERT PRESTON, biomedical plastics engineer; b. Cambridge, Mass., July 25, 1949; s. Fred Nelson and Myra Roxanne (Preston) K. BS in Plastics Engring., U. Mass., Lowell, 1971; MBA, Pepperdine U., Malibu, Calif., 1982. Cert. biomed. engr., Calif.; lic. real estate sales person, Calif. Product devel. engr., plastics divsn. Gen. Tire Corp., Lawrence, Mass., 1976-77; mfg. engr. Am. Edwards Labs. divsn. Am. Hosp. Supply Corp., Irvine, Calif., 1978-80, sr. engr., 1981-82; mfg. engring. mgr. Edwards Labs., Inc. subs. Am. Hosp. Supply Corp., Añasco, P.R., 1983; project mgr. Baxter Edwards Critical Care divsn. Baxter Healthcare Corp., Irvine, 1984-87, engring. and prodn. mgr., 1987-93; pres. Kinsman & Assocs., Irvine, Calif., 1993—, 2001—; expert/auditor Med. Device Certification GmbH, Memmingen, Germany, 1995—; dir. engring. CardioVascular Dynamics, Inc., Irvine, 1997-2000, HemoDynamics, Inc., Irvine, 1999-2000; dir. biomaterials engring. Anchor Med. Tech., Inc., Irvine, 2000—01; dir. opers. Triage Med., Irvine, 2001. Mgmt. adv. panel Modern Plastics mag., N.Y.C., 1979-80; elected Nat. Hon. Soc., 1967. Vol. worker VA, Bedford, Mass., 1967-71; instr. first aid ARC, N.D., Mass., Calif., 1971-82; pres., bd. dirs. Lakes Homeowners Assn., Irvine, 1985-91; chmn., bd. dirs., newsletter editor Paradise Park Owners Assn., Las Vegas, Nev., 1988-99; bd. dirs. Orange County (Calif.) divsn. Am. Heart Assn., 1991-2001, chmn. devel. com., 1993-95, v.p. bd. dirs., 1993-94, chmn.-elect bd. dirs., 1994-95, chmn. bd. dirs., 1995-96, adv. coun. rep., 1994-96, immediate

past chmn. bd. dirs., 1996-97, nominating com., 1995-98, chmn. nominating com., 2000-01, strategic planning com., 1998-2001, Golden Gavel emeritus mem. bd. dirs., 2001; steering com. Heart and Sole Classic fundraiser, 1988-2001, event chmn., 1991-92, 2001, devel. com. Calif. affiliate, 1993-95; bd. dirs. Billerica Hist. Soc., Mass., 2001-, treas., 2001-02, pres., 2002—; mem. Town of Billerica 350th Anniversary Celebration Com., 2003—, co-treas., 2003—. Capt. USAF, 1971-75, USAFR, 1975-81. Recipient Cert. of Appreciation, VA, 1971, Am. Heart Assn., 1991-95, Outstanding Svc. award., 1996; selected Community Hero Torchbearer 1996 Olympic Games, United Way Am. and Atlanta Com. for Olympic Games. Baxter/Allegiance Found. Community Svc . grantee, Deerfield, Ill., 1992, 93. Mem. Soc. Plastics Engrs. (sr., Mem. of Month So. Calif. sect. 1989), Soc. for Biomaterials, Soc. Mfg. Engrs. (sr.), Am. Mgmt. Assn., Am. Soc. Quality, Arnold Air Soc. (comptr. 1969, pledge tng. officer 1970), Plastics Acad., Demolay, Profl. Ski Instrs. Am., Mensa (life), Am. Legion, Elks, Phi Gamma Psi. Avocations: skiing, scuba diving, marathon running, golfing, music. Office: Kinsman & Assocs PO Box 505 Billerica MA 01821-0505 E-mail: kinsmanassociates@attbi.com.

KINSMAN, STEPHEN L. research scientist; BA, Columbia U., New York, 1979; MD, SUNY, Buffalo, 1983. Head, divsn. of pediatric neurology U. Md. Sch. of Medicine, Baltimore, 2002—. Office: U Md Sch of Medicine 22 S Greene St N5W66 Baltimore MD 21201

KINSOLVING, AUGUSTUS BLAGDEN, lawyer; b. Boston, Jan. 19, 1940; s. Arthur Lee and Mary Kemp (Blagden) K.; m. Monique Berard, Dec. 21, 1974; children: Isabelle, Arthur. BA, Yale U., 1961; MA, Oxford U., 1963; LLB, Harvard U., 1965. Bar: N.Y. 1965. Assoc. Davis Polk & Wardwell, N.Y.C., 1965-70; v.p. Donaldson Lufkin & Jenrette Inc., N.Y.C., 1970-74; v.p., gen. counsel Asarco Inc., N.Y.C., 1975-99; ptnr. Brock Ptnrs. LLP, N.Y.C., 2002—; mng. dir. Brock Capital Group LLC, 2002—. Dir. Adobe Air, Inc., 2000—, Equipment Support Svcs., Inc., 2000—. Trustee Down Town Assn., 1975-91. Rhodes scholar, 1961. Mem. Am. Assn. Rhodes Scholars (dir. Claremont, Calif. chpt. 1975-90), Assn. Gen. Counsel (emeritus mem.), Coun. of the Ams. (adv. bd. 1991-99), Nat. Ctr. for State Cts. (corp. counsel com. 1997-99), Warren E. Burger Found., N.Y. Yacht Club, Cruising Club of Am. Avocation: sailing.

KINSOLVING, CHARLES MCILVAINE, JR., marketing executive; b. N.Y.C., Jan. 27, 1927; s. Charles McIlvaine and Florence Natalie (Hogg) K.; m. Coral May Eaton, July 13, 1963 (dec. Jan. 1988); m. Jolie Brockman Hammer, Apr. 26, 1993 (dec. Aug. 1995); m. Jacqueline Wolf Vogelstein, Aug. 22, 1998. Student, U. Paris, 1948; AB, U. Pa., 1949; postgrad., Harvard Med. Sch., 1949-50, Columbia U., 1951-53. Stockholder rels. AT&T, N.Y.C., 1950-51; rsch. assoc. Young & Rubicam, Inc., N.Y.C., 1951-53; asst. mgr. media rsch. McCann-Erickson, Inc., N.Y.C., 1953-58; mgr. plans devel. Nat. Broadcasting Co., N.Y.C., 1958-60; v.p., mktg. new tech. Newspaper Advt. Bur., N.Y.C., 1960-87, sr. v.p. mktg. group, 1987-92; ind. comm. investor N.Y.C., 1992—. Media cons. U.K., Belgium, South Africa; speaker Internat. Fedn. of Editors and Jours. Contbr. articles to profl. jours. Dem. candidate for State Assembly, Manhattan, 1954, 98; 1st vice chmn. N.Y. County Dem. Exec. Com., N.Y.C., 1963-71; mem., chmn. Planning Bd. #6 Manhattan, N.Y.C., 1969-84. Served with U.S. Army, 1945-46. Mem. Am. Mktg. Assn., Am. Assn. pub. Opinion Rsch., Nat. Cable TV Assn., Am. Newspaper Assn. (tech. com. 1983-92, telecom. com. 1982-92), Union Club, Century Assn., Dutch Treat Club (bd. govs. 1994-99), City Club (v.p. 1987-89), Coffee House Club (bd. dirs. 1984—), St. Anthony Club Phila., St. Paul's Sch. Alumni Assn. (exec. com. 1994-99, v.p. 1995-99), Phi Beta Kappa, Delta Psi. Episcopalian. Avocations: travel, photography, philately. Home: 1107 5th Ave New York NY 10128-0145 Mailing: 27 Horseshoe Dr N East Hampton NY 11937 E-mail: cjkinsolving@nyc.rr.com.

KINSOLVING, SYLVIA CROCKETT, musician, educator; b. Berkeley, Calif., Sept. 30, 1931; d. Harold Waldo and Louise (Effinger) Crockett; m. Charles Lester Kinsolving, Dec. 18, 1953; children: Laura Louise, Thomas Philip, Kathleen Susan. AA in Voice, Piano magna cum laude, No. Va. Community Coll., 1983; BA, U. Calif., Berkeley, 1953. Solo vocalist various chs., Va., 1982—; pvt. tchr. piano, 1983—. Singer, soloist Unity Ch., Oakton, Va., 1980—, St. Andrew's Anglican Ch., Alexandria, Va., 1985—; active numerous local musical prodns., 1959—. Tour leader Vienna Newcomers, 1980. Mem. PEO, U. Calif. Alumni Club, Fairfax West Music Fellowship (sec. 1990—), Phi Theta Kappa, Pi Beta Phi. Democrat. Episcopalian. Avocations: walking, swimming, music, reading. Home: 1517 Beulah Rd Vienna VA 22182-1417

KINSTLER, EVERETT RAYMOND, artist; b. N.Y.C., Aug. 5, 1926; s. Joseph E. and Essie K.; m. Lea C. Nation, June 23, 1958 (div. 1984); children: Katherine G., Dana C.; m. Peggy Chartier, 1996. Ed., Art Students League, NYC, 1943—45; D (hon.), Rollins Coll., 1983, Lyme Acad. Art, 2002. Started career as illustrator, N.Y.C., 1943; began specializing in portraiture, 1955; instr. Art Students League, N.Y.C., 1969-74. Portraits include over 35 U.S. cabinet officers, ofcl. White House portrait former Pres. Gerald R. Ford, former Pres. Ronald Reagan, former Pres. Richard Nixon, J. Edgar Hoover, Richard K. Mellon, Mrs. Irenee duPont, Jr., Kurt Waldheim, sec.-gen. UN, Casper Weinberger, sec. of def., William Casey, dir. CIA, Cyrus Vance, sec. of state, Astronaut Alan B. Shepard, Jr., William Bowen, pres. Princeton U., James Cagney, John D. Rockefeller III, Byron Nelson, Frank Cary, pres. IBM, Charles Scribner, Jr., John Wayne, John Kemeny, pres. Dartmouth Coll., William Simon, sec. Treasury, Elliot Richardson, ambassador to Gt. Britain, Tennessee Williams, John Connally, gov. of Tex., Charles Brown, CH., ATT, Russel Long, U.S. Senator, Morris Udall, mem. U.S. Congress, Katharine Hepburn, Gregory Peck, former Pres. Richard M. Nixon; Bartlett Gramatti, pres. Yale U., George P. Shultz, former U.S. Sec. of State, Paul Newman, Thomas Kean, former Gov. N.J., former Pres. George Bush, Arthur Ashe, Tony Bennett, Carol Burnett, Elizabeth Dole, Betty Ford, Lady Bird Johnson, William Webster, Ruth Simmons Pres. Smith Coll., former dir. CIA, Harry Blackmun, U.S. Supreme Ct. Justice, former U.S. Sec. of State Warren Christopher, Placido Domingo, President Bill Clinton, Gene Hackman, Ruth Bader Ginsburg, U.S. Supreme Ct. Justice, Donald Rumsfeld U.S. Sec. Def., U.S. Senator Daniel Patrick Moynihan, NY Gov. George Pataki, Peter O'Toole, Sen. Robert Dole, also numerous others; represented in permanent collections, Butler Inst. Am. Art, Nat. Portrait Gallery, Washington, Nat. Acad. Design, Mus. City N.Y., Met. Mus. Art, N.Y.C., The Pentagon, Am. Embassy, Paris, Carnegie Mus., N.Y. Stock Exchange, Bklyn. Mus., White House, Smithsonian Instn., Retrospective Exhibition Boston U., Butler inst. Am. Art, Fairfield, Conn., 1999; numerous colls., univs., bus. firms; Author: Painting Portraits, 1971, Painting Faces, Figures, Landscapes, 1981; (documentary) An Artists Journey, PBS, 2001. Recipient Artists' Fellowship Medal, 1986, Nat. Arts Club medal, 1993, Allied Artists medal, 1997, Copley medal Nat. Portrait Gallery, 1999, Lifetime Achievement medal Salmagundi Club, 2002, medal honoree Nat. Acad. Design, 2002. Mem. Allied Artists Am. (dir. 1958-60), Artists Fellowships, Inc. (pres. 1967-70), Am. Watercolor Soc., Pastel Soc. Am., Audubon Artists, NAD, Actor's Fund Am. (life), Soc. Illustrators (hon.), Copley Soc. Boston (life), Lambs Club (N.Y.C.) (life),), Century Assn. Club (N.Y.C.), Lotos Club (N.Y.C.) (life), Nat. Arts Club (N.Y.C.), Dutch Treat Club (N.Y.C.), Players Club (life), Yale Club N.Y. (life). Office: care Nat Arts Club 15 Gramercy Park S New York NY 10003-1705

KINSTLINGER, JACK, engineering executive, consultant; b. Antwerp, Belgium, Mar. 2, 1931; came to U.S., 1939; s. Joseph and Rose (Lichtblau) K.; m. Marilyn Wiseman, July 16, 1967; children: Michael, Jeremy. BSCE, Rensselaer Polytechnic Inst., 1952; MSCE, MIT, 1954. Registered profl. engr., N.Y., Pa., Wash., N.H., Colo., Del., Md., Mass., Fla., N.J. Assoc. Tippetts, Abbett, McCarthy, Stratton, N.Y.C., 1957-68; dep. sec. Pa. Dept. Transp., Harrisburg, 1968-75; state hwy. dir. State of Colo., Denver, 1975-82; v.p. Daniel-Mann-Johnson-Mendenhall, Denver, 1982-84; CEO KCI Techs., Inc., Balt., 1984-99, chmn. bd. dirs., chmn. emeritus, 2000—. Bd. dirs. Am. Jewish Com., Balt.; mem. Adv. Bd. Rensselaer Poly. Inst.; chmn. Md. Coun. on Mgmt. and Productivity. Fellow ASCE, Am. Cons. Engrs. Coun.; mem. Am. Inst. Cert. Planners, Engring. Soc. Balt., Greater Balt. Com., Greater Washington Bd. Trade, Am. Rds. and Transp. Builders Assn. (vice chair, bd. dirs.), High Speed Ground Transp. Assn. (bd. dirs.). Office: KCI Techs Inc 10 N Park Dr Hunt Valley MD 21030-1841 E-mail: jkinstlinger@kci.com.

KINTNER, PHILIP L. history educator; b. Canton, Ohio, Jan. 23, 1926; s. William Wagner and Effie (Erwin) K.; m. Anne Genung, Dec. 27, 1951; children: Karen, Judith, Jennifer. BA, Wooster Coll., 1950; MA, Yale U., 1952, PhD, 1958. Instr. Trinity Coll., Hartford, Conn., 1954-56, Reed Coll., Portland, Oreg., 1957-58, Trinity Coll., 1958-59, asst. prof., 1959-64; vis. assoc. prof. U. Iowa, Iowa City, 1964-65; assoc. prof. Grinnell (Iowa) Coll., 1964-69; coll. entrance bd. exam commissioner European History, Princeton, N.J., 1968-70; chief reader advanced placement European history, 1969-72; ACM prof. Florence (Italy) Program, 1989-90; prof. Grinnell Coll., 1970-96, Rosenthal prof. humanities, 1976-96; prof. emeritus, 1996—. With U.S. Army, 1944-46. Recipient numerous travel/study grants for rsch. in Germany. Mem. Sixteenth Century Studies Conf. Avocations: woodworking, gardening, cooking, mineral hunting. Home: 716 Broad St Grinnell IA 50112-2226 Office: Grinnell Coll PO Box 805 Grinnell IA 50112-0805 E-mail: kintner@grinnell.edu.

KINTSCH, WALTER, psychology educator, director; b. Temesvar, Romania, May 30, 1932; arrived in US, 1955; s. Christof and Irene (Hollerbach) Kintsch; m. Eileen Hoover, June 27, 1959; children: Anja, Julia. PhD, U. Kans., 1960. Prof. U. Colo., Boulder, 1968—. Editor: Pyschol Rev, 1989—94; author: books. Office: U Colo Dept Psychology Institute Cognitive Scis Boulder CO 80309-0344 Business E-Mail: wkintsch@psych.colorado.edu.

KINTZEL, ROGER, publishing executive; b. July 9, 1943; m. Lee; 2 children. BA, Wright State U., 1970. Reporter Xenia (Ohio) Daily Gazette, 1970-72; from police reporter to bus. editor Richmond (Va.) News-Leader, 1973-79; fin. editor Dayton (Ohio) Jour.-Herald Cox Enterprises, 1979-81, bus. mgr. Dayton Newspapers, 1981-83, publ. Springfield (Ohio) News-Sun, 1983-85, pres. Cox Ariz. Publs., publ Mesa Tribune, 1985-86, publ. Austin Am.-Statesman, 1986-95, publ. Atlanta Jour.-Constitution, 1995—. S.E. rep. Assoc. Press Nominating Com. Bd. dirs. Newspaper Assn. Am. Found., Rsch. Atlanta; bd. councilors Carter Ctr.; mem. exec. com. Ctrl. Atlanta Progress. Mem. Atlanta C. of C. (mem. exec. com.), So. Newspaper Publ. Assn. (bd. dirs.). Office: Cox Newspaper Inc 72 Marietta St NW Atlanta GA 30303-2804*

KINTZELE, JOHN ALFRED, lawyer; b. Denver, Aug. 16, 1936; s. Louis Richard and Adele H. Kintzele; children: John A., Marcia A., Elizabeth A.; m. Suzanne Hinsberger; stepchildren: William Karp III, Christopher Karp. BS in Bus., U. Colo., 1958, LLB, 1961. Bar: Colo. bar 1961. Assoc. James B. Radetsky, Denver, 1962-63; pvt. practice law Denver, 1963—. Corp. officer, dir. Kintzele, Inc.; rep. 10th cir. U.S. Ct. of Claims Bar. Chmn. Colo. Lawyer Referral Service, 1978-83, Election commr., Denver, 1975-79, 83-86. Mem. ABA, Colo. Bar Assn., Denver Bar Assn., Am. Judicature Soc. Democrat. Roman Catholic. Home: 10604 E Powers Dr Englewood CO 80111-3957 Office: 1317 Delaware St Denver CO 80204-2704 E-mail: kintzeles@aol.com., jkintlaw@aol.com.

KINZELL, LA MOYNE B. school health services administrator, educator; b. Melstone, Mont., May 4, 1930; d. William Edward and Iro Millicent (Keeton) Berger; m. Les Kieth Kinzell, Sept. 18, 1954; children: Yvette Li Goins, Anitra Elise Chew, Antony Mikhail Kinzell. BS, Mont. State U., 1954; MA, Calif. State U., Northridge, 1982. RN Calif. Instr. surg. nursing Mont. Deaconess Hosp., Great Falls, 1954-55; instr. nursing arts St. Patrick's Hosp., Missoula, Mont., 1957-59; instr. sci. Palmdale (Calif.) Sch. Dist., 1966-86, dir. health svcs., 1986-2000. Adv. bd. facilitator Palmdale Healthy Start, 1992-2000; com. mem. Am. Cancer Soc., 1986—, United Way, 1991—; bd. dirs. A.V. Ptnrs. in Health, 2000—. Mem. Citizen Amb. Sch. Nursing Del. to Europe, 1994; treas. campaign sch. bd. mem., Palmdale, 1989, 93, 97; bd. dirs. A.V. Symphony Orch. and Master Choral, 2000—, A.V. Light Found., 2001-. Recipient Tchr. of Yr. award Palmdale, 1985-86, Los Angeles County Sheriffs Dept. award, 1985, Nat. Every Child by Two, Immunization Ptnrs. award, 1995; grantee Drug, Alcohol and Tobacco Edn., 1987, Healthy Start Planning, 1994, 95, Healthy Start Operational award, 1996, 98. Mem. Am. Heart Assn. (bd. dirs. 1997-2001), Am. Lung Assn. (chair edn. 1988-94), Calif. Sch. Nurse Orgn. (sec. 1992-95), Health Careers Acad. (adv. com. 1995—), Phi Kappa Phi (health careers acad. adv. bd., 1995—), Alpha Tau Delta, Sigma Theta Tau, Delta Kappa Gamma (area IX chair legislature 1993-95, area IX dir. 1995-97, area IX sec. 2001—03, mem. Chi state expansion com. 1997-99, leadership com. 1999-2001, chair leadership com. 2001-03, profl. affairs com., 2003—). Democrat. Episcopalian. Avocations: traveling, gardening, geology, marine biology, swimming. Home: 38817 2nd St E Palmdale CA 93550-3201 E-mail: l.kinzell@worldnet.att.net.

KINZER, CHARLES EDWARD, music educator; b. Charlottesville, Va., Dec. 17, 1959; s. Earl Thomas and Mary Jane Kinzer; m. Lisa Ann Baker, June 9, 1990; children: Sarah, Christian, Rachel. MusB, Auburn U., 1983; MusM, U. Ala., 1985; PhD in Music, La. State U., 1993. Asst. prof. Longwood Coll., Farmville, Va., 1992—98, assoc. prof., 1998—2002, Longwood U., Farmville, Va., 2002—. Saxophone and leader Southside Jazz Quartet, Va., 1996—. Contbr. articles to profl. jours. Recipient Cmty. Achievement in the Arts award, Longwood Ctr. for Visual Arts, 2000. Mem.: Am. Musicol. Soc., Soc. for Am. Music, Va. Hist. Soc. Roman Catholic. Avocations: jazz, history, auto mechanics. Office: Longwood Univ Dept Music Farmville VA 23909 Business E-Mail: ckinzer@longwood.edu.

KINZER, JAMES RAYMOND, retired pipeline company executive; b. Pampa, Tex., Sept. 14, 1928; s. William Graham and Leota (Gott) K.; m. Billy June Chesher, June 30, 1956 (dec.); children— Mark William, Kandice Ann, Karen June, Kourtney Margaret, John Richard. BBA, So. Methodist U., 1950, LL.B., 1952. Bar: Tex. bar 1952. Asso. firm Locke, Purnell, Boren, Laney & Neely, Dallas, 1955-59; counsel Tex. Industries, Inc., 1960-63; atty. Mobil Oil Corp., 1964-65; asst. gen. counsel Mobil Pipe Line Co., Dallas, 1966-70, gen. counsel, 1970-92. Served with AUS, 1952-55. Roman Catholic.

KINZER, WILLIAM LUTHER, lawyer; b. Mifflintown, Pa., Jan. 25, 1929; s. John Raymond and Ethel Naomi (Sellers) K.; m. Ann Marie Rosato, May 3, 1958; children: Karen, Carolyn, Cynthia, Matthew, Mark. BA, Dickinson Coll., Carlisle, Pa., 1950; LLB, Temple U., 1956; LLM, Georgetown U., 1961. Bar: D.C. 1957, Ga. 1962. Atty. IRS, Washington, 1956-62; assoc. Powell, Goldstein, Frazer & Murphy, Atlanta, 1962-65, ptnr., 1965-2000, of counsel, 2000—. Author miscellaneous tax articles, 2 BNA Tax Portfolios. Capt. USAF, 1951-53. Mem. ABA (com. chmn. 1987-89), Fed. Bar Assn., Ga. Bar Assn., Atlanta Bar Assn., Atlanta Tax Forum (pres. 1980, trustee 1978-81), Cherokee Town and Country Club (Atlanta). Roman Catholic. Avocation: golf. Home: 904 Spring Valley Woodstock GA 30189-6102 Office: Powell Goldstein Frazer & Murphy 191 Peachtree St NE Ste 16 Atlanta GA 30303-1740 E-mail: wkinzer@pgfm.com.

KINZIE, BRENDA ASBURRY, counselor; b. Roanoke, Va., Oct. 25, 1945; d. Omar Lee and Nadine Myrl (Sublett) Asburry; m. Samuel Joseph Kinzie, Mar. 30, 1973. BA, Hollins (Va.) U., 1990; MS, Radford (Va.) U., 1991. Case mgr./counselor Total Action Against Poverty, Roanoke, 1993-95; interagy. case coord. City of Roanoke, 1995-98. Mem.: ACA, Hunting Hills Garden Club. Democrat. Divine Sci. Ch. Avocations: music, reading, walking, flower gardening. Home: 1051 Starmount Ave Roanoke VA 24019-3135

KINZIE, JEANNIE JONES, radiation oncologist, nuclear medicine physician; b. Great Falls, Mont., Mar. 14, 1940; d. James Wayne and Lillian Alice (Young) Jones; m. Joseph Lee Kinzie, Mar. 26, 1965 (div. Sept. 1982); 1 child, Daniel Joseph; m. Johnson Wachira, Oct. 7, 1991. Student, Oreg. State U., 1960; BS, Mont. State U., 1961; MD, Washington U., 1965; MBA, U. Phoenix, 1997. Diplomate Am. Bd. Radiology; diplomate Am. Bd. Nuclear Medicine; cert. advanced master gardener Colo. State U., 1997. Intern. in surgery U. N.C., Chapel Hill, 1965-66; resident in therapeutic radiology Washington U., St. Louis, 1968-71, instr. in radiology, 1971-73; asst. prof. in radiology Med. Coll. of Wis., Milw., 1973-75, U. Chgo., 1975-78, assoc. prof. in radiology, 1978-80; assoc. prof. of radiation oncology Wayne State U., Detroit, 1980-85; prof. radiology U. Colo., Denver, 1985-95; dir. radiation oncology U. Hosp., Denver, 1985-91; fellow in nuclear medicine U. Colo., 1996-98, asst. clin. prof. nuclear medicine, 1998—; staff radiologist Denver Vets. Hosp., Denver, 2003—. Cons. Denver Vets. Hosp., 1985-98, Denver Gen. Hosp., 1985-95, Rose Med. Ctr., 1986-95, FDA Ctr. for Devices and Radiologic Health, 1986-; mem. sci. adv. bd. Cancer League Colo., 1985-88; examiner Am. Bd. Radiology, 1985-88; adv. physician Colo. Med. Found., 1988-98; chmn. faculty promotion com. U. Colo. Health Scis. Ctr., 1988-89. Assoc. editor Internat. Jour. Radiation Oncology Biology and Physics, 1985-95; contbr. articles to profl. jours.; chpts. to books. Mem. Faith Bible Chapel Ch. NIH grantee, 1973-75. Fellow Am. Coll. Radiology; mem. AMA, Am. Coll. Nuclear Physicians, Colo. Med. Soc., Denver Med. Soc. (del. to Colo. Med. Soc. Ho. of Dels. 1989—), Colo. Radiol. Soc., Soc. Nuclear Medicine, Rocky Mountain Oncology Soc. (bd. dirs. 1989-93, pres. 1991-93), Am. Soc. Therapeutic Radiologists, Am. Cancer Soc. (bd. dirs. Denver unit 1986-87), Wilderness Med. Soc. Republican. Avocations: stamp collecting, gardening, rug latching, mountain climbing. E-mail: jeannie.kinzie@worldnet.att.net.

KINZIE, MARY, poet, educator; b. Montgomery, Ala., Sept. 30, 1944; d. Harry Ernst Kinzie and Mary Louise Huey; divorced; 1 child. BA in German, Northwestern U., 1967; MA in Fiction Writing Seminars, Johns Hopkins U., 1970, PhD in English, 1980. Dir. creative writing program Northwestern U., Evanston, Ill., 1979—, assoc. prof. English, 1985-90, prof. English, 1990—. Lit. executor Estate of Louise Bogan, 2001—. Author: A Poet's Guide to Poetry, 1999; editor critical anthology Prose for Borges, 1972. Recipient Devins award U. Mo. Press, 1982; Guggenheim fellow in poetry, 1986. Office: Northwestern U English Dept University Hall 215 Evanston IL 60208-2240 E-mail: mkinzie@northwestern.edu.

KINZIE, RAYMOND WYANT, banker, lawyer; b. Chgo., Oct. 20, 1930; s. Raymond Allen and Florence (Wyant) K.; m. Dorothy Cherry Beek, Sept. 17, 1955; children: Diana K. Wieczorek, Dorothy K. Tedeschi, Raymond Wyant Jr., Susan Hawthorne (dec.). BA, Carleton Coll., 1952; LLB, Yale U., 1955, JD, 1964. Bar: Ill. 1956, U.S. Dist. Ct. (no. dist.) Ill. 1959, U.S. Ct. Appeals (7th cir.) 1961, U.S. Supreme Ct. 1964. Assoc. McBride and Baker, Chgo., 1955-56; atty. Continental Ill. Nat. Bank & Trust Co. (now Bank Am. Chgo.), Chgo., 1956-59; trust officer Lake View Trust and Savs. Bank, Chgo., 1959-65, asst. v.p. loans and credit, 1965-71, v.p., trust officer, 1971-82, sr. v.p., sr. trust officer, 1982-88; sr. v.p., sr. trust officer LaSalle Bank Lake View subs. Algemene Bank Nederland (now known as ABN-AMRO Bank), Chgo., 1988-90; sr. v.p. trust svcs. ABN-AMRO Bank subs. LaSalle Nat. Trust, N.A., Chgo., 1990-92; sr. v.p. wealth mgmt. group LaSalle Nat. Trust, N.A., Chgo., 1992-97, sr. v.p. Wealth Mgmt. Group LaSalle Nat. Bank, Chgo., 1997-98, cons., 1998—. Mem. adv. bd. Nat. Coll. Edn. (Lewis U.), Evanston, Ill., 1975—; commentator radio editl. rebuttals Sta. WBBM; talk shows commentator WLS. Contbr. Bd. dirs., sec.-treas. Ravenswood Hosp. Med. ctr., Chgo., 1975-85; bd. dirs., sec. Ravenswood Health Care Found., 1975-80. Mem. Am. Mgmt. Assn., Ill. State Bar Assn., Chgo. Bar Assn., Chgo. Estate Planning Coun., Land Trust Coun. Ill. Home: 1027 N Marion St Oak Park IL 60302-1374 E-mail: kinzie@ameritech.net. *Motto: Alle Anfang ist Schwer (All beginning is difficult.). A happy home, a career that's fun plus health and wealth and time enough to enjoy them is paradise found on earth - greater pleasure than these will not be found even in the Elysian Fields.*

KINZLER, PETER, lawyer; b. N.Y.C., Apr. 18, 1943; s. I. George Kinzler and Isabelle (Schlivek) Kinzler Feher; m. Virginia L. Smith, June 20, 1982; children: Samantha, Jason, Valerie, Kit. BA, Trinity Coll., 1964; JD, Columbia U., 1967. Bar: N.Y. 1967. Atty. NLRB, Washington, 1967-69; legis. asst. U.S. Rep. Thomas L. Ashley, Washington, 1969-74; atty. Fed. Trade Commn., Washington, 1974-75; counsel consumer protection & fin./oversight and investigations Commerce Com./Ho. of Reps., Washington, 1975-81; minority counsel then staff dir. consumer affairs subcom. Senate Banking Com., Washington, 1981-89, counsel, 1992; legis. dir. Sen. Christopher J. Dodd, Washington, 1989-92; staff dir. subcom. Fin. Instns. Supervision Regulation and Deposit Ins. House Banking Com., Washington, 1993-95; ptnr. Kinzler & Swab, Alexandria, Va., 1995-98; sole practitioner Alexandria, 1998—. Pres. Coalition for Auto-Ins. Reform, 1996—; adv. bd. Am. Acad. Developmental Medicine and Dentistry, 2003—. Pres. River Park Mut. Homes, Inc., Washington, 1976, Hollin Hills Swim Club, Alexandria, Va., 1988, Hollin Hills Tennis Club, 1994; v.p. Parent and Assoc. No. Va. Tng. Ctr., Fairfax, 1982; bd. dirs. HALT-Am. for Legal Reform, Washington, 1983-86, Voice of the Retarded, 1994—. Democrat. Avocations: folk music, crafts, tennis. Office: 7310 Stafford Rd Alexandria VA 22307-1807 E-mail: pkinzler@cox.net.

KINZLER, THOMAS BENJAMIN, lawyer; b. N.Y.C., June 19, 1950; s. David and Rhoda Lenore (Wolgel) K.; m. Carol Ada Loebel, Aug. 24, 1975; children: Katherine Diane, David James. BA, Columbia Coll., 1971; JD, Boston U., 1975. Bar: N.Y. 1976, U.S. Dist. Ct. (no., so., ea. and we. dists.) N.Y. 1976, U.S. Ct. Appeals (2d cir.) 1976. Assoc. Kreindler, Relkin & Goldberg, N.Y.C., 1975-77, Arthur, Dry & Kalish, N.Y.C., 1977-80, Kelley Drye & Warren LLP, N.Y.C., 1980-85; ptnr. Kelley Drye & Warren, N.Y.C., 1985—. Mem. ABA, Assn. of the Bar of City of N.Y.C. (products liability com. 1983-86, com. on state legis. 1978-80). Office: Kelley Drye & Warren 101 Park Ave Fl 30 New York NY 10178-0062

KIOK, JOAN STERN, lawyer; b. N.Y.C., Dec. 19, 1929; d. Milton William and Pauline (Bauer) Stern; children: Paul, Pter. BA, Cornell U., 1951; LLB, Columbia U., 1954. Bar: N.Y. 1955, Colo. 1958, U.S. Dist. Ct. (so. and ea. dists.) N.Y., U.S. Ct. Appeals (2d cir.) 1961, U.S. Supreme Ct. 1961, 1968-78. Assoc. gen. counsel D.C.37 AFSCME, AFL-CIO, N.Y.C.; sole practitioner N.Y.C., 1978—. Gen. counsel Mgr. Employees Assn., N.Y.C., 1980-02, Uniformed Sanitation chiefs Assn., N.Y.C., 1988—, EMS Chiefs Assn., N.Y.C., 1986—, Orgn. Staff Analysts, N.Y.C., 1985—, Fire Alarm Dispatchers, N.Y.C., 1988—; chair bd. dirs. MFY Legal Svcs., N.Y.C., 1980-85. Mem. N.Y. County Lawyers Assn. (labor law com. 1975—). Home and Office: 442 E 20th St New York NY 10009-8120 E-mail: kiok@earthlink.net.

KIPLINGER, KNIGHT A. journalist, publisher; b. Washington, Feb. 24, 1948; s. Austin Huntington and Mary Louise (Cobb) K. BA, Cornell U., 1969; postgrad., Princeton U., 1969-70. Reporter Montgomery County Sentinel, Rockville, Md., 1970; Washington corr. Griffin-Larrabee News Bur., Washington, 1970-73, bur. mgr., 1976-78; Washington bur. chief, chief news svc. Ottaway Newspapers div. Dow Jones & Co., Washington, 1978-83; with Kiplinger Washington Editors, Washington, 1983—, v.p. for publs., 1983-89, exec . v.p., 1989-92, pres., 1992—; assoc. editor The Kiplinger Letter, Washington, 1983-99, editor-in-chief, 1999—; editor in chief Kiplinger's Personal Fin. Mag., Washington, 1985—, pub., 1988—. Author: World Boom Ahead, 1998; co-author: Washington Now, 1975, The New American Boom, 1986, America in the Global '90s, 1989. Bd. dirs. The Washington Chorus, 1975-85, chmn., 1991-99; mem. adv. bd. Levine Sch. Music, Washington, 1975—, Mount Vernon Ladies' Assn., 1986-92—; mem. nat. adv. bd. Nat. Mus. Women in the Arts, Washington, 1988-92; trustee Greater Washington Rsch. Ctr., 1992-99. Mem. Soc. Profl. Journalists, Soc. Am. Bus. Editors and Writers, Nat. Press Club. Office: Kiplinger Washington Editors 1729 H St NW Washington DC 20006-3925

KIPNIS, DAVID MORRIS, physician, educator; b. Balt., May 23, 1927; s. Rubin and Anna (Mizen) Kipnis; m. Paula Jane Levin, Aug. 16, 1953; children: Lynne, Laura, Robert. AB, Johns Hopkins U., 1945, MA, 1949; MD, U. Md., 1951. Intern Johns Hopkins Hosp., 1951—52; resident Duke Hosp., Durham, NC, 1952—54, U. Md. Hosp., 1954—55; asst. prof. medicine Washington U. Sch. Medicine, St. Louis, 1958—63, assoc. prof., 1963—65, prof., 1965—, Busch prof., chmn. dept. medicine, 1973—92; disting. prof. medicine Washington U. Sch. of Medicine, St. Louis, 1992—; asst. physician Barnes Hosp., assoc. physician, 1963—72, physician-in-chief, 1973—93, distinguished prof., 1993—. Chmn. endocrine study sect. NIH, 1963—64, diabetes tng. program com., 1970—; chmn. Nat. Diabetes Adv. Bd. Editor: Diabetes, 1973; mem. editl. bd.: Am. Jour. Medicine, 1973, Am. Jour. Med. Scis.; contbr. articles to profl. jours. Served with U.S. Army, 1945—46. Named Bating lectr., Brit. Diabetes Assn., 1972; scholar Markle scholar in med. scis., 1957—62. Mem.: NAS (coun. mem. 1997—), Nat. Acad. Scis., Inst. Medicine, Am. Acad. Arts and Scis., Am. Soc. Biol. Chemists, Endocrine Soc. (Oppenheimer award 1965), Am. Diabetes Assn. (Lilly award 1965, Banting medal 1977, Best medal 1981), Am. Fedn. Clin. Rsch., Assn. Am. Physicians (Kober medal 1994), Am. Soc. Clin. Investigation. Home: 7200 Wydown Blvd Saint Louis MO 63105-3023 Office: Barnes Hosp Dept Medicine PO Box 8212 660 S Euclid Ave Saint Louis MO 63110-1010

KIPNISS, ROBERT, artist; b. N.Y.C., Feb. 1, 1931; s. Sam and Stella Anita K.; m. Jean Elizabeth Prutton, July 6, 1954 (div. 1982); children: Max, Ivan, Ruby, Benjamin; m. Laurie Lisle, 1994. Student, Wittenberg Coll., 1948-50; PhD (hon.), Wittenberg U., 1980; BA, U. Iowa, 1952, MFA, 1954; PhD (hon.), Ill. Coll., 1989. One man exhbns. include Museo de Arte Moderno, Cali, Columbia, 1977, Kalamazoo Art Inst., Canton Art Inst., Fnatsu Galerie, Tokyo, Gallery New World, Dusseldorf, Germany, Redfern Gallery, London, Venable Neslage, Washington, Hexton Gallery, N.Y.C., Tyler (Tex.) Mus., 1999, Butler Art Inst., Ohio, 1999, Bassenge Gallery, Berlin, 1999, Beadleston Gallery, N.Y.C., 1999, 2001, 2003, Weinstein Gallery, 1999, 2000, 2001, 2002; represented in permanent collections Chgo. Art Inst., Whitney Mus. Am. Art, N.Y.C., Nat. Collection Fine Arts, Victoria and Albert Mus., London, Libr. of Congress, L.A. County Mus., Detroit Inst. Art, Cleve. Mus., N.Y. Pub. Libr., Butler Art Inst., De Young Mus., Fogg Mus., Cambridge, Mass., Boston Mus. Fine Arts, Indpls. Mus. Art, Portland Mus. Art, Yale Mus., New Haven, Conn., Brit. Mus., London, The Fitz William Mus., Cambridge, U.K., New Orleans Mus. Art, Met. Mus. Art., Biblioteque Nat. France, Paris, Carnegie Mus., Pitts., Fine Arts Mus. San Francisco, Everson Mus., Syracuse, N.Y., Nelson-Atkins Mus., Kansas City, Mo., Pinakothek der Moderne, Munich. Served with U.S. Army, 1956-58. Recipient Ralph Fabri prize in lithography Nat. Acad. Design, 1976, James R. Marsh Meml. award in lithography Audubon Artists, 1978, Charles M. Lea prize Print Club Phila., 1978, prize for lithography Soc. Am. Graphic Artists, 1979, Medal of Honor in Graphics Audubon Artists, 1983, Childe Hassam purchase award Am. Acad. Arts and Letters, 1988, The Cannon prize Nat. Acad. Design, 1999, Graphics award Boston Printmakers, 1999, Daniel Serra-Badue Meml. award Audobon Artists, 1998, Medal of Honor, Audobon Artists, 1999, 2000, Purchase prize Delta Nat., 2001, Ark. State U., Prints U.S.A., 2001, Springfield Mus. of Art, Mo., Leo Meissner award Nat. Acad., 2003. Mem. Nat. Acad. Design, The Century Assn., Soc. Am. Graphics Artists, Royal Soc. Painter Printmakers (London), The Boston Printmakers.

KIPNISS MACDONALD, BETTY ANN, artist, educator; b. Bklyn., Aug. 1936; d. Samuel Simon and Stella Anita (Blackton) Kipniss; m. Gordon James MacDonald; divorced; children: Gordon, Maureen, Michael, Bruce. BA, Adelphi U., 1958; MA, Columbia U., 1960. Instr. Montshire Mus., Hanover, N.H., 1979-84, Lebanon (N.H.) Coll., 1984, Smithsonian Instn., Washington, 1985-95. Instr. Corcoran Mus. Art, 1996-98; pres., bd. dirs. Washington Printmakers Gallery; bd. dirs. Washington Print Club. Exhbns. include Nat. Mus. Women in the Arts, Washington, 1994, 95; in permanent collections at Community for Creative Nonviolence, Washington, 1989, Mus. of Modern Art, Buenos Aires, 1988, Am. Cultural Ctr., New Delhi, India, 1992, Pa. State U., 1992, New Orleans Mus. Art, 2002; featured in William and Mary Review, 1992, 93, 94, 95, 96. Grantee Giorgio Cini Found., 1962, NEA, 1981; recipient 1st prize printmakers Washington Women's Art Ctr., 1986, Past Pres.'s award Mus. Fine Arts, Springfield, Mass., 1982, de Cordova Mus., Soc. Am. Graphic Artists N.Y., Merit award Currier Gallery of Art, 1987, Purchase prize Print Club Albany, N.Y., 1998, Purchase award, Permanent Collection Ark. State U., 2001, Mus. Graphics award Washington County Mus. Fine Arts, Md., 2003, others. Mem. L.A. Printmaking Soc., Soc. Am. Graphic Artist, Boston Printmakers. Home: 7222 Vistas Ln Mc Lean VA 22101-5076

KIPP, JOHN THEODORE, lawyer, rancher; b. Guadalajara, Mex., Apr. 19, 1932; (parents Am. citizens); s. Eugene Harvey and Theresa (Greer) K.; 1 child, John Grant. BBA, U. Tex., 1954, JD, 1958. Bar: Tex. 1958, U.S. Dist. Ct. (no. dist.) Tex. 1962, U.S. Supreme Ct. 1964. Assoc. Gardere & Wynne, LLP and predecessor, Dallas, 1958-63, ptnr., 1964-98, of counsel, 1998—. Past chmn. Dallas County chpt. Am. Heart Assn.; trustee, treas. Dallas Hist. Soc. Lt. USN, 1954-56, Korea; mem. USNR (ret.). Mem. State Bar Tex. (chmn. corp. law com. 1973-75, bus. law sect. 1976-77), Dallas Bar Assn. Avocations: hunting, fishing, ranching, photography, golfing. Home: 3823 Hawthorne Ave Dallas TX 75219-2212 Office: Gardere & Wynne LLP 1601 Elm St Ste 3000 Dallas TX 75201-4761

KIPPENHAN, CHARLES JACOB, mechanical engineer, retired educator; b. Middle Amana, Iowa, Nov. 8, 1919; s. Adam John and E. L. (Heinemann) K.; m. Jane Elizabeth Munsinger, Dec. 18, 1941; children— Judith Evans (Mrs. James R. Halstead II), Kurt Alfred. BS in Mech. Engring, State U. Iowa, 1940, MS, 1946, PhD, 1948. Instr. mech. engring. State U. Iowa, 1941-42; from asst. prof. mech. engring. to prof., head dept. Washington U., St. Louis, 1948-64; prof. mech. engring. U. Wash., Seattle, 1963-88, chmn. dept. mech. engring., 1964-73, adj. prof. architecture, 1973-88; prof. emeritus, 1988. Cons. to industry, 1949— Contbr. profl. jours. Served to lt. USN, 1942-46. AEC-Am. Soc. Engring. Edn. fellow nuclear energy seminar Cornell U., summer 1959, direct energy conversion U. Ill., summer 1963; NSF sci. tchr. fellow TH Munich, Germany, 1960-61 Mem. ASHRAE, Am. Soc. Engring. Edn., ASME, Sigma Xi, Theta Tau, Pi Tau Sigma, Tau Beta Pi. Home: 3908 NE 38th St Seattle WA 98105-5416 E-mail: cjkip@comcast.net., cjkip@u.washington.edu.

KIPPER, BARBARA LEVY, corporate executive; b. Chgo., July 16, 1942; d. Charles and Ruth (Doctoroff) Levy; m. David A. Kipper, Sept. 9, 1974; children: Talia Rose, Tamar Judith. BA, U. Mich., 1964. Reporter Chgo. Sun-Times, 1964-67; photo editor Cosmopolitan Mag., N.Y.C., 1969-71; vice chmn. Chas Levy Co., Chgo., 1984-86, chmn., 1986—. Trustee Spertus Inst. Jewish Studies, Chgo. Hist. Soc., Golden Apple Ind., Joffrey Ballet of Chgo.; bd. dirs. Lincoln Park Zoo. Recipient Deborah award Com. Women's Equality, Am. Jewish Congress, 1992, Shapiro Human Rels. award The Anti-Defamation League of B'nai B'rith, Personal PAC's Leadership award, 1996, Disting. Cmty. Leadership award, ADL, 1999; named Nat. Soc. Fund Raising Exec.'s Disting. Philanthropist, 1995. Mem.: Chgo. Network, Chgo. Coun. on Fgn. Rels., Com. of 200, Coun. on Founds., Internat. Women's Forum, Econ. Club of Chgo., Execs. Club of Chgo., The Standard Club. Jewish. Office: Chas Levy Co 1200 N North Branch St Chicago IL 60622-2449

KIPPERMAN, LAWRENCE I. lawyer; b. Chgo., Nov. 22, 1941; s. Solomon and Idelle (Goldman) K.; m. Carol A. Kipperman, Jan. 29, 1967 (div. Sept. 1985); children: Anna, Lynne. BA, U. Ill., 1963, JD, 1966; LLM, George Washington U., 1968. Bar: Ill. 1966, U.S. Dist. Ct. (no. dist.) Ill. 1966, U.S. Supreme Ct. 1968, Ohio 1970, U.S. Ct. Appeals (7th cir.) 1973, U.S. Ct. Appeals (8th cirs.) 1986. Atty. NLRB, Washington, 1966-70; assoc. Burke, Haber & Berick, Cleve., 1970-71, Sidley & Austin, Chgo., 1971-73, ptnr., 1973-2000, sr. counsel, 2000—. Lectr. Ill. Continuing Legal Edn., 1985, Am. Arbitration Assn. Mem. Chgo. Bar Assn., Legal Club Chgo. Jewish. Avocations: architectural history, baseball, basketball, jazz. Office: Sidley Austin Brown & Wood Bank One Plz Chicago IL 60603-2000 E-mail: lkipperman@sidley.com.

KIPPERT, ROBERT JOHN, JR., lawyer; b. Detroit, Aug. 29, 1952; s. Robert John Sr. and Jeanne Marcella (DeYonker) K.; m. Dorothy Marie Cunningham, Oct. 28, 1978 (div. June 1988); 1 child, Cristie; m. Kim Denise Katherine Greenhan, Feb. 10, 1990; adopted children: Antonio, Jacob, Nicholas. BBA, U. Mich., 1974; JD, Wayne State U., 1977, LLM in Taxation, 1994. Bar: Mich. 1979; CPA. Tax staff acct. Arthur Young & Co., Bloomfield Hills, Mich., 1977-78; tax staff sr., mgr. McEndarffer, Hoke & Bernhard, P.C., Bloomfield Hills, 1978-84; tax supr. Cen. Transport, Inc., Sterling Heights, Mich., 1984-85; tax atty. Chrysler Fin. Corp., Southfield, Mich., 1985-89, mgr. non-income taxes and licensing, 1989-95, staff tax counsel, 1995-99; sr. tax couns. Chrysler Svcs. N.Am. LLC, Farmington Hills, Mich., 1999—. Charter pres. Sterling Heights Jaycees. Mem. ABA, Mich. Bar Assn., Mich. Assn. CPA's, Am. Arbitration Assn. (panel mem.). Republican. Roman Catholic. Avocations: softball, basketball coaching, music. Home: 48736 Ben Franklin Dr Shelby Township MI 48315-4026 Office: DaimlerChrysler Svcs NAm LLC 27777 Inkster Road Farmington Hills MI 48334-5326

KIPPING, HANS F. dermatologist, educator; b. Chgo., Jan. 8, 1924; s. Johaanes and Johannah (Rauch) K.; m. Rosemary New, Jan. 3, 1928 (dec.); children: Susan, John, David. MD, U. Buffalo, 1947. Intern Buffalo Gen. Hosp., 1947-48; resident in indsl. medicine Millard Fillmore Hosp., Buffalo, 1948-49; resident in dermatology E.J. Meyer Meml. Hosp., Buffalo, 1953-56; practice medicine specializing in dermatology, Buffalo, 1945—; clin. prof. dermatology SUNY, Buffalo, 1979, dermatologist Buffalo Gen. Hosp., 1980—; cons. dermatology Roswell Park Meml. Inst., 1980—. Cons., lectr. in field. Contbr. articles and rsch. studies to profl. jours. Served to capt. USAF, 1950-52. Fellow Am. Soc. Dermatopathology; mem. AMA, Profs. Dermatology, Soc. Investigative Dermatology, Am. Acaad. Dermatology, Dermatology Found., Toronto Dermatology Soc., Buffalo-Rochester Dermatology Soc. (pres. 1962-63), N.Y. State Dermatology Soc. (pres. 1974-75), Youngstown Yacht Club. Republican. Methodist. Home: 192 Castlebrook Ln Buffalo NY 14221-4475 Office: 4444 Main St Buffalo NY 14226-4420

KIPPUR, MERRIE MARGOLIN, lawyer; b. Denver, July 24, 1962; d. Morton Leonard and Bonnie (Seldin) Margolin; m. Bruce R. Kippur, Sept. 7, 1986. BA, Colo. Coll., 1983; JD, U. Colo., 1986. Bar: Colo. 1986, U.S. Dist. Ct. Colo. 1986, U.S. Ct. Appeals (10th cir.) 1987. Assoc. Sterling & Miller, Denver, 1985-88, McKenna & Cuneo, Denver, 1989-94; sr. v.p., gen. counsel, dir. First United Bank, Denver, 1994-96; prin. Merrie Margolin Kippur Assocs., PC, Denver, 1997—2002. Lectr. in field; clk. Hon. Elizabeth E. Brown, 2001—. Author: Student Improvement in the 1980's, 1984; (with others) Ethical Considerations in Bankruptcy, 1985, Partnership Bankruptcy, 1986, Colorado Methods of Practise, 1988. Pres.-elect, then pres. Jr. League Denver, 2001—03; bd. mgrs. Met. Mayors and Commrs. Youth Award; active Jr. League Denver, 1992—. Mem. ABA, Colo. Bar Assn. (ethics com.), Denver Bar Assn., Gamma Phi Beta, Phi Delta Phi, Pi Gamma Mu. Democrat. Avocations: reading, scuba diving, wine collecting. E-mail: merrie_kippur@cob.uscourts.gov.

KIRBERGER, ELIZABETH, lawyer, consultant; b. Tulsa, 1965; d. Robert Earl Jr. and Phyllis Kirberger. BA in Philosophy and lit., Wheaton Coll., 1987; JD, Georgetown U., 1990; MPH, Columbia U., 1997. Bar: N.Y. 1991. Law clk. to chief justice Okla. Supreme Ct., Oklahoma City, 1989; dir. contracts Herbert Barrett Mgmt. Inc., N.Y.C., 1990-93; cons. Population Coun., N.Y.C., 1993-94, Columbia U. Ctr. for Study of Human Rights, N.Y.C., 1995, Internat. Planned Parenthood Fedn., N.Y.C., 1996-98, AVSC Internat., N.Y.C., 1998-99; pres. Kirberger & Assocs., N.Y.C., 1998—. Editor Georgetown Internat. Environ. Law Rev., 1988-90; contbr. articles to profl. jours. Mem. ABA, N.Y. State Bar Assn., Assn. Bar City N.Y., Am. Immigration Lawyers Assn. Office: Kirberger & Assocs 81 Washington St Brooklyn NY 11201-1459 E-mail: k@immigration-lawyer.com.

KIRBY, ALLAN PRICE, JR., investment company executive; b. Wilkes-Barre, Pa., June 18, 1931; s. Allan Price and Marian (Sutherland) K.; children: Jessie Ann, Allan Price III, Slater Baran, Coray Sutherland, Milan Stanton. BA, Lafayette Coll., 1953. Pres. Liberty Sq., Inc., Mendham, N.J.; dir., chmn. exec. com. Alleghany Corp. Chmn. bd. dirs. A.P. Kirby Jr. Found. Inc.; chmn. bd. mgrs. Allan P. Kirby Ctr. for Free Enterprise and Entrepreneurship. Trustee Fred M. and Jessie A. Kirby Episcopal House, Wilkes U.; trustee, treas. Angeline Elizabeth Kirby Meml. Health Ctr. Lt. (j.g.) USNR, 1953-55. Mem. Delta Kappa Epsilon. Clubs: Mendham (N.J.) Golf and Tennis; Morris County Golf (Convent, N.J.); Yale (N.Y.C.); Black River Fish and Game (Pottersville, N.J.). Office: 14 E Main St PO Box 90 Mendham NJ 07945-0090

KIRBY, AMY ELIZABETH, microbiologist, researcher; b. Atlanta, May 28, 1976; d. Thomas Russell and Sharron Stevens Kirby. BS in Agr., U. Ga., Atlanta, 1997; PhD, SUNY, Buffalo, 2003. Emerging infectious disease fellow Ctrs. for Disease Control and Prevention, Atlanta, 1997—98. Recipient Erwin Neter award, Western NY ASM, 2002; Presdl. fellow, U. Buffalo, SUNY, 1999—2002, HOPE scholar, State of Ga., Alumni Merit scholar, U. Ga. Office: Univ Buffalo SUNY 138 Furber Hall 3435 Main St Buffalo NY 14214

KIRBY, CHARLES WILLIAM, JR., dancer, choreographer; b. Little Rock, Apr. 28, 1926; s. Charles William and Eva Rose (Horton) K. AA, Little Rock Jr. Coll., 1945. Adv. bd. George Brown Coll. Tech., Toronto; exec. com. Canadian Actors Equity Assn.; pres. Southeastern Regional Ballet Festival Assn., 1965; co-founder, co-owner (with Jacques Wensvoort) Abundance Restaurant, Inc., Toronto, 1980— Prin. soloist Ballet Soc. Ark., 1947, assoc. dir. Acad. Ballet Arts, Little Rock, 1948-50, prin. dancer Ark. State Musicals, 1949, Memphis Open Air Theatre, 1950, co-dir. Acad. Dance Arts, Memphis, 1950-65, prin. dancer, costume designer, choreographer Front St. Theatre, Memphis, 1954-64, choreographer Memphis Opera Theatre, 1954-64, performer Dallas Summer Musicals, 1964; co-organizer, choreographer ballets Memphis Civic Ballet, 1953-65; mem. Nat. Ballet Can., 1965-72, soloist, 1972-76, prin. dancer, 1976-85, prin. character artist, 1985-98; appeared: CBS-TV spls. Swan Lake, 1967, Cinderella, 1968 (Emmy award), Sleeping Beauty, 1972 (Emmy award), Giselle, 1975, La Fille Mal Gardee, 1979, Onegin, 1985, The Merry Widow, 1987, The Planets, 1994; choreographer: CBC-TV spls. CBC Opera prodn. La Rondine, 1971, Maurice Ravel Centennial Concert, 1975, summer opera festivals, Nat. Arts Centre, Ottawa, Can., Canadian Opera Co.; co. mgr. Dance Repertory Co., N.Y.C., 1972; author:, dir., choreographer, narrator: spl. ednl. program Spectrum: A Retrospective Look at Dance, 1973. Served with AUS, 1944. Recipient key to City of Little Rock, 1965 Mem. Assn. Canadian TV and Radio Artists. Episcopalian. Home: 7518 Silver Trumpet Ln # 101 Naples FL 34109

KIRBY, DOROTHY MANVILLE, social worker; b. Burke, SD, Oct. 23, 1917; d. Charles Vietz and Gail Lorena (Coonen) Manville; m. Sigmund Kirby, July 11, 1941 (div. 1969); children; Paul Howard, Robert Charles. BA, Wayne State U., 1970, MSW, 1972. Cert. social worker, Mich.; lic. marriage and family therapist, Mich. Pvt. practice social work, Allen Park, Mich., 1973—. Conduct seminars on stress, personal effectiveness and communication for various orgns., hosps. and bus. Pres. Allen Park Symphony Orch., 1990-92. Mem.: LWV (pres. Allen Park 1965—66), NASW (clin.), AAUW, Mich. Assn. Marriage and Family Therapy (sec. 1982), Nat. Assn. Marriage and Family Therapy. Presbyterian. Avocation: playing violin. Home and Office: 15720 Wick Rd Allen Park MI 48101-1535 E-mail: dmkirby@ameritech.net.

KIRBY, FRANK EUGENE, musicology educator, author, editor; b. N.Y.C., Apr. 6, 1928; s. Russell Thorp and Dorothy (Clement) K.; m. Emily Baruch, Aug. 17, 1952; children: Russell, Nicholas, Paula, Nathaniel. BA, Colo. Coll., 1950; PhD, Yale U., 1957. Music cataloguer Peabody Inst. Libr., Balt., 1956-57; Ford Found. teaching intern Williams Coll., 1957-58; vis. asst. prof. U. Va., 1958-59; guest asst. prof. U. Tex., Austin, 1959-60; asst. prof. W.Va. U., 1961-63; asst. prof. music Lake Forest (Ill.) Coll., 1963-66, assoc. prof., 1967-76, prof., 1977-93. Author: A Short History of Keyboard Music, 1966, An Introduction to Western Music, 1970, Music in the Classic Period, 1979, Music in the Romantic Period, 1986, Music for Piano, A Short History, 1995; contbr. numerous articles to profl. jours. Grantee W.Va., 1962, Lake Forest Coll., 1965-66, 68, Alexander von Humboldt-Stiftung grantee, 1966, 79, 87. Mem. Am. Musicological Soc.

KIRBY, FRED MORGAN, II, corporation executive; b. Wilkes Barre, Pa., Nov. 23, 1919; s. Allan P. and Marian G. (Sutherland) K.; m. A. Walker Dillard, Apr. 30, 1949; children: Alice Kirby Horton, Fred Morgan III, Dillard, Jefferson. Grad., Lawrenceville Sch., 1938; AB, Lafayette Coll., Easton, Pa., 1942; postgrad., Harvard Grad. Sch. Bus., 1947; LLD, Lafayette Coll., 1984; LHD, Drew U., 1997; LLD, St. Joseph's U., 1981, Wake Forest U., 2002. From v.p. to pres., bd. dirs. Allan Corp., 1953-75, pres., chmn. bd. dirs. Filtration Engrs., Inc., 1951-56; dir. Alleghany Corp., 1958-61, 63—, v.p., 1961, exec. v.p., 1963-67, chmn. bd., 1967—, pres., 1968-77, mem. exec. com., 1968—. Pres., bd. dirs. F.M. Kirby Found., Inc.; bd. dirs. Nat. Football Found. and Coll. Hall of Fame, Inc. Served to lt. (s.g.) USNR, 1942-46. Recipient 25th Anniversary citation NCAA, 1966, Silver Anniversary All-Am. award Sports Illustrated, 1966, Gold medal Pa. Soc., 1982, Gold medallion Internat. Swimming Hall of Fame, 1989, Gold medal Nat. Football Found. and Coll. Hall Fame, Inc., 2000, Lawrenceville medal Lawrenceville Sch., 2001. Mem. Westmoreland Club, (Pa.), Spring Valley Hounds (N.J.), Treyburn Country Club (N.C.), Morris County Golf Club (N.J.), Zeta Psi. Office: PO Box 151 17 Dehart St Morristown NJ 07963-0151

KIRBY, HARMON E. retired ambassador; b. Hamilton, Ohio, Jan. 27, 1934; s. Cecil and Julia Catherine (Tucker) Kirby; m. Françoise Rolande Chatelain, Dec. 26, 1963; children: Caroline Patricia, Christopher Harmon. AB, Harvard U., 1952; MA, George Washington U., 1977. With pers. and labor rels. Diamond Nat. Corp., Middletown, Ohio, 1959-60; exec. asst. to exec. v.p. Hudson Pulp and Paper Co., N.Y.C., 1960-61; joined Fgn. Svc., Dept. State, 1961; vice consul U.S. Mission, Geneva, 1961-63, U.S. Consulate Gen., Madras, India, 1964-66; internat. rels. officer Dept. State, 1966-69; polit. officer U.S. Embassy, New Delhi, 1969-72, Micronesia Status Negotiations, 1973; Turkish desk officer Dept. of State, 1974-76, dir. Pakistan/Afghanistan/Bangladesh affairs, 1982-84, dir. UN polit. affairs, 1987-89, dir., performance evaluation, 1989-90; polit. counselor U.S. Mission European Cmtys., Brussels, 1976-79; counselor, dep. chief of mission U.S. Embassy, Khartoum, 1979-81, min.-counselor dep. chief of mission Rabat, Morocco, 1984-87; sr. seminar Nat. and Internat. Affairs, Washington, 1981-82; amb. to Togo, 1990-94; ret., 1994. Bd. dirs. Internat. Eye Found. Fellow: Tangier Am. Legation Mus. Soc.; mem.: DACOR, Am. Fgn. Svc. Assn., Phi Beta Kappa. Avocations: travel, photography, tennis, swimming. Home: 6811 Barrett Ln Bethesda MD 20814-1205

KIRBY, H(ARRY) SCOTT, priest; b. Richmond, Va., May 6, 1938; s. William Alphus and Lucille Viola (Patterson) K.; m. Heather Patricia Roberts, June 22, 1963; children: Cheryl Christine, Robert Bruce. BA, U. Richmond, 1960; MDiv, Gen. Theol. Sem., N.Y.C., 1963. Ordained priest Episcopal Ch., 1963. Asst. to rector Cathedral of St. Luke and St. Paul, Charleston, S.C., 1963; curate Ch. of the Advent, Kenmore, N.Y., 1963-66; rector Ch. of St. John the Bapt., Dunkirk, N.Y., 1966-73, Ch. of St. John on the Mountain, Bernardsville, N.J., 1973-79; resident dir., dir. devel. St. Francis Acad., 1979-89; canon Christ Ch. Cathedral, Salina, Kans., 1979—, dean Eau Claire, Wis., 1989—. Devel. cons. St. Francis Acad., Salina, 1991—; chmn. long range planning Diocese of Eau Claire, 1989—, dean Chippewa Valley, 1990-96, mem. coun. of advice to the pres., ho. of deps., 1994-2000, chair com. on state of the ch., 1994-97; mem. com. elect presiding bishop, 1997-2000, mem. title IV com., 1997—, mem. exec. coun. visitation com.; chaplain Eau Claire Police Dept. Contbr. articles to mags. Bd. dirs. Episcopal Relief and Devel. Recipient Bishop's Svc. award Diocese of Western Kans., 1980. Mem. Anglican Soc. Home: 1712 Lehman St Eau Claire WI 54701-7524 Office: Christ Ch Cathedral 510 S Farwell St Eau Claire WI 54701-3723 E-mail: snhkirby@aol.com.

KIRBY, JAMES EDMUND, JR., theology educator; b. Wheeler, Tex., June 24, 1933; s. James Edmund and Mamie (Helton) K.; m. Patty Ray Boothe, July 22, 1955; children: David Edmund, Patrick Boothe. BA cum laude, McMurry Coll., 1954; B.D., Perkins Sch. Theology, 1957, S.T.M., 1959; PhD, Drew U., 1963; postgrad., Cambridge (Eng.) U., 1957-58. Ordained to ministry United Meth. Ch., 1959; pastor First Meth. Ch., Roby, Tex., 1958-59, Milford (Pa.) Meth. Ch., 1960-61; asst. prof. Bible, McMurry Coll., Abilene, Tex., 1959-60; asst. prof. religion Sweet Briar Coll., Va., 1963-67; prof. religion, head dept. religion Okla. State U., Stillwater, 1967-70; head Sch. Humanistic Studies, 1970-76; dean, Prof. Ch. History Sch. Theology, Drew U., Madison, N.J., 1976-81; dean Perkins Sch. Theology So. Meth. U., Dallas, 1981-94, pres. ad interim, 1994-95, prof. ch. history, 1995—. Teaching asst. Drew Theol. Sem., Madison, N.J., 1960-61; cons. bd. missions United Meth. Ch., South Africa, 1968 Co-author: The Methodists, 1996; author: Brother Will, 2000, The Episcopacy in American Methodism, 2000; contbr. articles to profl. jours.; bd. dirs., pres. Wesley Works Editl. Project. John M. Moore fellow, 1957-58; Dempster fellow, 1962 Mem. Am. Acad. Religion, Am. Soc. Ch. History, Alpha Chi, Omicron Delta Kappa. Home: 9235 Windy Crest Dr Dallas TX 75243-6222 Office: So Meth U Selecman Hall Perkins Sch Theology Dallas TX 75275-0001

KIRBY, JOHN JOSEPH, JR., lawyer; b. Washington, Oct. 22, 1939; s. John Joseph and Rose Elizabeth (Mangan) Kirby; children: John Pickens, Timothy James, Perrin Patricia Lucia. BA, Fordham Coll., 1961; BA (Rhodes scholar), Oxford U., 1964, MA, 1967; LLB, U. Va., 1966. Bar: Va 1966, NY 1969. Asst. prof. law U. Va., 1966-67; spl. asst. civil rights divsn. U.S. Dept. Justice, Washington, 1967-68; assoc. Mudge Rose Guthrie Alexander & Ferdon, N.Y.C., 1968-70, ptnr., 1971-95, chmn., 1991-95; ptnr. Latham & Watkins, N.Y.C., 1995—. Dep dir Pres's Comn Campus Unrest, 1970. Bd dirs Georgetown Univ, 1976—92, Fordham Univ, 1994—2000, Merton Col Charitable Corp, 1995—, Fund Modern Cts, 1998—. Mem.: ABA, DC Bar, Va State Bar, Asn Bar City NY. Home: 115 E 87th St Apt 6F New York NY 10128-1101 also: 64 Beach Rd Westhampton Beach NY 11978-2339 Office: Latham & Watkins 885 3d Ave Ste 1000 New York NY 10022-4834

KIRBY, KENT BRUCE, artist, educator; b. Fargo, N.D., Dec. 31, 1934; s. Harold Ely and Vida Nicola (Vennerstrom) K.; m. Lynn Rennetha Schutte, Sept. 1, 1956 (div. 1981); children: Kalin Louise, Jeffrey Bruce, Kristin Beth, m. Carrie Anne Parks, 1983 BA, Carleton Coll., 1956; MA, U. N.D., 1959; M.F.A., U. Mich., 1970. Tchr. Benjamin Franklin Jr. High Sch., Fargo, 1956-59; instr. in art, acting head dept. art Muskingum Coll., 1959-61; instr. Wilkes Coll., 1961-62; faculty art Alma (Mich.) Coll., 1962-90, prof., 1971—, chmn. dept. art and design, 1962—, chmn. div. fine arts, 1973-75, Charles A. Dana prof. art, 1976. One-man shows Grand Rapids Art Mus., 1981, U. N.Mex., 1980, Ctr. for Creative Studies, Detroit, 1982, Ctrl. Mich. U., Mt. Pleasant, 1990, New Eng. Sch. Photography, Boston, 1992; group shows include, 2d Internat. Exhbn. Prints and Drawings, Wesleyan U., 1982, Color Print U.S.A., Tex. Tech. U., Lubbock, 1983, 20th Bradley Nat. Print and Drawing Exhbn., 1985, 4th Rockford Internat. Biennale, 1985, Nat. Invitational Print Exhbn., U. Ala., 1988; exhibited Nat. Mus. Am. History, Washington, 1988-89, Stockton Nat. Print and Drawing Exhbn., Haggin Mus. of Art, 1990, " A Decade of Mich. Printmaking", Detroit Inst. of Art, 1992, 2001, Nat. Small Print Exhbn., U. of Wis., Parkside, 1994, 95, 97, 2002, 2003, Fla. Nat., 1997, Art Link Nat. Exhib., 2001, 2002; represented in permanent collections, Chgo. Art Inst., Detroit Art Inst., Smithsonian Inst., Brit. Mus., London; author: Studio Collotype: Continuous Tone Printing for the Artist, Printmaker and Photographer, 1988. Chmn. museums com., mem. Mich. State Council for Arts, 1966-68. Research fellow Newberry Library, 1974; Mich. Council for Arts grantee, 1975, 78; Nat. Endowment for Arts grantee, 1976 Mem. AAUP, Coll. Art Assn., Mid-Am. Print Coun. Home: 9667 W Van Buren Rd Riverdale MI 48877-9707 E-mail: kirby@alma.edu.

KIRBY, ODELL, retired small business owner, retired newswriter, writer; b. Vivan, Okla., 1921; s. Auda and Matilda (Brasfield) Kirby. Student, Inst. of Children's Lit., West Redding, Conn. Printer's devil Indian Jour., Eufaula, Okla., 1936; with various newspapers, 1936—72; owner vacuum cleaner sales and svc. bus., 1972—97. Home: 2701 N B St McAlester OK 74501

KIRBY, ORVILLE EDWARD, potter, painter, sculptor; b. Wichita, Kans., Jan. 31, 1912; s. Charlie and Elizabeth J. (Sage) K. Student, U. Utah, 1935-36, U. So. Calif., L.A., 1934-35, St. Paul Sch. Fine Art, 1933-34. Owner Orville Kirby Pottery, L.A., 1941-47, Sleepy Hollow Pottery, Laguna Beach, Calif., 1948-54, Monroe, Utah, 1955-2001; ret. Republican. Mem. Lds Ch. Avocation: collecting old coins. Home and Office: 95 W Center St Monroe UT 84754-4159

KIRBY, PETER CORNELIUS, lawyer, policy analyst; b. N.Y.C., Mar. 25, 1950; s. Cornelius Carroll and Anne (Pracny) K. B.A., Yale U., 1971; J.D., Harvard U., 1975. Bar: U.S. Dist. Ct. D.C. 1975, U.S. Ct. Appeals (D.C. cir.) 1975. Asst. Law Sch., Harvard U., 1975-76; law clk. U.S. Ct. Appeals (D.C. cir.), 1976-77; counsel Nat. Wildlife Fedn., Washington, 1977-80, Wilderness Soc., Washington, 1980—; mem. faculty Nat. Law Ctr., George Washington U., Washington, 1978-87, Vt. Law Sch., South Royalton, 1979-83; mem. Appalachian Trail Adv. Com., 1979-81. Contbr. numerous articles on natural resources law and policy to profl. jours. Mem. ABA (natural resources section forest resources com., 1984), Soc. Am. Foresters, Scroll and Key, Phi Beta Kappa. Democrat. Roman Catholic. Home: 1616 Piedmont Rd NE Apt L-4 Atlanta GA 30324-5270 Office: Wilderness Soc 1447 Peachtree St NE Ste 812 Atlanta GA 30309-3029

KIRBY, RONALD EUGENE, fish and wildlife research administrator; b. Angola, Ind., Nov. 26, 1947; s. Robert Waye and Lorraine Alice (Hoag) Kirby; m. Dona J. Kirby; children: Cyrus Robert, William Emil, Peter Waye, Joshua M. Brosten, Emily A. Brosten, Andrew J. Brosten. BS, Duke U., 1969; MA, So. Ill. U., 1973; PhD, U. Minn., 1976. Staff biologist Coop. Wildlife Rsch. Lab., So. Ill. U., Carbondale, 1969-72; collaborating biologist U.S. Forest Svc., St. Paul and Cass Lake, Minn., 1970-72; rsch. biologist Antarctic Rsch. Program NSF, McMurdo Station, Antarctica, 1974; NIH rsch. trainee dept. ecology and behavioral biology U. Minn., Mpls., 1972-76; wildlife biologist, Patuxent Wildlife Rsch. Ctr. U.S. Fish and Wildlife Svc., Laurel, Md., 1976-80, population mgmt. specialist div. refuge mgmt. Washington, 1980-82, rsch. coord. Nat. Wildlife Refuge System, 1982-83, regional assistance biologist, office info. transfer Ft. Collins, Colo., 1983-88, leader info. transfer sect., 1988-90; asst. dir. No. Prairie Wildlife Rsch. Ctr., Jamestown, N.D., 1991-92, dir., 1993; dir. U.S. Nat. Biol. Svc. No. Prairie Sci. Ctr., Jamestown, N.D.,

1993-96; dir. U.S. Geol. Survey No. Prairie Wildlife Rsch. Ctr., Jamestown, N.D., 1997-2001; dir. U.S. Geol. Survey Forest and Rangeland Ecosys. Sci. Ctr., Corvallis, Oreg., 2001—03; sr. biologist strategic devel. We. regional office U.S. Geol. Survey, Seattle, 2003—. Mem. waterfowl adv. com. Minn. Dept. Natural Resources, 1970—72; mem. black duck subcom. Atlantic Flyway Coun., 1976—80; mem. tech. sect. Central Flyway, 1991—. Editorial referee to sci. jours. and profl. reports; contbr. to numerous profl. publs. Active Boy Scouts Am., 1984—. Grantee AEC, 1972—76. Mem.: The Wildlife Soc., Lambda Chi Alpha. Avocations: hiking, camping, birdwatching, motorcycling, hunting. Office: Western Regional Office US Geol Survey 909 1st Ave Ste 800 Seattle WA 98104 E-mail: ronald_kirby@usgs.gov.

KIRBY, RUSSELL STEPHEN, epidemiologist, statistician, geographer; b. New Haven, June 8, 1954; s. Frank Eugene and Emily (Baruch) K.; m. Elizabeth Margaret Ivens, July 9, 1977; children: Rachel Anne, Amelia Jeanne, Jocelyn Eileen. BA, U. Wis., 1974, MS, 1977, PhD, 1981, MS, 1991. Lectr. U. Wis., Madison, 1980, 82-83; rsch. analyst 3 Wis. Ctr. for Health Stats., Madison, 1981-83, rsch. analyst 5, 1983-85, rsch. analyst 6 maternal and child health statistician, 1985-88; sr. rsch. analyst maternal and child health Ark. Ctr. Health Statistics, Little Rock, 1988-91; instr. dept. pediat. U. Ark. Med. Scis., Little Rock, 1989-93, asst. prof., 1993-96; assoc. prof. dept. ob.-gyn. Milw. Clin. Campus U. Wis. Med. Sch., 1996-01, prof., 2001—02; prof., vice chair dept. maternal and child health, dept. of pediat. Sch. Publ. Health U. Ala. at Birmingham, 2002—. Vis. asst. prof. Beloit Coll., 1987—88; adj. asst. prof. U. Ark., Little Rock, 1988—95; adj. assoc. prof. Coll. Bus. and Mgmt. Cardinal Stritch U., 2000—02; sci. dir. Ark. Reproductive Health Monitoring Sys., 1991—94, dir., 1994—96, cons., 1996—. Bd. editors: Jour. Perinatology, 1997-99; book rev. editor Jour. of Childs Health, 2003—; contbr. articles to profl. jours. Recipient Callon-Leonard award Wis. Assn. for Perinatal Care, 1994, Byron L. Hawks award Ark. Perinatal Assn., 1995, Fraternalist of Yr. award Ct. Razorback Ind. Order Foresters, 1996; named Vol. of Yr. SE chpt. Wis. March of Dimes Birth Defects Found., 1998, Outstanding Advocate for Maternal and Child Health Wis. Maternal and Child Health Coalition, 1999. Fellow Am. Coll. Epidemiology; mem. APHA, Assn. Am. Geographers (life), Agrl. History Soc. (life), So. Hist. Soc. (life), Wis. Assn. for Perinatal Care (bd. dirs. 1990-2002, pres.-elect 1998-99, pres. 1999-2000, past pres. 2000-01, prog. award prenatal care, 2003), Perinatal Found. (bd. dirs. 1996-2002, treas. 2000-2002), Ark. Perinatal Assn. (pres. 1991-92), Soc. for Epidemiologic Rsch., Nat. Perinatal Assn. (bd. dirs. 1990-92, 95-98, ann. conf. chair 1999), Nat Birth Defects Prevention Network (pres. 1999, past pres. 2000, exec. com. 1997—), Soc. for Pediatric and Perinatal Epidemiologic Rsch. (exec. com. 2000—), Teratology Soc., Ala. chpt. Mar. of Dimes (bd. dirs. 2002—). Avocations: camping, writing book reviews, computer cartography and graphics, used books. Home: 713 Kendall Dr Vestavia Hills AL 35226 Office: RPHB 320 1530 3rd Ave S Birmingham AL 35294-0022 E-mail: rkirby@uab.edu.

KIRCH, DARRELL GENE, academic administrator, dean; b. Denver, May 3, 1949; m. Deborah M. Kirch; children: Samantha M., MAdeline A. BA in Philosophy, U. Colo., 1973, MD magna cum laude, 1977. Diplomate Am. Bd. Psychiatry and Neurology. Resident in psychiatry U. Colo. Health Scis. Ctr., Denver, 1977—82; med. staff fellow adult psychiatry br. NIMH, Washington, 1982—84, sr. staff fellow neuropsychiatry br., 1984—87, med. dir. Neuropsychiat. Rsch. Hosp., 1987—89, dep. scientific dir. Bethesda, Md., 1992—93; prof. Sch. Grad. Studies, prof. dept. psychiatry Med. Coll. Ga., Augusta, 1994—2000, dean Sch. Medicine, 1994—2000, dean Sch. Grad. Studies, 1995—99, sr. v.p. for clin. activities, 1998—2000; prof. dept. psychiatry, sr. v.p. for health affairs Pa. State U., Hershey, 2000—, dean Coll. Medicine, 2000—; CEO Milton S. Hershey Med. Ctr., 2000—. Examiner Am. Bd. Psychiatry and Neurology, Deerfield, Ill., 1985—; chaor sec. on med. schs. AMA, 1998—99; mem. coun. deans adminstrv. bd. Assn. Med. Colls., 2000—. Assoc. editor: Psychopharacology Bull., 1990—98, Schizophrenia Bull., 1989—95. Capt. USPHS, 1986—94. Decorated Commendation medal. Mem.: AMA, Assn. of Am. Med. Coll. (chair 2003), Soc. for Exec. Leadership in Acad. Medicine, Pa. Psychiat. Soc., Pa. Med. Soc., Am. Soc. Clin. Psychopharmacology, Am. Psychiat. Assn. Home: 564 Olde Course Rd Hershey PA 17033-1337 Office: Pa State U H162 P O Box 850 500 University Dr Hershey PA 17033*

KIRCH, PATRICK VINTON, anthropology educator, archaeologist; b. Honolulu, July 7, 1950; s. Harold William and Barbara Ver (MacGarvin) Kirch; m. Debra Connelly, Mar. 3, 1979 (div. 1990); m. Therese Babineau, Feb. 6, 1994. BA, U. Pa., 1971; MPhil, Yale U., 1974, PhD, 1975. Assoc. anthropologist Bishop Mus., Honolulu, 1975-76, anthropologist, 1976-82, head archaeology div., 1982-84, asst. chmn. anthropology, 1983-84; dir., assoc. prof. Burke Mus. U. Wash., Seattle, 1984-87, prof., 1987-89, U. Calif., Berkeley, 1989—, prof. anthropology, endowed chair, 1994—; curator Hearst Mus. Anthropology, 1989—, dir., 1999—2002. Adj. faculty U. Hawaii, Honolulu, 1979—84; mem. lasting legacy com. Wash. State Centennial Commn., 1986—88; pres. Soc. Hawaiian Archaeology, 1980—81; vis. prof. Ecole des Hautes Etudes en Scis. Sociale, Paris, 2002. Assoc. editor Internat. Encyclopedia of the Behavioral and Social Scis., 2002; editor: Island Societies, 1986, Historical Ecology in the Pacific Islands, 1997; co-editor (with Terry L. Hunt): Historical Ecology in the Pacific Islands: Prehistoric Environmental and Landscape Change, 1997; co-author (with Peter S. Chapman): Archaeological Excavations at Seven Sites, Southeast Maui, Hawaiian Islands, 1979; co-author: (with Terry L. Hunt) Archaeology of the Lapita Cultural Complex: A Critical Review, 1989; co-author: (with Marshall Sahlins) Anahulu: The Anthropology of History in the Kingdom of Hawaii, Vol. 1: Historical Ethnography, 1992, Anahulu: The Anthropology of History in the Kingdom of Hawaii, Vol. 2, 1992; co-author: (with Roger C. Green) Hawaiki, Ancestral Polynesia: An Essay in Historical Anthropology, 2001; author: Marine Exploitation in Prehistoric Hawaii: Archaeological Investigations at Kalahuipua'a Hawaii Island, 1979, Island Societies: Archaeological Approaches to Evolution and Transformation, 1986, Niuatoputapu: The Prehistory of a Polynesian Chiefdom, 1989, The Evolution of the Polynesian Chiefdoms, 1989, Wet and the Dry: Irrigation and Agricultural Intensification in Polynesia, 1994, Anahulu: The Anthropology of History in the Kingdom of Hawaii, 1994, Feathered Gods and Fishhooks: An Introduction to Hawaiian Archaeology and Prehistory, 1995, Legacy of the Landscape: An Illustrated Guide to Hawaiian Archaeological Sites, 1996, Lapita Peoples: Ancestors of the Oceanic World, 1996, On the Road of the Winds: An Archaeological History of the Pacific Islands Before European Contact, 2000; contbr. articles to profl. pubs. Trustee Berkeley Art Mus. and Pacific Film Archives, 1999—. Recipient J.I. Staley prize in anthropology, Sch. Am. Rsch., 1998; fellow, Ctr. for Advanced Study in Behavioral Scis., 1997—98; grantee, NSF, 1974, 1976, 1977, 1982, 1987, 1988, 1989, 1993, 1996, 1998, 2001, NEA, 1985, NEH, 1988, 1999, Hawaii Com. for Humanities, 1981; rsch. grantee, Nat. Geog. Soc., 1986, 1989, 1996, Wenner-Gren Found. for Anthropol. Rsch., 1998. Fellow: NAS (John J. Carty medal for the advancement of sci. 1997), AAAS, Calif. Acad. Scis. (trustee 1999—), Am. Philos. Soc., Am. Anthrop. Assn., Am. Acad. Arts and Scis.; mem.: Polynesian Soc., Assn. Field Archaeology, Sigma Xi. Democrat. Avocations: cross-country skiing, gardening. Office: U Calif Dept Anthropology 232 Kroeber Hall Berkeley CA 94720-3710

KIRCHER, JOHN JOSEPH, law educator; b. Milw., July 26, 1938; s. Joseph John and Martha Marie (Jach) K.; m. Marcia Susan Adamkiewicz, Aug. 26, 1961; children: Joseph John, Mary Kathryn. BA, Marquette U., 1960, JD, 1963. Bar: Wis. 1963, U.S. Dist. Ct. (ea. dist.) Wis. 1963, U.S. Ct. Appeals (7th cir.) 1992. Sole practice, Port Washington, Wis., 1963-66; with Def. Research Inst., Milw., 1966-80, research dir., 1972-80; with Marquette U., 1970—, prof. law, 1980—, assoc. dean acad. affairs, 1992-93. Chmn. Wis. Jud. Council, 1981-83. Author: (with J.D. Ghiardi) Punitive Damages: Law and Practice, 1981, 2d edit (with C.M. Wiseman), 2000; editor Federation of Defense and Corporate Counsel Quarterly; mem. editorial bd. Def. Law Jour.; contbr. articles to profl. jours. Recipient Teaching Excellence award Marquette U., 1986, Disting. Service award Def. Research Inst., 1980, Marquette Law Rev. Editors' award, 1988. Mem. ABA (Robert B. McKay Professor award 1993), Am. Law Inst., Wis. Bar Assn., Wis. Supreme Ct. Bd. of Bar Examiners (vice chair 1989-91, chair 1992), Am. Judicature Soc., Nat. Sports Law Inst. (adv. com. 1989—), Assn. Internationale de Droit des Assurances, Scribes. Roman Catholic. Office: PO Box 1881 Milwaukee WI 53201-1881

KIRCHHEIMER, ARTHUR E(DWARD), lawyer, business executive; b. N.Y.C., June 26, 1931; s. Arthur and Lena K.; m. Esther A. Jordan, Sept. 11, 1965. BA, Syracuse U., 1952, LL.B., 1954. Bar: N.Y. 1954, Calif. 1973. Ptnr. Block, Kirchheimer, Lemax & Failmezger, Syracuse, N.Y., 1954-70; corp. counsel Norwich Pharmacal Co., N.Y., 1970-72; sr. v.p., gen. counsel Wickes Cos., Inc., San Diego, 1972-84; prin. Arthur E. Kirchheimer, Inc., P.C., San Diego, 1984-90; writer, cons. in bus. matters La Jolla, Calif., 1990—. Sec., dir. Corp. Fin. Council San Diego, 1975 Pres. Mental Health Assn. Onondaga County, 1970; chmn. Manlius (N.Y.) Planning Commn., 1969-72; mem. Alternatives to Litigation Spl. Panel, 1984—; mem. San Diego County Grand Jury, 1991-92. Mem. ABA, Calif. Bar Assn. Home and Office: 2876 Palomino Cir La Jolla CA 92037-7066

KIRCHHOFF, MICHAEL KENT, economic development executive; b. Effingham, Ill., Apr. 3, 1963; s. Robert D. and Violet M. (Baumann) K; m. Lynn Reilly, May 27, 1989; children, Amelia Elizabeth, Caroline Rebekah. BA in Econ., BS in Bus., East Ill. U., 1986; postgrad., U. Okla., 1995. Cert. econ. developer; cert. Ill. Assessing Officer. Owner, mgmt. cons. Spectrum Cons., Springfield, 1985-90; intern govs. office Ill. Dept. Revenue, Springfield, 1986-87, property tax analyst, 1987-89; econ. devel. prof. Dept. Commerce and Community Affairs, Springfield, 1989-92; data analyst Ill. Dept. Pub. Aid, Springfield, 1992; mkt. devel. rschr. Ill. Power Co., Decatur, 1992-95; joint purchasing coord. State of Ill., Springfield, 1995-96; owner Phoenix Assocs., Springfield, 1995-96; exec. dir. Tuscola (Ill.) Area Improvement Assn., 1996-97, program mgr. Mainstreet Tuscola, 1996-97; exec. dir. Jacksonville (Ill.) Area Econ. Devel. Coun., 1997-99, Jacksonville (Ill.) Regional Econ. Devel. Corp., 2000—. Asst. scoutmaster, asst. explorer advisor, scoutmaster, dist. chmn. Okaw dist. Boy Scouts Am., 1997, dist. chmn. Honest Abe dist., 1998—, exec. bd. mem. Abraham Lincoln coun., 1998—, coun. commr., 2003--; mem. Big Bros./Big Sisters, I-Search for Children, Project Safeplace; v.p. Sangamon County Reps., Operation Snowball; treas., bd. dirs. Ctrl. Ill. Youth Svc. Bur., Ctrl. Ill. Workforce Prep.; vice chair Douglas County Tourism Com.; advisor Tuscola Tourism Com.; mem. Ill. Enterprise Zone Assn., Nat. Main St. Network, bd. mem. Ill. Rural Ptnrs., membership chair, 1997-99; bd. dirs. Jacksonville Main St., 1998—; bd. dirs. Ill. Devel. Coun., 2000—, chair edn. com., 2003—; bd. dirs. Am. Econ. Devel. Coun., 2000-2001. Recipient Charles Carter Meml. award InterFraternity Coun., 1984; named one of 40 Under 40 Springfield Bus. Jour., 2000. Mem. Am. Soc. Pub. Adminstrn., Am. Econ. Devel. Coun. (bd. dirs. 2000-2001), Internat. Economic Devel. Coun. (mem. cert. bd. 2002--), Cmty. Devel. Soc., Ill. Devel. Coun. (bd. dirs. 2001-03, chmn. govt. affairs com. 1998-2000, chair edn. com. 2003), Mid-Am. Econ. Devel. Coun., Jacksonville Area Indsl. Corp. (sec. 1997-99), Acad. Polit. Sci., Mid Am. InterFraternity Coun. Assn. (Outstanding State Coord. 1984, Outstanding Area V.P. 1985), Nat. Trust for Hist. Preservation, Springfield Jaycees, Jacksonville Country Club, Rotary, Order of Omega, Omicron Delta Epsilon, Beta Sigma Psi. Lutheran. Home: 1225 W College Ave Jacksonville IL 62650-2214 Office: Jacksonville Regional Econ Devel Corp 200 W Douglas Ave Jacksonville IL 62650-2012 E-mail: mike@jredc.org.

KIRCHICK, WILLIAM DEAN, lawyer; b. Oceanside, N.Y., Nov. 20, 1950; s. Julian Gilbert and Jean (Kostinsky) K.; m. Carol Bonnie Rudnick, May 29, 1977; children: James Rory, Jeffrey Scott. BA in Polit. Sci. magna cum laude, U. Mich., 1973; JD cum laude, Boston Coll., 1976. Bar: Mass. 1978, Ill. 1976, U.S. Dist. Ct. Mass. 1978, U.S. Ct. Appeals (1st cir.) 1978, U.S. Tax Ct. 1976, U.S. Supreme Ct. 1982; accredited estate planner designation. Assoc. Arnstein, Gluck, Lehr & Milligan, Chgo., 1976-77; assoc., ptnr. Peabody & Brown, Boston, 1977-88; ptnr. Bingham Dana LLP, Boston, 1988—2002, Bingham McCutchen LLP, Boston, 2002—. Mem. Boston Probate and Estate Planning Forum, 1987—, program events coord., 1989-90, moderator, 1990-91; mem. Boston Estate Planning Coun., 1986—, mem. exec. com., 1989-92, sec. 1995-96, treas., 1996-97, v.p. 1997-98, pres.-elect, 1998-99, pres. 1999-2000; mem. Norfolk and Plymouth Bus. and Estate Planning Coun., 1990—; mem. Planned Giving Group of New Eng., Inc., 1997-2001; mem. curriculum adv. com. for Mass. Continuing Legal Edn., Inc. Contbg. author: Estate and Protective Planning Techniques in Massachusetts, 1990, A Practical Guide to Estate Planning in Massachusetts, 1996, Preparing Estate Tax Returns, 1997, Drafting Wills and Trusts in Massachusetts, 2002; contbr. articles to profl. jours. Chmn. young lawyers team spl. events com. Combined Jewish Philanthropies of Greater Boston, Inc., 1982-84, chmn. young lawyers team, 1984-85, mem. lawyers team cabinet, 1985-89, 91-94; trustee The CJP Disabilities Trust, 1998--, The Acorn Found., 2000--. Recipient Campaign Leadership award Combined Jewish Philanthropies of Greater Boston, Inc., 1984. Fellow Am. Coll. Trust and Estate Counsel; mem. ABA (mem. sect. probate, trusts and real property), Mass. Bar Assn. (mem. tax sect. exec. com. 1989-92, probate sect. exec. com. 1992-93), Boston Bar Assn. (mem. estate planning com. 1981—, chmn. 1984-88, chmn. subcom. to study income, gift and estate tax proposals of Tax Reform Act of 1986 1985-86, chmn. subcom. on proposed temporary regulations concerning Chpt. 13 Internal Revenue Code 1988-89, mem. probate sect. 1978—), U. Mich. Club Greater Boston, Boston Coll. Law Sch. Alumni Assn. Phi Beta Kappa, Phis Eta Sigma. Avocations: jogging, swimming, walking, skiing. Office: Bingham McCutchen LLP 150 Federal St Fl 15 Boston MA 02110-1726 E-mail: wdkirchick@bingham.com.

KIRCHKNOPF, MATTHEW BELA, research laboratory manager; b. Yonkers, N.Y., Jan. 25, 1960; s. Matthew and Mary. (Nemeth) K.; m. Gloria N. Muscardin, Mar. 5, 1994. BSME, Northeastern U., 1983; MBA, U. Md., 1993. Project/program mgr. Naval Rsch. Lab., Washington, 1985—. With USCGR, 1986—. Republican. Roman Catholic. Avocations: jogging, skiing, sports, golf, aerobics. Home: 5917 Berwyn Rd Berwyn Heights MD 20740 E-mail: kirchknopf@ncst.nrl.navy.mil.

KIRCHMAN, ERIC HANS, lawyer; b. Washington, May 2, 1962; s. Charles Vincent and Erika Ottilie (Knoeppel) K.; m. Hillary Bronkie Hutson, Apr. 19, 1991; children: Erika B., Thomas E. BA, Univ. Md., 1985; JD, Univ. Balt., 1990. Bar: Md. 1990, U.S. Dist. Ct. Md. 1991. Assoc. Hillel Abrams, Rockville, Md., 1990-92; ptnr. Kirchman & Kirchman, Wheaton, Md., 1992—. Of counsel Md. Coun. for Gifted and Talented Children, Inc., Silver Spring, 1994. With U.S. Army Reserve, 1985-98. Mem. ATLA, Md. Criminal Def. Attys. Assn., Montgomery County Bar Assn. Office: Kirchman & Kirchman 11141 Georgia Ave Ste 403 Wheaton MD 20902-4659

KIRCHNER, JAMES WILLIAM, retired electrical engineer; b. Cleve., Oct. 17, 1920; s. William Sebastian and Marcella Louise (Stuart) K.; m. Eda Christene Landfear, June 11, 1950 (dec. May 1977); children: Kathleen Ann Kirchner Duda, Susan Lynn Kirchner Buonpane. BS in Elec. Engring., Ohio U., 1950, MS, 1951. Registered profl. engr., Ohio. Instr. elec. engring. Ohio U., Athens, 1950-52; mgr. liaison engring. Lear Siegler Inc., Maple Heights, Ohio, 1952-64; coordinator engring. services Case Western Res. U., Cleve., 1964-72, gen. mgr. Med. Ctr. Co. (CWRU), 1972-91; ret., 1991; sec. of corp. Thermagon, Inc., Cleve., 1992. Mem. Portage County Republican Exec. Com., 1961-62; treas. PTA, Aurora, Ohio, 1963-65, v.p., 1965-66; mem. The Ch. in Aurora, 1956—. Served with USAAF, 1942-45, PTO Mem. NSPE (life), IEEE (life), VFW (life), Ohio Soc. Profl. Engrs. (life), Cleve. Engring. Soc. (chmn. environ. com. 1976), Am. Soc. Engring. Edn. (life). Home: Reserves of Aurora 535 Treetop Ct Aurora OH 44202-7317 E-mail: jwkfph@aol.com.

KIRCHNER, JOHN ALBERT, retired otolaryngology educator; b. Waynesboro, Pa., Mar. 27, 1915; s. Francis Edward and Jessie Cecilia (Cameron) K.; m. Aline Legault, Oct. 11, 1947; children: John C., Thomas L., Paul E., Marie Cecile, Christine A. MD, U. Va., 1940; MS, Yale U., 1952. Intern Charity Hosp., New Orleans, 1940-41; resident in otolaryngology Johns Hopkins Hosp., 1946-50; mem. faculty Sch. Medicine Yale U., New Haven, 1951—, prof. otolaryngology, 1962-85, prof. emeritus, 1985—; with Conn. Acad. of Arts and Scis., 1999—. Rsch. cons. NIH, 1966; spl. rschr. pathology and physiology of larynx and pharynx NINCDS. Editor: Yearbook Ear, Nose and Throat, 1969-75. Capt. inf. AUS, 1942-46. Decorated Bronze Star; recipient Harris P. Mosher rsch. award Am. Trilogical Soc., 1958, Semon medal in laryngology U. London, 1981; Commonwealth Fund fellow, 1963-64, fellow Silliman Coll., Yale U., 1977—. Mem. Am. Laryngol. Assn. (pres. 1979-80, Casselberry award 1966, Newcomb award 1969, de Roaldes medal 1985, Merit award 1988), Am. Acad. Otolaryngology (v.p. 1978-79), Am. Laryngol., Rhinol. and Otolaryn. Soc. (pres. 1981-82), Am. Assn. Head and Neck Surgery (pres. 1977-78), New Eng. Otolaryn. Soc. (pres. 1965-66), European Laryngological Soc. (hon.), Japan Broncho-Esophagological Soc. (hon.), German Soc. Otolaryngology, Head and Neck Surgery (corr.), Italian Soc. Otolaryn. (corr.), Coll. Oto-Rhino-Laryngologium Amicitae Sacrum. Home: 12 Rimmon Hill Rd Woodbridge CT 06525-1324 Office: Yale Sch Medicine Dept Surgery 333 Cedar St PO Box 208041 New Haven CT 06520-8041

KIRCHNER, LISA BETH, vocalist, actress; b. L.A. d. Leon and Gertrude (Schoenberg) K. BA, Sarah Lawrence Coll., N.Y., 1975. Picture rschr. McGraw-Hill, 1985-87, John Wiley & Sons, 1988, Simon & Schuster/Globe Book Co., 1992—2000, Chelsea House Pubs., 1987-94, Oxford Univ. Press, 1997, Facts on File, 2001—02, Greenwood Pub. Co., 1997, Lazard Freres, 1998—, The Oryx Press, 1999—, Abbeville Press, 2001—02. Songwriter, BMI. Broadway appearances include The Threepenny Opera, 1975, The Human Comedy, 1985; off-Broadway appearances include the Radiant City, 1993, Hotel for Criminals, 1974, The American Imagination, others; TV shows include Songs From the Heart, Another World, The Guiding Light, As The World Turns, Out of Our Father's House; appearances at The White House and Gracie Mansion; performed as featured soloist and back-up singer with Judy Collins (numerous TV appearances); prodr., solo vocalist CD releases (Albany Records) entitled One More Rhyme, 1999, When Lights Are Low, 2002. Mem. AFTRA, SAG, BMI, Equity, Actor's Equity Assn. Avocations: painting, crafts, poetry. E-mail: kirchl@aol.com.

KIRCHNER, RICHARD JAY, retired physical education educator; b. Schenectady, N.Y., Feb. 17, 1930; s. Richard Jacob and Leah (Williams) K.; m. Barbara Ann Crane, Feb. 2, 1952; children: Richard Alec, Barbara Jayne, Carolyn Diane, Robert Jay, Kathleen Kay. BS, U. Wis., 1952, MS, 1955, postgrad., 1956; EdD, Mich. State U., 1962. Instr. wrestling and track coach St. Cloud (Minn.) Tchrs. Coll., 1955-56; asst. prof., coaching staff Ctrl. Mich. U., Mt. Pleasant, 1956-62, prof. recreation, chmn. dept., 1962-87, with Office of Dean sch. edn., health and human svcs., 1987-88, sr. prof., 1988-92; ret., 1992. Chmn. pres.'s adv. com.; camp program dir., camp dir. Elkton-Pigeon-Bayport Sch. Camp, Caseville, Mich., 1962; mcpl. recreation dir. Petoskey (Mich.), 1963, cons., 1964-74; vice chmn. citizens adv. com. Recreation Svcs. divsn. Mich. Dept. Conservation, 1966-67. Pres. Mt. Pleasant Intermediate Sch. PTA, 1968-69; chmn. tech. planning com. Mt. Pleasant Recreation Commn. Capt. USMCR, 1952-54. Mem. AAHPER (v.p. Mich. 1966-67, v.p. Midwest dist. 1973-74), Nat. Recreation and Parks Assn., Am. Assn. Leisure and Recreation (nat. pres. 1976-77, nat. accreditation coun. 1978-83, vice chmn. 1979-81, chmn. 1981-83), Am. Camp Assn., Mich. Soc. Arts, Sci. and Letters, Mich. Soc. Gerontology, Outdoor Edn. and Camping Coun. (charter), Mich. Recreation and Parks Assn. (v.p. 1968-70), Phi Eta Sigma, Phi Epsilon Kappa, Phi Delta Kappa. Home: 6953 Riverside Dr Mount Pleasant MI 48858-7930

KIRDAR, NEMIR AMIN, banker; b. Kirkuk, Iraq, Oct. 28, 1936; s. Amin and Nuzhet (Mohamad Ali) K.; m. Nada Adnan Shakir, Feb. 1, 1967; children: Rena, Serra. BA, Coll. of the Pacific, 1960; MBA, Fordham U., 1972; postgrad., Harvard U., 1979. Trainee, asst. treas., asst. v.p. Allied Bank Internat., N.Y.C., 1969-73; v.p. Nat. Bank N.Am., N.Y.C., 1973-74; v.p., head Gulf Div., Chase Manhattan Bank, N.Y.C., 1974-81; pres., chief exec. officer INVESTCORP Bank E.C., Manama, Bahrain, 1982—; also bd. dirs. Chmn. Advisory Council Center for Contemporary Arab Studies, Georgetown U. Contbr. articles to profl. jours. Trustee London Philharmonic Trust, London. Mem. Overseers Committee on University Resources, Harvard U., Bd. Advs. World Economic Forum, Switzerland, Internat. Bd. Councillors Center for Strategic and Internat. Studies, Washington, D.C., Visiting Committee Fordham U., visiting committee JFK Sch. of Govt., Harvard U., bd. Trustees Heart Research Found. N.Y.C.; Friend of Somerville, Somerville Coll. Oxford U. Clubs: Metropolitan. Office: Investcorp 37th Fl W 280 Park Ave Rm 37W New York NY 10017-1216 also: Investcorp 65 Brook St London W1Y 1YE England also: Investcorp PO Box 5340 Manama Bahrain

KIRGIS, FREDERIC LEE, law educator; b. Washington, Dec. 29, 1934; s. Frederic Lee Sr. and Kathryn Alice (Burrows) K.; children: Julianne, Paul Frederic. BA, Yale U., 1957; JD, U. Calif.-Berkeley, 1960. Bar: Colo. 1961, Va. 1983. Atty. Covington & Burling, Washington, 1964-67; from asst. prof. to prof. law U. Colo., Boulder, 1967-73; prof. law UCLA, 1973-78, Washington & Lee U., Lexington, Va., 1978—, dir. Frances Lewis Law Ctr., 1978-83, dean law sch., 1983-88. Author: International Organizations in their Legal Setting, 1977, 2d edit. 1993, Prior Consultation in International Law, 1983; contbr. articles to profl. jours. Pres. Maury River Soccer Club, Lexington, 1978-85. Served to capt. USAF, 1961-64 Recipient Deak award 1974; research fellow NATO, Brussels, 1978 Mem. Am. Soc. Internat. Law (v.p. 1985-87, sec. 1994—), Am. Law Inst., Internat. Law Assn. (Am. br.), Am. Jour. Internat. Law (bd. editors 1984-96, 98-2003, hon. editor 2003—), State Bar Va., Order of Coif. Democrat. Presbyterian. Home: 15 Grey Dove Rd Lexington VA 24450-2269 Office: Washington and Lee U Sch of Law Lexington VA 24450

KIRIAKOPOULOS, GEORGE CONSTANTINE, dentist; b. Derby, Conn., June 3, 1926; s. Constantine Elias and Rose (Yerontakis) K.; AA, U. Paris (France), 1947; AB, Bklyn. Coll., 1950; DDS, Columbia, 1954; m. Virginia Demos, June 3, 1956; 1 dau., Stephanie. Pvt. practice gen. dentistry, Fort Lee, N.J., 1955—; assoc. dir. dept. dentistry St. Giles Hosp., Bklyn., 1955-60; attending dept. oral surgery Lenox Hill Hosp., N.Y.C., 1956-60, adj. oral surgeon, 1960-64; assoc. prof., then prof. dept. pedodontics Columbia, 1956—; attending in dentistry Presbyn. Hosp., 1986—; mem. adv. com. Columbia Presbyn. Hosp. Med. Ctr.; mem. adv. com. to dean Sch. Dental and Oral Surgery Columbia U. Served with AUS, 1943-46. Decorated Bronze Star, Silver Star, D.S.M.; recipient Medal of Meritorious Service, Lenox Hill Hosp., 1964. Fellow Royal Soc. Health; mem. ADA, Am. Assn. Hosp. Dentists, N.Y. State Dental Soc., Columbia U. Alumni Assn., Psi Omega. Greek Orthodox (pres. Parish Coun., Cathedral St. John, Tenafly, 1980-83). Author: Your Child's Teeth - the Layman's View, 1966; Who Wants to Be a Dentist?, 1968; The Modern Thermopylae—Battle of Crete, May 1941, 1978; Portrait of a Cretan Hero, 1978; Cyprus and the Polish Connection, 1980; Ten Days to Destiny, 1985, Paperback edit., 1986, The Nazi Occupation of Crete: 1941-45, 1995, others. Home and Office: 2205 Mackay Ave Fort Lee NJ 07024-5034

KIRICK, DANIEL JOHN, agronomist; b. Port Jervis, N.Y., Nov. 8, 1953; s. Daniel and Mary Theresa Kirick; m. Jean Marie Guse, Sept. 27, 1986; children: Nicholas, John, Kristina, Kimberly. BA in Biology, History, U. Minn., Duluth, 1976; BS in Agronomy, U. Minn., St. Paul, 1977. Cert. profl. agronomist. Agronomist Delft (Minn.) Farm Chems., 1978, Skelly Fertilizer, Trimont, Minn., 1978-80, Mower County Svc. Co., Sargeant, Minn., 1980-86, Cenex Supply, Ellis, S.D., 1986-88, Rice (Minn.) Farm Supply, 1988-91, Kirick Agronomy Svcs., St. Cloud, Minn., 1992—. Mem. Comty. Edn. Devel. Adv. Coun., Sauk Rapids, Minn., 1990-94, Youth Devel. Bd., Sauk Rapids, 1990, Benton County Ext. Com., 1993-98, Ctrl. Minn. Forage Coun., 1994—. Mem. AAAS, Weed Sci. Soc. Am., Soil Sci. Soc. Am., Crop Sci. Soc. Am., Am. Soc. Agronomy. Roman Catholic. Home: PO Box 206 Rice MN 56367-0206 Office: Kirick Agronomy Svcs 9144 County Road 4 Saint Joseph MN 56374-9748

KIRIHATA, TOSHIAKI, VLSI design engineer, researcher; b. Siga, Japan, Apr. 10, 1961; came to U.S., 1990; BS in Precision Engring., Shinshu U., Nagano, Japan, 1984, MS in Precision Engring., 1986. Rschr. IBM Japan Ltd., Tokyo, 1986-87, IBM Yasu Tech. Applications Lab., Japan, 1987-89, lead engr., 1989-91, IBM Microelectronics Divsn., Burlington, Vt., 1991-93, IBM, Hopewell Junction, N.Y., 1993-96, project leader, 1996-97; product design team leader IBM T.J. Watson Rsch. Ctr. IBM Rsch., Hopewell Junction, N.Y., 1997-99; product design mgr. IBM Microelectronics, Hopewell Junction, N.Y., 2000—. Mem. IEEE (sr.). Office: IBM 2070 Rte 52 Bldg 630 Hopewell Junction NY 12533 E-mail: kirihata@us.ibm.com.

KIRILA, CAROL ELIZABETH, osteopathic physician, internist; b. Mount Clemens, Mich., Oct. 28, 1952; d. Andrew William and Mary Margaret (Schmeltz) K. Diploma, Rsch. Med. Ctr. Sch. Nursing, Kansas City, Mo., 1974; BS in Biology, U. Mo., Kansas City, 1987; DO U. Health Scis., Coll. Osteo. Medicine, 1991. RN, Mo. Lab. asst. Lakeside Hosp., Kansas City, 1969-74, RN, inservice instr., 1976-87, part time staff nurse, relief supr., 1988-91; staff nurse Children's Mercy Hosp., Kansas City, 1974, U. Health Scis. Hosp., Kansas City, 1974-76, Rsch. Med. Ctr., Kansas City, 1976; part time staff nurse Kendallwood Pvt. Duty, 1988-91; intern Still Regional Med. Ctr., Jefferson City, Mo., 1991-92; resident internal medicine U. of Mo. Kansas City Sch. of Medicine, 1992-95; staff physician Internal Medicine Assocs. St. Joseph, Mo., 1995—96,

Permante Med. Group, Kansas City, Mo., 1996-98; mem. faculty U. of Health Scis., Coll. Osteo. Medicine, 1998—. Catechumenate sponsor St. James Ch., Kansas City, 1982; mem. Manheim Park Neighborhood Assn., Kansas City, 1982-91. Recipient cert. of recognition U. Health Scis. Coll. Osteo. Medicine, 1988-89, Outstanding Svc. and Achievement award U. Mo.-Kansas City, 1986, Pres.'s award Mo. Assn. Osteo. Physicians and Surgeons, 2000, 02 Mem.: Mo. Assn. Osteo. Physicians and Surgeons (Medallion award 2002), Am. Osteo. Assn. Democrat. Episcopalian. Avocations: plants, reading, music, cooking, fitness.

KIRILOVA, SVETLANA NIKOLOVA, psychologist, consultant; b. Vetrino, Bulgaria, Feb. 14, 1962; d. Nikola Stanev Nedelchev and Bistra Stankova Bodurova; m. Stanimir Naskov Kirilov, Nov. 12, 1990; 1 child, Atanas. MA in Psychology, Sofia U., 1988. Psychologist, cons. House of Creativity, Sofia, 1988-90; h.s. tchr. Vetrino, Bulgaria, 1990-93; psychologist Roli OOD, Sofia, 193-94, United Avio-Med. Rsch. Inst., Sofia, 1995-97; chief psychologist Bulgarian Air Forces, Sofia, 1997—. Psychology advisor Ministry of Def. Hdqrs. of Bulgarian Army, 1996—. Cons., image maker Presdl. Elections, Sofia, 1995; mem. Mensa Internat. 1st lt. Air Force, 1997-2000. Mem. AAAS. Avocations: archaeology, Eastern philosophy, martial arts. Home: 15127 NE 24th St PMB #484 Redmond WA 98052 E-mail: svetlanakirilova@hotmail.com.

KIRITANI, SAERI, artist; b. Osaka, Japan, June 12, 1970; came to U.S., 1988; d. Kazuyoshi and Reiko Kiritani. BA in Painting and Drawing, San Francisco State U., 1992; BFA in Painting and Drawing, San Francisco Art Inst., 1993; MFA in Painting and Drawing, U. Pa., 1997; postgrad., Skowhegan Sch., Maine, 1998. Price and quality investigator Kanazawa City Govt., Ishikawa, Japan, 1985-86; tel. operator MRO Home Shopping Network, Ishikawa, 1986-87; art coord. Japanese Newcomer Svc., San Francisco, 1992; docent San Francisco Mus. Modern Art, 1992-95; illustrator bio-chem. computer lab. U. Pa., Phila., 1995-97, tchg. asst., 1996-97; translator Yutaka Electronics and Stirus R&D, N.Y.C., 1997; translator, coord. for fashion designer Hiroko Koshino, 1997-98; artist asst. to Roxy Paine, 1999; sales supr. Whitney Mus. Am. Art, N.Y.C., 1998—99; translator Gregory and Gregory, NY, 2000—01; freelance translator, 2002—. Asst. to Gabrielle Bakker, Italian Stret Painting Festival, San Rafael, Calif., 1994; vis. artist Keystone Boys and Girls Club in Mission Dist., San Francisco, 1994; instr. Japanese lang. Berlitz Lang. Schs., San Francisco, 1994-95. One-woman shows include San Francisco Art Inst. Cafe, 1993, Irving Street Gallery, San Francisco, 1994, Live Art Gallery, San Francisco, 1995, U. Pa., 1998; 2-person show Diego Rivera Gallery, San Franciscco Art Inst., 1994; exhibited in group shows at Tesori Gallery, San Mateo, Calif., 1992 (2d place award), Miss. State U., Jackson, 1993, San Francisco Art Inst., 1993, Wells Fargo Bank, San Francisco, 1993, Somar Gallery, San Francisco, 1994, Borowsky Gallery, Phila., 1994, Club 1915 Folsom, San Francisco, 1994, Matrix Gallery, Sacramento, 1995, U. Pa., 1995, 96, 97, Park Avenue Armory, N.Y.C., 1995, Nexus Found. for Today's Art Gallery, Phila., 1995, Silvermine Guild Arts Ctr., New Canaan, Conn., 1996, Meyerson Hall Gallery, Phila., 1997, Arthur Ross Gallery, Phila., 1997, A.I.R. Gallery, N.Y.C., 1998, Jack Tilton Gallery, N.Y.C., 1998, Exit Art Gallery, N.Y.C., 1998, Key Bank Bldg., Skowhegan, Maine, 1998, First World Gallery, 1998, Cynthia Broan Gallery, N.Y.C., 1999, Thompson Gallery, N.Y.C., 1999, Contemporary Mus., Balt., 2000, The Fist World Gallery, N.Y.C., 2000, Para/Site Art Space, Hong Kong, 2000, The Art Fashion Mag. Collesioni EDGE, Italy, 2001, Knoedler Gallery, N.Y.C., 2001, Contaninazioni Gallery, Italy, 2001-2002, Williamsburg Art Hist. Ctr., Bklyn., 2002; represented in permanent collections San Francisco Mus. Modern Art, U. Pa., also pvt. collections. Scholar Japan Found. Ctr. for Global Partnership, San Francisco Art Inst., U. Pa.; grantee, Post-Art, Chgo., 1999, Pola Art Found., Japan, 2000, Japanese Agy. for Cultural Affairs, 2003—. Avocation: travel.

KIRK, BALLARD HARRY THURSTON, architect; b. Williamsport, Pa., Apr. 1, 1929; s. Ballard and Ada May (DeLaney) K.; m. Vera Elizabeth Kitchener, Mar. 13, 1951; children: Lisa Lee, Kira Alexandria, Dayna Allison, Courtlandt Blaine. BArch, Ohio State U., 1959. Pres. Kirk Assocs., Architects, Columbus, Ohio, 1963—. Mem. Ohio Bd. Bldg. Standards, Columbus, 1973-78, 92-99; pres. Nat. Coun. Archtl. Registration Bds., Washington, 1983-84, Ohio Bd. Examiners Architects, Columbus, 1973-93; bd. dirs. Nat. Archtl. Accrediting Bd., Washington, 1986-89. Mem. AIA (bd. dirs. Columbus chpt. 1988-92), Coll. of Fellows. Republican. Mem. Brethern Ch. Home: 2557 Charing Rd Columbus OH 43221-3673

KIRK, CARMEN ZETLER, data processing executive; b. Altoona, Pa., May 22, 1941; d. Paul Alan and Mary Evelyn (Pearce) Zetler. BA, Pa. State U., 1959-63; MBA, St. Mary's Coll. Calif., 1977. Cert. in data processing. Pub. sch. tchr. State Ga., 1965-66; systems analyst U.S. Govt. Dept. Army, Oakland, Calif., 1967-70; programmer analyst Contra Costa County, Martinez, Calif., 1970-76; applications mgr. Stanford (Calif.) U., 1976-79; pres. Zetler Assocs., Inc., Palo Alto, Calif., 1979—. Cons. State Calif., Sacramento, 1985-88. Office: Zetler Assocs Inc PO Box 50395 Palo Alto CA 94303-0395

KIRK, CAROL, lawyer; b. Henry, Ill., Dec. 23, 1937; d. Howard P. and Mildred Root McQuilkin; m. Robert James Kirk, Aug. 20, 1961; children: Kathleen, Nancy, Sally. BS in Music Edn., U. Ill., 1960; JD, Ind. U., Indpls., 1989. Bar: Ind. 1989. Pvt. piano tchr., 1957-85; pub. sch. music tchr., 1960-62; dir. Ind. State Ethics Commn., Indpls., 1989-97; atty. and investigator Disciplinary Commn., Supreme Ct. Ind., Indpls., 1997—. Pres. Coun. on Govtl. Ethics Laws, (Internat.), 1993-94. Exec. editor Articles & Prodn. Ind. Law Rev., 1988-89. Mem. Met. Devel. Commn., Indpls., 1982-87; chairperson Pub. Radio Adv. Bd., Indpls., 1983-84, treas. Cmty. Svc. Coun., Indpls., 1988-91. Invitee to Nat. 4H Congress, Chgo., 1956; named 4H Family of Yr., Washington Twp., 4-H, Indpls., 1980, Vol. of Week, Voluntary Action Ctr., Indpls., 1980. Mem. LWV (pres. Indpls. 1979-83), Ind. Bar Assn., Indpls. Bar Assn., Phi Alpha Delta, Mu Phi Epsilon. Avocation: choir singing. Office: Discip Commn Supreme Ct Ind 1165 South Tower 115 W Washington St Indianapolis IN 46204-3420 E-mail: rkirk1937@aol.com.

KIRK, CASSIUS LAMB, JR., retired lawyer, investor; b. Bozeman, Mont., June 8, 1929; s. Cassius Lamb and Gertrude Violet (McCarthy) K. AB, Stanford U., 1951; JD, U. Calif., Berkeley, 1954. Bar: Calif. 1955. Assoc. Cooley, Godward, Castro, Huddleson & Tatum, San Francisco, 1956-60; staff counsel for bus. affairs Stanford U., 1960-78; chief bus. officer, staff counsel Menlo Sch. and Coll., Atherton, Calif., 1978-81; chmn. Eberli-Kirk Properties, Inc. (dba Just Closets), Menlo Park, 1981-94; ret. Faculty Coll. Bus. Adminstrn. U. Calif., Santa Barbara, summers 1967-73; past adv. bd. Allied Arts Guild, Menlo Park; past nat. vice-chmn. Stanford U. Annual Fund; past pres. Menlo Towers Assn. Past v.p. Palo Alto C. of C. With U.S. Army, 1954-56. Mem. VFW, Stanford Faculty Club, Order of Coif, Menlo Towers Assn. (pres. 2000-02), Phi Alpha Delta. Republican. Home: 1330 University Dr Apt 52 Menlo Park CA 94025-4241

KIRK, COLLEEN JEAN, retired conductor, educator; b. Champaign, Ill., Sept. 7, 1918; d. Bonum Lee and Anna Catherine (Hoffert) K. BS with high honors, U. Ill., 1940, MS, 1945; Ed.D., Columbia U., 1953. Tchr. music pub. schs., Danvers, Ill., 1940-44; tchr. music pub. schs. Watseka, Ill., 1944-45; instr. Univ. H.S., Urbana, Ill., 1945-49; asst. prof. edn. and music U. Ill., 1949-58, assoc. prof., 1958-64, prof., 1964-70, Fla. State U., Tallahassee, 1970-90, condr. choral union, 1970-90. Choral clinician, condr., adjudicator. Dir. music Wesley United Meth. Ch., Urbana, 1947-70; dir. jr. chorus, Ill. Summer Youth Music, Urbana, 1963-71; co-dir. Fla. Honors Choral Ensemble, Tallahassee, 1980-81; dir. Fla. Jr. High Sch. Choral Ensemble, Tallahassee, 1983; author: (with others) Modern Methods in Elementary Education, 1959; (with Harold Decker) Choral Conducting: Focus on Communication, 1988, Choral Music Education in America (1892-1992), 1992; contbr. numerous articles to Choral Jour. Recipient Pres.'s Award for Excellence in Teaching, Fla. State U., 1979, Disting. Svc. award U. Ill. Sch. Music Alumni Assn., 1991; named to Fla. Music Educators Hall of Fame, 1992. Mem. Am. Choral Dirs. Assn. (life, pres. So. divsn. 1971-75, nat. pres. 1981-83, Wayne Hugoboom award for Disting. Svc. 1988, Harold A. Decker Choral award 1981, So. divsn. conv. award Excellence in Choral Art 1994, Robert Lawson Shaw citation 2001), Am. Choral Found., Inc., Music Educators Nat. Conf., Assn. Profl. Vocal Emsembles, Fla. Music Educators Assn., Internat. Fedn. Choral Music, AAUP, Coll. Music Soc., Fla. Vocal Assn., Fla. Coll. Music Educators Assn., Sonneck Soc., Pi Kappa Lamdba, Kappa Delta Pi, Sigma Alpha Iota. Home: Heartland Health Care Ctr 1001 E Pells Paxton IL 60957

KIRK, CONNIE ANN, English educator, writer; b. Wellsville, N.Y., Feb. 14, 1957; d. Leonard A. and Mary Arlene Lewis; m. Kenneth Andrew Kirk, May 21, 1983; children: Benjamin Lewis, Johnathan Patrick. BA in English and Creative Writing, Binghamton U., 1986, MA in English and Creative Writing, 1988, postgrad., 1999—. Adj. prof. English Mansfield (Pa.) U., 1988—. Designer, tchr. 1st online English course Mansfield U. Author: (children's nonfiction) First Peoples: The Mohawks of North America, 2001, (young adult biography) J. K. Rowling: A Biography, 2003. Mem.: MLA, Soc. of Children's Book Writers and Illustrators, Am. Lit. Assn., Emily Dickinson Internat. Soc. Office: P O Box 337 Painted Post NY 14870

KIRK, DANIEL LEE, retired physician, consultant; b. Alliance, Ohio, Aug. 1, 1919; s. John Lee and Olive (Strine) K.; m. Betty Kathryn Blair, Sept. 9, 1942, children— Daniel Lee, Nancy Jayne. Student, Gettysburg Coll., 1940; MD, George Washington U., 1943; certificate in Clin. Psychiatry, U. Pa., 1955; certificate, U. Wis., 1963. Intern Harrisburg (Pa.) Hosp., 1943-44; resident psychiatry Harrisburg State Hosp., 1944-45; practice medicine, specializing in psychiatry Waynesboro, Pa., 1945-50; staff physician Elwyn (Pa.) Sch., 1950-52, clin. dir., 1952-57; asst. supt. Pennhurst State Sch. and Hosp., Spring City, Pa., 1957-59; supt. Selinsgrove (Pa.) State Sch. and Hosp., 1959-68, ret., 1990. Former med. dir., research chmn. South Mountain (Pa.) Restoration Center; cons. in geriatric medicine; adj. prof. dept. spl. edn. Pa. State U., 1965— ; adviser Smith Kline & French film Toymakers; cons. Comprehensive Mental Health/Mental Retardation Program Region IV. Contbr. articles med. jours. Served with M.C. AUS, 1945. Fellow Am. Geriatrics Soc., Am. Assn. Mental Deficiency, N.Y. Acad. Scis., Nat. Bd. Med. Examiners; mem. AMA, Pa. Med. Soc., Med. Club Phila., Assn. Med. Supts. Mental Hosps., Nat., Pa. assns. retarded children. Clubs: Mason, Rotarian. Home: 201 N Church St Waynesboro PA 17268-1117

KIRK, DENNIS DEAN, lawyer; b. Pittsburg, Kans., Dec. 13, 1950; s. Homer Standley and Maida Corena (Rouse) K.; 1 child, Dennis Dean II. AA, Hutchinson Cmty. Jr. Coll., 1970; BS with distinction, No. Ariz. U., 1972; JD, Washburn U., 1975. Bar: Kans. 1975, U.S. Dist. Ct. Kans. 1975, D.C. 1977, U.S. Ct. Appeals (D.C. cir.) 1978, U.S. Supreme Ct. 1979, U.S. Ct. Appeals (5th cir.) 1981, U.S. Dist. Ct. Md. 1984, U.S. Tax Ct. 1984, U.S. Claims Ct. 1984, U.S. Ct. Appeals (fed. cir.) 1984, U.S. Ct. Mil. Appeals 1984, Va. 1990, U.S. Ct. Appeals (4th cir.) 1990; lic. pvt. investigator; lic. personal protection specialist. Trial atty. ICC, Washington, 1975-77; assoc. Goff, Sims, Cloud & Stroud, Washington, 1977-82; pvt. practice Washington, 1982-90; ptnr. Slocum, Boddie, Murry & Kirk, Falls Church, Va., 1990-93; pvt. practice Falls Church, Va., 1993—. Pres. Law Facilities, Inc., Washington, 1982—. Vol. parole and probation officer Shawnee County, Kans., 1973-74; citizens adv. task force group Md. Nat. Park and Planning Commn., 1978-80; citizens task force on gen. plan amendments study Fairfax County coun., Va., 1981-82; active Seven Corners Task Force, Fairfax County, 1981-82, chmn. transp. and housing subcoms.; pres. Seven Springs Tenants Assn., College Park, Md., 1976-80, Ravenwood Park Citizens Assn., 1981-82; dir. Greenwood Homes, Inc., Fairfax County Dept. Housing and Cmty. Devel., 1983—; active Gala Com. Spotlight the Kennedy Ctr. Pres. Adv. Com. on the Arts, 1986-87, Mason Dist. Rep. Com., 1981-91, Fairfax County Young Reps., Fairfax County Rep. Com., 1982—; founding chmn., charter mem. Mason Dist. Jaycees, 1984-86; sec., gen. counsel, bd. dirs. U.S. Assocs. for the Cultural Triangle in Sri Lanka, 1983-90; commr. Consumer Protection Commn., Fairfax County, 1982—, chmn., 1996-97; towing adv. bd. Fairfax County, 1993-; Ravenwood precinct chmn. Rep. Orgn., Falls Church, Va., 1982-90, 97-2003; bd. dirs. PTA Baileys Elem. Magnet Sch., 1995-99, v.p., 1996-97. Named to Honorable Order Ky. Cols. Mem. ABA, NRA (life), Am. Fedn. Musicians (life, emeritus), Assn. Former Intelligence Officers, Masons (Grand Sword Bearer 1992), Shriners, Tall Cedars, Scottish Rite, Moose, Royal Arch, Phi Kappa Phi, Phi Alpha Delta (nat. capital area alumni chpt. justice 1984-86, 94-96). Methodist. Avocation: music. Home: 6315 Anneliese Dr Falls Church VA 22044-1620 Office: 5201 Leesburg Pike Ste 1108 Falls Church VA 22041-3268 E-mail: kirklaw@fcc.net.

KIRK, DONALD, journalist; b. New Brunswick, N.J., May 7, 1938; s. Rudolf and Clara (Marburg) K.; m. Susanne Smith, May 31, 1965 (div.); m. Emiko Hayashi, Dec. 12, 1985 (div.); children: James Paul, John Winston, Christian Daryl. AB, Princeton U., 1959; MA, U. Chgo., 1965; postgrad. (Ford Found. fellow), Columbia U., 1964-65. Reporter Chgo. Sun-Times, 1960-61, N.Y. Post, 1961-64; free lance corr., writer, 1965—; Asia corr. Washington Star, 1967-70; Far East corr. Chgo. Tribune, 1971-74, N.Y. and UN corr., 1975-76; world editor, spl. corr. USA Today, 1982-90; Seoul corr. Internat. Herald Tribune, 1998—. Vis. fellow Cornell U., Ithaca, N.Y., 1986-88; Fulbright rschr., Philippines, 1995-96. Author: Wider War: The Struggle for Cambodia, Thailand and Laos, 1971, Tell It To The Dead: Memories of a War, 1975, Korean Dynasty: Hyundai and Chung Ju Yung, 1994, Tell It To The Dead: Stories of a War, 1996, Looted: The Philippines After the Bases, Business Guide to the Philippines, 1998, Korean Crisis: Unraveling of the Miracle in the IMF Era, 2000. Recipient Page One award Chgo. Newspaper Guild, 1960; citations Overseas Press Club, 1967, 72, 73, Best Asia article award 1974; George Polk Meml. award for fgn. reporting, 1975, Fulbright scholar, New Delhi, India, 1962-63; Edward R. Murrow fellow Coun. Fgn. Rels., N.Y.C., 1974-75. Mem. Am. Soc. Journalists and Authors, Soc. Profl. Journalists. Clubs: Nat. Press (Washington); Overseas Press (N.Y.C.); Fgn. Corrs. (Hong Kong); Internat. House of Japan. Home: 4343 Davenport St NW Washington DC 20016-4513 E-mail: kirkdon@attglobal.net.

KIRK, DONALD EVAN, electrical engineering educator, dean; b. Balt., Apr. 4, 1937; m. Judith Ann Sand, Sept. 4, 1962; children: Kara Diane, Valerie Susan, Dana Elizabeth. BSEE, Worcester Poly. Inst., 1959; MSEE, Naval Postgrad. Sch., Monterey, Calif., 1961; PhD in Elec. Engring., U. Ill., 1965. From asst. to full prof. Naval Postgrad. Sch., Monterey, Calif., 1965-87; assoc. dean engring. San Jose (Calif.) State U., 1987-90, prof. elec. engring., 1990-93, dean engring., 1994—2002. Vis. scientist MIT Lincoln Lab., Lexington, Mass., 1981-82; program officer NSF, Arlington, Va., 1993-94. Author: Optimal Control Theory: An Introduction, 1970; co-author: First Principles of Discrete Systems and Digital Signal Processing, 1988, Contemporary Linear Systems, 1994. Bd. dirs. Carmel (Calif.) Sanitary Dist., 1973-77. Fellow IEEE, ASEE; mem. Sigma Xi, Tau Beta Pi, Eta Kappa Nu. Office: San Jose State Univ Dept Elec Engring San Jose CA 95192-0084

KIRK, DONALD JAMES, accountant, consultant; b. Cleve., Nov. 28, 1932; s. John James and Helen Anna (Pilskaln) K.; children: J. Alexander, Bruce D.; m. Mary (Mimi) Colgage Bullock, Jan. 31, 1998. BA, Yale U., 1959; MBA, NYU, 1961; LLD (hon.), Lycoming Coll., 1979. Acct. Price Waterhouse & Co., N.Y.C., London and Washington, 1959-73, ptnr., 1967-73; from mem. to chmn. Fin. Acctg. Stds. Bd., Stamford, Conn., 1973-86; prof. acctg. Columbia U. Grad. Sch. Bus., N.Y.C., 1987-94, exec.-in-residence, 1995-2000; cons., corp. dir. Trustee Fidelity Group Mut. Funds, 1987—; dir. Gen. Re Corp., 1987-98, Valuation Rsch. Corp., 1993-95; pub. gov. Nat. Assn. Securities Dealers, Inc., 1996-2002, Am. Stock Exch., 2001—. Officer, bd. dirs. Urban League of Southwestern Fairfield County, Conn., 1971-77; mem. Greenwich (Conn.) Rep. Town Mtg., 1971-77, Greenwich Bd. of Estimate and Taxation, 1977-89; bd. dirs. Nat. Arts Stabilization Fund, 1983-2002, chmn., 1995-2000, bd. overseers NYU Schs. Bus., 1985-89; bd. trustees The Greenwich Hosp. Assn., 1989—, chmn., 1996-2000, Greenwich Found. for Comty. Gifts, 1991-93; bd. dirs. Yale-New Haven Health Sys., 1998—. Recipient Alumni Achievement award NYU Grad. Sch. Bus. Adminstrn., 1980; named to Acctg. Hall of Fame Ohio State U., 1996. Mem. AICPA (governing coun. 1987-90, pub. oversight bd. of SEC practice sect. 1995-2002, vice-chmn. 1999-2002, Gold medal for disting. svc. 1986), Am. Acctg. Assn., Fin. Execs. Inst. (bd. dirs. N.Y.C. 1990-94), Yale Alumni Assn. Greenwich (bd. dirs. 1988-91), Stanwich Club (past pres.), Yale Club N.Y.C. E-mail: djkirk@optonline.net.

KIRK, EDGAR LEE, musician, educator; b. Harrisburg, Pa., May 28, 1923; s. Arthur Lee and Bertha May (Berthel) K.; m. Ellen Calhoun Gray, June 18, 1947; children: Arthur Lee, Douglas Gray. MusB, Eastman Sch. Music, U. Rochester, 1947, MusM, 1948, PhD, 1957. Mem. faculty Mich. State U., East Lansing, 1948-89, now emeritus, prof. bassoon, chmn. applied music, 1973-89, chmn. grad. studies, 1978-87, dir. admissions dept. music, 1982, assoc. chmn., 1987-88; prof. bassoon Eastman Sch. Music, U. Rochester, summers, 1954-65; instr. bassoon Interlochen Arts Acad., 1975-79. Bassoonist, Rochester (N.Y.) Philharmonic Orch., 1946-47, 54-55, staff bassoonist, radio sta. WHAM, Rochester, 1947-48, 1st bassoonist, Lansing (Mich.) Symphony Orch., 1960-73, 87-89, mem., Richards Woodwind Quintet, 1965-88; Rec. artist: Wind Quintets of Peter Muller, Crystal Records, Anton Reicha, Wind Quintets Opus 99, No. 2 and Opus 100, No. 6, Mus. Heritage Soc. With U.S. Army, 1943-46. Mem. Internat. Double Reed Soc. (pres. 1973-74) Home: 1281 Scott Dr East Lansing MI 48823-5213

KIRK, HENRY PORT, academic administrator; b. Clearfield, Pa., Dec. 20, 1935; s. Henry P. and Ann (H.) K.; m. Mattie F., Feb. 11, 1956 (dec. July 1996); children: Mary Ann, Rebecca; m. Jenny Sheldon, Dec. 13, 1997. BA, Geneva Coll., 1958; MA, U. Denver, 1963, EdD, U. Southern Calif., 1973. Counselor, ednl. Columbia Coll., Columbia, Mo., 1963-65; dean Huron (S.D.) Coll., 1965-66; assoc. dean Calif. State U., L.A., 1966-70; dean El Camino Coll., Torrance, Calif., 1970-81; v.p. Pasadena (Calif.) City Coll., 1981-86; pres. Centralia (Wash.) Coll., 1986—. Contbr. articles to profl. jours. Mem. hist. commn., City Chehalis, 1990, pres. econ. devel. coun., 1992; campaign chmn., United Way, Centralia, 1989-90. Recipient PTK Bennett Disting. Pres. award, 1990, Exemplary Contbn. to Resource Devel. award Nat. Coun. Resource Devel., 1993, Earl Norman Leadership award, 2000. Mem. Wash. Assn. Community Colls. (pres. 1998-99), C. of C. (pres. 1998) Torrance Rotary Club (pres. 1977-78), Centralia Rotary Club (pres. 1990-91), Phi Theta Kappa, Phi Delta Kappa. Presbyterian. Avocation: antique restoration. Office: Centralia Coll 600 W Locust St Centralia WA 98531-4035 E-mail: hkirk@centralia.ctc.edu.

KIRK, IVAN WAYNE, agricultural engineer; b. Lark, Tex., Jan. 25, 1937; s. Percy Lee and Annie B. Kirk; m. Latrelle Venable, May 3, 1960; children: Kimberly Westbrook, Kendal. BS, Tex. Tech U., 1956—59; MS, Clemson U., 1959—60; PhD, Auburn U., 1965—67. Profl. Engr., 1968. Agrl. engr. USDA Ars, Lubbock, Tex., 1960—65, Auburn, Ala., 1965—67, Lubbock, Tex., 1967—71, supervisory agrl. engr. Mesilla Park, N.Mex., 1971—76; assoc. dir. USDA Ars Srrc, New Orleans, 1977—80, dir., 1982—87; agrl. engr. USDA Ars Sparc, College Station, Tex., 1987—2002. Coord. for byssinosis rsch. Usda Ars, New Orleans, 1978—80; adodr Niosh, Morgantown, W.VA., 1979—85, USEPA & SDTF, Washington, 1994—2001; tech. advisor Naaa Naaref Paass, Washington, 1996—2002. Contbr. over 100 articles to profl. jours. Recipient Arthur S. Fleming award, Wash. Jaycees, 1975, Alumni Citation award, Abilene Christian U., 1978, Eagle Mgmt. award, New Orleans Fed. Bus. Assn., 1980, Outstanding Svc. award, Nat. Agrl. Aviation Assn., 1999. Mem.: NAAA, CAST, AAAS, ESA, ASTM, ASAE. Home: 2903 Camille Dr College Station TX 77845-7723 Office: US Department of Agriculture 2771 F&B Rd College Station TX 77845-4966 Office Fax: 979-260-9386. Personal E-mail: i-kirk@tca.net. Business E-Mail: i-kirk@tamu.edu.

KIRK, JAMES ALLEN, mechanical engineering educator; b. Cleve., Nov. 3, 1944; s. Charles J. and Helen T. (Tulas) K.; m. Cynthia L. Ambler, Feb. 6, 1976; 1 child, Heather E. BSEE, Ohio U., 1967; MSME, MIT, 1969, PhD, 1972. Registered prof. engr., Md., Ohio. Rsch. engr. Ford Motor Co., Dearborn, Mich., 1966-67; rsch. assoc. MIT, Cambridge, Mass., 1968-72; asst. prof. mech. engring. U. Md., College Park, 1972-77, assoc. prof. mech. engring., 1977-86, prof. mech. engring., 1986-98, prof. emeritus mech. engring., 1998—; pres. Flywheel Sys., Inc., 1997-2000. Pres. FARE, Inc., College Park, Md. 1988—; owner Kirk Cons. Co., College Park, Md., 1977-88. Author: Scientific Automobile Accident Reconstruction, 1992, Vehicle Dynamics and Tire Forces, 1993, Forensic Engineering, 1993; contbr. articles to profl. jours. Mem. ASME, ASM Internat., Am. Soc. Engring. Edn. (Dow Outstanding Young Faculty award 1977), Soc. Automotive Engring. (Ralph Teetor award 1975), Nat. Assn. Profl. Accident Reconstrn. Specialists, Soc. Mfg. Engrs. Achievements include designed magnetically suspended flywheel for NASA and emergency stopping system for U.S. capitol-house subway system. Home: 7210 Windsor Ln Hyattsville MD 20782-1045 Office: Fare Inc 7210 Windsor Ln Hyattsville MD 20782-1045 E-mail: jkirk@eng.umd.edu.

KIRK, JAMES BARRETT, III, humanities educator, language educator; b. Somers Point, N.J., Nov. 5, 1958; s. James Barrett, II and Audrey Sophia (Cramer) Kirk; m. Patricia Elizabeth Winn; children: Elizabeth Barrett, Ellis James. BA, Stockton State Coll., Pomona, N.J., 1981; MA, U. N.H., Durham, 1985. Faculty Richard Stockton Coll., Pomona, NJ, 1985—. Lifeguard Ocean City Beach Patrol, 1977—98; curator Linwood Hist. Soc. Author (editor): (book) Golden Light, 2003; contbr. Mem.: N.J. Coun. of the Arts, N.J. Inst. Tchrs. Poetry. Avocations: birdwatching, surfing. Home: 306 Davis Ave Northfield NJ 08225-1908 Office: Richard Stockton College Dr Pomona NJ 28234

KIRK, JANE SEAVER, municipal government administrator; b. Boston, May 12, 1928; d. Howard Wesley and Ruth (Seaver) K. BA, Duke U., 1950; MS, Springfield (Mass.) Coll., 1956. Ctr. dir. ARC, Korea, Japan, France, Morocco, 1951-60; dep. dir. internat. group YMCA of the U.S.A., Chgo., 1961-93; chair selectmen Town of Nelson, NH, 1997—2004. Bd. dirs. N.E. Delta Dental, Concord, NH, 1998—2005; incorp Monadnock Family Svcs., 2001—02. Trustee Hist. Soc. Cheshire County, Keene, NH, 1995—2001, Springfield Coll., 1973—2000; pres. Granite Lake Assn., Munsonville, NH, 1995—2000; bd. dirs. Duke Ctr. for Living, Durham, NC, 1995—2001. Recipient Fundraising Achievement award N.Am. YMCA Devel. Officers, 1991. Mem. AAUW, DAR, ARCOA, NAFYR, Daus. of Founders and Patriots, Order Eastern Star, Union League Club Chgo., Coll. Club of Boston, Descendants of Colonial Clergy, Women's Aux., Mass. Ancient and Honorable Artillery Co., Edmund Rice (1638) Assn., Boston Alliance, Ladies Charitable Soc., Internat. Assn. of Women, Bay State African Violet Soc., Walpole Hist. Soc., Am. Orchid Soc., Rotary Club of Keene (Paul Harris fellow), Phi Beta Kappa. Republican. Baptist. Avocations: photography, gardening, travel, walking. Home: HC 33 Munsonville NH 03457-9801 Fax: 603-847-9647. E-mail: janekirk@msn.com.

KIRK, JOHN MACGREGOR, lawyer; b. Flint, Mich., Mar. 9, 1938; s. R. Dean and Berenice E. (Mac Gregor) K.; m. Carol Lasko, June 8, 1971; children: John M. Jr., Caroline Dwyer. BA, Washington & Lee U., 1960, LLB, 1962; LLM in Taxation, NYU, 1967. Bar: Mich. 1962, U.S. Ct. Mil. Appeals 1966, U.S. Supreme Ct. 1966, U.S. Tax Ct. 1969, U.S. Dist. Ct. (ea. dist.) Mich. 1982, U.S. Ct. Appeals (6th cir.) 1983. Trial atty. tax divsn. U.S. Dept. Justice, Washington, 1967-72; assoc. Boyer & Briggs, Bloomfield Hills, Mich., 1972-74; ptnr. Butzel, Long, Gust, Klein & Van Zile, Detroit, 1975-78; mem. Meyer, Kirk, Snyder & Lynch P.L.L.C., Bloomfield Hills, 1978—. Mem., past pres. Friends of Baldwin Pub. Libr., Birmingham, Mich., 1972—. Mem. ABA, State Bar Mich., Oakland County Bar Assn., Detroit Bar Assn., Birmingham Rotary, Walloon Yacht Club (treas., past commodore 1960—). Republican. Presbyterian. Home: 4350 Yale Ct Bloomfield Hills MI 48302-1669 Office: Meyer Kirk Snyder and Lynch PLLC 100 W Long Lake Rd Ste 100 Bloomfield Hills MI 48304-2773 E-mail: jkirk@meyerkirk.com.

KIRK, JOHN ROBERT, JR., lawyer; b. Stuart, Va., June 21, 1935; s. John Robert and Mary Elise (Mustaine) K.; m. Margarite Conover Kirk; children: Karen Louise, Laura Elise, Rebecca Elizabeth. Student, Rice Inst., 1953-56; BSChemE, U. Tex., 1959; JD, U. Houston, 1966. Bar: Tex. 1966, U.S. Patent and Trademark Office 1967, U.S. Supreme Ct. 1973, U.S. Dist. Ct. (so. dist.) Tex. 1974, U.S. Ct. Claims 1975, U.S. Dist. Ct. (no. dist.) Tex. 1977, U.S. Ct. Appeals (5th cir.) 1980, U.S. Ct. Appeals (11th cir.) 1981, U.S. Ct. Appeals (Fed. cir.) 1983. Patent atty. Jefferson Chem. Co., Houston, 1966-69; mgr. patent divsn., 1969-72; mem. Pravel, Gambrell, Hewitt, Kirk & Kimball, P.C., Houston, 1972-84; ptnr., 1973-84, Baker & Kirk, P.C., 1984-87, Baker, Kirk & Bissex, P.C., 1987-90, Baker, Kirk & Lindsay, P.C., 1990-93, Jenkens & Gilchrist, 1993—. Dir. Nat. Inventors Hall of Fame Found, Inc., 1979-82, 87-97, treas., 1983-84, v.p., 1984-86, pres., 1986-87; adv. bd. Intellectual Property Law Program U. Houston, 1991-2000, John Marshall Law Sch., 1999—, chair; adv. bd. Gulf Coast Regional Small Bus. Devel. Ctr., 1994—, Tex. Mfg. Assistance Ctr., Inc., 1995—. Lt. USMCR, 1958-60. Fellow: Coll. State Bar Tex., Houston Bar Found. (life), Tex. Bar Found. (life); mem.: ABA (com. chair 1982—90, intellectual property law sect. coun. 1990—94, vice chmn. 1994—95, chmn. 1996—97, standing com. on specialization 2002—),

Am. Intellectual Property Law Assn., State Bar Tex. (chair intellectual property law sect. 1977—78), Nat. Inventive Thinking Assn. (adv. dir. 1990—2000), Licensing Exec. Soc., Houston Bar Assn., Houston Intellectual Property Law Assn. (bd. govs. 1986—92, pres. 1990—91), Commn. of Patents Edn. Roundtable (commr. 1987—95), Nat. Coun. Intellectual Property Law Assns. (vice chmn. 1986—87, chmn. 1987—88), Garden of the Gods Club, Lakeside Country Club, Union League Club Chgo. Republican. Baptist. Office: 1100 Louisiana St Ste 1800 Houston TX 77002-5215 E-mail: jkirk@jenkens.com.

KIRK, LYNDA POUNDS, biofeedback therapist, neurotherapist, counselor; b. Corpus Christi, Tex., Dec. 17, 1946; d. James Arthur and Elizabeth Pauline (Sanders) Pounds; children: Leslie Jennifer, Edward Christopher. BA, U. Tex., Austin, 1977; MA, St. Edwards U., 1996. Lic. profl. counselor. Therapist Austin (Tex.) State Hosp., 1977-80; dir. stress mgmt. The Hills Med./Sports Complex, Austin, 1980-82; founder, owner Austin Biofeedback Ctr., 1982—, Health Mastery Concepts, Austin, 1982—, Optimal Performance Inst., 2000—; CEO Healthy Life Options, Inc., Austin, 1998—. Cons. State of Tex., Austin, 1983—, City of Austin, 1985—, Lower Colo. River Authority, Austin, 1984—. Author: (book/cassette series) Regenerative Relaxation, 1981; Urological Applications of Biofeedback, Stress Mastery and Peak Performance, 1986. Bd. dirs. South Austin Civic Club, 1983—, pres., 1987; bd. dirs., treas. Texans for the Preservation of Hist. Structures, 1990—; bd. dirs. Austin Ctr. for Attitudinal Healing, 1992—. Fellow Biofeedback Cert. Inst. Am. (sr.); mem. Assn. Applied Psychophysiology and Biofeedback (pres. 2003—), Internat. Soc. for Study of Subtle Energies and Energy Medicine, Biofeedback Soc. Tex. (pres. 1995-97, exec. bd., citation award 1989), Behavioral Medicine Soc. Am., Am. Holistic Med. Assn., Assn. Cert. QEEG Technologists, Internat. Soc. for Neuronal Regulation (pres. 1997-98), Acad. Cert. Neurotherapists, Phi Beta Kappa. Episcopalian. Avocations: jogging, snorkeling, mountain biking, designs for world peace. Home: 420 Brady Ln Austin TX 78746-5502 Office: Austin Biofeedback Ctr 3624 N Hills Dr Ste B205 Austin TX 78731-3061 E-mail: lkirk@austinbiofeedback.com.

KIRK, MARK STEVEN, congressman; b. Champaign, Ill., Sept. 15, 1959; s. Francis Gabriel and Judith Ann (Brady) K. BA, Cornell U., 1981; MS, London Sch. of Econs., 1982; JD, Georgetown U., 1992. Bar: Ill. 1992, D.C. 1993. Parliamentary aide Julian Critchley, London, 1982-83; chief of staff U.S. Rep. John Porter, Washington, 1984-90; officer World Bank, Washington, 1990; spl. asst. to asst. sec. of state State Dept., Washington, 1991-93; atty. Baker & McKenzie, Washington, 1993-95; counsel Ho. Internat. Rels. Com., Washington, 1995-99; mem. U.S. Congress from 10th Ill. dist., Washington, 2001—; mem. armed svcs. com., transp. and infrastructure com., budget com.; mem. Ho. Appropriations Com. Bd. dirs. Population Resource Ctr., Princeton, N.J. Contbr. articles to various newspapers. Organizer Bush/Quayle Campaign, No. Ill., 1988, Dole for Pres., 1988, various states; campaigner Porter for Congress, No. Ill., 1984-90. Lt. USNR, 1989—. Kellogg Fellow, Chgo., 1980, Radm James Fellow, Washington, 1984; recipient Coun. of Jewish Fedn. award Washington, 1988. Mem. Navy League, Naval Res. Assn., New Trier Rep. Orgn. Republican. Presbyterian. Avocations: backpacking, skydiving. Office: 1531 Longworth Ho Office Bldg Washington DC 20515 Home: 275 Whistler Rd Highland Park IL 60035-5947*

KIRK, PAUL GRATTAN, JR., lawyer, administrator; b. Newton, Mass., Jan. 18, 1938; s. Paul Grattan and Josephine Elizabeth (O'Connell) K.; m. Gail Ellen Loudermilk, May 11, 1974. AB, Harvard Coll., 1960, LLB, 1964; LLD (hon.), Stonehill Coll., 2002, So. New Eng. Sch. Law, 2003. Dir. ITT Corp., N.Y.C., 1989-98, Bradley Real Estate, Inc., Northbrook, Ill., 1990-2000, Rayonier Inc., Jacksonville, Fla., 1994—, Hartford (Conn.) Fin. Svcs. Group, 1994—, Hartford Life Ins. Co., Inc., 1994-2000; chmn., CEO Kirk and Assocs., Inc., Boston, 1990—; ptnr., of counsel Sullivan & Worcester, LLP, Boston, 1977-98. Trustee Stonehill Coll., 1984—, St. Sebastian's Sch., 1990—; treas. Dem. Party U.S., Washington, 1983-85, chmn., 1985-89; co-chmn. Commn. on Presdl. Debates, Washington, 1987—; chmn. John F. Kennedy Libr. Found., Boston, 1990—, Nat. Dem. Inst. for Internat. Affairs, Washington, 1992-2001; chmn. nominating com. Harvard Bd. Overseers, 1992-93, chmn. com. to visit dept. athletics, 2003—. Capt. U.S. Army, 1961-68. Recipient W. Averell Harriman Democracy award Nat. Dem. Inst. for Internat. Affairs, 1988. Roman Catholic. Home: PO Box 1433 Marstons Mills MA 02648-5433 Office: Sullivan & Worcester LLP One Post Office Sq Boston MA 02109

KIRK, REA HELENE (REA HELENE GLAZER), special education educator; b. N.Y.C., Nov. 17, 1944; d. Benjamin and Lillian (Kellis) Glazer; 3 stepdaughters. BA, UCLA, 1966; MA, Ea. Mont. Coll., 1981; EdD, U. So. Calif., 1995. Life cert. spl. edn. tchr., Calif., Mont. Spl. edn. tchr., L.A., 1966-73; clin. sec. speech and lang. clinic Missoula, Mont., 1973-75; spl. edn. tchr. Missoula, Gt. Falls, Mont., 1975-82; br. mgr. YWCA of L.A., Beverly Hills, Calif., 1989-91; sch. adminstrn., ednl. coord. Adv. Schs. of Calif., 1991-94; dir. Woman's Resource Ctr., Gt. Falls, Mont., 1981-82, Battered Woman's Shelter, Rock Springs, Wyo., 1982-84, Battered Woman's Program, Sweetwater County, Wyo., 1984-88, San Gabriel Valley, Calif., 1988; with Spl. Edn., Pasadena, 1994-96, prin., 1995; asst. prof. U. Wis., Platteville, 1996—2003, assoc. prof., 2003—. Mem. Wyo. Commn. on Aging, Rock Springs; mem. Cmty. Action Bd. City of L.A. Pres., bd. dirs. battered woman's shelter, Gt. Falls; pres. Women's Resource Ctr., Falls, Religious Congregation, Rock Springs; founder, advisor Rape Action Line, Gt. Falls; founder Jewish religious svcs., Missoula; 4-H leader; hostess Friendship Force; Friendship Force ambassador, Wyo., Fed. Republic Germany, Italy; mem. YWCA Mont. and Wyo.; v.p. Coun. Devel. Disabilities, Wis.; bd. dirs. Coun. Children with Behavior Disorders, Wis., Family Advocates, Platteville, 1996—; organizer Women's Readers Theater, Platteville, Wis.; advisor Pioneer Svc. Club, Platteville. Recipient Gladys Byron scholar U. So. Calif., 1993, Dept. Edn. scholar U. So. Calif., 1994, honors Missoula 4-H, Underkoffler Tchg. Excellence award U. Wis., 2000, named advisor of yr., 2000; recognized as significant Wyo. woman as social justice reformer and peace activist Sweetwater County, Wyo.; nominated Wyo. Woman of the Yr., 1981, 82; honored by L.A. Mayor Bradley for Anti-Poverty work. Mem. Coun. for Exceptional Children (v.p. Gt. Falls 1981-82, bd. dirs., Professionally Recognized Spl. Educator 1998), Wis. Coun. Exceptional Children (bd. dirs., pres. S.W. region), Wis. Divsn. Mentally Retarded/Developmentally Disabled), Wis. Assn. Children with Behavior Disorders, Assn. for Children with Learning Disabilities (Named Outstanding Mem. 1982), Pioneer Svc. Club (adv.), Phi Delta Kappa, Delta Kappa Gamma (sec. 2002-03), Kappa Delta Pi (co-counselor 2000-03, sec. 2002--), Pi Lamda Theta. E-mail: Kirkr@uwplatt.edu.

KIRK, RICHARD DILLON, lawyer; b. Washington, Jan. 23, 1953; s. William Edward and Mary Elizabeth (Dillon) K.; m. Bridget Louise Stillwagon, June 27, 1981; children: Catherine Dillon, Suzanne Grace. AB, Georgetown U., 1975; JD, U. Va., 1978. Bar: Del. 1978, U.S. Dist. Ct. Del. 1980, U.S. Ct. Appeals (3rd cir.) 1984, U.S. Supreme Ct. 1984. Law clk. Del. Supreme Ct., Wilmington, 1978-79; assoc. Richards, Layton & Finger, Wilmington, 1979-82; dep. atty. gen. Del. Dept. Justice, Wilmington, 1982-84; assoc. Morris, James, Hitchens & Williams, Wilmington, 1984-86, ptnr., 1987—. Mem. Del. State Bar Assn. (pres. 1993-94, New Lawyers Disting. Svc. award 1988). Democrat. Roman Catholic. Office: Morris James Hitchens & Williams 222 Delaware Ave Wilmington DE 19801-1621 E-mail: rkirk@morrisjames.com.

KIRK, SHERWOOD, librarian; b. Kermit, W.Va., July 12, 1924; s. James Douglas and Magdalene (Elkins) K.; m. Ora Ward, Jan. 9, 1958; children: Diana, James Sherwood, Philip Lindsey. Student, Mich. State U., 1944; AB, U. Ky., 1949; postgrad., U. Ill., 1949-50. Student asst. U. Ky., 1946-49; circulation asst. U. Ill., 1949-51; head reference and circulation Marshall U., 1951-52; sr. asst., agrl. libr. U. Neb., 1952-54; spl. project asst. Nat. Agr. Libr., Washington, 1954-55; reference asst., liaison loan div. Libr. Congress, 1955-56, catalog asst., 1956-57; coord. pub. libr. svcs. Ky. Dept. Librs., Frankfort, 1957-63, asst. state libr., 1963-69; state libr. Fla., 1969-71; assoc. dir. libr. ops. Ill. State Libr., Springfield, 1971-82; exec. dir. Western Ill. Libr. System, Monmouth, 1982-94; delivery cons. Alliance Libr. Sys., 1994-95, 1994-95; dir. Aledo-Mercer Carnegie Pub. Libr. Dist., 1996—. Mem. Ky. Gov.'s Planning Com. on Librs., 1968; chmn. Fla. Sec. of State's Com. Libr. Svc. to State Govt., 1970; adv. com. libr. svcs. and constrn. Fla. State Libr.; bd. dirs. Friends of Lincoln Libr., Springfield, Ill., 1977— ; sec. Resource Sharing Alliance West Central Ill.; mem. Adv. Com. on Edn. in Ill. Author publs. Mem. Ill. State Libr. subcom. for Pub. Libr. Svcs., Ill. State Libr. Scholarship Com.; pres. Ill. Book Pac; vol. cataloger Bartow Fla. Pub. Libr. Recipient plaque for outstanding libr. Ky. Libr. Trustee Assn., 1968. Mem. ALA (coun. 1967-69), Ky. Libr. Assn. (pres. 1965-66), Fla. Libr. Assn., Ill. Libr. Assn. (chmn. local arrangement 1974, conv., mem. Bicentennial, com. 1974—, legis.-libr. devel. com., Robert R. McClarren legis. award 1990, chair pub. policy com. 1991), Assn. State Libr. Agys. Methodist (adminstrv. bd.). Clubs: Mason (Frankfort) (Shriner), Optimist (Frankfort); Springfield Lit. (pres. 1972). Home: 527 Eastlake Dr Haines City FL 33844-6339 E-mail: kirk@ithink.net., sherd@copper.net.

KIRK, SUSANNE SMITH, editor; b. Washington; d. Harold Clair and Theodora Smith; m. Donald Kirk, 1965 (div. 1985); m. Samuel Alexander Tomlinson III, 1989. Student, Kaiserin-Theophanu Sch., Cologne, W.Ger., 1958; AB, Smith Coll., 1963; cert., Goethe Inst., Berlin, 1963; MS, Columbia U., 1965. Reporter South China Morning Post, Hong Kong, 1965-67; corr. German News Agy., Saigon, Vietnam, 1968-69; editor Charles Tuttle Pubs., Tokyo, 1972-74; freelance journalist, 1965-74; asst. editor Charles Scribner's Sons (now Scribner div. Simon & Schuster), N.Y.C., 1975, editor, 1976-80, asst. v.p., 1977-98, fgn. rights dir., 1978-82, sr. editor, 1980-85, exec. editor, 1985-98, v.p., sr. editor, 1998—. Spkr. various writers' confs. Contbr. articles to newspapers. Mem. Mystery Writers Am. (Ellery Queen award 2000), Crime Writers Assn. (U.K.), Internat. Assn. Crime Writers, Snarks Ltd. (N.Y.C., v.p. 1983-84, pres. 1985-86), Columbia Club, Pilgrimage Garden Club (Natchez), Smith Coll. Club (N.Y.C.). Home: PO Box 2056 Natchez MS 39121-2056 Office: Scribner Simon & Schuster 1230 Avenue Of The Americas New York NY 10020-1513

KIRK, THOMAS GARRETT, JR., librarian; b. Phila., Aug. 2, 1943; s. Thomas Garrett and Bertha (C.) K.; m. Elizabeth B. Walter, Aug. 29, 1964; children: Jennifer E., Cynthia M., Kristen A. BA, Earlham Coll., Richmond, Ind., 1965; MA, Ind. U., 1969; postgrad., Drexel U., 1987-88. Sci. libr. Earlham Coll., 1965-79; libr. cons. Richmond, Ind., 1972—; acting dir. librs. U. Wis., Parkside, Kenosha, 1979-80; dir. libr. Berea (Ky.) Coll., 1980-94, Earlham (Ind.) Coll., 1994-2000, dir. librs., coord. info. svcs., 2001—. Vis. instr. Ind. U. Libr. Sch., summers 1977, 78; bd. dirs SOLINET, 1981-84, 85-86, treas., 1982-84; bd. dirs. Ky. Libr. Network, 1985-87, 91-93, OCLC Mems. Coun., 1986-92, 99—, chmn. exec. com. 2001-02, Pvt. Acad. Libr. Network Ind., v.p. 1995-96, pres., 1996-97, OCLC Strategic Directions and Governance Adv. Com., 2000-2001; adv. bd. OCLC Coll. and Univ. Librs., 1995-98. Author: Library Research Guide to Biology, 1978; editor: Course-related Library and Literature Instruction, 1979, Increasing the Teaching Role of Academic Libraries, 1984; editl. bd. Coll. and Rsch. Librs., 1996-2002, Internet Reference Svcs. Quar., 1996—, Info. Literacy Adv. Comm., 2000-02. Mem. ALA (coun. 1986-90), Assn. Coll. Rsch. Librs. (v.p., pres.-elect 1992-93, pres. 1993-94, past pres. 94-95, exec. com. 1984-85, 86-90, 92-95, rep. to Coalition for Networked Info. 1990-95, Miriam Dudley Bibliographic Instrn. Libr. of Yr. award 1984), Inst. for Info. Literacy (adv. com. 1998—, chair 2001-03), Ind. Libr. Fedn., Ind. Coop. Libr. Svcs. Authority (exec. com. 1999-2001), Ky. Libr. Assn. (Acad. Libr. of Yr. award 1984), Phi Kappa Phi. Mem. Soc. Of Friends. Office: Earlham Coll Lilly Libr Richmond IN 47374

KIRK, WILEY PRICE, JR., physics and electrical engineering educator; b. Joplin, Mo., July 24, 1942; s. Wiley Price Sr. and Inez Isabel (Watson) K.; m. Sally Ann Stoots, June 13, 1964; children: Camille Maura, Alexander Price. BS, Washington U., St. Louis, 1964; MS, SUNY, Stony Brook, 1967, PhD, 1970. Tech. collaborator Brookhaven Nat. Lab., Upton, NY, 1969-70; postdoctoral fellow U. Fla., Gainesville, Fla., 1970-72, asst. prof., 1972-75, Tex. A&M U., Coll. Sta., 1975-77, assoc. prof., 1978-83, prof., 1984-99, also bd. dir.; prof. U. Tex. at Arlington, 1999—. Dir. NanoFAB ctr. TEES, 1990-2002. Editor: Nanostructure Physics and Fabrication, 1989, Nanostructures and Mesoscopic Sys., 1992; mem. editl. bd. Superlattices and Microstructures, 1991—; contbr. over 90 articles to profl. jour. Grantee NSF, 1973—, Rsch. Corp,. 1974; recipient Nat. Bur. Standards Precision Measurements award Nat. Inst. Standards and Tech., 1987, Tex. Engring. Experiment Sta. Rsch. Fellow award Tex. Engring. Exptl. Sta., 1992. Mem. AAAS, Am. Phys. Soc., Am. Vacuum Soc., Materials Rsch. Soc. Achievements include patent for gate adjusted resonant tunnel diode device and method of manufacture. Office: U Tex at Arlington Nano FAB Bldg Box 19072 Arlington TX 76019

KIRKBY, MAURICE ANTHONY, oil company executive; b. Southwell, Notts, U.K., Apr. 12, 1929; emigrated to Can., 1983; s. George Sydney and Rose (Marson) K.; m. Muriel Beatrice Longmire, 1954; children: Peter Michael, Susan Margaret. BA with 1st class honors in Mech. Sci., King's Coll., Cambridge, Eng., 1952, MA, 1955. Chief petroleum engr. Brit. Petroleum Co. p.l.c., London, 1969-74, gen. mgr. exploration and prodn. dept., 1976-80, dirs.' support staff, 1982-83; gen. mgr. BP Petroleum Devel., Aberdeen, Scotland, 1974-76; sr. v.p. oil and gas Standard Oil Co., Cleve., 1980-82; pres., chief exec. officer, dir. BP Can. Inc., Calgary, Alta., Can., 1983-88; chmn., chief exec. officer Hope Brook Gold Inc., Calgary, Alta., Can., 1986-88; dep. chmn. N.Am. Gas Investment Trust, London, 1989-95. Contbr. articles to profl. jours. Mem. Bus. Council on Nat. Issues, Ottawa, Ont., Can., 1983-88. Served with RAF, 1947-49. Fellow Inst. Mining and Metallurgy (dir. 1980), Royal Acad. Engring.; mem. Inst. Mech. Engrs., Soc. Petroleum Engrs. (dir. 1980, 81-83).

KIRK-DUGGAN, CHERYL ANN, religious studies educator; b. Lake Charles, La, July 24, 1951; d. Rudolph Valentino and Naomi Ruth (Mosely) Kirk; m. Michael Allan Duggan, Jan. 1, 1983. BA, U. S.W. La., 1973; MM, U. Tex., 1977; MDiv, Austin Presbyn. Theol. Sem., 1987; PhD, Baylor U., 1992. Ordained minister Christian Meth. Episcopal Ch., 1984. Instr. Prairie View A&M U., Tex., 1977-78; pvt. music instr. NYC, Austin, Tex., 1979-85; core doctoral and in residence faculty Meredith Coll., Raleigh, 1993-97; dir. Ctr. for Women and Religion, asst. prof. Grad. Theol. Union, 1997—. Organist, music dir. Russell Meml. Christian Meth. Episcopal Ch., Durham, NC, 1993-96, assoc. pastor, 1993; assoc. pastor Phillips Temple CME Ch., 1997—. Author: African American Special Days: 15 Complete Worship Services, 1996, It's In the Blood: A Trilogy of Poetry Harvested from a Family Tree, 1996, Exorcizing Evil: A Womanist Perspective on the Spirituals, 1997, Refiner's Fire: A Religious Engagement with Violence, 2000, The Undivided Soul: Helping Congregations Connect Body and Spirit, 2001, Misbegotten Anguish: A Theology and Ethics of Violence, 2001, Soul Pearls: Resources for African American Congregations, 2003; Mary Had a Baby: An Advent Study Based on African Am. Spirituals, 2003; mem. editl. bd. Contagion: Jour. Violence, Mimeses and Culture, 1994—; assoc. editor Semeia, an Experimental Journal in Biblical Studies 2000—; sr. editor Womanist Perspectives. Former denom. rep. Nat. Coun. Chs.; mem. Faith and Order Com.; mem. standing com. Inclusiveness and Justice. Named Womanist Scholar of Yr., AAR Womanist Approaches Group, 2001, a Woman Spiritual Leader in Am., White Fire, 2002; Coolidge scholar Assn. for Religion and Intellectual Life rsch. colloquium Yale, 1996; Lily scholar, 1994-96, Named Woman Spiritual Leader in Am. in White Fire, 2002. Mem. Am. Soc. Aesthetics, Am. Acad. Religion (past pres., program chair We. region), Soc. Christian Ethics, Ctr. Black Music Rsch., Soc. Bibl. Lit., Colloquium on Violence and Religion, Soc. Study Black Religion, Golden Key Honor Soc. (W.T. and Ethel L. Burton Scholarship), Sigma Alpha Iota. Avocations: sports, cross cultural music performing, triathlon, nature, travel. Office: 4872 Reno Ln Richmond CA 94803-3850

KIRK-DUGGAN, MICHAEL ALLAN, retired law, economics and computer sciences educator; b. Stevens Point, Wis., Dec. 15, 1931; s. Frank E. and Dorothy Ada (Darrow) Duggan; married July 1956 (div. Jan. 1981); children: Michelle, Cheryl, Michael, Christopher, Robert, Siobhan, Mary; m. Cheryl Ann Kirk, Jan. 1, 1983. BS in Math., Coll. Holy Cross, 1953; postgrad., U. Minn., 1953—56; JD, LLB, Boston Coll., 1956; M in Patent Law, Georgetown U., 1959. Bar: Mass. 1956, U.S. Supreme Ct. 1961; qualified trial/def. counsel Gen. Cts. Martial, 1965; cert. cmty. based conflict resolution, 1994. Sr. engr. Sylvania Programming Lab., Needham, Mass., 1960—61; trial atty. antitrust divsn. U.S. Dept. Justice, 1961—67; asst. prof. econs. Whittemore Sch., U. N.H., Durham, 1967—69; comdr. U.S. Naval Intelligence Res., 1956—78; adminstrv. judge Atomic Safety and Licensing Bd. Panel, Washington, 1972—89; prof. bus. law and computer scis. U. Tex., Austin, 1969—93, prof. emeritus, 1993—. Apptd. adv. procurator Tribunal, Diocese of Raleigh, 1995-97; editor-in-chief Computing Revs., N.Y.C., 1969-74. Author: Antitrust & U.S. Supreme Court, 1829-1984, 1984, Computer Utility, 1972, Law and the Computer, 1973, Paul Robeson Movies and Discography, 1998, Amazon Reviews; editor: Legal Developments, J. Marketing, 1967-93, Legal Comments; contbr. numerous articles to profl. jours. Head Profs. for Johnson, Durham, 1968; eucharistic min., lector, lay pres. St. Columba Cath. Ch., Oakland, Calif., 1997—; del. Tex. Dem. Com., Austin, 1972; IRS Vol. Income Tax Assistance, 1993-97. Mem. Mensa, Friend of Bill W. Democrat. Avocations: computer guru/hacker, semi-pro photographer, choral. Home: 4872 Reno Ln Richmond CA 94803-3850 E-mail: kirkdugg@attbi.com.

KIRKEGAARD, R. LAWRENCE, architectural acoustician; b. Denver, Dec. 11, 1937; s. Raymond Lawrence and Frances Jean (Stocking) K.; m. Joslyn Ann Hills, Mar 23, 1959; children: Dana Lawrence, Jonathan Eric, Bradford Andrew. AB cum laude, Harvard U., 1960, MArch, 1964. Cons. archtl. acoustics Bolt, Beranek & Newman, Cambridge, Mass., 1962-64; supervisory cons., regional mgr. Chgo., 1964-75; pres., prin. cons. R. Lawrence Kirkegaard & Assocs., Inc., Chgo., Ill., 1976—. Frequent panelist for Nat. Endowment for Arts Design Arts Challenge Grant program. Prin. archtl. acoustics works: new projects include new Concert Hall for Tanglewood, Ordway Music Theatre, St. Paul, new performing arts cts. in Denver, Fort Lauderdale, Charlotte, N.C., Maui, Portand, Oreg., L.A., Greenville, S.C., Cin., New Concert Hall for Atlanta, Ga.; internat. projects include performing arts ctrs. in Taipei and Tainan, Taiwan, Bergamo, Italy, Edmonton, remodeling of the Tyl Theatre, Prague, Royal Philharmonic Hall, Liverpool, Eng., Barbican Concert Hall, London, Maison de Musique, Toulose, France; remodeling projects include Carnegie Hall (post-renovation), Orch. Hall, Chgo., Davies Symphony Hall, San Francisco, Heinz Hall, Pitts., Mahaffey Theatre, St. Petersburg, Fla., Guthrie Theatre, Oreg. Shakespeare Festival, Stratford Shakespeare Festival, Ont., Young Peoples' Theatre, Toronto; new schs. of music include Rice U., Northwestern U., U. Ala., Iowa State U., Pacific Luth. U., Red Deer Coll., Alta., Cin. Convervatory Mus., Luther Coll., N.D. State U.; remodeling projects include U. Chgo., Carleton Coll., Oberlin Conservatory. Co-founder Chestnut Hill Mental Health Ctr., Greenville, S.C. Mem. AIA (hon., nat. com. on arts and recreation), Acoustical Soc. Am., Harvard Grad. Sch. Design Alumni Coun., U.S. Inst. Theatre Tech., Am. Symphony Orch. League, Harvard Club (Chgo.). Home: 5200 Brookbank Rd Downers Grove IL 60515-4544 Office: R Lawrence Kirkegaard & Assocs Inc 801 W Adams St Fl 8 Chicago IL 60607-3013

KIRKENDALL, THOMAS D. aerospace engineer, materials scientist; b. Columbus, Ohio, Sept. 8, 1937; s. Ben R. and Louise Dodge Kirkendall; m. Dorothy Boynton, July 27, 1939; children: Thomasin, Edward, Robert. BA, Colby Coll., Waterville, Maine, 1961; postgrad., Middlebury Coll., Vt. 1961—62. Asst. in physics Middlebury Coll., Vt., 1961—62; prin. scientist Raytheon Co., Stamford, Conn., 1962—69; mgr. failure analysis and reliability Comm. Satellite Corp., Clarksburg, Md., 1969—93; cons. materials and reliability Potomac, Md., 1993—. Contbr. Recipient Tech. Excellence award Comsat Labs., Clarksburg, Md., 1981. Mem.: Soc. for Applied Spectroscopy (B-W sect. chmn. 1980, named Outstanding Mem. 1980). Achievements include patents for in field. Avocations: sailing, gardening, music. Home: 8610 Camille Dr Potomac MD 20854

KIRKGAARD, VALERIE ANNE, retired media group executive, syndicated talk radio host, writer, producer, consultant; b. Merced, Calif., Aug. 18, 1940; d. Basil Stuart and Audrey (Thompson) Coghlan; m. Alonzo Bryson Kirkgaard, Oct. 6, 1962 (div. Aug. 1983); children: Jennifer Alexandra, John Erik. AA, Santa Monica City Coll., 1961; BA, UCLA, 1968; M of Counseling, Goddard Coll., L.A., 1982; M. of Enlightenment, Sci. of Mind Ch., San Diego, 1992; PhD, Harrington U., 1999. Bd. and care organizer Norwalk State Hosp., L.A. 1976-78; liaison to bd. dirs. Gay and Lesbian Cmty. Svcs. Ctr., 1976—79; therapist in pvt. practice Kirkgaard & Assocs, Pasadena, Pacific Palisades, Santa Monica, Calif., 1975—; pvt. practice matrimonial cons., 1976—; CEO Laughing Dragon Entertainment. Ear coning educator, mfr., 1992—; prodr., host radio and TV Waking Up In America, 1987—; radio prodr. Terry Cole Whittaker radio prodr./host Open Forum, Waking Up In America, 2 programs for KFNX Phoenix, Ariz., others; spkr. in field; also VoiceAmerica.com. Author: Breakfast At Bob's, 1982, Take Two Breaths and Call Me in the Morning, 1988, Making Room for Love: A Primer for Causing Powerful Relationships, 2001; environ. editor United Fitness Mag., 1992; columnist Hollywood Times, 1976, Century City News, 1990-92, Topanga Messenger, 1996—; author numerous articles, numerous appearances and interviews; inventor in field. Founder Golden Hearts Found. Olympic Torch bearer Olympic Com., Santa Fe Springs, Calif., 1984. Mem. Calif. Assn. Marriage Family and Child Counselors, Women's Mus. of Art, Los Angeles County Mus. Art, World Vision, State of the World Forum, The Hunger Project, Cousteau Soc., Mus. of Tolerance, Greater L.A. Press Club, Scriptwriters Network, Pacific Palisades C. of C., Roar Found. Avocations: polo, horseback riding, hiking, racquetball, reading, gardening. Office: Kirkgaard & Assocs 869 Via De La Paz Ste F Pacific Palisades CA 90272-5202 E-mail: elvenears2@aol.com.

KIRKHAM, JAMES ALVIN, manufacturing executive; b. Sumner County, Tenn., June 18, 1935; s. Shirley Barnes and Ouida Redempta (Bursby) K.; m. Shirley Ann Clouse, Sept. 3, 1954; children: Denise Anne, James Alvin II, Hughe Allan. Welder Ind. Wire Co., 1952-54; driver Arthur Lowe Cigar & Candy Co., 1954-56; time study Insley Mfg. Co., 1957; salesman Am. Chicle Co., 1958-59; mgr. Ace Battery, Inc., Indpls., 1967—; v.p. L P Industries, Inc., Indpls., 1977—; pres. Rubber Recycling Corp., 1989—; ptnr. TKT Leasing, Indpls., 1978—, LDJ Leasing, Indpls., 1979—, Vets. Interstate Plan, Inc. Sec. Johnson County Pk. Bd.; bd. dirs. English Ave. Boys Club, State 4-H Horse and Pony Orgn.; pres. bd. dirs. Ind. Horse Coun. Found., Inc.; pres. PTO, Clark Twp. Sch. Dist.; v.p. Johnson County 4-H Fairboard; active Boy Scouts Am.; chmn. fundraising equestrian events 10th Pan Am. Games; treas. Ind. Horse Coun. Inc. Recipient Golden Boy award Indpls. Boys Club Alumni Assn., 1970; named Outstanding Show Mgr., Ind. State Fair, 1971; named to Ind. Horseman Hall of Fame, 1998. Mem. Am. Horse Show Assn., Ind. Saddle Horse Assn., Ind. Motor Truck Assn., Indpls. Motor Truck Assn., U.S. C. of C., Indpls. C. of C., Masons, Shriners, Moose Lodge, Ind. Pony Exhibitors Club, Am. Hackney Club, Ind. Pony of Am. Club, Ind. Shetland Pony Breeders Club. Home: 1217 N Matthews Rd Greenwood IN 46143-8343 Office: 2166 Bluff Rd Indianapolis IN 46225-1983

KIRKHAM, JOHN SPENCER, lawyer, director; b. Salt Lake City, Aug. 29, 1944; s. Elbert C. and Emma Kirkham; m. Janet L. Eatough, Sept. 16, 1966; children: Darcy, Jeff, Kristie. BA with honors, U. Utah, 1968, JD, 1971. Bar: Utah 1971, U.S. Dist. Ct. Utah 1971, U.S. Ct. Appeals (10th cir.) 1990, U.S. Supreme Ct. 1991. Assoc. Senior & Senior, Salt Lake City, 1971-73; ptnr. VanCott, Bagley, Cornwall & McCarthy, Salt Lake City, 1973-92, Stoel Rives LLP, Salt Lake City. Mem. exec. bd. Great Salt Lake coun. Boy Scouts Am., 1987—; mem. Utah Statewide Resource Adv. Coun., 1995-97; trustee Met. Water Dist. Salt Lake and Sandy, 2003—. Mem. Utah Bar Assn., Utah Mining Assn. (bd. dirs. Salt Lake City chpt. 1987—), Rocky Mountain Mineral Law Found. (trustee 1989-92). Republican. Mem. Lds Ch. Office: Stoel Rives LLP 201 S Main St Ste 1100 Salt Lake City UT 84111-4904 E-mail: jskirkham@stoel.com.

KIRKHAM, M. B. plant physiologist, educator; b. Cedar Rapids, Iowa; d. Don and Mary Elizabeth (Erwin) K. BA with honors, Wellesley Coll.; MS, PhD, U. Wis. Cert. profl. agronomist. Plant physiologist U.S. EPA, Cin., 1973-74; asst. prof. U. Mass., Amherst, 1974-76, Okla. State U., Stillwater, 1976-80; from assoc. prof. to prof. Kans. State U., Manhattan, 1980—. Guest lectr. Inst. Water Conservancy and Hydroelectric Power Rsch., Inst. Farm Irrigation Rsch., China, 1985, Inst. Exptl. Agronomy, Italy, 1989, Agrl. U. Wageningen, Inst. for Soil Fertility, Haren, The Netherlands, 1991, Massey U., New Zealand, 1991, Lincoln U., New Zealand, 1998, Environ. and Risk Mgmt. Group HortResearch, 1998, Palmerston North, New Zealand, 1998, U. Hannover, Germany, 2003; William A. Albrecht seminar spkr. U. Mo., 1994; vis. scholar Biol. Labs. Harvard U., 1990; vis. scientist environ. physics sect. dept. sci and indsl. rsch. Palmerston North, New Zealand, 1991, The Horticulture and Food Rsch. Inst. New Zealand, Ltd., Crown Rsch. Inst., Palmerston North, 1998, Landcare Rsch., Lincoln, New Zealand, 1998; participant Internat. Grassland Congress, New Zealand, 13th Internat. Soil Tillage Rsch. Orgn. Conf., Aalborg, Denmark; spkr. Internat. Conf. Vadose Zone Hydrology, Davis, Calif., 1995, 4th Congress European Soc. for Agronomy, Veldhoven, The Netherlands, 1996, Internat. Workshop Characterization and Measurement of Hydraulic Properties of Unsaturated Soil, Riverside, Calif., 1997, Internat. Symposium on Plant Growth and Environ., Seoul, 1993, 15th Internat. Congress of Soil Sci., Acapulco, 1994, 16th Internat. Conf., Montpellier, France, 1998; invited paper Internat. Grass

ands Congress, New Zealand; invited keynote spkr. 5th Internat. Conf. on Biogeochemistry Trace Elements, Vienna, Austria, 1999, 2d Internat. Conf. on Contaminants in Soil Environ. in Australasia-Pacific Region, New Delhi, 1999, Chem. Bioavailability in Terrestrial Environ. Workshop, Adelaide, Australia, 001; peer rev. panel mem. USDA/Nat. Rsch. Initiative, Washington, 1994; mem. rev. panel USDA Office Sci. Quality Rev. Water Quality Nat. Program, 001, appt. mem. U.S. Nat. Com. for Soil Sci. of the Nat. Acad. Scis., 2001-. Editor: Water Use in Crop Production, 1999; co-editor: (with I.K. Iskandar) Trace Elements in Soil, 2001; cons. editor Plant and Soil Jour., 1979-; mem. editl. bd. BioCycle, 1978-82, Field Crops Rsch. Jour., 1983-91, Soil Sci., 1997-, Jour. Crop Prodn., 1998-, Jour. Environ. Quality, 2002-; mem. editl. adv. bd. International Agrophysics, 2000-; contbr. more than 220 articles and papers to sci. jours. Recipient Best Reviewer award, Water Resources Engring. divsn. Jour. Irrigation and Drainage Engring., ASCE, 1996, scholar award, 2000, grad. faculty tchg. award, Coll. of Agr., Kanas State Univ., 2001; fellow NSF postdoctoral fellow, U. Wis., 1971—73, NDEA fellow, E.I. du Pont de Nemours and Co. summer faculty fellow, 1976; grantee, NSF, USDA, U.S. Dept. Energy, Dept. Sci. and Indsl. Rsch., New Zealand. Fellow AAAS, Am. Soc. Agronomy (editl. bd. 1983-90), Soil Sci. Soc. Am. (travel grantee to internat. congress Japan 1990), Royal Meteorol. Soc., Crop Sci. Soc. Am. (editl. bd. 1980-84); mem. Am. Soc. Plant Physiology (editl. bd. 1982-87), Am. Soc. Hort. Sci., Internat. Soil Tillage Rsch. Organ., Internat. Union Soil Sci. (1st vice chmn. commn. soil physics 1994-98, sec. commn. on soils, food security and human health 2002—), Bot. Soc. Am., Am. Meteorol. Soc., Société Française de Physiologie Végétale, Japanese Soc. Plant Physiology, Scandinavian Soc. Plant Physiology, N.Y. Acad. Sci., Soc. for Exptl. Biology (London), Growth Regulator Soc. Am., Water Environment Fedn., Phytopathological Soc., Internat. Assn. Vegetation Sci., Am. Geophysical Union, Internat. Water Resources Assn., Royal Soc. New Zealand, Internat. Assn. Hydrolics Sci., Am. Physical Sci., Am. Math. Assn., Am. Chemical Soc., Phi Kappa Phi (scholar award 2000), Gamma Sigma Delta (Disting. Faculty award Kans. State U. chpt., 2001), Sigma Xi (sec. Kans. State U. chpt. 1997-99, Outstanding Sr. Scientist award 2002). Home: 1420 McCain Ln Apt 244 Manhattan KS 66502-4680 Office: Kans State U Dept Agronomy Throckmorton Hall Manhattan KS 66505-5501 E-mail: mbk@ksu.edu.

ZIRKHAM, PERRY M. immunologist; b. Crawfordsville, Ind., June 23, 1960; s. Gary D. and Mary Jo Kirkham; m. Lisa P. Horrall; children: Emily, Alison, MacKenzie. BS, Purdue U., 1983; PhD, U. Ala., 1995. Post-doctoral fellow Med. Rsch. Coun., Centre for Protein Engring., Cambridge, England, 1996—97; post-doctoral rsch. U. Ala., Birmingham, 1997—2000, rsch. asst. prof., 2000—02. Dir. Bacteriophage Display Core Facility, Birmingham, 1999—2001; vis. scientist Eli Lilly and Co., Indpls., 2001—02. Grantee Hitchings-Elion Fellowship, Burroughs-Wellcome Trust, 1996—99. Home: 119 Oak Grove Rd Birmingham AL 35209 Office: 6700B Rockledge Dr Bethesda MD 20892 Personal E-mail: eamkirkham@charter.net. Business E-Mail: pkirkham@niaid.nih.gov.

KIRKLAND, BERTHA THERESA, project engineer; b. San Francisco; d. Lawrence and Theresa (Kanzler) Schmelzer; m. Thornton C. Kirkland, Jr., Dec. 7, 1937 (dec. July 1971); children: Kathryn Elizabeth, Francis Charles. Ed. pub. schs., Calif. Supr. hosp. ops. Am. Potash & Chem. Corp., Trona, Calif., 953 51; office mgr., estimator T.C. Kirkland Elect. Contractor, San Bernardino, Calif., 1954-58, estimator, sec./treas., bd. dir., 1958-74; estimator design-installation engr. Add-M Electric, Inc., San Bernardino, 1972-82, v.p., 1974-82; estimator, engr. Corona (Calif.) Indsl. Electric, Inc., 1982-83; project engr. Fischbach & Moore, Inc., L.A., 1984-91; project engr. cons. Fischbach & Moor, Inc., L.A., 1993-94. Home: 526 Sonora St San Bernardino CA 92404-1762

KIRKLAND, GEOFFREY ALAN, motion picture production designer; b. Derby, Eng., Oct. 7, 1939; came to U.S., 1980; s. Cyril George and Florence Kathleen Kirkland; m. Elspeth Mary Kennedy, Mar. 23, 1970. AA, Royal Coll. of Art, London, 1961. Designer BBC, London, 1961-66; freelance art dir. London, 1966-75; freelance prodn. designer L.A., 1975—. Prodn. designer : (films) Bugsy Malone, 1975 (British Film Academy award, 1975); Midnight Express, 1978; Fame, 1980; Shoot the Moon, 1982; The Right Stuff, 1983 (Academy award nomination best art direction, 1983); Birdy, 1984; Leonard Part 6, 1987; Journey to the Center of the Earth, 1987; Mississippi Burning, 1988; Wildfire, 1989; Come See the Paradise, 1990; Renaissance Man, 1994; Space Jam, 1996; Desperate Measures, 1998; Angela's Ashes, 1998; The Life of David Gale, 2001. Nominee Best Art Direction award, British Acad.

KIRKLAND, JOHN C. lawyer; b. Omaha, Nebr., Dec. 28, 1963; s. John and Marilou (Witt) K. AB, Columbia U., 1986; JD, UCLA, 1990. Bar: Calif. 1990. Assoc. Cadwalader Wickersham & Taft, L.A., 1990-97; of counsel Weissmann Wolff Bergman Coleman & Silverman, LLP, Beverly Hills, Calif., 1997-2000; ptnr. Brown Raysman Millstein Felder & Steiner LLP, L.A., 2000-01; shareholder Greenberg Traurig LLP, L.A., 2001—. Bd. dirs. Oaktree Found., Inc. Mem. ABA, L.A. County Bar Assn., Beverly Hills Bar Assn. Home: 754 Swarthmore Ave Pacific Palisades CA 90272-4355 Office: 2450 Colorado Ave Ste 400E Santa Monica CA 90404 E-mail: kirklandj@gtlaw.com.

KIRKLAND, JOHN DAVID, oil and gas company executive, lawyer; b. McAllen, Tex., June 6, 1933; s. O.D. and Daisy (Donohoe) K.; m. Ann Wales, June 15, 1957 (div. Feb. 1985); children: David, Solace, Robert; m. Kate Sayen, May 15, 1993. BA, Yale U., 1955, LLB, 1958. Bar: Tex. 1958. Atty. Baker, Botts, Shepherd & Coates, Houston, 1958-67; v.p. in charge fin. Pennzoil Co., Houston, 1967-73, exec. v.p., dir., 1973-78; dir. exec. edn. Jones Sch. Mgmt. and Adminstrn. Rice U., Houston, 1978-79; vice chmn., dir. Sandefer Oil & Gas, Inc., Houston, 1980; exec. v.p., dir. Roy M Huffington, Inc., Houston, 1980-86; chmn. Heritage Trust Co., Houston, 1986-89; chmn., CEO Antara Resources Inc., Houston, 1996-2000; chmn. Huntington Exploration, Inc., 2002—. Bd. dirs. Mesa Petroleum Co., 1967-73, Jupiter Corp., 1962-67, Downtown Bank, 1965-70, Pogo, Inc., 1970-77, Plato, Inc., 1973-78. Pres. Houston Ballet Found., 1972-74, trustee, 1979—, chmn., 1979-84; treas., chmn. n. com. United Way of Houston, 1983-84; trustee Chinquapin Sch., 1991-94; d. dirs. Houston chpt. Juvenile Diabetes Found., 1995-97. Mem. Tex. Bar Assn. Home: 989 S Post Oak Ln Houston TX 77056-2203 E-mail: kirkland.johnd@sbcglobal.net.

KIRKLAND, JOHN LEONARD, lawyer; b. Elgin, Ill., Aug. 8, 1926; s. Alfred Hines and Elizabeth Aurelia (Younges) Kirkland; m. Harriet Grose, Oct. 4, 1950; children: Karen Emily Kirkland Lazos, Kevin Grose, Robert John, Melissa Caroline Kirkland Glyman. BA, Lake Forest Coll., 1948; JD, Chgo.-Kent Coll. Law, 1952. Bar: Ill. 1951, U.S. Dist. Ct. (no. dist.) Ill. 1952. Assoc. Hinshaw, Culbertson, Moelmann, Hoban & Fuller, Chgo., 1952-60, ptnr., 1960-90, mng. ptnr., 1979-84; of counsel Hinshaw and Culbertson, Chgo., 1991—. Lectr. Inst. Continuing Legal Edn. Ins. Law, 1968—75. Mem. Cook County Zoning Bd. Appeals, Ill., 1968—73, Arlington Heights Zoning Bd. Appeals, 1961—68, chmn., 1965—68; hon. life trustee Union League Boys and Girls Clubs. With USN, 1944—46. Fellow: Am. Coll. Trial Lawyers, Am. Bar Found.; mem.: Fedn. Ins. Counsel, Trial Lawyers Club Chgo. (pres. 1961), Soc. Trial Lawyers, Ill. State Bar Assn. (bd. govs. 1975—79, editor Policy ins. law bul. 1976—90), Big Foot Country Club (pres. 1978—79), Union League Club (Chgo.). Home: 7040 Pelican Bay Blvd # D303 Naples FL 34108-5520 Office: Hinshaw & Culbertson 222 N La Salle St Ste 300 Chicago IL 60601-1081

KIRKLAND, REBECCA TRENT, pediatric endocrinologist; b. Durham, N.C., Dec. 27, 1942; d. Josiah Charles Trent and Mary Duke (Biddle) Trent-Semans; m. John Lindsey Kirkland III, June 24, 1965. BA, Duke U., 1964, MD, 1968. Intern Baylor Coll. Medicine, 1968-69, resident in pediatrics, 1969-70, fellow in pediatric endocrinology, 1971-73, asst. prof. dept. pediatrics, 1975-81, assoc. prof., 1981-88, prof., 1988—, sr. assoc. dean med. edn., 2000; registrar Guy's Hosp., Hosp. for Sick Children, London, 1970; with U. Pa. Sch. Medicine, 1973-74, fellow, 1974-75. Asst. physician divsn. endocrinology Children's Hosp. Phila., 1973-75; mem. staff Tex. Children's Hosp., 1975—, Harris County Hosp. Dist., 1975—; head ambulatory svcs. Tex. Children's Hosp., 1984—, dir. jr. league outpatient dept., 1984—. Contbr. articles and revs. to profl. jours. Active Leadership Tex., Leadership Houston; pres. Greater Houston Women's Found., 1994—96; bd. dirs. AVANCE, Inc., 1992, YWCA, 1992; trustee Mus. Med. Sci., 1984—88; pres. Josiah C. Trent Meml. Found., Inc., 1983—, v.p., 1977—83; bd. dirs. Am. Leadership Forum, 1991, mem. selection com., 1989, 1990, sec. bd. dirs. Houston/Gulf Coast chpg., 1989, 1990, pres.-elect, 1991, pres., 1991—93; bd. dirs. Mus. Health and Med. Scis., 2001—. NIH fellow, 1971-73; recipient Alumnae award Baldwin Sch., 1983, Disting. Alumni award Durham Acad., 1984, Goodheart Humanitarian award B'nai B'rith, 1986, Disting. Svc. award Duke U. Med. Alumni Assn., 1992, Recognition award Ctr. for Interaction: Man, Sci. and Culture, 1993, One Voice for Children award Tex. Network for Medically Fragile and Chronically-Ill Children, 1993; named one of five Outstanding Women of Yr. Channel 13, Houston, 1984, Woman on the move Houston Post, 1989. Fellow Am. Acad. Pediatrics; mem. Endocrine Soc., Am. Fedn. For Clin. Rsch., So. Soc. for Pediatric Rsch., Lawson-Wilkins Pediatric Endocrine Soc., Houston Pediatric Soc., Tex. Pediatric Soc., Tex. Med. Assn., Soc. for Pediatric Rsch., Pediatric Endocrinology Soc. Tex., Ambulatory Pediatric Assn., Am. Pediatric Soc., Am. Acad. Pediatrics (pediatric endocrine sect.) 1990), Tex. Diabetes and Endocrine Assn. Office: Baylor Coll Medicine 1 Baylor Plz Houston TX 77030-3411

KIRKLAND, VIRGIL WAYNE, electrical engineer; b. Carthage, Tex., July 29, 1939; s. J.B. and Evelyn Virginia K.; 1 child, Olga Lynn. BSEE, Lamar State U., 1962. With Hughes Aircraft Co., Fullerton, Calif., 1962-94, mgr. tech. staff, 1979 94, asst. program mgr., 1995; with Butler Svc. Group Consulting, Orange, Calif., 1995; ret. Hughes Aircraft Co., Orange, 1995. Republican. Baptist.

KIRKLEY, D. CHRISTINE, non-profit organization administrator; b. Horton, Ala., Aug. 28, 1932; d. Vester Boyd and Josephine Prumrytle (Parrish) K.; m. Jack Stanley I, July 4, 1952; 1 child, Jack Stanley II. Student, U. Ala., 1951-52, Samford U., 1963-65, Cathedral Coll., 1982. Svr. rep. South Ctrl. Bell, Birmingham, Ala., 1984—; dir. Helpline Christian Outreach Ministries Inc, Birmingham, 1991—. Area mgr. Operating Blessing, Birmingham, 1989—; mem. Christian Helplines Internat., 1990—, sec. exec. com., 1994—. Mem. Telephone Pioneers Am. (fund raiser 1976-78, pres. 1979, cmty. edn. coord. 1982-83, drug abuse chairperson 1982-83). Mem. Assemby of God Ch. Avocations: reading, bowling, crocheting, swimming. Office: Helpline Christian Outreach Ministries Inc 8 Roebuck Dr Birmingham AL 35215-8046

KIRKLIN, JOHN WEBSTER, surgeon; b. Muncie, Ind., Aug. 5, 1917; m. Margaret Katherine Kirklin; 3 children. BA summa cum laude, U. Minn., 1938; MD magna cum laude, Harvard U., 1942; MD (hon.) (hon.), U. Munich, 1961; DSc (hon.) (hon.), Hamline U., 1966, U. Ala., Birmingham, 1978, Ind. U., Bloomington, 1983; hon. degree (hon.), U. Bordeaux, France, 1982, Universidad de la Republica, Uruguay, 1982. Diplomate Am. Bd. Surgery. Intern Hosp. U. Pa., 1942-43; resident in surgery Mayo Clinic and Mayo Grad. Sch. Medicine, Rochester, Minn., 1943-44, 46-48, first asst. in surgery, 1949-50, chmn. dept. surgery, 1964-66; asst. resident in surgery Children's Hosp., Boston, 1948-49; surgeon Mayo Clinic, 1950-66, instr. surgery, 1951-53, asst. prof., 1953-57, asso. prof., 1957-60, prof., 1960-66, bd. govs., 1965-66; surgeon-in-chief U. Ala., Birmingham, 1966-82; Fay Fletcher Kerner prof. surgery U. Ala.-Birmingham Sch. Medicine and Med. Ctr., 1966—; assoc. chief staffy U. Ala.-Birmingham Hosps., 1966—; chmn. dept. surgery U. Ala.-Birmingham Sch. Medicine and Med. Ctr., 1966-82, dir. div. cardiothoracic surgery, dir. Congenital Heart Disease Research and Tng. Ctr., 1982-84, prof. surgery, 1990-98, prof. emeritus, 1998—. Mem. task force on prevention and treatment of cardiovascular disease in the young Nat. Heart, Lung and Blood Inst., 1977—78; mem. policy adv. bd. for coronary artery surgery, mem. adv. com. crippled children services regional program NIH. Author (with R.B. Karp)): The Tetralogy of Fallot from a Surgical Viewpoint, 1970; author: (with others)) Cardiac Surgery and the Conduction System, 1983; contbr. ; mem. editl. bd.: Am. Heart Jour., 1974—76, Am. Jour. Cardiology, 1974—80, Circulation, 1967—78, Jour. Thoracic and Cardiovascular Surgery, 1971—83, Year Book Cardiovascular Medicine and Surgery, corr. mem. editl bd.: European Jour. Intensive Care Medicine, 1974—, former editl. bd.: Jour. French Soc. Thoracic Surgery. Capt. U.S. Army, 1944—46. Fellow: Assn. Surgeons Gt. Britain and Ireland (hon.), Royal Coll. Surgeons Eng. (hon.), Royal Coll. Surgeons Edinburgh (hon.), Royal Coll. Surgeons Ireland (hon.), Royal Australasian Coll. Surgeons (hon.); mem.: NAS, AAUP, AMA, ACS, So. Surg. Assn., So. Soc. Clin. Investigation, Soc. Vascular Surgery, Soc. Univ. Surgeons, Soc. Thoracic Surgeons, Soc. Surg. Chairmen, Soc. Critical Care Medicine, Soc. Clin. Surgery, Royal Soc. Medicine (affiliate), N.Y. Acad. Scis., Mayo Found. Alumni Assn., Jefferson County Med. Soc., Internat. Surg. Group, Harvard Med. Alumni Assn., Deutsche Gesellschaft Fur Chirurgie, Cardiac Soc. Australia and N.Z. (corr.), Birmingham Surg. Soc., Am. Surg. Assn. (recorder 1967—71), Am. Soc. Critical Care Medicine, Am. Soc. Artificial Internal Organs, Am. Heart Assn., Am. Coll. Cardiology (v.p. bd. govs. 1973—74), Am. Assn. Thoracic Surgery (pres. 1978—79), Am. Acad. Pediatrics, Ala. Heart Assn., Ala. Acad. Sci., Am. Bd. Thoracic Surgery (mem. exam. and tng. programs coms., diplomate), N.Y. Soc. Thoracic Surgery (hon.), Mexican Soc. Cardiology (hon.), European Soc. Cardiovascular Surgery (hon.), Surg. Biology Club. Office: U Ala Sch Medicine & Med Ctr Dept Surgery Ctr 701 S 19th St Dept S Birmingham AL 35294-0001*

KIRKORIAN, DONALD GEORGE, retired college official, management consultant; b. San Mateo, Calif., Nov. 30, 1938; s. George and Alice (Sergius) K. BA, San Jose State U., 1961, MA, 1966, postgrad., 1968, Stanford U., 1961, U. So. Calif., 1966; PhD, Northwestern U., 1972. Producer Sta. KNTV, San Jose, Calif., 1961; tchr. L.A. City Schs., 1963; instrnl. TV coord. Fremont Union High Sch. Dist., Sunnyvale, Calif., 1963-73; assoc. dean instrn. learning resources Solano C.C., Fairfield, Calif., 1973-85, dean instrnl. services, 1985-89, dean learning resources and staff devel., 1989-99; exec. dir. Learning Resources Assn. of Calif. Cmty. Colls., 1976—. Owner, CEO The Cruise Doctor travel agy., 1999—; owner, pres. Kirkorian and Assocs., Fairfield; field cons. Nat. Assn. Edn. Broadcasters, 1966-68; adj. faculty San Jose State U., 1968-69, U. Calif., Santa Cruz, 1970-73, U. Calif., Davis, 1973-76; chmn. Bay Area TV Consortium, 1976-77, 86-87; mem. adv. panel Speech Comm. Assn./Am. Theater Assn. tchr. preparation in speech., comm., theater and media, N.Y.C., 1973-77. Author: Staffing Information Handbook, 1990, National Learning Resources Directory, 1991, 93; editor: Media Memo, 1973-80, Intercom: The Newsletter for Calif. Community Coll. Librs., 1974-75, Update, 1980-90, Exploring the Benicia State Recreation Area, 1977, California History Resource Materials, 1977, Time Management, 1980; contbr. articles to profl. jours. Chmn. Solano County Media Adv. Com., 1974-76; bd. dirs. Napa-Solano United Way, 1980-82; mem. adv. bd. Calif. Youth Authority, 1986-93. Mem. Nat. Assn. Ednl. Broadcasters, Assn. for Edn. Comm. and Tech., Broadcast Edn. Assn., Calif. Assn. Ednl. Media and Tech. (treas.), Western Ednl. Soc. for Telecomm. (bd. dirs. 1973-75, pres. 1976-77, State Chancellor's com. on Telecomm. 1982-86), Learning Resources Assn. Calif. Comm. Colls. (sec.-treas., pres.), Assn. Calif. C.C. Adminstrs. (bd. dirs. 1985-91), Cmty. Coll. Instrnl. Network. Home: 1655 Rockville Rd Fairfield CA 94534-1373 Office: PO Box 298 Fairfield CA 94533-0029

KIRKPATRICK, ANDREW BOOTH, JR., lawyer; b. Asheville, N.C., Jan. 16, 1929; s. Andrew Booth and Gertrude Elizabeth (Ingle) K.; m. Frances Gordon Cone, Oct. 9, 1954; children: Christine, Melissa, Charles. BS cum laude, Davidson Coll., 1949; LLB magna cum laude, Harvard U., 1954. Bar: Del. 1954, Fla. 1955. Law clk. U.S. Ct. Appeals 3d Cir., 1954-55; assoc. Morris, Nichols, Arsht & Tunnell, Wilmington, Del., 1955-58, ptnr., 1958-95, of counsel, 1995—. Chmn. censor com. Supreme Ct. Del., 1970-78. Trustee U. Del.; trustee Unidel Found., Inc.; pres. Young Republicans of New Castle County, 1957-58; chmn. Kennett Pike Assn., Wilmington, 1967-68; chmn. Gov.'s Comm. on Organized Crime, 1972-73; trustee Tatnall Sch., Inc., 1972-82. 1st lt. inf. U.S. Army, 1951-53. Fellow Am. Coll. Trial Lawyers; mem. Del. Bar Assn. (pres. 1978-79), Wilmington Club, Wilmington Country Club, Vicmead Hunt Club, Phi Beta Kappa. Presbyterian. Home: 9 Barley Mill Dr Wilmington DE 19807-2217 Office: Morris Nichols Arsht & Tunnell PO Box 1347 Wilmington DE 19899-1347

KIRKPATRICK, ANNE SAUNDERS, systems analyst; b. Birmingham, Mich., July 4, 1938; d. Stanley Rathbun and Esther (Casteel) Saunders; children: Elizabeth, Martha, Robert, Sarah. Student, Wellesley Coll., 1956-57, Laval U., Quebec City, Can., 1958, U. Ariz., 1958 59; BA in Philosophy, U. Mich., 1961. Systems engr. IBM, Chgo., 1962-64; sr. analyst Commonwealth Edison Co., Chgo., 1981-97. Treas. Taproot Reps., DuPage County, Ill., 1977-80; pres. Hinsdale (Ill.) Women's Rep. Club, 1978-81. Mem.: Wellesley of Chgo. (bd. dirs. 1972-73). Home: 222 E Chestnut St Unit 8B Chicago IL 60611-2376 E-mail: a.kirkpatrick@sbcglobal.net.

KIRKPATRICK, CHARLES HARVEY, physician, immunology researcher; b. Topeka, Nov. 5, 1931; s. Hazen Leon and Clarice Opal (Privott) K.; m. Janice Faye Fosha, July 11, 1959; children: Heather, Michael, Brian. BA, U. Kans., 1954; MD, U. Kans., Kansas City, 1958. Diplomate Am. Bd. Internal Medicine, Am. Bd. Allergy and Immunology. Asst. prof. U. Kans., Kansas City, 1965-68. assoc. prof., 1967; sr. investigator Nat. Inst. Allergy and Infectious Diseases, NIH, Bethesda, Md., 1968-79; dir. allergy and clin. immunology Nat. Jewish Ctr., Denver, 1979-93; prof. U. Colo., Denver, 1979—; dir. rsch. Innovative Therapeutics, Inc., 1993-96; pres. Cytokine Sci., Inc., Denver, 1996-99. Active NIH study sects., Bethesda. Editor: 4 books; contbr. numerous articles to profl. jours. NIH research grantee, 1981-86. Fellow ACP, Am. Acad. Allergy and Immunology, Molecular Med. Soc.; mem. Am. Soc. Clin. Investigation, Am. Assn. Immunologists. Episcopalian. Avocations: enology, antique corkscrews, antique automobiles. Home: 295 Leyden St Denver CO 80220-5951 Office: U Colo Health Sci Ctr 1899 Gaylord St Denver CO 80206-1210 E-mail: ckirkpat@cri.uchsc.edu.

KIRKPATRICK, DAVID WARREN, educational researcher, writer; b. Bennington, Vt., Apr. 19, 1929; s. David Warren and Minerva Kirkpatrick. BS in Edn., North Adams (Mass.) State Coll., 1959; MA in History, Lehigh U., 1964. Cert. social studies tchr., Mass., Pa. High sch. history tchr. Easton (Pa.) Area Sch. Dist., 1961-71; pres. Pa. State Edn. Assn., Harrisburg, 1969-71; comms. dir. Pa. Gov., Harrisburg, 1971-73; cons., sr. staff mem. Pa. Senate Edn. Commn., Harrisburg, 1973-77; sr. staff mem. Pa. Senate and Rural Affairs Commn., 1977-80; exec. dir. Assn. Pa. State Colls. and Univs., Harrisburg, 1980-85; comms. dir. Pa. Auditor Gen., Harrisburg, 1985-86; exec. dir. Pa. Assn. Rural and Small Schs., Harrisburg, 1987-91, The Reach Alliance, Harrisburg, 1992-95; ednl. rschr., writer, cons., 1995—. Founder Pa. Rural Coalition, Harrisburg, 1980, bd. dirs., 1980—87, chmn., 1980—82; mem. consumer adv. coun. Pa. Pub. Utility Commn., 1985—87, chmn., 1986—87; sr. fellow Allegheny Inst., Pitts., 1998—2000, Options for Youth, Pasadena, Calif., 1999—2000; fellow Pub. Svc. Rsch. Fedn., Vienna, 1999—; fellow, then sr. fellow for tchr. choice Alexis de Tocqueville Instn., Arlington, Va., 1999—2001; columnist Express-Times, Easton, Pa., 1992—95. Author: Choice in Schooling, 1990, School Choice: The Idea That Will Not Die, 1997; education writer: IUniverse.com, 2000—02; editor: Schoolreformers.com, 2001—02; contbr. Pub. rels. chair Vote Yes for Water, Harrisburg, 1981; participant in numerous polit. campaigns. Named Alumnus of Yr., North Adams State Coll., 1971; Disting. fellow The Blum Ctr., Marquette U., 1995-99; Wm. Robertson Coe fellow Stanford U., 1965; Grad. scholar Lehigh U., 1959 61; sr. edn. fellow U.S. Freedom Found., 2002. Avocations: reading, travel, music collection. Home: 108 Highland Ct Douglassville PA 19518-9240 E-mail: tchrwrtr@aol.com.

KIRKPATRICK, DONALD ROBERT, secondary school educator; b. Ft. Belvoir, Va., Aug. 15, 1956; s. Robert Wilbur and Marsha Beatrice (Watson) K. BS, James Madison U., 1979; postgrad., U. Kans., 1979-81; MEd, U. S.C., 1994. Aid dept. paleobiology Nat. Mus. Natural History, Washington, 1979; rsch. asst. U. Kans., Lawrence, 1979-81; sci. tchr. 8th grade Johnakin Mid. Sch., Marion, SC, 1989—2003; sci. tchr. grades 9-12 Marion HS, 2003—. Rsch. assoc. Horry County Mus., Conway, 1990—; fossil collector/donor Nat. Mus. Natural History, 1979—; presenter in field; instr. part-time Coastal Carolina U., Conway, S.C., 1992—, Francis Marion U., Florence, S.C., 1998—. Lt. USNR, 1981-89. Mem. NEA, ASCD, Nat. Assn. Geosci. Tchrs., Nat. Sci. Tchrs. Assn., Nat. Assn. Biology Tchrs., SC Sci. Coun., SC Acad. Sci., Astronomical Soc. Pacific, Paleontological Rsch. Inst., Soc. Vertebrate Paleontology, Nat. Ctr. Sci. Edn., Assn. for Curriculm Devel. Episcopalian. Avocations: collecting fossils, walking, reading, swimming. Home: 1321 Snider St Conway SC 29526-3120 Office: Marion High Sch 1205 S Main St Marion SC 29571 Business E-Mail: dkirkpatrick@marion1.k12.sc.us. E-mail: drki@sccoast.net.

KIRKPATRICK, EDWARD THOMSON, college administrator, mechanical engineer; b. Cranbrook, B.C., Can., Jan. 15, 1925; came to U.S., 1954, naturalized, 1981; s. John Thomson and Mary Pauline (Jones) K.; m. Barbara Jane Kelsberg, May 22, 1948; children— Allan, Karen, Ann, Keith. B.A. in Sci., U. B.C., 1947; M.S., Carnegie Inst. Tech., 1956, Ph.D., 1958. Registered profl. engr., N.Y., Ohio. Sales engr., mgr. F.D. Bolton, Ltd., Vancouver, B.C., 1948-54; asst. prof. Carnegie Inst. Tech., Pitts., 1954-58; dept. head U. Toledo, 1958-63; engring. dean Rochester Inst. Tech., N.Y., 1963-71; pres. Wentworth Inst. Tech., Boston, 1971-90. Author: 1620 Fortran II-D Program, 1963. Contbr. articles to profl. publs. Recipient Outstanding Civilian Service medal U.S. Army, 1971. Fellow Am. Soc. Engring. Edn. (bd. dirs. 1982-86); mem. ASME, Nat. Soc. Profl. Engrs. Republican. Episcopalian. Avocations: homebuilt aircraft, flying, foreign travel. Home: 40 Radcliffe Rd Weston MA 02493-1024 Office: Wentworth Inst Tech Office of Pres 550 Huntington Ave Boston MA 02115-5998

KIRKPATRICK, FRANCIS H(UBBARD), biophysicist, intellectual property practitioner, consultant; b. Laurel Hill, N.C., Nov. 7, 1943; s. Francis Hubbard and Jean Orr Kirkpatrick; m. Cornelia Ewart Goodreds, Aug. 30, 1969; 1 child, Adam. BA Physics, Harvard Coll., 1964; PhD Biophysics, Stanford U., 1970. Registered U.S. patent agent, 1992. Postdoctoral Wash. State U., Pullman, 1969-71, U. Rochester Sch. Medicine, 1972-74, asst. prof. dept. biophysics, 1974-80; mgr. Pall Corp., Glen Cove, N.Y., 1980-84; tech. dir. FMC BioProducts, Rockland, Maine, 1984-93; dir. intellectual property Focal, Inc., Lexington, Mass., 1993-2000; ind. cons. in mgmt. of intellectual property startup cos., 2000—. Mem. Genetics Small Bus. Innovative Rsh. Spl. Study Sect., 1988-99; cons., lectr. in field. Contbr. articles to sci. jours.; patentee in field. Chair First Parish Ch., Chelmsford, Mass., 1999-2000. Recipient Rsch. Career Devel. award NIH, 1975-80. Mem. Optical Soc. Am., Am. Chem. Soc., Patent and Trademark Office Soc. Avocation: gardening. Address: 37 Clover Hill Dr Chelmsford MA 01824-2611

KIRKPATRICK, GARLAND PENN, pediatrician; b. Chgo., Aug. 23, 1932; m. Dorothy Ann McCluster, Jan. 31, 1958; children: Garland Penn, Dawn Annette. AB, Talladega (Ala.) Coll., 1954; BS, U. Ill., Chgo., 1956, MD, 1958. Diplomate Am. Bd. Pediatrics. Fellow in devel. and behavioral pediatrics U. N.C., Chapel Hill; clin. instr. pediatrics U. Ill. Coll. Medicine, Chgo., 1959-64; pvt. practice pediatrics Kirkpatrick & Germain, Chgo., 1963-89; clin. asst. prof. pediatrics U. Chgo., 1983; clin. assoc. prof. pediatrics Northwestern Med. Sch., Chgo., 1985; clin. asst. prof. pediatrics U. Mich. Sch. Medicine, Ann Arbor, 1995, asst. clin. prof. pediatrics, 1996—. Chmn. dept. pediatrics USAF Hosp., Richards Gebaur AFB, 1961-63; cons. Chgo. Bd. Edn., 1983-84; spkr. in field. Contbr. articles to profl. jours. Capt. USAF Med. Corps. Fellow Am. Acad. Pediatrics (exec. com. Ill. chpt. 1984); mem. AMA, Nat. Med. Assn., Soc. for Behavioral and Devel. Pediatrics. Baptist. Avocations: chess, gardening, reading, music: classical, jazz and gospel. Home: 1365 Folkstone Ct Ann Arbor MI 48105-2845

KIRKPATRICK, JEANE DUANE JORDAN, political scientist, government official; b. Duncan, Okla. d. Welcher F. and Leona (Kile) Jordan; m. Evron M. Kirkpatrick; children: Douglas Jordan, John Evron, Stuart Alan. AA, Stephens Coll.; AB, Barnard Coll.; MA, PhD, Columbia U.; postgrad. (French govt. fellow), Inst. Polit. Sci., U. Paris; LHD (hon.), Georgetown U., U. Pitts., U. Charleston, Hebrew U., Colo. Sch. Mines, St. John's U., Universidad Francisco Marroquin, Guatemala, Coll. of William and Mary, U. Mich., Syracuse U.; hon. degree, Loyola U., U. Rochester, Chgo. Asst. prof. polit. sci. Trinity Coll., 1962-67; assoc. prof. polit. sci. Georgetown U., Washington, 1967-73, prof., 1973—, Leavey prof., 1978—2002, prof. emeritus, 2002—; sr. fellow Am. Enterprise Inst. for Pub. Policy Rsch., 1977—; mem. cabinet U.S. permanent rep. to UN, 1981-85; mem. Def. Policy Rev. Bd. (DPB), 1985-93; chair Commn. on Fail Safe and Risk Reduction (FARR), 1990-92; mem. Pres.'s Fgn. Intelligence and Adv. Bd. (PFIAD), 1985-89; head U.S. Delegation to Human Rights Commn., 2003. Author: Elections USA, 1956, Perspectives, 1962, The Strategy of Deception, 1963, Mass Behavior in Battle and Captivity, 1968, Leader and Vanguard in Mass Society; The Peronist Movement in Argentina, 1971, Political Woman, 1974, The New Presidential Elite, 1976, Dismantling the Parties. Reflections on Party Reform and Party Decomposition, 1978, The Reagan Phenomenon, 1983, Dictatorships and Double Standards, 1982, Legitimacy and Force (2 vols.), 1988, The Withering Away of the Totalitarian State, 1990; syndicated columnist, 1985-97; contbr. articles to profl. jours.; editor, contbr. various pubs. Trustee Helen Dwight Reid Ednl. Found., 1972—, pres., 1990—. Recipient Disting. Alumna award Stephens Coll., 1978, B'nai B'rith

Humanitarian award, 1982, Award of the Commonwealth Fund, 1983, Gold medal VFW, 1984, French Prix Politique, 1984, Dept. Def. Disting. Pub. Svc. medal, 1985, Bronze Palm, 1992, Disting. Svc. medal Mayor of N.Y.C., 1985, Presdl. Medal of Freedom, 1985, Jamestown Freedom award, 1990, Centennial medal Nat. Soc. DAR, 1991, Disting. Svc. award USO, 1994, Laureate of the Lincoln Acad. of Ill., Medallion of Lincoln, 1996, Jerusalem 2000 award, 1996, Casey medal of hon., 1998, Tomas Garrigue Masaryk Order, 1998, Chauncey Rose award Rose-Hulman Inst. Tech., 1999, Hungarian Presdl. Gold medal, 1999, Living Legends medal Libr. Congress, 2000, Grand Officier du Wissam Al Alaoui medal King of Morocco, 2000; Kirkpatrick professorship of internat. affairs chair established in her honor Harvard U., 1999; Coun. on Fgn. Rels. established Jeane Kirkpatrick chair in nat. security, 2002. Mem. Internat. Polit. Sci. Assn. (exec. coun.), Am. Polit. Sci. Assn. (Hubert Humphrey award 1988), So. Polit. Sci. Assn. Office: Am Enterprise Inst 1150 17th St NW Washington DC 20036-4603 E-mail: jkirkpatrick@aei.org. *My experience demonstrates to my satisfaction that it is both possible and feasible for women in our times to successfully combine traditional and professional roles, that it is not necessary to ape men's career patterns,— -starting early and keeping one's nose to a particular grindstone, but that, instead, one can do quite different things at different stages of one's life. All that is required is a little luck and a lot of work.*

KIRKPATRICK, JOHN ELSON, retired oil company executive, retired naval reserve officer; b. Oklahoma City, Feb. 13, 1908; s. Elmer Elsworth and Claudia (Spencer) K.; m. Eleanor Blake, June 20, 1932; 1 child, Joan Elson. Student, U.S. Mil. Acad., 1925-26; BS, U.S. Naval Acad., 1931; postgrad., Harvard U. Grad. Sch. Bus. Adminstrn., 1935-36; LLD, Oklahoma City U., 1963; HHD, Bethany Nazarene Coll., 1967. Founder, v.p., treas. Allied Steel Products Corp., Tulsa, 1936-41; v.p., treas. Kirkpatrick & Bale Oil Co., Oklahoma City, 1945-50; ptnr. Kirkpatrick Oil Co., Oklahoma City, 1950-95. Emeritus dir., Bank One, Okla. Chmn. Kirkpatrick Found.; hon. consul Republic of Korea, 1974—; life trustee Okla. Zool. Soc.; mem. life bd. Oklahoma City Mus. Art; mem. Okla. Heritage Assn., Allied Arts Found.; hon. dir. Okla. State Fair; former mem. sr. adv. bd. Frontiers of Sci. Found.; hon. chmn. bd. dirs.; past pres. Presbyn. Homes, founder, bd. dirs. Oklahoma City Cmty. Found.; former mem. Bus. Com. for Arts, Inc.; hon. chmn. Lyric Theatre Okla.; hon. life trustee, dir. emeritus Nat. Cowboy and Western Heritage Mus.; trustee Falcon Found., donor Kirkpatrick Auditorium at Oklahoma City U., 1965; dir. Kirkpatrick Sci. and Air Space Mus. at Omniplex; mem. adv. bd. Okla. Health Scis. Ctr.; hon. trustee Tulsa Cmty. Found. Decorated Bronze Star with V; recipient Disting. Svc. award Okla. U., 1959, Sweet Success vol. award, 1998, Nat. Brotherhood citation NCCJ, 1962, AIA award, 1963, Outstanding Okla. Oil Man award Okla. Petroleum Coun., 1974, Merit award Okla. Hosp. Assn., 1974, Esquire/Bus. Com. for the Arts award, 1974, 75, Evergreen Disting. Svc. award for pub. svc., 1982, Okla. Charitable Achiever awards cert. of recognition Pearl M. & Julia J. Harmon Found., 1988, Patrick Henry medal Mil. Order of World Wars Okla. City chpt., 1989, Ptnrs. award World Neighbors, 1991, Henry G. Bennett Distng. Svc. award Okla. State U., 1992, Achievement award Okla. City Fedn. of Colored Womens Clubs, 1992; named to Okla. Hall of Fame, 1962, Okla. Commerce and Industry Hall of Fame, 1985, Wall of Fame Okla. City Pub. Sch. Found., 1990, Humanitarian award Nat. Arthritis Found. Okla. Chpt., 1993; named Outstanding Philanthropist, Okla. chapter Nat. Soc. Fund Raising Execs., 1986, Arts Advocate of Yr., SW Theatre Assn. Performing Arts for Children Divsn., 1993, Disting. Philanthropy award Am. Assn. Mus., 1995, Disting. Friends award Okla. City U., 1997; named Hon. USN Master Chief Petty Officer, 2000; donor Kirkpatrick Ctr. bldg. Okla. Ctr. Sci. and Arts, 1978; John E. Kirkpatrick Horticulture Ctr. Okla. State U. Tech. named in his honor, 1990; recognized by Profl. Photographers of Am. Inc. for meritorious contributions to profl. photography Nat. award; recipient John E. Kirkpatrick Humanitarian Oklahoma City Rotary, 1994; honored by Kappa Sigma; named to The Okla. Mil. Hall of Fame, 1999, Tulsa Hall of Fame, 1999, Okla. Higher Edn. Hall of Fame, 2000. Mem. Ind. Petroleum Assn. (past dir.), Oklahoma City C.of C. (life dir.), Okla. Hist. Soc. (dir. emeritus), Okla. County Hist. Soc. (Cardinal Svc. award 1989), Harvard Area Group, Asia Soc. Okla. (Civic Leader award 1991), 45th Inf. Divsn. Mus. (hon. life, bd. dirs.), Assn. Grads. USAF Acad. (hon.), Rotary, Oklahoma City Petroleum Club (pres. 1959-60). Office: Kirkpatrick Oil Co PO Box 268822 Oklahoma City OK 73126-8822

KIRKPATRICK, JOHN EVERETT, lawyer; b. Meadville, Pa., Aug. 20, 1929; s. Francis Earl and Marjorie Eloise (Roudebush) K.; m. Patricia Ann Benkert, Aug. 9, 1952 (div. June 1963); children: Amy Kirkpatrick Fidler, John Scot, Ann Kirkpatrick Mullen; m. Phyllis Jean Daeuble, Aug. 31, 1963. AB, Amherst Coll., 1951; JD, Harvard U., 1954. Bar: Ohio 1955, Ill. 1962. Assoc. Squire, Sanders & Dempsey, Cleve., 1954-61, Kirkland, Ellis, Hodson, Chaffetz & Masters, Chgo., 1962-64; sr. ptnr. Kirkland & Ellis, Chgo., 1965—. Contbr. articles on tax and estate planning to profl. jours. Mem. Cen. DuPage Hosp. Devel. Commn., Winfield, Ill.; elder 1st Presbyn. Ch., Wheaton, Ill., 1983—. Mem. ABA, Ill. State Bar Assn., Chgo. Bar Assn., Chgo. Golf Club, Mid Am. Club, Glen Oak Club, Lago Mar Club. Republican. Avocation: golf. Office: Kirkland & Ellis 200 E Randolph St Fl 54 Chicago IL 60601-6636

KIRKPATRICK, LAIRD CLIFFORD, law educator; b. Mpls., Aug. 8, 1943; s. Clifford and Marjorie (Dietz) K.; children: Duncan (dec.), Ryan, Morgan. AB cum laude, Harvard U., 1965; JD, U. Oreg., 1968. Instr. U. Mich., Ann Arbor, 1968-69; Reginald Heber Smith fellow OEO, Portland, Oreg., 1969-70; pvt. practice law Eugene, Oreg., 1970-72; exec. dir., dir. litigation Legal Aid Svc., Portland, 1972-74; asst. U.S. atty. U.S. Atty.'s Office, Eugene, 1978-80; prof. law U. Oreg., Eugene, 1974—, Hershner prof. jurisprudence, 1993—, assoc. dean, 1986-89, dean, 2002—, dean Law Sch., 2002—; counsel to asst. atty. gen. criminal divsn. U.S. Dept. Justice, 1999-2001; commr. ex-officio U.S. Sentencing Commn., 1999-2001. Chmn. task force on corrections Gov.'s Office, Salem, 1987-88. Author: Evidence Under the Rules, 4th edit., 2000; Oregon Evidence, 4th edit., 2002, Modern Evidence, 1995, Evidence, 1999, 3d edit., 2003, Federal Evidence, 5 vols., 2d edit., 1994. Mem. Oreg. Criminal Justice Coun., 1987-89. Fellow Am. Bar Found.; mem. ABA (ho. of dels. 1994-96), Am. Law Inst., Am. Judicature Soc. (bd. dirs. 1993-99), Am. Assn. Law Schs. (chair evidence sect. 1998), Oreg. Bar Assn. (Pres.'s award 1991), Order of Coif. Office: U Oreg School of Law 1515 Agate St Eugene OR 97403-1221 E-mail: lkirkpat@law.uoregon.edu.

KIRKPATRICK, ROBERT HUGH, communications executive; b. Kingston, NY, Mar. 3, 1954; s. Oscar Hugh and Ann (Page) K.; m. Debra Cook, Oct. 25, 1986; 1 child, Page. BA in Polit. Sci. with high honors, SUNY, Oneonta, 1977; M in Pub. and Pvt. Mgmt., Yale U., 1979. Cert. comml. pilot. Policy analyst edn. com. N.Y. State Assembly, 1977; mgr. mktg. Cummins Engine Co., Columbus, Ind., 1980-81, mgr. mktg. ops., 1982-83, dir. electronics mktg., 1984-86, dir. bus. devel. Svc. Products Co. subs., 1987-89; pres. Intelesis Inc., Columbus, 1989-97, CEO, 1996-97; pres. transp. and power divsn. AFFINA Corp., Columbus, 1998-2000; ptnr. Intelesis LLC, Columbus, 2001—; COO, Servco LLC, Indpls., 2002—. Cons. in field. Contbr. articles to bus. jours. Trustee SUNY, Albany, 1975-76; pres. Student Assn. State Univ., Inc., 1975-76, v.p. 1974-75; vice-chmn. Nat. Student Lobby, 1976-77; pres. Columbus Arts Guild, 1981-82; treas. San Souci, Inc., Columbus, 1983-85; allocations com. United Way, 1990-92; mem. City Transp. Commn., Oneonta, N.Y., 1973-74; bd. dirs. Leadership Bartholomew County Alumni Assn., 1991-92, Young Mothers' Ednl. Devel., Inc., 1994-96; adminstrv. bd. First United Meth. Ch., 1994-96, trustee 1997-99; exec. com. ABC-Stewart Montessori Sch., 1996-99, sec. 1997; vol. pilot Angel Flight Am., 2001—, Ind. Wing Leader, 2003—. Mem. Yale Club Ind. (treas. 1981-85), Rotary (bd. dirs. 1994-2000, pres. 1996-97, treas. 1997-99). Methodist. Home: 9727 Summerlakes Dr Carmel IN 46032 Office: Servco LLC 720 N High School Rd Indianapolis IN 46214

KIRKPATRICK, R(OBERT) JAMES, geology educator; b. Schenectady, N.Y., Dec. 31, 1946; s. Robert James and Audrey (Rech) K.; m. Susan A. Wilson, Sept. 4, 1968 (div. 1984); children: Gregory Robert, Geoffrey Stephen; m. Carol A. Hanna, Sept. 3, 1985. AB, Cornell U., 1968; PhD, U. Ill., 1972. Asst. U.S. Geol. Survey, Denver, 1968; rsch. and teaching asst. U. Ill., Urbana, 1968-72, asst. prof. dept. geology, 1978-80, assoc. prof., 1980-83, prof., 1983-88, prof., head dept., 1988-97, exec. assoc. dean Coll. Liberal Arts & Scis., 1997—; sr. rsch. geologist prodn. rsch. div. Exxon, Houston, 1972-73; rsch. fellow in geophysics Harvard U., Cambridge, 1973-75; asst. rsch. geologist Scripps Instn. Oceanography, La Jolla, Calif., 1976-78. Mem. ocean crust panel Joint Oceanographic Instns. for Deep Earth Studies, 1977-78, active margin panel, 1978, downhole measurements panel, 1977-78; cons. various corps. Editor: Initial Reports of the Deep Sea Drilling Project, Vols. 46 and 55, 1979, 80; co-editor: Kinetics of Geochemical Processes, 1981; assoc. editor American Mineralogist, 1987-90; contbr. over 200 articles to profl. jours. Overseas fellow Churchill Coll., Eng., 1985-86; rsch. grantee NSF, 1977—, Dept. Energy, 2000—, various other orgns., 1978—. Fellow Geol. Soc. Am., Mineral. Soc. Am. (councillor 1990-93); mem. Am. Geophys. Union (VGP award com. 1985-88, chmn. 1986-88), Am. Cer. Soc., Internat. Mineral. Assn. (alt. U.S. del. 1982, coord. com. 1986 meeting, chmn. program com. 1986, U.S. rep. Commn. on Crystal Growth, v.p. 1986-90, sec. Commn. on Mineral Physics 1986-91). Office: U Ill Dept Geology Urbana IL 61801 E-mail: kirkpat@uiuc.edu.

KIRKSEY, AVANELLE, nutrition educator; b. Mulberry, Ark., Mar. 23, 1926; BS, U. Ark., Fayetteville, 1947; MS, U. Tenn., Knoxville, 1950; PhD, Pa. State U., 1961; postdoctoral, U. Calif., Davis, 1976; DSc honoris causa, Purdue U., 1997. Assoc. prof. Ark. Polytechnic U., Russellville, 1950-55; research asst. Pa. State U., University Park, 1956-58, fellow Gen. Foods, 1958-60; assoc. prof. Purdue U., West Lafayette, Ind., 1961-69, prof. nutrition, 1970-85, disting. prof., 1985-96, disting. prof. emeritus, 1997. Prin. investigator nutrition project in rural Egypt; coord. nutrition program Indonesian Univs., 1987-91 Contbr. articles to profl. jours. Recipient Borden award Am. Home Econs. Assn., 1980. Fellow Am. Inst. Nutrition (Lederle award 1994); mem. N.Y. Acad. Scis., Phi Kappa Phi, Sigma Xi. Office: Purdue U Dept Food Nutrition West Lafayette IN 47907

KIRKWOOD, DAVID HERBERT WADDINGTON, Canadian government official; b. Toronto, Ont., Can., Aug. 8, 1924; s. William Alexander and Mossie May (Waddington) K.; m. Diana Thistle Gill, June 6, 1953; children: Peter, Gill, Melissa, John. BA, U. Toronto, 1945, MA, 1950. Research physicist Can. Atomic Energy Program, Chalk River, Ont., Canada, 1945-48; fgn. service officer Can. Dept. External Affairs, Ottawa, Ont., 1950-69; asst. sec. to cabinet Privy Council Office, Ottawa, 1969-72; asst. dep. minister Dept. Nat. Def., Ottawa, 1972-75; sr. asst. dep. minister Dept. Transport, Ottawa, 1975-78; chmn. Anti Dumping Tribunal, Ottawa, 1978-80; dep. minister Services Dept. Supply and Services, Ottawa, 1980-83; dep. minister Can. Dept. Nat. Health and Welfare, Ottawa, 1983-86; pres. Can. Mediterranean Inst., Ottawa, 1986-90; apptd. chmn. environ. assessment panel on air transp. devel. in So. Ontario, 1990-94. Chmn. environ. assessment panel on decommissioning of Elliot Lake Uranium Mines, 1993-96 Bd. dirs. Can. Med. Inst., 1986-96, Royal Can. Geog. Soc., 1987-97, Hospice of All Sts., 1987-97, 2002—, Ctrl. Children's Choir of Ottawa/Carleton, 2000-2003. Home: Apt 1B 260 Metcalfe St Ottawa ON Canada K2P 1R6 E-mail: dianakirkwood@sympatico.ca.

KIRKWOOD, JOHN ROBERT, neuroradiologist; b. Albany, N.Y., Mar. 19, 1941; s. John Kinloch and Rita Arline (Schwick) K.; m. Norma Starr Miller, June 17, 1967 (dec. Mar. 1973); 1 child, Timothy; m. Gale Arcuni Duncan, Aug. 3, 1974; children: James Duncan, Christopher, Allison. BA in Psychology magna cum laude, Yale U., 1963, MD, 1967. Diplomate Am. Bd. Med. Examiners; diplomate in diagnostic radiology and neuroradiology Am. Bd. Radiology. Intern Children's Hosp. Med. Ctr., Boston, 1967-68; resident in diagnostic radiology U. Calif. Med. Ctr., San Francisco, 1968-71; fellow, instr. neuroradiology Brigham Hosp., Boston, 1971-72; chief neuroradiology Walter Reed Army Med. Ctr., Washington, 1972-73; asst. prof. radiology George Washington U. Hosp., Washington, 1973-74; from asst. prof. to assoc. prof. radiology Tufts U. Sch. Medicine, Boston, 1974—. Vice chmn. dept. radiology, Baystate Med. Ctr., Springfield, Mass., 1987-95, chmn. dept., 1997—, pres. Baystate Radiology and Imaging, Inc., 1997—; pres. Radiology and Imaging, Inc., Springfield, 1995-97, chmn., 2000—. Author: Essentials of Neuroimaging, 1990, 2d edit., 1995; contbr. rsch. articles to profl. jours. Major U.S. Army, 1972-73. Fellow Am. Coll. Radiology (councilor 2001—); mem. AMA, Am. Soc. Neuroradiology, Mass. Radiology Soc. (sec. 1995, v.p. 1998, pres.-elect 1999, pres. 2000—). Avocations: sailing, skiing, golf, art, music. Office: Dept Radiology Baystate Med Ctr 758 Chestnut St Springfield MA 01199-0001 E-mail: robert.kirkwood@bhs.org.

KIRKWOOD, ROBERT KEITH, applied physicist; b. Santa Monica, Calif., Mar. 10, 1961; s. Robert Lord and Patricia Cathrine (Keith) K.; m. Kimberly DeNeve Saunders, May 2, 1991; children: Rebekah Marie, Rachel Kathryn. BS, UCLA, 1982, MS, 1984; PhD, MIT, 1989. Rsch. asst. dept. elec. engring. UCLA, 1982-84; mem. tech. staff TRW Space and Tech. Group, Redondo Beach, Calif., 1984-85; rsch. asst. MIT, Cambridge, 1985-89, vis. scientist Plasma Fusion Ctr., 1992-94; postdoctoral fellow Calif. Inst. Tech., Pasadena, 1989-91; rsch. assoc. geophysics div. Air Force Phillips Lab., Hanscom AFB, Mass., 1991-92, physicist, 1992-94, Lawrence Livermore (Calif.) Lab., 1994—. Contbr. articles to Nuclear Fusion, Physics of Plasmas, Rev. Sci. Instruments, Physics Letters A, Physical Review Letters. Recipient Rsch. Associateship award NRC, 1991; postdoctoral fellow Dept. Energy, 1989; doctoral fellow TRW Space and Tech. Group, 1985. Mem. Am. Phys. Soc. (Simon Ramo award in plasma physics 1991), Am. Geophys. Union. Achievements include development of wave transmission diagnostics for plasmas and demonstration of the interaction between multiple laser beams in plasmas. Office: Lawrence Livermore Lab L-399 PO Box 808 Livermore CA 94551-0808

KIRMAN, CHARLES GARY, photojournalist; b. Chgo., Feb. 2, 1949; s. Irving A. and Sylvia Lea K.; m. Heidemarie Mocker, Nov. 15, 1976 (div.); children: Christian, Courtney. BS in Profl. Photography, Rochester (N.Y.) Inst. Tech., 1972. Staff photographer Chgo. Sun-Times, 1972-81; pres. European Beauty Culture Coll., Phoenix, 1982-86; owner Phoenician Grill, Phoenix, 1987-88; admissions dir. Al Collins Graphic Design Sch., Tempe, Ariz., 1988-92; staff photographer Ventura County (Calif.) Newspapers, 1992—. With USNR, 1966-68. Recipient Nat. Headliner award for spot news photography, 1977; named Ill. Press Photographer of Year, 1975, Chgo. Press Photographer of Year, 1974 Mem. Ill. Press Photographers Assn., Chgo. Press Photographers Assn., Nat. Headliner Club. Office: 5250 Ralston St Ventura CA 93003-7318 Home: 1300 Saratoga Ave #309 Ventura CA 93003-6403

KIRMSE, SISTER ANNE-MARIE ROSE, nun, educator, researcher; b. Bklyn., Sept. 23, 1941; d. Frank Joseph Sr. and Anna (Keck) K. BA in English cum laude, St. Francis Coll., 1972; MA in Theology with honors, Providence Coll., 1975; PhD in Theology, Fordham U., 1989. Joined Sisters of St. Dominic, Roman Cath. Ch., 1960; cert. elem. tchr., N.Y. Tchr. elem. sch. Diocese Bklyn., 1962-73; instr. adult edn. Diocese Rockville Centre, N.Y., 1974—; dir. religious edn. St. Anthony Padua Parish, East Northport, N.Y., 1975-83; dir. spiritual programs Diocese of Rockville Centre, 1979—. Demonstration tchr. Paulist Press, N.Y.C., 1968-70; cons. Elem. Sch. Catechetical Assocs., Bklyn., 1971-73; mem. adj. faculty grad. program Sem. Immaculate Conception, Huntington, N.Y., 1979-80; adj. instr. Molloy Coll., Rockville Centre, 1985, St. Joseph's Coll., Patchogue, N.Y., 1990-91; adj. asst. prof. Ignatius Coll., Bronx, N.Y., 1996-98; adj. assoc. prof. Fordham Coll. Liberal Studies, 1998—; asst. to Card. Avery Dulles, Fordham U., Bronx, 1988—, rsch. assoc. Laurence J. McGinley chair in religion and society, 1989-2003. Recipient Kerygma award Diocese of Rockville Centre, 1980; Dominican scholar Providence Coll., 1973, Presdl. scholar Fordham U., 1988; McGinley fellow Fordham U., 1988. Mem. Cath. Theol. Soc. Am., Coll. Theology Soc., Amnesty Internat., Kiwanis (pres. Fordham U. 1997-2000, Tablet of Honor 2000, N.Y. dist. chmn. Internat. Understanding/Student Exch., 2001-03, lt. gov. Bronx-Westchester South divsn. 2003—, KPTC fellow 2001). Democrat. Roman Catholic. Avocations: swimming, needlework, cooking, traveling, reading. Office: Fordham U Faber Hall 255 Bronx NY 10458 E-mail: kirmse@fordham.edu. *With Saint Irenaeus, I believe that "the glory of God is a person fully alive!" Life is meant to be lived to the full, with passion and extravagance, with commitment and the courage of one's convictions. As with love, the more of our lives we give away, the more life we find we have.*

KIRNER, PAUL TIMOTHY, lawyer; b. Cleve., July 1, 1947; s. Paul F. and Anna M. (Christy) K.; m. Deborah J. Horvat, July 25, 1970; children: Paul James, Peter S. BS, Marquette U., 1969; JD cum laude, Cleve. State U., 1972. Bar: Ohio 1972, US Supreme Ct. 1976. Assoc. Buckingham & Doolittle, Akron, Ohio, 1972-73, Quandt & Giffels, Cleve., 1973-74, Leary & Schifko, Parma, Ohio, 1974-89, Kirner & Boldt, North Royalton, Ohio, 1989—. Spl. counsel to atty. gen. State of Ohio, 1982-96. Mem. Cuyahoga County Ctrl. Com., Ohio, 1974—; councilman City of Parma, 1987-99; pres. pro tem Parma City Coun., 1988-99; chmn. Parma Fair Housing Com., 1983-88; pres. St. Anthony's Parish Coun., 1981-84, Athletic Assn. St. Anthony, 1986-93; bd. dirs. St. Ignatius Fathers Club, Cleve., 1987-88; chmn. design rev. com. City of Parma, 2000—. Served to 1st lt. C.E., U.S. Army, 1969-73. Mem. ABA, ATLA, Ohio Trial Lawyers Assn., Ohio State Bar Assn., Cuyahoga County Bar Assn., Cleve. Bar Assn., Parma Bar Assn. (pres. 1979-80, trustee 1980-83, 95-97), Cleve. State U. Coll. Law Alumni (trustee 1969-70), Elks, Lions (treas. Parma 1982-84), Am. Legion. Democrat. Roman Catholic. Avocation: photography. Office: 8025 Corporate Cir Cleveland OH 44133-1257 E-mail: ptkirner@aol.com.

KIRSCH, ARTHUR WILLIAM, financial consultant; b. Bklyn., Jan. 22, 1941; s. Joseph and Helen (Silverstein) K.; m. Isabel Leader, Sept. 20, 1965 (div. 1980); children: Deborah Beth, Gabrielle, Alexandra, Andrew; m. Denise McLaughlin, May 15, 1982. BA, Washington Sq. Coll., NYU, 1962; postgrad., Grad. Sch. Pub. Adminstrn., NYU, 1962-68. Program budget dir. N.Y.C. Human Resources Adminstrn., 1966-68; sr. assoc. E.F. Shelley & Co., N.Y.C., 1968-73; v.p. Citibank, N.A., N.Y.C., 1973-80; sr. mng. dir. Marine Midland Bank, N.A., N.Y.C., 1980-91; pres. Paradigm Mgmt. Inc., N.Y.C., 1991-93; dir. Pricewaterhouse Coopers, N.Y.C., 1993-2000, Pershing, L.L.C., 2000—. Pres. Kirsch Bros., Inc., Bklyn., 1978—. Author: (with William Grinker and Don Cooke) Climbing the Job Ladder, 1968, (with Cooke) Upgrading the Work Force, 1971, Manpower Services in the Workplace, 1980. Served with U.S. Army, 1962-65. Office: Coopers & Lybrand 1301 Avenue Of The Americas New York NY 10019-6022

KIRSCH, DONALD, financial consultant, writer; b. N.Y.C., Oct. 9, 1931; s. William and Eva (Wasserman) K.; m. Dorothy Ann Tejw, June 6, 1959; children: Mark Adam, Karen Rebecca Hoffman, Jonathan Bradford. BS, NYU, 1952. Editorial staffer Wall Street Jour., N.Y.C., 1952-53; writer AP, N.Y.C., 1954-55; pres. Wall Street Cons., N.Y.C., 1955—; chmn. Wall St. Group, Calif., Inc., Los Angeles, 1963—; chmn., pres. The Wall Street Group, Inc., N.Y.C., 1959—. Adj. assoc. prof. NYU Grad. Sch. Arts and Sci., 1974-79; founding chmn. Typesetting Products, Inc., Talleres Graficos de Interamericanos, Inc. San Juan, P.R., 1962-80; chmn. Eurofinancing Ltd., 1968; bd. dirs. Co*star Entertainment Inc., MedNet Inc. (chmn. strategic planning com.), Medi-Mail Inc., Dialscan Systems, Audiofidelity Enterprises Inc., Interstate Nat. Dealers Svcs. Inc. Author: FInancial and Economic Journalism: Analysis Interpretation and Reporting, 1978 (Librarians Assn. award 1978), Investor Relations for the Over-the-Counter or Newly Public Company, (with others) The Handbook of Investor Relations; contbr. numerous articles to profl. jours. Trustee Nat. Symphony Orch. of the John F. Kennedy Ctr. for Performing Arts, treas. bd. trustees, 1996-98; trustee Big Bros.; mem. bd. mgrs. Episcopal Social Svcs. N.Y. Mem. N.Y. Soc. Security Analysts, Met. Pres'. Orgn., Young Pres. Orgn. (chmn. met. chpt. 1976-77), Chief Execs. Orgn., Am. Assocs. Royal Acad. Trust (mem. nat. coun.), Econs. Club N.Y., Friar's Club, The Metropolitan (N.Y.C.), Masons. Office: The Wall St Group Inc 32 E 57th St New York NY 10022-2513 E-mail: dkirsch1@aol.com.

KIRSCH, JEFFREY SCOTT, securities executive; b. Chgo., Nov. 11, 1947; s. Norton M. and Estelle (Kaufman) K.; m. Jodi Lynn Spak, May 20, 1985; children: Alexandra J., Jonathan Peter. BSBA, Babson Coll., 1970. Registered securities dealer. V.p. Auto Gard Inc., Chgo., 1970-90; securities dealer Chgo. Bd. Option Exchange, 1973—, mem. arbitration com., 1978-79, mem. system and facilities com., 1980-81, mem. nominating com., 2002—03, mem. lessors com., 2003; pres. Kirsch Inc., Chgo., 1981-99, Fromex One Hour Photo Sys. Chgo., 1990-99. Bd. dirs. Young Men's Jewish Council, Chgo., 1978; mem. New Warrior Chgo., counselor Hales Franciscan H.S., Chgo. Mem.: Automotive Parts and Accessories Assn., Babson Coll. Alumni Com., Pottawattomie Country Club, East Bank Club of Chgo., Standard Club (Chgo.). Avocations: boating, tennis, polo, windsurfing. Home: 442 W Wellington Ave Chicago IL 60657-5804

KIRSCH, LAURENCE STEPHEN, lawyer; b. Washington, July 20, 1957; s. Ben and Bertha (Gomberg) K.; m. Celia Goldman, Aug. 19, 1979; children: Rachel Miriam, Max David. BAS, MS, U. Pa., 1979; JD, Harvard U., 1982. Bar: D.C. 1982, U.S. Ct. Appeals (3d cir.) 1983, (5th cir.) 1997, (9th cir.) 2001, U.S. Dist. Ct. D.C. 1985, U.S. Ct. Appeals (D.C. cir.) 1985, U.S. Supreme Ct. 1987; registered environ. assessor, Calif. 1988. Law clk. to presiding judge Pa. Dist. Ct., Phila., 1982-83; vis. asst. prof. law U. Bridgeport (Conn.) Law Sch. 1983-84; assoc. Cadwalader, Wickersham & Taft, Washington, 1984-90, ptnr. 1991—2002; with Shea Gardner, Washington, 2002—. Chmn. steering coms. Superfund. *Mr. Kirsch is an environmental litigator, counselor and transactional attorney. His litigation victories include three appellate decisions overturning site listings on the National Priorities List, including the first such decision in the history of the Superfund program, and opinions on the interaction of bankruptcy and environmental law. He negotiates with government agencies and private parties, advises on environmental implications of real estate and corporate transactions, and performs environmental assessments. Mr. Kirsch lectures widely on environmental law subjects and taught a law school course on Law, Science and Technology. He was interviewed as an expert in environmental law by CBS News, the MacNeil-Lehrer Report, and numerous radio shows and newspapers.* Editor-in-chief Indoor Pollution Law Report, 1987-91; mng. editor Harvard Environ. Law Rev., 1981-82; contbr. articles to profl. jours. Mem. ABA, Fed. Bar Assn., AAAS, Air and Waste Mgmt. Assn. (indoor air quality com.), Environ. Law Inst., Nat. Inst. Bldg. Scis. (indoor air quality com.), Am. Soc. Testing and Measurement (indoor air quality com.), Phi Beta Kappa. Home: 7212 Longwood Dr Bethesda MD 20817-2122 Office: Shea & Gardner 1800 Massachusetts Ave NW Washington DC 20036 E-mail: lkirsch@sheagardner.com.

KIRSCH, MARILYN, artist; b. Mar. 21, 1950; BFA, Mass. Coll. Art, 1972; MFA, Sch. Mus. Fine Arts, Boston, 1976. One-woman shows include The Germantown Acad. Arts Ctr. Gallery, Ft. Washington, Pa., 1998, Phila. Art Alliance Members' Gallery, 1999, DeBottis Gallery, West Chester, Pa., 1999, 2001, 2003, Akar Arch. & Design, Iowa City, 1999, exhibited in group shows at N.C. Mus. Art, Raleigh, 1975, Inst. Contemporary Art, Boston, 1975, Nielsen Gallery, 1976, Katonah (NY) Gallery, 1977, U. Art Mus., Santa Barbara, Calif., 1978, Bertha Urdang Gallery, NYC, 1978, Jessica Berwind Gallery, Phila., 1987—88, 1990, 1993—94, Phila. Art Alliance, 1988, 1997, 2001, Art in the Armory, Phila., 1990, DeBottis Gallery, West Chester, Pa., 1999—2002, Tufts U. Alumni Exhbn., Medford, Mass., 2001, represented in numerous pvt. and corp. collections. Home and Studio: 10 Park Ave 26K New York NY 10016-4338 E-mail: mkirsch@earthlink.net.

KIRSCH, ROSLYN RUTH, art educator, painter, printmaker; b. N.Y.C., Dec. 30, 1928; d. Harry Morris and Lillian (Zemachson) Friedenberg; m. Louis Kirsch, Dec. 26, 1948; children: Libby Ann, Andrew Lawrence. Student Queens Coll., 1946-48; BA, Hunter Coll., 1950. Art dir. Ladies' Ready-to-Wear Buying Office, N.Y.C., 1948-50; profl. artist, self employed, 1965—; art educator Armory Art Ctr., West Palm Beach, Fla., 1987—, Boca Raton Mus. Art Sch., Boca Raton, Fla., 1990—. One-person shows include J&W Gallery, New Hope, Pa., Capitol Gallery, Tallahassee, Fla., S&W Gallery, New Hope, Pa., Peter Drew Galleries, Fla., Ken Elias, Habitat Gallery, West Palm Beach, Fla., Joel Kessler Gallery, Fla., Indigo Gallery, Fla., Palm Beach Internat. Airport; exhibited in group shows Ann. Hortt Exhbn., Mus. of Art, Ft. Lauderdale, 199[illegible] (award), Nat. Assn. Women Artists, West Palm Beach, 1995 (award), Mus. Art (invitational exhibit), Ft. Lauderdale, 1998, Boca Raton Mus. Art, Fla., 1999; represented in permanent collections including Mus. Art., Ft. Lauderdale, Boca Raton Mus. Art. Recipient Honorable Mention award Mus. Art, Ft. Lauderdale, 1994, others. Mem. Nat. Assn. Women Artists, Boca Raton Mus. Artists Guild, others. Avocations: golf, fundraising. E-mail: kirschfineart@yahoo.com.

KIRSCH, SCOTT DOUGLAS, family practice physician; b. Bronx, N.Y., Nov. 4, 1946; s. Max Milton Kirsch and Linda Paley Sokoloff; m. Bonnie B. Becker; children: Geoffrey Z., Laura G. BA, Queens Coll., 1967; MD, SUNY, Buffalo, 1971. Diplomate Am. Bd. Family Practice. Asst. dir. family practice residency program South Nassau Cmtys. Hosp., Oceanside, NY, 1980—82, dir. 1982—99, dir. dept. family practice, 1989—99, emeritus mem. dept. family practice, 2001—; assoc. dir. family practice residency program Southside Hosp., Bayshore, NY, 1999—. Pres. N.Y. State Acad. Family Physicians, 2001—02; del. to nat. conv. Am. Acad. Family Physicians, 1999—, mem. commn. on continuing med. edn., 2002—. Exec. v.p. Kings Pk. Jewish Ctr. 2001—03. Recipient award for dedication to Hispanic Cmty., Nat. Hispanic Med. Assn., 2002, legis. resolution for disting. svc., N.Y. State Senate, 1999

Avocations: reading history, travel, baseball. Home: 63 Crossbow Ln Commack NY 11725 Office: Southside Hosp 301 E Main St Bay Shore NY 11706 Office Fax: 631-968-3210. E-mail: scottkirsch@optonline.net.

KIRSCH, STEPHEN AUGUSTINE, retired geology educator; b. Lancaster, Pa., Apr. 28, 1939; s. Stephen John and Loretta Genevieve (Tremmel) K. BS in Geology & Mineralogy, Pa. State U., 1961; PhD in Geology, U. Calif., Berkeley, 1968. Asst. prof. geology emeritus San Francisco State U., 1969-89. Vol. geology curator North Mus., Lancaster, Pa., 1993—. Contbr. articles to profl. jours. Mem. Geol. Soc. Am., Planetary Soc., Esmeralda Soc. Avocation: winemaking. Home: 405 Lampeter Rd Lancaster PA 17602-4007

KIRSCH, THORSTEN, cell biologist, educator; s. Heinz and Ingeborg Kirsch; m. Renee Jun Yue, Aug. 17, 2002. PhD, Friedrich-Alexander U., Erlangen, Germany, 1992. Asst. prof. Pa. State Coll. of Medicine, Hershey, 2000—02, assoc. prof. U. Md. Sch. Medicine, Baltimore, 2002—, dir. orthopaedic rsch. Rsch. grant, NIH, 1999, 2003, Arthritis Found., 2003. Mem.: Orthop. Rsch. Soc. (life). Office: Univ Md Sch of Medicine 22 S Greene St Baltimore MD 21201 Office Fax: 410-706-0028. E-mail: tkirsch@umoa.umm.edu.

KIRSCHBAUM, ALAN IRA, air force officer, systems integration specialist; b. Balt., Oct. 3, 1948; s. Marvin and Nadine (Gross) K.; m. Cheryl Louise Demming, Sept. 2, 1984. BME, U. Md., 1971; MBA, N.Mex. Highlands U., 1984; diploma, Def. Systems Mgmt. Coll., Alexandria, Va., 1981, Nat. Def. U., Washington, 1986. Registered profl. engr., Ohio. Commd. 2d lt. U.S. Air Force, 1971, advanced through grades to col., 1993, engine performance analyst aero. systems div., 1971-76, space def. project mgr., space div. L.A., 1976-79, satellite integration mgr., space div., 1979-81, concept devel. br. chief, weapons lab. Albuquerque, 1981-84, advanced systems integration chief, rsch. office Washington, 1985-89; chief seismic systems acquisition div. USAF Tech. Applications Ctr., Melbourne, Fla., 1989-93; dep. dir. Acquisitions Tech. Applications Ctr., Melbourne, Fla., 1991-93; dep. dir. tech. Ballistic Missile Def. Orgn., Washington, 1993-95; dir. systems engring. Space and Missile Systems Ctr. USAF, L.A., 1995—98; program mgr. space sys. and tech. AT&T Govt. Solutions, Santa Barbara, Calif., 1999—. Adviser Program Mgmt. Assistance Group, Dayton, 1981, Launch Readiness Rev., L.A., 1977. Contbr. articles to profl. jours. Big brother, Big Bros. Am., L.A., 1978; judge Internat. Sci./Engring. Fair, L.A., 1978; assoc. Kennedy Ctr. Performing Arts, Washington, 1985; grant evaluation panel United Way Santa Barbara County Cmty., 2001-03. Decorated Legion of Merit. Fellow AIAA (assoc., orgn. rep. 1977-79); mem. ASME, Air Force Assn., Mil. Ops. Rsch. Soc., Bard House Officers Club, Temple Beth Torah Brotherhood, Tau Beta Pi, Pi Tau Sigma, Omicron Delta Kappa. Home: 2102 Fox Den Ct Oxnard CA 93030-7701

KIRSCHBAUM, MYRON, lawyer; b. N.Y.C., Nov. 20, 1949; s. Jonas and Doris (Rose) K.; m. Esther Weiner, June 23, 1971; children: Rachel, Shoshana Stein, Yisrael. BA, Yeshiva U., 1971; JD, Harvard U., 1974. Bar: N.Y. 1975, U.S. Dist. Ct. (so. dist.) N.Y. 1975, U.S. Dist. Ct. (no. dist.) Calif. 1989, U.S. Ct. Appeals (2d cir.) 1975, U.S. Ct. Appeals (9th cir.) 1990, U.S. Ct. Appeals (fed. cir.) 1994, U.S. Ct. Appeals (3d cir.) 2001. Law clk. U.S. Ct. Appeals (2d cir.), N.Y.C., 1974-75; assoc. Kaye, Scholer, Fierman, Hays & Handler, N.Y.C., 1975 82, ptnr., 1983 . Editor Harvard Law Rev., 1972-73, case and comment editor, 1973-74. Mem. ABA, Assn. Bar City N.Y. Office: Kaye Scholer LLP 425 Park Ave New York NY 10022-3506 Business E-Mail: mkirschbaum@kayescholer.com.

KIRSCHENBAUM, HOWARD, educator; b. N.Y.C., Oct. 6, 1944; s. Abraham Irving and Theone (Hamburger) K.; m. Barbara Linell Glaser, Mar. 2, 1972 (div. 1985); 1 child, Kimara Linell; m. Mary M. Rapp, July 30, 1988. BA, New Sch. for Social Rsch., 1966; MS, Temple U., 1968, EdD, 1975. Tchr. Abington (Pa.) H.S., 1966-68, New Lincoln Sch., N.Y.C., 1968-69; instr. Temple U., Phila., 1969-71; exec. dir. Nat. Humanistic Edn. Ctr., Upper Jay, N.Y., 1971-77, Sagamore Inst., Raquette Lake, N.Y., 1977-90; pres. Values Assocs., Rochester, N.Y., 1990-97; prof. Warner Grad. Sch. Edn. U. Rochester, 1997—, chair counseling and human devel. dept., 2000—. Adj. faculty SUNY Brockport, 1992-97; dir. White Pine Camp Mus., Paul Smiths, N.Y., 1994-97. *Considered one of the world's leading authorities on the life and work of pioneer psychologist/psychotherapist Carl R. Rogers (e.g., Roger's biography; co-editor Carl Rogers Reader and Carl Rogers: Dialogues; video "Carl Rogers and The Person-Centered Approach," 2003). Also a leading authority on values and character education.* Author: 100 Ways to Enhance Values and Morality in Schools and Youth Settings, 1995, On Becoming Carl Rogers, 1979; co-author: Values Clarification, 1972, 3rd edit., 1995, 20 others; contbr. articles to profl. jours. Founder, pres. Adirondack Archtl. Heritage, Keeseville, N.Y., 1990-97; former bd. dirs., v.p. Adirondack Nature Conservancy and Land Trust, Keene Valley, N.Y. Mem. ACA, Author's Guild, Assn. Counselor Edn. and Supervision, Character Edn. Partnership, Nat. Eagle Scout Assn. Avocations: hiking, travel, historic preservation. Office: Warner Grad Sch Edn Univ Rochester Rochester NY 14627 E-mail: Howard.Kirschenbaum@rochester.edu.

KIRSCHENFELD, J. J. retired physician, educator; b. Austria, Feb. 8, 1919; came to U.S., 1923; s. Samuel and Helen Kirschenfeld; m. Helen Chapin, Sept. 1944; children: Sherry, Trudy, Debbie, Jeffrey, Kimberly. BS magna cum laude, Bklyn. Coll., 1940; MD, NYU, 1943; DHum (hon.), Huntington Coll., 2000. Diplomate Am. Bd. Internal Medicine, Am. Bd. Family Practice, Nat. Bd. Med. Examiners. Intern Queens Gen. Hosp., Jamaica, N.Y., 1944; resident in medicine USAF Regional Hosp., Montgomery, Ala., 1944-45; tng. as flight surgeon USAF Sch. Aviation Medicine, Randolph Field, Tex., 1945; practice family practice/internal medicine, Ft. Deposit, Ala., 1946-60, gen. internal medicine, Montgomery, 1960-99; prof. medicine U. Ala. Sch. Medicine, Birmingham, 1979-99, assoc. clin. prof. rehab. medicine, 1977-99, assoc. dean for Montgomery affairs Montgomery, 1974-99; ret. from med. practice, 1999; emeritus prof. of medicine U. Ala. Sch. Medicine, Montgomery, 1999—. Chmn., dir. med. edn. Montgomery Area Cmty. Health Scis. Inst., 1972—, prog. dir. UAB Montgomery Internal Med. Residency Prog., 1968-99. Contbr. numerous articles to profl. jours. Capt. USAF, 1944-46. Recipient Alpha Omega Alpha, NYU Med. Sch., 1943, Buford Word award Med. Assn. State of Ala., 1999, Ralph O. Claypoole Meml. awd. of Am. Coll. of Physicians, 1997. Fellow ACP (laureate award Ala. chpt. 1991), Am. Coll. Chest Physicians, Am. Coll. Cardiology; mem. AMA, Ala. Soc. Internal Medicine, Am. Soc. Internal Medicine, Ala. Med. Assn., Montgomery County Med. Soc., Ala. Heart Assn., Ala. Thoracic Soc., Ala. Diabetic Soc., Assn. Program Dirs. in Internal Medicine (program dir. residency program 1968-99). Office: 4371 Narrow Lane Rd Ste 200 Montgomery AL 36116-2975

KIRSCHENMANN, HENRY GEORGE, JR., management consultant, former government official, accountant; b. Bklyn., June 11, 1930; s. Henry Godfrey and Eva Helen (Gellert) Kirschenmann; m. Pam Hirst; children: Victoria Mary, Henry George III, Ronald William. BS, Md. U.; MPA, Am. U. CPA; cert. gov. fin. mgr. Mem. auditor staff Price Waterhouse & Co., Washington; mem. auditor staff U.S. Army Audit Agy.; mem. internal auditor staff Martin-Marietta Co., Orlando, Fla.; various fin. and adminstrv. positions HEW, Washington; dep. asst. sec. HHS, Washington; assoc. cons. Bearing Point, Inc., Tyson's Corner, 1988—. Bd. dirs., assoc. dir. tng. Pub. Svc. Inst., Silver Spring, Md.; exec. dir. Nat. Edn. Inst., Rockville, Md.; instr. Sch. Continuing Edn. U. Va., Fairfax; lectr. in field. Pres. Support Groups, Inc.; dir. Soc. Not for Profit Orgns.and Cmtys., Inc. Recipient Superior Svc. award, HHS, Disting. Svc. award, Presdl. Rank award. Mem.: AICPA, Md. Assn. CPA, Inst. Cost Analysis (bd. dirs. 1981—84), Assn. Govt. Accts. (Recognition of Achievement award 1968, 1972, 1977), Nat. Grants Mgmt. Assn. (bd. dirs., bus. officer 1997—), Soc. rsch. Adminstrs., Pi Alpha Alpha.

KIRSCHNER, BARBARA STARRELS, pediatric gastroenterologist; b. Phila., Mar. 23, 1941; m. Robert H. Kirschner. MD, Women's Med. Coll. Pa., 1967. Diplomate Am. Bd. Pediatrics; cert. in pediatric gastroenterology and nutrition. Intern U. Chgo., 1967-68, resident, 1968-70; mem. staff U. Chgo. Children's Hosp., 1977-83, asst. prof. pediatrics, 1984-88, prof. pediatrics and medicine, 1988—, mem. com. on nutrition and nutritional biology. Contbr. articles to profl. jours. Pediatric Gastroenterology fellow U. Chgo., 1975-77; recipient Davidson award in Pediatric gastroenterology Acad. Pediatrics, 1993, Joseph Brenneman award Chgo. Pediat. Soc., 2001. Mem. Am. Gastroenterologic Assn., N.Am. Soc. Pediatric Gastroenterology, Soc. Pediatric Rsch., Alpha Omega Alpha. Office: U Chgo Med Ctr 5839 S Maryland Ave # MC 4065 Chicago IL 60637-5417

KIRSCHNER, ESTHER GREEN, social worker; b. N.Y.C., Oct. 3, 1928; d. Harry and Rose (Meyerson) Green; m. Stanley Kirschner; children: Susan, Daniel. BA, Bklyn. Coll., 1950; MSW, Simmons Coll., 1952. Lic. clin. social worker, Mich.; lic. marriage and family counselor, Mich.; diplomate Am. Bd. Examiners in Social Work. Clin. social worker Inst. of Juvenile Rsch., Urbana, Ill., 1952-54, Mich. Dept. Social Svcs., Pontiac, 1954, Wayne State U., Detroit, 1956-58, Oakland Child Guidance Clinic, Birmingham, Mich., 1958-72, Children's Ctr., Detroit, 1972-74, Bloomfield Hills (Mich.) Schs., 1975-91. Lectr. on learning disabilities and problems relating to depression, 1965—; part-time clin. social worker in pvt. practice. NIMH scholar, 1951—. Fellow: Am. Orthopsychiat. Assn.; mem.: NASW, DCSW, ACSW, Oakland County Sch. Social Workers (pres. 1986—87), Mich. Clin. Social Work Soc. (bd. dirs. Detroit chpt. 1985—92). Avocations: swimming, bicycling, folk dancing, traveling. Home: 25615 Parkwood Dr Huntington Woods MI 48070-1424 E-mail: skirsch@sun.science.wayne.edu.

KIRSCHNER, KENNETH HAROLD, lawyer; b. Bklyn., Dec. 1, 1953; s. Samuel and Stella K.; m. Andrea Chase, Feb. 8, 1997. BS, Cornell U., 1975; JD, NYU, 1978, LLM, 1981. Bar: N.Y. 1979, U.S. Ct. Appeals (2d, 5th and D.C. cirs.), 1979, U.S. Dist. Ct. (so. and ea. dists.) N.Y., 1979, U.S. Supreme Ct. 1982. Assoc. Kelley Drye & Warren, N.Y.C., 1978-82, Breed Abbott & Morgan, N.Y.C., 1982-86, ptnr., 1986-93, Kelley Drye & Warren LLP, N.Y.C., 1993—. Adj. asst. prof. mgmt. NYU, 1988—. Contbr. articles to profl. jours. Office: Kelley Drye & Warren 101 Park Ave Fl 30 New York NY 10178-0062

KIRSCHNER, PHILIP, lawyer; b. Phila., July 11, 1952; s. Herbert and Ruchel Kirschner; m. Janet C. Kirschner, Aug. 8, 1973. BA, Am. U., Washington, 1973; JD, Rutgers U., 1976. Bar: N.J., Pa.; cert. assn. exec. Dir. govt. rels. N.J. Assn. of Sch. Adminstrs., Trenton, 1977-81; exec. dir., legis. counsel N.J. State Bar Assn., New Brunswick, 1981-88; dir. govt. rels. N.J. Sch. Bd. Assn., Trenton, 1988-90; sr. exec. v.p., 1st v.p. N.J. Bus. Industry Assn., Trenton, 1990—. Vice chair zoning bd. of adjustment Morristown, N.J., 1993-97; mem. N.J. Commn. on Holocaust Edn., 1990—; mem. Leadership N.J., 1993. Mem. N.J. Soc. of Assn. Execs. (bd. dirs.), N.J. State Bar Assn., Am. Soc. of Assn. Execs., Camden County Bar Assn. Office: NJ Bus and Industry Assn 102 W State St Trenton NJ 08608-1102 E-mail: pkirschner@njbia.org.

KIRSCHNER, RICHARD MICHAEL, naturopathic physician, speaker, writer; b. Cin., Sept. 27, 1949; s. Alan George and Lois (Dickey) K.; 1 child, Aden Netanya; m. Lindea Bowe. BS in Human Biology, Kans. Newman Coll., 1979; D in Naturopathic Medicine, Nat. Coll. Naturopathic Medicine, 1981. Vice pres. D. Kirschner & Son, Inc., Newport, Ky., 1974-77; co-owner, mgr. Sunshine Ranch Arabian Horses, Melbourne, Ky., 1975 77; pvt. practice Portland, Oreg., 1981-83, Ashland, Oreg., 1983—. Seminar leader, trainer Inst. for Meta-Linguistics, Portland, 1981-84; cons. Nat. Elec. Contractors Assn., So. Oreg., 1985-86, United Telephone N.W., 1986; spkr. Ford Motor Co., Blue Cross-Blue Shield, Balfour Corp., NEA, AT&T, Triad Sys., Supercuts, 1986-89, Hewlett-Packard, Pepsi Co., George Bush Co., 1990-91, Goodwill Industries Am., Motorola, 1992, The Homestead T.V.A., Federated Ambulatory Surg. Assn., V.H.A. Satellite Broadcast, 1993, Oreg. Dept. Edn., Anaheim Meml. Hosp., 1994, Inc. 500 Conf., U.S. C. of C., Inst. Indsl. Engrs., 1995, EDS, ASFSA, Safeco Ins., Fairfax County, Va.; spkr., trainer Careertrack Seminars, Boulder, Colo., 1986-93; owner, spkr., trainer R & R Prodns., Ashland, Oreg., 1984-2001. Co-author: (audio tape) How to Deal with Difficult People, 1987, (video tape), 1988; (CD-Rom) The Leadership Series: Difficult People, 1997, Living Your Life by Design, 2003; author: (audio tape) How to Find and Keep a Mate, 1988; (video tape) How to Find a Mate, 1990, The Happiness of Pursuit, 1994, How to Deal with Difficult People, Vol. II, 1992; (book) Dealing With People You Can't Stand, 1994, 2d edit., 2002, Digital Publishing on e World, Discussions of Problem People and Happiness, 1995, Life By Design, 1999, Dealing with Relatives, 2002; (7 vol. video) Telecare: Exceptional Service on the Phone, 1998. Spokesman Rogue Valley PBS, 1986, 87. Mem.: Am. Assn. Naturopathic Physicians (bd. dirs. 1995—2000, chmn. pub. affairs 1989—93, webmaster 1996—2000), Wilderness Soc. Office: Talk Natural Prodns PO Box 896 Ashland OR 97520-0030

KIRSCHNER, ROD, secondary education educator; b. St. Joseph, Mo., May 1, 1949; s. Jasper Jordan and Betty June (Newman) K.; m. Lelia Jane Huff, July 25, 1981; children: Bryce, Matthew, Rodney II. BA, Coll. of Emporia, 1972; MS, Northwest Mo. State U., 1977. Cert. secondary tchr., Ohio, Mo., Ky., Kans. Dir. high sch. rels. So. Ohio Coll., Cin.; asst. basketball coach St. Mary of Plains Coll., Dodge City, Kans.; tchr., Am. history, head basketball coach Dodge City Sr. High Sch.; tchr., basketball/soccer coach Summit County Day Boys Middle Sch., Cin.; tchr., dept. chair history and social studies, head basketball coach Beechwood High Sch., Ft. Mitchell, Ky., 1990-94; head basketball coach Horton H.S., 1994-2000; phys. edn. tchr. Everest Mid. Sch., Horton, M.S., 1995-2000; head basketball coach, health tchr., tech. asst. Nickerson (Kans.) H.S., 2000—. Head track coach Horton H.S., 1997-99; conducted basketball camps in Antwerp, Ronse, Belgium, 1999, 2000; owner Rocket Enterprises. Contbr. to 40 Winning Strategies by 40 Winning Coaches. Mem. ASCD, NEA, AAHPERD, Nat. Assn. Basketball Coaches, Nat. Fedn. Interscholastic Coaches Assn., Kans. Coaches Assn., Kans. Edn. Assn., Kans. Assn. Health, Phys. Edn., Recreation, and Dance, Kans. Basketball Coaches Assn., KC, Lions Internat. (past pres.). Office: 305 S Nickerson St Nickerson KS 67561 E-mail: rocketet@cox.net., rkirschner@usd309.k12.ks.us.

KIRSCHNER, RONALD ALLEN, osteopathic plastic surgeon, otolaryngologist, educator; b. N.Y.C., Jan. 18, 1942; s. Hyman C. and Eleanor (Pinkus) K.; m. Olivia Barbara Schlesinger, June 27, 1964; children: Andrew Scott, Julie Renee. AB, NYU, 1962; DO, Phila. Coll. Osteo. Medicine, 1966, MS in Otolaryngology, 1972. Diplomate Am. Osteo. Bd. Otolaryngology. Intern LeRoy Hosp., N.Y.C., 1966-67; resident Grandview Hosp., Dayton, Ohio, 1967-68, Phila. Coll. Osteo. Medicine, 1970-72, asst. prof., 1972-74, assoc. prof., 1974-76, clin. assoc. prof., 1976-85, clin. prof., 1985-90, prof., chmn. dept. otolaryngology, bronchoesophalogy and facial plastic surgery, 1990-92, dir. emerging tech., 1992—; pvt. practice in plastic, otolaryngology and laser surgery Bala Cynwyd, Pa., 1976—. Dir. neurosensory unit, 1973-76; chmn. laser surgery City Ave. Hosp., Grad. Health System, 1994—; NIH fellow Armed Forces INst. Pathology, Washington, 1971; attending physician Grad. Hosp., 1991—, Suburban Gen. Hosp., chief ear, nose, and throat and plastic surgery, 1976-96, chmn. divsn. surgery, 1983-89, exec. com., 1983-89; attending physician, cons. Del. Valley Med. Ctr., 1985-92, Presbyn.-U. Pa. Med. Ctr., 1987—, Hosp. of Phila. Coll. Osteo. Medicine, chmn. laser and endoscopy com., 1987-89, 91—, mem. exec. com., 1990-92; v.p., chief med. adv. Courtlandt Group, 1979-85, exec. v.p., 1985-86, also dir. rsch. and edn., 1986; otolaryngologist Pa. Hearing Assn., 1986—; preceptor Xanar Laser Divsn., Johnson & Johnson, 1982; design cons. Philling Inc., 1982-87, Inframed Inc., 1985-97, Sigma Dynamics Inc., Rhein Med., Inc., 1988-97; otologic cons. Children's Hearing Aid Bank; pres. Kirschner Design Group, Inc., 1987—; bd. dirs. KDG-Rotem U.S.A., Pa. Acad. Cosmetic Surgery; dir. head and neck YAG laser protocol Cooper Lasersonics, 1983-88; chmn. med. symposium Internat. Conf. on Applied Laser Electro Optics, 1986, 87, 91; session chair Medtech '89, Freie Univ., Berlin, 1989; vis. prof. internat. sch. for quantum electronics Etore Majorana Nato, Ericc, Sicily, 1990; cons. Bur. Vocat. Rehab., Imunodiagnostics Lab., Allergy Mgmt. Systems Inc., dir. 1st World Congress on Cosmetic Laser Surgery, 1992; workshop dir. Internat. Conf. on Occuloplastic Surgery, 1995. Med. editor Med. Portfolio, 1980-85; guest editor Surg. Clinics of N.Am., 1984; monthly columnist Photonics Spectra, 1987-91; contbg. editor Photonics Spectra, 1988-94; med. editl. bd. Pa. Osteo. Med. Jour., Laurin Publs., 1987-94, Laser Applications; contbr. articles to med. jours., chpts. in med. texts; developer various med. instruments. Served with M.C., USN, 1968-70; lt. comdr. Res. Recipient award for disting. tchg. Lindbach Found., 1973, Legion of Honor, Chapel of Four Chaplains, 1982; Survivor of Yr. award, 1984; named Disting. Practitioner Am. Acads. of Practice. Fellow Pan Am. Allergy Assn., Phila. Acad. Facial Plastic Surgery, Phila. Laryngologic Soc., Phila. Coll. Physicians, Am. Soc. Lasers in Medicine and Surgery, Am. Auditory Soc., Am. Acad. Otolaryngology-Head and Neck Surgery, Soc. Ear, Nose, and Throat Advances in Children, Am. Acad. Facial Plastic Surgery (assoc.), Soc. Photo Optical Engrs., Osteo. Coll. Ophthalmology and Otorhinolaryngology, Am. Acad. Cosmetic Surgery; mem. AMA, Am. Osteo. Assn. (editl. cons. Jour. 1977—, editl. referee 1980—), Am. Soc. Esthetic and Reconstructive Surgery, Pa. Med. Soc., Pa. Acad. Otolaryngology, Pa. Acad. Cosmetic Surgery (bd. dirs. 1990—), Internat. Soc. Cosmetic Plastic Surgeons (bd. dirs. 1990-94), Internat. Soc. Cosmetic Plastic Surgery, Philadelphia County Osteo. Med. Assn. (chair laser com.), Centurian Club of Deafness Rsch. Found., Internat. Assn. Logopedics and Phoniatrics, Midwestern Biolaser Inst., Inst. for Applied Laser Surgery (pres.), Pa. Osteo. Med. Assn. (chmn. com. otolaryngology 1984-88, 90-92, chmn. com. promotion of rsch. 1985-88), Am. Acad. Osteopathy Survivors Club of Phila. Coll. Osteo. Medicine (pres. 1981-82), Internat. Soc. for Optical Engring., AAAS, AMA, Acad. Surg. Rsch., N.Y. Acad. Scis., Am. Soc. Liposuction Surgery, Laser Assn. Am. (sec. 1985-88), Laser and Electro Optics Mfs. Assn., Am. Assn. Advancement Med. Instrumentation, Am. Soc. Cosmetic Surgeons, Pa. Hearing Aid Soc. (otologist), Pa. Am. Assn. Otolaryngology and Bronchoesophagology, Pa. Acad. Ophthalmology and Otolaryngology, Pa. Osteo. Med. Soc. (chmn. com. otolaryngology 1984-88, 90—, chmn. med. adv. bd.), Del Valley Tinnitus Assn., Laser Inst. Am. (sr. Outstanding Svc. award 1986, chmn. lasers 1987-89, bd. dirs. 1989—, dir., chmn. com. on biology and medicine 1989-92), Pa. Acad. Cosmetic Surger (bd. dirs.), Am. Acad. Cosmetic Laser Surgery (bd. dirs. 1991-94), Pa. Med. Soc., Montgomery County Med. Soc., Variety Club, NYU Club, Vesper Club, Pickwick Club of Phila., Masons, Shriners, Sigma Xi, Sigma Chi, Lambda Omicron Gamma (pres. 1981-82), Disting. Svc. award Caduceus chpt. 1982). Jewish. Office: 2 Bala Cynwyd Plz Ste 17il Bala Cynwyd PA 19004

KIRSCHNER, STANLEY, chemist; b. N.Y.C., Dec. 17, 1927; s. Abraham and Rebecca K.; m. Esther Green, June 11, 1950; children— Susan Joyce, Daniel Ross. BS magna cum laude, Bklyn. Coll., 1950; AM, Harvard U., 1952; PhD, U. Ill., 1954. Research chemist Monsanto Chem. Co., Everett, Mass., 1951; teaching asst. in chemistry Harvard U., 1950-52, U. Ill., Urbana, 1952-54; mem. faculty dept. chemistry Wayne State U., Detroit, 1954—, prof., 1960—, prof. emeritus, 1992—. Vis. prof. U. London, 1963-64, U. Florence, Italy, 1976, U. Sao Paulo, Brazil, 1969, Tohoku U., Sendai, Japan, 1978, Tech. U. Lisbon, Portugal, 1984, U. Porto, Portugal, 1984 Author: Advances in the Chemistry of Coordination Compounds, 1961, Coordination Chemistry, 1969, Inorganic Syntheses, Vol. 23, 1985; contbr. articles to profl. jours. Served with USN, 1945-46. Recipient Pres.'s award for excellence in teaching Wayne State U., 1979, Gold award Engring. Soc. of Detroit, 1995, Heyrovsky medal Czechoslovak Acad. Scis., 1978, Catalyst award in chem. edn. Chem. Mfrs. Assn., 1984, Faculty Svc. award Wayne State U. Alumni Assn., 1986; fellow Fulbright Found., 1963-64, NSF, 1963-64, Ford Found., 1969-70. Fellow AAAS, Am. Inst. Chemists, N.Y. Acad. Scis.; mem. AAUP, Am. Chem. Soc. (chmn. divsn. edn., bd. dirs. 1985-93, Henry Hill award 1995, Brazilian Acad. Scis., Internat. Conf. Coordination Chemistry (permanent sec. 1966-89, emeritus 1990), Internat. Union Pure and Applied Chemistry (com. nomenclature of inorganic chemistry 1991-93), Chem. Soc. Chile (hon.), Chem. Soc. (London). Home: 25615 Parkwood Dr Huntington Woods MI 48070-1424 Office: Dept Chemistry Wayne State Univ Detroit MI 48202

KIRSCHSTEIN, RUTH LILLIAN, physician; b. Bklyn., Oct. 12, 1926; d. Julius and Elizabeth (Berm) Kirschstein; m. Alan S. Rabson, June 11, 1950; 1 child, Arnold. BA magna cum laude, L.I. U., 1947; MD, Tulane U., 1951, LLD, PhD, Tulane U., 1997; DSc (hon.), Mt. Sinai Sch. Medicine, 1984; LLD, Atlanta U., 1985; DSc (hon.), Med. Coll. Ohio, 1986; LHD (hon.), L.I. U., 1991; PhD (hon.), U. Rochester Sch. Medicine, 1998, Brown U., 1999; DSc (hon.), Spelman Coll., 2001, Georgetown U., 2001. Intern Kings County Hosp., Bklyn., 1951-52; resident pathology VA Hosp., Atlanta, Providence Hosp., Detroit, Clin. Ctr., NIH, Bethesda, Md., 1952-57; fellow Nat. Heart Inst. Tulane U., 1953-54; asst. dir. div. biologics standards NIH, 1971-72; dep. dir. Bur. Biologics, FDA, 1972-73, dep. assoc. commr. sci., 1973-74; dir. Nat. Inst. Gen. Med. Scis., 1974-93; acting assoc. dir. woman's health NIH, Bethesda, 1974-93, acting dir., 1993, 2000—, dep. dir., 1993—, acting dir., 2000. Chmn. grants peer rev. study team NIH; mem. Inst. Medicine NAS, 1982—; co-chair, sec. Spl. Emphasis Oversight com. on Sci. and Tech., 1989—; mem. Office Tech. Assessment Adv. Com. on Basic Rsch., 1989—; co-chair PHS Coordinating Com. on Women's Health Issues, 1990—. Recipient Superior Svc. award, 1980, 1993, Presdl. Disting. Exec. Rank award, 1985, 1995, Pub. Svc. award, Fedn. Am. Soc.s Exptl. Biology, 1993, Nat. Pub. Svc. award, Am. Pub. Adminstrn./Nat. Acad. Pub. Adminstrn., 1994, Roger W. Jones award for exec. leadership, Am. U., 1994, Georgeanna Seegar Jones Women's Health Lifetime Achievement award, 1995, Albert Sabin Hero of Sci. award, 2000, Women Achievement award, Anti-Defamation League, 2001, J. Richard Nesson award, Harvard Med. Sch., 2002, Pub. Svc. award, Am. Soc. for Biochemistry and Molecular Biology, 2003. Mem.: NAS-IOM, AMA (Dr. Nathan Davis award 1990), Am. Acad. Arts and Scis., Am. Acad. Microbiology, Am. Assn. Pathologists, Am. Assn. Immunologists. Home: 6 West Dr Bethesda MD 20814-1510 Office: NIH 1 Center Dr Msc 0148 Rm 158 Bethesda MD 20892-0001 E-mail: rk25n@nih.gov.

KIRSH, HERB, state legislator; b. N.Y.C., May 17, 1929; s. Isadore and Yetta K.; m. Sue Kirsh; children: Mike, Kevin. BA with honors, Duke U., 1949. With Kirsh's Dept. Store, Clover, S.C., 1949-95; mayor pro tem Clover, S.C., 1971-75; mayor, 1975-79; mem. S.C. Ho. of Reps., 1979—; mem. several coms. Chmn. bd. Clover Cmty. Bank. Past pres. Clover C. of C.; tchr. Sunday Sch. With USNR, 2 yrs. With USNR, 1949—50. Named Clover Man of Yr., 1976, S.C. Legislator of Yr. S.C. County Govts., 1994, S.C. Firemen's Assn., 1994, Legislator of Yr. S.C. Recreation and Park Assn., 1989; recipient Disting. Svc. award S.C. Mcpl. Assn., 1985, Legis. award S.C. Commn. on Alcohol and Drug Abuse, 1985, Leadership award S.C. State Office Adult Edn., 1987, Svc. award Carolina Men's Apparel Club, 1992, S.C. Assn. Taxpayers, 1993, Svc. and Leadership award Carolina and Va. Fashion Exhibitors Inc., 1989. Mem. Clover Jaycees (charter), Clover Optimists (charter), Clover Rotary (charter), Mason, Shriners, Lions (nat. del.). Office: SC Ho of Reps PO Box 31 Clover SC 29710-0031

KIRSH, MICHAEL ALAN, financial estate planner; b. Bklyn., Aug. 3, 1952; s. Lawrence and Pauline (Goldberg) K.; m. Marcia Beth Fabrikant, Sept. 11, 1976; children: Jordana Erin, Ross Morgan. Grad. high sch., Bklyn. CFP; CLU; accredited estate planner. Prin. Kirsh Fin. Svcs., Inc., N.Y.C., 1978—. Mem. Nat. Assn. Estate Planners, Nat. Assn. Ins. and Fin. Advisors, Fin. Planning Assn., Soc. Fin. Svc. Profls., Assn. Advanced Life Underwriting, Million Dollar Roundtable (Honor Roll, Top of the Table award), The Internat. Forum. Republican. Jewish. Avocations: tennis, skiing, reading. Office: 21 E 40th St New York NY 10016 0501 E-mail: mkirsh@highland.com.

KIRSHBAUM, HOWARD M. retired judge, arbiter; b. Oberlin, Ohio, Sept. 19, 1938; s. Joseph and Gertrude (Morris) K.; m. Priscilla Joy Parmakian, Aug. 15, 1964; children— Audra Lee, Andrew William. BA, Yale U., 1960; AB, Cambridge U., 1962, MA, 1966; LL.B., Harvard U., 1965. Ptnr. Zarlengo and Kirshbaum, Denver, 1969-75; judge Denver Dist. Ct., Denver, 1975-80, Colo. Ct. Appeals, Denver, 1980-83; justice Colo. Supreme Ct., Denver, 1983-97; arbiter Jud. Arbiter Group, Inc., Denver, 1997—, sr. judge, 1997—; adj. prof. law U. Denver, 1970—. Dir. Am. Law Inst. Phila., 1982-2002, Am. Judicature Soc., Chgo., 1979-2002, Colo. Jud. Inst. Denver, 1979-89; pres. Colo. Legal Care Soc., Denver, 1974-75. Bd. dirs. Young Artists Orch., Denver, 1976-85; pres. Community Arts Symphony, Englewood, Colo., 1972-74; dir. Denver Opportunity, Inc., Denver, 1972-74; vice-chmn. Denver Council on Arts and Humanities, 1969 Mem.: ABA (standing com. pub. edn. 1996—2001), Soc. Profls. in Dispute Resolution, Denver Bar Assn. (trustee 1981—83), Colo. Bar Assn. Avocation: music performance. Office: Jud Arbiter Group Inc 1601 Blake St Ste 400 Denver CO 80202-1328

KIRSHBAUM, JON ALAN, information systems consultant, retired educational administrator; b. L.A., Nov. 5, 1942; s. George Alexander and Mary Elizabeth (Ball) K.; m. Anne Nofrey, Aug. 11, 1961 (div.); 1 child, Warren Ashley (dec.); m. Linda Louise Carl, Dec. 15, 1976; stepchildren: Gary Nicholas, Grant Adam. BS in Comprehensive Mktg., No. Ill. U., 1965, MBA in Fin., 1971, postgrad., 1988-93; MDiv, McCormick Theol. Seminary, Chgo., 1980. Cert. chief sch. bus. ofcl. IRD sales/DPD br. office adminstr. IBM Corp., Chgo., 1965-67, systems analyst/sr. assoc. planner Endicott, N.Y., 1967-71; seminary asst. Lincoln Park Presbyn. Ch., Chgo., 1972-73; team/project leader Chgo. Pub. Schs., 1974-89, data base adminstr., 1989-92, supr. desktop pub.,

1992-94, core team mem., Time re-engring. project, 1994-95; project leader Info. Technologies, Chgo., 1995-96; prin. cons. Keane, Inc., Lisle, Ill., 1996-99; sr. analyst Mantiss a Dynegy Co., Chgo., 2000-2001. Freelance travel writer and editor, 1998—. Mng. editor: Today's Traveler Mag., Chgo., 1991-92, exec. editor/v.p. mktg., 1992-97. Mem. DuPage Art League, DuPage County (Ill.) Handweavers Guild of Am., Geneal. Soc. (bd. dirs. 1986-89, pres. 1989-90), DuPage County Hist. Soc., Glen Ellyn (Ill.) Hist. Soc., Morton Arboretum, Salem (Ohio) Hist. Soc., Project Mgmt. Inst. (Chicagoland chpt.), Soc. Profl. Journalists, Chgo. Headline Club, N.Am. Travel Journalists Assn. (regional v.p. 1993-94), East West News Bur. Internat., Vernon County (Mo.) Hist. Soc., U.S. Lighthouse Soc., New Dungeness Light Sta. Assn., Preservation Soc. of Newport County, Rainshadow Natural Sci. Found., Friends of Port Angeles Fine Arts Ctr., The Wheaton History Ctr., Near East Archaeol. Soc., Nat. Trust Historic Preservation, Orgn. Mondiale de la Press Périodique Republican. Presbyterian. Avocations: fishing, genealogy, travel, weaving. E-mail: jon_kirshbaum@usa.net.

KIRSHBAUM, LAURENCE J. book publishing executive; Degree, U. Mich., 1966. Reporter Newsweek Mag., Detroit and San Francisco, 1966—69; asst. sales mgr. Random House, 1970—74; dir. mktg. Ballantine Books, 1970—74; from v.p. mktg. to pres. Warner Books, Warner Pub. Svcs., 1974—82; v.p., circulation dir. Conde Nast Pubs., 1982—83; pub., COO Warner Books, 1983—84, pres., 1984—95, chmn., 1996—. Co-author: Is the Library Burning?, 1970. Office: Warner Books Inc 1271 Avenue Of The Americas New York NY 10020-1300

KIRSHENBAUM, RICHARD IRVING, public health physician; b. Bklyn., Aug. 19, 1933; s. Joseph and Anne (Hantman) K.; m. Jean Shicher, Aug. 17, 1957; children: Miriam, Susan, Rachel. AB, Temple U., 1955; DO, Phila. Coll. Osteo. Medicine, 1959; MPH, Columbia U., 1971. Diplomate Am. Bd. Preventive Medicine. Resident intern Met. Hosp., Phila., 1959-60; pvt. practice medicine Bklyn., 1960-70; resident in pub. health N.Y.C. Dept. Health, 1970-73, pub. health physician, 1973-81, regional health dir. for Queens County, 1977-80, chief epidemiologist for Manhattan Borough, 1980-81; pub. health physician N.Y. State Dept. Health, N.Y.C., 1981-98; retired, 1998. Contbr. articles to profl. jours. Lt. col. Med. Corps N.Y. Army NG, 1981-91, USAR, 1991-93. Recipient Physician's Recognition award AMA 1973, 76, 79, 82, 85, 88, 90, 93, 96, 98. Home: 313 Whitman Dr Brooklyn NY 11234-6935 E-mail: bd67124@optonline.net.

KIRSHNER, HOWARD S, neurologist, medical educator; b. Bryn Mawr, Pa., July 11, 1946; s. Jacob Joseph and Estelle Varbalow Kirshner; m. Carol Adams, July 27, 1969; children: Joshua, Jode. BA, Williams Coll., Williamstown, MA, 1964—68; MD, Harvard Medical Sch., Boston, MA, 1968—72. Prof. and vice-chmn. Vanderbilt U. Sch. of Med., Nashville, 1978—. Dir. Vanderbilt Stroke Ctr., Nashville; prof. & vice chmn./dept. of neurology Vanderbilt Med. Ctr., Nashville; program dir. Vanderbilt Stadium Rshab. Hosp., Nashville. Mem. Am. Heart Assoc., Nat. MS Soc., Nat. Assoc. Lt. Comdr. USN, 1973—75. Named one of Alpha Omega Alpha, 1972, Phi Beta Chi, 1968. Home: 4616 Chalmers Dr Nashville TN 37215 Office: Nashville Univ Med Ctr 2100 Pierce Ave Nashville TN 37212

KIRSNER, JOSEPH BARNETT, physician, educator; b. Boston, Sept. 21, 1909; s. Harris and Ida (Waiser) K.; m. Minnie Schneider, Jan. 6, 1934; 1 son, Robert S. MD, Tufts U., 1933; PhD in Biol. Scis., U. Chgo., 1942; DSc (hon.), Tufts U., 1993. Intern Woodlawn Hosp., Chgo., 1933—34, resident in internal medicine, 1934—35; asst. in medicine U. Chgo., 1935—37, from asst. prof. to assoc. prof., 1937—51, prof., 1951—, Louis Block Disting. Service prof. medicine, 1968—, chief of staff, also dep. dean for med. affairs, 1971—76. Cons. NIH, 1956-69; hon. pres. Gastrointestinal Research Found., 1961— ; mem. drug efficacy adv. com. to NRC; chmn. adv. group Nat. Commn. on Digestive Diseases, 1978; chmn. emeritus sci. adv. com. Nat. Found. Ileitis and Colitis. Editor, author: Inflammatory Bowel Disease, 5th edit., 1999, The Growth of Gastroenterologic Knowledge During the 20th Century, 1994, Early Days of American Gastroenterology, 1996; contbr. more than 735 articles to profl. publs. Served with M.C. AUS, 1943-46, ETO; PTO. Recipient Julius Friedenwald medal disting. work gastroenterology, 1975, Horatio Alger award, 1979, hon. Gold Key for Disting. Service U. Chgo. Med. Alumni Assn., 1979, Alumni medal U. Chgo. Alumni Assn., 1989, Disting. Educator award Am. Gastroenterological Assn., 1999; Joseph B. Kirsner award for excellence in rsch. in clin. gastroenterology established in his honor, Am. Gastroent. Assn., 1990; G. Brohée lectr. World Cong. Gastroenterology, 1994, Laureate award Lincoln Acad. Ill. Mem. Am. Assn. Physicians, ACP (master, John Phillips award), Am. Gastroent. Assn. (past pres., governing bd.), Am. Gastroscopic Soc. (past pres.), Am. Soc. Gastrointestinal Endoscopy (past pres., Rudolf Schindler award), Am. Soc. Clin. Investigation, Ctrl. Soc. Clin. Rsch., Chgo. Soc. Internal Medicine (past pres.), Inst. Medicine Chgo. (George H. Coleman medal) Achievements include rsch. in gastrointestinal disorders, inflammatory disease of gastrointestinal tract. Home: 5805 S Dorchester Ave Chicago IL 60637-1730 Office: U Chgo Med Ctr 5841 S Maryland Ave Chicago IL 60637-1470 *We need a return to higher standards, personally and professionally. Striving for personal excellence and achievement promotes universal excellence and peace.*

KIRST, MICHAEL WEILE, education educator, researcher; b. Westreading, Pa., Aug. 1, 1939; s. Russell and Marian (Weile) K.; m. Wdndy Burdsall, Sept. 6, 1975; children: Michael, Anne. AB summa cum laude, Dartmouth Coll., 1961; MPA, Harvard U., 1963, PhD, 1964. Budget examiner U.S. Bur. Budgets, Office of Edn., Washington, 1964-64; assoc. dir. President's comsn. on White House fellows Nat. Adv. Coun. on Edn. Disadvantaged Children, Washington, 1966; dir. program planning and evaluation Bur. Elem. and Secondary Edn., U.S. Office Edn., Washington, 1967; staff dir. U.S. Senate Subcommittee Manpower, Employment and Poverty, Washington, 1968-69; with Ca. State Bd. Edn., Sacramento, 1975-77, pres., 1977-81; prof. edn. Stanford (Calif.) U., 1969—. Prin. investigator Policy Analysis for Calif. Edn., Berkeley, 1984—, Ctr. Policy Rsch. in Edn., Rutgers U., Stanford U., Mich. State U., 1984—, Reform Up Close, 1988-92; chmn. bd. comparative studies in edn. U.S. Nat. Acad. Scis., 1994—. Author: Government Without Passing Laws, 1969, (with Frederick Wirt) The Political Web of American Schools, 1972, (with Joel Berke) Federal Aid to Education: Who Governs, Who Benefits, 1972, State School Finance Alternatives, 1975, (with others) Contemporary Issues in Education: perspectives from Australia and U.S.A., 1983, (with others) Who Controls Our Schools: American Values in Conflict, 1984, (with Frederick Wirt) Schools in Conflict: Political Turbulence in American Education, 1982, 3d edit., 1992, Political Dynamic of American Education, 2001, Betraying the College Dream, 2003; editor: The Politics of Education at the Local, State, and Federal Levels, 1970, State, School and Politics, 1972; author numerous monographs; contbr. numerous articles to profl. jours., newspapers and mags. Pres. Calif. State Bd. Edn., Sacramento, 1977-80. Mem. NAS (chmn. bd. international comparative studies in edn.), Nat. Acad. Edn., Am. Edn. Rsch. Assn. (v.p.), Internat. Acad. Edn., Phi Beta Kappa. Office: Stanford U Sch Edn MC 3096 Stanford CA 94305

KIRST-ASHMAN, KAREN KAY, social work educator; b. Milw., Dec. 29, 1950; d. Gary A. and Ruth G. Kirst; m. Nicolas H. Ashman, June 5, 1982. BA in Social Work, U. Wis., 1972, MS in Social Work, 1973; PhD, U. Ill., 1983. Lic. ind. clin. social worker Wis. Social worker Curative Workshop, Milw., 1973-75; pvt. therapist Juneau Acad. Residential Treatment Ctr., Milw., 1975-76; social work therapist Juneau Acad. Day Svcs., Milw., 1975-76, social svc. dir., 1976-77, asst. dir., 1977-78; teaching asst. U. Ill. Sch. Social Work, Urbana-Champaign, 1978-80; prof. U. Wis., Whitewater, 1980—, coord. sexual harassment awareness program, 1983-85, chairperson women's studies dept., 1985-88, chairperson social work dept., 1988-91. Mem. bd. Coun. on Social Work Edn., 1998—2001. Author: Understanding Human Behavior and the Social Environment, 1987, 5th edit., 2000, Understanding Generalist Practice, 1993, 3d edit., 2002, Generalist Practice with Organizations and Communities, 1997, 2d edit., 2001, The Macro Skills Workbook, 1998, 2d edit., 2000, Human Behavior, Communities, Organizations, and Groups in the Macro Social Environment, 2000, Introduction to Social Work and Social Welfare: Critical Thinking Perspectives, 2003; mem. editl. bd. Affilia: Jour. Women and Social Work, 1990—96. Mem.: NASW, Wis. Coun. Social Work Edn. (exec. bd. mem. 1989—), Coun. on Social Work Edn., Acad. Cert. Social Workers (bd. dirs.). Home: 4945 Riverside Rd Waterford WI 53185-3329 Office: U Wis Social Work Dept Whitewater WI 53185

KIRSTEIN, PHILIP LAWRENCE, lawyer, investment company executive; b. N.Y.C., May 29, 1945; s. Paul H. and Marie (Erdreich) Kirstein. AB, U. N.C., 1967; JD, U. Syracuse, 1973; LLM in Taxation, NYU, 1974. Bar: N.Y. 1974, Fla. 1974. Assoc Townley & Updike, N.Y.C., 1974—80; atty. Merrill Lynch Asset Mgmt., LP, N.Y.C., 1980—83, v.p., 1983—84, sr. v.p., gen. counsel, 1984—98; gen. counsel Merrill Lynch Asset Mgmt. Group, 1998—. Mem. Mercer County Dem. Com., 1992—97; bd. dirs. N.J. Race for the Cure, 1996—, Jug Tavern Sparta, Inc., ICI Mutual Ins. Co.; mem. Zoning Bd. Appeals, Ossining, NY, 1983—85, N.Y.-N.J. Trail Conf., N.Y.C., 1978—82. Served to capt. USNR, 1967—94. Mem.: Assn. Bar City N.Y., Fla. Bar Assn., ABA. Democrat. Jewish. Home: 71 Brooks Bnd Princeton NJ 08540-7554 Office: 800 Scudders Mill Rd PO Box 9011 Princeton NJ 08543-9011

KIRSTEUER, ERNST KARL EBERHART, biologist, curator; b. Vienna, Sept. 28, 1933; came to U.S., 1965; s. Ernst and Barbara (Reichhalter) K.; m. Erika Stepnitz, Jan. 18, 1958. PhD (research fellow 1958-60), U. Vienna, 1961. Instr. U. Vienna, 1961-62; prof. marine biology U. Cumana, Venezuela, 1963-65; asst. curator Am. Mus. Natural History, N.Y.C., 1965-70, assoc. curator, 1970-75, curator, 1975-87, chmn., 1977-84, ret., 1987. Contbr. articles in field to profl. jours. NSF grantee, 1968-71

KIRTLEY, JANE ELIZABETH, law educator; b. Indpls., Nov. 7, 1953; d. William Raymond and Faye Marie (Price) K.; m. Stephen Jon Cribari, May 8, 1985. BS in Journalism, Northwestern U., 1975, MS in Journalism, 1976; JD, Vanderbilt U., 1979. Bar: N.Y. 1980, D.C. 1982, Va. 1995, U.S. Dist. Ct. (we. dist.) N.Y. 1980, U.S. Dist. Ct. D.C. 1982, U.S. Ct. Claims 1982, U.S. Ct. Appeals (4th cir.) 1982, U.S. Ct. Appeals (D.C. cir.) 1985, U.S. Ct. Appeals (10th cir.) 1996, U.S. Ct. Appeals (5th cir.) 1997, U.S. Ct. Appeals (6th cir.) 1998, U.S. Ct. Appeals (6th and 11th cir.) 1998, U.S. Supreme Ct. 1985. Assoc. Nixon, Hargrave, Devans & Doyle, Rochester, N.Y., 1979-81, Washington, 1981-84; exec. dir. Reporters Com. for Freedom of Press, Arlington, Va., 1985-99; Silha prof. media ethics & law U. Minn. Sch. Journalism & Mass Comm., Mpls., 1999—; dir. Silha Ctr. for Study of Media Ethics and Law, Mpls., 2000 ; mem. affiliated faculty U. Minn. Law Sch., 2001—. Mem. adj. faculty Am. U. Sch. Comm., 1988-98; mem. affiliated law faculty U. Minn., 2001—. Exec. articles editor Vanderbilt U. Jour. Transnat. Law, 1970 79; editor The News Media and the Law, 1985—, The First Amendment Handbook, 1987, 4th edit., 1995, Agents of Discovery, 1991, 93, 95, Pressing Issues, 1998-99; columnist NEPA Bull., 1988-99, Virginia's Press, 1991-99, Am. Journalism Rev., 1995—, W.Va.'s Press, 1997-99, Tenn. Press, 1997-99; mem. editl. bd. Comm. Law and Policy. Bd. dirs. Sigma Delta Chi Found., Indpls. Mem. ABA, N.Y. State Bar Assn., D.C. Bar Assn., Va. State Bar Assn., Sigma Delta Chi. Home: 3645 46th Ave S Minneapolis MN 55406-2937 Office: 111 Murphy Hall 206 Church St SE Minneapolis MN 55455-0488 E-mail: kirtl001@tc.umn.edu.

KIRTON, JENNIFER MYERS, artist; b. Berwick, Pa, Sept. 16, 1949; d. Fred H. and Jean I. Myers; m. Timothy Kirton, Aug. 8, 1970; children: Timothy James, Andrea Jolene, Andrew Joseph. Diploma, Orange Meml. Sch. Nursing, Orlando, Fla., 1970. RN. Galleries in Paris; represented by Mt. Dora Creative Framing Gallery, Met. Art and Antiques Gallery, art-exchang.com, IRRA Registry, Ormond Beach, Leesburg Ctr for Arts. Tchr. drawing Leesburg Ctr. for Arts; overseas prod. exhibitor, Paris, 1992—; lectr. in field; chair, judge juried art shows. Exhibited in group shows at Nat. Red Cross Scholastic (Nat. award, 1961), Apopka Art & Foliage (1st Place, 1975, 1982, Purchase award, 1978, 3rd Place, 1983, Hon. Mention, 1980, 1986), Winter Park Mall (Best of Show, 1977), Longwood ALOC/CFA (3rd Place, 1980), Colonial Plz. (Hon. Mention, 1982, 1st Place, 1988, 1989), Springs Plz. (Hon. Mention, 1983), Howell Branch Plz. (1st Place, 1984), Under the Trees (2nd Place, 1984, Special Judges award, 1985), Fashion Sq. (Hon. Mention, 1986), Artist League (Hon. Mention, 1986), Centrust (1st Place, 1988), Lake County Art Show (Hon. Mention, 1992), Working Area Artist, Altamonte Library, Pine Hills, Fiesta in the Park, Art Addiction Sweeden, Mount Dora Ctr. for the Arts, MDCA Permanent Collection, Artists of Fla., Vol. IV, 1994—95, one-woman shows include Meritor Bank, Seminole C.C., Fifth Street, Overseas European Corp., Mayor's Show Apopka City Hall, Fruitland Park Libr., mural, Apopka H.S. Stadium, Represented in permanent collections City of Apopka, Mt. Dora Ctr. for Arts. Recipient art awards including 1st, 2d, and 3rd Art Works, 2000. Mem. Orange County League of Artists (past pres.), Ctrl. Fla. Artists, Nat. Mus. Women in the Arts (Fla. com.), Leesburg Art Assn., Art Exch. Baptist. Avocation: collecting fine art. Home: 4700 Meadowland Dr Mount Dora FL 32757-9661 E-mail: kirtonart@aol.com.

KIRTON, ORLANDO CECILIO, surgeon, educator; b. Gamboa, Panama, Sept. 14, 1958; s. Leafton and Ruth Isabel (Atkinson) K.; m. Jillian Euphemia, July 4, 1987; children: Phillip, Briana, Emily. BA in Biochemistry, Brown U., 1978; MD cum laude, Harvard U., 1983. Diplomate Am. Bd. Surgery. Intern SUNY Health Sci Ctr., Bklyn., 1983-84; resident in surgery SUNY, Bklyn., 1984-85, 87-89, chief resident in surgery, 1989-90; clin. instr., rsch. fellow dept. pathology Children's Hosp., Boston, 1985-87; fellow surg. critical care dept. surgery Jackson Meml. Hosp./U. Miami Sch. Medicine, 1990-91; fellow surgery trauma Jackson Meml. Hosp./U. Miami, 1991-92, med. dir. advanced trauma life support, 1996—; asst. prof. clin. surgery dept. surgery U. Miami, 1992-97, assoc. prof. surgery, 1997-99; assoc. dir. surg. intensive care Jackson Meml. Med. Ctr., 1992—; assoc. dir. dept. surgery, chief gen. surgery Hartford (Conn.) Hosp., 1999—; assoc. prof. surgery, assoc. program dir. dept. surgery U. Conn. Health Ctr., Hartford, 1999—. Attending physician trauma & surg. care Jackson Meml. Hosp., 1992—, mem. faculty gen. surg. & trauma critical care, 1992—, mem. faculty anesthesia critical care, 1992—, attending nutritional and metabolic support svcs., 1993—, attending physician dept. hyperbaric medicine, 1995—; attending surgeon VA Hosp., Miami, 1995—; med. dir. trauma ICU Jackson Meml. Med. Ctr., 1997—. Cons. editor Chest, 1996—; contbr. articles to profl. jours. Spkr. 4th Ann. Black History Month program Miami Arena, 1995; mem. Dade County Trauma adv. com., 1996—. Maj. U.S. Army Res., 1992—. Recipient H. Quillian Jones award Fla. Com. Trauma, 1991, Disting. Svc. award South Fla. Coalition Black Trade Unionists, 1993, DuPont Critical Care Rsch. award Am. Coll. Chest Physicians, 1995, Young Investigator award, 1993; grantee Nat. Rsch. Svc., 1985-87, Merck & Co., 1993, Zeneca Pharms., 1995—; rsch. fellow N.Y. Dept. Health, 1979. Fellow ACS (candidate group 1984-92), Am. Coll. Critical Care Medicine; mem. AMA, Nat. Med. Assn., Am. Trauma Soc., Am. Assn. Surgery Trauma, Assn. Acad. Surgeons, Soc. Critical Care Medicine (abstract reviewer 1994-96, editor surg. sect. newsletter 1995—), So. Med. Assn., Eastern Assn. Surgery Trauma, Assn. Surg. Edn., Alpha Omega Alpha. Office: Hartford Hosp Dept Surgery PO Box 5037 80 Seymour St # B501C Hartford CT 06102-5037

KIRVEN, GERALD, lawyer; b. Augusta, Ga., Apr. 26, 1922; s. Ceil LaCoste and Miriam Creber (Gerald) K.; m. Cara Carter Fisken, Sept. 11, 1948; children: James F., Cara M. Kirven Cox, Christine Y., Alfred C., Mary Lea. AB, U. Va., 1944; LLB cum laude, U. Louisville, 1948. Bar: Ky. 1948, U.S. Dist. Ct. (we. dist.) Ky. 1949, Calif. 1953, U.S. Dist. Ct. (ea. dist.) Ky. 1954, U.S. Ct. Appeals (6th cir.) 1954, U.S. Supreme Ct. 1975. Assoc. Bullitt, Dawson & Tarrant, Louisville, 1948-50; law clk. U.S. Dist. Ct. (we. dist.) Ky., 1953; assoc. Middleton, Seelbach, Wolford, Willis & Cochran, Louisville, 1953-80, ptnr., 1958-80; sr. ptnr. Baird, Kirven, Westfall & Talbott, Louisville, 1980-85; of counsel Greenebaum, Treitz, Brown & Marshall, 1985-93; appointed spl. justice Ky. Supreme Ct., 1990, 92. Instr. law U. Louisville, 1959, 64, 85-91. Bd. dirs., v.p. Arthritis Found., 1960; v.p., bd. dirs. Mental Health Assn., Ky., 1970—, pres., 1980-81; v.p., vice chmn., bd. dirs. Seven Counties Svcs., 1978-81, Living Supports, Inc., 1987-90; vice chancellor Episcopal Diocese of Ky., 1979-94; bd. dirs. Transit Authority River City, 1995-2003, sec.-treas., 1996-2003. Lt. comdr. USNR, 1943-46, 50-53. Recipient Disting. Svc. award Arthritis Found., 1961, Alumnus of Yr. award U. Louisville Law Sch., 1993, Vol. of Yr. award Mental Health Coalition, 1998. Mem. ABA, Ky. Bar Assn. (hon. life, sr. counselor), State Bar Calif., Jud. Conf. U.S. 6th Cir. (life), Brandeis Soc. (comty. mem.), Univ. Club, Phi Beta Kappa, Omicron Delta Kappa. Democrat. Episcopalian.

KIRVEN, TIMOTHY J. lawyer; b. Buffalo, Wyo., May 26, 1949; s. William J. and Ellen F. (Farrell) K.; m. Elizabeth J. Adams, Oct. 31, 1970; 1 child, Kristen B. BA in English, U. Notre Dame, 1971; JD, U. Wyo., 1974. Bar: Wyo. 1974. Ptnr. Kirven & Kirven, PC, Buffalo, 1974—. Author Rocky Mountain Mineral Law, 1982. Mem. Johnson County Libr. Br., Buffalo. Mem. ABA (ho. of dels. 2002—), Wyo. State Bar (pres. 1998-99), Johnson County Bar Assn., Western States Bar Conf. (pres. 1998-99), Rotary (pres. Buffalo club 1988-89, youth exch. program chmn. 1993-98). Home: PO Box C Buffalo WY 82834-0060 Office: Kirven & Kirven PC PO Box 640 Buffalo WY 82834-0640

KIRWAN, KATHARYN GRACE (MRS. GERALD BOURKE KIRWAN JR.), retail executive; b. Monroe, Wash., Dec. 1, 1913; d. Walter Samuel and Bertha Ella (Shrum) Camp; m. Gerald Bourke Kirwan Jr., Jan. 13, 1945. Student, U. Puget Sound, 1933-34; BA, BS, Tex. Woman's U., 1937; postgrad., U. Wash., 1941. Libr. Brady (Tex.) Sr. High Sch., 1937-38, McCamey (Tex.) Sr. High Sch., 1938-43; mgr. Milady's Frock Shop, Monroe, 1946-62, owner, mgr., 1962-93. Meml. chmn. Monroe chpt. Am. Cancer Soc., 1961-93; mem. Snohomish County Police Svcs. Action Coun., 1971; mem. Monroe Pub. Libr. Bd., 1950-65, pres. bd., 1964-65; mem. Monroe City Coun., 1969-73; mayor City of Monroe, 1974-81; commr. Snohomish County Hosp. dist. 1, 1970-90, chmn. bd. commrs., 1980-90; mem. East Snohomish County Health Planning Com., 1979-81; mem. Snohomish County Law and Justice Planning Com., 1974-78, Snohomish County Econ. Devel. Coun., 1975-81, Snohomish County Pub. Utility Dist. Citizens Adv. Task Force, 1983; sr. warden Ch. of Our Saviour, Monroe, 1976-77, 89, sr. warden, 1976-77, 89-90; mem. Monroe Breast Cancer Screening Project community planning group Fred Hutchinson Cancer Rsch. Ctrs., 1991-93. With USNR, 1943-46. Recipient Malstrom award for Hist. Homes and Bldgs. of Monroe, 2000, award of project excellence Washington Mus. Assn., 2000. Mem. AAUW, U.S. Naval Inst., Ret. Officers Assn., Naval Res. Assn., Bus. and Profl. Women's Club (2d v.p. 1980-82, pres 1983-84), Washington Gens., Snohomish County Pharm. Aux., C. of C. (pres 1972), Valley Gen. Hosp. Guild (pres. 1994, 95, 96), Valley Gen. Hosp. Found (sec. 1993-97). Episcopalian. Home: 538 S Blakeley St Monroe WA 98272-2402

KIRWAN, R. DEWITT, lawyer; b. Albany, Calif., Aug. 30, 1942; s. Patrick William and Lucille Anne (Vartanian) K.; m. Betty-Jane Elias, June 29, 1969 (div. 1982); children: Katherine DeWitt, Andrew Elias; m. Nancy Jane Evers, Oct. 27, 1984; 1 child, Fletcher Evers. BA, U. Calif., Berkeley, 1966; JD, U. San Francisco, 1969. Bar: Calif. 1971, U.S. Dist. Ct. (ctrl. dist.) Calif. 1971, U.S. Ct. Appeals (9th cir.) 1971. Assoc. Schell & Delamer, L.A., 1971-73; ptnr. Lillick & McHose, L.A., 1973-90, Pillsbury Madison & Sutro, L.A., 1990-98, Akin Gump, Strauss, Hauer & Feld, L.A., 1998—. Chmn., exec. bd. U. Calif., Berkeley, 1988-97, trustee U. Calif. Berkeley Found., 1995-98; bd. dirs., trustee Pacific Crest Outward Bound Sch., 1993-99; bd. dirs. L.A. Philharm. Assn., 1985-89, pres., 1986-88, mem. bus. and profl. com.; bd. dirs. Pasadena (Calif.) Symphony Assn., 1978-82; adv. bd. OpusAlliance.com., 1999-2001. Capt. USAR, 1966-71. Mem.: ABA, Am Bd. Trial Advs., Calif. Club. Democrat. Roman Catholic. Avocations: fly fishing, mountaineering, hunting, skiing. Office: Akin Gump Strauss Hauer & Feld Ste 2400 2029 Century Park E Los Angeles CA 90067-3012

KIRWAN, WILLIAM ENGLISH, II, mathematics educator, university official, academic administrator; b. Louisville, Apr. 14, 1938; s. Albert Dennis Kirwan and Elizabeth (Heil) Kirwan; m. Patricia Ann Harper, Aug. 27, 1960; children: William English III, Ann Elizabeth. BA, U. Ky., 1960; MS (NDEA fellow 1960-63), Rutgers U., 1962, PhD, 1964. Instr. Rutgers U., 1963—64; mem. faculty U. Md., College Park, 1964, prof. math., 1972, chmn. dept. 1977—81, vice chancellor for acad. affairs, 1981—86, provost, 1986—88, acting pres., 1988—89, pres., 1989—98, Ohio State U., Columbus 1998—2002; chancellor Univ. of Maryland, 2002—. Vis. lectr. London U. 1966—67; program dir. NSF, 1975—76. Contbr. articles to profl. jours. MS 2000 Com. for NRC; mem. adv. bd. Montgomery County (Md.), 1975—79; bd. dirs. Nat. Assn. State Univs. and Land Grant Colls., 1995—, Greater Washington YMCA, 1994—; World Trade Ctr. Inst., 1990—. Decorated officer Order King Leopold II (Belgium); named Disting. Alumnus, U. Ky., 1989. Mem. NCAA (pres. commn. 1995—), Coun. for the Internat. Exch. of Scholars, Math Assn. Am., Am. Assn. Colls. and Univs. (bd. dirs. 1993—, 1994—), Am. Math Soc. (coun. 1980—82, editor Proc. 1977—82). Office: University System of Maryland Chancellor's Office 3300 Metzerott Rd, Suite 2C Adelphi MD 20783

KIRWIN, KENNETH FRANCIS, law educator; b. Morris, Minn., May 10 1941; s. Francis B. and Dorothy A. (McNally) K.; m. Phyllis J. Hills, June 2 1962; children— David, Mark, Robert. BA, St. John's U., 1963; JD, U. Minn. 1966. Bar: Minn. 1966, U.S. Dist. Ct. Minn. 1968, U.S. Ct. Appeals (8th cir.) 1969. Law clk. to assoc. justice Supreme Ct., Minn., 1966-67; assoc. Lindquist & Vennum, Mpls., 1967-70; prof. law William Mitchell Coll. Law, St. Paul 1970—. Staff dir. Uniform Rules Criminal Procedure, 1971-74, reporter 1982-87; reporter Uniform Victims of Crime Act, 1991-92; adj. prof. U. Minn Law Sch., 1977, 80; active Minn. Lawyers Profl. Responsibility Bd., 1975-81 Minn. Bd. Continuing Legal Edn., 1975-83. Author: (with Maynard E. Pirsig) Cases and Materials on Professional Responsibility, 1984. Mem. Ramsey County Bar Assn., Minn. State Bar Assn. (chair rules of profl. conduct com. 2002-), ABA (mem. standing com. on discipline 1983-89), Am. Law Inst Home: 1418 Brookshire Ct New Brighton MN 55112-6390 Office: William Mitchell Coll Law 875 Summit Ave Saint Paul MN 55105-3030 E-mail kkirwin@wmitchell.edu.

KIRZ, JANOS, physicist; b. Budapest, Hungary, Aug. 11, 1937; came to U.S. 1957; s. Andras and Emma (Teller) K.; m. Micheline Barthez, Dec. 19, 1964 (div. Aug. 1985); 1 child, Steven; m. Regina Moreno, Jan. 5, 1988. BA, U Calif. Berkeley, 1959; PhD, U Calif., 1963. Physicist Lawrence Berkeley Lab. Berkeley, Calif., 1964-67; lectr. U. Calif., Berkeley, 1967; assoc. prof. SUNY Stony Brook, 1968-72, prof., 1973—, Disting. prof., 1995—, chmn. dept physics and astronomy, 1988—2001. Contbr. articles to profl. jours. Fellow Woodrow Wilson Found., 1959, A.P. Sloan Found., 1970, Guggenheim Found. 1985. Fellow AAAS, Am. Physical Soc.; mem. Optical Soc. Am. Achievements include development of scanning X-ray microscope. Office: SUNY Dep Physics and Astronomy Stony Brook NY 11794-3800

KISABETH, TIM CHARLES, obstetrician, gynecologist; b. Fostoria, Ohio Oct. 29, 1957; s. Donald C. and Doris J. (Smith) K. BA in Chemistry, Capita U., 1979; MD, Ohio State U., 1982. Diplomate Nat. Bd. Med. Examiners, Am Bd. Obstetrics and Gynecology. Resident in ob-gyn Oakwood Hosp., Dearborn Mich., 1982-86, chief resident, 1985-86; pvt. practice Alton, Ill., 1986—; lab dir. Alton Multispecialists, 1995—; also bd. dirs.; chmn. ob-gyn. dept. Alton (Ill.) Meml. Hosp., 1991—93, 1995—97, 2001—; chmn. ob-gyn dept. St Anthony's Hosp., Alton, Ill., 1999—2001. Mem. Riverbend Growth Assn. 1987—; bd. dirs. Pride, Inc., 1992—, chmn. Alton Lake com., 1993-95. Fellow Am. Coll. Ob-Gyn.; mem. AMA (del. resident sect. 1984-86, del. young physicians sect. 1990-92), Ill. Med. Soc. (ho. of dels. 1987-2001, young physicians com. 1987-92, com. on pub. rels. and membership 1992-99, chmn Coun. on Membership and Advocacy 1999—), Madison County Med. Soc (pres. 1994-95), Masons, DeMolay (Legion of Honor award 1988). Lutheran Avocations: travel, photography. Home: 3312 Rosenberg Ln Godfrey Il 62035-1172 Office: Alton Multispecialists Ste 311 2 Saint Anthonys Way Alton IL 62002-4569

KISAK, PAUL FRANCIS, venture capitalist, consultant; b. Pitts., July 15 1956; s. Paul F. and Catherine M. (Svaranowic) K.; married. BSE in Nuclea Engring., Engring. Physics and Engring. Sci., U. Mich., 1982; MBA, Ea. Mich U., 1984; postgrad., U. Va., 1986, George Washington U., 1985-87, UCLA Naval Postgrad. Sch., Argonne Nat. Lab., Los Alamos Nat. Lab., Sandia Nat lab., Lawrence Livermore Nat. Lab. Lic. realtor, contractor. Intelligence officer engr. CIA, Langley, Va., 1983-86; engr., diplomat U.S. Dept. of State Washington, 1986-87; engr., program mgr. Space Applications Corp., Vienna Va., 1987-88; founder, pres. KKI, Inc., Middletown, Va., 1986—; sr. scientist program mgr. Info. Tech. & Application Corp., Reston, 1987-89; cons. devel PFK Enterprises, Washington, 1986—. Pub., editor, author, mem. mgmt. adv group CIA; mem. working group Strategic Def. Initiative, 1986—; ind. pub. editor, writer. Holder software copyrights and trademarks. Caseworker U.S Senator John Glenn, Columbus, Ohio, 1979; trustee League of Student Orgns. regent Colloquy Mega Found.; del. Loudoun County Rep. Nat. Party, 1988— Cpl., Va. State Guard. Corp. Va. State Guard. Ea. Mich. U. scholar, Ohio State U. scholar; recipient Presdl. Sports awards, George P. Schultz U.S. Dept. State Tribute of Appreciation award, Cold War cert.; named to NRA Legion of Honor Fellow: Sigma Soc.; mem.: ISPE, ASME, AIAA, Poetic Genius Soc., Marine Corp. League Det. #890, Naval Intelligence Profls., Cerebral Soc., Thinker Internat., Colloquy, Camelopard Socs., The Ultranet, Texnikoi, Intertel, Mensa

Bioengring. Soc., Assn. Former Intelligence Officers, Assn. MBA Execs., Am. Mgmt. Soc., Am. Astronautical Soc., Am. Nuc. Soc., Am. Math. Soc., Am. Phys. Soc., Internat. Soc. Profl. Engrs., Sigma Soc., Pi Mu Epsilon, Beta Gamma Sigma. Avocations: reading, sports, movies, woodworking, music. E-mail: kki@visuallink.com.

KISCADEN, SHEILA M. state legislator; b. St. Paul, Apr. 21, 1946; d. Harvey Richard and Bea Mae (Conway) Martineau; m. Richard Craig Kiscaden, Sept. 12, 1970; children: Michael, Karen. BS in Edn., U. Minn., 1969; MS in Pub. Adminstrn., U. So. Calif., L.A., 1986. Tchr. So. St. Paul Secondary Schs., Minn., 1969-70, Jobs 70, Rochester, Minn., 1970-71; regional coord. Planned Parenthood, Rochester, Minn., 1971-76; vol. svc. coord. Olmsted County, Rochester, Minn., 1977-80, human svc. planner, 1980-82, legis. liaison, 1982-85; prin. Cons. Collaborator, Rochester, Minn., 1987—; mem. Minn Senate from 30th dist., St. Paul, 1992—. Bd. dirs. Ability Bldg. Ctr. Found. Bd., Rochester, Minn., 1989-94, Dyslexia Inst. Minn., Rochester, Minn., 1989-94; team leader Global Vols., 1989—. Fulbright scholar, 1970. Mem. Phi Beta Kappa. Republican. Office: Minn State Senate 143 State Office Bldg Saint Paul MN 55155-0001

KISCHER, CLAYTON WARD, human embryologist, educator; b. Des Moines, Mar. 2, 1930; s. Frank August and Bessie Erma (Sawtell) K.; m.Linda Jese Espejo, Nov. 7. 1964; children: Cynthia Ann, Eric Armine, Frank Henry. BS in Biology, U. Omaha, 1953; MS, Iowa State U., 1960, PhD, 1962. Asst. prof. biology Ill. State U., 1962-63; rsch. assoc. Argonne (Ill.) Nat. Lab., 1963; asst. prof. zoology Iowa State U., 1963-64; NIH postdoctoral fellow in biochemistry M.D. Anderson Hosp, Houston, 1964-66; chief sect. electron microscopy S.W. Found. Rsch. and Edn., San Antonio, 1966-67; assoc. prof. anatomy U. Tex. Med. Br., Galveston, 1967-77, U. Ariz. Coll. Medicine, Tucson, 1977—95, prof. emeritus, 1995—. Dir. Scanning electron microscopy lab. Shrine Burns Inst., Galveston, 1969-73, cons. Am. Life League, Stafford, Va., other right to life groups; chmn. Am. Bioethics Adv. Commn. Co-author: The Human Development Hoax: Time to Tell the Truth; author sci. and pub. policy; contbr. articles to profl. jours. Cubmaster pack 107 Island Dist., Galveston, 1974-76; bd. dirs. YMCA. With USN, 1947-49. NIH Rsch. grantee, 1968-89; Morrison Trust grantee, 1975-76. Mem. SAR, Galveston Rsch. Soc. (pres. 1971-72), Am. Soc. Cell Biology, Electron Microscopy Soc. Am., Am. Assn. Anatomists, Tex. Soc. Electron Microscopy (hon.) (editor newsletter 1969-73, pres. 1975-76), Ariz. Soc. Electron Microscopy (pres. 1980-81), Gamma Pi Sigma. Home: 6249 N Camino Miraval Tucson AZ 85718 3024 Office: U Ariz Coll Medicine Dept Cell Biology and Anatomy Tucson AZ 85724-0001 E-mail: wkisch@netzero.net.

KISCHUK, RICHARD KARL, insurance company executive; b. Detroit, Mar. 14, 1949; s. Russell and Aubrey Ann (Artt) K.; m. Sandra Jean Dierkes, June 26, 1971; children: Robert Charles, Kirsten Grace, Erin Michelle, Danielle Laraine, Russell Olan, Erika Anne. BS, U. Mich., 1969, M in Actuarial Sci., 1971; MS in Bus. Adminstrn., Ind. U., 1979. Enrolled actuary. Actuarial trainee Lincoln Nat. Life, Ft. Wayne, Ind., 1971-72, actuarial asst., 1972-1973, asst. actuary, 1973-77, asst. v.p., 1977-80, 2d v.p., 1980-82; v.p. Lincoln Nat. Corp., Ft. Wayne, Ind., 1982-86; v.p., dir. Lincoln Nat. Health and Casualty Ins. Co., 1985-87, Lincoln Nat. Life Reins. Co., 1985-87, Lincoln Nat. Adminstrv. Service; chief operating officer, dir. Lincoln Intermediaries, Inc., 1985-87, Spl. Pooled Risk Adminstrs., Inc., 1985-87, Underwriters and Mgmt. Services, Inc., 1985-87, pres. Crown Point Mgmt. Cons., Inc., 1987—, Beneficient Solutions, Inc., 1998—. Mem. editorial adv. bd. CLU Jour., 1983-91; contbr. articles to profl. jours. Fellow Soc Actuaries (chmn. fin. reporting sect. 1982-85, bd. govs. 1986-89), mem. Am. Acad. Actuaries. Avocations: camping, backpacking, canoing, photography. Office: Crown Point Mgmt Cons Inc PO Box 355 Pendleton IN 46064-0355

KISCIRAS, ROSS PETER, chemical engineer, plant manager; b. Passaic, N.J., Apr. 15, 1962; s. Paul George and Pandora (Peterson) K.; m. Pamela Regina Comune, Aug. 22, 1992; 1 child, Zackary. BChemE, Villanova U., 1985. Plant mgr. H&S Chem. Co., Wallington, N.J., 1986—. Contbr. articles to profl. jours. Nat. merit scholar, 1980. Avocations: table tennis, golf, sports, music. Office: H&S Chem Co 5264 Van Dyke St Wallington NJ 07057 E-mail: kisciras@aol.com.

KISE, JAMES NELSON, architect, urban planner; b. Trenton, May 2, 1937; s. Charles Richard and Gladys May (Doll) K.; m. Rachel Bok, Dec. 20, 1958 (div.); children: Jefferson Bok, Charles Curtis; m. Sarah Ludlow Ogden Smith, June 15, 1974; children: Laura Ludlow Susanna, Anthony Lawrence Triplett. BArch, U. Pa., 1959, MArch, 1963, M in City Planning, 1964; postgrad., U. Rome, 1959-60. Registered architect, Pa., N.J., Maine, Del. New town planner Harvard-MIT Joint Ctr. of Urban Studies Ciudad Guayana Project, Caracas, Venezuala, 1961-62; ctr. city planner Phila. City Planning Commn., 1962-66; project dir. Wallace McHarg Roberts & Todd, Phila., 1966-67; dir. urban design ctr. Nat. Urban Coalition (formerly Urban Am., Inc.), Washington, 1967-70; ptnr. Kise Straw & Kolodner, Phila., 1970—. Lectr. U. Pa., 1962-67, 95—; adj. instr. urban design Drexel U., 1974-76; dir. Curtis Pub. Co., 1970-75. Work includes master plans for Schukill River Park, Phila., 1965, Downtown Harrisburg, Pa., 1975, Sadat City, Egypt, 1977, Acad. Ctr. for Performing Arts, 1981, Atlantic City Master Plan, 1986, South Broad St. Design, Phila., 1991, Schuylkill Heritage Corridor Plan, 1995, Lakewood Ranch Town Ctr. Plan, Fla., 1996, Independence Mall Masterplan, 1997, Riverside, Jefferson Co., Ky., 2001. Pres. Fleisher Art Meml., 1982—94, Historic Rittenhouse Town, 2000—; bd. overseers Grad. Sch. Fine Arts U. Pa., 2002—; Bd. dirs. Settlement Music Sch., 1963—83, Phila. Mus. Art, 1975—, Ebenezer Maxwell Mansion, 1980—93, Ctrl. Phila. Devel. Corp., 1989—, The Found. for Architecture, 1991—2002, Preservation Pa., 1991—, Phila. Soc. Preservation of Landmarks, 1993—99; Fleisher Art Meml., 1970—; bd. dirs. Washington Cmty. Sch. Music, 1967—70, pres. bd., 1968—70. Mem.: AIA, Am. Inst. Planners, Grad. Sch. Fine Arts U. Pa. Alumni Assn. (pres. 2000—02), Phila. Cricket Club, Phila. Club, Tau Sigma Delta, Franklin Inn. Democrat. Episcopalian. Home: Lane's End 8031 W School House Ln Philadelphia PA 19144-5431 Office: 123 S Broad St Ste 1270 Philadelphia PA 19109-1024 E-mail: JKise@ksk1.com.

KISELIK, PAUL HOWARD, manufacturing executive; b. Newark, Nov. 29, 1937; s. Jerome W. and Rose Kiselik; m. Teri Nimaroff, Sept. 6, 1959; children: Daniel, Jonathan. BS in Indsl. Engring., Lehigh U., 1960; MS in Mgmt. Engring., N.J. Inst. Tech., 1965. Registered profl. engr., N.J., Pa. V.p. Nimrow Carton Co., Elizabeth, NJ, 1961-71; pres. Sebro Packaging Corp., South Hackensack, NJ, 1971—. Pres. Rayart Folding Box Co., South Hackensack, 1971—, Lane Graphics, South Hackensack, 1984—; sr. ptnr. Green St. Assn., South Hackensack, 1979—. Author: (book) Equity Financing of a Small Business, 1965. Lt. U.S. Army, 1960—61. Mem.: TAPPI, Asa Packer Soc., Morristown-Beard Sch. Alumni Assn. (v.p. 1979—81), Newtonian Soc., Alpha Pi Mu, Tau Beta Pi. Avocation: raising dogs.

KISER, BRENDA HATHAWAY, freelance/self-employed writer, editor; b. Corpus Christi, Tex., Mar. 13, 1944; d. Loren Hall and Marjorie Hathaway Kiser; life ptnr. David Lubman. BA, Fla. State U., 1966. Asst. editor Lippincott-Raven Pubs., Brea, Calif., 1993—. Editor: The Guide to Biomedical Standards, 21st edit., (newsletter) Clinical Lab Letter; contbr. articles to mags. and newsletters, columns to newspapers. Coord. Self-Help Interfaith Program, Huntington Beach, 2000—02; sec. Profl. Writers of Orange County, Orange, Calif., 1997—99. Episcopalian. Avocations: music, travel, crafts. Home Fax: 714-373-3050. Personal E-mail: brendakiser@ix.netcom.com.

KISER, DANIEL, music educator, musician; s. Howard Wayne and Ruth Ann Kiser; m. Ruth Witter. MusB, So. Ill. U., 1982, MusM, 1983; Dr. of Musical Arts, U. of Ill., 1987. Cert. tchr. music State of N.C., 1993. Asst. prof. of music N.D. State U., Fargo, ND, 1985—92; chair of the sch. of fine arts and prof. of music Lenoir-Rhyne Coll., Hickory, NC, 1992—. Orchestral musician Western Piedmont Symphony, Hickory, NC, 1995—. Office: Lenoir-Rhyne College Sch of Fine Arts PO Box 7355 Hickory NC 28603

KISER, GLENN AUGUSTUS, retired pediatrician, investor; b. Bessemer City, N.C., July 13, 1917; s. Augustus B. and May (Carpenter) K.; m. Katherine Parham, June 13, 1941 (dec. 1972); m. Muriel Coykendall, Feb. 4, 1973. BS, MD, Duke U., 1941. Diplomate Nat. Bd. Med. Examiners. Resident physician Duke Hosp., Durham, N.C., 1946-48, Johns Hopkins U., Balt., 1946; pvt. practice Salisbury, N.C., 1947-55; freelance investor, 1955—. Founder stockholder Food Lion, Inc.; med. cons. State of N.C., Raleigh, 1961-64, 75-76, New River Mental Health Ctr., Boone, N.C., 1976-77; chief pediat. dept. Rowan Meml. Hosp., Salisbury, 1947-55, chief of staff, 1951-52, pres. Watauga County (N.C.) Med. Soc., 1978. Author: The Good Doctor--The Life and Times of Dr. Glenn A. Kiser, 1999. Bd. advisors Chowan Coll., Murfreesboro, N.C., 1977-78; trustee Rowan Regional Med. Ctr. Found., Salisbury, Kiser Med. Office Bldg. at Rowan Regional Med. Ctr., Kiser Welcome Ctr. at Duke U. Children's Hosp. Surgeon USPHS, 1941-46. Recipient Exemplary Life Svc. award Catawba Coll., 1995, N.C.'s Philanthropist of Yr. award, 1996, Order of the Long Leaf Pine award State of N.C., 1996, Disting. Svc. award Duke U. Med. Ctr., 2000; named Salisbury's Man of Yr., 1998. Mem. AMA, N.C. Med. Soc., Pinnacle Club Duke Med. Ctr. (charter), Duke Med. Ctr. Alumni Assn. (coun. 1988), Duke U. Founders Soc., Lions (dep. dist. gov. N.C. chpt. 1959), James B. Duke Soc. (pres. Milford Hills chpt. 1959, zone chmn. 1959, dep. dist. gov. 1960, internat. amb. 1961), Salisbury Country Club. Presbyterian. Achievements include Achievements include development of the concept of childproof safety caps; one of the first pediatricians to point out the extreme danger of lye poisoning in children. Avocations: photography, boating, music, bicycling. Home: PO Box 68 Spencer NC 28159

KISER, JO ANN, editor; b. Penny, Ky., Nov. 9, 1940; d. Ezra and Hazel (Bartley) Kiser. BA, CUNY, 1967; MA in English, U. Chgo., 1968, PhD in Comm. on Social Thought, 1993. Editl. asst. Charles E. Merrill Books, Columbus, Ohio, 1960—61; sec. Hawthorn Books, N.Y.C., 1962—63; typist, rschr., reader New Yorker mag., N.Y.C., 1963—78; manuscript editor U. Chgo. Press, 1989—97; instr. Morehead (Ky.) State U., 1997—98; quality editor Lexis-Nexis, Dayton, Ohio, 1999—2000; assoc. editor lit. Ency. Britannica, Chgo., 2000—03; copy editor Am. Jour. Sociology, 2003—. Book reviewer Whitesburg, Ky. Mountain Eagle, 1993—. Author: short stories, poems. Democrat.

KISER, JOY MARIAN, librarian, writer, historian; b. Akron, Ohio, Jan. 29, 1947; m. James R. Kiser, Jan. 27, 1968 (div. Oct. 1978); children: Heather Joy, Adam James. BA in Art History/English/Photography, U. Akron, 1988; MA in Art History, Case Western Res. U., 1990; MLS, Kent State U., 1994. Med. libr. Wooster Cmty. Hosp., Wooster, Ohio, 1992-95; head libr. Cleve. Mus. Natural History, 1995-98, 1998-01; head librarian Nat. Endowment for Arts, Washington, 2001—. Contbr. articles to profl. jours. Mem. Ohio Preservation Coun., Soc. for the History of Natural History (London), Spl. Librs. Assn. (natural history caucus), Washington Rare Book Group. Avocations: gardening, carpentry, dressage riding, photography, writing. Office: National Endowments for the Arts Rm 213 1100 Pennsylvania Ave NW Washington DC 20506 Office Fax: 202-682-5651.

KISER, KENNETH M(AYNARD), chemical engineering educator; b. Detroit, Nov. 28, 1929; s. Kenneth Chapman and Emma (Kutkuhn) K.; m. Florence Mary Sclafani, June 26, 1954; children: David, Thomas, James, John, Melissa. BS in Chem. Engring., Lawrence Tech. U., 1951; MS in Chem. Engring., U. Cin., 1952, D.Engring., Johns Hopkins U., 1956. Registered profl. engr., N.Y. Chem. engr. Gen. Electric Co., Schenectady, N.Y., 1956-64; asst. prof. chem. engring. SUNY-Buffalo, 1964-65, assoc. prof., 1965 80, prof., 1980—, acting chair chem. engring. dept., 1977, 78, assoc. dean engring., 1978-95, chair chem. engring. dept., 1995-97, prof. emeritus, 1997—; adj. prof. Rensselaer Poly. Inst., Troy, N.Y., 1962-64; chem. engring. cons., 1965—. Contbr. articles to profl. jours., 1957—. Patentee in field. Recipient Chancellor's award SUNY-Buffalo, 1974; grantee NSF, Heart Assn., others, 1965-80. Mem. Am. Inst. Chem. Engrs., Am. Soc. Engring. Edn., Alpha Chi Sigma, Sigma Xi, Tau Beta Pi (Tchr. award 1973). E-mail: ken_kiser@hotmail.com.

KISER, M.L. computer programmer, freelance artist, writer, poet; b. Lexington, Ky., Oct. 28, 1957; AA, Fugazzi Jr. Coll., 1985; grad., Inst. Children's Lit., Writer's Digest. I.S. tech, database, systems analyst/programmer Chandler Med. Ctr. U. Ky., Lexington, 1997-99; with I.S. Tech, NT/ Novell, 1999—2002; freelance writer, artist, poet, 2002—. Contbr. poems to Internat. Libr. of Poetry, Poetry.com, Sparrowgrass, German Publs. Poetry Plus, World of Poetry, short stories to publs. in U.S. and Can. Mem. Native Am. Rights Found. Recipient awards Internat. Libr. of Poetry, Poetry.com, Sparrowgrass, World of Poetry. Mem.: Nat. Mus. of Am. Indian, John Wayne Cancer Found. (life). Avocations: poetry, writing, painting. E-mail: mlkiser42@aol.com.

KISER, MOLLY, musician; b. Dec. 15, 1971; d. Loren Hall and Yoko Tajima Kiser. Student, Tokyo Nat. U. of Fine Arts and Music, 1990; BM, Curtis Inst. Music, 1994; MM, New Eng. Conservatory, 1996; DMA, Juilliard Sch., 2003. Performer: Beethoven's 5th concerto "Emperor" with Rosenkranz Orch., Tchaikovsky's 1st Piano Concerto with NHK secondary Orch., Aspen Music Festival Student Orch., 1992, Salem Philharm. Orch., 1995, New Eng. Conservatory Symphony Orch., 1994, 1996, Ft. Collins Symphony Orch., 1996, Corpus Christi Symphony Orch., 1997, World Festival Orch., 1999, Westchester Symphony Orch., 2001, Tokyo City Orch., 2002. Recipient piano hons. audition, New Eng. Conservatory, 1991, winner concerto competition, Aspen Music Sch., 1992, New Eng. Conservatory, 1994, 1996, 1st prize, 41st Ft. Collins Symphony Orch. Young Artist Competition, 1996, 15th Kingsville Internat. Young Performers competition, 1996, Bronze medal, 6th San Antonio Internat. Piano competition, 1997, Silver medal, 47th Nina Widemann Piano competition, 1997, gold medal, World Piano competition, 1999, numerous others; fellow Tanglewood Music Festival fellow, 1993. Avocations: dancing, reading. Home: 47-35 39th Pl 2d flr Sunnyside NY 11104 Office: The Juilliard Sch 60 Lincoln Center Plz New York NY 10023

KISER, MOSE, III, small business owner; b. Raleigh, N.C., Nov. 14, 1956; s. Mose Jr. and Joyce Ann (Carpenter) K.; m. Jean Louise Charles, May 15, 1982; children: Taylor Forbes, Margaret Stewart. BA in Psychology, N.C. State U., 1980. Sales trainee Odell Sentry Hardware, Greensboro, N.C., 1980, Wrangler Menswear, Greensboro, 1981-82, sales rep. Knoxville, Tenn., 1982-84; pres., owner, operator AuraTech, Inc., Greensboro, 1986—. Bd. dirs. Greensboro Ice Sports. Adult dir. Greensboro Ice Sports, Inc., 1990; mem. Greensboro Sports Coun., 1990, also bd. dirs. Mem. HemoCue Assn. Regional Distbrs., Health Industry Distbrs. Assn., Biomktg. assn., N.C. State U. Athletic Aid Assn., Greensboro Sports Coun., N.C. State U. Alumni Assn., Greesboro Country Club. Republican. Methodist. Avocations: ice hockey, golf, running, dirt biking. Home: 3106 Solara Trce Greensboro NC 27410 9053 Office: AuraTech Inc 7349 W Friendly Ave Greensboro NC 27410-6255

KISER, NAGIKO SATO, retired librarian; b. Taipei, Republic of China, Aug. 7, 1923; came to U.S., 1950; d. Takeichi and Kinue (Soma) Sato; m. Virgil Kiser, Dec. 4, 1979 (dec. Mar. 1981). Secondary teaching credential, Tsuda Juku U., Tokyo, 1945; BA in Journalism, Trinity U., 1953; BFA, Ohio State U., 1956, MA in Art History, 1959; MLS, cert. in library media, SUNY, Albany, 1974. Cert. community coll. librarian, Calif., cert. jr. coll. tchr., Calif., cert. secondary edn. tchr., Calif., cert. tchr. library media specialist and art, N.Y. Pub. rels. reporter The Mainichi Newspapers, Osaka, Japan, 1945-50; contract interpreter U.S. Dept. State, Washington, 1956-58, 66-67; resource specialist Richmond (Calif.) Unified Sch. Dist., 1968-69; editing supr. CTB/McGraw-Hill, Monterey, Calif., 1969-71; multi-media specialist Monterey Peninsula Unified Sch. Dist., 1975-77; librarian Nishimachi Internat. Sch., Tokyo, 1979-80, Sacramento City Unified Sch. Dist., 1977-79, 81-85; sr. librarian Camarillo (Calif.) State Hosp. and Devel. Ctr., 1985-93. Editor: Short Form Test of Academic Aptitude, 1970, Prescriptive Mathematics Inventory, 1970, Tests of Basic Experience, 1970. Mem. Calif. State Supt.'s Regional Coun. on Asian Pacific Affairs, Sacramento, 1984-91. Library Media Specialist Tng. Program scholar U.S. Office Edn., 1974. Fellow Internat. Biog. Assn. (life); mem. ALA, Am. Biog. Inst. (life, dep. gov. 1988—), Libr. Congress (nat. mem.), Calif. Libr. Assn., Med. Libr. Assn., Asunaro Shogai Kyoiku Kondankai (Lifetime Edn. Promoting Assn., Japan), The Mus. Soc., Internat. House of Japan, Matsuyama Sacramento Sister City Corp., Japanese Am. Citizens League, Japanese Am. Nat. Mus., Japanese Am. Cultural and Cmty. Ctr., Ikenobo Ikebana Soc. Am., L.A. Hototogisu Haiku Assn., Ventura County Archeol. Soc., Internat. Platform Assn., Internat. Soc. Poets, AAUW, Ventura County Chpt. Mem. Christian Science Ch. Avocations: flower arranging, ballroom dance, classical music.

KISER, ROBERTA KATHERINE, medical records administrator, education educator; b. Alton, Ill., Aug. 13, 1938; d. Stephen Robert and Virginia Elizabeth (Lasher) Golden; m. James Robert Crisman, sept. 6, 1958 (div. May 1971); 1 child, Robert Glenn; m. James Earl Kiser, Dec. 19, 1971; 1 child, James Jacob. BEd, So. Ill. U., 1960. Cert. tchr., Ill., Calif. Librarian Oaklawn (Ill.) Elem. Sch., 1960-62, Alsip (Ill.) Elem. Sch., 1966-69; tchr. Desert Sands Unified Sch. Dist., Indio, Calif., 1969-79; prin. Mothercare Infant Sch., Rancho Mirage, Calif., 1980-89; substitute tchr. Greater Coachella Valley Sch., Calif., 1989-91; med. acct. Desert Health Care, Bermuda Dunes, Calif., 1990-92; mentor tchr., computing, typing skils Wilde Woode Children's Ctr., Palm Springs, Calif., 1990-92; chiropractic asst. Rapp Chiropractic Health Ctr., Palm Desert, Calif., 1992-93; sr. med. records clerk Eisenhower Med. Ctr., Rancho Mirage, Calif., 1993-2000, transcription coord., 2000—. V.p. Palm Desert (Calif.) Community Ch. Montessori Sch. Bd., 1982-85; mem. choir Cmty. Ch. of Joy. Republican. Home: 39-575 Keenan Dr Rancho Mirage CA 92270-3610 Office: Eisenhower Med Ctr 39000 Bob Hope Dr Rancho Mirage CA 92270-3221 E-mail: Rkgkiser@aol.com.

KISER, SHARON ANN, health facility professional; b. Dayton, Ohio, Aug. 2, 1945; d. Charles Russell and Louise Matilda (Baer) Warner; m. Peter Joseph D'Onofrio, Oct. 16, 1971 (div. June 1976); m. Ronald Eugene Kiser, June 14, 1986; 1 stepchild, Rebecca Erin (dec.). Degree in secretarial sci., Miami Jacobs Jr. Coll., 1971; AS in Bus. Adminstrn., Sinclair Community Coll., 1986; BA in Mgmt., Antioch U., 1990. Cert. dir. volunteer resources, Ohio. Exec. sec. NCR Corp., Dayton, 1963-78; dir. vol. services Grandview Hosp. and Med. Ctr., Southview Hosp. and Family Health Ctr., Dayton, 1978—. Speaker Nat. Osteo. Guild Assn., Dayton, 1981; nat. speaker Am. Soc. Dirs. Vol. Services Ednl. Conf., Houston, 1983, Cin., 1984, Phila., 1986; mem. tng. com., human resources com. Voluntary Action Ctr. United Way, Dayton, 1983, 86. Contbr. articles to profl. jours. V.p. Sulphur Grove United Meth. Women, 1993-95; loaned exec. United Way, 1999, chmn. Grandview Hosp. United Way, 1983. Recipient Pam Fenn award for outstanding vol. adminstr. United Way of Dayton, 1999. Mem. Am. Soc. Dirs. Vol. Svcs. (innovative programming com. 1987, Creative Achievement award 1983, 84, 86), Ohio Soc. Dirs. Vol. Svcs. (bylaws com. 1980-81, mentor membership com. S.W. Ohio chpt. 1981-85, newspaper rep. 1982-84, co-chmn. award for creative achievement 1991-92). Avocations: reading, hiking, camping. Home: 7201 Claircrest Dr Huber Heights OH 45424-2912 Office: Grandview Med Ctr 405 W Grand Ave Dayton OH 45405-4796 E-mail: sharon.kiser@kmcnetwork.org.

KISER, STEPHEN, artist, educator; b. Koloa, Hawaii, Feb. 4, 1944; s. Mary A. Kiser; m. Kathleen A. Cahill, Jan. 14, 1973; children: Lisa, Kari. Cert., Brooks Inst. Photography, 1965; BA, San Jose State U., 1976, MA, 1978. Freelance photojournalist, 1964-66, 72-74; photographer Pace Publs., L.A. and N.Y.C., 1966-68; exec. and artistic dir. Tidewater Young Performers, Norfolk, Va., 1968-69; owner Steve Kiser Prodns., Orange, Calif., 1970-72; coord. dir. Ctr. for Creative Arts and Scis., San Francisco, 1976-78; owner Steve Kiser Studios, Palo Alto, Calif., 1995—; assoc. prof. Foothill Coll., Los Altos Hills, Calif., 1974—2000; prof. City Coll. San Francisco, 1995—. Trustee, v.p. Am. Indian Contemporary Arts, San Francisco, 1988—. Exhibiting artist with numerous one man and group shows, 1970—. Event coord. Calif. Winter Spl. Olympics, Momouth, Calif., 1975-80; v.p. Hands Across the Water, U.S./Indonesia, 1984-93; advisor Leadership Mid-Peninsula, 1995. With USN, 1968-69. Fellow Rotary, Brazil, 1970; Arts fellow for Contemporary Native Am. Artist, Ednl. Found. Am., 1996. Mem. Am. Soc. Media. Photographers, Internat. Sculpture Assn., Soc. for Photog. Edn., Coll. Art Assn., Hale Naua III. Avocation: exploring new places and concepts. Home: 3302 Vernon Ter Palo Alto CA 94303-4203 Office: 4000 Middlefield Rd # 3 Palo Alto CA 94303-4739 E-mail: Steve@SteveKiser.com.

KISH, ELISSA ANNE, educational administrator, consultant; b. Bklyn., Sept. 29, 1934; d. Robert Joseph and Yolanda Filomina (Romano) Lucadamo; m. Joseph Laurence Kish Jr., Oct. 16, 1955; children: Grace Edna Kish, Joseph Robert, Frances Caroline Kish Burrell. BA, CUNY, 1956; EdM, Rutgers U., 1965. Elem. tchr. N.Y. City Pub. Schs., Bklyn., 1956-57, U.S. Army Dependent Schs., Hanau, West Germany, 1958, Piscataway (N.J.) Pub. Schs., 1961-62, New Brunswick (N.J.) Pub. Schs., 1965, 71-76; vice prin. Hopatcong (N.J.) Pub. Schs., 1977-78; asst. supt. Dunellen (N.J.) Pub. Schs., 1978-80; supr. K-12 instrn. Elmwood Park (N.J.) Pub. Schs., 1980-90; interim high sch. adminstr. Dunellen Pub. Schs., 1991-92; adminstr. ctrl. office Elmwood Park Pub. Schs., 1992-96. Cons. Newark Pub. Schs., 1976-77; evaluator Middle States Assn., Navesink, N.J., 1988; cons. State U. N.Y., Garden City, 1992, Mt. Vernon Pub. Schs., N.Y., 1992; mem. fine arts & humanities coun. Town of Wareham, Mass., 1996—. Author: Nutrition Program For Schools, 1979; contbng. author: Curriculum & Values: An Inquiry, 1976. Mem. strategic planning team Town of Elmwood Park, 1993-95; officer, mem. Westfield Coll. Women's Club, Westfield, N.J., 1969-92; founder, 1st pres. Vocational Adv. Coun., Elmwood Park, 1980-90; trustee Christopher Montessori Acad., Westfield, 1968-72. Recipient numerous grants for rsch. and curriculum devel., 1979—. Mem. ASCD, NEA, Elmwood Park Prins. and Suprs. Assn. (pres. 1989-90), Elmwood Park Adminstrs. Assn. (pres. 1986-89), Nat. Geographic Soc., Smithsonian Assocs., Kappa Delta Pi, Alpha Epsilon Phi. Avocations: theatre, opera. Home and Office: 635 4th Ave Lindenwold NJ 08021

KISH, GEORGE FRANKLIN, thoracic and cardiovascular surgeon; b. Toledo, Ohio, Mar. 30, 1944; s. George F. and Ann (Kucharski) K.; m. Joann Mata Kish, Mar. 16, 1968; children: Jeremy, Nathan. BS, Ohio State U., 1966, MD, 1970. Surg. intern George Washington U. Med. Ctr., 1970-71, surg. resident, 1971-74, surg. rsch. fellow, 1974-75, chief surg. resident, 1975-76, thoracic and cardiovascular surgery resident, 1976-78; asst. prof. surgery W.Va. U. Med. Ctr., Morgantown, 1978-80; cardiovascular surgeon Flagship CVTS, Erie, Pa., 1980—, Flagship Cardiac, Vascular, Thoracic Surgery, Erie. Chief cardiovascular surgery Hamot Med. Ctr., Erie, 1982-93. Contbg. author International Trends in General Thoracic Surgery, Vol. 7, 1991; contbr. articles to profl. jours. Dr. I.S. Grisoff fellow cardiovascular surgery George Washington U., 1974-75; affiliate rsch. grantee Am. Heart Assn., W.Va. Med. Ctr., 1979. Fellow ACS, Internat. Soc. Cardiovascular Surgeons, Soc. Thoracic Surgeons, Am. Coll. Cardiology, Am. Coll. Chest Physicians, Southeastern Surg. Congress, Internat. Coll. Angiology. Avocations: downhill skiing, tennis. Home: 218 Frontier Dr Erie PA 16505-2506 Office: Flagship CVTS 104 E 2nd St Erie PA 16507-1532 Fax: (814) 456-1859.

KISKADDEN, ROBERT MORGAN, artist, educator; b. Tulsa, Dec. 6, 1918; s. William Walter and Irene Sylvia (Price) K.; m. Barbara Jane Meyer, Dec. 23, 1948; children: Kathryn Ann Kiskadden McMurray, Jayne Ann Kiskadden Bechtel. BFA, U. Kans., 1947; MA, Ohio Wesleyan U., 1949. Tchg. fellow Ohio Wesleyan U., Delaware, 1947-49; asst. prof. art Wichita (Kans.) Mcpl. U., 1949-57; assoc. prof. art Wichita State U., 1958-66, prof. art, 1967-68, prof. and acting chmn., 1969, prof., chmn. dept. art, 1970, asst. dean divsn. art, 1971-84, prof., asst. dean emeritus, 1984 . One man shows include Ohio Wesleyan, Delaware, 1949, Estes Park, Colo., 1950, 51, Wichita State U., 1958, Petroleum Club, Wichita, 1958, Hutchinson (Kans.) Art Assn., 1961, 77, Studio Gallery, Topeka, 1962, Wichita Art Mus., 1965, Melody Art Mart, Paducah, Ky., 1966, Wichita State Bank, 1967, Hays (Kans.) State Coll., 1967, Wichita Art Assn., 1972, 84, Bethel Coll., Newton, Kans., 1974, Ellington Gallery, Wichita, 1979, Carmel (Calif.) Fine Art Gallery, 1988, Mus. of the S.W., Midland, Tex., 1993; exhibited in group shows at U. Wichita Gallery, 1949, 60, William Rockhill Nelson Gallery, Kansas City, 1952-55, 57, 59, 63, Wichita Art Mus., 1953-70, Mulvane Art Mus., 1957, 72, 74, Blue Door Gallery, Taos, N.Mex., 1958, Mus. N.Mex., Santa Fe, 1959, Springfield (Mo.) Art Mus., 1965, U. Tex.-El Paso, 1969, Sacred Heart Coll., 1969, So. State Coll., Springfield, S.D., 1971, Birger Sandzen Meml. Gallery, Lindsborg, 1981, McFarland Gallery, Wichita, 1969, Raven Art Gallery, Wichita, 1972, Ulrich Mus., 1977, 79, Ellington Gallery Oils and Watercolors, Wichita, 1979, annually Wichita Art Assn., Wichita State U., others; works in permanent collections Am. Embassy, Cairo, Peking U., Art of Emprise, Emprise Bank, Wichita, 2000, others; contbr., worked on Joan Miro Mosaic Project facade of Ulrich Mus. Art, 1976-78. Chmn. bdlg. com. McKnight Art Ctr., Wichita, 1974, ex-officio mem. Wichita Art Mus., Wichita Art Assn.; adv. coun. Kans. Cultural Arts Commn., Topeka, 1969, 75. Sgt. C.E. U.S. Army, 1942-45. Recipient numerous awards of merit, best of show, cash, purchase awards, popular, hon. mention, 1st, 2d, 3rd prizes, 1949-93; Kiskadden Scholarship for Studio Art Majors established by Wichata State U., 1984—. Mem. Srs. in Retirement, Chisholm Trail Antique Gun Assn. (life), Wichita Art

Assn. (adv. bd.), Wichita Artist Guild (past pres., bd. dirs.), Kans. Watercolor Soc. (charter), Kans. Acad. Oil Painters (charter), Nat. Assn. Mus., Nat. Cowboy Hall of Fame, Sigma Alpha Epsilon. Avocations: golf, fly fishing.

KISKER, CARL THOMAS, physician, medical educator; BA, Johns Hopkins U., 1958; MD, U. Cin. Coll. Medicine, 1962. Diplomate Am. Bd. Pediatrics, Am. Bd. Pediatric Hematology-Oncology. Lic. physician Ohio, Iowa. Intern U. Oreg. Coll. Medicine, 1962-63; sr. asst. surgeon NIH, 1963-65; jr. resident pediat. Children's Hosp., Cin., 1965-66, sr. resident pediat., 1966-67, fellow pediat. hematology, 1967-69, asst. attending pediatrician, 1968-69, attending pediatrician, 1969-73, dir. hemophilia project, 1971-73, dir. clin. hematology lab., 1972-73; asst. prof. pediat. U. Cin., 1969-72, assoc. prof. pediat., 1972-73, U. Iowa, Iowa City, 1973-79, dir. divsn. pediat. hematology-oncology, 1973-97, prof. pediat., 1979—. Med. lectr. various student and profl. groups; active mem. Pediat. Hematology-Oncology Group, Cin., Children's Cancer Study Group, L.A.; pres. Midwest Blood Club.; mem. adv. coun. Nat. Hemophilia Ctrs., 1979—.$D Mem. editl bd. Pediat. Today; contbr. numerous sci. papers to profl. jours. and chpts. in books. Mem. Iowa Found. Fund Raising Com. Lederle Med. Student Rsch. fellow, 1959; recipient state and fed. grants, Alumni of Yr. award U. Cin. Coll. Medicine, 2002. Mem. Am. Soc. Hematology, Mid-west Soc. for Pediat. RSch., Am. Fedn. for Clin. RSch., Am. Heart Assn., Internat. Soc. Thrombosis and Haemostasis (sub-com. on neonatal hemostasis), Ctrl. Soc. for Pediat. Rsch., Soc. Pediat. Rsch., Johnson County Med. Soc., Prairie Region Affiliated Blood Svcs., Am. Pediat. Soc. Office: Univ of Iowa Hosp 2520 Jcp Iowa City IA 52242 E-mail: c-kisker@uiowa.edu.

KISLAK, JEAN HART, art director; b. 1931; d. Frank Ernest and Isabelle Tayor (Ellis) Hart; m. William I. Herendeen, Aug. 23, 1952 (div. Feb. 1956); m. Louis G. Johnson, Jan. 31, 1959 (div. Feb. 1975); 1 child, Jennifer Taylor Johnson; m. Jay Kislak, Apr. 7, 1985. Student, Peace Jr. Coll., Raleigh, N.C., Queens Coll., Charlotte, N.C. With Storer Broadcasting Co., Miami, Fla., S.E. Banks, N.A., Miami, 1974-84, art dir., 1974-84; mem. Gov. Fla. Panel Visual Arts, 1979-81; art cons., 1974—. Internat. rep. Christies, Inc., 1998—2001; mem. art and architecture com. Libr. of Congress, Washington, 2003. Bd. dirs. Viscaya Mus., Miami, 1963, Beaux Arts, U. Miami, 1968, Theatre Art Patrons, Miami, 1968, Theatre Art Patrons, Miami, 1965, NEH, Fla., 1992; trustee Dade County Zool. Soc., 1988—, Miami Art Mus., Barry Coll. Charter Sch.; mem. Bacardi Imports Art Bd., 1983-89, 98—, Fla. State Bd. Art Coun., 1987, Miami Art Mus. (formerly Dade County Ctr. for the Arts Bd.), 1989-99; bd. dirs. Nat. Wildflower Assn., 1991; mem. exec. bd. Zool. Soc. Fla., 1994; mem. Fla. Humanities Bd., 1994; mem. visual arts com. Libr. Congress, 2002. Recipient Gov. Fla. award art, 1976, 79, Miami Dade Pub. Libr. award, 1978, Bus. Com. for Arts award, 1975-79, WPBT Pub. TV award, 1976, 77, 80, Lowe Gallery, U. Miami cert. recognition, 1980, Dade County Art in Pub. Places cert. recognition, 1981, 82. Mem. 1805 Club (London) (hon. v.p. 1993—), Kislak Found. (bd. dirs. 1997—). Address: 720 NE 69th St Miami FL 33138-5738

KISLIK, RICHARD WILLIAM, publishing executive; b. N.Y.C., Oct. 31, 1927; s. Louis K. and Isabelle (Deutelbaum) K.; m. Audrey Gerber, June 19, 1949; children: Nancy J., Andrew R., Laurie S., Wendy J. AB, Harvard U., 1948, MBA, 1949. Rsch. asst. Bus. Sch. Harvard U., 1949-50; asst. contr. Maidenform Brassiere Co., 1950-54; contr. Doubleday & Co., Inc., 1954-60; treas., dir. Ziff-Davis Pub. Co., 1960-61; v.p. fin., dir. Random House, Inc., 1961-68; cons., 1968; v.p. Intext Ednl. Pubs., Inc., 1968-69, pres., 1969—; exec. v.p. Intext, Inc., 1970-71, pres., 1971-77, chmn. bd., chief exec. officer, 1972-80, cons., 1980; pres., dir. W.H. Smith Pubs. Inc., 1981-86; pvt. practice, 1986—2001. Bd. dirs., v.p. fin. Chelsea Green Pub. Co., White River Junction, Vt. Mem. Players Club, Dutch Treat Club, Harvard Club (N.Y.C.), Pubs. Lunch Club, Harvard Bus. Sch. Club Greater N.Y. Home: 176 E 71st St New York NY 10021-5159 E-mail: rwkislik@interport.net.

KISNER, JACOB, poet, editor, publisher; b. Chelsea, Mass., Apr. 30, 1926; s. Louis and Sarah (Kotel) K.; m. Gladys Selma Feinstein, May 29, 1947; 1 daughter, Lesley Kisner Cafarelli. Student, Calvin Coolidge Coll., 1945-46, Burdett Coll., 1943-45, Harvard Univ. Extension, 1944-48, Mass. State Univ. Extension, 1944-50, Cambridge Ctr. for Adult Edn., 1946-51. With Boston American advt. dept., 1943; Sunday dept. writer Boston Globe, 1943-45; local news editor Jewish Advocate, Boston, 1945-46; founder, editor, pub. Dorchester (Mass.) Herald, 1946-47; copywriter Harold Cabot & Co. Advt. Agy., Boston, 1948; trade reporter Fairchild News Svc., Boston, 1948-49; with Boston Pub. Libr. Cataloguing Dept., 1949; sr. proof-reader Rec. and Statis. Corp., Boston, 1950-54; participant NBC Comedy Writers Devel. Project, 1956; editor Crossroads, Toronto, Ont., Can., 1964-67; Am. editor View, Can., 1967—; rsch. dir. N.Y. bur. Moneytree Publs., N.Y.C., 1972—; stamp and autograph dealer, 1973-82; owner, operator Penthouse F Stamps, 1982—. Discoverer Lord and Taylor find of Finnish postal hist.; free-lance writer, 1943—. Author: (plays) First Came Paula, 1954, Speak of the Devil, 1955, The Monkey's Tail, 1956; (TV plays): The Late Mr. Honeywell, 1957, A World Apart, 1957; (poetry) I Am Hephaestus, 1966; numerous pub. articles, revs., rsch. on stamps and postal hist.; contbr. poetry to various lit. jours. and anthologies; included in Anthology of American Poetry, Vol. X, 1970, Vol. XI, 1971. Saxophonist, leader big band Jack Kenton, 1943-46; philatelic journalist; discussion moderator Great Books Found., Boston, 1948-51; judge of poetry contests, Rochester, N.Y., also N.Y. Poetry Forum, 1969—; sec. Am.-European Friendship Assn., 1948-51; chmn. Nat. Poetry Day Com., 1970; N.Y. State dir. and N.Y.C. chmn. World Poetry Day Com., 1971—; v.p., bd. dirs., incorporator N.Y. Poetry Forum, 1973-75; founder postmaster Park Ave Local Post, 1978—. Recipient Spl. Commendation for poem on death of Martin Luther King, Jr., So. Christian Leadership Conf., 1968, Internat. Who's Who in Poetry award, London, 1969, World Peace award Ky. State Poetry Soc., 1970, Gold Medal award Internat. Poets' Shrine, Hollywood, 1971, Radio award for Poetry of Superior Broadcast Quality, Sta. WEFG-FM, Winchester, Va., 1970, Spl. Citation award Poetry Pageant, 1970, Writer's Digest award, 1971. Mem. Am. Newspaper Guild, Acad. Am. Poets (founder), Wilson MacDonald Poetry Soc. Can. (exec. com. 1967-77, v.p. 1977—), Am. Philatelic Soc., Trans-Miss. Philatelic Soc., Soc. Philatelic Ams., Soc. Israel Philatelists, Am. Revenue Assn., Confederate Stamp Alliance, United Postal Stationery Soc., Scandinavian Collectors Club, Perfins Club, Am. Philatelic Rsch. Libr., Scandinavian Philatelic Libr. So. Calif., N.Mex. Philatelic Assn., Finnish Study Group, Scandinavian Philatelic Found. Address: Penthouse F 254 Park Ave S Ph F New York NY 10010-7208

KISNER, WENDELL HOWARD, JR., plastic surgeon; b. L.A., Dec. 5, 1939; s. Wendell Howard Sr. and Jennie Junkin Kisner; m. Jane Johnsey, June 26, 1957; children: Wendell, Aaron, Meg, Walter. BS, Tulane U., 1961, MD, 1965. Diplomate Am. Bd. Plastic and Reconstructive Surgery. Intern in surgery U. Kans. Med. Ctr., 1965-66; resident in gen. surgery LDS Hosp., Salt Lake City, 1966-67, Ochsner Clinic, New Orleans, 1969-71; resident in plastic surgery U. Miss., 1971-72; chief resident in plastic surgery U. Tenn., 1972-73; pvt. practice Salem, Oreg., 1973-75, Baton Rouge, 1975—. Rsch. fellowship microvascular surgery Ochsner Clinic, 1970; instr. surgery U. Miss., 1971-72, U. Tenn., 1972-73; clin. instr. surgery U. Oreg., 1973-75; clin. asst. prof. plastic surgery dept. surgery La. State U. Med. Sch., 1975—, assoc. med. dir. Our Lady of the Lake Regional Med. Ctr., 2002—, dir. wound clinic, 2001—, chief-of-staff, 1986; lectr. in field. Contbr. articles to profl. jours., poetry to anthologies. Charter mem. bd. mem. Baton Rouge Opera, 1983; bd. mem. Baton Rouge Symphony, 1998—2001; meet physician, head NCAA Track and Field Championship, Baton Rouge, 1982, 1987. Capt. USAF, 1967—69. Mem. Am. Assn. Hand Surgery, Am. Coll. Surgeons, Am. Soc. Plastic and Reconstructive Surgeons (sports medicine com., mktg. com., panel mem. sports injuries 1986), Southeastern Soc. Plastic and Reconstructive Surgeons (chmn. pub. rels. com., historian 1990-91, trustee 1992-94, asst. sec. 1994-96, v.p. 1996-97, pres.-elect 1997-98, pres. 1998-99), Baton Rouge Surg. Soc. (pres. 1989), Costa Rica Plastic Surgery Soc. (corr.), La. Soc. Plastic Surgery, La. State Med. Soc., East Baton Rouge Parish Med. Soc., Surg. Assn. La., Undersea and Hyperbaric Med. Soc., Am. Coll. Hyperbaric Medicine, Am. Soc. Aesthetic Plastic Surgery, Mardi Gras Krewe of Bacchus. Avocations: hunting, fishing, golfing, camping, naturalist studies. Office: 7777 Hennessy Blvd Ste 5001 Baton Rouge LA 70808-4368 E-mail: trotman@earthlink.net.

KISON, CAROL, nursing educator, critical care nurse; b. Milw. Diploma, Sacred Heart; AAS in Mgmt., Milw. Area Tech. Coll.; BSN in Mgmt., Alverno Coll.; MSN in Edn. and Critical Care Splty., Clayton U., 1988; MSM, Cardinal Stritch, 1987; MSN, U. Wis., Milw., 1990; PhD in Nursing, Walden U., Minn. RN, Wis. Prof. nursing Concordia U., Mequon, Wis., MATC, Milw., Cardinal Stritch Coll., Milw.; RN, mgr. Medicare unit Marriewa Inn., Milw. Adj. asst. prof. nursing Marian Coll., Fond du Lac, Wis.; DON long-term care U. Wis., Milw.; clin. assessments Nations Care Link. Contbr. articles to profl. jours. Mem.: AACN, ANA, Doctorate Assn. N.Y. Educators, Greater Milw. Area Chpt., Wis. Nurses Dist., Nat. League for Nursing, Sigma Theta Tau.

KISOR, HENRY DU BOIS, newspaper editor, critic, columnist, writer; b. Ridgewood, N.J., Aug. 17, 1940; s. Manown and Judith (Du Bois) K.; m. Deborah L. Abbott, June 24, 1967; children: Colin, Conan. BA, Trinity Coll., 1962, LittD (hon.), 1991; MS in Journalism, Northwestern U., 1964. Copy editor Wilmington News-Jour. (Del.), 1964-65, Chgo. Daily News, 1965-73, book editor, 1973-78, Chgo. Sun-Times, 1978—. Adj. prof. Medill Sch. Journalism Northwestern U., Evanston, Ill., 1979-82 Author: What's That Pig Outdoors?: A Memoir of Deafness, 1990, Zephyr: Tracking a Dream Across America, 1994, Flight of the Gin Fizz; Midlife at 4,500 Feet, 1997, Season's Revenge, 2003. Bd. dirs. Chgo. Hearing Soc., 1975-76. Recipient Stick-O-Type award Chgo. Newspaper Guild, 1981, 85, Outstanding Achievement award Ill. UPI, 1983, 85, 1st pl. award Ill. UPI columns divsn., 1985, James Friend Meml. Critic award Friends of Lit., 1988, Best Non-fiction award, 1991; finalist Pulitzer Prize nomination in criticism Columbia U., 1981; named to Chgo. Journalism Hall of Fame, 2001; NEH seminar fellow, 1978. Office: Chgo Sun-Times 401 N Wabash Ave Chicago IL 60611-5642

KISS, BOGLARKA, music educator; b. Pecs, Hungary, Apr. 19, 1974; d. Tibor Kiss and Boglarka Torma. BA in Econs., Whittier Coll., Calif., 1996; MFA in Flute Performance, U. of Calif., Irvine, 2000. Bus. analyst McKinsey & Co., LA, 1996—98; instr. Cerritos Coll., Norwalk, Calif., 2000—. Adjudicator Music Tchrs. Assn. of Calif., Whittier, 2000—. Musician: (cds of flute works) Air, 2002. Recipient Yamaha prize, Julius Baker Masterclasses, Danbury, Conn., 2000; scholar Academic Scholarship, Whittier Coll., 1992—96, Grad. Scholarship, U. of Calif., Irvine, 1998—2000. Mem.: Mu Phi Epsilon. Office: Cerritos Coll 11110 Alondra Blvd Norwalk CA 90650 Personal E-mail: boglarka@fuvola.com.

KISS, ELIZABETH, philosophy educator; d. Sandor and Eva Ilona Kiss; m. Jeffrey Holzgrefe, Mar. 18, 1989. BA magna cum laude, Davidson Coll., NC, 1983; B. of Philosophy, Oxford U., UK, 1985, D. Philosophy, 1990. Instr. in politics Princeton U., NJ, 1988—89; vis. prof. of humanities Deep Springs Coll., Deep Springs, Calif., 1990—91; fellow, ethics prog. Harvard U., Cambridge, Mass., 1992—93; asst. prof. Princeton U., 1990—96; fellow Nat. Humanities Ctr., NC, 1995—96; vis. prof. Deep Springs Coll., Deep Springs, Calif., 1999; assoc. prof. Duke U., Durham, NC, 1997—; dir. Kenan Inst. for Ethics, Duke U., Durham, NC, 1997—. Bd. of directors Ctr. for Documentary Studies, Durham, NC, 1997—2003; dean's adv. com. on svc. learning Duke U., Durham, NC, 1997—; co-chair Academic Integrity Assessment Com., Durham, NC, 1999—. Author: (article) Moral Ambition within and beyond Political Constraints: Reflections on Restorative Justice, Democracy and the Politics of Recognition, In Praise of Eccentricity: Character, Moral Education, and Democracy, Alchemy or Fools Gold: Assessing Feminist Doubts and Rights. Represented Hungarian Human Rights Found. Conf. on Non-Governmental Organizations and Human Rights, UN, Geneva, 1987—87; Martin Luther King day planning com. Duke U., Durham, NC, 2000—01; interpreter at Hungarian elections Alliance of Free Democrats, Budapest, Hungary, 1990—90. Recipient Bowen Presdl. Preceptorship, Princeton U., 1994-1997; grantee Postdoctoral grant, Am. Coun. of Learned Societies, 2000-2001; scholar Rhodes Scholarship, Oxford U., 1983-1986. Mem.: N. Am. Soc. for Social Philosophy, NAS (treas.), Ctr. for Academic Integrity (bd. of directors 1997—2003), Davidson Coll. (bd. of trustees 1997—2003), NC Rhodes Scholarships (sec., selection com. 1998—2003). Office: Kenan Institute for Ethics Po 90432 Durham NC 27708

KISS, MARY CATHERINE CLEMENT, writer; b. Johnson City, Tenn., July 28, 1928; d. Hugh Wilfred and Ruby Pearl (Sammons) Clement; m. Alvin Ferencz Josef Kiss, Feb. 27, 1954 (dec. 1998); children: Tony, Stephen, Mary Margaret. Student, St. Mary-of-the-Woods Coll., Terre Haute, Ind., 1946-47; BA in Journalism, U. Mich., 1950. Staff writer Kingsport (Tenn.) Times News, 1950-90; video co-producer, script writer, cons. Get The Picture, Kingsport, 1990—; owner Mary Kiss Media Svcs., Kingsport, 1990—; staff writer The Independent, Bluff City, Tenn., 1994-95; freelance writer, rschr., cons., 1996—. Recipient 1st Pl. award Best Local Feature Tenn. Press Assn., 1970, 1st Pl. award Pub. Svc. Features, 1978. Mem. Investigative Reporters and Editors. Avocation: social service. Home and Office: Mary Kiss Media Svcs 100 Edmond Cir Kingsport TN 37663-2612 E-mail: mckiss_1999@yahoo.com.

KISS, ROBERT, state legislator; s. Matthew J. Sr. and Catherine E. (Schnarr) K.; m. Melinda Ashworth. BA, Ohio State U., 1979, JD, 1982. With firm Gorman, Sheatsley & Co., L.C.; mem. W.Va. Ho. of Dels., 1988-99, chmn. subcom. on ways and means, 1989, vice chair fin. com., chmn. fin. com., 1993, speaker of the house, 1996—. Bd. dirs. Beckley Renaissance, Raleigh County Hospice. Bernard Levy scholar, 1980-82. Mem. Fla. State Bar Assn., Ohio Bar Assn., W.Va. Bar Assn., Raleigh County Bar Assn., Beckley Bus. and Profl. Women's Club. Office: W Va State Legislature Rm 234 M Bldg 1 1900 Kanawha Blvd E Charleston WV 25305*

KISSA, ERIK, retired chemist, consultant; b. Apr. 7, 1923; came to U.S., 1951, naturalized, 1956; s. Mats and Selma (Jakobson) K.; m. Selma Alide Tamm, Sept. 6, 1952; children: Erik Harold, Karl Martin. MS, Tech. U., Karlsruhe, Germany, 1951; PhD, U. Del., 1956. Rsch. chemist E. I. du Pont de Nemours & Co. Inc., Wilmington, Del., 1951-67, sr. rsch. chemist, 1967-74, rsch. assoc. Jackson Lab., 1974-86, sr. rsch. assoc., 1986-90, rsch. fellow, 1990-93; ret., 1994. Cons., 1994—; UN tech. expert, India, 1978, 79, China, 1982, Korea, 1986-88. Author: Fluorinated Surfactants, 1993, Dispersions, 1999, Fluorinated Surfactants and Repellents, 2001; editor: Detergency Theory and Technology, 1987; contbr. articles, chpts. on surface chemistry, textile chemistry, and analytical chemistry to profl. pubs.; U.S. and internat. patentee in field. Recipient Soap and Detergent Assn. award, 1991. Fellow Am. Inst. Chemists; mem. Am. Oil Chem. Soc., Am. Chem. Soc., Internat. Assn. Colloid and Interface Scientists, Del. Photographic Soc., Du Pont Country Club. Lutheran. Home and Office: 1436 Fresno Rd Wilmington DE 19803-5122 E-mail: ekissa@aol.com.

KISSA, KARL MARTIN, electrical engineer; b. Wilmington, Del., June 5, 1961; s. Erik and Selma (Tamm) Kissa; m. Wendy Sue Earle, Mar. 8, 2003. BS, Duke U., 1982; MEE, U. Del., 1986, PhD, 1989. Tech. staff C.S. Draper Lab., Cambridge, Mass., 1989-94; photonic device engr. United Techs. Photonics, Bloomfield, Conn., 1994-95; sr. optical engr. JDS Uniphase, Bloomfield, 1995—. Vol. Harvard Sq. Meals Program, Cambridge, Mass., 1991-94. Mem. IEEE, Phi Beta Kappa, Tau Beta Pi, Eta Kappa Nu. Congregationalist. Home: 9 Rebecca Ln Simsbury CT 06070-1424 Office: JDS Uniphase 45 Griffin Rd S Bloomfield CT 06002-1302

KISSANE, DANIEL, school librarian; b. Bklyn., May 23, 1963; s. James and Carol (Tietgen) Kissane. BA in English, Sonoma State Coll., 1989; MLS with distinction, La. State U., 1995; MEd, McNeese State U., 1997. English tchr. Enterprise (Oreg.) Sch. Dist., 1995—96; libr. McNeese State U., Lake Charles, La., 1996—97, SUNY, Oneonta, 1997—. Active Ea. Oreg. Spl. Edn. Adv. Com., 1993—94. Mem.: ALA. Democrat. Office: SUNY 109 Milne Libr Oneonta NY 13820 Business E-Mail: kissandf@oneonta.edu.

KISSANE, MARY ELIZABETH, communications executive, consultant; b. Westchester, N.Y. d. Thomas Patrick and Marion (O'Shea) K. BA, Iona Coll., MS in Corp. Comms. with honors, 1990; JD, N.Y. Law Sch., 1996. Asst. to CFO Aspen Systems Corp., 1984; acct. supr. Charles Barker, Inc., 1984-86; comm. mgr. BET Fin., Inc., 1987; assoc. Bliss, Barefoot & Assocs., 1988; asst. v.p. Georgeson & Co., 1989-92, v.p., 1992-95, dir. investor rels. divsn., 1995-98; sr. mng. dir. Hill and Knowlton, N.Y.C., 1998-2000; sr. v.p. Abernathy MacGregor Group, N.Y.C., 2000—02; pres. Corp. Perception Rsch. LLC, N.Y.C., 2003—. Adj. asst. prof. mass comm. Grad. Sch. Arts Sci., Iona Coll., New Rochelle, N.Y.; adj. prof. prof. Sch. Continuing Profl. Studies NYU. Mem. N.Y. Law Sch. Jour. Internat. and Comparative Law, 1994-95. Recipient Am. Jurisprudential prizes for legal writing and rsch., 1992-93. Mem.: ABA, Nat. Investor Rels. Inst. (sec. bd. dirs. N.Y. chpt.).

KISSANE, SHARON FLORENCE, writer, consultant, educator; b. Chgo., July 2, 1940; d. Bruno William and Agnes Evelyn (Payne) Mrotek; m. James Quin Kissane, July 2, 1966 (dec. June 1989); children: Laura Janine Ehrke, Elaine Marie Kissane. BA, De Paul U., 1962; MA, Northwestern U., 1963; PhD, Loyola U., 1970. Cert. tchr., Ill. Tchr. Notre Dame H.S., Chgo., 1959-61, Our Lady of Solace Sch., Chgo., 1961-62; tech. writer, editor Commerce Clearing House, Chgo., 1962-63; tchr. U. Ill., Chgo., 1963-66; mgr. Amalgamated Ins. Co., Chgo., 1966-68; writer Herald Newspapers, Des Plaines, Ill., 1968-69; assoc. dir. Montague Coll. Psycho-Ednl. Clinic, Chgo., 1970-72; dir. Learning Ctr., libr. Stevenson Elem. Sch., Des Plaines, 1972-73; dir. Park Ridge (Ill.) Reading Ctr., 1973-78; pres. Kissane Comms. Ltd., Barrington, Ill., 1979—. Learning disabilities specialist Montessori Sch., Lake Forest, Ill.; gifted coord. Winfield Pub. Schs. Author: What is Child Abuse?, 1993, 2001, Gang Awareness, 1995, 2001; co-author: Polish Biographical Dictionary, 1992, Career Success for People With Physical Disabilities, 1996, Autobiography of Mousie Garner, Vaudeville Stooge; contbr. articles to profl. jours. and encyclopedia of advt. Bd. dirs. Barrington (Ill.) Children's Choir, 1984-85, LA FEF Student Exch. Program, Barrington, 1983-84, Barrington Area United Way Operation Smile Internat., Chgo.; mem. task force Dist. # 220, Barrington 1983-86; founding mem. Barrington Area Arts Coun., 1980, Park Ridge Hist Soc., 1972; mem. curriculum com. Barrington H.S., 1981-84; elections judge South Barrington Precinct, 1989—; mem. bus. adv. coun. Nat. Rep. Congl. com Recipient Dale Carnegie Speech scholarship Jr. Achievement, 1958; named Hon. Citizen of Korea, 1965; recipient La Città del Sole, Italy, Disting. Bus Leader award, 2001, Ill. Businessman of Yr. award, 2003; honored as local author, Ill. Assn. Conv., 1999; Literacy grantee, 2000. Mem. Nat. Assn. Women Bus. Owners (bd. dirs. 1982-83), Internat. Platform Assn., MIT Forum, Ill. Libr Assn. (Conn. chpt.), Barrington Profl. Women, Midwest Soc. Profl. Cons. Northwestern U. Entertainment Alliance, Authors Guild, Writers Guild Am., Ph Delta Kappa, Kappa Gamma Pi. Republican. Avocations: painting, post-card art, music, sports. Office: Kissane Comms Ltd 15 Turning Shore Dr South Barrington IL 60010-9597

KISSEBERTH, PAUL BARTO, retired publishing executive; b. Tiffin, Ohio July 5, 1932, s. Roscoe Paul and Mary Margaret (Barto) K.; m. Ann Capps Grinton, June 26, 1954; children: Mary, Katharine, Michael, John. BA, Ohio Wesleyan U., 1954. With McGraw Hill Inc., 1956-89, Western field sales mgr Fleet Owner Mag., Chgo., 1974-76, advt. sales mgr. N.Y.C., 1976-78, pub. 1978-89, v.p., pub., 1986-89; chmn. McGraw-Hill Pubs., 1981-82; v.p., assoc pub. Aviation Week & Space Tech., 1987-89; sr. v.p., pub. Fleet Owner Mag. FM Bus. Publs., 1989, pres. transp. and trucking divsn., 1989-91; pub. Fleet Owner mag. Intertec Pub. Inc., White Plains, N.Y., 1992-96; ret., 1996. Lay leader First United Methodist Ch., Stamford, Conn., 1980-83. Served to 1st lt USAF, 1954-56. Mem. Associated Bus. Press, Beta Theta Pi. Home: 39 Happy Hill Rd Stamford CT 06903-1203 E-mail: kissyl@juno.com.

KISSEL, HOWARD WILLIAM, drama critic; b. Milw., Oct. 29, 1942; s. Leo and Ruth (Miletzky) K.; m. Christine Buck, May 5, 1974. BA, Columbia U. 1964; MS in Journalism, Northwestern U., 1966. Arts editor Women's Wear Daily, N.Y.C., 1971-86; drama critic N.Y. Daily News, 1986—97, 2001— columnist, 1997—2001. Juror Pulitzer Prize for Drama, 1994; bd. dirs. Theater Devel. Fund., 1982--; adj. prof. Marymount Manhattan, 1998-01. Author: David Merrick, The Abominable Showman; Dictionary of Literary Biography, 1982-97; editor: Stella Adler: The Art of Acting. Named to Hall of Achievement Northwestern U., 1997. Mem. N.Y. Drama Critics Circle (pres. 1984-86), N.Y. Film Critics Circle (chmn. 1975, 82), Players Club. Jewish. Home: 275 Central Park W New York NY 10024-3015 Office: NY Daily News Inc 450 W 33rd St Fl 3 New York NY 10001-2681

KISSEL, KEVIN KARL, freelance/self-employed writer; b. Lincoln Park Mich., Feb. 3, 1965; s. Fay Leroy and Phyllis Mae Kissel. A in Bus., Henry Ford CC, Dearborn, Mich., 1986. Bartender Lincoln Park Eagles, sec.; collector DMR Fin. Svcs., Farmington Hill, Mich., Mortgage Ctr. Inc., Southfield, Mich. freelance writer Lincoln Park. Contbr. articles to mags. Mem.: KC, Eagles (little bro. 2002—03, trustee Mich., chmn. E. Ctrl. Regional Henry Ford chpt., chmn Mich. Henry Ford chpt., state chaplain 2002—03). Democrat. Roman Catholic Avocations: golf, softball. Home and Office: 2082 Champaign Rd Lincoln Park MI 48146-2506

KISSEL, PETER CHARLES, lawyer; b. Watertown, N.Y., Sept. 29, 1947; s. Laurence Haas and Catherine Cantwell (Weldon) Kissel; m. Sharon Darlene Murphy, June 14, 1970. AB, Syracuse U., 1969; JD, Am. U., 1972. Bar: DC 1973, US Court Claims 1976, US Court Appeals (3d cir) 1976, US Supreme Court 1978, US Dist Ct DC 1979, US Ct Appeals (9th cir) 1979, US Ct Appeals (DC cir) 1983, US Ct Appeals (5th cir) 1988. Atty.-advisor Fed. Power Commn., Washington, 1972-74; atty. pub. utilities, 1974-77; assoc. O'Connor & Hannan, Washington, 1977-79, ptnr., 1979-87, Baller Hammett, Washington 1987-93; ptnr., CFO, Grammer, Kissel, Robbins, Skancke & Edward (GKRSE), Washington, 1993—. Co-bus mgr Energy Law Jour, Washington 1981, asst editor, 1982—89, bus. mgr., 1989—92. Contbr. articles profl jours Mem Washington adv. bd. Syracuse U., 1995—; mem. adv. bd. Maxwell Sch Citizenship and Pub. Affairs, 2002—; bd. dirs. Episcopal Caring Response to AIDS Inc., 1988—93, v.p., 1990—91, pres., 1992, mem. exec. com., 1990—93 mem vestry St Patrick's Episcopal Ch, Washington, 1975—78, chmn. ann fundraising campaign, 1987—89; bd. dirs. PRISM, 1996—97, Waterpower XI Steering Com., 2000—01. Recipient Spl Award, Fed Power Comn, 1973. Mem. Syracuse Univ. Soc. Fellows, Bar Assn. DC, John Sherman Myers Soc., Nat Hydropower Assn., Energy Bar Assn. (vice chmn com on publs 1984—85 chmn com on hydroelectric regulation 1991—92), Phi Kappa Psi. Democrat Episcopalian. Avocations: gardening, American history, Irish history. Home 5604 Utah Ave NW Washington DC 20015-1230 Office: GKRSE 1500 K St NW Ste 330 Washington DC 20005 E-mail: pckissel@GKRSE-law.com.

KISSEL, RICHARD JOHN, lawyer; b. Chgo., Nov. 27, 1936; s. John and Anne T. (Unichowski) K.; m. Donna Lou Heidersbach, Feb. 11, 1961; children Roy Warren, David Todd, Audrey Anne. BA, Northwestern U., 1958; JD Northwestern U., Chgo., 1961. Assoc. Peterson, Lowrey, Rall, Barber & Ross Chgo., 1961-65; divsn. counsel Abbott Labs., North Chicago, Ill., 1965-70 mem. Pollution Control Bd., Chgo., 1970-72; adminstrv. asst. Gov.'s Staff Chgo., 1972; ptnr. Martin, Craig, Chester & Sonnenschein, Chgo., 1973-88 Gardner, Carton & Douglas, Chgo., 1998—2000, chmn. mgmt. com., 1996-98 of counsel, 2000—. Adj. prof. U. Ill. Sch. Pub. Health, Chgo., 1973-76; inst Kent. Sch. Law, Ill. Inst. Tech., Chgo., 1974-78; mem. vis. com. Northwestern U. Law Sch., 1996-99. Recipient Ill. award IAWA, 1996. Contbr. articles to legal jours. Mem. Lake Forest (Ill.) Sewer Adv. Com. Fellow Internat. Soc Barristers; mem. Ill. State Bar Assn., Chgo. Bar Assn., Ill. State C. of C. (chmn environ. affairs 1973-76), Com. on Cts. for 21st Century, Knollwood Club (Lake Forest; gov. 1976-82), Lake Forest/Lake Bluff Sr. Citizens Found (bd. dirs.), Harbour Ridge Yacht & Country Club. Roman Catholic. Office: Gardner Carton & Douglas 191 N Wacker Dr Chicago IL 60606-1698 E-mail rkissel@gcd.com.

KISSEL, WILLIAM THORN, JR., sculptor; b. Feb. 6, 1920; s. William Thorn and Frances A. (Dallett) K.; m. Barbara Eldred Case, June 17, 1943 (dec. June 1978); children: William Thorn III (dec.), Michael C. Grad., Choate Sch 1939; BA, Harvard U., 1944; postgrad., Pa. Acad. Fine Arts, 1951-53; grad Barnes Found., 1953, Rinehart Grad. Sch. Sculpture, Balt., 1958; BFA (hon. Md. Inst. Coll. Art, 1996. T. Exhibited sculpture Lever House, N.Y.C., N.A.D. N.Y.C., Balt. Sculptor's Exhibit, York, Pa., Beverly, Mass., Gloucester, Woodmere Gallery, Germantown, Pa.; represented in pvt. collections, U.S.; executed large granite meml., Montclair, N.J.; also many animal sculpture studies and commns. Pilot, lt. (j.g.) USNR, 1943-45. Recipient Mass. Sculptor's award Regional Exhibit, 1958, Speyer award NAD, 1966, 68, Am. Artists Profl League award, 1966; fellow Pa. Acad. Fine Arts, 1951-53. Fellow Am. Artists Profl. League, Nat. Sculpture Soc. Republican. Episcopalian. Home: 60 Brightwood Club Dr Lutherville MD 21093

KISSELEV, KATE, economist; b. Oct. 1972; d. Edmond and Elaine Schneider; m. Alec Kisselev. BS in Fgn. Svc./Econs. magna cum laude Georgetown U., 1994; MPhil in Econs., NYU, 2001, PhD in Econs., 200 Rsch. asst. U.S. Dept. State, Washington, 1991-94; drill instr. Russian lang Georgetown U., Washington, 1993-94; economist Fed. Res. Bank N.Y., N.Y.C 1994—99. Nat. Merit scholar, 1990. Mem. Phi Beta Kappa, Phi Alpha Theta

KISSIN, YURY VIKTOR, chemist, geochemist; b. Moscow, Feb. 17, 1937; came to U.S., 1980; s. Viktor and Rosa Kissin; m. Natalie Kissin, Dec. 3, 1960; 1 child, Anna. MD in Chemistry, Lomonosov Inst. Chem. Tech., Moscow, 1960; PhD in Polymer Chemistry, Semenov Inst. Chem. Physics, Moscow, 1966. Sr. rschr. Semenov Inst. Chem. Physics, 1960-79; rsch. assoc. Gulf R & D Co., Pitts., 1980-85, Mobil Chem. Co., Edison, N.J., 1985-2000; vis. scientist dept. chemistry Rutgers U., Piscataway, N.J., 2000—. Author: Isospecific Olefin Polymerization, 1985, Polymers of Higher Olefins, 1997; contbr. over 185 articles and reviews to profl. jours.; 25 patents in field. Avocation: painting. Office: Rutgers U Dept Chemistry 610 Taylor Rd Piscataway NJ 08854-8087 E-mail: ykissin@rutchem.rutgers.edu.

KISSINGER, HENRY ALFRED, former secretary of state, international consulting company executive; b. Fuerth, Germany, May 27, 1923; came to U.S., 1938, naturalized, 1943; s. Louis and Paula (Stern) K.; m. Ann Fleischer, Feb. 6, 1949 (div. 1964); children: Elizabeth, David; m. Nancy Maginnes, Mar. 30, 1974. AB summa cum laude, Harvard U., 1950, MA, 1952, PhD, 1954. Exec. dir. Harvard Internat. Seminar, 1951-69; mem. faculty dept. govt., Ctr. for Internat. Affairs Harvard U., 1954-69; dir. def. studies program Harvard Internat. Seminar, 1958-69, assoc. prof. govt., 1959-62, prof., 1962-69; faculty Ctr. Internat. Affairs, Harvard U., 1960-69; asst. to Pres. for Nat. Security Affairs, 1969-75; Sec. of State, 1973-77; founder, chmn. Kissinger Assocs., Inc., N.Y.C. Chmn. Nat. Bipartisan Commn. on Ctrl. Am., 1983-84; study dir. nuclear weapons and fgn. policy Coun. Fgn. Rels, 1955-56; dir. spl. studies project Rockefeller Bros. Fund, Inc., 1956-58; cons. Ops. Rsch. Office, 1950-61; cons. to dir. Psychol. Strategy Bd., 1952; cons. Ops. Coordinating Bd., 1955, Weapons Systems Evaluation Group, 1959-60, Dept. State, 1965-69; trustee Ctr. Strategic and Internat. Studies; hon. chmn. World Cup USA, 1994; adv. bd. dirs. Am. Express Co., Forstmann Little & Co.; internat. adv. coun. J.P. Morgan Chase, Am. Internat. Group; trustee Ctr. Strategic and Internat. Studies; exec. com. Trilateral Commn.; chair Eisenhower Exch. Fellowship; chancellor Coll. William & Mary; bd dirs. Internat. Rescue com.; Hollinger Internat. Inc., U.S. Olympic com. Author: Nuclear Weapons and Foreign Policy, 1957, A World Restored: Castlereagh, Metternich and the Restoration of Peace, 1812-22, 1957, The Necessity for Choice: Prospects of American Foreign Policy, 1961, The Troubled Partnership: A Reappraisal of the Atlantic Alliance, 1965, White House Years, 1979, For the Record, 1981, Years of Upheaval, 1982, Observations: Selected Speeches and Essays, 1984, Diplomacy, 1994, Years of Renewal, 1999, Does America Need A Foreign Policy?, 2001, Ending the Vietnam War, 2003, Crisis, 2003; Editor: Problems of National Strategy: A Book of Readings, 1965, Confluence, An Internat. Forum, 1951-58; contbr. to profl. jours. Hon. mem. Internat. Olympic Com. Recipient citation Overseas Press Club, 1958, Woodrow Wilson prize for best book fields of govt., politics, internat. affairs, 1958, Disting. Pub. Svc. award Am. Inst. Pub. Svc., 1973, Nobel Peace prize, 1973, Presdl. Medal of Freedom, 1977, Medal of Liberty, 1986; named Hon. Knight Comdr. of St. Michael and St. George, 1995; Guggenheim fellow, 1965-66. Mem. Am. Polit. Sci. Assn., Council Fgn. Relations, Am. Acad. Arts and Scis., Phi Beta Kappa. Clubs: Metropolitan (Washington); Century, River Club, Brook Club (N.Y.C.), Bohemian (San Francisco). Republican.

KISSINGER, WALTER BERNHARD, retired automotive test and service equipment manufacturing executive; b. Furth, Germany, June 21, 1924; came to U.S., 1938, naturalized, 1939; s. Louis and Paula (Stern) K.; m. Eugenie Van Drooge, July 4, 1958; children: William, Thomas, Dana Marie, John. BA, Princeton U., 1951; MBA, Harvard U., 1953; PhD (hon.), Hofstra U., 2001. Asst. to v.p. fgn. operations Gen. Tire & Rubber Co., Akron, Ohio, 1953-56; pres. Advanced Vacuum Products Co., Stamford, Conn., 1957-62; exec. v.p., dir. Glass-tite Industries, Providence, 1960-62; asst. to pres. Jerrold Corp., 1963-64; exec. v.p., Chmn. exec. com., dir. Jervis Corp., Hicksville, N.Y., 1964-68; chmn., pres., chief exec. officer Allen Group Inc., Melville, N.Y., 1969-88; pres. WBK Assocs., Melville, N.Y., 1988—. Chmn. bd. of the Long Island Res. Inst., Melville, NY, 1992-98; vice chmn. bd. of trustees & chmn. of academic affairs comm., Hofstra U. Dir. Kissinger Family Found., mem. bd. Stony Brook Found.; served to capt. AUS, 1943-46, 50. Decorated Commendation medal. Mem.: The Lakes (Palm Desert, Calif.), Princeton Club of N.Y. Home: Lower Dr Huntington Bay NY 11743 also: Lazy K Ranch Divide CO 80814 Office: WBK Assocs 200 Broadhollow Rd Melville NY 11747-4806 E-mail: ludwigwbk@aol.com.

KISSLING, FRED RALPH, JR., publishing executive, insurance agency executive; b. Nashville, Feb. 10, 1930; s. Fred Ralph and Sarah Elizabeth (FitzGerald) K.; m. Mary Jane Gallaher (dec. 1999); children: Sarah FitzGerald, Jayne Kirkpatrick. BA, Vanderbilt U., 1952, MA, 1958. Spl. agt. Northwestern Mut. Life Ins. Co., Nashville, 1953-58, gen. agt. Lexington, Ky., 1962-80, New Eng. Mut. Life Ins. Co., 1981-87; mgr. life dept. Bennett & Edwards, Kingsport, Tenn., 1958-62; pres. Employee Benefit Cons., Inc., Lexington, 1961—. Owner Lexington House, Inc., 1966—, Kennington Assocs., 1967—; prin. Kissling Orgn., 1980—, pub. Leader's mag., 1967—, editor, 1996—; owner, editor Fin. and Estate Planners Quar., 1993—; owner and pub. Fin. Svcs. Advisor, 1993—, Fraternal Monitor, 1999—; owner, pub., editor Probe Pub. Inc., 1997—; pub. Estate Rsch. Inst. Inc. Author: Sell and Grow Rich, 1966; editor: Questionnaire in Pension Planning, 1970, Questionnaire in Estate Planning, 1971. Adv. bd. Salvation Army, Lexington, 1971—, chmn., 1988-91; gen. chmn. United Way of Blue Grass, 1975, bd. dirs., 1975-78, 80-83; trustee, chmn. bd. Lexington Children's Theatre, 1979-81, pres., 1981-83. Mem. Am. Soc. CLU's (chpt. pres. 1969-70, 80-81, 2001-02, regional v.p. 1971-73), Ky. Gen. Agts. and Mgrs. Assn. (pres. 1965-66), Million Dollar Round Table (life mem., v.p., program chmn. 1976), Assn. for Advanced Underwriting (bd. dirs. 1976-84, pres. 1982-83), Am. Soc. Pension Actuaries (bd. dirs. 1971-78, pres. 1974-90), U. Akron Sales Insts. (adv. dir. 1996—), Am. Philatelic Soc., Sigma Chi, Lexington Club, Iroquois Hunt Club, Lafayette Club, Spindletop Hall, Masons, Shriners, Jefferson Club, Thoroughbred Club Am. Office: 98 Dennis Dr Lexington KY 40503-2915

KISSLING, PAUL JOSEPH, academic administrator, religious studies educator, minister; b. Toledo, Ohio, Aug. 3, 1957; s. Carl J. and Margaret E. Kissling; m. Catherine Diane Kissling, June 23, 1979; children: Joshua Ryan, Jeremiah David. BA, Gt. Lakes Christian Coll., 1980; MDiv, Lincoln (Ill.) Christian Sem., 1984; ThM, Trinity Evang. Divinity Sch., Deerfield, Ill., 1985; PhD, U. Sheffield, Eng., 1991. Ordained 2001. Youth Min. Fist Ch. of Christ, Niles, Mich., 1978—80; Min. Ch. of Christ, Ancona, Ill., 1980—84, Chester, England, 1985—91; prof. of Old Testament Gt. Lakes Christian Coll., Lansing, Mich., 1991—2000, v.p. acad. affairs, 2000—, provost, 2003—. Adj. prof. TCM Internat., Vienna, 1994—; prof. of record Ea. Mich. Perspectives, Lansing, 1998—. Author: Reliable Characters in the Primary History, 1996, A Sketch of Old Testament Theology, 1998; editor: (book series) College Press NIV Old Testament Commentary, 1997—; mem. editl. bd. Stone-Campbell Jour., 1997—. Fellow: Inst. Biblical Rsch.; mem.: Soc. Biblical Lit. Office: Gt Lakes Christian Coll 6211 W Willow Hwy Lansing MI 48917 Business E-Mail: pkissling@glcc.edu.

KISSLINGER, CARL, geophysicist, educator; b. St. Louis, Aug. 30, 1926; s. Fred and Emma (Tobias) K.; m. Millicent Ann Thorson, Mar. 27, 1948; children: Susan, Karen, Ellen, Pamela, Jerome. BS, St. Louis U., 1947, MS, 1949, PhD, 1952. Faculty St. Louis U., 1949-72, prof. geophysics, geophys. engring., 1961-72, chmn. dept. earth and atmospheric scis., 1963-72; prof. geophysics U. Colo., Boulder, 1972-94; dir. Coop. Inst. for Rsch. in Environ. Sci., 1972-79, 93-94; emeritus U. Colo., Boulder, 1994—; UNESCO expert in seismology, chief tech. adviser Internat. Inst. Seismology and Earthquake Engring., Tokyo, 1966-67; chmn. com. seismology NRC-Nat. Acad. Scis., 1970-72. Mem. U.S. Geodynamics Com., 1975-78; U.S. nat. corr. Internat. Assn. Seismology and Physics of Earth's Interior, 1970-72; mem. Internat. Union Geodesy and Geophysics, bur., 1975-83, v.p., 1983-91; mem. Gov.'s Sci. Adv. Council, State of Colo., 1973-77, com. on scholarly communication with People's Republic of China, Nat. Acad. Scis., 1977-81, NRC/Nat. Acad. Scis. adv. com. to U.S. Geol. Survey, 1983-88; governing bd. Am. Inst. Physics, 1989-95; chair NRC/Nat. Acad. Scis. panel on seismic hazard evaluation, 1992-96. Recipient Alumni Merit award St. Louis U., 1976, Alexander von Humboldt Found. Sr. U.S. Scientist award, 1979, U.S. Geol. Survey's John Wesley Powell award, 1992, Disting. Svc. award U. Colo., 1993, Commemorative medal USSR Acad. Scis., 1985. Fellow Am. Geophys. Union (bd. dirs. sect. seismology 1970-72, fgn. sec. 1974-84), Geol. Soc. Am., Assn. Exploration Geophysics (India), AAAS; mem. Soc. Exploration Geophysicists, Seismol. Soc. Am. (dir. 1968-74, pres. 1972-73), Austrian Acad. Sci. (corr.), Ret. Faculty Assn. U. Colo. (v.p./pres. elect 2001-02, pres. 2003-04), Phi Beta Kappa, Sigma Xi. Clubs: Cosmos. Home: 4165 Caddo Pky Boulder CO 80303-3602 E-mail: kissling@cires.colorado.edu., kissling@frii.com.

KISTER, JAMES MILTON, retired mathematician, educator; b. Cleve., June 29, 1930; s. James Leonard and Katherine Alice (Sherrick) K.; m. Susan Spence, 1956; 1 dau., Karen Lynn; m. Jane Bridge; 1978. BA, Coll. of Wooster, 1952; MA, U. Wis., 1956, PhD, 1959. Rsch. asst. Los Alamos (N.Mex.) Sci. Lab., 1953-55; mem. faculty U. Mich., Ann Arbor, 1959-98, prof. math., 1966-98, chmn. dept., 1971-73; ret., 1998. Assoc. Office Naval Rsch., U. Va., 1960-61; mem. Inst. Advanced Study, Princeton, N.J., 1962-64; vis. prof. UCLA, 1967; vis. fellow Clare Hall, Cambridge (Eng.) U., 1970; vis. mem. Institut des Hautes Etudes Scientifique, 1974; vis. prof. U. Calif. at Berkeley, summer 1975; vis. fellow Wolfson Coll., Oxford U., 1977, 85-86. Assoc. editor: Duke Math. Jour, 1972-75; assoc. editor: Mich. Math. Jour, 1976-78, mng. editor, 1978, 82-88. Hon. rsch. fellow Univ. Coll., London, 1993. Mem. Am. Math. Soc., Math. Assn. Am.

KISTIAKOWSKY, VERA, physics researcher, educator; b. Princeton, N.J., Sept. 9, 1928; d. George Bogdan and Hildegard (Moebius) K.; m. Gerhard Emil Fischer, June 16, 1951 (div. 1970); children: Marc Laurenz Fischer, Karen Marie Fischer. AB, Mt. Holyoke Coll., 1948, ScD (hon.), 1978; PhD, U. Calif.-Berkeley, 1952. Staff scientist U.S. Naval Rsch. Def. Lab., San Francisco, 1952-53; fellow U. Calif.-Berkeley, 1953-54; rsch. assoc. Columbia U., N.Y.C., 1954-57, instr., 1957-59; asst. prof. Brandeis U., Waltham, Mass., 1959-62, adj. assoc. prof., 1962-63; staff mem. MIT, Cambridge, 1963-69, sr. rsch. scientist, 1969-72, prof. physics, 1972-94, prof. emerita, 1994—. Author: Atomic Energy, 1959, One Way Is Down, 1967; contbr. articles on nuclear and elem. particle physics and astrophysics to profl. jours. Dir. Coun. for a Liveable World, 1983—, dir. Edn. Fund, 1983—2001, pres., 1997—2000. Recipient Centennial award Mt. Holyoke Coll., 1972. Fellow AAAS, Am. Phys. Soc. (councilor 1974-77); mem. Assn. for Women in Sci. (pres. 1982-83), Phi Beta Kappa (vis. scholar 1983-84, senator 1988-96), Sigma Xi (lectr. 1990-92). Office: MIT 77 Massachusetts Ave Rm 6-108 Cambridge MA 02139-4307 E-mail: verak@mit.edu.

KISTNER, RICHARD WARREN, university administrator; b. Bloomington, Ill., Feb. 11, 1961; s. Richard Loren and Patricia Ann Kistner. BA, Ill. Wesleyan U., 1983; MS, Ill. State U., 1991. Food svc. dir. ARA Svcs., Phila., 1984-89; tchg. asst. Ill. State U., Normal, 1989-91; assoc. dir. career svcs. Ea. Ill. U., Charleston, 1991-95; dir. career svcs. Ill. Wesleyan U., Bloomington, 1995—. Bd. dirs. ARC, Bloomington, 2000—; vol., VIP St. Jude Midwest Affiliate, Peoria, Ill., 2000—. Mem. Nat. Bd. for Cert. Counselors (nat. cert. 1993), Nat. Assn. Colls. and Employers, Midwest Assn. Colls. and Employers (com. work 1991—, mem. assembly, 2002—), Ill. Small Coll. Placement Assn. (various offices, com. chair 1996—, pres. 1998-99), Ill. Assn. for Sch., Coll. and Univ. Staffing (pres. 1995-96), Rotary (Bloomington program chairperson 1999-2000, bd. dirs. 2000 03), Theta Chi (mem. alumni bd.) Democrat. Roman Catholic. Avocations: travel, biking, exercise, reading, antiques. Home: 3504 Ballyford Dr Bloomington IL 61704 Office: Ill Wesleyan U Career Ctr Gulick Hall 109 E University Bloomington IL 61701 E-mail: wkistner@titan.iwu.edu.

KIT, SAUL, biochemist, educator; b. Passaic, N.J., Nov. 25, 1920; s. Isadore and Minnie (Darvick) K.; m. Dorothy Anken, Sept. 28, 1945; children: Sally, Malon, Gordon. AB, U. Calif.-Berkeley, 1948, PhD, 1951. Post-doctoral fellow U. Chgo., 1951-52; rsch. assoc. biochemistry dept. U. Tex./M.D. Anderson Hosp. and Tumor Inst., Houston, 1953-55, asst. biochemist dept. biochemistry, 1956-57, assoc. biochemist, 1957-60, biochemist and chief sect. nucleoprotein metabolism, 1961-62; asst. clin. prof. biochemistry Baylor U. Coll. Medicine, Houston, 1956-57, assoc. clin. prof., 1957-58, vis. prof. virology and epidemiology dept., spring 1962, prof. biochemistry and head divsn. biochem. virology, 1962-92, prof. emeritus, 1993—. Vis. prof. Inst. Venez Olano, Caracas, Venezuela, 1971, U. Buenos Aires, 1971, Calouste Gulbenkian Found., Lisbon, 1973; disting. vis. prof. La Trobe U., Victoria, Australia, 1982; mem. del. U.S.-Soviet Health Exch. in Virology, 1967; mem. del. on indsl. biochemistry Program to People's Republic of China, 1990; chmn. pathobiol. chemistry study sect., 1975-79; cons. NIH, 1970-92; sci. adv. bd. Am. Genetics Internat., Inc., 1981-84, Novagene Inc., 1983—. Assoc. editor: Cancer Research, 1960-79; mem. editorial bd. Intervirology, 1972-85, Internat. Jour. Cancer, 1964-90; contbr. 250 articles to profl. jours.; holder 12 U.S. patents, 15 fgn. patents in field. With AUS, 1942-46. Recipient Rsch. Career award NIH, 1962-88, Disting. Inventor of 1987 award Intellectual Property Owners, Inc. Mem. Am. Soc. Cell Biology (treas. 1965-68, pres. 1970), Am. Assn. Cancer Rsch. (pres. S.W. sect. 1965-66), Am. Soc. Biol. Chemists, Am. Chem. Soc., Am. Soc. Microbiology, Am. Soc. Virology, Argentine Soc. Virology (corr.), Am. Assn. Vet. Lab. Diagnostics. Home: 11935 Wink Rd Houston TX 77024-7134 E-mail: saulkit@aol.com.

KITADA, SHINICHI, biochemist; b. Osaka, Japan, Dec. 9, 1948; came to U.S., 1975; s. Koichi and Asako Kitada. MD, Kyoto U., 1973; MS in Biol. Chemistry, UCLA, 1977, PhD, 1979. Intern Kyoto U. Hosp., Japan, 1973-74; resident physician Chest Disease Research Inst., 1974-75; rsch. scholar lab. nuclear medicine and radiation biology UCLA, 1979-87, rsch. scholar Jules Stein Eye Inst., 1988-91; rsch. biochemist La Jolla (Calif.) Cancer Rsch. Found., 1992—. Author papers in field. Japan Soc. Promotion Sci. fellow 1975-76. Mem. Am. Oil Chemists Soc., N.Y. Acad. Scis., Sigma Xi. Home: 920 Kline St Ste 301 La Jolla CA 92037-4320 Office: The Burnham Inst 10901 N Torrey Pines Rd La Jolla CA 92037-1062 E-mail: skitada@ljcrf.edu.

KITAO, T. KAORI, art history educator; b. Tokyo, Jan. 30, 1933; came to the U.S., 1952; d. Harumichi and Aiko (Yoshida) K.; 1 child, Giulio K. BA, U. Calif., Berkeley, 1958, MA, 1961; PhD, Harvard U., 1966. Asst. prof. RISD, Providence, 1963-66, Swarthmore (Pa.) Coll., 1966-68, assoc. prof., 1968-75, prof., chairperson art dept., 1975-81, prof. art history, 1981-93, William R. Kenan prof., 1993-00; ret., 01—. V.p. Internat. Soc. for the Comparative Study Civilizations, 1980-84. Andrew Mellon grantee, 1977-78, Sloan Found. grantee, 1986; NEH Younger Humanist fellow, 1973-74. Mem. Soc. Archtl. Historians. Office: Swarthmore Coll 500 College Ave Swarthmore PA 19081-1306

KITATANI, KENJI, electronics executive; MA in Comm. Policy, Law and Mgmt., PhD in Comm. Policy, Law and Mgmt., U. of Wisc. Spl. corr., U.S. presdl. elections TV Asahi Network, 1980; prodr. PBS documentaries, 1980; scriptwriter Nippon TV Network, 1981—82; pres. media rsch. inst. Tokyo Broadcasting Sys., 1984—99, counsel on internat. affairs, 1984—99; exec. strategist, media content, broadcasting and comm. Sony Corp. of Am., 1999—2001; group exec. officer Sony Corp., 2001—; exec. v.p., bus. planning Sony Corp. of Am., 2001—. Bd. directors Tokyo Dome Corp., 1991—; pres. Tokyo Dome Enterprises Corp.; lectr., media law and mgmt. Sony U., Tokyo; adj. prof. of telecom. Ind. U., Wash. State U. Author: (book) Am. CATV, 1991, The Entertainment Bus., 1999. Trustee Wash. State U. Found.; sr. advisor Sports and Entertainment Acad., Grad. Sch. of Bus., Ind. U. Office: Sony Corp of Am 550 Madison Ave New York NY 10022*

KITAY, HARVEY ROBERT, lawyer, investment manager; b. Bklyn., Oct. 16, 1931; s. David and Celia (Sherman) K.; m. Betty Finkelstein, Sept. 3, 1956; children: Robin Ann, William Douglas. BA, NYU, 1953; JD, Harvard U., 1956. Bar: N.Y. 1957. Acct. Peat Marwick Mitchel, N.Y.C., 1956-57; assoc. Law Office Gustave Simons, N.Y.C., 1957-70; ptnr. Kolleeny, Kitay & Hort, N.Y.C., 1970—. Mgr. Sahabe Securities Co., Scarsdale, N.Y., 1960—. Mem. ABA, N.Y. State Bar Assn., N.Y. Co. Bar Assn., Assn. of Bar of City of N.Y. Home: 38 Montrose Rd Scarsdale NY 10583-1127 Office: Kolleeny Kitay & Hort 500 Fifth Ave Ste 1610 New York NY 10110 E-mail: hkitayesq@aol.com.

KITCH, EDMUND WELLS, lawyer, educator, private investor; b. Wichita, Kans, Nov. 3, 1939; s. Paul R. and Josephine (Pridmore) K.; m. Joanne Steiner, 1966 (div. 1976); 1 child, Sarah; m. Alison Lauter, Jan. 29, 1978 (div. 2000); children: Andrew, Whitney; m. Gail Lettwich Apr. 26, 2003. BA, Yale U., 1961; JD, U. Chgo., 1964. Bar: Kans. 1964, Ill. 1966, U.S. Supreme Ct. 1973, Va. 1986. Asst. prof. law Ind. U., 1964-65; mem. faculty U. Chgo., 1965-82, prof., 1971-82; prof., mem. Ctr. Advanced Studies U. Va., Charlottesville, 1982-85, Joseph M. Hartfield prof., 1985—2003, Sullivan and Cromwell rsch. prof., 1996-99, Mary and Daniel Loughran prof., 2003—, E. James Kelly Jr. Class of 1965 rsch. prof., 2003—. Vis. prof. Bklyn. Law Sch., 1995, Northwestern U., 1996, Georgetown U., 2002, U. Nebr., 2002; spl. asst. solicitor gen. U.S. Dept. Justice, 1973-74; exec. dir. Adv. Com. on Procedural Reform CAB, 1975-76; reporter Com. on Pattern Jury Instruction, Ill. Supreme Ct., 1966-69; mem. com. on pub.-pvt. sector rels. in vaccine innovation Inst. of Medicine, NAS, 1982-85, mem. com. on evaluation polio vaccine, 1987-88. Author: (with Harvey Perlman) Intellectual Property, 5th edit., 1997; Regulation, Federalism and Interstate Commerce, 1981. Contbr. articles to profl. jour. Mem. Va. Bar Assn., Am. Law Inst., Order of Coif, Phi Beta Kappa. Office: U Va Sch Law 580 Massie Rd Charlottesville VA 22903-1738

KITCHEN, CAROL ANNE, social worker; b. Buffalo, July 4, 1941; d. Denis A. and Norma (Caton) K.; m. Robert L. Magee, Apr. 24, 1965 (div. 1981); 1 child, Bruce. AB, Marietta Coll., 1964; MLS, U. Pitts., 1965; MSW, Ohio State U., 1973, PhD, Drew U., 1991. Cert. clin. social worker. Supervising social worker Salvation Army Family Svc. Bur., Cin., 1974-78; counselor Ctr. for Mental Health, Anderson, Ind., 1978 81, Genesee Coun. on Alcoholism, Batavia, N.Y., 1982-85; supervising social worker Geneva B. Scruggs ICF, Buffalo, 1985-86; counselor United Labor Agy., Newark, 1988-90; clin. supr. Livingston County Coun. on Alcoholism, Lakeville, NY, 1991—93; crisis therapist Strong Meml. Hosp., 1994—99; counselor Cath. Family Ctr., Rochester, NY, 2001—. Co-coord. Unitarian Universalists for Lesbian & Gay Concerns, Boston, 1987-89. Scholar Unitarian Universalist Assn., Boston, 1989-90; fellow Congregational History Project U. Chgo., 1990-91. Mem.: NASW, AAUW. Green Peace Party. Mem. Soc. Of Friends.

KITCHEN, CHARLES WILLIAM, lawyer; b. July 17, 1926; s. Karl K. and Lucille W. (Keynes) K.; m. Mary Applegate, July 22, 1950; children: Kenneth K., Guy R., Anne Kitchen Campbell. BA, Western Res. U., 1948, JD, 1950. Bar: Ohio 1950, U.S. Dist. Ct. Ohio 1952, U.S. Ct. Appeals (6th cir.) 1972, U.S. Supreme Ct. 1981. Ptnr. Kitchen, Derry & Barnhouse Co., LPA, Cleve., 1950-97, sr. ptnr., 1972, ret., 1997; life mem., exec. com. 8th Jud. Dist. Ct., 1988-91. Mem. Regional Coun. on Alcoholism, 1981-86, chmn., 1985-86; bd. dirs. Scarbourgh Hall, 1992-94. With A.C., U.S. Army, 1944-45. Fellow Internat. Acad. Trial Lawyers, Am. Coll. Trial Lawyers (sr. mem.); mem. Am. Bd. Advocates, Ohio State Bar Assn. (coun. of dels. 1985-86), ABA (sect. tort and ins. practice, sec. litigation), Am. Arbitration Assn. (panelist 1961-91), Am. Bd. Trial Advocates (advocate), Cleve. Assn. Civil Trial Attys. (pres. 1971-72), Ohio Assn. Civil Trial Attys. (pres. 1975-76), Greater Cleve. Bar Assn. (chmn. med.-legal com. 1974-75, chmn. lawyers assistance program 1981-83, chmn. mentor com. 1988-95, jud. campaign com. chmn. 1993-95, trustee 1984-87, coun. of dels. 1985-86), Am. Legion, Order of Coif, Beta Theta Pi, Phi Delta Phi. Presbyterian. Home: 8755 E Old Spanish Ter Dr Tucson AZ 85710 E-mail: ckitch26@aol.com.

KITCHEN, CHESTER, toxicologist, forensic specialist; s. Chester Kitchen and Judith Womelsdorf; m. Leslie Kitchen. BA, U. South Fla., 1995. Forensic toxicologist/investigator/autopsy technician Hillsborough County Med. Examiner Dept., Tampa, Fla., 1993—96; forensic toxicologist/investigator Broward County Med. Examiner Dept., Ft. Lauderdale, Fla., 1996—98; toxicologist/devel. chemist II United Chem. Techs., Bristol, Pa., 1998—99; rsch. chemist Merck & Co., Inc., West Point, Pa., 1999—. Contbr. articles to profl. jours. Eucharistic min. Cath. Ch., Pa., 2002. Mem.: Am. Acad. Forensic Scis. (assoc.), Am. Assn. Pharm. Scientists (assoc.). Republican. Roman Catholic. Achievements include patents for Extraction Material Comprising Treated Silica and Method for Determination of Gamma-Hydroxybutyrate. Avocations: travel, volleyball, scuba diving.

KITCHEN, JOHN MARTIN, historian, educator; b. Nottingham, Eng., Dec. 21, 1936; s. John Sutherland and Margaret Helen (Pearson) K. BA with honors, U. London, 1963, PhD, 1966. Mem. Cambridge Group Population Studies, Eng., 1965-66; mem. faculty Simon Fraser U., Burnaby, B.C., Can., 1966—. Author: The German Officer Corps 1890-1914, 1968, A Military History of Germany, 1975, Fascism, 1976, The Silent Dictatorship, 1976, The Political Economy of Germany 1815-1914, 1979, The Coming of Austrian Fascism, 1980, Germany in the Age of Total War, 1981, British Policy Towards the Soviet Union During the Second World War, 1986, The Origins of the Cold War in Comparative Perspective, 1988, Europe Between the Wars, 1988, A World in Flames, 1990, Empire and After: A Short History of the British Empire and Commonwealth, 1994, Nazi Germany at War, 1994, The Cambridge Illustrated History of Germany, 1996, Empire and Commonwealth, 1996, Kaspar Hauser, 2001, The German Offensives of 1918, 2001. Fellow Royal Hist. Soc., Royal Soc. Can. Home: 24B-6128 Patterson Ave Burnaby BC Canada V5H 4P3 Office: Simon Fraser U Dept History Burnaby BC Canada V5A 1S6 E-mail: kitchen@sfu.ca.

KITCHEN, OTIS DORSEY, music educator; b. Williamsport, Md., July 5, 1931; s. Paul Dorsey Kitchen and Estella Oneil Byers; m. Alma Irene Phibbs, June 18, 1955 (div. Mar. 13, 1979); children: Sharon Lynn Cole, Gary Wayne. BS, Bridgewater Coll., Bridgewater, VA, 1953; AG, Navy Sch. of Music, Washington, DC, 1955; MusD (hon.), Nat. Conservatory of Mex., Mexico City, 1982. Pub. sch. tchr. Greensville County Schools, Emporia, Va., 1953—54; dir. army band sch. U.S. Army Ft. Jackson, Columbia, SC, 1954—55; pub. sch. tchr. William Fleming H.S., Roanoke, Va., 1956—65; coll. prof. Elizabethtown Coll., Elizabethtown, Pa., 1965—96; ch. organist St. Paul's United Meth., Lancaster, Pa., 1966—; prof. emeritus Elizabethtown Coll., Elizabethtown, Pa., 1966—, free lance music dir., 1966—. Music dir. All Am. Honors Musicians, Worldwide, 1980—98, Mexican Invitational Festival, Mexico City, Mexico, 1978—88, London and Vienna Festivals, London, 1987—99; dir. of lancaster youth symhony Musical Art Soc., Lancaster, Pa., 1966—85. Dir. of music Elizabethtown Music Found., Elizabethtown, Pa., 1966—71; music cons. For Kids' Sake (Messiah Benefit), Hershey, Pa., 1985—98, Rotary Club, Elizabethtown, Pa., 1996. Specialist U.S. Army, 1954—56, U.S.A. Recipient Citation of Excellence, Nat. Band Assn., 1979, Phi Beta Mu Band Frat., 1985, Music Educators Assn., 1996. Mem.: Am. Band Masters Assn., Nat. Music Educators Assn. (Citation 1996), Elizabethtown PA Rotary Club (Citation 1975), Nat. Band Assn. (bd. of directors 2002—02). R-Consevative. Protestant. Achievements include Founder of Elizabethtown College Community Symphony Orchestra; Founder of Lancaster County Music Camp; Director of Music for festivals held in Mexico, Europe, China, Rusia and the United States. Avocations: travel, tennis, elderhostel teaching, guest conducting and adjudicating. Office: Elizabethtown College 1 Alpha Drive Elizabethtown PA 17022 Office Fax: 717-361-1187. E-mail: kitcheod@etown.edu.

KITCHEN, PAUL HOWARD, hockey historian; b. Toronto, Ont., Can., Nov. 14, 1937; s. Percy Floyd and Mary Henrietta (Price) K.; m. Anne Margaret Heaney, Aug. 23, 1963; children: Kevin, Peter. BA, Carleton U., 1963; BLS, U. B.C., 1964. Librarian Nat. Library Can., Ottawa, 1964-66, chief bibliography div., 1966-70, spl. asst to nat. librarian, 1970-72, liaison officer govt. libraries, 1972-75; exec. dir. Can. Library Assn., Ottawa, 1975-85; pres. Paul Kitchen and Assocs., Ottawa, 1986-98. Dir. Book and Periodical Devel. Council, Toronto, 1975-85. Ann. contbr. Am. Library Assn. Yearbook, 1975-85. Recipient Brian McFarlane award for outstanding rsch. and writing (hockey), 2000. Mem. Soc. for Internat. Hockey History Rsch. (pres. 1996-2000). E-mail: pkitchen@magma.ca.

KITCHENS, CLARENCE WESLEY, JR., technology administrator; b. Panama City, Fla., Nov. 8, 1943; s. Clarence Wesley and Voncile (Rudolph) K.; m. Terry Lee Worsley, Dec. 26, 1966; children: Kathy Lee, Mark Wesley. BS, Va. Poly. Inst. and State U., 1966, MS, 1968; PhD, N.C. State U., 1970. Registered profl. engr., Md. Aerospace engr. U.S. Army Ballistic Rsch. Lab., Aberdeen Proving Ground, Md., 1972-77, asst. to dir., 1977-78, leader fluid dynamics analysis team, 1978-80, chief blast dynamics br., 1980-83, chief penetration mechanics br., 1983-85, chief terminal ballistics divsn., 1985-92, dir. Army Rsch. Lab. Transition Office, 1992-93, chief terminal effects divsn., 1992-93; dir. Benét Labs., Watervliet Arsenal, N.Y., 1993-96; dir. weapons techs. Office Sec. Def., Washington, 1997-98, prin. dep. for tech. Army Material Command, Alexandria, Va., 1998—2000; chief scientist Weapon Sys. Tech. Info. Analysis Ctr., Alexandria, 2000—03; v.p. Hicks and Assocs., Inc., McLean, Va., 2003—. U.S. nat. leader tech. panel The Tech. Coop. Program, 1986-92; U.S. nat. leader, sr. nat. rep. Future Tank Main Armament Interoper-

ability Working Group, 1993-96, chmn. reliance sub-panel on conventional guns, 1994-95; army prin. for conventional weapons panel, 1996; U.S. leader conventional weapons tech. cooperation program, 1997-98; mem. U.S./Chile sci. and tech. com., 1997-98; chair U.S./France Tech. Working Group, 1998-2002; chmn. bd. dirs. Army Rsch. Lab., 1998-2000; exec. co-chair U.S./U.K. Tech. Working Group, 1998-2000, U.S./Germany Tech. Working Group, 1998-2000, SAIC Exec. Sci. and Tech. Coun., 2003—. Contbr. articles to profl. jours. Treas. Edgewood (Md.) Meadows Civic Improvement Assn., 1975-76; dir. Aberdeen Proving Gound Fed. Credit Union, 1980-85. Capt. U.S. Army, 1970-72. Recipient Meritorious Civilian Svc. award U.S. Army, 1986, 2000, Exceptional Civilian Svc. award, 1989, 2000, Presdl. Meritorious Exec. Rank award, 1991, Presdl. Exceptional Exec. Rank award, 2000, Superior Civilian Svc. award, 1997; Ford Found. fellow, 1966-67, NASA fellow, 1967-69; named to Hon. Order of Saint Barbara Field Artillery, 1996. Fellow AIAA (assoc.), U.S. Army Rsch. Lab. (emeritus), Ballistic Rsch. Lab. (emeritus); mem. Nat. Def. Indsl. Assn., Assn. of U.S. Army, Tau Beta Pi, Pi Mu Epsilon, Phi Kappa Phi, Omicron Delta Kappa. Democrat. Methodist. Avocations: fly fishing, fly tying, cross-country skiing, reading. Home: 7915 Hollington Pl Fairfax Station VA 22039-3162 Office: Hicks and Assocs Inc Ste 1300 1710 SAIC Dr McLean VA 22102 Office Fax: 703-676-5813. E-mail: kitchenscl@saic.com.

KITCHENS, FREDERICK LYNTON, III, education educator, researcher; s. Frederick Lynton Kitchens, Jr. and Carol Ann (Crane) Kitchens. BBA, Ga. So. U., 1984—88, MBA, 1991—92; PhD, U. of Miss., 1994—2000. PIA; Comml. Ins. Profl. Ins. Agents, 1988, Ins. Inst. of Am., 1988. Grad. instr. The U. of Miss., Oxford, 1986—2000; am. scholar Lloyd's of London, 1987—87; comml. underwriter Fireman's Fund Ins. Co., Atlanta, 1988—90; temp. instr. Ga. So. U., Statesboro, 1993—94; asst. prof. Ball State U., Muncie, Ind., 2000—. Asst. underwriter Cherokee Ins. Co., Nashville, 1984—84; mgmt. trainee Hamilton-Lines Mfg., Bognor, England, 1985—85; asst. agt. Coastal Plains Ins. Assoc, Jacksonville, Fla., 1986; v.p. to pres. Doctoral Student Orgn., Oxford, Miss., 1998—99; dir. Cluster Computing Rsch. Project, Muncie, Ind., 2001—; advisor Assn. of Info. Tech. Professionals, Muncie, 2001—. Author: (book chapter) Neural Networks in Bus.: Techniques and Applications, (papers) S.W. Decision Sciences Inst. (Student Paper Award, 1988, Disting. Paper Award, 2002, Innovative Edn. Award, 2003); advisor (software development) FSA-Based Lang. Translator (First Pl., Ind. Cyberstar Awards, 2002); author: (papers) Internat. Jour. of Innovation and Learning, Jour. of Info. Tech. and Tourism, Internat. Jour. of Mobile Comm. Recipient Eagle Scout, Boy Scouts of Am., 1982; grantee George A. and Frances Ball Rsch. Grant, Ball State U., 2001. Mem.: Omicron Delta Kappa (assoc.), Mu Kappa Tau (assoc.), Beta Gamma Sigma (assoc.). Avocation: travel. Office: Ball State U WB 203 Muncie IN 47306

KITCHENS, JOYCE ELLEN, lawyer; b. Jesup, Ga., Oct. 8, 1948; d. Arthur Ellis and Ray Lucille (Burton) K.; m. Larry Keith Brumfield, Aug. 23, 1969 (div. July 1973); m. Jerry Baxter Barnes; stepchildren: Craig Randall Barnes, Suzanne Cynthia Barnes. BA in English Lit., Purdue U., 1970, MA in English Lit., 1972; JD, Emory U., 1982. Bar: Ga. 1982, U.S. Dist. Ct. (no. dist.) Ga. 1982, U.S. Dist. Ct. (mid. dist.) Ga. 1992, U.S. Ct. Appeals (11th cir.) 1982, U.S. Ct. Mil. Appeals 1996, U.S. Tax Ct. 1995, U.S. Ct. Appeals (fed. cir.), 1999. Staff atty. Dept. Vet. Affairs, Atlanta, 1982-89, asst. dist. counsel, 1989-91; pvt. practice Atlanta, 1991—. Adj. faculty Emory U. Sch. Law Mem. Fed. Bar Assn. (pres. Atlanta chpt. 1991-92, 11th cir. officer 1992-98, dep. sec. 1998-99, sec. 1999-2000, pres.-elect, 2002, pres. 2003--), Ansley Kiwanis (past pres. 1992-93, Disting. Svc. award 1991). Democrat. Methodist. Avocations: reading, travel, adventure. Office: 2973 Hardman Ct Atlanta GA 30305

KITCHENS, LARRY EDWIN, university administrator; b. San Angelo, Tex., Dec. 7, 1940; s. Otis Paul and Hazel May (Hodgin) K.; m. Carolyn Kay Young, June 7, 1963; children: Kathy, David, Mark. BS in Social Sci. and Phys. Edn., Tex. Wesleyan Coll., 1963; MEd in Secondary Sch. Adminstrn., Tex. Christian U., 1969; postgrad., East Tex. State U., 1973-76. Tchr. history, golf coach, bldg. coordinator audio-visual services Ft. Worth Ind. Sch. Dist., 1963-67; dir. instructional media, instr. Tex. Wesleyan Coll., Ft. Worth, 1967-77; dean edni. resources, chmn. various coms. Richland Coll., Dallas, 1977-86, acting v.p. student devel., 1986-87; dir. instrnl. svcs. Tex. Christian U., Ft. Worth, 1987—. Mem. sch.-industry coop. com. Tex. State Tech. Inst., 1977-79; mem. campus speaker's bur. Richland Coll. Chmn. citizens adv bd. Hurst-Euless-Bedford Ind. Sch. Dist., Hurst, Tex., 1982—83; vice chmn. parks and recreation bd. Hurst Parks, 1982—2001; mem. City Coun. of Hurst. Named one of Outstanding Young Men in Am., 1970, 71. Mem. Assn. Ednl. Communications and Tech. (bd. dirs. 1976-79, div., pres. 1989-90, pres.-elect 1991-92, pres. 1992-93, William A. Fulton award for outstanding leadership), Tex. Assn. Ednl. Tech. (past v.p., bd. dirs., pres. 1976-77), Tex. Ednl. TV Assn. (chmn. various com.), Tex. Libr. Assn., Nat. Soc. for Supervision and Curriculum Devel. Lodges: Optimists. Democrat. Methodist. Avocations: photography, skiing, hiking, camping. Home: 624 Post Oak Dr Hurst TX 76053-6520 Office: Tex Christian U PO Box 298390 Fort Worth TX 76129-0001 E-mail: L.Kitchens@tcu.edu.

KITCHENS, WILLIAM H. lawyer; b. Newnan, Ga., Aug. 3, 1948; BA with high honors, Emory U., 1970; JD, U. Ga., 1973. Bar: Ga. 1973. Mng. ptnr. Arnall Golden Gregory, LLP, Atlanta. Adj. prof. food and drug law Emory U. Sch. Law, 1979—. Notes editor Ga. Law Review, 1972-73; mem. editl. adv bd. Food and Drug Law Jour., 1981-87, 96-2001; author: Georgia Jurisprudence Environmental Law, 1995, 96, The Georgia Environmental Law Handbook, 1996, FDA Regulation of Tissue Engineering in Synthetic Biodegradable Polymer Scaffolds, 1997; contbr. articles to profl. jours. Mem. Leadership Atlanta. Mem. ABA, Am Judicature Soc., State Bar Ga., Lawyers Club Atlanta, Atlanta Bar Assn, Food and Drug Law Inst., Ga. Biomed. Partnership, Met. Atlanta C. of C. (bd. advisors, biosci. coun.), Omicron Delta Kappa Office: Arnall Golden & Gregory LLP 1201 W Peachtree St NW Ste 2800 Atlanta GA 30309-3454

KITCHIN, JOHN JOSEPH, lawyer; b. Kansas City, Mo., Mar. 23, 1933; s. John Bernard and Delia Clare (White) K.; m. Mary A. Medill, Feb. 15, 1958; children: Teresa M., Nancy J., John T., Barbara A. BA, Rockhurst Coll., 1954; JD cum laude, St. Louis U., 1957. Bar: Mo. 1957. Assoc. Swanson, Midgley Law Firm, Kansas City, 1961-65; ptnr. Swanson, Midgley, Gangwere, Kitchin and McLarney, Kansas City, 1966—, mng. ptnr., 1983—2001. Gen. counsel Nat. Collegiate Athletic Assn. Contbr. articles to profl. jours. Chmn. Kansas City Bd. Liquor Rev.; mem. Avila Coll. Bd. Councillors, Kansas City, 1972-90, pres., 1989-90; trustee Avila Coll., 1991-2000; mem. Seton Ctr., Inc., Kansas City, 1980-99; trustee St. Joseph Health Ctr. Found., 1994-2000, chmn., 2000. Capt. USAF, 1957-61. Mem. ABA, Kansas City Bar Assn., Lawyers Assn. of Kansas City, Am. Judicature Soc., Mo. Bar Assn., Nat. Sports Law Inst. (bd. advisors), Sports Lawyers Assn., Serra Club (pres. 1978-79), St. Teresa Acad. Club (pres. 1976-77), Rotary. Democrat. Roman Catholic. Avocations: golfing, travel, reading. Home: 11548 Baltimore Ave Kansas City MO 64114-5554 Office: Swanson Midgely LLC 2420 Pershing Rd Ste 400 Kansas City MO 64108 E-mail: jkitchin@swansonmidgley.com.

KITE, LEWIS DONALD, pharmaceutical executive; b. Houston, June 14, 1945; s. Lewis Dutch and Blanche Linelle K.; m. Anita Cole, Apr. 17, 1993. BA, Hardin-Simmons U., 1968; MS, Stephen F. Austin State U., 1971; PhD, La. Christian U., 1998; D in Christian Counseling, Internat. Christian Inst., 1998. Rschr. Baylor Coll. Medicine, Houston, 1974-81; med. lab. dir. Brennan Preventive Medicine Ctr., Houston, 1981-90; contractor, rschr. Med. Rsch. Br. NASA, Houston, 1982-84; v.p. Life Clin. Lab., Houston, 1982-84; pres. Kite Labs., Inc., Houston, 1990—; prof. psychology Internat. Christian Inst. & Grad. Sch., Houston, 1998—; dir. counseling svcs. Providian Health Care, Inc., Houston, 2001—. Chmn. bd. dirs. Kite Labs., Inc., Houston; cons. Chemedic, Inc., Houston, 1989—. Patentee in field. Recipient Undergrad. Rsch. grant NSF, 1968. Mem. Am. Counseling Assn., Am. Assn. Clin. Chemistry, Internat. Assn. Addiction and Offender Counselors, Cert. Christian Counselors Assn., Nat. Guild of Hypnotists, Houston Inventors Assn. Avocations: hunting, fishing. Office: Kite Labs Inc 8323 Wilcrest Dr Apt 13010 Houston TX 77072-3747 E-mail: LDKite@aol.com.

KITE, MARILYN S. state supreme court justice, lawyer; b. Laramie, Wyo., Oct. 2, 1947; BA with honors, U. Wyo., 1970, JD with honors, 1974. Bar: Wyo. 1974. Mem. Holland & Hart, Jackson, Wyo., 1979—2000; justice Wyo. Supreme Ct., 2000—. Contbr. articles to profl. jours. Mem. ABA (nat. resources sect., litigation sect.), Wyo. State Bar. Address: Wyo Supreme Ct 2301 Capitol Ave Cheyenne WY 82002*

KITE, RICHARD LLOYD, lawyer, real estate development company executive; b. Chgo., Jan. 26, 1934; s. Leonard Robert and Idelle (Berss) K.; m. Iris Goldberg, Aug. 26, 1984; children: Larry, Daniel, Jill. BSBA in Acctg. with highest honors, UCLA, 1955, JD, 1958. Bar: Wis. 1964, Calif. 1959. Sole practice, Beverly Hills, Calif., 1959-64; pres. Marcus Theatres Corp., Milw., 1964-80, Kite Devel. Corp., Milw., 1980—. Sec.-treas., trustee Regency Investors, 1982-83; v.p., sec., dir., chief legal counsel Marcus Corp., 1964-81; dir. Mid-Continental Bancorp., Milw., Am. Hampton Bank, Milw., Guardian State Bank, Milw., Continental Bank and Trust, Milw., Mid-Am. Bank, Milw. Editor UCLA Law Rev., 1957-58. Pres. Variety Club of Wis., 1978-79, bd. dirs. 1964—; sec., bd. dirs. Mt. Sinai Glendale Health Ctr., Milw.; hon. bd. dirs. Ballet Found., Milw., Inc.; bd. govs. Wis. Israel Bonds Com., Milw., Jewish Fedn.; pres., bd. dirs. Wis. chpt., trustee Am. Friends Hebrew U. Mem. Young Pres.'s Orgn., Internat. Coun. Shopping Ctrs., Order of Coif. Office: 1031 Cove Way Beverly Hills CA 90210-2818 E-mail: rlkite@pacbell.net.

KITE, STEVEN B. lawyer; b. Chgo., May 30, 1949; s. Ben and Dolores (Braver) K.; m. Catherine Lapinski, Jan. 13, 1980; children: David, Julia. BA, U. Ill., 1971; JD, Harvard U., 1974. Bar: Ga. 1974, U.S. Dist. Ct. Ga. 1974, U.S. Ct. Appeals (5th and 11th cirs.) 1981, Ill. 1985, Fla. 1986. Ptnr. Kutak Rock, Atlanta, 1974-84, Gardner, Carton & Douglas, Chgo., 1984—. Author, editor: Law For Elderly, 1978; author: Tax-Exempt Financing for Health Care Organizations, 1996; co-author: Bond Financing, 1994. Bd. dirs. Atlanta Legal Aid Soc., 1979-84; trustee Sr. Citizens Met. Atlanta, 1980-83. Mem. ABA, Ill. Bar Assn., State Bar Ga., Chgo. Bar Assn., Fla. Bar Assn., Nat. Assn. Bond Lawyers. Avocations: travel, sports, reading. Office: Gardner Carton & Douglas LLC 191 N Wacker Dr Ste 3700 Chicago IL 60606 E-mail: skite@gcd.com.

KITE, THOMAS O., JR., professional golfer; b. Austin, Tex., Dec. 9, 1949; m. Christy Kite; 3 children. Student, U. Tex. Profl. golfer PGA, 1972-2000, PGA Srs., 2000—. Mem. Ryder Cup Team, 1979,81,83,85,87,89,93., Capt., 1997. Named PGA Rookie of Yr., 1973, PGA Player of Yr., 1989; winner Air New Zealand Open, 1974, European Open (Eur), 1980, Oki Pro-Am (Spain), 1996; winner numerous golf tournaments including Bicentennial, 1976, B.C. Open, 1978, Inverrary Open, 1981, Bay Hill Open, 1982, Tournament Players Championship, 1985, 89, 91, Western Open, 1986, Kemper Open, 1987, Nestle Invitational, 1989, Nabisco Championship, 1989, Atlanta Classic, 1992, U.S. Open, 1992, L.A. Open, 1993, The Countrywide Tradition, 2000; recipient Vardon trophy, 1981, 82, Achievements include being the PGA leading money winner, 1981, 89.

KITHIER, KAREL, pathologist, educator; b. Prague, Czechoslovakia, Dec. 6, 1930; came to U.S. 1968, naturalized, 1978; s. Karel and Marie (Bohackova) K.; m. Viktorie Svecova, May 6, 1961; 1 child, Karel. MD, Charles U., Prague, 1962, PhD, 1967. Rsch. scientist Rsch. Inst. for Child Devel., Prague, 1967-68, Child Rsch. Ctr. of Mich., Detroit, 1968-71, Mich. Cancer Found., Detroit, 1972-74; asst. prof. pathology Wayne State U Sch. Medicine, Detroit, 1974-78, assoc. prof. pathology, 1978-95; chief, clin. immunology Detroit Receiving Hosp. and Univ. Health Ctr., Detroit, 1978-89, assoc. head clin. chemistry, 1978-89, med. dir. spl. chemistry, 1989-96; staff pathologist VA Med. Ctr., Allen Park, Mich., 1976—2001. Contbr. articles to profl. jours. Fellow Nat. Acad. Clin. Biochemistry; mem. Am. Assn. Cancer Research, Am. Assn. Immunologists, Am. Assn. Clin. Chemists, Internat. Soc. Oncodevelopmental Biology and Medicine. Avocation: fishing. E-mail: K.Kithier@wayne.edu. Office: Wayne State U Sch Medicine 540 E Canfield St Detroit MI 48201-1928

KITNA, JON, football player; b. Tacoma, Washington, Sept. 21, 1972; m. Jennifer Kitna; children: Jordan, Jada, Jalen. Postgrad in math edn., Ctrl. Wash. Quarterback Cin. Bengals, 2001—, Seattle Seahawks, 1997—2000. Office: Cin Bengals One Paul Brown Stadium Cincinnati OH 45202

KITNER, DAVID N. lawyer; b. Brownwood, Tex., Aug. 25, 1948; BA, Rice U., 1970; JD with honors, U. Tex., 1973. Bar: Tex. 1973; bd. cert. labor and employment law, Tex. Bd. Specialization. Mem. Strasburger & Price L.L.P., Dallas. Instr. trial advocacy So. Meth. U., 1982-86. Fellow Am. Coll. Trial Lawyers; mem. ABA, Tex. Assn. Def. Counsel, Dallas Bar Assn., Order Coif, Defense Rsch. Inst.; fellow Tex. Bar Found. Office: Strasburger & Price LLP 901 Main St Ste 4300 Dallas TX 75202-3724 E-mail: david.kitner@strasburger.com.

KITNER, HAROLD, artist, educator; b. Cleve., May 18, 1921; s. Isaac and Frieda Kitner; m. Joyce Lapaz, Nov. 30, 1946; children: Jon, Ann, Kathi. MA, Case Western Res. U., 1947; postgrad., Cleve. Inst. Art, Ohio U., Cleve. Coll., Washington and Lee U.; D Equivalency, Kent State U., 1949. Chmn. fine arts Kent (Ohio) State U., 1950-74, dean Honors Coll., 1970-72, prof. emeritus, 1980. One-man shows include Cleve. Mus., Kent State U. Mus., Libr. Congress; represented in permanent collections at Akron Art Mus., Canton Art Inst., Cleve. Mus., Dayton Art Inst., Akron U., Kent State U. Negotiator, pres. faculty union AAUP, Kent., 1977-80; founder Blossom Festival Sch., Cleve., 1967. Jewish. Home: 2274 Ashley River Rd Apt 1007 Charleston SC 29414

KITNER, JON DAVID, art educator; b. El Paso, Tex., Oct. 26, 1946; s. Harold C. and Joyce M. (LaPaz) K.; m. Debra S. Johnsen, June 12, 1976; 1 child, Jason R. BFA, Kent State U., 1969, MA, 1971. Instr. Stark Campus, Kent State U., Canton, Ohio, 1970-73, Broward Community Coll., Ft. Lauderdale, Fla., 1973-76; instr. Miami (Fla.)-Dade Cmty. Coll., 1973-76; assoc. prof. fin art Miami (Fla.)-Dade Community Coll., 1976-91, prof., 1991—, chmn. dept., 1988—94, mem. honors faculty, 1981-86, dir. art gallery, 1985-86. Ofcl. evaluator Fla. Internat. U., Fla. Endowment for Humanities, Miami, 1987; arts program coord. Visual Arts Honors Conservatory, 2002—. One-man shows include Meeting Point Gallery, Miami, 1981, Green Gallery, Miami, 1984, Wakefield Galleries, Yorkshire, Eng., 1989; exhibited in group shows Mus. Art, Ft. Lauderdale, Fla., 1984 (award of Merit), Barbara Scott Gallery, 1993; monthly columnist Miami-Herald, 1988-89. Recipient U.S. Disting. Tchr. award U.S. Dept. Edn., 1986, Outstanding Faculty award Miami-Dade C.C., 1988, Nat. Tchg. Excellence award U. Tex. Nat. Inst. for Staff Devel., 1989, Arthur Hertz Endowed Tchg. Chair for Fine Arts and Humanities, 1994-97, Nat. Inst. for Staff and Orgnl. Devel. award for ednl. excellence 2d superior leadership U. Tex., 1995, Miami-Dade County Arts Educator of Yr. award Children's Cultural Coalition, 1999, Simon Bolivar Endowed Tchg. chair, 2000-03, award Nat. Inst. for Staff and Devel., 2001; Fulbright scholar, 1988-89. Mem.: Miami Art Mus., Fulbright Alumni Assn. Office: Miami-Dade CC North Campus Dept Art & Philosophy 11380 NW 27th Ave Miami FL 33167-3418 E-mail: jkitner@mdcc.edu.

KITNER, KATHI R. anthropologist; d. Harold C. and Joyce M. Kitner; m. Denzil Weitz, Apr. 7, 1998; children: Gabriela Salazar Kitner, Alehna Kitner Weitz. BA, Kent State U., 1979; MA, U. Fla., 1986, PhD, 1996. Asst. rsch. prof. U. Miami, Fla., 1997—99; cultural anthropologist South Atlantic Fishery Mgmt. Coun., Charleston, SC, 1999—. Author: (ethnographic report) Ethnographic Social Network Tracing among South Atlantic Commercial Fishermen; contbr. journal article; author: (journal article) Journal of Substance Use and Misuse, Human Organization. Grantee Doctoral Rsch. grant, Fulbright Committe, Internat. Inst. of Edn., 1992, Exploratory Rsch. Award, US Census, Dept. of Commerce, 2000-2001. Fellow: Soc. for Applied Anthropology (hon.); mem.: Nat. Assn. Practicing Anthropologists (sec. 2001—), Soc. of Econ. Anthropology, Am. Anthrop. Assn. (sec. 2001—). Achievements include research in Ethnographic assessments of US fishing industry in federal managemen policies; street ethnography among drug users at risk for HIV infection; tourism and culture change; Latin America; Caribbean. Avocations: writing, travel, sailing, cooking, gardening. Office: South Atlantic Fishery Management Counci One Southpark Circle Ste 306 Charleston SC 29407 Office Fax: 843-769-4520. E-mail: kathi.kitner@safmc.net.

KITSANTAS, ANASTASIA, educational psychologist; PhD in Edn. Psychology, CUNY, 1996. Asst. prof. James Madison U., Harrisonburg, Va., 1997—99, Fla. State U., Tallahassee, 1999—2000; asst. prof., edn. psychology program coord. George Mason U., Fairfax, Va., 2001—. Assoc. dir. Hellenic Inst. Psychology & Health, Greece, 1999—. Contbr. articles to profl. jours. Mem.: APA, Fla. Rsch. Assn., Am. Ednl. Rsch. Assn. (chair, spl. interest group officer 2001—). Office: George Mason Univ Grad Sch Edn MSN 4B3 Fairfax VA 22030-4444 Business E-Mail: akitsant@gmu.edu.

KITSON, JOHN RICHARD, musicologist; b. Vancouver, BC, Can., Aug. 7, 1932; arrived in U.S., 1987; s. George Richard and Elizabeth Lilian Kitson. Assoc., Royal Conservatory Music, Toronto, 1967; lic., Trinity Coll., London, 1966; MusB, U. B.C., 1971, MusM, 1973, PhD, 1986. Prof. Music Douglas Coll., New Westminster, Canada, 1972—87; rsch. assoc., sr. editor Repertore Internat. de la Presse Musicale U. Md., College Park, 1987—2000; assoc. editor Retrospective Index to Music Periodicals, Balt., 2000—. Author: Dwight's Journal of Music, 1991, The Musical World, 1996—97, Quar. Musical Mag. and Rev., 1989. Recipient Vincent H. Duckles award, Music Libr. Assn., 1993. Mem.: Am. Musicol. Soc. Home: 17 F Hamill Rd Baltimore MD 21210 Office: RIPM Consortium Ltd 3100 Saint Paul St #511 Baltimore MD 21218

KITSOPOULOS, SOTIRIOS C. electrical engineer, management consultant; b. Athens, Greece, Feb. 12, 1930; came to U.S., 1958; s. Constantine S. and Maria (Lymberea) K.; m. Antonia Mitsakou, Dec. 7, 1957 (dec.); children: Constantine A., Nicholas, Maria, Andrew T.; m. Karen Hall Siegel, Nov. 30, 1998. Diploma, Swiss Fed. Inst. Tech., Zurich, 1952, PhD, 1955; MSW, Rutgers U., 1978. Cert. mgmt. cons.; lic. clin. social worker, N.Y. Instr. U. Md., overseas, 1956-57; asst. prof. Rensselaer Poly. Inst., Troy, N.Y., 1958-59; with AT&T Bell Labs., Murray Hill, N.J., 1959-69, 70-89, IBM Rsch. Lab., Zurich, Switzerland, 1969-70; sr. ptnr. Euclid Cons., Internat. Mgmt. Consul, NY, Athens, Greece and Zurich, 1989—; sr. advisor Inst. for Cross Cultural Comms., Zug, Switzerland, 1992-98. Author: Mesanastasis, 1986, Metonomasies, 1995; editor: (textbook) Einfuehrung in die Fernmeldetechnik, 1954; editor Consulting to Management Jour., 2001—; contbr. articles to profl. jours. Mem. IEEE (sr.), N.Y. Acad. Scis., Swiss Electrotech. Soc. (life), Inst. Mgmt. Consul. Achievements include 12 patents in field. Home and Office: 10 Park Ave 16S New York NY 10016 E-mail: sotiris@euclidconsulting.com.

KITT, EARTHA MAE, actress, singer; b. St. Matthews, S.C., Jan. 17, 1927; d. John and Anna K.; m. William McDonald, June 1960 (div.); 1 child, Kitt Shapiro. Grad. high sch. Soloist with Katherine Dunham Dance Group, 1948; night club singer, 1949—, appearing in France, Turkey, Greece, Egypt, N.Y.C., Hollywood, Las Vegas, London, Stockholm; actress: (plays) Dr. Faustus, Paris, 1951, New Faces of 1952, N.Y.C., Mrs. Patterson, N.Y.C., 1954, Shinbone Alley, N.Y.C., 1957, Timbuktu, 1978, Blues in the Night, 1985, (films) including New Faces, 1953, Accused, 1957, Anna Lucasta, 1958, Mark of the Hawk, 1958, St. Louis Blues, 1957, Saint of Devil's Island, 1961, Synanon, 1965, Up The Chastity Belt, 1971, Dragonard, Ernest Scared Stupid, 1991, Boomerang, 1992, Fatal Instinct, 1993, Harriet the Spy, 1996, Ill Gotten Gains (voice), 1997, (TV) The Wild Thornberrys (voice), 1998, The Emperor's New Grove (voice), 2000, Feast of All Saints, 2001, Santa Baby!, 2001, Standard Time, 2002, Holes, 2003, also 2 French films, also numerous TV appearances including Cat Woman role in Batman series, (broadway shows) The Wizard of Oz, 1998, The Wild Party, 2000 (Tony nominee), Rodgers & Hammerstein's Cinderella, 2001; star: (documentary film) All By Myself, 1982; albums include In Person at the Plaza, 1987, My Way: A Musical Tribute to Rev. Dr. Martin Luther King Jr., 1987; author: Thursday's Child, 1956, A Tart Is Not a Sweet, Alone With Me, 1976, I'm Still Here, 1990, Confessions of a Sex Kitten, 1991; co-author: Down to Eartha, 2000, How to Rejuvenate: It's Not Too Late, 2000; albums: Best of Eartha Kitt, 1983, Miss Kitt, To You, 1992, Back in Business, 1994, Standard/Live, 1998, The Best of Eartha Kitt: Where Is My Man, 1998, Thinking Jazz, 1998, Purr-fect: Greatest Hits, 1999, Where Is My Man: The Best of Eartha Kitt, 1999. Named Woman of Yr. Nat. Assn. Negro Musicians, 1968; nominated 2 Grammys, 2 Tony awards, 1 Emmy. Office: care Provident Fin Mgmt 1185 Sixth Ave 19th Fl New York NY 10036*

KITT, OLGA, artist; b. N.Y.C., July 29, 1929; d. Elias and Mary (Opiela) K.; m. Nicholas Rawluk, Aug. 6, 1955 (div. 1960); 1 child, Wade. BA, Queens Coll., 1951; MA, State U. Iowa, 1952; studied with Meyer Schapiro, N.Y.C., 1954; studied with Hans Hofmann, N.Y.C., Provincetown, 1954-55; postgrad., Inst. Fine Arts, NYU, 1955, NYU, 1960-62; studied with Robert Beverly Hale, N.Y.C., 1979. Gallery asst. Chappellier Gallery, N.Y.C., 1952—53; asst. to Walter Pach NY, 1953—56; tchg. asst. CCNY, 1953—58; tchr. art NY, 1962—80. One-person shows include CCNY, 1957, Manhattan Coll., Riverdale, N.Y., 1980, Blackout Gallery, N.Y.C., 1997, Coll. Mt. St. Vincent, N.Y.C., 2001, 02, 03, The Corridor Gallery of Riverdale Temple, N.Y.C., 2001, 2002, The Corridor Gallery of Interchurch Ctr., N.Y.C., 2002; exhibited in group shows at Whitney Mus., N.Y.C., 1954, Bronx County Hist. Soc., 1978, Mus. Modern Art, N.Y.C., 1978, Art Students League, N.Y.C., 1979, Bronx Mus. Arts, 1979, Coll. Mt. St. Vincent, N.Y., 2000, Broome Street Gallery, N.Y.C., 2002, 03; represented in permanent collections including Bronx Arts Ensemble, Riverdale Press, Riverdale YM-YWHA, U. Iowa, Iowa City, Fordham U., Fordham Prep. Sch., Hostos Coll., N.Y.C., Harris Sch. of Art, Tenn., Broome St. Gallery, N.Y.C., 2002, 2003; represented in pvt. collections. Home: Apt 4D 5610 Netherland Ave Bronx NY 10471-1703 Studio: 495 S Broadway Yonkers NY 10705-3221 E-mail: olgakitt2@cs.com.

KITT, SANDRA ELAINE, writer, librarian; b. N.Y.C., June 11, 1947; d. Archie Benjamin Nathaniel and Annabelle Clementine (Wright) Kitt. AA, Bronx (NY) C.C., 1968; BFA, CCNY, 1970, MFA, 1975. Sec., asst. Philip Gips Design Studio, N.Y.C., 1970—73; info. operator NY Telephone Co., N.Y.C., 1965—67; part-time asst. Am. Mus., N.Y.C., 1969—71; freelance graphic designer N.Y.C., 1971—90; libr. specialist Am. Mus. Natural History, N.Y.C., 1973—2003. Author: Rites Of Spring, 1984, Adam and Eva, 1984, All Good Things, 1984, Perfect Combination, 1985, Only With The Heart, 1985, With Open Arms, 1987, An Innocent Man, 1989, The Way Home, 1990, Someone's Baby, 1991, Lover Everlasting, 1993, Love Is Thanks Enough, 1993, Serenade, 1994, Sincerely, 1995, The Color of Love, 1995, Someone's Baby, 1996, Sweet Dreams, 1996, Suddenly, 1996, Significant Others, 1996, Celebration, 1996, Homecoming, 1996, Adam and Eva, 1997, Family Affairs, 1999, Heart of the Matter, 1999, Close Encounters, 2000, She's the One, 2001, Just Passing Through, 2002. Recipient Keys to the city of East Orange, Women of Excellence, Mayor of N.Y.C., Lifetime Achievement award, Romantic Times. Mem.: Novelist Inc., Romance Writers Am. (Spl. Svc. award), Spl. Librs. Assn. (pres. NY chpt. 1999—2000). Avocations: travel, cooking. Office: PO Box 403 New York NY 10024 E-mail: sandikitt@hotmail.com.

KITT, WALTER, psychiatrist; b. NYC, Dec. 18, 1925; s. Elias and Mary (Opiela) K.; m. Terry Escorcia, May 15, 1955 (dec. 1974); 1 child, Gregory; m. Sally Anderson Chappell, June 22, 1977. Student, CCNY, 1942-44; AB magna cum laude, Syracuse U., 1948; MD, Chgo. Med. Sch., 1952. Diplomate Am. Bd. Psychiatry and Neurology. Resident Neuropsychiat. Inst., Chgo., 1953-56; practice medicine specializing in psychiatry Chgo., 1956—62, Park Ridge, Ill., 1992—97; psychiatrist Lakeside VA Med. Ctr., Chgo., 1981-92, acting chief psychiat. svcs., 1986-87; ret., 1998. Asst. prof. clin. psychiatry U. Ill. Med. Ctr., Chgo., 1958-64, Northwestern U., Chgo., 1974-96, asst. prof. emeritus 1996-2003; chmn. divsn. psychiatry Our Lady of Mercy Hosp., Dyer, Ind., 1970-72; practice medicine specializing in Psychiatry, Munster, Ind., 1962-80. Mem. Am. Psychiat. Assn.

KITTA, JOHN NOAH, lawyer; b. San Francisco, Aug. 26, 1951; s. John E. and Norma Jean (Noah) K. BS, U. Santa Clara, 1973, JD, 1976. Bar: Calif. 1976. Asst. mgr. Transamerica Title Co., Dublin, Calif., 1977-78; assoc. Rhodes, McKeehan & Bernard, Fremont, Calif., 1978-79, sr. atty., 1979—. V.p. Californians Against Fraud, 1996—. Author: Wrongful Discharge...Look Before You Leap, 1990. Commr. Calif. Crime Resistance Task Force, Sacramento; trustee Alameda County Bd. Edn.; del. Dem. Cen. Com., Alameda County, 1980-81, 83-84. Democrat. Home: 2135 Ocaso Camino Fremont CA 94539-5645 Office: 39560 Stevenson Pl Ste 217 Fremont CA 94539-3074 E-mail: jkitta@aol.com.

KITTEL, PETER, research scientist; b. Fairfax, Va., Mar. 23, 1945; s. Charles and Muriel K.; m. Mary Ellen, Aug. 12, 1972; 1 child, Katherine. BS, U. Calif., Berkeley, 1967; MS, U. Calif., La Jolla, 1969; PhD, Oxford U., 1974. Rsch. asst. U. Calif., La Jolla, 1967-69, Oxford (Eng.) U., 1969-74; rsch. assoc., adj. assoc. prof. U. Oreg., Eugene, 1974-78; rsch. assoc. Stanford (Calif.) U., 1978; rsch. assoc. Nat. Rsch. Coun. Ames Rsch. Ctr. NASA, Moffett Field, Calif., 1978-80, rsch. scientist, 1980—. Dir. Internat. Cryogenic Engrng. Conf., 1998—, Cryogenic Engrng. Conf., 1983-89, 92—. internat. CryoCooler conf., 1996—; co-chmn. Internat. CryoCooler conf., 1996-98. Adv. editor: Cryogenics, 1987—; editor: Advances in Cryogenic Engineering, 1992-98; contbr. articles to profl. jours. Fellow Oxford U., 1972-74, Nat. Rsch. Coun., 1978-80; recipient medal for Exceptional Engrng. Achievement NASA, 1990, Space Act award NASA, 1989, 91. Fellow: Cryogenic Soc. Am.; mem.: AAAS, Am. Phys. Soc. Home: 3132 Morris Dr Palo Alto CA 94303-4037 Office: NASA 244-10 Ames Research Ctr Moffett Field CA 94035-1000 E-mail: peter.kittel@nasa.gov.

KITTELSEN, RODNEY OLIN, lawyer; b. Albany, Wis., Mar. 11, 1917; s. Olen B. and Nellie Winifred (Atkinson) K.; m. Pearle M. Haldiman, Oct. 12, 1940; children: Gregory S., James E., Bradley J. PhB, U. Wis., 1939, LLB, 1940. Spl. agt. FBI, Washington, 1940-46; ptnr. Kittelsen, Barry, Ross, Wellington & Thompson, Monroe, Wis., 1946—. Dist. atty. Green County, Monroe, 1947-53; pres. State Bar Wis., Madison, 1976-77, 83-85; dir. Wis. Law Found., Madison, 1992—. Pres. Monroe Police and Fire Comm., 1947—; legal counsel X-FBI Inc., Quantico, Va., 1986—; mem. Am. Coll. Trust and Estate Coun., Chgo., 1983—. Recipient Outstanding Citizen award Monroe Jaycees, 1977, Outstanding Svc. award Albany FFA, 1991, Hon. Am. Famer award, 2003, Disting. Svc. award U. Wis. Law Sch., 1995, Disting. Svc. award U. Wis. Law Alumni Assn., 1995. Fellow: Am. Bar Found.; mem.: Wis. Bar Found., Wis. Law Found. (life), Wis. Bar Assn. Home: 708 26th Ave Monroe WI 53566-1620 Office: 916 17th Ave Monroe WI 53566-2003

KITTERMAN, JOAN FRANCES, education educator, educator; b. Muncie, Ind., July 27, 1951; d. Thomas Harvey and Ruth (Jackson) K. BS in Elem. Edn. magna cum laude, Ball State U., 1973, MA in Elem. Edn., 1976, EdD in Spl. Edn., 1984. Cert. gen. elem. edn., reading; cert. tchr. learning disabled/neurologically impaired, Ind. Tchr. phys. edn. and music Morrison Christian Schs., Taiwan, 1973-74, tchr. 4th grade, 1974-75; title I reading tchr. Blackford County Schs., Hartford City, Ind., 1976-77, Liberty-Perry Community Schs., Selma, Ind., 1977 81; doctoral fellow Ball State U., Muncie, Ind., 1981-83; asst. prof. English as a fgn. lang. Seoul (Korea) Theol. Sem., 1984-86; asst. prof. spl. edn. and reading Ohio No. U., Ada, 1986-88; asst. prof. grad. studies Georgetown (Ky.) Coll., 1988-90, interim dean grad. studies, 1990-91, dean grad. edn., 1991-93; assoc. prof. edn. Ind. Wesleyan U., Marion, 1993-94, Taylor U., Upland, Ind., 1994-96, chair edn. dept., 1996-2000, prof. edn., dir. tchr. edn., 1997-2000, prof. edn., 2000—. Workshop presenter in field. Mem.: TESOL, Internat. Reading Assn., Coun. for Exceptional Children, Phi Delta Kappa. Avocations: reading, cross-stitching. Office: Taylor U 236 W Reade Ave Upland IN 46989-1002 E-mail: jnkitterm@tayloru.edu.

KITTINGER, THOMAS W. retired music educator; b. Gettysburg, Pa., Nov. 21, 1947; s. James Merle and Marie Seifert Kittinger; m. Denise A. Nagle, May 31, 1969; children: Thomas Jr., Gina, Kristy. BA in Music Edn., Anderson U., 1969; M Music Edn., Towson U., 1978. Cert. tchr. Pa. Vocal music instr. (5 - 12 grade) Littlestown (Pa.) Area Sch. Dist., 1969—99; adj. prof. of music Harrisburg (Pa.) Area CC, 2000—. Ch. organist/choir dir. Bart's Centenary United Meth. Ch., Littlestown, 1971—. Mem.: NEA, Music Educators Nat. Conf., Pa. State Edn. Assn. Ret. Home: 11 Mummert Dr Littlestown PA 17340 Office: Harrisburg Area CC One HACC Dr Harrisburg PA 17110 E-mail: twkittin@hacc.edu.

KITTLE, CHARLES FREDERICK, surgeon; b. Athens, Ohio, Oct. 24, 1921; s. Frederick F. and Ida (Falls) K.; m. Jeane Mignon Groenier, 1945 (div. 1973); children: Candace Mignon, Bradley Dean, Leslie Jeane, Brian David; m. Ann Catherine Bates, 1981. AB with honors, Ohio U., Athens, 1942, LLD, 1967; MD with honors, U. Chgo., 1945; MS in Surgery, U. Kans., 1950. Diplomate Am. Bd. Surgery, Am. Bd. Thoracic Surgery (mem. bd. 1967-75, chmn. 1973-75). Intern U. Chgo. Clinics, 1945-46; resident gen. and thoracic surgery U. Kans. Med. Center, 1948-52; spl. tng. radio-isotopes for med. use Oak Ridge Inst. Nuclear Studies, 1950, cons. med. div., 1950-55; mem. faculty U. Kans. Sch. Medicine, 1950-66; assoc. prof. surgery, lectr. history medicine, 1959-66; cons. thoracic surgery VA Hosp., Wadsworth, Kans., 1954-57, cons. gen. surgery, 1957-60; attending gen. surgery VA Hosp. Kansas City, Mo., 1954-66, Wichita, Kans., 1955-62; prof. surgery, head sect. thoracic and cardiovascular surgery U. Chgo. Clinics, 1966-72; prof. surgery, dir. thoracic surgery sect. Rush Med. Coll. and Presbyn.-St. Luke's Hosp., 1973-92, prof. emeritus, 1992—; dir. Rush Cancer Ctr., 1978-86; mem. staff McNeal Hosp., Berwyn, Ill., 1986-92. Cons. Mcpl. TB Sanatorium, Chgo., 1968-74, Hines VA Hosp., Maywood, Ill., 1973-92; spl. rsch. cardiovascular surgery, control of blood flow. Life trustee Newberry Libr., Chgo. Served as lt. (j.g.) USNR, 1946-48. Clin. fellow Am. Cancer Soc., 1950-52; Markle scholar med. scis., 1952-58. Mem. AAAS, ACS (bd. dirs. Kans. 1965-68), Am. Assn. History Medicine, Am. Assn. Thoracic Surgery, Am. Coll. Cardiology (bd. dirs. Kans. 1963-66), Chgo. Surg. Soc. (pres. 1972-73), Am. Heart Assn. (chmn. program com. cardiovasc. surgery 1965-88, exec. com. cardiovasc. surgery coun. 1962-74, chmn. coun. 1972-74), Am. Physiol. Assn., Cen. Surg. Soc., Chgo. Med. Soc., Am. Surg. Assn., Internat. Cardiovasc. Soc. (sec. 1965-71), Internat. Soc. Surgery, Soc. Med. Hist. (pres. Chgo. 1983-85), N.J. Thoracic Surgery Soc., Ill. Thoracic Surgery Soc. (pres. 1983-84), Soc. Clin. Surgery, Soc. Surg. Oncology, Soc. Vascular Surgery, Soc. Univ. Surgeons (pres. 1966-67), Soc. Thoracic Surgery, Univ. Village Assn. (bd. dirs. 1986-89, pres. 1989), Arthur Conan Doyle Soc., Caxton Club (pres. 1999-2001), Chgo. Literary Club, Hounds of Baskerville, Baker Street Irregulars, Grolier Club, Phi Beta Kappa, Sigma Xi, Alpha Omega Alpha. Home: 856 S Laflin St Chicago IL 60607-4026

KITTLE, JIM, JR., state representative, political party administrator; m. Sherry Kittle; children: Sawyer, Kenzie. Postgrad, Ind. Univ., Ind. Univ. Sch. law. Chmn., CEO Kittle's Furniture Group, 1979—; state chmn. Ind. Republican State Ctrl. Com., 2002—. Vice chair Bush for Pres. Team, 2000; delegate Three National Conventions; fin. chmn. McIntosh Campaign, 2000. Chmn. Retail Divsn. United Way Ctrl. Ind.; bd.dirs. Human Soc. Indpls.; adv. bd. St. Vincent Hosp.; bd. dirs. Ind. Chamber Commerce, Better Bus. Bur., Nat. Retail Fedn. Republican. Office: Ind State Rep Party 47 S Meridian St 2nd Fl Indianapolis IN 46204*

KITTLE, JOSEPH S. science administrator, consultant; b. Clarksburg, W.Va., June 19, 1939; s. Harry Maurice and Florence Louise (Stealey) Kittle; m. Mary B. Kittle, Dec. 27, 1961; children: Adam, Andrew. BS, The Citadel, Charleston, S.C.; MBA, Auburn U., 1973. Lt. col. USAF, 1961—81; sr. assoc. CACI, Arlington, Va., 1981—83; pres. Synergetics, Alexandria, Va., 1983—89; bus. devel. dir. Aeroflex Sys. Divsn., Mclean, Va., 1988—89; program devel. dir. S.W. Rsch. Inst., San Antonio, 1989—. Program dir. Resource Cons., Mclean, 1983—87; mem. faculty continuing engring. studies U. Tex., Austin, 1996—. Cmty. leader Cub Scouts, Alexandria, 1975—80; music dir. Shrine Mt. Family Conf., 1978—; vol. Samm Homeless Shelter, San Antonio, 1992—, bd. dirs.; mentor Holmes Bus. Careers H.S., 1993—96; mem. vestry St. Mark's Ch., Alexandria, 1961—81, warden, 1961—81. Mem.: World Trade Assn., Plz. Club, Am. Def. Preparedness Assn. Episcopalian. Avocations: music, guitar, soccer, skiing. Home: 103 Ivy Ln San Antonio TX 78209-5446 Office: SW Rsch Inst PO Box 28510 San Antonio TX 78228-0510

KITTLESON, HENRY MARSHALL, lawyer; b. Tampa, Fla., May 13, 1929; s. Edgar O. and Ardath (Ayers) K.; m. Barbara Clark, Mar. 20, 1954; 1 dau., Laura Helen. BS with high honors, U. Fla., 1951, JD with high honors, 1953. Bar: Fla. 1953. Ptnr. Holland & Knight, Lakeland and Bartow, Fla., 1955—. Mem. adv. bd. Fla. Fed. Savs. & Loan Assn., 1974-86; mem. Fla. Law Revision Commn., 1967-76, vice chmn., 1969-71; mem. Gov.'s Property Rights Study Commn., 1974-75, Nat. Conf. Commrs. Uniform State Laws, 1982—. Mem. council U. Fla. Law Center, 1974-77. Served to maj. USAF, 1953-55. Fellow Am. Bar Found.; mem. ABA (chmn. standing com. on ethic and profl. responsibility 1980-81), Am. Law Inst., Am. Coll. Real Estate Lawyers, Fla. Bar (chmn. standing com. profl. ethics 1965-66, tort litigation rev. commn. 1983-84), Blue Key, Sigma Phi Epsilon, Phi Delta Phi, Phi Kappa Phi, Beta Gamma Sigma, Lakeland Yacht and Country Club. Presbyterian. Home: 5334 Woodhaven Ln Lakeland FL 33813-2656 Office: Holland & Knight PO Box 32092 92 Lake Wire Dr Lakeland FL 33815-1510

KITTLESON, MARK DOUGLAS, veterinary cardiologist, veterinary medicine educator; b. Sherburn, Minn., Sept. 21, 1950; s. Norman Leonard and Lavonne Elaine Kittleson; m. Judith Ann Knobloch, June 11, 1972; children: Ashlie Ann, Natalie Jean. BS, U. Minn., 1972, DVM, 1974; PhD, Ohio State U., 1982. Diplomate Am. Coll. Vet. Internal Medicine. Staff veterinarian Westfield (N.J.) Vet. Group, 1974-76; resident in vet. internal medicine Kans. State U., Manhattan, 1976-78; rsch. assoc. Ohio State U., Columbus, 1978-80; asst. prof. Mich. State U., East Lansing, 1980-84; from asst. prof. to assoc. prof. U. Calif., Davis, 1984-92, prof., 1992—. Cons. Vet. Info. Network, Davis, Calif.; Buchanan lectr. Coll. Vet. Medicine, Mich. State U., 2005; assoc. dir. Vet. Med. Tchg. Hosp., 1996-2000. Author: (book) Small Animal Cardiovascular Medicine, 1998, (website) www.vnth.ucdavis.edu/cardio/cases Case Studies in Small Animal Cardiovascular Medicine; assoc. editor: Jour. Vet. Internal Medicine, 1986-90; contbr. over 75 articles to sci. jours., chpts. in books. Recipient Small Animal Rsch. award Ralston Purina, 1989. Mem. Am. Coll. Vet. Internal Medicine (bd. cert. in cardiology, pres. 1984-87, v.p. 1998-99, pres.-elect 1999-2000, pres. 2000-01, chmn. bd. 2001-2002). Avocations: basketball, computers.

KITTLITZ, RUDOLF GOTTLIEB, JR., chemical engineer, researcher; b. Waco, Tex., Apr. 19, 1935; s. Rudolf Gottlieb and Lena Hulda (Landgraf) K.; children: Lenell, Theresa, Liesel, Rolf. BSChemE, U. Miss., 1957; MS in Engring., U. Ala., 2003. Registered profl. engr., Calif. Engr., polychems. research E.I. du Pont de Nemours & Co., Wilmington, Del., 1957-60, engr., textile fibers dept. Seaford, Del., 1960-62, sr. engr., textile fibers dept., 1962-67, Chattanooga, 1967-68, sr. research engr., 1968-83, sr. research engr. textile fibers, 1983-87, research assoc. textile fibers, 1987-92, sr. rsch. assoc. fibers, 1992-94, Chattanooga, 1995—2000; statis. cons. Rudy Kittlitz & Assocs., Alpine, Tex., 2001—. Lectr. in field; adj. prof. U. Tenn.-Chattanooga, 1980—82, Sul Ross State U., 2001—; Citizen Am. Program del. to Russia, 1991. Co-author: Quality Assurance for the Chemical and Process Industries--A Manual of Good Practices, 1987, 2d edit. 1999, ANSI/ASQC Q90/ISO 9000: Guidelines for Use by the Chemical and Process Industries, 1992, Specifications for the Chemical and Process Industries--A Manual for Development and Use, 1996. Vice chmn. Cmty. Action Com., Seaford, 1966; mem. Alpine Pks. Bd., 2001—; chmn. U.S. tech. adv. group to tech. com. Internat. Orgn. Standardization, 2001—. Fellow: Am. Soc. for Quality (cert. quality and reliability engr., chmn. Chattanooga sect. 1975—76, councilor region 11 chem. divsn. 1975—80, chmn. Del. sect. 1984—85, exec. regional dir. 1987—91, dir.-at-large 1991—93, parliamentarian 1993—99, 2000—, W.G. Hunter award 1989); mem.: Internat. Orgn. for Standardization, Am. Statis. Assn. Democrat. Baptist. Home: 2006 Ceredo Dr Alpine TX 79830 Office: 117 N 2d St # 2207 Alpine TX 79830-4701

KITTO, FRANKLIN CURTIS, computer systems specialist; b. Salt Lake City, Nov. 18, 1954; s. Curtis Eugene and Margaret (Ipson) K.; m. Collette Madsen, Sept. 16, 1982; children: Melissa Erin, Heather Elise, Stephen Curtis. BA, Brigham Young U., 1978, MA, 1980. Tv sta. operator Sta. KBYU-TV, Provo, Utah, 1973-78; grad. teaching asst. Brigham Young Univ., 1978-80, cable TV system operator Instructional Media U. Utah, Salt Lake City, 1980-82, data processing mgr., 1982-83, media supr., 1983-85, bus. mgr., 1985-87; dir. computer systems tng. MegaWest Systems, Inc., Salt Lake City, 1987-90, dir. new product devel., 1990-91, mgr. tng. and installation, 1991-93, mgr. rsch. and devel., 1993; tng. and installation mgr. Total Solutions, American Fork, Utah, 1993-95, tng., support and installation mgr., 1995; EDI programmer Megawest Systems, Inc., Salt Lake City, 1996; EDI supervisor Companion Technologies (formerly Megawest Systems, Inc.), Midvale, Utah, 1996-99; software developer Nuskin Internat., Provo, Utah, 1999—2001, sr. programmer, analyst, 2001—. Recipient Kiwanis Freedom Leadership award, Salt Lake City, 1970, Golden Microphone award, Brigham Young U., 1978, Summit award, Nuskin Internat., 2002. Mem. Assn. Ednl. Communications and Tech., Utah Pick Users Group (sec. 1983-87, pres. 1987-89, treas. 1989-90), Am. Soc. Tng. and Devel., Assn. for Computer Tng. and Support, Phi Eta Sigma, Kappa Tau Alpha. Mem. Lds Ch. Home: 10931 S Avila Dr Sandy UT 84094-5965 Office: NuSkin Internat IT Dept 75 W Center St Provo UT 84601-4432 E-mail: fckitto@nuskin.net., fkitto@iname.com.

KITTO, JOHN BUCK, JR., mechanical engineer; b. Evanston, Ill., Dec. 22, 1952; s. John Buck and Marie (Comstock) K.; children: Christopher Daniel, Andrew Comstock. BSME, Lehigh U., 1975; MBA, U. Akron, 1980. Reg. profl. engr., Ohio, Pa. Sr. engr. McDermott Tech. Inc. subs. Babcock & Wilcox Co., Alliance, Ohio, 1975-80, research engr., 1980-81, program mgr., 1981-94, bus. devel. specialist, 1995-99; bus. devel. mgr. The Babcock and Wilcox Co., Barberton, Ohio, 1999—. Editor: Heat Exchangers for Two Phase Flow, 1983, Two-Phase Heat Exchanger, 1985, Maldistribution of Flow, 1987, Steam: Its Generation and Use, 1992; author and patentee in field. Fellow ASME (chmn. chpt. 1983-84, chmn. exec. com. of heat transfer divsn. 1992-93, v.p. region V 1992-95, officer bd. comms. 1991-95, sr. v.p. 1995-98, mem. bd. govs. 1998—, Prime Movers award 1992, Dedicated Svc. award 1992, George Westinghouse Silver medal 1991); mem. Air Waste Mgmt. Assn., Tau Beta Pi, Pi Tau Sigma, Beta Gamma Sigma, Sigma Iota Epsilon. Republican. Avocations: reading, hiking, board games, coaching soccer. Home: 1225 Arrowhead Dr SW Dellroy OH 44620 Office: Babcock & Wilcox Co PO Box 351 20 S Van Buren Ave Barberton OH 44203-0351 Fax: 330-860-1409.

KITTREDGE, JOHN RUSSELL, physician; b. Ellsworth, Maine, Apr. 17, 1950; s. Russell Millard and Florence Elizabeth (Davis) K.; m. Carol Kittredge; children: Crichton, Russa, Olivia, Clare, Clive. AB in Biology cum laude, Boston U., 1972; MD, Albany Med. Coll. Union U., 1976. Resident Overlook Hosp., Summit, N.J., 1976-79; staff physician Indian Health Svc., Shawnee, Okla., 1979-80, clin. dir., 1980-89, Tucson, Ariz., 1989-92, coord. med. contracts, 1992—, acting chief med. officer, 1993-2000, acting dep. assoc. dir., 1996-99, chief med. officer, 2000—. Capt. USPHS, 1979—. Mem. Am. Coll. Physician Execs., Am. Acad. Family Practice, Ariz. Acad. Family Practice, Officers Assn. USPHS. Independent. Avocations: classical music, reading, hiking. Office: Indian Health Svc 7900 S J Stock Rd Tucson AZ 85746-7012 Home: 4910 N Via Serenidad Tucson AZ 85718-5718 E-mail: john.kittredge@mail.ihs.gov.

KITTREDGE, WILLIAM ALFRED, humanities educator; b. Portland, Oreg., Aug. 14, 1932; s. Franklin Oscar and Josephine (Miessner) K.; m. Janet O'Connor, Dec. 8, 1952 (div. 1968); children: Karen, Bradley. BS, Oreg. State U., 1953; MFA in Creative Writing, U. Iowa, 1969. Rancher Warner Valley Livestock, Adel, Oreg., 1957-67; prof. U. Mont., Missoula, 1969—, now Regents Prof. emeritus. Author: The Van Gogh Field, 1979, We Are Not In This Together, 1984, Owning It All, 1987, Hole in the Sky, 1992, Who Owns the West, 1996, The Portable Western Reader, 1997, Taking Care, 1999, Balancing Water, 2000, The Nature of Generosity, 2000, Southwestern Homelands, 2002, The Best Stores of William Kittredge, 2003. With USAF, 1954-57. Recipient award for lit. Gov. of Mont., 1988, Charles Frankel prize in Humanities, NEH, 1994; named Mont. Humanist of Yr., 1989. Home: 143 S 5th St E Missoula MT 59801-2719

KITTRELL, PAMELA R. lawyer; b. Athens, Ga., June 15, 1965; d. John Edison and Anne (Hagins) K. AB summa cum laude, U. Miami, 1987; JD, U. Mich., 1990. Bar: Fla. 1990, U.S. Dist. Ct. (so. dist.) Fla. 1991, D.C. 1992, Colo. 1994, U.S. Ct. Appeals (11th cir.) 1994, U.S. Dist. CT. (mid. dist.) Fla. 1995. Assoc. Stearns, Weaver, Miller, Weissler, Alhadeff & Sitterson, PA, Miami, 1990-93; sr. assoc. Cooney, Mattson, Lance, Blackburn, Richards & O'Connor, P.A., Ft. Lauderdale, Fla., 1994-98. Mem. Fla. Bar (appellate practice sec.), Fla. Def. Lawyers Assn. Democrat.

KITTRIE, NICHOLAS, lawyer, international consultant, writer; b. en route Bilgoraj, Poland, Mar. 26, 1930; (parents Brit. citizens); s. S.K. Kronenbergh and Perla F. (Ver Standijk) K.; m. Sara Yudovic de Burak, June 1, 1962; children: Orde Felicien, Norda Nicole, Zachary McNair. Student, U. Cairo, 1946, U. London, 1947; LLB, U. Kans., 1950, MA, 1951; postgrad., U. Chgo., 1954-55; LLM, Georgetown U., 1963, SJD, 1968. Bar: Kans. 1953, D.C. 1958, U.S. Supreme Ct. Rsch. asst. U. London, 1947; instr. Western civilization dept. U. Kans., 1948-50; legal analyst Kans. Govt. Rsch. Ctr., 1951-54; asst. to dir. legis. svc. ABA, 1955-56, project dir., 1956-58; rsch. assoc. Yale Law Sch., 1958; legal counsel to U.S. Senator Wiley, 1959; counsel to U.S. Senator Estes Kefauver, antitrust and monopoly subcom. U.S. Senate, 1959-62; ptnr. DeGrazia & Kittrie, Washington, 1962-67; prof. criminal and comparative law Washington Coll. Law, Am. U., 1963—, dir. Inst. for Advanced Studies in Justice, 1970-78, dean, 1977-79, Mooers scholar and prof. law, 1983—; univ. prof. Am. U., Washington, 1994—. Lectr. U. Ottawa, summer 1966; vis. lectr. Salzburg Law Sch., summers 1999—; rsch. scholar Univs. Warsaw and Berlin, summers 1967, 68; rsch. assoc. Ctr. Studies Criminal Justice U. Chgo., 1967-68; dir. Law and Policy Inst., Jerusalem, summers 1970-76, Inst. Law and Mass Media, 1978—; chmn. Eleanor Roosevelt Inst. for Justice and Peace, 1989—; vis. fellow Inst. Advanced Legal Rsch. U. London, 1973-74, Nat. Inst. Justice U.S. Dept. Justice, 1979-80; vis. prof. London Sch. Econs., 1974; prof. internat. criminal law, Salzburg Law Sch., 2000-; cons. Pres.'s Commn. Marijuana and Drug Abuse, 1972, v.p.'s commn. to combat terrorism, 1985; permanent rep. of AIDP to UN Social and Econs. Coun., 1975—; mem. task force on role of psychology in criminal justice Am. Psychol. Assn.; dir. Dulles Internat. Bank, 1998-, Bank of Chios, Athens, Greece; dir., gen. counsel Liberty House Investments; chmn. KVK Communications Ltd.; chmn. finance com. U. Bridgeport, 1998- Author: International Legal Responsibility for Colonial People, 1951, The Mentally Disabled and the Law, 1959, The Right to be Different: Deviance and Enforced Law, 1971, The Comparative Law of Israel and the Middle East, 1971, The Real Estate Settlement Process and Its Cost, 1972, Crescent and Star: Arab-Israeli Perspectives on the Middle East Conflict, 1972, Medicine, Law and Public Policy, 1975, The Tree of Liberty: Rebellion and Political Crime in America, 1986, 2d edit., 1998, The Uncertain Future: Gorbachev's Eastern Bloc, 1988, The War Against Authority: From the Crisis of Legitimacy to a New Social Contract, 1995, Rebels With a Cause: The Minds and Morality of Political Offenders, 2000, Sentencing, Sanctions and Corrections: Federal and State Law, Policy and Practice, 2002, The Future of Peace in the 21st Century, 2003, Crimes and Punishments: International Criminal Law and Procedure, 2003; chmn. editl. bd. Jour. Criminology, 1973-75; mem. editl. bd. Law and Human Behavior, 1976-80; mem. editl. adv. bd. The Washington Times; mem. exec. bd. Paragon House Pubs.; sr. cons. U.S. News and World Report Books; contbr. articles to profl. jours. Chmn. UN Alliance of NGOs on Crime Prevention and Criminal Justice, 1998—, sci. com. U. Messina, Italy. Served with Brit. Middle East Command. Raymond fellow U. Chgo., 1954-55; rsch. fellow Yale Law Sch., 1955; sr. fellow NEH, 1973-74. Mem. ABA, AAAS (mem. coun. 1972—), Am. Soc. Criminology (pres. 1975), Internat. Assn. Penal Law (v.p. Am. sect., sec.-gen. 1975-80), Internat. Assn. Comparative Pub. Law (bd. dirs. 1976—), Am. Soc. Pub. Adminstrn., Am. Soc. Internat. Law, Internat. Inst. Space Law, Inter-Am. Bar Assn., Kans. Bar Assn., D.C. Bar Assn., Rose Haven Yacht Club (bd. dirs.), Cosmos Club, Phi Delta Phi (Sam Green award 1989). Home: 6908 Ayr Ln Bethesda MD 20817-4902 also: Ramsbridge Farm Cochran Mill Rd Leesburg VA 20175-4617 Office: Am U Sch Law 4801 Massachusetts Ave NW Ste 354 Washington DC 20016 Fax: 202-387-3629.

KITTROSS, JOHN MICHAEL, retired communications educator; b. NYC, Apr. 25, 1929; s. John H. and Lucile S. (Vossen) K.; m. Sally Sprague, Dec. 27, 1951; children— David M., Julia Ann. AB, Antioch Coll., 1951; MS, Boston U., 1952; PhD, U. Ill., 1960. Various positions broadcasting, summer stock, motion picture prodn., 1946-52; rsch. asst. U. Ill. Inst. Comm. Rsch., Urbana, 1955-59; from instr. to assoc. prof. dept. telecomm. U. So. Calif., Calif., 1959-68; prof. comm. Temple U., 1968-85, asst. dean Sch. Comm. and Theater, 1971-73, assoc. dean, 1973-80; dean Emerson Coll., Boston, 1985, provost, v.p. acad. affairs, 1985-87, prof. dept. mass comm., 1987-93. Vis. prof., dir. Temple U. Sch. Comms. and Theater London Programme, 1994; mng. dir. K.E.G. Assocs., 1995—. Author: Television Frequency Allocation Policy in the United States, 1979; co-author: Stay Tuned: A Concise History of American Broadcasting, 1978, 3d edit., 2002, Controversies in Media Ethics, 1996, 2nd edit., 1999; editor: Free and Fair: Courtroom Access and the Fairness Doctrine, 1970, Jour. Broadcasting, 1960-72, Documents in American Telecommunications Policy, 1977, Administration of American Telecommunications Policy, 1981; editor: Media Ethics, 1989—; compiler: Bibliography of Theses and Dissertations in Broadcasting, 1920-73, 1978; contbg. editor: Comm. Booknotes Quar., 1997—; contbr. articles to profl. jours. Trustee Upper Moreland Free Pub. Library, 1976-82. Served with AUS, 1952 54. Mem. AAUP, Broadcast Edn. Assn. (Disting. Broadcast Edn. award 1990), Assn. Edn. in Journalism and Mass Comm., Radio-TV News Dirs. Assn., Soc. Profl. Journalists, ACLU. Unitarian (trustee ch. 1966-68). Home: 164 High St Acton MA 01720-4218

KITZ, RICHARD JOHN, anesthesiologist, educator; b. Oshkosh, Wis., Mar. 25, 1929; s. Edward G. and Lona M (Schneider) Kitz; m. Jeanne Hogan, Feb. 27, 1954; 1 child, Anne Marie. BS, Marquette U., 1951, MD, 1954; MA (hon.), Harvard U. Med. Sch., 1969; DSc (hon.), Marquette U., 2000. Diplomate Am. Bd. Anesthesiology (dir.). Intern in surgery, Columbia U., 1954—55; resident in surgery, 1956—57; resident in anesthesiology Columbia U., 1958—60, instr. in anesthesiology, 1960—61, NIH spl. rsch. fellow, 1961—62, asst. prof. anesthesiology, 1962—66, assoc. prof., 1966—69; prof. rsch. and tchg. in anesthesia Harvard U.-MIT, co-dir. divsn. health scis. tech., 1985—91; anaesthetist-in-chief Mass. Gen. Hosp., Boston, 1969—94; prof. Harvard U. Med. Sch., 1969—70, Henry Isaiah Dorr prof. anaesthesia, 1970—98, Henry Isaiah Dorr Disting. prof., 1998—, faculty dean clin. affairs, 1994—99. Cons. FDA; prin. investigator Harvard Anaesthesia Rsch. and Rsch. Tng. Ctr., 1969—93. Editor: This is No Humbug! Reminiscences of the Department of Anesthesia at the Massachusetts General Hospital, 2002; editor: (with E.M. Papper) Uptake and Distribution of Anesthetic Agents, 1963; editor: (with M.B. Laver) Sci. Basis of Anesthesia; editor-in-chief Jour. Clin. Anesthesia, 1987—95; contbr. articles to profl. jours. Served with M.C. USN, 1955—57. Fellow: Coll. Anesthesiologists; mem.: Harvard Club (Boston), Royal Coll. Surgeons Ireland (hon. mem. faculty anesthetists), Mass. Soc. Anesthesiologists, Am. Soc. Anesthesiologists, Royal Coll. Anesthetists Eng. (hon.), Japan Soc. Anesthesiologists (hon.), German Soc. Anesthesiologists and Intensive Care (hon.), Australian Soc. Anesthetists (hon.), Assn. Univ. Anesthetists, AMA, Inst. Medicine, NAS, Blue Water Sailing Club, Beverly Yacht Club. Roman Catholic. Home: 6 Pond St Dover MA 02030-2432 Office: Mass Gen Hosp Dept Anesthesia Boston MA 02114 E-mail: richard_kitz@hms.harvard.edu., rkitz@partners.org.

KITZES, ARNOLD S. retired chemical engineer, retired nuclear engineer; b. Boston, Sept. 21, 1917; s. Isidore and Yetta (Weiss) Kitzes; m. Esther Grossman (dec.); children: Judith A., David H.; m. Helen L. Knox. BSChemE, CCNY, 1939; MSChemE, U. Minn., 1941, PhD, 1948. Registered profl. engr., Pa. Engr. Park-Leggett Altman, Mpls., 1941—42; chief chemist Sangamon Ordnance Plant, Springfield, Ill., 1942—45; rsch. assoc. U. Minn., St. Paul, 1945—48; sr. engr. Oak Ridge (Tenn.) Nat. Lab., 1948—57; adv. engr. Westinghouse Comml. Atomic Power, Pitts., 1948—50, mgr. test engring., 1950—72, adv. engr., 1972—87, chmn. patent com., 1978—86. Contbr. articles to profl. jours. Pres. Group Against Smog and Pollution, Pitts., 1972—73, Pitts. Opera Theater, 1978—. Fellow: AAAS; mem.: ANS, ASME (chmn. subcom. 1976—77), AIChE, Phi Lambda Upsilon, Sigma Xi. Democrat. Achievements include patents for spray drying; volume reduction of radioactive liquid, solid wastes, comml. welding; high tech heater design. Avocations: fishing, camping, dogs. Home: 9 Hearthstone Dr Pittsburgh PA 15235-4530

KITZES, DAVID LOUIS, cardiologist, educator; b. Bklyn., May 27, 1938; s. Samuel and Evelyn Kitzes; m. Mary Evelyn Kitzes; children: Benjamin, Sydney, Madeline. BA, Cornell U., 1959; MD, SUNY, 1963. Diplomate Am. Bd. Internal Medicine. Intern Ind. U. Med. Ctr., Indpls., 1963-64, resident, 1966-68, fellow in cardiology, 1968-70; from clin. asst. to clin. assoc. prof. Brown U., Providence, 1970—; physician Miriam Hosp., Providence, 1970—, treas. med. staff, 1992-94, v.p. med. staff, 1994-96, pres. med. staff, 1996-98; physician Meml. Hosp., Pawtucket, R.I., 1970—. Capt. U.S. Army, 1964-66. Fellow Am. Coll. Cardiology; mem. Am. Soc. Internal Medicine, Am. Med. Soc., Providence Med. Soc., R.I. Med. Soc. Avocations: running, golf, tennis, swimming. Office: 1 Randall Sq Ste 307 Providence RI 02904-2774

KITZES, WILLIAM FREDRIC, lawyer, safety analyst, consultant; b. Bklyn., Nov. 24, 1950; s. David Louis and Rhoda Rachel (Feldman) K; m. Sandra Shimasaki, Apr. 7, 1979: children: Justin, Dana. BA, U. Wis., 1972; JD, Am. U., 1975. Bar: D.C. 1977. Legal advisor on product recalls U.S. Consumer Products Safety Commn., Washington, 1975-77, program mgr., 1977-80, regulatory counsel, 1980-81; v.p., gen. mgr. Inst. for Safety Analysis, Rockville, Md.,

1981-83; prin. Consumer Safety Assocs., Potomac, Md., Boca Raton, Fla., 1983—. Cons. Toro Co., Bloomington, Minn., 1987, Vendo Co., Fresno, Calif., 1987, Nat. Assn. Attys. Gens., Washington, 1987, Arctic Cat, Inc., Thief River Falls, Minn., 1995—, Global Furniture, Toronto, Ont., 1997, Product Safety Online, Boca Raton, 1997—, Cisco Sys., Inc., San Jose, Calif., 2001-. Contbg. columnist CCH Product Safety Guide and Products Liability Reporter, 2000-01. Counsel Friends of Charlie Gilchrist, Montgomery County, Md., 1983; chmn. Fla. Consumers Coun., 1995—. Recipient silver medal for distinguished svc. U.S. Consumer Products Safety Commn., 1976. Mem. Am. Soc. Safety Engrs., Human Factors Soc., System Safety Soc., Nat. Safety Coun., Internat. Consumer Product Health and Safety Orgn. Home and Office: Consumer Safety Assocs 4501 NW 25th Way Boca Raton FL 33434-2506

KITZHABER, JOHN ALBERT, former governor, physician, former state senator; b. Colfax, Wash., Mar. 5, 1947; s. Albert Raymond and Annabel Reed (Wetzel) K.; m. Sharon Lacroix; 1 child, Logan. BA, Dartmouth Coll., 1969; MD, U. Oreg., 1973. Intern Gen. Rose Meml. Hosp., Denver, 1976-77; Emergency physician Mercy Hosp., Roseburg, Oreg., 1974-75; mem. Oreg. Ho. of Reps., 1979-81, Oreg. Senate, 1981—93, pres., 1985—93; former gov. State of Oregon, 1995—2003; pres. Estes Park Inst., Englewood, Colo., 2003—; endowed chair Found. for Med. Excellence, Portland, Oreg., 2003—. Assoc. prof. Oreg. Health Sci. U., 1989-1995; MD chmn. health policy Found. Med. Excellence, 2003-. Pres. Estes Park Inst., Colo., 2003—. Mem. Am. Coll. Emergency Physicians, Douglas County Med. Soc., Physicians for Social Responsibility, Am. Council Young Polit. Leaders, Oreg. Trout. Democrat. Office: Found Med Excellence Ste 800 1 SW Columbia St Portland OR 97258*

KITZKE, EUGENE DAVID, research and development company executive; b. Milw., Sept. 2, 1923; s. Leo R. and Regina R. (Tomczyk) Kitzke; m. Lorraine Grace Shummon, Sept. 2, 1946; children: Mary Victoria, Paul Simon, Patrice Lynn, Jerome Peter. BS, Marquette U., 1945, MS, 1947; diploma in basic clin. sci., Med. Coll. Wis., 2002. Instr. microbiology St. Mary's Sch. Nursing, Grand Rapids, Mich., 1946-47; assoc. prof. Aquinas Coll., 1947-51; lab researcher S.C. Johnson & Son, Inc., Racine, Wis., 1951-57, research mgr., 1957-76, v.p. corp. R&D, 1976-81; pres. Oak Crete Block Corp., South Milwaukee, Wis., 1900 , developer Wind Crest Subdiv., Wind Lake, Wis., 1993. Asst. clin. prof. dept. environ. medicine Med. Coll. Wis., Milw., 1973—81; owner Danel Enterprise, South Milwaukee; judge Marquette U. Sci. Fair; bd. dirs. Songcards, inc. Author: (book) For the Next Generation, 1986; contbr. articles to tech. jours., fiction and poetry to mags.;, author pubs. in field. Mem. pres.' coun. Alverno Coll., 1979—87. Recipient H. F. Johnson Cmty. Svc. award, 1996; Disting. scholar, Marquette U., 1995. Mem.: AAAS, Hist. Sci. Soc., Palm Soc. (exec. bd., past pres.), Sigma Xi, Sigma Tau Delta, Phi Sigma. Roman Catholic. Achievements include patents in field. Home: 616 Aspen St South Milwaukee WI 53172-1702 Office: PO Box 413 South Milwaukee WI 53172-0413 also: 7101 S Pennsylvania Ave Oak Creek WI 53154-2439 *Honor thyself. Be in control. Be paid.*

KITZMAN, JERRY MATSON, pharmaceutical executive; b. Elkhorn, Wis., Dec. 11, 1947; s. Walter Eugene and Florence Leona (Knilans) K.; m. Renate Ulrike Bernold, Dec. 29, 1981; 1 child, Daniela Helen. BA, Northwestern U., 1970; MA, UCLA, 1978, postgrad., 1979. Tchg. asst., assoc., fellow UCLA, 1978-79; tchr. Latin Marlborough Sch., L.A., 1981-82; supr., planner Schein Pharms., Phoenix, 1983—. Contbr. article to profl. jour. Lt. j.g. USN, 1970-74. Fulbright fellow, 1980-81; recipient award for excellent damage control USS Cook USN. Mem. AAAS, N.Y. Acad. Scis., Planetary Soc. Republican. Baptist. Avocations: astronomy, fossil and rock collecting, stamp collecting, national parks. Home: 4665 W Desert Crest Dr Glendale AZ 85301-4116 Office: Schein Pharm 620 N 51st Ave Phoenix AZ 85043-2702

KITZMILLER, HOWARD LAWRENCE, lawyer; b. Shippensburg, Pa., May 6, 1930; s. Franklin Leroy and Emma Corrinna (Bedford) K.; m. Shirley Mae Pine, Apr. 4, 1953; children: David Lawrence, Diane May. BA summa cum laude, Dickinson Coll., 1951; JD, Dickinson Sch. of Law, 1954; LLM, George Washington U., 1958. Bar: Pa. 1955, D.C. 1984. Commr. U.S. Ct. Mil. Appeals, Washington, 1958-59; various positions to assoc. gen. counsel FCC, Washington, 1959-80; various positions to dir., sr. v.p. and sec. Washington Mgmt. Corp., 1983—. Editor Dickinson Law Rev., 1954. Deacon, elder Westminster Presbyn. Ch., Alexandria, Va.; bd. dirs. S.E. Fairfax Devel. Corp., Fairfax County, Va., 1977-98, also past pres.; various positions including pres., parents adv. coun., bd. assocs., trustee, investment com. Randolph-Macon Coll., Ashland, Va., 1984-95. Capt. JAGC, U.S. Army, 1955-58. Mem. ABA, FBA, City Club Washington, Masons, Phi Beta Kappa. Republican.

KITZMILLER, W. JOHN, plastic, reconstructive and hand surgeon, educator; b. Cin., May 17, 1957; m. Sarah Kitzmiller, Sept. 23, 1989; children: Jacqueline, Mary Katherine. BS in Engring., Duke U., 1979, MD, 1983. Diplomate Am. Bd. Surgery, Am. Bd. Plastic Surgery. Resident in gen. surgery U. Cin., 1983-87, chief resident in gen. surgery, 1987-88, resident in plastic surgery, 1988-90; microvascular and hand surgery fellow Davies Med. Ctr., San Francisco, 1990-91; from asst. to assoc. prof. U. Cin. Coll. Medicine, 1991—. Contbr. articles to profl. jours., chpts. to books. Recipient award Aesthetic Edn. and Rsch. Found., 1999. Office: Divsn Plastic Surgery U Cin Coll Medicine 231 Bethesda Ave Cincinnati OH 45267-0001

KIVETZ, MICHAEL ADAM, artist, sculptor; b. N.Y.C., Sept. 29, 1963; s. Jack Harold Kivetz and Delores Luchs. BA, Hobart Coll., 1986; postgrad., Studio Art Ctr. Internat., Florence, Italy, 1986-87, U. Ga., 1988-89. Tchg. asst. U. Ga., Athens, 1988-89; mold maker MJM Studios, South Kearny, N.J., 1990; graphic artist DataFax, N.Y.C., 1991; freelance artist N.J., 1990—; new media artist Telcordia Techs., Piscataway, N.J., 1994—. Cons. mobeus.net, Warren, N.J., 1997—. Author: (online publ.) Technology and Me, 1999—; sculptor Bent Bar, 1991. Mem. Electronic Freedom Found., N.Y. New Media Assn., Sierra Club. Avocations: rock climbing, photography, travel. Office: Telcordia Techs Inc 33 Knightsbridge Rd Piscataway NJ 08854-3925

KIVIKOSKI, ASKO ILMARI, retired obstetrician, gynecologist; b. Helsinki, Finland, Aug. 3, 1932; came to U.S., 1984; MD, U. Turku, Finland, 1958, DSc, 1967. Diplomate Am. Bd. Ob-gyn. Intern U. Turku, 1962, resident in ob/gyn., 1962-65, asst. prof., 1966-76; resident in surgery City Hosp., Turku, 1965-66; researcher Washington U., St. Louis, 1971-72; fellow in perinatology Mt. Sinai Hosp., N.Y.C., 1978-79; head dept. ob/gyn. Ctrl. hosp., Lahti, Finland, 1976-84; staff Barnes Hosp., St. Louis, 1984-87, 97—; chief gynecol. svcs. St. Louis Regional Med. Ctr., 1987-97; Connect Care, 1998-2001; asst. prof. Washington U., St. Louis, 1984-92, assoc. prof., 1992-2001, assoc. prof. emeritus, 2001—. Author articles on anatomy, obstetrics and perinatology. Mem. ACOG, Am. Inst. Ultrasound in Medicine, N.Y. Acad. Sci.

KIVULS, JURIS, plastic surgeon; b. N.Y.C., July 18, 1952; s. Arvids and Alma Kivuls; m. Sarma Kreismanis, Oct. 20, 1984; children: Andris, Aleks, Kristine. BS in Chemistry, CUNY, 1973; MD, U. Pa., 1977. Diplomate Am. Bd. Plastic Surgery. Intern Hosp. U. Pa., 1977-78, resident in gen. surgery, 1978-83, resident in plastic surgery, 1983-85; plastic surgeon Kaiser Permanente, Bellflower, Calif., 1985—. Soccer coach, referee Am. Youth Soccer Orgn., 1995—. Fellow ACS; mem. AMA, Am. Soc. Plastic Surgeons, Am. Soc. Aesthetic Plastic Surgery, Liploplasty Soc. (bd. dirs. 1996-2000, chair rsch. com. 1994-2000), Am. Cleft Palate Assn., Calif. Soc. Plastic Surgeons. Avocations: skiing, volleyball, running, soccer. Office: Kaiser Permanente Dept Plastic Surgery 9400 Rosecrans Ave Bellflower CA 90706-2200 E-mail: juris.x.kivuls@kp.org.

KIYANITZA, LUBOV DENISOVNA, library director; b. Kiev, Ukraine, May 30, 1943; d. Denis Vasilievich and Maria Ivanovna (Shepelenko) K.; m. William Konstantinovitch Kuindzhy, dec. 12, 1995; children: Violetta, Sviatoslav. Grad. commodity expert, Book-Trade Coll., 1971; library bibliographer, State Krupskaya Inst. of Culture, 1980. Instr. periodical press dissemination City Press Agy., Uman, 1967-71; libr. supr. Chem. Engring. Coll. Libr., Novocherkassk, 1971-78; sector supr. Libr. of Novocherkassk, 1978-83; dep. dir. for rsch. work Politechnical Inst., Novochercassk, 1983-86; dir. libr. South-Russia State Tech. U., 1986—. Supr. methodic ctr. univ. librs. Rostov region, 1994; supr., participant practical sci. seminars, 1990—; lectr. Libr. Politechnical Inst., 1979-83. Mem. Russian Libr. Assn., Nat. Libr. Trade Union (Medal of Honour 1985), North Caucasus Assn. Univ. Librs. Avocations: history of arts, philately, travel. Home: 7-3 Galina Petrova str 346409 Novocherkassk Russia Office: Libr State Tech Univ Prosveschenia str 346400 Novocherkassk Rostov Russia Address: 132 Prosveschenyia Str 346428 Novocherkassk Russia E-mail: library@srstu.novoch.ru.

KIYONAGA, JOHN CADY, lawyer; b. Atsugi, Japan, Dec. 27, 1953; s. Joseph Yoshio and Bina Mary (Cady) Kiyonaga; m. Susan Marie Fraser, Dec. 5, 1980 (div. Oct. 1990); children: Joseph Yoshio, Anastasia, Clayton Cady, Catherine Bina; m. Nan Catherine Schnell, Sept. 13, 1997. BA, Georgetown U., 1976; JD, MS in Journalism, Columbia U., N.Y.C., 1980. Bar: N.Y. 1981, D.C. 1990, Va. 1990. Assoc. Brown & Wood, N.Y.C., 1980-83; ins. officer Overseas Pvt. Investment Corp., Washington, 1984; ptnr. Kiyonaga & Kiyonaga, Alexandria, Va., 1990—2001; sole practice Law Office of John C. Kiyonaga, Alexandria, Va., 2001—. Contbr. articles and editl. writings to profl. publs. With U.S. Army, 1985-89. Mem. Nat. Assn. Criminal Def. Lawyers, Alexandria Bar Assn., Japanese Am. Vets. Assn. (v.p.), Columbia Country Club, 5th Chukker Polo Club, Army and Navy Club. Roman Catholic. Avocations: polo, wing shooting. Office: Law Office John C Kiyonaga 526 King St Ste 213 Alexandria VA 22314-3143

KIYOTA, HEIDE PAULINE, clinical psychologist; b. Bamberg, Germany, July 6, 1942; came to U.S., 1970; d. Fritz and Marcella (Schropfer) S.; m. Ronald Masaki Kiyota, Dec. 26, 1982; children: Heather E., Catherine M., Michelle H. BS, U. Md., 1975, MA, 1979; PhD, U. Hawaii, 1986. Lic. psychologist, Hawaii; accelerated hypnotherapy cert. The Wellness Inst., 1996. Counselor-trainee Regional Inst. for Children & Adolescents, Balt., 1976-77; supr.-counselor Multiple Offender Alcoholism Program, Balt., 1977-80; therapist-intern VA, Honolulu, 1983-84; clin. psychologist Kalihi-Palama Counseling Svcs., Honolulu, 1987-89; pvt. practice psychologist Honolulu, 1988—. Presenter in field. Contbr. articles to profl. jours. Mem. Am. Psychol. Assn., Hawaii Psychol. Assn., Phi Kappa Phi. Home: 1812 Nahenahe Pl Wahiawa HI 96786-2627 Office: 410 Kilani Ave Ste 219 Wahiawa HI 96786-1844

KIZER, CAROLYN ASHLEY, poet, educator; b. Spokane, Wash., Dec. 10, 1925; d. Benjamin Hamilton and M. (Ashley) K.; m. Stimson Bullitt, Jan., 1948 (div.); children: Ashley Ann, Scott, Jill Hamilton; m. John Marshall Woodbridge, Apr. 11, 1975. BA, Sarah Lawrence Coll., 1945; postgrad. (Chinese govt. fellow in comparative lit.), Columbia U., 1946-47; studied poetry with Theodore Roethke, U. Wash., 1953-54; LittD (hon.), Whitman Coll., 1986, St. Andrew's Coll., 1989, Mills Coll., 1990, Wash. State U., 1991. Specialist in lit. U.S. Dept. State, Pakistan, 1964-65; first dir. lit. programs Nat. Endowment for Arts, 1966-70; poet-in-residence U. N.C. at Chapel Hill, 1970-74; Hurst Prof. Lit. Washington U., St. Louis, 1971; lectr. Spring Lecture Series Barnard Coll., 1972; acting dir. grad. writing program Columbia U., 1972; poet-in-residence Ohio U., 1974; vis. poet Iowa Writer's Workshop, 1975; prof. U. Md., 1976-77; poet-in-residence, disting. vis. lectr. Centre Coll., Ky., 1979; disting. vis. poet East Wash. U., 1980; Elliston prof. poetry U. Cin., 1981; Bingham disting. prof. U. Louisville, Ky., 1982; disting. vis. poet Bucknell U., Pa., 1982; vis. poet SUNY, Albany, 1982; prof. Columbia U. Sch. Arts, 1982; prof. poetry Stanford U., 1986; sr. fellow in humanities Princeton U., 1986; vis. prof. writing U. Ariz., 1989, 90, U. Calif., Davis, 1991; Coal Royalty chair U. Ala., 1995. Participant Internat. Poetry Festivals, London, 1960, 70, Yugoslavia, 1969, 70, Pakistan, 1969, Rotterdam, Netherlands, 1970, Knokke-le-Zut, Belgium, 1970, Bordeaux, 1992, Dublin, 1993, Glasgow, 1994; sr. fellow humanities council Princeton U., 1986. Author: Poems, 1959, The Ungrateful Garden, 1961, Knock Upon Silence, 1965, Midnight Was My Cry, 1971, Mermaids in the Basement: Poems for Women, 1984 (San Francisco Arts Commn. award 1986), Yin: New Poems, 1984 (Pulitzer prize in poetry 1985), The Nearness of You, 1987 (Theodore Roethke prize, 1988); Proses: On Poems & Poets, 1994, Picking & Choosing: Prose on Prose, 1995, Harping On: Poems 1985-1995, 1996, The Complete Pro Femina, 2000, Cool, Calm and Collected Poems, 1960-2000; editor: Woman Poet: The West, 1980, Leaving Taos, 1981, The Essential Clare, 1993, 100 Great Poems by Women, 1995; translator Carrying Over, 1988; founder, editor: Poetry N.W., 1959-65; contbr. poems, articles to Am. and Brit. jours. Recipient award Am. Acad. and Inst. Arts and Letters, 1985, Pres.'s medal Ea. Wash. U., 1988, 5 Gov.'s awards State of Wash., 1965, 85, 95, 98, 2001, Silver medal Commonwealth Club, 1997, 2001, Aiken Taylor prize Sewanee Rev., 1998, Patterson prize, 2002, Western State Lifetime Achievement award, 2002, 1st prize Ind. Pub. Book award, 2002, L.A. Times Top Ten Books award, 2002, Acad. prize, 2003, Poets' prize, 2003. Mem. PEN, Amnesty Internat., Poetry Soc. Am. (Masefield prize 1983, Frost medal 1988). Episcopalian. Address: 19772 8th St E Sonoma CA 95476-3849

KIZER, JORGE R. cardiologist, epidemiologist; arrived in U.S., 1979; s. Saul Kizer and Fanny Dejman; m. Carol A. Lillienstein, May 28, 2000. BS, SUNY, Stony Brook, 1990; MD, U. of Pa., 1994; MSc, Harvard U., 1999. Diplomate internal medicine Am. Bd. of Internal Medicine, cardiovasc. disease Am. Bd. of Internal Medicine. Medicine intern and resident Brigham and Women's Hosp./Harvard Med. Sch., Boston, 1994—97; fellow in cardiovasc. medicine U. of Pa. Med. Ctr., Phila., 1997—2001; asst. prof. medicine and pub. health Weil Med. Coll. of Cornell U., N.Y.C., 2001—. Recipient Mentored Patient-Oriented Rsch. Career Devel. award, NIH, 2002—07. Mem.: Phi Beta Kappa, Alpha Omega Alpha. Achievements include peer-reviewed publs. association between pulmonary fibrosis and coronoary artery disease; role of cardiac troponin T in the long-term risk stratification of patients undergoing percutaneous coronary intervention; limitations of current risk-adjustment models in the era of coronary stenting. Avocations: jogging, swimming, languages, travel.

KIZER, KENNETH WAYNE, physician, educator, researcher, consultant, administrator; b. Decatur, Ind., May 28, 1951; s. Homer Martin Kizer and Ellen Hope Howland; m. Suzanne A. Stoddard, Aug. 26, 1972; children: Kelli Christina, Kimberly Casey. BS with honors, Stanford U., 1972; MD with honors, MPH in Epidemiology, UCLA, 1976. Rotating internship Naval Regional Med. Ctr., Portsmouth, Va., 1977; undersea medicine fellowship Naval Undersea Med. Inst., Groton, Conn., 1977; resident in diagnostic radiology U. Calif, San Francisco, 1980-81, resident in occupational medicine, 1982-83; firefighter; emergency physician; dir. Emergency Med. Svcs. Authority State of Calif., 1983-84; chief dep. dir. and chief of pub. health Calif. Dept. Health Svcs., Sacramento, 1984-85, dir., 1985-91; prof., chmn. dept. community and internat. health U. Calif., Davis, 1991-94; undersec. for health Dept. Vets. Affairs, Washington, 1994-99; dir. Health Sys. Internat., Inc., 1994-97; pres. Nat. Quality Forum, Washington, 1999—. Contbr. numerous articles to profl. jours., chpts. to books. Chair Radiation Emergency Screening Team, 1988-91, Hazardous Waste Appeal Bd., 1990; co-chair Calif. AIDS Leadership Com.; mem. Diving Control Bd. U. Calif., 1980-91, Gov.'s Emergency Ops. Exec. Coun., 1984-91, Governing Bd. Calif YMCA Model Legislature Program, 1986-90, Chem. Emergency Planning and Response Commn., 1988-90; chair S.W. Low Level Radioactive Waste Compact Commn., 1990-91, tobacco edn. oversight com. State Calif., 1990-91, bd. dirs. Calif. Wellness Found., 1992—, Matthews Found., 1991-94, Ctr. for AIDS Rsch., Edn. and Svcs., 1992-94, Infection Control Coun., 1991-94; mem. adv. bd. Preventive Sports Medicine Inst., 1991-94. Lt. USN, 1976-80. Recipient Humanitarian Svc. medal Dept. of Def., 1979, Spl. Recognition award No. Calif. Emergency Med. Care Coun., 1984, Golden State Med. Assn., 1986, Calif. Div. Am. Lung Assn., 1988, Calif. Health Fedn., 1988, cert. of Recognition Calif. Asian Pacific Health Coalition, 1989, Spl. Achievement award Calif. Emergency Physician Med. Group, 1989, Jean Spencer Felton award for Excellence in Scientific Writing, 1989, spl. awards from March of Dimes, Am. Cancer Soc., Calif. State Senate, Calif. Conf. Local Health Officers, others, 1991—, Healthcare Heroes award Calif. State Assembly, 1996, Cert. of Recognition award, 1996, Dr. Nathan Davis award AMA, 1998, Literacy Achievement award Am. Coll. Physician Execs., 1998, Founders award Wilderness Medical Soc., 1998; named Toll fellow Coun. State G ovts., 1987. Fellow Am. Coll. Preventive Medicine, Am. Coll. Emergency Physicians, Am. Coll. Occupational Environ. Medicine, Am. Acad. Clin. Toxicology, Royal Soc. Health, Royal Soc. Medicine, Am. Coll. Med. Toxicology, Am. Coll. Physician Execs., Am. Acad. Med. Adminstrs., Explorers Club; mem. APHA, Internat. Soc. Toxicology, Inst. Medicine NAS, Wilderness Med. Soc., Undersea and Hyperbaric Med. Soc., Nat. Soc. YMCA Youth Govs., Nat. Assn. Underwater Instrs. (Outstanding Contribution to Diving award 1984), Inst. Medicine, Nat. Acad. Scis., Delta Tau Delta (Beta Rho chpt. Hall of Fame 1987), Alpha Omega Alpha, Delta Omega. Independent. Avocations: scuba diving, hiking and backpacking, photography, racquet sports, book collecting. Office: Nat Quality Forum Ste 500 North 601 13th St NW Washington DC 20005 E-mail: kwkizer@qualityforum.org.

KJELLMARK, ERIC WILLIAM, JR., management consultant, opera company director; b. New Rochelle, N.Y., May 14, 1928; s. Eric William and Anna Sophia (Fogelstrom) K. BCE, Cornell U., 1950. Mgr. mktg. planning E. I. DuPont de Nemours, Wilmington, Del., 1980-87, dir. Far East task force, 1987-89; gen. dir. Opera Del., Inc., Wilmington, 1985-95; cons. Condux, Inc., Wilmington, 1985-94. Cons. Monkman-Rumsey, Inc., Wilmington, 1986-92. Treas., v.p. Grand Opera House, Inc., Wilmington, 1971-91, bd. trustees 1992—; panelist Del. State Arts Coun., Wilmington, 1987-89, 96, 97; sec.-treas. Opera Del., 1994-96, bd. dirs., 1956—, Wilmington Waterways, Inc., 1985-89; chmn. oversight com. Delaware Art Stabilization, 1993-96, chmn. level IV cos. Opera Am., 1989-91, bd. dirs., 1991-94; panelist Mid-Atlantic States Arts Consortium, 1990, NEA, 1991-94; pres. Opera for Youth, 1997-2000; bd. dirs. Nat. Opera Assn., 1998, 99. Recipient W.W. Laird award DE, 1992, Partners in Excellence award Opera Guild Internat., 1994. Mem. Am. Chem. Soc., Am. Inst. Chem. Engrs., Alpha Chi Sigma. Republican. Episcopalian. Office: Opera Del PO Box 432 Wilmington DE 19899-0432

KJELSTRUP, CHERYL ANN, librarian; b. Madison, Wis., Sept. 23, 1947; d. Robert A. and Katherine E. (Benish) Heiman; m. Glen W. Wildenberg, Apr. 6, 1968 (div. June 1984); 1 child, William G. Wildenberg; m. Rod R. Kjelstrup, Jan. 3, 1987; children: Christopher M., Andrew J. BA in Social Scis., Kans. State U., 1970; student, U. Wis., Oshkosh, 1983; M of Libr. and Info. Sci., U. Wis., Milw., 1997. Cert. K-12 libr. and computer instr., Wis. Libr. aide Two Rivers (Wis.) Pub. Schs., 1976-88; libr. Wrightstown (Wis.) Cmty. Schs., 1988-90; libr., computer coord. Brillion (Wis.) Schs., 1990—. Bd. dirs. Cmty. Concerts Assn., Manitowoc, Wis., 1980-88, Manitowoc-Calumet County Libr., 2001—; long-rang planning com. Brillion Pub. Libr., 1993-94. Delta Kappa Gamma Sigma scholar, 1994-95. Mem. Wis. Ednl. Media Assn. (mem. info. literacy com. 1992-93), Brillion Fedn. Tchrs. (pres. local 1994-96, 98-2000), Delta Kappa Gamma (pres. 1992-94). Avocations: competitive pistol shooting, deer hunting, needlework, sewing. E-mail: kjelstrup@lakefield.net' ckjelstr@brillion.k12.wi.us. Home: 14415 Jambo Creek Rd Mishicot WI 54228-9734 Office: Brillion Pub Schs 315 S Main St Brillion WI 54110-1294

KJOK, SOL, artist, art historian, linguist, government authorized translator; b. Lillehammer, Norway, Mar. 16, 1968; d. Erik and Ingunn (Haugsrud) K. BA in French Lit., U. Vienna, Austria, 1991; M in French Lit., U. Paris, 1992; MA in Romance Lang. and Lit., U. Cin., 1993, MA in Art History, 1996; MFA in Painting, Parsons Sch. Design, N.Y.C., 1998. Cert. govt. authorized transl. and interpreter. Graphic designer Agence Karen, Paris, 1988; tchg. asst. art history U. Cin., 1995-96, dir. ind. studies of Norwegian lang./culture, 1993-96; resident Larroque Artists' Colony, Urt, France, 1997-98; tchg. asst. painting Parsons Sch. Design, N.Y.C., 1997-98. Lectr. in field. Contbr. articles to profl. jours.; translator: French/Norwegian, Paris, 1988; Spanish/Norwegian translator/interpretor Medellin, Bogota, Colombia, 1993; translator English, German novels, articles, short stories into Norwegian, various pub. houses, 1985—; one-woman shows include Brodie Gallery, Cin., 1996, Kreditkassen, Bagn, Norway, 1987, Tegnerforbundet Gallery, Oslo, 2001; exhibited in group shows at Gjensidigegården, Fagernes, Norway, 1985, Valdrestunet, Bagn, 1987, Art et Dessin, Paris, 1988, Mus. of U. Medellin, 1993, KZF Gallery, Cin., 1994, 840 Gallery, Cin., 1995, 96, Machina dell'Arte, Cin., 1996, Schoharie County Arts Coun., 1996, Gallery Alexy, Phila., 1996, Glenn Eure's Ghost Fleet Gallery, Nags Head, N.C., 1996, Amos Joseph Fine Art, Santa Fe, 1996, N.J. Ctr. Visual Arts, 1997, Pleiades Gallery, N.Y.C., 1997, Viridian Artists, Inc., 1997, Akademie der bildenden Künste Munich, 1997, A.I.R. Gallery, N.Y.C., 1997, Artists' Space, N.Y.C., 1997, Brenda Taylor Gallery, N.Y.C., 1998, Cmty. Cultural Ctr., Phila., 1998, Manefisken Galleri, Oslo, 1998, Valdres Kunstforening's Gallery, Norway, 1998, PS 122 Gallery, N.Y.C., 1998, Cameron/Weiland Gallery, N.Y.C., 1998, Galeri Steen, Oslo, Norway, 1999, Painted Bride Art Ctr., Phila., 2002, others; works in pvt. and pub. collections. Mem. Cin. Artists Group Effort, 1994—. Recipient Alpha Kappa Alpha Grad. Merit award; grantee Ga. Rotary Student Program, 1989, Lise & Arnfinn Heje's Legacy, Oslo, 1990, Thom Wilhelmsen's award, Oslo, 1991, Knut Hamsun's Legacy, Oslo, 1992, Olav and Lizzie Juvkam's legacy, 1990-94, Einar Storsveen's Legacy, 1992-94; Cin. Women's Club scholar, 1995, U. Cin. scholar, 1993-96, Parsons scholar, 1997-98; AAUW fellow, 1997-98; Joahn Jorgen Brochs Legat. grant, 1998, Rsch. grant Astrup-Fearnley, Oslo, 1996, Thesis Rsch. grant Astrup-Fearnley Found., Oslo, 1996, Artist grant Norwegian Ministry Culture, 1998; recipient Edwin Gould Found. award Nat. Arts Club, N.Y.C., 1998, Excellence in Drawing award Internat. Icarus Exhbn., 1998, Spl. Gallery prize Contemporary Realism III Exhibit, Phila., 1998, others. Mem. Internat. Assn. Univ. Women, Coll. Art Assn., Norwegian Soc. Young Artists, Norwegian Visual Artists, Drawing Assn. Norway. Avocation: long distance running. Home: 44 Eagle St Brooklyn NY 11222-1013 E-mail: solveig.kjok@rcn.com.

KJOS, VICTORIA, lawyer; b. Fargo, N.D., Sept. 17, 1953; d. Orville I. and Annie J. (Tanberg) K. BA, Minot State U., 1974; JD, U. N.D., 1977. Bar: Ariz. 1978. Assoc. Jack E. Evans, Ltd., Phoenix, 1977-78, pension and ins. cons., 1978-79; dep. state treas. State of N.D., Bismarck, 1979-80; freelance cons. Phoenix, 1980-81, Anchorage, 1981-82; asst. v.p., v.p., mgr. trust dept. Great Western Bank, Phoenix, 1982-84; assoc. Robert A. Jensen P.C., Phoenix, 1984-86; ptnr. Jensen & Kjos, P.C., Phoenix, 1986-89; assoc. Allen, Kimerer & LaVelle, Phoenix, 1989-90, ptnr., 1990-91; dir. The Yoga and Fitness Inst., Phoenix, 1994-97; mem. faculty Maricopa County C.C., 1997—. Freelance cons., Phoenix, 1999—2003; lectr. in domestic rels. Contbr. articles to profl. jours. Bd. dirs. Arthritis Found., Phoenix, 1986-89, v.p. for chpt. devel., 1988-89; bd. dirs. Ariz. Yoga Assn., 1993-95, v.p., 1993-95. Mem. ABA, ATLA, Am. Coll. Sports Medicine, Am. Alliance Health, Phys. Edn., Recreation & Dance, Ariz. Bar Assn. (exec. coun. family law sect. 1988-91), Maricopa Bar Assn. (sec. family law com. 1988-89, pres. family law com. 1989-90, judge pro tem 1989-91), Ariz. Trial Lawyers Assn.

KLAAS, NICHOLAS PAUL, management and technical consultant; b. Kieler, Wis., June 25, 1925; s. Paul Francis and Ida Klaas; m. Ruth Elizabeth Barry, Nov. 5, 1949; children: Paul, Patricia, Kathleen, James. BA, Loras Coll., 1945; PhD, U. Notre Dame, 1948. Registered to practice before U.S. Patent Office, 1970. Product mgr. Rohm & Haas Co., Phila., 1948-52; mgr. research and devel. 3M Co., St. Paul, 1952-65; exec. v.p., dir. Wyomissing Corp., West Reading, Pa., 1965-71; group v.p. chems. GAF Corp., N.Y.C., 1971-77; gen. mgr. splty. chems. Ga. Pacific Corp., Portland, Oreg., 1977; pres. J.T. Baker Chem. Co., Phillipsburg, N.J., 1977-84; chmn. bd. J.T. Baker B.V., Deventer, Netherlands, 1978-84; pres. Klaas Assocs., 1984—. Adj. prof. chemistry San Diego State U., 1985-98; mem. bd. visitors U. N.C., Asheville, 1986-91, Council for Chem. Research, 1987-98. Patentee in field; contbr. articles to profl. jours. Trustee St. Joseph Hosp., Reading, Pa., 1968-71; bd. regents Loras Coll., Dubuque, Iowa, 1974-76. Mem. AAAS, Synthetic Organic Chem. Mfg. Assn. (dir. 1974-77), Asphalt Roofing Mfrs. Assn. (dir. 1974-77), Am. Chem. Soc. Clubs: Smoke Rise. Address: 51 Hoot Owl Ter Kinnelon NJ 07405-2409 E-mail: npaulklaas@aol.com.

KLAAS, OTTMAR, software engineer; b. Boerger, Germany, Jan. 22, 1967; came to U.S., 1996; s. Wilhelm and Sigrid Klaas; m. Lisa Ann Easterly, Apr. 14, 1961. MSCE, U. Hanover, Germany, 1992, PhD in Civil Engring., 1996. Rsch. engr. U. Hanover, 1992-96; postdoctoral rsch. assoc. Sci. Computation Rsch. Ctr. Rensselaer Poly. Inst., Troy, NY, 1997-98, rsch. assoc. Sci. Computation Rsch. Ctr., 1998—2002; sr. software engr. Simmetrix Inc., Troy, 2002—. Co. owner Comscience Engring., Hanover, 1992-97; educator U. Hanover, 1994-95, Profl. Sch. Hanover, 1993-95. Reviewer profl. jours., 1998—; contbr. articles to profl. jours. Fellow World Innovation Found.; mem. ASME, Assn. for Computing Machinery, U.S. Assn. for Computational Mechanics, Chamber of Engring. (Germany). Address: 8 Locust Park Albany NY 12205 E-mail: oklaas@scorec.rpi.edu.

KLAAS, PAUL BARRY, lawyer; b. St. Paul, Aug. 9, 1952; s. N. Paul and Ruth Elizabeth (Barry) K.; m. Barbara Ann Bockhaus, July 30, 1977; children: James, Ann, Brian. AB, Dartmouth Coll., 1974; JD, Harvard U., 1977. Bar: Minn. 1977, U.S. Dist. Ct. Minn. 1977, U.S. Ct. Appeals (8th cir.) 1979, U.S. Ct. Appeals (10th cir.) 1980, U.S. Supreme Ct. 1982, U.S. Ct. Appeals (9th cir.) 1989, U.S. Ct. Appeals (fed. cir.) 1994. Assoc. Dorsey & Whitney, Mpls.,

1977-82, ptnr., 1983—. Chair trial dept., co-chair Internat. Arbitration and Litigation Practice Group; adj. prof. William Mitchell Coll Law, St. Paul, 1980-85. Fellow: Am. Coll. Trial Lawyers. Office: Dorsey & Whitney 50 S 6th St Ste 1500 Minneapolis MN 55402-1498 E-mail: klaas.paul@dorseylaw.com.

KLACHKO, DAVID MAX, physician, educator; b. Durban, South Africa, Apr. 8, 1932; came to U.S., 1963; s. Joshua and Dora (Epstein) K.; m. Hanna Margot Wolff, Sept. 15, 1963; children: Susan Miriam Holmes, Ruth Marian Limon. MB BCh, U. Witwatersrand, South Africa, 1955; MS in Edn., U. So. Calif., 1974. Cert. physician, Mo. Intern, resident Johannesburg Gen. Hosp. and Baragwanath Hosp., 1955-60; sr. registrar various hosps., London, 1960-61; asst. surgeon P&O-Orient Lines, London, 1961-62; med. officer Baragwanath Hosp., Johannesburg, 1962-63; rsch. fellow U. Mo., Columbia, 1963-65, instr. internal medicine, 1965-67, asst. prof., 1967-73, assoc. prof., 1973-79, prof., 1979-99, prof. emeritus, 1999—. Assoc. dir. for clin. svcs. Cosmopolitan Internat. Diabetes Ctr., Columbia, 1985-99. Editor: Comparative Endocrinology of Prolactin, 1977, Hormone Receptors, 1978, Hormones and Energy Metabolism, 1979, The Endocrine Pancreas and Juvenile Diabetes, 1979. Fellow ACP, Coll. Physicians South Africa; mem. Endocrine Soc., Am. Diabetes Assn. (pres. Mo. regional affiliate 1982-84, Disting. Svc. award 1990, bd. dirs. emeritus 1997), Boone County Med. Soc. (pres. 1986-87), Am. Fedn. for Med. Rsch., Internat. Brotherhood Magicians (pres. ring 8, Columbia 1993-96), Sigma Xi, Alpha Omega Alpha. Avocations: magic, origami, dancing, barbershop singing. Home: 407 Westwood Ave Columbia MO 65203-2867 Office: Cosmopolitan Internat Diabetes Ctr 1 Hospital Dr Columbia MO 65212 E-mail: dklachko@pol.net.

KLADIVA, JASON LOUIS, historian, writer; b. Melrose Pk., Ill., Jan. 17, 1973; s. Robert Louis and Susan Theresa Kladiva. Hist. cons. "Andersonville" - Turner Pictures, Atlanta, 1994, "Legends of the Old Northwest", History Channel; hist. interpreter LaFox Corp., Geneva, Ill., 1994—2001, Mackinac State Hist. Parks, Mich., 2000—01. Dir. Am's. Back Pages Children's Mus., Grand Haven, Mich., 1998—99. Author: (book) Gleanings of Mackinac, 2001, "Journals of an American Traveler", 2002. Mem.: Nat. Trust Hist. Preservation, Nat. Assn. for Interpretation. Avocations: photography, travel, reading, civil war reeinacting. Personal E-mail: jasonlkladiva@yahoo.com.

KLAEHNE, EBERHARD O W, pharmaceutical executive, chemist; b. Hamburg, Germany, Jan. 31, 1951; arrived in U.S., 1993; s. Walter and Hedwig (Jaster) Klaehne; m. Soumontha Phommachack, Dec. 21, 1987; m. Gabriele Jacobsen; children: Maurice Nicolas, Somsay Phommachack. Diploma in chemistry, U. Hamburg, 1977, Dr. rer. nat., 1982. Dir. quality control Ichthyol Gesellschaft Cordes, Hermanni and Co., Hamburg, 1982—85; dir. quality control/quality assurance LTS Lohmann Therapie Systeme AG, Neuwied, Germany, 1985—93; dir. quality assurance LTS Lohmann Therapy Systems Corp., West-Caldwell, NJ, 1993—96; dir. quality control, clin. supply LTS Lohmann Therapie Systeme AG, Andernach, Germany, 1996—2001, dir. quality assurance, 2001—02; exec. dir. quality Mylan Technologies Inc., St. Albans, Vt., 2002—. Rsch. assoc. DFG German Rsch. Soc., U. of Hamburg, Hamburg, Hamburg, Germany, 1977—77; sci. asst. lectr. U. of Hamburg, Hamburg, Hamburg, Germany, 1977—78; predoctoral rsch. assoc. CEN Centre d'Etudes Nucléaires de Saclay, Saclay, France (incl. Monaco), 1979—79; rsch. assoc. DFG, German Rsch. Soc., Hamburg, Hamburg, Germany, 1980—80; sci. asst. U. of Hamburg, Hamburg, Hamburg, Germany, 1979—81; presenter in field. Contbr. articles to profl. jours. Leader table tennis sporting group Glashuetter (Germany) Sporting Club, 1968—74. Scholar, DAAD German Academic Exch. Svc., 1978, DAAD German Academic Exch. Svc., CEN Centre d' Etudes Nucléaires de Saclay, Paris, France, 1979. Mem.: Verband Angestellter Akademiker Assn. Acad. Employees (assoc.). Achievements include research in synthesization and characterisization of novel class of neutral, anionic and cationic trigonal-bipyramidal coordinated Uranium(IV) organyls; photo reduction of Uranium(IV) to U(III) organyls with Trispentahaptocyclopentadienyl U(IV)alkyls; Homolytic cleavage of U(IV)-C bonds with excess of Li-organyls.

KLAERNER, CURTIS MAURICE, former oil company executive; b. Fredericksburg, Tex., Sept. 7, 1920; s. Elgin and Irene (Wagner) K.; m. Aileen E. Eitt, Sept. 4, 1942 (dec. Oct. 1998); children: Sherilyn Kay, Curtis Elgin; m. Jean L. Patton, Aug. 26, 2000. BS in Chem. Engring, U. Tex., 1942; grad. program sr. execs., Mass. Inst. Tech., 1956. Process engr., then chief process engr. Magnolia Petroleum Co., 1942-53; refinery mgr., then mgr. Eastern region mfg. Socony Mobil Oil Co., 1953-59; regional exec., then regional v.p. Mobil Internat. Oil Co., 1959-61; pres. Mobil Inner Europe, Geneva, Switzerland, 1962-65; corp. v.p. charge marine transp. and internat. sales Socony Mobil Oil Co., 1965-69; exec. v.p. internat. div. Mobil Oil Corp., 1969-72, pres., 1972-79, also exec. v.p., dir., mem. exec. com. corp.; vice chmn., dir. Commonwealth Oil Refining Co., San Antonio, 1979, pres., chief operating officer, 1979-83; ret., 1983; pres. Klaerner Enterprises, 1984—; vice chmn. Weed Instrument Co.; dir. Belgian Refining Corp., Antwerp, 1984—, W.I. Oil Corp., Antigua, 1984—, Nat. Petroleum Ltd., Bermuda, 1986—. Mem. adv. coun. Engring. Found., U. Tex., Austin. Recipient Disting. Grad. award Coll. Engring., U. Tex., 1983 Mem. Phi Eta Sigma, Omega Chi Epsilon, Phi Kappa Sigma. Clubs: Circumnavigators (N.Y.C.); Oak Hills Country, Optimists, Exchange, Petroleum (San Antonio), Country Club San Antonio. Republican. Episcopalian. Home: 144 Cas Hills Dr San Antonio TX 78213-3322

KLAES, JAMES GRAHAM, III, advertising executive; b. Mt. Vernon, N.Y., Nov. 21, 1945; s. James Graham, Jr. and Frances Imelda (Barker) K.; m. Geraldine Margaret Romitti, Jan. 27, 1968 (div. Dec. 1984); children: Ian Christopher, Brian Jeremy. BA in English, U. San Francisco, 1968. Writer, prodr. White & Shuford Advt., El Paso, Dallas, 1971-73, Mithoff Advt., El Paso, 1973-75, Chapman Advt., El Paso, 1976-78; creative dir., prodr. Paragon Advt., El Paso, 1978-79; prodr., news reporter KDBC-TV, El Paso, 1980-83; creative dir., prodr. Knight & Co. Advt., El Paso, 1983-84; freelance writer and prodr., 1984-95; mgr., prodr. RXL-Pulitzer, Spokane, Wash., 1995-97; writer El Paso Inc., 1997—99; assignment editor KVIA-TV News, El Paso, 1999—2000; gen. mgr. Results video, El Paso, 2000—02; exec. dir. Insights, El Paso Sci. Mus., 2003—. Dir., prodr. (TV show) Contact, KDBC-TV, El Paso, 1980-82; prodr., writer (video) The Murals of El Paso, 1993, Carlos Callejo Fresco, 1995; host (TV show) Mayor's Spotlight, Paragon TV, El Paso, 1997-99. Bd. dirs. El Paso Tourist Attractions Promotions, 1983-88, Mexican Food Capitol of World, El Paso, 1985-90, Goodwill Industries, 1990-96, El Paso Ctr. Children, 1991-97. With U.S. Army, 1968-70, Germany. Mem. Advt. Fedn. El Paso (Topps award 1973, Vision award 1993). Avocations: rock climbing, archaeology, local history, arts. E-mail: jimklaes@aol.com.

KLAFF, LESLIE J. physician, research company executive; b. Durban, South Afric, Mar. 7, 1948; s. Jacob B. and Marjorie P. (Levey) K.; m. Denise G. Melman, Mar. 26, 1972; children: Lindy S., Jeffrey B. MB BCh, U. Witwatersrand, South Africa, 1971; PhD, U. Cape Town, South Africa, 1981. Diplomate in internal medicine and endocrinology Am. Bd. Internal Medicine. Lectr. in medicine U. Cape Town, 1981-82, sr. lectr. in medicine, 1982-83; asst. prof. medicine U. Wash., Seattle, 1983-88, assoc. prof. medicine, 1988-89; physician Valley Diabetes and Endocrine Ctr., Renton, Wash., 1989-96, Valley Internal Medicine, Renton, 1997—. Dir., ptnr. Rainier Clin. Rsch. Ctr., Renton, 1992—. Fellow Royal Coll. Physicians Edinburgh, Am. Coll. Endocrinologists; mem. Am. Diabetes Assn., Endocrine Soc., King County Med. Soc. Jewish. Office: Valley Internal Medicine 4033 Talbot Rd S Ste 500 Renton WA 98055-5704

KLAFTER, CARY IRA, lawyer; b. Chgo., Sept. 15, 1948; s. Herman Nicholas and Bernice Rose (Maremont) K.; m. Kathleen Ann Kerr, July 21, 1974; children: Anastasia, Benjamin, Eileen. BA, Mich. State U., 1968, MS, 1971; JD, U. Chgo., 1972. Bar: Calif. 1972. Assoc. Morrison & Foerster, San Francisco, 1972-79, ptnr., 1979-96; v.p. legal and govt. affairs, dir. corp. affairs, corp. sec. Intel Corp., Santa Clara, Calif., 1996—. Lectr. law Stanford Law Sch., 1990-99. Capt. USAR, 1971-78. Mem. Am. Soc. Corp. Secs. (bd. dirs.).

KLAFTER, CRAIG EVAN, university administrator, legal historian; b. N.Y.C., Aug. 2, 1958; s. Gerald and Lenore (Schiener) K.; m. Catriona Susan Walker, Aug. 24, 1985 (div. May 1999). BA with honors, U. Chgo., 1980, MA, 1983; DPhil, Oxford (Eng.) U., 1991. Lectr. Am. history and instns. U. Manchester, Eng., 1990-91; lectr. modern history U. Southampton, Eng., 1991-92, rsch. fellow modern history, 1992-93; assoc. historian Jud. Br. U.S., Washington, 1993-94; adj. prof. law Boston U., 1994—2002, asst. to prov., 1994-95, asst. to pres., 1995—2002; treas. U. Birmingham Found., 2003—. Author: Reason Over Precedents: Origins of American Legal Thought, 1993, Essays on English Law and the American Experience, 1994, Legal Practice Management and Quality Standards, 1995. V.p., treas., trustee St. Catherine's Coll. (Oxford) Found., Washington, 1993-2000—, pres., 2000—, dir., KVC Inc., Boca Raton, 2000-; mem. convocation Oxford U. Mem. Oxford Soc., Am. Soc. Legal History, Hist. Soc. Avocations: skiing, squash, swimming. Home: 66 Kenrick St Boston MA 02135-3805 E-mail: cklafter@stcatz.org.

KLAFTER, GEORGE, urologist; b. Malmo, Sweden, Apr. 7, 1948; came to U.S., 1954; s. Abraham and Rachel K.; m. Roberta Teller, Oct. 26, 1980; children Farrah Elyse, Carly Samantha. BA, Yeshiva U., 1970; MD, N.Y. Med. Coll., 1974. Diplomate Am. Bd. Urology. Resident in surgery Montefiore Hosp. & Med. Ctr., Bronx, 1974-76; resident in urology N.Y. Med. Coll., N.Y.C., 1976-78, NYU Med. Ctr., N.Y.C., 1978-80; urologic oncology fellow Roswell Park Meml. Cancer Inst., Buffalo, 1977, Meml. Sloan Kettering Hosps., N.Y.C., 1979; urologic surgeon Ross Loos Med. Group, L.A., 1980-81, Health Ins. Plan of Greater N.Y., Bronx, 1981-83, George Klafter, M.D., P.C., Cliffside Park, N.J., 1981-99, The Urology Ctr., 1999—. Chief dept. urology St. Barnabas-Union Hosps., Bronx, 1986-98. Exec. bd. Israel Bonds, 1993—. Recipient Leonard Wershub Meml. Prize in urology N.Y. Med. Coll., 1974; Mosby Books scholar, 1974. Avocations: playing guitar, stamp and coin collecting, automobiles. Office: 663 Palisade Ave Ste 304 Cliffside Park NJ 07010-3012 also: 75 S Dean St Englewood NJ 07631 also: 2371 Arthur Ave Bronx NY 10458-8113 E-mail: klafter04@aol.com.

KLAHR, GARY PETER, retired lawyer; b. N.Y.C., July 9, 1942; s. Fred and Frieda (Garson) K. Student, Ariz. State U., 1958-61; LL.B. with high honors, U. Ariz., 1964. Bar: Ariz. 1967, U.S. Dist. Ct. Ariz. 1967. Assoc. Brazlin & Greene, Phoenix, 1967-68; sr. ptnr. Gary Peter Klahr, P.C., Phoenix, 1968—2002. Asst. editor Ariz. Law Rev., 1963-64; contbr. articles to profl. jours. Bd. dirs. CODAMA, 1975-89, pres., 1980-81; bd. dirs. Tumbleweed Runaway Ctr., 1972-76; mem. bd. dirs. Internat. Found. Anti-Cancer Drug Discovery, 1998-2002, chair exec. com., 1999-2002; chmn. Citizens Criminal Justice Commn., 1977-78; elected Phoenix City Coun., 1974-76; co-chmn. delinquency subcom. Phoenix Forward Task force; vol. referee Juvenile Ct., 1969; mem. City Coun., Phoenix, 1974-1976; vol. adult probation officer; vol. counselor youth programs Dept. Econ. Security and Dept. of Corrections, Phoenix; ex-officio mem., spl. cons. Phoenix Youth Commn.; mem. citizen adv. coun. Phoenix Union H.S. Dist., 1985-90, 95-99, co-chmn. 1998-99, elected governing bd., 1991-95, 2000—, v.p., 1992-95, co-chmn. citizens adv. com., 1970-72; mem. rev. bd. Phoenix Police Dept., 1985-94; bd. dirs. Metro Youth Ctr., 1986-87, Svc./Employment/Redevel. (SER) Jobs for Progress, Phoenix, 1985-90, pres., 1986-87; bd. dirs. East McDowell Youth Assn., 1992-94; v.p. local chpt. City of Hope, 1985-86; Justice of the Peace pro tem Maricopa County Cts., 1985-89, City License Appeals Bd., 1987-97, vice chmn. 1988-93, chmn. 1993-97; juvenile hearing officer Maricopa County Juvenile Ct., 1985-89; v.p., co founder Cmty. Leadership for Youth Devel. (CLYDE); del. Phoenix Together Town Hall on Youth Crime, 1982. Named 1 of 3 Outstanding Young Men of Phoenix, Phoenix Jaycees, 1969; recipient Disting. Citizen award Ariz. chpt. ACLU, 1976. Mem. ACLU (v.p. ctrl. chpt. Ariz. 1990-95, pres. 1995-2001, mem. state bd. 1990-2001), Ariz. State Bar (past sec., bd. dirs. young lawyers sect., co-chmn. unauthorized practice com. 1988-89, mem. other coms.), Maricopa County Bar Assn. (past sec., bd. dirs. young lawyers sec., vice-chmn. juvenile practice com. 1998-99), Am. Judicature Soc., Jewish Children's and Family Svc., Common Cause, NAACP, Ariz. ConsumersCoun., Phoenix Jaycees, Order of the Coif, Phi Alpha Delta. Democrat. Jewish. Office: 317 E Berridge Ln Phoenix AZ 85012

KLAIDMAN, STEPHEN DAVID, writer; b. N.Y.C., May 28, 1938; s. Moe Klaidman and Pauline Hinerfeld; m. Kitty Cecile Ehrenreich, Dec. 27, 1959; children: Elyse Suzanne, Daniel Marc. Student, CCNY, 1955-59. Copy editor N.Y. Times, N.Y.C., 1962-69; dep. fgn. editor The Washington Post, 1970-75, reporter, 1976-77; news editor, chief editl. writer Internat. Herald Tribune, Paris, 1977-82; sr. rsch. fellow Kennedy Inst. Ethics, Georgetown U., Washington, 1982-2001. Cons. Dept. of Def., Washington, 1982-83, Dept. of Edn., Washington, 1998-99; counselor Adv. Com. on Human Radiation Experiments, Washington, 1995-97. Author: The Virtuous Journalist, 1987, Health in the Headlines, 1991, Saving the Heart, 2000. Recipient 1st prize Woodrow Wilson Internat. Ctr. for Scholars, Media Studies Competition, 1991, Lowell Mellett award Pa. State U., 1992; grantee NEH, Washington, 1985. Avocations: reading, listening to music, basketball, tennis. E-mail: sklaid@aol.com.

KLAIN, DAVID RICHARD, naval officer; b. Caracas, Venezuela, June 21, 1967; s. Richard Morris and Carol (Piccoli) K.; m. Kimberly Kay Evans, Dec. 15, 1990; 1 child, Douglas. BS in Polit. Sci., U.S. Naval Acad., 1989; MA in Internat. Affairs, Cath. U. Am., 1997. Main propulsion asst. USS Thach, Yokosuka, Japan, 1989-91; combat info. ctr. officer USS Thach, 1991-92; anti-submarine warfare officer USS Vella Gulf Norfolk, Va., 1993-95; policy and joint doctrine officer Office of Chief Naval Ops. USN, Washington, 1995-96, adminstrv. asst. Office Chief Naval Ops., 1996-97; weapons officer USS The Sullivans Mayport, Fla., 1997-99; combat sys. officer USS The Sullivans USN, Mayport, Fla., 1999-2000; mil. legis. fellow Office of Senator Mary Landrieu, Washington, 2001; exec. officer USS Thorn, Norfolk, Va., 2002—. Rep. com. terminology to NATO Dept. Def. USN, Washington, 1995-96. Contbr. articles to profl. jours. Mem. U.S. Naval Inst. (Author of Yr. group award 1998), Surface Navy Assn. Avocations: sailing, flying, travel, golf. Home: 1640 Pocahontas St Norfolk VA 23511 E-mail: drklain@iname.com.

KLAIN, JANE, editor, critic, research administrator; b. N.Y.C., Jan. 05; 1 child. BA, MA in Theater and Film, postgrad. in film studies, NYU. Film reviewer, reporter Motion Picture Herald, Motion Picture Daily; assoc. editor Motion Picture Almanac and TV Almanac; listings editor, assoc. editor, theater/film critic Where Mag.; editor Exec. Dining, N.Y., 1982-83, Quigley Pub. Co., Inc., 1986-90; theater editor, researcher, biographies editor Baseline, N.Y.C., 1990-92; sr. editor The Mus. of TV & Radio, N.Y.C., 1994-99, mgr. rsch. svcs., 1999—. Editor: International Motion Picture Almanac, 1989, 90, International TV and Video Almanac, 1989, 90; assoc. editor: The Encyclopedia of Film, 1991; contbg. writer Show Music mag., The Sondheim Rev.; contbg. theater, film critic Good Times, 1985—. Mem. Phi Beta Kappa. Office: Museum of TV and Radio 25 W 52nd St New York NY 10019-6104 E-mail: jklain@MTR.org.

KLAIN, RONALD ALAN, lawyer; b. Indpls., Aug. 8, 1961; s. Stanley Hugh and Sarann (Horwitz) K.; m. Monica Medina, June 22, 1986; children: Hannah, Michael, Daniel. BA, Georgetown U., 1983; JD, Harvard U., 1987. Bar: Pa., 1992, D.C. 1999. Law clk. Hon. Byron R. White, Washington, 1987-89; spl. asst. Senate Judiciary Com., Washington, 1986-87, chief counsel, 1989-92; dir. Washington issues Clinton/Gore Campaign, 1992; assoc. counsel to Pres. The White House, Washington, 1993-94; chief of staff for Atty. Gen., Dept. Justice, Washington, 1994-95; staff dir. Senate Dem. Leadership Com., Washington, 1995; chief of staff Vice President Gore, The White House, Washington, 1995-99; ptnr. O'Melveny & Myers, Washington, 1999-2000, 01—; gen. counsel Gore-Lieberman Recount Com., Tallahassee, 2000. Commr. Pres.'s Commn. on Fed. Appointments Process, Washington, 1990. Democrat. Jewish. Home: 3912 Rosemary St Chevy Chase MD 20815 E-mail: rklain@omm.com.

KLAINBERG, MARILYN BLAU, community health educator; b. N.Y.C., Jan. 6, 1942; d. George Blau and Etta (Nagel) Konrad; m. Bernard Klainberg, June 3, 1961; children: Dennis, Danielle, Gregory, Joshua. BS, Adelphi Coll., 1963; MS, Adelphi U., 1977; EdD, Columbia U., 1994. RN, N.Y. From mem. adj. faculty to assoc. prof. Adelphi U., Garden City, NY, 1977—2002, assoc. prof., 2002—; asst. prof., dir. continuing edn. SUNY Health Sci. Ctr., Bklyn., 1989—97, chmn. undergrad. faculty, 1999—, faculty officer, 1992—93, dir. continuing edn., assoc. prof. Coll. Nursing, 1995—97; assoc. dean Adelphia U. Sch. of Nursing, 2002—, interim dean, 2003. Summer program nurse, dir. Manhasset (N.Y.) Pub. Schs., 1974-88, cons. health promotion programs, 1991-92, chmn. substance abuse com., 1991; edn. dir. Friends of Hospice, Manhasset, 1990-98, chmn. rsch. grant com.; cons. on drugs and alcohol Manhasset Youth Coun.; presenter in field. Newspaper columnist: Manhasset Press, 1980—84; co-author: A Guidebook for the Prevention of Substance Abuse, 1990; lead author: Community Health Nursing: An Alliance for Health, 1998, mem. editl. bd.: NACLI, chair editl. bd.:, 2001—, pub.: Nursing Spectrum, 1999—, Am. Jour. Nursing, 1999—, Am. Liver Found. Newsletter, 2000—; author: (jour. article) The Ann. Rev. of Nursing Edn. Mem. Manhasset Student Com., 1989-96, mem. exec. bd., 1990-95, Manhasset Schs. Parent Coun.; chmn. Safe Homes, 1988; edn. chair exec. bd. Friends of Hospice, 1993-98, rsch. grant chair, 1994-95, adv. bd. mem., 1998—; mem. Manhasset Park Dist. Adv. Bd., 1997—; mem. Plandome Rd. Commn.; appointed mem. adv. bd., bd. dirs. Queens Theater in the Pk., 1999—; adv. bd. Am. Liver Found. L.I. Coalition, 1999—; bd. dirs. Queens Theater Pk., 1999—. Recipient Ruth W. Harper Disting. Svc. award, Nurses Assn. of Counties of LI, 1995, Nurse of Excellence award, Spectrum, NY, 1997, Presdl. Citation award, NACLI, 2001, Helene Fuld Scholar Leadership devel. award, AACN, 2002; grantee New Faculty rsch., SUNY, 1991. Fellow: AACN; mem.: AAUP (mem. steering com. rep., mem. Adelphi com. 1999—), ANA, Nurses Assn. Counties of L.I. (membership com., exec. bd. 1992—93, editl. bd. 1993—, chair editl. bd. 2001—, nominating com. 1998—99, web adv. com., Presdl. citation 2001), Sigma Theta (exec. bd. by-laws com. 1990—93, chmn. fundraising com. 1989, nominating com. 1994, dist. 14 editl. bd. 1993, co-chmn. spring conf. and 1995 25th anniversary celebration, co-chmn. by-laws com., pres. Alpha Omega chpt. 1996—2000, webmaster 1999—), Kappa Delta Pi. Avocations: travel, knitting. Home: 14 Short Dr Manhasset NY 11030-3421 Office: Sch Nursing Adelphi U Garden City NY 11530 E-mail: nursemarilyn@prodigy.net., klainberg@adelphi,edu.

KLAITS, JOSEPH AARON, education program director, historian; b. N.Y.C., Sept. 23, 1942; s. Julius Klaits and Beatrice Spielman; m. Sondra G. Stein, 1994; m. Barrie Gelbhaus, 1965; children: Frederick, Alexander. AB, Columbia U., 1964; MA, U. Minn., 1966, PhD, 1970. Prof. history Oakland U., Rochester, Mich., 1969-91; dir. Jennings Randolph Program for Internat. Peace U.S. Inst. Peace, Washington, 1991—. Vis. prof. history Cath. U. Am., Washington, 1982-83; Fulbright program acad. liaison U.S. Info. Agy., Washington, 1983-86; cons. Woodrow Wilson Internat. Ctr. for Scholars, Washington, 1985-91. Author: Servants of Satan: The Age of the Witch Hunts, 1985, Printed Propaganda under Louis XIV: Absolute Monarchy and Public Opinion, 1976; editor: Liberty/Liberté: The French and American Experiences, 1991, The Global Ramifications of the French Revolution, 1994. Fulbright fellow, France, 1967-68; NEH fellow, 1982-83; Am. Coun. Learned Socs. fellow, 1986-87. Home: 2737 Woodley Pl NW Washington DC 20008-1518 Office: US Inst Peace 1200 17th St NW Washington DC 20036-3006 Fax: 202-429-6063. Business E-Mail: jklaits@usip.org.

KLAKEG, CLAYTON HAROLD, cardiologist; b. Big Woods, Minn., Mar. 31, 1920; s. Knute O. and Agnes (Folvik) K.; student Concordia Coll., Moorhead, Minn., 1938-40; BS, N.D. State U., 1942; BS in Medicine, N.D. U., 1943; M.D., Temple U., 1945; MS in Medicine and Physiology, U. Minn.-Mayo Found., 1954; children: Julie Ann, Robert Clayton, Richard Scott. Intern, Med. Ctr., Jersey City, 1945-46; mem. staff VA Hosp., Fargo, N.D., 1948-51; fellow in medicine and cardiology Mayo Found., Rochester, Minn., 1951-55; internist, cardiologist Sansum Med. Clinic Inc., Santa Barbara, Calif., 1955—; mem. staff Cottage Hosp., St. Francis Hosp. Bd. dirs. Sansum Med. Rsch. Found., pres., 1990. Served to capt. M.C., USAF, 1946-48. Diplomate Am. Bd. Internal Medicine. Fellow ACP, Am. Coll. Cardiology, Am. Coll. Chest Physicians, Am. Heart Assn. (mem. council on clin. cardiology); mem. Calif. Heart Assn. (pres. 1971-72, Meritorious Service award 1968, Disting. Service award 1972, Disting. Achievement award 1975), Santa Barbara County Heart Assn. (pres. 1959-60, Disting. Service award 1958, Disting. Achievement award 1971), Calif. Med. Assn., Los Angeles Acad. Medicine, Santa Barbara County Med. Assn., Mayo Clinic Alumni Assn., Santa Barbara Soc. Internal Medicine (pres. 1963), Sigma Xi, Phi Beta Pi. Republican. Lutheran. Club: Channel City. Contbr. articles to profl. jours. Home: 5956 Trudi Dr Santa Barbara CA 93117-2175 Office: Sansum Med Clinic Inc PO Box 1239 Santa Barbara CA 93102-1239

KLAMANN, JOHN MICHAEL, lawyer; b. Fresno, Calif., Aug. 23, 1952; s. Michael J. and Jacqueline C. K.; m. Brigid A. Cleary, Apr. 17, 1982; children: Conor, Seth, Zachary, Hannah, Kaitlin, Abbye. BS in Psychology, Kans. State U., 1974; JD, U. Kans., 1978. Bar: Mo. 1978, Kans. 1979. Atty. Popham Law Firm, Kansas City, Mo., 1978-88, Payne and Jones, Overland Park, Kans., 1989-96, Klamann and Hubbard, P.A., Overland Park, 1996—. Adj. prof. U. Mo., Kansas City Sch. of Law, 1998-2001. Author: (with others) Am Jur Trials, 1988, 90, 92. Mem. ABA, ATLA, Mo. Assn. Trial Attys., Kans. Trial Lawyers Assn., Mo. Bar Assn., Kans. Bar Assn. Home: 4105 W 123rd St Leawood KS 66209 Office: Klamann and Hubbard PA 7101 College Blvd Ste 120 Overland Park KS 66210 Fax: 913-327-7800. E-mail: jklamann@kh-law.com.

KLAMERUS, KAREN JEAN, pharmacist, researcher; b. Chgo., Aug. 10, 1957; d. Robert Edward and Jane Mary (Nawoj) Klamerus; m. Frederick P. Zeller. BS in Pharmacy, U. Ill., 1980; PharmD, U. Ky., 1981. Registered pharmacist Ky., Ill., Pa. Staff pharmacist Haggin Meml. Hosp., Harrodsburg, Ky., 1980-81, Regional Med. Ctr., Madisonville, Ky., 1982, critical care liasion, 1982; clin. pharmacist resident U. Nebr., Omaha, 1983; clin. pharmacist cardiothoracic surgery U. Ill., Chgo., 1983-88, clin asst. prof. dept. pharmacy practice, 1983-86, asst. prof., 1986-88, departmental affiliate dept. pharmaceutics, 1986-88; sr. pharmacokineticist Wyeth-Ayerst Rsch., Phila., 1988-91, asst. dir. clin. pharmacology, 1991-95, assoc. dir. clin. pharmacology, 1995-97; dir. med. rsch. Roche Global Devel., Palo Alto, Calif., 1997—2001; dir. clin. rsch. Vical, Inc., San Diego, 2002, Pfizer, 2002—. Fellow: Am. Coll. Clin. Pharmacology (indsl. rels. com. 1995); mem.: Mid-Atlantic Coll. Clin. Pharmacology (sec. 1991, pres. 1992—94), Am. Soc. Clin. Pharmacology and Therapeutics. Avocations: softball, scuba diving, gardening, sewing. Office: Pfizer-La Jolla 10777 Science Center Dr B85 San Diego CA 92121 E-mail: kjklamerus@yahoo.com.

KLAMMER, JOSEPH FRANCIS, management consultant; b. Omaha, Mar. 25, 1925; s. Aloys Arcadius and Sophie (Nadolny) K. BS, Creighton U., 1948; MBA, Stanford U., 1950; cert. in polit. econs. Grad. Inst. Internat. Studies, U. Geneva, 1951. Cert. mgmt. cons. Adminstrv. analyst Chevron Corp., San Francisco, 1952-53; staff asst. No. Natural Gas Co., Omaha, 1953-57; mgmt. cons. Cresap, McCormick and Paget, Inc., N.Y.C., 1957-75, v.p., mgr. San Francisco region, 1968-75, bd. dirs.; mgmt. cons., prin. J.F. Klammer Assocs., San Francisco, 1975-2000; semi-ret. practice mgmt. cons., San Francisco, 2000— CEO, pres. Isabelle Towers Homeowners Assn., 1993—94, also bd. dirs., mem. fin. com., 1994—95, 1996—2001, mem. rules com., 1995—96, mem. maintenance com, 2000—, bd. dirs., Conard House. Apptd. and attended U.S. Mil. Acad., West Point, N.Y.; mem. adv. coun. Creighton U. Coll. Arts and Scis. 1st lt. USAAF, 1943-46, lt. col. USAF, ret. Recipent Sovereign Mil. Hospitaller Order of St. John of Jerusalem of Rhodes and of Malta, Alumni Merit award Creighton U. Coll. Arts and Scis., 1998. Mem. Plaza Club, Knights of Malta, Alpha Sigma Nu. Republican. Roman Catholic. Home: 1998 Broadway San Francisco CA 94109-2281

KLAMON, LAWRENCE PAINE, lawyer; b. St. Louis, Mar. 17, 1937; s. Joseph Martin and Rose (Schimel) K.; m. Jo Ann Karen Beatty, Nov. 1957 (div. Feb. 1974); children: Stephen Robert, Karen Jean, Lawrence Paine; m. Frances Ann Estes, Mar. 1980. AB, Washington U., St. Louis, 1958; JD, Yale U., 1961. Bar: N.Y. 1964, Ga. 1992. Confidential asst. Office Sec. Def., Washington, 1961-62, spl. asst. to gen. counsel, 1962-63; asso. Cravath, Swaine & Moore, N.Y.C., 1963-67; v.p., gen. counsel Fuqua Industries, Inc., Atlanta, 1967-73, sr. v.p. fin. and adminstrn., 1971-81, pres., 1981-89, chief exec. officer, 1989-91; chmn., 1991; sr. counsel Alston & Bird, Atlanta, 1991-95; pres., CEO Fuqua Enterprises, Inc., Atlanta, 1995-97. Chmn. Gov.'s Internat. Adv. Coun., 1992-95. Mem. bd. editors Yale Law Jour., 1959-61. Mem. State Bar Ga., Order of Coif, Phi Beta Kappa, Omicron Delta Kappa. Home: 2665 Dellwood Dr NW Atlanta GA 30305-3519

KLAMPE, CRAIG ALLEN, composer; b. San Diego, Apr. 14, 1957; s. Dean Gordon and Shirley Lorraine Klampe; m. Katherine Anne Kampmann, July 22, 1978; children: Gordon Dean, Ian Joseph. BA, U. Calif., San Diego, 1978; MA, Claremont Grad. U., 1983. Choirmaster All Saints Luth. Ch., San Diego, 1988—; co-dir. St. Anthony Antiochian Orthodox Ch., La Jolla, Calif.,

1995—2000. Composer: (choral) O Lord, teach me to seek, 1995, Intimam, 2001, O splendor of the Father's light, 2002, I will sing, 2002, Ely Canticles, 1996. Mem.: Am. Choral Dirs. Assn. (life).

KLANG, MARY MARGARET, secondary school educator; b. Butte, Mont., Mar. 22, 1949; d. James J. and Eileen T. O'Brien; m. Donald L. Klang; children: Evangeline, Alexia, Jesse. BA, San Francisco State U., 1974; Master Herbalist, Emerson Coll. Herbology Ltd., Mont., Que., Can., 1981. Cert. tchr. Mont., Calif. Tchr. Laguna Salada Sch. Dist., Pacifica, Calif., 1973—79; substitute tchr. Sch. Dist. 5, Kalispell, Mont., 1990—95; tchr., tutor Linderman Mid. Sch., Kalispell, 1995—2002; tchr. English and math. Linderman Sch., Kalispell, 2002—. Dir. summer sch. Linderman Sch., Kalispell, 1998—2002; pvt. tutor, Kalispell, 1995—2002. Author: (pamphlet) Steps to Success: A Tutoring Program, 1998, Seeing, 1985. Grantee travel grantee as mem. of Reading Delegation, China, Alpha Delta Kappa, 2001. Mem.: ASCD, Internat. Reading Assn., Phi Delta Kappa, Alpha Delta Kappa (sec. 2002—02). Democrat. Avocations: literacy, gardening, travel. Office: Linderman Mid Sch 124 3rd Ave E Kalispell MT 59901 Personal E-mail: klang@digisys.net. Business E-Mail: klangm@sd5.k12.mt.us.

KLAPER, MARTIN JAY, lawyer; b. Chgo., Jan. 12, 1947; s. Carl and Kate F. (Friedman) K.; m. Julia Warner, Nov. 14, 1973. BS in Bus. summa cum laude, Ind. U., 1969, JD summa cum laude, 1971. Bar: Ind. 1971, U.S. Dist. Ct. (no. and so. dists.) Ind. 1971, U.S. Ct. Appeals (7th cir.) 1972, U.S. Supreme Ct. 1979. Law clk. to justice U.S. Ct. Appeals (7th cir.), 1971-72; ptnr. Ice Miller, Indpls., 1972—. Mem. ABA, Ind. Bar Assn. Office: Ice Miller PO Box 82001 Indianapolis IN 46282-2001 E-mail: Klaper@comcast.net., Klaper@Icemiller.com.

KLAPMEIER, JOLIE BLEEKER, lawyer; b. Mpls., Mar. 7, 1961; m. Steven James Klapmeier, June 14, 1986. BA in Internat. Rels., Carleton Coll., 1983; JD, Am. U., 1987, MA in Internat. Affairs, 1988. Bar: Minn. Pro bono legal asst. to VISTA atty. Lao Family Cmty., St. Paul, 1982; asst. to mem. of parliament West German Parliament, Bonn, 1983; legal intern U.S. Treasury Dept., Office Fgn. Assets Control, Washington, 1985; summer assoc. Fredrikson & Byron, P.A., Mpls., 1986; prin. Klapmeier & Assocs. Internat., Mpls., 1988—; exec. v.p., gen. counsel Bluewater Yachts, Mora, Minn., 2002—. Pres. U.S.-China Peoples Friendship Assn. Minn., 1991-95, chair Sister-City and strategic planning coms., 1995-2000; gen. legal counsel Orgn. Chinese Ams. Minn., 1992-99; mem. adv. com. for trade with China, Minn. Trade Office, 1993-2000; mem. Mpls.-St. Paul Com. on Fgn. Rels., 1996—; bd. dirs. State Minn. Export Fin. Authority, Minn. World Trade Ctr. Corp. Chief editor U.S.-China Rev., 1997-99. Mem. Minn. Internat. Ctr., 1987—; class agt. Carleton Coll. Alumni Annual Fund, 1988-94; mem. exec. com. Midwest Asia Ctr., 1993-96; mem. planning com. Twin Cities Internat. Citizens Awards, 1993-2002, chair award selection com., 1997, chair corp. award com., 1997-98; bd. dirs. WAMSO Minn. Orch. Vol. Assn., 1993-2001, v.p. comm., 1996-99, pres., 1999-2001; bd. dirs. Young Audiences Minn., 2001--, WCCO Good Neighbor Awards, 2000--; Minn. v.p., bd. dirs. UN Assn., 1994-96, mem. adv. com., 1997—, chair nominating com., 1997-99. Recipient Nat. Svc. award Nat. US China Peoples Friendship Assn., 1993, Hon. Chinese award Orgn. Chinese Ams. Minn., 1994, Gov.'s Commendation for Outstanding Pub. Svc., State Minn., 1994, Good Neighbor award for cmty. svc. WCCO Radio, 1995, Twin Cities Internat. Citizen award Cities of Mpls. and St. Paul, 1995, CitiBus. Unsung Heroes award, 2000. Mem. Am. Soc. Internat. Law, Minn. Women Lawyers Assn., Minn. Advs. for Human Rights, Minn. State Bar Assn. (David Graven Pub. Svc. award 1998), Hennepin County Bar Assn., Nat. U.S.-China Peoples Friendship Assn. (chair internat. exchs. 1995-99, chair U.S. China Rev. editl. com. 1996—). Office: Klapmeier & Assocs Internat 4151 Dynasty Dr Minnetonka MN 55345-1812 Fax: 612-935-8918. E-mail: jolie_klapmeier@msn.com.

KLAPPER, ANDREW, computer scientist, educator; b. White Plains, N.Y., Feb. 26, 1952; s. Morris and Marion Klapper; life ptnr. Judy Goldsmith. BA in Math., NYU, 1974; MS in Applied Math., SUNY, Binghamton, 1974; MS in Math., Stanford U., 1977, PhD in Math., Brown U., 1981. Postdoctoral fellow Clark U., Worcester, Mass., 1981—84; asst. prof. Northeastern U., Boston, 1984—91, U. Man., Winnipeg, Canada, 1991—93, U. Ky., Lexington, 1993—97, assoc. prof., 1997—2001, prof., 2001—. Gen. chair Crypto '98, Santa Barbara, Calif., 1997—98. Foreman/squire Squash Beetle Morris Dancers, Lexington, 1994—. Mem.: Internat. Assn. Cryptologic Rsch. (bd. dirs. 1997—99, assoc. editor for rsch. Cryptologia Jour. 1999—2001), IEEE Info. Theory Soc. (assoc. editor for sequences IEEE Transactions on Info. Theory 2000—), Lexington Traditional Dance Assn. (bd. dirs. 2000—). Avocations: dancing, birdwatching. Office: U Ky Dept Computer Sci 779a Anderson Hall Lexington KY 40506-0046 Personal E-mail: klapper@cs.uky.edu. Business E-Mail: klapper@cs.uky.edu.

KLAPPER, BYRON D. financial company executive; b. NYC, May 2, 1938; s. Irving and Lottie K.; m. Karin I. Klapper, June 28, 1964; children: Kimberly, Lonn-Eric. BS in Journalism, U. Kans., 1964; cert. Wharton Sch., U. Pa., 1974. Reporter Topeka Daily Capitol, Kans., 1963, U.P.I., Kans. City, Mo.; editor Am. Cyanamid Co., Wayne, NJ, 1964-67; media rels. staff Bethlehem Steel Corp., NYC, 1968; speech writer Burlington Ind., Inc., NYC, 1969; reporter Wall St Jour., NYC, 1970-80; sr. v.p. Std. and Poors Corp., NYC, 1980-90; mng. dir. Fitch Investors Svc., NYC, 1990-98, Am. Capital Access, Inc., 1998—2001. Columnist skiing Morristown Daily Record, 1988-2001, Editor-in-chief, Sno-Sports., Internet Ski Mag.; bd. dir. Powell Techs., Inc., Visions West, Inc. Contbg. editor Barron's NYC, 1967-69; pub. S&P's Creditweek, 1981-90; publ. Creditweek Internat., 1983, Mcpl. Bond Book, 1984, S&P's Creditwire, 1986; original author of the anticipated novel: "Fuel or Fool Your Mind". Recipient Nat. Journalism award, William Randolph Hearst Found., 1960, 62, New Products award, McGraw Hill, 1986. Mem. Ea. Ski Writers Assn. (dir. 1985-91), Govt. Fin. Officers Assn., Pub. Securities Assoc., Bond Market Assn., Downtown Athletic Club, Fgn. Corres. Club Japan (hon.), N.Am. Snowsports Journalists Assn. (dir. 1998-2001). Avocations: writing, photography, skiing, computers, triathlon. Home: 37 Tara Ln Montville NJ 07045-9699

KLAPPER, MOLLY, lawyer, educator; b. Berlin; came to U.S., 1950; d. Elias and Ciporah (Weber) Teicher; m. Jacob Klapper; children: Rachelle Hannah, Robert David. BA, CUNY, MA, 1964; PhD, NYU, 1974; JD, Rutgers U., 1987. Bar: N.J. 1987, U.S. Dist. Ct. N.J. 1987, N.Y. 1989, U.S. Dist. Ct. (so. and ea. dists.) N.Y. 1989, D.C. 1989, U.S. Supreme Ct. 1991, U.S. Ct. Appeals (2d cir.) 1992; cert. arbitrata, Better Bus. Bur., 2000, cert. arbitrator (NASD) Nat. Assn. of Security Dealers, 2003. Prof. English Bronx C.C., CUNY, 1974-84; law intern U.S. Dist. Ct. N.J., Newark, 1987; law sec. to presiding judge appellate div. N.J. Supreme Ct., Springfield, 1987-88; assoc. Wilson, Elser, Moskowitz, Edelman and Dicker, N.Y.C., 1988-96; adminstrv. law judge Dept. Finance, N.Y.C., 1997—; adj. prof. law Touro Law Ctr., Huntington, N.Y., 2001—. Small claims ct. arbitrator, 1994—; mediator N.Y. State Supreme Ct., comml. divsn., 2000—; jud. nominee State Supreme Ct., 2d dist., 1999; mediator Nat. Assn. Sec. Dirs., 2002—. Author: The German Literary Influence on Byron, 1974, 2d edit., 1975, The German Literary Influence on Shelley, 1975; contbr. to profl. publs. NEH fellow, 1978; grantee Am. Philos. Soc., 1976. Mem. Assn. Bar of City of N.Y., Adminstr. Law Com., 2003. Avocations: bicycling, skiing, roller skating, walking, hiking. Office: 720 Ft Washington Ave New York NY 10040-3708

KLAPPERICH, FRANK LAWRENCE, JR., investment banker; b. Oak Park, Ill., Oct. 11, 1934; s. Frank Lawrence and Marjorie (Doan) K.; m. Margaret Monroe Touborg, Mar. 9, 1957; children: Margaret Friis, Susan Doane, Frank Lawrence III, Elizabeth Monroe. AB, Princeton U., 1956; MBA, Harvard U., 1961, postgrad., 1979. With Kidder, Peabody & Co., Inc., Chgo., 1961—, v.p., 1964—, dir., 1972-86, mng. dir., 1986-88, sr. v.p., 1988-90, ret., 1990; pres. Charter Capital Corp., 1991—. Governing mem. Orchestral Assn. Chgo. Symphony Orch., 1995—; vice chmn. governing mems., 1996-98. With USN, 1956—59, ret. LCDR USNR. Mem. Investment Analysts Soc. Chgo., Securities Industry Assn. (chmn. Ctrl. States dist. 1986-87), Inst. Chartered Fin. Analysts, Harvard Bus. Sch. Assn. Chgo., Princeton Club (Chgo., pres. 1970-71), Charter Club (governing bd. 1987-97), Chgo. Club, Mid-Day Club (trustee 1987-90), Bond Club (pres. 1983-84), Econ. Club, Forum Club S.W. Fla. (bd. dirs. 2002—), Harvard Club of Naples (Fla., bd. dirs. 1999-2000, v.p. 2000-01, pres. 2001-03), Princeton Club of S.W. Fla. (bd. dirs. 2003—), Indian Hill Club (Winnetka, Ill.), Hole-in-the-Wall Golf Club (Naples). Home: 345 Woodley Rd Winnetka IL 60093-3740

KLARE, GEORGE ROGER, psychology educator; b. Mpls., Apr. 17, 1922; s. George C. and Lee (Launer) K.; m. Julia Marie Price Matson, Dec. 24, 1946; children: Deborah, Roger, Barbara. Student, U. Nebr., 1940-41, U. Minn., 1941-43, U. Mo., 1943; BA, U. Minn., 1946, MA, 1947, PhD, 1950. Instr. U. Minn., 1948-50; staff psychologist Psychol. Corp., N.Y.C., 1950-51; research assoc. U. Ill., 1952-54; asst. prof. dept. psychology Ohio U., Athens, 1954-57, assoc. prof., 1957-62, prof., 1962-79, Disting. prof., 1979-89, Disting. prof. emeritus, 1989—, chmn. dept., 1959-63, acting dean Coll. Arts and Sci., 1965, 85-86, dean, 1966-71, media coordinator, 1972-75, acting assoc. provost for grad. and research programs, 1986-87; research assoc. Harvard U., 1968-69; vis. prof. State U. N.Y. at Stony Brook, 1971-72, U. Iowa, 1979-80. Staff mem. N.Y.C. Writers Conf., 1956-57; cons., lectr. Nat. Project Agr. Communication, 1957-59, Com. on World Literacy and Christian Lit., 1958-62; exec. asst., sr. rsch. engr. Autonetics, 1960-61; cons. Resources Devel. Corp., 1962-65, Boston Pub. Sch., 1968, D.C. Heath Co., 1971, Western Electric, 1973, Westinghouse, 1975, Human Resources Rsch. Orgn., 1978-79, U.S. Navy, 1975, Armed Svcs. Readability Rsch., 1975, Center for Ednl. Exptl., Devel. and Evaluation, 1978-79, 81, U.S. Army, 1979, Bell System Center for Tech. Edn., 1975-80, Time, Inc., 1977-79, AT&T, 1979-81, 83,84, Coll. Osteo Medicine, Ohio U., 1987-89; lectr. Open Univ., Eng., 1975, NATO Conf. Visual Presentation of Info., The Netherlands, 1978, Beijing Normal U., 1990. Author: (with Byron Buck) Know Your Reader, 1954, The Measurement of Readability, 1963, (with Paul A. Games) Elementary Statistics: Data Analysis for the Behavioral Sciences, 1967, A Manual for Readable Writing, 1975, 4th edit., 1980, How to Write Readable English, 1985, Assessing Readability-Citation Classic, 1988; mem. editorial bd. Info. Design Jour., 1979—, Instrl. Sci., 1975-93, Reading Tchr., 1981-82, Reading Rsch. and Instrn., 1985-87, The Literacy Dictionary, 1993 (invited essay 1995). Served to 1st lt. USAAF, 1943-45. Decorated Air medal, Purple Heart; Fulbright travel grantee U.S.-U.K. Ednl. Commn. to Open U., 1977-81 Fellow Am. Psychol. Assn.; mem. Nat. Reading Conf. (invited address 1975, Oscar Causey award for outstanding contbns. to reading research 1981), Internat. Reading Assn. (elected to Hall of Fame 1997), Am. Ednl. Research Assn., Phi Beta Kappa, Delta Phi Lambda, Psi Chi, Phi Delta Kappa. Home and Office: 8800 Johnson Rd Ste 108 The Plains OH 45780-1277 E-mail: klare@chiou.edu.

KLARE, MICHAEL THOMAS, social science educator, program director; b. N.Y.C., Oct. 14, 1942; s. Charles and Mildred (Smith) K. BA, Columbia U., 1963, MA, 1968; postgrad., Yale U., 1963-65; PhD, Union Inst., 1976. Instr. Parsons Sch. Design, N.Y.C., 1967-70; research dir. N.Am. Congress on Latin Am., Berkeley, Calif., 1970-76; vis. lectr. Tufts U., 1973; vis. fellow Center of Internat. Studies, Princeton U., 1976-77; program dir. Inst. Policy Studies, Washington, 1977-84; prof. peace & world security studies Hampshire Coll., Amherst, Mass., 1985—, dir. 5 colls. program in peace and world security studies, 1985—. Vis. assoc. prof. of peace studies Wellesley Coll., 1992-93; def. corr. The Nation, 1983—. Author: War Without End, 1973, Supplying Repression, 1978, Beyond the Vietnam Syndrome, 1981, American Arms Supermarket, 1985, Rogue States and Nuclear Outlaws, 1995, Resource Wars, 2001; co-author: A Scourge of Guns, 1996; editor: Peace and World Security Studies: A Curriculum Guide, 6th edit., 1994; co-editor: Low Intensity Warfare, 1988, Peace and World Security Studies: A Curriculum Guide, 5th edit., 1989, World Security: Challenges for a New Century, 1991, 3d edit., 1998, Lethal Commerce: The Global Trade in Small Arms and Light Weapons, 1995, Light Weapons and Civil Conflict, 1999; contbg. editor Current History. Bd. dirs. Arms Control Assn., 1994—. Mem.: Fedn. Am. Scientists (bd. dirs. 1999—), Am. Acad. Arts and Scis. (internat. security studies com.). Home: 17 Columbus Ave Northampton MA 01060-4252 Office: Hampshire Coll Sch Social Sci Amherst MA 01002 E-mail: mklare@hampshire.edu.

KLARFELD, JONATHAN MICHAEL, journalism educator; b. Springfield, Mass., Dec. 11, 1937; m. Patricia Holland, Sept. 7, 1974; children: Victoria, Alexander. AB, Colgate U., 1960. Reporter, editor Holyoke (Mass.) Transcript-Telegram, 1962-65, UPI, Springfield, Boston, 1965-66, Boston Globe, 1966-68; press sec. Boston Parks/Redevel. Auth., 1968-70; reporter, writer Boston Record-Am., 1970-72; mgr. pub. info. Mass. Blue Cross, 1972-74; assoc. professor journalism Boston U., 1975—, dir. print journalism, 1979-96, dir. print and online journalism program, 1996—. Editl. cons. Lawyers Weekly Pubs., Boston, Lansing, Mich., Richmond, Va., Providence, 1983-92; press analyst Oxbow Corp., West Palm Beach, Fla., 1984-96; news media critic/columnist Boston Herald, 1994, 95; cons. in libel and invasion of privacy cases. Contbr. articles to numerous newspapers, periodicals. Mem. New Eng. Gilbert and Sullivan Soc., Sorcerers Rugby Club (pres. 1974-80), Newton Squash and Tennis Club (bd. govs. 1999-2003), Delta Kappa Epsilon. Unitarian Universalist. Avocations: squash, tennis, Gilbert and Sullivan. Office: Boston U Sch Journalism Boston MA 02215 E-mail: jklar@bu.edu.

KLARFELD, PETER JAMES, lawyer; b. Holyoke, Mass., Aug. 19, 1947; s. David Nathan and Gloria (Belsky) K.; m. Mary Myrtle, July 7, 1985; children: Peter Marcus (dec.), Mary Elizabeth, Louis Edward. BA, U. Va., 1969, JD, 1973; MA, U. Chgo., 1970. Bar: Va. 1973, D.C. 1975, U.S. Dist. Ct. D.C. 1977, U.S. Dist. Ct. (ea. dist.) Va. 1977, U.S. Dist. Ct. (ea. dist.) Wis. 1987, U.S. Dist. Ct. (no. dist.) Calif. 1990, U.S. Ct. Appeals (4th cir.) 1978, U.S. Ct. Appeals (3rd & 9th cirs.) 1986, U.S. Ct. Appeals (2d cir.) 1998, U.S. Ct. Appeals (7th cir.) 2003, U.S. Supreme Ct. 1977. Law clk. to Hon. Robert R. Merhige, Jr. U.S. Dist. Ct. (ea. dist.) Va., Richmond, 1973-74; atty., office of legal counsel U.S. Dept. Justice, Washington, 1974-76; ptnr. Brownstein Zeidman & Lore, Washington, 1977-96, Wiley, Rein &Fielding LLP, Washington, 1996—. Editor: Covenants Against Competition in Franchise Agreements, 2002; contbr. articles to profl. jours. Trustee Dalkon Shield Other Claimants Trust, Richmond, 1990-96, chmn., 1991-96. Mem. ABA. Home: 434 E Columbia St Falls Church VA 22046-3501 Office: Wiley Rein & Fielding 1776 K St NW Washington DC 20006-2304 E-mail: pklarfeld@wrf.com.

KLARICH, DAVID JOHN, political organization executive, lawyer; b. Hamilton, Ohio, July 17, 1963; s. Victor Martin and Janet Dawn (Carlson) K.; m. Cheryl Ruth O'Donnell, June 18, 1988. BA in Biology and Chemistry, U. Mo., 1985; MA in Pub. Policy, JD, Regent U., 1990. Bar: Mo. 1990. Mem. Mo. Ho. of Reps. from 92nd & 94th dists., Jefferson City, 1990-94, Mo. Senate from 26th dist., Jefferson City, 1994—2002, Riezman and Berger, P.C., Clayton, Mo., 1995—2002; apptd. commr. Mo. Indsl. Rels., 2002—; mng. mem. Citizens for Policy Reform, LLC. Chmn. judiciary com. Mo. State Senate, 2001—02. Trustee Logan Coll. Chiropractic, 1998. Recipient Adminstrn. of Justice award Jud. Conf. Mo., 1991, 99, Mo. Bar award, 1993, 97, 2000, 01, Mo. Hosp. Assn. award, 1995, Jud. Conf. award, 2000, 02, Legal Svcs. award, 2000, award Mo. Assn. Probate and Assoc. Cir. Judges, 2001; named Mo. Bar Outstanding Legis. of Yr., 1996, Voice of Bus. award Assoc. Industries, 1998. Mo. Lawyers weekly v.p. and coming Lawyer Mem. Bar Assn. Met. St. Louis, Young Lawyers Assn., Vol. Lawyers Assn., St. Louis Lawyers Assn., Mo. Assn. Trial Attys., ABA, St. Louis Eagle Scout Assn., Nat. Eagle Scout Assn., Jaycees, Lions, Mo. C. of C. (Spirit of Enterprise award 1997), Theta Xi. Mem. Assembly of God Ch. Fax: 636-230-8116. E-mail: dklarich@sbcglobal.net.

KLARIK, BELA WILLIAM JAMES CLARK, retired school system administrator; b. Masontown, Pa., Aug. 7, 1931; s. Louis Klarik and Margaret Irma (Soltesz) Clark; children from previous marriage: Frank, Roxana, Steven, Louis M. AB in Edn. cum laude, Fairmont State Coll., 1957; postgrad., Antioch Coll., 1960, U. Md., 1965—75, W.Va. U., 1958—59; MEd, U. Ga., 1961. Cert. ednl. supr. and adminstr., math. sci. and phys. edn. tchr. Ohio, Md. Profl. baseball player minor leagues Bklyn. Dodgers, 1953-55; tchr. math., coach Madison (Ohio) Meml. HS, 1957-60; tchr. math. and sci. Euclid (Ohio) City Schs., 1961-62; head dept. math. Richard Montgomery High Sch., Montgomery County Pub. Schs., Rockville, Md., 1962-65; Nat. Assn. Secondary Sch. Prins. adminstrv. intern John F. Kennedy HS, Silver Spring, Md., 1965-66; vice-prin. Col. E. Brooke Lee Jr. HS, Silver Spring, 1966-67; supr. math. Montgomery County Pub. Schs., Rockville, 1967-75, dir. dept. acad. skills, 1975-91; ret., 1991. Staff sgt. U.S. Army, 1949—52. NSF Summer Inst. fellow, Antioch Coll., 1960, NSF Acad. Yr. Inst. fellow, U. Ga., 1960—61, NSF fellow, W.Va. U., 1963, U. Ga. fellow, 1961. Mem.: ASCD, Inst. for Ednl. Leadership, Burnt Store Isles (Fla.) Assn., Montgomery County Ret. Tchrs. Assn., Md. Ret. Tchrs. Assn., Burnt Store Isles Boat Club, Am. Legion. Democrat. Roman Catholic. Avocations: travel, boating, sports, gourmet cuisines and wines. Home: 5006 Ovideo St Punta Gorda FL 33950-8000 E-mail: ldsleigh@comcast.net.

KLARQUIST, KENNETH STEVENS, JR., lawyer; b. Washington, Aug. 18, 1948; s. Kenneth S. and Lois M. (Boening) K.; m. Linda L. Arndt, Sept. 18, 1971; children: Josef, Peter, Jared. AB, Princeton U., 1970; JD, U. Oreg., 1973. Bar: Va. 1974, Oreg. 1975, Wash. 2003, U.S. Supreme Ct. 1980. Atty. estate tax U.S. Dept. Treasury, Richmond, Va., 1973-76; assoc. McMurry & Nichols, Portland, Oreg., 1976-77, Dahl, Zalutsky, Nichols & Hinson, P.C., Portland, Oreg., 1977-80; shareholder Zalutsky & Klarquist, P.C., Portland, Oreg., 1980—. Dir., past pres. Oreg. Wildlife Heritage Found., Portland, 1981—; dir., treas. KBPS Pub. Radio Found., Portland, 1991-99; bd. dirs. Nat. Alliance for Mentally Ill-Oreg., 1999—, pres., 2001—, Mem. Rotary (Rotarian of Month Portland 1996). Avocation: competitive rowing. Office: Zalutsky & Klarquist PC 215 SW Washington St Portland OR 97204-2636

KLASCO, RICHARD, emergency physician, information technology executive; b. New York, NY, June 4, 1953; MD, Harvard Med. Sch., Boston, MA, 1986—90. Diplomate Am. Bd. of Emergency Medicine/MI, 1996, Fellow of the American College of Emergency Physicians ACEP/TX, 2002. Chief med. officer Micromedex, Greenwood Village, Colo., 1996—; asst. clin. prof., dept. of surgery, divsn. of emergency medicine U. of Colo. Sch. of Medicine, Denver, 1999—. Office: Micromedex 6200 S Syracuse Way Greenwood Village CO 80111-4740 E-mail: rich.klasco@mdx.com.

KLASEEN-EAGLE, VIRGINIA, retired volunteer; b. Alameda, Calif., Dec. 23, 1927; d. Theodore Alexander Klaseen and Audrey Mackey Pepper-Klaseen; m. Donald Lloyd Eagle, June 9, 1957; children: Kathryn Anne, Robert Steven, John David. BS in Home Econs., U. Calif., Berkeley, 1950. Tchr. Lassen H.S., Susanville, Calif., 1950-54, Chester (Calif.) Jr./Sr. H.S., 1956-57, Susanville Elem. Sch., 1957-58; cons. Lassen County Welfare Dept., Susanville, 1971; tchr. Shaffer Union Elem., Litchfield, Calif., 1977-85; trustee Lassen C.C., Susanville, 1987—2000; ret., 2000. Mem. AAUW. Avocations: reading, hiking, gardening, crafts. Home: PO Box 396 Standish CA 96128-0396

KLASING, JOHN CHRISTOPH, manufacturing executive; b. Joliet, Ill., Sept. 19, 1948; s. Charles Louis Jr. and Betty Marion (Gill) K.; m. Deborah Sue Hull, June 7, 1969; children: Juliet Elizabeth, John Christoph Matthew. BS in Mech. Engring., U. Tex., 1970; MBA, U. Chgo., 1980. Registered profl. engr., Va. Project engr. Amoco Oil Co., Chgo., 1975-77, supt. marine ops. Texas City, Tex., 1977-79, project mgr. Chgo., 1981-85, mgr. refining projects, 1985-88, gen. mgr. environ., health and safety, 1988-93; v.p. Amoco Pipeline Co., Oak Brook, Ill., 1993-96; plant mgr. BP-Amoco, Greenville, S.C., 1996—. Mem. mech. engring. vis. com. U. Tex., Austin, 1995-98; commr. Donaldson Ctr. Fire Dist., Greenville, 1996—; dir. Jr. Achievement Greenville, 1996—, Greenville County chpt. ARC, 1997—. Lt. (j.g.) USNR, 1971-75. Episcopalian. Avocations: golf, fly fishing. Home: 102 Walnut Trace Ct Simpsonville SC 29681-4767 Office: BP Amoco Polymers PO Box 849 Greenville SC 29602-0849 Fax: 864-299-9451. E-mail: JCKlasing@aol.com., klasinjc@bp.com.

KLASING, SUSAN ALLEN, environmental toxicologist; b. San Antonio, Sept. 10, 1957; d. Jesse Milton and Thelma Ida (Tucker) Allen; m. Kirk Charles Klasing, Mar. 3, 1984; children: Samantha Nicole, Jillian Paige. BS, U. Ill., 1979, MS, 1981, PhD, 1984. Staff scientist Life Scis. Rsch. Office, Fedn. Am. Socs. Exptl. Biology, Bethesda, Md., 1984-85; assoc. dir. Alliance for Food and Fiber, Sacramento, 1986; postgrad. rschr. U. Calif., Davis, 1986-87, 94-96; project dir. Health Officers Assn. Calif., Sacramento, 1987-89; cons. Klasing and Assocs., Davis, Calif., 1989-2000; staff toxicologist Calif. Environ. Protection Agy., 2000—. Mem. expert com. for substances-of-concern San Joaquin Valley Drainage Program, Sacramento, 1987, follow-up task force, 1990-91, drainage oversight com., 1992-94. Author: (chpt.) Consideration of the Public Health Impacts of Agricultural Drainage Water Contamination, 1991. Office: Klasing and Assocs 515 Flicker Ave Davis CA 95616-0178

KLASKO, HERBERT RONALD, lawyer, law educator, writer; b. Phila., Nov. 26, 1949; s. Leon Louis and Estelle Lorraine (Baratz) K.; m. Marjorie Ann Becker, Aug. 27, 1977; children: Brett Andrew, Kelli Lynn. BA, Lehigh U., 1971; JD, U. Pa., 1974. Bar: Pa. 1974, U.S. Dist. Ct. (ea. dist.) Pa. 1974, U.S. Ct. Appeals (3d cir.) 1981. Assoc. Fox, Rothschild, O'Brien & Frankel, Phila., 1974-75; ptnr., chmn. immigration dept. Abrahams & Loewenstein, Phila., 1975-88, Dechert, Price & Rhoads, Phila., 1988—. Instr., mem. adv. bd. Inst. for Paralegal Tng., Phila., 1974-81; instr. Temple Law Sch. Grad. Legal Studies, Phila., 1984; adj. prof. Villanova U. Law Sch., Pa., 1985-90. Co-author: (with Matthew Bender and Hope Frye) Employer's Immigration Compliance Guide, 1985; bd. editors: Immigration Law and Procedure Reporter. Exec. committeeman, bd. dirs. Jewish Community Rels. Coun., Phila., 1977—; chmn. exec. com., com. on unprosecuted Nazi war criminals Nat. Jewish Community Rels. Adv. Coun., N.Y.C., 1983-90; v.p. Hebrew Immigrant Aid Soc., Phila., 1977—; pres. Coun. of Tenants Assn., Southeastern Pa., 1980-81. Recipient Legion of Honor award Chapel of Four Chaplains, 1977. Mem. ABA (coordinating com. on immigration), Phila. Bar Assn., Am. Immigration Lawyers Assn. (chmn. Phila. chpt. 1980-82, bd. govs. 1980—, nat. sec. 1984-85, 2d v.p. 1985-86, 1st v.p. 1986-87, pres.-elect 1987-88, pres. 1988-89, exec. com. 1984-90, 96-99, gen. counsel, 1996-99, Founders award 1999), Am. Immigration Law Found. (bd. dirs. 1987-90). Avocations: politics, sports, traveling, organizations. Office: Dechert Price & Rhoads 4000 Bell Atlantic Tower 1717 Arch St Lbby 3 Philadelphia PA 19103-2713 E-mail: ronald.klasko@dechert.com.

KLASONS, ILONA, accountant, consultant; b. Riga, Latvia, June 15, 1939; arrived in U.S., 1950; d. Evalds and Lize (Planics) Kaufert; m. Visvaldis Klasons, Apr. 23, 1960; 1 child, Erik. BS, Towson State U., 1974. Cert. ins. examiner Ins. Regulatory Examiners Soc. Ins. examiner State of Md. Ins. Dept., Balt., 1975-92; mgr. KPMG Peat Marwick, Dallas, 1992-93; assoc. commr. Md. Ins. Adminstrn., Balt., 1993—2000; regulatory cons., 2000—. Mem. Soc. Fin. Examiners (v.p. 1991-92, cert.), Nat. Assn. Managed Care Regulators (pres. 1992-94). Home: 22 Ballybunion Ct Lutherville Timonium MD 21093-6711

KLASS, PHILIP JULIAN, technical journalist, electrical engineer; b. Des Moines, Nov. 8, 1919; s. Raymond N. and Ann (Traxler) K.; m. Nadya Boriss Boboschevska. BSEE, Iowa State U., 1941. Engr. GE, Schenectady, N.Y., 1941-52; sr. avionics editor Aviation Week & Space Tech., N.Y.C., 1952-58, Washington, 1958-86, contbg. avionics editor, 1986—. Author: UFOs—Identified, 1968, Secret Sentries in Space, 1971, UFOs—Explained, 1975, UFOs: The Public Deceived, 1983, UFO—Abductions: A Dangerous Game, 1988, The REAL Roswell Crashed-Saucer Cover-up, 1997. Recipient writing awards Aviation/Space Writers Assn., 1973, 75, 77, 80, Lauren D. Lyman award, 1989, Profl. Achievement in Enging. award Iowa State U., 1988, aerospace journalist award Royal Aero. Soc., 1998, Boeing Decade of Excellence award for lifetime achievement, Royal Aeronautical Soc., 1998; asteroid named in his honor, 1999. Fellow IEEE, Com. Sci. Investigation Claims of Paranormal (founder); mem. Nat. Press Club. Home and Office: 404 N St SW Washington DC 20024-3702 E-mail: philklass@aol.com.

KLASSEK, CHRISTINE PAULETTE, behavioral scientist; b. Chgo., Dec. 28, 1947; d. Walter and Pauline (Bogolin) Strom; m. Alexander George Klassek, June 14, 1969; 1 child, Margaret Mary. BA in Applied Behavioral Sci., Nat. Louis U., 1989, cert. in leadership, 1993. Asst. juvenile libr. Bolingbrook (Ill.) Fountaindale Libr., 1974-79; behavior modification counselor, dir. vol. svcs. J.P. Kennedy Sch. for Exceptional Children, Palos Park, Ill., 1982-86; tchr. spl. edn. Little Friends Orgn., Downers Grove, Ill., 1986-89; program dir. Carmelite Carefree Village, Darien, Ill., 1989—, adminstrv. liaison, 1997—. Bd. mem. Benedictine Univ. Adv. Bd. for Sr. Programs and Issues, 1996; dep. registrar for Carefree Village, Dupage County, 1998—; notary public, 1999—; panelist Long Term Care Forum by Congresswoman Judy Biggert and Ill. Dept. of Aging, 2000. Treas. Young Democrats Will County, 1972; chmn., pres. bd. dirs. Dem. Women's Com. DuPage Twp., Ill., 1973-76; leader Campfire Girls Assn.; mem. adv. coun. case mgmt. Little Friends Assn., 1988; cert. pastoral min. care St. Charles Borromeo Pastoral Ctr.; vol. Pub. Action to Deliver Svc., Helping Hands Rehab. Ctr., Ray Graham; active Cath. Coun. Women; bd. dirs., mem. human rels. com. J.P. Kennedy Sch. Exceptional Children. Recipient Cert. of

Appreciation, Am. Cancer Soc., 1991, Achievement award Life Svcs. Network Ill., 1995, DuPage County Consortium Intergenerational Task Force, 1996, 2000 Nat. award for sr. program devel. Sr. Network, Inc. Mem. LWV, Assn. Sr. Svc. Providers, Ill. Activity Profl. Assn., Surburban Activity Therapists Assn., Notary Public Assn. Am., Jaycees. Roman Catholic. Avocations: arts and crafts, reading, walking, classical music, writing poetry, needle point. Home: 240 Davis Ln Bolingbrook IL 60440-2369 Office: Carmelite Carefree Village 8419 Bailey Rd Darien IL 60561-5361

KLASSEN, HENRY JOHN, ophthalmologist; b. Sonoma, Calif., June 2, 1957; s. Herbert John and Magrita Freie Klassen; m. Mary Kazanecki Klassen-Fischer, Aug. 10, 1989 (div. 1996). BA, U. Calif., Berkeley, 1979; MS, U. Calif., Santa Cruz, 1983; PhD, U. Pitts., 1989, MD, 1991. Diplomate Am. Bd. Medicine. Sr. scientist Children's Hosp. Orange (Calif.) County, 1998—, dir. stem cell rsch., 2000—. Cons. RCT, Tucson, 2002—. Contbr. articles to profl. jours. Named Yale Alumni in Ophthalmology Rsch. prize, New Haven, 1994; recipient Outstanding Presentation award Ea. Students Rsch. Forum, U. Miami, 1989, Cert. Recognition for Excellence, AMA, Chgo., 1989. Mem.: Soc. for Neurosci., Assn. for Rsch. in Vision and Ophthalmology, Sigma Xi. Avocations: art, literature. Home: 21052 Raquel Rd Laguna Beach CA 92651 Office: Childrens Hosp Orange County 455 S Main St Orange CA 92862

KLASSEN, PETER JAMES, academic administrator, history educator; b. Crowfoot, Alta., Can., Dec. 18, 1930; came to U.S., 1955; s. John C. and Elizabeth (Martens) K.; m. Nancy Jo Cooprider, Aug. 1, 1959; children: Kenton, Kevin, Bryan. BA, also cert., U. B.C., Can., 1955; MA, U. So. Calif., 1958, PhD, 1962. Cert. secondary tchr. Lectr. U. So. Calif., Los Angeles, 1957-62; prof. history Fresno (Calif.) Pacific Coll., 1962-66, Calif. State U., Fresno, 1966—, dean sch. social scis., 1979-97, dir. internat. programs, 1992—2001. Author: The Economics of Anabaptism, 1964, Europe in the Reformation, 1979, Reformation: Change and Stability, 1980, A Homeland for Strangers, 1989; contbr. articles to jours. Pres. West Fresno Home Improvement Assn., 1966-70, Fresno Sister Cities Coun., 1987-90; mem. Calif. Coun. for Humanities, 1987-92. Research grantee Deutscher Akademischer Austauschdienst, 1975. Mem. Am. Hist. Assn., Am. Soc. Ch. History, Fresno City and County Hist. Soc. (pres. 1983-85), Soc. Reformation Rsch., German Studies Assn., Sixteenth Century Studies Assn., Assn. Advancement Slavic Studies, Golden Key, Phi Alpha Theta, Phi Kappa Phi, Phi Beta Delta. Home: 1838 S Bundy Dr Fresno CA 93727-6201 E-mail: peterk@csufresno.edu.

KLATELL, JACK, dentist, department chairman; b. N.Y.C., July 15, 1918; s. Meyer and Jennie (Merin) Klatsky; m. Arline Bragin, Aug. 9, 1944; children: Robert E., David A. Dental. BS, Coll. City N.Y., 1938; D.D.S., Columbia U., 1941. Intern Mt. Sinai Hosp., N.Y.C., 1941-42; sr. resident dental and oral surgery Seaview Hosp., S.I., N.Y., 1942-43; pvt. practice dentistry N.Y.C., 1943-93; dir. dept. dentistry, dentist-in-chief Mt. Sinai Hosp., 1965—; assoc. clin. prof. N.Y.U. Coll. Dentistry, 1967—; prof. dentistry Mt. Sinai Sch. Medicine, 1966—2002, emeritus prof., 2002—, emeritus chmn. dept.; clin. prof. dentistry Columbia U. Sch. Dental and Oral Surgery, 1994—. Cons. Bronx VA Hosp., 1972—, Goldwater Meml. Hosp., 1974-80 Author: The Mt. Sinai Medical Center Family Guide to Dental Health; contbr. profl. jours. Served to capt. Dental Corps AUS, 1943-46. Fellow Acad. Gen. Dentistry Internat. Coll. Dentists, Am. Coll. Dentists (life); mem. ADA (life), Am. Acad. Oral Pathology, N.Y. Inst. Clin. Oral Pathology, Met. Conf. Hosp. Dental Chiefs, Am. Assn. Hosp. Dentists, Phi Beta Kappa, Omicron Kappa Upsilon, Alpha Omega. Home: 8 E 83rd St New York NY 10028-0418

KLATELL, ROBERT EDWARD, lawyer, electronics company executive; b. Tampa, Fla., Dec. 11, 1945; s. Jack S. and Arla M. (Bragin) K.; m. Penelope E. Manegan, June 14, 1970; children: Christopher J., James M., Jeremy N. BA, Williams Coll., 1968; JD, NYU, 1971. Bar: N.Y. 1972. Asso. Kramer, Lowenstein, Nessen, Kamin & Soll, N.Y.C., 1970-76; gen. counsel Arrow Electronics, Inc., N.Y.C., 1976—2002, v.p., 1979-88, sr. v.p., 1988-93, treas., 1990-96; CFO, 1992-96; exec. v.p. Arrow Electronics, Inc., Melville, N.Y., 1993—. Mem. ABA, Assn. Bar City N.Y., Fin. Execs. Inst. Office: Arrow Electronics Inc 25 Hub Dr Melville NY 11747-3509

KLATT, MELVIN JOHN, library consultant; s. John Edward and Marie Barbara K.; m. Shirley Ann Ryan, Aug. 31, 1957; children: Mary, John, Peter. BS in History and Econ., U. Wis., 1956; MA in Libr. Sci., U. Denver, 1958; postgrad., Ind. U., 1969-72. Circulation asst. Wis. State Hist. Soc., Madison, 1955; head br. librs. Milw. Pub. Libr., 1958-62; head acquisitions dept. U. Ill., Chgo., 1962-65; head tech. svcs. U. Denver, 1965-67, dir. librs., 1967-69; asst. dean Dominican U. Grad. Sch. Libr. Sch., River Forest, Ill., 1972-74; head Libr. Elmhurst (Ill.) Coll., 1974-94; prof. emeritus Elmhurst Coll., 1997. Chair Suburbia and the Am. Dream Conf., Elmhurst, 1977; cons. St. Xaviers Coll., Chgo., 1982. Author-contbr.: Dictionary of Wisconsin Biography, 1960; book compiler Directory of Human Resources, 1979; co-editor Colo. Acad. Librs., 1968. Chmn. S.W. Denver Human Rels., Denver, 1968-69, v.p. polit. action com., 1968-70; judge, visual arts com. Ill Arts Coun., Chgo., 1979-81. With U.S. Army, 1951-53, Korea. City of Milw. scholar, 1957, Ill. Acad. Libr. of the Yr. award Ill. Assn. Coll. and Rsch. Librs., 1994; recipient Mel George award LIBRAS, 1996; NDEA fellow, 1969, 70, 71. Mem. ALA, LIBRAS Consortium (pres. 1979-81, Libr. of Yr. Ill. consortium 1994), AAUP (exec. com. 1964-65), North Ctrl. Accreditation Assn. (chair resources com. 1979), Ill. Libr. Assn., Pvt. Acad. Librs. Ill. (pres. 1979-81), Chgo. Libr. Club (v.p. 1979-80, pres. elect 1983-85), Beta Phi Mu, Omicron Delta Kappa. *Reading allows the imagination to take the side roads not possible with the visual effects of television. Reading remains one of the most powerful educational and recreational tools of all time.*

KLATT, WAYNE ROY, editor, writer; b. Chgo., Sept. 11, 1940; s. Waldemar George Klatt and Agnes Sophie Scannell; m. Marilyn Louise Koeppel, Aug. 7, 1965; children: Theresa Ann, Catherine Louise, Jennifer Marie. BS in Comm., U. Ill., 1962. Reporter City News Bureau of Chgo., 1963—64, editor, 1965—. Co-author: Freed to Kill, 1990, I Am Cain, 1994, Homicide: 100 Years of Murder in America, 1998; contbr. articles to mags. Recipient Short Story Contest awards, U. Ill., 1958, 1st prize, Nit & Wit Mag., 1983. Mem.: Chgo. Press Vets. Assn. Avocations: reading, history, literature, films, psychology. Home: 4722 N Avers Ave Chicago IL 60625-6201 Office: City News Service Tribune Tower 435 N Michigan Ave Chicago IL 60611

KLAUBERG, WILLIAM JOSEPH, technical services company executive; b. N.Y.C., June 30, 1926; s. Leo V. and Marian (Casey) K.; m. Kathleen Kelly, Feb. 18, 1950; children: Christine Anne, Kathleen Noel, Angela Ellen, William Jr. BS in nautical sci., Merchant Marine Acad., 1947; BS in fgn. svc., Georgetown U., 1949. Mgr. US Lines, Inc., Japan, 1949-65, v.p., 1965-68, v.p. European Div. London, 1968-71, v.p. West Coast Div. San Francisco, 1971-73, v.p. East Coast Div. N.Y.C., 1973-81; project mgr. Vinnell Corp., Balt., 1981-82, v.p. Fairfax, Va., 1982-83, exec. v.p., 1983-88, pres., CEO, 1988-93, chmn., chief exec. officer, 1993-94; chmn., 1994-97. Lt. (j.g.) USNR, 1947-52.

KLAUS, CHARLES, retired lawyer; b. Freiburg, Baden, Germany, Feb. 11, 1935; came to U.S., 1939; children: Charles, Kathryn, Richard; m. Elaine S. Jones, Jan. 6, 2002. BA, Cornell U., 1956, MBA, JD with distinction, 1961; postdoctoral, Case Western Res. U., 1964, Lakeland Community Coll., 1976. Bar: Ohio 1961, U.S. Dist. Ct. (no. dist.) Ohio 1962. Assoc. Baker & Hostetler, Cleve., 1961-71, ptnr., 1972-94, formerly mng. ptnr. Cleve. office, retired, 1995. Past hon. trustee and pres. Cleve. Music Sch. Settlement; past trustee Cleve. Audubon Soc.; past trustee, sec. Cleve. Area Arts Coun., Lake Erie Opera Theatre, N.E. Ohio chpt. Arthritis Found.; former mem. Group Svc. Coun. Welfare Fedn. Cleve.; corp. mem. Holden Arboretum, 1993—; mem. Coun. of Holden Arboretum, 2003—. Recipient Award of Merit, Cleve. Audubon Soc., 1979. Mem. Millard Fillmore Soc., Rowfant Club (past sec.), Kirtland Country Club (past dir., past sec., Willoughby, Ohio).

KLAUS, SUZANNE LYNNE, horticulturist, production specialist; b. Kansas City, Mo., May 2, 1956; d. John Wallace and Shirley Jane (Hoffman) K.; m. William D. Luebbert, Nov. 4, 1989. BS in Agr., U. Mo., 1978, MS in Horticulture, 1980. Prodn. mgr., owner John Klaus & Sons Greenhouses, Greenwood, Mo., 1972—. Tchr. horticulture Longview C.C., Lee's Summit, Mo., 1979-81, 99—; guest spkr., panel mem. Mo. State Florists Convs., 1981, 92, 86, 89; guest spkr. St. Louis Growers Assn., 1985, Ohio Florists' Conf., 1986, Ball's Grow Show, 1987, Kans. State Growers Conf., 1988; pharmacy technician HyVee, Lee'sSummit, Mo., 2002—. Floriculture judge for nat. conv. Future Farmers Am., 1984-98. Mem. Mo. State Florists' Assn. (bd. dirs. 1980-89, pres. 1987-88), Floral Acad. Mo. (bd. dirs. 1986-87, pres.-elect 1988-89), Nat. Assn. Women in Horticulture (pres. 1989-90), Ohio Florists' Assn., Pointsettia Growers Assn., Nemokan Floral Assn. (bd. dirs. 1987-89). Republican. Roman Catholic. Avocations: swimming, water skiing, computer science, piano and organ playing, pharmacy. Home: PO Box 376 Greenwood MO 64034-0376

KLAUS, WILLIAM ROBERT, lawyer; b. Phila., Jan. 19, 1926; s. William Anthony and Amanda (Pusey) K.; m. Janet Lois Scoggins, Aug. 18, 1951; 1 child, Kenneth Springfield. LLB, Temple U., 1951. Bar: Pa. 1952. Assoc. Pepper, Hamilton & Scheetz, Phila., 1952-59, ptnr., 1959—95, retired, chmn. emeritus, 1995—. Bd. dirs. Pa. Warehousing, Co., Phila. Co-author: Practical Guide to U.C.C., 1969. Chmn. Phila. Comm. Legal Svcs., Inc., 1966-83, Phila. Legal Assistance Corp., 1995-2000. Staff sgt. U.S. Army, 1943-46, ETO. Faculty fellow U. Pa. Law Sch., 1973. Mem. ABA (chmn. com. legal aid 1978-79), Nat. Legal Aid Defenders Assn. (pres. 1978), Pa. Bar Assn., Phila. Bar Assn. (chancellor 1974), Phila. Club (chmn. house com. 1979-2002), Little Egg Harbor Yacht Club (commodore 1991), Merion Cricket Club. Avocations: skiing, sailing, archeology, music, antiques.

KLAUSMEYER, DAVID MICHAEL, scientific instruments manufacturing company executive; b. Indpls., Aug. 29, 1934; s. David M. and V. Jane (Donnellan) K.; m. Julie Ann Johnson, Oct. 29, 1955; children: Kathleen M., Kevin M., Gregory J. BSS, Georgetown U., 1955. Asst. to pres. White Cons. Ind., Cleve., 1957; auditor Ernst & Ernst, Cleve., 1957-59; pres. Photopipe, Inc., Cleve., 1960-63; v.p. McGregor & Werner Internat., Inc., Washington, 1964-70; internat. cons. Stratford of Tex., Houston, 1971-72; pres. FLR Corp., Houston, 1972-74, Southwest Cons., Houston, 1981-86, Imaging Products, Houston, 1987-90; sec. Nanodyanmics, Inc., N.Y.C., 1988—, also bd. dirs.; pres. Corp. Devel., Houston, 1974-81; ptnr. Klausmeyer & Assoc., Houston, 1970—2001; ret., 2001. Dir. U.S. investment banking Secured Electronic Global Order Execution Sys. Securities, Grand Cayman Island, 1995—2001; bd. dirs. S.ure Reification, Houston. Bd. dirs. Catholic Endowment Found. Galveston-Houston, 1999—. With USCG, 1955-57. Republican. Roman Catholic. Home: 288 Litchfield Ln Houston TX 77024-6035 Office: Nanodynamics Inc 10878 Westheimer Rd # 178 Houston TX 77042-3202

KLAUSNER, JACK DANIEL, lawyer; b. N.Y.C., July 31, 1945; s. Burt and Marjory (Brown) K.; m. Dale Arlene Kreis, July 1, 1968; children: Andrew Russell, Mark Raymond. BS in Bus., Miami U., Oxford, Ohio, 1967; JD, U. Fla., 1969. Bar: N.Y. 1971, Ariz. 1975, U.S. Dist. Ct. Ariz. 1975, U.S. Ct. Appeals (9th cir.) 1975, U.S. Supreme Ct. 1975. Assoc. counsel John P. McGuire & Co., Inc., N.Y.C., 1970-71; assoc. atty. Hahn & Hessen, N.Y.C., 1971-72; gen. counsel Equilease Corp., N.Y.C., 1972-74; assoc. Burch & Cracchiolo, Phoenix, 1974-78, ptnr., 1978-98; judge pro tem Maricopa County Superior Ct., 1990—, Ariz. Ct. Appeals, 1992—; ptnr. Warner Angle Roper & Hallam, Phoenix, 1998—. Bd. dirs. Hunter Contracting Co. Bd. dirs. Santos Soccer Club, Phoenix, 1989-90; bd. dirs., pres. south Bank Soccer Club, Tempe, 1987-88. Home: 9146 N Crimson Canyon Fountain Hills AZ 85268 Office: Warner Angel Roper & Hallam 3550 N Central Ave Ste 1500 Phoenix AZ 85012 2112

KLAUSNER, JEFFREY, dean; married; 2 children. BS, U. Md.; MS, U. Minn. Vet. medicine resident U. Minn. Coll. Vet. Medicine, St. Paul, 1974, prof., chair dept. small animal clin. scis., 1992—, interim dean, 1998—2000, dean, 2000—. Contbr. articles to peer-reviewed jours. Office: U Minn Coll Vet Medicine 1365 Gortner Ave Saint Paul MN 55108

KLAUSNER, RICHARD D. cell biologist, researcher; b. New York, N.Y., Dec. 22, 1951; BS, Yale U., 1973; MD, Duke U. Med. Sch., 1976. Rsch. assoc. Harvard Med. Sch., 1977-79; rscher., med. officer, mathematical biology program Nat. Insts. Health, Bethesda, Md., 1979-84; branch chief, cell biology, metabolism branch Nat. Inst. of Child Health and Human Develop., Bethesda, Md., 1984-95; dir. Nat. Cancer Inst., Bethesda, Md., 1995—2001; exec. dir. Global Health (Bill and Melinda Gates Found.), Seattle, 2002—. Chrm., Scientific Advisory Bd., Ariad Pharmaceuticals, 1991. Medicine, 1976; numerous articles in prof. journals. Recipient Meritorious Svc. Award, 1986, PHS, Damashek Prize, 1992, Am. Soc. for Hematology Mem. NAS, Am. Soc. for Clinical Investigation, Inst. Medicine. Office: PO Box 23350 Seattle WA 98102

KLAUSNER, SAMUEL ZUNDEL, sociologist, educator; b. Bklyn., Dec. 19, 1923; s. Edward Solomon and Bertha (Adler) K.; m. Bracha Turgeman, Oct. 26, 1948 (div. 1960); children: Rina Ellen Klausner Spence, Jonathan David; m. Madeleine Suringar, Feb. 20, 1964 (div. 1982); children: Daphne Klausner Genyk, Tamar; m. Roberta Sands, Nov. 26, 1992. BS, NYU, 1947; MA, Columbia U., 1951, EdD, 1952, PhD, 1963. Cert. psychologist, N.Y., D.C. Lectr. edn. CCNY, 1951-52, 55-57; lectr. sociology Columbia U., 1957-63; instr. psychology Hebrew U., Jerusalem, 1952-53; lectr. religion and psychiatry Union Theol. Sem., 1961-63; assoc. prof. sociology U. Pa., Phila., 1967-70, prof., 1970-96; dir. Ctr. for Rsch. on the Acts of Man, 1971-88, chmn. grad. group in sociology, 1984-86; prof. emeritus U. Pa., Phila., 1996—. Clin. psychologist Govt. Mental Hosp., Jerusalem, 1954-55; program dir. Bur. Applied Social Rsch., Columbia U., 1956-61; sr. rsch. assoc. Bur. Social Sci. Rsch., Washington, 1964-67; exec. sec. Soc. for Study of Religion, 1964-70; cons. U.S. Dept. Commerce, 1968-69, U.S. Naval Chaplains Sch., 1973-81, Nat. Libr. Medicine, 1969, NRC, 1967-81, others; vis. prof. Al Mansoura U., Egypt, 1983, Muhammad V. Univ., Morocco, 1986. Author: Psychiatry and Religion, 1964, The Quest for Self-Control, 1965, The Study of Total Societies, 1967, Why Man Takes Chances, 1968, Society and Its Physical Environment, 1970, On Man in His Environment, 1971, Eskimo Capitalists, 1981; author, editor: The Nationalization of the Social Sciences, 1986; also articles. With USAAC, 1943-45; with Israel Air Force, 1947-48. Ford Found. area rsch. fellow, 1952-53; Fulbright scholar, 1983. Mem. APA, AAAS, Am. Sociol. Assn., Assn. Sociol. Study of Jewry (pres. 1980), Soc. Sci. Study of Religion (v.p. 1974), Am. Vets. Israel (pres. 1951, 98-2000, newsletter editor 1998—). Jewish. Home: 7055 Greenhill Rd Philadelphia PA 19151-2322 Office: Univ Pa Dept Sociology Philadelphia PA 19104 E-mail: sklausner@ucwphilly.rr.com. *My ideals of social conduct have not been designed to assist in attaining professional success. Judaism is a central guiding reference and though I may deviate from its principles in my daily behavior for reasons of good sense and self interest, they remain normative. My professional station arises from an obsession with the requirements of scholarship. A willingness to be critical of current social institutions has brought social attention but not professional advancement.*

KLAUSS, KENNETH KARL, composer, educator; b. Parkston, S.D., Apr. 8, 1923; s. Christian and Paulina (Engel) Klauss. MusB in Composition, U. So. Calif., 1946. Tchr. composition and piano, L.A., 1946 50; composer Lester Horton Theater, L.A., 1949-50; tchr. music San Francisco, 1950-61; composer, educator L.A., 1961—; lectr. in music for dance Idyllwild (Calif.) Sch. Music and Arts, 1967-74; lectr. in music history So. Calif. Inst. Architecture, Santa Monica, 1970-76. Composer in residence Perry/Mansfield Camp, Steamboat Springs, Colo., 1966; guest performer, composer, lectr. Libr. Congress, Am. U., Washington, 1996; guest lectr. U. S.D., Vermillion, 2002. Composer: (opera) Fall of the House of Usher, 1952, harpsichord/violin composition commd. by U. S.D., 2001; author, composer: (poetry/music orchestration) Story of the World Vols. I to VIII, 1952-86. Founder, patron Klauss/James Archive and Art Mus., Parkston, 1995—. Recipient hon. mention opera competition Ohio U., Athens, 1954. Democrat. Avocations: history, poetry. Home: 440 Wren Dr Los Angeles CA 90065-5040 E-mail: kkennkarl@aol.com.

KLAVANO, ANN MARIE, school librarian; b. Pullman, Wash., Oct. 8, 1956; d. Paul Arthur and Martha Emma Klavano. M in Libr. and Info. Studies, U. Tex., 1986; BA, Washington State University, Pullman WA, 1976. Reference libr. Mercy Coll. Librs., Dobbs Ferry, NY, 1986—97; reference libr. external scvs. Buena Vista U., Storm Lake, Iowa, 1997—. Chair social concerns ministry St. Mark Luth. Ch., Storm Lake, 2000—01; bd. dirs. Midnight Run, Dobbs Ferry, 1994—97. Lutheran. Office: Buena Vista U Libr 610 W 4th St Storm Lake IA 50588

KLAVITER, HELEN LOTHROP, magazine editor; b. Lima, Ohio, Mar. 5, 1944; d. Eugene H. and Jean (Walters) Lothrop; m. Douglas B. Klaviter, June 7, 1969 (dec. 1982); 1 child, Elizabeth BA, Cornell Coll., Mt. Vernon, Iowa, 1966. Communication specialist Coop. Extension Service, Urbana, Ill., 1969-71; mng. editor Poetry Mag., Chgo., 1973—. Editorial cons. Harper & Row, N.Y.C., 1983 87. Bd. dirs. Ill. Theatre Ctr., 1989-95, St. Clement's Open Pantry, 1990—, Episc. Diocese of Chgo. Hunger Commn., 1992—, Comms. Commn., 1993—. Episcopalian. Office: Poetry Mag The Poetry Found 1030 N Clark St Ste 420 Chicago IL 60610 E-mail: hklaviter@poetrymagazine.org.

KLAW, SPENCER, writer, editor, educator; b. N.Y.C., Jan. 13, 1920; s. Alonzo and Alma (Ash) K.; m. Barbara Van Doren, July 5, 1941; children: Joanna Klaw Schultz, Susan Klaw (Del Tredici), Rebecca Klaw (Feldman), Margaret Klaw (Metcalfe). AB, Harvard U., 1941. Reporter San Francisco Chronicle, 1941; Washington corr. Raleigh (N.C.) News and Observer, and United Press, 1941-43; reporter United Press, N.Y.C., 1946, The New Yorker, 1947-52; asst. to Sunday editor New York Herald Tribune, 1952-54; asso. editor Fortune, 1954-60; free-lance writer, 1960—; lectr. in journalism U. Calif., Berkeley, 1968-69, Grad. Sch. Journalism, Columbia U., N.Y.C., 1970-87; editor Columbia Journalism Rev., 1980-89. Author: The New Brahmins: Scientific Life in America, 1968, The Great American Medicine Show, 1975, Without Sin: The Life and Death of the Oneida Community, 1993; contbr. to publs. including American Heritage, Esquire, Fortune, Saturday Evening Post, Natural History, Playboy, Harper's, The Reporter. With U.S. Army, 1943-45. Home and Office: 280 Cream Hill Rd West Cornwall CT 06796-1207

KLAWANS, STUART, film critic, writer; Film critic The Nation, 1988—; of counsel Kreisberg Group, 1984—, sr. writer, v.p., 1995—. Tchr. film divsn. Columbia U.; mem. selection com. N.Y. Film Festival. Fil critic, commentator: publs. including N.Y. Times Arts & Leisure sect., Newsweek, Fresh Air program, Nat. Pub. Radio; author: (book) Film Follies: The Cinema Out of Order (Nat. Book Critics Cir. Awards criticism category finalist, 1999). Recipient Guggenheim fellowship, 2003—04. Office: The Kreisberg Group Ste 800 130 W 25th St New York NY 10001*

KLAWITER, DONALD CASIMIR, lawyer; b. Phila., Feb. 26, 1950; s. Joseph C. and Frances J. (Koniecki) K.; m. Marie M. Gabuzda, Jan. 2, 1982; children: Joseph, Jeffrey. BA, MA, U. Pa., 1972, JD, 1975. Bar: Pa. 1975, U.S. Supreme Ct. 1979, D.C. 1987, U.S. Dist. Ct. D.C. 1987, U.S. Ct. Appeals (4th and 8th crcts.) 1988, U.S. Ct. Appeals (9th crct.) 1993. Trial atty. antitrust div. U.S. Dept. Justice, Phila., 1975-78, spl. asst. operations antitrust div. Washington, 1978-80, chief antitrust Dallas, 1980-82, sr. trial atty. Washington, 1982-86; of counsel Morgan, Lewis & Bockius LLP, Washington, 1986-88; ptnr. Morgan, Lewis & Bockius, Washington, 1988—. Chair bd. dirs. Pinecrest Sch., Annandale, Va., 1998—; chair bd. trustees Commonwealth Acad., Alexandria, Va., 2001—. Mem. ABA (litigation, antitrust law and bus. law sects., chair criminal practice and procedure com. sect. antitrust law 1995-97, mem. governing coun. sect. antitrust law 1997--, sec. sect. antitrust law 2000-01, program officer sect. antitrust law 2001-03, vice chmn., 2003—), Internat. Bar Assn. (sect. bus. law, antitrust coms). Roman Catholic. Home: 5930 Munson Ct Falls Church VA 22041-2443 Office: Morgan Lewis & Bockius 1111 Pennsylvania Ave NW Washington DC 20004 E-mail: dklawiter@morganlewis.com.

KLAY, ANNA NETTIE, lawyer; b. Palo Alto, Calif., Aug. 27, 1940; BA, U. Colo., Boulder, 1962; JD, Golden Gate Law Sch., 1976. Bar: Calif. 1976. Ptnr. Edson & Klay, Eureka, Calif., 1977-82; atty. Anna N. Klay Law Firm, 1982-87, Conrad F. Gullixson Law Firm, Palo Alto, 1987-93; sole practice, 1993—. Vol. chaplain Stanford U. Hosp., Palo Alto, 1996—. Named one of Silicon Valley's Best Lawyers, San Jose Mag., 1999, 2000, 2001, 2002. Democrat. Episcopalian. Avocations: music, opera, gardening. Office: 550 Hamilton Ave Ste 300 Palo Alto CA 94301 Office Fax: 650-326-2404.

KLAYMAN, BARRY MARTIN, lawyer; b. Montclair, N.J., Sept. 26, 1952; s. Max M. and Sylvia (Cohen) K.; m. Anna Kornbrot, June 8, 1975; children: Alison Melissa, Matthew Daniel. BA magna cum laude, Columbia U., 1974; JD cum laude, Harvard U., 1977. Bar: Pa. 1977, Del. 1998, U.S. Dist. Ct. (ea. dist.) Pa. 1977, U.S. Dist. Ct. Del. 1998, U.S. Ct. Appeals (3d cir.) 1978. From assoc. to ptnr. Wolf, Block, Schorr & Solis-Cohen LLP, Phila., 1977—. Bd. dirs. BBYO, Inc., 2001—. Contbr. articles to profl. jours. Bd. dirs. Akiba Hebrew Acad., 1991—, sec., 1994-95, v.p., 1995-96, 98-2000, treas. 1996-98, pres. 2000-03; mem. cmty. planning and allocations com. Jewish Fedn. Greater Phila., 1997—, trustee, 2000-03, mem. com. on nat. svcs., 1991—, chair, 1998—, mem. com. on formal Jewish edn., 2000-; exec. com. United Jewish Communities Nat. Funding Coun., 2002-. Mem. ABA (litig. sect., torts and ins. practice sect.), Del. Bar Assn., Phila. Bar Assn., Pa. Bar Assn., Assn. Trial Lawyers Am., B'nai B'rith Youth Orgn. (bd. dirs. Phila. region 1984—, chmn. 1991-95, mem. Internat. Youth Commn. 1991-2001, exec. com., 1996-01), B'nai B'rith (coun. v.p. 1996-97, mem. Justice Lodge 1992—), Phi Beta Kappa. Office: Wolf Block Schorr & Solis-Cohen LLP 1100 N Market St Ste 1001 Wilmington DE 19801 E-mail: bklayman@wolfblock.com.

KLAYTON, RONALD JAY, physician; b. Long Beach, Calif., Oct. 12, 1943; s. Thurston and Evelyn Geraldine (Gruber) K.; m. Janet Sue Lindsey, July 30, 1977; 1 child, Tracy Lea. BA in Biology, Lehigh U., 1965; MD, SUNY, Bklyn., 1969. Diplomate Am. Bd. Internal Medicine. Intern U. Pitts., 1969-70, resident in internal medicine, 1970-72; fellow in pulmonary disease U. Calif., San Francisco, 1972-74; pulmonary physician U.S. Naval Hosp., Portsmouth, Va., 1974-85, head, pulmonary div., 1982-85, chief medicine Oakland, Calif., 1985-87, dir. internal medicine residency program, 1985-87; lead physician in pulmonary medicine Kaiser Penderbrook, Fairfax, Va., 1995—2003; pulmonary medicine svc. chief Kaiser Mid-Atlantic, 2003—. Asst. prof. Eastern Va. Sch. Medicine, Norfolk, 1974-83, assoc. prof., 1983-85; assoc. clin. prof. Sch. Medicine, San Francisco, 1985-95. Contbr. articles to profl. jours. Capt. USN, 1974-95. Recipient Excellence in Teaching award Kaiser Found., 1994. Fellow Am. Coll. Physicians, Am. Coll. Chest Physicians; mem. Am. Thoracic Soc., Assn. Mil. Surgeons U.S., Am. Fedn. Clin. Research. Home: 10207 Oakton Station Ct Oakton VA 22124-2643 Office: Kaiser Penderbrook 12011 Lee Jackson Hwy Fairfax VA 22033-3310

KLEBANER, BENJAMIN JOSEPH, economics educator; b. Bklyn., Oct. 30, 1926; s. Simon and Pearl (Yollis) K.; m. Ruth Perlman, Jan. 20, 1963; children: Simeon Nathan, Josiah Abraham. BS magna cum laude, CCNY, 1945; MA, Columbia U., 1947, PhD, 1952. Instr. Rutgers U., Newark, 1951-54; asst. prof. econs. CCNY, 1954-59; from assoc. to prof. econs. CUNY, 1959—, chmn. MA Com. in Econs., 1971—2003. Regional economist, Second Nat. Bank Region Office of the Comptroller of Currency, N.Y.C., 1966-82. Author: American Commercial Banking, 1990, Public Poor Relief in America 1790-1860, 1952, Commercial Banking in the United States, 1974; editor: New York City's Changing Economic Base, 1981; contbr. articles to prof. jours. With U.S. Army, 1945 46. Am. Econ. History fellow Columbia U., 1949-50. Mem.: Kappa Delta Pi, Phi Beta Kappa. Office: CCNY Econs Dept New York NY 10031

KLEBANOFF, MARK A. epidemiologist, physician; s. Sam D. and Gertrude Klebanoff. AB, Johns Hopkins U, 1976; MD, Johns Hopkins U., 1979, MPH, 1983. Diplomate Am. Bd. Pediat., 1984. Intern in pediat. U. Rochester, NY, 1979—80, resident in pediat., 1980—82; staff fellow Nat. Inst. of Child Health and Human Devel., Bethesda, Md., 1983—87, med. officer, 1987—. Pres. Soc. for Pediatric and Perinatal Epidemiologic Rsch., Bethesda, Md., 2000—01. Recipient Spl. Recognition award, USPHS, 1991, Dir.'s award, NIH, 2001. Fellow: Am. Coll. of Epidemiology; mem.: Am. Epidemiol. Soc., Johns Hopkins Soc. of Scholars. Achievements include research in Infections and preterm birth. Avocation: private pilot. Office: NICHD NIH 6100 Bldg Rm 7B05 Bethesda MD 20892 E-mail: mk90h@nih.gov.

KLEBANOFF, SEYMOUR JOSEPH, medical educator; b. Toronto, Ont., Can., Feb. 3, 1927; s. Eli Samuel and Ann Klebanoff; m. Evelyn Norma Silver, June 3, 1951; children: Carolyn, Mark. MD, U. Toronto, 1951; PhD in Biochemistry, U. London, 1954. Intern Toronto Gen. Hosp., 1951—52; postdoctoral fellow dept. path. chemistry U. Toronto, 1954—57; postdoctoral fellow Rockefeller U., N.Y.C., 1957—59, asst. prof., 1959—62, 1959—62; assoc. prof. medicine U. Washington, Seattle, 1962—68, prof., 1968—2000, prof. emeritus, 2000—. Mem. adv. coun. Nat. Inst. Allergy and Infectious Diseases, NIH,

1987—90. Author: The Neutrophil, 1978; contbr. over 200 articles to profl. jours. Recipient Merit award, NIH, 1988, Mayo Soley award, Western Soc. for Clin. Investigation, 1991, Bristol-Myers Squibb award for Disting. Achievement in Infectious Disease Rsch., 1995. Fellow: AAAS; mem.: NAS, Am. Acad. Arts and Scis., Inst. of Medicine, Soc. for Leukocyte Biology (Marie T. Bonazinga rsch. award 1985), Endocrine Soc., Infectious Diseases Soc. Am. (Bristol award 1993), Assn. Am. Physicians, Am. Soc. Biol. Chemists, Am. Soc. Clin. Investigation. Home: 509 Mcgilvra Blvd E Seattle WA 98112-5047 Office: U Wash Dept Medicine Div Al & Infectious Disease PO Box 357185 Seattle WA 98195-7185

KLEBBA, RAYMOND ALLEN, property manager; b. Chgo., Apr. 16, 1934; s. Raymond Aloysius and Marie Cecelia (Tobin) K.; m. Barbara Ann Gurbal, Oct. 7, 1961; children: Anne, Daniel, Mary, Theresa. Student, Loyola U., Chgo., 1954-56; cert. property mgr., Inst. Real Estate Mgmt., 1970. Corr., rep. Western R.R. Assn., Chgo., 1956-61; pres. Midland Warehouses, Chgo., 1961-68; v.p., gen. mgr. Strobeck, Reiss Sch. Mgmt. Co., Chgo., 1968-70, real estate mgr. and broker, 1970-83; v.p., dir. Mid-Am. Nat. Bank, Chgo., 1983-90; br. mgr. Bank of Highwood/Deerfield, Ill., 1990-94; v.p. sales First Colonial Mortgage Corp., Chgo., 1994-95; bus. mgr. St. Matthias Parish, Chgo., 1995-98. Mem. Chgo. Bd. Realtors (vice chmn. comml. and indsl. leasing and property mgmt. coun.), Inst. Real Estate Mgmt. (life; chmn. chpt. of yr. com. 1975-76), Rotary, Moose, KC. Avocations: bowling, golf, gardening, fishing (Chicagoland individual casting champion 1999. Home: 4933 N Leavitt St Chicago IL 60625-1308

KLEBER, HERBERT DAVID, psychiatrist, educator; b. Pitts., June 19, 1934; s. Max J. and Dorothea (Schulman) K.; m. Joan Louise Fox, Sept. 9, 1956 (div. Jan. 1988); children: Elizabeth, Marc, Pamela. BA in Psychology cum laude, Dartmouth Coll., 1956; MD, Jefferson Med. Coll., 1960; MA (hon.), Yale U., 1975; PhD (hon.), N.Y. Med. Coll., 1990. Lederle rsch. fellow Jefferson Med. Coll., 1959-60; rotating intern Health Ctr. Hosps. of U. Pitts., 1960-61; resident in psychiatry Yale U., New Haven, 1961-64; surgeon, chief receiving svc. USPHS Hosp., Lexington, Ky., 1964-66; asst. chief Hill-West Haven divsn. Conn. Mental Health Ctr., 1966-67, outpatient and admissions coord., 1967-68, dir., founder drug dependence unit, 1968-75, dir. substance abuse treatment unit, 1975-89; exec. dir. psychiatry emergency rm. svc. Yale-New Haven Hosp., 1967-68; from asst. prof. to assoc. prof. Yale U. Sch. Medicine, New Haven, 1966-75; prof. Yale U., 1975-91; exec. v.p., med. dir. Ctr. on Addiction and Substance Abuse Columbia U., 1992—; prof., dir. divsn. substance abuse N.Y. State Psychiat. Inst., 1991—; prof. psychiatry Columbia U. Coll. Phys. and Surg., N.Y.C., 1991—; attending psychiatrist Columbia-Presbyn. Med. Ctr., 1992—. U.S. presdl. appointee Office Nat. Drug Control Policy, dep. dir., 1989-91; founder APT Foudn., Inc., 1970, CEO, 1982-89; dir. NIDA Clin. Rsch. Ctr. for Treatment of Opioid and Cocaine Abuse, Yale U., 1986-89, dir. rsch. tng. fellowship in substance abuse, 1988-89; mem. drug abuse adv. com. FDA, 1987-90; mem. bd. of sci. counselors Addiction Rsch. Ctr, Nat. Inst. on Drug Abuse, 1982-85; mem. exec. instns. rev. groups NIMH and Nat Inst. on Drug Abuse; Nolan D.C. Lewis vis. prof. Carrier Found., 1985; dir. Nat. Inst. Drug Abuse Medication Devel. Ctr., 1994—, Columbia U., Rsch. Training Fellowship program, Columbia U., 1993—; lectr. and presenter in field. Contbr. chpts.: Opiate Addiction: Origins and Treatment, 1973, Treatment Aspect of Drug Dependence, 1978, Clinical Psychiatric Medicine, 1981, Cocaine: Scientific and Social Dimensions, 1992, Drugs, Alcohol and Tobacco: Making the Science and Policy Connections, several others; editor: APA Treatment Manual for Substance Abuse Disorders, APA Textbook of Substance Abuse Treatment, Clinician's Guide to Cocaine Abuse Treatment; (with others) APA Textbook-Treatment of Psychiatric Disorders: Treatment of Substance Abuse; assoc. editor Am. Jour. Drug and Alcohol Abuse and Addictive Behaviors, mem. edit. bd.; rsch. editor Jour. Substance Abuse Treatment, mem. edit. bd. Am. Jour. Addictions, Advances in Alcohol Actions/Misuse, Harvard Rev. of Psychiatry; edit. cons. Archives Gen. Psychiatry, Conn. Medicine, Med. Letter, Jour. Maintenance in the Addictions, Sci.; contbr. over 200 articles to profl. jours. Exec. com. Com. on Problems of Drug Dependence, Inc.; co-chmn. Mayor's Task Force on Drugs, City of New Haven; mem. adv. bd. Rand Drug Policy Rsch. Ctr.; mem. Gov.'s Drug Adv. Coun., State of Conn., 1970-76; mem. nat. adv. coun. Nat. Inst. of Drug Abuse, Alcohol, Drug Abuse and Mental Health Adminstrn., 1975-79, NIMH, 1977-79. Recipient Meritorious Svc. award Lapides Found., 1979, Families in Action Drug Prevention award, 1990, Gov.'s award for outstanding svc. in field of substance abuse State of Conn., 1987, Nyswander and Dole award, 1986, Alcohol, Drug Abuse, Mental Health Agy. award for pub. svc., 1986. Fellow ACP, Am. Psychiat. Assn. (mem. coun. on addiction, cons. joint commn. on pub. affairs, task force on benzodiazepine dependency, Gold award 1975, Found.'s Fund prize 1981), Am. Coll. Neuropsychopharmacology (Eddy award of Coll. on Problems of Drug Dependence 1995), N.Y. Acad. Medicine, Am. Acad. Psychiatrists in Alcoholism and Addictions (founding, Founders award 1987); mem. Inst. of Medicine (substance abuse coverage com., medication devel. for substance abuse com.). Republican. Jewish. Avocations: swimming, cross-country skiing. Office: Columbia U Coll Phys/Surgns 1051 Riverside Dr New York NY 10032-1013

KLECK, ROBERT ELDON, psychology educator; b. Archbold, Ohio, Aug. 3, 1937; AB in Philosophy, Denison U., 1959; PhD in Social Psychology, Stanford (Calif.) U., 1963. Postdoctoral fellow Stanford U., 1963-64; asst. prof. Williams Coll., Williamstown, Mass., 1964-66; asst. to assoc. prof. Dartmouth Coll., Hanover, N.H., 1966-75, prof. psychology, 1975—, John Sloan Dickey Third Century Prof. of Social Scis., 1985-90, chmn. dept. psychology, 1993-99. Vis. rsch. prof. Boy's Town Ctr. Study of Youth Devel., Stanford U., 1974-75; cons. VA Stroke Project, 1983-86, Disadvantaged Children in N.H., 1974, Bur. Devel. Disabilities, Concord, N.H., 1975-80, Crotchet Mountain Rehab. Ctr., 1973, Abilities, Inc., Albertson, N.Y., 1979-81, Can. Rsch. Coun., NSF, USPHS; faculty sponsore USPHS Post-doctoral fellowship, 1977-78. Cons. editor Jour. Personality and Social Psychology, 1974-78, assoc. editor 1971-72; mem. editorial bd. Jour. Nonverbal Behavior, 1990-93; mem. editorial adv. bd. Action for Children's TV, 1975-79; editorial cons.various jours.; contbr. articles to profl. jours. Danforth fellow, 1959-63; Gen. Motors scholar, 1955-59. Mem. Am. Psychol. Soc., Internat. Soc. Rsch. on Emotion, Soc. Experimental Social Psychology, New Eng. Psychol. Assn., Soc. Kent and Danfoth Fellows, Sigma Xi, Phi Beta kappa. Home: 6207 Moore Hall Hanover NH 03755-3578 Office: Dartmouth Coll Dept Of Psychology Hanover NH 03755 E-mail: r.kleck@dartmouth.edu.

KLECKNER, ROBERT GEORGE, JR., lawyer; b. Reading, Pa., Mar. 14, 1932; s. Robert George and Elizabeth (Endlich) K.; m. Carol Espie, June 15, 1955; children: Anthony Savage, Susan Duffield. BA, Yale U., 1954; LLB, U. Pa., 1959. Bar: Pa. 1960, N.Y. 1964. Pvt. practice, Reading, 1960-63; assoc. Sullivan & Cromwell, N.Y.C., 1963-70; house counsel Goldman, Sachs & Co., N.Y.C., 1970-78; cons. N.Y.C., 1978-80; house counsel Johnson & Higgins, N.Y.C., 1980-97; sr. atty. legal dept. Marsh & McLennan Cos., Inc., N.Y.C., 1997; ret., 1997. 1st lt. USAR, 1955-57, Korea. Mem. ABA, Assn. Bar City N.Y., Berks County Bar Assn., Union Club, Univ. Club, Mill Reef Club, Phi Beta Kappa. Republican. Lutheran. Home: 80 East End Ave New York NY 10028-8004

KLECKNER, SIMONE MARIE, law librarian; b. Bucharest, Romania, Mar. 7, 1927; came to U.S., 1966; d. George Vrabiescu and Clementa (Cionea) Radian; m. Rudolf Kleckner, Apr. 23, 1960. JD, Bucharest U., 1953; MLS, Columbia U., 1969; LLM, NYU, 1973. Asst. curator NYU Sch. Law Libr., 1969-74; legal libr. UN Dag Hammarskjold Libr., N.Y.C., 1975-86, chief reference and biblio. sect., 1986-87; chief libr. U.S. Ct. Internat. Trade, N.Y.C., 1987-96; pers. counselor Pres. of Romania, 1999—2000. Author: International Legal Bibliography, 1983, Settlement of Disputes in International Law Bibliography, 1985; translator Romanian Penal Code, 2001; lic, 1976; compiler UN Juridical Yearbook, 1974-84. Pres. ad hoc com. Orgn. Romanian Democracy, 1997—. Mem. Am. Soc. Internat. Law, Am. Fgn. Law Assn. Republican. Ea. Orthodox. Avocation: travel. Home: 110 W 69th St New York NY 10023-5116

KLECZEK, DAVID A. lawyer; b. Chgo., Apr. 28, 1972; s. Andrew J. Kleczek and Rebecca Mellander; m. Jana K. Payne, May 10, 2003. BA in Econs., U. Ill., 1996; JD, U. Chgo., 2002. Bar: Ill. 2002. Benefits cons. Hewitt Assocs., Lincolnshire, Ill., 1997—2000; law clk. Levenfeld Pearlstein, Chgo., 2000—02, assoc., 2002—. Mem.: Adv. Soc. Avocations: tennis, running. Office: Levenfeld Pearlstein Ste 1300 2 N LaSalle St Chicago IL 60602

KLECZKA, GERALD D. congressman; b. Milwaukee, Wis., Nov. 26, 1943; m. Bonnie L. Scott, 1978. Ed., U. Wis., Milw. Mem. Wis. Assembly, 1968-74; mem. Wis. Senate, 1974-84, U.S. Congress from 4th Wis. dist., Washington, 1984—. Mem. ways and means com., ways and means health subcom., house budget com. Mem. Wis. Dem. Com., Milwaukee County Dem. Com. With Air N.G., 1963-69. Mem. LaFarge Lifelong Learning Inst., Thomas More Found., Polish Am. Alliance-Milw. Soc., Polish Am. Congress. Democrat. Office: 2301 Rayburn Bldg Washington DC 20515-4904*

KLEE, CLAUDE BLENC, medical researcher; MD, U. Marsailles, France, 1959. Chief lab. chemistry, chief protein biochemistry sect. Nat. Cancer Inst., 1974—. Recipient Women's Excellence in Scis. award, Fedn. Am. Soc. for Exptl. Biology, 1997. Mem.: Inst. Medicine of NAS. Office: Nat Cancer Inst-Biochem Lab 9000 Rockville Pike Bethesda MD 20892-0001

KLEE, VICTOR LA RUE, mathematician, educator; b. San Francisco, Sept. 18, 1925; s. Victor La Rue and Mildred (Muller) K.; BA, Pomona Coll., 1945, DSc (hon.), 1965; PhD, U. Va., 1949; Dr. honoris causa, U. Liège, Belgium, 1984, U. Trier, Germany, 1995. Asst. prof. U. Va., 1949-53; NRC fellow Inst. for Advanced Study, 1951-52; asst. prof. U. Wash., Seattle, 1953-54, assoc. prof., 1954-57, prof. math., 1957-97, adj. prof. computer sci., 1974—98, prof. applied math., 1976-84; prof. emeritus, 1998—. Vis. assoc. prof. UCLA, 1955-56; vis. prof. U. Colo., 1971, U. Victoria, 1975, U. Western Australia, 1979; cons. IBM Watson Research Center, 1972; cons. to industry; mem. Math. Scis. Research Inst., 1985-86; sr. fellow Inst. for Math. and its Applications, 1987. Co-author: Combinatorial Geometry in the Plane, 1963, Old and New Unsolved Problems in Plane Geometry and Number Theory, 1991, Convex Polytopes, 2003; contbr. more than 200 articles to profl. jours. Recipient Rsch. prize U. Va., 1952, Vollum award for disting. accomplishment in sci. and tech. Reed Coll., 1982, David Prescott Burrows Outstanding Disting. Achievement award Pomona Coll., 1988, Max Planck rsch. prize, 1992; NSF sr. postdoctoral fellow, Sloan Found. fellow U. Copenhagen, 1958-60, fellow Ctr. Advanced Study in Behavioral Scis., 1975-76, Guggenheim fellow, Humboldt award U. Erlangen-Nürnberg, 1980-81, Fulbright fellow U. Trier, 1992. Fellow AAAS (chmn. sect. A 1975), Am. Acad. Arts and Scis.; mem. Am. Math. Soc. (assoc. sec. 1955-58, mem. exec. com. 1960-70), Math. Assn. Am. (pres. 1971-73, L.R. Ford award 1972, Disting. Svc. award 1977, C.B. Allendoerfer award 1980, 99), Soc. Indsl. and Applied Math. (mem. coun. 1966-68), Internat. Linear Algegra Soc., Phi Beta Kappa, Sigma Xi (nat. lectr. 1969). Home: 13706 39th Ave NE Seattle WA 98125-3810 Office: U Wash Dept Math PO Box 354350 Seattle WA 98195-4350 E-mail: klee@math.washington.edu.

KLEEBLATT, NORMAN L. museum curator; AB in Art History, Rutgers U., 1971; diploma in conservation, MA, NYU, 1975. Conservator The Jewish Mus., N.Y.C., 1975-80, curator collections/conservator, 1981-87, curator collections, 1987-94, Susan and Elihu Rose curator fine arts, 1995—. Mem. sci. coun. Mus. Art and History of Judaism; cons. Montclair (N.J.) Art Mus., 1975. Contbg. author: Gonn Mosny: Atmen und Malen, 1989, Pre-Raphaelite Art in its European Context, 1995, L'Affaire Dreyfus de A & Z: histoire et dictionnaire, 1994, L'Affaire Dreyfus et l'opinion publique en France et à l'étranger, 1995, Diaspora and Modern Visual Culture: Representing African and Jewish Diaspora, 1998; reviewer in field. Recipient Hon. Mention, Henry Allen Moe Prize, 1985, 88, Nat. Jewish Book award, 1992, Second prize Henry Allen Moe Prize, 1992, Présidence d'honneur Com. Sci. Soc. Internat. d'Histoire de l'Affaire Dreyfus, 1994—; post-grad. fellow Nat. Mus. Fellowship Act, 1975-76; fellow mus. profls. Nat. Endowment Arts, 1996. Mem. Internat. Assn. Art Critics (Am. sect.), Am. Assn. Mus., Coll. Art Assn. Office: The Jewish Mus 1109 5th Ave New York NY 10128-0118

KLEEMAN, CHARLES RICHARD, medical educator, nephrologist, researcher; b. L.A., Aug. 19, 1923; m. 1945; 3 children. BS, U. Calif., 1944, MD, 1947. Rotating intern San Francisco City Hosp., 1947-48; asst. resident pathology Mallory Inst.-Boston City Hosp., 1948-49; resident in medicine Newington VA Hosp., 1949-51; from instr. to asst. prof. metabolism Yale U. Sch. Medicine, 1953-56; assoc. prof. UCLA Sch. Medicine, 1956—60, prof. medicine Cedars-Sinai Med Ctr., 1961—72, prof., dir. dept. internal medicine, 1972—94, prof. emeritus, 1994—. Nephrologist VA Med. Ctr., West L.A., 1993—; prof. medicine, dept. chief Hadassah Med. Sch.-Hebrew U., Israel, 1972-75; vis. prof. Beilinson Hosp.-Tel Aviv U., 1968, St. Francis Hosp., Honolulu, 1968, U. Queensland, 1966; chief metabolic sect. VA Hosp., L.A. 1956-60, cons., 1962—; chief metabolic sect. Wadsworth VA Med. Ctr., L.A., 1956-60. Upjohn-Endocrine Soc. scholar U. London, 1960-61. Mem. AMA, Am. Physiol. Soc., Inst. Medicine-NAS, Am. Soc. Clin. Investigation, Endocrine Soc., Am. Assn. Physicians. Office: VAMC West LA Med Divsn Nephr W111L, 11301 Wilshire Blvd Los Angeles CA 90073 Business E-Mail: ckleeman@ucla.edu.

KLEEMAN, NANCY GRAY ERVIN, retired special education educator; b. Boston, Feb. 19, 1946; d. John Wesley and Harriet Elizabeth (Teuchert) Ervin; m. Brian Carlton Kleeman, June 27, 1969. BA, Calif. State U., Northridge, 1969; MS, Calif. State U., Long Beach, 1976, cert. resource specialist, 1982. Cert. spl. edn., learning disabilities and resource specialist tchr., Calif. Tchr. spl. edn., resource specialist Downey (Calif.) Unified Sch. Dist., 1972-86; tchr. spl. day class Irvine (Calif.) Sch. Dist., 1986-2001. Tutor in field; spkr. Commn. for Handicapped, L.A., 1975; advisor Com. to Downey Unified Sch. Dist., 1976-82; owner ISIS Design Publs. Author: Rhyme Your Times, 1990; author numerous greeting cards. Vol. sec. UN, L.A., 1980—83; vol. coord., art dir., educator Sierra Vista Mid. Sch., Irvine, 1986—88; liaison Tustin (Calif.) Manor Convalescent Home and Regents Point Retirement Home, Irvine, 1988—2000; fundraiser Ronald McDonald House, Orange, Calif.; vol. Sr. Cheer Project, 1986—2001, Vets. Cheer Project, 1996—2001, Make-A-Wish Found., Children in Crisis, Alexander Cohen Hospice, Modesto, Calif.; vol. horticulture program Sierra Vista Mid. Sch., 1999—2001; mem. Nat. Youth Svc., Washington. Recipient award Concerned Students Orgn., Downey, 1984; named Tchr. Yr. Sierra Vista Middle Sch., 1988. Mem.: Nat. Hist. Soc., Save Our Strays, Yankee Golden Retriever Rescue, Dogs for the Blind. Avocations: restoring antique carousel horses, canoeing, numerology, stained glass design, sculpting.

KLEESCHULTE, CHARLES A. communications director; b. St. Charles, Mo., Feb. 18, 1952; s. Elmer A. and Mildred Grace Kleeschulte; m. Penelope Victoria Kelly, June 23, 1987. BA in Polit. Sci., U. Mo., St. Louis, 1974; M of Journalism, U. Mo., Columbia, 1975; cert., Oxford (Eng.) U., 1991. Editor County Tribune Newspaper, O'Fallon, Mo., 1968-76; reporter Juneau (Alaska) Empire Newspaper, 1976-80, 84-89; press sec. to Gov. Jay Hammond Juneau, 1980-83; reporter Anchorage Daily News, 1983-84; pub. info. specialist Alaska Dept. Environ. Conservation, Juneau, 1989-91; comm. dir. to U.S. Sen. Frank Murkowski Washington, 1991—2002; comm. dir. to U.S. Senator Lisa Munkowski, 2003—. Journalism instr. U. Alaska S.E., Juneau, 1978-81, 85-90; freelance writer, 1976-90; bus. reporter Alaska Bus. Monthly Mag., 1984-90. Contbr. articles to profl. jours. Mem. reporters com. Alaska chpt. Freedom of the Press, 1977-90. Roman Catholic. Avocations: hiking, tennis, photography. Home: 14900 Poplar Hill Rd Accokeek MD 20607 Office: Sen Lisa Murkowski 322SH Washington DC 20510

KLEESE, WILLIAM CARL, genealogy research consultant, financial services representative; b. Williamsport, Pa., Jan. 20, 1940; s. Donald Raymond and Helen Alice (Mulberger) K.; m. Vivian Ann Yeager, June 12, 1958; children: Scott, Jolene, Mark, Troy, Brett, Kecia, Lance. BS in Wildlife Biology, U. Ariz., 1975, MS in Animal Physiology, 1979, PhD in Animal Physiology, 1981. Sales rep. Terminix Co., Tucson, 1971-72; pest control operator, 1973-75; fire fighter Douglas Ranger Dist. Coronado Nat. Forest U.S. Forest Svc., 1975, biol. technician Santa Catalina ranger dist., 1975-76; lab. technician dept. animal scis. U. Ariz., 1977-78, rsch. technician dept. pharmacology and toxicology, 1978, rsch. asst. dept. biochemistry, 1979-81, rsch. specialist muscle biology group, 1981-91; genealogy rsch. cons. Tucson, 1988—; fin. svcs. rep. World Fin. Group, Tucson, 1999—. Author: Introduction to Genealogy, 1988, Introduction to Genealogical Research, 1989, The Genealogical Researcher, Neophyte to Graduate, 1992, Genealogical Research in the British Isles, 1991; contbr. numerous articles to profl. jours. Chaplain Ariz. State Prisons, Tucson, 1988—. Mem. Nat. Assn. Securities Dealers, Ariz. Geneaolgy Adv. Bd. (com. chmn. 1990-92), Herpetologists League, Lycoming County Geneal. Soc., Nat. Geneal. Soc., Nat. Wildlife Fedn., Pa. Geneal. Soc., Soc. for the Study of Amphibians and Reptiles, Soc. of Vertebrate Paleontology, Ariz. State Geneal. Soc. (pres. 1990-93). Republican. Mem. Lds Ch. Avocation: photography. Home: 6521 E Fayette St Tucson AZ 85730-2220 Office: 6121 E Broadway Blvd Ste143 Tucson AZ 85711-4026 E-mail: wmkleese@familyhistoryland.com.

KLEFFMAN, KEN, small business owner, rancher; b. Chgo., Apr. 30, 1935; s. Elmer Owen and Mildred Eleanor Kleffman; m. Betty J. Kleffman, Nov. 17, 1957; children: Todd, Thad, Troy, Tara, Tori. BS, We. Ill. Univ., Macomb, Ill., 1957; MA, Univ. Chgo., Ill., 1962. Tchr., coach Argo Cmty. H.S., Argo, Ill., 1957—64; acct. exec. Warner Jenkinson Mfg., St. Loius, Mo., 1964—72; cattle rancher Pana-Sea Ranch, Middleburg, Ky., 1973—; restaurateur Whiskers's Q, Liberty, Ky., 1992—96; ptnr., owner Power Logistics, Lexington, Ky., 1996. Found. Casey County Basketball program for Youth, 1987—. Mem.: Great Lakes Table Tennis Tourament (dir., pres. 1967—69, State of Ill. Table Tennis Champion 1961, Ky. State Table Tennis Champion 1992), Blue Grass State Games, Table Tennis (chrmn., dir. 1985—), Chgo. Land Table Tennis Club (found. 1961, pres. 1961—64). Independent. Avocations: tennis, racquetball, basketball, kayaking, table tennis. Home: POB 8 629 Mill Dam Rd Middleburg KY 42541

KLEIKAMP, BEVERLY, poet, writer, publisher; b. Iron Mountain, Mich., Apr. 15, 1953; d. Hector Joseph and Lorraine Agnes (Frisque) Dugree; m. Vernon Lee Kleikamp, Feb. 5, 1972; children: Henry J., Richard V., Carl A. Freelance writer U.P. Horse News, Florence, Wisc., 1984-91; pub. North Star Pub., 1998—. Editor: (mag.) Northern Stars, 1997—; author: (book) Fifth Season, 1997, Of Higher Powers, 1998; pub.: (book) Best of 98 Anthology, 1999, Old Century/New Millennium Anthology, 2000, Shining Stars Anthology, 2001, Stars of Wonder Anthology, 2002, Stars I, 2003, Stars II, 2003 (book) Stories for Children, 2002. Tracy and The Shadow Horse (book), 2003. Recipient 8th Honorable Mention, Poets' RoundTable 59th Internat. Poetry Contest, 1999, 6th Hon. Mention 63d ann. contest, 2003. Mem. Upper Peninsula Publs./Authors Assn., Upper Peninsula Writers Assn. Avocations: camping, fishing, hunting, photograpy. Home: N17285 County Road 400 Powers MI 49874 9758

KLEIM, E. DENISE, city official; BA in Econs. cum laude, San Jose State U., 1975; MBA, Willamette U., 1982. Mgmt. asst. Urban Renewal Agy. City of Salem, Oreg., 1976-78, grant adminstr. dept. cmty. devel., 1978-80, asst. to dir. dept. cmty. devel., 1981-84, lobbyist, 1980-83; sr. mgmt. analyst Bur. Bldgs., City of Portland, Oreg., 1984-86, adminstrv. mgr., 1986-99, mgr. adminstrv. svcs. bur. devel. svcs., 1999—. V.p. Montclair After Sch. Care Assn., Portland, 1995-96; mem. Atkinson Soc., Salem, 1995-97. Office: City of Portland Bur Devel Svc 1120 SW 5th Ave Portland OR 97204-1912

KLEIMAN, ALAN BOYD, artist; b. Bklyn., Feb. 20, 1938; s. Louis and Alfreda (Belowsky) K.; m. Audrey Barbara Code, Feb. 9, 1963; 1 dau., Andrea Kristin. B.F.A., Va. Commonwealth U., 1951; M.F.A., Cranbrook Acad. Art, 1953. Asst. publicity dir. Artist Tenents Assn., 1960-67; v.p. Grand St. Artist Group, 1970-75; chmn. Soho Artifacts, 1971-75. Author: Painting Provincetown Water, 1961, Investigations into the Light of Red Color, 1968, Light, Dazzle and Glow, 1970; one-man show includes Elizabeth Harris Gallery, N.Y.C., 1995, Ohara Gallery, N.Y.C., 1996, Robert Steel Gallery, N.Y.C., 1997, Kouros Gallery, N.Y.C., 2000; group shows include Nexus Gallery, Boston, 1959, Betty Parsons Gallery, N.Y.C., 1961, 79, Sun Gallery, 1962, New Gallery, Provincetown, Mass., 1961-62, Marino, N.Y.C., 1966, Warren Benedek, N.Y.C., 1972, Landmark Gallery, N.Y.C., 1975-76, Renaissance Soc., Chgo., 1979, Art U.S.A. '80, U.S., Can., Sweden, Siegel Gallery, N.Y.C., 1983, Michael Walls Gallery, N.Y.C., 1989, Robert Steel Gallery, N.Y.C., 1997; represented in permanent collections Mus. Modern Art, Whitney Mus., Am. Arts, Met. Mus. Art, N.Y.C., Carnegie Mus., Pitts., Boston Mus. Fine Arts, William Patterson Coll., Wayne, N.J.; 169 self portraits at Clocktower, N.Y.C., 1985—; retrospective 1960-86 at P.S.I., N.Y.C., 1986. Served with U.S. Army, 1953-55. Recipient 1st prize Boston Arts Festival, 1954; N.Y. State Council Arts grantee, 1977-78; Curtral Council Found. awardee, 1978; Esther and Adolph Gottleib Found. grantee, 1985, Pollack-Krasner Found. grantee, 1987. Mem. Theatre of Artists League (v.p. 1972), Orgn. Ind. Artists, Am. Abstract Artists, Nat. Endowment for Arts. *My creative drive has at times thrived on procrastination, anger, jealousy, rage, talent and plain hard work. Balancing emotion and intelligence make the tension expressed in my painting. I want to make more and better art.*

KLEIMAN, BERNARD, lawyer; b. Chgo., Jan. 26, 1928; s. Isidore and Pearl (Wikoff) Kleiman; m. Gloria Baime, Nov. 15, 1986; children: Leslie, David. BS, Purdue U., 1951; JD, Northwestern U., 1954. Bar: Ill. 1954. Practice law in assn. with Abraham W. Brussell, 1957-60; dist. counsel United Steel Workers Am., 1960-65, spl. counsel, 1997—, gen. counsel, 1965-97; ptnr. Kleiman, Cornfield & Feldman, Chgo., 1960-75; prin. B. Kleiman (P.C.), 1976-77, Kleiman, Whitney, Wolfe & Elfenbaum, P.C., 1978-99. Mem. collective bargaining coms. for nat. labor negotiations in basic steel, tire mfg., and shipbuilding industries. Contbr. articles to legal jours. Served with U.S. Army, 1946—48. Mem.: ABA, Allegheny County Bar Assn.

KLEIMAN, DAVID HAROLD, lawyer; b. Kendallville, Ind., Apr. 2, 1934; s. Isadore and Pearl (Wikoff) K.; m. Meta Dene Freeman, July 6, 1958; children: Gary, Andrew, Scott, Matthew. BS, Purdue U., 1956; JD, Northwestern U., 1959. Bar: Ind. 1959. Assoc. firm Bamberger & Feibleman, Indpls., 1959-61; ptnr. Bagal, Talesnick & Kleiman, Indpls., 1961-73, Dann Pecar Newman & Kleiman, Indpls., 1973—; dep. pros. atty., 1961-62; counsel Met. Devel. Commn., 1965-75; Ind. Heartland Coordinating Commn., 1975-81. Editor: Jour. of Air Law and Commerce, 1958-59. Chmn. Young Leadership Coun., 1967; v.p. Indpls. Hebrew Congregation, 1973, bd. dirs., 2003—; pres. Jewish Cmty. Ctr. Assn., 1972-75; pres. Jewish Welfare Fedn., 1981-84; v.p. United Way Ctrl. Ind., 1982-86, pres., 1986, chmn. bd. dirs., 1987; bd. dirs. Jewish Fedn., 1972—, Ind. Symphony Soc., 1991-96; bd. dirs. Ind. Repertory Theatre, 1986—, pres. 1991-94; trustee Indpls. Found., 2000—; bd. dirs. Ctrl. Ind. Cmty Found., 2000—, English Found., 2000—. Recipient Young Leadership award, 1968, Isadore Fiebleman Man of Yr. award, 1987, Mossler Cmty. Svc. award, 1988, Chalfie Cmty. Svc. award, 1998. Mem. ABA, Ind. State Bar Assn., Indpls. Bar Assn., Comml. Law League Am., Am. Coll. Bankruptcy, Columbia Club, Skyline Club (bd. dirs. 1993—), B'nai B'rith, Broadmoor Country Club. Office: Dann Pecar Newman & Kleiman One American Square PO Box 82008 Indianapolis IN 46282-2008

KLEIMAN, GARY HOWARD, broadcast, advertising and cellular communications consultant; b. Phila., Jan. 24, 1952; s. Leon and Martha (Rubin) K.; m. Annette Suzanne Vranich, Sept. 23, 1978; children: Aaron Jay, Jared Adam. Diploma, Am. Acad. Broadcasting, Phila., 1969, Pa. State Fire Sch., Media, 1969; BS, Temple U., 1972. Cert. radio mktg. cons., Radio Advt. Bur., N.Y.C. Gen. mgr. Sta. WFEC, Harrisburg, Pa., 1974-75; local sales mgr. Sta. WYSP-FM, Phila., 1976-79; pres. A.S.K. Advt., King of Prussia, Pa., 1976-80; v.p., gen. mgr. Sta. WGLU-FM, Johnstown, 1980-82, Sta. WAJE, Edensburg, Pa., 1982-84, Sta. WSBY-WQHQ-AM-FM, Salisbury, Md., 1984-86; mgr. Sta. WJDY, Salisbury, 1986-87; pres. IDEAS Unltd. Mktg. and Advt. Co., Salisbury, 1986—; gen. mgr. Sta. WACS-FM, Schenectady, 1988-89; v.p., gen. mgr. Sta. WDLE-FM, Federalsburg, Md., 1989-91. Media cons. Sta. WMDT-TV, Salisbury, 1988; dir., tchr. Am. Acad. Broadcasting, Phila., 1976-79; area mgr. Bell Atlantic Mobile Sys., 1992-93; pres. CellComm Mobile/Cellular One, 1993—. Contbr. articles to profl. publs. Com. chmn. Salisbury Revitalization, 1984—; mem. Bennett Mid. Sch. Parents, Tchrs., Students Assn., pres., 1994-95; bd. dirs. Salisbury Regional Urban Design Action Team, 1984-89, Deers Head Hosp. Found., Am. Heart Assn.; co-sponsor projects Lower Shore Easter Seals, Salisbury, 1985, Am. Cancer Soc., 1984-85, Kidney Found., 1985, Epilepsy Assn., 1985, Johnstown Area Regional Industries, 1981-84; promotion coord. Salisbury Festival com., 1985, 87, 88, 89, 90, 91, vice chmn., 1985-90; mem. exec. com. Lower Shore chpt. March of Dimes, 1984-89; scout leader Boy Scouts Am., 1988-90; adult leader 4-H, 1988-2001; mgr. area Little League; active campaigner Cambria County Dem. Com., 1982-84, Wicomico County Dem. Com., 1991—. Squadron comms. officer, pub. affairs officer, mem. air crew and ground team search and rescue MDWG USAF aux./CAP, 1997—; mem. adv. bd. Wicomico Mentoring Project, 1994—, co-chair, 1996-2001, chmn. 2000-01; vice chmn. bd. dirs. Jr. Achievement, 2000-01. Recipient numerous awards from local civic orgns., 1981—. Mem. Downtown Salisbury Assn. (bd. dirs., v.p. 1997-98, pres. 1999-00), Fruitland C. of C. (bd. dirs. 1996-2000, v.p. 1999-2000), Salisbury Area C. of C. (bd. dirs. 1989-92,

98-2001), Caroline County C. of C. (bd. dirs. 1989), Salisbury Jaycees (Springboard award 1985), Johnstown Jaycees, Salisbury State U. Athletic Club (pres. 1985), Tall Timber Park Assn. (pres. 1992-94). Democrat. Jewish. Avocations: photography, camping, skiing, softball, volleyball. Home: 115 Tall Timber Ln Fruitland MD 21826-1318 Office: CellComm Mobile Ste 103 City Ctr on Plaza Salisbury MD 21801 also: IDEAS Unltd Broadcast Cons City Center Ste 103 Salisbury MD 21801 E-mail: phoneman@cellcomm-mobile.com. *To me success is not measured in money, it's measured in how other perceive you in your community. To me, a business day starts at 7:30 and ends when all of my clients and customers are happy and all problems have been solved.*

KLEIMAN, KELLY (RUTH B. KLEIMAN), journalist, lawyer; b. Balt., Feb. 17, 1955; d. Allen and Jeanette (Albert) K.; m. Ronald D. Falzone, Sept. 4, 1978 (div. Sept. 1989). AB, U. Chgo., 1975, JD, 1979. Bar: Ill. 1979. Dep. dir. Pub. Funding for the Arts, Chgo., 1978-79; assoc. Rudnick & Wolfe, Chgo., 1979-81; asst. dean Chgo. Kent Coll. Law, Chgo., 1981-86; exec. dir. Chgo. Children's Choir, 1986-87; prin. NFP Cons., Chgo., 1987—2002. Faculty Coll. of DuPage Bus. and Profl. Inst., 1989—97. Contbr. articles to mags. and jours. Tech. assistance com. Chgo. Women in Philanthropy, 1992-95, 2000—; vol. reader Rec. for Blind, Chgo., 1992—; bd. dirs. Lincoln-Belmont YMCA, Chgo., 1992-95. Mem. Assn. Cons. to Nonprofits (bd. dirs. 1989-93, 97-2000, pres. 1998-2000). Democrat. Jewish. Avocations: writing fiction, theater directing. Home and Office: Apt 16 2103 N Seminary Ave Chicago IL 60614-4176 E-mail: kellynfp@aol.com.

KLEIMAN, VIVIAN ABBE, filmmaker; b. Phila., Oct. 11, 1950; d. Philip and Hilda Kleiman. BA, U. Calif., 1974. Filmmaker; lectr. Grad. Program in Documentary Film Stanford U., 1995—2002. Bd. dirs. Cultural Rsch. and Comm., Berkeley, Jewish Film Festival, 1981—85, Assn. Ind. Video and Filmmakers, N.Y.C., 2000—02; v.p. Frameline, San Francisco, 1995—2001; pres. Signifyin' Works, Berkeley, 1991—94; v.p. Fine Arts Found., San Francisco, 1983—93; cinematographer Tongues United, 1999. Exec. prodr. First Person Plural, 2000, Hope Along the Wind, 2001; prodr., dir. films including Judy Chicago: The Birth Project, 1985, Ein Stehaufmannchen, 1991, My Body's My Business, 1992, Of Rights and Wrongs, 2002; co-prodr. films including Routes of Exile: A Moroccan Jewish Odyssey, 1982, California Gold, 1984, Color Adjustment, 1992, Roam Sweet Home, 1996, (with Michael Chandler) Forgotten Fires, 1998; assoc. prodr. The Disney Channel, 1982-83; rschr. for various films including A Woman Named Golda, 1982. Recipient George Foster Peabody award Sundance Film Festival, Outstanding Achievement award Internat. Documentary Assn., Nat. Emmy award nominee, The Eric Barnouw awards Orgn. Am. Historians, Red ribbon Am. Film and Video Festival, Best of Festival award Black Maria Festival, Black Internat. Cinema Berlin, Gold Plaque, Social/Polit. Documentary Chgo. Internat. Film Festival, N.C. Silver Juror's prize. Mem. Assn. of Ind. Video and Filmmakers, Film Arts Found., Internat. Documentary Assn. Office: 2600 10th St Berkeley CA 94710-2522

KLEIN, ABRAHAM, physics educator, researcher; b. Bklyn, Jan. 10, 1927; s. Philip and Ida (Warshofsky) K.; m. Murielle Pollack, June 18, 1950; children—Julia, Hilary BA, Bklyn. Coll., 1947; MA, Harvard U., 1948, PhD, 1950; DSc (hon.), U. Frankfort, 1995. Instr. physics Harvard U., Cambridge, Mass., 1950-52, jr. fellow, 1952-55; assoc. prof. physics U. Pa., Phila., 1955-58, prof., 1958-94, prof. emeritus, from 1994. Vis. prof. U. Paris, 1961-62, Princeton U., NJ, 1969-70, MIT, Cambridge, 1975-76, Yale U., New Haven, 1983; disting. vis. prof., Drexel U., 1994—. Assoc. editor Phys. Rev., 1965-68; contbr. articles to profl. jour. Served with USAF, 1946 Sr. postdoctoral fellow NSF, 1961-62, fellow Alfred P. Sloan Found., 1961-63, Guggenheim Found., 1975; recipient Disting. Alumnus award Bklyn. Coll., 1966, Hunboldt Sr. Scientist award, 1987, 95, Lifetime Achievement award, 2002. Fellow Am. Phys. Soc.; mem. AAUP, Am. Assn. Physics Tchr. Avocations: gardening, theater, films, reading. Home: Wynnewood, Pa. Died Jan. 19, 2003.

KLEIN, ANNE SCEIA, public relations executive; b. Phila., Apr. 25, 1942; d. Charles B. and Kathryn L. (Lucas) Sceia; m. Gerhart L. Klein, June 19, 1976. BS in Econs., U. Pa., 1964, MA in Communications, 1965. Promotion asst. S.E. Pa. Transit Authority, Phila., 1965; pub. rels. dir. Pa. Lung Assn., Phila., 1965-68; info. dir. H2L2 Architects, Phila., 1968; pub. rels. officer Girard Bank, Phila., 1969-76; acct. exec. Aitkin-Kynett Co., Inc., Phila., 1977; mgr. media rels. Sun Co., Radnor, Pa., 1978-80, mgr. exec. communications, 1980-82; pres. Anne Klein & Assocs., Inc., Mt. Laurel, N.J., 1982—. Mem. Ethics Com., Mt. Laurel, 1988-92; mem. Citizens Adv. Com., Mt. Laurel, 1988-92; mem. water quality com. Old Taunton Colony Club, Medford, N.J., 1995—. Recipient Super Communicator of 80's award Women in Comm., 1987, Tribute to Women in Industry award YMCA, 1990, Hale's Legacy award Women in Comm., 1996, Sarah award Women in Comms., 1998; named Small Bus. Person of Yr. So. N.J. C. of C., 1991. Fellow: Pub. Rels. Soc. Am. (accredited, pres. Phila. chpt. 1979, mid-Atlantic chmn. 1984, assembly del. 1980—82, 1988—94, exec. com. Counselors Acad. 1990—91, Coll. of Fellows 1991, Maxine Elkin award Phila. chpt. 2001, Pepperpot awards, PR Profl. of Yr. N.J. chpt. 2002); mem.: Forum Exec. Women (sec. bd. dirs. 1981—83), Pub. Rels. Profls. So. N.J. (chmn. 1987—, pres. 1985—87), U. Pa. Faculty Club, Harbor League Club, Kappa Delta. Avocations: skiing, boating. Office: Anne Klein & Assocs 10 Lake Ctr Ste 108 Marlton NJ 08053-3215

KLEIN, ARNOLD SPENCER, lawyer; b. N.Y.C., Mar. 10, 1951; s. Paul and Ethel (Cooper) K.; m. Arlene Sandra Feinberg, Aug. 14, 1977; children: Jeffrey Daniel, Rachel Pauli. BA, SUNY, Stony Brook, 1974; JD cum laude, N.Y. Law Sch., 1977. Bar: N.Y. 1978, Fla. 1984, U.S. Dist. Ct. (so. and ea. dists.) N.Y., U.S. Dist. Ct. (so. dist.) Fla., U.S. Ct. Appeals (2d cir.), U.S. Supreme Ct. Mem. Kelley, Drye & Warren, N.Y.C., 1977-85, ptnr., 1986-94, Meltzer, Lippe & Goldstein, LLP, Mineola, 1994—. Mem. ABA, N.Y. State Bar Assn., Nassau County Bar Assn. Office: Meltzer Lippe 190 Willis Ave Mineola NY 11501-2693 E-mail: aklein@mlg.com.

KLEIN, ARNOLD WILLIAM, dermatologist; b. Mt. Clemens, Mich., Feb. 27, 1945; s. David Klein; m. Malvina Kraemer. BA, U. Pa., 1967, MD, 1971. Intern Cedars-Sinai Med. Ctr., Los Angeles, 1971-72; resident in dermatology Hosp. U. Pa., Phila., 1972-73, U. Calif., Los Angeles, 1973-75; pvt. practice dermatology Beverly Hills, Calif., 1975—. Prof. dermatology/medicine U. Calif. Ctr. for Health Scis; mem. med. staff Cedars-Sinai Med. Ctr.; asst. clin. prof. dermatology Stanford U., 1982-89; asst. clin. prof. to prof. dermatology/medicine, UCLA; trustee David Geffen Sch. Medicine UCLA, UCLA Med. Ctr., 2003-; mem. Calif. State Adv. Com. on Malpractice, 1983-89; med. adv. bd. Skin Cancer Found., Lupus Found. Am., Botox, Allergan; presenter seminars in field. Assoc. editor Jour. Dermatologic Surgery and Oncology; reviewer Jour. Sexually Transmitted Diseases, Jour. Am. Acad. Dermatology; mem. editorial bd. Men's Fitness mag., Shape mag., Archives of Dermatology; contbr. numerous articles to med. jours. Founder R. Tarlow/Dr. Arnold Klein Fund for Breast Cancer Treatment. Mem. AMA, AFTRA, Calif. Med. Assn., Am. Soc. Dermatologic Surgery, Internat. Soc. Dermatologic Surgery, Am. Assn. Cosmetic Surgeons, Assn. Sci. Advisors, L.A. Med. Assn., Am. Coll. Chemosurgery, Met. Dermatology Soc., Am. Acad. Dermatology, Dermatology Found., Scleroderma Found., Internat. Psoriasis Rsch. Inst., Lupus Found., Discovery Fund for Eye Rsch. (dir.), Hereditary Disease Found. (dir.), Jennifer Jones Simon Found. (trustee), Am. Venereal Disease Assn., Soc. Cosmetic Chemists, L.A. Mus. Contemporary Art (founder), Dance Gallery L.A. (founder), Am. Found. AIDS Rsch. (founder, dir.), Children's Mus. L.A. (founder), Friars Club, Phi Beta Kappa, Sigma Tau Sigma, Delphos. Office: 435 N Roxbury Dr Ste 204 Beverly Hills CA 90210-5004 E-mail: awkleinmd1@aol.com. *The sincerest form of respect is trust. Being a Physician is all about serving this trust. Also, it is about dedication, observation, obsession and creative intelligence. Who and what I am...where I begin and where I end...is all about being a physician.*

KLEIN, ARTHUR, foundation executive; b. Phila., June 27, 1934; s. Philip and Esther (Moyerman) K.; m. Marilyn A. Burnett, Mar. 12, 1961 (dec. Dec. 1990); children: Joshua, Rebecca Rose Clark, Alexander, Judith Amy Francis. AB, Haverford Coll., 1955; MS, U. Pa., 1958; DHL, Combs Coll. Music, Bryn Mawr, Pa., 1983. Editor Phila. Jewish Times, 1958-71; pres. Rittenhouse Found., Phila., 1963-96, chmn., 1996—. Pres. Phila. Meml. Park, 1965-85, Gt. Valley Pet Cemetery, Frazer, Pa., 1968-85, Bristol Gardens, Inc., 1981—; trustee Mikveh Israel Cemetery Trust, Phila., 1977—. Treas. Found. Big Bros./Big Sisters Am., 1989—, Big Bros./Big Sisters Am., 1976—94; chmn. Phila. Art Alliance, 1968—71; trustee The Provincial Found., Phila., 1965—, Friends of Independence Nat. Hist. Pk., 1989—96; mem. exec. bd. Com. of Seventy, 1989—2002; treas. Independence Hall Preservation Fund, 1991—99, pres., 1992—99; sec. Am. Revolution Patriots Fund, 1992—2002; committeeman 8th Ward Rep. Exec. Com., Phila., 1979—; hon. v.p. Temple Beth Zion-Beth Israel; bd. dirs. Mann Ctr. for Performing Arts, 1989—98, Pan Am. Assn., 1991—96, English Speaking Union Phila., 1991—96; trustee Combs Coll. Music, 1983—85, Pa. Coll. Podiat. Medicine, Phila., 1983—98; mem. bd. visitors Temple U. Sch. Podiat. Medicine, 1998—; chmn. Found. for Temple U. Sch. Podiat. Medicine, 2001—03; trustee Harcum Coll., Bryn Mawr, 1976—; chmn. Harcum Coll., Bryn Mawr, 1982—95; trustee Temple U. Hosp., 2001—. Recipient Eyerman award Pa. Jaycees, 1962. Mem.: Soc. Profl. Journalists (pres. Phila. chpt. 1968), Jewish Cemetery Assn. Phila. (pres. 1970), Union League of Phila., Barnegat Light Yacht Club (commodore 1977), Plays and Players (hon.). Republican. Home: 2023 Pine St Philadelphia PA 19103-6522 Office: The Rittenhouse Found 225 S 15th St Ste 2034 Philadelphia PA 19102-3979

KLEIN, AUGUST STONE, retired physicist; b. Newton, Mass., Aug. 31, 1924; s. August Clarence and Maree Keeling Klein; m. Abigail Banghart, Apr. 27, 1957; children: Susan Mckenna, August, Jr, Franklin. BS, Williams Coll., Williamstown, Mass., 1948; MS, Harvard U., 1950. Registered mech. engr. D.C. rep atomic power divsn. Westinghouse Electric Corp., Washington, 1950—57; v.p. Nuclear Sci. and Engring. Corp, Pitts., 1957—59; West Coast regional mgr. High Voltage Engring. Corp, Walnut Creek, Calif., 1959—63; mgr. spl. products divsn. Tech. Measurement Corp, San Mateo, Calif., 1963—67; pres. Nuclear Engring. Corp, Palo Alto, Calif., 1967—80; exec. v.p. envirotech. divsn. Baker Hughes Corp, Palo Alto, 1980—84; pres., CEO Ion Implant Corp, Santa Clara, Calif., 1985—91; pres. Savel Circuits Corp, Sunnyvale, Calif., 1991—94; ret. Cons. Nanometrics, San Jose, 1994—. Contbr. papers to profl. jours. (IR 100 award, 1972). Mem.: Am. Vacuum Soc. Episcopalian. Achievements include development of energy dispersive x-ray spectromeer. Avocations: tennis, skiing, private flying, guitar. Home: 160 La Questa Way Woodside CA 94062 Home Fax: 650-529-1068. Personal E-mail: akleinsr@aol.com.

KLEIN, BENJAMIN, economics educator, consultant; b. N.Y.C., Jan. 29, 1943; s. Hyman and Beartha (Kristel) K.; m. Lynne Schneider; children: Franz, Emily, Amanda. ABA in Philosophy, Bklyn. Coll., 1964; MA in Econs., U. Chgo., 1967, PhD in Econs., 1970. Asst. prof. UCLA, 1968-72, assoc. prof., 1973-78, prof. econs., 1978—; faculty research fellow Nat. Bur. Econs., N.Y.C., 1971-72, research assoc., 1976-77; pres. Econ. Analysis Corp., Los Angeles, 1980—. Vis. prof. U. Wash., Seattle, 1978; cons. FTC, Washington, 1976-86, bd. govs. FRS, Washington, 1973-75. Contbr. articles to profl. jours. Ford Found. fellow, 1967-68, Scaiffe Found. fellow, 1975-76, Law and Econs. fellow U. Chgo. Law Sch., 1979; grantee Sloan Found., 1981-87; recipient ann. prize for disting. scholarship in law and econs. U. Miami Law and Econ. Ctr., 1978-79. ann. award for best articles Western Econ. Assn., 1979. Mem. Am. Econs. Assn. Office: UCLA Dept Econs 405 Hilgard Ave Los Angeles CA 90095-9000

KLEIN, BERNARD, publishing company executive; b. N.Y.C., Sept. 20, 1921; s. Joseph J. and Anna (Wolfe) K.; m. Betty Stecher, Feb. 17, 1946; children: Cheryl Rona, Barry Todd, Cindy Ann. BA, CCNY, 1942. Founder, pres. U.S. List Co., Boca Raton, Fla., 1946—; founder, pres., chief editor B. Klein Publs., Delray Beach, Fla., 1953—. Cons. direct mail advt. and reference book pub. to pubs., industry, 1950— Author: all biennials Ency. of American Indian, 1954— ; Guide to American Directories. Served with AUS, 1942-45, ETO. Mem. Direct Mail Advt. Assn. Lodges: Masons. Home: 12727 Coral Lakes Dr Boynton Beach FL 33437-4143

KLEIN, BERNARD, clinical chemist; b. N.Y.C., Sept. 16, 1914; s. Samuel Klein and Mamie Cohen; m. Rose Shweitzer, Aug. 8, 1942; children: David Andrew, Peter Alan. BS, Bklyn. Coll., 1934; PhD, Polytech. U., 1950. Diplomate Am. Bd. Clin. Chemistry. Chief biochemistry, dept. of pathology VA Hosp., Bronx, N.Y., 1948-67; asst. dir. diagnostic rsch. Hoffmann-LaRoche Inc., Nutley, N.J., 1967-80; visiting prof. Dept. Lab. Med. Albert Einstein Coll. Medicine, Bronx, N.Y., 1980-85; tech. dir. Lakeville Lab., New Hyde Park, N.Y., 1985-95. Contbr. 100 articles to profl. jours.; patentee in field. Mem. Am. Chem. Soc., Am. Soc. for Clin. Chemistry (Ames award 1975, Van Slyke award 1969). Avocations: baking, gardening, pictorial photography. Home: 129 Patton Blvd New Hyde Park NY 11040-1726 E-mail: bernardkleinusa@netscape.net.

KLEIN, CALVIN RICHARD, fashion designer; b. N.Y.C., Nov. 19, 1942; s. Leo and Flore (Stern) K.; m. Jayne Centre, Apr. 26, 1964 (div. 1974); 1 dau., Marci; m. Kelly Rector, Sept. 1986 (div. 1996). AA, Fashion Inst. Tech., 1962. Pres., designer Calvin Klein, N.Y.C., 1969—. Critic Parsons Sch. Design; critic, cons. Fashion Inst. Tech., dir., 1975—. Recipient Coty award, 1973, 74, 75, Woolmark award for Career Achievement, 1987; named Outstanding Am. talent in women's fashion design Coun. Fashion Designers of Am., 1981, 83, 87; Womenswear/Menswear Designer of the Year, Coun. Fashion Designers of Am., 1993. Mem. Council Fashion Designers, Mus. Modern Art, Met. Mus. Art, Whitney Mus., Guggenheim Mus. Office: Calvin Klein Inc 205 W 39th St 4 New York NY 10018-3102 Address: Calvin Klein Europe Via Montenapoleone 29 20121 Milano Italy

KLEIN, CECELIA F. art historian, educator; d. William H. and Eleanor Pollock Ford; children: Stefyn Mikaela, Sacha Klein Martin. PhD, Columbia U., N.Y.C., 1972. Prof. Oakland U., Rochester, Mich., 1972—76, UCLA, 1976—. Author: (edited conf. vol.) Gender in Prehispanic America. Mem.: Soc. for Ethnohistory, Soc. for Am. Archaeology, Am. Anthrop. Associaton, Coll. Art Assn. (assoc. Achievement award). Office: University of California Los Angeles 405 Hilgard Ave Los Angeles CA 90095

KLEIN, CERRY MARTIN, operations research and industrial engineering educator, consultant; b. Kansas City, Mo., Dec. 11, 1955; BS, Northwest Mo. State U., Maryville, 1977; MS, Purdue U., West Lafayette, 1980, PhD, 1983. Tchr. Cen. Sch. Dist. #1, Kansas City, 1977-78; prof. U. Mo. Columbia, 1984—, dir. undergrad. studies, 1991-92; dir. grad. studies U. Mo., Columbia, 1992—. Cons. in field. Contbr. articles to profl. jours., chpts. to books. Counselor Big Bros., Maryville, 1975-77; mem. Ptnrs. in Edn. Columbia Sch. Dist. Recipient Outstanding Engring. Prof. award U. Mo., Ralph R. Teetor Ednl. award, Soc. Automotive Engrs., 1989, Young Investigator award Office Naval Rsch., William T. Kemper Fellow award, Kemper Found., 1992; David Ross fellow Purdue U., 1982, rsch. fellow U. Mo., 1986, 88—. Mem. Ops. Research Soc. Am., Soc. Indsl. and Applied Maths, Math. Programming Soc., Pi Mu Epsilon, Sigma Xi. Avocations: paleontology, raquetball, basketball, bicycling, astronomy. Home: 7751 W Old Barclay Creek Ln Columbia MO 65202-9594 Office: E3437 Engring Bldg E U Mo Columbia MO 65211

KLEIN, CHARLES HENLE, lithographing company executive; b. Cin., Oct. 5, 1908; s. Benjamin Franklin and Flora (Henle) K.; student Purdue U., 1926-27, U. Cin., 1927-28; m. Ruth Becker, Sept. 23, 1938 (dec. 1997); children— Betsy (Mrs. Marvin H. Schwartz), Charles H., Carla (Mrs. George Fee III). Pres., Progress Lithographing Co., Cin., 1934-59, Novelart Mfg. Co., Cin., 1960— ; dir. R.A. Taylor Corp. Founding mem. Chief Execs. Orgn., Losantiville Country Club, Queen City Club, Bankers Club. Home: Amberley Village 6754 Fair Oaks Dr Cincinnati OH 45237-3606 Office: Amberley Village 2121 Section Rd Cincinnati OH 45237-3509

KLEIN, CHARLOTTE CONRAD, public relations executive; b. Detroit, June 20, 1923; d. Joseph and Bessie (Brown) K. BA, UCLA, 1945. Corr. UPI, Los Angeles, 1945-46; staff writer CBS, Los Angeles, 1946-47; publicist David O. Selznick Studios, Culver City, Calif., 1947-49, Foladare and Assocs., Los Angeles, 1949-51; publicist to v.p. Edward Gottlieb & Assocs., N.Y.C., 1951-62; v.p. to sr. v.p. Harshe Rotman & Druck, N.Y.C., 1962-78; dir. press/govt. affairs Sta. WNET-TV, N.Y.C., 1978-79; pres. Charlotte C. Klein Assocs., N.Y.C., 1979-84; sr. v.p., group supr. Porter Novelli, N.Y.C., 1984-89; prin. Charlotte Klein Assocs., N.Y.C., 1989—. Adj. prof. pub. rels. NYU; bd. dirs. U.S. Trademark Assn., 1959-62, Am. Arbitration Assn., 1970-80 (exec. com. 1980-82); mem. adv. bd. Coll. and Cmty. Fellowship Grad. Ctr., CUNY, 2002—; cons. Ctr. for Advancement of Women, 2003—. Contbr. articles to profl. jours. Bd. dirs. Manhattan chpt. Am. Cancer Soc., 1988-92. Recipient Cine Golden Eagle, 1977, Matrix award Women in Communications, 1975. Mem. Pub. Rels. Soc. Am. (accredited; pres. N.Y. chpt. 1985-86, Silver Anvil award 1978, John Hill award 1988), Women's Forum (bd. dirs. N.Y. chpt. 1986-87, 96-98), Internat. Women's Forum (leadership com. chair dialogue for democracy 1993-98, co-chair task force on violence against women globally, 1998-2001), Women Execs. in Pub. Rels. (pres. 1965), cons., Center for Advancement of Woman, 2002—. Avocations: painting, stamp collecting, tennis, kite flying. E-mail: kleintravis@earthlink.net.

KLEIN, CHRISTOPHER CARNAHAN, economist; b. Anniston, Ala., July 5, 1953; s. Wallace Carnahan and Frances Luvona (Meaders) K.; m. Vicki Lynn Brown, May 7, 1983; children: Hannah Marie Brown, Colin Christopher Brown. BA in Econs., U. Ala., 1976; PhD in Econs., U. N.C., 1980. Economist FTC, Washington, 1980-86, Tenn. Pub. Svc. Commn., Nashville, 1986-93, rsch. dir., 1993-94, dir. utility rate div., 1994-95, chief utility rate divsn. Tenn. Regulatory Authority, Nashville, 1995-97, chief econ. analysis divsn., 1997—2002; assoc. prof. econ. and fin. dept. Mid. Tenn. State U., Murfreesboro, 2002—. Mem. adj. faculty Mid. Tenn. State U., Murfreesboro, 1990-94; adj. assoc. prof. Vanderbilt U., 1998-2002; mem. Fed.-State Joint Bd. Staff, 1994-96; mem. rsch. adv. com. Nat. Regulatory Rsch. Inst., Columbus, Ohio, 1990-95, chmn., 1993-95; mem. staff subcom. on gas Nat. Assn. Regulatory Utility Commrs., 1990-94. Contbr. articles to profl. jours. Recipient cert. of commendation FTC, 1985. Mem. Am. Econ. Assn., So. Econ. Assn., Indsl. Orgn. Soc., Transp. and Pub. Utilities Group, Alpha Pi Mu. Avocations: writing poetry, tube hi-fi, photography. Office: Econ and Fin Dept Middle Tenn State U PO Box 27 Murfreesboro TN 37132 E-mail: cklein@mtsu.edu.

KLEIN, CHUCK, private investigator; b. Cin., 1942; s. Charles H. and Ruth Emily Klein; m. Annette Margolis Levine, Aug. 18, 1996; children: Trey, Jay, Todd, Amy, Brad. LLB, Blackstone Law Sch., 1972. Cert. police officer, Ohio; cert. fire fighter, Ind.; cert. firearms instr. NRA; lic. pvt. investigator; cert. instinct shooting instr. Tactical Def. Inst., Ohio. Firearms editor P.I. Mag., Toledo, Ohio, 1988—. Author: (fiction) Circa 1957, 1990, (non-fiction) Instinct Combat Shooting, 1986, Klein's Firearm Manual, 1997, Klein's C.C.W. Handbook, 1998, (fiction) The Power of God, 1999, (non-fiction) Lines of Defense, 2000, (fiction) The Way it Was, 2003. Mem. Am. Soc. Law Enforcement Trainers, Internat. Assn. Law Enforcement Firearms Instrs., Fairfield Sportsman Assn., Kiwanis Club of Cin. (pres. 2002-03). Avocations: golf, skeet.

KLEIN, COLEMAN EUGENE, lawyer; b. Chgo., Apr. 8, 1938; BBA, Wayne State U., 1960, JD magna cum laude, 1967. Bar: Mich. 1968, U.S. Dist. Ct. (ea. dist.) Mich. 1968, U.S. Tax Ct. 1968, U.S. Ct. Appeals (6th cir.) 1970, U.S. Supreme Ct. 1989. Ptnr. Shere & Klein, Detroit, 1968-82; pvt. practice Southfield, Mich., 1982-2000, Bloomfield Hills, Mich., 2000—. Contbr. articles to profl. jours. Recipient Disting. Cmty. Svc. award Alzheimer's Assn., Detroit, 1984, 91. Mem. ABA, State Bar of Mich., Oakland County Bar Assn. Office: 39533 Woodward Ave Ste 210 Bloomfield Hills MI 48304-5103

KLEIN, DALE EDWARD, federal agency administrator; b. Cooper County, Mo., July 6, 1947; BS, U. Mo., 1970, MS, 1971, PhD in Nuclear Engring., 1977. Design engr. Procter & Gamble Co., 1970-72; teaching and rsch. asst. nuclear engring. U. Mo., Columbia, 1973-77; asst. prof. U. Tex., Austin, 1977-82, assoc. prof., 1982-90, prof., 1990—, dir. nuclear engring. teaching program, 1988-94, assoc. dean rsch. coll. engring.; asst. secy. for nuclear, chem. and bio. defense programs U.S. Dept. Defense, Washington, 2001—. Named Young Engr. of Yr., Travis chpt. Tex. Soc. Profl. Engring., 1982, Engr. of Yr., 1990, Tex. Engr. of Yr., 1992. Mem. ASME (Edwin F. Church award 1988, Gustus L. Larson Meml. award 1990). Achievements include research in thermal analysis of nuclear shipping containers, heat transfer augmentation for flow over rough surfaces, liquid metal flows through a packed bed under the influence of a transverse magnetic field, and nuclear waste disposal. Office: US Dept Defense Nuclear Chem and Bio Defense Programs 3150 Defense Pentagon Washington DC 20301-3150

KLEIN, DEBORAH RAE, health facility administrator; b. Detroit, Mar. 29, 1951; d. Chester Anthony and E. Jacquelyn (Hollenbeck) Simpson; m. Robert Joseph Klein, Apr. 15, 1977; 1 child, Jeffrey. BS in Nursing, Mich. State U., 1974; MS in Health Adminstrn., U. Houston, 1984. Grad. nurse St. Mary's Hosp., Livonia, Mich., 1974; RN U.S. Army, Ft. Polk, La., 1974-78; DON Byrd Meml. Hosp., Leesville, La., 1978-79, Alvin (Tex.) Cmty. Hosp., 1979-83; adminstrn. resident Katy (Tex.) Med. Ctr., 1983-84, DON, 1984-85, COO, DON, 1985-90; v.p. Doctors' Hosp., Tulsa, 1990-97; dir. ops. improvement Okla. divsn. Columbia HCA, 1997-98; v.p., COO SouthCrest Hosp., Tulsa, Okla., 1998—2001; chief nursing officer Vaughn Regional Med. Ctr., Selma, Ala., 2002—03; dir. Tulsa Regional Med. Ctr., Tulsa, Okla., 2000—01; v.p. clin. integration Hillcrest HealthCare Sys., Tulsa, 2000—01. Cons. in field; diplomat Am. Coll. Healthcare Execs.; adj. faculty Bartlesville Wesleyan Coll., 1999-2001. Sec., treas. Sam Houston coun. Boy Scouts Am., 1984-88. Capt. U.S. Army, 1972-78. Republican. Roman Catholic. Avocation: reading. Home: 107 Al Jo Curve Selma AL 36701-6502

KLEIN, DONALD CHARLES, psychologist; b. Worcester, Mass., Aug. 10, 1923; s. Abraham Albert and Anne (Shapero) K.; m. Lola Perl, Mar. 31, 1946; children: Stefan, Jonathan, Alan, Jeremy. AB, Roosevelt U., Chgo., 1947; PhD, U. Calif., Berkeley, 1952. Cert. psychologist, Md. Sr. psychologist Berkeley (Calif.) State Mental Hygiene Clinic, 1950-53; exec. dir. Human Rels. Svc., Wellesley, Mass., 1953-63; dir. Human Rels. Ctr. Boston U., 1963-67, assoc. prof. dept. psychology, 1963-67; program dir. NTL Inst. for Applied Behavioral Sci., Washington, 1967-72; adj. prof. Johns Hopkins U. Evening Coll., Balt., 1972-81; core faculty mem. The Union Inst. and U., Cin., 1981—. Tng. cons. The Race Inst., Washington, 1970. Author: Community Dynamics and Mental Health, 1968, (with M. Broom) Power: The Infinite Game; editor: Psychology of the Planned Community, 1978, Community Research, 1985, New Vision, New Reality, 2001. Bd. mem. NTL Inst. Applied Behavioral Sci., Washington, 1960, Black Family Life Ctr., Columbia, Md., 1975. With U.S. Army, 1943-46. Fellow Am. Psychol. Assn. (disting. practice award div. community psychology 1987), Am. Pub. Health Assn., Am. Orthopsychiat. Assn., OD Network. Office: Union Inst and U 440 E Mcmillan St Cincinnati OH 45206-1925 Home: 4730 Sheppard Ln Ellicott City MD 21042-1441 E-mail: dklein@tui.edu.

KLEIN, DONALD FRANKLIN, psychiatrist, scientist, educator; b. N.Y.C., Sept. 4, 1928; s. Jesse and Rose K.; m. Rachel Gittelman, Dec. 29, 1968; children: Beth, Geri, Hilary, Michelle, Erika. BA magna cum laude, Colby Coll., Waterville, Maine, 1947; MD, SUNY, Bklyn., 1952, DSc, 1998. Rotating intern USPHS Hosp., S.I., N.Y., 1952-53; resident in psychiatry Creedmoor State Hosp., 1953-54, 56 58; dir. rsch. and evaluation, dept. psychiatry L.I. Jewish-Hillside Med. Center, 1972-76; prof. psychiatry SUNY Med. Sch., Stony Brook, 1972-76; dir. rsch. and therapeutics N.Y. State Psychiat. Inst., N.Y.C., 1976—; attending psychiatrist N.Y. Presbyn. Hosp., N.Y.C., 1977—; prof. psychiatry Columbia U. Coll. Physicians and Surgeons, N.Y.C., 1978—. Chmn. clin. psychopharmacology study sect. NIMH, 1973-75; sr. sci. advisor Alcohol Drug Abuse Mental Health Adminstrn., 1989-91; cons. Nat. Inst. Drug Abuse, 1991—, Nat. Inst. Alcoholism and Alcohol Abuse, 1996—. Co-author: Diagnosis and Drug Treatment of Psychiatric Disorders: Adults and Children, 2d edit., 1980, Mind, Mood and Medicine, 1981, Understanding Depression, 1993; co-editor: Critical Issues in Psychiatric Diagnosis, 1978, Anxiety: New Research and Changing Concepts, 1980; contbr. articles to med. jours. Sr. asst. surgeon USPHS, 1954-56. Recipient A.E. Bennett Neuropsychiat. Rsch. award, 1964, Nat. Assn. Pvt. Psychiat. Hosp. Rsch. award, 1965, 1971, Samuel W. Hamilton award, APPA, 1980, William R. McAlpin award for rsch. in achievement, NAMH, 1988, Found.'s Fund prize for rsch. in psychiatry, Am. Psychiat. Assn., 1988, Gold medal, Soc. Biol. Psychiatry, 1990, Heinz Lehmann award, N.Y. State Office of Mental Health, 1991, Thomas W. Salmon award for disting. svc. in psychiatry, N.Y. Acad. Medicine, 1993, Lifetime Achievement award, Soc. Biol. Psychiatry, 1996, Exemplary Psychiatrist award, Nat. Alliance for the Mentally Ill, 1997, Castillo del Pino prize for achievement in psychiatry, 1999. Fellow Psychiat. Rsch. Soc., Am. Psychopathol. Assn. (past pres., Hamilton award 1980), Am. Coll. Neuropsychopharmacology (life, past pres., Paul Hoch award 1991), Royal Coll. Psychiatry (founding); mem. Am. Soc.

Clin. Psychopharmacology (pres. 1993-97, v.p. 1997—), Phi Beta Kappa. Home: 1016 5th Ave Apt 14D New York NY 10028-0132 Office: NY State Psychiat Inst 1051 Riverside Dr New York NY 10032-1013 also: 182 E 79th St Ste E New York NY 10021-0422 E-mail: donaldk737@aol.com., dfk2@columbia.edu.

KLEIN, DONALD LOUIS, retired air transportation executive; s. Richard Louis and Bertha Martha Klein, William and Thelma Hardy Bell; children: Clare Joslin, Karol Dickerson. Asst. v.p. sales Pacific Airlines, San Francisco, 1957—63; dir. transp. LA Helicopters Airlines, 1963—68; dir. customer svc. SFO Helicopter Airlines, San Francisco, 1967—68; pres. Pacific Airlines, San Francisco, 1969—74, ret., 1974. Composer: (march and song) San Diego's Calling Me, 1998; author: (novels) Cradle in the Sky, 2002. 1st lt. U.S. Army, 1951—53. Mem.: Am. Legion - Post 201 (judge adv., fin. mgr. 1997—99). Home: 311 Mill Dam Rd New Bern NC 28560 Personal E-mail: dklein@lpmonline.net.

KLEIN, EDWARD JOEL, editor, author, lecturer; b. Yonkers, N.Y., Oct. 19, 1936; s. Meyer I. and Gertrude (Axelrod) K.; m. Emiko Oshikiri, June 25, 1963 (div. 1975); children: Karen, Alec; m. Tessa Namuth, Mar. 20, 1978 (div. 1981); m. Dolores Jones Barrett, Oct. 24, 1987. BS, Columbia U., 1960, MS, 1961. Copy boy, feature writer N.Y. Daily News, N.Y.C., 1957-60; reporter World Telegram & Sun, N.Y.C., 1960-61; reporter, editor Japan Times, Toyko, 1961-63; fgn. corr. UPI, Tokyo, 1963-64; editor The Shipping and Trade News, Toyko, 1964-65; assoc. editor Newsweek Mag., N.Y.C., 1965-69, fgn. editor, 1969-76, asst. mng. editor, 1976-77; editor N.Y. Times Mag., N.Y.C., 1977-87; contbg. editor Vanity Fair, N.Y.C., 1988—, Parade, N.Y.C., 1991—; columnist Walter Scott's Personality Parade, 1991—. Author: (with Robert Littell and Richard Chesnoff) If Israel Lost the War, 1969, The Parachutists, 1981, All Too Human: The Love Story of Jack and Jackie Kennedy, 1996, Just Jackie: Her Private Years, 1998, The Kennedy Curse: Why Tragedy Has Haunted America's First Family for 150 Years, 2003; editor: (with Don Erickson) About Men. Mem. Coun. on Fgn. Rels., PEN Am. Ctr., Am. Motorcyclist Assn., The Oversease Press Club N.Y. E-mail: meiji@aol.com.

KLEIN, ELEANOR (MARY KLEIN), retired clinical social worker; b. Luzon, Philippines, Dec. 13, 1919; came to U.S., 1921; (parents Am. citizens); d. Roy Edgar and Edith Lillian Hay; m. Edward George Klein, June 24, 1955. BA, Pacific Union Coll., 1946; MSW, U. So. Calif., 1953. Lic. clin. social worker. Social worker White Meml. Hosp., Los Angeles, 1948-56; clin. social worker UCLA Hosp. Clinics, 1956-65, supr. social worker, 1965-67, assoc. dir., 1967-73, dir., 1973-82. Bd. dirs., treas. Los Amigos de la Humanidad, U. So. Calif. Sch. Social Work; hon. life mem. bd. dirs. Calif. div. Am. Cancer Soc., mem. vol. bd. Calif. div., 1964—, del. nat. dir., 1982-84, chmn. residential crusade for Orange County (Calif.) unit, 1985-86; bd. dirs. Vol. Exchange, 1988-97, sec., 1991-96, v.p., 1996-97; v.p. Dem. Club West Orange County, 1996-98, 2003, pres., 1998-99, sec., 1999-2002. Recipient Disting. Alumni award Los Amigos de la Humanidad, 1984, Outstanding Performance award UCLA Hosp., 1968, various service awards Am. Cancer Soc., 1972-88. Fellow Soc. Clin. Social Work; mem. APHA, NASW (charter), Soc. Social Work Leadership in Health Care (formerly Soc. Hosp. Social Work Dirs.) (nat. pres. 1981, bd. dirs. 1978-82, life mem. local chpt.), Assn. Oncology Social Work (charter). Democrat. Avocations: travel, gardening. Home: 1661 Texas Cir Costa Mesa CA 92626-2238

KLEIN, GABRIELLA SONJA, retired communications executive; b. Chgo., Apr. 11, 1938; d. Frank E. Vosicky and Sonja (Kosner) Becvar; m. Donald J. Klein. BA in Comm. and Bus. Mgmt., Alverno Coll., 1983. Editor, owner Fox Lake (Wis.) Rep., 1962-65, McFarland (Wis.) Comty. Life and Monona Cmty. Herald, 1966-69; bur. reporter Waukesha (Wis.) Daily Freeman, 1969-71; cmty. rels. staff Waukesha County Tech. Coll., Pewaukee, Wis., 1971-73; pub. rels. specialist JI Case Co., Racine, Wis., 1973-75, corp. publs. editor, 1975-80; v.p., bd. dirs. publs. Image Mgmt. Valley View Ctr., Milw., 1980-82; pres. Comm. Concepts Unltd., Racine, 1983-98; ret., 1998. Past pres. Big Bros./Big Sisters Racine County; past v.p. devel. Girl Scouts Racine County, bd. dirs.; steering com. Racine Cmty. Coalition for Youth; bd. dirs., 2d v.p. Homeward Bound; bd. dirs., v.p. mktg. Racine Cmty. Found. Recipient awards Wis. Press Assn., Nat Fedn. Press Women; named Wis. Woman Entrepreneur of Yr., 1985, Vol. of Yr. Racine Area United Way, 1994, Woman of Distinction Bus., Racine YWCA, 1995, Silver medal Ad Club Racine, 1998, Edn. Cmty. Leader of Yr., Racine Area Mfrs. and Commerce, 2000, Thanks Badge Girl Scouts of Racine County, 2000, Outstanding Alumna award Alverno Coll., 1999. Silver medal, Ad Club of Racine, 1998 Home: 3045 Chatham St Racine WI 53402-4001

KLEIN, GARNER FRANKLIN, cardiologist, internist; b. San Pedro, Calif., June 21, 1933; s. John William and Anna Louise K.; m. Nancy Shank, Aug. 19, 1985; children: Kevin Wayne, Samuel Kyle, Lisa K., Garner F. BA in Biology, North Tex. State U., 1953; MA in Anatomy, U. Tex. Med. Br., Galveston, 1956, MD, 1958. Diplomate Am. Bd. Internal Medicine. Intern U.S. Naval Hosp., Camp Pendleton, Calif., 1958—59; resident in internal medicine VA Hosp./Southwestern Med. Sch., Dallas, 1962—66; cardiologist Valley Diagnostic Clinic, Harlingen, Tex., 1966—2002, Valley Bapt. Med. Ctr., Harlingen, 1966—, chief medicine dept., 1982—84, 1992—94, 2002—, chief med. staff, 1994—96; pres. Valley Diagnostic Med. and Surg. Clinic, 1992—96; med. dir. Valley Health Plans, 2002—. Cons. in cardiology Dolly Vinsant Meml. Hosp., San Benito, Tex., 1966-2000, South Tex. Hosp., Harlingen, 1966-2000; med. dir. South Tex. Emergency Care Found., 1991—, Valley Diagnostic Clinic, 1996-99, Los Fresnos Rural Health Clinic, 1996-2000; clin. prof. medicine U. Tex. Health Sci. Ctr., San Antonio, 1999—. Mem. Wesley United Meth. Ch., Harlingen. Lt. comdr. M.C., U.S. Navy, 1958-66. Named Profl. Vol. of Yr., Tex. affiliate Am. Heart Assn., 1983. Fellow ACP, Am. Coll. Cardiology; mem. Nat. assn. EMS Physicians, Nat. Assn. Managed Care Physicians, Am. Coll. Managed Care Medicine, Tex. Soc. Internal Medicine (Ambassador Leadership award 1998), Am. Heart Assn. (pres. Tex. affil. 1980-81), Cameron-Willacy County Med. Soc. (pres. 1978), Sigma Xi, Alpha Omega Alpha. Avocations: hunting, fishing, gardening. Office: Valley Health Plans 2005 Ed Carey Dr Harlingen TX 78550 E-mail: garner.klein@valleybaptist.net.

KLEIN, GEORGE, manufacturing company executive, microcomputer system and engineering consultant; b. Budapest, Hungary, Aug. 4, 1934; came to U.S., 1950; s. Louis and Sue (Fleiner) K.; m. Marcella E. Baum, Aug. 23, 1964; children: Diane L., Elliot C., Louis H., David A. BEE, CUNY, 1964; MBA, Hofstra U., 1971. Registered profl. engr., N.Y. Gen. mgr. Alphanumerics, Inc., Lake Success, N.Y., 1967-70; founder, officer, dir. Catoptrics, Inc., New Hyde Park, N.Y., 1970-72; consulting engr. G. Klein & Assocs., New Hyde Park, 1972-77, 78-81; v.p. engring. Codata Corp., Larchmont, N.Y., 1977-78; founder, sr. v.p., CEO DCS Controls Corp., Great Neck, N.Y., 1981-86; founder, pres., dir. Landmark Systems, Inc., N.Y.C., 1986—; pres. Klein and Labiak, Inc., 1992, Dura BioMed., Inc.; founder, pres., dir. GPK Technologies Corp., New Hyde Park, N.Y., 1986—; co-founder, dir. SatQuest.com; prin. Stack, Klein and Labiak Fin. and Mgmt. Cons. Contbr. articles to profl. jours. Patentee signal measurement system, 1972, communications network, 1979, universal input/output device, 1983. Served with U.S. Army, 1957-59. Mem. IEEE, ASHRAE, Am. Energy Engrs. Avocations: weight lifting, racquetball, squash, reading. Home: 159 Robby Ln New Hyde Park NY 11040-1105

KLEIN, GERHART LEOPOLD, public relations executive; b. Phila., July 24, 1948; s. Joseph G. and Liselotte M. (Peschke) K.; m. Anne Sceia, July 19, 1976. BS cum laude, Temple U., 1970, JD, 1980. Bar: Pa. 1980, N.J. 1980, U.S. Dist. Ct. (ea. dist.) Pa. 1980, U.S. Dist. Ct. N.J. 1980, U.S. Ct. Appeals (3d cir.) 1982, U.S. Supreme Ct. 1985, U.S. Tax Ct. 1985. News anchor WAMS, Wilmington, Del., 1967-68; news anchor, disc jockey WRCP AM & FM, Phila., 1968-70, news dir., 1970; editor, writer, reporter, news anchor WCAU (CBS) Radio, Phila., 1970-72; dir. pub. info., press sec. Pa. Dept. Pub. Welfare, Harrisburg, 1972-73; freelance journalist Phila., 1973-75; asst. editor Focus Mag., Phila., 1974-75; editor, writer, reporter, news anchor KYW Newsradio, Phila., 1975-77; atty. Montgomery, McCracken, Walker & Rhoads, Phila., 1980-85; v.p., gen. mgr. to exec. v.p. Anne Klein & Assocs., Inc., Marlton, NJ, 1985—. Mem. Environ. Commn., Mt. Laurel Twp., N.J., 1988-92; mem. water quality com. Old Taunton Colony Club, 1995—. Recipient Phila. Trial Lawyers Assn. Barrister award, 1980. Mem. Pub. Rels. Soc. Am. (chmn. task force on ethics bd. confidentiality 1991-92, mem. body of knowledge bd. 1994-98, author PR Law Sect. of Accreditation Handbook 1990, Phila. chpt. Pepperpot awards, Presdl. citation 1991, 92), Pub. Rels. Soc. Am. Counselors Acad. (chmn. tech. com.), Pub. Rels. Profls. So. N.J. (treas. 1990-92), Soc. Profl. Journalists, Broadcast Pioneers, Pinnacle Worldwide (treas. 1994-96, pres.-elect 1996-98, pres. 1998-2000, chmn. 2000-02, chmn. emeritus 2002-). Office: Anne Klein & Assocs Inc 10 Lake Ctr Ste 108 Marlton NJ 08053-3215

KLEIN, GLORIA, artist, retired educator; b. Bklyn., Sept. 12, 1936; d. Nathan and Mary Klein. BA, Bklyn. Coll.; MA, Hunter Coll., 2002. Tchr. N.Y.C. Bd. Edn., 1963-98. Painter acrylic on canvas. Democrat. Jewish. Avocations: reading, walking, computer games, movies. Home: 16 Monroe St Apt 4A New York NY 10002-7604

KLEIN, GLORIA RITTERBAND, social worker; b. N.Y.C. d. Max and Sara (Abelson) Ritterband; m. Morton Klein; children: Lisa, Melanie. MSW, Adelphi U., 1976. Lic. clin. social worker, sch. social worker; cert. social worker Acad. Cert. Social Workers. Social worker St. Mary's Hosp., Hoboken, N.J., 1976-85; supr. family therapy, psychiat. social worker St. Joseph's Hosp., Paterson, NJ, 1985—2001; clin. project assoc. Ackerman Inst. for Family Therapy, N.Y.C., 1993—; pvt. practice, 2002—. Mem. Nat. Assn. Social Workers.

KLEIN, HARVEY, physician, educator; b. N.Y.C., Aug. 29, 1937; s. Emanuel and Rose (Sanderman) K.; m. Phyllis Levine, Sept. 22, 1963; children: Laura, Daniel. SB, U. Chgo., 1959; MD, Harvard U., 1963. Diplomate Am. Bd. Internal Medicine. Intern N.Y.-Cornell, N.Y.C., 1963-64, asst. resident, 1964-65, sr. resident, 1967-68, chief resident, 1968-69, fellow in medicine, 1969-70; asst. prof. medicine Cornell U. Med. Coll., N.Y.C., 1970-75, assoc. prof., 1975-88, William S. Paley prof. clin. medicine, 1992—. Capt. USAF, 1965-67. Office: Cornell U Med Coll 525 E 68th St New York NY 10021-4870

KLEIN, HEINZ KARL, information systems researcher; b. Germany, Nov. 25, 1939; arrived in U.S., 1984; s. Karl K. and Waltraud Franzl; m. Nora E., 1972 (div. 1986); children: Charlotte, Thomas, Ellen; m. Linda F., 2002. Dipl.-Kfm., U. Munich, Germany, 1965, Dr.rer.publ., 1969; Dr.h.c., Oulu U., Finland, 1998. Rsch. assoc. Econ. Rsch. Inst., Munich, Germany, 1965-66, faculty asst. U. Regensburg, Germany, 1967-69; asst. rschr. U. Mannheim, Germany, 1969-70, rsch. assoc., 1970-77; asst. prof. mgmt. sci. McMaster U., Hamilton, Ont., Can., 1978-83; assoc. prof. SUNY, Binghamtom, 1984-2000, Temple U., Phila., 2001—. Vis. assoc. prof. SUNY, Buffalo, 1972-73, McMaster U., 1973-74. Author: Heuristic Decision Models, 1971, Business Logistics Systems, 1973, Information Systems Development for Human Progress, 1989, Information Systems Research: Contemporary Approaches and Emergent Traditions, 1991, Information Systems Development and Data Modeling: Conceptual and Philosophical Foundations, 1995, Signs of Work, Semiosis and Information Processing Organisations, 1996; contbr. articles to scholarly jours. (MISQ Best Paper award 1999). Vis. scholar, London Sch. Econs., 1982, U. Jyäskylä, 1985, 1989, U. Aalborg, 1990, Auckland U., 1994, U. Pretoria, 1995, 2002. Avocations: sailing, skiing, tennis, travel. E-mail: hkklein@temple.edu.

KLEIN, HENRY, architect; b. Cham, Germany, Sept. 6, 1920; came to U.S., 1939; s. Fred and Hedwig (Weiskopf) K.; m. Phyllis Harvey, Dec. 27, 1952; children: Vincent, Paul, David. Student, Inst. Rauch, Lausanne, Switzerland, 1936-38; BArch, Cornell U., 1943. Registered architect, Oreg., Wash. Designer Office of Pietro Belluschi, Architect, Portland, Oreg., 1948-51; architect Henry Klein & Assoc., Architects, Mt. Vernon, Wash., 1952—78; pvt. practice architect Henry Klein Partnership, 1978—. Bd. dirs. Wash. Pks. Found., Seattle, 1977-92, Mus. N.W. Art, 1988-95. With U.S. Army, 1943-46. Recipient Louis Sullivan award Internat. Union Bricklayers and Allied Craftsmen, 1981; Presdl. Design award Nat. Endowment Arts, 1988; George A. and Eliza Howard Found. fellow. Fellow AIA (Seattle chpt. medal 1995). Jewish. Home: 21625 Little Mountain Rd Mount Vernon WA 98274-8003 Office: Henry Klein Partnership 314 Pine St Mount Vernon WA 98273-3852

KLEIN, HERBERT GEORGE, newspaper editor; b. L.A., Apr. 1, 1918; s. George and Amy (Cordes) K.; m. Marjorie Galbraith, Nov. 1, 1941; children: Joanne L. (Mrs. Robert Mayne), Patricia A. (Mrs. John Root). AB, U. So. Calif., 1940; Hon. Doctorate, U. San Diego, 1989. Reporter Alhambra (Calif.) Post-Advocate, 1940-42, news editor, 1946-50; spl. corr. Copley Newspapers, 1946-50, Washington corr., 1950; with San Diego Union, 1950-68, editl. writer, 1950-52, editl. page editor, 1952-56, assoc. editor, 1956-57, exec. editor, 1957-58, editor, 1959-68; mgr. communications Nixon for Pres. Campaign, 1968-69; dir. comm. Exec. Br., U.S. Govt., 1969-73; v.p. corp. rels. Metromedia, Inc., 1973-77; media cons., 1977-80; editor-in-chief, v.p. Copley Newspapers, Inc., San Diego, 1980—2003, cons., 2003—. Publicity dir. Eisenhower-Nixon campaign in Calif., 1952; asst. press. sec. V.P. Nixon campaign, 1956; press sec. Nixon campaign, 1958; spl. asst., press sec. to Nixon, 1959-61; press sec. Nixon Gov. campaign, 1962; dir. comm. Nixon presdl. campaign, 1968; mem. Advt. Coun., N.Y. Author: Making It Perfectly Clear, 1980. Trustee U. So. Calif.; past chmn. Holiday Bowl; bd. dirs. Greater San Diego Internat. Sports Coun.; mem. com. Super Bowls XXII, XXIII, and XXXVII; chair internat. com. Scripps Health and Sci. Found.; active Olympic Tng. Site Com.; trustee U. So. Calif.; trustee U. Calif. San Diego Found; bd. dirs. San Diego Econ. Devel. Com. With USNR, 1942-46; comdr. Res. Recipient Fourth Estate award U. So. Calif., 1947, Alumnus of Yr. award U. So. Calif., 1971, Gen. Alumni Merit award, 1977, Spl. Svc. to Journalism award, 1969, Headliner of Yr. award L.A. Press Club, 1971, San Diego State U. First Fourth Estate award, 1986, Golden Man award Boys and Girls Club, 1994, Newspaper Exec. of Yr. award Calif. Press Assn., 1994; named Community Champion, Hall of Champions, 1993, Mr. San Diego, 2001. Mem. Am. Soc. Newspaper Editors (past dir.), Calif. Press Assn., Pub. Rels. Seminar, Gen. Alumni U. So. Calif. (past pres.), Alhambra Jr. C. of C. (past pres.), Greater San Diego C. of C. (mem. exec. com.), Bohemian Club, Fairbanks Country Club, Kiwanis, Rotary (hon.), Sigma Delta Chi (chmn. nat. com., chmn. gen. activities nat. conv. 1958), Scripps Inst. (chair internat com.), Delta Chi. Presbyterian. Home: 5110 Saddlery Sq PO Box 8935 Rancho Santa Fe CA 92067-8935 Office: Copley Press Inc 350 Camino De La Reina San Diego CA 92108-3003 *As I look back on a lifetime in journalism and politics, the thesis which has most effected my career has been a desire to be a thoughtful "man in the arena". To leave a legacy, you cannot be bland. I believe one must develop a philosophy endowed with principle which allows him to take a stand, popular or not, on issues in which he or she believes.*

KLEIN, HOWARD BRUCE, lawyer, law educator; b. Pitts., Pa, Feb. 28, 1950; s. Elmer and Natalie (Rosenzweig) K.; m. Lonnie Jean Wilets, Dec. 12, 1977; children: Zachary B., Eli H. Student, Northwestern U., 1968-69; BA, U. Wis., 1972; JD, Georgetown U., 1976. Bar: Wis. 1976, Pa. 1981, U.S. Ct. Appeals D.C., 1978, U.S. Dist. Ct. Pa. 1981, U.S. Ct. Appeals (3rd cir.) 1982, U.S. Supreme Ct. 1983. Law clk. to justice Robert Hansen Wis. Supreme Ct., Madison, 1976-77; asst. atty. gen. dept. justice State of Wis., 1977-80; chief criminal divsn. U.S. Atty.'s Office, Phila., 1980-87; ptnr. Blank, Rome & McCauley, Phila., 1987-96, chmn. litigation dept., 1991-94; prin. Law Offices of Howard Bruce Klein, Phila., 1996—; dir. in house tng. Am. Law Inst.-ABA, 1996—. Regional, nat. instr. Nat. Inst. Trial Advocacy, Phila. and Boulder, Colo., 1987-98; adj. prof. evidence and trial advocacy Temple U. Law Sch., 1984—; instr. Atty. Gen. Advocacy Inst., Washington, 1983-87; lectr. pub. corruption and trial advocacy; cons. Pa. Valley Neighborhood Assn., 1984—. Contbr. to profl. jours. Advisor Phila. Police Dept. Reform Commn., 1986—; campaign issues dir. Pa. Atty. Gen. campaign, Phila., 1988, 92; bd. dirs. Citizens Crime Commn. Delaware Valley, Phila. Mem. Fed. Bar Assn. (chmn. criminal law com.), Phila. Bar Assn., Wis. Bar Assn., D.C. Bar Assn., U.S. Attys. Alumni Assn. (co-founder, exec. bd.), Vesper Club (Phila.). Democrat. Jewish. Avocations: golf, basketball, hiking. Office: 1700 Market St Ste 2632 Philadelphia PA 19103-3903 E-mail: howbrklein@aol.com.

KLEIN, HUBERT, accountant; b. Englewood, N.J., Apr. 3, 1964; s. Alfred and Margaret (Wilson-Reynolds) K.; m. Marilyn Donato, May 16, 1992; children: Matthew C., Allison M. AS in Computer Sys. Mgmt., Johnton & Wales Coll., 1984, BS in Acctg., 1986. CPA, N.J.; cert. valuation analyst; diplomate Am. Bd. Forensic Accts. CPA Tobin & Collins CPA's, River Edge, N.J., 1986-89, Burton, CiErie, Delfordi, Montclair, N.J., 1989-92; ptnr. Marchionda & Ferrer PA, Clifton, N.J., 1992—. Trustee Bergen Pines Hosp. Found., Paramus, N.J., 1993-98; pres. New Milford (N.J.) Rep. Club, 1994-98; dep. chmn. Rep. County Com., New Milford, 1996-98. Mem. AICPA, N.J. Soc. CPA's, Assn. Cert. Fraud Examiners (cert. fraud examiner), Nat. Assn. CVA's. Republican. Roman Catholic. Avocations: scuba diving, fishing, hunting. Office: Marchionda & Ferrer PA 66 Mount Prospect Ave Clifton NJ 07013-1987

KLEIN, IRWIN GRANT, lawyer; b. Bklyn., June 6, 1949; s. Melvin Morton and Gladys (Mandel) K.; m. Charlene Elena Perez, July 31, 1988; children: Robert Matthew Perez, Gabriella Margaux Perez. BS, U. Wis., 1971; JD, Vt. Law Sch., 1977. Bar: N.Y., 1977, U.S. Dist. Ct. (so. & ea. dist.) N.Y., 1977, Vt., 1977, U.S. Supreme Ct., 1988. Assoc. atty. Hein, Waters, Klein & Zurkow, Far Rockaway, N.Y., 1977-78; asst. dist. atty. Queens County Dist. Atty., Kew Gardens, N.Y., 1979-82; ptnr. Hein, Waters & Klein, Cedarhurst, NY, 1982—89, Lapp & Klein, Cedarhurst, 1989-91, Hein, Waters & Klein, Cedarhurst, 1991—. Mem. Vt. Law Rev., N.Y. State Defenders Assn., N.Y. State Bar Assn., Nassau County Bar Assn., Queens County Bar Assn., Phi Delta Phi. Office: Hein Waters & Klein 123 Grove Ave Cedarhurst NY 11516-2302 E-mail: igkny@earthlink.net.

KLEIN, JAMES MIKEL, music educator, associate dean; b. Greenville, S.C., Aug. 27, 1953; s. Rubin Harry Klein and Billie (Mikel) Newton. BM, U. Tex., 1975, MM, 1977; MusD, U. Cincinnati, 1981. Prin. trombone player Austin (Tex.) Symphony Orch., 1973-77; conducting asst. U. Tex., Austin, 1975-77, U. Cin., 1977-78; dir. instrumental music Valparaiso (Ind.) U., 1978-84; prof. music Calif. State U. Stanislaus, Turlock, 1984-99; spkr. of faculty Calif. State U., Turlock, 1997-98, assoc. dean Coll. Arts, Letters, Scis., 1999—2003, dir. Sch. Fine and Performing Arts Coll. Arts, Letters, Scis., 1999—, exec. asst. to pres. Coll. Arts, Letters, Scis., 2002—03, dean Coll. Arts, Letters, Scis., 2003—. Mem. faculty Nat. Luth. Music Camp, Lincoln, Nebr., 1985-86, 95-97; guest conductor, clinician, adjudicator various states, internationally, 1978—; trombone player Modesto (Calif.) Symphony Orch., 1984—; conductor Stanislaus Youth Symphony, Modesto, 1985; music dir. Modesto Symphony Youth Orch., 1986-2002; site adminstr. Nat. Honors Orch., Anaheim, Calif., 1986, Indpls., 1988, Cin., 1992, asst. condr., Kansas City, 1996, Phoenix, 1998; faculty, coord. instrumental music Calif. State Summer Sch. of Arts, 1987-88. Pres. Turlock Arts Fund for Youth, 1986-88; mem. internat. Friendship Com., subcom., City of Modesto, 1990-92; vol. Big Bros. Am. Recipient Meritorious Prof. award Calif. State U., Stanislaus, 1988, Outstanding Young Man of Am. award, 1990, Orch. Dir. of Yr. award, Calif., 1994, Outstanding Arts Educator award, Stanislaus County, Calif., 2000. Mem. Music Educators Nat. Assn., Nat. Sch. Orch. Assn. (pub. rels. chair 1994-96), Am. Fedn. Musicians (local 1), Condrs. Guild, Am. Symphony Orch. League, Calif. Orch. Dir.'s Assn. (pres.-elect 1988-90, pres. 1990-92, Orch. Dir. of the Year, 1994). Avocations: sailing, racquetball, reading, skiing. Home: 565 N Daubenberger Rd Turlock CA 95380-9144 Office: Calif State U Coll of ALS 801 W Monte Vista Ave Turlock CA 95382-0256 Business E-Mail: jklein@stan.csustan.edu.

KLEIN, JASON EVAN, magazine publishing executive; b. N.Y.C., May 11, 1960; s. William Louis and Bernice Carol (Tick) K.; m. Robin Fern Nash, July 23, 1989; children: Michael Louis, Jill Lauren. AB, Dartmouth Coll., 1982; MBA, Harvard U., 1986. Assoc. cons. Bain & Co., Palo Alto, Calif., 1982-84; sr. engagement mgr. McKinsey & Co., N.Y.C., 1986-93; dir. strategy Times Mirror, N.Y.C., 1993-95; pres., group pub. Field & Stream/Outdoor Life and Today's Homeowner, N.Y.C., 1995—99; pres., CEO, Times Mirror Mags., N.Y.C., 1999—2001, Healthy Living Media, N.Y.C., 2001—03, Newspaper Nat. Network, N.Y.C., 2003—. Bd. dirs. Mag. Pub. of Am. Trustee N.Y.C. Police Found.; mem. Recreation Roundtable. Mem. Am. Sportfishing Gov. Affairs, Phi Beta Kappa. Office: Newspaper Nat Network 20 W 33d St 7th Fl New York NY 10001 E-mail: jklein@mba1986.hbs.edu.

KLEIN, JEFFREY HOWARD, oncologist, internist; b. Cleve., Jan. 24, 1943; s. Joseph Bart and Tillie Alice Klein; m. Nancy Klein, June 5, 1971; 1 child, Bart Edward. Student, Brown U., 1961-64; BS in Medicine, Northwestern U., 1966, MD, 1968. Diplomate Am. Bd. Internal Medicine, Am. Bd. Med. Oncology, Am. Bd. Hospice & Palliative Medicine. Intern Cleve. Met. Gen. Hosp., 1968-69, resident, 1969-70, Rush-Presbyn. St. Luke's Med. Ctr., Chgo., 1970-71, Am. Cancer Soc. clin. fellow, 1971-72; pvt. practice internist, oncologist Lombard Med. Group, Thousand Oaks, Calif., 1974-2000; chief of medicine Los Robles Regional Med. Ctr., Thousand Oaks, 1976-77, chief of staff, 1979-81; med. dir. hospice San Fernando office Vitas Healthcare Corp., 2000—. Trustee Columbia/Los Robles Med. Ctr., Thousand Oaks, 1995-98. Maj. USAF, 1972-74. Mem. Am. Soc. Clin. Oncology, So. Calif. Acad. Clin. Oncology (charter), Am. Acad. of Hospice and Palliative Medicine, Phi Beta Kappa, Pi Kappa Epsilon, Alpha Omega Alpha. Avocations: philosophy, tennis, skiing, music. E-mail: jeffrey.klein@vitas.com.

KLEIN, JEFFREY PETER, investor; b. NYC, June 29, 1943; s. Seymour M. and Ruth (Liberman) Klein. BA, Colgate U., 1965; MBA, Columbia U., 1967. Exec. Mr. Ephram, Inc., N.Y.C., 1967—69; account exec. Thomson-Leeds Co., 1969—79; officer M.K.B. Group, Inc., N.Y.C., 1979—2000. Trustee, com. chmn. Collegiate Sch., N.Y.C., 1976—85, 1991—98, pres. bd. trustees, 1994—98; bd. dirs., com. chmn. 92d St. YMHA, 1980—; chmn. bd. dirs. NY Chamber Symphony, 1993—2002; pres. Bertha & Isaac Liberman Found., 1983—. Mem.: Mus. Modern Art, Conservation Com., Contemporary Arts Coun., Arch. and Design Com., Colgate Club (N.Y.C.), Harmonie Club (bd. dirs. 2002—), Sunningdale Country Club (Scarsdale, N.Y.) (bd. dirs. 1980—85). Avocations: golf, photography, travel, reading. Home: 480 Park Ave New York NY 10022-1613 Office: 200 Park Ave S Ste 1018 New York NY 10003-1503 E-mail: jpk480@aol.com.

KLEIN, JEFFREY S. lawyer, media executive; b. Los Angeles, Apr. 15, 1953; s. Norman and Shirlee Klein; m. Karyn Kitson, Sept. 29, 1984; 3 children. BA suma cum laude, Claremont Mens Coll., 1975; M in Journalism, Columbia U., 1978; JD, Stanford U., 1980. Assoc. Kaplan, Livingston, Goodwin, Berkowitz & Selvin, Beverly Hills, Calif., 1980-81, Garey, Mason & Sloane, Santa Monica, Calif., 1981-83; weekly contbr. UPI-Radio, L.A., 1983-84; sr. staff counsel Times Mirror, 1983-87, asst. to pres., 1987-90; asst. to pub. L.A. Times, 1989-91; pres. L.A. Times Valley and Ventura County edits., 1991-96; v.p. L.A. Times, 1991-96, sr. v.p. consumer mktg., 1996-97, sr. v.p., gen. mgr. news, 1997-98; pres. COO 101 Comms. LLC, 1999—2001, CEO, 2002—. Pres., CEO Calif. Cmty. News Corp., 1995-97; adj. prof. journalism U. So. Calif., 1985-87, 2002; adv. Gov. Bruce Babbitt, Phoenix, 1980. Author weekly column Legal View, L.A. Times, 1985-93, various book revs., contrb. Online Journalism Review 1999, Columbia Journalism Rev., 2000. Bd. dirs. Meet Each Need With Dignity, Gould Ctr. for Humanities, Claremont McKenna Coll. Recipient Angel award Vol. League of San Fernando Valley, Disting. Cmty. Svc. award Anti-Defamation League, 1994, Visionary award United Way North Angeles Region, 1995, Premiere Parents award March of Dimes, 1996. Mem. Calif. Bar Assn. Office: 101 Comm 9121 Oakdale Ave Ste 101 Chatsworth CA 91311-6517

KLEIN, JERRY EMANUEL, insurance and financial planning executive; b. Cin., Apr. 4, 1933; s. Milton H. and Ida S. (Dunsker) K.; m. Arlene Ruth Rosen, July 3, 1957 (dec. Nov. 1974); children: Marjorie, Bradley, Amy; m. Nancy Cohen Hahn, Aug. 7, 1982. BMech. Engring., Cornell U., 1956; MBA, Ohio State U., 1959. CLU, ChFC. Fin. engring. Avco Electronics, Cin., 1959-61; fin. rep. Northwestern Mut. of Milw., Cin., 1961—. Vice chmn. Am. Jewish Com., 1978; pres. Social Health Assn., 1964-66, Jewish Vocat. Svc., 1978-80, Cancer Family Care, 1981-83, chmn. fin. com. Jewish Fedn., 1981-83, treas., mem. exec. com., 1981-84; bd. dirs. Children Psychiat. Ctr., 1973-86, Jewish Family Svc., 1984-94, Jewish Vocat. Svc., 1964-92, Cin. Jewish Fedn., 1972-92, Halom House, 1992, treas., 1998—; chmn. HILB Scholarship Com., 1985—; bd. dirs. Radio Reading Svc., 1997; bd. dirs. Cin. Assn. Blind, 1999—. 1st lt. USAF, 1956-58. Recipient Kate S. Mack award Jewish Fedn., 1975, Human Rels. award NCCJ, 1992. Mem. Million Dollar Round Table (life), Nat. Assn. Life Underwriters, Estate Planning Coun. Cin., Assn. CLUs. Jewish. Office: Northwestern Mut Fin Network Rookwood Tower 2d Fl 3805 Edwards Rd Cincinnati OH 45209

KLEIN, JERRY LEE, SR., religion educator, minister; b. Walters, Okla., Oct. 25, 1947; s. Rudolf Anton and Mable Eula (Elliott) K.; m. Jane Ellen Keeth, Apr. 20, 1969; children: Jerry, Jr., John AA, Cameron U., 1967; BA, Okla. Christian Univ. of Sci. and Arts, 1969; MA, Harding U., 1974; postgrad., N.Y. Inst., 1988-91, Tex. Tech U., 1994. Instr. Bible, Henderson State Coll., Arkadelphia, Ark., 1970-71; pulpit min. Ch. of Christ, Comanche, Okla.,

1971-75; instr. Greek Prairie Hill Sch. of Bible, Comanche, 1974-75; pulpit minister Main St. Ch. of Christ, Lockney, Tex., 1975-82; prof. religion Amarillo (Tex.) Coll., 1982-95, instr. part-time, 1995—; dir. Amarillo Bible Chair, 1982-94; min. Comanche Trail Ch. of Christ, Amarillo, 1995—; tchr. Bible, Caprock H.S., Amarillo, 1995—96, 2001—02. Edn. dir. Mountain Terrace Ch. of Christ, Memphis, Tenn., 1969-70, San Jacinto Ch. of Christ, Amarillo, 1984-89; campus coun. Amarillo Coll., 1982-94, chaplain, 1990-91; steering com. Amazing Grace Campaign, Amarillo, 1990. Author: Training Leaders for Christ I, 1998, Training Leaders for Christ II, 1998, True Worship, 1989, (children's songs) Bible Teachers Mailbox, 1988; contbr. articles to religious jours. Dir. vols. Ark. Children's Colony, Arkadelphia, 1970-71; bd. dirs. VICA, Tascosa H.S., 1983-94; city chmn. Heart Fund and Kidney Found., Comanche, 1974-75; cubmaster Boy Scouts Am., Lockney, 1978-82; coach Little League Baseball, Lockney, 1978-82; mem. child welfare bd., Floyd County, Tex., 1980-82; bd. dirs. Samaritan Pastoral Counseling Ctr., 1998-99. Recipient spl. citation Ark. Children's Colony, 1971, certs. appreciation Tex. Dept. Health, 1982, Tex. Dept. Human Resources, 1983; named Favorite Prof. Bapt. Student Union, Amarillo Coll., 1989, 93. Mem. Christian Edn. Assn., Soc. Bibl. Lit., Am. Acad. Religion, Lions (pres. Comanche 1974-75), Rotary, Kappa Chi (sponsor 1982-95). Republican. Home: 5614 Purdue St Amarillo TX 79109-5823 Office: Comanche Trail Ch of Christ 2700 E 34th Ave Amarillo TX 79103-4700 E-mail: jjklein@arn.net. *Life itself can't give me joy—unless I really will it. Life just gives me time and space—it's up to me to fill it.*

KLEIN, JOHN JACOB, retired economist; b. Chgo., Aug. 30, 1929; s. John and Mathilda (Keller) K.; m. Sylvia Elvine Knauss, Nov. 25, 1953; children: Leslie Klein Funk. BA cum laude, Northwestern U., 1950; MA, U. Chgo., 1952, PhD, 1955. Asst. prof. econs. Okla. State U., Stillwater, 1957-60; assoc. prof. econs. Fordham U., N.Y.C., 1960-67; prof. econs. Ga. State U., Atlanta, 1967—94, prof. econs. emeritus, 1994—. Author: (with M. Friedman) Studies in the Quantity Theory of Money, 1956, (with Leftwich, Trenton, Poole) The Oklahoma Economy, 1963; author: Money and the Economy, 6th edit. 1986; contbr. articles to profl. jours. With U.S. Army, 1955-57. Mem. Am. Econ. Assn., So. Econ. Assn., Phi Beta Kappa, Pi Mu Epsilon. Republican. Avocation: music. Home: 855 Oakhaven Dr Roswell GA 30075-1248

KLEIN, JONATHAN D. finance company executive; Various Hambros Bank Ltd., 1983-93; co-founder Getty Investment Holdings L.L.C., 1993-95; joint chmn., co-founder Getty Commns. plc, 1995-96, CEO, dir., 1996-98; co-founder, CEO, dir. Getty Images, 1998—. Dir. Hambros Bank Ltd., 1989-98; bd. dir. Getty Investments L.L.C., A Contemporary Theatre, Realnetworks. Office: Getty Images 601 N 34th St Seattle WA 98103

KLEIN, JONATHAN DAVID, physician, researcher; s. Harvey and Tobey Klein; m. Susan Ellen Cohn; children: Daniel, Amanda. MD, UMDNJ-New Jersey Med. Sch., 1984. Bd. Cert. in Pediat. and Adolescent Medicine Am. Bd. of Pediat., 1988. Asst. prof. pediat., cmty. and preventive medicine U. of Rochester, NY, 1992—98, assoc. prof. pediat., cmty. and preventive medicine, 1998—. Mem. U.S. Preventive Svcs. Task Force, Rockville, Md., 2000—. Mem., com. on adolescence Am. Acad. of Pediat., Elk Grove Village, Ill., 1998—. Generalist Faculty Scholars award, Robert Wood Johnson Found., 1992—96. Mem.: Soc. for Adolescent Medicine. Achievements include research in Adolescent health svcs., quality, access, and prevention effectiveness. Office: Univ of Rochester 601 Elmwood Ave #690 Rochester NY 14642 Personal E-mail: jonathan_klein@urmc.rochester.edu. E-mail: jonathan_klein@urmc.rochester.edu.

KLEIN, JOSEPH MARK, retired mining company executive; b. N.Y.C., Nov. 9, 1921; s. Erwin Wolffe and Ada (Black) K.; m. Betty Evelyn Northington, Dec. 24, 1948; children: Kathryn Ann Zornes, Elizabeth Ellen Scahill, Joseph Mark, Jr., Timothy N. Certificate in fgn. trade, Am. Grad Sch. Internat. Mgmt., 1947; D Internat Laws (hon.), Am. Grad. Sch. Internat. Mgmt., 1993. Vice pres. internat. ops. Clary Corp., San Gabriel, Calif., 1948-60, dir., 1967-70; dir. internat. ops. Remington Rand Corp., N.Y.C., 1961-62; pres. NBC Internat. Ltd.; v.p. NBC News, N.Y.C., 1962-66; exec. v.p., dir. Cyprus Mines Corp., Los Angeles, 1966-79; chmn. bd. Hawaiian Cement Corp., 1969-79; ret. pres., dir. Pluess-Staufer Industries, Inc., Los Angeles, 1979-91, sr. fin. cons., bd. dirs., 1991-99. Dir. Mission Ins. Group, Inc.; mem. Pres.'s Export Expansion Council, 1971-74; Vice-chmn. bd. trustees Am. Grad. Sch. Internat. Mgmt., 1975-83, chmn. bd. trustees, 1983-88. Served pvt. to capt. U.S. Army, 1940-46. Decorated Silver Star, Bronze Star with oak leaf cluster, Purple Heart, Combat Inf. Badge, Croix de Guerre; recipient Jonas B. Mayer Outstanding Alumni award, Am. Grad. Sch. Internat. Mgmt., 1974, So. Calif. Alumni Assn. award, 1974. Mem. AIME, The Ret. Officers Assn. (pres. dir. west L.A. area chpt.), Town Hall, Mil. Order Purple Heart (comdr. Ariz. 1949-50, Hollywood chpt. 1987-88), Am. Legion (post comdr. 1990-91, trustee 1991—), Riviera Country Club, Elks. Republican. Presbyterian. Home: 1071 Villa View Dr Pacific Palisades CA 90272-3949

KLEIN, JULIA MEREDITH, freelance/self-employed journalist; b. Phila., Dec. 11, 1955; d. Abraham and Murielle (Pollack) K. BA magna cum laude, Harvard U., 1977. Copy editor J.B. Lippincott, Phila., 1977; features reporter The Oakland Press, Pontiac, Mich., 1978; freelance writer, researcher, editorial cons., 1978—; reporter, critic and editor The Phila. Inquirer, 1983-2000. Nat. Arts Journalism Program fellow, 1996-97, John J. McCloy fellow in journalism, 1998, Alicia Patterson Found. fellow, 2000, Western Knight Ctr. fellow for Specialized Journalism, 2001. Mem. Soc. Profl. Journalists (2d Pl. award for criticism 1998, 3d Pl. award for criticism 1999), Am. Soc. Journalists and Authors, N.Am. Travel Journalists Assn., Journalism and Women Symposium, Phi Beta Kappa. Home and Office: 307 Monroe St Philadelphia PA 19147-3211 E-mail: julklein@juno.com.

KLEIN, KATHRYN ANN, social worker; b. Milw., Aug. 25, 1961; d. Lawrence and Marilyn Frieda (Denney) K.; m. Frederick Pickering, Feb. 14, 1988 (div. Apr. 1992). BS in Psychology, Sociology, Carroll Coll., 1983; MSW, SUNY, Stony Brook, 1986. Lic. clin. social worker. Case mgr. YMCA Family Svcs., Bayshore, N.Y., 1986, project dir. Mastic, N.Y., 1986-88; area mgr. Cmty. Health and Counseling Svcs., Millinocket, Maine, 1988-93, therapist, 1993-94, program svcs. coord., 1994-95; pvt. practice clin. social worker East Millinocket, Maine, 1993—. Mem. adv. bd. Children's Emergency Response, Millinocket, 1992-97. Co-chair svc. provision, mem. com. Katahdin Area Response Effort for Family Violence, Millinocket, 1990—; mem. MADE-IT Team-youth substance abuse prevention, Millinocket, 1993-96; social work rep. Commn. to Evaluate Adequacy of Aid to Families with Dependent Children Need and Payment Standards, Augusta, 1990-91; bd. dirs., treas. Katahdin Friends, Inc., East Millinocket, 1990-97. Mem. NASW. Democrat. Avocations: cross country skiing, tennis, shoto kan karate (1st Dan black belt). Office: HC 69 Box 38 Medway ME 04460 E-mail: kathyk@kai.net.

KLEIN, KENNETH MICHAEL, pathologist; b. N.Y.C., Jan. 31, 1941; s. Joseph Bernard and Bess (Goldfeder) K.; m. Constance Randolph Wise, Mar. 3, 1972; children: Ariel Stran, Noah Benjamin, Liam Randolph, Anina Sarah. BA, NYU, 1961; MD cum laude, Cath. U., Leuven, 1967. Diplomate Am. Bd. Pathology. Asst. prof. pathology NYU Sch. of Medicine, 1972-76; asst. attending pathologist Bellevue Hosp. Ctr., N.Y.C., 1972-76; asst. prof. of pathology CMDNJ - N.J. Med. Sch., Newark, 1976-82, assoc. prof. pathology, 1982-88, prof. pathology and lab. medicine, 1988—; acting chmn. pathology UMDNJ - N.J. Med. Sch. and Grad. Sch., 1988-89, 92-94; pathologist Martland Coll., Univ. Hosp., Newark, 1976—, acting chief of pathology svcs., 1988-89, 92-94; chief of anatomic pathology Bergen Regional Med. Ctr., Paramus, N.J., 1997-98. Mid. Atlantic regional commr. Lab. Accreditation Program Coll. Am. Pathologists, Northfield, Ill., 2001—. Co-author: (book) Handbook of Pathology, 1987; contbr. articles to profl. jours. Trustee Norwood Pub. Libr., N.J., 1983-97, pres. 1986-91. Fellow Coll. of Am. Pathologists, mem. Hans Popper Hepatopathology Soc., AMA, AASS, Gastrointestinal Pathology Soc., N.J. Soc. Pathologists, Essex County Med. Soc., N.Y. Pathol. Soc. Avocations: reading, travel. Office: UMDNJ - NJ Med Sch Dept Path and Lab Medicine 185 S Orange Ave Newark NJ 07103-2757 E-mail: kklein@umdnj.edu.

KLEIN, LAURA, publishing executive; With Levine, Huntley, Schmidt & Beaver Advt., N.Y.C., 1985—86; nat. sales mgr. Andrew's Mag., 1986—89; acct. mgr. ELLE Mag., 1989—92; Ea. sales mgr. Woman's Day, N.Y.C., 1992—96, v.p., ad dir., 1996—2000, v.p., pub., 2002—; pub. Family Life, 2000. Office: Womans Day 1633 Broadway 42d Fl New York NY 10019

KLEIN, LAWRENCE ROBERT, economist, educator; b. Omaha, Sept. 14, 1920; s. Leo Byron and Blanche (Monheit) Klein; m. Sonia Adelson, Feb. 15, 1947; children: Hannah, Rebecca, Rachel, Jonathan. BA, U. Calif.-Berkeley, 1942; PhD, MIT, 1944; MA, Lincoln Coll., Oxford U., 1957; LLD (hon.), U. Mich., 1977, Dickinson Coll., 1981; ScD (hon.), Widener Coll., 1977, Elizabethtown Coll., 1981, Ball State U., 1982; ScD (hon.), Technion, 1981; ScD (hon.), U. Nebr., 1983; D (hon.), U. Vienna, 1977; EdD, Villanova U., 1978; D (hon.), Bonn U., 1974; D (hon.), Free U. Brussels, 1979, U. Paris, 1979, U. Madrid, 1980; DSc, Nat. Central Univ. Taiwan, 1985; DHC, So. Helsinki Sch. Econs., 1986; Dr. Humane Letters, Bard Coll., 1986, Bilkent U., 1989, St. Norbert Coll., 1989; DHC, Univ. Lodz, 1990; D. Litt, Univ. Glasgow, 1991; DSc, Rutgers Univ., 1992; PhD (hon.), Bar Ilan U., 1994; D. honors (hon.), Carleton Univ., 1997; DHC, U. Piraeus, 1999, Acad. Economic Studies, Romania, 1999. Faculty U. Chgo., 1944—47; research assoc. Nat. Bur. Econ. Research, 1948—50; faculty U. Mich., 1949—54; research assoc. Survey Research Center, 1949—54, Oxford Inst. Stats., 1954—58; faculty U. Pa., Phila., 1958—, prof., 1958—, Univ. prof., 1964—, Benjamin Franklin prof., 1968—, prof. emeritus; vis. prof. Osaka U., Japan, 1960, U. Colo., 1962, CUNY, 1962-63, 82, Hebrew U., 1964, Princeton U., 1966, Stanford U., 1968, U. Copenhagen, 1974; Ford vis. prof. U. Calif. at Berkeley, 1968, Inst. for Advanced Studies, Vienna, 1970, 74; hon. prof. Shanghai Jiao Tong Univ., 1984; honorary prof. Nankai Univ., 1993, Shanghai Acad. Soc. Sci., 1994; dir. W.P. Carey & Co., 1984—; adv. State Information Ctr., Beijing, 1992—; hon. chmn. Pa. Inst. for Econ. Rsch. Adv. Bd., 2002—. Cons. Can. Govt., 1947, UNCTAD, 1966, 75, 77, 80, McMillan Co., 1965—74, E.I. du Pont de Nemours, 1966—68, State of N.Y., 1969, AT&T, 1969, Fed. Res. Bd., 1973, UNIDO, 1973—75, Congl. Budget Office, 1977—, Coun. Econ. Advisers, 1977—80; chmn. bd. trustees Wharton Econometric Forecasting Assocs., Inc., 1969—80, chmn. profl. bd., 1980—; trustee Maurice Falk Inst. for Econ. Rsch., Israel, 1969—75; adv. coun. Inst. Advanced Studies, Vienna, 1977—; chmn. econ. adv. com. Gov. of Pa., 1976—78; mem. com. on prices Fed. Res. Bd., 1968—70; prin. investigator econometric model project Brookings Instn., 1963—72, Project LINK, 1968—; sr. adviser Brookings Panel on Econ. Activity, 1970—; mem. adv. com. Inst. Internat. Econs., 1983; hon. mem. Chinese Bd. Soc. Scis., 1997, Romanian Acad., 1999—; coord. Jimmy Carter's Econ. Task Force, 1976; mem. adv. bd. Strategic Studies Ctr., Stanford Rsch. Inst., 1974—76; corr. fellow Brit. Acad., 1991—. Author: The Keynesian Revolution, 1947, Textbook of Econometrics, 1953, An Econometric Model of the United States, 1929-1952, 1955, Wharton Econometric Forecasting Model, 1967, Essay on the Theory of Economic Prediction, 1968, An Introduction to Econometric Forecasting and Forecasting Models, 1980; author, editor: Brookings Quar. Econometric Model of U.S., Ecometric Model Performance, 1976, Lectures in Econmetrics, 1983; editor: Internat. Econ. Rev., 1959—65; assoc. editor:, mem. editl. bd.: Empirical Econs., 1976—. Recipient William F. Butler award, N.Y. Assn. Bus. Economists, 1975, Golden Slipper Club award, 1977, Pres.'s medal, U. Pa., 1980, Alfred Nobel Meml. prize in econs., 1980. Fellow: Nat. Assn. Bus. Economists, Am. Acad. Arts and Scis., Econometric Soc. (past pres.); mem.: NAS, Ea. Econ. Assn. (pres. 1974—76), Am. Econ. Assn. (exec. com. 1966—68, pres. 1977, John Bates Clark medalist 1959), Social Sci. Rsch. Coun. (fellow 1945—46, 1947—48, com. econ. stability, dir. 1971—76), Am. Philos. Soc. Office: U Pa Mc Neil Bldg Rm 335 3718 Locust Walk Philadelphia PA 19104-6209 Address: WP Carey 50 Rockefeller Plaza New York NY 10020

KLEIN, LAWRENCE ALLEN, accounting educator; b. Harrisburg, Pa., Jan. 14, 1946; s. Samuel Edward and Ella Violet (Loeb) K. AB, Franklin and Marshall Coll., 1969; MBA, Pa. State U., 1974, PhD, 1978. Adminstrv. asst. dept. acctg. and mgmt. info. sys. Pa. State U., State College, 1975-76; asst. prof. acctg. U. Houston, 1978-79, U. Wyo., Laramie, 1982-84; asst. prof. bus. adminstrn. Franklin and Marshall Coll., Lancaster, Pa., 1979-82; assoc. prof. accountancy Bentley Coll., Waltham, Mass., 1984—. Vis. prof. econ. and mgmt. Vesalius Coll., Brussels, 1996; presenter in field. Author study guides for books in field; co-editor conf. procs., 1976. Program/conf. coord. N.E. Am. Acctg. Assn., State College, 1976; small bus. coun. Laramie Area C. of C., 1973-74. With USAF, 1969-70. Grantee Am. Acctg. Assn., Hasking & Sells Found. Mem. AICPA, NRA (life), AARP, Nat. Retired Tchrs. Assn., Inst. Mgmt. Accts. (I. Wayne Keller award, Ray E. Longnecker award 1980, Cert. Merit Manuscript award), Am. Acctg. Assn. (Sectional Best Paper award 1987), Inst. Internal Auditors, Decision Scis. Internat. (chmn. acctg. track N.E. sect. 1992), Mass. Soc. CPAs (acad. assoc.), Fin. Execs. Internat., Am. Legion (life), Am. Inst. Physics, U.S. Golf Assn., U.S. Tennis Assn. (life), Elks (permanent benefactor), Marine Meml. Club (perpetual benefactor), Jewish War Vets. (life), Beta Gamma Sigma, Beta Alpha Psi, Omicron Delta Kappa. Republican. Jewish. Avocations: tennis, golf, reading, swimming. Home: 521 Katahdin Dr Lexington MA 02421-6452 E-mail: lklein@bentley.edu.

KLEIN, LINDA ANN, lawyer; b. N.Y.C., Nov. 7, 1959; d. Gerald Ira Klein and Sandra Florence (Kimmel) Fishman; m. Michael S. Neuren, Sept. 23, 1985. BA cum laude, Union Coll., 1980; JD, Washington & Lee U., 1983. Bar: Ga. 1983, D.C. 1984, U.S. Dist. Ct. (no. and mid. dist.) Ga. 1985, U.S. Ct. Appeals (11th cir.) 1986. Assoc. Nall & Miller, Atlanta, 1983-86, Martin, Cavan & Andersen, Atlanta, 1986-90, ptnr., 1990-93; mng. ptnr. Gambrell & Stolz, 1993—. Instr. Nat. Ctr. Paralegal Tng., Atlanta, 1986. Mem.: ABA (editor Trial Techniques newsletter 1989, vice chmn. trial techniques com. 1989—90, chair 1991—92, vice chair fidelity and surety com. 1994—97, chair am. meeting 1996—97, mem. coun. tort and ins. practice sect. 1998—, ho. of dels. 1998—, chair elect tort and ins. practice sect. 2002—), Am. Law Inst. (mem. 2003—), Coun. of Superior Cts. Judges (ex-officio uniform rules com.), Atlanta Bar Assn. (chair commn. on uniform rules of ct. 1986, bd. dirs. Atlanta Coun. on Young Lawyers 1986—89), Inst. for CLE (chair Ga. br. 1998—2000), Nat. Conf. Bar Pres. (exec. coun. 1998—2001), State Bar of Ga. (chair study com. on rules of practice 1987—94, bd. govs. 1989—, mem. exec. com. 1992—99, sec. 1994—96, pres. 1997—98, vice chair prof. liability com.), Pi Sigma Alpha, Phi Alpha Delta.

KLEIN, LLOYD, college educator; b. Bklyn., Feb. 20, 1951; s. Theodore and Rosalyn (Chozick) K. PhD, CUNY Grad. Sch., 1993. Asst. prof., criminal justice U. Tenn., Chattanooga, 1999-2000, La. State U., Shreveport, 2000—03, Bemidji (Minn.) State U., 2003—. Adj. prof. Medgar Evers Coll., Bklyn., 1986-99. Author: (book) It's in the Cards; Consumer Credit and the American Experience, 1999. Mem. Soc. for Study of Social Problems.

KLEIN, LUELLA VOOGD, obstetrics-gynecology educator; b. Walker, Iowa, Oct. 24, 1924; d. Elmer De Witt and Leah (Stunkard) Bare; m. Alfred O. Colquitt. BA, U. Iowa, 1947, MD, 1949. Diplomate Am. Bd. Ob-Gyn. Intern Western Res. U., Cleve., 1949—50; resident in medicine, surgery and ob-gyn Cleve. City Hosp., 1950—55; U.S. Sr. Fulbright Rsch. scholar U. London Postgrad. Med. Sch., 1955—57; obstetric cons. Ga. Dept. Pub. Health, Atlanta, 1958—60; pvt. practice Atlanta, 1960—65; asst. dir. clin. rsch. Bristol Labs., Syracuse, NY, 1965—67, prof., dir. maternal and infant care project Emory U. Grady Meml. Hosp., Atlanta, 1967—; co-dir. Regional Perinatal Ctr., Charles Howard Candler prof., chmn. dept. ob-gyn Emory U. Sch. Medicine, Atlanta, 1986—93. Gen. bd. dirs., bd. dirs. divsn. maternal-fetal medicine Am. Bd. Ob-Gyn.; bd. dirs. Alan Guttmacher Inst., N.Y.C., chmn., vice chmn.; Maternal and Child Health Care governing coun. Am. Hosp. Assn., Chgo.; chmn. FDA Ob-Gyn Device Com., Washington, 1986—88. Recipient Elizabeth Blackwell award, Am. Women's Med. Assn., 1986, Atlanta Woman History Maker award, Am. Women's Assn., 1987, Daggett Harvey award, Chgo. Maternity Ctr., Northwestern U., 1991, 40th Anniversary award, FIGO, 1994. Fellow: ACOG (pres., v.p., asst. sec. 1982—85, Disting. Svc. award 1994); mem.: AMA, Inst. Medicine, Med. Assn. Ga. (chair maternal and child health care com.), Atlanta Obstet. and Gynecol. Soc. (pres.), Ga. Obstet. and Gynecol. Soc. (pres.), Marietta (Ga.) Country Club. Office: Grady Meml Hosp Dept Gyn/Ob 69 Butler St SE Atlanta GA 30303-3033

KLEIN, LYNN ELLEN, artist; b. San Francisco, Apr. 14, 1950; BA in Studio Arts, U. Minn., 1974, MFA in Design, 1976. Instr. art edn. U. Minn., Mpls., 1976-78, lectr. in design, 1974-84; vis. artist U. Iowa, Ames, 1984—, Textile Ctr. of Minn., 2003. Resident Cité Internat. des Arts, Paris, summer 1998, vis. artist Textile Arts Ctr. of Minn., 2003. One woman shows include Rochester (Minn.) Fine Arts Ctr., 1976, Northrup Gallery, U. Minn., Mpls., 1976, Allrich Gallery, San Francisco, 1982, 88, Coffman Gallery, U. Minn., 1982, The Print Club, Phila., 1985, Foster-White Gallery, Seattle, 1989, Carolyn Ruff Gallery, Mpls., 1994, Robert Green Fine Arts, 2000; exhibited in group shows at Mpls. Inst. Arts, 1976, 88, Franklin Inst. Sci. Mus., Phila., 1984, Minn. Mus. Art, St. Paul, 1990, Textile Arts Internat., 1990, San Francisco Bay Area Women Artists Mentors, San Francisco, 1994, USART San Francisco Internat. Art Expo, I. Wolk Gallery, St. Helena, Calif., 1996, Robert Green Fine Arts, Mill Valley, Calif., 1996, 2002, Craftsman's Guild and Calif. Heritage Gallery, 1998, Ren Brown Collection, Bodega Bay, Calif., 1998, Gensler Architecture-Material Matters, San Francisco, 1998, San Jose Mus. Art, Visible Rhythm, 2001, 2003, Achenbach Collection Fine Arts Mus., San Francisco, 2001, Kala Art Inst., 2002; represented in permanent collections Mpls. Inst. Arts, Oakland (Calif.) Mus., Bibliotéque Nat., Dept. des Estampes et de lá Photographie, Paris, Phila. Mus. Art, Walker Art Ctr., Mpls., Achenbach Found., Fine Arts Mus. San Francisco, San Jose Mus. Art., Calif. Recipient J.D. Phelan award World Print Coun., 1983; Minn. State Arts Bd. Grantee, 1978; Photography fellow, St. Paul, 1984; Rockefeller Found. fellow, Am. Ctr., 1984-86, Jerome Found. Printmaking fellow, Kala Inst., Berkeley, 1989; Amity Art Found. grant, Woodbridge, Conn., 2003. Mem. Achenbach Graphic Arts Coun.

KLEIN, MARJORIE HANSON, psychiatry educator; b. Milw., Sept. 13, 1933; d. Norman Richard and Anna (Emery) Hanson; m. William A. Klein, June 26, 1956 (div. 1968); children: Jennifer K. Thompson, Susan E. Burns; m. Norman S. Greenfield, May 17, 1969; 1 stepchild, Ellen G. Simmons. BA in Psychology, Wellesley Coll., 1955, MA in Psychology, 1957; PhD in Psychology, Harvard U., 1964. Lic. psychologist, Wis. Lab. asst. Wellesley (Mass.) Coll., 1955-57; rsch. asst. sect. on personality NIMH, Bethesda, Md., 1957-59; project asst. psychotherapy rsch. group Wis. Psychiat. Rsch. Inst., U. Wis., Madison, 1962-64, postdoctoral rsch. fellow, 1964-65, rsch. assoc., 1965-66, 67-72; postdoctoral rsch. fellow NIMH, Bethesda, 1966-67; asst. prof. psychiatry U. Wis., Madison, 1972-75, assoc. prof. psychiatry, assoc. prof. women's studies prog., 1975-80, prof. psychiatry, prof. women's studies program, 1980—. Mem. spl. rev. com. Psychotherapy of Depression Collaborative Program, NIMH, 1979-80, 83, mem. treatment devel. and assessment rsch. rev. com., 1977-81, 84-86, chmn., 1986-88, mem. treatment devel. and assessment rsch. rev. com., clin. rsch. ctrs. subcom., 1986-89, chmn., 1990-97, 99-2000, mem. sci. adv. bd. depression awareness, recognition and treatment, 1989-91, mem. psychosocial rsch. adv. com., 1991; mem. spl. rev. com. Nat. Inst. Alcohol Abuse and Alcoholism, 1989. Editor: (with others) Personality and Depression: A Current View, 1992, Research in Mental Health Computer Applications: Directions for the Future, 1987; author: (with others) Research in Mental Health Computing: The Next Five Years, Computers in Human Services, 1987; contbr. articles to profl. jours.; editorial bd. Psychiatry, 1978—, Jour. Marital and Family Therapy, 1978-90, Clin. Psychology Rev., 1978-93, Computers in Human Behavior, 1984-94, Jour. Psychotherapy Practice and Rsch., 1989—, Current Opinion in Psychiatry, 1995-97, Jour. Personality Disorders, 1992—. Grantee Nat. Libr. Medicine, 1980-85, NIMH, 1980—. MacArthur Found., 1991—, Upjohn Pharms., 1990-91, Nat. Inst. Aging, 1985-86, 91-93, others. Mem. APA (editorial bd. div. 29 1976-79), Soc. Psychotherapy Rsch., Phi Beta Kappa, Sigma Xi. Office: U Wis 6001 Research Park Blvd Madison WI 53719-1176

KLEIN, MARTIN, ocean engineering consultant; b. N.Y.C. s. Allen and Muriel Klein. SBEE, MIT, 1962. Program mgr. sonar systems EG&G Internat., Bedford, Mass., 1962-67; pres. Klein Assocs., Inc., Salem, N.H., 1968-89; cons. Andover, Mass., 1989—. Mem. mgmt. coun. Project Urquhart (Loch Ness), London, 1992-2000; mem. bd. advisors B.Engring. Tech. program U. N.H., Durham, 1988-2003; mem. adv. bd. MIT Sea Grant, Cambridge, 1989—; adv. bd. U N.H. Sea Grant, Durham, 1999—; bd. dirs. Marine Archaeol. and Hist. Rsch. Inst., Elliot, Maine, 1990-98; pres. The Bear Trap Investment Co., 1995-96; mem. vis. com. R.S. Peabody Mus. Archaeology, 1995-98; assoc. mem. Adv. Coun. Underwater Archaeology, 1992-2002. Contbr. articles to mags. Mem. min. search com., publicity dir. Unitarian Universalist Ch., Andover, 1990-91, chair publicity com., 1991-93; trustee Andover Pub. Libr., 1992-98; founding dir. Parent-to-Parent, Andover, 1989-91. Recipient Small Bus. Person of Yr. award SBA, 1983, Merit award Soc. Hist. Archeology, 2003; inducted into Hall of Fame, A.B. Davis H.S., Mt. Vernon, NY, 1984. Fellow Marine Tech. Soc. (dir. budget and fin. 1991-93, chair fellows com. 1998-99), Explorers Club; mem. IEEE, Instrument Soc. Am., Acoustical Soc. Am., Am. Bonsai Soc. (v.p. 1993-95, pres. 1995-97). Achievements include patents in field; development of first commercially successful side scan sonar; designed and manufactured sonar that helped locate most famous shipwrecks, including Titanic; found famed Loch Ness Wellington bomber.

KLEIN, MARTIN I. lawyer; b. N.Y.C., Nov. 12, 1947; m. Diane Levbarg. BA, Lehigh U., 1969; JD, Am. U., 1972. Bar: N.Y. 1973, Fla. 1978, Calif. 1981, D.C. 1981; solicitor Supreme Ct. Eng., 1996—. Mem. profl. staff U.S. Senate Com. on Labor and Pub. Welfare, 1969-72; legis. aide U.S. Senator Jacob K. Javits, 1969-72; ptnr., head creditors' rights dept. Dreyer & Traub, N.Y.C., 1980-93; ptnr., head dept. bankruptcy Shea & Gould, N.Y.C., 1993—95; pvt. practice Martin I. Klein, P.C., 1995—. Lectr. Am. Law Inst.-ABA Com. on Continuing Profl. Edn., 1975—, The Practising Law Inst., 1975—, Mathematica, 1981—; adj. assoc. prof. law Benjamin Cardozo Sch. Law, Yeshiva U., 1980—; lectr. Columbia U. Sch. Law, 1980—; mem. med. malpractice mediation panel appellate div. Supreme Ct. State N.Y. 1980—; trustee, treas., pres. Cen. Synagogue, N.Y.C., 1986-2000; arbitrator, N.Y.C. Small Claims Ct. Contbr. articles on fin. real estate and comml. law to profl. jours. Del. White House Conf. on Youth, 1971; chmn. Town of Palm Beach Zoning Commn., 1994-2001. Mem. ABA, N.Y. State Bar Assn., Fla. Bar Assn., Calif. Bar Assn., D.C. Bar Assn., N.Y. County Lawyers Assn. (mem. com. on bankruptcy), Am. Arbitration Assn. (mem. comml. panel). Address: 21st Fl 780 Third Ave New York NY 10017

KLEIN, MARTIN JESSE, physicist, educator, science historian; b. N.Y.C., June 25, 1924; s. Adolph and Mary (Neuman) K.; m. Miriam June Levin, Oct. 28, 1945 (div. 1973); children: Rona F., Sarah M. Klein Zaino, Nancy R. Klein; m. Linda L. Booz, Oct. 8, 1980; 1 child, Abigail M. AB, Columbia U., 1942, MA, 1944; PhD, MIT, 1948. With OSRD for USN, 1944-45; research assoc. in physics MIT, Cambridge, 1946-49; instr. physics Case Inst. Tech., Cleve., 1949-51, asst. prof., 1951-55, assoc. prof., 1955-60, prof., 1960-67, acting dept. head, 1966-67; prof. history physics Yale U., New Haven, 1967-74, Eugene Higgins prof. history physics and prof. physics, 1974-91, 95-99, Bass prof. history sci., prof. physics, 1991-95, chmn. dept. history sci., 1971-74, William Clyde De Vane prof., 1978-81, prof. emeritus, 1999—. Van der Waals guest prof. U. Amsterdam, 1974, Pieter Zeeman guest prof., 1993; vis. prof. Harvard U., 1989-90, Rockefeller U., 1975, adj. prof. 1976-79. Author: Paul Ehrenfest, Vol. I: The Making of a Theoretical Physicist, 1970; editor: Collected Scientific Papers of Paul Ehrenfest, 1959; sr. editor The Collected Papers of Albert Einstein, 1988-97; editorial adviser Ency. Brit, 1956-76; translator: Letters on Wave Mechanics, 1967; contbr. articles to profl. jours. NRC fellow Dublin (Ireland) Inst. Advanced Studies, 1952-53; Guggenheim fellow Leyden, Netherlands, 1958-59; Guggenheim fellow Yale, 1967-68 Fellow Am. Acad. Arts and Scis., Am. Phys. Soc.; mem. NAS, AAUP, History of Sci. Soc., Am. Assn. Physics Tchrs., Internat. Acad. History of Sci., Phi Beta Kappa, Sigma Xi. Home: 44 N Lake Dr Apt B-1 Hamden CT 06517-2419 Office: Yale U Dept Physics PO Box 208120 New Haven CT 06520-8120

KLEIN, MARTIN SAMUEL, management consulting executive; b. N.Y.C., Dec. 8, 1932; s. David and Dorothy (Manheim) K.; m. Elizabeth Jann Perks, Dec. 19, 1964 (dec. Aug. 1994); children: Sarah Madeline, Dorothy Ann. AB, Harvard U., 1954, MBA, 1962. V.p. United Rsch., Cambridge, Mass., 1962-69, Boston Cons. Group, 1969-73; pres. Instnl. Strategy Assocs., Belmont, Mass., 1973—. Cons. Brookings Instn., Washington, 1963-64. Author: (with others) Impact of Transportation on Development, 1964, Combining Public Health Nursing Agencies, 1964; contbr. articles to profl. jours. Bd. dirs. Vis. Nurse Assn., Boston, 1972-82, Harvard Cmty. Health Plan, Boston, 1978-93; vice chmn. Harvard Cmty. Health Plan Found., 1986-93, Cambridge Ctr. for Adult Edn., 1983-85; sec.-treas. Ctr. for Effective Philanthropy, Cambridge, 1982-98; trustee Mt. Auburn Hosp., Cambridge, 1995-, Big Sister Assn. Greater Boston, 1996-99; counselor to bd. trustees Aga Khan U., Karachi, 1993-2002. Sr. fellow

Cheswick Ctr., 1980—, trustee; Harvard Coll. scholar, 1954, Fulbright scholar, Australia, 1954-55, George F. Baker scholar Harvard Bus. Sch., 1962. Mem. Am. Hosp. Assn. (com. on governance 1998-2001), Mass. Hosp. Assn. (trustee adv. coun. 2002-), Harvard Club (N.Y.C. and Boston), Belmont Hill Club (treas. 1979-80), Harvard Travellers Club (Boston), Kirribilli Club (Sydney, Australia). Jewish. Office: Instl Strategy Assocs Inc 43 Village Hill Rd Belmont MA 02478-2117

KLEIN, MARY ANN, special education educator; b. Ridgewood, N.J., Jan. 31, 1956; d. Julius R. and Nancy M. Pascuzzo; m. Thomas F. Klein, July 16, 1983. B in Elem. Edn. & Spl. Edn., Adelphi U., Garden City, N.Y., 1978; M in Spl. Edn. & Reading, Adelphi Univ., Garden City, N.Y., 1980. Cert. in spl. edn. Learning disabilities specialist Merrick UFSD, Merrick, NY, 1978—. Swimming instr. disabled children and adults Village of Garden City, 1974—79; pvt. piano instr., NY, 1978—82; clinician & diagnostician Adelphi U. Reading Clinic, Garden City, 1980—84; ednl. cons. BOCES of Nassau County, Merrick, NY, 1993—94, SETRC of Nassau County, Westbury, NY, 1995—96; founder peer tutoring program Birch Sch., Merrick, NY; spl. edn. rep. Birch Child Study Team, Merrick, NY. Co-author: (curriculum guide) Foundations for Learning, 1991; author: (resource guide) Strategies to Assist Learning Disabled Children in the Classroom Setting, 1995. Mem. Merrick PTA, 1978—, tchr. liaison, 1994—97; mem. Merrick SEPTA, 1983—, Com. on Spl. Edn., 1983—, Nassau Reading Coun., 1996—; co-founder Students Against Destructive Decision-Making, Birch Sch., Merrick, NY; apptd. Crisis Mgmt. Team, Birch Sch. Mem.: State Congress of Parents & Tchrs. (hon.), Coun. for Exceptional Children, Kappa Delta Pi. Avocations: piano, travel.

KLEIN, MAURICE (MAURY) NICKELL, education educator, writer; b. Memphis, Tenn., Mar. 14, 1939; s. Harry Klein and Alice Lena Nickell. BA, Knox Coll., 1956—60; MA, Emory U., 1960—61, PhD, 1961—64; LHD (hon.), Knox Coll., 2001. Instr. in history Emory U., 1963—64, U. of RI, 1964—65, asst. prof. history, 1965—73, prof. history, 1973—. Author: (book) The Great Richmond Terminal, Days of Defiance: Secession, Slavery, and the Civil War, The Life and Legend of E. H. Harriman, Rainbow's End: The Crash of 1929, Edward Porter Alexander, History of the Louisville & Nashville Railroad, The Life and Legend of Jay Gould, Union Pacific: The Birth, 1862-1893, Union Pacific: The Rebirth, 1894-1969, The Flowering of the Third America, Unfinished Business: The Railroad in American Life; author: (co-author) Prisoners of Progress: American Industrial Cities 1850-1920. Recipient Best Article in Bus. History Rev., Newcomen Soc., 1967, Disting. Alumni Award, Knox Coll., 2001; Newcomen Fellow in Bus. History, Harvard Bus. Sch., 1966—67, Advanced Rsch. Fellowship, NEH-Mellon Found., 1988. Independent. None. Avocations: acting, basketball, music, softball. Home: 167 Pine Glen Drive East Greenwich RI 02818 Office: U of Rhode Island History Dept Kingston RI 02818 Home Fax: 401-885-0316. E-mail: mauryk@uri.edu.

KLEIN, MICHAEL CLARENCE, lawyer; b. Kearney, Nebr., July 16, 1952; s. Milton N. and Mary E. (Moore) Klein; m. Jacqueline A. McGuigan, Aug. 14, 1971; children: Andrew M., Benjamin P., Molly E., Katherine A. BA, Kearney State Coll., 1974; JD, U. Nebr., 1977. Bar: Nebr. 1977, U.S. Dist. Ct. Nebr. 1977, U.S. Supreme Ct. 1987. Ptnr. Anderson, Klein, Peterson & Swan, Holdrege, Nebr., 1977—; chmn. 10th Jud. Dist. Mental Health Bd., Holdrege, 1981—90. Editor: Nebr. Law Rev., 1975—77. Bd. dirs. Child Saving Inst., Omaha, Phelps County Cmty. Found., Holdrege. Mem.: ABA, Phelps County Bar Assn. (pres. 1981), 10th Jud. Dist. Bar Assn. (sec. 1981—82), Nebr. Bar Assn., Elks. Republican. Roman Catholic. Home: 820 Hancock St Holdrege NE 68949-2146 Office: Anderson Klein Peterson & Swan 417 East Ave Holdrege NE 68949-2216

KLEIN, MICHAEL D. lawyer; b. Wilkes-Barre, Pa., June 9, 1951; BA magna cum laude, King's Coll., 1973; JD, Dickinson Sch. Law, 1976. Bar: Pa. 1976, U.S. Ct. Appeals (3rd cir.) 1984, U.S. Dist. Ct. (mid. dist.) Pa. 1984, U.S. Dist Ct. (ea. dist.) Pa. 1994. Asst. atty. gen. Commonwealth of Pa., Harrisburg, 1976-82; mgr. corp. affairs, corp. sec. Pa. Am. Water Co., Hershey, 1982-89; ptnr. LeBoeuf, Lamb, Greene & MacRae LLP, Harrisburg, Pa., 1991—. Mem. Pa. Bar Assn., Am. Water Works Assn. Office: LeBoeuf Lamb Greene & MacRae LLP PO Box 12105 Harrisburg PA 17108-2105 E-mail: mklein@llgm.com.

KLEIN, MICHAEL ELIHU, physician; b. NYC, Apr. 6, 1946; s. Leo and Edith (Rigrod) K.; m. Elizabeth Angela McGehee, Oct. 8, 1988; children: Michael, Debra, Daniel. BA, Wesleyan U., Middletown, Conn., 1967; MD, MPH, Yale U., 1972. Diplomate Am. Bd. Internal Medicine. Asst. dir. hematology U. Md., Balt., 1979-83; sr. investigator U. Md. Cancer Ctr., Balt., 1979-83; pvt. practice specializing in hematology/oncology Cowley Assocs., Camp Hill, Pa., 1983-97, Ctrl. Pa. Hematology & Oncology, Lemoyne, 1997—; chief hematology Pinnacle Health Systems, Harrisburg, Pa., 2002—. Cons. in hematology and oncology Holy Spirit Hosp., Camp Hill, Pa., 1983—, chmn. blood usage com., 1998—2000, Camp Hill, 2003—; cons. in hematology and oncology Pinnacle Health System, Harrisburg, 1983—, chief hematology, 2002—, chmn. blood utilization com., 1988—. Author: Political Dynamics National Health Insurance in New York, 1972; contbr. articles to profl. jours., chpts. to books. Founder, bd. dirs. Number Nine, New Haven, 1971. Comdr. lt. USPHS, 1974-77. Mem. AMA, Am. Soc. Clin. Research, Am. Soc. Clin. Oncology, Am. Soc. Hematology, Am. Legion, Balt. Blood Club (pres. 1979-83). Avocations: stamp collecting, baseball, reading. Office: Ctrl Pa Hematology & Oncology 50 N 12th St Ste 100 Lemoyne PA 17043-1440

KLEIN, MICHAEL ROGER, lawyer, business executive; b. N.Y.C., Apr. 10, 1942; s. Jesse and Stephanie (Siegel) K.; m. Joan Ilona Fabry, Feb. 19, 1977; children: Nicholas Jesse, Alexander Fabry. BBA, U. Miami, Coral Gables, Fla., 1963, JD, 1966; LLM, Harvard U., 1967. Bar: Fla. 1966, D.C., 1969, U.S. Dist. Ct. (D.C. cir.) 1970, U.S. Supreme Ct. 1970. Asst. prof. law La. State U., Baton Rouge, 1967-69; assoc. Wilmer, Cutler & Pickering, Washington, 1969-74, ptnr., 1974—. Chmn. Zenith Gallery, Inc., Washington, 1978—, LePavillon of D.C., Washington, 1983-89; co-founder, chmn. bd. CoStar Group Inc., 1988—, vice-chmn. bd. dirs. Perini Corp. 1991—; bd. dirs. SRA Internat. Inc.; co-founder, chmn. bd. Precept Corp., 1999—. Author: Eminent Domain, 1969; contbr. articles to profl. jours. Trustee Ctr. for Law in the Pub. Interest, L.A., 1975-91, Am. Himalayan Found., 1996—, Pen Faukner Found., 2002--; chmn. bd. trustees Advocates for Pub. Interest, Washington, 1986-89; dir. Support Ctr. of D.C., Inc., 1991-95. Mem. Am. Law Inst. Jewish. Office: Wilmer Cutler & Pickering 2445 M St NW Ste 500 Washington DC 20037-1487

KLEIN, MICHAEL TULLY, university dean, chemical engineer, consultant; b. Wilmington, Del., Mar. 15, 1955; s. Donald Michael and Nancy (Tully) K.; m. Elizabeth Thompson, Aug. 7, 1976; children: Jennifer, Michael, Lisa. BSChemE, U. Del., 1977; ScD, MIT, 1981. Asst. prof. chem. engring. U. Del., Newark, 1981-85, assoc. prof., 1985-89, prof., 1989—, dept. chmn., 1991-96, assoc. dean Coll. Engring., 1987-88, dir. Catalysis Ctr., 1988-91, Elizabeth Inez Kelley prof., 1994-98; dean Sch. Engring., Rutgers U., Piscataway, N.J., 1998—, bd. govs. prof., 1998—. Contbr. more than 200 articles to profl. jours. Named Presdl. Young Investigator NSF, 1985. Achievements include development of Detailed Molecular reaction modeling software. Office: Rutgers U Sch Engring Office of Dean 98 Brett Rd # B204 Piscataway NJ 08854-8058

KLEIN, MILES VINCENT, physics educator; b. Cleve., Mar. 9, 1933; s. Max Ralph and Isabelle (Benjamin) K.; m. Barbara Judith Pincus, Sept. 2, 1956; children: Cynthia Klein-Banai, Gail. BS, Northwestern U., 1954; PhD, Cornell U., 1961. NSF postdoctoral fellow Max Planck Inst., Stuttgart, Germany, 1961; prof. U. Ill., Urbana, 1962—. Co-author: Optics, 1986; contbr. articles to profl. jours. A.P. Sloan Found. fellow, 1963. Fellow AAAS, Am. Phys. Soc. (Frank Isakson prize 1990), Am. Acad. Arts and Scis.; mem. IEEE (Sr.), Nat. Acad. Scis. Office: Materials Rsch Lab 104 S Goodwin Ave Urbana IL 61801-2902

KLEIN, MILTON MARTIN, history educator; b. N.Y.C., Aug. 15, 1917; s. Edward and Margaret (Greenfield) K.; m. Margaret Gordon, Aug. 25, 1963; children: Edward Gordon, Peter Gordon. BSS, CCNY, 1937, MS in Edn., 1939; PhD, Columbia U., 1954. Historian, USAAF, 1944-47; tchr. N.Y.C. pub. schs., 1947-57; vis. prof. Columbia U., summers 1959, 60, lectr. history, 1954-58; prof. history, chmn. dept. L.I. U., 1958-62, dean Coll. Liberal Arts and Sci., 1962-66; dean grad. studies and research SUNY-Fredonia, 1966-69; prof. history U. Tenn., 1969-84, alumni disting. service prof., 1977-84, Lindsay Young prof., 1980-84, prof. emeritus, 1984—, univ. historian, 1988-97. Walter E. Meyer vis. prof. N.Y. U. Law Sch., 1976-77; chmn. Columbia U. Faculty Seminar on Early Am. History and Culture, 1971-72 Author: Social Studies for the Academically Talented Student, 1960, The Politics of Diversity: Essays in the History of Colonial New York, 1974, New York in the American Revolution: A Bibliography, 1974, The American Whig: William Livingston of New York, 1990, 93, Vol. Moments: Vignettes of the History the University of Tennesse, 1794-1994, 1994; editor: Independent Reflector (William Livingston), 1963, A History of the American Colonies, 13 vols., 1973-86, New York-The Centennial Years, 1676-1976, 1976, Courts and Law in Early New York, 1978, The Twilight of British Rule in Revolutionary America: The New York Letter Book of General James Robertson, 1983, North America in Colonial Times, 4 vols., 1998, The Empire State: A History of New York, 2001; mem. editl. bd. Am. Jour. Legal History, 1970-76, N.Y. History, 1973-2000, Soundings, 1985-2000, U. Tenn. Press, 1972-75, Presidl. Studies Quar., 1992-96; adv. editor: Eighteenth-Century Studies, 1975-83, 93-95; adv. bd. America: History and Life, 1982-96; contbr. articles to profl. jours. Lt. col. USAF Res. Recipient Outstanding Teaching award U. Tenn. Alumni, 1974, Kerr History prize N.Y. State Hist. Assn., 1975, 92, Articles prize Am. Soc. 18th Century Studies, 1976; Fulbright lectr. U. Canterbury, Christchurch, N.Z., 1962; Ford Found. traveling fellow, 1955-56, Lilly Found.-Clements Libr. fellow, 1961; Am. Philos. Soc. grantee, 1973. Mem. Am. Hist. Assn., Orgn. Am. Historians, Am. Soc. 18th Century Studies (articles prize 1976), Southeastern Am. Soc. 18th Century Studies (dir. 1978-81, v.p. 1982-84, pres. 1984-85), AAUP (nat. coun. 1978-80, Claxton award for Outstanding Contbn. to Higher Edn. 1997), Am. Soc. Legal History (chmn. membership com. 1969-74, dir. 1971-76, 84-86, sec. 1975-77, v.p. 1978-80, pres. 1980-82), Am. Antiquarian Soc., Mass. Hist. Soc., Phi Beta Kappa, Sigma Alpha Mu, Phi Alpha Theta, Phi Kappa Phi, Omicron Delta Kappa, Golden Key. Home: 7103 Rotherwood Dr Knoxville TN 37919-7413 E-mail: mklein@usit.net.

KLEIN, NANCY HESS, interior designer; b. Cin., Aug. 31, 1950; d. Stanley Edward and Ruth (Wood) Hess; m. Thomas Michael Klein, July 3, 1987. BS, Syracuse U., 1972. Assoc. interior designer Armstrong World Industries, Lancaster, Pa., 1972-78; dir. interior design Haak, Kaufman, Reese & Beers, Lancaster, 1978-81; interior designer Janet Schirn Interiors, Chgo., 1981-82, Midwest interior textiles specialist The Wool Bur., Inc., Chgo., 1983—91; interior design textiles, adj. faculty Internat. Acad. of Merchandising and Design, Chgo., 1986—91; pres. Nancy Klein Design & Mktg., 1992—. Recipient Citation for Design Excellence Pa. and Cen. Pa. State chpt. AIA, 1980; named One of Outstanding Young Women of Am., 1981. Mem. Am. Soc. Interior Designers (profl. mem., cert. by NCIDQ), Chgo. Hist. Soc., Art Inst. of Chgo., Nat. Trust for Hist. Preservation, Chgo. Bot. Garden, Friends of Colonial Williamsburg, Friends of Montpelier, Alpha Chi Omega. Avocations: singing, traveling, bicycling, cross country skiing. Home and Office: 823 Michigan Ave Evanston IL 60202-5428

KLEIN, NEIL CHARLES, physician; b. N.Y.C., Jan. 6, 1935; s. Martin and Jeannette F. (Pazow) K.; divorced; children: Lisa, Susie, David; m. Phyllis Klein, Nov. 26, 1989. AB, Columbia U., 1956; MD, Cornell U., 1960. Diplomate Am. Bd. Internal Medicine, Am. Bd. Gastroenterology, Nat. Bd. Med. Examiners. Intern N.Y. Hosp., 1960-61, resident, 1964-67; fellow in medicine Cornell Med. Coll., 1965-67, clin. instr. in medicine, 1967-70, asst. clin. prof. medicine, 1970-77; assoc. clin. prof. medicine N.Y. Med. Coll., 1977-84, clin. prof. medicine, 1984—98, Columbia U., N.Y.C., 1998—; asst. clin. attending physician N.Y. Hosp., 1970-77, St. Joseph's Hosp., Stamford, Conn., 1967-72; from asst. to assoc. attending physician Stamford (Conn.) Hosp., 1967—, assoc. chief medicine, 1972-75, chief divsn. gastroenterology, 1978-84. Bd. dirs. Conn. Med. Ins. Co., 1988-2002, fin. com., 1988-2002, sec., 1990-2002; bd. dirs. Stamford Health Network, 1987-93, chmn. fin. com., 1994-2001; mem. sci. adv. coun. Fairfield-Westchester Ileitis-Colitis Found., 1982—; mem. Commn. of Aging, Stamford, 1971-82. Fellow ACP, Am. Coll. Gastroenterology, Royal Soc. Tropical Medicine and Hygiene; mem. Fairfield County Med. Assn. (trustee 1980-87, chmn. bd. trustees 1984-85, pres. 1985-86), Conn. State Med. Assn., Am. Soc. Gastrointestinal Endoscopy, Am. Gastrointestinal Assn., Cornell Med. Coll. Alumni Assn. (pres. 1976-78, sr. advisor 1978—), Stamford Med. Soc. (pres. 1990-91). Office: Shoreline Med Group 1450 Washington Blvd Stamford CT 06902-2451 E-mail: neilklein@shorelinemedicalllp.com.

KLEIN, OTTO GEORGE, III, lawyer; b. Berkeley, Calif., Dec. 7, 1950; BA, U. Wash., 1973; JD, Yale U., 1976. Bar: Wash. 1976. Atty. Perkins Coie, 1976-81; ptnr. Syrdal, Danelo, Klein, Myre & Woods, 1981—88, Heller Ehrman, 1988-97; mem. Summit Law Group, Seattle, 1997—. Office: Summit Law Group Ste 1000 315 5th Ave S Seattle WA 98104-2679

KLEIN, PAUL E. lawyer; b. N.Y.C., Apr. 26, 1934; AB, Cornell U., 1956; JD, Harvard U., 1960. Bar: Mich. 1960, Ill. 1965, N.Y. 1967, U.S. Supreme Ct. 1977, U.S. Ct. Appeals (2d cir.) 1980. Atty. Dow Chem. Co., Midland, Mich., 1960-65; assoc. Gunther & Choka, Chgo., 1965-66; atty. Esso Rsch. & Engring. Co., Linden, N.J., 1966-67; sr. mng. editor Matthew Bender & Co., N.Y.C., 1967-72; assoc. gen. counsel N.Y. Life Ins. Co., N.Y.C., 1972-80, v.p., assoc. gen. counsel, 1980-84; v.p., counsel Huggins Fin. Svcs., Inc., N.Y.C., 1984-86; exec. corp. tax. div. Ernst & Young, N.Y.C., 1986-95; pvt. practice White Plains, N.Y., 1995—. Adj. asst. prof. L.I. U., 1972-79, adj. assoc. prof., 1979-80; adj. assoc. prof. acctg. and taxation, Fordham U. at Lincoln Ctr. grad. sch. of bus. adminstrn., 1995—. Former columnist Jour. Real Estate Taxation; writer; editor. Mem. ABA (past chmn. subcom. on life ins. products/ins. cos. com., sect. taxation), Assn. Bar City N.Y. (past chair subcom. on life and health ins. of the com. on ins. law), Assn. Life Ins. Counsel (sec.-treas. 1979-83, bd. govs. 1983-87), N.Y. State Bar Assn. Office: 58 Midchester Ave White Plains NY 10606-3817 E-mail: pek34@optonline.net.

KLEIN, PERRY IAN, electronics engineer; b. Balt., Nov. 15, 1942; s. Samuel C. and Vivian (Elkin) K.; m. Susan Shurberg, June 20, 1965; 1 child, Sherry. BSEE, U. Pa., 1964, MSE, 1965, PhD in Engring., 1968. Mem. tech. staff Comms. Satellite Corp., Washington, 1968-71; pres., gen. mgr. Radio Amateur Satellite Corp., Washington, 1971-80; v.p. Washington Cable Sys., Inc., 1979—. Pres. Shurberg-Klein Found., Washington, 1997—; founder Radio Amateur Satellite Corp., Washington, 1969. Patentee in field. Dir. Md. Brass Ensemble, 1986—. Mem. IEEE (sr.). Avocations: amateur radio, composing music, creating neon art. Home: 700 7th St SW Washington DC 20024-2438 Office: Washington Cable 700 7th St SW Washington DC 20024-2484 E-mail: pk@ieee.org.

KLEIN, PETER MARTIN, lawyer, retired transportation company executive; b. N.Y.C., June 2, 1934; s. Saul and Esther (Goldstein) K.; m. Ellen Judith Matlick, June 18, 1961; children: Amy Lynn, Steven Ezra. AB, Columbia U., 1956, JD, 1962. Bar: N.Y. 1962, D.C. 1964, U.S. Supreme Ct. 1966. Asst. proctor Columbia U., 1959-62; asst. counsel Mil. Sea Transp. Svc., Office Gen. Counsel, Dept. Navy, Washington, 1962-65; trial atty. civil div. U.S. Dept. Justice, N.Y.C., 1966-69; gen. atty. Sea-Land Svc., Inc., Menlo Park, N.J., 1969-76, v.p., gen. counsel, sec., 1976-79, Sea-Land Industries, Inc., Menlo Park, 1979-84; assoc. gen. counsel R.J. Reynolds Industries, Inc., Winston-Salem, N.C., 1978-84; sr. v.p., gen. counsel, sec. Sea-Land Svc., Inc. (formerly Sea-Land Corp.), Charlotte, N.C., 1984-94, sr. v.p.-law, sec., 1994-95, ret., 1996—. Mem. adv. com. on pvt. internat. law Dept. State, 1974-95; mem. U.S. delegation UN Conf. of Trade and Devel., UN Commn. on Internat. Trade Law, 1975-76, trade regulation adv. bd. Bur. Nat. Affairs, 1986-88; alt. mem. N.Am. coun. London Ct. of Internat. Arbitration, 1988-95. Trustee Jewish Edn. Assn. Met. N.J., 1973-76; trustee Temple B'nai Abraham of Essex County, N.J., 1973—, v.p., 1976-81, pres. 1981-83; mem. Essex County Dems. Com., 1986-88; mem. Livingston Twp. Planning Bd., 1996—, vice chmn. 1997-99, chmn., 2000—. With USN, 1956-59, Antarctica. Mem. ABA, FBA, Am. Maritime Assn. (bd. dirs., chmn. coms. on law and legis. 1974-78), Am. Polar Soc. (life), Navy League U.S. (life), U.S. Naval Inst. (life), N.Y. State Bar Assn., D.C. Bar Assn., Internat. Bar Assn., Maritime Law Assn. Home: 22 Sandalwood Dr Livingston NJ 07039-1409

KLEIN, PETER WILLIAM, lawyer, corporate officer, investment company executive; b. Lorain, Ohio, Sept. 22, 1955; s. Warren Martin Klein and Barbara (Lesser) Pomeroy; m. Jennifer Lynn Ungers, Aug. 3, 1984. Student, U. Sussex, 1975-76; BA, Albion Coll., 1976; JD, Cleve. Marshall Coll. Law, 1981; LLM, NYU, 1982. Bar: Ohio 1981, Ill. 1984. Assoc. Guren, Merritt, Feibel, Sogg & Cohen, Cleve., 1982-84, Siegan, Barbakoff, Gomberg & Gordon, Ltd., Chgo., 1984-86; mng. dir., gen. counsel Trivest Inc., Miami, Fla., 1986-2000; ptnr., gen. counsel Brockway, Moran & Ptnrs., Inc., Boca Raton, Fla., 2000—. Mem. ABA (taxation sect., corp. sect., banking and bus. law). Home: 541 Hardee Rd Coral Gables FL 35146 Office: Brockway Moran & Ptnrs Inc 7th Fl 225 NE Mizner Blvd Fl 7 Boca Raton FL 33432-4078

KLEIN, PHILIP ALEXANDER, economist; b. Austin, Tex., Oct. 8, 1927; s. David Ballin and Rose (Schaffer) K.; m. Margaret A. McCormack, May 20, 1961; children— Kathleen Monico, Lisa Schaffer BA, U. Tex., 1948, MA, 1949; PhD, U. Calif., Berkeley, 1958. Instr. Carleton Coll., Northfield, Minn., spring 1955; mem. faculty Pa. State U., State College, 1955—, prof. econs., 1965—2000, emeritus prof. econs., 2000—; rsch. assoc. Nat. Bur. Econ. Rsch., 1955-70, 73-79, Ctr. Internat. Bus. Cycle Rsch., Columbia U., 1979-96, Econ. Cycle Rsch. Inst., 1996—. Vis. prof. San Francisco State U., summer 1963, U. Hawaii, summer 1967, Inst. Europeen D'Adminstrn. des Affairs, Fontainbleau, France, 1963-64, 65, 66, 67, U. Osijek, Yugoslavia, 1970, Mills Coll., spring 1982; acad. visitor London Sch. Econs., 1973-74, 81; disting. Fulbright fellow U. Siena, Italy, 1989; adj. scholar Am. Enterprises Inst., Washington, 1976—; cons. UN, Ctr. Devel. Planning Projections Policies, 1973, OECD, Paris, 1978-81, EEC, Brussels, 1979-82, World Bank, Washington, 1986, 87, 88 Mem. editorial bd. Internat. Jour. Forecasting, 1986—, Jour. Econ. Issues, 1976-81, 85-87; author books in field; contbr. articles to profl. jours., chpts. to books. With M.C., AUS, 1946-47. Recipient Distinction in Social Scis. award Pa. State U., 1981, Veblen-Commons award Assn. Evolutionary Econs., 1990; Fulbright fellow France, 1963, Yugoslavia, 1970, Italy, 1989. Mem. Econs. Assn., Assn. Evolutionary Econs. (pres. 1977, Veblen-Commons award 1990), Assn. Comparative Econs., Phi Beta Kappa (pres. chpt. 1981). Home: 719 S Sparks St State College PA 16801-4114 Office: Pa State U Dept Econs 516 Kern Grad Bldg University Park PA 16802

KLEIN, PHILIPP HILLEL, electronic materials consultant; b. N.Y.C., Sept. 14, 1926; s. Raphael and Lillian Rae (Wald) K.; m. Charlotte Feuerstein, June 21, 1953; children: Joshua David, Daniel William, Jonathan Henry. BS in Chemistry, Syracuse U., 1948, MS in Phys. Chemistry, 1951, PhD in Phys. Chemistry, 1953. Rsch. assoc. Knolls Atomic Power Lab., Schenectady, N.Y., 1952-56; phys. chemist GE Electronics Lab., Syracuse, N.Y., 1956-61; mem. rsch. staff Sperry Rand Rsch. Ctr., Sudbury, Mass., 1961-66; rsch. chemist NASA Electronics Rsch. Ctr., Cambridge, Mass., 1966-70; sect. head U.S. Naval Rsch. Lab., Washington, 1970-87, rsch. cons., 1987-90; prin. Philipp Klein Cons., Washington, 1990—. Assoc. editor Materials Letters, 1985-89; editor Advanced Energy Conversion, 1962; contbr. articles to profl. jours. With USNR 1945-46. Fellow: Am. Inst. Chemists; mem.: IEEE (life; chmn. com. on solid state devices 1962—63), Materials Rsch. Soc., Am. Phys. Soc., Am. Assn. for Crystal Growth (program chmn. 1985—87), Am. Ceramic Soc. (electronics com. 1968—70), Sigma Xi. Achievements include patents on the purification of fluorides, preparation of laser hosts, and deposition of silicon carbide shapes. Office: Philipp Klein Cons 2017 Hillyer Pl NW Washington DC 20009-1005

KLEIN, R. KENT, lawyer; b. Richmond, Mo., Feb. 11, 1944; BA with distinction, U. Ariz., 1965, JD, 1968. Bar: Ariz. 1968. Atty. State Compensation Fund Ariz., 1968-74, Lewis & Roca, Phoenix, 1974—2002, Klein, Lundmark, Barberich & La Mint, P.C., Phoenix, 2002—. Mem. State Bar Ariz. Office: Klein Lundmark Barberich & La Mont PC 702 E Oberon Ste 180 Phoenix AZ 85067

KLEIN, RICHARD G. anthropologist, educator; PhD, U. Chgo., 1966. Prof. U. Chgo.; prof. and head human biocultural evolution program dept. anthrop. scis. Stanford U., Calif., 1993—, Anne T. and Robert M. Bass prof. Sch. Humanities and Scis. Author: Man and Culture in the Late Pleistocene: A Case Study, 1969, Ice-Age Hunters of the Ukraine, 1973; co-author: The Analysis of Animal Bones from Archaeological Sites, 1984; author: The Human Career; co-editor: Quaternary Extinctions: A Prehistoric Revolution, 1984; editor: Southern African Prehistory and Paleoenvironments, 1984, Jour. Archaeol. Sci. Mem.: NAS. Office: Dept Anthrop Scis Stanford U Mail Code 2117 Bldg 360 Stanford CA 94305-2117*

KLEIN, ROBERT, manufacturing company executive; b. Phila., Dec. 3, 1924; s. Julius and Eleanor (Arons) K.; m. Judith Auritt, June 30, 1946; children: William J., Sally G., Anne L. BA, Pa. State U., 1948. From indsl. engr. to pres. Caloric Corp., Topton, Pa., 1948-69; pres. Samuel Klein Corp., Alburtis, Pa., 1969-74, Alliance Wall Corp., Atlanta, 1963-78, chmn. bd., 1978-85, dir., 1985-87; chmn. bd. Eichler Wood Products Co., Laury's Station, Pa., 1971-78; dir. John M. Spiegel Co., Allentown, Pa., 1972-78; mng. dir. Alliance Europe, Genk, Belgium, 1971-85, gen. mgr., 1985-87; chmn. bd., CEO, 3 Springs Water Co., Laurel Run, Pa., 1988—. Bd. dirs., v.p. Nat. Bank Topton, 1960-67; mng. dir. Alliance Pentagon, Odense, Denmark, 1972-85; trustee Albert Einstein Med. Ctr., Phila., 1989—. Chmn. adv. com. Good Shepherd Home Workshop, 1967-85; mem. bd. assocs. Muhlenberg Coll., 1969-72, pres. bd. assocs., 1969-70, trustee, 1970-82, life trustee, 1982; trustee Jewish Fedn., Allentown, 1970-74, 78-81, Boca Raton, Fla. and Phila., 1990; bd. dirs. Porcelain Enamel Inst., 1974-89, treas. 1986-89, Nat. Foundry Assn.; pres. alumni trustees, sec. Coll. Bus. Adminstrn., Pa. State U., 1977-85, pres. Alumni Assn., 1987-89; mem. exec. bd. Disting. Alumni Assn., Penn State, 1997; vice chmn. nat. campaign, 1998—. With USMCR, 1943-45. Decorated Purple Heart; recipient Alumni Achievement award Muhlenberg Coll., 1976, Alumni Achievement award Pa. State U., 1978, Disting. Alumni award, 1994; Alumni fellow Pa. State U., 1981; named Pa. State U. Vol. of Yr., 2002. Home: 500 SE 5th Ave Apt 901S Boca Raton FL 33432-5515 E-mail: jak21klein@aol.com. *Work hard, think smart, and work with and encourage your associates. Always remember that every decision you make includes and affects people. This should not decrease aggressiveness but instead make your decisions "people sensitive.".*

KLEIN, ROBERT DALE, lawyer; b. Balt., July 29, 1951; s. James Robert and Madeline Margaret (Horak) K.; m. Patricia Kay Purvis, May 6, 1978; children: Morgan Elizabeth, Patrick Jameson, Evan Robert. Student, U. Durham, Eng., 1971-72; BS, MIT, 1973; JD, Columbia U., 1976. Bar: Md. 1976, U.S. Dist. Ct. Md. 1977, U.S. Ct. Appeals (4th cir.) 1978, U.S. Dist. Ct. D.C. 1983, D.C. 1983. Assoc. Piper & Marbury, Balt., 1976-84, ptnr., 1984-87; shareholder Wharton Levin Ehrmantraut Klein, PA, Annapolis, Md., 1987—. Mem. Product Liability Adv. Coun., chmn. rules of procedure and practice com., 1991-98, exec. com., 1997-2000; standing com. rules of practice and procedure Ct. Appeals Md. 1994—. Author: Maryland Civil Procedure Forms: Practice, 1984—, annual supplements; editor Def. Line Jour., 1983-84; contbr. articles to profl. jours. Bd. dirs., pres. Am. Found. for the U. Durham, Inc., 1992—. Alfred P. Sloan Found. scholar, 1969-73. Mem. ABA, Md. State Bar Assn. (chmn. product liability com. litigaton sect. 1991-95), Balt. City Bar Assn. (chmn. com. on long range planning 1986-87, chmn. product liability law com. 1987-88, chmn. spl. com. on video 1983-84, chmn. standing com. on pub. rels. 1984-86), Md. Def. Counsel (bd. dirs. 1984-91, v.p. 1985-86, pres. 1986-87, chmn. product liability law com. 1989-91, chmn. standing com. on the rules of practice and procedure 1992-94), Anne Arundel County Bar Assn., D.C. Bar Assn., Def. Rsch. Inst. (Exceptional Performance award 1987), Chi Phi (sec. Beta chpt.). Roman Catholic. Home: 302 Rugby Cv Arnold MD 21012-2131 Office: Wharton Levin Ehrmantraut & Klein PO Box 551 Annapolis MD 21404-0551 E-mail: rdk@wlekn.com.

KLEIN, ROBERT MARSHALL, lawyer; b. Chgo., Mar. 21, 1957; s. Ronald Shevre and Jacqueline Carol (Margolin) K.; m. Cynthia Lynn Martin, Dec. 2, 1983; children: Brian, David, Jacob. BBA, U. Wis., 1979, JD, 1982. Bar: Wis. 1982, U.S. Dist. Ct. (we. dist.) Wis. 1982, Ill. 1982, U.S. Dist. Ct. (no. dist.) Ill. 1982, U.S. Ct. Appeals (7th cir.) 1982, U.S. Supreme Ct. 1985. Assoc. Laner, Muchin, Donbrow, Becker, Levin & Tominberg, Ltd., Chgo., 1982-88, ptnr., 1988-95, Coffield, Ungaretti & Harris, Chgo., 1995-96, Klein, Dub & Holleb, Chgo., 1997—. Mem. Ill. Atty. Registration and Disciplinary Commn., Ill. Supreme Ct., Chgo., 1987-94. Contbr. articles to profl. jours. Mem. Ill. Bar Assn. (employee benefits sect. coun. 1989—, chmn. 1993-94), Lake County Bar Assn. (chair employment law 1999—), Chgo. Bar Assn., Internat. Found. Employee Benefit Plans, Mensa. Avocations: swimming, piano, coin collecting. Home: 1152 Norman Ln Deerfield IL 60015-3114 Office: Klein Dub & Holleb 222 N La Salle St Ste 1900 Chicago IL 60601-1110

KLEIN, SAMI WEINER, librarian; b. Worcester, Mass., July 6, 1939; d. Phillip and Barbara Rose (Ginsberg) Weiner; m. Eugene Robert Klein, Oct. 22, 1961; children: Pamela, Jeffrey, Elizabeth. BS, Simmons Coll., 1961; MLS, U. Md., 1973; postgrad., Johns Hopkins U., 1976-78. Chemist Hercules, Wilmington, Del., 1961-62, FDA, Washington, 1965-66; libr. NSWC, White Oak, Md., 1973-78; chief Hdqs. Libr. EPA, Washington, 1978-82; chief rsch. info. svcs. Nat. Inst. Svcs. and Tech., Gaithersburg, Md., 1982-95; chief rsch. libr. and info. program, rsch. libr. Nat. Inst. Stds. and Tech., Gaithersburg, Md., 1995-99; retired Nat. Inst. Svcs. and Tech., Gaithersburg, Md., 1999. Cons. in field; mem. librs. exec. coun. Met. Washington Coun. of Govts., 1981-82; elected mem. com. Fed. Libr. Info. Ctr., 1993-95, chair, budget and fin. working group, 1994-98. Editor OIS Sci.-Tech Info, 1982-95; mem. editorial bd. Assn. Ofcly. Analyt. Chemists, 1985-92, Sci. and Tech. Librs., 1996—. Fed. govt. rep. Inst. for Sci. Info. Internat. Users Group, 1985—86; mem. info. tech. com. Candlelight Concert Soc.; chmn. Howard County Holocaust Remembrance Program, 2003; 2d v.p. Bet Aviv Congregation; mem. edn. com. Fed. Libr. and Info. Ctr. Com., 1987—91. Recipient Gold medal Am. Soc. Chemists, 1961, Engring. award Govt. Inidustry Data Exch. Program, 1997. Mem. ALA (sec.-treas. Fed. Librs. Round Table 1983-84, rep. to NTIS 1984-90, bd. dirs. 1986-89, v.p. 1991, pres. 1991-92, nominations chair 1992-93, scholar 1994-96, chair privatization com. 1995-97, chair co-awards com. 1996—, 1st FLRT Disting. Svc. award 1995), Spl. Librs. Assn. (treas. info.-tech. group 1986-87, student loan com. 1984-85), D.C. Law Librs. Soc. (NIST v.p. standards com. for women 1988, pres. 1989, bd. dirs. Comstar Credit Union 1994-2000), Fed. Libr. and Info. Network (exec. adv. com. 1989-91, sec. 1989, vice chair 1990-91), Jewish Mus. Md. (bd. dirs. 1999—), Beta Phi Mu. Democrat. Jewish. Home: 11041 Wood Elves Way Columbia MD 21044-1002 E-mail: swklein@comcast.net.

KLEIN, SCOTT RICHARD, acting and directing educator; b. Aberdeen, South Dakota, June 2, 1959; s. Richard Lewis and Jalois Mae (Janish) K. BA, Gustavus Adolphus Coll., 1981; MFA, Mankato State U., 1983. Actor, tchr. Ark. Arts Ctr., Little Rock, 1983-84; assoc. dir. Permian Playhouse, Odessa, Tex., 1984-89; instr. acting and directing, coach Cameron Univ., Lawton, Okla., 1989-92, asst. prof., 1992-95, chmn., 1994—, assoc. prof., 1997—. Directed plays including Echoes, 1983; Vanities, 1985; A.B.C., 1986; Wiley and the Hairy Man, 1988; Night of January 16th, 1988; The Foreigner, 1989; The Barber of Seville, 1991; The Lion in Winter, 1992; Seascape, 1993; Betty the Yeti, 1995; Night Sky, 2002 (ACTF OK I Respondent's Choice Award); appeared in plays The Glass Menagerie, 1989; Anything Goes, 1989; A Funny Thing Happened, 1989; Charley's Aunt, 1986; The Crucible, 1991; Christopher Columbus: The Gypsy's Fortune, 1992; Guys and Dolls, 2000; comml. for Kent Kwik, 1987 (Addy Award). Rep., United Way, Lawton, Okla., 1989-2000. Recipient Excellence in Direction Award, ACTF region V north, 1983; Best Dir. Award, Kaleidoscope Co., 1988; Alpha Psi Omega, 1990; Outstanding Rsch. Performance, C.U. Sch. Fine Arts, 1994; OK I Excellence in Direction Award ACTF, 2001; named Vol. of Yr. Arts for All S.W. Okla. Opera Guild, 1997; Vol. of Yr. S.W. Theatre Assn., 2000; Lawton Arts and Humanities Educator in the Arts, 2002. Mem. Tex. Non-Profit Theatres (cons. 1984—, adjudicator 1995, 97-99); Assn. Theatre in Higher Edn., S.W. Theatre Assn. (v.p. promotions 1997-2000, webmaster 2000—); Okla. Cmty. Theatre Assn., S.W. Okla. Opera Guild, 1994— (pres. 1995-96); Arts for All, Inc. (bd. dir. 1996-99); Lawton Cmty. Theatre (bd. dir. 1995-); Phi Kappa Phi. Avocations: music, dancing, books, videotapes. Home: 717 N W 36th St Lawton OK 73505-5123 Office: Cameron Univ 2800 W Gore Blvd Lawton OK 73505-6377 E-mail: scottk@cameron.edu.

KLEIN, SHELDON, computational linguist, educator; b. Chgo., May 15, 1935; s. Joseph and Bertha (Stone) K.; m. Carol Wallace, Oct. 20, 1955; 1 child, Jahna (Mrs. Paul N. Antoniades). BA in Anthropology, U. Calif., Berkeley, 1956, PhD in Linguistics, 1963. With Artificial Intelligence Research Group, System Devel. Corp., Santa Monica, Calif., 1961-64; asst. prof. linguistics and computer sci. Carnegie-Mellon U., Pitts., 1964-66; assoc. prof. computer sci. and linguistics U. Wis., Madison, 1966-73, prof., 1973—2003, chmn. dept. linguistics, 1974-76, prof. emeritus, 2003—. Vis. dir. studies L'Ecole des hautes etudes en sciences sociales, Paris, 1976-77; vis. prof. Fakultät für Linguistik und Literaturwissenschaft, U. Bielefeld, Fed. Republic Germany, 1977-78; vis. fellow Clare Hall and Dept. Archaeology U. Cambridge, 1988; life mem. Clare Hall, 1988—; linguistic fieldwork with Kawaiisu Indians, U. Calif. Survey of Calif. Indian Langs., Cen. Calif., 1958, Wenner-Gren Found. Anthrop. Research, 1981-86; archaeological fieldwork, Kebara cave, Mt. Carmel, Israel, 1990; cons. System Devel. Corp., 1965, 67. Contbr. articles to books and profl. jours. Life mem. in residence Clare Hall, Cambridge U., 1995. NSF grantee, 1969-73; Internat. Rsch. and Exchs. Bd. sr. scholar Soviet Ministry of Higher Edn., Fgn. Langs. Inst., Moscow, 1973. Fellow Am. Anthrop. Assn., Royal Anthrop. Inst. Gt. Britain and Ireland; mem. Am. Assn. Artificial Intelligence, Assn. Computational Linguistics, Cognitive Sci. Soc., Soc. Study on Indigenous Langs. of Americas, Linguistics Soc. Am. (life mem. 1997), Soc. Linguistic Anthropology, Sigma Xi. Office: U Wis Dept Computer Sci 1210 W Dayton St Madison WI 53706-1613

KLEIN, SHIRLEY ANN, educator; b. Sioux Center, Iowa, Sept. 20, 1953; d. Charles L. and Grace (Blom) K. BA, Dordt Coll., Sioux Center, 1975. Cert. tchr., Iowa, Minn., N.J. Classroom tchr. Terra Ceia (N.C.) Christian Sch., 1975-78; tchr. biology Eastern Christian High Sch., North Haledon, N.J., 1979-84; sci. tchr. Des Moines Christian Sch., 1986-87; tchr. sci. Faith Christian High Sch., Bigelow, Minn., 1987-91; asst. editor God's World Publs., Inc., Asheville, N.C., 1991-92; adj. instr. sci. N.W. Iowa C.C., Sheldon, 1992—. Republican. Christian Reformed. Avocations: photography, reading, camping, wood carving.

KLEIN, SHIRLEY SNYDERMAN, retail executive; b. Balt., Oct. 23, 1929; d. Julius Herman and Fannie (Dannenberg) Snyderman; m. Ralph Lincoln Klein, Jan. 4, 1953; children: Andrew P., Michael J., Howard S. BA, Towson State Tchr.'s Coll., 1951. Office staff accts. receivable, jr. controller Klein's Tower Plz., Inc., Forest Hill, Md., 1952-60, jr. buyer, 1960-70, v.p., buyer children's, ladies, linens, 1970—; bd. mem. Ben Chesapeake Health Sys. (2 Hosp.), 1994; chmn. Upper Chesapeake Health Found., 1995—2001. Treas. Mortgage Svc. Co., Inc., 1956—64; v.p. Klein's Supermarkets, 1979—, Colgate Investments, 1970—; bd. dirs. Upper Chesapeake Health Systems, found. chair, 1993—2001. Pres. Hadassah Harford County, 1966-68; v.p.; adv. bd. John Carroll Sch., Md. Diocese, 1967, bd. mem., 1970; chmn. Retinitis Pigmentosa Found., Harford County, Md., 1971; bd. dirs. Harfard Opera Theatre Guild, 1976-79; treas. Harford County Commn. for Women, 1977-82; v.p. Jewish Nat. Fund., Balt., 1990-95, bd. dirs., 1993-2000; vice chair Israel Bonds Balt., 1980-97. Recipient Goldie Myeir award, 1996. Mem.: LWV. Home: 109 W Jarrettsville Rd Forest Hill MD 21050-1319 Office: 2101 Rockspring Road Forest Hill MD 21050 Fax: 410-515-9305.

KLEIN, SOPHIA H. entrepreneur; b. Dayton, Ohio, Aug. 17, 1915; d. Felix Frank Borkowski, Helen Marie Sichujainska; children: Helen Marie, Betty Jean. Owner Oak Hill Optical, Dayton, Town & Country Water Softener, Dayton, Klein Enterprises, Dayton, Country Squire Supper Club, Dayton, Bagel Connection, Dayton, Exquisitely Yours Jewelers, Dayton. Mem.: Dayton Cath. Bus. Women's Club (pres., Dayton Woman of Yr. 1988), Holy Seplecher (Lady of the Cross 1987—, U.S. Rep. Millennium visit to Vatican 2000). Democrat. Roman Catholic. Avocation: golf. Home: 20 Oak Knoll Dr Dayton OH 45419

KLEIN, STEPHEN THOMAS, performing arts executive; b. Cleve., Mar. 9, 1947; s. Howard B. and Lilly (Gatchell) K.; m. Mary Ussery, Nov. 19, 1972; children— William Howard, Sarah Katherine. B.F.A., Boston U., 1970. Orch. Mgr. Cleve. Orch., 1978-82; exec. dir. Denver Symphony Orch., Colo., 1982-85, Nat. Symphony Orch., Washington, 1985-94; mng. dir. Pitts. Pub. Theater, 1994—.

KLEIN, STEVEN GEORGE, osteopathic physician; b. Phila., Mar. 21, 1943; s. William Klein and Vivian (Korostoff) Fingerhood; m. Shoshana Nevo, May 2, 1991. BA, Temple U., 1965; cert., U. Heidelberg, Germany, 1966; grad., Calhoon M.E.B.A. Marine Engring. Sch., 1975; MA, U. Pa., 1976; DO, U. Osteo. Medicine, Des Moines, 1984; MPH, Med. Coll. Wis. Diplomate Am. Bd. Family Practice; cert. tchr., marine engr., physician. Tchr. Phila. Sch. Sys. North Pa. Schs., Lansdale, 1971-72; tchr. North Penn Schs., Lansdale; pvt. practice Gloucester City, N.J., 1987—. German-English translator, interpreter Northwest Industries, Lone Star, Tex., 1976; translator U. Heidelberg, 1965-66. With U.S. Mcht. Marine, 1973-80. Mem. Rotary. Avocations: short wave radio, photography. Office: PO Box 208 104 S Broadway Gloucester City NJ 08030-0208

KLEIN, T(HEODORE) E(IBON) D(ONALD), writer; b. N.Y.C., July 15, 1947; s. Richard and Norma (Kashins) K. AB, Brown U., 1969; M.F.A., Columbia U., 1972. Asst. story editor Paramount Pictures, N.Y.C., 1972-75; editor-in-chief Twilight Zone Mag., N.Y.C., 1981-86; editor CrimeBeat mag., N.Y.C., 1991-93; editor mag. Sci-Fi Entertainment, Herndon, Va., 1995. Author: (novel) The Ceremonies, 1984, (story collection) Dark Gods, 1985; screenwriter: (feature film) Trauma, 1994; contbr. fiction to anthologies; author articles in mags., newspapers. Recipient novel award Brit. Fantasy Soc., 1985, novella award World Fantasy Soc., 1986. Mem. Phi Beta Kappa Home: 210 W 89th St New York NY 10024-1805 E-mail: theodoreklein@att.net.

KLEIN, VERLE WESLEY, retired corporate executive, retired naval officer; b. Stickney, S.D., Apr. 7, 1933; s. Albert and Kate (Notcboom) K., children by previous marriage: Pamela Louise, Janice Lynn; m. Marjorie Nancy Hagan, Apr. 29, 1989; children: Tia Leigh, Nelson Hoffman. BS, U.S. Naval Postgrad. Sch., 1962; MBA, George Washington U., 1975. Commd. ensign U.S. Navy, 1954, advanced through grades to rear adm., 1980; assigned to (Patrol Squadron 22), 1955-58; flight instr. (Naval Air Sta.), Corpus Christi, Tex., 1958-60; with (Air Antisubmarine Squadron 22), 1963-65; test pilot (Naval Air Test Center), Patuxent River, Md., 1967-69; comdg. officer (Light Attack Squadron 4), 1969-70; ops. officer (USS Wasp), 1971-72; asst. aviation comdr. detailer (Bur. Naval Personnel), 1972-74; head major procurement programs and budgeting br. (Naval Material Command), 1975-76; exec. asst. and naval aide to asst. sec. (Dept. Navy), 1976-78; comdr. (Naval Air Station), Patuxent River, 1978-80; dep. dir. Office Budgets and Reports, also fiscal mgmt. div. (Office of Chief Naval Ops.), 1980-85; v.p. BDM Corp., McLean, Va., 1985-87; cons., 1987-2000. Decorated Silver Star, Legion of Merit with four gold stars, D.F.C., 24 Air medals with two gold stars, Navy Commendation medal, Gallantry Cross Republic Vietnam, numerous others. Mem. Am. Soc. Mil. Comptrollers. Home: 12324 Birchfalls Dr Raleigh NC 27614

KLEIN, WILLIAM BRENT, surgeon; s. John and Sylvia Klein; m. Donna Marie Blazer, Sept. 19, 1987; children: Jordan, Steven. BS, Tulane U., 1982, MPH&TM, 1992; MD, La. State U., 1986; MBA, Regis U., 2002. Cert. advanced trauma life support ACS, 2002, ACLS Am. Heart Assn., 2002. Flight surgeon, med. dir. 2d aeromed. staging facility David Grant Med. Ctr., Travis AFB, Calif., 1987—89; chief aeromed. svcs. 57th Fighter Interceptor Squadron, Keflavik Naval Air Sta., Iceland, 1989—91; comdr. 366 aero. medicine squadron, chief aeromed. svcs. 366 Med. Group, 389th Fighter Squadron, Mountain Home AFB, Idaho; dep. comdr., chief aero. medicine 31st Med. Group, Aviano, Italy, 1996—99; chief aero. medicine br. Hq Afrc, Robins AFB, Ga., 1999—2002, chief aero. medicine divsn., chief, profl. svcs., 2002—. Col. USAF. Decorated Commendation medal USAF, Achievement Medal, Achievement medal, Aerial Achievement medal, Meritorious Svc. medal. Fellow: Am. Coll. Preventive Medicine (specialist occupl. medicine, specialist aero. medicine), Aero. Med. Assn. (assoc.); mem.: AMA, Am. Soc. Tropical Medicine Hygiene, Assn. Mil. Surgeons, Air Force Assn. (life), Soc. USAF Flight Surgeons, Am. Coll. Physician Executives (cert.), Sigma Chi (life). Office: Hq Afrc/Sgp 135 Page Road Warner Robins GA 31098 Personal E-mail: wbklein@aol.com.

KLEIN, WILLIAM DAVID, lawyer; b. St. Cloud, Minn., Oct. 30, 1954; s. Wilfred George and Rita Christina (Gottwalt) K.; m. Rebecca Lynn Ready, May 26, 1979; children: Michaela Laine, Caitlin Brianne. BA summa cum laude, St. Olaf Coll., 1976; JD magna cum laude, U. Mich., 1979. Bar: Minn. 1979, U.S. Dist. Ct. Minn. 1979, U.S. Claims Ct. 1983, U.S. Tax Ct. 1985. Law clk. to presiding justice Minn. Supreme Ct., St. Paul, 1979-80; assoc. Gray, Plant, Mooty, Mooty, & Bennett P.A., Mpls., 1980-84, ptnr., 1985—, CFO, 1990-98, also bd. dirs. Bd. dirs. Katahdin Inc., chmn. bd., 1992-94. Author: (with others) Case Studies in Tax Planning--Partnerships, 1987, PPC Tax Planning Guide--Partnerships, 1990, S Corporations and Life Insurance, 1992, 2d edit., 1999. Bd. dirs. Highland Dist. Coun., St. Paul, 2002—, sec., 2003—. Mem.: ABA (chair subcom. revenue rulings, S Corps. com. tax sect. 1996—), Hennepin County Bar Assn., Minn. State Bar Assn. (sec. tax sect. 2000, coun. mem. 2000—, treas. 2001, vice chmn. 2001—02, chmn. 2002—03), Rotary (bd. dirs. 1999—2002, pres. Found. 1999—2002). Office: Gray Plant Mooty Mooty & Bennett 33 S 6th St Ste 3400 Minneapolis MN 55402-3796 E-mail: william.klein@gpmlaw.com.

KLEIN, WILLIAM FRANCIS, social ecologist, multimedia publisher, producer, musician, writer; b. Glendale, Calif., June 8, 1953; s. Richard Edward and Arlene May Klein. BA in Sociology, U. Calif., Santa Barbara, 1976; MPA, Calif. State U., Long Beach, 1978; MS in Sys. Mgmt., U. So. Calif., L.A., 1981; MA in Writing and Consciousness, New Coll. Calif., 1999. Cert. Am. Inst. Cert. Planners. Sr. mgr. Deloitte Haskins & Sells, San Francisco and L.A., 1982-91; dir. Capital Partnerships, San Francisco, 1991-95; sr. mgr. Merill & Assocs., San Francisco, 1995-97; prodr. Metal House, Beverly Hills, Calif., 1997-98, Atomic Pest, Walnut Creek, Calif., 1998—. Musician: various groups. Bd. dirs. Shared Living Resource Ctr., Berkeley, 1986-96. Mem. Green Party. E-mail: gfrancisous@yahoo.com.

KLEINBARD, EDWARD D. lawyer; b. N.Y.C., Nov. 6, 1951; s. Martin L. and Joan K.; m. Norma F. Cirincione, Oct. 17, 1947. BA, MA, Brown U., 1973; JD, Yale U., 1976. Bar: N.Y. 1977. Ptnr. Cleary, Gottlieb, Steen & Hamilton, N.Y.C. Book rev., article editor Yale Law Jour., 1975-76; contbr. articles to profl. jours. Fellow Am. Coll. Tax Counsel; mem. ABA, N.Y. State Bar Assn. (co-chmn. fin. instruments com. 1989-91), Assn. Bar City of N.Y., Internat. Assn. Fin. Engrs., Internat. Fiscal Assn. Office: Cleary Gottlieb Steen & Hamilton 1 Liberty Plz Fl 38 New York NY 10006-1470

KLEINBERG, DAVID LEWIS, education administrator; b. San Francisco, Feb. 28, 1943; s. Moe and Lilyan (Abrams) K.; m. Gay Buros, Mar. 21, 1970 (div. 1983); children— Leah, Rebecca; m. Patrice Ellen Greenwood, Apr. 29, 1984; stepchildren: Aaron, Brian, Jesse. BA, San Francisco State U., 1970. Prodr. Sta. KTVU TV, Oakland, Calif., 1978-79, 89-90; writer, editor San Francisco Chronicle, 1960-80, editor Sunday Datebook, 1980-94; co-dir. Bay Area Classic Learning, San Francisco, 1994—. Served with U.S. Army, 1965-67, Vietnam Decorated Bronze Star Jewish. Avocations: basketball, post card collecting, stand-up comic, producer of comedy. Office: 300 Taravac St San Francisco CA 94116-1953 E-mail: bael@bael.com.

KLEINBERG, LAWRENCE H. investor, consultant; b. N.Y.C., Dec. 20, 1943; s. Paul and Gertrude (Voron) Kleinberg; m. Lois Helene Kass, June 10, 1967; children: Brian Andrew, Rachel Adele. BA in Econs., Adelphi U., 1965, MBA, 1969. Analyst, Pfizer, Inc., N.Y.C., 1965-69; various fin. mgmt. positions Beech-Nut, Inc., N.Y.C., 1969-73; v.p., controller Life Savers, Inc., N.Y.C., 1973-79, sr. v.p. fin., 1979-83, exec. v.p., 1983, pres., 1984, divsn. pres. Nabisco Brands, Inc., 1984-87; v.p., corp. controller Nabisco Brands, Inc., Parsippany, NJ, 1987-88; sr. v.p. fin. Nabisco Foods Group, Parsippany, 1988-94; sr. v.p. planning Nabisco, Inc., Parsippany, 1995 96; pvt. investor, cons., 1996—. Bd. dirs. Old London Foods, Stravina Oper. Co. Home: 13285 Verdun Dr Palm Beach Gardens FL 33410 E-mail: lhk43@aol.com.

KLEINBERG, NORMAN CHARLES, lawyer; b. Phila., July 18, 1946; s. Frank and Mildred Brosnan (Hill) K.; m. Marcia Sue Topperman, Jan. 31, 1971; children: Lauren Blythe, Joanna Leigh. AB, Tufts U., 1968; JD, Columbia U., 1972. Bar: N.Y. 1973, U.S. Supreme Ct., U.S. Ct. Appeals (1st, 2d, 3d, 5th, and fed. cirs.), U.S. Dist. Ct. (so. and ea. dists.) N.Y., U.S. Tax Ct., U.S. Dist. Ct. (ea. dist.) Wis., U.S. Dist. Ct. (no. dist.) Calif., U.S. Dist. Ct. (ea. dist.) Mich. Law clk. to judge U.S. Dist. Ct. (so. dist.) N.Y., N.Y.C., 1972-74; assoc. Hughes Hubbard & Reed, N.Y.C., 1974-80, ptnr., 1980—. Articles editor Columbia Jour. Law and Social Problems, 1971-72. Served to staff sgt. USAR, 1968-74. Fellow Am. Coll. Trial Lawyers; mem. ABA, Fed. Bar Coun., Assn. Bar of City of N.Y. (com. on state cts. of superior jurisdiction, com. profl. responsibility, com. profl. and jud. ethics., com. on jud., coun. on jud. adminstrn.), Internat. Bar Assn., N.Y. State Bar Assn., Def. Rsch. Inst. Home: 460 E 79th St New York NY 10021-1443 Office: Hughes Hubbard & Reed 1 Battery Park Plz Fl 12 New York NY 10004-1482 E-mail: kleinber@hugheshubbard.com.

KLEINBERG, ROBERT IRWIN, lawyer; b. Bronx, N.Y., Sept. 10, 1937; s. Abraham and Lillian (Fox) K.; m. Luise Bitterman, Oct. 27, 1962; children: Andrew, Jeanine. BA, U. Mich., 1958; LLB, Columbia U., 1961. Bar: N.Y. 1962. Mng. dir., gen. counsel Merrill Lynch, Pierce Fenner & Smith, Inc. (subs. Merrill Lynch Capital Mkts. Group), N.Y.C., 1978-80; gen. counsel, exec. v.p. Oppenheimer & Co. Inc., N.Y.C., 1980-98, Nat. Fin. Ptnrs. Corp., 1999—. Arbitrator Am. Stock Exch. Mem. ABA, N.Y. State Bar Assn., Nat. Assn. Securities Dealers (arbitrator, dist. com. 12, bd. govs. 1992—, chmn. nat. bus. conduct com. 1993), Securities Industry Assn. (pres. legal and compliance divsn. 1990-91, chmn. bus. com. dist. 10 1991). Home: 1016 5th Ave # 11D New York NY 10028-0132 Office: Oppenheimer & Co Inc Oppenheimer Tower World Fin Ctr New York NY 10281 E-mail: rkleinberg@nfp.com.

KLEINE, HERMAN, economist; b. N.Y.C., Mar. 6, 1920; s. Max and Fannie (Schechter) K.; m. Paula Stein, June 16, 1962; children— Joseph, Michael. BS, State U. N.Y. at Albany, 1941, MA, Clark U., 1942, PhD, 1951. Researcher for Nat. Indsl. Conf. Bd., 1946; instr. to asst. prof. Worcester Polytech. Inst., 1946-49; economist ECA, Mut. Security Agy., The Hague, Netherlands, 1949-53; internat. relations and econs. FOA, ICA, Washington, 1953-57; dir. U.S. Ops. Mission to Ethiopia, ICA, 1957-59, asst. dep. dir. for ops., 1959-61; Nat. War Coll., 1961-62; AID adviser U.S. Mission to UN, N.Y.C., 1962-64; dep. asst. adminstr. for Africa AID, Washington, 1964-67; dep. dir. U.S. AID mission to Brazil, 1967-69; asso. U.S. coordinator Alliance for Progress, 1969-70; dep. U.S. coordinator, asst. adminstr. Latin Am. Bur. AID, Washington, 1971-76; advisor to controller Interam. Devel. Bank, 1976-84; dir. internship programs Ctr. Immigration Policy and Refugee Assistance, Georgetown U., 1984-86; cons., mediator, 1986—. Mem. U.S. delegation UN Gen. Assembly, 1962, 63 Served from pvt. to capt. USAAF, 1942-46. Recipient AID Distinguished honor award, 1973, Adminstrs. Distinguished Career Service award, 1976, Superior Honor award Dept. State, 1976, Distinguished Alumnus award State U. N.Y. at Albany, 1977; duPont fellow, 1948; named to Hempstead, N.Y. Sch. Dist. Hall Fame, 1986. Mem. Kappa Phi Kappa. Jewish. Home and Office: 100 Hilary Cir Fairfield CT 06825

KLEINER, ELAINE LAURA, English literature educator; b. Portland, Oreg., May 2, 1942; d. Eugene Michael and Florence Isabelle (Hoffman) K. BA, Oreg. State U., 1964; MA, U. Chgo., 1966, PhD, 1971. Tchg. asst. U. Wis., Madison, 1966-67; instr. English Wis. State U., Whitewater, 1966, 67; asst. prof. English Ind. State U., Terre Haute, 1969-76, assoc. prof., 1976-81, acting dir. honors, 1977-78, dir. univ. studies, 1976-85, prof. English, 1981—2002, prof. emerita, 2002—; adj. prof. Jackson Cmty. Coll., 2002—. Mng. editor Sci.-Fiction Studies, Terre Haute, 1967-69. Author: This Sacred Earth and Other Poems, 1997, Beside Great Waters: Poems of the Highlands and Islands, 1997; co-editor: Sacramental Acts: The Love Poems of Kenneth Rexroth, 1997. Mem., patron Terre Haute Choral Assn., 1980-95; bd. dirs. United Ministries for Higher Edn., Terre Haute, 1978-85. Fulbright sr. scholar USIA, Romania, 1989; NEH summer fellow, 1979; Ind. Arts Commn. grantee, 1983, Ind. Humanities grantee, 1985. Mem. W.B. Yeats Soc., Assn. for Study of Lit. and Environment, Soc. for Romanian Studies. Democrat. Eastern Orthodox. Avocations: sailing, creative writing, cycling, swimming, hiking. Home: 808 S West Ave Jackson MI 49203 E-mail: ejek@yahoo.com.

KLEINER, FRED SCOTT, art historian, archaeologist, educator, editor; b. N.Y.C., Apr. 29, 1948, m. Diana Elizabeth Edelman, Dec. 22, 1972; 1 child, Alexander Mark. BA with honors, U. Pa., 1968; MA, Columbia U., 1969, PhD, 1973. Agora fellow Am. Sch. Classical Studies, Athens, Greece, 1973-75; asst. prof. art history and archaeology U. Va., Charlottesville, 1975-78; asst. prof. Boston U., 1978-81, assoc. prof., 1981-86, prof., 1986—, dir. grad. studies dept. art history, 1979-81, 99, chmn. dept. art history, 1981-85, sr. fellow Soc. Fellows Humanities, 1985-86. Excavator, Cosa, Italy, 1969-70; vis. prof. Yale U., New Haven, 1997. Author: Greek and Roman Coins in the Athenian Agora, 1976, The Early Cistophoric Coinage, 1977, Medieval and Modern Coins in the Athenian Agora, 1978, The Arch of Nero in Rome, 1985, Art Through the Ages, 10th edit., 1996, Art Through the Ages, 11th edit., 2001 (Texty Prize, 2001, McGuffey Prize, 2001), Art Through the Ages-The Western Perspective, 2003; editor-in-chief: Am. Jour. Archaeology, 1985—98, mem. adv. bd.: Archaeol. News, 1980—; contbr. articles to profl. jours. Bd. dirs. Yale Youth Hockey Assn., 1994-97, v.p., 1996-97; co-founder, mgr. Conn. Ice Dogs, 1997-2001. Grantee Am. Philos. Soc., 1971, 80, Am. Coun. Learned Socs., 1978, 82; Guggenheim fellow, 1988-89. Mem.: Tex. and Acad. Authors Assn. (awards com. 2002—), Soc. Acad. Authors (awards com. 2002—), Coll. Art Assn. (Morey Book award com. 1999—2000, chair 2001—03), Archaeol. Inst. Am. (chmn. fellowship com. 1985, publs. com. 1985—98, numismatics com. 2000—). Home: 102 Rimmon Rd Woodbridge CT 06525-1941 Office: Boston U Dept Art History Boston MA 02215 E-mail: fsk@bu.edu.

KLEINER, HEATHER SMITH, retired academic administrator; b. N.Y.C., Mar. 31, 1940; d. Henry Lee Smith and Marie (Ballou) Edwards; m. Scott Alter Kleiner, Mar. 20, 1961; children: Greta (dec.), Catherine. BA in Sociology, Smith Coll., 1961; MAT in Edn., Lynchburg Coll., 1969; postgrad., U. Ga., 1974-82. Rsch. analyst Edward Weiss Advt., Chgo., 1963-65; acad. advisor U. Ga. Coll. Arts and Scis., Athens, 1982-88; asst. dir. womens studies program U. Ga., Athens, 1988-90, assoc. dir. womens studies program, 1990-2000. Co-founder, 1st pres. Jeannette Rankin Found., Athens, 1976-77, bd. dirs., hon. dir., 1977—, chair capital fund drive 1993-96; trustee Unitarian Universalist Fellowship of Athens, Ga., 2003—. Mem.: LWV, AAUW, Jeannette Rankin Found. Avocations: reading, swimming.

KLEINFELD, ANDREW J. federal judge; b. 1945; BA magna cum laude, Wesleyan U., 1966; JD cum laude, Harvard U., 1969. Law clk. Alaska Supreme Ct., 1969—71; U.S. magistrate U.S. Dist. Ct. Alaska, Fairbanks, 1971—74; pvt. practice law Fairbanks, 1971—86; judge U.S. Dist. Ct. Alaska, Anchorage, 1986—91, U.S. Ct. Appeals (9th cir.), San Francisco, 1991—. Contbr. articles to profl. jours. Mem.: Tanana Valley Bar Assn. (pres. 1974—75), Alaska Bar Assn. (pres. 1982—83, bd. govs. 1981—84), Phi Beta Kappa. Republican. Office: US Ct Appeals 9th Cir Courthouse Sq 250 Cushman St Ste 3-a Fairbanks AK 99701-4665

KLEINFELD, DENIS ALAN, lawyer; b. Chgo., Feb. 10, 1946; s. J. Laurence and Helen Kleinfeld; m. June Kleinfeld; children: Harrison, Jaclene. BS Accountancy, U. Ill., 1967; JD, Loyola U., Chgo., 1970. CPA; Bar: Ill., 1970, Fla., 1983. Atty. IRS, Chgo., 1970-74, Denis Kleinfeld & Assocs., Chgo., 1974-83, Kleinfeld & Assocs., Miami, Fla., 1983-97, Kleinfeld Law Firm, Miami, Fla., 1997—2003, spl. counsel to, 2003—. Author: Offshore Trusts, 2000; co-author: Estate Planning for Florida Resident, 2001, Practical International Tax Planning, 2003, Offshore Asset Protection Trusts, 2003; contbr. editor: Offshore Investment Mag.; mem. editl. bd. Offshore Fin. USA Mag., Estate Planning mag.; contbr. articles to profl. jours. Mem. ABA (asset protection com.), Internat. Tax Planning Assn., Soc. Trust and Estate Practitioners, Fla. Bar Assn., Ill. Bar Assn., Am. Assn. Attys.-CPAs, Fla. Soc. CPAs, Estate Planning Coun. Miami. Avocations: work, reading, travel. Office: Four Point Mgmt LLP Grand Galleria Ste 220 43-46 Norre Gade St Thomas VI 00802

KLEINFELD, ERWIN, mathematician, educator; b. Vienna, Apr. 19, 1927; came to U.S., 1940; s. Lazar and Gina (Schönbach) K.; m. Margaret Morgan, July 2, 1968; children— Barbara, David. BS, CCNY, 1948; MA, U. Pa., 1949; PhD, U. Wis., 1951. Instr. U. Chgo., 1951-53; asst. prof. Ohio State U., 1953-56, assoc. prof., 1957-60, prof., 1960-62; prof. math. Syracuse U., 1962-67, U. Hawaii, 1967-68, U. Iowa, 1968—2002, prof. emeritus, 2002—. Vis. lectr. Yale, 1956-57; cons. Nat. Bur. Standards, summer 1953; research specialist U. Conn., summer 1955; research mathematician Bowdoin Coll., summer 1957; research asso. Cornell U., summer 1958, U. Calif. at Los Angeles, summer 1959, Stanford, summer 1960, Inst. Def. Analysis, summer 1961, 62, AID-India, summer 1964, 65; vis. prof. Emory U., 1976-77; Cons. Edn. IX Project, World Bank, U. Indonesia, 1985-86, Mucia/Ind. U.-(ITM) Shah Alam, Malaysia Project, 1988 89. Editorial bd. Jour. Algebra-Academic Press; cons. editor, Merrill Pub. Co.-Div. Bell & Howell. Contbr. articles research jours. Served with AUS, 1945-46. Wis. Alumni Rsch. Found. fellow, 1949-51, vis. rsch. fellow U. New Eng., Australia, 1992; grantee U.S. Army Rsch. Office, 1955-70, NSF, 1970-75. Mem. Am. Math. Soc., Sigma Xi. Home: 1555 N Sierra 120 Reno NV 89503 E-mail: kleinfld@math.uiowa.edu.

KLEINGARTNER, ARCHIE, founding dean, educator; b. Gackle, N.D., Aug. 10, 1936; s. Emanuel and Ottile (Kuhn) K.; m. Dorothy Jean Hanselmann, Sept. 21, 1957; children: Elizabeth, Thomas. BA, U. Minn., 1959; MS, U. Oreg., 1961; PhD, U. Wis., 1965. Asst. and assoc. prof. UCLA, 1964-69, assoc. dean, chmn., 1969-71, prof., 1971-75, 83—, dir. entertainment mgmt. program, 1988—, founding dean Sch. Pub. Policy and Social Rsch., 1994—; v.p. U. Calif. Sys., Berkeley, 1975-83. Cons. in field, 1967—; arbitrator in field, 1971—; chmn. Global Window Ptnrs., Inc., 1998—. Mem. labor mgmt. disputes panel City of L.A., 1978—. With U.S. Army, 1954-56. Mem. London Sch. Econs., Alpha Kappa Psi. Republican. Methodist. Avocations: tennis, biking, gardening. Home: 12258 Montana Ave #103 Los Angeles CA 90049 Office: UCLA Sch Pub Policy Social Rsch PO Box 951656 Los Angeles CA 90095-1656 E-mail: archie.kleingartner@anderson.ucla.edu.

KLEINHENZ, CHRISTOPHER, foreign language educator, researcher; b. Indpls., Dec. 29, 1941; s. John Emory and Louise Eleanor (Ross); m. Margaret Ellen Zechiel, Aug. 1, 1964; children: Steven Russell, Michael Thomas. BA, Ind. U., 1964, MA, 1966, PhD, 1969. Asst. prof., dir. Bologna program Ind. U., 1970-71; instr. U. Wis., Madison, 1968-69, asst. prof., 1969-70, asst. prof., dept. French and Italian, 1971-75, assoc. prof., 1975-80, chmn. medieval studies program, 1975-80, 81-84, 89-95, 96—, prof., 1980—, chmn. dept., 1985-88, Carol Mason Kirk prof. Italian, 2000—. Dir. devel. grant NEH, Madison, 1976-79, co-dir. rsch. tools grant, 1980-84. Author: The Early Italian Sonnet, 1986; editor: Medieval Manuscripts and Textual Criticism, 1976, Medieval Studies in North America, 1982, Routledge Studies in Medieval Literature, 1986-2002, Dante Studies, 1988-2003, Medieval Italy: An Encyclopedia, 2003; co-editor: Saint Augustine the Bishop: A Book of Essays, 1994, Routledge Medieval Casebooks, 1991—, Fearful Hope: Approaching the New Millennium, 1999; assoc. editor: Dante Ency., 2000; chmn. editl. bd. Medieval Acad. Reprints for Teaching, 1981-93; bibliographer MLA, N.Y.C., 1981-88, BIGLLI, Rome, 1994—, Dante Studies, 1984-, ICLS, 2002—; book rev. editor Italica, 1984-93; co-translator: Dante Alighieri, Il Fiore and the Detto d'Amore, 2000. Chmn. com. on ctrs. and regional assns. Medieval Acad., 1993-99. Newberry Libr./NEH grantee, 1988-89. Mem. Medieval Assn. of Midwest (pres. 1984-85, 2003—), Dante Soc. Am. (mem. coun. 1985-91), Am. Boccaccio Assn. (v.p. 1987-93, pres. 1993-97), Am. Assn. Tchrs. of Italian (v.p. 1997-98, pres. 1999-2003). Avocations: sports, stamp collecting, photography, travel. Home: 2247 Fox Ave Madison WI 53711-1922 Office: U Wis Dept French and Italian 1220 Linden Dr Madison WI 53706-1525 E-mail: ckleinhe@wisc.edu.

KLEINKNECHT, JOCHEN, management consultant; Vordiplom Math., U. of Stuttgart, Germany, 1992—94; MSc Engring., Ecole Centrale Paris, Chatenay-Malabry, France, 1994—96; MSc Ops. Rsch., Stanford U., 1996—97, PhD Mgmt. Sci., 1997—2002. Rechr. Stanford U., 1997—2002; cons. The Boston Consulting Group, San Francisco, 2002—. Cons. LSI Logic, Milpitas, Calif., 1997—99, Booz Allen & Hamilton, Munich, 1998—98, A.T. Kearney, San Francisco, 1999, Gen. Motors, Warren, Mich., 1999—2001. Pres. Stanford German Student Assn., 1998—2000. Recipient Dept. Svc. Award, Dept. of Mgmt. Sci. & Engring., Stanford U., 2002; grantee ERP Fellowship, German Ministry of Commerce, 1998-2001; German Nat. Merit Scholar, German Nat. Merit Found., 1992-2001, Program TIME Scholar, Ecole Centrale Paris, France, 1994-1996, Tech. Scholar Group, Daimler-Chrysler Group, Stuttgart Germany, 1995-1998. Mem.: INFORMS. Achievements include research in First mathematical model to jointly optimize valuation of supply contracts with and without options and inventory policy in the presence of a spot market. Office: The Boston Consulting Group Two Embarcadero Ctr San Francisco CA 94111 E-mail: kleinknecht.jochen@bcg.com.

KLEINKNECHT, KENNETH SAMUEL, retired aerospace company executive, former federal space agency official; b. Washington, July 24, 1919; s. Christian Frederick and Nell May (Barr) K.; m. Patricia Jean Todd, May 24, 1947; children: Linda May, Patricia Ann, Frederick William. BSM.E., Purdue U., 1942. Project engr. NACA Lewis Research Center, Cleve., 1942-51; aero. research scientist NASA Flight Research Ctr., Edwards AFB, Calif., 1951-59; successively mgr. Mercury Project, dep. mgr. Gemini Program, mgr. command and service modules NASA Johnson Space Ctr., 1959-70, mgr. Skylab Program, 1970-74, dir. flight ops., 1974-76, asst. mgr. Orbiter Project, 1976-77; head constrn. space shuttle orbiter NASA Johnson Space Center, 1979-81; dep. assoc. adminstr. for space transp. systems European ops. to European Space Agy., Paris NASA Hdqrs., Washington, 1977-79; mgr. program engring., sr. space transp. system tech. adviser Denver div. Martin Marietta Aerospace, 1981-83, mgr. mfg. procurement and testing, 1983-84, dir. design to cost/productivity Space Sta. Project, 1984-88; mgr. laser project Zenith Star Program, 1988-90, ret., 1990. Exec. bd. Sam Houston Area council Boy Scouts Am., Houston, 1972-77. Recipient (with others) Group Achievement award for Mercury Project NASA, 1962, NASA medal for outstanding leadership Pres. of U.S., 1963, 81, John J. Montgomery award San Diego chpt. Nat. Soc. Aerospace Profls., 1963, with others) Group Achievement award for X-15 Research Airplane Flight Test Orgn., 1964, for Gemini Program, 1966, NASA Exceptional Service medal, 1969, NASA Disting. Service medal, 1969, 73 Fellow Am. Astron. Soc. (W. Randolph Lovelace II award 1975); assoc. fellow AIAA; mem. Internat. Acad. Astronautics. Clubs: Masons. Home: 825 Front Range Rd Littleton CO 80120-4005 *As a member of the team that made lunar and space shuttle missions successes, I believe that my "formula for success" is one part high goal and one hundred parts persistence. I have always believed in establishing principles, high ideals of conduct as structures to direct our lives. It is voluntary total dedication to valid ideals, attention to detail, discipline and accepting accountability that will bring success on every level. To reach beyond one's present grasp is to assure ever higher attainments in the future.*

KLEINKORT, JOSEPH ALEXIUS, physical therapist, consultant; b. Bronxville, N.Y., Jan. 28, 1946; s. Joseph P. and Marie C. (Richter) K.; m. Kathleen J. Kleinkort, Oct. 3, 1953; children: Pat, Mike, Kelly, Kristin, Kevin. BS in Phys. Therapy, St. Louis U., 1968; MA in Psychology, Ball State U., 1977; PhD (hon.), Medicina Alternativa, Copenhagen, 1983; PhD in Safety Mgmt., Western States U., 1998. Registered safety dir. World Safety Orgn.; registered phys. therapist, Tex., Fla.; cert. indsl. ergonomist. Dir. phys. therapy Phys. Therapy, Inc., Ft. Lauderdale, Fla., 1970—72; commd. officer USAF, 1972; dir. phys. therapy USAF Hosp.-Barksdale, Bossier City, La., 1972-74, USAF Hosp.-Torrejone, Madrid, 1974-78; asst. dir. Wilford Hall Med. Ctr., San Antonio, 1980-83; res. at rank of maj. USAF, 1983; pres. Chronic Pain Assn., Inc., San Antonio, 1983-88; exec. dir. Ft. Worth Back Inst., 1988-90; pres. Joseph A. Kleinkort, P.C., Roanoke, Tex., 1983—. Sr. v.p., 1995—96; exec. v.p., 1996—; COO, 1997—; cons. Dynatronics Corp., Salt Lake City, 1985—; bd. dirs. Sci. Cons. Magnetherapy; mem. Applied Biomed. Rsch. Inst., 1996—2001; v.p. clin. rsch. Health Rsch. and Clin. Assoc., 1996—; COO Worksteps Inc., 1997—; pres. Ergosteps, 1999—; liaison officer UN for World Safety Orgn. Author: Therapeutic Medical Devices, 1983, Thermal Agents Rehabilitation, 1985, Laser Application Technology, 1986. Precinct judge, San Antonio, 1988; precinct chmn. Denton County Rep. Party, 1996—98; sr. elder First Bapt. Ch., Roanoke, 2001—03; bd. dirs. Arlington Philharm. Symphony, 1993—94. Recipient Alumni Merit award St. Louis U., 1983; named Outstanding Phys. Therapist of Tex., Tex. Phys. Therapy Bd., 1985. Fellow Am. Coll. Orthopedics (membership sec. 1988-90); mem. Internat. Soc. Lasers in Medicine and Sci., Am. Assn. Phys. Medicine and Rehab., Am. Coll. Occupl. and Environmental Medicine, Am. PHys. Therapy Assn., Am. Phys. Therapy Assn., Tex. Phys. Therapy Assn., Am. Platform Soc. Avocations: sailing, gospel teaching. Home and Office: 303 Inverness Dr Roanoke TX 76262-5561 E-mail: indusrehab@aol.com.

KLEINLEIN, KATHY LYNN, training and development executive; b. S.I., N.Y., May 2, 1950; d. Thomas and Helen Mary (O'Reilly) Perricone; m. Kenneth Robert Kleinlein, Oct. 30, 1983. BA, Wagner Coll., 1971, MA, 1974; MBA, Rutgers U., 1984; MA in Theology, Barry U., 1998. Cert. secondary tchr., N.Y., N.J., Fla. Tchr. English N.Y.C. Bd. Edn., S.I., 1971-74, Matawan (N.J.) Bd. Edn., 1974-79; instr. English Middlesex County Coll., Edison, N.J., 1978-81; med. sales rep. Pfizer/Roerig, Bklyn., 1979-81, mgr. tng. ops. N.Y.C., 1981-86; dir. sales tng. Winthrop Pharms. divsn. Sterling Drug, N.Y.C., 1986-87; dir. tng. Reuters Info. Sys., N.Y.C., 1987-90; pres., dir. tng. Women in Transition career counseling firm, 1990-98; pastoral min., dir. religious edn. St. Raphael's Ch., 1998-2001; diocesan dir. catechetical ministry Diocese of Venice (Fla.), 2001—. Pres. Kleinlein Cons.; pers. mgmt. officer USAR, N.J., 1981-86; cons. Concepts & Prodrs., N.Y.C., 1981-85; bd. regents Blessed Edmund Rice Sch. for Pastoral Ministry; bd. dirs. Campaign for Human Devel. Trainer United Way, 1982-83, mem. polit. action com., 1982—85; mem. Rep. Presdl. Task Force, Washington, 1983—; chair Sarasota Library Adv. Bd.; sec. Intracoastal Civic Assn.; mem. Reinventing Govt. Coun., Sarasota County Planning Commn., exec. bd. Edn. Found., St. Joseph Bon Secours Hosp.; mem. grievance com. Fla. Bar; bd. regents Blessed Edmund Rice Sch. for Pastoral Ministry. Mem. Sarasota County Sch. Bd., 2002—. Capt. U.S. Army, 1974—78. First woman in N.Y. N.G., 1974; first woman instr. Empire State Mil. Acad., Peekskill, N.Y., 1976. Mem.: Sarasota Women's Alliance, Rep. Women's Club, Alpha Omicron Pi. Republican. Roman Catholic. Office: Diocese Venice Cath Ctr 1000 Pinebrook Rd Venice FL 34292 E-mail: kleinlein@dioceseofvenice.org.

KLEINMAN, ANDREW YOUNG, plastic surgeon; b. Bklyn., July 2, 1953; s. Hyman Jack and Ruth Young K.; m. Elizabeth Wofsey, June 3, 1979 (div. 1998); m. Noela MacGinn, June 8, 2003; children: Julia, Alexander. BS, MIT, 1975; MD, U. Rochester, 1979. Diplomate Am. Bd. Plastic Surgery. Gen. surg. resident George Washington U. Hosp., Washington, 1979-81; resident in surgery Harvard Surg. New Eng. Deaconess Hosp., Boston, 1981-82; rsch. fellow Mass. Gen. Hosp., Boston, 1982-83; resident in plastic surgery Baylor Coll. Medicine, Houston, 1983-85; pvt. practice New Rochelle, NY, 1985—. Mem.: Am. Soc. Plastic and Reconstructive Surgery, Med. Soc. Westchester (chpt. bd. dir. 1997—, chmn. peer rev. 1997—2002, v.p. 2002—03, pres. 2003—), Med. Soc. State NY, Phi Beta Kappa, Phi Lambda Upsilon. Avocations: sailing, audiophile. Office: 175 Memorial Hwy New Rochelle NY 10801-5635 also: 50 E 69th St New York NY 10021 E-mail: AKleinman@aol.com.

KLEINMAN, ARTHUR MICHAEL, medical anthropologist, psychiatrist, educator; b. N.Y.C., Mar. 11, 1941; s. Marcia F. (Kaplan) K.; m. Joan Andrea Ryman, Mar. 20, 1965; children: Peter John, Anne Simone. AB, Stanford U., 1962, MD, 1967; MA, Harvard U., 1974; LLD (hon.), Miscolc U., Hungary, 1999. Diplomate: Nat. Bd. Med. Examiners, Am. Bd. Neurology and Psychiatry. Med. intern Yale New Haven Hosp., 1967-68; surgeon USPHS, Bethesda, Md., Taiwan, 1968-70; resident in psychiatry Mass. Gen. Hosp., Boston, 1972-73; assoc. prof. U. Wash., Seattle, 1976-79, prof. psychiatry and anthroplogy, 1979-82; prof. med. anthropology and psychiatry Harvard U., Cambridge, Mass., 1982—, chmn. dept. social medicine, dir. Ctr. for Study Culture and Medicine, 1991-2000, Maude and Lillian Presley prof. med. anthropology and psychiatry, 1993—2002, Esther and Sidney Rabb prof. anthropology, 2002—. Co-chair com. on culture, health and devel. Social Sci. Rsch. Coun., 1990. Author: Patients and Healers in the Context of Culture, 1980 (Wellcome medal Royal Anthrop. Inst.), Social Origins of Distress and Disease, 1986, The Illness Narratives, 1988, Rethinking Psychiatry, 1988, Writing at the Margin, 1995; co-editor: Relevance of Social Science for Medicine, 1981, Culture and Depression, 1985, Pain as Human Experience, 1992; editor-in-chief: Culture, Medicine and Psychiatry: A Jour. of Internat. Cross-Cultural Rsch., 1976-86. Recipient Rsch. award NIMH, 1977-79, Rockefeller Found., 1983-86, 88-89, NSF,1983-86, R.W. Johnson Found., 1988-89; grantee NIMH, 1984—, Carnegie Corp., 1990-92, MacArthur Found., 1992-94, Rockefeller Found., 1992-94; Guggenheim fellow, 1992. Fellow AAAS, Am. Psychiat. Assn., Am. Anthrop. Assn., Inst. Medicine of Nat. Acad. Scis. (chmn. com. on chronic pain, illness behavior and disability), Royal Anthrop. Inst., Am. Acad. Arts and Scis. (Franz Boas award), Am. Anthrop. Assn. Office: Harvard U 330 William James Hall 33 Kirkland St Cambridge MA 02138-2019 E-mail: Kleinman@wjh.harvard.edu.

KLEINMAN, BURTON HOWARD, real estate investor; b. Chgo., Nov. 19, 1923; s. Eli I. and Pearl (Cohan) K.; m. Shirley A. Freyer, Sept. 6, 1950 (div. Oct. 1969); children: Kim, Lauri. BS in Engring., U.S. Naval Acad., 1948. Commd. ensign USN, 1948, resigned, 1949; v.p. C.F. Corp., Chgo., 1958-80, pres., 1980-85; owner B.H. Kleinman Co., Northfield, Ill., 1955—. Bd. dirs. United Way Northfield, 1970-72, North Shore Mental Health Assn., 1978-82. Mem. Northfield C. of C. (bd. dirs. 1976-81), Kenosha Pilots Assn. Clubs: Deerfield Singles (pres. 1974-75), Winnetka Tennis Assn., Ridge & Valley Tennis. Libertarian. Unitarian Universalist. Avocations: tennis, scuba diving, sailing, flying. Home: 570 Happ Rd Northfield IL 60093-1112 Office: BH Kleinman Co 456 W Frontage Rd Northfield IL 60093-3034

KLEINMAN, CHARLES STEPHAN, physician, medical educator; b. N.Y.C., Mar. 12, 1947; s. Meyer and Dora (Levine) K.; m. Jessica Sue Pollack, June 14, 1969; children: Ari David, Joshua Michael. BA, NYU, 1967; MA, Rutgers U., 1968; MD, N.Y. Med. Coll., 1972; MA (hon.), Yale U., 1986. Diplomate Am. Bd. Pediatrics. Instr. pediatrics Cornell U. Med. Coll., N.Y.C., 1974-76; from asst. prof. pediat. to prof. pediat., diagnostic imaging and ob-gyn. Yale U., New Haven, 1977—99; chief pediatric cardiology Yale U./Yale-New Haven Med. Ctr., 1986-99; courteous clin. prof. pediat. U. Fla. Coll. Medicine, 2000—02; prof. clin. pediat. and ob-gyn. Columbia U. Coll. Physicians and Surgeons, 2002—. Office: Morgan Stanley Childrens Hosp NY Presbyn Hosp Babies Hosp 2-N 3959 Broadway New York NY 10032

KLEINMAN, NOELA MACGINN, family nurse practitioner; b. Mar. 17, 1961; m. Andrew Y. Kleinman M.D., June 8, 2003. BSN, SUNY, Stony Brook, 1983, MS, Nurse Practitioner, 1989. RN, N.Y., 1983; cert. family nurse practitioner, N.Y., 1989, Am. Bd. Occupl. Health Nurse, 1994, Am. Acad. Nurse Practitioners, 1995, ANA family nurse practitioner, 1993. Occupl. health nurse practitioner L.I. Jewish Med. Ctr., Lake Success, NY, 1989-93; clin. mgr. for employee health NYU Med. Ctr., 1993-96; dir. Sound Shore Health Sys., New Rochelle, NY, 1996-99; nurse practitioner, officer Med. Dept. J.P. Morgan Chase, N.Y.C., 1999—2002; cosmetic nurse practitioner Dr. Andrew Kleinman Plastic Surgery Practice, Westchester, NY, 1998—; skincare practitioner Skin-Klinic, N.Y.C., 2002. Home: 4D Weavers Hill Greenwich CT 06831

KLEINMAN, WAYNE ALAN, research scientist; b. N.Y.C., June 29, 1953; s. Martin and Sarah (Schiffman) K. BS, Herbert H. Lehman Coll., N.Y.C., 1975. Asst. editor World Tech., Willow Grove, Pa., 1972-76; health sci. specialist Berson Yalow Lab., VA Med. Ctr., Bronx, 1976-80; lab. mgr. Clin. Sci. Yalow Lab., Montefiore Med. Ctr., Bronx, 1980-85; health sci. specialist Berson Yalow Lab., VA Med. Ctr., Bronx, 1985-91; pres. Techno Ventures Inc., Nanuet, NY, 1991—; rsch. scientist Am. Health Found., Valhalla, NY, 1991—. Cons. in field. Contbr. articles to profl. jours. Avocation: sculpting. Office: Inst for Cancer Prevention 1 Dana Rd Valhalla NY 10595 E-mail: wkleinma@ifcp.us.

KLEINPELL-NOWELL, RUTH, nursing educator and researcher, medical writer; b. Cleve., Mar. 29, 1960; d. George John and Margaret Ann Sweeney; m. Horace Mann Nowell, Nov. 4, 1989; 1 child, Horace. RN, Luth. Med. Ctr. Sch. Nursing, Cleve., 1981; MSN, U. Ill. Coll. Nursing, 1987, PhD in Nursing, 1991. Cert. ACNP, NP, 1995. Staff nurse ICU/stepdown Deaconess Hosp., Cleve., 1981-84; clin nurse SICU U. Ill. Hosp., Chgo., 1984—2000, tchg./rsch. asst., 1987-99; asst. to dir. nursing rsch. support svcs. Rush U. Coll. of Nursing, Chgo., 1991—, assoc. prof., 1992—; nurse practitioner Our Lady of the Resurrection MC, Chicago, 2000—. Adj. faculty U. Ill. Coll. Nursing, Chgo., 1992—; mem. continuing edn. adv. bd. Nurseweek, 2003—. Editor: (book) Outcome Assessment in Advanced Practice Nursing, 2000, Practice Issues for the Acute Care Nurse Practitioner, 1999; mem. editl. bd. AACN Clinical Issues: Advanced Practice in Acute and Critical Care, 1996—99, Critical Care Nursing Clinics of North America, 1999—2002. Recipient Disting. Writer award Sigma Theta Tau, Indpls., 1999, Luther Christman award for Excellence in Pub. Writing, 1999, others. Fellow: Am. Acad. Nursing; mem.: ACNP, ANA, NONPF (mem., chair acute care spl. interest group, cons.), AANP (mem., chair acute care spl. interest group), AACN (mem. advanced practice adv. team Aliso Viejo, Calif. 1996—99, CE test writer 1998—, Wyeth-Ayerst Mentor award 1994), Am. Heart Assn. (coun. CV nursing), Soc. Critical Care Medicine (mem. membership com., mem. rsch. com.), Midwest Nursing Rsch. Soc., Sigma Theta Tau (pres./v.p. 1995—97, Nursing Recognition award 1999, Outstanding Rsch. Achievement awrad Acute Care Nursing Rsch. sect. 2003). Avocation: writing. Office: Rush Univ Coll Nursing 600 S Paulina St Rm 1062B Chicago IL 60612-3806 E-mail: ruth_m_kleinpell@rush.edu.

KLEINROCK, VIRGINIA BARRY, public relations executive; b. Boston, Nov. 5, 1947; d. Robert Edmund and Anne Marie (Crowley) Barry; m. Lewis James Kleinrock, Dec. 15, 1984. AS, Garland Jr. Coll., Boston, 1967; BS, East Carolina U., 1969; MS, Simmons Coll., 1973; postgrad. Sch. Bus. Communications, Boston U., 1973, 86, 88. Tchr. Somerville (Mass.) Pub. Schs., 1969-70, Newton (Mass.) Pub. Schs., 1970-84, career edn. program coord., 1978-83; pres. Infinite Energy, Belmont, Mass., 1982-95; prin. The Kleinrock Group, Naples, Fla., 1996—. Cons. McKnight Pub. Co., Bloomington, Ill., 1976-82; publicity coord./intern Impact Communications, Boston, 1982. Contbr. articles to profl. jours. Recipient Commendation for Excellence for Pilot Occupational Training Program, New Eng. Assn. of Schs. and Colls., 1969. Mem. Pub. Rels. Soc. Am., Counselors Acad., The Fashion Group, Fla. Pub. Rels. Assn., Advt. Fedn. of S.W. Fla., Internat. Women's Writing Guild, Pub. Rels. Assn. of Collier County, Naples C. of C., Naples Press Club. Office: The Kleinrock Group 853 Vanderbilt Beach Rd Ste 10 Naples FL 34108-8746 E-mail: vkleinrock@aol.com.

KLEIN-SCHEER, CATHY ANN, social worker; b. Hicksville, N.Y., Jan. 23, 1951; d. Louis and Dorothy (Levine) Klein; m. Barry Scheer, Oct. 23, 1983; 1 child, Danielle. AA, Nassau Community Coll., Garden City, N.Y., 1971; BSW, SUNY, Buffalo, 1973, MSW, 1976. Cert. social worker R-ACSW; diplomate Register Clin. Social Work. Coord. vol. svcs. Erie County Rehab. Ctr., 1972-73; alcoholism cons. Buffalo Gen. Hosp. Community Mental Health Ctr., 1976-77; psychiat. social worker Pilgram State Hosp., 1978; asst. coord. Plainview Rehab. Ctr. Family Svcs., 1978-79; psychiat. social work Beth Israel Med. Ctr., 1979-86; pvt. practice Kew Gardens, N.Y., 1984—, Croton-on-Hudson, N.Y., 1994—. Mem. NASW, EAPA. Office: 80-59 Lefferts Blvd Kew Gardens NY 11415-1715 also: 40 Irving Ave Croton On Hudson NY 10520-2644 E-mail: cathycsw@bestweb.net.

KLEINSCHMIDT, CAROL C. (CAROL C. FIELEKE), pianist, educator; b. Richland, N.Y., Mar. 21, 1936; d. R. Burkett and Kathleen (Healy) Curtiss; m. Norman S. Fieleke, June 16, 1962 (div. Dec. 1984); children: Andrew, Eric, Michael; m. Klaus Kleinschmidt, Sept. 9, 1995; stepchildren: Erich, David, Alexander, Deirdre. Student, Middlebury Coll., 1953-55; BS, Syracuse U., 1957; MA Tchg., Columbia U., 1962. Tchr. elem. schs. Chgo. Pub. Schs., 1957-59, Edn. Authority, Roxburghshire, Scotland, 1959-61, Arlington (Va.) County Pub. Schs., 1962-64; pvt. piano tchr. Winchester, Mass., 1969—; adjudicator Nat. Guild Piano Tchrs., Austin, Tex., 1980—; piano tchr. Rivers Music Sch., Weston, Mass., 1985-92. Trustee, advisor Winchester (Mass.) Cmty. Music Sch., 1981—; collector, coord. Books for Belize, 1988-91. Mem. Nat. Guild Piano Tchrs. (local chmn. 1990-95, 97—), New Eng. Piano Tchrs. Assn. (bd. dirs., sec., v.p. 1976-87, pres. 1987-89), Winchester Music Club (program planner 1970—). Avocations: Spanish language, travel, study and service in Latin America, outdoor activities. Home and Office: Kleinschmidt Piano Studio 5 Canterbury Rd Winchester MA 01890-3812

KLEIN-SEETHARAMAN, JUDITH, biochemist; b. Cologne, Nord-Rhein Westfalen, Germany, May 30, 1971; d. Clementine Klein; m. Sridhar Seetharaman, Mar. 5, 1971; 1 child, Roshan. PhD, MIT, 1996—2000. Humboldt fellow Goethe Universitaet Frankfurt, Frankfurt/Main, Germany, 2001—; rsch. scientist Carnegie Mellon U., Pittsburgh, 2001—; asst. prof. U. Pitts., Pa., 2002—. Co-director Ctr. Biol. Lang. Modeling, Pittsburgh, 2002—; vis. rschr. Forschungsinstitut Juelich, Nordrhein-Westfalen, Germany, 2002—. Author: (computer game) Biomedical Problem Solving Environment. Recipient Sofja Kovalevskaja Prize, Humboldt-Found. and Bundesregierung Deutschland, 2001; fellow Predoctoral Fellowship, Howard Hughes Med. Inst., 1996-2000; grantee Computational Learning and Discovery in Biol. Sequence, Structure and Function Mapping, NSF, 2002-2007. Mem.: Biophysical Soc., Protein Soc. Achievements include research in analysis of conformational changes in g protein coupled receptors and other signaling proteins using biochemical, biophysical and computational approaches; use of analogy between language and biology for the mapping of sequence to structure, function and dynamics of proteins. Office: Univ Pitts Med Sch 200 Lothrop St Pittsburgh PA 15261 Office Fax: 412-648-1945.

KLEINSORGE, WILLIAM PETER, metallurgical engineer; b. San Francisco, Feb. 10, 1941; s. William P. Kleinsorge; m. Kathryn Deane Vincent, Nov. 14, 1966; children: Elizabeth Louise, Victoria Anne. BS in Metall. Engring., U. Nev.-Reno, 1964. Registered profl. engr., S.C., Calif. Welding engr. Mare Island Naval Shipyard, Vallejo, Calif., 1965—69, Charleston-Naval Shipyard, 1969—70; supervisory welding engr. U.S. Naval Ship Repair Facility, Subic Bay, Philippines, 1970—72; head welding engr. Charleston Naval Shipyard, 1972—79; metall. engr. U.S. Nuc. Regulatory Commn., Atlanta, 1979—99; ret., 1999. With Nat. Guard U.S. Army, 1965—72. Mem.: Am. Soc. Mil. Engrs., Am. Welding Soc., Am. Soc. Metals, Masons.

KLEIN-SZANTO, ANDRES J. P. pathologist; b. Buenos Aires, Apr. 25, 1943; s. Geza and Madeleine Klein-S.; m. Maria U. Weyrauch, Dec. 29, 1972; children: Walter, Matias, Julian. MD, U. Buenos Aires, 1965, D.Med.Sci., 1970. Chief instr. dept. pathology U. Buenos Aires, 1967-73; staff scientist Argentine AEC, Buenos Aires, 1970-77; sr. med. scientist Oak Ridge (Tenn.) Nat. Lab., 1978-82; prof. U. Tex. M.D. Anderson Cancer Ctr., Smithville, Houston, 1982-86; sr. pathologist and head exptl. histopathology service Fox Chase Cancer Ctr., Phila., 1986—. Chief asst. dept. oral structural biology U. Zurich, 1974-76; chem pathology study sect., 1986, 87-91; mem. environ. health scis. com. NIH, 1993-96. Assoc. editor: Acta Odontologica Latonoamericana, 1984—, Molecular-Carcinogenesis, 1995—; assoc. editor Jour. of Cutaneous Pathology, 1981, editor-in-chief, 1981-83; editor 4 books in field; contbr. numerous articles to profl. jours., chpts. to books. Mem. AAAS, Am. Assn. Cancer Rsch., Radiation Rsch. Soc., Internat. Acad. Pathology (divsn. sec. 1978), European Soc. Pathology, Am. Assn. Pathologists. Office: Fox Chase Cancer Ctr 7701 Burholme Ave Ste 2 Philadelphia PA 19111-2497

KLEMA, DONALD DAVID, architect; b. Oak Ridge, Tenn., June 28, 1956; s. Ernest Donald and Virginia Clyde (Carlock) K.; m. Martha Louise Wetherill, May 22, 1994; 1 child, Madeleine Wetherill. BA with honors, Princeton U., 1978; postgrad., Rice U., 1978-79; MArch, MIT, 1982. Registered architect, Mass. Intern Morris-Aubry Architects, Houston, 1979-80; architect Ann Beha Assocs., Boston, 1982-86; assoc. William Rawn Assocs., Boston, 1986-89; sr. assoc. Kallmann, McKinnell & Wood Architects, Boston, 1989—. Design studio instr. Boston Archtl. Ctr., 1989-90; thesis advisor, 1990; vis. archtl. critic MIT, Boston Archtl. Ctr., Mass. Coll. Art, Roger Williams Coll., Wentworth Inst. Tech., 1982—. Prin. works include Charlestown Navy Yard Rowhouses (AIA Honor award 1994), Marx Hall, Princeton (NJ) U., (Boston Soc. Archs. award 1996), Miller Performing Arts Ctr., Alfred U., (AIA/Brick Inst. Am. award 2001, Boston Soc. Archs. award 1999), Ewing Marion Kauffman Found Hdqs., Kansas City, Mo., World Trade Ctr. West, Boston. Grantee Travel grant, Aga Khan Found., 1982. Mem. AIA (found. scholarship 1981-82), Boston Soc. Architects, Phi Beta Kappa. Democrat. Home: 26 Butman St Beverly MA 01915-4649 Office: Kallmann McKinnell & Wood Architects 939 Boylston St Boston MA 02115-3104 E-mail: dklema@comcast.net.

KLEMA, ERNEST DONALD, nuclear physicist, educator; b. Wilson, Kan., Oct. 4, 1920; s. William W. and Mary Bess (Vopat) K.; m. Virginia Clyde Carlock, May 23, 1953; children: Donald David, Catherine Marion. AB in Chemistry, U. Kans., 1941, MA in Physics, 1942; postgrad., Princeton U., 1942, U. Ill., 1946-49; PhD in Physics, Rice U., 1951. Staff scientist Los Alamos Sci. Lab., 1943-46; sr. physicist Oak Ridge Nat. Lab., 1950-56, prin. physicist, 1958; assoc. prof. nuclear engring. U. Mich., 1956-58; prof. nuclear engring. Northwestern U., 1959-68, chmn. dept. engring. scis., 1960-66; prof. engring. sci. Tufts U., 1968-86, dean Coll. Engring., 1968-73, adj. prof. internat. politics Fletcher Sch. Law and Diplomacy, 1973-83, dean emeritus, prof. emeritus Coll. of Engring., 1987—. Vis. scholar physics Harvard U., 1985-86; chmn. subcom. on neutron standards and measurements NRC, 1958-62; del. Internat. Atomic Energy Agy. symposium neutron detection, dosimetry and standardiazation, Harwell, Eng., 1962; cons. Oak Ridge Nat. Lab., Argonne Nat. Lab. Author articles fission cross-sects., gamma-gamma angular correlations, empirical nuclear models, thermal neutron measurements, semi-conductor radiation detectors.;patentee purification hydrogen-argon mixtures. Fellow Am. Phys. Soc., Am Nuclear Soc.; mem. IEEE (sr.), Phi Beta Kappa, Sigma Xi, Pi Mu Epsilon, Alpha Chi Sigma. Clubs: Harbor (Seal Harbor, Me.).

KLEMAN, CHARLES J. finance company executive; With various acctg. firms; v.p., contr. Electronic Monitoring & Controls, Inc., 1986—88; ind. acctg. cons., 1988; contr. Chico's, 1989—91, v.p., asst. sec., 1991—92, CFO, 1992—, sec., treas., 1993—, sr. v.p. finance, 1996, exec. v.p. finance, 1996—. Office: 11215 Metro Pkwy Fort Myers FL 33912

KLEMANN, GILBERT LACY, II, lawyer; b. New Rochelle, N.Y., July 26, 1950; s. N. Robert and Rosemary Virginia (Gerard) K.; m. Patricia Louise Hild, June 16, 1973; children: Tricia Rosemary, Gilbert Hild. AB, Coll. Holy Cross, 1972; JD, Fordham U., 1975. Bar: N.Y. 1976, U.S. Dist. Ct. (so. and ea. dists.) N.Y. 1976, Conn. 1988, U.S. Supreme Ct. 1991. Assoc. Chadbourne & Parke, N.Y.C., 1975-83, ptnr., 1983-90, of counsel, 2000; sr. v.p., gen. counsel Fortune Brands, Inc. (formerly Am. Brands Inc.), Old Greenwich, Conn., 1991-97, exec. v.p. strategic and legal affairs, 1998, exec. v.p. corp., mem. bd. dirs., 1999; sr. v.p., gen. counsel, sec. Avon Products, Inc., N.Y.C., 2001—. Editor Fordham Law Rev., 1974-75. Mem. Conn. Bar Assn., Greenwich (Conn.) Country Club, Nassau Club (Princeton, N.J.), Longboat Key Club (Fla.). Republican. Roman Catholic. Avocation: golf. Home: 25 Hope Farm Rd Greenwich CT 06830-3331 also: 415 L'Ambiance Dr Longboat Key FL 34288 Office: Avon Products Inc 1345 Ave of the Americas New York NY 10105-0196 E-mail: gilbert.klemann@avon.com.

KLEMENS, JONATHAN MARK, pharmacy educator, writer; b. Tarentum, Pa., July 3, 1948; s. Stanley Daniel Klemens and Winona Katherine Klemens (Wilcox); m. Linda Ellen Bailich, Sept. 9, 1972; children: Lauren Morelli, Aaron. BS in Pharmacy, Duquesne U., 1976, BS in Biol. Rsch., 1970; postgrad., Univ. Ark., 1998—2000. Registered pharmacist. Dir. of pharmacy Highlands Hosp., Connellsville, Pa., 2000—02, Dept. of Veterans Affairs Med. Ctr., Butler, Pa., 2002—. Adj. instr., pharmacy Duquesne U. Mylan Sch. of Pharmacy, Pitts., 1994—; instr. in pharmacy practice CC Allegheny County, 1979; instr. in sterile products U. Pitts., 1976—81. Author: Mountains and Rivers: Complementing your Healthcare with Alternative Medicine, 2003; contbr. articles to profl. jours. Korean martial arts instr. (black belt) Taekwon-Do; bd. dirs. Assn. for Integrative Medicine, 2001. Named to Director's Club, Medicine Shoppe Internat., Inc., 1978. Mem.: Nat. Writers Assn., Am. Med. Writers Assn., Am. Assn. of Oriental Medicine, Assn. for Integrative Medicine, UK Psychiat. Pharmacy Group, Pa. Soc. of Health-System Pharmacists. Avocations: writing, martial arts, oriental medicine, intergrative medicine, photography. Home: 3298 Cramlington Dr Gibsonia PA 15044 Office: Dept Vet Affairs Med Ctr 325 New Castle Rd Butler PA 16001 Personal E-mail: jksamurai@alumni.duq.edu. E-mail: jonathan.klemens@med.va.gov.

KLEMENS, PAUL GUSTAV, physicist, educator; b. Vienna, May 24, 1925; came to U.S., 1959, naturalized, 1968; s. Walter and Ida (Klug) K.; m. Ruth Hannah Wiener, July 30, 1950; children: Michael Walter, Susan Margaret. BSc, U. Sydney, 1946, MSc, 1948; PhD, Oxford U., 1950. With Nat. Standards Lab., Sydney, Australia, 1950-59, research officer, 1950-52, sr. research officer, 1952-57, prin. research officer, 1957-59; physicist Westinghouse Research Lab., Pitts., 1959-64, mgr. transport properties of solids dept., 1964-67; prof. physics U. Conn., 1967-91, prof. emeritus, 1991—, head dept. physics, 1967-74. Vis. prof. Leiden (The Netherlands) U., 1963-64, City U., London, 1989, U. Nottingham, Eng., 1992; mem. adv. bd. on heat Nat. Bur. Standards, 1967-70, mem. adv. bd. on cryogenics, 1974-79; mem. governing bd. Internat. Thermal Conductivity Confs., 1973—; mem. adv. bd. associateship program NRC, 1983-87; mem. standing com. on accreditation Conn. Bd. Higher Edn., 1980-86, cons. Los Alamos Nat. Lab., 1972-97. Contbr. articles to sci. jours. Recipient Y.S. Touloukian award Heat Transfer div. ASME, 1988. Fellow Am. Phys. Soc.; mem. Conn. Acad. Sci. and Engring. (fin. com.) Clubs: Cosmos Washington. Achievements include The Internat. Conference on Phonon Scattering in Condensed Matter decided in 2001 to name its triennial award the Klemens Award, to recognise his early work in the field. Home: 21 Timber Dr Storrs Mansfield CT 06268-1210 Office: U Conn Dept Physics Storrs Mansfield CT 06269-3046 E-mail: klemens@rcn.com.

KLEMENS, THOMAS LLOYD, editor; b. Pitts., Mar. 28, 1952; s. Robert F. and Ann E. (Lacy) K.; m. Norreen McLellan, Aug. 4, 1973; children: Jonathan, Zachary. BFA, Carnegie-Mellon U., 1974; BSCE, U. Pitts., 1983; postgrad., Roosevelt U., Chgo., 1990-91. Registered profl. engr., Ill. Choir dir., tchr. Wellsville (Ohio) H.S., 1975-76; asst. band dir., tchr. North Hills H.S., Ross Twp., Pa., 1976-79; field engr. S.J. Groves & Sons, Pitts., 1983; structural engr. Sargent & Lundy, Chgo., 1983-87; field engr. Structural Preservation Systems, Inc., Margate, N.J., 1987; project mgr. Northwest Group, Inc., West Chicago, Ill., 1987; engr., purchasing agt. L.J. Keefe Co., Mt. Prospect, Ill., 1987-89; from assoc. editor to editor Hwy. & Heavy Constrn. Cahners Pub., Des Plaines, Ill., 1989-91, editor Hwy. & Heavy Constrn. Products, 1991-93, sr. editor Consulting/Specifying Engr., 1993-94; co-owner Wordwright, Palatine, Ill., 1993—. Instr. Motorola U., 1996-98; com. on constrn. equipment Transp. Rsch. Bd., Washington, 1991-93 adj. faculty William Rainey Harper Coll., Palatine, 1997—. Author Hwy. and Heavy Constrn., 1989-91, editor, 1991-92; author, editor Infrastructure, 1992-93; sr. editor Cons./Specifying Engr., 1993-94; editor PM Engr., Bus. News Pub., 1994-96, Plumbing Engr., TMB Pub., 1996-2003; sr. editor engring. Hanley-Wood LLC, 2003—. Mem. ASCE, Am. Concrete Inst., Am. Soc. Testing and Materials. Office: 426 S Westgate Addison IL 60101-4546 E-mail: tklemens@hanley-wood.com.

KLEMENT, VERA, artist; b. Gdansk, Dec. 14, 1929; d. Klement and Rose (Rakovchik) Shapiro; divorced; 1 son, Max Klement Shapey. Cert. in fine arts, Cooper Union Sch. Art and Architecture, 1950. Prof. art U. Chgo., 1969-95. One woman shows include RoKo Gallery, N.Y.C., 1958, 60, Bridge Gallery, N.Y.C., 1965, Artemisia Gallery, Chgo., 1974, Chicago Gallery, 1976, Marianne Deson Gallery, 1979, 81, Goethe Inst., 1981, CDS Gallery, N.Y.C., 1981, 84, Roy Boyd Gallery, Chgo., 1983, 85, 87, 89, 90, 91, 92, 93, Spertus Mus., Chgo., 1987, retrospective exhbn., 1953-86, Renaissance Soc., Chgo., 1987, Brody's Gallery, Washington, 1992, Fassbender Gallery, Chgo., 1994, 95, 96, 97, Chgo. Cultural Ctr., 1999, retrospective exhbn., 1965-99, Fassbender, 1999, 2001, Ft. Wayne Mus. Art, Ind., 2001, Block Mus., Northwestern U., Evanston, Ill., 2001, U. Ariz. Mus. Art, Tucson, 2001, Tarble Arts Ctr., Ea. Ill. U., Charleston, 2002, Ea. Ill. U., Charleston, 2002, Brauer Art Mus., Valparaiso U., Ind., 2002; group shows include Mus. Modern Art, N.Y.C., 1954, 55, Bklyn. Mus., 1950-60, Dallas Mus. Fine Arts, 1954, Tate Gallery, London, 1956, Museo de Arte Moderno, Barcelona, Spain, 1955, Musee d'Arte Moderne, Paris, 1955, U. Ky., 1959, Art Inst. Chgo., 1967, Walker Art Center, Mpls., 1977, U. Mo., 1978, Detroit Inst. Arts, 1978, Ukrainian Inst. Art, Chgo., 1978, Jewish Mus., N.Y.C., 1982, Kunstverein, Munich, Germany, 1987, Amerika Haus, Berlin, 1987, Terra Mus. Am. Art, Chgo., 1988, Corcoran Gallery, Washington, 1994, Cultural Ctr., Chgo., 1994, former IBM Gallery, N.Y.C., 1995, Va. Beach Cu. Arts, 1995, Fischer Art Gallery at U. So. Calif., 1995, Portland (Oreg.) Mus. Art, Evanston (Ill.) Art Ctr., Mus. Contemporary Art, Chgo., 1996, Block Gallery Northwestern U., Evanston, Ill., 1996, Fort Wayne Museum of Art, 2001, Riva Yares Gallery, Santa Fe, N.Mex., 2002, Klein Artworks, Chgo., 2002, Maya Polsky Gallery, Chgo., 2002, many others; represented in permanent collections Mus. Modern Art, N.Y.C., Phila. Mus. Art, Print Club, Phila., Ill. State Mus., Springfield, U. Tex., Nat. Mus. Am. Art, Washington, Jewish Mus., N.Y.C., Art Inst. Chgo., Philip Morris, N.Y.C., Smart Mus. U. Chgo., Sch. Social Svc. Adminstrn. U. Chgo., Mus. Contemporary Art, Chgo., Mary & Leigh Block Gallery, Evanston, Ill., Mus. Art U. Ariz., Tucson, Union Club League Chgo., Daum Mus. Contemporary Art, Sedalis, Mo.; also pvt. collections. Recipient Pollock/Krasner Found. award, 1998, others; Louis Comfort Tiffany Found. fellow, 1954, Guggenheim fellow, 1981-82, Nat. Endowment for the Arts fellow, 1987; Ill. Arts Coun. grantee, 1988. E-mail: veraklement@aol.com.

KLEMIN, LAWRENCE R. lawyer; b. New Rockford, N.D., Mar. 31, 1945; s. Lawrence R. Klemin and Carol M. (Cook) Roaldson; m. Rita R. DiPalma, Sept. 2, 1970; children: Laura K., Peter L. BA in English, U. N.D., 1967, JD with distinction, 1978. Bar: N.D. 1978, U.S. Dist. Ct. N.D. 1978, U.S. Ct. Appeals (8th cir.) 1987, U.S. Supreme Ct. 1988. Hearing officer N.D. Employment Security Bur., Bismarck, 1971-75; assoc. Atkinson & Dwyer, Bismarck, 1978-81; ptnr. Atkinson, Dwyer & Klemin, Bismarck, 1981-82, Dwyer & Klemin, Bismarck, 1982-86; pres. Lawrence R. Klemin, P.C., Bismarck, 1986-92, Bucklin & Klemin, P.C., Bismarck, 1992-96, Bucklin, Klemin & McBride, P.C., Bismarck, 1996—. Pres. Title and Escrow Co., Bismarck, 1988-98, Litigation Svcs., Inc., Bismarck, 1995—; state rep. N.D. legis assembly, 1998—; commr. Nat. Conf. of Commrs. on Uniform State Laws, 1999—; mem. state adv. coun. N.D. Office Adminstrv. Hearings, Bismarck, 1993-98; lectr. on real property law Nat. Bus. Inst., 1989—. Author, editor Civil Practice of North Dakota, 1993—. Bd. dirs. N.D. March of Dimes, Bismarck, 1994-2002, Burleigh-Morton chpt. Am. Red Cross, 2002—; mem. Corpus Christi Parish Coun., Bismarck, 1996-2002. With U.S. Army, 1967-70, Vietnam. Mem. State Bar Assn. N.D. (chair adminstrv. law com. 1996-98), N.D. Land Title Assn. (legis. com. 1990-99), Bismarck Mandan C. of C. (bd. dirs. 1996-98), Optimist Internat. (bd. dirs. 1985-86), Elks, Eagles. Roman Catholic. Avocations: antique auto restoration, astronomy, camping. Home: 1709 Montego Dr Bismarck ND 58503-0856 Office: Bucklin Klemin & McBride PC 400 E Broadway #500 PO Box 955 Bismarck ND 58502-0955 E-mail: lklemin@bkmpc.com.

KLEMME, CARL WILLIAM, banker; b. Ft. Wayne, Ind., Sept. 11, 1928; s. Ludwig and Marianne (Rupil) K.; m. Ann Elise Wichman, Sept. 11, 1954; children: Ellen Elise Taylor, Sarah Ann Melamed, Carl Andrew. BS, Yale U., 1950; MBA, NYU, 1956; postgrad. mgmt., Harvard U., 1971. With Morgan Guaranty Trust Co., N.Y.C., 1950-80, v.p., 1961-70, sr. v.p., 1970-72, exec. v.p. 1972-80, Russell Reynolds Assocs., Inc., N.Y.C., 1981-82, Nat. Westminster Bancorp, N.Y.C., 1982-93. Arbitrator NASD, N.Y.C., 1975—, NYSE, N.Y.C., 2002—; mgmt. cons. Nat. Exec. Svc. Corps., N.Y.C., Internat. Exec. Svc. Corps, Stamford, Conn. Mem. Millburn Bd. Edn., 1967-73; trustee Howard U., 1975-91, Millburn (N.J.) Pub. Libr., 1979-84, Wittenberg U., 1983-96, New Eyes for the Needy, 1980-86, Twp. Beautification League, 1998—; bd. dirs. Downtown-Lower Manhattan Assn., 1972-80; bd. dirs. Bank Adminstrn. Inst., 1975-81, chmn., 1979-80. With U.S. Army, 1950-52. Mem. Phi Beta Kappa. Republican. Episcopalian. Home: 35 Woodfield Dr Short Hills NJ 07078-1609

KLEMP, HAROLD, minister, writer; Student, U. Ind. Spiritual leader Eckankar Religion of the Light and Sound of God, Mpls., 1981—. Spkr. in field. Author: The Wind of Change, 1980, The Book of ECK Parables, Vols. 1-4, 1986, 4th edit., 1994, Soul Travelers of the Far Country, 1987, The ECK Dream 1 Discourses, 1987, 2d edit., 1989, Child in the Wilderness, 1989, The Living Word, Books 1 and 2, 1989, 2d edit., 1996, Letters of Light & Sound 1 and 2, 1991, The Easy Way Discourses, 1992, The Spiritual Exercises of ECK, 1993, Ask the Master, Books 1 and 2, 1993; : 2d edit., 1994, The Dream Master, 1993, We Come as Eagles, 1994, The Master 3 Discourses, 1994, The Drumbeat of Time, 1995, The Slow Burning Love of God, 1996, A Modern Prophet Answers Your Key Questions About Life, 1998; The Art of Spiritual Dreaming, 1999; author: Autobiography of a Modern Prophet, 2000, How to Survive Spiritually in Our Times, 2001, The Spiritual Laws of Life, 2002, Past Lives, Dreams, and Soul Travel, 2003. Office: Eckankar PO Box 27300 Minneapolis MN 55427-0300

KLEMPERER, WILLIAM, chemistry educator; b. N.Y.C., Oct. 6, 1927; s. Paul and Margit (Freund) K.; m. Elizabeth Cole, Jan. 12, 1949; children: Joyce Hillary, Paul, Wendy Judith AB, Harvard U., 1950; PhD, U. Calif., Berkeley, 1954; DSc, U. Chgo., 1996. Instr. chemistry Harvard U., Cambridge, Mass., 1954-57, asst. prof., 1957-61, assoc. prof., 1961-65, prof., 1965—. Asst. dir. NSF, Washington, 1979-81; vis. scientist Bell Telephone Lab., 1963-83; Evans lectr. Ohio State U., 1981, Pratt lectr. U. Va., 1984, Rollefson lectr. U. Calif., 1985, Oesper lectr. U. Cin., 1987, Kolthoff lectr. U. Minn., 1987, Mary E. Kapp lectr. Va. Commonwealth U., 1987, Linus Pauling Disting. lectr. Oreg. State U., 1988, Harry Emmett Gunning lectr. U. Alta., Can., 1988, Fritz London Meml. lectr. Duke U., 1989, Hinshelwood lectr. Oxford U., Eng., 1989, Neckers lectr. So. Ill. U., 1990; George C. Pimentel meml. lectr. U. Calif., Berkeley, 1992, vis. Miller prof., 1998; Joe L. Franklin meml. lectr. Rice U., 1994, E.K.C. Lee Fellowship lectr. U. Calif., Irvine, 1994; Richard C. Lord lectr. MIT, Cambridge, Mass., 1997; Bernstein lectr. UCLA, 1997. Served with A.C., USN, 1944-46 Recipient Wetherill medal Franklin Inst., 1978, Disting. Svc. medal NSF, 1981, Bomem Michelson award Coblentz Soc., 1990, Faraday Medal and Lectureship Royal Soc. Chemistry, 1995; named hon. citizen City of Toulouse, France, 2000. Fellow Am. Phys. Soc. (Earle Plyler prize 1983); mem. NAS, Am. Acad. Arts and Scis., Am. Chem. Soc. (Irving Langmuir award 1980, Peter Debye award in phys. chemistry 1994, E. Bright Wilson award in spectroscopy 2001, Remsen award Md. sect. 1992), Achievements include research in molecular structure, energy transfer and intermolecular forces using experimental spectroscopic methods; modelling molecule formation and detection in the interstellar medium. Home: 53 Shattuck Rd Watertown MA 02472-1310 Office: Harvard U Dept Chemistry and Chem Biology 12 Oxford St Cambridge MA 02138-2902 E-mail: klemperer@chemistry.harvard.edu.

KLENE, MARY JEAN, nun, English educator; b. Hannibal, Mo., Sept. 8, 1929; d. Othmar Carl and Ada Blanche (Ridder) K. BA, St. Mary's Coll., Notre Dame, Ind., 1959; MA, Notre Dame U., 1966; PhD, U. Toronto, Ont., Can., 1970. Tchr. St. Mary's Sch., Alexandria, Va., 1951-53; H.S. tchr. high schs., South Bend, Ind., 1953-61; tchr., counselor Sisters of the Holy Cross, Notre Dame, Ind., 1961-63; H.S. tchr. h.s., Flint, Mich., 1963-64; dean students St. Mary's Acad., South Bend, 1964-65; lectr. St. Mary's Coll., Notre Dame, 1965—. Chair dept. English St. Mary's Coll., 1973—78, 1980—85; lectr. in field. Contbg. author: New Dictionary of National Biography; editor, transcriber: The Southwell-Sibthorpe Commonplace Book, 1997 (Josephine Roberts award for Best Edition), Instructor's Guide for the Slide Set Shakespeare: New Productions, 1975-80, The Royal Shakespeare Company, 1981; contbr. articles to books, jours. in field, women writer's database and ren. women online, Brown Univ. Fellow NEH, 1978-79, 1980, 83, 84, Faculty fellow Lilly Endowment, London, 1985-86. Mem. MLA, Renaissance English Text Soc., Renaissance Soc. Am., Shakespeare Assn. Am. Avocations: swimming, designing shakespeare multimedia programs and website for children. Office: St Mary's Coll Notre Dame IN 46556

KLENK, JAMES ANDREW, lawyer; b. Evergreen Park, Ill., July 18, 1949; s. Paul Theodore and Joan (Launspach) K.; m. Carol Evans, Aug. 26, 1972; children: Paul Andrew, Matthew Evans. BA, Beloit Coll., 1971; JD, U. Wis., 1974. Bar: Ill. 1974, Wis. 1974, U.S. Supreme Ct. 1978. Law clk. to Judge Thomas E. Fairchild U.S. Ct. Appeals (7th cir.), Chgo., 1974-75; assoc. Kirkland & Ellis, Chgo., 1975-78; ptnr. Reuben & Proctor, Chgo., 1978-86, Isham, Lincoln & Beale, Chgo., 1986-88, Sonnenschein, Nath & Rosenthal, Chgo., 1988—. Articles editor Wis. Law Rev. Mem. ABA (litigation sect., torts and ins. practice sect., bus. law sect.), Ill. Bar Assn. (anti-trust law sect., litigation sect., torts and ins. practice sect., intellectual prop.), Libel Def. Resource Ctr. (def. counsel sect.), Order of Coif, Phi Beta Kappa. Office: Sonnenschein Nath & Rosenthal 8000 Sears Tower Chicago IL 60606

KLENKE, DEBORAH ANN, band director, choral director, department chairman; b. Oak Park, Ill., May 20, 1958; d. Myron and Rita Frances Joshel; children: S. Joel, Jeremy. BS, Elmhurst Coll., 1986. Dir. music, dept. chmn. Faith Christian Elem.- Jr. HS, Geneva, Ill., 1987—2003; dir. bands St. Peter Sch., Geneva, Ill., 1991—99. Prin. flutist West Suburban Symphony, Hinsdale, 1991—2003; freelance flutist. Mem.: Ill. Grade Sch. Music Assn., Ill. Music Educators Assn., Chgo. Flute Club. Office: Faith Christian Elem - Jr HS 1745 Kaneville Rd Geneva IL 60134 Personal E-mail: debklenke@yahoo.com.

KLEPINGER, JOHN WILLIAM, trailer manufacturing company executive; b. Lafayette, Ind., Feb. 7, 1945; s. John Franklin and R. Wanda (North) K.; m. Mary Patricia Duffy, May 1, 1976; 1 child, Nicholas Patrick. BS, Ball State U., 1967, MA, 1968. Sales engr. CTS Corp., Elkhart, Ind., 1969-70; exec. v.p. Woodlawn Products Corp., Elkhart, 1970-78; v.p. Period Ind., Henderson, Ky., 1976-78, Sotebeer Constrn. Co., Inc., Elkhart, 1978-81; gen. mgr. Wells Industries Inc., Ogden, Utah, 1981—2000; regional mgr. Wells Cargo, Inc., Phoenix, 1995—, Carbondale, Pa., 1999—2003. Regional dir. Zion's First Nat. Bank, Ogden, 1986-99. Bd. dirs. St. Benedict's Hosp., Ogden, 1986-94, chmn., 1987-94; bd. dirs. Weber County Indsl. Devel. Corp., Nat. Job Tng. Partnership Inc., 1986-89; mem. Weber-Morgan Pvt. Industry Coun., 1983-96, Utah Job Tng. Coordinating Coun., 1988-96, chmn. 1993-94. Named Ogden Bus. Man of Yr., Weber County Sch. Dist., 1984. Mem. Nat. Assn. Trailer Mfrs. (bd. dirs., vice chmn. 1994-95, chmn. 1995-97, sec., treas. 1998-99, mem. tech. and maintenance coun. task force 1999--), Weber County Prodn. Mgrs. Assn. (pres. 1984-85, 92-93), Nat. Assn. Pvt. Industry Couns. (bd. dirs. 1986-96, pres. 1988-92), Nat. Alliance Bus. (bd. dirs. 1987-90), Ogden Area C. of C. (bd. dirs. 1986-96, treas. 1986-89), Phoenix C. of C., Exch. Club (bd. dirs. Ogden 1984-86), Soc. of Automotive Engrs. (trailer com. 1999--), others. Roman Catholic. Avocations: finance, community service, leadership, sports, travel. Office: Wells Cargo Inc 6902 W Hadley St Phoenix AZ 85043-4300

KLEPPA, OLE J. chemistry educator; b. Oslo, Feb. 4, 1920; married; 2 children. MS, Norwegian Inst. Tech., 1946, DS, 1956. Union Carbon and Carbide postdoctoral fellow, instr. U. Chgo. Inst. Study of Metals, 1948-50; rsch. supr. divsn. chemistry and metallurgy Norwegian Def. Rsch. Establishment, 1950-51; asst. prof. U. Chgo., 1952-57, assoc. prof., 1958-62, prof. dept. chemistry, 1962-90, prof. dept. geophys. scis., 1968-90, prof. emeritus, 1990—, assoc. dir. James Franck Inst., 1968-71, dir., 1971-77, dir. materials rsch. lab., 1984-87. Cons. Argonne Nat. Lab., 1959-71; dir. The Calorimetry Conf., 1963-69, chmn., 1966-67; vis. prof. Japan Soc. Promotion of Sci., 1975, U. Paris, Orsay, 1977; presenter confs. in field. Bd. editors Jour. Chem. Physics, 1965-67, Jour. Chem. Thermodynamics, 1981-87, Jour. Phase Equilibria, 1995—; contbr. articles to profl. jours. Recipient Huffman Meml. award, 1982, U.S. Sr. Sci. Humboldt award, 1983-84. Fellow AAAS, Am. Soc. Metals; mem. Am. Chem. Soc., Am. Ceramic Soc., Soc. Norwegian Engrs., Royal Norwegian Soc. Sci. and Letters, Norwegian Acad. Tech. Scis., Minerals, Metals, and Materials Soc. (Hume-Rothery award 1994). Achievements include pioneering development of new technique of high-temperature oxide melt solution calorimetery; being the first person to extensively apply the Calvét-type twin microcalorimeter in high temperature thermochemistry; originator of a novel high-temperature reaction calorimeter suitable for continuous use at temperatures up to about 1500K; applying new calorimeter in extensive studies of binary alloys of early transition metals and rare earth metals with Group VIII transition metals and with noble metals. Office: U Chgo James Franck Inst 5640 S Ellis Ave Chicago IL 60637-1433 E-mail: Kleppa@control.uchicago.edu.

KLEPPE, JOHN ARTHUR, electrical engineering educator, business executive; b. Oakland, Calif., Feb. 21, 1939; s. Arthur William and Musa (Anderson) K.; m. Julianna Marie Galli, Aug. 12, 1961; children: John Frederick, Johanna Beth, Judith Anne. BSEE, U. Nev., 1961, MSEE, 1967; PhD, U. Calif., Davis, 1970. Registered profl. engr., Nev., Calif. Prof. elec. engring. U. Nev., Reno, 1970—, dir. Engring. Research and Devel., 1976-88; pres., research cons. Sci. Engring. Instruments, Inc., Reno, 1968 97; pres. Klepco, Inc., 1976—. Cons.; chief engr. NSF weather expdn. to Antarctica, 1977; del. White House Conf. Small Bus., 1980 Author: (textbook) Engineering Applications of Acoustics, 1989; contbr. articles, papers to publs. and confs. around the world. Served to lt. C.E. USN, 1961-65. Recipient Outstanding Engring. Achievement award for Nev., 1981, 84; Inventor of Yr. award, 1985 Mem. IEEE, Nev. Innovation and Tech. Coun. (pres. 1981-93, pres. 1996-97), Sigma Xi, Tau Beta Pi. Home: 2776 Spinnaker Dr Reno NV 89509 Office: U Nev Dept Elec Engring MS 260 Reno NV 89557-0153 E-mail: kleppe@ee.unr.edu.

KLEPPE, SHIRLEY R. KLEIN, artist; b. Sedalia, Mo., Sept. 29, 1946; d. Benjamin Eades Klein and Clara Louise Shirley; m. Stephen Douglas Kleppe, Nov. 22, 1968; children: Clinton Douglas, Nicole Lynne. BS in Edn., Ctrl. Mo. State U., 1967; postgrad., Ariz. State U., 1988. Art tchr. Benton County R#1 Sch. Dist., Cole Camp, Mo., 1967-68, Turner (Kans.) Unified Sch. Dist., 1968-69; graphic designer Menorah Med. Ctr., Kansas City, Mo., 1969-70; freelance graphic designer, illustrator Kansas City, 1970-75; advt. dir. Gorges Wholesale Meats, Inc., Harlingen, Tex., 1975-76; art instr. City of Phoenix, 1979-82; owner Ariz. Restaurant Sys. Inc., Scottsdale. Sponsor vis. artist program Ctrl. Mo. State U., Warrensburg, 1993—; pres. Outrageous Red LLC, Scottsdale, Ariz., 1994—; pres. Outrageous Red Studio and Gallery at Grayhawk, 2003. Exhibited in shows at Western Fedn. Watercolor Socs., El Cajon, Calif., 1990 (Best of Show), Salmagundi Club, N.Y.C., 1990 (Thomas Moran award for watercolor), Rocky Mountain Nat. Watermedia, Golden, Colo., 1994 (3d Pl. award), Ky. Watercolor Soc., 1995 (Top award for watercolor); contbr. watercolor painting articles to profl. publs. Pres. Edmond (Okla.) Iris Soc., 1986-87. Mem. Nat. Watercolor Soc. (signature mem., 2d pl. award 1997), Watercolor West, Pa. Watercolor Soc., Ky. Watercolor Soc., Western Fedn. Watercolor Socs., Ariz. Watercolor Soc. (Royal Scorpion mem.), Ariz. Artists Guild (v.p. membership 1983-84, scholarship chmn. 1990-95, bldg. fund 1998—), Western Colo. Watercolor Soc. (Past Pres. award 1992, 97), Western Fedn. of Watercolor Socs., Exhbn. of Watermedia 2000 (signature mem.). Avocations: Porsche Club racing, skiing, scuba diving, photography. Studio: 7950 E Thompson Peak Pky Scottsdale AZ 85255

KLEPPER, ANNE, journalist, speechwriter; b. Denver, Sept. 19, 1920; d. Max and Ethel (Perlstein) Lopatin; m. Sidney Lester Klepper, Feb. 3, 1951; 1 child, Leslie Klepper Arkin. BA magna cum laude, U. Colo., 1942. Intern Nat. Inst. Pub. Affairs, Washington, 1942; panel asst. disputes Nat. War Labor Bd., Washington, 1942-45; dep., chief of agy. Nat. Railway Labor Panel, Washington, 1946-47; researcher, reporter Time, N.Y.C., 1948-54; speechwriter, spl. asst. to pres., dir. corp. contbns. Time Inc., 1955-73; sr. rsch. assoc., dir. contributions mgmt. inst. Conf. Bd., N.Y.C., 1974-93. Bd. dir. Nat. Charities Info. Bur., N.Y.C., 1969-81, WNYC Found., N.Y.C., 1984-97; trustee WNYC Radio, N.Y.C., 1997—. Mem. Phi Beta Kappa. Avocations: piano, opera. Home: 520 E 90th St New York NY 10128-7850

KLEPPER, CAROL HERDMAN, mental health therapist; b. Wagner, S.D., July 17, 1933; d. Forrest Glenwood and Augusta Wilhamina (Mills) Herdman; m. Albert Raymond Klepper, May 14, 1955; children: James David, Leesa Lynn, Krista Patrice. BS in Psychology cum laude, South Oreg. State Coll., 1987; MS in Counseling, Oreg. State U., 1989. Nat. cert. counselor, lic. profl. counselor; cert. diplomate in psychotherapy. Dir. counseling Klamath Hospice, Klamath Falls, Oreg., 1990-91; staff therapist Klamath Mental Health Ctr., 1991-94; in-house counselor Wednesday's Child, 1995-2001, title 19 supv., 1996-99; pvt. practice Klamath Falls, Oreg., 2000—. Data rschr. Rich Pickett and Co., Klamath Falls, 1986—90; pre-commitment investigator Klamath Mental Health Ctr., 1991—94; EPSDT coord. County of Klamath, 1991—94; affil. Big Sage Counseling, 2000—02. Mem. youth svcs. team local mid-schs, Klamath Falls, 1992—94; juv. fire-setters network Klamath Falls Fire Dist. #1, 1992—95; head start health bd. Klamath Falls, 1991—2001; adv. bd. Klamath Falls Gospel Mission, 2000—; RAPP Team Mem., 1995—; program therapist KAP, 1995—2000; abuse therapist Klamath County Juvenile Dept., 2000—02; child and family counselor Head Start, 2000—01. Mem. Psi Chi. Home and Office: 8926 Highway 66 Klamath Falls OR 97601-9519 Office: 2960 Maywood Dr # 10 Klamath Falls OR 97602 E-mail: klepper@cvc.net.

KLEPPER, ELIZABETH LEE, physiologist; b. Memphis, Mar. 8, 1936; d. George Madden and Margaret Elizabeth (Lee) K. BA, Vanderbilt U., 1958; MA, Duke U., 1963, PhD, 1966. Research scientist Commonwealth Sci. and Indsl. Research Orgn., Griffith, Australia, 1966-68, Battelle Northwest Lab., Richland, Wash., 1972-76; asst. prof. Auburn (Ala.) U., 1968-72; Plant physiologist USDA Agrl. Research Service, Pendleton, Oreg., 1976-85, research leader, 1985-96. Assoc. editor Crop Sci., 1977-80, 88-90, tech. editor, 1990-92, editor, 1992-95; mem. editl. bd. Plant Physiology, 1977-92, Irrigation Sci., 1987-92; mem. editl. adv. bd. Field Crops Rsch., 1983-91; contbr. articles to profl. jours., chpts. to books. Marshall scholar British Govt., 1958-59; NSF fellow, 1964-66. Fellow AAAS, Crop Sci. Soc. Am. (fellows com. 1989-91, pres.-elect 1995-96, pres. 1996-97, past pres. 1997-98), Soil Sci. Soc. Am. (fellows com. 1986-88), Am. Soc. Agronomy (monograph com. 1983-90, bd. dirs. 1995-98); mem. Agronomic Sci. Found. (bd. dirs. 1993-99), Sigma Xi. Home: 1454 SW 45th Pendleton OR 97801 Office: USDA Agrl Rsch Svc PO Box 370 Pendleton OR 97801-0370 E-mail: klepperb@uci.net.

KLESKO, RYAN, baseball player; b. Westminster, Calif., June 12, 1971; Right field San Diego Padres, 2000—, Atlanta Braves, 1992—99. Spokesperson Make-A-Wish Found. Avocations: hunting, fishing. Office: San Diego Padres Qualcomm Stadium 8880 Rio San Diego Dr Ste 400 San Diego CA 92112-2000

KLETSCHKA, HAROLD DALE, cardiovascular surgeon, biomedical company executive; b. Mpls., Aug. 26, 1924; s. Herbert Leland and Emma Elizabeth (Kopf) K. AS, Brainerd (Minn.) Jr. Coll., 1943; BS, U. Minn., 1946, MB, 1947, MD, 1948; LLB, Blackstone Sch. Law, Ill., 1970; grad., Air War Coll., 1972. Diplomate Am. Bd. Surgery, Am. Bd. Thoracic Surgery, Am. Bd. Forensic Medicine. Intern Kings County Hosp., Bklyn., 1947-49; asst. resident surgery Univ. Hosp., Ann Arbor, Mich., 1950-51; resident gen. surgery State U. N.Y. Downstate Med. Center, 1953-54, chief resident thoracic surgery, 1952-53, 54-55; thoracic and gen. surgeon Bratrud Clinic, Thief River Falls, Minn.,

1951-52; asst. chief, acting chief neurosurgery 3275th and 2349th USAF hosps., Parks AFB, Calif., 1955-56, asst. chief thoracic surgery, 1956, chief thoracic surgery, 1956-57; founder, chief USAF Cardiovascular Research Center, 1957-58; practice medicine specializing in thoracic and cardiovascular surgery San Francisco and San Jose, Calif., 1958-59; thoracic surgeon VA Hosp., Syracuse, N.Y., 1959-60; chief thoracic surgery, 1960-67; asst. prof. surgery SUNY Upstate Med Center, Syracuse, 1959-67, cons. thoracic surgery, 1959-67, USAF med service liaison officer for surgeon gen., 1964-67; dep. comdr., chief hosp. services 102d TAC Hosp., Phalsbourg Air Base, France, 1961-62; mil. cons. to surgeon gen. USAF; surgeon Hdqrs. Command USAF, 1965-73; aerospace med. cons. to dir. Aerospace Med. Services, Malcolm Grow USAF Med. Center, 1965-73; thoracic surgeon VA Hosp., Houston, 1967-68, Montgomery, Ala., 1968-72, dir. cardiopulmonary labs., 1970-72; co-founder, incorporator, 1st chmn. bd., pres., chief exec. officer Bio-Medicus, Inc., Minn., 1972—; founder, chmn . bd., pres., ceo K-Heart Indrusties Inc., Mpls., 1990—. Mem. Nat. council on U.S.-USSR Health Care, Citizen Exchange Corps, N.Y.C., 1976— ; exec. com. Council for U.S.-USSR Health Exchange, Boston, 1976— Contbr.: chpt. to Progress in Surface and Membrane Science, 1973; Bd. editors: Minn. Medicine, 1960-82, editor charge spl. issue, 1966; contbr. articles to profl. jours.; collaborator liturg. mus. composition dedicated to Cardinal Spellman: Pater Noster, 1961, internat. TV performance, 1962; patentee in field. Campaign mgr. Ind. Republican candidate Dist. 43B, Minn. Ho. of Reps.; mem. nat. adv. bd. Am. Security Council.; mem. Reagan-Bush '84 Election Com., Reagan Presdl. Campaign Task Force, Reagan Nat. Adv. Bd.; spl. advisor U.S. Congl. Adv. Bd. Recipient Hon. Sci. award Bausch & Lomb, 1941, IR-100 award for devel. Rafferty-Kletschka artificial heart, 1972, Worldwide Symbolic grad. Air War Coll., 1973, 1st pl. award Med./Analytical div. Plastics World, 1976, 1st prize in Med. div. 8th Bachner award competition, 1976, eminent Churchill fellow, Winston Churchill medal Wisdom Soc., 1988; named to Wisdom Hall of Fame, 1979, Brainerd H.S. Acad. Hall of Fame, 2000. Fellow ACS; mem. Am. Heart Assn. (coun. on basic scis., coun. on cardiovascular surgery), Am. Med. Writers Assn., AAUP, U. Minn. Alumni Assn., Am. Soc. Artificial Internat. Organs, Twin City Thoracic and Cardiovascular Surgs. Soc., VFW, Am. Legion,, European Soc. Artificial Organs, Internat. Soc. Heart Transplantation, European Acad. Arts, Scis. and Humanities, Clarence Dennis Soc., K.C. (4 deg.). Achievements include co-inventor Kletschka/Rafferty Blood Pump, heart assist device and artificial heart; pioneer non-pulsatile blood flow field with contbns. of discoveries and devices, Kletschka-Levowitz fracture; discovery of medical spallation phenomenon; first to successfully perform world's 1st clin. use of constrained force vortex artificial heart blood pump, first to identify relationship of restenosis to distal embolization; inventor Kletschka blood pump, heart assist device and artificial heart, Kletschka angioplasty trap/barrier device. Home: 1925 Noble Dr N Minneapolis MN 55422-4158 *In the beginning, be disposed interiorly so as to be receptive to the whispers of God regarding His plans. Listen attentively until those designs are clearly perceived, and then follow them. Truth is the indispensable guiding beacon for life's journey. Be fearless in making decisions based on independent personal judgements, honestly founded on trying to be right. Failure is not to be feared. Success is measured by a dedicated effort without compromising truth, honesty, and fairness in the process.*

KLETT, EDWIN L. lawyer; b. Clearfield, Pa., Dec. 8, 1935; s. John L. and Gertrude Elizabeth (Larson) K.; m. Janis Lynn Gibson; children: David, Lauren, Krista, Kirklin, Keenan. BS in Commerce and Finance, Bucknell U., 1957; JD, Dickinson Sch. Law, Carlisle, Pa., 1962. Bar: Pa. 1963, U.S. Dist. Ct. (we. dist.) Pa. 1963, U.S. Dist. Ct. (mid. dist.) Pa. 1995, U.S. Dist. Ct. (ea. dist.) Pa. 2000, U.S. Ct. Appeals (3d cir.) 1967, U.S. Ct. Appeals (6th cir.) 1985, U.S. Ct. Appeals (11th cir.) 2001, U.S. Supreme Ct. 1983. Assoc. Eckert, Seamans, Cherin & Mellott, Pitts., 1962, ptnr., 1969; sr. ptnr., chmn. Klett Rooney Lieber & Schorling P.C., Pitts., 1989—. Trustee Dickinson Sch. Law, 1982—; mem. civil procedural rules com. Pa. Supreme Ct., 1986-99, vice chair, 1989-92, chair, 1993-99. Mem. Pa. State Transp. Adv. Bd., Harrisburg, Pa., 1985-88, Rep. State Fin. Com., Harrisburg, 1986-91, Allegheny County Rep. Fin. Com., Pitts., 1987-92. Fellow Internat. Acad. Trial Lawyers, Am. Coll. Trial Lawyers (Pa. state com. 1994-99, state chair 1996-98), Am. Bd. Trial Advs., Am. Bar Found., Am. Bar Inst., Pa. Bar Found., Alletheny County Bar Found.; mem. ABA (ho. dels. 1999-2000), Am. Bd. Trial Advs., Acad. Trial Lawyers Allegheny County (bd. govs. 1986-89, pres. 1988-89), Am. Judicature Soc., Allegheny County Bar (bd. govs. 1989-92, 99-02, pres. 1999-01). Home: 151 Ordale Blvd Pittsburgh PA 15228-1525 Office: Klett Rooney Lieber & Schorling 1 Oxford Ct Fl 40 Pittsburgh PA 15219-1407 E-mail: elklett@klettrooney.com.

KLETT, GORDON A. retired savings and loan association executive; b. Galva, Iowa, Apr. 29, 1925; s. Ernest and Frieda (Gutknecht) K.; m. Edna Mae Klett, June 11, 1950; children: Joel G., Kristin F., Andrea E. BA, Valparaiso U., 1949; MA, UCLA, 1951. With U.S. Weather Bur., St. Paul, 1941-42; vis. lectr. U. Ceylon, Colombo, 1951-52; fgn. service officer U.S. Dept. State, Mex., 1956-58; with Glendale (Calif.) Fed. Savs. and Loan Assn., 1953-56, 59-84, pres., chief operating officer, 1980-84. Served with USAAF, 1943-46.

KLEY, JOHN ARTHUR, banker; b. Jericho, NY, Oct. 24, 1921; s. John and Annie (Upton) K.; m. Florence Elizabeth Cannon, Sept. 1, 1945 (dec. Apr. 1983); 1 dau., Martha Anne; m. Edna C. Dornhoefer, June 1984 (div. June 1987); m. Lorelei W. Lasecki. Apr. 1989. Grad., Stonier Grad. Sch. Banking, Rutgers U., 1952; B.P.S., Pace U., 1974. With Washington Irving Trust Co. (and successor County Trust Co.), White Plains, N.Y., 1937-76, asst. treas., asst. v.p., v.p., 1947-57, exec. v.p., 1957-60, pres., 1960-72, chmn. bd., 1972-76; v.p. Bank N.Y. Co., 1968-74, vice chmn., 1974-77; dir. Bank of N.Y., 1973-77. Past chmn. bd. trustees, trustee emeritus Westchester C.C.; past pres., chmn. Westchester C.C. Found.; past pres. Legal Aid Soc. West County; past chmn. bd. regents Stonier Grad. Sch. Banking, Rutgers U. Served from pvt. to maj. USAAF, 1942-46; lt. col. Res., 1946-51. Recipient Leffingwell medal, 1960 Mem. ABA (com. on mechanization of check handling, chmn. tech. com. 1954-64, NY State Bankers Assn. (pres. 1969-70), Imperial Golf Club (Naples), Whippoorwill Club (Armonk, N.Y.). Episcopalian. Home: 7515 Pelican Bay Blvd Apt 303 Naples FL 34108-6518

KLIEBENSTEIN, DON, lawyer; b. Marshalltown, Iowa, May 3, 1936; s. Donald B. and Gertrude E. (Skeie) K.; m. Mary L. Delfs, June 11, 1960; 1 child, Julie Ann. Student, Grinnell Coll., 1953-55; BA, U. Iowa, 1957, JD, 1961. Bar: Iowa 1961, U.S. Dist. Ct. (no., so. dists.) Iowa 1961, U.S. Supreme Ct. 1971. Pvt. practice, Grundy Center, Iowa, 1961-67; ptnr. Kliebenstein & Heronimus, Grundy Center, 1967-77, Kliebenstein, Heronimus & Schmidt, Grundy Center, 1977-98, Kliebenstein Heronimus Schmidt and Harris, Grundy Center, 1999—. Bd. dirs. Grundy Nat. Bank, Grundy Ctr.; county atty. Grundy County, 1965-98. Mem. ABA, Iowa State Bar Assn., Grundy County Bar Assn. (pres. 1979-80), 1st Jud. Dist. Bar Assn. (pres. 1975-76). Republican. Methodist. Home: 701 9th St Grundy Center IA 50638-1238 Office: Kliebenstein Heronimus Schmidt & Harris 630 G Ave Grundy Center IA 50638-1500

KLIEBHAN, SISTER M(ARY) CAMILLE, academic administrator; b. Milw., Apr. 4, 1923; d. Alfred Sebastian and Mae Eileen (McNamara) K. Student, Cardinal Stritch Coll., Milw., 1945-48; BA, Cath. Sisters Coll., Washington, 1949; MA, Cath. U. Am., 1951, PhD, 1955. Joined Sisters of St. Francis of Assisi, Roman Catholic Ch., 1945; legal sec. Spence and Hanley (attys.), Milw., 1941-45; instr. edn. Cardinal Stritch Coll., 1955-62, assoc. prof., 1962-68, prof., 1968—, head dept. edn., 1962-67, dean students, 1962-64, chmn. grad. div., 1964-69, v.p. for acad. and student affairs, 1969-74, pres., also bd. dirs., 1974-91, chancellor, 1991—. Mem. TEMPO, 1982—2001; bd. dirs., 1986—89; bd. govs. Wis. Policy Rsch. Inst., 1987—97; bd. dirs. Goals for Milw. 2000, 1980—83; treas. Wis. Found. Ind. Colls., 1974—79, 1987—90, v.p., 1979—81, pres., 1981—83; bd. dirs. DePaul Hosp., 1982—91, Sacred Heart Sch. Theology, 1983—, Viterbo Coll., 1990—98, Milw. Cath. Home, 1991—2001, St. Ann Ctr. for Intergenerational Care, 1991—99, Wis. Psychoanalytic Found., 1989—96, St. Coletta's of Mass., 1995—98, Internat. Inst. Wis., 1984—94, Milw. Achiever Program, Inc., 1983—2003, Franciscan Pilgrimage Programs, Inc., 1997—, Friends of Internat. Inst. Wis., 1994—, Mental Hea.th Assn. Milwaukee County, 1983—87, Pub. Policy Forum, 1987—90, Better Bus. Bur. of Wis., Inc., 1989—2001, YWCA Greater Milw., 1996—2001, St. Camillus Campus, 1996—2001, mem. adv. bd., 1989—96. Mem. Am. Psychol. Assn., Rotary Club of Milw. (v.p., pres. elect 1992-93, pres. 1993-94), St. Mary's Acad. Alumnae Assn., Phi Delta Kappa, Delta Epsilon Sigma, Psi Chi, Delta Kappa Gamma, Kappa Delta Pi. *It is because of my faith that I can meet every condition with courage.*

KLIEFOTH, A(RTHUR) BERNHARD, III, neurosurgeon; b. San Antonio, Nov. 26, 1942; S. Arthur Bernhard, Jr. and Pauline (Gray) K.; m. Ingrid R. Kunde, Apr. 22, 1968; children: Karena, Tanya. AB in Chemistry, Princeton U., 1965; MD, U. Tex., 1970. Diplomate Am. Bd. Neurol. Surgery. Intern Naval Hosp., Oakland, Calif., 1970-71, resident gen. surgery San Diego, 1972-73; neurosurg. tchr. Washington U., St. Louis, 1973-78, rsch. fellow dept. radiation scis., 1977-78; commd. ensign USN, 1969, advanced through grades to comdr., 1977; staff neurosurgeon Naval Regional Med. Ctr., Oakland, 1978-81; resigned, 1981; capt. USNR, 1985; practice medicine specializing in neurosurgery Knoxville, Tenn., 1981—; mem. staff U. Tenn Hosp., St. Mary's Hosp.; chmn. dept. surgery, 1989-90; clin. assoc. prof. surgery U. Tenn. Bd. dirs. Tenn. Donor Svcs., Cole Neurosci. Found., Knoxville Donor Svcs., Epilepsy Found. Ea. Tenn. Pres. Princeton Alumni Assn. Knoxville and Ea. Tenn Recipient Dist. Southern Neurosurgeon, So. Neurosurgery Soc., 2003—. Fellow ACS, Stroke Coun. Am. Heart Assn.; mem. AMA, Am. Assn. Neurol. Surgeons, Am. Soc. Stereotactic and Functional Neurosurgery, Tenn. Neurosurg. Soc., World Soc. Stereotactic and Functional Neurosurgery, Congress Neurol. Surgeons, So. Neurosurg. Soc., So. Med. Assn., Tenn. Med. Assn., Knoxville Acad. Medicine, San Francisco Neurol. Soc., Soc. Med. Cons. to Armed Forces, Assn. Mil. Surgeons U.S., Soc. Neurosci. Office: 6901 Office Park Cir Knoxville TN 37909-1162 Address: PO Box 51648 Knoxville TN 37950-1648

KLIESCH, WILLIAM FRANK, retired physician; b. Franklinton, La., Nov. 4, 1928; s. Edward Granville and Elsie Jeni (Sylvest) K.; m. May Virginia Reid, Dec. 17, 1955; children: Thomas Karl, William August, John Francis. BS, La. State U., 1949, MD, 1953. Intern Valley Forge Hosp., Phoenixville, Pa., 1953-54; intern in med. rsch. Charity Hosp., New Orleans, 1956-57; resident, fellow in internal medicine Ochsner Found. Hosp., New Orleans, 1957-59; pvt. practice New Orleans, 1959-69, Jackson, Miss., 1969-99; dir. spinal injury svc. Miss. Meth. Rehab. Ctr., Jackson, 1980-99; ret., 1999. Capt. U.S Air Force, 1953 56. Fellow Am. Coll. Emergency Physicians; mem. Am. Spinal Injury Assn., Internat. Paraplegia Soc. Episcopalian. Avocations: gardening, farming. Home: 0092 Oury Rd Jackson MS 39272

KLIGER, MILTON RICHARD, financial services executive; b. N.Y.C., Sept. 26, 1922; s. David and Sadie (Zelikow) K.; m. Ruth Salkind, Jan. 30, 1944 (dec. July 1991); children: Alan S., Sandra F.; m. Gladys Duarte, Sept. 26, 1992. BBA, Bernard Baruch Coll., 1947. Acct. Shipowners Agy. Inc., N.Y.C., 1946-48; chief acct. Am.-Israeli Shipping Co. Inc., N.Y.C., 1948-53; exec. v.p. Maritime Overseas Corp., N.Y.C., 1953-87, also bd. dirs.; sr. v.p., treas. Overseas Shipholding Group Inc., N.Y.C., 1970-87, also bd. dirs.; pres. OSG Internat. Inc., 1980-87; sr. v.p. Argent Group, Ltd., N.Y.C., 1988-89; pres. Milton Kliger Mgmt. Svcs., Inc., N.Y.C., 1989-93, Marine Equity Corp., N.Y.C., 1990—. Home: 7000 Island Blvd Apt 909 Aventura FL 33160

KLIGERMAN, MORTON M. radiologist; b. Phila., Dec. 26, 1917; s. Samuel and Dorothy (Medvene) K.; m. Barbara B. Coleman, Mar. 14, 1956; children: Hilary, Thomas A., Valli á Court. BS, Temple U., 1938, MD, 1941, M.Sc., 1948; MA (hon.), Yale U., 1958; D.F.A. (hon.), New Sch. Music, 1985; MA (hon.), U. Pa., 1986. Instr. radiology Temple U., Phila., 1947-48, Columbia U., N.Y.C., 1948-50, asst. prof. radiology, 1950-53, assoc. prof., 1953-58; Robert E. Hunter prof. radiology, chmn. dept. radiology Yale U., New Haven; also radiologist-in-chief Yale-New Haven Hosp., 1958-72; dir. Cancer Research and Treatment Center U. N.Mex., Albuquerque, 1972-80, prof. radiology, 1972-80; asst. dir. for radiation therapy Los Alamos Sci. Lab., 1972-80; chief div. radiation oncology Bernalillo County Med. Center, Albuquerque, 1972-80; prof. radiation oncology U. Pa., Phila., 1980—, Henry K. Pancoast prof. research oncology, 1984-88; prof. emeritus, 1988—. Cons. on staff Presbyn. Hosp., Lovelace-Bataan Med. Center, St. Joseph Hosp., VA Hosp., all Albuquerque, Los Alamos Med. Center. Contbr. articles to profl. jours. Bd. dirs. Santa Fe Opera, 1975-80, mem. nat. adv. bd., 1980-89; bd. dirs. Santa Fe Opera Found., 1976-80, also pres.; bd. dirs. N.Mex. divsn. Am. Cancer Soc., 1972-76, Phila. divsn., 1985-89, Pa. Ballet, 1985-89; bd. advisors Annenberg Ctr., U. Pa., 1987-2001, bd. overseers, 2001—, Phila. Scholar Fund, 1992—. With M.C., U.S. Army, 1944-47. Recipient Disting. Alumni award Temple U., 1964; Silver Medallion Columbia U., 1967; Grubbe Gold Medal award Chgo. Med. Soc.-Chgo. Radiol. Soc., 1976; Disting. Alumnus award Temple U. Med. Sch., 1986; named Med. Alumnus of Yr. Temple U. Med. Sch., 1989. Fellow Am. Coll. Radiology, Coll. Physicians Phila.; mem. Pa. Med. Soc., Philadelphia County Med. Soc., Am. Assn. Cancer Rsch., Am. Radium Soc. (v.p. 1976-77, pres. 1982-83, Janeway medal 1981), Am. Soc. Therapeutic Radiologists (pres. 1968-69, Gold medal 1982), Am. Legion, Alpha Omega Alpha. Home: 220 W Rittenhouse Sq Philadelphia PA 19103-5737 Office: Hosp of Univ Pa Dept Radiation Oncology 3400 Spruce St Philadelphia PA 19104-4283 E-mail: kligerman@xrt.upenn.edu.

KLIGFIELD, PAUL DAVID, physician, medicine educator; b. N.Y.C., Dec. 20, 1945; s. Irving and Yetta (Blumenstein) K.; m. Mary Susan Winters, Dec. 16, 1978; 1 child, Benjamin Winters. BA, Queens Coll., N.Y.C., 1966; B in Med. Sci., Dartmouth Coll., 1968; MD, Harvard U., 1970. Diplomate Am. Bd. Internal Medicine, Am. Bd. Cardiovascular Diseases. Intern and resident in medicine Beth Israel Hosp., Boston, 1970-72; rsch. fellow St. Georges Hosp., London, 1972-73; fellow in cardiology N.Y. Hosp., 1973-75, dir. cardiac graphics lab., 1977—; asst. prof. medicine Med. Coll., Cornell U., N.Y.C., 1977-83, assoc. prof., 1983-92, prof., 1992—. Cons. Rockefeller U. Hosp., N.Y.C., 1977—. Contbr. articles to profl. jours. Lt. comdr. USNR, 1975-77. Fellow Am. Coll. Cardiology, N.Y. Acad. Medicine (trustee 1990-97), N.Y. Cardiologic Soc. (sec.-treas. 1997—); mem. Am. Osler Soc. (pres. 1991-92), N.Y. Heart Assn. (bd. dirs. 1988-94), Internat. Soc. for Computerized Electrocardiography (bd. dirs. 1984—), Grolier Club. Office: Cornell Med Ctr 525 E 68th St New York NY 10021-4870

KLIM, CHRISTOPHER, editor, publishing executive, writer; b. Trenton, N.J., Sept. 8, 1962; s. Eugene and Margaret Klim; m. Karin S. Seidel, Apr. 19, 1994. BS in Computer Sci. and Physics, Rutgers U., 1984; MS in Computer Sci. and Physics, N.J. Inst. Tech., 1988. Aerospace engr. RCA/GE, Hightstown, NJ, 1984—88; comm. engr. Xpedite, Eatontown, NJ, 1988—96; editor, pub. Writers Notes Mag., Titusville, NJ, 2002—. Writing mentor, NJ, 1998—2003. Author: (novels) Jesus Lives in Trenton, 2002; : Write to Publish, 2003. Office: Hopewell Publs LLC PO Box 11 Titusville NJ 08560

KLIMA, ROGER RADIM, physiatrist; b. Prague, Czechoslovakia; came to U.S., 1982, naturalized, 1988; s. Josef and Radka Klima. BA, Zatlanka Coll., Prague, 1971; MD, Charles U., Prague, 1978. Diplomate Am. Bd. Phys. Medicine and Rehab., Am. Bd. Electrodiagnostic Medicine. Resident in surgery Charles U., 1978-79, resident in orthopedic surgery, 1979-81; fellow, clin. clk. Beverly Hills Med. Ctr. and Cedars-Sinai Med. Ctr., L.A., 1984-86; resident in surgery U. Medicine and Dentistry-N.J. Med. Sch., Newark, 1986-87; resident in phys. medicine and rehab. U. Medicine and Dentistry-N.J. Med. Sch./Kessler Inst., Newark and West Orange, 1987-90; mem. phys. medicine and rehab. faculty Stanford (Calif.) U. and affiliated hosps., 1990—; dir. phys. medicine and rehab. outpatient svcs. Palo Alto (Calif.) VA Health Care Sys., 1992—, also co-dir. comprehensive pain mgmt. Clin. instr. in phys. medicine and rehab. U. Medicine and Dentistry-N.J.Med. Sch., 1989-90; clin. instr. in phys., medicine and rehab. Stanford U. Sch. Medicine, 1990-96, asst. prof., 1996—. Contbr. articles to profl. jours. Recipient first ann. Thompson Humanitarian award Stanford U. Phys. Medicine and Rehab., 1994, 97, 2000. Mem. Am. Acad. Phys. Medicine and Rehab. (liaison resident physician coun. 1989-90), Assn. Acad. Physiatrists, Am. Assn. Electrodiagnostic Medicine. Office: Stanford U Med Ctr Divsn Phys Medicine and Rehab Rm NC 104 Stanford CA 94305

KLIMAN, GERALD BURT, electrical engineer; b. Boston, July 28, 1931; s. Milford and Minnie (Savits) K.; m. Edith Vivian Moses, Aug. 21, 1960; children: Jonathan Meir, Daniel Joseph. SB, MIT, 1955, SM, 1959, ScD, 1965. Electronics technician meteorology dept. MIT, Cambridge, 1950-55, instr., tchg. asst. elec. engring. dept., 1957-65; asst. prof. elec. engring. Rensselaer Poly. Inst., Troy, N.Y., 1965-71; elec. engr. transp. divsn. GE, Erie, Pa., 1971-76; elec. engr. Advanced Nuclear Systems GE, San Jose, Calif., 1976-78, Corp. Rsch. and Devel. GE, Schenectady, NY, 1978—2001; rsch. prof. Rensselaer Poly. Inst., Troy, NY, 2001—. Assoc. editor Electric Machines and Power Systems Jours., 1976—; contbr. articles to profl. jours. Mem. exec. bd. Interfaith Community, Schenectady, 1983; pres., v.p., concertmaster Music Co. Orch., Schenectady, 1978—; chmn. Agudat Achim Sch. Com., Schenectady, 1990-91; Capt. USAF, 1955-57. Fellow IEEE, mem. Sigma Xi, Tau Beta Pi, Eta Kappa Nu. Achievements include 85 patents on electromagnetic pumps, permanent magnet motors, incipient fault diagnostics, electron beam and laser cutting; switched reluctance motors, high speed motors, generator core quality, superconducting magnets, and soft magnetic composites. Office: Rensselaer Poly Tech JEC 5008 116 8th St Troy NY 12180

KLIMAN, SYLVIA MAY STERN, film executive, editor, realtor; b. Boston, July 16, 1934; d. Edward I. and Bernice Stern; m. Allan Kliman, June 24, 1956; children: Gilbert Harrow, Douglas Hartley. AB, Vassar Coll., 1956. Editl. asst. Harvard Law Sch. profs., Cambridge, Mass., 1956-58; editor Vassar Micellany News, Poughkeepsie, N.Y., 1953-56; editor, founder Park Parent, Brookline, Mass., 1968-73; pres. Sylvia S. Kliman Real Estate Brokerage, Brookline, 1971—. Pres. Dunewind Films, 1979—, creative cons. for feature films & TV, 1977—. Vol. Mass. ARC blood program, 1970-73; polit. speechwriter, 1960—; mem. Barn Gallery, Ogunquit Mus. of Art, Friends of Vassar Art Gallery; trustee Park Sch., Brookline, 1970-73; bd. friends Peter Bent Brigham Hosp., 1970-75; bd. dirs. Spl. Com. to Restore Ogunquit Dunes, 1975—. Mem. Park Sch. Parents Assn. (pres. 1968-70), Norfolk Dist. Med. Soc. Womens Aux., Boston Mus. Fine Arts, Vassar Club (bd. dirs.), Coll. Club. Unitarian Universalist. Home: 40 Newton St Brookline MA 02445-7407 also: Dunewind Ogunquit ME 03907

KLIMCZUK, STEPHEN JOHN, business executive, foundation director; b. North Hollywood, Calif., Jan. 14, 1963; s. Leon and Wanda (Kotowicz) K.; m. Iris C.B. Massion, Sept. 6, 1991; children: Caroline, Julia, Christina, Isabella (dec.). BA in Econs., UCLA, 1983; MBA, Harvard U., 1987. Assoc. cons. Bain & Co., Palo Alto, Calif., 1983-84; fin. analyst John Nuveen & Co. Inc., San Francisco, 1984-85; assoc. Goldman, Sachs & Co., N.Y.C., 1987-88; mgr. Nat. Review Inc., N.Y.C., 1988-89; dir., mem. bd. World Economic Forum, Geneva, 1989 95; dir. global bus. policy coun. A.T. Kearney, Inc., Alexandria, Va., 1996—. Mng. dir. World Link Publs. S.A., Geneva, 1991-92. Freeman, City of London, 1990. Recipient Cavaliere, S.M.O. Constantiniano di San Giorgio, 1987; named officer Most Venerable Order of St. John, 1994; invested Knight of Malta, 1996. Fellow: Salzburg Seminar, Royal Soc. Arts (London); mem.: Travellers Club (London), Harvard Club of N.Y.C., Phi Beta Kappa. Roman Catholic. Avocations: travel, history, visual arts, mountain walking. Home: 9801 Georgetown Pike Great Falls VA 22066-2617

KLIMEK, JOSEPH JOHN, physician, educator; b. Wilkes-Barre, Pa., Sept. 14, 1946; s. Joseph John and Frances Carol (Pavloski) K.; m. Jane Marie Stout, June 26, 1971 (div.); 1 child, Adam. AB cum laude, Princeton U., 1968; MD, Pa. State U., 1972. Diplomate Am. Bd. Internal Medicine, Am. Bd. Infectious Diseases. Intern, resident in internal medicine Hartford (Conn.) U., then fellow in infectious disease, 1972-76, chief epidemiology, 1976-87, dir. subsplty. medicine, 1985-87, assoc. dir. medicine, 1987-90, assoc. dir. dept. medicine and chmn. AIDS program, 1987-90, dir. dept. medicine, 1990—, chmn. AIDS task force, 1985-90, assoc. chmn. dept. medicine, 1995—; asst. prof. medicine U. Conn., Farmington, 1977-84, assoc. prof., 1984-90, prof., 1990—; assoc. chmn. dept. medicine U. Conn. Sch. Medicine, 1995—. Conn. mem. numerous faculties pharm. industry. Sr. assoc. editor Am. Jour. Infection Control, 1980-95; med. editor Asepsis, The Infection Control Forum; also mem. numerous editl. bds. in field; contbr. articles to med. jours. Recipient Disting. Alumnus award, 1978, ARC award, 1986. Fellow ACP, Infectious Disease Soc. Am.; mem. APHA, AAAS, Am. Profls. in Infection Control, Am. Soc. Microbiology, Am. Fedn. Clin. Rsch., Soc. Hosp. Epidemiologists Am., Am. Venereal Disease Assn., Am. Med. Writers Assn. Achievements include integrated internal medicine residency of Hartford Hospital with University of Connecticut School of Medicine; developed hospital community linkage network for AIDS care in Greater Hartford; introduced primary care medicine practice model to all ambulatory services; expanded care to indigent with two bilingual satellite practices; developed hospital cardiac services product line; initiated formal hospitalist program for care of inpatients. Home: 31 Main St Farmington CT 06032-2229 Office: Hartford Hosp 80 Seymour St Hartford CT 06115-2701 E-mail: jklimek@harthosp.org.

KLIMENT, ROBERT MICHAEL, architect; b. Prague, Czechoslovakia, June 9, 1933; came to U.S., 1950; s. Felix and Sophie (Baltinester) K.; m. Janet McClure, Sept. 12, 1959 (div. 1968); 1 child, Nicholas McClure; m. Frances Halsband, May 1, 1971; 1 child, Alexander Halsband. BA, Yale U., 1954, MArch, 1959. Registered architect Penn., N.Y., N.J., Mass., Conn., Ohio, Va., D.C., N.C., N.H., Md., Ill., Miss.; cert. Nat. Coun. Archtl. Registration Bds. Architect Mitchell/Giurgola Architects, Phila., 1961-66, architect, assoc. N.Y.C., 1967-71; ptnr. R.M. Kliment Architect, N.Y.C., 1972-78, R.M. Kliment & Frances Halsband Architects, N.Y.C., 1978—. Instr. U. Pa., Phila., 1963-66, vis. prof., 1972-73; asst. prof. Columbia U., N.Y.C., 1966-70, vis. prof., 1977, 84; vis. prof. MIT, Cambridge, Mass., 1970, Yale U., New Haven, 1972-74, N.C. State U., Raleigh, 1978, Rice U., Houston, 1979, U. Va., Charlottesville, 1979-80, Harvard U., Cambridge, 1980-81. Works include Computer Sci. Bldg. Princeton U. (Nat. Honor award AIA 1994), U. Va. Life Scis. Bldg., Columbia U. Computer Scis. Bldg. (Nat. Honor award AIA 1987, award NYSAA 1985, Tucker award Bldg. Stone Inst. 1985, other awards), Mercantile Exch. Bldg., N.Y. (Bard award for excellence in architecture City Club N.Y. 1989), Burke Chemistry Bldg., Dartmouth Coll., Adelbert Adminstrn. Bldg., Case Western Res. U. (AIA Nat. honor award 1994), Sudikoff Computer Sci. Bldg., Dartmouth Coll., MTA/L.I. R.R. Entrance Bldg., Penn Sta., N.Y. (Bard award for excellence in architecture City Club N.Y. 1995, AIA nat. honor award 1996, NYSAA & NYC AIA awards 1995), Ebert Art Ctr., Coll. of Wooster, U.S. Courthouse and post office, Bklyn., U.S. Courthouse Gulfport, Miss., Yale Divinity Sch., Franklin and Marshall Coll. Roschel Performing Arts Ctr., N.Y.C. Primary Sch. 54, N.Y.C. Priamry Sch. 178, N.Y.C. Monroe H.S.; exhibited in group shows at Bklyn. Mus., 1977, The Drawing Ctr., 1977, Cooper Hewitt Mus., 1977-78, Mus. Finnish Architecture, Helsinki, Finland, 1980, Harvard Grad. Sch. Design, 1981, NAD, 1981, 87, Smith Coll. Mus. Art, 1981, Rice U. Farrish Hall Gallery, 1983, Columbia U. Low Libr., 1986, Parrish Art Mus., 1987, German Architecture Mus., Frankfurt, 1989, Rotunda Gallery, Bklyn., 1995. With U.S. Army, 1955-57. Fulbright scholar, Italy, 1959-60; AIA Archtl. Firm award, 1997, Medal of Honor NYC AIA, 1998. Fellow AIA, Century Assn. Office: R M Kliment & Frances Halsband Architects 255 W 26th St New York NY 10001-8001

KLIMENT, STEPHEN ALEXANDER, architect, editor, journalist; b. May 24, 1930; s. Felix and Sophia (Baltinester) K.; m. Felicia Drury, Dec. 24, 1957; children: Pamela Drury, Jennifer Anne. Student, Ecole Speciale d'Architecture, Paris, 1948-49; BArch, MIT, 1953; MFA in Arch., Princeton U., 1957. Draftsman Jean Labatut, Princeton, N.J., 1957; designer Skidmore, Owings & Merrill, N.Y.C., 1957-59, Reeb-Draz Assos., Cleve., 1959-60; editor Archtl. and Engring. News, 1961-69; v.p. Caudill Rowlett Scott, N.Y.C., 1969-72; architect, cons., 1972-78; editor in chief Advt. & Pub. News, 1978-80; exec. editor Whitney Libr. of Design, 1981-85; v.p., editl. dir. Practice Mgmt. Assocs., Ltd., 1985-87; editor sci. and tech. div. John Wiley & Sons, 1987-90; editor-in-chief Archtl. Record, 1990-96; arch., journalist, writer, 1996—. Adj. prof. Sch. Architecture and Environ. Studies, City Coll. of CUNY, 1997—; lectr. U. Oreg., Carnegie-Mellon U., U. Ariz., Yale U., Harvard U., Washington U., St. Louis, U. Tex., U. Nebr., Ariz. State U., N.C. State U., Tex. A&M U., Miss. State U. Author: Writing for Design Professionals, 1998, Creative Communications for a Successful Design Practice, Into the Mainstream: Syllabus for a Barrier-Free Environment, Architectural Sketching and Rendering: Techniques for Designers and Artists; (with R.H. McNulty) Neighborhood Conservation; editor: Design Principal's Report and Design Firm Management & Administration Report, 1998—; founding editor Building Type Basics Series, John Wiley & Sons, Inc.; contbr. articles to profl. jours. Chmn. adv. coun. Princeton Sch. Architecture and Urban Planning, 1973-84. With AUS, 1953-55. Fellow AIA, Univ. Club (N.Y.C.). Episcopalian. Home and Office: 1255 5th Ave New York NY 10029-3850

KLIMLEY, NANCY LEE, volunteer; b. Chgo. d. William Peter and Flora (Sutherland) Enzweiler; m. Francis Joseph Klimley; children: Lisa, Brooks. BA, St. Mary's Coll., Notre Dame, Inc., 1951. Asst. fashion coord., dir. Carson Pirie

Scott, Chgo.; asst. social dir. Lake Shore Club, Chgo., editor mag. Chmn. women's divsn. Chgo. Heart Assn., 1958—, pres. women's coun., 3 times. Bd. dirs. Chgo. Boys and Girls Club, 1970—, Brookfield Zoo, 1982—, Libr. of Internat. Rels., 1980-92, Northwestern U. Settlement, 1962-78, Great Lakes Hosp. League, 1962, Boy Scouts Am., 1965, Aides to the Handicapped, 1965, ARC, Mus. of Scis.; bd. dirs. Children's Home and Aid Soc., 3-time pres. woman's bd., sponsor parent bd. 1962—; bd. dirs. Fashion Group, treas., 1958; bd. dirs. Am. Opera Soc., 1962-76, Ill. Opera Guild, 1962-76, Artists Adv. Coun., 1970-80, Republican Women Vols., 1958; bd. dirs., mem. exec. com. USO, 1980—, benefit chmn. 5 years, founder, pres. woman's adv. bd.; founding mem., benefit chmn. Joffrey Ballet, vice chmn. emeritus of benefits; chmn., hon. chmn. The Consular Ball. Recipient Golden Heart award, Heart of Yr. award Am. Heart Assn., Fund Raising award Children's Home and Aid Soc., Golden Eagle award USO, others. Mem. Chgo. Hist. Soc., Guild of the Chgo. Hist. Soc., Antiquarians of the Art Inst. (life), Woman's Athletic Club (bd. dirs.), Saddle and Cycle Club. Republican. Roman Catholic. Avocations: antiques, collecting and reading books, world of fashion as an art form, interior decorating. Home: 3240 N Lake Shore Dr Chicago IL 60657-3954

KLINCEWICZ, JOHN GREGORY, deacon, mathematician; b. Bkyln., Mar. 4, 1954; s. John James and Matilda Sophia (Gerlowski) K.; m. Kristine Ann Zagrobelny, Sept. 20, 1986. SB, MIT, 1975; MA, PhD, Yale U., 1979. Prin. mem. tech. staff AT&T Labs., Middletown, NJ, 1979—; deacon Holy Innocents Roman Cath. Ch., Neptune, 1990—. Office: AT&T Labs Laurel Ave Middletown NJ 07748

KLINCEWICZ, STEPHEN LOUIS, preventive medicine physician; b. Jersey City, Aug. 18, 1956; s. Watson L. and Gisele H. (Luipersbeck) K.; m. Leslie A. Devine, Jan. 12, 1985. BA with honors, McGill U., Montreal, Can., 1977; DO, U. Osteo. Medicine, Des Moines, 1983; MPH, Med. Coll. Wis., Milw., 1991; JD, Widener U., 1996. Diplomate Am. Bd. Preventive Medicine (occupl.), Am. Osteo. Bd. Preventive Medicine (occupl. and environ. medicine). Asst. dir. emergency svcs. USAF Hosp., Homestead, Fla., 1984-87; med. officer Ctr. Disease Control/ Nat. Inst. Occupl. Safety & Health, Cin., 1987-89; dir. occupational and environ. medicine Sacred Heart Hosp., Allentown, Pa., 1989-91; dir. occupational health Brandywine Hosp., Exton, Pa., 1991-95, med. dir. drug safety and pharmacoepidemiology Zeneca Pharms., Wilmington, Del., 1995-99; sr. med. dir. R&D Johnson & Johnson Pharm. Rsch., 1999—. With USPHS, 1987—, USAFR, 1979-87. Mem. Am. Acad. Pharm. Physicians, Animal Legal Def. Fund. Avocations: jazz, langs., bass, psitacine behavior. Home: PO Box 232 Carversville PA 18913-0232 Office: Janssen Rsch Found 1125 Trenton Harbourtown Rd Titusville NJ 08560-0200 E-mail: stephenk@justice.com.

KLINCK, CYNTHIA ANNE, library director; b. Salamanaca, N.Y., Nov. 1, 1948; d. William James and Marjorie Irene (Woodruff) K.; m. Andrew Clavert Humphries, Nov. 26, 1983. BS, Ball State U., 1970; MLS, U. Ky., 1976. Reference/ young adult libr. Bartholomew County Libr., Columbus, Ind., 1970-74; dir. Paul Sawyier Pub. Libr., Frankfort, Ky., 1974-78, Washington-Centerville Pub. Libr., Dayton, Ohio, 1978—. Libr. bldg. cons.; libr. cons., trainer OPLIN Task Force. Contbr. articles to profl. jours. Bd. dirs. Bluegrass Comty. Action Agy., Frankfort, Ky., 1971-73; founder, bd. dirs. FACTS, Inc. (info. & referral), Frankfort, 1972-74; co-founder, bd. dirs. Seniors, Inc., Dayton, Ohio, 1980-81, 91—; trustee, officer South Comty., Inc. Mental Health Ctr., Dayton, 1980-89; pres. Miami Valley Librs.; mem. govt. affairs com., ann. conf. planning com., fin. resources task force conf. presenter Ohio Libr. Coun.; program presenter Ohio Libr. Coun. Confs.; del. to Am. Libr. Assn. Congress on Profl. Edn. Recipient Vol. of Yr. So. Metro Regional C. of C. Mem. ALA, Am. Soc. for Info. Sci., Am. Soc. for Pers. Adminstrn., Ohio Libr. Assn. (chmn. legis. com.), South Metro Regional C. of C. (exec. com., bd. dirs., chmn. edn. com., 1st v.p.), Rotary (bd. dirs.), Pub. Libr. Assn. Mng. for Results (trainer). Office: Washington-Centerville Pub Libr 111 W Spring Valley Rd Dayton OH 45458-3761

KLINCK, JAMES WILLIAM, insurance company executive; b. Kitchener, Ont., Can., Dec. 12, 1951; s. Armand Adam and Imogene (Sim) K.; m. Viola Mary Wright, Sept. 17, 1977; childen: David James, Bonnie Ann. B in Math. with honors, U. Waterloo, Ont., Can., 1974. Cert. info. sys. profl. V.p., chief info. officer Metlife-Can. Ops., Ottawa, Ont., Can., 1991-96; v.p. applications devel. Met. Life, N.Y.C., 1996—. Named One of Top 10 Can. Chief Info. Officers Toronto, 1994. Mem. Can. Info. Processing Soc. Home: 18 Le Parc Ct West Windsor NJ 08550-5130 Office: Met Life Ins Co 501 Rte 22 Bridgewater NJ 08807 E-mail: jklinck@comcast.net.

KLINE, ADRIENNE MARIE, news producer; b. Lynn, Mass., June 23, 1977; d. Wesley Earl and Patricia Ann Kline. AS in Telecom., BS in Comms. Arts and Scis., Lyndon State Coll., 2000. News prodr. WPTV News Channel 5, West Palm Beach, Fla., 2000—. Mem.: Soc. Profl. Journalists. Home: 1900 N Estrella Ct # 107 Palm Beach Gardens FL 33410

KLINE, ALLEN HABER, JR., lawyer; b. Houston, June 17, 1954; s. Allen H. Sr. and Maude Rose (Brown) K.; m. Barbara Ann Byrd, July 24, 1982; children: Allison Ashley, Allen III. BA, U. Denver, 1976; JD, U. Miami, 1979. Bar: Tex. 1980, U.S. Dist. Ct. (so. dist.) Tex. 1980, U.S. Ct. Appeals (5th cir.) 1980, U.S. Ct. Appeals (11th cir.) 1983, U.S. Supreme Ct. 1985; bd. cert. personal injury trial law Tex. Bd. Legal Specialization. Sole practice, Houston, 1980—. Mem. Houston Bar Assn., Coll. of the State Bar of Tex. Clubs; City Wide (Houston) (life). Avocations: tennis, water, snow skiing. Office: 440 Louisiana St Ste 2050 Houston TX 77002-4205

KLINE, DANIEL THOMAS, English educator; b. San Bernardino, Calif., May 4, 1961; s. Danny Joe Kline and Shirley Josephine Tubiola; children: Samuel Thomas Holley-Kline, Jacob Daniel Holley-Kline. BA, U. of Ala., Huntsville, 1983, MA, 1985; MDiv, So. Bapt. Theol. Sem., 1989; PhD, Ind. U., 1997. Assoc. prof. English Jefferson C.C. SW, Louisville, 1990—97, U. Alaska, Anchorage, 1997—. Asst. dean Ky. Gov.'s Scholars Program, Danville, 1992—94. Author: (textbook) Responding to Literature: A Writer's Journal, 2001, Teaching Literature Online: A Guide to Teaching with Technology in the Literature Classroom, 2002; co-author: (computer handbook) SQL in a Nutshell, 2001; editor: Medieval Literature for Children, 2003; contbr. articles to profl. jours. Recipient Summer Seminar for Coll. and U. Faculty fellowship, NEH, 2000, Summer Inst. for Coll. and U. Faculty fellowship, 1997. Office: U Alaska 3211 Providence Dr Anchorage AK 99508 Office Fax: 907-786-4383. E-mail: afdtk@uaa.alaska.edu.

KLINE, DAVID ADAM, lawyer, educator, writer; b. Keota, Okla., Sept. 27, 1923; s. David Adam and Lucy Leila (Wood) K.; m. Ruthela Deal, Aug. 25, 1947; children: Steven, Timothy, Ruthanna. JD, Okla. U., 1950. Bar: Okla. 1949. Law clk., spl. master U.S. Dist. Ct. Okla., 1952-61; 1st asst. U.S. atty. We. Dist. Okla., 1961-69; judge We. Dist. Okla. U.S. Bankruptcy Ct., Oklahoma City, 1969-82; sr. shareholder Kline Kline Elliott Castleberry & Bryant, P.C., Oklahoma City, 1983—. Pres. Nat. Conf. Bankruptcy Judges 1977-78; mem. arbitration panel program U.S. Dist. Ct. (we. dist.) Okla., 1985— mem. faculty Fed. Jud. Ctr., Washington, Nat. Seminar Bankruptcy Judges, 1971-86; adj. prof. law Oklahoma City U., 1980-84; cons. Norton Bankruptcy Law and Practice, 1986, Callaghan & Co.; bd. dirs. Consumer Credit Counseling Svc. Ctr., Okla., 1973-2001, chmn., 1992. Author: A Little Book (A New Thing in the Earth), 1993, A Little Book II (The Blood of the Lion), 1995, A Little Book III (The Revelation), 1997, A Little Book IV (A Still Small Voice), 1998, A Little Book V (Law and Liberty), 2003; digest editor Am. Bankruptcy Law jour., 1974—77; contbr. ; co-author: Briefcase, 1888—2000. Fellow Am. Coll. Bankruptcy. Office: Kline Kline Elliott Castleberry & Bryant PC Kline Law Bldg 720 NE 63rd St Oklahoma City OK 73105-6405 E-mail: dkline@klinefirm.org.

KLINE, DAVID GELLINGER, neurosurgery educator; b. Phila., Oct. 13, 1934; s. David Francis and Lois Ann (Gellinger) K.; m. Carol Anne Loewen, Mar. 1, 1958 (div.), children: Susan, Robert, Nancy. AB in Chemistry, U. Pa., 1956, MD, 1960. Diplomate Am. Bd. Neurol. Surgery (sec.-treas. 1978-83, chmn. 1983-84, adv. bd. 1984-90, chmn. 50th anniversary celebration 1990). Intern and resident in gen. surgery U. Mich., Ann Arbor, 1960-62; research investigator Walter Reed Army Inst. Research and Walter Reed Gen. Hosp., 1962-64; resident in neurosurgery and teaching instr. U. Mich., Ann Arbor, 1964-67; instr. neurosurgery and surgery Sch. Medicine La. State U., New Orleans, 1967-68, asst. prof., 1968-70, assoc. prof., 1970-75, prof., 1976, head sect. of neurosurgery, 1971, chmn. dept. neurosurgery, 1976—, Boyd prof., chmn. neurosurgery, 1995—. Cons. USPHS Health Center Hosp., New Orleans VA Hosp., Kessler AFB Hosp.-Lederle Labs.; vis. investigator Delta Regional Primate Center, Covington; mem. Am. Bd. Med. Specialists, 1978-86, mem. residency rev. com., 1977-84; lectr. in field. Contbr. articles to sci. jours., also mem. numerous editorial bds. Capt. M.C. AUS, 1962-64. Recipient Frederick Coller Surg. prize, 1967; numerous grants. Mem.: ACS, AMA, Soc. Univ. Surgeons, Assn. Acad. Surgery, Congress Neurol. Surgeons, Soc. Univ. Neurosurgeons, Am. Assn. Neurol. Surgeons (bd. dirs. 1985—89), So. Neurol. Surgery Soc. (sec. 1976—79, pres. 1985—86), Soc. Neurol. Surgeons (treas. 1986—91, v.p. 1994—95, pres. 1996—97), Am. Acad. Neurol. Surgery, New Orleans Neurol. Soc., La. State Med. Soc., Orleans Parish Med. Soc., Am. Assn. Hand Surgery (hon.), German Neurosurg. Soc. (hon.), Can. Neurosurg. Soc. (hon.), Sunderland Soc. (pres. 1981), Surg. Biol. Club II, Phi Chi, Phi Beta Kappa, Alpha Omega Alpha, Kappa Sigma. Episcopalian (vestry and lay reader). Home: 307 Fairway Dr New Orleans LA 70124-1020 Office: La State U Med Ctr Dept Neurosurgery 1542 Tulane Ave New Orleans LA 70112-2825 *Success, whether defined by the individual who believes he or she has achieved it or 'granted' by others has little meaning unless it is accompanied by happiness. To have both, one must not only enjoy his or her life's work but also life as a whole and particularly people and specifically working hard with and interacting well with others. Honesty about one's own efforts as well as those of others, a large measure of perseverance, a sense of humor, and a degree of courage as well as a certain amount of realistic optimism are very necessary to survive let alone flourish.*

KLINE, DENNY LEE, hazardous devices and explosives consultant; b. Boston, Jan. 31, 1939; s. Francis Marion and Sylvia Lee (Denny) K.; m. Sadie Mae Thompson, June 14, 1963; 1 child, Hank Von. Student, Vanderbilt U., 1957-58, Mid. Ga. Coll., 1959-61; BS, Ga. So. Coll., 1963; M. Forensic Sci., George WashingtonU., 1981. Cert. explosives and hazardous devices specialist. Tchr., coach football Harlem (Ga.) High Sch., 1963-65; tchr., coach Butler High Sch., Augusta, Ga., 1966-69; spl. agt., supr. FBI, Newark, 1970-76, supr.-examiner lab. explosives unit Washington, 1976-88, spl. investigator background investigation contract svc., 1995—; faculty instr. forensic sci. tng. and rsch. unit FBI Acad., Quantico, Va., 1988-90; pres., chief exec. officer ETA Consultants, Inc., Stafford, Va., 1990—. Cons. Nuclear Diagnostic Sys., Inc., Lorton, Va., 1991-93; cons., v.p. Gen. Nucleonics, Tucson, 1994; course dir. anti-terrist assistance U.S. Dept. State, Baton, Rouge, 1990—; mem. exch. faculty Police Staff Coll., Bramshill, Eng., 1989; bomb technician FBI Hazardous Devices sch., Huntsville, Ala., 1976—; spl. investigator background investigation contract svcs. program FBI, 1995—; contract investigator Govt. Bus. Svcs. Group, 2001—. Contbr. articles to profl. jours. Mem. Internat. Assn. Bomb Technicians and Investigators, Am. Soc. for Indsl. Security, Internat. Assn. Chiefs of Police, Assn. Former Spl. Agts. of the FBI. Episcopalian. Avocations: golf, tennis, fishing, sailing. Office: ETA Cons Inc 1335 Aquia Dr Stafford VA 22554-2037 E-mail: dennylkline@aol.com.

KLINE, DONALD, food company executive; b. Chgo., July 6, 1948; s. Ralph Waldo and Theresa (Donato) K.; m. Christine Janet Kennedy, Aug. 23, 1972; children: Bethany Amber, Torah-Ann Shiloh, Nathaniel Darwin Kennedy, Abraham Newton Kennedy, Seth-Andrew Brigham Kennedy. AA, Thornton C.C., 1969; AS, Kishwaukee Coll., 1971; BS, Roosevelt U., 1974, No. Ill. U., 1974; cert. thermal process control of low-acid canned foods, U. Wis., 1974. Quality control chemist Syntex Labs., Elgin, Ill., 1972-75; quality control mgr. Gt. China Food Products Co., Chgo., 1975; quality assurance mgr. TV Time Foods, Inc. subs. McCormick & Co., Inc., Bremen, Ind., 1975-80; pres. Abinadi Enterprises Internat. Corp., Nappanee, Ind., 1980-82; quality assurance/rsch. and devel. mgr. Snyder's of Hanover, Inc., Hanover, Pa., 1982-92; sr. rsch. assoc. Nabisco Biscuit Co., East Hanover, N.J., 1992-94; dir. quality assurance and tech. svcs. Hanover (Pa.) Foods Corp., 1994-95; dir. quality assurance UTZ Quality Foods, Inc., Hanover, 1995—2002, dir. tech. svcs., 2002—. Elder Ch. Jesus Christ of Latter-day Saints, 1976—, pres. Sunday sch., 1979-80, project coord., purchasing agt. ch. fund raising projects, 1980-82, exec. sec., 1981-82, pub. rels. dir., 1982-83, 91-92, mission leader for Gettysburg-Hanover, Pa., 1983-85, Gettysburg ward mission leader, 2000-03, Gettysburg ward fin.clk., 2003—; chmn., pack and troop treas. Boy Scouts of Am., 1985-92, Webeloes leader, 1987-89, merit badge counselor, 1988-92; citizen adv. coun. Spring Grove Area Sch. Dist., 1988-92, ch. employment dir., 1991-92, ch. phys. facilities fin. clk. for York, Pa., 1992-93; dir. Hanover/Gettysburg, Pa. Church Family History Ctr., 1996-2000. Mem. Inst. Food Technologists (profl.), Snack Food Assn. (sci. rev. 1996—), Am. Assn. Nutritional Cons. (cert. nutritional cons.), Nat. Assn. Cert. Natural Health Profls. Republican. Achievements include development of snack foods of nutritionally beneficial marketed U.S. and fgn. countries, development first product line of flavored sour-dough pretzels. Home: PO Box 68 New Oxford PA 17350-0068 Office: Utz Quality Foods Inc 900 High St Hanover PA 17331-1639 E-mail: donkcncfoodtec@yahoo.com., dkline@utzsnacks.com.

KLINE, DONNA S. musician, educator; b. Ottawa, Kans., Dec. 23, 1934; d. Ellis Wayne and Mabel Josephine Staley; m. Sylvan Harris Kline Jr., Oct. 14, 1966; children: Marilyn Louise, Joanne Rae. BA, Tex. Woman's U., 1957; MA, San Francisco State U., 1989. Pianist, tchr., lectr. Author: (book) Olga Samaroff Stokowski—An American Virtuoso on the World Stage, 1996. Chairperson Heritage Arts Commn., Tiburon, Calif., 1998-00. Mem. Music. Tchrs. Nat. Assn., Music Tchrs. Assn. Calif. Democrat. Presbyterian. Home: 672 Hilary Dr Belvedere Tiburon CA 94920-1446

KLINE, EUGENE MONROE, lawyer; b. N.Y.C., May 22, 1914; s. Lewis R. and Hattie (Wachter) K.; m. Harriet Meyer, July 2, 1939; children: Robert A., Thomas R. AB, Columbia U., 1933, LLB, 1935. Bar: N.Y. 1935, U.S. Dist. Ct. (so. dist.) N.Y. 1945, U.S. Dist. Ct. (ea. dist.) N.Y. 1955, U.S. Supreme Ct. 1973. Atty. Charter Rev. Commn., N.Y.C., 1935; assoc. Greenbaum, Wolf & Ernst, N.Y.C., 1935-37, Wagner, Quillinin and Rifkind, N.Y.C., 1937-40; atty. SEC, N.Y.C. and Washington, 1941-43; from assoc. to ptnr. Phillips Nizer LLP, N.Y.C., 1943—. With U.S. Army, 1943. Home: 390 Heathcote Rd Scarsdale NY 10583-7538 Office: Phillips Nizer LLP 666 5th Ave New York NY 10103-0084 E-mail: ekline@phillipsnizer.com.

KLINE, EVA JANE, library services administrator, educator; b. Duncannon, Pa., Oct. 11, 1942; d. Stanley L. and Grace (Louden) Peters; m. Glenn N. Kline, Sept. 24, 1963 (div. 1971); 1 child, Kent K. Kline. BS in Edn., Kutztown (Pa.) U., 1963; MLS, U. Pitts., 1978. Libr., tchr. West Perry High Sch., Elliottsburg, Pa., 1963-64; libr. Westerly Pkwy. High Sch., State College, Pa., 1964-65, various 13 schs., State College, 1965-66, Susquenita High Sch., Duncannon, Pa., 1966-68, McConnellsburg (Pa.) Elem. Schs., 1970-71; dir. libr. svcs. Somerset (Pa.) State Hosp., 1971—96; libr. Crown Am., Johnstown, Pa., 1997—2000; adminstr. Somerset County Federated Libr. Sys., 1999—; tchr. speech, lit. and composition Mt. Aloysius Jr. Coll., Cresson, Pa., 1989—. Cons. N.W. Ga. Regional Hosp., Rome, Ga., 1990-92, Killam Assocs., Somerset, 1994—; consortium dir. HI RESCUE, Somerset, 1978—. Recipient Cert. of Merit award Pa. Libr. Assn., 1996; named Outstanding Instl. Librarian, Pa. Spl. Librs., 1983. Mem. Med. Libr. Assn. (Pitts. regional chair 1994-95, Scroll of Exemplary Svc. 2002). Avocations: taxidermy, reading, traveling. Home: PO Box 47 Sipesville PA 15561 Office: Somerset County Federated Libr Sys 6022 Glades Pike Ste 120 Somerset PA 15501-4300

KLINE, FAITH ELIZABETH, college official; b. Lake Charles, La., Dec. 22, 1937; d. Walter Raymond and Erma Ruth (Gilbert) McClung; m. George Ellis Kline, Nov. 26, 1959; children: Alexandra M., George E. IV, Elizabeth A. BA, So. Nazarene U., 1960. Owner, ptnr. Country Peddler Gift Shop, Jackson, Mich., 1972-75; asst. dir. admissions Spring Arbor (Mich.) Coll., 1976-80; exec. sec. to pres. Camp Internat., Inc., Jackson, Mich., 1980-85; registered rep. IDS/Am. Express, Jackson, 1985-86; investment broker A. G. Edwards & Sons, Inc., Jackson, 1986-89; dir. trust and investment svcs., corp. asst. sec. The Free Meth. Found., Spring Arbor, 1989-92; dir. trusts and investments Hillsdale (Mich.) Coll., 1992—. Mem. Jackson County (Mich.) Hosp. Fin. Authority, 1987-92; pres. Hearthstone Enterprises, Inc., 1996—; co-owner Idyll Hour Coffeehouse, Spring Arbor, Mich., 1997-99. Author: The Klines of Evanston: 1848 to 1968, 1970. Trustee Concord (Mich.) Bd. Edn., 1979-95, v.p., 1991-93, pres., 1993-94; sec. Jackson County (Mich.) County Reps., 1984-85, mem. exec. com., 1993-96; mem. Spring Arbor Twp. Hist. Com., Jackson Area Estate Planning Coun.; mem. Nat. Com. on Planned Giving, 1993—. Presbyterian. Avocations: 19th century american antiques, piano music. Home: 223 Wickenham Dr Spring Arbor MI 49283 Office: Hillsdale Coll 33 E College St Hillsdale MI 49242-1205

KLINE, FRANK MENEFEE, psychiatrist; b. Cumberland, Md., May 14, 1928; s. Frank Huber and Margaret (Menefee) K.; m. Shirley Steinmetz, June 27, 1953; children: Frank F., Margaret L. BS, U. Md., 1950, MD, 1952; PhD, So. Calif. Psychoanalytic Ins., 1977. Diplomate Am. Bd. Psychiatry and Neurology (examiner 1970—). Intern Cin. Gen. Hosp., 1952-53; resident Brentwood VA Med. Ctr., West L.A., 1955-58; Regional chief West Cen. Mental Svc., L.A. County Dept. Mental Health, L.A., 1967-68; assoc. dir. adult psychiatry out-patient dept. L.A. County, U. So. Calif. Med. Ctr., 1968-77, acting dir. adult psychiatric dept., 1977; chief psychiatry VA Med. Ctr., Long Beach, Calif., 1977-91. Clin. prof., vice-chair U. Calif., Irvine, 1978—91, prof. emeritus, 1995—; clin. prof. Drew King, 1992—; reviewer Hosp. Comty. Psychiatry, 1978—, Am. Jour. Psychiatry, 1978—, Readings, 1995—; cons. Los Angeles County Dept. Mental Health, 1992—. Editor: A Handbook of Group Psychotherapy, 1983, Readings, 1995-2002. 1st lt. M.C., U.S. Army, 1953-55. Office: San Pedro Cmty Mental Health Ctr 769 W 3d St San Pedro CA 90731 Fax: 310-325-3941.

KLINE, GEORGE LOUIS, author, translator, retired philosophy and literature educator; b. Galesburg, Ill., Mar. 3, 1921; s. Allen Sides and Wahneta (Burner) K.; m. Virginia Harrington Hardy, Apr. 17, 1943; children: Brenda Marie, Jeffrey Allen, Christina Hardy (Mrs. Francis C. Hanak). Student, Boston U., 1938-41; AB with honors, Columbia Coll., 1947; MA, Columbia U., 1948, PhD, 1950. Instr. philosophy Columbia U., 1950-52, 53-54, asst. prof., 1954-60; vis. asst. prof. U. Chgo., 1952-53; assoc. prof. philosophy and Russian Bryn Mawr Coll., 1960-66, prof. philosophy, 1966-81, Milton C. Nahm prof. philosophy, 1981-91, chmn. dept., 1977-82, chmn. dept. Russian, 1990-91, Milton C. Nahm prof. emeritus of philosophy, 1991—, Katharine E. McBride prof. of philosophy, 1992-93. Lectr. Free U., West Berlin, Heidelberg U., Marburg U., Germany, London Sch. Econs. and Polit. Sci., Mid East Tech. U., Ankara, Turkey, Oxford (Eng.) U., Queens U., Belfast, Trinity Coll., Dublin, U. Belgrade, U. Zagreb, Yugoslavia, U. P.R., Uppsala U., Sweden; participant internat. confs. Austria, Can., Denmark, France, Germany, The Netherlands, Italy, Mex., Eng., Scotland, Russia. Author: Spinoza in Soviet Philosophy, 1952, 1981, Religious and Anti-Religious Thought in Russia, 1968; author: (with others) Continuity and Change in Russian and Soviet Thought, 1955, Marx and the Western World, 1967, Hegel and the Philosophy of Religion, 1970, Sartre: A Collection of Critical Essays, 1971, Hegel and the History of Philosophy, 1974, Dissent in the USSR: Politics, Ideology, and People, 1975, Speculum Spinozanum, 1977, Western Philosophical Systems in Russian Literature, 1979, Vico and Marx: Affinities and Contrasts, 1983, Nineteenth Century Religious Thought in the West, 1985, Spinoza nel 350 anniversario della nascita, 1985, Hegel and Whitehead: Contemporary Perspectives on Systematic Philosophy, 1986, George Lukács and His World: A Reassessment, 1987, Dictionary of Literary Biography Yearbook, 1987, 1988, Europa und die Folgen: Castelgandolfo-Gespräche, 1987, 1988, Hegel and His Critics, 1989, Brodsky's Poetics and Aesthetics, 1990, Spinoza: Issues and Directions, 1990, Histoire de la littérature russe, 1990, The Trotsky Reappraisal, 1992, Metaphysics as Foundation: Essays in Honor of Ivor Leclerc, 1992, Philosophical Imagination and Cultural Memory, 1993, Hryhorij Savyč Skovoroda: An Anthology of Critical Articles, 1994, Phenomenology and Skepticism: Essays in Honor of James M. Edie, 1996, Russian Religious Thought, 1996, Iosif Brodskii: Trudy i dni, 1998, J. M. Bochenski: The Man and His Work, 2001; translator: History of Russian Philosophy (V.V. Zenkovsky), 1953, Boris Pasternak: Seven Poems, 1969, 1972, Joseph Brodsky: Selected Poems, 1973; co-translator: A Part of Speech (Joseph Brodsky), 1980, To Urania (Joseph Brodsky), 1988; editor: Soviet Education, 1957, Alfred North Whitehead: Essays on his Philosophy, 1963, 1989; editor, contbr.: European Philosophy Today, 1965; co-editor: Iosif Brodskii: Ostanovka v pustyne, 1970, 2000; co-editor, contbr.: Russian Philosophy, 1965, 1969, 1976, 1984, Explorations in Whitehead's Philosophy, 1983, Philosophical Sovietology, 1988; co-editor: Jour. Philosophy, 1959—64; cons. editor:, 1964—78, Ency. Philosophy, 1962—67, Studies in Soviet Thought (now Studies in East European Thought), 1962—, Jour. Value Inquiry, 1967—, Process Studies, 1970—, Soviet Union, 1975—80, Philosophy Research Archives (now Jour. Philos. Rsch.), 1975—, Jour. History of Ideas, 1976—86, 1988—98, Slavic Review, 1977—79, Soviet Studies in Philosophy (now Russian Studies in Philosophy), 1987—, History of Philosophy Quar., 1990—93, Skepsis, 1990—, Symposion: A Journal of Russian Thought, 1996—, cons. editor philosophy: Current Digest of Soviet Press, 1961—64; contbr. articles to nat. and internat. jours. and reference works. Served with USAAF, 1942-45. Decorated D.F.C; Cutting traveling fellow Paris, 1949-50; Fulbright fellow Paris, 1950, 79; Ford fellow Paris, 1954-55; Rockefeller fellow USSR and East Europe, 1960; Nat. Endowment for Humanities sr. fellow, 1970-71; Guggenheim fellow, 1978-79. Mem. Am. Philos. Assn. (exec. com. Ea. div. 1990-93), Metaphys. Soc. Am. (councillor 1969-71, 78-82, v.p. 1984-85, pres. 1985-86, del. to Am. Coun. Learned Socs., 1994-97), Philosophy Edn. Soc. (pub. Rev. Metaphys., dir. 1966-90), Soc. Phenomenology and Existential Philosophy, Am. Assn. Advancement Slavic Studies (dir. 1972-75, award for Disting. Contbns. to Slavic Studies 1999), Hegel Soc. Am. (councillor 1968-70, 74-78, v.p. 1971-73, pres. 1984-86), Soc. Advancement Am. Philosophy, Phi Beta Kappa. Achievements include works translated into numerous fgn. languages. Home: 632 Valley View Rd Ardmore PA 19003-1029

KLINE, HOWARD JAY, cardiologist, educator; b. White Plains, NY, Nov. 5, 1932; s. Raymond Kline and Rose Plane; divorced; children: Michael, Ethan; m. Ellen Sawamura, June 13, 1987; 1 child, Christopher. BS, Dickinson Coll., 1954; MD, N.Y. Med. Coll., 1958. Intern San Francisco Gen. Hosp., 1958—59; resident Mt. Sinai Hosp., N.Y.C., 1959—61; sr. resident U. Calif. Med. Ctr., San Francisco, 1961—62; cardiology fellow Mt. Sinai Hosp., N.Y.C., 1962—64; dir. cardiology tng. program St. Mary's Hosp., San Francisco, 1970—90, Calif. Pacific Med. Ctr., San Francisco, 1992—. Clin. prof. medicine and cardiology U. Calif. Med. Ctr., San Francisco, 1984—; vis. prof. Nihon U., Tokyo, 1986; dir. cardiology Valley Forge Gen. Hosp. Cardiology editor Hosp. Practice, Cardiology, 1992—; contbr. articles to profl. jours. Lt. col. U.S. Med. Corps, 1967-69. Fellow ACP, Am. Heart Assn., Am. Coll. Cardiology, Am. Coll. Chest Physicians; mem. Burkes Tennis Club, U. San Francisco Masters Swim Team. Avocations: painting, reading, running, skiing, tennis. Office: 2100 Webster St Ste 516 San Francisco CA 94115-2382

KLINE, JAMES EDGAR, actor; b. Beach Grove, Ind., Feb. 22, 1932; s. Charles Raymond and Edna Marie (Pollack) K.; m. Phyliss Dawn Schneider, Nov. 8, 1952; children: Timson, James Jr., Peggy, Daniel, Andrew, Mary, Jon. Lectr. in field; judge Nat. Prospectors and Treasure Convention, 1989-90. Appeared in films Coming Home, 1978, Comes A Horseman, 1979, Electric Horseman, 1980, China Syndrome, 1981, Tom Horn, 1982, Weekend in the Country, 1997, It's My Party, 1997, City of Angels, 1998, various other films, TV programs, commls.; screenwriter, exec. prodr., actor motion picture Father Dad; author (as James Klein): Where to Find Gold in Southern California, 1975, Where to Find Gold in the Desert, 1977, Where to Find Gold in Nevada, 1985, How to Find Gold, 1997, Gold Rush (childrens), 1998, Follow the Padres (childrens), 1999; other mag. articles and short stories. With U.S. Army, 1952-53. Recipient Cert. of Achievement, Am. Cancer Soc., 1977, Disneyland, 1983, City of Anaheim, 1984, also various schs.

KLINE, JAMES EDWARD, lawyer; b. Fremont, Ohio, Aug. 3, 1941; s. Walter J. and Sophia Kline; m. Mary Ann Bruening, Aug. 29, 1964; children: Laura Anne Kline, Matthew Thomas, Jennifer Sue. BS in Social Sci., John Carroll U., 1963; JD, Ohio State U., 1966; postgrad., Stanford U., 1991. Bar: Ohio 1966, NC 1989, US Tax. Ct. 1983. Assoc. Eastman, Stichter, Smith & Bergman, Toledo, 1966-70; ptnr. Eastman, Stichter, Smith & Bergman (name now Eastman & Smith), Toledo, 1970-84, Shumaker, Loop & Kendrick, Toledo, 1984-88; v.p., gen. counsel Aeroquip-Vickers, Inc. (formerly Trinova Corp.), Toledo, 1989-99; exec. v.p. Cavista Corp., 2000—01; dir. devel. Toledo Mus. Art, 2002—03; v.p., gen. counsel, sec. Cooper Tire and Rubber Co., Findlay, Ohio, 2003—. Corp. sec. Shelle-Globe Corp., 1977—84; adj. prof. U. Toledo Coll. Law, 1988—94; bd. dirs. Plastic Techs., Inc.; trustee Promedica Health

Edn. and Rsch. Corp., 2002—. Author: (with Robert Seaver) Ohio Corporation Law, 1988. Trustee Kidney Found. of Northwestern Ohio, Inc., 1972-81, pres., 1979-80; bd. dirs. Toledo Botanical Garden (formerly Crosby Gardens), 1974-80, pres., 1977-79; bd. dirs. Toledo Zool. Soc., 1983-96, 99—, pres., 1991-93; bd. dirs. Toledo Area Regional Transit Authority, 1984-90, pres., 1987-88; bd. dirs. Home Away From Home, Inc. (Ronald McDonald House NW Ohio), 1983-88; trustee Toledo Symphony Orch., 1981—, St. John's H.S., 1988-91, Lourdes Coll., 1988-96, chmn., 1994-96,Ohio Found. Ind. Colls., 1991-2000, ProMedia Health, Edn. and Rsch. Corp., 2002—, Toledo Opera, 2003—. Fellow Ohio Bar Found.; mem. ABA, Nat. Assn. Corp. Dirs., Ohio Bar Assn. (corp. law com. 1977—, chmn. 1983-86), NC Bar Assn., Toledo Bar Assn., Mfrs. Alliance (chair Law Coun. II 1997-99), Toledo Area C. of C. (trustee 1994—, chmn. 2000-01), Inverness Club, Toledo Club (trustee 1990-97), Stone Oak Country Club, Ottawa Skeet Club, Answer Club. Roman Catholic. Home: 216 Treetop Pl Holland OH 43528-8451 Office: Cooper Tire & Rubber Co 701 Lima Ave Findlay OH 45840 E-mail: jekline@coopertire.com.

KLINE, JERRY ROBERT, government official, ecologist; b. Mpls., May 20, 1932; s. Frederick Andrew and Margaret (Wicklund) K.; m. Alice Nell Reed, Sept. 4, 1954; children: Steven, Jennifer, Robert, Neil, Daniel. BS, U. Minn., 1957, MS, 1960, PhD, 1964. Postdoctoral rsch. assn. Argonne Nat. Lab., Ill., 1964-65, group leader rsch., 1968-74; scientist, dir. Rainforest Project P.R. Nuclear Ctr., 1965-68; sr. scientist Nuclear Regulatory Commn., Washington, 1974-80, adminstrv. judge, 1980-98. Contbr. articles to profl. jours., chpts. to books. Bd. dirs., chmn. Cedar Lane Unitarian Ch. Served with U.S. Army, 1950-53. Recipient NRC Spl. Achievement award, 1979. Mem. Nature Conservancy, Sigma Xi. Avocations: travel, gardening. Home: 13624 Middlevale Ln Silver Spring MD 20906-2123 E-mail: KJerry@verizon.net.

KLINE, JOHN, congressman; b. Allentown, Pa., Sept. 6, 1947; m. Vicky Kline; children: Kathy, Dan. BA, Rice U.; MPA, Shippensburg U. Mem. U.S. Ho. Reps. from Minn. 2nd dist., 2003—. Active USMC. Office: 1429 Longworth House Office Bldg Washington DC 20515*

KLINE, JOHN ALVIN, academic administrator; b. Marshalltown, Iowa, July 24, 1930; s. Laurence Alvin Kline and Kathryn White; m. Ann Louise Henry; children: Teri, Marc, David, Nanette, Melissa. BS, Iowa State U., 1967; MS, U. Iowa, 1968, PhD, 1970. Sr. exec. service, U.S. Govt. Asst. prof. speech U. N.Mex., Albuquerque, 1970-71; assoc. prof. speech communication U. Mo., Columbia, 1971-75; dean communication skills Air U., Maxwell AFB, Ala., 1975-82, ednl. adv., 1982-86, dir. academic affairs, 1986—90, sr. exec. provost, 1990—2000; prof. edn. Troy State U., 2000—, dir. Inst. Leadership Devel., 2003—. Conf. leader; motivational spkr. Author: Guide to Air Force Speaking, 1980, Speaking Effectively, 1989, Listening Effectively, 1996, Listening Effectively: Achieving High Standards in Communication, 2003, Speaking Effectively: Achieving Excellence in Presentations, 2003; co-author: Orientations to Interpersonal Communication, 1976; contbr. articles to profl. jours. Named Outstanding Tchr. Ctrl. States Speech Assn., 1972, Fed. Employee of Yr. Montgomery Fed. Adminstrs., 1979; recipient Award for Meritorious Civilian Svc., 1985, Decoration for Exceptional Civilian Svc., 1988, Outstanding Civil Svc., 2000, Career Civilian Svc. award, 2000; NDEA Title IV fellow U. Iowa, 1967-70. Mem. Internat. Listening Assn., Speech Comm. Assn., Air Force Assn., Rotary, Phi Delta Kappa. Methodist. Home: 8418 Shaffer Ridge Ct Montgomery AL 36117-7402 E-mail: john@klinespeak.com.

KLINE, JOHN WILLIAM, retired air force officer, management consultant; b. Zanesville, Ohio, June 26, 1919; s. Gerry William and Lillian Elizabeth (Scheiderer) K.; m. Katherine Edmond Winton, Oct. 24, 1942; children: Susan Isabel (Mrs. John Farris Morehead), Flora Edmond (Mrs. Richard Crandall Creighton), Elizabeth Gerry (Mrs. Paul Sweeney). Student, Ohio U., 1937-40; grad., Primary, Basic and Advanced Flying Schs., 1941, Air Command and Staff Sch., 1949, Air War Coll., 1959; BA, La. Tech. U., 1971. Commd. 2d lt. USAAF, 1941; advanced through grades to maj. gen. USAF, 1968; comdr. (2d Bomb Wing), Hunter AFB, Ga., 1961-63, (397th Bomb Wing), Dow AFB, Maine, 1963-64; dir. operations, chief staff Hdqrs. 8th Air Force, Westover AFB, Mass., 1964-66; vice comdr. 3d Air Div., Andersen AFB, Guam, 1966-68; asst. dep. chief staff ops. Hdqrs. SAC, Offutt AFB, Nebr., 1968-69; vice-comdr. 2d Air Force, Barksdale AFB, La., 1969-72; ret., 1972; v.p., mgmt. cons. Paul R. Ray, Inc., Ft. Worth, 1972—; pres. Mapotec, Inc., Daytona Beach, Fla., 1974, Precision Aerial Surveys, Inc., 1975-85; v.p. ops. Aero Service, Houston, 1976-80, v.p. new ventures and planning, 1980-82. Decorated D.S.M., Legion of Merit with 3 oak leaf clusters, Air medal with oak leaf cluster, Air Force Commendation medal; Air Force Distinguished Service Order Republic Vietnam). Mem. Oak Hills Golf Club, Guadalajara Golf Club, Beta Theta Pi. Presbyterian. Home: One Towers Park Ln # 912 San Antonio TX 78209-

KLINE, KENNETH ALAN, mechanical engineering educator; b. Chgo., July 11, 1939; s. George Lester and Beverly Gretchen (Hanson) K.; m. Nancy Ann Bixler, June 25, 1960; children: Lisa Suzanne, John Kenneth, Jeffery Eastbury, Gretchen Mary. BS, U. Minn., 1961, PhD, 1965. Rsch. asst. U. Minn., Mpls., 1961-62, rsch. fellow, 1962-65; sr. rsch. engr. Esso Prodn. Rsch. Co., Houston, 1965-66; assoc. prof. Wayne State U., Detroit, 1966-73, prof. mech. engring., 1973—, interim chair dept. mech. engring., 1986-87, chair, 1987-95, interim dean of engring., 1996—, chair mech. engring., 1997—. Cons. Ford Motor Co., Detroit, 1976—, vis. scientist, 1984-85; vis. prof. U. Munich, 1972-73. Editor Proc. 6th Internat. Conf. Vehicle Structures, 1986; contbr. articles to profl. jours. Patentee ops. in submarine wells, layng pipes in water. Rep. precinct del., Grosse Pointe Park, Mich., 1982-84; vol. Grosee Pointe Neighborhood Club, 1973-82. A.P. Sloan Found. nat. scholar, 1959-61; NSF fellow 1961-64, NASA fellow 1964-65; recipient Sr. U.S. Sci. award Alexander von Humboldt-Stiftung, Fed. Republic Germany, 1972; prin. investigator NSF Rsch. Experiences for Undergrad. Sites, 1995—. Fellow ASME (chair 1974-75, 89-91, program chair winter ann. meeting 1993, gen. chair internat. mech. engring. congress & expo. 1994, nat. nominating com. 1997—, chair nat. dept. heads com., 1998—, Dedicated Svc. award 1996), AIAA, Soc. Automotive Engrs. (chair 1984-86, Forest R. McFarland award 1993), Soc. Rheology, Engring. Soc. (vice chair Detroit 1988—). Avocations: bird watching, tree farming, reading, swimming. Office: Wayne State U Engring Rm 2105 Detroit MI 48202

KLINE, KEVIN DELANEY, actor; b. St. Louis, Oct. 24, 1947; s. Robert Joseph and Peggy (Kirk) K.; m. Phoebe Cates, Mar. 5, 1989; 2 children: Owen, Greta. BA in Speech and Theatre, Ind. U.; adv. program diploma, Juilliard Sch. Drama Divsn., N.Y.C., 1972. Founding mem. The Acting Co., N.Y.C., 1972-76. Apptd. artistic assoc. N.Y. Shakespeare Festival, 1993. Actor Broadway prodns.: On the Twentieth Century, 1978 (Tony award), Loose Ends, 1979, Pirates of Penzance, 1980 (Tony award, Obie award), Arms and the Man, 1985, The Play What I Wrote, 2003; off-Broadway: Richard III, 1983, Henry V, 1984, Hamlet, 1986 (Obie award), Much Ado About Nothing; actor, dir. off-Broadway: Hamlet, 1990; actor, dir. TV special: Hamlet, 1990; actor (off-Broadway) Measure for Measure, 1993, (Broadway) Ivanov, 1997, (off-Broadway) The Seagull, 2001; motion picture appearances include: Sophie's Choice, 1982, Pirates of Penzance, 1983, The Big Chill, 1983, Silverado, 1985, Violets are Blue, 1985, Cry Freedom, 1987, A Fish Called Wanda, 1988 (Academy award Best Supporting Actor 1989), The January Man, 1989, I Love You To Death, 1989, Soapdish, 1991, Grand Canyon, 1991, Consenting Adults, 1991, Chaplin, 1992, Dave, 1993, George Balanchine's The Nutcracker (voice only), 1993, Princess Caraboo, 1994, French Kiss, 1995, The Hunchback of Notre Dame (voice only), 1996, Fierce Creatures, 1997, In & Out, 1997, The Ice Storm, 1997, A Midsummer Night's Dream, 1999, Wild Wild West, 1999, The Road to El Dorado (voice), 2000, The Anniversary Party, 2001, Life as a House, 2001, The Emperor's Club, 2002, (film) DeLovely, 2003; dir. Hamlet, 1990. Office: William Morris Agy 1325 Avenue Of The Americas New York NY 10019-6026

KLINE, LEE B. retired architect; b. Renton, Wash., Feb. 2, 1914; s. Abraham McCubbin and Pearl (Davidson) K.; m. Martha Myers, Aug. 29, 1936 (div. Oct. 1995); children— Patricia, Joanne Louise Kline Kresse; m. Marilyn Gibson, May 7, 1997. B.Arch., U. So. Calif., 1937. Draftsman, designer, 1937-43; pvt. archtl. practice, 1943-2001; ret., 2001. Instr. engring. extension U. Calif., 1947-53; mem. panel arbitrators Am. Arbitration Assn., 1964— Pres. LaCanada Irrigation Dist., 1966-96, dir., 1963-96; bd. dirs. Foothill Mcpl. Water Dist., 1980-96, LaCanada br. ARC, 1959-81. Recipient Disting. Service citation Calif. council AIA, 1960, honor awards AIA, 1957, 59, Sch. of Month awards Nation's Schools, 1964, 71 Fellow AIA (pres. Pasadena chpt. 1957, pres. Calif. council 1959) Home: 526 W Huntington Dr Unit F Arcadia CA 91007-3443 Office: Kline Enterprises Inc 969 Colorado Blvd Los Angeles CA 90041-1773

KLINE, LINDA, employment consultant; b. Boston, Aug. 8, 1940; d. George and Eva (Weiner) Kline. BA in Biology, Boston U., 1962, postgrad. in Biochemistry, 1964—66. Pers. dir. Block Engring. Inc., Cambridge, Mass., 1964-66; brokerage mgr. Eastern Life Ins. Co. N.Y., Boston, 1966-68; mgr. direct placement Lendman Assocs., N.Y.C., 1968-72; dir. women-in-mgmt. divsn. Roberts-Lund, Ltd., N.Y.C., 1972-77; exec. dir. Majority Money, women's network, 1976-79; tchr. fin. planning for women Marymount-Manhattan Coll., 1977; pres. Maxima Consulting, Inc., New York, 1978—80; prin. Kline-McKay, Inc. (name changed to Kline Cons., Inc. 1991), 1978-93; pres. Kline Consulting, Inc., Kline McKay, Inc., New York, 1980—93; pres., mng. dir. Ptnrs. in Human Reosurces Internat. (formerly the Arbor Group, Inc.), N.Y.C., 1993—98; pres. Bus. & Human Resources Consulting, Tannersville, NY, 1998—. Treas. Lower East Side Print Shop, N.Y.C., 1997-99, bd. advisors, 1999—; lectr. and/or cons. women's programs at several colls. and univs. and corps. Co-author: Career Changing: The Worry-Fee Guide, 1982. Bd. dirs. Women Bus. Owners Edn. Fund, 1982-86, Mom's Amazing, 1985-88; cmty. bd. dirs. Mt. Sinai Med. Ctr., 1984-1899; adv. counselor U.S. Small Bus. Adminstrn. WNET Program. Mem. Internat. Assn. Outplacement Profls., Women Bus. Owners N.Y. (bd. dirs. 1978-84), Nat. Coalition Women's Enterprise (adv. bd. 1988-89), Town of Hunter C. of C. (v.p. 1999—). Democrat. Avocations: antiques, gourmet cooking, reading, photography, travel. Office: Business & Human Reosurces Cons PO Box 124 Tannersville NY 12485

KLINE, LOWRY F. food products executive, lawyer; Sr. v.p., gen. counsel Coca-Cola Enterprises, Atlanta, 1996-97, exec. v.p., gen. counsel, 1997-99, exec. v.p., chief adminstrv. officer, 1999-2001, elected to bd., vice chmn., 2000—02, vice chmn., CEO, 2001—02, chmn., CEO, 2002—. Office: Coca-Cola Enterprises 2500 Windy Ridge Pkwy SE Atlanta GA 30339-5677

KLINE, NORMAN DOUGLAS, federal judge; b. Lynn, Mass., Dec. 28, 1930; s. Samuel and Ida (Luff) K.; m. Betty Toba Feldman, Feb. 27, 1966; children: Sarah, Samuel. AB, Harvard Coll., 1952, postgrad., 1952-53; JD, Boston U., 1959. Bar: Mass. 1959. Pvt. practice, Boston, 1959-60; atty. U.S. Dept. Army, Cleve., 1960; trial atty. FMC, Washington, 1960-72, adminstrv. law judge, 1972-92, chief adminstrv. law judge, 1992—. With U.S. Army, 1953-55. Mem. Fed. Adminstrv. Law Judges Conf. Avocations: classical music, collecting cds. Office: Fed Maritime Commn 800 N Capitol St NW Washington DC 20573-0001 E-mail: normank@fmc.gov.

KLINE, PAUL CONLEY, lawyer; s. Joseph Nathaniel and Florence (Conley) Kline; m. Martha Elena Morales, Nov. 22, 1975; children: Samara Kathryn, Paul Conley Jr., Joseph Nathaniel IV. BA in Latin Am. Studies, Monterey Inst. Internat. Studies, Calif., 1974; MPA, Harvard U., Cambridge, 1990; JD, U. San Diego, 1994. Bar: Calif. 1999. Fgn. svc. officer U.S. Dept. State, 1976—99; founder, atty. Calif. Bus. Immigration, Bonita, 1999—. Bd. dirs. San Diego-Shannon Partnership, 2002—. Editor: (book) Perspectives on Change in Contemporary Mexico, 1974. Recipient Meritorious Hon. Award, U.S. Dept. State, 1986, 1998, Commendation, Drug Enforcement Adminstrn., Mex., 1989, Certificate of Appreciation, U.S. Southern Command, Panama, 1998. Mem.: Am. Immigration Lawyers Assn., Diplomatic Consular Officers, San Diego County Bar Assn., Am. Fgn. Svc. Assn., Harvard Club of San Diego. Republican. Roman Catholic. Avocations: genealogy, hiking. Office: Calif Bus Immigration 5035 Central Ave #F Bonita CA 91902 Office Fax: 619-479-4612. E-mail: paulckline@aol.com.

KLINE, PHILLIP D. state attorney general; b. Kansas City, Kans., Dec. 31, 1959; s. James R. and Janet S. (Shirley) K.; m. Deborah Suzanne Shattuck, July 22, 1989; 1 child, Jacqueline Hillary. BS in Pub. Rels. and Polit. Sci., Cen. Mo. State U., 1982; JD, U. Kans., 1987. Bar: Kans. 1987, U.S. Ct. Appeals (10th cir.), U.S. Dist. Ct. Kans. News reporter WHB Radio, Kansas City, Mo., 1981-82; pub. rels. rep. Mid-America, Inc., Kansas City, Mo., 1982-84; assoc. Blackwell, Sanders, Matheny, Weary & Lombardi, Overland Park, Kans., 1987—95; legislator State of Kans., 1992—2000, atty. gen., 2003—. Nominee Kans. 2d Congl. Dist., 1986; former chmn. taxation com.; fin. chmn. Johnson County Reps., 1990-91; chmn. Shawnee Reps., 1991-92; chmn., co-chmn. Corp. Woods Charity Jazz Festival, Overland Park, 1991-95; bd. dirs. Shawnee Mission Edn. Found., 1994-95, Rep. Ho. Campaign Com. Mem. Johnson County Bar Assn., Kans. Bar Assn., Rotary (bd. dirs., v.p. 1991-93, pres. 1994-95, Disting. Svc. award 1991). Republican. Methodist. Avocations: history, reading, athletics. Office: Atty Gen 120 SW 10th Ave, 2nd Fl Topeka KS 66612*

KLINE, RAYMOND ADAM, professional organization executive; b. New Ringgold, Pa., Sept. 14, 1926; s. Raymond Adam and Helen Marie (Herb) K.; m. Jeanelle Batley, Apr. 26, 1958; children— Robin Jeanelle, Raymond Ashley. AB, Lebanon Valley Coll., 1950, LLD (hon.), 1990; LLB, George Washington U., 1957, JD (hon.), 1982. Bar: D.C. 1958. Mgmt. analyst Army Missile Command, Huntsville, Ala., 1958-61; chief mgmt. devel. office Marshall Space Flight Ctr., Huntsville, 1961-66; asst. adminstr. for systems mgmt. NASA Hdqrs., Washington, 1967-75, asst. adminstr. instl. mgmt., 1975-77, assoc. adminstr. mgmt. ops, 1977-79; dep. adminstr. GSA, 1979-84, acting adminstr., 1981, 1984-85; pres. Nat. Acad. Pub. Adminstrn., 1985-92. Instr. in polit. sci. U. Ala., 1958-63 Served with U.S. Army, 1944-46, 50-51. Mem. D.C. Bar, Phi Delta Phi, Pi Gamma Mu. Home: 15432 Carrolton Rd Rockville MD 20853-1703

KLINE, RICHARD L. retired music educator; b. West Reading, Pa., Feb. 11, 1930; s. Leroy C. and Elda R. Kline; m. Barbara Sue Metzger, June 13, 1953; children: Susan K. Liberati, David R. BS in Music Edn., Lebanon Valley Coll., 1951; MA in Music Edn., Columbia U., 1952. Music educator Pequea Valley H.S., Intercourse, Pa., 1956—57, Hempfield Sch. Dist., Landisville, Pa., 1957—87; musical dir. Actors County Pa., Lancaster, 1989—97; ret. Organist Grace Luth. Ch., Lancaster, 1959—78; substitute organist local chs. With USAF, 1952—56. Recipient Red Rose award, The Lancaster New Era, 2000. Mem.: Pa. State Educators Assn., Pa. Music Educators Assn. (chmn. Ret. Music Educators 2002—, Disting. Svc. award Dist. 7 2000). Democrat. Lutheran. Avocations: travel, ballroom dancing, exercise, theater, reading. Home: 18 St Peter Cir Lititz PA 17543

KLINE, RICHARD STEPHEN, public relations executive; b. Brookline, Mass., June 20, 1948; s. Paul and Helen (Chartoff) K.; m. Carroll Potter, (dec. Apr. 1984); m. Sharon Tate, June 16, 1985; stepchildren: Allison, Kevin. BA, U. Mass., 1970. Reporter, photographer Worcester (Mass.) Telegram & Gazette, 1970-71; account exec. Wenger-Michael Advt., L.A., 1971; pub. rels. dir. Oakland (Calif.) Symphony Orch., 1972; asst. v.p., dir. promotions Gt. Western Savs. and Loan, Beverly Hills, Calif., 1972-75; v.p., dir. mktg. Union Fed. Savs. and Loan, L.A., 1975-78; chmn. bd. dirs. Berkhemer & Kline, L.A., 1978-88, Berkhemer Kline Golin/Harris, L.A., 1988-93; COO Golin/Harris Comm., Chgo., 1992-95; pres. Shandwick U.S.A., N.Y.C., N.Y., 1995-96, Kline Consulting Group, L.A., 1997; regional pres., sr. ptnr. Fleishman-Hillard, Inc., L.A., 1997—. Former instr. Am. Savs. and Loan Inst.; bd. dirs. Golin/Harris Communications; exec. com. Santa Barbara Old Spanish Days Fiesta Rodeo, 1992. Past pres., mem. exec. com. Big Bros. L.A.; bd. dirs. Am. Cancer Soc., L.A., Solvang (Calif.) TheatreFest; mem. Town Hall Forum, L.A.; commr. Parks and Recreation, City of Oakland, 1973-74; bd. dirs. United Way, 1988-93, TheaterFest, 1990-94.. Recipient Pres.'s Club award Big Bros. Greater L.A., 1987, 88, Best in West Pub. Svc. award Am. Advt. Fedn., San Francisco, 1975, Commitment to Youth award Big Bros. Greater L.A., 2001. Mem. Nat. Investor Rels. Inst., Pub. Rels. Soc. Am. (Disting. Cmty. Svc. award 1987), Internat. Assn. Bus. Communicators, Motor Press Guild, Newcomen Soc., Nat. Cattlemen's Assn., Arthur W. Page Soc., Calif. Cattlemen's Assn., Am. Quarter Horse Assn., Rancheros Visitadores, Vaqueros de Los Ranchos, Publicity Club L.A., Jonathan Club. Avocations: horseback riding, fishing. Office: Fleishman-Hillard Inc 515 S Flower St Ste 700 Los Angeles CA 90071-2209

KLINE, RONALD ALVIN, vascular surgeon, educator; b. Johnstown, PA, May 5, 1957; s. Alvin J. and Margaret C. (Batulis) K.; m. Denise Ann Budzinski, Sep. 14, 1991; 1 child, Katherine. BS summa cum laude, U. Pitts., Johnstown, Pa., 1979; MD, U. Pitts., 1983. Diplomate Am. Bd. Surgery, Nat. Bd. Med. Examiners. Intern in gen. surgery Wayne State U., 1983-84, resident in gen. surgery, 1984-86, chief surgery resident, 1988-90, vascular surgery fellow, 1990-91, asst. prof. surg., 1991-97, assoc. prof. surgery, 1997—; program dir. vascular surgery Harper Hosp., Detroit, 2000—, vascular rsch. fellow, 1985-88, chief surgery resident, stroke fellow, 1985-88, vascular surgeon, 1991—, Detroit Receiving Hosp., Detroit, 1991—, Hutzel Hosp., Detroit, Mich., 1991—, Huron Valley Hosp., Commerce Twp., Mich., 1996—, Cons. staff Rehab. Inst., Detroit, 1991—, Children's Hosp, 1991—; vascular faculty, lectr. Nat. Ctr. for Advanced Med. Edn., Chgo., 1992-98; presenter in field. Asst. editor Annals of Vascular Surgery, 1991—; contbr. articles to profl. jours. including Transplantation, Am. Jour. Surgery, others; co-author: (in French) Aspects Techniques de la Chirurgie Carotidienne, 1987, Indications et Resultats de la Chirurgie Carotidienne, 1988, Vertebrobasilar Arterial Disease, 1992, Le Remplacement Arteriel: Principes et Applications, 1992, also video tapes. Recipient Peter B. Samuels award Soc. Clin. Vascular Surgery; Scientific Rsch. Soc. of N.Am. grantee, 1978, Baxter Pharmaceuticals Rsch. grantee, Round Lake, Ill., 1992, 94. Fellow ACS; mem. AMA, Acad. Surg. Rsch., Midwestern Vascular Surg. Soc., Mich. Vascular Soc., Southeastern Mich. Surg. Soc., Wayne County Med. Soc., Detroit Surg. Assn. Home: 14413 24 Mile Rd Shelby Township MI 48315-2417 Office: Harper Hosp Divsn Vasc Surg 3990 John R St Detroit MI 48201-2097 E-mail: aa2290@wayne.edu.

KLINE, SUSAN ANDERSON, medical school official and dean, internist; b. Dallas, June 4, 1937; d. Kenneth Kirby and Frances Annette (Demorest) Anderson; m. Edward Mahon Kline, Dec. 26, 1964 (dec. July 1990). BA, Ohio U., 1959; MD, Northwestern U., 1963. Diplomate Am. Bd. Internal Medicine, Nat. Bd. Med. Examiners (bd. dirs. 1977-81). Asst. physician NY Hosp., 1967—68, physician-to-outpatients, 1968—69, electrocardiographer, 1968—70, asst. attending physician, 1969—76, physician-in-charge cardiopulmonary lab., 1970—71, dir. adult cardiac catheterizaion lab., 1970—71, dir. adult cardiac catheterization lab., 1971—79, assoc. attending physician, 1976—85, emeritus attending physician, 1985—, emeritus dir. adult cardiac catheterization lab., 1985—; assoc. dean student affairs Cornell U. Med. Coll., N.Y.C., 1974—78; assoc. dean admissions and student affairs Cornell Med. Sch., Ithaca, NY, 1978—80, mgr. occupl. med. programs GE Co., 1980—84, sr. assoc. dean student affairs N.Y. Med. Coll., Valhalla, 1984—94, interim dean, v.p. med. affairs, 1994—96, exec. vice dean acad. affairs, vice provost univ. student affairs, 1996—. Chmn. unmatched student com. Nat. Residency Matching Program, 1998—2000; mem. test com. Ednl. Commn. on Fgn. Med. Grads., Phila., 1985—92; mem. U.S. med. licensing exam test accommodations com. Nat. Bd. Med. Examiners, Phila., 1992—; bd. dirs. Nat. Resident Matching Program, 1996—, bd. dirs., mem. exec. com., 2003—; mem. Liaison Com. on Med. Edn., 1998—, chair ad hoc subcom. rev. accreditation stds., 2000—01, exec. com., 2002—; policy com. Liaiaon Com. on Med. Edn/, 2003—; chmn. adv. com. Electronic Residency Application Svc., 1996—2001. Bd. visitors Coll. Arts, Ohio U., Athens, 1981—91; bd. dirs. Burke Rehab. Hosp., White Plains, 1997—. Recipient Leaders of the Future award, Nat. Coun. Women, N.Y.C., 1978, Cert. of Appreciation, Ohio U., 1978. Fellow: ACP, Am. Soc. Internal Medicine, Am. Coll. Cardiology; mem.: Phi Kappa Phi, Am. Assn. Med. Colls. (chmn. 1989—93, chmn. N.E. group on student affairs, mem. sr. mgmt. adv. com. 2001—), N.Y. Cardiologists Soc., Am. Heart Assn. (fellow coun. on clin. cardiology), Cruising Club Am., Alpha Omega Alpha, Phi Beta Kappa. Avocation: sailing. Home: 561 Pequot Ave Southport CT 06490-1366 Office: New York Medical College Sunshine Cottage Valhalla NY 10595 E-mail: kline@nymc.edu.

KLINE, TIMOTHY DEAL, lawyer; b. Oklahoma City, July 16, 1949; s. David Adam and Ruthela (Deal) K.; m. Alyssa Lipp Krysler, Aug. 29, 1985. BA, U. Okla., 1971, JD, 1976. Bar: Okla. 1976, U.S. Dist. Ct. (we. dist.) Okla. 1977, U.S. Ct. Appeals (10th cir.) 1977; cert. in bus. bankruptcy law and consumer bankruptcy Am. Bankruptcy Bd. of Certification. Law clk. to presiding justice U.S. Dist. Ct. (we. dist.) Okla., Oklahoma City, 1976-80; assoc. Linn, Helms, Kirk & Burkett, Oklahoma City, 1980-83; ptnr. Kline & Kline, Oklahoma City, 1983—2001; shareholder Kline, Kline, Elliott, Castleberry & Bryant PC, Oklahoma City, 2001—. Adj. prof. law Oklahoma City U., 1980-84, 90. Mem. Am. Coll. Bankruptcy, Okla. County Bar Assn. (pres. 1998-99), Phi Delta Phi. Democrat. Office: Kline Kline Elliott Castleberry & Bryant PC 720 NE 63rd St Oklahoma City OK 73105-6405 E-mail: tkline@klinefirm.org.

KLINEDINST, JOHN DAVID, lawyer; b. Washington, Jan. 20, 1950; s. David Moulson and Mary Stewart (Coxe) K.; m. Cynthia Lynn DuBain, Aug. 15, 1981. BA cum laude in History, Washington and Lee U., 1971, JD, 1978; MBA in Fin. and Investments, George Washington U., 1975. Bar: Calif. 1979, U.S. Dist. Ct. (so. dist.) Calif. 1979, U.S. Ct. Appeals (9th cir.) 1987. With comml. lending dept. 1st Nat. Bank Md., Montgomery County, 1971-74; assoc. Ludecke, McGrath & Denton, San Diego, 1979-80; ptnr. Whitney & Klinedinst, San Diego, 1980-83, Klinedinst & Meiser, San Diego, 1983-86; mng. ptnr. Klinedinst PC, San Diego, 1986—. Mem. law coun. Washington and Lee U., 1993-97, vice chmn. law campaign, 1991-94, bd. trustees, 2001—; vice chmn. bd. dirs. ARC of San Diego/Imperial, 1991-97; pres. House Corp. Calif. Lambda, Phi Kappa Psi, 1999—. Recipient Disting. Alumnus award Washington and Lee U., 1993. Mem. ABA (standing com. on legal profl. liability), Calif. Bar Assn., San Diego Bar Assn., San Diego Def. Lawyers, San Diego/Tijuana Sister Cities Soc., Washington Soc. (bd. dirs. 1997—), Washington and Lee U. Alumni Assn. (bd. dirs. 1986-90, pres. 1989-90), Washington and Lee U. Club (pres. San Diego chpt. 1980-87, San Diego Dialogue of U. Calif. San Diego), La Jolla Beach and Tennis Club, Fairbanks Ranch Country Club, Phi Kappa Psi. Republican. Episcopalian. Home: 6226 Via Dos Valles Rancho Santa Fe CA 92067-9999 Office: Klinedinst PC 501 W Broadway Ste 600 San Diego CA 92101-3584 E-mail: jdk@kfmlaw.com.

KLINEFELTER, JAMES LOUIS, lawyer; b. L.A., Oct. 8, 1925; s. Theron Albert and Anna Marie (Coffey) K.; m. Joanne Wright, Dec. 26, 1957 (div.); children: Patricia Anne, Jeanne Marie, Christopher Wright; m. Mary Lynn S. Klinefelter, Aug. 19, 1971; 1 child, Mary Katherine. BA, U. Ala., 1949, LLB, 1951. Bar: Ala. 1951, U.S. Dist. Ct. (no. dist.) Ala. 1959, U.S. Ct. Appeals (11th cir.) 1983. Regional claims rep. State Farm Mut. Auto Ins. Co., Anniston, Ala., 1951-54; ptnr. Burnham & Klinefelter, Anniston, 1954—2003; mem. Sides, Oglesby, Held and Picks, 2003—. Mem. adv. com. Supreme Ct. Ala. Mem. Ala. Dem. Exec. Com., 1964—, chmn. legis. rev. com., 1964—; past chmn. Calhoun County Dem. Exec. Com., 1964—; mem. Anniston City Sch. Bd. Lt. (j.g.) USNR, 1943-46. Mem. ABA, Assn. Def. Trial Attys., Ala. Bar Assn. (mem. task force on jud. selection, mem. long-range planning task force), Calhoun County Bar Assn., Ala. Def. Lawyers Assn. (past pres.), Ala. Law Inst. (bd. dirs.), Ala. Sch. Bd. Attys. (past pres.), Internat. Assn. Def. Counsel, Kiwanis (past pres.), Anniston Country Club, Phi Kappa Sigma, Phi Alpha Theta. Avocations: tennis, swimming, reading. Home: 1412 Christine Ave Anniston AL 36207-3924 Office: Burnham & Klinefelter So Trust Nat Bank Bldg PO Box 1618 Anniston AL 36202-1618 E-mail: jlk@cableone.net. *When obligations or obnoxious tasks are accepted gratefully as opportunities, one's life can be turned about, and bitterness and resentment changed into joyful satisfaction. Hard tasks are the food of growth.*

KLINE-KOENIG, BARBARA A. nursing case manager; b. Pitts., July 11, 1958; d. Robert T. and Janet (Falkenstein) K. BSN, Cedar Crest Coll., Allentown, Pa., 1982; MSA in Health Adminstrn., West Chester U., 1988; postgrad., U. Pa., 1995—, postgrad. Cert. med.-surg. nurse, ACLS. Staff nurse Crozer-Chester Med. Ctr., Upland, Pa.; primary nurse Paoli (Pa.) Meml. Hosp.; mktg. dept. liaison U. Pa. Med. Ctr.; clin. resource mgr. adminstrn. Hosp. of U. Pa., Phila., 1994—, mgr. denials and appeals. Named Nurse of Hope, Am. Cancer Soc., 1984.

KLINETOB, CARSON WAYNE, retired physical therapist; b. Berwick, Pa., Feb. 8, 1922; s. Dalbys Bryan and Margaret Jeannette (Hampton) K.; m. Edna Mae Ginader (dec.); children: Sandra Lynne, Diane Beth. BS, East Stroudsburg U., 1946; cert. phys. therapy, U. Pa., 1948; postgrad., NYU, Kingston, Pa., 1949. Lic. phys. therapist Pa., Ill., Wis., Ala. Staff phys. therapist VA Hosp., Wilkes-Barre, Pa., 1948, chief phys. therapist, 1949, Downey (Ill.) VA Hosp., 1953; owner Phys. Rehab. Ctr., Waukegan, Ill., 1955-60; co-owner, bd. dirs. Tri W-G Inc., Valley City, N.D., 1968-86; phys. therapist Wausau (Wis.) Med. Ctr.

1969—; ret., 1997. Contbr. articles to profl. jours. With U.S. Army, 1943-45, ETO. Mem. Am. Phys. Therapy Assn., Wis. Phys. Therapy Assn., Am. Legion, DAV (life), Masons, Shriners, Acacia. Avocations: golf, sports. E-mail: res0v7f5@verizon.net.

KLING, MERLE, political scientist, university official; b. Russia, June 15, 1919; came to U.S., 1921, naturalized, 1927; s. Saul and Dina (Hoffman) K.; m. Ann Ruth Yasgur, Jan. 1, 1948 (dec. June 1976); 1 child, Arnold Saul; m. Sandra Perlman, Aug. 26, 1978 (dec. Aug. 1990). AB, Washington U., St. Louis, 1940, MA, 1941, PhD, 1949; DHC (hon.), Washington U., 1983; LLD (hon.), Mercy Coll., 1985. Mem. faculty Washington U., 1946—, asst. prof. polit. sci., 1950-54, asso. prof., 1954-61, prof., 1961-83, prof. emeritus, 1983—; dean Washington U. (Faculty Arts and Scis.), 1966-69, 73-76, provost, 1976-79, exec. vice chancellor, provost, 1979-83, acting chmn. dept. polit. sci., 1970-71; pres. Mercy Coll., Dobbs Ferry, N.Y., 1984-85. Vis. prof. U. Ill., 1961; research asso. Center Internat. Studies, Princeton U., 1964-65 Author: The Soviet Theory of Internationalism, 1952, A Mexican Interest Group in Action, 1961; contbr. articles to profl. jours. Served with AUS, 1942-45. Merle Kling professorship of Modern Letters established in honor, Washington U., 1983. Mem. Am. Polit. Sci. Assn. (council 1967 69), Midwest Polit. Sci. Assn. (editor jour. 1965-66, pres. 1969-70), Phi Beta Kappa, Alpha Kappa Delta, Omicron Delta Kappa. Home: 20 N Kingshighway Blvd Saint Louis MO 63108-1366

KLING, PHRADIE (PHRADIE KLING GOLD), small business owner, educator; b. NYC, July 2, 1933; d. Samuel A. and Mary Leah (Cohen) K.; m. Lee M. Gold, Sept. 5, 1955 (div. 1976); children: Judith Eileen, Laura Susan, Stephen Samuel, James David. BA, Cornell U., 1955; MA in Human Genetics, Sarah Lawrence Coll., 1971. Genetic counselor assoc. Coll. Medicine and Dentistry N.J., Newark, 1970-73; assoc. genetic counselor Sarah Lawrence Coll., Bronxville, N.Y., 1970-73; genetic counselor N.Y. Fertility Rsch. Found., N.Y.C., 1971-73; staff assoc., genetic counselor depts. pediatrics, ob-gyn and neurology Columbia U. Coll. Physicians and Surgeons, N.Y.C., 1973-78; asst. in genetics St. Luke's Hosp. Ctr., N.Y.C., 1977-79; health program assoc. Conn. Dept. Health Svcs., Hartford, 1978-84; edn. cons. Conn. Traumatic Brain Injury Assn., Rocky Hill, 1984-85; office mgr. Anderson Turf Irrigation Inc., Plainville, Conn., 1986-92; owner, mgr. KlingWorks, contract adminstrn., Avon, Conn., 1992—. Speaker, instr. on health and health ethics issues, Conn., N.Y., N.J., 1971-85; dir. confs. on genetics and traumatic brain injury, 1980-85; project dir. ednl. field testing Biol. Scis. Curriculum Study, 1981-83; scientist AAAS Sci.-by-Mail, 1991-2000. Active Farmington River Watershed Assn., Simsbury, Conn., 1988—; docent Sci. Mus. Conn., West Hartford, 1989-90. Recipient citation for dedicated svc. Conn. Safety Belt Coalition, 1985. Mem. Am. Human Genetics Soc., Bus. and Profl. Microcomputer Users Group (bd. dirs.), Conn. Assn. for Jungian Psychology (bd. dirs.), Am. Mensa (chpt. coord. gifted children 1985—), Cornell Club Greater Hartford. Home and Office: 33 Hunter Rd Avon CT 06001-3618

KLING, S(TEPHEN) LEE, banker; b. St. Louis, Dec. 22, 1928; m. Ann Hemingway (div. 1958); m. Rosalyn H. Kling, May 3, 1962; children: Stephen L., Frank Frederick, Lee C., Allan B. BBA, Washington U., St. Louis, 1950. Chmn. bd., CEO Landmark Bancshares Corp., St. Louis, 1971—91; asst. spl. counselor on inflation White House, Washington, 1978—79; adv. vice-chmn. bd. U.S. divsn. Reed Stenhouse, Inc., 1978—79; chmn. bd. Kling Rechter & Co., 1991—2001, The Kling Co., 2002—. Bd. dirs. Kupper Parker Comms. Inc., Engineered Support Systems Inc., N.Y.C., Falcon Products, Inc., St. Louis, Bernard Chaus Inc., N.Y.C., Nat. Beverage Co., Ft. Lauderdale, Fla., Electro Rent Corp., L.A. Trustee Barnes-Jewish Found., St. Louis and Coro Midwestern area NCCJ; chmn. Wyman Ctr., The Moog Oral Sch., St. Louis; trustee Truman Libr. Inst., Independence, Mo., St. Louis Zoo Found.; St. Louis U.-Mo.; trustee Chancellors Coun. Washington U., St. Louis; co-chmn. Citizens Com. for Ratification of Panama Canal Treaties;, 1977; treas. Dem. Nat. Conv., 1976; nat. treas. Carter-Mondale Re-election Com., Gephardt for Pres. Com.; U.S. econ. advisor representing pvt. sector during peace negotiations between Israel and Egypt; co-chmn. Coalition for Enactment of Caribbean Basin Initiative Legis., 1982—83; apptd. to Def. Base Closure and Realignment Commn., 1995, Mo. State Hwy. and Transp. Commn., 1995, apptd., 1995, chmn., 1997. Mem. Sr. Execs. Orgn., Burning Tree Club (Bethesda, Md.), Westwood Country Club. Home: Grayling Farm 5751 Robertsville Rd Villa Ridge MO 63089-2535 also: Ste 800 1401 S Brentwood Blvd Saint Louis MO 63144-1440 E-mail: sleekling@aol.com.

KLING, WILLIAM, economist, retired foreign service officer; b. N.Y.C., May 8, 1915; s. Irving and Sophie (Kling) K.; m. Suzanne Kaufman (M.D.), June 28, 1940; children: Robert Irving, Michael Paul, Virginia Airini Susan. BS, CCNY, 1937; MS, Mass. State Coll., 1938; PhD, Clark U., 1943. Grad. asst. Mass. State Coll., 1937-38, Clark U., 1938-39; instr. CCNY, 1939-40; agrl. economist Dept. Agr., also War Food Adminstrn., 1940-45; agrl. attache Bucharest, Rumania, Budapest, Hungary, Belgrade, Yugoslavia, Sofia, Bu, Albania, 1945-47; first sec., consul Am. embassy, London, 1948-54, 1st sec., consul Wellington, New Zealand, 1954-60; assigned Dept. of State, Washington, 1960-68, chief div. of functional intelligence, 1961-63, dep. dir. and acting dir. Office of Functional and External Research, 1962-63, econ. adviser to asst sec. for African Affairs, 1963-66, dep. dir. econ. affairs Office Inter African Affairs, 1966-68; dir. govt. affairs Uniroyal, Inc., Washington, 1968-73; Washington rep. Am. Soybean Assn., 1973-79; prin. William Kling Assos. (consultants), Falls Church, Va., 1979—; cons. Japanese Fedn. Agrl. Coop. Assns., 1979; dir. econs. and stats. div. Distilled Spirits Council U.S., Inc., Washington, 1979-86, dir. industry stats. div., 1986-97; ret. Mem. Nat. Def. Exec. Rsc., 1970—; cons. Fed. Emergency Mgmt. Agy., 1970—; mem. export policy task force U.S. C. of C., 1978-79, mem. multilateral trade negotiation task force and chmn. agr. subgroup, 1978-79. Editor: DISCUS UPC News, Annual Statis, Rev. Distilled Spirits Industry, Pub. Revenues from Alcohol Beverages, Tax Briefs, 1980-85, Retail Outlets for the Sale of Distilled Spirits, 1992, 97, Distilled Spirits Brand Directory, 1993, 95, 97; contbr. articles to profl. jours. Recipient Meritorious Honor award State Dept., 1968 Mem. Am. Fgn. Service Assn., Soc. Govt. Economists., Diplomatic and Consular Officers Ret. Clubs: Nat. Economists, Internat. Economists. Home and Office: Summerville 11215 Seven Locks Rd Potomac MD 20854-3260

KLING, WILLIAM HUGH, broadcasting executive; b. St. Paul, Apr. 29, 1942; s. William Conrad and Helen A. (Leonard) K.; m. Sarah Margaret Baldwin, Sept. 25, 1976. BA in Economics, St. John's U., 1964; postgrad., Boston U., 1964-66. Pres. Minn. Pub. Radio, Inc., St. Paul, 1966—, Greenspring Co., 1986—, Am. Public Media Group, 1999—; founding dir. Nat. Pub. Radio, 1968-70, dir., 1977-80; founding pres. Public Radio Internat., 1982-86; vice chmn. Pub. Radio Internat., 1986-93. Bd. dirs. St. Paul Cos., Wenger Corp., Irwin Fin.; mem. various fund bds. Capital Group Am. Funds. Bd. dirs. Minn. Orch., 1987-93; trustee J.L. Found., 1988—; bd. dirs., chmn. Fitzgerald Theater Corp., 1983—; mem. The James Madison Coun. of Libr. of Congress, 1992-94. Recipient Edward R. Murrow award, 1981, award for Excellence Channels Mag., 1987; named Twin Citian of Yr., Twin Citian mag., 1987, Disting. Minnesotan, 1995, One of 100 Disting. Minnesotans of the Century, Mpls. Star Tribune, 2000. Mem. Mpls. Club. Office: Am Pub Media Group 45 7th St E Saint Paul MN 55101-2274

KLINGBIEL, PAUL HERMAN, retired information science consultant; b. Watertown, Wis., Nov. 3, 1919; s. Herman Carl and Elsa Helen (Zilisch) K.; m. Mildred Louise Wells, Nov. 30, 1968; stepchildren: Alice J. Blessley, Jo Ann Grayson. PhB, U. Chgo., 1948, BS, 1950; MA, Am. U., 1966. Abstractor Armed Svcs. Tech. Info. Agy., Dept. Def., Washington, 1953-58; editor Tech. Abstract Bull., 1958-60; dir. Office of Lexicography, 1960-66; phys. sci. adminstr., linguistics rsch. Def. Documentation Ctr., 1966-79; sr. cons. Aspen Systems Corp., 1979-81; systems analyst PRC Data Svcs. Co., Linthicum Heights, Md., 1981-82; lectr. Am. U., Washington, 1966-69; cons. divsn. med. scis. NAS, 1969-70. Contbr. articles to profl. jours. With AUS, 1943-46. Recipient Meritorious Civilian Svc. award, 1974, Disting. Career award, 1979. Fellow AAAS; mem. Assn. Computational Linguistics, N.Y. Acad. Scis. Lutheran. Achievements include research in the field of computational linguistics. Home: 700 Mease Plz Apt 417 Dunedin FL 34698-6629

KLINGEISEN, RICHARD HERMAN, priest; b. Manitowoc, Wis., Aug. 25, 1946; s. Lester Reinard and Dolores Mary (Binversie) Klingeisen. BA in Philosophy, St. Paul Sem., 1968. Cert. chaplain Nat. Assn. Cath. Chaplains, Wis. Parochial vicar SS Peter & Paul, Green Bay, Wis., 1972—76, St. Jude, Green Bay, 1976—78, St. John Nepumocene, Little Chute, Wis., 1978—81; staff chaplain Holy Family Meml., Manitowoc, 1981, team leader pastoral care, 1998, dir. pastoral care, coord. health affairs, 1998; coord. health affairs Diocese of Green Bay, 1998. Mem.-at-large Manitowoc AIDS Task Force, 1999, Coalition on Care of Dying, Manitowoc, 2000—, Dementia Task Force, Manitowoc, 2000—. Recipient Leadership award, Nat. Assn. Cath. Chaplains Region VII, 1991, Low Income Housing Improvement Project award, Appalachian R&D Fund Ky., Inc., 1999. Mem.: Daus. of Isabella (Mystical Rose Cir., chaplain 1996-), Daus. of Isabella (chaplain 1996—), Travellers Protective Assn. (chaplain 1998—), KC (chaplain 1998—). Roman Catholic. Avocations: bowling, golf, walking, reading, playing card games. Office: Holy Family Meml Inc PO Box 1450 Manitowoc WI 54221-1450

KLINGEL, PATTI JEAN, health facility administrator; b. Marion, Ohio, Dec. 28, 1955; d. Elmer N. and Reba J. (Freeman) Noe; m. Jeffrey J. Klingel, Aug. 16, 1974; children: Shane, Seth, Bethann. Grad. LPN program, Marion Gen. Hosp. Sch. Nursing, 1975; student, Ohio State U., 1984-85; AD in Bus. Adminstrn. magna cum laude, Marion Tech. Coll., 1993; BA in Mgmt. and Orgnl. Devel. (summa cum laude), Spring Arbor Coll., 1966; MBA in Healthcare Adminstrn. (summa cum laude), Baker Coll., 2003. Cert. profl. in healthcare quality. Assembler Whirlpool Corp., Marion, 1974; nurse Marion Gen. Hosp., 1975-79; childbirth educator, 1977-92; nurse Cmty. Med. Ctr., Marion, 1981-83; instr., cons. Tri-Rivers Joint Vocat. Sch., Marion, 1996; office mgr., adminstrv. asst. J.T. Spare M.D., Inc., Marion, 1986-94; quality improvement coord. MedCtr. Hosp., Marion, 1994-98, Smith Clinic, Marion, 1998-99; dir. quality mgmt. No. Va. Cmty. Hosp., Arlington, 1999—2001, Foote Health Sys., Jackson, Mich., 2001—03, Bucyrus Cmty. Hosp., Ohio, 2003—. Cons. Marion Tech. Coll., 1991. Contbr. articles to profl. jours. Spokesperson Nurse Hope-Am. Cancer Soc., Marion, 1982; advisor 4-H, Marion, 1986-93; bus. adminstr. United Way, Marion, 1989. Recipient scholarship Ohio State U., Columbus, 1985, Marion (Ohio) Tech. Coll., 1991, Walters scholarship, 1992-93, Wall St. Jour. award. Mem.: Mich. Assn. Healthcare Quality, LPN Assn. (sec. 1975—76), Am. Assn. Office Nurses, Internat. Childbirth Edn. Assn., Ohio Soc. Risk Mgrs., Mich. Soc. Infection Control, Mich. Hosp. Assn., Va. Assoc. Healthcare Quality (editor), Parents Assn. Childbirth Edn. (pres., instr. rep. 1976—92, top instr. 1989), Nat. Assn. Health Quality. Avocations: sewing, cooking, crafts. Home: 1512 Gallery Pl Dr # 4 Jackson MI 49201 Office: 205 N East St Jackson MI 49201

KLINGENSMITH, ARTHUR PAUL, industrial and organizational psychologist, consultant; b. L.A., May 23, 1949; s. Paul Arthur and Hermine Elinore K.; m. Donna J. Bellucci, Apr. 26, 1976 (div. Jan. 1981). AA in Social Sci., Indian Valley Jr. Coll., 1976; BA in Indsl. Psychology, San Francisco State U., 1979; MA in Indsl. Psychology, Columbia Pacific U., 1980. Enlisted USAF, Biloxi, Miss., advanced through grades to staff sgt., instr. radio ops., 1968-72, air traffic control operator Hamilton AFB Novato, Calif., 1972-74, resigned, 1974; elec. technician Calif. Dept. Transp., Oakland, 1975-78, right of way agt. San Francisco, 1978-85, sr. right of way agt. Sacramento, 1985-87, computer researcher, 1985-87; v.p., cons. Associated Right of Way Svcs., Inc., 1989-92; pvt. practice relocation and redevel. cons., 1987-96; bus. and pers. devel. cons., 1996-2000; tech. and info. psychologist, cons. V.p. bd. dirs. PAST Found. Mem. Inst. Noetic Scis., World Future Soc. Independent. Avocations: automobile restoration, painting, writing. Home and Office: Arthur P Klingensmith & Assocs PO Box 574 Sausalito CA 94966-0574

KLINGENSMITH, JAMES M. health insurance executive; b. Pitts., Apr. 17, 1947; s. James H. and Patricia J. K.; m. Linda K. Klingensmith, June 16, 1984; children: James M. Jr., Katherine E. BA, Colby Coll., 1969; MBA, U. Pitts., 1971, MPH, 1977, ScD, 1987. Asst. adminstr. Castle AFB Hosp., Calif., 1971-75; sr. v.p., chief operating officer Allegheny Gen. Hosp., Pitts., 1977-84; dir. health adminstrv. program U. Pitts., 1985-97; group exec. v.p. Highmark Blue Cross Blue Shield, Pitts., 1997—. Prin. Klingensmith Assocs., Pitts., 1987-96. Chair bd. dirs. Keystone Health Plan West, Pitts., 1998—. Capt. USAF, 1971-75.

KLINGENSMITH, MICHAEL, publishing executive; Pres., pub. Entertainment Weekly Mag. Time Inc., N.Y.C., 1990—96, pres. Entertainment Weekly, 1996—98, pres. Sports Illustrated, 1998—2001, exec. v.p., 2001—. Office: Time Inc 1271 Avenue of the Americas New York NY 10020-1300

KLINGENSTEIN, R. JAMES, physician; b. NYC, Oct. 30, 1948; s. Paul and Selma (Feldman) Klingenstein; m. Susanne Klingenstein, 1993; children: Rachel J., R. Julia. AB magna cum laude, Case Western Res. U., 1970; MD with honors, NYU, 1974; JD, Boston Coll., 1989; student, Harvard Sch Pub. Health, 1988. Intern Mt. Sinai Hosp., N.Y.C., 1974-75, resident, 1975-76, Bellevue Hosp., N.Y.C., 1976-77; clin. assoc. immunology br. Nat. Cancer Inst. NIH, HEW, Bethesda, Md., 1977-79; fellow in gastroenterology Mass. Gen Hosp., Boston, 1979-82; clin. research fellow Harvard U., Boston, 1979-82; clin. assoc. medicine Mass. Gen. Hosp., 1982—. Instr. in medicine Harvard Med. Sch., 1982-83, Tufts U. Sch. Medicine, 1983-87; asst. prof. Tufts U., 1987—. Assoc. editor: Internat. Jour. of Risk and Safety in Medicine; contbr. articles to profl. jours. Fellow: ACP; mem.: Am. Gastroenterol. Assn., Phi Beta Kappa. Home: 2000 Washington St Ste 543 Newton MA 02462-1608 Office: Mass Gen Hosp GI Unit Boston MA 02114

KLINGER, ALLEN, engineering and applied science educator; b. N.Y.C., Apr. 2, 1937; s. Benjamin and Evelyne Klinger; m. Judith Theresa Flesch, Aug. 31, 1958 (div. Dec. 1980); children: Deborah, Richard; m. Dorothy Joy Fisher, Feb. 14, 1988; stepchildren: Elisa, Laura Duncan, Kevin. BEE, The Cooper Union, 1957; MS, Calif. Inst. Tech., 1958; PhD, U. Calif., Berkeley, 1966. Mem. tech. staff Hughes Aircraft Co., Culver City, Calif., 1957; teaching asst. Calif. Inst. Tech., Pasadena, 1957-58; electronics engr. ITT Labs., Nutley, N.J., 1958-59; electronics system engr. System Devel. Corp., Santa Monica, Calif., 1959-62; rsch. asst. U. Calif. Electronics Rsch. Lab., Berkeley, 1962-64; sr. rsch. engr. Jet Propulsion Lab., Pasadena, Calif., 1964-65; researcher Rand Corp., Santa Monica, Calif., 1965-67; prof. UCLA, 1967—. Mem. L.A. County Data Processing and Telecom. Adv. Com., 1994-95; cons. in pattern recognition, image analysis, computer systems and math. modeling; expert witness, 1990—. Author: Data Structures, in Ency. Phys. Sci. and Tech., 1987, 92, 2001; editor: Soviet Image Pattern Recognition Research, 1989, Human Machine Interactive Systems, 1991; co-editor: Data Structures, Pattern Recognition and Computer Graphics, 1977 Structured Computer Vision, 1980; co-guest-editor Jour. Theoretical Computer Sci., 2003; contbr. 11 chpts. to books; contbr. articles to profl. jours. Fulbright fellow India, 1990. Fellow IEEE (Disting vis. 1975-76, 88-90), Tau Beta Pi (nat. dist. dir. 2001—). Office: UCLA Computer Sci Dept 4531-C Boelter Hall Los Angeles CA 90095-1596 E-mail: klinger@cs.ucla.edu.

KLINGER, MARILYN SYDNEY, lawyer; b. N.Y.C., Aug. 14, 1953; d. Victor and Lillyan Judith Klinger. BS, U. Santa Clara, 1975; JD, U. Calif., Hastings, 1978. Bar: Calif. 1978. Assoc. Chickering & Gregory, San Francisco, 1978-81, Steefel, Levitt & Weiss, San Francisco, 1981-82, Sedgwick, Detert, Moran & Arnold, San Francisco and L.A., 1982-87, ptnr. San Francisco, 1988-98, L.A., 1998—. Guest lectr. Stanford U. Sch. Engring. Vol. atty. Lawyers Commn. on Urban Affairs, San Francisco, 1978-80. Mem. ABA (tort and ins. practice sect., chair-elect surety and fidelity com.2003-2004, chair-elect constrn. forum, pub. contracts sect.), Internat. Assn. Def. Counsel (chmn. fidelity and surety com. 1996-98, chair-elect 2003—), Nat. Assn. Bond Claims (spkr.), Surety Claims Inst. (spkr.), No. Calif. Surety Underwriters Assn., No. Calif. Surety Claims Assn. (lectr., pres. 1989-90), Surety Assn. L.A. (spkr.). Avocations: reading, hiking, golf. Home: 939 15th St # 10 Santa Monica CA 90403-3146 Office: Sedgwick Detert Moran & Arnold 801 S Figueroa St Fl 18 Los Angeles CA 90017-2573 E-mail: marilyn.klinger@sdma.com .

KLINGERMAN, KAREN NINA, elementary school educator, teacher consultant, course coordinator; b. Rahway, N.J., Sept. 12, 1952; d. Nelson Randolph and Alma Margaret (Magnani) Terry; m. William Robert Klingerman, May 25, 1975; children: Bryan William, Brad Nelson. BS in Secondary Edn., Bloomsburg (Pa.) U., 1974; MEd, Trenton State Coll., 1977; Elem. Edn. Cert., Holy Family Coll., Phila., 1992. Cert. secondary edn. educator, elem. edn. educator, Pa. Tchr. Bensalem (Pa.) Sch. Dist., 1974—; tchr. cons., course coord., asst. dir. for new fellows Pa. Writing Project West Chester (Pa.) U., 1988—; instrnl. facilitator to improve students' writing Bensalem Twp. Sch. Dist., 2002—, tchr. on spl. assignment, 2002—. Assoc. dir. New Fellows Pa. Writing Project, 2003. Contbr. articles to Pa. Writing Project Newsletter. Mem. James A. Michener Art Museum, Doylestown, 2001-. Grantee Just for the Kids Edn. Found., 2001; recipient Bucks County IU # 22 grant, 1986, Award for Innovative Teaching, Pa. State Educators Assn., 1988. Fellow Pa. Writing Project; mem. NEA, Pa. State Edn. Assn. Avocations: colonial crafts, antiques, sports spectator, summers at N.J. shore. Home: 49 Sharon Dr Richboro PA 18954-1049 Office: Bensalem Sch Dist 3000 Donallen Dr Bensalem PA 19020-1829

KLINGERMAN, ROBERT HARVEY, manufacturing company executive; b. Freeland, Pa., Nov. 10, 1939; s. Thomas Van and Emma Yeager (Hoffman) K.; m. Eleanor Jean Deemer, Aug. 31, 1963; children: Jeffrey Allen, Timothy Scott. BS in Chem. Engring., Lehigh U., 1961. Sr. applications engr. Elliott Co. div. Carrier Corp., Jeannette, Pa., 1961-66; project mgr. Stokes div. Pennwalt Corp., Phila., 1966-70, Cragmet Corp., Rancocas, N.J., 1970-74; v.p. engring. Cheston Co. (now Consarc Corp.), Rancocas, 1974-78; dir. ops. Inducto Heat, Madison Heights, Mich., 1978-82; pres. W.J. Savage Co., Knoxville, Tenn., 1982—, also bd. dirs. Bd. dirs. Metl-Saw, Inc., Benecia, Calif. Patentee in field. Mem. Abrasive Engring. Soc., Am. Soc. Metals, Nat. Machine Tool Bldrs., Soc. Mfg. Engrs. Republican. Methodist. Avocations: little theater, gourmet cooking. Home: 700 Chateaugay Rd Knoxville TN 37923-2014 also: WJ Savage Co 1255 Proctor St Knoxville TN 37921-5734 E-mail: rhkling@savagesaws.com.

KLINGHOFFER, DAVID, journalist; b. Santa Monica, Calif., Oct. 31, 1965; s. Paul and Carol (Bernstein) Kaye. AB magna cum laude, Brown U., 1987. Film and TV critic Washington Times, 1990-92; editl. asst. Nat. Rev., N.Y.C., 1987, asst. book editor, 1987-89, lit. editor, 1992-98, sr. editor, 1998-99, contbg. editor, 2000-01; editl. dir. Toward Tradition, 2001—02. Author: The Lord Will Gather Me In: My Journey to Jewish Orthodox, 1998, The Discovery of God: Abraham and the Birth of Monotheism, 2003. Jewish.

KLINGHOFFER, JUNE FLORENCE, physician, educator; b. Phila., Feb. 12, 1921; d. Harry and Esther (Uram) K.; m. Sidney U. Wenger, June 24, 1947; 1 child, Robert Klinghoffer Wenger. BA, U. Pa., 1941; MD, Woman's Med. Coll. Pa., Phila., 1945. Diplomate Am. Bd. Internal Medicine, Am. Bd. Rheumatology. Intern, then resident Albert Einstein Med. Ctr., Phila., 1945-47; fellow in pathology Woman's Med. Coll. Pa., 1947-48; prof. medicine Med. Coll. Pa., Phila., 1969—87, Ethel Russell Morris prof. medicine, 1987—2000, emeritus prof. medicine, 2000—. Contbr. articles to med. jours. Recipient Lindback award for disting. teaching, 1965, Alumnae Achievement award Med. Coll. Pa., 1978. Fellow ACP, Phila. Coll. Physicians; mem. AMA, AAUP, Am. Med. Women's Assn., Assn. Am. Med. Colls., Am. Coll. Rheumatology, Alpha Omega Alpha. Home: 356 Meadow Ln Merion Station PA 19066-1331 Office: Med Coll Pa 3300 Henry Ave Philadelphia PA 19129-1191

KLINGLE, PHILIP ANTHONY, law librarian; b. Bklyn., July 24, 1950; s. Lorin Russell and Therese Margaret (Meehan) K.; m. Rachelle Phyllis Miller, Nov. 20, 1977; children: David Adam, Michael Matthew, Anne Elizabeth. BA, Fordham U., 1971; MA, NYU, 1973; MS, Columbia U., 1976. Asst. reference libr. N.Y. Hist. Soc., N.Y.C., 1973-77; libr. Bklyn. Pub. Libr., 1977-78; reference libr., asst. prof. John Jay Coll. Criminal Justice CUNY, 1978-81; libr. Inst. Jud. Adminstrn. Sch. of Law NYU, 1981-82; sr. law libr ct. libr. N.Y. State Supreme Ct., S.I., 1982—. Editor: jour. The Literature of Criminal Justice, 1980-81, IJA Report, 1981-82. Mem. ALA, Am. Assn. Law Librs., Law Libr. Assn. Greater N.Y., Libr. Assn. CUNY (mem. exec. coun. 1978-81). Office: NY State Supreme Ct Libr Richmond County Courthouse Staten Island NY 10301

KLINGNER, DONALD E. educator, consultant; b. San Francisco, Oct. 27, 1946; s. Evans N. and Ruth Biebesheimer Klingner; m. Janette Kettmann Klingner, Nov. 14, 1953; children: Christian Hardy Fanning, Amy Elizabeth, Heidi Warden, John Gerard. BA in Polit. Sci., U. Calif., Berkeley, 1968; MA in Govt., George Washington U., 1971; PhD in Pub. Adminstrn., U. So. Calif., L.A., 1974. Mgmt. intern, staffing specialist U.S. CSC, Washington, 1968—73; asst. prof. Sch. Pub. and Environ. Affairs Ind. U., Indpls., 1974—80; prof. Coll. Urban and Pub. Affairs Fla. Internat. U., Miami, 1980—2001; prof. Grad. Sch. Pub. Affairs U. Colo., Colorado Springs, 2001—. Adv. panel mem. fed. classification reform Nat. Acad. for Pub. Adminstrn., Washington, 1990—92, adv. panel mem. jud. salary reform; vis. prof. Universidad Nacional Autonoma de Mex., Mexico City, 1999—; editor in chief Comparative Tech. Transfer and Soc., Johns Hopkins U. Press, Colorado Springs, Colo., 2001—; disting. prof. in residence US HHS, Washington. Author: (textbook) Administracion del Personal Publico (McGraw-Hill Interamericana, Mex. City), Public Personnel Management (Renmin U. Press, Beijing); co-author: Public Personnel Management: Contexts and Strategies. NDEA Title IV fellow, US Govt., 1971—74. Mem.: ASPA (life; chair sect. on pers. and labor rels. 1983—84, chair sect. on internat. and comparative adminstrn. 2001—), Phi Beta Kappa. Avocations: backpacking, folk music, kayaking, travel. Home: 50 Buckthorn Dr Littleton CO 80127-4311 Office: GSPA Univ Colo 1420 Austin Bluffs Pkwy PO Box 7150 Colorado Springs CO 80933-7150 Office Fax: 719-262-4183. Personal E-mail: deklingner@aol.com. E-mail: dklingne@uccs.edu.

KLINGSBERG, DAVID, lawyer; b. N.Y.C., Feb. 4, 1934; m. Fran Sue Morganstern, Aug. 16, 1959; 3 children. LL.B., Yale U., 1957; BS, NYU, 1954. Bar: N.Y. 1958. Law clk. to U.S. Dist. Judge, N.Y., 1957-58; atty. U.S. Dept. Justice, Office Dep. Atty. Gen., Washington, 1958-59; asst. U.S. atty. criminal div. So. Dist. N.Y., 1959-61; chief appellate atty. U.S. Atty. Office, NY, 1961-62; assoc. Kaye Scholer LLP, N.Y.C., 1962—65, ptnr., 1966—, chmn. exec. com., 1999—. Contbr. articles to legal jours.; mem. editorial bd. Yale Law Jour, 1956-57. Bd. dirs. Legal Aid Soc. NY, 2001—. Recipient Pub. Interest Leadership award, Legal Aid Soc., 2001. Fellow Am. Coll. Trial Lawyers; mem. ABA, Assn. Bar City N.Y. (chmn. anti-trust and trade regulation com. 1986-89, mem. com. on diversity in legal profession 1998—, Thurgood Marshall award for representation in death sentence cases 1998), N.Y. State Bar Assn., Fed. Bar Coun. Office: Kaye Scholer LLP 425 Park Ave New York NY 10022-3506

KLINK, FREDRIC J. lawyer; b. N.Y.C., Oct. 4, 1933; s. Frederick Carl and Sophia Adelaide (Wolf) K.; m. Sandra Scott, 1979; children: Christopher, Charles; stepchildren: Kirsten Morehouse, Trina Morehouse. AB, Columbia U., 1955, LL.B., 1960. Bar: N.Y. 1960. Practiced in, N.Y.C.; ptnr. firm Dechert, Price & Rhoads, 1989—. Editor: Columbia U. Law Rev., 1959-60. Served as lt (j.g.) USNR, 1955-57. Mem. Am. Law Inst., Am., Internat., N.Y. C. bar assns. Office: Dechert LLP 30 Rockefeller Plz New York NY 10021 Home: 265 Riverside Dr New York NY 10024

KLINK, KARIN ELIZABETH, medical communications company executive, writer; b. Nov. 12, 1937; d. Nils Gustaf and Mary Josephine (Crowley) Hernblad; m. Fredric J. Klink, Nov. 28, 1958 (div. Apr., 1979); children: Christopher Frederick, Charles Gustaf. BA in Geology, Barnard Coll., 1958; MFA in Film Making, Columbia U., 1963; MS in Counseling and Art Therapy, U. Bridgeport, 1977, grad. cert. in corp. video Fairfield U., 1983. Film editor, writer Eye Gate House, N.Y.C., 1966-68; sr. editor Starting Tomorrow, N.Y.C., 1968-70; dir. creative therapies Hall-Brooke Hosp., Westport, Conn., 1978-83; mgr. editorial devel. New Eng. Advt. Assn., Norwalk, Conn., 1984-85; editorial dir. Logical Communications, Norwalk, 1985; pres. Creative Word & Image, Rowayton, Conn., 1985—. Freelance med. writer, editor for various cos., 1984—. Artist; author films, filmstrips and videotapes; designer, animator The Stage Evolves, 1964; writer, photographer slide tapes, 1985. Sec., bd. dirs. aerial photographer Preserve the Wetlands, Rowayton, 1983-91; bd. dirs. Inst. Visual Artists, Silvermine Guild, New Canaan, Conn., 1984-2002. Mem. Am. Med. Writers Assn. (sec./treas. bd. dirs. N.Y. chpt. 1989-90, treas., 1990-93, del. to nat. meetings 1990-97, recipient disting. svc. award 1992, pres.-elect 1993-94, pres. 1994-95, exec. com., adminstr. pub. rels. 1995-96, adminstr. chpts. 1996-97, Fellow award 1996), Am. Art Therapy Assn. (profl.), Silvermine Guild Artists (artist mem., various awards), So. Conn. Art Therapy Assn. (art therapist, pres. 1982-83). Democrat. Episcopalian. Achievements include painted Easter egg in White House collection at Smithsonian Inst. Avocations: drawing, painting, aerial photography, sailing. Home and Office: 1521 Sabatini Dr Henderson NV 89052-4132

KLINK, PAUL LEO, business executive; b. Auburn, N.Y., July 28, 1965; s. Charles Lawrence and Regina Joyce (Maniscalco) K. Student, SUNY, Cayuga, 1979-85. Pres., CEO Aloha Direct divsn. of Klink, Inc., Honolulu, 1979—; pres. http://www.hawaiian.com/ Inc., 1995—, Viva Japan, Inc., 1998—. Pres. Info. Tech., 1979, Aloha Direct, 1995, Hawaii Visitors Database Bur., 1997, First Class Mailing Svcs., 1997; v.p. PhytoTech U.S.A., 1996; pres., CEO Katana Mktg., 1998. Contbr. and edited articles for profl. jours. Co-chmn. direct mktg. com. Aloha United Way, Honolulu, 1988—, bd. dirs. Student Aloha; mem. Friends of Hawaii State Congressman, Ewa Beach, 1988—, Friends of State of Hawaii Gov., Honolulu, 1988—, Friends of the Mayor of the City of Honolulu, 1988—; bd. dirs. Postal Customer Coun., 1992—, Kids Voting Hawaii, 1997—; founder Rock 'n Vote, Aloha Found.; co-founder Live Aloha: attendee inauguration of U.S. Pres. William J. Clinton and U.S. V.p. Albert Gore, 1993, 97; bd. dirs. First Night Honolulu, Student Aloha/Aloha United Way, 1998—.. Mem. Direct Mktg. Assn., Chinese C. of C., Korean C. of C., Filipino C. of C., C. of C. of Hawaii, Ad 2 (pres. 1995-96, chmn. bd. dirs. 1996-97), Japanese C. of C., Am. Mktg. Assn., Honolulu Publs. Assn., Honolulu Advt. Fedn., Pacific Club, Rotary. Avocations: surfing the internet, movies, world travel, hawaiiana research, photography. Office: Klink Inc Box 8578 330 Saratoga Rd Honolulu HI 96815-1945

KLINK, ROBERT MICHAEL, consulting engineer, management consultant, financial consultant, property developer; b. Hamilton, Ind., Sept. 5, 1939; s. Robert Eli and Marie Ann Klink; m. Jesse Joyce Plummer, Sept. 10, 1960 (dec. Feb. 1966); children: Kevin Mark, Kent Michael, Kelly Martin, Kris Montgomery, Jeffrey Arthur; m. Mary Louise Mauldin, Oct. 30, 1999. Student, Tri State Coll., Angola, Ind., 1957; degree in Hwy. Engring., Purdue U., 1959; cert. in grad. sch. mgmt., Harvard U., 1976. Cert. behavorial cons. Hwy. engr. Ind. State Hwy. Commn., Ft. Wayne, 1959-65; staff engr. Cities Svc. Oil Co., Inc., South Bend, Ind., 1965-66; client svcs. mgr., asst. to v.p. Clyde E. Williams & Assocs., South Bend, 1966-72; pres. Alpha Devel. Corp., South Bend, 1970-72; sr. v.p., CFO Snell Environ. Group, Inc., Lansing, Mich., 1972-77; pres. Klink Devel. Co., Dayton, Ohio, 1972-91; pres., chmn. Solar GeoThermo Energy Systems, Inc., Dayton, 1982—; pres., mng. ptnr. Klink Enterprises Co., Dayton, 1977—; pres., chmn. bd. Design Enterprise, Ltd., Dayton, 1977-91; chmn., pres Cons Info Agy, Chattanooga, 1991—. Cons. engr. in mech., elec., civil, hwy., environ., sanitary, transp., archtl., planning and surveying engring., bd. dirs. Pono Kai Resort, Kapaa, Kauai, Hawaii, Imperial Hawaii, Honolulu; cons. World Bank/USAID, Dacca, Bangladesh, Country of Brazil, Rio de Janeiro; cons. engr., mgmt. cons., project developer, cons. to govtl. agys. and Fortune 500 cos.; lectr., spkr. in field. Patentee Solar and Geo Thermo Energy System; co-author: Water Handling Handbook, 1977. Trustee Centerville (Ohio) Cmty. Ch., 1982-88, Okemos (Mich.) Cmty. Ch., 1972-77; mem. The Presdl. Roundtable, Washington, 1989—, Rep. Senatorial Inner Circle, Washington, 1985—, Nat. Rep. Congrl. Com., 1986—, The Presidents Assn.; tchr. Woodland Park Bapt. Ch., Chattanooga; mem. Woodland Park Bapt. Ch. Chattanooga, 1998—; mem. Downtown Kiwanas Club Chattanooga. Recipient Outstanding Citizen award Am. Legion, Butler, Ind., 1953, Resolution of Appreciation Centerville City Coun., 1978, Resolution of Appreciation Greene County, 1989; named Hon. Citizen of Tenn., Nashville, 1989. Mem. Am. Water Works Assn. (life), Nat. Water Pollution Control Fedn., Profl. Svcs. Mgmt. Assn. (com. chair), Soc. for Mktg. Profl. Svcs. (com. chair), Ind. Hoosier Assocs., Ohio Early Birds. Christian and Missionary Alliance. Avocations: gardening, landscaping, woodworking, classic automobiles, golf.

KLINK, RON, former congressman, reporter, newscaster; b. Canton, OH, 1951; m. Linda Hogan; children: Matthew, Juliana. Broadcast newsman, ctrl., southwest Pa., W.V., Ohio; TV news reporter, anchorman KDKA-TV, Pitts., 1978-92; ptnr. Dagwood's, Pitts.; mem. 103rd-106th Congress from 4th Pa. dist., Washington, 1993-2001; lobbyist, owner of Bucephalus LLC, Pitts., 2001—. Vol. local fire dept.; bd. dirs. Vocat. Tech. High Sch.; active com. on commerce, subcom. on telecom., trade and consumer protection, and energy and power, and oversight and investigations. Democrat. Mem. United Ch. Of Christ. Office: Bucephalus LLC 3824 Northern Pike Ste 925 Monroeville PA 15146

KLINMAN, JUDITH POLLOCK, biochemist, educator; b. Phila., Apr. 17, 1941; d. Edward and Sylvia Pollock; m. Norman R. Klinman, July 3, 1963 (div. 1978); children: Andrew, Douglas. BA, U. Pa., 1962, PhD, 1966; PhD (hon.), U. Uppsala, Sweden, 2000. Postdoctoral fellow Weizmann Inst. Sci., Rehovoth, Israel, 1966—67; postdoctoral assoc. Inst. Cancer Rsch., Phila., 1968—70, rsch. assoc., 1970—72, asst. mem., 1972—77, assoc. mem., 1977—78; asst. prof. biophysics U. Pa., Phila., 1974—78; assoc. prof. chemistry U. Calif., Berkeley, 1978—82, prof., 1982—, prof. molecular and cell biology, 1993—, chair dept., 2000—03. Mem. ad hoc biochemistry and phys. biochemistry study sects. NIH, 1977—84, phys. biochemistry study sect., 1984—88. Mem. editl. bd.: Jour. Biol. Chemistry, 1979—84, Biofactors, 1991—98, European Jour. Biochemistry, 1991—95, Biochemistry, 1993—, Ann. Rev. Biochemistry, 1996—2000; contbr. Fellow, NSF, 1964, NIH, 1964—66, Guggenheim, 1988—89. Mem.: NAS, Am. Philos. Soc., Am. Soc. Biochemistry and Molecular Biology (membership com. 1984—86, pub. affairs com. 1987—94, program com. 1995, pres.-elect 1997, pres. 1998, past pres. 1999), Am. Acad. Arts and Scis., Am. Chmn. Soc. (exec. coun. biol. divsn. 1982—85, chmn. nominating com. 1987—88, program chair 1991—92, Repligen award 1994), Sigma Xi. Office: U Calif Dept Chemistry Berkeley CA 94720-0001

KLINT, RONALD VERNON, secondary school educator, financial consultant; b. Chgo., Feb. 11, 1939; s. Charles W. and Claire P. (Buente) K.; m. Carol L. Rodningen, Oct. 13, 1984; children: Matthew, Andrew. AA, Glendale (Calif.) C.C., 1958; BA, UCLA, 1960; MA, Calif. State U., L.A., 1964. Cert. tchr. and admin., Calif. Tchr. math. Glendale Schs., 1961—, mentor tchr., 1988-94. Pres. Profl. Edn. Glendale., 1967-70; instr. Glendale C.C., 1970—. Vol. Glendale Rep. Party, various time. Mem. Foothill Math. Coun., Calif. Math Coun. Avocations: gardening, photography. Home: 2900 Community Ave La Crescenta CA 91214-3461 E-mail: ronklint@earthlink.net.

KLIPHARDT, RAYMOND A. engineering educator; b. Chgo., Mar. 18, 1917; s. Adolph Lewis and Hortense Marietta (Brandt) K.; m. Rhoda Joan Anderson, May 5, 1945; children: Janis Kliphardt Emery, Judith Kliphardt Ecklund, Jill Kliphardt White, Joan Kliphardt Quinn, Jennifer Kliphardt Miller. BS, Ill. Inst. Tech., Chgo., 1938, MS, 1948. Instr. North Park Coll., Chgo., 1938-43; asst. prof. Northwestern U., Evanston, Ill., 1945-51, assoc. prof., 1952-63, prof. engring. scis., 1964-87, prof. emeritus, 1987—, dir. U. Khartoum project, 1964-68, dir. focus program, 1975-78, chmn. engring. scis. and applied maths. dept., 1978-87. Cons. applied maths. div. Argonne Nat. Lab., Lemont, Ill., 1962-63; cons. on patent litigation Kirkland and Ellis, Chgo., 1976-77. Author: Analytical Graphics, 1957; Program Design in Fortran IV, 1970. Mem. bd. edn. Morton Grove, Ill., 1952-55, Niles Twp., Ill., 1957-58. Served as ensign USNR, 1943-45. Recipient Western Electric Fund award for excellence in instrn. of engring. students, Am. Soc. Engring. Edn., 1967. Office: Northwestern U Technol Inst Evanston IL 60208-0001

KLIPPERT, RICHARD HOBDELL, JR., engineering executive; b. Oakland, Calif., Jan. 25, 1940; s. Richard Hobdell and Carol Ione (Knight) K.; m. Penelope Ann Barker, Sept. 5, 1979; children: David, Deborah, Candice, Kristina. BS in Bus., Oreg. State U., 1962; postgrad. in polit. sci., U. Calif., Berkeley, 1968-69; postgrad. in polit. sci. and mgmt., George Washington U., 1972-73; grad., Naval War Coll., 1973. Commd. ensign USN, 1962, advanced through grades to comdr., 1971, ret., 1982, expert Antisubmarine Warfare; mem. Combat Search and Rescue, Southeast Asia, 1964-67; exec. officer H.S. Squadron, 1974; mem. Flag Staff, 1974-79; chief engr. Light Airborne Multipurpose Sys. MK-III, Washington, 1979-82; sr. engr., mgr. IBM, 1982-83, engring. mgr., 1983-84, mgr. HH-60 sys. engring., 1984-85, mgr. V-22 engring., 1985-88, program mgr. Document Mgmt. Sys. Integration, 1988—, dir. publ. solutions, 1990—; program mgr. USDA SCOAP/ASCS Programs, 1992, SAIC, Sacramento, 1997—, dir. instructional tech. Capture mgr. WARSIM Program, 1994; loaned exec. Boulder County United Way, 1993; dir. USDA FSA programs Unisys Fed. Sys., 1995-97; acct. exec. FDA. Author: The Moon Book, 1971; contbr. articles to profl. jours. Decorated Silver Star, Navy Commendation; recipient Outstanding Achievement and golden Circle awards IBM, 1986, Cert. Program Mgr., 1993, Answer Group Mgr., 2003. Mem. Soc. Naval Engrs., Assn. Image and Info. Mgmt., Soc. Automotive Engrs., Naval inst., Sigma Chi. Republican. Avocations: golf, tennis, photography, bridge. Office: SAIC 111 Telegraph Ste 100 Carson City NV 89703 E-mail: rklippert@earthlink.net.

KLIPPING, ROBERT SAMUEL, geophysicist; b. Glaston, N.D., Dec. 5, 1928; s. Roy Samuel and Marie (Peterson) K.; m. Gayle Cleone Swanson, Sept. 29, 1951; children: Barbara, Sharon, Joan. BS in Geology, Colo. Coll., Colorado Springs, 1953. Geophys. computer scientist Gen. Geophys. Co., Denver, 1953-57; geophys. supr. Mandrel Indsl. Inc., Denver, 1957-65, area mgr., 1965-69; geophys. Pennzoil Co., Denver, 1969-72, exploration mgr., 1972-78; geophys. cons., owner Klipping & Assocs., Denver, 1978—. Author: American Association of Petroleum Geologists, 1976, Montana Geological Society, 1978. Staff sgt. U.S. Army, 1946-48. Mem. Am. Assn. Petroleum Geologists, Soc. Exploration Geophysicists, Denver Geophys. Soc. (treas. 1972-73, sec. 1973-74). Republican. Methodist. Avocations: woodworking, antique cars, golf, fishing. Home: 14645 Sterling Rd Colorado Springs CO 80921-2618 Office: Klipping & Assocs 518 17th St Denver CO 80202-4130

KLIPSTEIN, ARNOLD LLOYD, gastroenterologist; b. Bklyn., June 9, 1939; s. Harold David and Hyacinth (Levin) K.; children: William, Linda. BA cum laude, Columbia Coll., 1961; MD, NYU, 1965. Diplomate Am. Bd. Internal Medicine, Am. Bd. Gastroenterology. Med. intern Bellevue Hosp., N.Y.C., 1965-66, resident in medicine, 1966-67, Yale-New Haven Hosp. and West Haven VA Hosp., 1969-70, fellow in gastrointestinal disease, 1970-71; physician, gastroenterologist Manchester (Conn.) Meml. Hosp., 1971—, Rockville Gen. Hosp., Vernon, Conn., 1971—, Hartford (Conn.) Hosp., 1987—; pvt. practice Manchester, Conn., 1971—; physician, gastroenterologist Johnson Meml. Hosp., Stafford Springs, Conn., 1971—; chief, sect. gastroenterology Manchester Meml. Hosp./Rockville Gen. Hosp., 2001—. Mem. Phi Beta Kappa, Alpha Omega Alpha. Avocations: tennis, working out at health clubs, travel, computers. Home: 333 Kennedy Rd Manchester CT 06040-2251 Office: 272 Main St Manchester CT 06040-3536 E-mail: alklipstein@aol.com.

KLIPSTEIN, ROBERT ALAN, lawyer; b. N.Y.C., Sept. 23, 1936; s. Harold David and Hyacinth (Levin) K. AB, Columbia U., 1957, JD, 1960; LLM in Taxation, NYU, 1965. Bar: N.Y. 1960, U.S. Supreme Ct. 1964. Practice of law Saxe Bacon & O'Shea, N.Y.C., 1961—, assoc., 1961, Rosenman, Colin, Kaye, Petschek & Freund, 1962-63; law sec. to justice N.Y. County Supreme Ct., 1963-64; assoc. Bernays & Eisner, 1965-70; ptnr. Eisner, Klipstein & Klipstein, 1971-77, Danziger, Bangser, Klipstein, Goldsmith, Greenwald & Weiss (now Bangser Klein Rocca & Blum), N.Y.C., 1977-92; counsel Sullivan & Donovan, 1992—2001; ptnr. Ballon, Stoll, Bader & Nadler, N.Y.C., 2002—. Arbitrator City of N.Y. Small Claims Ct., 1971—. With U.S. Army, 1960—62. Mem. ABA, N.Y. State Bar Assn., Assn. Bar City of N.Y., N.Y. County Lawyers Assn., Am. Immigration Lawyers Assn., Westchester County Bar Assn., Am. Judges Assn., Univ. Glee Club (N.Y.C.), Phi Alpha Delta. Home: 401 E 74th St Apt 6G New York NY 10021-3931 Office: Ballon Stoll Bader & Nadler 1450 Broadway New York NY 10018 E-mail: raklip@aol.com.

KLIR, GEORGE JIRI, systems science educator; b. Prague, Czechoslovakia, Apr. 22, 1932; arrived in U.S., 1966, naturalized, 1972; s. Jan and Emilie (Přitasilová) K.; m. Milena Řeholová, Jan. 26, 1962; children: Jane, John. MSEE, Czech Tech. U., Prague, 1957; PhD, Czechoslovak Acad. Scis., Prague, 1964; D (hon.), Prague U. Econs., Prague, 1994, Tech. U. in Brno, Moravia, 1997, Czech Tech. U., Prague, 1998. Rsch. fellow Inst. Computer Research, Prague, 1960-64; lectr. U. Baghdad, Iraq, 1964-66, UCLA, 1966-68; assoc. prof. Fairleigh Dickinson U., 1968-69, Sch. Advanced Tech., SUNY, Binghamton, 1969-72, prof. systems sci., 1972—, disting. prof. T.J. Watson Sch., 1984—, chmn. dept. systems sci., 1977-94. Dir. Internat. Conf. Applied Gen. Systems Rsch., 1977, Ctr. for Intelligent Systems, T.J. Watson Sch., 1995-2000. Author: Cybernetic Modelling, 1967, An Approach to General Systems Theory, 1969, Methodology of Switching Circuits, 1972, Architecture of Systems Problem Solving, 1985, 2d edit., 2003, Fuzzy Sets, Uncertainty, and Information, 1988, Facets of Systems Science, 1991, 2d edit., 2001, Fuzzy Measure Theory, 1992, Fuzzy Sets and Fuzzy Logic, 1995, Uncertainty-Based Information, 1998, 2d edit., 1999, Fuzzy Sets, 2000; author, co-author or editor other books; editor-in-chief: Book Series on Basic and Applied General Systems Research, 1978-82, Book Series on Frontiers in System Science: Implications for the Social Sciences, 1978-84, International Jour. Gen. Systems, 1974—, IFSR Book Series on Systems Science and Engineering, 1984—; mem. editl. bds. other profl. jours.; contbr. numerous articles to profl. jours. Recipient award for outstanding contbns., Austrian Soc. Cybernetics, 1976, award, Netherland Soc. Sys. Rsch., 1976, Bernard Bolzano gold medal in math. scis., Czech Acad. Scis., 1994, Lotfi A. Zadeh Best Paper award, 1994, Disting. Leadership award, ISSS, 1994, award for highest achievement in scholarship, Simon Bolivar U. in Caracas, 1997, Arnold Kaufmann's Gold Medal prize for excellence in uncertainty rsch., 2000, award, Internat. Conf. on Computing Anticipatory Sys., 2001, CASYS award for outstanding work on anticipatory and intelligent sys.; fellow rsch., IBM, 1969, Netherlands Inst. Advanced Studies, 1975—76, 1982—83, Japan Soc. for Promotion of Sci., 1980. Fellow IEEE (life), Internat. Fuzzy Systems Assn(pres. 1993-95)); mem. AAAS, Internat. Soc. Sys. Scis. (mng. dir., v.p. 1978-80, pres. 1980-81, disting. leadership award 1994), Internat. Fedn. Sys. Rsch. (pres. 1980-84), N.Am. Fuzzy Info. Processing Soc. (pres. 1988-91). Home: 401 Manchester Rd Vestal NY 13850-3606 Office: SUNY/Dept Sys Sci/Indsl Eng Thomas J Watson Sch Engring and Applied Sci Binghamton NY 13902-6000 E-mail: gklir@binghamton.edu. *The main force behind my intellectual development has been my passion for discovery and integration in science and technology. The most precious values in professional life are for me scientific honesty and tolerance.*

KLITZKE, THEODORE ELMER, former college dean, arts consultant; b. Chgo., Nov. 4, 1915; s. John Frederick and Edith (Bachmann) K.; m. Margaret Bridget Gaughan, Feb. 23, 1946; children: Annetta, Margaret. B.F.A., Chgo. Art Inst., 1940; BA, U. Chgo., 1941, PhD, 1953; D.F.A. (hon.), Kansas City Art Inst., 1980, Md. Inst., Coll. Art, 1982. Instr. art history U. Chgo., 1946-47; edn. adviser U.S. Armed Forces in Germany, Nurnberg, 1948-51; asst. prof. art history N.Y. State Coll. Ceramics, SUNY, Alfred, 1953-59; prof. art history, chmn. dept. U. Ala., 1959-68; v.p. acad. affairs, dean Md. Inst., Coll. Art, 1968-82, pres., 1977-78, Balt. News Network, 1989-97; mem. accessions com. Balt. Mus. Art, 1978-82. Author: Melville Price Retrospective, 1970; contbg. author: Festschrift Ulrich Middeldorf, 1968, Lothar Strauch: 1907-91, Plastik und Graphik, 1993; contbr. articles to profl. jours. and ency. Bd. dirs. Ala. chpt. ACLU, 1965-68; bd. dirs. S.W. Ala. Self-Help Housing, 1966-68. Served with AUS, 1942-46. Recipient First Annual Peace and Freedom award Democratic Student Orgn., U. Ala., 1968; citation Civil Liberties Union Ala. Mem. AAUP, Southeastern Coll. Art Conf. (pres. 1961-62), Coll. Art Assn., Nat. Assn. Schs. Art (dir. 1971-74, mem. commn. on accreditation 1975-78, treas. 1980-82, fellow 1981), Print and Drawing Soc. of Balt. Mus. Art (pres. 1974-76), Union Ind. Colls. Art (chmn. planning com. 1977-80), Am. Studies Assn., Coll. Art Assn. Am., Johns Hopkins Club (Balt.). Home: 7918 Sherwood Ave Baltimore MD 21204-3600 E-mail: tklitzke@bcpl.net.

KLITZMAN, BRUCE, physiologist, plastic surgery educator, researcher; b. Dayton, Ohio, Nov. 4, 1951; m. Hardee Burt Brown; children: Rachel Hardee, Page Hardee. BS in Biomed. Engring. cum laude, Duke U., 1974; PhD, U. Va., 1979. Rsch. assoc. physiology U. Ariz. Coll. Medicine, Tucson, 1979-81; asst. prof. physiology, biophysics La. State U. Sch. Medicine, Shreveport, 1981-85; assoc. prof., 1985; sr. dir. Kenan plastic surgery rsch. labs., asst. rsch. prof. surgery and biomed. engring., assoc. prof. cell biology and biochem. engring. Duke U. Med. Ctr., Durham, NC, 1985—. Adj. prof. biomed. engring. La. Tech. U., Ruston, 1982-86; session chmn. Third, Fourth and Fifth World Congresses for Microcirculation, 1984, 87, 91; speaker, lectr. various symposia and seminars. Contbr. articles to profl. jours., chpts. to books; assoc. editor Jour. Reconstructive Microsurgery; editl. bd. Cell Transplantation, Am. Jour. Physiology, Jour. Reconstructive Microsurgery, Microvascular Rsch., Microcirculation. Recipient Instl. Nat. Rsch. Svc. award NIH, 1974-81, Machiko-Kuno Med. Student Rsch. award, U. N.C. at Chapel Hill, 1992, first prize investigator category, Plastic Surgery Ednl. Found., 1988; fellow U. Va., 1979, NATO, 1980; grantee Am. Heart Assn., 1982-85, NIH, 1985—. Mem. Am. Physiol. Soc., Am. Heart Assn. (circulation coun. 1984, grantee 1982-85, rsch. com. La. chpt. 1985), Am. Soc. Reconstructive Microsurgery (chmn. sci. session), Microcirculatory Soc. (sec. 1993-97, program com. 1983-84, mem. com. 1984-87, pres. 1998-99), Soc. Biomaterials, Plastic Surgery Rsch. Coun. (sci. adv. bd. 1998), European Soc. Microcirculation (travel award 1980), Internat. Soc. Oxygen Transport to Tissue, Controlled Release Soc.. Home: 3015 Wade Rd Durham NC 27705-5630 Office: Duke U Med Ctr Plastic Surgery Rsch Lab PO Box 3906 Durham NC 27710-0001 E-mail: Klitz@duke.edu.

KLITZMAN, ROBERT LLOYD, physician, author; b. N.Y.C., July 1, 1958; s. Joseph Arthur and Joan Marilyn (Kahn) K. AB, Princeton U., 1980; MD, Yale U., 1985. Diplomate Am. Bd. Psychiatry and Neurology. Rsch. asst. Nat. Inst. Health, Bethesda, Md., 1980-81; researcher Papua New Guinea Inst. Med. Rsch., 1980-81; intern The N.Y. Hosp. Cornell U. Med. Ctr., N.Y.C., 1985-86, resident, 1986-89; fellow Columbia Presbyn. Med. Ctr., N.Y.C., 1989-96, asst. prof. clin. psychiatry, 1996—, asst. prof. Sch. Pub. Health, 2000—, co-dir. Ctr. for Bioethics, 2001—. Author: A Year-long Night, 1989, In a House of Dreams and Glass, 1995, Being Positive: The Lives of Men and Women with HIV, 1997, The Trembling Mountain, 1998, Mortal Secrets: Truth and Lies in the Age of AIDS, 2003; contbr. articles to profl. jours., chpts. to books. Recipient Keese prize Yale U., 1985, NIMH Career Devel. award, 1996-99; Robert Wood Johnson Found. clin. scholar U. Pa., 1991-93; DuPont fellow, 1982, Burroughs-Wellcome fellow Am. Psychiat. Assn., 1987, MacDowell Colony fellow, 1991, Aaron Diamond Found. fellow, 1993-96, Merck Co. Found. fellow Corp. of Yaddo, 1994, 2001; Picker-Commonwealth scholar, 1996-98, vis. scholar Russell Sage Found., 1999-2000, Rockefeller Found. fellow, Bellagio, Italy, 2003. Mem. PEN, Am. Psychiat. Assn. (mem. N.Y. County dist. br. com. on AIDS 1989—, commn. on AIDS 1988-89, steering com. of AIDS edn. project 1987-88).

KLOBASA, JOHN ANTHONY, lawyer; b. St. Louis, Feb. 15, 1951; s. Alan R. and Virginia (Yager) K. BA in Econs., Emory U., 1972; JD, Wash. U., 1975. Bar: Mo. 1975, U.S. Dist. Ct. (ea. dist.) Mo. 1975, U.S. Ct. Appeals (8th cir.) 1976, U.S. Supreme Ct. 1979, U.S. Tax Ct. 1981, U.S. Ct. Appeals (9th cir.) 1990, U.S. Ct. Appeals (10th cir.) 1993. Assoc. Kohn, Shands, Elbert, Gianoulakis & Giljum LLP, St. Louis, 1975—80, ptnr., 1981—. Spl. counsel City of Town and Country, Mo., 1987; spl. counsel City of Des Peres, Mo., 1987, alderman, 1989-91. Mem.: ABA, Met. St. Louis Bar Assn., Mo. Bar Assn., Order of Coif, Phi Beta Kappa. Republican. Office: Kohn Shands Elbert Gianoulakis & Giljum LLP One US Bank Plz Ste 2410 Saint Louis MO 63101-1643 E-mail: jklobasa@ksegg.com.

KLOBE, TOM, art gallery director; b. Mpls., Nov. 26, 1940; s. Charles S. and Lorna (Effertz) K.; m. Delmarie Pauline Motta, June 21, 1975. BFA, U. Hawaii, 1964, MFA, 1968; postgrad., UCLA, 1972-73. Vol. peace corps, Alang, Iran, 1964-66; tchr. Calif. State U., Fullerton, 1969-72, Santa Ana (Calif.) Coll., 1972-77, Orange Coast Coll., Costa Mesa, Calif., 1974-77, Golden West Coll., Huntington Beach, Calif., 1976-77; art gallery dir. U. Hawaii, Honolulu, 1977—. Acting dir. Downey (Calif.) Mus. Art, 1976; exhibit design cons. Honolulu Acad. Arts, 1998-, Hawaii State Art Mus., 2002; exhibit designer John Young Mus., U. Hawaii, 1998; cons. Judiciary History Mus., Honolulu, 1982-96, Maui (Hawaii) Arts and Cultural Ctr., 1984-94, curator Keia Wai Ola: This Living Water, 1994; exhbn. coord. Schaefer Portrait Challenge, 2003; exhibit designer Inst. for Astronomy, Honolulu, 1983-86; exhibit design cons. Japanese Cultural Ctr. Hawaii, 1993—; juror Print Casebooks; project coord. Crossings '97: France/Hawaii, Crossings 2003: Korea/Hawaii. Recipient Best in Exhbn. Design award Print Casebooks, 1984, 86, 88, Vol. Svc. award City of Downey, 1977, Chevalier l'Ordre des Arts et des Letters, France, 2000, Robert W. Clopton award for Disting. Cmty. Svc.; Exhbn. grantee NEA, 1979-93, State Found. Culture and the Arts, 1977—. Mem. Hawaii Mus. Assn. Roman Catholic. Office: U Hawaii Art Gallery 2535 The Mall Honolulu HI 96822-2233 E-mail: gallery@hawaii.edu. *Personal philosophy: Nothing is impossible. Believe in yourself and in each other. Each of us has the ability to shape our destiny.*

KLOBUTCHER, LAWRENCE ANTHONY, molecular biologist, educator; b. Kankakee, Ill., Nov. 18, 1952; s. Lawrence Matthew and Lucy Joan K.; m. Ann Elizabeth Cowan, Aug. 19, 1979; children: Lauren Stephany, Julia Maria. BS with honors, Loyola U., 1974; MPhil, Yale U., 1976, PhD, 1979. Postdoctoral fellow U. Colo., Boulder, 1980-83; asst. prof. biochemistry U. Conn. Health Ctr., Farmington, 1984-90, assoc. prof., 1990-97, prof. biochemistry, 1997—2003. Mem. adv. panel eukaryotic genetics, NSF, Washington, DC, 1993-96, 2001. Mem. bd. reviewers Jour. Eukaryotic Microbiology, 1989-95, 97-99; assoc. editor Jour. Eukaryotic Microbiology, 2000—; contbr. articles, book chaps. to profl. pubs. Mem. Friends of Farmington Edn., 1998-2000. Fellow, NIH, 1980-83; grantee NIH, 1984, 87, 91, NSF, 1994, 99, Basil O'Connor Starter Rsch. March of Dimes, 1984, The Robert Leet and Clara Guthrie Patterson Trust, 2001, 2002. Mem. AAAS, Am. Soc. for Biochemistry and Molecular Biology, Blue Key, Sigma Xi. Avocations: tennis, travel. Office: U Conn Health Ctr Dept Biochemistry Farmington CT 06030-0001 Fax: 860-679-3408. E-mail: klobutcher@NS02.uchc.edu.

KLOCEK, GARY RICHARD, apparel company executive; b. Phila., Aug. 15, 1950; BS, Rider U., Lawrenceville, N.J., 1972. Mgr. cost and inventory control ChemLink divsn. Arco Chem. Co., Phila., 1983-87; contr. Jones Apparel Group USA, Inc., Bristol, Pa., 1987-99, v.p., controller, 1999—. Office: Jones Apparel Group USA Inc 180 Rittenhouse Cir Bristol PA 19007-1618

KLOCK, JOHN HENRY, lawyer; b. Gouverneur, N.Y., Mar. 29, 1944; s. John F. and Patricia M. (Chateau) K.; m. Connie E. McLaughlin, May 31, 1969; children: Thomas, Jacqueline. BA, St. Bonaventure U., 1966; postgrad., U. Va., 1967; MA, NYU, 1970; JD, Rutgers U., 1976. Bar: N.J. 1976, U.S. Dist. Ct. N.J. 1976, N.Y. 1977, U.S. Ct. Appeals (3d cir.) 1979, U.S. Dist. Ct. (ea. dist.) N.Y. 1981, U.S. Supreme Ct. 1981, U.S. Dist. Ct. (so. dist.) N.Y. 1982, U.S. Dist. Ct. (no. dist.) N.Y. 1988, U.S. Dist. Ct. (we. dist.) N.Y. 2002; cert. civil trial atty. N.J. Law clk. to judge U.S. Dist. Ct. N.J., Newark, 1976-77; assoc. Gibbons, Del Deo, Dolan, Griffinger & Vecchione, Newark, 1977-83, ptnr., 1983—. Author: New Jersey Practice Court Rules (5th edit.), vol. 1, 1A, 2, 2A, 2000, New Jersey Practice Evidence Rules, 4th edit., 2002, New Jersey Practice Trial Lawyers Manual, vol. 2E, 2003; contbr. articles to profl. jours. Active Scotch Plains Hist. Commn. Mem. ABA, N.J. Bar Assn., N.Y. Bar Assn., U.S. Supreme Ct. Hist. Soc., N.J. Hist. Soc., Plainfield Country Club. Roman Catholic. Achievements include patents for quick release automatic chaulk gun. Avocations: golf, gardening. Home: 1800 Lake Ave Scotch Plains NJ 07076-2920 E-mail: jklock@gibbonslaw.com.

KLOCK, JOSEPH PETER, JR., lawyer; b. Phila., Mar. 14, 1949; s. Joseph Peter and Mary Dorothy (Fornace) K.; m. Susan Marie Girsch, Mar. 17, 1979; children: Susan Elizabeth, Kathleen Marie, Robert Charles, Peter Joseph II. BA in Philosophy with honors, LaSalle Coll., 1970; JD cum laude, U. Miami, Fla. 1973; DHL (hon.), LaSalle U., 1999. Bar: Fla. 1973, Pa. 1973, D.C. 1978. Ptnr. Steel, Hector & Davis LLP, Miami, Fla., 1977-79, adminstrv. ptnr., 1978-82, chmn., mng. ptnr., 1983—; gen. counsel, chief legal officer Flo-Sun, Inc. 1991—. Adj. prof. U. Miami Law Sch., 1974-84; bd. dirs. Nat. Beverage Corp., Premier Hotel Corp., Fla. Partnership for the Americas, FTAA Adminstrv. Secretariat, Inc., St. Thomas Human Rights Inst.; vice chmn. bd. dirs. Baypoint Sch., Inc.; mem. Fed. Jud. Nominating Com. of Fla., 1993-97. Trustee Belen Jesuit Prep. Sch., St. Joseph's Preparatory Sch., Barry U., Collins Ctr., Miami Art Mus., Fundacion Mir, New Hope Charities, Inc.; chmn. bd., trustee Carrollton Sch., 1982-98. Fellow Am. Bar Found.; mem. ABA (chmn. Caribbean law com. internat. law sect. 1991-92), Fla. Bar (chmn. civil procedure rules com. 1979-82), D.C. Bar, Dade County Bar Assn., Assn. Bar City of N.Y., Am. Law Inst., Am. Assn. Sovereign Mil. Order Malta, Iron Arrow Honor Soc. Westview Country Club, Sailfish Club Palm Beach, Govs. Club West Palm Beach, Miami City Club (pres. 1994-97), Phi Alpha Delta, Phi Kappa Phi, Omicron Delta Kappa. Democrat. Roman Catholic. Home: 5095 SW 82nd St Miami FL 33143-8503 Office: 200 S Biscayne Blvd Fl 41 Miami FL 33131-2398 also: Ste 200 One North Clematis St West Palm Beach FL 33401 E-mail: klock@steelhector.com.

KLODNICKI, RICHARD HENRY, military officer, systems analyst; b. Swindon, Wiltshire, U.K., Mar. 15, 1963; s. Richard H. and Veda W. Klodnicki; 1 child, Aubrey. Bachelors, USAF Acad., Colo. Springs, 1985; Masters, Lesley Coll., Cambridge, 1990; PhD, U. Of Denver, 2003. Dept. chair, mil. tng. USAF Acad., Colo. Springs, 1993—98; test dir., space systems Air Force Operational Test And Evaluation Ctr., Colo. Springs, 2002—. Editor: (text books) Cadet Professional Military Education. Sub-deacon St Mary Holy Dormition Orthodox Ch., Calhan, Colo., 1997—2003; pres. Higher Edn. Student Assn., Denver, 1999—2002; exec. v.p. Rocky Mountain Orthodox Christian Charities & Missions, Denver, 2000—03. Maj. USAF, 1981—2003. Decorated Meritorious Svc. medal USAF Acad.; recipient Outstanding Comdr., 1997, Gen. J. F. O'Malley Leadership award, 1997; scholar, USAF Acad., 1981. Mem.: Assn.

for Study of Higher Edn., Am. Polit. Scientist Assn., USAF Acad. Assn. of Graduates, Assn. for Instl. Rsch., Am. Ednl. Rsch. Assn., Air Force Assn. Conservative. Orthodox Christian. Achievements include research in Phd student motivation scale. Home: 7522 Madrid Ct Colorado Springs CO 80920-4113 Home Fax: 719-277-7292. Personal E-mail: richard@klodnicki.net. E-mail: richard.klodnicki@afotec.af.mil.

KLODT, GERALD JOSEPH, product development executive; b. Ottumwa, Iowa, Feb. 6, 1949; s. Edward William and Isabelle Margaret (Herrmann) K.; m. Menzi Louise Behrnd, May 26, 1979. BFA, U. Iowa, 1971, MA, 1972; MFA, U. Ill., 1974, U. Wis., 1979. Designer Tevcin, Inc., Perry, Iowa, 1972-75; assoc. designer William Stumpf & Assocs., Middleton, Wis., 1975-77; prof. design U. Wis., Madison, 1977-84; pres., chief exec. officer Klodt & Assocs., Madison, 1977—; engr. Fel-Pro Energy Inc., Lake Geneva, Wis., 1982-83; v.p. research and devel., product engring., product design, product packaging, product quality W.T. Rogers Co., div. Newell, Madison, 1984-91; dir. for product and graphic design Nordic Design Ltd. subs. of Nordic Group of Cos. Corp., Baraboo, Wis., 1994-95. Cons. engr. Linton Assocs., Chesieres, Switzerland, 1984; project dir., engr. U.S. Dept. Energy, Madison, 1980-83; bd. dirs. XYTE Inc., v.p. bus. and tech. devel., 1999-2000, pres., 2001, CEO, 2001—. Author: Earth Sheltered Housing, 1985; mech. and design patentee for office products, creator The Klodt Collection. Bd. dirs. Energy Idea Exchange, Madison, 1978-80; mem. Wis. State Resources Advisory Panel, 1978-80; leader, educator Am. Youth Found., Camp Miniwanca, Mich., 1977. Named Tchr Yr. dept. engring. and applied sci. U. Wis., 1982. Mem. Kappa Sigma. Home: 7422 Longmeadow Rd Madison WI 53717-1067 Office: Klodt & Assocs 7422 Longmeadow Rd Madison WI 53717-1067

KLOEPPER, DAVID ALAN, retired management consultant; b. Colby, Kans., Dec. 8, 1945; s. Robert Mayer and Justine (Peterson) K.; m. Evelyn Maria Gritzbach, June 27, 1969. BS in Metallurgy, MIT. Process devel. engr. Grumman Aerospace, Bethpage, N.Y., 1968-72; mgr. svc. engring. Hilti, Inc., Stamford, Conn., 1972-79; nat. sales mgr. F & S Cen. Mfg., Bklyn., 1979-82; v.p. ops. and adminstrn. Imperial Bolt & Mfg. Co., South Plainfield, N.J., 1982-85; nat. sales mgr. Indsl. Bolt & Nut, Irvington, N.J., 1985-86, T.A. & D.A. Troy, Fairfield, N.J., 1986-87; project mgr. Don Aux Assocs., Hasbrouck Heights, NJ, 1987—2001, practice leader, 1992—2001; ret., 2001. Pres. Van Vorst Park Neighborhood Assn., Jersey City, 1981-82; bd. dirs. Los Alamos Concert Assn., 2002-, Citizen Support for Civic Ctr., Inc., 2003-; adv. com. Los Alamos Planning and Zoning Commn., Los Alamos Comprehensive Plan, 2002—03. Republican. Avocations: movies, classical music. Home: 570 Rim Rd Los Alamos NM 87544 E-mail: kloepper@earthlink.net.

KLOER, PHILIP BALDWIN, popular culture critic; b. Honolulu, Sept. 13, 1955; s. Baldwin Ernest and Betty Louise (Burger) K.; m. Heather Ann Windsor, May 14, 1976; 1 child, Amanda Cynthia. BA, Ind. U., 1976. Writer Stillwater (Okla.) News-Press, 1976-78; film critic, columnist Fla. Times-Union, Jacksonville, 1978-85; arts editor Atlanta Constitution, 1985-87, TV critic, 1987—. Contbr. TV Guide, 1990. Recipient Olive Br. award Ctr. for War, Peace & Media, NYU, 1991, finalist Green Eyeshade award Sigma Delta Chi, 1986; named TV Critic of Yr., Nat. TV Movie Festival, 1990, Critic of Yr., Fla. Soc. Newspaper Editors, 1985. Office: Atlanta Constitution 72 Marietta St NW Atlanta GA 30303-2804

KLOESS, LAWRENCE HERMAN, JR., retired lawyer; b. Mamaroneck, N.Y., Jan. 30, 1927; s. Lawrence H. and Harriette Adelia (Holly) K.; m. Eugenia Ann Underwood, Nov. 10, 1931; children: Lawrence H. III, Price Mentzel, Branch Donelson, David Holly. AB, U. Ala., 1954, JD, 1956; grad., Air Command & Staff Coll., 1974, Air War Coll., 1976; grad. Indsl. Coll. of the Armed Forces, Nat. Def. U., 1977. Bar: Ala. 1956, U.S. dist. Ct. (no. dist.) Ala. 1956, U.S. Ct. Appeals (5th cir.) 1957, U.S. Ct. Mil. Appeals 1971, U.S. Supreme Ct. 1971, U.S. Ct. Appeals (11th cir.) 1981. Sole practice, Birmingham, Ala., 1956-60, 62-66; corp. counsel Bankers Fire and Marine Ins. Co., 1961-62; dist. counsel for Ala. Office Dist. Counsel U.S. Dept. Vets. Affairs, Montgomery, 1966-95. Contbr. articles on law to profl. jours. Vice chmn. Salvation Army adv. bd., 1981, mem. bd., 1978-81; mem. nat. conf. bar pres.'s ABA, 1981—; mem. adminstrn. bd. Frazer Meml. United Meth. Ch., 1987-90, 92—; mem. adv. coun. Ret. and Sr. Vol. Program, Montgomery, 1997—; mem. Montgomery Symphony League, 2000—. Col. Judge Adv. Gen. USAFR, 1954-86, ret. Bd. dirs., sec. Air Force Judge Adv. Gen. Sch. Found., 1996—. Decorated Legion of Merit, Meritorious Svc. medal with oak leaf cluster, USAF Commendation medal; named Outstanding Judge Advocate USAFR, 1977, 79. Mem.: ABA (pres. nat. conf. bar 1981—), Wynlakes Residential Homeowners Assn. (bd. dirs), English Speaking Union (bd. dirs. 1997), Ala. Spl. Camp for Children and Adults (bd. dirs. 1999), Svc. Corps of Ret. Execs. Assn. (bd. dirs. 1996—), Farrah Law Soc., Citizens Conf. on Criminal and Juvenile Justice (staff mem. 1974), Citizens Conf. on Ala. Ct. (exec. com., sponsor new jud. article to state constitution 1973), Fed. Bar Assn. (pres. Montgomery chpt. 1973), Montgomery County Bar Assn. (chmn. law day com. 1972, chmn.state bar liason com. 1975, chmn. bd. dirs. 1977, bd. dirs. 1979, chmn. and editor Montgomery County Bar Jour. (ABA Merit award) 1979—80, v.p. 1980, pres. 1981), Ala. Law Found. (trustee), Ala. State Bar Assn. (editl. bd. 1970—82, chmn. law day com. 1973, chmn.citizen edn. com. 1974, chmn. editl. adv. bd. Ala. Lawyer 1975—79, mem. adv. com. CLE 1983, character and fitness com.), Mystic Soc. (krewe of phantom host), Blue-Gray Cols. Assn., Montgomery Country Club, Maxwell-Gunter Officers, Montgomery, Res. Officers Assn. of U.S. (chpt. pres. 1978, state pres. 1982), Ret. Officers Assn. (life), Air War Coll. Alumni Assn. (life), Air Force Ret. Judge Advocate Assn., Capital City Club, The Club, Inc Birmingham, Montgomery Rotary Club (v.p. 1996, pres. 1998), Montgomery Capital Rotary Club (pres. 1979, Paul Harris fellow), Hon. Order Ky. Cols., Theta Chi (Outstanding Alumni award 1976), Sigma Delta Kappa (pres. U. Ala. chpt.). Republican. Home: 7157 Pinecrest Dr Montgomery AL 36117-7413 E-mail: kloess2@aol.com.

KLOHN, EARLE JARDINE, retired engineering company executive, consultant; b. Winnipeg, Man., Can., Aug. 14, 1927; s. August Frank and Florence (McLeod) K.; m. Beryl MacRae, Aug. 8, 1950 (dec. Nov. 19, 1963); children: James Kimberley, Douglas Alan, Barbara Marjorie; m. Lorna Charles, Oct. 2, 1964; 1 child, Michael. BSCE with distinction, U. Alta., Edmonton, Can., 1950, MSCE, 1952. Registered profl. civil engr., Can. Found. engr. O.J. Porter & Co. Ltd., Sacramento, Calif., 1950, R.M. Hardy and Assocs. Ltd., Edmonton, 1951, Klohn Leonoff Ltd., Vancouver, 1952-55, sr. engr., 1955-60, ptnr. Richmond, B.C., Can., 1960, pres., 1970-87, chmn., CEO, 1987-93; pres., CEO Klohn-Crippen Cons. Ltd., Vancouver, B.C., 1988-97, chmn. emeritus, 1997-2000; ret., 2000. Past chmn. Can. Nat. Com. on Large Dams; past mem. com. on tailing dams Internat. Commn. on Large Dams; mem. numerous cons. rev. bds. for earthfill dams; geotech. cons. Revelstoke Dam, Site C Dam, Stikine-Iskut devel. for BC Hydro, numerous others; internat. cons. design and constrn. tailing dams; past chmn. Vancouver Geotech. Group; presenter papers at various seminars, profl. meetings and confs. Contbr. numerous articles to profl. publs. Recipient Alfred A. Raymond award Raymond Internat., 1960, award Vancouver Geotech. Soc., 1988, Legget award Can. Geotech. Soc., 1990, McPartland Meml. medal, 1992, Pub. Paper award Can. Dam Safety Assn., 1995, Meritorious Achievement award Cons. Engrs. of B.C., 2002. Fellow ASCE, Engring. Inst. Can. (past chmn. Vancouver br., Leonard medal 1972), Can. Acad. Engring.; mem. Assn. Cons. Engrs. Can., Can. Inst. Mining and Metallurgy, Assn. Profl. Engrs. B.C. (Meritorious Achievement award 1982), Wash. Soc. Profl. Engrs., Minn. Soc. Profl. Engrs., Yukon Terr. Soc. Prof. Engrs., Alaska Soc. Profl. Engrs., Colo. Soc. Profl. Engrs., Wyo. Soc. Profl. Engrs., Can. Sect. Internat. Soc. Soil Mechanics and Found. Engring., Morgan Creek Go. and Country Club (Surrey, B.C.). Mem. United Ch. Can.

KLONER, ROBERT A. cardiologist, researcher, educator; b. Buffalo, Oct. 8, 1949; s. Philip and Shirley (Miller) K.; m. Judith A. Kloner, July 24, 1977; children: Alissa, Susan. BS, Northwestern U., 1971, PhD, 1974, MD, 1975. Med. house officer Peter Bent Brigham Hosp., Boston, 1975-76, from asst. resident to sr. resident, 1976-78, rsch. clin. fellow in cardiology, 1979; clin. fellow in medicine Harvard Med. Sch., Boston, 1975-78, rsch. fellow in medicine, 1978-79, asst. prof. medicine, 1979-81, assoc. prof. medicine, 1984; prof. medicine Wayne State U., Detroit, 1985-88, U. So. Calif., L.A., 1988—. Dir. rsch. Heart Inst. Hosp. of Good Samaritan, L.A., 1988—. Author: The Beta Virus, 1996, Mind Cure, 1998, Viagra, 1998, The Deity Genes, 2001; editor: The Guide to Cardiology, 1984, 3d edit., 1995; editor Cardiovascular Trials Review, 1996-2003; co-editor: Stunned Mycardium, 1993, Ischemic Preconditioning, 1994; mem. editl. bd. Circulation, Circulation Rsch., Jour. Am. Coll. Cardiology, Am. Jour. Cardiology, Am. Heart Jour., Heart Disease, Heart, Jour. Molecular and Cellular Cardilogy, Am. Jour. Geriat. Cardiology; contbr. over 600 articles and chpts. to profl. jours., books, monographs. Recipient Sheard-Sanford award ASCP, 1976, Merck award, 1975; named highlycited.com Inst. Sci. Info., 2002. Fellow Am. Coll. Cardiology; mem. Am. Heart Assn. (established investigator award 1981-86), N.Y. Acad. Scis., Am. Fedn. Clin. Rsch., Am. Soc. Clin. Investigators, Alpha Omega Alpha. Office: Hosp Good Samaritan Heart Inst 1225 Wilshire Blvd Los Angeles CA 90017 E-mail: rkloner@goodsam.org.

KLONGLAN, GERALD EDWARD, sociology educator; b. Nevada, Iowa, Apr. 1, 1936; s. Bernie R. and Willene Rebecca (Maland) K.; m. Donna Eileen Becvar, June 29, 1960; children: Jason, Suzanne. BS, Iowa State U., 1958, MS, 1962, PhD, 1963. Mem. faculty Iowa State U., Ames, 1963—2001, prof. sociology, 1972—2001, chmn. dept. sociology and anthropology, 1976-90, interim assoc. dean Coll. Sci. and Humanities, 1988-89; asst. dir. Iowa Agr. and Home Econ. Expt. Sta., 1990—2001; assoc. dean nat. programs Coll. Agr., 1995—2001; staff sociologist U.S. Dept. Agr., Coop. State Rsch. Svc., Washington, DC, 1991-93. Evaluation rschr. AID, Malawi, 1967, project cons., Ghana, 1976; ednl. cons. King Saud U., Saudi Arabia, 1981-83, Peking U., People's Republic of China, 1984-85; project implementor U. Zambia, Lusaka, 1982-83; family rsch., Norway, 1988, Czech Republic, 1995; project dir. mgmt. tng. Czech Republic and Slovak Republic, 1991-96; project dir. agr. rsch., Russia, Ukraine, other countries of former Soviet Union, 1992-99. Author: Social Indicators, 1972; (research monographs) Adoption Diffusion of Ideas, 1967; Creating Interorganizational Coordination, 1975, Communication Policy, 1983. Vol. scientist Am. Cancer Soc., 1969—; bd. dirs. Luth. Campus Ministry, Ames, 1972-78, chmn. bd., 1974-76; pres. Bethesda Luth. Ch., Ames, 1994-95. Recipient Wilton Park award Iowa State U., 1983 Mem. Rural Sociol. Soc. (coun. 1974-76, 91-92, v.p. 1977-78, pres. 1985-86), Am. Sociol. Assn. (com. on internat. sociology 1993-96), Midwest Sociol. Soc. (tng. com. 1975-78), Sigma Xi (pres. Iowa State U. chpt. 1983-84). Home: 1622 Maxwell Ave Ames IA 50010-5536 Office: Iowa State U Coll Agr 138 Curtiss Hl Ames IA 50011-0001 E-mail: klonglan@iastate.edu.

KLONSKY, BRUCE GARY, educator; b. N.Y.C., Sept. 30, 1950; s. Sam and Gertrude (Dogin) K. AB in Psychology, Lehman Col., 1971; MA in Psychology, Fordham U., 1973, PhD in Psychology, 1978. Tchg. fellow Fordham U., Bronx, N.Y., 1974-76; vis. asst. prof. W.Va. U., Morgantown, 1978-79; prof. SUNY, Fredonia, 1979—; vis. rsch. assoc. Purdue U., West Lafayette, Ind., 1988-89; vis. scholar Inst. for Rsch. on Human Devel. U. Ill., Urbana, 1988-89; vis. prof. W.Va. U., Morgantown, 1995-96. Cons. editor Genetic, Social, and Gen. Psychology, Jour. Genetic Psychology, Washington, 1984—; cons. Chautauqua Opportunities, Dunkirk, N.Y., 1995—; co-tchr. workshop on aggression, expression and mgmt. Chautauqua County Family Day Care Providers, Fredonia, 1994; vol. counselor SUNY Fredonia Counseling Ctr., 1997—; sport psychology cons. SUNY-Fredonia Varsity Athletic Teams, 1998—; workshop leader on sport psychology for youth sport coaches, Fredonia, 1999. Contbr. chpts. to books, articles to profl. jours. Vol., cons. Fredonia Hotline for Rape and Battering, 1985-87. Recipient rsch. grant SUNY Rsch. Found., 1982, rsch. opportunity award NSF, 1988-89; Evaluation and Assessment grantee U.S. HHS, 1997 99. Mem. APA, Am. Psychol. Soc., Am. Edn. Rsch. Assn., Am. Sociol. Assn., Assn. for Advancement of Applied Sport Psychology (tchr. cert. cons. assn. 2003-), Soc. for Rsch. in Child Devel., Soc. for Advancement of Social Psychology, Assn. for Study of Play, Sigma Xi, Psi Chi. Office: SUNY Psychology Dept Thompson Hall W339 Fredonia NY 14063 E-mail: klonsky@fredonia.edu.

KLOOS, HELMUT, geographer; b. Steinbach, Hessen, Germany, Aug. 9, 1939; s. Karl and Auguste K.; m. Diana Kloos, June 13, 1970; children: Jasmin, Benjamin. BA, Fresno State Coll., 1968; MA, Calif. State U., Fresno, 1974; PhD, U. Calif., Davis, 1977. Rsch. assoc. Inst. of Pathobiology Addis Ababa U., Addis Ababa, Ethiopia, 1972-73, 75-76, assoc. prof., 1983-91; asst. prof. U. Calif., San Francisco, 1978; rschr. Univ. Federal de Minas Gerais, Belo Horizonte, Brazil, 1999—. Vis. prof. Univ. Federal Minas Gerais, Belo Horizonte, 1996-98; cons. Awash Valley Authority, Addis Ababa, 1972-73, WHO, Geneva, 1979, 80, 82, 85, Cambridge U., Ministry of Health, Nairobi, 1985-87; mem. tech. rev. com. U.S. Agy. for Internat. Devel., Cairo, 1990-98. Editor/author: The Ecology of Health in Ethiopia, 1993; compiler/author: (book) Health, Disease, Medicine and Famine in Ethiopia: A Bibliography, 1991. Bd. dirs. Ptnrs. Against HIV/AIDS in Ethiopia. With U.S. Army, 1963-65. Rsch. grantee Edna McConnell Clark Found., N.Y.C., 1978-80. Mem. Ethiopian Am. Found., Ethiopian Pub. Health Assn., Ethiopian Med. Assn., Arbeitsgemeinschaft Ethnomedizin, Med. Geography Specialty Group, Assn. of Am. Geographers. Avocations: skiing, hiking, travel. Office: Univ Calif Parnassus San Francisco CA 94143-0650 E-mail: hk035@cvip.fresno.com.

KLOOSTER, JUDSON, academic administrator, dentistry educator; b. La Combe, Alta., Can., Dec. 24, 1925; s. Henry J. and Evelyn Mae (Eglin) K.; m. Arlene Jean Madsen, Nov. 28, 1948; children: Cherylin Klooster Peach, Lynette Carol Tibbetts, Terrill Ann Klooster McClanahan Hannum. Student, Andrews U., 1942-43, Pacific Union Coll., 1943-44; DDS, U. Pacific, 1947; MMS, Tulane U., 1968. Pvt. practice dentistry, San Francisco, 1947-49, Escondido, Calif., 1949-67; part-time mem. faculty Loma Linda (Calif.) U. Sch. Dentistry, 1956-67, full-time prof. restorative dentistry, 1967—, dir. continuing edn., 1968-72, dean, 1971-94, dean emeritus, 1994—, emeritus prof. dentistry, 1997—. Mem. faculty U. Pacific Sch. Dentistry, 1947-49; cons. USPHS, VA. Treas. Am. Fund for Dental Health, 1987-89, v.p. 1990-91, pres., 1992-93. Lt. Dental Corps USNR, 1953-55. Fellow Am. Coll. Dentists, Internat. Coll. Dentists (councillor); mem. ADA, Calif. Dental Assn. (chmn. coun. dental edn. 1972-75), Tri-County Dental Soc. (ex officio dir. 1971-94, pres.-elect 1978-79, pres. 1979-80), Rotary (pres. San Bernardino S. club 1977-78), Xi Psi Phi. Republican. Mem. Seventh Day Adventist Ch. (elder 1969—). Home: 25131 Crestview Dr Loma Linda CA 92354-3508

KLOOSTER, WILLEM WUBBO, historian; b. Groningen, Netherlands, Sept. 10, 1962; s. Jakob and Doetje Jantina Klooster; m. Aviva Ben-Ur, June 17, 2001. MA, U. Groningen, Netherlands, 1987; PhD, U. Leiden, Netherlands, 1995. Asst. prof. Clark U., Worcester, 2003—. V.p. Forum on European Expansion and Global Interaction, Providence, 2002—. Author: (monographs) Geschiedenis van Albanie; The Dutch in the Americas, 1600-1800; Illicit Riches: Dutch Trade in the Caribbean, 1648-1795; (with Alfred Padula:) The Atlantic World: Essays on Slavery, Migration, and Imagination. Recipient Charles Warren fellowship, 1997, NWO-Talent award, 1996, Alexander O. Vietor Meml. award, 1996, award, John Carter Brown Libr., 1995; fellow, Nat. U. of Ireland, Galway, Ireland, 2002, Fulbright Found., 1996, Centre for the Study of Human Migration and Historical Change. Mem.: Forum on European Expansion and Global Interaction, Soc. for Netherlandic History, Am. Hist. Assn. Office: Clark Univ 950 Main St Worcester MA 01610 Office Fax: 207-780-5571. E-mail: wklooster@clarku.edu.

KLOPACK, KENNETH BARTHON, art educator, artist; b. Chgo., Dec. 31, 1949; s. Barthon R. Klopack and Cecilia L. (Wojtkiewicz) Wojcik; m. Gaye Lee Green, Feb. 12, 1971; children: Kristin, Lauren, Kenneth R. BA in Art Edn., Northeastern Ill. U., 1971, MA in Spl. Edn. Gifted, 1989. Cert. art edn. K-12, Ill.; cert. type 75 adminstrn., Ill. Art educator Funston Elem. Sch. Chgo. Pub. Schs., 1972—; part-time art educator Sch of the Art Inst., Chgo., 1997-99. Tchr. to tchr. presenter Chgo. Found. Edn., 1994—; artist mem. Artists of Rogers Park, Chgo., 1997—2002, Galerie de Hamptons, West Hamptons Beach, L.I., NY, 1994—2000; mem. faculty Peninsula Art Sch., Fish Creek, Wis., 2002—. Author (Randi Stone): Best Classroom Practices, What Award-Winning Teachers Do, 2000; contbr. ; author: Show Off Your Art, 1984; illustrator Show Off Your Art, 1984, artist contbr. Chicago Art Scene, 2000, polit. cartoonist Nadig Newspapers, 1978—, book reviewer Corwin Press, 2002—; one-man shows include Northeaster Ill. U. Libr., 2002. Art adjudicator Old Town Art Fair, Chgo., 2000; art judge Waupaca (Wis.) Art Festival, 2003, Chgo. Art Open, 2003. Recipient Golden Apple award, Golden Apple Found., 1989, Kohl Internat. Tchg. award, Kohl Found., 1993. Mem.: Chgo. Art Inst., Mus. Contemporary Art, Chgo. Artists' Coalition, Ill. Arts Edn. Assn. (Art Educator of Yr. 1996), Ill. Arts Coun., Nat. Arts Edn. Assn. Avocations: running, sports, reading. Home: 4443 N Tripp Ave Chicago IL 60630-4207 E-mail: gkklopack@ameritech.net.

KLOPATEK, JEFFREY MATTHEW, ecology educator; b. Milw., Dec. 5, 1944; s. Raymond Matthew and Clare Louise (Seramur) K.; m. Carole Coe, July 18, 1984; children: Joshua Matthew, Sarah Barbara. BS, U. Wis., Milw., 1971, MS, 1974; PhD, U. Okla., 1978. Cert. sr. ecologist. Rsch. asst. U. Wis., 1971-73, U. Okla., Norman, 1973-76; rsch. ecologist Oak Ridge (Tenn.) Nat. Lab., 1976-81; asst. prof. Ariz. State U., Tempe, 1981-86, assoc. prof. botany, 1986-93, prof. botany, 1993—. Cosn. U.S. EPA, 1988-91, U.S. Dept. Justice, Washington, 1988-90. Editor: Landscape Ecological Analysis, 1999; co-editor: Energy and Ecological Modelling, 1981; contbr. articles to Biol. Conservation, Climate Change, Biogeochemistry Ecological Applications, Plant and Soil, Environ. Conservation, Soil Sci. Soc. Am., Environ. Mgmt., Ecology. 1st lt. U.S. Army, 1966 69. Fulbright scholar, 1990-91, grantee USDA, NSF, U.S. Dept. Energy, U.S. EPA, Nat. Geographic Soc. Mem. Ecol. Soc. Am., Am. Inst. Biol. Scis., Soil Sci. Soc. Am., Internat. Assn. Landscape Ecology, Internat. Soc. Ecological Model.

KLOPFENSTEIN, REX CARTER, electrical engineer; b. Pittsfield, Mass., Mar. 3, 1938; s. Glenn A. and Jasmine V. (Carter) Klopfenstein; m. Linda Gilgore, Oct. 6, 1962; children: Mark W., Eric G. BSEE, U. Conn., 1959; MEE, Syracuse U., 1963. Engr. GE, Syracuse, N.Y., 1959-63; lab. mgr. Melpar Divsn. E Sys., Falls Church, Va., 1963-70; mgr. hardware engring. Logicon Inc., Fairfax, Va., 1977-78; software and test mgr. Acuity Sys. Inc., Reston, Va., 1978-81; engring. mgr. AMF Electronic Rsch. Lab., Sterling, Va., 1981-82; tech. staff The MITRE Corp., McLean, Va., 1970-77, lead engr., 1982-96, Mitretek Sys., Inc., McLean, Va., 1996—. Sec. tech. com. X3K5 Am. Nat. Standards Inst., Washington, 1992-94. Co-author: Microcomputer Design and Application, 1977; contbr. articles to profl. jours. Mem. Rep. Nat. Com., chmn. honor roll, 1997. Named Engr. of Yr., D.C. Coun. Engring. and Archtl. Socs., 2000. Fellow: IEEE (No. Va. sect. sec. 1991—92, vice-chmn., treas. 1992—93, chmn. 1993—94, nat. area coun. vice-chmn. 1994—95, chmn. 1995—96, web site mgr. 1997—, editor 1998—99, bd. dirs. 2002—, assoc. editor, Third Millennium medal 2000), Washington Acad. Scis. (bd. mgrs. 1996—98, pres.-elect 1998, pres. 1999—2000); mem.: Assn. for Computing Machinery, Chi Phi, Tau Beta Pi. Avocation: photography. Home: 4224 Worcester Dr Fairfax VA 22032-1140 Office: Mitretek Systems Inc 3150 Fairview Pk Dr S Mc Lean VA 22042 4519

KLOPFLEISCH, STEPHANIE SQUANCE, social services agency administrator; m. Randall Klopfleisch; children: Elizabeth, Jennifer, Matthew. BA, Pomona Coll., 1962; MSW, UCLA, 1966. Social worker Los Angeles County, 1963-67, program dir. day care, vol. svcs., 1968-71; divsn. chief children's svcs. Dept. Pub. Social Svcs., Los Angeles County, 1971-73, dir. bur. social svcs., 1973-79; chief dep. dir. dept. cmty. svcs. Los Angeles County, 1980-96, dir., 1996-2001. With Area 10 Devel. Disabilities, 1981-82; bd. dirs. L.A. Fed. Emergency Mgmt. Act, 1985-91, pres., 1987; bd. dirs. L.A. Shelter Partnership, Pomona Coll. Assocs., 1988—. Mem. Calif. Commn. on Family Planning, 1976-79; chmn. L.A. Commn. on Children's Instns., 1977-78; bd. dirs. United Way Info., 1978-79; chmn. L.A. County Internat. Yr. of Child Commn., 1978-79; bd. govs Sch. Social Welfare, UCLA, 1981-84; bd. dirs. Calif. Soc. Welfare Archives, 1999—, pres.2002--; mem. Brentwood Symphony, 1999—. Mem. NASW, L.A. Philharm. Affiliates, Soroptimist Internat. (bd. dirs. 1989—, pres. L.A. chpt. 1993).

KLOPMAN, GILLES, chemistry educator; b. Brussels, Feb. 24, 1933; came to U.S., 1965; s. Alge and Brana (Brendel) Klopman; m. Malvina Pantiel, Sept. 5, 1957. BA, Athenee d'Ixelles, Belgium, 1952; lic. chemistry, U. Brussels, 1956, D in Chemistry, 1960. Rsch. scientist Cyanamid European Rsch. Inst., Geneva, 1960-67; postdoctoral fellow U. Tex., 1964-65; assoc. prof. Case Western Res. U., Cleve., 1967-69; prof. chemistry Case We. Res. U., Cleve., 1969—, chmn. dept., 1981—86, interim dean sci. and math., 1986—88, C.F. Mabery prof. of rsch., chmn. dept., 1988—2003, C.F. Mabery prof. rsch. emeritus, 2003—. V.p. Biofor, Ltd., PA, 1986-95; pres. Discovery Software Inc., 1991-93, Multicase, Inc., 1995—. Author: All Valence Electrons SCF Calculations, 1970, Chemical Reactivity and Reaction Paths, 1974; contbr. articles to profl. jours. Recipient Kahlbaum prize Swiss Chem. Soc., 1971; grantee NSF, NIH, EPA, PRF, ONR. Mem. AAUP, Am. Chem. Soc. (Morley medal 1993), Brit. Chem. Soc., Belgium Chem. Soc., Sigma Xi. Home: 22 Hyde Park Cleveland OH 44122-7536 Office: Case Western Res U 10900 Euclid Ave Cleveland OH 44106-1712 E-mail: gxk6@po.cwru.edu.

KLOPPENBERG, LISA A. law educator; b. L.A., Feb. 27, 1962; d. Edwin Francis and Angeline Stella K.; m. Mark Robert Zunich, Apr. 8, 1989; children: Nicholas Steven, Timothy Sean, Kellen Sun-Hee. Diploma (hon.), U.. Kent, Canterbury, Eng., 1983; BA magna cum laude, U. So. Calif., 1984, JD, 1987. Bar: Calif. 1987, DC 1988. Editor-in-chief So. Calif. Law Rev., L.A., 1986-87; law clk. to Hon. Dorothy Nelson U.S. Ct. Appeals (9th cir.), Pasadena, Calif., 1987-88; assoc. Kaye, Scholer, Fierman, Hays & Handler, Washington, 1988-92; law prof. U. Oreg., Eugene, 1992—; dean and law prof. U Dayton, Dayton, Ohio, 2001—. Vis. prof. U. San Diego, Trinity Coll., Dublin, Magdalen Coll., Oxford, Eng.; mem. local rules com. U.S. Dist. Ct., Oreg., 1995—. Author: Oregon Rules of Civil Procedure: 1994 Handbook, Oregon Rules of Civil Procedure: 1995-96 Handbook, Oregon Rules of Civil Procedure: 1997-98 Handbook, Oregon Rules of Civil Procedure: 1999-2000 Handbook, Playing it Safe, 2001; contbr. articles, revs. to profl. jours. Bd. dirs. Amigos de los Sobrevivientes, Eugene, 1993-96, Relief Nursery, Eugene, 1999-2001; pro bono lawyer Guatemalan Human Rights Commn. USA, Washington, 1990-92. Mem. ABA (site evaluator), Am. Judicature Soc., Lane County Bar Assn. (bd. dirs. 1999-2001), Eugene Inn of Ct. (sec. 1998—), Order of the Coif. Democrat. Roman Catholic. Office: U Dayton Sch Law 300 College Park Dayton OH 45469

KLOR DE ALVA, JORGE, education company executive; JD, U. Calif., Berkeley; PhD in History/Anthropology, U. Calif., Santa Cruz. Prof. anthropology Princeton (N.J.) U., 1989-94; prof. ethnic studies and anthropology U. Calif., Berkeley, 1994-96; v.p. bus. devel. Apollo Group Inc., 1996-98; pres. U. Phoenix, 1998—2001; chmn., CEO Apollo Internat., Inc., 2000—. Bd. dirs. Apollo Group Inc., 1991—, U. Phoenix, 1991—. Co-author: (novels) Interethnic Images: Discourse and Practice in the New World, 1993. Office: Apollo Internat Inc 4635 E Elwood St Phoenix AZ 85040-1958

KLOS, JEROME JOHN, lawyer, director; b. La Crosse, Wis., Jan. 17, 1927; s. Charles and Edna S. (Wagner) K.; m. Mary M. Hamilton, July 26, 1958; children— Bryant H., Geoffrey W. BS, U. Wis., 1948, JD, 1950. Bar: Wis. 1950. Pres. Klos, Flynn and Papenfuss, La Crosse, 1950—. Bd. dirs. Union State Bank, West Salem, Wis. Mem. LaCrosse County Bd., 1957-74, vice chmn., 1972 74; pub. adminstr. La Crosse County, 1962-73, bd. dirs. West Salem Area Growth, Inc., La Crosse Area Growth, Inc.; trustee Sander and McKinly Scholarship Funds of West Salem Sch. Dist. Fellow Am. Coll. Real Estate Lawyers, Am. Coll. Probate Counsel, Wis. Law Found.; mem. Wis. Bar Assn., Elks, KC. Home: 346 N Leonard St West Salem WI 54669-1238 Office: 800 Lynn Tower Bldg La Crosse WI 54601 E-mail: kfpatts@aol.com.

KLOSE, KEVIN, broadcast executive; b. Toronto, Ont., Can., Sept. 1, 1940; came to U.S., 1942; s. Willard and Virginia Taylor K.; m. Eliza Kellogg, Sept. 1964; children: Nina, Brennan, Chandler. BA in English Lit., Harvard U., 1962; DHL (hon.), Union Coll., 2000. Staff reporter Washington Post, 1967-77, Moscow bur. chief, 1977-81, midwest corr., 1983-87, deputy nat. editor, 1987-91; dir. Radio Free Europe/Radio Liberty, Munich, 1992-94, pres. Prague, Czech Republic, 1994-97; dir. U.S. Internat. Broadcasting Bur., Washington, 1997-98; assoc. dir. U.S. Info. Agy., Washington, 1997-98; pres., CEO Nat. Pub. Radio, Washington, 1998—, bd. dir. ind. sector, 2002—. Bd. dirs. Eurasia Found. Independent Sector, Washington; trustee Arthur F. Burns Fellowship Program, 1999-2002; mem. Internat. Rsch. & Exchs. Bd., Washington, 1999— Author: Russia and The Russians, 1984; co-author: I Will Survive, 1962, The Typhoon Shipments, 1974, Surprise! Surprise!, 1977, Freedom's Child, 1987. With USN, 1962—64. Woodrow Wilson Nat. fellow, 1983-87. Mem. Harvard Club N.Y. Avocations: skiing, sailing. Office: Nat Pub Radio 635 Massachusetts Ave NW Washington DC 20001-3753

KLOSINSKI, DEANNA DUPREE, medical educator, consultant; b. Goshen, Ind., Dec. 28, 1941; d. George C. and Gertrude (Todd) Dupree; m. William L. Collins, Jan. 2000; children from previous marriage: Elizabeth, John, Robert, Lara. BS, Ind. State U., 1964; MS, Purdue U., 1972; PhD, Wayne State U., 1990. Cert. med. technologist. Lab. specialist Home Hosp., Lafayette, Ind., 1968-74; program dir. Ind. Vocat. Tech. Coll., Lafayette, 1968-75; clin. asst. prof. Oakland U., Rochester, Mich., 1985-97; med. technologist South Bend (Ind.) Med. Found., 1959-68; cons. Delta Initiatives, Bloomfield Hills, Mich., 1999—. Program dir., asst. adminstr. William Beaumont Hosp., Royal Oak, Mich., 1979—96, chair adv. com. Schs. Allied Health, 1990—92, 1996; adj. assoc. prof. Mich. State U., East Lansing, 1991—96, 2000—; asst. prof. Sch. Medicine Wayne State U., Detroit, 1996—98, adj. asst. prof. Coll. Pharmacy and Allied Health, 1999—2000; cons., dir. benchmarking svcs. Chi Lab. Sys., Ann Arbor, Mich., 1998; adj. online instr. Baker Coll., Owosso, Mich., 2001—; cons. in field. Co-author: (videotape) Routine Venipunture, 1989, (book) Molecular Biology and Pathology, 1993, Clinical Laboratory Science Education and Management, 1997; author: (videotape) Blood Collection: The Difficult Draw, 1992; contbg. editor: (book) Outline Review of Clinical Laboratory Science, 2001. Websit chair Women's Com. for Hospice Care, 2003—; mem. pastoral coun. St. Hugo Cath. Ch., Bloomfield Hills, 1991—94. Named Outstanding Bus. Person, Mich. Coun. Vocat., 1992, Mich. Clin. Lab. Scientist, 1993; recipient Donna M. Duberg Mentorship award, Mich., 1997; Rsch. grantee, William Beaumont Hosp., 1989—90. Mem.: Wayne State U. Alumni Assn. (leadership devel. com. 2001—, dir., v.p. comm. 2003—), Mich. Soc. Clin. Lab. Sci. (treas. 1984—86, 1988—92, pres. 1995—96, past pres. 1996—97, ann. meeting gen. chair 1996—97), Internat. Fedn. Clin. Chemistry (edn. and mgmt. divsn. com. programs and courses 1996—98), Assn. Women in Sci., Am. Soc. Clin. Lab. Sci. (mem. edn. sci. assembly, co-chairperson clin. lab. edn. conf. 1991, bd. dirs. edn. and rsch. fund 1996—98), Am. Assn. Clin. Chemistry (mem. mgmt. edn. group 1995—98, mgmt. scis. divsn. com. 1997, faculty, mgmt. course com. 1997), Am. Soc. Clin. Pathologists (chmn. tech. sample 1984—93, editor Profl. Perspectives 1993—94, mem. editl. bd. Lab. Medicine 1993—96, Technologist of the Yr. 1994, diplomate in lab. mgmt.), Sigma Xi (sec. Oakland U. chpt. 1994—96), Delta Gamma Regional (4), Delta Gamma Alumnae (treas. 1978—81, v.p. 1991—93, pres. 1993—95, Region IV housing dir. 2003—, women's com. for hospice care, website chair 2003—), Alpha Mu Tau (scholar 1985, 1987, 1990). Office: Delta Initiatives 715 Brockmoor Ln Bloomfield Hills MI 48304-1416 E-mail: ddkdeltai@aol.com.

KLOSINSKI, LEONARD FRANK, mathematics educator; b. Michigan City, Ind., July 16, 1938; s. Frank and Helen (Podgorna) K. BS, U. Santa Clara, 1961; MA, Oreg. State U., 1963. Programmer NASA Ames Rsch. Ctr., Mountain View, Calif., 1963; instr. math. Santa Clara (Calif.) U., 1964-68, asst. prof., 1968-76, assoc. prof., 1976—. Dir. Nat. Sci. Found. Insts., 1969-74; mng. editor, treas. Fibonacci Assn., 1975-80, v.p., 1980-83; v.p., Fibonacci Assn., 1980-83; dir. William Lowell Putnam Math. Competition, 1978—. Author: Santa Clara Silver Anniversary Contest Book/ Problems and Solutions of the University of Santa Clara High School Mathematics Contests, 1985, Students' Solutions Manual to Accompany Lynn E. Garner's Calculus and Analytical Geometry, 1988; editor: William Lowell Putnam Mathematical Competition Problems and Solutions, 1965-84, 1985, From Galileo (1939) to Santa Clara (2001), 2001; contbr. articles to profl. jours. Mem. Math. Assn. Am. (coun. on competitions 1992—, Putnam prize com. 1975—, adv. bd. Math. Horizons 1993-2000, sec.-treas. No. Calif. sect. 1979-2000, vice-chair No. Calif. sect. 1999, chair No. Calif. sect. 2000, program chair No. Calif. sect. 2001, bd. govs. 2002--, award for disting. coll. or univ. tchg. math. No. Calif. sect. 1999, Deborah and Franklin Tepper Haimo award for Disting. Coll. or Univ. Tchg. of Math. 2001). Democrat. Roman Catholic. Avocation: art collecting. Office: Santa Clara U Math Dept Santa Clara CA 95053-0001

KLOSK, IRA DAVID, lawyer; b. N.Y.C., Nov. 9, 1932; s. Isidore and Freda (Braunstein) K. B.A., CCNY, 1955; LL.B., Bklyn. Law Sch., 1957. Bar: N.Y. 1958. Sole practice, Bklyn., 1958-81; sr. ptnr. firm Klosk and Ray, Mineola, N.Y., 1981— . Pres. Herricks Citizens Com. Better Schs., N.Y., 1970; mem. Herricks Citizens Budget Adv. Com., 1970, Herricks Sch. Bd., 1971-74; v.p. Hometown Party Mineola, 1979. N.Y. State scholar CCNY, 1951; recipient Richard R. Bowker Meml. award CCNY, 1954, Kupferman-Helm award, 1955. Hon. life mem. N.Y. PTA.

KLOSK, RUSSELL MARTIN, human resources executive; b. N.Y.C., Sept. 23, 1969; s. Michael J. Klosk and Laurie Beth (Wendel) Klosk-Gazzale; m. Carolyn E. Ford. BA, U. So. Calif., 1991. Cert. profl. project lead, Peoplesoft, sr. profl. human resources. Acct. exec., exec. recruiter Culver Personnel Svcs., Sherman Oaks, Calif., 1991—94; asst. mgr., exec. recruiter Ajilon, Burbank, 1994—95; corp. recruite, staffing Strategic Support Unit Electronic Data Sys., Florham Park, NJ, 1996—97; mgr. profl. staffing Price Waterhouse Coopers, LLP, N.Y.C., 1997-98; sr. human resources/reg. recruiting mgr. Microsoft Corp., Washington, 1998; dir. corp. recruiting Gannett Co., Inc., McLean, Va., 1998-99; prin. cons. Human Capital Strategists, Fairfax, Va., 1999—2002; dir. human resources/staffing NJVC LLC, Vienna, Va., 2002—. Career transition advisor cmty. outreach YMCA, Bernardsville, N.J., 1997; chmn. Fairfax County Transp. and Land Use Com., 2002—; v.p. Middleridge Civic Assn., 2003—. Event coord. Rep. Party Somerset County, Somerville, N.J., 1996, 97, Arlington County, Va., 1998-2000, Fairfax County (Va.) Rep. Party, 2000—; mem. Project SAVE, Project SAME, Middleridge Civic Assn., 2000—; v.p., 2003—; mem. legis. subcom. chmn. Fairfax County Transp. and Land Use Com., 2002-2003. Mem. Internat. Inst. Human Resources, Human Resources Exec. Mgmt. Assn., Am. Mgmt. Assn., Soc. Human Resources Mgmt., Human Resources Assn. Nat. Capital Area (membership chmn. 2002—), U. So. Calif. Nations Capital Alumni Club (v.p.), U. So. Calif. Gen. Alumni Assn., Magnolia Lodge (Master Mason), Phi Alpha Delta, Kappa Alpha Order, Order of Omega. Avocations: scuba diving, softball, golf, travel, motorcycling, reading. Office: NJVC LLC 8614 Westwood Ctr Dr Vienna VA 22182 Personal E-mail: russell.klosk@alumni.usc.edu.

KLOSKA, RONALD FRANK, manufacturing company executive; b. Grand Rapids, Mich., Oct. 24, 1933; s. Frank B. and Catherine (Hilaski) K.; m. Mary F. Minick, Sept. 7, 1957; children: Kathleen Ann, Elizabeth Marie, Ronald Francis, Mary Josephine, Carolyn Louise. Student, St. Joseph Sem., Grand Rapids, Mich., 1947-53; PhB, U. Montreal, Que., Can., 1955; MBA, U. Mich., 1957. Staff acct. Coopers & Lybrand, Niles, Mich., 1957, staff to sr. acct., 1960—63; treas. Skyline Corp., Elkhart, Ind., 1963, v.p., treas., 1964—67, exec. v.p. fin., 1967—74, pres., 1974—85, pres., chief ops. officer, 1985—91, vice chmn., chief adminstrn. officer, 1991—94, vice chmn., chief adminstrn. officer, sec., 1994—95, vice chmn., dep. CEO, chief adminstrn. officer, 1995—98, vice chmn., CEO, chief adminstrn. officer, 1998—2001, dir., cons., 2001—. With U.S. Army, 1957—60. Mem. Mich. Soc. CPAs, Ind. Soc. CPAs, South Bend Country Club. Roman Catholic. Home: 1329 E Woodside St South Bend IN 46614-1455 Office: Skyline Corp 2520 Bypass Rd Elkhart IN 46514-1584

KLOSKOWSKI, VINCENT JOHN, JR., educational consultant, writer, educator; b. Sept. 30, 1934; s. Vincent and Mary Kloskowski; m. Gerri K.; 1 child, Vincent John III. B.S. with honors, Seton Hall U., N.J., 1960, M.A., 1971; postgrad. Newark State Coll., 1960-62, Trenton (N.J.) State Coll., 1961-64; M.Ed. (Asian Found. scholar), Rutgers U., 1964; Ph.D., Philathea Coll., Western Ont., 1971; postdoctorate Harvard U., 1975, Appalachian State U., 1975; Ed.D. in Ednl. Adminstrn., Nova S.E. U., Fla., 1976. Substitute tchr. South River (N.J.) High Sch., 1958-60; tchr. Madison Twp. (N.J.) Pub. Schs., 1960-64; co-adj. mem. staff Rutgers U., 1961-64; remedial specialist North Brunswick (N.J.) Public Schs., 1964-65; vice prin. Jamesburg (N.J.) High Sch., 1965-66; asst. supt., child study coord., curriculum coord., fed. coord. urban funding Pub. Schs. Jamesburg, 1966-77, prin. elem., jr. high sch. and spl. edn. bldg., 1966-77; ednl. specialist N.J. Dept. Edn., 1977-91; cons. to para-profls. Mercer County Community Coll., Trenton, 1972; pvt. practice ednl. counseling, 1973—; speaker ann. conf. on incoming students Seton Hall U., Jamesburg Pub. Schs. In-Service Program, Middlesex County Child Study Team, PTA Jamesburg Pub. Schs., 1970, 72, Middlesex County Curriculum Council, East Brunswick Vocat. Sch., Holy Innocence Soc., Avenel, N.J., St. Catherines PTA, Clayton, N.J.; panelist child study devel. Madison Twp. Pub. Schs.; participant Internat. Reading Assn., Somerville, N.J., 42d Summer Sch. Conf. Sch. Adminstrn., Harvard U., Scott Foresman New Programs in Reading, Freehold, N.J., Ann. Reading Inst., Rutgers U., McGraw-Hill-Sullivan Reading Program, Hightstown, N.J., use of para-profls. in pub. schs. N.J. State Dept.-Middlesex County Community Coll., Edison; cons. Setting Up Pvt. Spl. Edn. Facility, South Brunswick, Ednl. Cons. Service N.J., 1971—, reading techniques for para-profl. Mercer County Community Coll., Trenton, 1971; merit badge counselor Boy Scouts Am.; mem. alumni resource bank counsel, mem. staff and adv. bd. transition program Rutgers U. Coll. Kettering Found. fellow. Mem. MENSA, Acad. Fellows (speaker nat. confs.), Am. Assn. Sch. Adminstrs., N.J. Assn. Sch. Prins., NEA (life), N.J., Middlesex County, Jamesburg edn. assns., Nat. Ednl. Assn. Sch. Prins., N.J. Classroom Tchrs. Assn., N.J. Assn. Retarded Children, Internat., N.J. reading assns., Middlesex County Audio-Visual Assn., Am. Soc. Notaries, Phi Delta Kappa, Alpha Epsilon Mu, Kappa Delta Pi. Author: Didacticism-Montessori and the Special Child, 1969; Amish School System and Special Education; asst. editor Seton Hall U. Newspaper and Coll. Yearbook, 1959-60; book reviewer Narod Polski, nat. Polish-Am. newspaper, 1976— . Home and Office: Hart Brook Farm PO Box 194 Hampshire Rd Brownfield ME 04010-0194

KLOSSON, MICHAEL, foreign service officer; b. Washington, Aug. 22, 1949; s. Boris Hansen and Harriet Fraser (Cheston) K.; m. Bonita L. Bender; children: Emily C., Karen Lee Bender. BA, Hamilton Coll., 1971; M.P.A., Woodrow Wilson Sch., Princeton U., 1974; MA, Princeton U., 1975. Asst. lectr. Hong Kong Baptist Coll., 1971-72; commd. fgn. service officer Dept. State, 1975, staff asst. to asst. sec. of state for East Asian affairs, 1975-77; Chinese Lang. trainee Fgn. Service Inst., Taichung, Taiwan, 1977-78; polit. officer Am. embassy, Taipei, Taiwan, 1978-80; polit. officer office Japanese affairs Dept. State, Washington, 1980-81, spl. asst. to sec. of state, 1981-83; Pearson fellow U.S. Senate, 1983-84; dep. dir. for polit. affairs Office European Security and Polit. Affairs Dept. State, Washington, 1984-87, dir., secretariat staff, 1987-90; dep. chief of mission Am. Embassy, Stockholm, 1990-92, chargé d'affaires, 1992-93, charge d'affaires The Hague, 1993-94, dep. chief of mission, 1994-96; dep. asst. sec. of state for legis. affairs Dept. of State, Washington, 1996-99; cons. genl. U.S. Consulate, Hong Kong, 1999—2002; amb. Republic of Cyprus, 2002—. Herbert H. Lehman fellow, 1971, Winston Churchill fellow, 1972-74. Mem. Am. Fgn. Svc. Assn., Phi Beta Kappa. Home: Psc 815 Fpo AE 09836

KLOSTER, SHERRY ANN, language educator; b. Carthage, N.Y., Feb. 5, 1972; d. John Robert and Cora Jane Kloster. BA in Multi-Lang., St. Lawrence U., 1994; MEd, SUNY, Potsdam, 2000. French tchr. Clifton-Fine H.S., Star Lake, NY, 1996—97, Carthage (N.Y.) H.S., 1997—2001, Beaver River Ctrl. Sch., Beaver Falls, NY, 2001—. Recipient Premier Degré, U. Mont St. Aignan, France, 1992, Cert. de Langue, École des Langues à Trois-Pistoles, Que., Can., 2000; scholar Augsburg North County scholar, St. Lawrence U., Canton, N.Y., 1990. Mem.: Am. Tchrs. French (pres. Pays du Nord chpt. 1999—2002), N.Y. State Assn. Fgn. Lang. Tchrs. (study scholar 2000). Avocations: reading, writing, art, music, gardening.

KLOTE, JAMES DENVER, financial consultant; b. Detroit, June 9, 1964; s. James Denver Klote Sr. and Gloria Ann DeVos; m. Mary McNerney, Apr. 12, 1999. BA, Capital U., 1987. Divsn. dir. United Way, Columbus, Ohio, 1987-90; sr. cons. Ward Dreshman & Reinhardt Inc., Worthington, Ohio, 1990-97, pres., 1997-98, James D. Klote & Assocs. Inc., Bethesda, Md., 1998—. Cons. Va. State Golf Assn., Richmond, 1997-98. Vol. Ark. Rep. Party, Little Rock, 1994-96; candidate U.S. Ho. of Reps., 1996; bd. dirs. Wesley Sem. Found. Mem. Nat. Soc. Fundraising Execs., Army and Navy Club (Washington). Episcopalian. Avocations: investing, boating, golf. Home: 1413 Grady Randall Ct Mc Lean VA 22101 Office: James D Klote & Assocs Inc 6905 Rockledge Dr Ste 600 Bethesda MD 20817-1878

KLOTH, CAROLYN, meteorologist; b. Lakewood, Ohio, Apr. 22, 1954; d. James Albert and Marian Lucille (Fiske) K. BS in Meteorology, Fla. State U., 1976; MS in Meteorology, U. Okla., 1980. Lic. pvt. pilot. Meteorologist intern Nat. Weather Svc., Louisville, 1980-82; meteorologist Nat. Severe Storms Forecast Ctr., Kansas City, 1982-95, Aviation Weather Ctr., Kansas City, 1995—. Part-time student scientist, coop. student Nat. Severe Storms Lab., Norman, Okla., 1977-80. Mem. Nat. Weather Assn. (Aviation Meteor. award 2000, co-chmn. aviation weather com. 1997-2002, v.p. 2002), Nat. Weather Svc. Employees Orgn. (sec. Kansas City chpt. mid 1980s), Am. Meteorol. Soc., 99s Internat. Women Pilots Orgn., Aircraft Owners and Pilots Assn., Am. Air Mus. in Britain (founding mem.), Fla. State U. Alumni Assn., U. Okla. Alumni Assn. Democrat. Avocations: gardening, needlework, reading, history. Office: Aviation Weather Ctr 7220 NW 101st Ter Rm 105 Kansas City MO 64153-2371

KLOTMAN, ROBERT HOWARD, music educator; b. Cleve., Nov. 22, 1918; s. Louis Klotman and Pearl (Warshawsky) Kaplan; m. Phyllis Helen Rauch, Apr. 4, 1943; children: Janet Lynn, Paul Evan. BS in Music Edn., Ohio No. U., 1940; MA in Music, Case-Western Res. U., 1950; EdD, Columbia U., 1956; MusD (hon.), Ohio No. U., 1984. Supr. music pub. schs., Dola, Ohio, 1940-42; tchr. instrumental, vocal music pub. schs. Euclid, Ohio, 1942, 46; tchr. instrumental music pub. schs. Cleveland Heights, Ohio, 1946-59; dir. music edn. pub. schs. Akron, Ohio, 1959-63; divisional dir. music edn. pub. schs. Detroit, 1963-69; prof., chmn. dept. music edn. Ind. U., Bloomington, 1969-83, prof. emeritus, 1987—. Vis. prof. Shanghai Conservatory of Music, 1985, U. Alta., Edmonton, Can., summer 1991; guest lectr. U. Bar-Ilan, Israel, 1984; ednl. dir. firm Scherl & Roth (string importers), Cleve., 1956-70; mem. adv. bd. Contemporary Music Project, Ford Found., 1964-65; ednl. cons. Summy-Birchard Co. (music pubs.); mem. bicentennial com. J. C. Penney Co., 1974-76. Condr., Akron Youth Symphony Orch., 1959-63, Oak Park (Ill.) Symphony, 1967-69, Bloomington Youth Symphony Orch., 1969-75, Terre Haute Youth Symphony, 1992, Great Lake Music Camp Orch., 1982-96; author: Learning to Teach Through Playing: String Techniques and Pedagogy, 1971, The School Music Administrator and Supervisor: Catalysts for Change in Music Education, 1973, Teaching Strings, 1988, 2d. edit. 1996, (with others) Humanities Through the Black Experience, Foundations of Music Education, 1983, 2d edit., 1988; co-author: Administrating and Supervising Music, 1991; contbg. author: Ency. of Edn., 1971; editor: Orch. News, 1959-70; mem. editorial bd. Music Educators Jour., 1962-64, Instrumentalist, 1974-91; editor (with others) Scheduling Music Classes, 1968; editor, contbg. author: Music Performance Trust Funds Guide; composer: Action with Strings, 1962, Renaissance Suite, 1964, String Literature for Expanding Technique, 1973. Bd. dirs., sec. Ind. U. Credit Union, 1974-87; chmn. ednl. com. Chamber Music Am., 1993-95. With inf. AUS, 1942-46, ETO, PTO. Recipient citation Nat. Assn. Negro Musicians Inc., 1966, citation Black Music Caucas, 1978, Outstanding Hoosier Musician award, 1986, Disting. Service award Am. String Tchrs. Assn., 1987, Sagamore of the Wabash Govs. award, 1991. Mem. Chamber Music Am. (chair edn. com. 1993-95), Am. String Tchrs. Assn. (pres. 1962-64, dir. pubs. 1985-94, chmn. past pres. coun. 1998-2000), Music Educators Nat. Conf. (chmn. commn. on tchr. edn. 1968-72, pres. 1976-78, Disting. Svc. award 1989, chmn. Hall of Fame com. 1996-2002), Rotary, Phi Mu Alpha Sinfonia, Phi Delta Kappa. Democrat. Jewish. Avocations: tennis, swimming, reading mystery novels. Home: 1234 Fenbrook Ln Bloomington IN 47401-4285 Office: Ind U Sch Music Bloomington IN 47405 E-mail: Klotman@indiana.edu.

KLOTSCHE, CHARLES MARTIN, real estate development company executive, photographer, writer, financial columnist; b. Milw., Jan. 30, 1941; s. J.M. and Roberta; m. Christine Klotsche, Feb. 13, 1972; children: Lyna, Kelly, Kay. BA in Econs., Babson Coll., 1962; postgrad., U. Wis., Madison, 1963—64; grad., NY Inst. Finance, 1965; MBA in Fin., U. Wis., Milw., 1968. Account exec. Harris-Upham and Co., 1963-65; chmn. bd. First Equity Corp., 1980—; pres. N.Am. Yachtshares, Inc., 1981—, Pan Am. Publs., Inc., 1982—, Trans Pacific Investments, Inc., 1986—; chmn. bd., CEO Klotsche Properties, Inc., 1983—; pres., CEO Pacific Continental Holdings, Inc., 1992—, Blue Moon Charter Co., 1992—; CEO Pan Am. Press, Inc., 1996—. Adv. dir. Bank of Santa Fe; bd. dirs. Visa Internat. Bank, Granada; lectr. Marquette U., 1967, Babson Coll., 1991, U. Calif., Irvine, 1992, Santa Monica Coll., 1993, The Explorers Club, 2001, Barnes and Noble Bookstores, 2001-2003, Four Arts Soc., 2003. Author: The Encumbered Perceptive and the Intrepid, 1978, The Real Estate Revolution, 1979, Real Estate Investing, A Practical Guide to Wealth Building Secrets, 1980, Real Estate Syndications, the Complete Handbook, 1983, Real Estate Development and Fin. Handbook, 1986, The 49th Vibration, 1989, Color Vibrational Healing, 1993, Omega Point, 1993, Delta Raven Four, 1994, The Silent Victims, 1997, Continents in the Mist, 1997 (screenplays) Capture, 1996, Provenduce, 1997, (travel books) Journeys, 1999, Crossings, 2000, Passages, 2002, Travels with Charlie, 2003; travel writer Christian Sci. Monitor, 1988, Gannet and Cox Newspapers; featured in numerous profl. and popular mag. Bd. dirs. N.Mex. Spl. Olympics for Mentally Retarded, Orch. Santa Fe, Santa Fe Assn. Retarded Citizens, St. Elizabeth Shelter; pres. Santa Fe Bus. Cmty. for Arts, 1986—, Palm Beach Sailing for the Disadvantaged, Inc. Served with Officer Corps USMC, 1964-67. Recipient 3 nat. awards for excellence Nat. Assn. Homebuilders; featured on NBC Evening News, Dateline, Hardcopy. Mem. US Mortgage Brokers Assn., Nat. Assn. Realtors, Fla. Assn. Realtors, Urban Land Inst., N.Mex. Gen. Contractors Assn., Rocky Mountain Outdoor Writers and Photographers Assn., Internat. Assn. Resort Developers, Timesharing Internat., Rotary, Gentlemen of the Garden Soc., Circumnavigators Club Internat., Palm Beach Sailing Club, Palm Beach Yacht Club, Southshore Yacht Club, Milw. Athletic Club, Palm Beach Pundits Club, Sons of Civil War Vets. Club, Miami Press Club, Palm Beach Maritime Mus., The Lord's Place, Sierra Club, Audubon Soc., Sci. Mus. of Palm Beach, Mental Health Assn. of Palm Beach, Arthur Marshall Found., Miami Internat. Press Club, Hospice of Palm Beach County. Republican. Lutheran. Office: PO Box 2603 Palm Beach FL 33480-2603 E-mail: panamericanpress@aol.com.

KLOTT, DAVID LEE, lawyer; b. Vicksburg, Miss., Dec. 10, 1941; s. Isadore and Dorothy (Lipson) Klott; m. Maren J. Randrup, May 25, 1975. BBA summa cum laude, Northwestern U., 1963; JD cum laude, Harvard U., 1966. Bar: Calif. 1966, U.S. Ct. Claims 1968, U.S. Supreme Ct. 1971, U.S. Tax Ct. 1973, U.S. Ct. Appeals (fed. cir.) 1982. Ptnr. Pillsbury Winthrop, San Francisco, 1966—. Mem. tax adv. group to sub-chpt. C J and K, Am. Law Inst.; instr. Calif. Continuing Edn. Bar, Practising Law Inst., Hastings Law Sch.; bd. dirs., counsel Marin Wind and Food Soc.; exec. v.p., sec. Global Ctr. Inc., 2000—01; vice-chmn. HL Ventures, LLC, 2000—. Commentator Calif. Nonprofit Corp. Law. Mem.: ABA, San Francisco Bar Assn., Calif. State Bar Assn., Internat. Wine and Food Soc. (coun. mgmt., bd. dirs., exec. com., sr. vice chmn., bd. govs. Ams.), Am.-Korean Taekwondo Friendship Assn. (1st dan-black belt), Harbor Point Racquet and Beach Club, Olympic Club, Harvard Club, Northwestern Club, Beta Alpha Psi, Beta Gamma Sigma (pres. local chpt.). Office: Pillsbury Winthrop 50 Fremont St San Francisco CA 94105-2230

KLOTTER, JAMES C. historian, educator; b. Lexington, Ky., Jan. 17, 1947; s. John Charles K. and Marjorie Virginia (Gibson) Gabbard; m. Freda Jean Campbell, Dec. 28, 1966; children: Karen, Christopher, Katherine. BA, U. Ky., 1968; MA, 1969; PhD, 1975; LittD, Ea. Ky. U., 1997, Union Coll., 1998. Rsch. analyst Ky. Hist. Soc., Frankfort, 1973-75, asst. editor, 1975-78, mng. editor, 1978-80, state historian, 1980-88, asst. dir., 1988-90, dir., state historian, 1990-98; state historian, prof. history Georgetown Coll., 1998—. Chmn. bd. dirs. Farmers State Bank, Booneville, Ky.; bd. dirs. Hyden (Ky.) Middlefork Fin., 1985—; chmn. bd. Collaborative Tchg. and Learning, 2000—. Author: William Goebel: Politics of Wrath, 1977, co-author: A New History of Kentucky, 1997; editor: Our Kentucky: Study of Blue Grass State, 2000. Sec. Ky. Civil War Roundtable, Lexington, 1984-94, pres. 1994—. Mem. So. Hist. Assn., Ky. Assn. Tchrs. History (pres. 1986-87), Ky. Coun. on Archives (chmn. 1980-81), Ky. Oral History Commn. Bd., Ky. Hist. Soc. Found., U. Ky. Libr. Assn. (pres. 1984-85). Office: 400 E College St # 244 Georgetown KY 40324-1628 E-mail: james_klotter@georgetowncollege.edu.

KLOTTER, JOHN CHARLES, retired legal educator; b. Louisville, Nov. 6, 1918; s. John J. and Lillie R. (Fischer) K.; m. Jane Riddle, Nov. 2, 1954 (dec.); children: James C., Douglas A., Ronald L. AB, Western Ky. U., 1941; JD, U. Ky., 1948. Bar: Ky. 1948, U.S. Supreme Ct. 1967. Tchr. pub. schs., Louisville, 1941-42; spl. agt. FBI, 1948-50; legal officer Ky. State Police, 1951-52; dir. divsn. probation and parole State of Ky., Frankfort, 1952-56; assoc. dir. So. Police Inst., U. Louisville, 1957-71, dir. So. Police Inst., prof., dean Sch. Justice Adminstrn., So. Police Inst., 1971-81. Editorial dir. criminal justice text series W.H. Anderson Co., 1970-76; chmn. Louisville-Jefferson County Criminal Justice Commn., 1974-76; mem. Ky. Crime Commn., 1971-75, Ky. Law Enforcement Coun., 1971-81, Atty. Gen.'s Prosecutors Adv. Coun., 1970-82. Author: Techniques for Police Instructors, 1963; (with Kanovitz) Constitutional Law, 1968, 8th edit., 1998, Criminal Evidence, 1971, 7th edit., 2002, Legal Guide for Police, 1978, 6th edit., 2002, Criminal Justice Instructional Techniques, 1979, Legal Aspects of Private Security, 1981, Criminal Law, 1983, 8th edit., 2003. Capt. U.S. Army, 1942-46; col. Res. ret. Ford Found. grantee, 1968 Mem. Ky., Louisville bar assns., Res. Officers Assn., Soc. Former Spl. Agts. FBI. Home: 2103 Starmont Rd Louisville KY 40207-1140 E-mail: jk40207@aol.com.

KLOTZ, CHARLES RODGER, shipping company and investment company executive; b. Englewood, N.J., Apr. 14, 1942; s. George Edward and Beryl Edith (Cullingford) K.; m. Deborah Goodwin, June 25, 1966; children: Christine, Suzanne. BS, Trinity Coll., Hartford, Conn., 1964; MBA, Dartmouth Coll., 1966. Officer Bank of Boston Corp., 1969—85; pres., chief exec. officer Gulf Resources & Chem. Corp., Boston, 1985—89, also bd. dirs.; chmn. bd., CEO Spartan Madison Corp., 1991—2002. Chmn. bd. G.L. Holdings Corp., 1988—; chief exec. officer, chmn. bd. Gotaas Larsen Shipping Corp., 1988-97, also bd. dirs.; pres., bd. dirs. Tec Capital Ltd., 2000—. Lt. USCG, 1966-69. Mem. Flyfisher's Club (London), Wellesley Country Club, Coral Beach and Tennis Club (Bermuda), Pocasset Golf Club. Episcopalian. Office: Bingham McCutchen 150 Federal St Fl 15 Boston MA 02110-1726

KLOTZ, DAVID WAYNE, executive, civil engineer; b. Victoria, Tex., Sept. 20, 1952; s. Bill W. and Dorothy (Brubaker) K.; m. Karen Wilson, July 20, 1974; children: Katheryne, David, Bradley, Valerie. BS in Civil Engring. with honors, Tex. A&M U., 1974; MS in Civil Engring., U. Houston, 1976. Registered profl. engr., Tex., La. Civil engr. Turner Collie & Braden, Houston, 1974-79; project mgr. Rady & Assocs., Ft. Worth, 1979-82, Dannenbaum Engring., Houston, 1982-85; pres., chief exec. officer Klotz Assocs., Inc., Houston, 1985—, Epilepsy Assn. Greater Houston, 1992-98. Bd. dirs. Harris-Galveston Coastal Subsidence Dist., 1998—; mem. Harris County Flood Control Task Force, Houston, 1987—, chmn., 1993-94; chmn. Clear Creek Parks Steering Com., Houston, 1987-91; adult tchr., deacon,chmn. 2003-2004, fin. com. properties com., mission statement task force Tallowood Bapt. Ch.; umpire Bear Creek Little League, 1987-92; coach Katy Basketball, 1992-93; bd. dirs., mem. exec. com. Astros golf tourney chair Epilepsy Assn. Greater Houston, 1992-; mem. U. Houston Civil Engring. Adv. Com., 1996-03, chmn., 2002-03; mem. Greater Houston Partnership, 1985—, mem. pres.'s adv. coun., 1999—, mem. trans. and infrastructure adv. com., 1997—, chmn. local appointments taskforce. Fellow ASCE (employment conditions com. 1989-92, sec. 1991-92, vice chair 1992-93, chair 1993-94, corr. mem. com. engring. mgmt./orgnl. level 1988-92, com. on convs. and confs. 1998—, chair 2001 Nat. Conf., Nat. Dir. 2001-, Nat. Policy Com. 2002, Hawley Fund trustee 1996-2002, chair 1999-2002, state dir. Tex. sect. 1988-90, pres. 1990-91, pres. Houston br. 1987-88, nat. bd. dirs. 2001—, Houston br. Award of Honor 1993, dir. Ft. Worth br. 1981-82, Hawley fellow 1976, Daniel Mead prize 1975, Tex. sect. Honor award 1994); mem. Cons. Engrs. Coun. Tex. (chmn. membership com. 1989-90, 98—, state legis. com. 1993—, treas. 1995-97, bd. dirs. 1993-97, mem. benefits task force chair 20032, New Prin. of Yr. award 1987), Greater Houston Builders Assn. (cmty. devel. coun. 1983—), Assn. Cons. Mcpl. Engrs. (v.p. 1992-93, pres. 1994-95, govt. steering com. 1996-98, 2003-), Houston Engring. and Scientific Soc. (bd. dirs. 1996-98), Am. Water Works Assn., Houston C. of C., "C" Club. Republican. Avocations: golf, reading. Office: Klotz Assocs Inc 1160 Dairy Ashford St Ste 500 Houston TX 77079-3098 E-mail: email@klotz.com.

KLOTZ, EDNA MAY, retired librarian; b. Corry, Pa., July 20, 1922; d. Milton Edward and Ethyl May Robbins; m. Donald L. Klotz, Sept. 9, 1950. BA, Hiram Coll., 1944; BSLS, Western Reserve U., Cleve., 1945. Student asst. Hiram (Ohio) Coll., 1941-44; head cataloguer Baldwin Wallace Coll. Library, Berea, Ohio, 1945-48; circulation librarian Ohio State U., Columbus, 1948-52, special collection librarian, 1952-57; asst. librarian Worthington Pub. Library, Worthington, 1957-68; circulation librarian Capital U. Library, 1968-80, acquisitions librarian, 1980-89; libr. emeritus, 1989—. Methodist. Home: 1937 Harwitch Rd Columbus OH 43221-2812

KLOTZ, IRVING MYRON, chemist, educator; b. Chgo., Jan. 22, 1916; s. Frank and Mollie (Nasatir) K.; m. Mary Sue Hanlon, Aug. 7, 1966; children: Edward, Audie Jeanne, David. BS, U. Chgo., 1937, PhD, 1940. Rsch. assoc. in chemistry Northwestern U., 1940-42, instr., 1942- 46, asst. prof., 1946-47, assoc. prof., 1947-50, prof., 1950-63, Morrison prof. chemistry, 1963-86, prof. emeritus, 1986—. Lalor fellow Marine Biol. Lab., Woods Hole, Mass., 1947-48, corp. mem., 1947—, trustee, 1957-65 Author: Chemical Thermody-

namics, 4th rev. edit., 1986, 5th rev. edit., 1994, 6th rev. edit., 2000, Energies in Biochemical Reactions, rev. edit., 1967, Introduction to Biomolecular Energetics, 1986, Diamond Dealers, Feather Merchants, 1986; Ligand-Receptor Energetics: A Guide for the Perplexed, 1997; contbr. articles to sci. and other jours. Recipient Army-Navy cert. of appreciation for wartime research, 1948, William C. Rose award biochem. Am. Soc. Biochem. and Molecular Biology, 1993. Fellow Royal Soc. Medicine, Am. Acad. Arts and Scis., AAAS; mem. Nat. Acad. Scis., Am. Soc. Biochemistry and Molecular Biology, Am. Chem. Soc. (Eli Lilly award 1949, Midwest award 1970), Phi Beta Kappa, Sigma Xi, Phi Lambda Upsilon, Alpha Chi Sigma. Home: 1500 Sheridan Rd # 7D Wilmette IL 60091 E-mail: i-klotz@northwestern.edu.

KLOTZ, LEORA NYLEE, retired music educator, vocalist; b. Canton, Ohio, Oct. 17, 1928; d. Clarence Karl and Nellie (Jacoby) Dretke; m. Kenneth Gordon Klotz, June 29, 1963. BMus and B.Pub. Sch. Music, Mount Union Coll., Alliance, Ohio, 1950; MA, Western Res. U., Cleve., 1954. Cert. vocal music tchr. Ohio. Elem. music supr. Canton City Schs., Ohio, 1950—60, h.s. vocal dir., 1955—60; elem. music tchr. Louisville City Schs., Ohio, 1960—71, h.s. vocal dir., 1960—81; adult choir dir. Perry Christian Ch., Canton, 1959—87; ret., 1987; mem. young artists competition com. Canton Symphony Orch. Bd., 1981—89; dir. Trirosis choir. Soprano soloist The Messiah Canton Symphony Orch., 1954—55; soprano soloist First Christian Ch., 1946—65, North Canton Cmty. Christian Ch., numerous vocal (solo) appearances N.E. Ohio. Composer choral octavos. Soprano soloist Rep. Civic Celebration, Canton, Ohio, 1950—60. Recipient Outstanding Young Ohio Composer, Ohioana Libr. Assn., 1959. Mem.: Mount Union Women, Canton Symphony League, Am. Guild Organists, ASCAP, Ohio Ret. Tchrs. Assn., Am. Choral Dirs. Assn. (life), Stark County Ret. Tchrs. Assn. (life), MacDowell Chorale (hon.), Canton Woman's Club, MacDowell Music Club (hon.), Order Ea. Star, PEO Sisterhood, Mu Phi Epsilon, Delta Kappa Gamma. Republican. Avocations: collecting Hummel figurines, reading, cooking. Home: 5036 Parkhaven Ave NE Canton OH 44705

KLOTZ, LOUIS HERMAN, structural engineer, educator, consultant; b. Elizabeth, N.J., May 21, 1928; s. Herman Martin and Edna Theresa (Kloepfer) K.; m. Virginia Helen Roll, Apr. 3, 1966 (dec. Oct. 1995); Emily Louise, Jennifer-Claire Virginia. BSCE, Pa. State U., 1951; MCE, N.Y.U., 1956; PhD, Rutgers U., 1967. Registered profl. engr., N.J., N.H. Structural engr. various firms, N.Y., N.J. metro area, N.Y., N.J., 1951-65; asst. prof. civil engring. U. N.H., Durham, 1965-69, assoc. prof. civil engring., 1969-86, chmn. dept. civil engring., 1971-74; spl. projects dir. ASCE, N.Y.C., 1986-87; cons. Klotz Assocs., Inc., New Castle, N.H., 1987-88; project mgr. Universal Engring. Corp., Boston, 1988-91; exec. dir. New Eng. States Earthquake Consortium, 1991-94; pres. Klotz Consultants Group, Inc., New Castle, N.H., 1994—; reservist FEMA, 1999—2002. Cons., evaluator Office of Energy Related Inventions, Gaithersburg, Md., 1978—; mem. energy policy adv. group N.H. Ho. of Reps., Concord, 1979-82; founding mem. N.H. Legis. Acad. Sci. & Tech., Concord, 1980-83. Editor: Energy Sources, The Promises and Problems, 1980; author: Users Manual Small Hydroelectric Financial/Economic Analysis, 1983; (monograph) Water Power, Its Promises and Problems; contbr. articles to Procs. of 1st Internat. Conf. on Computing in Civil Engring., Hydro Rev. Advisor Environ. Protection div. N.H. State Atty. Gen.'s Office, Concord, 1972-76; mem. New Castle (N.H.) Budget Com., 1977-79; tech. reviewer N.E. Appropriate Tech. Small Grants program Dept. Energy, Boston, 1979-80; bd. dirs. Family Svcs. Assn. Portsmouth, 1995 98, Seacoast Hospice, 1996-98. Ford Found fellow, 1962-65, Ford Found. grant, 1968, Systems Design fellow, NASA, Assn. for Engring. Edn., Houston, 1975; named Gen. Acctg. Office Faculty Fellow, U.S. Gen. Acctg. Office, Washington, 1975-76. Mem. AAAS, ASCE (com. on coordination outside ASCE 1978-86), Am. Assn. Engring. Edn., N.Y. Acad. Scis. Republican. Episcopalian. Home: 90 Mainmast Cir New Castle NH 03854 Office: Klotz Consultants Group Inc PO Box 204 New Castle NH 03854-0204 E-mail: lhk@comcast.net.

KLOWDEN, MICHAEL LOUIS, think-tank executive; b. Chgo., Apr. 7, 1945; s. Roy and Esther (Siegel) K.; m. Patricia A. Doede, June 15, 1968; children: Kevin B., Deborah C. AB, U. Chgo., 1967; JD, Harvard U., 1970. Bar: Calif. 1971. From assoc. to ptnr. Mitchell, Silberberg & Knupp, L.A., 1970-78; mng. ptnr. Morgan, Lewis & Bockius, L.A., 1978-95; vice chmn. Jefferies & Co., Inc., L.A., 1995-96; pres., COO Jefferies Group, Inc. and Jefferies Co., Inc., L.A., 1996-2000, vice chmn., 2000—01; pres., CEO Milken Inst., 2001—. Trustee U. Chgo., 1986—. Office: Milken Institute 1250 Fourth St Santa Monica CA 90401 Office Fax: 310-998-2695. E-mail: mklowden@milkeninstitute.org.

KLUBEK, BRIAN PAUL, science educator, researcher; b. Buffalo, Ny, Apr. 21, 1948; s. Bronislaus and Barbara Mary Klubek; m. Vickie Gail Campbell; children: Jill, Peter, Bethany. BS, Colo. St U., Ft Collins, CO, 1971; MS, Oreg. St U., Corvallis, OR, 1974; PhD, Utah St U., Logan, UT, 1977. Rsch. assoc N Carolina St U., Raleigh, NC, 1977—78; asst. prof. So. Ill. U., Carbondale, Ill., 1978—83, assoc prof., 1983—91, prof., 1991—. Cons. Savannah River Ecology Lab, Aiken, SC, 1989—89, Aiken, 1993—93. Contbr. articles to profl. sci. jours. Mem.: Soil Sci. Soc. of Am., Am. Soc. of Agronomy, Am. Soc. for Microbiology. Office: Southern Illinois University Dept Plant and Soil Science Carbondale IL 62901 Office Fax: 618-453-7457. E-mail: bklubek@siu.edu.

KLUCK, CLARENCE JOSEPH, physician, health facility administrator; b. Stevens Point, Wis., June 20, 1929; s. Joseph Bernard and Mildred Lorraine (Helminiak) Kluck; children from previous marriage: Paul Bernard, Annette Louise Kluck Winston, David John, Maureen Ellen. BS in Med. Sci., U. Wis., 1951, MD, 1954. Resident San Joaquin Hosp., French Camp, Calif., 1955-56; asst. instr. medicine Ohio State U., Columbus, 1958-60; physician, chief of medicine Redford Med. Ctr., Detroit, 1960-69; pvt. practice specializing in internal medicine Denver, 1969-83; med. dir. Atlantic Richfield Co., Denver, 1983-85; corp. med. dir. Cyprus Minerals Co., Englewood, Colo., 1985-92; pres. Kluck Med. Assocs., Englewood, 1992—. Pres., CEO, chmn. bd. Corpcare, Inc., Englewood, 1992—97; pres., CEO Corpcare Med. Assocs., P.C., 1992—97, Denver Occupl. Med. Examiners, P.C., 2001—; pres. Denver Occupl. and Aviation Medicine Clinic, P.C., 1995—. Contbr. articles to profl. jours. Served to capt. U.S. Army, 1956—58. Named Physician of Yr., Nat. Rep. Congl. Com., 2002; recipient Century Club award, Boy Scouts Am., 1972. Fellow: Am. Coll. Occupl. Medicine, Am. Coll. Occupl. and Environ. Medicine, Am. Occupl. Med. Assn.; mem.: Colo. Soc. Internal Medicine, Am. Soc. Internal Medicine, Am. Mining Congress Health Commn., Colo. Med. Soc. (del. 1973—74, 1981—87), Denver Med. Soc. (bd. dirs. 1973—74, coun. mem. 1981—87), Arapahoe County Med. Soc., Rocky Mountain Acad. Occupl. Medicine (bd. dirs. 1985—88), Am. Acad. Occupl. Medicine, Castle Pines Country Club, Met. Club, Flatirons Club (Boulder, Colo.). Roman Catholic. Avocations: fishing, hiking, skiing, flying, golf. Office: 3700 Havana St Ste 200 Denver CO 80239-3242

KLUEH, RONALD LLOYD, metallurgist; b. Ferdinand, Ind., Oct. 23, 1936; s. Gilbert Joseph and Virginia Mary (Schum) K.; m. Helen Louise Kays, Sept. 7, 1959; children: Rona Ann, Kevin Gilbert. BS, Purdue U., 1961; MS, Carnegie-Mellon U., 1964, PhD, 1966. Rsch. staff Oak Ridge (Tenn.) Nat. Lab., 1966-78, sr. rsch. staff, 1978—. Author: (ASTM monograph) High Chromium Ferritic and Martensitic Steels for Nuclear Applications, 2001, (novels) The Pittsburgh Stealers, 2002; editor: Reduced Activation Materials, 1990, Fusion Reactor Materials, 1992, International Fusion Reactor Materials, 1996; contbr. articles to profl. jours. With U.S. Army, 1954—56. Fellow Alcoa, Carnegie-Mellon U., 1961-63, Union Carbide Corp., 1963-64; recipient Best Paper awards Am. Nuclear Soc., San Diego, 1978, Washington, 1979. Fellow: ASM Internat.; mem.: Am. Soc. Metals. Roman Catholic. Achievements include invention of manganese stainless steel, 1989; patents for chromium-tungsten ferritic steel, 1994. Home: 4709 Guinn Rd Knoxville TN 37931-2022 Office: Oak Ridge Nat Lab PO Box 2008 Oak Ridge TN 37831-6138

KLUG, AARON, molecular biologist; b. Aug. 11, 1926; s. Lazar and Bella (Silin) Klug; m. Liebe Bobrow, 1948; 2 children. B.Sc., U. Witwatersrand; M.Sc., U. Cape Town; PhD, DSc, Cambridge U.; DSc (hon.), U. Chgo., 1978, Columbia U., 1978; D (hon.), U. Strasbourg, 1978; DSc (hon.), Stockholm U., 1980, U. Witwatersrand, 1984, Hebrew U., Jerusalem, 1984, Hull U., 1985, U. St. Andrews, 1987, U. Western Ont., 1991, Warwick U., 1994, Capetwon U., 1997; D Litt, Cambridge U., 1998, Stirling U., 1998; DSc (hon.), London, 2000, Oxford, 2001. Jr. lectr., 1947-48; rsch. student Cavendish Lab. Cambridge (Eng.) U., 1949-52; Rouse-Ball rsch. student Trinity Coll., 1949-52; Colloid Sci. dept., 1953; Nuffield rsch. fellow Birkbeck Coll., London, 1954-57, dir. virus structure rsch. group, 1958-61; mem. staff Med. Rsch. Coun. Lab. Molecular Biology, Cambridge U., 1962—, joint head div. structural studies, 1978-86, dir., 1986-96. Leeuwenhoek lectr. Royal Soc., 1973; Dunham lectr. Harvard U. Med. Sch., 1975; Harvey lectr., N.Y.C., 1979, Lane lectr. Stanford U., 1983; Silliman lectr. Yale U., 1985; Cetus lectr. Berkeley U., 1986; Pauli lectr., Zürich, 1986; Nishina Meml. lectr., Tokyo, 1986; J. T. Baker lectr. Cornell U., 1987; Jean Weigle lectr., Geneva, 1989, Steenbock lectr. U. Wis., Madison, 1989; Innovators in Biochem. lectr. U. Va., Richmond, 1990; Calbiochem. lectr. U. Calif., San Diego, 1991; Neurath lectr. U. Wash., Seattle; Blackett lectr. Delhi, 1997. Contbr. articles to sci. jours. Recipient Heineken prize Royal Netherlands Acad. Sci., 1979, Louisa Gross Horwitz prize Columbia U., 1981, Nobel prize in chemistry, 1982, Gold medal of Merit, U. Cape Town, 1983, Copley medal Royal Soc., 1985, Harden medal Biochem. Soc., 1985; Knight, 1988, Order of Merit, 1995. Fellow Royal Soc. (pres. 1995-2000), Peterhouse (Cambridge hon.), Royal Coll. Physn. (hon., Baly medal 1987), Royal Coll. Pathologists (hon.), Trinity Coll. (Cambridge, hon.), Birkbeck Coll. (London, hon.); mem. Am. Acad. Arts and Scis. (fgn. hon.), French Acad. Scis. (fgn. assoc.), Max-Planck-Gesellschaft (fgn. assoc.), NAS (fgn. assoc.), Am. Philos. Soc. (fgn. mem.). Office: Med Rsch Coun Lab Molecular Biology, Hills Rd Cambridge CB2 2QH England

KLUG, JOHN JOSEPH, secondary education educator, director of dramatics; b. Denver, Apr. 27, 1948; s. John Joseph Sr. and Dorthea Virginia (Feely) Carlyle. BA in English, U. N.C., 1974; MA in Theatre, U. Colo., 1984. Tchr. Carmody Jr. High Sch., Lakewood, Colo., 1976-78, Golden (Colo.) High Sch., 1978—, dir. of dramatics, 1978—; producer, dir. Children's Theatre Tours, 1978—. Theatrical cons., 1983—; improvisational workshop leader, 1983—. Playwright, editor: Children's Theatre scripts, 1982—; producer, dir. Denver Theatre Sports, 1993—. Recipient Bravo/TCI Theatre award, 1995. Home: 4565 King St Denver CO 80211-1357 Office: Golden HS 701 24th St Golden CO 80401-2379

KLUG, SCOTT LEO, former congressman; b. Milwaukee, Wis., Jan. 16, 1953; s. Ralph William Klug and Josephine (Farrell) Weber; m. Tess Summers, Mar. 4, 1978; children: Keefe, Brett, Collin Phillip. BA, Lawrence U., 1975; MS in Journalism, Northwestern U., 1976; MBA, U. Wis., 1990. Reporter TV sta., Wausau, Wis., 1976-78; reporter Sta. KING-TV, Seattle, 1978-81; investigative reporter Sta. WJLA-TV, Washington, 1981-88; anchor, reporter Sta. WKOW-TV, Madison, Wis., 1988 90; v.p. pub. fin. dept. Blunt, Ellis & Loewi, Madison, 1990; mem. 102nd-105th U.S. Congress from 2d Wis. dist., Washington, D.C., 1991-98, mem. commerce com.; publ., CEO Trails Media Group Inc., Madison, 1999—; pub. affairs counsel Foley and Lardner, Washington, 1999—. Reporter, producer documentaries (Emmy awards 1989, 90). Named Nat. Humanitarian of Yr., Humane Soc., 1986; John McCloy fellow Columbia U. Sch. Journalism, 1987. Republican. Avocations: tennis, basketball, cooking. Office: Trails Media Group PO Box 317 Black Earth WI 53515 also: Foley and Lardner Verex Plaza 150 E Gilman St Madison WI 53703

KLUGE, JOHN WERNER, broadcasting and advertising executive; b. Chemnitz, Germany, Sept. 21, 1914; s. Fritz and Gertrude (Donj) K.; children: Samantha, Joseph B. Student, Wayne U.; BA (4 year honor scholar), Columbia, 1937. Vice pres., sales mgr. Otten Bros., Inc., Detroit, 1937-41; pres., dir. radio sta. WGAY, Silver Spring, Md., 1946-59, St. Louis Broadcasting Corp., Brentwood, Mo., 1953-58, Pitts. Broadcasting Co., 1954-59; pres., treas., dir. Capitol Broadcasting Co., Nashville, 1954-59, Asso. Broadcasters, Inc., Ft. Worth-Dallas, 1957-59; partner Western N.Y. Broadcasting Co., Buffalo, 1957-60; pres., dir. Washington Planagraph Co., 1956-60, Mid.-Fla. Radio Corp., Orlando, 1952-59; treas., dir. Mid-Fla. Television Corp., 1957-60; owner Kluge Investment Co., Washington, 1956-60; partner Nashton Properties, Nashville, 1954-60, Texworth Investment Co., Ft. Worth, 1957-60; chmn. bd. Seaboard Service System, Inc., 1957-58; chm. bd., pres., CEO Metromedia Inc., Secaucus, N.J., 1959-86; former gen. ptnr., chm. bd., pres., CEO Metromedia Co., now chmn. and pres.; now pres., chmn. bd. Benale Holdings Corp., Dallas; also chmn., dir. LDDS Comm., Jackson, Miss.; investor, operator N.Y./N.J. Metro Stars, Secaucus, N.J., 1995. Pres. New Eng. Fritos, Boston, 1947-55, N.Y. Inst. Dietetics, N.Y.C., 1953-60; chmn. bd., pres., dir. Metromedia, Inc., N.Y.C., Metromedia, Inc. (including met. broadcasting div., world wide broadcasting div. and Foster & Kleiser div., outdoor advt.); chmn. bd., treas., dir. Kluge, Finkelstein & Co. (food brokers), Balt.; chmn. bd., treas. Tri-Suburban Broadcasting Corp., Washington, Kluge & Co.; chmn. bd., pres., treas. Washington, Silver City Sales Co., Washington; dir. Marriott-Hot Shoppes, Inc., Chock Full O' Nuts Corp., Nat. Bank Md., Waldorf Astoria Corp., Just One Break, Inc., Belding Heminway Co., Inc.; mem. adv. council Mfrs. Hanover Trust Co.; Mem. Washington Bd. Trade. Bd. dirs. Brand Names Found., Inc., Shubert Found.; v.p., bd. dirs. United Cerebral Palsy Research and Ednl. Found., 1972— ; trustee Strang Clinic Miliken U.; bd. govs. N.Y. Coll. Osteo. Medicine. Served to capt. U.S. Army, 1941-45. Mem. Nat. Food Brokers Assn., Washington Food Brokers Assn. (pres. 1958), Grocery Wheels Washington, Grocery Mfrs. Reps. Washington, Advt. Club Washington, Nat. Assn. Radio and Television Broadcasters, Advt. Council N.Y.C., Nat. Sugar Brokers Assn. Clubs: Army and Navy (Washington), University (Washington), Figure Skating (Washington), National Capital Skeet and Trap (Washington), Broadcasters (Washington); Metropolitan (N.Y.C.), Columbia Associates (N.Y.C.), University (N.Y.C.); Olympic (San Francisco); Marco Polo (N.H. gov.). Office: Metromedia One Meadowlands Plaza East Rutherford NJ 07073*

KLUGE, LEN H. director, actor, theater educator; b. Lakeview, Mich., Oct. 28, 1945; s. Leland H. and Edna Alvena (Paris) Kluge; m. Heather Lenartson, 2002. Diploma, Am. Acad. Dramatic Arts, 1967; student, Actors Studio, N.Y.C., 1968-69; BFA, Cen. Mich. U., 1977, MA in Counseling, 1978. Actor various mediums, N.Y., Calif., 1967-75; therapist Ionia County Mental Health Dept., Mich., 1978-79; exec. dir. Nat. Coun. on Alcoholism, Lansing, Mich., 1979-81; artistic dir. Spotlight Theatre, Grand Ledge, Mich., 1982—; prof. theater Spring Arbor Coll., 1993-95. Dir. The Actors Workshop and Ensemble Acting Co., Lansing, 1986—. Appeared in: (soap opera) Another World, 1968-69, (off-Broadway play) Man with the Flower in His Mouth, 1969, (film) Rennaisance Man, 1994, spl. performance as Clarence Darrow for Do the Right Thing program, Punta Gorda, Fla., 1996, 97, 98; performed for Boarshead Pub. Theatre, 1997-2001. Mem. Ctr. for the Arts, Lansing; bd. dirs. Child Abuse Prevention Svcs., 1993—; spl. Recipient Obie award, 1969, Thespie X award Lansing State Jour., 1982, 84, 86-90, 2001, Decade of Excellence award for body of work, 1993, Barney award Okemos Barn Theatre, Lansing, 1984, Riverwalk Theater, 91, 95, 96, 99, Star X award Spotlight Theatre, 1984-97. Lutheran. Avocations: baseball, writing, teaching, lecturing, travel, cigars. Home: 1937 Byrnes Rd Lansing MI 48906-3402 E-mail: wilieloman@aol.com.

KLUGER, RICHARD, author, editor; b. Paterson, N.J., Sept. 18, 1934; s. David and Ida (Abramson) K.; m. Phyllis Schlain, Mar. 23, 1957; children—Matthew Harold, Leonard Theodore. AB cum laude, Princeton, 1956. Copy editor Wall St. Jour., 1956-57; editor, pub. county Citizen, New City, N.Y., 1958 60; staff writer N.Y. Post, 1960-61, asso. editor Forbes mag., 1962; gen. books editor N.Y. Herald Tribune, 1962-63, book editor, 1963-66; editor Book Week, 1963-66; sr. editor Simon and Schuster, 1966-68, mng. editor, 1968, exec. editor, 1968-70; editor-in-chief Atheneum Pubs., 1970-71; pres., pub. Charterhouse Books, 1971-73. Author: When the Bough Breaks, 1964, National Anthem, 1969, Simple Justice, 1976, Members of the Tribe, 1977, Star Witness, 1979, Un-American Activities, 1982, The Paper: The Life and Death of the New York Herald Tribune, 1986, The Sheriff of Nottingham, 1992, Ashes to Ashes: America's Hundred-Year Cigarette War, 1996; co-author: (with Phyllis Kluger) Good Goods, 1982, Royal Poinciana, 1988. Recipient George Polk award, 1987, Pulitzer prize Gen. Non-Fiction, 1997; Nat. Am. Book Non-Fiction award nominee, 1976, 86, Nat. Book Critics Cir. award nominee, 1997. Home: 29 Mayhew Dr South Orange NJ 07079*

KLUGMAN, PETER JAY, psychologist, consultant; b. Bklyn., May 19, 1942; s. Joseph and Shirley (Rich) K.; m. Marthanne Hamlin, Oct. 29, 1964 (dec. Dec. 1979). BA, U. Miami, 1961, MEd, 1965; MA, U. Fla., 1974, PhD, 1978. Diplomate Am. Acad. Pain Mgmt.; lic. psychologist, N.J., Pa. Commd. 2d lt. U.S. Army, 1966, advanced through grades to lt. col., 1983, ret., 1986; chief Community Mental Health Svc., Ft. Dix, N.J., 1976-86; clin. dir. Biofeedback Ctr. of South Jersey, Willingboro, N.J., 1986-99; pres. Orgnl. Potential, Medford, N.J., 1986—. Cons. Pub. Svc. Electric and Gas, N.J., 1984—, Office Surgeon Gen. U.S. Army, 1986—, USAF, 1994—. Psychology editor Medicine of the Ams., 1999—; contbr. articles to profl. jours. Bd. dirs. Girl Scouts of South Jersey Pines, 1981-2002, Lenape Regional H.S. Bd. Edn., N.J.; v.p. Medford Bd. Edn., N.J. Decorated Bronze Star, Legion of Merit, Army Commendation medal, Vietnam Svc. medal, Civilian Achievement medal Dept of the Army, N.J. Disting. Svc. medal. Mem. APA, N.J. Psychol. Assn. (South Jersey rep. 1990-93), South Jersey Psychol. Assn. (bd. dirs. 1989-93). Jewish. Office: Orgnl Potential PO Box 1551 Medford NJ 08055-6551

KLUGMAN, STEPHAN CRAIG, newspaper editor; b. Fargo, N.D., May 11, 1945; s. Ted and Charlotte (Olson) K.; m. Julie Sue Terpening, Sept. 18, 1971; children: Josh, Carrie. BA in Journalism, Ind. U., 1967. Copy editor Chgo. Sun-Times, 1967-68, asst. telegraph editor, 1968-72, telegraph editor, 1972-74, city editor, 1974-76, asst. mng. editor features, 1976-78; asst. prof. Medill Sch. Journalism, Northwestern U., Evanston, Ill., 1978-79, dir. undergrad. studies, 1979 82; editor Jour.-Gazette, Ft. Wayne, Ind., 1982—. Mem. Am. Soc. Newspaper Editors. Office: Jour-Gazette 600 W Main St Fort Wayne IN 46802-1408

KLUKA, DARLENE ANN, human performance educator, researcher; b. Berwyn, Ill., Oct. 6, 1950; d. Aloysius Louis and Lillian (Malkovsky) K. BA, Ill. State U., 1972, MA, 1976; PhD, Tex. Woman's U., 1985. Educator, coach Fenton High Sch., Bensenville, Ill., 1972-73, New Trier East High Sch., Winnetka, Ill., 1973-80; coach Bradley Univ., Peoria, Ill., 1980-82; grad. teaching asst. Tex. Woman's Univ., Denton, 1982-85; prof. Newberry (S.C.) Coll., 1985-86; prof., rschr., dir. Human Performance Ctr., Grambling (La.) State U., 1986-90; asst. prof. human studies and sport adminstrn. U. Ala., Birmingham, 1990-94, rschr., dir. Motor Behavior and Sports Vision Lab., 1990-94; dir. grad. program U. Ctrl. Okla., Edmond, 1994-97; prof., coord. kinesiology and sport studies Grambling (La.) State U., 1997—. Head of del. Internat. Olympic Acad., Olympia Greece, 1990; dep. del. U.S. Olympic Com., 1996-2000; adv. bd. Women's Sports Found., 1992—; U.S.A. Volleyball Sports Medicine and Performance Commn., 1994—; bd. dirs. U.S.A. Volleyball, v.p. rels. and human resources, 1996-2000. Author: Visual Skill Enhancement for Sport Exercises, 1989, Volleyball Drills, 1990, Volleyball, 4th edit., 2000, Motor Behavior: From Learning to Performance, 1999; founding co-editor Internat. Jour. Sports Vision, 1991-97; founding editor Internat. Jour. Volleyball Rsch., 1997—, mem. editl. bd., Coaching Volleyball Jour., 1988—. ICHPERSD dir. Girls and Women in Sport Commn., 1993—2001; mem. La. Gov.'s Coun. on Phys. Fitness and Sports, 2003—. Recipient Rsch. award So. Assn. Phys. Edn. Coll. Women, 1994, 96, USA Volleyball Leader award, 1998, Joseph Andera Rsch. award Internat. Acad. of SportsVision, 1999, Disting. Svc. award AAALF Internat. Rels. Coun., 1999, Disting. Achievements award Ill. State U. Alumni Assn., 1997; LAHPERD scholar, 1999-2000, Honor award 2002, So. Dist. Honor award 2003. Mem. AAHPERD (rsch. fellow, bd. govs. 1993-96, So. dist. scholar 2001. So. Dist. Honor award 2003), AAUP (Disting. scholar award 1997), Nat. Assn. for Girls and Women in Sport (bd. dirs., exec. com. 1989-92, 93-96, pres. 1990-91, Honor award 1996), Internat. Coun. for Sport Sci. and Phys. Edn. (exec. bd. 1997-02, treas. 2002—, editl. bd. 1998—), Internat. Acad. Sports Vision (adv. bd. 1989-98, v.p. 1993-01), Am. Volleyball Coaches Assn. (mem. editl. bd. Coaching Volleyball Jour., 1988 , bd. dirs. 2003—, chmn. edn. and publs. com. 2003—, Disting. Scholar in Sport award 1995, Excellence in Edn. award 1999, Kluka/Love Young Rsch. Award named in her honor 2001), Women's Sports Found. (internat. coun. 1993—, edn. & rsch. coun. 1995—, Pres.'s award 1996, Darlene A. Kluka rsch. award named in her honor 2001), Internat. Assn. Phys. Edn. and Sports for Girls and Women, Girls and Women in Sport (bd. cons. 2000—). Roman Catholic. Avocations: jogging, photography, collecting olympic games memorabilia, bicycling.

KLUNZINGER, THOMAS EDWARD, writer, actor, director; b. Ann Arbor, Mich., Sept. 11, 1944; s. Willard Reuben and Katherine Eileen (McCurdy) Klunzinger. BA in Advt. cum laude, Mich. State U., 1966. Copywriter Campbell-Ewald Advt. Co., Detroit, 1966-70; travel cons. Moorman's Travel Svc., Detroit, 1973-74; media dir. Taylor for Congress Campaign, East Lansing, Mich., 1974; comms. specialist House Republican Staff, Lansing, Mich., 1975-80; trustee Meridian Twp., Ingham County, Mich., 1980-84; vice chmn. Econ. Devel. Corp., 1982-84; compliance officer The Eyde Co., Lansing, 1985-88; legis. aide Mich. Ho. of Reps., Lansing, 1988-90; comm. officer Ingham Regional Med. Ctr., 1994—96, 2000—03, Schultz Investment Advisors, 2003—. Author: Chester!, 1981, Heavy Lady, 1983, Double Standards, 1985, A Villa in Unadilla, 1985, Losing It, 1987, The Wizards of Kyshtym/Deine Kleine Beine, 1988, Lounge Lizards/Managing Gran, 1989, Like A Brother, 1989, Loose Dogs Will Bite, 1990, Beloved Friend, 1990, To Be Announced, 1991, Okemos Passing, 1992, Song of the Whale, 1993, Mimsy Borogroves and the Tooth Fairy, 1993, What About the Hungarian?, 1995, The Passion of Richard II, 1996, The Hunchback of Notre Dame, 1997, Out at Home, 1998, The Real Boy's Pirate Show, 1998, As I Was Saying..., 1999, Breakfast in Berlin, 1999, Folles, 2000, Blond Ambition, 2000, Rock the Cradle, 2000, In Pain, 2001, Butterknife, 2002, Better Than Never, 2003, American Burkha, 2003, Rush Limbaugh in Hell, 2003. Mem. Ingham County Bd. Canvassers, 1993—96; treas. Meridian Twp., 1996—2000; pres. Riverwalk Theatre, 1990—92, sec., 1993—95; mem. Ingham County Rep. Com., 1976—, sec., 1986—88, 1991—92, 1996, treas., 2001—02, Mich. Rep. State Com., 1981—85, 6th Dist. Rep. Com. sec., 1989—93; bd. dirs. Capital Area Transp. Authority, 1999—2001. Mem.: Mich. Numis Soc. (sec. 1991—96, editor 1993—, 1st v.p. 2003—), Am. Numis. Assn., Dramatists Guild. Address: PO Box 585 Okemos MI 48805-0585

KLURFELD, DAVID MICHAEL, nutritionist, pathologist; b. N.Y.C., Feb. 22, 1951; s. Lester and Ethel (Wagner) K.; m. Esther Margiloff, Jan. 14, 1973; children: Jonathan Alan, Michael Eric. BS, Cornell U., 1972; MS, Med. Coll. Va., 1975, PhD, 1977. Lab. specialist, blood bank Med. Coll. Va., Richmond, 1976-77; postdoctoral fellow The Wistar Inst. Anatomy and Biology, Phila., 1977-79, rsch. assoc., 1979-82, asst. prof., 1982-86, assoc. prof., 1987-92; assoc. prof. nutrition in surgery U. Pa. Sch. Medicine, Phila., 1989-92; prof. dept. nutrition and food sci. Wayne State U., Detroit, 1992—, chmn. dept. nutrition and food sci., 1992—2003. Cons. numerous food cos., 1985—. Editor-in-chief Jour. of Am. Coll. Nutrition, 1999—; contbr. over 145 articles to profl. jours. Recipient Nutrition Rsch. award Nutrition Rsch. Editl. Bd., 1982. Fellow Am. Coll. Nutrition; mem. Am. Soc. Investigative Pathology, Am. Soc. Nutritional Sci. (mem. editl. bd. 1992-96), Soc. for Exptl. Biology and Medicine (mem. editl. bd. 1985-91). Achievements include research on fat energy and dietary fiber in cancer development, cholesterol and lipid metabolism, atherosclerosis. Office: Wayne State U 3009 Science Hall Detroit MI 48202 E-mail: david.klurfeld@wayne.edu.

KLUTE, ALLAN ALOYS, physicist, economist; b. St. Louis, July 19, 1916; s. Aloys J Henry and Noelie Constance (Jeep) Klute; m. Mary Eileen Zeni, June 5, 1993. AB, Washington U., St. Louis, 1949, postgrad., 1949-50. Supr. technics office Aero. Chart and Info. Ctr., St. Louis, 1951-72. 2d lt USAF, 1942—45, prisoner-of-war, 1944—45, Germany. Decorated Air medal, Purple Heart; recipient Orgn. Excellence award, USAF, 1970. Mem.: Air Force Assn., Mil. Order World Wars. Achievements include co-development of system of mapping surface of moon; development of a system for determining accurate geodetic positions within strategic areas.

KLUTH, FREDERICK JOHN, computer consultant, artist; b. Charleston, W.Va., Nov. 13, 1942; s. Fred Carl and Edna Adrienne (Overbeke) K.; m. Martha Starrow Schaffer, Sept. 5, 1964; 1 child, Thomas William. BA, Johns Hopkins U., 1964; MA in Edn., U. Akron, 1987. Cartographer USAF, 1964—67; secondary sch. tchr. Mo., Ohio, 1972—78; antique restorer, 1978—88; staff Nat. Machine Co., 1988—97; computer cons. F.J. Kluth Co., Kent, Ohio, 1997—2001; owner Open Space Gallery, Kent, 2001—. Artist of drawings and prints, various internat. exhbns., 1993-99; contbr. articles to profl. jours.; author web site: http://apk.net/nfjk. Mem. tech. adv. coun. Summit County (Ohio) Solid Waste Policy Com., 1989-92; resource mem. infrastructure com. Akron Reg. Devel. Bd., 1991-92. Fellow Ohio Acad. Sci. (coord. 1993-03); mem. Ohio Math. and Sci. Coalition. Unitarian-Universalist. Avocations: tennis. Office: Open Space Gallery 612 N Mantua St Kent OH 44240

KLUTHO, MARK PAUL, landscape architect, educator; b. St. Louis, Feb. 20, 1949; s. Paul Ralph and Mary Lee Klutho. Sgt. U.S. Army, 1968—71, Vietnam. Home: 14496 120th Ave N Largo FL 33774

KLUTZ, ANTHONY ALOYSIUS, JR., health, safety and environmental manager; b. Wilkes-Barre, Pa., Dec. 2, 1954; s. Anthony A. Klutz and Matilda (Konopka) Weigand; m. LetaMarie A. Rydzewski, July 15, 1978; children: Athena Marie, Anthony A. III. BS, Kings Coll., Wilkes-Barre, 1976; MS, Rensselaer Poly. Inst., 1978; MBA, Clemson U., 1988. Material devel. engr. Sangamo Capacitor-Schlumberger, Pickens, S.C., 1978-87, product devel. engr., 1986-87; mgr. process engring. Sangamo Weston-Schlumberger, West Union, S.C., 1987-90; safety and environ. mgr. Schlumberger Industries, West Union, 1990-94, health, safety and environ. mgr. Electricity N.Am., 1994-98, health, safety environ. N. Am., 1998—. Vice chmn. Oconee County Local Emergency Planning Com., Walhalla, S.C., 1988—; mem. coun. Holy Cross Parish, Pickens, 1986-87. Mem. Am. Vacuum Soc., Electro Chem. Soc., Am. Soc. Materials, S.C. C. of C. (tech. com.), Mgmt. Club (pres. 1985, 92, v.p. 1991), KC (Knight of Mo. award Pickens 1988, Grand Knight 1994-97). Avocations: reading, computing, travel. Home: 398 Chinquapin Rd Easley SC 29640-7053 Office: Sangamo Weston-Schlumberger Hwy 11 West Union SC 29696-9610

KLUTZOW, FRIEDRICH WILHELM, neuropathologist; b. Bandoeng, Preanger, Dutch East Indies, Aug. 6, 1923; came to U.S., 1953; s. Rudolph F.W. and Pauline (Van Thiel) K.; m. Apr. 2, 1954; children: Judith A., Michael J.; m. Merlene Hutto Byars, Dec. 10, 1999. MD, U. Utrecht, Netherlands, 1951. Diplomate Am. Bd. Neuropathology and Anatomic Pathology. Chief of staff Cmty. Meml. Hosp., Oconto Falls, Wis., 1965-68; pathology resident U. Wis., Madison, 1968-71, Armed Forces Inst. Pathology, Washington, 1971-72; neuropathologist VA Hosp., Mpls., 1972-75, dir. pathology dept. Brockton, Mass., 1975-83, Wichita, Kans., 1983-87, chief of staff Bath, N.Y., 1987-90, neuropathologist Bay Pines, Fla., 1991—. Clin. assoc. prof. pathology U. Rochester (N.Y.) Sch. Medicine, U. South Fla., Tampa; cons. in neuropathology Minn. Bd. Med. Practice, 1999—; invited spkr. 24th Internat. Congress on Arts & Comm. seminar on medicine Oxford (Eng.) U., 1997, 26th Internat. Congress, Lisbon, Portugal, 1999, 28th Internat. Congress, Cambridge, England, 2001. Prin. author: Neuropathology Manual: The Practical Approach, 1996, contbr. articles to profl. jours. Col. USAR, 1979 85. Recipient Paul Harris fellowship, Rotary Internat., Bath, 1990, Outstanding Career award, Dept. Vet. Affairs, Washington, 1990. Fellow: Coll. Am. Pathologists, mem.. Internat. Soc. Neuropathology, Am. Assn. Neuropathologists. Republican. Achievements include research in persistent vegetative state and practical approach to lesions in neuropathology. Home: PO Box 3387 West Columbia SC 29171-3387 Fax: 803-794-4869.

KLYATIS, LEV MATUSOVICH, test engineer; b. Kiev, Ukraine, Mar. 4, 1933; came to U.S., 1993; s. Matus I. Klyatis and Dina Sifry; m. Nellya V. Klyatis, Aug. 31, 1956; children: Irina, New York, Evgeny, Karmiel. MS, Agrl. Inst., Dnepropetrovsk, Ukraine, 1958; PhD in Engring. Tech., Belorussia State U., Minsk, 1963; Hab. Dr.Ing., Latvia State U., Jelgava, 1993; D of Tech. Scis., Leningrad Agrl. U., Pushkin, Russia, 1982. Test engr. Govtl. Test Ctr., Kiev, 1958-62, prin. engr. Kalinin, Russia, 1962-65; prin. specialist Ministry of Agrl., Moscow, 1965-68, head of dept., 1968-73; lead scientist, head of dept. All-USSR Agrichem. Inst., Moscow, 1973-86, All-USSR Industry Inst., Moscow, 1986-90; head of dept., prof. engring. U. Agrl., Moscow, 1988—90; chmn. State Enterprise Testmash, Moscow, 1990-93; head of dept. ECCOL Inc., N.Y.C., 1997—. Bd. dirs. Internat. Assn. Arts and Scis. Inc., N.Y.C.; academician Acad. for Quality Russian Fedn., 1998—; expert. U.S. tech. adv. group to Internat. Electrotech. Commn., 2000—. Author: Methods of Accelerated Testing, 1969, Accelerated Evaluation of Farm Machinery, 1985, Trends in the Development of Testing Technique, 1991, Step-by-Step Accelerated Testing, 1999, Successful Accelerated Testing Part 1, 2002, Foundation of Farm Machinery Accelerated Testing, 1980, The Strategy of Accelerated Reliability Testing for Car Components, 2000, Equipment for Accelerated Reliability Testing of Cars and Their Components, 2001; over 30 patents in field; contbr. over 200 articles to profl. books, papers and jours. Mem. Am. Soc. Quality (rsch. grantee 1998, Spl. Svc. award 2002, Allen Chop award 2003), Soc. Automotive Engrs. Internat. Achievements include development of 14 advanced technological systems of simulation and 12 new types of testing equipment research in application of new approach accelerated testing techniques in reliability engineering; invention of cost-effective technology of accelerated quality improvement, including high correlation between accelerated testing results and field results. Home: 72 Montgomery St Apt 1311 Jersey City NJ 07302-3827 E-mail: lklyatis@agoron.com.

KLYBERG, ALBERT THOMAS, historical society administrator; b. Hackensack, N.J., Aug. 8, 1940; AB, Coll. Wooster, 1962; MA in History, U. Mich.; LHD (hon.), R.I. Coll., 1985. Asst. curator manuscripts William L. Clements Libr., Ann Arbor, Mich., 1963-68; libr. R.I. Hist. Soc., Providence, 1968-69, exec. dir., 1969-99, Heritage Harbor Mus., Providence, R.I., 1999—; dir. mus. and programs Heritage Harbor, Providence, 2001. Adj. prof. history U. R.I., 1974-93, Providence Coll., 1986-93; project mgr. Woonsocket Visitors Ctr., Mus. Work and Culture. Compiler, bibliographer March of America series Univ. Microfilms, Inc., 1966; editor R.I. History; project dir. Papers of Gen. Nathanael Greene. Mem. R.I. Hist. Soc. Office: Heritage Harbor 222 Richmond St Providence RI 02903

KLYM, KENDALL, journalist, dancer, educator, choreographer; b. Hartford, Conn., Feb. 9, 1964; s. Nicholas and Lillian (Ostrowski) K. BA magna cum laude, Baylor U., 1994; postgrad., S.W. Tex. State U., 2002—. Classical ballet dancer Kansas City (Mo.) Ballet, 1984—86; soloist ballet dancer Chgo. City Ballet, 1976—87; classical ballet dancer Dallas Ballet, 1987—88; pantomime dancer Tivoli Pantomine Theatre, Copenhagen, 1988; prin. dancer State Ballet of Mo., Kansas City, 1988—89; ballet dancer Louisville Ballet, 1990—91; editl. intern Seeds Mag., Waco, Tex., 1992; assoc. editor Adventure West Mag., Incline Village, Nev., 1993; editor The Baylor Corral, Waco, 1993—94; city coun. reporter, feature writer Neighbors publ. of The Fresno (Calif.) Bee; staff reporter Carmel (Calif.) Pine Cone/Monterey Times; copy editor, page designer North County Times, Oceanside, Escondido, Calif.; tchr. of record Dept. English S.W. Tex. State U., 2001—. Dancer, choreographer, tchr. Tapestry Dance Co., Austin, Tex.; pub. rels. cons. Seeds Mag., Waco; freelance writer Presbyn. Today mag.; guest ballet tchr. Danse Sedona (Ariz.), Dance Inc., Phoenix, Tucson Regional Ballet, Sierra Vista (Ariz.) Ballet, 1997; choreographer, mktg. dir. Ballet Fantasque, Monterey, Calif., 1997; ballet tchr. Austin Musical Theatre Performing Arts Acad. Editor: The Asian Cultural Review, 1993, The Baylor Corral, 1993-94; freelance dance reviewer The Fresno Bee, Presbyterians Today mag.; freelance arts reviewer, features and travel writer Austin Am.-Statesman; contbr. articles to profl. jours. Group organizer Highland Presbyn. Ch., Louisville, 1990-92, Ctrl. Presbyn. Ch., Waco, 1992-94, fellowship group 1992-94; participant Habitat for Humanity, Waco, 1992. Recipient Fresno-Madera Area Agy. on Aging award for media coverage of sr. issues, 1995; acad. scholar S.W. Tex. State U., 2002. Mem. Alpha Chi. Avocations: spelunking, hangliding, canoeing, camping. Home: # A 816 Patterson Ave Austin TX 78703-4726

KLYMAN, FRED IRWIN, healthcare executive; b. Memphis, Feb. 23, 1946; s. Joseph and Lena (O'Mell) K.; m. Suzanne Bowman; children: Marnie O'Mell, Alicia Catherine. AA, Memphis State U., 1966, BS, 1967, MEd, 1970; EdD, Okla. State U., 1973. Instr. dept. sociology Memphis State U., 1970-71; asst. prof. dept. adminstrn. of justice Wichita (Kans.) State U., 1971-75; assoc. prof. crime study ctr. So. Ill. U., Carbondale, 1976-78; tng. comdr. police acad. Memphis Police Dept., 1978-86; asst. program dir., prof. Health Care Adminstrn. Baccalaureate program Tusculum Coll., Memphis, 1986-89; dir. provider rels. CIGNA Health Plan, Memphis, 1989-92; regional dir. provider rels. Healthsource Tenn., Inc., Memphis, 1993-97; exec. dir. The Stern Cardiovascular Ctr., Memphis, 1997—. Cons. police tng. Kans. Atty. Gen., Topeka, 1973-76; cons. Wichita Police Dept., 1974-76; lectr. Nat. Acad. FBI, Quantico, Va., 1975-76; adj. lectr. Shelby County Sheriff's Acad., Memphis, 1988-93. Editor: POlice Roles in a Changing Community, 1972, Accountability and the Criminal Justice Instructor, 1973, Introduction to Law Enforcement, 1975, Introduction to Police Administration, 1978. Tng. officer res. bur. Shelby County Sheriff's Dept., Memphis, 1987-93. Recipient Police Neighborhood Svc. Ctr. award U.S. Dept. Justice, 1973, Police Community Rels. Inst. award U.S. Dept. Justice, 1974, Community-Centered Crime Prevention award U.S. HUD, 1978, Police Roles in Sch. Crime Prevention award U.S. Dept. Justice, 1975, Crime Prevention Tng. award U.S. Dept. Justice, 1985. Mem. Mid-South Med. Mgmt. Assn. Jewish. Avocation: raising american kennel club registered carin terrier dogs. Home: 2269 Lansingwood Dr Germantown TN 38139-5242 Office: 80 Humphreys Ctr Memphis TN 38120-2353

KLYOSOV, ANATOLE ALEX, biochemist, researcher; b. Chernyakhovsk, Russia, Nov. 20, 1946; came to US, 1990; s. Alexey Ivan and Tamara Michael (Kuz) K.; m. Gail Michael Muratov, Dec. 28, 1967; children: Svetlana, Yuri. MS, Moscow State U., 1969, PhD, 1972, DSc, 1978. Scientist Moscow State U., 1969—72, asst. prof., 1972—75, sr. scientist, 1975—79, prof., 1979—81; prof., head Carbohydrate Rsch. Lab. Acad. Sci. USSR, Moscow, 1981—92; prof. biochemistry Harvard Med. Sch., Boston, 1990—; mgr. biochem. rsch., v.p. Kadant Composites, 1996—; chief scientist Pro-Pharmaceuticals, Inc., Boston, 2000—. Vis. lectr. biochemistry Harvard U., 1974-75; adv. bd. Coun. Biotech. Acad. Sci. USSR, 1981-90, chmn. commn. cellulose bioconversion, 1982-90; expert panel Biofocus Found., Stockholm, Washington, 1991—. Author: The Practical Course of Chemical and Enzyme Kinetics, 1976, Enzyme Catalysis, 1980, Enzymatic Degradation of Polymers, 1984, Enzyme Engineering at the Industrial Level, 1989. Recipient Lenin Komsomol Nat. prize USSR in Sci. USSR Govt., Moscow, 1978, Nat. prize in Sci., 1984, Sci. and Tech. Gold medal, 1988. Mem. Am. Chem. Soc., Internat. Orgn. Biotech. Bioengring., World Acad. Art and Sci. Avocations: science, tennis, running. Home: 36 Walsh Rd Newton MA 02459-3529 Office: Kadant Composites 8 Alfred Cir Bedford MA 01730-2340 also: Pro-Pharmaceuticals 189 Wells Ave Newton MA 02459 E-mail: aklyosov@comcast.net., aklyosov@kadantcomposites.com.

KMENTA, JAN, economics educator; b. Prague, Czechoslovakia, Jan. 3, 1928; came to U.S., 1963; m. Joan Helen Gaffney, Aug. 9, 1959; children: David, Steven. B in Econs. with 1st class honors, Sydney U., 1955; MA, Stanford U., 1959, PhD, 1964; hon. doctorate, U. Saarland, Germany, 1989. Lectr. U. N.S.W., Sydney, 1957-61; sr. lectr. Sydney U., 1961-63; asst. prof. U. Wis., Madison, 1963-65; prof. Mich. State U., East Lansing, 1965-73, U. Mich., Ann Arbor, 1973—. Vis. prof. U. Bonn, Germany, 1971-72, 1979-80, U. Saarland, Saarbrucken, Germany, 1984, 85, 86. Author: Elements of Econometrics, 2d edit., 1986; editor: (with others) Evaluation of Econometric Models, 1980, Large-Scale Macro-Econometric Models, 1981; contbr. articles to profl. jours. Recipient U.S. Sr. Scientist Prize, Humboldt Found., Bonn, 1979; Fulbright scholar, 1957-59. Fellow Am. Statis. Assn., Econometric Soc.; mem. Am. Econ. Assn., Czechoslovak Soc. Arts and Scis. in Am. Home: 2511 Londonderry Rd Ann Arbor MI 48104-4017 Office: U Mich Dept Econs Ann Arbor MI 48109

KMETY-STEVENSON, CARMEN RAMONA, physicist; b. Arad, Romania, May 9, 1964; came to U.S., 1989; d. Samuil and Viorica Kmety; m. Kenneth Lee Stevenson, May 9, 1992; 1 child, Sarah Ann. BS, MS in Physics, U. Bucharest, Romania, 1987; MS in Math., Purdue U., 1994; PhD in Physics, Ohio State U., 2000. Grad. tchg. asst. Ohio State U., Columbus, 1994-96, grad. lab. supr., 1996-97, grad. rsch. asst., 1997-2000; postdoctoral appointee Argonne (Ill.) Nat. Lab., 2000—02. Contbr. articles to sci. jours. Mem. Am. Phys. Soc., Assn. Women Mathematicians (hon.). Avocations: traveling, photography, aerobics, jogging. Home: 8214 Black Oak Ct Fort Wayne IN 46825 E-mail: ckmety@netscape.net.

KMETZ, DONALD R. retired academic administrator; Dean Sch. Medicine U. Louisville, 1981-98; ret.; v.p. health affairs U. Louisville, 1992-98; ret. Office: U Louisville Sch Medicine Health Scis Ctr 323 E Chestnut St Louisville KY 40202-1823

KMIEC, DOUGLAS WILLIAM, law educator, columnist; b. Chgo., Sept. 24, 1951; s. Walter and Beatrice (Neumann) K.; m. Carolyn Keenan, June 2, 1973; children: Keenan, Katherine, Kiley, Kolleen, Kloe. BA, Northwestern U., 1973; JD, U. So. Calif., L.A., 1976. Bar: Ill. 1976, Calif. 1980, U.S. Supreme Ct. 1986. Assoc. Vedder, Price, et al, Chgo., 1976-78; prof. law Valparaiso U., Ind., 1978-80, Notre Dame U., 1980-99; Caruso family chair in constitutional law Pepperdine U., 1999-01; dean, St. Thomas More prof. Cath. U., Washington, 2001—. Dir. Thomas J. White Ctr. on Law and Govt., 1983-88; dep. asst., atty. gen. Ofice of Legal Counsel, Dept. Justice, Washington, 1985-87; asst. atty. gen., 1988-89; vis. scholar Stanford U., 1985; spl. asst. to sec. HUD, Washington, 1982-83; disting. chair Dorothy & Leonard Straus, Pepperdine U. Sch. Law, 1995-96, 97-98; mem. pres.'s Commn. on Manufactured Housing, Washington, 1984-85, 89-92; mem. adv. com. Civil Rights Commn., bd. trustees Housing Allowance Program, Ind., 1983-85; state chmn. Scholars for Reagan and Bush, Ind., 1984. Author: Recharting Criminal Procedure, 1984, Zoning and Planning Desk Book, 1986, The Attorney General's Lawyer, 1992, Cease-fire on the Family, 1995, (with Stephen B. Presser) The American Constitutional Order, 1998, Individual Rights and the American Constitution, 1998, The History, Philosophy and Structure of the American Constitution, 1998; host, exec. prodr. Forefront TV series WNIT-TV, 1984-85; radio commentator The American Family Perspective, 1994-96; columnist Chgo. Tribune, 1996-99. Recipient Clark Boardman prize, 1983, 87, 90, Disting. Svc. award HUD, 1983, Disting. Svc. award Dept. Justice, 1987, Edmund J. Randolph award Dept. Justice, 1989; White House fellow, Washington, 1982-83, 40th Anniversary Fulbright Disting. fellow, 1987. Mem. U.S. Supreme Ct. Bar, Ill. Bar Assn., Calif. Bar Assn., Notre Dame Club (Washington). Republican. Roman Catholic. Office: Cath U Sch of Law Washington DC 20064

KMIEC, EDWARD URBAN, bishop; b. Trenton, N.J., June 4, 1936; s. John and Thecla (Czupta) K. Ed., St. Charles Coll., Catonsville, Md., 1956, St. Mary's Sem., Balt., 1958; STL, Gregorian U., Rome, 1962. Ordained priest Roman Cath. Ch., 1961. Ordained titular bishop Simidicca and aux. bishop Trenton, 1982-92; bishop of Nashville, 1992—. Roman Catholic. Address: The Catholic Center 2400 21st Ave S Nashville TN 37212-5302

KNAB, KAREN MARKLE, lawyer; d. Joseph George and Mary (Kelly) Markle. BA, St. Marys Coll., South Bend, Ind., 1970; JD, U. Chgo., 1975. Bar: Ill. 1975, U.S. Dist. Ct. (no. dist.) Ill. 1981, U.S. Ct. Appeals (7th cir.) 1981. Dep. dir. state cts. Wis. Supreme Ct., Madison, 1977-80; dep. dir. Dept. Revenue, State of Ill., Chgo., 1980-81; dir. family divsn. D.C. Superior Ct., Washington, 1981-84; dir. adminstrn. Pepper, Hamilton & Scheetz, Washington, 1984-86, chief adminstrv. officer Phila., 1988-2000; chief oper. officer Shaw Pittman, Washington, 2000—. Cir. exec. U.S. Ct. Appeals (D.C.) Cir., 1986-88; pres., cons. Knab Assocs., Chgo., 1980-81. Author: Courts of Limited Jurisdiction, 1977, Alternatives to Litigation, 1978; contbr. articles to profl. jours. Mem. Nat. Assn. Trial Ct. Adminstrs., Assn. Legal Adminstrs. Office: 2300 N St NW Washington DC 20037-1122 E-mail: karen.knab@shawpittman.com.

KNABE, GEORGE WILLIAM, JR., pathologist, educator; b. Grand Rapids, Mich., June 29, 1924; s. George William and Dorothy Emma (Fischofer) K., m. Lorine Jeanette Moffit, Jan. 16, 1954; children: Katharine J., Elizabeth J., Ann C., Dorothy M. Student, Mich. State U., 1942-43, The Citadel, Charleston, SC, 1943-44, Johns Hopkins U., 1944-45; MD, U. Md., 1949. Diplomate Am. Bd. Pathology. Intern Balt. City Hosp., 1949-50; resident pathology Cleve. Clin. Found., 1950-51, Henry Ford Hosp., Detroit, 1953-54; chief lab. svc. VA Ctr., Dayton, Ohio, 1955-57; vis. prof. pathology U. El Salvador Sch. Medicine, 1957-59; asst. prof. pathology U. P.R. Sch. Medicine, 1959-60; prof., chmn. dept. pathology Sch. Medicine, U. S.D., 1960-68, dean., 1967-72; dir. med. edn. St. Luke's Hosp., Duluth, 1972-78; prof. pathology U. Minn.-Duluth Sch. Medicine, 1972—, assoc. dean clin. affairs., 1972-76; chief. dept. pathology Virginia (Minn.) Regional Med. Ctr., 1978-98; pres. Range Pathology, 1998—. Bd. dirs Health Sys. Agy. of Western Lake Superior, Duluth 1975-82, No. Lakes Health Care Consortium, 1984—, U. Minn. Health and Med. Sch. Adv. Groups 1972—. 1st lt. to capt. M.C., USAF, 1951-53; surgeon to capt., USPHS Res., 1957—. Mem. AMA, U.S. and Can. Acad. Pathology, Am. Soc. Clin. Pathologists, Coll. Am. Pathologists. Avocations: art, horticulture, photography. Home: 1008 S 7th Ave Virginia MN 55792-3151 Office: Range Pathology 1008 7th Ave S Virginia MN 55792-3151

KNACHEL, PHILIP ATHERTON, librarian; b. Indpls., June 23, 1926; s. Firman F. and Mary Esther (Atherton) K.; m. Pierrette Annie Roy, July 1, 1955; children— Sylvette, Eric BS, Northwestern U., 1948; cert., Institut de Tours, France, 1951; MA, Johns Hopkins U., 1952, PhD, 1954; MSL.S., Syracuse U., 1959; Litt.D. (hon.), Amherst Coll., 1984. Instr. history Hunter Coll., N.Y.C., 1954-57; historian Rome Air Devel. Ctr., N.Y., 1957-59; chief tech. services Folger Shakespeare Library, Washington, 1959-61, asst. dir., to 1969, assoc. dir., 1969-93; freelance French translator, 1993—. Adj. prof. history U. Md., College Park, 1967-69; French translator cons. Author: England and the Fronde, 1967; editor: Eikon Basilike, 1966, The Case of the Commonwealth of England Stated, 1967 Served with USN, 1944-46 Mem. ALA, Am. Translators Assn. Clubs: Cosmos (Washington). Avocations: piano, travel. Home: 5807 Phoenix Dr Bethesda MD 20817-3401

KNACKSTEDT, MARY V. interior designer; b. Harrisburg, Pa., Oct. 26, 1940; d. Harry and Veronica Knackstedt. Student, Pratt Inst., 1957-59, Cooper Union, Phila. Coll. Art. Pres. Knackstedt Inc., Harrisburg, N.Y.C., 1958—. Mem. adv. bd. PNC Bank, N.A., Camp Hill, Pa., 1981—; pvt. practice cons.; speaker in field; lectr. bus. practices Harvard U., 1988—. Author: Interior Dsign for Profit, 1980, Profitable Career Options for Designers, 1985, The Interior Design Business Handbook, 1988, 92, Marketing and Design Services: The Designer Client Rlationship, 1993, Interior Design and Beyond, 1995; interior design projects include Hershey Med. Ctr., Milton Hershey Sch., founder's Hall, Hershey, Pa., The Hershey Pub. Libr. Bus. devel. program founder Riverfront Peoples Park, Harrisburg, 1980-90; bd. dirs. Harrisburg Symphony Assn., 1983-89; founder, pres. Profl. Cath. Women's Forum; devel. coun. Bishop McDevitt Sch., Harrisburg. Fellow Internat. Interior Design Assn., Am. Soc. Interior Designers (past officer); mem. Internat. Furnishings and Design Assn., Illuminating Engring. Soc. N.Am., Interior Design Soc., Pres.'s Assn., Am. Mgmt. Assn. Home and Office: 2901 N Front St Harrisburg PA 17110-1223 Address: 161 E 61st St New York NY 10021-8125

KNAG, PAUL EVERETT, lawyer; b. Flushing, N.Y., Feb. 26, 1948; s. Howard Alf and Charlotte (Rausch) K.; m. Maryann McCaffrey, June 27, 1970; children: Paul Everett, Peter, Kathleen, John. BA magna cum laude, Queens Coll., 1967; JD cum laude, Harvard U., 1970. Bar: N.Y. 1970, Conn. 1971, D.C. 1983. Law clk. U.S. Ct. Appeals (2nd cir.), N.Y.C., 1970-71; ptnr. Cummings & Lockwood, Stamford, 1979—2002, Murtha Cullina LLP, New Haven, 2002—. Author: HIPAA: A Guide to Healthcare Privacy and Security Law, 2002. Mem. Mass. Bar Assn., Boston Bar Assn., Conn. Bar Assn., Regional Bar Assn., Am. Health Lawyers Assn., Conn. Health Lawyers Assn., Officer's Club Hartford, Dunes Club (Naragansett, R.I.), Middlesex Club Darien, Harvard Club Fairfield County, Quinnipiack Club. Republican. Office: Murtha Cullina LLP Box 704 2 Whitney Ave New Haven CT 06503-0704 also: 99 High St Boston MA 02110-2320

KNAPE, HERBERT FRITZ, business executive; b. Grand Rapids, Mich., Dec. 24, 1922; s. John C. and Mayme J. Knape; m. Glenna S. Knape, Feb. 12, 1950; children: John, Judy, Mary Lou, Jim, Bill, Betsy, Robert. BS in Engring., MIT, 1944. Process engr. Jarecki Machine & Tool, Grand Rapids, Mich., 1945-55; v.p. engring. Knape and Vogt Mfg., Grand Rapids, 1955-65; pres. Knape Industires, Inc., Rockford, Mich., 1965—2001, chmn. bd., 2001—. Mem. Soc. of Vacuum Coaters (bd. dirs.), Am. Welding Soc. (bd. dirs.), Employers Assn. (bd. dirs.), Spring Lake Yacht Club (bd. dirs.), Grand Rapids Yacht Club, Spring Lake Country Club. Roman Catholic. Avocations: sailing, yachting. Home: 435 Edgemere Dr SE Grand Rapids MI 49506-2904 Office: Knape Industries Inc 10701 Northland Dr NE Rockford MI 49341-8008 E-mail: knapeindincnancy@wmis.net.

KNAPIK, JOSEPH JOHN, research physiologist; BS in Phys. Edn., BA in Psychology, Calif. State U., Hayward, 1970, MS in Phys. Edn., 1974; ScD in Applied Anatomy and Physiology, Boston U., 1984. Instr. phys. edn. St. Clement's Elem. Sch., Hayward, 1969-72; grad. asst., intr., intramural sports dir. Calif. State U., Hayward, 1971-73; asst. dir. Mariner Sailing Sch., Alameda, Calif., 1973-74; rsch. technician U.S. Army Rsch. Inst. Environ. Medicine, Natick, Mass., 1975-83; physiologist U.S. Army War Coll., Carlisle, Pa., 1984-88; rsch. physiologist U.S. Army Inst. Environ. Medicine, Natick, 1988-93; exercise physiologist U.S. Army War Coll., Carlisle, 1993-94; rsch. physiologist U.S. Army Rsch. Lab., Aberdeen Proving Ground, Md., 1994-97, U.S. Army Ctr. for Health Promotion and Preventive Medicine, Aberdeen Proving Ground, Md., 1997—. Adj. assoc. prof. indsl. engring. N.C. Agrl. and Tech. State U., Greensboro, 1996—. Contbr. articles to sci. and profl. jours. Grantee U.S. Army Human Factors Engring., 1993, Army Med. Rsch. and Devel. Command, 1992, Def. Women's Health Rsch., 1994, Pvt. Industry, 1998. Avocations: hiking, mountaineering, long distance running, bicycling, home brewing. E-mail: Joseph.knapik@apg.amedd.army.mil.

KNAPP, ALBERT BRUCE, gastroenterologist; b. N.Y.C., Aug. 9, 1955; s. Russell Sage and Bettina (Liebowitz) K.; m. Alice Anne Cohen, Sept. 7, 1986. BA, Columbia U., 1975, MD, 1979. Intern, resident Albert Einstein Med. Ctr., N.Y.C., 1979-82; fellow in gastroenterology Brigham & Women's Hosp. and Harvard Med. Sch., Boston, 1982-85; assoc. attending Lenox Hill Hosp., N.Y.C., 1985—, St. Vincent's Hosp., N.Y.C., 1985—; asst. prof. NYU Med. Sch., N.Y.C., 1990—; asst. attending NYU Med. Ctr., N.Y.C., 2002—. Author textbook in field, 1982; contbr. numerous articles to profl. jours. Trustee N.Y. Police Found., N.Y.C., 1991—. NIH rsch. grantee, 1982. Fellow ACP (jour. reviewer Annals of Internal Medicine 1985—); mem. Am. Gastroenterol. Assn. (jour. reviewer Gastroenterology 1985—), Am. Assn. Gastrointestinal Endoscopy, Am. Assn. for Study of Liver Disease (Rsch. award 1984). Office: 21 E 79th St New York NY 10021-0125 E-mail: scopeu@attglobal.net.

KNAPP, CANDACE LOUISE, sculptor; b. Benton Harbor, Mich., Feb. 28, 1948; d. Claire Warren and Frances Mary (Collins) K.; m. Björn Andrén, Mar. 3, 1988. BFA, Cleve. Inst. Art, 1971; MFA, U. Ill., 1974. Sculptures exhibited in numerous galleries; represented in permanent collections including Northwood Inst. Collection, West Palm Beach, Fla., Memphis Brooks Mus. Art, Mobil Oil Co., Stockholm, HageGården Music Ctr., Edane, Sweden, others; included in book Contemporary American Women Sculptors; numerous commns. including St. Peter and Paul Cath. Ch., Orlando, Fla., Padre Pio Found., Cromwell, Conn., Temple Emanuel, Dallas, West Haven, Conn., Tampa (Fla.) Gen. Hosp., Pub. Art Commn. City of St. Petersburg, Fla., Pub. Art Commn. Hillsborough County Courthouse, Tampa, Fla. Helen Greene Perry traveling scholar, 1971. Fax: 813-654-6572. E-mail: aok@andoknap.com.

KNAPP, CHARLES BOYNTON, economist, educator, university president; b. Ames, Iowa, Aug. 13, 1946; s. Albert B. and Anne Marie (Taff) K.; m. Lynne Vickers, Aug. 25, 1967; 1 dau., Amanda. BS, Iowa State U., 1968; MA, PhD, U. Wis., 1972. Asst. prof. econs., research assoc. Ctr. for Study of Human Resources, U. Tex., Austin, 1972-76; spl. asst. to Sec. of Labor Dept. Labor, Washington, 1977-79, dep. asst. sec. labor, 1979-81; assoc. prof. pub. policy George Washington U., 1981-82; assoc. prof. econs. Tulane U., New Orleans, 1982-87, sr. v.p., 1982-85, exec. v.p., 1985-87; pres., prof. econs. U. Ga., Athens, 1987-97; pres. Aspen Inst., 1997-99; ptnr. Heidrick & Struggles Internat., Inc., Atlanta, 2000—. Bd. dirs. AFLAC Inc. Contbr. articles to profl. jours. Office: Heidrick & Struggles Internat Inc 303 Peachtree St NE Ste 3100 Atlanta GA 30308-3200

KNAPP, CHARLES LINCOLN, law educator; b. Zanesville, Ohio, Oct. 22, 1935; s. James Lincoln and Laura Alma (Richardson) K.; m. Beverley Earle Trott, Aug. 23, 1958 (dec. 1995); children: Jennifer Lynn, Liza Beth. BA, Denison U., 1956; JD, NYU, 1960. Bar: N.Y. 1961. Assoc. Paul, Weiss, Rifkind, Wharton & Garrison, N.Y.C., 1960-64; asst. prof. law NYU Law Sch., N.Y.C., 1964-67, assoc. prof., 1967-70, prof. law, 1970-88, Max E. Greenberg prof. contract law, 1988-98, Max E. Greenberg prof. emeritus contract law, 1998—, assoc. dean, 1977-82. Vis. prof. law U. Ariz. Law Sch., Tucson, 1973, Harvard U. Law Sch., Cambridge, Mass., 1974—75, Bklyn. Law Sch., 2003, Hastings Coll. Law, San Francisco, 1996—97, disting. prof. law, 1998—2000, Joseph W. Cotchett Disting. prof. law, 2000—. Author: Problems in Contract Law, 1976, (with N. Crystal and H. Prince) 5th edit., 2003; editor-in-chief: Commercial Damages, 1986. Mem. Am. Law Inst., Order Coif, Phi Beta Kappa. Office: Hastings Coll Law 200 McAllister St San Francisco CA 94102-4707 E-mail: knappch@uchastings.edu.

KNAPP, DAVID HEBARD, banker; b. N.Y.C., May 22, 1938; s. Alfred John and Doris (Hebard) K.; m. Letitia Lykes, Aug. 18, 1959; children— Genevieve, Christopher, Breckenridge. BA, Williams Coll. With Rotan, Mosle, Houston, 1960-62; asst. cashier, mgr. credit dept. Fannin Bank, Houston, 1962-64, asst. v.p. comml. loans, 1964-66, v.p. comml. loans, 1968-70, vice chmn. bd., 1970-82; co-chmn. exec. com. Interfirst Bank Fannin, 1982-83. Devel. loan

officer AID, Rio de Janeiro, Brazil, 1966-68; pres. Penta Internat., Inc., Houston, 1979-82; dir. Lykes Bros. Inc., Tampa, Fla., First Fla. Banks, Tampa, Interocean Steamship Co., Tampa, Lykes Bros. Steamship Co., New Orleans Trustee St. Lukes Episcopal Hosp., Houston, St. John's Sch., Urban Affairs Corp.; trustee Armand Bayou Nature Center, Pasadena, Tex., pres., 1977-79. Mem.: Houston Country (Houston). Home: 2328 Timber Ln Houston TX 77027-4129 Office: 2807 Bammel Ln Houston TX 77098-1105

KNAPP, EDWARD ALAN, retired government agency administrator, scientist; b. Salem, Oreg., Mar. 7, 1932; s. Gardner and Lucille (Moore) K.; m. Jean Elaine Hartwell, June 27, 1954; children: Sandra, David, Robert, Mary. AB, Pomona Coll., 1954; PhD, U. Calif., Berkeley, 1958; D.Sc. (hon.), Pomona Coll., 1984, Bucknell U., 1984. With Los Alamos Sci. Lab., U. Calif., 1958-82, dir. accelerator tech. div., 1977-82; asst. dir., then dir. NSF, Washington, 1982-84; sr. fellow Los Alamos Nat. Lab., 1984; pres. Univs. Rsch. Assn., Washington, 1985-89; sr. fellow Los Alamos Nat. Lab., 1990, dir. Los Alamos meson physics facility, 1990-91; pres. Santa Fe Inst., 1991-96, prof., 1996. Bd. trustee Coll. Santa Fe; bd. dirs. K/P Corp.; cons. in field Contbr. articles to profl. jours. Fellow AAAS, Am. Phys. Soc.; mem. IEEE, Sigma Xi. Methodist. Office: 1399 Hyde Park Rd Santa Fe NM 87501-8943

KNAPP, GEORGE GRIFF PRATHER, retired insurance executive; b. New Rochelle, N.Y., June 26, 1923; s. Griff Prather and Lucy Chadbourne (Norvell) K.; m. Eva Witte, May 30, 1953; children: Edward, Wesley, Helen, Elizabeth. BA, Harvard U., 1945; postgrad., Law Sch., 1946. With Chubb & Son, N.Y.C., 1947-88, mgr. personal lines dept., 1966-73, asst. to pres., 1973, Can. zone officer, 1974-78, N.Y. zone officer, 1978-83, sr. v.p., 1968-88, nat. producer liaison, 1984-88; sr. v.p. Fed. Ins. Co., 1968-88, dir., 1970-88; exec. dir. Excess Line Assn. N.Y., 1988-90; cons. ins. advisor Westchester County vol. hosp. Arbitrator for major property/casualty ins. co. Gov. Lawrence Hosp., 1968-75. Served with U.S. Army, 1943-46. Mem.: Harvard (N.Y.C.); Bronxville Field. Republican. Roman Catholic. Home: 23500 Cristo Rey Dr Unit 312D Cupertino CA 95014-6527

KNAPP, GEORGE M. lawyer; b. Inglewood, Calif., June 19, 1954; BA magna cum laude, UCLA, 1975; JD, George Washington U., 1978. Bar: Calif. 1978, D.C. 1979. Law clk. to Hon. Jon G. Lotis Fed. Energy Regulatory Commn., 1978-79, dep. asst. gen. counsel, 1980; ptnr. Squire, Sanders & Dempsey L.L.P., Washington. Mem. ABA (vice chmn. alt. energy sources com. sect. of environ., energy, and resources, 1980-85, chmn. 1985-89, mem. coun. 1989-92, chmn. membership com. 1992-94, chmn. strategic planning com. 1994-96, vice chmn. sect. 1996-97, chmn.-elect sect. 1997-98, chmn. sect. 1998-99), State Bar Calif., D.C. Bar, Energy Bar Assn. (chmn. program com. 1991-92, chmn. internat. energy transactions com. 1995-97), Phi Beta Kappa. Office: Squire Sanders & Dempsey LLP 1201 Pennsylvania Ave NW Washington DC 20044 E-mail: gknapp@ssd.com.

KNAPP, HOWARD RAYMOND, internist, clinical pharmacologist; b. Red Bank, N.J., Oct. 5, 1949; s. Howard Raymond and Jane Marie (Ray) K.; m. Brenda Louise Carr, 1984; 1 child, Matthew. AB in Biology, Washington U., St. Louis, 1971; MD, Vanderbilt U., 1977, PhD in Pharmacology, 1984. Diplomate Am. Bd. Internal Medicine. Asst. prof. medicine and pharmacology Vanderbilt U., Nashville, 1984-89, assoc. prof., 1990, assoc. prof. internal medicine and pharmacology U. Iowa, Iowa city, 1990-97, prof. internal medicine and pharmacology, 1997-2000, assoc. dir. NIH Clin. Rsch. Ctr., 1997-2000; exec. dir. Deaconess Billings (Mont.) Clin. Res. Divsn., 2000—. Mem. NIH Nutrition Study Sect., Bethesda, Md., 1994—96; cons. pharm. firms, grant orgns. and govtl. entities ; mem. applied pharmacol. task force Nat. Bd. Med. Examiners, 1997—2000; mem. expert panel on cardiovasc. and renal drugs U.S. Pharmacopeia, 2000—. Editor-in-chief Lipids, 1995—; contbr. numerous articles to profl. jours., chpts. to books. Grantee NIH, Am. Heart Assn., others. Fellow ACP, Am. Heart Assn. (vascular biol. rsch. rev. com. 1993-95, arteriosclerosis coun.); mem. Ctrl. Soc. for Clin. Rsch. (chair clin. pharmacol. sect. 1992-95), Am. Soc. for Clin. Pharmacology and Therapeutics. Achievements include first demonstration that calcium ionophores stimulate eicosanoid synthesis; first evidence that N-3 fatty acids reduce platelet activation and blood pressure in patients; first demonstration of the effects of 5-lipoxygenase inhibition in humans. E-mail: hknapp@billingsclinic.org.

KNAPP, JAMES IAN KEITH, judge; b. Bklyn., Apr. 6, 1943; s. Charles Townsend and Christine (Grange) K.; m. Joan Elizabeth Cunningham, June 10, 1967 (div. Mar. 1971); 1 child, Jennifer Elizabeth; m. Carol Jean Brown, July 14, 1981; children: Michelle Christine, David Michael Keith AB cum laude, Harvard U., 1964; JD, U. Colo., 1967; M in Law in Taxation, Georgetown U., 1989. Bar: Colo. 1967, Calif. 1968, U.S. Supreme Ct. 1983, D.C. 1986, Ohio 1995. Dep. dist. atty. County of L.A., 1968-79; head dep. dist. atty. Pomona br. office, 1979-82; dep. asst. atty. gen. criminal divsn. U.S. Dept. Justice, Washington, 1982-86, dep. assoc. atty. gen., 1986-87, dep. asst. atty. gen. tax divsn., 1988-89, acting asst. atty. gen. tax divsn., 1989, acting dep. chief organized crime sect. criminal divsn., 1989-91, dep. dir., asset forfeiture office criminal divsn., 1991-94; adminstrv. law judge Social Security Adminstrn., 1994—. Editor: California Uniform Crime Charging Standards and Manual, 1975 Vice chmn. Young Reps. Nat. Fedn., 1973-75; pres. Calif. Young Reps., 1975-77; mem. exec. com. Rep. State Ctrl. Com., Calif., 1975-77. Mem.: DC Bar Assn., Calif. Bar Assn. Episcopalian. Avocations: travel, reading. Office: Office of Hearings & Appeals 110 N Main St Suite 800 Dayton OH 45402-1786

KNAPP, JOHN ANTHONY, lawyer; b. Mason City, Iowa, June 14, 1949; s. John Emmett and Lois Jane (Feeney) K.; m. Maureen Ann Jacobs, Dec. 20, 1972; children: Christopher John, Kevin Anthony, Elizabeth Lael. BA, St. John's U., Collegeville, Minn., 1971; JD, U. Iowa, 1974. Bar: Iowa 1974, Minn. 1974, D.C. 1982, U.S. Dist. Ct. Minn. 1974. Asst. revisor of statutes Minn. Legislature, St. Paul, 1974-76; v.p. Hessian, McKasy & Soderberg, Mpls., 1976-85; ptnr. Winthrop & Weinstine, St. Paul, 1985—. Adj. asst. prof. St. Mary's Coll. Grad. Ctr., Mpls., 1985—. Contbr. articles to profl. jours. Mem. ABA, Iowa Bar Assn., Minn. Bar Assn., D.C. Bar Assn., Ramsey County Bar Assn., Min. Govt. Rels. Coun. (pres. 1993-94), Citizens League, Mortgage Bankers Assn. Minn. (chmn. law com. 1984—), Town and Country Club. Mem. Democratic Farmer Labor Party. Roman Catholic. Home: 2193 Sargent Ave Saint Paul MN 55105-1130 Office: Winthrop & Weinstine 3200 Minnesota World Trade Ctr 30 7th St E Saint Paul MN 55101-4914 E-mail: jknapp@winthrop.com .

KNAPP, JUDITH ANN, computer information systems educator; b. Ft. Wayne, Ind., July 6, 1943; d. Walter Fredrick Jr. and Margaret June (Houk) Nagel; (div. June 1979); 1 child, Kathryn Louise. Student, Earlham Coll., 1961-62; BS in Bus., Ind. U., 1965, MBA in Mktg., 1967. Retail intern F&R Lazarus, Columbus, Ohio, 1964; acct. Wible & Adams, Bloomington, Ind., 1964-66; systems analyst Eli Lilly & Co., Indpls., 1967-68; sr. systems engr. Quaker Oats Co., Chgo., 1969; systems and program mgr. Androcor, Inc., Hammond, Ind., 1969 73; sr. systems analyst Boeing Computer Svcs., Calumet City, Ill., 1973-75; pvt. practice Hammond, 1976-83; assoc. prof. computer info. sys. Ind. U. N.W., Gary, Ind., 1983—. Author: Data Structures for Business Programming, 1989. Bd. dirs. Girl Scouts of the Calumet coun., Highland, Ind., 1983—. Mem. Assn. Info. Tech. Profls., Am. Mktg. Assn., Midwest and N.Am. Case Writers Assn., Assn. MBA Execs. Office: Ind U NW 3400 Broadway Gary IN 46408-1101

KNAPP, JUDY ANN, pharmacist; b. Cin., July 21, 1952; BS in Pharmacy, U. Cinn., 1975. Registered pharmacist, Ohio. Pharmacy intern Jewish Hosp., Cin., 1970-75; pharmacist Children's Hosp. Med. Ctr., Cin., 1975—. Item writer, reviewer Pharmacy Technician Certification Bd., Washington, 1996, 97, 98, 99, 2002. Editor: Drug Formulary, 1989-93, 98, 2001-02; contbr. articles to profl. jours. Recipient Dupont Pharm. Innovative Pharmacy Practice award, 1998, Star award Am. Pharm. Assn., 1987, 88, 89, APPM Presentation award, 1992. Office: Childrens Hosp Med Ctr 3333 Burnet Ave Cincinnati OH 45229-3026

KNAPP, LONNIE TROY, elementary education educator; b. Charles City, Iowa, Dec. 2, 1948; s. Troy Leroy and Anna Mildred (Conner) K.; m. Nancy Maureen Godfrey, Aug. 19, 1972; children: Eric Lonnie, Jamie Troy, Dusty Mack. BA, U. No. Iowa, 1972. Elem. tchr., Clear Lake, Iowa, 1972-92, Palm Springs (Calif.) Unified Sch. Dist., 1992—. Contbr. articles to profl. jours. Recipient Outstanding Tchr. award, Conservation Tchr. award, Iowa, North Cen. U.S. Mem. NEA, Iowa Edn. Assn., Calif. Tchrs. Assn., Clear Lake Edn. Assn. (various offices). Home: 42360 Minto Way Hemet CA 92544-9038

KNAPP, LUCRETIA A, artist, educator; b. Wheeling, W.Va., July 28, 1956; d. Charles Freeman and Mary Evelyn Knapp; life ptnr. Lynne M Yamamoto, Oct. 3, 1961. BA in Photography, Ohio State U., 1979, MA in English Lit., Woman's Studies, Photography and Video, 1985, Master of Liberal Studies, 1990; MFA, U. of Mich., 1997. Adj. faculty Sch. of Visual Arts, N.Y.C., 2000—, NYU, N.Y.C., 2000—, Internat. Ctr. of Photography, N.Y.C., 2000—. Screening of film casting stones, Away From Home at the Wexner Center, Columbus, OH, ghost of a flea (video loop), B-Hotel exhibition at P.S. 1 Contemporary Art Center, LIC, NY, yellow light (video), Akihabara-TV, Tokyo, Japan, Davina Knapp (photograph), Our Grandmothers: 75 Women Photographers; author: (the queer voice in marnie (article) Out in Culture: Gay, Lesbian and Queer Essays on Popular Culture (originally pub. in Cinema Jour., 1993). Recipient Best Interactive Program, Film and Video Festival, U. of Mich., 1999, Saturday Night Audience award, Media City II, Windsor, Ont., 1995. Mem.: Coll. Art Assn. Personal E-mail: lucretia@umich.edu.

KNAPP, MARK LANE, communication educator, consultant; b. Kansas City, Mo., July 12, 1938; s. Herbert H. and Mary Ellen (Coleman) K.; m. Cynthia Lackie Dennis, Jan. 27, 1963 (div. Aug. 1974); children: Hilary A. Cellard, Eric C.; m. Lillian J. Davis, Aug. 8, 1975 (div. July 2002); 1 child, Avery K. Davis. BS, U. Kans., 1962, MA, 1963; PhD, Pa. State U., 1966. From instr. to asst. prof. U. Wis., Milw., 1965-70; from assoc. prof. to prof. Purdue U., West Lafayette, Ind., 1970-80; prof. SUNY, New Paltz, N.Y., 1980-83; disting. vis. prof. U. Vt., Burlington, 1983; vis. prof. U. Tex., Austin, 1983-85, sr. lectr., 1985-87, prof., 1987-89, Jesse H. Jones Centennial prof. in comm., 1989—, U. Tex. Disting. Tchg. prof., 1999—. Cons., lectr. in field. Author: Nonverbal Communication in Human Interaction, 1972, 5th edit. (with J. Hall), 2001, Japanese edit., 1979, Spanish edit., 1980, Chinese edit., 1999, Portuguese edit., 1999, Polish edit., 2000, Social Intercourse: From Greeting to Goodbye, 1978, Essentials of Nonverbal Communication, 1980, Interpersonal Communication and Human Relationships, 1984, 4th edit. (with A. Vangelisti), 2000, (with J.C. McCroskey and C.E. Larson), An Introduction to Interpersonal Communication, 1971; editor: (with G.R. Miller) Handbook of Interpersonal Communication, 1985, 2d edit., 1994, 3d edit. (with J.A. Daly), 2002; contbr. articles to profl. jours., chpts. to books. With U.S. Army, 1957-59. Recipient Outstanding Young Tchr. award Ctrl. States Speech Assn., 1969; Ea. Comm. Assn. scholar, 1982-83. Fellow Internat. Comm. Assn. (pres. 1975-76); mem. Nat. Comm. Assn. (pres. 1989-90, Golden Anniversary award 1974, Disting. Scholar award 1993, Robert J. Kibler Meml. award 1993), Assn. Comm. Adminstrs. (pres. 1997), Coun. Comm. Assns. (vice chair 1997). Achievements include research in interpersonal communication, nonverbal communication, communication in developing and deteriorating relationships, lying and deception, communication and the process of aging, communication behavior in organizational settings. Home: 5804 Rising Hills Dr Austin TX 78759-5513 Office: U Tex Dept Comm Studies Austin TX 78712 E-mail: mlknapp@mail.utexas.edu.

KNAPP, MILDRED FLORENCE, retired social worker; b. Detroit, Apr. 15, 1932; d. Edwin Frederick and Florence Josephine (Antaya) K. BBA, U. Mich., 1954, MA in Cmty. and Adult Edn., 1964, MSW, 1967. Dist. dir. Girl Scouts Met. Detroit, 1954-63; planning asst. Coun. Social Agys. Flint and Genessee County, 1965; sch. social worker Detroit Pub. Schs., 1967-98; field instr. grad. social workers. Mem. alumnae bd. govs. U. Mich., 1972-75, scholarship chmn., 1969-70 76-80, chair spl. com. women's athletics, 1972-75, class agt. fund raising Sch. Bus. Adminstrn., 1978-79; mem. Founders Soc. Detroit Inst. Art, 1969—, Friends Children's Mus. Detroit, 1978— Women's Assn., Detroit Symphony Orch., 1982-89, Mich. Humane Soc., 1991—; vol. Coun. Detroit Symphony Orch., 1990—; trustee, fin. chmn. Children's Mus. Recipient Appreciation cert.; Mott Found. fellow, 1964; HEW grantee, 1966. Mem. NASW, Acad. Cert. Social Workers, Nat. Cmty. Edn. Assn. (charter), Sch. Social Work Assn. Am. (charter), Outdoor Edn. and Camping Coun. (charter), Mich. Sch. Social Workers Assn. (pres. 1980-81), Detroit Sch. Social Workers Assn. (past pres.), Detroit Assn. U. Mich. Women (pres. 1980-82), Detroit Fedn. Tchrs., Madame Alexander Doll Club. Methodist. Home: 702 Lakepointe St Grosse Pointe Park MI 48230 1706

KNAPP, RICHARD MAITLAND, association executive; b. Hartford, Conn., July 23, 1941; s. Maitl K.; m. Elizabeth Burgoyne, Apr. 1969; children—Heather, Peter. BA, Marietta (Ohio) Coll., 1963; MA, U. Iowa, 1965, PhD in Hosp. and Health Adminstrn., 1968. Trainee USPHS, 1964-65; Project dir. Teaching Hosp. Info. Ctr., Council of Teaching Hosps., Assn. Am. Med. Colls., Washington, 1968-69; dir. div. teaching hosps. Assn. Am. Med. Colls., Washington, 1969-73, dir. dept. teaching hosps., 1973-87, sr. v.p., 1987-93, exec. v.p., 1994—; mem. adv. com. ambulatory dental services program Robert Wood Johnson Hosp., 1978-83. Bd. dirs. Nat. Assn. Biomed. Rsch., chmn. exec. com. 1993-95; chmn. exec. com. Ad Hoc Group for Med. Rsch., 1992—. Contbr. articles to profl. jours.; mem. editorial bd. Inquiry, 1983-88. Bd. dirs. Hosp. Fund, Inc., 1984-2000; adv. com. The Commonwealth Fund Exec. Nurse Devel. Program, 1984-93; trustee Inova Health Sys. Bd., 1986—, chmn., 1999—; trustee Inova Health Care Svcs. Bd., 1982-98, chmn. 1993-98; mem. operating bd. Fairfax Hosp., 1987-92, sec. bd., 1987-89, chmn. bd., 1990-92; mem. vestry St. Anne's Episc. Ch., Reston, Va., 1979-83. Mem.: Va. Hosp. and Health Care Assn. (bd. dirs. 2001—), NAS-Inst. of Medicine, Am. Hosp. Assn., Assn. Univ. Programs in Health Adminstrn., W.Va. Thoroughbred Breeders Assn., Throughbred Owners and Breeders Assn., Md. Horse Breeders Assn., Hidden Creek Country Club, Cosmos Club, Delta Upsilon. Office: Assn Am Med Colls 2450 N St NW Washington DC 20037-1167 E-mail: rmknapp@aamc.org.

KNAPP, ROBERT CHARLES, retired obstetrics and gynecology educator; b. NYC, Jan. 19, 1927; s. Jack and Hilda (Knapp); m. Miriam Hermanos, Nov., 1955; children: Louise, Jennifer, Michael. AB, Columbia U., 1949; MD, SUNY Downstate Med. Center, Bklyn., 1953; MA, Harvard U., 1982; DSc (hon.), SUNY, Bklyn., 2003. Diplomate Am. Bd. Ob-Gyn. Intern Kings County Hosp., Bklyn., 1953-54, resident, 1954-58; instr. ob-gyn SUNY, Bklyn., 1958-62, Am. Cancer Soc. fellow, 1962-63, asst. prof. ob-gyn, 1962-63; asst. prof. Cornell U., 1963-69, assoc. prof., 1969-70; chmn. dept. ob-gyn. Nassau County Med. Center, East Meadow, N.Y., 1967-70; assoc. prof. ob-gyn. Harvard Med. Sch., Boston, 1970-75, William H. Baker prof. gynecology, 1975-93, William H. Baker prof. emeritus, 1993—; asso. chief of staff Boston Hosp. for Women, 1975-80; dir. gynecology surgery and oncology Brigham and Women's Hosp., Boston, 1980-89. Dir. gynecology Sidney Farber Cancer Inst., 1975-89. Served with U.S. Army, 1944-46. Fellow ACOG, ACS; mem. AAAS, Am. Soc. Clin. Oncology, Am. Fedn. Clin. Rsch., Obstet. Soc. Boston, Am. Radium Soc., Boston Surg. Soc. Soc. Gynecologic Oncology, Am. Assn. for Cancer Rsch., Soc. Surg. Oncologists, Internat. Soc. Gynecologic Oncologists. Home: 20 Sutton Pl S New York NY 10022-4165 E-mail: robert_knapp_ma82@post.howard.edu.

KNAPP, ROSALIND ANN, lawyer; b. Washington, Aug. 15, 1945; d. Joseph Burke and Hilary (Eaves) K. BA, Stanford U., 1967, JD, 1973. Bar: Calif. 1973, D.C. 1980. With U.S. Dept. Transp., Washington, 1973—, asst. gen. counsel legislation, 1979-81, dep. gen. counsel, 1981—. Mem. D.C. Bar Assn., Calif. Bar Assn. Office: Dept Transp Office of the General Counsel 400 7th St SW Washington DC 20590-0003 E-mail: lindy.knapp@ost.dot.gov.

KNAPP, STEPHEN JOHN, English educator; b. Phila., Apr. 8, 1954; s. William Frederick and Elizabeth Staats Knapp; m. Linda Jensen, Apr. 29, 1978; children: Caroline, Christiana. BA in Humanities, Hofstra U., 1975, MA in English, 1978; PhD in English, U. Toronto, Ont., Can., 1987. Commd. 2d lt. USAF, 1980, advanced through grades to capt.; prof. English USAF Acad., Colo., 1982-86; instr. adminstrn. USAF, Biloxi, Miss., 1990-93, resigned, 1993; asst. prof. English Ark. State U., Beebe, 1994—. Contbr. essays to profl. pubs. Mem. Two-Yr. Coll. Assn. Home: 1803 Orangewood Cove Beebe AR 72012 Office: Ark State U at Beebe Box 1000 Beebe AR 72012 E-mail: sjknapp@asub.edu.

KNAPP, WHITMAN, federal judge; b. N.Y.C., Feb. 24, 1909; s. Wallace Percy and Caroline Morgan (Miller) K.; m. Ann Fallert, May 17, 1962; 1 son, Gregory Wallace; children by previous marriage— Whitman Everett, Caroline Miller (Mrs. Edward M. W. Hines), Marion Elizabeth. Grad., Choate Sch., 1927; BA, Yale, 1931; LLB, Harvard U., 1934; LLD (hon.), CUNY City Coll., 1992. Bar: N.Y. 1935. With firm Cadwalader, Wickersham & Taft, N.Y.C., 1935-37; dep. asst. dist. atty. N.Y.C., 1937-41; with firm Donovan, Leisure, Newton & Lumbard, N.Y.C., 1941; mem. staff dist. atty. N.Y.C., 1942-50; chief indictment bd., 1942-44; chief, appeal bur., 1944-50; partner firm Barrett Knapp Smith Schapiro & Simon (and predecessors), 1950-72; U.S. dist. judge So. Dist. N.Y., 1972-87, sr. dist. judge, 1987—. Spl. counsel N.Y. State Youth Commn., 1950-53; Waterfront Commn. N.Y. Harbor, 1953-54; mem. temp. commn. revision N.Y. State penal law and criminal code, 1964-69; chmn. Knapp Commn. to Investigate Allegations of Police Corruption in N.Y.C., 1969-72; gen. counsel Urban League Greater N.Y., 1970-72. Editor: Harvard Law Rev, 1933-34. Sec. Community Council Greater N.Y., 1952-58; pres. Dalton Schs., N.Y.C., 1950-53, Youth House, 1967-68; Trustee Univ. Settlement, 1945-64, Moblzn. for Youth, 1965-70. Mem. ABA, Am. Law Inst., Am. Bar Found., Am. Coll. Trial Lawyers, Assn. Bar City N.Y. (sec. 1946-49, chmn. exec. com. 1971-72). Office: 1201 US Courthouse 40 Foley Sq New York NY 10007-1502

KNAPPENBERGER, PAUL HENRY, JR., science museum director; b. Reading, Pa., Sept. 5, 1942; s. Paul Henry and Kathryn (Medrick) K.; m. Naomi Knappenberger; children— Paul Charles, Timothy Alan, Shannon Rose Lalor, Heidi Kathrin. AB in Math, Franklin and Marshall Coll., 1964; MA in Astronomy (NASA fellow), U. Va., 1966, PhD in Astronomy, 1968. Astronomer Fernbank Sci. Center, Atlanta, 1968-72; instr. Emory U. and Ga. State U., Atlanta, 1970-72; dir. Sci. Mus. of Va., Richmond, 1973-91; pres. The Adler Planetarium, Chgo., 1991—. Asst. prof. Va. Commonwealth U., U. Richmond, 1973-81; bd. dirs. Assn. Sci. and Tech. Centers, pres., 1985-87; instr. astronomy Yellowstone Inst.; former v.p. Midlothian Athletic Assn.; mem. council Nat. Mus. Act, 1984-86. Former mem. bd. dirs. Mus. Film Network, Exhibit Research Collaborative; co-founder Planetarium Show Network; dir. Informal Sci. Instructional Services, Ltd. NSF Sci. Edn. grantee, 1971-72; grantee NEH, Inst. Mus. Services. Mem. Am. Astron. Soc., AAAS, Internat. Planetarium Soc., Va. Acad. Sci., Va. Assn. Museums (council 1979-91), Am. Assn. Museums, Great Lakes Planetarium Assn. Home: 6n488 Splitrail Ct Saint Charles IL 60175-6928 Office: Adler Planetarium 1300 S Lake Shore Dr Chicago IL 60605-2489

KNAPSTEIN, MICHAEL, advertising executive; BS in Comm./Advt. and Pub. Rels., U. Wis., Stevens Point, 1979. Copywriter TAM Advt., Wausau, Wis., creative dir.; copy/contact Waldbillig & Besteman, Inc., Madison, Wis., 1979, co-owner, 1988, CEO, 1993—. Represented in permanent collections Nikon, Eastman Kodak. Active Start Smart, United Way Dane County. Mem. Madison Advt. Fedn. (bd. dirs.), Am. Advt. Fedn. (bd. dirs., chair exec. com. ctrl. region). Home: 1528 Red Oak Ct Middleton WI 53562 Office: Waldbillig and Besteman Inc 7633 Ganser Way Madison WI 53719-2092 Fax: 608-829-0901.

KNAUER, GEORG NICOLAUS, classical philologist; b. Hamburg, Germany, Feb. 26, 1926; came to U.S., 1975; s. Georg A. and Ilse M. (Groothoff) K.; m. Elfriede Regina Overhoff, Aug. 3, 1951; 1 child, Georg Lorenz. DrPhil, U. Hamburg, 1952. Research asst. Thesaurus Linguae Latinae, Munich, 1952-54; asst. Freie U., Berlin, 1954—61, privatdozent, 1961-64, assoc. prof., 1964-66, prof., 1966-74; prof. classical studies U. Pa., Phila., 1975-88, prof. emeritus, 1988—, chmn. dept. classical studies, 1978-79, 80-82, 85-88; resident Rockefeller Found., Bellagio Study and Conf. Ctr., Como, Italy, 1989. Brit. Council scholar U. London, 1957-58; vis. prof. Yale U., 1965 66; Nellie Wallace lectr. Oxford (Eng.) U., 1969; mem. Inst. Advanced Study, Princeton, N.J., 1973-74; vis. prof. Columbia U., fall 1976; mem. Notgemeinschaft für eine freie Universität, Berlin, 1969-90; mem. Bund Freiheit der Wissenschaft, Bonn, 1970—; mem. Internat. Council on Future of Univ., N.Y.C. Author: Psalmenzitate in Augustins Konfessionen, 1955, 2d edit. under title Three Studies, 1987, Die Aeneis und Homer, 1964, 2d edit. 1979. Served with German Army, 1944-45. Guggenheim fellow, 1979-80, NEH fellow, 1984-85, Herzog August Bibliothek fellow, Germany, 1991, 97, 2002; vis. scholar Am. Acad., Rome, 1979-80, 90, 97, 2003, resident in classics, 1985 Mem. Am. Philol. Assn., Berliner Wissenschaftliche Gesellschaft, Am. Renaissance Soc. Home: The Quadrangle Apt 3314 3300 Darby Rd Haverford PA 19041-1070 Office: U Pa Dept of Classical Studies Logan Hall Philadelphia PA 19104-6304 E-mail: gknauer@sas.upenn.edu.

KNAUER, JAMES A. lawyer; b. Terre Haute, Ind., Sept. 18, 1946; s. Eugene A. and Dorothy R. K.; m. Jill A. Knauer, Apr. 25, 1988. BS, Ind. U., Bloomington, 1968; JD, Ind. U., Indpls., 1972. Bar: Ind. 1972, U.S. Dist. Ct. (so. dist.) Ind. 1972, U.S. Ct. Appeals (7th cir.) 1972, U.S. Supreme Ct. 1977. Assoc. Kroger Gardis & Regas, Indpls., 1972-70, mng. ptnr., 1979—. Adj. prof. law Ind. U., 1987-88, 90-91; trustee U.S. Bankruptcy panel, 1980-88; pres. bd. dirs. Alpha Tau Omega, Inc., 1997-99; pres. The Lakeridge Group, 1998-2003; SEC receiverships Heartland Fin. Svcs., Wellington Bank, Concord Devel., About Trading. Contbr. articles to profl. jours. Capt. U.S. Army, 1971-72. Mem. ABA, ATLA, Comml. Law League of Am., Indpls. Bar Assn., Am. Bankruptcy Inst., Columbia Club, Woodstock Club. Republican. Office: Kroger Gardis & Regas 900 Bank One Ctr Indianapolis IN 46204 E-mail: jak@kgrlaw.com.

KNAUER, JAMES PHILIP, physicist; b. Sandusky, Ohio, May 12, 1950; s. William David Sr. and Alice Roselyn (Mowry) Knauer; m. Susan Diana Holmes, Apr. 8, 1974. BS, MIT, 1972; MS, U. Hawaii, 1974, PhD, 1977. Rsch. asst. MIT, Cambridge, Mass., 1971-72; grad. tchg. asst. U. Hawaii, Honolulu, 1972-74, 74-77, jr. researcher, 1978-79; rsch. investigator U. Pa., Phila., 1977-78; assoc. rsch. scientist Lockheed Missiles & Space Co., Palo Alto, Calif., 1979-86, rsch. scientist, 1979-86; scientist Lab. Laser Energetics U. Rochester, NY, 1986-99, sr. scientist, 1999—. Mgr. Nat. Laser Users Facility, Rochester, 1986—96. Leader 4-H Club, Monroe County, NY, 1987—. Mem.: Carriage Assn. Am., Am. Driving Soc., Am. Phys. Soc. (Excellence in Plasma Physics Rsch. award 1995), N.Y. State Horse Coun., Sigma Xi. Republican. Avocation: riding and driving horses. Office: Lab for Laser Energetics Univ of Rochester 250 E River Rd Rochester NY 14623-1212 E-mail: jkna@lle.rochester.edu.

KNAUER, LEON THOMAS, lawyer; b. N.Y.C., July 16, 1932; s. Lawrence R. and Loretta M. (Trainor) K.; m. Traude Kunz, Sept. 11, 1976; children: Robert A., Katrine M. BS in Math., Fordham U., 1954; JD, Georgetown U., 1961. Bar: Conn. 1961, D.C. 1961, U.S. Supreme Ct. 1965. Law clk. U.S. Dist. Ct. (D.C.), 1960-61; assoc. Wilkinson, Barker & Knauer LLP, Washington, 1961-68, ptnr., 1968-82, Wilkinson Barker Knauer, LLP, Washington, 1982—. Instr. Georgetown U. Law Center, 1964-65. Editor: Telecommunications Act Handbook: A Complete Reference for Business, 1996, Telecommunications Act of 1996-A Domestic and International Prospective for Business, 1998. Pres. Catholic Apostolic Mass Media, 1974-76, Knights of Malta, 1979—, Thomas More Soc. of U.S., 1984-85. Lt. USMC, 1954-57. Recipient award for outstanding legal svc. in media area NAACP, 1973, Officer's Cross for legal svcs. to Austria, 1992. Mem. Fed. Comms. Bar Assn. (editor Comms. Bar Jour. 1960-69, treas. 1980-82, mem. exec. com. 1982-84), Washington Golf and County Club, Cosmos Club Washington, Fordham U. Alumni of Washington (pres. 1982-85). Republican. Roman Catholic. Office: 2300 N St NW Ste 700 Washington DC 20037-1122

KNAUER, VIRGINIA HARRINGTON (MRS. WILHELM F. KNAUER), consumer consultant, former government official; b. Phila., Mar. 28, 1915; d. Herman Winfield and Helen (Harrington) Wright; m. Wilhelm F. Knauer, Jan. 27, 1940; children: Wilhelm F., Valerie H. (Mrs. I. Townsend Burden III). BFA, U. Pa., 1937; grad., Pa. Acad. Fine Arts, 1937; postgrad., Royal Acad. Fine Arts, Florence, Italy, 1938-39; LL.D. (hon.), Phila. Coll. Textiles and Sci., St. Francis de Sales, Widener Coll., Chester, Pa., Tufts U.; Litt.D. (hon.), Drexel U.; L.H.D. (hon.), Russell Sage Coll., Pa. Coll. Podiatric Medicine; L.H.D., Jacksonville U.; LLD (hon.), U. Pa., 1971. Dir. Pa. Bur. Consumer Protection, 1968-69; spl. asst. to Pres. for consumer affairs The White House, 1969-77; dir. U.S. Office Consumer Affairs, Washington, 1971-77, 81-88; spl. adv. to Pres. for consumer affairs The White House, 1981-88; chair ABRH Inc., Washington, 1988-91; consumer cons. Haney and Knauer, Inc., Washington, 1991-93. Pres. Virginia Knauer & Assocs., Inc., Washington, 1977-81; chmn. Coun. for Advancement of Consumer Policy, 1979-81; U.S. rep., vice chmn. consumer policy com. OECD, 1970-77, 81-88; mem. Coun. Wage and Price Stability, 1974-77; vice-chmn. Philadelphia County Rep. Com., 1958-77; pres. Phila. Congress Rep. Women's Councils, 1958-77; dir. Pa. Coun. Rep. Women, 1963-80;

founder N.E. Phila. Coun. Rep. Women, pres., 1956-68 Bd. dirs. Hannah Penn House, 1956—, v.p., 1971; chmn. Knauer Found. Hist. Preservation, 1963—; nat. chmn. to promote no fault automobile ins. Project New Start, 1988-91; bd. dirs. Nat. Coalition for Cancer Survivorship; mem. city coun., Phila., Pa., 1960-68. Recipient Gimbel-Phila. award, 1977, Ind. Achievement in Govt. award Soc. Consumer Affairs Profls., 1983; named Disting. Dau. Pa., 1969; named to Disting. Women's Com., Northwood U., 1997. Mem. Nat. Trust Hist. Preservation, Am. Assn. Ret. Persons, Internat. Neighbors Club, Exec. Women in Govt., Penn Women (trustees coun.), Consumers for World Trade (bd. dirs.), Zeta Tau Alpha, Kappa Delta Epsilon (hon.). Episcopalian.

KNAUS, TIM, political organization administrator; Chmn. Jefferson County Dem. Com., Colo. State Dem. Party, 1999—. Office: Colo Dem Party 5200 E Colfax Ave Denver CO 80220-1304 also: Ste 200 770 Grant St Denver CO 80203-3517

KNAUSS, DAVID EUGENE, music educator; b. Lewisburg, Pa., May 29, 1951; m. Joanne Lynn Mattern, July 30, 1951; children: Sarah E., Anna A., William A. BS in Music, West Chester U., 1973; MEd in Music, Mansfield U., 1981, Orff-Schulwerk cert. Level III, 1991; postgrad., Pa. State U., 1997—. Cert. supr. music I, music educator nat. cert. Classroom music and choral music tchr. Williamsport (Pa.) Area Sch. Dist., 1973—99; prof., supr. music student tchrs. Mansfield (Pa.) U., 1999—2001; classroom music and choral music tchr. So. Tioga Sch. Dist., Liberty, Pa., 2001—02, No. Tioga Sch. Dist., Elkland, Pa., 2002—03. Author: of 5 scope and sequenced classroom music curriculum books for grades K-12. Grantee, Arts Spl. Edn. Project, 1992. Mem.: Pa. Music Educators Assn., Am. Orff-Schulwerk Assn., Music Educators Nat. Conf. Home: RR #3 Box 87B Columbia Cross Roads PA 16914

KNAUSS, JOHN ATKINSON, former federal agency administrator, oceanographer, educator, former university dean; b. Detroit, Sept. 1, 1925; s. Karl Ernst and Loise (Atkinson) K.; m. Marilyn Mattson, Sept. 6, 1954; children: Karl, William. BS, MIT, 1946; MS, U. Mich., 1949; PhD, U. Calif., 1959; DSc (hon.), U R.I., 1992. Oceanographer Navy Electronics Lab, San Diego, 1947, Office Naval Rsch., 1949-51, Scripps Instn. Oceanography, 1951-52, 55-62; prof. Grad. Sch. Oceanography, U. R.I., Narragansett, 1962-90, dean, 1962-87, provost for marine affairs, 1969-82, v.p. marine programs, 1982-87, prof., dean emeritus, 1990—; undersecretary for oceans and atmosphere Dept. Commerce, Washington, 1989-93; adminstr. Nat. Oceanic and Atmospheric Adminstrn., Washington, 1989-93; U.S. commr. Internat. Whaling Commn., 1991-93; rsch. assoc. Scripps Inst. Oceanography U. Calif., San Diego, 1993—. Leader 10 oceanographic expdns to study oceanic circulation, 1955-65; chair U.S. phys.-chem. panel Internat. Indian Ocean Expdn., 1959-62; mem. Pres's. Commn. on Marine Scis., Engring. and Resources, 1967-68; mem. State Dept. Pub. Adv. Com. on Law of Sea, 1970-82; chair sr. adv. com. on environ. scis. Ctr. for Energy and Environ. Rsch., U. P.R., 1977-80; mem. Nat. Adv. Com. on Oceans and Atmosphere, 1978-85, vice chair, 1979-81, chair 1981-85; chair bd. govs. Joint Oceanographic Instns., Inc., 1978-80; co-founder Law of Sea Inst., mem. exec. bd. 1965-76, 82-87; bd. dirs. Coun. for Ocean Law, 1983-89, 94-2001; chair marine divsn. Nat. Assn. State U. and Land Grant Colls., 1984-85; chair Joint Oceanographic Instns. for Deep Earth Sampling, 1984-86; bd. dirs. Harbor Br. Oceanographic Instn., 1987-89; 1st vice chmn. Intergovernmental Oceanographic Commn., 1991-93; mem. bd. trustees Bermuda Biological Sta. for Rsch., 1995—; mem. ocean rsch. adv. panel Nat. Oceanographic Rsch. Leadership Coun., 1998-02, chair, 1998-2002, Sea Grant adv. com., 2003—. U.S. Congress renamed its Sea Grant fellowship the Dean John A. Knauss Fellowship program in 1987. With USNR, 1943-46, 53-54. Named to R.I. Heritage Hall of Fame, 1983; recipient Albatross award Am. Miscellaneous Soc., 1959, Nat. Sea Grant award, 1974. Fellow AAAS (v.p. 1972-73), Am. Geophys. Union (pres. oceanography sect. 1965-67, pres-elect 1996-98, pres. 1998-2000, Ocean Sci. award 1988); mem. Am. Meteorol. Soc. (hon., coun. 1980-82). Home: 126 Willett Rd Saunderstown RI 02874-3810 also: 2634 Ellentown Rd La Jolla CA 92037

KNAUSS, ROBERT LYNN, international business educator, corporate executive; b. Detroit, Mar. 24, 1931; s. Karl Ernst and Loise (Atkinson) K.; m. Angela Tirola Lawson, Feb. 21, 1973; children by previous marriage: Robert B., Charles H., Katherine E.; 1 stepson, Ian T. Lawson. AB, Harvard U., 1952; JD, U. Mich., 1957. Bar: Calif., Tenn., Tex. Assoc. Pillsbury, Madison & Sutro, San Francisco, 1958-60; prof. law U. Mich., 1960-72, v.p. student svcs., 1970-72; dean, prof. law Vanderbilt U., Nashville, 1972-79; dean U. Houston Law Ctr., 1981-93, disting. univ. prof., 1981-95. Vis. prof. Vt. Law Sch., South Royalton, Amos Tuck Sch. Bus. Adminstrn., Dartmouth Coll., Hanover, NH, 1979—81; chmn., CEO Baltic Internat. USA/Inc., 1994—2003; chmn., PEO Phillips Svcs. Corp., 2002—; bd. dirs. Mex. Fund, Equus II, Inc., Seitel Inc. Editor: Small Business Financing, 4 vols., 1966, Securities Regulation Sourcebook, 1970-71, (with others) Cases and Materials on Enterprise Regulations, 1987; contbr. articles to profl. jours. Regent Nat. Coll. Dist. Attys., 1981-95. Lt. (j.g.) USN, 1952-55. Fellow Tex. Bar Found., Am. Bar Found; mem. Calif. Bar Assn., Tenn. Bar Assn., Tex. Bar Assn. (chmn. corp. coun. sect. 1991), Am. Law Inst. (life), Order of Coif. Home: PO Box 40 ThreeCreek Ranch Burton TX 77835-0040 Office: 5151 San Felipe St Ste 1661 Houston TX 77056-3646

KNAUST, CLARA DOSS, retired elementary school educator; b. Freistatt, Mo., Feb. 18, 1922; d. John Fredrick and Hedwig Louise (Brockschmidt) Doss; m. Donald Knaust, July 7, 1946 (dec.); children: Karen Louise, Ramona Elizabeth, Heidi Marie. BS in Edn., S.W. Mo. State U., 1969. Elem. tchr. Trinity Luth. Sch., Freistatt, 1942-46; tchr. kindergarten Trinity Luth Ch., Springfield, Mo., 1961-65, Redeemer Luth Ch., Springfield, 1962-63, 66-69, Springfield R-12 Sch. System, 1969-70, 73-84, elem. tchr., 1970-73; elem. and kindergarten tchr. Springfield Luth. Sch., 1984-88. Mem. planning bd. Early Childhood Conf., U. Mo., Columbia, 1977-80. Pres. Springfield Gen. Hosp. Guild, 1969-71; local and zone pres. Luth. Women's Missionary League, Springfield, 1986-94; historian Trinity Luth. Ch., 1985-94; chair bd. edn. Grace Luth. Ch., Tulsa. Mem. Assn. for Childhood Edn. Internat. (br. state pres. 1980-84, president's coun. 1983-85, Hall of Fame plaque 1988, state pres. 1989-93), Springfield Edn. Assn. (life), Springfield Luth. Sch. Assn. (pres. 1992-94), S.W. Dist. Kindergarten Assn. (pres. 1978-79), Alpha Delta Kappa. Avocations: painting, crafts, collecting, music. Home: Univ Club 1722 S Carson Ave Apt 1710 Tulsa OK 74119-4641

KNAUTH, STEPHEN CRAIG, poet; b. Milw., Dec. 5, 1950; s. Henry Martin and Dorothy Ruth K.; m. Sara Cox K., Feb. 5, 1975; children: Elizabeth, Walker, Benjamin. BS in Psychology summa cum laude, Ohio U., 1972. Assoc. editor So. Poetry Rev. U. N.C., Charlotte, 1987-96. Author: The River I Know You By, 1999 (Roanoke-Chowan award 1999), Twenty Shadows, 1995, The Pine Figures, 1986, Night-Fishing on Irish Buffalo Creek, 1982; contbr. poetry to profl. publs. including The N.M. Rev., Pacifi Rev., Va. Quar. Rev., Seneca Rev., Manhattan Poetry Rev., Kans. Quar., others. Creative Writing fellow Nat. Endowment for the Arts, 1984, 96, N.C. Arts Coun. writer's fellow, 1986, 90; recipient Roanoke-Chowan award N.C. Literary Hist. Assn., 1999, Anniversary award for poetry Associated Writing Programs, 1984, Brockman-Campbell Book award N.C. Poetry Soc., 1983. Mem. N.C. Writers Conf. Home: 805 E Worthington Ave Charlotte NC 28203

KNEAVEL, ANN CALLANAN, humanities educator, communications consultant; b. Balt., Oct. 29, 1946; d. James Michael and Ann (Ijams) Callanan; m. Thomas Charles Kneavel, Jr., Dec. 18, 1970; children: Meredith Elizabeth, Thomas Charles III, Rebecca Ann. BA, Coll. Notre Dame Md., 1968; MA in Am. Lit., U. Md., 1970; PhD in Modern Brit. Lit., U. Ottawa, Ont., Can., 1979. Instr. U. Md., College Park, 1968-71, U. Ottawa, 1971-72, Wilmington (Del.) Coll., 1976-79, Del. Tech. and C.C., Dover, 1975-79; asst. prof. Widener U., Chester, Pa., 1981-82; prof. Goldey-Beacom Coll., Wilmington, Del., 1981—; dir. satellite campuses Total Quality Master's Program, Falmouth, Mass., 1995—. Contbr. articles to profl. jours. Trustee Hockessin (Del.) Pub. Libr., 1981-93, Alpha Tau Omega Fraternity, Wilmington, 1994—; mem. Friends of Hockessin Libr., 1981—. Mem. MLA, Nat. Coun. Tchrs. English, Conf. on Christianity and Lit., Am. Culture Assn., C.C. Humanities Assn., Alpha Chi (faculty sponsor, Svc. award 1994, v.p. region VI 2000—). Roman Catholic. Home: 7 Arthur Dr Hockessin DE 19707-1012 Office: Goldey-Beacom Coll 4701 Limestone Rd Wilmington DE 19808-1927 E-mail: kneavela@gbc.edu.

KNEAVEL, THOMAS CHARLES, JR., psychologist, educator; b. Balt., Oct. 30, 1941; s. Thomas Charles and Caroline Frances (Noha) K.; m. Ann Callanan, Dec. 18, 1970; children: Meredith, Thomas, Rebecca. BS, Loyola Coll., Balt., 1963, MEd, 1968; PhD, U. Ottawa, 1979. Diplomate Am. Bd. Forensic Examiners; lic. psychologist, Del. Tchr. Ridge Sch., Towsen, Md., 1961-65; psychologist Balt. City Schs., 1965-69; clin. psychologist D.C. Children's Ctr., Laurel, Md., 1969-70; cons. Joseph House, Balt., 1969-70; psychology intern Child Study Ctr. U. Ottawa, 1970-71; psychology intern Child Diagnostic and Devel. Clinic Children's Hosp. of Ea. Ont., Ottawa, 1971-72; sch. psychologist Cape Henlopen Sch. Dist., Nassau, Del., 1972-79; psychologist Comty. Mental Health Clinic, Beebe Hosp., Lewes, Del., 1973-79; program dir. child crisis unit Terry Children's Psychiat. Ctr., New Castle, Del., 1979-86, chief psychologist, 1982-86; pvt. practice, 1983—; psychologist Thomas A. Edison Charter Sch., Wilmington, Del., 2000—. Mem. adj. faculty dept. psychiatry and human behavior Thomas Jefferson U. Med. Sch., 1980-86; psychologist Christina Sch. Dist., 1986-98; clin. cons. Turnabout Counseling Ctr., Seaford, Del., 1987-91; clin. dir. adolescent programs Meadow Wood Hosp., New Castle, Del., 1993-94; dir. psychol. svcs. Med. Ctr. Del. Dept. Adolescent Medicine 1st State Sch., 1995-99; adj. prof. Widner U., 1995-99; cons. on compulsive gambling to dir. divsn. mental health, frequent nat. presenter on treating oppositional disorders in children and adolescents, 1980-82; apptd. by Gov. DuPont and Gov. Castle to Del. Devel. Disabilities Planning Coun., 1982-94, vice chmn., 1983-85, chmn., 1985-87; mem. citizens adv. bd. Comty. Mental Health Clinic, Beebe Hosp., 1974-79; state rep. Nat. Assn. Devel. Disabilities, Washington, 1984-87, mem. child devel. com.; mem. state genetics adv. coun. A.I. DuPont Inst. and State of Del., 1986-94; apptd. by Gov. Castle to State Bd. Psychol. Examiners, 1989, v.p., 1991-92, pres., 1992-94; bd. dirs., networking dir. Assn. Comprehension Energy Psychology, 2001-2002. Mem. APA, Del. Psychol. Assn., Falmouth Inst. Quality Sys. Mgmt. (bd. dirs. 1997—), Nat. Assn. Sch. Psychologists (charter), Del. Sch. Psychologists Assn. (pres. 1976-77), Del. Psychol. Inc. (bd. dirs. 1987-89), Nat. Grad. Sch. for Quality Mgmt. (bd. dirs. 1997-, bd. chair 2003-), Nat. Eagle Scout Assn. Roman Catholic. Home: 7 Arthur Dr Hockessin DE 19707-1012 Office: 17-C Trolley Sq Wilmington DE 19806 E-mail: dockneavel@yahoo.com.

KNEBEL, CONSTANCE, potter, ceramist; b. Nov. 2, 1934; Student, Northeastern U., 1953-54, Boston Sch. Art, 1954-55. Asst. to editor Esquire Mag. N.Y.C., 1961-70; photographer Time, Inc., N.Y.C., 1971-83; freelance potter, ceramicist Honolulu, 1983-97, Canaan, N.Y., 1997—. Home: 271 Tunnel Hill Rd Canaan NY 12029-2706 E-mail: cknebel@taconic.net.

KNEBEL, DONALD EARL, lawyer; b. Logansport, Ind., May 26, 1946; s. Everett Earl and Ethel Josephina (Hultgren) K.; m. Joan Elizabeth Vest, June 5, 1976 (div. 1980); 1 child, Mary Elizabeth; m. Jennifer Colt Johnson, Sept. 25, 1999. BEE with highest distinction, Purdue U., 1968; JD magna cum laude, Harvard U., 1974. Bar: Ind. 1974, U.S. Ct. Appeals (7th cir.) 1980, U.S. Ct. Appeals (3rd cir.) 1986, U.S. Ct. Appeals (6th cir.) 1987, U.S. Ct. Appeals (fed. cir.) 1988. Assoc. Barnes, Hickam, Pantzer & Boyd, Indpls., 1974-81; ptnr. Barnes & Thornburg, Indpls., 1981—. Contbr. articles on intellectual property, antitrust and distbn. law to profl. publs. Trustee Indpls. Civic Theatre, 1986—95, chmn., 1988—91, hon. trustee, 1995—2002, Trustee, 2002—, chmn., 2002—. Mem.: ABA, TechPoint (dir. 2003—), TechLaw Group (v.p. 2002—), 7th Cir. Bar Assn., Indpls. Bar Assn., Ind. Bar Assn., Columbia Club, Kiwanis (pres. 1991—92). Presbyterian. Office: Barnes & Thornburg 11 S Meridian St Ste 1313 Indianapolis IN 46204-3535

KNEBEL, JACK GILLEN, lawyer; b. Washington, Jan. 28, 1939; s. Fletcher and Amalia Eleanor (Rauppius) K.; m. Linda Karin Ropertz, Feb. 22, 1963; children: Hollis Anne (dec.), Lauren Beth. BA, Yale Coll., 1960; LLB, Harvard U., 1966. Bar: Calif. 1966, U.S. Dist. Ct. (no. dist.) Calif. 1966, U.S. Ct. Appeals (9th cir.) 1966. Assoc. McCutchen, Doyle, Brown & Enersen, San Francisco, 1966-74, ptnr., 1974-94, of counsel, 1994-99; owner Artema, 1999—; lectr. in law Stanford Law Sch., 1998-2001, Harvard U. Sch. Law, 2002—; dir. litigation tng. Brigham, McCutchen, San Francisco, 2002—. Exec. com. San Francisco Lawyers Com. for Urban Affairs, 1991-93; adv. coun. Hastings Coll. Trial Advocacy, San Francisco, 1981-91, chair, 1990-91; mediator, arbitrator Am. Arbitration Assn., 1989—. Bd. dirs., pres. Orinda (Calif.) Assn., 1972-74, Sea Ranch (Calif.) Assn., 1978-79; co-chmn. Citizens to Preserve Orinda, 1983-85. Lt. (j.g.) USN, 1960-66. Fellow Am. Coll. Trial Lawyers (mem. com. on fed. rules civ. pro 1990-93); mem. ABA, Maritime Law Assn. of U.S. Democrat. Home: PO Box 1133 Gualala CA 95445 Office: Bingham McCutchen Three Embarcadero Ctr Ste 1800 San Francisco CA 94111 E-mail: jknebel@Bingham.com., knebeljack@juno.com.

KNEBEL, JOHN ALBERT, lawyer, former government official; b. Tulsa, Oct. 4, 1936; s. John Albert and Florence Julia (Friend) K.; m. Zenia Irene Marks, June 6, 1959; children— Carrie, John Albert III, Clemens. BS, U.S. Mil. Acad., 1959; MA in Econs, Creighton U., 1962; JD, Am. U., 1965. Bar: D.C. bar 1966, U.S. Ct. Appeals bar 1966. Asst. to Rep. J.E. Wharton of N.Y., Washington, 1963-64; asso. mem. law firm Howrey, Simon, Baker & Murchison, Washington, 1965-68; asst. counsel Com. on Agr., U.S. Ho. Reps., Washington, 1968-71; gen. counsel SBA, Washington, 1971-74, U.S. Dept. Agr., Washington, 1973-75; under sec. Dept. Agr., 1975-76, sec. of agr., 1976-77; ptnr. firm Baker & McKenzie, Washington, 1977-86; pres. Am. Mining Congress, Washington, 1986-95; exec. v.p. Nat. Assn. Broadcasters, Washington, 1995—. Served to 1st lt. USAF, 1959-62. Mem. Fed. Bar Assn. (past pres.), Am., D.C. bar assns., Delta Theta Phi, Omicron Delta Gamma. Home: 1418 Laburnum St Mc Lean VA 22101-2523 Office: Nat Assn Broadcasters 1771 N St NW Washington DC 20036-2891

KNECHT, BEN HARROLD, surgeon; b. Rapid City, SD, May 3, 1938; m. Jane Bowles, Aug. 27, 1961; children: John, Janelle. BA, U. S.D., 1960; MD, U. Iowa, 1964; cert. total quality mgmt., U. Wash., 1998. Diplomate Am. Bd. Surgery. Intern Los Angeles County Gen. Hosp., 1964-65; resident in surgery U. Iowa Sch. Medicine, Iowa City, 1968-72; surgeon Wenatchee Valley Clinic, Wash., 1972—; med. dir. Wenatchee Valley Hosp., 1997—; chmn. med. informatics Wenatchee Valley Clinic, 1995—2000, chmn. gen.-vasc. surg. dept., 1996—2001. Dir. emergency rm. Ctrl. Wash. Hosp., Wenatchee, 1972-79, chmn. libr., 1976-86, chief surgery, 1983-86; chmn. claims rev. panel Wash. State Med. Assn., Seattle, 1979-82, prof. liability com. risk mgmt., 1985-90; clin. prof. surgery U. Wash.; mem. adv. risk mgmt. com. Wash. State Physicians Ins. Subscribers, 1990-98, regional adv. com. Nat. Libr. Medicine, 1991-93. Fundraiser Cen. Wash. Hosp. Found., 1987; del. Gov.'s Conf. on Libr., 1991; bd. dir. United Way, 1974-77; mem. founding bd. Cascade Unitarian Fellowship, 1986-88; mem. ad hoc com. on tchg./learning Wenatchee HS, 1999-2002, mem. prin.'s adv. com., 2002--; post leader Med. Explorers, 1973-76. Lt. comdr. USN, 1965-68, Vietnam. Recipient AMA Physicians Recognition Award, 1992—2006. Mem. AMA (alt. del. 1985-87, del. 1988-98, surg. caucus exec. com. 1991-94), ACS (bd. dir. Wash. chpt. 1981-84), Am. Coll. Physician Exec., Am. Soc. Quality, North Pacific Surg. Assn., Wash. State Med. Assn. (trustee 1979-98), Chelan-Douglas County Med. Soc., Am. Soc. Gen. Surgery (founding bd. 1994—, bd. dir.1992—), Henry A. Harkins Surg. Soc., Rotary (chmn. youth com. 1976-78), Alpha Tau Omega. Avocations: snow and water skiing, reading, hiking, computing. Office: Wenatchee Valley Clinic 820 N Chelan Ave Wenatchee WA 98801-2028 E-mail: bknecht@wvclinic.com.

KNECHT, CHARLES LEWIS, III, retired radiologist; b. Phila., 1931; MD, Jefferson Med. Coll., 1957. Cert. in radiology. Intern Germantown Disp-Hosp., 1957-58, resident in radiology, 1958-61; with Good Shepherd Rehab. Hosp., Pa., 1961-99, Lehigh Valley Hosp., Allentown, Pa., 1961-92, pvt. rad. prac., 1970-96.; ret., 1999. Mem. ACR, AMA, Soc. Breast Imaging, Soc. Radiologists in Ultrasound.

KNECHT, JAMES HERBERT, lawyer; b. Los Angeles, Aug. 5, 1925; s. James Herbert and Gertrude Martha (Morris) K.; m. Margaret Paton Vreeland, Jan. 3, 1953 (dec. 1994); children— Susan, Thomas Paton, Carol. BS, UCLA, 1947; LLB, U. So. Calif., 1957. Bar: Calif. bar 1957, U.S. Supreme Ct. bar 1969. Mem. firm Forster, Gemmill & Farmer, Los Angeles, 1957-84; sole practice, 1985—. Chmn. bd. Templeton (Calif.) Nat. Bank, 1992-95. Fellow Am. Bar Found. (life); mem. ABA, San Luis Obispo County Bar Assn., Legion Lex, Caltech Assocs., L.A. Area C. of C. (dir. 1979-83), Beta Theta Pi. Home: 5030 Vineyard Dr Paso Robles CA 93446-9682 Office: PO Box 2280 Paso Robles CA 93447-2280 E-mail: jknecht@ccaccess.net.

KNECHT, MELISSA, music educator, musician; b. Wooster, Ohio, Feb. 23, 1954; d. Richard Boid and Joy (Brand) Gerber; m. John David Robinson, Aug. 20, 1985 (div. Dec. 12, 1988); m. Sam James Knecht, Nov. 28, 1998; children: Lydia Joy, Katherine Ruth. MM, Ind. U., 1979; BME, U. Mich., 1976, PhD, 1992. Tchg. asst. U. Mich., Ann Arbor, 1986—90; adj. prof. U. Toledo, 1995—96, Siena Heights Coll., Adrian, Mich., 1996—97, Hillsdale Coll., Mich., 1993—97, vis. prof., 1997—98, asst. prof., 1998—2002, assoc. prof., 2002—. Music dir. Tampa Theatre, Fla., 1980—81; orch. conductor Livonia Youth Philharm. Orch., Mich., 1991—96; dir. edn. and outreach Toledo Symphony, 1999—; presenter in field; violinist/violist Spoleto Festival, Italy, 1978, Philharmonica de Caracas, Venezuela, 1981, Jacksonville Symphony, 1978—89, Fla. Philharmonic, 1979—82, Am. Chamber Orch., Chgo., 1983—84, Toledo Symphony, 1991—2001. Grantee, CETA, 1978—79. Mem.: Coll. Music Soc., Am. String Tchrs. Assn. Avocation: running. Office: Hillsdale Coll 81 E College Hillsdale MI 49242

KNECHT, RICHARD ARDEN, family practitioner; b. Grand Rapids, Mar. 7, 1929; s. Fredrick William and Eva Rae (Blakley) K.; m. Joan Matson, Dec. 26, 1951 (div. 1975); children: Richard Arden, Karrie Jo, Jeffrey Paul; m. Patricia Irene Gilmore, Aug. 14, 1976; 1 child, Kimberly Kahler. BS, U. Mich., 1951, MD, 1955. Diplomate Am. Bd. Family Practice, Am. Bd. Geriatric Medicine; cert. med. dir. Intern St. Mary Hosp., Grand Rapids, Mich., 1955-56; pvt. practice, Fife Lake, Mich., 1956—. Fellow Am. Acad. Family Physicians, Am. Geriatric Soc., Royal Soc. Medicine; mem. Mich. Med. Soc. (com. on aging 1988—), Mich. Acad. Family Practice (chmn. com. on aging 1986-88, pub.'s award 1988), Mich. Med. Dirs. Assn. (pres. 1996-97). Avocations: archaeology, motorcycling, geology, hunting, fishing. Home and Office: PO Box 130 125 Morgan St Fife Lake MI 49633

KNECHT, WILLIAM L. lawyer; b. Lock Haven, Pa., Jan. 15, 1946; s. Clair N. and Betty R. (Harter) K.; m. Margaret E. O'Malley, June 10, 1972; children: William E., Jennifer M. BA, Pa. State U., 1967; JD, Dickinson Sch. Law, 1970. Bar: Pa. 1970, U.S. Supreme Ct. 1976, U.S. Tax Ct. 1981, U.S. Dist. Ct. (middle dist.) Pa. 1973, Ct. Common Pleas 1970. Assoc. McCormick, Lynn, Reeder, Nichols & Sarno, Williamsport, Pa., 1973-76; ptnr. McCormick, Reeder, Nichols, Dahl, Knecht & Person, Williamsport, 1976-96; ptnr. McCormick Law Firm, Williamsport, 1996—. Bankruptcy trustee U.S. Justice Dept., Williamsport, Pa., 1978-91. Editor Lycoming Reporter, 1976—. 1st lt. U.S. Army, 1971-73. Fellow Pa. Bar Found. (life); mem. ABA, Pa. Bar Assn., Lycoming County Law Assn. (exec. com. 1976—), Lycoming Law Assn. (pres. 1995), Ross Club. Republican. United Ch. of Christ. Avocation: stamps and first day cover collecting. Home: 253 Lincoln Ave Williamsport PA 17701-2237 Office: McCormick Law Firm 835 W 4th St Williamsport PA 17701 E-mail: bknecht@mcclaw.com.

KNEE, MICHAEL J. science librarian, consultant; s. Teddy and Minerva Knee; m. Karen R. Kirchofer; children: Margaux, Amber. BA, Montclair State U., 1971, MA, 1975; MLS, Rutgers U., 1977. Serials, reference libr. Rutgers U., Piscataway, NJ, 1977—78; info. scientist Knoll Pharm. Co., Whippany, NJ, 1978—79; pub. services libr. U. N.D., Grand Forks, 1979—81; sci. bibliographer U. Albany, SUNY, 1981—. Author: The Reference Librarian, 1987, Collection Management, 1990, Hypertext/Hypermedia: An Annotated Bibliography, 1990, Library Acquisitions: Theory & Practice, 1992, Reference Services Review, 1995, Wolves: A Bibliography and Guide to the Literature, 1968-1987, 1995, Issues in Science & Technology Librarianship, 1997, College & Research Libraries News, 2001. Mem.: SUNY Libr. Assn., Am. Chem. Soc., Spl. Libr. Assn. Office: Univ Albany SUNY Sci Libr Albany NY 12222 Office Fax: 518-437-3952. E-mail: knee@albany.edu.

KNEE, RUTH IRELAN (MRS. JUNIOR K. KNEE), social worker, health care consultant; b. Sapulpa, Okla., Mar. 21, 1920; d. Oren M. and Daisy (Daubin) Irelan; m. Junior K. Knee, May 29, 1943 (dec. Oct. 1981). BA, U. Okla., 1941, cert. social work, 1942; MA in Social Svcs. Adminstrn., U. Chgo., 1945. Psychiat. social worker, asst. supr. Ill. Psychiat. Inst., U. Ill., Chgo., 1943-44; psychiat. social worker USPHS Employee Health Unite, Washington, 1944—49; social work assoc. Army Med. Ctr., Walter Reed Army Hosp., Washington, 1949-54; psychiat. social work cons.. HEW, Region III, Washington, 1955-56; with NIMH, Chevy Chase, Md., 1956-72; chief mental health care adminstrn. br. Health Svcs. and Mental Health Adminstrn., 1967-72, USPHS assoc. dep. adminstr., 1972-73; dep. dir. Office of Nursing Home Affairs, 1973-74; long-term mental health care cons.; mem. com. on mental health and illness of elderly HEW, 1976-77; mem. panel on legal and ethical issues Pres.'s Commn. on Mental Health, 1977-78; liaison mem. Nat. Adv. Mental Health Coun., 1977-81. Mem. editl. bd. Health and Social Work, 1979-81. Bd. dirs. Hillhaven Found., 1975-86, governing bd. Cathedral Coll. of the Laity, Washington Nat. Cathedral, 1988-94, Cathedral Fund Com., 1997—,bd. of visitors sch. of social work, Univ. of Okla., 2000— Recipient Edith Abbott award, U. Chgo. Sch. Social Svc. Adminstrn., 2001, Disting. Alumna award, U. Okla. Coll. Arts and Scis., 1999. Fellow APHA (sec. mental health sect. 1968-70, chmn. 1971-72), Am. Orthopsychiat. Assn. (life), Gerontol. Soc. Am., Am. Assn. Psychiat. Social Workers (pres. 1951-53); mem. Nat. Conf. Social Welfare (nat. bd. 1968-71, 2d v.p. 1973-74), Inst. Medicine/NAS (com. study future of pub. health 1986-87), Coun. on Social Work Edn., Nat. Assn. Social Workers (sec. 1955-56, nat. dir. 1956-57, 84-86, chmn. competence study com., practice and knowledge com. 1963-71, presdl. award for exemplary svc. 1999), Acad. Cert. Social Workers (NASW Found. co-chair social work pioneers 1993—), Am. Pub. Welfare Assn., DAR, U. Okla. Assocs., Woman's Nat. Dem. Club (mem. gov. bd. 1992-95, ednl. found. bd. 1992-2000), Cosmos Club (Washington, chair program com. 1998-2001), Phi Beta Kappa (fellow), Psi Chi. Address: 8809 Arlington Blvd Fairfax VA 22031-2705

KNEE, STEPHEN H. lawyer; b. Newark, Oct. 15, 1940; s. Simon E. and Mollie (Liest) K.; m. Carole Leibowitz, Feb. 17, 1984; children: Robert A., David E., Dana R. AB, Duke U., 1962; JD, N.Y.U., 1965. Bar: N.J. 1965, N.Y. 1981, U.S. Ct. Appeals (3rd cir.) 1981, U.S. Supreme Ct. 1969, U.S. Dist. Ct. (so. dist.) N.Y. 1999. Law sec. Superior Ct. of N.J., Paterson, 1965-66; ptnr. Stryker, Tams & Dill, LLP, Newark, 1966-98, Saiber, Schlesinger, Satz & Goldstein, LLC, Newark, 1998—. Author: Buying and Selling Businesses, 1996. Trustee N.J. Shakespeare Festival, 1988—, Jewish Family Services of Metrowest, 1988-2002, 2003—. Mem. ABA (com. on negotiated acquistions, subcom. on uniform securities act of state regulation of securities com.), N.J. Bar Assn. (dir. corp. and bus. law sect. 1979—, chmn. 1984-86, program com. 1991-97), Inst. for Continuing Legal Edn. (past mem. adv. com.), Essex County Bar Assn., Am. Coll. Investment Counsel. Office: Saiber Schlesinger Satz & Goldstein LLC One Gateway Ctr Newark NJ 07102 E-mail: shk@saiber.com.

KNEEDLER, RICHARD (ALVIN KNEEDLER), former academic administrator; b. Ruffsdale, Pa., Apr. 8, 1943; s. Alvin Raymond and Louise (Mac Innes) Kneedler; m. Suzette Gallagher, June 17, 1967; children: Eric, Rebecca. AB, Franklin and Marshall Coll., 1965; MA in French Lang. and Lit., U. Pa., 1967, PhD in French Lang. and Lit., 1970; cert. in Ednl. Mgmt., Harvard U., 1975; DHL (hon.), Tohoku Gakuin U., 1993. Instr. French Franklin and Marshall Coll., Lancaster, Pa., 1968—70, asst. prof. French, 1970—72, asst. to. dean, 1971—74, asst. to pres., 1974—77, sec. coll., 1977—79, v.p. adminstrn., 1979—84, v.p. devel., 1984—88, sec. bd. trustees, 1974—88, pres., 1988—2002; cons. Coun. of Ind. Colleges, 2002—. Mem. exec. com. Assn. Ind. Colls. and Univs. Pa., 1989—98, 2000—, chmn., 1996—97; exec. com. Nat. Assn. Ind. Colls. and Univs., 1999, chair policy & pub. rels. com., 99, mem. coun. ind. coll. dir., 2000—. Mem. Lancaster City Planning Commn., 1980—85, chmn., 1983—85; v.p., bd. dirs. Hist. Preservation Trust, Lancaster, 1984—87; sec., bd. dirs. Pa. Sch. Arts, 1985—89; bd. dirs. St. Joseph Hosp., 1991—95, Lancaster Area Arts Coun., 1967—91, Louise Von Hess Found. for Med. Edn., 1990—, Urban League Lancaaster County, 1991—93, United Way, 1993—98, Urban Alliance, 1998—; chmn. Cmty. Cultural Planning Com., 1989—90; mem. Downtown Task Force, 1989—90; trustee Kiski Sch., 1988—95; chmn. exec. bd. Commonwealth Partnerships, 1997—98; mem. adv. bd. PRIME, Inc., 1991—98. Mem.: Am. Soc. 18th Century Studies, Am. Assn. Tchrs. French, Lancaster C. of C. and Industry (bd. dirs. 1990—92), Phi Alpha Theta, Phi Beta Kappa. Republican. Presbyterian. Home: 1416 Newton Rd Lancaster PA 17603-2461

KNEELAND, DOUGLAS EUGENE, retired newspaper editor; b. Lincoln, Maine, July 27, 1929; s. Vernis Bruce and Sadie Jane (Curtis) K.; m. Anne Packard Libby, Sept. 8, 1951 (dec. Nov. 1989); children: Debra Jo Kneeland Wentz, Libby Kneeland Williams, Bruce, Wayne; m. Barbara Jordan Lees, May 24, 1997. BA in Journalism, U. Maine, 1953. Reporter Bangor Daily News, Maine, 1951-53, Worcester Telegram, Mass., 1953-56; city editor, news editor Lorain Jour., Ohio, 1956-59; copy editor, nat. corr., dep. nat. editor N.Y. Times, N.Y.C., Kansas City, San Francisco and Chgo., 1959-81; nat.-fgn. editor Chgo. Tribune, 1981-82, assoc. mng. editor, 1982-87, assoc. editor, 1987-90, pub. editor, 1990-93; vis. lectr. journalism U. Maine, Orono, 1993—. Columnist Lincoln News, Maine, 1995—2001. Served with AUS, 1947-49, Korea, Japan. Home: 31 Albert Dr Lincoln ME 04457-9601 E-mail: dougk@midmaine.com.

KNEEN, JOHN W. venture capitalist; b. Detroit, Sept. 3, 1952; s. Russell Packard and Joyce (Knapper) Kneen; m. Mary Ellen Raphael, June 18, 1983 (div. Sept. 1998). BA, Coll. Wooster, 1974; MBA, Northwestern U., Evanston, Ill., 1976. CPA Ill., 1978. CPA Coopers & Lybrand, Chgo., 1976—88; v.p. Prime Group, Inc., Chgo., 1988—89; sr. v.p. devel. Evergreen Healthcare, Inc., Carmel, Ind., 1990—96; CFO Alterra Healthcare, Inc., Brookfield, Wis., 1996—97; mng. dir. Beecken Petty & Co., Chgo., 1997—. Bd. trustees Wooster Coll., 2003—. Mem.: Western Golf Assn. (bd. dirs. 1995—), Coll. Wooster Alumni Assn. (pres. 1999—2000), Union League Club Chgo., Medinah Country Club (bd. dirs. 1994—96). Republican. Methodist. Avocations: golf, skiing. Home: 2337 N Cambridge Chicago IL 60614 Office: Beecken Petty & Co 200 W Madison Chicago IL 60606 Office Fax: 312-435-0371. Business E-Mail: jkneen@bpcompany.com.

KNEIPPER, RICHARD KEITH, lawyer; b. Kenosha, Wis., June 18, 1943; s. Richard F. and Esther E. (Beaster) K.; m. Sherry Hayes, Dec. 16, 1977; children: Ryan Hayes, Lindsey Merrill. BS, Washington and Lee U., 1965; JD, Cornell U., 1968. Bar: Tex. 1982, U.S. Dist. Ct. (so. dist.) N.Y. 1968, U.S. Ct. Appeals (2d cir.) 1971. Atty. Chadbourne & Parke, N.Y.C., 1968-81, Jones, Day, Reavis & Pogue, Dallas, 1981-99; chief adminstrv. officer Provider HealthNet Svcs. Inc., Dallas, 1999—. Mem. adv. com. Nat. Mus. Am., Smithsonian, Nat. Arts Edn. Initiative, Nat. Mus. Am. Art, Smithsonian Instn. Contbr. numerous articles to profl. jours. Bd. trustees The Dallas Parks Found.; mem. profl. adv. group Save Outdoor Sculpture!; chmn. Dallas Adopt-a-Monument; bd. dirs., mem. adv. coun. Appalachian Coll. Assn., Inc., Sch. Visual Arts, U. North Tex.; former mem. new bus. task force, former mem. internat. task force Health Industry Coun. Dallas-Ft. Worth Region. Mem. ABA, N.Y. Bar Assn., Tex. Bar Assn., Tex. Sculpture Assn., Assn. of Bar of City of N.Y. Episcopal. Office: Provider HealthNet Svcs Inc 15851 Dallas Pkwy Ste 925 Addison TX 75001-6022

KNEISEL, EDMUND M. lawyer; b. Atlanta, Feb. 21, 1946; s. John F. and Mary E. (Moore) K.; m. Leslie A. Jones, June 19, 1976; 1 child, Mary Kathleen. AB, Duke U., 1968; JD, U. Ga., 1974. Bar: Ga. 1974, U.S. Dist. Ct. (no. and mid. dists.) Ga., U.S. Ct. Appeals (2d, 4th, 5th, 6th and 11th cirs.), U.S. Supreme Ct. 1984. Law clk. to Hon. R.C. Freeman U.S. Dist. Ct. (no. dist.) Ga., Atlanta, 1974-76; assoc. Kilpatrick & Cody, Atlanta, 1976-82; ptnr. Kilpatrick Stockton LLP, 1982—. Mng. editor Ga. Law Rev., Athens, 1973-74; contbr. articles to profl. jours. Lt. USNR, 1968-71. Mem. ABA, Lawyers Club Atlanta, Druid Hills Golf Club. Office: Kilpatrick Stockton LLP 1100 Peachtree St NE Ste 2800 Atlanta GA 30309-4530 E-mail: ekneisel@kilstock.com.

KNEISER, RICHARD JOHN, accountant; b. Milw., Nov. 20, 1938; s. Frank Edward and Esther (Sobek) K.; m. Caroline Irene Stahl, Aug. 22, 1959; children: Richard J. Jr., Ronald V., Robert C. BS in Acctg., Marquette U., 1960. CPA. Staff mem. Arthur Andersen & Co., Milw., 1960-65, audit mgr., 1965-73, ptnr., 1973-94. Mem. exec. bd. Wis. Pub. Utility Inst., Madison, 1982-94; advisor acctg. practices com. U.S. Cath. Conf., 1989-2001; mem. adv. bd. Biltmore Investors Bank, 1995-97, N.Am. Clutch Corp., 1995-2003, dir., 2003—; pres. The Carowoods Corp., 1990—. Dir. Skylight Opera Theatre, Milw., 1987-95; active Marquette U. Pres. Exec. Senate, Milw. 1987-94; trustee Village of Oconomowoc Lake, Wis., 1991-95, 97—, mem. planning commn., 1989-93, 97—, chmn. fin. com., 1991-93, mem., 1993—; bd. dirs. Oconomowoc Meml. Hosp. Found., Inc., 1996-99, treas., 1997-98, v.p., 1998-99. Mem. AICPA, Wis. Inst. CPA, Oconomowoc Lake Club (bd. dirs. 1988-97, officer, 1989-95, commodore 1994-95), Lac LaBelle Golf Club, Beta Gamma Sigma, Beta Alpha Psi. Avocations: antiques, fishing, tennis, golf, gardening. Home: 35920 Pabst Rd Oconomowoc WI 53066-4519

KNELLER, JOHN WILLIAM, academic administrator, retired French language and literature educator; b. Oldham, Eng., Oct. 15, 1916; s. John William and Margaret Ann (Truslove) K.; m. Alice Bowerman Hart, Apr. 30, 1943; 1 dau., Linda Hart. AB, Clark U., 1938, LittD, 1970; AM, Yale U., 1948, PhD, 1950; French Govt. and Fulbright fellow, U. Paris, France, 1949-50. Asst. in instrn. Yale U., 1947-49; instr. French Oberlin Coll., 1950-52, asst. prof., 1952-55, assoc. prof., 1955-59, prof. French, 1959-65, chmn. dept. Romance langs., 1958-65, dean Coll. Arts and Scis., 1967-68, provost, 1965-69; pres. Bklyn. Coll., CUNY, 1969-79, pres. emeritus, 1979—. Univ. prof. humanities and arts Hunter Coll. and Grad. Ctr., CUNY, 1979-95, prof. emeritus, 1995—; mng. editor French Rev., 1962-65, editor-in-chief, 1965-68; co-chair bd. dirs. Henri Peyre Inst. for the Humanities, 1980-2001; cons. NEH; chmn. subcom. on enrollment goals and projections N.Y. State Edn.; Commr.'s Adv. Coun. on Higher Edn., Adv. Coun. on Higher Edn. Co-author: Initiation au francais, 1963, Introduction a la poesie francaise, 1962; assoc. editor Yale French Studies, 1948-50; contbr. articles to jours. in field. Bd. dirs. Independence Savs. Bank. With AUS, 1942-46. Decorated comdr. Ordre des Palmes Académiques (France). Mem. Am. Assn. Tchrs. French (exec. council 1962-68), Modern Lang. Assn. (exec. council 1965-69), Yale Grad. Sch. Assn. (exec. com. 1967, 71), Bklyn. C. of C. (dir.), Kappa Delta Pi (hon.), Alpha Sigma Lambda (hon.) Clubs: Century (N.Y.C.), Yale (N.Y.C.), Southport Racquet.

KNEPPER, EUGENE ARTHUR, realtor; b. Sioux Falls, S.D., Oct. 8, 1926; s. Arlie John Knepper, May (Crone) Knepper; m. LaNel Strong Knepper, May 7, 1948 (div. Sept. 1996); children: Kenton Todd, Kristin Rene. BSc in Acctg., Drake U., 1951. Acct. G.L.Yager CPA, Estherville, Iowa, 1951—52; auditor R.L. Meriwether, CPA, Des Moines, 1952—53; acct. Govt. Renegotiation Dept. Collins Radio Co., Cedar Rapids, Iowa, 1953—54; head acctg. dept. Hawkeye Rubber Mfg. Co., Cedar Rapids, 1954—56; asst. contr. United Fire & Casualty Ins. Co., Cedar Rapids, 1956—58; sales assoc. Equitable Life Assurance Soc. U.S., Cedar Rapids, 1958—59; contr. Gaddis Enterprises, Inc., Cedar Rapids, 1959—61; sales assoc., mgr. comml. investment divsn. Tommy Tucker Realty Co., Cedar Rapids, 1961—74; owner Real Estate Investment Planning Assocs, Cedar Rapids, 1974—. Owner Estherville Laundry Co., 1959—64; treas. Investment Properties Inc., Cedar Rapids, 1994—; div. fin. acct., Cedar Rapids, 2000—; controlling ptnr. numerous real estate syndicates; cons. in field; fin. spkr.; guest lectr. Kirkwood C.C., Cedar Rapids, Mt. Mercy Coll., Cedar Rapids, Cornell Coll., Mt. Vernon, Iowa. Contbr. Patron Cedar Rapids Symphony, 1983—86, mem. exec. com., bd. dirs.; bd. dirs. Oak Hill-Jackson Outreach Fund, 1970—83, pres., 1973—74; bd. dirs., pres. Consumer Credit Counseling Svc., Cedar Rapids, Marion, 1974—80; mem. pub. rels. com., vol. newsletter contbr. Cedar Valley Habit for Humanity, 1991—95, vol. mental health adv., 1991—. With USN, 1945—46. Recipient Storm Manuscript award, 1976. Mem.: Cedar Rapids Bd. Realtors, Internat. Inst. Valuers, Real Estate Securities and Syndication Inst. (steering com. 1985, small group investment coun., vice chmn. regional officers and state officers devel. com., gov. Iowa divsn., regional v.p.), Nat. Inst. Real Estate Brokers (Iowa membership chmn. 1972—73), Nat. Assn. Accts., Nat. Assn. Realtors (state mcpl. legis. com., subcom. multi-family housing), Iowa Assn. Realtors (life; pres. comml. investment divsn. 1973, 1980, state legis. com., savs. and loan formation feasibility com., instr. creative financing Iowa Real Estate Commn., mcpl. and county legis. com.), Internat. Platform Assn., Cedar Rapids Optimist Club (past chmn. boys work com.), Ea. Iowa Execs. Club (bd. dir., pres. 1981—82). Methodist. Home: 283 Tomahawk Trl SE Cedar Rapids IA 52403-2037

KNEPPER, GEORGE W. history educator; b. Akron, Ohio, Jan. 15, 1926; s. George W. and Grace (Darling) K.; m. Phyllis Watkins, Aug. 21, 1949; children— Susan Lynne, John Arthur. BA, U. Akron, 1948; MA, U. Mich., 1950, PhD, 1954. Mem. faculty U. Akron, 1948-49, 54-92, assoc. prof. history, head dept., 1959-62; dean U. Akron (Coll. Liberal Arts), 1962-67, prof. history, 1964-88, disting. prof. history, 1988-92. Author: New Lamps for Old, One Hundred Years of Urban Higher Education at the University of Akron, 1970, An Ohio Portrait, 1976, Akron: City at the Summit, 1981, Ohio and Its People, 1989, Summit's Glory: Sketches of Buchtel Coll. and the University of Akron, 1990; editor: Travels in the Southland; The Journal of Lucius Verus Biérce 1822-23, 1966. Served to ensign USNR, 1943-46. Fulbright fellow U. London, Eng., 1953-54 Mem. Am., So. hist. assns., Orgn. Am. Historians, Ohio Acad. History, Omicron Delta Kappa, Alpha Tau Omega, Phi Alpha Theta, Alpha Sigma Lambda. Home: 88 Ridge Side Ct Munroe Falls OH 44262-1076 Office: Univ Akron Coll Liberal Arts Dept History Akron OH 44325-0001

KNERR, ANTHONY DAVID, strategic consultant; b. Bellefonte, Pa., Dec. 7, 1938; s. Henry William Knerr and Catherine Margaret Conner; m. Katrina Ely Carter, June 22, 1963 (div. July 1974); children: Christopher Hamilton, Theodore Gabriel; m. Susanne E. Kastler, Apr. 20, 2002. BA magna cum laude, Yale U., 1960, MA cum laude, 1964; PhD, NYU, 1978. Tchr. Milton (Mass.) Acad., 1961-63; program officer Internat. Exchange Program, N.Y.C., 1965-67; assoc., cons. Booz Allen & Hamilton, N.Y.C., 1967-70; vice chancellor for budget and planning CUNY, N.Y.C., 1970-77; spl. asst. to acting pres. Yale U., New Haven, 1977-78; exec. v.p. fin., treas. Columbia U., N.Y.C., 1978-88; pres. Publ. Group Inc., N.Y.C., 1988-90; mng. dir. Anthony Knerr & Assocs., N.Y.C., 1990—. Lectr. Columbia U., N.Y.C., 1986-88; pres. emeritus Caribbean Conservation Corp., 1993-2001; vice chmn. Humanity in Action, 2000—; bd. dirs. Del. Mut. Funds. Author: Shelley's Adonais: A Critical Edition, 1984. Bd. dirs. N.Y. Soc. Libr., 1983—.; pres. emeritus United Neighborhood Houses, 1994—; vice chmn. Humanit in Action, 1997—. Mem. The Century Assn., Keats-Shelley Assn. (bd. dirs. 1983—), Grolier Club, Phi Beta Kappa. Home: 115 E 70th St New York NY 10021-5020 Office: Anthony Knerr & Assocs 500 5th Ave Ste 3600 New York NY 10110-3699

KNESEL, ERNEST ARTHUR, JR., diagnostic company executive; b. New Orleans, Dec. 11, 1945; s. Ernest Arthur and Catherine Charlotte (Maier) K.; m. Lavina Lynn Menge, June 2, 1968; children: Eric Ernest, Tami Lynn, Bradley William. Student, Armstrong Coll., 1963-64; BS, Fairleigh Dickinson U., 1968, MS, 1970. Cert. clin. chemist. Technologist Am. Biol. Control Lab., Tenefly, N.J., 1966-68; sr. technologist Englewood (N.J.) Hosp., 1968-69; founder, v.p. Biomed. Reference Labs., Inc., Burlington, N.C., 1969-82; sr. v.p. Roche Biomed. Labs., Inc., Burlington, 1982-95; pres., founder Roche Image Analysis Sys., Inc., Elon College, N.C., 1989-96; exec. v.p., founder Autocyte, Inc., Elon College, 1996-99; v.p., founder TriPath Imaging, 1999-2000; cons. True North Group, 2000—01; founder, pres. Select Diagnostics Inc., 2001—, Sydermed Select Ptnrs., Inc., 2003—. Inventor serum filter/dispenser vial, automated aliquoting system, cyto-rich automated cytology preparation system and simultaneous machine and human interactive cytology evaluation system. Mem. Am. Assn. Clin. Chemistry, Am. Soc. Clin. Pathologists (assoc.). Roman Catholic. Avocation: magic. Office: AutoCyte Inc PO Box 1029 Burlington NC 27216-1029

KNEZO, GENEVIEVE JOHANNA, science and technology policy researcher; b. Aug. 8, 1942; d. John and Genevieve (Sadowski) K.; 1 child, Alexandra M. AB in Polit. Sci., Rutgers U., 1964, MA in Sci., Tech. and Pub. Policy, George Washington U., 1981; grad., Nat. Def. U., 1989. With Congl. Rsch. Svc. Libr. of Congress, Washington, 1967—, specialist in sci. and tech., 1979—, head sci., rsch. and tech. sect., 1986-88, sr. level specialist in sci. and tech. policy, 1991—. Author profl. publs. Mem. Phi Beta Kappa, Pi Sigma Alpha. Avocations: white-water canoeing, hiking, gymnastics, classical music, community volunteer activities. Home: 606 Oakley Pl Alexandria VA 22302-3611 Office: Libr of Congress Congl Rsch Svc Resources Sci/Indust Divsn Washington DC 20540-7450 E-mail: gknezo@crs.loc.gov.

KNICKERBOCKER, ROBERT PLATT, JR., lawyer; b. Hartford, Conn., Sept. 23, 1944; s. Robert P. and Audrey Jane (Stempel) K.; m. Kathleen A. Sakal (div. May 1985); children: Sarah, Abigail, Jonathan; m. Barbara Denise Whinnem, Oct. 3, 1987. BA, Cornell U., 1966; JD, U. Conn., 1969. Bar: Conn. 1969, U.S. Dist. Ct. Conn. 1969, U.S. Ct. Appeals (2d cir.) 1970. Law clk. to presiding justice Conn. Supreme Ct., Hartford, 1968-69; ptnr. Day, Berry & Howard, Hartford, 1969—. Mem. State Implementation Plan Regulation Adv. Commn., 1979-90. Chmn. Town Plan and Zoning Commn., Glastonbury, Conn., 1975-79, Glastonbury Bd. Edn., 1982-86. Mem. Conn. Bar Assn., Greater Hartford C. of C. (state legis. com.). Republican. Episcopalian. Office: Day Berry & Howard Cityplace Hartford CT 06103-3499 E-mail: rpknickerbocker@dbh.com.

KNICKREHM, GLENN ALLEN, management executive; b. L.A., Mar. 27, 1948; s. Allen F. and Evelyn Knickrehm. BA magna cum laude, Occidental Coll., 1971; BS, Columbia U., 1971, MBA, 1973. Analyst Exxon Co., N.Y.C. and L.A., 1971-72; cons. Boston Cons. Group, Boston and Munich, 1973-77, mgr. Boston, 1977-83; pres., chmn. Our Market Supermarket, Inc., 1980-81; pres. Bay Resource Corp., 1983—. Chmn. Apex Internat. Alloys, Inc., 1986-89; pres. Mashamoquet Holdings, Inc., 1995—; adv. Beach Brook Prodns., 1995—; pres. Constellation Prodns., Inc., 1996—; dir. Scuola il Bisonte, Florence, Italy, 1998—; bd. dirs. Am. Repertory Theatre, Mus. Fine Arts; trustee Westfield Ctr. for Early Keyboard Studies, 1999—. Dir. New Eng. Theater Guild, Inc., 1985-89, Samuel Bronfman fellow, 1972; pres. Constellation Charitable Found., 2001—. Mem. Boston Anthenaeum, Columbia U. Faculty Club, Phi Beta Kappa, Tau Beta Pi, Beta Gamma Sigma, Sigma Pi Sigma, Pi Mu Epsilon, Kappa Mu Epsilon. Office: 1280 Massachusetts Ave Cambridge MA 02138-3840

KNIES, ROBERT CARL, JR., critical care nurse; b. Wilkes-Barre, Pa., Sept. 7, 1960; s. Robert Carl and Alice Ann (Swartman) K.; m. Lisa Ann Stumhofer, May 17, 1986; 1 child, Kayleigh Ann Elisabeth. Diploma, St. Joseph Hosp. Sch. Nursing, Reading, Pa., 1983; BSN, Pa. State U., 1990; MSN, Villanova U., 1996. Cert. emergency nurse, CPR instr., emergency med. technician, instr., ACLS. Staff nurse St. Joseph Hosp., Reading, 1983-84; clin. nurse Community Gen. Hosp., Reading, 1984-89; nurse Med. Pers. Pool, Allentown, Pa., 1989-91, Pottstown (Pa.) Meml. Med. Ctr., 1990-96; clin. nurse specialist emergency svcs. Health Sys. Minn., 1996-2000; clin. mgr. emergency svcs. Stevens Hosp., Edmonds, Wash., 2000—, dir. emergency svcs., 2001—. Adj. faculty Reading Area C.C., 1991-95, Seattle Pacific U., 2001. Mem. Nat. Assn. Clin. Nurse Specialists (bd. dirs. 1999-01), Emergency Nurses Assn. (pres. Twin-Cities chpt. 2000, pres.-elect Minn. coun. 2000), Sigma Theta Tau, Alpha Sigma Lambda. E-mail: rck_cns@hotmail.com.

KNIESER, CATHERINE, music educator; b. Seoul, Republic of Korea, Aug. 12, 1974; d. Thomas and Susan Knieser. MusB, U. Del., 1997; MusM, Ithaca Coll., 2000. Cert. tchr. N.Y., Nat. Bd. Early Adolescent through Young Adulthood, 2003. Tchr.-in-charge, secondary music Wappingers Ctrl. Sch. Dist., Wappingers Falls, NY, 1999—. Grantee Latin Percussion Mini grant, Wappingers Ctrl. Sch. Dist., 1998—99, African Music Mini grant, Mid Hudson Tchr. Ctr., 1999—2000, Tech. Digital grant, Wappingers Ctrl. Sch. Dist., 2002—. Mem.: N.Y. State Sch. Music Assn., Music Educators Nat. Conf., Am. Orff-Schulwerk Assn., Sigma Alpha Iota (life). Personal E-mail: krabaple@vh.net.

KNIESLER, FREDERICK CORNELIUS, retired municipal official; b. Trenton, N.J., Feb. 2, 1930; s. Frederick Edward and Mary Ellen (Hanheen) K.; m. Bernice Rottkamp, Aug. 17, 1929; children: Frederick C. Jr., Christopher D., Gregory B., Maria E. AA, Rider U., 1970, BS, 1973, MA, 1980. Lic. pub. acct. N.J.; cert. mcpl. fin. officer N.J. Spl. dep. clk. Monmouth County, NJ, 1969-75; project coord., sec. treas Manasquan River Regional Sewerage Authority, NJ, 1975-77; from clk. bd. chosen freeholders to dep. county clk. Monmouth County, 1977-82; asst. commr. N.J. Dept. Labor, 1982-90; twp. adminstr. Manalapan Twp., 1990-94; dep. commr. N.J. Dept. Labor, 1994-97. Commr. Monmouth County Bd. Parks & Recreation, 1991—; NJ rep. Mid Atlantic Regional Conf. Nat. Recreation and Pk. Assn., 2001—; past chair policy com. N.J. Unemployment Ins. Reemployment Demonstration Project, Mgmt. Com. Disability Automated Benefits sys., evaluation com. Mail Claims Pilot Program; past mem. Gov.'s Mgmt. Improvement Program; part-time cons. Fred Kniesler & Assocs.; owner Dusty Pages Book Shop. Twp. clk. Upper Freehold Twp., N.J., 1954-57, treas., 1975-86; county chmn. Rep. Com., Monmouth County, 1981-86, mcpl. chmn. Upper Freehold; del. Rep. Nat. Convention, Kansas City, 1976. Served in USAR, 1949-81. Recipient Pres.'s Disting. Svc. award N.J. State League of Municipalities. Mem. Am. Soc. Profl. Adminstrs., Nat. Assn. Govt. Labor Ofcls. (pres. 1996-97), Interstate Conf. Employment Security Adminstrs. (sec. 1987-89), N.J. Conf. of Mayors (charter), Assn. U.S. Army, Internat. Assn. Employees in Employment Security, KC, Knights of Columbus. Republican. Roman Catholic. Avocations: thomas merton, collecting am flyer trains, gray iron toy soldiers. Fax: 609-208-0482. E-mail: Kniesler1@aol.com.

KNIFFEN, DONALD AVERY, astrophysicist, educator, researcher; b. Kalamazoo, Apr. 27, 1933; s. Frederick Bowerman and Eva Virginia (Arp) Kniffen; m. Janis Kay Nesom, June 14, 1952; children: Karyol Kniffen Poole, Donald Avery Nesom Jr., Kimberly Kniffen Giesbrecht. BS magna cum laude, La. State U., 1959; AM, Washington U., St. Louis, 1960; PhD, Cath. U. Am., 1967. Astrophysicist Goddard Space Flight Ctr., Greenbelt, Md., 1960-91; lectr. physics U. Md., College Park, 1978-87; project scientist Compton Gamma Ray Obs., 1979-91; William W. Elliott prof., chmn. dept. physics and astronomy Hampden-Sydney Coll., Va., 1991-2001; rsch. prof. George Mason U., 2002—. Vis. scientist NASA/USRA, Greenbelt, 1997—98; astrophysics cons. NASA/HSTX, NASA/USRA, 1991—98; program scientist NASA Hdqrs., 1999—. Contbr. articles to profl. jours. Served with USN, 1952-56. Recipient Medal for Outstanding Leadership NASA, 1992, Laurel award Space/Missiles, Aviation Week & Space Tech., 1991. Fellow Royal Astron. Soc.; mem. AAUP, Am. Phys. Soc., Am. astron. Soc., Internat. Astron. Union, Sigma Xi. Democrat. Avocations: travel, reading, gardening. Home: 2814 Andy Ct Crofton MD 21114-3157 also: Code SE NASA Hdqs Office Space Scis Washington DC 20546-0001 Personal E-mail: donk@annapolis.net. E-mail: donald.a.kniffen@nasa.gov.

KNIFFIN, PAULA SICHEL, insurance sales executive; b. N.Y.C., Oct. 2, 1941; d. Harold M. and Edith (Sachnoff) Sichel; m. Richrd G. Kniffin, Aug. 3, 1963; children: Douglas, Kelly. BA, Bucknell U., 1963. CLU; cert. fin. planner. Tchr. New Cumberland (Pa.) Jr. High Sch., 1963-64, Meadowbrook Jr. High Sch., East Meadow, N.Y., 1964-67; real estate salesperson Claire Sobel Real Estate, Syosset, N.Y., 1979-80; sales force recruiter Mut. of N.Y. Life Ins. Co., Jericho, 1981-82; head of life and health ins. dept., employee benefit cons. The Viking Agy., Inc., Syosset, N.Y., 1983—. Mem. Soc. Fin. Svc. Profls., Fin. Planning Assn., Women Life Underwriters Conf. (pres. 1988-89), Nat. Assn. Ins. and Fin. Advisors (bd. dirs. 1988-89), Nat. Assn. Ins. and Fin. Advisors, Ladies Golf Com. (chair 1990-93), Nassau Country Club, Mayacoo Lakes Country Club. Republican. Avocations: golf, tennis, bridge, reading. Office: The Viking Agy 117 Oak Dr Syosset NY 11791-4625 E-mail: paula@vikingagency.com.

KNIGHT, ALEXA DAVEY, real estate company executive, real estate broker; b. Denver, Aug. 1, 1949; d. F. Norton and Margaret E. (Monaghan) Davey; m. G. Kent Knight, Dec. 11, 1971 (div. May 1976); m. James R. Duley, June 27, 1998. BS in Occupational Therapy with honors, Colo. State U., 1973; MBA, U. Denver, 1979. Lic. real estate broker. Geophys. tech. asst. Husky Oil Co., Denver, 1974-77, assoc. landman, 1977-80; tech. sales rep. Eastman Kodak Co., San Francisco, 1980-84, regional bus. and mktg. specialist, 1984; systems sales rep. Control Data Corp., Sunnyvale, Calif., 1984-85; asst. adminstr. The Sequoias, Portola Valley, Calif., 1985-87, San Francisco, 1987-88; assoc. Coldwell Banker Real Estate, San Mateo, Calif., 1988-91; real estate broker RE/MAX Mid-Peninsula Realtors, San Mateo, Calif., 1991-96; ptnr., broker Real Estate Connection, Foster City, Calif., 1996-2000, RE/MAX Today, Foster City, 2000—. Del. Colo. Assembly, 1978; mem. Met. League San Francisco Symphony, Peninsula Humane Soc., Menlo Park Presbyn. Ch.; dir. Women's Recovery Assn. Recipient Gold Circle award, Gold and Silver Achievement awards, numerous others. Mem.: San Mateo County Assn. Realtors (MLS governing com.), San Mateo-Burlingame Bd. Realtors (chair edn. com., mem. computer users planning com., pub. svc. com., Realtor of Yr. 1994), Calif. Assn. Realtors (dir., mem. real estate fin. com.), Nat. Assn. Realtors, Foster City C. of C. (amb. 1998, chief amb. 1999, dir. exec. com. 2000—), San Mateo C. of C., Phi Theta Epsilon. Presbyterian. Avocations: sailing, skiing, camping, music, travel. Home: 2790 Belmont Canyon Rd Belmont CA 94002-1248 Office: RE/MAX Today 1098 Foster City Blvd # 205 San Mateo CA 94404 E-mail: alexaknight1@comcast.net.

KNIGHT, ANDREW KONG, visual artist, educator; b. Seattle, July 5, 1964; s. Richard Ivan Cook and Clara Kun Nai Kong; m. Julie Anne McLean, Feb. 2, 1991. Student, Calif. Coll. Arts and Crafts, 1978; BFA, San Francisco Art Inst., 1986; postgrad., Nat. U., 1996. Cert. tchr., Calif. Staff illustrator Western Ind. Bankers, Oakland, Calif., 1984-88, Western assn. Equipment Lessors, Oakland, 1989-94; art educator Kenneth C. Aikin Cmty. Ctr., Castro Valley, Calif., 1986-96; art educator, mural supr. Hayward (Calif.) Unified Sch. Dist., 1992—; prof. art Acad. Art Coll., San Francisco, 2002. Freelance illustrator Miller Freeman Pubs., San Francisco, Hewlett Packard, Palo Alto, Calif., New United Motor Co., Fremont, Calif., 1983—, Island/Mercury Records, N.Y.C.; guest lectr. Stanford U., Palo Alto, 1996, Calif. State U., Hayward, 1992-96, guest prof. art, 2001; spkr. in field. Exhibited in at Art of Calif., 1993, 94 (Silver award 1993, Gold award 1994), Am. Illustration 13, 1994 (award), Airbrush-Action Mag. (1st Pl. Fine Art award 1993), 3 Dimensional Art Dirs. and Illustrators Awards Show, 1996 (Gold award). Mem. adv. Hayward Arts Coun., 1994-95. Mem. NEA, Nat. Assn. Artists' Orgns., Calif. Tchrs. Assn., Precita Eyes Muralists. Home: 5181 Chesney Glen Dr Castro Valley CA 94552-5514

KNIGHT, ARTHUR WINFIELD, English educator; b. San Francisco, Dec. 29, 1937; s. Walter Arthur and Irja Blomquist K.; m. Glee Marquardt, Sept. 27, 1966 (dec. Oct. 1975); m. Kit Duell, Aug. 25, 1976; 1 child, Tiffany Carolyn. BA, San Francisco State U., 1960, MA, 1962. Tchr. English Anderson (Calif.) Union H.S., 1963-64; instr. journalism Riverside (Calif.) City Coll., 1964-65; instr. English Delta Coll., University Center, Mich., 1965-66; prof. English California U. Pa., 1966-93; film critic Anderson Valley Advertiser, Boonville, Calif., 1992—. Adj. prof. profl. studies U. San Francisco, 1995—2000; adj. prof. English Western Career Coll., 2001—02; co-entertainment editor Am. River Sentinel, 2003—. Author: All Together, Shift, 1972, Who Moved Among the Others as They Walked, 1974, The Secret Life of Jesse James, 1996, The Darkness Starts Up Where You Stand, 1996, The Cruelest Month, 1997, Johnnie D., 2000, Blue Skies Falling, 2001, The Erotic Life of Billy the Kid, 2003; contbr. articles to profl. jours.; author poems; author (plays): King of the Beatniks, 1985, 1988, 1993, Blue Earth, 1986, The Abused, 1986, Burning Daylight, 1987. Recipient 1st Pl. prize Joycean Lively Arts Guild, East Douglas, Mass., 1982. Mem. Western Writers Am. Avocation: photography. Office: PO Box 544 Citrus Heights CA 95611

KNIGHT, ATHELIA WILHELMENIA, journalist; b. Portsmouth, Va., Oct. 15, 1950; d. Daniel Dennis and Adell Virginia (Savage) K. BA with honors in English, Norfolk State Coll., 1973; MA with honors in Journalism, Ohio State U., 1974. Cert. tchr., Va. Aide D.C. Coop. Extension Service, 1969-72; sub. tchr. Portsmouth Pub. Schs., 1973; reporter Virginian Pilot, Norfolk, 1973, Chgo. Tribune, 1974; met. desk reporter Washington Post, 1975-81, investigative reporter, 1981-94, sports writer, 1994-2000; asst. dir. Washington Post Young Journalists, 2000—03, dir., 2003; adj. prof. Georgetown U., 2002—. Vis. prof. journalism Hampton U., 2001. Recipient Mark Twain award, 1982, 87, Front Page award Washington-Balt. Newspaper Guild, 1982, Nat. award for edn. Edn. Writers Assn., 1987, Pub. Svc. award Md.-Del.-D.C. Press Assn., 1990, 93, 1st Pl. award for spot news, 1997; Ohio State U. fellow, 1974, Nieman fellow Harvard U., 1985-86. Maynard Mgmt. at the Kellogg Sch. of Mgmt. N.W. U., 2003. Mem.: Assn. Women in Sports Media, Investigative Reporters and Editors, Nat. Assn. Black Journalists, Women in Comm., Herb Black Found. Methodist. Office: Washington Post 1150 15th St NW Washington DC 20071-0002

KNIGHT, BRIAN, writer; b. Lewiston, Idaho, Apr. 30, 1973; Author: (novels) Feral. Home: 618 3rd St Clarkston WA 99403 Personal E-mail: wickedman@cableone.net.

KNIGHT, CHARLES FIELD, electrical equipment manufacturing company executive; b. Lake Forest, Ill., Jan. 20, 1936; s. Lester Benjamin and Elizabeth Anne (Field) Knight; m. Joanne Parrish, June 22, 1957; children: Lester Benjamin III, Anne Field Knight Davidson, Steven P., Jennifer Lee. BSME, Cornell U., 1958, MBA, 1959. Mgmt. trainee Goetzewerke A.G., Burscheid, Germany, 1959—61; pres. Lester B. Knight Internat. Corp., 1961—63; from exec. v.p. to pres., CEO Lester B. Knight & Assocs., Inc., Chgo., 1963—73; from vice-chmn. bd. to CEO Emerson Electric Co., St. Louis, 1973—2000,

chmn. bd., 2000—. Bd. dirs. Southwestern Bell Corp., Caterpillar Inc., Baxter Internat. Inc., Anheuser Busch Cos., Inc., The Brit. Petroleum Co. plc. Active Civic Progress, 1973; bd. dirs., trustee Washington U., St. Louis, Olin Found.; bd. dirs. Arts and Edn. Coun. Mem.: Glen View Golf Club (Ill.), Cristal Downs Club (Traverse City, Mich.), Log Cabin Club (St. Louis), St. Louis Country Club, Chicago Club, Sigma Phi. Office: Emerson Electric Co 8100 W Florissant Ave Saint Louis MO 63136-1494*

KNIGHT, CHERYL DUBOIS, library director; b. Mar. 2, 1950; BA, SUNY, New Paltz, 1973; MSLS, L.I. U., 1988. Head children's svcs. Hicksville (N.Y.) Pub. Libr., 1987-92; libr. dir. Brandywine Cmty. Libr., Topton, Pa., 1997—. Office: 60 Tower Dr Topton PA 19562-1301 E-mail: brandywinecl@berks.lib.pa.us.

KNIGHT, CHRISTOPHER NICHOLS, lawyer; b. New Haven, Sept. 7, 1946; s. Douglas Maitland and Grace Wallace (Nichols) K.; m. Emily Byrn Turner, Oct. 20, 1979; children: Ethan Douglas, Benjamin Walker Lester, Christopher N. Jr. BA, Yale U., 1968; JD, Duke U., 1971. Bar: Wis. 1971, U.S. Dist. Ct. (ea. dist.) Wis. 1973, U.S. Ct. Appeals (7th cir.) 1977, N.C. 1979, U.S. Dist. Ct. (mid. dist.) N.C. 1979, Minn., 1980, U.S. Supreme Ct. 1980, U.S. Ct. Appeals (4th, 8th cirs.) 1980, U.S. Dist. Ct. Minn. 1980, Ill. 1982, N.Y., 1996. Assoc. Quarles & Brady, Milw., 1971-78, ptnr., 1978-79, Smith Helms Mulliss & Moore, Greensboro, N.C., 1979-80, Kutak Rock, Mpls., 1980-82, Isham Lincoln & Beale, Chgo., 1982-88, Hopkins & Sutter, Chgo., 1988-2001, Foley & Lardner, Chgo., 2001—, mng. ptnr., 2003—. Bd. dirs. Lyric Opera Chgo., 2003—. Mem. ABA, Ill. State Bar Assn., Minn. State Bar Assn., N.Y. State Bar Assn., N.C. State Bar Assn., State Bar Wis., Nat. Assn. Bond Lawyers. Congregationalist. Office: Foley & Lardner Ste 2800 321 N Clark St Chicago IL 60610-4764 E-mail: cknight@foleylaw.com.

KNIGHT, CONSTANCE BRACKEN, writer, realtor, corporate executive; b. Detroit, Oct. 30, 1937; d. Thomas Francis and Margaret (Kearney) Bracken; m. James Edwards Knight, June 14, 1958 (div. Feb. 1968); children: Constance Lynne Knight Campbell, James Seaton, Keith Bracken. Student, Barry Coll., 1955-56, Fla. State U., 1958-60; AA, Marymount Coll., 1957. Columnist, feature writer Miami Herald, Ft. Lauderdale, Fla., 1954-55, 79-80; pub. rels. dir. Lauderdale Beach Hotel, 1965-67; columnist, feature writer Ft. Lauderdale News/Sun-Sentinel, 1980-81; owner Connie Knight and Assoc. Pub. Rels., Ft. Lauderdale, 1981-85; editor, pub. Vail (Colo.) Mag., 1986-89, contbg. freelance writer, 1989—; editorial cons. Vail Valley Mag., 1993; pres. Knight Enterprises, Vail, 1994—; photojournalist Denver Post, 1999—. Instr. Colo. Mountain Coll., Vail, 1979. Mem. Planning and Environ. Commn., Vail, 1990-92, Vail Licensing Authority, 1995—. Mem. N.Am. Snowsport Assn. Journalists (treas. 1990-93). Office: 385 Gore Creek Dr Ste 201 Vail CO 81657-3606 Fax: 970-477-7475. E-mail: cknight@vail.net.

KNIGHT, DAVID CLOUGH, physician; b. Worcester, Mass., Mar. 28, 1950; s. Carleton and Mary (Burnett) K.; m. Francine Charles, Aug. 23, 1975; children: Jessica, Emily, Abigail, Charles. BA, Harvard U., 1972; MBBCh, Royal Coll. of Surgeons, Dublin, Ireland, 1981. FACS. Physician Surg. Assocs. of Waterbury, P.C., Conn., 1986—. Pres. GWHN and Physicians, Inc., Waterbury, 1994-98; trustee Waterbury Hosp., 1995—. Fellow Am. Coll. Surgeons. Office: Surg Assocs of Waterbury PC 1211 W Main St Waterbury CT 06708-3106

KNIGHT, DIANE, special education educator; b. De Ridder, La., Dec. 2, 1955; BS, McNeese State U., 1976; MEd, Northwestern State U., Natchitoches, La., 1980, EdD, 1986. Cert. tchr., La., Ga. Tchr. English Vernon Parish Sch. Bd., Leesville, La., 1976-77; tchr. spl. edn. Natchitoches Parish Sch. Bd., La., 1978-80, ednl. diagnostician, 1985-88; tchr. spl. edn. Sabine Parish Sch. Bd., Many, La., 1983-85; dir. pupil appraisal Red River Parish Sch. Bd., Coushatta, La., 1988-89; asst. prof. Ga. Southwestern Coll., Americus, 1989-90, U. Southwestern La., Lafayette, 1990-95; assoc. prof. U. Ga., Athens, 1995-96; ednl. diagnostician Spl. Sch. Dist. 1, 1996—2002; assoc. prof. La. State U., Shreveport, 2002—03. Ednl. cons. and evaluator, Lafayette, 1990-95, Athens, Ga., 1995-96, Baton Rouge, 1996-2002, Shreveport, 2002—; presenter in field. Contbr. articles to profl. jours., chapters to books. Mem.: Coun. for Exceptional Children (learning disabilities divsn., tchr. edn. divsn., La. state sec., v.p., pres., past pres.), La. Assn. Evaluators, Am. Coll. Forensic Examiners, Rotary, Phi Delta Kappa, Kappa Delta Pi, Phi Kappa Phi. Republican. Mem. Unity Ch. Home: 9000 W Wilderness Way Apt 24 Shreveport LA 71106

KNIGHT, DORIS RATHBUN, retired government and history educator; b. N.Y.C., Feb. 22, 1936; d. Roger E. and Armenia (Bertoli) Rathbun; m. Paul R. Knight, Apr. 19, 1958; 1 child, Roger. BA, U. Mass., 1957, MA, 1962, postgrad., 1962-63, 72-73. Editl. asst. Merriam-Webster Unabridged Dictionary, 3d edit., Springfield, Mass., 1958-60; prof., chair social sci. divsn. Holyoke (Mass.) C.C., 1963-94. Guest columnist: Jour.-Tribune, 1994—97; editor: Strolling Through the Port, 2001. Mem., chair. planning bd., Southampton, Mass., 1977—82; mem., 1983—92; mem. planning bd. Kennebunkport, Maine, 1995—99; vice chmn., 1998—99; mem. zoning bd. appeals, 1999—, chair, 2000—02; mem. adminstrv. code com., 2003—; vice chair Dem. Town Com., Southampton, 1990—94, R.S.V.P. So. Maine Adv. Coun., 1998—99, chair, 1999—2000. Mem. Newcomers Club (pres. 1997-98), Kennebunkport Hist. Soc. (pub. chair 1999). Avocations: reading, writing, travel, local history research.

KNIGHT, DOUGLAS MAITLAND, educational administrator, optical executive, writer; b. Cambridge, Mass., June 8, 1921; s. Claude Rupert and Fanny Sarah Douglas (Brown) K.; m. Grace Wallace Nichols, Oct. 31, 1942; children: Christopher, Douglas Maitland, Thomas, Stephen. AB, Yale U., 1942, MA, 1944, PhD, 1946; LLD (hon.), Ripon Coll., Knox Coll., Davidson Coll., 1963, U. N.C., 1965, Ctr. Coll., 1973, Ohio Wesleyan U., 1971; LHD (hon.), Lawrence U., 1964, Carleton Coll., 1966, Emory U., 1968; LittD (hon.), St. Norbert Coll., Wake Forest Coll., 1964. Instr. English, Yale U., 1946-47, asst. prof., 1947-53; vis. asst. prof. English, U. Calif., Berkeley, summer 1949; Morse rsch. fellow, 1951-52; pres. Lawrence U., Appleton, Wis., 1953-63, Duke U., Durham, N.C., 1963-69, pres. emeritus, 1992—; v.p. divsn. ednl. devel. RCA, N.Y.C., 1969-71, v.p. divsn. edn. svcs., 1971-72, staff v.p. edn. and community rels., 1972-73, cons., 1973-75; pres. RCA Iran, 1971-72, dir., 1971-73; pres. Social Econ. and Ednl. Devel., Inc., 1973-76, Questar Corp., 1976-99, chmn., 1999—2001, sr. cons. R & D, 2001—. Assoc. fellow Saybrook Coll., Yale U., 1954—; U.S. del. SEATO Conf. Asian U. Pres., Pakistan, 1961; mem. nat. commn. UNESCO, 1965-67; chmn. Nat. Adv. Commn. Librs., 1966-68; advisor Imperial Orgn. for Social Svc., Govt. of Iran; mem. Nat. Commn. Sci. and Engring. Manpower, 1959-61. Author: Pope and the Heroic Tradition, 1951, (poetry) The Dark Gate, 1971, Journeys in Time, 1993, Close Encounters, 2003; editor, contbr.: The Federal Government and Higher Education, 1960, Iliad and Odyssey, Twickenham edit., 1967, Medical Ventures and the University, 1967, Libraries at Large, Tradition, Innovation and the National Interest, 1970, Street of Dreams: The Nature and Legacy of the 1960's, 1989, Education and the Civil Order: A Memoir of the Woodrow Wilson National Fellowship Foundation, 1996, The Dancer and the Dance, One Man's Chronicle 1938-2001, 2003; co-inventor the Questar long-distance microscope, 1981; co-patentee the Questar stereo microscope, 2001. Trustee Edward W. Hazen Found., 1951-63; corp. mem. MIT, 1965-70; bd. dirs., chmn. Woodrow Wilson Nat. Fellowship Found., 1957-93, emeritus, 1993—; bd. dirs. CEEB, 1955-59, Catalyst, 1961-73, United Negro Coll. Fund, 1967-72, Near East Found., 1975-84, Internat. Schs. Svcs., 1976-82, Solebury Sch., 1975-83; program chmn. Salzburg Seminar, 1971, mem. adv. coun., 1997; founding trustee Questar Libr. Sci. and Art, 1982—, pres., 1996-99, 2002—; pres. Delaware River Mill Soc., 1992-97, emeritus, 1997. Mem. Am. Assn. Advancement of Humanities (bd. dirs. 1979-83), Grolier Club, Century Assn. (N.Y.C.), Cosmos Club (Washington), Elizabethan Club, Berzelius (New Haven), Phi Beta Kappa. Home: Heritage Towers #816 200 Veterans Ln Doylestown PA 18901 Office: Questar Corp 6204 Ingham Rd New Hope PA 18938-9663

KNIGHT, EDWARD HOWDEN, retired hospital administrator; b. Vancouver, BC, Can, Apr. 13, 1933; s. Edward Allen and Helen Blackley (Howden) K.; m. Glenda Carol Wiggins, Mar. 6, 1964; children: Carolyn, Patricia, Brett. B of Commerce, diploma in hosp. adminstrn., U. B.C., 1956. Adminstrv. asst. Vancouver Gen. Hosp., 1956-57; adminstr. Prince Rupert Gen. Hosp., 1957-61, Red Deer Gen. Hosp., 1961-72, Dr. Richard Parsons Aux. Hosp., 1963-72, Valley Pk. Manor Nursing Home, 1969-72; dep. exec. dir. Calgary Gen. Hosp., Calgary, Canada, 1972-74, exec. dir., 1974-83, pres., 1983-88, E.H. Knight & Assoc. Inc., Calgary, Canada, 1988-92. Lectr. Red Deer Coll., 1968-72; adj. asst. prof. faculty medicine U. Calgary, 1978-91; trustee Alta. Blue Cross Plan, 1963-68; mem. Fed. Task Force on Cost of Health Svc. in Can., 1969 Recipient Queen's Silver Jubilee medal, 1977. Fellow Can. Coll. of Health Svc. Exec. (dir. 1972-74, founding charter mem.), Am. Coll. Healthcare Exec. (regent for Alberta. 1973-76, 79-82); mem. Can. Hosp. Assn. (dir. 1981-83), Alta. Hosp. Assn. (dir. 1977-84, pres. 1983), Assn. Can. Tchg. Hosp. (pres. 1986-87), Rotary, Rancho Bernardo (pres. 2003-2004), Kinsmen Club (pres. 1971-72), Phi Delta Theta. Home: 820 Windridge Cir San Marcos CA 92078-7917 E-mail: ehknight@adelphia.net.

KNIGHT, EDWARD R. judge, lawyer, educator, psychologist; b. Milw., Oct. 5, 1917; s. Harry and Lillian (Bachman) K.; m. Judith A. Weidberg, July 6, 1941; 1 child, Barbara Jane. AB, U. Wis., 1940, JD, 1941; AM, NYU, 1942, PhD, 1943. Bar: Wis. 1941, N.J. 1976; diplomate Am. Bd. Profl. Psychology. Master Oxford Acad., Pleasantville, NJ, 1941, psychologist, 1942, head psychologist, 1943, asst. headmaster, 1945-47, headmaster, 1947-73, emeritus, 1973—. U.S. magistrate judge, 1976—; judge Mcpl. Ct., Margate City, N.J., 1976-81; ptnr. Fox, Rothschild, Atlantic City, N.J., 1976—; dir. First Fidelity Bank, 1950-90. Pres., bd. govs. Atlantic City Med. Ctr., 1973-87, chmn. emeritus, 1987—; chmn. Master Planning Bd., Egg Harbor Twp., N.J., 1961-73; chmn. Atlantic County (N.J.) Charter Study Commn., 1973-74, treas. bd. Atlanticare, 1993—. Author: Self-Discipline and Academic Failure; mem. editl. bd. Parental Delinquency; contbr. articles on edn. and psychology to profl. jours. Capt., USAAF, 1943-45; personnel com., personnel div. ATSC, Wright Field. Fellow APA (sch. psychologists div.); mem. Ea. N.J. psychol. assns., Nat. Assn. Ind. Schs., N.J. Assn. Sch. Psychologists, Interam. Soc. Psychology, Boarding Sch. Headmasters Assn. Mid. States (pres. 1966-67), Wis. Alumni Assn., U. Wis. Mem. Union (life), Atlanticare Health Sys. (vice-chmn. bd.), Phi Delta Kappa, Kappa Delta Pi. Home: 7 N Thurlow Ave Margate City NJ 08402-1213 Office: US Dist Ct 1301 Atlantic Ave Fl 3 Atlantic City NJ 08401-7207

KNIGHT, FAITH TANYA, lawyer; b. N.Y.C., Oct. 20, 1969; d. Ernest L. and Marion L. K. AB in Sociology, Dartmouth Coll., 1991; JD cum laude, Tulane U., 1996. Bar: Ga. 1996, U.S. Dist. Ct. (no. dist.) Ga. 1997. Assoc. Alston & Bird, Atlanta, 1996-99, The McDowell Law Group, 1999-2000, Smith, Gambrell and Russell LLP, 2000—02; assoc. gen. counsel Emory U., Atlanta, 2002—. Temp. in house counsel Charter Behavioral Health Svcs., Atlanta, 1998, 99. Mem. Am. Health Lawyers Assn., Ga. Assn. Black Women Attys. Avocations: photography, travel.

KNIGHT, FRANK BARDSLEY, mathematics educator; b. Chgo., Oct. 11, 1933; s. Frank Hyneman and Ethel Eunice (Verry) K.; m. Ingeborg G. Belz, Aug. 30, 1971; children: Marion A., Marc A., Ellen D. BA, Cornell U., 1955; PhD, Princeton U., 1959. Instr. math. U. Minn., Mpls., 1960-61, asst. prof., 1962-63; asst. prof. math. U. Ill., Urbana, 1964-66, assoc. prof., 1967-71; prof. U. Ill, Urbana, 1971-91, prof. emeritus, 1991—. Author: Essentials of Brownian Motion and Diffusion, 1981, Essays on the Prediction Process, 1981, Foundations of the Prediction Process, 1992. Sloan fellow, 1968-71; NSF grantee, 1981-89. Mem. Am. Math. Soc., Inst. Math. Stats., Am. Alpine Club. Office: U Ill 1409 W Green St Urbana IL 61801-2943 E-mail: f-knight@math.uiuc.edu.

KNIGHT, FRANK JAMES, pharmaceutical marketing professional; b. L.A., July 17, 1947; s. George Orlando Jr. and Virginia Clarabelle (Seig) K.; m. Mary Jane Vargo, Aug. 7, 1977 (div. July 1989); children: Cheryl Lynne, Michael Scott; m. Barbara Lorrene Garlick, June 19, 1993. BS, Okla. State U., 1970. Mktg. rep. Mobil Oil Corp., N.Y.C., 1971-73; sales rep. Monarch Crown Corp., N.Y.C., 1974-78; territory mgr. V.H. Monette, Inc., Smithfield, Va., 1978-81; profl. rep. Dermik Labs., Blue Bell, Pa., 1981-83; nat. bus. rels. mgr. Novartis Oncology, East Hanover, N.J., 1983—. Capt. U.S. Army, 1970. Mem. Am. Motorcycle Assn., Harley Owners Group (dir.), Elks. Home: 8768 Banyan St Alta Loma CA 91701-3355 Office: Novartis Pharmaceuticals 59 State Route 10 East Hanover NJ 07936-1005 E-mail: Frank.Knight@pharma.novrtis.com.

KNIGHT, FRANKLIN W. history educator; b. Mile Gully, Manchester, Jamaica, Jan. 10, 1942; came to U.S., 1964; s. Willis Jefferson and Irick May (Sanderson) K.; m. Ingeborg Bauer, June 11, 1965; children: Michael, Brian, Nadine. BA with honors, U. West Indies, Jamaica, 1964; MA, U. Wis., 1965, PhD, 1969. From asst. to assoc. prof. SUNY, Stony Brook, 1968-73; assoc. prof. Johns Hopkins U., Balt., 1973-77, prof., 1977-91, Stulman prof. History, 1991—, dir. Latin Am. Studies Program, 1992-95; v.p. Latin Am. Studies Assn., 1997-98; pres., 1998-00. Author: Slave Society in Cuba, 1970 (Black Acad. award 1971), The Caribbean, 1990; co-editor: The Modern Caribbean, 1989, Atlantic Port Cities, 1991; editor: Caribbean Slave Societies, 1997. Active Md. Quincentenary Com., 1992. Named Disting. Grad. U. West Indies, Jamaica, 1992. Mem. The Hist. Soc., Latin Am. Studies Assn., Assn. Caribbean Historians. Office: Johns Hopkins U 3400 N Charles St Baltimore MD 21218-2680 E-mail: fknight@jhu.edu.

KNIGHT, FRED BARROWS, forester, entomologist, educator; b. Waterville, Maine, Dec. 12, 1925; s. Stephen Cecil and Mildred Evelyn (Barrows) K.; m. Jane Wooster, Dec. 18, 1945; children: Mary Jane Knight Cushman, Susan L. Knight Hughes, James Wooster. BS with distinction, U. Maine, 1949; M in Forestry, Duke U., 1950, D in Forestry, 1956. Lic. forester, Maine. With Bur. Entomology and Plant Quarantine, U.S. Dept. Agr., Asheville, N.C., 1950-51; rsch. entomologist Forest Service, Ft. Collins, Colo., 1951-60; assoc. prof. to prof., chmn. dept. U. Mich., Ann Arbor, 1960-72; prof. forest resources, dir. Sch. Forest Resources, U. Maine, Orono, 1972-82, Dwight B. Demeritt prof. forest resources, 1972-90, interim dean Coll. Forest Resources, 1982-83, assoc. dean, 1983-88, acting dean, 1986-88, dean, 1988-90, dean, prof. emeritus in forestry, 1991—. Dir. seven Islands Land Co., 1984-97; mem. State Bd. Licensing Prof. Foresters, 1990-98. Author: Principles of Forest Entomology, 4th edit., 1965, 5th edit., 80; also numerous articles. Comdr. USNR, 1943-85, ret., 1985. Fellow AAAS, Soc. Am. Forester (assoc. editor, past sect. officer); mem. Entomol. Soc. Am., Am. Forestry Assn., Soc. Les Voyageurs, Sigma Xi, Phi Kappa Phi (pres. U. Maine chpt. 1991-93), Alpha Zeta, Xi Sigma Pi. Congregationalist. Home: 16 Cortland Cir Bangor ME 04401 E-mail: fknight@maine.edu.

KNIGHT, GARY, lawyer, educator, publisher; b. St. Joseph, Mo., Dec. 8, 1939; s. Herbert S. and Iris (Crawford) K.; m. Rebecca Emelie Forrester, Nov. 24, 1962; children: Kevin Crawford, David Forrester, Jonathan Gary. Student, Westminster Coll., 1957-59; AB in Polit. Sci., Stanford U., 1961; JD, So. Meth. U., 1964. Bar: Calif. 1965. Assoc. Nossaman, Thompson, Waters and Moss, L.A., 1964-68; mem. faculty La. State U. Law Center, Baton Rouge, 1968-85, assoc. prof., 1971-75, prof. law, 1975-85, Campanile prof. marine resources law, 1971-85; owner Jonathan Pub. Co., 1981—. Mem. adv. com. on law of sea Nat. Security Council Inter-Agy. Law of Sea Group, 1972-81; cons. CIA, 1977-85; mem. Gulf of Mex. Fishery Mgmt. Coun., 1981-84. Author: The Future of International Fisheries Management, 1975, Managing the Sea's Living Resources, 1977, The International Law of the Sea: Cases, Documents and Readings, 1991, Marine Fisheries Management Reporter, 1981-94; assoc. editor: Ocean Development and International Law: A Jour. of Marine Affairs, 1972-85. Mem. ABA (com. on law of sea 1971-80, com. marine resources 1967-71), Am. Soc. Internat. Law (bd. rev. and devel. 1975-80, panel on law of sea 1972-80), Internat. Law Assn. (com. on law of sea 1974-81), Law of Sea Inst. (exec. bd. 1975-81), Order of Coif, Phi Alpha Delta, Omicron Delta Kappa, Beta Theta Pi.

KNIGHT, GEORGE B. corporate executive, lawyer; b. 1923; married. B.B.A., U. Wis., 1948, J.D., 1950. Bar: Wis. With Arthur Andersen & Co., C.P.A.s., Milw., 1950-51; with Northwestern Mut. Life Ins. Co., 1951-56; asst. counsel H. K. Porter Co., 1956-60; corp. atty. Mead Johnson & Co., 1960-65; sec., gen. counsel Harnischfeger Corp., Milw., 1965-84, chief counsel products liability, asst. sec., 1984— . Served to maj. USAAF, 1943-46. Office: Harnischfeger Corp PO Box 554 Milwaukee WI 53201-0554

KNIGHT, GLADYS (GLADYS MARIA KNIGHT), singer; b. Atlanta, May 28, 1944; d. Merald and Elizabeth (Woods) Knight, Sr.; m. Barry Hankerson, Oct. 1974 (div. 1979); 1 child, Shanga Hankerson; m. William McDowell, Apr. 2001. Grad. coll.; degree (hon.), Shaw U. Author: lyrics Way Back Home, others; first pub. recital, Mt. Mariah Bapt. Ch., Atlanta, 1948; toured with Morris Brown Choir, 1950-53, recitals local chs. and schs., 1950-53; winner grand prize Ted Mack's Amateur Hour 1952; jazz vocalist, Lloyd Terry Jazz Ltd., 1959-61, mem. Gladys Knight and the Pips (formerly Pips Quartet), 1953—, concert appearances in Eng., 1967, 72, 73, 76, Australia, Japan, Hong Kong, Manila, 1976; rec. artist, Brunswick, 1957-61, Fury, 1961-62, Everlast, 1963, Maxx and Bell, 1964-66, Motown, 1966-73, Buddah, Capitol, Columbia, MCA, 1988; albums with the Pips include Best of Gladys Knight and the Pips, All the Great Hits, If I Were Your Woman, 1989, Soul Survivors: The Best of Gladys Knight and the Pips 1973-1988, 1990, Blue Lights in the Basement, 1996, Imagination, 1996, The Lost Live Albums, 1996; solo album Good Woman, 1991; TV appearance Charlie & Co., 1985; produced, appeared in HBO film Sisters in the Name of Love, 1986. Winner 6 gold Buddah records, 1 gold, 1 platinum Buddah album; 4 Grammy awards; named Top Female Vocalist, Blues and Soul mag. 1972; spl. award Washington City Coun. for inspiration to youth in city, 1972; other awards include Clio, AGVA, NAACP Image, Ebony Music, Cashbox, Billboard, Record World, Rolling Stone, Ladies Home Jour., Am. Music award (with Pips), 1984, 1988, Core award B'nai B'rith award; inducted into Rock and Roll Hall of Fame, 1996. Address: Care Shakeji Inc 3221 LaMirada Ave Las Vegas NV 89120

KNIGHT, H. STUART, law enforcement official, consultant; b. Sault St. Marie, Ont., Can., Jan. 6, 1921; s. Alexander G. and Muriel C. (Breathwaite) K.; m. Betty Cooley, June 29, 1946; children: Suzanne Cawley, Bill, Bob, John, Barbara Powell. BS, Mich. State U., 1948; postgrad., Princeton U., 1965-66. With U.S. Secret Svc., 1950-82, dir., 1973-82. Vice chmn. Guardsmark Inc., Memphis, 1984—; v.p. Interpol, Paris, 1974-81; disting. faculty fellow Fed. Execs. Inst., Charlottesville, Va., 1981; mem. adv. bd. Am. Products Devel. Co.; mem. steering com. Ctr. for Strategic and Internat. Studies. Bd. dirs. Falls Church (Va.) Homeowners Assn., 1982-84; bd. dirs., pres. INKODE Govt. Sys.; mem. lottery bd. State of Va. Staff sgt. U.S. Army, 1942-46, PTO. Decorated Silver Star, Bronze Star, Purple Heart; named original mem. Gallery of Fame, Mich. State U., to Wall of Fame, 2001; recipient Mr. Sam award, Touchdown Club, Washington, 1979. Mem. Internat. Assn. Chiefs of Police (life, mem. bd. officers 1974-81), Nat. Sheriffs Assn. (life), Civitan. Avocations: bicycling, golf, puzzles. Office: Guardsmark Inc 22 S 2nd St Memphis TN 38103-2695

KNIGHT, HENRY L. minister; b. Monroville, Ala., Nov. 10, 1933; s. Cullin Knight, Queen (Bolar) Knight; m. Carrie Mural Agee, Apr. 9, 1955 (div. May 2002); 1 child, Darlene Marie Knight Wooten;children: Karen L. Knight Mayo, Darryl D. Mayo. BA, L.I.F.E. of L.A., 1975; MA, Azusa Pacific U., 1984; HDL (hon.), St. Stephens Ednl. Coll., 1994. Cert. Pastoral cert., Ordination bd. cert. U.S. Chaplain Assn. Tchr. Lockhaven Christian Sch., Inglewood, Calif., 1975—76; tchr., counselor West Angeles Ch., L.A., 1977—89; pastor, counselor Greater True Light Tabernacle, L.A., 1989—. Hosp. med. coord. L.A. County Health Dept., 1958—93; tchr., chaplain Union Rescue Mission, L.A., 1993—95; care giver Feed the Children, L.A., 1998—. Author: What is Preaching, 1999, Unique Bible Study, 1987, The Solution, 1986. E-5 U.S. Army, 1956—58. Recipient Good Conduct medal, U.S. Army, 1958. Democrat. Mem. Ch. Of God In Christ. Avocations: singing, walking, skating. Home: 3618 Buckingham Rd Los Angeles CA 90016-5710 Office: Greater True Light Tabernacle 5426 S Vermont Ave Los Angeles CA 90037-3532

KNIGHT, HERBERT BORWELL, manufacturing company executive; b. Oak Park, Ill., July 4, 1928; s. Herbert Alfred and Bessie Carne (Borwell) K.; m. Nancy Gordon, June 29, 1963; children: Sharon and Tom (twins). AB, Dartmouth Coll., 1951, MBA, 1952. V.p. mktg. B.K. Johl, Allsteel Equipment Co., Aurora, Ill., 1966-69; asst. to pres. Bliss & Laughlin Industries, Oak Brook, Ill., 1969-71; sr. v.p. First Health-Care, Chgo., 1972-75; pres. Newport News Indsl. Corp., Va., 1975-80; dir. planning Tenneco Inc., Houston, 1980-86; treas., owner A.E. Bogott & Sons, Inc., Sterling, Ill., 1988-98; venture capitalist, real estate investor, 1998. Past bd. overseers C. Everett Koop Inst., Dartmouth Med. Sch., Hanover, N.H.; trustee Rush Presbyn. St. Lukes Hosp., Chgo., Rush-Copley Med. Ctr., Aurora, Ill., Copley Healthcare Found. Mem.: Dunham Woods Riding Club, Geneva Golf Club, Union League Club (Chgo.). Episcopalian.

KNIGHT, IDA BROWN, retired elementary educator; b. Macon, Ga., Aug. 8, 1918; d. Morgan Cornelius and Ida (Moore) Brown; m. Dempsey Lewis Knight, Apr. 11, 1942; children: Lavera Knight Hughes, Eugene Charles. BS, Spelman Coll., 1940; MS, SUNY, Fredonia, 1958; postgrad., SUNY, 1974, U. Manchester, Eng., 1974. Cert. tchr. home econs. Clothing tchr. Bibb County Vocat. Sch., Macon, 1940-42; tchr. home econs. Ballard Normal Sch., Macon, 1943-45; elem. tchr. Jamestown (N.Y.) Pub. Schs., 1955-77; ret., 1977. Bd. dirs. Jamestown Girls Club, 1970-78, Jamestown Cmty. Schs., 1989-97; ch. organist, 1974-82; jr. bd. Elizabeth Marvin Cmty. House, 1994-2001, gov. bd. dirs., 1998-2000. Mem. AAUW, Chautauqua County Ret. Tchrs. Assn., N.Y. State Congress Parents and Tchrs. (hon. life), Links, Inc. (past pres. Jamestown chpt.), Delta Kappa Gamma (corr. sec. 1963-64). Avocations: flower gardening, hand crafts, playing piano, reading. Home: 5573 Place Dr South Bend IN 46614

KNIGHT, JACK VERNON, medicine and microbiology educator; b. Osceola, Mo., Sept. 6, 1917; m. Elizabeth Gordon; 4 children. AB, William Jewell Coll., 1939, DSc (hon.), 1982; MD, Harvard U., 1943. Diplomate Am. Bd. Internal Medicine. Intern Mass. Meml. Hosp., Boston, 1943; resident Cornell U.-N.Y. Hosp. Med. Ctr., N.Y.C., 1946-47, from asst. in medicine to asst. prof., 1948-54; assoc. prof. medicine Vanderbilt U. Sch. Medicine, Nashville, 1954-59; clin. dir. Nat. Inst. Allergy and Infectious Diseases, NIH, Bethesda, Md., 1959-66; prof., chmn. dept. microbiology and immunology Baylor Coll. Medicine, Houston, 1966-88, prof. infectious disease sect. dept. medicine, 1966—, prof. biotech., dir. Ctr. for Biotech., 1989-94, prof., acting chmn. dept. molecular physiology-biophysics, 1994-99, prof. molecular physiology and biophysics, 1994—, Kyle and Josephine Morrow disting. prof., 1984. Sr. attending physician Meth. Hosp., Houston, 1966—; attending physician Ben Taub Gen Hosp., Houston, 1966—; physician, cons. VA Hosp., Houston; bd. dirs. Viratek, Inc., Costa Mesa, Calif., 1980-94; mem. med. scis. rev. panel to NASA, Am. Inst. Biol. Scis., 1976-80; profl. cons. U.S. Army Med. Rsch. Inst. Infectious Diseases, 1962-81. Patentee on small particle aerosol generator for treatment respiratory disease including lungs; patentee for small particle aerosol liposome and liposome-drug combinations for med. use. Bd. dirs. Contemporary Arts Mus., Houston, 1977-82, Gorgas Meml. Inst. Tropical and Preventive Medicine, Washington, 1977-91. With M.C., USN, 1944-46, ETO. Recipient Guy R. Odum, Jr. award M.D. Anderson Hosp. and Tumor Inst., 1986; Disting. Svc. Prof. award Baylor Coll. Medicine, 1986, Disting. Faculty award, 1987. Mem. ACP, Am. Clin. and Climatol. Assn., Am. Fedn. for Clin. Rsch., Am. Soc. for Clin. Investigation, Am. Soc. for Microbiology, Am. Soc. for Virology, Assn. Am. Physicians, Assn. Med. Sch. Microbiology Chairmen (pres. 1981), Infectious Diseases Soc. Am. (emeritus), Internat. Assn. Aerobiology, Internat. Leprosy Assn., Soc. for Exptl. Biology and Medicine, Tex. Med. Assn., Harris County Med. Soc., Sigma Xi, Alpha Omega Alpha. Office: Baylor Coll Medicine 1 Baylor Plz Rm T-434 Houston TX 77030-3411 E-mail: knight@bcm.tmc.edu.

KNIGHT, JAMES ATWOOD, manufacturing executive; b. Providence, Apr. 26, 1954; s. Richard Brayton and Louise (Atwood) K.; m. Cynthia Forbes Olney, June 11, 1983; children: Hilary Atwood, James Atwood Jr., Remington Forbes, William Olney, Elsie Lawson. BS, Boston U., 1975; MBA, Dartmouth Coll., 1984. Sr. assoc. Strategic Decisions Group, Menlo Park, Calif., 1984-88; mgr. Apple Computer, Cupertino, Calif., 1988-90; with Holt, Chgo., 1990, Boston Cons. Group, Chgo., 1991-95; v.p. SCA Consulting L.L.C., Chgo., 1995-97, mng. ptnr., 1997—2001; ptnr. Mercer Cons., 2001—02; chmn. Knight Industries, Northfield, Ill., 2002—, Knight-Celotex, 2002—; chmn., CEO Knight-Rikett, LLC, 2002—. Author: Value Based Management, 1997; contbr. chpt. to book. Avocations: skiing, squash. Home: 606 Tiverton Rd Lake Forest IL 60045-1655 Office: Knight Industries LLC One Northfield Plz Ste 210 Northfield IL 60093 E-mail: jknight@aknightcompany.com.

KNIGHT, JANE MILLER, nurse midwife, retired air force officer; b. Hampton, Va., Oct. 8, 1950; d. Donald Alexander and Elizabeth Harriet (Wilgus) Miller; m. David Ray Knight, Nov. 12, 1988. BSN, Med. Coll. Va.

1972; MA in Guidance and Counseling, Hampton (Va.) Inst., 1984. RN, Va.; cert. nurse-midwife, legal nurse cons. Staff nurse Mary Immaculate Hosp., Newport News, Va., 1972, Potomac Hosp., Woodbridge, Va., 1973, N.E. Bapt. Hosp., San Antonio, 1973-74, Hampton Gen. Hosp., 1974-76; commd. 1st lt. USAF, 1976, advanced through grades to lt. col., 1993, ret., 1996; staff nurse USAF Hosp., Barksdale AFB, La., 1976-78, staff nurse, midwife Langley AFB, Va., 1979-84; instr. USAF Nurse-Midwifery program Malcolm Grow USAF Med. Ctr., 1984-91; staff nurse-midwife 416th Med. Group, Griffiss AFB, N.Y., 1991-94; maternal child flight leader 10th Med. Group, USAF Academy, Colo.; nurse-midwife Lasky, Knoeller, Dexter and Slatch, MDs, P.C., Saratoga Springs, NY, 1996—2001; asst. nurse mgr. The Birth Place Albany (N.Y.) Med. Ctr., 2003—. Speaker on women's health issues; workshop leader; ind. cons. and bereavement svcs. Decorated Air Force Commendation medal, Meritorious Svc. medal. Mem. Am. Coll. Nurse-Midwives, Am. Assn. Legal Nurse Consultants, Air Force Assn., Assn. Women's Health, Obstetric and Neonatal Nurses. Episcopalian. Avocations: reading, camping, needlework. Home: 546 Acland Blvd Ballston Spa NY 12020-3079

KNIGHT, JEFFREY RICHARD, information technology specialist; b. Salt Lake City, Apr. 22, 1962; s. Richard M. and Donna H. (Hallman) K.; m. Carrie Lyn Jackson; 1 child, Jessica Lyn. BBA, Calif. State Poly. Inst. U., 1984, MBA, 1986. With Lockheed Martin, Camarillo, Calif., 1985-96; prin. engr., sr. mgr. info. tech. DirecTV, 1996—; owner KD Enterprises, 1995—2002. Owner, KD Enterprises, pres. Co. Activities Coordinating Com., Camarillo, 1991-93. Treas. Hillcrest Park Home Owners Assn., 1990-92, pres., 1992-93; chmn. Calif. State Poly. Inst. U. Rose Float Com., 1984-85; gen. sec. Evangel. Free Ch. Conejo Valley Men's Ministry, 2000-02, dir. men's ministry, 2002--; mem. Fin. Integrity Team, 2002. Mem. Rose Float Alumni Assn. (treas. 1985-86, bd. dirs. 1987-88, pres. 1991-93, historian/archivist 1994—, chmn. 50th float activities com.), Nat. Employee Svcs. and Recreation Assn. (pres. Gold Coast chpt. 1994-95), Toastmasters Internat. (chpt. treas. 1996, v.p. pub. rels. 1996, v.p. membership 2000, Competent Toastmaster award 1996), Santa Clara River Valley R.R. Hist. Soc., Calif. Poly. Inst. Pomona Alumni Assn. (bd. dirs. 2000). Republican. Avocations: philately, softball, darts. Home: 2143 Saxe Ct Thousand Oaks CA 91360-3148 E-mail: jrknight@directv.com.

KNIGHT, JOHN ALLAN, clergyman, philosophy and religion educator; b. Mineral Wells, Tex., Nov. 8, 1931; s. John Lee and Beulah Mae (Bounds) K.; m. Justine Anne Rushing, Aug. 22, 1958; children— John Allan, James Alden, Judith Anne. BA, Bethany Nazarene Coll., 1952; MA, Okla. U., 1954; B.D., Vanderbilt U., 1957, PhD, 1966. Ordained to ministry Ch. of Nazarene, 1954; pastor Tenn. Dist. Ch. of Nazarene, 1953-61, 71-72; prof., chmn. dept. philosophy and religion Trevecca Nazarene Coll., Nashville, 1957-69; chmn. dept. philosophy and religion Mt. Vernon (Ohio) Nazarene Coll., 1969-71, pres., 1972-75; pastor Grace Nazarene Ch., Nashville, 1971-72; pres. Bethany (Okla.) Nazarene Coll., 1976-85; gen. supt. Internat. Ch. of the Nazarene, 1985—2001, vice chair Bd. Gen. Supts., 1990-92, chair Bd. Gen. Supts., 1992-94; ret., 2001. Coordinator U.S. Govt. Project Studying Possible Coop. Ventures for Tenn. Colls. and Univs., 1969; mem. gen. bd. Internat. Ch. of Nazarene, 1980-85. Author: Commentary on Philippians, 1968, The Holiness Pilgrimage, 1971, In His Likeness, 1976, Beacon Bible Expositions, Vol. 9, 1985, What the Bible Says About Tongues - Speaking, 1988; co-author: Sanctify Them -- That the World May Know, 1987; co-author: Go -- Preach, The Preaching Event in the 90s; author: All Loves Excelling, 1995, Bridge to Our Tomorrows, 2000; editor-in-chief: Herald of Holiness, Kansas City, Mo., 1975-76. Pres. bd. govs. Okla. Ind. Coll. Found., 1979-81; trustee So. Nazarene U., Okla. Recipient Lily Found. Theology award Vanderbilt U., 1958-59; Carré fellow Vanderbilt U., 1960-62 Mem. Soc. Sci. Study Religion, Am. Acad. Religion, Wesley Theol. Soc. (pres. 1979), Evang. Theol. Assn. Clubs: Kiwanis Internat. Mem. Ch. Of Nazarene. Home: PO Box 368 Bethany OK 73008-0368 Office: Internat Ch of the Nazarene 6401 Paseo Blvd Kansas City MO 64131-1213 E-mail: jkharlo@aol.com.

KNIGHT, JOHN FRANCIS, retired insurance company executive; b. N.Y.C., Sept. 30, 1919; s. Samuel F. and Abigail (Sullivan) K.; m. Marilyn Rockefeller, Oct. 30, 1948; children: Jeffrey J., Melanie K. Eggers, John Mark, Jane M., James M. BBA cum laude, St. John's U., 1952. With Republic Fin. Svcs. Inc., Republic Ins. Group, Dallas, 1939-88, agy. supr., 1950-56, asst. v.p., 1956-60, v.p., 1960-67, sr. v.p., 1967-69, exec. v.p., 1969-71, sr. exec. v.p., 1971-72, pres., 1972-83, vice chmn., bd. dirs., 1983-88. Served to maj. AUS, 1942-46. Decorated Bronze Star. Republican. Roman Catholic. Home: 16 Coolidge St Malverne NY 11565-1808

KNIGHT, JOSEPH ADAMS, pathologist; b. Provo, Utah, Dec. 22, 1930; s. John Clarence and Martha Maude (Adams) K.; m. Pauline Brown, Oct. 18, 1949; children: David Paul, Leigh Knight Smith. BS in Chemistry, Brigham Young U., 1955, MS in Organic Chemistry, 1957; MD, U. Utah, 1963. Diplomate Am. Bd. pathology; lic. Utah, Calif., Nev., Wyo. Intern U. Utah Hosp., Salt Lake City, 1963-64, residency in pathology, 1964-67; instr. pathology Sch. Medicine U. Utah, Salt Lake City, 1966-67, clin. instr. pathology, 1967-70; assoc. pathologist Holy Cross Hosp., Salt Lake City, 1967-70; asst. clin. prof. pathology Sch. Medicine U. Utah., Salt Lake City, 1970-75; assoc. Health Svcs. Corp., Salt Lake City, 1969-75; assoc. pathologist Santa Rosa Med. Ctr., San Antonio, 1975-76; assoc. clin. prof. pathology Sch. Medicine U. Tex., San Antonio, 1975-76; dir. clin. labs. Primary Children's Med. Ctr., Salt Lake City, 1976-79; assoc. clin. prof. Sch. Medicine U. Utah, Salt Lake City, 1977-79, assoc. prof. pathology, 1979-88, prof. pathology, 1988—; head div. edn. VA Med. Ctr., Salt Lake City, 1986-98, chief lab. svc., 1990-97. Vis. prof. pathology Sch. Medicine U. Conn., Farmington, 1985-86; mem. admissions com. Sch. Medicine U. Utah, 1981-82, 2000—, mem. grad. sch. com. Sch. Med. Technologists U. Utah, 1981-85. Author: (with others) Laboratory Examination of Cerebrospinal, Synovial and Serous Fluids: A Textbook Atlas, 1982, Body Fluids: A Textbook Atlas, 2nd edit., 1986, 3d edit., 1993; author: Laboratory Medicine and the Aging Process, 1996, Free Radicals, Antioxidants, Aging and Disease, 1999; reviewer Clin. Chemistry, 1971, 77, 84, 86—; contbr. articles to profl. jours. Served with U.S. Navy, 1948-52, Korea. Fellow Am. Soc. Clin. Pathologists, Coll. Am. Pathologists, Nat. Acad. Clin. Biochem.; mem. AMA, Am. Assn. Clin. Chemists, Utah Soc. Pathologists (pres. 1968-70, 79-80), Am. Bd. Pathology (test com. 1987-92), Am. Soc. Clin. Pathology (editl. rev. bd. 1987—, numerous other coms., chmn. coun. on edn. and rsch. 1996—), Assn. Clin. Scientists (membership com. 1985—, v.p. 1995, pres. 1996, Diploma of Honor 1997), Coll. Am. Pathologists (insp. 1978-2000), Alpha Omega Alpha. Republican. Mem. Lds Ch. Avocations: jogging, cycling, hiking, tv/radio/local sports. Office: U Utah Sch Medicine Dept Pathology 50 N Medical Dr Salt Lake City UT 84132-0001

KNIGHT, KENNETH GEORGE, retired aerospace and defense company executive; b. Flint, Mich., Dec. 13, 1956; s. George and Elvira (Haas) K.; m. Dianne Virginia Dickson, July 12, 1980; children: Aimee, Rachelle, Christina. Student in bus. adminstrn., Cen. Mich. U., 1975; student in psychology, Concordia Coll., Seward, Nebr., 1975-76; BA in Psychology, U. Nebr., 1978; postgrad. in law, U. Calif., Santa Barbara, 1978-79; Grad. Real Estate (GRE), Jones Coll., Colo. Springs, Colo., 1981; MS in Aerospace Systems, Ctrl. Fla. U./Loyola U., Orlando, 1987. Cert. real estate broker. Prodn. control planner Computer Communications Tech. Corp. div. Info. Magnetics, Santa Barbara, 1979-80; prodn. control specialist Martin Marietta Corp., Denver, 1980-83; prodn. ops. controller Thorn EMI Corp. div. Inmos Microelectronics, Colorado Springs, Colo., 1983-85; planning specialist Martin Marietta Corp., Orlando, Fla., 1985-90, sr. planning mgr., 1990-95, continuing edn. services, 1985-95; CEO Sonic/Morning Star Corp., Wilmington, Del., 1994—96. Owner, cons. Property Mgmt. and Investments, Colorado Springs, 1980-95, Sonic/Morning Star, 1974-95; realtor Reel C. Davis Co., Colorado Springs, 1983-86; amateur radio sta. operator. Bd. dirs. Youth Ctr. Coffee House, Seward, Nebr., 1977; cons. to numerous vol. orgns. and cmty. support activities. Regent's scholar U. Calif., 1978. Mem. AMSAT, IEEE Computer Soc., Am. Radio Relay League (charter bd. mem. 1995-), Nat. Bd. Realtors, SETI League, Inc., Izaak Walton League Am., Nat. Rifle Assn. (voting 1981—, life). Republican. Baptist. Avocations: amateur radio, music. Home: 5815 Eldora Dr Colorado Springs CO 80918-1709

KNIGHT, KENNETH VINCENT, leisure company executive, entrepreneur, venture capitalist; b. Jersey City, Mar. 30, 1944; s. Julian (Konopacki) and Ellen (Gordon) Knight; m. Karen Keenan, June 1, 1968 (div. June 1978); 1 child, Karisa M.; m. Maria H. Herrera, June 17, 1983; children: Alexander, (adopted) Maria B. Barroso, Christina M. Barroso. Student, Northwestern Coll., Iowa, 1962-65; BS in Mgmt., N.Y. Inst. Tech., N.Y.C., 1973; MBA, Nova Southeastern U., Ft. Lauderdale, Fla., 1977; grad., Officer Candidate Sch., FARNG, 1968. Mgr., customer/corp. rels. Cavanaugh Corp., Miami, Fla., 1968; asst. dir. corp. svcs. Burger King Corp., Miami, 1968-70; asst. to sr. v.p. investor rels. Deltona Corp., Miami, 1970-74; dir. corp./investor rels. Gen. Devel. Corp., GDV Corp., Miami and N.Y.C., 1974-78; v.p. resort affiliations, stockholder Interval Internat., Miami, 1978-79, sr. v.p. mktg., 1979-82, exec. v.p., chief ops., 1983-84; pres., chief ops. Interval Internat. & Worldex, Miami, 1984-87, pres. and major shareholder, 1987-89, vice chmn., 1989-92; founder, gen. ptnr. Leisure Fund, Ltd., Miami, 1992—95; founder, pres., CEO Leisure Founders, Inc., 1992—96; founder, sr. ptnr. Leisure Fund Assoc., L.P., 1995—; founder, chmn., CEO Leisure Corp. Internat., 1996—; pres. KFH Mgmt., Inc., 1995—. Founder, chmn, CEO, dir., co-founder Worldex Corp., Miami, 1982-92, Worldex Travel Ctrs., 1983-92, Leaguestar Plc, London, 1988-92; co-founder Worldex Corp., Denver and L.A., Worldex Europe Ltd., London, Intercambico Internat. de Vacienes, SA, Mexico City, 1985-92, Interval Austrailasia Pty. Ltd., Sydney, 1980-91, Leisurecorp Internat., 1992—; bd. advisors Property Planning, Inc., 1972-75, Interval Internat., 1975-78; founder, spkr., forum participant Time Share Inst., 1978-92; sr. founder, spkr., forum participant, Moderator Am. Resort Developers Assn., Washington, 1978-91; Ecotourism Natureshare Assn., Stowe, Vt., 1990, Interval/CUC Internat. Merger Aquasition, Stamford and London, 1992; II Merger, 1994, Vacation Accommodation Directory, Tampa, 1992, Condo Network, Inc., Kansas City, 1992, Brentwood Equities/ALA Healthcare, L.A., 1993-95, Nextec Corp./Erose Capital, L.A., 1997—, Voice Track Corp., Dallas, 1997, InterLink Acquisition Restructure, Denver, 1999; bd. govs. Nova U. Grad. Sch. Bus. Century Found., 1987-91, Nova Southeastern Wayne Hurizenga Grad. Sch. Bus. and Entrepreneurship, 1992—, adv. bd.; spkrs. forum Dave Thomas's Ambs. Enterprise Program, Nova Southeastern U., 1995, bd. dirs. South Fla. Alumni; mem. Farquhar Undergrad. Pres. Search Com., 1998, bd. trustees audit com., 1998—; trustee Nova Southeastern U., 1994, vice chair strategic planning, 1996; Fla. venture forum Fla. Internat. U., 1995—, Small Bus. Devel. Ctr., U. Ctrl. Fla., 1996—, Assoc. Gov. Bds. Univs. and Colls., 1995—; guest spkr./lectr. in field. Founder: (mags.) The Leisure Society, Dreamweavers; exec. pub.: (newspaper) Timesharing Times, 1980; (mag.) Timeshare Traveler, 1984-90, Directory Resorts, 1980-90; mem. editl. bd. Vacation Industry Rev., 1985— (most traveled exec. 1984, spkr. worldwide); author: Best Use for Resort Condominiums, 1972, Time Sharing—What It Is and How It Works, 1974, MBA Mag., Timesharing for Land Devel. Industry, 1974, Timesharing—Alternatives for Low Cost Vacations and Second Homes, NSU Graduate Business Jour., 1977, Timesharing Times, Quality First for Interval and Knight, 1980, Travelmost Mag., 1982, Fla. Trend, The Achievers Sharing the Honors in a Time-Share Success, 1982, Timesharing Institute, The State of the Industry, 1983, Timeshare Encyclopedia, Volume II, Marketing & Sales, 1979, Volume IV, Finance & Servicing, Receivables, 1980, U.S. Congressional Record, 1987, Leisure Sharing for the 21st Century, NYU Hospitality Conference, 1992. 2d lt. U.S. Army, 1966-67; 1st lt. Fla. Army N.G., 1970-72, ret. 1993. Recipient Achievers award Fla. Trend mag., 1983, 88, Inc. 500 award Inc. mag., 1984, The Capital award Nat. Leadership Coun., 1991, Nova U. Alumni award, 1992; named Fla.'s Best Internat. Co., Prestige Internat. mag., 1985, Alumni of Yr., Nova Southeastern U., 1993. Roman Catholic. Avocations: adventure travel, cruising, skiing. Office: LeisureCorp Internat 6278 N Federal Hwy #294 Fort Lauderdale FL 33308 E-mail: knightnsu@aol.com, leisurefund@aol.com.

KNIGHT, KIT MARIE, poet, writer, movie critic; b. North Kingston, R.I., Sept. 21, 1952; d. Basil Arthur and Helen (Swerdi) Duell; m. Arthur Winfield Knight, Aug. 25, 1976; 1 child, Tiffany Carolyn. BA in Comm., California U. Pa., 1975. Co-editor, co-pub. the unspeakable visions of the individual, lit. mag., California, 1976-84; poet, columnist Russian River News, weekly newspaper, Guerneville, Calif., 1988-92; poet, columnist, film critic Russian River Times, Guerneville, 1997-98; film critic Citizens' Echo, American Canyon, Calif., 1999—; film critic, reporter City Times, Citrus Heights, Calif., 2002—03; film critic, reporter, columnist Am. River Sentinel, Citrus Heights, 2003—. Author: (book of poetry) Women of Wanted Men, 1994 (Perry award James-Younger Gang 1995); co-editor: (anthologies) The Beat Diary, 1977, Beat Angels, 1982, The Beat Vision, 1987, Kerouac and The Beats, 1988. Docent Petaluma (Calif.) Hist. Libr. and Mus., 1998-99. Mem.: Sacramento Civil War Roundtable (v.p. 2001—), North Bay Civil War Roundtable (charter, v.p.). Avocation: research and writing about the war between the states. Home and Office: PO Box 544 Citrus Heights CA 95611

KNIGHT, LINDA K. financial company executive; With Fed. Nat. Mortgage Assn., Washington, 1982—, v.p., asst. treas., 1986—92, sr. v.p., treas., 1993—. Office: Fed Nat Mortgage Assn 3900 Wisconsin Ave NW Washington DC 20016-2806

KNIGHT, LOUISE OSBORN, lawyer; b. June 17, 1944; d. Newell Sloss and Helen (Willis) Knight. AB, Wellesley Coll., 1966; JD, George Washington U., 1969. Bar: Mo. 1969, D.C. 1970, Pa. 1972, U.S. Dist. Ct. D.C. 1970, U.S. Dist. Ct. (mid. dist.) Pa. 1972, U.S. Ct. Appeals (D.C. cir.) 1976, U.S. Ct. Appeals (5th cir.) 1971, U.S. Ct. Appeals (3d cir.) 1976. Staff atty. Nat. Assn. Broadcasters, 1969—70, asst. gen. counsel, 1970—72; assoc. Kury & Kury, Sunbury, Pa., 1972—74; ptnr. Clement & Knight, Lewisburg, Pa., 1974—98; adj. assoc. prof. Bucknell U., 1975—99. Chair Hearing Com. 3.04, Disciplinary Bd. Pa. Supreme Ct. Contbr. articles to profl. jours. Solicitor Lewisburg Area Sch. Dist., 1975—99, Lewisburg Borough Zoning Hearing Bd., 1985—99. Mem.: Nat. Assn. Women Judges (Pa. conf. state trial judges), Pa. Sch. Bd. Solicitors Assn. (pres. 1986), Pa. Bar Assn., D.C. Bar Assn., Mo. Bar Assn. Republican. Episcopalian. Office: Union County Courthouse 103 South Second St Lewisburg PA 17837

KNIGHT, MARGARET ELIZABETH, music educator; b. Biddulph, Staffordshire, Eng., July 3, 1938; came to U.S., 1972; d. William Bateman and Amy Elizabeth (Willshaw) Whitehurst; m. Richard Alan Scudder, Apr. 5, 1972 (div. Mar. 1979); m. Rev. Arthur James Knight, May 26, 1979. Grad., No. Sch. of Music, Manchester, Eng., 1959; Assoc. in Piano Teaching, Royal Coll. Music. Lic. in voice culture, aural tng., sch. music and psychology. Asst. to head dept. music Thistley Hough Sch., Stoke, Eng., 1959-65; head dept. music Macclesfield (Eng.) H.S., 1966-72; pvt. piano tchr. Shamong, N.J., 1972—. Adj. mem. faculty dept. music Crewe (Eng.) Tchrs. Coll., 1963-72; dir. student activities South Jersey Music Tchrs. Assn., 1986-88; N.J. state rep. for Assoc. Bd. Royal Schs. Music, London, 1993—, developmental cons., 1994—; presenter in field. Sec. Conservative Party, Congleton, Eng., 1968-71, active Town Coun., Congleton, 1971-72. County Music scholar Cheshire County Coun., Chester, Eng., 1955. Mem. Music Tchrs. Nat. Assn., Nat. Guild Piano Tchrs. (judge 1987—), N.J. Music Tchrs. Assn. (dir. student activities 1988-92, pres. 1992-94). Episcopalian. Avocation: travel. Home: 3 Blueberry Rd Shamong NJ 08088-8627 E-mail: margaretknight@prodigy.net.

KNIGHT, MARGARET L. librarian, educator; b. Rochelle, Ill., Feb. 13, 1920; d. Burton Eugene and Viola Amelia (Harter) K. BS in Edn., No. Ill. U., 1943; MLS, U. Ill., 1956. Rural sch. tchr. Ogle County, Rochelle, 1939-42; tchr. 6th grade, librarian Lee County, Dixon, Ill., 1943-56; librarian jr. high sch. Cook County, Park Ridge, Ill., 1956-57, dist. supr. libr.-media ctrs., 1957-75; librarian elem. sch. Ogle County, Lindenwood, Ill., 1994—, piano, organ tchr., 1976—. Mem. bd. dirs. League of Women Voters, Rochelle, Ill., 1977—, mem. bd. dirs., sec.-treas. Lindenwood Water Assn., 1977—. Mem. No. Ill. Botanical Soc. (librarian 1990—), Ogle County Hist. Soc. (bd. dirs. 1977—), Ogle County Genealogical Soc., Prairie Preservation Soc. of Ogle County (treas. 1980—), Des Plaines Valley Geological Soc. (librarian 1994-98, treas. 1998—), Flagg Twp. Hist. Soc. (bd. 1990—). Avocations: creation of jewelry, geology, music, gardening.

KNIGHT, MONTGOMERY, JR., lawyer; b. Atlanta, Nov. 1, 1932; s. Montgomery and Emily (Millner) K.; m. Jeraline Seelinger, Aug. 7, 1954; children: Paul, Kimberly Anne. AA, Coll. William and Mary, Norfolk, Va., 1952; AB, Coll. William and Mary, Williamsburg, Va., 1954, JD, 1956. Bar: Va. 1956, U.S. Ct. Appeals (4th cir.) 1960. Ptnr. Knight, Clarke, Dolph & Rapaport, P.L.C., Norfolk, 1960-98; mem. Hofheimer Nusbaum, P.C., Norfolk, 1998—. Life mem. Jud. Conf. of U.S. Ct. Appeals for 4th Cir. Pres. Norfolk Sports Club, 1966, Chesapeake Athletic Club, 1963; bd. dirs. Norfolk Tides. Fellow Am. Coll. Trust and Estate Counsel (fiduciary litig. com. 1992-2001). Episcopalian. Avocations: golf, tennis, cars. Office: 1700 Dominion Tower 999 Waterside Dr PO Box 3460 Norfolk VA 23514-3460

KNIGHT, NORMAN, philanthropist, former broadcast executive; b. July 24, 1924; LLD (hon.), Northeastern U.; DBA (hon.), Nathaniel Hawthorne Coll.; DCS (hon.), Merrimack Coll.; DHL (hon.), Suffolk U.; DCC (hon.), Anna Maria Coll. News reporter, scriptwriter Sta. WEW, WIL, WTMV, 1938-41; Announcer, host-producer Sta. WTMV, 1942; announcer, promotion mgr., news reporting continuity dir. Sta. KTHS, 1943; announcer Sta. WMC, 1943; announcer, news writer, reporter, salesman Sta. WMMN, 1944; gen. mgr. Sta. WAJR, 1944-46; Eastern dir. sta. relations MBS, 1946-49; v.p. sales, advt. and promotion Sponsor Publs., Inc., 1950-53; gen. mgr. Sta. WABD (now WNYW-TV), 1953-54; exec. v.p., gen. mgr. Yankee Network div. RKO Teleradio Pictures, Inc. (operating Yankee Network WNAC, WRKO, WNAC-TV); also dir. Yankee Network; v.p. RKO Teleradio Pictures, 1954-60; pres. Yankee div. RKO Teleradio Pictures, Inc., 1957-60, Yankee div. RKO Gen., Inc., 1958-60; treas., chmn. Knight Sales, Inc.; chmn., treas. Knight Radio, Inc. (WEZF, WGIR and WGIR-FM), Knight Broadcasting N.H, Inc. (WHEB-FM, WXHT, WTMN); pres., treas. Knight Communications Corp. (WTAG and WSRS). Chmn. Caribbean Communications Corp.; tv and radio advisor John F. Kennedy. Established first complete TV sta.; pub. affairs film unit which produced Brotherhood Series: River of Life, Wershmeitz (only film 1956 Hungarian revolt), Suffer the Little Children, Breast Cancer, over 100 programs Dangers of Apathy; TV documentaries, 1953-60; Author: (sales techniques radio/TV) The Cause of All Mankind, (film and TV) A Storm is Always a Challenge, Awake America, others. Radio-TV chmn. United Fund Greater Boston, Mass. Cancer Soc., ARC chpt. Met. Boston, Met. Boston chpt. ARC; bus. chmn. Easter Seal Soc.; radio chmn. Salvation Army; dir. Strawberry Banke; bd. dirs. New Eng. Nephrosis Found.; pres., founder New Eng. Kidney Disease Found.; founder, chmn. Nat. Kidney Disease Found.; pres. Norman Knight Charitable Found.; trustee Mass. Bd. Regional Community Colls., Agassiz Village Camps, Crippled Children's Non-Sectarian Fund, Boys and Girls Camps, Inc.; mem. nat. council, exec. com. New Eng. council Boy Scouts Am.; exec. com., dir. Rescue, Inc.; exec. com. The Jimmy Fund; exec. com., trustee Children's Cancer Research Found., Dana Farber Cancer Inst.; mem. fin. com. Com. Econ. Devel.; mem. devel. council Boston U.; mem. pres.'s council Boston Coll.; bd. dirs. Freedoms Found.; also nat. co-chmn. Am. Freedom Ctr.; chair, pres. Mass. Fallen Firefighters Meml. Fund, 2001. Recipient Americanism award Am. Heritage Com., 1959, awards from VFW, Am. Legion, Amvets, Am. Legion Aux., 1959-60, award for contbn. to radio and TV industry Alpha Epsilon Rho; Golden Mike award Broadcasters Found., 1996; named one of ten Outstanding Yougn Men, Boston Jr. C. of C., 1956, Man of Yr., Italian-Am. Police Assn., Humanitarian award ARC, 1998; Norman Knight Camping Fund for less priviledged established in his honor, 1958, Norman Knight Hyperbaric Medicine Ctr., Mass. Eye and Ear Infirmary established in his name, 1999, Norman Knight Endowment Fund for batter women and children established in his honor, 1999, chair and pres. Mass. Fallen Firefighters Memorial, Inc., 2001-. Mem. Radio-TV Execs. Sec., Young Pres.'s Orgn., Broadcast Pioneers, AIM, Alpha Epsilon Rho. Clubs: Variety (Boston); Broadcasting Execs. New Eng, 100 of Mass. (co-founder, pres., dir.), 100 of N.H. (life), 100 of Vt. (life). Office: 63 Bay State Rd Boston MA 02215 1802

KNIGHT, PATRICIA MARIE, medical device researcher, consultant; b. Schnectady, N.Y., Jan. 25, 1952; BS in Engring. Sci., Ariz. State U., 1974, MSChemE, 1976; PhD in Biomed. Engring., U. Utah, 1983. Teaching and rsch. asst. Ariz. State U., Tempe, 1974-76; product devel. engr. Am. Med. Optics, Irvine, Calif., 1976-79, mgr. materials rsch., 1983-87; rsch. asst. U. Utah, Salt Lake City, 1979-83; dir. materials rsch. Allergan Surg. Products, Irvine, 1987-88, dir. rsch., 1988-91, v.p. rsch., devel. and engring., 1991—2002; v.p. rsch., devel. Advanced Med. Optics, Santa Ana, Calif., 2002—03; cons. biomed. product rsch. and devel. Laguna Niguel, Calif., 2003—. Contbr. articles to profl. jours. Mem. Soc. Biomaterials, Am. Chem. Soc., Soc. Women Engrs., Assn. Rsch. in Vision and Opthalmology, Biomed. Engring. Soc. E-mail: pfbiomed@cox.net.

KNIGHT, PHILIP H(AMPSON), apparel executive; b. Portland, Oreg., Feb. 24, 1938; s. William W. and Lota (Hatfield) Knight; m. Penelope Parks, Sept. 13, 1968; children: Matthew, Travis. BBA, U. Oreg., 1959; MBA, Stanford U., 1962. CPA Oreg. Chmn., CEO, past pres. Nike, Inc., Beaverton, Oreg., 1967—. Bd. dirs. U.S.-Asian Bus. Coun., Washington. 1st lt. AUS, 1959—60. Named Oreg. Businessman of Yr., 1982; named one of 1988's Best Mgrs., Bus. Week Magazine. Mem.: AICPA. Republican. Episcopalian. Office: Nike Inc One Bowerman Dr Beaverton OR 97005

KNIGHT, ROBERT EDWARD, banker; b. Alliance, Nebr., Nov. 27, 1941; s. Edward McKean and Ruth (McDuffee) K.; m. Eva Sophia Youngstom, Aug. 12, 1966. BA, Yale U., 1963; MA, Harvard U., 1965, PhD, 1968. Asst. prof. U.S. Naval Acad., Annapolis, Md., 1966-68; lectr. U. Md., 1967-68; fin. economist Fed. Res. Bank of Kansas City (Mo.), 1968-70, rsch. officer, economist, 1971-76, asst. v.p., sec., 1977, v.p., sec., 1978-79; pres. Alliance (Nebr.) Nat. Bank, 1979-94, also chmn., 1983-94; pres. Robert Knight Assocs., banking and econ. cons., Cheyenne, 1979—2003. Chmn. Eldred Found., 1985—; vis. prof., chmn. banking and fin. East Tenn. State U., Johnson City, 1988; faculty Stonier Grad. Sch. Banking, 1972-2002, Colo. Grad. Sch. Banking, 1975-82, Am. Inst. Banking, U. Mo., Kansas City, 1971-79, Prochnow Grad. Sch. Banking, U. Wis., 1980-84; extended learning faculty Park Coll., 1996—; mem. Coun. for Excellence for Bur. Bus. Rsch. U. Nebr., Lincoln, 1991-94, mem. Grad. Sch. Arts and Scis. Coun., Harvard, 1994—; chmn. Taxable Mcpl. Bondholders Protective Com., 1991-94. Contbr. articles to profl. jours. Bd. dirs. People of Faith (Royal Oaks) Found., 2000—, Stonier Grad. Sch. Banking, 1979-82, Nebr. Com. for Humanities, 1986-90; trustee Knox Presbyn. Ch., Overland Park, Kans., 1965-69; bd. regents Nat. Comml. Lending Sch., 1980-83; mem. Downtown Improvement Com., Alliance, 1981-94; trustee U. Nebr. Found., 1982-94; mem. fin. com. United Meth. Ch. Alliance, 1982-85, trustee, 1990-93; mem. Box Butte County Indsl. Devel. Bd., 1987-94. Woodrow Wilson fellow, 1963—64. Mem. Am. Econ. Assn., Am. Fin. Assn., So. Econ. Assn., Nebr. Bankers Assn. (com. state legis. 1980-81, com. comml. loans and investments 1986-87), Am. Inst. Banking (state com. for Nebr. 1980-83), Am. Bankers Assn. (econ. adv. com. 1980-83, cmty. bank leadership coun.), Western Econ. Assn., Econometric Soc., Rotary, Masons. Home and Office: 429 W 5th Ave Cheyenne WY 82001-1249

KNIGHT, ROBERT G. mayor, investment banker; b. Wichita, Kans., July 31, 1941; s. Edwar G. and Melba (Barbour) K.; m. Jane Carol Benedick, Aug. 12, 1967; children— Jennifer, Amy, Kristin BA, Wichita State U. Rep. First Securities Co., Wichita, Kans., 1970-76, v.p., 1984—; Mid-Continent Mcpls., Wichita, Kans., 1977-82, Ranson & Co., Wichita, Kans., 1982-84; mayor City of Wichita, 1980-81, 84—. Trustee Salvation Army, Wichita, 1980—, Urban Ministeries, Wichita, 1980—, Southwestern Coll., Winfield, Kans., 1980—; bd. dirs. Kans. Water Authority, Topeka, 1983—; commr. City of Wichita, 1979—. Served with USMCR, 1962-66 Recipient award of honor Concerned Citizens for Community Standards, 1982 Mem. Nat. League Cities, Kans. League Municipalities Republican. Methodist. Avocation: sports. Office: Mayors Office City Hall 1st Fl 455 N Main St Wichita KS 67202-1600

KNIGHT, ROBERT HUNTINGTON, lawyer, bank executive; b. New Haven, Feb. 27, 1919; s. Earl Wall and Frances Pierpont (Whitney) K.; m. Rosemary C. Gibson, Apr. 19, 1975; children: Robert Huntington, Jessie Valle, Patricia Whitney, Alice Isabel, Eli Whitney. Grad., Phillips Acad., Andover, Mass., 1936; BA, Yale, 1940; LL.B., U. Va., 1947, LLM, 1949. Bar: N.Y. bar 1950. With John Orr Young, Inc. (advt. agy.), 1940-41; asst. prof. U. Va. Law Sch., 1947-49; assoc. firm Shearman & Sterling & Wright, N.Y.C., 1949-55, ptnr., 1955-58; dep. asst. sec. def. for internat. security affairs Dept. Def., 1958-61; gen. counsel Treasury Dept., 1961-62; ptnr. firm Shearman & Sterling, N.Y.C., 1962-80, sr. ptnr., 1980-85, of counsel, 1986—; dep. chmn. Fed. Res. Bank N.Y., 1976-77, chmn., 1977-83. Counsel to bd. United Technologies Corp., 1974-85; dir. internat. bd. Owens-Corning Fiberglas Corp., 1989—; dir. I-Corps, Nat. Leadership Bank, Mercator, Inc., Citizen Exchange Coun.; mem. Intelsat Arbitration Panel, 1971-91. Bd. dirs. Internat. Vol. Services; chmn. bd. dirs. U. Va. Law Sch. Found., 1970-90; bd. dirs. Asia Found.. Served to lt. col. USAAF, 1941-45. Mem. ABA, Fed. Bar Assn., Internat. Bar Assn., Inter-Am.

Bar Assn., Assn. of Bar of City of N.Y., N.Y County Lawyers Assn., Internat. Law Assn., Washington Inst. Fgn. Affairs, Council Fgn. Relations, Pilgrims Club, Links Club, World Trade Ctr Club, River Club (N.Y.C.), Army and Navy Club, Met. Club (Washington), Round Hill Club (Greenwich, Conn.), Ocean Club (Ocean Ridge, Fla.), Farmington Club (Va.). Home: 12 Knollwood Dr Greenwich CT 06830-4733 also: 570 Park Ave New York NY 10021-7370 also: 6767 N Ocean Blvd Ocean Ridge FL 33435-3314 Office: 599 Lexington Ave New York NY 10022-6030

KNIGHT, SANDRA NORTON, civil engineer; b. Chattanooga, Mar. 2, 1962; d. Johnny Lee Norton and Wanda Dean (Pledger) Weaver. Student, Chattanooga State Tech. C.C., 1980-82; BSCE, U. Tenn., 1986; postgrad., Fla. State U., 1990. Registered profl. engr., Tenn. Traffic engr. technician City of Knoxville; project mgr. Fla. Dept. Transp., Tallahassee, 1987-93, Cook & Spencer Cons., Chattanooga, 1993-96; engr. design mgr. City of Chattanooga, 1996; county engr. Bradley County, Cleveland, Tenn., 1996—. Bldg. inspector Town of Decatur, Tenn., 1996-99, alderman, 1995-99. Named Engr. of Yr., Chattanooga Area Engr.'s Week, 2002. Mem.: Indsl. Tech. Adv. Coun., Tenn. Soc. Profl. Engrs. (sec. Chattanooga chpt. 1998—99, v.p. 1999—2000, prof. engr. in govt. Tenn. sect. 2000, pres.-elect Tenn. sect. 2000—01, pres. 2001—02, v.p. 2001—02, pres.-elect 2002—03, pres. 2003—, Outstanding Engr. of Yr. 2003), ASCE (sec.-treas. 1994—95, v.p. 1995—96, pres. 1996—97, v.p. Tenn. sect. 1998—99, pres.-elect 1999—2000, pres. 1999—2001, dist. 9 sec., treas. 2003—, Young Engr. of Yr. 1991, 1996, 1997, Govt. Engr. of Yr. 2000, Engr. of Yr. award 2002, Disting. Svc. award 2003). Republican. Baptist. Avocations: siberian huskies, reading. Office: Bradley County Engr PO Box 1167 Cleveland TN 37364-1167

KNIGHT, THOMAS JEFFERSON, JR., technology consultant, trainer; b. San Antonio, Oct. 21, 1955; s. Thomas Jefferson and Martha Lena (Craig) K.; m. Lois Ann Simmons, July 13, 1985 (div. Jan. 1993); 1 child, Thomas Jefferson III. BS, Baylor U., 1978; M. Pub. Adminstrn., Golden Gate U., 1988. Commd. 2d lt. USAF, 1978, advanced thru grades to capt., 1988; chief of adminstrn. USAF 780th Radar Squadron, Fortuna AFB, N.D., 1978-79; squadron sect. comdr. USAF 325th Component Repair Squadron, Tyndall AFB, Fla., 1979-82; protocol officer USAF HQ Tactical Air Command, Langley AFB, Va., 1982-85; exec. officer USAF 487th Tactical Missile Wing, Comiso AS, Italy, 1985-86, USAF 57th Fighter Weapons Wing, Nellis AFB, Nev., 1986-90; resigned, 1990; cons., 1990; dir. tech. svcs. Entré Computer Ctr., Waco, 1990-99, ClearSource, Inc., Waco, 1999—2001; cons., 2001—. Local commr. Panama City (Fla.) Boy Scouts Am., 1979-80. Mem. Air Force Assn. Presbyterian. E-mail: tknight55@yahoo.com.

KNIGHT, TOWNSEND JONES, lawyer; b. N.Y.C., Aug. 10, 1928; s. Jesse and Marguerite H. (Jones) K.; m. Elise Heck; children: Margaret Knight Dudley, Elise Knight Wallace, Jessica Knight Casoni. BS, Harvard U., 1949; JD, Columbia U., 1952. Bar: N.Y. 1952. Assoc. Curtis, Mallet-Prevost, Colt & Mosle, N.Y.C., 1953-65, ptnr., 1965—2001, of counsel, 2001—. Trustee Metropolitan Coll. of NY, 1969—, Cold Spring Harbor (N.Y.) Lab., 1970-76, 82-88, 89-95, hon. trustee, 1995—. Mem. ABA, N.Y. State Bar Assn., Assn. of Bar of City of N.Y., Downtown Assn., Harvard Club, Cold Spring Harbor Beach Club. Episcopalian. Avocation: photography. Office: Curtis Mallet-Prevost Colt & Mosle 101 Park Ave Fl 35 New York NY 10178-0061

KNIGHT, WALKER LEIGH, editor, publisher, clergyman; b. Henderson, Ky., Feb. 6, 1924; s. Cooksey Bennett and Rowena (Henderson) K.; m. Iva Nell Moseley, Nov. 10, 1943; children: Walker Leigh, Kenneth Wayne, Nelda Denise, Emily Jill. BA, Baylor U., 1949. Reporter Henderson Gleanor and Jour., 1942; ordained to ministry Bapt. Ch., 1948; pastor in Dale, Tex., 1948-49; editor Falls County Record, Marlin, Tex., 1948-49; assoc. editor Bapt. Std., Dallas, 1950-59; editl. dir. So. Bapt. Home Mission Bd., Atlanta, also editor Missions U.S.A. mag. and Atlanta bur. chief Bapt. Press News Service, 1959-83; editor, pub. Bapts. Today (formerly SBC Today), 1983-89, pub., 1989-93, pub. emeritus, 1994—. Editor The Whitsitt Jour., 1995-98. Author: Panama, The Land Between, 1965, Struggle for Integrity, 1969, See How Love Works, 1971, Seven Beginnings, 1976, Chaplaincy, Love on the Line, 1978, Tell the People, 1986; contbr. to Southern Baptists Observed, 1992, Struggle for the Soul of the SBC, 1993. With USAAF, 1943-45. Home and Office: 1008 Forrest Blvd Decatur GA 30030-4732

KNIGHT, WILLIAM D., JR., lawyer; b. Rockford, Ill., May 18, 1925; s. William D. and Lela Mae (Clark) K. AB, Dartmouth Coll., 1949; JD, Northwestern U., 1952. Bar: Ill. 1953, U.S. Dist. Ct. (no. dist.) Ill. 1957, U.S. Ct. Appeals (7th cir.) 1959. Ptnr., Knight & Knight, Rockford, 1953—. Bd. dirs. Boys Club Assn. of Rockford, 1959-75. Served to 1st lt., inf., U.S. Army, 1943-46. Mem. Ill. Bar Assn., Winnebago County Bar Assn., Internat. Assn. Ins. Counsel, Fedn. Ins. Counsel, Assn. Ins. Attys., Def. Rsch. Inst., Rockford Country Club. Republican. Methodist. Home: 1205 Lundvall Ave Rockford IL 61107-3341 also: 575 S Lake Shore Dr Lake Geneva WI 53147-2126 Office: Knight and Knight 1111 Talcott Bldg 321 W State St Rockford IL 61101-1137

KNIGHT, WILLIAM J. (PETE KNIGHT), state legislator, retired air force officer; b. Noblesville, Ind., Nov. 18, 1929; s. William T. and Mary Emma (Illyes) K.; m. Helena A Stone, June 7, 1958; children: William Peter, David, Stephen; m. Gail A. Johnson, Sept. 3, 1983. BS, Air Force Inst. Tech., 1958; student, Indsl. Coll. Armed Forces, 1973-74. Commd. 2d lt. USAF, 1953, advanced through grades to col., 1971; fighter pilot Kinross AFB, Mich., 1953-56; exptl. test pilot Edwards AFB, Calif., 1958-69; exptl. test pilot, 1969-70; dir. test and deployment F-15 program, 1976; dir. Flight Attack System Program Office, 1977-79; vice comdr. Air Force Flight Test Ctr. Edwards AFB, 1979-82; ret. USAF, 1982; mayor City of Palmdale, Calif., 1988-92; mem. Calif. Assembly, Sacramento, 1992-96, Calif. Senate, Sacramento, 1996—. V.p. Eidetics Internat., Torrance, Calif., 1988-92. Decorated D.F.C. with 2 oak leaf clusters, Legion of Merit with 2 oak leaf clusters, Air medal with 11 oak leaf clusters, Astronauts Wings; recipient Octave Chanute award, 1968, Harmon Internat. trophy, 1968, citation of honor Air Force Assn., 1969 winner Allison Jet Trophy Race, 1954; named to Nat. Aviation Hall of Fame, 1988, Lancaster Aerospace Walk of Honor, 1990, Internat. Space Hall of Fame, 1998. Fellow AIAA (assoc.), Soc. Exptl. Test Pilots (past pres.); mem. Air Force Assn., Internat. Order of Characters, Aerospace Primus Club, Daedalians, Elks, Shriners. Holder world's speed record for winged aircraft, 4520 m.p.h., 1967. Home: 220 Eagle Ln Palmdale CA 93551-3613 Office: 2196 State Capital Sacramento CA 95814

KNIGHTON, BARBARA MCLEOD, occupational health specialist, risk specialist; b. Regina, Sask., Can. d. Alan Donald and Jeanne-Marie (Smith) McLeod; m. James Edward Knighton, Feb. 9, 1979; children: Skye Alan, Aren James, Taylor William. BS, U. B.C., Vancouver, Can., 1976; MS, Calif. State U., Northridge, 1992. Tchg. asst. U. Wash., Friday Harbor, 1976; rsch. asst. Controlled Environ. Pollution Expt., Vancouver, 1976, Can. Fisheries and Marine Svc., Vancouver, 1977-78, U. Tex. Med. Br., Galveston, 1979-80; mem. tech. staff Los Angeles County Dept. Pub. Works, Alhambra, Calif., 1992-95, safety officer, 1995-97, risk mgr., 1997—. Asst. scoutmaster Boy Scouts Am., La Crescenta, Calif., 1996—. Mem. Am. Soc. Safety Engrs., Am. Indsl. Hygiene Assn., Am. Conf. Govtl. Indsl. Hygienists. Avocations: camping, hiking. Office: Los Angeles County Dept Pub Works 900 S Fremont Ave Alhambra CA 91803-1331

KNIGHTS, EDWIN MUNROE, pathologist; b. Providence, Dec. 25, 1924; s. Edwin Munroe and Viola Ruth (Koreb) K.; m. Ruth Lindsay Currie, Sept. 23, 1961; children— Edwin B., Jessie B., Ross D., David J. (dec. 1979). AB, Brown U., 1948; MD, Cornell U., 1948. Intern Bellevue Hosp., N.Y.C., 1948-49; resident in pathology R.I. Hosp., Providence, 1949-50, Henry Ford Hosp. Detroit, 1952-54; assoc. pathologist Harper Hosp., Detroit, 1954; dir. labs. Hurley Hosp., Flint, Mich., 1957-62, Providence Hosp., Southfield, Mich., 1963-75; dir. Northland Oakland Med. Labs., Southfield, Mich., 1964-75, Bio Sci. Labs., Detroit, 1975-85, Smith Kline Bio-Sci. Labs., Detroit, 1985-89; dir. labs. Kern Hosp., Warren, Mich., 1977-81; pres. Coll. Terr. Inc., Flint, Mich., 1968—; dir. Performance Assurance Profls., Bloomfield Hills, 1988-94; pres. Life Sci. Inc., Flint, 1971-72, Vet. Med. Labs., 1973-75; clin. prof. pathology Mich. State U., 1974-75; rep. Comprehensive Health Planning Council S.E. Mich., 1973-85, trustee, 1986-87; mem. lab peer rev. com. Mich Dept. Social Services, 1979-84; med. dir. Smith Kline Beecham Labs., Detroit, 1990-92, Nat. Health Labs., Flint, Mich., 1992-94. Pres. Life Sci. Inc., Grantham, 1996-98; pathologist Project Hope, Indonesia and Vietnam, 1961, Peru, 1962, Ecuador, 1964; bd. dirs. GeneSaver DNA Preservation Svcs., 1996—. Author: Ultramicro Methods for Clinical Laboratories, 1957, 2d edit., 1962; editor: Minicomputers in the Clinical Laboratory, 1970, Lifelines, 1971-75; contbg. editor Jour. Foot Surgery, 1983-89; contbr. numerous articles to profl. jours. and mags.; patentee in field. Emeritus mem. adv. coun. New Eng. Hist. Geneal. Soc., trustee, 2001—; mem. long range planning com. Ea. Cmty. Assn., 1997—. Lt. USNR, 1944-46, 50-52, ETO, Korea USPHS grantee, 1957-66 Fellow ACP, Coll. Am. Pathologists, Am.Soc. Clin. Pathologists (Mich. councillor 1966-68); mem. AMA, Oakland County Med. Soc. (pres. 1974), Mich. Soc. Pathologists (pres. 1970, del. Mich. State Med. Soc. 1986-93), Internat. Acad. Pathology, Mich. State Med. Soc., Assn. Clin. Scientists, Gen. Soc. Mayflower Descs., Roger Williams Family Assn. Home and Office: 164 Top O'World Rd Box 1303 Grantham NH 03753-1303

KNIJFF, JAN-PIET, musician, educator; b. Haarlem, Netherlands, May 8, 1966; m. Brigitte Pohl. MM, Conservatory of Amsterdam; studied, The Grad. Ctr., CUNY. Organist-in-residence Aaron Copland Sch. of Music, Queens Coll., CUNY, N.Y.C.; adj. prof. Fairfield U., Conn.; concert organist in residence St. Paul's Ch. Nat. Hist. Site, Mount Vernon, NY; dir. of music St. Michael's Luth. Ch., New Canaan, Conn.; music dir. St. Boniface's Ch., De Rijp, Netherlands, 1990—94; adj. prof. Inst. for Early Music, Music Acad. Trossingen, Germany, 1994—97. Mem. Arts Com., City Coun., Haarlem, Netherlands, 1993—98. Author: (journal) The Tracker, Het Orgel, (jounal) Pianowereld; musician: (cd) Schnittke, Symphony 5/Concerto grosso 4, Goldberg Variations (collaborative artist). Recipient First Prize and Audience Prize, Internat. Bach Competition, Lausanne, Switzerland, 1997, Second Prize, Hindemith-Micheelsen Competition, Rotterdam, 1996, Third Prize, Hendrik Andriessen Competition, Utrecht, 1992, Finalist, Tournemire-Langlais Competition, Haarlem, 1992. Mem.: Royal Dutch Soc. Organists, Am. Guild Organists, Organ Hist. Soc. Home: 12 Salem Ln South Salem NY 10590 Personal E-mail: jp@music.org.

KNILANS, MICHAEL JEROME, supermarkets executive; b. Columbus, Ohio, Mar. 3, 1927; s. Alfred Sidney and Bernice (Meyers) K.; m. Anne Eberhardt, June 15, 1947; children: Michael, Kyleen, Christine, Timothy, Suzanne. BS, Ohio State U., 1949. With Big Bear Stores Co., Columbus, 1942-89, mdse. mgr., 1952-61, v.p., 1961-70, exec. v.p., 1970-76, pres., 1976-89, also dir. Bd. dirs. Price Chopper Supermarkets, Schenectady, N.Y. Chmn. bd. Ohio Workers Compensation Bd., 1989-95; bd. dirs. Children's Hosp., Columbus, Mt. Carmel Coll. Nursing, Columbus; v.p. East Ctr. region Boy Scouts Am. With USNR, 1944-46, PTO. Mem. Ohio Coun. Retail Mchts. (treas.), Better Bus. Bur. (pres. 1978), C. of C., Masons, Shriners, Jesters, Rotary (pres. 1981—, dist. gov. 1993-94). Republican. Home: 1119 Kingsdale Ter Columbus OH 43220-4946

KNILANS, TIMOTHY KEVIN, pediatrician; b. Columbus, Ohio, Oct. 6, 1957; s. Michael Jerome and Anne Marie (Eberhardt) K.; m. Teri Marie Grunewald, June 28 1986. AB, Wittenberg U., 1979; MD, U. Cin., 1983. Diplomate Am. Bd. Pediatrics, Am. Bd. Pediatric Cardiology. Intern in pediatrics Children's Hosp. Med. Ctr., Cin., 1983-84, resident in pediatrics, 1984-86, fellow in pediatric cardiology, 1986-89; fellow in cardiac electrophysiology St. Vincent Hosp., Indpls., 1990-91; fellow in pediatric electrophysiology Tex. Children's Hosp., Houston, 1991; dir. cardiac electrophysiology Children's Hosp. Med. Ctr., Cin., 1991—, med. dir. cardiac exercise lab., 2001—. Contbr. to textbooks. Fellow Am. Coll. Cardiology; mem. AMA, Acad. of Medicine of Cin., Ohio State Med. Assn., N.Am. Soc. Pacing and Electrophysiology, Pediatric Electrophysiology Soc. Office: Children's Hosp Med Ctr 3333 Burnet Ave Cincinnati OH 45229-3026 E-mail: knilans@cchmc.org.

KNIPPERS, DIANE LEMASTERS, association executive; b. Rushville, Ind., Jan. 6, 1952; m. Edward C. Knippers, Jr. BA in History, Asbury Coll., 1972; MA in Sociology, U. Tenn., 1974. Teaching asst. U. Tenn., 1972-73; assoc. editor, asst. editor, editorial asst. Good News Mag., 1974-80, assoc. exec. sec., editor, 1980-82; exec. v.p., deputy dir., program dir., dir. orgn. IRD, 1982-93; pres. Inst. Religion and Democracy, 1993—. Office: Inst Religion and Democracy 1110 Vermont Ave NW Ste 1180 Washington DC 20005-3544

KNIPSCHILD, ROBERT, artist, educator; b. Freeport, Ill., Aug. 17, 1927; s. Leon Francis and Alice (Walsh) K.; m. Patricia Ann O'Connor, Sept. 1, 1949; children— Abby Clare Knipschild Weber, Amy Louise Knipschild Wermeling, John Eliot, Jill Anne Knipschild Harsch, Sarah Kate. BA, U. Wis., 1950; M.F.A., Cranbrook Acad. Art, 1951. Tchr. Balt. Mus. Art, 1951-52, Am. U., 1952, U. Conn., 1954-56, U. Wis., 1956-60, U. Iowa, 1960-66; prof. art, dir. grad. studies fine arts U. Cin., 1966-90, prof. emeritus fine arts, 1990—. Exhbns. include, Mus. Modern Art, Whitney Mus., Met. Mus., Corcoran Mus., Boston Mus., Carnegie Inst., also in Europe, Japan and, Australia. Served with AUS, 1945-47. Office: 1159 Hill Crest Rd Cincinnati OH 45224-3223

KNISELEY, RALPH MARION, pathologist, nuclear medicine physician; b. Swissvale, Pa., Dec. 26, 1920; s. Ralph MacGregor and Mary Margaret (Smith) K.; m. Helen Sutton, July 20, 1947 (dec. May 1961); children: Susan, Lucy, Greg, Martha, Julie; m. Frances Sutton, 1963 (div. 1973); m. Joan Y. Silva, Oct. 16, 1973. BS, U. Pitts., 1942, MD, 1943. Diplomate Am. Bd. Pathology, Am. Bd. Nuclear Medicine (founding mem.). Intern St. Margaret's Meml. Hosp., Pitts., 1944; resident Mayo Found., Rochester, Minn., 1944-46, 48-49; dir. labs. Lovelace Clinic, Albuquerque, 1949-51; pathologist Oak Ridge (Tenn.) Assoc. Univs., 1951-55, chmn. clin. rsch. and tng., 1959-63, assoc. chair, 1963-73; pathologist Eden Hosp., Castro Valley, Calif., 1955-59; dir. life scis. divsn. Internat. Atomic Energy Agy., Vienna, 1973-75; pvt. practice Emmett and Boise, Idaho, 1975-94; gen. practice Oak Ridge, 1994—2001. Cons. Donner Lab., U. Calif., Berkeley, 1955-59; mem. pathology grants com. NIH, Bethesda, Md., 1966-69; vis. prof. Internat. Atomic Energy Agy. to Nt. Inst. Radiol. Sci., Chiba, Japan, 1962. Contbr.a rticles to profl. jours., chpts. to books. Bd. dirs., exec. com. Nat. Planned Parenthood, N.Y., 1973; bd. trustees, pres. Unitarian Ch., Oak Ridge, 1960s to 1970s; bd. dirs. Mental Health Ctr., Oak Ridge, 1950s, Oak Ridge Art Ctr., 1950s. Capt. M.C. U.S. Army, 1946-48. Recipient Commr.'s medal Commr. on Continuing Edn., Am. soc. Clin. Pathologists; named Hevesy Pioneer in Nuclear Medicine, Am. Soc. Nuclear Medicine, 1995. Democrat. Avocation: professional painting.

KNISELY, CHARLES WILLIAM, JR., engineering educator, researcher, consultant; b. Johnson City, N.Y., Dec. 29, 1952; s. Charles William and Hattie Elnora (Miller) K.; m. Karin Ingrid Wegener, May 21, 1983; children: Katrina Marie, Carleton Perry, Brian Frederick. BSME, Bucknell U., 1975, MSME, 1978; PhD in Mech. Engring., Lehigh U., 1980. Rsch. engr. Sulzer Bros., Inc., Winterthur, Switzerland, 1980-83, U. Karlsruhe, Fed. Republic of Germany, 1983-85, David Taylor Naval Ship R & D Ctr., Bethesda, Md., 1985-87; lectr. Kyoto (Japan) U., 1987-90; asst. prof. Bucknell U., Lewisburg, Pa., 1990-94, assoc. prof., 1994—. Vis. prof. Osaka (Japan) Electro-Comm. U., summer, 1995, U. Siegen (Germany), 2002; dir. Bucknell Small Bus. Devel. Ctr., 1997—99. Inventor in field. Western Electric Co. scholar, 1972-75. Mem.: AIAA, ASME, Internat. Conf. Bluff Body Aerodynamics and its Applications (sec. Kyoto meeting 1988), Am. Soc. Engring. Edn. Avocations: gardening, travel, photography, squash. Office: Bucknell U Mech Engring Dept Lewisburg PA 17837

KNISELY, RALPH FRANKLIN, retired microbiologist; b. Altoona, Pa., Mar. 30, 1927; s. Calvin Ross and Frieda Pauline (Neher) K.; m. Joan Marie Fitzgerald, Jan. 29, 1949 (div. 1955); 1 child, Patricia Ann; m. Ann Martin, May 21, 1960. BS, postgrad., Pa. State U., 1953. Bacteriologist Altoona Hosp., 1953-56, adminstrv. asst. to pathologist, 1957-59; microbiologist Chem. Corps Dept. Army, Ft. Detrick, Md., 1959-72; rsch. microbiologist Edgewood Arsenal, Aberdeen Proving Ground, Md., 1972-86. Contbg. author: Rapid Identification of Biological Agents, 1966; contbr. articles to Jour. Bacteriology, European Jour. Microbiology. Pres. Eastview Civic Assn., Frederick, Md., 1968-69; mem. Srs. and Lawmen Together Coun., Frederick City Police and Frederick County Sheriffs Office. With USN, 1945-46, 50-51; capt. Res. ret., 1945-87. Mem.: AARP (bd. dirs. chpt. 636 1990—92, chpt. pres. 1995—96, bd. dirs. chpt. 636 1997—98), Rsch. Soc. Am. (emeritus), Am. Soc. for Microbiology (emeritus), N.Y. Acad. Sci. (life), Assn. Mil. Surgeons U.S. (life), Legion of Honor (comdr. 2002—), Knisely Reunion Assn. (historian 1993—, pres. 1994—95), Internat. Platform Assn., Ret. Officer's Assn. (chpt. v.p. 1969—70, pres. 2002—03), Nat. Assn. Ret. Fed. Employees (life; pres. chpt. 409 1995—97, bd. dirs. 1997—98), Am. Philatelic Soc. (life), Sampson WWII Vets. (life; Md. dir.), Fleet Res. Assn., Nat. Sojourners (pres. chpt. 354 1965, 1981, sec. 1986—), Am. Legion, Korean Vets., Philalethes Soc. Quatour Coronati Corr. Cir. (London), Masonic Rsch. Soc., Keystone Kopps (pres. 2002), George Washington Masonic Stamp Club (pres. 1978—80, sec. 1988—98), KT, Scottish Rite, Order of Quetzalcoatl, Tall Cedars of Lebanon, Elks, Shriners, Masons. Republican. Lutheran. Avocations: family genealogy, amateur radio. Home: 7400 Skyline Dr Frederick MD 21702-3652

KNISKERN, JOSEPH WARREN, lawyer; b. Coral Gables, Fla., July 7, 1951; s. Kenneth Felix and Elise (Scofield) K.; m. Cheryl Rybka. BSBA, U. Fla., 1973, JD cum laude, 1976. Bar: Fla. 1976; cert. real estate atty., Fla.; cert. family mediator, Fla.; registered real estate salesperson, Fla. Assoc. Smathers & Thompson, Miami, Fla., 1976-83, ptnr., 1983-87, Kelley Drye & Warren, Miami, 1987-93; pvt. practice Coral Gables, Fla., 1993-2000, Weston, Fla., 2000—. Authorized agt. Attys. Title Ins. Fund, Lawyers Title Ins. Corp. Author: When the Vow Breaks: A Survival and Recovery Guide for Christians Facing Divorce, 1993, Courting Disaster: What Runaway Litigation is Costing You and What Can Be Done to Stop the Fallout, 1995, Making a New Vow: A Christian Guide to Remarriage and Blended Families, 2003. Trustee Miami-Gables Ch. of Christ, 1979-86. Mem. ABA, Nat. Lawyers Assn., Fla. Bar, Dade County Bar Assn., Broward County Bar Assn., Christian Legal Soc., Cmty. Assns. Inst., Inst. for Christian Conciliation, Am. Assn. Christian Counselors. Republican. Office: 17190 Arvida Pkwy Ste 2 Weston FL 33326-2379 E-mail: kniskern1w@aol.com.

KNITTEL, JANNA MARIE, literature educator; b. Corvallis, Oreg., May 16, 1967; d. Martin Dean Knittel and Marjorie Claire Knittel (Swanson). BA, U. Oreg., Eugene, 1989, MA, 1991, PhD, 1995; MA, U. Kans., Lawrence, 2001. Lectr. English U. Kans., Lawrence, 1999—, vis. lectr. in women's studies, 2000—. Author: (poetry) Sonnet for Depression, Parnassus Literary Review, Impasse, Apostrophe; contbr. articles to profl. jours. Rudolf Ernst Grad. fellowship, U. Oreg., 1993. Mem.: MLA, Soc. for Study of Multi-Ethnic Lit. of US. Office: Univ Kans Dept English 1445 Jayhawk Blvd Rm 3116 Lawrence KS 66045-7590 E-mail: knittel@ku.edu.

KNITTLE, WILLIAM JOSEPH, JR., media executive, psychologist, religious leader, management and marketing consultant, educator; b. Santa Monica, Calif., June 11, 1945; s. William Joseph Knittle and Lahlee (Duggins) Morrell; m. Linda Catherine Black, Apr. 19, 1969 (div. Aug. 1977); 1 child, Kristen Elizabeth; m. Alexis Carrell Upton, Sept. 30, 1977 (div. Aug. 1996); 1 child, Jonathan Kynan. Student, Inst. for Japanese Culture, 1960, Am. Nat. Theater and Acad., 1962-64; BA in English, Loyola U., L.A., 1966, MA in Comm. Arts, 1970, MA in Counseling Psychology, 1973; PhD in Communication Theory and Social Psychology, Lawrence U., Santa Barbara, Calif., 1976; D of Dharma in Asian Religion and Philosophy, U. Oriental Studies, L.A., 1980; MBA, U. La Verne, 1983; grad., Grantsmanship Ctr., L.A., 1980. Ordained Sramanera, Buddhist monk, 1976; ordained Bikkhu, Vietnamese lineage, 1977, Chinese lineage, 1977; ordained Zen Master and High Tchr. in all Buddhist Traditions, Fo Kuang Shan Monastery, Taiwan, 1977. Assoc. editor Black Belt mag., 1960—65; pub. lectr. on current world affairs and fraudulent holistic healing practices, 1965—; acting news dir., pub. affairs/continuity acceptance coord. Sta. KHJ-TV, L.A., 1966—67; news editor Sta. KFWB Radio, L.A., 1967—69; profl. photographer, 1969—80; dir. news and media rels. Loyola Marymount U., L.A., 1969—75; pvt. therapist, hypnotherapist L.A., 1974—; gen. mgr., dir. televised studies Media Five Film and TV Prodns., L.A., 1976—79, v.p., 1981—83; prof. acupuncture, traditional Chinese medicine and hypnosis U. Oriental Studies, L.A., 1976—83, chmn. East-West psychology dept., 1976—; sex therapist and educator L.A., 1979—83; assoc. dir. divsn. of continuing edn. U. La Verne, Calif., 1979—81, adj. prof., 1980—; pres. Western News Assocs., L.A., 1983—; asst. to dean UCLA Sch. Medicine, 1985—86; advt./mktg. dir. summer sessions UCLA, 1986—98; prof. Coll. Buddhist Studies, L.A., 1991—. Co-creator, instr. 1st accredited unscreened film, dir. interview grad. course UCLA, 1965; govt. liaison Loyola U. Credit Union, L.A., 1971-75; chief instr. martial arts Loyola Marymount U., 1963-74; lectr. L.A. Police Dept., 1978; founder Realization Therapy, 1976; host Campus report, KHJ-AM/KRTH-FM, L.A., 1973-74, At Your Leisure program KXLU-FM, L.A., 1972-76; dir. film segments KCOP-TV, L.A., 1966; tech. dir. Quien Lo Sabe program KMEX-TV, L.A., 1964; instr. systematic theology and sacred scripture L.A. Archdiocese, 1969-72; cons. Yu Shing Corp. Taiwan, 1992, Zhong Shan (Sun Yat Sen) Victory Ship (Nat. Treas.) Mem. Complex, Peoples Republic of China, 1997, CITIC Pharms. Co., Peoples Republic of China, 1998—, Purex Corp., 1980; profl. ventriloquist, singer, actor 1955-66; co-founder L.A. Film Tchrs. Assn., 1970; founder Ann. Psychology Film awards So. Calif. Psychol. Assn., 1980; cons. in field, 1976— Author: Survival Strategies for the Classroom Teacher, 1982; syndicated columnist various newspapers, mags., 1970—; Hollywood corr. Columbia mag., 1974-87; contbr. articles to profl. jours.; writer/cinematographer On Campus series KNBC-TV, L.A., 1974; speechwriter Chinese Democracy Advocates, 1996—. Media spokesman Am. Cancer Soc., 1960-62; media teenage coord. Los Angeles County March of Dimes, 1961-68; assoc. dir. Pasadena/San Gabriel Valley Counseling Ctr., Pasadena, 1973-74; assoc. abbot Internat. Buddhist Med. Ctr., L.A., 1976-81; bd. dirs. Dharma Vijaya Buddhist Vihara, L.A., 1985—; founding mem. So. Calif. Buddhist Sangha Coun., L.A. Buddhist Union, So. Calif. Interreligious Coun.; host, announcer Karate Championship Tournament, 1975, 5th ann. open Am. Tae Kwon Do-Kung Fu Championship Tournament, 1976; host, announcer Dedication of Wat Thai Buddhist Temple, North Hollywood, 1980; martial arts instr. Santa Monica (Calif.) Police Dept., 1961-63, Santa Monica Dept. Recreation & Parks, 1961-63. Recipient Martial Arts Pioneer award Am. Tae Kwon Do-Kung Fu Assn., 1976, Nat. Headliners award Wash. Press Club, 1968, Internat. Journalism award Sigma Delta Chi, 1968; inducted into Motion Pictures Pioneers, Hollywood, Calif., 2003. Mem.: NATAS, AAAS, Nat. Acad. TV Arts and Scis., Nat. Police Acad., Am. Fedn. Police (chaplain 1985—), Investigative Reporters and Editors, Nat. Book Critics Circle, Am. Soc. Tng. and Devel., Internat. Imagery Assn., Internat. Brotherhood of Magicians, L.A. Film Critics Cir., Soc. Interdisciplinary Study of Mind, Inst. for Holistic Edn., Assn. for Transpersonal Psychology. Avocations: martial arts, magic, pseudoscience, religious history, qigong. Home and Office: Western News Assocs PO Box 24130 Los Angeles CA 90024-0130 E-mail: LAShrink@earthlink.net.

KNIZE, DAVID MAURICE, plastic surgeon; b. Ennis, Tex., Apr. 2, 1938; s. Joseph Fred and Mary Elizabeth (Vavra) K.; m. Barbara Ruth Reed BA, Tex. U., 1959; MD, Southwestern Med. Coll., 1963. Resident in Orthopedic surgery Duke U., Durham, N.C., 1964-66; resident gen. surgery U. Colo., Denver, 1966-68; resident plastic surgery N.Y.U., 1970-74; assoc., prof. surgery U. Colo., Denver, 1974--. Contbr. articles to profl. jours. Lt. Comdr. USN, 1969-71. Mem. Am. Soc. Plastic and Reconstructive Surgeons, AMA, Colo. State Soc. Republican. Avocations: bicycling, wind surfing, scuba diving, R.C. glider flying. Office: 3555 S Clarkson St Englewood CO 80110-3909

KNIZESKI, JUSTINE ESTELLE, insurance company executive; b. Glen Cove, N.Y., June 4, 1954; d. John Martin and Elsie Beatrice (Gozelski) Knizeski. BA, Conn. Coll., 1976; M in Mgmt., Northwestern U., 1981. Customer svc. supr. Brunswick Savs., Freeport, Maine, 1977-79; investment analyst Bankers Life and Casualty Co., Chgo., 1980-83, dir. corp. planning and analysis, 1983-87; dir. budgets, cost acctg. Blue Cross/Blue Shield of Ill., 1987-97, dir. planning, budgets and analysis, 1997—, exec. dir. budgets and analysis, 2002—. Chmn. bd. dirs. Alternatives, Inc., Chgo., 1984—87, vice chmn., 1987—91, 2002—, sec., 1991—92, bd. dirs., 1983—84, 2001—02, mem. ad hoc fin. com., 1998—2001; mem. Chgo. Coun. Fgn. Rels., 1984—85, 2002—; bd. dirs. Non-Profit Fin. Ctr., 2000—, treas., 2002—. Mem. Planning Forum. Avocations: travel, sailing, bicycling, traveling, painting.

KNOB, STEVEN EDWARD, band director, composer; b. Bowling Green, Ky., Dec. 27, 1959; s. Edward A. and Nancy Jackson Knob; m. Sherrie Lynn Reese; children: Sarah, Stuart, Stephanie. B of Music Edn., U. Fla., 1985; M of Music Edn., U. Ark., 1994. Dir. of bands Hamiltion County H.S., Jasper, Fla., 1986—88, Lake Worth (Fla.) H.S., 1988—92; grad. asst. U. of Ark., Fayetteville, 1992—94; dir. of bands Mariner H.S., Cape Coral, Fla., 1994—97, Hopkinsville H.S., Hopkinsville, Ky., 1998—2002. Judge Drum Corps Midwest, 2000—, Drum Corps Internat., 2001—; bd. dirs. Tri-State Circuit for the

Pagentry Arts. Composer, arranger: marching band show music various bands, musician, arranger: Walt Disney World, 1988. Mem. local planning commn. Christian County Sch. Bd., Hopkinsville, 2000—02. Recipient Excellence in Tchg. Color Guard award, Ky. Gen. Assembly, 1999. Mem.: Nat. Band Assn., Internat. Assn. of Jazz Educators, Music Educators Nat. Conf., Ky. Music Educators Assn. (band pres dist. 3 2002—), Lambda Kappa Alpha, Phi Mu Alpha. Avocations: golf, aviation. Home: 203 Hunting Creek Rd Hopkinsville KY 42240 Office: Hopkinsville HS 430 Koffman Dr Hopkinsville KY 42240 Personal E-mail: sknob@charter.net.

KNOBBE, LOUIS JOSEPH, lawyer, educator; b. Carroll, Iowa, Apr. 6, 1932; s. Louis C. and Elsie M. (Praeger) Knobbe; m. Jeanette M. Sganga, Apr. 3, 1954; children: Louis, Michael, Nancy, John, Catherine. BSEE, Iowa State U., 1953; JD, Loyola U., L.A., 1959. Bar: Calif. 1960, U.S. Supreme Ct. 1963, U.S. Patent and Trademark Office. Tech. staff Bell Tel. Labs., 1953-54; patent engr. GE, Washington, 1955—56, N.Am. Aviation, Downey, Calif., 1956-59; patent lawyer Beckman Instruments, Fullerton, Calif., 1959-62; co-founder, ptnr. Knobbe, Martens, Olson & Bear, Newport Beach, Calif., 1962—2002, of counsel, 2003—. Lectr. Computer Law Assn., Inc., L.A., L.A. Intellectual Property Law Assn., San Diego Bar Assn., adj. prof. Sch. Law San Diego U., 1987—; mem. engring. adv. bd. U. Calif., Irvine. Co-author: (book) Attorney's Guide to Trade Secrets, 1972, 2d edit., 1996, update, 2002, How to Handle Basic Patent, 1992; contbg. author (book) Using Intellectual Property Rights to Protect Domestic Markets, 1986; contbr. articles to profl. jours. Bd. dirs. Orange County (Calif.) Performing Arts Ctr., 1975—83; past pres. Philharm. Soc. Orange County; past bd. mem., past v.p. Opera Pacific, Orange County; bd. visitors Loyola Law Sch., 2000—. Recipient Jurisprudence award, Anti-Defamation League, 1988. Fellow: Inst. Advancement Engring.; mem.: IEEE (past chmn. Orange County sect., Centennial medal 1984), ABA, Licensing Execs. Soc., San Diego Patent Law Assn., Orange County Patent Law Assn. (lectr.), Orange County Bar Assn., State Bar Calif., Am. Arbitration Soc. (panel neutrals), Am. Intellectual Property Law Assn. (lectr.), Balboa Yacht Club, First Friday Friars, Santa Ana North Rotary, Pacific Club, Eta Kappa Nu, Tau Beta Pi, Phi Kappa Phi. Avocations: boating, still and video photography, travel and exploration in lake powell, death valley, deserts of Arizona and Baja California. Office: 2040 Main St Fl 14 Irvine CA 92614 E-mail: LKnobbe@kmob.com.

KNOBEL, DALE THOMAS, history educator, university administrator; b. East Cleveland, Ohio, Sept. 14, 1949; s. Harry Spencer and Gwynne Ann K.; m. Tina Hess Jamieson, June 19, 1971; children: Allison Hess. BA, Yale U., 1971; PhD, Northwestern U., 1976. Asst. prof. history Northwestern U., Evanston, Ill., 1976-77, Tex. A&M U., College Station, 1977-84, assoc. prof. history, 1984-96, dir. univ. hons. prog., 1987-92, exec. dir. honors programs and acad. scholarships, 1992-95, assoc. provost for undergrad. programs, 1995-96; provost, dean of faculty, prof. history Southwestern U., Georgetown, Tex., 1996-98; pres., prof. history Denison U., Granville, Ohio, 1998—. Author: America for the Americans: The Nativist Movement in the United States, 1996, Paddy and the Republic: Ethnicity and Nationality in Antebellum America, 1985; co-author: Prejudice, 1982; book rev. editor Jour. of Early Republic, 1987-89; contbr. articles to profl. jours. Chmn. Bryan Hist. Landmark Commn., 1987-93; trustee Bryan Tx.Pub. Libr., 1989-92, Brazos Valley Mus. of Natural History, 1994-96, Inst. for Internat. Edn. Students, Chgo., 1999—, trustee, Newark Midland Theater Assn.,1999., vice chmn. Ohio Found of Ind. Coll., 2002-, v.p. North Coast Athletic Conf., 2002-, Am. Assn. State and Local History grantee, 1981; NEH grantee, 1978; NSF grantee, 1972-74; W.K. Kellogg Found. grantee, 1985-87. Mem. Nat. Collegiate Hons. Coun., Orgn. Am. Historians, Immigration History Soc., Soc. for Hist. of the Early Am. Republic, Univ. Club Chgo., Rocky For Hunt and Country Club, Phi Alpha Theta, Omicron Delta Kappa, Phi Kappa Phi, Phi Beta Delta. Methodist. Home: 204 Broadway W Granville OH 43023-1120*

KNOBLER, ALFRED EVERETT, ceramic engineer, manufacturing company executive, publisher; b. N.Y.C., Mar. 4, 1915; s. Samuel and Mildred (Weisz) K.; children— Peter Stephen, Joanna Gabin. BS in Ceramic Engring, Va. Poly. Inst., 1938. Engr. U.S. War Dept., Phila., 1942-44, Fed. Tel. & Tel. N.Y.C., 1944-45; CEO Pilgrim Glass Corp., Ceredo, W.Va., 1949—; pres. Knobler Internat. Ltd., Moonachie, N.J., 1950—, Knobler Energy Assocs., Inc., West Hamlin, W.Va., 1976—. Home: 301 W 57th St New York NY 10019-3114 E-mail: alfknobler@aol.com.

KNOBLOCH, FERDINAND J. psychiatrist, educator; b. Prague, Czechoslovakia, Aug. 15, 1916; emigrated to Can., 1970; s. Ferdin and Marie (Verunac) K.; m. Susana Hartman (dec. 1944 victim of Holocaust); m. Jirina Skorkovska, Sept. 5, 1947; children: Katerina, Yohana. Maturity degree, Realgymnasium, Prague, 1927-35; student med. sch., Charles U., Prague, 1935-46; psychoanalytic tng., 1945-53. Successively lectr., asst. prof., assoc. prof. psychiatry Charles U., 1946-70; mem. faculty U. B.C., Vancouver, Can., 1970—, prof. psychiatry, 1971-83, prof. emeritus, 1983—; clin. dir. Day House Univ. Hosp., 1972-90. Vis. prof. U. Havana, 1963, U. Ill., Chgo., 1968-69, Columbia U., 1969-70, Albert Einstein Med. Coll., 1970; pres. European seminar mental health and family WHO, 1961, 3d Internat. Congress Psychodrama, 1968; co-chmn. Internat. Symposium Non-Verbal Aspects and Techniques of Psychotherapy, 1974; hon. dir. psychodrama Moreno Inst., N.Y.C., 1974. Author: (with Jirina Knobloch) Forensic Psychiatry, 1967 (award Czechoslovak Med. Soc. 1968), Psychotherapy, 1968, Neurosis and You, 1962, 63, 68, Integrated Psychotherapy, 1979 (transl. into German 1983, Japanese 1984, Czech 1993, Chinese, 1995), Integrated Psychotherapy in Action, 1999; contbr. articles on psychotherapy integration, psychology of music and evolutionary psychology to profl. jours. Political prisoner of Gestapo, 1943-45. Mem. Czechoslovak Soc. Advancement Psychoanalysis and Integration of Psychotherapy (pres. 1968-72), Am. Acad. Psychoanalysis, Polish Psychiat. Assn. (corr.), Am. Psychiat. Assn., Can. Psychiat. Assn., Am. Group Psychotherapy Assn., Can. Soc. for Integrated Psychotherapy and Psychoanalysis (pres. 1972—), World Psychiat. Assn. (co-chmn. sect. psychotherapy 1983-93, chmn. 1993-96). E-mail: knobloch@interchange.ubc.ca.

KNODT, ELLEN ANDREWS, English language educator, writer; b. Mpls., Jan. 14, 1943; d. Jack Dunlap Andrews and Betty Louise (Johnson) Andrews Locke; m. Kenneth S. Knodt, June 20, 1964; 1 child, Andrew Snowden. BA, Northwestern U., 1964; MA, Purdue U., 1971; ArtsD, Carnegie-Mellon U., 1982. Tchr. English Valparaiso (Ind.) Cmty. Schs., 1964-67, Williamsburg (Va.) Schs., 1967-70; grad. asst. Purdue U., West Lafayette, Ind., 1970-71; lectr. Montgomery County C.C., Blue Bell, Pa., 1972—76; instr. English Pa. State U., Abington, 1976—82, asst. prof. English, 1982-89, assoc. prof. English, 1989—2003, head divsn. arts and humanities, 1997—2003, prof. English, 2003—. Author: Writing: Process and Purpose, 1986, Making Progress: From Paragraph to Essay, 1991; review editor Teaching English in the Two-Year College, 1994—2000; editor: Understanding Ourselves: Readings for Developing Writers, 1996; contbr. articles. Ednl. adv. coun. Upper Dublin Township, Ft. Washington, Pa., 1995-2000. Mem. Nat. Coun. Tchrs. of English, Conf. Coll. Composition and Comm., Ernest Hemingway Soc. Office: Pa State U 1600 Woodland Rd Abington PA 19001-3918 E-mail: eak1@psu.edu.

KNOEBEL, SUZANNE BUCKNER, cardiologist, medical educator; b. Ft. Wayne, Ind., Dec. 13, 1926; d. Doster and Marie (Lewis) Buckner. AB, Goucher Coll., 1948; MD, Ind. U.-Indpls., 1960. Diplomate: Am. Bd. Internal Medicine. Asst. prof. medicine Ind. U., Indpls., 1966-69, assoc. prof., 1969-72, prof., 1972-77, Krannert prof., 1977—. Asst. dean rsch. Ind. U., Indpls., 1975-85; assoc. dir. Krannert Inst. Cardiology, Indpls., 1974-90; asst. chief cardiology sect. Richard L. Roudebush VA Med. Ctr., Indpls., 1982-90; editor-in-chief ACC Current Jour. Rev., 1992-2000. Fellow Am. Coll. Cardiology (v.p. 1980-81, pres. 1982-83); mem. Am. Fedn. Clin. Research, Assn. Univ. Cardiologists Office: Krannert Inst 1701 N Senate Ave Indianapolis IN 46202 E-mail: sknoebel@iupui.edu.

KNOEDLER, ELMER L. retired chemical engineer; b. Gloucester, N.J., Feb. 12, 1912; s. Elmer L. and Carolyn (Belle) K.; m. Mabel Dyer Todd, Jan. 15, 1966; children: Dianne, Homer. ME, Cornell U., 1934, MS, 1936; PhD, Columbia, 1952. Registered profl. engr., 3 states. With Atlantic Mfg. Co., 1934-35; asst. supt. charge Davis Emergency Equipment Co., 1937-38; charge research and devel. metal powder process Metals Disintegrating Co., 1939-41, cons. chem. engr., sr. field engr., 1941-82; partner Sheppard T. Powell & Assocs., Balt. Past mem. Md. Bd. for Registration Engrs. and Land Surveyors. Contbr. numerous articles tech., profl. jours. Fellow Am. Inst. Chemists, ASME (past chmn. com. water conditioning and indsl. waste); mem. Am. Inst. Chem. Engrs. (chmn. Balt. sect. 1953), Am. Chem. Soc., Am. Inst. Cons. Engrs., Sigma Xi, Phi Lambda Upsilon. Home: 400 Avinger Ln Apt 321 Davidson NC 28036-9759 Office: 1915 Aliceanna St Baltimore MD 21231-3014

KNOEPFLMACHER, ULRICH CAMILLUS, literature educator, educator; b. Munich, June 26, 1931; U.S. citizen; s. George A. and Hilde (Weiss) K.; married; 4 children. AB, U. Calif., Berkeley, 1955, MA, 1957; PhD, Princeton U., 1961. From instr. to assoc. prof. U. Calif., Berkeley, 1961-69, Humanities Rsch. prof., 1966-67, 77; asst. dean U. Calif. Coll. Letters and Sciences, Berkeley, 1967-71; prof. U. Calif., Berkeley, 1969-79; prof. English Princeton U., 1979—, now William and Annie S. Paton Found. prof. ancient and modern lit. Vis. prof. Harvard U., 1971; Grad. prof. Tulsa U., 1979, Bread Loaf Sch. English, 1981, 83, 85, 87, NYU, 1982, Johns Hopkins U., 1983; adv. bd. Publs. MLA, 1977-81, SEL, 1979— VIJ, 1982—, Children's Lit., 1987—; dir. NEH summer seminars, 1975, 84, 86, 89, 90, 91, 95, 99. Author: Religious Humanism and the Victorian Novel, 1965, George Eliot's Early Novels: The Limits of Realism, 1968, Laughter and Despair: Readings in Ten Novels of the Victorian Era, 1971, Emily Bronte's Wuthering Heights, 1988, Wuthering Heights: A Study, 1994, Ventures into Childland: Victorians, Fairy Tales, and Femininity, 1998; editor: Francis Newman: Phases of Faith, 1970, George MacDonald's Fairy Tales, 1999, Frances Hodgson Burnett's A Little Princess, 2002; co-editor: Nature and the Victorian Imagination, 1977, The Endurance of Frankenstein: Essays on Mary Shelley's Novel, 1978, Forbidden Journeys: Fairy Tales and Fantasies by Victorian Women Writers, 1992, Cross-Writing the Child and the Adult, 1997; cons. editor Teaching Children's Literature: Issues, Pedagogy, Resources, 1992; edit. bd. publs. MLA, 1981-83. Recipient Disting. Tchg. award Acad. Senate U. Calif., 1977; Am. Coun. Learned Soc. fellow, 1965, Guggenheim fellow, 1969-70, 87-88, sr. fellow NEH, 1972-73, 91-92, sr. fellow Humanities Coun., Princeton U., 1975, Rockefeller Found. sr. fellow, 1983-84, Nat. Humanities Ctr. fellow, 1996. Mem. MLA, Nat. Coun. Tchrs. English, N.E. Victorian Assn., Children's Lit. Assn. Office: Princeton U Dept English McCosh Hall Princeton NJ 08544-1016 E-mail: uknopf@princeton.edu.

KNOKE, DAVID HARMON, sociology educator; b. Phila., Mar. 4, 1947; s. Donald Glenn and Frances Harriet (Dunn) Knoke; m. Joann Margaret Robar, Aug. 29, 1970; 1 child, Margaret Frances. BA, U. Mich., 1969, MSW, 1971, PhD, 1972; MA, U. Chgo., 1970. Asst. prof. sociology Ind. U., Bloomington, 1972-75, assoc. prof., 1975-81, prof., 1981-85, dir. Inst. Social Rsch. and Ctr. for Survey Rsch., 1982-84; prof. sociology U. Minn., Mpls., 1985—, chmn., 1989-92, undergrad. dir., 1995-98, grad. dir., 1998—2002. Mem. sociology program rev. panel NSF, 1981-83; mem. sociology rev. panel Fulbright Scholars, 1993-95; mem. sociology com. Grad. Records Exams., 1998-2000. Author: Change and Continuity in American Politics, 1976, (with Peter J. Burke) Log-Linear Models, 1980, (with James R. Wood) Organized for Action, 1981, (with George W. Bohrnstedt and Alisa Potter Mee) Statistics for Social Data Analysis, 1982, 4th edit., 2002, (with James H. Kuklinski) Network Analysis, 1982, (with Edward O. Laumann) The Organizational State, 1987, Organizing for Collective Action, 1990, Political Networks, 1990, (with George W. Bohrnstedt) Basic Social Statistics, 1991, (with Franz Pappi, Jeffrey Broadbent and Yutaka Tsujinaka) Comparing Policy Networks, 1996, (with Arne Kalleberg, Peter Marsden and Joe Spaeth) Organizations in America, 1996, (with Peter Capelli, Laurie Bassi, Harry Katz, Paul Osterman and Michael Useem) Change at Work, 1997, Changing Organizations, 2001. Recipient NIMH Rsch. Scientist Devel. award, 1977-82; 11 rsch. grants NSF. Mem. Merit scholar, 1965-69, Fulbright Sr. Rsch. scholar, Germany, 1989, scholar of the Coll. U. Minn., 1996-99; Ctr. for Advanced Study in the Behavioral Scis. fellow, 1992-93. Mem. Am. Sociol. Assn. (chair orgns. and occupation sect. 1992-93), Sociol. Rsch. Assn., Acad. of Mgmt., Internat. Network for Social Network Analysis, European Group for Orgnl. Studies. Unitarian Universalist. Home: 7305 Wooddale Ave S Minneapolis MN 55435-4157 Office: U Minn Dept Sociology Minneapolis MN 55455 E-mail: knoke@atlas.socsci.umn.edu.

KNOLL, ANDREW HERBERT T. biology educator; b. West Reading, Pa., Apr. 23, 1951; s. Robert Samuel and Anna Augusta (Meyer) K.; m. Marsha Craig, June 22, 1974; children: Kirsten C., Robert A. BA with highest honors, Lehigh U., 1973; MA, Harvard U., 1974, PhD, 1977; PhD (hon.), Uppsala U., Sweden, 1996; DSc (hon.), Lehigh U., 1998. Asst. prof. geology Oberlin Coll., Ohio, 1977-82; assoc. prof. Harvard U., Cambridge, Mass., 1982-85, prof. biology, 1985-2000, curator bot. mus., 1985—, prof. earth and planetary sci., 1985—, chmn. dept. organismic and evolutionary biology, 1992-98, Fisher prof. natural history, 2000—, assoc. dean faculty Arts and Scis., 2000—03. Mem. com. on planetary biology U.S. Space Sci. Bd., 1982-88, NRC Bd. on Earth Scis., 1987-88, 92-95, space studies bd., 1989-90, 97-2000; Crosby vis. lectr. MIT, 1999; mem. sci. team NASA MER 2003 Mars Mission. Assoc. editor Paleobiology, 1980-92, Precambrian Rsch., 1985—, Trends in Ecology and Evolution, 1987-92, Rev. of Palaeobotany and Palynology, 1987—, Am. Jour. Sci., 1990—, Geology, 1992-98, Palaios, 1996-2002, Palaeography Palaeoclimatology Palaeocology, 1997—, Internat. Jour. Plant Scis., 1998—; contbr. articles to profl. pubs. Bd. dirs. U.S. Nat. Mus. Nat. Hist., 1993-97. Named one of Time/CNN America's Best Scientists, 2002; recipient Walcott medal, Nat. Acad. Scis., 1987, Chang prize in paleontology, Am. Mus. Natural History, 2001; fellow, Geol. Soc. Am., Linnean Soc., London, Am. Acad. Arts and Scis., 1987, Guggenheim, 1987, AAAS; Vis. fellow, Gonville and Caius Coll., Cambridge, Eng., 1991—92. Fellow AAAS, European Union Geoscis. (hon.); mem. NAS, Bot. Soc. Am., Am. Philos. Soc., Paleontol. Soc. (Schuchert award 1987), Soc. Study Evolution, Phi Beta Kappa, Sigma Xi. Avocations: travel, reading, cooking, choral music. Office: Harvard Univ Botanical Museum 26 Oxford St Cambridge MA 02138-2902

KNOLL, AUGUST E. retired music educator; b. Des Moines, 1942; s. Ernest August and Edna Alberta Knoll. BME in Music Edn., Wartburg Coll., Waverly, IA, 1964; MA in Music Edn., U. Of Iowa, 1971. Instrumental music Wheatland Sch., Wheatland, Iowa, 1964—85, Calamus-Wheatland Sch., Wheatland, Iowa, 1985—2003; ret., 2003. Ch. musician St. Paul's United Ch. of Christ, Wheatland, Iowa, 1975, St. James Cath. Ch., Toronto, Iowa, 1994; performing musician Quad City Wind Ensemble, Davenport, Iowa, 1999. Recipient Karl L. King Disting. Svc. award, Iowa Bandmasters Assn., 1990, Phillip Sehmann Disting. Tchg. Award, North East Iowa Bandmasters Assn., 1994. Lutheran. Avocations: travel, camping, reading. Home: PO Box 486 Wheatland IA 52777

KNOLL, FLORENCE SCHUST, architect, designer; b. Saginaw, Mich., May 24, 1917; d. Frederick E. and M. Haisting Schust; m. Hans G. Knoll, July 1, 1946 (dec. 1955); m. Harry Hood Bassett, June 22, 1958 (dec. 1991). Student, Cranbrook Art Acad., Bloomfield Hills, Mich., 1935-37, Archtl. Assn., London, 1938-39; B.Arch., Ill. Inst. Tech., Chgo., 1941; D.F.A. (hon.), Parsons Sch. Design, 1979. Archtl. draftsman, designer Gropius & Breuer, Boston, 1941; design dir. Knoll Planning Unit, 1942-55; pres. Knoll Internat., N.Y.C., 1955-65; pvt. practice architecture and designer Coconut Grove, Fla., 1965—. Named to Ill. Inst. Tech. Hall of Fame, 1982; recipient Athena award R.I. Sch. Design, 1982, Nat. Medal of Arts, 2003. Mem. AIA (Gold medal 1961), Indsl. Designers Am. (hon.)

KNOLL, GREGG A. artist, printmaker, educator; b. Milw., May 10, 1949; s. Gilbert Alan and Helen A. (Burek) K. BFA with honors, Layton Sch. Art & Design, 1973; MA, U. Iowa, 1977, MFA, 1979. Founder and master printer Green River Press, Iowa City, 1976—, profl. artist, 1985—; founder handpapermaking facility U. Iowa, Iowa City, 1979-84, vis. artist (faculty), 1979-84. Juror Graham Scholarship com. U. Iowa, 1980-83; head press restoration team Smithsonian Instn., Washington, 1982; cons. Grand Valley State Coll., Allendale, Mich., 1984, Graphic Chem. and Ink Co., Villa Park, Ill., 1999-2000; participant watercolor workshops Wustum Mus. Fine Arts, Racine, Wis., 1990, Mount Mercy Coll., Cedar Rapids, 1976, Sioux City Art Ctr., 1977. Exhibited in group shows at Chautauqua (N.Y.) Art Assn. Galleries, 1978, Cheney Cowles Meml. Mus., SPokane, Wash., 1979, Farthing Art Gallery, Boon, N.C., 1980, Nicolet Coll. and Tech. Inst., Rhinelander, Wis., 1989, Wustum Mus. Fine Arts, 1989, Wausau (Wis.) Ctr. for Visual Arts, 1991, Eau Claire (Wis.) Regional Arts Ctr., 1993, Regional Art Exhbn., Kenosha, Wis., 1993, Appalachian State U., Boone, N.C., 1995, North Valley Art League Gallery, Redding, Calif., 1996, others; represented in permanent collections at L.L. Pelling Co., Iowa City, U. Iowa hosps. and clinics, U. Iowa Mus. Art, Northwestern Mutual Ins. Co., Milw., Wustum Mus. Fine Arts; author: (with others) Papermaking, 1977, Handmade Paper Today, 1979. Recipient Grumbacher Gold Medallion Mdse. award Wustum Mus. Fine Arts, 1989, 2d Pl. award 1998, Mary Ann Naczinski Meml. Purchase award, 1989, S.C. Johnson Wax Purchase award, 1990, 1st Place award 7th Annual Regional Art Exhbn. Gallery Ten, Rockford, Ill., 1993, No. Nat. Art Competition Rotary Club, 1993, 1st place Best of Show award Anderson Arts Ctr., Kenosha, Wis., 2001, Thomas Newman Meml. Purchase award Wustum Mus. Fine Arts, 2001, others; grantee U. Iowa, 1975. Mem. U. Iowa Alumni Assn., Coll. Art Assn. Am., Milw. Art Mus. Avocations: billiards, fishing, archaeology, astronomy. Office: Green River Press PO Box 356 South Milwaukee WI 53172-0356

KNOLL, JEANNETTE THERIOT, state supreme court justice; b. Baton Rouge; m. Jerold Edward Knoll; children: Triston Kane, Eddie Jr., Edmond Humphries, Blake Theriot, Jonathan Paul. BA in Polit. Sci., Loyola U., 1966, JD, 1969; LLM, U. Va., 1996; studied with Maestro Adler, Mannes Coll. of Music, 1962-63. Criminal defense atty., first asst. dist. atty. Twelfth Jud. Dist. Ct. Avoyelles Parish, 1972-82; gratuitous atty., advisor U.S. Selective Svc., Marksville, La.; judge (3d cir.) U.S. Ct. of Appeal, 1982-93; justice La. Supreme Ct., 1997—. Instr. La. Jud. Coll.; chair CLE La. Ct. of Appeal Judges; mem. vis. com. Loyola U. Sch. of Law, Loyola Music Sch.; bd. dirs. Loyola U. Alumni Assn.; former mem. state bd. of La. commn. on law enforcement and criminal justice. Past pres. Bus. and Profl. Women's Club; Marksville C. of C.; active Am. Legion Aux. Recipient scholarship Met. Opera Assn., New Orleans Opera Guild. Office: La Supreme Ct 301 Loyola Ave New Orleans LA 70112-1814*

KNOLL, ROBERT EDWIN, English educator; b. Liberty, Nebr., Feb. 3, 1922; s. Louis Jarrett and Marie (von Goetz) K.; m. Virginia Elizabeth Koehler, June 29, 1953; children: Elizabeth, Sarah, Benjamin. BA, U. Nebr., 1943; MA, U. Minn., 1947, PhD, 1950. From asst. prof. to prof. English U. Nebr., Lincoln, 1950-90, George Holmes prof., 1980-88, Paula and D.B. Varner prof., 1988-90, Varner prof. emeritus, 1990—. Founding fellow centennial ednl. program, a cluster coll. at U. Nebr., 1969-72. Author: Prairie University, A History of the University of Nebraska, 1995 (cert. Am. Assn. State and Local History 1997); editor: McAlmon and the Lost Generation, 1962, Landmark edit., 1976, Ben Jonson's Plays, An Introduction, 1964, Christopher Marlowe, 1969, Conversations with Wright Morris, 1977, Weldon Kees and the Midcentury Generation, Letters 1935-1955, 1986, 2d edit., 2003. Bd. govs. Willa Cather Pioneer Meml., 1974-95. 1st lt. U.S. Army, 1943-46. Woods fellow Warburg Inst., London, 1959-60; Fulbright prof., Graz, Austria, 1966-67; fellow Nat. Humanities Inst., Yale U., 1977-78; named Nebr. Prof. of Yr., 1988, Nebraskan of Yr., Rotary, 1989; recipient award for tchg. Coun. for Advancement and Support of Edn., 1988, others. Mem. AAUP, MLA, Nat. Coun. Tchrs. English, Shakespeare Assn. Am. (founding trustee 1972-76), Phi Beta Kappa. Democrat. Presbyterian. Home: 2818 S 24th St Lincoln NE 68502-4907

KNOLLENBERG, JOSEPH (JOE KNOLLENBERG), congressman; b. Mattoon, Ill., Nov. 28, 1934; m. Sandie Knollenberg; children: Martin, Stephen. Student, Eastern Ill. U. CLU. Agent, owner ins. co., 1960-93; mem. 103rd-106th Congresses from 9th Mich. Dist. (formerly 11th), 1993—, mem. budget com. appropriations, mem. stds. of offcl. conduct coms. Past chmn., Birmingham Cable TV Community Adv. Bd., 18th Dist. Rep. Com., Rep. Com. Oakland County, 1978-86; past pres. St. Bede's Parish Coun., Evergreen Sch. PTA (Birmingham Sch. Dist.), Bloomfield Glens Homeowner's Assn., Cranbrook Homeowner's Assn.; past coord. Southfield Ad Hoc Park and Recreation Devel. Com.; past mem. Southfield Mayor's Wage and Salary Com.; chmn. Candidate Assistance Com./State Com., Oakland County Campaign, 1978; former regional/vice chair 17th Dist. Com., 1975-77; mem. Rep. State Com.; exec. com. mem. and fin. com. Rep. Com. Oakland County; founder, mem. Rep. Leadership Com. Oakland County, 1984—; mem. Allstate Ins. Co's P.A.C.; del. Rep. Nat. Conv., 1980; del. to every state convention since 1974. Named chmn. of one of the top twenty-five counties in the country by Rep. Nat. Com. Mem. Am. Soc. Chartered Life Underwriters, Detroit Assn. Life Underwriters, Oakland County Lincoln Rep. Club, Troy C. of C. (current vice chmn.). Republican. Office: US Ho Reps 2349 Rayburn HOB Washington DC 20515-2211 also: 30833 Northwestern Hwy Ste 100 Farmington Hills MI 48334*

KNOLLENBERG, KIMBERLY See GOFF, KIMBERLY

KNOLLER, GUY DAVID, lawyer; b. N.Y.C., July 23, 1946; s. Charles and Odette Knoller; children: Jennifer Judy, Geoffrey David. BA cum laude, Bloomfield (N.J.) Coll., 1968; JD cum laude, Ariz. State U., 1971. Bar: Ariz. 1971, U.S. Dist. Ct. Ariz. 1971, U.S. Supreme Ct. 1976. Trial atty. atty. gen.'s hons. program Dept. Justice, 1971-72; atty., adv. NLRB, 1972-73, field atty. region 28, 1972-74; assoc. Powers, Ehrenreich, Boutell & Kurn, Phoenix, 1974-79; ptnr. Froimson & Knoller, Phoenix, 1979-81; sole practice Phoenix, 1985—; of counsel Burns & Burns. Mem. bd. visitors Ariz. State U. Coll. Law, 1975-76; pres. Ariz. Theatre Guild, 1990, 91. Fellow Ariz. Bar Found.; mem. ABA, State Bar Ariz. (chmn. labor rels. sect. 1977-78), Ariz. State U. Coll. Law Alumni Assn. (pres. 1977). Office: 2828 N Central Ave Ste 1110 Phoenix AZ 85004-1028

KNOOP, VERN THOMAS, civil engineer, consultant; b. Paola, Kans., Nov. 19, 1932; s. Vernon Thomas and Nancy Alice (Christian) K. Student, Kans. U., 1953-54; BSCE, Kans. State U., 1959. Registered profl. engr., Calif. Surveyor James L. Bell, Surveyors and Engrs., Overland Park, Kans., 1954; engr. asst. to county engr. Miami County Hwy. Dept., Paola, 1955; engr. State of Calif. Dept. Water Resources, L.A., 1959-85, sr. engr., 1986-88, chief, water supply evaluations sect. L.A., Glendale, 1989—. Hydrology tchr. State of Calif. Dept. Water Resources, L.A., 1984; mem. Interagency Drought Task Force, Sacramento, 1988-91. Mem. Jefferson Ednl. Found., Washington, 1988-91, Heritage Found., Washington, 1988—, Nat. Rep. Senatorial Com., Washington, 1990—, Rep. Presdl. Task Force, Washington, 1990-91. With U.S. Army, 1956-57. Decorated Good Conduct medal U.S. Army, Germany, 1957. Mem. ASCE (life, dir. L.A. sect. hydraulics/water resources mgmt. tech. group 1985-86, chmn. 1984-85), Profl. Engrs. Calif. Govt. (dist. suprs. rep. 1986—), Am. Assn. Individual Investors (life), L.A. World Affairs Coun., Singles Internat. Baptist. Home: 116 N Berendo St Los Angeles CA 90004-4711 Office: State Calif Dept Water Resources 770 Fairmont Ave Glendale CA 91203-1035 E-mail: vernk@msn.com.

KNOPF, ALFRED, JR., retired publisher; b. White Plains, N.Y., June 17, 1918; s. Alfred A. and Blanche (Wolf) K.; m. Alice Laine, July 27, 1952; children— Alison, Susan, David. Grad., Phillips Exeter Acad., 1937; AB, Union Coll., Schenectady, 1942. With Atheneum Pubs., N.Y.C., 1959-88, chm. bd., 1964-88. Vis. chmn. Scribner Book Cos.; sr. v.p. MacMillan Pub. Co. (ret.). Capt. USAAF, 1941-45. Mem. Delta Upsilon. Clubs: Dutch Treat (N.Y.C.); Tavern (Chgo.). Home: 530 E 72nd St Apt 18F New York NY 10021-4864

KNOPF, BARRY ABRAHAM, lawyer, educator; b. Passaic, N.J., May 11, 1946; s. Edward and Sonia (Sameth) K.; children: Elisa, Scott. Student, Rutgers U., 1968, JD, 1972. Bar: N.J. 1972, U.S. Dist. Ct. N.J. 1972, U.S. Tax Ct. 1975, U.S. Supreme Ct. 1975, U.S. Ct. Appeals (3d cir.) 1981; cert. civil trial atty. Nat. Bd. Trial Advocacy, N.J. Supreme Ct. Assoc. Cohn & Lifland, Saddle Brook, N.J., 1972-75, ptnr., 1975—. Instr. N.J. Inst. for Continuing Legal Edn., 1982—, Nat. Inst. Trial Advocacy, 1989—; adj. faculty Hofstra U. Sch. of Law, 2000. Co-author: Professional Negligence, Law of Malpractice in New Jersey, 1979, 5th edit., 2001, Personal Injury Litigation Practice in New Jersey, 1990, Civil Trial Preparation, Practical skills Series, 1992, 2d edit., 1996, New Jersey Product Liability Law, 1994. V.p. Temple Beth Tikvah, Wayne, N.J., 1985-93, pres. 1993-95. Mem. Morris Pashman Inn of Ct. (master 1998—). Home: 1014 Smith Manor Blvd West Orange NJ 07052-4227 Office: Cohn Lifland Pearlman Herrmann & Knopf Park 80 West 1 Saddle Brook NJ 07663 E-mail: bak@njlawfirm.com.

KNOPF, FRITZ L. biologist; b. Aurora, Ohio; s. Fred and Mary Knopf. BA, Hiram Coll., Hiram, OH, 1967; MS, Utah State U., Logan, Utah, 1973, PhD, 1975. Asst. prof. Okla. State U., Stillwater, Okla., 1976—76; sr. scientist US

Geol. Survey, Fort Collins, Colo., 1980—. Editor: (book) Ecology and Conservation of Great Plains Vertebrated, Prairie Conservation. With US Army, 1969—70. Office: US Geological Survey 2150 Centre Ave Fort Collins CO 80526-8118

KNOPF, KENYON ALFRED, economist, educator; b. Cleve., Nov. 24, 1921; s. Harold C. and Emma A. (Underwood) K.; m. Madelyn Lee Siddy Trebilcock, Mar. 28, 1953 (dec. June 1999); children— Kristin Lee, Mary George. AB magna cum laude with high honors in Econs., Kenyon Coll., 1942; MA in Econs.; PhD, Harvard U., 1949; LLD (hon.), Kenyon Coll., 1993. Mem. faculty Grinnell Coll., 1949-67, prof. econs., 1960-67, Jentzen prof., 1961-67, chmn. dept., 1958-60, chmn. div. social studies, 1962-64, chmn. faculty, 1964-67; dean coll. Whitman Coll., Walla Walla, Wash., 1967-70, prof. econs., 1967-89, Hollon Parker prof. econs., 1985-89, prof. emeritus, 1989—, provost, 1970-81, dean faculty, 1970-78, acting pres., 1974-75; pub. interest dir. Fed. Home Loan Bank, Seattle, 1976-83. Mem. council undergrad. assessment program Ednl. Testing Service, 1977-80 Author: (with Robert H. Haveman) The Market System, 4th edit, 1981; A Lexicon of Economics, 1991; editor: Introduction to Economics Series (9 vols.), 1966, 2d edit., 1970-71; co-editor: (with James H. Strauss) The Teaching of Elementary Economics, 1960. Mem. youth coun. City of Grinnell, 1957—59; mem. Walla Walla County Mental Health Bd., 1968—75, Walla Walla Civil Svc. Commn., 1978—84, chmn., 1981—84; mem. Grinnell City Coun., 1964—67; pres. Walla Walla County Human Svcs. Adminstrv. Bd., 1975—77; mem. Ia. adv. coun. SBA; tax aide AARP/IRS Tax Counseling for Elderly, 1987—98, local coord., 1990—91, assoc. dist. coord. S.E. Wash., 1991—94, assoc. dist. coord. tng., 1994—98; mem. planning commn. Swinomish Indian Tribal Cmty., 2002—; bd. dirs. Skagit County Boys & Girls Club, 2001—; mem. planning commn. Swinomish Indian Trial Cmty., 2002—; bd. dirs. Walla Walla United Fund, 1968—76, pres., 1973; bd. dirs. Shelter Bay Cmty., Inc., 1995—2003, v.p., 1995—97, pres., 1997—2003; bd. dirs. La Conner Cmty. Scholarship Found., 1997—, La Conner Boys and Girls Club, 1999—, pres., 2001—03; bd. dirs. Skagit County Boys and Girls Club, 2003—. With USAF, 1942—46, PTO. Social Sci. Rsch. Coun. grantee, 1951-52. Mem.: Am. Conf. Acad. Deans (exec. com. 1970—77, chmn. 1975), Am. Assn. Ret. Persons, LaConner Club, Kiwanis (pres. 2003—), Phi Beta Kappa. Office: 223 Skagit Way La Conner WA 98257-9602

KNOPF, TANA DARLENE, counselor, music educator; b. Des Moines, Oct. 19, 1951; d. Charles D. Sr. and Edith D. Smith; m. James E. Knopf, Aug. 7, 1982; children: Daniel P., Chandra D. BA, Met. State Coll., Denver, 1974; MEd, U. Colo., Denver, 1983. Instrumental music tchr. Denver Pub. Schs., 1974—2000, counselor, 2001—.

KNOPIK, CHRISTOPHER SCOTT, lawyer; b. South Bend, Ind., Nov. 8, 1959; s. Walter Michael and Ora Mae (Jones) K.; m. Andrea Kim Cheney, Nov. 12, 1988. BS, Fla. State U., 1980; JD, U. Va., 1983. Bar: Fla. 1983, U.S. Dist. Ct. (middle and so. dists.) Fla., U.S. Ct. Appeals (11th cir.), U.S. Supreme Ct. Law clk. U.S. Dist. Judge Hon. William Terrell Hodges, Middle Dist., Tampa, Fla., 1983-85; assoc. Holland and Knight, Tampa, Fla., 1985-86; shareholder Stagg, Hardy and Yerrid, Tampa, Fla., 1986-90, Yerrid, Knopik & Valenzuela, Tampa, Fla., 1990-96, Yerrid, Knopik & Mudano, Tampa, 1996-98, Yerrid, Knopik & Krieger, 1998-2000, KnopikKriegerVarner, Tampa, 2000—. Bd. cert. civil trial atty, Nat. Bd. of Trial Advocates, Am. Bd. of Trial Advocates, Million Dollar Advocates Forum. Dir., exec. com. YMCA of Hillsborough County, Tampa, 1983—, pres. downtown br., 1989-91; vol. Big Bros. of Hillsborough County, Tampa, 1982-97; prodr. Tampa Bay Performing Arts Ctr., 1990—; active Leadership Fla. Mem. Fla. Bar Assn. (bd. legal specialization and edn.), Hillsborough County Bar Assn. (trial lawyers sect., past chmn.), ATLA, Fed. Bar Assn. (pres.), Am. Inns of Ct. (master), Am. Judicature Soc., Maritime Law Assn. (proctor), Bay Area Vol. Lawyers Assn. Avocations: health and fitness, politics, reading, travel, sports. Office: KnopikKriegerVarner 406 S Morgan St Tampa FL 33602 E-mail: cknopik@kkvlaw.com.

KNOPIK, ROBERT, retail executive, consultant; b. Chgo., Nov. 29, 1945; s. Walter Robert and Josephine Kay Knopik; m. Penelope Gretchen Kraft, Nov. 13, 1993; children: Tracy, Cory, Kimberly. BS, Drake U., 1967. Tchr. Greenbrook North H.S., Northbrook, Ill., 1967—72; various mgmt. positions Inland Steel, Chgo., 1972—91; v.p. Inland Steel Industries, Chgo., 1991—98; exec. search cons. Boyden, Chgo., 1998; pres. Creative Apparel & Design, Rockford, Ill., 1999—2001, The Leadership Search Group, North Barrington, Ill., 2000—01, mng. dir., 2001—. Pres. Wynstone Homeowners Assn., Barrington, 1999—. Mem.: Wynstone Golf Club (bd. dirs. 2002—). Republican. Roman Catholic. Avocations: golf, skiing, gardening. Home: 19 Lakeside Ln North Barrington IL 60010 Office: The Leadership Search Group 300 Village Green Dr Lincolnshire IL 60069 Office Fax: 847-277-0436. E-mail: rwk72949@aol.com.

KNOPOFF, LEON, geophysics educator; b. L.A., July 1, 1925; s. Max and Ray (Singer) K.; m. Joanne Van Cleef, Apr. 9, 1961; children— Katherine Alexandra, Rachel Anne, Michael Van Cleef. Student, Los Angeles City Coll., 1941-42; BS in Elec Engring, Calif. Inst. Tech., 1944, MS in Physics, 1946, PhD in Physics, 1949. Asst., then assoc. prof. physics Miami U., Oxford, Ohio, 1948-50; mem. faculty UCLA, 1950—, prof. physics, 1961—, prof. geophysics, 1959—, rsch. musicologist, 1963—; assoc. dir. Inst. Geophysics and Planetary Physics, 1972-86; prof. geophysics Calif. Inst. Tech., 1962-63, research assoc. seismology, 1963-64; vis. prof. Technische Hochschule, Karlsruhe, Germany, 1966, Harvard U., 1972, U. Chile, Santiago, 1973. Chmn. U.S. Nat. Upper Mantle Com., 1963-71; sec. Internat. Upper Mantle Com., 1963-71; chmn. com. math. geophysics Internat. Union Geodesy and Geophysics, 1971-75; mem. Internat. Union Geodesy and Geophysics (U.S. nat. com.), 1973-75; vis. prof. U. Trieste, 1984. Recipient Wiechert medal German Geophys. Soc., 1978; Gold medal Royal Astron. Soc., 1979; NSF sr. postdoctoral fellow Cambridge (Eng.) U., 1960-61; Guggenheim Found. fellow, 1976-77; Selwyn Coll. Cambridge U. fellow. Fellow AAAS, Am. Acad. Arts and Scis., Royal Astron. Soc. (Jeffreys lectr.), Am. Geophys. Union (Gutenberg lectr. 1992), Nat. Acad. Scis., Seismol. Soc. Am. (hon., medal 1990); mem. Am. Phys. Soc., Am. Philosophical Soc., Phi Beta Kappa (hon.). Office: U Calif Dept Physics Los Angeles CA 90095-0001

KNOPP, MARVIN ISADORE, mathematics educator; b. Chgo., Jan. 4, 1933; s. Mitshel and Minnie (Israel) K.; m. Josephine Zadovsky, June 9, 1957 (div. 1998); children: Seth David, Yudah Benjamin, Abby Alissa, Elana Melissa. BS, U. Ill., 1954, A.M., 1955, PhD, 1958. Rsch. mathematician Space Tech. Labs., L.A., 1958-59; NSF postdoctoral fellow Inst. Advanced Study, Princeton, N.J., 1959-60; asst. prof. U. Wis., 1960-62, assoc. prof., 1962-67, prof., 1967-72; mathematician Nat. Bur. Standards, Washington, 1963-64; vis. prof. U. Basel, Switzerland, 1968-69; prof. U. Ill., Chgo., 1970-76, Temple U., Phila., 1976—, Bryn Mawr (Pa.) Coll., 1988-89. Mem. Inst. Advanced Study, Princeton, N.J., 1975, 78, 88; vis. prof. Ohio State U., spring 1979 Author: Theory of Area, 1969, Modular Functions in Analytic Number Theory, 1970, 2d edit., 1993; editor Ill. Jour. Math., 1971-78, The Ramanujan Jour., 1995—, Procs. of Conf. in Analytic Number Theory, 1981, others; contbr. articles to profl. jours. NSF grantee, 1960-90, Fulbright-Hays grantee NRC, 1975-76, Nat. Security Agy. grantee, 1990-93. Mem. Am. Math. Soc., London Math. Soc. Democrat. Jewish. Home: 410 Lancaster Ave Apt 221 Haverford PA 19041-1326 Office: Temple U Dept Math Philadelphia PA 19122

KNOPP, MICHAEL A. chemist, educator; b. Oswego, N.Y., Oct. 11, 1954; s. Neil James and Marlene Jeanette (Denbrock) Knopp. BA, Oswego State, N.Y., 1976, MS, 1980, PhD, Syracuse U., N.Y., 1989. Rsch. chemist Pfizer Ctrl. Rsch., Groton, Conn., 1980—82; tchg. asst. Syracuse (N.Y.) U., 1982—89; asst. prof. chemistry Miami U. of Ohio, Middletown, 1993—97, U. Maine at Presque Isle, 1997—. Asst. curator for chemistry Northern Maine Mus. Sci., Presque Isle, 1999—. Mem.: Am. Chem. Soc., Phi Kappa Phi. Democrat. Roman Catholic. Avocations: bicycling, history, literature, motorcycling. Home: 53 DuPont Dr Apt E3 Presque Isle ME 04769 Office: U Maine at Presque Isle 181 Main St Presque Isle ME 04769 E-mail: knoppm@polaris.umpi.maine.edu.

KNÖPPEL, HANS-ARMIN, librarian; b. Flensburg, Germany, Sept. 13, 1941; PhD, U. Kiel, Germany, 1969. Acquisition libr. Univ. Libr., Wuerzburg, Germany, 1972—91, chief libr. Greifswald, Germany, 1991—. Lutheran. Office: Greifswald Univ Bibliothek Friedrich Ludwig Jahn Str 14a D-17487 Greifswald Germany E-mail: knoeppel@mail.uni-greifswald.de.

KNORR, JOHN CHRISTIAN, entertainment executive, bandleader, producer; b. Crissey, Ohio, May 24, 1921; s. Reinhold Alfred and Mary (Rieth) K.; m. Jane Lucy Hammer, Nov. 8, 1941; children: Gerald William, Janice Grace Knorr Wilcox. Student, Ohio No. U., 1940-41. Violin soloist with Helen O'Connell, 1934-35; reed sideman Jimmy Dorsey, Les Brown and Sonny Dunham orchs., 1939-48; mem. theater pit orchs. and club shows, Ohio, 1949-57; leader Johnny Knorr Orch., Toledo, 1958—. Mgr. Centennial Ter.; owner Johnny Knorr Entertainment Agy.; bandleader, show producer; mem. Royal Ct. of Jesters #21, 1987. Recs. include Live at Franklin Park Mall, 1973, Let's Go Dancing, 1979, encore, 1984, (TV spl.) An Era of Swing, 1973, Live at Centennial Terrace, 1986, Let's Dance, 1989, Oh Johnny, 1997, One More Time, 2000. Trustee Presbyn. Ch. Served to cpl. AUS, 1944-45. Recipient outstanding dance band citations, Chgo., 1966, Des Moines, 1968, Las Vegas, 1969, Nat. Ballroom Operators Assn., Omaha, 1970, Entertainment Operators Assn., 1973; named Grand Duke of Toledo, King of the Hoboes, 1975; named to First Libbey H.S. Hall of Fame, 1994; winner in instrumental category Peoples Choice Awards for Performing Arts, 1997; inducted into Lake Erie West People's Choice Awards Hall of Fame, 1999. Mem. Am. Fedn. Musicians, Am. Legion, Exch. Club, Circus Fans Am., Masons, Shriners, Ind. Order Foresters. Home and Office: 1751 Fallbrook Rd Toledo OH 43614-3251

KNORTZ, HERBERT CHARLES, retired conglomerate company executive; b. Bklyn., Mar. 31, 1921; s. John Walter and Elizabeth (Grotyohann) K.; m. Lorraine Marion Kraut, Aug. 12, 1949; children: Steven Holbrook, Elizabeth Alyn, David Cartwright. BBA, St. Johns U., 1946, DCS (hon.), 1977; MBA, NYU, 1949. C.P.A., N.Y. Supervising clk. Bklyn. Trust Co., 1938-43; with Price Waterhouse & Co., N.Y.C., 1945-51; supr. standard costs Lever Bros. Co., 1951-55; mgr. cost dept. Crown Cork & Seal Co., 1955-56; asst. comptroller Royal McBee Corp., 1956-60; controller Mack Trucks, Inc., 1960-61; dep. comptroller ITT Corp., 1961-63, v.p., comptroller, 1963-66, sr. v.p., comptroller, 1966-73, exec. v.p., comptroller, 1973-85, exec. v.p., 1985-86. Ptnr. Cortina Shops, 1957-60, Lewisboro Tennis Club, 1971-72; trustee Corp. Property Investors, 1973-91; bd. dirs., nominating com., audit com. Xtra Corp., 1990-99; lectr. profl. meetings. Contbr. to jours.; also Financial Executives Handbook; Editor: Food for Thought. Trustee Vincent Ross Research Found.; mem. bus. adv. bd. St. John's U. Served with USAAF, 1943-45. Mem. Fin. Execs. Inst. (v.p. research found., mem. internat. com.), Am. Mgmt. Assn. (gen. mgmt council, audit com., trustee), Am. Contract Bridge League, Am. Inst. C.P.A.s, Nat. Assn. Accountants (nat. pres. 1985-86, nat. chmn. 1986-87), Inst. Mgmt. Accounting (bd. regents), Internat. Assn. Fin. Exec. Insts., Acad. Acctg. Historians, Delta Mu Delta, Beta Alpha Psi, Beta Gamma Sigma. Clubs: Economics, Accountants, Board Room, Armonk Tennis, Flint River Forests. Home: 14 Manor Rd Ridgefield CT 06877-4908 *The weak pursuit of small goals by little people produces little progress; but the intense pursuit of great goals by little people can achieve surprisingly great gains.*

KNORTZ, WALTER ROBERT, accountant, former insurance company executive; b. Bklyn., July 15, 1919; s. John Walter and Elizabeth Anna (Grotyohann) K.; m. Muriel Clancy, Oct. 14, 1950 (dec.); children: Deborah Ann, Kenneth Robert, Pamela Jane; m. Dorothy E. Lauterborn, Nov. 17, 1962. BBA, St. Johns U., 1942; MBA, N.Y. U., 1949. Former registered prin. Nat. Assn. Securities Dealers. C.P.A., N.Y. Acct. Consol. Edison Co., N.Y.C., 1936-45; mng. acct. S.D. Leidersdorf & Co., N.Y.C., 1945-53; with Equitable Life Assurance Soc. of U.S., N.Y.C., 1953-82, 2d v.p., 1969-73, v.p., assoc. controller, 1973-75, v.p., fin. officer investment ops., 1975-82; asst. treas., treas. Equitable Life Holding Corp., 1971-75; comptroller Equitable Life Mortgage & Realty Investors, 1970-75; v.p., treas. Equitable Life Community Enterprises Corp., 1970-75, Student Life Funding, Inc., 1970-75; v.p., dir. Equico Lessors, Inc., Mpls., 1974-78; v.p. Equico Securities, Inc., 1970-80, Planters Devel. Corp., St. Louis, 1972-81. Mem. Phila. Stock Exchange, Inc., 1971-78. Pres. Leisure Towne Civic League, 1983-84, treas., 1985-86; mem. bldg. fund com. Holy Eucharist Ch., chmn. fin. com., 1984-89. Served with AUS, 1942-45. Mem. AICPA, Tax Execs. Inst., Fin. Execs. Inst., Beta Rho Kappa, Delta Mu Delta. Roman Catholic. Home: 41 Finchley Ct Southampton NJ 08088-1006

KNOSPE, WILLIAM HERBERT, medical educator; b. Oak Park, Ill., May 26, 1929; s. Herbert Henry and Dora Isabel (Spruce) K.; m. Adris M. Nelson, June 19, 1954. BA, U. Ill., Chgo. and Urbana, 1951; BS, U. Ill., 1952; MD, U. Ill., Chgo., 1954; MS in Radiation Biology, U. Rochester, 1962. Diplomate Am. Bd. Internal Medicine and Subspecialty Bd. on Hematology. Rotating intern Upstate Med. Ctr. Hosps-SUNY-Syracuse, 1954-55; resident in medicine Ill. Central Hosp., Chgo., 1955-56, VA Research Hosp-Northwestern U. Med. Sch., Chgo., 1956-58; investigator radiation biology Walter Reed Army Inst. Research, Washington, 1962-64, investigator hematology, asst. chief dept. hematology, 1964-66; attending physician med. service Walter Reed Gen. Hosp., Washington, 1963-64, fellow in hematology, 1964-65; asst. chief hematology service, chief hematology clinic Walter Reed Army Inst. of Rsch., Washington, 1964-66; asst. attending staff physician Presbyn. St. Luke's Hosp., Chgo., 1967-68, asst. dir. hematology radiohematology lab., 1967-74, assoc. attending staff physician, 1968-74, sr. attending staff physician, 1974—; asst. prof. medicine U. Ill.-Chgo., 1967-69, assoc. prof., 1969-72; assoc. prof. medicine Rush Med. Coll., Chgo., 1971-74, prof. medicine, 1974—; dir. sect. hematology Rush-Presbyn.-St. Luke's Med. Ctr., Chgo., 1974-93; Elodia Kehm prof. hematology Rush-Med. Coll., Chgo., 1986-94, prof. emeritus, 1994—; prof. medicine U. N.Mex., Albuquerque, 1994—. Speaker at profl. confs. U.S. and abroad; vis. prof. medicine dept. hematology U. Basel, Switzerland, 1980-81, Cancer Ctr., U. N.Mex., 1992-93. Contbr. numerous articles to profl. pubs. Trustee Ill. chpt. Leukemia Soc. Am., 1977-88, v.p., 1979-80; trustee Bishop Anderson House (Rush-Presbyn.-St. Luke's Med. Ctr.), 1980-94. Served to capt. M.C., USAR, 1958-61, to lt. col., U.S. Army, 1961-66. Fellow ACP; mem. Am. Fedn. Clin. Research, AMA, Am. Soc. Hematology, Am. Soc. Clin. Oncology, Central Soc. Clin. Research, Chgo. Med. Soc., Inst. Medicine Chgo., Internat. Soc. Exptl. Hematology, Radiation Research Soc., Southeastern Cancer Study Group, Polycythemia Vera Study Group, Eastern Coop. Oncology Group, Ill. State Med. Soc., Assn. Hematology-Oncology Program Dirs., Sigma Xi, Chgo. Literary Club. Office: 310 Big Horn Ridge Dr NE Albuquerque NM 87122-1455

KNOTEK, ROBERT FRANK, management consultant, educator; b. Racine, Wis., May 10, 1945; s. Joseph Anthony and Josephine Marie (Lauer) K.; m. Janet Ilene Odegaard, Sept. 18, 1965; children: Kristine Margaret, Mikal Jon. LLB, LaSalle U., Chgo., 1973; MBA in Gen. Mgmt. with honors, Calif. Pacific U., 1987, MA in Human Behavior, 1988; postgrad., Harvard U., 1988, U. Autonoma Barcelona, Barcelona, 1997, Oxford U., 2002. Cert. profl. cons.; cert. econ. devel. fin. profl. Mdse. mgr. Schmitt Music Co., Mpls., 1966-74; founder, CEO Met. Music Corp., Richfield, Minn., 1974-87; prin. RFK-Bus. Cons., Eden Prairie, Minn., 1984-97; CEO Kaes Analytics, Inc., Eden Prairie, 1997—. Adj. faculty Hennepin Tech. Coll., Plymouth, Minn., 1985-92, U. Minn. Extension Svc., Mpls., 1990-92, Normandale C.C., Bloomington, Minn., 1992-95, U. St. Thomas, St. Paul, 1995-98, U. Iowa, Iowa City, 1996-99, Nat. Am. U., Bloomington, Minn., 1999-02; adj. prof. LaSalle U., Mandeville, La., 1995-96; vis. scholar U. Tver, Russia, 1994; hosted del. Universitat de La Habana, Cuba, 1998; CIEE guest U. Western Cape, U. Pretoria, 1999. Author: Cash Flow Paradox, 1990, Entrepreneurship Lite, 1998; host (TV series) QCTV: Business Profiles, 1987-88; co-anchor (TV series) Normandale News; contbr. articles to profl. jours. Mem. Eden Prairie Pub. Schs. Com., 1989-91, Hennepin Tech. Coll. Adv. Bd., Plymouth, 1989-91; nominee U.S. Peace Corps, Ea. Europe, 1994. Recipient Cert. Appreciation Minn. Bd. of Vocat. Edn., 1990, Minn. Bd. Tech. Colls., 1991, Am. Soc. for Indsl. Protection, 1992, Golden Apple award C. of C., 1992, Group Study Exch. to Australia Rotary Internat. Found., 1996. Mem. Am. Booksellers Assn., Upper Midwest Booksellers Assn., Internat. Coun. Small Bus., Acad. Entrepreneurship (charter), Nat. Assn. Music Mchts., Mensa, Alpha Psi Omega, Iota Omega Chi. Republican. Lutheran. Avocations: playing piano, jazz guitar. Home: 9813 Dorset Lane Eden Prairie MN 55347-3139 E-mail: rknote19@skypoint.com.

KNOTT, ALEXANDER WALLER, historian, educator; b. Chgo., Oct. 14, 1938; s. Alexander Knott and Constance Burtenshaw; m. Susan Jane Sheehan, Jan. 26, 1963; children: Alexander Christopher, Jefferson Sheehan. BA, U. Colo., 1961, MA, 1963, PhD, 1968. Asst. prof. history U. No. Colo., Greeley, 1968—74, assoc. prof., 1974—. Faculty cons. Advanced Placement, U.S. History, Ednl. Testing Svc., Princeton, NJ, 1991—. Co-editor: Essays in Twentieth Century American Diplomatic History, 1982. Mem.: Soc. for Historians of Am. Fgn. Rels. Republican. Congregationalist. Avocations: camping, tennis. Office: Univ of Northern Colorado Dept History 501 20th St Greeley CO 80639-6900 Home: 1316 45th Ave Greeley CO 80634

KNOTT, DOUGLAS RONALD, college dean, agricultural sciences educator, researcher; b. Fraser Mills, B.C., Can., Nov. 10, 1927; s. Ronald David and Florence Emily (Keeping) K.; m. Joan Madeline Hollinshead, Sept. 2, 1950 (dec.); children: Holly Ann, Heather Lynn, Ronald Kenneth, Douglas James (dec.); m. Pat Decker, June 1, 2002. BSA, U. B.C., 1948; MS, U. Wis., 1949, PhD, 1952. Asst. prof. U. Sask., Saskatoon, 1952-56, assoc. prof., 1956-65, prof., 1965-93, head dept. crop sci., 1965-75, assoc. dean rsch. Coll. Agr., 1988-93; prof. emeritus, 1993—. Author: The Wheat Rusts—Breeding for Resistance, 1989; also numerous papers. Named to Saskatchewan Agr. Hall of Fame. Fellow Am. Soc. Agronomy, Agrl. Inst. Can.; mem. Can. Soc. Agronomy, Genetics Soc. Can., Order of Can. Mem. United Ch. of Can. Avocations: squash, tennis. Office: U Sask Dept Plant Scis 51 Campus Dr Saskatoon SK Canada S7N 5A8 E-mail: dougknott@shaw.ca.

KNOTT, JOHN RAY, JR., language professional, educator; b. Memphis, July 9, 1937; s. John Ray and Wilma (Henshaw) K.; m. Anne Percy, Dec. 5, 1959; children: Catherine, Ellen, Walker, Anne. AB, Yale U., 1959, Carnegie fellow, 1960; PhD, Harvard U., 1965. Instr. Harvard U., 1965-67; mem. faculty U. Mich., Ann Arbor, 1967—, prof. English, 1976—, chmn. dept., 1982-87, assoc. dean Coll. Arts and Scis., 1977-80, acting dean Coll. Arts and Scis., 1980-81, interim dir. Inst. for Humanities, 1987-88, interim dir. Program in the Environment, 2001—02. Dir. region IV Mellon Fellowship Selection Com., 1989-94. Author: Milton's Pastoral Vision, 1971, The Sword of the Spirit, 1980, Discourses of Martyrdom in English Literature, 1563-1694, 1993, Imagining Wild America, 2002; editor: The Triumph of Style, 1967, Mirrors: An Introduction to Literature, rev. edit., 1987, The Huron River: Voices From the Watershed, 2000, Reimagining Place, 2001; contbr. articles on Abbey, Berry, Browne, Bunyan, Fox, Foxe, Milton, and Spenser to scholarly jours. Woodrow Wilson fellow, 1960-61; NEH fellow, 1974 Mem. MLA, Milton Soc., Renaissance Soc. Am., Sierra Club. Office: Univ Mich Dept English Ann Arbor MI 48109

KNOTT, KENNETH, engineering educator, consultant, expert witness; b. Dudley, Worcestershire, Eng., Mar. 6, 1929; came to U.S., 1977; s. John Peter Grainger and Sarah (Turner) K.; m. Margaret Knott, Apr. 22, 1957; children: DiLwyn John, Tracy James. Diploma in Grad. Studies, Engring. Prodn., U. Birmingham at Edgbaston, Eng., 1956; MS in Indsl. Engring., Pa. State U., 1966; PhD in Engring. Prodn., Tech. U. Loughborough, Eng., 1983. Apprentice British Thompson Houston Co. Ltd., Birmingham, 1944-48, Coventry, Eng., 1948-50; design draftsman New Conveyor Co. Ltd., Smethwick, Eng., 1952-53; tech. asst. to gen. mgr. N. Hingley and Sons, Netherton, Eng., 1953-55; prodn. engr. Chubb and Sons, Ltd., Wolverhampton, Eng., 1955-56; plant mgr. John Morris Electrical Engring., Bilston, Eng., 1956; lectr. in prodn. engring. Dudley and Staffordshire Tech. Coll., Dudley, Eng., 1956-63; instr. in indsl. engring. Pa. State U., State College, 1963-66; mng. dir. Maynard Tng. Ctr., Birmingham, 1966-70, Kenneth Knott Ltd., Birmingham, 1966-77, Work Study Contract Svcs., Birmingham, 1970-77; asst. prof. indsl. and mgmt. systems engring. Pa. State U., 1977-84, assoc. prof. indsl. and mgmt. engring., 1984-87, prof. indsl. and mgmt. engring., 1987-95, emeritus prof. indsl. engring., 1996—. Mem. editorial bd. Internat. Jour. Prodn. Rsch., Loughborough, 1984—; mem. robotics sub-com. Welding Rsch. Coun., N.Y.C., 1977-79, welding processes sub-com., 1977-83; mem. com. maintenance in mfg. Nat. Mfg. Engring. Ctr., Ann Arbor, Mich., 1989-90. Author: Job Analysis Procedure Manual, 1970, (with others) A Comparison of Alternative Time Slotting Systems for Indirect Time Standards Work Measurement, 1986, An Analytical Approach to Designing and Testing Time Slotting Systems, 1986; co-author: Laboratory Manual Manufacturing Processes, 1965, Principles and Practice of MTM-2, 1970, Principles and Practice of MTM-3, 1971, Manufacturing Processes Associate Degree Program, 1980; editor Metods Time Measurement Jour., 1982-90; contbr. tech. papers to profl. jours. Recipient AT&T Found. Outstanding Teaching award Am. Soc. Engring. Edn., 1991, Lenhard Teaching fellowship Lenhardt Ctr. Innovative Teaching Pa. State U., 1992. Fellow Inst. Indsl. Engrs. (panel rsch. in work measurement work measurement and methods engring. divsn. 1981-83, assoc. editor IIE Transactions 1982-92, program chmn. 1983-87, rsch. chmn. 1984-89, reorganization com. 1988, divsn. dir. 1982-83, honors chmn. 1991—, pres. Ctrl. Pa. chpt. 1982-83, Phil Carroll award 1986, Tech. Innovation in Indsl. Engring. award 1993), World Acad. Productivity Sci.; mem. NSPE, Am. Soc. Quality Control. Soc. Am. Magicians, Pa. Soc. Profl. Engrs., Fedn. Productivity Scis. (hon., London), Methods Time Measurement Assn. (editor Methods Time Measurement Jour., chmn. midland region United Kingdom divsn. 1967-72, internat. com. investigation into Application Handbook Requirements 1970, tech. panel United Kingdom divsn. 1969-77, tng. and qualifications com.), Soc. Mfg. Engrs. (continuing edn. chmn. Ctrl. Pa. chpt. 1987, sec. 1993—), Internat. Brotherhood Magicians (mem. Magic Circle), Kano Soc., Sigma Xi, Alpha Pi Mu. Avocations: magic, Judo. Home: PO Box 234 Pine Grove Mills PA 16868-0234 Office: Pa State U 207 Hammond Bldg University Park PA 16802-1401 E-mail: kok@psu.edu., k.knott@fimexpert.com.

KNOTT, WILEY EUGENE, electronic engineer; b. Muncie, Ind., Mar. 18, 1938; s. Joseph Wiley and Mildred Viola (Haxton) K.; 1 child, Brian Evan. BSEE, Tri-State U., 1963; postgrad., Union Coll., 1970-73, Ga. Coll., 1987. Assoc. aircraft engr. Lockheed-Ga. Co., Marietta, 1963-65; tech. publs. engr. GE, Pittsfield, Mass., 1965-77, sr. publs. engr., 1977-79, group leader, 1967-79; specialist engr. Boeing Mil. Airplane Co., Wichita, Kans., 1979-81, sr. specialist engr., 1981-84, 89-90, logistics mgr., 1984-85, customer support mgr., 1985-89, base mgr. Castle AFB, 1990-91; facilities plant ops. and maintenance engr. Boeing Comml. Airplane Co., Everett, Wash., 1991-92, lead engr., 1992-93, prin. engr., 1993-95; part-time bus. cons., 1972—. Active Jr. Achievement, 1978-79, Am. Security Coun., 1975-90, Nat. Rep. Snatori al Com., 1979-86, Nat. Rep. Congl. Com., 1979-87, Rep. Nat. Com., 1979-87, Rep. Presdl. Task Force, 1981-86, Joint Presdl./Congl. Steering Com., 1982-86, Rep. Polit. Action Com., 1979-86, Mus. of Aviation, 1987-95; state advisor U.S. Congl. Adv. Bd., 1981-86; adviser Jr. Achievement, 1978-79. With AUS, 1956—59. Mem.: AARP, Assn. U.S. Army, Amvets, Air Force Assn. (life), Heidelberg Am. H.S. Alumni Assn., Mil. Brats, Overseas Brats, Ill. Rlwy. Mus., U.S. Golf Assn., PGA Tour Ptnrs. (life). E-mail: wileyknott@cox.net.

KNOTT, WILLIAM ALAN, library director, management and building consultant; b. Muscatine, Iowa, Oct. 4, 1942; s. Edward Marlan and Dorothy Mae K.; m. Mary Farrell, Aug. 23, 1969; children: Andrew Jerome, Sarah Louise. BA in English, U. Iowa, 1967, MA in L.S., 1968. Asst. dir. Ottumwa (Iowa) Pub. Libr., 1968-69; libr. cons. Iowa State Libr., Des Moines, 1968-69; dir. Hutchinson (Kans.) Pub. Libr., S. Cen. Kans. Libr. Sys., 1969-71, Jefferson County Pub. Libr., Lakewood, Colo., 1971—. With USAR, 1965—67. Mem.: ALA, Urban Librs Coun., Colo. Libr. Assn. Office: Jefferson County Pub Libr 10200 W 20th Ave Lakewood CO 80215-1402 E-mail: wknott@jefferson.lib.co.us.

KNOTTS, ROBERT LEE, retired insurance company executive; b. Thornton, W.Va., Jan. 14, 1942; s. James Bailey and Lena Louise (Jacobs) K.; m. Dottie Lue Watts, Aug. 20, 1967; children: Brice Alan, Lance Eric, Chandra Marie. ChFC, CLU. Sales, truck driver Wholesale Grocery, Grafton, W.Va., 1960-67; lineman, crew leader Monongahela Power Co., Grafton, W.Va., 1967—78; agt. N.Y. Life Ins., N.Y. Life Ins. & Annuity Corp., Charleston, W.Va., 1978—2001, NYLIFE Securities Corp., Charleston, W.Va., 1978—2001; ret., 2001. Sec. bd. dirs. Grafton Homes, Inc., 1990-97. V.P. Taylor County Econ. Devel. Authority, Grafton, 1985-87; pres. Taylor Devel. Group, Inc., Grafton, 1987—. With USMC, 1960-64. V.p. Taylor County Econ Devel. Authority, Grafton, 1985-87, pres. Taylor Devel. Group, Inc., 1987—; treas. Taylor County Dem. Exec. Com., 1990-98. With USMC, 1960-64. Mem. Nat. Assn. Life Underwriters, Fairmont Assn. Life Underwriters, North Ctrl. W.Va. Chartered Fin. Cons., N. Ctrl. W.Va. Estate Planning Coun., Grafton Rotary (pres. 1979-81, 95-96, pres. edn. endowment 1991-96). Methodist.

KNOTTS, ROBERT SPENCER (BOB KNOTTS), writer, playwright; b. Detroit, Mich., Dec. 9, 1952; s. John William and Elizabeth Jeanette Knotts; m. Jill Kalber Knotts, Sept. 9, 1995. Writer various Vt. newspapers, Burlington, Vt., 1980—83; reporter, anchor WJOY Radio, Burlington, 1983—86; reporter

WCAX-TV, Burlington, 1986—89; writer, reporter South Fla. Sun-Sentinel, Fort Lauderdale, Fla., 1989—94; writer Fort Lauderdale, Fla., 1994—. Author: (book) Super Eight: Today's Hottest Sports Stars, 1999, (book) The Summer Olympics, 2000, Pocket Guide to the 2000 Olympics, 2000, Martial Arts, 2000, Equestrian Events, 2000, Weightlifting, 2000, Track and Field, 2000, Hard News, 2001, (book) Florida History, 2002, Florida Plants and Animals, 2002, Florida Native Peoples, 2002, All Around Florida, 2002, Uniquely Florida, 2002, People of Florida, 2002; contbg. editor: Arthur Frommer's Budget Travel; contbr. articles to mags. including Sports Illustrated, Travel & Leisure, USA Weekend, N.Y. Times, Family Circle, Reader's Digest; author: (plays) In Mordant Whispers, 2003, juvenile novels under pen name M.D. Spenser; : (plays) Never Nothin' Again No More, 2001. Recipient Various Writing & Journalism awards, Fla. Mag. Assn., 2001, Associated Press, 1984, 1985, 1986, Vt. Broadcasters Assn., 1984, 1985, 1986. Mem.: Poets, Playwrights, Editors, Essayists, Novelists, Authors Guild. Avocations: music, auto racing, weightlifting. Business E-Mail: bob@bobknotts.com.

KNOTTS, TAMI LEIGH, finance educator; b. Haynesville, La., July 27, 1971; d. Mack Daniel and JoNell Knotts. BS in acctg., La. State, Shreveport, 1994, MBA, 1995; DBA, La. Tech. U., Ruston, 2000. Tchr. Herndon Magnet Sch., Shreveport, 1995—97; tchg. asst. La. Tech. U., 1997—99, instr., 1999—2000; asst. prof. S.W. Mo. State U., Springfield, 2002—. Libr. rep. S.W. Mo. State U., 2002—; sec. bd. dirs. S.W. Mo. Humane Soc., 2000—. Contbr. articles to profl. jours. Mem.: Delta Sigma Pi, Omicron Delta Kappa, Beta Gamma Sigma. Office: Southwest Missouri St Univ 901 S National Ave Springfield MO 65804 Business E-Mail: tlk090f@smsu.edu.

KNOUS, PAMELA K. wholesale distribution executive; Student, Carleton Coll.; Degree in Math., Bus. Administrn., Acctg., U. Ariz. Ptnr. KPMG Peat Marwick, L.A.; exec. v.p., CFO, treas. The Vons Cos., Inc., 1991; exec. v.p., CFO Supervalu Inc., Mpls., 1994—. Office: Supervalu Inc PO Box 990 Eden Prairie MN 55344

KNOWLES, CHARLES TIMOTHY, lawyer, state legislator, military officer, educator; b. Providence, Aug. 21, 1949; s. Charles Timothy and Olga (Dower) K.; m. Sandra J. Bellem; children: Justin, Jennifer. BA, U. R.I., 1971; JD cum laude, New England Sch. Law, 1977; MSS, U.S. Army War Coll., 2000. Bar: R.I., U.S. Dist. Ct. (R.I.), U.S. Supreme Ct. Assoc. Robinson & Resnick, Warwick, R.I., 1977-79, Haronian & Paquin, Warwick, 1979-84; ptnr. Knowles & Bissonnette, Warwick, 1984—; mem. R.I. Ho. of Reps., Providence, 1989-97, chmn. jud. com., 1993-97; retired; legal counsel corp. com. R.I. Ho. of Reps., 2000—; adj. prof. Johnson and Wales U., 2001—. Sec. Narragansett (R.I.) Dem. Cen. Com., 1982-93; vice-chmn. Narragansett Zoning Bd., 1982-88; coach Narragansett Little League, 1982-88. 1st lt. U.S. Army, 1971-73; col. R.I. ARNG, 1974-99, brig. comdr., 1997-99; comdr. 1021st civil affairs group, 1999-2001. Decorated Legion of Merit, Meritorious Svc. medal (3); named to St. Andrew's Hall of Fame, 2002. Mem. R.I. Bar Assn., Am. Legion, Save the Bay, Lions, St. Andrew's Alumni Assn. (sec.). Episcopalian. Home: 56 Fowler St North Kingstown RI 02852-5010 Office: Knowles and Bissonnette 3214 Post Rd Warwick RI 02886-7129

KNOWLES, CHRISTOPHER ALLAN, healthcare executive; b. Washington, Oct. 24, 1949; s. Charles Edward and Eleanor Patricia (Murphy) K.; m. Mary Margaret O'Loughlin, Feb. 14, 1988; children: Sean Christopher, James Charles, Thomas Patrick. BA, U. Nebr., 1975; MPA, Drake U., Des Moines, 1982; postgrad., Fordham U., 1987-91. Adminstrv. asst. to dir. Nebr. Dept. Water Resources, Lincoln, 1976-78; environ. planner Iowa Natural Resources Council, Des Moines, 1978-81, Md. Environ. Trust, Balt., 1982; fin. analyst Norwest Corp., Des Moines, 1982-83; asst. dir., dir. fin. Hospice of Cen. Iowa, Des Moines, 1983-85; assoc. dir. home health svcs. dept. Hackensack Med. Ctr., N.J., 1985-86; fiscal mgr. Family Health Ctr. Montefiore Med. Ctr., N.Y.C., 1986-87; assoc. dir. and adminstr. Comprehensive Family Care Ctr., Albert Einstein Coll., N.Y.C., 1987-88; exec. dir. Hospice Care of L.I., 1988; assoc. dir. Bronx-Lebanon Hosp., N.Y.C., 1989; chmn., chief exec. officer Knowles Econometrics, Inc., Pelham Manor, N.Y., 1990-91; asst. controller N.Y.C. Health & Hosps. Corp., 1990; dep. dir. Coalition Vol. Mental Health Agys., N.Y.C., 1990-91; dir. Vis. Nurse Svc., Martha's Vineyard Cmty. Svcs., Oak Bluffs, Mass., 1991—; chief economist Knowles Econometrics, Vineyard Haven, Mass., 1994-96. Pres. The Wintertide Coffeehouse, Inc., Vineyard Haven, Mass., 1993-94; treas. AIDS Alliance of Martha's Vineyard (Mass.), Inc., 1992-93; chmn. Dukes County (Mass.) Health and Human Svcs. Adv. Com., 1995-96. Chmn. Barnstable County (Mass.) Health Human Svcs. Adv. Com., 1999-2001. U.S. Dept. Edn. grantee, 1981-82. Mem. Mason (32d deg.), Knight Templar, Pi Sigma Alpha, Pi Alpha Alpha Republican. Roman Catholic. Avocation: sailing. Office: PO Box 369 Vineyard Haven MA 02568-0369 E-mail: cknowles@tiac.net.

KNOWLES, ELIZABETH PRINGLE, museum director; b. Decatur, Ill., Jan. 9, 1943; d. William Bull and Elizabeth E. (Pillsbury) Pringle; m. Joseph E. Knowles; 1 child, Elizabeth Bakewell. BA in Humanities with honors, Stanford U., 1964; MA in Art History, U. Calif., Santa Barbara, 1968; grad., Mus. Mgmt. Inst., 1984; MBA, Rensselaer Poly. Inst., 1999. Cert. jr. coll. tchr. Calif. Instr. art history Murray State U., Murray, Ky., 1967-68; instr. Santa Barbara Art Inst., 1969, Santa Barbara City Coll., 1969-70, 76-78, instr. cont. edn., 1973-86; from staff coord. docents to curator edn. Santa Barbara Mus. Art, 1974-86; assoc. dir. Meml. Art Gallery, Rochester, N.Y., 1986-88; instr. mus. studies Calif. State U., Long Beach, 1989; exec. dir. Lyman Allyn Art Mus., New London, Conn., 1989-95; pres. Only In Conn. Spl. Interest Tours, Chester, 1995-97; supr. mus. edn. programs Mystic (Conn.) Seaport Mus., 1996-2001; exec. dir. Wildling Art Mus., Los Olivos, Calif., 2001—. Instr. continuing edn. Santa Barbara City Coll., 1973—86. Contbr. essays to art catalogues. Bd. dirs., chmn. Met. Transit Dist., Santa Barbara, 1978—80; commr. Santa Barbara City Planning Commn., 1975—77; founding pres. Santa Barbara Contemporary Arts Forum, 1976—78. Fellow Kellogg Found., Smithsonian Inst., 1985. Mem.: New Eng. Mus. Assn. (v.p. 1993—95), Coll. Art Assn., Am. Assn. Mus. (treas. edn. com. 1986—88). E-mail: Penny@wildlingmuseum.org.

KNOWLES, HARVARD VAUGHAN, literature educator; b. Newport, Maine, Mar. 11, 1935; s. Elbert Lowell and Bertie Elizabeth Knowles. BA, Tufts U., Medford, 1958; MA, Duke U., Durham, 1965. Loomis chaffee sch. Sch., Windsor, Conn., 1962—74; phillips exeter acad. Exeter, NH, 1974. Cons. Ednl. Testing Svc., Princeton, NJ, 1990—. Sp/4 U.S. Army, 1958—60. Recipient Brown Tchg. Award, Phillips Exeter Acad., 1993, Tchg. Award, Harvard Club of Boston, 1995, Outstanding Tchr. award, U.S. Dept. Edn., 1999; Klingenstein fellow Columbia U., 1978—79. Mem.: MLA. Home: 400 High Street #11 Hampton NH 03842 Office: Phillips Exeter Academy 20 Main Street Exeter NH 03833

KNOWLES, JAMES KENYON, applied mechanics educator; b. Cleve., Apr. 14, 1931; s. Newton Talbot and Allyan (Gray) K.; m. Jacqueline De Bolt, Nov. 26, 1952; children: John Kenyon, Jeffrey Gray, James Talbot. SB in Math., MIT, 1952, PhD, 1957; DSc (hon.), Nat. U. Ireland, 1985. Instr. math. MIT, Cambridge, 1957-58; asst. prof. applied mechanics Calif. Inst. Tech., Pasadena, 1958-61, assoc. prof., 1961-65, prof. applied mechanics, 1965—, William R. Kenan Jr. prof., 1991—, William R. Kenan Jr. prof. emeritus, 1996—. Vis. prof. MIT, 1993-94; cons. in field. Contbr. articles to profl. jours. Recipient Eringen medal Soc. Engring. Sci., 1991. Fellow: AAAS, ASME (Koiter medal 2002), Am. Acad. Mechanics. Home: 524 Michillinda Way Sierra Madre CA 91024-1066 Office: Calif Inst Tech Divsn Engring & Applied Sci 104-44 1201 E California Pasadena CA 91125-0001 E-mail: knowles@caltech.edu.

KNOWLES, JOCELYN WAGNER, health writer, women's health specialist; b. N.Y.C., Feb. 22, 1918; d. Frederick and Violet Alice (Swain) W.; m. Clive Dorman Knowles, 1950 (div. 1959); 1 child, Katherine Miranda. Student, London Sch. Econs., 1938; BS, Columbia U., 1939, MA, 1940; MPH, UCLA, 1970. Exec. dir. Nat. Physicians Forum, Inc., N.Y.C., 1945-49; West Coast editor Nat. Foremen's Inst. Prentice-Hall Co., L.A., 1959-68; writer, editor The Female Patient mag., 1980-81; dir. Planned Parenthood of S.W., Silver City, N.Mex., 1981-83; freelance writer, 1977—; asst. to pres., lit. agt. Writers House, Inc., N.Y.C., 1989-92. Book critic Kirkus Revs., 1989-90, Book of the Month Club, 1991-99, Pubs. Weekly, 1991-98. Contbr. articles to med. and consumer mags.; staff bookreviewer L.A. Times. First woman organizer Brotherhood of Railway Trainmen, 1945-47; publicist Farmers Union of Iowa, Des Moines, 1951, Golden Gate Arboretum, San Francisco, 1976; bd. dirs. Nat. Womens Health Network, 1981-85; apptd. to Sarasota (Fla.) Commn. on Status of Women, 1994-96; sec. Sarasota County Health Care Campaign, 1996-98, Howard County (Md.) Commn. on Women, 1999-2000; chmn. Adv. Commn. on Aging Columbia Assn., Md., 2000—; bd. dirs. LWV, Howard County, Md., 2001-03. NIH grantee U. Calif., L.A., 1968-70; Va. Ctr. for the Arts fellow, Charlottesville, 1976, Woolrich fellow Columbia U., N.Y.C., 1977, Wurlitzer Found. fellow, Taos, N.Mex., 1981. Jewish.

KNOWLES, JULIE NALL, secondary school educator; b. Webb, Ala., Nov. 5, 1941; d. Ealie Edward and Creola (Carter) Nall; m. William Durwood Knowles, Jan. 17, 1970. BS in Edn. magna cum laude, Troy State U., 1965; MA in English, Samford U., 1969; PhD in English, Auburn U., 1980; AA in Music, Chattahoochee Valley C.C., Phenix City, Ala., 1999. Cert. tchr. Ala., Ga., Fla. Tchr. Ahrens High Sch. Jefferson County Schs., Louisville, Ky., 1975-76; instr. Auburn (Ala.) U., 1981-82; assoc. prof. Stillman Coll., Tuscaloosa, Ala., 1983-85; asst. prof. Mercer U., Macon, Ga., 1986-87; prof. Troy State U., Phenix City, Ala., 1987-99; tchr. Camden County High Sch. Camden County Schs., Kingsland, Ga., 1999-2000; tchr. Paxon Sch. Advanced Studies Duval County Sch. Sys., Jacksonville, Fla., 2000—. Editor, creator: The Chariot, 1988-91; contbr. articles to mags. Ch. pianist Turners Station (Ky.) Bapt Ch., 1973—76, Union Grove Bapt. Ch., Opelika, Ala., 1976—82, Hatchechubbee (Ala.) Bapt. Ch., 1988—95; mem. choir Folkston (Ga.) Bapt. Ch., 2000—. Rsch. grantee Troy State U., 1992; recipient Woodrow Hale Meml. Prize # 1 Green River Writers, 1996. Mem. Profl. Assn. Ga. Educators, Phi Theta Kappa, Phi Kappa Phi, Kappa Delta Pi (counselor Rho Phi chpt. 1989-92, Point of Excellence award 1993). Democrat. Southern Baptist. Avocations: motorcycling, piano, fishing. Home: Rte 2 Box 1785 Folkston GA 31537

KNOWLES, MARJORIE FINE, lawyer, educator, dean; b. Bklyn., July 4, 1939; d. Jesse J. and Roslyn (Leff) Fine; m. Ralph I. Knowles, Jr., June 3, 1972. BA, Smith Coll., 1960; LLB, Harvard U., 1965. Bar: Ala., N.Y., D.C. Teaching fellow Harvard U., 1963-64; law clk. to judge U.S. Dist. Ct. (so. dist.), N.Y., 1965-66; asst. U.S. atty. U.S. Atty.'s Office, N.Y.C., 1966-67; asst. dist. atty. N.Y. County Dist. Atty., N.Y.C., 1967-70; exec. dir. Joint Found. Support, Inc., N.Y.C., 1970-72; asst. gen. counsel HEW, Washington, 1978-79; insp. gen. U.S. Dept. Labor, Washington, 1979-80; assoc. prof. U. Ala. Sch. Law, Tuscaloosa, 1972-75, prof., 1975-86, assoc. dean, 1982-84; law prof., dean Ga. State U. Coll. Law, Atlanta, 1986-91, law prof., 1986—. Cons. Ford Found., N.Y.C., 1973-98, 2000-03, trustee Coll. Retirement Equities Fund, N.Y.C., 1983-2002; mem. exec. com. Conf. on Women and the Constn., 1986-88; mem. com. on continuing profl. edn. Am. Law Inst.-ABA, 1987-93. Contbr. articles to profl. jours. Am. Council Edn. fellow, 1976-77, Aspen Inst. fellow, Rockefeller Found., 1976. Mem. ABA (chmn. new deans workshop 1988), Ala. State Bar Assn., N.Y. State Bar Assn., D.C. Bar Assn., Am. Law Inst., Tchrs. Ins. Annunity Assn. (trustee Coll. Equities Ret. Equities Fund 2002—). Office: Ga State U Coll Law University Plz Atlanta GA 30303

KNOWLES, RANDALL GENE, financial planner; b. Great Falls, Mont., Nov. 15, 1951; s. Vernon James and Joyce Ann (Zbinden) Knowles; m. Sheryl Jean Sanders, Jan. 2, 1971; children: Karen Angela Knowles Edgell, Jennifer Kim. BS in Econs., Mont. State U., 1974; ChFC, Am. Coll., 2002. Registered investment advisor, CFP. Banker First Bank & First Inter-State, Great Falls, Mont., 1976-81; ins. agt. Lincoln. Nat. Life, Ft. Wayne, Ind., 1981-2001; assoc., invesment advisor LNC Adv. Svcs., Ft. Wayne, Ind., 1990—; pres. Mont. Fringe Benefits, 1989—; with FSC Securities Corp., 2001—, Rocky Mountain Fin. Advisors, 2001—. Guest lectr. Coll. Gt. Falls Ins.; spkr. State of Mont. Pers. Dept., Mont. State U., Mont. Food Svc. Assn., 1996—, Mont. Edn. Assn., Mont. Tchrs. Assn.; tchr. Ctr. Fin. Tng., 1998—; adult edn. tchr. pub. sch. dists., Gt. Falls, Bozeman, 1990—; treas. Gt. Falls Sports Complex, Inc., 2002—03. Editor: Gt. Falls Pachyderm newsletter, 2001; contbr. articles to profl. jours. Vol. estate planner Spl. K Ranch, 1993; donor ARC, Gt. Falls, 1992; pres. Preservation Cascade, 2000; chair Ctrl. Christian Ch. Endowment and Trust, 1998—2002; treas. Christian Chs. Mont., 2002—; bd. dirs. Advs. Developmentally Disabled, 1986—94. Life Underwriters Tng. Coun. fellow, 1993. Mem.: S.C.O.R.E. (pres. 1996), NRA (estate planner 1989—), Nat. Assn. Ind. Fin. Advisors (chari IFA-PAC Mont. chpt. 2000—01, nat. com. 2000—03), Mont. Assn. Life Underwriters (pub. rels. chair 1996), Toastmasters (pres. 1986, lt. gov. 1987, Toastmaster of the Yr. 1987, CTM Toastmaster 1983, ATM Toastmaster 1984, DTM Toastmaster 1986, CL Toastmaster 2002), Kiwanis (pres. 1985), Scottish Rite, Shriners, Masons. Avocations: photography, hunting, fishing, writing, teaching. Home and Office: 3017 9th Ave S Great Falls MT 59405-3421 E-mail: KnowlesMT@Bigfoot.com.

KNOWLES, RICHARD ALAN JOHN, English language educator; b. Southbridge, Mass., May 17, 1935; s. Clarence Fay and Mildred Elizabeth (Branniff) K.; m. Jane Marie Boyle, Sept. 1, 1958; children: Jonathan Edwards, Katherine Mary. BA magna cum laude, Tufts U., 1956; MA, U. Pa., 1958, PhD, 1963. Physics asst. Tufts U., Medford, Mass., 1954-56; asst. instr. English U. Pa., Phila., 1956-60; from asst. prof. to prof. U. Wis., Madison, 1962-90, Dickson-Bascom prof. humanities, 1990—. Vis. lectr. U. Pa., 1967, George Washington U., Am. U., 1969, Cath. U., Washington, 1985; manuscript reader various univs., 1965—; cons. Am. Players Theater, Spring Green, Wis., 1980-83; poetry judge Brittingham Poetry Prize, Madison, 1986—, NEH referee, panelist, Washington, 1988—. Author: (with others) Shakespeare Variorum Handbook, 1971; author: Shakespeare Variorum Handbook,revised, 2003; 3editor: (with others) English Renaissance Drama, 1978; editor: New Variorum As You Like It, 1977; co-editor New Variorum Shakespeare, 1978—; mem. editl. bd. Shakespeare Notes, 1996—. Officer, producer Madison Savoyards, Wis., 1978—; pres. Friends U. Wis. Librs., Madison, 1982-84. Folger Libr. fellow, Washington, 1968, Guggenheim fellow, N.Y., 1976-77; NEH fellow 1983-87; Rsch. fellow Humanities Rsch. Inst., Madison, 1990. Mem. MLA, Shakespeare Assn. Am., Internat. Assn. Univ. Profs. English, Assn. Lit. Critics and Scholars, Nakoma Country Club. Democrat. Avocations: theater, chamber music, opera, gardening, carpentry. Home: 2226 Commonwealth Ave Madison WI 53726-5302 Office: U Wis Dept English 600 N Park St Madison WI 53706-1403 E-mail: rknowles@facstaff.wisc.edu.

KNOWLES, RICHARD NORRIS, chemist; b. Wilmington, Del., Aug. 8, 1935; s. Francis and Dorothy Edith Knowles; m. Alice Keith Pfohl, Aug. 30, 1957 (div. May 1987); children: Elizabeth Nelson, Dorothy Lawrence, Cynthia Norris; m. Claire Elaine Frerichs, Dec. 31, 1988; 1 stepchild, Christine J. Stoelting. BS, Oberlin Coll., 1957; PhD, U. Rochester, 1961. With DuPont Co., Wilmington, Del., 1960-96; asst. works mgr. Chambers Works, NJ, 1980-83, mgr. Niagara Falls (N.Y.) Plant, 1983, Belle (W.Va.) Plant, 1987-95; dir. cmty. awareness emergency response & industry outreach Wilmington, 1995-96; work with Chem. Mfrs. Assn. in Responsible Care; assoc. Dalmau Network; prin. Richard N. Knowles & Assocs.; advisor to mayor Niagara Falls, 1999—; founder, dir. Ctr. Self-Orgnl. Leadership, 2001—. Author: The Leadership Dance, Pathways to Extraordinary Organizational Effectiveness, 2002; (feaures include) The New Pioneers, 1998, The Soul at Work, 2000; contbr. articles to profl. jours. Elder Presbyn. Ch.; bd. dirs. Nat. Inst. Chem. Studies, Berkana Inst. Recipient Chem. Emergency Planning and Preparedness Ptnr. award, EPA, 1995, 1996. Mem.: Almost Heaven Hammered Dulcimer Soc., Nature Conservancy (DuPont Agrl. Products Crystal award 1991), Am. Chem. Soc. Achievements include 40 patents in field. Office: 6989 Rebecca Dr Niagara Falls NY 14304-3050 E-mail: rnknowles@aol.com.

KNOWLES, THOMAS WILLIAM, business educator, consultant; b. Chgo., June 2, 1941; s. Thomas Houlding and Dorothy (Lovell) K.; m. Fay Rosemary Bailey, June 18, 1966; children: Jennifer Lynn, Julie Bailey (dec.). BSChemE, Purdue U., 1963; MBA, U. Chgo., 1966, PhD, 1971. Prodn. engr. Lever Bros. Co., Hammond, Ind., 1963-64; prof. ops. mgmt. and mgmt. sci. Stuart Grad. Sch. of Bus., Ill. Inst. Tech., Chgo., 1969—. Vis. assoc. prof. U. Chgo. Grad. Sch. Bus., 1988; pres. Thomas W. Knowles and Assocs., Inc., Olympia Fields., Ill., 1976—. Author: Management Science: Building and Using Models, 1989; contbr. articles to profl. jours. Treas. BZ chpt. Sigma No Alumni Assn., 1967-73, Com. for Legis. Reform, Ill., 1978-80, Compassionate Friends, Ill., 1980-90; pres., v.p. Rich Twp. (Ill.) Reps., 1973-74; del. Rep. Nat. Conv., New Orleans, 1988; trustee Rich Twp., 1981-89, supr., 1989-93. Mem. Decision Scis. Inst. (Stanley T. Hardy award 1989), Inst. for Ops. Rsch. and Mgmt. Sci. (chmn. Chgo. 1975-78), Math. Programming Soc., Prodn. and Ops. Mgmt. Soc., Beta Gamma Sigma, Tau Beta Pi. Avocations: reading, fishing, travel, genealogy, boating. Home: 20440 Hellenic Dr Olympia Fields IL 60461-1438 Office: Stuart Grad Sch of Bus Ill Inst Tech 565 W Adams St Chicago IL 60661-3613 E-mail: knowles@stuart.iit.edu.

KNOWLES, TONY, former governor; b. Tulsa, Jan. 1, 1943; m. Susan Morris; children: Devon, Lucas, Sara. BA in Econs., Yale U., 1968. Co-owner Downtown Deli, Anchorage, 1976—; mayor Municipality of Anchorage, 1981-87; gov. State of Alaska, 1994—2002. Mem. citizen's com. to develop comprehensive plan for growth and devel., Anchorage, 1972; mem. Borough Assembly, Anchorage, 1975—79. With 82d Airborne U.S. Army, 1961—65, Vietnam. Named Child Advocate of the Yr., Child Welfare League Am., 1999; recipient Silver Medal of Merit, VFW, 2001. Democrat. Home: 1146 S Street Anchorage AK 99501

KNOWLES, WILLIAM LEROY (BILL KNOWLES), television news producer, journalism educator; b. L.A., June 23, 1935; s. Leroy Edwin and Thelma Mabel (Armstrong) K.; children from previous marriage: Frank, Irene, Daniel, Joseph, Ted; m. Sharon Weaver, Dec. 28, 1990. BA in Journalism, San Jose State Coll., 1959; postgrad., U. So. Calif., 1962-63. Reporter, photographer, producer KSL-TV, Salt Lake City, 1963-65; producer, editor, writer WLS-TV, Chgo., 1965-70; news writer ABC News, Washington, 1970-71, asso. producer, 1971-75, ops. producer, 1975-77, So. bur. chief, 1977-81, Washington bur. chief, 1981-82, West Coast bur. chief, 1982-85; prof. U. Mont., Missoula, 1986—; jazz writer and historian; chair radio-TV dept. U. Mon., 2000—. Advisor U. Mont. Student Documentary Unit; chair faculty senate, 2003—. Served with U.S. Army, 1959-62. Decorated Commendation medal; Gannett fellow Ind. U., 1987; Media Mgmt. fellow Poynter Inst. Media Studies, 1988. Mem. Assn. for Edn. in Journalism (head radio-TV divsn. 1995-96). Office: U Mont Radio-TV Dept Missoula MT 59812-6480 E-mail: bill.knowles@umontana.edu.

KNOWLES, WILLIAM S. retired chemist; b. 1917; BS in Chemistry, Harvard U., 1939; PhD in Steroid Chemistry, Columbia U., 1942. Chemist Monsanto, St. Louis, 1942—86, ret., 1986; postdoct. fellow Harvard U., Cambridge, Mass., 1951. Recipient St. Louis award, St. Louis sect. ACS, 1978, Nobel prize in chemistry, Royal Swedish Acad., 2001. Home: 661 E Monroe Ave Saint Louis MO 63122

KNOWLTON, GRACE FARRAR, sculptor, photographer, painter; b. Buffalo, Mar. 15, 1932; d. Frank Neff and Esther Sargeant (Norton) Farrar; m. Winthrop Knowlton, July 8, 1960 (div. 1980); children: Eliza, Samantha. BA, Smith Coll., 1954; MA, Columbia U., 1981. Asst. to curator of graphic arts Nat. Gallery of Art, Washington, 1955-57; tchr. art Arlington (Va.) Pub. Schs., 1957-60; sculptor, photographer, painter, 1960—; tchr. art Art Students League, N.Y.C., 1999—. Home: 67 Ludlow Ln Palisades NY 10964-1606

KNOWLTON, KEVIN CHARLES, lawyer; b. Syracuse, N.Y., Oct. 19, 1957; s. Erwin Leslie and Arlene Grace (Morgan) K.; m. Lois Jean Clair, July 21, 1979; children: Andrew, Keith, Lauren. BA cum laude, Houghton Coll., 1979; JD, Syracuse U., 1982. Bar: Fla. 1982, U.S. Dist. Ct. (mid. dist.) Fla. 1982, U.S. Ct. Appeals (11th cir.) 1982, U.S. Supreme Ct. 1986. Law clk. to judge 2nd Dist. Ct. Appeals, Lakeland, Fla., 1982-85; ptnr. Peterson & Myers P.A., Lakeland, 1985—, mgmt. com. Treas. Phoenix (N.Y.) Rep. Com., 1980-82, Planning Bd., 1980-82, Town of Schroeppel Planning Bd., 1980-82; chmn. bd. dirs. Lakeland Christian Sch.; chmn. pres.'s adv. bd. Houghton Coll.; vice-chmn. Fla. Bar 10th Jud. Cir. Grievance Com.; mem. instnl. rev. bd. Lakeland Regional Med. Ctr., mem. ethics com.; chmn. exec. bd. dirs. Lake Morton Cmty. Ch., 1995-99, elder. N.Y. State Regents scholar 1975-79. Mem. ABA, Fla. Bar Assn., Lakeland Bar Assn. (chmn. law day legal forum 1986), Fla. Acad. Healthcare Attys., Am. Health Lawyers Assn., Christian Legal Soc., Houghton Coll. Alumni Assn. (pres. Orlando, Fla. chpt. 1985, 91—), Willson Inn of Ct., Lakeland Yacht and Country Club, Phi Alpha Theta. Avocations: basketball, snow skiing. Home: 1143 E Highland Dr Lakeland FL 33813-1774 Office: Peterson & Myers PA 225 E Lemon St ste 300 Lakeland FL 33801-4655

KNOWLTON, LESLIE BROOKS, journalist; b. Orange, N.J., July 18, 1952; d. Bruce Douglas and Elizabeth (Snow) Knowlton; m. Charles Gottlieb Herzog, Dec. 27, 1979 (div. 1992); 1 child, Siri Whitney Herzog. BA, U. Conn., 1977; MA, Calif. State U., Long beach, 1983; postgrad., City Coll., 1998—. Dir. rsch. Grubb & Ellis Co., Newport Beach, Calif., 1985-87; reporter Orange County Businessweek, Irvine, Calif., 1987-89; reporter/desk asst. L.A. Times, Costa Mesa, Calif., 1989-90; free lance journalist L.A. Times, Psychiat. Times, Fitness Mag., other publs., N.Y.C., 1989—. U. Conn. Faculty scholar, 1976, Univ. scholar, 1976. Mem. Am. Soc. Journalists and Authors, Author's Guild, Nat. Writers Union, N.Y. Newswomen's Club, Deer Isle Yacht Club, Phi Kappa Phi, Psi Chi. Avocations: fiction, boating, hiking. Home (Summer): Dunham Point Rd Sunset ME 04683 E-mail: leslie.knowlton@verizon.net.

KNOWLTON, THOMAS A. university dean, retired food products executive; b. Toronto, Ont., Can., June 16, 1946; s. William George and Grace K.; m. Janice Elizabeth Knowlton, June 8, 1968; children: Kimberly, Tricia, Jeffrey, Andrea. BA, U. Windsor, Ont., 1968, MBA, 1970. Brand mgr. Colgate Palmolive, Toronto, 1970-73; product mgr. Gen. Foods, Toronto, 1973-75; v.p., dir. client services Leo Burnett, Toronto, 1975-79; sr. v.p. mktg. and sales Kellogg Salada Can. Inc., Rexdale, Ont., 1979-82, pres., chief exec. officer, 1983-88; v.p. Kellogg Co., 1984—; mng. dir. Kellogg Co. of Gt. Britain Ltd., 1989-90, chmn., 1990-94, exec. v.p., area dir. Europe, 1992-94; corp. exec. v.p., pres. Kellogg N.Am., 1994-99; ret., 1998; dean faculty bus. Ryerson U., Toronto, 2000—. Bd. dirs. Wm. Wrigley Jr. Co., AIM Trimark Funds Mgmt., Toronto, Sun Rype Products, Hudson's Bay Co. Mem. Young Pres.'s Orgn., York Downs Golf and Country Club (Unionville, Ont.), Sanctuary Golf Club (Sanibel, Fla.).Hudsons Bay Co. Home: 123 Cheltanham Ave Toronto ON Canada M4N 1R1

KNOWLTON, WILLIAM ALLEN, political and military consultant, educator; b. Weston, Mass., June 19, 1920; s. Frank Warren and Isabelle (Riese) K.; m. Marjorie Adams Downey, Nov. 27, 1943; children: William Allen, Davis Downey, Timothy Riese, Hollister Knowlton Petraeus. BS, U.S. Mil. Acad., 1943; MA, Columbia U., 1957; grad., Nat. War Coll., 1960; LLD (hon.), Akron U., 1972. Commd. 2d lt. U.S. Army, 1943, advanced through grades to gen., 1976; with 7th Armored Div., World War II, Army Gen. Staff, 1947-49, SHAPE, France, 1951-54; assoc. prof. social scis. U.S. Mil. Acad., 1955-58, supt., 1970-74; bn. comdr. 3d Armored Cav. Regt., 1958-59, mil. attache, 1961-63; brig. comdr. Ft. Knox, Ky., 1963-64; with Office Chief Staff U.S. Army, 1964-65; mil. asst. to spl. asst. to sec. and dept. sec. def. Office Sec. Def., 1965-66; sec. Joint Staff, dir. pacification support, dep. asst. chief staff for civil ops. revolutionary devel. support U.S. Mil. Assistance Command, Vietnam, 1966-67; asst. div. comdr. 9th Inf. Div., Vietnam, 1968; sec. gen. staff Office Chief Staff U.S. Army, 1968-70; chief staff hdqrs. U.S. European Command, Stuttgart, W.Ger., 1974-76; comdr. Allied Land Forces Southeast Europe, Izmir, Turkey, 1976-77; U.S. rep. NATO Mil. Com., Brussels, 1977-80; ret., 1980; cons. on internat. affairs and strategic intelligence R & D Assocs., Marina del Rey, Calif.; sr. assoc. Burdeshaw Assocs. Ltd., 1981-91; dir. Aeronca Inc., 1982-86, Chubb Corp., Fed. Ins. Co., Vigilant Ins. Co., Chubb Life Am., 1983-93; sr. fellow CAPSTONE course Nat. Def. U., 1984-95, sr. fellow emeritus CAPSTONE course, 1995—. Sr. rsch. fellow Inst. Advanced Technology U. Tex., Austin, 1998—; lectr. Am. U., 1995—1998 Contbr.: Ency. Americana and nat. mags. Trustee Davis and Elkins Coll., 1982-90. Decorated Def. D.S.M., Army D.S.M., Silver Star with 2 oak leaf clusters, Legion of Merit with oak leaf cluster, D.F.C., Bronze Star with V device, Air medal with 9 oak leaf clusters, Army Commendation medal with oak leaf cluster, knight comdr. cross Order Merit W. Ger., officer Legion of Honor France, Vietnamese Nat. Order and Gallantry Cross with palm; recipient George Washington honor medal Freedoms Found., Valley Forge, 1957, 58, Lemnitzer award, 1994; named Hon. Col. Regiment, 40th armor Berlin. Mem. Am. Mil. Inst., 7th Armored Divsn. Assn. (hon. pres.), Coun. Fgn. Rels., Soc. Mayflower Descs., Washington Inst. Fgn. Affairs (v.p. 1998), S.R., Soc. Colonial Wars, Univ. Club (N.Y.C.), Army and Navy Club (Washington), Phi Kappa Phi. Home: 4520 4th Rd N Arlington VA 22203-2343

KNOX, ARTHUR LLOYD, investor; b. Perkins, Okla., May 12, 1932; s. Myrl Frank and Margaret (Grant) K.; m. Earlene Lois Luff, Feb. 19, 1955; children: Arthur Earl, Angela Marie. BS, Okla. State U., 1955. With Lincoln Steel Corp., Nebr., 1957-84, exec. v.p., COO, 1979-81, pres., 1981-84. Sr. v.p. Commerce Capital Inc., 1984-90; ptnr. Reinox Devel., 1984-87; chmn. RF Investment Advisors, Inc., 1991-93; ptnr. 2LK Horse & Cattle Co., Knox Assocs.; adv. bd. Nebr. Dept. Econ. Devel., 1979-83; del. White House Conf. Small Bus., 1974—. Chmn. Lancaster County Young Reps., 1966-67, Nebr. Fedn. Young Reps., 1967-68, Lancaster County Rep. Com., 1972-76; asst. chmn. Nebr. Rep. Party, 1979-80; mem. Rep. Nat. Com., 1980-84; co-chmn. Gov. Charles Thone Campaign, 1978, Gov. Kay Orr Campaign, 1986-90; mem. adv. com. Nebr. Small Bus. Adminstrn., 1986; mem. adv. com. Nebr. Econ. Devel. Commn., 1987, chmn., 1988; bd. dirs. Lower Platte South Natural Resources Dist., 1974-2000, chmn., 1988-89; presdl. elector for Nebr., 1976—; del. Rep. Nat. Conv., 1988; mem. Nebr. Diplomats, 1987—; bd. dirs., pres. Peoples City Mission Found., 1995—. With AUS, 1955-57. Recipient various Rep., Jaycee and Rotary awards, 2001. Mem. Nebr. C. of C. and Industry, Lincoln C. of C. (dir. 1981-84), Rotary (bd. dirs.2001-2002, pres. 1993-94, dist. gov. 1997), Farmhouse. Presbyterian. Home: 920 Pine Tree Ln Lincoln NE 68521-4071 Office: 846 NBC Ctr Lincoln NE 68508 E-mail: alk.lnk@ispi.net.

KNOX, BRIAN VICTOR, newspaper publisher and editor; b. Madison, Wis., May 2, 1951; s. William David and Jane (Shaw) K.; m. Terrie Lynn Wyrick, Aug. 23, 1984; children: Jessica, Paris, Gillian, Brian. Editor, pub. Daily Jefferson County Union, Ft. Atkinson, Wis., 1977—; v.p. ops. W.D. Hoard & Sons Co., Ft. Atkinson, 1981—; editor, pub. Hometown News LLP, Ft. Atkinson, 1991—. Pres. South Ctrl. Publs., Stoughton, Wis., 1997-2001. Mem. Ft. Atkinson Sch. Bd., 1988-94. Mem. Wis. Newspaper Assn. (bd. dirs. 1998—, pres. 2003-). Republican. Episcopalian. Avocations: cross country skiing, book collecting, dairy farming. Office: WD Hoard & Sons Co 28 Milwaukee Ave W Fort Atkinson WI 53538-2096

KNOX, DEBORAH CAROLYN, state information systems administrator; b. Manchester, Tenn., Mar. 31, 1962; d. Eugene Clarke and Myrtle Carolyn (Bell) Knox. BBA in Acctg., Middle Tenn. State U., 1984. CPA, Tenn.; cert. govt. fin. mgr. Sr. fin. planner Lincoln Fin. Group, Brentwood, Tenn., 1986; staff acct. Charles Tharp & Assocs., Nashville, 1987; staff acct. dept. treasury State of Tenn., Nashville, 1984-85, supr. pension payroll dept. treasury, 1987, compliance analyst, policy planner, 1988, dir. program acctg. dept. fin., adminstrn., 1988-93; from data adminstr. to mgr. application devel. and support Dept. of Fin. and Adminstrn., Nashville, 1993-99, asst. dir. info. sys. mgmt., 1999—. Mem. Assn. Govt. Accts., Nat. Assn. CPAs (John Lewis award 1984). Avocations: snow and water skiing, raising and training horses and dogs.

KNOX, ELIZABETH LOUISE, community volunteer, travel consultant; b. Forest Hills, N.Y. d. Frederick Conrad and Emma M. Wissel; m. Rudolph T. Haas Jr., Feb. 1944 (div. June 1955); 1 child, Rudolph T. III; m. James Henry Knox, Aug. 22, 1956 (dec. Feb. 1987),; children: Julie Frances, Alice Carrie. Student, Hunter Coll. Ret. co-owner Del Mar (Calif.) Travel Bur. Mem. bd. trustees Salk Inst., La Jolla, 1994—; co-chair Salk Inst. Coun., 1995—; v.p. women's assn., 1969-70, pres., 1970-72, trustee, 1981-82, chmn. Andy Williams golf tournament benefit, 1969-70, chmn. 30th anniversary com., 1990-92; co-chmn. fashion show benefit Bishop's Sch., La Jolla, 1967, chmn., 1968, trustee, devel. chmn., 1971—, v.p., 1980-82, pres., 1982-86, headmaster's adv. coun., 1986—; bd. dirs. women's aux. Scripps Meml. Hosp., La Jolla, 1963-64, co-chmn. candlelight ball, 1963; charter mem. La Jolla unit Children's Hosp., San Diego, 1956, chmn. ways and means La Jolla unit, 1956-59, chmn. 10th annual fair benefit, 1963, pres. La Jolla unit, 1965, bd. dirs. women's auxiliary, 1962-64, chmn. San Diego stadium premiere benefit, 1967; bd. regents Calif. Luth. Univ., 1994—. Named Mother of Yr., March of Dimes, 2002; recipient Nat. Lane Bryant award, 1966, Woman of Valor award, Temple Beth israel, 1967, Jonas Salk award of Congress, Salk Inst., 1972, Pres' award, Women's Assn. Salk Inst., 1978, Woman of Dedication award, San Diego Door of Hope Aux/Salvation Army, 1986. Mem. La Jolla Beach and Tennis Club, Del Mar Turf Club. Home: 2688 Hidden Valley Rd La Jolla CA 92037-4025

KNOX, GERTIE R. company executive, accountant; b. Rossville, Tenn., Feb. 2, 1960; d. Columbus and Mabel (Strickland) K.; m. Micheal F. Coley, Sept. 1, 1990. BBA, U. Memphis, 1982; MBA, Colo. State U., 1998. CPA, Calif. Contracts and fin. adminstr. Textron Aerostructures, Nashville, 1983-86; ptnr. PricewaterhouseCoopers LLP, Irvine, Calif., 1986-2001; COO, Global Social Compliance LLC, L.A., 2001—. Mem.: AICPA. Avocations: reading, travel. Home: Irvine CA 92606 Office: Global Social Compliance LLC 801 S Figueroa St Ste 850 Los Angeles CA 90017 Fax: 213-362-6012. E-mail: gknox@gsocialc.com.

KNOX, GLENDA JANE, retired health and safety specialist, educator; b. Abernathy, Tex., Mar. 8, 1939; d. Raymond Arnold and Viola Jane (Melton) Boykin; m. William Gene Bright, Mar. 2, 1954 (dec. July 1974); children: Rocky Dwain, Jeannie Ann, Mary Jane, Tommy Lynn; m. Arthur Richard Knox, May 1, 1978; step-sons: Ricky Lynn Stinson, Tony Ray Knox; foster son, Roy David Haney. Grad., Comml. Coll., Baton Rouge, 1975; student, Odessa Coll., 1986-89. Cert. water safety instrn. trainer, health and safety specialist, infant, presch. and parent swimming instr. specialist. Sales clk. Flying B Western Wear, Odessa, Tex., 1975-76; mgr. Redondo Western Wear, Odessa, Tex., 1976-78, Andy's Western Wear, Odessa, Tex., 1978-79; owner Classy Original's Western Wear, Odessa, Tex., 1979-81; water safety instr. Odessa Family YMCA, 1979-82, Odessa Coll., 1981-83, water safety coord., 1983-96, health and safety instr., 1987-96, aquatics coord. continuing edn., 1983-92; ret., 1996. Owner Mydarn Barn Gallery, 2001; instr. Arthritis Found. YMCA Aquatics Program, Odessa, 1990—93, Aquatic Exercise Assn., Odessa, 1987—93; instr. specialist ARC Adapted Aquatics, Midland, Tex., 1986—93; lifeguard instr. trainer ARC, Odessa, 1979—83, CPR instr. trainer, 1981—93, 1st aid instr. trainer, 1981—93, canoeing instr., 1988—91; water safety specialist Boy Scouts and Girl Scouts Am., Odessa, 1980—93; 1st aid instr. Medic First Aid, Odessa, 1990—93. Author, editor, artist: Water Aerobics, 1986; author, editor: Food Safety Svc., 1992; designer logo and pin West Tex. Ter. Am. Red Cross, 1988. Vol. Salvation Army, Odessa, 1979-83; mem. exec. bd. ARC, Odessa, 1992, nat. awards chmn., 1992-95, health and safety chmn. region III, terr. 3, 1987-95. Recipient Outstanding Vol. Svc. award Commodore Longfellow Soc., 1994, 95, ARC, 1994, others. Mem. NAFE, Commodore Longfellow Soc. (Outstanding Svc. award 1990, 94), Smithsonian Inst., Nat. Trust for Hist. Preservation, Northshore Animal League (Benefactor award 1988, 89), Christian Cowboys Riding Assn. (awards chmn. 2001). Baptist. Avocations: doll collector, antique collector, swimming, artist, riding horses. Home: 10177 W 26th St Odessa TX 79763-6333

KNOX, HELENE MARGRETHE, writer; b. Sacramento, Calif., May 1, 1943; d. James Dale and Helen Margrete (Clemens) K. BA with honors, U. Calif., 1965, MA, 1968, PhD, 1979; MDiv, Starr King Sch. for Ministry, Berkeley, Calif., 1994. Assoc., instr., sect. leader dept. English U. Calif., Berkeley, 1972-74, 77-78; Fulbright lectr. in Am. studies U. Perpignan, France, 1972-73, U. Augsburg, Fed. Republic Germany, 1980-81; lectr. English U. San Francisco, 1979; vis. asst. prof. English Drexel U., Phila., 1981-82; asst. prof. English and creative writing Muhlenberg Coll., Allentown, Pa., 1982-86; ind. poet, essayist, tchr., scholar, editor, interviewer Oakland, Calif., 1986—; instr. Starr King Sch. for Ministry, 1991. Presenter pub. readings of original poetry, U.S., Europe and Tunisia, 1970—; lectr. on lit., U.S. and Europe, 1972-89; presenter papers at profl. meetings. Contbr. poetry to lit. mags. and anthologies; contbg. editor Standing Before Us: Unitarian Universalist Women and Social Reform, 1776-1936, 2000; contbr. stories, scholarly articles to various publs. Recipient Feminist Theology award Unitarian Universalist Women's Fedn., Boston, 1991. Mem.: PEN, Nat. Writers Union. Mem. Green Party. Unitarian Universalist. Avocations: music, organic gardening. Home: 331 62nd St Oakland CA 94618-1215

KNOX, JAMES EDWIN, lawyer; b. Evanston, Ill., July 2, 1937; s. James Edwin and Marjorie Eleanor (Williams) K.; m. Rita Lucille Torres, June 30, 1973; children: James Edwin III, Kirsten M., Katherine E., Miranda G. BA in Polit. Sci., State U. Iowa, 1959; JD, Drake U., 1961. Bar: Iowa 1961, Ill. 1962, Tex. 1982. Law clk. to Justice Tom C. Clark, U.S. Supreme Ct., Washington, 1961-62; assoc., then ptnr. Isham, Lincoln & Beale, Chgo., 1962-70; v.p. law N.W. Industries, Inc., Chgo., 1970-80; exec. v.p., gen. counsel Lone Star Steel Co., Dallas, 1980-86; sr. v.p. law Anixter Internat. Inc., Chgo., 1986—2002. Instr. contracts and labor law Chgo. Kent Coll. Law, 1964—69; arbitrator Nat. Ry. Adjustment Bd., 1967—68; ptnr. Mayer, Brown & Platt, Chgo., 1992—96; gen. counsel Arris Group, Inc., 1996—2002. Mem. ABA, Ill. Bar Assn., Order of Coif, Phi Beta Kappa. Office: Anixter Internat Inc 2301 Patriot Blvd Glenview IL 60025-8020 E-mail: jeknoxie@aol.com.

KNOX, JOHN, JR., philosopher, educator; b. Nashville, Mar. 5, 1932; s. John and Lois Adelaide (Bolles) K.; m. Alida van Bronkhorst, June 30, 1962 (div. 1978); children— Trevor McTaggart, Amethy Alida; m. Lois Marie Starner Uhlman, Jan. 7, 1990. Student, Cambridge U., 1952; BA, Emory U., 1953; PhD, Yale U., 1961. Instr. philosophy C.W. Post Coll., L.I. U., 1960, asst. prof. philosophy, 1961-67; from assoc. prof. philosophy to prof. emeritus Drew U., Madison, NJ, 1967—2002, prof. emeritus, 2002—. Vis. prof. philosophy U. Miami, spring 1981 Contbr. articles to philos. publs. Served to lt. (j.g.) USNR, 1953-56. Nat. Endowment for Humanities fellow, 1973-74 Mem. Am. Philos. Assn., Phi Beta Kappa, Phi Sigma Tau. Home: 4 Shadewood Ln Hilton Head Island SC 29926-2582 *I try to believe what, and only what, I consider to be objectively true. The objective truth is not, per se— indeed it is not likely to resemble— the comfortable certainties of fixed traditions or of passing fashions. Yet I think I should be happier if I had it; at least, I am unhappy in not having it. Hence I like cautious speculations better than unthinking certitudes, and I favor Reason's occasional glimmers over Faith's unending dream.*

KNOX, MICHAEL JOHN, academic administrator; b. Coleman, Tex., Sept. 4, 1971; s. Eldon Beck and Mary Margaret Korenek Knox; m. Erica Leigh Stocker, July 5, 2003. B in Edn., Tex. A&M U., 1994; MEd, U. Pa., 1999. Tchr. Huntington Indep. Sch. Dist., Tex., 1996—98; asst. dir. student activities U. Ky., Lexington, 1999—2002; asst. dean students, dir. student activities Bellarmine U., Louisville, 2002—. Mem.: Nat. Orienation Dirs. Assn., Nat. Assn. Student Pers. Adminstrs. Roman Catholic. Avocations: golf, travel. Office: Bellarmine Univ 2001 Newburg Rd Louisville KY 40205 Office Fax: 502-473-3196. E-mail: mknox@bellarmine.edu.

KNOX, PAUL L. architecture educator, dean; bachelor's, PhD in Geography, U. Sheffield, Eng. Prof. dept. urban affairs and planning Va. Tech, assoc. dean acad. affairs, 1993—98, dir. PhD program in environ. design and planning, univ. disting. prof., interim dean Coll. Architecture and Urban Studies, 1998—99. Lectr. in field. Author 12 books; contbr. articles to profl. jours. Mem.: Va. Soc. AIA (hon.). Office: Coll Architecture and Urban Studies Va Tech 202 Cowgill Hall 0205 Blacksburg VA 24061*

KNOX, ROBERT LEE, educator; b. Enid, Okla., Jan. 15, 1932; s. Beryl Leroy and Doris Ethel (Ulrey) K.; m. Mary Frances Kern, Aug. 16, 1958; children: Shelly L., Cynthia C. BS in Commerce, Okla. State U., 1954, MS in Econs., 1958; PhD in Econs., U. N.C., 1963. Asst. prof. econs. Coll. William and Mary, Williamsburg, Va., 1961-63, Ariz. State U., Tempe, 1963—66, assoc. prof. econs., 1966—71, prof. econs., 1971—97, prof. emeritus econs., 1997—. Cons. antitrust econs., 1971—. Contbr. articles to profl. jours. Capt. USAF, 1954-57, USAFR, 1958-63. Home: 46 W Caroline Ln Tempe AZ 85284-3035

KNOX, ROBERT SEIPLE, physicist, educator; b. Franklin, N.J., July 13, 1931; s. Harvey Stoll and Laura (Seiple) K.; m. Myrta I. Borges, Sept. 1, 1954; children: Bruce Robert, Wayne Harvey, Lee Benjamin. BS in Engring. Physics, Lehigh U., 1953; PhD in Physics and Optics, U. Rochester, 1958. Rsch. assoc. U. Ill., 1958-59, rsch. asst. prof., 1959-60; mem. faculty U. Rochester, N.Y., 1960—, assoc. prof. dept. physics, 1963-68, prof., 1968-97; sr. scientist Lab. for Laser Energetics, 1985—; chmn. dept. physics and astronomy U. Rochester, 1969-74, assoc. dean spl. programs Coll. Arts and Scis., 1982-87, faculty sr. assoc., 1997-2001, prof. emeritus, 1997—. Cons. solid state sci. divsn. Argonne Nat. Lab., 1959—69, Naval Rsch. Lab., 1960—70; NSF sr. fellow U. Leiden, 1967—68. Author: Theory of Excitons, 1963, (with A. Gold) Symmetry in the Solid State, 1964, (with D.L. Dexter) Excitons, 1965; also articles. Japan Soc. Promotion of Sci. fellow Kyoto U., 1979, Royal Soc. Guest Rsch. fellow, Fulbright fellow Imperial Coll. (London), 1993. Fellow Am. Phys. Soc. (Biol. Physics prize 1994), Am. Soc. Photobiology, Am. Assn. Physics Tchrs., Biophys. Soc., Internat. Soc. Photosynthesis Rsch.. Achievements include research in atomic spectra and structure, absorption and luminescence spectra ionic and molecular crystals, photosynthesis theory, picosecond spectroscopy. Office: U Rochester Dept Physics & Astronomy Rochester NY 14627-0171 E-mail: rsk@pas.rochester.edu.

KNOX, SARAH STUART, psychophysiologist, researcher; b. Cin., Nov. 21, 1946; d. Frank Samual and Mary Stuart (Duckworth) K.; m. Eje Thelin, Apr. 16, 1980 (div. 1986); 1 child, Vanessa Thelin-Knox. BA, U. N.H., 1968; MA and PhD, U. Stockholm, Sweden, 1981. Lic. psychologist, Sweden. Rsch. physiologist Nat. Inst. for Psychosocial Factors and Health, Stockholm, 1981-83; rsch. assoc. U. Stockholm, 1983-86, assoc. prof., 1986—; dir. rsch. group Karolinska Inst., Stockholm, 1983-87; assoc. prof. psychiatry Med. Sch. Wayne State U., Detroit, 1987-91; with Behavioral Medicine Br. Nat. Heart, Lung & Blood Inst., Bethesda, Md., 1991—. Rsch. cons. WHO, Lljubliana, Yugoslavia, 1985, Nordic Working Group on Noise, Bergen, Norway, 1986; co-chair nat. workshop on biobehavioral mechanisms of lipid metabolism and atherosclerosis, Nat. Inst. Heart, Lung and Blood; chmn. workshop on gender and heart disease, NATO, Hungary, 2000; lectr. in field. Grantee Swedish Work Environment Fund, 1981-82, 84, 85, 86, Swedish Dept. Environ. Conservation, 1983. Mem. AAAS, N.Y. Acad. Scis., Soc. Behavioral Medicine, Soc. Psychophysiol. Rsch. Achievements include research in stress and heart disease. Home: 205 Fairgrove Cir Gaithersburg MD 20877-3474 Office: Nat Heart Lung & Blood Inst II Rockledge Ctr 6701 Rockledge Dr Bethesda MD 20817-1813

KNOX, WILLIAM ARTHUR, judge; b. Fargo, N.D., Jan. 8, 1945; BS, N.D. State U., 1966; JD, U. Minn., 1968. Law specialist USCG, Boston, 1968—72, Juneau, Alaska, 1968—72; prof. U. Mo. Sch. Law, Columbia, 1972—85; magistrate judge U.S. Cts., Jefferson City, Mo., 1985—. Author: Federal Criminal Forms, 2002, Missouri Criminal Practice, 1995. Office: 131 W High St Jefferson City MO 65101-1557

KNOX, WILLIAM DAVID, publishing company executive; b. Sault Ste. Marie, Mich., June 9, 1920; s. Victor A. and Bertha V. (Byers) K.; m. Jane Edith Shaw, June 15, 1941; children: Georgia Knox Mode, William David II, Randall S., Brian V. BS, Mich. State U., 1941; postgrad., Harvard U., 1943-44; LLD (hon.), U. Wis., 1973. Youth editor Hoard's Dairyman mag., W.D. Hoard & Sons Co., Fort Atkinson, Wis., 1941-42, asso. editor, 1946-49, editor, 1949—, pres., treas., gen. mgr., 1972—. Pres. Nat. Brucellosis Com., 1955-66, chmn. Wis. com., 1951-60; mem. nat. agrl. adv. com., 1961-62, nat. adv. com. on trade negotiations, 1976-82; bd. dirs. First Am. Bank and Trust, D.C.I. Mktg., Inc. Pres. Fort Atkinson Bd. Edn., 1948-59; bd. visitors U. Wis., 1979-84; trustee Univ. Rsch. Park, Inc., 1984-93; bd. dirs. Wis. Taxpayers Alliance, 1976-98. Lt. USNR, 1942-46. Recipient Disting. Svc. award Nat. Brucellosis Com., 1957, Pure Milk Assn., 1966, Am. Dairy Sci. Assn., 1970, Wis. Farm Bur. Fedn., 1974, Nat. Assn. Animal Breeders, 1981, Nat. Assn. Livestock Records, 1983, Wis. Agri-Bus. Coun., 1992, Nat. Agri-Mktg. Assn., 1992, Outstandin ANR Patriarch award Alumni assn. Coll. of Agr. and Natural Resources, Mich. State U., 1992; service citations Fla. Dairy Farmers Fedn., 1962, Wis. Farm Bur. Fedn., 1956, Nat. Plant Food Coun., 1963, Dairy Coun. Ctrl. Ga., 1967, Mid-Am. Dairymen Salute award, 1977, Nat. 4-H Alumni award, 1965, Mich. State U. Disting. Alumnus award, 1966; named Tri-State Man of Yr., 1966, Milw. Milk Prodrs. Assn. Man of Yr., 1976. Fellow Am. Dairy Sci. Assn.; mem. Agrl. Publs. Assn. (pres. 1979-81), Am. Newspaper Pubs. Assn., Am. Vet. Med. Assn. (hon.), Am. Jersey Cattle Club (hon.), Am. Agrl. Econs. Assn., Wis. Vet. Med. Assn. (hon.), Rotary (Internat. Svc. citation 1956), Alpha Gamma Rho, Alpha Zeta (Centennial Honor Roll award 1997). Republican. Episcopalian. Home: 703 Robert St Fort Atkinson WI 53538-1150 Office: Hoard's Dairyman W D Hoard & Sons Co PO Box 801 Fort Atkinson WI 53538-0801

KNOXVILLE, JOHNNY, actor; b. Knoxville, Tenn., Mar. 11, 1971; m. Melanie Knoxville; 1 child, Madkson. Student, Am. Acad. Dramatic Arts. Actor: (films) Desert Blues, 1995, Coyote Ugly, 2000, The Tree, 2001, The Ringer, 2001, Life Without Dick, 2001, Don't Try This at Home, 2001, Big Trouble, 2002, Deuces Wild, 2002, Men in Black 2, 2002; creator : (TV series) Jackass, 2000. Office: Creative Artists Agy 9830 Wilshire Blvd Beverly Hills CA 90212

KNUDSEN, DEAN DEWAYNE, sociology educator; b. Harlan, Iowa, July 9, 1932; s. Arthur Stephen and Nina Surina (Christensen) K.; m. Ruth Lucille Dalton, June 9, 1956; children: Karen Elizabeth, Stephen Brent. BA, Sioux Falls Coll., 1954; BD, Berkeley Bapt. Div. Sch., 1957; MA, U. Minn., 1961; PhD, U. N.C., 1964. Instr. sociology Augsburg Coll., Mpls., 1960-61; asst. prof. Ohio State U., Columbus, 1964-69; assoc. prof. Purdue U., West Lafayette, Ind., 1969-88, prof., 1988—, head dept. sociology/anthropology, 1992-98. Cons. Tippecanoe County Welfare Dept., Lafayette, Ind., 1973-74. Author: Spindles and Spires, 1975, Child Protective Services, 1990, Abused and Battered, 1991, Child Maltreatment, 1992. Pres. bd. dirs. Cmty. and Family Resource Ctr., Lafayette, 1977-83; bd. dirs. United Way, Lafayette, 1980-81; mem. adv. bd. Cmty. Health Clinic, Lafayette, 1990-93; coord. child protection team State of Ind.-Tippecanoe County, 1979-83. NIMH postdoctoral fellow U. N.H., 1983-84. Mem. Am. Sociol. Assn. (sect. sec. 1961), Internat. Assn. Child Abuse, Soc. for Study of Social Problems (chairperson of chairpersons 1993-95), Soc. for Sci. Study of Religion (sec. 1972-73), North Ctrl. Sociol. Assn. (pres. 1977-78). Democrat. Baptist. Avocations: gardening, playing squash, woodworking. Home: 1805 Sheridan Rd West Lafayette IN 47906-2225 Office: Purdue Univ Dept Sociology/Anthropology 1365 Stone Hall West Lafayette IN 47907-1365

KNUDSEN, KERMIT BRUCE, physician; b. Mpls., Sept. 16, 1931; m. Karen Hansen, Mar. 27, 1954; children: Peter, Mark, John, Lisa, Karen. BS, Lawrence Coll., 1952; MD, U. Ill., 1956. Diplomate Am. Bd. Internal Medicine, Am. Bd. Gastroenterology. Intern St. Louis City Hosp., 1956-57; resident in internal medicine Henry Ford Hosp., Detroit, 1959-62, fellow in gastroenterology, 1962-63; cheif gastroenterology Wilford Hall USAF Hosp., San Antonio, 1963-67; pvt. practice specializing in internal medicine Boulder, Colo., 1967-68; gastroenterologist Scott & White Clinic and Hosp., Temple, Tex., 1968-96, dir. gastroentology divsn., 1972-74, chmn. edn. dept., 1974-78, assoc. clinic bd., 1975-92, chmn. dept. internal medicine, 1975-79, pres., 1979-92; chief of staff Scott & White Meml. Hosp., Temple, 1979-92; dir. Ctr. for Outcomes Studies Scott & Whtie Clinic and Hosp., Temple, Tex., 1992-96. Assoc. dean Tex. A&M U., Temple, 1975-79, prof. internal medicine, 1975-96; bd. dirs. Temple Indsl. Found., pres., 1985; bd. dirs. N.C.N. Bank, Temple. Bd. dirs. Temple Econ. Devel. Commn., 1985-88, Health Sys. Minn., Stratis Health. Fellow ACP; mem. Am. Gastroent. Assn., AMA, Am. Group Practice assn. (trustee 1983-90, sec. 1986-87, v.p. 1988, pres.-elect 1989, pres., 1989-90), Tex. Med. Assn., Alpha Omega Alpha. Lutheran. Home: 66 Ponderosa Park Dr Durango CO 81301-6908 Office: Scott & White Clinic 2401 S 31st St Temple TX 76508-0001 E-mail: kknudsen@mailbox.sw.org.

KNUDSEN, LAURA GEORGIA, linguist; b. Kenosha, Wis., Sept. 21, 1969; d. Richard Dennis and Georgia Elizabeth (Perrin) Wright; m. Martin Christian Knudsen, Aug. 20, 1994. BA in Linguistics, Ind. U., 1991, MA in Linguistics, 2001. Linguist Ind. U., Bloomington, 1987—, tchr. ESL, Ctr. for English Lang. Tng., 1995—; tchr. ESL Aichi U., Toyohashi, Japan, 1998, Ind. U./ Purdue U. Indpls., 2002; tchr. Aikido Ind. U., 2001—. Presenter in field Contbr. articles to profl. jours. Fulbright scholar IIE, Budapest, 1996-97; FLAS fellow U.S. Dept. Edn., Ind. U., 1993-94, GANN fellow, 1991-92. Mem. Linguistic Soc. Am., Ind. U. Linguistic Club (sec. 1996, pres. 1998), INTESOL (student rep. 1999, rec. sec. 2002-03). Avocation: Aikido. Office: Ind U Ctr English Lang Tng Meml Hall 317 Bloomington IN 47405

KNUDSEN, RUDOLPH EDGAR, JR., insurance company executive; b. Far Rockaway, N.Y., July 18, 1939; s. Rudolph Edgar and Katherine Elizabeth (Benham) K.; m. Margaret Rebecca Vreeland, June 10, 1961 (dec.); children— Peter, Kathryn. AB, Columbia Coll., 1961. Programmer Met. Life Ins. Co., N.Y.C., 1961-65, Am. Life Ins. Co. N.Y., N.Y.C., 1965-70, 2d v.p., 1971-72, v.p., 1973—. Served with USAR, 1961-62. Mem.: Broken Sound. Methodist. Home: 2436 NW 63rd St Boca Raton FL 33496-3626 Office: Mut of Am Life Ins Co 1150 Broken Sound Pkwy NW Boca Raton FL 33487-3525

KNUDSEN, WILLIAM CLAIRE, geophysicist, researcher; b. Provo, Utah, Dec. 12, 1925; s. Nels William and Julia A. (Brown) K.; m. Ruth Crandall, Aug. 31, 1948; children: Linda, Ruthanne, Guy, Grant. BS, Brigham Young U., 1950; MS, U. Wis., 1952, PhD, 1954. Sr. rsch. physicist Calif. Rsch. Corp., La Habra, 1954-62; staff scientist Lockheed Palo Alto Rsch. Lab., Palo Alto, Calif., 1962-84, Knudsen Geophys. Rsch. Inc., Monte Sereno, Calif., 1984-95; ret., 1995. Adj. prof. Brigham Young U., 1997, Utah State U., 1997. Patentee in field. With Signal Corps U.S. Army, 1944-46. Mem. Am. Geophys. Union, Sigma Xi. Mem. Lds Ch. E-mail: wcknudsen@msn.com.

KNUDSON, DUANE VICTOR, kinesiology education educator, researcher; b. West Allis, Wis., Oct. 1, 1961; s. Henry T. and Rosa Ellen (Shondel) K.; m. Lois Mary Reinders, Aug. 5, 1983; children: Joshua Thomas, Mandy Kay. BS, U. Wis., Oshkosh, 1983; MS, Baylor U., 1984; PhD, U. Wis., Madison, 1988. Grad. asst. U. Wis., Madison, 1985-88, Baylor U., Waco, Tex., 1983-84, lectr. phys. edn., 1984—97; assoc. prof. Calif. State U., Chico, 1997—. Contbr. articles on biomechanics rsch. to scholarly and profl. jours.; author two books; reviewer Phys. Therapy, Jour. Biomechanics. Rsch. grantee Victor Sports, Inc., 1986, Apple Computer, 1987, 88, U.S. Tennis Assn., 1987, 89, 92, 94, 96, 98, 2000, 01, 02. Mem. AAHPER and Dance, Am. Soc. Biomechanics, Internat. Soc.Soc. Biomechanics in Sports, Am. Coll. of Sports Medicine (USTA sport sci. com.). Office: Calif State Univ Dept PE and Exercise Sci Chico CA 95929-0330

KNUDSON, MARK BRADLEY, medical corporation executive, venture capitalist; b. Libby, Mont., Sept. 24, 1948; s. Melvin R. and Melba Irene (Joice) K.; m. Susan Jean Voorhees, Sept. 12, 1970; children: Kirstin Sue, Amy Lynn. BS, Pacific Luth. U., 1970; PhD, Wash. State U., 1974. Lectr. Wash. State U., Pullman, 1973-75; rsch. assoc. U. Wash., Seattle, 1976-78, asst. prof., 1976-79; physiologist Cardiac Pacemakers Inc., St. Paul, 1979-80, mgr. rsch., 1980-82, dir. applied rsch., 1982-83; pres., chmn. bd. SenTech Med. Corp., St. Paul, 1983-86; pres. Arden Med. Systems Inc. subs. Johnson & Johnson, 1986-89; pres., dir. Johnson & Johnson Profl. Diagnostics Inc., Raritan, N.J., 1988-89; ptnr. Med. Innovation Ptnrs., 1989-99; gen. ptnr. Med. Innovation Fund, 1999—; chmn., CEO Venturi Group LLC, 1999—; pres., CEO Pi Med., Inc., 1999—2002; exec. chmn. Restore Med., Inc., 2002—. Bd. dirs. Diametrics Inc.; lectr. in field. Contbr. articles to profl. jours.; patentee in field. Chmn., bd. dirs. Luth. Sem. Fellow, NIH, Wash. State U., 1974—75, U. Wash., 1975—76. Fellow Am. Heart Assn.; mem. AAAS, Sigma Xi. Republican. Lutheran. Office: Venturi Group LLC 2800 Patton Rd Saint Paul MN 55113-1100

KNUDSON, RUTH ESTHER, education educator; b. Phila., June 29, 1945; d. Robert J. and Ruth M. (Weisner) Rodisch; m. Karl J. Knudson, June 15, 1968; children: Robert K., Richard K. BA, Bryn Mawr Coll., 1967; MS, U. Wis., 1968; PhD, U. Calif., Riverside, 1988. Cert. secondary tchr., Calif. Tchr. English and reading, Calif., La., and Mass., 1969-77; supr. tchr. edn. Sch. Edn., U. Calif., Riverside, 1985-88, asst. head tchr. edn., 1988-89, mem. edn. faculty, 1989-95; assoc. prof. Calif. State U., Long Beach, 1995-99, prof., 1999—. Chair single subject com. Calif. State U., Long Beach, 1995—97, mem. human subjects rsch. rev. com., 1997—99, chair faculty merit increase com., 2000—01, chair retention, tenure and promotion com. Coll. Edn., 2002—03; cons. pub. sch. dists., Calif., 1984—92; chair tchr. edn. com. U. Calif., Riverside, 1992—94, mem. retention, tenure and promotion com., 1999—; local arrangements chair Nat. Reading Conf., 1991; evaluator Mid. Schs. Demonstration Programs, 1997—2000. Contbr. articles to profl. jours. Woodrow Wilson fellow, 1967-68; recipient Spencer award Spencer Found., Chgo., 1989-90. Mem. Nat. Conf. of Rsch. on Lang. and Literacy, Nat. Coun. of Tchrs. of English, Am. Ednl. Rsch. Assn. (program reviewer 1989—, Dissertation of Yr. award 1989), Internat. Reading Assn., Phi Delta Kappa. Avocations: reading, family vacations. Office: Calif State U Long Beach Coll Edn 1250 N Bellflower Blvd Long Beach CA 90840-0006 E-mail: rknuded@aol.com., knudson@csulb.edu.

KNUDSON, RUTHANN, environmental consultant; b. Milw., Oct. 24, 1941; d. Sidney Olaus and Clara Ruth (Tappe) K. BA magna cum laude, U. Minn., 1963, MA, 1966; PhD, Wash. State U., 1973; postgrad., U. Idaho, 1988. Seasonal ranger Nat. Park Svc., Bandelier Nat. Monument, N.Mex., 1963; instr. U. No. Colo., Greeley, 1966-68; asst. rsch. prof. U. Idaho, Moscow, 1974-79, assoc. rsch. prof., 1979-81; dir. cultural resource svcs. Woodward Clude Cons., San Francisco, 1981-86, v.p., shareholder, 1985-88; archeologist Nat. Park Svc., Washington, 1990—96; supr. Agate Fossil Beds Nat. Monument, 1996—; prin. Knudson Assoc. (formerly Paleo-Designs), 1974—. Vis. asst. prof. Wright State U., Dayton, Ohio, 1974; cons. Am. Folklife Ctr., Washington, 1981-83, NRC, Washington, 1982, 83; resource cons. Calif. Heritage Task Force, 1983-94, Office Tech. Assessment, Washington, 1986; Woodward lectr., 1985; mem. Nebr. Panhandle Tourism Coalition, 1996—. Author: Cambria Village Ceramics, 1967, Organizational Variability in Late Paleo-Indian Assemblages, 1983, Contemporary Cultural Resource Management, 1986; co-editor: The Public Trust and the First Americans, 1995, The 10,000 year old Lubbock Artifact Assemblage, 1998, Using Cultural Resources to Enhance Ecosystem Management, 1999, Using the Past to Shape National Park Service Policy for Wildlife, 1999, Cultural Resource Management in Context, 2000, Medicine Creek is a Paleoindian Cultural Ecotone: The Red Smoke Assemblage, 2002. Bd. dirs. Preservation Action, Washington, 1980-85, 89-90, Californians for Preservation Action, 1981-82; sec.-treas. Idaho NOW, 1977-78; co-chmn. Nebr. Panhandle Tourism Coalition, 2000-01. Recipient Preservation award Nat. Conf. State Historic Preservation Officers, 1981, Conservation award Am. Soc. Conservation Archaeology, 1981. Mem. Soc. Applied Anthropology, Am. Anthropol. Assn. (Margaret Mead award 1983), Soc. Am. Archaeology (exec. bd. 1979-81, exec. com. 1983-85, legis. coord. 1979-82, chmn. com. pub. archaeology 1980-82, 84-85), Women's Coun. Energy & Environ. (bd. dirs. 1994-96), Soc. Vert. Paleontology, Geol. Soc. of Am., Phi Beta Kappa. Home: 343 River Rd Harrison NE 69346-2734 Office: Agate Fossil Beds Nat Monument 301 River Rd Harrison NE 69346-2734 E-mail: paleoknute@aol.com.

KNUDSON, THOMAS JEFFERY, journalist; b. Manning, Iowa, July 6, 1953; s. Melvin Jake and Koreen Rose (Nickum) Knudson. BA in Journalism, Iowa State U., 1980. Reporter/intern Wall St. Jour., Chgo., 1979; staff writer Des Moines Register, 1980—99; sr. writer Sacramento (Calif.) Bee, 1999—. Office: Sacramento Bee PO Box 15779 Sacramento CA 95852-0779

KNULL, ERHARD, minister; b. Radomsko, Poland, June 25, 1929; came to U.S., 1952. s. Richard and Martha (Kamchen) K.; m. Lydia Penno, July 21, 1956; children: Carmen Ruth Knull Bloomster, Ralph Erhard Carl. BA, Sioux Falls Coll., 1960; BD, No. Am. Bapt. Seminary, 1961; post grad., U. Tuebingen, Fed. Republic Germany, 1961-62; MA, Kent state U., 1973; MDiv, North Am. Bapt. Seminary, 1984; postgrad., Chaplain Tng. Sch., St. Louis, 1974, Samaritan Counseling Ctr., Lakewood, Ohio, 1982-83. Ordained to ministry Bapt. Ch, 1963; cert. VA chaplain, Washington. Min. Rosenfeld Bapt. Ch., Drake, N.D., 1962-65, Missionary Bapt. Ch., Parma, Ohio, 1965-69; lectr. Kent (Ohio) State U., 1969; sr. staff chaplain Louis Stokes Cleve. Dept. of Veterans Affairs Med. Ctr., Brecksville, 1970—. Chaplain, counselor DVA Community Outreach program, Cleve., 1978—. Contbr. articles to profl. jours. Active Parma Heights Bapt. Ch., also tchr., advisor men's fellowship. Mem. North Am. Bapt. Conf. (endorsed chaplain), North Am. Bapt. Sem. Alumni Assn. Baptist. Avocations: reading, bicycling, traveling, walking, gardening. Office: Louis Stokes Cleve Med Ctr Dept Vets Affairs 10000 Brecksville Rd Dept Vets Cleveland OH 44141-3204

KNUPP, RALPH, information technology executive; Sr. v.p. human resources Reed Elsevier, Inc., Newton, Mass.; v.p. human resources & comm. Varian Semiconductor Equipment Assoc., Gloucester, Mass., 1999—. Office: Varian Semiconductor Equipment Assoc 35 Dory Rd Gloucester MA 01930-2236

KNUTESON, MILES GENE, advertising executive; b. Wisconsin Rapids, Wis., Aug. 18, 1952; s. Kenneth Thomas and Myrtle Lucille (Knoll) K.; m. Christine Marie Coleman, Aug. 18, 1979; children: Katherine Marie, Emily Melissa. BS, U. Wis., Stevens Point, 1974. News reporter Sta. WHBY, Appleton, Wis., 1974-77, acct. exec., 1977-79; gen. sales mgr. Sta. WAPL, Appleton, 1979-80, Stas. WHBY, WAPL-FM, Appleton, 1980-81, Sta. WGEE, Green Bay, Wis., 1981-83; v.p., gen. mgr. Stas. KIOA/KDWZ-FM, Des Moines, 1983-88; v.p. sales, mktg. Midwest Comm., Inc., Des Moines, 1988-89; gen. sales mgr. Sta. WMEE/WQHK, Ft. Wayne, Ind., 1988-89, Stas. WTTS/WGCL, Bloomington, Ind., 1989-90; v.p., gen. mgr. Stas. WFHR/WGLX, Wisconsin Rapids, Wis., 1990—. Bd. dirs. United Way, Wisconsin Rapids, 1991-92, campaign chairperson, 1992, pres., 1994; chmn. adv. bd. Salvation Army, Appleton, 1981-83, mem. adv. bd., Bloomington; chmn. Distributive Edn. Adv. Bd., 1980, chmn. pub. rels. com., Des Moines, 1987; pres. Immanuel Luth. Sch. Bd., 1995-2001. Recipient Pub. Affairs award N.W. Broadcast News Assn., 1976, Sch. Bell award Wis. Edn. Assn. Coun., 1976. Mem.: Wisconsin Rapids Area C. of C. (bd. dirs. 1994—2000, chmn. 1996), Fox Cities C. of C. (amb.), Wis. Broadcasters Assn. (bd. dirs. 1995—, chmn. 2001), Des Moines Radio Broadcasters Assn. (v.p., sec., chmn.), Rotary (bd. dirs. Wisconsin Rapids chpt. 1995—2002, pres. 2000—01, Paul Harris fellow). Lutheran. Avocations: golf, gardening. Home: 5411 Barberry Dr Wisconsin Rapids WI 54494-1524

KNUTH, DONALD ERVIN, computer sciences educator; b. Milw., Jan. 10, 1938; s. Ervin Henry and Louise Marie (Bohning) Knuth; m. Jill Carter, June 24, 1961; children: John Martin, Jennifer Sierra. BS, MS, Case Inst. Tech., 1960; PhD, Calif. Inst. Tech., 1963; DSc (hon.), Case Western Res. U., 1980, Luther Coll., Decorah, Iowa, 1985, Lawrence U., 1985, Muhlenberg Coll., 1986, U. Pa., 1986, U. Rochester, 1986; Docteur, U. Paris-Sud, Orsay, 1986; DSc (hon.), SUNY, Stony Brook, 1987, Oxford (Eng.) U., 1988, Brown U., 1988, Valparaiso U., 1988, Grinnell Coll., 1989, Dartmouth Coll., 1990; D Tech., Royal Inst. Tech., Stockholm, 1991; DSc (hon.), Concordia U., Montréal, 1991; Pochetnogo Doktora, St. Petersburg U., Russia, 1992; DSc (hon.), Adelphi U., 1993, Masaryk U., Brno, 1996, Duke U., 1998, St. Andrews U., 1998, Marne-la-Vallée, 1993; DLitt (hon.), U. Waterloo, 2000; DSc (hon.), Williams Coll., 2000, U. Tubingen, 2001, Athens U. Econ., 2001, U. Oslo, 2002, Harvard U., 2003, U. Thessaloniki, 2003, U. Antwerp, 2003. Asst. prof. Calif. Inst. Tech., Pasadena, Calif., 1963—66, assoc. prof., 1966—68; prof. Stanford U., Calif., 1968—92, prof. emeritus, 1993—. Cons. Burroughs Corp., Pasadena, Calif., 1960—68. Author: The Art of Computer Programming, 1968 (Steele prize, 1987), Computers and Typesetting, 1986. Recipient Nat. medal of Sci., Pres. James Carter, 1979, Disting. Alumni award, Calif. Inst. Tech., 1978, Priestly award, Dickinson Coll., 1981, Franklin medal, 1988, J.D. Warnier prize, 1989, Adelsköld medal, Swedish Acad. Sci., 1994, Harvey prize, Israel Inst. Tech., 1995, Kyoto prize, Inamori Found., 1996; fellow Guggenheim Found. fellow, 1972—73. Fellow: Am. Acad. Arts and Scis., The Computer Mus.; mem.: NAS, IEEE (hon. McDowell award 1980, Computer Pioneer award 1982, von Neumann medal 1995), Acad. Sci. (fgn. assoc. Paris, Oslo, Munich, London), Assn. for Computing Machinery (Grace Murray Hopper award 1971, Alan M. Turing award 1974, Computer Sci. Edn. award 1986, Software Sys. award 1986), Nat. Acad. Engring. Lutheran. Avocation: playing pipe organ. Office: Stanford Univ Computer Scis Dept Stanford CA 94305-9045

KNUTH, ELDON LUVERNE, engineering educator; b. Luana, Iowa, May 10, 1925; s. Alvin W. and Amanda M. (Becker) K.; m. Marie O. Parrat, Sept. 10, 1954 (div. 1973); children: Stephen B., Dale L., Margot O., Lynette M.; m. Margaret I. Nicholson, Dec. 30, 1973. BS, Purdue U., 1949, MS, 1950; PhD (Guggenheim fellow), Calif. Inst. Tech., 1953. Aerothermodynamics group leader Aerophysics Devel. Corp., 1953-56; asso. research engr. dept. engring. UCLA, 1956-59, asso. prof. engring., 1960-65, prof. engring. and applied sci., 1965-91, prof. emeritus, 1991—, head chem., nuclear thermal div. dept. engring., 1963-65, chmn. energy kinetics dept., 1969-75, head molecular-beam lab., 1961-88. Gen. chmn. Heat Transfer and Fluid Mechanics Inst., 1959; vis. scientist, von Humboldt fellow Max-Planck Inst. für Strömungsforschung, Göttingen, Fed. Republic Germany, 1975-76; mem. Internat. Adv. Com. Internat. Symposium Rarefied Gas Dynamics., 2000—. Author: Introduction to Statistical Thermodynamics, 1966; also numerous articles; patentee radial-flow molecular pump. Served with AUS, 1943-45. Recipient Fritz Reuter medal, Landsmannschaft, Mecklenburg, 2002. Mem. AIAA, Am. Soc. Engring. Edn., Am. Inst. Chem. Engrs., Combustion Inst., Soc. Engring. Sci., AAAS, Am. Phys. Soc., Am. Vacuum Soc., Sigma Xi, Tau Beta Pi, Gamma Alpha Rho, Pi Tau Sigma, Sigma Delta Chi, Pi Kappa Phi. Clubs: Gimlet (Lafayette, Ind.). Home: 18085 Boris Dr Encino CA 91316-4350

KNUTH, MARYA DANIELLE, special education educator; b. Bowling Green, Ohio, Apr. 27, 1971; d. Kerry Lee and Sandra Jean Knuth. BEd, U. Toledo, 1997; MEd (hon.), U Toledo, 2002; cert. in reading (hon.), U. Toledo, 2002. Cert. in tchg. Tchr. spl. edn. Jefferson Jr. H.S., Toledo, 1997—98, Washington Jr. H.S., Toledo, 1998—; promotion coord. J&L Mktg., 2002—. Coach intramurals Washington Local Schs., Toledo, 1998—2002; chairperson bldg. beautification com. Washington Jr. H.S., Toledo, 2001—, chairperson best practice com.; dem. exch. program Ohio - Ukraine- Hungary Ednl. Exch. Program in the Pub. Sch. Setting, Toledo, 1999—2000; reading tutor Read for Lit., Toledo, 2000—; co-chairperson 100% Homework Club, Washington Jr. High, 2002—03; promotion coord. J&L Mktg., 1999—; head coach freshman girls Whitmer HS. Author (editor): A Netherland Tour, 1998. Mem. Build Your Sch. Garden Com., 2003—; head coach freshman Broomball Team, Toledo, 2003—; mem. Sister Cities of Toledo, 2000—. Recipient Best Lesson Plans award, Teachers Orgn., 2000. Mem.: ASCD, Coun. Exceptional Children. Republican. Avocations: tutoring, travel, rollerblading. Home: 4812 W Bancroft St Apt 30 Toledo OH 43615 Office: Washington Jr HS 5700 Whitmer Dr Toledo OH 43613 Personal E-mail: MaryaK1999@aol.com.

KNUTH FISCHER, CYNTHIA STROUT, environmental consultant; b. Walpole, Mass. d. Harold A. and Doris A. (Kendall) Strout; m. Adam Knuth (dec.); m. Charles S. Fischer. BA, Middlebury Coll., 1948; MA in Internat. Law and Govt., NYU, 1965. Adminstrv. asst. FAO Mission to Iraq, Baghdad, 1950—53; internat. conf. precis-writer Copenhagen, 1954—56; exec. sec. to UN legal counsel, 1956—62; exec. sec. to pres. Gen. Assembly UN, N.Y.C., 1962—63; exec. sec. UN Devel. Program, N.Y.C., 1964—69; with Ctr. for Internat. Affairs, Harvard U., Cambridge, Mass., 1976—82; founder, pres. Friends of Native Ams., 1986—. Founder Menotomy Indian Day, Arlington, Mass., 1991, Aberjona Indian Day, Winchester, Mass., 1992; founder, pres. Ctr. for Environ. Edn., East Coast, 1990—; sec. to bd. dirs. UN Assn. Greater Phila., 1998—2002; publicity chair, bd. dirs. Valley Forge Audubon Soc., 1996—2000; environ chair Lions Club of West Chester, Pa., 1996. Vol. Chadds Ford Hist. Soc., Second Reading Bookstore to benefit Sr. Ctr. of West Chester, 1998—; founder Friends of Indigenous Peoples, 2000—; rep. Phila. Hospitality, 2002—. Mem. Common Cause (exec. bd. Mass. 1986), Mass. UN Assn. (exec. bd. 1970), Boston Jazz Soc. (exec. bd. 1975), Mystic River Watershed Assn. (exec. bd. 1991), Phi Delta Kappa (2d v.p. Harvard U. chpt. 1990-92), Sierra Club/Thoreau Group (chair 1993), Walden Forever Wild (exec. bd. 1993-95). Home: 956 Conner Rd West Chester PA 19380-1810

KNUTSON, DAVID HARRY, retired lawyer, banker; b. St. Paul, Dec. 17, 1934; s. Harry E. and Violet I. (Ekberg) K.; m. Kirsten Birgit Eriksen, Aug. 20, 1977; one child, Clara Elizabeth. AB Cum Laude, Harvard U., 1956, LLB, 1961; LLM in Corp. Law, NYU, 1990; LLM in Taxation, SUNY, 1994. Bar: Minn., 1962, N.Y., 1963. Assoc. Lord, Day, and Lord, N.Y.C., 1962-69; staff atty. Freeport Minerals Co., N.Y.C., 1969-70, asst. sec., 1970-75, sec., 1975-85, v.p., 1984-85, sr. atty., 1985-86; sec. Freeport McMoRan Inc., N.Y.C., 1980-85; v.p., sr. assoc. counsel The Chase Manhattan Bank, N.Y.C., 1986-96, securities law counsel, 1992-96. Dir., pres., treas., Roxbury Land Trust, Inc. Am. Scandinavian Found. Fellow U. Copenhagen, Fulbright travel grantee, 1961-62. Mem. Bar Assn., Assn. Bar City N.Y., N.Y.C. Harvard Club, N.Y.C. Lutheran. Home: 45 Davenport Rd Roxbury CT 06783-1001

KNUTSON, DAVID LEE, state legislator, lawyer; b. Mpls., Nov. 24, 1959; s. Howard Arthur and Jerroldine Margo (Sundby) K.; m. Laurie Sjoquist, June 25, 1983; children: Ann Marie, Timothy David. BA, St. Olaf Coll., 1982; JD, William Mitchell Coll. Law, 1986. Bar: Minn. 1986, U.S. Dist. Ct. Minn. 1986, U.S. Ct. Appeals (8th cir.) 1987, U.S. Tax Ct. 1989. Pvt. practice, Apple Valley, Minn., 1986—; mem. Minn. State Senate from Dist. 37, 1993—2002, asst. minority leader, 1995—2002. Bd. dirs. Our Saviour's Shelter for Homeless, Mpls., 1988-90, City Task Force on Arts, Burnsville, 1988, Legal Assistance Dakota County, Ltd., 1994—, Dakota County Tech. Coll. Found., 1994—; bd. dirs. Minn. Valley YMCA, 1988-2000, chmn., 1991-93, 99-00; bd. dirs. Serve Minn., 2003-. Named one of Ten Outstanding Young Minnesotans, Minn. Jaycees, 1993, Legislator of the Biennium, Minn. Retailers Assn.; recipient Lake Conf. Disting. Alumni award, 1996, Pro Bono Publico award Legal Svcs. Coalition, 1998, YMCA Disting. Vol. award, 1999, Outstanding Achievement award Burnsville H.S., 2001. Mem. Minn. Bar Assn., Dakota County Bar Assn., Burnsville Jaycees (bd. dirs. 1988-90), Apple Valley C. of C., Burnsville C. of C. (bd. dirs. 1990-92), No. Dakota County C. of C., Burnsville Breakfast Rotary. Republican. Avocations: reading, travel, sports. Office: Severson Sheldon Dougherty & Molenda PA Ste 600 7300 W 147th St Apple Valley MN 55124 E-mail: knutsond@seversonsheldon.com.

KNUTSON, GEORGIANNA (GEEGEE KNUTSON), retired small business owner; b. Mitchell, S.D., Sept. 9, 1937; d. Orwin Fredrick and Dorothy Jane (Fredericks) Johnson; m. Thomas Ray Knutson, Aug. 20, 1958 (div. Dec. 1981); children: Tami Ann Knutson Carter, Nancy Jo Knutson Gresham, Carey Lynn Knutson Clark. BFA in Music Edn., U. S.D., 1959. Tchr. music Rapid City (S.D.) Sch. System, 1959-60, Bedford (Ind.) Jr. High Sch., 1960-61, Redford Union Schs., Detroit, 1973-77; temp. office worker Olsten Temp., Atlanta, 1982-84; adminstr. customer support Harris Adacom, Atlanta, 1984-92; owner Word P Pro, Decatur, Ga., 1989-94; ret., 1994. Pub. I Can Color, 1993. Past adult leader, trainer, day camp dir., neighborhood chair Girl Scouts U.S., 1971-81; active Parents Without Ptnrs., 1982-91, state v.p. family activities, 1987-88; mem. Internat. K-Kids Com., 2003—. Mem. Kiwanis Internat. (sec. Northlake 1994-97, 99—, pres. 1997-98, divsn. sec. 1995-2003, Dist. Leadership award 1998, 2003, Hixson award Northlake-Dekalb 1999, adminstrv. asst. Builders Club/K-kids 1999—). Mem. Eckankar Ch. E-mail: geegeek@bellsouth.net.

KNUTSON, ROGER M. writer, retired science educator; b. Montevideo, Minn., Jan. 3, 1933; s. Melvin Arthur and Lydia Alvina Knutson; m. Sharon Louise Belding; children: Karin Grace, Anne Faith, Benjamin Will, Steven King, Samuel Prophet. BA, St. Olaf Coll., Northfield, MN, 1957; MS, Mich. State U., East Lansing, MI, 1961, PhD, 1965. Biology educator Luther Coll., Decorah, Iowa, 1964—95. Author: (book) Flattened Fauna, Furtive Fauna, Fearsome Fauna. Sn NAVY, 1953—55, Florida. Grad. fellow, NSF, 1963—65, Faculty fellow, 1971—72. Avocations: photography, fishing. Home: 408 Burns Street Charlevoix MI 49720

KNUTSON, RONALD DALE, economist, educator, academic administrator; b. Montevideo, Minn., July 12, 1940; s. Claus and Alice (Peterson) K.; m. Sharron DeGree, Sept. 16, 1961; children: Scott, Ryan, Nicole. BS, U. Minn., 1962, PhD, 1967; MS, Pa. State U., 1963. Prof. Purdue U., 1967-73; staff economist Agrl. Mktg. Svc., USDA, Washington, 1971-73; adminstr. Farmer Coop. Svc., 1973-75; prof. dept. agrl. econs. Tex. A&M U., Coll. Station, 1975—2001, dir. Agrl. Food Policy Ctr., 1989—2000, prof. emeritus, 2002—. Econ. cons. Kraft, Borden Inc., Sun-Diamond, Am. Bankers Assn., Milk Industry Found., GAO, U.S. Dept. Justice, Am. Farm Bur. Fedn., White House Food and Nutrition Study, NAS, U.S. Congress, Nat. Commn. on Productivity Exec. Office Pres.; project leader Rural Devel. Policy; chmn. milk pricing adv. com. U.S. Dept. Agr.; mem. Pres. Reagan's Transition Task Force for Agr., 1980-81; mem. agrl. policy adv. com. Sec. Agr. and Trade Rep., 1980-87; mem. agrl. group White House Partnership for Prosperity Conf., 2002; co-dir. Partnership for Prosperity, 2002- . Author: (with J.B. Penn and B.L. Flinchbaugh) Agricultural and Food Policy, 5th edit., 2003. Bd. dirs. Farm Found., vice chmn., 2000, chmn., 2001. Recipient Lifetime Achievement award So. Agrl. Econs. Assn., 1995, Faculty Disting. Achievement award in Ext., 1984, Former Students of Tex. A&M U., Faculty Disting. Achievement award in Tchg., 1998 Assn. Former Students of Tex. A&M U., Regents Prof. Svc. award The Tex. A&M U. Sys., 1999; Rsch. grantee Govt. of Trinidad and Tobago, 1999-2001. Mem. Am. Agrl. Econs. Assn. (bd. dirs. 1999-2002), So. Agrl. Econ. Assn. Home: 1011 Rose Cir College Station TX 77840-2327 Office: Tex A&M U Agrl Food Policy Ctr College Station TX 77843-2124

KNUTZEN, MARTHA LORRAINE, lawyer; b. Bellingham, Wash., Aug. 28, 1956; BA in Polit. Sci., Scripps Coll., 1978; MA in Polit. Sci, Practical Politics, JD, U. San Francisco, 1981. Bar: Calif. Lawyer, mgr. legal computer support svcs., San Francisco, 1981—. Mem. San Francisco Citizens' Adv. Com. on Elections, 1994-96; 3d vice chair Dem. Party, San Francisco, 1996-2000, mem. Resolution Com., Calif. Dem. Party, 2001—; chair San Francisco Human Rights Commn., 1996—; cmty. organizer. Recipient Civil Rights Leadership award, 1996. Office: Office Atty Gen 455 Golden Gate San Francisco CA 94102-2230 Home: Apt 44 601 Van Ness Ave San Francisco CA 94102-3263

KNYAZEV, ANDREW, mathematician, consultant; b. Moscow; BA and MS in Computer Sci. and Cybernetics, Moscow State U., 1981; PhD in Numerical Maths., Inst. Numerical Maths., Russian Acad. Scis., Moscow, 1985. Cert. senior scientist. Software engr. Kurchatov's Inst. Atomic Energy, Moscow, 1981—83; sr. scientist Inst. Numerical Maths., Russian Acad. Scis., Moscow, 1983—92; assoc. prof. dept. math. U. Colo., Denver, Ala., 1994—. Part-time asst. prof. Moscow Physico-Tech. Inst., Dolgoprudnii, Russia, 1985—91; vis. scientist Courant Inst. Math. Scis., NYU, 1992—94; dir. Ctr. for Computational Math. U. Colo., Denver, 1999—2001. Author: (book) Computation of eigenvalues and eigenvectors for mesh problems: algorithms and error estimates, 1986; contbr. articles to profl. jours. Recipient award DMS 9508328, Math. Scis. Computing Rsch. Environments., NSF, 1995, award DMS 9501507, Math. Scis.: Preconditioned Parallel Methods for Large Symmetric Eigenproblems, 1995—98, award DMS MRI 0079719, Acquisition of a High-Performance Parallel Computer for Math. Scis. and Applications, 2000—01; fellow faculty rsch. fellow, U. Colo., Denver, 2000. Office: U Colo Dept Math Campus Box 170 PO Box 173364 Denver CO 80217-3364 Office Fax: 303-556-8550.

KO, CHENG CHIA CHARLES, obstetrician-gynecologist; b. Taiwan, June 18, 1929; came to U.S., 1969; MD, Nat. Taiwan U., 1956. Diplomate Am. Bd. Ob-gyn. Intern Detroit Women's Hosp., 1964-65; resident in ob-gyn. Wayne U. Hosp., Detroit, 1969-73; ob-gyn. physician Planned Parenthood League, Detroit, 1973-74, Lakeside Med. Ctr., Detroit, 1974-76; mem. staff Garfield Med. Ctr., Monterey Park, Calif., San Gabriel Valley Med. Ctr., San Gabriel, Calif.; pvt. practice Monterey Park, Calif., 1978-93; ret., 1993. Mem. ACOG, AMA, Calif. Med. Assn. Home: 8353 Elm Ave San Gabriel CA 91775-2465

KO, CHIA-WEN, biostatistician, researcher; b. Changhua, Taiwan, Dec. 15, 1965; d. Wu-Hsiang Ko and Yen Lin; m. Christopher John Endres, May 22, 1993; children: Claire Yvonne Endres, Eleanor Marie Endres, Angela Anna Endres. BS, Nat. Ctrl. U., 1988, MS, 1990; PHD, U. Wis., 1996. Statistician Walter Reed Army Med. Ctr., Washington, 1998—99; rsch. biostatistician Organon Pharmaceuticals, Inc, West Orange, NJ, 2002—. Cons. Organon Pharmaceuticals, Inc, 2002—; reviewer Walter Reed Army Med. Ctr., 1998—99; mentor NIH, Bethesda, Md., 1999—2001. Recipient Excellent Tchg. asst., U. Wis., Madison, 1993—94, Intramural Rsch. Tng. award, Found. For Advanced Edn. In Sci., 1997—99; fellow, NIH, 1997—98, 1999—2002; scholar, Bd. Edn., 1985—89. Mem.: Internat. Chineses Statis. Assn., Soc. Clin. Trials, Internat. Biometrics Soc., Am. Statis. Assn. Achievements include research in Published Or Submitted 20 Scientific Articles In The Past Two Years; development of Quality Of Life Instruments To Be Used For Male Hypogonadism; discovery of The Genetic And Environmental Risk Factors For Birth Defects And Newborn Hearing Screening Failures. Avocations: reading, movies, travel. Office: Organon Pharmaceuticals Inc 375 Mt Pleasant Ave West Orange NJ 07052 Office Fax: 973-325-5292. Personal E-mail: c.ko@organonusa.com. E-mail: c.ko@organonusa.com.

KO, FRANK K. materials scientist, educator; b. Kwanteng, China, Aug. 5, 1947; s. Lun Hung and King Hin Ko; m. Catherine Lee, Dec. 21, 1971; children: Kara, Jana. BS, Phila. U., 1970; MS, Ga. Tech. U., 1971, PhD, 1977. Asst. prof., assoc. prof., lab. mgr. Phila. U., 1977—84; assoc. prof.,prof., dir. Rsch. Ctr. Drexel U., Phila., 1984—. Vis. scientist MIT, Boston, 1992, Hong Kong U. Sci. and Tech., 1993; vis. prof. Katholicke U. Leuven, Belgium, 1994; vis. fellow Hong Kong Polytech. U., 1996; vis. prof. UCLA, 2002. Author: Atkins and Pearce Handbook of Indian Braid, 1989; author: (in Chinese) Textile Structural Composite, 2001; editor (series): Textile Structure Composites, 1989; contbr. Fellow: Soc. for Advancement of Material and Processing Engrs. (nat. chair student chpts. 1987—); mem.: Am. Soc. Composites, Fiber Soc. (membership com. 1997—, Disting. Achievement award 1984). Achievements include patents in field. Avocations: painting, arachnology, calligraphy. Office: Drexel Univ 31st and Market St Philadelphia PA 19104*

KO, HYUNOK, artist, sculptor; b. Seoul, Korea, Aug. 29, 1962; came to U.S., 1975; d. Inshik and Ohi (Han) K.; m. James Steven Drage, Sept. 14, 1986. MFA, Columbia U., 1989; BA, U. Calif., Berkeley, 1993. Cert. substitute tchr., Calif. Instr. sculpture shop Buck's Rock, New Milford, Conn., summer 1994; translator Korean-English Alameda (Calif.) Sch. Dist., 1994-95; substitute tchr. Spectrum Ctr., San Lorenzo, Calif., 1995, summer 96; jeweler Koko Jewelry, Berkeley, Calif., 1996—. Exhibited in group shows Columbia (Mo.) Coll., 1992, SRW Gallery, Sierra Madre, Calif., 1995. Mem. Calif. Autism Found. (cert. appreciation 1996). Avocations: piano, visiting art galleries, reading biographies of famous people. Home: 34906 Seal Rock Ter Fremont CA 94555-3255

KO, LAN, molecular biologist, researcher; b. Beijing, May 6, 1963; MD, Beijing Med. U., 1987; PhD, SUNY, Bklyn., 1996. Asst. prof. Inst. Biophysics, Beijing, 1987—90; rsch. fellow Joslin Diabetes Ctr., Harvard Med. Sch., Boston, 1996—97, Brigham and Women's Hosp., Harvard Med. Sch., 1998—99, Eli Lilly and Co., Indpls., 1999—. Contbr. articles to profl. jours. Recipient Young Scientist award, Chinese Acad. Sci., 1990. Mem.: Am. Soc. for Microbiology, Endocrine Soc. (travel grant award 1999, 2001).

KO, SEUNG KYUN, educator, consultant; b. Seoul, Korea, July 13, 1936; came to U.S., 1957; s. Byong Ryon and Hung Sun (Song) K.; m. Sook Jin Bae, Aug. 29, 1972; children: Young Min, Young Eun. BA, Coll. of Wooster, Ohio, 1962; MA, U. Pa., 1963, PhD, 1969. Instr. Lake Superior State Coll., Sault Ste Marie, Mich., 1967-68; asst. prof. Maryville (Tenn.) Coll., 1968-69; rsch. commr. Ministry of Fgn. Affairs, Seoul, 1972; lectr. Seoul Nat. U., 1972; assoc. prof. Hawaii Loa Coll., Kaneohe, 1972-78, prof. internat. rels., 1978—. Contbr. articles to profl. jours. Pres. Korean Sr. Citizens Coll., Honolulu, 1985. Mem. United Korean Soc. Hawaii (v.p., pres. Honolulu chpt. 1984). Home: 45-209 Lilipuna Rd # A Kaneohe HI 96744-3106 Office: Hawaii Pacific U Hawaii Loa Campus 45-045 Kam Hwy Kaneohe HI 96744-5297

KO, WEN-HSIUNG, electrical engineering educator; b. Shang-Hong, Fukien, China, Apr. 12, 1923; came to U.S., 1954, naturalized, 1963; s. Sing-Ming and Sou-Yu (Kao) K.; m. Christina Chen, Oct. 12, 1957; children: Kathleen, Janet, Linda, Alexander. BSEE, Nat. Amoy U., Fukien, China, 1946; MS, Case Inst. Tech., 1956, PhD, 1959. Engr., then sr. engr. Taiwan Telecommunication Adminstrn., 1946-54; mem. faculty Case Inst. Tech., Cleve., 1956-93; prof. elec. and biomed. engring. Case Western Res. U., Cleve., 1967-93, prof. emeritus, 1994—, dir. engring. design center, 1970-82; pres., prin. Wen H. Ko & Assocs., Cleve., 1996—. Cons. NSF, N.Am. Mfg. Co., NIH, 1966-82; pres. Transducer Rsch. Found., 1986—; rschr. in med. implant electronics, telemetry and stimulation, microsensors and microactators, micro-electro-mech.-sys. Recipient career achievement award Transducer Internat. Conf., Chgo., 1997. Fellow IEEE, AIMBE; mem. Instrument Soc. Am., Bio-Med. Engring. Soc., Sigma Xi, Eta Kappa Nu. Home: 1356 Forest Hills Blvd Cleveland OH 44118-1359 Office: Case Western Res U Electronics Design Ctr Cleveland OH 44106

KO, WEN-HSIUNG, plant pathology educator; b. Chao Chow, Taiwan, May 14, 1939; came to U.S., 1963; s. Ming-chu and Wang (Huang) K.; m. Sachi Su, Jan. 12, 1968; children: Subo, Supin. BS, Nat. Taiwan U., Taipei, 1962; PhD, Mich. State U., 1966. Postdoctoral rsch. assoc. Mich. State U., East Lansing, 1966-69; asst. prof. U. Hawaii, Honolulu, 1969-72, assoc. prof., 1972-74, prof. plant pathology, 1976—. Assoc. editor Plant Disease, 1988-90, Phytopathology, 1980-82; mem. editorial bd. Bot. Bull. Academia Sinica, 1988—; contbr. articles to profl. jours. Mem. Am. Phytopath. Soc. (Ruth Allen award 1984, Fellow award 1990), Mycological Soc. Am., Phytopath. Soc. Japan. Buddhist. Achievements include patent in field; research in plant disease and phytopathology. Office: U Hawaii 461 W Lanikaula St Hilo HI 96720-4037

KOACH, STEPHEN FRANCIS, flight instructor, retired army officer; b. NYC, June 19, 1950; s. Harry Francis and Anna Nell (Burakowski) K.; m. Marie Annette Helms, Feb. 14, 1975; children: Sharon, Heather, Kristin. BS, St. John's U., 1972; MBA, Embry-Riddle Aero. U., 1988. Cert. master army aviator, comml. helicopter pilot. Asst. buyer J.W. Mays Inc., Bklyn., 1972-73;

commd. 2d lt. US Army, 1972, advanced through grades to maj., 1984; rifle platoon leader C Co. 2nd Bn. 503rd ABN Inf., Ft. Campbell, Ky., 1973-74; exec. officer HHC 2nd Bn. 503rd ABN Inf., Ft. Campbell, 1974; platoon comdr., ops. officer 1st Squadron, 17th Air Cavalry, Ft. Bragg, N.C., 1975-79; attack platoon comdr., exec. officer, ops. officer 501st AVN Bn., Katterbach, Fed. Republic Germany, 1979-82; brigade S-3, company comdr. Aviation Training Brigade, Ft. Rucker, Ala., 1982-86; sr. Army force planner ROK/US Combined Forces Command, Seoul, Republic of Korea, 1986-87; dir. plans, tng., moblzn. and security Ft. Monroe, Va., 1987-89; team chief hdqrs. US Army Aviation Tech. Assistance Fielding Team, King Khalid Mil. City, Saudi Arabia, 1989-90; instr. Enterprise (Ala.) State Jr. Coll., 1991-96, 2001—; chief evaluation div. US Army Aviation Ctr., Directorate of Evaluation and Standardization, Ft. Rucker, Ala., 1990-93; ret. US Army, 1993; traffic mgr. Collins Sign Co., Inc., Dothan, Ala., 1993-99; flight instr. U.S. Army Aviation Ctr., Ft. Rucker, Ala., 2000—03, tng. specialist Unmanned Aerial Vehicles, Directorate Tng., Doctrine and Simulation, 2003—. Mem. Hampton (Va.) Cup Regatta Com., Phoebus Celebration Com., Hampton, 1987-89, USS Newport News (Va.) Commissioning Com., 1988-89. Decorated Defense Meritorious Service medal. Mem. KC, Am. Legion, Army Aviation Assn. Am., Ret. Officers Assn., VFW. Republican. Roman Catholic. Avocations: golf, computers, photography. Home: 107 Lake Oliver Dr Enterprise AL 36330-1436 Office: US Army Aviation Ctr HQ Aviation Tng Brigade Fort Rucker AL 36362 E-mail: skoach@centurytel.net.

KOBAK, ALFRED JULIAN, JR., obstetrician, gynecologist; b. Chgo., Feb. 10, 1935; s. Alfred J and Rose B (Baron) Kobak; m. Sue B Stein, May 3, 1959; children: William, Steven, Jane, Deborah. BS, U. Ill., 1957, MD, 1959. Diplomate Am Bd Ob-Gyn. Intern Michael Reese Hosp., Chgo., 1959-60; resident Cook County Hosp., 1960-62, 64-65; practice medicine specializing in ob-gyn. Valparaiso, Ind., 1965—. Mem. med. staff Porter Meml. Hosp., Valparaiso, 1965—, pres. med. staff, 1981—82; asst. clin. prof. ob-gyn. Ind. U. Sch. Medicine; pres. Ob-Gyn. Assocs., 1970—. Contbr. articles to profl jours. Bd. dirs. N.W. Ind. Jewish Fedn., 1970—84, Porter County Bd. Health, 1991—, pres., 1997; bd. dirs., past pres. Porter County Health Dept. Capt USAF, 1962—64. Fellow: ACS, Am. Coll. Ob-Gyn., Internat. Coll. Surgeons; mem.: AMA, Chgo. Gynecol. Soc. (v.p. 1998—99), Porter County Med Soc (pres. 1979, 1986), Ctrl. Assn. Obstetricians and Gynecologists, Ind. Med. Assn., Am. Soc. Reproductive Medicine, Sand Creek Club. Office: 1101 Glendale Blvd Valparaiso IN 46383-3724

KOBAK, JAMES BENEDICT, management consultant; b. St. Louis, Mar. 4, 1921; s. Edgar and Evelyn (Hubert) K.; m. Hope McEldowney, June 13, 1942; children: James Benedict, John D. (dec.), Thomas M. BS, Harvard U., 1942; postgrad. in accounting, Pace Coll., 1946-49. CPA, N.Y., La., Union S.Africa. Assoc. J.K. Lasser & Co., N.Y.C., 1946-71, partner, 1954-64, adminstrv. partner, 1964-71; internat. adminstrv. partner Lasser, Harmood Banner, Dunwoody, N.Y.C., 1964-71; pres. James B. Kobak & Co., Darien, Conn., 1971—. Ptnr. James B. Kobak Bus. Models Co., 1972-82; founder Kobak Open. Author: How to Start a Magazine and Publish It Profitably, 2002. Chmn. mag. com., mem. bus. com. Nat. council Boy Scouts Am.; co-founder, sec.-treas. John D. Kobak Appalachian Edn. Found., Darien; trustee Hill Sch., Pottstown, Pa. Served to capt., F.A. AUS, 1942-46. Mem. AICPA, N.Y. State Soc. CPAs, Transvall Soc. Accts., Harvard Club (N.Y.C.), Wee Burn Country Club (Darien), Hapenny Bay Beach Club (St. Croix), Carambola Golf Club, St. Croix Country Club. Home and Office: 6 Hale Ln Darien CT 06820 Home: Sweet Lime Village # 29 Kingshill VI 00850

KOBAK, JAMES BENEDICT, JR., lawyer, educator; b. Alexandria, La., May 2, 1944; s. James Benedict and Hope (McEldowney) K.; m. Carol Johnson, June 11, 1966; children: James Benedict III, Katherine Jean, Marcie Ann. BA magna cum laude, Harvard U., 1966; LLB, U. Va., 1969. Bar: U.S. Dist. Ct. (so. and ea. dists.) N.Y. 1972, U.S. Supreme Ct. 1977, U.S. Ct. Appeals (2nd cir.) 1973, (5th cir.) 1982, U.S. Dist. Ct. (no. dist.) Calif. 1983, N.J. 1996. Asst. prof. U. Ala., 1969-70; assoc. Hughes Hubbard & Reed LLP, N.Y.C., 1970-77, ptnr., 1977—. Lectr. in law U. Va., 1986-2000; adj. assoc. prof. Fordham U., 1986—; arbitrator Am. Arbitration Assn. Editor: Misuse: Licensing and Litigation, 2000; mem. bd. editors Va. Law Rev., 1967-69, assoc. editor, 1968-69; contbr. articles to profl. jours., mags., treatises and newspapers. Trustee Morristown-Beard Sch., 1995—2001, Jersey City Mus., 2002—. Mem. ABA (antitrust sect., former chair intellectual property com.), Assn. Bar City N.Y., N.Y. County Lawyers Assn. (bd. dirs. 1988-93, 95-97, 2001—, chmn. trade regulation com. 1987-88, chmn. com. on changing trends in the profession 1990-93, chmn. com. on law reform 1994-98, exec. com. 1996-98, chair libr. com. 1998—), Order of Coif, Am. Law Inst., Adirondack 46ers Club, Keene Valley Country Club (trustee 1995-98), Harvard Club (N.Y.). Home: 206-95 W Shearwater Ct Jersey City NJ 07305 Office: Hughes Hubbard & Reed 1 Battery Park Plz Fl 12 New York NY 10004-1482 E-mail: kobak@hugheshubbard.com.

KOBAYASHI, ALBERT SATOSHI, mechanical engineering educator; b. Chgo., Dec. 9, 1924; s. Toshiyuki and Taka (Torii) K.; m. Elizabeth Midori Oba, Sept. 24, 1953; children: Dori Kobayashi Ogami, Tina, Laura. BS in Engring., U. Tokyo, 1947; MSME, U. Wash., 1952; PhD, Ill. Inst. Tech., 1958. Position II engr. Konishiroku Photo Industry, Tokyo, 1947-50; design engr. Ill. Tools Works, Chgo., 1953-55; rsch. engr. Armour Rsch. Found., Ill. Inst. Tech., Chgo., 1955-58; from asst. prof. to assoc. prof. dept. mech. engring. U. Wash., Seattle, 1958-64, prof., 1964-97, Boeing Pennell prof. structural mechanics, 1988-95, prof. emeritus, 1997—. Coll. faculty assoc.The Boeing Co. Seattle, 1958—76; cons. Math. Sci. Northwest, Bellevue, Wash., 1962—82, UN Devel. Program, NY, 1984; vis. scholar U. Tokyo, 1969, 77; program dir. mech., structural and materials engring. divsn. NSF, 1987—88. Contbr. over 480 papers to Fracture Mechanics, Exptl. Mechanics Biomechanics and numerical analysis. Recipient F. G. Tatnall award Soc. Exptl. Stress Analysis, 1973, B.J. Lazan award, 1981, R. E. Peterson award, 1983, William Murray Lecture medal, 1983, Burlington Resources Found. Faculty Achievement award, 1992, M. M. Frocht award, 1995, G. E. Sr. Rsch. award Am. Soc. Engring. Edn., 1995, Disting. Alumni award Univ. Student Club (UW), 1997; decorated Order of Rising Sun, gold rays with neck ribbons Emperor of Japan, 1997. Fellow ASME, Soc. Exptl. Mechanics (hon. life mem., pres. 1989-90); mem. NAE, Am. Ceramic Soc. Home: 15420 62nd Pl NE Kenmore WA 98028-4312 Office: U Wash Dept Mech Engring Box 352600 Seattle WA 98195-2600 E-mail: ask@u.washington.edu.

KOBAYASHI, HERBERT SHIN, electrical engineer; b. Webster, Tex., Feb. 6, 1929; s. Mitsutaro and Moto Kobayashi; m. Haruko Orita; children: June, Naomi, Ken. BSEE, U. Houston, 1951; MSEE, U. Mich., 1958, MS in Indsl. Engring., 1969. Design engr. SIE, Houston, 1960-61, Boeing Aerospace, Huntsville, Ala., 1961-62, New Orleans, 1962, Lockheed Electronics, Houston, 1963; aerospace technologist NASA, Houston, 1963—2002; pres. Kobayashi Inc., Webster, Tex., 1960—. Patentee in field. Mem. planning and zoning commn., Webster, 1993-94. With U.S. Army, 1954-56. Mem. IEEE, AIAA. Achievements include development of technique to make stronger concrete slabs, to separate dirt from rock by smaller, lighter machinery, pulse width modulation for servo loop (closed or open) more efficiency. Home: 1428 NASA Pkwy Webster TX 77598-4702

KOBAYASHI, IKUO, information systems engineer; b. Ogawa, Saitama, Japan, Oct. 12, 1959; s. Toshio and Teruko Kobayashi. B in Engring., Waseda U., Tokyo, 1984, M in Engring., 1986; PhD, U. Tokyo, 1998. Rschr. Sumitomo Electric Industries Ltd., Osaka, Japan, 1986-88; engr. Colin Electronics Co. Ltd., Komaki, Japan, 1988-92; pres. Signalysis Inc., 1996—. Vol. for literacy Divsn. Edn., Sandaun Province, Papua New Guinea, 1993-95. Mem.: IEEE. Avocations: skiing, scuba diving. Personal E-mail: ghf02120@nifty.ne.jp. Business E-Mail: kobayashi@signalysis.co.jp.

KOBAYASHI, NOBUHISA, civil and coastal engineer, educator; b. Osaka, Japan, May 4, 1950; came to U.S., 1976; s. Kazunobu and Shigeko Kobayashi; children: Sachi C., Orion A. BCE, Kyoto (Japan) U., 1974, MCE, 1976; PhD, MIT, 1979. Sr. cons. engr. Brian Watt Assocs., Inc., Houston, 1979—81; asst. prof. U. Del., Newark, 1981—86, assoc. prof., 1986—91, prof. dept. civil engring., 1991—, dir. Ctr. for Applied Coastal Rsch., 2001—. Mem. editl. bd. Jour. Coastal Rsch., 1987-99; assoc. editor Jour. Waterway, Port, Coast and Ocean Engring., 1990-92, editor, 1992-94; editor Rational Design of Mound Structures, 1990, Wave Forces on Inclined and Vertical Wall Structures, 1995; contbr. articles to profl. jours. Rsch. grantee NSF, 1984—, NOAA, 1983—, U.S. Army Coastal Engring. Rsch. Ctr., 1988—, U.S Army Cold Regions Rsch. and Engring. Lab., 1986-87, Army Rsch. Office, 1992-98. Mem. ASCE (J.G. Moffatt-F.E. Nicol Harbor and Coastal Engring. award 2003), Am. Geophys. Union, Japan Soc. Civil Engrs. Achievements include development of new numerical methods for rational design of breakwaters and revetments used to protect harbors and beaches, arctic engring., coastal sediment transport, coastal hydrodynamics, marina design and oil spills. Office: U Del Ctr for Applied Coastal Rsch Ocean Engring Lab Newark DE 19716

KOBAYASHI, ROGER HIDEO, allergy and immunology educator; b. Honolulu, May 21, 1947; s. Roy T. and Setsuko (Ebesugawa) K.; m. Ai Lan Doan, May 21, 1974; children: Lisa, Timothy. MS in Physiology, U. Hawaii, 1975; MD, U. Nebr., 1975. Diplomate Am. Bd. Allergy and Immunology, Am. Bd. Pediatrics, Nat. Bd. Med. Examiners. Asst. prof. pediatrics U. Nebr. Med. Ctr., Omaha, 1980-84, asst. prof. medical microbiology, 1980-85, dir. pediatric allergy and immunology, 1980-88, assoc. prof. pediatrics, 1984-88, assoc. prof. pathology and microbiology, 1985-88; assoc. prof. pediatrics UCLA, 1988-90, assoc. clin. prof. pediatrics, 1990-95, clin. prof. pediatrics, 1995—. Bd. dirs. Am. Lung Assn. Nebr., Asthma and Allergy Found. Am., Am. Lung Assn. Nebr.; cons. physician Children's Hosp., 1980—, Rare Antibody and Antigen Corp., Shanghai, ZLB Biologic Divsn., 1996—, Immune Deficiency Found., 1997—, Bayer Biologics, 2000—;mem. U. Nebr. Chancellor's Com. on Rural Health, 1982-88. Grantee Enzon Inc., 1986-88, Sandoz, Inc. 1986-87, 88-92, Schering Co. 1987-88, 90-93, NIH 1982, Mead-Johnson 1983-84, Fisons, Inc. 1990-92, Pfizer 1990-91, Rorer Pharm. 1993-97, Glaxo Inc., 1993-98, Genentech, 1994-96, Smith Kline Beecham, 1994-97, Miles Labs., 1995, Hoechst, 1995-96, McNiel, 1995, Muro, 1996—, Zeneca, 1996—, Bayer Pharm., 1996—. Fellow Am. Acad. Pediatrics (sec.-treas. Nebr. chpt. 1985-88), Am. Acad. Allergy and Immunology; mem. Nebr. Allergy Soc. (pres. 1981-84), Am. Fedn. Clin. Rsch., Am. Soc. Microbiology, Clin. Immunol. Soc. Avocations: fly fishing, wine collecting, tennis, med. economics, golf. Home: 9942 Lafayette Ave Omaha NE 68114-2132

KOBAYASHI, SEIEI, English literature educator; b. Maebashi, Gunma, Japan, Nov. 22, 1941; s. Mokuhci and Shizuko (Yamada) K.; m. Chieko Ohto, Apr. 4, 1970; children: Shigehisa, Naoki. BA, U. Tokyo, 1965, MA, 1969. Lectr. Kyoritsu Women's Jr. Coll., Tokyo, 1970-74, asst. prof., 1974-80; Hosei U., Tokyo, 1980-81, prof., 1981-93; prof. English lit. Chuo U., Tokyo, 1994—. Author: An Essay on Shakespeare's History Plays, 1981; contbg. author: The Discourse of Vision-The Meeting Point of Popular Culture and Art (ed. Y. Midzunoe), 1994, Essays on World Modern Drama (ed. M. Osada), 1996, Celtic Illusion (ed. Y. Midzunoe), 1998, A Dictionary of English and American Drama, 1999, The Kenkyusha Dictionary of Shakespeare, 2000, New Phases of Modern Drama (ed. M. Osada), 2001, The Still Centre: Reading English Literature (ed. A. Kudo), 2001.; co-editor: Kadokawa—Scott Foresman English-Japanese Dictionary, 1992; co-translator: Joseph Zsuffa, Béla Balázs The Man and Artist, 2000. Mem. English Lit. Soc. Japan, Shakespeare Soc. Japan, Renaissance Inst. Avocations: music, photography. Office: Chuo U Faculty Sci & Tech 1-13-27 Kasuga Bunkyo 112-0003 Japan

KOBAYASHI, SUSUMU, computer company executive; b. Kumamoto, Japan, Apr. 3, 1939; s. Senkichiro and Michiko Kobayashi. BS, Tokyo Inst. Tech., 1963. Programmer Osaka (Japan) Gas Co., Ltd., 1963-65, C. Itoh Computing Services Co., Ltd., Tokyo, 1965-67; applications analyst, systems engr. Control Data Far East, Inc., Tokyo, 1967-75; asst. gen. mgr. systems dept. JMA Sys., Inc., Tokyo, 1975-79; dir. Nuc. Data Corp., Tokyo, 1979-89, Yokogawa Supertek Corp., Tokyo, 1989-90; tech. advisor sales divsn. Yokogawa Cray ELS Ltd., Tokyo, 1990-92; tech. advisor Cray Rsch. Japan Ltd., Tokyo, 1990-96; advisor Tsukuba Press Ltd., Tsukuba-shi, Japan, 1996-97; pres. Tera Computer Japan (now called Cray Japan, Inc.), Tokyo, 1997—2000, 2000—02, chief scientist Tsukuba-shi, 2002—. Translator, editor: book Fortran 4 (D. D. McCracken), 1968, Lisp 1.5 Primer (C. Weissman), 1970, A Few Good Men from Univac (D. E. Lundstrom), 1992, The Official Computer Widow's (and Widower's) Handbook (by Experts on Computer Widow/Widowerhood), 1992, Future Computer Opportunities (Jack Dunning), 1993, Enabling Technologies for Petaflops Computing (T. Sterling, P. Messina, P. H. Smith), 1997, The Supermen (Charles J. Murray), 1998; contbr. articles to electronic mags. Mem.: IEEE, AIAA, Astron. Soc. Pacific, Am. Assn. Artificial Intelligence, Japan Info. Processing Soc., Japan Math. Soc., Assn. Computing Machinery. Avocations: motoring, audio/visual. Home: 85-2-206 Migawa 2-chome Mito Ibaraki 310-0912 Japan Office: Cray Japan Inc Tsukuba/Tohoku Ops 10-2-102 Matsushiro 2-chome Tsukuba-shi 305-0035 Japan Office Fax: (+81) 298-55-9010. Business E-Mail: skob@cray.com.

KOBDISH, GEORGE CHARLES, lawyer; b. Casper, Wyo., June 30, 1950; s. Richard Matthew and Jo Earl (Uttz) K.; m. Mary Ellen Griffith, Jan. 24, 1969; children: George Charles, Jr., Kelly Rebecca, Kimberlee Nelle. BBA with honors, U. Tex., 1971, JD, 1974. Bar: Tex. 1974, U.S. Dist. Ct. (no. dist.) Tex. 1975. Asst. atty. gen. State of Tex., Austin, 1974-76; assoc. McCall, Parkhurst & Horton LLP, Dallas, 1976-80, ptnr., 1981—. Bd. dir. North Dallas Shared Ministries, 1993—2000, pres., 1996—98; bd. dir. Notre Dame of Dallas Schs, Inc., 2000—; lay gen. chairperson Cath. Cmty. Appeal, 2000—01. Mem. Am. Coll. Bond Counsel, Nat. Assn. Bond Lawyers, Tex. Bar Assn., Dallas Bar Assn., Royal Oaks Country Club, Tower Club, Dallas Friday Group, Serra Internat. (Dallas bd. dirs., pres. 1998-99, U.S.A. coun., gov. Dist. 46, 2002-03), Phi Delta Theta. Roman Catholic. Home: 7147 Araglin Ct Dallas TX 75230-2097 Office: McCall Parkhurst & Horton LLP 717 N Harwood St Ste 900 Dallas TX 75201-6586

KOBE, LAN, medical physicist; b. Semarang, Indonesia; naturalized; d. O.G. and L.N. (The) Kobe. BS in Physics, IKIP U., Bandung, Indonesia, 1964; MS in Physics, IKIP U., 1967; MS in Med. Physics and Biophysics, U. Calif.-Berkeley, 1975. Physics instr. Sch. Engring. Tarumanegara U., Jakarta, Indonesia, 1968-72; rsch. fellow dept. radiation oncology U. Calif.-San Francisco, 1975-77; clin. physicist in residence dept. radiation oncology UCLA, 1977-78, asst. hosp. radiation physicist, 1978-80, hosp. radiation physicist, 1980—. Instr. radiation oncology physics to resident physicians and med. physics grad. students. Contbr. sci. papers to profl. publs. Newhouse grantee U. Calif.-Berkeley, 1974-75, grantee dean grad. divsn. U. Calif.-Berkeley, 1975; recipient Pres. Work Study award U. Calif., Berkeley, 1974-75, Outstanding Svc. award, 1986, devel. Achievement award, 1988, Ptnrs. in Excellence award UCLA, 1996. Mem. Am. Soc. for Therapeutic Radiology and Oncology, Am. Assn. Physicists in Medicine (nat. and So. Calif. chpts.), Am. Bd. Radiology (cert.), Am. Assn. Individual Investors (life). Office: UCLA Dept Radiation Oncology Los Angeles CA 90095-6951

KOBER, ARLETTA REFSHAUGE (MRS. KAY L. KOBER), supervisor; b. Cedar Falls, Iowa, Oct. 31, 1919; d. Edward and Mary (Jensen) Refshauge; m. Kay Leonard Kober, Feb. 14, 1944; children: Kay Mary, Karilyn Eve. BA, State Coll. Iowa, 1940; MA, U. No. Iowa. Tchr. HS, Sidler, Iowa, 1943—50, 1965—67; coord. Office Edn. Waterloo (Iowa) Cmty. Schs., 1967—84; head dept. coop. career edn. West HS, Waterloo, 1974—84. Mem. Waterloo Sch. Health Coun.; mem. nominating com. YWCA, Waterloo; Black Hawk County chmn. Tb Christmas Seals; ward chmn. ARC, Waterloo; co-chmn. Citizen's Com. Sch. Bond Issue; pres. Waterloo PTA Coun., Waterloo Vis. Nursing Assn., 1956—62, 1982—, Kingsley Sch. PTA, 1959—60; v.p. Waterloo Women's Club, 1962—63, pres., 1963—64, trustee bd. clubhouse dirs., 1957—58; mem. Gen. Fedn. Women's Clubs, Nat. Congress Parents and Tchrs.; bd. dirs. United Svcs. Black Hawk County, Broadway Theatre League, St. Francis Hosp. Found., Black Hawk County Rep. Women, 1952—53; del. Iowa Rep. Convs., 1996, 1998; Presbyterial world svc. chmn. Presbyn. Women's Assn.; deacon Westminister Presbyn. Ch., 1995—98. Mem.: LWV (dir. Waterloo 1951—52), NEA, AAUW (v.p. Cedar Falls 1946—47), Black Hawk County Hist. Soc. (charter), Internat. Platform Assn., Town Club (dir.), P.E.O., Elklets, Dleta Kappa Gamma, Delta Pi Epsilon (v.p. 1966—67). Home: 3436 Augusta Cir Waterloo IA 50701-4608 Office: 503 W 4th St Waterloo IA 50701-1554

KOBER, JANE, lawyer; b. Shamokin, Pa., May 17, 1943; d. Jeno Daniel and Angela Agnes (Kogut) DiRienzo; m. Arthur Kober, June 20, 1970 (div. 1975). AB, Pa. State U., 1965; MA, U. Chgo., 1966; JD, Case Western Res. U., 1974. Bar: Ohio, N.Y. Lectr. U. Baghdad, Iraq, 1966-67; editor, cons. Ernst & Young, Washington, 1968-70; law clk. to Hon. William K. Thomas, U.S. Dist. Ct. for No. Dist. Ohio, Cleve., 1974-75; atty., ptnr. Squire, Sanders & Dempsey, Cleve. and N.Y.C., 1975-87; ptnr. Shea & Gould, N.Y.C., 1987-89, LeBoeuf, Lamb, Greene & MacRae, L.L.P., N.Y.C., 1989-98; sole practitioner, 1998—; sr. v.p., gen. counsel, sec. Biopure Corp., Cambridge, Mass., 1998—. Mem. vis. com. Case Western Res. U. Sch. Law, Soc. of Benchers. Office: Jane Kober Law Offices 125 W 55th St New York NY 10019-5369 also: Biopure Corp 11 Hurley St Cambridge MA 02141-2110 E-mail: jkober@biopure.com.

KOBERNICK, SIDNEY D. pathologist, educator; b. Montreal, Que., Can., May 7, 1919; m. Isabelle Kobernick (dec. July 10, 1985); children: Allan, Michael, Joan. BSc, McGill U., 1941, MDCM, 1943, MSc, 1949, PhD, 1951. Diplomate pathol. anatomy Am. Bd. Pathology, clin. pathology Am. Bd. Pathology. Asst. prof. pathology McGill U., Quebec, Canada, 1951—52, Wayne State U. Sch. Medicine, 1953—60, clin. assoc. prof., 1960—79, coord. cancer tchg., 1960—63, clin. prof., 1979; adj. assoc. prof. Wayne State U. Sch. Pharmacy and Allied Health, 1978—79, adj. prof., 1979—. Acting pathologist Jewish Gen. Hosp., Montreal, 1950—51; prosector Royal Victoria Hosp., Montreal, 1951—52; cons. pathologist Verdun Protestant Hosp., 1951—52; chmn. dept. lab. medicine Sinai Hosp., Detroit, 1952, dir. Sinai Sch. Med. Tech., 62; cons. VA Hosp., Dearborn, Mich., 1963—64. Contbr. articles to profl. jours. User's group pres. Clin. Lab 12, 1971—73, labcom users group pres., 1975—76; insp. Nat. Accrediting Agy. Clin. Lab. Sciences, 1978; active Mich. State Med. Soc., Mich., 2002—02, Mich. Assn. Med. Edn., Mich., 1978, Wayne County Med. Soc., 1972—72; coeditor Detroit Med. News, Detroit, Mich., 1980—80; planning com. Seven-County Health Planning Adv. Com., Mich., 1980—80; lectr. Beaumont 60th Ann. Lecture Series, 1981—81; coun. NW Dist. Geog. Rep., 2002—02. Fellow Grad. Med. Rsch. Fellowship, NRC of Can. for Exptl. Pathology for Rsch. in the Field of Hypersensitivity, 2002, Tchg. fellow Pathology, McGill U., 1947-1948, Postdoctoral fellowship, Am. Life Ins. Med. Rsch. Fund, 1949-1951; grantee grant, Can. Def. Rsch. Bd. for Experiments on the Effect of Cold on Hypersensitivity Lesions of Rabbits, 1949-1952, grant award for Designing Specimen Collection Area in the Mich. fifth Ann. Search for New Hosp. Achievements, Mich. Hosp. Assn. (Mich. Blue Cross), 1963, grant for New Technique in Electron Microscope, Sinai Hosp. Rsch. Fund, 1970-1973. Fellow: Coll. Am. Pathologists; mem.: Mich. Hosp. Automated Computer Pilot Project (chmn. 2002), Internat. Acad. Pathology, NY Acad. Science, Wayne County Med. Soc., Soc. Exptl. Biology and Medicine, Am. Assn. Pathologists Bacteriologists, Clin. Lab 12 (exec. com. 1977—2002), Mich. Cancer Found. (cancer registry tech. adv. com. 1976—2002), Mich. Cancer Found. (cancer registry com. 1972—2002), Greater Detroit Area Hosp. Coun. Inc. (physician-hospital rels. com. 1980—2002), Med. Care Cost Com., Coun. WCMS (ex officio 1980—2002), Ad Hoc Detroit Sci. Ctr. Com. (chmn. 1978—2002), Ad Hoc Profl. Liability Com. (chmn. 1977—78), Comprehensive Health Planning Coun. Southeastern Mich. (vice chmn. high tech. services com. 1981—81), Comprehensive Health Planning Coun. Southeastern Mich. (subcommittee bed reduction 1980—2002), Comprehensive Health Planning Coun. Southeastern Mich. (tech. work group 1980—2002), Mich. Soc. Pathologists (med. care ins. com. 1968—72), Mich. Soc. Pathologists (program com. 1965—65), Sigma Xi, Alpha Omega Alpha. Achievements include patents for Tissue-Staining and Processing Machine; Microtome Assembly. Avocations: golf, tennis, painting, electronics, music recording. Home: 5627 Country Lakes Drive Sarasota FL 34243-3806 Office: Sinai Hospital Detroit 6767 West Outer Drive Detroit MI 48235

KOBERSTEEN, KENT, photographer, director, editor-in-chief; b. Minneapolis, Minn., 1948; Attended, Univ. of Minn. Staff photo. Minn. Tribune, 1965, editor, 1981; illus. editor Nat. Geo. mag., 1983, dir. of photog., 1998. Kobersteen's work for the Mpls. Tribune took him throughout the US and Canada and to more than 25 other countries. His duties at Nat. Geo. have sent him to Europe, Africa, the Arctic, Latin Am. and the Caribbean. He received recognition for his work on the drought in Africa's Sahel, Cuba under Castro, the major oil-producing nations and global poverty. Contbr. chapters to books picture books. Named recognition, Overseas Press Club, Nat. Press Photographers Assoc., dir. of photography and sr. asst. editor, Nat. Geo. Mag., 1998; recipient several Photography Awards, Minn. Tribune. Mem.: Bd. of Visitors of the Sch. of Journalism and Mass Comm. of the Univ. of NC at Chapel Hill. Achievements include He lectures andf participates regularly in workshops and seminars on photography, journalism ethics, editing and newspaper prod. throughout the world. Office: National Geographic Dir of Photography 1145 17th St NW Washington DC 20036-4688

KOBERT, JOEL A. lawyer; b. Newark, Oct. 4, 1943; BA, Norwich U., 1965; JD, Howard U., 1968. Bar: D.C. 1968, N.J. 1971. Atty. U.S. Dept. Justice, Washington, 1968; ptnr. Courter, Kobert, Laufer & Cohen P.C., Hackettstown, N.J. Active Supreme Ct. Ad Hoc Com. on Legal Svcs. 1982-88, Supreme Ct. Com. on Interests and Trust Accts., 1984-86, Supreme Ct. Com. on Computerization of Ct. System, 1984-86; chmn. bd. trustees Interest on Lawyers Trust Accts., 1988-91. Capt. U.S. Army, 1968-70. Reginald Heber Smith fellow, 1970-71. Fellow Am. Bar Found.; mem. ABA (mem. dist XIII ethics com. 1982-86), D.C. Bar, N.J. State Bar Assn. (treas. 1987, sec. 1988, 2d v.p. 1989, 1st v.p. 1990, pres. elect 1991, pres. 1992, bd. trustees 1981-87, bd. trustees N.J. Lawyer, bd trustees N.J. State Bar Found., 1986-93, mem. ops. com. 1985-91, chmn. com. law adminstrn. and econs. 1981-86, mem. membership com., 1986-87, mem. com. fin. and ops, 1990-93, mem. travel com. 1990-93), N.J. League Mcpl. Attys. Office: Courter Kobert Laufer & Cohen PC 1001 County Road 517 Ste 1 Hackettstown NJ 07840-2709

KOBERT, NORMAN NOAH, asset management consultant; b. N.Y.C., Apr. 15, 1929; s. Murray Hyman Kobert and Rose Winger; m. Natalie Toby Tanhauser, Nov. 23, 1955; children: Robyn Beth, Roy Scott, Jay Stuart, Lisa Ellen. B in Indsl. Engring., NYU, 1949; MBA, Marquette U., 1959; D in Comml. Sci. (hon.), London Sch. Econs., 1973. Chief indsl. engring. Consol. Ldries, Newark, 1949-52; chief mgmt. engring. svcs. Picatinny Arsenal, Dover, N.J., 1953-55; mgr. mgmt. engring. svcs. Ordnance Corps U.S. Army, Washington, 1955-57; asst. dir. Mgmt. Ctr. Marquette U., Milw., 1957-61; v.p. Bayer, Kobert & McElrath, Detroit, 1961-64; exec. v.p. Stevenson, Jordan & Harrison, N.Y.C., 1965-72; prin. N. Kobert & Assocs., Ft. Lauderdale, Fla., 1972—. Bd. dirs. Lexington Industries, N.Y.C.; dir. Entourage Broward Ctr. for Performing Arts. Author: Aggressive Management Style, 1980, Inventory Strategies, 1980, Managing Time, 1981, Managing Inventory for Cost Reduction, 1992, Cut the Fat Not the Muscle, 1995, Improving Management of the Manager's Time, 1996; editor-in-chief (newsletter) Workstyle; contbg. editor, columnist Inventory Outlook, Purchasing mag., Newton, Mass., 1989-92; mem. productivity panel Bottom Line Bus., 1979-84. Recipient Brampton Productivity Improvement award, 1995; Cyril Vanes grantee Indonesia Bjonct, Jakarta, 1978. Mem. Am. Inst. Indsl. Engrs., Soc. Advancement of Mgmt., Am. Prodn. and Inventory Soc., Harbor Beach Surf Club, Entourage (v.p.), Alpha Pi Mu, Beta Gamma Sigma. Jewish. Avocations: golf, dancing, trap-shooting, tennis, chess. Office: N Kobert & Assoc PO Box 460067 Fort Lauderdale FL 33346-0067 E-mail: nknkobert@cs.com.

KOBETZ, RICHARD WILLIAM, criminologist, consultant; b. Chgo., Oct. 23, 1933; s. Nestor Joseph and Mary (Zurek) K.; m. Eleanore Marian Sever, Oct. 8, 1960; children: Kevin, Kimberly and Candice (twins). AA, Chgo. City Jr. Coll., 1959; student, Ill. Tchrs. Coll., 1964-66; MS in Pub. Adminstrn., Ill. Inst. Tech., 1968; D of Pub. Adminstrn., Nova U., 1978. Diplomate Am. Bd. Forensic Examiners; cert. personal protection specialist. Police officer Winnetka (Ill.) Police Dept., 1954-55; from police officer to sgt. to lt. Chgo. Police Dept., 1955-68; asst. dir. Internat. Assn. Chiefs of Police, Washington, 1968-79. Exec. dir., trainer, cons. Exec. Protection Inst., Berryville, Va., 1979—; dir., trainer, cons. North Mountain Pines Tng. Ctr., Winchester, Va., 1979—; security cons. numerous U.S. corps., 1979—; active various security and enforcement agys., 1979—; del. Interpol; spkr. UN, Vienna. Author: The Police Role and Juvenile Delinquency, 1971, Juvenile Justice Administration, 1973, Target Terrorism: Providing Protective Services, 1979, Providing Executive Protection, 1990, Vol. II, 1994; contbr. articles to profl. jours., chpts. to books. Acad. Security Educators and Trainers disting. fellow, 1987. Mem. Acad. Security Educators and Trainers (pres., v.p. 1982—), Internat. Assn. Chiefs of Police (Achievement award 1979), Am. Soc. Indsl. Security, Am. Soc. Criminology, Am. Soc. for Pub. Adminstrn. Clubs: Nine Lives Assocs. (Berryville) (exec. sec. 1978—). Republican. Roman Catholic. Avocations: shooting, camping, travel. Home and Office: Highlander Lodge 276 Journeys End Ln Bluemont VA 20135-1862 E-mail: rwk@crosslink.net.

KOBLENZ, MICHAEL ROBERT, lawyer; b. Newark, Apr. 9, 1948; s. Herman and Esther (Weisman) K.; m. Bonnie Jane Berman, Dec. 22, 1973; children: Adam, Alexander, Elizabeth. B.A., George Washington U., 1969, LL.M., 1974; J.D., Am. U., 1972. Bar: N.J. 1972, D.C. 1973, N.Y. 1980, U.S. Dist. Ct. N.J. 1972, U.S. Dist. Ct. D.C. 1973, U.S. Dist. Ct. (so. dist.) N.Y. 1980, U.S. Ct. Appeals (7th cir.) 1976, U.S. Ct. Claims 1973, U.S. Tax Ct. 1973, U.S. Mil. Ct. Appeals 1974. Atty., U.S. Dept. Justice, Washington, 1972-75; lectr. Am. U., 1975-78; spl. asst. U.S. atty. Office of U.S. Atty., Chgo., 1976-78; atty. Commodity Futures Trading Commn., Washington, 1975-77; spl. counsel, 1977, asst. dir., 1977-78; regional counsel, N.Y.C., 1978-80; assoc. Rein, Mound & Cotton, N.Y.C., 1980-82, ptnr., Mound, Cotton & Wollan (and predecessor firms), 1983—. Contbr. articles to legal jours. Mem. bd. appeals Village of Flower Hill, Manhasset, N.Y., 1983-84, trustee, 1984-86; trustee Village of East Hills, 1988—, Dep. Mayor, 1993-94, Mayor, 1994—; mem. Roslyn Little League, 1991—, bd. dirs., 1992. Recipient Cert. of Appreciation for Outstanding Service U.S. Commodity Futures Trading Commn., 1977. Home: East Hills 20 Hemlock Dr Roslyn NY 11576-2303 Office: Mound Cotton & Wollan 1 Battery Park Plz New York NY 10004-1405

KOBLER, JOHN F. priest, researcher; b. Chgo., June 16, 1925; s. Leo Peter Kobler and Ella O'Donnell. MA, St. Louis U., 1957. Ordained Passionists, Louisville, 1954; cert. tchr. h.s. Mo., 1957. Sem. lector in Latin and Greek Mother of Good Coun. Sem., Warrenton, Mo., 1958—65; tchr. Latin Bellarmine Coll., Louisville, 1965—67; superior Immaculate Conception monastery, Chgo., 1968—71; cons. Nat. Method Inst., Charlottenlund, Denmark, 1972—75; superior Immaculate Conception Monastery, Chgo., 1975—79; fund raiser CP missions, Birmingham, Ala., 1972—75; rschr. Vatican II Chgo., 1979—. Tchr. med. ethics St. Mary's Infirmary, St. Louis, 1956—57; cons. Nat. Method Inst., Charlottenburg, Denmark, 1963—67; chaplain Fort Leonard Wood, Whiteman AFB, Fort Knox; fundraiser CP Monastery, Chgo., 1975—79; assoc. editor Soc. Justice Rev., St. Louis, 2001—; assoc. dir. Holy Cross Retreat House, Cin., 1971; mem. extraordinary chpt. acad. formation and fin. com. Senate of Holy Cross Province, 1969; trustee Cath. Theol. Union, Chgo., 1970—71. Author: (books) Vatican II and Phenomenology, 1985, Vatican II, Theophany and Phenomenon of Man, 1991; contbr. articles to religious jours. Recipient Golden Heart award, Immaculate Conception Monastery, 1975. Mem.: Soc. Cath. Social Scientists, Fellowship of Cath. Scholars, C.G. Jung Inst. of Chgo., Lumen Christi Inst. Cath. Faith, Thought and Culture, The Acton Inst. Study of Religion and Liberty, Cath. Hist. Soc., The Metaphysical Soc. Am. Achievements include research in use of a phenomenological style in Vatican II's reflection. Avocation: philosophy. Office: Immaculate Conception Monastery 5700 N Harlem Ave Chicago IL 60631 Office Fax: 773-631-8059.

KOBLINER, RICHARD, secondary school educator; b. Bronx, N.Y., May 29, 1935; s. Meyer and Celia (Kantner) K.; m. Suzanne, July 11, 1965. BA, CCNY, 1959, MS in Edn., 1962; postgrad., U. Wis. Cert. administr. and supr., social studies tchr., N.Y. Secondary sch. educator DeWitt Clinton, Bronx, N.Y., Hillcrest, Jamaica, N.Y., Cardozo, Bayside, N.Y. Mem. Nat. Coun. for Accreditation of Tchr. Edn.; supr., student tchr. Queens Coll., N.Y.C.; lectr. Elderhostel, Ret. Tchrs. Program. Author: Handbook for the Teaching of Social Studies, Middle Ages Workbook, History of Black Americans; mem. adv. bd. Wall St. Jour.; classroom edit., social studies publs.; contbr. Ency. of N.Y.C. Mem. ASCD, AFT, N.Y. SUT, UFT (chair innovations com.), ATSS, NCSS. Home: PO Box 740425 Boynton Beach FL 33474-0425

KOBRIN, JAY ARTHUR, interior designer, fiber artist; b. N.Y.C., Nov. 30, 1936; s. Irving and Hortense (Freezer) K. BA, Brandeis U., 1958; MFA, Yale U., 1961. Theatre designer, N.Y.C., 1961-64; prin. Jay Arthur Inc., N.Y.C., 1964-66; designer Bellciano Couture, N.Y.C., 1966-68, Masionette, N.Y.C., 1968-72, Malcolm Starr Boutique, N.Y.C., 1972, Damon Internat., N.Y.C., 1972-75, Goldworm Knits, N.Y.C., 1975-76; v.p. Gordon Micunis Designs, Inc., Stamford, Conn., 1976—. Artist, exhibitor Art of the N.E., 1990, Soc. of Conn. Craftsmen, 1991. Mem. bd. advisers Stamford Theatre Works, 1988-92; bd. dirs. Loft Artist Assn., Stamford, 1989—, Stamford Hist. Soc., 1985-87. Mem. Yale Club of Stamford (bd. dirs. 1983-85). Democrat. Jewish. Office: Gordon Micunis Designs Inc One Strawberry Hill Ave Stamford CT 06902

KOBRIN, LAWRENCE ALAN, lawyer; b. N.Y.C., Sept. 14, 1933; s. Irving and Hortense (Freezer) K.; m. Ruth E. Freedman, Mar. 5, 1967; children: Jeffrey, Rebecca, Debra. AB in History suma cum laude, Columbia U., 1954, JD, 1957. Bar: N.Y. 1957, U.S. Dist. Ct. (sou. dist.) N.Y. 1958, U.S. Dist. Ct. (ea. dist.) 1958, U.S. Ct. Appeals (2d cir.) 1959, U.S. Supreme Ct. 1966. Assoc. Cahill, Gordon, Reindel & Ohl, N.Y.C., 1958-59, Arthur D. Emil, N.Y.C., 1959-63; ptnr. Emil & Kobrin, N.Y.C., 1963-79, Milgrim, Thomajan, Jacobs and Lee, N.Y.C., 1979-83, Cahill Gordon & Reindel, N.Y.C., 1984—. Bd. dirs. Wurzweiler Sch. of Social Work, vice-chmn., 1994-98; dir. UMB Bank and Trust Co., 1978-91; treas. The Jewish Week, N.Y.C., 1992-96, chmn., 1996—. Notes editor Columbia U. Law Rev.; mng. editor Tradition, 1961-64, editl. com. 1964—; contbr. articles to profl. jours. V.p., assoc. treas., chmn. dist. com. Fedn. Jewish Philanthropies, N.Y.C., 1981-84, com. long range planning, 1985-86, com. inner city, 71-76; chmn. Ramaz Sch., N.Y.C., 1978-83; sec. to bd. Bar Ilan U., N.Y.C., 1972-80; pres. The Jewish Ctr., N.Y.C., 1987-90; dir. N.Y.C. UJA-Fedn., chmn. communal planning com., 1988-91, chmn. com. on cmty. couns., 1996-98; v.p. Union Orthodox Jewish Congregations, 1968-74, dir. 1962—; chmn. campus com., 1962-66, chmn. Israel com., 1967-72, chmn. pub. com., 1972-78; pres. Massad Camps, 1971-77; bd. dirs. Am. Friends Pardes, 1991-96, Histadrut Ivrit., 1991—; pres. Ariel Am. Friends of Midrasha and United Instns., 1991-95, chmn., 1995-2001; sec. Beth Din of Am., 1994-96, chmn. exec. com., 1997—02, exec. com. Orthodox Caucus, 1995—, bd., exec. com., Edah, 1994—; mem. exec. com. Columbia Barnard Hillel, 1995—. Kent scholar, 1954-55, Stone scholar, 1954-55. Mem.: N.Y. State Bar Assn. (com. coops.and condominiums), N.Y. County Lawyers Assn. (chmn. real property law sect. 1991—93), Assn. Bar City N.Y. (com. on philanthropic orgns. 1974—79, edn. and law com. 1985—88, com. on legal edn. 1988—91, com. on legal problems of elderly 1991—94), Coop. Housing Lawyers Group (exec. com. 1972—80), Am. Coll. Real Estate Lawyers, Cream Hill Lake Assn., The Down Town Assn., Columbia Coll. Alumni Assn. (bd. dirs. 1990—2001, v.p. 1996—98), Phi Beta Kappa. Home: 15 W 81st St New York NY 10024-6022 also: 8 Popple Swamp Rd Cornwall Bridge CT 06754-1135 Office: Cahill Gordon & Reindel 80 Pine St Fl 17 New York NY 10005-1790 E-mail: kobrinL@mindspring.com., Lkobrin@cahill.com.

KOBS, JAMES FRED, direct marketing consultant; b. Chgo., June 27, 1938; s. Fred Charles and Ann (Ganser) K.; m. Nadine Schumacher, May 18, 1963; children: Karen, Kathleen, Kenneth. BS in Journalism, U. Ill., 1960. Copywriter Rylander Co., Chgo., 1960 62; mng. dir. Success Mag., Chgo., 1963-65, mail order mgr. Am. Peoples Press, Westmont, Ill., 1966-67; exec. v.p. Stone & Adler Advt., Chgo., 1967-78; chmn. Kobs & Brady Advt., Inc. (now Draft Direct Worldwide), Chgo., 1978-88; vice chmn. Kobs & Brady Advt., Inc. (now Draft Worldwide), Chgo., 1988; chmn. Kobs Gregory & Passavant, Chgo., 1989—. Guest lectr. U. Wis., U. Ill., NYU; adj. prof. direct mktg. Northwestern U. Medill Sch. Journalism Grad. Program; instr. U. Chgo. Strategic Direct Mktg. Cert. Program; internat. lectr. in field. Author: Profitable Direct Marketing, 2d edit., 1991, 24 Ways to Improve Your Direct Mail Results, 99 Proven Direct Response Offers; contbr. articles to periodicals. Chmn.. Direct Mktg. Ednl. Found. Recipient numerous local and nat. advt. awards; named to Direct Mktg. Hall of Fame. Mem. Direct Mktg. Assn. (dir., sec., mem. exec. com., recipient Silver and Gold Mailbox, Gold Medallion, Gold Echo, Ed Mayer award), Chgo. Assn. Direct Mktg. (past pres., Direct Marketer of Yr.), Boys and Girls Clubs of Chgo. (corp. bd.), Alpha Delta Sigma. Office: Kobs Strategic Consulting 155 N Michigan Ave Chicago IL 60601

KOBSA, ALFRED, computer scientist, educator; b. Linz, Austria, Oct. 8, 1956; s. Franz and Susanne K.; m. Gloria Janet Mark; children: Michaela Grace, Natalie Claire. M in Computer Sci., M in Social and Econ. Sci., U. Linz, 1980; PhD, U. Vienna, 1985. Project dir. U. Saarbrucken, Germany, 1985-91; vis. researcher Internat. Computer Sci. Inst., Berkeley, Calif., 1988; assoc. prof. U. Konstanz, Germany, 1991-95; vis. rschr. Columbia U., N.Y., 1993; inst. dir. GMD, St. Augustin, Germany, 1995—; prof. U. Essen, Germany, 1995—2000; assoc. prof. U. Calif., Irvine, Calif., 2000—03, prof., 2003—. Cons. European Commn., Brussels, Belgium, 1994—. Editor: User Modeling in Dialog Systems, 1989, Adaptive Hypertext and Hypermedia, 1998; editor-in-chief User Modeling and User Adapted Interaction, 1991—. Recipient Theodor Korner award Republic of Austria, 1985, Heinz Zemanek award Austrian Computer Soc., 1985. Mem. Assn. for Informatik, User Modeling Inc. (pres. 1994—), Assn. of Computing. Office: U Calif Dept of Info and Comp Science Irvine CA 92697-3425

KOBUS, RICHARD LAWRENCE, architect, designer, executive; b. Chgo., Nov. 19, 1952; BS in Architecture, U. Ill., 1974; MArch, Harvard U., 1978. Registered architect, Mass., N.H., Maine, Ill., Pa., R.I., Ohio, N.J., Conn., Wash., Mo., N.Y., Vt. Designer Metz, Train, Olsen & Youngren, Chgo., 1974-75, Shepley, Bulfinch, Richardson & Abbott, Boston, 1978-79; assoc. Skidmore, Owings and Merrill, Boston, 1979-83; pres., prin., founder Tsoi/Kobus & Assocs., Inc., Cambridge, Mass., 1983—. Archtl. prin. healthcare acad., corp., and rsch. facilities U.S., Europe, Asia. Mem. permanent bldg. com. Town of Belmont, 1999—2002; bd. trustees Buckingham, Browne and Nichols, 1999—, Mass. Eye and Ear Infirmary, 1999—; pres. Major's Cove Assn., Edgartown, Mass., 1997—2001. Julia Amory Appleton fellow Harvard U., 1978-79; recipient Gov. Design award, 1986, Modern Healthcare Nat. Design award, 1988, 94, 98, AIA.Boston Soc. Architects Healthcare Assembly Design award, 1997, 98, 99, 2001, PCI Design award, 1995, 98, AIA Honor Design award, 1994, 97, 98, 99, Am. Sch. and Univ. Archtl. Portfolio award, 1989, 90, Small Bus. of Yr. award Greater Boston C. of C., 2000. Mem.: AIA (mem. Acad. on Arch. for Health 1997—, Healthcare Assembly Design award 1997, 1998, 1999, 2001), Soc. Campus and Univ. Planning, Urban Land Inst., Boston Soc. Archs. (sec. bd. dirs. 2000—01), Am. Coll. Healthcare Archs. (founding mem. and fellow), Nat. Assn. Indsl. and Office Parks. Avocations: sailing, rowing, photography, auto racing. Office: Tsoi/Kobus & Assocs Inc PO Box 9114 One Brattle Sq Cambridge MA 02238-9114 E-mail: rkobus@tka-architects.com.

KOBYLARZ, JOSEPH DOUGLAS, secondary education educator; b. Garfield, N.J., Dec. 18, 1948; s. Joseph H. and Josephine (Rys) K.; m. Joyce Ann Metzger, July 15, 1978; children: Lauren Ann, Kristen Ann. BS, Northwestern State Coll., 1970; MA, Montclair State Coll., 1976. Cert. tchr. indsl. arts, coord. C.I.E., supr., prin., N.J. Tchr. Garfield Bd. Edn., 1970—, master tchr., 1974-76, dept. chmn., 1976—, adminstrv. asst. to the supt., 1991—. Mem. Am. Indsl. Arts Safety Com., 1978-81, adv. Am. Indsl. Arts Student Assn., Garfield, 1980-85; adj. instr. Montclair State Coll., Upper Montclair, N.J., 1982-86; transcript reviewer Bennett Pub. Co., Peoria, Ill., 1985-87; mem. com. practitioners State N.J. Dept. Edn., 1996—. Co-author: (safety guide) New Jersey Industrial Arts Safety Manual, 1982; author (safety guide) Garfield District Safety Manual, 1981. County committeeman Garfield Dem. Orgn., 1972-75; bd. govs. Ocean Beach and Yacht Club, Lavallette, N.J., 1972-78, dir. beach security, 1989—; mem. Garfield Housing Authority, 1979-84, chmn., 1984; mem. Kinnelon Cmty. Edn. Adv. Com., 1994—, N.J. State Dept. Edn. Com. Practitioners, 1996—. Mem. Vocat. Edn. Assn. N.J. (rec. sec. 1982-88, pres.-elect 1986-87, pres. 1987-88, editor newsletter 1991, region I rep. to Am. Vocat. Assn. 1992—, focus and task force com. State Vocat. Safety Manual 1991-92), Am. Vocat. Assn. (N.J. rep. region I 1990-91), N.J. Vocat. Adminstrs. and Suprs. Assn. (pres. 1997-98, sec. 2000—, Supr. of Yr. 1993), Kinnelon Edn. Found., Phi Delta Kappa. Roman Catholic. Avocations: windsurfing, jogging, racquetball, hiking, wave riding. Home: 97 Miller Rd Kinnelon NJ 07405-3003 Office: Garfield High Sch 500 Palisade Ave Garfield NJ 07026-2546

KOBYLECKY, CAREY LYNN, elementary school educator, music educator; b. Chgo., Aug. 19, 1975; d. Joseph John and Elizabeth Kobylecky. BA in Edn., Ea. Ill. U., 1999. Elem. music tchr. Charlotte (N.C.) Mecklenburg Sch. Sys., 1999—99; performance singing Bravo! Restaurant, Charlotte, NC, 1998—2000. Pvt. piano tchr., Charlotte, 1992—. Mem.: Nat. Tchrs. Music Assn. (pres. 1994—96).

KOBZA, DENNIS JEROME, architect; b. Ullysses, Nebr., Sept. 30, 1933; s. Jerry Frank and Agnes Elizabeth (Lavicky) K.; m. Doris Mae Riemann, Dec. 26, 1953; children: Dennis Jerome, Diana Jill, David John. BS, Healds Archtl. Engring., 1959. Draftsman, designer B.L. Schroder, Palo Alto, Calif., 1959-60; sr. draftsman, designer Ned Abrams, Architect, Sunnyvale, Calif., 1960-61, Kenneth Elvin, Architect, Los Altos, Calif., 1961-62; ptnr. B.L. Schroder, Architect, Palo Alto, Calif., 1962-66; pvt. practice architecture Mountain View, Calif., 1966—. Served with USAF, 1952-56. Recipient Solar PAL award, Palo Alto, 1983, Mountain View Mayoral award, 1979. Mem. C. of C. (dir. 1977-79, Archtl. Excellence award Hayward chpt. 1985, Outstanding Indsl. Devel. award Sacramento chpt., 1980), AIA (chpt. dir. 1973), Constrn. Specifications Inst. (dir. 1967-68), Am. Inst. Plant Engrs., Nat. Fedn. Ind. Bus. Orgn., Rotary (dir. 1978-79, pres. 1986-87). Home: 3840 May Ct Palo Alto CA 94303-4545 Office: 2083 Old Middlefield Way Mountain View CA 94043-2465 E-mail: dkarch@kobza.com.

KOCAN, RONALD ROBERT, secondary school educator; b. Farrell, Pa., Sept. 26, 1937; s. William W. and Mary Kocan; m. Helen R. Rose, July 25, 1960; children: Kristine, Carolyn, Michael. BS in Edn., U. Mich., 1963; M, Ea. Mich. U., 1969. Tchr., coach Cherry Hill H.S., Inkster, Mich., 1963—64, St. Charles (Mich.) H.S., 1964—67, Chippewa Valley H.S., Clinton Twp., Mich., 1967—94; substitute tchr. East China Schs., St. Clair, Mich., 1998—. Author: In Their Own Words, 1997. With USMC, 1956—58. Named Outstanding Tchr., WDIV and Newsweek Mag., Detroit, 1994; named to Coaches Hall of Fame, Chippewa Valley H.S., 1998, Mercer County (Pa.) Hall of Fame, 2001. Mem.: NEA (life), Mich. Edn. Assn. (life). Avocations: working out, bicycling, fishing, writing, reading, Judo. Home: 611 Turnberry Dr Saint Clair MI 48079 E-mail: r/kocan@aol.com.

KOCAOGLU, DUNDAR F. engineering management educator, industrial and civil engineer; b. June 1, 1939; came to U.S., 1960; s. Irfan and Meliha (Uzay) K.; m. ALev Baysak, Oct. 17, 1968; 1 child, Timur. BSCE, Robert Coll., Istanbul, Turkey, 1960; MSCE, Lehigh U., 1962; MS in Indsl. Engring., U. Pitts., 1972; PhD in Ops. Rsch., 1976. Registered prof. engr., Pa., Oreg. Design engr. Modjeski & Masters, Harrisburg, Pa., 1962-64; ptnr. TEKSER Engring. Co., Istanbul, Turkey, 1966-69; project engr. United Engrs., Phila., 1964-71; rsch. asst. U. Pitts., 1972-74; vis. asst. prof., 1974-76; assoc. prof. indsl. engring., dir. engring. mgmt., 1976 87; prof., chmn. engring. and tech. mgmt. dept. Portland State U., 1987—. Pres., CEO TMA-Tech. Mgmt. Assocs., Portland, Oreg., 1973—; pres, CEO Portland Internat. Conf. Mgmt. Engring. and Tech., 1990—. Editor: Management of R&D and Engineering, 1992; co-editor: Technology Management-The New International Language, 1991, Technology and Innovation management, 1999, Innovation in Technology Management-The Key to Global Leadership; series editor: Wiley Series in Engring. and Tech. Mgmt., 1984-98; contbr. articles on tech. mgmt. to more than 100 profl. jours. Lt. C.E., Turkish Army, 1966-68. Fellow IEEE (Centennial medal 1984, Millenium medal, 2000); editor-in-chief trans. on engring. mgmt. 1986—, Millennium medal, 2000); mem. Informs (chmn. Coll. Engring. Mgmt. 1979-81), Am. Soc. Engring. Edn. (chmn. engring. mgmt. div. 1982-83), IEEE Engring. Mgmt. Soc. (fellow, publs. dir. 1982-85), ASCE (mem. engring. mgmt. bd. govs. 1988-93), Muhendis, Ilim Adamlari ve Mimarlar Dernegi Soc. Turkish Engrs. and Scientists (hon.), Am. Soc. Engring. Mgmt. (dir. 1981-86), Omega Rho (pres. 1984-86). Office: Portland State U Engring Mgmt Program PO Box 751 Portland OR 97207-0751

KOCAR, GEORGE FREDERICK, artist; b. Cleve., Sept. 28, 1948; s. George Lewis and Elizabeth Kocar; m. Bonnie Strunak, Feb. 11, 1972 (div. Sept. 1972); m. Kathleen Louise Kocar, Jan. 29, 1973; children: Diana, Allison. BA, Cleve. State U., 1977; MFA, Syracuse U., 1983. Artist Western Res. Printing, Macedonia, Ohio, 1978-80, Visacom, Willoughby, Ohio, 1980-82; owner Kocar Advt. Art, Cleve., 1981-84; artist Am. Greetings, Brooklyn, Ohio, 1984—2002; owner Flying Banana Studio, Bay Village, Ohio, 1984—. Instr. illustration U. Akron, Ohio, 2002—; instr. Ashland (Ohio) U., 2003—, Cuyahoga CC, Cleve., 2003—. Illustrator: Is That You Laughing, 1986, Cooking with Humor, 1992. With U.S. Army, 1969—72. Recipient Gold medal for painting Metro Art Gallery, 1986, Jurors award Butler Inst. Art, 1999. Mem. No. Ohio Illustrator Soc. (bd. dirs. 2001, officer 2001—), Spaces, Cleve. Mus. Art (Jurors award 1979), Cleve. Ctr. Contemporary Art. Democrat. Home: 24213 Lake Bay Village OH 44140 E mail: gkocar@aol.com.

KOCEN, LORRAINE AYRAL, accountant; b. Levittown, N.Y., July 20, 1956; d. Edward Joseph and Joan Dorothy (DeStefanis) Ayral; m. Ross Kocen, Oct. 4, 1981; 1 child, Daniel. BS, Hofstra U., 1978; MBA, U. Minn., 1985. Engr. Sperry Systems Mgmt., Great Neck, N.Y., 1978-81; fin. analyst ITT Consumer Fin. Corp., Mpls., 1981-84; cost acct. Mercy Med. Ctr., Mpls., 1984-85, contr., 1985-86; bus. segments acct. GTE, Thousand Oaks, Calif., 1986-88, Cerritos project acct., 1988-90, Cerritos project adminstr., 1990-92, fin. adminstr., 1992-93, sr. sales adminstr., 1993-94, adminstr. mobile comms., 1994-96; fin. mgr. Blue Cross of Calif., Newbury Park, 1996-97, bus. analyst GTE, Newbury Park, 1997-99; specialist regulatory Verizon/GTE, Thousand Oaks, Calif., 1999—. Asst. editor newsletter Healthcare Fin. Mgmt. Assn., Mpls., 1985-86. Mem. archtl. com. Foxmoor Hills Homeowners Assn.; bd. dir. Westlake, Calif., 1989, Parent Faculty Assn., 1998-2002, PTA, 2002—. Office: Verizon 112 S Lakeview Canyon Road Thousand Oaks CA 91362-3813 E-mail: lorraine@vcnet.com.

KOCH, ALBERT ACHESON, management consultant; b. Atlanta, May 16, 1942; s. Albert H. and Harriet M. (Acheson) K.; m. Bonnie Royce, June 6, 1964; children: Bradford Allen, David Albert, Robert Acheson, Donald Leonard. BS cum laude, Elizabethtown Coll., 1964. With Ernst & Young, 1964-88, nat. dir. client svcs. nat. office, 1977-81, mng. ptnr. Detroit office, 1981-88; mng. ptnr. Equity Ptnrs. Am., Troy, Mich., 1988-94; vice chair, mng. prin. Alix Ptnrs. LLC, Southfield, Mich., 1995—2001, chmn., 2002—; prin. mem., gen. ptnr. Questor Ptnrs., Southfield, Mich., 2002—; CFO, Kmart Corp., Troy, Mich., 2002—03. Bd. dirs. Numatics, Inc., Highland, Mich.; mem. adv. com. on replacement cost implementation SEC, 1976. Co-author: SEC Replacement Cost Requirements and Implementation Manual, 1976. Bd. dirs. Detroit Med. Ctr., 1990-94, Harper-Grace Hosps., 1982-91, DMC Health Care Ctrs., 1984-94, New Detroit, 1986-87, Elizabethtown Coll., 1981-93, Met. Detroit YMCA, 1982-94, Mich. Colls. Found., 1981-96, Detroit Symphony Orch., 1983-88, Detroit Receiving Hosp. Univ. Clinic, 1988-94, Grace Hosp., 1991-92; trustee Bloomfield Hills Bd. Edn., 1992-2000. 1st lt. Fin. Corps, USAR, 1966-72. Recipient Educate for Svc. award Elizabethtown Coll., 1966. Fellow Am. Coll. Bankruptcy, Life Mgmt. Inst.; mem. AICPA (Elijah Watt Sells Gold medal award 1965), Mich. Assn. CPAs, Bloomfield Hills Country Club, Orchard Lake County, The Sanctuary Golf Club. Office: Alix Partners LLC 2000 Town Ctr Ste 2400 Southfield MI 48075-1463

KOCH, BRUCE R. diplomat; b. Robesenia, Pa., Aug. 1, 1933; s. Mervyn R. and Sarah E. (Boyer) K.; m. Johanna Heinzel, Mar. 1, 1958; 1 child, Sigrid D. Assoc. degree in Chemistry, Wyomissing Polytech, 1954; BA in Polit. Sci., Ursinus Coll., 1961; MA in Internat. Affairs, George Washington U., 1971. Field officer Am. Embassy, Bonn, Germany, 1973-75, dep. cultural affairs officer London, 1975-77, counselor pub. affairs Prague, Czechoslovakia, 1978-81, Accra, Ghana, 1981-83, Lagos, Nigeria, 1985-88; min. counselor, 1987; counselor pub. affairs Am. Embassy, Belgrade, Yugoslavia, 1989-91; dir. European Affairs USIA, Washington, 1991-92, dir. African Affairs, 1992-94. Dir. German-Am. Inst., Tuebingen, Fed. Rep. Germany, 1970-73; dir., mgr. U.S. Nat. Exhibit, Romania, 1969; asst. cultural affairs officer, Am. Embassy, Bucharest, Romania, 1966-68; br. info. officer, Am. Embassy Consulate Gen., Zagreb, Yugoslavia, 1962-65. Bd. dirs. World Affairs Coun. of Berks County, Pa., 1999-2000; pres. Susquehanna Valley chpt. People to People Internat., 1998-2003; vol. tax counselor AARP. Recipient Youth Conservation award Pa. Fedn. Sportsmen, 1950; sr. rsch. scholar Atlantic Coun., Washington, 1984. Mem. German-Am. Soc., U.S. Humane Soc., Nat. Wildlife Fedn., Nature Conservancy, Landis Vly Assn., Pine Creek Preservation Assn., Am. Legion. Home and Office: CEE Consulting 105 E 3rd Ave Lititz PA 17543-2724

KOCH, CARL MARK, environmental engineering executive; b. Orefield, Pa., Apr. 29, 1944; s. Mark and Florence Viola (Hoffman) K.; m. Nancy Louise Varady, Aug. 10, 1966; children: Carcy, Roger, Janine. BSCE, U. Del., 1966, U. Pa., 1967, PhD in Water Resources, 1972. Registered profl. engr., Pa., Del.; cert. sewage plant operator, Pa. Hydraulic engr. U.S. Army C.E., Phila., summer 1966; rsch. fellow U. Pa., Phila., 1966-70; environ. engr. GE Reentry and Environ. Sys. Divsn., Phila., 1970-74, Greeley and Hansen, Phila., 1976—, ptnr., 1995—. Lectr. U. Del., Newark, 1992; spkr. in field. Contbr. articles to procs. and profl. jours. Chmn. bd. trustees Good Shepherd Luth. Ch., Wilmington, Del., 1995—. Mem. ASCE (com. chmn. 1966-82, chmn. residuals com. 1994—), Water Environ. Fedn. (contbg. author 1990), Am. Acad. Environ. Engring. (diplomate). Democrat. Avocations: bridge, volleyball. Home: Graylyn Crest 1919 Gravers Ln Wilmington DE 19810-3903 Office: Greeley and Hansen 1818 Market St Philadelphia PA 19103-3638

KOCH, CAROLE JACKSON, human resources executive; b. Evergreen Park, Ill., Feb. 25, 1951; d. Robert Lawrence Capman and Norma Gene (Benson) C.; m. Donald Charles Jackson, Sept. 24, 1976 (dec. Mar. 1984); m. Curtis Gerard Koch, Aug. 28, 1987. BA with honors, U. Ill., Chgo., 1972. Job analyst U. Ill., Chgo., 1973-76, personnel coordinator, 1976-80, assoc. personnel dir., 1980-83; dir. human resources U. Ill. Hosp. and Clinics, Chgo., 1983-96; assoc. hosp. dir./ dir. human resources U. Ill.-Chgo. Med. Ctr., 1996-2000; human resource mgmt. cons., 2000—. Mem. human resources coun. Met. Chgo. Healthcare Coun., 1987-2000. Mem. Am. Soc. Healthcare Human Resources Adminstrn., Soc. Human Resource Mgmt. E-mail: kochx2@aol.com.

KOCH, CATHERINE ANN, music educator, musician; b. Manchester, N.H., July 27, 1953; d. David Milton and Clarice Joyce Cargill; children: Christopher Lawrence, Gretchen Renate. B in Music Edn., Bucknell U., Lewisburg, Pa., 1975; MS in Music Edn., Syracuse U., 1976. Cert. tchr. N.Y. Pvt. piano, voice and guitar tchr., Fayetteville, NY, 1975—; choral and gen. music tchr. Smith Rd. Sch., N. Syracuse, NY, 1976—81, Manlius Pebble Hill Sch., DeWitt, NY, 1981—89, Eagle Hill Middle Sch., Manlius, NY, 1989—. Substitute organist, soloist various chs., NY, 1993—; organist U. Meth. Ch., Manlius, 1976—93; jr. choir dir. DeWitt Cmty. Ch., 1993—2000; accompanist Syracuse U. Oratorio Soc., 1975—82; mgr., accompanist Jr. High All-County Chorus, Onondaga County, NY, 1992, Onondaga County, 95, Onondaga County, 98, Onondaga County, 2001; chmn. elem. and jr. high vocal task com. Elem. and Jr. High Schs., Onondaga County, 2001—03. Author: (pocket card) Student's Prayer, 1995; musician (pianist): Purely Percussion, 1993, 1995. Recipient Music Masters Harmony award, Soc. Preservation and Encouragement Barbershop Quartet Singing in Am., 2003. Mem.: Am. Choral Dirs. Assn., Onondaga County Music Educators Assn. (pres.-elect), N.Y. State Sch. Music Assn. (presenter 1997, Presdl. Citation for Fayetteville-Manlius music program 1997), Music Educators Nat. Conf. Avocations: reading, swimming, biking. Home: 320 Highbridge St Fayetteville NY 13066 Office: Eagle Hill Middle Sch 4645 Enders Rd Manlius NY 13104

KOCH, CHARLES DE GANAHL, business executive; b. Wichita, Kans., Nov. 1, 1935; s. Fred Chase and Mary Clementine (Robinson) K. BS in Gen. Engring, MIT, 1957, MS in Mech. Engring., 1958, MS in Chem. Engring., 1959. Engr. Arthur D. Little, Inc., Cambridge, Mass., 1959-61; v.p. Koch Engring. Co., Inc., Wichita, 1961-63, pres., 63-71, chmn., 1967-78; pres. Koch Industries, Inc., Wichita, 1966-74, chmn., CEO, 1967—. Bd. dirs. Intrust Bank, N.A., Mercatus Ctr. Chmn. Inst. Humane Studies. Mem.: Flint Hills Nat., Mt. Pelerin Soc., The Vintage Club. Office: Koch Industries PO Box 2256 4111 E 37th St N Wichita KS 67220

KOCH, DAVID HAMILTON, chemical company executive; b. Wichita, Kans., May 3, 1940; BS in Chem. Engring., MIT, 1962, MS in Chem. Engring., 1963. Engr. Amicon Corp., Cambridge, 1963-64, Arthur D. Little, Inc., Cambridge, Mass., 1964-67, Halcon Internat., Inc., N.Y.C., 1967-70; with Chem. Tech Group of Koch Ind., Wichita, Kans., 1970—, exec. v.p., 1981—. Bd. trustees NYU Med. Ctr., N.Y.C.; gov. N.Y. Hosp., N.Y.C., chmn. devel. com.; trustee Meml. Sloan Kettering, N.Y.C., others; bd. dirs. Am. Mus. Natural History, N.Y.C., Aspen Inst., Colo., Earthwatch, Watertown, Mass., Inst. of Human Origins, Berkeley, Calif.; mem. bd. assocs. Whitehead Inst., Cambridge, Mass.; bd. overseers, WGBH, Channel 2, Boston; trustee Guggenheim Mus., N.Y.C., others; Libertarian Party Candidate for V.P. of U.S., 1980; bd. dirs. Reason Found., L.A., CATO Inst., Washington, Citizens for a Sound Economy, Washington. Mem. River Club (N.Y.), Racquet & Tennis Club (N.Y.), Explorers Club (N.Y.), numerous others. Avocations: skiing, tennis, golf. Office: Koch Engring 667 Madison Ave Fl 22D New York NY 10021-8029

KOCH, DONALD LEROY, retired geologist, state agency administrator; b. Dubuque, Iowa, June 3, 1937; s. Gregory John and Josephine Elizabeth (Young) K.; m. Celia Jean Swede, July 5, 1962; children: Kyle Benjamin, Amy Suzanne,

Nathan Gregory. BS, U. Iowa, 1959, MS in Geology, 1967, postgrad., 1971-73. Research geologist Iowa Geol. Survey, Iowa City, 1959-71, chief subsurface geology, 1971-75, asst. state geologist, 1975-80, state geologist and dir., 1980-86; state geologist and bur. chief Geol. Survey Bur., Iowa City, 1986—2002; ret., 2002—. Contbr. articles to profl. jours. Fellow Iowa Acad. Sci. (bd. dirs. 1986-89); mem. Geol. Soc. Iowa (pres. 1969), Iowa Groundwater Assn. (pres. 1986), Rotary, Sigma Xi. Avocations: bicycling, camping, chess, numismatics. Home: 1431 Prairie Du Chien Rd Iowa City IA 52245-5615 E-mail: statefossil@aol.com.

KOCH, DOUGLAS DONALD, ophthalmologist, educator; b. Port Huron, Mich., May 28, 1951; s. Donald Allen and Helen Baptie (Webster) K. BA, Amherst Coll., 1973; MD, Harvard U., 1977. Diplomate Am. Bd. Ophthalmology. Intern St. Luke's Episcopal Hosp., Houston, 1977—78; resident in ophthalmology Baylor Coll. Medicine, Houston, 1978—81, prof. ophthalmology, 1982—; ophthalmologist Cullen Eye Inst., Houston. Mem. River Oaks Breakfast Club, Phi Beta Kappa, Alpha Omega Alpha. Office: Cullen Eye Inst 6565 Fannin St # Nc205 Houston TX 77030-2704

KOCH, EDNA MAE, lawyer, nurse; b. Terre Haute, Ind., Oct. 12, 1951; d. Leo K. and Lucille E. (Smith) K.; m. Mark D. Orton. BS in Nursing, Ind. State U., 1977; JD, Ind. U., 1980. Bar: Ind. 1980, U.S. Dist. Ct. (so. dist.) Ind. 1980. Assoc. Dillon & Cohen, Indpls., 1980-85; ptnr. Tipton, Cohen & Koch, Indpls., 1985-93, LaCava, Zeigler & Carter, Indpls., 1993-94, Zeigler Cohen & Koch, Indpls., 1994—. Leader seminars for nurses, Ind. U. Med. Ctr., Ball State U., Muncie, Ind., St. Vincent Hosp., Indpls., Deaconess Hosp., Evansville, Ind., others; lectr. on med. malpractice Cen. Ind. chpt. AACCN, Indpls. "500" Postgrad. Course in Emergency Medicine, Ind. Assn. Osteo. Physicians and Surgeons State Conv., numerous others. Mem. ABA, ANA, Ind. State Bar Assn., Indpls. Bar Assn., Am. Soc. Law and Medicine, Ind. State Nurses Assn. Republican. Office: Zeigler Cohen & Koch 9465 Counselors Row Ste 104 Indianapolis IN 46240-3816

KOCII, EDWARD I. former mayor, lawyer; b. N.Y.C., Dec. 12, 1924; s. Louis and Joyce K. Student, Coll. City N.Y.; LLB, NYU, 1948. Bar: N.Y. State 1949. Pvt. practice, N.Y.C., 1949-64, democratic dist. leader Greenwich Village, 1963-65; sr. partner firm Koch Lankenau Schwartz & Kovner, N.Y.C., 1965-69; mem. N.Y.C. Council, 1967-68, 91st-92nd Congresses from 17th Dist. N.Y., 1969-72, 93d-95th congresses from 18th Dist. N.Y., 1973-77, mem. appropriations com., sec. N.Y. Congl. del.; mayor N.Y.C., 1978-89; ptnr. Bryan Cave, N.Y.C., 1990—. Author: Mayor, 1984, Politics, 1985, His Eminence and Hizzoner, 1989, All the Best, Letters from a Feisty Mayor, 1990, Citizen Koch, 1992, Ed Koch on Everything, 1994, Murder at City Hall, 1995, Murder on Broadway, 1996, Murder on 34th Street, 1997, The Senator Must Die, 1998, Giuliani Nasty Man, 1999, I'm Not Done Yet!, 1999. Served with AUS, World War II. Office: Bryan Cave 1290 Avenue Of The Americas Fl 33 New York NY 10104-3300

KOCH, EDWARD RICHARD, lawyer, accountant; b. Teaneck, N.J., Mar. 25, 1953; s. Edward J. and Adelaide M. K.; m. Cora Susan Koch, Apr. 12, 1997; children: Edward Peter, William John. BS in Econs. magna cum laude, U. Pa., 1975; JD, U. Va., 1980; LLM in Taxation, NYU, 1986. Bar: N.J. 1980, U.S. Dist. Ct. N.J. 1980, U.S. Tax Ct. 1981, U.S. Ct. Claims 1981. Staff acct. Touche Ross & Co. (now Deloitte & Touche), Newark, 1975-77; assoc. Winne, Banta & Rizzi, Hackensack, N.J., 1980-82; tax atty. Allied Corp. (now Honeywell Internat. Inc.), Morristown, 1982-87; asst. v.p. ChemBank (now Chase Manhattan), N.Y.C., 1987-90; tax mgr. Paul Scherer & Co. LLP, N.Y.C., 1990-97, ptnr., 1998—. Vice chmn. law and legis. com. U.S.A. Track and Field, Indpls., 1985-89, chmn., 1989-2000, chmn. ins. com., 1984-88, bd. dirs., 1989—, treas., 2000—; pres. N.J. Athletics Congress, Red Bank, 1986-90; mem. Jury of Appeals, 1988, U.S. Olympic Men's Marathon Trials, Holy Family Sch. Edn. Coun., 1992-96; Olympic Track and Field ofcl., 1996; chmn. tax com. Mag. Pub. of Am., 2002—. Mem. AICPA, N.J. Soc. CPAs, Am. Assn. Attys.-CPAs, N.J. State Bar Assn., N.J. Striders Track Club (chmn. 1981-96), Magazine Publishers Am. (chair tax comm., 2002-). Republican. Roman Catholic. Avocation: running track and field. Home: 130 Grant St Haworth NJ 07641-1951 Office: Paul Scherer & Co 335 Madison Ave Fl 9 New York NY 10017-4605 E-mail: ekoch@pscherer.com.

KOCH, EDWIN ERNEST, artist, interior decorator; b. Bronx, N.Y., Feb. 21, 1915; s. Henry Koch and Elsie Ziegenbalg. One-man shows include Mus. of Hudson Highlands, 1986; exhibited in group shows at Met. Mus. Art, 1952, Bklyn. Mus., 1953, Pa. Acad., 1953, NAD, 1958, Am. Watercolor Soc.; represented in permanent collections Butler Art Inst., Youngstown, Ohio. With AUS, 1942-46. Recipient Top Best in Show awrd Middle Town Art Soc., 1980's, Nat. Arts Club, 1989. Mem. Audubon Artists Am., Nat. Soc. Painters in Casein and Acrylic (bd. dirs. 1975-76), Painters and Sculptors Soc. N.J. (v.p. 1978), Knickerbocker Artists, Artists Equity. Home: 109 Old Hoagerburgh Rd Wallkill NY 12589-3430 E-mail: eek@frontier.net.

KOCH, GEORGE WILLIAM, lawyer; b. Cin., Apr. 8, 1926; s. George Earl and Lucille (Arnold) K.; m. Helen Lawton, July 29, 1950; children: Jorie, Danny, P.C., Bobby, Monte, Lucy. B.BS, U. Cin., 1948, LL.B., JD, 1950. Bar: Ohio 1950. Asst. city atty., Cin., 1950-54; assoc. dir. Ohio Council Retail Merchants, Columbus, 1954-59; dir. fed. affairs Sears, Roebuck & Co., Washington, 1959-65; pres., chief exec. officer Grocery Mfrs. Am., Inc., Washington, 1966-90; ptnr. Kirkpatrick Lockhart, 1990—. Chmn. Congl. Charity Tennis Tournament, Congl. Charity Golf Tournament. Served with USNR, World War II. Mem. Nat. Press Club, Union League, City Tavern Club, Congl. Country Club, Greenbrier Golf and Tennis Club. Home: 10837 Stanmore Dr Potomac MD 20854-1521 Office: Kirkpatrick & Lockhart 1800 Massachusetts Ave NW Fl 2 Washington DC 20036-1806

KOCH, JAMES VERCH, academic administrator, economist; b. Springfield, Ill., Oct. 7, 1942; s. Elmer O. and Wilma L. K.; m. Donna L. Stickling, Aug. 20, 1967; children: Elizabeth, Mark. BA, Ill. State U., 1964; PhD, Northwestern U., 1968. From asst. prof. to prof. econs. Ill. State U., 1967-78, chmn. dept., 1972-78; dean Faculty Arts and Scis., R.I. Coll., Providence, 1978-80; prof. econs., provost, v.p. acad. affairs Ball State U., Muncie, Ind., 1980-86; pres. U. Mont., Missoula, 1986-90, Old Dominion U., Norfolk, Va., 1990-2001, prof. econs., 2001—. Author: Industrial Organization and Prices, 2d edit, 1980, Microeconomic Theory and Applications, 1976, The Economics of Affirmative Action, 1976, Presidential Leadership, 1996, The Entrepreneurial President, 2003. Mem. Am. Econ. Assn. Lutheran. Home: 240 Keith Ave Missoula MT 59801-4308 Office: Old Dominion U Dept Econs Norfolk VA 23529 *Survival in the 21st century, whether in higher education or in automobile production, demands and requires quality. Excellence must be our goal in all that we undertake. This is an attitude that must be instilled in the home, in our schools, and throughout society so that it permeates our lives.*

KOCH, JAMIE, political party official; married; 2 children. BS in Edn., U. N.Mex., 1959. State legis. State of N.Mex., 1968—74; chmn. N.Mex. Game and Fish Bd., 1983—94; pres. Daniels Ins., Santa Fe; chmn. Dem. Party N.Mex., 2002—. Office: 5317 Menaul Blvd Albuquerque NM 87110

KOCH, JOANNE ELLEN, guidance counselor; b. Paterson, N.J., Dec. 28, 1962; d. Walter Ernest and Karen Gambert. BA in Early Childhood Edn., William Paterson Coll., 1984, MA in Social Sci., 1987, MEd in Counseling, 1988, MEd in Ednl. Adminstrn., 1991. Cert. tchr., supr., dir. student pers. svcs., N.J. Tchr. St. Andrew Sch., Westwood, N.J., 1985-86; guidance counselor DePaul High Sch., Wayne, N.J., 1986-87; county 4-H agt. Rutgers Coop. Extension Svc., New Brunswick, N.J., 1987-88; guidance counselor High Point Regional High Sch., Sussex, N.J., 1988—. Mem.: Sussex County Guidance Assn. (pres.), N.J. Edn. Assn. Avocations: swimming, bicycling, rollerblading, animals, travel.

KOCH, KATHERINE ROSE, communications executive; b. Pitts., Apr. 21, 1949; d. Irving Samuel Stapsy and Betty Ruth (Sachs) Blake; m. Stanley Christopher Brown, July 26, 1986; 1 child, Matthew. BFA, Rochester Inst. Tech., 1973. Instr. Sch. Profl. Art, Pitts., 1973-74; advt. dir. Buhl Optical Co., Pitts., 1974-77; pres., creative dir. Ambit Mktg. Comm., Ft. Lauderdale, Fla., 1977—. Instr. Point Park Coll., Pitts., 1977-78. Bd. dirs. Nat. Conf. Cmty. and Justice, 1999—, United Way, Broward County, 1995—, Broward C.C. Found., 2002; bd. dirs., chair Broward Coordinating Coun., 1994—; bd. dirs. Broward Alliance. Mem.: Tower Forum (bd. dirs. 1995—), Womens Exec. Club (pres. 1995—96). Office: Ambit Mktg Comm 2455 E Sunrise Blvd Ste 711 Fort Lauderdale FL 33304-3110

KOCH, MAGALY, geologist, researcher; b. Büderich, Germany, Mar. 2, 1959; d. Franz D. and Floralba (Mejia) K. MSc in Geology, U. Cologne, Germany, 1986; Diploma in Hydrology, Poly. U. Catalonia, Barcelona, Spain, 1987; PhD in Geology, Boston U., 1993. Rsch. assoc. Ctr. for Remote Sensing, Boston U., 1993-96, rsch. asst. prof., 1998—; rsch. fellow Earth Scis. Inst. "Jaume Almera", CSIC, Barcelona, 1996-98. Vis. scientist geography dept. U. Nottingham, Eng., 1996; vis. prof. geology dept. Autonomous U. Madrid, 2000-01; cons. UNDP-UNESCO Geo Devel. Project for Capacity Bldg. Egyptian Geological Survey & Mining Authority and Nat. Authority for Remote Sensing and Space Scis., Cairo, 1999. Contbr. articles to profl. jours. TMR Marie Curie Rsch. grantee Commn. of European Communities, 1995, Brit. Coun. Spl. Visit grantee, 1996. Mem. Remote Sensing Soc. U.K., Marie Cure Fellowship Assn., European Commn., Am. Soc. for Photogrammetry and Remote Sensing, Geol. Soc. Am. Avocations: film, travel, art. Office: Boston U Ctr Remote Sensing 725 Commonwealth Ave Boston MA 02215-1401 E-mail: mkoch@bu.edu.

KOCH, MARGARET RAU, writer, artist, historian; b. Sacramento; d. George James Rau and Callista Marie Martin; children: Edward James, Kathleen, Thomas C. Student, U. Calif., Berkeley, 1936-38. Mem. editl. staff Santa Cruz (Calif.) Sentinel, 1958-76. Author: Santa Cruz County, Parade of the Past, 1973, 74, 77, 81, 91, 99, They Called It Home, 1974, Walk Around Santa Cruz, 1978, Going To School in Santa Cruz County, 1978, The Pasatiempo Story, 1990, Santa Cat-Behind the Lace Curtains, 2001; exhibited in group shows at Sedona Arts Ctr., Yavapai County Arts Fair, Ft. Verde Art Show, 1997, 98, 99, 2000. Organizer, first pres. Santa Cruz Hist. Soc. Recipient 3 Mixed Media Watercolor awards Yavapai County Art Fair, Ariz., 2 Watercolor awards Fort Verde Art Show, Ariz. Mem. No. Ariz. Watercolo Soc., Pen Women, Santa Cruz Art League, Sedona Art Ctr.

KOCH, MICHAEL ARTHUR, music educator; b. Grand Island, Nebr., June 8, 1966; s. Everett Earl Koch and Connie Luann Biblan, m. Debra Kay Forsell, June 20, 1992. MusB, Hastings Coll., 1988; MusM, U.Nebr., Lincoln, 1998. Cert. tchr. Nebr. 5-12 instrumental music tchr. Milford (Nebr.) Pub. Schools, 1988—89; 5-12 instrumental & 7-12 vocal music tchr. Shickley (Nebr.) Pub. Schools, 1989—92; 5-12 instrumental music tchr. Bridgeport (Nebr.) Pub. Schools, 1992—98, Scottsbluff (Nebr.) Pub. Schools, 1998—. Mem.: NEA, Nebr. State Edn. Assn., Nebr. State Bandmasters Assn., Nebr. Music Educators Assn. (Jack R. Snider Young Band Dir. award 1994). Avocations: trumpet, golf.

KOCH, MITCHELL, information technology executive; married; 3 children. BA in Acct., Calif. State U. With Arthur Anderson & Co.; various positions including pres. Buena Vista Home Entertainment; corp. v.p. worldwide retail sales & mktg. for home & retail divsn. Microsoft, Redmond, Wash., 2000—. Office: One Microsoft Way Redmond WA 98052-6399

KOCH, RANDALL GLORY, hospital administrator; b. Passaic, N.J., Oct. 12, 1970; s. Gilbert William and Geraldine (Abruscato) K. BA, William Paterson Coll., 1993; postgrad., Seton Hall U., 1993-2000, MPA, 2000. Registration supervisor Kennedy Hosp., Saddlebrook, N.J., 1988-92; patient acct. supervisor Englewood (N.J.) Hosp., 1992-99; patient account mgr. Passaic Beth Israel Hosp., 1999-2000; dir. admission svcs. Jersey City (N.J.) Med. Ctr., 2000—02; credit mgr. Englewood Hosp. and Med. Ctr., Englewood, NJ, 2002—. Mem. Am. Coll. Healthcare Execs., Am. Soc. Pub. Adminstrn., U.S. Golf Assn., Am. Soc. Notaries. Office: Englewood Hosp and Med Ctr 350 Engle St Englewood NJ 07631

KOCH, RICHARD, retired pediatrician, educator; b. N.D., Nov. 24, 1921; s. Valentine and Barbara (Fischer) K.; m. Kathryn Jean Holt, Oct. 2, 1943; children: Jill, Thomas, Christine, Martin, Leslie. BA, U. Calif. at Berkeley, 1958; MD, U. Rochester, 1951. Mem. staff Children's Hosp., LA, 1952—75, mem. staff, 1977—2003, dir. child devel. div., 1955-75; dep. dir. Calif. Dept. Health, 1975-76; prof. pediatrics U. So. Calif., 1955-75, 77—; prof. clin. pediatrics U. So. Calif. Sch. of Medicine, L.A., 1958—; dir. Phenylketonuria Collaborative Study, 1966-82; med. dir. Spastic Children's Found., Los Angeles, 1980-85, ret., 2003—. Mem. Project Hope, Trujillo, Peru, 1970; dir. Regional Center for Developmentally Disabled at Children's Hosp., Los Angeles, 1966-75; mem. research adv. bd. Nat. Assn. Retarded Citizens, 1974-76; mem. Gov.'s Council on Devel. Disabilities, 1981-83; bd. dirs. Down's Syndrome Congress, 1974-76; prin. investigator Maternal Phenylketonuria Project Nat. Inst. Child Health and Human Devel., Washington, 1985-2003; mem. forensic assessment team South Ctrl. Regional Ctr. for Developmental Disabilities, 1999—. Author: (with James Dobson) The Mentally Retarded Child and his Family, 1971, (with Kathryn J. Koch) Understanding the Mentally Retarded Child, 1974, (with Felix de la Cruz) Downs Syndrome, 1975; contbr. articles to profl. jours. Recipient Albert L. Anderson award for outstanding health care profl., 1997, Homer Smith Rsch. award, 1998; Carrie D. Jones scholar, U. Calif., Berkeley, 1941. Mem. Am. Assn. on Mental Deficiency (pres. 1968-69), Am. Acad. Pediatrics, Western Soc. Pediatric Research, Soc. for Study Inborn Errors Metabolism, Soc. Inborn Metabolic Disorders, Sierra Club (treas. Mineral King task force 1972). Achievements include research in mental retardation, phenylketonuria and relation to pediatrics. Home: 2125 Ames St Los Angeles CA 90027-2902 Office: Children's Hosp of LA MPKU # 73 4650 Sunset Blvd Los Angeles CA 90027-6062 E-mail: rkoch8@earthlink.net.

KOCH, ROBERT CHARLES, lawyer, community activist; b. Berwyn, Ill., Apr. 7, 1947; s. Eugene William and Ellen Marie (Hudec) K.; m. Sharon Smith, June 27, 1970; children: Jason, Ryan, Lindsay. BS, Ill. Inst. Tech., 1969; JD, Coll. William and Mary, 1972. Bar: Ill. 1972, Okla. 1978, N.Y. 2003. Assoc. Bell, Boyd & Lloyd, Chgo., 1972-78; staff atty. Phillips Petroleum Co., Bartlesville, Okla., 1978-81, sr. atty., 1986-90, sr. counsel, 1990—2002; counsel Phillips Petroleum Co. Europe & Africa, London, 1981-86; mng.ptnr. Koch Law Office, 2002—. Author of Sunday sch. curriculums. Chmn. Washington County Dem. Party, Bartlesville, 1993-97; pres., dir. Westside Cmty. Assn., Bartlesville, 1997—2002. Mem. ABA, ATLA, Okla. Bar Assn., Am. Legion. Democrat. Presbyterian. Avocations: church youth ministry, travel. Home: 6972 Palmetto Circle S Apt 507 Boca Raton FL 33433 Office: 1699 W Adams Blvd Bartlesville OK 74004 Mailing: PO Box 81041 Boca Raton FL 33481-0841 E-mail: BobKoch@KochLawOffice.com.

KOCH, ROBERT LOUIS, II, manufacturing company executive, mechanical engineer; b. Evansville, Ind., Jan. 6, 1939; s. Robert Louis and Mary L. (Bray) K.; m. Cynthia Ross, Oct. 17, 1964; children: David, Kevin, Kristen, Jennifer. BSME, U. Notre Dame, 1960; MBA, U. Pitts., 1962; D of Tech. (hon.), Vincennes U., 1992. Registered profl. engr., Ind. V.p. Ashdee Corp., Evansville, 1962-68, pres., 1968-82; ptnr. Fesk Partnership, Evansville, 1964—; chmn., CEO Gibbs Die Casting Corp., Henderson, Ky., 1976—; pres., CEO Koch Enterprises, Inc., Evansville, 1982—; chmn., dir. UNISEAL, Inc., Evansville, 1984—; v.p., dir. Brake Supply Co., Evansville, 1986—; chmn. bd. Marco Sales, Inc., St. Louis, 1997—. Exec. in residence U. So. Ind., Evansville, 1967; bd. dirs. Fifth-Third Bacnorp, Cincinnati, Ohio, Bindley Western Industries, Indpls., So. Ind. Properties, Inc., Evansville, So. Ind. Minerals, Inc., N.Am. Green, Inc., Audubon Metals LLC, Vectren Corp.; chmn. bd. dirs. Uniseal Rubber Products, Inc., Arnold, Mo., 1988-95. Inventor, patentee water purifier, drying oven, powder coating booth, electro painting system. Contr., dep. mayor City of Evansville, 1976-80; active Gov.'s Fiscal Policy Adv. Com., Indpls., 1978-89, Pres. Adv. Coun. Indiana Univ., 1992—, Purdue U., 1992—, parents exec. com., West Lafayette, 1985-88, sch. bd. nominating com., 1987-89; vice-chmn. bd. trustees U. Evansville, 1985-92, chmn. bd. trustees, 1993-96; pres. Signature Learning Ctr. Inc., Evansville, 1994—; vice-chmn. bd. trustees Evansville Mus. Arts and Scis., 1982-92; bd. dirs. SW Ind. Pub. Broadcasting, 1985-89, Pub. Edn. Found., Evansville, 1986-88, Hoosiers for Higher Edn., 1991-98, Commit, Inc., Cmty. Alliance Found., 1991—, Ind. Colls. Ind., 1992—, Found. for Ind. Higher Edn., 1996—, Project E, 2000; treas. Vanderburgh County Rep. Com., Evansville, 1984-88; pres. Cath. Edn. Found., Evansville, 1978-82; chmn. Ind. Econ. Devel. Coun., 1991-92, Ind. Humanities Coun. Bus. Forum, 1999, United Way of Southwestern Ind. Campaign, 1998; co-chmn. Ind. Bus. Higher Edn. Forum, 1991-96; pres. Cath. Found. Southwestern Ind., 1992—; v.p. Ind. Acad., Indpls., 1999--; pres. Evansville Regional Bus. Com., 2002--. 1st lt. USAR, 1961-67. Recipient Challenger award Nat. Assn. Woodworking Machinery Mfrs., Louisville, 1980, Boy Scout's Disting. Citizen's award, 1991, Rotary Club Citizenship award, 1991, Sagamore of the Wabash, 1999; named Exec. of Yr. Profl. Secs. Assn., 1984, Knight of the Order of the Holy Sepulchre, 1996, Entrepreneur of Yr., Ind. Mfg., 1998, Ind. Bus. Leader of Yr. Ind. C. of C., 2002. Mem. Metro Evansville C. of C. (bd. dirs. Met. 1983-96, named Bus. Person of Yr. 1998), Ind. C. of C. (bd. dirs., chmn. 1991—), Young Pres. Orgn., World Pres. Orgn., Evansville Country Club, Victoria Nat. Golf Club. Avocations: golf, tennis, snow skiing. Office: Koch Enterprises Inc 10 S 11th Ave Evansville IN 47744-0001

KOCH, ROBERT MICHAEL, research scientist, consultant, educator; b. Mineola, N.Y., Apr. 19, 1964; s. Roy Arthur and Ellen Anne (Trimble) K.; m. Laureen Theresa Chase, July 6, 1991. BSME, Poly. U., Bklyn., 1986, PhD in Applied Mechanics, 1991. Profl. engr., R.I. Mech. engr. Vernitech Corp., Deer Park, N.Y., 1983-85; instr. Poly. U., Bklyn., 1986-91; chief rsch. scientist Naval Undersea Warfare Ctr., Newport, RI, 1991—. Cons. Beltran, Inc., Bklyn., 1988-91; adj. prof. Roger Williams U., Bristol, R.I., 1993—. Teaching fellow Poly. U., 1986-90, rsch. fellow, 1987, 90. Mem. AIAA, ASME, Acoustical Soc. Am., N.Y. Acad. Scis., Sigma Xi. Republican. Roman Catholic. Achievements include research in undersea propulsion, underwater shock analysis, underwater structural acoustics, adaptive procedures in h-and p-version finite element analysis, rapid prototyping with stereolithography, probabilistic structural mechanics, ultrasonic wave propagation in elastic solids. Home: 304 White Horn Dr South Kingstown RI 02881-1829 Office: Naval Undersea Warfare Ctr Code 8232 Bldg 1302 Newport RI 02841-0001

KOCH, ROBERT WOTRING, chemical engineer; b. St. Louis, Jan. 24, 1927; s. Robert Rudolph and Anne Lenore (Studt) K.; m. Beth A. Miller, June 1, 1951; children: Kathryn A., Wayne M., Donald L., Dorothy M. BSChemE, Washington U., 1949; MSChemE, MIT, 1950. Sr. rsch. engr. Gulf Rsch. and Devel. Co., Harmarville, Pa., 1950-85; chem. engr. U.S. Dept. Energy, Morgantown, W.Va., 1985-92, K&M Engring. and Cons. Corp., Washington, 1994-95, ret., 1995. Inventor 3 petroleum refining inventions. With U.S. Army, 1945-46. Mem. AIChE, Alpha Chi Sigma. Republican. Presbyterian. Avocation: gardening. Home: 1100 Hunter Rd Verona PA 15147-2602

KOCH, RONALD PETER, retired biologist; b. Buffalo, Oct. 27, 1932; s. Karl W. and Marian Elizabeth (Andrews) K.; m. Loraine M. May, July 26, 1958; children: Edna E. Haugland, Ronald P. Jr. BA in Biology, U. Buffalo, 1954, EdM in Secondary Sch. Tchg., 1955. Sci. tchr. Cleveland Hill H.S., Cheektowaga, N.Y., 1955-56; asst. dist. scout exec. Boy Scouts Am., Buffalo, 1959, dist. scout exec., 1960-64, Rochester, N.Y., 1964-66; asst. to chmn. biochemistry SUNY, Buffalo, 1966-69; rsch. analyst Roswell Park Cancer Inst., Buffalo, 1969-73; lab. technician Erie County Pub. Health Lab., Buffalo, 1975-94, ret., 1994. Author: Dress Clothing of the Plains Indians, 1977. Dist. positions Boy Scouts Am., Buffalo, 1966-74, dist. chmn., 1975-76, ecology-conservation dir. Nat. Camping Sch., N.E. region, 1977-2003. With U.S. Army, 1956-58. Recipient Silver Beaver award Boy Scouts Am., 1974. Mem. SAR (chpt. pres. 1984-85), Mass. Soc. Mayflower Descendants, Huguenot Soc. N.Y., Sons Union Vets, Civil War. Lutheran. Avocations: nature study, American Indian studies, genealogy. Home and Office: 2778 George Urban Blvd Depew NY 14043-2150

KOCH, TAD HARBISON, chemistry educator, researcher; b. Mount Vernon, Ohio, Jan. 1, 1943; s. Justin Louis and Mary Fosdick (Grove) K.; m. Carol Ann Kuban, May 28, 1976 BS, Ohio State U., 1964; PhD, Iowa State U., 1968. Asst. prof. chemistry U. Colo., Boulder, 1968-74, assoc. prof., 1974-82, prof., 1982—, chmn. dept. chemistry and biochemistry, 1983-86; fellow U. Colo. Cancer Ctr., 1997—; mem. grad. sch. faculty Sch. Pharmacy, U. Colo. Health Scis. Ctr., 1999—. Contbr. numerous articles to profl. jours.; patentee in field Grantee U.S. Army Med. Comd., 1998, 2001, NSF, 1985, 89, 92, NIH, 1985, 87, 93, 98, 2001, Coun. Tobacco Rsch., 1992, 96, Petroleum Rsch. Fund, 1997, Am. Cancer Soc., 1997. Mem. AAAS, Am. Chem. Soc., Am. Assn. Cancer Rsch., Am. Soc. Photobiology. Office: U Colo 215 UCB Boulder CO 80309-0215 E-mail: tad.koch@colorado.edu.

KOCH, THOMAS FREDERICK, lawyer; b. Hackensack, N.J., Nov. 24, 1942; s. Elmer J. and Evelyn (Zombeck) K.; m. Sally J. Tucker, June 6, 1970; children: Christine E., Donald T. AB, Middlebury Coll., 1964; JD, U. Chgo., 1967. Bar: Vt. 1967, U.S. Dist. Ct. Vt. 1971. Assoc. firm Free and Bernasconi, Barre, Vt., 1970-74; ptnr. Bernasconi & Koch, Barre, 1974—. Mem. jud. nominating bd. State of Vt., 1979-81; mem. Vt. Ho. of Reps., 1977-80, 97—, mem. mcpl. corps. and elections, judiciary, house rules and joint rules coms. health and welfare, chair, 2001—, joint com. on health access oversight; moderator Town of Barre, 1984— ; chmn. Vt. Rep. Platform com. 1984. Del. nat. convs. of Assn. of Evang. Luth. Chs., 1978, 84, 86; del. to constrn. conv. of Evang. Luth. Ch. in Am., 1987-94; mem. churchwide assemblies, 1991, 97, 99; mem. New Eng. synod coun. Evangelical Luth. Ch. Am., 1987-94; mem. churchwide assemblies, 1991, 97; scoutmaster Boy Scouts Am., Barre, 1989-93, dist. chmn. 1993-96, 98-2000; mem. exec. bd. Green Mountain Coun., 1997—, v.p. for dist. ops., 2002--. Mem. Vt. Bar Assn., Washington County Bar Assn., Barre Lions Club (pres. 1977-78). Republican. Home: 326 Lowery Rd Barre VT 05641-9090 Office: 107 N Main St PO Box 892 Barre VT 05641-0892 E-mail: tfklaw@aol.com.

KOCH, WILLIAM JOSEPH, public relations executive; b. Celina, Ohio, June 6, 1949; s. George Albert and Helen Marie (McKovich) K.; m. Susan Margaret Griffith, June 14, 1969; children: Brian William, Dana Marie. BA, U. Akron, 1974. Draftsman Summit County Engr.'s Office, Akron, Ohio, 1968-72; pub. info. officer Ohio Dept. Transp., Ravenna, Ohio, 1972-75; asst. dir. mktg. and pub. rels. Metro Regional Transit Auth., Akron, 1975-78; sr. acct. exec. Meeker-Mayer Agy., Akron, 1978—84; exec. v.p., COO David A. Meeker & Assocs., 1984—87; mgr. pub. affairs Tricil, Inc., Akron, 1987-90; dir. corp. comm. Laidlaw Inc., Akron, 1990-94; dir. comm./pub. rels. Laidlaw Passenger Svcs. Group, Fairlawn, Ohio, 1994-97, Laidlaw Inc., Fairlawn, Ohio, 1997-98; v.p. comm. Laidlaw Edn. Svcs., Naperville, Ill., 1998—. Co-author: No Surprises: The Crisis Communication Management System, 1988. Mem. pub. rels. adv. com. Kent State U. Fellow: Pub. Rels. Soc. Am.; mem.: Nat. Investor Rels. Inst., Nat. Sch. Pub. Rels. Assn., Arthur W. Page Soc., Akron Press Club, Jaycees (senator, disting. svc. award 1983). Democrat. Roman Catholic. Home: 1190 Arborside Dr Aurora IL 60504-7074 Office: 55 Shuman Blvd Ste 400 Naperville IL 60563-8248

KOCHAN, PATRICIA ANN, artist; b. Dallas, Oct. 29, 1938; d. William Reed and Elsie Irene Wheelis; m. John Robert Kochan, June 12, 1959; children: Curtis Michael, Christy S. Student, U. Colo., 1957-59. Judge Dallas Bus. Com for the Arts. One-woman shows include Med. City Hosp., Dallas, 1985, Cottonwood Art Festival, Richardson, Tex., 1985, Savs. of Am., Dallas, 1987, Housley-Hanson Fine Furniture, Dallas, 1988, Carol Richmind Interiors, Dallas, 1989, The Grand Kempenski Hotel, Dallas, 1990-91, Covins House and Table, Dallas, 1992, Kathleen's Art Cafe, Dallas, 1993, 95, Grand Prairie Women's League, Tex., 1994, Goodrich Gallery, Dallas, 1996, The Fish Restaurant, Dallas, 1997, North Dallas C. of C., 1997, 99, others; group shows include Farmers Br. Mansky Libr., Tex., 1986, Med. city Hosp., 1987, Hasgow Gallery, Dallas, 1987, Sheraton Gallery, Dallas, 1987, Irving Art Assn., Tex., 1988, The Grand Kempinski, Addison, 1989, Goodrich Gallery, 1989, Carold Richmond Interiors, 1989, Trammell Crow Co., Dallas, 1991, Suite X Gallery, Dallas, 1992, Gallery de hobieche Deep Ellum, Dallas, 1993-95, others; represented in permanent collections Belo Mansion, Dallas, Magnolia Hotel, Dallas, Allinz Bldg., Dallas, Edn. Ctr., FelCor Corp., Las Colinas, Irving, Tex., Dallas, Episcopal Ch. Good Shepherd, Dallas, Los Vaqueros, Dallas, Harvey House Hotel, Dallas, Arthur Andersen Assocs., Dallas, Smith, Underwood, Carmichael, Collins & Martin, Dallas, Casa Dominguez Restaurants, Dallas, Dallas Tortilla Factory, Lunas Tortilla Factory, Dallas, Crown Charter Nat. Bank, Dallas, Stature Field Corp., Richardson, The Fish Restaurant, Dallas, City of Dallas, others. Mem. Nat. Acrylic Painters Assn. (assoc.), Nat. Watercolor Soc. (assoc.), Allied Artists Am. (assoc.), Southwestern Watercolor Soc. (assoc., editor 1990-2001, chmn. artists in residence program 1990-91, chmn. signature exhbn. 1993-94), Tex. Visual Arts Assn. (bd.d irs. 1992-93, chmn. signature exhbn. 1992-93), Tex. Watercolor Soc. (del.-at-large 1991-95,

Purple Sage award), Dallas Visual Art Ctr. (assoc.), Dallas Hist. Soc. (assoc.), Artists and Craftsman Assn. (assoc.), Dallas Mus. Art (assoc.), Art Focus XC (founding mem.). Episcopalian. Avocation: golf. Home: 3727 Blue Trace Ln Dallas TX 75244 E-mail: patkart@aol.com.

KOCHAN, THOMAS A. business educator; b. Manitowoc, Wis., Sept. 28, 1947; s. Leo H. and Loretta M. K.; m. Kathryn A. Otis, Aug. 23, 1969; children: Andrew, Sarah, Samuel, Jacob, Benjamin. PhD, U. Wisc., 1973; hon. degree, U. San Martin de Porres, 1999. Asst./asoc. prof. Cornell U., Ithaca, N.Y., 1973-80; prof. MIT Sloan Sch. Mgmt., Cambridge, Mass., 1980—. Arbitrator Am. Arbitration Assn., Boston. Author: The Transformation of American Industrial Relations, 1986 (award Best Book on Mgmt. 1988), The Changing Nature of Work, 2000 (award Nat. Acad. Scis. Com. Report); editor: Perspectives on Work mag., 1997. Advisor AFL-CIO, Washington, 1983-88, Fed. Mediation and Conciliation Svc., Washington, 1993—; commn. mem. Nat. commn. on the Future of Worker Mgmt. Rels., Washington, 1993-95; cons. U.S. Sec. Labor, Washington, 1979-80. Recipient Cushing Gavin award Labor Guild of the Archdiocese of Boston, 1998. Mem. Indsl. Rels. Rsch. Assn. (pres. 1999-2000), Soc. Profls. Dispute Resolution (task force chair on workplace 1999, Bill Abner award 1974), Internat. Indsl. Rels. Assn. (pres. 1992-95), Nat. Acad. Human Resources. Democrat. Roman Catholic. Avocations: travel, vacationing in N.H., reading. Home: 136 Eliot St Chestnut Hill MA 02467 Office: MIT Sloan Sch Mgmt 50 Memorial Dr Cambridge MA 02142 Home Fax: 617 566 2394; Office Fax: 617 253 7696. E-mail: tkochan@mit.edu.

KOCHANEK, PATRICK MICHAEL, pediatrician, educator; b. Detroit, July 1, 1954; s. Julius E. and Stella A. (Mrowiec) K.; m. Denise Marie Kochanek; children: Ashley, Stanton, Jillian. BS, U. Mich., 1976; MD, U. Chgo., 1980. Intern, then resident U. Calif., San Diego, 1980-83; fellow pediatric critical care medicine Children's Hosp. Nat. Med. Ctr., Washington, 1983-86; guest scientist Naval Med. Rsch. Inst., Bethesda, Md., 1983-86; asst. prof. U. Pitts., 1986-91, assoc. prof., 1991—, dir. Safar Ctr. for Resuscitation Rsch., 1994—; dir. pediatric critical care medicine rsch. Children's Hosp. Pitts., 1992—. Editor in chief Pediatric Critical Care Medicine, 2000—. Recipient Investigator award Soc. Critical Care Medicine, 1994—. Office: Safar Ctr Resuscitation Rsch 3434 5th Ave Pittsburgh PA 15260 E-mail: kochanekpm@ccm.upmc.edu.

KOCHANSKI, LOIS WHIDDEN, foundation administrator; b. San Angelo, Tex., Aug. 21, 1923; d. James Edgar and Bessie Mae (Mullican) Whidden; m. Joseph Thaddeus Kochanski, Jan. 21, 1949; children: Mary Ann Daly, James T., Constance Wetterer. BA, U. Tex., 1945. Intelligence analyst U.S. Office of Naval Intelligence, Arlington, Va., 1960-64; asst. to v.p. for acad. affairs George Washington U., Washington, 1964-67; exec. dir. Found. for Advanced Edn. in Scis., Bethesda, Md., 1970—. Author: The Mullican Family of Warren County, Tennessee, 1991. Mem. AAUW, NIH Camera Club, Soc. of Mayflower Descendants. Avocations: photography, piano, genealogy, tennis, bridge. Home: 5301 Westpath Way Bethesda MD 20816-2212

KOCHAR, MAHENDR SINGH, physician, educator, administrator, scientist, writer, consultant; b. Jabalpur, India, Nov. 30, 1943; arrived in U.S., 1967, naturalized, 1978; s. Harnam Singh and Chanan Kaur Kochar; m. Arvind Kaur, 1968; children: Baltej (Baj), Ajay (Jay). MB, BS, All India Inst. Med. Scis., New Delhi, 1965; MSc, Med. Coll. Wis., 1972; MBA, U. Wis. Milw., 1987. Diplomate Am. Bd. Internal Medicine, Nephrology and Geriat., Am. Bd. Family Practice, Am. Bd. Mgmt., Am. Bd. Clin. Pharmacology. Intern All India Inst. Med. Scis. Hosp., New Delhi, 1966-67, Passaic (N.J.) Gen. Hosp., 1967-68; resident in medicine Allegheny Gen. Hosp., Pitts., 1968-70; fellow in clin. pharmacology Milw. VA Med. Ctr., 1970-71, attending physician, 1973; fellow in nephrology and hypertension Milw. County Gen. Hosp., 1971-73, attending physician, 1973-95, St. Michael Hosp., Milw., 1974—, dir. hemodialysis unit, 1975-80; clin. asst. prof. medicine and pharmacology and toxicology Med. Coll. Wis., Milw., 1973-75, asst. prof., 1975-78, assoc. prof., 1978-84, prof., 1984—, assoc. dean continuing med. edn., 1985-86, assoc. dean grad. med. edn., 1987-99, sr. assoc. dean acad. affairs, 1994-95, sr. assoc. dean grad. med. edn., 1999—. Attending physician St. Joseph's Hosp., Milw., 1975—; chmn. medicine Northpoint Med. Group, Milw., 1974-75; dir. Milw. Blood Pressure Program, 1975-78; dir. Hypertension Clinic, Milwaukee County Downtown Med. and Health Services, 1975-79; chief hypertension, VA Med. Cu., Milw., 1978-2000, assoc. chief staff for edn., 1979-2000; exec. dir. Med. Coll. Wis. Affiliated Hosps. Inc., Milw., 1987—. Author: Hypertension Control, 1978, 2nd rev. edit., 1985; editor: Textbook of General Medicine, 1983, Concise Textbook of Medicine, 2d edit., 1990, 3d edit. 1998, 4th edit., 2003. Recipient Grad. of Last Decade award U. Wis., Milw., 1998. Fellow ACP/Am. Soc. Internal Medicine (pres., gov. Wis. chpt. 1994-98, mem. bd. regents 1997-2003, chmn. bd. govs. 1998-99, Laureate award 2000, Key Contact award 2001), Am. Coll. Cardiology (gov. Am. Coll. Cardiology dept. vets. affair, 1999-2000), Am. Acad. Family Physicians, Royal Coll. Physicians Can., Am. Coll. Clin. Pharmacology, Am. Heart Assn. (high blood pressure coun.), Royal Coll. Physicians (London), Am. Coll. Physician Execs.; mem. AMA (alt. del. Wis.), Am. Assn. Physicians from India (pres. Wis. chpt. 1995-97), Am. Fedn. Med. Rsch., Milw. Acad. Medicine (pres. 1996-97, trustee 1997—03, pres.'s award 1998), Milw. County Med. Soc. (bd. dirs. 2000-2002, pres. elect 2002-03, pres. 2003), Wis. Med. Soc. (alt. del. ho. dels. AMA, Disting. Svc. award 2001), Mensa, Highlander Elite Tennis Club, Univ. Club Milw. Home: 18630 Le Chateau Dr Brookfield WI 53045-4924 Office: Med Coll Wis 8701 Watertown Plank Rd Milwaukee WI 53226 E-mail: kochar@mcw.edu.

KOCHARIAN, ARMEN, physicist; b. Yerevan, Armenia, Oct. 8, 1955; s. Karlen Kocharian and Ekaterina Poghosian; m. Marina Davtian; children: Anna, Mariam. PhD, Yerevan State U., 1980. Systems engr. GE Med. Systems, Milw., 2002—. Vis. scientist U. Wis., Madison, 1994—96. Recipient Sr. Scientist Crystallography, Higher Bd. Cert., Moscow, 1986; scholar Vis. Scientist Program, U. Oslo, Norway, 1986; rsch. fellow, Mayo Clinic and Found., Rochester, Minn., 1998—2002. Mem.: Internat. Union Crystallographers, Am. Assn. Physicists in Medicine, Internat. Soc. Magnetic Resonance in Medicine. Achievements include patents for X-ray Interferometry. Office: GE Med Systems 3200 North Grandview Blvd Waukesha WI 53188 E-mail: armen.kocharian@med.ge.com.

KOCH-EILERS, EVAMARIA WYSK, oceanographer, researcher; b. Porto Alegre, Brazil, May 11, 1961; came to U.S., 1985; d. Walter and Eva Margarethe Elsa Anna (Wysk) K. BS in Oceanography, U. Rio Grande, Brazil, 1984; MS in Botany, U. South Fla., 1988, PhD in Marine Sci., 1993. Rsch. asst. U. Rio Grande, 1980-85, U. South Fla., Tampa, 1985-89; biol. scientist Fla. Marine Rsch. Inst., St. Petersburg, 1988-89; rsch. scientist U. Conn./NOAA, Milford, 1993-95; asst. prof. Horn Point Lab., U. Md. Ctr. Environ. Sci., Cambridge, Md., 1995-2001, assoc. prof. 5, Md., 2001—. Contbr. to profl. publs. Mem. Estuarine Rsch. Fedn., Am. Soc. Limnology and Oceanography, Sigma Xi. Achievements include development of first culture media for tissue culture of seagrasses. Office: Horn Point Lab PO Box 775 Cambridge MD 21613-0775

KOCHEMS, ROBERT GREGORY, lawyer; b. Cleve., Aug. 6, 1951; s. Roy George and Virginia Mae (Budniak) K.; m. Georgann Ryan; 1 child, Alane Carin. BA cum laude, John Carroll U., 1973; JD, St. Louis U., 1976. Bar: Pa. 1976, U.S. Dist. Ct. (we. dist.) 1978. Sole practice, Mercer, Pa., 1976-81, 88-92; ptnr. Bogaty, McEwen, Sparks, & Kochems, P.C., Mercer, 1981-87, Nelson, Ryan & Kochems, 1992—. Asst. pub. defender Mercer County, 1977-88; asst. dist. atty., 1988—; sub-com. chairperson Mercer County Juvenile Ct. Adv. Com., 1986-88, chair child death rev. com., 1999—, leader dist. atty.'s child abuse prosecution unit, 1996-2001; solicitor Mercer County Regional Planning Commn., 1991—; law enforcement coord. Sharon/Farrell Weed and Seed Program, 2001--. Assoc. editor St. Louis U. Law Jour., 1975-76. Bd. dirs. Transfer Harvest Home Assn., 1986-88; solicitor Mcpl. Corp., 1996—; co-chairperson Mercer County Sexual Assault Response Team, 2000—. Mem. Pa. Bar Assn., Mercer County Bar Assn. (sec. 1977-79, bench bar com. 1982, 84), KC (adv. 1978-88). Republican. Home: PO Box 226 Mercer PA 16137-0226

KOCHENGIN, SERGEY ALEXANDROVICH, information technology consultant; b. Leningrad, Russia, May 16, 1970; arrived in U.S., 1994; s. Alexander Fedorovich Kochengin and Maria Kuzminichna Kochengina; m. Valeria Valerievna, Jan. 30, 1991; children: Tatiana, Alexander. Diploma higher edn., St. Petersburg State U., 1992; MS, Emory U., 1997, PhD, 1999. Info. tech. cons. Macquarium, Inc., Atlanta, 1999—. Contbr. Grantee, Russian Fund for Fundamental Rsch., 1992—94. Home: 320 Birch Rill Dr Alpharetta GA 30022 Office: Macquarium Inc 1800 Peachtree St NW Atlanta GA 30309-2519

KOCHER, CYNTHIA, investment specialist, financial executive; b. Lompoc, Calif., May 6, 1954; d. John Wayland and Marjorie (Bartle) K.; m. Bruce Abrahamson, June 25, 1993. BA in Asian Studies, U. Oreg., 1976; MBA in Internat. Mgmt., Am. Grad. Sch. Internat. Mgmt., 1978; MBA in Fin. Planning, City U., 2002. CFP. Comml. asst., mgr. Far East imports Barber S.S. Lines, N.Y.C., 1978-80; asst. sec. internat. cash mgmt. Mfrs. Hanover Trust Co., N.Y.C., 1980-84; sales staff Century 21-Gordon Agy., 1984-86; broker, sales-person Forest Hill Realty, Newark, 1986-90; owner, operator Oregon Cafe, Jersey City, 1988-90; comms. analyst and onboard svc. mgr. Northwest Airlines, N.Y., Minn., Japan, 1990-93; personal fin. advisor, project mgr., internat. promotions Am. Express Fin., Advisor, Inc., Mpls., 1993-98; pres. The Mil. Retirees' Bed and Breakfast Club, Inc., 1998-99; ind. distbr. Rexall Showcase Internat., 1998-99; sr. investment specialist Charles Schwab and Co., Inc., 2000—. Recipient 5th pl. award Internat. Speech Contest in Japanese, Asahi Shimbun, 1975. Mem. NAFE, DAR (geneal. records chmn. 1985 86, schs. chmn. 1985-86, yearbook co-chmn. 1983-87, rec. sec. 1986-87), Rotary (Maple Grove club chmn. com. internat. svc. 1998-99), Kiwanis (Bellevue Sunrise). Home: 1015 13th Pl SW North Bend WA 98045-9121 Mailing: 11100 NE 8th St Ste 250 Bellevue WA 98004 E-mail: bluejay1012001@yahoo.com.

KOCHER, JUANITA FAY, retired auditor; b. Falmouth, Ky., Aug. 9, 1933; d. William Birgest and Lula (Gillespie) Vickroy; m. Donald Edward Kocher, Nov. 18, 1953. Grad. high sch., Bright, Ind. Cert. internal auditor and compliance officer. Bookkeeper Mchts. Bank and Trust Co., West Harrison, Ind., 1952-56, teller, asst. cashier, 1962-87, br. mgr., 1979-87, internal auditor, 1987-96, ret., 1996; bookkeeper Progressive Bank, New Orleans, 1956-58; with proof dept. 1st Nat. Bank, Cin., Ohio, 1958-59, teller Harrison, Ohio, 1959-62. Bookkeeper Donald E. Kocher Constrn., Harrison, 1981—. Mem. Am. Bankers Assn., Ind. Bankers Assn. Home: 11277 Biddinger Rd Harrison OH 45030

KOCHER, MININDER SINGH, pediaric orthopaedic surgeon, epidemiologist; b. Rochester, N.Y., Dec. 23, 1966; s. Haribhajan Singh and Ranjit Kaur Kocher; m. Michele Mary Dupre, June 4, 1994; children: Sophia Dupre, Isabelle Dupre, Calvin Dupre. AB, Dartmouth Coll., 1989; MD, Duke U., 1993; MPH, Harvard U., 2000. Bd. cert. Am. Bd. Orthopaedic Surgeons, 2002. Intern Beth Israel Hosp./Harvard Med. Sch., 1993—94; resident Harvard Combined Orthop. Surgery Residency program, 1994—98; fellow pediat. orthop. surgery Boston Children's Hosp., 1998—99; fellow sports medicine Steadman Hawkin's Clinic, 1999—2000; pediatric orthop. surgeon Children's Hosp. Boston, 2000—; instr. orthop. surgery Harvard Med. Sch., Boston, 2000—; cons. Steadman Hawkins Sports Medicine Found., Vail, Colo., 2000—. Dir. Children's Hosp. Orthop. Inst. for Clin. Effectiveness, Boston, 2000—. Sci. adv. com. Steadman Hawkins Sports Medicine Found., Vail, Colo., 2000; med. adv. com. LeadingMD.com, L.A., 2001. Recipient Wilburt Davidson award, Duke U. Sch. Medicine, 1993, Harris Yett award, Harvard Combined Orthop. Program, 1994, Von Meyer award, Children's Hosp. Boston, 1998, Zimmer award, Am. Orthop. Assn., 1999, Richard Kilfoyle award, New Eng. Orthop. Soc., 1999, Clin. Rsch. prize, Arthroscopy Assn. N.Am., 2000, 2001, Vernon Thompson award, Western Orthop. Assn., 2000; Nat. Honor Soc. scholar, LG Balfour, 1985—89, Nat. Merit Scholarship, 1985—89, Rufus Choate scholar, Dartmouth Coll., 1988—99. Fellow: Am. Acad. Orthop. Surgeons; mem.: Am. Orthop. Soc. for Sports Medicine, Anterior Cruciate Ligament Study Group, Pediat. Orthop. Soc. N.Am. (clin. effectiveness com. 2002—), Phi Beta Kappa. Office: Childrens Hosp Boston 300 Longwood Ave Boston MA 02135 Office Fax: 617-739-3338.

KOCHHAR-BRYANT, CAROL ANNE, education educator; d. Edward James and Florence Eileen Newitt; m. John David Bryant, May 22, 1999; children: Anjali Carol Kochhar, Shawn Anil Kochhar. BS in Zoology and Psychology, U. Md., 1975; EdD in Spl. Edn. /Evaluation, George Washington U., 1987. Tech. services coord. Cmty. Services Bd., Fairfax-Falls Church, Va., 1982—87; prof. edn. George Washington U., Washington, 1987—. Cons. U.S. Dept. Edn., Washington, 2000—02, N.Mex. State Dept. Edn., Santa Fe, 1999—, Acad. for Ednl. Devel., Washington, World Bank, Washington, 1994—95. Author: Pathways to Successful Transition, 2003; contbr. poem; author: Aligning Transition and Standards-Based Education, 2003, Successful Inclusion: Strategies for a Shared Responsibility. Bd. mem. Mitsubishi Electric Am. Found., Washington, 1990. Grantee Numerous grants for leadership tng. projects, U.S. Dept. of Edn., 1987—. Mem.: Internat. Coun. for Exceptional Children (life; divsn. pres. 1997—2001, Oliver P. Kolstoe award 2001—02). Achievements include design of system of 6 Special Education Regional Resource Centers across the U.S; development of design, and funding for the Leaders for System Change Doctoral Program; design, and funding for an Education Specialist program in special education; design, and funding for a Masters Program in Traumatic Brain Injury; design, and funding for a Masters Training Program for Teachers of At-Risk Urban Youth. Avocations: writing, poetry, travel, photography, cooking. Home: 11026 Solaridge Dr Reston VA 20191 Office: George Washington U 2134 G St Rm 305 Washington DC 20052 Office Fax: 202-994-3365. E-mail: kochhar@gwu.edu.

KOCHI, JAY KAZUO, chemist, educator; b. Los Angeles, May 17, 1927; s. Tsuruzo and Shizuko (Moriya) K.; m. Marion Kiyono, Mar. 1, 1959; children: Sims, Julia. Student, Cornell U., 1945; BS, UCLA, 1949; PhD, Iowa State U., 1952. Faculty Harvard U., 1952-55; NIH fellow Cambridge U., Eng., 1956; mem. faculty Iowa State U., 1956; with Shell Devel. Co., 1957-61; mem. faculty dept. chemistry Case Western Res. U., Cleve., 1962-69, prof., 1966-69; prof. chemistry Ind. U., Bloomington, 1969-74, Earl Blough prof. chemistry, 1974-84; Robert A. Welch Disting. prof. chemistry U. Houston, 1984—. Cons. chemist, 1964— Mem. Am. Chem. Soc., Chem. Soc. (London), Nat. Acad. Scis., Sigma Xi. Achievements include research on mechanism of catalysis of organic reactions, organometallics, electrochemistry and photochemistry, time-resolved spectroscopy of reactive intermediates. Home: 4372 Faculty Ln Houston TX 77004-6601 Office: U Houston Dept Chemistry 4800 Calhoun Rd Houston TX 77204-5003 E-mail: jkochi@uh.edu.

KOCHTA, RUTH MARTHA, artist; b. N.Y.C., Jan. 5, 1924; d. Harry Joseph and Anna (Braun) Evers; m. Albert Emil Kochta, Nov. 7, 1948; children: Alan, Carol. Student, CUNY, Queens, 1965-68, Art Students League, 1970-75. Artist, Queens, N.Y. and Lenox, Mass., 1965—; dir. Imperial Gallery, N.Y.C., 1981; owner, dir. Clark Whitney Gallery, Lenox, 1983-2000. Work exhibited at Nat. Acad., N.Y.C. 1969, Audubon Artists, N.Y.C. 1971, Heckscher Mus., Huntington, N.Y., 1972, Elizabet Ney Mus., Austin, Tex., 1972, Wadsworth Atheneum, Hartford, Conn., 1975, Philathea Mus., Ont., Can., 1976, New Britain (Conn.) Mus., 1978, Guild Gallery, N.Y.C. 1979, other exhibits. Recipient over 50 awards in various competitions. Home and Office: Devonshire Estates 329 Pittsfield Rd Lenox MA 01240-2306

KOCK, ROBERT MARSHALL, investment banker; b. Middletown, N.J., Aug. 31, 1942; s. Winston Edward and Kathleen (Redmond) K.; m. Sherry Tranum, Feb. 3, 1968; children: Cristobel Kathleen, Kimberly Tranum, Caroline Redmond, Robert Marshall Jr. Student, U. Bristol, England, 1962, U. Mich., 1961, U. Colo., 1959-60. Mgr. Pan Am. Airways, N.Y.C., 1964-68, Goldman Sachs & Co., N.Y.C., 1968-71, v.p. London, 1971-80; managing dir. Smith Barney Harris Upham Internat., Paris, London, 1980-87; pres., C.E.O. RMK Internat. Securities Inc., Hilton Head, S.C., 1990-92; ptnr. Little & Co., London, 1990-91; bd. dirs. Recovery Ctr. of Hilton Head, 1991-96; with Morgan Keegan & Co., Inc., Atlanta, 1993-96, Intercapital Securities, Inc., N.Y.C., 1996-97; pres. Global Funding Resources, Darien, Conn., 1997—, Investors Capital Mgmt., Inc., Rowaton, Conn., 1998—. Cons., Club of Rome, 1974; lectr., The City U., London, 1977. Contbr. articles to profl. jours. Vestry St. Luke's Episc. Ch., Hilton Head Island, S.C., 1990-93, sr. warden, 1991. Mem. Assn. Internat. Bond Dealers (market practice com. 1975-76), The Bond Club London (chmn. 1983-84), Annabel's London, Hurlingham Club London. Republican. Avocations: sailing, golf, skiing.

KOCKA, FRANK EDWARD, microbiologist; b. Chgo., May 28, 1938; s. Francis James and Lucille Ella (Beck) K. BS in Biology, Ill. Inst. Tech., 1961, MS in Microbiology, 1966; PhD in Microbiology, Kans. State U., 1969. Rsch. assoc., lectr. Purdue U., West Lafayette, Ind., 1969-71; sr. microbiologist Searle Diagnostic, Columbus, Ohio, 1971-73; dir. rsch. Wilson Diagnostic, Glenwood, Ill., 1973; asst. prof., assoc. dir. clin. microbiology U. Chgo., 1973-76; assoc. prof. pathology and microbiology Chgo. Med. Sch., North Chicago, Ill., 1976-94, prof., 1995—; chief microbiology North Chicago VA Hosp., 1976-82; chmn. microbiology Cook County Hosp., Chgo., 1983-97; chief infectious disease lab. Ill. Dept. Pub. Health, Chgo., 1997 99, dir. Chgo. lab., 2000—. Fellow Am. Acad. Microbiology, Acad. Clin. Lab. Scientists and Physicians; mem. Am. Soc. Microbiology (mem. com. 1989-94), Ill. Soc. Microbiology (pres. 1977-78), South Ctrl. Assn. Clin. Microbiology (chair com.), Sigma Xi. Lutheran. Achievements include patent for inhibition of antibacterial action of blood. Home: 3200 N Lake Shore Dr Apt 1008 Chicago IL 60657-3931 Office: IDPH Lab 2121 W Taylor St Chicago IL 60612-7260 E-mail: fkocka@idph.state.il.us.

KOCKELMAN, KARA MARIA, engineering educator; b. Santa Fe, N.Mex., Apr. 1969; m. Steven G. Rosen. MS in City and Regional Planning and Civil Engr., U. Calif., Berkeley, 1996, PhD in Civil Engring., 1999. Registered profl. engr. Tchg./rsch. asst. U. Calif., Berkeley, 1994—98; asst. prof. U. Tex., Austin, 1998—. Project engr. U.S. Peace Corps, 1991—93; advisor SWE student chapter, 1999—. Contbr. papers to 43 confs. and 32 publs. (Transp. Rsch. Bd.'s Pedestrian com. award, 2002). Mem. Transp. Rsch. Bd. Coms., Washington, 1999—2002. Recipient Faculty Early Career Devel. award, NSF, 2000—04, Career Award, Ford Foundation, 2002. Fellow: The Henry Luce Found. (Clare Boothe Luce prof. 1999—2004). Office: U Tex Ste 6 9 ECJ Austin TX 78712

KOCUR, SEAN EDWARD, toxicologist; b. Beverly, Mass., Nov. 19, 1971; s. Edward Marshall Kocur and Carol Ann Marie Keith; m. Tara Lee Kocur, Dec. 30, 1994; children: Benjamin Aaron, Jonathan Patrick, Adam Matthew. BS in Chemistry summa cum laude, Salem (Mass.) State Coll., 2002. Cert. auto glass technician, Mass. Asst. mgr. Best Friends Pet Care, Boxford, Mass., 1988—95; preload supr. United Parcel Svc., Lynnfield, Mass., 1990—94; auto glass technician J.N. Philips Glass, Salem, 1995—98; auto glass shop mgr. New Angle Glass, Lynn, Mass., 1998—2002; forensic toxicologist Willow Labs and Med. Ctr., Lynn, Mass., 2002—. Pvt. 1st class USMC, 1994-95. Mem. Phi Kappa Phi. Republican. Congregationalist. Avocations: book collecting, basketball, football, baseball, kenpo karate (green belt). Home: 8 Sylvan St Danvers MA 01923 E-mail: sekocur@aol.com.

KODADEK, WILLIAM F(RANCIS), communication educator; b. Newark, July 27, 1950; s. Robert E. and Agnes T. (LaRossa) K.; m. Kathy M. Kodadek; children: Lori Anne, Kelly Jean. BA magna cum laude, York Coll. of Pa., 1993. Cert. tchr., Pa. Substitute tchr. York (Pa.) Sch. Dist., 1993-95; adult edn. instr. York County Sch. Tech., 1995—. Trevethan Meml. scholarship York Coll., 1992. Mem. Alpha Chi. Home: 221 Eberts Ln York PA 17403-1136 Office: 2179 S Queen St York PA 17402-4628

KODALI, DHARMA RAO, research scientist; s. Seetharamaiah and Venkata Subbamma Kodali; m. Suseela Karlapudi, Dec. 25, 1982; children: Harsha Sitharam, Sithara. PhD, Kurukshetra Universtiy, 1974—80. Fellow of American Institute of Chemists Am. Inst. of Chemists, 1986. Asst. prof. biophysics Boston U. Sch. Medicine, Boston, 1989—91; prin. / staff scientist Cargill Ctrl. Rsch., Minneapolis, 1991—2000; R & D mgr. Cargill Indsl. Oils and Lubricants, Minneapolis, 2001—. Mem., tech. adv. com. Ctr. Interfacial Engring., U. Minn., Minneapolis, 1993—98; mem., instl. rev. bd. Abbott Northwestern Hospitals, Minneapolis, 2003—. Editor (associate editor): (journal) Journal of American Oil Chemists Society (Indsl. Innovation Award, Am. Chem. Soc. Gt. Lakes Region, 2002, TL Mounts Award, Am. Oil Chemists Soc., 2003, Chairman's Innovation Award, Cargill Inc., 2001). Fellow, Am. Inst. Chemists, 1986; grantee Whitaker Rsch. Grant, Whitaker Health Sciences Fund, 1989. Mem.: FSCT, STLE, Indian Sci. Congress Assn., Am. Chem. Soc., Am. Oil Chemists Soc. (chair-person, indsl. oil products divsn. 2001—). Achievements include patents for 15 U.S. issued patents; research in pubs. more than 60 papers published. Home: 710 Olive Ln Plymouth MN 55447 Personal E-mail: kodali@qwest.net.

KODSI, SYLVIA ROSE, ophthalmologist; b. Boston, Nov. 13, 1962; BS, Stanford U., 1983; MD, NYU, 1987. Intern in internal medicine Beth Israel Med. Ctr., N.Y.C., 1987-88; resident in ophthalmology St. Vincent's Med. Ctr., N.Y.C., 1988-91; neuro-ophthalmology fellow Mayo Clinic, Rochester, Minn., 1991-92; pediat. ophthalmology fellow U. Minn., Mpls., 1992-93; chief pediat. ophthalmology L.I. Jewish Med. Ctr., New Hyde Park, NY, 1994—. Fellow Am. Acad. Ophthalmology; mem. Assn. Pediat. Ophthalmology and Strabismis, N.Y. Soc. Pediat. Ophthalmology and Strabismis. Office: 600 Northern Blvd Ste 214 Great Neck NY 11021-5200

KOECHEL, LORETTA, science educator; d. Edward Joseph Koechel and Catherine Loretta Woltal. BA, St. Josephs Coll., Bklyn., 1950; MS, Cath. U., 1963; PhD, NYU, 1971. Tchr. Good Shepherd Sch., Bklyn., 1944—46, Queen of the Rosary H.S., Amityville, NY, 1950—51, St. Agnes H.S., Rockville Centre, NY, 1952—59, Bishop McDonnell H.S., Bklyn., 1959—60, Molloy Coll., Rockville Centre, 1960—. Vol. Civil Def., Rockville Centre, NY. Mem.: Nat. Sci. Tchrs. Assn. Office: Molloy Coll Rockville Centre NY

KOEDEL, JOHN GILBERT, JR., retired metal products executive; b. Pitts., June 25, 1937; s. John Gilbert and Elizabeth Marie (Kramer) K.; m. Fay Birren, Dec. 21, 1963; 1 son, John III. BS in Commerce, Washington and Lee U., 1959. V.p. Pitts. Nat. Bank, 1960-68; various positions up to pres. Nat. Forge. Co., 1968-95. Bd. dirs. The RCR Group, Inc. Served to sgt., U.S. Army, 1960-65. Mem. Fishing Bay Yacht Club, Conenango Club, Masons. Republican. Presbyterian. Avocations: sailing, wood working. Home: PO Box 877 Deltaville VA 23043-0877

KOEDEL, ROBERT CRAIG, minister, historian, educator; b. Tarentum, Pa., July 1, 1927; s. Theodore and Evelyn (Dagan) K.; m. Barbara Ellen Wood, Jan. 6, 1962. BA, Wheaton Coll., Ill., 1949; M.Div., Pitts. Theol Sem., 1953; MA, U. Pitts., 1964; postgrad., Temple U., 1964-70. Ordained to ministry Presbyn. Ch. U.S.A., 1953. Pastor Monaghan Presbyn. Ch., Dillsburg, Pa., 1956-59; asst. pastor Mt. Calvary Presbyn. Ch., Corapolis, Pa., 1959-60; assoc. pastor Dormont Presbyn. Ch., Pitts., 1960-64; mem. faculty Atlantic Community Coll., Mays Landing, N.J., 1966-92, prof. social sci., history, religion, 1978-92, chmn. dept. history, 1969-70, 78-79, asst. dean instrn., 1970-72; lectr. in history Stockton State Coll., 1985-86; clergyman Pitts. Presbytery. Author: South Jersey Heritage: A Social, Economic and Cultural History, 1977, God's Vine in This Wilderness: Religion in South Jersey to 1800, 1980, Following the Water: The Shellfish Industry in South Jersey, 1983, Ships and the Sea Down Jersey, 1989, Becoming a Presbyterian, 1993, Letters from Wheaton by a Forty-Niner, 1997, The Sky Pilot Said It: Memoires of an Air Force Chaplain, 2001; contbr. articles to profl. jours., articles to newspapers. Mem. Atlantic County Cultural and Heritage Adv. Bd., 1991. Served as chaplain USAF, 1953-56. N.J. Hist. Commn. research grantee, 1974, 84. Mem. United Teaching Professions, N.J. Hist. Soc. (trustee 1985-88), Atlantic County Hist. Soc. (editor jour. 1983-91), Gloucester County Hist. Soc., Pitts. Presbytery, Hist. Soc. Western Pa. (rsch. historian). Home: 1 Unger Ln Pittsburgh PA 15217-1018

KOEGEL, WILLIAM FISHER, lawyer; b. Washington, Aug. 18, 1923; s. Otto Erwin and Rae (Fisher) K.; m. Barbara Bixler, Feb. 2, 1946 (dec. 1968); children: John Bixler, Robert Bartlett; m. Ruth Swan Boynton, June 21, 1969 (dec. 1983); m. Irene Lawrence, Aug. 4, 1984. BA, Williams Coll., 1944; LL.B., U. Va., 1949. Bar: N.Y. 1950. From assoc. to ptnr. Clifford Chance US LLP (formerly Rogers & Wells), N.Y.C., 1949—88, head litigation dept., 1977-88, sr. counsel, 1989—. Chmn. Scarsdale (N.Y.) Republican Town Com., 1965-71; pres. trustees Hitchcock Presbyn. Ch., Scarsdale, 1970-73, 78-79, 82-83. Served with AUS, 1943-45, ETO. Fellow ACTL; mem. ABA, N.Y. State Bar Assn., Bar Assn. City N.Y., Order of Coif. Clubs: Town (Scarsdale) (pres. 1976-77); Sky (N.Y.C.), Williams (N.Y.C.); Shenorock Shore, Fox Meadow Tennis, The Moorings. Home: 7 Chesterfield Rd Scarsdale NY 10583-1619 Office: Clifford Chance US LLP 200 Park Ave New York NY 10166-0005

KOEGEN, ROY JEROME, lawyer; b. Spokane, Wash., Mar. 1, 1949; s. Frank J. and Jeanne (Bardsley) K.; m. Ann Martinelli, Aug. 28, 1970; children: Jennifer, Christopher. BA, Gonzaga U., 1971; JD, U. Calif., San Francisco, 1974. Bar: Calif. 1974, Wash. 1979, U.S. Supreme Ct. 1982. Assoc. Wilson,

Jones, Morton & Lynch, San Mateo, Calif., 1974-78, Blair & Koegen, Spokane, 1978-80; ptnr. Preston, Thorgrimson, Ellis & Holman, Spokane, 1980-90, Perkins Coie LLP, Seattle, Spokane, 1990—2002, Lukins & Annis, PS, Spokane, 2002—. Author: Washington Municipal Financing Deskbook, 1992. Chmn. exec. com. Community Alcohol Ctr., Spokane, 1982-84, Century II Park Dist., Spokane, 1982-84; bd. dirs. Nature Conservancy. Mem. ABA, Wash. Bar Assn., Calif. Bar Assn., Nat. Assn. Bond Lawyers, The Nature Conservancy (bd. dirs.). Roman Catholic. Office: Lukins & Annis PS 1600 Washington Trust Fin Ctr 717 Sprague Ave Spokane WA 99201

KOEHL, CAMILLE JOAN, accountant; b. Chgo., Nov. 9, 1943; d. Alfonse James and Genevieve V. (Riche) Daurio; children: David A., Laura L., Robert M., Karen M. BS in Acctg., De Paul U., 1976; postgrad., Roosevelt U., 1987—. CPA, Ill.; CFP. Treas. Meritex Corp., Carpentersville, Ill., 1966-68; contr. Di Com Corp., Glenview, Ill., 1968-72; v.p., treas. Ridge Road Co., Northbrook, Ill., 1982-87, Decker Gardens, Inc., Northbrook, 1979-87, S&L Engring. Co., Northbrook, 1972-87; ptnr. HJS Constrn. Co., Barrington Hills, Ill., 1979—; pres. Lé Tan Ltd., Palatine, Ill., 1984—, CJK Enterprises Ltd., Lakemoor, Ill., 1985—; owner Camille J. Koehl & Assoc., Lakemoor, 1978—; pres. Koehl Constrn. and Devel. Corp., Lakemoor, 1990—, Pressing Matters Ltd., McHenry, Ill., 1990—. Mem. Internat. Bd. Cert. Fin. Planners, Ill. CPAs. Avocations: golf, reading. Home and Office: 2020 W Il Route 120 # A Mchenry IL 60050

KOEHLER, CAROL JEAN, nurse; b. Berlin, Wis., Apr. 26, 1943; d. Raymond H. Wendt and Lorna M.L. Kobiske; m. Ronald F. Koehler, Aug. 5, 1967; children: Catherine, Susan, Daniel, Angela, Ada, Aaron. Diploma, Inst. Children's Lit., 1987; grad. cert. nursing asst., Fox Valley Tech. Coll., 1993. LPN, Wis. Owner Bus. Builders, Manawa, Wis., 1974—; caregiver Waupaca (Wis.) County, 1984-90; news reporter Manawa Advocate and Appleton (Wis.) Post-Crescent, 1987-93; nursing asst. Manawa Nursing Ctr., 1991-93; staff nurse Wis. Vets. Home, King, 1993-94, St. Joseph's Residence, New London, Wis., 1994-96; agy. nurse STAT Temporary Svcs., Appleton, 1996—. Back fitness instr. Nat. Safety Coun., King, Wis., 1994. Host mother Am. Intercultural Student Exchange and Youth for Understanding, Manawa, 1982-86; foster mother, 1988-91. Republican. Lutheran. Avocations: German language, travel, walking, photography, baking. Home: PO Box 178 Manawa WI 54949-0178

KOEHLER, COLLEEN M. accountant; b. Belleville, Ill., June 7, 1972; d. Gerald Thomas Koehler and Susan Jane McEvilly. BBA in Acctg. and Mgmt. summa cum laude, McKendree Coll., 1998; MS in Taxation, Fontbonne U., 2002. CPA, Ill. Acct. The Salvation Army, Belleville, 1996-98; staff acct. Rice, Sullivan & Co., Ltd., Belleville, 1998—2000; acct. Nestle Purina Co., St. Louis, 2000—03, Drury Devel. Corp., St. Louis, 2003—. Mem. AICPA, Ill. CPA Soc., Sigma Beta Delta. Democrat. Roman Catholic. Avocations: reading, tennis, music, softball, swimming. Home: 117 Andrew Dr Swansea IL 62226-2453 Office: Drury Devel Corp 8315 Drury Industrial Pkwy Saint Louis MO 63114

KOEHLER, GEORGE APPLEGATE, broadcasting company executive; b. Phila., July 23, 1921; s. Herbert Jacques and Mildred Warrington (Applegate) K.; m. Jane Marie Caputi, Feb. 20, 1944; children: Eric George, Gary Stephen. BA, U. Pa., 1942. Various positions WFIL Stas., Phila., 1945-55; sta. mgr. WFIL Radio and TV, 1955-68; gen. mgr. radio and TV div. Triangle Pubs., Inc., Phila., 1968-72; pres. Gateway Communications, Inc., Cherry Hill, N.J., 1970-84, vice chmn. bd, 1985—2001. Mem. planning com. Phila. Commn. on Human Rels., 1957; mem. Adv. Com. on Naval Affairs, 1968-70; pub. rels. chmn. United Fund, 1965. Trustee Meth. Hosp., Phila., 1962-97, Salem County C.C., 1996-98; com. commn. United Meth. Ch., 1980-84; bd. dirs. Pennington (N.J.) Sch., 1973-80; elder Presbyn. Ch., 1992-2000. Capt. USAAF, 1942-45. Decorated D.F.C., Air medal with 3 oak leaf clusters; recipient Distinguished Service award Chapel of 4 Chaplains, 1969; named Man of Yr. TV and Radio Advt. Club, Phila., 1971; Broadcast Pioneer of Yr. Delaware Valley chpt. Broadcast Pioneers. Mem.: Relilgion in Am. Life (bd. dirs. 1986—87, inducted Phila. Broadcasting Hall of Fame 1994), Assn. Maximum Svc. Telecasters (bd. dirs. 1976—, sec.-treas. 1980—83, chmn. 1984—85, chmn. emeritus 1986), ABC-TV Affiliates Assn. (adv. bd. 1967—71, chmn. 1970—71), Pa. Assn. Broadcasters (pres. 1958—59), Union League Club (Phila.), Union League Club, Rotary (pres. 1960), Alpha Delta Sigma. Republican.

KOEHLER, HARRY GEORGE, real estate executive; b. Somerville, N.J., Jan. 10, 1954; s. Harry George and Lillian Elizabeth (Fischer) K.; m. Marylou Elizabeth Harrison, Aug. 21, 1976; children: Kristen, Kelly, Meghan. BS, Rutgers U., 1977; MCRP, U. Tex., 1985. Project mgr. Kupper Assocs., Piscataway, N.J., 1977-78; regional site planner JCPenney Co., Inc., N.Y.C. and Dallas, 1978-83; v.p. site planning May Realty Inc. (May Dept. Stores Co.), St. Louis, 1983—. Recipient Eagle Scout Boy Scouts Am., 1969; George H. Cook scholar Rutgers U., 1977. Mem. Alpha Zeta. Avocation: one-design sailing. Office: May Dept Stores Co 611 Olive St Saint Louis MO 63101-1721 E-mail: harry_koehler@may-co.com.

KOEHLER, MARTHA-KAYE, lawyer; b. Tampa, Fla., July 27, 1958; d. DeCarr Dowman and Joyce (Collier) Covington; m. Carl James Koehler, June 1, 1997; 1 child, Ryann Collier. BA, U. Fla., 1980; JD, Nova U., 1983. Atty. Hillsborough C.C., Tampa, 1985—. Mem. Jr. League of Tampa. Mem. Fla. Bar Assn., Hills County Bar Assn., Nat. Jud. Officers Assn., Nat. Assn. Coll. and Univ. Attys. Republican. Methodist. Office: Hillsborough Cmty Coll 39 Columbia Dr Tampa FL 33606 E-mail: mkoehler@hccfl.edu.

KOEHLER, PAUL BURRELL, retired medical administrator; b. New Haven, Apr. 1, 1925; s. Oscar Ernest and Isabel Lillian (Dilg) K.; m. Mary Lorraine Mahan, June 14, 1947 (dec. May 1988); children: Shawne K. Kaeser, Paul B. Jr., Kristin K. O'Connor, Thomas T.; m. Margaret Morgan Miller, May 20, 1989. BS, Yale U., 1945, MD, 1948. Diplomate Am. Bd. Pediat., Am. Bd. Allergy and Immunology. Assoc. med. dir. Nat. Drug Co. divsn. Richardson-Merrell, Phila., 1961-63; med. dir. biol. librs. Nat. Drug Co., Swiftwater, Pa., 1963-67; med. dir. Dome Labs. divsn. Miles Labs., West Haven, Conn., 1967-73; med. dir., v.p. Purdue Frederick Co., Norwalk, Conn., 1973-74; med. dir. Chesebrough-Pond's Inc., Trumbull, Conn., 1974-87. Pvt. practice specializing in pediat., Greenfield, Mass., 1952-61. Contbr. articles to profl. jours. Lt. USN, 1950-52. Republican. Roman Catholic. Home: 99 Mountainside Dr Newbury NH 03255-5205

KOEHLER, REGINALD STAFFORD, III, lawyer; b. Bellevue, Pa., Dec. 29, 1932; s. Reginald S. and Esther (Hawken) K.; m. Ann Ellsworth Rowland, June 15, 1956; children: Victoria Elizabeth, Cynthia Rowland, Robert Steven. BA, Yale U., 1956; JD, Harvard U., 1959. Bar: N.Y. 1960, Calif., Fla., D.C. 1979, Wash. 1984, Oreg. 1985, Alaska 1985, U.S. Supreme Ct. 1973. Assoc. Davis Polk & Wardwell, N.Y.C., 1959-68; ptnr. Donovan Leisure Newton & Irvine, N.Y.C., 1968-84, Perkins Coie, Seattle, 1984—. Author: The Planning and Administration of a Large Estate, 1982, 5th edit. 1986. Chmn. bd. trustees Fred Hutchinson Cancer Rsch. Ctr. With U.S. Army, 1952-54. Fellow Am. Coll. Trust and Estate Counsel; mem. N.Y. State Bar Assn., Calif. Bar Assn., D.C. Bar Assn., Wash. Bar Assn., Oreg. Bar Assn., Alaska Bar Assn., Chi Psi. Episcopalian. Office: Perkins Coie 1201 3rd Ave Fl 40 Seattle WA 98101-3029

KOEHLER, ROBERT BRIEN, priest; b. Hastings, Nebr., Aug. 26, 1950; s. Robert Joseph and Melba Deloris (Morey) K.; m. Terry Ellen Collins; children: Gregory, Michael, Louisa. BA cum laude, U. Dallas, 1972; postgrad., U. Wis., 1973; MDiv, Nashotah Ho., 1976. Chaplain DeKoven Found., Racine, Wis., 1976-81; Curate Emmanuel Ch., Rockford, Ill., 1978-81; Rector St. Raphael's Ch., Ft. Myers Beach, Fla., 1981-84; Vicar Ch. Holy Cross, Burleson, Tex., 1984-87; Canon to the Ordinary, Diocese of Ft. Worth, 1987-93; Rector St. Luke's Ch., Ft. Myers, Fla., 1993—2001, Baton Rouge, 2001—. Exec. dir. Episc. Synod Am., Ft. Worth, 1991-93. Dist. chmn. Boy Scouts Am., Ft. Myers, 1993-96; trustee Nashotah (Wis.) House, 1994—; bd. dirs. Interfaith Vol. Care Givers, 1996-99, Goodwill Industries, S.W. Fla., 1999-2001; instl. review com. Lee Meml. Health Sys., 1999-2001. Mem. SAR, Soc. Holy Cross, Soc. Colonial Wars. Office: St Luke's Episc Ch 8833 Goodwood Blvd Baton Rouge LA 70806 E-mail: frkoehler@stlukesbr.org.

KOEHLER, WALLACE, library and information scientist, educator, library and information scientist, researcher; b. Chgo., Ill., Apr. 2, 1945; s. Wallace and Mirjam Koehler; m. Vera Blair; children from previous marriage: Ingrid, William. PhD, Cornell U., 1973—77; MS, U. Tenn., 1993—97. Asst. prof. SLIS U. Okla., Norman, Ga., 1997—2001; assoc. prof., dir. MLIS program Valdosta State U., Valdosta, Ga., 2001—. Author: Fundamentals of Informational Studies: Understanding Information and Its Environment, 2003, (article) Library Management, 2000 (Highly Commended Paper award, 2000); contbr. articles to profl. jours. With U.S. Army, 1966—68. Office: Valdosta State U 1500 N Patterson St Valdosta GA 31698 Office Fax: 229-259-5055. Business E-Mail: wkoehler@valdosta.edu.

KOEHN, ENNO, engineering educator, researcher; b. Flushing, N.Y., Apr. 29, 1936; s. Theodore J. and Anna M. (Sievers) K.; m. Carol Ann Butcher, Nov. 25, 1967; children: William Enno, James Frederick. BCE, CUNY, 1958; MS, Columbia U., 1960; PhD, Wayne State U., 1975. Registered profl. engr., Tex., Ind., Ohio. Engring. inspector Bd. Water Supply, N.Y.C., 1957; rsch. engr. N.Am. Rockwell, Columbus, Ohio, 1958-59; asst. prof. L.I. U., Greenvale, N.Y., 1960-66; specialist IBM, Burlington, Vt., 1966-67; prof. civil engring. Ohio Northern U., Ada, 1967-79; assoc. prof. civil engring. Purdue U., West Lafayette, Ind., 1979-84; prof., chair dept. civil engring. Lamar U., Beaumont, Tex., 1984—. Rsch. cons. Atomic Internat., Canoga Park, Calif., 1962, GM Corp., Warren, Mich., 1973, Bechtel Corp., Ann Arbor, Mich., 1978-81, U.S. Army Rsch. Lab., Champaign, Ill., 1983-88; program evaluator Accreditation Bd. for Engring. and Tech. Contbr. articles to profl. jours. Active Alumni Rep. Com. Columbia U., N.Y.C., 1990—; sustaining mem. Boy Scouts Am. Troop Com., 1980—; pres., campaign chairperson United Way, Ada, 1975-77, Lamar Engring., Beaumont, 1984-86. Fellow ASCE; mem. NSPE, Am. Soc. Engring. Edn., Assn. Advancement Cost Engring. Internat., Rotary Internat. (dir. 1970-73), Tau Beta Pi, Sigma Xi, Chi Epsilon. Episcopalian. Avocations: reading, gardening, walking, traveling. Office: Lamar U Civil Engring Dept PO Box 10024 Beaumont TX 77710-0024

KOEHN, WILLIAM JAMES, lawyer; b. Winterset, Iowa, Mar. 24, 1936; s. Cyril Otto and Ilene L. (Doop) K.; m. Francia C. Leeper, Sept. 6, 1958; children: Cynthia Rae, William Fredric, James Anthony. BA, JD cum laude, U. Iowa, 1963. Bar: Iowa 1963, U.S. Ct. Appeals (8th cir.) 1971, U.S. Ct. Appeals (10th cir.) 1972, U.S. Ct. Appeals (2d cir.) 1972, U.S. Ct. Appeals (5th cir.) 1977, U.S. Supreme Ct. 1971. Mem. Davis, Brown, Koehn, Shors & Roberts, P.C., Des Moines, 1963—. Prof., lectr. in U.S., Can., Europe. Bd. editors Iowa Law Rev., 1961-63; contbr. articles to profl. jours. C0-founder Big Bros.-Sisters of Greater Des Moines, 1969, pres., 1976-77; chmn. Des Moines Friendship Commmn., 1970-71; bd. dirs. Greater Des Moines YMCA, 1983-90; co-chmn. Des Moines Bicentennial Commn., 1975-76; chmn. Environ. and Pub. Works Commn.; mem. adv. com. civil justice reform act, 1990; chmn. worldwide dispute resolution com., Lex Mundi, 1989-94, bd. dirs., 1992-96. Lt. USNR, 1958-61. Mem. ABA (environ. litigation sub-com., construction com., internat. lit. environ. commn.), Iowa Bar Assn. (environ. coun. 1989-92, 1999-2001, litigation com. 1992-95, proflism. com. 1994-2002), Polk County Bar Assn., Iowa Trial Lawyers Assn., Order of Coif. Republican. Office: Fin Ctr 666 Walnut St Des Moines IA 50309-3904 Home: Unit 1801 3305 Ep True Pkwy West Des Moines IA 50265-7677

KOEKEMOER, CARL LODEWICUS, college official, business consultant; b. Pretoria, South Africa, June 8, 1948; s. Petrus Philippus and Olga Koekemoer; m. Annette Moelich, Nov. 9, 1974; children: Minette, Carlé, Lize-Marie. B Commerce, U. Pretoria, 1969, MBA, 1971; PhD, Rhodes U., South Africa, 1976; B Commerce with honours, Rand Afrikaans U., Johannesburg, South Africa, 1978. Econs. rschr. South African Dept. Commerce, Pretoria, 1969-70; market rsch. mgr. Market Rsch. Africa (Pty) Ltd., Johannesburg, South Africa, 1971-72; account dir. VZ divsn. Otm, 1972-73; dir. market rsch. De V & S div. Young & Rubicam, Cape Town, South Africa, 1973-75; sr. lectr. Ft. Hare U., Alice, 1975-76, Rand Afrikaans U., Johannesburg, 1977-78; dep. mng. dir. Mortimer Tiley Group div. BBDO, Johannesburg, 1979-86; prof. U. Pretoria, 1986-90; sr. lectr. Rand Afrikaans U., Johannesburg, 1977-78, chmn., dir. dept. bus. mgmt., 1990-95, dir. sch. for devel. of bus. leaders, 1995-2000. Owner Checklist Mktg. Cons., 1986—; vis. prof. U. N.C. Kenan Flagler Bus. Sch., Chapel Hill, 1991; vis. prof. disting. lectr. series Calif. State U., 1996; mng. dir. Assn. of Advt. Agys. Sch. Advt., 1999—. Author: Print Media Advertising, 1978, Profit from Effective Advertising, 1991; author, editor: Marketing Communications Management, 1987, Promotional Strategy, Marketing Communications in Practice, 1998; co-author: Business Economics, 1991, Marketing Management, 1996, 99. Recipient Loerie award Asom Advt. Awards, 1983, recipient best paper of conf. award Internat. Coun. for Small Bus., 1992. Mem. AAA (exec. com. 1999—), Assn. Advt. Agys. Mem. Dutch Reformed Ch. Avocation: golf. Home: Northcliff 12 De La Rey Rd Johannesburg 2195 South Africa Office: AAA Sch Advt PO Box 2289 Parklands 2121 South Africa E-mail: ludi@aaaschool.co.za.

KOELLER, JEAN MARTHA, artist, librarian; b. Columbus, Ohio, May 24, 1958; d. Leslie Howard and Jone (Morris) Jones; m. Kenneth Allen Koeller, July 26, 1980. Student, Skowgegan Sch. Art, 1981; BFA, BS, Wright State U., 1982; MFA, Parsons Sch. Art, 1987. Instr. art Dayton (Ohio) Art Inst., 1987-90; artist in residence Colonel White H.S., Dayton, 1992-93; vis. artist Antioch U., Yellow Springs, Ohio, 1994-95; libr. visual resource U. Dayton, 1995—. Adj. prof. Sinclair C.C., Dayton, 1988-91, Wright State U., Dayton, 1989-90, U. Dayton, 1988-93. One-woman shows include Lakeland (Wis.) Coll., 1997, Wilmington (Ohio) Coll., 1996, U. Mass., Lowell, 1994, Austin Peay U., Clarksville, Tenn., 1997, Coleman Gallery, Albuquerque, 1998, Cox Arboretum, Kettering, Ohio, 1999, Archetype Gallery, Dayton, Ohio, 2001, Ohio Art League, Columbus, 2001, Franklin Pk. Conservatory, Riverbend Art Ctr., Dayton, others, Represented in permanent collections Mallinkrodt Corp., St. Louis, Vern Riffe Ctr. for Govt. and the Arts, Columbus, Kettering Hosp., Ohio, Ridgeleigh Terr, Kettering Residence, Dayton, Country Club of the North, First Nat. Bank of Western Pa., New Castle, Deloitte & Touche, Dayton, Art Source, Millikin U., Decatur, Ill., Wright State U. Sch. Bus., Dayton, Pub. Employees Retirement Sys., Columbus, others. Grantee Evansville Mus. Art, 1992, Springfield Mus. Art, 1990, Miami Valley Cultural Dist., 1993, Hoyt Inst. Fine Arts, 1993, Ohio Arts Coun. Individual Artist, 1998, Montgomery County Cultural Commn., 1999, 2003; U. Dayton travel grantee, France. Mem.: NOW, Dayton Visual Arts Ctr. (exhbn. com. 1990—92, chair bd. dirs. 2000—03). Home: 1220 Demphle Ave Dayton OH 45410-2215 Office: Univ Dayton Visual Arts Dept 300 College Park Ave Dayton OH 45469-0001 E-mail: jean.koeller@notes.udayton.edu.

KOELLER, LYNN GARVER, public defender; b. Portsmouth, Ohio, Dec. 4, 1943; d. Stanley Wayne and Ruth Louise (Garver) Paulson; m. Michael Koeller, Sept. 6, 1964 (div. July 1980); children: Kristin Schmid, Mark. BS, U. Dayton, 1977, JD, 1980. Bar: Ohio, 1980, U.S. Dist. Ct., 1980. Assoc. Denny, Malloy & Cox, Dayton, Ohio, 1980-82; asst. pub. defender Montgomery County Pub. Defender Office, Dayton, 1982-95, chief pub. defender, 1995—. Mem. Dayton Bar Assn. (criminal law com.), Dayton Women's Bar Assn. Montgomery County Criminal Justice Coun., Barbara Jordon/Thurgood Marshall Roundtable. Office: Office Pub Defender 14 W 4th St Ste 400 Dayton OH 45402-1883 Home: 19901 Forest Ave Castro Valley CA 94546-4516

KOELLER, ROBERT MARION, lawyer, director; b. Quincy, Ill., Apr. 8, 1940; s. Marion Alfred and Ruth (Main) K.; m. Marlene Meyer, June 1962; children: Kristin, Katherine, Robert. AB, MacMurray Coll., 1962; LLB, Vanderbilt U., 1965. Bar: Ind. 1968. Asst. gen. counsel Nat. Homes Acceptance Corp., Lafayette, Ind., 1967-70; gen. counsel, sec. Herff Jones Co., Indpls., 1970-74; ptnr. Warren, Snider, Koeller & Warren, Indpls., 1974-76; sole practice Indpls., 1976—; mem. Coons, Maddox & Koeller, Indpls., 1993-96, Maddox, Koeller Hargett & Caruso, 1996—2002, Sheeks Ittenbach Johnson Trettin & Koeller, Indpls., 2002—. Dir. various cos. Mem. ABA, Ind. Bar Assn., Indpls. Bar Assn., Hillcrest Country Club. Republican. Methodist. Office: Ste 4 6350 N Shadeland Ave Indianapolis IN 46220 E-mail: rkoeller@sheeks-ittenbach.com.

KOELLING, THOMAS WINSOR, lawyer; b. Jefferson City, Mo., Oct. 10, 1951; s. Oscar Alvin and Helen Louise (Shields) K.;m. Rebecca Ann Nentwig, Nov. 24, 1973; children: Zachary Thomas, Mathew Garret. BS in Criminal Justice Adminstrn., Ctrl. Mo. State U., Warrenburg, 1978; JD, U. Mo., 1981. Bar: Mo. 1981, Colo. 1982, U.S. Dist. Ct. (we. dist.) Mo. 1981, U.S. Dist. Ct. Colo. 1981, U.S. Ct. Appeals (8th cir.) 1982, U.S. Ct. Appeals (10th cir.) 1981, U.S. Supreme Ct. 1992. Assoc. Tinsley, Frantz et al, Lakewood, Colo., 1981-82, Rex Johnson Law Office, Colorado Springs, Colo., 1982-85; ptnr. Koelling & Crawford, P.C., Kansas City, Mo., 1985—. Legal advisor Kansas City Ski Club, 1987, Competitors Assn., Kansas City, 1995—; adj. prof. dept. criminal justice and legal studies Mo. Western State Coll., St. Joseph, Mo., 1998—. With USAF, 1972-76. Mem. ABA, Am. Coll. Legal Medicine, Am. Soc. Law, Medicine Ethics, Am. Trial Lawyers Assn., Mo. Assn. Trial Lawyers, Clay County Bar Assn. Roman Catholic. Avocations: snow skiing, fly fishing, backpacking. Home: 9617 N Campbell St Kansas City MO 64155-2056 Office: Koelling & Crawford PC 5950 N Oak Trfy Ste 202 Kansas City MO 64118-5164

KOELMEL, LORNA LEE, data processing executive; b. Denver, May 15, 1936; d. George Bannister and Gladys Lee Steuart; m. Herbert Howard Nelson, Sept. 9, 1956 (div. Mar. 1967); children: Karen Dianne, Phillip Dean, Lois Lynn; m. Robert Darrel Koelmel, May 12, 1981; stepchildren: Kim, Cheryl, Dawn, Debbie. BA in English, U. Colo., 1967. Cert. secondary English tchr. Substitute English tchr. Jefferson County Schs., Lakewood, Colo., 1967—68; sec. specialist IBM Corp., Denver, 1968—75, pers. administr., 1975—82, asst. ctr. coord., 1982—85, office systems specialist, 1985—87, backup computer operator, 1987—; computer instr. Barnes Bus. Coll., Denver, 1987—92; owner, mgr. Lorna's Precision Word Processing and Desktop Pub., Denver, 1987—89; computer cons. Denver, 1990—. Editor newsletter Colo. Nat. Campers and Hikers Assn., 1992-94. Organist Christian Sci. Soc., Buena Vista, Colo., 1963-66, 1st Ch. Christ Scientists Thornton-Westminster, Thornton, Colo., 1994—; chmn. bd. dirs., 1979-80. Mem. NAFE, Nat. Secs. Assn. (retirement ctr. chair 1977-78, newsletter chair 1979-80, v.p. 1980-81), Am. Theatre Organ Soc. (Rocky Mountain chpt.), Am. Guild Organists, U. Colo. Alumni Assn., Avon Ind. Sales Rep and Pres. Club, Alpha Chi Omega (publicity com. 1986-88). Clubs: Nat. Writers. Lodges: Job's Daus. (recorder 1953-54). Republican. Avocations: needlepoint, piano, bridge, reading, golf.

KOELTL, JOHN GEORGE, judge; b. N.Y.C., Oct. 25, 1945; s. John J. and Elsie (Bender) K. AB summa cum laude, Georgetown U., 1967; JD magna cum laude, Harvard U., 1971. Bar: N.Y. 1972, U.S. Dist. Ct. (so. and ea. dists.) N.Y. 1973, U.S. Ct. Appeals (2d cir.) 1973, U.S. Supreme Ct. 1978, U.S. Ct. Appeals (5th and 11th cirs.) 1981, U.S. Ct. Appeals (4th cir.) 1992, U.S. Dist. Ct. (no. dist.) N.Y. 1982. Law clk. to Judge U.S. Dist. Ct. (so. dist.), N.Y.C., 1971-72; law clk. to Justice Potter Stewart U.S. Supreme Ct., Washington, 1972-73; asst. spl. prosecutor Watergate Spl. Prosecution Force, Dept. Justice, Washington, 1973-74; assoc. Debevoise & Plimpton, N.Y.C., 1975-78, ptnr., 1979-94; judge U.S. Dist. Ct. (so. dist.), N.Y.C., 1994—. Adj. prof. law NYU Law Sch., 1999—. Mem. bd. editors Manual for Complex Litigation 4th edit.; contbr. articles to profl. jours. Mem.: ABA (bd. editors jour. 1991—97, vice chmn. securities com. adminstrv. law sect. 1979—81, co-dir. divsn. publs. litigation sect. 1982—84, coun. mem. litigation sect. 1984—87, assoc. editor Litigation jour. 1975—78, exec. editor 1978—80, editor-in-chief 1980—82, chmn. 1st amendment com. 1987—89, chmn. spl. pubs. com. 1989—92, dir. divsn. publs. litigation sect. 1992—93), Am. Law Inst., Harvard Law Sch. Assn. N.Y. (v.p. 1993—94), N.Y. County Lawyers Assn. (mem. fed. cts. com. 1984—87), N.Y. State Bar Assn., Assn. Bar N.Y.C. (mem. com. on fed. legislation 1976—78, sec. 1978—81, mem. com. profl. and jud. ethics 1981—84, fed. cts. com. 1984—86, chmn. 1986—89, mem. com. on profl. responsibility 1991—94, mem. com. on internat. dispute resolution 2000—). Office: US Courthouse 500 Pearl St Rm 1030 New York NY 10007-1316

KOELZER, GEORGE JOSEPH, lawyer; b. Orange, N.J., Mar. 21, 1938; s. George Joseph and Albertina Florence (Graul) K.; m. Patricia Ann Kilian, Apr. 8, 1967; 1 son, James Patrick. AB, Rutgers U., 1962, LLB, 1964. Bar: N.J. 1964, D.C. 1978, N.Y. 1980, Calif. 1993; registered fgn. lawyer, U.K., 2001. Assoc. Louis R. Lombardino, Livingston, N.J., 1964-66, Lum Biunno & Tompkins, Newark, 1971-73, Giordano, Halleran & McOmber, Middletown, N.J., 1973-74; asst. U.S. atty. for N.J. U.S. Dept. Justice, 1966-71; ptnr. Evans, Koelzer, Osborne & Kreizman, N.Y.C. and Red Bank, N.J., 1974-86, Ober, Kaler, Grimes & Shriver, N.Y.C., 1986-92, Lane Powell Spears Lubersky, L.A., 1993-97, Hancock, Rothert & Bunshoft, L.A., 1997-2000, Coudert Bros., L.A., London, 2000—. Adj. prof. Seton Hall U. Sch. Law, 1989-92; mem. lawyers adv. com. U.S. Ct. Appeals (3d cir.) 1985-87, vice chmn., 1986, chmn., 1987; mem. lawyers adv. com. U.S. Dist. Ct. N.J., 1984-92; permanent mem. Jud. Conf. of U.S. Ct. Appeals for 3d cir.; del. jud. conf. U.S. Ct. Appeals for 2d cir., 1987, 88, 89. Recipient Atty. Gen.'s award, 1970. Fellow Am. Bar Found.; mem. ABA (sect. litigation, co-chmn. com. on admiralty and maritime litigation 1979-82, 89-90, mem. coun. sect. litigation 1985-88, chmn. 9th ann. meeting sect. litigation 1984, dir. divsn. IV procedural coms. 1982-85, dir. divsn. I adminstrn. 1988-89, mem. nominating com. 1982, 84, 87, advisor standing com. lawyer competence 1986—), Civil Justice Inst., Maritime Law Assn. U.S. (ABA relations com., fed. procedure com., vice chmn. com. on maritime fraud and crime 1989-94, chmn. 1994-98, bd. dirs. 1998-2001), State Bar Calif., N.Y. State Bar Assn. (chmn. admiralty com., comml. and fed. litigation sect. 1989-92), Assn. of Bar of City of N.Y. (admiralty com. 1987-90), D.C. Bar Assn., Fed. Bar Assn. (mem. fed. practice com. 1994—), Fed. Bar Council, Comml. Bar Assn. (London), Assn. Average Adjustrs Gt. Britain, Assn. Average Adjusters U.S., Assn. Bus. and Trial Lawyers, L.A. World Affairs Coun.; Clubs: Mid-Ocean (Bermuda), Jonathan Club (L.A.). Roman Catholic. Republican. Home: 521 S Orange Grove Blvd 100 Pasadena CA 91105-3528

KOEMPEL, MICHAEL L. government official, researcher; b. Farmington, Minn., July 4, 1949; s. Willis Matthews and Marion (White) K.; m. Dianne Patricia Hunt, May 6, 1978; 1 child, Gabriel Mack. BS, Georgetown U., 1971; JD, Cath. U., 1974. Legis. dir. U.S. Rep. Albert H. Quie, Washington, 1974-78; spl. asst. Minn. Govr. Albert H. Quie, St. Paul, 1979; rsch. dir. Congl. Quar. Inc., Washington, 1979-85, dir. info. svcs., 1985-94; asst. dir. govt. and fin. Congl. Rsch. Svc., Washington, 1995—. Co-author: Congressional Deskbook, 2000, 2003. Mem. Am. Polit. Sci. Assn., D.C. Bar Assn. Home: 6612 Allegheny Ave Takoma Park MD 20912 Office: Congl Rsch Svc 101 Independence Ave SE Washington DC 20540 E-mail: mkoempel@crs.loc.gov.

KOEN, BILLY VAUGHN, mechanical engineering educator; b. Graham, Tex., May 2, 1938; s. Ottis Vaughn and Margaret (Branch) Koen; m. Deanne Rollins, June 3, 1967; children: Kent, Douglas. BA in Chemistry, BS in Chem. Engring., U. Tex., 1961; S.M. in Nuclear Engring., MIT, 1962, Sc.D. in Nuclear Engring., 1968; Diplome d'ingenieur en Genie Atomique, L'institut National des Scis. et Techniques Nucleaires, France, 1963. Registered profl. engr., Tex. Asst. prof. mech. engring. U. Tex., Austin, 1968-71, assoc. prof., 1971-80, Minnie S. Piper prof., 1980, prof., 1981—; dir. Bur. Engring. Teaching U. Tex.-Austin, 1973-76. Prof. Ecole Centrale, Paris, 1983; undergrad advisor mech. engring., 1988-92; vis. prof. Tokyo Inst. Tech., 1994 (summer), 1998-99, 2001 (summer); cons., lectr. in field. Author: Definition of the Engineering Method, 1985, Discussion of the Method, 2003; contbr. articles to profl. jours. Bd. dirs. Oak Ridge Associated Univs., 1975-76. Recipient Standard Oil Ind. award, 1970, W. Leighton Collins Distinguished and Unusual Service awd., Am. Soc. for Engineering Education, 1992. Fellow Am. Soc. Engring. Edn. (v.p. 1987-93, Chester Carlson award 1980, Ben Dasher best paper award 1985, 86, Helen Plants award 1986, William Elgin Wickenden best paper award 1986, Olmsted award, dir. 1982-84, W. Leighton Collins award 1992, Centennial medallion 1993), Am. Nuc. Soc.; mem. N.Y. Acad. Sci., Association des Ingenieurs en Genie Atomique, Rotary Club (Austin; Internat. fellow 1962), Phi Beta Kappa, Sigma Xi (disting. lectr. 1981-83), Tau Beta Pi. Mem. Soc. Of Friends. Achievements include development of computer algorithm for calculation of nuclear system reliability. Office: U Tex Dept Mech Engring Etc 5160 Austin TX 78712

KOENIG, ALLEN EDWARD, higher education consultant; b. Feb. 11, 1939; s. Edward and Eva (Barnes) Koenig; m. Judy Lynn Gill, June 8, 1969; children: Wendy, Jody, Mark. BA, U. So. Calif., L.A., 1961; MA, Stanford U., 1962; PhD, Northwestern U., 1964. Asst. prof. speech Ea. Mich. State U., Ypsilanti, 1964—65, U. Wis.-Milw., 1965—67, Ohio State U., Columbus, 1967—69; dir. comm. AAUP, Washington, 1969—70; v.p. devel. Capitol U., Columbus, 1970—74; exec. v.p. Marycrest Coll., Davenport, Iowa, 1974—75; assoc. dir. U. So. Calif.-Idyllwild Campus, 1975—76, exec. dir., 1976—79; pres. Emerson Coll., Boston, 1979—89, Chapman U., Orange, Calif., 1989—91; sr. assoc. Thomas H. Langevin & Assoc., 1992—2002; sr. cons. R.H. Perry & Assocs.,

1993—. Prof. cons. radio TV stas. Appalachia Ednl. Lab., Charleston, W.Va., 1967—69; mem. commn. on leadership devel. Am. Coun. on Edn., Washington, 1984—86; co-founder Registry Coll. and U. Pres., 1992; vis. prof. mass comm. Boston U., 1991—92. Sr. editor: The Farther Vision: Educational Television Today, 1967; editor: Broadcasting and Bargaining: Labor Relations in Radio and Television, 1970, Jour. Ednl. Broadcasting Rev., 1967—69; contbr. articles to profl. jours. Exec. bd. dirs. pres.'s steering com. Boston Pub. Schs., 1982—86; v.p., treas. Profl. Arts Consortium, 1988—89; trustee Marycrest Coll., Davenport, 1982—86. Recipient Broadcast Preceptor award, San Francisco State Coll., 1969, 1971. Mem.: NATAS (bd. govs. New Eng. chpg. 1980—84, pres. 1988—89), Mass. Corp. for Ednl. Telecomms. (chmn. 1989), Assn. Ind. Colls. and Univs. in Mass. (exec. com. 1983—89), Alpha Kappa Delta, Alpha Epsilon Rho. E-mail: akoenig@columbus.rr.com.

KOENIG, ELIZABETH BARBARA, sculptor; b. N.Y.C., Apr. 20, 1937; d. Hayward and Selma E. (Rosen) Ulman; m. Carl Stuart Koenig, Sept. 10, 1961; children: Katherine Lee, Kenneth Douglas. BA, Wellesley Coll., 1958; MD, Yale U., 1962; postgrad., Art Students League N.Y., 1963-64, Corcoran Sch. Art, 1964-67. One-woman shows include St. John's Coll., Annapolis, Md., 1974, Foxhall Gallery, Washington, 1977, 85, 99, also solo retrospectives Lyman Allyn Mus., New London, Conn., 1978, Rotunda of Pan-Am. Health Orgn., Washington, 1978, Gallery Metayer, Paris, 1999; exhibited in group shows at Internat. Dedication Nat. Bur. Stds., Gaithersburg, Md., 1966, Textile Mus., Washington, 1974-75, No. Va. Mus., Alexandria, 1975, Meridian House Internat., Washington, 1980; commd. works include Free Spirit marble carving Washington Hebrew Congregation, 1978, Monumental Torso bronze for grounds George Meany Ctr. for Labor Studies, 1982, desert stone marble carving Regional Ctr. for Women in Arts, Westchester, Pa., 2003; represented in pvt. collections, U.S. and Europe. Recipient 1st prize sculpture Tri-State Regional Exhbn., Md., 1970, 2d and 3d prize sculpture, 1971. Mem. Artists Equity Assn. (v.p. Washington 1977-83), Art Students League N.Y. (life), Internat. Sculpture Ctr., New Arts Ctr. Avocations: reading, gardening. Home: 9014 Charred Oak Dr Bethesda MD 20817-1924

KOENIG, HAROLD MARTIN, former United States Navy surgeon general; b. Salinas, Calif., Feb. 28, 1940; m. Deena Prescott; children: Steven Fillmore, Scott Osborne, Grant Matthew. BS, Brigham Young U., 1962; MD, Baylor U., 1966. Diplomate Am. Acad. Pediatrics, Pediatric Hematology and Oncology. Commd. lt. USN, 1958, advanced through grades to vice adm.; gen. med. officer Fleet Activities, Sasebo, Japan, 1967-69; resident, fellow Naval Hosp., San Diego, 1969-73, head pediatric, hematology-oncology div., 1973-80; chief pediatrics Naval Regional Med. Ctr., Oakland, Calif., 1980-83; dir. med. svcs. Naval Hosp., Oakland, 1983-84, exec. officer Portsmouth, Va., 1984-85, comdg. officer San Diego, 1985-87, Naval Health Scis. Edn. and Tng. Command, Bethesda, Md., 1987-88; dir. health care ops. div. Office of Surgeon Gen./Naval Medicine, Washington, 1988-90; dep. asst. sec. def. Health Svcs. Ops., Office of Sec. Def., Washington, 1990-94; surgeon gen. USN, Washington, 1994-98, ret., 1998. Contbr. articles to profl. jours. Decorated Def. Superior Svc. medal, Legion of Merit (2); recipient 4 other personal awards, Navy disting. svc. medal. Fellow Am. Acad. Pediatrics (chmn. mil. sect. 1982-84), Am. Soc. Hematology; mem. AMA, other med. socs. Home: 4933 Marlborough Dr San Diego CA 92116-2346

KOENIG, HAROLD PAUL, management consultant, ecologist, evangelist, writer; b. Mason City, Iowa, Apr. 22, 1926; s. Reuben Harold and Dorothea (Paule) K.; m. Barbara Anne Rucker, June 29, 1974; 1 child, Kimberley Anne. Student, Ohio Wesleyan U., 1944-45; BS, Iowa State U., 1947; MS, Ill. Inst. Tech., 1956. Registered profl. engr., Iowa, Minn., Ill., Ind., Fla.; ordained to ministry Bapt. Ch., 1994. Chief engr. Grain Processing Corp., Muscatine, Iowa, 1948-50; engr. mgr. Standard Oil Co. Ind., Whiting, Ind., 1953-56; with Booz, Allen & Hamilton, Chgo. and Genoa, Italy, 1956-64; v.p. Dresser Industries, Inc., Dallas, 1964-67; founder, chmn., pres., CEO Ecol. Sci. Corp., Miami and Lugano, Switzerland, 1967-73, Tele-Optics, Inc., West Palm Beach, Fla., 1986-90; chmn., pres., CEO Unionam., Inc. subs. Windham Power Lifts, Elba, Ala., 1974-76; dir. gen., CEO Matisa, S.A., Lausanne, Switzerland, 1977-78; dir. gen. Canron Pipe & Hydraulics, Montreal, Que., Can., 1978-80; COO Tel-Tech Devices, Inc., Ft. Lauderdale, Fla., 1984-86; chmn. H.P. Koenig Mgmt. Cons., Miami, 1980-84, Jupiter, Satellite Beach, Fla., 1990—. Cert. trainer Evang. Explosion Internat., Ft. Lauderdale, 1981—, cert. Evang. Explosion lectr., West Palm Beach, 1991—; advisor Citizens Democracy Corps, Russia, 1996-97, Ukraine, 1998; lectr. in field. Author: Winning Against Satan-Applying Military Principles to Spiritual Warfare, 1991; contbr. articles to profl. jours. Witness on environ. and ecol. matters U.S. Congress, Washington, 1969-71; adv. for founding Earth Day, 1970; mem. Citizens Democracy Corps, Khabarovsk, Sakhalin Island, Russia, 1996, Velikie Luki, Russia, 1997, Odessa and Nikolaev, Ukraine, 1998; adv. for Drug Treatment Fla., 1998-99; mem. Pres. Nixon's Com. on Environ. Quality, 1969-72; deacon Bapt. Ch., missionary to Kenya; founder, pres., CEO H.E.A.R.T. (Help Early Addicts Receive Treatment), 1999; scoutmaster, Iowa, 1949-50. Lt. comdr. USNR, 1943-46; PTO Seabees, 1951-53. Recipient Eagle Scout award, Boy Scouts Am., 1942, Meritorious Svc. award, Govt. of Italy, 1962. Mem. Phi Gamma Delta (Golden Owl award), Gideon. Republican. Avocation: tennis, bridge, Christian witnessing, golf, eagle scout. Home and Office: 341 Lanternback Island Dr Satellite Beach FL 32937-4708

KOENIG, JAMES BENNETT, geologist, consultant; b. New York, NY, Nov. 25, 1932; s. Philip and Lorraine Rose Koenigsfest; m. Deborah Libby Scolnick, Feb. 16, 1992; m. Anne Mariner Jennings, June 6, 1964 (div. Jan. 9, 1984); children: Laura Bethune, Andrea Croft, Cassandra Gregory. B.S. in geology, Bklyn Coll., 1950—54; MA in geology, Ind. U., 1954—56; Diploma in meteorology, U.S. Naval Postgraduate Sch., 1957—58; Candidate, PhD in geology/seismology, U. of Nev., 1963—65. Registered geologist State of Calif., 1972. Geologic aide Howe Sound Mining Co., Canada, 1953; ground-water geologist U.S. Geol. Survey, St. Paul, 1955—56; jr. and asst. geologist Calif. Divsn. of Mines and Geology, 1956—57, asst. geologist, assoc. and sr. geologist, 1960—63, sr. and supervising geologist, 1965—72; pres. and chmn. of the bd. GeothermEx, Inc., Richmond, Calif., 1973—96; pres. El Cerrito Consultants, Calif., 1996—. Cons. UN, 1971; chmn., fin. com. World Geothermal Congress, Italy, 1992—95, Japan, 1997—2000; cons. UN, 1981, Calif. Energy Co., Indonesia, 1992—94, World Bank, Kenya, 1987—93, InterAmerican Devel. Bank, Costa Rica, 1975—80, Caltex Petroleum, 1981—83, Amoseas Indonesia Inc., 1982—84; mem., bd. of dir. Geothermal Resources Coun., Calif., 1974—91, pres., 1989—91; mem. of bd. of dir. Internat. Geothermal Assn., Italy, 1989—95, gen. chmn. World Geothermal Congress, Turkey, 2000—. Contbr. over 70 papers and abstracts published. Lt. USN, 1957—60, Navy Weather Rsch. Facility, Norfolk, VA. Recipient Joseph Aidlin award, Geothermal Resources Coun., 1987; fellow NASA Fellowship, U. of Nev., 1963—65; NY State Scholarship, Regents of State of NY, 1950—54, Rsch. fellowship, Ind. U., 1956. Fellow: Geol. Soc. of Am.; mem.: Societe Canadienne d'Onomastique, Am. Name Soc., Internat. Geothermal Assn., San Francisco Bay Area Jewish Geneal. Soc. (mem., bd. of dir. 2000—). Independent. Jewish. Achievements include discovery of of miravalles geothermal field, Costa Rica, 1979; of Dixie Valley geothermal field, Nev., 1977; of Batong Buhay geothermal field, Philippines, 1983; research in numerical simulation of reserves at geothermal fields. Avocations: genealogy, onomastics, travel. Home and Office: 6332 Barrett Ave El Cerrito CA 94530 Home Fax: 510-234-3320. E-mail: jbkoenig6332@msn.com.

KOENIG, LEO JOHN, family practice physician; b. Chgo., June 15, 1948; s. Leo John and Veronica Theresa (Butryn) Koenigshofer; m. Karen Marie Jasaitis, Nov. 30, 1974; children: Monica, Cheryl, Rebecca. BS, Loyola U., 1970, MD, 1974. Diplomate Am. Bd. Family Practice. Resident in family practice Luth. Gen. Hosp., Park Ridge, Ill., 1974—77, faculty physician, 1977—78, Hinsdale (Ill.) Hosp., 1978—80, 1984—86; pvt. practice Fairbury, Ill., 1980—81; med. dir. Olin Corp., Joliet, Ill., 1981—84; v.p. med. svcs. Met. Life Ins. Co., Aurora, Ill., 1986—99; v.p., med. dir. First Penn-Pacific Life Ins. Co., Schaumburg, Ill., 1999—. Cons. occupl. medicine Olin Corp., Joliet, Ill., 1984—86; clin. preceptor in family medicine Hinsdale (Ill.) Hosp., 1978—. Named clin. preceptor of year Hinsdale Hosp. Family Practice Residency Prog., 1994, 96, 99. Fellow Am. Acad. Family Physicians; mem. AMA, Am. Acad. Ins. Medicine, Am. Acad. Occupl. and Environ. Medicine, Knights of Columbus (Bolingbrook Ill. chpt.). Republican. Roman Catholic. Office: First Penn-Pacific Life Ins Co 10 N Martingale Rd Ste 200 Schaumburg IL 60173-2268

KOENIG, MARIE HARRIET KING, public relations director, fund raising executive; b. New Orleans, Feb. 19, 1919; d. Harold Paul and Sadie Louise (Bole) King; m. Walter William Koenig, June 24, 1956; children: Margaret Marie, Susan Patricia. Major in Voice, La. State U., 1937-39; Pre-law, Loyola U., 1942-43; BS in History, U. LaVerne, 1986. Adminstrv. asst. to atty. gen. State of La., New Orleans, 1940-44, contract writer MGM Studios, Culver City, Calif., 1944-46; asst. sec., treas. Found. for Ind., L.A., 1950-56, Found. for Social Rsch., L.A., 1950-56; dir. communications Incentive Rsch. Corp., L.A., 1969-78; rsch. supr., devel. dept. Calif. Inst. Technology, Pasadena, Calif., 1969; dir. funding devel. Rep. Party of L.A. County, South Pasadena, 1989-92. Author: Does the National Council of Churches Speak for You?, 1978; delivered lecture series on U.S. fgn. policy. Named Hon. Citizen Colonial Williamsburg Found., 1987; active Nat. Trust for Historic Preservation, 1986, Friends of the Huntington Libr., 1986, Town Hall of L.A., 1986—, Pasadena City Women's Club, 1982-84; past mem. Coun. Women's Clubs; charter mem. Nat. Mus. of Women in Arts; bd. mem. Pasadena Opera Guild; contbg. mem. L.A. World Affairs Coun., 1990, L.A. County Mus. Art, 1999; past pres., pub. chmn., Pasadena Rep. Women Federated; charter mem. Freedoms Found. at Valley Forge L.A. County Chpt., Autry Mus. Western Heritage, 1986, Women of L.A.; pres. Greater L.A. Women's Coun., Navy League of the U.S. Recipient Pres.'s award So. Calif. Motion Picture Coun., 1996, Cert. Recognition Calif. State Assembly, 1989, 95, Recognition of Excellence, Achievement and Commitment U.S. Ho. Reps., 1989, Cert. Merit Rep. Presdl. Task Force, 1986, Cert. Appreciation U.S. Def. Com., 1984, Hon. Freedom Fighter award U.S. Def. Com., 1985, Cert. Appreciation Am. Conservative Union, 1983, Cert. Commendation Rep. Cen. Com. L.A. County, 1972, Cert. Appreciation Eisenhower-Nixon So. Calif. Com., 1952; named Disting. Citizen of Yr. L.A. Area Coun. Boy Scouts Am. Mem. Women in Communications, Greater L.A. Press Club, World War II Meml. (charter). Republican. Avocations: reading, music, opera. Home: 205 Madeline Dr Pasadena CA 91105-3311

KOENIG, MICHAEL EDWARD DAVISON, information science educator; b. Rochester, N.Y., Nov. 1, 1941; s. Claremont Judson and Mary Fletcher (Davison) K.; m. Nancy Crane Packard, 1966 (div. 1976); children: Christopher Wells Bowen, Davison Packard; m. Luciana Marulli, Feb. 2, 1980. BA in Psychology, Yale U., 1963; MLS, U. Chgo., 1968, MBA, 1970; PhD in Information Sci., Drexel U., 1982. Info. svcs. mgr. Pfizer, Inc., Groton, Conn., 1970-74; info. ops. dir. Inst. Scientific Info., Phila., 1974-77, devel. dir., 1977-78; v.p. ops. Swets N.Am., Berwyn, Pa., 1978-80; assoc. prof. Columbia U., N.Y.C., 1980-85; v.p. info. mgmt. Tradenet, Inc., N.Y.C., 1985-88; prof., dean sch. libr. and info. sci. Dominican U., River Forest, Ill., 1988-96, prof., dean emeritus, 1996-99; dean, prof. Coll. Info. and Computer Sci. Long Island U., Brookville, N.Y., 1999—. Chmn. editl. bd. Third World Librs., 1991-96. Contbr. more than 100 articles to profl. jours. Lt. USNR, 1963-65. Mem. ALA (councilor 1993-97, 2001—), Am. Soc. Info. Sci., Internat. Soc. Scientometrics and Informetrics (pres. 1995-97), Assn. Computing Machinery, Spl. Librs. Assn., Grolier Club, Caxton Club, Elizabethan Club. Home: 16 Buckwalter Farm Ln Phoenixville PA 19460-2317

KOENIG, ROBERT AUGUST, clergyman, educator; b. Red Wing, Minn., July 14, 1933; s. William C. and Florence E. (Tebbe) K.; m. Pauline Louise Olson, June 21, 1962. BS cum laude, U. Wis., Superior, 1955; MA in Ednl. Adminstrn., U. Minn., 1965, PhD, 1973; MDiv magna cum laude, San Francisco Theol. Sem., 1969; postgrad. (John Hay fellow), Bennington Coll., summer, 1965. Ordained to ministry Presbyn. Ch., 1970. Supr. music Florence (Wis.) H.S., 1955—56; dir. instrumental music Chetek (Wis.) Pub. Schs., 1958—62; tchr. instrumental music and humanities Palo Alto (Calif.) Sr. H.S., 1962—65; asst. to min. St. John's Presbyn. Ch., San Francisco, 1964—65; min. Sawyer County (Wis.) larger parish, 1969—74; tchr. gen. music Jordan Jr. H.S., Palo Alto, 1966—69; instr. Coll. Edn. U. Minn., 1969—71; adminstv. asst. to pres. Lakewood State C.C., White Bear Lake, Minn., 1971—72; asst. to exec. dir. Minn. Higher Edn. Coord. Bd., St. Paul, 1972, coord. commn. and pers. svcs., 1972—74; instr. Inver Hills C.C., Inver Grove Heights, Minn., 1974; pastor First Presbyn. Ch. of Chippewa Falls (Wis.), 1974—85; sr. pastor Grove Presbyn. Ch., Danville, Pa., 1985—88, First Presbyn. Ch., South St. Paul, Minn., 1988—98; supply pastor Couderay and Radisson Presbyn. Chs., Wis., 1999—. Mem. study com. Presbytery of Chippewa, 1973-74, mem. min. rels. com., 1974-77; adj. asst. prof. ednl. adminstrn. U. Minn., Mpls., 1976-77; mem. faculty U. Wis. Ext., Eau Claire, 1977, chmn. 3d Ann. Bibl. Seminar, 1977, mem. faculty Communiversity, 1977-85; mem. internat. coord. com. ch. mission Synod of Lakes and Prairies, 1978-79; mem. ministerial rels. com. Presbytery of No. Waters, 1977-82, chmn. ministerial rels. com., 1981-82, moderator, 1983; chmn. Synod Designation Pastor Plan Cabinet, 1982-84; chmn. Presbytery Coun., 1982-84; chairperson Christian edn. com. Presbytery of Northumberland, 1987-88, mem. Presbytery coun., 1987-88; mem. Christian edn. com. Synod of the Trinity, 1987-88, mem. com. on ministry Presbytery of the Twin Cities Area, 1999-2001, chairperson subcom. on presbytery membership; mem. com. on ministry Danville-Riverside Area Ministerial Assn., 1985-88, pres., 1987-88; mem. South St. Paul Ministerial Assn., 1988-98, pres., 1989-90. Contbr. articles to profl. jours. Bd. dirs. North Ctrl. Career Devel. Ctr., Mpls., 1978-84, chmn. fin. com., 1979-84, bd. dirs. devel. found., 1983-85; pres. Chippewa Valley Ecumenical Housing Assn., 1984-85; mem. alumni bd. U. Minn., 1999—; bd. dirs. Coll. Edn. and Human Devel. Alumni Soc. U. Minn., 1999—, exec. com., v.p., 2001-2002, pres., 2002—. With U.S. Army, 1956-58, Korea. Mem. Masons (grand chaplain Wis. chpt. 1977-80, 83-85), Elks (Danville chpt.), Phi Delta Kappa Internat. (U. Minn. Twin Cities chpt.). Home: 6045 Bowman Ave E Inver Grove Heights MN 55076-1502

KOENIG, ROBERT EMIL, clergyman; b. St. Louis, Aug. 31, 1919; s. Hermann Emil and Martha Ida (Baur) K.; m. Norma Caroline Evans, July 18, 1943; children: Elsa Koenig Weber, Robert, Richard, Martha Koenig Stone, Thea Koenig Burton, Laura Koenig Godinez. BS, U. Chgo., 1941; BD, Chgo. Theol. Sem., 1945; PhD, U. Chgo., 1953; DD, Elmhurst Coll., 1987. Pastor St. John's Evang. & Reformed Ch., Hinsdale, Ill., 1943-46; from instr. to assoc. prof. religion Elmhurst (Ill.) Coll., 1946-54; dir. curriculum Bd. Christian Edn., Phila., 1954-61; editor-in-chief United Ch. Bd. for Homeland Ministries, Phila., 1961-84; interim pastor St. Paul's United Ch. Christ, Fort Washington, Pa., 1985-87, Bethany United Ch. Christ, Phila., First United Ch. of Christ, Quakertown, Pa., St. Vincent United Ch. of Christ, Phoenixville, Pa., Collenbrook United Ch., Brownback's United Ch. of Christ, Spring City, Boehm's United Ch. of Christ, 1988—2003; adj. prof. Christian edn. Lancaster (Pa.) Theol. Sem., 1988-89; cons., dir. Koenig Ch. Edn. Cons., Inc., Havertown, Pa., 1988—. Adj. instr. Defiance Coll., 1995-2000. Mng. editor PRISM Mag., 1990—. Pres. Ardmore (Pa.) Jr. High Home and Sch. Assn., 1962-63; mem. Penn Wynne (Pa.) Libr. Bd., 1985-89; pres. Univ. Glee Club of Phila., 1987-88; mem. ElderNet, Lower Merion, Pa., 1986—, pres., 1988-89, treas., 1994-96. Mem. Haverford Twp. Clergy Assn. (treas. 1990—). Democrat. Avocations: singing, playing violin, hiking. Home and Office: 566 Haverford Rd Havertown PA 19083-2642 E-mail: reknek@compuserve.com.

KOENIG, RODNEY CURTIS, lawyer, rancher; b. Black Jack, Tex., Nov. 21, 1940; s. John Henry and Elva Marguerite (Oeding) K.; m. Mary Mishler, May 1, 1993; children: Erik Jason, Jon Todd. BA, U. Tex., 1962, JD with honors, 1969; postgrad., Auburn U., 1965-67. Bar: Tex. 1969, U.S. Dist. Ct. (so. dist.) Tex. 1970, U.S. Ct. Appeals (5th cir.) 1970, U.S. Tax Ct. 1980, U.S. Ct. Mil. Appeals 1986. Ptnr. Fulbright & Jaworski, LLP, Houston, 1969—. Lectr. State Bar Tex., various univs., local estate planning councils; asst. prof. Auburn U., 1965-67 Contbr. articles to profl. jours. Pres. Houston Navy League, 1979-81; commr. Battleship Texas Commn.; Houston Saengerbund; bd. dirs. Houston divsn. Am. Heart Assn., Fayette Heritage Mus.; dir. Advanced Estate Planning and Probate Course, 1988; trustee Luck and Loessin Collection Trust, Luth. Found. of the S.W., treas., exec. com.; active Tex. Luth. U. Corp. With USN, 1962-67; served to capt. JAGC, USNR, 1967-89. Recipient Fed. Republic of Germany Order of Merit, 1994. Fellow Am. Coll. Trust and Estate Counsel, Coll. State Bar Tex. (charter); mem. ABA, Internat. Acad. Estate and Trust Law (academician), Tex. Judge Adv. Res. Officers Assn., German Texan Heritage Soc. (pres. 1997-2000), Tex. German Soc. (founding dir.), Res. Officers Assn., Sons of Republic of Tex., Wednesday Tax Forum (past chmn.), German Gulf Coast Assn. (pres. 1989-93), Bach Soc. (bd. dirs.), English Speaking Union (bd. dirs.), Houston Early Music (pres. 2000—), Houston Karneval Verein (prince 1994-95), USS San Jacinto Com. (treas.), Houstonian Club, Houston Ctr. Club, Frisch Auf Valley Country Club, Order of Coif, U.S. Naval Order, Phi Delta Phi, Omicron Delta Kappa. Lutheran. Home: 2720 University Blvd Houston TX 77005-3440 Office: Fulbright & Jaworski LLP 1301 Mckinney St Fl 51 Houston TX 77010-3031 E-mail: rkoenig@fulbright.com.

KOENIGSBERG, JUDY Z. NULMAN, clinical psychologist; b. Bklyn., Apr. 21, 1951; d. Macy and Sarah (Rosenberg) Nulman; m. David I. Koenigsberg, June 18, 1972; children: Benjamin, Rachel. Grad. summa cum laude, Yeshiva U. Tchrs. Inst., N.Y.C., 1971; BA with honors, Bklyn. Coll., 1972; MA, Northeastern Ill. U., 1980; grad. study, U. Chgo., 1980—82; MEd, Loyola U., Chgo., 1985; PhD in Psychology, Northwestern U., 1990. Lic. and reg. clin. psychologist, Ill.; Nat. Register of Health Service Providers in Psychology. Clin. specialist Charter Barclay Hosp., Chgo., 1985-86; psychology extern Luth. Gen. Hosp., Park Ridge, Ill., 1987-88; psychol. testing extern Evanston (Ill.) Hosp., 1988-89, psychology intern, 1989-90; psychology postdoctoral resident Loyola U. Chgo., 1991-92; clin. psychologist U. Chgo., 1993-94; dir. Stats Unlimited, 1995—. Contbr. articles to profl. jours. & The Gale Encyclopedia of Mental Disorders. Recipient Outstanding Achievement award Nat. Culture Coun., 1972; scholarship award dept. modern langs. Bklyn. Coll., 1972, Kappa Delta Pi, 1972. Mem. APA, Ill. Psychol. Assn., Soc. for Computers in Psychology, Northwestern U. Alumni Assn. Sch. Edn. and Social Policy (dir. bd. 1993-94). Avocations: violin, Tae Kwon Do, table tennis, swimming. Office: 708 Church St Ste 250 Evanston IL 60201-3840 E-mail: jzok@earthlink.net.

KOENIGSKNECHT, ROY A. education administrator; b. Fowler, Mich., Dec. 27, 1942; s. Joseph I. and Katherine (Zimmermann) K.; m. Marilie A. Dani, Aug. 20, 1966; children: John, Adam, Amanda. AB in Psychology, Central Mich. U., 1964; MA in Speech and Lang. Pathology, Northwestern U., 1965, PhD in Communicative Disorders, 1968. Head speech and lang. pathology Northwestern U., Evanston, Ill., 1973-78, prof. speech and lang. pathology, 1975-85, chair communicative disorders, 1978-81, assoc. dean Grad. Sch., 1981-85; dean Grad. Sch. Ohio State U., Columbus, 1985-95; v.p. Ohio State U. Rsch. Found., Columbus, 1985-95. Mem. Grad. Record Exams. Bd., 1991-95, NIH adv. bd. on deafness and other communicative disorders, 1990-95; cons. evaluator Commn. on Instns. Higher Edn., 1996—. Author: Developmental Sentence Analysis, 1974; Interactive Language Development, 1975. Contbr. articles to profl. jours. Mem. adv. coun. on grad. study Ohio Bd. Regents, Columbus, 1985-95; bd. dirs. Friends of Evanston Pub. Libr., 1984, Evanston Pub. Libr., 1985. Recipient Disting. Alumni award Central Mich. U., 1977; Fulbright fellow, 1982. Fellow Am. Speech-Lang. Hearing Assn. (exec. bd. 1986-91, pres. 1990), AAU Assn. Grad. Schs.), Com. on Instnl. Cooperation Grad. Deans (chair 1985-86), Nat. Assn. State U. and Land Grant Colls.- Coun. Rsch. Pol. and Grad. Edn. (exec. com. 1995-96). Avocations: golf, skiing. Home: 720 Gatehouse Ln Columbus OH 43235-1732 Office: Ohio State U 105 Pressey Hall Columbus OH 43210-1335

KOENKER, DIANE P. history educator; b. Chgo., July 29, 1947; m. Roger Koenker; 1 child. AB in History, Grinnell Coll., 1969; AM in Comparative Studies in History, U. Mich., 1971, PhD in History, 1976. From asst. prof. to assoc. prof. in history Temple U., Phila., 1976-83; asst. prof. history U. Ill., Urbana-Champaign, 1983-86, assoc. prof., 1986-88, prof. history, 1988—, dir. Russian and East European Ctr., 1990-96, editor Slavic Rev., 1996—. Vis. lectr. history U. Ill., Urbana-Champaign, 1975; vis. fellow Australian Nat. U., 1989; Fulbright-Hays Faculty Rsch. Abroad, 1993; active Study Group on Russian Revolution, Study Group on Internat. Labor and Working-Class History; lectr. in field. Author: Moscow Workers and the 1917 Revolution, 1981, paperback edit., 1986, (with William G. Rosenberg) Strikes and Revolution in Russia 1917, 1989, editor: Tret'ya Vserossiiskaya Konferentsiya Professional'nykh Soyuzov 1917, 1982, (with William G. Rosenberg and Ronald Grigor Suny) Party, State and Society in the Russian Civil War: Explorations in Social History, 1989, (with Ronald D. Bachman) Revelations from the Russian Archives, 1997; editor, translator: (with S.A. Smith) Notes of a Red Guard, 1993; mem. editl. bd. Cambridge Soviet Paperbacks; mem. adv. bd. Soviet Studies in History, 1986-89; book reviewer to numerous jours.; contbr. articles to profl. jours. Rsch. fellow Temple U., 1977, 82, Sr. fellow Russian Inst.-Columbia U., 1977-78, Individual fellow NEH, 1983-84, Rsch. fellow NEH, 1984-85, 94-95, MUCIA Exch. fellow Moscow State U., 1991; grantee Am. Coun. Learned Socs.-Social Sci. Rsch. Coun., 1977-78, Temple U., 1979-81, 82-83, William and Flora Hewlett Internat. Rsch. grantee, 1986, 91, Nat. Coun. for Soviet and East European Rsch. grantee, 1989, IREX Travel grantee, 1993; recipient Fulbright-Hays Faculty Rsch. award for USSR, 1989, Arnold O. Beckman Rsch. Bd. award, 1990-91, 2002-. Mem. Am. Hist. Assn. (mem. membership com. 1996-98, European History sect. chair 2001), Am. Assn. Advancement Slavic Studies (bd. dirs. 1996—), Midwest Workshop of Russian and Soviet Historians, Assn. Women in Slavic Studies. Office: U Ill Slav Rev 57 E Armory Ave Champaign IL 61820-6601 also: U Ill Dept History 309 Gregory Hall 810 S Wright St Urbana IL 61801-3644

KOEP, RICHARD MICHAEL, lawyer; b. Mpls., Dec. 4, 1949; s. Clifford Michael and Mary Corrine (Narey) K.; children: Matthew, Theodore, John, Sarah. JD, William Mitchell Coll. Law, 1980. Bar: Colo. 1980, U.S. Dist. Ct. Colo. 1980, Calif. 1981, U.S. Dist. Ct. (cen. dist.) Calif. 1982. Dir. Crandall Wade & Lowe, Calabasas, Calif., 1982—. With USMC, 1968-70, Vietnam. Mem. Am. Bd. Trial Advocates, So. Calif. Defense Counsel, Ventura County Bar Assn. Roman Catholic. Office: Crandall Wade & Lowe 23901 Calabasas Rd Ste 1020 Woodland Hills CA 91302-1542

KOEPFINGER, JOSEPH LEO, retired utilities executive; b. Sewickley, Pa., May 6, 1925; s. Joseph P. and Mary M. (O'Hanlon) K.; m. Genevieve C. Strobel, Oct. 1, 1955; children: Nancy, Joseph, Margaret, Patricia, James, Paul. BSEE, U. Pitts., 1949, MSEE, 1953. Jr. devel. engr. Duquesne Light Co., Pitts., 1949-52, devel. engr., 1952-54, sr. devel. engr., 1954-57, project engr., 1957-61, sr. project engr., 1961-64, product and comml. engr., 1964-80, dir. project and comml. dept., 1980-85, dir. sys. studies and rsch., 1985-2000, ret., 2000, ind. cons., 2000—. Chmn. accredited std. com. C62, Am. Nat. Std. Inst.; bd. dirs. Mehta Tech. Inc.; U.S. tech. adv. SC 37A and 37B, Internat. Electrotech. Commn., 1979—, sec. for IEC C37, 1996—; mem. Lane dept. computer sci. and elec. engring. acad. W.Va. U. Prin. writer standard Guide for Surge Withstand Capability Test, 1974 Pres. Moon Area Sch. Dist., Moon Twp., Pa., 1978-79. With U.S. Army, 1943-45, ETO. Fellow IEEE (mem. emeritus stds. bd., Charles P. Steimetz award 1989), IEEE Power Engring. Soc. (Excellence in Power Distbn. Engring. award 1998). Democrat. Roman Catholic. Home: 119 Windy Willow Dr Coraopolis PA 15108-2945 E-mail: joseph_l_koepfinger@msn.com.

KOEPKE, JOHN ARTHUR, hematologist, clinical pathologist; b. Milw., Mar. 25, 1929; s. Elmer Paul and Meta Clara (Jennrich) K.; m. Evelyn Mae Lovekamp, June 18, 1955; children: Mary Evelyn, John Frederick, Mark David, James Robert. BA, Valparaiso U., 1951; MD, U. Wis., 1956; MS, Marquette U., 1964. Intern, resident in clin. pathology and internal medicine Milw. Hosp., 1956-60; mem. faculty U. Ky. Coll. Medicine, 1961-71, assoc. prof., 1965-71; dir. clin. pathology, prof. pathology U. Iowa, Iowa City, 1972-79, vice chmn. dept., 1972-79; prof. pathology, assoc. prof. internal medicine Coll. Medicine, Duke U., Durham, N.C., 1979-94; dir.clin. transfusion svc. hematology lab. Duke U. Med. Ctr., 1979-88, prof. emeritus, 1994—. Vis. scientist Karolinska Inst., Stockholm, 1967-68, Royal Postgrad. Med. Sch., London, 1978. Author 7 books in field; editor 6 books; bd. editors Am. Jour. Clin. Pathology, 1976—, Clin. and Lab. Hematology, 1978-94, Blood Cells, 1985-98; assoc. editor Cytometry, 1993—, Comms. in Clin. Cytometry, 1994-99, Lab. Hematology, 1994—; contbr. over 250 articles to profl. jours., 25 chpts. to books. Recipient Pres.'s award Valparaiso U., 1951, also Disting. Alumnus award, 1980 Fellow Am. Soc. Clin. Pathologists, Coll. Am. Pathologists; mem. AMA, Internat. Coun. for Standards in Hematology (secretariat 1978—, v.p. 1990-92, pres. 1992-94). Lutheran. Home: 3924 Saint Mark's Rd Durham NC 27707-5015 E-mail: nckoepke@mindspring.com.

KOEPP, DONNA PAULINE PETERSEN, librarian; b. Clinton, Iowa, Oct. 8, 1941; d. Leo August and Pauline Sena (Outzen) Petersen; m. David Ward Koepp, June 5, 1960 (div. June 1984). BS in Edn., U. Colo., 1967; MA in Libr., U. Denver, 1974; postgrad., U. Colo., 1984-85. Subject specialist govt. publs., map dept. Denver Pub. Libr., 1967-85; head govt. documents, map libr. U. Kans., Lawrence, 1985-2000, map and geomedia svcs. libr., 2000—02. Head govt. document, microforms, reference instrn. Soc. Sci. Program Harvard U., 2002-; apptd. Fed. Depository Libr. Coun. to Pub. Printer, 1998-2001. Prodn.

mgr. Meridian Jour., 1988-93, 96-99; editor: Index and Carto-Bibliography of Maps, 1789-1969, 1995. Recipient Documents to the People award Congl. Info. Svc./Govt. Documents Round Table/ALA, 1999. Mem. Map & Geography Round Table of Am. Libr. Assn. (chmn. 1986-87, Outstanding Contbn. to Map Librarianship 1991), Govt. Documents Round Table of Am. Libr. Assn., Western Assn. Map Libr. (sec. 1983-84). Office: Govt Documents Microforms Libr Lamont Libr Lower Level U Harvard College Libr Cambridge MA 02138- E-mail: koepp@fas.harvard.edu.

KOEPPE, EUGENE CHARLES, JR., electrical engineer; b. Chgo., Sept. 15, 1955; s. Eugene Charles and Lucille (Luczak) K. BSEE, Ill. Inst. Tech., 1977, MSEE, 1984. Registered profl. engr.-in-tng., Ill. R & D engr. Teletype Corp., Skokie, Ill., 1977-85; tech. staff AT&T Bell Labs., Skokie, 1985-90, Naperville, Ill., 1990-96, feature engr. svc. cir. system, 1993-94; tech. staff Lucent Field Sys. Engring. (formerly Bell Labs.), Naperville, 1996—, dept. webmaster, 1997, group webmaster, 2000—. Cert. TEMPEST engr., 1986-88; webmaster Adopt-A-School, 1998—. Mem. IEEE, NSPE, Am. Radio Relay League, Mensa, Tau Beta Pi. Achievements include patents for system and method for recording and controller on/off events of devices of a dwelling; expandable modular annunciation and intercom system. Office: Lucent Techs PO Box 3033 2000 N Naperville Rd Naperville IL 60566-7033 E-mail: centaur@mad.scientist.com.

KOEPPE, PATSY PODUSKA, internist, educator; b. Memphis, Nov. 18, 1932; d. Ben F. and Lily Mae (Reid) Poduska; m. Douglas F. Koeppe Sr., Sept. 8, 1967; 1 child, Douglas F. Jr. BA, Tex. Woman's U., 1954; MD, U. Tenn., 1957. Intern Roanoke (Va.) Meml. Hosp., 1960-61; resident in internal medicine VA Teaching Group Hosp., Memphis, 1961-62, Lahey Clinic, Boston, 1962-63; fellow in endocrinology and metabolism U. Tex. Med. Br., Galveston, 1963-65; pvt. practice Kingsville, Tex., 1972-73; dir. Women's Health Care Ctr., College Park, Md., 1974-77; instr. internal medicine and endocrinology U. Tex., Galveston, 1965-69; asst. prof. endocrinology Med. Br., U. Tex., Galveston, 1969-72, asst. prof. internal medicine, 1969-72, 78-87; assoc. prof. U. Tex., Galveston, 1987-93, prof., 1994-98; mem. grad. faculty biomed. sci. Med. Br., U. Tex., Galveston, 1988-90, acting dir. div. geriatrics, 1991-92. Hon. mem. med. staff Med. Br. U. Tex., 1998—. Mem. Am. Geriatric Soc., Tex. Med. Assn., Tex. Med. Found., Galveston County Med. Soc. Presbyterian. Home: 1101 Skyline Ridge Lookout Wimberley TX 78676-6041 E-mail: pkoeppe@pol.net.

KOEPPEL, GARY MERLE, publisher, art gallery owner, writer; b. Albany, Oreg., Jan. 20, 1938; s. Carl Melvin and Barbara Emma (Adams) K.; m. Emma Katerina Koeppel, May 20, 1984. BA, Portland State U., 1961; MFA, State U. Iowa, 1963. Writing instr. State U. Iowa, Iowa City, 1963-64; guest prof. English U. P.R., San Juan, 1964-65; assoc. prof. creative writing Portland (Oreg.) State U., 1965-68; owner, operator Coast Gallery, Big Sur, 1971—, Pebble Beach, Calif., 1986—, Maui, Hawaii, 1985—, Hana, Hawaii, 1991—, Carmel, Calif., 2003—; owner Coast Pub. Co., Coast Seri Graphics, Coast Advt., 1991—. Editor, pub. Big Sur Gazette, 1978-81; producer, sponsor Maui Marine Art Expo., 1984-95, Calif. Marine Art Expo., Paris Marine Art Expo., Hawaiian Cultural Arts Expo., 1993; founder, pres. Global Art Expos1994, Planet Big Sur, 1996, Coast Constrn., 1998; founder ideasbank.com, 1999, investmentart.com, 2001. Author: Sculptured Sandcast Candles, 1974, Henry Miller, The Paintings, 1991. Founder Big Sur Vol. Fire Brigade, 1975; chmn. coordinating com. Big Sur Area Planning, 1972-75; chmn. Big Sur Citizens Adv. Com., 1975-78. Mem. Am. Soc. Appraisers, Big Sur C. of C. (pres. 74-75, 82-84), Big Sur Grange, Phi Gamma Delta, Alpha Delta Sigma. Address: Coast Gallery PO Box 223519 Carmel CA 93922-3519 E-mail: gary@coastgalleries.com.

KOEPPEL, HARRY SAUL, interior designer, educator; b. Anniston, Ala., Feb. 6, 1942; s. Harry Saul Koeppel and Eula Jean (Griffen) Irish; m. Rita Ann Jezuit, Aug. 12, 1967; children: Brent Everett, Jill Christine. BFA, Syracuse U.; MA, SUNY New Paltz. Lic. interior designer, N.Y. Tchr. art N.Y. State Schs., 1964-73; furniture designer N.Y.C., 1972-74; interior designer, 1978-82; project mgr. N.Y. State Docs, 1983-95; interior design mgr. N.Y.C. Sch. Constrn. Authority, 1995-99. Design cons. N.Y.C., 1964—; instr. SUNY, Albany, 1972-95; profl. scouter Boy Scouts Am., 1974-78. Mem. Am. Soc. Interior Designers, Interior Design Soc. Home and Office: 501 Route 15 Elizaville NY 12523-1008

KOEPPEL, JOHN A. lawyer; b. Jersey City, Aug. 9, 1947; s. A.J. and Florence (McDonald) K.; m. Susan Lynn Rothstein, Nov. 12, 1972; children: Adam, Leah. BA in Govt. cum laude, U. Notre Dame, 1969; MA in Internat. Law, Tufts U., 1970; JD, U. Calif., San Francisco, 1976. Bar: Calif. 1976, D.C. 1980, U.S. Dist. Ct. (no. dist.) Calif. 1976, U.S. Supreme Ct. 1980. Assoc. Barfield, Barfield, Dryden & Ruane, San Francisco, 1976-80; from assoc. to shareholder Ropers, Majeski, Kohn & Bentley, San Francisco, 1980—, resident dir., 1992-95, 97-99. Arbitrator San Francisco Superior Ct., 1979—; legal counsel San Francisco Jaycees, 1980-81, Amigos de los Americas, San Francisco, 1982-84, St. Francis Homes Assn., 1987-89, treas.; instr. Hastings Coll. Advocacy, San Francisco, 1988-91; lectr. U. Calif., San Francisco, 1990-95; sec. San Francisco Casualty Claims Assn., 1993-95; bd. dirs. and legal counsel Or Shalom, 2002—; bd. dirs. Ropers Majeski Kohn & Bentley, 1992-99, 2003—. Bd. dirs. San Francisco Sch., 1998-2000, active youth sports coaching, 1990-2000. Mem. Nat. Bd. Trial Advocacy, Calif. State Bar (certificate of recognition for pro bono legal work, 1989), D.C. Bar, San Francisco Bar Assn. Avocations: running, skiing, hiking, rowing, travel. Office: Ropers Majeski Kohn & Bentley 333 Market St Ste 3150 San Francisco CA 94105-2132 E-mail: jkoeppel@ropers.com., johna1k@aol.com.

KOEPPEL, MARY SUE, communications educator; b. Phlox, Wis., Dec. 12, 1939; d. Alphonse and Emma Petronella Marx Koeppel; m. Robert B. Gentry, May 31, 1980. BA, Alverno Coll., 1962; MA, Loyola U., Chgo., 1968; postgrad., U. Wis., St. Louis U., U. N.H., U. Calif., U. North Fla., U. Minn., Jacksonville U. Tchr. St. Joseph H.S., Milw., 1962-68, Pius XI H.S., Milw., 1968-72; instr., head dept. comms., dir. learning ctr. Waukesha County Tech. Inst., Pewaukee, Wis., 1972-80; pres., exec. bd. West Suburban Coun. Tchg. Profession, 1976-80. Adv. Waukesha chpt. Parents Without Partners, 1975—80; cons. Learning Ctrs., 1976—, Coll. and Univ. Faculties; instr. comm. Fla. C.C., Jacksonville, 1980—; instr. (summers) Inst. for Tchrs. of Writing Westbrook Coll., Portland, Maine, 1980—84, instr. (summers) nat. master tchr. seminar, 1982—, TV interviewer, 1989—; instr. Nat. Inst. for Tchrs. Writing, Greenfield, Mass., 1987—94. Editor (-in-chief): Kalliope Jour. Women's Lit. and Art, 1988—, Lollipops, Lizards and Literature, 1994—; editor: Instructional Network Notes, 1982—85; co-editor: Women of Vision, 2000; author: Writing Resources for Conferencing and Collaboration, 1989, Writing Strategies Plus Collaboration, 1997, Writing Strategies Plus Collaboration. 3d edit., 2000, Write Your Life-The Memory Catcher, 1998, In the Library of Silences, Poems of Loss, 2001; contbr. ; contbg. editor: State St. Rev., 1992—. Mem. Sherman Park Cmty. Ctr., 1975—80; co-founder, bd. dirs. Instrnl. Network for coll. Faculty, 1981—85. Recipient Red Schoolhouse award for tchg. excellence, Assn. Fla. C.C., 1983, Faculty Excellence award, 2000, Frances Buck Sherman award, 2001, Educator of Yr. award, Cultural Coun. of Greater Jacksonville, 2001, Trustees award for Cmty. Svc., Fla. C.C. at Jacksonville, 2003; grantee, NDEA, 1968, Art Ventures, 1992, Tchg. and Learning Ctr., 1999; scholar, Fla. Humanities Coun., 1999. Mem.: Am. Pen Women, Nat. Coun. Tchrs. of English. Office: Kalliope 11901 Beach Blvd Jacksonville FL 32246 E-mail: skoeppel@fccj.edu.

KOEPPEL, NOEL IMMANUEL, financial planner, securities and real estate broker; b. NYC, Apr. 30, 1930; s. Eziel and Anna (Bodian) K.; divorced; children: Thomas Joseph, Elizabeth Mansfield, Roberta Sharon. BA, U. Wis., 1952; MBA, Wharton U. of Pa., 1957. CFP. V.p. E. Koeppel, Inc., Jamaica, N.Y., 1956-77; account exec. First Investors Corp., N.Y.C., 1977-79, Ross Stebbins Co., N.Y.C., 1980-82; account exec., CFP Advest Inc., Forest Hills, N.Y., 1982-83, Donald & Co. Securities Inc., Jersey City, N.J., 1983-90, Stuart Coleman Co. Inc., N.Y.C., 1990-97; account exec. Brill Sec. Inc., N.Y.C., 1998—. Lt. (j.g.) USN, 1952-56. Mem.: Fin. Planners Assn. N.Y., Inst. CFPs, Penn Club N.Y. Avocations: skiing, sailing, hiking, classical music and art. Home: 130 E End Ave New York NY 10028-7553 Office: Brill Sec Inc 152 W 57th St Fl 16 New York NY 10019-3310

KOEPPEN, RAYMOND BRADLEY, lawyer; b. Valparaiso, Ind., July 9, 1954; s. Raymond Carl August and Thelma Gleda (Moore) K.; m. Debra Gail Ray, Dec. 21, 1985. BS, Ball State U., 1976; MA, Kent (Ohio) State U., 1983; JD, Valparaiso U., 1983. Bar: Ind. 1984, Fla. 1984. Assoc. Sachs & Hess, P.C., Hammond, Ind., 1984-85, Lucas Holcomb Medrea, Merrillville, Ind., 1985; city atty. City of Valparaiso, 1985-88; ptnr. Clifford, Clauden, Alexa & Koeppen, Valparaiso, 1988-90; mng. ptnr. Douglas, Koeppen & Hurley, Valparaiso, 1991—. Mem. com. Valparaiso Popcorn Festival, 1985-97; mem. Valparaiso Econ. Devel. Corp., 1986, 87; mem. Valparaiso C. of C.; bd. dirs. Boys and Girls Club of Porter County, 1986—, chmn. bd. dirs., 1995-97. Greek Ministry of Culture and Sci. scholar, 1975; Fulbright scholar U.S. Ednl. Found., 1976. Mem. ABA, Ind. State Bar Assn., Porter County Bar Assn., Fla. Bar Assn., Phi Alpha Theta, Pi Gamma Mu, Beta Theta Pi. Presbyterian. Avocations: golf, basketball, reading, travel, community volunteering. Home: 2005 Beulah Vista Blvd Valparaiso IN 46383-2950 Office: Douglas Koeppen et al PO Box 209 14 Indiana Ave Valparaiso IN 46383-5634

KOEPSEL, WELLINGTON WESLEY, electrical engineering educator; b. McQueeney, Tex., Dec. 5, 1921; s. Wesley Wellington and Hulda (Nagel) K.; m. Dorothy Helen Adams, June 25, 1950; children: Kirsten Marta, Gretchen Lisa, Wellington Lief. BS in Elec. Engring., U. Tex., 1944, MS, 1951; PhD, Okla. State U., 1960. Engr. City Pub. Service Bd., San Antonio, 1946-47; research sci. Mil. Physics Research Lab., U. Tex., 1948-51; research engr. North Am. Aviation, Downey, Calif., 1951; asst. prof. So. Methodist U., 1951-59; assoc. prof. U. N.Mex., Albuquerque, 1960-63, Duke U., 1963-64; prof., head dept. elec. engring. Kans. State U., Manhattan, 1964-76, prof. elec. engring., 1976-84, prof. emeritus, 1984—; pres., owner, chief engr. Mutronic Systems, Austin, Tex. Contbr. articles profl. jours. Served from ensign to lt. (j.g.) USNR, 1944-46. Mem. IEEE (sr.), Sigma Xi, Eta Kappa Nu. Achievements include research on microcomputer simulation and modeling of electromagnetic (microwave) sensor systems; digital signal processing; development of R.F. wireless data transmission and computer software for systems simulation. Address: PO Box 26806 Austin TX 78755-0806 E-mail: wkoepsel@ieee.org..

KOEPSELL, PAMELA ANN, nursing educator; b. Brookings, S.D., Nov. 9, 1950; d. Paul Loel and Delores Lillian (Johnson) K. Diploma, Sioux Valley Hosp., Sioux Falls, S.D., 1981; BSN, S.D. State U., 1989, MS, 1999. Nursing case mgr. Midwestern Home Health Care Sioux Valley Hosp., Sioux Falls, 1988-91, charge nurse, 1982-87, neonatal flight nurse, 1982-93, primary nurse, 1986-93; clin. care coord., 1987—2001. Adj. instr. S.D. State U., 1999—2001, edn. tng. specialist, 2001—. Mem.: PEO, Sioux Valley Hosp. Nurses Alumni Assn. (2d v.p. 1985—86, 1st v.p. 1990—91, 1999—2000, pres. 2001—03), S.D. Perinatal Assn. (pres. 2001), Nat. Assn. Neonatal Nurses, Phi Kappa Phi, Sigma Theta Tau. Presbyterian. Avocations: collecting precious moments, sewing, counted cross-stitch. Home: 909 S Lowell Ave Sioux Falls SD 57103-2347 Office: Sioux Valley Hosp 1100 S Euclid Ave Sioux Falls SD 57105-0496 E-mail: koepselp@siouxvalley.org., pakoepsell@aol.com.

KOERBER, DOLORES JEAN, music educator, musician; b. Martins Ferry, Ohio, Apr. 7, 1936; d. Clarence Donald and Bertha Gail (Palmer) K. B in Religious Edn., Malone Coll., 1958, BS, 1965; MEd, Kent State U., 1972; D in Religious Edn., Massillon Baptist Coll., 2000. Cert. tchr. music grades K-12, Ohio. Tchr. Coun. Religious Edn., North Canton, Ohio, 1958-60, Shelby, Ohio, 1960-62, Garaway Local, Sugarcreek, Ohio, 1965-71, Fairless Local, Justus, Ohio, 1971-73, Massillon (Ohio) Christian Sch., 1973-75; prof. Massillon Bapt. Coll., 1973—. Choir dir. Evang. United Brethren Ch., Sugarcreek, 1965-68, Westminster Presbyn., Canton, 1973-75, organist, 1981-85, Christ United Meth., Louisville, Ohio, 1985-92, St. Paul's United Meth., Canton, 1993—. Performer in programs for schs., clubs and chs. Named first native Cantonian to graduate from Malone Coll. after its relocation in Canton, 1958. Mem. Fortnightly Music Club (pres. 1970-71), MacDowell Club (rec. sec. 2001-03, 1st v.p. 2003—), Am. Guild Organists. Republican. Avocations: doll collecting, handwork, swimming.

KOERBER, JOAN C. retired educator; b. Newark, Mar. 23, 1929; d. George Vincent and Catherine Rose (Donahue) Callanan; m. John Calvin Koerber, June 27, 1953; children: John C., Joanne C. BS in Elem. Edn., Newark State Coll., 1952; MA in Adminstrn., Kean Coll., Union, N.J., 1984. Tchr. 15th Ave Sch., Newark, 1952-71, Lincoln Sch., Newark, 1971-78, tchr. Chpt. I, 1978-79, coord. Chpt. I, 1979-84, basic skills tchr., 1984-95, ret., 1995. Summer sch. coord. Lincoln Sch., 1979-84; past pres. Kean Coll. Grad. Sch. Coun. Sec. Essex County PTA; rec. sec., dir. Crandon Lakes Country Club Inc. Property Owners Assn.; lector and eucharist minister Our Lady of Mt. Carmel Ch., Swartswood, N.J. Mem. ASCD, AAUW, PTA (hon. life), NEA, N.J. Edn. Assn., Essex County Edn. Assn., Newark Edn. Assn., Newark Tchrs. Union, N.J. State Columbiettes (supreme bd. dirs., past state pres.), Kappa Delta Phi (past pres.), Phi Delta Kappa (past pres.). Home: 17 N Bayberry Rd Newton NJ 07860-6570

KOERBER, MARILYNN ELEANOR, gerontology nursing educator, consultant, nurse; b. Covington, Ky., Feb. 1, 1942; d. Harold Clyde and Vivian Eleanor (Conrad) Hilge; m. James Paul Koerber, May 29, 1971. Diploma, Christ Hosp. Sch. Nursing, Cin., 1964; BSN, U. Ky., 1967; MPH, U. Mich., 1970. RN, Ohio, S.C.; cert. gerontologist. Staff nurse premature and newborn nursery Cin. Gen. Hosp., 1964-65; staff nurse, hosp. discharge planner Vis. Nurse Assn., Cin., 1967-69, asst. dir. Atlanta, 1976-78; instr. Coll. Nursing, U. Ky., Lexington, 1970-71; supr. Montgomery County Health Dept., Rockville, Md., 1971-74; asst. prof. Coll. Nursing, U. S.C., Columbia, 1979-86, instr., 1987-89; alzheimer's project coord. S.C. Commn. on Aging, Columbia, 1988-90; dir. edn. and tng. Luth. Homes S.C., White Rock, 1988-91; grad. asst. U. S.C. Sch. of Pub. Health, 1991-94; trainer for homemakers home health aides S.C. Divsn. on Aging, 1991-97; coord. to train homemakers home aides nursing assts. State Pilot Program, DSS and Divsn. on Aging, 1993-95; Alzheimer's trainer office aging, nurse mgr. Beaufort-Jasper Hampton Comprehensive Health, 1998—; allied health program mgr. Tech. Coll. of the Lowcountry, 1997—. Mem. utilization rev. bd. Palmetto Health Dist., Lexington, 1984-2000; test item writer, nurse aide cert. Psychol. Corp., San Antonio, 1989, 91, 92; bd. examiners Nursing Home Adminstrn. and Community Residential Care Facility Adminstr., chmn. of edn. com., Columbia, S.C., 1990-93; presenter gerontol. workshops and residential care facilities adminstrn. Contbg. editor: (handbook) Promoting Caregiver Groups, 1984; reviewer gerontology textbooks, 1983-91; contbr. tng. video and manuals on Alzheimers, 1988 (hon. mention Retirement Rsch. Found. 1989). Del. S.C. Gov. White House Conf. on Aging, Columbia, 1981; chmn. ann. meeting S.C. Fedn. for Older Ams., Columbia, 1989—91; v.p. Alzheimer's Family Services of Greater Beaufort, 1998—99, mem. adv. bd., 2002—; bd. dirs. Sr. Svcs. of Beaufort County, 1997—2002, Alzheimer's Family Services of Greater Beaufort, 1997—2002. USPHS trainee, 1965-67, Adm. on Aging trainee, 1969-70. Mem. ANA (cert. gerontol. nurse, cmty. health nurse), S.C. Nurses Assn., So. Gerontol. Soc., Gerontol. Soc. Am., S.C. Gerontol. Soc. (treas. 1989-91, Rosamond R. Boyd award 1986, Pres. award Mid State Alzheimers Chpt., 1993, Macy Scally Alzheimers award 2000), Soc. for Pub. Health Edn., Am. Soc. on Aging, Alzheimers Assn. (bd. dirs. Columbia chpt. 1988-93, sec. 1992, chmn. nominating com. 1991-92; bd. dirs. S.C. combined health appeal 1991-93), Nat. Coun. on Aging, Nat. Gerontol. Nursing Assn. Democrat. Unitarian Universalist. Avocations: interior decorating, wine tasting.

KOERNER, JO ELLEN, health facility administrator; b. Sioux Falls, S.D., Aug. 13, 1946; d. Reuben and Florence Carolyn (Gering) Goertz; m. Dennis J. Koerner, Feb. 17, 1967; children: Kristi Jo, Christopher John. Diploma, Sioux Valley Hosp. Sch. Nursing, Sioux Falls, 1967; BS, Mt. Marty Coll., 1980; MS, S.D. State U., 1982; PhD, Fielding Inst., 1993. RN, S.D. Nurse mgr. Sioux Valley Hosp., Sioux Falls, 1968-70; physicians asst. Rural Med. Clinics, Freeman, S.D., 1973-75; dir. nursing dept. Freeman Jr. Coll., 1975-82; exec. sec. S.D. Bd. of Nursing, Sioux Falls, 1982-84; v.p. patient svcs. Sioux Valley Hosp., Sioux Falls, 1984-98; sr. cons. Creative Health Care Mgmt., Mpls., 1998—99; pres. Global Nursing Acad., Boulder, Colo., 1998—2001; chief clin. officer Simulis, LLC, Houston, 2001—. Preceptor U. Minn., Mpls., 1985—; cons., New Zealand, Czechoslovakia, Germany, Australia, England; mem. PEW Health Professions Commn.; faculty Ctr. for Nursing Leadership and Inst. Health Care Execs. Co-author: for F.A. Davis Book Co., 1983, 94, 98; mem. editl. bd. Jour. Nursing Adminstrn., Nursing Outlook, Jour. Profl. Nursing, Nursing Adminstrn. Quarterly; editor book in field, 1994; contbr. articles to profl. jours. Task force mem. Nat. Commn. on Nursing, 1987—; v.p. S.D. Bd. Nursing, Sioux Falls, 1980-82; nursing rep. Gov.'s Task Force; treas., bd. dirs. Family Svcs., Sioux Falls, 1987—; mem. S.D. Women's Advocacy Network, Sioux Falls, 1985—; sec., bd. dirs. Freeman Hosp., 1980-86; chair Robert Wood Johnson nat. adv. bd. Colleagues in Caring, 1996—. Named S.D. Woman of Yr., Am. Adv. Bd., 1980; Top 10 Businesswoman of S.D., 1994; recipient Golden Heart award, 1985, Profl. Leader of Yr. award YWCA, 1992, Disting. Alumnni award profl. divsn. S.D. State U., 1993; fellow U. Pa. Wharton Sch., 1986. Fellow Am. Acad. Nursing; mem. S.D. Nurses Assn. (bd. dirs. 1985-87, Pres.'s award 1987), S.D. Orgn. Nurse Execs. (nat. bd. dirs. 1991, coun. rep. 1985—), Sioux Falls C. of C. (bd. dirs., treas. 1993), Profl. and Bus. Women's Assn., Am. Orgn. Nurse Execs. (pres. 1997-98), Dorcas Soc., Phi Kappa Gamma, Sigma Theta Tau (disting. lectr. award). Republican. Avocations: organ playing, weaving, reading. Office: Simulis LLC 10000 Memorial Dr Ste 250 Houston TX 77024 E-mail: jkoerner@virtualorg.com.

KOERNER, JOSHUA DAVID, foundation administrator; s. Howard and Naomi Koerner. BA, SUNY, Purchase, 1990. Exec. dir. CHOICE of New Rochelle, Inc., NY, 1996—. Freelance photographer. Contbr. Mem. NYAPRS, Albany, NY, 1998—2003. Recipient Art Lewis Award for Exemplary Achievement in Rehab. and Recovery, 2001. Mem.: Phi Theta Kappa. Taoist.

KOERNIG, STEPHEN K. marketing professional, educator; s. Sharon Beck and Neil Koernig; m. Lynn Marie Gross, Apr. 21, 2002. BS, U. Ill., 1989, PhD, 2000; MBA, DePaul U., Chgo., 1994. Assoc. prof. Calif. State U., Fullerton, 1999—2002; asst. prof. DePaul U., Chgo., 2002—. Author: (academic rsch.) Psychology & Mktg., Quar. Jour. of Electronic Commerce. Recipient Doctoral Consortium Fellow, Am. Mktg. Assn., 1997. Mem.: Mktg. Educators Assn., Acad. of Mktg. Sci., Am. Mktg. Assn. Office: DePaul Univ Ste 7500 1E Jackson St Chicago IL 60604 E-mail: skoernig@fullerton.edu.

KOESSEL, DONALD RAY, retired banker; b. Grand Rapids, Mich., May 15, 1929; s. Fred Christian and Erna Wilhelmina (Grein) K.; m. Jeannine C. Koessel; children: Martin, Kathryn. BA, Yale U., 1951; MBA, Harvard U., 1955. Copywriter Grand Rapids Press, 1951-52; public relations rep. Smith Kline & French Labs., 1952-53; money market analyst Nat. Shawmut Bank of Boston, 1955-58; asst. sec. 1st Bank System, Mpls., 1958-62, asst. v.p., 1962-63; with 1st Nat. Bank Mpls., 1963-85, exec. v.p., 1975-85, chmn. trust com., 1979-85. Home: 18064 N Somerset Dr Surprise AZ 85374-6446

KOESTEL, MARK ALFRED, geologist, photographer; b. Cleve., Jan. 1, 1951; s. Alfred and Lucille (Kemeny) Koestel; life ptnr. Jennifer E. Budzak; children: Jennifer Rose, Bonnie Leigh. BS, U. Ariz., 1978. Registered profl. geologist Wyo., Alaska, Ind.; registered environ. assessor, Calif. Sr. geologist Union Oil Co. of Calif., Tucson and Denver, 1978-86; mgr. geology Harmsworth Assocs., Laguna Hills, Calif., 1986-88; sr. project mgr. Applied GeoSystems, Irvine, Calif., 1988-90; cons. geologist, photographer Adventures in Geology/Outdoor Images, Chino, Calif., 1990—. Contbr. articles and photographs to profl. jours. and mags. N.Mex. state rep. Minerals Exploration Coalition, Tucson and Denver, 1982. Sci. Found. scholarship No. Ariz. U., 1969, Acad. Achievement scholarship, 1970, Disting. Scholastic Achievement scholarship, 1971. Mem. Am. Inst. of Profl. Geologists (cert.), Soc. of Mining Engrs., Aircraft Owners and Pilots Assn., Geol. Soc. of Am., Nat. Geographic Soc. Avocations: woodworking, sporting clays, backpacking, travel, scuba. Home and Office: 13214 Breton Ave Chino CA 91710-5952 Home Fax: 501-325-5851. E-mail: outdoorimages@post.com.

KOESTENBAUM, WAYNE, English educator, author; b. San Jose, Calif., Sept. 20, 1958; BA, Harvard U., 1980; MA, Johns Hopkins U., 1981; PhD, Princeton U., 1988. Assoc. prof. English, Yale U., New Haven, 1988-96; prof. English, CUNY Grad. Ctr., N.Y.C., 1997—. Author: Double Talk, 1989, Ode to Anna Moffo and Other Poems, 1990, The Queen's Throat, 1993, Rhapsodies of a Repeat Offender, 1994, Jackie Under My Skin, 1995, The Milk of Inquiry, 1999, Cleavage, 2000, Andy Warhol, 2001. Recipient Writer's award Whiting Found., N.Y.C., 1994. E-mail: wkoestenbaum@aol.com.

KOESTER, BERTHOLD KARL, lawyer, law educator, retired honorary German consul; b. Aachen, Germany, June 30, 1931; s. Wilhelm P. and Margarethe A. (Witteler) K.; m. Hildegard Maria (Buettner), June 30, 1961; children: Georg W., Wolfgang J., and Reinhard B. Doctor of Laws, U. Muenster, Fed. Republic Germany, 1957. Cert.in Real Estate Brokerage, Ariz. Asst. prof. civil and internat. law U. Muenster, Germany, 1957-60; v.p. Bank J. H. Vogeler and Co., Duesseldorf, Germany, 1960-64; atty. Ct. of Duesseldorf, Germany, 1960-82; pres. Bremer Tank-u, Kuehlschiffahrtsges, M.B.H., Germany, 1964-72; prof., internat. bus. law Am. Grad. Sch. Internat. Mgmt., Glendale, Ariz., 1978-81; of counsel Tancer Law Offices, Phoenix, 1978—86; chmn., CEO Arimpex, Inc., Phoenix, 1979—; ptnr. Applewhite, Laflin, and Lewis, Real Estate Investments, Scottsdale, Ariz., 1981-88; atty., trustee internat. corp. Duesseldorf, Germany and Phoenix, 1983—; chief exec. officer, chmn. bd. German Consultants in Real Estate Investments, Phoenix, 1988—; prof., internat. bus. law, chmn. dept. Western Internat. U., Phoenix, 1996—. Bd. dirs. Ariz. Partnership for Air Transp., 1988-92; chmn. Finvest Corp., Phoenix, 1990—; hon. German cons. for Ariz., 1982-92. Author: The Refinancing of the Banking System, 1963, Long Term Finance, 1968, International Joint Ventures, 1974, History and Economy of the Middle East, 1975, Bauhaus and the Expresssionism, 1983; contbr. articles to profl. jour. Pres. Parents Assn., Humboldt Gymnasium, Duesseldorf, Germany, 1971-78; active German Red Cross, from 1977. Mem. Duesseldorf Chamber of Lawyers, Bochum, Fed. Republic Germany, Assn. Tax Lawyers, Bonn German-Saudi Arabian Assn. (pres. 1976-79), Bonn German-Korean Assn., Assn. for German-Korean Econ. Devel. (pres. 1974-78), Ariz. Consular Corp. (sec., treas. 1988-89), Nat. Soc. Arts and Letters (Greater Ariz. chpt., bd. dirs. 1997—), German-Am. C. of C., Phoenix Met., C. of C., Rotary, Scottsdale, Ariz. Home: 6201 E Cactus Rd Scottsdale AZ 85254-4409 Office: PO Box 15674 Phoenix AZ 85060-5674

KOESTER, FREDERICK H. aviation systems engineer; b. Mt. Vernon, N.Y., Aug. 28, 1932; s. Frederick H. and Frances A. (Moore) K.; m. Eileen R. Bobb, Dec. 30, 1961; children: Robert J., John M., Thomas E. BS in Naval Sci., US Naval Acad., 1955; BSEE, Naval Postgrad. Sch., Monterey, Calif., 1962; MS in Adminstrn., Systems Mgmt., George Washington U., 1967. Commd. ensign USN, 1955, advanced through grades to lt. comdr., ret., 1975; sr. engr. Booz-Allen & Hamilton, Bethesda, Md., 1975-79, ManTech Internat., Washington, 1979-82, Raytheon Svc. Co., Washington, 1982-84, 86-90; task mgr., sr. engr. Quest Rsch. Corp., McLean, Va., 1984-86; sr. systems engr. MiTech Inc., Rockville, Md., 1990-93; knowledge strategist, systems engr. Titan Systems Corp., Washington, 1993—. Editor: Digital Symposium Proceedings, 1966; contbr. articles to profl. jours. Mem. Soc. Competitive Intelligence Profls. Republican. Roman Catholic. Avocations: golf, investing, history. Home: 7601 Gaylord Dr Annandale VA 22003 Office: 1500 K St NW Washington DC 20005

KOESTER, HELMUT HEINRICH, theologian, educator; b. Hamburg, Germany, Dec. 18, 1926; came to U.S., 1958; s. Karl and Marie-Luise (Eitz) K.; m. Gisela G. Harrassowitz, July 8, 1953; children: Reinhild, Almut, Ulrich, Heiko. Dr. theol., U. Marburg, Germany, 1954; Privatdozent, U. Heidelberg, Germany, 1956; Dr. theol. (hon.), U. Geneva. Ordained to ministry Luth. Ch., 1956; asst. pastor Hannover, Germany, 1951-54; teaching asst., then asst. prof. U. Heidelberg, 1954-56, 56-58, 59; mem. faculty Harvard U. Div. Sch., 1958-98, John H. Morison prof. N.T. studies, 1964-98, Winn prof. ecclesiastical history, 1968-98, rsch. prof., 2000—. Vis. prof. U. Heidelberg, 1963, Drew U., 1966, U. Minn., 1990, Free U. Amsterdam, 1992, Boston U., 2000, Williams Coll., 2001. Author: Synoptische Ueberlieferung bei den Apostolischen Vaetern, in Texte und Untersuchungen, 1957, (with James M. Robinson) Trajectories through Early Christianity, 1971, Einfuehrung in das Neue Testament, 1979, Introduction to the New Testament, 1982, Ancient Christian Gospels, 1990, (with Francois Bovon) Genèse de l'écriture chrètienne, 1991, History, Religion and Culture of the Hellenistic Age, 1995, History and Literature of Early Christianity, 2000; editor Harvard Theol. Rev., 1975-99, Hermeneia, Archaeol. Resources for New Testament Studies. Asso. trustee Am. Schs. Oriental Research, 1974-75; trustee William F. Albright Inst. Archaeol. Research, 1974-80. Served with German Navy, 1944-45. Guggenheim fellow, 1964-65; Am. Coun. Learned Socs. fellow, 1971-72, 78-79. Fellow Am. Acad. Arts and Scis.; mem. Soc. Bibl. Lit. (pres. 1990-91), Soc. Novi Testamenti Studiorum. Home: 12 Flintlock Rd Lexington MA 02420-1704 Office: 45 Francis Ave Cambridge MA 02138-1911 E-mail: helmut_koester@harvard.edu.

KOESTER, ROBERT JAMES, publishing executive, educational consultant; b. Pomona, CA, Dec. 31, 1962; s. Frederick Henry and Eileen Rose Koester; m. Emily V. Koester, May 11, 2003. BA, U of VA, Charlottesville, VA, 1985, MS, 1989. Cert. EMT-C VA, 1999. Tchr. asst. U of VA, Charlottesville, Va., 1985—88; tech. instr. VA Dept. of Emergency Mgmt., Richmond, Va., 1988—; pres. dbs Productions, Charlottesville, Va., 1989—; faculty Piedmont Va. Comm. Coll., Charlottesville, Va., 1990—92; sr. lab. spec. U of VA, Charlottesville, Va., 1992—95; spec. considerations liaison Fed. Emergency Mgmt. Agy., Phila., 1999—. Author: (jour. article) Wilderness and Environmental Medicine, 1995, Lost Alzheimer's Disease Search Mgmt., 1999, Man-Trackers & Doghandlers in SAR, 2000. Mem. Gov. Task Force/ Emergency Response to Disasters, Richmond, Va., 1988—89; pres. VA Search & Rescue Coun., Richmond, Va., 1993—; bd. of dir. Appalachian Search & Rescue Conf., Charlottesville, Va., 1985—; mem. Charlottesville Albemarle Rescue Squad, Charlottesville, Va., 1996—. Recipient Kepner, U of VA, 1988, Svc., VA Dept. Emergency Mgmt., 2001; grantee Alzheimer's Grant Award, VA Ctr. for Aging, 1996. Mem.: Blue Ridge Mountain Rescue Group Dir. (assoc.), Alzheimer's Assoc. (assoc.), Wilderness Med. Soc. (assoc.). Catholic. Achievements include first to Develop. behavioral profile for lost Alzheimer's disease subjects. Avocations: running, hiking, camping. Home: 2508-A Fontaine Ave Charlottesville VA 22903-2958 Office: dbs Productions PO Box 1894 Charlottesville VA 22903

KOFF, FRED WILLIAM, retired research chemist; b. Haapsalu, Estonia, July 21, 1922; s. Fritz and Matilde (Lindström) K.; m. Annemarie Fehmel, June 13, 1947 (div. Apr. 1989). Degree in marine navigation, Merchant Marine Acad., Tallinn, Estonia, 1944. Rsch. chemist Chem. Rsch. Ctr. Allied Chem. Corp., Morristown, N.J., 1959-84. Contbr. articles to profl. jours. including Hydrometallurgy, Jour. Am. Chem. Soc.; patentee in field. Freedom fighter against Russian encroachment into the affairs of the Baltic States, Ctrl. and East European Coalition in U.S., N.Y.C., 1994—. Lutheran. Avocations: sailing, classical music. Home: 19804 Rhea See Dr Lutz FL 33548-4281

KOFF, HOWARD MICHAEL, lawyer; b. Bklyn., July 25, 1941; s. Arthur and Blanche Koff; m. Linda Sue Bright, Sept. 10, 1966; 1 son, Michael Arthur Bright. BS, NYU, 1962; JD, Bklyn. Law Sch., 1965; LLM in Taxation, Georgetown U., 1968. Bar: N.Y. 1965, D.C. 1966, U.S. Supreme Ct. 1969, U.S. Ct. Appeals (2d, 3d, 4th, 5th, 7th, 9th and D.C. cirs.), U.S. Dist. Ct. (no. dist.) N.Y. 1981. Appellate atty. tax divsn. U.S. Dept. Justice, Washington, 1965-69; tax supr. Chrysler Corp., Detroit, 1969-70; chief tax counsel Conn. Gen. Life Ins. Co., Hartford, Conn., 1970-77, Rohm & Haas Co., Phila., 1977-78; ptnr. Dibble, Koff, Lane, Stern and Stern, Rochester, 1978—81; pres. Howard M. Koff, P.C., Albany, N.Y., 1981—. Lectr. tax matters. Editor-in-chief Bklyn. Law Rev., 1964-65; charter mem. editl. adv. bd. Jour. Real Estate Taxation; contbr. articles to legal jours. Chmn. pub. adv. coun. N.Y. State Ethics Commn. Recipient Founders Day award NYU, 1962, Lawyers Coop. award for gen. excellence Lawyers Coop. Pub. Co., 1965. Mem. ABA (past chmn. subcom. on partnerships tax sect.), FBA (past pres. Hartford County chpt.), Albany County Bar Assn., Estate Planning Coun. Ea. N.Y., Albany Area C. of C., Rotary, Colonie Guilderland N.Y. Club. Republican. Home: 205 W Bentwood Ct Albany NY 12203-4905 Office: 600 Broadway Albany NY 12207-2205

KOFF, ROBERT HESS, academic administrator; b. Chgo., June 5, 1938; s. Arthur Karl and Dorothy (Hess) K. BA, U. Mich., 1961; MA, U. Chgo., 1962, PhD, 1966. Lic. psychologist, Calif. Instr., counselor S. Shankman Orthogenic Sch. U. Chgo., 1961—64; tchr. U. Chgo. Lab. Sch., 1963—64; instr. U. Ill., Champaign, 1964, U. Chgo., 1964—66; vis. scientist, Lab. for Hypnosis Rsch., asst. prof. Stanford U., Calif., 1966—72; prof., dean Roosevelt U., Chgo., 1972—79; univ. dean SUNY, Albany, 1979—92; program dir., sr. v.p. Danforth Found., St. Louis, 1992—2003; prof. and dir. edn. skills initiative Washington U., St. Louis, 2003—. Vis. scholar Oxford U., Eng., 1965; chmn. N.Y. State Ednl. Conf. Bd., Albany, 1981-92. Mem. Nat. Adv. Coun. on Edn. of Disadvantaged Children, Washington, 1979-82, Gov.'s Adv. Commn. on Children and Youth, Albany, 1981-92. Mem. APA (com. chmn.), Am. Ednl. Rsch. Assn., Nat. Register Health Svc. Providers in Psychology. Home: 48 Kingsbury Pl Saint Louis MO 63112

KOFF, SHIRLEY IRENE, writer; b. Oakland, Calif., Aug. 31, 1948; d. Lawrence Ray and Stella Pauline (Durham) Butler; m. Robert Allen Koff, June 12, 1971; children: Jennifer, Katherine. BA, Calif. State U., 1971, MA, 1972. Adj. prof. Pellissippi State U., Knoxville, 1989-93; asst. mgr. Adolfo II, Pigeon Forge, Tenn., 1994-98. Poet, writer; tchr. adult religious edn. classes and seminars; expert info. provider internet resource AskAnything.com. Tchr., lay min., bd. dirs. First Assembly of God Ch., Sevierville, 1996-99; core group leader, founding mem. Wellspring Congregation, United Meth. Ch., 1999-2001. Mem.: AAUW, Knoxville (Tenn.) Writers Guild, Tenn. Writers Alliance, Appalachian Writers Assn., Mensa. Democrat. Avocations: writing, speaking, teaching. Home: 1214 Amber Ln Sevierville TN 37862-6101 E-mail: skoff@ix.netcom.com.

KOFFEL, MARTIN M. engineering company executive; b. 1939; MS, MBA, Stanford U., 1971. With Homestake Mining Co., 1974-81, Cooper Labs., Inc., 1981-84, Gilette Corp., 1984-86, Cooper Vision Inc., 1986-88; chmn. bd., pres., CEO URS Corp., San Francisco, 1989—. Adv. coun. McLaren Sch. Bus., U. San Francisco; trustee Am. Enterprise Inst. Pub. Policy, Washington; bd. dirs. James Hardie Industries NV. Office: URS Corp 600 Montgomery St 25th Fl San Francisco CA 94111-2727

KOFFLER, STEPHEN ALEXANDER, investment banker; b. Providence, R.I., Sept. 22, 1942; s. Irving I. and Jessie Lillian (Seltzer) K.; m. Enid Freya Mellion, June 15, 1963; children: Samara Rachel, Debra Lyn. BMetE, Rensselaer Poly. Inst., 1964, MS, 1967, PhD, 1968. Security analyst Auerbach Pollak & Richardson, N.Y.C., 1968-70; asst. v.p. investment banking A.G. Becker, Inc., N.Y.C., 1970-72; v.p., treas. Mattel, Inc., Hawthorne, Calif., 1972-74; sr. v.p., chief fin. officer Audio Magnetics, Inc., Gardena, Calif., 1974-75; cons. Koffler & Co., L.A., 1975-81; mng. dir. Becker Paribas, Inc., L.A., 1981-84, Merrill Lynch, L.A., 1984-91; exec. v.p., dir. investment banking divsn. Sutro and Co., Inc., L.A., 1991-94; mng. dir. Smith Barney Inc., L.A., 1994-96; pres. Koffler & Company, L.A., 1996—. Bd. dirs. Sandel Med. Industries, St. John's Health Ctr. Bd. dirs. L.A. Music Ctr. Opera, 1989—96. Mem. Am. Soc. for Metals, Nat. Assn. Securities Dealers Inc. (mem. corp. fin. com. 1994-95), Riviera Tennis Club, Regency Club, Teton Pines Country Club, Brentwood Country Club. Avocations: tennis, golf, hiking, opera. Office: Koffler & Co 11755 Wilshire Blvd Ste 2370 Los Angeles CA 90025-1569 E-mail: skoffler@kofflerco.com.

KOFFLER, WARREN WILLIAM, lawyer; b. N.Y.C., July 21, 1938; s. Jack and Rose (Conovich) K.; m. Barbara Rose Holz, June 11, 1959; m. Jayne Audri Goetzel, May 15, 1970; children: Kevin, Kenneth, Caroline. BS, Boston U., 1959; JD, U. Calif., Berkeley, 1962; LLD, NYU, 1972. Bar: D.C. 1962, N.Y. 1963, U.S. Dist. Ct. D.C. 1963, Fla. 1980, Va. 1981, Pa. 1982. Atty. FAA, Washington, 1964; pvt. practice law Washington, 1964, 78—, Hollywood, Palm Beach, Miami, Fla., 1978—; atty. Fed. Home Loan Bank Bd., Washington, 1964-66; ptnr. Koffler & Spivack, Washington, 1967-77. Mem. ATLA, ABA, FBA, Inter-Am. Bar Assn., D.C. Bar Assn., Fla. Bar Assn., Va. Bar Assn., Brit. Inst. Internat. and Comparative Law, Univ. Club (Washington), Bankers Club (Miami), Membership Club PGA Nat. (Palm Beach), City Club (Palm Beach), Circumnavigator's Club (N.Y./Palm Beach). Office: 4521 PGA Blvd Ste 361 West Palm Beach FL 33418 also: 1730 K St NW Washington DC 20006-3868 E-mail: wwkvip@msn.com.

KOFFMAN, MARTHA ALICE, communications and training executive, ergonomist; b. Boston; m. Philip J. Koffman, Apr. 26, 2002. BA, Clark U., 1981; MA, Columbia U., 1984. Cert. prof. ergonomist. Human factors engr. AT&T, Piscataway, N.J., 1984-87; mgr. govt. svcs. Dynamics Rsch. Corp., Andover, Mass., 1987—. Office: Dynamics Rsch Corp PO Box 93253 Phoenix AZ 85070

KOFINK, WAYNE ALAN, minister; b. Chgo., Apr. 21, 1949; s. Lawrence Howard and Catherine Elizabeth (Szlavik) K. MusB, Roosevelt U., 1971; MDiv, Luth. Sch. Theology, Chgo., 1976; BA in Philosophy, Fla. Internat. U., 1981, MS Adult Edn., 1985, EdD, 1991; postgrad., Westminster Choir Coll., 1982, St. Thomas U., 1984-85. Ordained to ministry Evang. Luth. Ch. in Am., 1977. Choir dir. Ascension Luth. Ch., Chgo., 1971-73; pastor Messiah Evang. Luth. Ch., Miami, Fla., 1977-98; lectr. religious studies Fla. Internat. U., Miami, 1986-98; interim pastor St. Thomas Luth. Ch., Miami, 1993; pastor Our Saviour Luth. Ch., Ocala, Fla., 1998—. Sec., v.p. Luth. Campus Ministry of Dade County, Miami, 1979-85; mem. Fla. Synod Worship Consultation, Tampa, 1988-2002; trustee Guardian Shepherd Luth. Sch., Coral Gables, Fla., 1990-98; adj. South Fla. Ctr. for Theol. Studies, Miami, 1995-98 ; chair Dade-Monroe conf. Evangelical Luth. Ch. Am., 1996-98; instr. Leadership Program for Musicians, 2000-02, Luther Hostel. Editor (newsletter) Doxology, 1986-87; contbr. articles to profl. jours. Mem. adv. com. Miami-Coral Pk. Adult Edn. Ctr., 1988-93; mem. Marion Oaks Civic Assn. Mem. Soc. Bibl. Lit., Liturgical Conf., Spiritual Dirs. Internat., Am. Soc. Ch. History, Greater Ocala Ministerial Assn. Home: 2901 SW 41st St Apt 2702 Ocala FL 34474-6207 Office: Our Saviour Luth Ch 260 Marion Oaks Ln Ocala FL 34473-2812 *God gives every person the ability to make a positive contribution to life. The difference our particular gifts and opportunities allow us to make may seem insignificant in a world needing radical transformation, but we must do what is in our power. Success isn't determined by the size of the results, but by loving faithfulness.*

KOFMAN, MIKHAIL, economist, engineering executive; b. Nikolaev, Ukraine, Oct. 14, 1961; s. Efim and Tatiana K.; m. Anna Barybina, Ju. 4, 1982; children: Julia, Yuri. Degree in Econs./Electronics, Nikolaev (Ukraine) C.C., 1981; BS in Econs., BSc Electronics/Digital Satellite Sys., Ukrainian State Maritime Tech., Nikolaev, 1990. Mgr., gen. mgr. Chernomorsky Shipbuilding Yard, Nikolaev, 1983-88; pres. Astra Inc., Nikolaev, 1988-94; prin., owner New EVE, Corp., Springfield, Mass., 1994-96; pres. Elithan United, Inc., Springfield, Mass., 1996-97; CEO 9 Net Ave, Inc., Fort Lee, N.J., 1997-99; dir. engrng. Concentric Network Corp., San Jose, Calif., 1999-2000; owner, founder, CEO, 3WCorp, Inc., Fort Lee, N.J., 2000—, Data Peer Inc., Fort Lee, 2000—. With USSR Army, Ukraine. Office: DataPeer Inc 2115 Linwood Ave 5th Fl Fort Lee NJ 07024 E-mail: mkofman@mkofman.com.

KOFORD, KENNETH JOHN, economics educator; b. Hollywood, Calif., Dec. 30, 1948; s. Kenneth Harold and Theresa Amelia (Sutton) K.; m. Blagovesta Dimitrova. BA, Yale U., 1970; MA, UCLA, 1973, PhD, 1977; D honoris causa, Sofia (Bulgaria) U., 2001. Asst. prof. econs. Vassar Coll., Poughkeepsie, N.Y., 1976-78; vis. asst. prof. Conn. Coll., New London, 1978-79; asst. prof. econs. U. Del., Newark, 1979-85; vis. assoc. prof. Washington U., St. Louis, 1985; vis. assoc. Calif. Inst. Tech., Pasadena, 1987; assoc. prof. econs. and polit. sci. U. Del., Newark, 1985-94, prof. econs. and polit. sci., 1994—, prof. legal studies, 1997—, dir. legal studies program, 2000—. Resident scholar Jerome Levy Econs. Inst., Annandale-on-Hudson, N.Y., 1991; instr., dir. in A.I.D. program, Bulgaria, 1991-92; Fulbright lectr. Sofia U., Bulgaria, 1997; bd. dirs. Ea. Econ. Assn. Editor: Keynes Economic Legacy, 1986, Social Norms and Economic Institutions, 1991, Eastern Econ. Jour., 1998—; contbr. articles on econs. and polit. sci. to profl. jours. Mem. Am. Econ. Assn., Am. Polit. Sci. Assn., Econometric Soc., Pub. Choice Soc. Office: U Del Dept Econs Newark DE 19716 E-mail: kofordk@lerner.udel.edu.

KOFORD, STUART KEITH, electronics executive; b. North Hollywood, Calif., Oct. 25, 1953; s. Kenneth Harold and Theresa (Sutton) K.; m. Gail Anne Joerger, Dec. 28, 1985; 1 child, Michelle Anne. BSME, Mich. Tech. U., 1976. Engr. Motorola, Schaumburg, Ill., 1976-77, sr. engr., 1977-79; engrng. project mgr. Amphenol, Cicero, Ill., 1979-80, mgr. R & D, 1980-82, mgr. engrng. Broadview, Ill., 1982—91; pres. Koford Engrng., Lisle, Ill., 1982-2001; product gen. mgr. MK-Koford, Des Plaines, Ill., 2001—; ptnr., sec.-treas. Micro-Lungo, 1998—. Contbr. articles to profl. jours.; patentee in field. Mem. IEEE (program com. Electronic Components Conf. 1979-91), Soc. Plastic Engrs., ASME, Electronic Connector Study Group (program chmn. 1982-84). Republican. Avocation: slot car racing (world champion 1989). Home: 1239 Cheshire Ave Naperville IL 60540-5724 Office: MK Koford 1776 Winthrop Dr Des Plaines IL 60018

KOFRANEK, ANTON MILES, floriculturist, educator; b. Chgo., Feb. 5, 1921; s. Antonin J. and Emma (Rehorek) K.; children— Nancy, John A. BS, U. Minn., 1947; MS, Cornell U., 1949, PhD, 1950. Asst. prof. to prof. U. Calif., Los Angeles, 1950-68, prof. hort. dept. Davis, 1968-87, ret. prof. emeritus, 1987. Vis. prof. U. Wageningen, Netherlands, 1958, Cornell U., 1966, Hebrew U., Rehovot, Israel, 1972-73, Lady Davis fellow, 1980; vis. prof. Glasshouse Crops Research Inst., Littlehampton, U.K., 1980, AID, Egypt, 1978-82, FAO-UN, India, 1985 Co-author: (with Hartmann, Rubatzky and Flocker) Plant Science— Growth, Development and Utilization of Cultivated Plants, 2d edit., 1981; co-editor: (with R. A. Larson) U. Calif. Azalea Manual, 1975; contbr. articles to profl. jours. Served with AUS, 1942-45, ETO; Served with AUS, PTO. Recipient rsch. awards of merit Calif. State Florist Assn., 1966, Garland award 1974; named Young Man of Yr. Westwood Jr. C. of C., 1956; recipient rsch. and tchng. award Soc. Am. Florists, 1993. Fellow Am. Soc. Hort. Sci (dir., sectional chmn. 1973-74); mem. Sigma Xi, Pi Alpha Xi. Office: U Calif Dept Environ Hort Davis CA 95616 *Always give dollar value for the work you promise to perform.*

KOFSKY, PHILLIP MARK, surgeon; b. Bklyn., June 12, 1956; m. Pamela Dana Furman. BS, Muhlenberg Coll., 1978; MD, Temple U., 1984. Diplomate Am. Bd. Surgery, Am. Bd. Colon and Rectal Surgery. Resident in gen. surgery Albert Einstein Med. Ctr., Phila., 1984-89; fellow in colon-rectal surgery Lehigh Valley Hosp. Ctr., Allentown, Pa., 1989-90; ptnr. Associated Surgeons, Norristown, Pa., 1990—; attending surgeon Montgomery Hosp., Norristown, Pa., 1990—, Mercy Suburban Hosp., Norristown, Pa., 1994—. Pres. med. staff Montgomery Hosp. Contbr. articles to profl. jours. Fellow Am. Coll. Surgeons, Pa. Soc. Colon and Rectal Surgeons, Am. Soc. Colon and Rectal Surgeons, Soc. Am. Gastrointestinal Endoscopic Surgeons, Pa. Med. Soc., Montgomery County Med. Soc. (bd. dirs.) Office: Associated Surgeons # 100 1330 Powell St Norristown PA 19401-3353 E-mail: pkofsky@aol.com.

KOGA, ROKUTARO (ROCKY KOGA), physicist; b. Nagoya, Japan, Aug. 18, 1942; came to U.S., 1961, naturalized, 1966; s. Toyoki and Emiko (Shinra) K.; m. Cordula Rosow, May 5, 1981; children: Evan A., Nicole A. BA, U. Calif., Berkeley, 1966; PhD, U. Calif., Riverside, 1974. Rsch. fellow U. Calif., Riverside, 1974-75; rsch. physicist Case Western Res. U., Cleve., 1975-79, asst. prof., 1979-81; physicist Aerospace Corp., L.A., 1981-96, sr. scientist, 1996-2000, dsting. scientist, 2000—. Contbr. articles to profl. confs. Mem. IEEE, Am. Phys. Soc., Am. Geophys. Union, N.Y. Acad. Scis., Sigma Xi. Achievements include research on gamma-ray astronomy, solar neutron observation, space sciences, charged particles in space and the effect of cosmic rays on microcircuits in space. Home: 29403 Stonecrest Rd Palos Verdes Peninsula CA 90275 Office: Aerospace Corp Space Scis Lab Los Angeles CA 90009 E-mail: rocky.koga@aero.org.

KOGAN, RICHARD JAY, former pharmaceutical company executive; b. N.Y.C., June 6, 1941; s. Benjamin and Ida K.; m. Susan Linda Scher, Aug. 29, 1965. BA, CCNY, 1963; MBA, NYU, 1968. V.p. planning and adminstrn. pharm. divsn. Ciba-Geigy Ltd., Summit, N.J., 1975-76, pres. Can. pharm. ops., 1976—79, pres. U.S. pharm. divsn., 1979—82; exec. v.p. pharm. ops. Schering-Plough Corp., Kenilworth, NJ, 1982—86, pres., COO, 1986-95, pres., CEO, 1996-98, chmn. bd. dirs., CEO, 1999—2001, chmn. bd. dirs., CEO, pres., 2001—03. Bd. dirs. Colgate-Palmolive Co., The Bank of N.Y. Co., Inc.; bd. trustees St. Barnabas Med. Ctr. and Corp.; bd. trustees NYU. Mem. Council Fgn. Rels., The Bus. Roundtable.

KOGAN, YAAKOV, mathematician, researcher; b. Moscow, May 15, 1941; m. Asya Rapaport, Oct. 28, 1975; children: Daniel, Gregory. MS in Probability and Stats., Moscow State U., 1963; PhD in Theoretical Cybernetics, USSR Acad. of Scis, Moscow, 1969; D in Computer Sci., USSR Acad. of Scis., Moscow, 1987. Prof. Technion U., Haifa, Israel, 1989—93; rsch. scientist Inst. of Control Scis., Moscow, 1963—89; tech. cons. AT&T Labs., Middletown, NJ, 1993—. Author: (book) Stochastic Analysis of Computer Storage, Queueing Analysis of Computer Networks, Analytical Methods for Performance Evaluation of High Speed Computers, Performance Evaluation and Optimization of Computer Systems, (book) Computer Resource Allocation: Algorithms and Models; contbr. articles to profl. jours. Fellow: IEEE. Achievements include patents for Dimensioning bandwidth and admission control for elastic traffic in high-speed communication networks. Office: AT&T Labs 200 S Laurel Ave Middletown NJ 07748

KOGER, DAVID GORDON, science administrator; b. Topeka, Apr. 27, 1951; s. John Marshall Sr. and Thurza Mae (Ellis) K. BS, Kans. State U., 1975. Agent contract surety dept. Hussey Agency Inc., Topeka, 1976-79; analyst remote sensing/image analysis, tech. support and customer tgn. Interpretation Systems Inc., Overland Park, Kans., 1979-83; rsch. assoc. geology and environ. sci. depts. Tex. Christian U., Ft. Worth, 1983-86; cons. Koger Remote Sensing and Image Analysis, Ft. Worth, 1983—. Image analyst Shroud of Turin Rsch. Project, Chgo., 1982, Mt. Ararat Rsch. Found. for Noah's Ark, Houston, 1985; enhanced video search for Titanic, Tex., 1983; organizer World Conf. Remote Sensing for Acid Rain, Germany, 1984; chmn. Geosat Com. Inc.; instr. tng. seminars Remote Sensing and Photogeology; frequent guest speaker in field. Mentor Big Brothers, Topeka, 1976-81. Cpl. USMC, 1969-71. Mem. Assn. Petroleum Geochem. Exploration, Geol. Remote Sensing Group, Ft. Worth Geol. Soc., Dallas Geol. Soc., Masons (32 degree), Shriners. Republican. Presbyterian. Avocations: tennis, running, reading, travel, rugby football. Office: Koger Remote Sensing 3150 Waits Ave Ste 2000 Fort Worth TX 76109-2330 E-mail: info@www.davekoger.com.

KOGER, MICHAEL PIGOTT, physician, writer; b. Balt., Jan. 20, 1953; s. Linwood Jr. and Margaret (Pigott) K.; children: Michael Pigott Koger Jr. Student, Morgan State U., 1970, Fisk U., 1971-73, MIT, 1973-74; MD, Meharry Med. Coll., 1979; BA Journalism, Ga. State U., 2001, BA in Spanish, 2002; postgrad. in Health Scis., U. Ala., 2003—. Internal med. resident Franklin Sq. Hosp., Balt., 1979—82; attending physician Provident Hosp., Balt., 1982-85, VA Hosp., Marion, Ill., 1986-88, Central State Hosp., Milledgeville, Ga., 1988—92, Northwest Ga. Regional Hosp., Rome, 1992—96, Complete Wellness Med. Ctr., Atlanta, 1997; news dir. Sta. WRAS, Ga. State U., Atlanta, 2000—02; with Applied Rsch. Ctr., Ga. State U., 1999—2002; announcer WVUA FM Tuscaloosa New Rock 90.7 FM, 2002—. Chmn. dept. quality assurance and utilization review Hancock Meml. Hosp., Sparta, Ga., 1985-86; mem. sci. adv. bd. Nutrition Superstore.com, 1999—. Columnist Sparta Ishmaelite, 1985-86, Signal (Ga. State U.), 2000. Vol. com. Olympic Games, Atlanta, 1996, Hands on Atlanta, 1996-97, Atlanta Cmty. Food Bank, 1996-97, organizing com. Atlanta Paralympic, 1996, Am. Heart Assn., Marietta, Ga., 1996. Mem. AMA, Soc. Profl. Journalists, Journalism History Soc. Home: PO Box 21260 Tuscaloosa AL 35402 Office: Inst for Social Science Rsch Univ Alabama Tuscaloosa AL 35402 E-mail: mkoger@alum.mit.edu.

KOGGE, PETER MICHAEL, computer scientist, educator; b. Washington, Dec. 3, 1946; s. Roy and Louise (McGrath) K.; m. Mary Ellen Clarke, June 12, 1971; children: Peter Michael, Mary Elizabeth, Timothy McGrath. BSEE, U. Notre Dame, 1968; MS in Systems Info. Scis., Syracuse U., 1970; PhDEE, Stanford U., 1973. Jr. engr. IBM, Owego, N.Y., 1968-72, staff engr., 1972-74, adv. engr., 1974-76, sr. engr., 1976-81, mem. sr. tech. staff, 1981-93; IBM fellow, 1993; McCourtney prof. computer sci. U. Notre Dame, Ind., 1994—2001, interim dept. chair computer sci. dept., 2000—01, prof. elec. engrng., assoc. dean rsch. Coll. Engrng, 2001—. Adj. prof. computer scis. SUNY, Binghamton, 1977—94; past mem. rev. com. NSF Computing Divsn.; program chair 6th Symposium on Frontiers of Massively Parallel Computation, 1996; disting. vis. scientist NASA Jet Propulsion Lab., 1997; program com. Supercomputing, 1998, 99, 2000, 02, Internat. Symposium on Computer Arch., 1999; program vice chair 7th Symposium on Frontiers of Massively Parallel Computation, 1999; program co-chmn. Great Lakes Conf. on VLSI, 2002. Author: Architecture of Pipelined Computers, 1980, Architecture of Symbolic Computers, 1991; editor conf. proc. Internat. Conf. on Parallel Processing, 1988. Recipient IBM Outstanding Innovation awards for Space Shuttle, IOP, 3838 Array Processor, AI Parallel Processor, Pres.'s award for patents, Daniel L. Slotnick award for most original paper Internat. Conf. Parallel Processing, 1994, Outstanding Computer Sci. and Engring. Dept. Instrn., 1999. Fellow IEEE; mem. Assn. for Computing Machinery, Am. Assn. Artificial Intelligence, IBM Acad. Tech. Roman Catholic. Office: U Notre Dame Dept Computer Sci and Engring 384 Fitzpatrick Hl Engrng Notre Dame IN 46556-5637 E-mail: kogge@cse.nd.edu.

KOGOVSEK, DANIEL CHARLES, lawyer; b. Pueblo, Colo., Aug. 4, 1951; s. Frank Louis and Mary Edith (Blatnick) K.; m. Patricia Elizabeth Connell, June 30, 1979; 1 child, Ryan Robert. BA, U. Notre Dame, 1973; JD, Columbia U., 1976. Bar: Colo. 1976, U.S. Dist. Ct. Colo. 1976, U.S. Ct. Appeals (10th cir.) 1978, U.S. Supreme Ct. 1983. Ast. atty. gen. Colo. Dept. Law, Denver, 1976-79; campaign mgr. Congressman Kogovsek, Pueblo, 1980, 82; dir. Office Consumer Svcs., Denver, 1981; mem. firm Fish & Kogovsek, Denver, 1983-84; sr. assoc. Petersen & Fonda, P.C., Pueblo, 1985-89; mem. firm Kogovsek & Higinbotham, P.C., Pueblo, 1989—2002; mem. firm. Kogovsek Law Firm, P.C., Pueblo, 2002—; county atty. Pueblo County, 2001—. Mem. ABA, Colo. Bar Assn., Pueblo Bar Assn. Home: 584 W Spaulding Ave S Pueblo West CO 81007-1874 Office: Ste 202 830 N Main St Pueblo CO 81003-0202 E-mail: kog-law@aculink.net.

KOGUT, JOHN ANTHONY, retail/wholesale executive; b. Lackawanna, N.Y., Dec. 8, 1942; s. John J. and Rose J. (Gaj) K.; m. Deborah A. Hillman; children: David J., Robert J., Katherine A., Lindsey A., Kimberly M. BS in Pharmacy, U. Buffalo, 1965; MBA, Syracuse U., 1978. Pharmacist, mgr. Fay's Drug Co., Liverpool, N.Y., 1969-75, v.p., 1975-82, sr. v.p., 1982-89, pres., 1989-95; pres. Health Mart divsn., v.p. Franchise Svcs. FoxMeyer Corp., 1995-96; pres. Health Mart Divsn., v.p. mktg. McKesson Corp., 1996-99; pres. pharmac ops. Cmty. Health Svcs., Inc., Chgo., 1999—. Mem. N.Y. State Bd. Pharmacy, 1987-95. Served to capt. U.S. Army, 1966-69 Mem. Am. Pharm. Assn., Pharm. Soc. of State N.Y., Am. Mgmt. Assn., Nat. Assn. Chain Drug Stores (pharmacy affairs com. chmn. 1982-83), N.Y. State Bd. Pharmacy. Republican. Roman Catholic.

KOGUT, KENNETH JOSEPH, consulting engineer; b. Chgo., Dec. 3, 1947; s. Joseph Henry and Estelle Theresa (Swiercz) K.; m. Darlene Agnes Jedlicka, June 15, 1974. Student, Lewis Coll., 1966-68; BME, U. Detroit, 1971, ME, 1972, postgrad., 1972—. Registered profl. engr., Ill.; cert. energy mgr. Mech. engr. Fluor Pioneer Inc., Chgo., 1972-73, cons. engr., 1973-75; project mgr. Engrng. Corp. Am., Chgo., 1976-77; sr. cons. pub. utilities DeLoitte, Haskins & Sells, Chgo., 1977-79; individual practice as energy and mgmt. cons., 1979—. Author: Energy Management for the Community Bank. Alfred P. Sloan fellow, 1971-73; reciepient award Pres.'s Program for Energy Efficiency, Corp. Energy Mgmt. award, 1981, Regional Energy Profl. Devel. award, 1984, Regional Energy Engr. of Yr. award, 1987, Ill. Energy award, 1988, Illiana Energy Mgmt. Exec. of Yr. award Assn. Energy Engrs., 1992, 96, Disting. Svc. award Assn. Energy Engrs., 1999, Excellence in Engring. award Am. Soc. Heating Refrigeration and Air-Conditioning Engrs. Ill. chpt., 1994, Energy Mgrs. Hall of Fame, 2002. Mem. Am. Nuclear Soc., Nat., Ill. socs. profl. engrs., Assn. Energy Engrs. (pres. Chgo. chpt. 1985, pres Ill. chpt. 1990-93, regional v.p. 1993-95, dir. chpt. devel., 1996, internat. pres-elect 1997, internat. pres. 1998, energy policy com.), Environ. Engrs. and Mgrs. Inst., Demand-Side Mgmt. Soc., Exec. Hosp. Engrs. Soc. Ill., Energy Svcs. Mktg. Soc., Blue Key, Tau Beta Pi, Pi Tau Sigma, Polish Nat. Alliance. Address: 5232 170th Pl Oak Forest IL 60452-4450

KOH, EUNMEE, mathematician, educator, consultant; b. Seoul, Korea (South), June 26, 1958; d. Jungsuk Koh and Junghee Yoo; m. Dongsoo Kim, Mar. 7, 1987; children: Raymond, Edmund. BS, Seoul Nat. U., Seoul, Korea, 1981; MS, U. Wisconsin-Madison, Madison, WI, 1985, PhD, 1988. Tchg. asst. U. Wis., Madison, Wis., 1981—85, rsch. asst., 1985—88; asst. prof. U. Colo., Health Sci. Ctr., Denver, 1989—90; assoc. prof. Teikyo Loretto Heights U., Denver, 1990—2002. Statis. cons. U. Wis., Madison, Wis., 1985—89, U. Colo., Health Sci. Ctr., Denver, 1989—90, Nat. Oceangraphic Atmospheric Assn., Boulder, Colo., 1990—95; vis. prof. Chosun U., 2003—. Contbr. articles to profl. jours. Korean lang. educator Denver Korean Cmty., Aurora, Colo., 1989—92; helping and interpreting koreans US Ct., Denver, Colo., 1996—99. Recipient Invited Spkr., Inst. Math. Stats., 1987, U. Denver, 1992-1994. Mem.: Rocky Mountain Math. Assn., Am. Statis. Assn. Jehovah'S Witness. Achievements include research in finding an omnibus test for the model adequacy in polynomial regression; an algorithm for the omnibus test based on smoothing spline. Avocations: hiking, cooking, reading. Home: 9608 W Dorado Drive Littleton CO 80123 Office: Teikyo Loretto Heights University 3001 S Federal Boulevard Denver CO 80236 Personal E-mail: eunmeekoh@yahoo.com.

KOH, MOON-SOO, urologist, researcher; MD, Chung-Ang Med. Sch., 1985. Rsch. assoc. Baylor Coll. of Medicine, Baylor, Tex., 2002—. Office: Baylor College of Medicine Urology Dept One Baylor Plz Houston TX 77030

KOHAN, BETSY BURNS, lawyer; b. La Mesa, Calif., Jan. 24, 1949; d. William Richard and Winifred Marion Burns; m. Dennis Lynn Kohan, Mar. 8, 1986; children: Toni Kick, Bart, Elyse, David Karowsky. BA, Stanford U., 1971; JD, U. Colo., 1974. Bar: Colo. 1974, Calif. 1985. Ptnr. Karowsky, Witwer & Oldenburg, Greeley, Colo., 1974-82; pvt. practice, Greeley, 1983-84; v.p., assoc. gen. counsel Sun Savs., San Diego, 1985-86; v.p., asst. gen. counsel Imperial Savs. & Loan Assn., San Diego, 1986-88, Am. Real Estate Group, Irvine, Calif., 1988-90, Columbia Savs. & Loan Assn., Irvine, 1990-91; staff atty. FDIC, Irvine, 1991-94; prof. Anhui Inst. Fin. and Trade, Bengbu, China, 1994, Guangzhou (China) Inst. Fgn. Trade, 1995; sr. counsel Nissan N.Am., Inc., Torrance, Calif., 1996—. Mem. Commn. on Legal and Jud. Edn., Colo. Supreme Ct., Denver, 1983-84. Contbr. articles to legal publs. Chmn. Colo. Commn. on Women, Denver, 1978-80; vice chmn. bd. trustees U. No. Colo., 1980-84. Named Outstanding Coloradoan, Colo. Jaycees, 1980, Outstanding Young Lawyer, Colo. Bar Assn., 1979. Mem. L.A. Bar Assn. (comml. law com. 1997—). Home: 525 E Seaside Way Unit 204 Long Beach CA 90802-8001 Office: Nissan NAm Inc 990 W 190th St Fl 8 Torrance CA 90502-1046 E-mail: kohanb@hotmail.com.

KOHAN, CAROL E. historical site administrator; b. Kingston, N.Y. BA, Union Coll., Schenectady, N.Y., 1974; MA, 1980. Curator Regional Pk. Svc., Iowa City, 1986-90, Martin Van Buren Birthplace Site, Kinderhook, Nev., 1990-93; supt. Herbert Hoover Nat. Hist. Site, West Branch, Iowa, 1993—. Office: Herbert Hoover Nat Hist Site Parkside Dr and Main St West Branch IA 52358

KOHAN, DENNIS LYNN, international trade educator, consultant; b. Kankakee, Ill., Nov. 22, 1945; s. Leon Stanley and Nellie (Foster) K.; m. Julianne Johnson, Feb. 14, 1976 (dec. Sept. 1985); children: Toni, Bart, Elyse; m. Betsy Burns, Mar. 8, 1986; 1 child, David. BA, Ill. Wesleyan U., 1967; MPA, Gov.'s State U., 1975; postgrad., John Marshall Law Sch., 1971-74. Police officer Kankakee County, 1967-75; loan counselor, security officer Kankakee Fed. Savs. & Loan, Kankakee, 1975-76; mgr. Bank Western, Denver, 1976-85; mgr. real estate lending dept. Cen. Savs., San Diego, 1985-87; maj. loan work-out officer Imperial Savs., San Diego, 1987-88; cons. Equity Assurance Holding Corp., Newport Beach, Calif., 1987-88; compliance officer Am. Real Estate Group and New West Fed. Savs. and Loan, Irvine, Calif., 1988-90; co-founder Consortium-Real Estate Asset Cons., Costa Mesa, Calif., 1990-91; investigator, criminal coord. Resolution Trust Corp., Newport Beach, Calif., 1991-94; instr. for Internat. Trade Anhui Inst. Fin. and Trade, Bengbu, People's Republic of China, 1994-95; instr. Guangzhou Inst. Fgn. Trade, People's Republic of China, 1995—; owner Kohan Internat. Bus. Forensics, 1995—; investigator Office Inspector Gen. L.A. Unified Sch. Dist., 2000—. Instr. U. No. Colo. Coll. Bus., Greeley, 1981-85; chmn. bd. North Colo. Med. Ctr., Greeley, 1983-85; pres. bd. Normedco, Greeley, 1984-85; part-time prof. bus. pub. adminstrn. So. Calif. Internat. Coll., 1998—. Vol. cons., chmn. ARC, Colo., 1979-85; campaign mgr. Donley Senatorial campaign, Colo., 1982, Kinkade City Coun. campaign, Colo., 1983; chmn. Weld County Housing Authority, 1981. Staff sgt. U.S. Army, 1969-71, Vietnam. Mem. Nat. Assn. Realtors, Shriners, Kiwanis. E-mail: dkohan@earthlink.net.

KOHAN, FEREYDOON, nuclear medicine physician; b. Shiraz, Iran, Aug. 4, 1963; arrived in U.S., 1983; s. Rahim Kohanfars and Ashraf Lalezari; m. Roya Zakanya; 1 child, Rebecca. MD, SUNY, Brooklyn, N.Y., 1992. Cert. Internal Medicine, 1999, Echocardiology, 2002, nuc. cardiology, 2002. Cardiologist Heart Ctr. of Jersey, Jersey City, 2002—. Office: Heart Ctr of Jersey 600 Pavonian Ave Jersey City NJ 07306

KOHAN, LOIS RAE, community health nurse; b. Paterson, N.J., Feb. 2, 1945; d. Raymond Cornelius and Margaret Gavina (Phillips) Englishman; m. Raymond Roy Kohan, Oct. 16, 1966; children: Jeffrey, Glenn, Sharon, Kevin, Craig. Diploma, Hackensack (N.J.) Sch. Nursing, 1966. Substitute sch. nurse Hillsdale (N.J.) Pub. Schs., 1976-80; phys. assessment nurse Phys. Measurements, Inc., Caldwell, NJ, 1978-81; pvt. duty nurse Charles Blando Family, Oradell, N.J., 1980-85, At Home Nursing Agy., Thells, N.Y., 1985-87; pub. health nurse Dumont (N.J.) Bd. Health, 1987-91, Hillsdale (N.J.) Bd. Health, 1992—; pediat. nurse Bergen Cmty. Health Care Nursing Agy., 1992—; parish nurse Hillsdale United Meth. Ch., 2003—. Den leader Boy Scouts Am., Hillsdale, 1975-85; counselor, dir., founder Helping Hand Food Pantry, Hillsdale, 1992—; mem. Drug Alliance Force, Hillsdale, 1996-97; adv. bd. Bergen County Juvenile Fire Prevention Program, Paramus, N.J., 1994-97; active ch. choir. Recipient Hillsdalean award Mayor and Coun. Hillsdale, 1992, Mayor's award Mayor and Coun. Hillsdale, 1995. Mem. N.J. State Nurses Orgn., Nurses Alumni Hackensack Med. Ctr., Bergen County Mcpl. Nurses Assn., Hillsdale Woman's Club. Methodist. Avocations: walking, hiking, tennis, gardening, crafts. Home: 45 Carlyle Pl Hillsdale NJ 07642-2805

KOHEL, RUSSELL JAMES, geneticist; b. Omaha, Nov. 30, 1934; married; 3 children. BS, Iowa State U., 1956; MS, Purdue U., 1958, PhD, 1959. Supervisory rsch. geneticist Argrl. Rsch. Svc. USDA, College Station, Tex., 1959—. Fellow Am. Soc. Agronomy; mem. Am. Soc. Plant Physiologists, Am. Genetic Assn., Genetics Soc. Am. Office: USDA So Plains Agrl Rsch Ctr Crop Germplasm Rsch Unit 2765 F&B Rd College Station TX 77845-9593

KOHGADAI, SHUKRULLAH, foundation administrator, editor; b. Kabul, Afghanistan, June 1, 1952; arrived in U.S., 1989; s. Mohammad Ayub Kohgadai; married; children: Abobaker, Freshta, Ali Baba, Beheshta. BA in Social Scis., Kabul U., 1974; MA in Journalism, Sch. Social Studies in Journalism, Kabul, 1988,, 1998, PhD in Journalism, 2002. Parliamentary news writer, youth newspaper editor, pub., 1969—73; dir. press and publ. Kabul U., 1973—78, lectr. dept. journalism, 1978—83; pres. Afghan Journalism Found.; chief editor Caravan Newspaper; analyzer Radio Afghanistan. Author: Afghanistan in the Bloody Grip of Communism, 2001. Cmty. work Festivals of Art and Culture, 1998, 2001. Achievements include speaking Farsi, Pashto, English, Spanish, Urda, and Arabic. Address: PO Box 205 Alameda CA 94501

KOHL, BENJAMIN GIBBS, historian, educator; b. Middletown, Del, Oct. 26, 1938; s. Victor Philip and Caterine B. (Carpenter) K.; m. Judith Ann Cleek, Jan. 2, 1961; children: Benjamin Gibbs, Laura Ann Kohl Ball. AB with honors, Bowdoin Coll., 1960; MA, U. Del., 1962; PhD, Johns Hopkins U., 1968. Adj. instr. Franklin and Marshall Coll., Lancaster, Pa., 1961-62; instr. history Johns Hopkins U., Balt., 1965-66, Vassar Coll., Poughkeepsie, NY, 1966-68, asst. prof., 1968-74, assoc. prof., 1974-81, prof., 1981-2001, chmn. dept. history, 1979-82, 88, 1993-96, Andrew W. Mellon prof. of humanities, 1994-2001, prof. emeritus, 2001—. Pres. Am. Friends of Warburg Inst., NYC, 1994-96; adv. bd. Renaissance Studies, 1988—; pres., Hedgelawn Found., Worton, Md., 2003—. Author: Renaissance Humanism, Bibliography of Materials in English, 1985, Padua Under the Carrara, 1998, The Records of the Venetian Senate on disk 1335-1400, 2000, Culture and Politics in Early Renaissance Padua, 2001; co-author: (with A.A. Smith), Major Problems in the History of the Italian Renaissance, 1995; co-editor: (with R.G. Witt) The Earthly Republic, 1978; co-editor Centennial Directory of the American Academy in Rome, 1995, Weyer on Witchcraft, 1998; contbr. more than 20 scholarly essays and more than 50 books revs. on medieval and Renaissance history to profl. jour. Historian, City of Poughkeepsie, 1971-77. Fulbright fellow, Padua, Italy, 1964-65; Am. Acad. fellow, Rome, 1970-71; Delmas fellow, Venice, 1978. Fellow Royal Hist. Soc.; mem. AAUP (pres. chpt. 1987-89, 95-98, Medieval Acad. Am. (life), Renaissance Soc. Am. (life), Am. Hist. Assn. (life). Democrat. Episcopalian. Avocations: cooking, farming in Delaware, reading. Home: PO Box 166 One Bayview Rd #8 Betterton MD 21610-0166 E-mail: kohlinmd@dmv.com.

KOHL, DAVID, dean,emeritus librarian; b. Grand Island, Nebr., July 31, 1942; s. D. Franklin and La Vern Harriet (De Long) K; m. Marilyn L. Kohl, Sept. 28, 1969 (div. 1986); 1 child: Nathaniel F. BA cum laude, Carleton Coll., 1965; ThM Divinity Sch., U. Chgo., 1967, DMn, 1969, MA, 1972. Asst. dir. Admission and Aid U. Chgo., 1969-72; Social Scis. reference librarian Washington State U., Pullman, 1972-77, head ctrl. circulation, 1977-80; undergrad librarian U. Ill., Urbana, 1980-86; asst. dir. Pub. Svcs. U. Colo., Boulder, 1986-91, head Norlin Libr., 1989-91; dean, univ. libr. U. Cin., 1991—2002, emeritus, 2002—; dir. U. Cin. Digital Press, 1996—. Assoc. prof. U. Ill. Urbana Libr. Sch., 1984-86, Emporia State U., 1991-92, Ind. U., Bloomington, 1992, U. Ky., 1994—. Author: Handbooks for Library Management (6 vols.), 1984-86, 12 Years 'Til 2000, 1990; editor-in-chief Jour. Acad. Librarianship, 2003; rev. editor RQ Reference Tools, 1988—; contbr. articles to profl. jours. Relief houseparent for Learning Disabled Student Whitman County Mental Health, Pullman, Wash., 1973-75; Koinonia House Bd. (pres. 1979-80), Pullman, 1975-81; mem. bd. Mental Health Found., Boulder County, 1986-91. Rockefeller fellow Rockefeller Found., 1965-66; Disciples House scholar Disciples Divinity House, Chgo., 1965-69. Mem. ALA (v.p., pres. reference and adult svc. divsn. 1993—), Libr. Guild. Presbyterian. Avocation: jogging. Home: 2929 Courtropes Ln Cincinnati OH 45244-3807 E-mail: david.kohl@uc.edu.

KOHL, HAROLD, missionary, educator; b. Linden, N.J., Dec. 13, 1923; s. Herman and Martha (Sperber) K.; m. Beatrice Minniebelle Wells, Mar. 21, 1946; children: Loren, Loretta, Lyndon. BA, Monmouth Coll., 1962; MA in Edn., NYU, 1968, postgrad., 1974; ThD in English Bible, Internat. Bible Inst., 1980. Ordained to ministry Assemblies of God Ch., 1948. Pastor, evangelist Assemblies of God Ch., W.Va., Md., 1944-50, pres. youth ministries Potomac Dist. Coun., 1947-48, fgn. missionary, 1950-56; pastor Assemblies of God Chs., N.J., 1956-61; missionary, tchr., educator Assemblies of God Ch., Far East, Pacific, Europe, 1961-94, ednl. cons., 1980-83; assoc. pastor Hayfield (Va.) Assembly of God, 1995-2000; ret., 2000. Pres. Bethel Bible Coll., Manila, 1963-68; pres., founder Far East Advanced Sch. Theology (now Asia Pacific Theol. Sem., Baguio City, The Philippines), Manila, 1964-73; adj. prof. Baguio City, 1991-2000; dean coll. divns. Internat. Corr. Inst. (now named Global U., Springfield, Mo.), Brussels, 1973-78, Belgium, 1983-88, Rhode St. Genese, Belgium, 1988-99, mem. external faculty, Brussels/Irving, Tex., 1988-94. Mem. Soc. Pentecostal Studies, Religious Edn. Assn., Phi Delta Kappa, Phi Theta Kappa. Republican. Avocations: photography, reading, walking. Home: 429 Superior Ave Winchester VA 22601-4253 *In a truly successful and satisfying life, the will of God is always paramount. At the heart of every personal decision there must be unreserved cooperation with the holy and wise will of God.*

KOHL, HERBERT, senator, professional sports team executive; b. Milw., Feb. 7, 1935; BA, U. Wis., 1956; MBA, Harvard U., 1956. Owner Milw. Bucks (NBA) Milw. Brewers; U.S. senator from Wis., 1989—; pres. Herbert Kohl Investments. State chmn. Dem. Party, Wis., 1975-77; mem. com. on aging, appropriations com., senate Dem. steering & coordination com., com. on judiciary, 1989; ranking minority mem. jud. subcom. on terrorism, tech. & govt. info. With USAR, 1958-64. Democrat. Office: US Senate 330 Hart Senate Office Bldg Washington DC 20510-0001 also: Milw Bucks Bradley Ctr 1001 N 4th St Milwaukee WI 53203-1314*

KOHL, JOHN PRESTON, management educator; b. Allentown, Pa., Dec. 26, 1942; s. Claude Evan and Edna Lenoir (Woodland) K.; m. Nancy Ann Christensen, Mar. 11, 1967; children: John P. Jr., Mark C. BA, Moravian Coll., 1964; MDiv, Yale U., 1967; MS in Mgmt., Am. Tech. U., 1974, MS in Counseling, 1976; PhD in Bus. Adminstrn., Pa. State U., 1982. Ordained to ministry United Ch. of Christ, 1967. Minister Christ Congl. Ch., New Smyrna Beach, Fla., 1968-71, First Congl. Ch., Hutchinson, Minn., 1971-73; instr. Pa. State U., University Park, 1978-82; asst. prof. mgmt. U. Tex., El Paso, 1982-85; assoc. prof. mgmt. San Jose State U., 1985-87; prof. mgmt., chmn. dept. mgmt. U. Nev., Las Vegas, 1988-99; dean Grad. Sch. internat. Trade & Bus. Adminstrn. Tex. A&M Internat. U., Laredo, 1999—2003, interim provost, v.p. acad. affairs, 2002. Cons. in field. Co-author: (text) Personnel Management, 1986; contbr. articles to profl. jours. Capt. U.S. Army, 1973-78, to col. USAR, 1993-99, ret., 1999. Decorated Nat. Def. Svc. medal, Meritorious Svc. medal, Army Commendation medal. Mem. Am. Acad. Mgmt. Home: PO Box 450232 Laredo TX 78045-0232 Office: Coll Bus Adminstrn Tex A&M Internat U Laredo TX 78041-1900 E-mail: jkohl@tamiu.edu.

KOHL, KATHLEEN ALLISON BARNHART, lawyer; b. Ft. Leavenworth, Kans., Jan. 11, 1955; d. Robert William and Margaret Ann (Snowden) Barnhart. BS, Memphis State U., 1978; JD, Loyola U., New Orleans, 1982. Bar: La. 1982, U.S. Dist. Ct. (ea. dist.) La. 1982, U.S. Dist. Ct. (no. dist.) Tex. 1985, U.S. Ct. Appeals (5th cir.) 1986, U.S. Ct. Appeals (11th cir.) 1988, U.S. Supreme Ct. 1994. Assoc. Garrity & Webb, Harahan, La., 1982; revenue officer IRS, Dallas, 1984; sr. trial atty. EEOC, Dallas, 1984-86; sr. criminal enforcement counsel U.S. EPA, Dallas, 1986-91, chief water enforcement sect., office regional counsel, 1991-92, dep. dir. criminal enforcement counsel divsn. Washington, 1992-93, dir. criminal enforcement counsel divsn., 1993-94, sr. criminal enforcement counsel Dallas, 1994—99; spl. asst. U.S. atty. U.S. Atty.'s Office, Montgomery, Ala., 1988-89; chief, criminal enforcement unit Office of regional counsel, Dallas, 1999—. Vis. instr. Fed. Law Enforcement Tng. Ctr., Glynco, Ga., 1987—; adj. prof. environ. crimes seminar Cornell U. Law Sch., spring 1993, environ. law Sch. Law Tex. Wesleyan U., fall 1998; instr. EPA Nat. Acad., 1997—. Vol. instr. New Orleans Police Acad., 1981. Mem. La. Bar Assn. Office: EPA 1445 Ross Ave Ste 1200 Dallas TX 75202-2733

KOHL, STEVE, pediatrician, infectious disease physician; b. N.Y.C., Aug. 13, 1945; s. Moses Judah and Dorethy (Weisenfeld) Kohl; m. Sybil Janice Brandt, June 11, 1967; 1 child, Gwynne Odette. BS magna cum laude, CCNY, 1966; MD, Columbia U., 1970. Diplomate Nat. Bd. Med. Examiners, Am. Bd. Pediat., Am. Bd. Pediat. Infectious Diseases, lic. physician Oreg. Rsch. fellow Columbia Presbyn. Med. Ctr., N.Y.C., 1970-71; intern Babies Hosp., N.Y.C., 1972, resident in pediat., 1972-74; fellow in pediat. infectious diseases and immunology Emory U. Sch. Medicine, Atlanta, 1974-76; from asst. prof. to prof. pediat. U. Tex. Med. Sch., Houston, 1976-89; from asst. prof. infectious diseases to prof. U. Tex. Cancer Ctr., Houston, 1976-89; attending physician Hermann Hosp., Houston, 1976-89, Moffitt Long Meml. Hosp., San Francisco, 1989-99, San Francisco Gen. Hosp., 1989-99, Mt. Zion Hosp., San Francisco, 1989-99; prof. pediat., chief divsn. pediat. infectious diseases U. Calif. Med. Sch., San Francisco, 1989-99; clin. prof. pediatrics Oreg. Health Scis. U., Portland, 1999—. Cons. pediat. infectious diseases MD Anderson Hosp. and Timor Inst., Houston, 1976—89; mem. FDA Vaccine and Related Biologic Adv. Com., 1998—2001; presenter, spkr. and reviewer in field. Contbr. Adv. bd. Nat. Found. March of Dimes, Houston, 1978—79; adv. com. children's rsch. fund Pediat. AIDS Found., 1993—95. Named Best Doctor of Bay Area, 1988; grantee, NIH, 1975—76, 1978—95, Nat. Found. Rsch., 1977—78, March of Dimes Birth Defects Found., 1984—88, U. Calif., 1990—91; scholar James Donovan scholar, CCNY, 1966, N.Y. State Med. Regents scholar, 1966—70. Fellow: Infectious Diseases Soc. Am. (awards com. 1990—95, chmn. 1993—94); mem.: Physicians for Social Responsibility, We. Soc. for Pediat. Rsch. (coun. 1993—95), Pediat. Infectious Diseases Soc. (coun. 1990—97, chmn. sci. program com. 1993—95, nominations and awards com. 1995—97), Am. Assn. Immunologists, Am. Soc. for Microbiology (conf. moderator 1986), Soc. for Pediat. Rsch. (coun. 1986—88, abstract reviewer, moderator ann. meeting 1997, v.p. 1988—89, pres.-elect 1989—90, pres. 1990—91), Am. Soc. for Clin. Investigation, Am. Acad. Pediat. (infectious diseases com. 1991—97, coun. on govt. affairs 1988—92, pub. policy coun. 1988—92), Am. Pediat. Soc., Phi Beta Kappa, Alpha Omega Alpha. Avocation: Avocations: scuba diving, photography, hiking, Tai Chi. Office: Dept Pediat Oreg Health Scis Univ Portland OR 97201 E-mail: stkohl@msn.com.

KOHLER, DOLORES MARIE, gallery owner; b. Rochester, N.Y., June 26, 1928; d. Thomas Beranda and Kathryn (Held) White; m. Reuel S. Kohler, June 27, 1946; children: Richard, Kathryn Kohler Farnsworth, Linda Kohler Barnes, Pamela Kohler Conners. BMus, U. Utah, 1976. Lic. real estate broker, lic. cert. gen. real estate appraiser (emeritus). Broker Kohler Investment Realty, Bountiful, Utah, 1962—; registered rep. Frank D. Richards, Salt Lake City, 1986-93, Internmountain Fin. Svcs. Corp., Salt Lake City, 1996—; appraiser FHA/HUD, 1962-99; owner Marble House Gallery, Salt Lake City, 1987—. Owner Sandcastle Theaters, Bountiful, 1976-98. Composer songs, 1973—. Music chmn. N. Canyon Stake LDS Ch., Bountiful, 1989-93, sec. North Canyon 3d Ward Sunday Sch., 1993-98, music dir. Relief Soc., 1996-2000, primary pianist, 2000-03. Mem. Inst. Real Estate Mgmt. (pres. 1984), Salt Lake Bd. Realtors, Salt Lake Art Dealers Assn. (v.p. 1988-90, pres. 1990-91), U. Utah Coll. Fine Arts Alumni Assn. (coun. 1995-99, sec. 1997), Composers Guild, Mu Phi Epsilon (v.p. local chpt. 2000-2002). Avocations: music composing, travel, stained class creations. Home: 2891 S 650 E Bountiful UT 84010-4455 Office: Marble House Gallery 44 Exchange Pl Salt Lake City UT 84111-2713 E-mail: kohlerart@wmconnect.com.

KOHLER, HEINZ, economics educator; b. Berlin, Aug. 19, 1934; came to U.S., 1957, naturalized, 1960; s. Arthur Oskar and Gertrud (Förster) K.; m. Linda J. Maloney, Dec. 14, 1990. Student, Free U., Berlin, 1953-54, 55-57; MA, U. Mich., 1958, PhD, 1961; MA, Amherst Coll., 1969. Teaching fellow U. Mich., 1958-59, lectr., 1961; from asst. prof. to prof. emeritus Amherst (Mass.) Coll., 1961—97, prof. emeritus, 1997—. Vis. prof. econs. Smith Coll., U. Mass., Mt. Holyoke Coll., 1962-93 Author: Economic Integration in the Soviet Bloc, 1965, Welfare and Planning, 2d edit., 1979, Scarcity Challenged, 1968, Readings in Economics, 2d edit., 1969, Economics, the Science of Scarcity, 1970, What Economics is All About, 1972, Economics and Urban Problems, 1973, Scarcity and Freedom, 1977, Intermediate Macroeconomics: Theory and Applications, 3d edit., 1990, Statistics for Business and Economics, 3d edit., 1994, Essentials of Statistics, 1988, Comparative Economic Systems, 1989, Economics, including supplements, 1992, Economic Systems and Human Welfare: A Global Survey, 1997, Statistics for Business and Economics: MINITAB Enhanced, 2002, Statistics for Business and Economics, EXCEL Enhanced, 2002. Home: PO Box 147 Montague MA 01351-0147 E-mail: hkohler@amherst.edu.

KOHLER, HERBERT VOLLRATH, JR., diversified manufacturing company executive; b. Sheboygan, Wis., Feb. 20, 1939; s. Herbert Vollrath and Ruth Miriam (DeYoung) K.; children: Laura Elizabeth, Rachel DeYoung, Karger David; m. Natalie Black. Grad., The Choate Sch., 1957; BS, Yale U., 1965. With Kohler Co., Wis., 1965—, gen. supr. warehouse div., 1965-67, factory systems mgr., 1967-68, v.p. operations, 1968-71, exec. v.p., 1971-72, chmn. bd., chief exec. officer, 1972—, pres., 1974—, dir., 1967—68. Ret. chmn. Kohler Found.; dir. emeritus Harnischfeger Corp. Served with U.S. Army, 1957-58. Inductee Nat. Kitchen and Bath Hall of Fame, 1989, Nat. Housing Hall of Fame, 1993, Morgan Horse Hall of Fame, 1996. Mem. Am. Horse Show Assn., Am. Morgan Horse Assn. Clubs: Sheboygan Economic (pres. 1973-74). Republican. Episcopalian. Office: Kohler Co 444 Highland Dr Kohler WI 53044*

KOHLER, KATHRYN ALEXIS, epidemiologist; b. Taipei, Taiwan, Dec. 31, 1970; d. Fred Dean Kohler. AB, Stanford U., 1993; PhD, Emory U., 1999. Epidemic intelligence svc. officer Ctrs. for Disease Control, Atlanta, 1999—2001, epidemiologist, 2001—. Recipient Fgn. Duty award, USPHS, 2000, Achievement award, 2001, Bicentennial Unit Commendation, 2001, Outstanding Unit Citation, 2000, U.S. Presdl. scholarship, U.S. Presdl. Scholars, 1989, Fgn. Duty award, USPHS, 2002. Mem.: Commd. Officers Assn. of the USPHS, Internat. Epidemiol. Assn.

KOHLER, PETER OGDEN, physician, educator, university president; b. Bklyn., July 18, 1938; s. Dayton McCue and Jean Stewart (Ogden) K.; m. Judy Lynn Baker, Dec. 26, 1959; children: Brooke Culp, Stephen Edwin, Todd Randolph, Adam Stewart. BA, U. Va., 1959; MD, Duke U., 1963. Diplomate Am. Bd. Internal Medicine and Endocrinology. Intern Duke U. Hosp., Durham, N.C., 1963-64, fellow, 1964-65; clin. assoc. Nat Cancer Inst., Nat Inst. Child Health and Human Devel., NIH, Bethesda, Md., 1965-67, sr. investigator, 1968-73, head endocrinology service, 1972-73; resident in medicine Georgetown U. Hosp., Washington, 1969-70; prof. medicine and cell biology, chief endocrinology divsn. Baylor Coll. Medicine, Houston, 1973-77; prof., chmn. dept. medicine U. Ark., 1977-86, interim dean, 1985-86; chmn. Hosp. Med. Bd., 1980-82, chmn. council dept. chmn., 1979-80; prof., dean Sch. Medicine, U. Tex., San Antonio, 1986-88; pres. Oreg. Health Scis. U., Portland, 1988—. Cons. endocrinology merit rev. bd. VA, 1985—86; mem. endocrinology study sect. NIH, 1981—85, chmn., 1984—85; mem. bd. sci. counselors NICHD, 1987—92, chair, 1990—92; mem. Nat. Adv. Rsch. Resources Coun. NIH, 1998—; chair task force on health care delivery AAHC, 1991—92; Inst. Medicine bd. dirs. Stds. Ins. Co.; bd. dirs. Portland br. Fed. Res. Bank of San Francisco; chair Task Force on Improving Quality of Long-Term Care, 1994; bd. dirs. Assn. Acad. Health Ctrs., chair, 1998—99; OHSU bd. Northwest Health Found., 1997—2001; mem. adv. bd. Loaves and Fishes, 1989—99; mem. Gov.'s adv. com. Commn. on Tech. Edn., 1989—92; chair Oreg. Health Coun., 1993—95; mem. bd. govs. Am. Bd. Internal Medicine, 1987—93, mem. endocrinology bd., 1983—91, chmn., 1987—91, 1997. Editor: Current Opinion in Endocrinology and Diabetes, 1994-97, Diagnosis and Treatment of Pituitary Tumors, (with G. T. Ross), 1973, Clinical Endocrinology, 1986; assoc. editor: Internal Medicine, 1983, 87, 90, 94, 98; contbr. articles to profl. jours. Mem. campaign cabinet United Way, 1999—; bd. dirs. Portland C. of C., 1997—. With USPHS, 1965-68. NIH grantee, 1973—; Howard Hughes Med. Investigator, 1976-77; recipient NIH Quality awrds, 1969, 71, Disting. Alumnus award Duke Med. Sch., 1992, MRF Mentor award, Med. Rsch. Found., 1994, Humanitarian award Am. Lung Assn., 1996, Jewish Nat. Fund Tree of Life award, 1998. Fellow ACP; mem. AMA (William Beaumont award 1988), Inst. Medicine, Am. Soc. Clin. Investigation, Am. Fedn. Clin. Rsch. (nat. coun. 1977-78, pres. so. sect. 1976), So. Soc. Clin. Investigation (coun. 1979-82, pres. 1983, Founder's medal 1987), Am. Soc. Cell Biology, Assn. Am. Physicians, Am. Diabetes Assn., Endocrine Soc. (coun. 1990-93), Raven Soc., Phi Beta Kappa, Sigma Xi, Alpha Omega Alpha, Omicron Delta Kappa, Phi Eta Sigma. Methodist. Office: Oreg Health Scis U Office of Pres 3181 SW Sam Jackson Park Rd Portland OR 97201-3011

KOHLER, SHEILA M. humanities educator, writer; b. Johannesburg, Nov. 13, 1941; arrived in U.S., 1981; d. Max Kohler and Sheila M. Bodley; m. William M. Tucker; children: Sasha T., Cybele, Brett. BA, Sorbonne, Paris; MA, Inst. Catholique, Paris; MFA, Columbia U., 1983. Prof. New Sch., N.Y.C., 1996—99, CCNY, 2001, Bennington Coll., 2001—03. Author: The Perfect Place, 1987, Miracles in America, 1990, The House on R Street, 1994, Cracks, 1999, The Children of Pithiviers, 2001, One Girl, 1999, Stories From Another World, 2002. Recipient O'Henry Prize, 1999; Lewis B. Cullman Libr. Fellowship, N.Y. Pub. Libr. Ctr. for Scholars and Writers, 2003—.

KOHLER, WILLIAM CURTIS, sleep specialist, neurologist; b. Wharton, N.J., May 22, 1942; s. Walter Henry and Elizabeth (Curtis) K.; m. Barbara Bauman, Sept. 1, 1962; children: Jonathan, Kristina, Elizabeth. AB, Oberlin Coll., 1964; MD, U. Fla., 1968. Diplomate Am. Bd. Pediats., Am. Bd. Neurology with spl. competence in child neurology, Am. Bd. Electroencephalography and Neurophysiology, Am. Bd. Sleep Medicine; cert. in clin. hypnosis. Asst. prof. pediatrics U. Fla., Gainesville, 1973-76; neurologist Tallahassee Neurol. Clinic, 1976-94, Billings (Mont.) Clinic, 1994-96, The Sleep Ctr. of Mont., Billings, 1996—2001; med. dir. The Sleep Ctr. at St. Vincent, 1996—2001; dir. pediatric sleep svcs. Univ. Cmty. Hosp., Tampa, Fla., 2002—. Staff neurologist Wilford Hall Med. Ctr., USAF, San Antonio, 1973-75; from clin. asst. to clin. assoc. prof. pediatric neurology U. Tex., San Antonio, 1973-75; cons. child neurology Divsn. Children's Med. Svcs. Fla., Tallahassee, 1973-94; med. dir. Lancaster Youth Devel. Ctr., Trenton, Fla., 1975-76. Bd. dirs. United Cerebral Palsy Assn., 1977-84, Big Bend Epilepsy Assn., 1977-92. Recipient Humanitarian Svc. award United Cerebral Palsy Assn., Physician's Recognition award, AMA. Fellow Am. Acad. Neurology, Am. Acad. Sleep Medicine; mem. Am. Med. EEG Assn., Am. Soc. Clin. Hypnosis. Office: The Sleep Ctr Univ Cmty Hosp 3100 E Fletcher Ave Tampa FL 33613 E-mail: kohler2@bellsouth.net.

KOHLHEPP, EDWARD JOHN, financial planner; b. Phila., Aug. 11, 1943; s. Edward H. and Helen Kathleen (Egan) K.; m. Elizabeth A. Bretschneider, June 21, 1969; children: Edward Joseph, Karen Ann, Mary Beth. BS in Acctg., LaSalle U., 1967; MBA in Mgmt., Temple U., 1969. Cert. pension cons.; CLU, CFP; registered prin. NASD; chartered fin. cons.. Instr. Bucks County C.C., Newtown, Pa., 1969-72, asst. prof., 1976-79, assoc. prof., 1979-83, sr. assoc. prof., 1983-86; sec.-treas. Lincoln Investment Planning, Inc., Jenkintown, Pa., 1972-75; cons. Neil G. Kyde, Inc., Yardley, Pa., 1975-79; v.p. William L. Marshall Assocs., Inc., Doylestown, Pa., 1979-80; pvt. practice as fin. planner, 1980-87; pres. Van Buren & Kohlhepp, Ltd., 1987-94; prin. Manchester Benefits Group, Ltd., 1994-98; pres. Manchester Advisers, 1994-98, Manchester Fin. Svcs., 1994-98, Kohlhepp Investment Advisors, 1998—. Adj. faculty

Bucks County C.C. Mem. Fin. Planning Assn., Am. Acad. Actuaries, Am. Soc. Pension Actuaries, Bucks County Estate Planning Coun., Beta Gamma Sigma, Beta Alpha. Office: 150 E State St Doylestown PA 18901-4313 E-mail: ejk1@voicenet.com.

KOHLI, HARINDER S. business executive, development economist; b. Apr. 11, 1945; s. Ujagar Singh and Jogingar (Anand) Kohli; m. Paulina Ledergerber; children: Harpaul Alberto, Monica Sarita. BSc, Punjab (India) U., 1966; MBA, Harvard U., 1972. Mktg. exec. Union Carbide India, New Delhi, 1967-70; dir. The World Bank, Washington, 1986-93, sr. adv., 1994-98; pres., CEO Centennial Group, Inc., Washington, 1998—. Spkr., author (books, articles) fin., infrastructure. energy, litig. and econ. devel. Baker scholar, Harvard U., 1972. Mem.: First Ea. Investment Group (Hong Kong), Optimos and Internat. Devel. Bus. Cons. Home: 6516 Deidre Ter Mc Lean VA 22101-1605 E-mail: harinder@centennial-group.com.

KOHLMEIER, LOUIS MARTIN, JR., newspaper reporter; b. St. Louis, Feb. 17, 1926; s. Louis Martin and Anita (Werling) K.; m. Barbara Anne Wilson, Nov. 15, 1958; children— Daniel Kimbrell, Ann Werling. B.Journalism, U. Mo., 1950. Staff writer Wall St. Jour., St. Louis and Chgo., 1952-57, Washington, 1960—; staff writer St. Louis Globe-Democrat, 1958-59. Author: The Regulators Watchdog Agencies and the Public Interest, 1969. Served with AUS, 1950-52. Recipient Nat. Headliners Club award nat. reporting, 1959, Sigma Delta Chi award Washington corr., 1964, Pulitzer prize nat. reporting, 1964 Home: # 105 11400 Strand Dr Apt 105 Rockville MD 20852-2942

KOHLOSS, FREDERICK HENRY, retired consulting engineer; b. Ft. Sam Houston, Tex., Dec. 4, 1922; s. Fabius Henry and Rowena May (Smith) K.; m. Margaret Mary Grunwell, Sept. 9, 1944; children: Margaret Ralston, Charlotte Todesco, Eleanor. BS in Mech. Engring, U. Md., 1943; M.Mech. Engring., U. Del., 1951; JD, George Washington U., 1949. Engring. faculty George Washington U., Washington, 1946-50; devel. and standards engr. Dept. Def., 1950-51; chief engr. for mech. contractors Washington, 1951-54, Cleve., 1954-55; chief engr. for mech. contractor Honolulu, 1955-56; cons. engr., 1956-61; pres. Frederick H. Kohloss & Assocs., Inc., Cons. Engrs., Honolulu, 1961-91; chmn. Lincolne, Scott & Kohloss Inc, Cons. Engrs., Honolulu, 1991-97, sr. cons., 1997-2001, cons. engr., 2001—03, ret., 2003. Contbr. articles to profl. jours. Served with AUS, 1943-46. Fellow ASME, ASHRAE, Chartered Inst. Bldg. Svcs. Engrs., Instn. Engrs. Australia, Australian Inst. Refrigeration, Air Conditioning, Heating; mem. IEEE (sr.), NSPE, Soc. Fire Protection Engrs. Clubs: Oahu Country (Honolulu). Home: 1645 Ala Wai Blvd Penthouse 1 Honolulu HI 96815

KOHLSTEDT, JAMES AUGUST, lawyer; b. Evanston, Ill., June 1, 1949; s. August Lewis and Deloris (Weichelt) K.; m. Patricia Ann Lang, Oct. 8, 1977; children: Katherine, Matthew, Lindsey, Kevin. BA, Northwestern U., 1971; JD, MBA, Ind. U., 1976. Bar: U.S. Dist. Ct. (no. dist.) Ill. 1976, U.S. Tax Ct. 1978. Tax specialist Peat Marwick, Mitchell & Co., Chgo., 1976-77; assoc. Bishop & Crawford Ltd., Oak Brook, Ill., 1977-83, 1984-85; ptnr. Arnstein, Gluck, Lehr & Milligan, Oak Brook, 1985-87, Keck, Mahin and Cate, Oak Brook, 1987-96, McBride Baker & Coles, 1996-2001, mem. mgmt. com., 1997; chair McBride Baker & Coles Trade and Profl. Assn. Practice Group; sr. ptnr. Kohlstedt and Teske LLC, 2001—. Bd. dirs. Nat. Entrepreneurship Found., Bloomington, Ind., 1981-92, Camp New Hope Devel. Bd., Oak Brook, 1983; mem. sch. bd. Lyons Twp. H.S. Dist. 204, La Grange, Ill., 1985—, Hinsdale (Ill.) Cmty. House Coun., 1991-94; mem. area leadership com. Superconducting Super Collider, 1987-88; mem. citizens adv. com. on edn. to U.S. Congressman Harris Fawell, 1986-93; bd. dirs. Ill. Corridor Partnership for Excellence in Edn., 1988-94, DuPage Conv. and Visitors Bur., 1997-2001; mem. exec. bd. Visit Ill., 1997-2003; mem. planned giving com. Elmhurst Coll., 1986—; mem. citizens adv. panel U.S. Army ROTC Cadet Command, 1991-94; bd. dirs. Ill. Math and Sci. Acad. Alliance, 1989—; del. White House Conf. Travel and Tourism, 1995; mem. allied adv. bd. midwest chpt. Am. Soc. Travel Agents, 1995; Collegiate Edn. adv. com. Dept. Def., 1995. Recipient Outstanding Young Citizen of Chgo. award 1987. Mem. ABA, Ill. Travel and Tourism Assn., Ill. Bar Assn., DuPage Estate Planning Coun., Oak Brook Jaycees (pres. 1984—, chmn. bd. 1985, trustee 1985-86), Beta Gamma Sigma. Republican. Lutheran.

KOHLSTEDT, SALLY GREGORY, history educator; b. Ypsilanti, Mich., Jan. 30, 1943; BA, Valparaiso U., 1965; MA, Mich. State U., 1966; PhD, U. Ill., Urbana, 1972. Asst. prof. Simmons Coll., Boston, 1971-75; assoc. prof. to prof. Syracuse (N.Y.) U., 1975-89; prof. history of sci. U. Minn., Mpls., 1989—; dir. Ctr. for Advanced Feminist Studies, 1997-98. Vis. prof. history of sci. Cornell U., 1989, Amerika Inst. U. Munich, 1997; lect. univs. in U.S. and abroad; mem. nat. panels. Author: The Formation of the American Scientific Community: AAAS, 1848-1860, 1976; editor: (with Margaret Rossiter) Historical Writing on American Science, Osiris, 2d Series, 1, 1985, (with R.W. Home) International Science and National Scientific Identity: Australia between Britain and America, 1991, The Origins of Natural Science in the United States: The Essays of George Brown Goode, 1991, (with Barbara Haslett et al.) Gender and Scientific Authority, 1996, (with Helen Lonino) The Women, Gender, and Science Question, 1997, The History of Women in Science: An Isis Reader, 1999, (with Bruce Leavenstein and Michael Sokal) The Establishment of Science in America: The American Association for the Advancement of Science, 1999; contbr. articles to profl. jours.; mem. editl. bd. Signs, 1980-88, 90-93, Sci., 1980-81, News and Views: History of Am. Sci. Newsletter, 1980-86, Sci., Tech. and Human Values, 1983-90, Syracuse Scholar, 1985-88, chair, 1988, Isis, 2002-; assoc. editor Am. Nat. Biography, 2d edit., 1988-98, consulting edit., 1993—; Gruphon Press Reprints in the History of Science, 1993-98; reviewer books, articles, proposals for NSDF, NEH, U. Chgo. Press, numerous other pub. cos.; editor sci. biography series Cambridge U., 1997—. NSF grantee, 1969, 78-79, 84, 93-95, Smithsonian Instn. predoctoral fellow, 1970-71, Danforth Assoc., 1975-82, Syracuse U. grantee, 1976, 82, Am. Philos. Soc. rsch. grantee, 1977, Haven fellow Am. Antiquarian Soc., 1982, Fulbright Sr. fellow U. Melbourne, Australia, 1983, Woodrow Wilson Ctr. fellow, 1986, Smithsonian Instn. Sr. fellow, 1987. Fellow AAAS (nominating com. 1980-83, 96-98, sect. chair 1986, bd. dirs. 1998—2002, coun. 2004—), Am. Hist. Assn. (profl. com. 1974-76, rep. U.S. Nat. Archives Adv. Coun. 1974-76), Berkshire Conf. Women Historians (program com. 1974), Forum on the History Sci. in Am. (coord. com. 1980-86, chair 1985, 86), History of Sci. Soc. (sec. 1978-81, coun. 1982-84, 89-91, 94-96, com. on publs. 1982-87, chair nominating com. 1985, 99, women's com. 1972-74, vis. lectr. 1988-89, chair edn. com. 1989, pres. 1992, 93), Internat. Congress for History of Sci. (U.S. del. 1977, 81, vice chair 1985) Orgn. Am. Historians (chair com. on status of women 1983-85, endowment fund drive, auction subcom. 1990-91) Lutheran. Home: 4140 Edmund Blvd Minneapolis MN 55406-3646 E-mail: sgk@tc.umn.edu.

KOHMSTEDT, JEFFERY JOHN, literature educator, political consultant; s. Harold James and Barbara Francis Kohmstedt. AA, William Rainey Harper Coll., 1993; BA, Ea. Ill. U., 1995, MA, 1997. Instr. English U. Ill., Champaign, 1999—2002; mktg. rsch. asst. Grad. Sch. of Polit. Mgmt., Washington, 2001—02; instr. of English George Washington U., Washington, 2001—02; lectr. English Howard U., Washington, 2002—. Polit. cons. David Mills for Congress, Nashville, 2002. Recipient ADEC award, Am. Distance Edn. Consortium, 1999. Mem.: MLA, Nat. Coun. Tchrs. English, Am. Assn. Polit. Consultants. Home Fax: 775-898-2024. E-mail: kohm@gwu.edu.

KOHN, A. EUGENE, architect; b. Phila., Dec. 12, 1930; s. William Bernard and Hannah (Steinberg) K.; m. Barbara S. Kohn; children: Brian, Steve, Laurie. BArch, U. Pa., 1953, MArch, 1957. Registered architect Ala., Calif., Colo., Conn., Del., D.C., Fla., Ga., Idaho, Ill., Kans., Ky., Md., Mass., Mich., N.J., N.Y., N.C., Ohio, Okla., Pa., Tenn., Tex., Va., Wis., Minn., U.K., Japan; lic. profl. planner, N.J. With Nolan Swinburne, 1957-60; project designer, project mgr. Nolan & Swinburne, Architects, Phila., 1958-60; project designer, studio designer head Vincent G. Kling Architects, Phila., 1960-64; designer Kahn & Jacobs Architects, N.Y.C., 1964-65; dir. design Welton, Becket & Assocs., N.Y.C., 1965-67; pres., prin. John Carl Warnecke & Assocs., N.Y.C., Los Angeles, San Francisco, 1967-76; founder, pres. Kohn Pedersen Fox Assocs. PC, Architects and Planners, N.Y.C., 1976—. Mem. archtl. rev. panel N.Y. Port Authority; guest lectr. Bucknell U., U. Ky., UCLA, U. Pa., Miami U., Oxford, Ohio, Kent State U., U. Tenn., N.Y. Inst. Tech., Clemson U., Pa. State U., U. Fla., Washington U., St. Louis, U. Chgo., Ill. Inst. Tech., U. Wis., Pratt U., Harvard U., Kuala Lumpur, Australia, New Zealand, Japan, Russia, Hong Kong; spkr. in field; archtl. critic various univs.; exec. fellow Harvard Design Sch. Former bd. dirs. Sheltering Arms Children Svc., Archtl. League, Chgo. City Ballet; chmn. bd. overseers Grad. Sch. Fine Arts, trustee U. Pa., adv. bd. MS in Real Estate Devel.; trustee Columbia U. Grad. Sch. Arch. and Planning, Silvermine Art Guild; mem. bd. advisors com. on the Art Gallery and Brit. Arts Ctr. Yale U.; bd. trustees Mus. African Art, N.Y.C., Nat. Bldg. Mus. Lt. comdr. USN, 1953—56. Recipient Receiving the Flame of Truth award, Fund for Higher Edn., 1987, GSA award, Ellis Island Medal of Honor, 1998; Theopolis Parsons Chandler fellow. Fellow: AIA (pres. N.Y. chpt. 1987—88, internat. steering com., honor design awards 1962, 1984, 1987); mem.: Mcpl. Art Soc. N.Y., Nat. Coun. Archtl. Registration Bds., N.Y. State Assn. Archs., N.Y. Bldg. Congress, Urban Land Inst. (trustee), Royal Inst. Brit. Architects, Octagon Soc. of the AIA, University (N.Y.C.), City Club N.Y., TAu Sigma Delta. Avocations: painting, music, tennis, golf, skiing. Home: 570 Park Ave New York NY 10021 Office: Kohn Pedersen Fox Assocs PC 111 W 57th St New York NY 10019-2211

KOHN, ALAN CHARLES, lawyer; b. St. Louis, Feb. 14, 1932, s. William Kohn and Rose Kohn (Steinberg) K.; m. Joanne J. Kohn, Aug. 29, 1954; children: Tom, Jim, John. AB, Washington U., 1953, LLB, 1955. Law clk. to assoc. justice Charles E. Whittaker U.S. Supreme Ct., 1957-58; assoc. William Kohn, St. Louis, 1958-59, Coburn, Croft & Kohn, St. Louis, 1959-62, ptnr., 1962-70, Kohn, Shands, Elbert, Gianoulakis & Giljum, St. Louis, 1970—. Mem. Mo. Bd. Law Examiners, 1969-79, pres., 1975-79; mem. U.S. Dist. Ct. (ea. dist.) Mo. Bd. Admissions, 1969-72, chmn., 1970-72; mem. fed. practice com. U.S. Dist. Ct. (ea. dist.) Mo., 1987-2003. Editor-in-chief Washington U. Law Quarterly, 1955; contbr. articles to profl. jours. Chmn. Mo. Housing Devel. Com., 1975-79; treas. University City (Mo.) Bd. Edn., 1970-71. 1st lt. U.S. Army Security Agy., 1955-57. Fellow Am. Coll. Trial Lawyers; mem. ABA, ABA Found., Am. Law Inst., Mo. Bar Assn., St. Louis Bar Assn., Am. Bd. Trial Advocates (advocate), Order of Coif, Phi Beta Kappa, Omicron Delta Kappa, Phi Eta Sigma. Republican. Avocation: tennis. Home: 40 Upper Ladue Rd Saint Louis MO 63124-1630 Office: Kohn Shands Elbert Gianoulakis & Giljum One US Bank Plaza Suite 2410 Saint Louis MO 63101 E-mail: akohn@kseeg.com.

KOHN, ART, education educator; b. Detroit, Oct. 28, 1957; s. Art and Margaret Kohn. BA, Oakland U., 1980; postgrad. in Japanese Studies, Nagoya U., Japan; PhD, Duke U. Prof. N.C. State U., Raleigh, 1987-88, Duke U., Durham, N.C., 1986-91, Meredith Coll., Raleigh, 1989-91, N.C. Ctrl. U., Durham, 1990-91, Janis Panngis U., Pecs, Hungary, 1992-93, Pacific U., Forest Grove, Oreg., 1993—97, Portland State U., 1997—. Author: Communicating Psychology, 1989, 3d edit., 95; integrator for Introductory Psychology CD-ROM, Personal Health CD-ROM; film dir., Life Span Development, Faces of Abnormal Psychology I and II, Learning of Psychology; contbr. articles to profl. jours. Recipient Fulbright award Pecs, 1992, Internat. Study award Rotary, France, 1990. Mem. Am. Psychol. Soc., Am. Psychol. Assn. (Nat. Tchng. award 1989). Avocations: travel, constrn., computers, camping, cooking. Mailing: 5508 N Detroit Ave Portland OR 97217 E-mail: artkohn@darkbluemorning.com.

KOHN, IMMANUEL, lawyer; b. Jerusalem, Dec. 6, 1926; came to U.S., 1934; s. Hans and Yetty (Wahl) K.; m. Vera Sharpe, July 22, 1950; children: Gail, Peter, Sheila, Robert. Grad., Deerfield Acad., 1944; BA summa cum laude, Harvard U., 1949; LL.B cum laude, Yale U., 1953. Bar: N.Y. 1955, U.S. Dist. Ct. (ea. dist.) N.Y. 1955, U.S. Dist. Ct. (so. dist.) N.Y. 1957, U.S. Ct. Appeals (2d cir.) 1966, U.S. Supreme Ct. 1972. Assoc. Gordon & Reindel, N.Y.C., 1953-62, ptnr., 1962, mem. exec. com., 1972—, chmn. exec. com., 1991—. Trustee Inst. Advanced Study, Princeton, NJ, 1997—; nat. gov. Shaw Festival Niagra-on-the-Lake, Ontario, Canada, 1999—. Editor, Yale U. Law Jour., 1951-53. Served as ensign U.S. Maritime Service, 1946. Sheldon travelling fellow, 1949-50 Mem. Downtown Assn., Met. Opera Club, Sky Club, Bedens Brook Club (N.J.), Order of Coif, Phi Beta Kappa. Home: 34 Puritan Ct Princeton NJ 08540-2416 Office: Cahill Gordon & Reindel 80 Pine St Fl 17 New York NY 10005-1790

KOHN, JEAN GATEWOOD, medical facility administrator, physician, retired; b. Chgo., July 8, 1926; d. Gatewood and Esther Lydia (Harper) Gatewood; m. Martin M. Kohn, Feb. 10, 1951; children: Helen, Joel, Michael, David. BS, U. Chgo., 1948, MD, 1950; MPH, U. Calif., Berkeley, 1973. Diplomate Am. Bd. Pediatrics. Physician Permanente Med. Group, San Leandro, Calif., 1953-60; pediatric cons. Calif. Children Svcs., 1961-72; lectr. maternal and child health U. Calif., 1973-91; med. advisor rehab. engring. ctr. Packard Children's Hosp. at Stanford, Calif., 1976-97, med. dir. child prosthetic clinic, 1977-97, ret., 1997, pediatrician Mary L. Johnson Infant Devel. Unit, 2000—. Asst. neurologic diagnostic ctr. U. Calif., San Francisco, 1960-72; pediatric cons. Project HOPE, Nicaragua, 1966, Peru, 1962; pediatric cons. sch. pub. health U. Hawaii, Okinawa, 1975. Contbr. chpts. to books and articles to profl. jours. Mem. adv. panel State of Calif. Dept. Spl. Edn., Calif. Children Svcs.; bd. dirs. Mental Health Assn., United Cerebral Palsy Assn., Head Start, San Mateo County, 1993—. Recipient Lyda M. Smiley award Calif. Sch. Nurses Orgn., 1987. Fellow Am. Acad. Pediats., Am. Acad. Cerebral Palsy and Devel. Medicine; mem. Project HOPE Alumni Assn. (pres. 1988-92).

KOHN, JOSEPH JOHN, mathematician, educator; b. Prague, Czechoslovakia, May 18, 1932; came to U.S., 1945, naturalized, 1953; s. Otto and Emilie (Schwarz) K.; m. Anna DiCapua, Dec. 15, 1966; children: Edward, Emma, Alicia. S.B., Mass. Inst. Tech., 1953; MA, Princeton, 1954, PhD, 1956; hon. degree, U. Bologna, 1990. Instr. Princeton U., 1956-57; mem. Inst. Advanced Study, 1957-58, 62-63, 76-77, 80-81, 88-89; mem. faculty Brandeis U., 1958-68, prof. math., 1965-68, chmn. dept., 1964-68, Henry Burchard Fine prof. math., 2002; prof. math. Princeton U., 1968—, chmn. dept., 1973-76, 93-96. Vis. prof. U. Florence, Italy, 1972-73, Harvard U., 1996-97; mem. U.S. pure and applied math. del. to People's Republic of China, 1976; chmn. com. math. NRC, mem. Bd. Math. Scis. Editor: Annals of Mathematics, 1977-88, University Series in Mathematics; contbr. articles to profl. jours. Bd. dirs. Am., Czech and Slovak Edn. Fund. Recipient L.P. Steele prize, 1979, Bolzano medal Czechoslovak Union Mathematicians and Physicists, 1990, first degree medal Union of Czech Mathematicians and Physicists, 1993; named NSF fellow, 1954, Sloan fellow, 1964, Guggenheim fellow, 1976-77; named to Bklyn. Tech. Hall of Fame, 2000. Mem. NAS, Am. Acad. Arts and Scis., Am. Math. Soc. (trustee 1976-81), Czechoslovak Soc. Arts and Scis. (v.p. 1992-94). Home: 32 Sturges Way Princeton NJ 08540-5335 E-mail: kohn@princeton.edu.

KOHN, JULIEANNE, travel agent; b. Detroit, Apr. 15, 1946; d. Ralph Merwin and Jane Tacke (Meyers) K. BA, Heidelberg Coll., Tiffin, Ohio, 1968; postgrad., Eastern Mich. U., 1969-70; diploma, Inst. Cert. Travel Agts., 1979. Travel agt. Am. Express Co., Detroit, 1970-73, Thomas Cook Inc., Detroit, 1973-75; mgr. Island Traveller, Grosse Ile, Mich., 1975-76; pres., owner Flying Suitcase, Inc., Grosse Ile, Mich., 1976-99; travel agt. AAA of Mich., Southgate, 1999—. Mem. Am. Soc. Travel Agts., Inst. Cert. Travel Agts. (life), Grosse Ile Golf and Country Club, Circum navigators Club. Episcopalian. Home: Unit 1 8365 Colony Dr Grosse Ile MI 48138-1739 Office: AAA of Mich 15150 Fort St Southgate MI 48195-1399 E-mail: jqkohn@aaamichigan.com.

KOHN, MARY LOUISE BEATRICE, nurse; b. Yellow Springs, Ohio, Jan. 13, 1920; d. Theophilus John and Mary Katherine (Schmitkons) Gaehr; m. Howard D. Kohn, 1944; children: Marcia R., Marcia K. Epstein. AB, Coll. Wooster, 1940; M in Nursing, Case Western Res. U., 1943. Nurse, 1943-44, Atlantic City Hosp., N.J., 1944, Thomas M. England Gen. Hosp., U.S. Army, Atlantic City, N.J., 1945-46, Peter Bent Brigham Hosp., Boston, 1947, Univ. Hosps., Cleve., 1946-48; mem. faculty Frances Payne Bolton Sch. Nursing Case We. Res. U., Cleve., 1948-52; vol. nurse Blood Svc. ARC, 1952-55; office nurse Cleve., 1955-94; freelance writer. Author: Berry and Kohn's Operating Room Technique, 10th edit., 2003; asst. editor: Cleve. Physician Acad. Medicine, 1966-71. Bd. dirs. Aux. Acad. Medicine Cleve., 1970-72, officer, 1976; mem. Cleve. Health Mus. Aux., Am. Cancer Soc. vol.; mem. women's com. Cleve. Orch., 1970; mem. women's com. Sta. WVIZ-TV. Mem. ANA, Ohio, Greater Cleve. Nurses Assn., Alumni Assns. Wooster Coll., Frances P. Bolton Sch. Nursing (pres. 1974-75, bd. dirs. 1997-2000), Assn. Oper. Rm. Nurses, Assn. Oper. Rm. Nurses of Greater Cleve., Antique Automobile Assn. Am., Western Res. Hist. Soc., Am. Heart Assn., Cleve. Playhouse, Internat. Fund for Animal Welfare, Cleve. Animal Protective League, U.S. Humane Soc., Friends of Cleve. Ballet, Smithsonian Instn., Coun. World Affairs, Cleve. Children's Mus., Cleve. Zool. Soc., Cleve. Racquet Club (social com. 1999-2000), Women's City Club (Jewel award 1992), Internat. Honor Soc. Nursing. Home: 28099 Belcourt Rd Cleveland OH 44124-5615

KOHN, RICHARD H. historian, educator; b. Chgo., Dec. 29, 1940; s. Henry L. and Kate K.; m. Lynne Holtan, Aug. 15, 1964; children: Abigail, Samuel. AB, Harvard U., 1962; MS in History, U. Wis., 1964, PhD in history, 1968. Asst. prof. history CCNY, 1968-71; from asst. prof. to prof. Rutgers U., New Brunswick, N.J., 1971-84; Harold Keith Johnson vis. prof. mil. history U.S. Army Mil. History Inst., Army War Coll., Carlisle Barracks, Pa., 1980-81; chief Office Air Force History, USAF, Washington, 1981-91; adj. prof. Nat. War Coll., Washington, 1985-90; from assoc. prof. to prof. history U. N.C., Chapel Hill, 1991—, chair, curriculum in peace, war and defense, 1992—. Expert witness U.S. Indian Claims Commn., Washington, 1974; cons. to various def. and hist. agys. and orgns., 1972 ; vis. scholar strategic studies Johns Hopkins U. Sch. Advanced Internat. Studies, 1991; exec. sec. Triangle Inst. for Security Studies, 1992 2000; bd. visitors Air Univ. USAF, 1996 2001. Author: Eagle and Sword: The Federalists and the Creation of the Military Establishment in America, 1783-1802, 1975; co-author: The Exclusion of Black Soldiers from the Medal of Honor in World War II, 1997; editor (reprint series) The American Military Experience, 1979; editor: The U.S. Military under the Constitution of the United States, 1789-1989, 1991; co-editor: (books) Air Superiority in World War II and Korea, 1983, Air Interdiction in World War II, Korea, and Vietnam, 1986, Strategic Air Warfare, 1988, Soldiers and Civilians, 2001; contbr. articles to profl. jours., chpts. to books. Recipient cert. for patriotic civilian service Dept. of Army, 1981, 96, Orgnl. Excellence award Dept. Air Force, 1990, Exceptional Civilian Svc. award Dept. Air Force, 1991. Mem. Air Force Hist. Found. (Pres.' award 1987), Am. Antiquarian Soc., Am. Hist. Assn. (coun. 1986-89), Orgn. Am. Historians (Binkley-Stephenson award 1973, pub. history com. 1989-92, chair 1991-92), Soc. for Mil. History (trustee 1981-89, 95-99, parliamentarian 1982-89, pres. 1989-93, chair nom. com. 2000-2003), World War II Studies Assn. (bd. dirs. 1985-88, 91-94). Office: U NC Curriculum Peace War Defense Cb # 3200 Chapel Hill NC 27599-3200

KOHN, RITA, writer, playwright, journalist, educator; b. South Fallsburg, N.Y., Oct. 10, 1933; d. William and Molly Tevelowitz; m. Walter S.G. Kohn, June 19, 1955 (dec. Nov. 1998); children: Sharon Ruth, Martin Steven, Thomas David. BS summa cum laude, Buffalo State Coll., 1955; MS, Ill. State U., Normal, 1968. Cert. tchr., N.Y. Tchr. Tonawanda (N.Y.) Jr. H.S., 1955-56, Metcalf Lab. Sch., Normal, 1963-68, 78-79; from instr. to asst. prof. Ill. State U., Normal, 1969-73, 87-88, dir. mktg., CEPS, 1980-83; dir. continuing edn. Butler U., Indpls., 1983-84; adj. prof. journalism Ind. U., Indpls., 1984—. Coord. Always A River Project, Ind. Humanities Coun., NEH, Indpls., 1988-91, 93; editor Ohio River Valley Books, Univ. Press. of Ky., Lexington, 1991—; columnist, feature writer NUVO News Weekly, Indpls., 1997—, Arts Indiana mag., 1998-2001, arts4all.com/newsletter, 2001—; cons. Indpls. Children's Mus., 1988-93, Corn Belt Libr. Sys., Normal, 1974-79; cons. to Office of Devel., Ill. Wesleyan U., Bloomington, 1967-74; co-founder Heartland Theatre, Normal, Ill., 1985, Am. Indian Theatre Co., 2000, Beckmann Theatre Co., 2003. Author: (picture books) Spring Planting, 1995, Celebrating Summer, 1995, Fall Gathering, 1995, Winter Storytime, 1995, Always A People: Oral Histories of Contemporary Woodland Indians, 1997, (co-producer documentary) Long Journey Home: Delaware Indians of Indiana, PBS, 2003; playwright: Necessities, 1984, numerous other publs. Precinct committeeman, asst. committeeman Dem. Party, Normal, 1960s-80s; vol. Ind. Repertory Theatre, Phoenix Theatre, Civic Theatre, Indpls., 1983—; bd. dirs., vol. Indpls. Hebrew Congregation, 1983—; co-founder Heartland Theatre, Normal, Ill., 1985, The Beckmann Theatre Co., 2003. Recipient Spirit of Philanthropy award Ind. U.-Purdue U., 1996, Mitzvah award Indpls. Hebrew Congregation, 1996, award Festival Emerging Am. Theatre, 1984, Individual Artist award Ind. Arts Commn., Nat. Endowment for Arts, 2000, others; Land Salzburg rsch. grantee, 1982; Ind. Humanities Coun./NEH grantee, 2001. Mem. Authors Guild, Dramatists Guild, Soc. Profl. Journalists, Hoosier Folklore Soc., Ind. Theatre Assn. Avocations: reading, gardening, travel, volunteering. E-mail: rKohn@nuvo.net.

KOHN, ROGER ALAN, surgeon, b. Chgo., May 1, 1946, s. Arthur Jerome and Sylvia Lee (Karlen) K.; m. Barbara Helene, Mar. 30, 1974; children: Bradley, Allison. BA, U. Ill., 1967; MD, Northwestern U., 1971. Diplomate Am. Bd. Ophthalmology. Internship UCLA, 1971-72; residency Northwestern U., Chgo., 1972-75; fellowship U. Ala., Birmingham, 1975, Harvard Med. Sch., Boston, 1975-76; chmn. dept. ophthalmology Kern Med. Ctr., Bakersfield, Calif., 1978-87; asst. prof. UCLA Med. Sch., 1978-82, assoc. prof., 1982-86, prof., 1986—. Author: Textbook of Ophthalmic Plastic and Reconstructive Surgery, 1988; contbr. numerous articles to profl. jours.; author chpts. in 16 additional textbooks; patentee in field. Bd. dirs. Santa Barbara (Calif.) Symphony, 1990—. Capt. USAR, 1971-77. Name applied to med. syndrome Kohn-Romano Syndrome. Mem. Am. Soc. Ophthalmic Plastic and Reconstructive Surgery (cert.), Am. Acad. Ophthalmology (Honor award 1995), Santa Barbara Ophthalmologic Soc. (pres. 1998), Pacific Coast Ophthal. Soc. (bd. dirs. 1986—, 1st v.p. 1990). Jewish. Avocations: guitar, tennis. Office: 525 E Micheltorena St Ste 201 Santa Barbara CA 93103-4212

KOHN, SHALOM L. lawyer; b. Nov. 18, 1949; s. Pincus and Helen (Roth) K.; m. Barbara Segal, June 30, 1974; children: David, Jeremy, Daniel. BS in Acctg. summa cum laude, CUNY, 1970; JD magna cum laude, MBA, Harvard U., 1974. Bar: Ill. 1975, U.S. Dist. Ct. (no. dist.) Ill. 1975, U.S. Ct. Appeals (7th cir.) 1976, U.S. Supreme Ct. 1980, N.Y. 1988, U.S. Dist. Ct. (so. dist.) N.Y. 1988, others. Law clk. to chief judge U.S. Ct. Appeals (2d cir.), N.Y.C., 1974-75; assoc. Sidley & Austin, Chgo., 1975-80, ptnr., 1980—. Exec. com. Adv. Coun. Religious Rights in Eastern Europe and Soviet Union, Washington, 1984-86; bd. dirs. Brisk Rabbinical Coll., Chgo. Contbr. articles to profl. jours. Mem. ABA, Chgo. Bar Assn. Office: Sidley Austin Brown & Wood Bank One Plz 10 South Dearborn Chicago IL 60603 also: 787 Seventh Ave New York NY 10019

KOHN, STEPHEN MARTIN, lawyer; b. Plainfield, N.J., Sept. 6, 1956; s. Arthur and Corinne Kohn; m. Leslie M. Rose, Oct. 23, 1988; children: Nataleigh Rose, Max Simon. BS magna cum laude, Boston U., 1979; MA, Brown U., 1981; JD, Northeastern U., Boston, 1984. Bar: Pa. 1985, N.J. 1986, D.C. 1988, U.S. Supreme Ct. 1987. Law clk. U.S. Ct. Appeals (3d cir.), Phila., 1983-84; dir., corp litigation Govt. Accountability Project, Washington, 1984-88; ptnr. Kohn, Kohn & Colapinto, Washington, 1988—. Adj. prof., clin. supr. Antioch Sch. Law, Washington, 1984-88; chmn. bd. Nat. Whistleblower Ctr., Washington, 1988 . Author: Protecting Environmental and Nuclear Whistleblowers: A Litigation Manual, 1985, Jailed for Peace: The History of American Draft Law Violators, 1986, The Whistleblower Litigation Handbook: Environmental, Health and Safety Claims, 1990, American Political Prisoners: Prosecutions Under the Espionage & Sedition Act, 1994, Concepts and Procedures in Whistleblower Law, 2001; co-author: (with Michael D. Kohn) The Labor Lawyer's Guide to the Rights and Responsibilities of Employee Whistleblowers, 1988, Federal Whistleblower Laws and Regulation, 2003; contbr. articles to profl. jours. Fellow Nat. Endowment for the Humanities, 1981. Mem. D.C. Bar Assn. Office: Kohn Kohn & Colapinto PC 3233 P St NW Washington DC 20007-2756

KOHN, WALTER, educator, physicist; b. Vienna, Mar. 9, 1923; m. Mara Schiff; children: J. Marilyn, Ingrid E.Kohn Katz, E. Rosalind. BA, U. Toronto, Ont., Can., 1945, MA, 1946, LLD (hon.), 1967; PhD in Physics, Harvard U., 1948; DSc (hon.), U. Paris, 1980; PhD (hon.), Brandeis U., 1981, Hebrew U. Jerusalem, 1981; DSc (hon.), Queens U., Kingston, Can., 1986, Fed. Inst. of Tech., Zurich, 1994, U. Wuerzburg, 1995, Tech. U. Vienna, 1996; PhD (hon.), Weizmann Inst., Israel, 1997. Indsl. physicist Sutton Horsley Co., Canada, 1941—43; geophysicist Koulomzine, Canada, 1944—46; instr. physics Harvard U., Cambridge, Mass., 1948—50; asst. prof. physics Carnegie Mellon U., Pitts., 1950—60, assoc. prof. physics, 1953—57; prof. physics U. Calif., San Diego, 1960—79, chmn. dept. physics, 1961—63; dir. Inst. for Theoretical Physics, U. Calif., Santa Barbara, 1979—84; prof. dept. physics U. Calif., Santa Barbara, 1984—91, prof. of physics emeritus, rsch. prof. of physics, 1991—; rsch. physicist Ctr. for Quantized Electronic Structures, U. Calif., Santa Barbara, 1991—. Vis. scholar U. Pa., U. Mich., U. Wash., U. Paris, U. Copenhagen, U. Jerusalem, Imperial Coll., London, ETH, Zurich, Switzerland; cons. Gen. Atomic, 1960—72, Westinghouse Rsch. Lab., 1953—57, Bell Telephone Labs.,

1953—66, IBM, 1978; mem. or chmn. rev. coms. Brookhaven Nat. Labs., Argonne Nat. Labs., Oak Ridge Nat. Labs., Ames Lab., Tel Aviv U. (physics dept.), Brown U., Harvard U., U. Mich., Simon Frazer U., Tulane U., Reactor Divsn. NIST, Gaithersburg, Md.; chmn. S.D. divsn. Acad. Senate, 1968—69; dir. NSF Inst. Theoretical Physics U. Calif. Santa Barbara, 1979—84; mem. senate rev. com. U. Calif. Mgmt. Nat. Labs., 1986—89; adv. bd. Statewide Inst. Global Conflict and Cooperation, 1982—92; mem. bd. govs. Weizmann Inst. Sci., 1996—. Contbr. over 200 sci. articles and revs. to profl. jours. With Can. Army Inf., 1944—45. Recipient Buckley prize, 1960, Davisson-Germer prize, 1977, Nat. medal of Sci., 1988, Feenberg medal, 1991, Niels Bohr/UNESCO Gold medal, 1998, Nobel prize in Chemistry, 1998; fellow Lehman, Harvard U., 1946, NRC, 1950—51, sr., NSF, 1958, Guggenheim, 1963, sr. postdoctoral, NSF, 1967. Fellow: AAAS, Am. Acad. Arts and Scis., 1963, Am. Phys. Soc. (counselor-at-large 1968—72); mem.: NAS, 1969, Royal Soc. of London, 1998, Am. Philos. Soc., Internat. Acad. Quantum Molecular Scis., 1991. Achievements include research in electron theory of solids and solid surfaces. Office: U Calif Dept Physics Santa Barbara CA 93106*

KOHN, WILLIAM IRWIN, lawyer; b. Bronx, N.Y., June 27, 1951; s. Arthur Oscar and Frances (Hoffman) K.; m. Karen Mindlin, Aug. 29, 1974; children: Shira, Kinneret, Asher. Student, U. Del., 1969—71; BA with honors, U. Cin., 1973; JD, Ohio State U., 1976. Bar: Ohio 1976, U.S. Dist. Ct. (no. dist.) Ohio 1982, Ind. 1982, U.S. Dist. Ct. (no. and so. dists.) Ind. 1982, D.C. 1992, U.S. Supreme Ct., 1992, Ill. 1994; cert. Bus. Bankruptcy Law Am. Bankruptcy Bd. Cert. Ptnr. Krugliak, Wilkins, Griffith & Dougherty, Canton, Ohio, 1976-82, Barnes & Thornburg, Chgo., 1982—2001, Sachnoff & Weaver Ltd., Chgo., 2002, Schiff Harden & Waite, Chgo., 2002—. Adj. prof. law U. Notre Dame, Ind., 1984—90. Author: West's Indiana Business Forms, West's Indiana Uniform Commercial Code Forms; contbr. articles to profl. jours. Bd. dirs. Family Svcs., South Bend, 1985-94, Jewish Fedn., Highland Park United Way, Jewish Family and Cmty. Svcs. Mem. ABA (bus. bankruptcy subcom.), Am. Bankruptcy Inst. (insolvency sect., bd. dirs.), Ill. Bar Assn., Chgo. Bar Assn., Comml. Law League, Am. Bd. Certification (dir., std. com.). Office: Schiff Hardin & Waite 6600 Sears Tower Chicago IL 60606 E-mail: wkohm@schiffhardin.com.

KOHNEN, CAROL ANN, librarian; b. St. Louis, Apr. 8, 1948; d. Joseph William and Josephine (Strenfel) Licavoli; m. Richard Joseph Kohnen, May 9, 1970; children: Jill Patricia, Douglas Richard. BA, St. Louis U., 1970; MA in Libr. Sci., U. Mo., 1994. Cert. tchr. secondary English, Mo.; cert. libr. K-12, Mo. Programmer, cons., Creve Coeur, Mo., 1981-90; audio-visual technician Parkway Schs., Chesterfield, Mo., 1989-92; libr. St. Joseph's Acad., Frontenac, Mo., 1992-98, Parkway North H.S., 1998—. Co-chair telecomms. users group Coop. Sch. Dists., St. Louis County, 1995-99; dept. leader Parkway North H.S., 1999—, mem. Profl. Devel. com., 2000—; Parkway Sch. Dist. Tech. Coun., 2002—. Am. memory fellow Libr. Congress, 1998-99. Mem. ALA, ASCD, Am. Assn. Sch. Librs., Mo. Assn. Sch. Librs. (webmaster, bd. dirs. 2003—), St. Louis Suburban Sch. Librs. Assn. (sec. 1993-95, membership chmn. 2001-03), Parkway Sch. Dist. Librs. Tech. Com. (chmn. 1999—), Phi Beta Kappa, Beta Phi Mu. Avocations: reading, genealogy, web browsing. Office: Parkway North HS 12860 Fee Fee Rd Saint Louis MO 63146-4431 E-mail: ckohnen@pkwy.k12.mo.us.

KOHOUT, LADISLAV JAN, computer science educator; b. Prague, Czechoslavakia, Jan. 22, 1941; s. Ladislav Petr Kohout and Ruzena Anastazia Kohoutova; m. Isabel Maria Stabile, Oct. 3, 1987; children: Eva Maria, Peter Jan, James Wyllis. Diploma in Elec. Engring., Czech Tech. U., Prague, 1963; PhD, U. of Essex, U.K., 1977. Cert. Chartered Engr. U.K. Rsch. asst. Charles U., Prague, Czech Republic, 1961—63; dept. head of hardware group Inst. of Physics, Czechoslovak Acad. of Scis., Prague, Czech Republic, 1965—67; dept. head, computing ctr. Inst. of Astronomy, Czechoslovak Acad. of Scis., Ondrejov Observatory, Czech Republic; asst. prof. bio-med computing Med. Sch., Univ. Coll., London, 1974—79; assoc. prof. Brunel U., London, 1983—85, reader, 1985—88; prof. computer sci. Fla. State U., Tallahassee, 1988—. Bd. dirs. Internat. Inst. for Sys. Rsch. and Cybernetics, Windsor, Canada, 1984—; mem. of the bd. of directors Assn. for Intelligence Machinery, Durham, NC, 1997—. Author: (rsch. monograph) A Perspective on Intelligent Systems (Best book award in AI by Internat. Inst. of Advanced Studies in Systems Rsch., 1991), (book) Knowledge-Based Systems for Multiple Environments (Outstanding Scholarly Contbn. award, 1993); editor: Knowledge Representation in medicine and Clinical Behavioral Sciences; author: (math. paper) Fuzzy Sets and Systems: an Internat. Jour.; contbr. book chpt.; editor: Jour. of Intelligent Sys., 1994; assoc. editor Inform. Scis.: An Internat. Jour., 1997, editl. bd. Internat. Jour. of Gen. Sys., 1995. Nominee Japan Prize in Info. Tech., Govt. of Japan, 1996; recipient Outstanding Contr. Recognition award, World Aviation Congress Expn., 1997, The William R. Jones Most Valuable Mentor award, Fla. Edn. Fund, 1998, Profl. Excellency Program award, State U. Sys. of Fla., 1999; fellow Fellow, Internat. Inst. for Advanced Studies in Systems Rsch. and Cybernetics, 1992; grantee Decision Making Under Uncertainity, NSF, 1995—2001. Mem.: Czech Assn. to the Club of Rome (hon.). Achievements include first to Activity structures methodology; design of Med. knowledge based sys., CLINAID; discovery of Fast Fuzzy relational algorithms and BK-products of relations. Used for knowledge representaton in medicine, engring. commerce. Office: Fla State Univ Dept of Computer Sci Tallahassee FL 32306-4530 Office Fax: 850-644-0058. E-mail: kohout@cs.fsu.edu.

KOHRING, VICTOR H. state legislator; b. Waukegan, Ill., Aug. 2, 1958; s. Heinz H. and Dolores E. Kohring. AAS in Bus. Adminstrn., Matanuska-Susitna C.C., Palmer, Alaska, 1985; BA in Mgmt. Sci., Alaska Pacific U., 1987, MBA, 1989. State legislator Ho. of Reps., Dist. 26 Wasilla and Peters Creek/Chugiak, AK, 1994, re-elected 1996, 98—; mem. ho. fin. com. Ho. of Reps., 1994, 96, 98—. Chmn. house budge subcoms. for dept. edn., 1995-96, adminstrn., 1995-96, environ. conservation, 1997-98, cmty. and regional affairs, 1997-98, commerce and econ. devel., 1997-98, law, 1999—, natural resources, 1999—; constn. exec., 1978—; real estate developer, 1978-82. Bd. dirs. Alaska Housing Fin. Corp., Anchorage, 1991-94; vice chmn., mem. Iditarod Trail Com.; mem. Matanuska-Susitna Borough Econ. Devel. Commn., 1993-94; mem. Wasilla Planning and Utilities Commn., 1991-94; chmn., mem. Alaska del. Rep. Nat. Conv., Dallas, 1984, dist. del. rep., 1984, 86, 90, 92; treas. Rep. Party Alaska, Mat-Su, 1990, fin. chmn., 1990-91. Mem. NRA, Christian Businessman's Assn., Greater Wasilla C. of C., Chugiak-Eagle River C. of C., Anthony J. Dimond H.S. Alumni Assn., Pioneers of Alaska. Republican. Home: PO Box 870515 Wasilla AK 99687-0515 Office: Alaska Ho of Reps State Capitol Bldg Juneau AK 99801

KOHRMAN, ARTHUR FISHER, pediatrics educator; b. Cleve., Dec. 19, 1934; s. Benjamin Myron and Leah (Fisher) K.; m. Claire Hoffenberg, Nov. 10, 1955; children: Deborah, Benjamin, Ellen, Rachel. BA, BS, U. Chgo., 1955; MD, Western Res. U., 1959. Diplomate Am. Bd. Pediatrics. Lic. Ill., Ind. Intern Cleve. Met. Gen. Hosp., 1959-60; resident in pediatrics Case Western Res. U., Cleve., 1960—62; post doctoral fellow Stanford U., Palo Alto, Calif., 1965-68; from asst. prof. to prof. Mich. State U., East Lansing, 1968—81, assoc. chmn. dept. human devel., 1968—78, assoc. dean Coll. Human Medicine, 1977—81; prof., assoc. chmn. dept. pediatrics U. Chgo., 1981-96; pres. La Rabida Children's Hosp. and Research Ctr., Chgo., 1981-96; prof. pediatrics, assoc. chmn. Northwestern U. Sch. Medicine and Children's Meml. Hosp., Chgo., 1997—2002; prof. preventive medicine Sch. Medicine, Northwestern U., Chgo., 2000—02, prof. emeritus pediatrics and preventive medicine, 2003—. Congl. fellow Office Tech. Assessment, U.S. Congress, 1980-81; pres. Children's Hospice Internat., 1983-86; chmn. instl. rev. bd. U. Chgo., 1986-96. Contbr. numerous scholarly articles to profl. jours. Served to capt. USAF, 1962-65. Recipient Outstanding Service award Am. Diabetes Assn. Mich. chpt., 1977. Fellow Am. Acad. Pediatrics (chmn. com. on bioethics 1990-94); mem. Am. Pediatric Soc., Ambulatory Pediatric Assn., Soc. Pediatric Rsch., Lawson Wilkins Pediatric Endocrine Soc., Alpha Omega Alpha.

KOHUT, ROBERT IRWIN, otolaryngologist, educator; b. Chgo., Nov. 29, 1932; s. Emil and Ruth Irene Kohut; m. Joanne Kay Hughes, Dec. 26, 1953 (dec. Oct. 1982); children: James, Paul, Robert, John; m. Frances Irene Speas, June 6, 1983 (div. 1999). BA, Wittenburg Coll., 1956; MD, U. Chgo., 1960. Diplomate Am. Bd. Otolaryngology (bd. dirs. 1979). Intern U. Chgo., 1961-62, resident in otolaryngology, 1962-65, NIH fellow, 1965-66, instr. in otolaryngology, 1965-66; assoc. prof. U. Fla., Gainesville, 1966-68, 1968-71, assoc. prof., acting chmn., 1971-72; prof., chief otolaryngology U. Calif., Irvine, 1972-79; prof., chmn. otolaryngology Wake Forest U. Sch. Medicine, Winston-Salem, 1979-99, prof. emeritus, chair, 1999—. Mem. study sect. Nat. Insts. Neurol. and Communicative Disorders and Stroke/NIH, Bethesda, Md., 1981—86; cons. NASA, 1982—84; mem. adv. bd. Nat. Inst. Deafness and Other Comm. Disorders, 1991—94; exec. v.p. med. affairs, med. dir. Deafness Rsch. Found., 1999—2001. Contbr. numerous chpts. to books and articles to profl. jours.; editor otology divsn. Head and Neck Surgery-Otolaryngology; mem. editorial bd. Am. Jour. Otology, 1992-2000, Am. Jour. Otolaryngology, 1982-2000, Archives of Otolaryngology, 1980-2000, Laryngoscope, 1976-2000. With USAF, 1950-53. Recipient Norvel Pierce award Chgo. Laryngological Soc., 1965, Basic Rsch. award Acad. Ophthalmology and Otolaryngology, 1968. Mem. ACS, Soc. Univ. Otolaryngologists (pres. 1978-79), Barany Soc., Am. Laryngological, Rhinological and Otological Soc. (exec. coun. 1987-90, Edmund Fowler award 1974, Guest of Honor, So. sect. 1996), Am. Broncho-Esophagological Ass., Am. Neurotology Assn., Otosclerosis Study Group, Am. Otological Soc. (sec.-treas. 1987-92, pres.-elect 1992-93, pres. 1993-94), Assn. Acad. Depts. Otolaryngology, Pacific Coast Oto-Ophthalmol. Soc., Forsyth County Med. Soc., N.C. Med. Soc., N.C. Soc. Otolaryngology Head and Neck Surgery (v.p. 1985, pres. 1986-87), Assn. for Rsch. in Otolaryngology, Am. Acad. Otolaryngology-Head and Neck Surgery, Am. Soc. Head and Neck Surgery, Internat. Fedn. Oto-Rhino-Laryngological Soc. (chmn. standing com. edn.), others. Avocations: fishing, hunting, sailing. Office: Wake Forest U Sch Medicine Dept Otolaryngology Medical Center Blvd Winston Salem NC 27157-0001 Office Fax: 704-278-4813. E-mail: rikohut@direcway.com.

KOIDE, FRANK TAKAYUKI, electrical engineering educator; b. Honolulu, Dec. 25, 1935; s. Sukeichi and Hideko (Dai) K.; children: Julie Anne M., Cheryl Lynne K. BSEE, U. Ill., 1958; MEE, Clarkson U., Potsdam, N.Y., 1961; PhD (NIH predoctoral fellow), U. Iowa, 1966. Publs. engr. to electronics engr. Collins Radio Co., Cedar Rapids, Iowa, 1958-61; tchr. Cedar Rapids Adult Edn. Sch., 1960-61; lab. instr. U. Iowa Coll. Medicine, 1963-64; asst. prof. Iowa State U., 1966-69; prin. biomed. engr. Tech., Inc., San Antonio, 1968-69; mem. faculty U. Hawaii, 1969—2002, prof. elec. engring. and physiology, 1974—95, prof. emeritus, 2002—. Cons. in field. Author papers, reports in field. NASA-Am. Soc. Engring. Edn. Space systems Design Inst. fellow, 1967; NSF Digital and Analogue Electronics Inst. fellow U. Ill., 1972 Mem. IEEE. Office: U Hawaii Dept Electrical Engring 2540 Dole St Honolulu HI 96822-2303

KOIDE, SAMUEL SABURO, biomedical researcher, researcher, physician; b. Honolulu, Oct. 6, 1923; s. Sukeichi and Hideko (Dai) Koide; m. Sumi Mitsudo, Nov. 29, 1960; children: Mark K., Eric A. BS, U. Hawaii, Honolulu, 1945; MD, Northwestern U., 1953, PhD, 1960. Diplomate Am. Bd. Internal Medicine. Assoc. Sloan-Kettering Meml. Cancer Ctr., N.Y.C., 1960-65; sr. scientist Ctr. Biomed. Rsch. Population Coun., N.Y.C., 1965—. 1st lt. inf. U.S. Army, 1945—47, CBI. Recipient Joseph A. Capps prize, Inst. Medicine, 1958; grantee, NIH. Mem.: ACP, Am. Soc. Biochemistry and Molecular Biology, Alpha Omega Alpha. Achievements include patents for on Beta-hCG preparation and methods. Office: Ctr Biomed Rsch Population Coun 1230 York Ave New York NY 10021-6307 E-mail: koide@popcbr.rockefeller.edu.

KOIRALA, HARI PRASAD, mathematics educator; b. Pokhara, Nepal, June 3, 1956; arrived in came to U.S., 1995; s. Ved Nidhi and Sumitra Koirala; m. Sita Koirala; children: Shrijana, Pratistha. PhD, U. B.C., 1995. Asst. prof. Ea. Conn. State U., Willimantic, 1995-2000, assoc. prof., 2000—. Contbr. articles to profl. jours. Mem. Internat. Group for Psychology of Math. Edn. Office: Ea Conn State U 83 Windham St Willimantic CT 06226 Fax: (860) 465-5099. E-mail: koiralah@easternct.edu.

KOISTINEN, PAUL ABRAHAM CARL, historian, educator; b. Wadena, Minn., Mar. 27, 1933; s. Alfred Kaleb and Hilma Effina (Torstrom) Koistinen; m. Carolyn Miriam Epstein, Sept. 17, 1961; children: David Joshua, Janice Hilma. BA in History, English, U. Calif., Berkeley, 1956, MA in History, 1959, PhD in History, 1964. Reader to assoc. instr. U. Calif., Berkeley, 1959—62; asst. prof. to prof. dept. history Calif. State U., Northridge, 1963—. Vis. scholar U.S. Mil. Acad., West Point, NY, 1979, USAF Acad., Colorado Springs, Colo., 1982, German Hist. Inst., Augsburg, 1994; assoc. editor Am. Nat. Biography, 1989—99; bd. editors, patron Pacific Hist. Rev., L.A., 1977—; cons. Ctr. for Nat. Securities Studies, Los Alamos Nat. Lab., 1991; cons., participant video WWII, Breadlines to Boomtimes, 3 vols., L.A., Monterey, 1994; lectr. in field; referee for pubs. and grants for scholarly pubs. and orgns. Author: (book) The Hammer and the Sword, 1920-1945, 1979, The Military-Industrial Complex: A Historical Perspective, 1980 (Univ. Scholarly Pub. award, 1981), Beating :Powshares into Swords: The Political Economy of American Warfare, 1606-1865, 1996 (Univ. Scholarly Pub. award, 1997), Mobilizing for Modern Warfare: The Political Economy of American Warfare, 1865-1919, 1997 (Univ. Scholarly Pub. award, 1999), Planning War, Pursuing Peace: The Political Economy of American Warfare, 1920-1939, 1999 (Univ. Scholarly Pub. award, 1999); contbr. With U.S. Army, 1956—58. Recipient Disting. Prof. award for outstanding tchg., Calif. State U. Northridge, 1982; fellow Rsch. fellow, Charles Warren Ctr., Harvard U., 1974—75, Am. Coun. Learned Socs., 1975, NEH, 1988; grantee Rsch. grantee, Calif. State U., 1964—2002. Mem.: Inter-Univ. Seminar on the Armed Forces and Soc., World War II Studies Assn. (com. on bibliography), Peace History Soc., Orgn. Am. Historians, Am. Hist. Assn. Democrat. Avocations: travel, theater, hiking, woodworking, literature. Office: California State Univ History Dept Northridge CA 91330-8250

KOJAC, JEFFREY STANLEY, military officer; b. L.A., Nov. 30, 1967; BA, St. John's Coll., Annapolis, Md., 1989; cert., Amphibious Warfare Sch., 1992, Marine Aviation Tactics Sch., 1997, MIT, 1998; MA, U. Pa., 2000. Commd. 2d lt. USMC, 1989, advanced through grades to maj., 1999; instr. Marine Corps Comm.-Electronics Sch., 1993-96; comdr. Tactical Air Ops. Ctr., 1997-99; speech writer Comdt. of the Marine Corps, 1999, 2001—02; dir. def. policy Nat. Security Coun. Staff, 2003; fellow Internat. Affairs Ctr. Strategic and Internat. Studies, 2003—. Mem. Coun. on Fgn. Rels. Contbr. articles, revs. to U.S. Naval Inst. Procs., Mil. Rev., Airpower Jour., Parameters, Talon, Marine Corps Gazette, Naval War Coll. Rev., Joint Force Quar. Participant Pacific Coun. on Internat. Policy, L.A., 1995-96, Coun. on Fgn. Rels., 2002—. Recipient Navy Commendation medal (2), Navy Achievement medal, Meritorious Svc. medal, 2003, Joint Svc. Commendation medal, 2003. Mem. U.S. Naval Inst., Marine Corps Assn., Soc. for Mil. History.

KOJEVNIKOV, BORIS OLEG, lawyer, foreign legal consultant; b. Rome, Oct. 16, 1950; came to U.S., 1977; s. Oleg Vladimir and Oxana (Artem) K.; m. Irina Maxim Baranova, Aug. 8, 1974; children: Oxana, Oleg. Law Degre, Inst. Fgn. Rels., Moscow, 1972, Cand Legal Scis., 1984. Legal adviser USSR Ministry Fgn. Trade, Moscow, 1972-77, Amtorg Trading Corp., N.Y.C., 1977-82, Comecon, Moscow, 1982-84; dir. legal dept. Chamber Commerce and Industry, Moscow, 1984-91; v.p. Prosystem GmbH, Vienna, 1991-96; v.p., mem. Golubov & Tiagai, N.Y.C., 1996—; mng. dir. Inhorn GmbH, Vienna, 1999—. Arbitrator Internat. Comml. Arbitration ct., Moscow, 1984—, Internat. Arbitration Ctr., Vienna, 1989-94. Author 4 books; contbr. more than 20 articles to U.S., Russian and German periodicals. Fellow Chartered Inst. of Arbitrators; mem. Assn. Bar City N.Y., U.S.-USSR Trade and Econ. Coun. Inc. (USSR co-chmn. legal com. 1989-91), Canada-USSR Bus. Coun. (USSR co-chmn. legal com. 1989-91), Internat. Chamber of Commerce (USSR coord. ICC-USSR joint task force, 1989-90). Avocations: tennis, squash. Home: 7 Summit St Englewood Cliffs NJ 07632-1443 Office: Golubov & Tiagai PLLC 475 5th Ave Rm 1112 New York NY 10017-6220

KOJIMA, AKINORI, public health counselor, pathologist; b. Yao, Osaka, Japan, Nov. 2, 1943; s. Takaji and Kazuko Taguchi K.; m. Yukiko Tanaka, Nov. 2, 1973; children: Tomoko, Reishi. MD, Kyoto U., 1968, D.Med.Sci., 1977. Rschr. Aichi Cancer Ctr. Rsch. Inst., Nagoya, Japan, 1971-77, sr. rschr., 1977-90; dir. Environ. Health Dept. Nagoya City Pub. Health Rsch. Inst., 1990-93; dir. Nagoya City Moriyama Health Ctr., 1993-94; counselor pub. health Pub. Health Bur., City of Nagoya, 1994-97; dir. Nagoya City Pub. Health Rsch. Inst., 1997—. Vis. investigator Jackson Lab., Bar Harbor, 1978-80. Recipient Eleanor-Roosevelt fellowship UICC, 1978. Achievements include establishment of exptl. models of organ-specific autoimmune diseases in mice. Office: Nagoya City Pub Health Rsch Inst 1-11 Hagiyama-cho Mizuho-ku 467-8615 Nagoya Aichi Japan

KOJIMA, TAKESHI, law educator, arbitrator, writer; b. Yokohama, Japan, Sept. 1, 1936; s. Buzaemon and Maki Kojima; m. Shigeko Niwa, May 3, 1966; children: Natsuko, Haruka. BA, Chuo U., Tokyo, 1959, LLM, 1961, LLD, 1978; qualified lawyer, Inst. Legal Tng. and Rsch., Tokyo, 1963. Rschr. U. Mich., Ann Arbor, 1966-68; asst. prof. law Chuo U., 1960-64, assoc. prof., 1964-71, prof., 1971—, councilor, 1995—, chmn. grad. sch., 1997—. Vis. prof. U. Florence, Italy, 1974, Columbia U., N.Y.C., 1988; guest prof. Aix-Marseille (France) U., 1983, Frankfurt (Germany) Goethe U., 1991-92; examiner nat. jud. exam. Ministry Justice, Tokyo, 1984-90, acting chmn. Study Commn. on Issue Fgn. Lawyers (with Ministry Justice, Japan Fedn. Bar Assns.), 1992-94, chmn. Study Commn. on Representation in Internat. Arbitration (with Ministry Justice, Japan Fedn. Bar Assns.), 1994-95; chmn. Study Commn. on Fgn. Lawyers (with Ministy Justice, Japan Bar Assns.), 1996—, acad. councillor Ctr. Internat. Civil & Comml. Law, 1996—; trustee Ctr. Automobile Product Liability, 1995—; chmn. study commn. on issue fgn. lawyers Ministry of Justice, Japan Fedn. Bar Assns., 1996—; legis. coun. Ministry of Justice, 1997—; expert mem. coun. for screening newly founded univs. and other schs., Ministry Edn., 1990-95; dir. Japan Inst. Comparative Law, Tokyo, 1987-90. Co-author: Access to Justice, Vol. I, 1978, Small Claims Courts, 1991; editor: Perspectives on Civil Justice and ADR, 1990, The Grand Design of America's Justice System, 1995; contbr. articles to profl. jours. Spl. arbitrator Ctrl. Tribunal, Ministry Constrn., Tokyo, 1990—; spl. mem. coun. on indsl. structure Ministry Internat. Trade and Industry, Tokyo, 1991-94; mem. Nat. Tribunal Constrn. Procurement, Office of Prime Min., Tokyo, 1991-96; insp. Govtl. Sch. Insp., Ministry Edn., Tokyo, 1993—, chmn. collaborators conf. for rsch. legal edn. reform; coun. legis. on civil procedure, Ministry Justice, 1997—. Mem. Japanese Assn. Civil Procedure Law (pres. 1995-98), Japanese Assn. Pvt. Law (bd. dirs. 1983-87), Japan Legal Aid Assn. (mng. trustee 1993—), Japan Negotiation Assn. (v.p. 1993—), Japan Assn. Lawyers (trustee 1975—), Japanese-Am. Assn. for Legal Studies (councilor 1991—), Am. Law Inst. Buddhist. Avocations: golf, travel. Home: 1013 Shinyoshida-machi Yokohama Kohoku 223 Japan Office: Chuo U 742-1 Higashinakano Hachioji Tokyo 192-03 Japan

KOJOUHAROV, HRISTO VENELINOV, mathematician, educator, mathematician, researcher; b. Razgrad, Bulgaria, Sept. 21, 1971; arrived in U.S., 1995; s. Venelin Hristov Kojouharov and Jordanka Petkova Kojouharova; m. Daniela Ilia Stoevska, Oct. 16, 1971; 1 child, Velin Hristov. MS in Secondary Math. Edn., MS in Math., U. Sofia, Bulgaria, 1994; PhD in Applied Math., U. Wyo., 1998. Vis. asst. prof. Ariz. State U., Tempe, 1998—2000; asst. prof. U. Tex., Arlington, 2000—. Math. webmaster U. Tex., Arlington, 2000—02, founding mem. Multidisciplinary Analysis Inverse Design and Optimization Inst., 2002—, founding mem. Ctr. for Numerical Simulation and Modeling. Contbr. chapters to books, articles to profl. jours. Grantee, Sci. Found. Eureka, Bulgaria, 1995, Am. Math. Soc. and NSF, 2000, Inst. for Math. and its Applications and NSF, 2000, NSF, 2001—02, U. Tex., Arlington, 2001—02; Grad. Rsch. and Tchg. fellow, U. Wyo., 1995—98. Mem.: Soc. for Indsl. and Applied Math., Soc. for Math. Biology. Home: 2504 Early Bird Dr Arlington TX 76001 Office: Univ Tex Arlington 411 S Nedderman Dr 478 Pickard Hall Arlington TX 76019

KOK, A. GURHAN, industrial engineer, consultant; b. Izmir, Turkey, Apr. 17, 1975; s. Recep and Habibe Kok. BS in Indsl. Engring., Bilkent U., Ankara, Turkey, 1996, MS in Indsl. Engring., 1998; MA in Applied Economics, U. Pa., 2000, PhD, 2003—03. Rschr., tchg. asst. Bilkent U., 1996—98; rschr., tchg. fellow Wharton Sch., Phila., 1998—. Mem. acad. team Harvard-Wharton Consortium for Operational Excellence in Retailing, Boston, 1999—; cons. Ahold, NV., Zaandam, Netherlands, 2000—02. Grantee, Sci. and Tech. Rsch. Coun. of Turkey, 1998; scholar, Bilkent U., 1992—96, 1996—98. Mem.: Mfg. and Svc. Ops. Mgmt. Soc., Inst. Ops. Rsch. and Mgmt. Sci. Achievements include research in developed the concept of heuristic equilibrium, a novel way to evaluate the robustness of heuristics. Avocations: basketball, bridge, hiking, literature, films. E-mail: kokg@wharton.upenn.edu.

KOK, HANS GEBHARD, consulting engineer; b. Potshausen, Germany, Apr. 5, 1923; came to U.S., 1951, naturalized, 1959; s. George J. and Anitina K. (Janssen) K.; m. Roselle V. Venier, June 22, 1960; Children: George H., Karen R. Student, Sudberg Engring. Coll., Germany, 1940-42, Hamburg Engring Coll., 1945-46; Dipl.Ing, Technische Hochschule, Aachen, Germany, 1950. Registered profl. engr., N.Y., Pa., Ind., Mich., Calif., Fla., N.J., Ariz., Md. Design engr. Lummus Co., N.Y.C., 1951-53; structural engr. M.H. Treadwell Co., N.Y.C., 1953-56, head structural engring. sect., 1956-62, chief structural engr., 1962-63; mgr. plant design divsn. Treadwell Corp., N.Y.C., 1963-69, asst. v.p. engring., 1969-73, v.p. engring., 1973-83; pres. Treadwell Corp. Mich., Inc., 1974-83; dir. BassetMiller Treadwell Pty. Ltd., 1973-83; cons. engr., 1983—. Chmn. exec. com. Coun. Engring. Laws, 1976. Contbr. articles to profl. jours. Recipient 1st award James F. Lincoln Arc Welding Found., 1966. Fellow ASCE; mem. Nat. Soc. Profl. Engrs., N.Y. State Soc. Profl. Engrs., Am. Inst. Mining, Metall. and Petroleum Engrs. (chmn. materialshandling com.), Am. Mining congress, Am. Mgmt. Assn. Home: 4438 Meager Cir Port Charlotte FL 33948-9495

KOK, LAI CHOW, physician, medical educator; b. Alor Star, Kedah, Malaysia, Oct. 26, 1965; m. Wendy Su Khim Chan, Oct. 2, 1993; 1 child, Marcus Shih En. MB, BChir, Nat. U. Singapore, 1990. Diplomate Am. Bd. Internal Medicine, 1997, cardiovascular disease Am. Bd. Internal Medicine, 2000, cardiac electrophysiology Am. Bd. Internal Medicine, 2001. Intern U. Hawaii, Honolulu, 1994—95, resident, 1995—97; fellow U. Va., Charlottesville, 1997—2001; co-dir. cardiac electrophysiology McGuire VA Med. Ctr., Richmond, Va., 2002—; asst. prof. medicine Med. Coll. Va./VCU Sch. Medicine, Richmond, 2002—. Recipient Nancy Sachiko Ikeda Med. Edn. award, Kuakini Med. Ctr., Honolulu, 1997, Assn. ACP award for Abstract Presentation, ACP-Hawaii Chpt., 1996; ASEAN scholar, Ministry Edn., Singapore, 1981. Mem.: ACP-Am. Soc. Internal Medicine. Office: McGuire VA Med Ctr 1201 Broad Rock Blvd Richmond VA 23249 Office Fax: 804-675-5467. E-mail: laichow.kok@med.va.gov.

KOKALJ, JAMES EDWARD, retired aerospace administrator; b. Chgo., Oct. 29, 1933; s. John and Antoinette (Zabukovec) K. AA in Engring., El Camino Coll., Torrance, Calif., 1953. Dynomometer lab. technician U.S. Electric Motors, L.A., 1953-54; devel. lab. technician AiResearch divsn. Garrett, L.A., 1956-59; tech. rep. McCulloch, L.A., 1959-65; dist. mgr. Yamaha Internat., Montebello, Calif., 1965-67; salesman Vasek Polak BMW, Manhattan Beach, Calif., 1967-68; sr. svc. rep. Stratos-We. div. Fairchild, Manhattan Beach, 1968-70; asst. regional mgr. we. states J.B.E. Olson div. Grumman, L.A., 1970-71; gen. mgr. Internat. Kart Fedn., Glendora, Calif., 1971-73; logistics support data specialist Mil. Aircraft divsn. Northrop Grumman, Hawthorne, Calif., 1974-95; ret., 1995. Author: Technical Inspection Handbook, 1972; contbr. articles to profl. jours. With USN, 1954-56. Mem. U.S. Naval Inst., Internat. Naval Rsch. Orgn., Nat. Maritime Hist. Soc., So. Calif. Hist. Aircraft Found., Found. L.A. Maritime Mus. Republican. Roman Catholic. Avocations: woodworking, ship modeling, maritime history, auto and aircraft restoration. Home: 805 Bayview Dr Hermosa Beach CA 90254-4147 E-mail: jekokalj@netzero.net.

KOKAME, GREGG TAKASHI, medical educator, researcher; s. Glenn and Takako Kokame; m. Carol Liu Kokame. MD, UCLA Sch. of Medicine, 1978—82. Cert. Am. Bd. of Ophthalmology, 1989. Assoc. clin. prof. U. of Hawaii Sch. of Medicine, 1991—. Med. dir. The Retina Ctr. at Pali Momi, Aiea, Hawaii, 1993—. Contbr. jours. Recipient Honor Award, Am. Acad. of Ophthalmology, 1999, Vitreous Soc., 2001, Sr. Honor award, 2003. Mem.: Retina Soc., Macula Soc. Office: The Retina Center at Pali Momi 98-1079 Moanalua Rd Ste 470 Aiea HI 96701 Office Fax: 808-487-3699.

KOKE, RICHARD JOSEPH, author, exhibit designer, museum curator; b. N.Y.C., Sept. 19, 1916; s. Joseph and Emily Josephine (Chevrolet) K.; m. Mary A. Kimbley, Jan. 1, 1955. Student, Art Students League, 1935, Cooper Union Art Inst., 1935-37; AB, NYU, 1941; MA, Columbia U., 1947. Historian, Bear Mountain (N.Y.) Trailside Hist. Mus., 1935-37; curator Stony Point (N.Y.) Battlefield Mus., summers 1937-41; research cons. Hudson Valley Survey, 1946-47; historian Saratoga Nat. Hist. Park, 1947; curator mus. N.Y. Hist. Soc., 1947-83, curator emeritus, 1983—. Conducted archaeol. investigations on Revolutionary War mil. sites in Highlands of the Hudson, N.Y., 1935-41 Author: Accomplice in Treason; Joshua Hett Smith and the Arnold Conspiracy,

1973, Corridor Through the Mountains, 1998; editor: Scenic and Historic America, 1938; contbr. mags. and revs.; compiler American Landscape and Genre Painting in the New York Historical Society, 3 vols., 1982. Served with AUS, 1942-45; art dir, in charge cartographic dept. M.C. 1942-44; battlefield history research analyst. hist. sect. Hdgrs. 1944-45; engaged in collection and editing of mil. data pertaining to tactical operations Am. forces, preparation ofcl. army histories of Services of Supply, 1st, 3d, 7th, 9th, 15th armies World War 11, Western European Front. Recipient 1st prize hist. essay contest sponsored by Colonial Dames of N.Y., 1940 Home: PO Box 700 Peru NY 12972-0700 Office: 170 Central Park W New York NY 10024-5152

KOKKO, JUHA PEKKA, physician, educator; b. Helsinki, Finland, Mar. 26, 1937; came to U.S., 1949; s. U. Pentti and Kirsti (Taskinen) K.; m. Nancy Radford, June 21, 1961; children: Kenneth E., Karl R. BA, Emory U., 1959, MD, PhD, Emory U., 1964. Intern in medicine Johns Hopkins Hosp., Balt., 1964-65, resident, 1965-66, clin. assoc. Nat. Heart Inst., Bethesda, Md., 1966-69, chief resident, NIH, 1968-69; asst. prof. medicine U. Tex. Health Sci. Ctr., Dallas, 1969-72, assoc. prof., 1972-74, prof., 1974-86, chief nephrology dept., 1973-86; prof., chair medicine dept. Emory U. Sch. Medicine, Atlanta, 1986-99, Asa G. Candler prof. medicine, assoc. dean clin. rsch., 1999—. Author: Fluids and Electrolytes. Chmn. Planning and Zoning Com., Addison, Tex., 1975-80, Airport Commn., Addison, 1984-86. Comdr. USPHS, 1966-69. Fellow ACP; mem. Am. Soc. Nephrology (pres. 1984-85), So. Soc. Clin. Investigators (pres. 1989-90), Assn. Profs. Medicine. Lutheran. Office: Emory U Dept Medicine H153 Emory Hosp 1364 Clifton Rd NE Atlanta GA 30322-1061 E-mail: juha_kokko@emory.org.

KOKOTOVIC, PETAR V. electrical and computer engineer, educator; b. Mar. 18, 1934; Dipl.Eng., U. Belgrade, Yugoslavia, 1958, Magistar (Elec. Engring.), 1963; Candidate of Tech. Scis., Russian Acad. Scis., Moscow, 1965. Prof. elec. engring. U. Ill., Urbana, 1966-91, Grainger prof. emeritus, 1991—; prof. elec. and computer engring. U. Calif., 1991—; dir. Ctr. for Control Engring. and Computation. Recipient Quazza medal Internat. Fedn. Automatic Control, 1990, IEEE Control Sys. Field award, 1995. Fellow: IEEE (Engring. Outstanding AC Transactions Paper award 1982—83, Axelby Outstanding Paper award 1991—92, H. Bode Prize lecture 1991, James H. Mulligan, Jr. Edn. medal 2002, Richard E. Bellman Control Heritage award 2002); mem.: NAE. Office: U Calif Electrical & Comp Eng Dept Santa Barbara CA 93106

KOKOWSKI, PALMA ANNA, nurse consultant; b. New Brighton, Pa., Aug. 15, 1947; d. William M. and Steffa A. (Zaleski) Mangine; m. Clifford M. Kokowski, Oct. 2, 1971; 1 child, Bonnie A. RN, South Side Hosp., Pitts., 1968. RN. W.Va., Pa., Md., Ohio, Mass.; cert. disability mgmt. specialist, rehab. RN. cert. case mgr., Rehab. Nursing Certification Bd.; diplomate Am. Bd. Forensic Nursing. Real estate sales Marsh Realty, Pitts.; staff nurse South Side Hosp., 1968-73; field nurse Upjohn Healthcare Svcs., Pitts., 1975-77, field supr., 1977-78, field nurse rehab., 1978-81, rehab. coord., 1981-82; charge nurse Greater Pitts. Guild for Blind, Bridgeville, Pa., 1977-79; med. and rehab. specialist Champion Claim Svc., Pitts., 1982-87; owner, rehab. nurse cons. Palma Kokowski Rehab., South Park, Pa., 1988—. Mem. ANA, Pa. Nursing Assn., NARPPS, Assn. Rehab. Nurses (treas. 1982), Western Pa. Assn. Rehab. Nurses. Home and Office: Palma Kokowski Rehab 1188 Mike Reed Dr South Park PA 15129 9157 E mail: rnermcdms@attbi.com.

KOKTVEDGAARD, MOGENS, education educator; b. Vejle, Denmark, Nov. 18, 1933; s. Olaf and Ida (Holst) K.; m. Hanne Tolboll, June 26, 1965; children: Olaf, Kristian. Cand.jur., Univ. Copenhagen, 1957, Dr. jur., 1965; Dr.jur. (hon.), Univ. Stockholm, 1993. Lectr. Univ. Copenhagen, 1961-66, prof., 1966, dean of law sch., 1971, vice-rector, 1972-81; chmn. Danish Radio and TV Bd., 2000—. Chmn. Monopolies Commn., Denmark, 1980-89; editor: Weekly Law Report, Denmark, 1976—. Author: Immaterialretspositioner, 1965, Danish Patent Law, 1979, Intellectual Property, 2001, Danish Trademark Law, 1998, Law of Competition, 2002. Decorated knight 1st Order, Queen of Denmark; recipient Gold medal Univ. Copenhagen, 1959. Mem. Danish Copyright Soc. (chmn. 1968), Royal Acad. Fine Arts, Acad. Tech. Scis., Academia Europaea. Office: Inst Legal Sci Studiestraede 6 DK 1455 Copenhagen Denmark E-mail: mogens.koktvedgaard@jur.ku.dk.

KOKUBUN, RUSSELL S. state senator; BBA, So. Methodist U., 1971. In agr., 1974—88; mem. Hawaii County Coun., 1984—88, chmn., 1988—92; proj. dir. Hilo Main St. prog., 1992—95; exec. asst. to mayor County of Hawaii, 1995—97, dep. planning dir., 1997—2000; senator dist. 2 Hawaii State Senate, 2000—. Vice chair ways and means com. Hawaii State Senate, 2003—, vice chair energy and environment com., 2003—, mem. health com., 2003—, senate vice chair, joint senate-house investigative com. for Felix consent decree, 2003—. Mem. nat. bd. adv. Nat. Trust for Hist. Preservation, 1996—2002; trustee Hist. Hawaii Found, 1995—2002. Democrat. Avocations: farming, hiking, camping, reading. Office: Hawaii State Senate State Capitol Rm 207 415 S Beretania St Honolulu HI 96813 Fax: 808 586-6689. Business E-Mail: senkokubun@capitol.hawaii.gov.*

KOLA, ARTHUR ANTHONY, lawyer; b. New Brunswick, N.J., Feb. 16, 1939; s. Arthur Aloysius and Blanche (Raym) K.; m. Jacquelin Lou Draper, Sept. 3, 1960; children— Jill, Jean, Jennifer; m. Anna Molnar, Apr. 15, 1977 AB, Dartmouth Coll., 1961; LLB, Duke U., 1964. Bar: Ohio 1964, U.S. Dist. Ct. (no. dist.) Ohio 1969, U.S. Ct. Appeals (6th cir.) 1971, U.S. Supreme Ct. 1972. Assoc. Squire, Sanders & Dempsey, Cleve., 1964-65, assoc., 1968-74, ptnr., 1974-94; pvt. practice Kola Law Office, Cleve., 1994—. Asst. prof. law Ind. U., Bloomington, 1967-68; instr. labor law Case Western Res. U., Cleve., 1976 Bd. visitors Duke U. Sch. Law, 1985—. Served to capt. U.S. Army, 1965-67 Mem. Ohio Bar Assn., Cleve. Bar Assn. (chmn. labor and employment law sect. 1993-94), Am. Arbitration Assn. (bd. dirs. 1991-97). Office: Kola Law Office Park Ctr I Ste 200 6100 Oak Tree Blvd Cleveland OH 44131

KOLAKOWSKI, DIANA JEAN, county commissioner; b. Detroit, Aug. 28, 1943; d. Leo and Genevieve (Bosh) Zyskowski; m. William Francis Kolakowski, Jr., Oct. 22, 1966; children: Wiliam Francis III, John. BS, U. Detroit, 1965. Lab. asst. chemistry dept. U. Detroit, 1961-65; rsch. chemist Detroit Inst. Cancer Rsch., Mich. Cancer Found., 1965-70; substitute tchr. Warren (Mich.) Consol. Schs., 1979-81; mem. Macomb County Bd. Commrs., Mt. Clemens, Mich., 1983—, vice chmn., 1993-95, chmn., 1995-97. Dir. S.E. Mich. Transp. Authority, Detroit, 1983—85; trustee Macomb County Ret. System, Mt. Clemens, 1988—91, 1992—95; chmn. Regional Transit Coord. Coun., 1995—97; del. S.E. Mich. Coun. Govts., Detroit, 1987—, vice chmn., 1995—99, chmn., 1999—2000, Regional Transit Coord. Coun., 1995—97; bd. dirs. Creating a Healthier Macomb, 1996—2001, Macomb Bar Found., 1996—. Contbr. articles to sci. jours. Trustee Myasthenia Gravis Found., Southfield, Mich., 1964-71; dir. Otsikita coun. Girl Scouts Am., 1995-96; mem., sec. Sterling Heights (Mich.) Bd. Zoning Appeals, 1978-83; mem. Macomb County Dem. Exec. Com., Mt. Clemens, 1982—, 10th and 12th Dem. Congl. Dist. Exec. Com., Warren, 1982—, del. 1996 Dem. Nat. Conv.; mem. behavioral medicine adv. coun. St. Joseph Hosp. GM scholar U. Detroit, 1961-65; named Woman of Distinction Macomb County Girl Scouts U.S.A., 1996; recipient Leadership award Cath. Social Svcs. Macomb, 1997, Polish Pride award Polish Am. Citizens for Equity, 1997, Excellence in County Govt. award, 1997, others. Mem. Nat. Assn. Counties, Mich. Assn. Counties, Mich. Assn. Planning Ofcls., Am. Polish Cultural Ctr., Polish Am. Congress, Alpha Sigma Nu. Roman Catholic. Avocations: singing, piano, crossword and jigsaw puzzles. Home: 33488 Breckenridge Dr Sterling Heights MI 48310-6082 Office: Office Bd Commrs Macomb Co Adminstrn Bldg 1 S Main St Fl 9 Mount Clemens MI 48043-2306 E-mail: dianakolakowski1@comcast.net.

KOLANOSKI, THOMAS EDWIN, financial company executive; b. San Francisco, Mar. 1, 1937; s. Theodore Thaddeus and Mary J. (Luczynski) K.; m. Sheila O'Brien, Dec. 26, 1960; children: Kenneth John, Thomas Patrick, Michael Sean. BS, U. San Francisco, 1959, MA, 1965. Cert. fin. planner. Educator, counselor, adminstr. San Francisco Unified Sch. Dist.; adminstr. Huntington Beach Union, HSD, Calif., 1965—79; regional v.p. fin. svcs. Waddell & Reed, Inc., Ariz., Nev., Utah, So. Calif., 1979-94, retired, 1994; registered investment advisor Locust St. Securities Inc. Fellow NDEA, USC, 1965. Mem. Nat. Assn. Secondary Sch. Prin., Fin. Planners Assn., Nat. Assn. Securities Dealers; mem. ING Fin. Adv. Network. Republican. Roman Catholic. Avocation: fly fishing. Home: 1783 Panay Cir Costa Mesa CA 92626-2348 Fax: 714-434-9425. E-mail: teksok@pacbell.net.

KOLANSKY, DANIEL M. cardiologist; b. Phila., Oct. 1, 1958; s. Harold and Elsa K.; m. Ana Salazar; children: David, Jonathan, Matthew. AB, Stanford U., 1980; MD, Yale U., 1984. Diplomate Am. Bd. Internal Medicine, Am. Bd. Cardiovasc. Disease. Intern, resident Yale New-Haven (Conn.) Hos0p., 1984-87; fellow in cardiovasc. disease Yale U., New Haven, 1987-92; assoc. prof. U. Pa., Phila. Office: Hosp of the Univ of Pa 9th Fl Founders Pavilion 3400 Spruce St Philadelphia PA 19104-4206

KOLANSKY, HAROLD, physician, psychiatrist, psychoanalyst; b. Carbondale, Pa., Aug. 15, 1924; s. Abe and Miriam (Raker) K.; m. Elsa Harwitz, June 8, 1948; children: Jeffrey, Betta, Daniel. Student, U. Scranton, 1942-44; MD cum laude, Georgetown U., 1948. Rotating intern Walter Reed Army Hosp., Washington, 1948-49; resident Coatesville (Pa.) VA Hosp. and Deans' Com. Program, Phila., 1949-52; practice medicine specializing in psychiatry and psychoanalysis Phila., 1952—, Elkins Park, Pa., 1959—; clin. assoc. prof. psychiatry U. Pa. Sch. Medicine, 1972-77, clin. prof., 1977, 91—, mem. steering com. Psychoanalytic Cluster, 1991—, chair steering com. Psychoanalytic Cluster, 1997-99; prof. psychiatry and human behavior Jefferson Med. Coll., Thomas Jefferson U., Phila., 1977-91, dir. sect. child and adolescent psychoanalysis, 1980-90, dir. sect. psychoanalysis, 1982-90. Mem. psychiatry staff Albert Einstein Med. Ctr., 1952-69, 82—, sr. attending, 1983—, dir. divsn. child psychiatry, 1955-69, acting chmn. dept. psychiatry, 1968-69, dir. child psychiatry fellowship, 1960-69, dir. ctr. for psychoanalysis, 1991—, mem. exec. com., ednl. com. and curriculum com., 1991—; mem. faculty Inst. Phila. Assn. Psychoanalysis, 1960—, chmn. adminstrv. bd., 1966-69, dir. divsn. childrn and adolescent psychoanalysis, 1975-84, tng. and supervisory analyst, 1976—, chmn. tng. analyst com., 1982-83, 93-94, 95-96, chmn. curriculum com., 1982-88, dir. consultation and evaluation divsn., 1988-89, mem. ednl. com., 1989-94, mem. ednl. com., vice chmn., 1997, mem. ednl. com., 1997-2000, chmn. edn. com., 2000-2001, vice-chmn., 1997-2001, chmn. faculty com., 1997—, chmn., liaison com. med. edn., 1994—, chair ednl. com., 2000-01; mem. staff psychiatry Phila. Psychiat. Ctr., 1952-81; pres. Regional Coun. Child Psychiatry, Pa., S.E. N.J., Del., 1967-68, 72-73, chmn. exec. com., 1970-73; chmn. med. bd. Ea. State Sch. and Hosp., Trevose, Pa., 1966-69; asst. prof. psychiatry Hahnemann Med. Coll. and Hosp., Phila., 1952-60; mem. Pa. Task Force on Mental Health Children, 1971-74; vis. prof. psychiatry U. P.R. Sch. Medicine, 1982—; mem. steering com. psychoanalytic cluster U. Pa. Sch. Med., 1991—, chmn., 1997-99. Contbg. author to numerous texts on psychoanalysis and psychiatry including: A Handbook of Child Psychoanalysis, 1968, Behavior Pathology of Childhood and Adolescence, 1973, Controversy in Psychiatry, 1978, Prognosis, 1981; contbr. numerous articles on child and adult psychiatry and psychoanalysis to profl. jours. Capt. M.C., U.S. Army, 1950-51, Korea. Recipient 1st prize biochemistry Georgetown U., 1945, Robert Waelder award for Teaching Excellence in Psychiatry Thomas Jefferson Med. Coll., 1987, Dedication to Edn. award, 1990, award for teaching excellence dept. psychiatry Albert Einstein Med. Ctr., 1993, award for tchg. excellence, 1996, 2000, 02; 1st pl. U.S. in Surgery Nat. Bd. Med. Examiners, 1948. Fellow: Phila. Coll. Physicians, Am. Acad. Child Psychiatry (chmn. com. continuing med. edn. 1974—82, councillor, citation for developing continuing med. edn. program 1976), Am. Psychiat. Assn.; mem.: AMA, Phila. County Med. Soc., Pa. Med. Soc., Am. Psychoanalytic Assn. (exec. counselor 1969—73, 1977—82, fellow bd. profl. standards 1983—89, 1992—98, mem. com. on child and adolescent analysis 1984—90, 1999—, acting fellow bd. on profl. standards 1989, mem. univ. and med. edn. com. 1995—2000, budget and fin. com. 1996—98, all exec. counselor 1999—2001, Edith Sabshin Teaching award 2000), Internat. Psychoanalytic Assn., Phila. Psychiatric Soc., Assn. Child Psychoanalysis, Phila. Assn. Psychoanalysis (bd. dirs. 1984—86, pres. 1984—86, Gersld Pearson prize award 1960).

KOLAPARTHI, VENKATASUBBARAO, oncologist; s. Gopala Krishnaiah and Pushpavalli Kolaparthi; m. Savitri Devi Bhogavilli; 1 child, Krishna. BSc, U. Madras, 1981, MSc, 1983, MPhil in Genetics, 1984, PhD in Genetics, 1989. Sr. rsch. fellow Tamil Nadu Agrl. U., Coimbatore, India, 1990—92; rschr. Thomas Jefferson U., Phila., 1992—93, Cancer Inst. N.J., Piscataway, 1993—94; sr. rsch. assoc., postdoctoral scholar U. Ky., Lexington, 1994—98; rsch. faculty U. Tex. Health Sci. Ctr., San Antonio, 1998—. Contbr. articles to profl. jours. Judge Fayette County Pub. Schs., Lexington. Named Fgn. External Examiner, U. Madras, 2000—; recipient Best Rsch. award, Hoffman-LaRoche, 1997; Jr. Rsch. fellow, Dept. Atomic Energy, Govt. India, 1984—88. Mem.: AAAS, Am. Soc. for Microbiology, Am. Assn. for Cancer Rsch. Achievements include research in invention of the underlying molecular mechanisms of the loss of growth factor (TGF-ß) signaling in human pancreatic cancer. Office: Univ Tex Health Sci Ctr 7703 Floyd Curl Dr San Antonio TX 78229-3900 Office Fax: 210-567-6687. Personal E-mail: kolaparthi@hotmail.com. E-mail: kolaparthi@uthscsa.edu.

KOLAR, MARY JANE, trade and professional association executive; b. Benton, Ill., Aug. 9, 1941; d. Thomas Haskell and Mary Jane (Sanders) Burnett; m. Otto Michael Kolar, Aug. 13, 1966; children: Robin Lynn, Deon Michael. BA with high honors, So. Ill. U., 1963, MA with highest honors, 1964. Tchr. pub. schs., Benton and Zeigler, Ill., 1960-63; grad. asst. and grad. fellow So. Ill. U., Carbondale, 1963-64; instr. Ridgewood High Sch., Norridge, Ill., 1964-67, Maine Twp. High Sch., Des Plaines, Ill., 1967-70; freelance writer plumbing, heating & cooling industry couns. Chgo., 1970-71; ednl. coord. Am. Dietetic Assn., Chgo., 1971-72; dir. profl. devel. Am. Dental Hygienists Assn., Chgo., 1972-78; dir. Learning Ctr. div. Am. Coll. Cardiology, Bethesda, Md., 1978-80; dir. edn. Nat. Moving and Storage Assn., Alexandria, Va., 1980-82; exec. dir. Women in Communications, Inc., Austin, Tex., 1982-84, Altrusa Internat., Chgo., 1984-87, Assn. Govt. Accts., Alexandria, Va., 1987-90, Bus./Profl. Advt. Assn., Alexandria, 1991-92, Am. Assn. Family and Consumer Scis., Alexandria, 1992-96, dir. Project Taking Charge Adolescent Pregnancy Prevention Program, 1993-95; pres., CEO The Alexandria Group, Inc. (charter accredited co., Am. Soc. Assn. Execs.), 1996—. Mem. Accreditation Commn. for Assn. Mgmt. Cos.; cons. spkr. various profl. assns., ednl. instns. and fed agys. Contbr. articles to profl. jours. and assn. mags., chpts. to books. Mem. adv. council Accrediting Commn., Assn. of Ind. Colls. and Schs., 1980-88; treas. Pub. Employees Roundtable, 1988-90, Hollin Hills Civic Assn., 1989-90. Fellow Am. Soc. Allied Health Professions (dir. 1978-79), Am. Soc. Assn. Execs. (charter accredited; cert. commr. accreditation commn. for assn. mgmt. cos. 2002—, Key Profl. Assn. coun. 1994-96, Peer Rev. Com., 1997-2000, rsch. com. 1996-2000, strategic leadership forum com. 1996 97, awards com. 1992 93, univ. affairs commn. 1986-92, chair 1990-91, found. bd. 1987-91, chmn. edn. sect. 1982-83, bd. dirs. 1983-86, chair higher edn. task force 1990-91, chair fellows 1987, Educator of Yr. award 1978, Key award 1990, pres., CEO), Assn. Mgmt. Cos. (commr. accreditation commn. 2002--); mem. Greater Washington Soc. Assn. Execs. (edn. com. 1979-82, CEO com. 1990-92, 94-96, vice chair 1995-96, strategic planning com. 1994-95, exec. search com. 1994-96), Assn. Mgmt. Cos. (commr. accreditatin commn. 2003—), Future Home Makers Am. (bd. dirs. 1992-96), Alexandria C. of C. (assn. coun. 1990-96, steering com. 1993-96), Women in Comm. (newsletter editor, legis. and career re-entry chair, chair ERA task force, dir. Washington profl. chpt. 1981-83, program com. Chgo. chpt. 1984-86), So. Ill. U. Alumni Assn. (bd. dirs. 1984-89, v.p. 1986-89, presdl. search com. 1986-87). Office: 526 King St Ste 423 Alexandria VA 22314-3143 E-mail: mjkolar@alexandriagroup.com. *Being a professional means many things. It means adhering to an ethical code, having high standards of quality, striving toward excellence through basic and ongoing preparation for the profession I have chosen to practice. It means having goals and being willing to contribute to solving the social, economic and political problems of the society of which I am a part. Professionalism is more than acceptance of responsibility, more than doing one's duty, more than being good at what one does. Professionalism requires a commitment to what you do and to the future. It carries with it obligation and risk. It necessitates service to the profession— a willingness to be a leader— and a desire to meet the needs of others.*

KOLAROV, NICKOLAI ATANASSOV, musician, educator; b. Sofia, Bulgaria, July 10, 1963; arrived in U.S., 1995; s. Atanas Ivanov Kolarov and Stefka (Russeva) Kolarova; m. Aurora Gueorguieva Moussorlieva, Jan. 20, 1996; children: Radha, Mary-Rose, Stephanie. Diploma, Bulgarian Acad. Music, 1989; MusM, U. Mo., 1997; DMA, U. Minn., 2002. Cellist Bulgarian Nat. Theater of Music, Sofia, 1990—95; instr. Strings Heart of Am. Coll., Kansas City, Mo., 1998—2000; prof. Cello St. Thomas U., St. Paul, 2001—. Tchr. Music St. Bernadette Sch., Kansas City, 1998—99; founder, pres. Art Salon Zora, Sofia, 1993—. Performer (solo recital): Nat. Palace of Culture, 1994; performer: Bulgarian Contemporary Music, 1999. Mem.: Am. Fedn. Musicians. Avocations: yoga, hiking, vegetarianism. Home: 1314 Gibbs Ave Saint Paul MN 55108 Office: Saint Thomas Univ 2115 Summit Ave BEC9 Saint Paul MN 55105-1048*

KOLASINSKI, JOHN RICHARD, electrical engineer; m. Hilda L. Cooper. BSEE, U. Md., 1985. Sys. engr. Litton Industries, College Park, Md., 1985-89; elec. sys. engr. NASA, Greenbelt, Md., 1989—, sr. engr. spaceflight fiber optic devel., 1993—. Evaluator NASA patents, Nat. Sci. and Engring. Coun. of Can. rsch. grants; leader NASA fiber optic devel., including Hubble Space Telescope, Internat. Space Sta., Space Shuttle. Patentee in field. Mem. Telecom. Industry Assn., Soc. Automotive Engrs. Office: NASA/Goddard Space Flight Ctr Code 565 Greenbelt MD 20771-0001 E-mail: john.kolasinski@gsfc.nasa.gov.

KOLATCH, ALFRED JACOB, publisher; b. Seattle, Jan. 2, 1916; s. Sander and Yetta (Jacobs) K.; m. Thelma Rubin, June 16, 1940; children: Jonathan, David. BA, Yeshiva U., 1937; Rabbi, Jewish Theol. Sem., 1941. Ordained rabbi, 1941; rabbi, 1941-43, Kew Gardens, N.Y., 1946-48; founder, pres. Jonathan David Pubs., Middle Village, N.Y., 1949—. Author: These Are the Names, 1948, Who's Who in the Talmud, 1964, The Name Dictionary, 1967, Jewish Information Quiz Book, 1967, The Family Seder, 1968, Names for Pets, 1971, JD Dictionary of First Names, 1980, Jewish Book of Why, 1981, Complete Dictionary of English and Hebrew First Names, 1984, The Second Jewish Book of Why, 1985, Today's Best Baby Names, 1986, This Is the Torah, 1987, The New Name Dictionary, 1989, The Jewish Home Advisor, 1990, The Jewish Child's First Book of Why, 1992, The Jewish Mourner's Book of Why, 1992, Classic Bible Stories for Jewish Children, 1994, The Jewish Heritage Quiz Book, 1995, Great Jewish Quotations, 1996, Let's Celebrate Our Jewish Holidays, 1997, A Child's First Book of Jewish Holidays, 1997, Best Baby Names for Jewish Children, 1998, What Jews Say About God, 1999, The Presidents of the United States and the Jews, 2000, The Masters of the Talmud, 2003, (paperback edit.) The Jewish Book of Why, 2003. Served as chaplain U.S. Army, 1943-46. Mem. Rabbinical Assembly, Assn. Jewish Chaplains (past pres.), Mil. Chaplains Assn. (past v.p.) Home: 72-08 Juno St Forest Hills NY 11375-5930 Office: 68-22 Eliot Ave Middle Village NY 11379 E-mail: rabbiajk@aol.com.

KOLATCH, MYRON, magazine editor; b. Bklyn., Sept. 26, 1929; s. Philip S. and Rebecca (Langberg) K.; m. Francine Ruth Miller, Jan. 28, 1951; children: Barry Steven, Jonathan Lee, Sari Elana. B.A, N.Y. U., 1950, postgrad in English, 1950-51. Mem. staff New Leader, 1953—, mng. editor, 1960-61, exec. editor, 1961—. Bd. dirs. Tamiment Inst. Served with AUS, 1951-53. Home: 18622 Radnor Rd Jamaica NY 11432-5829 Office: 275 7th Ave New York NY 10001-6708 E-mail: mkolatch@thenewleader.com.

KOLAYA, MARGARET HELEN BOUTWELL, librarian; b. Concord, N.H., Apr. 15, 1947; d. Harvey B. and Margaret A. Boutwell; m. John L. Kolaya, June 20, 1970; children: Lauren B., Timothy A. BA in History, Bucknell U., 1969; MLS, Rutgers U., 1979. Manuscripts asst. Yale U. Libr., New Haven, 1969-70; head libr. The Wardlaw-Hartridge Sch., Edison and Plainfield, N.J., 1983-96; supervising libr. Rockwood Meml. Libr., 1996-97; dir. Clark Pub. Libr., 1997—2002, Scotch Plains (NJ) Publ Libr., 2002—. Bd. dirs. Hist. Soc. Plainfield, 1973-97, pres., 1987-88; bd. dirs. Catherine Webster Home, Inc., Plainfield, 1993-2002. Mem. ALA, N.J. Libr. Assn., Third N.J. Regiment (Brigade of the Am. Revolution). Home: 1081 Oakland Ave Plainfield NJ 07060-3411 Office: Scotch Plains Pub Libr 1927 Bartle Ave Scotch Plains NJ 07076-

KOLB, BERTHA MAE (BERTHA MAE RAGSDALE), travel agency administrator; b. Dumas, Ark., Nov. 3, 1925; d. Harold Dewey and Hallie Eugenia (Muskelley) Ragsdale; m. Charles Rudolph Kolb, Oct. 9, 1951 (dec. 1982); 1 child, Charles Harold. Student, La. State U., 1959-61. Sec. Le Tourneau Co., Vicksburg, U.S. Govt. Waterways Experiment Sta.; travel agt. Am. Internat. Travel, Inc., 1983—. Pres. Vicksburg Coun. of Garden Clubs, 1972; bd. dirs. Garden Clubs of Miss., 1977-89, 91-2000; active numerous Vicksburg civic svc. clubs, 1953-. Mem. Vicksburg Country Club (pres. ladies orgn. 1969-70), Town and Country Garden Club (pres. Vicksburg chpt. 1973-75). Episcopalian. Avocations: theater, travel, gardening. E-mail: bkhr981@cablelynx.com.

KOLB, CHARLES EUGENE, research and development company executive; b. Cumberland, Md., May 21, 1945; s. Charles Eugene and Doris Helen (McFarland) Kolb; m. Susan Marie Foote, Aug. 19, 1965; children: Craig E., Amy C. BS, MIT, 1967; MA, Princeton U., 1968, PhD, 1971. Sr. rsch. sci. Aerodyne Rsch. Inc., Burlington, Mass., 1971-74, prin. rsch. sci. Bedford, Mass., 1975-76, dir. Ctr. Chem. and Environ. Physics, 1977-79, tech. dir. applied scis. div., 1979-80, dir. applied scis. div., v.p., 1981-84, exec. v.p. and dir. rsch. Billerica, Mass., pres., CEO, 1985—. Assoc. atmospheric chemistry Harvard U., 1976—85; rsch. affiliate Spectroscopy Lab. MIT, 1981—92, rsch. affiliate dept. aeronautics and astronautics, 1993. Editor: Geophys. Rsch. Letters, 1996—99; mem. editl. bd. Internat. Jour. Chem. Kinetics, 1990—92; contbr. chapters to books, articles to profl. jours. Fellow: AAAS, Am. Geophys. Union, Am. Phys. Soc., Optical Soc. Am.; mem.: Union Concerned Scientists, Combustion Inst., Am. Chem. Soc. (chmn. northeastern sect. 1991, trustee 1994—96, com. environ. improvement 2002—, Creative Advances in Environ. Sci. and Tech. award 1997), MIT Alumni Assn. (Bronze Beaver award 1987, Lobdell award 1981). Home: 8 Stearns Rd Bedford MA 01730-1077 also: 46 Oak Grove Ave East Falmouth MA 02536-7431 Office: Aerodyne Rsch Inc 45 Manning Rd Billerica MA 01821-3976 E-mail: kolb@aerodyne.com.

KOLB, CHARLES CHESTER, humanities administrator; b. Erie, Pa., Sept. 4, 1940; s. John Christian and Edna Lucille (Church) K.; m. Joy Bilharz, June 3, 1972 (div. Mar. 1991); 1 child, Nancy Gwenyth; m. P. Jean Drew, July 20, 1991; 1 child, Catherine Claire Fraley. BA in History, Pa. State U., 1962, PhD in Archaeology and Anthropology, 1979. Instr. anthropology Pa. State U., University Park, 1966-69, Bryn Mawr (Pa.) Coll., 1969-73; from instr. to asst. prof. anthropology Pa. State U., Erie, 1973-84; dir. rsch. and grants Mercyhurst Coll., 1984-89, asst. dir. Hammermill Libr., 1989; humanities adminstr. program officer divsn. state programs NEH, Washington, 1989-91, program officer divsn. preservation and access, 1991-96, sr. program officer, 1997—. Manuscript reviewer Holt, Rinehart and Winston, Inc., 1977-89, Prentice-Hall, Inc., 1979-85, William C. Brown, Pubs., 1982-85, U. Tex. Press, 1988—, U. Utah Press, 1991—, U. Press of Fla., 1994—, AltaMira Press/Sage, 1995—, U. Pa. Mus. Applied Sci. Ctr. Archaeology, 1996—, Dover Pub., 1996—, U. Press of Colo., 2003—; grant proposal reviewer NEH, 1981-89, NSF, 1982—, Wenner-Gren Found. for Anthropol. Rsch., 1987-89; co-founder, ann. symposium co-organizer Ceramic Studies Interest Group, 1986—. Author: Marine Shell Trade and Classic Teotihuacan, 1987, editor: A Pot for All Reasons, 1988, Ceramic Ecology, 1988, 89, 97; contbr. articles to profl. jours., chpts. to books; book and film reviewer Sci. Books and Films, 1977—; manuscript reviewer Am. Antiquity, 1978—, Current Anthropology, 1979—, Ancient Mesoamerica, 1990—, Ethnohistory, 1995—, Jour. Material Culture, 1995—, Hist. Archaeology, 1995—, L.Am. Antiquity, 1995—, H-Net Revs., 1996-, Jour. Archaeol. Sci., 1998—, Jour. Am. Inst. for Conservation, 2001—; abstractor Ceramic Abstracts, 1990-96, Art and Archaeology Technical Abstracts, 1996—; regional editor La Tinaja: Newsletter of Archaeol. Ceramics, 1991—; N.Am. corr. Old Potter's Almanack, 1992—; reviewer CHOICE, 1992—, ScienceNETLinks, 1999—, Transoxiana: E-journal de Estudios Orientales, 2003—, Central Asian Rsch. Rev., 2003—; contbr. Encyclopedia of Modern Asia, 2002, Encyclopedia World's Minorities, 2003, Dictionary of American History, 2002. Mem. Commonwealth Pa., Gov.'s Conf. on Librs. and Info. Systems, 1989. Fellow AAAS (panelist sci. journalism awards 2003—), Royal Anthrop. Inst. Gt. Britain and Ireland, Am. Anthrop. Assn.; mem. Am. Ceramic Soc., Am. Chem. Soc., Am. Ethnological Soc., Am. Soc. Ethnohistory, Archaeol. Inst. Am., Assn. Field Archaeology, Coun. Mus. Anthropology, Materials Rsch. Soc., Prehist. Ceramic Rsch. Group, Soc. Am. Archaeology, Soc. Archaeol. Scis. (life, bd. dirs. 1998—, assoc. editor for archaeol. ceramics Bull. 1997—), Soc. Hist. Archaeology, Soc. Am. Archivists, Register Profl. Archaeologists, U.S. Naval Inst. (life), Soc. for Pa. Archaeology, N.Y. State Archaeol. Assn., Paleopathol-

ogy Assn., Assn. Moving Image Archivists, Pearl Harbor History Assocs. (life), Naval Hist. Found., Ctrl. Eurasian Studies Soc., Sigma Xi, Alpha Kappa Delta, Phi Kappa Phi, Pi Gamma Mu. Achievements include rsch. in tech. and cultural interpretations of archaeol. ceramics by using physiochem. analyses and petrographic microscopy, ceramics from Afghanistan, Ctrl. Asia, Mexico, Guatemala, East Africa, Great Lakes Basin. Home: 1005 Pruitt Ct SW Vienna VA 22180-6429 Office: NEH Divsn Preservation & Access 1100 Pennsylvania Ave NW Washington DC 20004-2501 E-mail: ckolb@neh.gov.

KOLB, DAVID ALLEN, psychology educator; b. Moline, Ill., Dec. 12, 1939; s. John August and Ethel May (Petherbridge) K.; m. Alice Yoko; 1 son, Jonathan Demian. AB cum laude, Knox Coll., 1961; PhD, Harvard U., 1967; ScD (h.c.), U. N.H., 1984; PhD (h.c.), Internat. Mgmt. Ctr., Buckingham, 1988; LittD (h.c.), Franklin U., 1994; DHL (h.c.), SUNY, 1996. Asst. prof. organizational psychology MIT, Cambridge, 1965-70, assoc. prof., 1970-75; prof. organizational behavior and mgmt. Case Western Res. U., Cleve., 1976—, deWindt Prof. Leadership and Enterprise Devel. Weatherhead Sch. Mgmt., 1992-97, chmn. dept., 1984-90. Vis. prof. mgmt. London Grad. Sch. Bus., 1971; dir. Devel. Research Assos., 1966-80; mgmt. cons., U.S., Australia, N.Z., Indonesia, Singapore, Malaysia, Thailand, Japan. Author: Experiential Learning: Experience as the source of learning and development, 1984; co-author: Organizational Behavior: An Experiential Approach, 7th edit, 2001, Organizational Behavior: A Book of Readings, 7th edit, 2001, Changing Human Behavior: Principles of Planned Intervention, 1974, Innovation in Professional Education: Steps on Journey from Teaching to Learning, 1995, Conversational Learning: An Experiential Approach to Knowledge Creation, 2002. Woodrow Wilson fellow, 1962 Mem. Internat. Assn. Applied Social Scientists (charter), Soc. Intercultural Edn., Tng. and Rsch. (charter), Coun.l Advancement of Experiential Learning (Research Excellence award 1984, Morris T. Keaton Adult and Experiental Learning award 1991, Case Weatherhead Rsch. Recognition award 2002-03). Office: Case Western Res U Dept of Orgn Behavior Cleveland OH 44106 E-mail: dak5@msn.com.

KOLB, DOROTHY GONG, elementary education educator; b. San Jose, Calif. d. Jack and Lucille Gong; m. William Harris Kolb, Mar. 22, 1970. BA with highest honors, San Jose State U., 1964; postgrad., U. Hawaii, Calif. State U., L.A.; MA in Ednl. Tech., Pepperdine U., 1992. Cert. in elem. edn., edn. for mentally retarded, edn. for learning handicapped pre-sch., adult classes, resource specialist, English lang. devel., specially designed acad. instrn. in English, 2000. Tchr. Cambrian Sch. Dist., San Jose, 1964-66, Ctrl. Oahu Sch. Dist., Wahiawa, Hawaii, 1966-68, Montebello (Calif.) Unified Sch. Dist., 1968—. Recipient Very Spl. Person award, Calif. PTA, 1998, Hon. Svc. award, 2003; Walter Bachrodt Meml. scholar. Mem.: Tau Beta Pi, Pi Tau Sigma, Kappa Delta Pi, Pi Lambda Theta.

KOLB, FELIX OSCAR, physician; b. Vienna, Nov. 12, 1921; arrived in U.S., 1938; s. Leon and Hilde (Grunwald) K.; m. Susan L. Goldberger, July 1, 1966; children: Lisa F., Marc E. AB, U. Calif., Berkeley, 1941; MD, U. Calif., San Francisco, 1943. Diplomate Am. Bd. Internal Medicine, Am. Bd. Endocrinology and Metabolism. Intern San Francisco Gen. Hosp., 1943-44; clin. asst. U. Calif. Med. Ctr., San Francisco, 1946-47; med. resident VA Hosp., U. Calif., San Francisco, 1947-49, New Eng. Ctr. Hosp., Boston, 1949-50; grad. asst. endocrine svc. of Dr. Fuller Albright Mass. Gen. Hosp., Boston, 1950-51; attending physician U. Calif. Hosp., San Francisco, 1952—; asst. chief, assoc. chief, sr. dept. of medicine Mt. Zion Hosp., San Francisco, 1952-98, emeritus, 1998—; asst. assoc. dir. metabolic rsch. unit U. Calif., San Francisco, 1952-85, clin. prof. medicine, 1969-99, clin. prof. medicine emeritus, 1999—, asst. assoc. dir. metabolic rsch. unit, 1952-85; pvt. practice in endocrinology and metabolism San Francisco, 1952-99; retired. Cons. physician Shriners Hosp., San Francisco, VA Hosp., San Francisco, Children's Hosp., San Francisco, Letterman Hosp., San Francisco, Marshal Hale Hosp., San Francisco, Calif. Pacific Med. Ctr., San Francisco. Co-author, author 3 text book chpts.; contbr. numerous articles to profl. jours.; editl. bd. Metabolism, Reviewer for Ann. and Arch. Internal Medicine, Calcified Tissue Internat. Capt. U.S. Army, 1944-46. Fellow ACP; mem. AMA, Calif. Med. Assn., San Francisco Med. Assn., Am. Diabetes Assn., Endocrine Soc., Am. Fedn. for Clin. Rsch., We. Soc. for Clin. Rsch., Am. Soc. Internal Medicine, Calif. Soc. Internal Medicine, San Francisco Soc. Internal Medicine, Am. Soc. for Bone and Mineral Rsch., Alpha Omega Alpha (sec.-treas. 1955-56), Phi Delta Epsilon. Democrat. Jewish. Avocations: piano, golf. Home: 9 Starboard Ct Mill Valley CA 94941-3210 Fax: (415) 383-1013. E-mail: FOKolb@pol.net.

KOLB, GWIN JACKSON, language professional, educator; b. Aberdeen, Miss., Nov. 2, 1919; s. Roy Rolly and Nola Undine (Jackson) K.; m. Ruth Alma Godbold, Oct. 11, 1943; children: Gwin Jackson II, Alma Dean. BA, Millsaps Coll., 1941; MA, U. Chgo., 1946, PhD, 1949; LHD, Millsaps Coll., 1991. Editorial asst. Modern Philology, 1946-56; mem. faculty U. Chgo., 1949-89, prof. English, 1961-77, Chester D. Tripp prof. humanities, 1977-89, emeritus, 1990—, chmn. dept., 1963-72, chmn. coll. English staff, 1958-60, head humanities sect. in coll., 1960-62. Vis. assoc. prof. Northwestern U., winter 1958, Stanford U., spring 1960; vis. prof. U. Wash., summers 1967, 73, Ohio State U., spring 1987, Peking U., fall 1994, U. Evansville, winter, spring 1996, Huntingdon Coll., winter, spring 1997, U. Ga., winter 1998, Berry Coll., winter, spring 2000. Co-author: Dr. Johnson's Dictionary, 1955, Reading Literature: A Workbook, 1955; editor: (Samuel Johnson) Rasselas and Other Tales, 1990; co-editor: A Bibliography of Modern Studies Complied for Philological Quarterly, 1951-65, 3 vols., 1962, 72, Modern Philology, 1973-89, Approaches to Teaching the Works of Samuel Johnson, 1993. Served with USNR, 1942-45. Frederick A. and Marion S. Pottle fellow Beinecke Libr. Yale U., 1993; recipient Quantrell award U. Chgo., 1955, Medal of Honor U. Evansville, 1992, Alumni award Millsaps Coll., 1967; Guggenheim fellow, 1956-57; grantee Am. Coun. Learned Socs., 1961-62. Mem. MLA, Midwest MLA (pres. 1964-65), Johnson Soc. Ctrl. Region (pres. 1965-66), Nat. Coun. Tchrs. English (bd. dirs. coll. sect. 1966-68), Am. Soc. 18th Century Studies (exec. bd. 1973-76, pres. 1976-77), The Johnsonians, Assn. Depts. English (pres. 1968), Caxton Club, Quadrangle. Home: 5819 S Blackstone Ave Chicago IL 60637-1855

KOLB, HAROLD HUTCHINSON, JR., English language educator; b. Boston, Jan. 16, 1933; BA in English with honors, Amherst Coll., 1955; MA in Am. Studies, U. Mich., 1960; PhD in British and Am. Lit., Ind. U., 1968. Instr. English Valparaiso U., 1960-62; teaching assoc. Ind. U., 1962-65; from asst. prof. to prof. English U. Va., Charlottesville, 1967-99, prof. emeritus, 2000—, dir. Ctr. for Liberal Arts, 1984-99. Project dir. NEH, 1972-76, 85-99; dir. Canadian Judicial Writing Program, 1981-84; guest prof. Am. studies U. Bonn, 1982; chmn. MLA Delegate Assembly Steering Com., 1984-85. Author: The Illusion of Life-American Realism as a Literary Form, 1969, A Field Guide to the Study of American Literature, 1976, A Writer's Guide: The Essential Points, 1980; co-author: A Handbook for Research in American Literature and American Studies, 1994; contbr. articles to scholarly and other publs. Naval aviator, 1955-59. Recipient Armstrong prize in English, Amherst Coll., 1952, James A. Work prize U. Ind., 1965, Guggenheim fellowship, 1970-71, Faculty Leadership award Am. Assn. Higher Edn., Carnegie Found. for Advancement of Teaching and Change mag., 1986, Citation for Leadership in Rejuvenation of Secondary and Elem. Edn., Va. Bd. Edn., 1987, Phillip E. Frandson award for Innovation and Creative Programming, Nat. U. Continuing Edn. Assn., 1988, Outstanding Faculty award Va. Coun. Higher Edn., 1988.

KOLB, JERRY WILBERT, accountant; b. Chgo., Dec. 22, 1935; s. Herman and Myrtle (Richter) K.; m. Marlene Joyce Tipp, Feb. 3, 1957 (div. July 1986); children: Bradley, Steven, Lisa; m. Carol Ann Fleming, Dec. 14, 1986. BS in Acct. with high honors, U. Ill., 1957; MBA, DePaul U., 1962. CPA, Ill., N.Y., Iowa. Acct. Deloitte Haskins & Sells CPAs, Chgo., 1957-68, ptnr., 1968-76, ptnr.-in-charge Chgo. Office, 1976-83; ptnr.-in-charge profl. svcs. Deloitte & Touche CPAs (formerly Deloitte Haskins & Sells), N.Y.C., 1983-86, CFO, 1986-92, vice-chmn., 1992-98; dir. New Skies Satellites N.V., 1998—. Lectr. DePaul U., Chgo., 1962-76, mem. adv. council dept. acctg., 1981-83; mem. profl. adv. bd. dept. accountancy U. Ill., Urbana, 1979-82; mem. adv. council Sch. Accountancy, Northwestern U., Evanston, 1980-83. Recipient Disting. Alumni award DePaul U., 1970. Mem. AICPA (Sells Gold Medal award 1957), Ill. CPA Soc. (bd. dirs. 1973-77, v.p. 1976-77), Am. Acctg. Assn., N.Y. Yacht Club, Tampa Yacht and Country Club. Home: 308 W Lyon Farm Dr Greenwich CT 06831-4356 E-mail: nquest1@aol.com.

KOLB, JOHN CONNER, financial markets executive; b. Dallas, Apr. 29, 1965; s. Nathaniel Key and Catherine Lou (Conner) K.; 1 child, Jane Catherine. BS in Econs., So. Meth. U., 1988. Spl. projects coord. Cystic Fibrosis Found., Bethesda, Md., 1988-90; head trader, securities lending Baring Securities, N.Y.C., 1990-93; regional head (Ams.) equity fin. Paribas Corp., N.Y.C., 1993-95; global head equity fin. Banque Paribas, London, 1995-98; head U.K., Europe Securities Fin. Commerzbank, London, 1998-2001; head, Americas Securities Fin. Commerzbank Capital Mkts. Corp., N.Y.C., 2001—. Bd. mem. Equity Borrowers Working Com., London Investment Banking Assn., 1996-97. Com. mem. Cystic Fibrosis Found., N.Y.C., 1990-95; mem. Oaklawn Tex. Found., Dallas, 1987—. Mem. Phi Theta Kappa. Avocations: skiing, jogging, tennis, motorcycling. Office: Commerzbank Capital Markets Corp 1251 Ave of the Americas New York NY 10020 Home: 84 Chapel Road Waccabuc NY 10597

KOLB, JOHN E. lawyer; b. Argenta, Tex., Aug. 19, 1928; s. Luther T. and Gladys (Bomer) K.; m. Joy Voltz, Aug. 16, 1947; children: Susan Kolb Dunwoody, Jay T., Paul M., Ellen Kolb Klepacki, Ann Kolb Cuclis. BBA, U. Tex., 1949; LLB, U. Houston, 1955. From assoc. to ptnr. Vinson & Elkins, Houston, 1955—. Bd. dirs. Adobe Resources Corp., N.Y.C. Regent U. Houston System, 1981-87; bd. dirs. W.M. Keck Found., Los Angeles, 1986—. Recipient Disting. Alumnus award U. Houston Alumni Assn., 1984. Mem. ABA, Tex. Bar Assn., Houston Bar Assn. Mem. Disciples of Christ Ch. Clubs: Ramada (Houston), River Oaks Country. Address: 10 S Briar Hollow Apt 59 Houston TX 77027

KOLB, JOYCE DIANA, artist, educator; b. Detroit, Nov. 28, 1942; d. David Victor and Jean (Silber) Howell; m. Gary Jack Kolb, June 15, 1963; 1 child, Michael Daniel. BFA, Corcoran Sch. Art, Washington, 1981. Legal sec. Advance Mortgage Co., Detroit, 1961-63; profl. artist Arnold, Md., 1981—; founder, facilitator Healing Through Art, Arnold, 1995—; facilitator Natural Healing, Inc., Severna Park, Md., 1997—, Unity By-the-Bay, Severna Park, 1996—, Psyche's WEll, Easton, Md., 1998—, Art Inst. Gallery, Salisbury, Md., 1998—, Sunrise Assisted Living, Severna Park, 1998—, Innersource, Annapolis, Md., 1998—, art educator home sch. for children Arnold, 1996—. Founder, facilitator Healing Through Art workshops, Arnold, 1995—. Exhibited sculpture, Flint, Mich., 1976 (3-Dimension Design award 1976), painting, Glen Echo, Md., 1981 (artist-in-residence 1981); represented in permanent collection Nat. Mus. of Women in Arts, Washington. Recipient 1st pl. award 23d Invitational Art Exhibit, Towson Bus. Assn., 1990, Best of Show Annapolitan Gallerie, 1994. Mem. Women's Caucus for Arts (participating artist D.C. chpt. Beijing 1996), Md. Fedn. Art, Corcoran Alumni Assn. Avocations: promoting positive energy, traveling, friends, animal lover, appreciation of outdoors. Office: Healing Through Art PO Box 163 Arnold MD 21012-0163 E-mail: joyce@art-kolb.com.

KOLB, KEITH ROBERT, architect, educator; b. Billings, Mont., Feb. 9, 1922; s. Percy Fletcher and Josephine (Randolph) K.; m. Jacqueline Cecile Jump, June 18, 1947; children: Brooks Robin, Bliss Richards. Grad. basic engring., US Army Specialized Training Rutgers U., 1944; BArch cum laude, U. Wash., 1947; MArch, Harvard U., 1950. Registered architect, Wash., Mont., Idaho, Calif., Oreg., Nat. Council Archtl. Registration Bds. Draftsman, designer various archtl. firms, Seattle, 1946-54; draftsman, designer Walter Gropius and Architects Collaborative, Cambridge, Mass., 1950-52; prin. Keith R. Kolb, Architect, Seattle, 1954-64, Keith R. Kolb Architect & Assocs., Seattle, 1964-66; ptnr. Decker, Kolb & Stansfield, Seattle, 1966-71, Kolb & Stansfield AIA Architects, Seattle, 1971-89; pvt. practice Keith R. Kolb FAIA Architects, Seattle, 1989—. Instr. Mont. State Coll., Bozeman, 1947-49; asst. prof. arch. U. Wash., Seattle, 1952-60, assoc. prof., 1960-82, prof., 1982-90, prof. emeritus, 1990—. Design architect Dist. II Hdqrs. and Comm. Ctr., Wash. State Patrol, Bellevue, 1970 (Exhbn. award Seattle chpt. AIA), Hampson residence, 1970 (nat. AIA 1st honor 1973, citation Seattle chpt. AIA 1980), Acute Gen. Stevens Meml. Hosp., 1973, Redmond Pub. Libr., 1975 (jury selection Wash. coun. AIA 1980), Tolstedt residence, Helena, Mont., 1976, Herbert L. Eastlick Biol. Scis. Lab. bldg. Wash. State U., 1977, Redmond Svc. Ctr., Puget Sound Power and Light Co., 1979, Computer and Mgmt. Svcs. Ctr., Paccar Inc., 1981 (curatorial team selection Mus. History and Industry exhbn. 100th anniversary of AIA 1994), Seattle Town House, 1960 (curatorial team selection Mus. History and Industry exhbn. 100th anniversary of AIA 1994), Comm. Tower, Pacific N.W. Bell, 1981 (nat. J.F. Lincoln bronze), Forks br. Seattle 1st Nat. Bank, 1981 (commendation award Seattle chpt. AIA 1981, nat. jury selection Am. Architecture, The State of the Art in the '80's 1985, regional citation Am. Wood Coun. 1981), Reg. ops. Control Ctr. Sacramento Dist. Corps Engrs. McChord AFB, Wash., 1982, Puget Sound Blood Ctr., 1983-88, expansion vis./dining/recreation facilities Wash. State Reformatory, Monroe, 1983, Univ. Sta. P.O., U.S. Postal Svc., Seattle, 1983, Guard Towers, McNeil Island Corrections Ctr. Wash., 1983, Magnolia Queen Anne Carrier Annex, U.S. Postal Svc., Seattle, 1986, Tolstedt residence, Seattle, 1987, Maxim residence, Camano Island, Wash., 1991, Carmean residence alterations/additions, Seattle, 1995, 96, 97, 2001, 2002, Susanna Burney and Bliss Kolb residence, Seattle, 2001-03. Pres. Laurelhurst Cmty. Club, Seattle, 1966. Served with U.S. Army, 1943-45, ETO. Decorated Bronze Star medal ETO; recipient Alpha Rho Chi medal; selected Am. Architects, Facts on File, inc., 1989. Fellow AIA (dir. Seattle chpt. 1970-71, sec. Seattle chpt. 1972, Wash. state coun. 1973, pres. sr. coun. Seattle chpt. 1994-96, trustee Seattle Archtl. Found. 1994-96, Citation award Seattle chpt. for a Seattle 1960 Town House, 1990, honored Living Legends Series 2002); mem. U. Wash. Archtl. Alumni Assn. (pres. 1958-59), Phi Beta Kappa, Tau Sigma Delta. Home and Office: 3379 47th Ave NE Seattle WA 98105-5326

KOLB, KEN LLOYD, writer; b. Portland, Oreg., July 14, 1926; s. Frederick Von and Ella May (Bay) K.; m. Emma LaVada Sanford, June 7, 1952; children: Kevin, Lauren, Kimrie. BA in English with honors, U. Calif., Berkeley, 1950; MA with honors, San Francisco State U., 1953. Cert. jr. coll. English tchr. Freelance fiction writer various nat. mags., N.Y.C., 1951-56; freelance screenwriter various film and TV studios, Los Angeles, 1956-81; freelance novelist Chilton, Random House, Playboy Press, N.Y.C., 1967—. Instr. creative writing Feather River Coll., Quincy Calif., 1969; minister Universal Life Ch. Author: (teleplay) She Walks in Beauty, 1956 (Writers Guild award 1956), (feature films) Seventh Voyage of Sinbad, 1957, Snow Job, 1972, (novels) Getting Straight, 1967 (made into feature film), The Couch Trip, 1970 (made into feature film), Night Crossing, 1974; contbr. fiction and humor to nat. mags. and anthologies. Foreman Plumas County Grand Jury, Quincy, 1970; chmn. Region C Criminal Justice Planning commn., Oroville, Calif., 1975-77; film commr. Plumas County, 1986-87. Served with USNR, 1944-46. Establishment Ken Kolb Collection (Boston U. Library 1969). Mem. Writers Guild Am. West, Authors Guild, Mensa, Phi Beta Kappa, Theta Chi. Clubs: Plumas Ski (pres. 1977-78). Democrat. Avocations: skiing, tennis, traveling. Home and Office: PO Box 30022 Cromberg CA 96103-3022 *The true measure of success is not the attainment of great wealth or a position of power over others, but the quality of one's own life. I'm grateful for the money and honors I've had from writing, but more important to me is my ongoing love affair with my wife and the loving friendship of my grown children. I believe in God and a sense of humor as guiding principles, but I can't explain either one.*

KOLB, NATHANIEL KEY, JR., architect; b. Sherman, Tex., Aug. 17, 1933; s. Nathaniel Key and Nelcine (Dial) K.; m. Catherine Conner, Nov. 24, 1958; children: Nathaniel Key, Mary Catherine, Amy Monica, Peter Paul, John Conner, Elizabeth Dial. BArch, Tex. A&M U., 1957; MArch, U. Pa., 1960. Registered architect, Tex. With CRSS, Houston, 1955-58, Vincent G. Kling, Phila., 1958-61, William B. Tabler, N.Y.C., 1961-63; chmn. bd., pres. Omniplan, Inc., Dallas, 1963-99. Instr. Tex. A&M Univ., Coll. Station, 1957-58; adj. asst. prof. Columbia U., N.Y.C., 1961-62; bd. dirs. Fidelity Bank, Dallas, 1985-98; mem., chmn. Urban Design Task Force, Dallas, 1974-83; dir., mem. exec. com. Greater Dallas Planning Coun., 1982-85; mem. adv. coun. Ryan Real Estate Coun., U. Tex., Arlington, 1985-88; bd. dirs. Peacock Alley, 1998—. Chmn. Hist. Landmarks Com., Dallas, 1977-79; pres., dir. Dallas Ballet, 1982-87. Recipient Outstanding Alumni award, Coll. of Architecture, AEM U./Tex., 2003, Disting. Alumni award, Sherman HS, 2002. Fellow AIA; mem. Tex. Soc. Architects, Dallas chpt. AIA (dir. 1976-80, pres. 1979), Dallas Club (pres., dir. 1980-86) Office: Omniplan 1845 Woodall Rogers Fwy Dallas TX 75201

KOLB, RAINER, chemist; b. Hamburg, Germany, Dec. 1, 1965; came to U.S., 1997; s. Peter and Brigitte K.; m. Sabine Entzian, Aug. 22, 1997. Diploma, U. Hamburg, 1994, PhD, 1997. Asst. scientist U. Hamburg, 1994-97; vis. scientist Nat. Inst. STandards Tech., Gaithersburg, Md., 1997-98; sr. chemist Exxon Mobil Rsch. Engring., Annandale, N.J., 1998—. Contbr. articles to profl. jours. Mem. ACS, Am. Phys. Soc. Avocations: scuba diving, marathons. Office: Exxon Mobil Chem Co 5200 Bayway Drive Baytown TX 77520-2101

KOLB, RICHARD MAURICE, sports writer, sportscaster; b. Washington, Feb. 17, 1951; s. Maurice Woodrow and Dorothy Evelyn (Taylor) K.; 1 child, Michael Richard. Student, U. Md., 1969-71; AA, Prince George's Coll., 1971; AS, No. Va. Coll., 1978. Lic. radio operator, D.C. Pub. info. news specialist USDA, Washington, 1977-78; sports writer Tampa (Fla.) Tribune, 1988-89; pub. rels. dir. Brewster Tech. Ctr., Tampa, 1991; editor Sports Tampa Bay, 1993; sports columnist Bowl Mag., Washington, 1990—, Bowling World, Dublin, Calif., 1991—, Pinbuster, St. Petersburg, Fla., 1993—, Across the Lanes, San Antonio, 1996—; radio sports anchor WTAN, Clearwater, Fla. Writer-photographer Bowling Digest, Chgo., 1998—. Columnist Sports Time mag., 1999—; radio sports talk show host Sta. WWBA, St. Petersburg, Fla. Mem. Young Dems. of Am., College Park, Md., 1970-79. Recipient Best Sports Writer and Sportscaster, Tampa Tribune's Top Ten Award, 1994, Best Feature Story award Bowling Mag., 1998, Gen. Excellence award Pro Bowlers Assn. Tour, 2000. Mem. Bowling Writers Assn. Am. (Bowler of Mo. com. 1997—), Young Am. Bowling Alliance (mem. collegiate bowling poll 1995—), Bowling Writers Assn. Am. (Bowler of Year com. 2001-), Fla. Press Club. Democrat. Avocations: photography, videos, exercising, bowling, golf. Home: 5677 Sailfish Dr Lutz FL 33558-7108

KOLB, SHARON MARIE, educator, cognitive disabilities director; b. Kenosha, Wis., Sept. 6, 1966; d. Darrell Anthony and Colleen Faith Kolb; life ptnr. Britta Jan Johnson; 1 child, Kelly Kolb-Johnson;1 child, Shelby Kolb-Johnson. BS, U Wis., Eau Claire, 1988; MS, U Wis., Whitewater, 1993; PhD, U Wis., 2000. Tchr. Beaver Dam (Wis.) Unified Sch., 1988—2000; lctr. U Wis., Whitewater, 2000—01, asst. prof., coord. of Cognitive Disabilities Program, 2001—. Cons. Statewide Transition Consortium"Wis. Healthy and Ready to Work Project", Madison, 2002—; Spkr. in field. Contbr. chapters to books, articles. Mem. Am. Legion Auxiliary, Wis., 1973—, Rainbow Families of Wis., Madison, Wis., 1997—. Recipient Transition:18-21 Age Group, Dept. of Pub. Instr., 2002—03. Mem.: Council of Exceptional Children, Phi Kappa Phi. Democrat. Luth. Avocations: parent volunteer, volleyball, soccer, guitar. Home: 335 Huntsville Ridge Sun Prairie WI 53590 Office: Dept of Special Education 800 West Main Street Whitewater WI 53190

KOLB, WADE S., JR., lawyer; b. Sumter, S.C., Sept. 16, 1949; s. Wade S. and Rebecca (Bartlett) K.; m. Dorothy Skardon, May 17, 1975; children: Wade S., Sally S., Rebecca G. BS, U. S.C., 1971, JD, 1974. Bar: S.C. 1974, U.S. Dist. Ct. S.C. 1974. Asst. atty. gen. State of S.C., Columbia, 1974-77; asst. solicitor Sumter, 1977-82; solicitor 3d Jud. Cir. Ct. of S.C., Sumter, 1983-98; pvt. practice Sumter, 1998—. Pres. United Way of Sumter, 1977-82; chmn. ARC, Sumter, 1978-82. Recipient Silver Scales of Justice award State Victims' Assistance Network, 1990. Mem. ABA, S.C. Solicitors Assn. (sec.-treas. 1984-88, v.p. 1989-91, pres. 1991-92), Rotary. Office: 7 East Calhoun St Sumter SC 29150-4315

KOLBAS, ROBERT MICHAEL, electrical engineering educator; b. Syracuse, N.Y., Nov. 13, 1953; s. John Michael and Frances C. (Woityra) K.; children: Michael Thomas, Daniel Robert, Sarah Anne, Mary Chen; m. Dahua Zhang. BS in Engring., Cornell U., 1975; MS in Physics, U. Ill., 1977, PhD, 1979. Rsch., teaching asst. U. Ill., Urbana, 1975-79; prin. rsch. scientist Honeywell, Inc., Bloomington, Minn., 1979-83, sr. prin. rsch. scientist, 1983-85; assoc. prof. N.C. State U., Raleigh, 1985-90, prof. elec. and computer engring., 1990—, head elec. and computer engring. dept., 1995-2000. Contbr. articles to profl. publs.; patentee in field. Mentor to high sch. students, N.C. Sch. Sci. and Math., Durham, 1988-91. Kodak Doctoral fellow, U. Ill./Kodak, 1978. Fellow IEEE; mem. Am. Phys. Soc., Tau Beta Pi, Sigma Xi. Office: N C State U PO Box 7911 Raleigh NC 27695-0001

KOLBE, JAMES THOMAS, congressman; b. Evanston, Ill., June 28, 1942; s. Walter William and Helen (Reed) K. BA in Polit. Sci., Northwestern U., 1965; MBA in Econs., Stanford U., 1967. Asst. to coordinating architect Ill. Bldg. Authority, Chgo., 1970-72; spl. asst. to Gov. Richard Ogilvie Chgo., 1972-73; v.p. Wood Canyon Corp., Tucson, 1973-80; mem. Ariz. State Senate, 1977-83, majority whip, 1979-80; mem. U.S. Congress from 5th dist. Ariz., 1985—; mem. appropriations com.; chmn. appropriations subcom. treasury, postal svc., gen. gov. Trustee Embry-Riddle Aero. U., Daytona Beach, Fla.; bd. dirs. Community Food Bank, Tucson; Republican precinct committeeman, Tucson, 1974—. Served as lt. USNR, 1968-69, Vietnam. Republican. Methodist. Office: US Ho of Reps 2266 Rayburn Ho Office Bldg Washington DC 20515-0001*

KOLBE, KARL WILLIAM, JR., lawyer; b. Passaic, N.J., Sept. 29, 1926; s. Karl William Sr. and Edna Ernestine (Rumsey) K.; m. Barbara Louise Bogart, Jan. 28, 1950 (dec. Aug. 1992); children: Kim E., William B., Katherine B.; m. Patricia L. Coward, Apr. 30, 1994. BA, Princeton U., 1949; JD, U. Va., 1952. Bars: N.Y. 1952, D.C. 1976, U.S. Supreme Ct. 1966. Ptnr. Thelen, Reid & Priest, N.Y.C., 1966-92, of counsel, 1993—. Dir. Bessemer Trust Co. (N.A.), N.Y.C.,1977-97, Carolinas Cement Co., 1994-98, World Trade Corp., 1987-2002; vice-chmn. The Friends of Thirteen Inc. Bd. dirs. N.J. Ballet Co., West Orange, 1970-98, Ocean Liner Mus., 1992-2003. With USN, 1944-46. Mem. ABA (chmn. pub. utility law sect. 1984-85). Clubs: Univ. (N.Y.C.); Metro. (Washington). Republican. Episcopalian. Home: PO Box 278 111 Old Chester Rd Essex Fells NJ 07021-1625 Office: Thelen Reid & Priest 875 Third Ave New York NY 10022 E-mail: wkolbe@thelenreid.com.

KOLBE, LLOYD JOSEPH, health facility administrator; b. Balt., Oct. 13, 1948; s. Lloyd Arthur and Blanche (Cossentino) K. BS, Towson State U., 1973; MEd, U. Toledo, 1975, PhD, 1978. Asst. prof. U. No. Colo., Greeley, 1976-77; dir. evaluation Nat. Ctr. for Health Edn., San Francisco, 1978-79, dir., sch. health edn., 1980-81; chief, evaluation section U.S. Office Disease Prevention, Washington, 1982; assoc. dir. Ctr. Health Promotion Rsch. U. Tex., Houston, 1983-85, assoc. prof. Sch. Pub. Health, 1983-85; chief Sch. Health Ctr. U.S. Ctr. for Disease Control, Atlanta, 1986-87, dir., Div. Adolescent and Sch. Health, 1988—; dir. Ctr. for Sch. Health WHO, Atlanta, 1990—. Co-author: (book) School Health in America, 1988. Recipient Superior Svc. award USPHS, Washington, 1989, Disting. Svc. award State Dirs. of Health Edn., Washington, 1988, Honor award Eta Sigma Gamma, Muncie, Ind., 1989; named Outstanding Alumnus, U. Toledo, 1985. Fellow Am. Sch. Health Assn. (pres. 1989-90); mem. Assn. Advancement of Health Edn. (Scholar award 1989), APHA, Soc. for Pub. Health Edn., Internat. Union for Health Edn. (trustee 1986—). Office: Nat Ctr Chronic Disease Prevention 1041 Davidson Bldg Roger Ctr 2858 Woodcock Blvd Atlanta GA 30341-4002*

KOLBE, RONALD LYNN, research engineer; b. Washington, June 3, 1950; s. Casper Maul and Ruthlee (Cade) K.; m. Margaret Garret, Mar. 16, 1984; 1 child, Katharine Lynn. BSME, U. Md., 1973; MS in Nuclear Engring., Purdue U., 1976; PhD in ME, U. Tenn., 1986. Mech. engr. Burns & Roe, Oradell, NJ, 1981—84; asst. prof. engring. U.S. Mcht. Marine Acad., Kings Point, NY, 1984—87; asst. prof., dir. engr. Shepherd Coll., Sheperdstown, W.Va., 1987—88; staff scientist Berkeley Rsch. Assocs., Springfield, Va., 1989—91; mech. engr. Naval Rsch. Lab., Washington, 1991—97; sr. software engr. Mgmt. Tech., Lexington Park, Md., 1997—2000; sr. scientist Sci. Applications Internat. Corp., McLean, Va., 2000—. Mem.: ASME, AIAA, Sigma Xi. Republican. Methodist.

KOLBE, STEPHANIE JILL, artist; b. New Ulm, Minn., Feb. 7, 1947; d. Virgil and Arline (Blomguist) Schmiesing; m. Douglas Kolbe, Mar. 16, 1968; children: Justin, Erin. BS in English magna cum laude, Minn. State U., 1969. Tchr. Appleton (Minn.) H.S., 1969-70, Owatonna (Minn.) H.S., 1970-72; daycare provider Owatonna, 1973-83; artist, 1982—. Supt. Steele County Fair, Owatonna, 1984—; artist Minn. Wildlife Heritage Found., St. Paul, 1984-98, Festival Arts, Owatonna, 1994—. Exhibitions include Owatonna Festival of Arts, Steele Co. Fair. Mem., artist Owatonna Arts Ctr., 1982—; vol., presenter, tchr. Santa's Cellar, 1978—, Straight River Wood Carver's, Owatonna, 1982—,

Susquecnetennial Arts Com., 2003-04. Recipient Best of Show award Minn. Art Show, 1989, award Excellence, 1992, Best of Show award, 1995, People's Choice award Minn. Wildlife Heritage Art Show, 1997, Best of Show for sculpture Owatonna Festival of Arts. Mem. Nat. Wood Carver's Assn., Internat. Wood Carver's Assn., Minn. Wild Fowl and Decoy Club. Avocations: dancing, painting, sculpting, computer art, traveling.

KOLBER, RICHARD A. lawyer; b. Wantagh, N.Y., Aug. 2, 1961; s. Leonard and Yola Kolber. BA, SUNY, Binghamton, 1983; JD, U. Calif., 1986. Bar: Calif. 1986, U.S. Dist. Ct. (so. and ea. dists.) Calif. 1987. Assoc. Haight, Brown & Bonesteel, Santa Monica, Calif., 1986-88, Barash & Hill, L.A., 1988-93; pvt. practice Law Offices of Richard A. Kolber, L.A., 1993—. Office: Ste 900 2029 Century Park E Los Angeles CA 90067-2910 Fax: 310-203-0821.. E-mail: rakolber@pacbell.net.

KOLBERT, JACK, foreign language educator, French literature educator, humanities educator; b. Perth-Amboy, N.J., Apr. 25, 1927; s. Robert Kolbert-Kroop and Sophie (Burstein) Klobert- Kroop; m. Ruth M. Katz (dec. June 2003); children: Harry Jules, Shelley Robert. BA magna cum laude, U. So. Calif., 1948, MA; postgrad., U. Calif., Berkeley, 1949-51; PhD, Columbia U., 1957. Lectr. French Columbia U., N.Y.C., 1951-52; instr. French, Spanish Wesleyan U., Middletown, Conn., 1954-55; from asst., assoc. prof. to prof. Romance langs. U. Pitts., 1955-65, chmn. dept. of Romance and Modern langs., 1960-65; prof. U. N.Mex., Albuquerque, 1965-77; vis. prof. Pomona Coll., Claremont, Calif., 1970-71; pres. Monterey (Calif.) Inst. of Internat. Studies, 1977-80; dir. external rels. Calif. Acad. of Scis., San Francisco, 1980-82; div. chmn. Piedmont Community Coll., Charlottesville, Va., 1982-85; dept. chmn. Susquehanna U., Selinsgrove, Pa., 1985-92, prof., 1992-96, prof. emeritus, 1996—. Cons. City of Pitts. and Forest Hills Schs., Allegheny County, Pa., 1956-66; cons. Bucknell U. Press, Greenwood Friends Sch., Pa.; hon. fellow, mem. bd. advisors Inst. of Am. Univs., Aix-en-Provence, France; vis. prof. U. Kansas, 1968, Calif. State U., L.A., 1971, Am. Inst. Univs., Aix-En-Provence, France, 1995; cons. Dept. Edn. Commonwealth of Pa., 1985-96; mem. adv. bd. for French Lit., Contemporary Authors, Gale Rsch. Pubs., 2002—. Author: Edmond Jaloux, Critique Litteraire, 1962, The World of A. Maurois, 1986 (Choice Book award 1987); co-author: L'Art de Michel Butor, 1970, Vols. I and II French for Elementary Teachers, 1958, 60, The Worlds of Elie Wiesel, 2001; editl. bd. profl. jours.; contbr. more than 500 articles and reviews to profl. jours. Hon. Consul Gen. French Republic, N.Mex., No. Calif., 1965-80; pres. City Coun. Albuquerque, 1974-77; bd. dirs. St. Joseph's Med. Ctr., Albuquerque, 1974-77, Albquerque C. of C., 1974-77; co-chmn. Commonwealth of Va. Lang. Com., Richmond, 1983-85. Fulbright fellow, Pre, Post Doctoral Fulbright fellow, Paris, 1953-54, 63-64, Ford fellow, Ford Found., 1954-55, Camargo Found. fellow, France, 1992-93, fellow Cerisy-La-Salle Found. Elie Wiesel, 1995; hon. fellow Inst. Am. Univs., Aix-en-Provence, France; decorated knight and officer Acad. Palms, French Govt., Paris, knight Nat. Order of Merit, French Govt., Paris; named Pa. Lang. Prof. of Year, 1987. Mem. MLA (hon., life), Am. Assn. Tchrs. of French (bd. mem. 1967-75, hon. life). Democrat. Jewish. Avocations: classical music, gymnastics, travel, lecturing. Home: PO Box 271 Selinsgrove PA 17870-0271 E-mail: jackkolbert@hotmail.com.

KOLBESON, MARILYN HOPF, holistic practitioner, educator, artist, advertising executive; b. Cin., June 9, 1930; d. Henry Dilg and Carolyn Josephine (Brown) Hopf; children: Michael Llen, Kenneth Ray, Patrick James, Pamela Sue Kolbeson Lang, James Allan. Student, U. Cin., 1947-48, 50. Cert. holistic memory release practitioner. Interior decorator Metro Carpet, 1971-77; sales and mktg. mgr. Cox Patrick United Van Lines, 1977-80; sales mktg. mgr. Creative Incentives, Houston, 1980-81; pres. Ad Sense, Inc., Houston, 1981-87, M.H. Kolbeson & Assocs., Houston, 1987, Seattle, 1987—, The Phoenix Books, Seattle, 1987-90, METASELF Healing, Seattle, 1999—. Bd. dirs. Umbrella Prodns.; cons. N.L.P. Practitioner and Cons.; aircraft bus. mgmt. cons., Seattle, 1988—90; holographic memory release practitioner, 1996—; cooking demonstrator, nutritional advisor Puget Consumers Coop., Seattle, 1991—2002; lectr., cons. in field. Pub.: You Make the Difference in Nat. Lit. Poetry Anthology, Morning Song, 1996, : Moving On in Nat. Libr. Poetry, 1998; contbr. poetry to; originator : Heart Button Technique, 1995; mgr., assoc. prodr. (mus. comedy) Times Three, 1999; prodn. mgr. Of a Certain Age, 2002; instrument keeper (group shows) Gentle Wind Project, 1999—. Vol. Seattle Pub. Schs., 1992—; mem. citizens adv. bd. Arcola (Ill.) Sch. Dist., 1964—66; charter mem. Rep. Task Force; mem. adv. bd. Alief Ind. Sch. Dist., 1981—87, pres., 1983—84; bd. dirs. Santa Maria Hostel, 1983—86, v.p., 1983—84; mem. citizen's adv. bd. Am. Inst. Achievement, 1986—87; bd. dirs. The Breighton Found. Sr. Housing Devel., Seattle, 2000—, S.E. Seattle Sr. Found., 2000—; founder, pres. Mind Force, Houston, 1978—87, Seattle, 1987—95; founder META Group, Seattle, 1991—, Meta-Self Healing Ministries, Seattle, 1997—. Mem. ARC (Seattle), Nat. Assn. Mentally Ill (Wash.), Internat. Platform Assn., Houston Advt. Splty. Assn. (bd. dirs. 1984-87, treas. 1985, v.p. 1986-87), Inst. Noetic Scis. (charter), Galleria Area C. of C. (bd. dirs. 1986-87), Toastmasters (area gov. 1978), Grand Club (v.p. 1986), Lakewood Seward Park Cmty. Club (bd. dirs.), Fair and Tender Ladies Book Group, Internat. Soc. Poets, World Future Soc. Republican. Universalist. Office: 5253 S Brandon St Seattle WA 98118-2522 E-mail: mhk9@attby.com.

KOLBET, KEVIN MICHAEL, real estate company executive; b. Cresco, Iowa, Apr. 6, 1954; s. Paul M. and Geneva G. Kolbet; m. Janean S. Moore, June 6, 1981; children: Kyle J., Karen C. BA, St. Mary's U., 1976. Lic. real estate broker, Iowa. Owner Kolbet Realtors, Osage, Iowa, 1978—. Active Osage Devel. Corp.; pres. North Iowa area C.C. Bd., Mason City, 1999, Meals on Wheels Osage; ad altare Dei Archdiocese of Dubuque (Iowa), 1967; eagle scout Boys Scouts Am., Cresco, 1968. Mem. Kiwanis, Osage C. of C. (pres. 1981, Disting. Svc. medal 1981, Employer of Yr. 1987), Cedar Valley Bd. Realtors (pres.). Roman Catholic. Avocations: pheasant hunting, golf, baseball, basketball, bicycling. Home: 1985 Highway 9 Osage IA 50461-8155 Office: Kolbet Realtors 1429 Main St PO Box 245 Osage IA 50461-0245 E-mail: kevin@kolbetrealtors.com.

KOLBRENER, JONATHAN, lawyer; b. Newark, Feb. 18, 1957; s. Peter Denker and Sandra Lee (Heller) K. BA, Brandeis U., 1979; JD, Hofstra U., 1982. Bar: N.Y. 1983, U. S. Dist. Ct. (ea. and so. dists.) N.Y. 1983, U.S. Dist. Ct. (no. dist.) N.Y., 1998. Assoc. Bower & Gardner, N.Y.C., 1982-85, Sheft and Sheft, N.Y.C., 1986-90, Peter Kolbrener, Garden City, N.Y., 1991-93, Marshall, Conway & Wright, N.Y.C., 1993-94, Kelner & Kelner, N.Y.C., 1996-98, Patrick Colligan, Purchase, NY, 1999—. Mem. ABA, N.Y. Bar Assn. Avocations: bicycling, running, swimming, skiing, triathlons. Office: 450 Mamaroneck Ave Harrison NY 10528-2400

KOLDA, THOMAS JOSEPH, non-profit organization executive; b. Chgo., Dec. 1, 1939; s. Amos Joseph and Cecilia Marie (Baxa) K.; m. Gail Judith Kettler, June 30, 1962; children: Brian Joseph, Jeffrey Thomas. BA, Coe Coll., 1961, MA, 1984; PhD in Adminstrn. and Fin. Mgmt., Columbia Pacific U., 1986. Cert. fund raising exec. Dir. devel./pub. rels. Mt. Mercy Coll., Cedar Rapids, Iowa, 1965-69; v.p. devel. St. Mary's Coll., Orchard Lake, Mich., 1969-71; dir. devel. Roman Catholic Diocese, Tucson, 1971-74; dir. devel./pub. rels. The Pontifical Coll. Josephinum, Columbus, Ohio, 1975-77; dir. trusts and estates Ohio State U. Devel. Fund, Columbus, 1977-85; v.p. devel. Coe Coll., Cedar Rapids, Iowa, 1985-87; dir. trusts and estates Marquette U., Milw., 1987-92; pvt. practice cons. fin. and charitable gift planning, 1992-98; dir. Coll. Edn. Advancement and Univ. Planned Giving U. Wisc., Whitewater, 1999—. V.p. Whitewater City Coun., Wis. Mem. Nat. Soc. Fund Raising Execs. (past pres. Ctrl. Ohio chpt.), Internat. Assn. Fin. Planning (bd. dirs. 1991-95), Coun. Advancement and Support Edn., Nat. Com. on Planned Giving. Office: 2041 Winther Hall 800 W Main St Whitewater WI 53190-1705 E-mail: Koldat@mail.uww.edu., Koldat@charter.net.

KOLDE, RICHARD ARTHUR, insurance company executive, consultant; b. Pomona, Calif., Jan. 25, 1944; s. Arthur and Rosemary (Decker) K.; children: Nicole Rochelle, Eric Christian, Katarina R. AA, Mt. San Antonio Coll., 1963; BS, U. So. Calif., 1965; AS, Mira Costa Coll., 1979. Lic. CPCU. Asst. mgr., mgr. Lord Rebel Ind., Montclair, Costa Mesa and Carlsbad, Calif., 1971-74; agt. Conn. Mut. Life Ins. Co., San Diego and Carlsbad, 1974-77; pres., owner Investment Assocs., Carlsbad, 1977-82, 93—; mng. gen. agt. E.F. Hutton Life Ins. Co., San Diego, 1982—. Cons. Hansch Fin. Group, Laguna Hills, Calif., 1984; cons., recruiter Ky. Gen. Life Ins. Co., 1990-92; mng. gen agt. N.W. Life of Can. Ins. Co, 1991—. Bd. dirs. Boys Club Am., Carlsbad, 1980-84, adv. bd., 1984—; bd. dirs. YMCA, Pomona, 1960-64. With USAF, 1966-71. Decorated Outstanding Unit award Small Arms Expert award Security 1 & 2 Protection of Pres. U.S. award; named Largest Producing Mng. Gen. Agt. in Nation, E.F. Hutton Life Co., 1982, 83. Mem. Nat. Assn. Life Underwriters (legis. officer 1974—), Calif. Assn. Life Underwriters, Internat. Assn. Fin. Planners (Mem. of Yr. award 1977), U.S. Gymnastics Fedn. (coaching credentials, ofcl. judge collegiate level), VFW, Rotary, Phi Sigma Beta. Republican. E-mail: rkolde@surfbest.net.

KOLECKI, PAUL FRANCIS, emergency physician; b. Camden, N.J., Feb. 3, 1966; s. Richard and Phyllis Kolecki; m. Jennifer Taylor, May 3, 2003. BS, U. Notre Dame, 1988; MD, Jefferson Med. Coll., 1992. Cert. Am. Coll. Emergency Medicine, Am. Coll. Med. Toxicology, ATLS 1995, ACLS instr. 1995, Pediat. Advanced Life Support instr. 1994. Residency Med. Ctr. Del., Wilmington, 1992—95; resident emergency physician Newark Emergency Dept., Newark, 1994—95; emergency physician Samaritan Health Ctr., Ahwatukee, Ariz., 1995—97; asst. med. dir. North Tex. Poison Ctr. Parkland Health and Hosp. Sys., Dallas, 1997—98; asst. prof. Dept. Emergency Medicine Thomas Jefferson U., Phila., 1998—. Emergency physician Maricopa Med. Ctr. Emergency Dept., Phoenix, 1996—97; asst. prof. Dept. Surgery U. Tex. Southwestern Med. Ctr., Dallas, 1997—98; cons. Phila. Poison Control Ctr., Phila., 1998—; dir. med. student edn. Dept. Emergency Medicine Thomas Jefferson U., Phila., 2000—; lectr., presenter in field. Contbr. articles to profl. jours. including Jour. Emergency Medicine, Am. Jour. Emergency, Annals Emergency Medicine, Clin. Toxicology, Acad. Emergency Medicine, Critical Decisions in Emergency Medicine, others. Pianist St. John the Evangelist Ch., Phila., 1999—. Mem.: Am. Chpt. Emergency Medicine, Am. Acad. Emergency Medicine (bd. cert. 1997), Am. Coll. Med. Toxicology (bd. cert. 1999), Am. Acad. Clin. Toxicology, Alpha Omega Alpha. Home: 520 Lombard St Unit F Philadelphia PA 19147 Office: Thomas Jefferson Univ Thompson Bldg Rm 239 1020 Sansom St Philadelphia PA 19107-5004 Address: Phila Poison Control Ctr 3535 Market St #985 Philadelphia PA 19104 also: Children's Hosp Phila Clin Toxicology Sect 34th & Civic Center Blvd Philadelphia PA 19104

KOLEK, ROBERT EDWARD, lawyer; b. Chgo., June 1, 1943; s. Joseph and Mary Kolek; m. Linda L. Bernicchi, Aug. 27, 1966; children: Kimberley M., Robert E. Jr. BBA, Loyola U., Chgo., 1965, JD, 1968. Bar: Ill. 1968. Law clk. to Hon. Thomas Kluczynski, Ill. Supreme Ct., Chgo., 1968-70. Mem. ABA, Chgo. Bar Assn. Roman Catholic. Avocation: photography. Office: Schiff Hardin & Waite 6600 Sears Tower Chicago IL 60606 E-mail: rKolek@schiffhardin.com.

KOLENDA, PAULINE M. anthropology educator, researcher; b. Manchester, N.H., Feb. 4, 1928; d. Robert Fulton and Mary Paulina Moller; m. Konstantin Kolenda, June 9, 1962 (dec. Dec. 6, 1991); 1 child: Christopher George. BA, Wellesley Coll., 1949; PhD, Cornell U., 1955. Instr. Univ. Ariz., Tucson, 1959-61; asst. prof. Oakland Univ., Rochester, Mich., 1961-62; assoc. prof. Univ. Houston, 1963-69, prof., 1969-99; adj. prof. Univ. Tex., Austin, 1985-99; vis. scholar Univ. Calif., Berkeley, 1999—. Vis. prof., Univ. Tex., 1983, Univ. Calif. Berkeley, 1981. Author: Caste in Contemporary India, 1978, 85. Recipient scholarship Rockefeller Study Ctr., Bellagio, Italy, 1985; supercomputer grantee, Nat. Sci. Found., San Diego, 1986-89. Home: 206 Yale Ave Kensington CA 94708 E-mail: kolenda@uclink4.berkeley.edu.

KOLESAR, PETER JOHN, business and engineering educator, entrepreneur; b. N.Y.C., Nov. 25, 1936; s. John Michael and Agnes (Vajda) K.; m. Nicole Bordat, May 30, 1969 (div. 1981); children: Lara, Alexandre; m. Miriam Larsson, June 18, 1988; 1 child, Angelica. BA, Queens Coll., 1959; BS in Indsl. Engring., Columbia U., 1959, MS, 1962, PhD, 1964. Systems analyst Procter & Gamble, Cin., 1959-61; lectr. Imperial Coll., London, 1964-65; asst. prof. Sch. Engring. Columbia U., N.Y.C., 1965-70, prof. Grad. Sch. Bus., 1975—, rsch. dir. Deming Ctr. Quality Mgmt., 1990; sr. analyst Rand Corp., N.Y.C., 1971-74. Examiner Malcolm Baldrige Nat. Quality Award, 1990-91; chmn. mgmt. com. Mont. Fly Co., LLC, 1999—; pres., Montgomery Lake Assn., 2001—; cons. in field. Assoc. editor Mgmt. Sci.; editor-at-large Interfaces, 1991—; contbr. articles to profl. jours. Recipient Systems Sci. prize NATO, 1976 Fellow AAAS; mem. Ops. Research Soc. Am. (council 1980-83, Lanchester prize 1976), Inst. Mgmt. Scis., Am. Statis. Assn., Am. Soc. Quality Control. Home: 410 Riverside Dr New York NY 10025-7974 Office: Columbia U 408 Uris Hall New York NY 10027

KOLESKE, JOSEPH VICTOR, chemical engineer, consultant; b. Stratford, Wis., Jan. 23, 1930; s. Joseph John and Mary Helen (Jilek) K.; m. Mary Anne Casey, Nov. 3, 1951; children: Robert Casey, Krista Koleske Killmeier. BS in Chem. Engring., U. Wis., 1958; MS, Inst. Paper Chemistry, Appleton, Wis., 1960, PhD, 1963. Corp. rsch. fellow Union Carbide Corp., South Charleston, W.Va., 1963-88; sr. cons. Consolidated Rsch. Inc., Kingsford, Mich., 1988—. Short course lectr. radiation chemistry, N.D. State U., 1996-2002. Author: Free Radical Radiation Curing, 1997, Alkylene Oxides and Their Polymers, 1990, Poly Ethylene Oxide, 1976, Poly Vinyl Chloride, 1969, Cationic Radiation Curing, 1991, Radiation Curing of Coatings, 2002, others; editor: ASTM Paint and Coating Testing Manual, 1995; mem. editl. rev. bd. Jour. Coatings Tech., 1979—; contbg. editor Paint & Coatings Industry mag., 2000—; contbr. chpts. to books and more than 100 articles to profl. jours.; patentee in fields of chemistry, polymer blends, and coatings. With USAF, 1950-54. Recipient Interstab Award, U. So. Miss., 1981, Award for Sci. Achievement, Am. Chem. Soc., 1978. Mem. ASTM (Charles Dudley award, 2000), Radtech Internat., Fedn. Socs. for Coating Techs., Serra of Charleston. Roman Catholic. Avocations: philately, writing, reading. Home and Office: 1513 Brentwood Rd Charleston WV 25314-2307 E-mail: jvkoleske@aol.com.

KOLESNIK, GRIGORI, mathematician, educator, mathematician, researcher; b. Kiev, Ukraine, Apr. 17, 1937; arrived in U.S., 1975; s. Abram and Faina Kolesnik; m. Alexandra Kolesnik, Oct. 23, 1966; 1 child, Alexander. MS, Moscow State U., 1965, PhD, 1972. Visitor UCLA, 1975—76; instr. Caltech, Pasadena, Calif., 1976—77; asst. prof. SUNY, Buffalo, 1977—78, U. Tex., Austin, 1978—84; prof. Calif. State U., L.A., 1984—. Visitor Inst. for Advanced Study, Princeton, NJ, 1981, Brigham Young U., Provo, Utah, 1990—91. Author (with S.W. Graham): Van Der Corput's Method of Experimental Sums, 1991; contbr. articles to profl. jours. With Russian Mil., 1956—59. Independent. Jewish. Home: 24662 Calle Largo Calabasas CA 91302-3010 Office: Calif State Univ 5454 State University Dr Los Angeles CA 90032

KOLESON, DONALD RALPH, retired college dean, educator; b. Eldon, Mo., June 30, 1935; s. Ralph A. and Fern M. (Beanland) Koleson; children: Anne, David, Janet. BS in Edn., Ctrl. Mo. State U., 1959; MEd, So. Ill. U., 1973. Mem. faculty So. Ill. U., Carbondale, 1968—73; dean tech. edn. Belleville Area Coll., Ill., 1982—93; ret., 1993. Mem.: Nat. Assn. Two-Yr. Schs. of Constrn. (pres. 1984—85), Am. Welding Assn., Am. Vocat. Edn. Assn., Jesters, Shriners, Masons.

KOLFF, WILLEM JOHAN, retired internist, internist, educator; b. Leiden, Holland, Feb. 14, 1911; arrived in U.S., 1950, naturalized, 1956; s. Jacob and Adriana (de Jonge) Kolff; m. Janke C. Huidekoper, Sept. 4, 1937; children: Jacob, Adriana P., Albert C., Cornelis A., Gualtherus C.M. Student, U. Leiden Med. Sch., 1930—38; MD summa cum laude, U. Groningen, 1946; MD (hon.), U. Turin, Italy, 1969; MD (hon.), Rostock (Germany) U., 1975, U. Bologna, Italy, 1983; DSc (hon.), Allegheny Coll., Meadville, Pa., 1960; DSc (hon.), Tulane U., 1975; DSc (hon.), CUNY, 1982, Temple U., 1983; DSc (hon.), U. Utah, 1983; D. of Tech. Scis. (hon.), Tech. U. Twente, Enschede, The Netherlands, 1986; DSc (hon.), U. Athens, 1988, Aix-Marseille II, 1993. Internist, head med. dept. Mcpl. Hosp., Kampen, Holland; dir. divsn. artificial organs Cleve. Clinic Found., 1950—67; privaat docent, dept. medicine U. Leiden, 1950—67; prof. surgery U. Utah Coll. Medicine, Salt Lake City, 1967—. Disting. prof. medicine and surgery, 1979—, prof. internal medicine, 1981—, dir. Kolff's Lab., 1986—, dir. Inst. Biomed. Engring., dir. divsn. artificial organs, 1967—86, ret. Decorated commandeur Order Van Oranje Netherlands, Orden de Mayo al Merito en el Grade de Gran Official Argentina; named one of Utah's Most Disting. Achievers, 1996; named to, Nat. Inventors Hall of Fame, 1985, 1995, On the Shoulders of Giants Hall of Fame, Cleve., 1989; recipient Landsteiner medal for establishing blood banks during German occupation in Holland, Netherlands Red Cross, 1942, Cameron prize, U. Edinburgh, Scotland, 1964, Gairdner prize, Gairdner Found., 1966, Valentine award, N.Y. Acad. Medicine, 1969, 1st Gold medal, Netherlands Surg. Soc., 1970, Leo Harvey prize, Technion, Israel, 1972, Sr. U.S. Scientist award, Alexander Von Humboldt Found., 1978, Austrian Gewerbeverein's Wilhelm-Exner award, 1980, John Scott medal, City of Phila., 1984, Japan prize, Japan Found. Sci. and Tech., 1986, Rsch. prize, Netherlands Royal Inst. Engrs., 1986, 1st Jean Hamburger award, Internat. Soc. Nephrology, 1987, 1st Edwin Cohn-De Laval award, World Apheresis Assn., 1990, Fed. prize, Fedn. Sci. Med. Assn., 1990, Father of Artificial Organs award and medal, Internat. Soc. Artificial Organs, 1992, Christopher Columbus Discovery award in biomed. rsch., NIH, 1992, Legacy of Life award, LDS Deseret Found., 1995, Lifetime Achievement award, Ahmedabad, India, 1996, Russ prize, Ohio U. and Nat. Acad.of Engring., 2003. Mem.: ACP, NAE (City of Medicine award 1989), AAUP, AAAS, AMA (Sci. Achievement award 1982), European Dialysis and Transplant Assn., Nat. Kidney Found., Am. Soc. Artificial Internal Organs, N.Y. Acad. Scis., Soc. Exptl. Biology and Medicine, Am. Physiol. Soc., Academia Nacional de Medicine (hon.; Colombia), Austrian Soc. Nephrology (hon.), Rotary. Achievements include patents for ventricular assist device and method of manufacturing; collapsible artificial ventricle and pumping shell; ventricular assist device with volume displacement chamber; electrohydraulic heart with septum mounted pump; muscle and air powered left ventricular assist device; development of artificial kidney for clinical use, 1943; heart-lung machine, 1949; first membrane oxygenator, 1955; disposable twin-coil kidney, 1956; balloon pump, 1962; wearable artificial kidney (WAK), 1981; artificial heart, 1958; human implantation, Dr. Barney Clark, 1982.

KOLICK, DANIEL JOSEPH, lawyer; b. Lakewood, Ohio, May 12, 1950; s. Joseph Frank and Agnes Helen (Lusnak) K. BA, Holy Cross Coll., 1972; JD, Case Western Res. U., 1975. Bar: Ohio 1975. Sole practice, North Olmsted, Ohio, 1975-85; ptnr. Kolick & Kondzer, Westlake, Ohio, 1985—; acting law dir. City of Strongsville, Ohio, 2000—01, asst. law dir., 1978—2000, 2002—. Dir. law Village of Lindale, Cleve., 1975-76. Chmn. North Olmsted Charter Rev. Commn., 1981, 83; mem. council St. Richard's Parish Council, North Olmsted, 1980-82, tchr. Sch. Religion, 1979-81; mem. Strongsville Cmty. Improvement Corp., 2000-01. Mem. Cuyahoga County Bar Assn., Ohio Sch. Bd. Assn., Ohio State Bar Assn., ABA. Clubs: North Olmsted Exchange (trustee, treas. 1977-78). Roman Catholic. Avocations: basketball, tennis. Office: Kolick & Kondzer 24500 Center Ridge Rd Ste 175 Westlake OH 44145-5628 Home: 6579 Summer Wind Dr Brecksville OH 44141-3365

KOLINSKY, MICHAEL ALLEN, emergency physician; b. Phila., Dec. 23, 1947; s. Maurice and Lenore (Rose) K.; m. Barbara Victorine, June 20, 1981; children: Nicole, Daniel, Samuel. BA, U. Wis., 1970; MD, Rush U., 1979. Diplomate Am. Bd. Emergency Medicine. Staff physician emergency dept. River Parishes Hosp., LaPlace, La., 1982-85; co-med. dir. emergency dept. Meadowcrest Hosp., Gretna, La., 1985-92; co-med. dir. City of New Orleans Emergency Med. Svcs., 1987—; med. dir. emergency dept. Tulane U. Med. Ctr., New Orleans, 1992—. Fellow Am. Acad. Emergency Medicine. Office: Tulane Med Ctr Emergency Dept 1415 Tulane Ave New Orleans LA 70112-2600 E-mail: kolinsky@sstar.com.

KOLKER, ALLAN ERWIN, ophthalmologist; b. St. Louis, Nov. 2, 1933; s. Paul P. and Jean Kolker; m. Jacquelyn Krupin, Dec. 8, 1957; children: Robin, Marci, David, Scott. AB, Washington U., St. Louis, 1953, MD, 1957. Diplomate Am. Bd. Ophthalmology (dir. 1994-98). Intern St. Louis Children's Hosp., 1957-58; resident in ophthalmology Washington U./Barnes Hosp., St. Louis, 1960-65; glaucoma fellow Washington U., St. Louis, 1963—64, staff, faculty, 1964—, prof. ophthalmology, 1974-96, clin. prof. ophthalmology, 1996—. Med. dir. The Glaucoma Inst., St. Louis; mem. glaucoma com. Prevent Blindness Am. Author: (with J. Hetherington) Becker and Shaffer's Diagnosis and Therapy of the Glaucomas, 3d, 4th, 5th edit., 1983, (with T. Krupin) Complications in Ophthalmic Surgery, 1999; contbr. numerous articles to profl. jours., chpts. to books. Served with USPHS, 1958-60. NIH spl. fellow, 1963-65; grantee, 1969-80; 1st Disting. Eye Alumni award Washington U., 1990, Alumni/Faculty award Washington U. Sch. Medicine, 2002. Mem. AMA, Assn. Rsch. in Vision and Ophthalmology, Am. Acad. Ophthalmology (mem. coun. 1986-92, trustee 1994-98, Life Achievement award 2002), Am. Bd. Ophthalmology (dir. 1994-98), Am. Ophthal. Soc., Am. Glaucoma Soc. (founding mem., pres. 1992-94, Spl. Honor award 2002), Mo. Ophthal. Soc. (pres. 1986-87), St. Louis Med. Soc. Home: 176 Plantation Dr Saint Louis MO 63141-8352 Office: 12601 Olive Blvd Saint Louis MO 63141-6313

KOLKER, JAMES HAMILTON, architect; b. Phila., Oct. 27, 1962; s. Melvin Ira and Cynthia Weisman Kolker. BA, Columbia U., NYC, 1984, MArch, 1986. Cert. AIA, 1992, registered Pa., 1992. Archtl. intern Venturi, Scott Brown and Assoc., Phila., 1986—90; arch. Arkkitehtitoimisto Pekka Salminen, Helsinki, Finland, 1990—91, Venturi, Scott Brown and Assoc., 1991—92, assoc., 1992—94, sr. assoc., 1994—99, mng. dir., 1999—. Design com. mem. Germantown Jewish Centre, Phila., 1996—; design com. chair Hopkinson House, 2003—. Mem.: AIA. Democrat. Jewish. Avocations: travel, design, art. Office: Venturi, Scott Brown and Assoc 4236 Main St Philadelphia PA 19127 Business E-Mail: kolker@vsba.com.

KOLKER, LAWRENCE PAUL, lawyer; b. Huntington, N.Y., Aug. 1, 1956; s. Justin William and Sondra Geraldine (Budow) K.; m. Emily Diane Porter, June 14, 1981; children: Danielle, Jeremy, Madeline. BA, SUNY, Binghamton, 1978; JD, Bklyn. U., 1983. Bar: N.Y. 1984, U.S. Dist. Ct. (so. and ea. dists.) N.Y. 1984, U.S. Dist. Ct. (we. dist.) Mich. 1992, U.S. Ct. Appeals (2d cir.) 1989, U.S. Ct. Appeals (11th cir.) 1992. Clk. Hon. Henry F. Werker, N.Y.C., 1981-82; asst. corp. counsel N.Y.C. Law Dept., 1983-87; assoc. Hill, Betts & Nash, N.Y.C., 1987-89; ptnr. Wolf, Haldenstein, Adler, Freeman & Herz, LLP, N.Y.C., 1989—. Mem. N.Y. State Bar Assn., Assn. of Bar of City of N.Y. Avocations: carpentry, cooking, guitar, cross-country skiing, tennis. Office: Wolf Haldenstein Adler Freeman & Herz LLP 270 Madison Ave New York NY 10016-0601 E-mail: kolker@whafh.com.

KOLKER, ROGER RUSSELL, insurance executive; b. Guttenberg, Iowa, Aug. 14, 1929; s. Russell Edward and Olina Colby (Schwab) K.; m. Suzanne Chaddock Griffin, June 9, 1954; children: Roger Russell, Karolyn, Sara. Student, U. Iowa, 1947-50; BS, U.S. Mil. Acad., 1954. C.L.U., 1966. Field sales dir. Mut. of N.Y., Chgo., 1964-66, dir. mgmt. tng. N.Y.C., 1966-68, regional v.p. Atlanta, 1968-71; exec. v.p. N. Am. Life Ins. Co., Mpls., 1971-77, Monumental Life Ins. Co., Balt., 1978-79, pres., chief exec. officer, 1979-83; chmn., pres., chief exec. officer Monumental Gen. Ins. Group, Inc., Balt., 1983-84; pres., chmn., chief exec. officer Monumental Gen. Ins. Co., Balt., 1983-84. Bd. dirs. Equitable Bancorp N.A., Balt., French/Bray, Inc. Bd. dirs. Balt. Symphony Orch.; bd. dirs. South Balt. Gen. Hosp. Mem. Gen. Agts. and Mgrs. Assn., Balt. Life Underwriters Assn., Am. Coll. Life Underwriters (sponsor Gold Key Soc.), Legal Mut. Liability Ins. Soc. Md. (bd. dirs.). Lutheran. Home: PO Box 510124 Key Colony Beach FL 33051-0124 Office: The Kolker Consultancy 511 Chatterton Rd Lutherville Timonium MD 21093-1929

KOLKER, SCOTT LEE, lawyer; b. St. Louis, Dec. 31, 1968; s. Allan E. and Jacquelyn E. Kolker. BSBA, U. Mo., 1991; JD, Wash. U., 1994. Bar: Mo. 1994, Ill. 1995, U.S. Dist. Ct. (ea. dist.) Mo. 1995. Assoc. Holtkamp, Liese et al, St. Louis, 1994-95, Law Offices of Thomas M. Burke, P.C., St. Louis, 1995-99, The Hullverson Law Firm, St. Louis, 1999—. Mem.: ATLA, Lawyers Assn. St. Louis (exec. com. 1997—2002, treas. 2002—03, sec. 2003—), Ill. Trial Lawyers Assn., Bar Assn. Met. St. Louis, Mo. Assn. Trial Attys. Office: Hullverson Law Firm 1010 Market St Ste 1550 Saint Louis MO 63101-2091 E-mail: skolker@hullverson.com.

KOLKER, SONDRA G. fund raising, special events executive; b. N.Y.C., Nov. 30, 1933; d. Morris Henry and Alice (Cohen) Budow; m. Justin William Kolker, Aug. 23, 1953 (div.); children: Lawrence Paul, David Brett; m. David Kern, July 2000. Student, Hofstra U. Dir. N.Y.C. Office N.Y. State Dem. Com., 1977-79; v.p., exec. dir. Fund for Higher Edn., N.Y.C., 1980-88; pres. Sondra Kolker & Assocs., Halesite, N.Y., 1988-96, Miami, Fla., 1996-98, Ft. Lauderdale, Fla., 1998—. Spl. cons. Internat. Devel. Svcs. subs NMP of Am., Inc., 1989-90; dist. rep. Congressman Robert J. Mrazek, 1990-93. Speechwriter for numerous speakers at corp. banquets, 1980-88. Bd. dirs. Huntington (N.Y.) Townwide Fund, 1978-96, Single Family Homes at Sawgrass, treas., 1999--;

mem. adv. bd. Julia's Fund (divsn. Gilda's Club), 1999—; active Huntington Hosp. Aux., 1965-96, Great Gatsby Soc. for Multiple Sclerosis, 1988-96, Marble Hills Civic Assn., Halesite, 1955-96; committeewoman Huntington Dem. Com., 1974-82; fundraiser/dist. rep. Congressman Robert J. Mrazek, L.I., N.Y., 1991-93; banquet planner Temple Adath Or; active Temple Kol Ami; mem. Broward Guild, Miami City Ballet. Recipient Meritorious Svc. award Huntington Twp. C. of C., 1974, 76, 77, 78, Bicentennial Citation Town of Huntington, 1977. Mem. NAFE, MOMA, Met. Mus. Art, Nat. Mus. Women in the Arts, L.I. Crafts Guild, Huntington Twp. C. of C., Women's Econ. Round Table, Huntington Bus. and Profl. Women, Nature Conservancy, Sierra Club, World Wildlife Fund. Jewish. Avocations: fabric painting, writing poetry, nature study, travel, opera. Home and Office: Sondra Kolker & Assoc 12683 NW 11th Pl Sunrise FL 33323-3119

KOLKEY, DANIEL MILES, judge; b. Chgo., Apr. 21, 1952; s. Eugene Louis and Gilda Penelope (Cowan) K.; m. Donna Lynn Christie, May 15, 1982; children: Eugene, William, Christopher, Jonathan. BA, Stanford U., 1974; JD, Harvard U., 1977. Bar: Calif. 1977, U.S. Dist. Ct. (ea. dist.) Calif. 1978, U.S. Dist. Ct. (cen. dist.) Calif. 1979, U.S. Ct. Appeals (9th cir.) 1979, U.S. Dist. Ct. (no. dist.) Calif. 1980, U.S. Supreme Ct. 1983, U.S. Dist. Ct. Ariz. 1992, U.S. Dist. Ct. (so. dist.) Calif. 1994. Law clk. U.S. Dist. Ct. judge, N.Y.C., 1977-78; assoc. Gibson Dunn & Crutcher, L.A., 1978-84, ptnr., 1985-94; counsel to Gov., legal affairs sec. to Calif. Gov. Pete Wilson, 1995-98; assoc. justice Calif. Ct. Appeal, 3rd Appellate Dist., Sacramento, 1998—. Arbitrator bi-nat. panel for U.S.-Can. Free Trade Agreement, 1990—94; commr. Calif. Law Revision Commn., 1992—94, vice chair, 1993—94, chair, 1994; mem. Blue Ribbon Commn. on Jury Sys. Improvement, 1996; adj. prof. McGeorge Sch. Law, 2001—; mem. Calif. State-Fed. Jud. Coun., 2001—. Co-editor: Practitioner's Handbook on International Arbitration and Mediation, 2002; contbr. articles to profl. jours. Co-chmn. internat. rels. sect. Town Hall Calif., L.A., 1985—90; chmn. internat. trade legis. subcom., internat. commerce steering com. L.A. Area C. of C., 1983—91, law and justice com., 1993—94; adv. coun., exec. com. Asia Pacific Ctr. for Resolution of Internat. Bus. Disputes, 1991—94; mem. L.A. Com. on Fgn. Rels., 1983—95, Pacific Coun. Internat. Policy, 1999—; gen. counsel Citizens Rsch. Found., 1990—94; assoc. mem. ctrl. com. Calif. Rep. Party, 1983—94, mem. ctrl. com., 1995—98; dep. gen. coun. credentials com. Rep. Nat. Conv., 1992, alt. Calif. Delegation, 1992, Calif. del., 1996; bd. dirs. L.A. Ctr. for Internat. Comml. Arbitration, 1986—94, treas., 1986—88, v.p., 1988—90, pres., 1990—94. Master Anthony Kennedy Inns. of Ct., 1996-99. Mem. Am. Arbitration Assn. (panel of arbitrators, arbitrator large complex case dispute resolution program 1993-94), Chartered Inst. Arbitrators, London (assoc. 1986-94), Friends of Wilton Park So. Calif. (chmn. exec. com. 1986-94, exec. com. 1986—). Office: Calif Ct of Appeal 3d Appellate Dist 914 Capitol Mall Sacramento CA 95814-4802

KOLKEY, ERIC SAMUEL, customer service representative; b. Chgo., Sept. 30, 1960; s. Eugene Louis and Gilda P. (Cowan) K. Student, Columbia Coll., 1979-82. Booking agt. C.O.D. Club, Chgo., 1979—83; mgr. Video Plus, Chgo., 1984—90; freelance screenwriter, 1991—96; customer comm. specialist MCSI, Bensenville, Ill., 1997—. Lectr. Northwestern U., Evanston, Ill., 1982. Contbr. articles to profl. jours. Active Presdl. Trust, Washington, 1992, Nat. Rep. Senatorial Com., Washington, 1992, Rep. Party Platform Planning Com., Washington, 1992. Recipient Cert. of Recognition Rep. Nat. Com., 1991, Cert. of Award Rep. Presdl. Adv. Com., 1992. Avocation: weightlifting. Home: 750 N Dearborn St Apt 2302 Chicago IL 60610-5379 Office: MCSI 621 Busse Hwy Bensenville IL E-mail: eric.kolkey@mcsinet.com.

KOLKEY, GILDA, artist; b. Chgo. d. David and Evelyn (Jacobson) Cowan; m. Gene Kolkey (dec.); children: Daniel, Sandor, Eric. BA in Painting, U. Ill., Champaign; postgrad., Art Inst. Chgo., 1950, postgrad., 1978—79. Art tchr. Highland Park (Ill.) Recreational Ctr., 1976. Exhibited in group shows at Thompson Ctr., Chgo., 1998—99, ArtLink Gallery, Ft. Wayne, Ind., 1998, Art House, 2001, Mars Gallery, 2001, Jettsett Gallery, 2002, Chgo. Anthenaeum, Shaumburg, Ill., 2002, Art Inst. Chgo., Andersen Mus., Kenosha, Wis., 2003; featured in Chgo. Art Rev., 1989, ArtNetwork Ency. of Living Artists, 1997; Ency. of Living Artists, 1997. Named to Later Impressions, 2003; recipient award of Excellence, North Shore Art League, 1965—66, Painting award, New Horizons Painting, 1959, Scan Members Show, 1992, San Juried Show, 1992—2000, Hon. Mention, Women's Club Evanston, 1972. Mem.: Chgo. Artists Coalition, Chgo. Soc. Artists, Arts Club Chgo., Andersen Mus., Mid-Am. Club. Republican. Home: 1100 N Lake Shore Dr Apt 21B Chicago IL 60611-1088

KOLKHORST, KATHRYN MACKAY, lawyer; b. Richmond, NY, Sept. 21, 1949; d. Bernard Edwin and Jane Mackay (Shaw) K.; m. Mark Finks, 1968 (div. 1972); m. William George Ruddy, Mar. 31, 1979; children: Anna Caroll, Elena Jane. Student, Wellsley Coll., 1966-68; BA, So. Conn. State Coll., 1969; post grad., Yale U., 1975-77; JD, U. Conn., West Hartford, 1977. Bar: Alaska 1979, U.S. Dist. Ct. Alaska 1982. Reporter New Haven Jour. Courier, 1970-75; law clk. to presiding justice AK Supreme Ct., Juneau, Alaska, 1977-78; asst. atty. gen. State of AK, Juneau, Alaska, 1979-85; ptnr. Ruddy, Bradley, & Kolkhorst, Juneau, Alaska, 1986—. Active Juneau Arts Coun., 1979-82, Juneau Symphony, 1980-84; chairperson Juneau Jazz & Classics, 1987—. Mem. Alaska Bar Assn. Democrat. Presbyterian. Office: Ruddy Bradley & Kolkhorst PO Box 34338 Juneau AK 99803-4338 E-mail: kmk@pobox.alaska.net.

KOLKO, GABRIEL, historian, educator; b. Paterson, N.J., Aug. 17, 1932; s. Philip and Lillian Kolko; m. Joyce Manning, June 11, 1955. BA, Kent State U., 1954; MS, U. Wis., 1955; Ph.D, Harvard U., 1962. Assoc. prof. U. Pa., 1964-68; prof. history SUNY-Buffalo, 1968-70, York U., Toronto, Ont., Can., 1970-92, Disting. research prof., 1986-92, prof. emeritus, 1992—. Author: Wealth and Power in America, 1962; The Triumph of Conservatism, 1963; author: Railroads and Regulations, The Politics of War, 1968, The Roots of American Foreign Policy, 1969, The Limits of Power, 1972, Main Currents in Modern American History, 1976, Anatomy of a War, 1985, Confronting the Third World, 1988, Century of War, 1994, Vietnam, Anatomy of a Peace, 1997, Another Century of War?, 2002; contbr. articles to profl. jours. Fellow Social Sci. Research Council, 1963-64; Guggenheim fellow, 1966-67; fellow Am. Council Learned Socs., 1971-72; Killam fellow, 1974-75, 82-84 Fellow Royal Soc. Can. Home: Wittenburgergracht 53 1018 MX Amsterdam Netherlands E-mail: kolko@chello.nl.

KOLL, RICHARD LEROY, retired chemical company executive; b. Muscatine, Iowa, Mar. 16, 1925; s. Charles C. and Emma (Schafer) K.; m. Patricia Ann Grunder, Jan. 2, 1955; children: Craig, Christine, Cary. BSME, U. Iowa, 1951. Plant mgr. Grain Processing Corp., Muscatine, Iowa, 1971-72, v.p., 1972-77, sr. v.p., 1977-90, mem. exec. com., bd. dirs., 1989-90, ret., 1990. With USMC, 1944-46. Mem. Elks, Univ. Athletic Club (Iowa City), Geneva Golf and Country Club (Muscatine, Iowa), Seminole Lakes Country Club (Punta Gorda, Fla.). Home: Apt 323 1750 Jamaica Way Punta Gorda FL 33950-5170 also: 1317 Oakland Dr Muscatine IA 52761-5511

KOLLAER, JIM C. real estate executive, architect; b. Amarillo, Tex., Jan. 5, 1943; s. Walter W. and Margaret M. Kollaer; 1 child, Andrew N. Student, Amarillo Coll., 1960-62, La. State U., 1962-65; BArch, Tex. Tech. U., 1969. Lic. architect, Tex.; lic. broker, Tex. V.p., dir. urban design RKA Inc. Assoc., Dallas, 1969-75; sr. planner CRS Inc., Houston, 1975-76, assoc., 1976-77, v.p., dir. mktg., 1977-80; pres. Houston divsn. Henry Miller Co., Houston, 1980-85; pres. Henry S. Miller/Grubb & Ellis, 1985-89, Kollaer Internat., 1989-90; pres., CEO Greater Houston Partnership, 1990—. Past chmn. Tex. Bus. Hall of Fame; cons. and lectr. in field. Sr. fellow Am. Leadership Forum. Fellow AIA; mem. Assn. C. of C. Execs., Tex. Soc. Archs., Urban Land Inst., Tex. Assn. Realtors, Nat. Assn. Realtors, Coun. for Urban Econ. Devel., U.S. C. of C. (bd. dirs.), Chamber Found. (bd. dirs.), Coronado Club. Republican. Presbyterian. Office: Greater Houston Partnership 1200 Smith St Ste 700 Houston TX 77002-4400 E-mail: jkollaer@houston.org.

KOLLANDER, MEL, social scientist, statistician; b. N.Y.C., Dec. 10, 1939; s. Max and Gisella (Balin) K.; children: Steven B., Sondra L. BS, NYU, 1962; MA, New Sch. for Social Rsch., 1964, postgrad., 1967. Statistician AT&T, N.Y.C., 1964-68; economist, statistician Mitre Corp., McLean, Va., 1968-71; sr. statistician Social Security Adminstrn., Balt., 1971-77; mgr., sr. statistician Westat, Inc., Rockville, Md., 1977-79; prin. survey statistician U.S. EPA, Washington, 1979-94, mgr. small community info. and data program, 1992-94; dir. Washington office Inst. Survey Rsch. Temple U., Washington, 1995—. Advisor Govt. of Kuwait, 1991-92, 2000—, WHO, Geneva, 1987-92; lectr. WHO, USDA Grad. Sch., 1990-92. Chief editor, author: Survey Management Handbook, 1985; chief editor: Guidance on Survey Design for Human Exposure, 1993, (booklet) An Introductory Guide to Human Exposure Assessment Locations (Heals) Studies, Survey Methods and Statistical Sampling, 1992, Survey Management Handbook, 2003; contbr. chpt. to book. Mem. Citizen Taskforce on Property Assessment, Montgomery County, Md., 1978. Mem. ASTM (stats. methods sect., indoor air subcom. 1988-91), Internat. Statis. Inst. (elected mem.), Am. Statis. Assn., Internat. Assn. Survey Statisticians. Avocations: jogging, biking. Home: 4521 Saucon Valley Ct Alexandria VA 22312-3163 E-mail: mellk@erols.com.

KOLLER, JOHN DRYDEN, media educator, scriptwriter; b. Newton, Mass., Apr. 14, 1942; s. George Frank Koller and Charlotte Evelyn (Traylor) Clapper; m. Karen Elizabeth Anderson, Jan. 15, 1984; 1 child, Douglas Dryden. BA, Emerson Coll., 1964; MA, Suffolk U., 1966, Emerson Coll., 1971. Instr. speech & theatre, dir. theatre Suffolk U., Boston, 1966-68; asst. prof. speech & theatre Salem (Mass.) State Coll., 1970-73; founding ptnr. Phoenix Jazz Ltd. Records, Bergenfield, N.J., 1971—; founder, artistic dir. Am. Restoration Theatre Co., Inc., 1973-77; asst. prof. mass comms., dept. chmn. Ricker Coll., Houlton, Maine, 1977-78, Medaille Coll., Buffalo, 1979-82; asst. prof. journalism & broadcasting U. Maine at Orono, 1982-83; prof. broadcasting & TV Mt. Wachusett C.C., Gardner, Mass., 1983—. Bd. dirs. Opera Northeast, N.Y.C., 1993—. Recipient Excellence award Nat. Inst. for Staff and Orgnl. Devel., 1991. Mem. Nat. Broadcasting Soc. (chpt. advisor 1982—, Nat. Advisor of Yr. award 1987-88), Nat. Assn. Educators in Broadcasting, Internat. Assn. Jazz Educators. Office: Mt Wachusett CC 444 Green St Gardner MA 01440-1348

KOLLER, LOREN D. veterinary medicine educator; b. Pomeroy, Wash., June 16, 1940; s. Edwin C. and Doris K. (Shelton) K.; m. Kathleen Noel Ringness, Sept. 7, 1963; children: Susan E., Michael D., Christopher L. DVM, Wash. State U., 1965; MS, U. Wis., 1969, PhD, 1971. Head diagnostic and comparative pathology Nat. Inst. Environ. Health Scis., Research Triangle Park, N.C., 1971-72; rsch. assoc. dept. vet. medicine Oreg. State U., Corvallis, 1972-76, assoc. prof., 1976-78, prof., 1995—2001, dean Coll. Vet. Medicine, 1985-95; assoc. prof., asst. dean Dept. Vet. Medicine, U. Idaho, Moscow, 1978-81, assoc. prof., assoc. dean, 1981-82, prof., assoc. dean, 1982-85; owner Loren Koller & Assocs., LLC, 2001—. Research asst. Dept. Vet. Sci. U. Wis., Madison, 1968-71; assoc. veterinarian Blue Cross Vet. Clinic, Corvallis, 1965-66; mem. Nat. Adv. Com. to Establish Acute Exposure Guidelines for Hazardous Substances Commn. Contbr. articles to profl. jours., chpts. to books. Served to capt. M.C., U.S. Army, 1966-68. Grantee NIH, USDA, Dow Chem. Co., EPA, WHO, FDA, Merck Sharp & Dohme, Warner-Lambert, Pew Found. Fellow Acad. Toxicol. Sci.; mem. AVMA, NAS (mem. com. toxicology and Inst. of Medicine). E-mail: kollerl@pacifier.com.

KOLLER, MARITA ANN, accountant; b. Chgo., June 6, 1955; d. Frank J. and Jean J. Koller. BA, Western Ill. U., 1976; MPA, Am. U., 1980; AAS, Oakton Coll., 1989. Legis. asst. U.S. Congress, 1977-81; acct. UOP, Des Plaines, Ill., 1986—; UOP group leader Document Control-UOP Modular Tech. Ctr.; computer specialist Baxter Labs., Deerfield, Ill., 1985-86; actuarial asst. Towers, Perrin, Foster and Crosby, Chgo., 1981-85; instr. computer tech. Oakton Coll., Des Plaines, 1985—. U. Ill. scholar. Mem. Am. Mgmt. Assn., Am. Soc. Profl. and Women Execs., Nat. Soc. Pub. Accts. Home: 934 E Forest Ave Des Plaines IL 60018-1476

KOLLER, SHIRLEY LEAVITT, sculptor; b. Youngstown, Ohio, Apr. 6, 1921; d. Benjamin Harrison and Rose (Cohen) Leavitt; m. Herbert Richard Koller Mar. 7, 1943 (wid. June 1988); children: Donald Lee, Susan Koller Van Horne, Laura Frances. Diploma, Cleve. Inst. of Art, 1942; BS, Western Res. U., Cleve., 1942; MFA, The Am. U., 1972. Lectr. No. Va. C.C., Alexandria, Va., 1977-92; curator art program AAAS, 1997—. Lectr. sr. citizens Jewish Cmty. Ctr. of Greater Washington, Rockville, Md., 1990, 95, Washington Hebrew Congregation, Washington, 1995, Georgetown, 2001; appearance on Peter Jennings/ABC World News Tonight, 1991, Arlington Cable, 1990, Voice of Am. Radio, 1992; adj. faculty Md. Coll. of Art & Design, 1991-93; vis. artist Fairfax County Pub. Schs., 1982-85; visual art specialist, Fillmore Arts Ctr., Washington, 1977-81; spkr. in field. Artist: (3-D wall installation) The Joy of Transportation, 1989-93 (comm. 1989); writer: (newsletter) Eye Wash, 1990-92; curator Tri-State Ednl. Assn. exhibits, Washington; one-woman shows include Watkins Gallery, Am. U., 1972, Gate House Gallery, Washington, 1994, Mansion Art Gallery, Rockville, 1993, Friedholm Fine Arts Gallery, Asheville, N.C., 1991, O Street Studios, Washington, 1990, AAAS/Atrium Gallery, Washington, 1989-90, others; exhibited in group shows at Gallery 10, Washington, 1998, Tri-State Sculptors Ednl. Assn., Washington, 1997, Associated Artists of Winston-Salem, N.C., 1996, 99, Tri-State Sculptors Conf., U. S.C., Spartenburg, 1996, ARTS 901 E Street, Washington, 1996, AAAS, Washington, 1995-96, Newhouse Ctr. for Contemporary Art, S.I., N.Y., 1995-96, Mill River Gallery, Ellicott City, Md., 1999, Tysons Galleria II, Vienna, Va., 1999, Washington Sculptors Group, 1998-2000, Coastal Carolina U., Myrtle Beach, 1999, Grounds for Sculpture, Hamilton, NJ, 2000, 02, Mus. Art, Beijing, 2001, Brookside Gardens, 2002-03, Meridith Coll., Raleigh, NC, 2003, Artists In Our Midst, Washington, D.C., 2003, Meredith Coll., Raleigh, N.C., 2003, others; work collected at Ballston Metro Sta., Arlington, Va., First Am. Bank, Va. Commonwealth U., U. Md., AAAS/Washington, Akin Group, Law Offices, Washington, IBM Rsch. Hdqtrs., Durham, N.C., Internat. Sculpture Ctr., Hamilton N.J., Tri State Sculptors Edn. Assn., U. N.C., Brevard, others. Recipient Editor's Choice award Internat. Libr. Photography, 1998. Mem. Tri-State Sculptors Ednl. Assn. (life), Washington Sculptors Group. Democrat. Jewish. Avocations: travel, lecturing, gourmet cooking. Home: 2700 Virginia Ave NW Washington DC 20037-1908 E-mail: shirleyartkoller@metronets.com.

KOLLI, SAI, airline executive, educator; b. Hyderabad, India, July 28, 1966; came to U.S., 1989; s. Koteswara R. and Lakshmi B. Kolli; m. Rajeswari R. Rao, May 24, 1968; children: Vivek, Divya. M Mgmt. Studies, Birla Inst. Tech. and Sci., Pilani, India, 1987, M Engring., 1988; MS, U. Louisville, 1992, PhD, 1994. Grad. asst. U. Louisville, 1990-94; lectr. U. Tex., Dallas, 1995-2001; sr. analyst Am. Airlines, Ft. Worth, 1995-98, mgr. fin. analysis, 1998-2000, contr., 2000-01, dir., 2001—. Author: (books) Management Consulting, 2000, Production and Operations Management, 2000; editor: (book) Manufacturing Decision Support Systems, 1997. Recipient All Am. Scholar award U.S. Achievement Acad. Univs., 1993 Mem. INFORMS (cluster chmn. meeting 1999, sec. Dallas-Ft. Worth chpt. 1995-97, pres. Dallas-Ft. Worth chpt. 1998), Alpha Pi Mu (newsletter editor engring. economy divsn. 1993-94, sec. student chpt. 1991-92). Home: 437 Waterview Dr Coppell TX 75019 Office: Am Airlines MD 5494 PO Box 619616 Dallas TX 75261-9616 E-mail: kolli@dellepro.com., sai.kolli@aa.com.

KOLLIAS, JIM HARRY, music educator; b. Laguna Beach, Calif., Jan. 4, 1966; s. Harry D. and Linda Kollias; m. Doris C. Kateyiannis, Aug. 20, 1989; 1 child, Christina Eleftheria;1 child, Harrison James. BA in Music, UCLA, 1987; MS in Music Edn., U. Ill., Champaign-Urbana, 1996. Cert. profl. clear single subject instrn. credential, music Calif. Instrumental music dir. Vina Danks Mid. Sch., Ontario, Calif., 1988—94, Columbus Tustin Mid. Sch., Tustin, 1994—, C. E. Utt Mid. Sch., Tustin, 1994—96; orch. dir. Tustin H.S., Calif., 2000—. Guest condr. San Bernardino County H.S. Honor Orch., Calif., 1998, San Bernardino County Concert Orch., Calif., 2000; mentor tchr. Ontario Montclair Sch. Dist., Ontario, 1993—94, Tustin Unified Sch. Dist., 1996—97; chairperson Tustin Unified Sch. Dist. Facilities Com., 1995—96; presenter in field. Composer: (music) Everyone Can Play in Twelve Keys, 1990; contbr. articles to profl. jours. Named Toast of the Town, Town & Country Com., Orange County Philharm. Soc., 2001; recipient Pied Piper award, So. Calif. Sch. Band & Orch. Assn., 1996, PTSA Hon. Svc. award, Vina Danks Mid. Sch. PTSA, 1992; grantee, Orange County Philharm. Soc., Tustin Pub. Schs. Found. Mem.: Calif. Music Educators Assn., San Bernardino County Music Educators Assn. (secondary orch. rep. 1993—94), So. Calif. Sch. Band & Orch. Assn. (v.p. elem. & mid. sch. edn. 1999—2001). Office: Columbus Tustin MS/Tustin HS 17952 Beneta Way Tustin CA 92780 Office Fax: 714-730-7512. Personal E-mail: jhkollias@yahoo.com. Business E-Mail: jhkollias@yahoo.com.

KOLLINS, MICHAEL JEROME, automotive engineer, historian, writer; b. Mar. 20, 1912; s. Michael Arthur and Mary Ann (Peck) K.; m. Julia Dolores Advent, Jan. 16, 1934; children: Michael Lewis, Richard, Laura. Student, Coll. City Detroit, 1928—32. Chief sect. svc. engring. and tech. data Studebaker-Packard Corp., Detroit, 1945—55; mgr. tech. svcs. Chrysler Corp., Detroit, 1955—64, mgr. warranty adminstrn., 1964—68, mgr. Highland Park Svc. Ctr., 1968—75; pres. Kollins Design & Engring., Detroit, 1975—. Designer racing cars, 1932—39; designer sports cars, spl. luxury vehicles, 1951—; designer automotive performance and safety devices, 1946—. Author: Motor Torpedo Boat Engr.'s Manual, 1945; co-author: The Technology Century, 1995; author: Pioneers of the U.S. Automobile Industry, 2002; contbr. articles to profl. publs. Trustee Nat. Automotive Hist. Collection, 1982—; active Birmingham (Mich.) Chorale, Meadowbrook (Mich.) Festival Chorus; bd. dirs. Capuchin Charity Guild, 1983—; nat. advisor Motorsports Hall of Fame, 1988—. With USN, 1942—45. Mem.: Am. Automobile Assn. (contest bd.), Engring. Soc. Detroit (industry amb. 1972—), Soc. Automotive Historians, Soc. Automotive Engrs., U.S. Auto Club (vice-chmn. tech. com. 1971—82, dir. cert. com. 1983—). Home: 821 Highwood Dr Bloomfield Hills MI 48304-3024 Office: Kollins Design & Engring PO Box 214 Bloomfield Hills MI 48303-0214

KOLLMEYER, KENNETH ROBERT, surgeon; b. Berwyn, Ill., Feb. 1, 1947; BS in Biology-Chemistry, Randolph-Macon Coll., 1969; PhD in Physiology, U. Cin., 1973; MD cum laude, U. Colo., 1977. Diplomate Am. Bd. Surgery, Am. Sub-bd.Vascular Surgery. Head lab divsn. thoracic and cardiovascular surgery Med. Ctr. Va., Richmond, 1968-69; NIH rsch. fellow dept. clin. physiology Nat. Asthma Ctr., Denver, 1973-74; intern in surgery Parkland Meml. Hosp., Dallas, 1977-78, resident in surgery, 1978-80, chief resident in surgery, 1980-81; fellow in vascular surgery, instr. dept. surgery U. Tex. Southwestern Med. Sch., Dallas, 1981-82, clin. asst. prof. surgery, 1982—; dir. S.W. Vascular Lab., Dallas, 1982—. Attending vascular surgeon Meth. Med. Ctr., Dallas, 1982—, chief gen. surgery, 1997-99, sec. dept. surgery, 2000-; mem. staff Charlton Meth. Hosp., St. Paul Med. Ctr., Med. City Dallas Hosp.; teaching asst. dept. physiology U. Cin. Coll. Medicine, 1972-73; founder Dallas Surgery Group; chmn. Doctors Care PA, Dallas; presenter in field. Contbr. articles to profl. publs. Fellow ACS; mem. AMA, Tex. Med. Assn., Tex. Surg. Soc., Dallas County Med. Soc., Dallas Soc. Gen. Surgeons, Soc. for Non-Invasive Vascular Tech., Nat. Hon. Biol. Soc., Parkland Surg. Soc., Alpha Omega Alpha. Office: Dallas Surgical Group Meth Med Ctr Pavilion II 221 W Colorado Blvd Ste 625 Dallas TX 75208-2345

KOLLSTEDT, PAULA LUBKE, communications executive, writer; b. Cin., Aug. 27, 1946; D. Elmer George and Mary Margaret (Kelly) Lubke; m. Stephen Leonard Kollstedt, Jan. 21, 1968; children: Kelly, Lance, Stacey, Jonathan. BA, Xavier U., 1968, MEd, 1982. Cert. secondary tchr., Ohio. Editor, writer Shillito's Dept. Store, Cin., 1966-69; freelance writer Cin., 1969-74; pub. info. coord. Prince William County Parks and Recreatoin Com. (Va.), 1974-75; comm. coord. City of Cin. Recreation Com., 1975-78; cons. Warner Amex Cable TV, Cin., 1982-84, Moellers Assocs., Cin., 1982-84; writer Cin. Enquirer, 1982-83; exec. comm. specialist Gen. Electric Aircraft Engines, 1984-87, employee comm. specialist, 1987-90, mgr. comm., 1990-96, mgr. employee comm., 1996-99, mgr. cmty. and pub. rels., 1999—. Spkr. Cin. Presch. Coops., 1981, Cin. Women's Conf., 1984, lectr., presenter workshops on self-esteem for parents, 1975-86; lectr. bus. comm., 1992—. Author: Surviving the Crisis of Motherhood, 1982; contbr. articles to newspapers; writer, prodr. multi-media presentation Comm. Cin. (Unique Program award Ohio Parks and Recreation), 1978. Recipient Prism award Pub. Rels. Soc. Am., 1983, 85, 86, 87, 88, 92, 94, 95, 96, Pres.' award, 1995, 97, 98, Bronze Quill award Internat. Assn. Bus. Communicators, 1986, 87, 88, 90, 92, 95, 96, 97, 98, 99, Silver Quill award, 1989. Mem. Women in Comm. (v.p. programs 1981-82, v.p. corp. sponsorship 1998, 99, 2000, Gt. Lakes regional 1st pl. award 1984, 86, 87, 88, 95, recipient Nat. Clarion awards 1990, 98, Gem award 1992, Outstanding Communicator of Yr. 1999). Roman Catholic. Home: 5391 Haft Rd Cincinnati OH 45247-7419 Office: GE Aircraft Engines One Neumann Way Cincinnati OH 45215-1915

KOLM, PETTER N. investment advisor, mathematician; b. Stockholm, July 5, 1967; arrived in U.S., 97; s. Ake Nils and Gunilla Märta Kolm; m. Carmen Mauogan Kolm, Sept. 21, 2002. Diploma Math., ETH Zurich, Switzerland, 1996; MPhil, Royal Inst. Tech., Stockholm, 1999, Yale U., New Haven, 1999, PhD, 2000. Rsch. scientist Royal Inst. Tech., Stockholm, 1996—97, Yale U., New Haven, 1997—2000; assoc. Goldman Sachs & Co., NYC, 2000—. Contbr. chapters to books, articles to profl. jours. Grantee rsch. fellowship, Yale U., 1997—2000, rsch., DARPA/AFOSR. Mem.: NY Acad. Scis., Am. Math. Soc., Am. Fin. Assn., Soc. Applied and Indsl. Math., Sigma Xi. Home: 1 River Pl #2108 New York NY 10036 Office: Goldman Sachs & Co 32 Old Slip New York NY 10005

KOLM, RON, author, editor; b. Pitts., May 21, 1947; s. Roger Edward and Martyne (Akerson) K.; m. Donna Maxine Sterling, Sept. 5, 1984; children: Daniel, Gregory. BA, Albright Coll., Reading, Pa., 1970. Mgr. St. Marks Bookstore, N.Y.C., 1984-88, Coliseum Books, N.Y.C., 1988—. Flow mgr. Unbearables, N.Y.C., 1985—. Author: Welcome to the Barbecue, 1991; editor (anthologies) The Unbearables, 1995, Crimes of the Beats, 1998, Help Yourself!, 2001; contbr. articles, stories and poems to numerous mags. and anthologies; stories transl. into Czech and Japanese, 1 became movie; work reviewed in Village Voice, N.Y. Times, N.Y. Press, also others; manuscripts, books and mags. archived by Downtown Writers Group, placed in Fales Collection, NYU Libr. Home: 30-73 47th St Apt 3F Long Island City NY 11103

KOLMEN, SAMUEL NORMAN, retired consultant; b. Brownsville, Tex., Mar. 20, 1930; s. Joseph and Cyla (Gerson) K.; m. Barbara Kass, June 13, 1954; children: Benita Kolmen Solomon, Jeannette Kolmen Rosato. BA, U. Tex., Austin, 1954; PhD in Physiology, U. Tex. Med. Br., Galveston, 1957. James W. McLaughlin fellow in infection and immunology U. Tex. Med. Br., Galveston, 1955-57; Jeane B. Kempner postdoctoral fellow in medicine, London, 1957-58; asst. prof., assoc. prof., prof. U. Tex. Med. Br., Galveston, 1958-75; prof. physiology, chmn. dept. Coll. Sci. and Engring., Sch. Medicine Wright State U., Dayton, Ohio, 1975-84, prof., asst. dean Sch. Medicine, 1980-84, asst. to pres. in rsch., 1979-84; prof., assoc. dean, co-founder liaison com. for computing Hahnemann U. Sch. Medicine, Phila., 1984-89; dir. med. edn. and rsch. Mercy Hosp. Pitts., 1989-94; pres. Kolmen & Assocs., 1994—; ret. Rsch. coord. Shriners Burns Inst., Galveston, 1970-75; cons. Nat. Bd. Med. Examiners, Phila., 1989. Artist, painting in oils and acrylics; 20 juried shows in Phila. and Pitts.; contbr. over 35 articles to sci. jours. Pres. Congregation Beth Jacob, Galveston, 1970-72; bd. dirs. Jewish Assn. South Dayton, 1976-83; mem. sci. rev. coun. Miami Valley chpt. and Ohio Regional coun. Am. Heart Assn., 1981-83; vol. cons. Allegheny Policy Coun., 1994—, Coalition on Math. and Sci. (K-12), 1994-96; vol. Career and Passport Commn., 1994—, Operation Safety Net, 1994-96; a founder Nat. Campaign for Tolerance, 2002.. Recipient Disting. Alumnus award U. Tex. Med. Br., 1981. Mem.: Artist and Craftsmen Guild (bd. dirs. 2000—03, treas. 2003). Democrat. Achievements include development of technique for chronic lymphatic studies; research on erythocyte adsorption of fibrinolytic agents, vitamin K influence on fibrinogen metabolism, septicemia in burned animals by intestinal portal of entry, fibrinogen metabolic turnover and delivery. Office: Kolmen & Assocs 256 Sweet Gum Rd Pittsburgh PA 15238-1348

KOLMES, STEVEN ALBERT, biologist, educator; b. Poughkeepsie, N.Y., Sept. 17, 1954; s. Isaac and Beatrice (Stoller) K.; m. Linda Ann Fergusson, June 20, 1987; children: Sara Kjellaug, Elijah John. BS in Zoology, Ohio U., 1976; MS, U. Wis., 1978, PhD, 1984. Lectr. U. Wis., Madison, 1983-84; asst. prof. biology Hobart & William Smith Colls., Geneva, N.Y., 1984-89, chmn. biology dept., 1988-90, assoc. prof., 1989-94, prof., environ. studies coord., 1994-95; Molter chair sci., environ. studies dir., prof. biology U. Portland, Oreg., 1995—. Vis. scientist Univ. Coll., Cardiff, Wales, 1987, Simon Fraser U., Burnaby, B.C., 1985, B.C., 86; biology coord. Simcalc Project, Dartmouth, Mass., 1994—95, mem. adv. bd., 1993—95; mentor Oreg. Collaborative Excellence in Preparation of Tchrs., 1995—99; mem. Willamette River and Lower Columbia River Salmonid Tech. Recovery Team, 2000—, Tex. Tech. Adv. Com. Dept. Environ. Quality, 2001—03. Issue editor Coun. on Undergrad. Rsch. Quar., 1996-98; contbr. articles to profl. jours. Mem. vestry St. Peter's Ch., Geneva, 1992-95. Fulbright rsch. scholar, 1991; grantee USDA, 1993-95, NSF, 1996-98, NOAA, 2001-03. Mem. AAAS, Animal Behavior Soc. (mem. membership com. 1993-96), Entomol. Soc. Am., Fulbright Assn. (life). Democrat. Episcopalian.

Achievements include research in inactive constituents of pesticide formulations, honeybee colonies containing behaviorally distinct patrilines. Office: Univ Portland Dept Biology 5000 N Willamette Blvd Portland OR 97203-5743

KOLMIN, KENNETH GUY, lawyer; b. N.Y.C., Oct. 22, 1951; s. Frank William and Edith Kolmin; m. Suzan L. Frumm, Sept. 3, 1978; children—Stephen Todd, Jennifer Dana, Robert Scott. BS summa cum laude, SUNY-Albany, 1973; MS, Syracuse U., 1975, JD cum laude, 1975. Bar: Ill. 1976, U.S. Dist. Ct. (7th dist.) Ill. 1976, U.S. Tax Ct. 1980, U.S. Supreme Ct. 1985; CPA, Ill. Tax cons. Arthur Young and Co., Chgo., 1976-79; atty. Shefsky Saitlin & Froelich, Chgo., 1979-81; ptnr. Rooks Pitts & Poust, Chgo., 1981-84, Schwartz & Freeman, 1984-96, Sonnenschein, Nath & Rosenthal, Chgo., 1996—. Contbr. articles to profl. jours. Mem. ABA, AICPA, Ill. Bar Assn., Ill. Soc. CPAs. Home: 975 Eastwood Rd Glencoe IL 60022-1122 Office: Sonnenschein Nath & Rosenthal 8000 Sears Tower Chicago IL 60606

KOLODEY, FRED JAMES, lawyer; b. LaCoste, Tex., Mar. 5, 1936; s. Raymond and Mamie V. (Newman) K.; children: Trecia Anne Estep, Michele Leigh Kolodey; m. Helen Gable McIntosh, June 10, 1989. BA, Tex. Christian U., 1962; LL.B., So. Methodist U., 1964. Bar: Tex. 1964. Since practiced in, Dallas; ptnr. Kolodey & Thomas, 1975-83, of counsel, 1983-94, Thomas, Sheehan & Culp, 1994—2001, Kolodey, Thomas & Blackwood, 2001—. Pres. Dallas Jr. Bar Assn., 1969 Comments editor: Southwestern Law Jour, 1963-64. Mem. dist. hearing office panel Dallas Community Coll., 1974, Democratic precinct chmn., 1968-73. Mem. Tex., Dallas bar assns., Delta Theta Phi (pres. 1963, Nat. award 1964), Alpha Chi, Pi Sigma Alpha. Home: 540 Mariah Bay Dr Heath TX 75032-7626

KOLODNER, RICHARD DAVID, biochemist, educator, geneticist; b. Morristown, N.J., Apr. 3, 1951; s. Ignace Izack and Ethel (Zelnick) Kolodner; m. Karin Ann Gregory, Aug. 6, 1983 (div. May 1991). BS, U. Calif., Irvine, 1971, PhD, 1975; MS (hon.), Harvard U., 1988. Rsch. fellow Harvard U. Med. Sch., Boston, 1975-78; asst. prof. Dana Farber Cancer Inst. and Harvard U. Med. Sch., Boston, 1978-83, assoc. prof., 1983-88, prof. biochemistry, 1988-97; chmn. divsn. cellular molecular biology Dana-Farber Cancer Inst., Boston, 1991-94, head x-ray crystallography lab., 1991-97, chmn. divsn. of human cancer genetics, 1995-97; prof. medicine, mem. Cancer Ctr. U. Calif. Med. Sch., San Diego, 1997—; mem. Ludwig Inst. for Cancer Rsch., San Diego, 1997—. Editor: PLASMID Jour., 1986—95; editor: (assoc.) Cancer Rsch. Jour., 1995—2000, Cell jour., 1996—; mem. editl. bd. Molecular Cellular Biology Jour., 1999—, Jour. Biol. Chemistry, 2000—, DNA Repair Jour., 2003—; contbr. articles to sci. jours. Recipient Jr. Faculty Rsch. award, Am. Cancer Soc., 1981, Faculty rsch. award, 1984, Merit award, NIH, 1993, Charles S. Mott prize, GM Cancer Rsch. Found., 1996; grantee rsch. grantee, Am. Cancer Soc., 1980—82, NIH, 1978—. Fellow: Am. Acad. Microbiology; mem.: NAS, Am. Assn. Cancer Rsch., Genetic Soc. Am., Am. Soc. Microbiology, Am. Soc. Biochemistry and Molecular Biology. Home: 13468 Kibbings Rd San Diego CA 92130-1231 Office: Ludwig Inst for Cancer Rsch CMME 3080 9500 Gilman Dr La Jolla CA 92093-0669 E-mail: rkolodner@ucsd.edu.

KOLODNY, DEBRA RUTH, labor management and non-profit consultant; b. N.Y.C., Aug. 21, 1960; d. Sidney and Irma (Smith) Kolodny. BS, Cornell U., 1981; JD, U. Pa., 1985. Bar: DC 1985, Pa. 1985. Lawyer Fed. Election Commn., Washington, 1985-86; asst. counsel negotiations Nat. Treas. Employees Union, Washington, 1986-87, dir. coop. efforts, 1988-92; consulting assoc. Restructuring Assocs., Inc., Washington, 1992-94; labor mgmt. and non-profit assn. cons. Washington, 1995—; coord. workplace participation programs Svc. Employees Internat. Union, Washington, 1996. Spkr. in field; dir. organizing and devel. ALEPH: Alliance for Jewish Renewal, 2003—. Editor: (anthology) Blessed Bi Spirit: Bisexual People of Faith, 2000; contbr. articles to profl. jours. Nat. coord., lobbyist BiNet USA, 1992—94, 1996—98, adv. bd., 1998—; steering com. DC BiNetwork, Washington, 1989—92; co-founder core group AmBi, Washington, 1991—93; bd. dirs. Interfaith Alliance Montgomery County, 1998—99, v.p., 1999—2000; prison minister Adelphi Friends, Md., 1991—93. Mem. Assn. Quality and Participation (bd. dirs. 1991-94), Washington Bar Assn., Fabrangen Havurah, ALEPH: Alliance for Jewish Renewal (chair bd. dirs. 2002—). Democrat. Jewish. Avocations: bicycling, swimming, singing, tai chi. Home and Office: 631 Ritchie Ave Silver Spring MD 20910-5240 E-mail: debraruth@mac.com.

KOLODNY, EDWIN HILLEL, neurologist, geneticist, medical administrator; b. Boston, Mar. 15, 1936; s. Myer Zeman and Naomi Lillian (Zalkind) K.; m. Roselyn Leinwand, May 31, 1958; children: Nancy, Leonard Benjamin, Robin, Noah Jacob. AB in Econs. cum laude, Harvard Coll., 1957; MD with honors, NYU, 1962. Diplomate Am. Bd. Psychiatry and Neurology, Am. Bd. Med. Genetics. Intern, resident in internal medicine Bellevue Hosp., N.Y.C., 1962-64; resident in neurology Mass. Gen. Hosp., Boston, 1964-67; spl. fellow lab. neurochemistry Nat. Inst. Neurol. Diseases, Bethesda, Md., 1967-70; asst. prof. neurology Harvard Med. Sch., Boston, 1970-76, assoc. prof., 1976-85, prof., 1985-91; Bernard and Charlotte Marden prof., chmn. dept. neurology NYU Med. Ctr., N.Y.C., 1991—. Vice-chmn. exec. com. Med. Bd. Tisch Hosp., N.Y., 1993-97, chmn., 1997-99; vis. prof. Weizmann Inst. Sci., Rehovot, Israel, 1988, 90; assoc. dir. Eunice Kennedy Shriver Ctr., Mental Retardation, Inc., Waltham, Mass., 1976-83, acting dir., 1983-84, dir., 1984-90; assoc. neurologist Mass. Gen. Hosp., Boston, 1976-87, neurologist, 1988-91; chmn. com. Rsch. Ctrs. Forward Planning Mental Retardation, Nat. Inst. Child Health and Human Devel., 1983-84; cons. pres.'s com. Mental Retardation, 1982; adv. genetic svcs. Dept. Pub. Health Mass., 1977-80; mem. Mass. Nat. Inst. Health Centennial Com., 1987-88, profl. adv. bd. Internat. Rett Syndrome Assn., 1986-94, sci. adv. bd. United Leukodystrophy Found., 1986-94, sci. med. adv. com. Canavan Found., 1994—; med. adviser Gaucher Initiative Project Hope, 2000-02; mem. steering com. Global Orgn. for Lysosomal Diseases, 2002—. Mem. editl. bd. Annals of Neurology, 1984-89; contbr. articles to profl. jours. Mem. sci. adv. bd. Nat. Tay Sachs and Allied Diseases Assn., 1970—; mem. med. adv. bd. Dysautonomia Found., 2001—; v.p., trustee Temple Emanuel, Newton, Mass., 1983—89; trustee Hebrew Coll., Brookline, Mass. Recipient Solomon A. Berson Med. Alumni Achievement award clin. sci. NYU Sch. Medicine, 1993, Above and Beyond award, Nat. Tay sachs and Allied Dis. Assn., 2003. Fellow Am. Coll. Med. Genetics, Am. Acad. Neurology (S. Wier Mitchell award 1970); mem. Am. Assn. Neuropathology (Moore award 1975), Am. Neurol. Assn., Am. Soc. Human Genetics, Am. Soc. Neurochemistry, Child Neurology Soc., Harvard Varsity Club (Cambridge), Assn. for Rsch. in Nervous and Mental Diseases (bd. dirs. 1993—), Alpha Omega Alpha. Avocations: judaica, photography. Home: 110 Bleecker St Apt 24D New York NY 10012-2106 Office: NYU Med Ctr 550 1st Ave New York NY 10016-6402 E-mail: edwin.kolodny@med.nyu.edu.

KOLODNY, STANLEY CHARLES, oral surgeon, air force officer; b. N.Y.C., Feb. 22, 1923; s. Aaron and Lea (Stern) K.; m. Mary Kathryn Leigh, Feb. 22, 1947; children: Kathleen Susan, Carter Leigh, Stanley Charles. BA, U. Tex., 1944, D.D.S., Baylor U., 1947, MS, U. Ill., 1961. Diplomate: Am. Bd. Oral and Maxillofacial Surgery. Commd. 1st lt. USAF, 1951, advanced through grades to maj. gen., 1981; cons. in oral surgery Surgeon Gen. U.S. Air Force, 1966; chmn. dept. oral surgery Wilford Hall USAF Med. Center, San Antonio, 1969-75, dir. dental services, 1975-77; asst. surgeon gen. for dental services Bolling AFB, Washington, 1979-82. Clin. prof. dept. surgery U. Tex. Dental Br., Houston, 1969-77; clin. asso. prof. dept. surgery U. Tex. Med. Sch., San Antonio, 1969-77 Contbr. chpt. to book, articles to profl. jours. Bd. dirs. Am. Cancer Soc., 1970-77. Decorated D.S.M., Legion of Merit with oak leaf cluster, Air Force Commendation medal; recipient cert. of achievement for outstanding oral surgery USAF. Fellow Am. Coll. Dentists, Am. Assn. Oral and Maxillofacial Surgeons; mem. ADA, Soc. Air Force Clin. Surgeons. Home: 6401 Red Bud Dr Flower Mound TX 75022-5859

KOLODZEI, NATALIA A. art foundation administrator, art historian, curator; b. Moscow, Jan. 8, 1974; d. Tatiana A. and Alexander D. Kolodzei. BA in Art History with honors, State U. N.J., 1998. Exec. dir. Kolodzei Art Found., Inc., Highland Park, N.J., 1991—; curator Bergen Mus. Art and Sci. Mem. adv. bd. Russian Am. Forum, N.Y., 1995—. Contbr. articles to art mags. Art Chronika, Iskusstuo. Named Hon. Citizen of State of Okla., Gov. of Okla., 1993. Mem. Am. Assn. for Advancement of Slavic Studies, Internat. Salon Soc. (ambassador 1996—), Internat. Art Fund, Print Club N.Y. (bd. dirs.), N.Y. Russian Club (bd. dirs.), Golden Key Nat. Honor Soc., Phi Beta Kappa. Avocation: collecting russian and eastern european art. Home: 123 S Adelaide Ave Apt 1N Highland Park NJ 08904-1615 Fax: 732-545-8428. E-mail: kolodzei@kolodzeiart.org.

KOLODZIEJ, EDWARD ALBERT, political scientist, educator; b. Chgo., Jan. 4, 1935; s. Albert Stanley and Anna Caroline (Chudzik) K.; m. Antje Heberle, Aug. 15, 1959; children: Peter, Andrew, Matthew, Daniel. BS summa cum laude, Loyola U., Chgo., 1956; MA, U. Chgo., 1957, PhD, 1961. Analyst nat. security fgn. affairs div. Congl. Research Service, Library of Congress, Washington, 1960-62; asst. prof. polit. sci. U. Va., Charlottesville, 1962-67, assoc. prof., 1967-73, chmn. dept. govt. and fgn. affairs, 1967-69, prof. polit. sci., 1973-83; head dept. U. Ill., Urbana, 1973-77, dir. Office Arms Control, Disarmament and Internat. Security, 1983-86, research prof. polit. sci., 1983—, elected univ. scholar, 1988. Vis. prof. LaTrobe, Melbourne, 1999, Senshu U., Tokyo, 2001; cons. in field Author: The Uncommon Defense and Congress, 1966, French International Policy under de Gaulle and Pompidou: The Politics of Grandeur, 1974, Making and Marketing Arms: The French Experience and Its Implications for the International System, 1987; editor: American Security Policy, 1979, Security Policies of Developing States, 1981, Limits of Soviet Power in the Developing World, 1987, Security and Arms Control: Guide to National and International Policy-Making, 2 vols., 1989, Cold War as Cooperation, 1991, Coping with Conflict After the Cold War, 1996; mem. editl. bd. Internat. Studies Quar., Defence and Peace Econs., Contemporary Security Policy, European Security; contbr. articles on fgn. and security policy and decision-making to profl. jours., U.S., Europe; also contbg. author books. Mershon Postdoctoral fellow nat. security Ohio State U., 1964-65, Rockefeller Postdoctoral fellow in internat. rels., Paris, 1965-66, Ford Found. fellow in social sci., 1969-71, Fulbright Rsch. fellow, 1986; NSF grantee, 1971, Deutscher Akademischer Austauschdienst grantee, 1975, Ford Found. Internat. Arms Control Competition grantee, 1976, Ctr. for Advanced Study, U. Ill., 1979, 95—, Rockefeller Found. grantee, 1980, grantee NEH, 1981, Woodrow Wilson Ctr., 1987, U.S. Inst. Peace grantee, 1987, 91, grantee Ford Found., 1993; recipient Burlington award for outstanding tchg. and scholarship, 1985. Mem. Internat. Inst. Strategic Studies London, Council Fgn. Relations N.Y., Am., Midwest internat. polit. sci. assns., Internat. Studies Assn. Home: 711 W University Ave Champaign IL 61820-3919 Office: U Ill Dept Polit Sci Urbana IL 61801

KOLOMBATOVIC, VADJA VADIM, retired management consulting company executive; b. Belgrade, Serbia, Yugoslavia, Jan. 20, 1924; came to U.S., 1944; s. George Steven and Antigona (Kefala) K.; m. Virginia Doris Carter, 1946; children: Vadja Vadim Jr., Mimi Carter. BS, U. Ill., 1948; cert. in personnel mgmt., U. Richmond, Va., 1949. Office mgr. State Farm Ins. Co., Richmond, 1948-49; spl. agt. FBI, N.Y.C. and San Francisco, 1949-66, asst. legal attache Paris, 1966-69, legal attache Madrid, Spain, Paris, 1969-75, chief liaison sect. Washington, 1975-76; v.p. for internat. affairs Intertel, Washington, 1976-83, sr. v.p., 1983-85, exec. v.p. Rockville, Md., 1985-89, pres., 1989-92, pres., CEO, 1993-2000, also bd. dirs. V.p. Chalk's Internat., Miami, Fla., 1976-91; sr. internat. cons. Served to lt. U.S. Army, M.I., 1946-47. Mem. Am. Legion, Soc. Former Spl. Agts., Assn. Former Intelligence Officers, Assn. Former Legats, REs. Officers Assn., Masons (32 deg.), Shriners (Fairfax, Va.), McLean C. of C. Republican. Avocations: philately, gardening. Home: 1171 Dolley Madison Blvd Mc Lean VA 22101-3019

KOLOMIETS, ALEXEI, computer programmer; b. Simferopol, Ukraine, Sept. 23, 1970; came to U.S., 1992; s. Vladimir and Natalia Kolomiets; m. Elena Bespalova, May 3, 1994; 1 child, Alexei. BS in Physics, Simferopol (Ukraine) State U., 1992; PhD, Tex. A&M U., College Station, 1998. Grad. asst. Tex. A&M U., College Station, 1993-98, postdoctoral rsch. fellow, 1998-99; programmer Elite Software Devel. Inc., Bryan, Tex., 1999-2000; software engr. Critical Devices Inc., Dallas, 2000-01; software design engr. Microsoft Corp., Redmond, Wash., 2001—. Home: 17210 NE 33rd St Redmond WA 98052 E-mail: akolomiets@hotmail.com.

KOLOMYTKIN, OLEG, biophysicist, consultant; b. Kaunas, Lithuania, USSR, July 20, 1947; arrived in U.S., 1995; s. Vladimir and Evdokiya (Nekhaeva) Kolomytkin; m. Irinia Chernikova, Mar. 30, 1977; children: Rotislav, Dmitry, Igor. BS, Moscow Inst. Physics and Tech., 1972; PhD, Russian Acad. Scis., Pushchino, Moscow region, 1978; D in Phys. and Math. Scis., Russian Acad. Scis., 1990. Engr.; physicist. Rsch. scientist Inst. Biophysics, Moscow, 1972-78; sr. rsch. scientist Russian Acad. Scis., 1978-89, dir. lab. radiation biophysics Inst. Cell Biophysics, 1989-97; rsch. scientist La. State U. Health Sci. Ctr., Shreveport, 1995—. Mem. elected coun. Inst. Cell Biophysics, Pushchino, Russia, 1991—96; mem. organizing com. Internat. Symposium Va. Commonwealth U., 1991, 94. Contbr. articles to profl. jours., chapters to books. Grantee, Internat. Sci. Found., 1993, 1994, 1995. Mem.: Bioelectromagnetics Soc., European Bioelectromagnetics Assn. Achievements include visualization of ionic channels by a scanning tunneling microscope; finding response of brain receptor systesm to microwave energy exposure; finding switches of electrophysiological states of the cells by interleukin-1. Avocation: sports. Home: 1331 Woodrow St Shreveport LA 71103 E-mail: okolom@lsuhsc.edu.

KOLSBY, HERBERT F. lawyer, educator; b. Phila., July 10, 1926; s. Leonard H. and Josephine R. (Refsen) K.; m. Hermine W. Kolsby, Sept. 5, 1948; children: Dana Kolsby Edenbaum, Robert, Paul. JD, Temple U., 1951. Bar: Pa. 1951. Ptnr. Kolsby Gordon Robin & Shore, Phila., 1954—. Prof. law, dir. LLM in trial advocacy Temple U. Sch. Law, Phila., 1991-97. Gen. chmn. Fedn. Jewish Agys., Phila., 1989-90; pres. Temple Adath Israel, Phila., 1993-94. Recipient Justice Michael A. Musmanno award as outstanding trial lawyer Phila. Trial Lawyers Assn., 1993; Herbert F. Kolsby disting. lectureship in trial advocacy at Temple U. Sch. Law established in his honor, 2001. Fellow Am. Coll. Trial Lawyers, Internat. Acad. Trial Lawyers; mem. Inner Circle Advocats, White Manor Country Club (pres. 1968-69). Democrat. Avocation: golf. Office: Kolsby Gordon Robin Et Al 1650 Market St Fl 22D Philadelphia PA 19103-7301 Home: Apt 1612 9600 Atlantic Ave Margate City NJ 08402-2261

KOLSRUD, HENRY GERALD, dentist; b. Minnewaukan, N.D., Aug. 12, 1923; s. Henry G. and Anna Naomi (Moen) K.; m. Loretta Dorothy Cooper, Sept. 3, 1945; children: Gerald Roger, Charles Cooper. Student, Concordia Coll., 1941-44; DDS, U. Minn., 1947. Gen. practice dentistry, Spokane, Wash., 1953—. Bd. dirs. Spokane County Rep. Com., United Crusade, Spokane; at-large-del. Rep. Planning Com.; mem. Rep. Presdl. Task Force. Capt. USAF, 1950-52. Recipient Employer of the Yr. award Lilac City Bus. and Profl. Women, 1994. Mem. ADA, Wash. State Dental Assn., Spokane Dist. Dental Soc., Spokane Country Club, Masons, Shriners. Home: 2107 W Waikiki Rd Spokane WA 99218-2780 Office: 3718 N Monroe St Spokane WA 99205-2850

KOLTNOW, PETER GREGORY, engineering consultant; b. N.Y.C., Apr. 14, 1929; s. Harry George and Fay (Richman) Koltnow; m. Dorothy D. Witter, Oct. 27, 1950; children: Nan Koltnow Chase, Nina. BS, Antioch Coll., 1951; MS, U. Calif. at Berkeley, 1956. Engr. City of Dayton, Ohio, 1953-55; traffic engr. County of Fresno, Calif., 1956-62, Auto Club of So. Calif., 1962-67; dir. urban div. Automotive Safety Found., Washington, 1967-69, Hwy. Users Fedn., 1970-71, v.p., 1971-74, pres., 1974-84; counselor to pres. Am. Trucking Assns., 1985-90. Guest lectr. various univs., 1965—; chmn. Transp. Rsch. Bd., 1979. Contbr. Pres. Candlelighters, 1970—71. With Ordnance Corps U.S. Army, 1951—53, a. Recipient Disting. Svc. award, Transp. Rsch. Bd., 1982. Mem.: ASCE (apptd. nat. assoc. nat. academies 2002, James Laurie prize 1984). Unitarian Universalist. Home and Office: 9210 Fernwood Rd Bethesda MD 20817-3316

KOLVE, V. A. English literature educator; b. Taylor, Wis., Jan. 18, 1934; s. Amos and Gunda (Lien) K. BA, U. Wis., 1955; BA with honors, Oxford U., 1957, MA, D Philosophy, Oxford U., 1962. From asst. prof. to assoc. prof. English Stanford (Calif.) U., 1962-69; prof. English U. Va., Charlottesville, Va., 1969-78, Commonwealth prof. English, 1979-86, chmn. dept. English, 1979-81; found. prof. English UCLA, 1986—2001, prof. emeritus, 2001—. Guggenheim Found. ednl. adv. bd., 1988—; The Alexander Lectures, U. Toronto, 1993, The Clark Lectures, Cambridge U., 1994. Author: The Play Called Corpus Christi, 1966, Chaucer and The Imagery of Narrative, 1984; author, editor: (with Glending Olson) Norton Critical Edition: Chaucer: The Canterbury Tales, 1989. 1st lt. U.S. Army, 1959. Recipient Brit. Coun. Humanities prize, 1985, Harbison Teaching award Danforth Found., 1972, UCLA Disting. Teaching award, 1995, Disting. Faculty award, 1999; Jenkins Rsch. fellow Oxford U., 1958-62, Guggenheim fellow, 1968, Sr. fellow Ctr. Advanced Studies in Visual Arts, Nat. Gallery, 1984, fellow Ctr. Advanced Study in Behavioral Scis., Stanford U., 1985; Rhodes scholar, 1955-58. Fellow Medieval Acad. Am. (pres. 1992), Am. Acad. Arts and Scis.; mem. MLA (chair exec. com. Chaucer divsn. 1973-77, 86-90, James Russell Lowell prize 1985), New Chaucer Soc. (trustee 1988-92, pres. 1994-96), Early English Text Soc., AAUP, Phi Beta Kappa. Democrat. Home: 2034 Outpost Dr Los Angeles CA 90068-3726 Office: UCLA Dept English Los Angeles CA 90024

KOLVENBACH, PETER HANS, priest, religious order superior; b. Druten, The Netherlands, 1928. Student U. Nijmegen (Netherlands), theology St. Joseph U., Beirut, linguistics, Paris, 1963-67. Joined Jesuit Order Netherlands; ordained priest Roman Cath. Ch., 1961; prof. linguistics St. Joseph U., Beirut, 1968-81; provincial superior Beirut, 1974-81; rector Pontifical Oriental Inst., Rome, 1981-83; superior-gen. Soc. of Jesus, 1983—; consultor Congregation for Oriental Chs., mem. Congregation for Evangelization of Peoples, mem. Orthodox-Cath. dialogue, 1983—. Author: In Cammino Verso La Pasqua, 1988, Men of God: Men for Others, 1990, El Padre Kolvenbach en Colombia, 1990, Kolvenbach en México, 1990, Cinco mensajes universitarios, 1991, Seleccion de escritos 1983-90, also various articles and revs. in field of linguistics and spiritual theology; mem. of commns. Cath. Orthodox dialogue books. Address: Borgo Santo Spirito 4 00193 Rome Italy

KOLYER, JOHN MCNAUGHTON, materials specialist, chemist; b. East Williston, N.Y., June 30, 1933; s. John and Mildred (McNaughton) K.; children: Scott McNaughton, Paul Franklin, Craig David, Jeffrey John. BA, Hofstra U., 1955; PhD, U. Pa., 1960. Technician Olin-Mathieson Chem. Corp., Port Washington, N.Y., 1955-56; rsch. chemist FMC Corp., Princeton, N.J., 1960-62; tech. supr. Allied Chem. Corp., Morriston, N.J., 1964-71; mem. tech. staff Rockwell Internat., Anaheim, Calif., 1973-96; scientist, engr. Boeing Co., Anaheim, 1997—. Author: many articles and books; patentee in field. Mem.: N.Y. Acad. Scis., Soc. for Advancement Materials Processing and Engring., Am. Chem. Soc., Phi Lambda Upsilon, Kappa Mu Epsilon, Sigma Kappa Alpha. Home: 885 Seagull Ln Apt B311 Newport Beach CA 92663-6640

KOLZ, BEVERLY ANNE, publishing executive; b. Newark, Ohio, Dec. 25, 1946; d. Willard Joseph and Lydia Marie (Gaze) Kolz. BA, Ohio Dominican Coll., 1968; MBA, U. Iowa, 1991. Prodn. editor Merrill Pub., Columbus, Ohio, 1968-69, series editor, 1969-75, media buyer, 1975-76, prodn. buyer, 1976-78, mng. editor, 1978-80, adminstrv. editor, 1980-85, exec. editor, 1985-86; v.p., dir. of ops. and prodn. William C. Brown Pub. Co., Dubuque, Iowa, 1986-91; corp. v.p. ops. William C. Brown Comm., Inc., Dubuque, 1991-92; exec. v.p., gen. mgr. William C. Brown Pubs., Dubuque, 1992-94, CEO, pres., 1995-97; prin. Simon and Kolz Pub., Dubuque, 1997—. Mem. reader panel Dubuque Telegraph Herald, 1998—. Mem. 21st Century Adv. Coun., 2003—; v.p. Altrusa, Columbus, 1985—86; mem. after sch. mentor program St. Mark's Cmty. Ctr., 1998—, mem. edn. com., 2000—; vol. Dubuque Arboretum and Bot. Garden, 2001 . Mem.: Nat. Assn. Coll. Stores, Nat. Assn. Coll. Stores (trustee 1994—95), Am. Assn. Pubs. (exec. coun. higher edn. divsn. 1992—97), Chgo. Women in Pub. (Pub. Woman of the Yr. 1993), Women in Pub., Women in Comm. (pres. 1979—80, 1992—93), Am. Ednl. Rsch. Assn., U. Iowa Alumni Assn., Dubuque Area C. of C. (small bus. coun.). Avocation: bicycling. Office: Simon and Kolz Publishing 1631 Main St Dubuque IA 52001-4512 E-mail: bkolz@simon-kolz.com.

KOM, AMBROISE, literature educator; b. Yogam, Cameroon, Dec. 15, 1946; s. Defomamotcha and Marguerite Wayou; m. Dorothée Njuidje; children: Nouepeyiô, Messà, Ghainsom. Lic in letters, U. Yaounde (Cameroon), 1970, diploma higher studies, 197l; D 3d cycle, U. Pau (France), 1975; D Letters, U. Sorbonne, Paris, 198l. Instr. Brown U., Providence, 1972-75, asst. prof., 1975, Dalhousie U., Halifax, Canada, 1975—77; asst. prof., rschr. U. Sherbrooke, Canada, 1978-82; assoc. prof. U. Rabat, 1982-84; assoc. prof. lit. U. Yaounde, 1984-88, prof., 1988-97, Coll. of the Holy Cross, Worcester, Mass., 1997—. Author: Le Harlem de Chester Himes, 1978, Dictionnaire des Oeuvres Littéraires Négro-Africaines de Langue Française, 1983, George Lamming et le destin des Caraïbes, 1986, Littératures of africaines, 1987, Le Cas Chester Himes, 1990, Mongo Beti. Présence francophone 42, 1993, Education et démocratie en Afrique, 1996, Dictionnaire des oeuvres littéraires de langue française en Afrique au sud du Sahara, vol. 2, 1996, La Malédiction francophone, 2000, Francophonie et dialogue des cultures, 2000, Mongo Beti parle, 2002, Remember Mongo Beti, 2003. Home: 17 Merlin Ct Worcester MA 01602-1363 Office: Coll Holy Cross Dept Modern Lang/Lit Box 89A Worcester MA 01610-2395 E-mail: akom@holycross.edu.

KOMANDURI, RANGA, engineering educator; b. Jaggammapeta, Andhra Pradesh, India; arrived in U.S., 1972; s. Mangachary and Kanakavalli Komanduri; m. Srilakshmi Komanduri, Aug. 16, 1978; children: Sangeetha, Mukund. B Engring. in Mech. Engring., Osmania U., Hyderabad, India, 1964, M Engring. in Heat Power, 1966; PhD, Monash U., Melbourne, Australia, 1972, D Engring., 1992. Asst. prof. Carnegie-Mellon U., Pitts., 1972—77; mfg. engr. corp. R&D GE, Schenectady, NY, 1978—89; Regents prof., A.H. Nelson jr. endowed chair in engring. Okla. State U., Stillwater, 1989—. Adj. prof. Rensselaer Poly. Inst., Troy, NY, 1978—86; program dir. NSF, Washington, 1986—89. Contbr. articles to profl. jours.; author (with G. Lakshmi Bayi): The Splendor of Sree Padmanabha Swamy of Tiruvananthapuram, 1999; author: The Splendor of Sri Nava Narasimha of Ahobila Kshetram, 2000. Fellow: ASME (v.p. 1988—92), Soc. Mfg. Engrs. (pres. N.Am. Mfg. Rsch. Conf.); mem.: NAMRC/SME, Internat. Instn. for Prodn. Engring. Rsch. Avocations: cricket, tennis, swimming, photography, Hindu philosophy. Home: 4020 Timberline Dr Stillwater OK 74074 Office: Okla State Univ 218 Engr N Stillwater OK 74078 Business E-Mail: ranga@ceat.okstate.edu.

KOMAR, VITALY, artist; b. Moscow, Sept. 11, 1943; Student, Stroganov Inst. Art and Design, Moscow, 1967. Ptnr. Komar & Melamid Studio, N.Y.C., 1965—. Instr. visual art Moscow Regional Art Sch., 1968-76. Exhibitions include Wadsworth Atheneum, Hartford, Conn., 1978, Mus. Modern Art, Oxford Eng., Mus. Decorative Art, Paris, 1985, Neuen Gesellschaft fur Gildende Kunst, Berlin, 1988, Bklyn. Mus., 1990, Alternative Mus., N.Y.C., 1994, Storefront for art and architecture, N.Y.C., 1995, Ukraine State Mus., Kiev, 1995, Mus. Modern Art, Cologne, Germany, 1997, Kunsthalle, Vienna, Austria, 1998; exhibited in group shows at Met. Mus. Art, N.Y.C., 1982, 84, Chrysler Mus., Norfolk, Va., 1983, Sydney, Australia, 1986, Kassel, Documenta 8, Germany, 1987, Solomon R. Guggenheim Found., 1987, FIAC, Paris, 1989, Bklyn. Mus., 1990, Venice Bienalle, 1997, 99, Yeshiva U. Mus., N.Y.C., 2002-03; represented in permanent collections Whitney Mus. Am. Art, N.Y.C., Stedeliyk Mus., Amsterdam, The Netherlands, Guggenheim Mus., Mus. Modern Art, Met. Mus. Art; commns. include mural Unity, 1st Interstate Bank Bldg., L.A., 1993, murals Liberty as Justice, N.Y., Bronx Housing Ct., 1994-98. Grantee Nat. Endowment Arts, 1982.

KOMARA, EDWARD MICHAEL, musicologist; b. Buffalo, N.Y., Aug. 18, 1966; s. John Albert Komara and Anne Elizabeth Wing. BA, St. John's Coll., 1988; MLA, SUNY Buffalo, 1991, MA in Music History, 1992. Music libr., blues archivist U. Miss., Oxford, 1993—2001; Crane music libr. SUNY Potsdam, 2001—. Author: The Dial Recordings of Charlie Parker, 1998; author: (essay, discography) Charley Patton, Screamin' and Hollerin' the Blues, 2001; contbr. Recipient Eagle Scout award, Boy Scouts Am., 1982. Mem.: MLA (Walter Gerboth award 1995), Am. Musicol. Soc. Office: Crane Library SUNY Potsdam 44 Pierrepont Ave Potsdam NY 13676

KOMAROFF, ANTHONY LEADER, physician; b. Milw., June 7, 1941; s. Michael I. and Lillian J. (Leader) K.; m. Lydia Villa, June 18, 1970. AB, Stanford U., 1963; MD, U. Wash., 1967. Intern Cambridge Hosp., Cambridge, 1967-8; resident Beth Israel Hosp., Boston, 1970-72, asst. physician, 1971-79; sr. physician Brigham & Women's Hosp., Boston, 1992—, chief div. gen. medicine, 1982-97; prof. medicine Harvard Med. Sch., 1993—; editor-in-chief Harvard Health Publs., 1997—. Mem. nat. adv. coun. Reg. Med. Programs, Dept. HEW, Washington, 1971-76. Contbr. over 270 articles to profl. jours. Lt. col. USPHS, 1968-70. Grantee, HEW, Dept. Health and Human Svcs., 1976—. Achievements include development of field of clinical algorithms; applications of computers in medical care; studies of common illnesses. Office: Harvard Health Publs 10 Shattuck St Boston MA 02115-6011

KOMAROFF, STANLEY, lawyer; b. Bklyn, Apr. 1, 1935; s. William Ralph and Fanny (Wein) K.; m. Rosalyn Steinglass, Dec. 25, 1960; children: William Charles, Andrew Steven. BA, Cornell U., 1956, JD, 1958. Bar: N.Y. 1959. Assoc. Proskauer Rose LLP, N.Y.C., 1958-68, ptnr., 1968—, chmn., 1991-99. Mem. rev. and planning coun. N.Y. State Hosp., 1982-92; trustee Beth Israel Med. Ctr., 1984—, vice chair, 1999—; trustee St. Lukes-Roosevelt Hosp. Ctr., Continuum of Health Ptnrs. Inc.; mem. bd. regents L.I. Coll. Hosp., 2001—; bd. dirs. Edmond de Rothschild Found., Club Med, Inc., 1984-95, Overseas Shipholding Group, Inc., Westhampton Beach Performing Arts Ctr.; chmn. ann. fund Cornell U. Law Sch., 1991-93, mem. adv. coun. 1st lt. USAR, 1958. Fellow Am. Bar Found.; mem. N.Y. State Bar Assn., Assn. of Bar of City of N.Y., N.Y. County Lawyers Assn., Order of Coif, Sunningdale Country Club, Phi Kappa Phi. Home: 910 Park Ave Apt 5-s New York NY 10021-0255 Office: Proskauer Rose LLP 1585 Broadway New York NY 10036-8299 E-mail: skomaroff@proskauer.com.

KOMATSU, SHIGEGO RICHARD, architect; b. San Francisco, May 5, 1916; s. Denzo and Tome (Fujimoto) K.; m. Chisato Frances Kuwata, Aug. 6, 1943; children: Richard Shigeto, Kathryn Kay. BArch, U. Calif., Berkeley, 1938; cert. in interior design, San Francisco Archtl. Club, 1939; cert. in machine design, Lawrence Inst. Tech., Detroit, 1944. Registered architect, Calif.; cert. architect Nat. Coun. Archtl. Registration Bds. Landscape planner Golden Gate Internat. Expn., San Francisco, 1938-39; designer/architect Charles F. Strothoff, Architect, San Francisco, 1939-42, 46-52; asst. project engr. Fed. Pub. Housing Authority, Detroit, 1944; designer Harley, Ellington & Day, Architects, Detroit, 1944; assoc./architect Donald L. Hardison & Assocs., Richmond, Calif., 1952-57; sec./prin. Hardison and Komatsu Assocs., San Francisco, 1957-79; pres./prin. Hardison Komatsu Ivelich & Tucker, San Francisco, 1979-88, cons., 1988—; pvt. practice cons. S. Richard Komatsu, Architect, El Cerrito, Calif., 1988—. Invited speaker nat. conv. Nat. Assn. Home Builders, Chgo., 1966, confs. ASCE, San Francisco, 1972, Calif. and Nev. Water Pollution Control Assn., South Lake Tahoe, Calif., 1972; vis. archtl. adviser Cogswell Coll., San Francisco, 1981-82; initiated formation of Design Rev. Bd., City of El Cerrito, Calif., 1968; mem. seismic safety study Gen. Plan for Cities of El Cerrito, Richmond, and San Pablo, State of Calif. Prin. works include 47 water treatment plants and related facilities, East Bay Mcpl. Utility Dist., 1964-84 (Gov.'s award 1974), Advanced Wastewater Treatment Plant, Clark County Sanitation Dist., Las Vegas, Nev., 1979, South Valley Water Reclamation Facility, Midvale, Utah, 1987, East Bank Wastewater Treatment Plant, Metairie, La., 1988, main office complex, Turlock (Calif.) Irrigation Dist., 1988, 24 water treatment plants and related facilities, Contra Costa Water Dist., Concord, Calif., 1967-88 (Concord award 1972), pre-design of 6 water reclamation plants, 3 pumping plants, 1 dechlorination facility for Clean Water Program Greater San Diego, 1990-92; design advisor adminstrn., ops., and lab. bldg., wastwater treatment plant City of Santa Rosa, Calif., administrn. bldg. Dublin San Ramon (Calif.) Svcs. Dist., plant ops. ctr. Delta Diablo Sanitation Dist., Calif., 1991-92; design developer adminstrn.-opers. bldgs, treatment facilities Jones Island Wastewater Treatment Plant Milw. Met. Sewage Dist., 1980-82; contbr. articles to jours. in field. Bd. dirs. Richmond (Calif.) Art Ctr., 1956-60, City of Richmond Ballet Co., 1956-60; mem. El Cerito Planning Commn., 1962-75, chmn., 1966-67; mem. El Cerrito Design Rev. Bd., 1969-78, chmn., 1973-77; mem. Contra Costa chpt. Japanese Am. Citizens League, 1950—, pres., 1957, bd. dirs., 1956-60 (silver pin achievement award 1966). Master sgt. Mil. Intelligence Svc., U.S. Army, 1944-46. Recipient Eminent Conceptor award Consulting Engrs. Assn. Calif., 1974, Cons. Engrs. award Fairfield-Suisun Wastewater Mgmt. Facilities, 1978, AIA award Student Ctr. Complex U. Calif., 1978, Gold Nugget award Southeast Water Pollution Control Plant, 1984. Fellow (emeritus) AIA (East Bay chpt., bd. dirs. 1968-69, chmn. numerous coms.); mem. Am. Water Works Assn. (cert. life mem., invited speaker various confs.) Republican. Presbyterian. Avocations: water color painting, archtl. delineating, golf. Address: 1323 Devonshire Dr El Cerrito CA 94530-2572 *I was blessed with perseverence, thirst for knowledge and a will to nurture aptitude. However, my humble environment did not allow optimism for a meaningful future until an unexpected scholarship gave me the means to advance to a university. Still, adversities had to be overcome: World War II, the unconstitutional internment, military service and racial discrimination. Perhaps in spite of these, the meaningful accomplishments have been achieved with God and family, and the inspiring people who guided, encouraged and supported me.*

KOMEN, LEONARD, lawyer; b. St. Louis, May 31, 1943; s. Meyer and Yetta (Ellman) K.; m. Sandra Gail Cytron, June 8, 1969; children: Douglas Steven, Matthew Todd. BA, U. Mo., 1965, JD, 1970. Bar: Mo. 1970, U.S. Dist. Ct. (ea. dist.) Mo. 1971, U.S. Supreme Ct. 1973, U.S. Ct. Appeals (8th cir.) 1985, U.S. Claims Ct. 1992, U.S. Ct. Appeals (3d cir.) 1995. Assoc. Susman, Willer & Rimmel, St. Louis, 1970-74, Susman Schermer Rimmel & Parker, St. Louis, 1974-77, ptnr., 1977-80; prin., v.p. Selner, Glaser, Komen, Berger & Galganski, P.C., St. Louis, 1980-96; prin. mgr. Komen, Berger & Cohen, L.C., 1996-99; prin. Law Offices of Leonard Komen, P.C., 1999—. Ct.-apptd. trustee, examiner, receiver U.S. Bankruptcy Ct., 1988—. bd. dirs. Zeta Beta Tau Frat. Inc., 1984—, nat. sec., 1989-90, nat. v.p., 1990-92, nat. pres., 1992-94; mem. supervisory bd. Nat. Interfraternity Coun. Legal Advocacy Fund, 1993-98. Pres. Creve Coeur Hockey Club Inc., St. Louis, 1987-88, bd. dirs., 1989-93; coord. Parkway North Hockey Club, 1989-91; pres., bd. dirs. Roswell Messing Ednl. Found., 1989—; bd. dirs. Zeta Beta Tau Centennial Found. 1990-98. Recipient Merit citation Zeta Beta Tau Frat., Inc., 1977, 91, 92, 2002. Mem.: ATLA, Mo. Bankers Assn., Comml. Law League Am. Jewish. Home: 14385 Stablestone Ct Chesterfield MO 63017-2502 Office: Law Offices of Leonard Komen PC 7733 Forsyth Blvd Ste 300 Clayton MO 63105 E-mail: lenkomen@komenlaw.com.

KOMENSKY, PAUL LOUIS, music educator; b. Jenkins Township, Pa., Jan. 6, 1955; s. Paul John and Helen Claire Louise Komensky. BA, King's Coll., Wilkes-Barre, PA, 1973—77; bachelor music, Coll. Misericordia, Dallas, PA, 1978; masters music, Temple U., Philadelphia, PA, 1987. Music educator Parkland Sch. Dist., Allentown, Pa., 1978—93; music min. St. Dominic's Ch., Wilkes-Barre, Pa., 1993—2001, Immaculate Conception Ch., West Pittston, Pa., 2002—; music educator Dallas Sch. Dist., Dallas, Pa., 2000—01, St. Mary's Bzy Sch., Wilkes-Barre, Pa., 2001—. Recipient Excellence In Music Edn., Coll. Misericordia, 1989. Mem.: Pa, Music Educators Assn., Nat. Assn. for Music Edn. Home and Office: R 159 Oak Street Apt D Pittston PA 18640

KOMER, MATTHEW W. athletic director; b. Holy Oke, Mass., July 26, 1974; s. Gregory A. and Linda K. Komer. BS in Sports Mgmt., U. Mass., 1996, MEd, 1999. Grad. asst. athletics U. Mass., Amherst, 1996—98, dir. ops. men's basketball, 1998—2000, asst. athletic dir. acad./athletics, 2000—. Com. mem. troop 424 Boy Scouts Am. Mem.: KC. Avocations: travel, golf, reading. Office: Univ Mass Athletics 302 Mullins Ctr Amherst MA 01003

KOMINIS, KATHERINE ELIZABETH, librarian; d. George and Lucille Kominis. BA, SUNY, 1971; MLS, So. Conn. State U., 1981; MA, Boston (Mass.) U., 1988, cert., 1999. Rare book selector Spl. Collections Boston (Mass.) U., 1982—97, asst. dir. for rare books Spl. Collections, 1997—. Mem. women's coun. Boston (Mass.) U. Contbr. articles to profl. jours. Grantee, Chem. Heritage Found., 2003. Mem.: Mass. Friends of Librs. (sec. 2000—02, treas. 2000—02), Phi Delta Kappa (pres. 1997—99). Office: Boston University Special Collections 771 Commonwealth Avenue Boston MA 02215 E-mail: katkom@bu.edu.

KOMISAR, ARNOLD, otolaryngologist, educator; b. N.Y.C., Nov. 27, 1947; s. Samuel and Sonia (Schwartz) K.; m. Lenora I. Felderman, Dec. 23, 1984; children: Alexandra Danielle, Jonathan Reed. BS, Bradley U., 1968; DDS, NYU, 1972; MD, Hahnemann Med. Coll., 1975. Diplomate Am. Bd. Otolaryngology. Resident in surgery Beth Israel Med. Ctr., N.Y.C., 1975-76; resident in otolaryngology Mt. Sinai Med. Sch., N.Y.C., 1976-79; asst. prof. otolaryngology Albert Einstein Coll. Medicine, N.Y.C., 1979-85, assoc. prof., 1985-86, assoc. clin. prof., 1986-90; assoc. dir. head and neck surgery Albert Einstein Affiliated Hosps., N.Y.C., 1982-86; attending otolaryngologist Montefiore Hosp. and Med. Ctr., N.Y.C., 1979-90, Bronx Mcpl. Hosp. Ctr., N.Y.C., 1979-90, North Ctrl. Bronx Hosp., N.Y.C., 1979-90, N.Y. Hosp.-Cornell U. Med. Ctr., N.Y.C., 1997—; clin. assoc. prof. otolaryngology Cornell U. Med. Coll., N.Y.C., 1994—98, clin. prof., 1998—2000; attending otolaryngologist N.Y. Hosp.-Cornell U. Med. Ctr., N.Y.C., 1997—99; clin. prof. otolaryngology NYU, 2000—. Otolaryngologist Lenox Hill Hosp., N.Y.C., 1986—, asst to dir. resident edn. dept. otolaryngology, 1986—, adj. otolaryngologist, 1987—, attending otolaryngologist, 1989—, assoc. dir. otolaryngology, 1990—; cons. otolaryngology N.Y. Eye and Ear Infirmary, N.Y.C., 1986-89; courtesy staff surgery-otolaryngology Drs. Hosp., N.Y.C,, 1986-90; attending staff Manhattan Eye Ear and Throat Hosp., 1995—; attending otolaryngologist N.Y. Hosp. Cornell U. Med. Ctr., 1997-2000; presenter in field. Contbr. articles to profl. jours. Recipient Centurion award Bradley U., 1997. Fellow Am. Coll. Surgeons, Am. Soc. Head and Neck Surgery, Am. Acad. Facial Plastic and Reconstructive Surgery, Am. Acad. Otolaryngology/Head and Neck Surgery (Honor award), Triological Soc. (Mosher award), Am. Bronchoesophalogical Soc., N.Y. Acad. Medicine, Am. Laryngol. Assn.; mem. AMA, Pan-Am. Soc. Brochoesophagology, Soc. Univ. Otolaryngologists, N.Y. Head and Neck Soc., Med. Soc. N.Y., N.Y. Laryngol. Soc., N.Y. County Med. Soc. Avocations: reading, travel. Office: 1317 3d Ave New York NY 10021-2995 E-mail: axk2@aol.com.

KOMISAR, DAVID DANIEL, retired university provost; b. N.Y.C., July 20, 1917; s. Jacob and Yetta (Jacobson) K.; m. Beatrice Liebman, Aug. 15, 1940 (dec. Sept. 1981); children— Jack Lloyd, June Diana; m. Molly Komisar, Nov. 1984 BSS., Coll. City N.Y., 1937, MS, 1940; postgrad., U. Glasgow, 1945, Sorbonne, 1946; PhD, Columbia U., 1953. With Civil Service, N.Y.C., 1939-42; indsl. personnel work, 1943-44; counselor vocational rehab. U.S. Army, 1943-46; dir. guidance Mohawk Coll., 1946-48; dir. guidance, chmn. dept. psychology Champlain Coll., State U. N.Y., Plattsburg, 1948-53; chmn. dept. psychology U. Hartford, 1953—, pres. univ. faculty senate, 1964-65; dean U. Hartford (Sch. Arts and Scis.), 1966-67, dean of faculties, 1967-70, v.p. acad. affairs, 1970-71, provost, 1972-80, Univ. prof., 1980-84, prof. and provost emeritus, 1984—; mem. Conn. Civil Service Commn., 1980-84; pres. Emeriti Assn., 1989-91; cons. Palm Beach County Mental Health Assn., 1991—. Project dir. research in mental retardation Office Vocat. Rehab., Dept. Health, Edn. and Welfare, 1964-65, psycho-social com. social rehab. services, 1968-74; head New Eng. Conf. Mental Retardation, 1960, Conn. Task Force on Mental Retardation, 1960-61; Conn. rep. Nat. Def. Edn. Act, 1960-61; research fellow U.S. Office Vocational Rehab., 1962-63; Conn. Citizens Com. on State Welfare, 1967-69; mem. standing com. accreditation Conn. Commn. High Edn., 1969-75. Contbr. articles on testing, therapy, vocational selection to profl. jours. Co-chmn. Citizens Charter Com. Hartford, 1959; mem. bd. Hartford Jewish Cmty. Ctr., 1955-63, v.p., 1963-78, life officer 1978—; mem. bd. Mental Health Assn., 1959-62; bd. dirs. Inst. of New Dimensions, Palm Beach Cmty. Coll., 1994—. Recipient rsch. grant for study residential care retarded children HEW, 1965-69, Disting. Svc. medal U. Hartford, 1990, Univ. medal U. Hartford, 1991; elected to Townsend Harris Hall of Fame, 1998. Mem. Conn. Valley Assn. Psychologists (past pres.), Am. Psychol. Assn., Conn. Psychol. Assn. (council; pres.), Nat. Vocational Guidance Assn., Am. Personnel and Guidance Assn., Sigma Xi. Clubs: Connecticut Valley Torch (past pres.), Probus (past pres.) (Hartford).

KOMISARJEVSKY, CHRISTOPHER P.A. public relations executive; b. 1945; BS in Polit. Sci., MBA; postgrad. German Lit./Internat. Affairs, U.S./Europe. Hill and Knowlton, Inc., 1972-92, pres., CEO Europe, Mid. East and Africa ops., CEO Carl Byoir & Assocs.; pres., CEO Gavin Anderson & Co. Omnicom, 1992-95; pres., CEO Burson-Marsteller U.S., N.Y.C., 1995-99, Burson-Marsteller Worldwide, N.Y.C., 1998—. Chmn. Burson-Marsteller Global Corp. Practice, 1995-99. Co-author: Peanut Butter and Jelly Management, 2000; contbr. articles to profl. jours.; lectr. at Spain's Instituto de Empresa, Switzerland's Internat. Inst. for Mgmt. Devel., N.Y.U. Grad. Sch. Bd. dirs. several non-profit orgs.; trustee EQ Advisors Trust. Capt. U.S. Army, 1967-72 (Vietnam). Recipient Ellis Island Medal of Honor, 1996. Office: Burson Marsteller 230 Park Ave New York NY 10003-1566

KOMISSARCHIK, EDWARD, computer scientist; b. Moscow, July 5, 1949; came to U.S., 1990; s. Alexander and Riva (Zilberstein) K.; m. Stella Mnatsakanian, Sept. 5, 1969; 1 child, Julia. M in Math., Lomonosov U., Moscow, 1971; PhD of Computer Sci., Inst. Cybernetics, Russia, 1978. Rsch. scientist Inst. Control Scis., Acad. Scis., Moscow, 1971-77, Inst. Sys. Studies, Acad. Scis., Moscow, 1977-90; assoc. prof. computer sci. Inst. Radio Electronics and Automation, Moscow, 1978-90; pres., chief tech. officer Accent, Inc., San Francisco, 1993-96; dir. Aspect Telecomm., San Jose, 1996-2000; v.p. engring. Savvio.com, 2000—01; pres. Reactive Network Solutions, Redwood City, 2001—02; CEO Glenbrook Networks, 2002—. Contbr. articles to profl. jours. Mem. IEEE, ACM, Internat. Platform Assn., Russian Math. Soc., Scientists Club. Avocations: public speaking, medieval history, tennis. Home: 995 Parrott Dr Hillsborough CA 94010

KOMIVES, PAUL J. federal judge; b. 1932; AB, U. Detroit, 1954; JD, U. Mich., 1958. Bar: Mich. 1958, D.C. 1958, U.S. Ct. Appeals (6th cir.) 1961, U.S. Ct. Appeals (D.C. cir.) 1961, U.S. Supreme Ct. 1963. Asst. U.S. atty. U.S. Dist. Ct. (ea. dist.) Mich., 1961-66; spl. prosecutor Mich. Cir. Ct., Detroit, 1966-67; pvt. practice, 1967-71; magistrate judge U.S. Dist. Ct. (ea. dist.) Mich., Detroit, 1971—. Adj. prof. Detroit Coll. Law, 1972-2000; adj. prof. Wayne State U. Law Sch., Detroit, 1998—. Office: US Dist Ct Ea Dist Mich 629 US Courthouse 231 W Lafayette Blvd Detroit MI 48226-2700 Fax: 313-234-5497.

KOMLOS, PETER, violinist; b. Budapest, Hungary, Oct. 25, 1935; s. Laszlo and Franciska (Graf) K.; m. Edit Feher, 1960; 2 sons; m. Zsuzsanna Arki, 1984; 1 son. Educated, Budapest Music Acad. Founded Komlos String Quartet, 1957; 1st violinist Budapest Opera Orchestra, 1960; leader Bartok String Quartet, 1963; extensive concert tours to USSR, Scandinavia, Italy, Austria, W.Ger., Czechoslovakia, 1958-64, to U.S., Can., N.Z., Australia, 1970, Japan, Spain, Portugal, 1971; Far East, U.S., Europe, 1973; recordings include Beethoven's string quartets for Hungaroton, Budapest; Bartok's string quartets for Erato, Paris, all Bartok's Quartets, 1991-92, Different Haydn Quartets, Canyon Classic-Japan, Mendelssohn-Schonberg Pieces, Hunghroton, 1992. Recipient 1st prize Internat. String Quartet Competition, Liè ge, 1964, Liszt prize, 1965, Gramopone Record prize of Germany, 1969, Kossuth prize, 1970, second Kossuth prize, 1997, UNESCO Music Coun. placque, 1981; named Eminent Artist, 1980.

KOMMEDAHL, THOR, plant pathology educator; b. Mpls., Apr. 1, 1920; s. Thorbjørn and Martha (Blegen) K.; m. Faye Lillian Jensen, June 2, 1924; children: Kris Alan, Siri Lynn, Lori Anne. BS, U. Minn., 1945, MS, 1947, PhD, 1951. Instr. U. Minn., St. Paul, 1946-51, asst. prof. plant pathology, 1953-57, assoc. prof., 1957-63, prof., 1963-90, prof. emeritus, 1990—; asst. prof. plant pathology Ohio Agrl. Research and Devel. Ctr., Wooster, 1951-53, Ohio State U., Columbus, 1951-53; prof. Univ. Coll., U. Minn., St. Paul, 1990—. Cons. botanist and taxonomist Minn. Dept. Agr., 1954-60, Sci. Mus. Minn., 1990—; 7th A.W. Dimock lectr. Cornell U., 1979; external assessor U. Pertanian Malaysia, 1994-97. Author: Pesky Plants, 1989; co-author: Scientific Style and Format, 1994; editor Minn. Fulbright newsletter, 1995-2002, Procs. IX Internat. Congress Plant Protection, 2 vols., 1981, Corn Disease newsletter, 1970-76; assoc. editor The Boghopper, 1996—; cons. editor McGraw Hill Ency. Sci. and Tech., 1972-78; editor-in-chief Phytopathology, 1964-67; sr. editor: Challenging Problems in Plant Health, 1982, Plant Disease Reporter, 1979; contbr. articles to profl. jours. Bd. mem. Park Bugle, 1998—. Recipient Elvin Charles Stakman award, 1990, Award of Merit, Gamma Sigma Delta, 1994; Guggenheim fellow, 1961, Fulbright scholar, 1968. Fellow AAAS, Am. Phytopathol. Soc. (councilor 1958-60, pres. 1971, publs. coord. 1978-84, Disting. Svc. award 1984, 93, sci. adv. 1984—, adv. bd. office internat. programs 1987-93, editor Focus 1981—); mem. Am. Inst. Biol. Scis., Bot. Soc. Am., Coun. Sci. Editors, Internat. Soc. Plant Pathology (councilor 1971-78, sec.-gen. and treas. 1983-88, treas. 1988-93, editor newsletter 1983-93), Mycol. Soc. Am., Minn. Acad. Sci., N.Y. Acad. Scis., Weed Sci. Soc. Am. (award of excellence 1968), Fulbright Assn. (editor newsletter Minn. chpt. 1995-2002). Baptist. Home: 1666 Coffman St Apt 322 Saint Paul MN 55108-1340 Office: U Minn Dept Plant Pathology 495 Borlaug Hall 1991 Upper Buford Cir Saint Paul MN 55108-6030 Office Fax: 612-625-9728. E-mail: thork@umn.edu.

KOMOROWSKI, ANNE MARIE, freelance journalist, paralegal; b. Cleve., July 20, 1938; d. Frank Joseph Salaciak and Antonia Mental; m. Joseph A. Komorowski, June 5, 1965; children: Scott, Michael, Joseph F. Author: Woman to Woman, 2000. Avocations: cooking, baking, collecting buttons. Home: 129 E Canal St (rear) Newcomerstown OH 43832

KOMOSKI, PAUL KENNETH, community activist, educational research executive; b. Jersey City, Nov. 20, 1928; s. Louis Stanislaw and Stelle Marie (Norwich) K.; m. Isabel Jane Parrish, Mar. 24, 1952 (dec. Mar. 1970); children: Christina, William; m. Joanna Monica Anthony, June 15, 1972; 1 child, Mara Mia. BA, Acadia U., 1950, MA, 1952. Tchr. Morristown (N.J.) Sch., 1950-52; tchr., head mid. sch. Collegiate Sch., N.Y.C., 1952-60; pres. Ctr. for Programmed Instrn., N.Y.C., 1960-64; assoc. dir. Inst. for Ednl. Tech. Columbia U., N.Y.C., 1963-66; pres., exec. dir. Ednl. Products Info. Exch. Inst., Hampton Bays, N.Y., 1967—. Pres., founder Learning and Info. Networking Cmty. Tech. (LINCT) Coalition, Hampton Bays, 1994—, U.S. Environ. Protection Agy., Washington, 1986-88, NSF, Washington, 1992-93. Founder, exec. editor www.eLearningspace.org, 2000—. Bd. mem. Children Uniting Nations; overseer Friends World Program, Southampton Coll., LIU, 1992-. Mem. ASCD, Am. Edn. Rsch. Assn., Assn. Ednl. Comm. and Tech. (Lifetime Achievement 1981), Internat. Soc. for Performance and Instrn. (Lifetime Achievement award 1979). Mem. Soc. Of Friends. Avocations: tennis, jazz vocalist. Home: 355 Sebonac Rd Southampton NY 11968-2720 Office: EPIE Inst 103 W Montauk Hwy Hampton Bays NY 11946-4003

KOMP, RICHARD JOSEPH, solar scientist; b. Chgo., Aug. 7, 1938; s. Joseph C. and Rose Ann (Schatzman) K.; m. Vicky Patton, June 23, 1969 (div.); m. Mirdza Leskov, Oct. 24, 1983. BS, Loras Coll., Dubuque, Iowa, 1960; PhD, Wayne State U., 1964. Sr. physicist Xerox Corp., Webster, N.Y., 1964-68; assoc. prof. dept. physics and astronomy Western Ky. U., Bowling Green, 1968-73; v.p. Zip Svcs. div. Ednl. Act., Columbus, Ohio, 1973-75; rsch. assoc. dept. chemistry Wayne State U., Detroit, 1975-81; exec. dir. Skyheat Assocs., Jonesport, Maine, 1979—; v.p. R & D Sunwatt Corp., Jonesport, Maine, 1981-88, pres., 1988—. Adj. prof. Coll. of the Atlantic, 1991. Author: Practical Photovoltaics, 1981, 3d rev. edit. 1995, (with Joel Davidson) The Solar Electric Home, 1983; contbr. articles to profl. jours.; patentee photovoltaics and copying machines. Bd. dirs. Urban Alternative Homestead, Louisville, 1981-87, Ind. Solar Industries Assn., Indpls., 1982-85. Mem. AAAS, Am. Phys. Soc., Internat. Solar Energy Soc., N.E. Sustainable Energy Assn. (bd. dirs. 1990-94, 2001-), Maine Solar Energy Assn. (pres. 1989-93, 95—, v.p. 1994-95), Sigma Xi. Avocations: hiking, sailing, theater, model railroading. Home and Office: Sunwatt Corp 17 Rockwell Rd RR Jonesport ME 04649-9001

KOMPALA, DHINAKAR SATHYANATHAN, chemical engineering educator, biochemical engineering researcher; b. Madras, India, Nov. 20, 1958; arrived in U.S., 1979; s. Sathyanathan and Sulochana Kompala; m. Sushila Viswamurthy Rudramuniappa, Nov. 18, 1983; children: Tejaswi Dina, Chytanya Robby. BTech., Indian Inst. Tech., Madras, 1979; MS, Purdue U., 1982, PhD, 1984. Asst. prof. chem. engring. U. Colo., Boulder, 1985-91, assoc. prof., 1991—. Vis. assoc. chem. enging. Calif. Inst. Tech., 1991-92; vis. prof. Internat. Ctr. Biotech., Osaka U., Japan, 1999. Editor Cell Separation Sci. and Tech., 1991; contbr. articles to profl. jours.; mem. editl. bd. Jour. Biotech. Recipient NSF Presdl. Young Investigators award, 1988-93; NSF Biotech. Rsch. grantee, 95-99, 00-03; Dept. Commerce rsch. grantee, 1988; The Whitaker Found. grantee, 1990-93; USDA grantee 2000-03. Mem. Am. Inst. Chem. Engrs. (program chair 2000, 01), Am. Chem. Soc. (biotechnology program chair biochem. tech. divsn. 1993). Office: U Colo PO Box 424 Boulder CO 80309-0424

KOMPASS, EDWARD JOHN, consulting editor; b. Jersey City, Dec. 22, 1926; s. Edward F. and Margaret A. (Doran) K.; m. Amelia M. Heubel, Sept. 22, 1951; children: Christine (Mrs. Kevin Scully), Daniel E., Andrew J., Timothy M., Matthew P., Julie A. (Mrs. Matthew Wilhm). Degree in mech. engring., Stevens Inst. Tech., 1951. Jr. engr. Intelectron Inc., N.Y.C., 1951-52; engr. De Florez Co., N.Y.C., 1952-54; asst. editor control engring., McGraw-Hill Pub. Co., N.Y.C., 1954-60, assoc. editor, 1960-65; mng. editor control engring., Dun-Donnelley Pub. Corp., N.Y.C., 1965-72; editor control engring., Tech. Pub., Barrington, Ill., 1972-86; editorial dir. control engring. Cahners Publ., 1986-87, cons. editor, 1987—, forum discussions moderator, control engring online, 1997. Co-organizer ann. advanced control confs. Purdue U., Lafayette, Ind., 1974-77, 79-93; conf. dir. Internat. Control. Engring. Expn. and Conf., Chgo., 1992-94; mem. adv. coun. Indsl. Automation Conf., 1994, 95, 96. Editor, contbr. profl. articles and editorials to jours.; editorial advisor Detroit Engr. With USNR, 1944-46. Recipient 19th Ann. Crain award Assn. Bus. Pubs., 1987. Mem. IEEE, Am. Soc. Bus. Paper Editors, Instrument Soc. Am., Engring. Soc. Detroit, Am. Legion, VFW, Rotary Internat., Beta Theta Pi. Roman Catholic. Home and Office: 678 Cobb Hill Rd Lincoln VT 05443-9699 E-mail: ekompass@gmavt.net.

KON, MARK ANDREW, mathematics educator; b. Warsaw, Mar. 13, 1952; came to U.S., 1959; s. Steven H. and Christine Marie (Soltan) K. BA, Cornell U., 1974; PhD, MIT, 1979. Asst. prof. Boston U., 1979-88, assoc. prof., 1988—; asst. prof. Columbia U., N.Y.C., 1985-89, assoc. prof., 1989-90. Co-organizer N.E. Conf. Differential Equations, Boston, 1984; organizer Complexity Symposium, 1990; referee various jours., 1979—. Author: Probability Distributions, 1985; contbr. numerous articles to profl. jours. Grantee NSF, 1979, 80-87, 91—, Can. Math. Soc., 1986, Air Force Office Sponsored Rsch., 1990—; Fulbright fellow, 1996-97. Mem. Am. Math. Soc. (organizer spl. session 1984), Internat. Neural Network Soc. (conf. organizer 1988, 1993), Internat. Assn. Math. Physics, AAAS, Assn. for Computing Machinery. Avocations: tennis, studying history. Office: Boston U Dept Math Boston MA 02215

KONAR, NANDINI, research scientist; arrived in arrived in U.S., 1990; d. Debbindu Konar. B in pharmacy, B.I.T.S., Pilani, India; MS, U. Ohio, Toledo, OH.; PhD, Temple U., Phila. Rsch. scientist Wyeth, Marrietta, Pa., 1999—2000, sect. head, 2000—. Author: (jour. articles) Jour. of Continue Release, Polymer Prepr., 1991, J. Appl. Polymer Sci., J. Pharmacy Sci., 1997, PISCRBM (crs), 1997, Jour. of Continue Release, Polymer Prepr., 1998, J. Appl. Polymer Sci., J. Pharmacy Sci., 1998, PMSE(acs), 1998. Mem.: Am. Chemical Soc., Controlled Release Soc., Am. Assn. of Pharm. Scientists. Avocations: reading, writing, arithmetic.

KONCSOL, STEPHEN WAYNE, psychologist, educator; b. Elizabeth, NJ, July 28, 1948; s. Louis and Mary Helen Koncsol; m. Dorian F. Cirrone, Aug. 4, 1979; children: Siena Teresa, Blaise John. BA Clark U., 1970; MS, Rutgers U., 1973, PhD, 1976. Diplomate Am. Bd. Psychopharmacology; lic. Psychologist Fla. Asst. prof. Barry U., Miami, Fla., 1977—83, assoc. prof., 1983—; pvt. practice, 1982—; pres. Therapeutic Life Concepts, Miami, Fla., 2003—. Mem.: APA, Dade County Psychol. Assn., Fla. Psychol. Assn. Democrat. Roman Catholic. Avocations: wine, opera, running. Home: 13200 SW 32d Ct Fort Lauderdale FL 33330 Office: Dept Psychology Barry U 11300 NE 2d Ave Miami FL 33161

KONDAS, NICHOLAS FRANK, retired shipping company executive; b. Eger, Hungary, Sept. 26, 1929; came to U.S., 1957. s. Miklos and Ilona (Racz) K.; m. Elfriede O. Strauss; children: Walter, Nicolette. MS in Econs., Karl Marx U., Budapest, Hungary, 1952. Mgr. Szovosz Cent., Budapest, Hungary, 1952-56; assembler S. Goldberg Inc., Hackensack, N.J., 1957-67; supr. Alfred Industries, Richfield Park, N.J., 1967-68; mgr. C.R. Bard, New Providence, N.J., 1968-69; v.p. Seatrain Lines Inc., N.Y.C., 1969-81; gen. mgr. Harper Robinson Co., San Francisco, 1981-82; ret. v.p. Farrell Lines Inc., N.Y.C., 1982-2000; pres. Dionic Resources Inc., 1994—2001; ret., 2001. V.p. Transp. Sys. Internat., Washington, 1980—, Pacific Enterprises Inc., 1992—. Served to lt. Hungary Army Res., 1952-56. Mem. Nat. Def. Transp. Assn., 1982—. Avocation: photography.

KONDO, MASANOBU, investment company executive; CFO Nissho Iwai Corp., Tokyo. Office: Nissho Iwai Corp 2-3-1 Daiba Minato-Ku Tokyo 135-8655 Japan Office Fax: +81-3-3588-4136.

KONDONASSIS, ALEXANDER JOHN, economist, educator; b. Greece, Feb. 8, 1928; arrived in US, 1948, naturalized, 1960; s. John I. and Eve (Hatzistylianou) K.; m. Patricia Mundorff, Feb. 2, 1956; children: John, Yolanda. AB with distinction, DePauw U., 1952; MA, Ind. U., 1953, PhD, 1961. Teaching assoc. Ind. U., 1954-56, lectr., 1956-58; mem. faculty U. Okla., 1958—, prof. econs., 1964—, David Ross Boyd prof. econs., 1970—, chmn. dept., 1961-71, dir. div. econs., 1979-86, dir. advanced program in econs. bus. coll., 1971—, chmn. faculty senate, 1976-77, Regents prof., 1993. Lectr. Am.

participant program U.S. Info. Agy., Iceland, Greece, Yugoslavia, 1986; Fulbright prof. Athens (Greece) Sch. Econs. and Bus. Sci., 1965-66, vis. prof., 1971; assocs. disting. lectureship U. Okla., 1988; bd. dirs. Am. Bank of Commerce; mem. Gov. Okla. Adv. Coun. Export Expansion, 1964-65;adv. council Inst. E. Mediterranean Affairs, 1967-68; chmn. editorial policies com. S.W. Soc. Sci. Quar., 1974-77. Author: Concepts of Economic Development with Special Reference to Underdeveloped Countries, 1963, Monetary Policies of the Bank of Greece, 1949-1951, Contributions to Monetary Stability and Economic Development, 1961, (with others) An Economic Base Study of Lawton, Oklahoma, 1963, Economic Planning and Free Enterprise, 1966, The Role of Agriculture in a Developing Economy, 1973, The EEC and Her Association with Israel, Spain, Turkey and Greece, 1972, Some Recent Trends in Development Economics, 1972, Contributions of Agriculture to Economic Development: The Cases of U.K., U.S.A., Japan and Mexico, 1973, Mediterranean Europe and the Common Market, 1976, The European Economic Community in the Mediterranean: Developments and Prospects on a Mediterranean Policy, 1976, The European Economic Community and Greece: Toward a Full Membership, 1977, The Greek Inflation and the Flight from the Drachma: 1940-48, 1977, The Greek Economy: The Old and the New, 1979, The Bank of Greece, 1949-51: Credit Control Changes in An Inflationary Environment, 1979, The European Economic Community: Toward a Common Development Policy, 1980, Recent Trends in Development Assistance Committee Aid Programs, 1981, Economic and Non-Economic Aspects of Economic Development, the Less Developed Countries: A Synthesis, 1983, Some Internal Problems of Social Sciences with Special Emphasis on the Economics of Development, 1985, Agricultural Productivity and Economic Development: A Note on Japan and Taiwan, 1987 Approaches to Economic Development: Some Swings of the Pendulum, 1988, The European Economic Community and the Single European Act, 1989, The European Economic Community in 1992, 1991, The Economy of Cyprus, 1991, Major Issues of Global Development, 1991, German Unification: Problems and Prospects, 1993, Monetary Union and Economic Integration: The Less Developed Areas of the European Community. 1993, Toward Monetary Union of the European Community: History and Experiences of the European Monetary System, 1994, NAFTA: Old and New lessons from Theory and Practice with Economic Integration, 1996, The European Monetary Union in Transition, 1998, Strengthening the Global Financial Stability, 2001. Bd. dirs. Am. Friends Wilton Park, N.Y., 1967-68. Recipient U. Okla. Regents award excellence teaching, 1964, Merrick Found. Teaching award, 1977, DePauw U. Rector Scholar Alumni Achievement award, 1977; inducted Okla. Higher Edn. Hall of Fame, 1998. Mem. Am. Econ. Assn., So. Econ. Assn., Southwestern Econ. Assn. (pres. 1993-94), Mo. Valley Econ. Assn. (dir., exec. com. 1980—, pres. 1983-84), Southwestern Social Sci. Assn. (v.p. 1980-83, pres. 1983-84), AAUP (pres. 1977-78), Phi Beta Kappa, Omicron Delta Epsilon (pres.-elect internat. exec. bd. 1985-89, pres. 1989-92), Beta Gamma Sigma. Home: PO Box 695 Norman OK 73070-0695

KONDRACKI, EDWARD JOHN, lawyer; b. Elizabeth, N.J., Sept. 27, 1932; s. John and Catherine Chudio (Saas) K.; m. Barbara Terese Caruso; children: Carol Ann, Maryanne, Christopher. BSEE, N.J. Inst. Tech., 1959; JD with honors, George Washington U., 1963. Bar: Va. 1964, DC 1964, U.S. Dist. Ct. D.C. 1964, U.S. Dist. Ct. (ea. dist.) Va. 1964, U.S. Dist. Ct. (ctrl. dist.) Calif., U.S. Dist. Ct. (so. dist.) Ala., U.S. Dist. Ct. (no. dist.) Fla., U.S. Dist. Ct. (no. dist.) Ga., U.S. Dist. Ct. (we. dist.) La., U.S. Dist. Ct. (ea. dist.) Mich., U.S. Dist. Ct. (no. dist.) Okla., U.S. Dist. Ct. (ea. dist.) Pa., U.S. Dist. Ct. (no. dist.) N.Y., U.S. Dist. Ct. (ea. dist.) Tex., U.S. Dist. Ct. (no. dist.) Tex., U.S. Ct. Appeals (fed. cir.) 1983, U.S. Ct. Claims 1976, U.S. Ct. Customs and Patent Appeals 1976. Patent atty. Gen. Electric Co., Washington, 1959-63; assoc. Kerkam, Stowell Kondracki & Clarke, P.C. and predecessor, Arlington, Va., 1963-65; dir., prin. Kerkam, Stowell Kondracki & Clarke, P.C., Arlington, 1965-99; prin. Miles & Stockbridge, McLean, Va., 2000—. Owner, dir. Patmark Paralegal Svcs., 1975—90, chmn., 1999—, gen. counsel, 2003—. Author: Trademarks-Servicemarks, Use, Usage and Protection, 1990, Proper Use of Trademarks and Servicemarks, 1982, Common Pitfalls Encountered in Patenting Inventions, 1983, Copyright Protection of Computer Software, 1989, Intellectual Property, Rights Acquisition and Protection Conference World Trade Assn. N.J., 1989; contbr. article to Voice of Tech. Bd. dirs. The Amadeus Concerts, Inc., 2003—. Served with USN, 1951—55. Mem. ABA, Am. Intellectual Property Law Assn., Internat. Assn. Protection Indsl. Property, Fed. Bar Assn., Va. Bar Assn., Internat. Trademark Assn., Washington Patent Lawyers Club, D.C. Bar Assn. (chmn. com. internat. affairs 1973), Gt. Falls Hist. Soc., Marmota Farm Assn., KC, Tau Beta Pi, Eta Kappa Nu, Omicron Delta Kappa, Phi Eta Sigma. Office: 1751 Pinnacle Dr Ste 500 Mc Lean VA 22102-3833 Fax: (703) 610-8686. E-mail: ekondracki@milesstockbridge.com.

KONDZER, THOMAS ALLEN, lawyer; b. Cleve., Apr. 13, 1950; s. Andrew Francis and Ann (Ziegler) K.; m. Maureen Veronica Walsh, June 2, 1973; 1 child, Joseph Thomas. BBA, John Carroll U., 1972; JD, Case Western Res. U., 1975. Bar: Ohio 1975, U.S. Dist. Ct. (no. dist.) Ohio 1977, U.S. Ct appeals (6th cir.) 1980. Law clk. to presiding justice Ohio Ct. Appeals (8th dist.), Cleve., 1975-77; assoc. Amsdell and Slivka, Cleve., 1977-81; sole practice Cleve., 1981-85; prosecutor Village of Northfield, Ohio, 1981—; ptnr. Kolick and Kondzer, Cleve., 1985—. Lectr. Cleve. State U., 1981-82; coop. counsel Cath. League for Religious and Civil Liberties, Milw., 1981—. Mem. Westlake Civil Service Commn., 1986—. Mem. ABA, Ohio State Bar Assn., Greater Cleve. Bar Assn., North Olmsted C. of C., Order of Coif, Beta Gamma Sigma. Democrat. Roman Catholic. Home: 25668 Melibee Dr Cleveland OH 44145-5455 Office: Kolick and Kondzer 24500 Center Ridge Rd Ste 175 Cleveland OH 44145-5628

KONDZIOLKA, DOUGLAS, neurosurgeon; b. Montreal, Que., Can., Sept. 12, 1961; came to U.S., 1989; MD, U. Toronto, 1985; MSc, U. Pitts., 1991. Prof. neurol. surgery U. Pitts., 1992—. Recipient Lars Leksell award World Fedn. of Neurosurg. Socs., 197, Stephen Mahaley award Am. Assn. Neurol. Surgeons/Congress Neurol. Surgeons, 1997, 99. Mem. Am. Assn. Neurol. Surgeons, Congress Neurol. Surgeons. Office: U Pitts Med Coll 200 Lothrop St Ste B-400 Pittsburgh PA 15213-2546 Business E-Mail: kondziolkads@msx.upmc.edu.

KONE, BRUCE C. medical educator, nephrologist; b. Frankfurt, Germany, Jan. 29, 1958; s. Kenneth M. and Dorothy Kone; m. Daisy Linda Waller, June 10, 1992; children: Natalie Audrey, Justine Dorothy, Lindsey Jane. AB, Princeton U., 1975—79; MD, U. Fla., 1979—83. Internal Medicine Am. Bd. Internal Medicine, 1984, Nephrology Am. Bd. Internal Medicine, 1994. Resident Johns Hopkins Hosp., Baltimore, Md., 1983—86, chief, sect. of nephrology The U. of Tex. M.D. Anderson Cancer Ctr., Houston, 2000—; renal fellow Brigham and Women's Hosp., Boston, 1986—88; instr. medicine Johns Hopkins U. Sch. Medicine, Baltimore, Md., 1989—91; asst. prof. medicine U. Fla. Coll. Medicine, Gainesville, 1991—95; assoc. prof. medicine U. Tex. Med. School-Houston, 1995—99, prof. medicine, 2000—, dir., divsn. renal diseases and hypertension, 2000—, vice chair, dept. internal medicine, 2000—, the James T. and Nancy B. Willerson chair. Fellow Nat. Rsch. Svc. Award, NIH; grantee Clin. Investigator Award, RO1 Individual Rsch. Awards. Fellow: Molecular Medicine Soc., Am. Coll. Clin. Pharmacology, Am. Heart Assn. (Established Investigator Award), ACP; mem.: So. Soc. Clin. Investigation (councilor 2003—), Alpha Omega Alpha Honor Med. Soc. Office: U Texas Med Sch Houston 6431 Fannin MSB 4138 Houston TX 77030 Home Fax: 713-500-6882. Personal E-mail: bruce.c.kone@uth.tmc.edu.

KONECK, JOHN MICHAEL, lawyer; b. Mpls., Aug. 16, 1953; s. Robert W. and Bernice V.; m. Debra K. Plotz, Aug. 16, 1980; 1 child, Robert John. BS, N.D. State U., 1975; JD, Yale Law Sch., Mpls., 1978. Bar: N.D. 1978, Minn. 1979. Jud. law clk. N.D. Supreme Ct., Bismarck, 1978-79; ptnr. Fredrikson & Byron, Mpls., 1979—. Real property law specialist, mem. Minn. Bd. Legal Cert., Supreme Ct. Minn., 1994-99, chmn., 1996-99; mem. Vol. Lawyers Network; assoc. prof. William Mitchell Coll. Law, 1997—. Mem. ABA (chair litigation and dispute resolution, com. of sect. real property, probate and trust law 1995-98, chief editor newsletter of litigation and dispute resolution com. 1991-93, vice chair 1991-95), Minn. State Bar Assn. (co-chair real property cert. coun. 1990—, mem. rules of profl. conduct com.), State Bar Assn. N.D., Hennepin County Bar Assn. (co-chair rules of profl. conduct com. 1991-93). Office: Fredrikson & Byron 4000 Pillsbury Ctr 200 South 6th St Minneapolis MN 55402-1425 E-mail: jkoneck@fredlaw.com.

KONENKAMP, JOHN K. state supreme court justice; b. Oct. 20, 1944; m. Geri Konenkamp; children: Kathryn, Matthew. JD, U. S.D., 1974. Dep. state's atty., Rapid City; pvt. practice, 1977-84; former and presiding judge S.D. Cir Ct. (7th cir.), 1988-94; assoc. justice S.D. Supreme Ct., Pierre, 1994—. Bd. dirs. Alt. Dispute Resolution Com., Adv. Bd. for Casey Family Program. With USN. Mem. Am. Judicature Soc., State Bar S.D., Pennington County Bar Assn., Nat. CASA Assn., Am. Legion. Office: SD Supreme Ct 500 E Capitol Ave Pierre SD 57501-5070*

KONERKO, PAUL, baseball player; b. Providence, R.I., Mar. 2, 1976; 1st baseman Chgo. White Sox, 1999—. Host Starlight Children's Found., Comiskey Park. Office: Chgo White Sox 333 W 35th St Chicago IL 60616

KONETZNI, ALBERT H., JR., career officer; b. N.Y.C., Nov. 16, 1944; s. Albert H. Sr. and Adeline E. (Gergel) K.; m. Shirley A. Lane, Nov. 21, 1995; children: Albert H. III, Kristen, Kiera, Kyle. BS, U.S. Naval Acad., Annapolis, Md., 1966; MS in Pers. Adminstrn., George Washington U., 1972. Commd. ensign U.S. Navy, 1966, advanced through grades to vice adm., 2001; submarine office, comdr. U.S.S. Grayling, Charleston, S.C., 1981-84; comdr. Submarine Squadron 16, Kingsbay, Ga., 1987-89; asst. chief pers. for policy, plans, career progression U.S. Navy, Washington, 1994-95; comdr. Submarine Group Seven, Yokosuka, Japan, 1995-98; comdr. submarine force U.S. Pacific Fleet, Harbor, Hawaii, 1998-2001; dep. commdr. in chief, chief of staff U.S. Atlantic Fleet, 2001—. Co-author: Command At Sea, 1980. Office: USN 1562 Mitscher Ave Ste 250 Norfolk VA 23551-2489

KONG, DAVID FRANKLIN, cardiologist, educator; b. Durham, N.C., July 29, 1967; s. Yihong and Wen-chi (Kao) K. AB, Harvard U., 1988, AM, 1989; MD, Johns Hopkins U., 1993. Rsch. asst. Duke U. Med. Ctr., Durham, 1985-90; fellow in medicine Johns Hopkins U., 1993-96; fellow in cardiology Duke U. Med. Ctr., 1996—; intern in internal medicine Johns Hopkins Hosp., 1993-94, resident in internal medicine, 1994-96; fellow in cardiology Duke U. Med. Ctr., 1996—2001, assoc. of medicine, 2001—02, asst. prof. medicine, 2002—. Teaching fellow Harvard U., Cambridge, Mass., 1988-89; microcomputer cons., 1987—. Ford Program for Undergrad. Rsch. fellow, 1987-89; recipient Thomas Temple Hoopes prize for excellence in undergrad. work and the art of teaching, 1989. Republican. Presbyterian. Avocations: computers, racquetball, distance swimming, music, travel. Home: 2814 Dekalb St Durham NC 27705-5602 Office: Duke Univ Med Ctr Box 3850 Durham NC 27710

KONG, GAIL MILDRED, foundation executive; b. Calif. BA, Stanford U., 1967. Exec. dir. Coordinating Coun. Literary Mags., N.Y.C., 1970-75; dep. adminstr., child welfare agy. head Spl. Svcs. Children Human Resources Adminstrn., N.Y.C., 1978-84; exec. dir. Nat. Svc. Corp. for City of N.Y.C. City Vol. Corps, 1986-90; pres. StarServe Found., Santa Monica, Calif., 1990-93; pres., exec. dir. Asian Pacific Am. Cmty. Fund, San Francisco, 1993—. Contbr. articles to profl. jours.; editor: Elucidation Profiles to Understand the Role of Student Service in School Improvement, 1993; co-editor: Asian Pacific Am. Non-Profits: Perceptions and Realities, 1996. Bd. dirs. Chinatown Voter Edn. Alliance, N.Y.C., 1985-93; bd. dirs. United Way of the Bay Area, San Francisco, 1997, mem. Nat. Asian Pacific Am. Legal Consortium, 2003. Recipient Summer Program for Sr. Execs. award Harvard U. John F. Kennedy Sch. Govt., 1982. Office: Asian Pacific Fund 225 Bush St Ste 590 San Francisco CA 94104-4207 E-mail: info@asianpacificfund.org.

KONG, KENNETH SEHKIANG, software testing engineer; b. K. Terengganu, Terengganu, Malysia, Nov. 6, 1969; came to U.S., 1995; s. Seng Fook and Chiewsia (Ong) K. BSBA in Computer Info. Systems, Hawaii Pacific U., 1997, MBA in Fin., 1998. Asst. EDP adminstr. Schering Plough (m) Sdn Bhd, Kuala Lumpur, Malaysia, 1991; programmer, software support Syntex Computer (m) Sdn Bhd, Petaling Jaya, Malaysia, 1992; asst. sales mgr. Adlycom Sdn Bhd, Petaling Jaya, 1992-93; svc. mktg. exec. Unifloor (m) Sdn Bhd, Petaling Jaya, 1994; computer technician ISLE Computer Consulting, Honolulu, Hawaii, 1996-99; computer profl. Volt Svcs. Group, Redmond, Wash., 1999-2000; software test engr. Microsoft Corp., Redmond, Wa., 2000—. Mem. Hawaiian Island Investment Group, Delta Mu Delta, Epsilon Delta Pi. Home: 13711 NE 10th Pl # A3208 Bellevue WA 98005-2819 Office: Microsoft Corp Bldg 27/Room 3257 One Microsoft Way Redmond WA 98052-3863 E-mail: kenkong@e-mail.com.

KONG, LINGJU, mathematician, educator; b. Shenxian, China, Oct. 19, 1972; s. Qiangyin Kong and Huanchun Guo; m. Zhen Wang, Apr. 17, 1973. BS, Shandong Normal U., 1992; MS, Ocean U. Of Qingdao, 1999; PhD, No. Ill. U., 2001. Cert. Tchr. 1999. Asst. prof. Ocean U. Of Qingdao, China, 1999—2000; tchg. asst. No. Ill. U., Dekalb, Ill., 2000—. Contbr. scientific papers to jours. Recipient D.R. Ostberg award, 2003; Excellent Student scholar, Shandong Normal U., 1994, 1995, Sanhao Student scholar, 1994, 1995, Excellent Grad. scholar, Ocean U. Of Qingdao, 1998. Home: 746 N Annie Glidden Rd # 303 Dekalb IL 60115 Office: Dept Math Scis No Ill U Dekalb IL 60115 Personal E-mail: lkong@math.niu.edu.

KONG, NORMAN, chemist; b. Qufu, Shandong, China, Mar. 26, 1964; arrived in U.S., 1995; s. Fanyi Kong; m. Jingyi Li, Feb. 13, 1989; children: Eddie, Brandon. BSc, Shandong U., Jinan, China, 1984, MSc, 1989; PhD, U. Alta., Edmonton, Can., 1995. Postdoctoral fellow SUNY, Buffalo, 1995—96, sr. postdoctoral fellow, 1996—97; prin. scientist Hoffmann-La Roche, Nutley, NJ, 1997—2001, sr. prin. scientist, 2001—. Contbr. articles to profl. jours. Mem.: N.Y. Acad. Sci., Am. Chem. Soc. Achievements include patents in field. Avocations: music, fishing, hiking, golf. Office: Hoffmann-La Roche 340 Kingsland Nutley NJ 07110

KONG, XIANGLI (CHARLIE KONG), mechanical and control engineer, educator; b. Chifeng, China, Mar. 11, 1953; came to U.S., 1989; s. Fanxin Kong and Yuzhen Y.; m. Xiuxian H., Jan. 28, 1978; children: Ling Xin, Brian Lingyu. B of Engring., Shenyang (China) Poly. U., 1978; MSc, Xian (China) Jiaotong U., 1981, PhD, 1985. Lectr. Xian Jiaotong U., 1983-86, assoc. prof., 1986-89; engring. dir. Hill Equipment Corp., Whittier, Calif., 1990-92; pres., CEO MS-Tech Corp., La Mirada, Calif., 1992—. Vis. assoc. prof. UCLA, 1988-90, tchr. computer-controlled machines course, 1993-2000, team leader, key contbr. advanced PC-CNC sys. Contbr. articles to profl. jours. Named Outstanding Young Scientist, Chinese Sci. & Tech. Assn., 1987, Outstanding Young Educator, Fok Yingtong Found., 1988; recipient more than 10 rsch. achievement awards. Office: MS-Tech Corp 14770 Firestone Blvd Ste 208 La Mirada CA 90638-5944

KONIECZNY, SHARON LOUISE, insurance agency executive; b. Madison, Minn., July 2, 1952; d. Frank H. and Elenore A. (Mikkelson) K. Student, Dakota Wesleyan U., 1970-71, U. Minn., 1971-72. CLU. Sales rep. Advance Schs., Bloomington, Minn., 1972; sales agt. ITT Life Ins., Mpls., 1973-75, mktg. auditor, 1975-76, supr. new bus., 1976-79, mgr. UND Issue, 1979-81, asst. v.p. new bus., 1981-83, asst. v.p.sales support, 1983-87, v.p., sales mktg., 1987-94; nat. dir. new bus. devel. ITT-Hartford Life Ins., 1994-95; v.p. mktg. Minn. Chamber Bus. Svcs., St. Paul, 1995-2000; v.p. sales MARSH USA, Mpls., 2000—. Vice chmn. United Way, Mpls., 1984-85, chmn., 1985. Mem. Nat. Assn. Life Underwriters, Nat. Assn. Health Underwriters, Am. Mktg. Assn., Nat. Assn. Ins. Women, Soc. Ins. Trainers and Educators, Internat. Assn. Fin. Planners, Minn. Assn. Health Underwriters (pres.). Lutheran. Avocations: woodworking, swimming, reading, fishing. Home: 12610 50th Ave N Minneapolis MN 55442-2060

KÖNIG, PETER, pediatrician, educator; b. Cluj, Romania, Feb. 14, 1938; came to U.S., 1976; s. Rudolf and Irina (Grünwald) K.; m. Lea Schiffer, Sept. 30, 1965; 1 child, Orly. Graduate, Timisoara Med. Sch., Romania, 1959; MD, Hebrew U., Jerusalem, 1966; PhD, U. London, 1974. Resident Bikur Cholim Hosp., Jerusalem, 1970-71, staff, 1974-76; fellow in pulmonary diseases Brompton Hosp., London, 1971-74; asst. prof. child health U. Mo., Columbia, 1976-80, assoc. prof. child health, 1980-84, prof. in child health, 1984—. Fellow Am. Acad. Allergy; mem. Am. Thoracic Soc., Acad. Allergy, Soc. Pediatric Research, Chilean Asthma Found., Sigma Xi. Home: 1310 Vintage Dr Columbia MO 65203-4878 Office: U Mo Child Health 1 Hospital Dr Columbia MO 65212-5276 E-mail: KonigP@health.missouri.edu.

KÖNIG, ROLF, immunologist, educator; b. Saarbrücken, Saarland, Germany, July 4, 1953; came to the U.S., 1987—; s. Kurt Lothar König and Inge Kneip; m. Rita Müggler; children: Michael Christopher, Jessica Anita. MS, U. Bern, Switzerland, 1980, PhD, 1984. Rsch. assoc. U. Mass., Amherst, 1985, U. Bern, 1985-87; vis. fellow NIH, Bethesda, Md., 1987-91; vis. assoc. NIH/Nat. Inst. Allergy and Infectious Diseases, Bethesda, 1991-93; asst. prof. U. Tex., Galveston, 1993-99; assoc. prof. U. Tex. Med. Br., Galveston, 1999—. Assoc. editor Jour. Immunology, 1999—; contbr. articles to profl. jours. Mem. AAAS, N.Y. Acad. Sci., AAI. Office: U Tex Med Br 301 University Blvd Galveston TX 77555-1070 Fax: 409-747-6869. E-mail: rokonig@utmb.edu.

KONIGSBERG, ALLEN STEWART See ALLEN, WOODY

KONIGSBERG, ROBERT LEE, electrical engineer; b. N.Y.C., May 23, 1921; s. Max and Rose (Saper) K.; m. Helen Mae Aronson, June 11, 1950; children: Richard L., Jane F. BEE, Cooper Union, 1942; MAdE, NYU, 1948; MSE, Johns Hopkins U., 1954. Test/standardization engr. Western Electric Co., Kearny, N.J., 1942-46, product engr. filter dept., 1946-47; electronics engr. telemetering group Fairchild Engine & Aircraft Corp., Farmingdale, N.Y., 1947; electronic engr. radar component design DeMornay Budd Co., Bronx, N.Y., 1948; electronics engr. telemetering instrumentation Glenn L. Martin Co., Balt., 1948-51; rsch. assoc. radiation lab. Johns Hopkins U., Balt., 1951-56, prin. profl. staff engr. Applied Physics Lab., Laurel, Md., 1956-88, ret., 1988; part time cons., 1989—. Part-time instr. engring. Johns Hopkins U., 1965-71. Contbr. articles to profl. jours. Recipient Group Achievement award to MAGSAT Project Team NASA, 1979, Group Achievement award to AMPTE Project Team NASA, 1985. Mem. IEEE, Sigma Xi, Tau Beta Pi. Democrat. Jewish. Avocations: amateur radio, tennis. Home: 2218 Ridgemont Dr Finksburg MD 21048-1717 E-mail: robkon@ccpl.carr.org.

KONIGSBURG, ELAINE LOBL, writer; b. N.Y.C., Feb. 10, 1930; d. Adolph and Beulah (Klein) Lobl; m. David Konigsburg, July 6, 1952; children— Paul, Laurie, Ross. BS, Carnegie Mellon U., 1952; postgrad., U. Pitts., 1952-54; LHD (hon.), U. North Fla., 2001. Author: juveniles Jennifer, Hecate, Macbeth, William McKinley and Me, Elizabeth, 1967 (Newbery Honor Book), From The Mixed-Up Files of Mrs. Basil E. Frankweiler, 1967 (Newbery medal 1968), About the B'nai Bagels, 1969, (George), 1970, Altogether, One at a Time, 1971, A Proud Taste for Scarlet and Miniver, 1973 (Nat. Book award nominee), The Dragon in the Ghetto Caper, 1974, The Second Mrs. Giaconda, 1975, Father's Arcane Daughter, 1976, Throwing Shadows, 1979 (Am. Book award nominee), Journey to an 800 Number, 1981, Up From Jericho Tel, 1986, Samuel Todd's Book of Great Colors, 1990, Samuel Todd's Book of Great Inventions, 1991, Amy Elizabeth Explores Bloomingdale's, 1992, T-backs, T-shirts, COAT and Suit, 1993, TalkTalk, 1995, The View From Saturday, 1996 (Newbery medal 1997), Silent to the Bone, 2000. Recipient Regina medal, Cath. Libr. Assn., 2001; named to State of Fla. Hall of Fame, 2000.

KONIKIEWICZ, LEONARD WIESLAW, biomedical communications consultant; b. Lvow, Poland, July 24, 1928; came to U.S., 1959; s. Lubin Adolph and Melania (Rogozinska) K.; m. Antonina Kazimiera Grodowska; 1 child, Annette Melany. BS in Liberal Arts, SUNY, 1981; PhD in Natural Sci., Universitatis Polonorum, London, 1985. Registered biomed. photographer, illustrator. Med. photographer Cornell U., N.Y.C., 1960-67; dir. visual comm. Poly. Med. Ctr., Harrisburg, Pa., 1967-85; dir., clinics asst. prof. biomed. comm. James H. Quillen Coll. of Medicine, East Tenn. State U., Johnson City, Tenn., 1985-97, ret., 1997; sr. rsch. cons. Intertech Corp., Atkinson, N.H., 1997—. Export cons. in U.S.-Eastern Europe; cons. NASA Plant Space Biology Lab. Author: Bioelectrography, 1984, Career of Joanna Kurtz, 1995, Turin Shroud and Science, 1999; author, artist: The Price of Dissent, 1998; contbr. articles to profl. jours. and books; patentee in field. Vol. interpreter ARC, Harrisburg, 1979-85; mem. refugee com. Polish Cultural Assn., Harrisburg, 1982, v.p. 1978-79; vol. organist Our Lady Cath. Ch., Harrisburg, 1970-85; rschr. Cystic-Fibrosis, Cancer, Harrisburg, 1975-85; v.p. Polish Cultural Assn., 1978-79. Decorated Iron Crest of Merit of Home Army; recipient 2d prize Pa. Arts Coun., 1972, best cover award Lab World, 1975, best med. picture award Med. World News, 1977; rsch. grantee Pa. March of Dimes, 1976-78, Pa. Cystic Fibrosis Found., 1978-81, Betatron Corp., 1983-84. Mem. Biol. Photog. Assn., Assn. Biomed. Comm. Dirs., Internat. Assn. Polish Combat Vets. Avocations: organ music, oil painting. Home: 2023 Sundale Rd Johnson City TN 37604-3027 E-mail: konik@charterth.net.

KONING, HENDRIK, architect; came to the U.S., 1979; BArch, U. Melbourne, Australia, 1978; MArch II, UCLA, 1981. Lic. architect Calif., 1982, contractor, 1984; registered architect, Australia; cert. Nat. Coun. Archtl. Registration Bds. Prin. in charge of tech., code, and prodn. issues Koning Eizenberg Architecture, 1981—, v.p., 1990—. Instr. UCLA, U. B.C., Harvard U., MIT; lectr. in field. Exhbns. incl. "House Rules" Wexner Ctr., 1994, "The Architect's Dream Houses for the Next Millenium", The Contemporary Arts Ctr., 1993, " Angels & Franciscans", Gagosian Gallery, 1992, "Conceptual Drawings by Architects", Bannatyne Gallery, 1991, Koning and Eizenberg Projects Grad. Sch. Architecture & Urban Planning UCLA, 1990, others; prin. works include Digital Domain renovation and screening rm., Santa Monica, Lightstorm Entertainment offices and THX theater, Santa Monica, Gilmore Bank addition and remodel, L.A., 1548-1550 Studios, Santa Monica, (with RTA) Materials Rsch. Lab. U. Calif., Santa Barbara, Ken. Edwards Ctr. Cmty. Svcs., Santa Monica, Peck Park Cmty. Ctr. Gymnasium, San Pedro, Calif., Sepulveda Recreation Ctr. Gymnasium, L.A., (Nat. Concrete /Masonry award 1996, AIA Calif. Coun. Honor award 1996, AIA L.A. Chpt. Merit Award, 1997, L.A. Bus. Coun. Beautification awrd 1996, AIA/SFV Design award 1995), PS# 1 Elem. Sch., Santa Monica, Famers Market additions and master plan, L.A. (Westside Urban Forum prize 1991), Stage Deli, L.A., Simone Hotel, L.A. (Nat. Honor award AIA 1994), Boyd Hotel, L.A. Cmty. Corp. Santa Monica Housing Projects, 5th St. Family Housing, Santa Monica, St. John's Hosp. Replacement Housing Program, Santa Monica, Liffman Ho., Santa Monica, (with Glenn Erikson) Electric Artblock, Venice (Beautification award L.A. Bus. Coun. 1993), 6th St. Condominiums, Santa Monica, Hollywood Duplex, Hollywood Hills (Record Houses Archtl. Record 1988), Calif. Ave. Duplex, Santa Monica, Tarzana Ho. (Merit award L.A. chpt. AIA 1991, Merit Award AIA Calif. Coun., 1998, Sunset Western Home awards 1993-94), 909 Ho., Santa Monica (Merit award L.A. chpt. AIA 1991), 31st St. Ho., Santa Monica (Honor award AIACC 1994, Record House 1995, Nat. AIA Honor award 1996), others. Recipient 1st award Progressive Architecture, 1987; named one of Domino's Top 30 Architects, 1989. Fellow AIA (juror San Diego design awards 1992, panelist honor awards 1994, Calif. coun. spl. awards 1997, nat. interior design awards 1997), Royal Australian Inst. Archs.; mem. Nat. Trust for Hist. Preservation, So. Calif. Assn. Non-Profit Housing, L.A. Conservancy. Office: Koning Eizenberg Architecture 1454 25th St Santa Monica CA 90404-3008

KONISKY, JORDAN, microbiology educator; b. Providence, Apr. 8, 1941; s. George Martin and Norma Virginia (Storti) K.; m. Judith Esther Wax, June 25, 1967; children: Daniel L., David M. BA, Providence Coll., 1963; PhD, U. Wis., 1968. Asst. prof. U. Ill., Urbana, 1970-75, assoc. prof., 1975-81, prof., 1981—, chmn. dept. microbiology, 1984-89, dir. Sch. Life Scis., 1989-94, dir. Biotech. Ctr., 1995-96; vice provost for rsch. and grad. studies Rice U., Houston, 1996—, prof. biochemistry and cell biology, 1996—. Postdoctoral fellow NIH, 1968-70, Yale U.; cons. in field. Contbr. articles to profl. jours. Recipient Research Career Devel. award NIH, 1975-80. Fellow AAAS; mem. Am. Soc. Microbiology, Fedn. Am. Socs. Exptl. Biology, Am. Acad. Microbiology, Am. Chem. Soc. Office: Rice U Off Vice Provost Rsch Grad Stud MS13 Houston TX 77025

KONKEL, HARRY WAGNER, civic volunteer, retired career officer; b. Jackson, Wyo., July 11, 1935; s. Maurice and Beatrice Helen (Nelle) Wagner; m. Susan Donnell Konkel, June 3, 1960; children: James Donnell Konkel, Susan Konkel. Student, U. Wyo., 1953—54; BS, U.S. Naval Acad., 1958; BS in Elec. Engring., Naval Postgrad. Sch., 1965; MA, Naval War Coll., 1974. Commd. ensign USN, 1958, advanced through ranks to capt., 1979, ret., 1985, elecs. material officer, comms. officer, weapons officer USS Trathen, 1959-63, engr. officer USS Richard E. Byrd, 1965-67, asst. fleet elecs. maintenance officer US Atlantic Fleet, 1967-70, exec. officer USS Keppler, 1970-71, commdr. USS Laffey, 1971-72, commdr. USS DAmato, 1972-73, engr. officer USS America, 1978-79, head availabilities sect., maintenance policy and progamming branch Ships Maintenance and Modernization Divsn. Office

Chief of Naval Opers., 1979-81, commdr. USS Yellowstone, 1982-84; dir. electronic and spl. warfare divsn. Naval Electronic Systems Command, 1974-77; head surface ship fleet modernization program design mgmt. divsn. Naval Sea Systems Command, 1984; dep. dir. ship maintenance and modernization divsn., head ships maintenance and modernization branch Office of Chief of Naval Ops., 1984-85. Bd. trustees Gunston Sch., Centreville, Md., 1981-91, Gould Acad., Bethel, Me., 1987-93, Osher Libr. Assoc., 1993—; bd. dirs. Humane Soc. Hancock County, Findlay, Ohio, 1986-87; nat. dir. Navy League US, 1989-97, Portland Mus. Art, fellow 1993-96, trustee, 1996—; pres. Osher Libr. Assocs., Osher Map Libr., 1995-98, USNA Blue and Gold, 1994—. Decorated Legion of Merit, Meritorious Svc. medal with one gold star, Navy Commendation Medal with two gold stars. Mem. Am. Soc. Naval Engrs., Am. Inst. Conservation of Historic and Artistic Works, Am. Philatelic Soc., Am. Numismatic Assn., Am. Orchid Soc., U. Wyo. Alumni Assn., US Naval Acad. Alumni Assn., Naval Postgrad. Sch. Alumni Assn., Naval War Coll. Aluni Assn., US Naval Inst., Navy League US, Mil. Officers Assn. Am., Surface Navy Assn. (lifetime plankowner mem.), USS Damato Assn., USS Laffey Assn., USS Trathen Assn., USS Keppler Assn., USS Am. Assn., Bohemian Club, Portland Country Club. Republican. Episcopalian. Avocations: golf, stamp and coin collecting. Home: 71 Carroll St Portland ME 04102-3522

KONKEL, MARY SUSAN, library administrator; b. Portland, Oreg., Jan. 7, 1957; d. William Eugene Konkel and Carole Barbara Lehman; m. Steven Andrew Balcken, Dec. 19, 1981; 1 child, Dianna Lynn Balcken. BA in Spanish and Portuguese, U. Wis., Milw., 1979, MLS, 1981; MA in Comm. Studies, Governors State U., University Park, 1992; cert. in Computer Info. Systems, Coll. of DuPage, Ill., 2003. Libr. tech. asst. U. Wis., Milw., 1976-81, original cataloger, acad. specialist, 1982-85; fieldworker Am. Geog. Soc. Collection, Milw., 1980-81; head monographic cataloging unit, asst. libr. U. Cin., 1985-87; head cataloging, libr., univ. prof. Governors State U., 1987-92; head cataloging, asst. prof. bibliography U. Akron, Ohio, 1992-98, assoc. prof. bibliography, 1999-2001; head tech. svcs. Coll. of DuPage, Ill., 2001—. Pres. Online Audiovisual Catalogers, Inc., 1994-95, mem. cataloging policy com., 1989-93; presenter in field. Contbr. articles to profl. jours. Vol. Inventure Pl. Nat. Inventors Hall of Fame Mus., Akron, 1995-2000; bd. dirs. Suburban Libr. Sys., Burr Ridge, Ill., 1989-92; trustee Richton Park (Ill.) Pub. Libr., 1989-92; founding mem. YMCA Trailblazers Oreg. Trail Bunkhouse, 1993-96. Mem. ALA (Video Round Table), Assn. Coll. and Rsch. Librs. (chair media resources com.), Assn. Libr. Collections and Tech. Svcs., Acad. Libr. Assn. Ohio (pres. 1998-99, bd. dirs. 1995-97, chair pub. rels. com. 1996-97, archivist 1999-2001). Avocations: camping, mall shopping, movies, music, reading. Office: Library Coll of DuPage 425 Fawell Blvd Glen Ellyn IL 60137-6599 E-mail: konkel@cdnet.cod.edu.

KONKOWSKI, DEBORAH ANN, mathematics educator; b. Akron, Ohio, Mar. 3, 1955; d. Daniel J. and Dorothea A. K. BS in Physics, Harvey Mudd Coll., 1977; PhD in Physics, U. Tex., 1983. Asst. prof. U.S. Naval Acad., Annapolis, Md., 1987-91, assoc. prof., 1991-97, prof., 1997—. Vis. assoc. prof. U. London, 1995. Contbr. articles to profl. jours. NSF grantee, 1989—, U.S. Naval Acad., 1987-89; Rsch. fellow U.Md., College Park, 1983-85, U. London, 1985-87. Mem. AAAS, Am. Phys. Soc., Am. Math. Soc., Math. Assn. Am., N.Y. Acad. Scis., Internat. Soc. Gen. Relativity & Gravitation. Office: U S Naval Acad Dept Math Annapolis MD 21402

KONNER, JOAN WEINER, university administrator, educator, publisher, broadcasting executive, television producer; b. Paterson, N.J., Feb. 24, 1931; d. Martin and Tillie (Frankel) Weiner; children: Rosemary, Catherine; m. Alvin H. Perlmutter. Student, Vassar Coll., 1948-49; BA, Sarah Lawrence Coll., 1951; MS, Columbia U., 1961. Editorial writer, columnist, reporter Hackensack (N.J.) Record, 1961-63; producer, reporter WNDT Ednl. Broadcasting Corp., N.Y.C., 1963-65; producer, writer, reporter NBC News, N.Y.C., 1965-77; exec. producer nat. pub. affairs programs WNET Ednl. Broadcasting Corp., N.Y.C., 1977-78, exec. prodr. Bill Moyers Jour., 1978-81, up met. programming, 1981-84; exec. prodr., pres. Pub. Affairs TV with Bill Moyers PBS; prof. broadcast and journalism, dean Grad. Sch. Journalism Columbia U., N.Y.C., 1988-97, pub. Columbia Journalism Rev., 1988-99. Prof. Grad. Sch. Journalism, Columbia U., N.Y.C., 1988—; bd. dirs. Providence Jour. Past trustee Columbia U. Rockland Ctr. for Arts, Sarah Lawrence Coll., Religion Writers Found., Contemplative Mind in Soc., Radio and TV News Dirs. Found., Pulitzer Prize Bd. Recipient 12 Emmy awards NATAS, Columbia-du Pont award, Peabody award, Gavel award ABA, Edward R. Murrow award, others. Mem. Dirs. Guild, Writers Guild, Soc. Profl. Journalists, Newspaper Women's Club of N.Y.C., Century Assn., Cosmopolitan Club. Office: Columbia U Grad Sch Journalism Journalism Bldg New York NY 10027

KONNICK, DIANNE CHERYL, financial executive; b. New Brunswick, N.J., Feb. 11, 1961; d. Richard Edward and Cathleen Gladys (Bickler) Readdy; m. Christopher Matthew Konnick, Aug. 14, 1982; children: Matthew Roy, Allison Marie. BBA in Fin. with highest honors, Shippensburg State, 1982. Cert. mgmt. acct. Comml. loan examiner Am. Bank & Trust, Reading, Pa., 1982-83; analyst, asst. fin. officer Meridian Bancorp, Reading, 1983-86; fin. analyst Am. Chem. Soc., Washington, 1986-88, sr. budget analyst, 1988-89; fin. analyst Dietrich's Milk Products, Reading, Pa., 1989-93; mgr. budgeting and acctg. Citizens Utilities Water, 1993-99; dir. fin., treas. Bollman Hat Co., Adamstown, Pa., 1999—2003. Past treas. Shillington Pool and Park Assn., 1996—2002; treas. Shillington Legion Baseball Assn. Mem. Inst. Cert. Mgmt. Accts., Inst. Mgmt. Accts. Republican. Roman Catholic. Avocations: reading, hiking, all sports. Home: 36 Glennola Dr Mohnton PA 19540-9002

KONNYU, ERNEST LESLIE, former congressman; b. Tamasi, Hungary, May 17, 1937; arrived in US, 1949; s. Leslie and Elizabeth Konnyu; m. Lillian Muenks, Nov. 25, 1959; children: Carol, Renata, Lisa, Victoria. Student, U. Md., 1960-62; BS in Acctg., Ohio State U., 1965. Mem. Calif. Assembly, Sacramento, 1980-86, 100th Congress from 12th Calif. dist., 1987-89; CEO Konnyu Financials and Taxes, Inc. Chmn. Assembly Rep. Policy Com. of State Assembly, Sacramento, 1985-86; vice chmn. Assembly Human Svcs., Sacramento, 1980-86; vice chmn. Policy Rsch. Com., Sacramento, 1985-86. Mem. Rep. State Cen. Com., Calif., 1977-88, Rep. Cen. Com., Santa Clara County, Calif., 1980-88; mem. adv. bd. El Camino Hosp., Mountain View, Calif., 1987-89. Served to maj. USAF, 1959-69. Recipient Nat. Def. Medal, 1968, Disting. Service award U.S. Jaycees, 1969, Nat. Security award Am. Security Council Found., 1987; named lifetime senator U.S. Jaycees, 1977. Mem. Am.-Hungarian C. of C. (v.p. 1995-97). Republican. Roman Catholic. Avocations: politics, golf. E-mail: konnyu@sbcglobal.net.

KONO, JUNICHIRO, adult education educator; b. Osaka, Osaka, Japan, Apr. 14, 1966; s. Atsuo and Chieko Kono; m. Yuko Mori; children: Renee Miki, Alissa Yuki. PhD physics, SUNY at Buffalo, Buffalo, NY, 1992—95; MS applied physics, U of Tokyo, Tokyo, Japan, 1990—92, BS applied physics, 1985—90. Asst. prof. Rice U, Houston, 2000—; fellow W.W. Hansen Exptl. Physics Lab, Stanford U, Stanford, Calif., 1997—2000; postdoctoral rsch. assoc. U of Calif., Santa Barbara, Calif., 1995—97. Recipient CAREER Award, NSF, 2002; fellow Fellowship, W.W. Hansen Exptl. Physics Lab., Stanford U, CA, 1997—2000; scholar Scholarship, Ishizaka Found., 1992—94. Mem.: IEEE, SPIE, Optical Soc. of Am., Am. Phys. Soc. Office: Rice U 6100 Main St Houston TX 77005 Office Fax: 713-348-5686. E-mail: kono@rice.edu.

KONO, ROBERT HIROSHI, writer, educator; b. L.A., Aug. 31, 1932; s. Isamu and Mildred Masuko Kono; m. Carol Louise Lippold, May 9, 1959; children: David Masaru, Kevin Hisashi. BA, U. Wash., 1963, PhD, 1971. Asst. prof. U. Oreg., Eugene, 1974—76, dept. dir. Innovation Ctr., 1976—80; columnist Pacific Citizen, Japanese Am. Citizens League, San Francisco, 1980—82; translator and freelance writer Eugene, 1982—92. Mem.: Japanese Am. Assn. (cmty. rels. Asian coun. 1992—, bd. dirs. 1995—2001), N.W. Assn. Book Publ., Willamette Writers, Phi Beta Kappa. Independent. Avocations: photography, travel, music. Office: Abe Publishing PO Box 5226 Eugene OR 97405 Fax: 541-485-3893. Personal E-mail: hiroshicarob@aol.com.

KONO, TETSURO, biochemist, physiologist, educator; b. Tokyo, May 17, 1925; s. Ichiro and Hiroko (Sasaki) K.; m. Seiko Kanda, Dec. 18, 1961; children: Michiko, Masahiro, Kenji. BA, U. Tokyo, 1947, PhD, 1958. Research assoc. Johns Hopkins U., Balt., 1958-59; research assoc. Vanderbilt U., Nashville, 1959-60, mem. faculty, 1963—, prof. physiology, 1974-85; prof. molecular physiology and biophysics, 1985-92; prof. emeritus molecular physiology and biophysics, 1992—. Instr. Univ. Tokyo, 1960-63 Contbr. articles to profl. jours. NIH grantee, 1961-92. Mem. Am. Diabetes Assn. Am. Soc. Biol. Chemists, Sigma Xi. Home: 505 Belair Way Nashville TN 37215-6108 Office: Vanderbilt Med Sch Dept Molecular Physiol 209 Oxford House Nashville TN 37232-4245 E-mail: tetsuro.kono@vanderbilt.edu., tetsuro.kono@comcast.net.

KONO, TOSHIHIKO, cellist; b. Ashiya, Japan, Nov. 8, 1930; came to U.S., 1966; m. Edna Libby, June 20, 1968; children: Miyo, Kaori. LLB, Kyoto (Japan) U., 1953; postgrad, Mannes Coll. Music, Stanford U., Kneisel Hall Sch.; DFA (hon.), London Inst. Applied Rsch.; studied with, Gaspar Cassado, Zara Nelsova. Mem. faculty Sch. for Strings, N.Y. Conservatory of Music, S.I. Conservatory of Music; hon. prof. Alliance Universelle pour la Paix par la Connaissance. Appearances throughout world in recitals, concerto solos, chamber music, and with symphony orchs.; also radio, TV and festival concerts; prin. cellist Kyoto Symphony Orch., ASO In-sch. Concerts, Philharm. Symphony of Westchester (N.Y.), 1971-73, 87-90, Rockaway Five Towns Symphony Orch., 1989-91, S.I. Symphony Orch., 1990—, Drs. Orch. Soc. N.Y., 1991—, Ctr. Symphony Orch., 1992—, Yonkers Philharm. Orch., 1997—, Northern Westchester Symphony Orch., 2002—; asst. prin. cellist New Orleans Philharm. Orch., 1967-68; cellist Am. Symphony Orch. (Leopold Stokowski, Carnegie Hall), N.Y.C., 1968-90, trustee, 1975-90; participant Salud Casals, 100 Cello Orch., N.Y.C., 1970; resident artist and mem. Acadia String Quartet, Bar Harbor (Maine) Festival, 1971—, also prin. cellist Festival String Orch., 1984—, trustee, 1988-90, chmn. adv. bd., 1990—; artistic dir. Mid-Summer Festival for Chamber Music, Osaka, Japan, 1981; mem. Bangor Symphony String Quartet, A.R.T. Trio of N.Y., Richmond Quartet, Clover Quintet, Kono-Levinson Trio, Bklyn. Coll. I.R.P.E. Trio, Gordon-Kono-Tsukikawa Piano Trio, Pro Musica Ensemble, Kyoto Quartet, Kyoto Solisten; freelance musician Bklyn. Philharm. Orch., Westchester Symphony Orch., White Plains Symphony Orch., Queens Symphony Orch., Naumburg Symphony Orch. (asst. prin.), Pan-Am. Symphony Orch., Philharmonia Orch. of N.Y. (prin.), Down Town Symph. Orch. (prin.), Little Orch. Soc., N.J. Pops Orch., N.Y.C. Ballet Orch., Dance Theater of Harlem Orch., Manhattan Plaza Chamber Orch. (prin.), Am. Chamber Orch. (soloist), Bklyn. Chamber Orch. (prin.), Slavic Arts Ensemble, N.Y. String Soc. (prin.), Arcady Chamber Players, Rochester Baroque Sinfonia (soloist), St. Petersburg Chamber Orch. USSR, St. George's Sinfonia, Oratorio Soc. N.Y., St. Cecilia Chorus and Orch., Met. Greek Chorale and Orch., Collegiate Chorale and Orch., Naumburg Messiah Orch. (prin.), Mt. Desert (Maine) Chorale and Orch. (prin.), Regina Opera Orch. (prin.), Bklyn. Lyric Opera Orch. (prin.), Island Lyric Opera Orch. (prin.), Long Island Opera Orch. (prin.), Dicapo Opera Orch. (prin.), Kor-Am Opera Orch. (prin.), Am. Chamber Opera Orch. (prin.), Opera Amici Orch. (prin.), Surry (Maine) Opera Orch. (prin.), N.Y. Grand Opera Orch., Pax Opera Orch. (prin), Empire State Opera Orch. (prin.), Riverside Opera Orch. (prin.); contbr. numerous articles to profl. jours. and periodicals. Decorated Knight Comdr. Lofsensic Ursinius Order; baron Royal Order of Bohemian Crown; Count Order of San Ciriaco; Fromm fellow Festival Contemporary Music, Tanglewood, 1970, 71; recipient The van Beethoven medal, diploma of honor and Silver medal for Disting. Svc. to Music, 1974, award for Contemporary Achievement, 1975, U.S. Pres.'s medal of merit, 1990, Legion of Merit, 1991, ABI Gold Medal of Honor, 1991, Svc. award BHF, 1991, Internat. Peace prize United Cultural Convention, 2003; named Man of Yr. ABI, 1991, others; given lifetime royal patronage The Principality of Hutt River Province, Highland Laird of Camster Burn, Caithness. Mem.: IBC (dep. dir. gen. 1997—, Gold medal 1991, Order Internat. Fellowship 1998—), Internet Cello Soc., N.Y. Com. for Young Audiences, Internat. Platform Assn., Violoncello Soc., Am. Fedn. Musicians, Assoicated Musicians Greater N.Y., Acad. Maison Internat. des Intellectuels. Home: 400 W 43rd St New York NY 10036-6312 E-mail: libtok@aol.com.

KONOLA, CLAUDETTE JUNE, finance company executive, financial consultant; b. Deadwood, S.D., Sept. 2, 1948; d. Donald John Konola and Rose Marie Larive-Konola. BSc, Univ. Colo., 1981. Mgmt. trainee Am. Nat. Bank, Denver, 1974-80; training coord. loan analysis United Bank Denver, 1980-81; asst. v.p. Canadian Commercial Bank, Denver, 1981-83, First Interstate Bank of Denver, 1983-88; v.p. Ctrl. Bank Denver, 1988-93; revolving loan fund adminstr. Mesa county Western Colo. Bus. Devel. Corp., Grand Junction, Colo., 1994-96; southwest regional dir. Cmty. Reinvestment Fund, Inc., Mpls., 1996—2002, nat. dir. tng. and assistance, 2002—. Pres. Downtown Denver Bus. and Profl. Women, Denver, 1985-87; treas. Women's Bean Project, Denver, 1991-93; sec., treas. Riverside Task Force, Grand Junction, 1995-98; co-founder Colo. Women's Hall of Fame, 1986. Democrat. Office: Cmty Reinvestment Fund PO Box 552 Clifton CO 81520-0552 E-mail: claudette@crfusa.com.

KONOLD, KYLE BRIAN, educational consultant, grant project director; b. McHenry, Ill., Aug. 12, 1969; s. Pearce and Marilyn Konold; children: Emily, Adam. Ednl. Specialists Degree, So. Ill. U., 1996. Adj. prof. U. of Nev., Las Vegas, 1999—, project dir., 2000—; sch. psychologist Odyssey Charter Sch., Las Vegas, 2000—, Andre Agassi Coll. Prep. Acad., Las Vegas, 2001—; edn. cons. Collaborative Autism Resources and Edn., Las Vegas, 2002—. Ednl. specialist Ctr. for Ednl. Enhancement, Las Vegas, 2000—02. Recipient Cert. of Distinction, U. of Nev., 2001; Grant, U.S. Dept. Health and Human Svcs., 2001—, U. of Nev., 2001, 2002. Mem.: NASP. Personal E-mail: kkonold@odysseycs.org.

KONON, NEENA NICHOLAI, design strategist; b. Chgo., Dec. 4, 1951; d. Nicholas Alexander and Marie G. (Korotkoff) K. BFA cum laude, Ohio U., 1973. Interior designer Architectonics, Inc., Chgo., 1973-75, sr. interior designer, 1978-82; interior designer Space Mgmt. Assoc., Inc., Chgo., 1975-78; design prin. Borkon & Konon Assoc., Inc., Chgo., 1982-84; dir. interiors Perkins & Will, Chgo., 1984-91; pres. Nicholai Ltd., Chgo., 1991—; assoc. Woman Bus. Enterprise (WBE), Chgo. Founding mem. Orthodox Christian Synergy, 1988—. Mem. Chgo. Real Estate Exec. Women. Republican. Avocations: drawing, gourmet cooking. E-mail: neena@nicholaistudio.com.

KONOPINSKI, VIRGIL JAMES, industrial hygienist, consultant; b. Toledo, July 11, 1935; BSChemE, U. Toledo, 1956; MSChemE, Pratt Inst., 1960; MBA, Bowling Green State U., 1971. Registered profl. engr., Ohio, Ind., Calif., cert. indsl. hygienist, safety profl. Assoc. engr. Owens Ill., Toledo, 1956, 60; real estate developer Grand Rapids, Ohio, 1961; chem. engr. USPHS, Cin., 1961-64; sr. environ. engr. Vistron Corp., Lima, Ohio, 1964-67; environ. specialist, asst. to dir. environ. control Owens Corning Fiberglas, Toledo, 1967-72; gen. mgr. Midwest Environ. Mgmt., Maumee, Ohio, 1972-73; staff specialist, indl. hygienist Williams Bros. Waste Control, Tulsa, 1973-75; dir. divsn. indsl. hygiene and radiol. health Ind. State Bd. Health, Indpls., 1975-87; exec. v.p. ACT Ind., Indpls., 1987-89; sr. cons. Occusafe, Chgo., 1990-91; regional safety engr., human resources analyst/safety U.S. Postal Svc., Bloomingdale, Ill., 1991—2003. Bd. dirs. IOSHA Indsl. Hygiene, 1975—83; cons. indoor air, radon, occupl. health, Zionsville, 1987—91, Cary, 1991—2003, Maumee, Ohio, 2003—. Contbr. articles to profl. jours. With USNR, 1956—59. Mem.: Am. Soc. Safety Engrs., Am. Indsl. Hygiene Assn., Ret. Oficers Assn., Naval Res. Assn. Republican. Roman Catholic. Home and Office: 7206 Lonewater Dr Maumee OH 43537

KONOWITZ, HERBERT HENRY, textile company executive; b. Brookline, Mass., Feb. 13, 1937; s. Robert Isaac and Sarah (Freedman) K.; m. Linda Phyllis Swartzman, Dec. 20, 1958; children: Cindy Lee, Jeffrey Scott. BSBA, Babson Coll., 1958. V.p. Vita Rest Sales Co., N.y.C., 1958-63, Lady Linda Covers Inc., N.Y.C., 1963—; pres. Milford Stitching Co., Del., 1968—. V.p. Comml. Drapery Contractors, Inc., Silver Springs, Md., 1976-81; dir. Greater Del. Corp., Dover, Del. Nat. Life, Yankee Land, Inc., Reclamation Center, Inc., 1972-75, G.L.K., Inc.; trustee, chmn. fin. com. Congregation Beth Sholom, 2002-. Mem. Gov. Del. Coun. Consumer Affairs, 1971-76; commr. State Lottery Commn., 1978-81; bd. dirs. Jobs for Del. Grads. Inc., 1979, health Plan of Del.; chmn. local Rep. dist. com., 1971-75; dir. Del. Dept. Tourism, 1988-96; mem. Del. Rep. Dtrl. Com., 1971—; vice chmn. Kent County Rep. com., 1975-79, chmn. 1979-81; v.p. Kent County chpt. Am. Heart Assn., 1974-75, pres., 1975-76; mem. State Coun. Tourism, 1988, 96; trustee Broadmeadow Sch., 1980-84; trustee Congregation Beth Sholom, 1980-86, 2001—, chmn. fin. com.; mem. parent's coun. Northfield-Mt. Hermon Sch., 1984-86; mem. Del. Devel. Coun., 1991; county chmn. Gov.'s Election Com., 1984; mem. adv. coun. Goldey Beacon Coll., 1987. Mem. Masons, Elks, Shriners. Home: 55 Beloit Ave Dover DE 19901-5704 Office: Milford Stitching Co S Marshall St Milford DE 19963

KONRAD, ADOLF FERDINAND, artist; b. Bremen, Germany, Feb. 21, 1915; came to U.S., 1925, naturalized, 1931; s. Roman and Katherine Heidientje (Engelken) K.; m. Adair Watts, Apr. 26, 1980. Student, Newark Sch. Fine and Indsl. Art, 1930-34, Cummington (Mass.) Sch., 1936-37; DFA, Kean U., 1971. Tchr., advisor N.J. State Council on Arts, 1971-74; artist-in-residence Everhart Mus., Scranton, Pa., 1973, Somerset County Coll. (now Raritan Valley Coll.), Somerville, N.J., 1977-80. Lectr., panelist. One-man shows include Newark Mus., 1966, Everhart Mus., Scranton, Pa., 1973, Mus. Fine Arts, Springfield, Mass., 1973, Montclair Art Mus. and N.J. State Mus., Trenton, 1980, The Newark Mus., 1997; represented in permanent collections Newark Mus., Montclair Art Mus., Mus. Fine Arts, Everhart Mus., N.J. State Mus., NAD, N.Y.C., Newark Public Library, The Forbes Collection, N.Y.C, Ct. Gen. Sessions Painting Collection, Washington, CIBA Geigy, Basle, Switzerland, AT&T, Bedminster, N.J., Crum & Forster Ins. Co., Morristown, N.J., Bell Labs. Murray Hill, N.J., N.J. Public Service, Newark, Schering-Plough Corp., Liberty Corner, N.J., Geraldine R. Dodge Found., Morristown, N.J., Somerset Art Assn., Bedminster, N.J., 2000; mural executed N.J. Vets. Meml. Home, Paramus, 1986; retrospective exhbn. The Morris Mus., Morristown, N.J., 1992, Hunterdon Art Mus., Clinton, N.J., 1996. Louis Comfort Tiffany fellow, 1937; Tiffany Found. fellow, 1961; resident fellow Yaddo, Saratoga Springs, 1956; winner grand prize Atlantic City Fine Arts Festival, 1961, 63; first prize Montclair Art Mus. Ann. Exhbn., 1963; Andrew Carnegie prize NAD Ann., 1967; Audience Choice award Marietta (Ohio) Coll., 1969; Gov.'s citation; N.J. Symphony Ann. Arts award, 1969; David Humphreys Meml. prize Allied Artist of Am., 1971; Artist of Year award Art Educators N.J., 1973; Fellowship award in Painting N.J. State Council on Arts, 1982. Mem. Associated Artists N.J. (pres. 1960-65), Artists Equity Assn. N.J. (pres. 1952-60, NAD (academician; Thomas B. Clark prize 1956). Home: 9 Hillside Dr Annandale NJ 08801

KONRAD, AGNES CROSSMAN, retired real estate agent, retired educator; b. Rutland, Vt., Nov. 26, 1921; d. Warren Julius and Susan Anna (Cain) Crossman; children: Suzanne Martha, Dianna Marie; m. Henry Konrad, Nov. 27, 1954. Assoc. degree in Edn., Castelton Coll., 1943; BS in Edn., Castelton State Coll., 1951; postgrad., SUNY, New Paltz, 1969-70, Fla. Atlantic U., 1973; grad., Realtors Inst. Fla., 1981. Cert. realtor. Tchr. 1st to 8th grades Pittsford (Vt.) Pub. Schs., 1943-44, tchr. 1st grade, 1950-52; tchr. 3d grade Ralph Smith Sch.-Hyde Park (N.Y.) Ctrl. Schs., 1952-69, Violet Ave. Sch.-Hyde Park Sch. Sys., 1969-73; realtor Four Star Realty of Boca Raton (Fla.), 1974-93; ret., 1993. Inducted into Golden Alumni Soc. of Castleton State Coll., 2001. Mem. AAUW (life), N.Y. State Ret. Tchrs. Assn. (life), Castleton Vt. State Coll. Alumni. Avocations: painting, travel, reading, poetry, computer art painting. Home: 1229 SW 13th St Boca Raton FL 33486-5307 E-mail: Henag40@aol.com.

KONSCHNIK, DAVID MICHAEL, lawyer; b. Weston, Pa., Apr. 21, 1948; s. Frank Joseph and Margaret (Broyan) K.; m. Maureen Anne Talty, June 26, 1970; children: Katherine Erin, David Michael Jr. BS, Georgetown U., 1970, JD, 1975; MA in Teaching, Howard U., 1971. Bar: Md. Ct. Appeals 1975, D.C. Ct. Appeals 1980. Teaching intern Urban Tchr. Corps., Washington, 1970-71; math. tchr. Ballou Sr. High Sch., Washington, 1971-76; atty. advisor sect. of fin. proceedings ICC, Washington, 1976-79, atty. advisor office of commr. Clapp, 1979-82, atty. advisor sect. of rates, office of proceedings, 1982, atty. advisor office of commr. Gradison, 1982-85, chief of staff, 1985-90, dir. office of procs., 1990-95, Surface Transp. Bd., Washington, 1996—. Roman Catholic. Home: 3510 Horseman Way Davidsonville MD 21035-2423 Office: Surface Transp Bd 1925 K St NW Washington DC 20423-0001

KONSIS, KENNETH FRANK, forester, educator; b. Danville, Ill., Dec. 3, 1952; s. Frank John and Regina Ann (Stefaniak) K.; m. Lorna Jean Wiesemann, May 6, 1978. AS, Danville Area Community Coll., 1972; BS in Forestry, So. Ill. U., 1974. Park ranger Vermilion County Conservation Dist., Danville, 1974-84, dist. forester, 1984-87, rsch. forester, instr. in outdoor edn., 1987-91, dep. dir., 1991-92, exec. dir., 1992—. State del. Ill. Conservation Congress, 1993, 94, 97; mem. Lake Vermilion Water Quality Coalition, 1996—, treas., 2000—; mem. Vermilion River Ecosys. Partnership, 1997—. Mem. VOTEC Agr. and Horticulture Adv Com.; mem. external adv. coun. dept. natural resources and environ. scis. U. Ill., 1993—; v.p. Walnut Coun. Found., 2001—; mem. retail task force com. City of Danville, 2001—, mem. river front task force com., 2001—; mem. Interstate 74 Corridor Planning Com.; mem. nat resources com. Danville Halo Project. Mem.: Ill. Assn. Conservation Dists. (v.p. 1995—96, pres. 1996—2000, Ill. trails and greenways coun. 1997—, v.p. 2001—), Am. Forestry Assn., Shiitake Growers' Assn. Wis., Ill. Tree Farm Com., Ill. Walnut Coun. (regional bd. dirs. 1989—92, v.p. 1991—92, pres. 1992—93, treas. 1994—), Soc. Am. Foresters (comm. chair 1997—98), Am. Chestnut Soc., Ill. Lake Mgmt. Assn. (charter), Ill. Woodland Owners and Users Assn., Internat. Walnut Coun. (nat. meeting program chair 1998, v.p. 1998, pres. 1999, immediate past pres. 2000, v.p. Walnut Coun. Found. 2000—), Ill. Native Plant Soc. (pres. 1986—93, exec. com. 1986—). Roman Catholic. Avocations: photography, gardening, travel, biking, nature. Home: 234 S Walnut St Westville IL 61883-1664 Office: Vermilion Co Conservation Dist 22296-A Henning Rd Danville IL 61834-5336 E-mail: kkonsis@vccd.org.

KONSTAN, DAVID, classics and comparative literature educator, researcher; b. N.Y.C., Nov. 1, 1940; s. Harry and Edythe (Wahrman) K.; m. Pura Nieto; children: Eve Anna, Geoffrey Theodore. Instr. Bklyn. Coll., 1965-67; prof. Wesleyan U., Middletown, Conn., 1967-87; prof. classics and comparative literature Brown U., Providence, R.I., 1987—. Author: Epicurean Psychology, 1973, Roman Comedy, 1983, Simplicius Physics 6, 1989, Sexual Symmetry, 1994, Greek Comedy and Ideology, 1995, Friendship in The Classical World, 1997, Philodemus on Frank Criticism, 1998, Pity Transformed, 2001. Mem. Am. Philol. Assn. (pres. 1999). Avocation: cooking. Home: 70 Westford Rd Providence RI 02906-2515 Office: Brown U 48 College St Providence RI 02912-1856 E-mail: dkonstan@brown.edu.

KONSTANTINOV, TZVETAN KRUMOV, musician, concert pianist, educator; b. Bulgaria; came to U.S., 1979; s. Krum Christov and Maria Apostolov (Veselkov) K.; m. Lee-Ann Larson, Mar. 7, 1980; children: Alexander, Christian. MusM, State Acad Music, Sofia, Bulgaria, 1974; postgrad., U. Music & Performing Arts, Vienna, Austria, 1979. Prof. State Acad. Music, Sofia, Bulgaria, 1974-77, Levine Sch. Music, Washington, 1984-89, George Washington U., Washington, 1989—. Bd. dirs. Met. Chorus; lectr. in field. Am. debut at Meany Hall, Seattle, 1980; performer TV documentary Music To Promote Democracy, 1990, Spotlight, 1988, Capital Concerts, 1989, Voice of Am., 1999; performances at Carnegie Hall and Kennedy Ctr., Strathmore Hall; recs. with Centauer Records. Organizer tours throughout Europe, Asia and U.S. Recipient Diploma for Highest Achievements Fifth All-Bulgarian Competition, 1969, Laureate Second Nat. Competition, 1970. Mem. AAUP, Am. Liszt Soc., Am. Assn. for Promoting Bulgarian Culture, Am. Beethoven Soc., Friday Morning Music Club. Avocations: arts, hiking, languages, golfing, jogging. Home: PO Box 554 Mc Lean VA 22101-0554 Office: George Washington U Dept Music Washington DC 20052-0001 E-mail: tzvetan@tzvetankonstantinov.com.

KONSTANTINOV, VASSIL ALEXANDROV, finance educator; b. Plovdiv, Bulgaria; arrived in U.S., 1990; s. Alexander Konstantinov and Elenka Konstantinova. BA, MA, Yale U., 1994; AM, PhD, Harvard U., 2000. Cert. pilot FAA, scuba diver PADI. Asst. prof. U. Wyo., Laramie, 1999—. Referee (jour.) Jour. Econs. and Bus., 2001, Fin. Rev., 2001 (finalist Pan Agora prize, 2002). Mem.: Rocky Mountain Harvard U. Club, Yale Club Colo. Home: 1706 Sherman Hill Rd Apt B Laramie WY 82070-5304 Office: U Wyo Dept Econs and Fin PO Box 3985 Laramie WY 82071-3985

KONTNY, VINCENT L. rancher, engineering executive; b. Chappell, Nebr., July 19, 1937; s. Edward James and Ruth Regina (Schumann) K.; m. Joan Dashwood FitzGibbon, Feb. 20, 1970; children: Natascha Marie, Michael Christian, Amber Brooke. BSCE, U. Colo., 1958, DSc honoris causa, 1991. Operator heavy equipment, grade foreman Peter Kiewit Son's Co., Denver, 1958-59; project mgr. Utah Constrn. and Mining Co., Western Australia, 1965-69, Fluor Australia, Queensland, Australia, 1969-72; sr. project mgr. Fluor

Utah, San Mateo, Calif., 1972-73; sr. v.p. Holmes & Narver, Inc., Orange, Calif., 1973-79; mng. dir. Fluor Australia, Melbourne, 1979-82; group v.p. Fluor Engrs., Inc., Irvine, Calif., 1982-85, pres., chief exec. officer, 1985-87; group pres. Fluor Daniel, Irvine, Calif., 1987-88, pres., 1988-94, Fluor Corp., Irvine, 1990-94, vice chmn., 1994; ret., 1994; bd. dirs. Chgo. Bridge & Iron Co., Plainfield, Ill., 1997—; COO Washington Group Internat., Inc., Boise, Idaho, 2000—. Purchased Last Dollar Ranch, Ridgway Co. 1989, Centennial Ranch, Colona Co., 1992, owner Double Shoe Cattle Co. Contbr. articles to profl. jours. Mem. engring. devel. coun., U. Colo.; mem. engring. adv. coun., Stanford U. Lt. USN, 1959-65. Mem.: Ctr. (Costa Mesa, Calif.). Republican. Roman Catholic. Avocation: snow skiing.

KONTOS, GEORGE JOHN, JR., surgeon; b. Chgo., May 26, 1958; s. George John and Sherry Knox Kontos; m. Sherry Knox Reed, Aug. 24, 1991; children: Alexis Reed, Nicholas John. BA, Northwestern U., Evanston, Ill., 1977—79; MD, Loyola U., Maywood, Ill., 1979—82. Diplomate Am. Bd. Thoracic Surgery, 1992, Am. Bd. Surgery, 1988. Resident, gen. surgery Mayo Clinic, Rochester, Minn., 1982—88; resident, cardiac surgery U. Ala., Birmingham, 1988—91; cardiovasc. and thoracic surgeon Midwest Cardiovasc. Ctr., Sioux Falls, SD, 1992—94, Ctrl. Ala. Thoracic and Cardiovasc. Surgery, Montgomery, 1994—2002; surgeon U. Tenn., Memphis, 2002—. Guest reviewer Jour. Applied Physiology, Houston, 1991—92, Transplantation, Boston, 1991—97, Am. Jour. Cardiology, Dallas, 2001—02. Mem. Am. Hellenic Philanthropic Orgn., Montgomery, Ala., 1994—2002. Grantee, Am. Heart Assn., 1992. Fellow: Am. Coll. Chest Physicians, Am. Coll. Cardiology, Southeastern Surg. Congress, Am. Coll. Surgeons; mem.: Johns Hopkins Med. and Surg. Assn., Priestly Soc., Mayo Clinic, N.Y. Acad. Scis., Soc. Thoracic Surgeons. Greek Orthodox. Avocations: fountain pen collector, water sports, sailing. Home: 429 Greenfield Rd Memphis TN 38117 Office: Univ Tenn 7945 Wolf River Blvd Ste 290 Germantown TN 38138-1733 Office Fax: 901-347-8295. E-mail: geokontos@earthlink.net.

KONTOS, GREGORY EDWARD, film company executive, sculptor; b. Teaneck, N.J., June 4, 1977; s. Kenneth Edward and Elaine May Kontos. BS in Anthropology, Coll. of William and Mary, 1999. Pres. Etehigraphy Films, Inc, Richmond, Va., 1998—, Kontos Trading Co., Richmond, Va., 2001—. Dir.: (films) More, Tribute to Dziga Vertov, The Tarot Reader; exhibitions include Frames and Mugs. Founder Richmond Libertarian Party, 2003; min. Universal Life Ch., Richmond, 2000—02; chatecist St. Francis of Assisi Cath. Ch., Quantico, Va., 1993—95. Scholar Merit Scholarship, Anthropology Film Ctr., 1999, 2000. Libertarian. Buddist. Avocations: travel, motorcycles, horticulture, botanical medicine, electrical engineering.

KONTOS, HERMES APOSTOLOU, retired academic administrator; b. Lefka, Cyprus, Dec. 13, 1933; married; 3 children. MD, U. Athens, 1958; PhD, Med. Coll. Va., 1967. Resident Nocosia (Cyprus) Gen. Hosp., 1959; intern Md. Gen. Hosp., 1959—60; jr. asst. resident Med. Coll. Va., Richmond, 1960—61, asst. resident, 1961—62, rsch. fellow, 1962—64, from instr. medicine to asst. prof., 1964—70; from assoc. prof. medicine to prof. Va. Commonwealth U., Med. Coll. Va., Richmond, 1970, from co-chmn. divsn. cardiology to chmn., 1977-86, 86-91, vice chmn. dept. internal medicine, 1984—91, acting chmn. dept. internal medicine, 1988—93, acting chmn. dept. pathology, 1991—93, interim dean sch. medicine, 1993—94, dean sch. medicine, 1994—95, dean sch. medicine, sr. assoc. v.p. health svcs., 1995—97; v.p. health svcs., dean Sch. Medicine, Va. Commonwealth U., Richmond, 1997—2000; CEO, v.p. health scis. VCU Health Sys. Authority, Richmond, 2000—02; ret.

KONWIN, THOR WARNER, financial executive; b. Berwyn, Ill., Aug. 17, 1943; s. Frank and Alice S. (Johnson) K.; m. Carol A. Svitak, Aug. 2, 1967 (div. Feb. 1990); 1 child, Christopher Vernon; m. Virginia Colburn, May 21, 1993 (div. Mar. 2002). AA, Morton Jr. Coll., 1966; BS, No. Ill. U., 1967; MS, Roosevelt U., 1971. Acct. Beckerman & Terrill, CPA's, Chgo., 1967-68; cost acct. Sunbeam Corp., Chgo., 1968-72; CFO Gen. Molded Products, Inc., Chgo., 1972-75; controller Sunbeam Appliance Co., Chgo., 1975-81; chief fin. officer Bear Med. System, Inc., Riverside, Calif., 1981-84, Bird Products Corp., Palm Springs, Calif., 1984—; gen. ptnr., 1985—; pres. B&B Ventures Ltd., Riverside, 1987—; chief exec. officer Med One Fin. Group, Salt Lake City; pres. Tags Antiques, Inc., Palm Springs. Bd. dris. Bird Med. Techs., Inc., Palm Springs, Bird Products Corp., Palm Springs, Bird Internat., Inc., Riverside, B&B Ventures, Inc., Riverside, Equilink, Inc. Riverside, Stackhouse, Inc., Riverside, Med One Fin. Group, Salt Lake City; CEO Equitable Inc., Palm Springs, Calif., 1990—; adv. coun. U. Calif. Grad. Bus. Sch., Riverside, 1988—; CEO Entertainment Leader Inc., Cathedral City, Calif., 1995—. Served with U.S. Army, 1969-71. Home: 36564 Camino Del Mar Cathedral City CA 92234-1586 E-mail: thorkonwin@aol.com.

KONZ, GERALD KEITH, retired manufacturing company executive; b. Racine, Wis., Apr. 3, 1932; m. Marianne Bubolz; children: Richard C., Brenda S. BS in Econs., U. Wis., 1957, LLB, 1960. V.p. in charge corp. tax dept. S.C. Johnson & Son, Inc., Racine, 1982-98, chmn. bd. trustees pension trust, employee profit sharing and savs. plan, 1982-98. Bd. dirs. Johnson Family Funds, Inc., Racine, Wis. Pub. Expenditure Survey, Madison, 1982-92; mem. adv. bd. Venture Investors, Inc., Madison, Wis., 1997—. Treas. St. Catherines H.S. Found., Racine, 1994—97, pres., 1997—2001; bd. dirs. YMCA, Racine, 1988—98. Mem. ABA, Tax Execs. Inst. (pres. Wis. chpt. 1972), Wis. Bar Assn., Racine-Kenosha Estate Planning Coun. (pres. 1980). Office: 3515 Taylor Ave Racine WI 53405-4727 E-mail: gkkonz@execpc.com.

KOO, ANTHONY YING CHANG, economist, educator; b. Shanghai, Nov. 22, 1918; came to U.S., 1940; s. Vee-Sing and Tseng (Soo) K.; m. Delia Zung-Fung Wei, June 6, 1943; children: Victoria M., Margery E., Emily D. BA, St. John's U., Shanghai, 1940; MS, U. Ill., 1941; MA, Harvard U., 1943, PhD, 1946. Prof. econs. U. Mich., Ann Arbor, 1964-67; from asst. prof. to prof. Mich. State U., East Lansing, 1950-64, prof. econs., 1967—. Cons. The East-West Ctr., Honolulu, 1963, Internat. Labor Orgn., Geneva, 1965-66, U.S. Dept. Energy, Washington, 1980-82; vis. prof. Nat. Taiwan U., 1969-70, Indonesia 2d U. Project, 1989, Wuhan U. and Zhongshan U., China, 1990; adj. prof. econs. Fla. State U., 1990—. Author: Land Market Distortion and Tenure Reform, 1982; editor: Selected Essays of Gottfried Haberler, 1986; editor/author: The Liberal Economic Order, 1993; contbr. articles to profl. jours. Grantee Soc. Sci. Coun., 1953, 57, 64, 68, Ford Found., 1956-57, 61-62, NSF, 1965-67. Mem. Am. Econ. Assn., Econometric Soc., Acad. Sinica. Home: 4554 Sequoia Trl Okemos MI 48864-2044 Office: Mich State U Dept Of Econs East Lansing MI 48824 also: Fla State U Dept Econs Tallahassee FL 32306

KOO, EUN-HEE, education educator; b. Seoul, Korea (South), Apr. 30, 1967; d. Jaduk Koo and Junja Kim; m. Jae K Wi, June 17, 2000. BA, Sungshin Women's U., Seoul, Korea, 1987—91; MA, Adelphi U., 1992—93; EdD, U. of Houston, 1994—98. Cert. of Task Based Lang. Tchg. Workshop Nat. Fgn. Lang. Resource Ctr., 2001, Cert. of Recognition Hope Internat. U., 2001. Edtl. dir. Found. for SATII Korean, LA, Calif., 1999; prof. Hope Internat. U., Fullerton, Calif., 1999—2001, La Sierra U., Riverside, Calif., 2001—. V.p. Found. for SAT II Korean, LA, 2001—. Author: (poetry) Dear King Sejong, (test preparation book) Preparation Book of SATII Korean. Recipient New Poet Award, Moon Yae Un Dong (The Lit. Movement), 1999. Master: Jiphyunjun; mem.: Korean Poet Assn. of Am. (la 1991—2003), Internat. Assn. of Korean Lang. Edn., Am. Assn. of Teachers of Korean. Protestant. Office: Foundation for SATII Korean 680 Wilshire Pl Suite 416 Los Angeles CA 90005 Office Fax: 213-380-5718. Personal E-mail: drkoo@sat2korean.com.

KOO, GEORGE PING SHAN, business consultant; b. Changting, China, June 4, 1938; came to the U.S., 1949, naturalized, 1955; s. Ted Swei Yen and Pei-Fen (Yang) K.; m. May Jen, May 5, 1962; children: Denise, Douglas, Alyssa. BS, MIT, 1960, MS, 1962; DSc, Stevens Inst. Tech., 1969; MBA, U. Santa Clara, 1975. Mgr. Allied Chem. Corp., 1963-71; assoc. dir. SRI Internat., 1972-78; v.p. Chase Manhattan Bank, 1978-79; mng. dir. Bear Stearns China Trade, 1979-82; v.p. Bear-Stearns & Co., 1982-83; pres. Microelectronic Bus. Internat., Inc., Mountain View, Calif., 1983-85; v.p. Tiara Computer Sys., Inc., 1985-86; mng. dir. internat. svcs. H&Q Tech. Ptnrs., Inc., 1987; mng. dir., CEO Internat. Strategic Alliances, Inc., 1988-99; dir. Chinese svcs. group Deloitte & Touche LLP, San Jose, Calif., 1999—. Cons., chair on Asian Fin. and Alliances, Santa Clara, Calif., 1990-93. Human rels. commr. City of Mountain View, 1994-98. Mem. Asian Am. Mfrs. Assn. (chmn. 1996-97), mem. com. of 100 (dir. 1998—). Home: 1819 Van Buren Cir Mountain View CA 94040-4054 E-mail: gemaykoo@comcast.net.

KOO, JOHN YING MING, dermatologist; b. Tokyo, Jan. 9, 1955; arrived in U.S., 1967; s. Kwang Ming Koo and Amy Tsai Ma; m. Nancy Chiang, July 7, 1978; children: Kathie, Jennifer, Jocelyn, Jonathan, Karina. BA in Biochemistry, U. Calif., Berkeley, 1977; MD, Harvard U., 1981. Cert. psychiatry and dermatology. Intern UCLA Ctr. Health Scis., 1981—82; resident in psychiatry UCLA Neuropsychiatric Inst., 1982—85; resident in dermatology U. Calif.-San Francisco Med. Ctr., 1985—88; dir. Psoriasis and Skin Treatment Ctr., U. Calif., San Francisco, 1988—; prof. and vice chmn. dept. dermatology, prof. U. Calif., San Francisco, 1989—. Cons. Novartis, NJ, 1988—, Allergan, Costa Mesa, Calif., 1990—, Roche, NJ, 1992—; cons. in field; med. adv. bd. Nat. Psioriasis Found., Portland, Oreg., 1995. Mem. editl. bd.. Jour. Am. Acad. Dermatology, 1994; editor: Psychosomatic Medicine, 1999. Scholar Harvard Nat. scholar, Harvard Med. Sch., Boston, 1981. Mem.: Am. Psychiat. Assn., Am. Acad. Dermatology, Assn. for Psychocutaneous Medicine N.Am. (founder). Avocations: creative writing, photography, military history. Office: U Calif San Francisco Psoriasis and Skin Treatment Ctr 515 Spruce St San Francisco CA 94118

KOO, SHOU-ENG, economics educator; b. Yenchen, Jiangsu, China, Jan. 13, 1911; arrived in U.S., 1945; s. Yun Peng Koo and Sze Chih; m. Ying-Zhen Xia, May 1938 (dec. Oct. 1975); children: Boping Gu, Zhong-ping Gu; m. Ailin Dong, Mar. 22, 1989. BA, Nat. Ctrl. U., Nanjing, China, 1931; MA, Columbia U., 1946, PhD, 1961. Asst. prof. John Carroll U., Cleve., 1961-66; vis. assoc. prof. U. Ga., Athens, 1966-67; assoc. prof. Ind. U., Indpls., 1967-74, prof., 1974-87, prof. emeritus, 1987—. Vis. prof. Taiwan U., Taipei, 1973-74, Nanjing U., 1980-81, Nankai U., Tianjian, China, 1983, Fudan U., Shanghai, China, 1985-86, U. Fin. and Econ., Shanghai, 1987-88; spl. lectr. Beijing U., 1999. Author: An Input-Output Study for Metropolitan Indianapolis, 1973, Foreign Investment and Industrialization in Taiwan, 1976, Tariff and the Development of the Cotton Industry in China: 1842-1937, 1982, China Opens to the Outside World, 1988. Mem. C.A. Nat. Ctrl. U. Alumni Assn. (pres. 1996—), N.Am. Inst. Internat. Comm. (v.p. 1992—), The 1990 Inst. Avocations: tennis, cruise tour, walking.

KOOB, CHARLES EDWARD, lawyer; b. Kansas City, Mo., Aug. 31, 1944; s. Charles H. and Adeline (Meinert) K.; m. Pamela Ann Nabseth, June 26, 1971; children: Jason Wyeth, Peter Nabseth. BA, Rockhurst Coll., 1966; JD, Stanford U., 1969. Bar: Calif. 1970, N.Y. 1972, U.S. Dist. Ct. (so. and ea. dists.) N.Y. 1973, U.S. Ct. Appeals (2d cir.) 1975, U.S. Ct. Appeals (5th cir.) 1979, U.S. Supreme Ct. 1988, U.S. Ct. Claims 1988, U.S. Ct. Appeals (3d cir.) 1985. Assoc. Simpson, Thacher & Bartlett, N.Y.C., 1970-76, ptnr., 1976—. Mem. ABA, N.Y. State Bar Assn., Calif. Bar Assn. Office: Simpson Thacher & Bartlett 425 Lexington Ave Fl 15 New York NY 10017-3954

KOOB, ROBERT DUANE, chemistry educator, educational administrator; b. Graetinger, Iowa, Oct. 14, 1941; s. Emil John and Rose Mary (Slinger) Koob; m. E. Yvonne Ervin, June 9, 1960; children: Monique, Gregory, Michael, Eric, David;children: Angela, Julie. BA in Edn., U. No. Iowa, 1962; PhD in Chemistry, U. Kans., 1967. From asst. prof. to prof. chemistry N.D. State U., Fargo, 1967—90, chmn. dept. chemistry, 1974—78, 1979—81, dir. Water Inst., 1975—85, dean Coll. Sci. and Math., 1981—84, v.p., 1985—90, interim pres., 1987—88; v.p. for acad. affairs, sr. v.p. Calif. Poly. State U., San Luis Obispo, 1990—95; pres. U. No. Iowa, Cedar Falls, 1995—, prof., 1995—. Cons. TransAlta, Edmondton, Alta., Canada, Alta. Rsch. Coun., Mitre Corp., Washington; bd. dirs. State Bank Fargo, Fargo Cass County Econ. Devel. Corp.; chair bd. dirs. Cal Poly Found.; chair Iowa Coordinating Coun. for Post-H.S. Edn., 1996—97. Contbr. articles to profl. jours. V.p. Crookston Diocesan Sch. Bd., Minn., 1982; pres. elem. sch. bd., St. Joseph's Ch., Moorhead, Minn., 1982, parish coun., Moorhead, Minn., 1983; pres. bd. Shanley H.S., Fargo, 1985. Grantee in field. Mem.: Iowa Assn. Coll. Pres. (pres. 1996—). Roman Catholic. Avocations: reading, flying, sailing, racquet sports, water skiing . Office: Univ of Northern Iowa 1227 W 27th St Cedar Falls IA 50614-0001

KOODALI, RANJIT THAZHATHAVEETIL, chemist, researcher; b. Cannanore, Kerala, India, July 19, 1968; s. A.V.K. Nambiar and K.T. Vilasini; m. Seema T. Kannoth. BSc, Loyola Coll., Madras, India, 1988; MSc, Indian Inst. Tech., Madras, 1990, PhD, 1995. Postdoctoral fellow Hebrew U. Jerusalem, 1995-98, U. Houston, 1999—. Contbr. numerous articles to profl. jours.; patentee in field. Office: Kans State U 111 Willard Hall Manhattan KS 66506 Fax: (713) 743-2709. E-mail: ranju30@hotmail.com.

KOOIJMANS, PIETER HENDRIK, judge International Court of Justice; b. Heemstede, The Netherlands, July 6, 1933; m. A. Kooijmans-Verhage; 4 children. Degree, Free U., Amsterdam, The Netherlands, 1964. Mem. Faculty of Law Free U. of Amsterdam, 1960-65, prof. European law and pub. internat. law, 1965-73; state sec. for fgn. affairs Govt. of The Netherlands, 1973-77; prof. pub. internat. law U. Leiden, The Netherlands, 1978-92, 95-97; minister of fgn. affairs Govt. of The Netherlands, 1993-94; judge Internat. Ct. of Justice, The Hague, The Netherlands, 1997—. Author textbooks in field; contbr. articles to profl. jours. Head Netherlands del. to UN Commn. on Human Rights, 1982-85, 92, chair commn., 1984-85, spl. reporter on questions relevant to torture, 1985-92; mem. various UN and Orgn. on Security and Coop. in Europe missions to former Yugoslavia, 1991-92. Office: care Internat Ct of Justice Peace Palace 2517 KJ The Hague Netherlands

KOOIMA, LINDA KAY, neonatal and pediatrics nurse; b. Rock Valley, Iowa, Aug. 26, 1948; d. Thomas and Frances Mae (Harmelink) K.; m. Orlando Sabas Arroyo, Apr. 12, 1976; children: Annie Josephine, Solomon Jordan. Dipl. nursing, Northwestern U., 1969; BA in Spanish, S.D. State U., 1989. RN, Ill., S.D., Ariz., Calif., Fla. Critical care nurse Children's Meml. Hosp., Chgo., 1969-70; nurse neonatal ICU, Moffitt Hosp. U. Calif., San Francisco, 1970-76; clinic nurse S.D. State U., Brookings, 1985-88; mother and baby nurse Santa Barbara (Calif.) Cottage Hosp., 1988-89; neonatal nurse Santa Ana (Calif.) Hosp. and Med. Ctr., 1990, Hoag Presbyn. Meml. Hosp., Newport Beach, Calif., 1991; pediatric camp nurse Camp Gulliver, Coral Gables, Fla., 1993-95; utilization rev. nurse Initial Health Care, Miami, 1995-98; travel nurse mother/baby Star-Med Co., 1998-99, U.S. Nursing Corp., 2000—. Travel nurse mother-baby unit Cedars-Sinai Med. Ctr., L.A., 2002—03. Mem. Assn. Camp Nurses. Republican. Avocation: scuba diving. Home: 13890 SW 100th Ln Miami FL 33186-6869

KOOISTRA, ANDREW J. painter, sculptor; b. Whitinsville, Mass., July 8, 1924; s. Henry A. Kooistra and Tillie A. Frieswyck; m. Ingeberg H. Kooistra, May 30, 1968; children: Andrea, Katharine. BFA, Tufts U., Medford, Mass., 1951; postgrad., Harvard U., 1952; MFA, U. So. Calif., L.A., 1953. Tchr. art Ellenville Ctrl. Sch., NY, 1953. One-man shows include Woodstock (N.Y.) Artists Assn., 1953, Ellenville Pub. Libr. and Mus., 1987, Petrucci Gallery, Saugerties, N.Y., 1989, Schenectady Mus. and Planetarium, N.Y., 1989, Whitinsville Social Libr., Mass., 1989, Sullivan County Art Mus., Hurleyville, N.Y., 1990, Fletcher Gallery, Woodstock, N.Y., 1996, exhibited in group shows at Hawthorn Gallery, Woodstock, 1988, Provincetown Art Assn. and Mus. Bd. dirs. Woodstock Artists' Assn., 1985. With USAAF, 1943—46. Episcopalian. Avocation: book and print collecting. Home: PO Box 203 Napanoch NY 12458

KOOISTRA, WILLIAM HENRY, clinical psychologist; b. Grand Rapids, Mich., May 20, 1936; s. Henry P. and Marguerite (Brinks) K.; m. Jean Heynen, Aug. 24, 1957 (div. Dec. 1984); children: Kimberly Lynn, William Peter, Kristin Jean, Allison Carol; m. Carol Sue Smitter, Mar. 9, 1985. BA, Calvin Coll., 1957; PhD, Wayne (Mich.) State U., 1963. Diplomate Am. Bd. Prof. Psychology, Am. Bd. Forensic Examiners. Intern psychology Lafayette Clinic, Detroit, 1961-62; chief psychologist Pine Rest Christian Hosp., Grand Rapids, Mich., 1964-67; clin. psychologist Kooistra, Jansma, Teitsma, DiNallo & Van Hoek, Grand Rapids, 1967—. Instr. Wayne State U., 1959-63, Hope Coll., Holland, Mich., 1964, Calvin Coll., Grand Rapids, 1964-81, Grand Valley State U., 1987-92. Founder Project Rehab., Grand Rapids, 1968, bd. dirs., 1969—, pres., 1972-74; mem. Kent County Dem. Exec. Com., 1969-73, 79-82, 86—, mem. governing bd. Fountain Street Ch., 1989-95, pres. 1994; rep. 3d dist. Presl. Electoral Coll., 1992. Mem. Am. Psychol. Assn. (council rep. 1982-85), Am. Soc. Psychologists in Pvt. Practice (sec. 1973-75), Mich. Psychol. Assn.(pres. 1979), Mich. Soc. Forensic Psychology, Grand Rapids Area Psychol. Assn (pres. 1968). Avocations: golf, tennis, sailing. Home: 2946 Cascade Rd SE Grand Rapids MI 49506-1965 Office: 3330 Claystone St SE Grand Rapids MI 49546-7716

KOOKEN, JOHN FREDERICK, retired bank holding company executive; b. Denver, Nov. 1, 1931; s. Duff A. and Frances C. K.; m. Emily Howe, Sept. 18, 1954; children: Diane, Carolyn. MS, Stanford U., 1954, PhD, 1961. With Security Pacific Nat. Bank-Security Pacific Corp., L.A., 1960-92; exec. v.p. Security Pacific Corp., L.A., 1981-87, chief fin. officer Los Angeles, 1984-92, vice chmn., 1987-92. Bd. dirs. Golden State Bancorp., 1992-2002, ACE Ltd., 1985-91 Centris Group, 1986-99, Pacific Gulf Properties, 1994-2001, East West Bancorp, 2002-; lectr. Grad. Sch. Bus. U. So. Calif., 1962-67; chmn. Bank Adminstrn. Inst., 1989-90. Pres. bd. dirs. Children's Bur., L.A., 1981-84; bd. dirs. United Way, L.A., 1982-89, Huntington Meml. Hosp., Pasadena, 1985—, chmn., 1999—; bd. dirs. So. Calif. Healthcare Systems, 1993—, chmn. 2001—. Lt. (j.g.) USNR, 1954-57. Mem. Fin. Execs. Inst. (pres. Los Angeles chpt. 1979-80, dir. 1981-84)

KOOLURIS DOBBS, LINDA KIA, artist; b. Orange, N.J., Jan. 28, 1949; m. Kildare Dobbs, May 7, 1981. AA, Pine Manor Coll., 1968; Cert., Sorbonne, 1968-69; BFA with honors, Sch. Visual Arts, 1972. Tchg. staff various colls., 1975—, Ryerson U., 1980—, Ave. Rd. Art Sch., 1999—. Exhibitions include Mus. of Textiles, Toronto, ArtCanadiana.com, Gallery Sheila Roth, Bronxville Art and Frame Gallery, Atrium Gallery, Chubb Group of Ins. Cos., Warren, N.J., Vancouver Art Gallery, Newbury Fine Arts, Boston and Edgartown, Mass., Art Gallery of Hamilton, Toronto Watercolour Soc., Vancouver Maritime Mus., Ceperley House of Visual Arts Burnaby, B.C., Sutton Gallery, Carrier Gallery, Columbus Ctr., First Canadian Pl. Gallery, Toronto, Represented in permanent collections AT&T, Artform, Norway, Glaxo Wellcome Inc., Inland Pacific Enterprises, Temple Scott & Assocs., Uniglobe, Advance Travel, AGF Mgmt. Ltd., Toronto Stock Exch., Ont. Govt. Art Collection, Parliament Bldg., Queen's Park, Pine Manor Coll., U.S., Mt. Sinai Hosp., Merrill Lynch, Aon Reed Stenhouse, U. Toronto, Scotia McLeod, Probyn & Co., numerous others, prin. works include portrait commns. the Hon. Henry N. R. Jackman, the Hon. Edwin A. Goodman, the Hon. Barbara McDougall, others, the Hon. David Peterson ; contbr. to art periodicals and publications; featured in water color books, Splash 3, 4, 5 & &; photogopher The Nat. Post, The Fin. Post., Verve Mag. Recipient Ann. Art Purchase prize Pine Manor Coll., 1968, 2d prize Fin. Post Ann. Reports awards, 1981. Mem. Toronto Watercolour Soc. (Hon. Mention, Ann. Fall Show 1991, Best in Architecture 1994). Address: Published By Posters Internat North Light Books 330 Spadina Rd Ste 1005 Toronto ON Canada M5R 2V9

KOOMEN, CORNELIS JAN, telecommunications and electronics executive; b. Zaandam, The Netherlands, Sept. 25, 1947; s. C.J. and G. (Dykman) K.; m. Jantiena Catharina de Jong; children: Casper Jan, Jeroen. MS, Tech. U., Delft, The Netherlands, 1972, PhD, 1982. Rschr. RVO/TNO, The Hague, The Netherlands, 1973-74, Philips Rsch. Labs., Eindhoven, 1974-83; sys. engr. Philips Telecom. and Data Systems, Hilversum, The Netherlands, 1983-84; software coord. Philips Electronics, Eindhoven, 1984-86; mgr. Philips Rsch. Labs., Eindhoven, 1987-89; semiconductor exec., tech. mgr., dir. Philips Telecom. and Data Systems, Hilversum, 1989-90; dir. Philips Comm. Systems, Hilversum, 1990-91; dir., v.p. Philips Semiconductors, Eindhoven, 1991-94, exec. v.p., 1995-98, chmn., 1996-98; pres. and CEO digital video group Philips Consumer Electronics, Palo Alto, Calif., 1998-2000; chmn. Securealink, Los Gatos, Calif., 2000—02, SafeNet Europe, 2002—, sr. v.p., 2002—. Prof. Tech. U., Eindhoven, The Netherlands, 1984-2001; module dir. Found. Toptech Studies, Delft, 1987-92. Author: The Design of Communicating Systems; editor Internat. Fedn. of Info. Processing Computer Hardware Description Langs. conf. proc., 1985-87; patentee in field; contbr. articles to profl. jours. Chmn. Cultural Com., Waalre, The Netherlands, 1977-81. Named Prof. Bahlerprice, Royal Inst. Engrs., 1986. Mem. IFIP WG 10.2, Soc. for Gen. Edn. (chmn. 1985-88). Avocations: aguarel painting, sailing, tennis. Office: Securealink 20 S Santa Cruz Ave Ste 308 Los Gatos CA 95030 Home: 15415 Via Caballero Monte Sereno CA 95030

KOOMEY, RICHARD ALAN, lawyer; b. N.Y.C., Sept. 20, 1932; s. Garo H. and Ruth (Mushekian) K.; m. Cynthia C. Chaffee, Feb. 18, 1961 (div. 1974); children: Jonathan G., Gregory C., Christopher D. AB, Columbia Coll., 1957, MS, 1958; LLB, NYU, 1962. Bar: N.Y. 1962, U.S. Ct. Appeals (3d cir.) 1968, N.C. 1982. Assoc. Chadbourne, Parke, Whiteside & Wolf, N.Y.C., 1966-69; asst. gen. counsel Sperry & Hutchinson Co., N.Y.C., 1969-80; gen. counsel Sperry & Hutchinson Furniture Inc., High Point, N.C., 1980-82; of counsel Robert E. Sheehan Assocs., High Point, 1982-83, Contino, Ross & Benedict, N.Y.C., 1983-84; dep. gen. counsel Pechiney Corp. and Howmet Corp., Greenwich, Conn., 1984-97; semi-ret. pvt. practice, 1997—2001; ret., 2002. Adj. prof. law St. John's U. Sch. of Bus., Jamaica, N.Y., 1983-85. Trustee Union Free Sch. Dist. 3, Huntington Station, N.Y., 1966-67. Served to capt. USAF, 1952-56. Mem. N.C. Bar Assn.

KOON, RAY HAROLD, management and security consultant; b. Little Mountain, S.C., Nov. 19, 1934; s. Harold Clay and Jessie Rae (Epting) K.; m. Bertha Mae Gardner, Aug. 19, 1958; children: Shari Madilyn Koon Goode, Schyler Michele Koon Richards, Kamela Suzanne Koon Scott. BSBA, Old Dominion U., 1957; postgrad., Columbia (S.C.) Coll., 1957—58. Lic. pvt. pilot. Supr. office svcs. FBI, Norfolk, Va., 1953-61, Las Vegas, Nev., 1961-62; agt. State Gaming Control Bd., Carson City, Nev., 1962-64, coord., 1967-80, chief of investigations, 1980-83; prodn. control mgr. Colite Industries, Inc., West Columbia, S.C., 1964-67; pres. Assoc. Gaming Consultants, Las Vegas, 1983; dir. gaming surveillance Hilton Hotels Corp., Beverly Hills, Calif., 1983-86; pres. JRJ Enterprises, Las Vegas, 1986-88, Assoc. Cons. Enterprises, Las Vegas, 1983—, Assoc. Gaming Cons., 1983—, CEO, 1990—. Past sec. Sta. KNIS-FM. Editor, pub. Ray Koon's Gaming/Gram, 1986—; columnist Casino Gaming Internat., 1990-92. Chief vols. Warren Engine Co. 1, Carson City Fire Dept., 1962-83; mem. Carson City Sheriff's Aero Squadron, 1983—, past comdr.; past mem. exec. bd. Nev. Bapt. Conv. With U.S. Army, 1957-59. Mem. Nev. Arbitration Assn. (bd. dirs. 1986-90), Las Vegas C. of C. (mem. commerce crime prevention and legis. action coms. 1989-90), Zelzah Shrine Aviation Club (past comdr.), Nat. Intelligence and Counterintelligence Assn. (bd. dirs. 1995-99), Officers, Toastmasters, Masons. Republican. Avocations: flying, do-it-yourself projects. Office: Ste D 2815 S Jones Blvd Las Vegas NV 89146-5623 E-mail: consultace@aol.com.

KOON, WANG-SANG, mathematician, researcher; s. Ziang-Yuen Kuen and Soo-Wu Chow; m. Marilyn P. Wong, June 18, 1972; children: Jidan, Danfeng. BA in Math., U. Calif., Berkeley, 1968, MA in Econs., 1972, PhD in Math., 1997. Instr. City Coll., San Francisco, 1982—90, Caltech, Pasadena, Calif., 1997—, postdoctoral scholar, 1997—2002, sr. scientist, 2002—. Reviewer Report on Math. Physics, 1997, Soc. for Indsl. and Applied Math., Phila., 1999—, Math. Reviews, 2002, Celestrial Mechanics and Dynamical Astronomy, 2000—02, AIAA, 2000—02; presenter in field. Contbr. articles to profl. jours. Fellow Econ. fellow, Ford Found., U. Calif., Berkeley, 1969—72. Mem.: Soc. for Indsl. and Applied Math., Am. Math. Soc., Phi Beta Kappa. Achievements include mathematically proving the existence of an interplanetary transport network that will allow for low energy interplanetary space missions; design of Low Energy Lunar Transfer and Capture. Office: California Inst Tech Control and Dynamical Systems 81-107 Pasadena CA 91125-0001 Office Fax: 626-796-8914. E-mail: koon@cds.caltech.edu.

KOONCE, CALVIN SCOTT, brokerage firm executive, physicist; b. Columbus, Ga., Dec. 9, 1937; s. Loftin Burns and Virginia (Scott) K.; m. Janet Elizabeth Bell, July 22, 1967; children: Elizabeth Ann, Kathleen Sharon, Franklin Scott. BS, MIT, 1960; PhD, U. Calif., Berkeley, 1967. Physicist Nat. Bur. Standards, Gaithrsburg, Md., 1967-75; pres. Koonce Securities, Inc., Bethesda, Md., 1979-99, chmn., 1999—; pres. Montgomery Investment Mgmt., Bethesda, 1989—. Contbr. articles to profl. jours. Recipient Disting. Young Scientist award Md. Acad. Scis., 1969; fellow NSF, 1963. Mem. Am. Phys. Soc., Security Traders Assn. of Washington (pres. 1987), Beta Theta Pi. Republican. Presbyterian. Home: 9101 Kendale Rd Potomac MD 20854-4512 Office: Koonce Securities Inc 6550 Rock Spring Dr Ste 600 Bethesda MD 20817-1185 E-mail: calvin@koonce.net.

KOONCE, JOHN PETER, investment company executive, educator; b. Coronado, Calif., Jan. 8, 1932; s. Allen Clark and Elizabeth (Webb) K.; m. Marilyn Rose Campbell, Sept. 21, 1952; children: Stephen Allen, William Clark, Peter Marshall. BS, U.S. Naval Acad., 1954; postgrad., U. So. Calif., 1957, U. Alaska, 1961, U. Ill., 1968-69; MS in Ops. Rsch., Fla. Inst. Tech., 1970; postgrad., Claremont Grad. Sch., 1970. Indsl. engr. Aluminum Co. Am., Lafayette, Ind., 1954-56; electronic rsch. engr. Autonetics Divsn. N.Am. Aviation, Downey, Calif., 1956-57; sys. field engr. Remington Rand Univac, Fayetteville, N.C., 1957-59; project engr. RCA Svc. Co., Cheyenne, Wyo., 1959-60, project supr. Clear, Alaska, 1960-62, Yorkshire, Eng., 1962-64, re-entry signature analyst Patrick AFB, Fla., 1964-66; mem. tech. staff TRW Sys. Group, Washington, 1966-68; mgr. ops. rsch. sys. analysis Magnavox Co., Urbana, Ill., 1968-69; tech. advisor EDP, to USAF, Aeroject Electro Sys. Co., Azusa, Calif., Woomera, Australia, 1969-72; investment exec. Shearson Hammill, L.A., 1972-74, Reynolds Securities, L.A., 1974-75; v.p. investments Shearson Hayden Stone, Glendale, 1975-77; v.p. accounts Paine, Webber, Jackson & Curtis, Inc., L.A., 1977-82; pres. Argo Fin. Corp., Santa Monica, Calif., 1982-83, Fin. Packaging Corp., Flintridge, Calif., 1983—; dir. Republic Resources, Inc., 2001—02. Fin. lectr. Princess Line Cruise Ships; tchr. investments Citrus Coll., Azusa, Calif., Claremont (Calif.) Evening Sch.; host, commentator Sta. KWHY-TV, L.A., (weekly) West of Wall Street, 1986-87; bd. dirs. Republic Resources, Inc. Contbr. articles to bus. jours. V.p. Claremont Rep. Club, 1973, pres., 1974; chmn. Verdugo Hosp. Assos., 1979. Mem. Nat. Assn. Security Dealers, Santa Maria Valley C. of C., Navy League U.S., Naval Acad. Alumni Assn., La Can. Flintridge Tournament Roses Assn. (patron), Masons (32d degree, master 1987, pres. dist. officers assn.), Shriners, Kiwanis (pres. La Canada 1995-96, Hixson fellow 2001), Marbella Golf and Country Club (founding). Home: 415 Foxenwood Dr Santa Maria CA 93455-4228 Office: 15233 Ventura Blvd Ste 404 Sherman Oaks CA 91403-2218

KOONCE, NEIL WRIGHT, lawyer; b. Kinston, N.C., July 8, 1947; s. Harold Wright and Edna Earle (Regan) K.; m. Virginia Gayle Evans, Feb. 27, 1993; children: Channing, Carl Younger, Ginny Younger. AB, U. N.C., 1969; JD, Wake Forest U., 1974; postgrad. exec. program, U. Va., 1983. Bar: N.C. 1973, U.S. Dist. Ct. (mid. dist.) N.C. 1975, U.S. Ct. Appeals (4th cir.) 1978, U.S. Supreme Ct. 1981. Atty. Cone Mills Corp., Greensboro, N.C., 1974-81, sr. atty., 1981-83, asst. gen. counsel, 1983-87, gen. counsel, 1987—, v.p., 1989—, v.p., gen. counsel, corp. sec., 1999—. Bd. dirs. Family and Children's Svcs., Greensboro, 1981-89, S.C. Energy Users Com., Columbia, S.C., 1984-89, Carolina Utility Customer's Assn., Raleigh, 1983-90, 94—, N.C. Found. for Rsch. and Econ. Edn., 1986-87, 93—, Electricity Consumers Resource Coun., Washington, 1987, 92—, vice chmn., 1990, chmn., 1991; bd. dirs. N.C. Citizens for Bus. and Industry, Raleigh, 1991-96, Met. YMCA, Greensboro, 1991-95, Salvation Army Boys and Girls Clubs, Greensboro, 1996—, S.C. Mfrs. Alliance, 1998—, N.C. Mfrs. Assn., 1998—. With AUS, 1970-71. Mem. ABA, N.C. Bar Assn., N.C. Textile Mfrs. Assn., Greensboro Bar Assn., Rotary (sec. 1983-86, bd. dirs. 1985-90, pres. 1988). Democrat. Presbyterian. Home: 200 Irving Pl Greensboro NC 27408-6510 Office: Cone Mills Corp # 300 804 Green Valley Rd Greensboro NC 27408-7020

KOONIN, STEVEN ELLIOT, physicist, educator, academic administrator; b. Bklyn., Dec. 12, 1951; BS, Calif. Inst. Tech., 1972; PhD, MIT, 1975. Asst. prof. Calif. Inst. Tech., Pasadena, Calif., 1975-78, assoc. prof., 1978-81, prof., 1981—, provost, 1995—. Cons. Inst. for Def. Analysis, MITRE Corp., Lawrence Livermore Nat. Lab., Argonne Nat. Lab., Sci. Applications Internat. Corp. Author: Computational Physics, 1985, Computational Nuclear Physics, vol. 1, 1991, vol. 2, 1993. Recipient Green Prize for Creative Scholarship, Calif. Inst. Tech., 1972, Assoc. Students Teaching award Calif. Inst. Tech., 1975-76, Sr. U.S. Scientist award Humboldt Found., 1985-86, Fusion Power Assocs. Leadership award, 1994, E.O. Lawrence award U.S. Dept. Energy, 1998; Alfred P. Sloan fellow, 1977-81. Fellow: AAAS, Am. Phys. Soc. (chmn. divsn. nuclear physics 1988—89, exec bd. dirs. 1994—96), Am. Acad. Arts and Scis.; mem.: Coun. Fgn. Rels., Calif. Coun. on Sci. and Tech. Office: Calif Inst Tech Office Of Provost 206-31 Pasadena CA 91125-0001 E-mail: koonin@caltech.edu.

KOONS, IRVIN LOUIS, design and marketing executive, graphic artist, consultant; b. Harrisburg, Pa., Mar. 14, 1922; s. Frank and Rose (Silver) K.; m. Leah Fay, Dec. 25, 1949; children: Adam, Jonathan, Joshua. Grad., Pratt Inst., 1942, New Sch., N.Y., 1946; student and instr., Ecole Des Beaux Arts, Fontainebleau, France, 1948-50; student, others schs. in France, Switzerland and Italy, 1947-49. Designer, chief exec. officer Irv Koons Assocs. (subs. Saatchi and Saatchi Worldwide, since 1983), N.Y.C., 1950-89; sr. advisor to adminstr. UN Devel. Program, N.Y.C., 1989—. Sr. advisor Div. for Pvt. Sector in Devel. and UNISTAR, UNDP; founder, co-dir. Internat. Design Assistance Commn., 1984—; sr. advisor to adminstr. UN Devel. Programme, 1989—; past cultural attache, spl. cons. U.S. Dept. State, India; dir. 1st internat. packaging exhbn. USIA; tchr. various art schs.; advisor Inferential Focus Forum; lectr. mktg. NYU, U. Pa., Columbia U., U. Tel Aviv, Northwestern U. and others in Eng., Holland, France, Switzerland, Brazil, India; expert legal witness corp. and product image/identity. Exhibited paintings and drawings in group shows in U.S. and France, represented in permanent collections including Mus. Modern Art, Cooper Hewitt Nat. Design Mus., the Jewish Mus., Yeshiva U. Mus.; complete collection of works on 7,000 slides plus several thousand sketches and finished items at Hagley Mus. and Libr., Wilmington, Del.; slides also available on CD-Rom; prin. works include Life of Moses series, 1975-78, stained glass wall for Fedn. Jewish Philanthropies, 1975, series coord. Torah ornaments for Temple Emmanuel, N.J., 1986; designed stage sets for traveling shows of original broadway casts: Harriette, Three Sisters, Blythe Spirit, Springtime for Henry, others; illus. many books and mags. including Ladies Home Jour., Good Housekeeping, Forturne, Seventee, Sports Illustrated; designer 1st Daily offset newspaper in world, Middletown Daily Record, 1956 (Ayer Cup best design 1957, 58), redesign Washington Star, 1969; cons. editor Graphis Packaging, Switzerland, 1970; art critic The Statesman newspaper, India, 1946; contbr. articles on mktg. to profl. jours.; subject one-man articles in mags. including Graphis, Idea, 1976, others; 40-min. multi-image show of life and work produced by PDC, 1982. Founder, co-dir. Internat. Design Assistance Commn.; bd. dirs., exec. com. Found. for Future Generations; past bd. dirs. Am.-Israel Cultural Found.; bd. dirs., trustee Temple Emanuel, Englewood N.J., 1987; trustee Art Ctr. No. N.J., Englewood, 1960-68; artist in residence Melton Orgn., 2003; contbr. logo and trade mark designs to non-profit civic orgns. including Am. Cancer Soc., Fedn. Jewish Philanthropies, World Hunger, Sloan-Kettering Meml. Hosp., United Cerebral Palsy, Jewish Theol. Sem., many others. With inf. U.S. Army, 1942-46, CBI. Recipient Clio award, 1976, 77, 81, Gold Clio award, 79, 84, 88, Best ann. report design, 1957, 59, 61, Silver award Variety Store Merchandisers, 1967, Gold award Variety Store Merchandisers, 1970, Gold award Internat. Folding Carton Competition, 1964, Gold award Paperboard Packaging Council, 1974, awards N.Y. Art Dir.'s Club, 1958, 59, 63, 76, 77, 79 (2), awards Am. Inst. Graphic Arts, 1955, 58, 59, 60 (3), 61, 65 (2), 72, awards Package Design Mag., 1963-68, 70 (3), Gold awards Package Design Council, 1977, 79, 80 (2), 87 (2); Best of Best 1985 (2); Desi award 1981, Indsl. Design awards, 1968, 75, Package of Yr. award, 1968, Nat. Printing award, 1981, Communication Arts awards, 1960, 64, 66, 67, 71, Best Bottle of Yr. award, 1975, awards Soc. Illustrators, 1959, 68, awards N.J. Art Dir.'s Club, 1962, 65 (3), 68, awards NYU, 1973, 74, Pratt. Inst. Alumni Achievement award, 1998, others. Mem. Package Designers Coun. (Person of Yr. 1982, bd. dirs. 1962—), Indsl. Design Soc. Am., Packaging Inst., Am. Inst. Graphic Arts. Avocations: collecting historical packages, rewriting and illustrating legends, fables and fairy tales. Home: 213 Engle St Tenafly NJ 07670-2139 Office: Irv Koons Assocs 213 Engle St Tenafly NJ 07670-2139 E-mail: ikadesign@aol.com.

KOONTS, JONES CALVIN, retired education educator; b. Lexington, N.C., Sept. 19, 1924; s. Harvey Hill and Elsie (Tussey) K.; m. Cortlandt Morper, Sept. 6, 1953; children: Carlisle Woodson, Camille Walton. AB in History and English magna cum laude, Catawba Coll., Salisbury, N.C., 1945; MA in Sociology, George Peabody Coll., Vanderbilt U., Nashville, 1949, PhD in Edn., 1958; Lit.D., Catawba Coll., 1979. Tchr. English and social studies Boyden High Sch., Salisbury, 1945-48; dir.-asst. student teaching George Peabody Coll., 1951-52; mem. faculty Erskine Coll., Due West, S.C., 1949-90, prof. edn., 1949-90, prof. emeritus, 1990—, chmn. dept. edn., 1949-87. Tchr. adult edn. Abbeville (S.C.) County Community Ctr., 1955; tchr. grad. courses Coastal Carolina Coll., U. S.C., 1971-78; also Clemson U., 1956; postdoctoral researcher UCLA, 1977. Author: (poetry) Since Promontory, 1967, Straws in the Wind, 1968, Under the Umbrella, 1971, A Slice of the Sun, 1976, A Stone's Throw, 1986, Lines: Opus 8, 1994; editor: (poetry) Green Leaves in January, 1972, Inklings, 1983. Rep. S.C. Bd. Edn., 1966-71; bd. commrs. Piedmont Tech. Coll., 1972-75; alumni bd. dirs. Catawba Coll., 1966; bd. advisers Gardner-Webb Coll., 1981-89; bd. dirs. Due West Retirement Ctr., 1993-99. Jesse H. Jones scholar, 1951; Algernon Sydney Sullivan scholar, 1951; fellow Council So. Univs., 1957-58; Peabody-Harvard scholar, 1960; Fulbright grantee, 1964; fellow, seminarist Worcester Coll., Oxford U., Eng., 1985; recipient Disting. Service key Phi Delta Kappa. Mem. N.C. Edn. Assn. (chpt. sec. treas. 1946-47), S.C. Assn. Student Teaching (founder, 1st pres. 1955-56), S.C. Council Tchr. Edn., S. Atlantic Philosophy Edn. Soc., Poetry Soc. S.C. (bd. dirs., William Gilmore Simms poetry prize 1973, Unicorn Poetry prize 1974, Lyric Poetry prize, 1975, Elizabeth B. Coker Poetry award 1977), Nat. Assn. Tchr. Educators (del S.C.), Am. Assn. Colls. for Tchr. Edn. (rep. S.C.), S.C. Assn. of Tchr. Educators (pres. 1979-80, SCATE Life Membership award 1999), Acad. Am. Poets, S.C. Acad. of Authors, Am. Poets and Writers (dir. 2001—). Presbyterian. Home: PO Box 163 Due West SC 29639-0163 *My philosophy of life is from Salutation to the Dawn, written in Sanskrit: "Yesterday is but a dream, tomorrow only a vision; but today well lived makes every yesterday a dream of happiness and every tomorrow a vision of hope".*

KOONTZ, ALFRED JOSEPH, JR., financial and operating management executive, consultant; b. Balt., Mar. 6, 1942; s. Alfred J. and Mary Agnes (Valis) K.; m. Kay Francis Frank, Aug. 4, 1962; children— Debbie Kay, Denise Marie, Stacey Lynn, Alfred Joseph, III. BSBA, Pa. State U., 1964. CPA, Md. Mgr. Price Waterhouse & Co., Balt., 1964-73, sr. mgr. N.Y.C., 1973-74, Morristown, N.J., 1974-75; v.p. fin Piper Aircraft Corp., Lock Haven, Pa., 1975-80, sr. v.p. fin., 1980-85, sr. v.p. fin., treas., 1985-86, exec. v.p., chief operating officer, 1987-88; pres., dir. Piper Acceptance Corp., Lakeland, Fla., 1985-88; sr. v.p. fin. and adminstrn., treas., bd. dirs. Todd Shipyards Corp., Seattle, 1988-91; exec. v.p., CFO Pay'N Pak Stores Inc., Bellevue, Wash., 1992-93; pres. Alfred J. Koontz & Assoc., Vero Beach, 1993—; co-owner, CFO Pub. Telecomm. Providers, Inc., Vero Beach, 1993-97; co-owner, operator A&K Enterprises of Vero, Inc., 1994—. Client rels. exec. Diamond Cluster Internat., Chgo., 1998—; CFO Wannabe's, LLC, 1999. Mem. AICPA, Md. Assn. CPAs, Inst. Mgmt. Accts. Home: 1790 Sand Dollar Way Vero Beach FL 32963-2723 Fax: 772-234-6077. E-mail: akcov1@aol.com.

KOONTZ, CARL LENNIS, II, investment counselor; b. Oct. 28, 1942; s. Carl Lennis and Jessie Marie (Rhodes) K.; m. Rose Marie Catalano, May 6, 1978. BS, U. Tenn., 1964, MS magna cum laude, 1968. Quality control analyst Ford Motor Co., Cin., 1965-66; mgmt. trainee Abbott, Procter & Paine, Richmond, Va., 1968-70; v.p. pension cons. Paine, Webber, N.Y.C., 1970-76; asst. v.p. Scudder, Stevens & Clark, N.Y.C., 1976-78, v.p. investments, 1978-85, mng. dir., 1985-87; v.p. Scudder, Stevens & Clark of Can., Toronto, Ont., 1984-87, Smith Barney Capital Mgmt., 1987-92; v.p. investment policy com. Capital Mgmt. Assocs., N.Y.C., 1992, sr. v.p., 1993; pres. Capital Mgmt. Mid-Cap Fund, 1994, co-head equity investments, 1996, co-chief investment officer, mng. dir., 1998; pres. Capital Mgmt. Small-Cap Fund, 1998; mng. dir. Weiss, Peck & Greer, 2000—; head Large Cap Growth Group, 2001—. Mgr. WPG Large-Cap Growth Fund, 2001—; dean's adv. coun. Coll. of Bus., U. Tenn. With U.S. Army ANG, 1965-70. Fellow Fin. Analysis Fedn. (chartered fin. analyst); mem. Investment Counsel Assn. Am. (chartered investment counselor), N.Y. Soc. Security Analysts, Madison Ave. Sports Car Driving and Chowder Soc., Holland Lodge, Univ. Club, Antique Automobile Club Am., Pontiac Oakland Club Internat., Bond Club N.Y. Avocations: antique cars, model railroading, photography, swimming, tennis. Home: 373 Middlesex Rd Darien CT 06820-2518 E-mail: Lennis.Koontz@robecousa.com.

KOONTZ, DEAN RAY, writer; b. Everett, Pa., July 9, 1945; s. Raymond and Florence (Logue) K.; m. Gerda Ann Cerra, Oct. 15, 1966. BS, Shippensburg U., 1966, LittD (hon.), 1989. Tchr. Appalachian Poverty Program, Saxton, Pa., 1966-67, Mechanicsburg (Pa.) Sch. Dist., 1967-69; freelance writer Orange, Calif., 1969—. Author of over 59 novels including Star Quest, 1968, The Fall of the Dream Machine, 1969, Fear That Man, 1969, Anti-Man, 1970, Beastchild, 1970 (Hugo award nomination 1971), Dark of the Woods, 1970, The Dark Symphony, 1970, Hell's Gate, 1970, The Crimson Witch, 1971, A Darkness in My Soul, 1972, The Flesh in the Furnace, 1972, Starblood, 1972, Time Thieves, 1972, Warlock, 1972, A Werewolf Among Us, 1973, Hanging On, 1973, The Haunted Earth, 1973, Demon Seed, 1973, rev. edit., 1997, After the Last Race, 1974, Nightmare Journey, 1975, Night Chills, 1976, The Vision, 1977, Whispers, 1980, Phantoms, 1983, Darkfall, 1984, Twilight Eyes, 1985, Strangers, 1986, Watchers, 1987, Lightning, 1988, Servants of Twilight, 1989, The Bad Place, 1990, Cold Fire, 1991, Hideaway, 1992, Dragon Tears, 1993, Mr. Murder, 1993, Winter Moon, 1994, Dark Rivers of the Heart, 1994, Strange Highways, 1995, Intensity, 1996, Santa's Twin, 1996, Fear Nothing, 1997, Tick Tock, 1997, Sole Survivor, 1997, From the Corner of His Eye, 2000, Icebound, 2000, False Memory, 2000, One Door Away from Heaven, 2001, By the Light of the Moon, 2002, The Face, 2003, others under pseudonyms David Axton, Brian Coffey, Deanna Dwyer, K.R. Dwyer, John Hill, Leigh Nichols, Anthony North, Richard Paige, and Owen West. Office: William Morris Agy 1325 Avenue Of The Americas New York NY 10019-6026*

KOONTZ, LAWRENCE L., JR., state supreme court justice; b. Roanoke, Va, Jan. 25, 1940; BS, Va. Polytech. U., 1962. Asst. commonwealth's atty., Roanoke, 1967—68; judge Va. Juvenile & Domestic Rels. Dist. Ct., 1968—76, Va. Cir. Ct. (23rd cir.), 1976—85, Ct. Appeals of Va., 1985—95, Supreme Ct. of Va., 1995—. Mem.: ABA. Office: PO Box 687 Salem VA 24153-0687

KOOP, CHARLES EVERETT, surgeon, educator, former surgeon general; b. Bklyn., Oct. 14, 1916; s. John Everett and Helen (Apel) K.; m. Elizabeth Flanagan, Sept. 19, 1938; children: Allen van Benschoten, Norman Apel, David Charles Everett, Elizabeth. AB, Dartmouth Coll., 1937, DSc (hon.) (hon.), 1989; MD, Cornell U., 1941; DSc in Medicine, U. Pa., 1947, DSc (hon.) (hon.), 1990; LLD (hon.) (hon.), Ea. Bapt. Coll., 1960, Phila. Coll. Osteo. Medicine, 1979, LaSalle Coll., 1983, Colby-Sawyer Coll., 1988, Princeton U., 1989, Hahnemann U., 1989, U. Miami, 1991, U. Cin., 1991; MD (hon.) (hon.), U. Liverpool, Eng., 1968; LHD (hon.) (hon.), Wheaton Coll., 1973, Phila. Theol. Sem., 1980, Chgo. Med. Sch., 1988, Brown U., 1990; DSc (hon.) (hon.), Gwynedd Mercy Coll., 1978, Washington and Jefferson Coll., 1979, Marquette U., 1983, Ea. Mich. U., 1985, N.Y. Med. Coll., 1985, Ball State U., 1987, Kirskville Coll. Osteo. Med., 1988, Albany Med. Coll., 1988, Colby Coll., 1988, Yeshiva U., 1988, Phila. Coll. Pharmacy and Sci., 1988, Baylor Coll. Medicine, 1988, U. Mass., Boston, 1989, Brandeis U., 1990, Northwestern U., 1990, U. New England, 1991; D. Pub. Svc. (hon.) (hon.), George Washington U., 1991; DPH, Cedar Crest Coll., 1995; D in Humanities, So. Utah U., 1997; LLD, Med. Coll. Pa., 1997. Diplomate Am. Bd. Surgery, Nat. Bd. Med. Examiners. Intern Pa. Hosp., Phila., 1941-42; fellow in surgery U. Pa. Hosp., Phila., 1942-47; fellow in pediat. surgery Children's Hosp., Boston, 1946; surgeon-in-chief Children's Hosp. of Phila., 1948-81; with U. Pa. Sch. Medicine, 1942-85, prof., 1959-85; former dep. asst. sec. for health HHS; surg. gen. of U.S., 1981-89; former dir. internat. health USPHS, from 1982; chair Safe Kids Nat. Campaign, Washington; dir. Elizabeth De Camp McInery prof. surgery C. Everett Koop Inst. Dartmouth-Hitchkock Med. Ctr., Hanover, N.H., 1993—. Cons. USN, 1964—81; sr. scholar C. Everett Koop Inst. at Dartmouth; dir. Ready to Learn Program Carnegie Found., 1993—95; McEnerny prof. surgery Dartmouth Med. Sch. Author: Visible and Palpable Lesions in Children, The Right to Live, The Right to Die, 1976, The Right to Live, The Right to Die, rev. edit., 1980, Smoking: The New Book of Knowledge, 1989; author: (with E. Koop) Sometimes Mountains Move, 1979; author: (with F. A. Schaeffer) Whatever Happened to the Human Race?, 1979; author: Koop: The Memoirs of America's Family Doctor, 1991; author: (with T. Johnson) Let's Talk, 1992; editor: surgery sect. Jour. Clin. Pediatrics, 1961—64; mem. editl. bd.: Zeitschrift fur Kinderchirurgie and Grenzqebiete, 1964—81, editor-in-chief: Jour. Pediatric Surgery, 1965—77, editl. cons.: Japanese Jour. Pediatric Surgery and Medicine, 1970—81, chmn. editorial bd.: PHS Reports, 1982—89, mem. editorial adv. bd.: Tobacco Control: An Internat. Jour.; contbr. Bd. dirs., pres. Nat. Health Mus. Inc.; bd. dirs., chmn. sci. adv. com. Biopure; chmn. Patient Med. Edn., 1993—96, Patient Med. Record, Inc., 1997—; Bd. dirs. Med. Assistance Programs, Inc., Brunswick, Ga., Friends Nat. Libr. of Medicine. Decorated chevalier Legion of Honor France, Order Duarte, Sanchez and Mella Dominican Republic, Chevalier French Legion of Honor; named Hon. Citizen, City of Balt., 1985; recipient medal, City of Marseille, Presbyn. Man of Yr. award, Presbyn. Social Union Phila., 1975, Super Achiever of Yr. award, Phila. chpt. Juvenile Diabetes Found., 1975, Man of Yr. award, Jewish Community Chaplaincy Svc. Phila., 1975, Copernicus medal, Polish Surg. Soc., 1977, Gold medal, Children's Hosp. Phila., 1981, Sec. of Health of Commonwealth of Pa. award, 1981, Thomas Linacre award, Nat. Fedn. Cath. Physicians Guild, 1981, Key to City of St. Louis, 1985, Award of Distinction, Alumni Assn. Cornell U. Med. Coll., 1988, Humanitarian Svc. award, City of Boston, 1989, Harry S. Truman award, City of Independence, Mo., 1990, Daniel Webster award, Dartmouth Coll., 1990, John Wiley Jones Disting. Lectr. award, Rochester Inst. Tech., 1990, NAS Public Welfare medal, 1990, Tyler prize, U. So. Calif., 1991, Albert Schweitzer prize, Johns Hopkins U., 1991, Person of Yr. award, Nat. Hosp. Orgn., 1991, C. Everett Koop Hon. Lectr. medal named in his honor, Anchor & Caduceus Soc., 1991, C. Everett Koop Health Adv. award named in his honor, Am. Soc. for Health Care Mktg. and Pub. Rels., Gustav O. Lienhard award, Inst. Medicine, 1992, Presdl. medal of Freedom, 1995, Heinz Found. award, 1995, Medal of Honor, Am. Cancer Soc., 2000, Presdl. Medal of Freedom; scholar Disting. scholar to Carnegie Found. for advancement of teaching. Fellow: ACS, Am. Acad. Pediatrics (William E. Ladd Gold medal), Royal Coll. Physicians and Surgeons of Glasgow (hon.), Royal Coll. Surgeons Eng. (hon.); mem.: AMA, Societé Suisse De Chirurgie Infantile, Deutschen Gesselschaft für Kinderchirugi, Societé Française de Chirurgie Infantile, Assn. Mil. Surgeons U.S. (pres. 1982, 1987, Founders medal), Internat. Soc. Surgery, Brit. Assn. Pediatric Surgeons (Dennis Browne Gold medal), Soc. U. Surgeons, Royal Soc. Medicine, Am. Surg. Assn., Sigma Xi. Office: Dartmouth Coll Dartmouth-Hitchcock Ctr C Everett Koop Inst Hanover NH 03755*

KOOPMAN, BARBARA GOLDENBERG, psychiatrist; b. Boston; d. Morris and Fannie (Goretsky) Goldenberg; m. Philip Koopman, Dec. 19, 1967 (div. Oct. 1981); m. Morris Klein, Dec. 30, 1985 (dec.). BS, Simmons Coll., 1944; MA, Smith Coll., 1945; PhD in Lit., Columbia U., 1951; MD, Tufts U., 1957. Diplomate Am. Bd. Psychiatry and Neurology. Lecturer Columbia U., N.Y.C., 1948-50; sr. psychiatrist Manhattan State Hosp., N.Y.C., 1961-62; clinical asst. psychiatry Mt. Sinai Hosp., N.Y.C., 1961-66; attending staff psychiatry Brookdale Hosp., Bklyn., 1962-71; faculty Inst. Short-Term Dynamic Psychotherapy St. Clare's Hosp., Denville, NJ, 1991—95. Translator: The Impulsive Character, 1974; editor Jour. Orgonomy, 1967-92; editor, co-translator: The Final Appeal to Mankind, 1997; contbr. articles to profl. jours. Fellow Mt. Sinai Hosp., 1959-61, Columbia U., 1948-51. Mem. Am. Psychiatric Assn. (life), Am. Coll. Orgonomy (pres. 1986-87). Avocations: fine arts, alternative healing. Home: 222 Riverside Dr New York NY 10025-6809 Office: 222 Riverside Dr New York NY 10025-6809 E-mail: MOZG7@aol.com.

KOOPMAN, RICHARD NELSON, engineer, consultant; b. Buffalo, N.Y., Nov. 26, 1945; s. Richard John Walter and Nellie Elkins (Wisbrock) K.; m. Mary Margaret Blume, July 17, 1970; Anthony Blake, Laura Nicole. BSME, Washington U., 1968; MSME, U. Minn., 1969, PhD, 1975. Registered profl. engr., Ill., Minn. Engr. Honeywell, Inc., Mpls., 1973-75, Argonne (Ill.) Nat. Lab, 1975-80; mem. tech. staff, supr. Bell Labs, Naperville, Ill., 1980-85; sr. cons. Engring. Sys. Inc., Aurora, 1996—2002, dir. mech. and elec. engring., 2002—; dir. McDonald's Corp., Oakbrook, Ill., 1985-96; v.p. Fla. Plastics Internat., Inc., Evergreen Park, Ill., 1999—2001. Contbr. articles to profl. jours.; patentee in field. Mem. Hinsdale (Ill.) Planning Commn., 1992-95, Zoning Bd. Appeals, 1995-96; bd. dirs. Bradley U. Parents Orgn., 1995-99, career com. chair, 1996-98. Named Supr. of Yr., INROADS-Chgo., 1991. Mem. ASME (section chmn. 1980-81), Nat. Soc. Profl. Engrs., Hinsdale Jaycees (treas. 1980-83), Woodlands Home Owners Assn. (treas. 1998—), Tau Beta Pi, Omicron Delta Kappa, Pi Tau Sigma. Mem. United Ch. of Christ. Office: Engring Sys Inc 3851 Exchange Ave Aurora IL 60504 E-mail: rnkoopman@prodigy.net.

KOOPMAN, WILLIAM JAMES, medical educator, internist, immunologist; b. Lafayette, Ind., Aug. 19, 1945; s. William James and Barbara Mary (Morehouse) K.; m. Lilliane Kathryn Desimone, June 15, 1968; children: Benjamin, Anna, Rebecca, Steven. BA, Washington and Jefferson U., 1967; MD, Harvard U., 1972. Diplomate Am. Bd. Internal Medicine. Intern/resident in medicine Mass. Gen. Hosp., Boston, 1972-74; rsch. fellow NIH, Bethesda, Md., 1974-77; from asst. prof., assoc. prof. to prof. medicine specializing in rheumatology and clin. immunology U. Ala., Birmingham, 1977—, Howard L. Holley prof. medicine, 1988-95, dir. Multipurpose Arthritis Ctr., 1983-96; chmn. Dept. Medicine, 1995—. Mem. nat. adv. coun. Nat. Inst. Arthritis, Musculo-skeletal and Skin Diseases, 1987-90; chmn. bd. sci. counselors, NIH, NIAMS, 1991-95. Editor: Arthritis and Rheumatism jour., 1985—90, Arthritis and Allied Conditions, 14th edit.; contbr. more than 250 articles to profl. jours. Recipient Carol Nachman Rsch. prize Fed. Republic Germany, 1982. Fellow ACP (master), Am. Coll. Rheumatology (pres. Southeastern region 1986-87, treas. 1992-94, 2nd v.p. 1994-95, pres.-elect 1995-96, pres. 1996-97); mem. ACP (master), Am. Soc. Clin. Investigation (pres. 1990-91), Assn. Am. Physicians, Am. Assn. Immunologists, Inst. of Medicine, Birmingham Area C. of C. Presbyterian. Avocations: fishing, gardening. Office: U Ala Sch Medicine DERB 1808 7th Ave S # Bdb420 Birmingham AL 35233-1912

KÖÖRNA, ARNO, economist, educator; b. Tallinn, Estonia, Feb. 2, 1926; s. Artur and Anna-Helena (Schultz) K.; m. Eha Lind, Dec. 28, 1946; children: Silvia, Vello. PhD, Tartu U., Estonia, 1955; academician, Estonian Acad. Scis., Tallinn, 1973, PhD in Econs., 1970. Prof. Tartu U., 1972-75; sec. gen. Estonian Acad. Scis., 1973-82, v.p., 1982-91, pres., 1991-94, ex-pres., 1995. Author: Economic Motivation of Quality, 1978, Science in Estonia, 1993, Estonian Science in Transition, 1994; contbr. articles to profl. jours. Mem. Estonian Parliament, Tallinn, 1985-90; chmn. Estonian Sci. Coun., Estonia, 1992-94. Mem. Internat. Assn. IUS Primi Viri (mem. standing com.), World Futures Studies Fedn., Russian Acad. Humanities, Ctrl. European Acad. Sci. and Art (hon.). Home: Kapi 9-22 10136 Tallinn Estonia Office: Estonian Acad Scis Kohtu 6 10130 Tallinn Estonia E-mail: arno.koorna@mail.ee.

KOOS, GREG, museum director; b. Bloomington, Ill., Sept. 26, 1949; s. Anthony Oscar and Catherine (Rodgers) K.; m. Carol Lynn, Oct. 26, 1985. BA, The Union Inst., Cincinatti, 1995. Archivist McLean Co. Hist. Soc., Bloomington, Ill., 1977-87, exec. dir., 1987—. Bd. dirs. Bloomington-Normal Black History Project, 1992—; adj. asst. prof. history Ill. State U. Author: Bloomington's C&A Shops, 1987; editor: Irish Immigrants in McLean County, Illinois, 2000; contbr. articles to Material Culture, Historic Ill., New Hibernia Rev., Labor's Heritage, History News. Pres. Union Inst. Alumni Assn., 1998-2002; bd. dirs. Bloomington Downton Commn., 1999—; faculty McLean Co. C. of C., 1994—. Mem. Am. Assn. Museums (vis. com.), Am. Assn. State and Local History (award of merit 1981, 93, 99, certificate of commendation 1983), Am. Com. Irish Studies, Soc. Commercial Archeology. Democrat. Avocations: reading, cooking, walking, banjo, art. Office: McLean Co Museum of History 200 N Main St Bloomington IL 61701-3912 E-mail: gregkoos@McHistory.org.

KOPAC, ANDREW JOSEPH, automotive executive; b. Hackensack, N.J., May 21, 1947; s. Andrew S. and Mary C. (Spacek) Kopac; children from previous marriage: Andrew, Jeffrey. BA, Rutgers U., 1969; AAS in Mgmt., Middlesex County Coll., Woodbridge, N.J., 1981, AAS in Mktg., 1982. Quality control supr. Delco-Remy, New Brunswick, NJ, 1972-74, gen. foreman quality control, 1974-76; quality engr. Delco-Remy divsn. GM, New Brunswick, 1976-81, gen. supt. mfg., 1981-83, supt. quality control Fitzgerald, Ga., 1983-85, 1985-86, mgr. mfg. ops., 1988-91, supt. material control, 1991-93; pers. dir. Delco-Remy/Delphi Automotive Sys., Olathe, Kans., 1993—. With U.S. Army, 1969—71. Decorated Bronze Star; recipient Frank M. Chambers award, Middlesex County Coll., 1981—82. Mem.: VFW, Am. Legion. Roman Catholic. Avocations: coaching, youth soccer, coaching youth baseball, golf, gardening. Home: 12473 S Acuff Ct Olathe KS 66062 E-mail: andrewj.kopac@delphi.com.

KOPACK, PAMELA LEE (PAMELA LEE MACMINN), business services executive; b. Portland, Maine, July 25, 1951; d. Everett John Foye and Lois Florence (Loveland) MacMinn; m. Charles Thomas Kopack, Apr. 2, 1971. Student, Sears, Roebuck Ext. Inst., 1969-73, Newspaper Inst. Am., 1979-85. Sales staff Sears Roebuck & Co., Cleve., 1966-69, credit collector, 1972-75; exec. sec., asst. Cole Nat. Corp., Cleve., 1976-79; pres. Kopack Svc. Bur., Cleve., 1979—. Contbr. Poetry-People, 1975, Recollections of Yesterday, 1996, Call Me Jackie, 1997, Poets Elite - The Best Poems of 2000; author numerous poems; lyrics for songs recorded on single records and albums, 1974-79; author greeting cards, articles, short stories. Recipient Poetry award for Facets of a Housewife, 1977. Mem. NAFE, Career Guild (New Feature award 1982), Secs.

Workshop, P.S. for Profl. Secs. (Bur. Bus. Practice, article award 1979), Internat. Platform Assn., Ohio Women Bus. Leaders, Internat. Soc. Poets, Women's Opportunity Workshop Club.

KOPACZYNSKI, GERMAIN, priest; b. Chelsea, Mass., Apr. 24, 1946; s. Edmund Kopaczynski and Eleanor Szczepaniak. PhD, Boston Coll., 1977; STD, Alphonsianum, Rome, 1992. Philosophy prof. Saint Hyacinth Coll., Granby, Mass., 1976—, pres., 1982-91; dir. edn. Nat. Cath. Bioethics Ctr., Boston, 1993—. Mem. Franciscan Order, 1964—. Author: No Higher Court, 1995, Linguistic Ramifications, 1978. Adam Zajdel fellowship St. Hyacinth Coll., 1990. Mem. Am. Philos. Assn., Am. Cath. Philos. Assn., Cath. Theol. Soc. of Am., Soc. of Christian Ethics, Soc. of Christian Philosophers, Fellowship of Cath. Scholars. Roman Catholic. Office: Nat Cath Bioethics Ctr 159 Washington St Boston MA 02135-4325 E-mail: Frgermai@ncbcenter.org.

KOPCHINSKI, ANITA FRANCINE, pharmaceutical executive; b. Staten Island, N.Y., July 8, 1965; BS in Chemistry and Nuc. Medicine Tech., Wagner Coll., Staten Island, 1987; PhD in Analytical Chemistry, Kans. State U., Manhattan, 1994. Nuc. medicine technologist Mountainside Hosp., Montclair, NJ, 1987—89; sr. rsch. chemist Ashland Chem., Drew Divsns., Booton, NJ, 1994—95; rsch. scientist Pfizer Inc., Groton, Conn., 1995—98; sr. rsch. scientist Pfizer Inc, Groton, Conn., 1998—2001; sr. rsch. investigator, strategic external alliance mgmt. Pfizer Inc., Groton, Conn., 2001, prin. III, strategic alliances, 2001—. Contbr. articles to profl. jours. and conf. procs. Mem.: Am. Chem. Soc., Am. Assn. Pharm. Scientists. Office: Pfizer Inc Eastern Point Rd Groton CT 06340 Office Fax: 860-715-7266. E-mail: anita_f_kopchinski@groton.pfizer.com.

KOPE, JOSEPH B. retired humanities educator, consultant; b. Youngstown, Ohio, Aug. 5, 1926; s. Joseph Bartholomew and Veronica Pauline Kope. AB Hist., Univ. PA, Philadelphia, PA, 1951; BS Educ., Youngstown Univ., Youngstown, OH, 1961; MA English educ., Ohio State Univ., Columbus, OH, 1971. Educator English, social studies Youngstown Ohio Bd. of Ed., 1962—89; tchr. Savs. and Loan Inst. Pres. Youngstown Teachers of English, Youngstown, Ohio, 1967—69; chmn. dept. english Woodrow Wilson H.S., Youngstown, Ohio, 1969—79; chmn. history dept. Volney Rogers H.S., Youngstown, Ohio, 1984—89; adv. Jr. Achievement. Cpl. U.S. Army, 1945—46, W. Pacific & Philippine Islands. Martha Holden Jennings scholar. Mem.: Nat. Coun. Tchrs. English, Mahoning County Ret. Teachers, Polish-Am. Hist. Assn., Am. Coun. of Polish Culture, Butler Mus. of Am. Art, Kosciuszko Found. of NYC, Cleve. Mus. of Art, Mahoning Valley Hist. Soc., Saybrook Beach Club, Sr. Citizens Club, Polish Arts Club (bd. of dirs. 1992—96), Saxon Club, Alpha Phi Omega, Kappa Delta Pi. Roman Catholic. Avocations: gardening, reading, art & stamp collecting, piano, accordion. Home: 284 Wilcox Road Austintown OH 44515

KOPEC, JOHN WILLIAM, research scientist; b. Chgo., Nov. 5, 1936; s. John Frank and Marie Eva (Wreshnig) K.; m. Jean Elois Prather, Dec. 28, 1958 (div. June 1977); children: Brian More, Vaune Estra. AA, Chgo. City Coll., 1974; student, Ill. Inst. Tech., Chgo., 1974 80. Systems analyst Motorola, Chgo., 1959-61; asst. exptl. engr. Ill. Inst. Tech. Rsch. Inst., Chgo., 1961-68, extpl. engr., 1968-74, liaison engr. Chgo. and Geneva, Ill., 1974-81; supr. Riverbank Acoustical Labs., Ill. Inst. Tech. Rsch. inst., Chgo. and Geneva, Ill., 1986-94, lab. mgr., 1994—, ret., 1998. Author: The Sabines at Riverbank, 1997, contbr. articles to Jour. Acoustical Soc. Am.; paper reviewer, contbr. articles Internat. Noise Control Engrs. With USAF, 1955-59. Fellow: Acoustical Soc. Am. (chmn. archives and history 1992—94, sec. tech. com. 1991—94, mus. curator 1985—98, co-chmn. tech. program 2001, Silver cert. 2002); mem.: ASTM (chmn. awards com., sec. E 33.01 1980—98, appreciation award 1994), Can. Acoustical Soc., Soc. Automotive Engrs. (task group, paper reviewer), N.Y. Acad. Scis. Achievements include one of first smokeless fires for firefighters of U.S. Navy and U.S. Air Force; one of first to discover ionization of turbulent flow in a hypersonic wind tunnel; discovered Wallace Clement Sabine files previously thought destroyed; developed one of first rapid transit speech noise floor's, also an industrial colored noise floor map. Home: 5206 S Lotus Ave Chicago IL 60638-1632

KOPECEK, JINDRICH, biomedical scientist, biomaterials and pharmaceutics educator; b. Strakonice, Bohemia, Czechoslovakia, Jan. 27, 1940; came to U.S., 1986; s. Jan and Herta Zita (Krombholz) K.; m. Marie Porcari, Aug. 11, 1962 (Div. 1984); 1 child, Jana; m. Pavla Hrušková, Apr. 27, 1985. MS in Polymer Chemistry, Inst. Chem. Tech., Prague, Czechoslovakia, 1961; PhD in Polymer Chemistry, Inst. Macromolecular Chemistry, Prague, 1965; DSc in Chemistry, Czechoslovak Acad. Scis., Prague, 1990. Rsch. sci. officer Inst. Macromolecular Chemistry, Prague, 1965-67, 68-72, head lab. of med. polymers, 1972-80; postdoctoral fellow NRC, Ottawa, Can., 1967-68; head lab. of biodegradable polymers Inst. Macromolecular Chemistry Czechoslovak Acad. of Scis., Prague, 1980-88; co-dir. Ctr. Controlled Chem. Delivery U. Utah, Salt Lake City, 1986—, prof. bioengring., pharmaceutics and phamaceutical chemistry, 1989—2001, chair dept. pharmaceutics and pharmaceutical chemistry, 1999—, disting. prof. bioengring., pharmaceutics and pharm. chemistry, 2002—. Vis. prof. U. Paris-Nord, Paris-Villetaneuse, 1983, 2000, U. Utah, 1986-88, Tokyo Med. Women's U., 1999; adj. prof. material sci. U. Utah, 1987—; disting. lectr. Nagai Found., Tokyo, 1997; lectr. in field. Mem. editl. bd. 13 sci. jours., U.S., U.K., The Netherlands, 1973—; contbr. over 300 articles to sci. publs. Recipient Best Sci. Paper award Presidia of the Czechoslovak and USSR Acads. of Sci., 1977, awards Chem. Sec. Czechoslovak Acad. Scis., 1972, 75, 77-78, 85, J. Heller award Jour. Controller Release, 1999, Millennial Pharm. Scientist award Millennial World Congress Pharm. Scis., 2000, Paul Dawson Biotech. award Am. Assn. Colls. Pharmacy, 2001, J. Heyrovsky hon. medal for merit in the chem. scis. Acad. Scis. Czech Republic, 2003; Rsch. grantee NIH, U. Utah, industry, 1986—, Czechoslovak Acad. Sci., 1970-88. Fellow Am. Assn. Pharm. Sci., Am. Inst. Med. and Biol. Engring.; mem. AAAS, Am. Chem. Soc., Am. Assn. Cancer Rsch., Soc. Biomaterials (Clemson award for basic rsch. 1995), Soc. for Molecular Recognition, Controlled Release Soc. (bd. govs. 1988-91, v.p. 1993-94, pres.-elect 1994-95, pres. 1995-96, Founders award 1999), Czech Learned Soc. (hon.). Achievements include 37 patents in biomedical field; formulation and development of comprehensive approach to the problems of designing macromolecular carriers to modulate the pharmacokinetics and tissue localization of therapeutic agents; research in synthesis and physical characterization of hydrogels, in biocompatibility of biomedical polymers; design of genetically engineered biomaterials. Office: U Utah Dept Pharm and Pharm Chemistry 30 S 2000 E Rm 301 Skaggs Hall Salt Lake City UT 84112-5820 E-mail: jindrich.kopecek@m.cc.utah.edu.

KOPEL, DAVID BENJAMIN, lawyer; b. Denver; s. Gerald Henry and Dolores B. Kopel; m. Deirdre Frances Dolan, Apr. 5, 1987. BA in History, Brown U., 1982; JD, U. Mich., 1985. Bar: Colo. 1986, N.Y. 1986, U.S. Dist. Ct. (ea. and so. dists.) N.Y. 1986, U.S. Ct. Appeals (2d cir.) 1988, U.S. Dist. Ct. Colo. 1988, U.S. Ct. Appeals (10th cir.) 1988, U.S. Ct. Appeals (D.C. cir.) 1997, U.S. Ct. Appeals (5th cir.) 1999, U.S. Ct. Appeals (4th cir.) 2003. Assoc. Sullivan & Cromwell, N.Y.C., 1985-86; asst. dist. atty. Manhattan Dist. Atty., N.Y.C., 1986-88; asst. atty. gen. Colo. State Atty. Gen., Denver, 1988-92; rsch. dir. Independence Inst., Golden, Colo., 1992—. Adj. prof. NYU Sch. of Law, 1998-99. Democrat. Avocations: skiing, ham radio, golf. Office: Independence Inst Ste 185 14142 Denver West Pkwy Golden CO 80401-3119

KOPEL, STEPHEN, educator; b. Dallas, June 11, 1940; s. Solomon and Frances Kopel. BA, UCLA, 1962; MA, San Francisco State U., 1970. Cert. tchr., Calif. Tchr. San Mateo (Calif.) Sch. Dist., 1965-80; co-producer Poetry in Motion TV show San Francisco. Author: (poetry collections) Crux, 2001, Spritz, 2003; contbr. poetry to numerous lit. jours. Mem. Poets and Writers Inc., Acad. Am. Poets. Avocations: travel, dance, theater. Home: 187 Beaver St San Francisco CA 94114-1516

KOPELMAN, HARRY ARVIN, physician; M.D., Georgetown U. Sch. of Med., Washington, D.C., 1976—80. Cardiac Electrophysiology The Am. Bd. of Internal Medicine, 1992, Cardiovascular Diseases The Am. Bd. of Internal Medicine, 1985, Internal Medicine The Am. Bd. of Internal Medicine, 1983. Physician & prtnr. The Atlanta Cardiology Group, P.C., Atlanta, Ga., 1989—. Fellow: Coun. on Clin. Cardiology of the Am. Heart Assn., Am. Coll. of Cardiology; mem.: North Am. Soc. of Pacing and Electrophys. Office: The Atlanta Cardiology Group PC 5665 Peachtree Dunwoody Road Suite 172 Atlanta GA 30342 Office Fax: 404-851-5401.

KOPELMAN, LARRY GORDON, lawyer; b. Charleston, W.Va., Apr. 20, 1949; s. Leo G. and Ruby Jean (Webb) K.; m. Mary Christine Kessler, June 28, 1975; children— Emily Nicole, Justin Gordon. B.S.E.E., W.Va. U., 1971, J.D., 1975. Bar: W.Va. 1975, U.S. Dist. Ct. (no. and so. dists.) W.Va. 1975, U.S. Ct. Appeals (4th cir.) 1984, U.S. Dist. Ct. D.C. 1986, U.S. Ct. Appeals (D.C. cir.) 1986. Tax analyst W.Va. Tax Dept., Charleston, 1975 76; asst. atty. gen. W.Va. Air Pollution Control Commn., 1976-79; spl. asst. atty. gen., 1979— ; pvt. practice, Charleston, 1979; pres. Larry G. Kopelman, L.C., Charleston, 1984—, Amity Real Estate Ltd., Charleston, 1979—; city atty. Town of Handley, 1980—, Town of Pratt, 1988—. Mem. W.Va. Bar Assn., Kanawha County Bar Assn., W.Va. Trial Lawyers, Assn. Trial Lawyers Am. Republican. Jewish. Club: South Charleston Rotary (pres. 1983-84). Office: 9 Pennsylvania Ave Charleston WV 25302-2313

KOPELMAN, LEONARD, lawyer; b. Cambridge, Mass., Aug. 2, 1940; s. Irving and Frances Estelle (Robbins) K.; m. Carol Hunsberger. BA cum laude, Harvard U., 1962, JD, 1965. Bar: Mass. 1966. Assoc. Warner & Stackpole, Boston, 1965-73; sr. ptnr. Kopelman and Paige, Boston, 1974— Lectr. Harvard U., 1965— ; permanent master Mass. Superior Ct., 1971— ; gen. counsel Emerson Coll.; hon. consul gen. of, Finland, Mass., 1975— ; U.S. del. Soc. for Internat. Devel.; Chmn. Mass. Jud. Selection Com. for the Fed. Judiciary, 1971— ; chief counsel AAUP; dean consular corps of Boston, 2001—. Trustee Cathedral of the Pines, 1972; pres. Hillel Found. of Cambridge, Inc., 1973— ; trustee Faulkner Hosp., 1974—, Parker Hill Med. Ctr., 1976—; dir. gen. Consular Corps Coll. NEH grantee, 1975; named one of the 12 most powerful lawyers in Mass. Nat. Law Jour. Mem. ABA (exec. coun. 1969—), Mass. Bar Assn. (chmn. mcpl. law sect.), Am. Judges Assn., Mass. C. of C. (pres. 1974-77), Harvard Faculty Club, Algonquin Club (pres.), Harvard Club, Union Club, Hasty Pudding Club, St. Botolph Club. Home: 33 Yarmouth Rd Chestnut Hill MA 02467-2815 Office: Kopelman and Paige 31 St James Ave Boston MA 02116-4101

KOPELMAN, LORETTA MARY, philosophy educator; b. N.Y.C., Sept. 5, 1938; d. Frank M. and Gertrude Mae (Vietch) Criden; m. Arthur E. Kopelman; children: Elizabeth Palumbo, William. BA in Philosophy, Syracuse U., 1960, MA in Philosophy, 1962; PhD in Philosophy, U. Rochester, 1966. Asst. lectr. U. Rochester, N.Y., 1965-66, assoc. lectr., 1971-73, instr., 1974-76, asst. prof., 1976-78; lectr. U. Tenn., Nashville, 1967-68, New Haven Coll., 1968-69, U. Md., 1969-71; assoc. prof. med. humanities, founding dir. Brody Med. Sch. East Carolina U., Greenville, NC, 1978-85, prof. med. humanities, 1985—, founding chair med. humanities dept., 1984—, mem. Inst. Medicine com. on clin. rsch. with children, 2003—. Co-chair ad hoc human growth hormone rev. com. NIH, 1992; cons. in filed. Editor: (with others) The Rights of Children and Retarded Persons, 1978, Ethics and Mental Retardation, 1984, Ethics and Critical Care Medicine, 1985, Children and Health Care: Moral and Social Issues, 1989, Building Bioethics: Conversations with Clouser and Friends, 1999, Physician Assisted Suicide: What Are the Issues?, 2001; mem. editl. bd. Jour. Medicine and Philosophy, 1984—, Clin. Med. Ethics, 1986—, Ency. of Bioethics, 2d and 3d edits., Developing World Bioethics; contbr. articles to profl. jours. Grantee NEH, 1983-84, U. Rochester, 1976-78, N.C. Humanities Com., 1980-87, AMA Edn. and Rsch. Found., 1982-84, Ross Labs., 1986-87, GTE, 1992-93. Fellow Assn. for the Advancement Philosophy and Psychiatry; mem. AAUP, Am. Philos. Assn. (com. 1982), Soc. for Health and Human Values (pres. 1997-98, chair program dir. 1990 91, editor essays and letters 1984 86), Am. Soc. Bioethics and Humanities (founding pres. 1997-98, founding bd. mem. 1997-99), Hastings Ctr., Kennedy Inst. Ethics, European Soc. for Philosophy Medicine and Health Care, Soc. Law and Medicine, Phi Beta Kappa, Phi Kappa Phi, Theta Beta Phi. Democrat. Mem. Soc. Of Friends. Avocations: painting, piano. Home: 411 Queen Annes Rd Greenville NC 27858-6306 Office: East Carolina U Dept Med Humanities 2517 Brody Med Scis Bldg Greenville NC 27858

KOPELMAN, RICHARD ERIC, management educator; b. N.Y.C., May 31, 1943; s. Seymour H. and Leona L. (Quint) K.; m. Carol Fialkov, June 7, 1970; children: Joshua Marc, Michael Adam. BS, U. Pa., 1965, MBA, 1967; DBA, Harvard U., 1974. Instr. bus. C.C. Phila., 1967-69; instr. mgmt. Baruch Coll./CUNY, N.Y.C., 1973-74, asst. prof., 1974-77, assoc. prof., 1978-80, prof., 1981—. Cons. in field; corp. dir. Aleph Null Corp., 1979-88, Applied Photonics, Inc., 1986-91, Infodex Sys., Inc., 1986-88, EMS Devel. Corp., 1992-96; pres. Cube One, Inc., 1998—; acad. co-dir. MS in Indsl. Rels. program Baruch/Cornell U., 1985-97, acad. co-dir. Baruch exec. MS in Indsl. Rels. program, 1994-2000; acad. dir. Baruch exec. MS in Indsl. and Labor Rels. program, 2000—. Author: The Management of Productivity: A Practical People-Oriented Perspective, 1986; mem. editl. rev. bd. Jour. Social Behavior and Personality, 1985-89, Nat. Productivity Rev., Jour. Orgnl. Behavior Mgmt., Perceptions, 1991-94, Jour. Psychology, 1999—, Jour. Orgnl. Excellence, 2000—; contbr. numerous articles to profl. and acad. jours. Bd. dirs. Day Care Council, Nassau County, 1979-82; Nassau Symphony Orch., 1984-85. Recipient Teaching award Baruch Coll., 1987, Teaching Excellence award, 1989, 91, 92, 93, CUNY Excellence Award for Rsch., Tchg. and Svc., 1999; William B. Harding fellow Harvard U. Mem. APA, Acad. Mgmt., Decision Scis. Inst., Soc. for Human Resource Mgmt. (accredited pers. diplomate, sr. profl. in human resources), Am. Compensation Assn., Met. N.Y. Assn. for Applied Psychology (sec. 1986-87, treas. 1987-88, v.p. 1988-89, pres. 1989-90), Sigma Iota Epsilon. Home: 65 Colgate Rd Great Neck NY 11023-1501 Office: Baruch Coll Zicklin Sch Bus/Dept Mgmt 17 Lexington Ave New York NY 10010-5518 E-mail: rekopelman@managingperformance.com.

KOPELSON, ARNOLD, film producer; b. New York, NY, Feb. 14, 1935; BS, N.Y.U.; JD, N.Y. Law Sch., 1959. Prodr. (film) Foolin' Around, 1980, Dirty Tricks, 1981, Gimme an F, 1984, Platoon, 1986 (Acad. awd Best Picture), Triumph of the Spirit, 1989, Out for Justice, 1991, Falling Down, 1993, The Fugitive, 1993 (Acad. award nom Best Picture), Outbreak, 1995, Seven, 1995, Eraser, 1996, Murder at 1600, 1997, Mad City, 1997, The Devil's Advocate, 1997, U.S. Marshals, 1998, A Perfect Murder, 1998, Don't Say A Word, 2001, Joe Somebody, 2001; exec. prodr. (film) Lost and Found, 1979, The Legacy, 1979, Night of the Juggler, 1980, Final Assignment, 1980, Dirty Tricks, 1981, Model Behavior, 1984, Warlock, 1989, Fire Birds, 1990; exec. prodr. (TV) Past Tense, 1994, The Fugitive, 2000, Thieves, 2001.*

KOPENHAVER, LILLIAN LODGE, journalism educator; b. Linden, N.J., Jan. 25, 1941; d. Thomas J. and Angela T. (Wolczanski) Lodge; m. David Arthur Kopenhaver. BA, Glassboro (N.J.) State Coll., 1962; MA, U. Wis., 1967; EdD, Nova U., 1980. Cert. English and journalism tchr., N.J., Fla. Tchr. English and journalism Brick Twp. High Sch., Bricktown, N.J., 1962-67; asst. prof. humanities Ocean County Coll., Toms River, N.J., 1967-71; asst. prof. journalism Miami-Dade Community Coll., Fla., 1971-73; dir. student activities Fla. Internat. U., Miami, 1971-73, asst. v.p. student affairs, 1976-78, dir. pub. relations, 1978-81, assoc. dean, prof. sch. Journalism/Mass Comm., 1981—2003, interim dean, 2003—. Corp. bd. Student Press Law Ctr., 1976—; reporter, editor Ocean County Daily Observer, Toms River, 1962 68; pres. Student Press Law Ctr., Washington, 1987-89; cons. in field. Author (with J.W. Click): College Media Advising: Ethics and Responsibilities, 4th edit., 2003; contbr. articles. Recipient Gold Key award Columbia Scholastic Press Assn., 1980, Pioneer award Nat. Scholastic Press Assn., 1983, Gold Medallion award Fla. Scholastic Press Assn., 1986, Fla. Internat. U. Outstanding Faculty Svc. award, 1996, Torch Award/Outstanding Faculty Mem., 2000, Joseph M. Murphy award for outstanding svc. CSPA, 2003; named to C.C. Journalism Assn. Hall of Fame, 1994. Mem. Coll. Media Advisers (pres. 1975-79, dir. Spring Coll. Media Conv., N.Y. 1983-2001, Disting. Svc. award 1987, Svc. Achievement award 1989, Hall of Fame 1994), Soc. Profl. Journalists (chmn. profl. devel. com. 1983-94, 2001-02, chmn. internat. journalism com. 1994-98, Outstanding Svc. award 1986, Wells Meml. Key 1987), Assn. Edn. Journalism and Mass Comm. (pres.elect 1997-98, pres. 1998-99 chmn. coun. affiliates 1987-88, chair adv. bd. 1988-89, chair newspaper divsn. 1991-92, chair pubs. com. 1992-95, vice-chair teaching standards com. 1992-93, chair membership com. 1995-96, honors lectr. 2000, Disting. Svc. award 1990, 2000, Disting. Leadership award 2001, others), Pub. Rels. Soc. Am., Women in Comm., Inc., Greater Miami Soc. Profl. Journalists (bd. dirs. 1981-94), Miami Internat. Press Club (founding bd. mem. 1986-88). Home: 2642 Nassau Dr Miramar FL 33023-4625 Office: Fla Internat U Sch Journalism/Mass Comm North Miami FL 33181 E-mail: kopenhav@fiu.edu.

KOPENHAVER, PATRICIA ELLSWORTH, podiatrist; Student, Columbia U., 1950-53; BA, George Washington U., 1954; MA, Columbia U., 1956; Dr. Podiatric Medicine, N.Y. Coll. Podiatric Medicine, 1963, postgrad., 1980; LLD (hon.), Barry U., 1998; MD (hon.) (hon.), Internat. U. Health Scis. Sch. Medicine, 2001; MD (hon.), Internat. Univ. of the Hlth. Sci., 2001. Diplomate Nat. Bd. Podiatry Examiners. Pvt. practice podiatry, Greenwich, Conn., 1964— ; staff podiatrist Havenhealth Care Ctr., Greenwich, 2003—. Mem. staff Laurelton Convalescent Hosp., Greenwich; trustee N.Y. Coll. Podiatric Medicine, 1998. Bd. dirs. Monmouth Opera Guild, 1965; trustee Monmouth Opera Festival, 1966, v.p., 1964; mem. Greenwich Arts Coun.; program chmn. Greenwich Women's Rep. Club, 1983-84, 4th dist. rep., 1984-85, 87—; trustee N.Y. Coll. Podiatric Medicine, 1998—. Recipient Hosp. Fund award for med. research translations ARC, Alumni award of distinction N.Y. Coll. Podiatric Medicine, 1997; scholarship named in her honor N.Y. Coll. Podiatric Medicine, 1997. Mem. AAUW (v.p. 1991, pres. Greenwich br. 1992-94, bd. dirs. 1996), NOW, Conn. Podiatric Med. Assn., Hist. Soc., Asian Soc., Fairfield Podiatry Assn., Am. Assn. Women Podiatrists (charter pres. 1969-78), Acad. Podiatry, Am. Podiatry Coun., UN Assn. U.S.A., Acad. Podiatric Medicine (chmn. nominating com. 1981, 1st v.p. 1983-84, chmn. fundraising 1984-85, chmn. women's issues 1985, chmn. cmty. edn. 1989), Am. Acad. Sports Medicine, Am. Acad. Podiatric Sports Medicine (assoc. 1989), George Washington U. Alumni Assn., Columbia Alumni Assn., Fairfield County Alumni Assn. Columbia U., Coast Soc. of Founders Barry U. (treas. 1998), Nat. Fedn. Rep. Women, Bruce Mus., Nature Conservancy, Federated Garden Club Conn., St. Mary Ladies Guild, Greenwich Gardeners, Womans' Club (ways and means com. 1989, pres.), Soroptimists Internat. Am. (pres. Greenwich br. 1990—, bd. dirs. 1997-98), Inc. (vice chmn. program com. 1985—, regional med. scholarship chmn. 1987, med. scholarship chmn. N.E. region 1988, program dir. 1988—, pres. Greenwich br. 1990-92), Toastmasters, Travel Club (program com. 1984—), Soroptimist (bd. dirs. 1997, 2000—), Greenwich Woman's Club (chair gardeners judges 2001—), Pi Epsilon Chi. Home: 2 Sutton Pl S New York NY 10022-3070 Office: 8 Dearfield Dr Greenwich CT 06831-5348 Fax: 203-869-5096.

KOPERSKI, NANCI CAROL, health care administrator, women's health nurse; b. Omaha, Sept. 14, 1962; d. William S. Jr. and Ethel A. (Friday) Koperski; divorced. Student, Marquette U.; BSN cum laude, Creighton U., 1984; MBA, MHSA, Ariz. State U. RN, Ariz.; cert. women's health nurse. Staff nurse Phoenix Meml. Hosp., Phoenix Gen. Hosp., Community Hosp., Phoenix, Phoenix Indian Med. Ctr.; clin. care coord. Ahwatukee Foothills Samaritan Health Ctr., 1992—2001; staff nurse Bergan Mercy Hosp., Omaha, 2001—. Mem. AWHONN, Ariz. Nurse's Assn., Sigma Theta Tau. Home: 1929 S 35th Ave Omaha NE 68105

KOPF, DAVID HEATH, economic consultant; b. Salem, Mass., Mar. 18, 1932; s. Carl Heath and Mary FitzRandolph (Chalfant) K. AB, Oberlin Coll., 1953; MA, Princeton U., 1957, PhD, 1967. Asst. dept. polit. economy Edinburgh (Scotland) U., 1957-59; instr. dept. econs. Princeton (N.J.) U., 1959-62; economist, chief spl. asst. Fed. Res. Bank N.Y., N.Y.C., 1962-76; v.p., money mgmt. economist White Weld, N.Y.C., 1976-78; v.p., economist Purcell Graham, N.Y.C., 1978-80; v.p., chief fin. economist 1st Nat. Bank Chgo., 1981-83; econ. cons., Chgo., 1984—. With U.S. Army, 1953-55. Mem. Am. Econ. Assn., Nat. Assn. Bus. Economists, Chgo. Assn. Bus. Economists, Downtown Economists N.Y. Avocations: bridge, chess, skiing. Home and Office: 3219 N Kenmore Ave Chicago IL 60657-3306

KOPF, GEORGE MICHAEL, retired ophthalmologist; b. Chilton, Wis., Oct. 20, 1935; s. George and Mary (Schmid) K.; m. Sandra Mary Nolte, Dec. 29, 1962; children: Karen, Jennifer, Nancy. BS, U. Wis., 1958, MD, 1961. Diplomate Am. Bd. Ophthalmology. Intern Luther Hosp., Eau Claire, Wis., 1961-62; resident Milw. County Hosp., 1962-63, Detroit Gen. Hosp., 1965-68; ophthalmologist pvt. practice, Zanesville, Ohio, 1968—; ret., 1999. Mem. med. staff Bethesda Hosp., Zanesville; mem. med. Staff Good Samaritan Med. Ctr., Zanesville, pres., 1978, sec. bd. dirs., 1986-96. Capt. USAF, 1963-65. Fellow ACS, Am. Acad. Ophthalmology; mem. Ohio Ophthalmology Soc. (pres. 1976-77), Muskigum County Acad. Medicine (pres. 1983), Ohio State Med. Assn., Rotary. Republican. Roman Catholic. Avocations: tennis, swimming, hiking, reading, travel. Home: 2950 Ash Meadows Blvd Zanesville OH 43701-9081

KOPF, RICHARD G. federal judge; b. 1946; BA, U. Nebr., Kearney, 1969; JD, U. Nebr., Lincoln, 1972. Law clk. to Hon. Donald R. Ross U.S. Ct. Appeals (8th cir.), 1972-74; ptnr. Cook, Kopf & Doyle, Lexington, Neb., 1974-87; U.S. magistrate judge, 1987-92; fed. judge U.S. Dist. Ct. (Nebr. dist.), 1992—, chief judge, 1999—. Mem. ABA, ABA Found., Nebr. State Bar, Nebr. State Bar Found. Office: US Dist Ct 586 US Courthouse 100 Centennial Mall N Lincoln NE 68508-3859

KOPIT, ALAN STUART, lawyer; b. Cleve., Aug. 26, 1952; s. Irving and Claire (Smira) K. BA summa cum laude, Tufts U., 1974; JD, U. Chgo., 1977. Bar: Ohio 1977, U.S. Dist. Ct. (no. dist.) Ohio 1977, U.S. Ct. Appeals (6th cir.) 1979, U.S. Ct. Appeals (10th cir.) 1991, U.S. Ct. Appeals (4th cir.) 1996, U.S. Supreme Ct. 1988. Ptnr. Hahn, Loeser & Parks, LLP, Cleve., 1977—. Staff atty. Sta. WKYC-TV3 NBC, Cleve., 1982—92; White House fellow spl. asst. to sec. def. The Pentagon, Washington, 1987-88; commentator on nat. TV, 2000—. Mem. Leadership Cleve. Growth Assn., 1985-86; vice chair Cleve. Bicentennial Commn., 1992—; bd. dirs. Adam Walsh Child Resource Ctr., Cleve., 1984-87, Fairmount Theatre of Deaf, Cleve., 1984—, Am. Jewish Com., Cleve., 1985—. Named one of Cleve.'s Most Interesting People, Cleve. Mag., 1984; recipient Sec. of Def. Medal, 1988. Mem. ABA (chairperson young lawyers div. 1986-87, del. ho. of dels. 1987—), Cleve. Bar Assn. (merit svc. award 1978, 79, 81, bd. dirs. 1981-82, 91—, pres. 1996-97), Am. Bar Endowment (bd. dirs. 1987-88), Ohio Bar Assn. (coun. del. 1985-87). Home: 2780 Brainard Hills Dr Cleveland OH 44124-4544 Office: Hahn Loeser & Parks 3300 BP America Bldg 200 Public Sq Ste 3300 Cleveland OH 44114-2303 E-mail: askopit@hahnlaw.com.

KOPLAN, ANDREW BENNET, lawyer; b. Birmingham, Ala., Apr. 12, 1971; Student, U. Sidney (Australia), 1991; BS in Fin. cum laude, Birmingham-Southern Coll., 1993; JD, U. Ala., 1996. Bar: Ala. 1996, Ga. 1997, U.S. Dist. Ct. (so. dist.) Ga., U.S. Dist. Ct. (no. dist.) Ga., U.S. Dist. Ct. (so. dist.) Ala. 1997. Legal intern Ala. Supreme Ct., Montgomery, 1995, Ala. Dept. Fin., Montgomery, 1995; jud. extern U.S. Dist. Ct. (no. dist.) Ala., Birmingham, 1995-96; clk. for Hon. Assoc. Justice Janie Shores Supreme Ct. Ala., Montgomery, 1996-97; assoc. Post & Pond, LLP, Atlanta, 1997-98, Drew, Elkl, & Farnham, LLP, Atlanta, 1998—2000, Mathis & Adams, Atlanta, 2000—. Jr. editor: Law & Psychology Rev., 1995-96. Mem. ABA, Ga. Trial Lawyers Assn. Avocations: music, sports, art, cooking, exercising. Office: Mathis & Adams 100 Peachtree St Ste 1400 Atlanta GA 30303

KOPLAN, JEFFREY POWELL, physician; b. Boston, Jan. 3, 1945; s. Samuel R. and Kate G. K.; m. Carol R. Bassuk, May 18, 1969; children: Adam, Kate BA, Yale Coll., 1966; postgrad., Tufts U., 1966-68; MD, Mount Sinai Sch. Medicine, N.Y.C., 1970; M.P.H., Harvard U., 1978. Diplomate Am. Bd. Internal Medicine, Am. Bd. Preventive Medicine. Intern, resident Montefiore Hosp. and Med. Ctr., Bronx, N.Y., 1970-72; epidemic intelligence service officer Ctr. for Disease Control, Atlanta, 1972-74, med. officer Office of Program Planning, 1978-82, asst. dir. pub. health practice, 1982-88; dir. Nat. Ctr. Chronic Disease Prevention and Health Promotion, Atlanta, 1989-94; asst. surgeon gen., 1989-94; exec. v.p., dir. Prudential Ctr. for Health Care Rsch., Atlanta, 1994-95; pres., 1995-98; vis. prof. community health Emory U., 1986—; resident Stanford U. Hosp, Calif., 1974-75; med. epidemiologist Calif. State Dept. Health, Berkeley, 1975, Caribbean Epidemiology Ctr., Port of Spain, Trinidad, 1975-77; dir. Ctrs. for Disease Control and Prevention, Atlanta, 1998—2002; v.p., academic health affairs Emory U., Ga., 2002—. Cons. World Bank, Washington, AID, Washington Contbr. articles to profl. jours. With USPHS, 1970-94. Recipient Order of Bifurcated Needle WHO, 1979; Saul Horowitz award Mt. Sinai Sch. Medicine, 1983; Commendation medal USPHS, 1984 Fellow ACP, Am. Coll. Epidemiology; mem. Assn. Tchrs. Preventive Medicine, Am. Pub. Health Assn., Soc. Med. Decision Making Office: Emory Univ WHSCAB 410 Atlanta GA 30322*

KOPLEWICZ, HAROLD SAMUEL, child and adolescent psychiatrist; b. Bklyn., Jan. 12, 1953; s. Joseph and Romana (Magid) K.; m. Linda Jane Sirow, June 22, 1980; children: Joshua, Adam, Sam. BS, U. Md., 1973; MD, Albert Einstein Coll. of Medicine, 1978. Diplomate Am. Bd. Psychiatry and Neurology, Am. Bd. Child Psychiatry. Med. dir. preschool hyperactivity program N.Y. State Psychiat. Inst., N.Y.C., 1982-85, med. dir. children's anxiety clinic, 1983-86; dir. gen. residency tng. child psychiatry Columbia Coll. Physicians and Surgeons, N.Y.C., 1985-86; chief divsn. child and adolescent psychiatry Schneider Children's Hosp. and Hillside Hosp. of L.I. Jewish Med. Ctr., N.Y.C., 1986-96; editor Youth Mental Health Update, 1989-96; assoc. prof. psychiatry Albert Einstein Coll. Medicine, N.Y.C., 1991-96; prof. clin. psychiatry and pediatrics, vice chmn. psychiatry NYU Sch. Medicine, 1996—; dir. child and adolescent divsn. NYU Med. Ctr./Bellevue Hosp. Ctr., N.Y.C., 1996—; dir. NYU Child Study Ctr. NYU Sch. Medicine, N.Y.C., 1997—, Arnold & Debbie Simon prof. child & adolscent psychiatry, 2000—. Cons. Riverdale Cmty. Ctr., 1981-86, The Dalton Sch., 1991-96, The N.Y. Infirmary, 1991, The Family Acad., 1991-96, Jewish Child Care Assn., 1992-96, Health Edn. Task Force, Roslyn Sch. Dist., 1993-96; dir. Nat. Child Mental Health Inst., 1999—. Author: It's Nobody's Fault: New Hope and Help for Difficult Children and Their Parents, 1996, Childhood Revealed: Art Expressing Pain, Hope and Discovery, 1999, Trubulent Times Prophetic Dreams, 2000, More Than Moody: Recognizing and Treating Adolescent Depression, 2002; editor NYU Child Study Ctr. Letter, 1996—; editor-in-chief: Jour. Child and Adolescent Psychopharmacology, 1998—; mem. adv. bd. Parents Mag., 1996—, Parents In Action, 1996—; mem. profl. adv. bd. Big Apple Parent Paper, 1995—, N.Y.C. chpt. Nat. Alliance for Mentally Ill, 2001—. Bd. dirs. Raoul Wallenberg New Leadership Soc., 1983-87, Cmty. Mainstreaming Assocs., 1990; chmn. Simon Wiesenthal Ctr., 1984-86; commr. N.Y. State Commn. for Study of Youth Crime and Violence and Reform of the Juvenile Justice Sys., 1993-96; prin. investigator Developing Innovative Mental Health Care Delivery for Adolescents, Hewlett-Woodmere Sch. Dist., 1992; adv. bd. Our Children's Found., 1996-97. Recipient Hulse award N.Y. Coun. Child and Adolescent Psychiatry, 1995, Exemplary Psychiatrist award Nat. Alliance Mentally Ill, 1997, Contbns. to Humanity award Marymount Manhattan Coll., 1999, Am. Grand Hope award 2000. Fellow Am. Acad. Child and Adolescent Psychiatry (Reiger award 1997), Am. Psychiat. Assn.; mem. Soc. Profl. Child and Adolescent Psychiatry, Am. Bd. Psychiatry and Neurology (examiner 1988-98), Nat. Bd. Med. Examiners (mem. psychiatry com. 1993-96), Nat. Found. Depressive Illness (nat. bd. dirs. 1992—), Mental Health Assn. of N.Y. (profl. adv. bd. 1997—). Office: NYU Child Study Ctr (NB21E7) 550 1st Ave New York NY 10016-6402 Fax: 212-263-0484. E-mail: harold.koplewicz@med.nyu.edu.

KOPLIK, JOEL, physicist, educator; b. Bklyn., Oct. 31, 1948; s. Abraham H. and Nettie (Cohen) K. BS, Cooper Union, N.Y., 1969; PhD, U. Calif., Berkeley, 1974. Rsch. assoc. Columbia U., N.Y.C., 1974-76; mem. Inst. for Advanced Study, Princeton, N.J., 1976-77, 78-79; charge de la recherche Ecole Normale Superieure, Paris, 1977-78; mem. profl. staff Schlumberger-Doll Rsch., Ridgefield, Conn., 1979-88; prof. physics CCNY, N.Y.C., 1989—. Assoc. editor Physics of Fluids, N.Y.C., 1990—; contbr. numerous publications to profl. jours. Fellow Am. Phys. Soc. Achievements include research in fluid mechanics, disordered systems and transport in porous media, non-equilibrium pattern selection, molecular dynamics, superfluidity, large scale computation. Office: CCNY Levich Inst T # 1M New York NY 10031 E-mail: koplik@sci.ccny.cuny.edu.

KOPLIK, MARC STEPHEN, lawyer; b. N.Y.C., Aug. 28, 1946; s. Arnold and Lillian (Weiner) K.; m. Deirdre Lee Henderson, May 30, 1970; children: Christopher Henderson, Timothy Henderson. AB cum laude, Brown U., 1968; JD, Yale U., 1971. Bar: N.Y. 1973. Assoc. Debevoise & Plimpton, N.Y.C., 1971-76; founder, mng. ptnr. Henderson & Koplik, N.Y.C., 1982—. Editor Yale Law Jour., 1970-71. Coll. scholar, Frances Wayland scholar. Mem. Assn. Bar City N.Y., N.Y. State Bar Assn., Old Chatham Hunt C. of C. Episcopalian. Club: Yale (N.Y.C.).

KOPLIK, MICHAEL R. durable goods company executive; Sales manager Castle & Overton Inc., N.Y.C., 1957-1960; dir., v.p. Perry H. Koplik & Sons Inc., N.Y.C., 1960-78, pres., CEO, 1978—. Office: Perry H Koplik & Sons Inc 505 Park Ave New York NY 10022-1106

KOPLIN, DONALD LEROY, health products executive, consumer advocate; b. Greenleaf, Kans., Dec. 31, 1932; s. Henry G. Koplin and Edith Mary Stevens; m. Patricia Joynes, June 2, 1962 (div. Aug. 1974); children: Marie Claire, Marie Joelle (adopted); m. Joan Freudenthal, June 28, 1997. Student, U. San Diego, 1956-59, 67-68. Electronics test insp. Gen. Dynamics, San Diego, 1956-59; cryptographer Dept. of State, Washington, 1959-67, communications program officer France, Angola, Madagascar, Qatar, India, Oman, Benin and the Bahamas, 1977-86; tech. writer Ryan Aero. Corp., San Diego, 1967-68; comml. dir., tech. advisor, pub. rels. officer Societe AGM, San Francisco, Athens, Greece, Antananarivo and Morondava, Dem. Republic of Madagascar, 1968-72; founder, dir. Soc. Bells, Cyclone & Akai, Antananarivo, 1972-74; founder, ptnr., assoc. editor Angola Report, Luanda, 1974-75; polit. reporter Angola Report, Reuters, AP, UPI Corr., BBC, Luanda; supr. Tex. Instruments, Lubbock, 1976-77; exec. Dial A Contact Lens, Inc., La Jolla, Calif., 1986-90, Assn. for Retarded Citizens, San Diego, 1991-92, Club Med, Copper Mountain, Colo., 1992-94; CEO Vient Inc., 1994-97, Koplin Kollection Fine Arts Gallery, La Jolla, Calif., 1996-98. Active San Diego Zool. Soc. With USN, 1951-55, Korea. Mem. Am. Fgn. Svc. Assn. Independent. Avocation: writing. Home: 6718 Evergreen Ave Oakland CA 94611-1518 E-mail: dojokop@webtv.net.

KOPLOVITZ, KAY, television network executive; b. Milw., Apr. 11, 1945; d. William E. and Jane T. Smith; m. William C. Koplovitz Jr., Apr. 17, 1971. BS, U. Wis., 1967; MA in Communications, Mich. State U., 1968. Radio and TV producer, dir. Sta. WTMJ-TV, Milw., 1967; editor Comm. Satellite Corp., Washington, 1968-72; dir. cmty. svc. UA Columbia Cablevision, Oakland, NJ, 1973-75; v.p., exec. dir. UA Columbia Satellite Services Inc., Oakland, NJ, 1977-80; founder, chmn., CEO USA Networks and Sci-Fi Channel, NYC, 1977—98; CEO Koplovitz & Co., NYC, 1998—. Founder Springboard 2000; bd. mem. Springboard Enterprises; bd. dir. Liz Claiborne, 1992—, Oracle, 1998—2001, Instinct, 2001, Nabisco, 1993—2000; Gen. re, 1991—2002. Mem. bd. overseers NYU Grad. Sch. Bus., 1984-90; bd. dir. Nat. Jr. Achievement, 1986-1996. Named Entrepreneur of Yr., Babson Coll., 2001; named to Cable Hall of Fame, 2001, Broadcasting Mag. Hall of Fame, 1992; recipient Outstanding Alumnus award, Mich. State U. Grad. Sch. Bus., 1985, Oustanding Corp. Social Responsibility, CUNY, 1986, Women Who Run the World award, Sara Lee Corp., 1987, Muse award, N.Y. Women in Film and TV, 1992, Ellis Island medal of honor, 1993, Crystal award, Women in Film, 1993. Mem.: Com. of 200, Nat. Acad. Cable Programming (bd. dirs. 1984—87), Cable Advt. Bur. (bd. dirs., exec. com., treas. 1981—87, Chmn.'s award for leadership 1987), Women in Cable (founding bd. dirs., membership chmn. 1979—80, v.p. 1981—82, pres. 1982—83), Nat. Acad. TV Arts and Scis. (chmn. 1994—97, bd. dirs. 1984—93), Internat. Coun., Advt. Coun. Inc. (chmn. 1992—93, bd. dirs. 1985—94), Nat. Cable TV Assn. (bd. dirs. 1984—98), N.Y.C. Partnership (bd. dirs. 1987—), Womens Forum. Avocations: tennis, skiing, travel.

KOPP, CHARLES GILBERT, lawyer; b. Hartford, Conn., Jan. 10, 1933; s. Henry and Grace (Goldberg) K.; m. Ann Weiss, June 10, 1962 (div. 1963) BA, Amherst Coll., 1955; JD, U. Pa., 1960. Bar: Pa. 1961. Sr. counsel Wolf, Block, Schorr and Solis-Cohen LLP, Phila., 1960—. Vis. lectr. Villanova (Pa.) Univ., 1981. Contbr. articles to profl. jours. Commr. Delaware River Port Authority, 1986-87; co-chmn. select com. of U.S. Embassy, Bern, Switzerland, 1985; mem. Pa. Gov.'s Spl. Tax Commn., 1980; mem. fin. com. Rep. State Com., 1984-98, mem. leadership com.; bd. dirs. Pennsylvanians for Effective Govt., Harrisburg, 1987-99; mem. Pa. Electoral Coll., 1988; mem. adv. bd. region I, Resolution Trust Corp., 1990-93; mem. coun. The Pa. Soc., 1991-98; trustee Thomas Jefferson U. Hosp., 1988—, Pop Warner Little Scholars; mem. adv. bd. PNC, Phila., 1992-2000. 1st lt. USAF, 1955-57. Recipient Pop Warner Gold Football award, 1988. Mem.: ABA, Phila. Bar Assn., Pa. Bar Assn., Greater Phila. C. of C. (exec. com. 1988—96), Vesper Club, Pyramid Club. Republican. Jewish. Home: 210 W Rittenhouse Sq Apt 3306 Philadelphia PA 19103-5780 Office: Wolf Block Schorr and Solis Cohen LLP 1650 Arch St Fl 22 Philadelphia PA 19103-2003

KOPP, EUGENE HOWARD, electrical engineer; b. N.Y.C., Oct. 1, 1929; s. Jacob and Fanny (Lipschitz) K.; m. Claire Bernstein, Aug. 31, 1950; children: Carolyn, Michael, Paul. B.E.E., CCNY, 1950, M.E.E., 1953; PhD in Engring, UCLA, 1965. Registered profl. engr., Calif. Project engr. Polarad Electronics Corp., Long Island City, N.Y., 1950-53, Kaye Halbert Corp., Culver City, Calif., 1953-55; chief engr. Precision Radiation Instruments, Inc., Los Angeles, 1955-58; mem. faculty sch. engring. Calif. State U., Los Angeles, 1958-74, assoc. prof., 1962-66, prof., 1966-74, dean engring. Sch., 1967-73; v.p. acad. affairs West Coast U., Los Angeles, 1973-79; sr. scientist Hughes Aircraft Co., 1980-85, mgr. research and devel., 1985-93, dir. advanced programs, 1994-95; v.p. mobile satellites Boeing Satellite Systems, 1996-97, chief scientist comml. satellites, 1998—2002; chief scientist homeland security The Boeing Co., 2003—. Lectr. evening divsn. CCNY, N.Y.C., 1950-53; lectr. UCLA, 1979-91. Vis. research fellow U. Leeds, Eng., 1966-67 Mem. IEEE, AIAA, Tau Beta Pi, Eta Kappa Nu, Pi Tau Sigma. Office: The Boeing Co PO Box 1351 South Pasadena CA 91031-1351

KOPP, EUGENE PAUL, lawyer; b. Charleston, W.Va., Nov. 20, 1934; s. Eugene Alexander and Virginia Elizabeth (King) K.; m. Katherine Patricia Rogers, July 1, 1967; 1 son, Eugene Paul. BA, U. Notre Dame, 1957, MA, 1958; JD, W.Va. U., 1961. Ba: W.Va. 1961, D.C. 1977, Tex. 1980. Law clk. U.S. Dist. Ct. W.Va., 1961-62; trial atty. Dept. Justice, Washington, 1962-69; dep. dir. USIA, 1973-77, acting dir., 1976-77; assoc. gen. counsel Champlin Petroleum Co., Ft. Worth, 1977-81; v.p. Washington affairs Union Pacific Corp., Washington, 1981-87; dep. dir. U.S. Info. Agy., 1989-93; exec. dir. MFJ Task Force, 1993-94; of counsel Clarendon Assocs., Inc., 1995-97, Ruddy and Muir, 1998—; vice chmn. Nexphase Comms., Inc., 2000—01. Cons. nat. Security Council, Washington, 1981, mem. transition team, 1980. Mem.: Washington Inst. Fgn. Affairs, DC Bar Assn., Tex. Bar Assn., W.Va. Bar Assn., Dacor Club (Washington), Met. Club (Washington), Belle Haven Country Club. Roman Catholic. Home: 508 Cathedral Dr Alexandria VA 22314-4706

KOPP, GEORGE PHILIP, JR., minister; b. Cin., July 17, 1927; s. George Philip and Ann Elizabeth (Suffield) K.; m. Janet Marie Thompson Shultz, Oct. 13, 1956. BA, Heidelberg Coll., 1950; BD, Eden Sem., 1955, MDiv, 1969. Ordained to ministry United Ch. of Christ, 1955. Pastor St. John's Ch., Middlebrook, Va., 1955-60, 83-85, ret.; commd. ensign USN, 1954, advanced through grades to lt. comdr., 1976, served as chaplain; ret., 1976, ret., 1976. Dir. Ctr. Atlantic Conf. United Ch. Christ, 1983-88. With USN, 1945-51, USNR, 1952. Home and Office: 308 Valley View Dr Staunton VA 24401-2101

KOPP, ILYA ZINOVIJ, energy and environmental researcher; b. Tashkent, Uzbekistan, Aug. 1, 1929; s. Zinovij Il'ich and Anna Hanna-Bath Abramovna K.; 1 child, Victor. MS in Engring., Navy Architecture U., St. Petersburg, Russia, 1951; DSc, State Tech. U., Russia, 1961; PhD, Moscow (Russia) Aviation Inst., Tech. U., 1988. Head rsch. dept. North-West Politechnical Inst., St. Petersburg, 1957-86; prof. State Tech. U., St. Petersburg, 1986-97. Dep. dir., head theoretical dept. Sci. and Rsch. Inst. of Atmospheric Air Protection, St. Petersburg, 1988-97. Author: Effective Surfaces for Heat Transfer, 2002, Decline of the Nuclear Century or?, 2002, Power Installations for Energy Supply and Environment, 1992, Heat Power Installation for Energy Supply and Environment Protection, 1988, Foundation of the Theory of the Environmental Protection, 1993 (2nd prize 1994), Energy and Environment, 1982, Foundations of Thermodynamics and Energy Equipment for Nuclear Power Installations, 1989, others; contbr. over 170 articles to profl. jours.; patentee in field. Mem. AAAS, N.Y. Acad. Sci., Internat. Info. Acad. Home: 36-19 Bowne St #5F Flushing NY 11354 E-mail: ilkopp@hotmail.com.

KOPP, RICHARD EDGAR, electrical engineer; b. Bklyn., July 12, 1931; s. Edgar A. and Anna M. (Barto) K.; m. Elaine Hecker, June 14, 1953; children: Debra, Richard (dec.), Lisa, Barbara. BEE, Poly. Inst. Bklyn., 1953, MS, 1957, DEE, 1960. Rsch. engr. Grumman Aerospace Corp., Bethpage, N.Y., 1953-58, head computing rsch. group, 1958-65, head systems rsch. lab., 1965-70, dir. systems scis. rsch., 1970-89, dir. sci. adv. bd., 1989-90, pvt. cons., 1990—. Mem. adv. com. Poly. Inst. Imaging Scis.; adj. prof. Poly. Inst. Bklyn.,, 1961-70. Contbr. articles to profl. jours. Fellow AIAA (assoc.); mem. IEEE (sr.), U.S. Power Squadron, Mariners Landing Golf and Country Club. Home: 205 Sherwood Dr Huddleston VA 24104-3351

KOPP, ROBERT WALTER, lawyer; b. Boston, Feb. 21, 1935; s. Robert A. and Marie (Powers) K.; m. Carol A. Rosenberger, Aug. 22, 1959; children: Robert A., Christopher F., J. Brian, David W., Karen A. BS in Physics, Holy Cross Coll., 1957; LLB, Georgetown U., 1963. Bar: N.Y. 1963. Sr. ptnr. Bond, Schoeneck & King, Syracuse, N.Y., 1963—; gen. counsel Pay Bd. Econ. Stabilization Program Phase II, Washington, 1972-73. Lt. (j.g.) USN, 1957-62. Fellow Am. Bar Found., Coll. Labor and Employment Law (founding); mem. ABA (coun. sect. labor and employment law 1980-88, sect. governance liaison 1989-90, 94-2000, sect. del. to ho. of dels. 1990-93), N.Y. State Bar Assn. Roman Catholic. Home: 1 Lincoln Ctr Syracuse NY 13202-1324 Office: Bond Schoeneck & King 1 Lincoln Ctr Fl 18 Syracuse NY 13202-1324

KOPPE, WILLIAM PAUL, deputy sheriff; b. Chgo., May 7, 1949; s. Paul John and Dolores Imelda (Pritchett) K.; m. Cathy Urbaniak, Sept. 10, 1977; children: Carrie Jane, David William. BSBA, U. San Francisco, 1971. Dep. sheriff Cook County, Chgo., 1985—. World advisor, grandmaster Han Chakyo Universal Taekwondo, Wheeling, Ill., 1991-96. German-Greek liaison United Hellenic Voters of Am., Addison, Ill. With U.S. Army, 1983. Named Knight of the Blessed Virgin Mary, Cath. Ch., 1997; recipient degree of Wing Chun, Jun Fan, Calif., 1960's. Mem. Am. Legion, Teamsters, U. San Francisco Alumni Assn., Von Steuben, German-Am. Nat. Congress. Republican. Avocations: martial arts, writing, bowling, internet. Office: Cook County Sheriff Daley Ctr 50 W Washington St Chicago IL 60602-1305 Home: Apt 2 6920 N Rosemary Ln Niles IL 60714-4457 Home Fax: 847-647-8898.

KOPPEL, DONALD M(AURICE), internist; b. Chgo., July 13, 1927; s. Ben and Mignon (Gottlieb) K.; m. Nancy L. Spadafore, Sept. 11, 1987; children: Edward, Jennifer, Jill Tracy. BS, U. Ill., 1945; MD, U. Ill., Chgo., 1949. Diplomate Am. Bd. Internal Medicine. Intern Cook County Hosp., Chgo., 1949-50, resident, 1950-51, 53-55, fellow in hematology, 1955-56; internist Fairmont (W. Va.) Clinic, 1958—; clin. prof. medicine W. Va. U. Med. Sch., Morgantown, 1958—. With USAF, 1951-53. Fellow ACP. Democrat. Avocation: golf. Office: Fairmont Clinic Locust Ave Fairmont WV 26554

KOPPEL, LOWELL B. chemical engineer; b. Chgo., Sept. 13, 1935; s. Maurice G. and Mynn S. (Schultz) K.; m. Barbara Jane Parker, June 12, 1957; children: Steven P., Sharon M. Grottkau, Michael D., Lowell B. Jr. BS in Chem. Engring., Northwestern U., 1957, PhD, 1960; MS in Chem. Engring., U. Mich., 1958. Instr., fellow Calif. Inst. Tech., Pasadena, 1960-61; from asst. to prof. chem. engring. Purdue U., 1961-85, head Sch. Chem. Engring., 1973-81; sr. cons. Setpoint, Inc., Houston, 1985-90, dir., 1990-95; v.p. Aspen Tech., Inc., Cambridge, Mass., 1996-00; prin., owner Value Techniques, LLC, Winchester, Mass., 2000—. Author: Process Control, 1965, Control Theory, 1968; contbr. numerous articles to profl. jours. Recipient Lectureship award Am. Soc. Energy Edn., 1982, Outstanding Personal Achievement award McGraw-Hill Chem. Engring., 1994. Mem. AIChE. Home: 16 Hastings Rd Winchester MA 01890-3859 Office: Value Techniques LLC 16 Hastings Rd Winchester MA 01890-3859 E-mail: koppel@valuetechniques.com.

KOPPEL, TED, broadcast journalist; b. Lancashire, Eng., Feb. 8, 1940; arrived in U.S., 1953; m. Grace Anne Dorney; 4 children. BA in Liberal Studies, Syracuse U.; MA in Mass Comm. Rsch. and Polit. Sci., Stanford U. News corr., writer Sta.-WMCA, N.Y.C., 1963; with ABC News, 1963—, former gen. assignment corr., former corr. Vietnam, diplomatic corr. Hong Kong Bur., chief Miami, Fla. Bur., 1968, chief Hong Kong Bur., 1969—71, chief diplomatic corr., 1971—80; anchorman ABC News Nightline, 1980—, also editl. mgr., 1980—. Corr. for TV spls. including, The People of People's China, 1973, Kissinger: Action Biography, 1974, Second to None, 1979, The Koppel Reports, 1988—90. Author: The Wit and Wisdom of Adlai Stevenson, 1965; author: (with Marvin Kalb) (novels) In The National Interest, 1977; author: Nightline: History in the Making, 1996. Recipient Sol Taishoff award for excellence in broadcasting, Nat. Press Found., 1984, 2 George Polk award for network TV reporting, 18 Emmy awards, Acad. TV Arts and Scis., 3 George Foster Peabody awards, 8 duPont-Columbia awards, 7 Overseas Press Club awards, 2 Ohio State U. awards, 2 Soc. Profl. Journalism awards, numerous others. Office: Nightline 1717 Desales St NW Washington DC 20036-4401*

KOPPELMAN, CHAIM, artist, educator; b. Bklyn., Nov. 17, 1920; s. Samuel and Sadie (Mondlin) K.; m. Dorothy Myers, Feb. 13, 1943; 1 child, Ann. Student, Bklyn. Coll., 1938, Am. Artists Sch., 1939; student Aesthetic Realism, with Eli Siegel, 1940-78; student, Art Coll. Western Eng., Bristol, 1944, Ecole des Beaux-Arts, Rheims, 1945, Art Students League, 1946, Amedée Ozenfant Sch., 1946-49; student Aesthetic Realism, with Ellen Reiss, 1978—. Art instr. N.Y. U., 1947-55, N.Y. State U., New Paltz, 1952-58; instr. Sch. Visual Arts, N.Y.C., 1959—. Cons. Aesthetic Realism Found., N.Y.C., 1971— Author: This is the Way I See Aesthetic Realism, 1969; illustrator: Definition, 1972; contbr. articles to profl. jours.; Bibliographies of his work The Indignant Eye (Ralph Shikes), 1969, The New Humanism (Barry Schwartz), 1974, The Art of the Print (Fritz Eichenberg), 1976, American Prints and Printmakers (Una Johnson), 1980, Hilla Rebay: In Search of the Spirit in Art (Joan Lukach), 1983; one man shows include Asso. Am. Artists Gallery, 1973, Terrain Gallery, N.Y.C., 1974, 83, Warwick (Eng.) Gallery, 1975, Merida Rapp Graphics, Louisville, 1985, Print Club, Phila., Beatrice Conde Gallery, 2000, others; group shows include Purdue U., 1972, Utah State U., 1972, Arte Fiera, Bologna, 1978, NAD, N.Y.C., 1983, Print Club, Phila., 1988, Alternative Mus., N.Y.C., 1988, Art Mus., Bogota, 1996; represented in permanent collections Victoria and Albert Mus., London, Mus. Fine Arts, Caracas, Venezuela, Mus. Modern Art, N.Y.C., Met. Mus. Art, N.Y.C., Library of Congress, Washington, Los Angeles County Mus. Art, Phila. Mus. Art, Guggenheim Mus., others; sculptor Eli Siegel Meml., Druid Hill Park, Balt., 2002. Served with USAF, 1942-45. Decorated Bronze Star; recipient N.Y. State Creative Artists Pub. Svc. award, 1976, prize Soc. Am. Graphic Artists, Fabri prize Nat. Acad. Ann., 1989, Cook prize, 1998; Louis Comfort Tiffany grantee, 1956, 59. Mem. Nat. Acad. Design. Home and Office: 498 Broome St New York NY 10013-2213 E-mail: pierodella@aol.com. *I learned from Eli Siegel, the great American poet and critic, the most important thing an artist can know-this Aesthetic Realism statement: "All beauty is a making one of opposities and the making one of opposites is what we are going after in ourselves." Every artist is trying to put together opposites such as sameness and difference, warm and cool, freedom and order, and every person and artist is trying to put these same opposites together in his life.*

KOPPELMAN, DOROTHY MYERS, artist, consultant; b. N.Y.C., June 13, 1920; d. Harry Walter and May (Chalmers) Myers; m. Chaim Koppelman, Feb. 13, 1943; 1 child, Ann. Student, Bklyn. Coll., 1938-42, Am. Artists Sch., 1940-42, Art Students League, 1942; student of Aesthetic Realism, with Eli Siegel, 1942-78, with Ellen Reiss, 1978—. Instr. art Bklyn. Coll., 1952-75; dir. Terrain Gallery, N.Y.C., 1955-83, Visual Arts Gallery., Sch. Visual Arts, 1961-62; pres. Aesthetic Realism Found., 1973-85, cons., 1973—. Instr. Nat. Acad. Sch. of Design, 1988-89, 96, 98. One-woman shows include Terrain Gallery, 1961, Rina Gallery, Jersey City, 1963, Atlantic Gallery, 1999; exhibited in group shows at Mus. Modern Art, N.Y.C., 1962, Balt. Mus., 1962, Bklyn. Mus., 1962, N.J. State Mus., Jersey City, 1959, Butler Art Inst., Youngstown, Ohio, San Francisco Art Inst., 1961-62, 65, Nat. Acad. of Design Juried Ann., 1986, 90, 99, 2000, Swiss Inst., N.Y.C., Susan Teller Gallery, N.Y.C., 1993, 95, Drawing Ctr., N.Y.C., Audubon Soc. ann., N.Y.C., 1995-96, 98, Chuck Levitan Gallery, N.Y.C., 1996, Washington Square East Gallery, N.Y.C., 1992, 96, Am. Soc. Contemporary Artists Anns., 1994-96, 97, 98, 99, 2000, 01, 02, Atlantic Gallery, 1998—, Beatrice Conde Gallery, 2000, Terrain Gallery, 2001, Sarah Lawrence Gallery, 2001, Denise Bibro Gallery, 2001, Terrain Gallery, 2002, 2003; represented in permanent collections Hampton Inst., Nat. Mus. Women in the Arts, Mus. Jewish Family, Durham, N.C., Savannah Coll. Art and Design, Washington County Mus. Art, Md.; author Poems and Prints, 2000; co-author: Aesthetic Realism: We Have Been There - Six Artists, 1969; illustrator Children's Guide to Parents (by Eli Siegel), 1971, 2d edit., 2003. Recipient Theresa Lindner award for painting ASCA, 1996, Clara Shainness award for painting, 1999; Tiffany grantee for painting, 1965. Home: 498 Broome St New York NY 10013-2213 Office: Aesthetic Realism Found Inc 141 Greene St New York NY 10012-3201 E-mail: pierodella@aol.com.

KOPPELMAN, LEE EDWARD, regional planner, educator; b. NYC, May 19, 1927; s. Max and Madelyn Judith (Eisenberg) K.; m. Constance E. Lowinger, June 18, 1948; children: Leslie, Claudia, Laurel, Keith. BEE, CCNY, 1950; MS, Pratt Inst., 1964; D in Pub. Adminstrn., NYU, 1970; LLD, L.I. U., 1978; DHL, Dowling U., 1991. Cert. landscape architect, NY; cert. profl. planner, NJ. Cons. on site planning and landscape architecture, 1950-60; dir. planning Suffolk County Planning Dept., 1960-88; exec. dir. LI Regional Planning Bd., 1965—; leading prof. polit. sci., dir. ctr. regional policy studies SUNY, Stony Brook, 1967—. Adj. prof. environ. sci. Syracuse U., 1976-83; cons. US Dept. Housing and Urban Devel., 1972-78, UN on Land Use and Coastal Zone Planning; mem. Coastal Zone Mgmt. Adv. Com., 1973-75, Nassau/Suffolk Comprehensive Health Planning Council, Melville, NY, 1973-76, Nat. Shoreline Erosion Adv. Panel, 1974-81; exec. dir. tax relief on LI Bi-CountySte Commn., 1991-92; adv. coun. Sch. of Art, Architecture and Planning Cornell Univ., 1995—. Co-author: Planning Design Criteria, 1968 (3rd edit. 1981), Housing: Planning and Design, 1974, A Methodology to Achieve the Integration of Coastal Zone Science and Regional Planning, 1974, The Urban Sea: Long Island Sound, 1976, Site Planning Criteria, 1978, Long Island Comprehensive Waste Treatment Management Plan, Vol. 1 and 2, 1979, Time Saver Standards for Site Planning, 1982, Long Island Segment of the Nationwide Urban Runoff Program, 1982, Financing Government on Long Island, 1992, The Long Island Comprehensive Special Groundwater Protection Area Plan, 1992, Airport Joint Use Feasibility Study: Calverton Airport, 1993, Financing Government on Long Island, working paper, vols. 1, 2, and 3, 1993, Groundwater and Land Use Planning Experience from North Am., 1996, Town of East Hampton comprehensive Plan, 2002. Recipient cert. of tribute Temp. State Commn. on Water Resources Planning, 1964, career achievement medal Engring. and Archtl. Alumni CCNY, 1977, Disting Alumnus award NYU, 1985, medal of honor LI Assn., 1987, Lone Eagle award Pub. Rels. Soc. Am., 1987, Disting. Leadership award nat. honors program Am. Planning Assn., 1989, Disting. Svc. award NY met. chpt. Am. Planning Assn., 2000, Disting. Svc. medal Found. for LI State Parks, 2001; Paul Harris fellow, 2002; named Citizen of Yr. LI chpt. Nat. Soc. Profl. Engr., 1983. Mem. Am. Inst. Architects (hon.), Am. Inst. Planners, NY State County Planners Assn. (pres. 1967-68), Internat. Fedn. Planning and Housing, Assn. Architecture and Engr., Sigma Xi. Home: 2 Dune Ct East Setauket NY 11733-1527 Office: SUNY Ctr Regional Policy Studies Stony Brook NY 11794-0001

KOPPENBRINK, WALTER EDWIN, III, internist; b. Kansas City, Mo., July 18, 1950; s. Walter Edwin Jr. and Elizabeth (Wieman) K.; m. Joan Waisanen, May 27, 1972; children: Kristin Renée, Kimberly Diane. BA, U. Mo., 1972; MD, Washington U., St. Louis, 1976. Diplomate Am. Bd. Internal Medicine. Res., fellow Maricopa County Hosp., Phoenix, 1976-80; critical care physician John C. Lincoln Hosp., Phoenix, 1980-83; pvt. practice North Valley Med. Assocs., Phoenix, 1983-97; cons. physician Mayo Clinic, Scottsdale, Ariz., 1997-2000; pvt. practice North Phoenix Med. Specialists, 2001—. Med. dir. Bryans Ctr., Phoenix, 1988-90, Subacute unit, 1990-98, Hospice of Ariz., 1995-2000, Aerotech Labs., Inc., 2002—; adj. prof. Ariz. State U., Phoenix, 1994-95; med. dir. BTDX Analytical Laboratories, 2002—. Bd. dirs. Phoenix Youth at Risk, 1990-97, Phoenix Theatre, 1994-99, Ariz. Crohn's & Colitis Found., Phoenix, 1993-94, med. adv. bd., 1998-2003. Named Vol. of Yr., Phoenix Youth at Risk, 1997, Top Doc, Phoenix Mag., 1997; Guide to Am's Top Physicians, 2003; named one of Am.'s Top Physicians Consumer's Rsch. Coun. Am., 2003. Mem. Am. Med. Dirs. Assn., Ariz. Med. Assn., Phoenix Gastroenterology Soc. Presbyterian. Avocations: scuba, skiing, sailing, travel, oenology. Office: North Phoenix Med Specialists 9100 N 2nd St Phoenix AZ 85020

KOPPENHEFFER, JULIE B. lawyer; b. Lexington, Ky., July 14, 1945; d. Arthur S. and Mae (Bronfeld) Adler; m. Thomas Lynn Koppenheffer, Dec. 22, 1967; children: Michael, Alex. AB, Boston U., 1966, JD, 1969. Bar: Mass. 1969, U.S. Dist. Ct. Mass. 1970, U.S. Supreme Ct. 1976, Tex.1979. Pvt. practice law, Williamstown, Mass., 1974-79; sr. corp. atty. LaQuinta Motor Inn, San Antonio, 1979-83, assoc. gen. counsel, 1983-84; v.p., gen. counsel Texian Inns, San Antonio, 1984—; adj. prof. North Adams State Coll., Mass., 1977-79. Bd. dirs. Encino Park Homeowners Assn., San Antonio, 1984. Mem. Tex. Bar

Assn., ABA, San Antonio Bar Assn. (chmn. Corp. Com. 1984-86). Home: 20015 Park Bluff St San Antonio TX 78259-1930 Office: The New Texian Co 8000 W Ih 10 Ste 1500 San Antonio TX 78230-3883

KOPPES, STEVEN NELSON, science writer, editor; b. Manhattan, Kans., Aug. 28, 1957; awd; s. Ralph James and Mary Louise (Nelson) K.; m. Susan Camille Keaton, May 18, 1984, (div. July 2001). BS in Anthropology cum laude, Kans. State U., 1978; MS in Journalism, Kans. U., 1982. Rsch. asst. dept. anthropology Kans. State U., Manhattan, 1979; reporter The Morning Sun, Pittsburg, Kans., 1981-83; co-mgr. Doc's B.R. Others Restaurant, Tempe, Ariz., 1983-85; info. specialist Ariz. State U. New Bur., Tempe, 1985-87, asst. dir., 1987-96, interim dir., 1996-97; sci. writer-editor Office Rsch. Comms. U. Ga., Athens, 1997-98; sci. writer U. Chgo. News Office, 1998—. Cons. Ariz. Sci. Ctr., 1995-96. Contbr. to Ariz. State U. Rsch. Mag., 1984-99. Bd. dirs. Children's Mus. of Metro Phoenix, 1988. Recipient Excellence in Mktg. and Pubs. award, Univ. Continuing Edn. Assn., 2002, Excellence award Internat. Assn. Bus. Communicators, 1991-92, Merit award, 1989-93, Disting. Tech. Comm. award Soc. Tech. Comm. Phoenix Chpt., 1994-95, Spl. Merit award mag. pub. improvement and award of excellence Coun. for Advancement and Support of Edn. Dist. III, 1999. Mem. Nat. Assn. Sci. Writers, Ariz. Archaeol. Soc. (bd. dirs. Phoenix chpt. 1987-88), Rio Salado Rowing Club (charter mem. 1995-97). Avocations: long-distance running, backpacking, outdoor photography. Office: U Chgo News Office 5801 S Ellis Ave Rm 200 Chicago IL 60637-5418

KOPPLIN, DAVID F. music educator, composer; s. Edward Mortimer and Frances Ann Kopplin; m. Rebecca Steuermann, Sept. 12, 1992. PhD, UCLA, LA, CA, 1992—99; MusM, USC, LA, CA, 1988—90. U of Colo., Boulder, CO, 1986—88; BA, U of Colo., Denver, CO, 1981—82. Asst. prof. Cal Poly Pomona, Pomona, Calif., 2001—; writer and editor Hollywood Bowl and LA Philharm., LA, 1996—2001; composer Various, LA, 1990—, musician/performer Various, 1978—. Program annotator and music writer various, various, United States, 1996—. Composer: (concerto for double bass and orchestra) Fables, Farewells, and Flashbacks, (symphonic song cycle) From the Runes; musician: (recording) Wild Beast/Clubfoor Orchestra; composer: (feature film score) The Cool Surface. Bd. mem. Santa Monica Symphony Orch., Santa Monica, Calif. Fellow Jazz Study Fellowship, Nat. Endowment for the Arts, 1983-84; grantee Artists in Edn. Grant, Colo. Coun. on the Arts and Humanities, 1982-83; scholar Henry Mancini Award, UCLA, 1995, Collegium of U Tchg. Fellows. Mem.: Internat. Assn. of Jazz Educators, BMI, Coll. Music Soc. (so. pacific chpt. vp 2000—03). Democrat-Npl. Office: Cal Poly Pomona 3801 W Temple Ave Pomona CA 91768 E-mail: dfkopplin@csupomona.edu.

KOPPOLU, AJOY P.K. research scientist, chemical engineer; s. Venkatanarasamma Yerakaliah Koppolu; m. Lakshmi Vadde, Dec. 7, 1994. BS, R.V. Coll. Engring., 1990; MS, Indian Inst. Sci., 1993; PhD, U. Nebr., 1998. Rsch. assoc. U. Nebr., Lincoln, 1998—99; sr. process devel. scientist Novartis Consumer Health, Inc., 1999—. Cons. John Roth & Son, Omaha, 1998—98. Recipient U. 9th Rank, Bangalore U., India, 1990, Gold medal, Arya Vysya Trust, India, 1990; fellow, Dept. Chem. Engring., Indian Inst. Sci., 1990—92, Milton E. Mohr Rsch. fellow, Coll. Engring., U. Nebr., 1997; scholar, Dept. Biol. Systems Engring., Univ. Nebr., 1995—99, Merit scholar, R.V.College Engring., Bangalore U., India, 1986—90. Mem.: AIChE (assoc.), Am. Oil Chemists' Soc., Am. Assn. Pharm. Scientists, Am. Chem. Soc. Achievements include patents for Preparation of fatty acid metal salts and enzymes from ruminal fluid Patent No. 6391598, May 21, 2002; patents pending for Novel Enzymatic Approach for Analytical Method Development, Accepted for Publication; research in Recovery of volatile fatty acids and enzymes from dilute model aqueous and ruminal waste streams, PhD thesis, University of Nebraska-Lincoln, Lincoln, NE, 2002; Studies on the kinetics of calcium carbonate and calcium hydroxide for energy storage, MS thesis, Indian Institute of Science, India, 1990; 'Settling of solids in suspension formulations in Pharmaceutical Technology, Vol. 26, No. 12, 48-54, 2002; 'Investigation on the kinetics of calcium carbonate decomposition' in Chemical Engineering Science, Vol. 49, 2198-2207, 1994. Personal E-mail: ajoy_lakshmi@yahoo.com. E-mail: ajoy_lakshmi@yahoo.com.

KOPPUS, BETTY JANE, retired savings and loan association executive; b. Toledo, June 14, 1922; d. Carl Emerson and Hilda Sarah (Semlow) Koppus. Student, pub. schs. With United Savs. and Loan Assn. (now Sky Bank), Toledo, 1940—, asst. sec., 1943—62, treas., 1962—73, sec., 1973—78, v.p., 1978-84, ret., 1984. Former trustee, sec. Luth. Social Svc. Northwestern Ohio; mem. St. Mark Luth. Ch. Mem.: Zonta Toledo I, River Rd. Garden Club, Beta Sigma Phi. Address: 5709 Chardonnay Dr Toledo OH 43615-7312

KOPRIVICA, DOROTHY MARY, management consultant, real estate and insurance broker; b. St. Louis, May 27, 1921; d. Mitar and Fema (Guzina) K. BS, Washington U., St. Louis, 1962. cert. in def. inventory mgmt. Dept. Def., 1968. Mgmt. analyst Transp. Supply and Maintenance Command, St. Louis, 1954-57, Dept. Army Transp. Material Command, St. Louis, 1957-62; program analyst Dept. Army Aviation System Command, St. Louis, 1962-74, spl. asst. to comdr., 1974-78; ins. broker D. Koprivica, Ins., St. Louis, 1978-81; real estate broker St. Louis, 1978-81; ret., 2002. Mem. Bus. and Profl. Women (pres. 1974-75), Order Ea. Star. Eastern Orthodox.

KOPROSKI, ALEXANDER ROBERT, real estate executive; b. Stamford, Conn., Apr. 6, 1934; s. Alexander J. and Gladys J. (Kryger) K.; m. Patricia A. Velliquette; children: Lisa, Susan, Gregory, Beth. Student, U. Conn., 1952-54; BS in Mktg. and Fin., Tri-State U., Angola, Ind., 1959. Lic. real estate broker, Conn., N.Y. Comml. and indsl. broker S.H. Silberman, Inc., Stamford, 1960-73; owner, CEO, comml. and indsl. broker Al Koproski Realty, Stamford, 1973—. Mem. Coastal Mgmt. Adv. Com. Past pres. Holy Name Home and Sch. Assn.; past chmn. Poles for Ford Com., Kosciuszko Park Meml. Com., Stamford-(Conn.) Pulaski Meml. Com., Hartford; past mem. Stamford Bicentennial Com., Resource Recovery Task Force, Polish Am. Affairs Coun., Mayor's South End Adv. Com., Stamford C.E.T.A. Manpower Program; mem. Stamford Hist. Soc.; mem. South End Revitalization Com., Stamford, 1996—; past chmn. lay adv. bd., past chmn. 75th ann. yr. book Holy Name of Jesus Cath. Ch.; past bd. dirs. Polish Am. Congress Conn., Polish Am. Cen. Com. Stamford; bd. dirs. Polish Slavic Info. Ctr., Stamford, 1975—, Am. Ctr. Polish Culture, Washington, 1990—, reelected treas., fund raiser; mem. Polish studies adv. com. Ctrl. Conn. State U., 1994; chmn. Little League, Dzialdowo, Poland, nat. v.p. Polish Nat. Youth Baseball Found., 1997; elected lay adv. bd. Holy Name of Jesus Ch., Stamford, mem. 100th anniversary com., 2002-2003; grand marshal N.Y.C. Pulaski Parade, 2000; mem. Poles for Bush, 2000. With U.S. Army, 1955-57. Named Citizen of Yr., Polish Am. World, N.Y.C., 1978, Layman of Yr., Stamford Kiwanis Club, 1979; recipient Krzyżem Kawwalerskim Orderu Zaslugi Rzeczypospolitej Polskeij medal, Govt. of Poland, 1994, Ellis Island Medal of Honor, 1998, Excellence award Inst. for Religious Edn. and Pastoral Studies, Sacred Heart U., 2001, Polish Govt. medal, 2001, Urzad Kultury Fizcznej i Sportu award, Govt. of Poland, 2001, REAPS award for excellence, Sacred Heart U. Bapt. Ct., 2001, Baseball field in Dizialdowo, Poland named "Al Koproski Stadium", 2003. Mem. Stamford Bd. Realtors, Am. Coun. Polish Cultural Clubs (nat. fundraising chmn. Washington project), Kosciuszko Found. (co-chmn. nat. coun.), Polish Am. Cultural Soc. (historian, pres. 2002--, Citizen of Yr. 1975), Am. Assn. Mil. Order of Malta, Exch. Club, Holy Name Athletic Club (pres., CEO, Citizen of Yr. 1982, past pres.), Polish Am. Bus. and Profl. Club (past pres.), Oceanview Beach and Tennis Club (past treas.). Republican. Roman Catholic. Achievements include honor by dedication of Al Koproski Little League Baseball Stadium, Dzialdowo Poland. Avocations: swimming, fundraising, travel. Home: 222 Ocean Dr E Stamford CT 06902-8134 Office: Polish Slavic Info Ctr PO Box 631 Stamford CT 06904-0631

KOPROWSKI, HILARY, microbiologist, educator; b. Warsaw; s. Pawel and Sonia (Berland) K.; m. Irena Grasberg; children: Claude Eugene, Christopher Dorian. BA, Nikolaj Rej Gymnasium of Luth. Congregation, Warsaw; MD, U. Warsaw; grad., Warsaw Conservatory Music and Santa Cecilia Acad., Rome; DSc (hon.), Ludwig-Maximilian U., Munich, Widener Coll.; D of Medicine and Surgery, U. Helsinki, Finland; MD (hon.), U. Uppsala, Sweden; LittD (hon.), Thomas Jefferson U.; DMS (hon.), U. Lublin, Poland, Univ. Coll. Dublin, U. Poznan, Poland, U. Warsaw Acad. Medicine. Rsch. asst. dept. exptl. and gen. pathology U. Warsaw, 1936—39; staff Yellow Fever Rsch. Svc., Rio de Janeiro, 1940—44; staff rsch. divsn. Am. Cyanamid Co., 1944—46; asst. dir. viral and rickettsial rsch. Lederle Lab., Pearl River, NY, 1946—57; dir. Wistar Inst., Phila., 1957—91, prof., 1957—93, prof. laureate, 1993—; Wistar Inst. prof. of rsch. medicine U. Pa., 1957—; prof. microbiology and immunology Thomas Jefferson U., Phila., 1992—; dir. Ctr. Neurovirology, Biotech. Found. Labs., 1992—. Cons. WHO, 1950—; mem. microbiology study sect. NIH, 1956-60; mem. FAIIO, mem. adv. com. Nat. Multiple Sclerosis Soc., 1970-78, mem. immunobiology adv. com. NIH, USPHS, 1975-76; mem. bd. sci. counselors div. cancer etiology Nat. Cancer Inst., 1982-86, chmn., 1987-90; mem. biol. response modifiers program decision network com. NIH, 1985-87; mem. immunobiol. adv. com. NIH, USPHS, 1975-76. Co-editor: Methods in Virology, Viruses and Immunity, Current Topics in Microbiology and Immunology, 1965—. Hon. trustee Kosciuszko Found., 1993—. Decorated commandeur Order du Mérite pour la Rsch. et l'Invention, chevalier Order Royal De Lion Belgium, comdr. Order of The Lion of Finland, officer Order of the Polish Republic, Chevalier Legion d'honneur The French Govt., Greater Order of Merit Pres. Poland; named hon. trustee, Kosciuszko Found., 1993; recipient Lifetime Achievement award, Monte Jade Sci. and Tech. Assn. Mid-Atlantic, Alvarenga prize, Coll. Physicians Phila., 1959, Alfred Jurzykowski Found. Polish Millenium prize, 1966, Felix Wankel Tierschutz prize, 1979, Alexander von Humboldt Sr. U.S. Scientist award, Phila. Cancer Rsch. award, Phila. Cancer Club, 1989, San Marino award, 1989, Nicolaus Copernicus medal, Polish Acad. Scis., 1989, The Phila. award, 1990, John Scott award, 1990; scholar Fulbright scholar, Max Planck Inst. für Verhaltensphysiologie, Seewiesen, Fed. Republic Germany, 1971. Fellow AAAS, N.Y. Acad. Medicine, Phila. Coll. Physicians; mem. NAS, Nat. Acad. Arts and Scis., Yugoslavian Acad. Scis., Polish Acad. Scis., Russian Acad. Med. Scis., Finnish Acad. Arts and Scis., N.Y. Acad. Scis. (pres. 1959, trustee 1960-72). Achievements include development of first oral polio vaccine which ultimately led to elimination, in 1992 of polio from the Americas; development of new rabies vaccine for humans, reducing the number of injections and of oral vaccine in bait for immunization of wildlife; research on mechanism of damage of cells in brain in neurotropic virus infection; development of first monoclonal antibody for treatment and cure of colorectal cancer. Office: Thomas Jefferson U Dept Microbiology and Immun JAH-M85 1020 Locust Street Philadelphia PA 19107 E-mail: h_koprowski@lac.jci.tju.edu.

KOPUZ, KASIM, educator, consultant; b. Rize, Turkey, Feb. 1, 1965; s. Necmettin and Sadiye K.; m. Zumrut, Aug. 25, 1998; 1 child, Hafsa Nihal. MA in History, Binghamton (N.Y.) U., 1999, postgrad., 2002—. Imam, exec. dir. Islamic Org. So. Tier, Binghamton, 1993—. Lectr. on Islam and Muslim cultures; cons. in field. Active Broome County Coun. of Ch., Binghamton, 1999, Broome County Peace Action. Home: 23 Custer Ave Johnson City NY 13790 Office: Islamic Org So Tier 161 Grand Ave Johnson City NY 13790 E-mail: kkopuz@binghamton.edu.

KOPYTKO, EDWIN EDWARD, nursing administrator; b. Chgo., 1953; s. Kazimierz and Anna Kopytko; m. Therese Kuras, 1984; children: Alexander, Katherine. BA, Loyola U., 1974; diploma, Augustana Hosp. Sch. Nursing, 1980; MS, Rush U., 1983. Mental health worker Barclay Hosp., Chgo., 1977-78; staff nurse Rush-Presbyn.-St. Luke's Hosp., Chgo., 1980-83, asst. unit leader, 1983-88, unit leader, 1988-98, unit dir., 1998—; instr. Rush Coll. Nursing. Parish counselor St. Agnes/St. Kieran Roman Cath. Ch., Chicago Heights, Ill., 1992—97; legal cons. Contbr. articles to profl. jours. Grantee Sigma Theta Tau and Chgo. Cmty. Trust Fund, 1985-86. Mem. Ill. Nurses Assn. (dist. 20 bd. dirs. 1996—, membership chair 1996-98, sec. 1997-2001, 1st v.p. 2001—), St. Agnes Holy Name Soc. (rec. sec., bd. dirs. 1992-98). Avocations: fishing, books on tape, church choir. Office: Rush-Presbyn-St Lukes Med Ctr 1653 W Congress Pkwy Chicago IL 60612-3833 E-mail: Edwin_E_Kopytko@rush.edu.

KORABIC, EDWARD WALTER, medical educator, speech pathology/audiology services professional; s. Edward Stanley Korabic and Italia Lucy Parisi; m. Tracy Van Houten Korabic, Sept. 23, 1983; children: Justine Alexandra, Jordan Elizabeth. BS, Siena Coll., 1972; MA, Coll. St. Rose, 1974; PhD, Syracuse U., 1981. Cert. course dir. Coun. Accreditation Occupl. Hearing Conservation, 1974, cert. clin. competence audiology Am. Speech-Lang.-Hearing Assn., 1976. Assoc. prof., chair dept. speech pathology and audiology Marquette U., Milw., 1979—. Occupl. hearing conservation cons., Shorewood, Wis., 1974—. Contbr. articles. Mem. adv. bd. Shorewood (Wis.) Cmty. Fitness Ctr., 1999—. Fellow: Am. Acad. Audiology. Conservative. Roman Catholic. Avocations: travel, photography, computing. Office: Marquette Univ PO Box 1881 Milwaukee WI 53201-1881 Office Fax: 414-288-3980. E-mail: edward.korabic@marquette.edu.

KORAL, ALAN MAX, lawyer; b. N.Y.C., July 10, 1941; s. Max and Sylvia (Stoffman) K. AB with highest honors, U. Rochester, 1962; postgrad., Princeton U., 1962-65; JD, U. Chgo., 1975. Bar: Ill. 1975, N.Y. 1977, U.S. Dist. Ct. (no. dist.) Ill. 1975, U.S. Dist. Ct. (so. dist.) N.Y. 1978, U.S. Dist. Ct. (no. dist.) N.Y. 1981, U.S. Dist. Ct. (ea. dist.) N.Y. 1986, U.S. Ct. Appeals (11th cir.) 1987, U.S. Ct. Appeals (2nd cir.) 1990, U.S. Ct. Appeals (3d and 4th cirs.) 1995. Assoc. Vedder, Price, Kaufman & Kammholz, Chgo., 1975-76, Vedder, Price, Kaufman, Kammmholz & Day, N.Y.C., 1976-81, ptnr., 1982-2000, Vedder, Price, Kaufman & Kammholz, N.Y.C., 2000—. Author: Conducting the Lawful Employment Interview, 1st edit., 1984, 4th edit., 1992, Employee Privacy Rights, 1988. Mem. N.Y. State Human Rights Adv. Coun., N.Y.C., 1985. Recipient Cmty. Svc. award Bar Assn. Human Rights Greater N.Y., 1988. Mem. ABA, N.Y. State Bar Assn. (chair labor sec. EEO exec. com.), Assn. of Bar of City of N.Y. Office: Vedder Price Kaufman & Kammholz 805 3rd Ave New York NY 10022-7513 E-mail: akoral@vedderprice.com.

KORANYI, ADAM, mathematics educator; b. Szeged, Hungary, July 13, 1932; came to U.S., 1957, naturalized, 1963; s. Jeno and Vilma (Szigethy) K.; m. Anna Eiben, Mar. 16, 1968; children— Peter, Daniel. Diploma, U. Szeged, 1954; PhD, U. Chgo., 1959. Instr. Harvard, 1959-60; asst. prof. U. Calif. at Berkeley, 1960-64; vis. asst. prof. Princeton, 1964-65; faculty Belfer Grad. Sch. Sci., Yeshiva U., N.Y.C., 1965-79, prof. math., 1968-79, Washington U., St. Louis, 1979-85; Disting. prof. Lehman Coll. CUNY, 1985—. Contbr. articles to profl. jours. Mem. Am. Math. Soc., Acad. Scis. Hungary. Home: 26 Royden Rd Tenafly NJ 07670-1010 Office: CUNY Lehman Coll Bronx NY 10468

KORB, CHRISTINE ANN, music therapist, researcher, educator; b. Milw., Aug. 9, 1943; d. Carl William and Lucille (Bell) Knoernschild; m. Mark Lee Korb, June 3, 1967 (div. May 1991); children: Tracy Lee, Amy Elizabeth. BS, Mt. Mary Coll., Milw., 1965; MMus in Music Therapy, Colo. State U., Ft. Collins, 1988. Registered and bd. cert. music therapist. Field dir. Girl Scouts of Am., Ill. Wis., 1965-69; contractual swimming tchr. YMCA, Janesville, Wis., 1970-76; contractual music tchr. YWCA, Janesville, Wis., 1971-76; music therapist inpatient/outpatient psychiat. unit Poudre Valley Hosp., Ft. Collins, 1989-92; music therapist Mary Hill Retirement Ctr., Milw., 1992-93, VA Med. Ctr., Milw., 1992-98; vis. asst. prof. music therapy Willamette U., Salem, Oreg., 1998—2000; dir of music therapy Marylhurst Univ., Oreg., 2000—. Composer (musical works) Nazareth, 1988 (Art of Peace award 1985), We Are Your People of Love, 1981 (hon. mention Am. Song Festival 1981), Windseeker, 1988, Merry Christmas Day, 1994. Founding mem. Women in the Arts, Ft. Collins, 1987-88. Rsch. for music therapy grantee Helen Bader Found., Milw., 1994-95. Mem. Am. Music Therapy Assn., Music Tchrs. Nat. Assn., Amnesty Internat., Mu Phi Epsilon, Am. assoc. of univ. women. Democrat. Avocations: reading, spirituality, hiking, cross-country skiing, canoeing. Home: 13538 SW 63rd Pl Portland OR 97219-8122

KORB, JOAN, lawyer; b. Fond du Lac, Wis., Jan. 22, 1953; d. Allen Dale Korb and Evelyn A. Schmitz-Korb; m. Frederic B. Will, June 19, 1983. BS in Biology, U. Wis., Oshkosh, 1975; JD, John Marshall Sch. Law, Chgo., 1985. Bar: Wis. 1985, Ill. 1985. Asst. corp. counsel Racine County, Racine, Wis., 1985-89, asst. dist. atty., 1990-99, Door County, Sturgeon Bay, Wis., 1999—. Commentator on fetal abuse on TV, radio, in newspapers. Author novels. Mem. Mt. Pleasant (Wis.) Zoning Bd. Appeals, 1987-99; past pres. Wis. Profl. Soc. on Abuse of Children, Milw.; treas. Bd. Children Law Sec. of State Bar of Wis., 1998-2003. Mem. NOW, AAUW (pub. policy chmn. Racine 1995-99), Sierra Club (life). Avocations: lectr. children and legal issues, reading, scuba diving, sailing, travel. Office: Door County Dist Atty's Office 421 Nebraska St Ofc Sturgeon Bay WI 54235-2249

KORB, LAWRENCE JOHN, metallurgist; b. Warren, Pa., Apr. 28, 1930; s. Stanley Curtis and Dagna (Pedersen) K.; m. Janet Davis, Mar. 30, 1957; children: James, William, Jeanine. B in Chem. Engring., Rensselaer Poly. Inst., Troy, N.Y., 1952. Registered profl. engr., Calif. Sales engr. Alcoa, Buffalo, N.Y., 1955-59; metall. engr. N.Am. Rockwell Co., Downey, Calif., 1959-62; engring. supr. metallurgy Apollo program Rockwell Internat. Co., Downey, 1962-66, engring. supr. advanced materials, 1966-72, engring. supr. metals and ceramics space shuttle program, 1972-88; cons., 1988—. Mem. tech. adv. com. metallurgy Cerritos Coll., 1969—74; mem. forensic team Columbia Accident Investigation, 2003. Contbr. chpts. to books and articles to profl. jours. Served with USNR, 1952-55. Fellow Am. Soc. Metals (chmn. aerospace activity com. 1971-76, judge materials application competition 1969, handbook com. 1978-83, chmn. handbook com. 1983, chmn. publs. coun. 1984). Republican. Home: 251 S Violet Ln Orange CA 92869-3740

KORB, WILLIAM BROWN, JR., manufacturing company executive; b. Warren, Pa., Apr. 27, 1940; s. William Brown and Helen (Haslett) K.; m. Dorothy Wendell Trout, June 11, 1962; children: Karen Michel, David Wendell, Christine Leigh. BS in Indsl. Engring, Pa. State U., 1962; grad., Advanced Mgmt. Program, Harvard U., 1979. With Reliance Electric Co. div. Exxon, 1962-86, gen. mgr. mech. group, Mishawaka, Ind., 1977-79, operating v.p., Cleve., 1979-86; pres., CEO, bd. dirs. Gilbarco, Inc., Greensboro, N.C., 1987-99, Marconi Commerce Systems, Inc., 1999—2001; ret., 2001. Bd. dirs. Cambrex Corp., Wachovia Bank of N.C., Greensboro, Premier Farnell plc. Bd. visitors Greensboro Coll.; trustee Moses Cone Health Sys. Mem.: Greensboro Country. Home: 2704 Lake Forest Dr Greensboro NC 27408-3805

KORBA, ROBERT W. manufacturing executive; b. 1943; BA, U. Nebr., Omaha, 1965, JD, 1968. Of counsel Lifetime Security Life Ins., Denton, Tex., 1971-72; ptnr. Foxter & Korba. Inc. PC, Denton, Tex., 1972-73; gen. counsel LSL Corp., Denton, Tex., 1973; pres., CEO Sammons Enterprises, Inc., Dallas, 1973—. With U.S. Army, 1968-71. Office: Sammons Enterprises Inc 5949 Sherry Ln Ste 1900 Dallas TX 75225*

KORBANKA, JUERGEN ERICH, psychologist, educator; b. Riedlingen, Germany, Aug. 12, 1963; s. Reinhold Paul and Doris Elizabeth Korbanka, m. Ines Katharina Paul, Aug. 17, 1964; children: Judith Martha, Lucas Paul. BA, U. of Calif., Irvine, 1986—88; MA, Naropa Inst., Boulder, CO, 1988—90; PhD, Calif. Inst. of Integral Studies, 1991—95. Designated Examiner Dept. of Human Services, Utah, 1998, Psychologist Lic. State of Utah, 1997, Domestic Abuse Intervention for Men and Women Nat. Domestic Abuse Intervention Project, Minn., 1995, Approved Clin. Supr. CCE, N.J., 2002, Clin. psychologist Wasatch Mental Health, Provo, Utah, 1994—98; adj. faculty Calif. Inst. of Integral Studies, San Francisco, 1996—98; rsch./ outcome specialist Wasatch Mental Health, Provo, 1998—2001; adj. faculty U. of Phoenix, Salt Lake City, Utah, 1998—2000, asst. dept. chair, 2000—; program mgr. Wasatch Mental Health, Provo, 2002—. Chair Utah County Domestic Violence Coalition, Provo, 1997—98; conf. chair Utah Counseling Assn., Salt Lake City, 2000—; mem. Utah Domestic Violence Adv. Bd., Salt Lake City, 2001—. Author: (jour. article) Psychol. Reports, Jour. of Interpersonal Violence; presenter (profl. presentation) Am. Counseling Assn. Recipient Outstanding Contbn. as Chair of Utah County Domestic Violence Coalition Award, Utah County Domestic Violence Coalition, 1998, Outstanding Svc. Award, 2000. Mem.: Assn. for Counselor and Educator Supervision, Utah County Domestic Violence Coalition, Utah Domestic Violence Adv. Coun., Utah Counseling Assn., ACA, APA. Office: U of Phoenix Utah 5373 South Green St Salt Lake City UT 84123 Office Fax: 801-269-9766. E-mail: juergen.korbanka@phoenix.com.

KORBITZ, BERNARD CARL, retired oncologist, hematologist, educator, consultant; b. Lewistown, Mont., Feb. 18, 1935; s. Fredrick William and Rose Eleanore (Ackmann) K.; m. Constance Kay Bolz, June 22, 1957; children: Paul Bernard, Guy Karl. B.S. in Med. Sci., U. Wis.-Madison, 1957, M.D., 1960, M.S. in Oncology, 1962; LL.B., LaSalle U., 1972. Asst. prof. medicine and clin. oncology, U. Wis. Med. Sch., Madison, 1967-71; dir. medicine Presbyn. Med. Ctr., Denver, 1971-73; practice medicine specializing in oncology, hematology, Madison, 1973-76; med. oncologist, hematologist Radiologic Ctr. Meth. Hosp., Omaha, 1976-82; practice medicine specializing in oncology, hematology, Omaha, 1982-95, ret., 1995; sci. advisor Citizen's Environ. Com., Denver, 1972-73; mem. Meth. Hosp., Omaha, 1977—; dir. Bernard C. Korbitz, P.C., Omaha, 1983-96; bd. dirs., pres. B.C. Korbitz P.C., ret., 1996. Contbr. articles to profl. jours. Webelos leader Denver area Council, Mid. Am. Council of Nebr. Boy Scouts Am.; bd. elders King of Kings Luth. Ch., Omaha, 1979-80; bd. elders St. Mark Luth. Ch., Omaha, 1993-98; mem. People to People Del. Cancer Update to People's Republic China, 1986, Eastern Europe and USSR, 1987; mem. U.S. Senatorial Club, 1984, Republican Presdl. Task Force, 1984. Served to capt. USAF, 1962-64. Named Medford (Wis.) H.S. Athletic Hall of Fame, 1997. Fellow ACP, Royal Soc. Health; mem. Am. Soc. Clin. Oncology, Am. Soc. Internal Medicine, AMA, Nebr. Med. Assn., Omaha Med. Society, Omaha Clin. Soc., Phi Eta Sigma, Phi Beta Kappa, Phi Kappa Phi, Alpha Omega Alpha. Avocations: photography, fishing, travel. Home: 9024 Leavenworth St Omaha NE 68114-5150

KORBMAN, MEYER HYMAN, rabbi, public school administrator; b. Newark, Oct. 30, 1925; s. Abraham and Celia Korbman; m. Mildred Penn, Dec. 17, 1950; children: Marc, Riva, David. BA, Yeshiva U., 1949; MA, Seton Hall U., 1954. Ordained rabbi, 1952. Rabbi Congregation Beth El, Hightstown, N.J., 1951-70, Temple Israel, Union, N.J., 1970—; v.p. pub. schs. Newark, 1974-95. Mem. Coun. Congregations and Chs., Union, 1970—. Trustee Rabbinical Coll., N.J., 1952-54, Jewish Fedn., Union, 1970—; trustee, exec. bd. Grad. Inst. Talmudical Studies, 1954; apptd. mem. Sr. Citizens Adv. Commn., Union, 1976—. With U.S. Army, 1944-46. Recipient cert. of merit Newark Bd. Edn., 1978, Citizen of Yr. award B'nai Brith, 1986, award Union County Bd. of Chosen Freeholders, 1986, citation Union Twp., 1986, Gen. Assembly citation State of N.J., 1986, Notable Am. award of merit, 1987, cert. recognition Union Twp. Bd. Edn., 1987, Golden Circle award Israel Histadrut Found., 1988. Mem. NEA, Union County Bd. Rabbis, Essex County Bd. Rabbis, Newark Reading Resource Assn. (pres. 1969-72), City Adminstrs. and Suprs. Assn., Right to Read (N.J. bldg. dir. 1970-72), Internat. Reading Assn. Home: 2454 Ogden Rd Union NJ 07083-6526 Office: Temple Israel of Union 2372 Morris Ave Union NJ 07083-5785 E-mail: rmkorb18@aol.com. *Life is so tenuous that it would be most prudent to live it in such a way as to leave good memories to those who come after us.*

KORCHIN, JUDITH MIRIAM, lawyer; b. Kew Gardens, N.Y., Apr. 28, 1949; d. Arthur Walter and Mena (Levisohn) Goldstein; m. Paul Maury Korchin, June 10, 1972; 1 son, Brian Edward. BA with high honors, U. Fla., 1971, JD with honors, 1974. Bar: Fla. 1974, U.S. Ct. Appeal (2d, 5th and 11th cirs.), U.S. Dist. Ct. (so., mid. and no. dists) Fla. Law clk. to judge U.S. Dist. Ct., 1974-76; assoc. Steel, Hector & Davis, Miami, Fla., 1976-81, ptnr., 1981-87, Holland and Knight, Miami, 1987—. Author, exec. editor U. Fla. Law Rev., 1973-74. Mem. U. Fla. Law Ctr. Coun., 1980-83; pres. alumni bd. U. Fla. Law Rev., 1983; bd. dirs. Fla. Film & Rec. Inst., 1982-84. Recipient Trail Blazer Award The Women's Com. of 100, 1988. Fellow: Am. Bar Found.; mem.: ABA (sect. alternative dispute resolution, vice chmn. 1994—95, co-chmn. fed. ct. mediation com. 1995, sect. labor and employment law, sect. litig.), Fla. Bar Found. (subcom. legal assistance for poor 1988—90), Fla. Bar Assn. (vice chmn. jud. nominating procedures com. 1982, civil procedure rules com. 1984—89, 1993—95), Nat. Assn. Bank Women (TV panelist greater Miami chpt. 1987), Nat. Assn. Women Bus. Owners (adv. coun. 1987—88), Dade County Bar Assn. (bd. dirs. 1981—82, treas. 1982, sec. 1983, 3d v.p. 1984, 2d v.p. 1985, 1st v.p. 1986, pres. 1987), CPR Inst. for Dispute Resolution (nat. panelist 1994—, exec. com. 2003—), Am. Arbitration Assn. (employment law panel, s.e. 1993—, comml. law panel 1993—), Greater Miami C. of C. (com. profl. devel. 1988—90), Rabbinical Assn. Greater Miami (TV panelist Still Small Voice 1987), City Club (bd. dirs. 1988—93), Phi Kappa Phi, Phi Beta Kappa, Order of Coif. Office: Holland & Knight PO Box 015441 701 Brickell Ave Ste 3000 Miami FL 33131-2898

KORCHNAK, LAWRENCE C. educational administrator, consultant, writer; AB, Georgetown U., 1968; MEd, Duquesne U., 1974; PhD, U. Pitts., 1987. Tchr., basketball coach St. Vincent Prep. Sch., Latrobe, Pa., 1968-70; tchr., counselor St. Mary of the Mount H.S., Pitts., 1970-76; dir. of edn. Median Sch., Pitts., 1983-85; vocat. guidance coord., drug & alcohol coord., counselor

Hopewell Area Sch. Dist., Aliquippa, Pa., 1976-86; instr. Pa. State U., Beaver, 1990-99; adminstr., profl. devel. coord. Beaver (Pa.) Area Sch. Dist., 1986-98; asst. supt. Hampton Township Sch. Dist., 1998-2000, supt., 2000—. Cons. Ednl. Support Svcs., 1987—; lectr. U. Pitts. Grad. Sch. Edn., 1988—; continuing edn. adv. bd. Pa. State U., Beaver, 1993-99; student assistance adv. bd. Prevention Project, Monaca, Pa., 1990-99; sch. attendance task force Beaver County, 1996-99; mem. Teen Pregnancy Task Force of Beaver County; mem. Allegheny County Student Assistance Coordinating Coun., 1998—; mem. Hampton Alliance for Ednl. Excellence, 1998—, Spl. Edn. Family Tng. Task Force, 1999-2001; mem. early childhood edn. action com. Edn. Policy and Issues Ctr. Author: Case Law and Common Sense, 1998, 2002, Important Legal Issues..., 1987, Focus on Careers, 1978 (Outstanding Rsch. award, 1999); contbr. articles to profl. publs. Mem. Managed Care Task Force, Beaver County, 1996-99, Drug and Alcohol Planning Coun., Beaver County, 1991-96, chair, 1994-98; exec. bd. dirs. Ars Millenium, 1996—; mem. Exec. Com., 2001—, Tri-State Study Coun., 2001—; ednl. adv. bd. C.C. of Allegheny County, 2002—; adv. bd. Health South, 2002—; adv. coun. Pa. State Student Assistance Program, 2003—; coord. Allegheny county schs. United Way. Mem. ASCD, Am. Assn. Sch. Adminstrs., Pa. Assn. Sch. Adminstrs. (state del. 2001—, Region 3 exec. com., Pa. Assn. for Supervision and Curriculum Devel. (legis. com. 1986—, pre-conf. inst. chair 1996-97, state conf. com. 1995—, Svc. award 1994-98), Nat. Assn. of Secondary Sch. Prins., Nat. Sch. Bds. Assn., Pa. Sch. Reform Network, Pa. Assn. of Elem. and Secondary Sch. Prins. (legis. liason 1986-98), Pa. Sch. Bds. Assn., Middle Level Prins. of Beaver County (pres., v.p. 1994-98), Pa. Assn. of Student Assistance Profls., Pa. Assn. Pupil Svcs. Adminstrs., Phi Delta Kappa (exec. bd. 2003—). Avocations: numismatic research, writing, antiquities. Home: 4245 Old New England Rd Allison Park PA 15101-1533 Office: Hampton Township Sch Dist 2919 E Hardies Rd Gibsonia PA 15044-8423

KORCHYNSKY, MICHAEL, metallurgical engineer; b. Kiev, Ukraine, Apr. 11, 1918; arrived in U.S., 1950, naturalized, 1956; s. Michael and Jadwiga (Zdanowicz) K.; m. Taisija Lapin, Nov. 22, 1951; children: Michael, Marina, Roksana Dipl. Ing. in Metals Tech., Tech. U. Lviv, 1942. Lectr. Tech. U. Lviv, 1942-44; chief engr. C.E., U.S. Army, Fed. Republic Germany, 1945-50; rsch. metallurgist Union Carbide Co., Niagara Falls, NY, 1951-61; rsch. supr. Jones & Laughlin Steel Corp., Pitts., 1962-68, dir. product rsch., 1969-72; dir. alloy devel. metals divsn. Union Carbide Co., N.Y.C., 1973-77, Pitts., 1978-86; cons., prin. Korchynsky and Assocs., Pitts., 1986—. Metall. cons. Strategic Minerals Corp.-STRATCOR, 1986—; lectr. Niagara U., 1957—58. Author, patentee in field of alloy design and processing tech. of a family of micro-alloyed high-strength low alloy steel. Union Carbide sr. fellow, 1979. Fellow Am. Soc. Metals Internat. (Andrew Carnegie lectr. 1973, W.H. Eisenman medal 1984, F.C. Bain award 1986); mem. AIME (Howe meml. lectr. 1983, Robert Earll McConnell engring. achievement award 1991) Iron and Steel Soc., SAE Internat., Am. Iron and Steel Inst. (medalist), Acad. Engring. Scis. of Ukraine, Ukrainian Technol. Soc. Home: 2770 Milford Dr Bethel Park PA 15102-1763

KORDASH, DOROTHY MAE, artist; b. St. Joseph, Mo., Sept. 7, 1927; d. Perle Elisha and Carrie Allene (Womach) Reece; m. James A. Kordash, Apr. 20, 1956. Art studies, various workshops, U.S., Can., Eng. Acctg. clk. Interstate Bakeries, Kansas City, Mo., 1946-50; adminstrv. clk. Ford Motor Co., Lenexa, Kans., 1951-82; freelance artist Leawood, Kans., 1972—. Treas. Art Images Gallery, Kansas City, 1982-86. One-woman shows include Grand Opening Macy's Dept. Store, Overland Park, Kans., 1975, Arte Ctr., Plano, Tex., 1997, exhibited in group shows at Knickerbocker Artists, Salmagundi Club, N.Y.C., 1983, Art-A-Fair, Laguna Beach (Best Abstract award, 1997, 1998, 1999, Best Mixed Media award, 1999, 2000, 2001, 2003), Town Art Show, Leawood, Kans., 2002 (Best of Show in Two-Dimensional Art award, 2002); contbr. paintings to Pub. TV Art Auction, Kansas City; artist commemorative bicentennial book, Johnson County, Kans., 1975, invitation cover Truman Med. Ctr., Kansas City, 1988, Celebration of Fine Art, Scottsdale, Ariz., 1991—2002; Represented in permanent collections Ford Motor Co., Claycomo, Mo., Volume Shoe Co., Topeka. Mem. Kans. Watercolor Soc. (signature, Purchase awards 1973, 75, 77, 83), Greater Kansas City Art Assn. (Best of Show award 1983). Avocation: photography. Home: 8624 Reinhardt Ln Leawood KS 66206-1455

KORDE, UMESH ARVIND, ocean engineer, researcher, educator; b. Nagpur, India, June 13, 1960; s. Arvind Yeshwant and Sunanda Arvind K.; m. Toyomi Tanaka, Sept. 1, 1988. BTech with honors, Indian Inst. Tech., Kharagpur, 1982; MEng, U. Tokyo, 1988; PhD, U. Notre Dame, 1993. Sr. sci. officer Indian Inst. Tech., Madras, 1982-85, sr. project officer, 1989-90; Monbusho rsch. fellow Inst. Indsl. Sci.-U. Tokyo, 1986-88; rsch. asst. U. Notre Dame, 1990-93; asst. prof. mech. engring. Christian Bros. U., Memphis, 1993-96; sci. and tech. fellow Japan Marine Sci. and Tech. Ctr., Yokosuka, 1997-99, prin. investigator, 1997-99; from asst. to assoc. prof., chair dept. Ind. Inst. Tech., Ft. Wayne, 1999—2002; assoc. prof. St. Cloud State U., St. Cloud, Minn., 2002—. Contbr. articles to sci. jours. Rsch. grantee Japan Sci. and Tech. Agy/NSF, 1997, NSF, 1995; British Coun. fellow, U. Edinburgh, 1983, Queen's U., Belfast. Mem. ASME, Soc. Mfg. Engrs. (cert. mfg. technologist), Am. Geophys. Union, Soc. Naval Architects and Marine Engrs. Avocations: classical music, reading, meditation. Office: St Cloud Univ Dept Mech and Manufacaturing Engring 720 Fourth Ave S Saint Cloud MN 56301 E-mail: uakorde@stcloudstate.edu.

KORDINAK, IRMA L. piano teacher, musician; b. Buffalo, Feb. 27, 1930; d. Paul Eugene Kompalla and Pauline Beuter; m. Albert Andrew Kordinak, July 18, 1964. BM, Oberlin Coll. Consevatory Music, 1953; postgrad, Eastman Sch. Music, Rochester, N.Y., 1962. Nat. cert. tchr. music Music Tchrs. Nat. Assn. Pianist, singer Hormel All-Girl Orch., 1953—54; piano faculty Cmty. Music Sch., Buffalo, 1954-64; piano tchr. pvt. practice, 1954—. Pres. Music Forum for Piano Tchrs. of Western N.Y., 1970—72, social chmn., 2002—03; bd. dirs. Music Forum for Piano Tchr. of Western N.Y., 1959—91, 2002—; pres. dist. 8 N.Y. Fedn. Music Clubs, 1970—76; pres.-elect Amherst (N.Y.) Symphony Orch. (Women's Com.), 1999—2000, co-chair scholarship com., 2000—03; chmn. dist. 10 N.Y. State Music Tchrs. Assn., Buffalo, 1987—; bd. dirs. QRS Arts Found., Buffalo, 1991—98. Mem.: Music Tchrs. Nat. Assn., Am. Liszt Soc., Friends of Vienna in Buffalo, Opera Buffs of Western N.Y., Chromatic Club (hon.; life, past. pres. 1967—68). Avocations: photography, theater, concerts. Home and Office: Buffalo-Niagara Frontier MTA 265 Countryside Ln Buffalo NY 14221-1523

KORDONS, ULDIS, lawyer; b. Riga, Latvia, July 9, 1941; came to U.S., 1949; s. Evalds and Zenta Alide (Apenits) K.; m. Virginia Lee Knowles, July 16, 1966. AB, Princeton U., 1963; JD, Georgetown U., 1970. Bar: N.Y. 1970, Ohio 1978, Ind. 1989. Assoc. Whitman, Breed, Abbott & Morgan, N.Y.C., 1970-77, Anderson, Mori & Rabinowitz, Tokyo, 1973-75; counsel Armco Inc., Parsippany, N.J., 1977-84; v.p., gen. counsel, sec. Sybron Corp., Saddle Brook, N.J., 1984-88, Hillenbrand Industries Inc., Batesville, Ind., 1989-92; pres. Plover Enterprises, Cin., 1992-95, Kordons & Co., LPA, Cin., 1996—. Lt. USN, 1963-67. Mem. N.Y. Bar Assn., Ohio Bar Assn., Ind. Bar Assn. Office: 8238 Wooster Pike Cincinnati OH 45227-4010 E-mail: ukordlaw@aol.com.

KORDYLEWSKI, LESZEK, cell biologist, forensic scientist; b. Cracow, Poland, Aug. 6, 1947; came to U.S., 1982; s. Kazimierz and Jadwiga Kordylewski; m. Anna Maria Kordylewski, Apr. 4, 1970; children: Marek, Jan, Maria. MSc, Jagiellonian U., 1969, PhD, 1975, DSc, 1986. Lectr., adj. prof. Jagiellonian U., Cracow, 1969-99; rsch. assoc. U. Chgo., 1982-85, rsch. assoc., asst. prof., 1988-94; forensic scientist Forensic Sci. Ctr., Chgo., 1996—. Vis. prof. Winthrop U., Rock Hill, S.C., 1995-96; rsch. fellow Rush Presbyn. St. Luke's, Chgo., 1995-96. Author: Problemy Bioetyki, 1996. Mem. Am. Soc. for Cell Biology, Am. Acad. Forensic Scis., Midwestern Assn. Forensic Scientists, State Microscopical Soc. Ill., Universal Esperanto Assn. (del. 1963). Avocations: microscopy, stereo-vision, 3d imaging, international language esperanto. Home: U Chicago 5645 S Drexel Chicago IL 60637

KORELITZ, BURTON I. gastroenterologist, educator; b. Boston, Mass., June 30, 1926; s. Samuel and Ada (Reinhart) Korelitz; m. Ann Zabin; children: Nina, Jean. CE, U. Maine, 1946; AB, Duke U., 1947; MD, Boston U., 1951. Assoc. clin. prof. Mt. Sinai Sch. Medicine, N.Y.C., 1972—78; chief Gastroenterology Sect. Lenox Hill Hosp., N.Y.C., 1978—. Clin. prof. NYU Sch. Medicine, N.Y.C., 1992—; Dana Rsch. fellow in gastroenterology Harvard Med. Sch., Boston, 1953—54; asst. clin. prof., assoc. clin. prof. Mt. Sinai Sch. Medicine, N.Y.C., 1966—77; clin. prof. Medicine NYU Med. Ctr., Valhalla, 1980—90, Cornell U. Med. Sch., Ithaca, NY, 1992—93, NYU Med. ctr., 1993—; vis. prof. Medicine SUNY Downstate, Bklyn., 1998—; asst. attending, assoc. attending physician Mt. Sinai Med. Ctr., N.Y.C., 1956—78; dir. GI Rsch. Lenox Hill Hosp., N.Y.C., 1999—. Contbr. ; editor (textbook): Inflammatory Bowel Disease: Experience and Controversy, 1981; editor: (textbook with N. Sohn), 1985, The Management of Inflammatory Bowel Disease, 1992; editor: (textbook with C. Prantera) Crohn's Disease, 1996; contbr. With U.S. Army, 1944—46. Recipient Robert and Sue Ellen Schneider award, 1993; grantee, Crohn's and Colitis Found. Am. Mem.: ACP, N.Y. County Med. Soc., N.Y. Acad. Gastroenterology, N.Y. Gastroent. Assn., N.Y. Acad. Medicine, N.Y. Soc. Gastrointestinal Endoscopy, Am. Soc. Gastrointestinal Endoscopy, European Assn. Gastroent. and Endoscopy, Internat. Orgn. Inflammatory Bowel Diseases, Am. Gastroent. Assn., Am. Coll. Gastroenterology. Home: 965 Fifth Ave 10A New York NY 10021 Office: Lenox Hill Hosp Chief Gastroenterology Sect 100 E 77th St New York NY 10021 also: 45 E 85th St New York NY 10028

KOREMAN, DOROTHY GOLDSTEIN, physician, dermatologist; b. Bklyn., Nov. 1, 1940; d. Benjamin and Ida (Krenick) Goldstein; m. Neil M. Koreman, Aug. 16, 1964; children: Elizabeth Koreman Landau, Robert Stephen. BA, Bklyn. Coll., 1961; MD, SUNY, Bklyn., 1965. Diplomate Am. Bd. Dermatology. Intern pediatrics Kings County Hosp. Ctr., Bklyn., 1965-66; resident dept. dermatology Wayne State U. Sch. Medicine, Detroit, 1966-69; clin. instr. dermatology Sch. Medicine Wayne State U., Detroit, 1969-71; asst. clin. prof. dermatology U. Miami, 1971-75, assoc. clin. prof. dermatology, 1975-82, clin. prof. dermatology and cutaneous surgery, 1982—. Mem. Miami Dermatol. Soc. (pres. 1978-79). Avocations: traveling, cooking, reading, skiing, needlepoint. Office: 7100 W 20th Ave Ste 107 Hialeah FL 33016-1813 E-mail: skinkor40@aol.com.

KOREN, EDWARD BENJAMIN, cartoonist, educator; b. N.Y.C., Dec. 13, 1935; s. Harry L. and Elizabeth (Sorkin) K.; m. Catherine Curtis Ingham; children: Nathaniel, Alexandra, Benjamin. BA, Columbia U., 1957; student, Atelier 17, Paris, 1957-59; M.F.A., Pratt Inst., 1964; D.H.L. (hon.), Union Coll., 1984. Cartoonist New Yorker mag., N.Y.C., 1962—; mem. faculty Brown U., 1964—, asso. prof. art, 1969-77, adj. assoc. prof., 1977—. One-man travelling exhbn. Art Gallery, SUNY, Albany, 1982; exhibited in group shows including Expn. Dessins d'Humeur, Soc. Protectrice d'Humeur, Avignon, France, 1973, Biennale Illustration, Bratislav, Czechoslovakia, 1973, Art from the New York Times, Soc. Illustr., N.Y.C., 1973, Art from the New Yorker, Grolier Club, 1975, Terry Dintinfass Gallery, N.Y.C., 1975-77, 79, 91, Virginia Lynch Gallery, 1992, 94, 2000, 2002; work appears in Fogg Mus., Princeton U. Mus., RISD Mus., Fitzwilliam Mus., Swann Collection Cartoon and Caricature, Libr. of Congress; contbr.: drawings to various publs. including The Nation, Time mag., Newsweek mag., Fortune mag., N.Y. Times, Sports Illustrated mag., Vogue mag., Vanity Fair mag.; illustrator: Don't Talk to Strange Bears, 1969, The People Maybe, 1974, Cooking for Crowds, 1975, Noodles Galore, 1977, How to Eat Like a Child, 1978, Dragons Hate to be Discrete, 1978, Teenage Romance, 1981, Do I Have to Say Hello?. 1989, A Dog's Life, 1995, Dear Bruno, 1996, Pet Peeves, 2000, The New Legal Seafoods Cookbook, 2003, Travelling While Married, 2003; author, illustrator: Behind The Wheel, 1972; author: Do You Want to Talk About It?, 1977, Are You Happy?, 1978, Well, There's Your Problem, 1980, Caution, Small Ensembles, 1983, What About Me?, 1989, Quality Time, 1995, The Hard Work of Simple Living, 1998, Very Hairy Harry, 2003. John Simon Guggenheim fellow, 1970-71 Mem. Author's League, Soc. Am. Graphic Artists. E-mail: curtisk@sover.net.

KOREN, EDWARD FRANZ, lawyer; b. Eustis, Fla., Aug. 6, 1946; s. Edward Franz Sr. and Frances (Boyd) K.; m. Louise Poole, June 19, 1970; children: Daniel Edward, Susan Louise. BSBA, U. Fla., 1971, JD, 1974. Bar: Fla. 1975, U.S. Dist. Ct. (mid. dist.) Fla. 1977, U.S. Supreme Ct. 1980, U. S. Ct. Appeals (11th cir.) 1981, U.S. Tax Ct. 1985, U.S. Ct. Claims 1986. Instr. tax U. Fla., Gainesville, 1974-75; assoc. Holland & Knight, Lakeland, Fla., 1975-79, ptnr., 1980—, chmn. trusts and estates dept., 1983—. Adj. prof. graduate tax program U. Fla., Gainesville, 1996; adj. prof. grad. estate planning program U. Miami Law Sch., 2000—. Author: Estate and Personal Financial Planning (West), 1988, 13th edit., 2001; contbr. articles to profl. jours. Capt. U.S. Army, 1971-72. Capt. U.S. Army, 1971—72. Fellow: Am. Bar Found., Am. Coll. Tax Counsel, Am. Coll. Trust and Estates Counsel (mem. bus. planning com., bd. regents 1997—, chmn. estate and gift tax com. 2001—); mem.: ABA (chmn. marital deduction com. 1991—95, mem. exec. coun. 1995—, real property, probate and trust law sect. 2001—, vice chmn. probate and trust divsn. 2001—), Fla. Inst. CPAs, Am. Assn. Attys. and CPAs, Fla. Bar Assn. (chmn. real property, probate and trust law sect. 1988—89, chmn. tax sect. 1990—91, active various sects. and coms.), Centre Club, Lakeland Yacht and Country Club, Tampa Club, Order of Coif. Republican. Presbyterian. Home: 114 Hickory Creek Dr Brandon FL 33511-8012 Office: Holland & Knight 92 Lake Wire Dr PO Box 32092 Lakeland FL 33802-2092 E-mail: ekoren@hklaw.com.

KOREN, ISRAEL, electrical and computer engineering educator; s. Zahava Koren; children: Yuval, Yaron. BSc, Technion/Israel Inst. Tech., Haifa, 1967, MSc, 1970, DSc, 1975. Asst. prof. elec. and computer engring. U. Calif., Santa Barbara, 1976-78, U. So. Calif., L.A., 1978-79; sr. lectr. Technion/Israel Inst. Tech., Haifa, 1979-85, head VLSI Sys. Rsch. Ctr., 1985-86; prof. elec. and computer engring. U. Mass., Amherst, 1986—. Vis. prof. U. Calif., Berkeley, 1982-83; cons. Tolerant Sys., San Jose, Calif., 1986, Digital Equipment Corp., Hudson, Mass., 1991, Intel, Haifa, 1992, AMD, Austin, Tex., 1994, IBM, 1995-97, Analog Devices, 1998—. Author: (textbook) Computer Arithmetic Algorithms, 2nd edit., 2002; editor, co-author: Defect and Fault Tolerance in VLSI, 1989. Fellow IEEE, Computer Soc. of IEEE, Japan Soc. for Promotion of Sci.; mem. Computing Machinery (mem. spl. interest group on computer architecture 1990—). Office: U Mass Dept Computer & Elec Engrig Amherst MA 01003-4410

KORENBLIT, PEARL, internist; b. Toronto, Ont., Can., May 3, 1954; came to the U.S., 1982; d. Nathan and Helen (Lazarovitch) Lefkowitz; m. Mory Hiam Korenblit, Feb. 28, 1988; children: Sarah S., Hinda M., Rachel M., Malka D., Nechama D. Student, U. Toronto, 1973-75, MD, 1979. Diplomate Am. Bd. Preventive Medicine, Am. Bd. Internal Medicine. Intern in family medicine Women's Coll. Hosp. U. Toronto, Can., 1979-80; resident in internal medicine Jewish Gen. Hosp. McGill U., Montreal, Quebec, Can., 1980-82; resident in gen. preventive medicine Mount Sinai Sch. Medicine, N.Y.C., 1982-84; resident, chief resident primary care internal medicine St. Vincent's Hosp., N.Y.C., 1984-86; fellow in gen. preventive medicine Mount Sinai Sch. Medicine, N.Y.C., 1986-88, asst. prof. dept. cmty. medicine, 1988-95; clin. dir. grants mgmt. North Gen. Hosp., N.Y.C., 1988-92; cons. and dir. worksite TB screening program ILGWU Union Health Ctr., N.Y.C., 1992-95; sect. chief gen. internal medicine Bronx VA Med. Ctr., 1995-97; dir. primary care Trinitas Hosp., Elizabeth, N.J., 1997—. Asst. attending physician, Internal Medicine Assocs., Mt. Sinai Hosp., N.Y.C., 1988-95; asst. prof. Dept. Cmty. Medicine, preceptor, third-yr. clerkship in Cmty. Medicine, seminar leader, Mt. Sinai Sch. Medicine, 1988-97; bd. dirs., treas. Health Care Network N.J., LLC, 1997-2001; mem. residency evaluation com., residency planning com., curriculum com. Seton Hall Sch. Grad. Edn., 1997—; mem. cancer com., investigational rev. bd. com., ambulatory care com., residency evaluation com. Trinitaas Hosp., 1997—; mem. TB advisory com., Mt. Sinai Med. Ctr., 1993-95; lectr. in field. Peer reviewer Jour. Indsl. Medicine, 1992-95, Jour. AMA, 1992—; contbr. articles, papers to profl. pubs. Bd. mem. upper Manhattan Task Force on AIDS, East Harlem, N.Y., 1990-93; active East Harlem Health Com., 1989-92; mem. profl. adv. bd. Little Sisters of the Assumption, East Harlem, 1988-93; chmn. Assn. Orthodox Jewish Scientist Nat. Conv., 1990; bd. govs. mem. Assn. Orthodox Jewish Scientists, 1986—. Dr. John P. Hubbard scholar, 1976, Univ. Coll. scholar, 1975, Mitchell scholar, 1973, Ontario scholar, 1973; recipient Mel Orenstein Meml. award, 1975; grantee in field. Fellow: Am. Coll. Preventive Medicine, ACP; mem.: Soc. Gen. Internal Medicine, APHA. E-mail: pkorenblit@trinitas.org.

KORENIC, LYNETTE MARIE, librarian; b. Berwyn, Ill., Mar. 29, 1950; d. Emil Walter and Donna Marie (Harbutt) K. m. Jerome Dennis Reif, Dec. 31, 1988. BS in Art, U. Wis., 1977, MFA, 1979, MA in LS, 1981, MA in Art History, 1984. Asst. art libr. Ind. U., Bloomington, 1982-84; art libr. U. Calif., Santa Barbara, 1984-88, head Arts Libr., 1988-99; art libr. U. Wis., Madison, 1999—. Author articles. Mem. Art Librs. Soc. N.Am. (sec. 1983-84, v.p. 1989, pres. 1990), Beta Phi Mu. Office: U Wis Kohler Art Libr Madison WI 53706 E-mail: lkorenic@library.wisc.edu.

KORÉNYI-BOTH, ANDRAS LEVENTE, pathologist, educator; b. Mar. 30, 1937; came to U.S., 1974, naturalized, 1978; s. Erno Jozsef and Maria Amalia (Korody-Katona) K.-B.; m. Ildiko Örlos, July 18, 1964; children: András, György, Adám. MD, Szeged Albert Szent-Gyorgyi Med. U., Hungary, 1962; PhD, Nat. Acad. of Scis., Hungary, 1972. Intern Szeged Albert Szent-Györgyi (Hungary) Med. U., 1961-62; resident in pathology Town Coun. Hosp., Hodmezovasarhely, Hungary, 1962-63; rsch. assoc. pathology Imre Haynal Postgrad. Med. U., Budapest, 1963-68; asst. prof. 1st Inst. Pathology Semmelweis Med. U., Budapest, 1968-70, sr. lectr., 1970-74, acting chmn., 1972-73; dir. 8th County Cytodiagnostic Ctr., Budapest, 1972-74; assoc. dir. pathology Erie County Labs., Buffalo, 1975-76; dir. neuromuscular lab. E.J. Meyer Meml. Hosp., Buffalo, 1976-78; clin. to rsch. asst. prof. pathology SUNY, Buffalo, 1975-78; pathologist, dept. pathology, head electronmicroscopy, histochemistry and immunopathology labs., dept. rsch. Lankenau Hosp., Phila., 1978-81; owner, operator pathology lab. Havertown, Pa., 1981-87; dir. dept. pathology and lab. medicine Sidney Hillman Med. Ctr., Phila., 1981-90; comdr. 316th Sta. Hosp. (Op. Desert Shield/Storm), 1991-92; assoc. prof. pathology dept. pathology and lab. medicine Med. Coll. Pa. and Hahnemann U., Phila., 1992-93; mgmt. physician Dept. Mil. and Vet. Affairs The Commonwealth of Pa., 1993-96; med. dir. Comprehensive Med. Network, P.C., Old Forge, Pa., 1996—98; pres., dir. dept. R&D, Al Eskan Found., 1998—. Chief of lab. svc. 348th Gen. Hosp., USAR, Folsom, Pa., 1982-83, 86-87, comdr. 718th Med. Detachment, 1983-85, 86-87, comdr. 718th Med. Detachment, 1983-85, chief profl. svcs. 338th Med. Group, 1985-86; brigade surgeon 157th Separate Infantry Brigade, 1987-90; comdr. 108th Combat Support Hosp. Army N.G., 1991-95; state surgeon Pa. Army N.G., 1995-97; flight surgeon Ohio Army N.G., 1997-2002; adj. prof. microbiology and cell biology Pa. State U., 1978-83; assoc. prof. pathology Thomas Jefferson U., Phila., 1979-91; assoc. prof. pathology Med. Coll. Pa., Hahnemann U., Phila., 1992-93; Whipple fellow Genesee Hosp., Rochester, 1974-75; Buswell fellow SUNY, Buffalo, 1977-78. Author: Muscle Pathology in Neuromuscular Disease, 1983; contbr. articles to sci. jours. Col. Army N.G., ret. 2003. Recipient Order of Mil. Med. Merit, "A" Proficiency Designator award in Pathology U.S. Army, 1988, Legion of Merit, Meritorious Svc. medal with 2 oak leaf clusters, Kuwait Liberation medal, Garde Nationale trophy of Lafayette. Fellow Coll. Physicians of Phila., Am. Assn. Pathologists; mem. AMA (Physician Recognition award 1980, 83, 85), AAAS, NRA, Internat. Acad. Pathology, Hungarian Med. Assn. Am., Coll. Am. Pathologists, European Soc. Pathologists, N.Y. Acad. Sci., Pathology Soc. Phila., Fedn. State Med. Bds. U.S., Assn. Mil. Surgeons of U.S., Nat. Fedn. Cath. Physicians Guilds, Soc. Med. Cons. to the Armed Forces, Am. Hungarian Med. Rsch. Instn., Phila. and Vicinity Hungarian Sportsman, Delaware County Field and Stream Assn. Republican. Roman Catholic. Achievements include discovery of Al-Eskan disease, known as Persian Gulf Syndrome. Home: 202 Wickford Rd Havertown PA 19083-4741 Office: Al Eskan Found 202 Wickford Rd Havertown PA 19083-4741

KORETZ, PAUL, state representative; b. LA, Apr. 3, 1955; m. Gail Koretz; 1 child, Rachel. BA in History, UCLA, 1979. Owner bus.; mem. Calif. Assembly, 2000—. Mem. LA County Dem. Ctrl. Com., 1976—86; aide LA City Councilman Marvin Braude, 1984; mem. West Hollywood City Coun., 1988—; campaign mgr., coun. dep. Councilmember Alan Viterbi; mem. Calif. Pooled Investment Authority; founder Calif. for Safer Sts., Cynthia Alliance Neighborhood Watch; adminstrv. dir. Ecology Ctr. So. Calif.; mem. ins. commr.'s AIDS Discrimination Task Force; mem. LA County Libr. Commn.; founder West Hollywood Graffitti Removal Program; West Hollywood Pub. Safety Commn.; bd. dirs. Jewish Labor Com., 1999—2000, LA County Sanitation Dist. Mem.: AFSCME (founding), Internat. Network Gay and Lesbian Officials (founding). Democrat. Jewish. Office: PO 942849 Rm 2176 Sacramento CA 94249-0001 Address: 8490 Sunset West Hollywood CA 90069*

KOREVAAR, DAVID, musician, educator; b. Madison, Wis., July 25, 1962; s. Jacob Korevaar and Johanna Thompson, William Bell Thompson (Stepfather); m. Elizabeth Stahl, Aug. 21, 1988; children: Alice Eloise, Willem Breyer. MusB, Juilliard Sch.Music, 1982, MusM, 1983, DMA, 2000. Artist-tchr. of piano Westport (Conn.) Sch. of Music, 1987—2000; head of piano studies U. of Bridgeport, Bridgeport, 1995—2000; asst. prof. of piano U. of Colo. Coll. of Music, Boulder, 2000—. Musician: (CD rec.) Piano Music of Lowell Lieberman, Bach's Well-Tempered Clavier, Books 1 and 2, Ernst von Dohnanyi Piano Music, Brahms Piano Pieces. Candidate for mayor Dem. Party, Norwalk, Conn., 1997, mem. of Dem. town com., 1990—2000. Recipient C. V. Starr Doctoral fellowship, Juilliard Sch. Music, 1998—2000, Spl. prize for performance of French music, Robert Casadesus Internat. Competition, 1989, Peabody-Mason Found. Sponsorship for Pianists, 1985, Top prize, U. Md./William Kapell Internat. Competition, 1988. Mem.: Coll. Music Soc., Am. Musicol. Soc., Am. Liszt Soc., Music Tchr.'s Nat. Assn. Democrat. Avocations: running, hiking. Office: U Colo Coll Music 301 UCB Boulder CO 80309-0301 Personal E-mail: david.korevaar@colorado.edu. E-mail: david.korevaar@colorado.edu.

KOREVAAR, WILHELMINA C. anesthesiologist; b. Delft, The Netherlands, 1952; d. Jaap Korevaar and Johanna Elzelina Thompson; m. Robert W. Pearson; c. Jennifer Anne Freeberg, Max J. Freeberg. BA, U. Calif., San Diego, 1973; MD, Yale U., 1977; M of Med. Mgmt., Carnegie Mellon U., 1999. Diplomate Am. Bd. Anesthesiology; cert. pain mgmt. Intern N.C. Meml. Hosp., Chapel Hill, 1977-78, resident in anesthesiology, 1978-80, Mercy Hosp. Med. Ctr., San Diego, 1980-81; fellow in pain mgmt. U. N.C. Dental Rsch. Ctr., Chapel Hill, 1978-79; fellow in pediatric anesthesiology and intensive care Children's Hosp. of Phila., 1981-82; med. dir. employee disability program City of Phila. Mem. AMA, Am. Acad. Pain Mgmt. (cert.), Am. Soc. Anesthesiology, Internat. Assn. for Study of Pain, Pa. Soc. Anesthesiology, Alpha Omega Alpha. Office: City of Phila Divsn Risk Mgmt 1515 Arch St Philadelphia PA 19102 also: MDance 401 S Second St Ste N 100 Philadelphia PA 19147 E-mail: paindoc@concentric.net., Wilma.Korevaar@phila.gov.

KOREY, JOHN L. political scientist, educator; b. Bklyn., Nov. 20, 1944; s. Edward L. and Hazel (Murphy) K.; m. Mary Haggerty, Sept. 7, 1968; children: Meghan Korey Lukisik, David S. AB, Georgetown U., 1966; PhD, U. Fla., 1971. Instr. Calif. State Poly. U., Pomona, 1971-72, asst. prof. polit. sci., 1972-78, assoc. prof. polit. sci., 1978-80, prof. polit. sci., 1980—. Campus rep. Inter-Univ. Consortium for Polit. and Social Rsch., Ann Arbor, Mich, 1972—, gov. bd., 2000—; vis. prof. Calif. State U., LA, 1994-97. Author: California Government, 1995, 3d edit., 2002; co-author: SPSS for Windows version 9.0: A Basic Tutorial, 1999. Mem. Am. Polit. Sci. Assn., Western. Polit. Sci. Assn., U. Faculty for Life. Roman Catholic. E-mail: jlkorey@csupomona.edu.

KORF, CLIFFORD DEAN, physician assistant; b. Garden City, Kans., Jan. 10, 1951; s. Lloyd James and Virginia Lee (Thomas) K.; m. Lavetta Mae Ruth Whitesell, Mar. 19, 1977; children: Jonathan David, Benjamin Joseph, Rachel Elizabeth. A in nursing, Garden City Cmty. Jr. Coll., 1975; B in health sci., Wichita State U., 1980. Reg. nurse St. Catherine Hosp., Garden City, 1975-77; RN Wesley Med. Ctr., Wichita, 1977-80; physician asst., dir. Wichita County Med. Ctr., Leoti, Kans., 1980-81; physician asst., supr. Cardiovascular Med. Group, Wichita, Kans., 1981-93; physician asst. Cardiovascular Cons. of Kans., Wichita, 1993—. Clin. instr. Wichita State U., 1985-95; affiliate to med. staff St. Francis Reg. Med. Ctr., 1981—; instr. Adv. Cardiac Life Support, Wichita, 1983—; allied health profl. rev. com. Via Christi Reg. Med. Ctr. St. Francis campus, Wichita, 1986—. Den leader Boy Scouts Am., Wichita, 1994-97, adult scouter-leader, 1995-97, asst. leader Pathfinders, 1997—. Fellow Am. Acad. Physician Assistants; mem. Kansas Acad. Physician Assistants. Republican. Seventh-Day Adventist. Avocations: scouting, gardening, camping, family activities, flowers. Home: 6501 SW 40th St Lincoln NE 68523-9269 Office: Cardiovascular Cons Kans 1035 N Emporia St Ste 210 Wichita KS 67214-2992

KORF, GENE ROBERT, lawyer; b. Greenville, S.C., June 2, 1952; s. Norman and Paula (Heller) K.; m. Madeline Jane Hammer, June 20, 1976; children: Scott, Neil. BA summa cum laude, Hunter Coll., 1974; JD, Bklyn. Law Sch., 1977; LLM in Taxation, NYU, 1983. Dir. Korf & Rosenblatt, Morristown, N.J. Prodr. (mus. rev.) And the World Goes Round (Drama Desk award 1990, 91, Outer Critics Cir. award 1990, 91), The Kentucky Cycle, 1993 (Tony award, 1994), The Crucible, 2002 (Tony award nominee 2002). Long Day's Journey Into Night, revival, 2003 (Tony award nominee 2003). Trustee Roundabout Theatre Co., 1993—, Harold Wetterberg Found., 1991—, Blanche and Irving

Laurie Found., 1991—, Schulman Family Found., 1993. Recipient City Ctr./Leonard Harris award 2001. Jewish. Office: Korf & Rosenblatt 89 Hdqrs Plz North Tower 14th Fl Morristown NJ 07960-1734

KORF, JEAN PRINZ, retired theater educator; b. New Albany, Ind., Oct. 28, 1925; d. Winfield Henry and Waneta Sadler Prinz; m. Leonard Lee Korf, Aug. 15, 1949; children: Kerry Lee, William Milton, Geoffrey Leonard. BA, UCLA, 1947, MA, 1953; MS in Edn., U. So. Calif., 1963. Theater prodn. mgr. Whittier (Calif.) H.S., 1949-52; drama tchr. Calif. H.S., Whittier, 1953-66; theater arts prof. Rio Hondo Coll., Whittier, 1966-90. Founder TheaterCreations Unltd., 1990—; guest dir. La. State U., Baton Rouge, 1990, 91, St. Barts Playhouse, N.Y.C., 1992, U.S. State Dept. Arts Am., Bialystok, Poland, 1993. Commr. Whittier Cultural Arts Commn., 1993-2005; bd. dirs. Whittier Cultural Arts Found., 1990—. Fellow Coll. Fellows Am. Theater (dean 1994-96), Rio Hondo Coll.; mem. Los Angeles County Mus. Art, Nat. Mus. Women in the Arts, UCLA Theater Film & TV Alumni Assn. (bd. dirs. 1991-2000), Nat. Theatre Conf., Nature Conservancy, World Wildlife Fund. Democrat. Unitarian Universalist. Avocations: theatre going, attending cultural events, conservation, travel, genealogy. Home: 9811 Pounds Ave Whittier CA 90603-1616 E-mail: jeankorf@aol.com.

KORF, LEONARD LEE, theater arts educator; b. Chgo., Jan. 31, 1917; s. William Milton and Eva (Lewin) K.; m. Claire Jean Prinz, Aug. 15, 1949; children: William Milton II, Kerry Lee, Geoffrey Leonard. BA, UCLA, 1949; diploma, Harvard U., 1945; MA, UCLA, 1957, PhD, 1972. Lifetime tchg. credential, Calif. Prof. theatre arts, chmn. dept. Fullerton (Calif.) Coll., 1952-56, Cerritos (Calif.) Coll., 1956-82; CEO Korfco, Inc., Whittier, Calif., 1983—. Screen writer The AAF Comes of Age, 1945, The Lifemaker, 1956; exec. editor Ednl. Theatre News, 1956-93; book and theatre reviewer L.A. Times, 1972-73; rev. editor Calif. Ednl. Theatre Assn., L.A., 1993—; lead actor Space Chase. Maj. USAF, 1941-46. Decorated Disting. Flying Cross with two clusters USAF, 1943-44, Air medal with 5 clusters USAF, 1943-44. Fellow Am. Theatre Fellow Kennedy Ctr. (life); mem. Am. Theatre Assn. (bd. mem., pub. rels. dir. 1970-71), So. Calif. Ednl. Theatre Assn. (pres. 1975-76). Democrat. Agnostic. Avocation: national table tennis champion. Home and Office: Korfco Inc 9811 Pounds Ave Whittier CA 90603-1616

KORF, RICHARD PAUL, mycology educator; b. Bronxville, N.Y., May 28, 1925; s. Frederick and Evelyn F. (Krug) K.; m. Kumiko Tachibana, June 27, 1959; children: Noni, Mia, Ian, Mario. BSc, Cornell U., 1946, PhD, 1950. Lectr. botany U. Glasgow, Scotland, 1950-51; asst. prof. Cornell U., Ithaca, N.Y., 1951-55, assoc. prof., 1955-61, prof. mycology, 1961-92, chmn. theatre arts, 1985-86, prof. emeritus, 1992—. Fulbright rsch. prof. Yokohama (Japan) Nat. U., 1957-58; cons. prof. U. Ryukyus, Ryukyu Islands, 1969; adjunktvikar U. Copenhagen, 1973; Fulbright rsch. scholar U. Louvain, Belgium, 1972-73; dir. Exe Island Biol. Sta., Portland, Ont., 1973—; mem. sci. coun. Academia Sinica, Beijing, China, 1985-90. Editor Mycotaxon, 1974-91; book rev. editor Mycologia, 1972-80; corr. editor Mycological Rsch., 1996-98; mem. editl. bd. Persoonia, 1987—, Mycosystema, 1988-94. State vice chair Liberal party, N.Y., 1968. Sr. postdoctoral fellow NSF, Yokohama, 1957; recipient SUNY Chancellor's award for excellence in teaching, 1992. Fellow Br. Mycol. Soc. (Centennial); mem. Internat. Mycol. Assn. (nomenclature chmn. 1971-84), Internat. Assn. Plant Taxonomy (mem. gen. com. 1975-91); Mycol. Soc. Am. (pres. 1971, Disting. Mycologist Award 1991). Avocations: acting, contract bridge, naturism. Home: 316 Richard Pl Ithaca NY 14850-3129 Office: Cornell U Plant Pathology Plant Sci Bldg Ithaca NY 14853 E-mail: rpk1@cornell.edu.

KORFF, Y. A. grand rabbi; b. Boston, Aug. 30, 1949; s. Nathan and Helen (Pfeffer) Korff; children: Kimberlee A., Yaakov Yisroel, Dovid Yehoshua, Mordechai, Boruch, Yechiel Michel. BJE, Hebrew Coll., 1968; BA, Columbia U., 1969; DD, Rabbinical Acad., 1971; JD, Bklyn. Law Sch., 1972; MA in Internat. Rels., Fletcher Sch. Law and Diplomacy, Tufts U.-Harvard U., 1973, MA in Law and Diplomacy, 1975; PhD in Internat. Law, Tufts U.-Harvard U., 1976; grad. resident Divinity Sch., Harvard U., 1975; LLM, Boston U., 1980. Bar: Mass. 1974, U.S. Dist. Ct. Mass. 1975, U.S. Tax Ct. 1976, U.S. Ct. Appeals (1st cir.) 1976, U.S. Supreme Ct. 1978, D.C. 1980, U.S. Ct. Internat. Trade, 1981. Ptnr. Hill, Livingstone & Assocs. and Interprise Internat., Inc., Boston, 1974-81, Lewenberg & Korff, Boston, 1974-94; rabbi Beth Sholom, Hull, Mass., 1969-71, Charles River Pk. Synagogue, Boston, 1971-74, Beth Sholom, Providence, 1974-75, Temple Aliyah, Needham, Mass., 1975-83, Congregation B'nai Jacob, Newton, Mass., 1983—; Zvhil-Mezbuz Rebbe Zvhil-Mezbuz Beis Medrash, Boston and Newton, Mass., 1993—. Spl. cons. to dist. atty. Norfolk County, Mass., 1975-85; spl. asst. to atty. gen. Commonwealth of Mass., Boston, 1977-85; judge Rabbinical Ct. Justice, Boston, 1975—; hon. consul Austria, dir. Austrian Consulate, Boston, 1987—; sr. v.p., bd. dirs. Viacom, Inc., N.Y.C., 1987-94, Viacom Internat., N.Y.C., 1987-94; pres. Nat. Amusements Inc., Dedham, 1988-94, pres., mng. dir. Nat. Amusements (UK) Ltd., Dedham, 1987-94; bd. dirs. Coun. on Religion and Law, Boston, 1978-84; bd. dirs., mem. exec. com. Nat. Assn. Theatre Owners, 1988-94. Owner, pub. The Jewish Advocate, The Jewish Times, Guide to Jewish Boston and New England, Boston, 1990—. Mem. Friends of Fletcher Sch. Law and Diplomacy, Boston, 1974-94, Boston Consumers Coun., 1975-80; trustee Dana Farber Cancer Inst., Boston, 1990-95; bd. visitors Hebrew Coll. Boston, 1990—; Jewish chaplain City of Boston, 1974—. Mem.: Am. Arbitration Assn., Harvard U. Club (Boston). Office: 15 School St Boston MA 02108-4307

KORFMACHER, WALTER AVERILL, chemist, researcher; b. St. Louis, Nov. 6, 1951; s. William Charles and Louise Trowbridge (Averill) K.; m. Madeleine Marie Deutsch, June 1, 1974; children: Mary Averill, Joseph Deutsch. BS in Chemistry, St. Louis U., 1973; MS in Chemistry, U. Ill., 1975, PhD in Chemistry, 1978. Lab. instr. St. Louis U., 1970-72; teaching asst. U. Ill., Urbana, 1973-75; grad. rsch. asst. Colo. State U., Ft. Collins, 1976-78; rsch. chemist Nat. Ctr. for Toxicol. Rsch., Jefferson, Ark., 1978-91; prin. scientist dept. drug metabolism Schering-Plough Rsch. Inst., Kenilworth, N.J., 1991—. Adj. assoc. prof. U. Tenn. Coll. Pharmacy, Memphis, 1988-91; adj. asst. prof. dept. chemistry U. Ark., Little Rock, 1983-91; adj. assoc. prof. dept. toxicology U. Ark. Med. Scis., Little Rock, 1991. Contbr. more than 100 articles to profl. jours. Recipient Plaque award USPHS, 1989, Commendable Svc. award FDA, 1990. Mem. AAAS, Am. Chem. Soc., Am. Soc. Mass Spectrometry, Assn. Ofcl. Analytical Chemists, N.Y. Acad. Scis., Phi Beta Kappa, Sigma Xi. Roman Catholic. Achievements include research in area of analytical methods development, particularly trace organic analysis, utility of GC-MS and LC-MS as well as tandem mass spectrometry. Office: Schering Plough Rsch Inst Dept Drug Metabolism 2015 Galloping Hill Rd Dept Drug Kenilworth NJ 07033-1300

KORG, JACOB, English literature educator; b. N.Y.C., Nov. 21, 1922; s. Reuben and Mary (Lehrman) K.; m. Cynthia Stewart, Jan. 21, 1952; 1 dau., Nora Francis. BA, CCNY, 1943; MA, Columbia U., 1947, PhD, 1952. Instr. English Bard Coll., 1947-49, CCNY, 1950-55; from asst. prof. to prof. U. Wash., Seattle, 1955-68, prof. English, 1970-91, prof. emeritus, 1991—; prof. English U. Md., 1968-70. Vis. prof. Nat. Taiwan U., 1960. Author: George Gissing, A Critical Biography, 1963, Dylan Thomas, 1965, Language in Modern Literature, 1979, rev. edit., 1992, Browning and Italy, 1983, Ritual and Experiment in Modern Poetry, 1995, Winter Love: Ezra Pound and H.D., 2003, also articles, revs.; editor: London in Dickens' Day, 1960, George Gissing's Commonplace Book, 1962, The Force of Few Words, 1966, Twentieth Century Views of Bleak House, 1968, Poetry of Robert Browning, 1971; co-editor: George Gissing on Fiction, 1978; mem. editl. bd. Victorian Poetry, 1979-2002, Nineteenth-Century Lit., 1983-95, Rivista di Studi Vittoriani. Served with AUS, 1943-46. Mem. MLA, Assn. Literary Scholars and Critics. Home: 6530 51st Ave NE Seattle WA 98115-7741 Office: Univ Wash Dept English Seattle WA 98195-0001 E-mail: korg@u.washington.edu.

KORINOW, IRA LEE, rabbi; b. Newton, Mass., Feb. 14, 1951; s. Maurice and Freida (Pecker) K.; m. Gail Lynne Jaffe, Feb. 20, 1977; children: Morry Lev, Doron Ephraim, Raanan Meir. BA in Religion, Boston U., 1973; MA in Hebrew Lit., Hebrew Union Coll., 1976, cert. crisis counseling, 1989. Ordained rabbi, 1978. Prin. Rodeph Sholom Religious Sch., N.Y.C., 1975-77; rabbi Temple B'nai Israel, Laconia, N.H., 1977-78, North Shore Congregation Israel, Glencoe, Ill., 1978-81, Temple Emanu-El, Haverhill, Mass., 1981—. Bd. dirs. Union Coun. for Soviet Jews, Washington, 1984-87, Action for Soviet Jewry, Waltham, Mass., 1983-88; founder, chmn. Greater Haverhill Citizens' Civil Rights Commn., 1991—. Mem. Nat. Conf. Soviet Jewry (bd. dirs. 1985-88), Ctrl. Conf. Am. Rabbis (Soviet Jewry com. 1981-87, trustee 1999—, N.E. Region Ctrl. Conf. Am. Rabbis (treas. 1989-91, sec. 1991-93, v.p. 1993-97, pres. 1997-99, trustee 1999-2001), Rabbinical Assembly (corr. 1991—), Mass. Bd. Rabbis (sec. 1985-87, treas. 1987-89, v.p. 1989-95, pres. 1995-97), Greater Haverhill Clergy Assn. (pres. 1989-92), Coalition for the Advancement Jewish Edn., Rotary. Home: 23 Singingwood Dr Haverhill MA 01830-1452 Office: Temple Emanu-El 514 Main St Haverhill MA 01830-3293

KORINS, LEOPOLD, stock exchange executive; Pres. Pacific Stock Exch., San Francisco, chmn., chief exec. officer, 1990-96, Phila. Stock Exchange, Phila., Pa., 1997-98; pres., chief exec. officer Security Traders Assn., N.Y.C., 1999—.

KORKIN, STEVEN ARTHUR, industrial engineer, project manager; b. Pittsfield, Mass., Oct. 29, 1948; s. Alfred and Augusta (Lipschitz) K.; m. Denise T. Baer, Feb. 13, 1971 (div. June 1975); m. Carleen Adamski, Aug. 29, 1976; children: Jason, Matthew. AS in Elec. Engring. Tech., Wentworth Inst., 1969; BS in Indsl. Tech. and Bus. Adminstrn., Northeastern U., Boston, 1974; MS in Mfg. Engring. Mgmt., U. Mass., Lowell, 1994. Engr. New England Power Co., Worcester, Mass., 1969-70, New England Tele. Co., Framingham, Mass., 1971-73, Northern Telecom, Boston, 1973-76; sr. engr. Jerrold Electronics Corp., Chicopee, Mass., 1977-79; prin. engr. Digital Equipment Corp., Salem, N.H., 1979-92; v.p., gen. mgr. Parke Math. Lab. Inc., Lowell, 1992-97; contract prin. engr. Compaq Computer, Salem, N.H., 1997-98; facilities mgr. CTS Interconnect Systems, Londonderry, NH, 1999—2001; project mgr. BHD Corp., Palm Beach Gardens, Fla., 2001—03; self-employed engr. cons., 2003—. With USNG, 1970-76.

KORMAN, A. GERD, history, educator, writer; b. Elberfeld, Germany, July 24, 1928; came to U.S., 1940; m. Ruth R. Zloten, June 22, 1956 (dec. July 1989); children: Arona, Joshua, Ezra, Malka; life ptnr. Ann Sandford. BA, Bklyn. Coll., 1951; MA, U. Wis., 1953, PhD, 1959. Asst. prof. history Elmira (N.Y.) Coll., 1957-62, U. Rochester, 1964; from asst. prof. to prof. Cornell U., Ithaca, NY, 1962—93, prof. emeritus, 1993—; assoc. prof. history Tel Aviv U., Israel, 1968-69, 71-72. Author: Industrialization Immigrants and Americanizers: The View from Milwaukee 1866-1921, 1967; editor: Hunter and Hunted: Human History of the Holocaust, 1973; contbr. articles to profl. jours. including Wis. Mag. History, Yad Vashem Studies, Societas, Revs. in Am. History, Am. Jewish History, Modern Judaism, Leo Baeck Yearbook, among others. Fellow Soc. Sci. Rsch. Coun., 1955-56, 58-59; Holocaust fellow Oxford (Eng.) Ctr. for Postgrad. Hebrew Studies, 1979-80. Mem. Orgn. Am. Historians, The Hist. Soc., Immigration and Ethnic Hist. Soc. Democrat. Jewish. Avocations: walking, writing fiction and poetry. Home: PO Box 63 Sagaponack NY 11962 E-mail: agk1@cornell.edu.

KORMAN, EDWARD R. federal judge; b. N.Y.C., Oct. 25, 1942; s. Julius and Miriam K.; m. Diane R. Eisner, Feb. 3, 1979; children: Miriam M., Benjamin E. BA, Bklyn. Coll., 1963; LL.B., Bklyn. Law Sch., 1966; LL.M., NYU, 1971. Bar: N.Y. 1966, U.S. Supreme Ct. 1972. Law clk. to judge N.Y. Ct. Appeals, 1966-68, assoc. Paul, Weiss, Rifkind, Wharton and Garrison, 1968-70; asst. U.S. atty. Eastern Dist. N.Y., N.Y.C., 1970-72; asst. to solicitor gen. of U.S., 1972-74; chief asst. U.S. atty. Eastern Dist. N.Y., 1974-78, U.S. atty., 1978-82; ptnr. Stroock & Stroock & Lavan, N.Y.C., 1982-84; prof. Bklyn. Law Sch., 1984-85; U.S. dist. judge Eastern Dist. N.Y., 1985—, chief judge, 2000—. Chmn. Mayor's Com. on N.Y.C. Marshals, 1983-85; mem. Temporary Commn. of Investigation of State of N.Y., 1983-85. Jewish. Office: US Dist Ct US Courthouse 225 Cadman Plz E Brooklyn NY 11201-1818

KORMAN, JAMES WILLIAM, lawyer; b. Washington, Apr. 29, 1943; s. Milton D. and Bernice (Rosensweig) K.; m. Barbara Dale Lewis, June 11, 1967; 1 child, Katherine Korman Frey. AB, Coll. William & Mary, 1965; JD, George Washington U., 1968. Bar: Va. 1968, D.C. 1970, U.S. Supreme Ct. 1972, U.S. Ct. Appeals (4th cir.) 1974, U.S. Dist. Ct. (ea. dist.) Va. 1975. Assoc. Kinney, Smith and Barham, Arlington, Va., 1968-73, ptnr., 1973-78; pres. Bean, Kinney & Korman, Arlington, 1979—; neutral case evaluator Fairfax Cir. Ct., 1995—. Mem. Va. Bar Coun., 1983-89, 98—, 10th dist. grievance com., 1978-81; mem. adv. bd. Bank of Arlington, Va., 1977-78; lectr. various civil litgation topics continuing legal edn.; contbg. atty. Mathew Bender's Fed. Practice Forms, 1978; panelist Va. Conf. Nat. Assn. Bank Women, 1984; adj. prof. George Mason U. Law Sch., 1996—; mem. faculty Va. State Bar Profl. Course, 1998-2001. Contbr. articles to profl. jours. Bd. dirs. No. Va. Jewish Cmty. Ctr., 1985-91; mem. adv. bd. Sch. Contemporary Edn., Springfield, Va., 1985-91; mem. Va. Commn. on Women and Minorities in the Law, 1988-92. Capt. USAR, 1972-74. Recipient Meritorious Svc. award Legal Aid Bur., 1968, Adult Leadership award Boy Scouts Am., 1972; named One of 50 Top Divorce Lawyers Washingtonian Mag., 2000, One of Best Lawyers in Am., 1999--. Fellow: Am. Bar Found., Va. Bar Found., Va. Law Found., Am. Acad. Matrimonial Lawyers (Va. chpt. v.p. 1996—99, pres. 2001—, cert. arbitrator); mem.: ATLA, ABA, Plaintiffs Bar Ltd., Va. Trial Lawyers Assn. (jud. task force 1998—), Arlington Bar Found. (bd. dirs. 1990—, pres. 2000—01), Arlington Bar Assn. (bd. dirs. 1977—81, pres. 1981—82, Robert J. Arthur Disting. Svc. award 2002), Va. State Bar (pro bono steering com. 1992—93). Democrat. Avocation: collecting political buttons. Home: 2450 N Wakefield Ct Arlington VA 22207-3554 Office: Bean Kinney & Korman 200 14th N St Ste 100 Arlington VA 22201-2552

KORMAN, JESS J. writer; b. N.Y.C. s. Rubin and Beatrice K. BA, NYU. Freelance TV writer, playwright, 1963-69; v.p., assoc. creative dir. J. Walter Thompson Co., N.Y.C., 1969-77, sr. v.p., exec. creative dir. Los Angeles, 1978-81; sr. v.p., creative dir. DMB&B, N.Y.C., 1983-86; pres., creative dir. Air Korman Inc. Creative Avt. Services, N.Y.C., 1987—. Writer numerous TV shows, plays, radio, TV commls. and videos. Mem. Writers Guild Am.

KORMAN, LEWIS J. entertainment/media company executive, entrepreneur; b. N.Y.C., Feb. 18, 1945; s. Irving D. and Sylvia (Margolies) K.; m. Sharon G. Weiss, Aug. 20, 1967; children: Eric Andrew, Raina Allison. BS in Indsl. and Labor Rels., Cornell U., 1966; JD cum laude, NYU, 1969. Bar: N.Y. 1970. Assoc. Kaye, Scholer, Fierman, Hays & Handler, N.Y.C., 1969-77, ptnr., 1978-79; founding ptnr. Gelberg & Abrams, N.Y.C., 1979-84, cons., 1984-87; gen. ptnr. Delphi Film Assocs. Partnerships, N.Y.C., 1982-86; sr. exec. v.p. Tri-Star Pictures, Inc., N.Y.C., 1987; COO, chmn. motion picture group Columbia Pictures Entertainment, Inc., 1988-89; pres. Savoy Pictures Entertainment, Inc., 1990-96; vice chmn. R.A.B. Holdings, Inc., 1997—; pres. Delphi Film Enterprises, Ltd., 1997—; chmn. Ep.Com Media, 2002—. Co-author: A Day in the Life of the United States Armed Forces, 2003. Mem. Acad. Motion Pictures Arts and Scis. (exec. br.), Order of the Coif. Office: RAB Holdings Inc 444 Madison Ave Ste 601 New York NY 10022-6903

KORMAN, NATHANIEL IRVING, research and development company executive; b. Providence, Feb. 23, 1916; s. William and Tillie (Jacobs) K.; m. Ruth C. Kaplan, Apr. 6, 1941; children: Michael, Robert. BS summa cum laude, Worcester Poly. Inst., 1937; MS (Coffin fellow), MIT, 1938; PhD, U. Pa., 1958. Dir. advance mil. systems RCA Corp., 1958-67. Chmn. radar panel U.S. R&D Bd., 1948-56; lectr. U. Pa. Evening Grad. Sch., 1967-68; cons. in field Color Sci., 1968-83; pres. Ventures R&D Group; cons. to Satellite Wholesale of N.Mex., 1991—. Author: The Evolution of Human Society, 1998; patentee in field. Mem. Citizens Com. for Better Schs., Moorestown, N.J., 1958. Recipient Merit award RCA, 1951. Fellow IEEE; mem. Sigma Xi. Home: 5700 Teakwood Trl NE Albuquerque NM 87111-6225

KORMAN, NEIL J. dermatologist; b. N.Y.C., Oct. 20, 1955; s. Joseph and Shirley K.; m. Diane P. Korman, Dec. 31, 1978; children: Benjamin, Joanna, Amanda. BE, SUNY, Stony Brook, 1976, MS, 1977; PhD, Case Western Res. U., 1982, MD, 1984. Diplomat Am. Bd. Dermatology. Intern U. Hosps. of Cleve., 1984-85, dermatology resident, 1985-87; dermatology rsch fellow NIH, Bethesda, Md., 1987-90; asst. prof. Case Western Res. U., Cleve., 1990-98, assoc. prof., 1998—, dir immunodermatology lab., 1990—, dir. clin. trials unit dept. dermatology, 1997—. Referee various sci. jours.; editor Med. and Surg. Dermatology, 1993—; contbr. articles to profl. jours. Recipient Career award Dermatology Found., 1990-92, Nat. Rsch. Svc. award NIH, Cleve., 1977-82. Mem. Soc. for Investigative Dermatology, Am. Fedn. for Clin. Rsch., Am. Acad. Dermatology, Ohio Dermatol. Assn., Cleve. Dermatol. Soc. Office: Univ Hosp of Cleve/Derm 11100 Euclid Ave Cleveland OH 44106-1736 E-mail: njk2@po.cwru.edu.

KORMES, JOHN WINSTON, lawyer; b. N.Y.C., May 4, 1935, s. Mark and Joanna P. Kormes; m. Frances W. Kormes, Aug. 19, 1978; 1 child, Mark Vincent. BA in Econs., U. Mich., 1955, JD, 1959. Bar: Pa. 1961, D.C. 1961, U.S. Supreme Ct. 1968. With License and Inspection Rev. Bd. Phila., 1972-73; asst. dist. atty. City of Phila., 1973-74; pvt. practice Phila., 1961—. Moot ct. advisor. Mem. staff Re-elect the Pres. Com., 1972, Rizzo for Mayor Com., 1971, 75, Phila. Flag Day Assn., 1965—. Served with USAF, 1956-57. Recipient N.Y. Intercoll. Legis. Assmebly award, 1954, R.I. Model Congress award, 1954, Queens Coll. Speech Guild award; Eminent Wisdom fellow Wisdom Hall of Fame. Fellow Lawyers in Mensa (charter), Triple Nine Soc. (elections officer 1992-93, legal officer, new mem. welcome program officer 1993—, com. to revise constitition 1993—, ombudsman 1994—), Internat. Soc. Phlos Enquiry (sr. fellow, pub. Best Telicom 1986, 87, legal officer 1986-91, v.p. 1990-91), Wisdom Soc.; mem. Am. Legion (life mem.), Phila. Bar Assn., Phila. Trial Lawyers Assn., N.Y. State Trial Lawyers Assn., Am. Arbitration Assn., Fed. Bar Assn., Pitts. Inst. Legal Medicine, Assn. Trial Lawyers Am., Intertel, Internat. Platform Assn., Cincinnatus soc., Top One Percent Soc., Collegium Soc. 99.5 (charter), Poetic Genius Soc. 99.5 (charter), Masons, Shriners, KP, Lions, Delta Sigma Rho. Republican. Home: 1070 Edison Ave Philadelphia PA 19116-1342 Office: 8122 Lister St Philadelphia PA 19152

KORMONDY, EDWARD JOHN, retired academic administrator, retired science educator; b. Beacon, N.Y., June 10, 1926; s. Anthony and Frances (Glover) Kormondy; m. Peggy Virginia Hedrick, June 5, 1950 (div. 1989); children: Lynn Ellen, Eric Paul, Mark Hedrick. BA in Biology summa cum laude, Tusculum Coll., 1950, DSc (hon.), 1997; MS in Zoology, U. Mich., 1951, PhD in Zoology, 1955. Tchg. fellow U. Mich., 1952-55; instr. zoology, curator insects Mus. Zoology, 1955-57; from asst. prof. to assoc. prof. Oberlin (Ohio) Coll., 1957—67, prof., 1967-69, acting assoc. dean, 1966-67; dir. Commn. Undergrad. Edn. Biol. Scis., Washington, 1968-72; dir. Office Biol. Edn. Am. Inst. Biol. Scis., Washington, 1968-71; mem. faculty Evergreen State Coll., Olympia, Wash., 1971-79, interim acting dean, 1972-73, v.p., provost, 1973-78; sr. profl. assoc., directorate sci. edn. NSF, 1979; provost, prof. biology U. So. Maine, Portland, 1979-82; v.p. acad. affairs, prof. biology Calif. State U., L.A., 1982-86; sr. v.p., chancellor, prof. biology U. Hawaii-West, Oahu and U. Hawaii, Hilo, 1986-93, chancellor emeritus, 2000—; pres. U. West L.A., 1995-97; spl. asst. to pres. Pacific Oaks Coll., 2000—. Author: (book) Introduction to Genetics: A Program for Self Instruction, 1964, Readings in Ecology, 1965, General Biology, A Book of Readings, 1966, Concepts of Ecology, 1969, 1976, 1983, 1996, General Biology: The Integrity and Natural History of Organisms, 1977, Handbook of Contemporary World Developments in Ecology, 1981, International Handbook of Pollution Control, 1989, (textbook) Biology, 1984, 1988, Fundamentals of Human Ecology, 1998, University of Hawaii-Hilo: A College in the Making, 2001; contbr. articles to profl. jours. With USN, 1944—46. Postdoctoral fellow, U. Ga., 1963—64, Vis. Rsch. fellow, Georgetown U., 1978—79, Rsch. grantee, NAS, Am. Philos. Soc., NSF. Fellow: AAAS; mem.: So. Calif. Acad. Scis. (bd. dirs. 1985—86, 1993—97, v.p. 1995—96), Nat. Assn. Biology Tchrs. (pres. 1981), Ecol. Soc. Am. (sec. 1976—78), Sigma Xi (Rsch. grantee). E-mail: ekor@aol.com.

KORN, DAVID, educator, pathologist; b. Providence, Mar. 5, 1933; s. Solomon and Claire (Liebman) Korn; m. Phoebe Richter, June 9, 1955 (div. Dec. 1993); children: Michael Philip, Stephen James, Daniel Clair; m. Carol Scheman, Dec. 24, 1997. BA, Harvard U., 1954, MD, 1959. Intern Mass. Gen. Hosp., Boston, 1959—60, resident in Pathology, 1960—61; rsch. assoc. NIH, 1961—63, asst. pathologist, 1963—68; mem. staff Lab. Biochem. Pharmacology; prof. pathology Sch. Medicine, Stanford (Calif.) U., 1968—97, chmn. dept. pathology Sch. Medicine, 1968—84; physician-in-chief pathology Stanford Hosp., 1968—84, dean Sch. Medicine, 1984—95, v.p., dean, 1986—95; cons. pathology Palo Alto VA Hosp., 1968—84; sr. v.p. biomed. and health scis. rsch. Assn. Am. Med. Colls., 1997—. Sr. surgeon USPHS, 1961—66; mem. cell biology study sect. NIH, 1973—77, chmn., 1976—77; mem. bd. sci. counselors divsn. cancer biology and diagnosis Nat. Cancer Inst., 1977—82, chmn., 1980—82, Nat. Cancer Adv. Bd., 1984—91; disting. scholar-in-residence Assn. Am. Med. Colls., 1995—97; sr. fellow sci. and health policy Assn. Acad. Health Ctrs., 1995—97. Mem. editl. bd. Human Pathology, 1969—74, assoc. editor, 1974—88, mem. editl. bd. Jour. Biol. Chemistry, 1973—79. Recipient Young Disting. Scientist award, Md. Acad. Sci., 1967. Fellow: AAAS; mem.: Inst. of Medicine, Fedn. Am. Soc. Exptl. Biology (bd. dirs., mem. exec. com.), Am. Soc. Investigative Pathology, Am. Soc. Biochemistry and Molecular Biology. Home: 3827 Cathedral Ave NW Washington DC 20016 Office: AAMC 2450 N St NW Washington DC 20037-1167 E-mail: dkom@aamc.org.

KORN, JESSICA SUSAN, research scientist, educator; b. L.A., Aug. 16, 1968; d. Lester B. and Carolbeth (Goldman) K. BA in Sociology, UCLA, 1990, MA in Edn., 1992, PhD in Philosophy, 1996. Actor Curb-Esquire Films, Burbank, Calif., 1984; exec. asst. Korn Capital Group, Inc., L.A., 1991; tchg. asst. Grad. Sch. Edn. and Info. Studies UCLA, 1995, rsch. analyst Grad. Sch. Edn. and Info. Studies, 1992-96, postdoctoral fellow Higher Edn. Rsch. Inst., 1996-97, tchg. assoc., 1997; rsch. scientist, affiliate asst. prof. U. Wash., 1997-99; v.p. instnl. rsch. Eckerd Coll., St. Petersburg, Fla., 1999—. Internat. election observer Orgn. for Security and Cooperation in Europe, 1997, 98, 2000, 02. Contbr. articles to profl. jours. Jr. assoc. Big Sisters Am., L.A., 1994-98. Mem. AAUW, Am. Ednl. Rsch. Assn., Assn. Study of Higher Edn., Assn. for Instnl. Rsch., Nat. Coun. Rsch. on Women, Screen Actors Guild Am. Avocations: working with rape and other trauma survivors, humanitarian aid, travel, writing, yoga, acting. E-mail: kornjs@eckerd.edu.

KORN, JOSEPH HOWARD, physician, educator; b. Augsburg, Fed. Republic of Germany, Jan. 31, 1947; came to U.S., 1947; s. Leo and Rose Korn; m. Paulette Jeremias, June 26, 1971; children: Naomi, Jerald, Joshua, Jonathan. BS, CCNY, 1968; MD, Columbia U., 1972. Cert. rheumatology: internal medicine. Intern N.C. Meml. Hosp., Chapel Hill, 1972-73, resident, 1973-75; fellow Med. U. S.C., Charleston, 1975-77, asst. prof. medicine, 1977-78, U. Conn. Sch. Medicine, Farmington, 1978-84, assoc. prof., 1984-90, prof., 1990-93; assoc. chief of staff R&D VA Med. Ctr., Newington, Conn., 1982-93; prof. medicine and biochemistry Boston U. Med. Ctr., chief rheumatology sect., dir. arthritis ctr. Mem. biomedical grant adv. panel Arthritis Found., Atlanta, 1986—91; mem. sci. adv. bd. Scleroderma Found. Mem. editl. bd. Arthritis and Rheumatism, 1985—90, Clin. Exptl. Rheumatology, 1998—; contbr. over 100 articles to profl. jours. Named to NIH Review Group, 1984-85. Fellow Am. Coll. Rheumatology; mem. AAAS, Am. Soc. Clin. Investigation. Avocations: reading, investing. Office: Boston U Sch Medicine 80 E Concord St Boston MA 02118-2307

KORN, LESTER BERNARD, business executive; b. N.Y.C., Jan. 11, 1936; BS with honors, UCLA, 1959, MBA, 1960; postgrad., Harvard Bus. Sch., 1961. Mgmt. cons. Peat, Marwick, Mitchell & Co., L.A., 1961-66, ptnr., 1966-69; founder, CEO Korn/Ferry Internat., L.A., 1969-91, chmn. emeritus, 1991—; U.S. amb. and U.S. rep. Econ. and Social Coun. UN, 1987-88; chmn., founder Korn Tuttle Capital Group, Inc., 1991; alt. rep. 42d and 43d UN Gen. Assembly. Chmn., CEO Korn Tuttle Capital Group, Inc., 1991; bd. dirs. Continental Am. Properties, Coun. Am. Ambs., Music Ctr. Operating Co. L.A., Performing Arts Ctr., L.A., Tenet Healthcare Corp., RAND-Ctr. for Russian and Eurasian Studies; mem. U.S. Presdl. Del. to Observe Elections in Bosnia, 1996. Author: The Success Profile, 1989. Trustee UCLA Found.; bd. overseers and bd. visitors Anderson Grad. Sch. Mgmt., UCLA; trustee, founding mem. Dean's Coun. UCLA, Performing Arts Cen. L.A., 1999—; mem. adv. coun. Am. Heart Assn.; spl. advisor, del. UNESCO Inter-gov. Conf. on Edn. for Internat. Understanding, Coop., Peace, 1983; adv. bd. Women in Film Found., 1983-84; chmn. Commn. on Citizen Participation in Govt., State of Calif., 1979-82; bd. dirs. John Douglas French Found. for Alzheimer's Disease; mem. Republican Nat. Exec. Fin. Com., 1985, Pres.'s Commn. White House Fellowships, Republican Eagles; hon. chairperson 50th Am. Presdl. Inaugural, 1985; co-chmn. So. Calif. region NCCJ; mem. U.S. Presdl. Del. to observe elections in Bosnia, 1996. Recipient Alumni Profl. Achievement award UCLA, 1984, Superior Honor award U.S. Dept. State, 1988, Neil H. Jacoby Internat. award, 1990, Internat. Citizen of Yr. award Internat. Visitors Coun., 1991; Korn Convocation Hall at

UCLA dedicated in his honor, 1995. Mem. AICPAs, Calif. Soc. CPAs, Am. Bus. Conf. (founding mem.), Coun. Am. Ambs., Prodrs. Guild of Am., Hillcrest Country Club, Rockefeller Ctr. Club. Office: Korn Tuttle Capital Grp 468 N Camden Dr Beverly Hills CA 90210-4507

KORN, MICHAEL JEFFREY, lawyer; b. Jersey City, Dec. 22, 1954; s. Howard Leonard and Joyce Ellen K.; m. Pamela Ann (VanZandt), May 29, 1983; children: David Harold, Suzanne Faye. BA, U. Va., 1976; JD, U. Fla., 1979. Bar: Fla. 1980, U.S. Dist. Ct. (no. and mid. dist.); U.S. Ct. Appeals (5th and 11th cir.). Jud. law clk. Fla. 1st Dist Ct. Appeal, Tallahassee, 1980-81; assoc. Boyer, Tanzler, and Boyer, Jacksonville, Fla., 1981-84; pvt. practice Jacksonville, Fla., 1984-87; ptnr. Prom, Korn, and Zehmer, P.A., Jacksonville, Fla., 1987-95, Korn and Zehmer, P.A., Jacksonville, Fla., 1995—. Rules com., Fla. Appellate Ct., 1991-2002. Bd. dir. North Fla. coun. Camp Fire, 1983-86; Jacksonville Jewish Fedn., 1985; v.p., 1994-99, treas., 1999-2003, v.p. 2003-; bd. dir. Youth Leadership Jacksonville, 1989-93; Jacksonville Cmty. Coun., 1989-94, 96-98, pres., 1995; Mandarin Cmty. Club, Jacksonville, 1988-91; cmty. adv. bd. WJCT-TV, Jacksonville, 1996—, chmn., 1999-2000; bd. dir. United Way of N.E. Fla., 1999—; Nonprofit Ctr. of N.E. Fla., Inc., 2003; trustee North Fla. Family Housing Found., 1999-2003. Recipient Young Leadership Award, Jacksonville Jewish Fedn., 1992; Tree of Life Award, Jewish Nat. Found., 2001. Mem. Fla. Bar (litig., appellate and health law sect., grievance com. 2001, chair 2003), Jacksonville Bar Assn. (fee arbitration com. 1987-90, chair 1995-99, chair appellate practice sect. 2003-), Acad. Fla. Trial Lawyers. Jewish. Avocations: running, reading, golf. Office: Korn and Zehmer PA Ste 200 6620 Southpoint Dr S Jacksonville FL 32216-0940 Fax: 904-296-2111 904-296-0384.

KORN, NEAL MARK, painter, art educator; b. Nyack, NY, May 11, 1957; s. Jacob and Sylvia Korn; m. Patsy Anne Trine, Oct. 25, 1985; 1 child, Sasha Jaye. AA, Palm Beach Jr. Coll., Lake Worth, Fla., 1978; BS in Art, Bklyn. Coll./SUNY, 1983; MA in Studio Art, Kean U., 1998. One-person show Tomasulo Art Gallery, N.J., Arts Guild Rahway, N.J., 2000-02, Art Alliance, N.J., 2001, City Without Walls, N.J., 2001; exhibited in group shows Night Gallery, N.Y.C., 1987, La Mama's La Galleria, N.Y.C., 1988-89, Ape Gallery, N.Y.C., 1990, 92, Art et Industrie Gallery, N.Y.C., 1991, 148 Gallery, N.Y.C., 1992-95, City Without Walls, N.J., 1995-96, 99, Art Alliance, N.J., 1995-98, Art Ctr. No. N.J., 1998, Aljira, N.J., 1996, 98, Audart, N.Y.C., 1996, N.J. Ctr. for Visual Arts, 1997, Watchung Arts Ctr., N.J., 1997, William Paterson U., N.J., 1998, Gallery of South Orange, N.J., 1999, Kean U., N.J., 1998, Joan Prats Gallery, N.Y.C., 1998, Liquid Gallery, N.J., 1999, Art Alliance, N.J., 2000, N.J. Ctr. Visual Arts, N.J., 2000, Art Guild of Rahway, 2001 (Merit award), N.J. Ctr. Visual Arts, 2001 (Best of Show, Marian H. Anderson Award for Portraiture 2002), Art Alliance, 2002, Jersey City Mus., 2002, 2003. two person show, Arts Guild of Rahway, N.J. 2003. Recipient Shaw award for painting Bklyn. Coll., 1982, Best of Oil Painting-Book, Rockport Pubs., 1996, other awards; Heart grantee for Art, 1998, 2002; Geraldine R. Dodge fellow, 2000; recipient Geraldine R. Dodge scholarship, Fine Arts Works Ctr. Provincetown, 2002, minigrant, 2003. Address: 912 Pennsylvania Ave Union NJ 07083-6930 E-mail: Nealpaintbrush11@earthlink.net.

KORN, PETER A. arbitrator, mediator, educator; b. N.Y.C., Sept. 16, 1939; s. Samuel S. and Sylvia (Sachs) K.; m. Marian Bell, Dec. 24, 1967; 1 child, Sheryl Robin. BBA, CCNY, 1961; M.G.A., U. Pa., 1962. Exec. asst. City of Rochester, N.Y., 1962-64, budget dir., 1964-69, city mgr., 1980-85; mgr. City of Long Beach, N.Y., 1970-71; adminstr. Jersey City, 1972-75, Broward County, Fla., 1975-76; prof., asst. to pres. Nova U., Ft. Lauderdale, Fla., 1976-80; v.p. electronic tng. div. Kodak Corp., Rochester, 1986-87, cons. state and local services, electronic tng. div., 1987-89; prof. pub. adminstrn. SUNY, Brockport, 1987-90; city mgr. City of Peoria, Peoria, Ill., 1990-96, City of New Rochelle, 1996—2002; labor arbitrator, 2002—. Author: Financing City and Schools in Yonkers NY, 1976 Mem.: Indsl. Rels. Rsch. Assn., Am. Arbitration Assn., Internat. City Mgmt. Assn. Avocation: boating.

KORN, WILLIAM DAVID, technology executive; b. NYC, Apr. 12, 1957; s. Edward W. and Betty F. (Brown) K.; m. Elizabeth Amy Kron, Mar. 27, 1988; 1 child, Sandra Lynne. AB in Econs. magna cum laude, Harvard Coll., 1978; MBA, Harvard Bus. Sch., 1980. Mgr. ops. planning United Techs. subs. Mostek Corp., Dallas, 1980-81, dir. fin. planning, 1982, controller bus. devel. group, 1983; CFO Incomnet, Inc., Westlake Village, Calif., 1984-85; program mgr. computing systems Research div. IBM, Yorktown Heights, N.Y., 1986; mgr. plans, controls, automation Corp. Research div. IBM, Yorktown Heights, N.Y., 1987-88; leader info. systems investment strategies program IBM Mktg. and Svcs., Stamford, Conn., 1988-89, mng. cons., 1990-91; prin. IBM Cons. Group, White Plains, N.Y., 1991-93; strategy advisor IBM Corp. Strategy, Armonk, N.Y., 1993-94; dir. strategy and bus. devel. IBM Electronics Commerce Svcs., Thornwood, N.Y., 1994-95; ops. exec. interactive fin. svcs. IBM, White Plains, N.Y., 1995-96; CFO Integrion Fin. Network, L.L.C., White Plains, 1996-98, INFONXX, Inc., Bethlehem, Pa., 1998-2000, COO, 1999—2000; pres. Telelogue, Inc., Iselin, NJ, 2001; CFO Antenna Software, Inc., N.Y.C., 2002—, iRail, LLC, Parsippany, NJ, 2002—. Bd. dirs. Nerdy Books, LLC, Flemington, NJ. Author: A Model for the Analysis of Corporate Capital Structures, 1978. Bd. dirs. The Common Condominium Assn., Old Greenwich, Conn., 1987. Mem. Harvard Bus. Sch. Club N.Y., Harvard Club of N.J. Jewish. Avocations: tennis, sailing, chess, music, art. Home and Office: 61 Darren Dr Basking Ridge NJ 07920 E-mail: billkorn@optonline.net.

KORNATOWSKI, SUSAN CAROL, elementary education educator; b. Constableville, NY, Apr. 21, 1955; d. Anthony John and Estella Helen (Ward) K. BA, SUNY, Potsdam, 1977; MA, Cortland State U., 1984. Cert. elem. edn. tchr., N.Y. 2nd grade tchr. Adirondack Central Sch., West Leyden, N.Y., 1983—. Active PTA, Nat. Arbor Day, 1990—. Named to SUNY Potsdam Alumni Sports Hall of Fame, 1990, Excellent Tchr. of Yr., 1997, 99; recipient Nat. Citizenship Edn. Tchr. award VFW, 2002-03. Mem. VFW (Nat. Citizenship Ednl. Tchr. award 2002-03), West Leyden Free Reading Ctr. (librarian 1982-83, treas. 1983—), Roman Catholic. Avocations: ceramics, knitting, sewing, sports, volleyball. Home: PO Box 121 West Leyden NY 13489-0121 Office: West Leyden Elem Sch Fish Creek Rd West Leyden NY 13489

KORNBERG, ALAN WILLIAM, lawyer; b. N.Y.C., Dec. 11, 1952; s. Peter and Selma (Borden) K. AB, Brandeis U., 1974; JD, NYU, 1977. Bar: N.Y. 1978, D.C. 1993. Assoc. Milbank, Tweed, Hadley & McCloy, N.Y.C., 1977-86, ptnr., 1986-90, Paul, Weiss, Rifkind, Wharton & Garrison, LLP, N.Y.C., 1990—. Fellow Am. Coll. Bankruptcy, 1995; adj. instr. law Yeshiva U., N.Y.C., 1984-85. Bd. dirs. Lubovitch Dance Found., Inc., 1988-98, Photographers & Friends United Against AIDS, 1989-92, Classical Action, 1993-98. Mem. ABA, N.Y. Bar Assn., Assn. of Bar of City of N.Y., Akin Hall Assn. Home: 71 E 77th St New York NY 10021-1849 Office: Paul Weiss Rifkind Wharton & Garrison LLP 1285 Avenue Of The Americas New York NY 10019-6064 E-mail: akornberg@paulweiss.com.

KORNBERG, ARTHUR, biochemist, educator; b. N.Y.C., N.Y., Mar. 3, 1918; s. Joseph and Lena (Katz) Kornberg; m. Sylvy R. Levy, Nov. 21, 1943 (dec. 1986); children: Roger, Thomas Bill, Kenneth Andrew; m. Charlene Walsh Levering, 1988 (dec. 1995); m. Carolyn Frey Dixon, 1998. BS, CCNY, 1937, LLD (hon.), 1960; MD, U. Rochester, 1941, DSc (hon.), 1962, U. Pa., U. Notre Dame, 1965, Washington U., 1968, Princeton U., 1970, Colby Coll., 1970; LHD (hon.), Yeshiva U., 1963; MD honoris causa, U. Barcelona, Spain, 1970. Intern in medicine Strong Meml. Hosp., Rochester, NY, 1941—42; commd. officer USPHS, 1942, advanced through grades to med. dir., 1951; mem. staff NIH, Bethesda, Md., 1942—52, nutrition sect., div. physiology, 1942—45; chief sect. enzymes and metabolism Nat. Inst. Arthritis and Metabolic Diseases, 1947—52; guest research worker depts. chemistry and pharmacology coll. medicine NYU, 0466; dept. biol. chemistry med. sch. Washington U., 1947; dept. plant biochemistry U. Calif., 1951; prof., head dept. microbiology, med. sch. Washington U., St. Louis, 1953—59; prof. biochemistry Stanford U. Sch. Medicine, 1959—88, chmn. dept., 1959—69, prof. emeritus dept. biochemistry, 1988—. Mem. sci. adv. bd. Mass. Gen. Hosp., 1964—67; bd. govs. Weizmann Inst., Israel. Author: For the Love of Enzymes, 1989; contbr. Lt. (j.g.), med. officer USCGR, 1942. Co-recipient Nobel prize in medicine, 1959; named Arthur Kornberg Med. Rsch. Bldg. at U. Rochester in his honor, 1999; recipient Paul-Lewis award in enzyme chemistry, 1951, Max Berg award prolonging human life, 1968, Sci. Achievement award, AMA, 1968, Lucy Wortham James award, James Ewing Soc., 1968, Borden award, Am. Assn. Med. Colls., 1968, Nat. medal of sci., 1979, Gairdner Found. Internat. Awards, 1995. Mem.: NAS, Am. Philos. Soc., Am. Acad. Arts and Scis., Royal Soc., Harvey Soc., Am. Chem. Soc., Am. Soc. Biol. Chemists (pres. 1965), Alpha Omega Alpha, Sigma Xi, Phi Beta Kappa. Office: Stanford U Sch of Med Dept Biochemistry Beckman Ctr Rm B400 Stanford CA 94305-5307 E-mail: arthur.kornberg@stanford.edu.*

KORNBERG, SIR HANS LEO, biochemist, educator; b. Herford, Germany, Jan. 14, 1928; s. Max and Margarete (Silberbach) K.; m. Monica Mary King, Oct. 6, 1956 (dec. June 1989); children: Julia Margaret, Rachel Elizabeth, Jonathan Paul, Simon Alexander; m. Donna Haber, July 28, 1991. BSc, U. Sheffield, 1949, PhD, 1953, DSc (hon.), 1979; MA, Oxford U., 1959, DSc, 1961; ScD, Cambridge U., 1975; DSc (hon.), Warwick U., 1975, Leicester U., 1979, Bath U., 1980, Strathclyde U., 1985, South Bank U., 1994, Leeds U., 1995, La Trobe U., 1997; D.U. (hon.), Essex U., 1979; MD (hon.), Leipzig U., 1984; LLD (hon.), Dundee U., 1999. John Stokes rsch. fellow U. Sheffield, 1951-53; Commonwealth Fund fellow Yale U., U. Calif., Berkeley, Pub. Health Rsch. Inst., N.Y., 1953-55; mem. sci. staff M.R.C. cell metabolism rsch. unit Oxford, 1955-60; prof. biochemistry U. Leicester, 1960-75; Sir William Dunn prof. biochemistry Cambridge (Eng.) U., 1975-95, fellow Christ's Coll., 1975—, Master, 1982-95. Lectr. Worcester Coll. Oxford, 1958-60; Leeuwenhoek lectr. Royal Soc., 1972; Weizmann Meml. lectr., Rehovot, 1975; mem. Sci. Rsch. Coun., 1967-72, chmn. sci. bd., 1969-72; mem. U.G.C. Biol. Sci. Com., 1967-76; U.K. rep. NATO-ASI Panel, 1970-76, chmn., 1974-75; chmn. Royal Commn. on Environ. Pollution, 1976-81; mem. Agrl. Rsch. Coun., 1981-84; mem. Priorities Bd. for Rsch. and Devel. in Agr., 1984-90; chmn. adv. com. on Genetic Modification, 1986-95. Author: (with Hans Krebs) Energy Transformations in Living Matter, 1957; contbr. articles to profl. jours. Mng. trustee Nuffield Found., 1972-93; gov. Hebrew U. Jerusalem, 1976-97, hon. gov., 1997—; sci. gov. Weizmann Inst. Sci., Rehovot, Israel, 1981-90, emeritus gov., 1990—; trustee Marine Biol. Lab., Woods Hole, Mass., 1982-87, 88-93, Wellcome Trust, 1990-92; gov. Wellcome Trust Ltd., 1992-95; bd. dir. U.K. Nirex Ltd., 1986-95; pres. Biochem. Soc. U.K., 1990-95, Assn. Sci. Edn., 1991-92, Internat. Union of Biochemistry and Molecular Biology, 1991-94. Recipient Colworth medal Biochem. Soc., 1963, Otto Warburg medal German Biochem. Soc., 1973; created knight bachelor, 1978; hon. fellow Worcester Coll., Oxford, 1981, Brasenose Coll., Oxford, 1982, Wolfson Coll., Cambridge, 1990. Fellow Royal Soc. (coun. 1975-77), Inst. Biology (v.p. 1970-72), Royal Soc. Arts, Royal Coll. Physicians (London) (hon.), Am. Acad. Microbiology; hon. mem. Am. Soc. Biochemistry and Molecular Biology, Am. Acad. Arts and Scis. (fgn. assoc.), German Soc. Biol. Chemists, Japanese Biochem. Soc., Biochem. Soc. U.K., Brit. Assn. Advancement Sci. (hon., pres. 1984-85); mem. NAS (fgn. assoc.), Am. Philos. Soc., German Acad. Scis. (Leopoldina), Italian Nat. Acad. Sci. (Lincei), Phi Beta Kappa. Office: The University Professors Boston U 745 Commonwealth Ave Boston MA 02215-1401 E-mail: hlk@bu.edu.

KORNBERG, JOEL BARRY, lawyer, emergency physician; b. Bklyn., June 17, 1953; s. Bernard Fred and Ada (Ritterstein) K.; m. Melinda Michelle Kornberg;children: Dana Nicole, Jordan Reid. AB, Boston U., 1975; MD, N.Y. Med. Coll., 1980; JD, Nova U., 1989. Bar: Fla. 1989, D.C. 1990, U.S. Dist. Ct. (so. dist.) Fla. 1989, U.S. Supreme Ct. 1994; cert. mediator, Fla. 1995; cert. Am. Bd. Emergency Medicine, healthcare risk mgr., Fla. Resident Long Island Jewish-Hillside Med. Ctr., New Hyde Park, N.Y., 1980-81; emergency physician Emergency Med. Svcs. Assocs., Inc., Plantation, Fla., 1981-83, Joel B. Kornberg, M.D. P.A., Coral Springs, Fla., 1983-90, EMSA Ltd. Partnership, Plantation, 1990—; med. dir. Dept. Emergency Svcs. Humana Hosp., Pompano Beach, Fla., 1985-92, regional med. dir., 1992-94; pvt. practice Joel Kornberg, M.D., J.D., Boca Raton, Fla., 1994—; med. dir. dept. emergency medicine Cedars Med. Ctr., Miami, 1993-94; pvt. practice Joel Kornberg MD, JD, Boca Raton, Fla., 1994—. Mem. exec. com. Humana Hosp. Cypress, Pompano Beach, 1985-92, corp. counsel med. affairs; risk mgmt. cons. EMSA Ltd. Partnership, Plantation, 1989-94; dir. edn. Voice Billstat, Plantation, 1992-94. Head coach Coral Springs Youth Soccer Assn., 1989—, mgr. North Springs Little League, 1995-97. Fellow Am. Coll. Legal Medicine, Am. Coll. Emergency Physician; mem. ABA, Nat. Health Lawyers Assn., Am. Soc. Law and Medicine, Nat. Bd. Med. Examiners. Avocations: skiing, piano, tennis, baseball, bicycle. Office: Ste 305C 7301A W Palmetto Park Rd Boca Raton FL 33433-3466 E-mail: jkmdjd@aol.com.

KORNBERG, WARREN STANLEY, science journalist; b. N.Y.C., June 21, 1927; s. Murray and Helen (Blumberg) K.; m. Felice Sher, June 15, 1952; children: Lisa Kornberg, Jena Talarico, Eva Polston. BA, Adelphi Coll., 1950; MA, Columbia, 1952; postgrad., U. Mo., 1954-55. Reporter Fall River (Mass.) Herald News, 1955-58, Boston Herald, 1958-59, Washington Post, 1960-61; Washington corr.-sci. editor McGraw Hill Publs., Washington, 1962-66; editor Sci. News, Washington, 1966-70; writer syndicated column Warren Kornberg on Science, 1969-70; sci. editor pub. affairs NSF, Washington, 1970-75; editor NSF mag. Mosaic, Washington, 1975—93; book rev. editor Physics Today, 1993—2003. Home: 11017 Kenilworth Ave Garrett Park MD 20896-0153

KORNBLUM, SYLVAN, psychologist; b. Antwerp, Sept. 15, 1927; s. Bernard and Charlotte (Geldzahler) m. Elizabeth Dorothea Humes, Dec. 30, 1970; children: David Alan, Karen Elaine. BA, Washingto U., St. Louis, 1951; MA, U. Mich., Ann Arbor, 1953, PhD, 1960; MS, U. Mich, 1955. Asst. dir. Mental Health Rsch. Inst. U. Mich., Ann Arbor, 1962-64; assoc. rsch. scientist Mental Health Rsch. Inst., Ann Arbor, 1960-70; sr. rsch. scientist Mental Health Res. Inst., Ann Arbor, 1970; prof. of psychology U. Mich., Ann Arbor, 1970-97, prof., sr. rsch. scientist emeritus, 1997—. Post doctoral fellow Applied Psychology unit, Cambridge, 1960-62; vis. fellow Yale U., New Haven, 1976-77; resident vis. scientist Bell Lab., Murray Hill, 1976-77; vis. rsch. scientist Inst. Neurophysiology/CNRS, Marseille, France, 1984. Founding mem., sec., treas. Internat. Assn. for Study of Attention and Performance, 1973-98. Cpl. U.S. Army, 1946-47. Fellow AAAS, Am. Psychol. Assn., Psychonomic Soc., Soc. Math. Psychology Cognitive Sci. Soc, Sigma Xi. Home: 3541 Daleview Dr Ann Arbor MI 48105-9686 Office: U Mich Mental Health Rsch Inst 205 Zina Pitcher Pl Ann Arbor MI 48109-0720 E-mail: kornblum@umich.edu.

KORNBLUTH, FRANCES HELEN SCHACHTER, artist; b. N.Y.C., July 26, 1920; d. Jacob and Sarah (Goodstone) Schachter; m. Marvin Hubert Kornbluth, Nov. 21, 1942; children: Bruce Ian, Jane Allyse Cathy. BA, Bklyn. Coll., 1940; MA in Edn., Pratt Inst., 1962. Cert. early childhood tchr., N.Y., Conn. Painter and sculptor, 1958—; tchr. Mineola (N.Y.) Pub. Schs., 1959-67; supr. student tchrs. Mills Coll., N.Y.C., 1966-68; instr. Art Edn. Hofstra U., Hempstead, N.Y., 1967-68, Adelphi U., Garden City, N.Y., spring 1968; instr. Art Dowling Coll., Oakdale, N.Y., 1967, U. Conn., Storrs, spring 1970; tchr. dir. gifted Thompson (Conn.) Elem. Sch., 1972-75; instr. Annhurst Coll., Woodstock, Conn., spring 1980. Lectr. in field. One-woman shows include Works on Canvas Cambridge (Mass.) Art Assn., 1976, Landscape is Alive and Well in Northeastern Connecticut, Women's Ctr. U. Conn., 1978, Path Artworks Gallery, Hartford, 1981, Works on Paper Galeria Prin., Dominican Republic, 1985, Collages, 1986, Selections Artworks Gallery, Hartford, 1991, Visions of Our Land Legis. Office Bldg., Hartford, Conn., 1992, U. Mass. Med. Sch., Worcester, 1997, Showcase for Collage, Providence, Points of Departure, Slater Meml. Mus., Norwich, Conn., 2001, Edge of the Sea Arts, Worcester, Mass., 2002, Atrium Gallery, Danielson, Conn., 2003, exhibited in group shows at Small Works on Paper Concordia Gallery, Bronxville, NY, 1992, Art for AIDS Sake, Worcester, Mass. Mem. Thompson Hist. Soc., 1989—. With OSS, Army, 1943-45. Recipient Charles H. Woodbury Meml. Prize for a Landscape, 1975, Helen Henningson Meml. Prize for Oil, 1977, Elizabeth Morse Genius Found. Prize-Works on Paper, 1982, 1st prize, Collage N.E. Conn. Art Guild, 1992, Miriam E. Halpern Meml. award, 1992, Lifetime Achievement award, Bklyn. Coll., 2000, 1st prize painting, Slater Meml. Mus., Norwich, 2000. Mem. Conn. Acad. Fine Arts, Nat. Assn. Women Artists (2 Gold medals of Honor), Women Artists of Monhegan Island, Arts Worcester, ART XII. Democrat. Avocations: music, movies. Home: 134 Buckley Hill Rd North Grosvenordale CT 06255-1803 Studio: Monhegan Island Monhegan ME 04852

KORNBREKKE, RALPH ERIK, colloid chemist; b. Bklyn., Nov. 22, 1951; s. Henning Norman and Esther (Pedersen) K.; m. Annette Elizabeth Kingman, Aug. 17, 1974. BS, Rensselaer Poly. Inst., 1974, PhD, 1981. Chemist Petroleum Action Inc., Rensselaer, N.Y., 1974-75, Rensselaer Rsch. Corp. Internat., Latham, N.Y., 1975-76; sr. rsch. chemist The 3M Corp., St. Paul, 1980-84; project leader Std. Oil of Ohio, Warrensville Hts., 1984-87; rsch. chemist IV The Lubrizol Corp., Wickliffe, Ohio, 1987-90, sr. rsch. chemist, 1990-91, rsch. scientist, 1991-97, prin. rsch. scientist, 1998—. Session chmn. Am. Chem. Soc. Nat. Meeting Colloid Div., N.Y.C., 1986; chmn. the Interface Sci. chpt. of 3M Tech. Forum, St. Paul, 1982-84; staff mem. NBS Molton Salts Data Ctr., Troy, 1975-76. Contbr. articles to profl. jours.; patentee in field. Pres. Oakwood Lustre Townhome Assn., Oakdale, Minn., 1981-84; judge Reg. Sci. Fair, Mpls., Cleve., 1981—; team capt. Cleve. Orch. Campaign Fund Raising, 1988-90. N.Y. State Regents scholar 1970; named J. Willard Gibbs Rsch. fellow, 1979-80. Fellow Am. Inst. Chemists; mem. AAAS, Internat. Assn. Colloid and Interface Scientists, Am. Chem. Soc., Soc. Automotive Engrs., Soc. Tribologists and Lubrication Engrs., Sigma Xi, Phi Lambda Epsilon. Achievements include discovery of stochastic nature of emulsion-type inversion process, complex nature of wetting near the critical point, special expertise surfactant interactions at solid-liquid interfaces, nonaqueous colloidal properties regarding dispersions and lubrication. Home: 8340 Tulip Ln Chagrin Falls OH 44023-4675 Office: The Lubrizol Corp 29400 Lakeland Blvd Wickliffe OH 44092-2298 E-mail: rko@lubrizol.com., rkornbrekke@kornbrekke.com.

KORN-DAVIS, DOTTIE, artist, educator, consultant; b. L.A. d. William and Anne Miller. BA, UCLA, 1961; MA, San Diego State U., 1981. Artist-in-residence Laocheng Tchrs. U., Shandong, China, 1996 El Taller de Pubilla Kasas, Barcelona, Spain, 1998-99, 2002; active Art in the Cmty./Woman's Caucus for Arts, San Diego, 1994-97, Found. for Women, San Diego, Calif.; one-woman shows include Art Gallery Chula Vista (Calif.) Libr., Bard Hall Gallery, Hillcrest, Calif., San Diego (Calif.) Hospice Downstairs Gallery; open studio artist COVA, 1995, 99, Found. for Women. Solo shows include Art Gallery/Earl and Birdie Taylor Libr., San Diego, 2002-03, Bard Hall, Hillcrest, Calif., Mira Costa Coll., Oceanside, Calif., East County Performing Arts Ctr., El Cajon, Caif., Spectrum Gallery, San Diego, Imperial Valley Coll., Calif.; exhibited in group shows at Mus., Calif. Ctr. for the Arts, Escondido, Calif., Taos (N.Mex.) Hist. Mus., Centre for Arts, Pico Rivera, Calif.; Multicultural Arts Inst., San Diego, San diego Artists Guild, Spectrum Gallery, San Diego, Riverside (Calif.) Arts Mus., San diego Art Inst., Orange County Ct. for Contemporary Art, Santa Ana, Calif., L.A. Mcpl. Art Gallery, U. Wis. Ctr., Waukesha, Art Union Gallery, San Diego, Gallery Ten, Rockford, Ill., Next Door Gallery, San Diego, USCD Cross Cultural Ctr. Gallery, San Diego, numerous others. Bd. dirs. Artists Guild/Mus. Art, 1991-92. Recipient 1st Prize award San Diego Artists Guild, 1983. Avocations: travel, hiking, theatre, dance.

KORNDORFFER, WILLIAM EARL, forensic pathologist; b. Natchez, Miss., Feb. 5, 1930; s. William Earl and Caroline Elizabeth (Lapthorn) K.; m. Betty Blair Hughes, June 18, 1954; children: William III, James Blair, Robert Craig, Brenda Lea. BS, U. Miss., 1952; MD, Harvard U., 1956. Diplomate Am. Bd. Pathology. Dir. labs Griffin-Spalding Co. Hosp., Griffin, Ga., 1963-65; co-dir. of labs Galveston Co. Meml. Hosp., Tex. City, Tex., 1965-68; dir. labs Rimmer Med. Labs., Dickinson, Tex., 1968-74, Danforth Meml. Hosp., Tex. City, 1968-74, Alvin (Tex.) Gulfcoast Hosp., 1968-74, Alvin (Tex.) Meml. Hosp., 1968-74, Angleton (Tex.) Danbury Hosp., 1968-74; chief med. exam Med. Examiner's Office, Tex. City, 1972—; prof. pathology U. Tex. Med. Branch, Galveston, 1978—. Capt. USAF, 1958-60. Mem. AMA, Coll. Am. Pathologists, Am. Soc. Clin. Pathologists, Nat. Assn. Med. Examiners, Am. Acad. Forensic Scis., Soc. Nuclear Medicine, Elks, Moose. Roman Catholic. Home: 5000 Hwy 3 Dickinson TX 77539-6830 Office: Med Examiners Office 6607 Highway 1764 Texas City TX 77591

KORNEGAY, HORACE ROBINSON, trade association executive, former congressman, lawyer; b. Asheville, N.C., Mar. 12, 1924; s. Marvin Earl and Blanche Person (Robinson) K.; m. Annie Ben Beale, Mar. 25, 1950; children: Horace Robinson, Kathryn Elder Kornegay Cozort, Martha Beale Kornegay Howard. BS, Wake Forest U., 1947, JD, 1949. Bar: N.C. 1949, D.C. 1979, U.S. Supreme Ct 1959. Practice in, Greensboro; asst. solicitor Superior Ct. Guilford County, 1951-53; dist. solicitor 12th Solicitorial Dist., 1955-60; mem. 87th-90th Congresses from 6th Dist. N.C.; v.p., counsel The Tobacco Inst., Washington, 1969-70, pres., exec. dir., 1970-81, chmn., 1981-86; counsel Adams Kleemeier Hagan Hannah & Fouts, Greensboro, N.C., 1987-2000. Bd. dirs. Greensboro Mcht. Assn. Pres. Guilford Young Dem. Club, 1952, N.C. Young Dem. Clubs, 1953-54; chmn. bd. visitors Sch. Law, Wake Forest U., 1979-93; past chmn. adminstrv. bd. Concord-St. Andrew's United Meth. Ch., Bethesda, Md.; mem. adminstrv. bd. West Market St. United Meth. Ch., Greensboro. With AUS, 1943-46. Decorated Purple Heart, Bronze Star, Combat Inf. badge, Expert Infantryman's badge; recipient Americanism award Anti-Defamation League, B'nai B'rith, Washington, 1985. Mem. ABA, Fed. Bar Assn., N.C. Bar Assn. (chmn. dispute resolution com. 1989-92), Greensboro Bar Assn. (pres. 1992-93), D.C. Bar Assn., Am. Judicature Soc., Wake Forest Univ. Lawyers Alumni Assn. (past pres.), SAR (trustee), Alpha Sigma Phi Edn. Found. (trustee), Am. Legion, VFW, Royal Brit. Legion (hon.), Congl. Country Club, Greensboro Country Club, Masons, Shriners, Rotary, Phi Delta Phi, Alpha Sigma Phi. Home: 12 St Augustine Sq Greensboro NC 27408-3834 E-mail: HoKorn34@aol.com.

KORNEL, LUDWIG, medical educator, physician, scientist; b. Jaslo, Poland, Feb. 27, 1923; came to U.S., 1958, naturalized, 1970; s. Ezriel Edward and Ernestine (Karpf) K.; m. Esther Muller, May 27, 1952 (div. 1996); children: Ezriel Edward, Amiel Mark; m. Barbara Konaszewska, Mar. 18, 1997. Student, U. Kazan Med. Inst., USSR, 1943-45; MD, Wroclaw (Poland) Med. Acad., 1950; PhD, U. Birmingham, Eng., 1958. Intern Univ. Hosp., Wroclaw, 1949-50, Hadassah-Hebrew U. Hosp., Jerusalem, 1950-51, resident medicine, 1952-55; Brit. Council scholar, Univ. research fellow endocrinology U. Birmingham, 1955-57, lectr. medicine, 1956-57; fellow endocrinology U. Ala. Med. Ctr., 1958-59, from asst. prof. to prof. medicine, 1961-67; dir. steroid sect. U. Ala. Med. Center, 1962-67, assoc. prof. biochemistry, 1965-67; postdoctoral trainee in steroid biochemistry U. Utah, 1959-61; prof. medicine U. Ill. Coll. Medicine, Chgo., 1967-71; dir. steroid unit Presbyn.-St. Lukes Hosp., Chgo., 1967-93, assoc. biochemist, 1967-70, sr. biochemist on sci. staff, 1970-71, attending physician, 1967-71; prof. medicine and biochemistry Rush Med. Coll., 1970-93, prof. emeritus of internal medicine and biochemistry, 1993—; sr. attending physician, sr. scientist Rush-Presbyn.-St. Lukes Med. Ctr., 1971-96, dir. steroid hypertension rsch. lab., 1971-95; sr. endocrinologist KHK Endocrinology and Diabetes Outpatient Clinic, Jerusalem, Israel, 1996-98. Hon. guest lectr. Polish Acad. Sci., Warsaw, 1965; vis. prof. Kanazawa (Japan) U., 1973, 82, 88, 93. Mem. editl. bd. Clin. Physiol. Biochemistry, 1975-94, Endocrinology, 1994-98; co-editor: Yearbook of Endocrinology, 1986-90; co-author: Ency. of Human Biology, 1991, 96; contbr. articles on endocrinology and steroid biochemistry to profl.jours.; contbr. chpts to textbooks. Recipient Physicians Recognition award AMA, 1969, 73, 76, 81, 86, Outstanding New Citizen award Citzenship Council Met. Chgo., 1970 Fellow Am. Coll. Clin. Pharmacology and Chemotherapy, Nat. Acad. Clin. Biochemistry (bd. dirs. 1982-86), Royal Soc. health; mem. AMA, AAAS, AAUP, Endocrine Soc., Am. Fedn. Clin. Rsch., N.Y. Acad. Scis., Am. Physiol. Soc., Cen. Soc. Clin. Rsch., Israel Soc. for Biochemistry and Molecular Biology, Am. Acad. Polit. and Social Scis., Fedn. Am. Socs. for Exptl. Biology (nat. corr. 1975—), Fedn. Israel Socs. for Exptl. Biology, Am. Soc. Hypertension, Israel Soc. Hypertension, Sigma Xi. Office: 1 Yitzchak Sadeh 53467 Givatayim Israel *Nothing can be accomplished without a sense of purpose. A long-term goal in life is a sine qua non for creative productivity. When the latter is channeled towards achieving a better understanding of various phenomena around us, the process of learning is at its best and a progress in scientific investigation ensues.*

KORNELIS, BENJAMIN DOUGLAS, education educator; b. Bellingham, Wash., Jan. 30, 1963; s. Kenneth Samuel and Bertha Kornelis; m. Patricia Christine Korvemaker, Dec. 28, 1963; children: Jason Michael, Mia Shae. BA in music edn., Calvin Coll., 1981—86; MusM, Western Wash. U., 1989—90; MusD, Mich. State U., 1996—99. Dir. of choral activities Dordt Coll., Sioux Ctr., Iowa, 1994—. Composer: (choral music) Time Pieces. Choral dir. St. John's Luth. Ch., LeMars, Iowa, 1995—2002. Mem.: Am. Choral Directors Assn. (Iowa state repertoire and standards chair, colleges and universities 2002), Pi Kappa Lambda. Office: Dordt Coll 498 Fourth Ave NE Sioux Center IA 51250

KORNELL, RONALD FRANK, economist; b. Chgo., June 4, 1935; s. Benedyct John and Esther Klimek-Wiorski; m. Patty Wilson, Oct. 17, 1963 (dec.); 1 child, E. Michael; m. Alyne Vidal, Jan. 5, 1977; 1 child, Nathalie. BA Econs./Internat. Affairs, U. Ill., 1957, MA Econs., 1958; Ops. Rsch., U. Mich., 1966; postgrad., Am. U., 1969-71. Internat. banking officer Bank of Am., San Francisco, 1962; project fin. officer Export-Import Bank, Washington, 1962-65; economist/planner Litton Industries, L.A., Athens, 1965-69; dir. internat. fin. Northrop-Page Comms., Vienna, Va., 1971-77; economist/aid coord. O.E.C.D., Paris, 1977-79; dir. E. Africa Louis Berger S.A., Paris, 1979-80; v.p. East and Southern Africa Louis Berger Internat., Inc., Nairobi, Kenya, 1980-85, group v.p. Asia-Pacific ops. Bangkok, Thailand, 1985—. Mem. Am. Soc. Civil Engring., Am. Econ. Assn., Road Engring. Assn. Asia and Australaysia, Am. C. of C. in Thailand, Transp. Rsch. Bd., The Asia Soc.. Home: Jaspal Apt 7A 34 Soi 23 Sukumvit Rd Bangkok 10110 Thailand Office: Louis Berger Group Inc 38 Convent Rd Bangkok 10500 Thailand E-mail: rkornell@louisberger.com.

KORNFELD, ROBERT JONATHAN, playwright, photographer; b. Newtonville, Mass., Mar. 3, 1919; s. Lewis Felix and Lillian (Seiferth) K.; m. Celia Seiferth Kornfeld, Aug. 23, 1945; 1 child: Robert J. Jr. AB, Harvard Coll., 1941. Script writer Sta. XEQ, Mexico City, 1938-39; editor Fed. Writers Project, New Orleans, 1941-42; reporter The Examiner, San Francisco, 1942-43; copy writer Conner Co., San Francisco, 1944, Albert Frank Agy., N.Y.C., 1945-47, Agrl. Adv. & Rsch., N.Y.C., 1947-50, Knox Kornfeld & Smith, N.Y.C., 1950-60; writer Robert Kornfeld Assoc., N.Y.C., 1961-78, playwright, 1979—. Vis. artist Am. Acad. in Rome, 1996. Author: Landmarks of the Bronx, 1990, (plays) The Art of Love, 1988 (1st prize San Francisco Playwrights Ctr., 1988), 616 Royal Street, 1994, Matisse, 1995, The Hanged Man, 1996, Acting Out, 1996, Queen of Carnival, 1997, Father New Orleans, 1997, Hot Wind from the South, 1998, The Celestials, 1998, Retrospective, 1999, Passage in Purgatory, 2000, The Celestials, 2000, The Gates of Hell, 2000; photographer (group shows) The Mask, 2000, Photographs, 2001, The Gates of Hell, 2002; dir.: (plays) Theater for the New City; author (libretto): (Operas) A Dream Within a Dream, 1985. Chmn. Riverdale Hist. Dist., 1975—, Toscanini Collection, 1984—87, Landmarks Task Force, 1975—99; bd. dirs. Hist. Dist. Coun., 1978—; active Bronx County Dem. Com.; bd. dirs. Riverdale Neighborhood Ho., 1968—90, Theater for the New City, NYC, 1992, Met. Historic Structures Assn. Pvt. U.S. Army, 1939—40. Recipient proclamation of thanks N.Y. City Coun. for Toscanini Collection, 1984, Preservation award Met. Hist. Structures Assn., 1989, award for establishing Riverdale Hist. Dist. N.Y. City Coun., State Assembly, Riverdale Neighborhood House, 1990, Bronx Landmarks Guardian award Bronx Borough pres., 1995. Mem. Dramatists Guild, N.Y. Theatre League, PEN (freedom to write com.), Harvard Club (N.Y.C.), Riverdale Yacht Club, Nat. Arts Club (co-chair lit. com.), Harvard Ind. Film Group. Home: 5286 Sycamore Ave Bronx NY 10471-2838

KORNGUTH, STEVEN EDWARD, biologist; b. NYC, Dec. 1, 1935; s. Eugene Irving and Helen (Pardes) K.; m. Margaret Livens, Aug. 29, 1958; children: Ingrid Laura Taylor, David Gregory. BA, Columbia Coll., 1957; PhD, U. Wis., 1961. Rschr. Psychiat. Inst. Columbia U., N.Y.C., 1961-62; from asst. prof. to prof. neurology and physiol. chmn. U. Wis., Madison, 1963-98; dir. neurol. scis. NSF, Washington, 1981-83; dir. Biol. Scis. Inst. Advanced Tech., prof. pharmacy U. Tex., Austin, 1985—2003. Cons. Inst. Def. Analyses, Alexandria, Va., 1985—, Dept. Def., Alexandria, 2000. Editor: Prof. Scholar, 1991; contbr. over 110 articles to profl. jours.; patentee in field. Mem. Rotary. Avocations: piano, bicycling, reading. Business E-Mail: steve_kornguth@iat.utexas.edu.

KORNHABER, EUGENE, psychiatrist; b. Bronx, N.Y., Nov. 5, 1941; s. Samuel and Ida (Wiener) K.; divorced; children: Miriam, Sarah, Rachel. BA, Bklyn. Coll., 1965; MD, Med. Coll. Va., 1970. Bd. cert. in adult and child psychiatry. Attending psychiatrist NYU-Bellevue, N.Y.C., 1975-85, N.W. Hosp. Ctr., Mt. Kisco, N.Y., 1985—. Fellow in child psychiatry NYU-Bellevue, N.Y.C., 1973-75. Fellow Am. Acad. Child and Adolescent Psychiatry; mem. AMA, Am. Psychiat. Assn. Office: 10 W Hyatt Ave Mount Kisco NY 10549-2818

KORNHAUSER, KENNETH RICHARD, funeral director, executive; b. N.Y.C., Oct. 6, 1947; s. Martin and Gladys (Tuchman) K.; m. Ann Rona Morris, July 4, 1976; children: Evan Jason, Craig Morris. BS, Jacksonville U., 1969; MS, L.I. U., 1973; postgrad. in edn., N.Y.U., 1973-76; diploma, Am. Acad. McAllister Inst., 1977. Cert. corrective therapist, 1973. Phys. edn. tchr. Andrew Jackson High Sch., St Albans, N.Y., 1969-73, dean of boys, 1973-76; assoc. prof., dir. spl. phys. edn. Queens Coll., Flushing, N.Y., 1973-75; athletic trainer U.S. Merchant Marine Acad., Kings Point, N.Y., 1975-76; pres. I.J. Morris, Inc., Bklyn., 1976—, IJM Computer Sys., Inc., Hempstead, N.Y., 1985-95, Monuments by I.J. Morris, Inc., Bklyn., 1989—, I.J. Morris of Fla., Inc., 1993—. Pres. Temple Beth Torah, Westbury, NY, 1992—94; bd. dirs. Gurwin Jewish Geriatric Ctr., Commack, NY, 1989—; bd. dirs. Theodore Roosevelt coun. Boy Scouts Am., 1991—; bd. dirs. Metro N.Y. region United Synagogue Conservative Judaism, 1993—; bd. dirs. Suffolk Assn. Jewish Ednl. Svcs., 1993—, United Jewish Cmty. Ctr. Long Is., 1993, Suffolk Y-JCC, Commack, 1986—, v.p., 2001—02; bd. govs. Rabbinical Coll. Jewish Theol. Sem. Am., NY, 1995—. Named Man of Yr., Suffolk County region Women's Am. Orgn. Rehab. Tng., 1987. Mem.: Jewish Funeral Dirs. Am. (bd. govs, treas. 1999—2001, v.p. 2001—03, pres. 2003—), Nat. Eagle Scout Assn. (mem. exec. bd. Nassau chpt. 1990), Old Westbury Golf and Country Club (N.Y., bd. govs. 1997—, sec. 2000—01, v.p. 2003—), Knights of Pythias, Masons. Republican. Avocations: golf, tennis, skiing, juggling, photography. Home: 90 Wheatley Rd Old Westbury NY 11568-1212 Office: IJ Morris Inc 21 E Deer Park Rd Dix Hills NY 11746-4814 E-mail: Ken10647@aol.com., kenkornhauser@ijmorris.com.

KORNICKER, LOUIS SAMPSON, museum curator; b. N.Y.C., May 23, 1919; s. Howard and Lena (Cohen) K.; m. Beatrice Nyman; children: Lance, Steven, William. BS, U. Ala., 1941; BSChemE, 1942; MA, Columbia U., 1954; PhD, 1957. Tech. group supr. Hercules Powder Co., Chattanooga, Tenn., 1942-45; sr. process engr., pilot plant supt. Cities Svc. Refining Co., Lake Charles, La., 1945-48; sec., treas. Uncle Sam Chem. Co., N.Y.C., 1948-57; asst. dir. Inst. Marine Sci. U. Tex., Port Aransas, 1957-60; geologist Office Naval Rsch., Chgo., 1960-61; prof. oceanography Tex. A&M U., College Station, 1961-64; curator dept. invertebrate zoology Smithsonian Inst., Washington. Adj. prof. biology George Washington U., 1968—. Author: Antarctic Ostracoda (Myodocopina), 1975, Research: Revision, Distribution, Ecology and Ontogeny of the Ostracode Subfamily Cyclasteropinae, 1981, Antrctic and Subantarctic Myodocipina (Ostracoda), 1993; assoc. editor: Biology and Paleobiology of Ostracoda, 1975; mem. editl. bd. Palaeogeography, Palaeoclimatology and Palaeocology, 1960-87; mem. bd. assoc. editors Antarctic Research Series Am. Geophys. Union, 1978-90. Mem. Soc. Systematic Zoology, Crustacean Soc., Sigma Xi. Office: Smithsonian Instn Nat Mus Natural History Washington DC 20560-0001 E-mail: kornicker.louis@nmnh.si.edu.

KORNIEWICZ, DENISE M. nursing educator; b. Detroit, Dec. 21, 1951; d. Edward John and Roseline Marie (Luczak) K. BS, Madonna Univ., 1974, MS in Nursing, Tex. Woman's U., 1977; DNSc in Nursing, Cath. U. of Am., 1986; postdoctoral, Johns Hopkins U., 1989. RN, Mich., Md., D.C. Dir. nurse practitioner program East Carolina U., Greenville, N.C., 1978-82; rsch. assoc. Cath. U. of Am., Washington, 1984-87; postdoctoral fellowship Johns Hopkins U., Balt., 1987-89, dir. acute care program, 1989-92; assoc. dean for acad. devel. Georgetown U., Washington, 1992-98; rsch. prof. U. Md., Balt., 1999—. Adv. bd. Ansell Cares, Sydney, Australia, 1993—, Regent Hosp. Products, Greenville, 1992—; chair, cons. Johns Hopkins U., Balt., 1993-94. Author: Pocket Guide to Infection Control, 1995; contbr. articles to profl. jours. Vol. probation officer, Washington, 1991. Capt. U.S. Army, 1973-77. Fellow Am. Acad. in Nursing; mem. So. Coun. on Colls. and Edn. (mentor 1992-94, Cert. 1994), Madonna U. Alumni (Plaque 1992), Am. Nurse Assn. Coun. of Nurse Rsch., Sigma Xi. Democrat. Roman Catholic. Achievements include developing the standards for patient examination gloves, sterile and unsterile; achieved success in technology development of materials used for patient care practices. Home: 1569 Redhaven Dr Severn MD 21144-1032 Office: U Md Sch Nursing 655 W Lombard St Baltimore MD 21201-1512 E-mail: korniewd@erols.com.

KORNREICH, EDWARD SCOTT, lawyer; b. Brooklyn, Apr. 18, 1953; s. Lawrence and Selma K.; m. Shirley (Werner), Feb. 28, 1982; children: Mollie, Davida, Lawrence. BA(hon.), Columbia U., 1974; JD, Harvard U., 1977. Appellate atty. Legal Aid Soc., N.Y.C., 1977-79; assoc. atty. Rosenman and Colin, N.Y.C., 1979-84; v.p., legal affairs, gen. counsel St. Luke's-Roosevelt Hosp. Ctr., N.Y.C., 1984-87; mem. Garfunkel, Wild, and Travis, P.C., Gt. Neck, NY, 1987-90; ptnr. Proskauer and Rose, LLP, N.Y.C., 1990—. Joint com. on health care decisions near end of life ABA and Hastings Ctr., 1992-95; sr. adv. com. Robert Wood Johnson N.Y. Acad. Medicine Project. Trustee, post grad. Ctr. Mental Health, N.Y.C., 1992-99. Mem. Am. Health Lawyers Assn.; N.Y. State Bar Assn. (chair provider's com. health law sect. 2002—); Assn. of Bar City of N.Y. (com. on medicine and law 1985-88, chmn. health law com. 1991-94, AIDS com. 1986-97); Phi Beta Kappa. Avocations: running (completed N.Y.C. Marathon 1978, 83, 86, 95, 97). Office: Proskauer & Rose LLP 1585 Broadway Fl 27 New York NY 10036-8299

KORNS, LEOTA ELSIE, writer, mountain land developer, insurance broker; b. Canton, Okla., Jan. 19, 1916; d. James Abraham and Ida Agnes (Engel) Klopfenstine; m. Richard Francis Korns, July 1, 1943 (wid. Dec. 17, 1988); 1 child, Michael Francis. BS, Pitts. State U. of Kans., 1966. Sec. various firms, Kans. City, Mo., 1937-45; cons. Electrolux Corp., St. Paul, 1946-49; sec. health, safety and waste IAEA, Vienna, Austria, 1959-60; tchr. Montezuma-Cortez H.S., Cortez, Colo., 1966-67; ins. agent Korns Ins. Agy., Durango, Colo., 1968—; owner, pres. Korns Investments, Inc., Durango, Colo., 1970—. Bd. dirs. LaPlata County Landowners Assn., Durango, 1981-87; writer, instr. women's history course U. N.Mex., Albuquerque, Ft. Lewis Coll., Durango, Colo., and Mesa (Ariz.) C.C., 1970-75; also spkr. in field. Author: (novels) Yesterday Should Have Been Over, 1965, Somewhere Out in the West, 2002; (play) Angry Young Men, 1957; writer numerous short stories including The Combine, 1960. Convenor, mem. NOW, Durango, 1970—; precinct capt. La Plata County Rep. Party, 1981—. Mem. Unity Sch. Christianity, Trimble Hot Springs. Avocations: mountain walking, swimming, piano, cross-country skiing. Home: 556 2d Ave Durango CO 81301-5604 E-mail: leotakorns@frontier.net.

KORNSPAN, SUSAN FELISCHNER, lawyer; b. N.Y.C., Mar. 5, 1965; d. Leonard Fleischner and Loretta (Hekelman) Brown; m. Scott Alan Kornspan, May 17, 1992. BA, Georgetown U., 1987; JD cum laude, U. Miami, 1990. Bar: Fla. 1990, U.S. Dist. Ct. Md. 1990, D.C. 1990, U.S. Ct. Appeals (D.C. cir.) 1991, U.S. Dist. Ct. (so. dist.) Fla. 1991, U.S. Dist. Ct. (mid. dist.) Fla. 2002, U.S. Ct. Appeals (11th cir.) 1991, U.S. Supreme Ct. 1997. Assoc. Piper & Marbury, Washington, 1989-91, Nason Gildan, West Palm Beach, Fla., 1991-94, shareholder, 1994-96, Greenberg Traurig, West Palm Beach, Fla., 1997—. Admissions interviewer Georgetown U., 1999—; dir. U. Miami Law Alumni Assn., 2003—. Bd. Young Govs. of Govs. Club Palm Beaches, Fla., 1998—2001. Scholar Young Lawyers Divsn. Fla. Bar, 1988; named Best of the Bar, South Fla. Bus. Jour., 2003. Mem.: ABA, Palm Beach County Bar Assn. (client rels. com. 1998—2001), Fla. Bar (mem. jud. evaluation com. 1998—, fee arbitration com. 1998—, vice-chair 2003—04), U. Miami Law Alumni Assn. (dir. 2003—), Order of Barristers. Avocations: tennis, theatre, travel. Office: Greenberg Traurig PA 777 S Flagler Dr 3d Fl E West Palm Beach FL 33401

KORNSTEIN, MICHAEL ALLEN, lawyer; b. Bklyn., Feb. 7, 1951; s. Samuel and Goldie (Starker) K.; m. Margaret Ann Tomlinson, Jan. 2, 1983; children: Harris, Benjamin, Max. BS, Union Coll., Schenectady, N.Y., 1973; JD, Union U., Albany, N.Y., 1977. Bar: N.Y. 1978, U.S. Dist. Ct. (no. dist.) N.Y. 1978, U.S. Dist. Ct. (so., ea. and we. dists.) N.Y. 1984, U.S. Supreme Ct. 1982. Assoc. Cooper Erving & Savage, 1978-82, ptnr., 1983—. Mem. N.Y. State Bar Assn. Democrat. Jewish. Office: Cooper Erving & Savage LLC 39 N Pearl St Ste 4 Albany NY 12207-2797

KORNUC, BARBARA ANNE, business owner; b. Cleve., Nov. 7, 1952; d. Henry Anthony and Mildred Barbara (Grubich) Podsiadlo; m. Steve Robert Kornuc, Sept. 8, 1973; children: Lisa Barbara, Timothy. BS in Edn., Bowling Green State U., 1973; MEd, Cleve. State U., 1978. Kindergarten tchr. Shaker Heights (Ohio) City Schs., 1974-80; substitute tchr. Nordona Hills Schs., Northfield, Ohio, 1990-95, kindergarten testing cons., 1990-96; owner, cons. Unique Solutions, Macedonia, Ohio, 1996—2001. Organizer helmet safety program City of Macedonia, 1996—, coun. person, 1994—, coun. pres., 2001-2001, mayor, 2001—; com. chair Band Aides Nordona Hills Schs., 1993; mem. Future Growth Com., 1996—; local founder Classroom Gallery Arts Program Nordona Elem. Schs., 1991-95; North Summit County Multi Svc. trustee and pres. Nordonia Hills City Sch. Found., 1998—. Mem. PTA (state life, coun. pres. 1996-98, high sch. pres. 1999—). Avocations: boating, bicycling, travel, reading, cooking.

KOROBKIN, BARRY JAY, architect; b. N.Y.C., Dec. 9, 1949; s. Raymond Lawrence and Leanore Anne (Kaplan) K.; m. Laura Hanft, Aug. 27, 1977; children: Rachel Tess, Robert Benjamin. BA magna cum laude, Williams Coll., 1971; MArch, Harvard U., 1976. Registered architect, Mass., N.Y., Fla. Planner M. Paul Friedberg and Assocs., N.Y.C., 1972; architect Herman Hertzberger, Amsterdam, The Netherlands, 1976-77; lectr. Harvard Grad. Sch. Design, Cambridge, Mass., 1977-79; ptnr. KJA Architects, Somerville, Mass., 1979-89, Linden Properties Inc., Somerville, 1983—; prin. Korobkin Assocs., Somerville, 1990—. Author: Images for Design, 1974; prin. works include Eldridge House, 1981 (AIA award 1982, Mass. Gov.'s award 1987), Maxim House, 1984 (New England AIA award 1987). Recipient AIA medal Harvard U. Grad. Sch. Design, 1976; Sheldon fellow Harvard U., 1977. Mem. AIA (chmn. housing com. 1987-90, rsch. fellow 1973), Boston Soc. Architects (bd. dirs. 1990-92), Phi Beta Kappa. Democrat.

KOROI, MARK MICHAEL, lawyer; b. Grosse Pointe, Mich., May 22, 1963; s. Remus M. and Eleanor Barbara Koroi. AA, Macomb C.C., Warren, Mich., 1983; Assoc of Gen. Studies, Macomb C.C., Warren, Mich., 1984; BA in Psychology, Wayne State U., 1986; JD, Thomas M. Cooley Sch. Law, 1990. Bar: Mich. 1991, U.S. Dist. Ct. (ea. dist.) Mich. 1991. Law clk. Law Offices of Roger Leemis, Southfield, Mich., 1986-88, Samaan, Mashni & Assocs., Dearborn, Mich., 1988-89, Law Offices of Salem Samaan, Plymouth, Mich., 1989-91; atty. Law Offices of Mark Koroi, Plymouth, 1991—. Lectr. Mich. Head Injury Alliance, Ann Arbor, 1996. Recipient Prix d'Accessit, French Consulate, Detroit, 1985. Mem. State Bar Mich. Pentecostal. Avocations: weight lifting, reading. Home: 12131 Champaign Ave Warren MI 48089-1246 Office: 150 N Main St Plymouth MI 48170-1236

KOROLENKO, KYRILL V. electrical engineer; b. Kharkov, Russia, May 12, 1932; arrived in U.S., 1949; s. Vladimir G. and Nina V. Korolenko; m. Svetlana V. Korolenko, June 6, 1958; children: George, Alexandra. B in Electronics Engring., Syracuse U., 1959; MSEE, SUNY, Buffalo, 1967; diploma, U.S. Naval War Coll., 1979. Registered engr., R.I. Engr. GE Co., Syracuse, NY, 1959—67; sr. engr. Raytheon Co., Portsmouth, RI, 1967—72; chief scientist Naval Undersea Warefare Ctr., Newport, RI, 1972—. Cons. to naval industry on undersea warfare; spkr. in field. Translator: Hydroacoustics and the Ship, 1968; contbr. articles to profl. jours. Active YMCA, Boy Scouts Am., ch. activities. With USAF, 1951—55. Mem.: 7th Bomb Wing B-36 Assn., Naval War Coll. Fund. Achievements include patents in field; patents pending in field. Avocation: travel. Home: 128 Thayer Dr Portsmouth RI 02871 Office: Naval Undersea Warfare Ctr Code 309 Newport RI 02841

KOROLOGOS, ANN MCLAUGHLIN, public policy, communications executive; b. Newark, N.J., Nov. 16, 1941; d. Edward Joseph and Marie (Koellhoffer) Lauenstein; m. John McLaughlin, 1975 (div. 1992); m. Tom C. Korologos, 2000. Student, U. London, 1961-62; BA, Marymount Coll., 1963; postgrad., Wharton Sch., 1987. Supr. network comml. schedule ABC, N.Y.C., 1963-66; dir. alumnae relations Marymount Coll., Tarrytown, N.Y., 1966-69; account exec. Myers-Infoplan Internat. Inc., N.Y.C., 1969-71; dir. comm. Presdl. Election Com., Washington, 1971-72; asst. to chmn. and press sec. Presdl. Inaugural Com., Washington, 1972-73; dir. Office of Pub. Affairs, EPA, Washington, 1973-74; govt. rels. and comm. exec. Union Carbide Corp., N.Y.C. and Washington, 1974-77; pub. affairs, issues mgmt. counseling McLaughlin & Co., 1977-81; asst. sec. for pub. affairs Dept. of Treasury, Washington, 1981-84; under sec. Dept. of Interior, Washington, 1984-87; cons. Ctr. Strategic and Internat. Studies, Washington, 1987; sec. labor Dept. of Labor, Washington, 1987-89; vis. fellow Urban Inst., 1989-92; pres., CEO New Am. Schs. Devel. Corp., 1992-93. Mem. def. adv. com. Women in the Svcs., 1973—74; mem. Am. Coun. Capital Formation, 1976—78; mem. environ. edn. task force HEW, 1976—77; chair Pres.'s Commn. Aviation Security and Terrorism, 1989—90; bd. dirs. Fannie Mae, Kellogg Co., Host Marriott Corp., Vulcan Materials Co., AMR Corp., Harman Internat. Industries, Inc., Microsoft; pres. Fed. City Coun., 1990—95; chair Aspen Inst., 1996—2000, vice-chair, 1996; vice chair RAND. Bd. dirs. Charles A. Dana Found., Conservation Fund, Catalyst; trustee Urban Inst., 1989—96; mem. bd. overseers Wharton Sch. U. Pa. Mem.: Sulgrave Club, Met. Club, Cosmos Club. Republican. Roman Catholic.

KOROLOGOS, TOM CHRIS, government affairs consultant, former federal official; b. Salt Lake City, Apr. 6, 1933; s. Chris T. and Irene (Kolendrianos) K.; m. Carolyn Joy Goff, June 16, 1960 (dec. Jan. 1997); children— Ann, Philip Chris, Paula; m. Ann McLaughlin, Dec. 9, 2000. BA, U. Utah, 1955; MS (Grantland Rice Meml. fellow 1957; Pulitzer traveling fellow 1958), Columbia, 1958. Reporter Salt Lake Tribune, 1950-56, 59-60; reporter N.Y. Herald Tribune, 1958; account exec. David W. Evans & Assos., Salt Lake City, 1960-62; asst. to Senator Wallace Bennett of Utah, Washington, 1962-71; dep. asst. Pres. Nixon, 1971-74; asst. to Pres. Ford, 1974-75; cons. Timmons and Co., Washington, 1975—2003; sr. counselor to Amb. Paul Bremer Office of Coalition Provisional Authority, Baghdad, Iraq, 2003—. Dir. congl. rels. Pres.-Elect Reagan; former chmn. U.S. Adv. Commn. Pub. Diplomacy. Former chmn. bd. trustees Am. Coll. of Greece; former mem. bd. dirs. Internat. Media Fund; mem. Internat. Broadcasting Bd. Govs., 1995-2002. With USAF, 1956-57. Recipient Disting. Alumnus award U. Utah, 1989, Hon.Doctorate in Human Letters, 2003. Mem. Ahepa. Greek Orthodox. Home: 1155 23d St NW Apt 7A Washington DC 20037

KOROM, FRANK JOSEPH, religion educator; b. Kikinda, Serbia, Dec. 15, 1957; s. Frank Korom and Maria Kalatschan. BA in Religious Studies and Anthropology, U. Colo., 1984; MA in Folklore and Folklife, U. Pa., 1987, PhD in Folklore and Folklife, 1992. Postdoctoral fellow Smithsonian Instn., Washington, 1992-93; curator Museum of Internat. Folk Art, Santa Fe, 1993-98; asst. prof. religion and anthropology Boston U., 1998—. Adj. lectr. religion and anthropology, Santa Fe Cmty. Coll., 1994-98. Author: Pakistani Folk Culture: A Select Annotated Bibiography, 1988, Folkloristics and Indian Folklore, 1991, Gender, Genre and Power in South Asian Expressive Traditions, 1991, Tibetan Culture in the Diaspora, 1997, Constructing Tibetan Culture: Contemporary Perspectives, 1997, Hosay Trinidad: Muharram Performances in an Indo-Caribbean Diaspora, 2003; editor Religious Studies Rev., 2001-03; also contbr. articles to profl. jours. Grantee NEH, 2000, Boston U., 1997, 98, 99, Museum of N.Mex., 1997, Am. Philos. Soc., 1997, Smithsonian Instn., 1991, 93; fellowAm. folklife Ctr, 1987, Am. Inst. Indian Studies, 1988, Fulbright-Hays Found., 1990, Mellon Found., 1991, Smithsonian Instn., 1992, others. Mem. All-India Folklore Congress, Am. Acad. Religion, Am. Anthropol. Assn., Am. Folklore Soc., Assn. Asian Studies, Folklore Fellows of Finland, Internat. Assn. Tibetan Studies, Internat. Soc. Ethnology and Folklore, Internat. Soc. for Folk Narrative Rsch., Phi Beta Kappa.

KOROMA, ABDUL G. judge of international court of justice; b. Freetown, Sierra Leone, Sept. 29, 1943; Student, Kings Coll., U. London, Kiev State U. Bar: Lincoln's Inn, High Ct. Sierra Leone. Joined Govt. of Sierra Leone, 1964, various positions, 1964-69; with Ministry Foreign Affairs, 1969; del. UN Gen. Assembly; dep. permanent rep. to UN Govt. of Sierra Leone, 1978-81, permanent rep. to UN, 1981-85, former amb. to EEC, permanent rep. to UNESCO, 1985—88, amb. to Ethiopia and Orgn. African Unity, 1988—92; high commr. in Zambia and Tanzania, 1988; judge Internat. Ct. of Justice, The Hague, 1994—. Mem. Internat. Law Com., chair 43d session; mem. dels. to 3d UN Conf. on Law and the Sea, UN Conf. on Succession of States in Respect to Treaties, UN Commn. on Internat. Trade Law, Spl. Com. on the Rev. of UN Charter and on Strengthening Role of Orgn. Com. on Peaceful Uses of Outer Space; vice chair UN Charter Com., 1978; chmn. UN Spl. Com. of 24, UN 6th Com.; lectr. numerous univs.; mem. internat. planning coun. Internat. Ocean Inst. Contbr. articles to profl. jours. Pres. Henry Dunant Ctr., Geneva. Decorated insignia Comdr. of Rokel. Mem. Am. Soc. Internat. Law, Lincoln's Inn (hon. bencher). Office: Internat Ct of Justice Peace Palace Carnegieplein 2517 KJ The Hague Netherlands

KORONES, SHELDON BERNARR, physician, educator; b. N.Y.C., Apr. 26, 1924; s. Samuel Aaron and Estelle (Goldstein) K.; m. Judith Ann Kest, June 15, 1952; children: David N., Susan Gifford. BS, U. Tenn., 1944; MD, U. Tenn., Memphis, 1947. Diplomate Am. Bd. Pediatrics, Am. Bd. Neonatal/Perinatal Medicine. Intern Boston City Hosp., 1948-49; asst. resident pediat. Babies Hosp., N.Y.C., 1950-51, 53-54; asst. in pathology Children's Med. Ctr., Boston, 1949-50; asst. clin. prof. pediat. U. Tenn., 1961-68, assoc. prof. newborn svcs. dept. pediats., 1968-72, prof. pediats., dir. newborn svcs., 1972-89, prof. ob-gyn., 1982-89, alumni disting. svc. prof. pediat. ob-gyn., 1989—. Project dir., prin. investigator collaborative perinatal project NIH, Bethesda, 1960-75; dir. newborn ctr. Regional Med. Ctr. Memphis, 1968—; perinatal adv. com. State Tenn., 1974—, chmn. subcom. standards regionalization perinatal care, 1975—, subcom. liaison, legis. funding and cmty. edn., 1979—, subcom. perinatal transp., 1979-86, gov.'s task force prevention mental retardation, 1980-83, gov.'s task force healthy children, 1983-86, subcom. follow-up, 1983-86, subcom. evaluation, 1983-86, subcom. med. home., 1983-86, task force child devel. standards dept. human svcs., 1984-86; med. svc. adv. com. March of Dimes, 1974-78, edn. adv. com., 1979-1987, exec. com. west Tenn. chpt., 1986-92; bd. examiner oral exams maternal and fetal medicine Am. Bd. Ob-Gyn., Chgo., 1975; study panel bur. med. devices diagnostic products FDA, 1976-93; prin. investigator Nat. Heart, Lung, Blood Inst., Bethesda, Md., 1976-83, Coop. Multictr. Network Neonatal Intensive Care Rsch., Bethesda, 1986-2001; profl. edn. rsch. com. Am. Lung Assn. Tenn., 1977-81; pres.-elect med. staff Regional Med. Ctr. Memphis, 1982-83, pres. 1983-84; adv. bd. Office Drug Policy, Memphis, 1991; subcom. ob-gyn. newborn svcs. TLC Family Care Healthplan, Memphis, 1994—; mem. perinatal com. devel. clin. practice guidelines TennCare, First Mental Health, Inc., 1996; spkr., cons. in field. Author: High Risk Newborn Infants: The Basis for Intensive Nursing Care, 1972, 4th edit., 1986, Spanish translation, 1979, Russian translation, 1981; co-author: Neonatal Decision Making, 1993; author, co-author: (chpts.) Synopsis of Pediatrics, 1963, 6th edit., 1984, Resuscitation of the Newborn, 3d edit., 1973, Iatrogenic Problems in Neonatal Intensive Care, 1976, Current Diagnosis, 1977, Standards and Recommendations for Hospital Care of Newborn Infants, 6th edit., 1977, Current Therapy in Obstetrics and Gynecology, 1980, 83, Assisted Ventilation of the Newborn, 1981, The Use of Computers in Perinatal Medicine, 1982, Parent-Baby Attachment in Premature Infants, 1983, Infant Stress under Intensive Care, 1985, Gynecology and Obstetrics, Vol. 2, 1985, Teratogen Update: Environmentally Induced Birth Defect Risks, 1986, Assisted Ventilation of the Neonate, 1988, 4th edit., 2003, Comprehensive Pediatrics, 1990, author: (introduction) Planning and Design for Perinatal and Pediatric Facilities, 1977; editor Ross Labs., Columbus, Ohio, 1975-82, Perinatal Press, U. Tenn., Memphis, 1976-78, Brentwood Pub. Corp., L.A., 1977-88, Am. Baby Hosp. Network Adv. Bd., 1984—, Jour. Perinatology-Neonatology, 1988—, Am. Baby Mag., 1992—; reviewer C.V. Mosby Co., 1976-77, 81, 83, J.B. Lippincott Co., 1979, Williams and Wilkins Co., 1981, Polymorph films, 1985, Pediats., 1974—, New Eng. Jour. Medicine, 1975—, Am. Jour. Ob-gyn., 1979, 92, 97, Jour. Pediats., 1997, Pediat. Nephrology, 1997, 98, 2000, 01, 02, Pediat. Infectious Disease Jour. 1997, 98, 99, 2000, 2003, Jour. Perinatology, 2001, 2002; contbr. over 300 articles to profl. publs. Bd. dirs. Memphis Orch. Soc., 1961-70. With USPHS, 1951-53. Named Citizen of Yr. Newspaper Guild Memphis, 1974, Who's Who in Medicine, Memphis Mag., 1984-88, Top Doctors, 1996; recipient Myrtle Wreath award Hadassah, 1976, Contribn. to Perinatal Medicine commendation Commr. Pub. Health Tenn., 1978, Cmty. Svc. award Nat. Conf. Christians and Jews, 1982, City Coun. Memphis, 1982, L.M. Graves Meml. Health award Mid-South Med. Ctr. Coun., Inc., 1984, Cert. Appreciation, Gov. Lamar Alexander, 1986, Key to City Memphis, Mayor Richard Hackett, 1988, Alumni Svc. award U. Tenn. Nat. Alumni Assn., 1989, Themis award March of Dimes, 1991, Meritorious Svc. commendation State Tenn. Ho. of Reps., 1992, Person of Vision award Alliance for Blind Visually Impaired, 1994, Meritorious Svc. award Tenn. Hosp. Assn., 1995; Sheldon B. Korones Chair Neonatology U. Tenn. Coll. Medicine named in his honor, 1989; grantee NIH, 1960-75, 1971-75, 1985-2001, Merck, Sharpe and Dohme, 1970-73, Tenn. Dept. Health, 1970—, Memphis Regional Med. Program, 1972-75, Tenn. Dept. Human Svcs., 1972—96, March of Dimes, 1973-80, Nat. Heart, Lung, Blood Inst., 1976-83, Nat. Inst. Child Health Human Devel., 1986-91, 91-96, 96—, Tenn. Dept. Children's Svcs., 1996-. Fellow Am. Coll. Ob-Gyn. (assoc.); mem. So. Soc. Pediat. Rsch., Am. Acad. Pediats. (com. fetus and newborn 1969-75, liaison com. perinatal health Am. Coll. Ob-Gyn.

1965-74, rep. to joint com. newborn hearing Am. Speech Hearing Assn., Am. Acad. Ophthalmology Otolaryngology 1969-75, task force on circumcision 1973-74), Tenn. chpt. Pediatrician of Yr. 1994), Tenn. Pediat. Soc., Memphis Pediat. Soc., Am. Pediat. Soc., Tenn. Perinatal Assn. (bd. dirs. 1983—), Russian Perinatologists Assn. (hon. pres. 1996), Nat. Assn. Perinatal Social Workers (hon. 1980), Sigma Xi, Alpha Omega Alpha. Office: U Tenn 853 Jefferson Ave Rm 201 Memphis TN 38103-2807

KOROS, WILLIAM JOHN, chemical engineering educator; b. Omaha, Aug. 31, 1947; s. William Alexander and Mary Ellen (Roth) K.; m. Ann Marie Teahan, Dec. 19, 1970. BSChemE, U. Tex., 1969, MSChemE, 1975, PhD-ChemE, 1977. Registered profl. engr., Tex. Chem. engr. E.I. DuPont, Wilmington, Del., 1969-71, cons., 1982—, engr. Camden, S.C., 1971-73; research asst. U. Tex., Austin, 1973-77; asst. prof. chem. engring. N.C. State U., Raleigh, 1977-80, prof., 1980-83; prof. chem. engring. U. Tex., Austin, 1983—2001, B.F. Goodrich prof. material engring., 1986—2001, chmn. chem. engring., 1993-97, Roberto C. Goizueta chair in chem. engring., 2001—. Editor in chief Jour. Membrane Sci. Recipient Sigma Xi Research award, 1980, Young Investigators award NSF, 1983, Alcoa Found Research award N.C. State U., 1983. Fellow AIChE (Inst. award for excellence in indsl. gas separations 1995, Gerhold award 1999); mem. Am. Chem. Soc., Nat. Acad. Engring. Office: Ga Inst Tech Sch Chem Engring 778 Atlantic Dr Atlanta GA 30330-0100

KOROT, BERYL, artist; b. N.Y.C., Sept. 17, 1945; d. George and Frieda (Braunstein) K.; m. Steve Reich, May 30, 1976; 1 child, Ezra. Student, U. Wis., 1963-65; BA, Queens Coll., 1967. Chief, co-founder Radical Software, 1970-73; co-editor Video Art, 1976. Exhibitions include 4 channel video work Dachau, exhibitions include 5 channel video work, weavings, drawings Text and Commentary, Kitchen, N.Y.C., 1975, exhibitions include Everson Mus. Art, Syracuse, N.Y., 1975, 1977, Documenta 6, Kassel, Germany, 1977, Videopoints, Mus Modern Art, N.Y.C., 1978, Mickery Theatre, Holland, 1978, Whitney Mus., N.Y.C., 1980, San Francisco Art Inst., 1981, Leo Castelli Gallery, N.Y.C., 1977, Mus. Fine Arts, Montreal, 1979, John Weber Gallery, 1986, Jack Tilton Gallery, 1987, Carnegie Mus. Art, 1990, Long Beach Mus. Art, 1988, Jewish Mus., N.Y.C., 1988, Video Skuptur, Kunstverein, Koln, 1989, The Cave, 1993, Reina Sofia Mus., Madrid, 1993—94, Dusseldorf Kunsthalle, Whitney Mus. Am. Art, N.Y.C., Carnegie Mus. Art, ICC Gallery, Tokyo, 1997, Hindenburg, 1998, Bklyn. Acad. Music, 1998, Spoleto Festival, 1998, Mass. Coll. Art, 1999, Historischen Mus., Frankfurt, 2000—01, Whitney Mus., N.Y.C., 2000, 2001, Jewish Mus. Paris, 2002—03, short commd. work, Art 21, PBS, 2002; performer: (video opera) The Cave, 1993—96, Three Tales, 2002—03. Montgomery fellow Dartmouth Coll., 2000. Artist fellow NEA, 1975, 77, 79, N.Y. State Coun. on Arts, 1978, Creative Artist Pub. Svc., 1975, 79, Guggenheim fellow, 1995; grantee Rockefeller Found., 1989, 98, Andy Warhol Found., 1991, NEA, 1991-92. Home: 258 Broadway New York NY 10007-2315

KOROTKIN, FRED, writer, philatelist; b. Duluth, Minn., Oct. 25, 1917; s. Morris and Ethel (Billert) K. BA, U. Minn., 1949. Writer-instr. Palmer Writers Sch., Mpls., 1961-66; editor Finance & Commerce, and Daily Market Record, Mpls., 1966-67; stamp editor Mpls. Star, 1970-74, White Bear Press, 1976, Minn. Suburban Newspapers, Inc., 1983-85, The Enterpri$e, 1988-89, Post Publs. Weekend, 1989-91. Mem. philatelic adv. panel Am. Revolution Bicentennial Commn., 1971-74, Am. Revolution Bicentennial Adminstrn., 1974, philatelic advisor, 1974-76; regional rep. Interphil '76, 1974-76, USO, AARP, So. Poverty Law Ctr./Klanwatch Project. Contbr. revs., articles to popular mags., newspapers. Pres. North High Alumni Assn., Mpls., 1946-47; mem. nat. adv. bd. The Generation After; assoc. Simon Wiesenthal Ctr. for Holocaust Studies; mem. St. Louis Park Centennial Commn., 1985-86; charter mem. U.S. Holocaust Meml. Mus., U.S. World War II Meml., Air Force Meml. Found., Nat. D-Day Mus.; founding mem. F.D.R. Meml., Nat. Campaign for Tolerance, William J. Clinton Presdl. Found. Recipient Disting. Topical Philatelist Hall of Fame award and invited to sign Disting. Topical Philatelist scroll of honor, 1962, Silver medal for Keeping Posted column in Mpls. Star Am. Philatelic Soc.-Chgo. Philatelic Soc. Conv., 1974, Silver award for Keeping Posted column in Post Publs. Weekend, sponsored by Coun. Philatelic Orgns., 1989, True Grit award Grit Mag., 1997, 98. Mem. Am. Topical Assn. (founding pres. chpt. 1957-61, nat. pres. 1968-70, 70-72, dir., nat. adv. com.), Internat. Philatelic Press Club (gov.), Internat. Assn. Philatelic Journalists, Am. Philatelic Soc. (life; speakers' bur. 1977—, writers unit), New Zealand Stamp Collector's Club Inc. (hon., anonymously donated annual Fred Korotkin Cup for best thematic entry 1966—), Christchurch Philatelic Soc., Inc., Royal Philatelic Soc. New Zealand, Collectors Club N.Y., Manuscript Soc., Statue of Liberty-Ellis Island Found. Inc. (charter), Nat. Com. To Preserve Social Security, Am. United for Separation of Ch. and State, Holocaust Survivors Assn. USA (nat. adv. bd.), Keren Or, Inc., Jerusalem Instn. for the Blind, Internat. Platform Assn., People for the Am. Way, DAV (life; comdr. Mpls. chpt. No 1, 1986), Paralyzed Vets. Am. (hon.), Father Solanus Guild. Home: Apt 512 4925 Minnetonka Blvd Minneapolis MN 55416-2271 also: PO Box 11053 Minneapolis MN 55411-0053 *Ever since I was a youngster I've tried to determine what character traits help make a person successful. I've come to believe that the most important combination is still confidence in self, stick-to-itiveness, and that other winning ingredient which can be called aim, direction or goal.*

KOROTKIN, MICHAEL PAUL, lawyer; b. N.Y.C., Oct. 5, 1937; m. Marcia Ellen, Aug. 28, 1960; children: Darryl, Alan, Alyssa. AB, Duke U., 1959; LLB, NYU, 1962. Bar: N.Y. 1963. Ptnr. Kramer, Levin, Naftalis & Frankel LLP, N.Y.C., 1973—. Office: Kramer Levin Naftalis & Frankel LLP 919 3rd Ave New York NY 10022-3902 E-mail: mkorotkin@kramerlevin.com

KOROTKOV, ALEXANDER N. physicist, educator, researcher; b. Voronezh, Russia, Dec. 12, 1963; arrived in U.S., 1993; s. Nikolai Efimovich and Nelli Il'inichna Korotkov; m. Galina A. Korotkova, Oct. 23, 1982 (div. 1996); 1 child, Mariya; m. Julija Auzane, Aug. 2, 1997; children: Michael, Anna. MS in Physics, Moscow State U., 1986, PhD in Physics, 1991. Engr., scientist, sr. scientist Moscow State U., 1986-93, sr. scientist, 1996-98; postdoctoral rschr. SUNY, Stony Brook, 1993-96, rsch. scientist, rsch. asst. prof., 1998-2000; from asst. prof. to assoc. prof. U. Calif., Riverside, 2000—. Contbr. articles to profl. jours. Mem. Am. Phys. Soc., IEEE. Office: Dept Elec Engring U Calif Riverside Riverside CA 92521-0204 E-mail: korotkov@ee.ucr.edu.

KORPAL, EUGENE STANLEY, banker, former army officer; b. St. Louis, Sept. 1, 1931; s. Stanley Anthony and Mary Ann (Bronakowski) K.; m. Lily M. Alder, July 17, 1954; children: Teresa Kaye, Karla Jeannine. BS, U. Mo., 1953. Commd. officer U.S. Army, 1954, advanced through grades to maj. gen.; served with inf. div., 1964-67; comdr. 1st Bn., 29th Arty. Ft. Carson, Colo., 1969-70; comdr. 3d Bn., 319th Arty., 1970-71; comdr. 3d Inf. Div. Arty., 1973-75; chief Joint U.S. Adv. Group, 1978-80; asst. div. comdr. 25th Inf. Div.; comdg. gen. Ft. Sill, Okla., 1985-87; adv. dir., v.p. Ft. Sill Nat. Bank, 1987—2002, dir., 2002—. Decorated DSM, Legion of Merit with oak leaf cluster, Bronze Star, Air medal, others. Mem. Assn. U.S. Army, Field Arty. Assn.

KORRASIK, JASON J. social sciences educator, researcher; b. Cooperstown, N.Y., Dec. 7, 1970; s. Steven George Korrasik and Zosia Golaszewski; m. Irene Isabel Miranda, Aug. 8, 1998. Rotary exch. student, Surat, India, 1988—89; student, Tel Aviv U., 1994; BA, Syracuse U., 1995; MA in Psychology, George Mason U., 1999. Testing & assessment assoc. APA, Washington, 1997—98; rsch. psychologist Army Corps Engrs., Washington, 1998—99, Pentagon, Washington, 1999—2000; rsch. fellow George Washing U., Washington, 2000—01; adj. prof. Mary Washington Coll., Fredricksburg, Va., 2001—03. Cons. JAK Solutions.com, Alexandria, Va., 1998—2002; rsch. psychologist Pentagon, 1999—2000. Swim asst. coach Spl. Olympics, FCPA, Fairfax, Va., 2003. Mem.: APA (lobbyist 1998), Acad. Mgmt. Avocations: reading, writing, mathematics, philosophy, backpacking. E-mail: jasonk@gwv.edu.

KORS, R. PAUL, search company executive; b. Pontiac, Mich., June 12, 1935; s. Ralph Dewey and Lydia Elizabeth (Shavlik) K.; m. Carol Jayne Kullick, July 17, 1966; children: Kristen Patricia, Shannon Elizabeth. BBA, U. Mich., 1958; MBA, U. So. Calif., 1965. Salesman Nalco Chem. Co., Los Angeles, 1958-66; investment mgr. Dean Witter & Co., Los Angeles, 1966-73; sr. assoc. Korn Ferry Internat., Los Angeles, 1973-74, v.p. Houston, 1974-77, v.p., mgr., 1977-78; founder, pres., chief exec. officer Kors Montgomery Internat., Houston, 1978—. Served to 1st lt. U.S. Army, 1958. Mem. World Tech. Exec. Network (bd. dirs. 1985—). Clubs: Houston Racket, Galveston Country. Avocations: skiing, golf, tennis, films, reading. Home: 14306 Heatherfield Dr Houston TX 77079-7407 Office: Kors Montgomery Internat 14811 Saint Marys Ln # 280 Houston TX 77079-2908

KORSCH, BARBARA M. pediatrician; b. Jena, Germany, Mar. 30, 1921; arrived in U.S., 1940; 1 child. BA, Smith Coll., 1941; MD, Johns Hopkins U., 1944. Cert. Am. Bd. Pediat. Asst. resident Bellevue Hosp., 1945, Mary Imogene Basset Hosp., 1946, N.Y. Hosp., 1947, fellow Inst. Child Devel., 1948—49; asst. pediats. Med. Coll. Cornell U., 1949—50, from instr. to assoc. prof., 1950—61; assoc. clin. prof. preventive medicine Sch. Medicine UCLA, 1961—64; assoc. prof. U. So. Calif., L.A., 1964—69, prof. pediats. Sch. Medicine, 1969—. George Armstrong lectr. Ambulatory Pediatric Assn., 1973; Katherine D. McCormick Disting. lectr. Stanford U., 1977; Kathy Newman Meml. lectr. Tulane U., 1987; asst. outpatient pediatrician N.Y. Hosps., 1949—50, asst. attending pediatrician, 1950—55, clin. dir. pediatric outpatient dept., 1950—61, assoc. attending pediatrician, 1955—61; pediatric cons. Dept. Health, NY, 1949—51, Hosp. Spl. Surgery, 1955—61, Gen. Pediatric Childrens Hosp., L.A., 1961—65, Med. Ctr., U. So. Calif., 1969—74; coord. pediatric rehab. program Nat. Found. Infantile Paralysis, 1953—61; pediatric dir. Obs. Clinic Children L.A., 1961—64; assoc. attending pediatrician Cedars of Lebanon Hosp., 1961—; vis. prof. numerous U.S. and fgn. univs., 1973—89; hon. staff mem. dept. pediat. Cedars-Sinai Med. Ctr., 1976—. Author: Intelligent Patient's Guide to the Doctor-Patient Relationship, 1997; contbr. articles to profl. jours. Chmn. coun. Bayer Inst. for Health Comm., 1989—98. Recipient Disting. Career award, Ambulatory Pediatric Assn., 1991. Mem.: Soc. Pediatric Rsch., Soc. Behavioral Pediat. (pres. 1985), Am. Pediatric Soc., Am. Acad. Pediat. (C. Anderson Aldrich award 1988, Genesis award for med. ethics 1998), Inst. Medicine NAS, Sigma Xi. Office: Childrens Hosp Divsn Gen Pediats MB # 76 4650 W Sunset Blvd Los Angeles CA 90027-6062 E-mail: bkorsch@chla.usc.edu.

KORSCHOT, BENJAMIN CALVIN, investment executive; b. LaFayette, Ind., Mar. 22, 1921; s. Benjamin G. and Myrtle P. (Goodman) K.; m. Marian Marie Schelle, Oct. 31, 1941; children: Barbara E. Korschot Hoehlen, Lynne D. Korschot Gooding, John Calvin. BS, Purdue U., 1942; MBA, U. Chgo., 1947. V.p. No. Trust Co., Chgo., 1947-64; sr. v.p. St. Louis Union Trust Co., 1964-73; exec. v.p. Waddell and Reed Co., Kansas City, Mo., 1973-74, pres., 1974-79, vice-chmn. bd., 1979-85; pres. Waddell & Reed Investment Mgmt. Co., 1985-86; chmn. bd. Waddell & Reed Asset Mgmt. Co., 1973-86. Pres. United Group of Mut. Funds, Inc., Kansas City, Mo., 1974-85, chmn., 1985-86; vice-chmn. Roosevelt Fin. Group, St. Louis, 1968-91, chmn. adv. bd., 1991-92; treas. Helping Hand of Goodwill Industries, 1993-95, chmn. investment com., 1995—; bd. dirs. Mo. United Meth. Found., 1995—, chmn. investment com., 2001—; chmn. bd. govs. Investment Co. Inst., 1980-82; chmn. bd. Fin. Analyst Fedn., 1978-79. Contbr. articles on investment fin. to profl. publs.; author autobiography, 1997. Mem. Civic Coun. Greater Kansas City, Mo., 1974-85; chmn. fin. com. ARC Retirement Sys., 1986-87. With USN, 1942-45, 50-52. Mem. Inst. CFAs, Fin. Execs. Inst., Kansas City Soc. Fin. Analysts, Lakewood Oaks Golf Club. Republican. Home: 101 NW Hackberry St Lees Summit MO 64064-1477 E-mail: bckorschot@yahoo.com. *A happy Christian home environment, the adversity of the depression of the 30's, the challenges of competitive sports, the desire to achieve knowledge, recognition and responsibilities, a devoted wife and three children who made our marriage most meaningful have been the dominant influences of my life.*

KORSGAARD, CHRISTINE MARION, philosophy educator; b. Chgo., Apr. 9, 1952; d. Albert and Marion Hangaard (Kortbek) K.; m. Timothy David Gould, June 1980 (div. Sept. 1984). BA, U. Ill., 1974; PhD, Harvard U., 1981. Instr. Yale U., New Haven, 1979-80; asst. prof. U. Calif., Santa Barbara, 1980-83; from asst. prof. to prof. U. Chgo., 1983-91; prof. Harvard U., Cambridge, Mass., 1991—, chair philosophy dept., 1996—2002. Vis. assoc. prof. Berkeley, 1989, UCLA, 1990; Tanner lectr. human values, 1992, Locke lectrs., 2002. Author: The Sources of Normativity, 1996, Creating the Kingdom of Ends, 1996; editor: (with Andrews Reath and Barbara Herman) Reclaiming the History of Ethics: Essays for John Rawls, 1997; contbr. chpts. to books, articles to profl. jours. Whiting fellow, 1978-79; Ctr. for Human Values fellow, 1995-96. Fellow AAAS; mem. Am. Philos. Assn., N.Am. Kant Soc., Hume Soc., Am. Soc. for Polit. and Legal Philosophy.

KORSH, JAMES F. educator; m. Nina B. Korsh; children: Eric, Aaron, Joanna. PhD, U. Pa., Phila., 1966. Asst. prof. U. Pa., Phila., 1967—71; sr. rsch. assoc. Calif. Inst. Tech., Pasadena, 1971—72; assoc. prof. Temple U., Phila., 1972—77, prof., 1977—. Office: Temple Univ Broad and Montgomery Philadelphia PA 19122 E-mail: korsh@temple.edu.

KORSMO, JOHN THOMAS, federal agency administrator; children: Ted, Charlie, Joe. B cum laude, U. Minn., 1972; JD, Georgetown U., 1975. Mem. nat. adv. coun. U.S. Small Bus. Adminstrn.; mem. N.D. State Bd. Higher Edn.; co-founder Korsmo and Wheeler, Fargo, ND, 1988; pres., owner Cass County Abstract Co.; founder, pres. Red River Title Svcs., Moorhead, Minn., 1983—95, Korsmo cons. Svcs.; chmn. Fed. Housing Fin. Bd., Washington, 2001—. Nominee U.S. Ho. Reps., ND; policy/legis. dir. N.D. Gov. Ed Schafer, 1996—97; chmn. N.D. Rep. Party, 1993—95. Republican. Office: Fed Housing Fin Bd 1777 F St NW Washington DC 20006

KORST, HELMUT HANS, mechanical engineer, educator; b. Vienna, Jan. 4, 1916; came to U.S., 1948; married, 1942; 4 children. Diploma in Engring., Vienna Tech. U., 1941, Dr. Tech. Sci., 1947, Golden Dr. diploma, 1997. Rsch. engr. Maschinenfabrik Augsburg-Nurnberg AG, Germany, 1941-45; asst. prof. mech. engring. Vienna Tech. U., 1945-48, vis. lectr. gas dynamics, 1948-49; from assoc. prof. to prof. mech. engring. U. Ill., Urbana, 1949-84, head dept. mech. and indsl. engring., 1962-74, prof. emeritus, 1984—; chair naval air power engring. USN Postgrad. Sch., Monterey, Calif., 1979; Ebaugh Chair Mech. Engring. U. Fla., Gainesville, 1984; pvt. practice cons. Urbana, 1956—. Vis. prof. Kans. State U., Manhattan, 1950, Va. Poly. Inst. and State U., Blacksburg, 1954; design specialist Gen. Dynamics Convair, Ft. Worth, 1955; propulsion specialist Rocketdyne div. N.Am. Aviation, 1960, 65-68; cons. GE, 1959, Adv. Group Aeronautical R & D NATO, 1964, U.S. Missile Command, 1971—. Sr. postdoctoral fellow NSF, 1957; recipient ASEE Centennial medal 1993, Daniel Guggenheim medal in aviation, 1994. Fellow: AIAA, ASME; mem.: ASME Internat. (hon.), Am. Soc. Engring. Edn., Sigma Xi. Achievements include research on internal and external aerodynamics, jet and rocket propulsion, and heat transfer. Address: 3 Eton Ct Champaign IL 61820-7602 E-mail: H-korst@uiuc.edu.

KORSTAD, JOHN EDWARD, biology educator; b. Woodland, Calif., July 4, 1949; s. Vernon E. and Jeanette (Beard) K.; m. Shelly Diane Steffen, July 29, 1972; children: Shauna, Sarah, Joya, Janna. BA, BS, Calif. Luth. U., Thousand Oaks, 1972; MS, Calif. State U., Hayward, 1979, U. Mich., 1979, PhD, 1980. Postdoctoral fellow SINTEF, Trondheim, Norway, 1987-88; prof. biology Oral Roberts U., Tulsa, 1980—. Asst. dir., dir. collegiate acad. Okla. Acad. Sci., 1984-89. Bd. dirs. MEND Pregnancy Crisis Ctr. and Young Life, Broken Arrow, Okla., 1991—. Fulbright fellow in aquaculture rsch., Norway, 1993-94; named Carnegie Found. Prof. of Yr. for Okla., 1996. Mem. Am. Soc. Limnology and Oceanography, World Aquaculture Soc., Catfish Farmers of Okla., Am. Assn. of Zool. Parks and Aquariums (advisor marine fishes adv. com. 1991—), Beta Beta Beta (faculty advisor), Gamma Beta Phi (faculty advisor). Republican. Avocations: scuba diving, snow skiing, outdoor sports, basketball. Office: Oral Roberts U Dept Biology 7777 S Lewis Ave Tulsa OK 74171-0001

KORTE, GENEVIEVE L, music educator; b. Bluffton, OH, July 9, 1928; d. Orlin Schumacher and Kathryn Garber; m. Urban H Korte, Aug. 20, 1949; 1 child, Edward (dec.);children: Esther E Judson, Maria, Robert, James, Betty Jean, Janet Hill, Carol Bowmann, Susan Carter. B in music, U. of Dayton OH, 1980. Supr., admissions mail U. of Dayton OH, 1972—80; head sec. psychology dept. Va. Commonwealth U., Richmond, Va., 1980—81; music tchr. Dinwiddie Sch., Dinwiddie, Va., 1981—83, Dayton Christian Sch., Tipp City, Ohio, 1984—85; piano instr. Korte Keyboard, Vandalia, Ohio, 1985—2003. Organist Hillcrest Bapt. Ch., St. Christopher Ch. Recipient Merit award, Nat. Fedn. of Music Club, 1997—98. Mem.: Dayton Piano Teachers Study Club (v.p. 2002—), Dayton Music Club (3rd vice pres. 1999—2000), Ohio Music Teachers Assn. (dir. of student activities 1997—98). Home: 1071 Bosco Ave Vandalia OH 45377

KORTEBEIN, STUART ROWLAND, orthopedic surgeon; b. Evanston, Ill., Apr. 17, 1930; s. Rowland J. and Grace K.; m. Alice C. Johnson, July 10, 1954; children: William, David. AA, North Park Coll., 1950; BS, Wheaton Coll., 1952; postgrad., North Park Theol. Sem., 1952-53; MD, Loyola U., 1957; JD, Jefferson Coll. Law, 1983. Diplomate Nat. Bd. Med. Examiners, Am. Bd. Orthopaedic Surgery. Intern Akron (Ohio) Gen. Hosp., 1957-58, resident, 1961-64, Hines (Ill.) VA Hosp., 1960, Northwestern U., Chgo., 1964; pvt. practice medicine specializing in orthopedic surgery Arlington Heights, Ill., 1965-88; mem. orthopaedic surgeon staff U.S. Naval Regional Med. Ctr., Memphis, 1986-96; pvt. practice medicine specializing in orthopedic surgery Milw., 1988—; chief dept. orthopedic surgery U.S. Naval Hosp., Great Lakes, Ill., 1987; mem. orthopaedic surgeon staff Sinai-Samaritan Med. Ctr., Milw., 1988—. Attending surgeon N.W. Cmty. Hosp., Arlington Heights, 1965-90, chief orthopedics, 1976; v.p. Magnetrans Rsch. and Devel. Corp., 1972-84, Window Well Protectors, Inc., McHenry, Ill., 1983-86; coord. med. cons. Compusoft Corp., Darien, Ill., 1984—, Pomsoft Corp, Willowbrook, Ill.; instr. emergency medicine technician course Haper Coll., 1973-84; vis. instr. police self-def. tactics Oakton Cmty. Coll., 1984-88. Contbr. Tech. advisor Juko-Kai Internat., 1977—; water safety instr. ARC, 1949—54; aux. police officer City of Rolling Meadows, Ill., 1984—88; choir dir. First Bapt. Ch., Twenty Nine Palms, Calif., 1959—60; bd. dirs. Chicagoland Drug Prevention Program, 1971—84. Lt. M.C. USNR, 1958—60. Mem. Am. Acad. Orthopaedic Surgeons, Physicians Martial Arts Assn., Soc. Black Belts Am., Christian Med. Soc., State Med. Soc. of Wis., Hakko-Ryu Jitsu Fed., Jiu Jitsu Black Belt Fedn. Am. (pres. Ill., rep. 1971-74), Oikiru-Ryu Jitsu (Sandan instr. 1977-85), U.S. Judo Assn. (Sho Dan life mem.). Office: 2455 N 124th St Brookfield WI 53005-4630

KORTENHOF, JOSEPH MICHAEL, lawyer, educator; b. Kimberly, Wis., Aug. 18, 1927; s. Joseph Arthur and Marie Agnes (Probst) K.; m. Althea Hunting, June 7, 1952; children: Elizabeth Ann, Michael, Amy Jo. BA cum laude, Lawrence U., 1950; JD, U. Mich., 1953. Bar: Mo. 1953, U.S. Ct. Appeals (8th cir.) 1953, U.S. Dist. Ct. (ea. dist.) Mo. 1953. Assoc. Coburn, Storckman & Croft, St. Louis, 1953-60; sr. ptnr. Kortenhof & Ely, St. Louis, 1960—. Adj. prof. law Washington U., St. Louis, 1984—. Served with USAF, 1945-47. Recipient award of honor Lawyers Assn. St. Louis, 1990. Fellow Am. Coll. Trial Lawyers, Am. Bd. Trial Advs., Internat. Soc. Barristers; mem. ABA, Mo. Bar Found. (trial lawyer award 1962), St. Louis Bar Assn., Assn. Civil Def. Counsel, Am. Maritime Law Assn., Sigma Phi Epsilon. Democrat. Episcopalian. Home: 5340 N Kenrick Parke Dr Saint Louis MO 63119-5056 Office: Kortenhof & Ely 1015 Locust St Ste 300 Saint Louis MO 63101-1333

KORTH, CHARLOTTE WILLIAMS, furniture and interior design firm executive; b. Milw.; d. Lewis C. and Marguerite Peil Brooks; m. Robert Lee Williams, Jr., Oct. 25, 1944 (dec.); children: Patricia Williams, Melissa Williams O'Rourke, Brooks Williams; m. Fred Korth, Aug. 23, 1980. Student, U. Wis., 1941. Owner Charlotte's Inc., El Paso, Tex., 1951—, chmn., CEO, 1979—; pres. Paso del Norte Design, Inc., El Paso, 1978-81; mem. adv. com. for interior design program El Paso C.C., 1981—; mem. adv. bd. S.W. Design Inst., 1982—; ptnr. Wilko Partnership, 1981-98; mem. adv. bd. Mountain Bell Telephone Co., 1976-79; mem. Sch. Architecture Found. Adv. Coun. U. Tex. Austin, 1985-91. Charter mem. Com. of 200, 1982—, Nat. Mus. Women in the Arts, 1985—; mem. Renaissance 400, El Paso, El Paso Women's Symphony Guild, El Paso Mus. Art. Recipient of Silver plaque Gifts and Decorative Accessories Mag., 1978; named Woman of Yr. by El Paso Am. Bus. Women's Assn., 1978, Outstanding Woman of Yr. by Women's Polit. Caucus, 1979. Mem. Am. Soc. Interior Designers (bd. dirs. Tex. chpt. 1977-82), El Paso Women's C. of C. (hon.), El Paso C. of C. (dir. 1976-82), Coronado Country Club, Internat. Club, El Paso Country Club, Santa Teresa Country Club (N.Mex.). Avocations: travel, antiques, collectibles. Home: 6041 Torrey Pines Dr El Paso TX 79912-2029 Office: Charlotte's Inc 5411 N Mesa St Ste 7 El Paso TX 79912-5495

KORTH, FRITZ-ALAN, lawyer; b. Ft. Worth, Aug. 29, 1938; s. Fred and Vera (Connell) K.; m. Penne Percy, Dec. 15, 1965 (div. 1997); children: Fritz-Alan Jr., Maria Eleanor, James Frederick. AB, Princeton U., 1961; LLB cum laude, U. Tex., 1964; HHD (hon.), U. Americas, 1982. Bar: Tex. 1964, D.C. 1964. Asst. sec. OKC Corp., Dallas, 1964-65; ptnr. Korth & Korth, Washington, 1965—; pres. Wilmar Corp., Port Chester, N.Y., 1980—. Founder, sec., bd. dirs. Women's Nat. Bank, Washington, 1978-85, chmn. bd. First WNB Corp., 1982-85; bd. dirs. Trans Leisure Corp., N.Y.C., 1970-75, chmn. bd., 1973-75; bd. dirs. Del Norte Tech., Inc., Dallas., 1969—, chmn., 1982-98, vice chmn. bd. dirs., 1998—; bd. dirs. Del Norte Tech. Ltd., Swindon, Eng., Wilmar Corp.; trustee Meridian Internat. Ctr., 2003—. Registrar St. John's Episcopal Ch., Washington, 1968-70, vestryman, 1970-74, treas., 1973-77; chmn. fin. com., mem. diocesan coun. Episcopal Diocese Washington, 1973-77; trustee, treas. Cathedral chpt. Washington Nat. Cathedral, 1977-84; pres. U. Americas Found., 1969-84; bd. assocs. U. Americas, Puebla, Mex., 1969—; bd. dirs. Travelers Aid Soc. Washington, 1969-86, pres., 1973-75; dir. Southwestern Exposition and Livestock Show, 1987—; charter commr. U.S.-Mex. Commn. for Ednl. and Cultural Exch., 1991-97; pres. AMMA Found., Inc., 1994—, dir. 1989. Mem. ABA, Inter-Am. Bar Assn., D.C. Bar, Tex. Bar Assn., Am. Law Inst., Am. Soc. of Most Venerable Order of Hosp. of St. John of Jerusalem, Phi Delta Phi. Clubs: Met. (Washington), Chevy Chase (Washington); Argyle (San Antonio); Steeplechase (Ft. Worth); Princeton (N.Y.C.); Gymkhana Club (Mauritius). Mailing: PO Box 65482 Washington DC 20035-5482 also: 888 17th St NW Ste 208 Washington DC 20006-3313

KORTH, JAY THOMAS, lawyer; b. Rockville Centre, N.Y., Oct. 27, 1962; s. Jay Francis and Grace Marie (Miller) K. BS, St. John's U., 1984, JD, 1987. Bar: N.Y. 1988, N.J. 1989, U.S. Dist. Ct. N.Y. 1989. Ptnr. Korth & Korth, Lynbrook, N.Y. Mem. legal dept. Town of Hempstead Atty.'s Office, 1985-86; mem. Alt. Dispute Resolution Com.; mediator Family Arbitration and Mediation of L.I. Mem. KC (legal advocate 1994-95), Nassau County Bar Assn. (mem. trusts and estates com. 1992—, mem. environ. law com. 1993-95, mem. alternative dispute resolution com., mem. cmty. rels. and pub. edn. com.). Roman Catholic. Avocations: hiking, photography, foreign affairs, travel. Office: Korth & Korth 28 Forest Ave Lynbrook NY 11563-2634

KORTH, THOMAS A. musician, educator; b. Phila., Aug. 13, 1943; s. Hyman and Fannie (Silverblatt) Korth; m. Sandi L. Foreman (div. Jan. 1993); 1 child, Lori Ann Swim; m. Vera L. Katz, Mar. 20, 1993. MusB, Howard U., 1966, MusM, 1968; D in Musical Arts, U. Md., 1975. Profl. musician, Washington, 1959—; contract music specialist U.S. Info. Agy., Washington, 1968-89; prof. music Howard U., Washington, 1971—. Composer: chamber music, film music, theatre music. Home: 12305 Remington Dr Silver Spring MD 20902-1533 E-mail: tkorth1@comcast.net.

KORTHALS, CANDACE DURBIN, lawyer; b. Tampa, Fla., Oct. 3, 1948; d. Robert F. and Geraldine B. Durbin; children: John Kristofor, Kathryn Elizabeth. BA in Internat. Studies, Ohio State U., 1969, BS in Edn., 1970; JD cum laude, Nova U., 1982. Bar: Fla. 1982. Tchr. Palatka (Fla.) Mid. Sch., 1970-72, Dillard H.S., Ft. Lauderdale, Fla., 1974-79; atty. Broward County Pub. Defenders, Ft. Lauderdale, 1982-84, Grimmett & Korthals, Ft. Lauderdale, 1984-90, Gunther & Whittaker, Ft. Lauderdale, 1990-94, Law Office of John Camillo, Ft. Lauderdale, 1994-99, Neale & De Almeida, Ft. Lauderdale, 1999-2000, Heinrich, Gordon, Hargrove, Weihe & James, Ft. Lauderdale, 2000—02, Barnett & Barnard, Hollywood, Fla., 2002—. Staff mem. Nova Law Rev., 1981, 82. Office: Barnett & Barnard 4601 Sheridan St #505 Hollywood FL 33021 Business E-Mail: ckorthals@bbslawfirm.com.

KORVATSKA, ELENA, biologist, educator; b. Kiev, Ukraine, Mar. 15, 1963; d. Boris Korvatsky and Ludmila Korvatska; m. Konstantin Kiianitsa, Dec. 18, 1992. Diploma in Biology (summa cum laude), U. Kiev, Ukraine, 1985; PhD, U. of Lausanne, Switzerland, 1998. Vis. postdoctoral scholar U. of Calif., Berkeley, 1999—2000, postdoctoral rschr. Davis, 2001—. Recipient Alfred Vogt Prize for the Rsch. in Ophthalmology, Alfred Vogt Found., Montreaux-

Zurich, 1999, Finn Word Travel award, Protein Soc., 1999; fellow Marie Heim-Vogtlin postdoctoral fellowship, Swiss NSF, 1999. Office: Dept of Rheumatol U of Calif One Shields Ave Davis CA 95616

KORVER, GERRY R(OZEBOOM), business executive; b. Orange City, Iowa, June 17, 1952; BA, Northwestern Coll., 1977. Fin. aid officer Northwestern Coll., Orange City. Bd. trustees Northwestern Coll. Trustee Northwestern Coll. Mem. Nat. Assn. Purchasing Mgmt. (cert.). Avocations: athletics, fishing, huntinig, outdoor activities, woodworking. Home: 1602 Albany Ave NE Orange City IA 51041-2039 Office: Northwestern Coll Orange City IA 51041

KORVIN, CATHERINE MADELEINE, editor; b. Paris, May 7, 1954; arrived in U.S., 1982; d. Charles Guit and Madeleine Finkel; m. Andrew Peter Korvin, Dec. 18, 1981; children: David, Steven. BA in German Studies, U. Sorbonne, 1976, BA in Russian Studies, 1978, MA in Russian Studies, 1980; diploma, Inst. Nat. Technique Documentation (INTD), 1980; MLS, St. John's U., 1986. Tchr. French Rutgers U., Newark, 1983—86, Alliance Francaise, N.Y.C., 1983—86; asst. editor Pub. Affairs, Info. Svcs., Inc., 1986—90, assoc. editor, 1990—97, editor, dep. exec. dir., 1997—. Head info. svc. GFC-BTP, Paris, 1980—82. Trustee Demarest Pub. Libr., NJ, 1998—2000. Avocations: travel, reading. Office: OCLC Pub Affairs Info Svc 521 W 43d St New York NY 10036 Fax: 212-643-2848. E-mail: korvinc@oclc.org.

KORWEK, ALEXANDER DONALD, management consultant; b. Madison, Ill., Feb. 20, 1932; s. Alexander and Constance (Gulewicz) K.; m. Katherine Moore, Oct. 24, 1954 (div. Nov. 1974; dec.); children: Alexander D., Brian P., Lizabeth E.; M. Judith Joy, Jan. 11, 1975; 1 child, Theodore Sofianos. BSBA, Washington U., St. Louis, 1962; MBA, U. Utah, 1967. Cert. in data processing, 1962. Asst. sec., asst. treas. Hoechst (Hystron) Fiber, N.Y.C., 1966-72; v.p. fin. Reeves/Teletape, N.Y.C., 1972-76; prin. A.D. Korwek Cons., North Babylon, N.Y., 1975-77; bus. mgr., CFO Queens Coll., CUNY, Flushing, N.Y., 1977-79; mng. dir. ASCE, N.Y.C., 1979-81; sec., gen. mgr., CEO United Engring. Trustees, N.Y.C., 1981-90; prin. A.D. Korwek Mgmt. Cons., 1990—. Exec. sec. Engring. Found., N.Y.C., 1981-90, Engring. Socs. Library, N.Y.C., 1981-90; sec. Daniel Guggenheim Medal Bd., N.Y.C., 1981-90, John Fritz Medal Bd., N.Y.C., 1981-90, Frank F. Aplan Award Bd., N.Y.C., 1989-90; bd. dirs. Daytona Beach C.C. Author: Cost Estimating Relationships, 1967, A Dissertation on Management, 1978; author manuals in field. Commr. Norwalk-Wilton Conv. and Visitors Bur., Conn., 1985; vol. bd. bank mem., bd. instr. Volusia/Flagler United Way, Fla., 1992-95; bd. dirs. Marineland Found., Inc., 1988-2000; trustee Daytona Beach C.C., 1999—. Recipient award of Appreciation Queen's Coll. Student Body, 1979. Mem. ASCE, IAJBBSC (bd. dirs. dist. 10 1989-90), Coun. of Engr. and Sci. Soc. Execs., N.Y. Soc. Assn. Execs., N.Y. Acad. Sci., Assn. for a Better N.Y., N.Y.C. of C., Conn. Specialty Club (pres. Norwalk 1985-90), Elks (treas. lodge 2709 1992-94). Avocations: decanter collecting, golf, philately, numismatics.

KORY, MARIANNE GREENE, lawyer; b. N.Y.C., 1931; d. Hyman Louis and Belle (Rome) Greene; children: Erich Marcel, Lisa. BA, CCNY; JD, N.Y. Law Sch., 1976; LLM, U. Wash., 1986. Bar: Ohio 1977, D.C. 1979, N.Y. 1983, Vt. 1994, U.S. Dist. Ct. (so. and ea. dists.) N.Y. 1983, U.S. Dist. Ct. Vt. 1994. Hearing examiner Ohio Bd. Employee Compensation, Columbus, 1977; atty. advisor Office Hearings and Appeals Social Security Adminstrn., Cin. and N.Y.C., 1977-78; gen. atty. labor Office of Solicitor U.S. Dept. of Labor, N.Y.C., 1978-82; pvt. practice N.Y.C., 1983—; adminstrv. Seattle, 1989-91, Burlington, Vt., 1994—. Grad. faculty New SCh. Social Rsch. Founder Cin. chpt. Amnesty Internat., 1977. Alvin Johnson fellow in Philosophy; grad. faculty New Sch. for Social Rsch. Mem. Nat. Abortion Rights Action League, Feminist Majority Found., Vt. Bar Assn., Planned Parenthood, Wilderness Soc., Defenders of Wildlife, Ctr. for Marine Conservation, Nat. Wildlife Fedn., Audubon Soc., Emily's List, Phi Beta Kappa. Office: 1361 S Ocean Blvd #202 Pompano Beach FL 33062-8022

KORYTKOWSKI, MARY T. physician; b. Buffalo, Nov. 15, 1949; BSN, D'Youville Coll., 1971; MN, Emory Univ., 1976; MD, Univ. N.C., 1982. Diplomate Am. Bd. Internal Medicine, Diplomate Am. Bd. Endocrinology and Metabolism. Internship, residency Francis Scott Key Med. Ctr., Balt., 1982-85; fellow Sinai Hosp. Balt., Johns Hopkins Hosp., Balt., 1986-88; head nurse St. Joseph's Hosp., Asheville, NC, 1972-74; staff nurse Clinic for Migrant Health Workers, Hendersonville, NC, 1972; instr. dept. nursing Western Carolina Univ., Cullowhee, NC, 1974-75, asst. prof. nursing, 1976-78; instr. dept. medicine John Hopkins Hosp. Sch. Medicine, Balt., 1988-89; assoc. prof. med., dir. UPMC Ctr. for diabetes & Endocrinology, Univ. Pitts., Sch. of Med., Pa., 1989—2003; staff physician Wyman Pk. Hosp., Balt., 1985; staff physician endocrine cons. Chesapeake Physician's Profl. Assn., Balt., 1988-89. Speaker at various conf., lectr. in field; co-dir., speaker Women's Health Issues Conf., 1993; mem. planning com., speaker Women and Children with DM, 1994; task force for DKA, 1994; reviewer Jour. AMA, Annals of Internal Medicine, Metabolism. Contbr. numerous articles to profl. jour. Planning com. Am. Diabetes Assn. meeting. Recipient Mother D'Youville award, 1967, Rathburn award Francis Scott Key Medical Ctr., 1983; numerous rsch. grants. Mem. Am. Coll. Physicians, Am. Diabetes Assn., The Endocrine Soc., Sigma Theta Tau. Home: 5606 Woodmont St Pittsburgh PA 15217 Office: Univ Pitts Medical Ctr 3601 5th Ave Rm 588 Pittsburgh PA 15213-3403 E-mail: korytkowski@msx.dept-med.pitt.edu.

KORZENIK, ARMAND ALEXANDER, lawyer; b. Hartford, Conn., Oct. 31, 1927; s. Bernard and Dorothy (Goldman) K.; m. Ursula Guttmann, June 30, 1956; children: Peter Brent, Jeffrey Dean, Andrea Diane. AB magna cum laude, Harvard Coll., 1951; JD, Harvard U., 1951; LL.M., Yale U., 1952. Bar: Conn. 1951, U.S. Supreme Ct. 1959. Practiced in Hartford, 1951—; asst. corp. counsel, 1966-72; counsel Hartford Redevel. Agy., 1966-68, Hartford Bd. Edn., 1968-72; instr. bus. law Hartford Inst. Accounting, 1974-75. Editor: Amicus Curiae, 1956-59; bd. editors: Conn. Bar Jour., 1971-79. Mem. Hartford Bd. Edn., 1953-59, Hartford Zoning Bd. Appeals, 1960-66, Hartford Dem. Town Com., 1985-92; justice of peace, Hartford, 1960-73, 84—; Mayor's rep. to Libr. Bd., 1989-91; bd. dirs. YMCA, Boy Scouts Am., PTA, Urban League, Am. Youth Hostels, Jr. C. of C.; founder Blue Hills Civic Assn., West End Civic Assn., Hartford. With USAF, 1946-48, 50, Conn. Air Nat. Guard, 1953-82, brig. gen., 1982-. Mem. Conn. Bar Assn. (ho. of dels. 1975-78, 89-90, exec. com. gen. practice sect. 1983—, chmn. 1997-2001), Hartford County Bar Assn. (editor Bar-Fly 1976-78), Conn. Criminal Def. Lawyers Assn., Harvard Club, Yale Club, Mensa Internat., Phi Beta Kappa. Democrat. Home: 120 Terry Rd Hartford CT 06105-1111 Office: 436 Farmington Ave Hartford CT 06105-4423

KORZENIK, SIDNEY S. lawyer; b. N.Y.C., Jan. 12, 1909; s. Adolph and Sally (Seiden) K.; m. Emily Faust K., June 23, 1949; children: David, Jeremy, Deborah, Joshua. BA, Harvard U., 1929; MA, Columbia U., 1931; LLB, NYU, 1939. Bar: N.Y., Federal Bar, U.S. Supreme Ct. Pvt. practice, N.Y.C., 1946—. With N.Y. State Unemployment Adv. Coun., 1936-41; mem. U.S. Govt. Mgmt.-Labor Textile adv. com.; mem. gen. arbitration coun. of Textile Industry; counsel to various apparel, textile and fur interest orgns., including Nat. Knitted Outerwear Assn., Fedn. Apparel Mfrs., Knitted Textile Assn., Am. Transfer Printing Inst., others; formerly adj. asst. prof. NYU Law Sch.; advisor to govt. textile trade missions; adviser in field. Bd. dirs. Ednl. Found. of Fashion Inst. of Technology, N.Y.C. With U.S. Army, 1941-46. Mem. Phi Beta Kappa. Home: 120 Carthage Rd Scarsdale NY 10583-7202

KORZICK, KAREN ANNE, pulmonary, critical care physician; b. Balt., Oct. 23, 1963; d. Theodore and Sandra Charlene Korzick; children: Ellen Penn, Jessica Penn. BS, U. Conn., 1985; MD, Loyola U., Maywood, Ill., 1989. Diplomate Am. Bd. Internal Medicine, Am. Bd. Pulmonary Medicine, Am. Bd. Critical Care. Mem. staff emergency dept. Mercy Hosp., Balt., 1992-97, intensivist, 1997—; intern, resident internal medicine U. Md., Balt., 1989-92; fellow John's Hopkins U., Balt., 1993-97, asst. prof., 1997—. Adv. bd. bioethics com. Loyola Coll., Balt., 1992—94, mem. med. morals com. Mercy Hosp., Balt., 1998—. Contbr. articles. Fellow: Am. Coll. Chest Physicians; mem.: ACP, Am. Thoracic Soc. (Md. chpt.), Alpha Sigma Nu, Alpha Omega Alpha, Phi Beta Kappa. Democrat. Roman Catholic. Avocations: sewing, needlecrafts, cooking, gardening. Office: Mercy Med Ctr 11th Floor ICU 301 Saint Paul Pl Baltimore MD 21202-2147 E-mail: kkorzick@aol.com.

KOSA, NAMIR BAHJAT, physician; b. Baghdad, Iraq, Jan. 12, 1951; came to U.S., 1992; s. Bahjat Mansour and Warda Matti Kosa; m. Ilham Sabri Kosa, July 6, 1980; children: Sandra, Fadi, Milad. MD, Baghdad U., 1973. Diplomate Am. Bd. Internal Medicine. Physician Care Group, Phila., 1996—. Mem. ACP. Roman Catholic. Avocations: tennis, listening to music, reading. Home: 1827 Earlington Rd Havertown PA 19083-2522 Office: Care Group 1444 W Passyunk Ave Philadelphia PA 19145-2312 E-mail: Milad8y@aol.com.

KOSAKOW, JAMES MATTHEW, lawyer; b. New London, Conn., Apr. 12, 1954; s. Leonard Louis and Lois Ann (Rosen) K.; m. Yvonne Manijeh Bokhour, June 4, 1978; 1 child, Jonathan Daniel. BA, Conn. Coll., 1976; JD, Yeshiva U., 1984. Bar: N.Y. 1985, Conn. 1985, D.C. 1985, Fla. 1991, U.S. Dist. Ct. (so. and ea. dists.) 1985, U.S. Tax Ct. 1993. Assoc. Vittoria & Forsythe, N.Y.C., 1986-92, Gregory and Adams, Wilton, Conn., 1992-94; pvt. practice N.Y.C. and Westport, Conn., 1994-97; ptnr. Kove & Kosakow, LLC, 1997—; vice-chancellor Cambridge Theol. Seminary, Carthage, Ill., 1996—. Guardian and litem N.Y. County Surrogate's Ct., N.Y.C., 1987—, Norwalk Probate Ct., 1993—; mem. faculty, instr. estate planning & personal planning program Albertus Magnus Coll.; lectr. in field, arbitrator BBB, N.Y.C., 1988-89. Co-author: Handling Federal Estate and Gift Taxes, 6th edit., 2000; asst. editor Insights and Strategies; contbr. articles to profl. jours. Trustee, bd. dirs. Internat. Nursery Sch., Queens, N.Y., 1987-89; mem. estates & trusts specialty group lawyers divsn. United Jewish Appeal-Fedn. Jewish Philanthropies of N.Y., Inc., 1990-94; commr. Wilton Water Commn., 1995-96, Wilton Fire Commn., 1996-2000; ptnr. Creative Philanthropic Resources, 1995—; chmn. membership com. Mid-Fairfield Substance Abuse Coalition, 1995-96; dir. Thee Art Tree Source, Inc., 1995—; adv. com. The Unicorn Archive. Mem. N.Y. Bar Assn. (legis. com., trusts and estates sect. 1987—), Conn. Bar Assn. (elder law com.), Fla. Bar (real property, probate and trust law, out-of-state mem. rels. com. 1994—), Assn. of Bar of City of N.Y., Exch. Club (bd. dirs. Wilton club). Office: 265 Post Rd W Westport CT 06880-1261 also: 685 3d Ave 30th Fl New York NY 10013 E-mail: jmk@kovkos.com.

KOSARAJU, S. RAO, computer science educator, researcher; b. Pedapulivarru, Guntur, India, Feb. 20, 1943; came to U.S., 1966; s. Punnaiah and Dhanalakshmi K.; m. Padmaja Valluripalli, Aug. 20, 1970; children: Sheela, Akhila. B.E., Andhra U., (India), 1964; M.Tech., Indian Inst. Tech., Kharagpur, 1966; PhD, U. Pa., 1969. Vis. asst. prof. computer sci. Johns Hopkins U., Balt., 1969-70, asst. prof., 1970-75, assoc. prof., 1975-77, prof., 1977—, Kouwenhoven prof., 1981-87; Compere and Marcella Loveless prof. Purdue U., West Lafayette, Ind., 1986-87; Edward J. Schaefer prof. Johns Hopkins U., Balt., 1987—, chmn. computer sci., 2001—. Contbr. articles to profl. jours.; assoc. editor Jour. Computer Langs., 1976-89, Theory of Computing Systems, 1976—, Jour. Computer and System Scis., 1981—, Information and Computation, 1983-91. Fellow IEEE, Assn. for Computing Machinery; mem. Soc. Indsl. and Applied Math. (mng. editor SIAM Jour. on Computing 1980-89, assoc. editor 1975—). Home: 4 Woodward Ct Reisterstown MD 21136-1835 Office: Johns Hopkins U Dept Computer Sci Baltimore MD 21218 E-mail: kosaraju@cs.jhu.edu.

KOSARIN, JONATHAN HENRY, lawyer, consultant; b. Bklyn., Aug. 13, 1951; s. Lester and Norma (Higger) K., m. Gayle C. Skarupa, Nov. 27, 1982. BA in History magna cum laude, Syracuse U., 1973; JD, Bklyn. Law Sch., 1976; LLM in Govt. Contract Law, George Washington U., 1984; postgrad., U.S. Army Command and Gen. Staff Coll., 1990, U.S. Army War Coll., 1997. Bar: N.Y. 1977, D.C. 1978, U.S. Supreme Ct. 1980, U.S. Ct. Claims 1981, U.S. Ct. Appeals (Fed. cir.) 1982. Commd. 2d lt. U.S. Army, 1973, advanced through grades to col., 1997, prosecutor trial counsel, 1977-78, adminstrv. law officer, 1978-79, instr. law, 1979-80, trial atty. contract appeals div. Washington, 1980-84; contracts atty. U.S. Army Hdqrs., Heidelberg, Fed. Rep. Germany, 1985-87; assoc. gen. counsel, dir. procurement law Fed Home Loan Bank Bd., Washington, 1987-89; assoc. counsel USN, Washington, 1989-94, dep. counsel, 1994—. Adj. asst. prof. contract law JAG Sch., Charlottesville, Va., 1988—93, adj. assoc. prof., 1993—95, adj. prof., vice chmn., 1995—99, adj. prof., chmn., 1999—2002; dep. gen. counsel def. prisoner of war Missing Pers. Office, 2002—; acting chief contract law U.S. Army Europe, Heidelberg, Germany, 2003; adj. faculty contract law U. Va., 1989—; mem. faculty Fed. Publs. Seminars, 1995—, ESI Internat., 1999—2002. Vol. info. specialist Smithsonian Instn. Washington, 1993—, pres. Temple Rodef Shalom, Falls Church, Va., 2000-02; mem. Mid-Atlantic coun. Union of Am. Hebrew Congregations, 2002—; para-Rabinnic fellow Temple Rodef Shalom, Falls Church, 1998—. Mem. ABA, D.C. Bar Assn., Titanic Hist. Soc., No. Va. Football Ofcls. Assn., Nat. Assn. Sports Ofcls., Phi Alpha Delta, Phi Beta Kappa, Phi Kappa Phi, Phi Delta Kappa. Democrat. Office: USN Office Of Gen Counsel Washington DC 20350-0001

KOSASKY, HAROLD JACK, fertility researcher; b. Winnipeg, Man., Can., Oct. 19, 1927; s. Jack and Lillian (Resnick) K.; m. Shirley Anne Johnston, Sept. 3, 1955; children: Julia, Leah, Robert. BA, U. Manitoba, Can., 1948; MD, U. Manitoba, 1953. Diplomate Am. Bd. Ob-gyn.; lic. Coll Physicians and Surgeons Can., Med. Coun. Can., Ky. State Bd. Health, Idaho State Bd. Health, Mass. Bd. Registration in Medicine. Intern Deer Lodge VA and Grace Hosps., Winnipeg, Man., Can., 1952-53; resident in gen. surgery Col. Belcher Hosp., Calgary, Alta., Can., 1953-54; resident in psychiatry Warren (Pa.) State Hosp., 1955-56; jr. asst. resident, asst. resident, sr. resident in ob-gyn. Chgo. Lying-In Hosp., 1956-59; exch. fellow in ob-gyn. Newcastle Gen. Hosp., U. Durham, Eng., 1959-60; asst. and assoc. prof. U. Louisville Sch. Med., 1961-65; asst. and assoc. in ob-gyn. various hosps., Boston, 1966-81; gynecologist, obstetrician Boston Hosp. for Women, 1965-81; gynecologist Brigham & Women's Hosp., Boston, 1981—; instr. ob-gyn. Harvard U., 1965—; pres., CEO Boston Rheology, 2000—. Cons. Ovutime, Boston, 1972-82; pres. Saltime Co., 1994, chmn. 1999-2000; asst. vis. surgeon Boston City Hosp., 1967-69; mem. Ky. Govs. Task Force on Mental Retardation, 1964-65, Com. on Malignancy, chmn., 1963-65; CEO, pres. Boston Rheology, 2000—. Contbr. articles to profl. jours.; co-inventor Ovutime; inventor Saltime Ovulation group of instruments. Fellow ACS, Royal Coll. Surgeons of Can. (cert.), Royal Soc. Health, Boston Obstetric Soc. (emeritus); mem. AAAS, Gen. Med. Coun. Gt. Britain (lic.), Royal Coll. Obstetricans and Gynecologists, Assn. Prof. Ob-gyn., Louisville Obstet. and Gynecol. Soc. (sec., treas. 1962-65), Louisville Med. Forum (v.p.). Clubs: Harvard. Episcopalian. Office: Ste 207 830 Boylston St Chestnut Hill MA 02467

KOSCHMANN, J. VICTOR, history educator, academic program director; Student, Lewis and Clark Coll., 1960-62; BA in Social Scis., Internat. Christian U., Tokyo, 1965; MA in Internat. Studies, Sophia U., Tokyo, 1971; PhD in History, U. Chgo., 1980. Translator, assoc. editor Japan Interpreter, Tokyo, 1971-77; Asian studies instr. Sophia U., Tokyo, 1975-76; social sci. lectr. U. Chgo., 1978-80; asst. prof. Japanese history Cornell U., Ithaca, N.Y., 1980-86, assoc. prof. Japanese history, 1986-94, prof. Japanese history, 1994—, dir. East Asia program. Fulbright fellow, vis. rsch. assoc. faculty law and politics Rikkyo U., Tokyo, 1983-84; vis. lectr. Internat. U. Japan, Niigata, 1983-84; vis. prof. Kyoto Ctr. for Japanese Studies, 1990-91; guest prof. faculty lit., U. Kyoto, 1990-91; vis. rschr. Tokyo U. Fgn. Studies, 1995-96; vis. prof. Japanese studies Nat. U. Singapore, 1999; cons. CBS News, N.Y. Times, Tokyo Broadcasting Sys.; manuscript and proposal reader for numerous instns., including Cambridge U. Press, Princeton U. Press, Cornell U. Press, Calif. U. Press, N.C. U. Press, Cornell East Asia Papers series, Sociol. Forum, East Asia Cultures Critique, Jour. Asian Studies, Pacific Affairs, Jour. Japanese Studies, Columbia East Asian Inst., Social Scis. and Humanities Rsch. Coun. Can., NEH, others; lectr., panel mem., participant NEH Seminar on Japanese Intellectual History, Hawaii, 1976, SSRC/ACLS, Monterey, 1978, Assn. for Asian Studies conv., Toronto, 1981, Cornell U., 1981-83, 85, 87-89, U. Chgo., 1982, 85, McGill U., Montreal, 1982, Harvard U., 1983, U. Calif., Berkeley, 1983, Hokkaido Nat. U., Sapporo, Japan, 1984, Japan Fgn. Svc. Tng. Inst., Tokyo, 1984, U. Seiji Kenkyukai, Atami, Japan, 1984, Rikkyo U. Internat. Symposium, Tokyo, 1985, Am. Hist. Assn., N.Y.C., 1985, San Francisco, 1989, Assn. Asian Studies, Boston, 1987, Chgo., 1990, Duke U., 1988, Smithsonian Instn., Airlie, Va., 1988, Sweet Briar Coll., 1989, Harvard U., 1989, U. Calif., San Diego, 1989, Columbia U., 1989, SUNY, Binghamton, 1990, Hokkaido U., 1991, U. Mich., 1993, Princeton U., 1994, U. Wash., 1995, Heidelberg, 1995, Rikkyo U., Tokyo, 1996, UCLA, 1997, Nat. U. Singapore, 1999, Australia Nat. U., 2001, others. Author: The Mito Ideology: Discourse, Reform and Insurrection in Late Tokugawa Japan, 1790-1864, 1987, Revolution and Subjectivity in Postwar Japan, 1997; editor: Authority and the Individual in Japan: Citizen Protest in Historical Perspective, 1978, Conflict in Modern Japanese History: The Neglected Tradition, 1982, International Perspectives in Yanagita Kunio and Japanese Folklore Studies, 1985, Total War and Modernization, 1998; contbr. articles to profl. jours. Fellow U. Chgo., 1976-79, Ctr. for Far Eastern Studies, 1978, 1979-80, Japan Found., 1979, 95-96, Cornell U., 1985-86; grantee Social Sci. Rsch. Coun., 1983-84, NEH, 1987-88, 92, 1983, Japan-U.S. Edn. Commn., 1983-84, Cornell U., 1984-85, 91, Japan Found., 1989, 94, Assn. for Asian Studies, 1985. Office: Cornell Univ Hist Dept 320 Mcgraw Hall Ithaca NY 14853-4601

KOSCIELAK, JERZY, scientist, science administrator; b. Lodz, Poland, Sept. 6, 1930; s. Jozef and Regina (Pokrzywa) K.; m. Anna Kitaszewska, 1969 (div. 1974); 1 child, Katarzyna. MB, Med. Acad., Warsaw, Poland, 1953, MD, 1960, DrSci, 1966. Asst. dept. physiol. chemistry Med. Acad., Warsaw, 1950-51; asst. and sr. asst. dept. biochemistry Inst. of Hematology, Warsaw, 1951-67; rsch. fellow Harvard Coll., Cambridge, 1964-65; head immunochem. lab. Inst. of Hematology, Warsaw, 1968-69, head dept. biochemistry, 1969—2002. Sci. sec. Inst. of Hematology, Warsaw, 1969-97, dir., rsch. 1997—, prof., 1973—. Editor-in-chief Acta Haematologica Polonica jour., 1976-85; contbr. articles to profl. jours. Mem. Polish Biochem. Soc. (chmn. Warsaw divsn. 1967-69), Forum of Carbohydrates Coming of Age (FCCA), Polish Acad. Sci., N.Y. Acad. Scis., Internat. Glycoconjugate Orgn. (Polish rep. 1988—, pres. 1993-95), Found. for Glycobioloby Glyco XII (founder, pres. 1993—). Avocation: history. Office: Inst of Hematology Chocimska 5 00957 Warsaw Poland E-mail: kosci@atos.warman.com.pl.

KOSEL, RENÉE, state representative; b. Chgo., Apr. 3, 1943; m. Alfred Kosel; 3 children. BS in Edn., Western Ill. U. Bd. dirs. Lincoln-Way H.S. Dist. Recipient Ednl. Excellence award, Lincoln-Way Found., New Lenox Twp. Steering Com. award, United Way. Mem.: Ill. Assn. Sch. Bds. (dir.), Edn. Commn. States (commr.), Nat. Sch. Bd. Assn. (fed. rels. rep.). Republican. Lutheran. Office: 221-N Stratton Office Bldg Springfield IL 62706 Address: 19201 S LaGrange Rd Ste 204B Mokena IL 60448*

KOSHAR, LOUIS DAVID, civil engineer; b. N.Y.C., Aug. 19, 1928; s. Benjamin and Edna K.; m. Marion Webber, Sept. 12, 1954; children: Richard E., Laurie D. BCE, CCNY, 1949, MCE, 1957. Registered profl. engr., N.Y., Fla., W.Va., Conn., Ohio, Del. Civil engr. Bur. Reclamation, Coulee Dam, Wash., 1949; bridge designer Madigan Hyland, N.Y.C., 1952-55; structural designer Tams, N.Y.C., 1955-57; bridge engr.-ptnr. Barstow, Mulligan, Korogodon & Koshar, N.Y.C., 1957-71; v.p. Pavlo Engring. Co., N.Y.C., 1971-93; pres. Ysrael A. Seinuk, P.C., 1993—2001. Designer numerous bridge and hwy. projects including Gramercy Bridge over the Mississippi river in La., Harvard Bridge over the Charles river from Boston to Cambridge, Mass.; presenter papers on bridge design at profl. confs. Recipient (as engr. in charge of design) award for Goose Hollow Bridge in N.H., Am. Inst. Steel Constrn., 1982, Merit award for Piney Creek Bridge in W.Va., 1989. Fellow ASCE; mem. NSPE, Am. Soc. Hwy. Engrs., N.Y. State Soc. Profl. Engrs. (sec. Nassau County chpt. 1961-66), Chi Epsilon. Home: 6029 Sandy Ln Tobyhanna PA 18466-9129 Office: Ysrael A Seinuk PC 228 E 45th St 3rd Floor New York NY 10017

KOSHI, ANNIE K. education educator, researcher; b. Changanacherry, Kerala, India, Apr. 30, 1934; came to U.S., 1969; d. Chacko Varkey and Thresiakutty Karickampally; m. Mathew Koshi, Dec. 28, 1978; children: Sarita, Anita, Mathew. MA, DePaul U., 1971; MEd, Columbia U., 1976, EdD, 1977. Sr. lectr. Assumption Coll., Changanachey, Kerala, India, 1958-69; adj. lectr. CUNY, N.Y.C., 1971-77; assoc. prof. City Coll., 1982—; tchr. LL Brandeis H.S., N.Y.C., 1977-82. Author: Discoveries, 1992. Named Outstanding Cmty. Leader Edn. Fedn. Kerala Assn. N. Am., 1994, Editor's Choice award Nat. Libr. Poetry, 1993, city Woman of Yr., CCNY, 2003. Mem. Asian-Am. Higher Edn. Coun. (bd. dirs. 1995—), soc. Indian Academics in Am. (culture com. 1990-96, sec. 1992-94, chair membership 1994-96, treas. 2002—). Avocation: walking. Home: 2621 Palisade Ave Apt 10H Bronx NY 10463-6110 Office: City Coll 138th St at Convent Ave New York NY 10031 E-mail: karickampa@aol.com.

KOSHKARIAN, GREGORY MERRILL, physician; b. Davenport, Iowa, June 30, 1962; s. Haig Aram and Susan Maxine (Rosenthal) K.; m. Sujatha Reddy, May 20, 1995. BS with honors, Stanford U., 1984; MD, Yale U., 1985-89. Diplomate Am. Bd. Internal Medicine, Am. Bd. Cardiovasc. Disease. Resident in internal medicine Mt. Sinai Hosp., N.Y.C., 1989-92; clin. rsch. fellow Columbia-Presbyn. Med. Ctr., N.Y.C., 1992-93; fellow in gen. cardiology Georgetown Hosp., Washington, 1993-95, fellow in interventional cardiology, 1995-96; attending cardiologist Desert Cardiology of Tucson, 1996—, dir. rsch., 1996—99, 2002—, physician mgr., 1999—; dir. heart failure clinic Desert Cardiology of Tucson, N.W. Med. Ctr., 1999—. Fellow Am. Coll. Cardiology; mem. Phi Beta Kappa. Avocations: music, theater, wine, travel. Office: Desert Cardiology of Tucson 6080 N La Cholla Blvd Tucson AZ 85741-3533

KOSHKIN-YOURITZIN, VICTOR, art educator; b. NYC, Dec. 20, 1942; s. Basil and Tatiana (Koshkin) Y.; m. Glenda Allen Green (div. 1980); m. Cynthia Lee Kerfoot (div. 1997). BA in Art History cum laude, Williams Coll., 1964; MA in Art History, Inst. Fine Arts, NYU, 1967; cert. in Mus. Tng., Met. Mus. Art, NYU, 1969. Instr. art history Vanderbilt U., Nashville, 1968-69, Newcomb Coll., Tulane U., New Orleans, 1969-72; asst. prof. art history U. Okla., Norman, 1972-80, assoc. prof., 1980-94, prof., 1994-97, David Ross Boyd disting. prof. history of art, 1997—. Lectr. in field; panelist program art on film Met. Mus. Art and J. Paul Getty Trust, N.Y.C., 1987, NEH, 1984; trustee Mabee-Gerrer Mus. Art, Shawnee, Okla., 1995-2002, chmn. bd. trustees, 1996-99, mem. adv. bd., 2002—; mem. coun. advisors Ogden Mus. So. Art, U. New Orleans, 1995—; trustee Okla. Mus. Art, Oklahoma City, 1978-84; mem. acquisitions com. Oklahoma City Art Mus., 1992-96; guest lectr. South African Dept. Nat. Edn., 1986; lectr. Met. Mus. Art, Art Students League N.Y., Dallas Mus. Art, other instns. in Eng., France, Africa, the Caribbean; cruise guest lectr. masterpieces of French impressionist and post impressionist painting Cunard Line, 1993. Author: Oklahoma Treasures, 1986, Five Contemporary Russian Artists, 1992, Twentieth-Century Russian Art, 1994, Paintings, Drawings, and Prints from the Late 19th and Early 20th Centuries, 1996, Twentieth-Century Russian Drawings, 1997, Modern Masters, 1998, Pavel Tchelitchew, 2002; author introduction: American Watercolors from The Metropolitan Museum of Art, 1991; contbr. articles to profl. jours. including Art Jour. and Gazette des Beaux-Arts; represented in collections including Nat. Libr. France, Paris, Beinecke Libr., Yale U., Wallach Divsn. Art, Prints, and Photographs, NY Pub. Libr., Wadsworth Atheneum Mus. Art. Ford Found. fellow Inst. Fine Arts, NYU, 1967-69, IBM and Noble fellow Columbia U., 1964-65; recipient Baldwin award Excellence in Teaching, U. Okla., 1987, Gov.'s Arts and Edn. award, Oklahoma City, 1992, Hon. citation State of Okla. House Reps., 1993. Mem. Koussevitzky Recs. Soc., Inc. (v.p. 1992—). Avocations: tennis, music. Home: 1721 Oakwood Dr Norman OK 73069-4449 Office: U Okla 520 Parrington Oval Rm 202 Norman OK 73019-0555 E-mail: vky@ou.edu.

KOSHLAND, DANIEL EDWARD, JR., biochemist, educator; b. N.Y.C., Mar. 30, 1920; s. Daniel Edward and Eleanor (Haas) Koshland; m. Marian Elliott, May 25, 1945 (dec. 1997); children: Ellen, Phyllis, James, Gail, Douglas; m. Yvonne Cyr, Aug. 27, 2000. BS, U. Calif., Berkeley, 1941; PhD, U. Chgo., 1949, Weizmann Inst. Sci., 1984; ScD (hon.), Carnegie Mellon U., 1985; LLD (hon.), Simon Fraser U., 1986; LHD (hon.), Mt. Sinai U.; LLD (hon.), U. Chgo., 1992; PhD (hon.), U. Mass., 1992, Ohio State U., 1995, Brandeis U., 2000. Chemist Shell Chem. Co., Martinez, 1941—42; rsch. assoc. Manhattan Dist. U. Chgo., 1942—44; group leader Oak Ridge Nat. Labs., 1944—46; postdoctoral fellow Harvard, 1949—51; 51staff Brookhaven Nat. Lab., Upton, NY, 1951—65; affiliate Rockefeller Inst., N.Y.C., 1958—65; prof. biochemistry U. Calif., Berkeley, 1965—97, prof. molecular biology, 1997—, chmn. dept., 1973—78. Fellow All Souls Oxford U., 1972; Phi Beta Kappa lectr., 76; John Edsall lectr. Harvard U., 1980, Robert Woodward vis. prof., 86; William H. Stein lectr. Rockefeller U., 1985; G. N. Lewis lectr.U U. Calif., Berkeley. Author: Bacterial Chemotaxis as a Model Behavioral System, 1980; mem. editl. bd. jours.: Accounts Chem. Rsch., Jour. Chemistry, Jour. Biochemistry; editor: jour. Procs. NAS, 1980—85, Sci. mag., 1985—95. Recipient T. Duckett Jones award, Helen Hay Whitney Found., 1977, Nat. Medal of Sci., NSF, 1990, Merck award, Am. Soc. Biochemistry and Molecular Biology, 1991, Clark Kerr award, U. Calif., 1994, Lasker Found. award, 1998; fellow Guggenheim Found., 1972.

Mem.: Acad. Forum (chmn.), Am. Acad. Arts and Scis. (coun.), Am. Philos. Soc., Am. Chem. Soc. (Edgar Fahs Smith award 1979, Pauling award 1979, Rosentiel award 1984, Waterford prize 1984, Seaborg medal 2000), Royal Swedish Acad. Scis. (hon.), Japanese Biochem. Soc. (hon.), NAS, Am. Soc. Biol. Chemists (pres.), Alpha Omega Alpha (hon.). Home: 3991 Happy Valley Rd Lafayette CA 94549-2423 Office: U Calif Dept Molecular Cell Biology 406 Barker Hall #3202 Berkeley CA 94720-3202 E-mail: dek@uclinic4.berkeley.edu.

KOSHY, VETTITHARA CHERIAN, chemistry educator, technical director and formulator; b. Kumbanad, Kerala, India, Jan. 5, 1952; arrived in U.S., 1984; s. Vettithara and Mariamma Cherian; m. Valsamma Koshy, Jan. 31, 1983; children: Rincy Mary, John Cherian. BSc in Chemistry, Kerala U., India, 1973; MSc in Chemistry, Ravishankar U., India, 1975, PhD in Chemistry, 1983; MS in Econ. Aspects of Chemistry, U. Detroit, 1992. Rsch. fellow chemistry Ravishankar U., Raipur, 1976-81; lectr., head dept. chemistry J.M. Patel Coll., 1981-83; lectr. dept. chemistry D.B. Sci. Coll., Gondia (India) Edn. Soc., India, 1983-84; group leader and evening supr. in R & D Widger Chem. Corp., Warren, Mich., 1984-87; mgr. automotive divsn., R & D Croda Caourep Corp., Westland, Mich., 1987-89; dir. R & D, quality control and mfg. Autotek, inc., Farmington Hills, Mich., 1989-94; pres. Koshy Speciality Products, Inc., Bloomfield Hills, Mich., 1994—; engr. Dale Packaging Inc., Livonia, Mich., 1994-95; sr. chemist Novamax Techs. (U.S.) Inc., Warren, 1995-96; tech. mgr. Henkel Corp. Novamax Techs., 1996-98; sr. rsch. scientist Henkel Surface Techs., Madison Heights, 1998—. Contbr. articles to Jour. Chem. Engring., Croatica Chemica Acta, Indian Acad. Scis., NAS Sci. Letters, others. Pres. sci. assn. J.M. Patel Coll., Bhandara, India, 1981-82; pres. chem. soc. Ravishankar U., Raipur, 1977-78, pres. rsch. scholars assn., 1979-81. Recipient numerous grants. Mem. Am. Chem. Soc., Am. Inst. Chemists, Soc. Automotive Engrs. (assoc.), Fedn. Kerala Assns. N.Am. (region 7 v.p. 1998-2000). Achievements include development of a formula for a universal sealer for automotive application; the first two component thermosettable composition system based on epoxy resins used in all robotics application to inject the foam. Home: 7030 White Pine Dr Bloomfield Hills MI 48301-3715 Office: Henkel Surface Techs 32100 Stephenson Hwy Madison Heights MI 48071-5514 E-mail: vkoshy@aol.com.

KOSINSKI, JOHN AUGUST, electrical engineer, civilian military employee; b. Hoboken, N.J., Aug. 26, 1958; m. Marisa Sigano Kosinski, June 15, 1985; children: Eric, Andrew. AA, Ocean County Coll., 1978; BS, Montclair State U., 1980; MS, Monmouth U., 1988; PhD, Rutgers U., 1993. Physicist Electronics Tech. and Devel. Lab., Ft. Monmouth, NJ, 1981—87; electronics engr. U.S. Army Rsch. Lab., Ft. Monmouth, 1987—95, U.S. Army Comm. Electronics Command, Ft. Monmouth, 1995—97, br. chief, 1997—98, sr. technologist, 1998—. Cubmaster Boy Scouts Am. Pack 333, Wall Township, NJ, 2000—. Fellow: IEEE (sr.), Internat. Soc. for Philos. Enquiry (sr.); mem.: IEEE Ultrasonics, Ferroelectrics and Frequency Control Soc. (assoc. editor IEEE UFFC Trans. 1995—, adminstrv. com. mem. 2002—), Assn. Old Crows. Office: US Army RDECOM CERDEC AMSEL-RD-IW-I Fort Monmouth NJ 07703-5211

KOSINSKI, RICHARD ANDREW, public relations executive; b. Chgo., Aug. 12, 1951; s. Andrew Ignatius and Olga Sophia (Janusz) K.; m. Susan M. Mark, Oct. 13, 1974 (div. June 1985). BS, Loyola U. Chgo., 1974; MPA, Roosevelt U., 1979. From dir. parents assocs. to dir. dental devel. Loyola U. Chgo., 1976-79; assoc. dir. devel. Am. Fund for Dental Health, Chgo., 1979-80; dir. devel. & pub. rels. Niles Twp. Sheltered Workshop, Skokie, Ill., 1985-88; assoc. exec. dir. Leukemia Soc. Am., Chgo., 1988-93; mgr. major gifts Prevent Blindness Am., Schaumburg, Ill., 1993-97; dir. devel. Youth Found. Skokie Park Dist., 1997-99; dir. devel. Alexian Bros. N.W. Mental Health Ctr., Palatine, Ill., 1999-2000; subs. tchr. Cmty. Consol., 2001—, Sch. Dist. 59, Elk Grove Twp., Ill., 2001—. Mem. svc. and rehab. com. Am. Cancer Soc., 1986-88. Recipient Tribute U.S. Ho. of Reps., 1986. Roman Catholic. Avocations: travel, photography, writing. Home: 7409 N Oconto Ave Chicago IL 60631-4441 E-mail: RAKosinski@hotmail.com.

KOSKI, CHRISTINE L. consulting firm executive; BS in Chemistry, St. Lawrence U., 1975—79; Exec. MBA, Cox Sch., So. Meth. U., 1999—2001. Purchasing project mgr. Celanese, AG, Dallas, 1999—2000; pres. Koski Consulting Group, Inc., Dallas, 2001—. Various sales & mktg. Celanese Chem. Co., Dallas, St. Louis, & Cleveland, 1980—87; purchasing mgr. Hoechst Celanese Chem. Co., Dallas, 1987—88; west coast sales mgr. Hoechst Celanese Co., Chem. Divsn., San Francisco, 1988—92; global mktg. mgr. Hoechst AG/Hoechst Celanese Chem., Frankfut am Main, Hessen, Germany, 1992—96, Celanese, AG, Dallas, 1996—99. Mem.: AMA, NAFE. Office: Koski Consulting Group Inc 3525 Turtle Creek Blvd Suite 19B Dallas TX 75219 Office Fax: 214-559-2977. E-mail: clkoski@swbell.net.

KOSKI, DONNA FAITH, poet; b. Wildwood, NJ, Aug. 18, 1935; d. Sebastian and Mildred (Shastany) Rossitto; m. Paul A. Koski, May 5, 1968 (div. June 1982); children: Danita Swift-Stearns, Darla Swift, Deanna Swift-Everett, Deena Swift Bauer, Charles Swift. Student, San Diego Jr. Coll., 1955-58, Mesa Jr. Coll, San Diego, 1993. With Pacific Telephone, San Diego, 1954-68; credit clk. Norwich (Conn.) Gas & Lights, 1968-70; clk. Navy Exch., New London, Conn., 1969-70; front desk clk. Del Webb's, San Diego, 1971-72; payroll clk. U.S.I.U., San Diego, 1974-76; facility mgr. Price Costco, San Diego, 1978-94, Price Enterprises, Inc., San Diego, 1994-97, Price Smart Vacations (Costco Travel), 1997—99; facility and maintenance mgr. The Price Club, 1999—2000; quality control and support agent Club 4 U. Worker Diversified Copier Products in San Diego, Price's, PAcific bell, Westgate (C Arnolt Smith), Alvin Strep Interiors, USIU, Norwich Gas and Electric, John Myers of Norwich, Navy Exch.-New London, Conn, several hotels and motels. Author: The Power of Love, 1995, Nights in Sedona, 1995, Faces in the Clouds, 1994, Dream Catcher, 2001, The New Heros, 2003, numerous poems. Vol. Nat. Multiple Sclerosis Soc., San Diego, 1995, React-Telecom. Emergency Svcs., San Diego, 1985-93, Perot Hdqrs., San Diego, 1992, 96, Social Svcs., San Diego, 1980-82, Project Oz (runaway kids). Recipient Editor's Choice award Nat. Libr. of Poetry, 1995, Accomplishment of Merit, Creative Arts and Sci., 1994, 1st Place Browning Competition award Iliad Press, 1998, Presdl. Recognition award, 1998-99, Outstanding Achievement in Poetry award Famous Poets Soc., 1998, others. Mem. Internat. Soc. Poets, Internat. Soc. Authors and Artists, Blind Soc., Multiple Sclerosis Soc., Moose. Mem. Unity Ch. Avocations: writing, poetry, computers, music, sports. Home: 8661 Winter Gardens Blvd # 45 Lakeside CA 92040 E-mail: koski_donna@aol.com., k78@yahoo.com.

KOSKINEN, JOHN ANDREW, government executive; b. Cleve., June 30, 1939; s. Yrjo Alfred and Irja (Danska) K.; m. Patricia Salz, June 15, 1963; children: Jeffrey, Cheryl. BA magna cum laude, Duke U., 1961; JD cum laude, Yale U., 1964; postgrad., Cambridge U., Eng., 1964-65. Bar: Calif. 1965, Conn. 1972. Clk. to presiding judge U.S. Ct. Appeals, Washington, 1965-66; lawyer Gibson, Dunn & Crutcher, L.A., 1966-67; spl. asst. to dep. exec. dir. Nat. Adv. Commn. Civil Disorders (also called Kerner Commn.), Washington, 1967-68; legis. asst. to Mayor John Lindsay N.Y.C., 1968-69; adminstrv. asst. to Senator Abraham Ribinoff, 1969-73; v.p. Palmieri Co., Washington, 1973-77, pres., chief operating officer, 1977-79, pres., chief exec. officer, 1979-94; dep. dir. for mgmt. Office of Mgmt. and Budget, Washington, 1994-97; asst. to Pres., chmn. President's Coun. on Year 2000 Conversion, Washington, 1998-2000; dep. mayor, city adminstr. Dist. of Columbia, 2000—. Mem. Pres.'s Mgmt. Improvement Coun., 1979-80; bd. dirs. Nat. Captioning Inst., 1979-91, chmn., 1986-87, vice-chmn., 1979-86; trustee Coop. Assistance Fund, 1982-93; trustee Duke U., 1985-97, vice chmn. 1993-94, chmn. 1994-97; chmn. Washington 1994 World Cup Commn., 1989-94, Washington Olympic Football Organizing Com., 1993-96; vice chmn. Am. Soccer League, 1987-91; trustee U.S. Soccer Found., 1993-94, 2001—; pres. Washington Met. Area Coun. Govt., 2003—. Fellow Nat. Acad. Pub. Adminstrn., Phi Beta Kappa; mem. Duke U. Gen. Alumni Assn. (pres. 1980-81), Soccer Hall of Fame, Va. Avocations: soccer, tennis, music. Office: Exec Office of the Mayor 1350 Pennsylvania Ave NW Washington DC 20004

KOSKO, GEORGE CARTER, lawyer; b. Tampa, Fla., Apr. 14, 1944; s. George and Margaret Elizabeth (Rea) K.; m. Polly Spann, Dec. 7, 1974. B.S., Univ. S.C., 1966, J.D., 1971; postgrad. Nat. Inst. Trial Advocacy, 1972. Bar: S.C. 1971, U.S. Supreme Ct. 1976, D.C. 1981, U.S. Customs Ct. 1976, U.S. Ct. Internat. Trade 1981, Fourth Circuit Court of Appeals Judicial Conference. Ptnr. Kosko, Coffas & Sipes, 1975-82, sr. ptnr., 1976— . Mem. ABA (state reporter aviation com. sect. litigation). S.C. Bar Assn. Clubs: De Bordieu, Palmetto, Sertoma (gov. Wade Hampton dist.), Quiet Birdmen (Columbia). E-mail: george_kosko@scd.uscourts.gov. Home: 21 Lakeview Cir Columbia SC 29206-3222 Office: 4910 Trenholm Rd Columbia SC 29206-4709

KOSLOW, SALLY, editor-in-chief; BA, U. Wis. Editor-in-chief McCall's mag., N.Y.C., 1994—2001; editor-in-chief Lifetime mag. The Hearst Corp., N.Y.C., 2002—, editor Mary Emmerling's Country, 2002—. Office: Lifetime mag The Heart Corp 1790 Broadway New York NY 10019*

KOSLOW, STEPHEN HUGH, science administrator, pharmacologist; b. N.Y.C., Oct. 14, 1940; s. Julius and Lillian (Kaye) K.; m. Diane Heisler, Aug. 18, 1962; children: Karin, James. BS, Columbia U., 1962; PhD, U. Chgo., 1967. Internat. postdoctoral fellow Swedish Med. Rsch. Coun., Karolinski Inst., 1968-69; pharmacologist, chief neurobiology unit St. Elizabeth's Hosp., Washington, 1970-77; chief biol. rsch. sect. Clin. Rsch. Br., Rockville, Md., 1975-81; chief div. Extramural Rsch. Neurosci. Rsch. Br. NIMH, Rockville, 1981—99, chief div. Basic Scis. Neurosci. Rsch. Br., 1985-88, dep. dir. divsn. Basic Brain and Behavioral Scis., 1990—99; dir. divsn. Basic and Clin. Neurosci. Rsch. NIMH-NIH, Rockville, 1996-99; assoc. dir., dir. office neuroinformatics NIMH, Rockville, Md., 1999—. Project dir. NIHM-CRB Collaborative Program on Psychobiology of Depression-Biol. Study, 1975-85; mem. adv. bd. Tourette Syndrome Assn., Bayside, N.Y., 1984; chair fed. coordinating com. on the Human Brain Project, 1991—; chair neuroinformatics subgroup of Office Econ. Coop. & Devel., Megasci. Forum, Biol. Working Group, 1996-99; co-chair US/EC com. on neuroinformatics, 1998—, chair global sci. forum neuroinformatics working group, 2000-2002. Mem. editl. bd. Neuropsychopharmacology, 1987-92, Critical Revs. in Neurobiol., 1991—, Human Brain Mapping, 1993—, Psychopharm. Bull., 1989-99, Neuroimage; series editor Progress in Neuroinformatics Rsch., 1996-2001, Neuroimage, 1995-2001, CNS Drug Revs., 1995-99, Biomednet, 1999-2003. Recipient NIMH Quality Increase award, 1977-78, Health Adminstr.'s award for Meritorious Achievement, 1986, Pub. Health Svc. Spl. Recognition award, 1992, Alumni Achievement award U. Chgo. Club of Washington, 1995, two Dir.'s awards NIH, 1996, Pres. award Internat. Neural Network Soc., 2001; Swedish Med. Rsch. Coun. internat. postdoctoral fellow, 1968-69, Spl. NATO fellow, 1969. Fellow AAAS, Am. Coll. Neuropsychopharmacology, Am. Coll. Med. Informatics; mem. Am. Soc. for Neurochemistry, Am. Soc. Pharmacology and Exptl. Therapeutics, Collegium Internat. Neuro Psychopharmacologium, Soc. for Neurosci., Soc. Biol. Psychiatry. Office: NIMH 6001 Executive Blvd Rm 6167 Bethesda MD 20892-0001 Fax: 301-443-1867. E-mail: koz@helix.nih.gov.

KOSMIDER, ALEXIA M. language educator; b. Toledo, Ohio, July 12, 1953; d. John Joseph and Barbara Jean Kosmider. BA, Miami U., Oxford, Ohio, 1975; MA, U. N.Mex., 1980, Brown U., 1994; student, U. RI, 1994. English instr. Dean Coll., Franklin, Mass., 1987—90; lectr. Roger Williams U., Bristol, RI, 1990—95, U. RI, Providence, 1995—. Faculty advisor U. RI, 2000—01. Author: Tricky Tribal Discourse, 1998; editor: Am. Trans Quar., 2000. Grantee, Philos. Soc., 1996, 1998. Mem.: New Eng. Native Am. Inst., Fulbright Assn. (grantee 1999—2000), Modern Lang. Assn. Home: 41 Stadden Street Providence RI 02907 Office: CCE URI Academic Skills Ctr 80 Washington Providence RI 02907 E-mail: akosmo@etal.uri.edu.

KOSMOWSKI, AUDRA MICHELE, lawyer; b. Cleve., Apr. 9, 1968; d. Warren M. and Kathleen T. Krueger; m. Michael F. Kosmowski, 1993. BA in Polit. Sci., John Carroll U., 1990; JD, U. Akron, 1993; LLM, Case Western Res. U., 2000. Bar: Pa. 1993, Ohio 1995. Assoc. Evans, Garvey, Lackey & Ochs, Sharon, Pa., 1995—. Tutor Sharon Literacy Coun., 1997-98; mem. Pa. Econ. League, Sharon, 1996—; bd. dirs. Aware, Inc., Sharon, 1997-99, Diversified Family Svcs., 1999—, treas., 2001. Mem. Ohio Bar Assn., Pa. Bar Assn., Mercer County Commn. for Women (vice chair 1998-99), Nat. Acad. Elder Law Attys. Office: Evans Garvey Lackey & Ochs PO Box 949 19 Jefferson Ave Sharon PA 16146-3342

KOSNER, EDWARD A(LAN), editor and publisher; b. N.Y.C., July 26, 1937; s. Sidney and Annalee (Fisher) Kosner; m. Alice Nadel, Feb. 1, 1959; children: John Robbins, Anthony William; m. Julie Baumgold, Nov. 19, 1978; 1 child, Lily. BA, CCNY, 1958. CCNY corr. N.Y. Times, 1957—58; rewriteman, asst. city editor N.Y. Post, 1958—63; assoc. editor Newsweek Mag., N.Y.C., 1963—67, gen. editor, 1967—69, nat. affairs editor, 1969—72, asst. mng. editor, 1972, mng. editor, 1973—75, editor, 1975—79, New York Mag., N.Y.C., 1980—93, editor, pub., 1986—91, editor, pres., 1991—93; editor-in-chief Esquire Mag., N.Y.C., 1993—97; editor N.Y. Sunday Daily News, N.Y.C., 1998—99; editor-in-chief N.Y. Daily News, N.Y.C., 2000—. Recipient various journalism awards. Mem.: Am. Soc. Mag. Editors (pres. 1984—86, exec. com.), Century Club. Home: 180 E 79th St New York NY 10021-0437 Office: 450 W 33rd St New York NY 10001-2603 E-mail: ekosner@edit.nydailynews.com.

KOSOVICH, DUSHAN RADOVAN, psychiatrist; b. Trepca, Niksic, Yugoslavia, Dec. 23, 1926; came to U.S., 1967, naturalized, 1972; s. Radovan Dj and Djurdja K. (Bacovic) K.; children— Jasmine, Nicholas. MD, Belgrade U., 1954, postgrad., 1954-57; certificate, Am. Inst. for Psychoanalysis and Postgrad. Center, 1972. Resident in neuropsychiatry, Belgrade, Yugoslavia, 1954-57; resident in psychiatry Bellevue Med. Center, N.Y.C., 1957-59, McGill U., Montreal, Que., Can., 1965-67; founder, chief neuropsychiatric service for inpatient and outpatients Gen. Hosp., Titograd, Montenegro, Yugoslavia, 1960-65; staff psychiatrist Bellevue Med. Center, N.Y.C., 1967-73; dir. inpatient psychiat. service Lincoln Hosp., Bronx, N.Y., 1973-75; chief inpatient services Methodist Hosp., Bklyn., 1975-76, acting dir. psychiat. dept., 1976-78, dir., 1978-84; pvt. practice N.Y.C., 1984—. Clin. asso. prof. dept. psychiatry Downstate Med. Center, State U. N.Y., 1975— ; Psychoanalyst Karen Horney Psychoanalytic Inst., N.Y.C. Author: Stress, 1989, Optimistic Psychoanalysis, 1989, It Drives Me Crazy, 1997, The Stress in the Vortex of Global Anomie, 2000, The Paradoxes of Dushan Kosovich, 2003; contbr. articles to profl. jours. Served with Yugoslavian Army, 1944-46. Recipient City of Titograd award for best sci. achievement, 1964 Fellow Assn. for Advancement Psychoanalysis, Karen Horney Psychoanalytic Inst. and Ctr., Am. Acad. Psychoanalysis; mem. Am. Acad. Clin. Psychiatrists, N.Am. Acad. for Auricular Medicine, Am. Acad. Psychiatry and Law, World Psychiat. Assn., Am. Yugoslav Med. Soc. Home: Trump World Tower Apt 21D 845 United Nations Plz New York NY 10017 Office: 333 E 46th St Apt 1E New York NY 10017 Office Fax: 212-661-1882. E-mail: DKosovich@msn.com.

KOSOWSKI, MARY, artist, educator; b. Pawtucket, R.I., Dec. 7, 1927; d. Marlin Padykula and Constance Trzuskowski; m. Alfred Kosowski, Oct. 14, 1950 (dec. July 1989); children: Eileen, Linda. BFA, R.I. Sch. Design, 1949; B in Tchg., R.I. Coll., 1970. Fabric designer Decorative Fabrics, Pawtucket, R.I., 1949-52; children's wear designer Healthtex, Pawtucket, 1964-67; tchr. Cumberland (R.I.) Sch. System, 1967-90. Mem. pres. club R.I. Sch. Design, 1996—. Recipient many awards for art works. Mem. Rockport Art Assn., Attleboro Mus., Providence Art Club (mem. providence art on art qualifications com. 1975—), Met. Mus. Art, Nat. Mus. for Women in Arts, Boston MFA, Copley Soc., others. Avocation: travel. Home: 76 Orchard Meadows Dr Smithfield RI 02917-1846

KOSOWSKY, DAVID I. retired biotechnical company executive; b. N.Y.C., Feb. 27, 1930; m. Ingrid M. Mehlstaeubl; children: Michael, Richard P., Steven A. BEE summa cum laude, CUNY, 1951; SM, MIT, 1952, ScD, 1955. Chmn. emeritus Damon Corp., Needham Heights, Mass. Speaker, lectr. on policy developments and trends in the health care industry. Patentee in field. Mem. Corp. MIT, mem. vis. com. dept. biology; trustees Beth Israel Hosp., U. Hosp., New Eng. Aquarium, Children's Hosp.; mem. exec. group Harvard Med. Ctr. bd. trustees; mem. Corp. Joslin Diabetes Ctr., Inc., Corp. Mus. Sci.; mem. Commn. on Acad. Health Ctrs., Economy of New Eng. for the New Eng. Bd. of Higher Edn. Mem. N.Y. Acad. of Scis., IEEE, Sigma Xi, Tau Beta Pi, Eta Kappa Nu, Order of St. John, Knights of Malta. Home: 403D Dedham St Newton MA 02459-3300 E-mail: dkosowsky@alum.mit.edu.

KOSOY, MICHAEL Y. biomedical researcher; b. Odessa, Ukraine, Feb. 12, 1953; s. Yefim Kosoy and Olga Dainzon; m. Olga Kosoy, Aug. 4, 1976; children: Roman, Jenia Michelle. PhD, Gamaleya Inst., Moscow, 1987. Mem.: Am. Soc. of Tropical Medicine and Hygiene. Achievements include research in Plague, tularemia, Bartonella, hantaviruses; Ecology of zoonotic and vector-borne infectious diseases. Home: 3244 Reedgrass Ct Fort Collins CO 80521 Office: CDC Rampart Rd Foothills Campus Fort Collins CO 80521 Office Fax: 970-221-6476. E-mail: mck3@cdc.gov.

KOSS, LEOPOLD G. physician, pathologist, educator; b. Gdansk, Poland, Oct. 2, 1920; arrived in U.S., 1947, naturalized, 1952; s. Abram and Rose (Merenholc) Kon; m. Lydia Palla; children: Michael S., Andrew C., Richard P. MD, U. Berne, Switzerland, 1946; Doctorate (hon.), Pomeranian Med. Acad., Poland, 2002. Intern, Lincoln Hosp., NYC, 1947-48; tng. pathology St. Gallen, Switzerland, 1946-47, Kings County Hosp., Bklyn., 1949-52; instr. pathology LI U. Coll. Medicine, NY, 1949-52; mem. staff Meml. Hosp. Cancer and Allied Diseases, NYC, 1952-70, attending pathologist, 1961-70, chief cytology svc., 1961-70; pathologist-in-chief Sinai Hosp. Balt., 1970-73; prof., chmn. dept. pathology Montefiore Hosp., Med. Ctr. Albert Einstein Coll. Medicine, Bronx, NY, 1973-92, prof., chair emeritus, 1993—. Hon. prof. pathology Severance Med. Coll., Seoul, Korea, 1956; assoc. mem. Sloan-Kettering Inst. Cancer Research, NYC, 1957-70; assoc. prof. pathology Sloan-Kettering div. Postgrad. Sch. Med. Sci., Cornell U., 1957-70; prof. pathology Jefferson Med. Coll., Phila., 1970-73; clin. prof. pathology U. Md. Med. Sch., 1971-73; vis. pathologist James Ewing Hosp., NYC, 1952-60; former cons. pathologist NY State Dept. Health, Hosp. Spl. Surgery, NYC; cons. pathologist Walter Reed Army Med. Ctr., Nassau County Med. Ctr.; Frost lectr., Balt., 1999. Author: Diagnostic Cytology and Its Histopathologic Bases, 4th rev. edit. 1992, Tumors of the Urinary Bladder, 1975, Supplement, 1984, Aspiration Biopsy: Cytologic Interpretation and Histologic Bases, 2nd rev. edit. 1992, Introduction to Gynecologic Cytology, 1999; editor: Advances in Clinical Cytology, Vol. I, 1981, Vol. II, 1984, Papillomaviruses and Human Diseases, 1987, Errors and Pitfalls in Diagnostic Cytology, 1997; contbr. over 365 articles to profl. jour. and 40 chpts. to books also monographs. Served to maj. M.C., AUS, 1955-57. Recipient Wien award Papanicolaou Cancer Inst., 1963, Alfred P. Sloan award cancer rsch., 1964, Fred Stewart award, 1984, Vandenberghe-Hill award, 1984, Meritorious medal U. Brussels, 1987, Jurzykowski award, 1991, Disting. Pathologist award US and Can. Acad. Pathology, 2001, Disting. Pathologist award Assn. Pathology Chairs, 2002, Doctor Honoris Causa, Pomeranian Med. Acad., Poland, 2002. Fellow: AAAS, Internat. Acad. Cytology (Goldblatt award 1962, Kazumasa Masubuchi Life-Time Achievement award in clin. cytology 1995), Coll. Am. Pathologists, Am. Soc. Clin. Pathology, Royal Coll. Pathologists (hon. Found. lectr. 1997), Royal Coll. Pathologists (hon.); mem.: AMA, Am. Soc. for Colposcopy and Cervical Pathology (Disting. Svc. award 1996), Internat. Soc. of Urol. Pathology (F.K. Mostofi Disting. Svc. award 1995), German Acad. Sci. (Leopoldina), Peruvian Soc. Ob-Gyn., Polish Soc. Pathology, Japanese Soc. Pathology, Argentinian Soc. Cytology, Mex. Soc. Cytology, Brit. Soc. Clin. Cytology (hon.), Royal Acad. Medicine Spain (corr.), Korean Med. Assn., NY State Soc. Pathology (Lansky-Ratner award 1989), NY Pathology Soc. (pres. 1985—87, Middleton-Goldsmith lectr. 1992), Internat. Acad. Pathology (Maude Abbott lectr. 1989), Am. Soc. Cytology (pres. 1962, Papanicolaou award 1966), James Ewing Soc., Am. Soc. Exptl. Pathology (Gold Cane award 1993). Office: Montefiore Medical Ctr 111 E 210th St Bronx NY 10467-2401

KOSS, RICHARD ALLEN, JR., economist; b. Cleve., Aug. 5, 1954; s. Richard Allen Sr. and Mary Ann (Minich) K.; m. Lee Marston Glendening, Oct. 8, 1977; children: Laura Jean, Daniel Walter. BS in Math., Case Western Res. U., 1976; PhD in Econs., U. Pa., 1985. Staff economist Coun. Econ. Advisers, Washington, 1976-78, Wharton Econometric Forecasting Assocs., Washington, 1978-80; sr. advisor GM, N.Y.C., 1985-91; v.p. CIBC, N.Y.C., 1991-93, mng. dir., 1993-95, Internat. Strategist Mfr. Inc., N.Y.C., 1995—98; sr. v.p., dir. global fixed income Brown Bros. Harriman, N.Y.C., 1998—. Cons. The World Bank, Washington, 1982-85; instr. econs. U. Pa., Phila., 1982-83. Co-author: Industrial Policy: Empirical Studies, 1985. Mem. Am. Econ. Assn., Nat. Assn. Bus. Economists, Internat. Economists Club N.Y. (pres. 1988-90), Conf. Bus. Economists.. Home: 11 Reeve Cir Millburn NJ 07041-1913 Office: Brown Bros Harriman 140 Broadway New York NY 10005

KOSS, ROSABEL STEINHAUER, retired health and physical education educator; b. Phila., Sept. 3, 1913; d. Arthur H. and Agnes (Temple) Steinhauer; m. Franklyn C. Koss, July 6, 1947 (dec. 1987); children: C. Lynn Knauff, Susan Kreiner, Carolyn Ruef, Rosalind Diehl. BS, Coll. of N.J., 1935; MA, Columbia U., N.Y.C., 1942; DEd, Columbia U., 1964; diploma, Hasmors Gym Leaders Inst., Lilsved, Sweden, 1970, Pensioner's Program, Lilsved, 1972. Cert. health edn. specialist, 1989. Supr. health and phys. edn. Flemington (N.J.) Pub. Schs., 1935-37; tchr. health and phys. edn. Ridgewood (N.J.) High Sch., 1937-40, Passaic Valley Regional High Sch., Little Falls, N.J., 1940-48; asst. prof. Montclair State Coll., Upper Montclair, N.J., 1958-61, Upsala Coll., East Orange, NJ, 1964—71; assoc. to full prof. Ramapo Coll of N.J., Mahwah, N.J., 1971-84, dir. tchr. edn., 1974-79, prof. emeritus, 1985; adj. prof. Richard Stockton Coll. of N.J., Pomona, 1985-95. Asst. sport attachee Royal Swedish Embassy, N.Y.C., 1964-74. Author: (with others) Dance for Older Adults, 1988, Mature Stuff. Physical Activity for Older Adults, 1989, Exercise for the Older Adult, 1998; contbr. articles profl. jours. Mem. Little Falls (N.J.) Bd. Edn., 1954-63; trustee, treas. Bergen County (N.J.) Ret. Sr. Vol. Program, 1979-84; mem. recreation adv. com. Stone Harbor Bd. Health, v.p., 1995; mem. Cape May County Freeholders Adv. Commn. on Women, 1986—, Cape May County Human Svcs. Adv. Coun., 1989—; vestrywoman St. Mary's Episcopal Ch., Stone Harbor; mem. N.J. Commn. on Aging, 1992-98, chmn., 1996-98; mem. Health Promotion and Planning Lab, State of N.J., 1998; del. White House Conf. on Aging, 1995; mem. adv. com. Cape May Human Svcs. Named Gerontologist of Yr., Soc. on Aging N.J., 1993; named to Athletic Hall of Fame Coll. N.J., 1980, Trenton State Coll. Alumni Athletic Hall of Fame, 1987, Nat. Women's Wall of Fame, 1994, Athletic Hall of Fame Ramapo Coll. N.J., 2003; recipient Work Study grants to Sweden, The Royal Swedish Consulate, N.Y.C., 1968, 1970, 1972, Athletic Alumni women's award, Trenton State Coll., 1976, State of N.J. Senate and Gen. Assembly citation, 1994, Cape Women's Resource Honor award, 1994. Fellow: Assn. for Gerontology in Higher Edn.; mem.: AAUW, AAHPERD (life; coun. on aging and adult devel., profl. achievement award, N.J. 1973, honor award fellow 1979, merit award Ea. Dist. 1980, disting. leadership award 1996, Rosabel Koss award named in her honor), Vols. in Medicine, Internat. Soc. Comparative Phys. Edn. and Sport, Nat. Coun. on Aging, N.J. AHPERD (Disting. Leadership award), Gerontol. Soc. N.J. (parliamentarian 1988—89), Wetlands Inst. (docent), Cape May County LWV, Stone Harbor Women's Civic Club, Garden Club. Avocations: travel, gardening, salt marsh ecology, swimming. Home: 150 91st St Stone Harbor NJ 08247-2016 Home (Winter): 30 Andrews Ave The Grove # 6 Delray Beach FL 33483

KOSSAR, RONALD STEVEN, lawyer; b. Ellenville, N.Y., May 30, 1948; s. Emanuel and Helen (Panken) K.; m. Sandra Perlman, Aug. 25, 1973. BA cum laude, Boston U., 1970; JD, Am. U., 1973. Bar: N.Y. 1974, D.C. 1974, U.S. Dist. Ct. (no. dist.) N.Y. 1974, U.S. Tax Ct. 1974, U.S. Ct. Appeals D.C. 1974. Tax law specialist Office Asst. Commr. (Tech.), IRS, Washington, 1973-75; sole practice Middletown, NY, 1976—. Dir. Newburgh (N.Y.) Realty Corp. Mem. ABA, N.Y. State Bar Assn., Orange County Bar Assn., Middletown Bar Assn., D.C. Bar. Jewish. Office: 402 E Main St Middletown NY 10940-2516 Office Fax: 845-343-5222. E-mail: rsklaw@warwick.net.

KOSSIAKOFF, ALEXANDER, chemist, researcher; b. St. Petersburg (formerly Leningrad), Russia, June 26, 1914; m. Arabelle Davies, Feb. 18, 1939; children: Tanya Ann, Anthony. BS in Chemistry, Calif. Inst. Tech., 1936, postdoctoral fellow, 1939; PhD in Chemistry, Johns Hopkins U., 1938. Instr. chemistry Catholic U. Am., 1939-42; tech. aide Office Sci. Research and Devel. also Nat. Def. Research Council, Washington, 1942-43; dep. dir. research Allegany Ballistics Lab., George Washington U., Cumberland, Md., 1944-46, with Applied Physics Lab., Johns Hopkins U., Silver Spring, Md., 1946—, asst. dir. tech. ops., asso. dir., 1961-66, head surface missile systems dept., 1965-69, dep. dir., 1966-69, dir. lab., 1969-80, chief scientist, 1980—, chmn. MS Tech Mgmt./MS Sys. Engring. program, Sch. Enring. Chmn. launching and handling panel research and devel. bd. U.S. Dept. Def., 1948-51; cons. Tech. Adv. Panel on Aeros., 1954-60; mem. com. on nat. labs. Office Sci. and Tech., 1969-73. Contbr. articles to profl. jours. Bd. dirs. Montgomery Gen. Hosp., 1979-85

mem. Gov.'s Sci. Adv. Council, 1979— . Recipient Navy Disting. Public Service award, Def. Dept. medal for disting. public service, Pres.'s Cert. of Merit, other awards. Fellow Am. Inst. Chemists; mem. AAAS, INCOSE, Phi Beta Kappa, Sigma Xi, Tau Beta Pi, Phi Lambda Upsilon. Clubs: Cosmos. Home: 120 Haviland Mill Rd Brookeville MD 20833-2308 Office: Johns Hopkins Rd Laurel MD 20723 E-mail: a.kossiakoff@jhuapl.edu.

KOSSIN, SANFORD MARSHALL, illustrator; b. L.A., June 4, 1926; s. Leo and Clara Kossin; m. Josephine Koscomb; children: David, James. Student, Jepson Sch. Art, L.A., 1946-50. Freelance illustrator, N.Y.C., 1952—; tchr. life drawing and documentary art Fashion Inst. Tech., N.Y.C., 2002—. Drawing instr. Parsons Sch. Art, N.Y.C., 1977-87; advanced illustraton instr. Pratt Inst., Bklyn., 1988-90. Illustrator paper back book covers Bantam Books, Pocket Books, New Am. Libr., Ballantine Books, Berkley Books, St. Martins Press, Harper Collins, Pyramid Books, 1950's-1999, children's books Houghton Mifflin Pubs., 1963-85, mags. Life Mag., Readers Digest, Saturday Eve Post, Good Housekeeping, Boys Life, Red Book, Argosy, Cavalier, Galaxy, 1963-85; movie posters for United Artists, Columbia, Paramount, 20th Century Fox, RKO; commd. by Bantam Books to do court room drawings of Sam Shepard murder trial #2; paintings represented in permanent collection Airforce Art Collection, MacArthur Mus. Sonarman 2nd class USNR, 1944-46, PTO. Mem. N.Y. Soc. Illustrators (life mem. Illustrations of Yr. ann. exhbn. 1956-80), NCS Berndt Toast Gang. Avocations: cartooning, portrait painting, oil and watercolor painting. Home and Office: Sandy Kossin Illustration 143 Cow Neck Rd Port Washington NY 11050-1143 Fax: 516-883-3038.

KOSSL, THOMAS LEONARD, lawyer; b. Oshkosh, Wis., Oct. 21, 1952; s. Leonard N. and Elaine M. (Noak) K.; m. Jacqueline E. Saco, Sept. 5, 1981; children: Kenzie, Clayton. AB, U. Chgo., 1974; JD, Georgetown U., 1978, MS in Fgn. Svc., 1994. Bar: D.C. 1979, U.S. Dist. Ct. D.C. 1979, N.J. 1992. Assoc. Daniels, Houlihan and Palmeter, Washington, 1978-80, Arent, Fox, Kintner, Plotkin and Kahn, Washington, 1980-83; asst. corp. counsel, then div. counsel Corning (N.Y.), Inc., 1983-86, assoc. internat. counsel, 1984-86; v.p., gen. counsel, asst. sec. MetPath Inc., Teterboro, N.J., 1986-92; v.p., gen. counsel, sec. Unilab Corp. and MetWest, Inc., Teterboro, 1988-92; assoc. gen. counsel Corning Lab. Svcs., Inc. and MetPath Inc., Teterboro, 1992-94; pvt. practice Kinnelon, NJ, 1994—2001; sr. v.p., gen. counsel, CCO, DIANON Systems Inc., Stratford, Conn., 2002—. Exec. com., policy com. MetPath, Inc., 1988-92. Mem. ABA, Am. Health Lawyers Assn. Office: DIANON Systems Inc 200 Watson Blvd Stratford CT 06615

KOST, GERALD JOSEPH, biomedical researcher physician; b. Sacramento, July 12, 1945; s. Edward William and Ora Imogene K.; m. Angela Louise Baldo, Sept. 9, 1972; children: Christopher Murray, Laurie Elizabeth. BS in Engring., Stanford U., 1967, MS in Engring.-Econ. Systems EEP, 1968; PhD in Bioengring., U. Calif., San Diego, 1977; MD, U. Calif., San Francisco, 1978. Diplomate Nat. Bd. Med. Examiners Am. BD. Pathology. Resident dept. medicine UCLA, 1978-79, resident dept. neurology, 1979-80; resident dept. lab. medicine U. Wash., Seattle, 1980-81, chief resident dept. lab. medicine, 1981-82, cardiopulmonary-bioengring. and clin. chemistry researcher, 1982-83; asst. prof. pathology U. Calif., Davis, 1983-87, assoc. prof., 1987-93, prof., dir. clin. chemistry, faculty biomed. engring., 1993—, dir. point-of-care testing ctr for tchg. and rsch., 1995—. Vis. prof. and Lilly scholar, 1990; numerous sci. cons., nat. and internat. speaker, invited lectr. Editor: Handbook of Clinical Automation Robotics and Optimization, 1996, Principles and Practice of Point-of-Care Testing, 2002; editl. bd. mem., contbr. numerous articles to profl. and sci. jours.; editor, author various monographs, video, audio and internet prodns. Recipient awards, honors and rsch. grants including Bank Am. Fine Arts award, 1963, Millberry Art award, 1970, Nat. Rsch. Svc. award Nat. Heart, Lung and Blood Inst., 1972-77, Young Investigator award Acad. Clin. Lab. Physicians and Scientists, 1982, 83, Nuclear Magnetic Resonance award U. Calif., Davis, 1984-88; S.A. Pepper Collegiate scholar, 1963; fellow Stanford U., 1967-68, Internat. scholar MOP, Venezuela, 1967, NIH fellowship, 1970, Highest Honor Calif. Scholarship Fedn.; grantee Am. Heart Assn., U. Calif., Davis, Lawrence Livermore Nat. Lab., others. scholar, Fulbright Found. Thailand, 2003-04 Mem.: Nat. Acad. Clin. Biochemistry, Mu Alpha Theta, Phi Kappa Phi, Sigma Xi. Avocations: trumpet, photography, art, outdoor sports.

KOST, WAYNE L. business executive; b. Chgo., Feb. 8, 1951; m. Denice Lee Eslinger, Nov. 24, 1979. BS, Northwestern U., 1973; M.P.A., Syracuse U., 1974. Adminstrv. asst. Chgo. Crime Commn., 1973; staff asso. Va. Mcpl. League, Richmond, 1975-77; dir. inst. affairs Am. Public Works Assn., Chgo., 1977-79; exec. dir. Am. Soc. Quality Control, Milw., 1980-82; sr. v.p. Philip Crosby Assocs., Winter Park, Fla., 1982-85; mng. dir. Crosby Assocs. Internat., Brussels, 1985-87, dir. Can. Region Winter Park, 1987-89, pres. Ams. div., 1989-95; CEO Internat. Computer Negotiations, Inc., Winter Park, 1995-97; pres., CEO, Philip Crosby Assocs. II, Inc., Winter Park, Fla., 1997—. Lectr. public adminstrn. Golden Gate U., 1976-78 Bd. dirs. Nat. Council YMCAs, 1970-73, Ill. Commn. on Children, 1969-73; chmn. Gov.'s Com. on Age of Majority, 1972. Gov.'s fellow, 1972 Mem. Am. Soc. Assn. Execs., Nat. Soc. YMCA Youth Govs. Office: PO Box 2687 Winter Park FL 32790-2687

KOSTECKE, B. WILLIAM, utilities executive; b. Caro, Mich., Aug. 1, 1925; s. Steve and Stella (Telewiek) K.; m. Lo Rayne M. Smith, Mar. 25, 1950; children: Diane, Keith. BS, U.S. Mcht. Marine Acad., 1947, Mich. State U., 1951. Controller Miller Brewing Co., Milw., 1963-66, treas., chief financial officer, 1966-70, pres., 1970-72; v.p., treas., dir. Wis. Gas Co., Milw., 1972-88; v.p., treas., sec., dir. WICOR, Inc., Milw., 1980-88. Gen. chmn. Milw. Nat. Alliance Businessmen, 1972. Recipient Dean Mellencamp award U. Wis., Milw., 1967, Outstanding Profl. Achievement award Kings Point Alumni Assn., 1972 Mem. Financial Execs. Inst. Clubs: Blue Mound Golf and Country. Home: 10200 W Bluemound Rd # 132 Wauwatosa WI 53226-4371

KOSTECKI, MARTIN PAUL, industrial engineer; b. St. Louis, Feb. 21, 1944; s. William Valentine and Anna Bernadette (Smugala) Kostecki; m. Mary Jacqueline Davis, Aug. 29, 1970; children: Christina, Daniel, Timothy. Cert. Indsl. Mgmt., Washington U., St. Louis, 1970, BS in Indsl. Mgmt., 1971; MS in Indsl. Adminstrn., Purdue U., 1972. Mgr. indsl. engirng. Wagner Electric Co., St. Louis, 1972-73; dir. indsl. engring. Combustion Engring., St. Louis, 1974-79; v.p. ops. Colt Industries, Inc., St. Louis, 1980-81; dir. engring. Food Ctr. Stores, St. Louis, 1981-82; sr. dir. ops. svcs. ConAgra, Inc., Omaha, 1982—2001; bus. cons. Nebr. Bus. Devel. Ctr., 2001—. Advisor Trend Mfg., Chesterfield, Mo., 1978-82; cons. Futura Coatings, Florissant, Mo., 1980-84. Author: (manuals) Regression Used in Production Standards, 1977, Forecasting Grocery Checkout Activity, 1981; editor: (manual) G.E. Regrssion Analysis Model, 1974. Corp. USMC, 1961-64. Mem. Am. Legion, Oddfellows Club (sec. 1970), Olympia Soccer Club (pres. 1991). Roman Catholic. Avocations: coaching soccer, mentoring youth, fitness. Home: 1217 N 123rd St Omaha NE 68154-1415

KOSTEL, LAURA EVERITT, social worker; b. Des Moines, Dec. 24, 1934; d. Sibley Ferry and Etta Elizabeth (Schoan) Everitt; m. Harry James Kostel, June 14, 1958; children: Laura Julia, George Everitt. BA, William and Mary Coll., 1955; M Social Work, Norfolk State U., 1981. Social worker, family therapist, Hampton, Va., 1981—. Vol. Peninsula Council on Domestic Violence, Hampton, 1981—. Mem. Nat. Assn. Social Workers, Va. Council Social Welfare, Jr. League of Hampton Rds. (trea., v.p.). Office: 2211 W Queen St Hampton VA 23666-3144

KOSTELANETZ, BORIS, lawyer; b. St. Petersburg, Russia, June 16, 1911; came to U.S., 1920, naturalized, 1925; s. Nachman and Rosalia (Dimschetz) K.; m. Ethel Cory, Dec. 18, 1938; children: Richard Cory, Lucy Cory. B.C.S., N.Y. U., 1933, BS, 1936; JD magna cum laude, St. John's U., 1936, LL.D. (hon.), 1981. CPA N.Y.; bar: N.Y. 1936. With Price, Waterhouse & Co., C.P.A.'s, N.Y.C., 1934-37; asst. U.S. atty. So. Dist. N.Y.; also confidential asst. to U.S. atty, 1937-43; spl. asst. to atty. gen. U.S., 1943-46; chief war frauds sect. Dept. Justice, 1945-46; spl. counsel com. investigate crime in interstate commerce U.S. Senate, 1950-51; ptnr. Kostelanetz Ritholz Tigue & Fink, N.Y.C., 1946-89, of counsel, 1990-94, Kostelanetz & Fink, N.Y.C., 1994—. Instr. acctg. N.Y. U., 1937-47, adj. prof. taxation, 1947-69; Mem. com. on character and fitness Appellate div. Supreme Ct. N.Y., 1st dept., 1974—, chmn., 1985-98. Author: (with L. Bender) Criminal Aspects of Tax Fraud Cases, 1957, 2d edit., 1968, 3d edit., 1980; Contbr. articles to legal, accounting and tax jours. Chmn. Kefauver for Pres. Com. N.Y. State, 1952. Recipient Meritorious Svc. award NYU, 1954, John T. Madden Meml. award, 1969, Pietas medal St. John's U., 1961, medal of honor, 1983, James Madison award, 1988, Torch of Learning award Am. Friends of Hebrew U. Law Sch., 1979, N.Y.U. Presdl. citation, 1990, N.Y. State Bar Assn. Fifty-Yr. Lawyer award, 1990, ABA Sect. Taxation Distinguished Svc. award, 1999. Fellow Am. Coll. Trial Lawyers, Am. Coll. Tax Counsel, Am. Bar Found.; mem. ABA (coun. sect. taxation 1978-81, ho. of dels. 1984-89), Fed. Bar Assn., Internat. Bar Assn., Soc. King's Inn, Ireland (hon. bencher 1995), N.Y. State Bar Assn., N.Y. State CPAs, N.Y. County Lawyers Assn. (v.p. 1966-69, pres. 1969-71, bd. dirs. 1958-64, 66-69, 71-74, chmn. judiciary com. 1965-69), Assn. of Bar of City of N.Y., NYU Sch. Commerce Alumni Assn. (pres. 1951-52), NYU Alumni Fedn. (pres. 1989-92), St. John's U. Law Sch. Alumni Assn. (pres. 1955-57), India House. Home: 37 Washington Sq W New York NY 10011-9181 Office: Kostelanetz & Fink 530 5th Ave Fl 22 New York NY 10036-5101

KOSTELANETZ, RICHARD, writer, media and visual artist; b. N.Y., May 14, 1940; s. Boris and Ethel (Cory) K. AB with honors, Brown U., 1962; postgrad. (Fulbright scholar), King's Coll., U. London, 1964-65; MA, Columbia U., 1966. Program assoc. thematic studies John Jay Coll. CUNY, 1972-73; sr. staff Ind. U. Writers' Conf., 1976; vis. prof. English and Am. studies U. Tex. at Austin, 1977; vis. prof. of theater Hunter Coll., CUNY, 2002; guest Mishkenot Sha'ananim, Jerusalem, 1979, 86, DAAD Berliner Kunstlerprogramm, 1981-83; master artist Atlantic Ctr. for the Arts, 2001. Co-propr. Assembling Press, 1970-82; lit. dir. The Future Press, 1976—; propr. Wordsand Music (ASCAP), 1982—; Archae Editions, 1978— guest artist WXXI-FM, Rochester, 1975, 76, Synapse, Syracuse U., 1975, Cabin Creek Ctr. for Work and Environ. Studies, 1978, Electronic Music Studio of Stockholm, 1981, 83, 84, 86, 88, Bklyn. Coll. Ctr. for Computer Music, 1984, Dennis Gabor Lab. Mus. of Holography, 1985, 89, Exptl. TV Lab., Owego, N.Y., 1985, 86, 87, 89, 90, 91, Real Art Ways, 1988, Film/Video Arts, 1989. Author: Music of Today, 1967, The Theatre of Mixed Means, 1968, 81, Master Minds: Portraits of Contemporary American Artists & Intellectuals, 1969, Visual Language, 1970, In the Beginning, 1971, The End of Intelligent Writing, 1974; 2d edit. as Literary Politics in Am, 1977; I Articulations/Short Fictions, 1974, Recyclings, vol. 1, 1974, complete text, 1984, Openings & Closings, 1975, Extrapolate, 1975, Come Here, 1975, Modulations, 1975, Portraits from Memory, 1975, Constructs, 1976, Rain Rains Rain, 1976, Numbers: Poems and Stories, 1976, Numbers Two, 1977, Illuminations, 1977, One Night Stood, 1977, Grants & the Future of Literature, 1978, Constructs Two, 1978, Tabula Rasa, 1978, Inexistences, 1978, Wordsand, 1978, Twenties in the Sixties, 1979, "The End" Appendix, 1979, "The End" Essentials, 1979, And So Forth, 1979, Exhaustive Parallel Intervals, 1979, More Short Fictions, 1980, Metamorphosis in Arts, 1980, The Old Poetries and the New, 1981, Autobiographies, 1981, Reincarnations, 1982, Turfs/Arenas/Fields/Pitches, 1983, American Imaginations, 1983, Epiphanies, 1983, Autobiographien New York Berlin, 1986, Prose Pieces/After Texts, 1987, The Old Fictions and the New, 1987, The Grants-Fix, 1987, Conversing with Cage, 1988, rev. edit., 2002, On Innovative Music(ian)s, 1989, Unfinished Business, 1990, The New Poetries and Some Olds, 1991, Politics in the African-American Novel, 1991, Constructs Three, 1991, Constructs Four, 1991, Constructs Five, 1991, Constructs Six, 1991, Fifty Untitled Constructivist Fictions, 1991, Intermix, 1991, Flipping, 1991, Published Encomia, 1991, Solos, Duets, Trios & Choruses, 1991, On Innovative Art(ist)s, 1992, A Dictionary of the Avant-Gardes, 1993, 2d edit., 1999, Wordworks: Poems New & Selected, 1993, On Innovative Performance(s), 1994, One Million Words of Booknotes 1958-1993, 1996, Minimal Fictions, 1994, Crimes of Culture, 1995, Fillmore East: Recollections of Rock Theater Twenty-Five Years After, 1995, Radio Writings, 1996, Openings, 1997, Thirty Years of Critical Engagements with John Cage, 1997. An ABC of Contemporary Reading, 1995, John Cage (Ex)plain(ed), 1996, 3-Element Stories, 1998, Vocal Shorts: Collected Performance Texts, 1998, Which Witch?, 1999, Political Essays, 1999, 3 Canadian Geniuses, 2001, More Wordworks, 2003, 35 Years of Visible Writing, 2003, More Opening and Closings, 2003, SoHo: The Rise and Fall of an Artists Colony, 2003, numerous others, works included in various anthologies; editor, contbr.: On Contemporary Literature, 1964, 69, The New American Arts, 1965, Twelve from the Sixties, 1967, The Young American Writers, 1967, Beyond Left & Right: Radical Thought for Our Times, 1968, Imaged Words & Worded Images, 1970, Moholy-Nagy, 1970, 91, John Cage, 1970, 91, Possibilities of Poetry, 1970, Social Speculations, 1971, Human Alternatives: Visions for Us Now, 1971, Future's Fictions, 1971, Seeing Through Shuck, 1972, Breakthrough Fictioneers, 1973, The Edge of Adaptation, 1973, Essaying Essays, 1975, Language & Structure, 1975, Younger Critics in North America, 1976, Esthetics Contemporary, 1977, 88, Assembling Assembing, 1978, Visual Literature Criticism, 1979, Text-Sound Texts, 1980, Scenarios, 1980, The Yale Gertrude Stein, 1980, A Critical Assembling, 1980, Aural Literature Criticism, 1981, American Writing Today, 1981, The Avant-Garde Tradition in Literature, 1982, Gertrude Stein Advanced, 1990, Merce Cunningham, 1992, 98, John Cage: Writer, 1993, Writings AboutJohn Cage, 1993, 2000, Nicolas Slonimsky: The First 100 Years, 1994, A Portable Baker's Biographical Dictionary of Musicians, 1995, AnOther E.E. Cummings, 1998, Writing on Glass, 1997, Classic Essays on 20th Century Music, 1996, A B.B. King Companion, 1997; A Frank Zappa Companion, 1997, Virgin Thomson: A Reader, 2002, The Gertrude Stein Reader, 2002, An Aaron Copland Reader, 2003, others; composer: Praying to the Lord, 1977, 81, Invocations, 1981, 84, The Gospels/Die Evangelien, 1982, The Eight Nights of Hanukah, 1983, New York City, internat. version, 1984, Am. version, 1987, A Special Time, 1985, Baseball: Americas' Game, 1988, 2nd edit., 1998, Onomatopoeia, 1988, Kaddish, 1990, Acoustic Fiction I: Ululation, 1992, No, I'm Not Richard Kostelanetz, 1993; producer numerous audiotapes, films, videotapes, extended radio features for stas. in Australia, Fed. Republic Germany, Sweden, U.S.; filmmaker: (with others) Openings & Closings, 1978, Constructivist Fictions, 1978, Epiphanies, 1981-94, Ein Verlorenes Berlin/A Berlin Lost/Berlin Perdu/Ett Forlorat Berlin/El Berlin Perdido/Berlin Sche-Einena Jother, 1984-88 (prizewinner Ann Arbor, Mich., Film Festival); video art: Three Prose Pieces, 1975, Kinetic Writings, 1989, Video Strings, 1989, Stringsieben, 1989, Turfs/Grounds/Lawns, 1989, Invocations, 1988, Seductions, 1988, The Gospels Abridged, 1988, Relationships, 1988, Two Erotic Videotapes, 1988, Two Sacred Texts, 1988, Partitions, 1986, Onomatopoeia, 1989, Kaddish, 1991, Openings & Closings, 1975, Video Writing, 1987, Declaration of Independence, 1979, Epiphanies, 1980, Home Movies Reconsidered, 1992, Americas' Game. 2001; contbg. editor: Pushcart Prize; writer, narrator: Camera Three, WCBS-TV, 1974; co-founder, compiler Assembling, 1970-82; co-pub., editor: Precisely, A Critical Jour., 1977—; contbr. articles, poems, revs., photographs and essays to mags.; numerous group exhbns. visual poetry, visual fiction, audiotapes, videotapes, films, holograms and numerical art; comprehensive exhbn.: Wordsand, at Simon Fraser U., U. Alta., Cornell Coll., Vassar Coll., U. N.D., Calif. State U., Bakersfield, Dade County C.C., Miami, Fla., 1978-81; retrospectives of video art: Anthology Film Archives, 1994, Bumbershoot, Seattle, 1991, Festival de la Baite, Geneva, 1989, U. of S.C., 1978. Woodrow Wilson fellow, 1962-63, Pulitzer fellow in critical writing, 1965-66, fellow Guggenheim Meml. Found., 1967-68, Fund for Investigative Journalism, 1980, Vogelstein Found., 1980, Internat. fellow Columbia U., 1963-64, Editors fellow CCLM, 1983, Ivri-Nasawi fellow, 2000—; Visual Arts grantee Nat. Endowment of Arts, 1976, 78, 79, 85, 86, 90, Media Arts grantee Nat. Endowment of Arts, 1981, 82, 84, 91; N.Y. State Regents scholar, 1963-64, Am. Pub. Radio Program Fund, 1984; Pollock-Krasner fellow, 2001; recipient Standard award ASCAP, 1983-92, 94— (annually). Mem. Nat. Coalition Ind. Scholars, Internat. Assn. Art Critics, Soc. for Origination of Horspiel in Am., Phi Beta Kappa. Address: PO Box 454 Prince St Rockaway Beach NY 11693 *To do what has not been done in several domains and in the course of that adventure to discover new possibilities in art, in writing, and in myself.*

KOSTELNIK, MICHAEL CHARLES, retired air force major general; b. Harlingen, Tex., May 15, 1946; s. Michael and Nita Louise K.; m. Barbara Lynn Brychta, Dec. 23, 1966; 1 child, Khristine Lynn Kostelnik Carlson. BS in Mech. Engring., Tex. A&M U., 1969; MS in Indsl. and Mgmt. Engring., U. Iowa, 1970; grad., USAF Test Pilot Sch., 1977; post grad., U. Fla., 1980; grad., Nat. Def. U., 1981, USAF Instrument Pilot Instrs. Sch., Indsl. Coll. of Armed Forces, 1986, Def. Sys. Mgmt. Coll., 1989; grad. sr. exec. devel. program, U. NH, 1993. Commd. 2nd lt. USAF, 1969, advanced through grades to maj. gen., 1994; pilot trainee Vance AFB, Okla., 1970-71; with 18th Tactical Reconnaissance Squadron, Shaw AFB, SC, 1971-72; aircraft comdr. 10th Tactical Reconnaissance Wing, Alconbury, England, 1972-75; ctr. test project pilot 4485th Test Squadron, Tactical Air Warfare Ctr., Eglin AFB, Fla., 1975-76; squadron ops. officer 3246th Test Wing, Eglin AFB, 1977-81; tactical fighter requirements officer Office Dep. Chief of Staff for Rsch., Devel. and Acquisition, Washington, 1981-85; dir. combined test forces Edwards AFB, Calif., 1986-87; comdt. USAF Test Pilot Sch., Edwards AFB, 1987-89; dep. program dir. F-16 Sys. Program Office, Wright-Patterson AFB, Ohio, 1989-91; program dir. Short Range Attack Missile II, SRAM-Tactical Sys. Program Office Aero. Sys. Divsn., Air Force Sys. Command, Wright-Patterson AFB, 1991-92; First Sys. Program dir., Aircraft Sys. Program Office Aero. Sys. Ctr., Air Force Material Command, Wright-Patterson AFB, 1992-93; vice comdr. Warner Robins Air Logistics Ctr., Robins AFB, Ga., 1993-94; dir. spl. programs Office Under Sec. of Def., The Pentagon, Washington, 1994-95; dir. plans Hdqs. Air Force Materiel Command, Wright-Patterson AFB, Ohio, 1995—97; comdr. Air Force Devel. Test Ctr. Air Force Materiel Command, Eglin AFB, Fla., 1998—99, comdr. Air Armanent Ctr., 1999—2002; apptd. mem. Sr. Exec. Svc. De. Assoc. Adminstr. for Space Shuttle & Internat. Space St., NASA; dep. assoc. adminstr. for space shuttle and internat. space sta. Hdqs. NASA, Washington; vice commdr. Air Force Materiel Command, Wright Paterson AFB. Assoc. editor Whispering Wind, 1992—; contbr. articles to profl. mags. Decorated Def. Disting. Svc. medal, Air Force Disting. Svc. medal with oak leaf cluster, Legion of Merit, Meritorious Svc. medal with two oak leaf clusters, Air Force Commendation medal with oak leaf cluster; recipient Marie Radice award Am. Indianist Soc., 1985, Les Bircher award, 1987, Nat. Def. Indsl. Assoc. gold medal, 2001, Air Force Assoc. Jerry Forman award, 2001, NAACP Cleophs McIntosh Armed Svcs. award, 2000, NDIA Moseley Munitions Mgmt. award, 2000, NASA Outstanding Leadership award, 2002. Mem. Soc. Experimental Test Pilots (sect. chmn.), Order of Daedalions. Roman Catholic. Avocations: golf, alpine skiing, Native American crafts and culture, fishing. Office: NASA 300 E Str SW Washington DC 20546

KOSTELNY, ALBERT JOSEPH, JR., lawyer; b. Phila., July 11, 1951; s. Albert Joseph and Margaret (Naile) K. BA, U. Pa., 1973, MA, 1974; JD, Fordham U., 1979. Bar: N.Y. 1980, U.S. Dist. Ct. (so. dist.) N.Y. 1983, U.S. Ct. Claims 1983, U.S. Supreme Ct. 1983, U.S. Ct. Internat. Trade 1985, U.S. Ct. Appeals (2d cir.) 1985. Atty. N.Y. State Divsn. Human Rights, N.Y.C., 1980-81, sr. atty., 1981-89, acting chief adminstrv. law judge, 1989-91, adjudication counsel to commr., 1990-98, supr. atty., dir. prosecutions unit, 1998—2001, assoc. atty., 2001—. Mem. ABA, N.Y. State Bar Assn., N.Y. County Lawyers Assn., Assn. Trial Lawyers Am. Republican. Roman Catholic. Office: NY State Div Human Rights One Fordham Plz Bronx NY 10458-5871 E-mail: kostelna@nysnet.net.

KOSTEN, THOMAS R. psychiatrist, educator; b. Bklyn., Feb. 16, 1951; s. Richard Kosten; m. Therese Kosten, Aug. 12, 1978; children: Molly, Neal. MD, Cornell, N.Y., 1977. Lic. Psychiatry Am. Bd. Psychiatry And Neurology, 1984, Addiction Psychiatry Am. Bd. Of Psychiatry And Neurology, 1993. Chief of psychiatry VA Conn., West Haven, Conn., 1996—2000; prof. Yale U., New Haven, 1983—. Congl. fellow, u.s. ho. of rep. Ho. Subcommittee on Human Resources (Christopher Shays, Chair), Washington, 1998—99. Recipient America's Top Drs., Second Edit.; Top Doctors: N.Y., Sixth Edit., Castle Connolly Med. Ltd., 2002. Fellow: Am. Acad. of Addiction Psychiatry (pres. 1998—2000). Achievements include research in 1993 Joel Elkes Internat. award for outstanding contrb. to Psychopharmacology, American Coll. of Neuropsychopharmacology 2000-on Sr. Scientist Award, Nat. Inst. on Drug Abuse. Avocations: tennis, ice skating. Office: VA Conn- Psychiatry 151D 950 Campbell Ave - Bldg 35 New Haven CT 06511

KOSTER, ELAINE LANDIS, publishing executive; b. N.Y.C. BA, Barnard Coll., 1962. Pres., pub. Dutton Signet, N.Y.C.; head Elaine Koster Literary Agy. LLC, N.Y.C. Office: Elaine Koster Literary Agy LLC 55 Central Park W Ste 6 New York NY 10023-6003

KOSTER, EMLYN HOWARD, geologist, educator; b. Suez Canal Zone, Egypt, Mar. 18, 1950; arrived in England, 1953, Canada, 1971, came to U.S., 1996; s. Douglas Albert and Dorothy Muriel (Roberts) Koster; m. Maryse Rémillard Koster, May 22, 1974; children: Véronique Justina, Simon Emlyn. BSC with spl. honours in Geology, U. Sheffield, Eng., 1971; PhD in Geology, U. Ottawa, 1977. Rsch. scientist terrain scis. divsn. Geological Survey of Can., Ottawa, 1973-74; cons. Geo-Analysis Ltd., Ottawa, 1975-76; asst. prof. dept. geology Concordia U., Montreal, Can., 1976-77; asst. prof. dept. geological scis. U. Saskatchewan, Saskatoon, Can., 1977-80; rsch. officer, project mgr. Alberta Geological Survey, Alberta Rsch. Coun., Edmonton, Can., 1980-86; dir. Royal Tyrrell Mus. of Palaeontology, Drumheller and Field Sta., Dinosaur Provincial Park, UNESCO World Heritage Site, Alberta, 1986-91; dir. gen. Ontario Sci. Centre, Agy. Govt. Ontario, Toronto, 1991-96; pres., CEO Liberty Sci. Ctr., N.J., 1996—. Mem. Challenger Ctr. for Space Sci. Edn., Va., 1993—2002, Can.-China Dinosaur Expdn. to Gobi Desert, China, 1987; vis. prof. U. Buenos Aires, 1988; pres. Geol. Assn. Can., 1996—97; mem. adv. com. Mus. Mgmt. Inst., Getty Leadership Inst., Calif., 1997—99; bd. dirs. Assn. Sci.-Tech. Ctrs., Washington, 1993—2001; v.p. Giant Screen Theatre Assn., Minn., 2003—; mem. Interdisciplinary Planning Com. for Liberty State Park, NJ, 1999—; Prin.-for-a-Day NY Pub. Schs., 2001; mem. sr. adv. bd. Flandrau Sci. Ctr., Ariz., 2002—; vis. prof. Inst. Marine and Coastal Studies, Rutgers U., NJ, 2002—; bd. dirs. Prosperity N.J.; mem. adv. coun. Met. Waterfront Alliance for N.Y. Harbor. Contbr. papers in sci. jours.; author numerous field guidebooks, book reviews; many interviews in field; internat. speaker at more than 125 sci. confs., assn. events, convs., workshops. Mem. leadership council UNA of the USA; advisor NJ Gov.'s Commn. on Victims Meml. to the World Trade Ctr. disaster, 2001; bd. dirs. Hudson County C. of C., 1997—, Save Ellis Island! Found., NJ, 2000—; mem. bd. regents St. Peter's Coll., NJ, 1998—2003. Decorated chevalier Ordre des Palmes Academiques (France); recipient Tracks award Can. Soc. Petroleum Engrs., 1984, John Cotton Dana award N.J. Assn. Mus., 2003. Fellow: Explorers Club; mem.: AAAS (com. on pub. awareness of sci. 2003—). Avocations: ecology, culture, tourism. Office: Liberty Sci Ctr Liberty State Pk 251 Phillip St Jersey City NJ 07305-4600

KOSTER, KIM RICHARD, anesthesiologist; b. Bottineau, N.D., Jan. 22, 1961; s. Richard A. and Alice (Neumann) K.; m. Lesa Ann Lohmoeller, Dec. 6, 1986; children: Ashley, Lynsey, Erick. BS, U. Kans., Lawrence, 1984; MD, U. Kans., Kansas City, 1991. Diplomate Am. Bd. Anesthesiology. Commd. 2d lt. USAF, 1987, advanced through grades to maj.; intern in internal medicine Wilford Hall Med. Ctr., Lackland AFB, Tex., 1991-92, resident in anesthesiology, 1992-95, staff anesthesiologist, 1995-99, asst. chmn. clin. affairs SAA, 1997-99; pvt. practice pediat. anesthesiologist, 1999—. Contbr. chpts. to books. Mem. AMA, Am. Soc. Anesthesiologists, Internat. Anesthesia Rsch. Soc., Tex. Soc. Anesthesiologists, Christian Med. and Dental Soc., Bexar County Med. Soc. Avocations: boating, bicycling. Office: 3838 Medical Dr Ste 204 San Antonio TX 78229 E-mail: KKoster@satx.rr.com.

KOSTERE, KIM MARTIN, psychologist, consultant; b. Detroit, Jan. 22, 1954; d. Walter Thomas and Shirley Marian (Goebel) K. BA, Mercy Coll., 1977; MA, Ctr. Humanistic Studies, Detroit, 1983; PsyS, Ctr. Humanistic Studies, 1986; PhD, Union Inst., Cin., 1989. Therapist Metro T.A.G., Livonia, Mich., 1978-81, Highland Waterford Ctr., Waterford, Mich., 1981-83; psychologist, v.p. substance abuse svcs. Square Lake Counseling Ctr., Bloomfield Hills, Mich., 1983-90; psychologist, co-dir. Counseling Ctr., P. C., Bloomfield Hills, Mich., 1991-99; cons., 1999—. Co-founder, dir. Ont. (Can.) NLP Inst., 1979-80; adj. faculty in psychology Edison C.C., Naples, Fla., 1999—, Capella U., Mpls. Author: A Brief Account of the Center for Humanistic Studies, 1987; co-author: Get the Results You Want, 1987, Maps, Models and the Structure of Reality, 1989, Utilizing the Metaphor: An Ericksonian/NLP Approach, 1992. Democrat. Roman Catholic. E-mail: kimk@cyberisle.com.

KOSTEREV, ANATOLIY A. research scientist; b. Semiluki, Voronezh Region, Russia, Sept. 7, 1962; arrived in U.S., 96; s. Anatoliy G. Kosterev and Tamara A. Zviagina; m. Yelena V. Shabanova, Oct. 11, 1988; children: Tatiana A. Kostereva, Maxim A. Grad., Moscow Inst. for Physics and Tech., 1985; PhD in Physics, Russian Acad. Scis., 1996. Rsch. scientist Inst. Spectroscopy, Russian Acad. Sci., Troitsk, Russia, 1985—98, Rice U., Houston, 1998—. Leading rsch. in quantum cascade lasers applications Rice U., Houston, 1998—. Contbr. articles to profl. jours. Mem.: Optical Soc. Am. Achievements include invention of quartz-enhanced photoacoustic spectroscopy. Office: Rice Univ 6100 S Main St MS 366 Houston TX 77005

KOSTICK, ALEXANDRA, ophthalmologist; BSc, MD, U. Man., Winnipeg, Can., 1990. Surg. intern St. Boniface Hosp./U. Man., Winnipeg, 1990-91; rsch. fellow in ocular pathology Storm Eye Inst./Med. U. S.C., Charleston, 1991-92; resident in ophthalmology U. Sask., Saskatoon, Can., 1992-95; fellow corneal diseases U. Mo., Columbia, 1995-96; practice ophthalmology specializing in cornea and external diseases, Ormond Beach, Palm Coast, Fla., 1996—. Contbr. articles to profl. jours. Fellow ACS, Am. Acad. Ophthalmology; mem. Am. Soc. Cataract and Refractive Surgeons, European Soc. Cataract and Refractive Surgeons, Royal Coll. Physicians and Surgeons Can., Castroviejo Corneal Soc., Paton Eye Bank Soc., Can. Ophthalmology Soc., Royal Acad. Dancing (London).

KOSTKA, ROBERT ANTON, artist, educator; b. Chgo., Sept. 11, 1928; s. Anton Miles and Marion Anna Kostka. BA,BS in Visual Design, Inst. Design, Chgo., 1951; MS in Art Edn., Ill. Inst. Tech., 1956. Art dir. WTTW/Chgo. Ednl. TV, 1956—67; prof. U. Ill., Chgo., 1967—69, U. Wis., Green Bay, 1967—70, U. Oreg., Eugene, 1970—77. Exhibitions include Brauer Mus. Art, Valparaiso, Ind., 1999, Rogue Valley Art Ctr., Medford, Oreg., 1992, Asian Arts, Ashland, Oreg., 1988, Mundelein Coll., Chgo., 1984, Tex. A&M U., College Station, 1974, Wurlitzer Found., Taos, N.Mex., 1980—85, Yaddo Found., Saratoga, N.Y., 1979, Ragdale Found., Lake Forest, Ill., 1989, JEGA Gallery, Ashland, Oreg., 1994, Meridian Gallery, San Francisco, 2001, Davis Gallery, Ashland, Oreg., 2001, Represented in permanent collections Mus. Contemporary Religious Art, St. Louis, Univ. Art Mus., U . Calif., Berkeley, Brauer Mus. Art, Valparaiso, Ind., Chgo. Hist. Soc., Harwood Mus. Art, Taos, 15 pvt. collections. Home and Studio: PO Box 1213 Ashland OR 97520-0041

KOSTKA, RONALD WAYNE, marketing consultant; b. Chgo., Sept. 13, 1931; s. James V. and Marie (Zvolanek) K.; m. Madonna Lou Miller, June 8, 1957 (div. Dec. 1980); children: Paul, Daniel, Jane; m. Irene Mary Harnett, Sept. 14, 1991. BS in journalism, U. Ill., Urbana, 1957. Reporter Champaign News Gazette, Champaign, Ill., 1956-57; copy editor Mpls. Tribune, Mpls., 1957-58; pub. rels. mgr. 3M Co., St. Paul, Minn., 1958-92; cons. mktg. Pub. Rel., Minnetonka, Minn., 1992—. Contbr. articles to profl. jours. Firearms safety instr. State of Minn., Minnetonka, 1967-77. Staff Sgt. USAF, 1951-55, Korea. Decorated Air medal (4 OLC), Purple Heart, Hwarang (Republic of Korea). Mem. DAV, Nat. Muzzle Loading Rifle Assn., NRA, Soc. of Profl. Jours. (cert 1957), Minnetonka Game & Fish Club. Avocations: canoeing, hunting, competitive skeet shooting. Home: 1004 Sunset Dr S Minnetonka MN 55305-1164

KOSTOFF, RONALD NEIL, aerospace scientist; b. Phila., Apr. 26, 1938; s. David and Fannie (Weisbrod) K. BSME, Drexel U., 1961; MA, Princeton U., 1963, PhD, 1967. Mem. tech. staff Bell Labs, Murray Hill, N.J., 1966-75; divsn. head Dept. Energy, Washington, 1975-83; dir. tech. assessment Office of Naval Rsch., Arlington, Va., 1983—. Editor Rsch. Evaluation, 1994, Scientometrics, 1996, Jour. Tech. Transfer, 1997; editl. bd. Scientometrics, 1995—, Jour. Tech. Transfer, 1996—; reviewer R&D Mgmt., 1993—, IEEE Trans. on Engring. Mgmt., 1996—; contbr. articles to profl. jours. Achievements include patent on database tomography for data mining; pioneered aerobraking subfield of orbit to orbit transfer; invented Wake Shield for high vacuum in low orbit. Home: 307 Yoakum Pky Alexandria VA 22304 Office: Office of Naval Rsch 800 N Quincy St Arlington VA 22217-0002 E-mail: kostofr@onr.navy.mil.

KOSTOULAS, IOANNIS GEORGIOU, physicist; b. Petra, Pierias, Greece, Sept. 12, 1936; came to the U.S., 1965, naturalized, 1984; s. Georgios Ioannou and Panagiota (Zarogiannis) K.; m. Katina Sioras Kay, June 23, 1979; 1 child, Alexandra. Diploma in physics, U. Thessoloniki, Greece, 1963; MA, U. Rochester, 1969, PhD, 1972; MS, U. Ala., 1977. Instr. U. Thessaloniki, 1963-65; tchg. asst. U. Ala., 1966-67, U. Rochester, 1967-68; guest jr. rsch. assoc. Brookhaven Nat. Lab., Upton, N.Y., 1968-72; rsch. physicist, lectr. UCLA, U. Calif.-San Diego, 1972-76; sr. rsch. assoc. Mich. State U., East Lansing, 1976-78, Fermi Nat. Accelerator Lab., Batavia, iLL., 1976-78; rsch. staff mem. MIT, Cambridge, 1978-80; sr. sys. engr., physicist Hughes Aircraft Co., El Segundo, Calif., 1980-86; sr. physisict electro-optics and space sensors Rockwell Internat. Corp., Downey, Calif., 1986-96, Boeing Corp., Downey, 1996-98; scientist Raytheon Sys. Co., El Segundo, Calif., 1998-2000; engring. specialist Northrop-Grumman Corp., Azusa, Calif., 2000—. Contbr. articles to profl. jours. With Greek Army, 1961-63. Rsch. grantee U. Rochester, 1968-72. Mem. Am. Phys. Soc., N.Y. Acad. Scis., Internat. Soc. Optical Engring., Pan Macedonian Assn., Sigma Pi Sigma, Hellenic U. Club, Ahepa Lodge. Home: 2404 Marshallfield Ln # B Redondo Beach CA 90278-4406 Office: Northrop-Grumman Corp Bldg 59 Dept 8510 1100 W Hollyvale St Azusa CA 91702-3305 E-mail: katinakay@earthlink.net.

KOSTREVA, MICHAEL MARTIN, mathematics educator; b. Pitts., May 9, 1948; s. Leonard Bernard and Leona Agnes (Staublin) K.; m. Barbara Louise Hatfield, July 17, 1971; children: Mark, Anna, Julia. BA, Clarion State Coll., 1971; MS, Rensselaer Poly. Inst., 1973, PhD, 1976. Asst. prof. U. Maine, Orono, 1976-78; rsch. scientist Gen. Motors Rsch. Labs., Warren, Mich., 1978-84; prin. mem. tech. staff GTE Labs., Inc., Waltham, Mass., 1984-86; mem. tech. staff Alphatech, Inc., Burlington, Mass., 1986; assoc. prof. Clemson (S.C.) U., 1986-89, prof., 1989—. Cons. Gen. Motors Corp., Troy, Mich., 1987—, Gillette Rsch. Inst., Gaithersburg, Md., 1990—; pres. Systematica Inc. of Clemson, 1989—. Contbr. articles to Math. Programming, Ops. Rsch., Internat. Jour. Game Theory. Mem. Informs, Soc. for Indsl. and Applied Math. Office: Clemson U Dept Math Scis Clemson SC 29634-0001

KOSTRZEWA, RICHARD MICHAEL, pharmacology educator; b. Trenton, NJ, July 22, 1943; s. John Walter and Wladyslosa (Wnuk) K.; m. Florence Agnes Palmer, Sept. 4, 1965; children: Theresa, Richard, Joseph, Maria, Krystyna, Thomas, John Palmer, Francis, Roseanna, Monica. BS, Phila. Coll. Pharmacy and Sci., 1965, MS, 1967; PhD, U. Pa., 1971. Rsch. pharmacologist VA Hosp., New Orleans, 1971-75; asst. prof. pharmacology Tulane Med. Ctr., New Orleans, 1972-76; asst. prof. physiology La. State U. Med. Ctr., New Orleans, 1975-78; assoc. prof., then prof. pharmacology East Tenn. State U. Med. Sch., Johnson City, 1978—. Vis. prof. Silesian Acad. Medicine, Katowice, Poland, 1997—. Author: Pharmacology, 1995, Highly Selective Neurotoxins, 1998; editor-in-chief Neurotoxicity Rsch., mem. editl. bd. Peptides, 1980—2000, Nutritional Neurosci., 1997—, Amino Acids, 1998—, Jour. Neural Transon, 2003—; contbr. articles to profl. jours. Recipient Rsch. award, East Tenn. State U. Found., 1981. Fellow: Japan Soc. Promotion of Sci.; mem.: Neurotoxicity Soc. (pres. 2001—03, past pres. 2003—), Internat. Brain Rsch. Orgn., Soc. for Neurosci., Am. Soc. Pharmacology. Roman Catholic. Achievements include research in NIMH project on tardive dyskinesia; Scottish Rite project on schizophrenia; NINDS project on Parkinson's disease. Office: East Tenn State Univ PO Box 70577 Johnson City TN 37614-1708 E-mail: kostrzew@etsu.edu.

KOSTYO, JACK LAWRENCE, physiology educator; b. Elyria, Ohio, Oct. 1, 1931; s. Louis and Matilda (Thomasko) K.; m. Shirlianne Guth, June 10, 1953; children: Cecile A., Louis C. AB, Oberlin Coll., 1953; PhD, Cornell U., 1957; MD (hon.), U. Göteborg, 1978. NRC fellow Harvard Med. Sch., Boston, 1957-59; asst. prof., then prof. physiology Duke U., 1959-68; prof., chmn. dept. physiology Emory U., Atlanta, 1968-79; prof. physiology U. Mich. Med. Sch., Ann Arbor, 1979-94, chmn. dept. physiology, 1979-85, active prof. emeritus in internal medicine, 1995—; assoc. dir. Mich. Diabetes Rsch. and Tng. Ctr., Ann Arbor, 1986-97, dir. grants program, 1997—. Mem. endocrinology study sect. NIH/USPHS, 1967-71, internat. and coop. projects study sect., 1992-96; mem. physiology test com. Nat. Bd. Med. Examiners, 1974-77, mem. comprehensive part II com., 1986-91, U.S. Med. Licensure Examination Step 2 Com., 1990-91. Editor in chief Endocrinology, 1978-82; sect. editor Ann. Rev. Physiology, 1982-86; mem. editorial bd. Growth Regulation, 1990-97; contbr. articles to profl. jours. Mem. adv. bd. Searle Scholars. Recipient Lederle Med. Faculty award, 1961, Ernst Oppenheimer Meml. award Endocrine Soc., 1969 Mem. Endocrine Soc. (editl. bd., coun., chmn. awards com.), Am. Physiol. Soc. (editl. bd., coun., chmn. standing com. on edn., mem. coun. of endocrinology and metabolism sect., chmn. endocrinology and metabolism sect. 1990-91, rep. to Coun. Acad. Socs. of Assn. Am. Med. Colls., mem. AAAS sect. on med. scis., Editor Handbook of Physiology sect. 7, Endocrinology, vol. 5), Soc. for Exptl. Biology and Medicine (editl. bd.), Internat. Union Physiol. Scis. (commn. on med. edn.), Assn. Chmn. Depts. Physiology (pres. 1979, coun.), Am. Diabetes Assn., Coun. Acad. Socs. (adminstrv. bd. 1983-86), Sigma Xi. Home: 1100 Highway 98 E Unit B304 Destin FL 32541-8516 Office: Mich Diabetes Rsch-Tng Ctr U Mich Med Sch 1331 E Ann St 0580 Ann Arbor MI 48109 E-mail: jkostyo@umich.edu.

KOSUB, JAMES ALBERT, lawyer; b. San Antonio, Jan. 8, 1948; s. Ernest Pete and Lonie (Doege) K.; divorced; 1 child, James Jr.; m. Jane Stevens Cain, Aug. 11, 1979; children: Kathryn, Nicholas (dec.). Student, East Carolina U., 1970, San Antonio Coll., 1971-72; BS, SW Tex. State U., 1974; JD, St. Mary's U., San Antonio, 1977. Bar: Tex. 1978, U.S. Dist. Ct. (we. dist.) Tex. 1980, U.S. Ct. Appeals (5th cir.) 1981, U.S. Dist. Ct. (so. dist.) 1986, U.S. Supreme Ct. 1988, U.S. Dist. Ct. (no. and ea. dists.) Tex. 1990. Ptnr. Kosub & Langlois, San Antonio, 1978-79, Kosub, Langlois & Van Cleave, San Antonio, 1979-83; mng. ptnr. Kosub & Langlois, San Antonio, 1983-86; sr. ptnr. James A. Kosub, San Antonio, 1986-94; pvt. practice Eldorado, Tex., 1994—2002; sr. ptnr. Kosub & Griffin, 2002—. Bd. dirs. Judson Ind. Sch. Bd. Trustees, Converse, Tex., 1975-81, Bexar County Fedn. Sch. Bds., San Antonio, 1977-80. Sgt. USMC, 1966-70. Fellow Tex. Bar Found., San Antonio Bar Found.; mem. ABA (EEOC liaison com. San Antonio chpt. 1987-93), San Antonio Bar Assn. (bd. dirs. 1990-92, sec. 1992-93), Fed. Bar Assn. 5th Cir. Bar Assn., Coll. State Bar Tex., State Bar Tex. (coun. labor and employment sect. 1993-97, sec. 1997-98, vice chair 1998-99, chair 1999-2000), Schleicher County C. of C. (pres. 1998-2000), Schleicher County Lions Club (v.p. 2003—). Episcopalian. Avocations: carpentry, gardening, golf. Office: 105 S Main Eldorado TX 76936-0460

KOSZARSKI, RICHARD, film historian, writer; b. N.Y.C., Dec. 18, 1947; s. Casimir and Janina (Orzechowski) K.; m. Diane Kaiser, 1975; 1 child, Eva. BA, Hofstra U., 1969; MA, NYU, 1974, PhD, 1977. Lectr. Sch. Visual Arts, N.Y.C., 1974-84, NYU, 1976, 97, Columbia U., N.Y.C., 1980-86; historian Astoria Motion Picture & TV Found., N.Y.C., 1977-81; curator of film Am. Mus. Moving Image, N.Y.C., 1981-92, exhbn. curator Masterpieces of Moving Image Tech., 1988, head collections and exhbns., 1992-96, sr. historian, 1996-97; assoc. prof. English Rutgers U., 1998—. Author: (books) Hollywood Directors 1914-40, 1976, The Rivals of D.W. Griffith, 1976, Hollywood Directors 1941-76, 1977, Universal Pictures: 65 Years, 1977, The Man You Loved to Hate, 1983, The Astoria Studio and Its Fabulous Films, 1983, An Evening's Entertainment: The Age of the Silent Feature Picture, 1915-1928, 1990, Von: The Life and Films of Erich von Stroheim, 2001; (documentary films) Roger Corman, Hollywood's Wild Angel, 1978, The Man You Loved to Hate, 1979; editor-in-chief Film History, An Internat. Jour., N.Y.C., 1986—. Mem. Ft. Lee Film Commn. Rsch. associateship Am. Film Inst., 1971, 72; rsch. grantee Am. Coun. Learned Socs., 1978; recipient Nat. Film Book award Nat. Film Soc., 1984, award Prix Jean Mitry, 1991; NEH fellow, 2003. Mem. Polish Inst. Arts and Scis., Antique Wireless Assn., Domitor, Assn. Moving Image Archivists.

KOSZEWSKI, BOHDAN JULIUS, retired internist, medical educator; b. Warsaw, Dec. 17, 1918; Came to U.S., 1952; s. Mikolaj and Helen (Lubienski) K.; children Mikolaj, Joseph, Wanda Marie, Andrzej Bohdan. MD, U. Zurich, Switzerland, 1946; MS, Creighton U., 1956. Resident in pathology U. Zurich, 1944-46, resident in internal medicine, 1946-50, assoc. in medicine, 1950-52; intern St. Mary's Hosp., Hoboken, N.J., 1953; practice medicine specializing in internal medicine Omaha, 1956-90. Mem. staff St. Joseph's Hosp., Mercy and Meth. Hosps.; instr. internal medicine Creighton U., 1956-57, asst. prof., 1957-65, assoc. prof. internal medicine, 1965-90; cons. hematology Omaha VA Hosp., 1957-90. Author: Prognosis in Diabetic Coma, 1952; contbr. numerous articles to profl. jours. Served with Polish Army, 1940-45. Fellow ACP, Am. Coll. Angiology; mem. AAAS, Am. Fedn. Clin. Research, Internat. Soc. Hematology, Polish-Am. Congress Nebr. (pres. 1960-68, 82-92). Home: Remington Hts 12606 W Dodge Rd Omaha NE 68154-2857

KOTA, VENKATA RANGAIAH, research scientist, researcher; s. Parijatha and Venkata Krishnaiah Kota; m. Pavithrini Pullumati, June 13, 1993; children: Rasagnya, Nikhil Krishna. M in pharm. sci., Birla Inst. of Tech., 1990—92. Sr. scientist Ranbaxy Rsch. Labs, Gurgaon, India, 1993—99; scientist Pentech Pharm., Inc, Wheeling, Ill., 1999—2000; sr. scientist Ivax Pharm., Inc, Northvale, NJ, 2000—. Cultural sec. in sch. Annamalai U., Annamalai Nagar, India, 1986—90. Fellow: Inst. of Chemists (India) (hon.); mem.: Am. Assn. of Pharm. Sciences (assoc.). Achievements include research in novel drug delivery models development. Home: 103 17th Ave Elmwood Park NJ 07407 Office: Ivax Pharmaceutical Inc 140 Legrand Ave Northvale NJ 07407 Office Fax: 201-767-8206. Personal E-mail: rangaiahkv@hotmail.com. E-mail: venkata_kota@ivax.com.

KOTAMARTHI, V. RAO, meteorologist; b. Kovvur, Andhar Pradesh, India, June 4, 1963; arrived in U.S., 2001, naturalized; s. S. and L. Kotamarthi; m. Sujatha Karoor, Dec. 12, 1989; children: Janavi, Anjali. PhD, U. of Iowa, 1991. Sr. rsch. assoc. Atmospheric and Environ. Rsch., Cambridge, Mass., 1991—94, staff scientist, 1994—96; spl. term appointee Environ. Rsch., Argonne (Ill.) Nat. lab., 1996—98, meteorologist, 1998—; sr. fellow Environ. Sci. Ctr., U. of Chgo., 2002—. Vis. rsch. fellow dept. atmospheric scis. U. Ill., Urbana-Champaign, 1996—98; conf. presenter in field. Contbr. articles and abstracts to profl. jours. Recipient Nat. Merit scholorship, Govt. of India, 1978—84. Mem.: Am. Geophys. Union. Achievements include research in Tropospheric Chemistry and Transport. Office: Argonne Nat Lab 9700 S Cass Ave Kinsman IL 60437 E-mail: vrkotamarthi@anl.gov.

KOTAN, RICHARD MARVIN, engineer; b. Omaha, Nebr., Apr. 30, 1949; s. Robert and Bernadine Joyce (Johnson) K.; m. Joann E. Fuchs, Apr. 20, 1974; children: Cheryl Ann, Sara Ann. BS, U. Nebr., Omaha, 1980; MS, U. Nebr., 1986. Registered profl. engr., Nebr. Engr. Blue Cross Blue Shield, Omaha, 1973-80, Omaha Pub. Power Dist., 1980-82, sr. engr., 1982-97, mgr. rail ops. & maintenance, 1997—. Contbr. articles to profl. jours. Mem. Omaha 2000 Edn. Initiative, 1991—, Omaha Pub. Schs. Math./Sci. Coord. Com., 1991-92, Omaha C. of C. Engring. Task Force, 1990-92; pres. Met. Sci. & Engring. Fair, 1995—. With USN, 1967—73. Mem. ASCE (Nebr. pres. 1989-90), NSPE (state dir. 1993-94, ea. chpt. pres. 1998—99), Am. Welding Soc. (subcom. on design chair 1991—02), Am. Inst. Steel Constrn. (task com. on welds 1993—02), Am. Railway Engring. & Maintenance of Way Assn. (com. 15 steel bridges 1997—). Republican. Avocations: golf, family. Home: 12706 Patrick Cir Omaha NE 68164-3900 Office: Omaha Pub Power Dist 444 S 16th St Omaha NE 68102-2247

KOTAS, ROBERT VINCENT, research physician, educator; b. Buffalo, Nov. 26, 1938; s. Vincent John and Regina Agnes (Hadynka) K.; m. Ilona Rae Fielding, Mar. 2, 1968; children: Nicole, Timothy, Robert, Rebecca. BS, Canisius Coll., 1959; MD, U. Buffalo, 1963. Diplomate: Am. Acad. Pediatrics. Research assoc. McGill U., 1969-70; intern Buffalo Children's Hosp., 1963-64; resident in pediatrics Johns Hopkins Hosp., Balt., 1964-66; asst. prof. pediatrics U. Okla. Med. Sch., 1970-72, dir. newborn services, 1970-72; dir., div. devel. physiology; career investigator W.K. Warren Med. Research Center, Tulsa, 1972-76, sci. dir., 1976-80; dir. William and Natalie Warren Med. Inst., Tulsa, 1980-83; chief pediatrician Ella Austin Health Ctr., San Antonio, 1989-95, med. dir., 1993-95; lab. dir., 1993-95; pediatrician UTHSC-SA Primary Care Cmty. Pediat., San Antonio, 1995-98, Minor Emergency Ctr., San Antonio, 1998-99; assoc. Fernando A. Guerra, MD, San Antonio, 1998-99, Lonestar Pediats., Kaufman, Tex., 1999—2002; lead staff physician Cmty. Outreach Clinic/Bluitt-Flowers, Dallas, 2002—; assoc. Antonia Bronstein MD, Hurst, Tex., 2003. Clin. prof. pediats. U. Okla. Med. Sch., Tulsa, 1977-99; clin. instr. pediats. U. Tex. Southwestern Med. Ctr., Dallas, 2002—; assoc. prof. pediats. U. Tex. Health Sci. Ctr., San Antonio, 1983-98, dir. rsch. devel., 1993-94, also med. dir.; guest scientist Nat. Inst. Child Health and Human Devel., Bethesda, Md., 1975-77, also cons.; cons. Am. Lung Assn., others; cons. pediatrician San Antonio Ind. Sch. Dist. Contbr. articles to profl. jours. and books. Served as capt. USAF, 1966-68. Recipient continuing edn. awards AMA; Best M.D. Written Book award Am. Med. Writers Assn., 1980; Mosby scholar, 1963; grantee NIH, 1969-70, 75-79, 84-88; grantee USPHS, 1968-69, 91-95; others. Fellow Am. Coll. Obstetricians and Gynecologists (assoc.); mem. Johns Hopkins Med. and Surg. Assn., So. Soc. Pediatric Rsch., Soc. Pediatric Rsch., Am. Physiol. Soc., Soc. Gynecol. Investigation. Home: 604 Courageous Dr Rockwall TX 75032-5768 Office: 1832 Norwood Plaza Ct S-A Hurst TX 76054-3783 E-mail: bnd562000@yahoo.com. *Grateful for the excitement of impending discovery which characterizes my work with its promise of surprise in the midst of daily routine, I am indebted for the guidance and inspiration that my present and past associates have given me to deal effectively with the diversity and perversity of experience.*

KOTASKA, GARY F. lawyer, partner; b. Flint, Mich., Oct. 20, 1949; s. Joseph Robert and Lillian (Ondrus) K.; m. Kathleen Sharon Marsden, June 10, 1972; children: Jonathan, Robert, Andrew, Kathleen. B.A. in History, Canisius Coll., Buffalo, 1971; J.D. magna cum laude, Bklyn. Law Sch., 1974. Bar: N.Y. 1975, U.S. Dist. Ct. (we. dist.) N.Y. 1975, U.S. Ct. Appeals (2nd cir.) 1986, U.S. Ct. Appeals (11th cir.) 1990. Ptnr. Moot & Sprague, Buffalo, 1974-90, Phillips, Lytle, Hitchcock, Blaine & Huber, Buffalo, 1990—; dir. Naylon Cos., Inc.; United bd. dirs. Battenfield-Am., Buffalo. W.N.Y. United Against Drug & Alcohol Abuse, Inc. Mem. Erie County Bar Assn. Democrat. Roman Catholic. Home: 143 Devonshire Rd Buffalo NY 14223-1946 Office: Phillips Lytle Hitchcock Blaine & Huber 3400 Marine Midland Ctr Buffalo NY 14203-2887

KOTCHER, RAYMOND LOWELL, public relations executive; b. N.Y.C., Nov. 19, 1951; s. Richmond and Elaine (Germain) Kotcher; m. Betsy Kasper, Sept. 10, 1978; children: Maris, Gregory. BS, SUNY, Geneseo, 1973; MS in Comm., Boston U., 1983. Account exec. Burson Marsteller, N.Y.C., 1978—79; v.p., mgmt. supr. J. Walter Thompson Co., N.Y.C., 1979—82; v.p. Ketchum Pub. Rels., N.Y.C., 1982—84; exec. v.p. G.S. Schwartz & Co., N.Y.C., 1984—85; exec. v.p., chief U.S. ops. pres. pub. rels. divsn. Ketchum Comm., N.Y.C., 1986—, also bd. dirs.; pres., CEO Ketchum PR, N.Y.C., 1990—; pres., sr. ptnr. Ketchum PR Worldwide, N.Y.C. Mem. exec. com. Boston U. Coll. Comm., 1988—. Mem.: Pub. Rels. Soc. Am., Old Westbury Country Club, Board Room Club, Princeton Club. Avocations: tennis, sailing, golf. Office: Ketchum Pub Rels 292 Madison Ave New York NY 10017-6307

KOTCHER, SHIRLEY J. W. lawyer; b. June 6, 1924; m. Harry A. Kotcher; children: Leslie Susan, Dana Anne. BA, NYU; JD, Columbia U. Bar: N.Y. In-house counsel Booth Meml. Med. Ctr., Flushing, N.Y., 1975-83, gen. counsel, 1983-91; v.p., gen. counsel the N.Y. Hosp. Med. Ctr. Queens 1991-97; advisor health care Borough Pres. Queens, 1978. Author: Hidden gold and Pitfalls in New Tax Law, 1970. Mem. North Hempstead Sr. Citizen Commn., Manhasset, NY, 1999—; mem. affordable sr. housing endowment adv. com. Town of North Hempstead, 1999—; bd. dirs. Denton Green Housing Co. Inc., Garden City Park, NY, 1999—. Mem. ABA (health law forum com.), Nat. Health Lawyers Assn., Am. Acad. Hosp. Attys., Am. Soc. Law and Medicine, Am. Soc. Health Care Risk Mgmt., Assn. for Hosp. Risk Mgmt. N.Y., Greater N.Y. Hosp. Assn. (legal adv. com. 1976-97).

KOTEFF, ELLEN, periodical editor; b. Harvey, Ill. d. Walter Peter and Florence (Walz) K. BS in Journalism, U. Fla. Editor Palm Beach (Fla.) Daily News; met. editor Daily Record, Parsippany; exec. editor Nation's Restaurant News, N.Y.C. Bd. dirs. Women's Foodservice Forum; v.p. Internat. Foodservice Editl. Coun. Bd. dirs. Women's Foodservice Forum, 2003. Recipient Jesse H. Neal award, 2002, McAllister Editl. fellowship award, 2002. Office: Nations Restaurant News 425 Park Ave New York NY 10022-3506

KOTELLY, GEORGE VINCENT, editor, writer, electrical engineer; b. Boston, Aug. 27, 1931; s. James Visar and Pauline (Plaha) K.; m. Shirley Elizabeth Mullo, June 14, 1959; children— Kenneth James, William John, Douglas George, Joanne Elizabeth BSE.E., Tufts U., 1953. Publs. engr. Raytheon, Burlington, Mass., 1970-73; tech. writer USM Corp., Beverly, Mass., 1973-75; engring. writer Analogic, Wakefield, Mass., 1975-77; tech. editor Computer Design Mag., Littleton, Mass., 1977-79; sr. editor Edn. Mag., Boston, 1979-83; editor-in-chief Mini-Micro Systems Mag., Cahners Pub. Co., Boston, 1983-88; mng. editor Lightwave Jour. PennWell Pub. Co., Westford, Mass., 1988-89; sr. editor Lincoln Lab. MIT, Lexington, 1989-91; editor COMDEX Preview and Show Daily The Interface Group, Needham, Mass., 1991-93; exec. editor Lightwave Jour. PennWell Pub. Co., Nashua, N.H., 1993-97; editor-in-chief Vision Systems Design Mag., Image Processing Europe, 1997—. Contbr. numerous articles to tech. jours. Sgt. U.S. Army, 1954-56. Mem. IEEE. Republican. Mem. Albanian Orthodox Ch. Avocations: golf, bowling, chess, jogging, baseball. Home: 12 Scotch Pine Ln Merrimack NH 03054-3900 E-mail: georgek@pennwell.com.

KOTELMAN, LAURA MARY, lawyer; b. Chgo., Apr. 5, 1972; Student, Am. U., 1992; BA, Lake Forest Coll., 1993; JD, U. Ill., 1997. Bar: Ill. 1997. Legis. analyst Ill. Senate Majority Staff, Springfield, 1993-94; program legal specialist Ill. Atty. Gen., Chgo., 1997-98; counsel Nat. Assn. Ind. Insurers, Des Plaines, Ill., 1998—. Mem. Ill. State Bar Assn., Federalist Soc. (chpt. pres. 1996-97), Phi Delta Phi (chpt. pres. 1995-96, Most Active Chpt. award 1996). Roman Catholic. Office: Nat Assn Ind Insurers 2600 S River Rd Des Plaines IL 60018-3203

KOTHARI, AMITAV, accountant; b. Calcutta, India, Dec. 10, 1952; s. Bijay singh and Puspa (Doogar) K.; m. Lata Mogha, Feb. 24, 1978; children: Yasaswy, Manaswy. M. Commerce, Calcutta U., 1975, LLB, 1977. Chartered acct. Sr. ptnr. Kothari & Co., Calcutta, 1975—; dep. chmn. Kothari Fiscal Svcs. (P) Ltd., Calcutta, 1995—. Pres. Merchants C. of C., India, 1989-90; mng. com. mem. Associated C. of C. and Industry, New Delhi, 1993—, co-chmn. expert com. on direct taxes, 1990-91; mem. commn. on taxation Internat. C. of C., Paris; chmn., mem. faculty more than 300 seminars and confs.; mem. State Consumer Protection Coun., 1989-90; mem., regional dir. Tex. Adv. Com.; mem. panel of arbitrators Indian Coun. Arbitration; registered valuer Ctrl. Bd. Direct Taxes, Govt. India, New Delhi; bd. dirs., chmn. audit com., shareholder/investors grievance com. Allahabad Bank, India. Contbr. articles to fin. newspapers, mags. and profl. jours.; mem. ctrl. adv. bd. Taxation, 1983-93. Mem. State Com. on Indsl. Devel. for large and medium industries under charimanship of Chief Min. of West Bengal, 1989-90; trustee Kothari Lok Kalyan Trust. Named Outstanding Young Person in field of law and law and taxation Indian Jaycees of West Bengal, 1988, Internat. Man of Yr. Internat. Biog. Ctr., Cambridge, Eng., 1995-96; recipient Global Distinction award Internat. Biog. Rsch. Inst., Edmonton, Can., 1994-95, Twentieth Century award for achievement Internat. Biog. Ctr., Cambridge; rsch. fellow Am. Biog. Inst., Inc. Fellow Inst. Chartered Accts. India (pres. 1986-87, mem. acctg. stds. bd.), Assn. Co. Secs., Execs. and Advisors (pres. 1985-86); chmn. co. law com. Indian C. of C., Rotary Club Calcutta, Calcutta Club Ltd., Calcutta Swimming Club. Hindu. Avocations: swimming, debating, travel, photography. Home: Flat 8-E, 8th Fl 26-B Camac St Neelkanth Apt Calcutta 700016 India Office: Kothari & Co 71 Ganesh Chandra Ave Calcutta 700013 India

KOTHARI, PURNIMA, obstetrician/gynecologist; b. Cambay, India, Aug. 16, 1950; MD, B.J. Med. Coll./Gujarat U., Ahmedabad, 1974. Diplomate Am. Bd. Ob-Gyn. Intern St. Alexis Hosp., Cleve., 1976-77; resident in ob-gyn Mt. Sinai Med. Ctr., Cleve., 1977-80; ob-gyn Fairview Gen. Hosp., Cleve. Office: 20800 Westgate Mall Fairview Park OH 44126-1318

KOTHARI, SRIPRAKASH, business educator; b. Gulbarga, India, June 7, 1957; s. Prakash Chandra and Sarojini K.; m. Vicky Burrowes, May 24, 1984 (div. Nov. 1989); 1 child, Kavita Charul; m. Dafni Botsis, Aug. 26, 1990; 1 child, Monica Priti. BE with hons., Birla Inst. of Tech. and Sci., Pilani, India, 1979; MBA, Indian Inst. Mgmt., Ahmedabad, India, 1980-82; PhD, U. Iowa, 1986. Asst. prof. Simon Sch./U. Rochester, N.Y., 1986-91, assoc. prof., 1991-96, prof., 1996-97, 98-99; vis. prof. Sloan/MIT, Cambridge, 1997-98, Gordon Y. Billard prof., 1999—. Contbr. articles to profl. jours. Home: 11 Walnut St Lexington MA 02421-8219 Office: Sloan/MIT E52-325 50 Memorial Dr Cambridge MA 02142-1347 E-mail: kothari@mit.edu.

KOTHARY, PIYUSH C. research scientist; b. Yangon, Myanmar, Sept. 4, 1940; s. Chamanlal D. and Labhuben C. Kothary; m. Sarla P. Parekh, Feb. 21, 1943; children: Shilpa, Priya. PhD magna cum laude, La Salle U., 1994. Demonstrator St. Xavier's Coll., Bombay, 1963—71; sr. rsch. assoc. U. Mich., Ann Arbor, 1971—. Dir. rsch. Skillman Lab. Kellogg Eye Ctr., Ann Arbor, 1994—. Grantee, NIH, 1990—95, 1993. Mem.: ARVO (Presented papers 1994-2002). Office: 521 Kellogg Eye Ctr 1000 Wall St Ann Arbor MI 48105 Home Fax: 734-647-0228; Office Fax: 734-647-0228. Personal E-mail: Piyush0940@aol.com. Business E-Mail: kotha@umich.edu.

KOTHBAUER, KARL F. neurosurgeon, researcher; b. St. Polten, Austria, Apr. 9, 1962; arrived in U.S., 1996, permanent resident, 1997; m. Ingrid J. Kothbauer-Margreiter, June 19, 1993. MD, U. Vienna, Austria, 1980—88. Cert. Austrian Med. Chamber, 1996. Neurosurgeon Neurochirurgische Klinik, Inselspital, Bern, Switzerland, 1995—99; neurophysiologist, Inst. Neurology and Neurosurgery Beth Israel Med. Ctr., Singer Divsn., N.Y.C., 1996—98, fellow in pediat. neurosurgery, 1998—99, pediat. neurosurgeon, Inst. Neurology and Neurosurgery, 1999—; asst. prof. neurosurgery Albert Einstein Coll. Medicine, N.Y.C., 2000—. Mem.: AAAS, Austrian Soc. for Neurol. Surgery, European Neurol. Soc., New York Acad. of Scis., Congress of Neurol. Surgeons. Avocations: sailing, running, travel. Office: Beth Israel Medical Center Singer Div 170 East End Ave New York NY 10128 Office Fax: 212-8709810. Business E-Mail: kkothbau@bethisraelny.org.

KOTHEIMER, WILLIAM CONRAD, consulting engineer; b. Louisville, May 26, 1925; s. Joseph Herman and Mary Julia (Bohan) K.; m. Anne Sheila Collins, Sept. 3, 1960; 1 child, William Conrad B.E.E., U. Louisville, 1951. Registered profl. engr., Pa. Sr. engr. Gen. Electric Co., Phila., 1951-65, mgr. devel. engring., 1965-80, cons. engr., 1980-82, Malvern, Pa., 1982-83, Kotheimer Assocs., Lansdowne, Pa., 1983-86; dir. engring. ABB Power T & D Co., Allentown, Pa., 1986-91, tech. dir. Coral Springs, Fla., 1991—. Contbr. articles of profl. jours. Patentee in field. Served with U.S. Army, 1943-45 Recipient Power Systems sector engring. award Gen. Electric Co., 1980 Fellow IEEE (best paper award power system relaying com. 1979); mem. NSPE, Roselawn Civic Assn. Republican. Roman Catholic. Avocations: astronomy; personal computing. Home: 5900 NW 99th Ave Coral Springs FL 33076-2566

KOTHERA, LYNNE MAXINE, clinical psychologist; b. Cleve., Dec. 18, 1938; d. Leonard Frank and Lillian (Shackleton) K.; m. Richard Litwin, Oct. 24, 1965 (dec.). BA with hons., Denison U., Granville, Ohio, 1960; MA, NYU, 1983; PhD, L.I. U., Bklyn., 1989; postgrad. psychotherapy/psychoanalysis, NYU, 2003. Dancer Martha Graham Dance Co., N.Y.C., 1961-62, Carmen DeLavallade Dance Co., N.Y.C., 1965-68, Glen Tetley Dance Co., N.Y.C., 1965-69; prin. dancer John Butler's, N.Y.C., 1971; artist-in-residence Boston High Schs. - Title III, 1969-71, Hobart-Smith Coll./Denison U., 1973; auditor N.Y. State Council of the Arts, N.Y.C., 1974-78; predoctoral fellow clin. psychology Yale-New Haven Hosp., 1987-88; postdoctoral fellow neuropsychology Inst. of Living, Hartford, Conn., 1989-91; with dept. rehab. medicine Mt. Sinai Med. Ctr., N.Y.C., 1991—, co-dir. tng. in-patient, 1995—; adj. asst. prof. Hunter Coll., N.Y.C., 1998-99. Mem.: APA. Democrat. Avocation: the arts. Home: 23 E 11th St New York NY 10003-4450 Office: Mt Sinai Med Ctr Rehab Med KCC-365-G PO Box 1674 1 Gustave L Levy Pl New York NY 10029-6500 E-mail: Lynne_Kothera@mssm.edu.

KOTHS, KIRSTON EDWARD, biochemist; b. La Fayette, Ind., Dec. 24, 1948; s. Jay Sanford and Margaret Louise (Edwards) K.; m. Catherine Elizabeth Lutes, Aug. 24, 1985. BS, Amherst Coll., 1971; PhD, Harvard U., 1979. Scientist Cetus Corp., Emeryville, Calif., 1979-82, dir. protein chemistry, 1982-91, sr. scientist, 1984-89, sr. dir., 1989-91; dir. protein therapeutics rsch. Chiron Corp., Emeryville, 1991—2001, cons., 2002—. Patentee in field. Avocations: gold prospecting, photography, fly fishing, teaching dance. Home: 2646 Mira Vista Drive El Cerrito CA 94530 E-mail: kkoths@sbcglobal.net.

KOTIN, PAUL, pathologist; b. Chgo., Aug. 13, 1916; s. Elias and Rose (Spunt) K.; m. Pauline H. Stephan, Dec. 12, 1970; children: Joel Tepper, David Bernard. BS, U. Ill., 1937, MD, 1940. Intern Deaconess Hosp., Chgo., 1939-40, resident pathology, 1940-41; pvt. practice pathology and internal medicine San Luis Obispo, Calif., 1946-48; researcher pathology U. So. Calif., 1949-50; med. microbiologist Los Angeles County Hosp., 1950-51, attending staff pathologist, 1951-62; mem. faculty U. So. Calif., 1951-62, prof. pathology, 1959-60, Paul Pierce prof. pathology, 1960-62; chief carcinogenesis studies br. Nat. Cancer Inst., 1962-63, asso. dir. for field studies, 1963-64, sci. dir. for etiology, 1964-66; dir. div. environ. health scis. NIH, 1966-69; dir. Nat. Inst. Environ. Health Scis., 1969-71; v.p. for health scis., dean Sch. Medicine, Temple U., Phila., 1971-74; sr. v.p. health, safety and environment Johns-Manville Corp., 1974-81. Edgar Allen Meml. lectr. Yale Sch. Medicine, 1957; vis. prof. oncology U. Wis., 1959-60; vis. prof. pathology U. N.C., also Duke U., 1967-71; Harry Shay Meml. lectr. Temple U., 1964; Sappington Meml. lectr. Am. Occupational Medicine Assn., Anaheim, Calif., 1979, Gehrmann lectr., Nashville, 1981; chmn. Gordon Research Conf. Cancer, 1965, Beryllium Industry Sci. Adv. Com., 1995—; adj. prof. pathology U. Colo., 1974—; Cons. air pollution med. program, div. spl. health service USPHS, 1958-62; mem. sci. adv. bd. Council Tobacco Research-U.S.A., 1952-65; adv. com. r.r. diesel gases and dust Calif. Pub. Utilities Commn., 1956-62; adv. com. research pathogenesis cancer Am. Cancer Soc., 1962-65; pathology study sect. NIH, 1962-66, lung cancer task force, 1967-68; corr. mem. permanent European com. Research Chronic Hazards, 1960— ; cancer prevention com. UICC, 1962-66, com. on exptl. design and methodology in carcinogenesis, 1967-70; sci. com. Inst. Occupational and Environ. Health, Quebec. Asbestos Mining Assn., 1966-75; mem. Fed. Com. Pest Control, 1964-71; program com. Tenth Internat. Congress, 1967-70; mem. Expert Panel on Carcinogenicity, 1962-70, Nat. Environ. Health Scis. Center, 1965, Nat. Adv. Com. Occupational Safety and Health, 1975-78, Armed Forces Epidemiol. Bd., 1976-80; chmn. Beryllium Industry Sci. Adv. Com., 1990—. Editorial adv. bd.: Cancer Research, 1957-61, Internat. Rev. Exptl. Pathology, 1968— ; editorial bd.: AMA Archives Pathology, 1965-71, Environ. Research, 1966—, Am. Jour. Pathology, 1971-82; Contbr. articles to med. jours. Served with AUS, 1941-46. Recipient Superior Service award HEW, 1966, Disting. Service award, 1969; Sr. postdoctoral fellow NSF, 1959-60; named Alumnus of Yr. U. Ill. Coll. of Medicine, 1990. Fellow Coll. Am. Pathologists, N.Y. Acad. Scis., Am. Acad. Occupational Medicine; mem. AMA (com. research on tobacco and health 1966-78), Am. Assn. Cancer Research (dir.), Am. Assn. Pathologists and Bacteriologists, AAAS, Am. Indsl. Hygiene Assn. (hon.), Am. Occupational Medicine Assn. (Knudsen award 1981), Sigma Xi, Alpha Omega Alpha. Home: 540 Camino Los Altos Santa Fe NM 87501

KOTKER, ZANE HICKCOX, writer; b. Waterbury, Conn., Jan. 2, 1934; d. Edward Scovill Hickcox and Jean Cadwallader; m. Norman R. Kotker, June 7, 1965 (dec. Feb. 1999); children: David, Ariel. BA, Middlebury (Vt.) Coll., 1956; MA, Columbia U., 1960. Reading specialist Baldridge Reading Svcs., Conn., 1961—63; editor Silver-Burdett, NJ, 1963—65, Harcourt, Brace, Jovanovitch, N.Y.C., 1966—69. Vis. writer Mt. Holyoke Coll., 1983, U. Mass., Amherst, 1984, Smith Coll., 1990, 91. Author (as Zane Kotker): Bodies in Motion, 1972, A Certain Man, 1976; author: White Rising, 1981, Try to Remember, 1997; author: (as Maggie Strong) Mainstay: For the Well Spouse of the Chronically Ill, 1988, 1989, 1997. (as Maggie Strong) founder Well Spouse Found. Fiction grant Nat. Endowment for the Arts; 5 fellowships MacDowell Colony; fellowship Yaddo. Mem. Authors Guild. Home: 45 Lyman Rd Northampton MA 01060 E-mail: zane@crocker.com.

KOTKOV, BENJAMIN, clinical psychologist; b. Boston, Apr. 8, 1910; s. Moses and Annie (Hopner) K.; m. Sally B., Jan. 28, 1941; children: Ralph, Frank. AB, Cornell U., 1929; MA, Harvard U., 1934; PhD, Ottawa U., Ont., Can., 1954. Diplomate Am. Bd. Clin. Psychology, Am. Bd. Profl. Psychology, Am. Bd. Med. Psychotherapists, Am. Bd. Disability Cons., Am. Bd. Prescribing Psychologists, Am. Coll. Forensic Examiners, Serious Mental Illness, Am. Coll. Advanced Practice Psychologists, Am. Bd. Psychologist-Physicians, Am. Bd. Psychotherapy, Am. Bd. Hypnotherapy. Staff to chief Nerve Clinic, New Eng. Med. Ctr., Boston, 1934-42, VA Mental Hygiene Unit, Boston, 1946-52; chief psychologist Mental Hygiene Clinics, State of Del., 1952-53; clin. exec. Child Guidance Ctr., Brattleboro, Vt., 1954-64; staff to prof. and faculty head Windham Coll., Putney, Vt., 1964-76; pvt. practice Brattleboro, 1976—. Internat. adv. bd. Acad. of Psychoanalysis, Germany, 1969-86. Contbr. numerous articles to profl. jours. Lt. U.S. Army, 1942-46. Recipient Editor's award Internat. Jour. Profl. Hypnosis, 1977, medallion Acad. Psychosmatic Medicine, 1979, Membership Leader award Vt. Lions, 1993-94, Outstanding Premier Leadership award in psychopharmacology for professional psychologists, 1998; NEA grantee, 1956-57. Fellow Am. Psychol. Soc., Internat. Soc. Profl. Hypnosis, Acad. Sci. Hypnotherapy, Am. Assn. Applied and Prevention Psychology, Acad. Clin. Psychology; mem. AAUP (emeritus), APA (life), Am. Philos. Assn., Soc. Personality Assessment (life), Vt. Psychol. Assn. (pres. 1968-69, chmn. cert. bd. 1974-76), New Eng. Soc. Clin. Hypnosis (pres. 1988), DAV (life), Lions (pres. 1973-74, 84-85, 94-97), Elks, Am. Legion. Home and Office: 70 Orchard St Brattleboro VT 05301-2678 E-mail: bkotkov2@juno.com.

KOTLARCHUK, IHOR O. E. lawyer; b. Ukraine, July 31, 1943; came to U.S., 1946, naturalized, 1957; s. Emil and Lidia N. (Maceluch) K. BS in Fin., Fordham U., 1965, JD, 1968; LLM, Georgetown U., 1974, MA in Govt., 1982. Bar: N.Y. 1969, D.C. 1972, Va. 2001, U.S. Ct. Mil. Appeals, U.S. Tax Ct., U.S. Supreme Ct. Sr. trial atty. criminal sect. tax divsn. U.S. Dept. Justice, Washington, 1973-78, civil sect. tax divsn., 1978-80, fraud sect. criminal divsn., 1980-84, internal security sect. criminal divsn., 1984-97; ret., 1999; sr. internat. law enforcement adv. on tax policy/enforcement U.S. Treasury Dept., 2000—; pvt. practice law Alexandria, Va., 2001—. Pres. The Washington Group, 2001—. With U.S. Army, 1969-73, Vietnam; judge advocate gen.; ret. col. USAR. Decorated Bronze star, Legion of Merit. Mem. ABA, N.Y. State Bar Assn., Va. State Bar Assn., Va. Trial Lawyers Assn., D.C. Bar Assn., Res. Officers Assn., Ukrainian Assn. Washington D.C. (pres. 2000-01), Phi Alpha Delta. Ukrainian Catholic. Address: 205 S Lee St Alexandria VA 22314-3307 Office: 109 S Fairfax St Alexandria VA 22314-3307 Fax: 703-548-1861.

KOTLER, MILTON, marketing company executive; b. Chgo., Mar. 15, 1935; s. Maurice and Betty (Bubar) K.; m. Greta Smith, July 11, 1976; children: Anthony, Joshua, Jonathan, Rebecca. BA, U. Chgo., 1954, MA in Polit. Sci, 1957, postgrad. (Jane Morton fellow), 1957-59. Asst. prof. Chgo. City Coll., 1961-63; resident fellow Inst. for Policy Studies, Washington, 1963-77; exec. dir. Inst. Neighborhood Studies, Washington, 1972-75, Nat. Assn. Neighborhoods, Washington, 1975-81; v.p. Ctr. for Responsive Governance, Washington, 1981—, treas., 1980—; pres. Kotler Mktg. Group, Washington, Chgo., London, 1984—. Vis. prof. Univ. Calif., Berkeley, 1968, Washington U., 1985; adj. prof. Am. Univ., Washington, 1976—, Univ. Md., 1980— Author: Neighborhood Government, 1969, Building Neighborhood Organization, 1983; co-editor: Jour. Community Action, 1981—; contbr. chpts. to books. Vice-pres. Alliance for Voluntarism, 1979-80; chmn. bd. Washington Symphony Orchestra, 1992—; bd. dirs. Nat. Com. Responsive Philanthropy, Washington, 1980—. With USAFR, 1959-60. Office: 925 15th St NW 4th Flr Washington DC 20005 *I have sought in all my work to empower the neighborhood community as a sphere of our personal responsibility. I have done this so that we may become more human through that responsibility, and with the hope that this responsibility will be guided by biblical faith.*

KOTLER, STEVEN, investment banker; b. N.Y.C., Jan. 9, 1947; s. Louis and Etta (Smeltzer) K.; m. Carolyn Miller, Sept. 26, 1973; children: William, Thomas. BBA, CCNY, 1967. V.p. N.Y. Hanseatic Corp., N.Y.C., 1967-74; with Schroder Wertheim & Co. Inc., N.Y.C., 1974—, gen. ptnr., 1979—, mng. dir., 1981—, pres., 1987—, CEO, 1996-99; vice chmn. Gilbert Global Equity Capital, LLC, N.Y.C. Chmn. exec. com., dir. Moore Med. Corp., Del Labs., Inc.; bd. govs. Am. Stock Exch., 1992-97; coun. pres. The Woodrow Wilson Internat. Ctr. for Scholars; mem. infrastructure & housing task force N.Y.C. Partnership, N.Y.C. C. of C. Trustee Columbia Grammar and Prep Sch. Served with USAR, 1967-72. Mem.: Coun. on Fgn. Rels.

KOTLIAR, B. GABRIEL, physics educator; b. Feb. 26, 1957; BSc in Physics and Math., Hebrew U., 1979, MSc in Physics, 1980; PhD in Physics, Princeton U., 1983. Postdoctoral fellow Inst. for Theoretical Physics U. Calif., Santa Barbara, 1983—85; asst. prof. MIT, 1985—88; assoc. prof. Rutgers U., Piscataway, NJ, 1988—92, prof. I, 1992—96, prof. II, 1996—. Assoc. editor Phys. Rev. Letters, 1996—97; cons. ATT Bell Labs., 1988—97, Los Alamos Nat. Labs., 1991—98. Editor (with D. D. Sarna and Y. Tokura): (book) Monographs in Condensed Matter Science, 1997. Recipient Guggenheim fellowship, 2003, Alfred P. Sloan rsch. fellowship, 1986—88, Presdl. Young Investigator award, 1987—92, Lady Davies fellowship, 1994—95. Fellow: Am. Phys. Soc. Office: Rutgers U Serin Physics Lab Piscataway NJ 08855-0849*

KOTLOWITZ, ALEX, writer, journalist; Student, Wesleyan U. Former prodr. segments TV series MacNeil/ Lehrer NewsHour; former reporter The Wall Street Jour.; former contbr. NPR. Writer-i-residence Northwestern U.; Welch chmn. in Am. studies U. Notre Dame, South Bend, Ind. Author: There Are No Children Here: The Story of Two Boys Growing Up In the Other America, 1991 (Helen Bernstein award Excellence Journalism N.Y. Pub. Libr. 1992), The Other Side of the River: A Story of Two Towns, a Death and America's Dilemma, 1998 (Heartland prize for nonfiction Chgo. Tribune 1998); contbr. various mags., including The New Yorker, The N.Y. Times Mag., This Am. Life. Recipient George Polk award TV reporting Long Island U. Journalism dept. work on MacNeil/Lehrer NewsHour, 1984, Robert F. Kennedy award Coverage of Disadvantaged, George Foster Peabody award 2003.

KOTLOWITZ, ROBERT, writer, editor; b. Paterson, N.J., Nov. 21, 1924; s. Max and Debra (Kaplan) K.; m. Carol Naomi Leibowitz, Oct. 15, 1950; children— Alexander William, Daniel Justin. BA, Johns Hopkins, 1947; preparatory diploma, Peabody Conservatory Music, 1941. Asso. editor Pocket Books, Inc., 1950-55, Discovery, 1952-55; mgr. press and information RCA Victor Records, 1955-60; sr. editor Show mag., 1960-64, Harper's mag., 1965-67, mng. editor, 1967-71; sr. v.p., dir. programming Sta. WNET/ Channel 13, N.Y.C., 1971-91, editorial advisor, 1991—. Guest lectr. Queen's Coll., 1954-55; author monthly column Performing Arts, 1966— Author: novel Somewhere Else, 1972, The Boardwalk, 1977, Sea Changes, 1986, His Master's Voice, 1992, (memoire) Before Their Time, 1997; Contbg. editor: Atlantic Monthly, 1971-74; Contbr. nat. publs. Served with inf. AUS, 1943-46. Recipient Edward Lewis Wallant award for novel, 1972, Nat. Jewish Book award, 1972, Nat. Emmy award, 1973; sr. fellow Freedom Forum, Columbia U., 1993; fellow Am. Acad., Berlin, 1998. Mem. Century Assn. Home: 54 Riverside Dr New York NY 10024-6509

KOTOSKE, ROGER ALLEN, artist, educator; b. South Bend, Ind., Jan. 4, 1933; s. Michael and Louise (Gallo) K.; 1 child, Tamara. Student, U. Notre Dame, 1950-52; BFA, U. Denver, 1955, MA, 1956. Instr. Fitzsimons Army Hosp., Denver, 1956-58, U. Denver, 1958-68; mem. faculty U. Ill., 1968— ; now assoc. prof. Vice pres., artist Denver Nat. Sculpture Symposium, 1968 One man shows James Yu Gallery, N.Y.C., 1974, Hiestand Gallery, Miami U., Oxford, Ohio, 1978, Hilton Center for Performing Arts, St. Louis, 1979, group shows include, Galex Nat. 23, Galesburg, Ill., 1989, Greater Midwest Internat. III, Warrensburg, Mo., 1988, SUNY, Potsdam, 1975, Grey Gallery, N.Y.C., 1976, Illinois Painters III, 1980; exhibited in group show U. Del., Newark, 1986, U. of Ill. Faculty Internat. Exchange Exhbn., Chinese Fine Arts Mus., Beijing, China, 1987, Art Yard, Denver, 1996, Vanguard Art in Colo. 1940-1970, Boulder Mus. Contemporary Art, 1999; represented in permanent collections Rock Hill Nelson Gallery, Kansas City, Mo., SUNY, Oswego, Denver Art Mus., others. Ford Found. grantee, 1975-78 Home: 1611 W White St Champaign IL 61821-3017

KOTRICH, ALEXANDRA, writer; b. Chgo., Nov. 8, 1962; d. Charles James Kotrich III and Irene G. Kotrich. Pres. Andrich Pub., Inc., Wilmington, 1994—2002; founder, chmn. The Children's Writing Found., Wilmington, Del., 1996—2002. Participating judge quality of life rsch. competition Salomon Smith Barney/Citicorp, N.Y.C., 2000. Author: (book) The Killing Game, 1994, (novels) The Croatian, 1995, The Composer, 1996, (screenplays) Fool's Game, 1998, The Chiliad Project, 1999. Recipient Best N.Y. Website for Publishers award, Best of NY, 1998. Mem.: Publisher's Mktg. Assn., Internat. Women's Writing Guild, Nat. Writers Union. Office: A Kotrich Ste 200 163 Amsterdam Ave New York NY 10023 Business E-Mail: andrich@andrichinc.com.

KOTSAY, MARK STEVEN, baseball player; b. Woodler, Calif., Dec. 2, 1975; Student, Calif. State U., Fullerton. Ctr. field, right field Fla. Marlins, 1996—. Named Most Outstanding Player Coll. World Series, 1995; recipient Golden Spikes award, USA Baseball, 1995. Achievements include being a mem. of U.S. Olympic Baseball Team, 1996; being tied for Ea. League for double plays by outfielder with four, 1997. Office: Florida Marlins 2267 NW 199th St Opa Locka FL 33056-2664

KOTT, ALAN, state agency administrator; b. Bronx, N.Y., Mar. 8, 1948; s. Murry and Lee (Raffelson) K.; m. Carol Mary Portanova, Nov. 4, 2000; children: Joni, Amy, Greg, Tyler, Corbin. BA in Psychology, Queens Coll., Flushing, N.Y., 1970; MA in Psychology, New Sch. for Social Rsch., N.Y.C., 1972; PhD, NYU, 1990. Psychometrician L.I. Jewish-Hillside Med. Ctr., Glen Oaks, N.Y., 1971-74; from rsch. scientist to unit chief Office of Alcoholism and Substance Abuse Svcs. State of N.Y., N.Y.C., 1974-86, asst. dir., 1987—. Prin. investigator Narcotic and Drug Rsch., Inc., N.Y.C., 1985-87; chmn. Evaluation Subcom. Task Force on Integrated Projects, N.Y.C., 1987-94; mem. Task Force Youth Substance Abuse State of N.Y., Albany, 1986-87, Combined Psychiat. and Addictive Disorders, N.Y.C., 1986-88; mem. rsch. Task Force Mentally Impaired Chem. Abusers, 1989-93; chmn. Evaluation Systems Program Adv. Com., 1995—; project dir. N.Y. State Treatment Outcomes and Performance Pilot Studies II, 1998-2002; chmn. N.Y. State Office of Alcoholism and Substance Abuse Svcs. IMPALA Adv. Com., 1999-2002. Mem.: AIAA, AAAS, Nat. Space Soc., Banner House. E-mail: alankott@oasas.state.ny.us

KOTT, BEVERLY PARAT, financial counselor, community activist; b. Chgo., Sept. 7, 1936; m. Russell Kott; children: Vinson V., Donna M., James L., Michael A. Grad., Life Underwritr Tng. Coun., Washington, 1977. Mem. mgmt. ea. region Met. Life Ins. Co., Balt., 1977; ins. broker, 1979-85; pres. Kott & Assocs. Fin. Counseling Svc., Joppa, Md., 1985—. Fin. counselor coop. extension svc. U. Md., Bel Air, 1987-2000, mem. Harford extension adv. coun., 1988-93; dir. Prison Ministry, 1983—; lay minister Roman Catholic Ch., 1995—. Commr. Harford County Commn. for Women, Bel Air, 1981-87; v.p. Joppa Friends of the Libr., 1988—; mem. Rumsey Island Civic Assn., 1980—; dir. Joppatowne Civic Assn., Joppa, 1990—, Padre Rio Rosary Makers, 1993—, Postal Adv. Coun., 1992-2000; sec. Harford County Libr. Coun., 1999—. Named one of Most Beautiful People, Harford County, 1990. Mem. Hunt Valley Bus. and Profl. Woman's Club (charter), Aux. VFW (pres. 1988-90, legis., youth, publicity and cancer aid coms. 1989, 90), Mensa Internat. Roman Catholic. Avocations: chess, bridge, writing, travel, volunteering. Office: 661 Towne Center Dr Joppa MD 21085-4439 E-mail: kottbev@aol.com.

KOTT, DAVID RUSSELL, lawyer; b. Trenton, N.J., Jan. 22, 1952; s. Maurice G. and Ruth (Shulman) K.; m. Lauren Handler, Aug. 24, 1980; children: Emily R., Adam J. BA, Am. U., 1973; JD, Rutgers U., 1977. Bar: N.J. 1977, U.S. Dist. Ct. N.J. 1977, U.S. Ct. Appeals (3d cir.) 1980, N.Y. 1984, U.S. Dist. Ct. (so. and ea. dists.) N.Y. 1985, cert. civil trial atty. Law clk. to justice N.J. Supreme Ct., Morristown, 1977-78; from assoc. to ptnr. McCarter & English LLP, Newark, 1978—. Sustaining mem. Product Liability Adv. Coun. Fellow Am. Coll. Trial Lawyers; mem. ABA, Am. Bd. Trial Advocates, N.J. Bar Assn., Essex County Bar Assn., Assn. Def. Trial Lawyers Attys., Trial Lawyers N.J., Fedn. Ins. and Corp. Attys., Def. Rsch. Inst., The Newark Club, Club at World Trade Ctr. Republican. Jewish. Office: McCarter & English LLP 4 Gateway Ctr 100 Mulberry St Newark NJ 07102-4004 E-mail: dkott@mccarter.com.

KOTT, JOSEPH, transportation executive, consultant, educator; b. Detroit, July 15, 1947; s. Joseph Frank and Catherine Marie (Szydlowski) K.; m. Katherine Babette Kitto, Sept. 28, 1973; children: Paul, Andrew, Amy. BA, Wayne State U., 1976; M of Regional Planning, U. N.C., 1979; M of Traffic Engring., Monash U., 2003. Planner Orange County, Hillsborough, N.C., 1979-80, transp. planner N.C. Dept. Transp., Raleigh, 1980-84, Ill. Commerce Commn., Springfield, Ill., 1984-86; planning coord. So. Ill. Sch. Medicine, Springfield, 1986-88; sr. transp. planner Androscoggin Valley Coun. Govts., Auburn, Maine, 1989-91; transp. planning mgr. Greater Portland (Maine) Coun. Govts., 1992-98; chief transp. ofcl. City of Palo Alto, Calif., 1999—. Adj. prof. cmty. planning & devel. Muskie Sch. Pub. Svc. U. So. Maine, Portland, 1997. Chair Auburn Maine Planning Bd., 1995-98, mem., 1992-98; adv. com. So. Maine Rideshare, Portland, 1993-98, Kids & Transp., Portland, 1994-98, Portland Area Clean Cities, 1996-98; bd. dirs. Western Maine Transp. Svcs., Mexico, 1994-98. Inst. Transp. Engrs. scholar, Washington, 1997, Eno Transp. Found. Can. Transit Studies Mission scholar, Washington, 1996; recipient Maine Environ. Citizen Yr. Natural Resources Coun. Maine, Augusta, 1995. Mem. AICP, Am. Planning Assn., Inst. Transp. Engrs. Democrat. Roman Catholic. Avocations: jogging, cross-country skiing, hiking. Home: 815 Santa Fe Ave Albany CA 94706-1823 Office: City of Palo Alto 250 Hamilton Ave Palo Alto CA 94301-2593

KOTT, PETE, state representative; b. Flint, Mich., Aug. 29, 1949; m. Lichine Kott; children: Peter, Pamela. BS in Criminal Justice, Fla. Internat. U., 1977, M in Pub. Adminstrn., 1979. With U.S. Air Force; co-owner Kott's Hardwood Flooring, Inc.; mem. Alaska Ho. of Reps., 1993—; select com. legis. ethics; legis. com. mil. vet. affairs. Former adj. prof. Wayland Bapt. U., 1986—95. Decorated 2 Commendation medals, Meritorious Svc. medal. Mem.: NRA, Am. Legion, Elks. Republican. Avocations: fishing, golf. Office: Rm 208 State Capitol Juneau AK 99801-1182 Address: 10928 Eagle River Rd Ste 141 Eagle River AK 99577*

KOTTAMASU, MOHAN RAO (K.V.R. MOHAN RAO), physician; b. Gudivada, India, Jan. 13, 1947; came to U.S., 1973; s. Janardana Rao and Kantharatnamma (Maddi) K.; m. Sarada Devi Vusirikala, Dec. 20, 1992; children: Pallavi, Aamani. MBBS, Gulbarga Med. Coll., 1972. House surgeon Govt. Gen. Hosp., Gulbarga, India, 1971-72; intern St. Vincent's Med. Ctr. of Richmond, S.I., N.Y., 1973-74, resident, 1974-76, chief resident, 1976-77; pulmonary diseases fellow Lahey Clinic and Deaconess Hosp., Boston, 1977-79; clin. fellow Harvard Med. Sch., Boston, 1978-79; assoc. Valley Pulmonary and Med. Assocs., Springfield, Mass., 1979-81, ptnr., v.p., 1981—. Adj. asst. prof. clin. pharmacy Mass. Coll. Pharmacy and Allied Health Scis., 1984—. Pres. house staff St. Vincent's Med. Ctr., 1976; founding pres. Indian Assn. Greater Springfield, 1985-86; pres. med. staff Mercy Hosp., Springfield, 1989-91. Fellow Am. Coll. Physicians, Am. Coll. Chest Physicians; mem. AMA, Am. Thoracic Soc., Mass. Med. Soc., Hampden Dist. Med. Soc. (pres.-elect 1999, pres. 2000-01, Cmty. Clinician of the Yr. 2001). Hindu. Avocations: chess, gardening. Home: 112 Twin Hills Dr Longmeadow MA 01106-2952 Office: Valley Pulmonary Med Assocs 222 Carew St Springfield MA 01104-4103

KOTTAS, JOHN FREDERICK, business administration educator; b. Hampton, Va., Apr. 18, 1940; s. Harry and Johnny (Edwards) K.; m. Betty Ann Hokenson, Aug. 7, 1965; children: John Bohlin, Ellen Elizabeth, Katherine Caroline, Paul Frederick. BS, Purdue U., 1962; MS, Northwestern U., 1964, PhD, 1968. Lectr. Wharton Sch., U. Pa., Phila., 1966-68; asst. prof. Sch. Bus. Adminstrn., U. N.C., Chapel Hill., 1968-73; adj. assoc. prof. Boston U. Overseas Grad. Program, Heidelberg, W. Ger., 1973-74; asso. prof. coordinator mgmt. sci. and info. systems Sch. Bus. Adminstrn., U. Mo., St. Louis, 1974-79; Zollinger prof. bus. adminstrn. Coll. William and Mary, Williamsburg, Va., 1979—. Presented three-day mgmt. seminar on Inventory Mgmt. and Control at numerous univs., U.S. and Can., 1976-78; cons. in field. Co-author: Production/Operations Management: Contemporary Policy of Managing Operating Systems, 1972, Cases and Applications in Lotus 1-2-3 (for DOS), 1995, Cases and Applications in Lotus 1-2-3 (for Windows), 1996, Cases and Applications in Microsoft EXCEL 5.0, 1996; contbr. articles to various publs. NDEA fellow, 1962-65; Walter P. Murphy fellow, 1962 Home: 109 Maxwell Pl Williamsburg VA 23185-5523 Office: Coll of William and Mary Sch Bus Adminstrn Williamsburg VA 23187 E-mail: jfkott@cox.net., john.kottas@business.wm.edu.

KOTTAYIL, SANTOSH GEORGE, pharmaceutical development executive; b. Manalady, Kerala, India, Apr. 18, 1963; arrived in U.S., 1987; s. Thuruthel Varkey and Grace (Joseph) Mani; m. Anita George, Dec. 30, 1993. BSc, U. Poona, Pune, India, 1983, MSc, 1985; PhD, U. Ky., 1993. Rsch. intern DuPont Merck, Wilmington, Del., 1991; sr. scientist Oramed, Mundelein, Ill., 1992; sr. scientist in pharm. devel. Unimed Pharms. Inc., Buffalo Grove, Ill., 1993-95, mgr., 1995-98, assoc. dir., 1998-99, dir. bus. ops., 1999—2002; pres. InSys Therapeutics, Inc., 2002—. Mem. selection com. for dean Coll. Arts and Scis., U. Ky., Lexington, 1991. Mem.: Am. Chem. Soc. Achievements include synthesis and evaluation of novel and improved chemical entities for the treatment of pain. Home: 8068 RFD Long Grove IL 60047-4814 Office: InSys Therapeutics Inc 25775 Hillview Ct Mundelein IL 60060 E-mail: gkottayil@insystherapeutics.com.

KOTTICK, EDWARD LEON, music educator, harpsichord maker; b. Jersey City, June 16, 1930; s. Hyman W. and Frieda M. (Stoller) K.; m. Gloria Astor, May 10, 1953; children: Judith, Janet AB, NYU, 1953; MA, Tulane U., 1959; PhD, U. N.C., Chapel Hill, 1962. Trombonist New Orleans Philharm., 1955-57; asst. prof. music Alma Coll., Mich., 1962-65; vis. prof. music U. Kans., Lawrence, 1965-66; assoc. prof. music U. Mo.-St. Louis, 1966-68; prof. music U. Iowa, Iowa City, 1968-92, prof. emeritus, 1992. Author: The Unica in the Chansonnier Cordiforme, No. 42 of Corpus Mensurabilis Musicae, 1967, Tone and Intonation on the Recorder, 1974, The Collegium: A Handbook, 1977, The Harpsichord Owner's Guide, 1987; author: (with G. Lucktenberg) Early Keyboard Instruments in European Museums, 1997; contbr. articles to profl. jours.; author: A History of the Harpsichord, 2003. With U.S. Army, 1953-55. U. Iowa grantee, 1975, 80, 85, 90, summer fellow, 1976; Galpin Soc. grantee, 1978. Mem. Am. Mus. Instrument Soc. (bd. govs. 1986-90, Am. Musicol. Soc. (chpt. sec. 1961-62, chpt. program com. 1964-66, chair com. 1972-73, 96-97, mem. nat. com. Collegium Musicum 1973-75), Fellowship Makers and Restorers of Hist. Instruments, Galpin Soc., Guild Am. Luthiers, Midwestern Hist. Keyboard Soc. (bd. dirs. 1980-90, 94-97). Home: 502 Larch Ln Iowa City IA 52245-3434 E-mail: edward-kottick@uiowa.edu.

KOTTLER, RAYMOND GEORGE MICHAEL, economist, researcher; b. Washington, Dec. 11, 1966; Diplomas, Goethe Inst., Staufen, Fed. Republic Germany, 1986, Tech. U. Dresden, German Dem. Republic, 1988, U. Vienna, Austria, 1988; BA in Econs., German, Rutgers U., 1989; postgrad. in Theology, St. Joseph's Sem., Inst. Religious Studies, Dunwoodie, 1995—97. Mgmt. trainee Met. Life Ins. Co., N.Y.C., 1989-90; environ. info. systems coord. Johnson & Johnson, New Brunswick, N.J., 1990-92; asst. economist Fed. Res. Bank N.Y., 1993-96; fin. analyst, client svcs. coord. Fed. Res. Bank of N.Y. - Rsch. and Market Analysis Group, 1996—. Mem. Rutgers First Aid Squad, 1985-89, crew chief, ambulance driver, 1987-89; cons. Literacy Vols. Am.-N.J., East Brunswick, N.J., 1991-93; mem. Pres.'s Com. on Edn. for Civic Leadership/Cmty. Svc. citizen edn. and cmty. svc. Project, Rutgers U., 1988-91, co-chair pres.'s mng./promoting diversity com. task force Com. to Advance Our Common Purposes, Rutgers U., 1990-91; co-chair cmty. svc. com. Rutgers Alumni Assn., 1991-94; mem. Rep. Presdl. Task Force, Rep. Senatorial Com., Rep. Presdl. Roundtable, Rep. Senatorial Com. Inner Circle. Recipient Merrill Lynch Disting. scholar, 1985—89, Garden State Disting. scholar, 1985—89, honoree Rep. Wall of Honor, Washington, 1993, Ronald Reagan Eternal Flame of Freedom award, 1994, Legion of Merit medal, 1995, 1999, Legion of Honor, 2002, Medal of Freedom, 2002; grantee Fed. Republic Germany Acad. Exch. Program scholar, 1986, German Dem. Republic Fgn. Ministry scholar, 1988, Austrian Ministry Sci. and Rsch. scholar, 1988. Mem. Rutgers Alumni Assn. (bd. dirs. 1988—, reunion chair 1989—, Rutgers Loyal Sons/Loyal Daus. award 2000, Rutgers Class of 1931 award 1999), Cap and Skull Soc., Phi Sigma Iota, Delta Phi Alpha, Omicron Delta Epsilon. Republican. Roman Catholic. Avocations: camping, swimming, boating, outdoor activities, gardening.

KOTTMEYER, MARTIN S. farmer, writer; b. Breese, Ill., Aug. 11, 1953; s. Martin and Alvera (Woker) K. AS, Kaskaskia Coll., Centralia, Ill., 1973. Engaged in farming, Carlyle, Ill., 1970s—. Contbr. articles to Magonia, The Reall News, Ency. of the Paranormal, Ency. of Extraterrestrial Encounters, others. Recipient Dr. Alexander Imich award Soc. for Enlightenment and Transformation of UN, 1995, Internat. Zurich prize, FundaciOn AnomalIa, 1999. Mem. Rational Exam. Assn. of Lincoln Land. Avocations: ufo culture, science fiction, bad movies. Home: 10501 Knolhoff Rd Carlyle IL 62231-3523

KOTTRABA, CARIN, psychologist; b. Balt., June 11, 1976; d. Robert Paul and Mary Brookes Kottraba. MA in Clin. Psychology, MS in Indsl./Orgnl. Psychology, Calif. Sch. Profl. Psychology, 2001, PhD in Clin. Psychology, PhD in Indsl./Orgnl. Psychology, 2003. Therapist Villa View Cmty. Hosp., San Diego, 2000—01, Pomerado Hosp., San Diego, 2001—, Palomar Hosp., San Diego, 2002—. Tchg. asst. and rschr. Calif. Sch. Profl. Psychology, San Diego, 2001—02; cons. Calif. State U., San Marcos, Calif., 1998—99, S. Ctrl. L.A. (Calif.) Regional Ctr., 2000—01, Bader Group Cons., San Diego, 2001—02; compensation cons. Bauer & Wilson, Ltd., Balt., 2002—03. Contbr. articles to profl. jours. Fellow, Orgnl. Cons. Ctr., 1998—2000; grantee, Calif. Sch. Profl. Psychology, 2001—03. Mem.: APA, Am. Psychol. Soc., Soc. for Indsl./Orgnl. Psychology, Ea. Psychol. Assn. Republican, Roman Cath. Avocations: travel, skiing, snorkeling, scuba diving, skydiving. E-mail: ckottraba@excite.com.

KOTUK, ANDREA MIKOTAJUK, public relations executive, writer; b. New Brunswick, N.J., Oct. 19, 1948; d. Michael and Julia Dorothy (Muka) Mikotajuk. BA, Douglass Coll., Rutgers U., 1970. Pub. relations asst. Wall St. Jour. Newspaper Fund, Princeton, N.J., 1970; editorial asst. Redbook mag., N.Y.C., 1970-71; asst. pub. relations dir. Children's Aid Soc., N.Y.C., 1971-75; assoc. pub. relations dir. Planned Parenthood, N.Y.C., 1975-80; pres. Andrea & Assocs., N.Y.C., 1980—. Writer publicist for non-profit agys.; contbg. editor Arts Mag., 1970-75. Office: Andrea & Assocs 112 E 23rd St New York NY 10010-4518

KOTULA, ANTHONY WILLIAM, retired research food scientist; s. Walenty and Katarzyna Kotula; m. Joan Dorothy Ryziewicz, Feb. 16, 1957; children: Kathryn, Louise, Valerie Ann. BS, U. Mass., 1951, MS, 1954; PhD, U. Md., 1964. Rsch. scientist UDSA, Washington, 1954—55, rsch. scientist and supr. Beltsville, Md., 1955—92. Editor: Muscle Foods. First lt. USAF, 1951—53, Korea. Fellow: Am. Soc. Animal Sci. (Meat Rsch. Award 1988); mem.: Poultry Sci. Assn. (rsch. award 1967), Am. Meat Sci. Assn. (Signal Svc. award 1983, R.C. Pollack award 2003, Disting. Rsch. Award 1992), Phi Kappa Phi, Gamma Sigma Delta, Sigma Xi. Roman Catholic. Achievements include determined criteria for the thermal destruction of Trichinella spiralis and Toxoplasma gondii. Developed procedures for the control of bacteria on meat. Avocations: gardening, fishing, hunting, reading, woodworking. Home: 135 Maple Road Storrs Mansfield CT 06268-2514 Home Fax: 860-429-9200. Personal E-mail: awkotula@msn.com.

KOTULAK, RONALD, newspaper science writer; b. Detroit, July 31, 1935; s. John and Mary (Roman) Kotulak; m. Jean Bond, May 6, 1961 (dec. July 1974); children: Jeffrey, Kerry, Christopher; m. Donna Clausonthue, July 19, 1980; stepchildren: Paul Clausonthue, Lisa Clausonthue. Student, Wayne State U., 1953—54; BJ, U. Mich., 1959. Mem. staff Chgo. Tribune, 1959—, sch. bd. reporter, 1961—63, writer, 1965—. Recipient 1st pl. sci. writing award, ADA, 1966, 1st pl. med. writing award, AMA, 1968, 1st pl. Howard Blakeslee Sci. Writing award, Am. Heart Assn., 1968, 1st prize Russell L. Cecil award, Arthritis Found., 1969, 1st pl. Claude Bernard Sci. Journalism award, Nat. Soc. Med. Rsch., 1971, James T. Brady award, Am. Chem. Soc., 1974, Lifeline award, Am. Health Found., 1976, Edward Scott Beck award, Chgo. Tribune, 1965, 1976, 1991, 1993, Outstanding Achievement award, U. Mich., 1978, Robert T. Morse Writers award, Am. Psychiat. Assn., 1982, 1989, Helen Carringer Nat. Mental Health Journalism award, Nat. Mental Health Assn., 1988, Excellence in Journalism award, Am. Aging Assn., 1992, Pulitzer Prize for explanatory journalism, 1994, others. Mem.: Nat. Assn. Sci. Writers (pres. 1972—73). Home: 737 N Oak Park Ave Oak Park IL 60302-1536 Office: The Chicago Tribune 435 N Michigan Ave Chicago IL 60611-4066

KOTYNEK, GEORGE ROY, mechanical engineer, educator, marketing executive; b. Lake Forest, Ill., Apr. 18, 1938; s. Anton Joseph and Zdenka K.; m. Virginia Jean Hyde, Sept. 4, 1965 (div. 1973); children: John Anton, Joseph George. BSME, Ill. Inst. Tech., 1960. Registered profl. engr., Ill. Efficiency engr. Commonwealth Edison Co., Chgo., 1959-63; instr. physics Glenbard East High Sch., Lombard, Ill., 1963-67; systems engr. Sargent and Lundy, Chgo., 1967-77; prin. engr. Fluor Corp., Chgo., 1977-85; mgr. fossil tech. Stearns Catalytic World Corp., Oak Brook, Ill., 1985-86; mgr. mktg. Volund USA Ltd., New Providence, N.J., 1986-94; tech. cons. VECTRA Techs., Inc., Lincolnshire, Ill., 1994-96; sr. tech. cons. Duke Engring. & Svcs., Inc., Naperville, Ill., 1996—2002, Framatome ANP, Naperville, 2002—. Mem. hazardous materials adv. com. Waubonsee C.C., Sugar Grove, Ill., 1992—. Contbr. articles to profl. publs. Mem. People to People Internat. Conventional and Nuclear Power Engring. Delegation to People's Republic of China, 1987. Mem. ASME (newsletter editor 1980-82, vice chmn. membership 1982-83, vice chmn. programs 1983-84). Achievements include the design of 2,700-MW electric generating station for cyclic service. Office: Framatome ANP 215 Shuman Blvd Ste 172 Naperville IL 60563-2580 E-mail: George.Kotynek@framatome-anp.com.

KOTYNEK, JAN GEORGE, surgeon; b. Chgo., Feb. 22, 1949; MD, U. Ill., 1975. Intern U. Wis., Madison, 1975-76, resident in pathology, 1976-78, resident in gen. surgery, 1978-82; with Wausau Hosp., 1983-90, Carle Found. Hosp., Urbana, Ill., 1990—. Clin. asst. prof. surgery U. Ill. Coll. Medicine, 1990—. Fellow ACS; mem. Ill. Surg. Soc., Alpha Omega Alpha. Office: Carle Clin Assocs 602 W University Ave Urbana IL 61801-2530 E-mail: jan.kotynek@carle.com.

KOTZ, SAMUEL, statistician, educator, translator, editor; b. Harbin, China, Aug. 28, 1930; s. Boris and Guta (Kahana) K.; m. Roselyn Greenwald, Aug. 6, 1963; children— Tamar Ann, Harold David, Pauline Esther. MSc with honors, Hebrew U., Jerusalem, 1956; PhD, Cornell U., 1960; Dr. honoris causa, U. Athens, 1995, Harbin Inst. Tech., 1984, Bowling Green State U., 1997. Rschr. Israel Meterol. Service, 1954-58; lectr. Bar-Ilan U., Israel, 1960-62; postdoctoral Ford fellow U. NC, 1962-63; asso. prof. U. Toronto, 1963-67; prof. math. Temple U., 1967-79; prof. stats. U. Md., Coll. Pk., 1979-97, disting. scholar-tchr., 1984-85. Disting. vis. prof. Bucknell U., 1977, Guelph (Can.) U., 1987; hon. prof. Harbin Inst. Tech., 1987; Eugene Lukacs disting. rsch. prof. Bowling Green (Ohio) State U., 1992; vis. prof. U. Luleå, Sweden, 1993, 95, Hong Kong U., 1994, U. Copenhagen, summer 1996, U. South Brittany, Vannes, France, 1998; vis. prof. econs. and fin. St. Petersburg (Russia) U., summer 1995; vis. rschr. Internat. Statis. Inst., The Hague, summer 1996, U. Paul Sabatier, Toulouse, France, summer 1998, U. York, Eng., U. Salford, Eng., 1999, 2000, Athens U. Econs., 1999, U. Lund, Sweden, 2000; vis. rsch. scholar George Washington U., 1997—, U. Trento, Italy, summers, 2001, 02, U. Padua, 2002. Author, editor 30 books, 4 Russian-English profl. dictionaries, also numerous rsch. papers; translator 18 books; co-editor-in-chief Encyclopedia of Statistical Sci., 9 vols. and supplement, 1982-89, editor-in-chief up-date vols. 1-3, 1994-98, Quality Control and Mgmt., 2000-; co-editor-in-chief Breakthroughs in Statistics, 3 vol., 1995-98; editor: Leading Statistical Personalities, 1997; co-author: Process Capability Indices, 1993, 98, Applied Bayesian Statistics (in Chinese), 2000, 2d edit., 2001, Extreme Value Distributions, 2000, Correlation and Dependence, 2001, Laplace Distribution and Applications, 2001, Strength-Stress Models, 2003, Statistical Size Distributions in Economics, 2003; mem. editl. bd. Soviet Jour. Applied Math. Stats, Jour. Quality Rsch. and Tech., coord. editor Jour. Statis. Planning and Inference, AIEE Transactions. Served with Israeli Army, 1950-52. Fellow Am. Statis. Assn., Inst. Math. Stat., Royal Statis. Soc., Washington Acad. Sci. (hon.); mem. Internat. Statis. Inst. (elected mem.). Office: George Washington U Dept Engring Management Washington DC 20052-0001 E-mail: kotz@seas.gwu.edu.

KOTZEN, MARSHALL JASON, mathematics educator; b. Malden, Mass., Dec. 29, 1942; s. Bernard and Regina (Katz) K.; m. Elizabeth Claudia Magner, Aug. 24, 1980. BS in Math., Tufts U., 1964; MS in Math., U. N.H., 1967. Grad. asst. in math. U. N.H., Durham, 1967-69; instr. of math. Worcester (Mass.) State Coll., 1969-74, asst. prof. math., 1974-89, assoc. prof. math., 1989—. Mem. Am. Math. Soc., Math. Assn. Am. Office: Worcester State Coll 486 Chandler St Worcester MA 01602-2597

KOUCHOUKOS, NICHOLAS THOMAS, surgeon; b. Grand Rapids, Mich., Dec. 26, 1936; s. Thomas Paul and Antoinette (Karver) K.; m. Judith Buell, Aug. 24, 1966; children— Nicholas Thomas, Robert Buell, Thomas Paul. Student (James B. Angell scholar), U. Mich., 1954-57; MD cum laude, Washington U., 1961. Diplomate Am. Bd. Thoracic Surgery (bd. dirs. 1989-96). Intern Barnes Hosp., Washington U. Med. Ctr., St. Louis, 1961-62, asst. resident in surgery, 1962-65, chief adminstrv. resident, 1965-66; sr. clin. trainee in surgery USPHS, 1966-67; asst. in surgery Sch. Medicine Washington U., St. Louis, 1961-65, instr. surgery, 1965-67, John M. Shoenberg prof. cardiovascular surgery, 1984-96, vice chmn. dept. surgery, 1993-96; research fellow surgery Sch. Medicine, U. Ala., Birmingham, 1967-68, instr. surgery, 1967-69, advanced trainee thoracic and cardiovascular surgery, 1968-70, asst. prof. surgery, 1969-71, assoc. prof., 1971-74, prof., vice-dir. div. thoracic and cardiovascular surgery, 1974-81, John W. Kirklin prof. cardiovascular surgery, 1981, clin. prof., 1981-84; cardiovascular surgeon-in-chief Jewish Hosp. of St. Louis, 1984-96, surgeon in chief, 1988-96; mem. cardiovascular research study com. Am. Heart Assn., 1977-79; surgery study sect. USPHS, Bethesda, Md., 1977-80; vice chmn. dept. surgery Washington U. Sch. Medicine, St. Louis, 1991-96. Ad hoc cons. Specialized Centers in Research Arteriosclerosis, Nat. Heart and Lung Inst., Bethesda, 1971-72, mem. ad hoc rev. com. for collaborative studies on coronary artery surgery, 1973-75, surgery A study sect., 1976-77; mem. merit rev. bd. in cardiovascular studies VA, Washington, 1976-78 Editorial bd. Jour. Cardiac Rehab., 1979-84, Current Topics in Cardiology, 1977-92, Circulation, 1978-81, 86-88, Cardiology Update, 1979-92, Annals Thoracic Surgery, 1980-89, Cardiosat, 1984-92; assoc. editor Jour. Thoracic and Cardiovascular Surgery, 1994-98. Fellow: ACS, Am. Coll. Cardiology (asst. treas. 1997—99, sec. 1999—2000, finalist Young Investigators award 1962); mem.: AAUP, AMA, Internat. Cardiovascular Soc., Soc. Vascular Surgery, Soc. Univ. Surgeons, So. Surg. Assn., So. Thoracic Surg. Assn., St. Louis Thoracic Surg. Soc. (pres. 1993—95), Soc. Thoracic Surgeons (treas. 1992—97, v.p. 1998, pres. 1999—2000), John Kirklin Soc., St. Louis Met. Med. Soc., Internat. Surg. Soc., Assn. Acad. Surgery, Assn. Clin. Cardiac Surgeons, Am. Surg. Assn., Am. Assn. Thoracic Surgery, Alpha Omega Alpha, Phi Beta Kappa. Home: 25 Picardy Ln Saint Louis MO 63124-1606 Office: Mo Bapt Hosp 3009 N Ballas Rd Ste 266C Saint Louis MO 63131-2308 E-mail: ntkouch@aol.com.

KOUCKY, FRANK LOUIS, geology educator, archeogeology researcher; b. Chgo., June 24, 1927; s. Frank Louis Sr. and Ella (Harshman) K.; m. Virginia Ruhl, Sept. 10, 1949; children: Frank Louis III, David, Walter, Jonathan. BPh, U. Chgo., 1949, MS, 1953, PhD, 1956. Instr. U. Ill., Chgo., 1949-55; asst. prof. Mont. Sch. of Mines, Butte, 1955-58, U. Ill., Urbana, 1958-60; assoc. prof. U. Cin., 1960-72; prof. Coll. of Wooster, Ohio, 1972-92; ret., 1992. Vis. prof. field camp U. Ill., Sheridan, Wyo., summers 1958-72; vis. prof. U. Swansea, Wales, 1968, MIT, Cambridge, Mass., 1978, 83, Am. Ctr. for Oriental Rsch., Ammon, Jordan, 1987; mem. archaeol. excavation in Cyprus, Jordan, Israel. Contbr. articles to profl. jours. With U.S. Army, 1945-47. Danforth fellow, 1965—, Bucher fellow U. Cin., 1968, NEH fellow, 1987. Fellow AAAS, Geol. Soc. Am., Ohio Acad. Sci.; mem. Mineral. Assn. Can., Geochem. Soc., Soc. Econ. Geologists, Am. Schs. of Oriental Rsch., Sigma Xi (pres. 1990-91). Avocations: archaeogeology, metallurgy. Home: 122 W Easton Rd Burbank OH 44214-9746

KOUCKY, JOHN RICHARD, metallurgical engineer, manufacturing executive; b. Chgo., Sept. 21, 1934; s. Frank Louis and Ella (Harshman) K.; m. Beverly Irene O'Dell, Aug. 16, 1958 (dec. May 1990); children: Deborah, Diane; m. Beverly Kay Cummins, Apr. 27, 1991 (dec. Jan. 1996); m. Mary Ann Hubbard, Jan. 4, 1997. BS in MetE., U. Ill., 1957; MBA, Northwestern U., 1959. Metallurgist, asst. plant mgr. Fansteel Metall. Corp., North Chicago, Ill., 1957-64; supr. production engring. cen. foundry div. Gen. Motors Corp., Saginaw, Mich., 1964-67; asst. gen. mgr. Marion (Ind.) Malleable Iron, 1967-68; mgr. production engring. tech., plant mgr., v.p. engr. Wagner Castings Co., Decatur, Ill., 1968-79, 83-91; v.p., gen. mgr. Pa. mall iron div. Gulf & Western, Lancaster, 1979-82; v.p. tech. Wagner Laser Techs., 1989-94; v.p. Decatur Mfg. Co., 1993-95, 300 Below, Inc., Decatur, 1993—. Served to 1st lt. U.S. Army, 1957-58. Mem. Am. Soc. Metals (local chmn. 1976—), Am. Foundrymans Soc. (local vice chmn. 1968—), Ductile Iron Soc. (nat. bd. dirs. 1983—), Iron Castings Soc., Soc. Automotive Engrs., U. Ill. Dept. Materials Sci. Alumni Assn. (bd. dirs. 1983-98, Loyalty award 1986), Gray Iron Founders Assn., Soc. for Advancement Material and Process Engring., Country Club Decatur, Decatur Tennis Club (pres. 1976-78), Decatur Racquet Club. Republican. Avocations: tennis, golf, bridge, gardening. Home: 510 Greenway Ln Decatur IL 62521-2533 Office: 300 Below Inc 2999 Parkway Dr Decatur IL 62526

KOUFARIS, MARIOS, information technology educator; b. Nicosia, Cyprus, Apr. 29, 1971; arrived in U.S., 1990; s. Andreas Koufaris, Elli Koufaris. BSc in Economics, BA in Psychology, U. Pa., 1994; PhD in Info. Sys., NYU, 2000. Tech. analyst Datacor, Inc., Florham Park, NJ, 1994—95; rsch. fellow Dynamic Logic, Inc., New York, NY, 1999—2000; asst. prof. SCIS dept. Baruch Coll., CUNY, New York, NY, 2000—. Contbr. articles to profl. jours. Fellow Nadler, NYU, 1998, Zicklin, CUNY, 2000-2001, Lang fellow, 2003—; scholar Benjamin Franklin, U. Pa., 1990-1994. Mem.: Inst. Ops. Rsch. and Mgmt. Scis., Assn. Computing Machinery, Beta Gamma Sigma, Delta Sigma Pi. Liberal. Avocations: travel, photography, art, literature, music. Office: CUNY Baruch Coll, SCIS Dept 55 Lexington Ave, Box B11-220 New York NY 10010 Business E-Mail: marios_koufaris@baruch.cuny.edu.

KOUFIS, JOHN THEODORE, accountant; b. East Lansing, Mich., June 28, 1965; s. Theodore John and Helen Constantinos (Athanasopoulos) K. BS in Acctg., DePaul U., 1987. CPA, Ill. Audit assoc. Coopers & Lybrand, Chgo., 1987-89, audit sr. assoc., 1989-93; asst. contr. NCH Promotional Svcs. divsn. Dun & Bradstreet, Lincolnshire, Ill., 1993-95, contr., 1995-98; CFO Croda Adhesives, Inc., Itasca, Ill., 1998—2001, Knights Apparel, LLC, Oakbrook, Ill., 2001—. Mem. AICPAs, Ill. CPA Soc. Avocations: ice hockey, music. Home: 1121 N Thackeray Dr Palatine IL 60067-2751 Office: Kinghts Apparel LLC 2221 Camden Ct # 390 Oak Brook IL 60523

KOUGH, ROBERT HAMILTON, retired clinical hematologist, consultant; b. Harrisburg, Pa., Feb. 19, 1921; s. Harry Milton and Olive Jane (Smith) K.; m. Nancy Jane Trunnell, June 18, 1943; 1 child, Elizabeth Trunnell Beiler. BS, Pa. State U., 1942; MD, U. Pa., 1945. Diplomate Am. Bd. Internal Medicine, Am. Bd. Hematology. Intern Hosp. of U. Pa., Phila., 1945-46; med. resident, Am. Cancer Soc. fellow in hematology Hosp. U. Pa., Phila., 1955-58; from asst. instr. to assoc. in pharmacology U. Pa. Med. Sch., Phila., 1949-52; mem. med. staff Carlisle (Pa.) Hosp., 1952-55; assoc. in hematology Geisinger Med. Ctr., Danville, Pa., 1958-65, head hematology, 1965-74, dir. dept. hematology and oncology, depts. medicine, 1974-86, sr. cons. in hematology and oncology, 1986-91. Mem. various coms. Geisinger Med. Ctr., 1959-91; affiliate Leukemia Group B Cancer Control Program, Cornell U., N.Y.C., 1974-78, Eastern Cooperative Oncology Group, Fox Chase, Pa., 1977-86, Mayo Clinic, 1986-87, North Ctrl. Cancer Treatment Group, Mayo Clinic, 1986-91; clin. prof. medicine Pa. State U., Hershey, 1975-87. Prin. author: Anemias Case Studies, 1981; contbr. articles to profl. jours. Active Mid Atlantic Oncology Program, 1984-86; corp. mem. Pa. Blue Shield, Camp Hill, 1972-87, mem. dental affairs com., 1977-79, med. affairs com., 1973-79, med. rev. com. 1980-86, corp. bd. nominating com., 1982-85, mem. profl. adv. coun., alt., 1985-86; bd. dirs. Capital Blue Cross, Harrisburg, Pa., 1969-93, hon. dir., 1993; cons. drug-related patient needs Dept. Health, Edn. and Welfare, NIH, Rockville, Md., 1971, med. surg. task force Dept. Health Commonwealth of Pa., Harrisburg, 1981; Pa. Liaison Coun. for Internal Medicine, 1980-87. Lt. (j.g.) M.C., USN, 1946-49. Recipient awards Pa. State chpt. Alpha Epsilon Delta, Phi Sigma Phi. Fellow ACP (life mem., regional planning com. 1964, program com. 1978, 79, 82, gen. chmn. 1981, book reviewer Annals of Internal Medicine 1964-74, manuscript reviewer Socioecons. 1981); mem. AAAS, AMA, Am. Cancer Soc. (chmn. profl. rels. com. Montour county unit 1959-64, Crusade award 1963), Am. Group Practice Assn. (editl. adv. com. Group Practice 1966-73), Am. Med. Writers Assn. (ad hoc com. on awards 1959), Am. Soc. Clin. Oncology, Am. Soc. Internal Medicine (ho. of dels. 1980-85, reference com. D 1980, meetings com. 1978-83, survey com. 1976, manpower pool 3d party payors 1980), Assn. Cmty. Cancer Ctrs. (Washington) (instl. rep. 1978), Am. Soc. Hematology, Pa. Med. Soc. (med. svcs. com. 1964-72, profl. liability commn. 1979-85, malpractice ins. task force 1966-71, Dept. Pub. Assistance com. 1966, profl. liability appeal com. 1986, pub. policy com. 1984, internal medicine adv. com. 1980-84, contbg. editor Pa. Medicine 1970-84), Pa. Soc. Internal Medicine (med. svcs. com. 1973-80, chmn. 1975-79, membership com. 1980-86, chmn. 1980-86, legis. com. 1981-83, peer rev. com. 1980-86, program chmn. 1978-79, chmn. nominating com. 1980, pres. 1979-80), Pa. Soc. Hematology and Oncology (organizing com. 1964-81, exec. com. 1982-95, pres. 1986-87), Montour County Med. Soc. (chmn. com. on comprehensive health planning 1970, censor, pres.-elect 1971-72, pres. 1972-73), Phila. Hematology Soc., Phi Eta Sigma, Phi Kappa Phi, Phi Beta Kappa, Alpha Omega Alpha. Republican. Lutheran. Achievements include pioneering rsch. with others in human vols. on the ctrl. control of respiration, cerebral blood flow and oxygen toxicity at 1 atm and 3.5 atm O2 partial press; author of 1st authenticated report of an unprovoked attack, with a bite, by a rabid insectivorous bat, alerting public to the insectivorous bat as a significant reservoir of rabies in spite of rarity of an obvious bite and in spite of fact that the method of transmission from bat to man and animals is not obvious; rsch. on recognition of membrane abnormalities of erythrocytes in myeloproliferative disorders by Merocyanine 540.

KOUL, HARI KRISHEN, research scientist, rights activist; b. Anantnag, Kashmir, India, Sept. 14, 1963; s. Soom Nath and Shyama (Dulari) K.; m. Sweaty Koul, Apr. 29, 1994; children: Neil, Kashyap. BS in Biology and Chemistry, Kashmir U., 1984, MS in Biochemistry, 1986; PhD in Biochemistry, Postgrad. Inst. Med. Edn. and Rsch., Chandigarh, India, 1990. Jr. rsch. fellow Postgrad. Inst. Med. Edn. and Rsch., 1986-88, sr. rsch. fellow, 1988-90, tutor in biochemistry, 1990-91; postdoctoral fellow in surgery and physiology U. Mass. Med. Sch., Worcester, 1991-94, sr. rsch. assoc. in surgery and physiology, 1994-96, instr. urologic and transplantation surgery, 1996-97; sr. staff scientist, prin. investigator Henry Ford Health Scis. Ctr., Detroit, 1997—2003; dir. rsch. divsn. urology U. Colo. Health Scis. Ctr., Denver, 2003—. Program dir. Urolithiasis Rsch. Project, NIH, 1997-2003; mem. NIH-Site visit com. U. Chgo. Program Project, Bethesda, Md., 1999, NIH-Gen. Medicine B-Study sect. and Urology Spl. Emphasis Panel (SEP), 2000. Author: (chpt.) Kidney Stones Medical and Surgical Management, 1996; editl. bd. (journal) Urol. Rsch., 2001; contbr. articles. Pres. Assn. Basic Med. Scientists, Chandigarth, India, 1990-91; mem. Kashmir Overseas Assn., 1991—, ACLU, 1997; founding exec. dir. Save Kashmir Movement, 1999; mem. Am. Friends of India, 2000, India Think Tank, 2000; coord. Panun Kashmir, 2000; mem. Oxalosis and Hyperoxaluria Found., 2001—. Recipient Jr. Rsch. fellowship Coun. Sci. and Indsl. Rsch., New Delhi, 1987, Internat. Scientist of Yr., 2002; Sr. Rsch. fellow Coun. Sci. and Indsl. Rsch., 1988, Postdoctoral fellow U. Mass. Med. Sch., 1991; Rsch. grantee NIH, 1997. Fellow: Am. Coll. Nutrition; mem.: AAAS, Am. Soc. Nephrology, Am. Soc. Biochemistry Molecular Biology, Molecular Medicine Soc., ROCK Soc., Urolithiasis Soc. India, N.Y. Acad. Sci., Am. Chem. Soc., Kashmir Overseas Assn. (bd. dirs. Mich. chpt. 2003, pres.). Avocations: cricket, soccer, international public policy analysis, reading, thinking. Office: Dir Rsch, Divsn Urology and Dept Surgery Univ Colo Sch Medicine 4200 E Ninth Ave, Box C319 Denver CO 80262 Home: 3162 Bloomfield Shr West Bloomfield MI 48323-3504 Office Fax: 303-315-7611. Business E-Mail: Hari.Koul@UCHSC.edu.

KOULOURIANOS, DIMITRI THEODORE, economist; b. Koroni, Greece, Dec. 4, 1930; s. Theodore and Paraskevi (Tsakonas) K.; m. Roula Varvoutsis, Sept. 2, 1966; children: Theodore, Athina. BBA, Athens (Greece) Econ. U., 1953; MA in Econs., U. Calif., Berkeley, 1964, PhD in Econs., 1967. Economist Bank of Greece, Athens, 1957-67, World Bank, Washington, 1968-81; min. of fin. Greek Govt., Athens, 1982-83; amb. OECD, Paris, 1986-90; bd. dirs. European Bank for Reconstrn. and Devel., London, 1991-93; cons. Athens, 1993-98; mem. European Parliament, 1999—. Pvt. Greek Army, 1953-55. Home: 8 Andrea Ghini St 15233 Halandri Athens Greece Office: 13 Rizari St Athens 11634 Greece E-mail: dkoulourianos@europarl.eu.int.

KOUNTAKIS, STILIANOS E, surgeon, otolaryngologist; BS, ChemE, U. Houston, Houston, Tex., 1983; MD, U Tex., Houston, Texas, 1988; resident in otolaryn. head and neck surgery, U Tex., Houston, 1993; PhD medicine, U. Crete, Heraklion, Crete, Greece, 1998. Diplomate Am. Bd. of Otolaryn., 1995. Chief of ENT LBJ Gen. Hosp., Houston, 1993—97; asst. prof. otolaryn. U Tex. Houston, 1993—99; assoc. prof. otolaryn. U. Va., Charlottesville, Va., 1999—, dir., rhinology U Va., Charlottesville, Va., 1999—. Recipient Honor Award, Am. Acad. of Otolaryn. Head and Neck Surgery, Found., 2002. Fellow: Am. Acad. of Otolaryn. (licentiate), ACS (licentiate), Am. Rhinol. Soc. (licentiate; bd. of directors 2001—). Office: U Va P O Box 800713 Charlottesville VA 22908 Office Fax: 434-982-3965.

KOURI, DONALD JACK, chemist, educator; b. Hobart, Okla., July 25, 1938; s. Eddie and Theresa LaJuan (Williams) K.; m. Shirley Ann Stewart, Apr. 9, 1965; children: Lisa Renee, David Matthew. BA, Okla. Bapt. U., 1960; MS, U. Wis., 1962, PhD, 1965. Postdoctoral fellow Joint Inst. Lab Astrophysics, U. Colo., 1965-66; asst. prof. chemistry Midwestern U., Wichita Falls, 1966-67, U. Houston, 1967-71, assoc. prof., 1971-73, prof., 1973—, Disting. Univ. prof., 1987-96, Cullen Disting. prof. chemistry, physics. Vis. lectr. U. Ill., 1972; vis. scientist Inst. for Strömungsforschung, Göttingen, Fed. Republic Germany, 1973-74; bd. dirs. Inst. for Digital Informatics and Analysis. Recipient U.S. Sr. Scientist award Alexander von Humboldt Found., 1973-74, Southwestern Tex. sect. award Am. Chem. Soc., 1981, Sigma Xi Rsch. award, 1995; fellow A.P. Sloan Found., 1972-74, Weizmann Inst., 1973, Inst. for Advanced Studies

Hebrew U. Jerusalem, 1978-79, Guggenheim Found., 1978-79. Fellow Am. Phys. Soc. (exec. com. mem., sec.-treas. Few Body Topical group); mem. IEEE, ASCAP, Am. Chem. Soc., Am. Assn. Physics Tchrs. Democrat. Baptist. Office: U Houston Dept Chemistry 4800 Calhoun Rd Houston TX 77004-2610 E-mail: kouri@uh.edu.

KOURIDES, IONE ANNE, endocrinologist, researcher, educator; b. N.Y.C., Sept. 1, 1942; d. Peter T. and Anne E. (Spetseris) K.; m. Charles G. Zaroulis, Nov. 30, 1974; children: Anna Larisa, Andrew, Christina, Peter. BA, Wellesley Coll., 1963; MD, Harvard U., 1967. Diplomate Am. Bd. Internal Medicine, Am. Bd. Endocrinology and Metabolism. Intern Jewish Hosp., Washington U., St. Louis, 1967-68; resident Montefiore, Albert Einstein Med. Sch., Bronx, N.Y., 1968-69; fellow Beth Israel, Harvard U., Boston, 1970-72; assoc. prof. medicine Cornell U. Med. Coll., N.Y.C., 1981—; sr. med. dir. diabetes team Pfizer Inc., N.Y.C., 1990—. Mem. editorial bd. Endocrinology, Jour. Clin. Endocrinol Metabolism, also others; contbr. over 100 articles to sci. jours., chpts. to books. Mem. nat. campaign Harvard Med. Sch., Boston, 1986-92; nat. bd. dirs. Philoptochos Soc. Greek Orthodox Archdiocese. Grantee NIH, 1979-84. Fellow ACP; mem. Am. Soc. Clin. Investigation, Am. Assn. Physicians, Am. Thyroid Assn. (coms.), Endocrine Soc. (coms.). Achievements include discovery of alpha-secreting pituitary tumors; demonstrated that measurement of amniotic fluid thyroid stimulating hormone can be used to diagnose hypthyroidism in utero; development of insulin secretagogue Glucotrol XL. Home: 1070 Park Ave New York NY 10128-1000 Office: Pfizer Inc 235 E 42nd St New York NY 10017-5755 E-mail: kourii@pfizer.com.

KOURIDES, PETER THEOLOGOS, lawyer; b. Istanbul, Turkey, July 24, 1910; came to U.S., 1912, naturalized, 1931; s. Theologos and Zafiro (Gurlides) K.; m. Anna E. Spetseris, Aug. 4, 1938; children— Ione A., P. Nicholas. BA, Columbia, 1931, JD, 1933; HHD (hon.), Hellenic Coll., 1985. Bar: N.Y. 1933. Mem. firm Seward, Raphael & Kourides, N.Y.C., 1935—; gen. counsel Greek Archdiocese of North and South Am., 1938-96; trustee Hellenic Cathedral City N.Y., 1938-98; trustee, counsel St. Basil's Acad., Garrison, N.Y., 1946-97, United Greek Orthodox Charities, 1965-70; counsel World Conf. Religion for Peace, 1970-82; dir., counsel Hellenic Am. C. of C., 1955—; dir. Atlantic Bank N.Y., 1974-97; counsel Consultate Gen. of Greece, N.Y.C., 1963-90. Nat. sec. Greek War Relief Assn., 1941-46; rep. Greek Archdiocese of North and South Am. at enthronement Athenagoras I, Istanbul, 1949; pres. Hellenic U. Club, 1951-52. Author: The Evolution of the Greek Orthodox Church in America and its Current Problems, 1959, The Centennial History of the Archdiocesan Cathedral of the Holy Trinity, 1992. Nat. v.p. Order of Ahepa, 1960; mem. gen. bd. Nat. Coun. Chs., 1960-82, v.p., 1969-72; counsel Columbia U. Cancer Clinic in Greece, 1965-70; del. 3d Assembly World Coun. Chs., New Delhi, India, 1961, 4th Assembly, Uppsala, Sweden, 1968, 5th Assembly, Nairobi, Kenya, 1975, World Conf. Religion on Peace, Kyoto, Japan, 1971; mem. internat. affairs com. World Coun. Chs., 1968-74; trustee Hellenic Coll., Brookline, Mass., 1968-97. Decorated Gold Cross Order of Phoenix by King Constantine II Greece, 1967, Titular Archon Megas Nomophylax by Ecumenical Partriarchate of Eastern Orthodox Ch., 1968, grand comdr. Knights of Holy Sepulchre Jerusalem Patriarchate of Eastern Orthodox Ch., 1961. Mem. ABA, N.Y. Bar Assn., Consular Law Soc., Am. Judicature Soc., Columbia Alumni Assn. Home: 46 Groton St Forest Hills NY 11375-5921 Office: 110 E 59th St New York NY 10022-1304

KOURILSKY, FRANÇOIS MICHEL, research scientist; b. Paris, Dec. 28, 1934; s. Raoul and Simone (Develay) K.; m. Colette Lucienne Bellegarde, Nov. 7, 1956 (div. Dec. 1985); children: Laurent, Michel; m. Françoise Marie-Noël Gauthier, Aug. 20, 1988. Cert. in Psychophysiology, Faculty Scis., Paris, 1961; Cert. in Immunology, Pasteur Inst., Paris, 1962; MD, Faculty Medicine, Paris, 1966; D (hon.), U. Buenos Aires, 1992. Sr. resident Paris Hosp., 1960-66; rsch. fellow Sch. Medicine, NYU, 1962-63; chef de clinique-attache Faculty Medicine, Paris, 1966-68; rschr. Nat. Inst. Health and Med. Rsch., France, 1967—88, emeritus rsch. dir., 2000—; dir. gen. Nat. Ctr. Sci. Rsch., France, 1988-94; dir. rsch. Inst. Gustave Roussy, Villejuif, France, 1995—2002, emeritus dir. rsch., 2001—. Dir. unit of tumor immunology Nat. Inst. Health and Med. Rsch., U. Paris 7, 1974-76; dir. Inst. Immunology Marseille, France, 1976-85; chmn. sci. coun. coord. Inst. Curie, Paris, 1983-87; dir. Federative Rsch. Inst., Inst. Gustave Roussy, 1996-2000; chmn. sci. coun. firms Immunotech SA, 1982, Epigene SA, 2000-01, IPSOGEN S.A., 2001—. Contbr. over 100 articles to profl. jours. V.p. superior coun. rsch. tech. French Ministry Rsch., 1983-87; chmn. commn. Plan Recherche, 1985; chmn. Rsch. Obs. Midi, Pyrenees, France, 2000-2003; pres. Mediterranean Techs., Provence, Alpes, Cote D'Azur, 2000-2003. Named officer Nat. Order of Merit, France, 1990, officer Legion D'Honneur, France, 1994, comdr. Order of Merit Fed. Republic of Germany, 1995 Home: 21 Blvd Du Montparnasse 75006 Paris France Fax: 33 1 42843226.

KOURKOUMELIS, NICK, financial analyst, consultant, finance educator; b. San Francisco, Mar. 1, 1948; s. Gerasimos A. and Ismini (Melissaratos) K.; m. Maria Demetriadou; 1 child, Effie Nicole. BS, Fairleigh Dickinson U., 1970, MBA with high honors, 1974; PhD in Bus. Adminstrn., Century U., 1990. Supr., fin. analyst comptr.'s office Texaco Inc., White Plains, N.Y., 1970-85, coord. human resources, 1986-88, sr. coord. human resource devel. comptr.'s office, 1988-93; fin. tng. cons. exec. dept., 1994-95; value analyst corp. planning and econs. dept. Texaco Inc., White Plains, N.Y., 1995-96, sr. fin. cons. human resources dept., 1997-98; pres., CEO The Melis Group, LLC, 1999—; mng. ptnr. Oher & Assocs., 2000—; mem. strategic planning program Calif. Inst. Tech., 1992; assoc. prof. bus. Am. Coll. Thessaloniki, 2002—. Adj. prof. econs. and fin. exec. MBA program Fairleigh Dickinson U., Teaneck, NJ, 1978—; fin. mgmt. cons. IBM Inst. for Advanced Bus., Calif. State Poly U., Bell Atlantic, USF&G Corp., Chase Manhattan Bank, Time, Inc., MCI Corp., Roche Lab., Allied Signal, Lockheed Martin, Pfizer, Fed. Home Loan Bank San Francisco, Hall Neighborhood House, Women and Minority Owned Bus., N.J. Ethnic Adv. Coun.; bus. mgr. various actresses; fin. cons. to celebrities and sports figures; exec. cons. The Sable Group, 1990—. Mem. nat. steering com. Clinton/Gore Presdl. Campaign, 1996; dir. Greek Orthodox Sunday Sch. Program; coun. mem., treas. St. Athanasios Ch. Texaco scholarship recipient Capitol award Nat. Leadership Coun., 1991, FDU Teaching Excellence award, 1994-96; named on Wall of Tolerance, 2002. Mem. ASTD (v.p. fin. Westchester chpt.), Internat. Econs. Honor Soc., Mgmt. Devel. Forum, The Planning Forum, Greek Am. Voters League N.J. (founder, dir.). Greek Orthodox. Home: 15 Fayette Pl Fair Lawn NJ 07410 Personal E-mail: nikolaos@ac.anatolia.edu.gr.

KOURLIS, REBECCA LOVE, state supreme court justice; b. Colorado Springs, Colo., Nov. 11, 1952; d. John Arthur and Ann (Daniels) Love; m. Thomas Aristithis Kourlis, July 15, 1978; children: Stacy Ann, Katherine Love, Aristithis Thomas. BA with distinction in English, Stanford U., 1973, JD, 1976; LLD (hon.), U. Denver, 1997. Bar: Colo. 1976, D.C. 1979, U.S. Dist. Ct. Colo. 1976, U.S. Ct. Appeals (10th cir.) 1976, Colo. Supreme Ct., U.S. Ct. Appeals (D.C. cir.), U.S. Claims Ct., U.S. Supreme Ct. Assoc. Davis, Graham & Stubbs, Denver, 1976-78, sole practice Craig, Colo., 1978-87; judge 14th Jud. Dist. Ct., Craig, Colo., 1987-94; arbiter Jud. Arbiter Group, Inc., 1994-95; justice Colo. Supreme Ct., 1995—. Water judge divsn. 6, 1987-94; lectr. to profl. groups. Contbr. articles to profl. jours. Chmn. Moffat County Arts and Humanities, Craig, 1979; mem. Colo. Commn. on Higher Edn., Denver, 1980-81; mem. adv. bd. Colo. Divsn. Youth Svcs., 1988-91; mem. com. civil jury instructions, 1990-95, standing com. gender and justice, 1994-97, chair jud. adv. coun., 1997-2002, chair com. on jury reform, 1996—; co-chair com. on atty. grievance reform, 1997-2002; mem. long range planning com. Moffat County Sch., 1990; bd. visitors Stanford U., 1989-94, Law Sch. U. Denver, 1997-2002; trustee Kent Denver Sch., 1996-2002. Named N.W. Colo. Daily Press Woman of Yr., 1993; recipient Trailblazer award AAUW, 1998, Mary Lathrop award Colo. Women's Bar Assn., 2001, Jud. Excellence award Acad. Matrimonial Lawyers, 2002, Champion for Children award Rocky Mountain Children's Law Ctr., 2003. Fellow: Colo. Bar Found., Am. Bar Found.; mem.: N.W. Colo. Bar Assn. (Cmty. Svc. award 1993—94), Dist. Ct. Judges' Assn. (pres. 1993—94), Colo. Bar Assn (bd. govs. 1983—85, mineral law sect. bd. dirs. 1985, sr. v.p. 1987—88), Rocky Mountain Mineral Found. Office: State Jud Bldg 2 E 14th Ave Denver CO 80203-2115

KOUSSER, J(OSEPH) MORGAN, history educator; b. Lewisburg, Tenn., Oct. 7, 1943; s. Joseph Maximillian and Alice Holt (Morgan) K.; m. Sally Ann Ward, June 1, 1968; children: Rachel Meredith, Thaddeus Benjamin. AB, Princeton U., 1965; M.Phil., Yale U., 1968, PhD, 1971; MA, Oxford U., Eng., 1984. Instr. Calif. Inst. Tech., Pasadena, 1969-71, assoc. prof. Padadena, 1975-79, prof., 1979—. Vis. prof. U. Mich., Ann Arbor, 1980, Harvard U., Cambridge, Mass., 1981-82, Oxford U., 1984-85, Claremont Grad. Sch., 1993; expert witness Minority Voting Rights Cases; researcher. Author: Shaping of Southern Politics, 1974, Colorblind Injustice: Minority Voting Rights and the Undoing of the Second Reconstruction, 1999. Recipient Lillian Smith award So. Regional Coun., 1999, Ralph J. Bunche award Am. Polit. Sci. Assn., 2000; Guggenheim Found. fellow, 1984-85, Woodrow Wilson Ctr. fellow, 1984-85; grantee NEH, 1974, 82. Mem. Orgn. Am. Historians, Am. Hist. Assn., Social Scis. History Assn., So. Hist. Assn. Democrat. Avocation: running. Office: Calif Inst Tech 228-77 Caltech Pasadena CA 91125-7700 E-mail: kousser@hss.caltech.edu.

KOUTOUJIAN, PETER JOHN, lawyer; b. Newton, Mass., Sept. 17, 1961; s. Peter and Cornelia (Cassidy) K. Student, U. Coll., Dublin, Ireland, 1981; BA in Psychology, Bridgewater (Mass.) State Coll., 1983; JD, New Eng. Sch. of Law, 1989. Rsch. asst. Commonwealth of Mass., Boston, 1984-86; pvt. practice Waltham, Mass., 1990—; asst. dist. atty. Mass. Ho. Reps., Boston, 1997-98, state rep. Bar adv. Middlesex County Bar Advs., Waltham, 1990—. Mem. Dem. City Com., Waltham, 1983—; big brother Big Bros. Assn. of Boston, 1990—. Roman Catholic. Avocations: tennis, basketball. Home: 154 Waltham St Newton MA 02465-1333 Office: Ho of Reps State House Rm 448 Boston MA 02133*

KOUTROULIS, ARIS GEORGE, artist, educator; b. Athens, Greece, May 14, 1938; came to U.S., 1953; s. George Aris and Julia (Eftimiades) K.; m. Mary Ann Schmid, 1964 (div. 1973); m. Jill Warren, July 4, 1982; 1 child, Georgina. BFA, La. State U., 1961; Master Printer, Tamarind Lithography Workshop, L.A., 1964; MFA, Cranbrook Acad. Art, Bloomfield Hills, Mich., 1966. Chmn. bd. Willis Gallery, Detroit, 1970-71; pres. Common Ground of the Arts, Detroit, 1969-72; guest artist Ox-Bow Summer Sch. Art, Saugatuck, Mich., 1973, co-dir., 1975; assoc. prof. art Wayne State U., 1966-75; head painting dept. Ctr. Creative Studies, Detroit, 1975-81, prof., chmn. Fine Arts Dept., 1981-2000. Exhibited in one-man shows Hanamura Gallery, Detroit, 1966, Montgomery Mus. Fine Arts, Ala, 1966, Va. Poly. Inst., 1968, Baton Rouge Gallery, 1968, Wayne State U., 1969, Mich. Coun. for Arts, 1969, Gertrude Kasle Gallery, Detroit, 1970, Detroit Artists Market, 1973, Klein-Vogel Gallery, Detroit, 1974, Detroit Inst. Arts, 1976, Gloria Cortella Gallery, N.Y.C., 1977, Gallery Renaissance, Detroit, 1980, Haber-Theodore Gallery, N.Y.C., 1980, OK Harris Gallery, N.Y.C., 1980, 81, 82, 83, 85, 87, 90, 92, 96, 98, Mich. Traveling Exhbn., 1981, Cantor/Cemberg Gallery, Birmingham, Mich., 1982, 88, Dubins Gallery, L.A., 1984, Nimbus Gallery, Dallas, 1986, Argo Gallery, Athens, Greece, 1988, Argo Gallery, Cypress, 1991, 94, OK Harris Works of Art, Birmingham, 1991, Art Gallery Registry Resort, Naples, Fla., 1992, Bell Gallery, B'haui, 1995, Ctr. Gallery, Detroit, 1996; exhibited in group shows Decorative Arts Ctr., N.Y.C., 1973, Detroit Inst. Arts, 1974, Bykert Gallery, N.Y.C., 1974, Bklyn. Mus., 1977, Brooks Meml. Art Gallery, Memphis, 1977, La. State U. Gallery, 1978, Tyler Sch. Art, Temple U., 1978, Mus. Fine Arts, Springfield, Mass., 1978, Van Doren Gallery, San Francisco, 1978, Consulate Gen. Greece, N.Y.C., 1978, Landmark Gallery, N.Y.C., 1978, Cranbrook Mus. Art, Bloomfield Hills, Mich., 1979, Detroit Inst. Arts, 1980, Mus. Fine Arts, Tampa, 1987, 51st nat. mid-yr. exhbn. Butler Inst. Am. Art, Youngstown, Ohio, 1987, Flint Mus. Art, Mich., 1989, Japan Expo, Tokyo, 1989, Ctr. Gallery Creative Studies, Detroit, 1989, 95, 97, Grove/Timmel Gallery, Naples, 2001; represented in pub. collections including Mus. Modern Art, Nat. Gallery Art, Detroit Inst. Arts, L.A. County Mus. Art Detroit Engring. Soc., Detroit Pub. Libr., U. Mich. Art Mus., Anglo-Am. Mus., Amon Carter Mus. Western Art, Ft. Worth, UCLA Grunwald Graphics Art Found., Ball State U. Art Mus., Vores Mus., Athens, The Goulandis Mus. Modern Art, Andros, Greece; represented in corp. collections; commd. Standard Oil Corp., San Ramon, Calif., Arbor Drugs, Inc., Bracewell/Patterson, Washington, Mich. Found for Arts, Detroit Engring. Soc., Art for Detroit, City of Detroit, WDIV-TV4, Detroit Tampa Mus. Collection, Criterion Ctr. N.Y.C., Masco Corp., Taylor, Mich. Address: PO Box 307 Denver NY 12421-0307 E-mail: akoutroulis@hotmail.com.

KOUTS, HERBERT JOHN CECIL, retired physicist; b. Bisbee, Ariz., Dec. 18, 1919; s. Oliver Allen and Lillian (Niemeyer) K.; m. Hertha Pretorius, Feb. 2, 1942; children: Anne Elizabeth, Catherine Jennifer; m. Barbara Stokes, Mar. 27, 1974; stepchildren: Francis Spitzer, Michael Spitzer, Daniel Spitzer. BS, La. State U., 1941, MS, 1946; PhD, Princeton U., 1952. With Brookhaven Nat. Lab., Upton, L.I., N.Y., 1950-73, 77-89, sr. scientist, asso. div. head, 1958-73, chmn. dept. nuclear energy, 1977-88; mem. Def. Nuclear Facilities Safety Bd., U.S. Govt., Washington, 1989-2000; ret. Dir. div. reactor safety rsch. AEC, Washington, 1973-75; dir. Office Nuclear Regulatory Rsch., U.S. Nuclear Regulatory Commn., Washington, 1975-76; mem. adv. com. reactor physics AEC, 1956-63, mem. adv. com. reactor safeguards, 1962-66; mem. European Am. Adv. Com. for Reactor Physics to European Nuclear Energy Agy., 1962-68; mem. internat. nuclear safety adv. group to IAEA, 1985-92. Served with USAAF, 1942-45. Recipient E. O. Lawrence award AEC, 1963, Disting. Service award, 1975; Disting. Service award NRC, 1976, Sec. Energy's Gold medal for achievement, 1999. Mem. Am. Nuclear Soc. (Theos Thompson award in nuclear reactor safety 1983), N.Y. Acad. Scis., Center Moriches Audubon Soc., Nat. Acad. Engring. Home: 249 S Country Rd Brookhaven NY 11719-9704 E-mail: hjckouts@erols.com.

KOUTSKY, DEAN ROGER, advertising executive; b. Omaha, Nov. 17, 1935; s. John Lewis and Ann Helen (Swan) K.; m. Kathryn Junette Strand; children: Linda, Lisa. BFA, Mpls. Coll. Art and Design, 1957. Art dir. Knox Reeves Advt., Inc., Mpls., 1958-65; v.p., exec. art dir. BBDO, Inc., Mpls., 1965-70; v.p., assoc. creative dir. Campbell-Mithun, Inc., Mpls., 1970-80, sr. v.p., creative dir., 1980-83, exec. v.p., exec. creative dir., 1983-85, vice chmn., 1985-89; exec. cons. Campbell-Mithun Esty, Inc., Mpls., 1989-90; ptnr., mgr. Harmon Ct., 1991-97. Bd. trustees Mpls. Coll. Art and Design, 1982-90, chmn., bd. trustees, 1985-89, adj. prof. advt./design divsn., 1995—. Office: 2005 James Ave S Minneapolis MN 55405-2404

KOUTSOGIANE, PHILLIP CHARLES, lawyer; b. Woonsocket, R.I., Sept. 26, 1944; m. Joyce Ann Hindle, July 28, 1984. BA, Brown U., 1966; JD, Boston U., 1973. Bar: R.I. 1973, Mass. 1973, U.S. Dist. Ct. R.I. 1974, U.S. Supreme Ct. 1980, U.S. Dist. Ct. Mass. 1996. Pvt. practice, Woonsocket. 1st lt. U.S. Army, 1968-70. Mem. ABA, R.I. Bar Assn., Pawtucket Bar Assn., Assn. Trial Lawyers Am., R.I. Trial Lawyers. Office: Stadium Bldg 313 Woonsocket RI 02895-3024

KOUTSTAAL, CORNELIS W. university administrator; b. Rotterdam, The Netherlands, May 10, 1935; came to U.S., 1961; s. Arie and Martina (Leentvaar) K.; m. Murilyn E. Graves, June 21, 1961; children: Robbert Willem, Stanley Wellington. Diploma, Inst. Gehrels, The Hague, The Netherlands, 1957, Logopedic Acad., 1960, Acad. Pedagogy, 1958, Clarke Sch. Deaf, 1963; MS, Springfield Coll., 1963; PhD, Western Res. U., 1966. Lic. speech pathologist, audiologist. Tchr. Effatha Sch. Deaf, Voorburg, The Netherlands, 1958-61, Clarke Sch. Deaf, Northhampton, Mass., 1961-63; fellow Western Res. U., Cleve., 1963-66; prof. Bowling Green (Ohio) State U., 1966-74; chmn., prof. CUNY, Bklyn., 1974-79; dean, prof. Ithaca (N.Y.) Coll., 1979-87; exec. dir. Delano Med. Mgmt. Corp., Pacific Palisades, Calif., 1987-91; prof. head divsn. human potential and performance Truman State U., Kirksville, 1991—2001; prof. emeritus, 2002. Lectr. U. Louvain, U. Groningen, 1969, Rotary Internat. project dir. for hearing impaired, Belize, 1997-2000. Author: Back to Basics, 1987; editorial cons. Williams and Wilkins Pub., Phila., 1975-80; editor-in-chief Spine Print Newsletter, Delano, 1987-90; contbr. 42 articles to profl. jours., also 2 films. Bd. dirs. Boy Scouts Am., Rye, N.Y., 1975, N.E.M.O. Health Coun., Chariton Valley Assn. for Handicapped Citizens, Continuing Med. Edn. Coney Island Hosp., Bklyn., 1974-78. Grantee NSF, 1967, NIH, 1979-81, U.S. Office Edn., 1970, 74-76, pvt. founds., 1979-86, corps., 1979—, Carl P. Miller Discovery Grant, 1996, Rotary Internat. matching grant, 1997-2000. Mem. APA, Am. Speech and Hearing Assn., Acoustical Soc. Am., Am. Assn. Phonetic Scis. (charter), Kirksville C. of C., Rotary (Paul Harris fellow), Phi Kappa Phi, Sigma Xi Rsch. Soc. Am. Avocations: music, reading, sports, travel. Home: 21495 Lake Wood Trail Lake Wood Estates #4 Kirksville MO 63501-9761 E-mail: keesusa@earthlink.net.

KOUVEL, JAMES SPYROS, physicist, educator; b. Jersey City, May 23, 1926; s. Spyros and Ifegenia (Cassianos) K.; m. Audrey Lumsden, June 26, 1953; children: Diana, Alexander. B.Engring., Yale U., 1946, PhD, 1951. Research fellow U. Leeds, Eng., 1951-53, Harvard, 1953-55; physicist Gen. Electric Co. Research and Devel. Center, 1955-69; prof. physics U. Ill.-Chgo., 1969—. Vis. scientist Atomic Energy Rsch. Establishment, Harwell, Eng., 1967-68; vis. prof. U. Paris, Orsay, France, 1981; cons. Argonne (Ill.) Nat. Lab., 1969-89, mem. rev. com., 1970-72, vis. scientist, 1973-74; mem. materials rsch. adv. com. NSF, 1980-82, mem. materials rsch. groups spl. emphasis panel, 1993; mem. evaluation panel NRC, 1981-85. Author papers in field.; Editor: Magnetism Conf. proc, 1965-67; editorial bd.: Jour. Magnetism and Magnetic Materials, 1975—. Served with USNR, 1944-46. Guggenheim fellow, 1967-68; NSF rsch. grantee, 1973-96. Fellow Am. Phys. Soc., AAAS Home: 223 N Euclid Ave Oak Park IL 60302-2107 Office: U Ill Physics Dept Chicago IL 60607-7059 E-mail: kouvel@uic.edu.

KOUWENHOVEN, GERRIT WOLPHERTSEN, retired museum director; b. Mt. Kisco, N.Y., May 8, 1939; s. John Atlee and Eleanor Warren (Hayden) K.; m. Ellen Mather Davis, June 17, 1961; children: Derek Gerritsen, Kirsten Elizabeth. BA in English, U. Colo., 1962, postgrad., 1962-64, Seattle Pacific U., 1975-76, Antioch, 1981-82. Human rights intern Eleanor Roosevelt Meml. Found., 1964-65; field rep., investigator equal opportunities divsn. State of Wis. Indsl. Commn., 1964-66; from employment specialist to asst. dir. Seattle Urban League, 1966-73; pvt. practice campaign cons., 1973-75; tchr. English, chair dept. English LaConner (Wash.) High Sch., 1976-78; tchr. English Arlington (Vt.) Meml. High Sch., 1978-79; pvt. practice rschr., 1979-80; dean Ethan Allen C.C., Manchester Center, Vt., 1981-82; with Friends of Hildene, Inc., Manchester, Vt., 1983—2001, exec. dir., 1986—2001, exec. dir. emeritus, bd. advisers, 2002—. Mem. allocations com. United Way Bennington County, 1992—95; mem. chancel choir First Congl. Ch., Manchester, 1979—, chair stewardship, 1980—82, 1991—93, bd. trustees, 1981—84, 1991—94, co-chair bicentennial steering com., 1983—84, bd. deacons, 1985—88, 1996—99, chair, 1986, chair search com., 1986—88, 1996—98; mem. exec. com. Vt. Conf. United Ch. of Christ, 1999—, chmn., bd. of dirs., 2002—; trustee Dorset (Vt.) Players, Inc., 1983—91, treas., 1986—91; bd. trustees Long Trail Sch., Dorset, 1988—98, vice chair, 1989—90, 1996—97, chair, 1990—96; bd. trustees Am. Theatre Works, Inc., Dorset, 1990—94, chair fin. com., 1992—94; bd. dirs. Preservation Trust Vt., Burlington, 1991—, v.p., 1993, pres., 1994—; bd. trustees United Counseling Svc. Bennington County, Inc., 1992—, sec., 1994—, v.p., 1995, pres., 1996—; bd. trustees Coll. St. Joseph, Vt., 1999—2002; bd. dirs. Vt. Conf. United Ch. of Christ, 1998—, Vt. Alliance of Conservation Voters, 2001—02. Recipient Cmty. Svc. award Manchester C. of C., 1994; recipient Cleveland E. and Phyllis B. Dodge award for Outstanding Cmty. Svc., United Counseling Svc. Bennington County, 2000. Mem. Dorset Nursing Assn. (bd. dirs. 1997—, sec. 1997-2000, pres. 2000-03, v.p. 2003—), Lions (Manchester chpt., bd. dirs. 1984-94, sec. 1984-88, pres. 1991-93). Office: 3768 Main Street PO Box 1233 Manchester VT 05254

KOUYATÉ, LANSANA, economist, international official, diplomat; b. Mali; Formerly economist, spl. rep. of UN Sec.-Gen. to Somalia and Rwanda; former exec. sec., now sec. gen. Econ. Cmty. of West African States, Abuja, Nigeria, 1997—2002. Office: ECOWAS 60 Yakubu Gowon Crescent Asokoro Dist PMB 401 Abuja Nigeria

KOUYMJIAN, DICKRAN, art historian, Orientalist, educator; b. Tulcea, Romania, June 6, 1934; (parents Am. citizens); s. Toros S. and Zabelle I. (Calusdian) K.; m. Angèle Kapoïan, Sept. 16, 1967. BS in European Cultural History, U. Wis., 1957; MA in Arab Studies, Am. U., Beirut, 1961; PhD in Near East Lang. and Culture, Columbia U., 1969. Instr. English Columbia U., N.Y.C., 1961-64; dir. Am. Authors, Inc., N.Y.C., 1965-67; asst. prof. and asst. dir. Ctr. for Arabic Studies Am. U., Cairo, 1967-71; prof., chmn. Armenian Studies dept. Haigazian U., Beirut, 1971-72; assoc. prof. history Am. U. Beirut, 1971-75; prof. art history Am. U., Paris, 1976-77; prof. history and art, dir. Armenian Studies program Calif. State U., Fresno, 1977—. Dir. Ctr. for Armenian Studies, Calif. State U., Fresno, 1990—; Fulbright disting. lectr., prof. Armenian and Am. Lit. Yerevan (Armenia, USSR), 1987; cons. archaeology UNESCO, Paris, 1976; prof., chairholder Armenian Sect., Inst. Nat. des Langs. et Civilisations Orientales, U. Paris, 1988—91; 1st incumbent Haig & Isabel Berberian endowed chair Armenian studies Calif. State U., Fresno, 1989—; 2nd incumbent William Saroyan endowed chair of Armenian studies U. Calif., Berkeley, 1996—97; vis. prof. Oriental Inst. U. Louvain-la-Neuve, Belgium, 2001. Author: Index of Armenian Art, part I, 1977, part II, 1979, The Armenian History of Ghazar P'arpetzi, 1986, Arts of Armenia, 1992; co-author: (with A. Kapoïan) The Splendor of Egypt, 1975, (with M. Stone, H. Lehmann) Album of Armenian Paleography, 2002, (with Giusto Traina, Carlo Franco, Cecilia Veronese Arslan) La Storia di Alessandro il Macedone. Codice miniato armeno del secolo XIV, 2003; author and editor: William Saroyan: An Armenian Trilogy, 1986, William Saroyan: Warsaw Visitor and Tales of the Vienna Streets, 1990; editor: (books) Near Eastern Numistatics, Iconography, Epigraphy and History, 1974, Essays in Armenian Numismatics in Honor of C. Sibilian, 1981, Armenian Studies: In Memoriam Haïg Berbèrian, 1986, Movses Xorenaci et l'histoiographie arméniennes des origines, 2000; editl. bd. Armenian Rev., 1974—, Ararat Lit. mag., 1975—, Revue des Etudes Arméniennes, 1978—, NAASR Jour. Armenian Studies, Jour. of the Soc. for Armenian Studies, 1995—; contbr. articles to profl. jours. Served with U.S. Army, 1957. Recipient St. Sahag and St. Mesrob medal His Holiness Karekin I, Catholics of All Armenians, 1996, Outstanding Prof. award Am. U., Cairo, 1968-69, 69-70, Hagop Kevorkian Disting. Lectureship in Near Eastern Art and Civilization, NYU, 1979, Arthur H. Dadian Armenian Heritage award Armenian Students Assn. Am., 2003; voted Outstanding Prof. of Yr., Faculty Senate, Calif. State U., Fresno, 1986-87; Fulbright fellow, USSR, 1986-87, Michael Dukakis fellow Am. Coll. Thessaloniki, 2003; grantee NEH, Paris, 1980-81, 95, Bertha & John Garabedian Charitable Found., 1994—; chosen Scholar of U. Phi Beta Phi Calif. State U., 1999; named Man of Yr. Armenian Nat. Com. Calif., 2000. Mem. Am. Oriental Soc., Am. Numismatic Soc., Mid. East Studies Assn. (charter), Coll. Arts Assn., Soc. Armenian Studies (charter, pres. 1985-86, 92-94), Société asiatique (Paris), Internat. Assn. of Armenian Studies, Mid. East Medievalist, Assn. Paléographique Internat., Phi Kappa Phi (nat. scholar Fresno chpt. 1998, Univ. Scholar award chpt. 962 1999). Achievements include selected to serve on jury for annual Francqui Fund Prize, Brussels, 2001. Avocations: music, films, bibliophile. Home: 54 rue Boussingault 75013 Paris France Office: Calif State U Armenian Studies Program 5245 N Backer Ave # PB4 Fresno CA 93740-8001 E-mail: dickrank@csufresno.edu.

KOVAC, F. PETER, advertising executive; Pres., CEO NKH&W, Inc., Kansas City, Mo. Office: NKH&W Inc 5th Fl 600 Broadway Kansas City MO 64105

KOVACEK, DUANE MICHAEL, secondary school educator; b. Lake Forest, Ill., Oct. 31, 1948; s. Albert G. and Katherine (Macinovich) K.; m. Kathy Ann Whitton, July 22, 1972 (dec. Sept. 1988); children: Kristin Ann; m. Diane M. Janis, Jan. 2, 2003. AA, Amundson-Mayfair Jr. Coll., 1969; BA, Western Ill. U., 1970; MA, Roosevelt U., 1977. Cert. secondary shc. tchr., spl. reading tchr., adminstr./supr., Ill. Computer operator Abbott Labs., North Chicago, Ill., 1971-72; tchr., coach, lang. arts liaison, drama dir. North Chicago H.S., 1972—. Tournament mgr. Warhawk Forensics Program, North Chicago, 1972—. Block capt. Neighborhood Watch Program, Gurnee, Ill., 1990—; prodr. performing arts/flower show, North Chicago, 1985—; coord. Studio 187 TV Studio. Named Tchr. of Yr., North Chicago VFW, 1990, Chicagoland Educator of Month, Coca Cola, 1995, Educator of Week, Chgo. Sun Times, 1997. Mem. Ill. Speech and Theater Assn. (contbr. to newsletter), Scotie Orgn. (commr. 1988-92), Nat. Fedn. Interscholastic Speech and Debate Assn., Nat. Coun. Tchrs. English, Croatian Fraternal Union Am., We. Ill. U. Alumni Assn. Avocations: fishing, gardening, amateur theater, television production, travel. Home: 1050 Ferndale Ave Gurnee IL 60031-2273 Office: North Chicago HS 1717 17th St North Chicago IL 60064-2052 E-mail: ncchsieteam@hotmail.com.

KOVACEVICH, RICHARD M. bank executive; BA, Stanford U., 1965, MBA, 1967. Exec. v.p. Kenner div. Gen. Mills, Inc., Mpls., 1967-72; prin. Venture Capital, 1972-75; v.p. consumer services Norwest Corp., Mpls., from 1975, then sr. v.p. N.Y.C. banking group, then exec. v.p., mgr. N.Y.C. bank div., then exec. v.p.. mem. policy com., vice-chmn., chief operating officer banking group, from 1986, now pres., chief oper. officer, vice chmn., 1989—93, CEO,

1993—96, chmn., 1995—96; chmn., CEO Wells Fargo & Co. (merged with Norwest Corp.), 1996—98, pres., CEO, 1998—2001, chmn., 2001—. Office: Wells Fargo & Co 420 Montgomery St San Francisco CA 94163-1205*

KOVACEVICH, ROBERT EUGENE, lawyer; b. Nov. 9, 1933; s. John Edward and Katrina Margaret K.; m. Yvonne R. Stokke; children: Tawni, Mark, Phillip, Bernhard. Grad., St. Martin's Coll., Lacy, Wash., 1955; JD with honors, Gonzaga U., Spokane, Wash., 1959; LLM in Taxation, NYU, 1960. Bar: Wash., 1960; U.S. Ct. Appeals (9th cir.) 1963, U.S. Ct. Appeals (fed. cir.) 1982, U.S. Ct. Appeals (11th cir.) 1988, U.S. Ct. Appeals (10th cir.) 1993, U.S. Dist. Ct. (ea. dist.) Wash. 1960, U.S. Dist. Ct. (we. dist.) Wash., 1976, U.S. Ct. Claims, 1973, U.S. Tax Ct., 1982, Wash. Supreme Ct., 1959, U.S. Supreme Ct., 1975. Lawyer U.S. Supreme Ct., Spokane, 1963-72; ptnr. Kovacevich & Algeo, Spokane, 1972-80; pvt. practice Spokane, 1980—. Instr. Gonzaga U. Sch. Bus., 1967-84; mgr. leasing co.; expert witness U.S. Senate Com. Appropriations, 1976. Mem. ABA, Assn. Trial Lawyers, Fed. Bar Assn. Ea. Wash., Spokane Co. Bar. Assn., Spokane Club. Office: 818 W Riverside Ave Ste 715 Spokane WA 99201-0910

KOVACH, ANDREW LOUIS, administrative executive; b. Greensboro, Pa., Feb. 4, 1948; s. Andrew and Pauline (Nassar) K.; m. Cindy Juliani, Nov. 28, 1970; 1 child: Courtney. BS in Indsl. Engineering, W.Va. U., 1969. Engr. DuPont, Martinville, Va., 1970-73; supt. engr. Allied Corp., Syracuse, N.Y., 1973-75, mgr. employee rels. Morristown, N.J., 1976-80, mgr. orgnl. devel., 1980, dir. human resources N.Y.C., 1981-82, dir. comml. devel., 1983-87; ptnr. Thomas Andrew Assoc., Morristown, N.J., 1987—; sr. v.p. human resources, info. systems Morristown Meml. Hosp., 1988-96; v.p. human resources and shared svcs. Atlantic Health Sys., Florham Park, N.J., 1996—. Chmn. bd. Morristown Meml. Physician Hosp. Orgn.; bd. dirs. Morristown Surgery Ctr. Mem. ethics com., Morris Twp.; co-compliance officer Atlantic Health Sys. Mem. Morristown Club (bd. dirs.), Park Ave. Club. Presbyterian.

KOVACH, BILL, educational foundation administrator; b. Greeneville, Tenn., Sept. 16, 1932; s. John and Olga (Sicos) K.; m. Lynne Marie Stamm, Jan. 11, 1956; children: Teresa, David, Charles, John. BS, East Tenn. State U., 1959; LLD (hon.), Colby Coll., 2000. Gen. assignment Press-Chronicle, Johnson City, Tenn., 1959-61; reporter Nashville Tennessean, 1961-68, N.Y. Times, N.Y.C., 1968-79, Washington bur. chief Washington, 1979-86; editor Atlanta Jour.-Constitution, 1986-88; curator Nieman Found., Harvard U., 1989-2000; chmn. Com. of Concerned Journalists, Washington, 1997—. Lectr. Ball State U., Muncie, Ind., 1981; chair adv. bd. Internat. Consortium Investigative Journalists; mem. adv. com. Ctr. for Pub. Integrity. Co-author: The Elements of Journalism, 2001, Warp Speed: America in the Age of Mixed Media, 1999; contbg. author: Assignment America, 1984, The Art of Writing Non-Fiction, 1986, Profiles in Courage for Our Time, 2002. With USN, 1951—55. Stanford Profl. Journalism fellow, 1967-68. Mem. AAAS. Office: Comittee Concerned Journalists 1850 K St NW Ste 210 Washington DC 20006-3508 E-mail: bkovach@journalism.org.

KOVACH, GEORGE DANIEL, writer, author; b. Fairfield, Calif., Dec. 29, 1951; s. George Elmer and Margaret Evelyn (Shaner) K.; m. Anne Marie Pleskovic, Jan. 23, 1980 (dec. Apr. 1993); children: Aria, Aura. Grad. high sch., Monaca, Pa. Author/writer ASCAP, N.Y.C., 1978—; one-man theater Versary Prodns., 1969—; Shakespearean poet Lundonia House, London, 1984—, FORGE Recording Studio, Valley Forge, Pa., 1993—. Rec. artist Eastern Recording, Richmond, Va., 1977-78; Shakespearean actor Coun. of the Arts, Trenton, N.J., 1985—; poet, actor Renaissance Faire, Mt. Hope, Pa.; artist in residence at several schs. Author: Passion of a Peasant, 1978, Three Dreams of Obsession, 1983, Tales and Legends of Immortality, 1983, Blessed Be Thine-...and Other Verses, 1989, Graveless, 1992, Poetry and Tales for the Little Ones, As Night Now Enters, George and the Jester, Candleberry Tale, Enchanted Melody, Love and the Wind, Poet and the Poetess, The Tale of Woodland Shire, Tale Bearer's Whimsical Tale, Omen from a Stranger, Rune of Rose Lee, Mistress of the Ravens, When White Roses Turn Brown, Mr. Velvet Ears and The Adventures of Thicket Hollow, Other Side of Darkness, Octobering Haunt, Among Tallowing Embers, Anytime! Bedtime! Rhymes!, From the Heart, A Basket Full of Six Tales, Fairytales of the Wintry Kind, Festoon Balloons, Forevermore!, Bough of Amenity, Quest for the Devil's Bones, Lore of Elizabeth Ann, Battlefields and Drum Sticks, From the Edge of Time, Words of The Spirits, Of Midnight Tales Obsessed, Allow Thy Candle to Light Up Yon Moon, Exquisite Rendezvous, January Rain; Smile Mag.; She's Crying My Tears, No One, As Night Now Enter/Silence, January Rain, Lorelei, 2003; contbr. columns in newspapers. Recipient Golden Poet award World of Poetry Press, 1989, 90, 91, 92, Outstanding Poet of 1994, 95 award, Nat. Libr. of Poetry, Man of the Year award, Internat. Biog. Ctr., 1996, Cambridge, Eng., 20th Century award for Achievement, Internat. Man of Yr., Order of Internat. Fellowship, 1996; Five Hundred Leaders of Influence Man of Yr., 1996, World Lifetime Achievement award, 1996; Platinum Record, 1996; named to 2000 Outstanding Writers of 20th Century, 2000, 2000 Outstanding Intellectuals of 20th Century, 2000, 2000 Outstanding People of 20th Century, 2000, Internat. Peace prize The United Cultural Convention of U.S., 2003. Mem. ASCAP, Internat. Platform Assn., Men's Inner Cir. of Achievement. Avocations: travel, fund raising, guest speaking. Address: 1503 Norwood House Rd Downingtown PA 19335-2530

KOVACH, JOSEPH WILLIAM, management consultant, psychologist, educator; b. Hammond, Ind., Oct. 4, 1946; s. William Charles and Florence (Miotke) K. BA in Speech, St. Joseph Coll., Whiting, Ind., 1969; MA in Psychology, Roosevelt U., 1974; PhD, Ill. Inst. Tech., 1981; PhD in Clin. Psychology, Chgo. Sch. Profl. Psychology, 1986. Diplomate Am. Bd. Psychological Specialties of Am. Coll. Forensic Examiners; lic. sch. psychologist, Ill., Ind., Mo.; cert. marriage & family therapist, Ind. Asst. corp. merchandising mgr. Kroch's & Brentano's, Chgo., 1965-70; regional ops. mgr. Interstate Dept. Stores, Inc., Highland, Ind., 1971-73; prof., chmn. psychology Calumet Coll. St. Joseph, Whiting, Ind., 1984—; dir. Ednl. Rsch. Exch., Calumet City, Ill., 1988—; pres. Joseph W. Kovach and Assocs., Ltd., Calumet City, 1969—; dir. Buzan Centre Ltd. of Chgo., 1992—. Sr. cons. Calumet City Youth Svc. Bur., 1973-75; supr. Loyola U. Med. Ctr., Maywood, Ill., 1980-83, Northwestern Meml. Hosp., 1973-83, rsch. assoc., 1979-81; pre-doctoral intern Chgo. Read Mental Health Ctr., 1983-84, asst. program dir., 1988-89; sch. psychologist intern Sch. Dist. 163, Park Forest, Ill., 1986; grad. asst. Roosevelt U., Chgo., 1970-71; rsch. assoc. Northwestern U. Med. Sch., 1974-76, Loyola U. Med. Ctr., Maywood, 1976-78; adj. faculty Thornton C.C. (now South Suburban Coll.), South Holland, Ill., 1976, 97-98, Purdue U. Calumet, Hammond, Ind., 1976-89; presenter Internat. Conf. of The Role of Social Science in the Devel. of Education, Business and Government Entering the 21st Century, Kaunas, (Lith.), 1998, 24th Internat. Congress on Arts and Comm., Oxford, Eng.; co-organizer USA Memory Championships; organizer Midwest Memory Championships; chief psychologist establishing nonmil. support svcs. for mil. and families, U.S. 8th Army, Korea, 2001. *Whether in front of a camera, on the radio, from behind a podium, or sitting in a chair, Professor Dr. Kovach has spent over thirty years working with the human condition. From consulting with business leaders to students, he is a world authority on whole brain thinking strategies and planning, learning techniques, and creativity, for the 21st century. He frequently speaks on stimulating and developing our natural genius. He is a columnist and has authored numerous articles, position papers, and books. As a visionary, he is paragidm shifter and an architect of the possibility. He was one of the original co-organizers for the first USA Memory Championships.* Columnist: Bus. in Rev./The Times, Munster, Ind., Executive Excellence and Personal Excellence, Provo, Utah., Talking to the Boss, Skokie, Ill. Bd. dirs. Milton H. Erickson Inst. No. Ill. Mem. APA, Midwest Psychol. Assn., Ill. Sch. Psychologists Assn. Office: PO Box 113 Calumet City IL 60409-0113

KOVACH, ROBERT LOUIS, geophysics educator; b. L.A., Feb. 15, 1934; s. Nicholas Arthur and Stefania Teresa (Rüssler) K.; m. Linda Elly Heyn, Dec. 23, 1960; children: Denise Lynn, Dianne Yvonne, John Robert, Robert John. Geophysical Engring Degree, Colo. Sch. Mines, 1955; MA, Columbia U., 1959; PhD, Calif. Inst. Tech., 1962. Registered geophysicist, Calif. Sr. scientist Jet Propulsion Lab., Pasadena, Calif., 1961-63; asst. prof. Calif. Inst. Tech., Pasadena, 1963-65, Stanford (Calif.) U., 1965-66, assoc. prof., 1966-70, prof. geophysics, 1970—. Prin. investigator Apollo Moon Seismic Expts., 1996-76; cons. DOE, 1996-97. Author: Earth's Fury, 1995, Conflict with the Earth, 1997. Lt. U.S. Army, 1956-58. Fellow John Simon Guggenheim Found., 1971; recipient Exceptional Sci. Achievement award NASA, 1973. Fellow Geol. Soc. Am.; mem. Am. Geophysical Union (pres. seismology sect. 1976-78), Can. Well Logging Soc., Seismol. Soc. Am., Soc. Exploration Geophysicists. Office: Dept Geophysics Stanford University Stanford CA 94305 E-mail: kov@pangea.stanford.edu.

KOVACHEV, LUBOMIR MILTCHEV, physicist, researcher; b. Dolna Bania, Bulgaria, July 19, 1955; s. Milcho Stoimenov Kovachev and Raina Dimitrova Kovacheva; m. Bonka Lubenova Stoeva, Oct. 1977; children: Miglena Lubomirova Kovacheva, Kamen Lubomirov. Ed, U. of Sofia, 1976—81; PhD, Inst. of Gen. Physics AN SSSR, 1988—90. Sci. rschr. Inst. of Electronics, BAS, Sofia, Bulgaria, 1985—. Contbr. articles to profl. jours. Ensign EARTH, 1974—76, Bulgaria. Mem.: Oprical Soc. Am. Orthodox. Achievements include research in parametric solitons; the interaction of solitons by cross-phase modulation; optical vortices with spin 1/2. Avocations: skiing, swimming, climbing. Home: Simeonovsko shossee 108 Sofia Bulgaria Office: Institute of Electronics BAS Tzarigradsko shossee 72 Sofia 1784 Bulgaria Home Fax: +359 2 9745493. E-mail: lkovach@ie.bas.bg.

KOVACHEVICH, ELIZABETH ANNE, judge; b. Canton, Ill., Dec. 14, 1936; d. Dan and Emilie (Kuchan) Kovachevich. AA, St. Petersburg Jr. Coll., 1956; BBA in Fin. magna cum laude, U. Miami, 1958; JD, Stetson U., 1961, LLD (hon.), 1993. Bar: Fla. 1961, U.S. Dist. Ct. (mid. and so. dists.) Fla. 1961, U.S. Ct. Appeals (5th cir.) 1961, U.S. Supreme Ct. 1968. Rsch. and adminstrv. aide Pinellas County Legis. Del., Fla., 1961; assoc. DiVito & Speer, St. Petersburg, Fla., 1961—62; house counsel Rieck & Fleece Builders Supplies, Inc., St. Petersburg, 1962; pvt. practice St. Petersburg, 1962—73; judge 6th Jud. Cir., Pinellas and Pasco Counties, Fla., 1973—82, U.S. Dist. Ct. (mid. dist.) Fla., Tampa, 1982—96, chief judge, 1996—. Chmn. St. Petersburg Profl. Legal Project-Days in Ct., 1967, Supreme Ct. Bicentennial Com. 6th Jud. Cir., 1975—76. Prodr., coord. (TV prodn.) A Race to Judgement. Bd. regents State of Fla., 1970—72; legal advisor, bd. dirs. Young Women's Residence, Inc., 1968; mem. Fla. Gov.'s Commn. on Status of Women, 1968—71; mem. Pres.'s Commn. on White House Fellowships, 1973—77; mem. def. adv. com. on Women in Svc. Dept. Def., 1973—76; Fla. publicity chmn. 18th Nat. Rep. Women's Conf., Atlanta, 1971; lifetime mem. Children's Hosp. Guild, YWCA of St. Petersburg; charter mem. Golden Notes, St. Petersburg Symphony; hon. mem. bd. of overeers Stetson U. Coll. of Law, 1986. Recipient St. Petersburg Panhellenic Appreciation award, 1964, Pinellas United Fund award in recognition of concern and meritorious effort, 1968, Disting. Alumni award, Stetson U., 1970, Woman of Yr. award, Beta Sigma Phi, 1970, 1970, Am. Legion Aux. Unit 14 Pres. award cmty. svc., 1970, Dedication to Christian Ideals award and Man of Yr. award, KC Dists. 20-21, 1972, USN Recruiting Command Appreciation award, 1975, Woman of Yr. award, Fla. Fedn. Bus. and Profl. Women, 1981, ann. Ben C. Willard Meml. award, Stetson Lawyers Assn., 1983, Alumni of Yr. award, St. Petersburg Jr. Coll., 1994, Cath. Law Person of Yr., Greater Tampa Cath. Lawyer's Guild, 1998, Disting. Svc. award, Fla. Coun. on Crime and Delinquency, 1999, J-Ben Watkins award, Stetson U. Coll. of Law, 1999, Woman of Achievement award, Delta Delta Delta, 2000, Outstanding Jurist award, Hillsborough County, 2000—01, Pub. Svc. award, William Reece Smith, Jr., 2001, Mrs. Charles Ulrick Bay award, St. Petersburg Rotary award, St. Petersburg Quarterback Club award, President's Award, Fed. Bar. Assn., 2001, Presidential Special Recognition Award, 2002. Mem.: ABA, St. Petersburg Bar Assn. (chmn. bench and bar com., sec. 1969), Am. Judicature Soc., Pinellas County Trial Lawyers, Fla. Bar Assn., ATLA. Office: US Dist Ct 801 N Florida Ave Tampa FL 33602-3849

KOVACHY, EDWARD MIKLOS, JR., psychiatrist, consultant; b. Cleve., Dec. 3, 1946; s. Edward Miklos and Evelyn Amelia (Palenscar) K.; m. Susan Eileen Light, June 21, 1981; children: Timothy Light, Benjamin Light. BA, Harvard U., 1968, JD, MBA, Harvard U., 1972; MD, Case Western Reserve U., 1977. Diplomate Nat. Bd. Med. Examiners. Resident in psychiatry Stanford U. Med. Ctr., Stanford, Calif., 1977-81; pvt. practice psychiatry, mediation, exec. coaching Menlo Park, Calif., 1981—. Presenter ann. meeting Am. Psychol. Assn., 1998, Calif. Assn. Marriage and Family Therapists, 1999. Co-prodr. Jolson and Company, Century Ctr. for the Performing Arts, N.Y.C., 2002; columnist The Peninsula Times Tribune, 1983-85. Trustee Mid-Peninsula H.S., Palo Alto, Calif., 1990-2001, mem. bd. advisors, 2001—; mem. gift com. Harvard Coll. Class of 1968, 25th reunion chmn. participation, San Francisco, 1993, 30th reunion chmn. participation, West Coast, 1998, nat. co-chmn. participation and assocs. giving, 1999—, nat. co-chmn. participation, 35th reunion, 2003. Recipient Albert H. Gordon award Harvard U., 2000; named to Hall of Fame, Shaker Heights Alumni Assn., 2003. Mem. Am. Psychiat. Assn. (presenter annual meetings 1984, 98), Physicians for Social Responsibility, Assn. Family and Conciliation Cts., No. Calif. Psychiat. Soc. Presbyterian. Avocations: personal activism, musical comedy, athletics. Office: 1187 University Dr Menlo Park CA 94025-4423 E-mail: edkovachy@aol.com.

KOVACIC, PETER, chemistry educator; b. Wylandville, Pa., Aug. 1, 1921; s. Marko and Barbara Kovacic; m. Dorothy A. Kovacic; 6 children. AB, Hanover Coll., 1943, DSc (hon.), 1964; PhD, U. Ill., 1946. Postgrad. MIT, Cambridge, Mass., 1947; instr. Columbia U., N.Y.C., 1948; rsch. chemist DuPont, Del., 1948-55; prof. Case Western Res. U., Cleve., 1955-68, U. Wis., Milw., 1968-87; vis. prof. various univs., 1987—. Guest editor Current Med. Chemistry, 1999-2001; contbr. articles to profl. jours. Fulbright fellow, 1983; NAS Exch. scholar, 1978. Office: San Diego State U Chemistry Dept San Diego CA 92182 E-mail: pkovacic@sundown.sdsu.edu.

KOVACIC, WILLIAM EVAN, law educator; b. Poughkeepsie, N.Y., Oct. 1, 1952; s. Evan Carl and Frances Katherine (Crow) K.; m. Kathryn Marie Fenton, May 18, 1985. AB with honors, Princeton U., 1974; JD, Columbia U., 1978. Bar: N.Y. 1979. Law clk. to sr. dist. judge U.S. Dist. Ct. Md., Balt., 1978-79; atty. planning office bur. competition FTC, Washington, 1979-82, atty. advisor to commr., 1983; assoc. Bryan, Cave, McPheeters & McRoberts, Washington, 1983-86; prof. George Mason U. Sch. Law, Arlington, Va., 1986-99, George Washington U. Law Sch., Washington, 1999—; gen. counsel U.S. FTC, 2001—. Cons. in field; mem. U.S. Senate Judiciary Subcom. on Antitrust and Monopoly, Washington, 1975-76. Contbr. legal articles to profl. jours. Assoc. Father Ford Found. Columbia U. Cath. Campus Ministry, N.Y.C. 1985—. Harlan Fiske Stone fellow Columbia U., 1976-78. Mem. ABA (antitrust law and pub. contract law sects.), Fed. Bar Assn. Roman Catholic. Avocations: hiking, camping, photography. Office: George Washington U Law Sch 720 20th St NW Washington DC 20052-0001 E-mail: wkovacic@main.nlc.gwu.edu.

KOVACIK, KAREN MARIE, university educator; b. East Chgo., Ind., July 21, 1959; d. Peter John and Frances Marie Kovacik; m. Daniel Carter Bourne, Dec. 10, 1983 (div. Dec. 1991). BA, Ind. U., 1981; cert., Sch. Art Inst. Chgo, 1988; MA, Cleve. State U., 1990; PhD, Ohio State U., 1997. Asst. prof. English Ind. U., Indpls., 1997—, Purdue U., Indpls., 1997—. Presenter in field. Author: Return of the Prodigal, 1991 (Poetry Atlanta prize, 1990), Nixon and I, 1998, Beyond the Velvet Curtain, 1999 (Wick prize, 1998). Sec. Etheridge Knight Poetry Festival Bd., Indpls., 2001—02. Recipient Fall Poetry Open prize, Glimmer Train, 1999, Fiction prize, Chelsea, 2001; fellow in poetry, U. Wis. Inst. Creative Writing, 1991—92. Mem.: Acad. Am. Poets, Poets & Writers, Modern Lang. Assn. Home: 1002 N New Jersey Street Indianapolis IN 46202 Office: IUPUI English Dept CA 502L 425 University Blvd Indianapolis IN 46202

KOVACIK, NEAL STEPHEN, hotel and restaurant executive; b. Toledo, Mar. 2, 1952; s. Albert Joseph and Phyllis (Lesinski) K.; m. Denise Reichert, Apr. 20, 1974 (div. June 1976). Student, Bowling Green State U., 1971-72, U. Toledo, 1973-74, Owens Tech. Coll., 1975. Dir. food and beverages Motor Inn of Perrysburg, Ohio, 1976-78; v.p. food and beverage ops. Bennett Enterprises, Perrysburg, 1978-82, v.p. hotel and restaurant ops., 1982—. Bd. dirs. Greater Toledo Office of Tourism and Convs., 1994—. Recipient Food and Beverage Dir. of Yr. award Holiday Inns. Inc. and Internat. Assn. Holiday Inns, 1976. Mem. Northwestern Ohio Restaurant Assn. (bd. dirs. 1980-84), Toledo Hotel and Motel Assn. Democrat. Roman Catholic. Avocations: art, wildlife photography. Home: 9640 Monclova Rd Monclova OH 43542-9709 Office: Bennett Enterprises Corp 27476 Holiday Ln Perrysburg OH 43551-3345 E-mail: neal_kovacik@bennett-enterprises.com.

KOVACS, BEATRICE, library studies educator; b. Seekirchen, Austria, June 2, 1945; came to U.S., 1948; d. Lorand and Helen (Magyary-Kossa) K.; m. Thomas Gordon Basler, Apr. 20, 1969 (div. 1979); m. Louis Edward Mitchum, Jan. 10, 1994. AB in English, Syracuse U., 1966; MLS, Rutgers State U., 1967; DLS, Columbia U., 1983. Libr. Nassau Acad. Medicine, Garden City, N.Y., 1967-70; cataloger, asst. acquisitions libr. Augusta (Ga.) Regional Libr., 1974-78; collection devel. libr. Med. Coll. Ga., Augusta, 1978-80; acct. specialist Readmore Publs., N.Y.C., 1982-83; chief collection devel. U. N.Mex. Med. Ctr. Libr., Albuquerque, 1984-85; asst. prof. U. N.C., Greensboro, 1985-91, assoc. prof., 1991—. Vis. instr. Pratt Inst. Grad. Sch. Libr., Bklyn., 1982-83; adj. prof. U. N.C. Chapel Hill Sch. Info. and Libr. Sci., 1997-98. Author: Decision-Making Process for Library Collections, 1990, ALA Fingertip Guide to National Health-Information Resources, 1995; co-author: Health Sciences Librarianship, 1977, Using Science and Technology Information Resources, 1991; contbr. articles to profl. jours. Bishop scholarship Med. Libr. Assn., 1966. Mem. ALA, N.C. Libr. Assn., Spl. Librs. Assn., N.C. Spl. Librs. Assn. (pres. 1992-93), Assn. Libr. & Info. Sci. Educators. Office: U NC Sch Edn PO Box 2617o Greensboro NC 27402-6170 E-mail: bea_kovacs@uncg.edu.

KOVACS, MALCOLM, sociology educator, religious studies educator; BA in Polit. Sci. with honors, Roosevelt U., 1965; cert., U. Geneva, 1966; MSc, London Sch. Econs., 1968; postgrad., Rabbinical Coll. Am., Morristown, N.J., 1972—75; PhD in Sociology, Union Grad. Sch., Cin., 1977. Spl. asst., overseas rep. U.S. Nat. Student Assn., Washington, 1966—68; assoc. dir. Washington Urban Coalition, 1967; prof. sociology Montgomery Coll., Rockville, Md., 1970—. Dir. Jewish Roots Ctr. Montgomery Coll., 1975—. Fax: 410-764-5088.

KOVACS, RYAN W. computer engineer; b. Saginaw, Mich., July 25, 1971; s. Ronald and Catherine (Sturgeon) Kovacs; m. Renee Alyce Clare, June 1, 1995; children: Sawyer Loyd, Isabella Diane Clare-Kovacs. AA, Delta Coll., Univ. Ctr., Mich., 1990—95. Network mgmt. Cox Cable, Saginaw, Mich., 1995—96; computer technician, network engr. Bethco/Inacom, Atlanta, 1996—99; infrastructure engr. First Franklin Fin., San Jose, Calif., 1999—, First Franklin Corp., San Jose, Calif., 1999—. Mem. Ga. Wireless Users Group, Atlanta, 2002—. Independent. Methodist. Avocation: travel. Personal E-mail: ryan@clarekovacs.com. E-mail: rkovacs@fffc.com.

KOVACS, WILLIAM LAWRENCE, lawyer; b. Scranton, Pa., June 29, 1947; s. William Lawrence and Jane Claire (Weiss) K.; m. Mary Katherine Maras, Dec. 2, 1979; children: Katherine Elizabeth, William Lawrence III, Margaret Ellen, Tyler Alexander. BS magna cum laude, U. Scranton, 1969; JD, Ohio State U., 1972. Bar: Pa. 1972, D.C. 1973, U.S. Ct. Appeals (D.C. cir.) 1974, U.S. Supreme Ct. 1976, Va. 1981. Legis. asst., staff atty. Congressman Fred B. Rooney, Washington, 1972-74; chief counsel U.S. Ho. of Reps. Subcom. on Transp. and Commerce, Washington, 1975-77; assoc. Liebert, Short, FitzPatrick & Lavin, Phila., 1977-78; environ., litigation atty. Nat. Chamber Litigation Ctr., Washington, 1979; ptnr. Abrams, Kovacs, Westermeier & Goldberg, Washington, 1980-84, Kovacs & Bury, Fairfax, Va., 1984-85, Jaeckle, Fleischmann & Mugel, Washington, 1986-87, Eckert, Seamans, Cherin & Mellott, Washington, 1987-89, Dunn, Carney, Allen, Higgins & Tongue, Portland, Oreg., 1990, Keller & Heckman, Washington, 1991-97; pres. Clean States Found., Inc., 1997-98; dir. legal affairs Worldwide Sunshine Makers, Inc., Washington, 1997-98; v.p. environ. tech. and regulatory affairs U.S. C. of C., Washington, 1998—. Contbr. articles to profl. jours. Mem. Hazardous Waste Facilities Siting Bd., Richmond, Va., 1984-86; vice chmn., 1984-85, chmn., 1985-86. Mem. ABA (vice chmn. energy resources law com. sect. on torts and ins. practice 1981-83, chmn. 1983-84), U.S. C. of C. (mem. environ. law adv. com. 1986-92). Roman Catholic. Home: 9805 Arnon Chapel Rd Great Falls VA 22066-3908 Office: 1615 H St NW Washington DC 20062-0001 E-mail: WKovacs@uschamber.com.

KOVALCHUK, ILYA, hockey player; b., Tver, Russia, Apr. 15, 1983; Right wing Atlanta Thrashers, 2001—. Achievements include the first Russian player to be selected first in an NHL Entry Draft. Office: Atlanta Hockey Club Inc 1 CNN Ctr 13 S Atlanta GA 30303

KOVALCIK, PAUL JEROME, surgeon; b. Buffalo, Apr. 16, 1943; s. Jerome G. and Dorothy I. (Kalinowski) K.; m. Janet I. Howe, Jan. 13, 1968; children: Julia, Peter, John, Matthew, Andrew. BA, CUNY, Flushing, 1965; MD, Georgetown U., 1969. Diplomate Nat. Bd. Med. Examiners, Am. Bd. Surgery, Am. Bd. Colon and Rectal Surgery; ATLS instr. Commd. ensign USN, 1969, advanced through grades to capt., 1984, ret. Med. Corps, 1989; intern medicine and surgery Naval Hosp., Boston, 1969-70, resident gen. surgery, 1970-73, Naval Regional Med. Ctr., Portsmouth, Va., 1973-74; fellow colon and rectal surgery Lahey Clinic, Boston, 1974-75; assoc. prof. surgery Ea. Va. Med. Sch., 1980—, Uniformed Svcs. U. Health Scis., 1986—; head dept. gen. surgery Naval Hosp. Portsmouth, 1985-87. Cons. Naval Hosp. Portsmouth; chmn. ethics com. Maryview Hosp., Portsmouth, 1992-2001, pres. med. staff, 2001-03; assoc. examiner Am. Bd. Colon and Rectal Surgery; vis. prof. Greenville (S.C.) Hosp. System, 1984, U. S.C., Columbia, 1984, W.Va. U. Med. Ctr., Charleston, 1986, East Carolina U., Greenville, 1991, 93; lectr. Georgetown U., Washington, 1985, U.S. Naval Hosp., Guantanamo Bay, Cuba, 1986, U.S. Naval Hosp., Roosevelt Roads, P.R., 1987, U.O.A. Mid-Atlantic Regional Conf., 1987, Acute Combat Symposium Tidewater chpt. AMSUS, Norfolk, 1987, Trauma Symposium Naval Hosp., Roosevelt Roads, 1988, Thomas Jefferson U. Med. Sch., 1988, 90, Acute Combat Trauma Symposium, Norfolk, 1988, Piedmont Soc. Colon and Rectal Surgeons, Williamsburg, Va., 1990, Sardestin, Fla., 1992, Kiawah Island, S.C., 1993, Joseph F. Mulach Med. Lectr. Series St. Clair Hosp., Pitts., 1991, Student Cancer Conf. Ea. Va. Med. Sch., Norfolk, 1994; Thordur Thordarson Meml. lectr., Reykjavik, Iceland, 1987; pres. Portsmouth Acad. Medicine, 1998-99; med. advisor Va. Tumor Registry; chmn. credentials appeals com. United Health Care Va., 2000-2002; lectr. U. Sienna, Italy, 1998, U. Copenhagen, 2002. Contbr. numerous articles to med. jours. Fellow: ACS (surveyor commn. on cancer 2000—), Am. Soc. Colon and Rectal Surgery; mem.: AMA, Va. Surg. Soc., Soc. Am. Gastrointestinal Endoscopic Surgeons (founder), Am. Soc. Colon and Rectal Surgeons (chmn. self-assessment com. 1988—92, mem.-at-large to exec. coun. 1992—, recert com.), Lahey Clin. Alumni Assn. Republican. Roman Catholic. Avocations: fishing, tennis, gardening, travel, collecting pipes. Home: 4762 River Shore Rd Portsmouth VA 23703-1518 Office: 3105 American Legion Rd Ste A Chesapeake VA 23321-5653 also: 667 Kinsborough Sq Ste 300 Chesapeake VA 23320 E-mail: pkovalcik@mindspring.com., colonandrectaldr@mindspring.com.

KOVALEFF, THEODORE PHILIP, financial consultant; b. N.Y.C., Feb. 8, 1943; s. Michael Oleg and Barbara Helen (Pointer) K.; m. Nancy Bowen Shepherd, Nov. 27, 1977; children: Kathryn, Theodore Jr. AB, Columbia U., 1964, MA, 1966; PhD in History, Legal and Econ., N.Y.U., 1972. Teaching asst Barnard Coll., N.Y.C., 1965-66, N.Y.U., 1966-68; instr. St. John's U., N.Y.C., 1969-72, asst. prof., 1972-75; lectr. Barnard Coll., 1975-77; dir. admissions Columbia U. Sch. of Law, N.Y.C., 1977-80, asst. dean, 1980-93. Asst. prof NYU, summers 1973, 75, 76; adv. bd. mem. The Antitrust Bull.; mem. Law Sch. Admission Coun., 1977-93; pres. Informed Sources Svc. Group. Mem. editl. bd. Presdl. Studies Quar., 1991-99, guest editor, 1998-99; author: Business and Government During the Eisenhower Administration, 1980, The Antitrust Impulse, 1994; co-author: Poland and the Coming of World War II, 1977; contbr. articles to profl. jours., chpts. to books. Mem. Morningside Renewal Coun., 1974-85, bd. dirs., 1976-85; mem. Cmty. Bd. 9, Manhattan, 1975—, officer, 1978-96, chair, 1981-82, 89-90, 92-96; mem. Broadway Malls Assn. 1989—, treas., 1990—; chair Borough Pres. of Manhattan's Com. on Pub. Safety, 1994-97; trustee Broadway Presbyn. Ch., N.Y.C., 1994-2000; mem. Silver Bay Coun., 1968—, v.p., 1999-2001, pres., 2001—; bd. dirs. Ecumenical Cmty. Devel. Orgn., 1999—. Summer rsch. grantee Eleuthrian Mills-Hagley Found., 1974; recipient Borough Pres.'s Cert. of Svc. award, 1977, Borough Pres.'s Citation for Svc. to Community, 1983, City of N.Y. Cert. of Appreciation for Svc. award Community Bds., 1987. Mem. Assn. Am. Law Schs. (sect. student svcs., program planning com. 1993). Avocations: tournament bridge, shuffleboard. Home: 454 Riverside Dr New York NY 10027-6845 Office: Cmty Bd 9 565 W 125th St New York NY 10027-3497

KOVALEV, ALEXEI, professional hockey player; b. Togliatti, Russia, Feb 24, 1973; Profl. hockey player N.Y. Rangers, 1992—98, Pitts. Penguins 1998—2003, N.Y. Rangers, 2003—. Recipient Olympic Gold medal, 1992. Office: New York Rangers 2 Pennsylvania Plz New York NY 10121

KOVALY, JOHN JOSEPH, consulting engineering executive, educator; b. McKeesport, Pa., June 12, 1928; s. Joseph and Mary (Demko) K.; m. Joan P. Misiewicz, June 16, 1957; children: Pamela Jane, Kurt David. BS, Muskingum Coll., 1950; MS, U. Ill., 1953. Research assoc. Coordinated Sci. Lab., U. Ill., Urbana, 1951-55; adv. research engr. Sylvania Electronic Products, Inc., Waltham, Mass., 1958-65; cons. engr., program mgr. Raytheon Co. Patriot Missile Sys. Engring. Svcs., Bedford, Mass., 1965-95. Lectr. Northeastern U., 1956-58, UCLA, 1977-87. Author: Synthetic Aperture Radar, 1976; contbr. articles profl. jours. Served to lt. U.S. Navy, 1955-58. Named to Hall of Fame, McKeesport High Sch., 1988. Fellow IEEE (pres. Boston sect. Aerospace and Electronic Systems Group 1972 contbn. award) Home: 3 Tubwreck Dr Dover MA 02030-1808

KOVALYOV, MIKHAIL, researcher, educator; b. Minsk, Belarus, Apr. 7, 1958; s. Alexander Kovalyov and Dora Mirkina. PhD, Courant Inst., NYU, 1981—86. Prof. U. of Alberta, Edmonton, Canada, 1986—; Gorentein prof. Queens Coll., CUNY, NY, 2002—. Author: (mathematical research) rsch articles & papers. Recipient Gorenstein Professorship, CUNY, Queens Coll., 2002-2003; grantee NSERC individual grants, 1986-present. Mem.: SIAM, Am. Math. Soc. Avocations: travel, Tae Kwon Do, photography. Office: Department of Mathematics Queens College CUNY Flushing NY 11367-1597

KOVANIC, PETER H. pathologist, educator; b. Prague, Czech Republic, Apr. 17, 1933; came to U.S., 1966; s. Luisa Kovanicova; m. Hana Dubovy, May 18, 1969; 1 child, Paula. MD, Charles U., Prague, 1958. Diplomate Am. Bd. Pathology, Czechoslovakia Bd. Pathology; lic. lab. dir., N.J.; lic. clin. lab. dir., N.Y.C.; lic. blood bank dir., N.Y.C.; cert. med. practitioner, Eng.; cert. physician, Southern Rhodesia. Intern, resident surg. dept. Sokolov Hosp, Czechoslovakia, 1958-60; intern, resident dept. medicine Marienbad Hosp., Czechoslovakia, 1958-60; resident, rsch. assoc. Inst. Pathology, Sch. Medicine, Charles U., Prague, 1960-64; registrar pathology Peace Meml. Hosp. Watford, Hertforshire, Eng., 1964-65; govt. med. officer pathology dept. Mpilo Gen. Hosp., Bulawayo, Rhodesia, 1965-66; sr. resident, asst. rsch. scientist dept. pathology NYU Med. Ctr., N.Y.C., 1966-70; assoc. pathologist Clara Maass Med. Ctr., Belleville, N.J., 1970-72, dir. clin. pathology and Blood Bank, 1972—99; dir. pathology Columbus Hosp., Newark, 1987—99; asst. clin. prof. pathology N.J. Coll. Medicine and Dentistry, Newark, 1976—; dir. pathology emeritus Columbus Hosp., 1999—; emeritus dir. clin. pathology Clara Maass Med. Ctr., 1999—. Lt. Czech Army, 1952-57. Fellow Am. Soc. Clin. Pathologists, Coll. Am. Pathologists; mem. N.Y. Path. Club, N.J. Path. Soc., N.J. Med. Soc. Republican. Home: 3610 Yacht Club Dr Aventura FL 33180 E-mail: phkovan@aol.com.

KOVARSKY, JOEL SEVERIN, rheumatologist, small business owner; b. Chgo., Aug. 16, 1947; s. Irving and Esther (Rabinovitz) K.; m. Deborah Barricks, Aug. 17, 1969; children: Lee B., Ian M. BS, U. Iowa, 1969, MD, 1972. Diplomate Am. Bd. Internal Medicine, Am. Bd. Rheumatology. Intern Duke U. Med. Ctr., Durham, N.C., 1972-73, fellow in rheumatology, 1974-76, jr. asst. resident in medicine, 1976-77; asst. resident neurology Strong Meml. Hosp., U. Rochester, N.Y., 1973-74; chief rheumatology William Beaumont Arym Med. Ctr., El Paso, Tex., 1977-79; rheumatologist Diagnostic Clinic Houston, 1979-80; asst. prof. medicine Baylor Coll Medicine, Houston, 1980-85, clin. asst. prof. medicine, 1985-96; pvt. practice Houston, 1985-96, Danville, Va., 1996—; dir. rheumatology Danville Regional Med. Ctr., 1996—; asst. cons. prof. med. Duke U. Rheumatology, 1998—; owner The Prime Meridian: Antique Maps and Books, 1998—. Asst. clin. prof. medicine Tex. Tech. U., Lubbock, 1977-79; cons. Meth. St. Luke's Episcopal Hosp., Houston, 1980-96; lectr. in field. Contbr. articles to profl. jours., chpts. to books. Mem. mus. adv. coun. Harwood Found., U. New Mexico, Taos, 1993-97. Maj. U.S. Army, 1977-79. Recipient Army Commendation medal, 1979. Fellow Am. Coll. Rheumatology; mem. Va. Med. Assn., Tex. Med. Assn., Med. Soc. Va., Internat. Antiquarian Mapsellers Assn. Jewish. Avocations: book collecting, racquetball, skiing. Office: Ste B 800 Memorial Dr Danville VA 24541

KOVAT, ROBIN M. secondary school educator; b. Bklyn., Sept. 8, 1957; d. Robert Sanford and Marilyn Kovat. BA in Politics and Sociology, Brandeis U., 1978; grad. cert. in arts mgmt., Adelphi U., 1982; MS in Journalism, Poly. Inst. U., Bklyn., 1991. Asst. to borough pres. Bklyn. N.Y. Borough Pres. Office, 1979—82; freelance writer, 1982—92; tchr. Riker's Island, N.Y.C. Bd. Edn., Elmhurst, 1992—95; scheduling coord., tchr. Job Corps, Bklyn., 1995—97; adj. prof. Touro Coll., N.Y.C., 1996—98; tchr. Sheepshead Bay H.S., Bklyn., 1998—, coord. rsch. program and law program, coach moot ct. and mock trial teams. Dir. cultural devel. and women's issues Bklyn. Borough Pres. Office, 1979—82; advisor Sheepshead Angels svc. orgn.; campaign coord. Judge Lila Gold, Bklyn., 1991—92; Bd. dirs. Rebecca Kelly Dance Co., N.Y.C., 1985—87. Recipient Sterling Quality of Life award, 2003. Democrat. Jewish. Avocations: running, reading, writing, bicycling, traveling. Home: 2662Ford St Brooklyn NY 11235 Office: Sheepshead Bay H S 3000 Ave X Brooklyn NY 11235

KOVATCH, JAK GENE, artist; b. Los Angeles, Jan. 17, 1929; s. Jack and La Vinia Blanche (Abernathy) K.; m. Carol Jean Wilhelm, Dec. 24, 1967; 1 son by previous marriage, Jason. Student, UCLA, 1946, Chouinard Art Inst., 1947-49, Calif. Sch. Art, L.A., 1949-50, U. So. Calif., 1951, L.A. City Coll., 1955-56, Art Students League, N.Y.C., 1972, 75. Student asst. Lynton Kistler Studio, L.A., 1952-53; staff animation dept. Walt Disney Prodns., Inc., Burbank, Calif., 1953. Instr. drawing and anatomy Famous Artists Schs., Westport, Conn., 1957-59; tchr. Roger Ludlowe H.S., Fairfield, Conn., 1959-60; extension instr. N.Y.C. Coll., 1959-60; instr. sculpture Fairfield U., 1967; mem. faculty U. Bridgeport, Conn., 1962-94, Ethyl prof. design, 1988-94, assoc. prof. dept. design, 1978-88, prof. design, 1988-94; mem. faculty Silvermine Sch. of Art, New Canaan, Conn., 1994—; vis. faculty mem. Aldrich Mus. Contemporary Art, Ridgfield, Conn., 1999; fellow Mellon Found.; Vis. Faculty Program Yale U., 1979-83; guest lectr. anatomy and figure drawing, 1953—. Stage designer for, Benjamin Zemach, L.A., 1953-54, freelance illustrator, N.Y.C., 1957-58; one-man show Monroe C. Gutman Libr., Harvard U., 2000; exhibited in some 650 group shows including Taipei Fine Arts Mus., Taiwan, R.O.C., 1987, 91, Tokyo Met. Mus., Japan, 1985-87, Barbican Arts Ctr., London, 1989, Legislative and State Office Bldgs., Hartford, 1991, Salford Mus., Eng., 1989, Inst. Tech. Aeroespacial, Sao Jose dos Campos, Brasil, 1987, U. Hawaii, 1985, Mus. Modern Art, Wakayama, Japan, 1987, Northeastern U., Boston, 1999, Butler Inst. Am. Art, Youngstown, Ohio, 2002, Boston Printmakers two-yr. traveling exhbn., 2002; represented in permanent collections Fogg Mus. Art, Cambridge, Mass., Library of Congress, Joseph Hirshhorn Collection, Greenwich, Conn., Fairfield Art Collection, John Slade Ely House Collections, New Haven, Bicentennial Art Collection, Westport (Conn.) Town Hall, U. Miss., Albert Dorne Collection, N.Y.C., others; artist project grant from Conn. Commn. on Arts, Hartford, 1984-85. Selection com. State of Conn. Commn. on Arts, Percent for Art Program, Hartford, 1987-88. Recipient award Boston Mus. Fine Arts, 1954, Wadsworth Atheneum, Hartford, Conn., 1958, 79, Mus. Art, Sci. and Industry, Bridgeport, 1962-63, 65-66, 75, 77, 79, 81-84, 22 awards Fairfield (Conn.) U., 1973-95, award New Haven Paint and Clay Club, 1976, 78, 81, 89-90, 97-98, spl. recognition award Print Club Albany, Schenectady Mus., 1992, John Taylor Arms Meml. award Audubon Artists, Inc., Nat. Arts Club, N.Y.C., 1993, etching award Stamford (Conn.) Mus., 1994, Painting award New Britain Mus. Am. Art, 1997, more than 170 others. Mem. Soc. Am. Graphic Artists, Boston Printmakers, N.Y. Artists Equity Assn., Audubon Artists (bd. dirs. for graphics 1995), Conn. Acad. Fine Arts, Greenwich Art Soc., L.A. Printmaking Soc., Phila. Print Club, Silvermine Guild Artists (trustee 1979-83), Westport-Weston Arts Coun., Graphic Arts Coun. N.Y. Home: 34 Sasco Creek Rd Westport CT 06880-6341 Office: Silvermine Sch of Art Inc 1037 Silvermine Rd New Canaan CT 06840-4398 E-mail: jakkovatch@aol.com. *I consider my concept of Image Continuum to be a significant consequence of 50 years of painting and printmaking. Six basic components form the foundation of this concept: 1. Use of former images to create new ones; 2. Repetition of a theme (subject matter and symbols repeated); 3. Use of modules; 4. Use of storyboards and grids; 5. Structuring forms transparently; 6. Use of abstraction, animation, distortion. An integral part of Image Continuum is persistent use of multiple images. This means of expression may be directly related to my personal impatience with dwelling too long on one image or idea. I have been able to temper this drive for immediacy and rapid image development by using images in a series or storyboard format.*

KOVATIS, PAUL EVANS, orthopedic surgeon, researcher, consultant; b. Cedar Grove, N.J., Apr. 17, 1963; s. Pericles Peter and Elizabeth Jane K. BS in Biology summa cum laude, Upsala Coll., East Orange, N.J., 1985; MD, U. Medicine and Dentistry N.J., 1989. Intern U. Medicine and Dentistry N.J., 1989-90, resident in orthopaedic surgery, 1990-95; fellow Hosp. Spl. Surgery, N.Y., 1996-97; attending orthopaedic surgeon Hackensack (N.J.) U., 1996—. Clin. cons. Capezio Balletmakers, Inc., N.J., N.Y., EBI Med. Sys. Inc., N.J., 1998—, Zimmer Orthopaedics, N.J., 1999—; clin. rschr. non-unions in fracture care FDA. Contbr. articles to profl. jours. Mem. nat. nominating com. Outstanding Young Women Am., 1998—. Named to Best Surgeons List, Better Living Mag., Best Doctors List, Consumer Health News. Mem. Am. Orthopaedic Foot and Ankle Soc., Am. Assn. Foot and Ankle Surgeons, Am. Hellenic Progressive Edn. Assn. (v.p. 1997—), Bergen County Med. Soc. (sec.-treas.), Phi Beta Kappa. Greek Orthodox. Avocations: baseball, physical fitness, theatre, travel. Home: 300 Prospect Ave Hackensack NJ 07601-7712 Office: Orthopedic Spine and Sports Medicine 2 Forest Ave Paramus NJ 07652-5214

KOVCHEGOV, YURI V. physicist, educator; b. Moscow, Dec. 3, 1973; arrived in U.S., 1993; s. Olga Kovtchegova, Vladislav Kovtchegov; m. Violita Jenniffer Hernandez. PhD, Columbia U., 1998; BSc, Moscow Inst. Phys. and Tech., 1993. Postdoctoral rsch. assoc. dept. physics U. Minn., Mpls., 1998—99; theoretical rsch. assoc. physics dept. Brookhaven Nat. Lab., Upton, NY, 1999—2000; rsch. asst. prof. dept. physics U. Wash., Seattle, 2000—. Fellow, Columbia U., 1993—98; grantee, Bi-National US-Israeli Sci. Found., 1999—2002, NSF, 2001. Mem.: Am. Phys. Soc. Achievements include invention of Balitsky-Kovchegov equation; Kovchegov regularization prescription. Office: U Wash Dept Physics Box 351560 Seattle WA 98195-1560

KOVE, MIRIAM, psychotherapist; b. Chotin, Romania, Feb. 17, 1941; came to U.S., Sept. 12, 1962; d. Avrum and Riva (Nussenbaum) Wolkove; m. Marc L. Kouffman, Aug. 16, 1964 (div. Oct. 24, 1989); children: Avra, Paulette. BA in English Lit., Sir George Williams U., 1962; MA in Early Childhood, Hunter Coll., 1975; Cert. in Psychoanalytic Psychotherapy, New Hope Guild, N.Y.C., 1979; MSW, Adelphi U., 1983. Tchr. various pub. schs., Montreal, Can., 1957-58; actress N.Y.C., 1962—; tchr. early childhood Emanuel Nursery Sch., N.Y.C., 1964-74; adj. lectr. early childhood Cmty. Coll., Bklyn., 1974-75; psychotherapist, clinician New Hope Guild Ctr., N.Y.C., 1979-81; intake dir., clinician Insts. of Religion and Health, N.Y.C., 1983-84; pschotherapist N.Y.C., 1984—; faculty, supr. New Hope Guild Ctr., N.Y.C., 1990—; dir. day care on-site therapy program C.I.S. Counseling Ctr., N.Y.C., 1992-94. Author: (book) Myths and Madness. Mem. People for the Am. Way, Warsaw Gathering of Holocaust Survivors. Recipient Hebrew prize Sir George Williams U., 1962; recommended for English prize Concordia U. Fellow Nat. Orgn. Social Work, Soc. for Clin. Social Work Psychotherapists (edn. com.); mem. New Hope Grad. Soc. (steering com.), Am. Bd. Examiners in Clin. Social Work. Jewish. Home and Office: 320 E 25th St Apt 8ee New York NY 10010-3100

KOVEL, RALPH M. writer, antiques expert; b. Milw. s. Lester and Dorothy K.; m. Terry Horvitz; children: Lee R., Karen. Attended, Ohio State U. Pres., chmn. U.S. Brands, Inc.; pres. Lucayan Aquaculture, Freeport, Bahamas. V.p., treas. Antiques, Inc.; trustee WVIZ-TV, Western Res. Hist. Soc., Cleve., Cleve. Pops Orch., Inc.; Hiram fellow course in antiques We. Res. U., John Carroll U. Writer: (with Terry Kovel) syndicated column Kovels Antiques and Collecting, 1955—, Ask the Experts, House Beautiful, 1979-2000, Medio, CD-Rom Mag., 1995, The Kovels on Collecting, Forbes Mag., 2000-02; editor: monthly newsletters Kovels on Antiques and Collectibles, 1974—, Kovels Sports Collectibles, 1992-97; Know Your Antiques, Pub. Broadcasting, 1969—; syndicated TV series Kovels on Collecting, 1981, 87, Collector's Journal, 1989-93, Flea Market Finds with the Kovels HGTV, 2000-; author: (with Terry Kovel) Kovels' Dictionary of Marks-Pottery and Porcelain, 1953, rev. edit., 1995, Directory of American Silver, Pewter and Silver Plate, 1958, American Country Furniture, 1780-1875, 1963, Kovels Know Your Antiques, rev. edit., 1993, Kovels Antiques and Collectibles Price List, 36th edit., 2003, Kovels American Art Pottery, 1993, Kovels' Bid, Buy & Sell Online, 2001, The Kovels Bottle Price List, 12th edit., 2002, Kovels Price Guide for Collector Plates, Figurines, Paperweight and Other Ltd. Editions, 1978, Kovels Collector's Guide to American Art Pottery, 1974, Kovels Collector's Guide to Limited Editions, 1974, Kovels Know Your Collectibles, 1981, 1992, Kovels Book Antique Labels, 1982, Kovels Depression Glass and Dinnerware Price List, 7th edit. 2001, Kovels Illustrated Price Guide to Royal Doulton, 2d edit., 1984, Kovels Organizer for Collectors, rev. edit., 1983, Kovels Collectors Source Book, 1983, Kovels New Dictionary of Marks Pottery and Porcelain, 1850 to the Present, 1986, Kovels Advertising Collectibles Price List, 1986, Kovels Guide to Selling Your Antiques and Collectibles, rev. edit., 1990, Kovels American Silver Marks 1650 to Present, 1989, Kovels Antiques and Collectibles Fix-It Source Book, 1990, Kovels Picture-a-Day Collectibles Calendar, 1990, 91, Kovels' Antiques & Collectibles 2003 Day-at-a-Time Calendar, Kovels Quick Tips: 799 Helpful Hints on How to Care For Your Collectibles, 1995, Kovels Guide to Selling, Buying and Fixing Your Antiques and Collectibles, 1995; (video tape series) Collecting With the Kovels, 1995—, Art Pottery I, Art Pottery II, 2003, The Label Made Me Buy It, 1998, Kovel's Yellow Pages 2d edit., 2003, also articles. Former mem. rev. and allocations com. United Torch Fund, Cleve.; past pres. E. End Neighborhood Settlement House; past chmn. adv. com. Woodhill Homes; past bd. dirs. Soc. Collectors, Silver Mus. Religious Art. Recipient Lane Bryant award, 1966; Peirce Award for Outstanding Cmty. Svc. Sta. WVIZ-TV, 1980, Cleve. Emmy award best entertainment, 1971, Cleve. Emmy award cultural affairs programming, 1987. Mem. Union League Club (Chgo.), Oakwood Club (Cleve.). Office: PO Box 22200 Cleveland OH 44122-0200

KOVEL, TERRY HORVITZ (MRS. RALPH KOVEL), writer, antiques authority; b. Cleve. d. Isadore and Rix Horvitz; m. Ralph Kovel; children: Lee R., Karen. BA, Wellesley Coll., 1950. Tchr. math. Hawken Sch. for Boys, Shaker Heights, Ohio, 1961-71; now pres. Antiques Inc.; past tchr. course in antiques Western Res. U., John Carroll U. Writer: (with Ralph Kovel) syndicated column Kovels Antiques and Collecting, 1955—, Ask the Experts, House Beautiful, 1979-2000, Medio, CD-Rom mag., 1995, The Kovels on Collecting, Forbes Mag., 2000-02; editor: monthly newsletters Kovels on Antiques and Collectibles, 1974—, Kovels Sports Collectibles, 1992-97; TV series Know Your Antiques, Pub. Broadcast, 1969—; syndicated TV Series Kovels on Collecting, 1981, 87, Collector's Journal, 1989-93, Flea Market Finds with the Kovels HGTV, 2000—; author: (with Ralph Kovel) Kovels' Dictionary of Marks-Pottery and Porcelain, 1953, rev. edit., 1995, Directory of American Silver, Pewter and Silver Plate, 1958, American Country Furniture, 1780- 1875, 1963, Kovels' Know Your Antiques, rev. edit, 1993, Kovels' American Art Pottery, 1993, Kovels' Antiques and Collectibles Price List, 36th edit., 2004, Kovels' Know Your Collectibles, 1981, 1992, Kovels' Bottle Price List, 12th edit., 2002, Kovels' Organizer for Collectors, 1978, revised, 1983, Kovels' Price Guide for Collector Plates, Figurines, Paperweights and Other Limited Editions, 1978, Kovels' Collector's Guide to American Art Pottery, 1974, Kovel's Collector's Guide to Limited Editions, 1974, Kovels' Price Guide to Depression Glass and Dinnerware, 7th edit., 2001, Kovels' Illustrated Price Guide to Royal Doulton, 2d edit., 1984, Kovels' Collectors' Source Book, 1983, Kovels' New Dictionary of Marks Pottery and Porcelain, 1850 to the Present, 1986, Kovels' Advertising Collectibles Price List, 1986, Kovels' Guide to Selling Your Antiques and Collectibles, 1987, 2d edit., 1990, Kovels' Book of Antique Labels, 1982, Kovels' American Silver Marks 1650 to the Present, 1989, Kovel's Antiques and Collectibles Fix-It Source Book, 1990, Kovels' Page-a-Day Collectibles Calendar, 1990, 91, Day-At-A-Time Calendar, 2003, Kovels' Guide to Selling, Buying and Fixing Your Antiques and Collectibles, 1995, Kovels' Quick Tips: 799 Helpful Hints on How To Care for Your Collectibles, 1995; (videotape series) Collecting With the Kovels, Art Pottery I, Art Pottery II, 1995—, The Label Made Me Buy It, 1998, Kovels' Yellow Pages, 2d. edit., 2003, Kovels' Bid, Buy and Sell Online, 2001; contbr. articles on antiques, numerous publs. Trustee Hiram Coll., 1989-99, hon. trustee, 2000; bd. mem. Shaker Hist. Soc. Hiram fellow; recipient Peirce award for outstanding cmty. svc. Sta. WVIZ-TV, 1980, Cleve. Emmy award for best entertainment, 1971, Cleve. Emmy award for cultural affairs programming, 1987; Laurel Sch. Alumanae of Yr. Office: 22000 Shaker Blvd Cleveland OH 44122-2644

KOVELESKI, KATHRYN DELANE, retired special education educator; b. Detroit, Aug. 12, 1925; d. Edward Albert and Delane (Bender) Vogt; m. Casper Koveleski, July 18, 1952; children: Martha, Ann. BA, Olivet Coll., 1947; MA, Wayne State U., 1955. Tchr. various schs., Mich., 1947-88, Garden City Schs., 1955-56, 59-88; resource and learning disabilities tchr., 1970-88; ret., 1988. V.p. Sch. Masters Bowling League, 1984—88; pres. Odd Couples Bowling League, 1982—83, treas., 1995—97; sec. bd. Christian edn. Congl. Ch., 1988—2001, chmn., 1988—90, sec., 1999—2001, mem. Christian svc. bd, 2003—. Mem. BPW (Woman of Yr. 1985-86), Mich. Assn. Ret. Sch. Pers., Wayne Hist. Soc. (trustee 1998, sec.-treas. 1998-2000—), Wayne Garden Club, Wayne Lit. Club (past pres., treas. 1988-89, historian 1998—), Savvy Wayne Srs. Investment Club (sec. 2003—).

KOVENOCK, DANIEL J. economist, educator; b. Madison, Wis., July 21, 1956; BSc, Hebrew U., Jerusalem, 1977; PhD, U. Wis., 1983. Asst. prof. econs. Purdue U., West Lafayette, Ind., 1983—89, assoc. prof. econs., 1989—94, prof. econs., 1994—, econs. policy chmn., 1997—2001; univ. docent Erasmus U., Rotterdam, Netherlands, 1989—90. Tinbergen Inst. prof. Erasmus U., Rotterdam, 1994; invited prof. U. Paris Panthéon-Sorbonne, 2002. Office: Purdue Univ Dept Econs 403 W State St West Lafayette IN 47907-2056

KOVNAR, EDWARD H. pediatric neurologist, medical educator; b. Denver, Jan. 6, 1951; BS in Elec. Engring., Washington U., St. Louis, MD, 1977. Diplomate in neurology and child neurology Am. Bd. Psychiatry and Neurology; diplomate Am. Bd. Pediatrics. Resident in pediatrics St. Louis Children's Hosp./Washington U., 1977-79, fellow in child neurology, 1980-82; resident in neurology Barnes Hosp./Washington U., 1979-80; asst. prof. neurology and pediatrics Med. Coll. Wis., Milw., 1982-85; asst. mem., head dept. neurology St. Jude Children's Rsch. Hosp., Memphis, 1985-90, assoc. mem., head dept. neurology, 1990-92; assoc. prof. neurology and pediatrics, divsn. head Med. Coll. Wis., Milw., 1992-2000. Med. dir. neurology Children's Hosp. of Wis., Milw., 1992-2000. Mem. editl. bd. Jour. Child Neurology, 1992-96; ad hoc reviewer jours. Mem. Child Neurology Soc. (rsch. com. 1994-97, councilor 1997-99), Pediatric Oncology Group (neurosci. com. 1985-2000, brain tumor core com.), Am. Acad. Neurology, Tau Beta Pi, Alpha Omega Alpha. Avocations: long-distance running, skiing, biking. Office: Pediat Neurology 3003 W Good Hope Rd Milwaukee WI 53209 E-mail: ekovnar@ah.com.

KOVNER, KATHLEEN JANE, civic worker, portrait artist; b. Cambridge, Mass., Nov. 25, 1919; d. David Leo and Kathleen Elizabeth (Lalley) Lane; m. Benjamin Kovner (dec.), June 20, 1938; children: Kathleen Barbara (dec.), Michael Anthony, Peter Christopher. Student, Art Students League, N.Y.C., 1937-40. Owner, CEO Helen Bennett Ltd., Stamford, Conn., 1948-59; cons. Bride's Mag., N.Y.C., 1967-70; co-chair membership com. Women's Nat. Rep. Club, N.Y.C., 1980-81, chmn. membership com., 1981-87, v.p., 1986-87, also bd. dirs. Ltd. ptnr. 519 8th Ave Corp., N.Y.C., 18-19th St. Corp., N.Y.C., Kaufman Arcade Bldg., N.Y.C., 19th St. Assn., N.Y.C., dir. Nelson Tower Assoc., N.Y.C., 1998, ptnr. 450 Seventh Ave Assoc., N.Y.C. Portrait artist in oils, with various portraits in pvt. collections. Fundraiser St. Ignatius Loyola, N.Y.C., 1960-61, Jeanine Pirro-Campaign for Dist. Atty., Westchester County, N.Y., 1993, 97. Republican. Roman Catholic. Home: 62 Brookridge Dr Greenwich CT 06830-4830 also: 923 5th Ave New York NY 10021-2649

KOVNER, VICTOR A. lawyer; b. N.Y.C., May 3, 1937; s. Harold and Eva (Eisenberg) K.; m. Sarah Schoenkopf, Oct. 9, 1964. B.A., Yale U., 1958; LL.B., Columbia U., 1961. Bar: N.Y. 1962, U.S. Supreme Ct. 1975. Assoc., Hays Sklar & Herzberg, now Botein Hays Sklar, 1963-66; ptnr. Lankenau Kovner & Bickford, N.Y.C., 1966— ; mem. adv. bd. Media Law Reporter; mem. faculty PLI Communications Law Inst. Contbr. articles to profl. jours. Mem., Mayor of N.Y.'s Com. on Judiciary, 1970-85, N.Y. State Commn. on Jud. Conduct, 1976— . Served with USAR, 1962. Mem. ABA, N.Y. State Bar Assn. (Ho. dels.), Bar Assn. City N.Y. (chmn. com. communications law 1983-86, chmn. judiciary com. 1986—). Office: Lankenau Kovner & Bickford 30 Rockefeller Plz New York NY 10112-0002

KOVTYNOVICH, DAN, civil engineer; b. Eugene, Oreg., May 17, 1952; s. John and Elva Lano (Robie) K. BCE, Oreg. State U., 1975, BBA, 1976. Registered profl. engr., Calif., Oreg. V.p. Kovtynovich, Inc., Contractors and Engrs., Eugene, 1976-80, pres., chief exec. officer, 1980—. Apptd. to State of Oreg. Bldg. Codes and Structures Bd., 1996—. Fellow ASCE; mem. Am. Arbitration Assn. (arbitrator/mediator 1979—, mem. dispute rev. bd. found.), N.W. China Coun., Navy League of U.S., Eugene Asian Coun. Republican. Avocations: flying, skiing, fishing, hunting. Office: Kovtynovich Inc PO Box 898 Lake Oswego OR 97034-0143

KOWAL, REBEKAH JANE, American Studies educator; b. Norfolk, Va., Aug. 24, 1966; d. Ira Joseph and Sheila (Slawsby) Kowal; m. David Scott Bullwinkle, Aug. 8, 1998; 1 child, Noah Kowal Bullwinkle. BA, Columbia U., 1988; PhD, NYU, 2000. Grad. tchg. asst. NYU, N.Y.C., 1992-98, lectr., 1995; asst. prof. English, Mellon fellow Haverford (Pa.) Coll., 1999-2000; asst. prof. dance U. Iowa, Iowa City, 2001—. Asst. prof. dance U. Iowa, reviews editor, Dance Rsch. Jour., 2002-. Regional fellow U. Pa. Humanities Forum, 2000. Mem.: Congress on Rsch. in Dance, Soc. Dance History Scholars, Am. Studies Assn. Avocations: modern dance, ballet, yoga, hiking, biking, swimming. Office: 114 Halsey Hall Iowa City IA 52242

KOWAL, RUTH ELIZABETH, library administrator; b. Amherst, Mass., Mar. 16, 1948; d. Alfred Alexander and Mary Arandale (Tomlinson) Brown; m. Harold F. Kowal, June 19, 1989; children: Elizabeth Ann, Susannah Terry. BS, Syracuse U., 1970; MLS, Simmons Coll., 1971. Reference libr. Falmouth (Mass.) Pub. Libr., 1971-74; sch. libr. Nauset High Sch., Eastham, Mass., 1974-75; asst. dir. Plymouth (Mass.) Pub. Librs., 1975, dir., 1976-83; exec. dir. Southeastern 3R's, Highland, N.Y., 1983-86; regional adminstr. Ctrl. Mass. Libr. System, Worcester, 1987-91, Ea. Mass. Libr. System, Boston, 1991-97, Boston Pub. Libr., 1997—, asst. dir., 1997-99; dir. ops. Boston Pub. Libr., 1999—. Instr. Northeastern U., Boston, 1980-83, SUNY, Albany, 1984-86. Mem. ALA. Office: Boston Pub Libr 700 Boylston St Boston MA 02117

KOWALCZYK, DAVID THEODORE, English language educator, poet; b. Batavia, N.Y., Nov. 22, 1952; s. Adam James Kowalczyk and Ida Marie Loranty. BA, SUNY, Buffalo, 1974; MA, SUNY, Brockport, 1988. Instr. English Ariz. State U., Tempe, 1983-84, Genesee Cmty. Coll., Batavia, 1987-88; lectr. Acad. Hspano Am., San Miguel De Allende, Mex., 1988; chmn. dept. English Herald Lang. INst., Changwon, Republic of Korea, 1996-97. Author: A Gentle Metamorphosis, 1993, Bless Me, Father, 1994, Still Waters, 1997, In Other Words, 1999, Stealing the Sky, 1999, Stainless Soul, 2001, Waltzing in Invisible Vienna, 2003. Recipient First Prize City Mag. Ann. Lit. Contest, Rochester, N.Y., 1984, Chatauqua Coun. on Arts, Jamestown, N.Y., 1990, Penhaligon Page Press, Wales, 1997. Mem. Just Buffalo Lit. Ctr. (Just Buffalo Writing award 2001), Grand Canyon Lit. Guild (v.p. 1981-82), Phi Beta Kappa, Sigma Tau Delta. Avocations: travel, numismatics.

KOWALCZYK, KIM JAN, editor, writer; b. Ellwood City, Pa., Aug. 20, 1952; d. Joseph and Josephine A. (Alexander) Januszkiewicz; m. Frank Joseph Kowalczyk, Aug. 26, 1972; children: Tanya Marie, Kelly Ann, Christopher Michael. BA in Gen. Arts and Sci., Pa. State U., 1989, postgrad., 1989-90. Office mgr. Ginther Wycoff Group, Denver, 1983-85; asst. to pres. Linguex Internat., Denver, 1985-86; sec., dir. engring. Locus, Inc., State College, Pa., 1987-89; tech. editor, writer Locus, Inc., Kaman Scis., State College, 1989-90; manuscript editor, writer Am. Philatelic Soc., State College, 1990-99, dir. edn., 2000—. Freelance editor, writer, Denver, State College, Pa., 1987—; cons. editor Real Time Devices, State College, 1990, Peter Jehrio Enterprises, State College, 1991-93, State College area YMCA, 1992-95. Editor The Battles of George S. Patton's Lowest Ranks, 1996-97; author, editor: (videos) Fish Day in Bellefonte, 1990, The Last Cruise, 1990, Welcome to Union Cemetery, 1996. Mem. State College Area H.S. Swim Team Boosters, sec., 1994-95; mem. YMCA swim team boosters, v.p., 1994-95. Mem. Kiwanis. Republican. Roman Catholic. Avocations: painting, drawing. Home: 504 N Burrowes St State College PA 16803-3506 Office: Am Philatelic Soc 100 Oakwood Ave State College PA 16803-1607 E-mail: kim@stamps.org.

KOWALCZYK, PAUL ALAN, civil engineer; b. Phila., Feb. 5, 1947; s. Andrew Paul and Bertha Florilla (Burnham) K.; m. Mary Jane Gresser, June 17, 1972; children: Andrew, Katherine, Benjamin, Sarah. BS, U.S. Mil. Acad., 1970; MS in Profl. Mgmt., Fla. Inst. Tech., 1979. Registered profl. engr., Colo.

Commd. 2d lt. U.S. Army, 1970, advanced through grades to capt., resigned, 1979; project engr. U.S. Army Engring. Dist., Seoul, Korea, 1974-75; project mgr. U.S. Army Corps of Engrs., Rock Island, Ill., 1976—99, asst. chief design br., 1999—. Soccer coach NE Family YMCA, Bettendorf, Iowa, 1981-82; treas. Boy Scouts Am., Bettendorf, 1983-85, com. chair 1986-96, commr., 1996—. Mem. Soc. Am. Mil. Engrs. (sec. 1977-78), Phi Kappa Phi. Roman Catholic. Avocations: biking, camping, skiing, reading, woodworking. Home: 4927 Greystone Dr Bettendorf IA 52722-6253 Office: US Army Corps of Engrs Clock Towers Bldg Rock Island IL 61204

KOWALKE, KIM H. music educator, musicologist, conductor, foundation executive; b. Monticello, Minn., June 25, 1948; s. Henry O. and Mayta M. (Schmidt) K.; m. Elizabeth Jane Keagy; 1 child, Kyle William Henry. BA, Macalester Coll., 1970; MA, Yale U., 1972, MPhil, 1974, PhD, 1977. Asst. prof. music Occidental Coll., L.A., 1977—82, assoc. prof., 1982—86; prof. music Eastman Sch. Music U. Rochester, N.Y., 1987—, chair dept. music, 1986—97, 2000—. Author: Kurt Weill in Europe, 1979 (Field prize 1978), Accounting for Success: Misunderstanding Die Dreigroschenoper (Deems-Taylor award 1990), Kurt Weill Modernism and Popular Culture, 1995 (Irving Lowens prize 1995); editor: A New Orpheus: Essays on Kurt Weill, 1986 (Deems-Taylor award 1987), A Stranger Here Myself: Kurt Weill Studien, 1993, Speak Low: The Letters of Kurt Weill and Lotte Lenya, 1996 (Freedley award 1997, Deems-Taylor award 1997), For Those We Love: Hindemith, Whitman, and 'An American Requiem'", 1997 (Irving Lowens prize 1998, Deems-Taylor award 1998), I'm An American!: Whitman, Weill and Cultural Identity, 2000 (Deems-Taylor award 2001); founding mem. editl. bd. Kurt Weill Edit., 1992—; contbr. articles to music and theater jours. Pres. bd. trustees Kurt Weill Found. for Music, N.Y.C., 1981—. Staff sgt. N.G., 1970-77. Recipient Graves Commn. award, Pomona Coll.; Martha Baird Rockefeller fellow, 1976, Whiting fellow, 1976-77, Am. Coun. Learned Socs. fellow, 1979. Mem.: Soc. for Am. Music, Internat. Brecht Soc., Am. Musicol. Soc. (coun. 1984—87, program com., 50 com.). Presbyterian. Avocations: tennis, bridge, running. Office: U Rochester 207 Todd Union PO Box 270052 Rochester NY 14627-0052 E-mail: kkwk@mail.rochester.edu.

KOWALOFF, DOROTHY RUBIN, retired lawyer; b. N.Y.C., May 8, 1917; d. Saul and Fannie (Romanoff) Roberts; m. Meyer Kowaloff, Mar. 18, 1945 (dec.); children: Arthur, Nina. BA, NYU, 1938; LLB, Columbia U., 1940. Bar: N.Y. Sole practice, N.Y.C., 1941-50; pres. Rokor Corp., 1950-67; atty., corp. counsel office Dept. Law, City of N.Y., 1967-86. Lawyer; b. N.Y.C., May 8, 1917; d. Saul and Fannie (Romanoff) Roberts; m. Meyer Kowaloff, Mar. 18, 1945 (dec.); children— Arthur, Nina. B.A., NYU, 1938; LL.B., Columbia U., 1940. Bar: N.Y. Sole practice, N.Y.C., 1941-50; pres. Rokor Corp., 1950-67; atty. corp. counsel office Dept. Law City of N.Y., 1967— . Mem. Women's Bar Assn. City of N.Y., N.Y. State Women's Bar Assn. Mem. Women's Bar Assn. City N.Y., N.Y. State Women's Bar Assn.

KOWALSKA, MARIA TERESA, research scientist, educator; b. Wielun, Poland, June 8, 1932; arrived in U.S., 1982, naturalized, 1991; d. Jozef Ozmina and Zofia Elzbieta Pecherska; m. Wielislaw Kowalski, Apr. 19, 1954 (dec. Nov. 1991); children: Jacek Kowalski, Beata Kowalska-Ellington. BA, Lyceum Gen. Edn., Lodz, Poland, 1950; MS in Pharmacy, Med. Acad., Poznan, Poland, 1954, PhD in Pharmacy, 1964; Dr. Hab., Med. Acad., Lodz, 1978. Asst. prof. pharmacy Med. Acad., Poznan, 1955—69; postdoctoral fellow in pharmacy U. Paris, 1969—70; assoc. prof. Acad. Agr., Poznan, 1970—80; prof. pharmacognosy Nat. U. Kinshasa, 1980—82; rsch. assoc. Rsch. Ctr. Fairchild Frop Garden, Miami, Fla., 1985—90. Adj. asst. prof. dept. biochemistry and molecular biology Sch. Medicine U. Miami, 1990—2000; counselor students Acad. Agr., Poznan, 1975—80; prin. investigator on grant Internat. Palm Soc., Miami, 1986, Miami, 87, World Wildlife Fund, Washington, 1988. Appeared (TV) ABC Miami News, 1992, CNN News, 1993; contbr. articles to profl. jours. Avocations: music, skiing, mountain climbing. Home: 6421 SW 106 St Miami FL 33156

KOWALSKI, ANTHONY ALBERT, music educator; b. Sandusky, OH, July 19, 1943; s. Albert Stanley and Virginia Rosemary (Passinissi) Kowalski; m. Linda Kay Montgomery, Aug. 31, 1968; children: Brian, Tiffany, Holly, Kristi, Lisa, Leslie. MusB ed., Bowling Green U, Bowling Green, OH, 1968, EdM, 1982. Music instr. Sandusky City Sch., Sandusky, Ohio, 1970—2002. Choir dir. Jackson Jr. High, Sandusky, Ohio, 1995. Author vocal and piano songs. Renovate bldg. and apart., Sandusky, Ohio, 1970. E-5 US Coast Guard, 1967—73, Toledo, OH. Mem.: Music Ed. Nat. Conf. Achievements include 3rd degree black belt in Shotokan Karate and instr. for more than 15 yr. Avocations: Karate, tennis, fishing, piano, performing and composition. Home: 3603 Ann Dr Sandusky OH 44870-2430 Office: Jackson Jr HS 314 W Madison St Sandusky OH 44870-2430

KOWALSKI, KAZIMIERZ, computer science educator, researcher; b. Turek, Poland, Nov. 7, 1946; arrived in U.S., 1986, naturalized, 1994; s. Waclaw and Helena K.; m. Eugenia Zajaczkowska, Aug. 5, 1972. MSc, Wroclaw (Poland) U. Tech., 1970, PhD, 1974. Asst. prof. Wroclaw U. Tech., 1970-76, assoc. prof., 1976-86, Pan Am. U., Edinburg, Tex., 1987-88; prof. computer sci. Calif. State U.-Dominguez Hills, Carson, 1988—, chmn. computer sci. dept., 1998—2001. Lectr. U. Basrah, Iraq, 1981-85; cons. XXCal, Inc., L.A., 1987-91; conf. presenter in field; rsch. fellow Power Inst. Moscow, USSR, 1978; info. sys. tng. UNESCO, Paris, 1978; cons. Tex. Instruments, Inc., 1999-2001. Co-author: Principles of Computer Science, 1975, Organization and Programming of Computers, 1976; also articles. Recipient Bronze Merit Cross, Govt. of Poland, 1980, Knights' Cross of the Order of Merit Republic of Poland, 1997. Mem. IEEE Computer Soc., Assn. for Advancement of Computing in Edn., Mensa, Sigma Xi. Avocations: travel, puzzles. Home: 3836 Weston Pl Long Beach CA 90807-3317 Office: Calif State U 1000 E Victoria St Carson CA 90747-0001 E-mail: kowalski@computer.org.

KOWALSKI, KENNETH LAWRENCE, physicist, educator; b. Chgo., July 24, 1932; s. Florian Lawrence and Emily Helen (Sinoga) K.; m. Audrey Bellin; children— Eric Clifford, Claudia Gail. BS, Ill. Inst. Tech., 1954; PhD (Universal Match Found. fellow), Brown U., 1963. Aero. research scientist Lewis Research Center, NACA, 1954-57; research asso. in physics Brown U., summer 1962, Case Inst. Tech., Cleve., 1962-63, asst. prof. physics, 1963-67, asso. prof., 1967-73, Case Western Res. U., 1967-73, prof., 1973—, exec. officer dept. physics, 1970-71, chmn. dept. physics, 1971-76. Vis. prof. Inst. Theoretical Physics U. Louvain, Belgium, 1968-69; scientist-in-residence Argonne Nat. Lab., 1986-87, User Fermilab, 1993—. Author: (with S.K. Adhikari) Dynamical Collision Theory and It's Applications, 1991; editor: (with W.J. Fickinger) Modern Physics in America, 1988; contbr. articles to profl. jours. NSF grantee, 1972-96. Mem. Am. Phys. Soc. Achievements include rsch. on theoretical physics. Home: 2275 S Overlook Rd Cleveland Heights OH 44106-3141 Office: Case Western Res U Dept Physics 10900 Euclid Ave Dept Physics Cleveland OH 44106-1712

KOWALSKI, RICHARD SHELDON, hospital administrator; b. Detroit, Feb. 18, 1944; s. Richard Joseph and Margaret Lucile (Sheldon) K.; m. Doris Kay Smith, Nov. 20, 1982; children: Renée Marie, Jerrod Patrick, Sterling Prescott. BBA, Ea. Mich. U., 1966; MS in Health Adminstrn., Trinity U., San Antonio, 1971. Adminstrv. asst. Univ. Hosp.-U. Wash., Seattle, 1969-70; med. facilities cons. Ill. Dept. Health, Des Moines, 1970-72; asst. adminstr. Mercy Hosp., Cedar Rapids, Iowa, 1972-79; chief exec. officer St. Mary Med. Ctr., Galesburg, Ill., 1979—. Mem. coun. for govt. rev. Crescent Counties Found. for Med. Care, Naperville, Ill., 1986—; bd. dirs. Assn. Venture Corp., Naperville; chmn. bd. dirs. United Health Properties, Galesburg, 1985—; mem. adv. bd. Physician Hosp. Inst.; mem. comty. bd. Wells Fargo. Mem. strategic planning steering com. City of Galesburg, 1986—; bd. dirs. Econ. Devel. Coun., Galesburg, 1986—, Knox County Devel. Corp., 1986, Civic Ctr. Authority, 2001—. Named hon. alumnus Grad. Program in Hosp. and Health Adminstrn., U. Iowa, 1990. Fellow Am. Coll. Healthcare Execs. (regent Ctrl. Ill.); mem. Ill. Hosp. Assn. (pres. region 1-B, bd. dirs. 1987—, Disting. Leadership award 1986), Galesburg Area C. of C. (chmn. 1990), Soangetaha Country Club (bd. dirs. 1990), Rotary. Avocations: golf, tennis. Office: St Mary Med Ctr 3333 N Seminary St Galesburg IL 61401-1251

KOWALSKI, STEPHEN WESLEY, retired chemistry educator; b. Bayonne, N.J., June 24, 1931; s. Steve J. and Anna (Gillack) K.; m. Evelyn L. Geiger, Apr. 2, 1955 (div. Apr. 1971); children: Lillian Ann, Kathryn Lynn, Kristina Eve, Stephen Edward; m. Barbara A. Soffe, Aug. 7, 1971; children— Brian Ashley, Scott William. BS, Fairleigh Dickinson U., 1953; MA, N.Y. U., 1954, PhD, 1964. Research chemist, cons. Shulton, Inc., Clifton, N.J., 1953-56; instr. chemistry Upsala Coll., East Orange, N.J., 1953-54, guest lectr., 1954-65; instr. sci. N.Y. U., 1954-55; tchr. sci. Kearny (N.J.) High Sch., 1955-56; research chemist Hoffman LaRoche, Nutley, N.J., 1956-57; prof., chmn. physics-geosci. dept. Montclair State U., Upper Montclair, NJ, 1956—94; also chmn. physics-geosci. dept. Montclair State Coll.; prof. emeritus, 1995—. Guest lectr. Fairleigh Dickinson U., 1955-69; coordinator, supr. AID Summer Sci. Insts., India and Ohio State U., 1966, NSF-AID Summer Sci. Insts., India, 1967; sci. coordinator master of arts in teaching program Fairleigh Dickinson U., 1968; vis. prof., cons. Interam U. P.R., 1983-84; internat. speaker on sci. in consumer edn.; mem. nat. edn. adv. com. Consumers Union. Author: Floridation of Polyethylenes, 1955, Chromotographic Separation of Xanthophylls, 1957, Laboratory Manual in Consumer Science, 1972, Consumer Science Text and Laboratory Manual, 1975, revised edit., 1978; contbr.: book Flavor Chemistry, 1959; patentee permeability of polyethylene, floridation. Bd. dirs. N.J. Consumers League, 1964-67, Montclair Athletic Commn.; sr. asso. Danforth Found., 1961— . Finished 3rd in archery, World Masters Games, Brisbane, Australia, 1994, 3rd in archery, U.S. Sr. Olympics, Baton Rouge, La., 1995, 5th in archery U.S. Sr. Olympics, Tucson, Ariz., 1997, 1st in archery in N.J. Masters State Championship, 1998, 1st in N.J. Sr. Games, 1999, 1st in Fla. Sr. Games, 1999, 5th in Sr. Olympics, 1999, 6th in U.S. Nat. Indoor Archery Championships, 1999, 3rd in Eastern Regionals, 1999. Mem. Am. Chem. Soc. (nat. com. confs. and insts., div. chem. edn. 1968—), N.E.A., N.J. Edn. Assn. (chmn. higher edn. com. 1968-70), Nat. Sci. Tchrs. Assn. (com. establishing goals sci. literacy), N.J. Sci. Tchrs. Assn., Assn. N.J. Coll. and Univ. Profs. (founder 1969), AAAS, Phi Delta Kappa (life) Clubs: Elk. Office: Montclair State University Montclair NJ 07043-1624 Home: 4 Manchester Ct Wayne NJ 07470-3304 *God works in strange ways. But whatever happens always happens for the best even though it may be hard to accept at the moment.*

KOWALSKI, SUSAN DOLORES, critical care nurse, educator; b. Aurora, Ill., Dec. 20, 1944; d. George Bernard and Dolores Ida (Smith) Bockman; m. Edgar Peter Kowalski, July 9, 1988. BSN, No. Ill. U., 1971; MSN, Boston Coll., 1976; MBA, Rockford Coll., 1987; PhD, Tex. Woman's U., 1994. Staff nurse ICU St. Joseph Hosp., Bloomington, Ill., 1971-72, St. Francis Hosp., Peoria, Ill., 1972-73; nursing instr. St. Francis Hosp. Sch. Nursing, Peoria, 1973-75, St. Anthony Med. Ctr. Sch. Nursing, Rockford, 1976-85; staff nurse ICU St. Joseph Hosp., South Bend, Ind., 1986-89; clin. instr. Ind. Vocat. Tech. Coll., South Bend, 1986-89; asst. prof. St. Mary's Coll., Notre Dame, Ind., 1987-89; sr. lectr. U. Tex., Tyler, 1990-94; assoc. prof. U. Nev., Las Vegas, 1994—. Contbr. articles to nursing jours. Mem.: ANA, Sigma Theta Tau. Republican. Roman Catholic. Home: 7736 Rye Canyon Dr Las Vegas NV 89123-0752 Office: U Nev 4505 S Maryland Pkwy Las Vegas NV 89154-9900

KOWALSKI, THADDEUS LAWRENCE, retired judge; b. Chgo., Aug. 10, 1931; s. Anton Kowalski and Victoria Gruszka; m. Patricia Anne Geraghty, Oct. 4, 1968; children: David Mark, Neil Patrick. AB, U. Ill., 1953; JD, Northwestern U., Chgo., 1958. Atty. Jaroszewski & Kowalski, Chgo., 1958-63, Ill. Atty. Gen.'s Office, Chgo., 1963-64; trial atty. Cook County Pub. Defender, Chgo., 1964-68, dist. chief 1st mcpl., 1969-80; assoc. judge Cir. Ct. of Cook County, Chgo., 1980—2001; ret., 2001. Author: Public Defenders Handbook, 1979. Bd. dirs. Nat. Polish Am. Jewish Am. Coun., Washington, 1985—; chmn. adv. bd. Felician-Montay Coll., Chgo., 1975-80; commr. Ill. Commn. on Human Rels., Chgo. and Springfield, Ill., 1974-80; pres. Polish Am. Congress, Chgo., 1974-78. 1st lt. U.S. Army, 1953-55. Recipient Advocates Soc. Disting. Svc. award, 1987, Creative Sentencing award N.W. Neighborhood Fedn., Chgo., 1993, appreciation award Gang Free/You and Me, Chgo., 1992, Street Intervention Program award YMCA, Chgo., 1996, cert. of appreciation Ravenswood Cmty. Coun., Chgo., 1998, Charter Mem. award Polish Am. Leadership Initiative, 2002, 1st Mcpl. Disting. Integrity award Cir. Ct. Cook County, 2001, Criminal Law Com. Award of Merit Chgo. Bar Assn., 2003, Recognition award, Chgo. Bar Assn., 2003, Cert. of Jud. Svc., 1980-2001, Chi Phi Parents Creativity award, 1993, Spirit of Rogers Park award, Chgo., 1994. Mem. Ill. Judges Assn. Avocations: sports cars, travel, flying. Home: 1917 N Cleveland Ave Chicago IL 60614-5215 E-mail: tedpatkow@hotmail.com.

KOWAL-VERN, ARETA, pathology and pediatrics educator; b. Weiden, Germany, Aug. 13, 1946; parents Am. citizens; d. Michael and Anna Kowal; m. Boris Vern; 3 children. BA cum laude, CUNY, 1968; MD with thesis honors, SUNY, Buffalo, 1972. Diplomate Am. Bd. Pediatrics; cert. in anat. pathology and hematopathology Am. Bd. Pathology. Resident in pediat. U. Iowa Hosps., Iowa City, 1972-74, staff physician, 1980-83; resident in pediat. Buffalo Children's Hosp., 1974-75; fellow in hematology and oncology Children's Nat. Med. Ctr., Washington, 1975-77; pvt. practice, Washington, 1978-79; pediatric hematologist and oncologist Luth. Gen. Hosp., Park Ridge, Ill., 1983-87, Loyola U. Med. Ctr., Maywood, Ill., 1987-88, fellow in hematopathology, 1988-90, resident in anatomic pathology, 1990-92, asst. prof. pathology and pediat., 1992-98, assoc. mem. Burn and Shock Trauma Inst., 1992-2000; dir. burn rsch. & tissue bank Cook County Hosp., Dept. Trauma, Chgo., 2000—. Contbr. articles to med. jours., including Blod, Cancer Rsch., Modern Pathology, Jour. Trauma, Burn Care and Rehab. Founder sibling support group Luth. Gen. Hosp., Loyola U. Med. Ctr. Mem. Am. Acad. Pediat., Am. Soc. Clin. Pathologists, Coll. Am. Pathologists, Am. Soc. Hematology, Shock Soc., Am. Burn Assn. Achievements include research on teratogenic effects of Trimethadione and Primidone for epilepsy; on subclassification of acute erythroleukemia, definitive study of Antithrombin concentrate in thermal injury. Office: John H Stroger Jr Hosp Cook County Chicago IL 60612-3834 E-mail: avern@rcn.com.

KOWARSKI, ALLEN AVINOAM, endocrinologist, educator; b. Tel Aviv, Dec. 30, 1927; s. Hanoch and Sima (Tkazh) K.; m. Hanna Rose Zas, Mar. 24, 1950; children: David, Ruth. Student, Hebrew U., Jerusalem, 1946-47, MD, 1955; student, U. Lausanne (Switzerland) Med. Sch., 1949-52. Academic physician Hebrew U., 1955-62; instr., fellow Johns Hopkins U., Balt., 1962-68, asst. prof., 1968-72, assoc. prof., 1972-81; prof. U. Md., Balt., 1981—; pres. Kay Labs., Inc., 1974—. Patentee in field; contbr. over 170 articles to profl. jours.; inventor nonthrombogenic blood withdrawal sys., nonthrombogenic glucose monitor; discovered DAWN phenomenon in diabetes and bioinactive growth hormone syndrome (Kowarski syndrome), also integrated concentration of growth hormone method for diagnosis of growth hormone deficiency. Grantee NIH, 1979-97, McNeil Pharm., 1984-86, DuPont Critical Care, 1985-90, Genentech Found. for Growth & Devel., 1994-95, Lilly Rsch. Lab. 1996-98. Mem. Am. Pediat. Soc., Soc. Pediat. Rsch., Lawson-Wilkins Pediat. Endocrine Soc., The Endocrine Soc., Am. Fedn. Clin. Rsch., Am. Diabetes Assn. (Diabetes Rsch. award 1983, Charles H. Best medal for disting. svc. 1994). Office: Kay Labs Inc 2405 Sugarone Rd Baltimore MD 21209

KOWEL, STEPHEN THOMAS, electrical engineer, educator; b. Phila., Nov. 20, 1942; s. Abraham and Anna (Forman) K.; m. Janis Zoltan, June 7, 1970; children: Ann, Eugene, Rose. BSEE, U. Pa., 1964; PhD in Elec. Engring., 1968; MSEE, Poly. Univ., 1966. Rsch. assoc. U. Pa., Phila., 1968-69; asst. prof. elec. and computer engring. Syracuse (N.Y.) U., 1969-74, assoc. prof., 1974-79, prof., 1979-84; prof. elec. engring. and computer sci. U. Calif., Davis, 1984-90, vice-chair dept., 1986-90, dir. organized rsch. program on polymeric ultrathin film systems, 1988-90; chmn. elec. and computer engring. U. Ala., Huntsville, 1990-97, dir. PhD program in optical sci. and engring., 1992-97, interim dean engring., 1997-98, dir., lab. for integrated computing and optoelectric systems, 1998-99, prof elec. and computer engring., 1998-99; dean engring. U. Cin., 1999—. Vis. prof. Cornell U., Ithaca, N.Y., 1982-83; cons. in field. Contbr. articles to profl. jours.; patentee in field. Grantee NASA, USAF, U.S. Army, NSF, Advanced Rsch. Projects Agy. Fellow OSA, IEEE (Centennial medal 1984); mem. AAUP, Am. Soc. Engring. Edn., Sigma Xi. Home: 11370 Brittany Woods Ln Cincinnati OH 45249-1634 Office: Univ Cin Coll Engring PO Box 210018 Cincinnati OH 45221-0018 E-mail: Stephen.Kowel@uc.edu.

KOWITZ, ALETHA AMANDA, retired dental librarian; b. Chgo., Sept. 26, 1925; d. William Carl and Amanda Hedwig (Ross) K. AA, Wright Jr. Coll., Chgo., 1945; BS, U. Chgo., 1951; MA, Rosary Coll., 1959. Rsch. chemist Synthetical Labs, Chgo., 1945-50, Glidden Co., Chgo., 1950-54, chem. libr., 1954-59; asst. circulation-reference libr. U. Ill. Med. Ctr., Chgo., 1959-67; periodicals libr. Northwestern U. Med. Libr., Chgo., 1967-70; reference libr. ADA, Chgo., 1970-76, asst. libr. dir., 1976-77, libr. dir., 1977-92; ret., 1992. Sec. St. Pauls House Corp., Chgo., 1979-95, bd. dirs. Author: Dentistry Journals and Serials, 1985; co-author: Dentistry on Stamps, 1990; contbr. articles to profl. jours. Fellow Am. Coll. Dentists (hon.); mem. Am. Chem. Soc., Am. Inst. Chemists, Am. Acad. History Dentistry, Med. Libr. Assn., Odontographic Soc. (hon., merit award 1985), Iota Sigma Pi. Mem. United Ch. of Christ. E-mail: lethalada@aol.com.

KOWLESSAR, MURIEL, retired pediatric educator; b. Bklyn., Jan. 2, 1926; d. John Henry and Arene (Driver) Chevious; m. O. Dhodanand Kowlessar, Dec. 27, 1952; 1 child, Indrani. AB, Barnard Coll., 1947; MD, Columbia U., 1951. Diplomate Am. Bd. Pediatrics. Instr. Downstate Med. Ctr., Bklyn., 1958-64, asst. prof., 1965-66; asst. prof. clin. pediatrics Temple U., Phila., 1967-70; assoc. prof. Med. Coll. Pa., Phila., 1971-83, dir. pediatric group svcs., 1975-90, acting chmn. pediatrics dept., 1981-83, vice chair pediatrics dept., 1982-91, prof., 1983-91, prof. emeritus, 1991—. Contbr. articles to med. jours. Mem. Pa. Gov.'s Task Force on Spl. Supplemental Food Program for Women, Infants and Children, Harrisburg, 1981-83, Phila. Bd. Health, 1982-86; vol. Phila. Com. for Homeless, 1991-92, Gateway Literacy Program, YMCA, Germantown Bridge, Pa., 1992-93. Fellow Am. Acad. Pediatrics (emeritus); mem. Phila. Pediatric Soc., Cosmopolitan Club Phila., Phi Beta Kappa. Democrat. Avocations: ballroom dancing, opera.

KOWROSKI, MARIA, dancer; b. Grand Rapids, Mich. Student, Sch. Grand Rapids Ballet, Sch. Am. Ballet, 1992. Apprentice N.Y.C. Ballet, 1994—95, mem. corps de ballet, 1995—97, soloist, 1997—99, prin., 1999—. Dancer (ballets) Agon, Apollo, Firebird, A Midsummer Nights Dream, The Nutcracker, Prodigal Son, Swan Lake, La Valse, The Waltz Project, Dances at a Gathering, Schoenberg/Wuorinen Variations, Sonatas and Interludes, Them Twos, Organon, Variations Sériuses. Recipient Princess Grace award, 1994. Office: NYC Ballet NY State Theatre 20 LIncoln Ctr Plz New York NY 10023-6913

KOZAK, ALEXANDER L. engineer; b. Kiev, Ukraine, June 16, 1951; arrived in U.S., 1996; s. Leonid Kozak and Evgenia Gerasimova; m. Evgenia I. Chakshova, Feb. 10, 1973; children: Natalia, Dmitry. MS in Structural Mechanics, Kiev Civil Engring. Inst., 1973, PhD in Structural Mechanics, 1981, DSc in Structural Mechanics, 1995. Sun cert. programmer Java platform. Engr., rschr., sr. rschr., prin. rschr. Struct. Mech. Inst. Kiev State Tech. U. Constrn. and Arch., 1973-95; sr. engr., prin. engr. SC Solutions, Inc., Sunnyvale, Calif., 1996—. Contbr. articles to profl. jours. Avocation: philately.

KOZAK, HARLEY JANE, actress; b. Wilkes-Barre, Pa., Jan. 28, 1957; d. Joseph Aloysius and Dorothy (Taraldsen) K.; m. Gregory Aldisert, 1997; children: Audrey, Lorenzo and Gianna. Cert., NYU, 1980. Appeared in films Parenthood, 1989, Arachnophobia, 1990, The Taking of Beverly Hills, 1990, The Favor, 1990, Necessary Roughness, 1991, All I Want for Christmas, 1991, Magic in The Water, 1995, TV series Harts of the West, 1993-94, Bringing Up Jack, 1995, You Wish, 1997. Office: United Talent Agy 9560 Wilshire Blvd Fl 5 Beverly Hills CA 90212-2400

KOZAK, JOHN W. lawyer; b. Chgo., July 25, 1943; s. Walter and Stella (Palka) K.; m. Elizabeth Mathias, Feb. 3, 1968; children: Jennifer, Mary Margaret, Suzanne. BSEE, U. Notre Dame, 1965; JD, Georgetown U., 1968. Bar: Ill. 1968, D.C. 1968. Patent advisor Office of Naval Rsch., Corona, Calif., 1968-69; assoc. Leydig, Voit & Mayer, Ltd. and predecessor firms, Chgo., 1969-74, ptnr., 1974—, chmn. mgmt. com., 1982-91, pres., 2001—. Mem. United Charities Legal Aid Soc., 1989-2002. Fellow Am. Coll. Trial Lawyers; mem. ABA, Am. Intellectual Property Law Assn., Licensing Execs. Soc., Chgo. Intellectual Property Law Assn., Univ. Club (Chgo.), The Lawyers Club Chgo., Winter Club (Lake Forest, Ill.), Knollwood Club (Lake Forest). Office: Leydig Voit & Mayer Ste 4900 2 Prudential Pla Chicago IL 60601 E-mail: jkozak@leydig.com.

KOZAREK, RICHARD ANTHONY, gastroenterologist, educator; b. Duluth, Minn., Apr. 22, 1947; s. Clarence Edward and Patricia Ann (Koors) K.; m. Linda Jane Cooper, June 9, 1973; children: Katherine, Ellen. BA in Philosophy U. Wis., 1969, MD, 1973. Diplomate Am. Bd. Internal Medicine; bd. cert. internal medicine and gastroenterology. Intern Dalhousie U., Halifax, N.S., Can., 1973-74; resident Good Samaritan Hosp., Phoenix, Ariz., 1974-76; fellow U. Ariz.-Phoenix VA Med. Ctr., Tucson, 1976-78; asst. chief gastroenterology Phoenix VA Med. Ctr., Tucson, 1978-83; asst. clin. prof. medicine U. Ariz., Tucson, 1978-83; with sect. gastroenterology Virginia Mason Med. Ctr., Seattle, 1983—; chief gastroenterology Va. Mason Med. Ctr., Seattle, 1989—; clin. prof. medicine U. Wash., Seattle, 1990—. Author 4 books, 65 book chpts., numerous sci. articles; mem. editl. bd. 8 med. jours., 1983—. Recipient Eddy D. Palmer award William Beaumont Soc., 1982. Fellow ACP, Am. Coll. Gastroenterology; mem. Am. Gastroenterology Assn., Soc. for Gastrointestinal Endoscopy (gov. bd. 1990-95, pres.-elect 1996-97, pres. 1998—), Pacific N.W. Gastroenterology Soc. (sec. 1990, pres. 1991), Federated Socs. Gastroenterology and Hepatology (chair 1998—), Orgn. Mondiale de GastroEnterologie (dep. sec.-gen. 2002--). Office: Virgina Mason Med Ctr 1100 9th Ave Seattle WA 98101-2756

KOZBERG, DONNA WALTERS, rehabilitation administration executive; b. Milford, Del., Jan. 1, 1952; d. Robert Glyndwr and Gailey Ruth (Bedorf) Walters; m. Ronald Paul Kozberg, June 8, 1974; 1 child, Mariel Gailey. BA, U. Fla., 1973, M in Rehab. Counseling, 1974; MFA, CUNY, 1979; MBA, Rutgers U., 1986. Cert. rehab. counselor. Rehab. counselor Office Vocat. Rehab., N.Y.C., 1975-81; area dir. Lift, Inc., Staten Island, N.Y., 1981-83, ea. region dir. pub. relations, advt. Mountainside, N.J., 1983-85, v.p., 1985—, v.p., chief fin. officer 1988, exec. v.p., 1991-93, pres., 1993; co-founder, mng. dir. Expert Strategies Inc., Mountainside, N.J., 1992—; self-employed writer, editor, 1975—. Adv. bd. Rutgers Exec. Master Bus. Adminstrn. Contbr. articles to profl. jours.; assoc. editor Parachute mag., 1978; editor-in-chief (newsletter) Counselor Adv, 1980. Pres. Com. on Employment of People with Disabilities; trustee Ctr. for Creative Living; bd. dirs. N.J. Adv. Coun. for Independent Living, adv. panel NYU. Mem. Nat. Rehab. Assn. (Spl. citation 1974, grantee 1973), Nat. Rehab. Adminstrs. Assn., Nat. Rehab. Counselors Assn., N.J. Rehab. Counselors Assn. (pres. 1996), Poets and Writers. Avocations: Tennis, English lit., Tae Kwon Do. Home: 45 Dug Way Watchung NJ 07069-6011 Office: Lift Inc PO Box 4264 Warren NJ 07059-0264 E-mail: dwkozberg@aol.com.

KOZBERG, RONALD PAUL, health and human services administrator; b. N.Y.C., Apr. 8, 1951; s. Raymond and Muriel (Tolmas) K.; m. Donna Lynn Walters, June 8, 1974; 1 child, Mariel Gailey. BA, Queens Coll., 1973; M of Rehab. Counseling, U. Fla., 1974; M of Pub. Health, Columbia U., 1986. Cert. rehab. counselor. Program dir. South Beach Psychiat. Ctr., S.I., N.Y., 1974-76, dir. rehab. svcs. Bklyn. Developmental Ctr., 1976-85; dir. stds. and compliance Bronx Developmental Svcs., 1985-91; pres. Expert Strategies, Inc., Warren, N.J., 1991—. Technology com. chairperson Union County Edn. Coun., Westfield, N.J., 1993—. Author: The Do's and Dont's of Interviewing, 1992. Recipient Dean's Coun. award Dean of Health Related Professions, 1974. Mem. Nat. Rehab. Adminstrs. Assn. (N.E. regional bd. mem. 1982), Nat. Rehab. Counselors Assn. (N.Y. state sec., treas. 1981-82), Nat. Rehab. Assn. (pres., Spl. Citation 1974), Am. Pub. Health Assn. Avocations: golf, tennis, photography. Home: 45 Dug Way Watchung NJ 07069-6011 Office: Expert Strategies Inc PO Box 4264 Warren NJ 07059-0264

KOZBIAL, RICHARD JAMES, retired elementary education educator; b. Toledo, Nov. 11, 1933; s. Phillip and Bernice Bronislawa (Durka) K.; m. Jane Ardys Verny, July 8, 1961 (dec. Nov. 1983); children: Ardys Jane, Beth Lynne. EdB, U. Toledo, 1957, EdM, 1976. Tchr. Toledo Pub. Schs., 1956-58, 1962-84, Van Dyke Sch. Dist., Warren, Mich., 1958-62; intern tchr. cons. Toledo Pub. Schs., 1984-87, cons., 1987-93; supr. student tchrs., course facilitator U. Toledo, 1987-97, vis. prof., 1997-99, mem. faculty, 1997-99; ESL tchr. Szeged, Hungary, 1993-95; supr. alt. plan U. Toledo, 1993-99, instr. integrated social studies/lang. arts/reading block, 1996-99, ret., 1999. Mem. textbook selection coms. Toledo Pub. Schs.; instr. student tchr. tng. programs Toledo U., 1962-84, instr. student tchr. tng. Bowling Green State U., 1962-84, Mich. State U., 1958-59; organizer Multi-Cultural Awareness Workshop Toledo Elem. Tchrs.

Internat. Inst., 1986-90; organizer Outdoor Edn. Program; participant Multi Unit Edn. Plan; mem. U. Toledo Internat. Edn. Com., 1997-98; mem. Eng. tour Canterbury Singers, 1989, 95, 2000. Author Spelling Curriculum Guide Toledo Pub. Schs., 1968; prodr. (TV programs) WGTE Famous Ams. Born in Feb., Israel. Up with People Host Family, Ohio Arab Affairs Coun., 1989—, ISS, USIA Host Family, 1986—; mem. Planned Parenthood N.W. Ohio, Toledo Mus. Modern Art, Nat. Trust Historic Preservation, 1988—; vestry mem. Trinity Episc. Ch., 1984-87, sesquicentennial com., chmn. music; baritone soloist Canterbury Choir; vocalist Hospice Meml. Svc., 1984—2001; bereavement vol. Hospice N.W. Ohio, Nat. Hospice Assn.; exec. bd. Toledo/Poznan Alliance, mem. Dozynki com. 1990-2002, chmn. 1990, 95, 2000; mem. Bedford Polish Culture Club, 1989-99; sponsor, coord. host families Zulu Choir, Durham, South Africa, Poznan (Poland) Nightengales. Named Outstanding Young Educator, Toledo C. of C., 1965-66; Jennings Founder scholar, 1979-80; recipient Miss Peach award Toledo Blade, 1963, Award of Excellence, 1983, Internat. Inst. Hall of Fame Disting. Svc. award, 1994, Letter of Commendation, Gov. of Ohio, 1994. Mem. Am. Fedn. Tchrs., Ohio Fedn. Tchrs., Toledo Fedn. Tchrs. (life), Internat. Inst. Inc. (life, chmn. edn. com., bd. dirs. 1985-91, pres. 1988-89), Assn. Two Toledos (bd. dirs., 1st v.p. 1990-91), U. Toledo Alumni Assn. (life), U. Mich. Alumni Assn., Am. Assn. Ret. Persons, Lucas County Ret. Tchrs. (life), Mid. East Affairs Coun. (bd. dirs.), Ellis Island Found., Smithsonian Assocs., Nat. Coun. Sr. Citizens, Toledo Sister Cities Internat. (bd. dirs., chmn. entertainment Masked Bash 1996, com. English lang. camp for students from Poland 1995, 96, chmn. host families), Am. Ctr. Polish Culture, Inc., Greenpeace, Phi Delta Kappa, Kappa Delta Pi (various offices including corr. sec., treas., v.p., pres., Point of Excellence award 1992). Democrat. Avocations: gardening, travel, reading, stained glass, calligraphy. Home: 1011 Fifth Ave Eau Claire WI 54703 E-mail: rkozbia@pop3.utoledo.edu.

KOZHEVNIKOV, MICHAEL BORIS, physicist, researcher; b. Abakan, Krasnoyarsk, Russia, Mar. 12, 1965; arrived in Israel, 1992; s. Boris Vasili and Rozaliya Michael (Orlov) K.; m. Maria Sigalov, Feb. 22, 1986; 1 child, Valeria. BSc in Physics, Moscow Inst. Physics & Tech., Moscow, 1986, MSc in Engring., 1988; MSc in Physics, Technion, Haifa, Israel, 1994, PhD in Physics, 1997. Engr./physicist Inst. Nuclear Rsch., Uzhgorod, Ukraine, 1988-92; adj. asst. tchr. Technion, Haifa, 1992-97; postdoctoral appointment U. Calif., Santa Barbara, 1997-99; rsch. assoc. Harvard U., Cambridge, Mass., 1999-2001; postdoctoral mem. tech. staff Bell Labs., Lucent Techs., Murray Hill, NJ, 2001—. Lt. Soviet Army, 1988. Miriam and Aaron Gutwirth Meml. fellow, 1995, Distinct fellow, 1996. Avocations: tennis, literature. Home: 88-2 Woodland Rd Short Hills NJ 07078 Office: Bell Labs Lucent Techs Rm 1D-465 600 Mountain Ave Murray Hill NJ 07974 E-mail: mk73@lucent.com.

KOZINSKI, ALEX, federal judge; b. Bucharest, Romania, July 23, 1950; came to U.S., 1962; s. Moses and Sabine (Zapler) K.; m. Marcy J. Tiffany, July 9, 1977; children: Yale Tiffany, Wyatt Tiffany, Clayton Tiffany. AB in Econs. cum laude, UCLA, 1972, JD, 1975. Bar: Calif. 1975, D.C., 1978. Law clk. to Hon. Anthony M. Kennedy U.S. Ct. Appeals (9th cir.), 1975-76; law clk. to Chief Justice Warren E. Burger U.S. Supreme Ct., 1976-77; assoc. Covington & Burling, Washington, 1979-81; asst. counsel Office of Counsel to Pres., White House, Washington, 1981; spl. counsel Merit Systems Protection Bd., Washington, 1981-82; chief judge U.S. Claims Ct., Washington, 1982-85; judge U.S. Ct. Appeals (9th cir.), 1985—. Lectr. law U. So. Calif., 1992. Office: US Ct Appeals 125 S Grand Ave Ste 200 Pasadena CA 91105*

KOZITKA, RICHARD EUGENE, retired consumer products company executive; b. Staples, Minn., Apr. 30, 1934; s. Michael V. and Luella H. (Drews) K.; m. Mary Elizabeth Juneau, Sept. 27, 1969; children: Michael Arthur, Laura Juneau Hensley. BA in Journalism, U. Minn., 1956. Program dir. Jr. Achievement of Chgo., 1961-63; mgr. publ./employee communications The Quaker Oats Co., Chgo., 1963-72, dir. employee and audio visual communications, 1972-78, v.p. corp. adminstrv. svcs., 1978-95. Trustee Luth. Social Svcs. Ill. Served with U.S. Army, 1957-61. Mem. Westmoreland Country Club (Wilmette, Ill.), Chgo. Curling Club (Northbrook, Ill.), Univ. Club Chgo., Pelican Strand Country Club (Naples, Fla.), La Playa Beach Club (Naples). Lutheran. Home: 9790 Gulf Shore Dr Unit 205 Naples FL 34108

KOZLIK, MICHAEL DAVID, lawyer; b. Omaha, Apr. 20, 1953; s. Otto John and Ella Mae (Slightam) K.; m. Emily C. Cunningham, Sept. 30, 1983; children: John E., Caroline C. BS in Bus., Creighton U., 1975, JD, 1979. Bar: Nebr. 1979, Iowa 2000, U.S. Dist. Ct. Nebr. 1979, U.S. Dist. Ct. Appeals (8th cir.) 1979, U.S. Tax Ct. 1991; CPA, Nebr. Acct. Peat Marwick, Omaha, 1979-84; v.p. fin. Emelco, Omaha, 1984-86; assoc. Nelson Morrow, Omaha, 1986-88; shareholder Schmid Mooney, Omaha, 1988-97, Croker Huck, Omaha, 1997—. Mem. Nebr. CPA Ethics Comm., 1984-85, Nebr. CPA Edn. Comm., 1988—. Contbr. articles to mags. Bd. dirs. Hugh O'Brian Found., Omaha, 1989—, Nebr. ACC Decathlon. Recipient Leadership Omaha award Omaha C. of C., 1989; named One of Ten Outstanding Young Omahans Jaycees, 1990, 92. Mem. Omaha Bar Assn., Nebr. Bar Assn., Optimists (pres. 1989-90, honor award 1990). Republican. Avocations: hunting, fishing, billiards, geneology. Home: 727 N 57th St Omaha NE 68132-2033 Address: Croker Huck DeWitt Anderson & Gonderinger 1250 Commerical Federal Tower 2120 S 72nd St Omaha NE 68124-2366 E-mail: mdkozlik@crokerlaw.com.

KOZLOFF, EUGENE NICHOLAS, zoologist, educator, author; b. Tehran, Iran, Sept. 26, 1920; came to U.S., 1921; s. Nicholas Emilianovich and Eugenie Afanasievna (Kuzenkova) K.; m. Anne Solomon, Oct. 20, 1944; 1 child, Rae Annette. AB in Zoology, U. Calif., Berkeley, 1942, MA in Zoology, 1946, PhD in Zoology, 1950. Lectr. U. Calif., Berkeley, 1945; from instr. to prof. Lewis and Clark Coll., Portland, Oreg., 1945-66; prof. zoology U. Wash., Seattle, 1966—; assoc. dir. Friday Harbor (Wash.) Labs., 1966-73, acting dir., 1979-81. Author: Essentials of Practical Microtechnique, 1964, 71; Seashore Life of Puget Sound, 1973, Keys to the Marine Invertebrates of Puget Sound, 1974, Plants and Animals of the Pacific Northwest, 1976, Seashore Life of the Northern Pacific Coast, 1983, Marine Invertebrates of the Pacific Northwest, 1987, Invertebrates, 1990, Plants of the San Francisco Bay Region, 1994, 2d edit., 2003. Guggenheim fellow, 1953-54. Mem. Am. Microscopical Soc. (editorial bd.), Soc. Protozoologists, Marine Biol.Assn., Western Soc. Naturalists (pres. 1962). Democrat. Home: 40 Hillcrest Pl S PO Box 37 Friday Harbor WA 98250 Office: U Wash Friday Harbor Labs Friday Harbor WA 98250

KOZLOFF, JESSICA S. university president; b. San Antonio, Mar. 29, 1941; d. Robert John and Ann (Acklen) Sledge; m. Stephen R. Kozloff, June 12, 1965; children: Kyle Schaller, Rebecca Esther. BS, U. Nev., 1963, MA, 1964; PhD, Colo. State U., 1983. Prof. polit. sci. U. Northern Colo., Greeley, 1976-89, exec. asst. to pres., 1985-89; v.p. acad. affairs State Colls. in Colo., Denver, 1989-94; pres. Bloomsburg U., 1994—. Mem. Middle States Commn. on Higher Edn., 2000—. Bd. dirs. United Way, Bloomsburg, 1994—2000, Boy Scouts Am., Bloomsburg, 1994—2000. Acad. Adminstrn. fellow Am. Coun. on Edn., 1985. Mem.: Bloomsburg C. of C., Nat. Collegiate Athletics Assn. (mem. pres. commn. 1996—2001), Am. Assn. State Colls. and Univs. (mem. nominating com. 1999—, pres. commn. policies and purposes 1995—97, commn. on intercollegiate athletics 1997—99, mem. Pa. campus compact bd. dirs. 1998—2001, chmn. com. undergrad. experience 2001—), Bloomsburg Rotary Club. Avocations: golf, tennis, skiing, biking, travel. Office: Bloomsburg U 400 E 2nd St Bloomsburg PA 17815-1399

KOZLOFF, LLOYD M. university dean, educator, scientist; b. Chgo., Oct. 15, 1923; s. Joseph and Rose (Hollobow) K.; m. Judith Bonnie Friedman, June 16, 1947; children— James, Daniel, Joseph, Sarah BS, U. Chgo., 1943, PhD, 1948. Asst., then assoc. prof. biochemistry U. Chgo., 1949-61, prof., 1961-64; prof. microbiology U. Colo., Denver, 1964-80, chmn. dept. microbiology, 1966-76, assoc. dean, prof., 1976-80; dean, prof. U. Calif., San Francisco, 1981-91, prof., dean emeritus, 1991—. Career investigator USPHS, U. Chgo., 1962 Founding editor Jour. Virology, 1966-76; contbr. articles to profl. jours., chpts. to books. Chmn. bd. dirs. Proctor Fund., 1981-91; v.p. San Francisco Alliance for Mental Illness, 1993-96; pres. emeritus U. Calif. San Francisco Faculty Assn., 1996-2000. With USN, 1944-46. Commonwealth Fund fellow, 1953, Lederle Found. fellow, 1954 Fellow AAAS, Am. Acad. Microbiol. (hon.); mem. Am. Soc. Biol. Chemistry, Am. Soc. Microbiology (head virology sect. 1974-76), Am. Chem. Soc., N.Y. Acad. Sci. Home: 43000 Lyndon Ln Fort Bragg CA 95437 Office: U Calif Grad Divsn San Francisco CA 94114-2732

KOZLOSKI, LILLIAN TERESE D. history of aerospace technology educator; b. Pitts., Sept. 11, 1934; d. Andrew and Juliana (Yevchak) Dzmura; m. Joseph Kozloski, May 22, 1956; children: Lisa, Cynthia, Charles, Christopher, Dolores Anne. AS, Mt. Aloysius Coll., 1954; BIS, George Mason U., 1981. Mus. technician Smithsonian Air & Space Instn., Washington, 1981-85, mus. specialist, 1985-95, ret., 1995; lectr. U.S. Space Gear Enterprises, Spotsylvania, Va., 1996—; docent James Monroe Mus., Fredericksburg, Va., 2001—. Cons. Smithsonian Instn., Washington, 1996, N.Y. Times, 1996; lectr. on living and working in space. Author: U.S. Space Gear History of Space Suit Technology, 1994, paperback edit., 2000; contbr. articles to profl. jours. Mem. AAUW, Am. Assn. Mus., N.Y. Acad. Scis., Soc. for History of Tech. Roman Catholic. Achievements include categorization and study of Nat. Air and Space Mus. collection of space suits; collected and organized space suit into loan collections and preservation and study collection. Home: 5035 Ridge Rd Spotsylvania VA 22553-6334 E-mail: lillkoz@rcn.com.

KOZLOV, SERGUEI V. medical researcher, consultant; b. Moscow, Russia, Apr. 20, 1969; s. Vladimir A. and Natalia P. (Nazarenko) Kozlov; m. Marina A. Dobrovolskaia, Sept. 25, 2002. PhD(hon.), U. of Zurich, Switzerland, 1994—99. Regulated surg. procedure lic. Home Office/ London, Eng., 1996. Rsch. and tchg. asst. U. of Zurich, Switzerland, 1994—99; rsch. scientist Nat. Cancer Inst., Frederick, Md., 1999—. Contbr. more than 40 pub. sci. papers and abstracts. Recipient Gold Medal, Internat. Chemistry Olympiad; grantee Rsch. Grant, European Union Committees. Mem.: Swiss Soc. for Neuroscience, Internat. Soc. for Neuroscience, Fedn. of European Biochemical Societies (assoc.). Achievements include patents for Structure of neuroserpin gene. Office: National Cancer Institute at Frederick 539 Boylest St Frederick MD 21702 E-mail: skozlov@mail.ncifcrf.gov.

KOZLOV, VYACHESLAV, hockey player; b. Voskresensk, Russia, May 3, 1972; Left wing Atlanta Thrashers, 2002—, Buffalo Sabres, 2001—02, Detroit Red Wings, 1991—2001; winner Stanley Cup, 1997—98; named Soviet league rookie of the yr., 1989—90. Office: Atlanta Thrashers 1 CNN Ctr 13 S Atlanta GA 30303

KOZLOWSKI, BETTE MARIE, accountant; b. Camden, N.J., Apr. 2, 1959; d. Joshua Ashley and Doris Annette (Saunders) Tobey. BS with honors in Acctg., Pa. State U., 1981. CPA Conn. Staff acct. Ernst and Whinney, Hartford, Conn., 1981-83; mid-Atlantic dir. univ. rels. KPMG LLP, Phila., 1983—. Fin. sec. St. Matthews United Meth. Ch., 1995—98; evangelism com., 2000—02; mem. career svcs. adv. coun. Widener U.; mem. adv. coun. acctg. dept. James Madison U. Mem.: AIPCA, Assn. to Advance Collegiate Schs. Bus. (acctg. accreditation com. 2002, accreditation quality com. 2003), Ea. Assn. Coll. and Univ. Bus. Officers, Am. Acctg. Assn. (tchg. and curriculum sect. vice chmn. practice 1998—2001, membership com. 2000, practice adv. com. 2001—02, membership com. 2002—03, edn. com. 2002—03, nomination com. 2003—), Nat. Assn. of Coll. Employers, Jules Link Inst. Accts., Friends of the Libr. U.S. (treas.), Pa. State U. Alumni Assn., Golden Key Nat., Phi Mu, Beta Alpha Psi, Beta Gamma Sigma. Republican. Methodist. Avocations: golf, running, gardening. Office: KPMG LLP 1601 Market St Philadelphia PA 19103-7279

KOZLOWSKI, CHERYL M. principal; b. Boston, July 19, 1974; d. Leo Dennis and Angeles Zenaida BA, Middlebury Coll., 1996; postgrad., Harvard Bus. Sch., 2000—02. Lic. pilot. Fin. analyst Merrill Lynch, N.Y.C., 1996-1998; prin. Clayton, Dubilier & Rice, Inc., N.Y.C., 1998-2000. Equity analyst Am. Express, 2002—. Treas. The Friends of Tolstoy Found., 1998—; chmn. Young New Yorkers of N.Y. Philharmonic, 1999—2002; bd. dirs. Shackleton Schs., 2000—. Avocation: skiing. Home: 610 Park Ave Apt 14A New York NY 10021-7080 E-mail: ckozlowski@mba2002.hbs.edu.

KOZLOWSKI, RONALD STEPHAN, librarian; b. Chgo., Oct. 18, 1937; s. Stephan James and Helen Marie Beck (Tancula) K.; m. Barbara Hartlein, Aug. 8, 1964; children: Ann, Keith, Ellen, Brent. BS in Edn, Ill. State U., 1961; MA in LS, Rosary Coll., 1968. Audiovisual libr. Triton Jr. Coll., River Grove, Ill., 1968-69; libr. Evansville (Ind.) Pub. Librs., 1969-70; asst. dir. Evansville (Ind.) Pub. Libraries, 1971-74; head reference and acquisitions dept. Ind. State U., Evansville, 1970-71; dir. West Fla. Regional Libr., Pensacola, 1974-77, Louisville Free Pub. Libr., 1977-83, Pub. Libr. Charlotte and Mecklenburg County, N.C., 1983-86; exec. dir. Cuyahoga County Pub. Libr., Cleve., 1986-89; dir. Miami-Dade Pub. Libr. System, Miami, Fla., 1989-1993; adminstr. Anne Arundel County Pub. Libr., Annapolis, Md., 1993—. Del. White House Conf. on Librs. Mem. ALA, Md. Libr. Assn. Home: 1160 Jeffery Dr Crofton MD 21114-1315 Office: Anne Arundel County Libr 5 Harry S Truman Pkwy Annapolis MD 21401-7084 E-mail: rsk@mail.aacpl.net.

KOZLOWSKI, THOMAS JOSEPH, JR., lawyer, trust company executive; b. Norristown, Pa., July 29, 1950; s. Thomas Joseph Kozlowski, Jr. and Mary Elisa (Alverez) Kozlowski; m. Michelle Mary Champagne, Jan. 9, 1971; children: Brian Christopher, Scott Michael, Mark Daniel. BSBA in Acctg., Georgetown U., 1971, JD, 1979; MBA, George Washington U., 1975. CPA Va.; bar: D.C. 1979, Va. 1980. Sr. acct. Touche Ross & Co., Washington, 1972-75; dir. internal audit Pentagon Fed. Credit Union, Arlington, Va., 1975-77; supr. acct. Snyder, Newrath & Co., Washington, 1977-79; v.p., sec. Owens & Co., Inc., Arlington, 1979-86; sr. v.p. fin. Realty Investment Co., Inc., Silver Spring, Md., 1986-89; sr. v.p., treas. The Selzer Group, Inc., N.Y.C., 1989-93; pres. The Collector's Gallery of Va. Inc., Alexandria, 1992-96; exec. v.p., dir. family office group Merrill Lynch Trust Co., Princeton, N.J., 1993—. Bd. dirs. Owens & Co., Inc., Alexandria, Va.; bd. advisors Unistates LLC, Alexandria, Cachet Media Inc., NY. Editor: Jour. Law and Policy in Internat. Bus., 1976—79. Arbiter Fairfax County Consumer Protection Commn., Va., 1977—95; treas. Commonwealth Found., Inc., Silver Spring, 1986—89; bd. dirs. Resdl. Youth Svcs., Inc., Alexandria, 1981—89, treas., 1982—84, v.p., 1984—85; treas. Coplex Found., N.Y.C., 1989—93; mem. planned giving adv. coun. Pa. State U., 2000—. Mem.: AICPA, ABA, Inst. Mgmt. Acctg. (cert. mgmt. acctg., cert. disting. performance 1975), Va. State Bar Assn., D.C. Bar Assn., D.C. Inst. CPA. Democrat. Roman Catholic. Avocations: reading, photography. Office: Merrill Lynch Trust Co 3d Fl 1300 Merrill Lynch Dr Pennington NJ 08534

KOZMA, ADAM, electrical engineer; b. Cleve., Feb. 2, 1928; s. Desire and Vera (Nagy) K.; m. Eileen Marie Somogyi, Oct. 24, 1956 (dec. Jan. 1978); children: Paul A. (dec.), Peter A.; m. Rebecca Chelius, Feb. 6, 1993. BSME, U. Mich., 1952, MS in Engring.-Instrumentation Engring., 1964; MS in Engring. Mechanics., Wayne State U., 1961; PhD in Elec. Engring., U. London, 1968; diploma of membership, Imperial Coll., 1969. Design engr. US Broach Co., Detroit, 1951-57; rsch. engr. Inst. Sci. & Tech., Willow Run Labs. U. Mich., Ann Arbor, 1958-69; gen. mgr. Electro Optics Ctr. Harris, Inc., Ann Arbor, 1969-73; sr. rsch. engr. radar div. Environ. Rsch. Inst. Mich., Ann Arbor, 1973-75, mgr. elec. and electromagnetics dept., 1975-76, mgr. tech. staff, 1976-77, v.p., dir. radar div., 1977 85, v.p., corp. devel., 1985-86; v.p., dir. def. electronics engring. div. Syracuse (N.Y.) Rsch. Corp., 1986-88; head intelligence systems dept. MITRE Corp., Bedford, Mass., 1988-89, head advanced systems dept., 1990-93; adj. prof. Coll. Engring. U. Mich., Ann Arbor, 1993—2002, vis. scholar, 2003—. Cons. Conductron Corp., Ann Arbor, 1966, IBM, Endicott, N.Y., 1967-68, U.S. Army Missile Command, Huntsville, Ala., 1974-76, MITRE Corp., 1993-2001, Veridian-ERIM-Internat., Inc., 1998-2001; lectr. various univs.; engring. cons., 1993—. Co-author: Hologram Visual Displays (Motion Picture TV Engrs. honorable mention 1977); patentee in field. With U.S. Army, 1946—47, with USAR, 1947—51, with reserve USAF, 1953—61. Fellow IEEE (life), Optical Soc. Am.; mem. Aero. and Electronics Systems Soc. of IEEE (radar systems panel 1984—, bd. govs. 91-93), Geoscience and Remote Sensing Soc. of IEEE, Am. Def. Preparedness Assn. (chmn. various coms. avionics sect. 1975-88, Ordnance medal 1984), Soc. Photo-Optical Instrumentation Engrs., Sigma Xi. Lutheran. Avocations: tennis, skiing, bicycling. Home and Office: 2996 Appleway Ann Arbor MI 48104-1808 E-mail: akozma@comcast.net.

KOZOBARICH, JERI L. director; b. Upper Darby, Pa., Jan. 27, 1945; d. Charles E. and Dorothy (Brown) Humphrey; children: Steven, Christine. BS cum laude in History, Muskingum Coll., 1967; MA, Ohio State U., 1986. Dir. develop., Coll. Social Work Ohio State U., Columbus, 1980—89, dir. advancement, Coll. Edn., 1989—. Contbr. chapters to books. Bd. dirs. Cmty. Resources Ctr., Columbus, 1986—91; bd. dir. Project Open Hand, Columbus, 1999—2001; vol. Riverside Hosp. Hospice, Columbus, 1996—. Democrat. Avocations: literature, history, visual & performing arts. Home: 150 Croswell Rd Columbus OH 43214 Office: Ohio State Univ Coll Edn 1945 N High St Columbus OH 43210

KOZOK, ULI, language educator; b. Hildesheim, Germany, May 26, 1959; s. Meinolf and Catharina Kozok; m. Febrina Marisyah, Feb. 14, 1964; 1 child, Nina Handayani. PhD, Hamburg U., Germany, 1994. Cert. Translator NZSTI, 1999. Sr. lectr., assoc. prof. U. Auckland, Auckland, New Zealand, 1994—2001; asst. prof., lang. co-ordinator U. Hawaii, Manoa, Honolulu, 2001—. Dir. Bahasa.Net, Honolulu, 1996—. Author: Surat Batak, Warisan Leluhur, Die Bataksche Klage. Mem.: Euroseas, Masyarakat Pernaskahan Nusantara, New Zealand Asian Studies Soc., Assn. for Asian Studies, Royal Inst. of Linguistics and Anthropology, Leiden, Netherlands, New Zealand Soc. of Translators and Interpreters. Office: U Hawaii at Manoa 2540 Maile Way Spalding 255 Honolulu HI 96822 Office Fax: 808-956-5978.

KOZOL, JONATHAN, writer; b. Boston, Sept. 5, 1936, s. Harry Leo and Ruth (Massell) K. BA, Harvard U., 1958; Rhodes scholar, Magdalen Coll., Oxford U., 1958-59. Tchr. Boston pub. schs., 1964-65, Newton pub. schs., 1966-68; dir., trustee Store-front Learning Center, 1968-74; vis. lectr. Yale U., 1969, numerous univs., 1971-2001; prof. edn. Trinity Coll., 1980. Cons. U.S. Office Edn., 1965-66; inst. Ctr. for Intercultural Documentation, Cuernavaca, Mex., 1969, 70, 74. Author: Death At An Early Age, 1967 (Nat. Book award, 1968), Free Schools, 1972, The Night Is Dark and I Am Far From Home, 1975, Children of the Revolution, 1978, Prisoners of Silence, 1980, On Being A Teacher, 1981, Illiterate America, 1985, Rachel and Her Children, 1988 (Robert F. Kennedy Book award, 1989), Savage Inequalities, 1991 (New Eng. Book award, 1992, Amazing Grace, 1995 (Anisfield-Wolf Book award, 1996), Ordinary Resurrections, 2000 (Christopher award, Harry Chapin award, 2001, Wilbur award, 2001); corr.: Los Angeles Times, USA Today, 1982-83; contbr. to N.Y. Times Book Rev., 1968-85; reporter-at-large The New Yorker mag., 1988. Trustee New Sch. for Children, Roxbury, Mass.; bd. dirs. Nat. Literacy Coalition, 1980-83. Recipient Olympia Thousand Dollar award, 1962, Lannan Literary award, 1994; Saxton fellow in creative writing Harper & Row, 1964; Guggenheim fellow, 1970, 84; Field Found. fellow, 1972; Ford Found. fellow, 1974; Rockefeller Found. fellow, 1978, fellow in humanities, 1983. Mem. Nat. Coalition for the Homeless, Fellowship of Reconciliation. Address: PO Box 145 Byfield MA 01922-0145 *My concerns are the education, health and housing of low income children.*

KOZOLCHYK, BORIS, law educator, consultant; b. Havana, Cuba, Cuba, Dec. 6, 1934; came to U.S., 1956; s. Abram and Chana (Brewda) D.; m. Elaine Billie Herman, Mar. 5, 1967; children: Abbie Simcha, Raphael Adam, Shaun Marcie. DCL, U. Havana, 1956; Diplome, Faculte Internat. de Droit, Luxembourg, 1958; LLB, U. Miami, 1959; LLM, U. Mich., 1960, SJD, 1966. Teaching asst. Sch. of Law U. Miami, Fla., 1957-59; asst. prof. law Sch. of Law So. Meth. U., Dallas, 1960-64; resident cons. The Rand Corp., Santa Monica, Calif., 1964-67; dir. Law Reform Project USAID, San Jose, Costa Rica, 1967-69; prof. law Coll. of Law U. Ariz., 1969—. Tchg. asst. Faculte Internat. de Droit Campare, 1958; vis. prof law Nat. U. of Mex., 1961; vis. exch. prof. law Nat. U. of Chile, Santiago, 1962; guest lectr. Latin Am. Law seminar Stanford (Calif.) U., 1964; guest lectr. extension grad. seminar on Latin Am. law UCLA, 1965; Bailey vis. prof., Tucker lectr. La. State U., 1979; vis. prof. U. Aix en Provence, France, 1985; cons. on legal sys. U.S. Agy. Internat. Devel., 1974-77, legal cons. Overseas Pvt. Investment Corp., 1974; cons. uniformity of comml. laws Orgn. Am. States and U.S. State Dept., 1974-77; expert witness on banking and comml. law and custom issues; advisor Libr. Congress Law divsn.; Joseph Bernfeld Meml. lectr. L.A. Bankruptcy Forum, 1989; magisterial lectr. Nat. U. Mex. Sch. Law, 1989; advisor Project Lao, 1991; lectr. in field. Author of books; bd. mem. Am. Jour. of Comparative Law; mem. editl. bd. Internat. Banking Law Jour.; founder, faculty advisor Ariz. Jour. of Internat. and Comparative Law, 1982-86; reporter Ency. Comparative Law, 1989; contbr. articles to profl. jours. and publs. Selected Nat. U. Mex. rep. First Mexican congress Comml. Law, 1974; pres. Ariz. Friends of Music, 1975-76; hon. chmn. community rels. com. Jewish Fedn. So. Ariz.; mem. adv. com. Ariz.-Mex. Commn. Govs.; legal advisor Ariz.-Mex. Banking com.; del U.S. Coun. on Internat. Banking to ICC; adv. mem. U.S. del. to UNCITRAL Internat. Contract Law, 1989-95; dir., pres., bd. dirs. Nat. Law Ctr. for InterAm. Free Trade, 1992—. Recipient Extraordinary Tchg. and Rsch. Merit award Coll. Law, U. Costa Rica, 1969, Cmty. Svc. award Tucson Jewish Cmty. Coun., 1979, Man of Yr. award, 1982, Commendation award U.S. Dept. Justice, 1979, Disting. Svc. award Law Coll. Alumni Assn., 1990, Commendation award U.S. Dept. State, 1990, Ptnrs. in Democracy award Am.-Israel Friendship League, 2003; named to Hall of Fame Profs. of Comml. Law, Nat. U., Mex., 1987; named One of Most Influential Hispanics, Hispanic Bus. Mag., 1991, Man of Yr., Hispanic Profl. Sch. Com., 1995; NSF grantee, 1973-75. Mem. ABA (task force for the revision of UCC article 5), State of Ariz. Bar (Honoree at 100 Women and Minority Lawyers Dinner), Inter-ABA (co-chmn. comml. law and procedure sec. 1973-78, Best Book award 1973), Am. Soc. of Internat. Law, Internat. Acad. Comml. and Consumer Law (pres. 1988-90), Am. Acad. Fgn. Law (founding), Am. Law Inst. (consultative com. to UCC articles 3, 4, 4a and 5), Nat. Mexican Notarial Bar Assn. (hon. life 1982), Internat. Acad. Comml. and Consumer Law (elected pres. 1988), Sonora Bar Assn. (1st Disting. Svc. award 1989). Home: 7401 N Skyline Dr Tucson AZ 85718-1166 Office: U Ariz Coll Of Law Tucson AZ 85721-0001 E-mail: b.kozolchyk@worldnet.att.net.

KOZSUCH, MILDRED JEANNETTE, librarian, archivist; b. Lynnville, Tenn., Dec. 3, 1928; d. Kenneth Carl and Minnie Kate (Shott) Spaulding; m. Paul James Kozsuch, Aug. 28, 1951 (div. Nov. 1959); 1 child, James Sandhi. BA, West Liberty State Coll., 1950; MA, East Tenn. State U., 1969. Tchr. Mt. Pleasant (Ohio) H.S., 1950-51; libr. clk. East Tenn. State U., Johnson City, 1956-60; libr., archivist, 1968-85; tchr., libr. Kingsport (Tenn.) City Schs., 1960-68; libr., archivist (part time) Milligan Coll. (Tenn.), 1992-99. Editor: Historical Reminiscenses of Carter County, Tenn., 1985. Co-chair Washington County Bicentennial Commn., Jonesborough, Tenn., 1994-96; vol. libr. First Christian Ch., Johnson City, Tenn., 1961-88. Mem. Tenn. Archivists, Watauga Assn. Genealogists (v.p.), Jonesborough Geneal. Soc., (v.p.), Washington County Hist. Assn. (pres., v.p.; editor Washington County Hist. Assn. Speeches 1987-1988, Samuel Cole Williams History award 2000, apptd. county historian 2002), Boone Tree Libr. Assn., Tenn. Hist. Soc., East Tenn. Hist. Soc., chmn., Washington Cty. records comm. 2002-, appointed to Washington County Archives Com. and Washington county Libr. Bd., 2003. Avocations: local history, genealogy, collecting postcards and books, collecting data for writing books. Home: 546 Matson Rd Jonesborough TN 37659-5767 E-mail: mildredJK@cs.com.

KOZUBOWSKI, TOMASZ J. mathematics and statistics educator, researcher; b. Warsaw, June 26, 1962; came to U.S., 1986; s. Jan A. Malgorzata Kozubowski; m. Agnieszka R. Riau, Sept. 14, 1982 (div. June 1986); 1 child, Kamil J.; m. Anna K. Panorska, Nov. 12, 1993; 1 child, Joseph A. Grad., U. Warsaw, 1986; MS, U. Tex., El Paso, 1988; PhD, U. Calif., Santa Barbara, 1992. Asst. prof. U. Tenn., Chattanooga, 1992-98, assoc. prof., 1998—. Vis. assoc. prof. U. Calif., Santa Barbara, 1999-2000; assoc. prof. U. Nev., Reno, 2003—; cons. Chattanooga Orthop. Group Found. for Rsch., 1997, Blue Cross Blue Shield Tenn., Chattanooga, 1997-2000; referee Am. Jour. Math. and Mgmt. Scis., Annals of Probability, Probability Theory and Related Fields, Jour. of Multivariate Analysis, Annals of the Inst. of Statis. Math., Comms. in Stats., Computational Stats.and Data Analysis, Math. and Computer Modeling, Statistics and Decisions, Math. Revs., Zentralblatt für Mathematik; presenter in field. Co-author: the Lapalce Distribution and Generalizations: A revisit with Applications to Communications, Economics, Engineering and Finance, 2001; contbr.: more than 30 articles to profl. jours.; contbr. Fellow U. Tenn. Fond., 1994, 97, faculty rsch. grantee, 1995, 98; Ctr. Excellence for Computer Applications Rsch. grantee, 1997, 98. Mem. Am. Math. Soc., Am. Statis. Assn., Bachelier Fin. Soc., Bernoulli Soc. for Math. Statistics and Probability, Inst. Math. Statistics, Actuarial Faculty Forum. Avocations: hiking, chess, photography. Office: Univ Nev Dept Math Reno NV 89557-0001

KOZUCH, JULIANNA BERNADETTE, librarian, educator; b. Wallis, Tex., Feb. 16, 1921; d. Felix Joseph and Agnes Mary (Vrana) K. BA in English, Our Lady of the Lake U., San Antonio, 1951; MEd, Our Lady of the Lake U., 1961, MLS, 1972. Joined Sisters of Divine Providence order, Roman Cath. Ch., 1936;

cert. tchr., Tex., Okla., La. Tchr. Sts. Cyril & Methodius, Granger, Tex., 1940-41, St. John's Sch., Fayetteville, Tex., 1941-42, 55-56, St. Ferdinand's Sch., San Fernando, Calif., 1942-43, Immaculate Conception, Houston, 1943-52, St. Joseph Meml., Enid, Okla., 1952-55, St. Mary's Sch., Natchitoches, La., 1956-57, St. Francis Sch., Iota, La., 1957-58, St. Joseph's Sch., Abilene, Tex., 1958-59, St. Genevieve, Lafayette, La., 1959-61, St. Peter and Paul Sch., New Braunfels, Tex., 1961-63, St. Pius, Pasadena, Tex., 1963-65, St. Anne's, Houston, 1965-70, Meml. High, Lafayette, La., 1972-73; tchr., libr. St. Mary's, San Antonio, Tex., 1970-72, St. Augustine, Laredo, Tex., 1973-77; with bookstore Our Lady of Lake U., San Antonio, 1977-78, ref. libr., 1978-85; head libr. Worden Sch., San Antonio, 1985—. Mem. ethnic affairs Tex. Cath. Conf., 1978—, treas., 1982—; speaker Tex. Inst. Texan Cultures, 1983; translator for Czechoslovakia refugees, 1981—, Dr. Denton Belk; interviewed on Channel 36 TV, 1982, Channel 12, 1979, 82. Mem. math. textbook com. Galveston (Tex.) Houston Diocese, 1968-70; rep. religious women Bishop's Coun., Corpus Christi (Tex.) Diocese, 1976-77; docent Luth. Youth Conf., Inst. Texan Cultures, 1983. Recipient Disting. Svc. award Bayanihan Dance Troupe, 1977, Margil award Tex. Cath. Conf. on Cmty. Ethnic Affairs, 1985, Papal medal, 1987. Mem. AAUP (sec. 1979-82), Nat. Coun. Math. Tchrs., Nat. Cath. Libr. Assn. (treas. Houston chpt. 1968-70, treas. San Antonio chpt. 1970-72, Community Leader of Am. award 1969), Tex. Libr. Assn., Bexar County Libr. Assn. (membership com. 1970-72), Teenage Libr. Assn. (bd. dirs Houston chpt. 1968-70), Southwestern Libr. Assn., Our Lady of the Lake U. Assn. (sec. San Antonio chpt. 1980-82, historian 1982—), Our Lady of the Lake Sisters Orgn. (social com. 1978-79), Czech-Am. Cultural and Edn. Found. (bd. dirs. 1982—, Svc. award 1987). Democrat. Roman Catholic. Home: 603 SW 24th St San Antonio TX 78207-4621 Office: Our Lady of the Lake U 411 SW 24th St San Antonio TX 78207-4666

KRA, ETHAN EMANUEL, actuary; b. Port Chester, N.Y., Mar. 26, 1948; s. Michael Aaron and Bessie (Shragowitz) K.; m. Madeline Rollhaus, Jan. 4, 1976; children: Joseph, Rachel, Joshua. BA summa cum laude, MA, Yale U., 1969, M of Philosophy in Math., 1973, PhD, 1974. Enrolled actuary. Prize teaching fellow Yale U., New Haven, 1972-73; with Prudential Ins. Co., Newark, 1973-77, asst. actuary, 1977; with Mercer Human Resource Cons. Inc., N.Y.C., 1977—, prin., 1984-89, mng. dir., 1989-94, mng. dir. and chief actuary-retirement, 1994—. Lectr. in field. Author: Infinitary Forcing for Languages with the Q-Quantifier, 1974; contbr. articles to profl. jours. Trustee Young Israel West Orange, N.J., 1987-89. Fellow Woodrow Wilson Found., 1969, NSF, 1969-72. Fellow: Conf. Cons. Actuaries, Soc. Actuaries (pension sect. coun. 1991—94, retirement sys. practice advancement com. 1992—, chair 1993—94, bd. govs. 1997—2000, chair 1997—2000, com. on discipline 2001—); mem.: Am. Acad. Actuaries (pension practice coun. 1993—94, 1997—, vice chair 2000—, pension com. 1994—, actuarial stds. bd. gen. com. 2002—), Am. Benefits Coun. (ret. and investment policy com. 1991—, retirement income task force 1995—), Phi Beta Kappa. Jewish. Avocation: bridge. Office: Mercer Human Resource Cons Inc 1166 Avenue Of The Americas 29th Floor New York NY 10036-2788

KRA, PAULINE SKORNICKI, French language educator; b. Lodz, Poland, July 30, 1934; arrived in US, 1950, naturalized, 1955; d. Edward and Nathalie Skornicki; m. Leo Dietrich Kra, Mar. 10, 1955; children: David Theodore, Andrew Jason. Student, Radcliffe Coll., 1951-53; BA, Barnard Coll., 1955; MA, Columbia U., 1963, PhD, 1968; MA, Queens Coll., 1990. Lectr. Queens Coll., CUNY, 1964-65; asst. prof. French Yeshiva U., N.Y.C., 1968-74, assoc. prof., 1974-82, prof., 1982-99, prof. emerita, 1999—; sr. programmer analyst Dept. Biomed. Informatics Columbia U., N.Y.C., 1998—. Author: Religion in Montesquieu's Lettres persanes, 1970; contbr. articles to profl. jours. Mem. MLA, Am. Assn. Tchrs. French, Am. Soc. 18th Century Studies, Société Française d'étude du XVIII Siècle, Soc. Montesquieu, Assn. for Computers and Humanities, Assn. for Lit. and Linguistic Computing, Phi Beta Kappa. Home: 10914 Ascan Ave Forest Hills NY 11375-5370 E-mail: kra@ymail.yu.edu.

KRABBENHOFT, KENNETH LESTER, radiologist, educator; b. Sabula, Iowa, Jan. 7, 1923; s. Lester Henry and Bessie Grant (Thompson) K.; m. Gloria Darlene Eriksen, June 17, 1944; children: Kenneth Lester, Douglas Harold, Karen Ann Krabbenhoft Graham. BA, State U. Iowa, 1943, MD, 1946. Diplomate: Am. Bd. Radiology. Intern Harper Hosp., Detroit, 1946-47, resident in radiology, 1949-52, assoc. radiologist, 1952-57, radiologist, 1957—; practice medicine specializing in radiology Birmingham, Mich., 1957—; prof., chmn. dept. radiology Wayne State U., Detroit, 1969-84; chief radiology Detroit Receiving Hosp.-Univ. Health Center, 1980-84. Cons. radiologist VA Hosp., Allen Park, Mich., Children's Hosp. Mich., Crittenton Gen. Hosp., Herman Kiefer Hosp., Nat. Cancer Inst.; mem. Nat. Cancer Adv. bd.,, 1970-73; pres. Affiliated Radiologists, Inc., Detroit, 1973-85, Detroit Gen. Hosp. Rsch. Corp., 1974-82; mem. Environ. Radiation Exposure Adv. Com., 1975-78; trustee Am. Bd. Radiology, 1971-93, sec., exec. dir., 1981-93, assoc. exec. dir., 1993-95; treas. Am. Bd. Med. Specialists, 1981-85; alt. del. Internat. Congress Radiology. Cons. editor: Am. Jour. Roentgenology, 1975-81. Served to lt. (j.g.), M.C. USNR, 1947-49. Recipient Disting. Alumnus award M.D. Anderson Cancer Ctr., 1988; Nat. Cancer Inst. grantee, 1971-75; Nat. Cancer Inst. Specialized Cancer Center grantee, 1973-75. Fellow Am. Coll. Radiology (Gold medal 1989); mem. Detroit Acad. Medicine, Detroit Med. Club, AMA (vice chmn. sect. council 1969-71), Mich., Wayne county med. socs., Mich. Radiol. Soc. (pres. 1969-70), Am. Radium Soc., Am. Roentgen Ray Soc. (Silver medal 1962, Gold medal 1983), AAAS, Radiol. Soc. N.Am., Chicago Radiol. Soc. (hon., Gold medal 1992), Inter-Am. Coll. Radiology, Friends of Detroit Public Library, Founders Soc. Detroit Inst. Art, State Hist. Soc. Iowa, Mich. Hist. Soc., Lost Lakes Woods Assn., Sigma Xi, Alpha Omega Alpha. Clubs: Masons. Achievements include exhibited portable radioactive istopes for radiography at Smithsonian Inst., 1964-67. Home: 52 Oxford Blvd Pleasant Ridge MI 48069-1111 E-mail: ae8724@wayne.edu.

KRACH, MITCHELL PETER, retired financial services executive; b. Westfield, Mass., Nov. 2, 1924; s. John Joseph and Sophie Mary (Swiatlowski) K.; cert. Mass. Extension U., 1944, Harvard U. Grad. Sch. Bus. Admnstrn., 1966; m. Theresa Florence Sanczuk, May 29, 1957; children— Susan, Gregory, Mitchell, Jonathan, Matthew. Auditor, H.F. Lynch Lumber Co., West Springfield, Mass., 1946-51, dir., 1951-79, sec. bd. dirs., 1951-79, mgr. purchasing, 1951-61, central mgr. purchasing, 1961-71, v.p. purchasing, 1971-76, v.p. purchasing and fin., 1976-79, treas. bd. dirs. 1976-79; treas., chmn. bd. dirs. Nat. Res. Corp., Longmeadow, Mass., 1957-93, ret., 1993; legal arbitrator bldg. materials. Exec. mem., vice-chmn. bd. govs. Shriners Hosp., Springfield, 1980. Cert. purchasing mgr.; notary public; registered and bonded real estate broker, Mass. Mem. Nat. Fedn. Ind. Bus. (nat. adv. council 1978), Nat. Assn. Purchasing Mgmt. (dir. nat. affairs 1965, nat. lumber chmn. 1970-80), Am. Soc. Notaries, Purchasing Mgmt. Assn. W. New Eng. (pres. 1963-64), Purchasing Mgmt. Assn. Worcester, Mfrs. Agts. Nat. Assn. Democrat. Roman Catholic. Clubs: Valley Press, 100 of Mass., Am. Turners, Elks (chmn. bd. trustees), Melha Temple, Masons, Shriners, K.T. Contbr. numerous articles to profl. jours. Home: 15 Woodhill Rd Monson MA 01057-9743

KRACKE, ROBERT RUSSELL, lawyer; b. Decatur, Ga., Feb. 27, 1938; s. Roy Rachford and Virginia Carolyn (Minter) K.; m. Barbara Anne Pilgrim, Dec. 18, 1965; children: Shannon Ruth, Robert Russell, Rebecca Anne, Susan Lynn. Student, Birmingham So. Coll.; BA, Samford U., 1962; JD, Cumberland Sch. Law, 1965. Bar: Ala. 1965, U.S. Tax Ct. 1971, U.S. Supreme Ct. 1971. Individual practice law, Birmingham, Ala., 1965—; founding ptnr. Kracke and Thompson, Birmingham, 1980—. Editor, Birmingham Bar Bull, 1974—; bd. editors Ala. Lawyer, 1980-86, 2003—; contbr. articles to profl. jours. Active Dem. Exec. Com., 1970-98; deacon Ind. Presbyn. Ch., Birmingham, 1973-76, elder, 1999-2003; bd. trustees Dirs. Found. of Ind. Presbyn. Ch., 2004—, pres. adult choir, 1968-99, chief adminstrv. officer, 1970-99, mem. Dirs. of Found., 2004—, pres., treas. Nov. Organ Recital Series, 1999—, Housing Agy. Retarded Citizens; pres. Ala. chpt. Nat. Voluntary Health Agys., 1988-89; mem. exec. com. legal counsel Birmingham Opera Theatre, 1983-95; bd. dirs. Ala. Assn. Retarded Citizens; bd. dirs. Jefferson County Assn. Retarded Citizens, 1983-91, pres.-elect, 1994-96, pres. 1996-98; mem. coordinating com. Nat. Conv. of the ARC of U.S., 1999—; bd. dirs., founding pres. Ala. chpt. Juvenile Diabetes Rsch. Found. Internat.; bd. dirs. The ARC of Ala., 1996-98, Found. of ARC, 1998—; v.p., bd. dirs.Mental Retardation/Devel. Disabilities Health Care Authority of Jefferson County, 2003—. With USNR, 1955-61. Mem. Birmingham (exec. com., law libr. chmn., law day 1976, bull., history and archives com.), Ala. Bar Assn., ABA (award merit law day 1976), Am. Judicature Soc., U.S. Supreme Ct. Hist. Soc., Ala. Hist. Assn., So. Hist. Assn., The Club, Phi Alpha Delta (pres. chpt. 1964-65), Rotary (pres. Shades Valley club 1988-89, Paul Harris fellow, sec. dist. 6860 1990-91, dist. coord. comm., bd. dir., sec. ednl. found.), Sigma Alpha Epsilon. Home: 4410 Briar Glen Dr Birmingham AL 35243-1743 Office: Kracke and Thompson Lakeview Sch Bldg 808 29th St S Birmingham AL 35205-1004 E-mail: rkracke@ktlegal.com.

KRAEHE, ENNO EDWARD, history educator; b. St. Louis, Dec. 9, 1921; s. Enno and Amelia Roth (Henckler) K.; m. Mary Alice Eggleston, May 25, 1946; children: Laurence Adams, Claudia. BA, U. Mo., 1943, MA, 1944; PhD, U. Minn., 1948. Instr. history U. Del., 1946-48; asst. prof. history U. Ky., 1948-50, asso. prof., 1950-63, prof., 1963-64, U. N.C., 1964-68, U. Va., 1968-71, Commonwealth prof., 1971-77, William W. Corcoran prof., 1977-91, William W. Corcoran prof. emeritus, 1991—. Vis. prof. U. Mo., 1946, U. Va., 1955, U. Tex., 1955, U. Minn., 1963; U.S. Dept. State Specialist in, Germany, 1953; mem. regional selection com. Woodrow Wilson fellowship Found., 1959-60; mem. Sr. Fulbright-Hayes History Screening Com., 1970-73 Author: Metternich's German Policy Volume I: The Contest with Napoleon 1799-1814, 1963; author: Volume II: The Congress of Vienna, 1814-1815, 1983; editor: The Metternich Controversy, 1971; mem. editl. bd. Ctrl. European History, 1967-72, Austrian History Yearbook, 1969-74; contbr. entries and articles to encys. and hist. jours., U.S. and Europe. Active Charlottesville Com. on Fgn. Rels.; mem. Nat. Coordinating Com. for Promotion of History, mem. policy bd., 1985-88; mem. Met. Opera Guild, Friends of Ky. Ctr. Recipient Best Book award Phi Alpha Theta; Fulbright scholar Austria, 1952-53; Guggenheim fellow, 1960-61, Am. Coun. Learned Socs. fellow, 1969, 73, resident fellow Rockefeller Ctr. in Bellagio, 1983; grantee NEH, 1973, 80, 83, NEH Libr. Preservation Screening Com., 1988 Mem. Am. Hist. Assn., Conf. Group for Ctrl. European History (mem. exec. bd. 1966-68), German Studies Assn. (mem. exec. coun. 1985—), So. Hist. Assn. (chmn. European sect. 1974, 75, Disting. Svc. award European sect.), Colonnade Club, Blue Ridge Swimming Club, Phi Beta Kappa. Episcopalian. Home: 130 Bennington Rd Charlottesville VA 22901-2653

KRAEMER, ALFRED ROBERT, school librarian; b. N.Y.C., Dec. 25, 1948; s. Philip George and Bernadette (Klein) K.; children: Sarah McCall, Philip Joseph. BA, Beloit Coll., 1973; MSLS, U. N.C., 1978; MA, N.C. State U., 1983; PhD, U. N.C., Greensboro, 1997. Cert. pub. libr., N.C.; lic. elem. and secondary tchr., N.C. Libr. asst. Duke Med. Ctr., Durham, N.C., 1976-78; English tchr. Patterson Sch., Lenoir, N.C., 1978-80; asst. prof. English St. Mary's Coll., Raleigh, N.C., 1980-88; asst. dir. tchg. fellows N.C. State U., Raleigh, 1989-92; sch. libr. Guilford County Schs., Greensboro, N.C., 1995--. Author: Malory's Grail Seekers and 15th Century English Hagiography, 1999. With USN, 1967-70. Mem. MLA, ALA. Democrat. Episcopalian. E-mail: jack_kraemer@yahoo.com.

KRAEMER, DAVID C. theology educator; b. Newark, Oct. 23, 1955; s. Paul William and Phyllis (Ferster) K.; m. Susan L. Boxerman, July 21, 1955; children: Talia, Liviya. BA, Brandeis U., 1977; MA, Jewish Theol. Sem., N.Y.C., 1978, PhD, 1984. Asst. prof. theology Jewish Theol. Sem., 1984-90, assoc. prof. theology, 1990-94, prof. theology, 1994—. Cons. The Jewish Mus., N.Y.C., 1990-92, Heritage/WNET, N.Y.C., 1997. Author: Reading the Rabbis, 1996, Responses to Suffering, 1995, The Mind of the Talmud, 1990, The Meanings of Death in Rabbinic Judaism, 2000; editor: The Jewish Family, 1989, Exploring Judaism, 1999. Assn. Jewish Studies, Soc. Bibl. Lit. Democrat. Jewish. Avocations: cooking, family care, pet care, running. Office: Jewish Theological Seminary 3080 Broadway New York NY 10027-4650

KRAEMER, HARRY M. JANSEN, JR., medical products executive; BA in Math. and Econs. summa cum laude, Lawrence U., 1977; M Mgmt. in Fin. and Acctg., Northwestern U., 1979. CPA Ill. With N.W. Industries, Bank of Am.; dir. corp. devel. Baxter Internat. Inc., Deerfield, Ill., from 1982, various positions in domestic and internat. ops., sr. v.p., CFO, 1993-97, mem. Office Chief Exec., 1995—, pres., 1997—, CEO, 1999—, also bd. dirs., chmn., 2000—. Bd. dirs. Comdisco, Inc., MedPtnrs., Inc., Sci. Applications Internat. Corp.; mem. coun. fin. execs. conf. bd. Bd. dirs. Highland Park Hosp., Ill.; mem. alumni adv. bd. Northwestern U. J.L. Kellogg Grad. Sch. Mgmt.; former mem. alumni bd. dirs. Lawrence U. Recipient Schaffner award, Northwestern U. J.L. Kellogg Grad. Sch. Mgmt., 1996. Mem.: Fin. Execs. Inst., Execs. Club Chgo., Mid-Am. Club, Comml. Club Chgo., Chgo. Club. Office: Baxter Internat Inc One Baxter Pky Deerfield IL 60015-4633

KRAEMER, KENNETH LEO, architect, educator, urban planner; b. Plain, Wis., Oct. 29, 1936; s. Leo Adam and Lucy Rose (Bauer) K.; m. Norine Florence, June 13, 1959; children: Kurt Randall, Kim Rene. BArch, U. Notre Dame, 1959; MS in City and Regional Planning, U. So. Calif., 1964, M of Pub. Adminstrn., 1965, PhD, 1967. From instr. to asst. prof. U. So. Calif., Los Angeles, 1965-67; asst. prof. U. Calif., Irvine, 1967-71, assoc. prof., 1971-78, prof., 1978—, dir. Pub. Policy Research Orgn., 1974-92, dir. Ctr. for Rsch. on Info. Tech. and Orgns., 1992—. Cons. Office of Tech. Assessment, Washington, 1980, 84-85; pres. Irvine Research Corp., 1978—. Author: Management of Information Systems, 1980, Computers and Politics, 1982, Dynamics of Computing, 1983, People and Computers, 1985, Modeling as Negotiating, 1986, Data Wars, 1987, Wired Cities, 1987, Managing Information Systems, 1989, Asia's Computer Challenge, 1998. Mem. Blue Ribbon Data Processing Com., Orange County, Calif., 1973, 79-80, Telecomm. Adv. Bd., Sacramento, 1987-92. Mem. Am. Soc. for Pub. Adminstrn. (Disting. Research award 1985), Internat. Conf. on Info. Systems, Am. Planning Assn., Assn. for Computing Machinery. Clubs: Notre Dame. Democrat. Roman Catholic. Office: U Calif Ctr Rsch Info Tech & Orgns Berkley Pl N Ste 3200 Irvine CA 92697-0001 E-mail: kkraemer@uci.edu.

KRAEMER, LILLIAN ELIZABETH, lawyer; b. N.Y.C., Apr. 18, 1940; d. Frederick Joseph and Edmee Elizabeth (de Watteville) K.; m. John W. Vincent, June 22, 1962 (div. 1964). BA, Swarthmore Coll., 1961; JD, U. Chgo., 1964. Bar: N.Y. 1965, U.S. Dist. Ct. (so. dist.) N.Y. 1967, U.S. Dist. Ct. (ea. dist.) N.Y. 1971. Assoc. Cleary, Gottlieb, Steen & Hamilton, N.Y.C., 1964-71, Simpson Thacher & Bartlett, N.Y.C., 1971-74, ptnr., 1974-99, of counsel, 2000—. Mem. vis. com. U. Chgo. Law Sch., 1988-90, 91-94, 97-99. Bd. mgrs. Swarthmore Coll., 1993—; warden St. Francis Episcopal Ch., Stamford, Conn., 2001—. Fellow Am. Coll. Bankruptcy; mem. Lawyers Alliance for N.Y. (bd. dirs. 1996-2001, co-chair capital campaign 2003—), Assn. of Bar of City of N.Y. (mem. various coms.), Coun. on Fgn. Rels., N.Y. State Bar Assn., Order of Coif, Phi Beta Kappa. Democrat. Avocations: travel, reading, word games. Home: 2 Beekman Pl New York NY 10022-8058 also: 62 Pheasant Ln Stamford CT 06903-4428 E-mail: lkraemer@stblaw.com.

KRAEMER, LISA RUSSERT, lawyer; b. Fayetteville, Ark., Dec. 6, 1954; d. William S. and Louise R. (Russert) K.; m. Richard S. Lang, Dec. 30, 1977; children: Jonathan Kraemer Lang, Katherine Kraemer Lang, William Kraemer Lang, Daniel Kraemer Lang. BA, Harvard U., 1976; JD, U. Cin., 1979; M in Conflict Resolution, Antioch U., 1996. Bar: Ohio 1979, U.S. Dist. Ct. (no. dist.) Ohio 1979. Staff atty. FTC, Cleve., 1980-85; assoc. Madorsky & Katz, Cleve., 1985-86; dir. CLE Case Western Law Sch., Cleve., 1986-88; assoc. Thomas and Boles, Chagrin Falls, Ohio, 1988-89; pvt. practice Cleve., 1989—. Contbg. author: Ohio Family Law Handbook-Mediation, 1996. Councilwoman Village of Chagrin Falls, 1989—; vol. magistrate juvenile divsn. program, 1999—. Mem. Cuyahoga County Bar Assn. Office: Three Commerce Park Square 23230 Chagrin Blvd Ste 740 Cleveland OH 44122-5499

KRAEMER, MICHAEL FREDERICK, lawyer; b. NYC, Jan. 21, 1947; s. Jerome W. and Honey (Dunner) K.; m. Ross Shepard, June 21, 1970; 1 child, Jordan Harriet. BA cum laude, Amherst Coll., 1969; JD, U. Pa., 1972. Bar: Pa. 1972, N.J. 1973, Mass. 2003, RI 2003, U.S. Dist. Ct. (ea. dist.) Pa. 1972, U.S. Dist. Ct. N.J. 1973, U.S. Ct. Appeals (3d cir.) 1974, U.S. Ct. Appeals (2d cir.) 1980, U.S. Ct. Appeals (4th and 7th cirs.) 1981, U.S. Ct. Appeals (6th cir.) 1990, U.S. Ct. Appeals (1st cir.) 2001. Assoc. Astor & Weiss, Phila., 1972-75, Pechner, Sacks, Dorfman, Rosen & Richardson, Phila., 1975-76; ptnr. Kleinbard, Bell & Brecker, Phila., 1976-85, White and Williams LLP, Phila., 1985—2002, Hinckley, Allen & Snyder LLP, Providence, 2002—. Bd. dirs. Ctr. City Residents Assn., Phila., 1976-78; Served to 2d lt. USAR, 1972-73. Recipient Disting. Svc. award Amherst Coll. Alumni Coun., 1994. Mem. Amherst Alumni Assn. Phila. (pres. 1977-79), Indsl. Rels. Rsch. Assn., Germantown Cricket Club (Phila.). Office: Hinckley Allen & Snyder LLP 1500 Fleet Ctr Providence RI 02903-

KRAETZER, MARY C. sociologist, educator, consultant; b. N.Y.C., Sept. 12, 1943; d. Kenneth G. and Adele L. Kraetzer; m. Kestas E. Silunas. AB, Coll. New Rochelle, 1965; MA, Fordham U., 1967, PhD, 1975. Instr. Mercy Coll., Dobbs Ferry, N.Y., 1969-70, asst. prof., 1970-75, assoc. prof., 1975-79, prof., 1979—, program dir. behavioral sci., 1997—, program dir. grad. programs in health svc. mgmt., 2001—. Rsch. asst. Fordham U., Bronx, N.Y., 1965-67, tchg. asst., 1967-68, tchg. fellow, 1968-69, adj. instr., 1971-75, adj. asst. prof., 1975-76; adj. assoc. prof. L.I. U. Grad. br. Campus Mercy Coll., 1976-79, adj. prof., 1979-81, coord. MS in Cmty. Health Program, 1976-81, adj. prof. Westchester campus, 1988-94; rsch. cons. elem. schoolbooks Nat. Coun. Chs./Ch. Women United Task Force on Global Consciousness, N.Y.C., 1971; mem. adv. com. edn. and society div. Nat. Coun. Chs., 1975-78; mem. evaluation team Middle States Assn. Colls. and Secondary Schs. Commn. on Higher Edn., Monmouth, N.J., 1976; presenter in field. Contbr. chpts. to books, articles to profl. jours. Recipient Tchg. Excellence award Mercy Coll., 1999; Bd. Regents scholar, 1961-65, 65-69; Fordham U. scholar, 1965-68; Fordham U. fellow, 1968-69; Mercy Coll. grantee, 1984, 85, 86, 88, 92; Mercy Coll. Faculty Devel. grantee, 1999; NSF summer intern, 1967. Mem. APHA (conf. presenter), Am. Sociol. Assn. (presenter). Office: Mercy Coll 555 Broadway Dobbs Ferry NY 10522-1134

KRAFFT, GEOFFREY ARTHUR, physicist; b. Enid, Okla., May 14, 1958; s. Gottfried Hermann George and Margaret Ellen (Kelly) K.; m. Alicia S. Hofler, May 21, 1994; children: Athena Margaret, Konrad Julian Jefferson. BA, Rutgers U., 1978; MA, U. Calif., Berkeley, 1980, PhD, 1986. Grad. student rsch. asst. Lawrence Berkeley Lab., 1979-85; staff scientist Thomas Jefferson Nat. Accelerator Facility, Newport News, Va., 1986—. Fellow: Am. Phys. Soc. Home: 136 Twin Lake Cir Newport News VA 23608-2434 Office: Thomas Jefferson Nat Accelerator Facility 12000 Jefferson Ave Newport News VA 23606-4323 E-mail: krafft@jlab.org.

KRAFKA, MARY BAIRD, lawyer; b. Ottumwa, Iowa, Jan. 4, 1942; d. Glenn Leroy and Alice Erna (Krebill) B.; m. Jerry Lee Krafka, Oct. 14, 1962; children: Lisa Krafka Piper, Gregory D., Jeffrey A., Amy Krafka Pittman. BA in English and Human Rels., William Penn Coll., Oskaloosa, Iowa, 1990; JD, U. Iowa, 1993. Bar: Iowa 1993. Vol. lawyer Legal Svcs. Corp., Ottumwa, 1993-94; pvt. practice, Ottumwa, 1994—. Mem. AAUW, ABA, Iowa Bar Assn., Wapello County Bar Assn., PEO Sisterhood (Iowa chpt. HC 1973). Lutheran. Avocations: sewing, walking and running, interior designing, church activities, reading. Home: 931 W Mary St Ottumwa IA 52501-4904 Office: 101 S Market St Ste 203 Ottumwa IA 52501-2933

KRAFT, ARTHUR, university dean; b. Eden, N.Y., May 7, 1944; s. Arthur Brauer and Mary Jane (Forti) K.; m. Joan Marie Brown, Sept. 3, 1966; children: Arthur G., Stephen Michael, Leigh Judith. BS, St. Bonaventure U., 1966; MA, SUNY, Buffalo, 1969, PhD, 1970. Asst. prof. Ohio U., Athens, 1969-72, assoc. prof., 1972-75; prof. U. Nebr., Lincoln, 1975-77, assoc. dean Coll. Bus., 1977-83; dean Coll. Bus. and Econs. W.Va. U., Morgantown, 1983-87; dean sch. bus. Rutgers U., New Brunswick, N.J., 1987-93; dean Sch. Mgmt. Ga. Inst. Tech., Atlanta, 1993-97; dean Coll. Commerce, Charles H. Kellstadt Grad. Sch. Bus., DePaul U., Chgo., 1997—. Pension adv. com. Monongalia County Hosp., Morgantown, 1985-87. Recipient NASA fellowship Stanford U., 1973, fellowship Sears-Roebuck Fellowship Found, Washington, 1974-75; named Outstanding Young Individual Jaycees, Lincoln, 1978. Mem. Am. Econ. Assn., Am. Assembly of Collegiate Schs. of Bus. (visitation com. 1977—, continuing accreditation com. 1987, bus. accreditation com. 1995—), North Ctrl. Assn. (evaluator 1986-87), Beta Gamma Sigma. Avocations: trivia, sports. Fax: 312-362-5198. E-mail: akraft@wppost.depaul.edu.

KRAFT, ELAINE JOY, community relations and communications official; b. Seattle, Sept. 1, 1951; d. Harry J. and Leatrice M. (Hanan) K.; m. Lee Somerstein, Aug. 2, 1980; children: Paul Kraft, Leslie Jo. BA, U. Wash., 1973; MPA, U. Puget Sound, 1979. Reporter Eastside Jour., Bellevue, Wash., 1972-76; editor Jour./Enterprise Newspapers, Wash. State, 1976; mem. staff Wash. State Senate, 1976-78, Wash. Ho. of Reps.,1978-82, pub. info. officer, 1976-78, mem. leadership staff, asst. to caucus chmn., 1980—; ptnr., pres. Media Kraft Communications; mgr. corp. info., advt. and mktg. communications Weyerhaeuser Co., 1982-85; dir. comms. Weyerhaeuser Paper Co., 1985-87; dir. cmty. rels. N.W. region Coors Brewing Co. 1987-95; comms. dir. King County exec. King County Ct. House, 1996—. Recipient state and nat. journalism design and advt. awards. Mem. Nat. Fedn. Press Women, Women in Comms., Wash. Press Assn. Home: 14329 SE 63d St Bellevue WA 98006-4802 Office: King County Courthouse 516 3d Ave Seattle WA 98104-2312

KRAFT, GEORGE HOWARD, physician, educator; b. Columbus, Ohio, Sept. 27, 1936; s. Glen Homer and Helen Winner (Howard) K.; children: Jonathan Ashbrook, Susannah Mary. AB, Harvard U., 1958; MD, Ohio State U., 1963, MS, 1967. Diplomate Am. Bd. Phys. Medicine and Rehab. (subspecialty in spinal cord injury medicine), Am. Bd. Electrodiagnostic Medicine. Intern U. Calif. Hosp., San Francisco, 1963-64, resident in phys. medicine and rehab., 1964-65, Ohio State U., Columbus, 1965-67; assoc. U. Pa. Med. Sch., Phila., 1968-69; asst. prof. U. Wash., Seattle, 1969-72, assoc. prof., 1972-76, prof., 1976—; chief of staff U. Wash. Med. Ctr., Seattle, 1993-95. Dir. electrodiagnostic medicine U. Wash. Hosp., 1987—, dir. Multiple Sclerosis Ctr., 1982—; co-dir. Muscular Dystrophy Clinic, 1974—; assoc. dir. rehab. medicine Overlake Hosp., Bellevue, Wash., 1989-2003; bd. dirs. Am. Bd. Electrodiagnostic Medicine, 1993-2000, chmn., 1996-2000. Co-author: Chronic Disease and Disability, 1994, Living with Multiple Sclerosis: A Wellness Approach, 2000; cons. editor: Phys. Medicine and Rehab. Clinics, 1990—, EEG and Clin. Neurophysiology, 1992-96; assoc. editor Jour. Neurol. Rehab. and Neurol. Repair, 1988-2000, Muscle and Nerve, 1998-2000; contbr. articles to profl. jours. Sci. peer rev. com. C Nat. Multiple Sclerosis Soc., N.Y.C., 1990-96, chmn., 1993-96, med. adv. bd., 1991—; bd. sponsors Wash. Physicians for Social Responsibility, Seattle, 1986—. Rsch. grantee Rehab. Svcs. Adminstrn., 1976-81, Nat. Inst. Handicapped Rsch., 1984-88, Nat. Multiple Sclerosis Soc., 1990-92, 94-95, Nat. Inst. Disability and REhab. Rsch., 1998—. Fellow Am. Acad. Phys. Medicine and Rehab. (pres. 1984-85, Zeiter award 1991, Krusen award 2002); mem. Am. Assn. Electrodiagnostic Medicine (pres. 1982-83), Assn. Acad. Physiatrists (pres. 1980-81), Am. Acad. Clin. Neurophysiology (pres. 1995-97), Am. Acad. Neurology, Internat. Rehab. Medicine Assn., Alpha Omega Alpha. Episcopalian. Office: Dept Rehab Med U of Wash PO Box 956490 Seattle WA 98195 E-mail: ghkraft@u.washington.edu.

KRAFT, GERALD, economist; b. Detroit, July 1, 1935; s. Jule and Shirley (Schwartz) K.; m. Sandra Doris Johnson, Aug. 7, 1955; children: Michael Stanton, Lynn Barbara. Student, U. Chgo., 1951-52; BA, Wayne U., 1955; MA, Harvard U., 1957. Mng. dir. Harvard U. Statis. Lab., Cambridge, Mass., 1957-58; prin. United Rsch. Inc., Cambridge, 1958-61; sr. rsch. assoc. Sys. Analysis and Rsch. Corp., Boston, 1961-64, Regional and Urban Planning Implementation, Inc., Cambridge, 1964-65; pres., CEO, chmn. Charles River Assocs. Inc., Boston, 1965-92; sr. v.p. The GSK Group, Ltd., 1994—; chmn. Modern Broadcast Prodns. Lectr. MIT, Harvard U., U. Pa., Northeastern U.; mem. planning com., dir. Maritime Transp. Rsch. Bd., NRC, 1976-79; mem. Group I Coun., mem. coms. Transp. Rsch. Bd., 1977-80; pres. Transp. Rsch. Forum, 1977, v.p. program, 1976; chmn. 2d Internat. Tungsten Symposium, 1982. Author: (with others) The Role of Transportation in Regional Economic Development, 1971; co-author: Report of Task Force on Transp. to Sci. Adv. panel to Com. on Pub. Works, U.S. Ho. of Reps, 1974; contbr. articles to profl. jours. Trustee, dir., fin. com., exec. com., former chmn. budget subcom., asst. treas. Beth Israel Hosp.; past dir. Beth Israel Corp.; trustee, fin. com., patient care and quality com., audit and compliance com. Beth Israel Deaconess Med. Ctr.; past dir. Med. Care Boston, Inc.; fin. com. Commonwell, Inc.; mem. Harvard U. Grad. Sch. Arts & Scis., adv. com. grad. student life Harvard U.; adv. bd. Medifile, Inc.; mem. allocation subcom. United Way. Mem. AAAS, Am. Econ. Assn., Econometric Soc., Am. Statis. Assn., Inst. Mgmt. Scis., Ops. Rsch. Soc. Am., Internat. Wine and Food Soc. (past treas., past pres., past chmn.), Confrerie des Chevaliers du Tastevin (past chef du protocole, comdr.), Grand Sénéchal (officier commandeur Sous-Commanderie de Mass.), Harvard

Club Boston, Univ. Club, Rotary (past bd. dirs., trustee student aid fund, Paul Harris fellow), Fine Wine Coun. Mass. (bd. dirs.), Beefeater Club, Chaine des Rotisseurs (vice echanson), L'ordre Mundial, Confraternita Enogastronomica Toscana, Phi Beta Kappa. Home: 60 Scotch Pine Rd Weston MA 02493-1405

KRAFT, HENRY ROBERT, lawyer; b. L.A., Apr. 27, 1946; s. Sylvester and Freda (Shochat) K.; m. Terry Kraft, July 21, 1968; children: Diana, Kevin. BA in History, San Fernando Valley State Coll., 1968; JD, U. So. Calif., 1971. Bar: Calif. 1972, U.S. Dist. Ct. (ctrl. dist.) Calif. 1985, U.S. Ct. Appeals (9th cir., fed. cir.) 1998, U.S. Dist. Ct. (so., ctrl. and no. dists.) Calif 1998. Dep. pub. defender San Bernardino (Calif.) County, 1972-78; pvt. practice, Victorville, Calif., 1979-96; city atty. Victorville, 1987—2002; of counsel Best Best & Krieger LLP, Victorville, 1996-98; assoc. Parker, Covert & Chidester, Tustin, Calif., 1999-2000; ptnr. Parker & Covert LLP, Tustin, 2000—. Atty. City of Barstow, Calif., 1980-97; instr. Victor Valley Coll., Victorville, 1986—. Atty. Barstow Community Hosp., 1980-88. Mem. FBA, San Bernardino Bar Assn. (fee dispute com., jud. evaluation com.), High Desert Bar Assn. (pres., v.p., sec. 1979-81), Calif. Soc. Health Care Attys., League Calif. Cities, Am. Arbitration Assn. (panel neutral arbitrators). Democrat. Jewish. Avocations: bicycling, travel, wine enthusiast. Office: Parker & Covert LLP East Bldg Ste 204 17862 E Seventeenth St Tustin CA 92780-2164 E-mail: hkraft@parkercovert.com.

KRAFT, IRVIN ALAN, psychiatrist; b. Huntington, W.Va., Nov. 20, 1921; m. Shirley Goldin, July 4, 1951; children: Karen Kraft Pennebaker, Joanna Kraft Katz, Elizabeth Kraft Schmachtenberger, Mark. BS, NYU, 1943, MD, 1949. Diplomate Am. Bd. Psychiatry and Neurology, Am. Bd. Child Psychiatry. Chief psychiatry Tex. Children's Hosp., Houston, 1958-65; prof. mental health U. Tex. Sch. Pub. Health, Houston, 1975-91; emeritus prof. mental health U. Tex., Houston, 1991—; assoc. clin. prof. pediatrics Baylor Coll. Medicine, Houston, 1977—, clin. prof. psychiatry, 1977—, U. Tex. Sch. Medicine, Houston, Galveston. Med. dir. Tex. Inst. Family Psychiatry, Houston, 1964-79; dir. Houston Heart Assn., 1969-70; med. dir. Adult Adolescent Rehab. Ctr., Houston, 1982-85; chmn. subcom. Mental Health Needs Coun., Houston, 1988-89. Author: (with others) Adolescent Group Psychotherapy, 1989, Bibliography of Child and Adolescent Psychiatry, 1990; co-editor: Child Group Psychotherapy: Future Tense, 1986; mem. editorial bd. Jour. Child and Adolescent Group Therapy, 1989—. Mem. drug prevention com. High Sch. for Health Professions, Houston, 1989-90; mem. Tex. House Rep. Com. on Edn., 1974. N.Y. Acad. Scis. fellow, 1971—; recipient Gold award Am. Acad. Pediatrics, 1969, cert. of award Am. Group Psychotherapy Assn., 1970. Fellow Am. Acad. Child and Adolescent Psychiatry (life), Am. Group Psychotherapy Assn. (life), Am. Acad. Psychoanalysis (life), Am. Psychiat. Assn. (life), Houston Group Psychotherapy Soc. (life), Southwestern Group Psychotherapy Soc. (life), Houston Psychiat. Soc. (life), Tex. Soc. Psychiat. Physicians (life), Tex. Soc. of Child and Adolescent Psychiatry (life), Am. Orthopsychiatry Assn. (life). Home: 2423 Gramercy Blvd Houston TX 77030-3105 Office: 4545 Post Oak Pl # 375 Houston TX 77027 Fax: 713-668-2555. E-mail: irvkraft@houston.rr.com.

KRAFT, KENNETH HOUSTON, JR., insurance agency executive; b. Chgo., Apr. 2, 1934; s. Kenneth Houston and Elizabeth (Preston) K.; m. Ruth Neely, Aug. 11, 1956 (div. Sept. 1979); children: Katherine Elizabeth, Carolyn Ruth, Kenneth Houston III; m. Kathleen Hartung, Mar. 16, 1985. BS in Fin., Purdue U., 1956. Pres., chmn. bd. Kraft Ins. Agy., Inc., Winter Park, Fla., 1960—, KHK Fin. Corp., Winter Park, 1974—; chmn. bd. Echo Pub. Co., Sulfur Springs, Tex., 1970—2000; owner Kraft Cattle Co., 1981—86. Sr. mem., exec., fin., comml. loan, audit and examining coms. Barnett Bank Cen. Fla., Orlando, 1965-98; founding dirs. Goodings Groceries of Fla., Altamonte Springs, Fla., Schwartz Electro-Optics, Orlando, Internat. Laser Sys., Orlando, KHK Fin. Corp., Carson City, Nev., Princeton Fin. Corp., Orlando, Falcon Aviation, Orlando, TV-9 Inc., ABC affiliate, Orlando, First Ctrl. Corp., Orlando, Inglewood Daily News, Inglewood Citizen Co., L.A. Bd. dirs. Winter Park C. of C., 1965-70, Orange County chpt. ARC, Orlando, 1963-65, Orange County chpt. United Way, Winter Park, 1970-72, Winter Park YMCA, 1972-75, citrus grower Kraft Groves, 1966-2000; mem. Fla. Citrus Mut., Lakeland, 1966-2000, Com. of 100 of Orange County, Inc., Orlando, 1983—; bd. trustees Winter Park Meml. Hosp., 1969-88, also exec. com., compensation com., chmn. long range planning com.; chmn. Winter Park Cmty. Trust Fund, 1981-92; mem. grievance com. 9th Jud. Cir., 1987-90; active Boy Scouts Am., Rollins Coll. Fiat Lux Soc., Corp. Coun., Crummer Grad. Sch. Bus., Winter Park, Fla.; mem. selection com. COMPUSA Fla. Citrus Bowl, 1999. Lt. (j.g.) USNR, 1956-58. Named Outstanding Young Man of Winter Park, Winter Park Jaycees, 1970, Citizen of the Yr., Winter Park, Fla., 2002. Mem.: U.S. Navy League, U.S. Naval Inst., So. Grand Bank Owners Assn., Nat. Assn. Ins. Agts., Fla. Assn. Ins. Agts., Ctrl. Fla. Assn. Ins. Agts. (pres. 1963—64), Purdue U. Alumni Assn. (pres. coun., dirs. cir. Krannert Grad. Sch. Mgmt., Deans Club Sch. Sci.), Rotary (bd. dirs. Winter Park Club 1968—74), All-Am. John Purdue Club, Gold Club Purdue Mus. Orgn., Country Club of Orlando (pres. 1994—95), Useppa Island Club, Captiva Island Yacht Club, U. Club, Masons, Delta Delta (chpt. pres. 1956, ctrl. Fla. alumni chpt.pres. 1960), Sigma Chi. Republican. Presbyterian. Home: 231 Chelton Cir Winter Park FL 32789-6004 also: 1765 Venus Dr Sanibel FL 33957-3427 Office: Kraft Ins Agy Inc PO Box 1443 Winter Park FL 32790-1443

KRAFT, MICHAEL EUGENE, political science educator; b. LA, Nov. 18, 1943; s. Louis and Pearl (Wiener) Kraft. BA, U. Calif., Riverside, 1966; MA, Yale U., 1967, PhD, 1973. Asst. prof. Vassar Coll., Poughkeepsie, N.Y., 1973-76, U. Wis., Green Bay, 1977-79, assoc. prof., 1979-82, prof., 1982—. Vis. disting. prof. Oberlin (Ohio) Coll., 1984-85, U. Wis., Madison, 1987-88. Author: Environmental Policy and Politics, 2001, 3d edit., 2003; co-author, editor: Technology and Politics, 1988, Public Reactions to Nuclear Waste, 1993, Environmental Policy, 5th edit., 2003, Toward Sustainable Communities, 1999, Public Policy, 2003. Bd. dirs. Lake Michigan Fedn., Chgo., 1986—. Yale U. fellow, 1966-69, Mem. AAAS, Am. Polit. Sci. Assn., Western Polit. Sci. Assn., Phi Beta Kappa, Phi Kappa Phi. Avocations: computers, running, music, gardening. Office: U Wis Pub & Environ Affairs/MAC B310 2420 Nicolet Dr Green Bay WI 54311-7001 E-mail: kraftm@uwgb.edu.

KRAFT, RICHARD LEE, lawyer; b. Lassa, Nigeria, Oct. 14, 1958; m. Tanya Kraft, July 14, 1984; children: Devin, Kelsey. BA in Fgn. Svc., Baylor U., 1980, JD, 1982. Bar: N.Mex. 1982, U.S. Dist. Ct. N.Mex., U.S. Ct. Appeals, U.S. Supreme Ct. Assoc. Sanders, Bruin & Baldock, Roswell, N.Mex., 1982-87, ptnr., 1987-98, Kraft & Stone, LLP, Roswell, 1998-2000; owner The Kraft Law Firm, 2000—. Vol. lawyer Ea. N.Mex. U. Roswell, 1984-98; bd. dirs. Roswell YMCA, 1983-87, Crimestopper, 1991-94; pres. Roswell Mens Ch. Basketball League; participant Roswell Mens Ch. Softball League; asst. chair legal div. United Way Drive, 1990. Recipient Outstanding Contribution award N.Mex. State Bar, 1987. Mem. ABA, N.Mex. Trial Lawyers Assn., N.Mex. Bar Assn. (bd. dirs. young lawyers div. 1983-91, pres. 1986-87, chmn. membership com., bar commr. 1986-87, 91- , pres. 1998-99, Outstanding Young Lawyer award 1990), Chaves County Bar Assn. (chair law day activities, chair ann. summer picnic com., rep. bench and bar com.), Roswell Legal Secs. Assn. (hon.), Roswell C. of C. (participant and pres. Leadership Roswell, exec. dir., bd. dirs. 1991-), Sertoma (bd. dirs. Roswell club 1989-91). Baptist. Office: The Kraft Law Firm 111 W Third St Roswell NM 88201-4783 E-mail: thekraftlawfirm@aol.com.

KRAFT, ROBERT ARNOLD, retired medical educator, physician; b. Seattle, Mar. 27, 1924; s. Vincent Irving and Blanche (Palmer) K.; m. Robby Lee Roberson, June 12, 1949 (dec. Aug. 2002); children: Angela Kraft Cross, Peter, Darius. BA, U. Wash., 1948, MD, 1954. Diplomate Am. Bd. Pathology, Am. Bd. Nuclear Medicine. Intern USPHS Hosp., Staten Island, N.Y., 1954-55; resident in Pathology Tacoma (Wash.) Gen. Hosp, 1958-60, U. Calif., San Francisco, 1960-62; staff pathologist Peninsula Hosp., Burlingame, Calif., 1962-90, dir. nuclear medicine, 1965-90; asst. clin. prof. nuclear medicine and pathology U. Calif., San Francisco, 1962-90. Bd. dirs. Am. Bd. Nuclear Medicine, L.A., 1990-95. Capt. USAF, 1943-45, ETO. Decorated DFC. Fellow Am. Coll. Nuclear Physicians (regent 1985-91), Coll. Am. Pathologists; mem. Am. Coll. Nuclear Physicians (pres. Calif. chpt. 1972-73), Soc. Nuclear Medicine (trustee 1982-85), South Bay Pathology Soc. (pres. 1966-67). Avocations: golf, astronomy, mining history, orchids. Home: 971 Baileyana Rd Hillsborough CA 94010-6173

KRAFT, ROBERT K. professional sports team executive; b. Brookline, Mass., July 5, 1941; m. Myra Kraft; 4 children. Grad., Columbia U.; MBA, Harvard U. Owner Foxboro (Mass.) Stadium; chmn. Chestnut Hill Mgmt.; pres. New England TV Corp., 1986-91; with Rand-Whitney Group, Inc., Worcester, Mass.; founder Internat. Forest Products, 1972; pres. Internat. Forest Products Group Cos.; chmn. Carmel Container Systems, Ltd., Israel; owner New England Patriots, 1994—. Mem. exec. com. Dana Farber Cancer Inst.; trustee Columbia U.; bd. dirs. Harvard Sch. Bus. Mem. bd. overseers Boston Symphony Orch., Boston Mus. Sci. Avocations: golf, tennis. Office: New England Patriots Gillete Stadium One Patriots Pl Foxboro MA 02035-1388

KRAFT, ROSEMARIE, dean, educator; b. Franklin, Pa., Nov. 18, 1936; d. Jack B. Harter and Romaine B. Shick; m. Louis R. Kraft; children: Louis W., Jack C. PhD, Ohio State U., 1976. Prof. U. Calif., Davis, 1977—, assoc. dean, 1994—. Dir., prof. for future fellowship U. Calif., Davis, 1995—. Author: Individual Differences in Cognition, 1998. Recipient McNair Scholars grant, U.S. Dept. Edn., 1995, 1999. Avocations: hiking, reading, traveling. Home: 1315 Lake Blvd Davis CA 95616 Office: U Calif Davis One Shields Ave Davis CA 95616

KRAG, MARTIN HANS, physician, orthopaedist, educator, researcher; b. St. Louis, Aug. 17, 1949; BA, Stanford U., 1970; MD, Yale U., 1975. Diplomate Am. Bd. Orthopaedic Surgeons. Resident in orthopaedics Yale U., New Haven, 1975-79, rsch. fellow, 1979-80, Ranchos Los Amigos Hosp., Downey, Calif., 1980-81; asst. prof. dept orthopaedics U. Vt., Burlington, 1981-89, assoc. prof., 1989-97, prof., 1997—; dir. Vt. Bank Rsch. Ctr., 1996—. Co-dir. Rehab. Engring. Ctr., Burlington, 1988—. Recipient spinal rsch. award Ea. Orthopaedic Assn., 1984; rehab. grantee Nat. Inst. Disability, 1988—, NIH, 1988-92. Fellow Am. Acad. Orthopaedic Surgeons; mem. Internat. Soc. for Study Lumbar Spine, Orthopaedic Rsch. Soc., Cervical Spine Rsch. Soc., N.Am. Spine Soc. Office: U Vt Dept Orthopaedics and Rehab Stafford Hl Burlington VT 05405-0001 E-mail: martin.krag@uvm.edu.

KRAG, OLGA, interior designer; b. St. Louis, Nov. 27, 1937; d. Jovica Todor and Milka (Slijpcevic) Golubovic. AA, U. Mo., 1958; cert. interior design, UCLA, 1979. Interior designer William L. Pereira Assocs., L.A., 1977-80; aassoc. Reel/Grobman Assocs., L.A., 1980-81; project mgr. Kaneko/Laff Assocs., L.A., 1982, Stuart Laff Assocs., L.A., 1983-85; restaurateur The Edge, St. Lois, 1983-84; pvt. practice comml. interior design, L.A., 1981—. Mem. invitation and ticket com. Calif. Chamber Symphony Soc., 1980-81; vol. Westside Rep. Coun., Proposition 1, 1971; asst. inaugural presentation Mus. of Childhood, L.A., 1985. Recipient Carole Eichen design award U. Calif., 1979. Mem. Am. Soc. Interior Designers, Inst. Bus. Designers, Phi Chi Theta, Beta Sigma Phi. Republican. Serbian Orthodox. Home and Office: 700 Levering Ave Apt 10 Los Angeles CA 90024-2797

KRAGEL, PETER J. academic administrator; BA, The Johns Hopkins U., Balt., 1977; MD, Georgetown U. Sch. Medicine, 1981. Cert. Clin. Pathology and Anatomic Pathology Am. Bd. Pathology. Resident U. Md. Hosp., College Park, 1981—85; prof. pathology and lab. medicine E. Carolina U., Greenville, NC, interim dean, Brody Sch. Medicine, 2001—. Contbr. articles to profl. jours. Office: Brody Sch Medicine E Carolina Univ 600 Moye Rd Greenville NC 27858

KRAGH, JOHN FREDERICK, JR., orthopedist, educator; b. Newburgh, N.Y., May 1, 1963; s. John Frederick and Maureen Ellen Kragh; m. Gretchen Dawn Garceau, Sept. 24, 1999. MD, Uniformed Services U. Health Scis., 1989. Diplomate Am. Bd. Orthop. Surgery. Officer US Army, 1985—, advanced through grades to lt. col.; orthop. surgeon Orthop. Dept., Fort Bragg, NC, 1997—2001; rsch. dir. Orthop. Residency, Fort Sam Houston, Tex., 2001—. Bn. surgeon 3d Ranger Bn., Fort Benning, Ga., 1990—93. Decorated Meritorious Svc. Medal U.S. Army; recipient Surgeon General's Physician Recognition Sabbatical fellowship, 1992, Eisenhower Army Med. Ctr. Rsch. award, 1993, Founders award, Soc. Mil. Orthopedic Surgeons. Fellow: Am. Acad. Orthop. Surgeons. Office: BAMC Orthopedics Rm 129-5 MCHE-SDR 3851 Roger Brooke Dr Fort Sam Houston TX 78234-6200

KRAHENBUHL, GARY STUART, university administrator; b. DeKalb, Ill., Sept. 11, 1943; s. Orville and Lillian (Wickness) K.; m. Richey Jane Krahenbuhl, Apr. 2, 1966; children: Lisa, Julie, Kevin, Michael. BS in Edn., No. Ill. U., 1965, MS in Edn., 1966; EdD, U. No. Colo., 1969. Asst. prof. U. Hawaii, Honolulu, 1969-73, Ariz. State U., Tempe, 1973-75, assoc. prof., 1975-79, prof. and chair, 1979-84, assoc. dean, 1984-90, dean liberal arts, 1990-2000, sr. v.p., 2001—. Contbr. articles to profl. jours. Convener, CEO, Coun. for the Arts and Scis. in Urban Univs., Wichita, Kans., 1993-98; mem. Higher Edn. Rsch. Adv. Bd., Phoenix, 1992-96; bd. dirs. Ariz. Sr. Olympics, Phoenix, 1985-87; chmn. adminstrv. bd. United Meth. Ch., Tempe, 1997-98. Recipient Award for Outstanding Contbn. to Edn., No. Ill. U., 1996, Difference Maker award Ariz. State U., 2001. Fellow Am. Acad. Kinesiology and Phys. Edn. (pres. 2000-2001), Am. Coll. Sports Medicine (bd. trustees 1988-91); mem. Coun. of Colls. of Arts and Scis. (pres. 1993-94), Am. Acad. Kinesiology and Phys. Edn. (pres. 2000-2001), Soc. for Coll. and Univ. Planning (editl. bd. 1997—). Republican. Avocations: photography, golf, travel, reading history and biographies. Home: 8822 S Oak St Tempe AZ 85284 Office: Ariz State Univ PO Box 872203 Tempe AZ 85287-2203 E-mail: gary.krahenbuhl@asu.edu.

KRAHL, ENZO, retired surgeon; b. Fiume, Italy, Apr. 22, 1924; came to U.S., 1951, naturalized, 1955; s. Massimiliano and Camilla (Aub) K.; m. Anne Katharine Ferbstein, June 14, 1958; children— Edward Alexander, Katharine Frances MD, U. Florence, Italy, 1948. Diplomate Am. Bd. Surgery. Asst. dept. surgery U. Rome, 1948-51; fellow in vascular surgery Columbia Presbyn. Med. Ctr., N.Y.C., 1951-52, fellow in surgery, 1954-55; resident in surgery St. Vincent's Hosp., N.Y.C., 1952-54; chief resident in surgery Akron City Hosp., Ohio, 1957-58; dir. grad. edn. Akron Gen. Hosp., 1959-60; practice medicine specializing in surgery Akron, 1958-60, Superior, Wis., 1960-84; ret., 1984. Mem. staff Superior Meml. Hosp., also bd. dirs.; founder Superior Clinic, 1964; past dir. Blue Cross-Blue Shield United of Wis. Contbr. articles to med. jours. Past v.p. Duluth-Superior Symphony; past mem. exec. com. bd. dirs. Health Systems Agy. Western Lake Superior. Served as capt. M.C., U.S. Army, 1955-57 Recipient United Fund award, 1965, cert. of merit N.Y.C. CD, 1953 Mem. Wis. State Med. Soc., Italian Heritage Soc., Am. Bridge League, Marshwood Country Club, AAD Temple Club, Masons, Shriners. Jewish. Home: 15 Cotton Xing Savannah GA 31411-2504 E-mail: anneandenzo@bellsouth.net.

KRAHMER, DONALD LEROY, JR., lawyer; b. Hillsboro, Oreg., Nov. 11, 1957; s. Donald L. and Joan Elizabeth (Karns) Krahmer; m. Suzanne M. Blanchard, Aug. 16, 1986; children: Hillary, Zachary. BS, Willamette U., 1981, MBA, 1987, JD, 1987. Bar: Oreg. 1988, Wash. 2003. Fin. analyst U.S. Bancorp, Portland, 1977-87; intern U.S. Senator Mark Hatfield, 1978; legis. aide State Sen. Jeannette Hamby, Hillsboro, Oreg., 1981-83, State Rep. Delna Jones, Beaverton, Oreg., 1983; bus. analyst Pacificorp, Portland, 1987; mgr. mergers/acquisitions Pacificorp Fin. Svcs., Portland, 1988-89, dir., 1990; CEO, pres. Atkinson Group, Portland, 1991—2002; ptnr. Black Helterline, LLP, Portland, 1991—2001; shareholder Schwabe Williamson & Wyatt, P.C., Portland, 2002—. Bd. dirs. Self-Enhancement, Inc.; chmn. Willamette Forum; with Oreg. Entrepreneur Forum, 1993, chmn. adv. bd., 95, chmn. bd., 98; founder, co-chmn. Oreg. Emerging Bus. Initiative, 1997—, New Economy Coalition, 2001—; bd. dirs. Portland Bus. Alliance, 2001—; chmn. audit com., chmn. corp. gov. com. Pacific Continental Bank, 2003—; chmn. Oreg. Tech. Alliance, 2002—03. Treas. Com. to Re-Elect Jeannette Hamby, 1986; bd. dirs. fin. com., devel. com. Am. Diabetes Assn., Portland, 1990—96; founder Needle Bros., 1994; chmn. Atkinson Grad. Sch. Devel. Com., Salem, 1989—92; bd. visitors Coll. Law Willamette U., 1997—2002; adv. bd. Ctr. for Law and Entrepreneurship U. Oreg. Sch. Law, 1997—2002; founder Conf. of Entrepreneurship, Salem, 1984; chmn. Entrepreneurship Breakfast Forum, Portland, 1993; chmn., founder Oreg. Conf. on Entrepreneurship and Awards Dinner, 1994—99, sr. v.p., 1999—; exec. com., bd. dirs. Cascade Pacific Coun. Boy Scouts Am., chmn. cmty. fund dir., 1997; chmn. Scoutrageous, 2000; vice-chmn. Gov.'s Coun. on Small Bus. State of Oreg.; mem. Gov.'s Econ. Devel. Joint Bds. Working Group, 1999—2002; co-chair Com. for Oreg.'s Future, 2002; steering com. Oreg. Opportunity; tech. advisor Oreg. Coun. on Knowledge and Econ. Devel., 2002—; mem. Greater Portland Innovation Network; mem. ch. coun. Our Savior Luth. Ch., 2000—01. Named one of Top 50 Leaders to Watch, Oreg. Bus. Mag., 2003; recipient Pub.'s award, 1987, Founders award, Willamette U., 1987, award, Scripps Found., 1980, 40 Under 40 award, Bus. Jour., 1996. Mem.: RAINS, ABA, Orgn. Tech. Alliance, Micro2Nano Collaborative, Am. Electronics Assn. (Oreg. coun.), Portland Soc. Fin. Analysts, Multnomah County Bar Assn., Software Assn. of Oreg., Oreg. Biotech. Assn., Japan-Am. Soc. Oreg., Oreg. Biosci. Assn., Oreg. Bar Assn. (sec. 1998, chmn. 1999, chmn. exec. com., fin. instns. com. sec., exec. com., bus. law sect., Pres.'s award 1999, James B. Castles Leadership award 2002), Assn. for Corp. Growth, Assn. Investment Mgmt. and Rsch., Arlington Club (treas. 2002, 1st v.p. 2003, bd. dirs.), Multnomah Athletic Club, City Club. Republican. Lutheran. Home: 16230 SW Copper Creek Dr Portland OR 97224-6500 Office: Schwabe Williamson & Wyatt 1211 SW 5th Ave Ste 1800 Portland OR 97204-3718

KRAHN, THOMAS FRANK, photographer; b. Racine, Wis., Feb. 14, 1941; s. Marvin Carl and Marie Mattie (Myers) K. Diploma, Control Data Inst., 1972; Doctorate (hon.), United World Assembly, 1984. Pres. Puget Sound Pub. Group, Everett, Wash.; photographer Arcturus Studio, Everett. Instr. Gay City U., 2001-03. Author: (novels) Atkar, The Norseman, 1998, Atkar in Africa, 1999, Atkar in Byzantium, 2001, Adventure at Whiterood, (novellas) The Boy on the Horse, 1994, The Naked Prey, 1994, Die Wolfenkindern, Vols. 1-3, 1994, The Indian Affair, 1998, The Dry Creek Canyon Incident, 1998, Something Lives Under the Porch, 10 Miles Hard, 1998, H.M.S. Futility, 1999, High Wind to Jamaica, Treasure of San Padre Island, 1999, The Northgate Affair, Dinner at Hosgroves, A Death in Academia, (nonfiction) Gay Ethics, Vols. 1 and 2, Vessels of Silver and Gold, 1994, Church, Children and Chicanery, A Biblical Approach to Modern Gay Living, 1989, The Complete Number Line and Introduction to the Algebraic Celestial Sphere, 1998, The Third Great Covenant, 2003, (booklets) The Seven Days of Wonder, 1996, How Do I Love Thee, 1996, Apertarian Everyday Prayer Book, 2000, Do You Believe...15 Questions About Gay Spirituality, 2002, Do You Believe...15 Questions about Nudist Spirituality, 2002, (plays) The Doughnut, The Dumpster, Witness for the Defense, Oz-Mosis (Oz Twenty Years Later), The Mystery of Edmund O'Shay, Every Man's Folly, also stories, poems; composer various works for piano, organ, vocal ensembles and solo works, including The Gay Hymnal, Vol I; editor Nudist N.W. Bus. Directory, 1999-2001. Pres. First All-Everett Foto Flea Market, 1996-97. Recipient Cert. of Appreciation Sta. KCTS-TV, 1991, award Exec. Coun. Selection Com., Everett C.C., 1988-89. Mem. Hist. Everett Theater Soc., Everet Photo Club (pres. 1996-2000), Tau Alpha Epsilon. Avocations: writing, composing. Home: 1321 Chestnut St Apt 1 Everett WA 98201-5203 Office: Arcturus Studio PO Box 754 Everett WA 98201 E-mail: tom_me_98@yahoo.com.

KRAICHNAN, ROBERT HARRY, physicist, consultant; b. Phila., Jan. 15, 1928; s. Robert Maxwell and Anna (Maximon) Kraichnan; m. Carol Gebhardt, May 22, 1954 (div. 1988); 1 child, John; m. Judy Ellen Moore, June 30, 1989. BS in Physics, MIT, 1947, PhD in Theoretical Physics, 1949. Mem., asst. to Albert Einstein Inst. Advanced Study, Princeton, NJ, 1949-50; mem. tech. staff Bell Tel. Labs., 1950-52; rsch. assoc. Columbia U., N.Y.C., 1952-56; rsch. assoc. Courant Inst. NYU, 1956-58, sr. rsch. scientist Courant Inst., 1958-62; pvt. practice physicist, 1962-80; pres., prin. Robert H. Kraichnan, Inc., Santa Fe, 1980—. Adj. assoc. prof. dept. grad. physics NYU, 1956—57; cons. Naval Rsch. Lab., 1957—59, Inst. Def. Analyses, 1967—70, Los Alamos Nat. Lab., 1979—, Princeton U., 1987—; cons. Inst. Space Studies NASA, 1961—69, contractor, 1967—69; assoc. in physics Woods Hole (Mass.) Oceanographic Inst., 1960—70; contractor Office Naval Rsch., 1962—80, rsch. affiliate meteorology MIT, 1963—. Contbr. articles to sci. jours. Recipient ADION medal, Observatoire de Nice; grantee, NSF, 1970—. Fellow: AAAS, Am. Phys. Soc. (Otto Laporte award 1993, Lars Onsager Meml. prize 1997); mem.: NAS. Avocations: mountain hiking, violin, carpentry.

KRAIG, ABE, psychoanalyst; b. Bklyn., Nov. 5, 1912; s. Herman and Sophia (Pulitzer) Krochmalnikoff; B.A., U. Chgo., 1943, M.A., 1945, Ph.D., 1947; Ph.D., Western U., 1951; pvt. studies Curtis Inst. Music, 1934-36, Met. Opera Co., 1936-37, Cooper Union, 1934-36; m. Zaira Astafiewa, 1955; children by previous marriage— Bruce, Karen, Frank, Dennis. Tenor, Met. Opera Co., 1936-37; allied arts tchr. N.Y.C. Bd. Edn., Ednl. Alliance, Henry St. Settlement House, Hull House, 1937-40; staff Jewish Bd. Guardians, Hawthorne Cedar Knolls Sch., 1940-44; exec. dir., pres. Pinehaven Sanitarium; exec. dir. Geriatric Ambulatory Care Clinic, Group Health Care Clinics; dir. Cytotest Corp.; dir. research Center for Study Paraphenomena, Internat. Soc. Psychic Research, Inst. Hypnologic Studies; cons. Cancer Cytology Found.; pres. advisor, 1969-74. Bd. dirs. Kraig House, 1946-50, N.J. Welfare Council, Cardio-Vascular Studies, Ocean County Rehab. Center, City of Pines Found., N.J. Heart Assn., Muscular Dystrophy Assn., Am. Geriatric Assn., Mexico Gen. Hosp., Parapsychology Found., Med. Assos. Clinic, Bd. Sr. Services; mem. Berkeley Psychodiagnostic Therapeutic and Research Center, Berkeley Home Health Agy., Berkeley Press, Berkeley Found., Berkeley Found. Center. Spiritual Frontiers fellow Princeton Inst. Metaphysical Studies, Cancer Detection Found. Recipient award of honor Wisdom Soc., cert. of merit in achievement in psychology award. Served with USN, 1930-33, as lt. (s.g.) USNR, 1934-46; comdr. Res. ret. Fellow Am. Schizophrenic Found., N.J. Acad. Scis., Brit. Coll. Psychic Research, Am. Soc. Psychic Research, Centro Studi E. Scambi Internazionali; mem. Brit. Assn. Advancement Sci., AAAS, Nat. Geriatric Soc., Am., N.J. hosp. assns., Adult Edn. Assn., Am. Acad. Polit. and Social Sci., Soc. Social Responsibility, Gt. Britain Spiritualist Assn., Assn. Research and Enlightenment, Inst. Gero-Psychiat. and Psychologic Studies, Inst. Cardiovascular Studies, Inst. Cytologic Studies, Inst. Studies in Phys. Medicine and Rehab., Inst. Bio-Engring. Studies, N.Y. Acad. Scis., Am. Acad. Med. Adminstrs., Smithsonian Instn. (charter nat. asso.), Internat. Platform Assn., U.S. Naval Inst. (bd. govs.). Clubs: KP, Lions. Author: Psychometric Testing and Mental Hygiene in Care of Aged, 1947.

KRAINC, DIMITRI, medical educator, researcher; m. Mili Krainc; children: Talia, Maya. MD, PhD, U. Zagreb, Croatia, 1992. Diplomate Am. Bd. Psychiatry and NeurologyBPN, 2001. Asst. prof. Harvard U., Boston, 2000—. Office: Harvard Univ 75 Fruit St ACC 835 Boston MA 02114 E-mail: krainc@helix.mgh.harvard.edu.

KRAININ, JULIAN ARTHUR, film director, producer, writer, cinematographer; b. N.Y.C., Jan. 24, 1941; s. David A. and Anne N. (Wineblatt) K.; m. Martha Wineblatt, June 17, 1967; 1 child, Todd Philip. BS, Allegheny Coll., 1962, HHD (hon.), 1993; MFA, Columbia U., 1965. Prodr. spl. projects Westinghouse Broadcasting Co., N.Y.C., 1967-69, also prodr., dir., writer, 1967—; v.p., exec. prodr. Krainin/Sage Prodns., Inc., N.Y.C., 1969-80, also dir., writer, 1969-80; pres. Krainin Prodns., Inc., N.Y.C., 1976—. Nat. lectr. motion pictures at various univs. and colls., 1967—; cons. on films U. Mass., 1973; juror Mid-West Film Makers and Graphic Arts Festival, 1971-72, Nat. Emmy Awards, 1975-82, 85-90, Dirs. Guild of Am. Awards, 1987-90; mem. journalism adv. bd. Queens Coll., 1987-90; bd. dirs. Bklyn. Ctr. for Families in Crises, 1986-90; journalism adv. bd. Queens Coll. Films include: The Reluctant Revolution, 1968, Exit to Nowhere, 1967, Promises to Keep, 1967, The March, 1965, Nowhere Fast, 1968, Hide and Seek, 1966, (with Jacques Cousteau) Oceans: The Silent Crisis, 1972, Art is (Acad. award nominee, hon. screenings White House, Mus. Modern Art), 1972, The Other Americans (Emmy award), 1969, Princeton: A Search for Answers (Acad. award), 1973, The American Experiment, 1974, Going Metric, 1975, To America, 1976, The Broken Silence, 1976, The World of James Michener: Hawaii Revisited, 1977, The World of James Michener: The South Pacific, End of Eden? (hon. screening Mus. Modern Art), 1978, (with Ed Asner) The Writer, 1980, The Making of an Opera, 1980, Luciano Pavorotti At Home, 1980, La Gioconda miniseries, 1980, Heritage: Civilization and the Jews (Peabody, Christopher awards), 1981-82, PBS series, CBS Reports: Don't Touch that Dial!: The Making of a Television Series (Emmy nominee, TV Guide citation, 1982, The Smithsonian Quadrangle: A View from the Castle, 1984, America Undercover: The Wrong Man, 1985-86, (with Tom Peters) The Power of Excellence, 1987; (with Abba Eban) Heritage: Civilization and the Jews, Disaster at Silo 7, 1988, Memory and Imagination, New Pathways to the Library of Congress, 1990; documentary film: The Television Quiz Show Scandal, 1991, Queen's College, 1993, (feature film) Quiz Show, 1994 (4 Acad. award nominations including Best Picture), The Unabomber: Deadly Mail!, 1996, The Thousand Acre Universe, 1996, George Wallace (Golden Globe, Humanitas, Cable Ace, Peabody awards), The John Glenn Story: Return to Space and Return of the Hero, 1998-99. Recipient numerous awards and citations including Acad. Award, 1973, Emmy Award,

1969, Chgo. Internat. Film Festival award, 1969, 77, 78, Florence Internat. Film Festival award, 1969, Cine Golden Eagle awards, 1969, 72, 73, 74, 76, 78, Photog. Soc. Am. award, 1968, Venice Film Festival award, 1970, Moscow Internat. Film Festival award, 1970, Cindy award Prodrs. Assn. Am., 1971, 76, San Francisco Internat. Film Festival award, 1972, Am. Film Festival award, 1974, 76, 78, Tel Aviv Internat. Film Festival award, 1970, Atlanta Internat. Film Festival award, 1969, 72, Festival of Ams. award, 1976, N.Y. Internat. Film and TV Festival award, 1969, 72, Gabriel award, 1968-70, Oberhausen Internat. Film Festival award, 1969, Columbus Film Festival award, 1973, Mannheim Internat. Film Festival award, 1969, U.S. Indsl. Film Festival award, 1973, Ohio State award, 1967, N.Y. Film Festival at Lincoln Center award, 1970. Mem. Writers Guild Am., Acad. Motion Picture Arts and Scis., Photog. Soc. Am., Dirs. Guild Am. (award 1973). Office: Krainin Prodns Inc 8 Century Rd Palisades NY 10964-1503 E-mail: krainin@rockland.net.

KRAIZER, SHERRYLL A. child safety and interpersonal violence prevention educator; b. San Antonio, June 12, 1948; d. Faye Burton and Phyllis Anne (Ringer) Graves; m. Alvin T. Kraizer, July 30, 1978; children: Charles, Ben. BS in Edn./Spl. Edn., Emporia State U., 1969, MS in Edn./Psychology, 1970; PhD in Edn., The Union Inst., 1991. Pres., exec. dir. Coalition for Children, 1983—. Presenter confs. in field; expert witness on child abuse, instnl. abuse, stds. and practices. Author: The Safe Child Book, 1985, 2d edit., 1995, Take A Stand: Prevention of Bullying and Interpersonal Violence, 2000; author (tng. programs) The Safe Child Program (pre-K-grade 3), 1989, 2d edit., 1994, Dating Violence: Prevention and Intervention, 1991, Domestic Violence Prevention and Intervention, 1991, Reach, 1992, Challenge, 1992, Recovery, 1992; adult mentor editor R.E.B.E.L. Youth Adv. Mag., 2001. Recipient Nat. Prog. award Child Abuse Prevention Coun., Houston, 1989, rsch. grant Nat. Ctr. on Child Abuse and Neglect, 1987, prog. devel. grant Small Bus. Adminstrn., 1988, Violence Against Women Act grantee, 1996-99, Aspen Inst. scholar, 1999. Mem. Internat. Soc. Prevention of Child Abuse and Neglect (peer reviewer). Office: Coalition for Children PO Box 6304 Denver CO 80206-0304 E-mail: kraizer@safechild.org.

KRAJEWSKI, MICHAEL, conductor; b. Detroit, Mich. m. Darcy Krajewski. Grad, Wayne State U., U. of Cinn Coll. Conservatory of Music. Music dir. Modesto Symphony Orch.; prin. pops condr. New Mex., Long Beach and Jacksonville Symphonies; asst. condr. Detroit Symphony Orch.; music dir. Detroit Symphony Civic Orch.; resident condr. Fla. Symphony Orch.; prin. pops condr. Houston Symphony Orch., 2000—. Fellowship condr. Detroit Symphony; artist intern Mich. Opera Theatre. Performed with Boston Pops Orch., San Francisco, St. Louis, Detroit, Balt., Atlanta, Minn., Oreg. et al. Recipient awards, Am. Soc. of Composers, Authors and Publishers. Office: Houston Symphony 615 Louisiana St Ste 102 Houston TX 77002

KRAJICK, KEVIN RUDOLPH, freelance/self-employed journalist; b. Camp Kilmer, N.J., Aug. 10, 1952; s. Rudolph Adam and Katherine Sarah (Distin) Krajick; m. Ruby Jean Kipniss, Sept. 8, 1996; children: Stella, Lydia. BA in Comparative Lit. cum laude, Columbia U., 1976, MS in Journalism, 1977. Assoc. editor Police and Corrections mags., N.Y.C., 1978-84; nat. editor Nat. Law Jour., N.Y.C., 1984-85; assoc. editor Newsweek, N.Y.C., 1988-96; freelance author N.Y.C., 1981—. Author: (book) Barren Lands: An Epic Search for Diamonds in the North American Arctic, 2001; contbr. articles to publs. Recipient Walter Sullivan award for excellence in sci. journalism, Am. Geophys. Union, 1998, Brock award for agrl. writing, Calif. Poly. U., 1998; Sci. Writing fellow, Marine Biol. Lab., 1996. Mem.: Nat. Assn. Sci. Writers. Home: 245 W 104th St Apt 14B New York NY 10025-4280 E-mail: krk4@columbia.edu.

KRAKAUER, THOMAS HENRY, museum director emeritus; b. Buffalo, Sept. 6, 1942; m. Janet MacColl, Dec. 20, 1968; 1 child, Alan Henry. AB, U. Rochester, 1964; MS, U. Miami, 1966; PhD, U. Fla., 1970. Asst. prof. biology Hollins Coll., Hollins College, Va., 1970-74; natural sci. chmn. Sci. Mus. Va., Richmond, 1974; sr. resident assoc. biology Hollins Coll., 1976-85; exec. dir. Sci. Mus. Assn. of Roanoke (Va.) Valley, 1976-85, N.C. Mus. Life and Sci., Durham, 1985—2003. Adj. asst. prof. Va. Poly. Inst. and State U., Blacksburg, 1973. Bd. dirs. Assn. Sci.-Tech. Ctrs., Triangle Land Conservancy; bd. dirs., pres. Grassroots Sci. Mus. Named Conservation Educator of Yr. Va. Wildlife Fedn., 1978, Profl. Svc. award N.C. Mus. Coun., 1998. Fellow: Assn. Sci.-Tech. Ctrs.; mem.: Am. Assn. Mus., Va. Assn. Mus. (past pres.), Assn. Sci.-Tech. Ctrs. (v.p. 1987, 1995, Lifetime Achievement award 2001). Home: 128 White Horse Run Bahama NC 27503-8980 Office: NC Mus Life and Sci PO Box 15190 Durham NC 27704-0190

KRAKOFF, KENNETH B. dentist, consultant; b. Columbus, Ohio, Apr. 13, 1925; s. Morris Joseph and Frieda (Cohen) K.; m. Corinne Bette Goldman, July 4, 1948; children: David M., Steven P. DDS, Ohio State U., 1949. Resident VA, L.A., 1949-50; pvt. practice, Toledo, 1950-51, 53—. Chief dental svc. Toledo Hosp., 1971-91; chmn. dentistry, program dir. gen. practice residency Med. Coll. Ohio, Toledo, 1975-79; pres. Depcon, Toledo, 1987—; dental cons. Owens Ill., Inc., Toledo, 1987-91; sec. Oral Health Assocs., Inc., Toledo, 1989—; mem. dean's adv. com. Ohio State U. Coll. Dentistry, Columbus, 1977-82; ProMedica, Toledo, 1994-97. Contbr. articles to profl. jours. Mem. dental adv. bd. Regional Med. Planning, Toledo, 1969-83; pres., bd. dirs. Health Planning Assn., Toledo, 1969-85; bd. dirs., v.p. Lucas County unit Am. Cancer Soc., Toledo, 1983-95; pres. N.W. Ohio Health Planning, Inc., Toledo, 1994-99, bd. dirs., 1983-2000; trustee Med. Mission Svcs. Found., Toledo, 1999—; bus. adv. coun. to Rep. Congl. com., 2002—; mem. Presdl. bus. com., 2002-03. With U.S. Army Air Force, 1943-46, USAF, 1951-53. Recipient Outstanding Svc. cert. Assn. for Retarded Children, Toledo, 1965, Disting. Svc. award Health Planning Assn., 1972, 73, 76, 81, 85; Pace Setter award Am. Cancer Soc., 1988, Life Saver award, 1993; Golden Buckeye award Ohio State U. Coll. Dentistry, 1999. Mem. ADA (del. 1973-76), Am. Assn. Hosp. Dentists, Pierre Fauchard Acad. (medal 1953), Am. Soc. Dentistry for Children (pres. Ohio unit 1972-73, 81-82), Ohio Dental Assn. (com. chmn., del. 1969-77), Toledo Dental Soc. (pres. 1969-70), Toledo Soc. Dentistry for Children (pres. 1965-66), Toledo C. of C. (health sys. study com. 1993-96). Avocations: photography, golf, tennis, skiing. Office: 2910 W Central Ave Toledo OH 43606-3026 E-mail: kbkrakoff@hotmail.com.

KRAKOFF, ROBERT LEONARD, publishing executive; b. Pitts., May 4, 1935; s. Frank and Della (Zionts) Krakoff; m. Sandra Gusky, June 22, 1958; children: Roger, Hope, Reed. BS with honors, Pa. State U., 1957; MBA, Harvard U., 1959. Staff v.p. mktg. planning TWA, N.Y.C., 1963—70; v.p., contr. consumer product div. Singer, N.Y.C., 1970—71; staff v.p. strategic planning RCA, N.Y.C., 1971—72; pres. Am. Internat. Travel Svc., Boston, 1972—73, Cahners Travel Group, N.Y.C., 1973—74, Cahners Expn. Group, N.Y.C., 1974—86; exec. v.p., COO Reed Pub. U.S.A., Newton, Mass., 1986—89, pres., COO, 1989—91, chmn., CEO, 1991—96, Advanstar, Inc. (formerly Advanstar Holdings, Inc.), Boston, 1996—. Bd. dirs. Reed Elsevier, 1990—96. With USAR, 1957—63. Office: Advanstar Inc 545 Boylston St Boston MA 02116-3606 E-mail: bkrakoff@advanstar.com.

KRAKOWER, BERNARD HYMAN, management consultant; b. N.Y.C., May 11, 1935; s. David and Bertha (Glassman) K.; m. Sondra Joan Fishbein, Apr. 14, 1968; children: Lorna, Victoria, Ariela Shauna. BA in Advt., UCLA, 1959; cert. in real estate, 1966, cert. in indsl. rels., 1972; MBA, Pepperdine U., 1979. Loan officer Lytton Fin. Corp., L.A., 1961-65; mgmt. cons. James R. Colvin & Assocs., L.A., 1965-67; sr. indsl. rels. rep. Sci. Data Systems (Xerox), 1967-68; dir. ops. Tratec, Inc., L.A., 1968-70; chmn. Krakower/Brucker Internat., Inc., L.A., 1970-88; sr. ptnr. Krakower Finnegan Assocs., L.A., 1988-90; pres. Krakower Group, Inc., 1990—. Bd. dirs. Columbia Nat. Bank, Santa Monica, Calif., Elings Park, Santa Barbara, Calif.; mem. adv. bd. Private Financing Group, 2000. Mem. citizens liaison com. L.A. Dept. Recreation and Parks, 1973; apptd. commr., v.p. L.A. Countywide Citizens Planning Coun. by L.A. County Bd. Suprs., 1988-97, v.p., 1991-93, pres. 1993-97; pres., bd. dirs. L.A. Bus. Coun.; mem. bd. visitors Pepperdine U. Graziadio Sch. Bus. and Mgmt., 1997—; leadership mem. Santa Barbara Region Econ. Cmty. Project, 1997; v.p. bd. dirs. Santa Barbara Newcomers, 1999; mem. adv. bd. Ctrl. Coast Venture Forum, 1999, co-chmn. Santa Barbara Region Tech. Coun., 1999; bd. dirs. Santa Barbara C. of C., 2001. Mem.: Santa Barbara Regional C. of C. (bd. dirs. 2001—, mem. fin. com. 2001—, mem. exec. com. 2003—, bd. dir. Elings Pk. chpt. 2003—).

KRALEWSKI, JOHN EDWARD, health service research educator; b. Durand, Wis., May 20, 1932; s. Joseph and Esther (Hetrick) K.; m. Marjorie L. Gustafson; Apr. 22, 1957; children: Judy, Ann, Sara. BS in Pharmacy, U. Minn., 1956, MHA, 1962, PhD, 1969. Asst. prof. U. Minn., Mpls., 1965-69, prof. health svcs. rsch., 1979—; prof. U. Colo., Denver, 1969-78. 1st lt. USAF, 1957-60. Kellogg fellow Kellogg Found., 1962-65, Valencia (Spain) Acad. Medicine fellow, 1993. Mem. APHA, Assn. Health Svcs. Rsch. Avocation: oenology. Office: U Minn Health Svc Rsch 420 Delaware St SE Box 729 Minneapolis MN 55455-0374

KRALJ, DEJAN, historian; b. Banja Luka, Bosnia-Herzegovina, Dec. 31, 1970; s. Nedeljko and Branka Kralj; m. Elanor Lorahn Horsley, Nov. 4, 1999. B, Ind. U. NW, 1990—93; MA, U. Ill. at Chgo., 1994—95; Doctoral Student, Loyola Univerisity Chgo., 2002—. Bassist, songwriter The Gufs, Milw., 1988—; musical rec. artist Red Submarine Records, Milw., 1991—, Atlantic Rec. Co., N.Y.C, 1995—99. Musician (song writer): (albums) Staring into the Sun, Songs of Life, Circa '89, Collide, The Gufs, Holiday from You. Mem.: ASCAP, Organizatin of Am. Historians, Am. Hist. Assn. Independent.

KRALLINGER, JOSEPH CHARLES, entrepreneur, business advisor, author; b. Lancaster, Pa., May 29, 1931; s. Ferdinand and Mathilde (Meyer) K.; m. Hilde Eisenhauer, Oct. 1, 1955; children— Joanne, Diane, Robert BS in Econs. cum laude, Franklin and Marshall Coll., 1953. C.P.A. Auditor GAO, Denver, 1953; auditor Army Audit Agy., 1953-55; ptnr. Arthur Andersen & Co., Phila., 1955-76; v.p. strategic planning and acquisitions, chief fin. officer Berwind Corp., Phila., 1976-88; cons. Palm Desert, Calif., 1988—. Dir., bus. advisor and investor various indsl., health care, mining, oil and gas cos., 1976—; cons. in field. Author: An Auditor's Approach to Statistical Sampling, 5 vols., 1967-72, Strategic Planning Workbook, 1989, 2d edit., 1993, How to Acquire the Perfect Business for Your Company, 1991; Planeacion Estrategica Practica, 1991; Mergers and Acquisitions: Managing the Transactions, 1997, Chinese and Spanish edits., 2000; contbr. articles to profl. jours. Bd. dirs. alumni coun. Franklin and Marshall Coll., Lancaster, 1969-75; pres., tchr. religious edn. St. Genevieve Cath. Ch., Flourtown, Pa., 1971-76; bd. dirs. Whitemarsh Twp. Citizens Coun., Plymouth Meeting, Pa., 1972-75; hon. life mem., past chmn. bd. dirs. Phila. chpt. Am. Cancer Soc. Recipient Nat. Vol. award Am. Cancer Soc., 1985, Crusade award Am. Cancer Soc., 1985, Teaching award St. Genevieve Ch., 1985, Cert. Merit Inst. Mgmt. Accts., 1998. Mem. AICPA (statis. sampling com.), Pa. Inst. CPAs, Nat. Assn. Accts. (past pres. Phila. chpt.), Planning Forum (past pres. Phila. chpt.), Soc. Children's Book Writers and Illustrators, Ironwood Country Club (bd. dirs. 1991-93). Avocations: golf, racquet sports, writing, reading. Home and Office: 48-120 Alder Ln Palm Desert CA 92260-6652

KRAM, HARRY BERNARD, surgeon; b. Newark, June 14, 1954; s. Philip and Bronya (Stein) K.; m. Leah Coone, June 15, 1986; children: Shayna, Yoseph, Eva, Dora. BS, U. Fla., 1977, MD, 1981. Diplomate Am. Bd. Surgeons, Am. Bd. Surgical Critical Care, Am. Bd. Gen. Vascular Surgery. Intern La. State U., New Orleans, 1982; resident in gen. surgery Harbor-UCLA Med. Ctr., Torrance, Calif., 1984; resident in trauma surgery Hollywood Presbyn. Med. Ctr., L.A., 1985; resident in gen. surgery King Drew Med. Ctr., L.A., 1987; fellow in vascular surgery Montefiore Med. Ctr., N.Y.C., 1991; pvt. practice surgery Torrance, Calif., 1992—; med. dir. LEGSAVERS, A Med. Corp. Hosp. appt. King: Drew Med. Ctr., L.A.; assoc. prof. surgery Drew U. Sch. Medicine. Contbr. over 100 articles to profl. jours, chpts. to ten books; mem. editl. bd. Jour. CC Medicine, 1981-83, Jour. Investigative Surgery, 1985-91, AMA Drug Evaluations, 1985-86. Fellow ACS (So. Calif. chpt.), Am. Coll. Critical Care Medicine; mem. Soc. Vascular Tech., L.A. County Med. Assn., Calif. Med. Assn., Torrance (Calif.) C. of C. Jewish. Office: Ste 230 3445 Pacific Coast Hwy Torrance CA 90505-6660 E-mail: kram@legsavers.com.

KRAM, PETER, lawyer; b. Chgo., Nov. 15, 1946; s. Paul Lauer and Nancy Ellen (Dineen) K. BA, St. Louis U., 1968; MA, U. Nev., 1972; JD, U. Puget Sound, 1976. Bar: Wash. 1977, U.S. Dist. Ct. (we. dist.) Wash. 1977, U.S. Ct. Appeals (9th cir.) 1977. Sole practice, Tacoma, Wash., 1977-78; ptnr. Lewis, Shillito et al, Tacoma, 1978; assoc. James F. Leggett, Tacoma, 1978-82; ptnr. Leggett & Kram, Tacoma, 1983—. Trustee North End Athletic Assn., Tacoma, 1981-88; mem. Charter Rev. Commn., Tacoma, 1983—. Served to capt. USAF, 1968-72. Mem. ABA, Wash. State Bar (corrections com., public rels. com., fee arbitration com.), Tacoma Pierce County Bar Assn. (trustee 1996-98), U.S. Tennis Assn. (pres. Pacific N.W. section, 2000—). Clubs: Lakewood Racquet; Tacoma Lawn Tennis (bd. dirs. 1981). Roman Catholic. Home: 414 Tacoma Ave N Tacoma WA 98403-2739 Office: Leggett & Kram 1901 S I St Tacoma WA 98405-3810

KRAM, RICHARD COREY, lawyer; b. N.Y.C., Oct. 8, 1942; BA in Polit. Sci., Syracuse U., 1964, MA in Polit. Sci., 1972, JD, 1973. Bar: N.Y. 1975, U.S. Dist. Ct. (no. dist.) N.Y. 1975, U.S. Ct. Appeals (2d cir.) 1980, U.S. Supreme Ct. 1982. Assoc. Nottingham Law Firm, Syracuse, N.Y., 1975-76; sole practice Syracuse, 1976—. Adj. prof. law Syracuse U., 1987-88, 89-90. Mem. Syracuse James Joyce Soc., 1996—. Fellow Am. Acad. Matrimonial Lawyers (N.Y. chpt. bd. mgr. 1993-97, 99-2001, v.p. 1997-98), Onondaga County Bar Assn. (bd. dirs. 1984-88, chair family law com. 1997-98). Avocations: reading, aerobics, bicycling, nordic skiing. Office: 120 E Washington St Syracuse NY 13202-4000

KRAMAN, CYNTHIA, language educator; BA summa cum laude in Comparative Lit., U. Mass., 1972; MA in Eng. Lit., Hunter Coll., 1990; PhD in Medieval Eng. Lit., U. London, 1998. Tutor math and writing Hudson Guild, N.Y.C., NY, 1972—73; tchr. writing U. Wash., Oberlin Coll. and Columbia U., 1975—77; adj. instr. composition Coll. New Rochelle, NY, 1987—91, adj. asst. prof. writing program, 1987—98, adj. asst. prof. creative writing, 1993—97, assoc. prof. Eng. dept., 1998—. Spkr. at confs., workshops and orgns., 1991—. Author: (collection) Taking on the Local Color, 1977, (poem) I land/Oregon, 1977, Club 82, 1980, You are like Me..., 1983, (collection) The Mexican Murals, 1986, (essay) On Style and Change, 1986, (short stories) Here, in This Sacred Grotto, 1987, (poem) Adelaide at Twilight, 1995, How Poetry Began, 1997, Rainbow over New Brunswick, 2000, Speak in the Dark, 2001, The Old Old Truth, 2001, The Touch, 2001, Ride to Manhattan with Rainbow, 2000; contbr. reviews and poems. Recipient Claire Woolrich Meml. award for poetry, 1974, Wesleyan Poetry prize, 1976; grantee, NEH, 1999; Commonwealth scholar, U. Mass., 1968—72. Mem.: Phi Beta Kappa. Office: Coll New Rochelle New Rochelle NY 10805

KRAMAR, JOHN SHAW, voice educator, vocalist; b. Washington, D.C., May 4, 1963; s. John Winston and Evelyn Shaw Kramar. MusB, Eastman Sch. of Music, 1987; MusM, Curtis Inst. of Music, Phila., 1989. Voice instr. Mid. Tenn. State U., Murfreesboro, 1996—98; asst. prof. voice, dir. of theater and opera East Carolina U. Sch. of Music, Greenville, NC, 1998—. Voice instr., dir. of opera workshop Tenn. Gov.'s Sch. of the Arts, Murfreesboro, 1998—; voice tchr., opera workshop dir. N.Y. State Summer Sch. of the Arts, Fredonia, 2002—. Singer: (profl. vocal chamber music ensemble) N.Y. Vocal Arts Ensemble, (solo recital) Carnegie Recital Hall. Mem.: Nat. Assn. of Tchrs. of Singing. Democrat. Episcopalian. Home: 2716-4 Meridian Dr Greenville NC 27834 Office: East Carolina U Sch Music 202A Fletcher Music Center Greenville NC 27858 Office Fax: 252-328-6258. Personal E-mail: kramarj@mail.ecu.edu. E-mail: kramarj@mail.ecu.edu.

KRAMARAE, CHERIS, educator; b. Brookings, S.D., Mar. 10, 1938; d. William H. Gamble and Deda Rae Smits; m. Dale V. Kramer, Dec. 21, 1960; children: Brinlee, Jana. BS, So. Dakota State, 1960; MS, Ohio Univ., 1963; PhD, U. Ill., Urbana-Champaign, 1975. Prof. communication Univ. Ill., Urbana, Ill., 1985-96, dir. women's studies, 1993-96, jubilee prof., 1993-96; researcher Ctr. for the Study of Women in Soc./U. Oregon, Eugene, 1996—. Internat. dean Internat. Women's Univ., Hamburg, Germany, 1998-00. Author: Women and Men Speaking, 1981; editor: Technology and Women's Voices, 1988; co-editor: The Knowledge Explosion, 1992 (Choice Outstanding Academic Books award, 1994), Routledge International Encyclopedia of Women, 2001. Rsch. scholar AAUW, 1999-2000. Mem.: AAUW. E-mail: cheris@uoregon.edu.

KRAMARIC, PETER STEFAN, lawyer; b. Ljubljana, Yugoslavia, Apr. 29, 1930; came to U.S., 1956; s. Stefan and Ana (Vidic) K.; m. Susan R. Little, Aug. 15, 1959; 1 dau., Karen Louise. Abs. Iur., Law Sch., U. Ljubljana, 1954; LL.B., Yale U., 1960. Bar: N.Y. 1962. Internat. atty. Union Carbide Corp., N.Y.C., 1961-70; gen. counsel internat. Gen. Foods Corp., White Plains, N.Y., 1970-73; dir. office of east-west trade devel. Dept. Commerce, Washington, 1973-74; asst. gen. counsel Am. Home Products Corp., N.Y.C., 1974—, also officer various subs. Mem. ABA, N.Y. State Bar Assn., Pharm. Mfrs. Assn. (legal com.). Republican. Club: Yale (N.Y.C.). Home: 12 Heatherbush Rd Essex Junction VT 05452-3828 Office: Am Home Products Corp 685 3rd Ave # 24th New York NY 10017-4024

KRAMARSIC, ROMAN JOSEPH, engineering consultant; b. Mokronog, Slovenia, Feb. 15, 1926; came to U.S., 1957; s. Roman and Josipina (Bucar) K; m. Joanna B. Ruffo, Oct. 29, 1964; children: Joannine M., Roman III. Student, U. Bologna, Italy, 1947-48; B of Applied Sci. in Mech. Engring., U. Toronto, 1954, M of Applied Sci., 1956; PhD, U. So. Calif., 1973. Registered profl. engr., Ont. Rsch. engr. Chrysler Rsch., Detroit, 1957-58; chief design engr. Annin Corp., Montebello, Calif., 1959-60; mgr. Plasmadyne Corp., Santa Ana, Calif., 1960-62; sr. rsch. engr. NESCO, Pasadena, Calif., 1962-64; asst. prof. U. So. Calif., L.A., 1971-77; mgr. engring. div. MERDI, Butte, Mont., 1977-78; sr. rsch. engr. RDA, Albuquerque, 1978-85; sr. staff mem. BDM, Albuquerque, 1985-90; owner Dr. R. J. Kramarsic's Engring. Svcs., Laguna Beach, Calif., 1985—. Cons. various tech. cos., So. Calif., 1964—; mem. various govt. coms. evaluating high power lasers. Author tech. presentations; contbr. articles to profl. jours. Violinist Albuquerque Civic Light Opera, 1980-85. Mem. ASME (life), AIAA (life; sr.), ASM Internat., Nat. Ski Patrol (aux. leader 1990-94). Roman Catholic. Avocations: classical music, violin, skiing.

KRAMB, AMY LYNN, environmentalist; b. Dublin, Ohio, July 16, 1976; d. Robert Joseph and Sharon L. Kramb. BA in History and Anthropology, Ohio State U., 1997. Cert. project mgmt. profl. Project Mgmt. Inst. Historian ASC Group Inc., Columbus, 1997—98; archtl. historian Applied Archaeol. Svcs., Worthington, Ohio, 1998—99; project mgr. Qwest Comms. Inc., Dublin, 1999—2002; environ. planner Parsons Brinckerhoff Inc., Dublin, 2002—. Vol. instr. First Aid Svc. Corp ARC, Columbus, 1998—; mentor Big Bros., Big Sisters, Columbus, 2000—. Mem.: Columbus Landmarks Found., Ohio Hist. Soc., Nat. Trust for Hist. Preservation. Avocations: camping, hiking, reading, nutrition and fitness, ballroom dancing. Office: Parsons Brinckerhoff Inc Enterprise Ct Dublin OH 43016

KRAMBERG, ROSS, arts administrator; b. N.Y.C., Apr. 29, 1955; s. Harold and Marilyn (Lief) K. BA in Theatre, Bklyn. Coll., 1980. House mgr. Bklyn. Ctr. for Performing Arts at Bklyn. Coll., 1976-78, assoc. artistic dir., program mgr., 1978-80; pub. rels. assoc. Jacob's Pillow Dance Festival, 1980; exec. asst. to exec. dir. The Joffrey Ballet, N.Y.C., 1981; company mgr. The Paul Taylor Dance Co., N.Y.C., 1982-89, gen. mgr., 1990, co-exec. dir., 1991, exec. dir., 1992—. Bd. dirs. Paul Taylor Dance Found., Inc. Bd. dirs. Broadway Cares/Equity Fights AIDS, 1994-98, Dance/USA. Office: Paul Taylor Dance Co 552 Broadway New York NY 10012-3922

KRAMER, ALAN SHARFSIN, lawyer; b. N.Y.C., Apr. 28, 1934; s. Michael and Alene (Sharfsin) K. BA, Dickinson Coll., 1956; LL.B., Columbia, 1962, JD, 1969. Bar: N.Y. 1962. Practice in, N.Y.C., 1962-69, 73—; sr. v.p. Am. Medicorp, Inc., N.Y.C., 1969-72; individual practice, 1974-78; pres. Alan S. Kramer (p.c.), 1978—; sr. mng. dir. Bear, Stearns & Co., Inc., 1990-96. Editor: Columbia Law Rev, 1960-62. Mem. nat. council Salk Inst. Served with M.I. AUS, 1956-58. Mem. Assn. of Bar of City of N.Y. Home: 315 E 86th St New York NY 10028-4714 Office: 780 3d Ave 16th Fl New York NY 10017

KRAMER, ALLAN FRANKLIN, II, researcher, botanical garden official; b. N.Y.C., Dec. 10, 1950; s. Walter Frederick and Dorothea (Russell-Hurley) K. AB, Coll. of Holy Cross, 1972; MS, Pratt Inst., 1979. Sr. document analyst Aspen Systems Corp., N.Y.C., 1979-81, team leader analyst, 1981-83, mgr. rsch. staff, 1983-86; sr. editor Bus. Guides, Inc. div., sr. rsch. mgr. Lebhar-Friedman, Inc., N.Y.C., 1987-91; conservator Bklyn. Botanic Garden, 1991—, trustee, 1995-97, 2000—. Mem. exec. com. Bklyn. Bot. Garden Aux., 1991—, v.p., 1993-95, pres. 1995-97, dir., 1997—; mem. pres.'s coun. Coll. Holy Cross, class chmn.; dir. Park Slope Geriatric Ctr., dir.Vol. Svcs. Opportunities Project; dir. Bklyn Conservatory of Music, chmn. devel. com., mem. exec. bd.; mem. Prospect Park Coun., The Woodlands Coun.; dir., treas. Park Slope Vol. Ambulance Corps.; dir. CAMBA; dir. Park Slope Neighborhood Family Ctr.; dir. Prospect Park YMCA. Gager fellow, 1991—. Mem. Am. Assn. Bot. Gardens and Arboreta, New Eng. Soc. in City of Bklyn. (v.p., dir.), Hundred Yr. Assn. N.Y., Royal Oak Found., Friendly Sons of St. Patrick (chmn.), Soc. Old Bklyn. (life), Battle of Bklyn. Conservancy (dir.), Assn. St. George the Martyr (Knight), Greek Order of St. Dennis of Zante (Knight), Montauk Club (pres.), Mcpl. Club Bklyn., Bklyn. C. of C., Surf Club of Quogue, English Speaking Union, Steuben Soc. Am., French-Am. Friendship Found., Beta Phi Mu (life). Avocations: sailing, travel, antiquing. Home: 35 Prospect Park W Brooklyn NY 11215-237[illegible] Office: Bklyn Botanic Garden 1000 Washington Ave Brooklyn NY 11225-1008

KRAMER, ANDREW JOSEPH, clergyman; b. Greensburg, Pa., May 31, 1954; s. Andy and Genevieve (Fultz) K.; m. Sandra Lee Hoy, June 7, 1975; children: Lauren Rae, Jenna Marie. BA in History summa cum laude, Grove City Coll., 1975; MDiv cum laude, Pitts. Theol. Sem., 1979. Ordained to ministry Presbyn. Ch. USA, 1979. Sales clk. H. Kimball Sportswear for Men, North Huntingdon, Pa., 1969-72; indsl. engr. Ft. Pitt Steel Casting, McKeesport, Pa., 1975-77; pastor 1st United Presbyn. Ch., Brilliant, Ohio, 1979-85, assoc. pastor Belleville, Ill., 1985—. Bd. dirs., sec., treas. Uni-Pres Kindercottage East St. Louis, Ill., 1985-96; developer, advisor Deacons Dental Grants Program, Belleville, 1992—; cons. ptnr. Belleville AmeriCorps Program, 1994—. Founder, pres. bd. dirs. Abraham Lincoln Neighborhood Assn., Belleville, 1993-99; coach West Pointe Lightning Select Soccer Team, Belleville, 1996-2000; developer, pres., bd. dirs. Neighbors for Renewal in Belleville, Inc., 1997—. Recipient Citizen of Yr. award Brilliant Lions Club 1984, Belleville Cmty. Devel. award, 2002; co-recipient Mildred Hagedorn award Giddings-Lovejoy Presbytery Coun. of Aging, 1993. Mem. Sundowner Club, Elks. Avocations: fishing, sports, reading. Home: 34 Char Claire D[illegible] Belleville IL 62226-1527 Office: 1st United Presbyn Ch 1303 Royal Heights R[illegible] Belleville IL 62223-5400 E-mail: VgerK2@aol.com., kramerAJ@juno.com.

KRAMER, ANDREW MICHAEL, lawyer; b. N.Y.C., Nov. 2, 1944; s. Irving and Ida (Kaplan) K.; m. Cheryle Lynn Safran, June 21, 1966; children: Howard, Jennifer; m. Nita Lynne Albert, Mar. 13, 1983; children: Samantha, Stephanie. BA cum laude, Mich. State U., 1966; JD cum laude, Northwestern U., 1969. Bar: Ill. 1969, D.C. 1977, U.S. Ct. Appeals (4th cir.) 1977, U.S. Ct. Appeals (5th cir.) 1972, U.S. Ct. Appeals (6th cir.) 1972, U.S. Ct. Appeals (7th cir.) 1970, U.S. Ct. Appeals (11th cir.) 1982, Ohio 1990. Assoc. firm Seyfarth, Shaw, Fairweather & Geraldson, Chgo., 1969-73, ptnr. Washington, 1974-83, Jones Day, Washington and Cleve., 1983. Exec. dir. Ill. Office Collective Bargaining, Springfield, 1973-74. Contbr. articles to profl. jours. Mem.: ABA, D.C. Bar Assn., Chgo. Bar Assn., Pepper Pike Club (Cleve.), Firestone Country Club, Congl. Country Club (Md.). Office: Jones Day 51 Louisiana Ave NW Washington DC 20001-2113

KRAMER, BARNETT SHELDON, oncologist; b. Balt., July 29, 1948; s. Mervin and Muriel Hannah (Woolf) K.; m. Ruth Solomon, June 25, 1972; 1 child, Jeremy. Student, Johns Hopkins U., 1966-69, MPH, 1991; MD, U. Md., 1973. Intern Washington U., St. Louis, 1973-74, med. resident, 1974-75; fellow Nat. Cancer Inst., Bethesda, Md., 1975-78, sr. investigator, 1986-90, assoc. dir., 1990-96, dep. dir. Divsn. Cancer Prevention and Control, 1996-97, dep. dir. Divsn. Cancer Prevention, 1997-2000; asst. prof. U. Fla., Gainesville, 1978-83, assoc. prof., 1983-86; editor-in-chief Jour. Nat. Cancer Inst., Bethesda; dir. Office Med. Applications of Rsch. NIH, 2000—, assoc. dir. for disease prevention, 2001—. Prof. medicine Uniformed Svcs. U. Health Scis., Bethesda, Md., 1989-90, clin. prof. medicine, 1990—. Co-editor: (with P. Greenwald and D. Weed) Cancer Prevention and Control, 1995; (with J. Gohagan and P. Prorok) Cancer Screening Theory and Practices, 1999, (with C. Allegra) Understanding Clinical Trials, 2000; assoc. editor Jour. Nat. Cancer Inst., 1988-94, editor-in-chief, 1994—; mem. editl. bd. Physicians Data Query, 1988—, chmn. bd. cancer prevention and screening, 1992—; contbr. articles to profl. publs., chpts. to books. With USPHS, 1975-78. Fellow ACP; mem. Am

Soc. Clin. Oncologists, Am. Assn. Cancer Rsch., Alpha Omega Alpha, Delta Omega. Avocation: fountain pen collecting. Office: NIH Office of Disease Prev Rm 1B-03 31 Center Dr Bldg 31 Bethesda MD 20892-2082 E-mail: bk76p@nih.gov.

KRAMER, BARRY ALAN, psychiatrist, educator; b. Phila., Sept. 9, 1948; s. Morris and Harriet (Greenberg) K.; m. Paulie Hoffman, June 9, 1974; children: Daniel Mark, Steven Philip. BA in Chemistry, NYU, 1970; MD, Hahnemann Med. Coll., 1974. Resident in psychiatry Montefiore Hosp and Med. Ctr., Bronx, N.Y., 1974-77; practice medicine specializing in psychigary, N.Y.C., 1977-82; staff psychiatrist L.I. Jewish-Hillside Med. Ctr., Glen Oaks, N.Y., 1977-82; asst. prof. SUNY, Stony Brook, 1978-82; practice medicine specializing in psychiatry, L.A., 1982—; asst. prof. psychiatry U. So. Calif., 1982-89, assoc. prof. clin. psychiatry, 1989-94, prof. clin. psychiatry, 1994-98; ward chief Los Angeles County/U. So. Calif. Med. Ctr., 1982-98. Med. dir. ECT, Cedars Sinai Med. Ctr., 1998—; cons. Little Neck Nursing Home (N.Y.), 1979-82, L.I. Nursing Home, 1980-82; dir. ECT U. So. Calif. Sch. Medicine, 1990. Reviewer Am. Jour. Psychiatry, Hosp. and Cmty. Psychiatry; mem. editl. bd. Convulsive Therapy; contbr. articles to profl. juors., papers to sci. meetings. Grantee NIMH, 1979-80, UCLA/U. So. Calif. Long-Term Gerontology Ctr., 1985-86, NARSAD, 2001--. Fellow Am. Psychiat. Assn., Assn. Convulsive Therapy (editl. bd.); mem. AMA, Soc. Biol. Psychiatry, Calif. Med. Assn., L.A. Med. Assn., Am. Assn. Geriatric Psychiatry, Gerontol. Soc. Am., So. Calif. Psychiat. Soc. (chair ETC com.). Jewish. Office: Cedars Sinai Med Ctr Thalians 155-W 8730 Alden Dr Los Angeles CA 90048 also: PO Box 5792 Beverly Hills CA 90209-5792 E-mail: krameb@cshs.org., barryakramer@yahoo.com.

KRAMER, BURTON, graphic designer, educator; b. NYC, June 25, 1932; s. Sam and Ida (Moore) K.; m. Irene Margarite Therese Mayer, Feb. 22, 1961; children: Gabrielle Kimberly, Jeremy Jacques. BS in Graphic Design, Ill. Inst. Tech., Chgo., 1954; postgrad. (Fulbright scholar), Royal Coll. Art, London, 1955-56; M.F.A., Yale U., 1957; D (hon.), Ontario Coll. of Art and Design, 2003. Registered graphic designer Ont. Designer Will Burtin, NYC, 1957-58; asst. art dir. Arch. Record, NYC, 1959; pres., creative dir. Kramer Design Assoc., Ltd., Toronto, Canada, 1967—2001; designer Geigy Chem. Corp., NYC, 1959-61; dir. corp. graphics Clairtone Sound Corp., Toronto, Canada, 1967; chief designer Halpern Advt., Zurich, Switzerland, 1961-65; instr. Ont. Coll. Art & Design, Ont., Canada, 1978—. Guest lectr. Rochester Inst. Tech., 1976, 81, designer-in-residence, 1981; vis. lectr. U. Cin., 1980; guest lectr., Arnhem, The Netherlands, 1994, Mexico City U. Autonoma, 1995; spkr. 1st Internat. Biennial of Symbols/Logotypes, Ostend, Belgium, 1994; mem. faculty Seneca Coll. Book designer The Art of Norval Morrisseau, 1979, Passionate Spirits, 1980; author Can. sect. Trademarks and Symbols of the World, 1973; co-author: Report on Canadian Road Sign Graphics, 1968; work pub. in numerous nat. and internat. jours., annuals and books; contbr. articles to profl. jours.; major works include signing-info. sys. CBC Broadcast Ctr., Toronto, IBM Tng. Ctr., Centenary Hosp., Scarborough, St. Lawrence Ctr. for Arts, Eaton Ctr., Erin Mills New Town, Mississauga, Metro Ctrl. YMCA, Copps Coliseum, Union Sta.; designer visual identity programs for CBC, N.Am. Life Assurance, Can. Imperial Bank Commerce, Reed Paper, ONEX Packaging Inc., Gemini, Vincor Internat., Can. Sys. Group, Nat. Rsch. Coun. Can., Centrestage, Royal Ont. Mus., Teknion Furniture Sys., Inc., Decoustics, Chartwell I.R.M., Scarborough Bd. Edn., Ont. Edn. Comm. Authority, Can. Crafts Coun., Ont. Guild Crafts, Zoomit Corp.; exhbn. paintings Pekao Gallery, Toronto, 1999, Peak Gallery, 2002, (Kahat Wrorel Gallery), 2003, Found. for Constructive Art, Calgary, 2002; work on website Canadian Ctr. for Contemporary Art, www.c-cca.ca, 2002. Bd. dir. Arts Toronto. Recipient gold medal Internat. Typographic Composition Assn., 1971, gold medal Art Dir. Club Toronto, 1973, medal Leipzig BookFair, Toronto Arts Lifetime Achievement award 1999, Order of Ont. award, 2003. Fellow Soc. Graphic Designers Can. (past pres.); mem. Alliance Graphique Internat., Royal Can. Acad. Arts, Assn. Registered Graphic Designers of Ont. (bd. dirs.), Nat. Yacht Club. Home: 101 Roxborough St W Toronto ON Canada M5R 1T9 Office: 103 Dupont St Toronto ON Canada M5R 1V4 E-mail: burton@kramer-design.com.

KRAMER, CAROL GERTRUDE, marriage and family counselor; b. Grand Rapids, Mich., Jan. 14, 1939; d. Wilson John and Katherine Joanne (Wassink) Rottschafer; m. Peter William Kramer, July 1, 1960; children: Connie R. Kramer Sattler, Paul Wilson Kramer. AB, Calvin Coll., 1960; MA, U. Mich., 1969; PhD, Holy Cross Coll., 1973; MSW, Grand Valley State U., 1985. Diplomate Internat. Acad. Behavioral Medicine, Counseling and Psychotherapy, cert. addictions/substance abuse counselor Mich., hypnotherapist/psychotherapist, clin. certified forensic counselor 2001. Elem. tchr. Jenison (Mich.) Pub. Sch., 1960-65; sch. social worker Grand Rapids Pub. Sch., 1964-81; pvt. practice marriage and family counselor Grand Rapids, 1973—; v.p. Human Resource Assocs., Grand Rapids, 1983-88; pres. bd. dirs. Telecounseling, 1996-99. Guest lectr. Calvin Coll., Mich. State U., Grand Valley State U., 1975-85; presenter in field. Co-author: Parent Involvement Program, 1993, Stop Sexual Abuse for Everyone, 1996. Ruling elder 1st Presbyn. Ch., Grand Rapids, 1975-78; mem. Gerald R. Ford Rep. Women, Grand Rapids, 1980-87; co-chair pastoral rels. com. Gun Lake Community Ch., 1989-91, v.p. consistory, 1991-93; apptd. fellow State Mich. Bd. Marriage Counselors, 1985-87; pres. bd. dirs. Stop Sexual Abuse for Everyone. Named one of Outstanding Young Women in Am., 1974; recipient Meritorious Svc. award Kent County Family Life Coun., 1983. Fellow Am. Assn. Marriage and Family Therapist; mem. NASW, Mich. Assn. Marriage Counselors (awards com. 1988, chmn. 1991, nominations com. 1992-95), Kent County Family Life Coun. (pres. 1975), Voters Against Sexual Abuse (pres., bd. dirs. 1992—). Home: 12622 Park Dr Wayland MI 49348-9085 Office: 1251 Century Ave SW Ste 107 Grand Rapids MI 49503-8047

KRAMER, CECILE E. retired medical librarian; b. NYC, Jan. 6, 1927; d. Marcus and Henrietta (Marks) K. BS, CCNY, 1956; MS in L.S., Columbia U., 1960. Reference asst. Columbia U. Health Scis. Library, N.Y.C., 1957-61, asst. librarian, 1961-75; dir. Health Scis. Libr. Northwestern U., Chgo., 1975-91, asst. prof. edn., 1975-91, prof. emeritus, 1991—. Instr. library and info. sci. Rosary Coll., 1981-85 ; cons. Francis A. Countway Library Medicine, Harvard U., 1974. Pres. Friends of Libr., Fla. Atlantic U., Boca Raton. Fellow Med. Libr. Assn. (chmn. med. sch. librs. group 1975-76, editor newsletter 1975-77, instr. continuing edn. 1966-75, mem. panel cons. editors Bull. 1987-90, disting. mem. Acad. Health Info. Profls. 1993—); mem. Biomed. Comm. Network (chmn. 1979-80). Home: 9184 Flynn Cir Apt 4 Boca Raton FL 33496-6675 E-mail: kramer@fau.edu.

KRAMER, DALE VERNON, retired English language educator; b. Mitchell, S.D., July 13, 1936; s. Dwight Lyman and Frances Elizabeth (Corbin) K.; m. Cheris Gamble Kramarae, Dec. 21, 1960; children: Brinlee, Jana. BS, S.D. State U., 1958; MA, Case Western Res. U., 1960, PhD, 1963. Instr. English Ohio U., Athens, 1962-63, asst. prof., 1963-65, U. Ill., Urbana, 1965-67, assoc. prof., 1967-71, prof. English, 1971-96; prof. emeritus, 1997—; acting head English dept. U. Ill., Urbana, 1982, 86-87, assoc. dean Coll. of Arts & Scis., 1992-95. Chmn. bd. editors Jour. English and Germanic Philology, 1972-95; mem. bd. editors Cambridge Edit. of the Works of Joseph Conrad, 1995—; assoc. vice provost, prof. English, U. Oreg., 1990. Author: Charles Robert Maturin, 1973, Thomas Hardy: The Forms of Tragedy, 1975, Thomas Hardy: Tess of the d'Urbervilles, 1991; editor: Critical Approaches to the Fiction of Thomas Hardy, 1979, Thomas Hardy, The Woodlanders, 1981, 85, Thomas Hardy, The Mayor of Casterbridge, 1987, Critical Essays on Thomas Hardy: The Novels, 1990, The Cambridge Companion to Thomas Hardy, 1999. Served to capt. U.S. Army, 1958-66. Mem. Center for Advanced Study, 1971; Am. Philos. Soc. grantee, 1969, 86, NEH grantee, 1986. Congregationalist.

KRAMER, DANIEL JONATHAN, lawyer; b. Cin., Dec. 20, 1957; s. Milton and Fradie (Ehrlich) K.; m. Judith L. Mogul; children: Ilona, Hannah, Joshua. BA magna cum laude, Wesleyan U., Middletown, Conn., 1980; JD, NYU, 1984. Bar: N.Y. 1985, U.S. Dist. Ct. (so. and ea. dists.) N.Y. 1985, U.S. Ct. Appeals (2d cir.) 1989. Assoc. Cravath, Swaine & Moore, N.Y.C., 1985-86; law clk. to Chief Judge Wilfred Feinberg, U.S. Ct. Appeals for 2d Cir., N.Y.C., 1986-87; assoc. Schulte Roth & Zabel LLP, N.Y.C., 1987-92, ptnr., 1993—2002, Paul, Weiss, Rifkind, Wharton & Garrison, LLP, N.Y.C., 2002—. Mem. pro se discretionary panel U.S. Ct. Appeals for 2d Cir., 1988—. Author: Federal Securities Litigation: Commentary and Forms, A Deskbook for the Practitioner, 1997, Regulation of Market Manipulation, Federal Securities Exchange Act of 1934, 2002; contbr. articles to law jours. and newspaper. Bd. dirs. Leukemia Soc., N.Y.C., 1995-98; Big Apple Greeter, 2001-03. Mem. ABA, Assn. Bar City N.Y., N.Y. Lawyers for Pub. Interest. Office: Paul Weiss Rifkind Wharton & Garrison LLP 1285 Avenue of the Ams New York NY 10019

KRAMER, DAVID J. state representative, lawyer; b. Omaha, Sept. 5, 1964; BA in Polit. Sci., Loyola Univ., 1987; JD, Georgetown Univ., 1990. Bar: Nebr. 1990, U.S. Dist. Ct. Nebr., U.S. Ct. Appeals (8th cir.). Atty. Baird Holm Law Firm, Omaha, 1990—96, 1999—; chmn. Nebr. Rep. Party, 2001—. Dir. resident program Internat. Rep. Inst., Luanda, Angola, 1997, Luanda, 98; chmn. Douglas County Rep. Party, 1995—96. Mem. Douglas County, 1991—, State Ctrl. Com., 1991—; vol. U.S. Senate Campaign, U.S. House Rep. Campaign, State Legislature Campaign, County Treas. Campaign, City Council Campaign, Sch. Bd. Campaign. Named One of Ten Outstanding Omahans, Jaycees, 1999. Mem.: ABA, State Ctrl. Com., Douglas County Com. (chmn. 1995—96). Republican. Office: Nebr Rep Party 421 S 9th St Ste 233 Lincoln NE 68508 Address: Baird Holm Mceachen Pedersen Hamann & St 1500 Woodmen Tower Omaha NE 68102 Office Fax: 402-475-3541. E-mail: dkramer@bairdholm.com.*

KRAMER, DENNY B. professional communication educator; b. Austin, Tex., Oct. 9, 1969; s. Dennis Lee and Margaret Helen (Anderson) K.; m. Deanne Michelle Seay, Nov. 11, 1995. BA in English, Baylor U., 1993, MA in Am. Studies, 1996; PhD, Okla. State U., 2003. Cert. tchr., Tex. Tchr. China Spring (Tex.) Ind. Sch. Dist., 1993-95; rsch. and editing asst. Inst. for Oral History at Baylor U., Waco, Tex., 1995-96; instr. English dept. Baylor U., Waco, Tex., 1996-97, Okla. State U., 1997—2001; prof. info. sys. dept. Baylor U., Waco, Tex., 2001—. Judge Heart of Tex. Regional History Fair, Waco, 1996. Pres. Lorena Ex-Students Assn., Lorena Ind. Sch. Dist., 1996-99, v.p. 1994-96; pres. Okla. State U. STC chpt., 1998-99. Young Scholar's symposium, Baylor U., 1995. Mem. Assn. Bus. Comm., Assn. Info. Systems, Assn. Profl. Comm. Cons., Soc. of Tech. Comm., Assn. Tchrs. of Tech. Writing, Knowledge and Innovation Mgmt. Profl. Soc., Sigma Tau Chi. Baptist. Avocations: reading, coaching little league, antiques, book collecting. Home: 1100 Del Mar Ct Waco TX 76706 E-mail: dkramer@hot.rr.com.

KRAMER, DONALD, insurance executive; b. N.Y.C., Nov. 17, 1937; s. Lawrence and Ruth Kramer; m. Elizabeth Gunderssen, June 1, 1982; children: Lauren Kramer Manino, Kim, Morten E., Christian Hoybye. BA in Econs., CUNY Bklyn. Coll., 1958; MBA, NYU, 1964. Chartered Fin. Analyst. Chmn. NAC RE Corp., Greenwich, 1984-93, Nat. Am. Ins. Co. Calif., Rancho Dominguez, 1986-91, Kramer Capital Cons. Inc., Greenwich, 1975-91, KCC Capital Mgrs., Greenwich, 1986-93; gen. ptnr. KCC Ptnrs. L.P., Greenwich, 1986-93; chmn. KCP Holding Co., Rancho Dominguez, Calif., 1986-91; pres., dir. Carteret Fed. Savs. Bank, Morristown, N.J., 1991-93; pres. Tempest Reins. Co. Ltd., Hamilton, Bermuda, 1993-99. Bd. dirs. Nat. Benefit Life Ins. Co., N.Y.C., mapfre Am. SA; vice chmn., dir. Ace Ltd., Bermuda, 1996—. Contbr. articles to jours. in field. Trustee Bklyn. Coll. Found. Mem. N.Y. Soc. Securities Analysts, Assn. for Investment Mgmt. and Rsch., Old Oaks Club (Purchase, N.Y.). Office: Ace Ltd 30 Woodbourne Ave Hamilton HM08 Bermuda

KRAMER, DONALD BURTON, lawyer; b. St. Louis, Oct. 21, 1928; s. Allen Samuel and Mae (Sachar) K.; m. Elaine Ruth Phillips, Sept. 7, 1952; children: Jeffrey Scott, Janet Sue. BBA, Wash. U., St. Louis, 1950, JD, 1952. Bar: Mo., 1952. Assoc. Kramer & Chused, St. Louis, 1954-60; ptnr. Kramer, Chused & Kramer, St. Louis, 1960-73; owner Kramer and Frank, St. Louis, 1974-86; pres. Kramer and Frank, P.C., St. Louis, 1987—, Attorneyfind Internet Dir., 1997—. Author: Mastering Commercial Collections, 1991; contbr. articles to profl. jours. Cpl. U.S. Army, 1952-54. Named Outstanding Trustee, Zeta Beta Tau, 1970. Mem. Bar Assn. Met. St. Louis, Mo. Bar Assn. (chmn. com. unauthorized practice of law 1969-73), Comml. Law League Am. (co-chmn. bankruptcy com. 1977-78, chmn. nominating com., 1985-86, chmn. midwest dist., 1982-83, practices com. fair debt collection 1986-88), Nat. Assn. Retail Collection Attys. (founder, pres. 1993-95). Office: Kramer & Frank PC 9300 Dielman Industrial Saint Louis MO 63132-3080 E-mail: dkramer@lawusa.com.

KRAMER, DONOVAN MERSHON, SR., newspaper publisher; b. Galesburg, Ill., Oct. 24, 1925; s. Verle V. and Sybil (Mershon) K.; m. Ruth A. Heins, Apr. 3, 1949; children: Donovan M. Jr., Diana Sue, Kara J. Kramer Cooper, Eric H. BS in Journalism, Pub. Mgmt., U. Ill., 1948. Editor, publisher, ptnr. Fairbury (Ill.) Blade, 1948-63, Forrest (Ill.) News, 1953-63; ptnr. Gibson City (Ill.) Courier, 1952-63; pres., publisher, editor Casa Grande (Ariz.) Valley Newspapers, Inc., 1963—; mng. ptnr. White Mt. Pub. Co., Show Low, Ariz., 1978—. Wrote, edited numerous articles and newspaper stories. Many award-winners including Sweepstakes award in Ill. and Ariz. Mem., chmn. Econ. Planning and Devel. Bd. State of Ariz., Phoenix, 1976-81; mem. Ctrl. Ariz. Coll. Found. Bd.; pres. Indsl. Devel. Authority of Casa Grande, 1977—; founding pres. Greater Casa Grande Econ. Devel. Found., exec. bd. dirs., 1982—; gov. apptd. bd. mem. Ariz. Dept. Transp., 1992-97, chmn., 1997; mem. adv. bd. dept. journalism U. Ariz.; bd. dirs. Ctrl. Ariz. Found. With USAAF, WWII, PTO. Recipient Econ. Devel. plaque City of Casa Grande, 1982, Lifetime Achievement award Greater Casa Grande Econ. Devel. Found., 1994. Mem. Ariz. Newspapers Assn. (pres. 1980, Master Editor-Pub. 1977, Hall of Fame, 1998), Cmty. Newspapers Ariz. (pres. 1970-71), Inland Newspapers Assn., Newspapers Assn. Am., Ctrl. Ariz. Project Assn., Nat. Newspapers Assn., Greater Casa Grande C. of C. (pres. 1981-82, Hall of Fame 1991), Soc. Profl. Journalists. Republican. Lutheran. Avocations: hiking, fishing, nature studies, travel, health awareness, econ. devel., military history.

KRAMER, EDWARD E. screenwriter, editor; b. Bklyn., Mar. 2, 1961; s. Leon A. and Helen M. Kramer. BS in Psychology, Emory U., Atlanta, 1983; MPH in Health Adminstrn. Planning, Emory U., 1994. Cert. addiction counselor - Level II 1987, nat. cert. addiction counselor Level II 1992. Program coord. Met. Atlanta Coun. on Alcohol and Drugs, Atlanta, 1985—87; tech. dir. Met. Regional Ednl. Svc. Agy., 1991—2001; pres. Ed Kramer & Assocs., Inc., Atlanta, 1998—, Psychiatric Healthcare Cons., Atlanta, 1987—98; dir. rsch. Talbott Recovery System, Atlanta, 1988—90; pub. Ora Press, Atlanta, 2003—. Pres. Dragon Con, Inc., Atlanta, 1986—2000; pub. Ora Press, Atlanta, 2003—. Editor: (anthology) Free Space, 1987 (Special Promethius Award Winner, 1998), The Sandman: Book of Dreams, 1996, Dark Love, 1996 (Deathrealm Award for Best Anthology, 1997), The Crow: Shattered Lives and Broken Dreams, 1998, Strange Attraction: Turns of the Midnight Carnival Wheel, 2000. Bd. dirs. Mayor's Taskforce on Domestic Violence, Atlanta, 1983—85; disaster action team mem. ARC, Decatur, Ga., 1982—88, CPR / multi-mediafFirst aid instr. Atlanta, 1980—87; foster care rev. panel co-chmn. Coun. of Juvenile Ct. Judges, Decatur, 1991—98. Fellow Melvin Jones fellow for humanitarian svc., Lions Club Internat. Found., 2000. Mem.: Sci. iction and Fantasy Writers Assn., Horror Writers Assn. (v.p. bd. trustees 1998—2001). Jewish. Avocation: Photography, Travel, Caving. Home: 2480 Honeycomb Way Duluth GA 30096 Personal E-mail: edkramer@edkramer.com.

KRAMER, EDWARD JOHN, materials science and engineering educator; b. Wilmington, Del., Aug. 5, 1939; s. Edward Noble and Irma (Nemetz) K.; m. Gail Allen Woodford, Aug. 24, 1963; children: Eric Woodford, Jeanne Noble. BChemE, Cornell U., 1962; PhD, Carnegie-Mellon U., 1967. Asst. prof. dept. materials sci. and engring. Cornell U., Ithaca, N.Y., 1967-72, assoc. prof., 1972-79, prof., 1979-88, Samuel B. Eckert prof. materials sci. and engring., 1988-97; prof. dept. materials & chem. engring. U. Calif., Santa Barbara, 1997—. Vis. scientist Argonne (Ill.) Nat. Lab., 1974-75; vis. prof. Akademie der Wissenschaften Inst. Metallphysik, Göttingen, Germany, 1979, Ecole Poly. Federale de Lausanne, Switzerland, 1982, Johannes Gutenberg U., Mainz, Germany, 1987-88. Contbr. over 300 articles to sci. jours. Recipient U.S. Sr. Scientist award Alexander von Humboldt Stiftung, 1987-88, Swinburne award Inst. Materials, U.K., 1996; NATO fellow, 1966-67, John Simon Guggenheim Found. fellow, N.Y.C., 1988. Fellow AAAS, Am. Phys. Soc. (High Polymer Physics prize 1985); mem. NAE, Materials Rsch. Soc., Am. Chem. Soc., Böhmische Phys. Soc. Avocation: masters swimming. Office: Univ Calif Materials Dept Engring II Santa Barbara CA 93106 Business E-Mail: edkramer@mrl.ucsb.edu.

KRAMER, ELEANOR, retired real estate broker, tax practitioner, financial consultant; b. N.Y.C., Feb. 18, 1939; d. Herman I. Kramer and Fay (Berger) Kramer-Levy; m. Richard H. Fitz-Gerald III, Dec. 24, 1959 (div.); m. Gregory F. Navarro, Oct. 1, 1975 (div. Mar. 1996); children: Brad, Cindy. BA in Speech and Theater, Bklyn Coll., 1975; MS in Urban Affairs, CUNY, Hunter Coll., 1976. Tchr. cultural arts Bronx (N.Y.) Bd. Edn., 1966-70; real estate broker, pres. Tritown Realty Corp., Mamaroneck, N.Y., 1978-83; pvt. practice tax cons. Mamaroneck, 1983—. Adj. prof. sociology Rockland Community Coll., Suffern, N.Y., 1979-85, Westchester Community Coll., Valhalla, N.Y., 1979-85; founder dance therapy St. Vincent's Hosp., N.Y.C.; lectr., demonstrator N.Y.C. Pub. Schs., author, producer, performer, co-creator child edn. programs, 1967-77. Mem. pub. relations com. Bicentennial commn. Village of Mamaroneck, 1976; bd. dirs. Community Action Program, Mamaroneck, 1977-79. Mem.: LWV (bd. dirs. 1977—80), NOW (ad hoc chmn. 1970, co-chair, co-author women's ednl. seminar Libr. of Congress), Nat. Soc. Tax Preparers, Lions (Larchmont, NY). Avocations: puzzles, tennis, antiques, jazz, theater. Office: PO Box 172 Bronx NY 10464-0172

KRAMER, ELISSA LIPCON, nuclear medicine physician, educator; b. N.Y.C., Feb. 22, 1951; d. Jules and Esther Ruth (Wagner) L.; children: Rachel, Aaron. BA, U. Pa., 1973; MD, NYU, 1977. Diplomate Am. Bd. Nuc. Medicine, Am. Bd. Radiology. Ob-gyn. intern Bellevue Hosp. Ctr./NYU Med. Ctr., 1977-78, resident in radiology, 1978-80, fellow in nuc. medicine, 1980-82; asst. prof. clin. radiology NYU, 1982-89, assoc. prof. clin. radiology, 1989-96, prof. clin. radiology, 1996—. Assoc. prof. radiology Cornell U. Med. Ctr., Ithaca, N.Y., 1989-90; assoc. Sloan-Kettering Cancer Ctr., N.Y.C., 1989-90; assoc. dir. nuc. medicine Tisch Hosp., N.Y.C., 1989-99; assoc. attending physician Tisch Hosp., 1990-99, Bellevue Hosp., N.Y.C., 1990—; dir. nuclear medicine Tisch Hosp./Bellevue Hosp., 1999—; master Lewis Thomas Soc. for the Arts and Humanities in Medicine, NYU Sch. Medicine. Author, editor: (book) Clinical SPECT Imaging, 1995; contbr. articles to profl. jours. Nat. Cancer Inst./NIG Rsch. grantee, 1993—. Mem. Am. Coll. Radiology, Am. Assn. Women Radiologists, Radiology Soc. N.Am., Soc. Nuc. Medicine (mem. brain imaging coun. 1982—, mem. bd. dirs. 1992-93). E-mail: elissa.kramer@med.nyu.edu.

KRAMER, ERNEST JOACHIM, music educator, composer; b. Huntsville, Ala., 1954; m. Ella Alexeeva. PhD, U. North Tex., 1989. Prof. Coll. St. Teresa, Winona, Minn., 1983—85, Northwest Mo. State U., Maryville, 1985—. Organist First United Meth. Ch., Maryville, 1986—2000. Composer: (book of piano solos) Romancing the Keys, 2001 (Tower Award, 2001), The Music Garden, 1999, The Musical Treasure Chest, 2002. Mem.: Music Tchrs. Nat. Assn. Office: Northwest Mo State Univ 800 University Dr Maryville MO 64468 Business E-Mail: kramer@mail.nwmissouri.edu.

KRAMER, EUGENE LEO, lawyer; b. Barberton, Ohio, Nov. 7, 1939; s. Frank L. and Portia I. (Acker) Kramer; m. JoAnn Stockhausen, Sept. 19, 1970; children: Martin, Caroline, Michael. AB, John Carroll U., 1961; JD, U. Notre Dame, 1964. Bar: Ohio 1964. Law clk. U.S. Ct. Appeals (7th cir.), Chgo., 1964-65; ptnr. Squire, Sanders & Dempsey, Cleve., 1965-91, Roetzel & Andress, A Legal Profl. Assn., Cleve. and Akron, Ohio, 1992-97; spl. counsel Ohio Atty. Gen., 2003. Cons. Ohio Constl. Revision Commn., Columbus, 1970—74. Trustee Regina Health Ctr., 1997—, pres., 2001—; past pres. HELP Found., Inc., HELP, Inc., Cleve., 1981—92, Playhouse Sq. Assn., Cleve., 1980—84; pres. N.E. Ohio Transit Coalition, 1992—; mem. policy com. Build-Up Greater Cleve. Program, 1982—98; mem. Greater Cleve. Growth Assn.; trustee Consultation Ct. Diocese Cleve., 1990—96, Citizens League Greater Cleve., 1984—90, 1993—, Citizens League Rsch. Inst., 1995—97, St. Ann Found., 1990—92, Lyric Opera Cleve., 1995—. Recipient Disting. Leadership award, HELP, Inc., 1986, Pioneer Achievement award, HELP-Six Chimneys, Inc., 1986, Disting. Svc. award, Assn. Retarded Citizens, 1990, Vol. Svc. award, City of Lakewood, 2001. Mem.: ABA, Cleve. Bar Assn., Ohio State Bar Assn. (chmn. local govt. law com. 1986—90), Club Key Tower. Democrat. Roman Catholic. Avocations: music, theater, sports, travel. Home and Office: 1422 Euclid Ave Ste 706 Cleveland OH 44115-2001

KRAMER, GEORGE P. lawyer; b. Holyoke, Mass., Feb. 22, 1927; m. Elizabeth M. Truax, Oct. 13, 1973; children: Alice S. Truax, R. Hawley Truax, Charles W. Truax. AB, Harvard U., 1950, LL.B., 1953; Cert., Sorbonne, 1948. Bar: N.Y. 1954. Assoc. Watson Leavenworth Kelton & Taggart, N.Y.C., 1953-59, partner, 1960-65, Conboy, Hewitt, O'Brien & Boardman, N.Y.C., 1965-86, Hunton & Williams (merger Conboy, Hewitt, O'Brien & Boardman), N.Y.C., 1986—. Lectr. Practising Law Inst.; bd. dirs. Burleson Corp.; mem. vis. com. Peabody Mus. of Harvard U., 1974-80; mem. N.Y. Cotton Exch., N.Y. Bd. Trade. Author: Misleading Trademarks and Consumer Protection. Trustee Hancock Shaker Village, 1982—; trustee Harvard U. Law Sch. Assn. of N.Y., 1985-87, v.p. 1987-89. Served to lt. USNR, 1945-46. Recipient Congl. Antarctic medal, 1977 Mem. ABA, Internat. Bar Assn., Assn. Bar City N.Y. (sec. 1963-65, exec. com. 1970-74, chmn. various coms.), Am. Law Inst., Internat. Trademark Assn. (dir. 1975-78), Assn. Internationale pour la Protection de la Propriete Industrielle, Harvard U. Alumni Assn. (bd. dirs. 1983-89), Mass. Speleological Soc. (pres.), Antarctican Soc., Am. Polar Soc., Century Assn., Harvard Club (sec. 1972-83, 88-90, bd. mgrs. 1983-86), Harvard Faculty Club. Home: 151 E 79th St New York NY 10021-0417 Office: Hunton & Williams 200 Park Ave Fl 43 New York NY 10166-0005

KRAMER, GERSON BALFOUR, lawyer; b. N.Y.C., June 12, 1925; s. Harry and Dora Bella K.; m. Beryl Joan Alpher, Feb. 10, 1952; children: Phyllis B., Arthur H., Rachel A. AB in Econs. with high honors, Rutgers U., 1951; LLB, George Washington U., 1955. Bar: Md. 1981, U.S. Dist. Ct. D.C. 1955, U.S. Ct. Appeals (D.C. cir.) 1955, U.S. Ct. Appeals (fed. cir.) 1981, U.S. Ct. Claims 1956, U.S. Supreme Ct. 1970. Trial atty. divil divsn. ct. claims sect. Justice Dept., Washington, 1956-66; appeals bd. Dept. Commerce, Washington, 1966-67; contract appeals bd. Dept. Transp., Washington, 1966-69, chmn., chief adminstrv. judge contract appeals bd., 1969-79; counsel Braude & Margulies PC, Washington, 1979—. Contbr. articles to profl. jours. V.p. Franklin Knolls Civic Assn., Md., 1982; sec., treas. Franklin Knolls Swim Assn., 1968-72. With USN, 1943-46. Mem. D.C. Bar Assn. (chmn. divsn. 10 steering com. 1977-81, chmn. procurement law com., sect. on govt. contracts and litigation 1983-86, chmn. ct. and bds. practice com., sect. on govt. contracts and litigation 1986-87), Fed. Bar Assn. (chmn. bd. contract appeals com. 1968-69), Bd. Contract Appeals (sec.-treas. nat. conf. 1969-72, v.p. 1973-74, pres. 1976-77), Selby Bay Yacht Club (comdr. 1987-88), Phi Beta Kappa. Home: 6 Mcalpine Ct Silver Spring MD 20901-4715 E-mail: bal4@starpower.net.

KRAMER, GILDA LEA, lawyer; b. N.Y.C., July 16, 1954; d. William W. and Sylvia (Steinberg) K. BA, Swarthmore Coll., 1976; JD, U. Va., 1979. Bar: D.C. 1979, Pa. 1982, N.J. 1989, D.C. Circuit Ct. 1980, Pa. Circuit Ct. (3d cir.) 1982, U.S. Dist. Ct. (D.C. dist.) 1980, U.S. Dist. Ct. (ea. dist.) Pa. 1982, U.S. Dist. Ct. N.J. 1989. Assoc. Pepper Hamilton & Scheetz, Washington, 1979-81; asst. city solicitor City of Phila., 1981-83, dep. city solicitor, 1983-84; assoc. Schnader, Harrison, Segal & Lewis, Phila., 1984-89; pvt. practice Phila., 1989—. Mem. ABA, Pa. Bar Assn., Phila. Bar Assn. (mem. bd. govs. 1992-94, judge pro tempore 1994—). Democrat. Jewish. Home: 127 Penarth Rd Bala Cynwyd PA 19004-2714 Office: 1500 Walnut St Ste 1100 Philadelphia PA 19102-3506 E-mail: Gilda_Kramer@yahoo.com.

KRAMER, GORDON, mechanical engineer; b. Bklyn., Aug. 1937; s. Joseph and Etta (Grossberg) K.; m. Ruth Ellen Harter, Mar. 5, 1967 (div. June 1986); children: Samuel Maurice, Leah Marie; m. Eve Burstein, Dec. 17, 1988. BS, Cooper Union, 1959; MS, Calif. Inst. Tech., 1960. With Hughes Aircraft Co., Malibu, Calif., 1959-63; sr. scientist Avco Corp., Norman, Okla., 1963-64; asst. divsn. head Batelle Meml. Inst., Columbus, Ohio, 1964-67; sr. scientist Aeroject Electrosystems, Azusa, Calif., 1967-75; chief engr. Beckman Instrument Co., Fullerton, Calif., 1975-82; prin. scientist McDonnell Douglas Microelectronics Co., 1982-83, Kramer and Assocs., 1983-85; program mgr. Hughes Aircraft Co., 1985-96, ret., 1996; personal fin. advisor Am. Express, 1999—. Cons. Korea Inst. Tech. NSF fellow, 1959-60. Mem. IEEE. Democrat. Jewish. Home: 153 Lake Shore Dr Rancho Mirage CA 92270-4055 E-mail: gordeve@aol.com., gordon.x.kramer@aexp.com.

KRAMER, GORDON EDWARD, manufacturing executive; b. San Mateo, Calif., June 22, 1946; s. Roy Charles and Bernice Jeanne (Rones) K.; m. Christina Hodges, Feb. 14, 1970; children: Roy Charles, Charlena. BS in Aero. Engring., San Jose State Calif., 1970. Purchasing agt. Am. Racing Equipment, Brisbane, Calif., 1970-71, asst. to v.p. mktg., 1971-72; founder, pres. Safety Direct, Inc., Sparks, Nev., 1972—. Manufacturing executive; b. San Mateo,

Calif., June 22, 1946; s. Roy Charles and Bernice Jeanne (Rones) K.; BS in Aero. Engring., San Jose State Coll., 1970; m. Christina Hodges, Feb. 14, 1970; children: Roy Charles, Charlena. Purchasing agent Am. Racing Equipment, Brisbane, Calif., 1970-71, asst. to v.p. mktg., 1971-72; founder, pres. Safety Direct Inc., hearing protection equipment, Sparks, Nev., 1972—; dir. Hodges Transp., Condor Inc.; mem. adv. bd. to pres. Truckee Meadows Community Coll., 1991—. Named Nev. Small Businessperson of Yr., Nev. Small Bus. Adminstrn., 1987, Bus. Person of Yr. Sparks Community C. of C., 1987. Mem. Am. Soc. Safety Engrs., Safety Equipment Distributors Assn., Indsl. Safety Equipment Assn., Nat. Assn. Sporting Goods Wholesalers, Nat. Sporting Goods Assn., Nev. State Amature Trapshooting Assn. (dir. 1978-79), Pacific Internat. Trapshooting Assn. (Nev. pres. 1979-80, 80-81), Nev. Mfrs. Assn. (dir. 1992—), Advanced Soccer Club (pres.1985-86). Republican. Methodist. Rotary Club (pres. Spark Club 1988-89). Named Nev. Small Businessperson of Yr., Nev. Small Bus. Adminstrn., 1987, Bus. Person of Yr., Sparks Cmty. C. of C., 1987. Mem. Am. Soc. Safety Engrs., Safety Equipment Distributors Assn., Indsl. Safety Equipment Assn., Nat. Assn. Sporting Goods Wholesalers, Nat. Sporting Goods Assn., Nev. State Amature Trapshooting Assn. (dir. 1978-79), Pacific Internat. Trapshooting Assn. (pres. Nev. chpt. 1979-81), Nev. Mfrs. Assn. (dir. 1992—), Advanced Soccer Club (pres. 1985-86), Rotary (pres. Spark Club 1988-89). Republican. Methodist. Office: Safety Direct Inc 56 Coney Island Dr Sparks NV 89431-6335 E-mail: gordonkramer@worldnet.att.net.

KRAMER, ILSE ELISABETH, rare book bibliographer; b. Duesseldorf, Germany, Feb. 16, 1936; d. Georg Friedrich Karl Kramer and Hilde Adele Emmi Schlieper. *Descendant of a line of royal counts (Gaugrafen) in Lower Saxony, Germany, 1605 through 18th century.* MLS, U. Cologne, 1959. Libr. Dept. German U. Bonn, Germany, 1952—62; rare book bibliographer John Carter Brown Libr., Brown U., Providence, 1962—91. Cons. Antiquarian Book Dealer Daniel Siegel, Providence, 1995—, Mrs. Robert H.I. Goddard, Providence, 2001—; translator John Carter Brown Libr., 1962—91. Author: Die Wunderbare Neue Welt, 1988, Pimpinella, 1996. Archivist Cen. Congrl. Ch., Providence, 1989—. Mem. German-Am. Friends Niederrhein, R.I. Libr. Assn., Writers Clan. Avocations: writing poetry and plays, hiking. Home: 248 Waterman St Providence RI 02906-5203 Office: Cen Congrl Ch 296 Angell St Providence RI 02906 E-mail: ilsekramer@aol.com.

KRAMER, JANE, writer; b. Providence, Aug. 7, 1938; d. Louis Irving and Jessie (Shore) K.; m. Vincent Crapanzano, Apr. 30, 1967; 1 dau., Aleksandra. BA, Vassar Coll., 1959; MA, Columbia U., 1961. Founder, writer Morningsider, N.Y.C., 1961-62; writer Village Voice, N.Y.C., 1962-63, New Yorker, N.Y.C., 1964—. Cons. German Marshall Fund; bd. dirs. East and Central European Pub. Project; mem. bd. adv. Daedalus. Author: Off Washington Square: A Reporter Looks at Greenwich Village, 1963, Allen Ginsberg In America, 1969, Honor to the Bride Like the Pigeon That Guards Its Grain Under the Clove Tree, 1970, The Last Cowboy, 1978, Unsettling Europe, 1980 (Am. Book award for non-fiction 1981), Europeans, 1988, Whose Art Is It?, 1994 (Nat. Mag. award 1993, Prix Européan de l'Essai 1993), Lone Patriot: The Short Career of an American Militiaman, 2002; contbr. to periodicals including N.Y. Times Book Rev., N.Y. Rev. of Books, others. Recipient Front Page award New Yorker, 1977, Overseas Press Club Am. award, 1979; named Woman of Yr. Mademoiselle, 1968. Mem. Council Fgn. Relations, Com. to Protect Journalists (bd. dirs.), Environ. Def. Fund, Authors Guild and League, Writers Guild, Nat. Book Critics Circle, Goethe Inst. (bd. dirs.). Office: New Yorker 25 W 43rd St New York NY 10036-7406*

KRAMER, JANET PHILLIPS, physician; b. Pottsville, Pa., Dec. 25, 1942; d. Earl Milton and Isabel (Price) Phillips; m. Brian Dale Kramer, June 10, 1967. BS in Pre-Medicine, Pa. State U., 1964; MD, Woman's Med. Coll., 1968. Diplomate Am. Bd. Family and CMty. Medicine, cert. Nat. Commn. Correctional Health Care. Resident in internal medicine Med. Ctr. Del., Wilmington, 1969—71; med. dir. Del. Divsn. Drug Abuse, Wilmington, 1971-75; fellow in adolescent medicine Med. Ctr. Del./Children's Hosp. Washington, D.C., 1971—72; dir. adolescent and young adult svcs. Christiana Care Health Sys., Wilmington, 1985-99, cons., 1999—; physician surveyor Nat. Commn. Correctional Health Care, 1999—. Developer 1st full svc. med. drug detox unit, Del., 1972; mem. 1st coun. grad. med. edn. U.S. Dept. Health, 1984—87; founder 1st sch. for chronically ill children and adolescents, 1985; bd. dirs. Del. Bd. Med. Practice, 1993—. Bd. dirs. Ctrl. YMCA, Wilmington, 1980—94; advisor Svcs. Overcome Drug Abuse, 1975—95; mem. edn. com. Del. Breast Cancer Coalition, 1999—; mem. alumni bd. Pa. State U. Eberly Coll. Sci., pres., 1999—2001; mem. alumni bd. MCP/Hahnemann Med. U., 1999—, chmn. fin. com., 2000—02, treas., 2002—. Recipient cmty. Svc. Assn., Am. Med. Women's Assn., 1992. Mem.: ACP, AOA, Phila. Coll. Physicians, Am. Coll. Clin. Toxicology, New Castle County LWV (pres. 2003—). Lutheran. Avocations: travel, public policy development, photography. Home: 3 Boysenberry Dr Hockessin DE 19707

KRAMER, JAY HARLAN, physiologist, researcher, educator; b. Bklyn., Dec. 26, 1952; s. Albert and Blossom K.; m. Aisar Atrakchi, Apr. 18, 1993; 1 child, Evan. BA with honors, Northeastern U., 1976; MS, Lehigh U., 1979, PhD, 1982. Clin. lab. technician Boston Med. Lab., Waltham, Mass., 1974-75; rsch. asst. Lehigh U., Bethlehem, Pa., 1979-81; rsch. assoc. Med. Coll. Va., Richmond, 1982-83; sr. rsch. assoc. Okla. Med. Rsch. Found., Oklahoma City, 1983-85; rsch. assoc. George Washington U., Washington, 1985-86, asst. rsch. prof. medicine, 1986-90, assoc. rsch. prof., 1990—, adj. assoc. prof. physiology, 1991—, assoc. rsch. prof. physiology, 1998—. Lectr. physiology George Washington U., Washington, 1987-89; cons. Squibb & Sons, Princeton, N.J., 1989, mem. George Washington U. Instl. Animal Care and Use Com., 1988—, mem. Basic Sci. Faculty Assembly and Inst. Biomed. Scis., 1996—. Contbr. more than 54 articles to profl. jours.; article referee profl. jours. Mem. basic sci. faculty assembly coun. George Washington U., 1992-94. Grad. sch. scholar Lehigh U., 1980; named one of Outstanding Young Men of Am., Jaycees, 1981, 82. Mem. Am. Heart Assn., Am. Physiol. Soc., N.Y. Acad. Scis. (invited speaker 1993, presenter various nat. scientific meetings), Internat. Soc. for Heart Rsch., Internat. Soc. for Free Radical Rsch., Soc. for Exptl. Biology and Medicine, Acad. Honor Soc., Phi Sigma. Achievements include first to demonstrate relationship between toxic free radical prodn. and severity of ischemia in heart; first to demonstrate superoxide anion prodn. in postischemic heart using ESR spin trapping; first to demonstrate free radical prodn. in regionally ischemic canine and post-ischemic swine heart models; first to demonstrate that excessive neuropeptide release during dietary magnesium restriction leads to reduced tolerance of animal hearts to ischemia/reperfusion injury; developed non-invasive ESR spin trapping technique for free radical detection; demonstrated occurrance of potentially toxic free radicals in human heart following open heart surgery. Office: George Washington U Dept Physiol and Exptl Med 2300 I St NW Washington DC 20037-2336 E-mail: phyjhk@gwumc.edu.

KRAMER, JOEL ROY, journalist, newspaper executive; b. Bklyn., May 21, 1948; s. Archie and Rae (Abramowitz) Kramer; m. Laurie Maloff, 1969; children: Matthew, Elias, Adam. BA, Harvard U., Cambridge, 1969. Editor-in-chief Harvard Crimson; reporter Sci. Mag., Washington, 1969—70; free lance writer Washington, 1970—72; from copy editor to news editor, exec. news editor, asst. mng. editor Newsday, L.I., NY, 1972—80; exec. editor Buffalo Courier-Express, 1981—82, Star Tribune, Mpls., St. Paul, 1983—91, pub., pres., 1992—98; sr. fellow Sch. Journalism and Mass Comms., U. Minn., Mpls., 1998—. Bd. dirs. Harvard Crimson Inc., World Press Inst. Chmn. bd. Mpls. Children's Theatre Co., 1994—96. Co-recipient Pulitzer Prize for pub. svc. for the Heroin Trail, Newsday, 1973; recipient Best Legal Writing on Large Daily award, N.Y. Bar Assn., 1974. Address: Sch Journalism U Minn 111 Murphy Hall 206 Church St SE Minneapolis MN 55455-0488

KRAMER, JOHN PAUL, entomologist, educator; b. Elgin, Ill., Mar. 13, 1928; s. Rutherford Hayes and Anna Maria (Burita) K.; m. Jean Kent Simpson, June, 1957 (div. 1973); children: Philip Simpson, Katherine Jean. BS, Beloit (Wis.) Coll., 1950; MS, U. Mo., 1952; PhD, U. Ill., 1958. Asst. prof. entomology N.C. State U., 1958-59; asso. entomologist Ill. Natural History Survey, Urbana, 1959-65; with Cornell U., 1965-90, prof. insect pathology dept. entomology, 1975-90, prof. emeritus, 1990—. WHO traveling cons., 1962, NSF vis. scientist, Japan, 1967; mem. study sect. for tropical medicine and parasitology NIH, 1966-68; vis. scientist Inst. Arctic Biology in Alaska, 1972; vis. prof. entomology Ohio State U., Columbus, 1984; collaborator in parasitology Oswaldo Cruz Inst., Brazil, 1999-2001. Contbr. articles to profl. jours. Served to 1st lt. U.S. Army, 1952-54. Decorated Bronze Star., Korean Svc. medal with 2 battle stars; NSF fellow, 1967; NIH research grantee, 1959-72; Office of Naval Research grantee, 1971-74; WHO research grantee, 1979-82; U.S. Dept. Agr. research grantee, 1980-90. Mem. Soc. Invertebrate Pathology, N.Y. Entomol. Soc., Am. English Spot Rabbit Club, Am. Cavy Breeders Assn., Am. Rabbit Breeders Assn., N.Y. State Rabbit Breeders Assn. (pres. 1989-90), Taughannock Area Rabbit Breeders Assn. (pres. 1983-84, 91-96), Am. Netherland Dwarf Rabbit Breeders Assn., N.Y. State Cavy Fanciers Club (v.p. 1973-75). Unitarian-Universalist. Home: 115 Hanshaw Rd Ithaca NY 14850-2207 Office: Cornell Univ Dept Entomology 3142 Comstock Hall Ithaca NY 14853-2601

KRAMER, JOHN C. pediatrician; MD, Harvard U., 1950. Diplomate in pediatrics and pediatric pulmonology Am. Bd. Pediatrics. Pediatrician, pres. Pediatric Clinic, Inc., 1983—; pediat.-pulmonologist T.L. Carey & Assocs., 1989—. Contbr. articles to profl. jours. Mem.: Okla. State Med. Assn. Office: 7125 S Braden Ave Ste A Tulsa OK 74136-6302

KRAMER, KAREN SUE, mind-body psychologist; b. L.A., Sept. 6, 1942; d. Frank Pacheco Kramer and Velma Eileen (Devlin) Moore; m. Stewart A. Sterling, Dec. 30, 1965 (div. 1974); 1 child, Scott Kramer Sterling. BA, U. Calif., Berkeley, 1966; MA, U.S. Internat. U., 1976; PhD, Profl. Sch. Psychology, 1980; MA in Asian Studies, U. San Francisco, 2003. Psychometrist U. Calif. Counseling Ctr., Berkeley, 1966-67; social worker Alameda County Welfare Dept., Oakland, Calif., 1967-69; vol. coord. San. Diego County Probation Dept., 1971-73; officer San Diego County Probation Dept., 1973-76; counselor and coord. clin. and outreach programs Western Inst., San Diego, 1976-77; program coord. and counselor Women's Resource Ctr., Oceanside, Calif., 1977-78; pvt. practice psychology San Diego, 1978-81; planner/analyst San Diego County Dept. Health Svcs., 1979-81; prof. psychology Nat. U., San Diego, 1979-81; social svcs. program cons. Calif. Dept. Social Svcs., Emeryville, 1981-83; affirmative action officer State Compensation Ins. Fund, San Francisco, 1983-87; cmty. psychologist Calif. Dept. Mental Health, 1987-89; pvt. practice psychology Berkeley, 1990—. Personal analyst State Comp. Ins. Fund, 1989-91; regional property mgr. State Compensation Ins. Fund, San Francisco, 1991-95; prof. Nat. U. San Diego, 1979-81; pres. North County Coun. Social Concerns, Vista, Calif., 1977-78; advisor USMC Camp Pendleton Human Svcs., 1977-79; mem. adv. bd. Chinatown Resources Devel. Ctr., San Francisco, 1984-87, 2000—, San Francisco Rehab., 1984-87; bd. dirs. Network Cons. Svcs., Napa, Calif.; founder Qi Gong in China-Ednl. Svcs., 1994; asst. dir. Qigong for Children, Am. Found. Traditional Chinese Medicine; cons. Am. Found. Traditional Chinese Medicine, 1999, Success Strategies, programs for Health, Sports, Tests, Life; prof. Psychology, Am. Coll. TCM, 1999; pub. chmn. Intuition Network Conf., 1997; advisor Calif.-Hawaii Inst., 1998—; apptd. Alameda County Mental Health Bd., 2000. Editl. advisor (website) Alternative Medicine, 1998. Clin. dir. Pathways to Wellness Clinics, Oakland, Calif., 2002—; chmn. pub. awareness com. Alameda County Mental Health Bd., 2000—03. Mem. Calif. Peer Counselors Assn. (adv. bd. 1987-90), Calif. Prevention Network (bd. dirs. 1989-93, editl. advisor jour. 1992-93). E-mail: K.Kramer@comcast.net.

KRAMER, KEITH ALLAN, music educator, composer; b. Baltimore, MD, Mar. 19, 1968; m. Li Chen Kramer. Doctor of Musical Arts, University of Miami, Coral Gables, Florida, 1995—99. Professor of Music Harford Community College, Bel Air, MD, 1998—2002; Graduate Assistant University of Miami, Coral Gables, FL, 1995—98. Composer: (Chamber Work for Clarinet and Piano) Uncertainty Principle, 1998 (Winner of the College Music Society Mid-Atlantic Chapter Student Composer Competition, 1999), (Concerto for Soprano Saxophone) Limits of Reason, 1996 (Winner of the University of Miami Symphony Orchestra Composition Competition, 1998). Recipient Winner Student Composer Competition, Coll. Music Soc. Mid-Atlantic Chpt., 1999, Symphony Orchestra Composition Competition, U. Miami, 1998. Mem.: Council for Higher Education in Music (CHEM), Society for Music Theory (SMT), College Music Society (CMS), BMI, American Composers Forum, Society of Composers Inc. (SCI). Home: 5714 Goldfinch Court Ellicott City MD 21043 Office: Harford Community College 401 Thomas Run Road, Harve de Grace Hall Bel Air MD 21015 Personal E-mail: kkramer@keithkramer.org.

KRAMER, KENNETH BENTLEY, federal judge, former congressman; b. Chgo., Feb. 19, 1942; s. Albert Aaron and Ruth (Pokrass) K.; m. Louise Kramer; children: Kenneth Bentley, Kelly J. BA magna cum laude in Polit. Sci., U. Ill., 1963; JD, Harvard U., 1966. Bar: Ill. 1966, Colo. 1969. Dep. dist. atty. El Paso County, Colo., 1970-72; pvt. practice law Colorado Springs, 1972-78; mem. Colo. Ho. of Reps., 1973-78, 96th-99th Congresses from 5th Colo. Dist., 1978-86; asst. sec. Dept. Army, Washington, 1988-89; judge U.S. Ct. of Appeals for Vets. Claims, Washington, 1989-2000, chief judge, 2000—. Chmn. com. on vets. benefits ABA, 1990-94. Bd. visitors U.S. Air Force Acad., 1979-86; bd. dirs. Pikes Peak Mental Health Ctr., 1976-78, Mountain Valley chpt. March of Dimes, 1983-85, U.S. Space Found., 1983—; founder U.S. Space Found.; commr. Nat. Coun. on Uniform State Laws, 1977-78. Capt. U.S. Army, 1967-70. Recipient Disting. Civilian Svc. medal. Mem. Phi Beta Kappa. Office: US Ct Appeals for Vets Claims 625 Indiana Ave NW Ste 900 Washington DC 20004-2923

KRAMER, KENNETH SCOTT, lawyer; b. Troy, N.Y., Nov. 7, 1957; s. David W. and Judith (Fell) Bernstein. BA, U. Pa., 1979; JD, U. So. Calif., 1982. Bar: Calif. 1982, N.Y. 1984. Assoc. Finley, Kumble, Wagner et al, Beverly Hills and Newport Beach, Calif., 1982-86, Pettit & Martin, Newport Beach and Los Angeles, 1986-89, ptnr., 1990-95, Paone, Callahan, McHolm & Winton, 1995-2000, Drummy, King, White, Parret & Joerger, 2000—. Sec. Pacific Basin Restaurant Concepts Inc., L.A., 1985-90; lectr. Continuing Edn. of Bar, Calif., 1986-87. Chmn. Measure M subcom. Indsl. League of Orange County, 1991; campaign organizer Citizens Against Proposition F, Beverly Hills, 1984. Named one of Outstanding Young Men of Am., 1983. Mem. ABA, Indsl. League Orange County (transp. com. 1990-93). Office: Drummy King et al Ste 1000 3200 Park Center Dr Costa Mesa CA 92626 also: 355 S Grand Ave Los Angeles CA 90071-1560 E-mail: kkramer@drummyking.com.

KRAMER, KEVIN WILLIAM, aerospace engineer; b. Southfield, Mich., Nov. 10, 1974; s. Kenneth Wayne and Roberta Ann Kramer; m. Amanda McKenzie Ross, Mar. 29, 2003. BS in Aerospace Engring., Embry-Riddle Aero. U., Prescott, Ariz., 1998. F/A18 E/F operational flight test engr. MOTSC/Boeing, Patuxent River, Md., 1998—2000; 727 avionics/powerplant engr. Champion Air, Mpls., 2000—01; project engr. Am. West Airlines, Phoenix, 2001—. Recipient F-18 E/F EMD award, USN, 1999. Mem.: AIAA. Republican. Roman Catholic. Home: 1609 W Musket Way Chandler AZ 85248-8406 Office: America West Airlines 4000 E Sky Harbor Blvd Phoenix AZ

KRAMER, LAWRENCE ELIOT, musicologist, composer; b. Phila., Aug. 21, 1946; s. Arthur Kramer and Charlotte (Epstein) Ernst; m. Nancy Scott Leonard, Mar. 3, 1973; 1 child, Claire Kramer Leonard. BA, U. Pa., 1968; MPh, Yale U., 1970, PhD, 1972. Prof. U. Pa., Phila., 1972-78, Fordham U., N.Y.C., 1978—. Author: Music and Poetry: The Nineteenth Century and After, 1984, Music as Cultural Practice: 1800-1900, 1990, Classical Music and Postmodern Knowledge, 1995, After the Lovedeath: Sexual Violence and the Making of Culture, 1997, Franz Schubert: Sexuality, Subjectivity, Song, 1998, Musical Meaning: Toward A Critical History, 2001; editor: Nineteenth Century Music; composer (mus. composition) Break of Day, 1987, Jornada del Muerto, 1988, Thresholds, 1989, Ursound, 1991, A Ring of Light, 1993, Revenants, 1995. Mem. Am. Mus. Soc. Office: Fordham U Lincoln Ctr New York NY 10023

KRAMER, LINDA KONHEIM, curator, art historian; b. N.Y.C., Nov. 8, 1939; d. Clarence John and May (Sternberg) Konheim; m. Samuel R. Kramer, Apr. 24, 1977; 1 child, Nicholas Clarence. BA in Fine Arts and Art History, Smith Coll., 1961; BFA in Painting and Graphic Design, Yale U., 1963; MA in 19th and 20th Century European and Am. Art, NYU, 1968, PhD, 2000. Program adminstr. Solomon R. Guggenheim Mus., 1973-76; cataloger modern drawings Sotheby Park-Bernet, N.Y.C., 1980-82; expert in modern drawings Sotheby's N.Y., 1982-85; curator prints and drawings, dept. head Bklyn. Mus., 1985-94. Tchr. Sch. Visual Arts, N.Y.C., 1977-80, Manhattanville Coll., summer 1995, 96; exec. dir. Nancy Graves Found., N.Y.C., 1996—; mem. adv. bd. Coll. Fine Arts, West Wash. U., Bellingham, 1987-95. Author books, pamphlets and catalogs; contbr. articles to profl. jours. Grantee Nat. Mus. Act, 1976, 78; Jane and Morgan Whitney fellow Met. Mus. Art, 1995-96. Mem. Am. Assn. Mus., Print Coun. Am., Art Table, Coll. Art Assn. Home: 372 Central Park W New York NY 10025-8240 Office: Nancy Graves Found 450 W 31st St 2d Fl New York NY 10001-4608 E-mail: mail@nancygravesfoundation.org.

KRAMER, MARY ELIZABETH, state legislator, health services executive; b. Burlington, Iowa, June 14, 1935; d. Ross L. and Geneva M. (McElhinney) Barnett; m. Kay Frederick Kramer, June 13, 1958; children: Kent, Krista. BA, U. Iowa, 1957, MA, 1971. Cert. tchr., Iowa. Tchr. Newton (Iowa) Pub. Schs., 1957-61, Iowa City Pub. Schs., 1961-67, tchr., asst. supt., 1971-75; dir. pers. Younkers, Inc., Des Moines, 1975-81; v.p. Wellmark, Inc., Des Moines, 1981-99; mem. Iowa Senate from 37th dist., Des Moines, 1990—; pres. of the senate, 1997—. Mem. Olympic adv. com. Blue Cross and Blue Shield Assn., Chgo., 1988—92; presdl. appointee White House Commn. on Presdl. Scholars, 2001, now chmn.; Bd. dirs. Polk County Child Care Rsch. Ctr., Des Moines, 1986—96, YWCA, Des Moines, 1989—94. Named Mgr. of Yr. Iowa Mgmt. Assocs., 1985, Woman of Achievement YWCA, 1986, Woman of Vision Young Women's Resource Ctr., 1989. Mem. Soc. Human Resource Mgmt. (Profl. of Yr. 1996), Iowa Mgmt. Assn. (pres. 1988), Greater Des Moines C. of C. (bd. dirs. 1986-96), Nexus, Rotary Internat. Republican. Presbyterian. Avocations: music, public speaking. Home: 13598 Village Ct Clive IA 50325 Office: Iowa State Senate State Capitol Des Moines IA 50319-0001 E-mail: mkramer@legis.state.ia.us., kaynmary@aol.com.

KRAMER, MEYER, lawyer, editor, clergyman; b. Russia, Feb. 4, 1919; came to U.S., 1927, naturalized, 1933; s. Chaim and D'vorah (Kotzin) K.; m. Rose Schnabel, Dec. 22, 1944; children: Doniel, Rena, Tamar, Shira. BA, Yeshiva Coll., 1940; postgrad., Rabbi Isaac Elchanan Theol. Sem., 1941; LL.B., U. Pa., 1944. Bar: Pa. 1944; ordained rabbi, 1941. Law clk. Superior Ct. Pa., 1944-45; atty. Opinion Writing Office, SEC, 1945-46; lectr. U. Pa. Law Sch., 1947-69; rabbi Adath Zion, Phila., 1951-67, Beth Tefilath Israel, Phila., 1967-72, Bustleton-Somerton Synagogue, Phila., 1972-75; editl. cons. The Orchard, 1988-2001. Dir. Office Periodicals, Am. Law Inst-Am. Bar Assn., Phila., 1972-84, dir. Office Publs., 1984-87; bd. dirs. Gratz Coll., Beth Jacob Schs., Phila., Talmudical Yeshiva Phila., Hapoel-Hamizrachi, Phila. Author: (with A. Leo Levin) Conservative Ketubah; editor Ali-ABA CLE Rev., 1972-84, ALI-ABA Course Materials Jour., 1976-84, CLE Register, 1979-84; assoc. editor Jewish Horizon, 1960-62, Practical Lawyer, 1972-84. Mem. Rabbinical Coun. Phila. (pres. 1966-68, 90-92), Rabbinical Coun. Am., Rabbinic Alumni Yeshiva U. (v.p. 1960-68). Home: 1401 Ocean Ave Brooklyn NY 11230-3971

KRAMER, MICHAEL STUART, pediatric epidemiologist; b. N.Y.C., July 8, 1948; arrived in Can., 1978; s. George and Beatrice (Jacobs) K.; m. Claire Yael Sasportas, June 14, 1981; children: Eric, Elise, Philippe. BA, U. Chgo., 1969; MD, Yale U., 1973. Diplomate Am. Bd. Pediatrics, Am. Coll. Epidemiology. Intern in pediat. Yale New Haven (Conn.) Hosp., 1973-74, resident in pediat., 1974-76; fellow clin. epidemiology Yale U., 1976-78; asst. prof. faculty medicine McGill U., Montreal, Que., Can., 1978-82, assoc. prof., 1982-87, prof., 1987—. Com. mem. U.S. Inst. of Medicine/NAS, Washington, 1986—; vis. scientist Nat. Perinatal Epidemiology Unit, Oxford, Eng., 1991-92; cons. WHO, Geneva, 1984—, Nat. Health Rsch. Scientist, Nat. Health R & D Program, Can., 1992-97; disting. scientist Can. Inst. Health Rsch., 1997—2002; sr. investigator Can. Inst. Health Rsch., 2002—. Author: Clinical Epidemiology and Biostatistics, 1988, Nutrition During Pregnancy, 1990, Adverse Events Associated With Childhood Vaccines, 1994. Violinist:New Haven Symphony, 1969-73, I Medici di McGill, Montreal, 1990-94. Nat. Health Rsch. scholar, 1982-88; recipient Prix d'excellence Insvc. Clubs Coun. Que., Montreal, 1987, Chercheur Boursier Sr. FRSQ, Que., 1988-91, Rsch. award Ambulatory Pediatric Assn., 1993. Mem. Soc. Pediatric Rsch. (coun. mem. 1986-89), Soc. Epidemiol. Rsch., Soc. Pediatric and Perinatal Epidemiol. Rsch. (pres. 1997-98). Avocations: chamber music (violin), skiing, hiking, tennis, squash. Office: McGill U 2300 Tupper St Montreal QC Canada H3H 1P3 E-mail: Michael.Kramer@mcgill.ca.

KRAMER, PAMELA KOSTENKO, librarian; b. Mar. 5, 1944; d. Barry Michael and Helene (Ullrich) Kostenko; m. Claude Richard Kramer, Aug. 17, 1966. AB, U. Ill., 1966; MALS, Rosary Coll., 1973. Tchr. English United Twp. H.S., East Moline, Ill., 1966-70, audiovisual libr., 1970-76; instr. Marycrest Coll., Davenport, Iowa, 1973-75; libr. United Twp. H.S., 1976-81, libr., audio visual dept. head, 1981-87; asst. libr. Libertyville (Ill.) H.S., 1987-92, Barrington (Ill.) H.S., 1992; dep. exec. dir. Am. Assn. Sch. Librs., 1993-97; owner Pamela K. Kramer and Assocs., Sch. Libr. Cons., 1997—. Sch. libr. cons.; instr. Virtual Ill. LTA program Coll. DuPage, 1999-2000; dir. youth and sch. and acad. svcs. DuPage Libr. Sys., 2000—. Author audiovisual software revs. for Previews mag., Sch. Libr. Jour., 1973-80; contbr. articles to Ill. Librs. mag. and Ill. English Bull. mag., Sch. Libr. Media Activities monthly mag.; prin. writer Linking for Learning, The Illinois School Library Media Guidelines. Trustee River Bend Libr. Sys., 1986-87; chair alumni bd. libr. and info. sci. Dominican U. Recipient Polestar award ISLMA, 1992, Exemplary Svc. award Dominican U., 2000; Edmund J. James scholar, 1962-66. Mem. ALA, NEA, Ill. Sch. Libr. Media Assn. (state pres. 1990-91, editor ISLMA news 1992-2000), Ill. State Libr. (adv. com. 1991-94, chair subcom. Interlibr. coop. 1993-94), Ill. Libr. Assn., Ill. Edn. Assn., Am. Assn. Sch. Librs., Young Adult Libr. Svcs. Assn., Beta Phi Mu. Home: 326 Stillwater Ct Wauconda IL 60084-2908 E-mail: pkramer@dupagels.lib.il.us.

KRAMER, PAUL R. lawyer; b. Balt., June 6, 1936; s. Philip and Lee (Labovitz) K.; m. Janet Amitin, Sept. 1, 1957; children: Jayne, Susan, Nancy. BA, Am. U., 1959, JD, 1961. Bar: Md. 1961, D.C. 1962, U.S. Supreme Ct. 1965, U.S. Ct. Appeals (6th cir.) 1992, U.S. Dist. Ct. 1963, U.S. Ct. Appeals (4th cir.) 1964, U.S. Ct. Appeals (9th cir.) 1996. Staff atty., dep. dir. Legal Aid Agy. Fed. Pub. Defender's Office, Washington, 1962-63; asst. U.S. atty. Dist. Md., 1963-69; dep. U.S. atty. Md. Balt., 1969-83; exec. bd. Balt. area coun. Boy Scouts Am., 1970-83, coun. adv. bd. Balt. area, 1983—, N.E. regional adv. bd., 1999—. Instr. U. Md. Sch. Law, 1975-80; assoc. prof. law Villa Julie Coll., 1976-80; assoc. professorial lectr. George Washington U., 1979; instr. Nat. Coll. Dist. Attys., 1979; permanent mem. 4th cir. fed. jud. conf. Mem. ABA, Fed. Bar Assn. (pres. Md. chpt. 1973-74, nat. dep. sec. 1981-82, nat. sec. 1982-83, nat. cir. v.p. 1973-81, 86-87, cir. officer 4th cir. 1992-93, v.p. 4th cir. 1996-02, chmn. nat. cir. v.p. 1978-80, nat. coun. 1973—, jud. selection com. 1971-79, 88-90, faculty Fed Practice Inst. 1981-86, strategic long range planning com. 1995-96), Md. Bar Assn. (subcom. litig. dist. ct. 1990—), Balt. Bar Assn. (jud. selection com. 1992—, chair judiciary sub-com. on policy 1993-94, criminal law com., 1990—, chair criminal law com. 1994-95, atty. grievance commn. of Md. 1993—, inquiry com., drug ct. com. 1994-95, dist. ct. com. 1990—), Nat. Assn. Criminal Trial Attys., Md. Trial Lawyers Assn., Md. Criminal Def. Atty.'s Assn., U.S. Atty. Alumni Assn. (bd. dirs. 2003), Barrister's Law Club (pres. 2003—) Masons (past master). Office: Jefferson Bldg 101 North Charles St #700 Baltimore MD 21201-3342

KRAMER, PETER ROBIN, computer company executive; b. N.Y.C., Sept. 29, 1951; s. Morris and Ruth (Soloway) K.; m. Gerry Festo, Aug. 25, 1985. BA in Fine Arts, SUNY, Stony Brook, 1973; MFA, L.I. U., 1975. Dir., gen. ptnr. Doll & Richards Gallery, Boston, 1979-81; exec. v.p. and dir. Zoom Telephonics, Inc., Boston, 1977—. Bd. dirs. Cambridge Art Assn., 1983-86, pres. 1986-88; mem. nat. adv. bd. Coll. Arts and Scis. SUNY, Stony Brook, 1999-; dir. Intermute, Inc., 2000-. Avocations: old houses, fine arts, antiques, tennis, golf.

KRAMER, PHILIP JOSEPH, lawyer; b. Binghamton, N.Y., May 1, 1936; s. Donald W. and Gladys M. (Dorion) K.; m. Barbara E. Fisher, July, 1960; children: Perry, Donald, Matthew, Sharon. BA, Yale U., 1958; LLB, Cornell U., 1961. Bar: N.Y. 1961, U.S. Dist. Ct. (no. dist.) N.Y. 1961. Assoc. Kramer, Wales & Robinson, Binghamton, 1961-64, ptnr., 1964-78; justice, 6th Jud. Dist. N.Y. Supreme Ct., 1978; ptnr. Kramer, Wales & McAvoy, Binghamton, 1979-84, Kramer, Wales & Wright, Binghamton, 1984-95, Kramer & Kenyon, 1996-98; spl. counsel Hinman, Howard & Kattell. Pres. Binghamton Local Devel. Agy., 1982-87. Fellow Am. Coll. Trial Lawyers; mem. N.Y. State Bar Assn., Broome County Bar Assn. (pres. 1982). Democrat. Roman Catholic. Avocations: fishing, hunting. Office: 700 Security Mut Bldg 80 Exchange St PO Box 5250 Binghamton NY 13902-5250 Fax: (607) 723-6605. E-mail: pkramer@hhk.com.

KRAMER, RANDOLPH JOHN, bank executive; b. Cin., July 14, 1955; s. Anthony and Gerda Margareta Kramer; m. Sally Jo Buchanan, Aug. 13, 1977. BA, Washington and Lee U., 1977. Salesman Color Tile Inc., Cin., 1978; loan officer Midland Guardian Fin., Cin., 1978—81; br. mgr. ITT Fin. Inc., Cin., 1981—85; mgr. ops. Glenway Loan and Deposit Co., Cin., 1985—86, v.p. ops., 1987—92; sr. v.p. ops. Centennial Savs. Bank, Cin., 1993—97; v.p. ops. Eagle Savs. Bank, Cin., 1998—. Dir. Oak Hills Coop. Bus. Assn., Cin., 1990—91, chmn. audit/compliance com. Tri-State League of Fin. Instns., Cin., 1999—2002. Mem. Delhi Bus. Assn., Cin., 1998—; treas. Lions Club Price Hill, Ohio, 1985—90, dir., 1990—94, treas., 1999—, v.p., 2003—. Avocations: collecting phonograph records, collecting board games, golf, tennis, travel. Office: Eagle Savs Bank 5148 Delhi Pike Cincinnati OH 45238

KRAMER, RICHARD JAY, gastroenterologist, educator; b. Morristown, N.J., Mar. 31, 1947; s. Bernard and Estelle (Mishkin) K.; m. Leslie Fay Davis, June 28, 1970; children: Bryan Jeffrey, Erik Seth Davis. Student, UCLA, 1965-68; MD, U. Calif., Irvine, 1972. Diplomate Am. Bd. Internat. Med., Am. Bd. Gastroenterology. Intern Los Angeles County Harbor Gen. Hosp., Torrance, Calif., 1972-73; resident Santa Clara Valley Med. Ctr., San Jose, Calif., 1973-76; fellow gastroent. Stanford (Calif.) U. Hosp., 1976-78; pvt. practice San Jose, 1978—2003; tchr. gastroenterology Santa Clara Valley Med. Ctr., San Jose, 2003—. Clin. assoc. prof. of medicine Stanford (Calif.) U., 1984—; chmn. med. dept. Good Samaritan Hosp., San Jose, 1988-90. Pres. Jewish Family Service Bd., San Jose, 1974. Recipient Regents scholarship U. Calif., 1965, 68, Mosby Book award, Mosby Books, Inc., Irvine, Calif., 1972. Mem. Am. Coll. Physicians, Calif. Med. Soc., Santa Clara County Med. Soc., No. Calif. Soc. Clin. Gastroenterologists, Internat. Brotherhood Magicians, Mystic 13 (pres. 1986-87, San Jose), Masons, Alpha Omega Alpha. Democrat. Jewish. Avocations: magic, piano, tennis, traveling. Office: 751 Bas Com Ave San Jose CA 95128

KRAMER, RONALD E. neurologist, neurophysiologist; b. Pitts., July 16, 1954; m. Leslie P. Kramer, Apr. 17, 1981. BA, Johns Hopkins U., 1976; MD, Pa. State U., 1981. Diplomate in neurology and in neurophysiology Am. Bd. Psychiatry and Neurology; diplomate Am. Bd. Sleep Medicine. Intern George Washington U., Washington, 1981-82; resident Georgetown U., Washington, 1982-85; fellow Cleve. Clinic, 1985-86, assoc. staff, 1986-87; staff Oreg. Epilepsy Program, Portland, 1987-90; dir. epilepsy and sleep programs Colo. Neurol. Inst., Denver, 1990—. Office: Colo Neurol Inst 701 E Hampden Ave Englewood CO 80110-2736

KRAMER, SHERRI MARCELLE, gemologist, jeweler; b. Phila., Apr. 14, 1954; d. Irvin and Rhoda Pearl (Levin) K.; m. Peter MacPhee, Oct. 18, 1997. Student, Montgomery C.C., 1971-73; BA, Rutgers U., 1975; paralegal asst., U. Md., 1977; MA in Bus. Adminstrn., Am. World U., 1999; postgrad., Gemological Inst. Am., 2000—03. Asst. to counsel U.S. Senator Jacob K. Javits, Washington, 1974-77; legis. asst. U.S. Senator Orrin G. Hatch, Washington, 1977-78; asst. project dir. Coun. Exceptional Children, Reston, Va., 1978-79; sr. legis. analyst Alliance Am. Insurers, Chgo., 1979-83; dir. legis. monitoring Ins. Svcs. Offices, N.Y.C., 1983-86; pres. Kramer Consulting, Ltd., Tampa, Fla., 1986-87; asst. dir. Tampa Jewish Fedn., 1987-89; assoc. exec. dir. Jacksonville (Fla.) Jewish Fedn., 1989-92; exec. dir. Ronald McDonald House of Jacksonville, 1992, Kramer Cons., Ltd., 1993, Dynamic Bus. Solutions, Milton Mills, NH, 1992—98; owner Regency Gems & Jewelry, 2000—. Dir. Dept. Econ. & Cmty. Devel., Farmington, N.H., 1998-2000; legis. and technical cons. Voc-Ed Handbook for Disabled, Univ. Wis., 1980; instr. Women's Bus. Ctr., Portsmouth, N.H., 1996-98; exec. bd. mem. York County Devel. Corp., 1996-2001; adv. com. on bus. adminstrn. York County Tech. Coll., Wells, Maine, 1996-2001; adj. instr. in small bus. York County Tech. Coll., 1999-2001. Co-author: Retraining Special Educators in Career Education, 1979. Del., Hillsborough County Human Rights Commn., Tampa, 1987-89, Interfaith Coun. Jacksonville, 1989-92; trustee Hillel Found. U. South Fla., Tampa, 1988-89; mem. Mayor's Coun. Reconciliation, 1992, Zoning Bd. Appeals, Acton, Maine, 1999-2001; bd. dirs. Jewish Family Svcs., So. Maine Econ. Devel. Dist., Sanford, 1999-2001. Mem. Orgn. for Rehab. and Tng., Greater Rochester C. of C., Women's Bus. Devel. Corp., Anti-Defamation League, Nat. Soc. Fundraising Execs., Montgomery County C.C. Alumni Assn. (bd. dirs. 1973-81), Gemological Inst. Am. Alumni Assn. Avocations: dogs, travel, politics, gemology. Home: 79 S Main St # 224 Rochester NH 03867 E-mail: info@regencygems.com.

KRAMER, SIDNEY B. publisher, lawyer, literary agent; b. N.Y.C., 1915; s. Louis and Mildred (Hindin) K.; m. Esther Schlansky, Nov. 23, 1939; children: Wendy Beth Kramer Posner, Mark William. BS, NYU, 1936; JD, Bklyn. Law Sch., St. Lawrence U., 1939. Bar: N.Y. 1940, Conn. 1962, U.S. Supreme Ct. 1975. Practice in, N.Y.C., 1940-45, Westport, Conn., 1963—; founder (1945), sr. v.p. Bantam Books, Inc., N.Y.C., 1945-67; founder (1950), mng. dir. Corgi Books, London, 1960-62; pres., dir. Remarkable Bookshop, 1960-95; pres. New Am. Library, N.Y.C., 1967-72, MEWS Books Ltd., Westport, Conn., 1975—. Mng. dir., cons. Cassell & Collier Macmillan Pubs. Ltd., London, 1973-74; chmn. Nat. Assn. Paperback Pubs., 1945-67 Chmn. Democratic Town Com., also justice peace, Westport, 1960—; chmn. Save Westport Now, 1981—. Recipient Westport Arts Heritage award for Lit., 2001. Mem. Conn. Bar Assn. Office: 20 Bluewater Hill Westport CT 06880-6504 E-mail: mewsbooks@aol.com.

KRAMER, SIMON PAUL, writer; b. Cin., Aug. 17, 1914; s. Simon Pendleton and Minnie (Halle) K.; m. Marie Louise Belden, Jan. 5, 1955 (div. 1968); 1 child, Theresa. BA, Princeton U., 1935; MLitt, Trinity Coll., Cambridge, Eng., 1938. Spl. asst. coord. Inter-Am. Affairs, Washington, 1940-43; staff CIA, Washington, 1947-51; ptnr. Auerbach, Pollak and Richardson, N.Y.C., 1954-57; pres. Conporacion Industrial, Panama, 1954-57, Panama Coop. Fisheries, 1957-60; staff cons. IGY-Nat. Acad. Scis., Washington, 1956-57, 60-62. Author: The Last Manchu, 1967, 2d edit. 1987, Latin American Panorama, 1968, The City in American Life, 1970, Nelson Rockefeller and British Security Coordination in Sage Readers in 20th Century History, 1982. Lt. USNR, 1943-46. Republican. Avocations: politics, gardening, bridge. Home and Office: 3023 Dent Pl NW Washington DC 20007-2916 E-mail: sptk@erols.com.

KRAMER, TIMOTHY EUGENE, lawyer; b. Cleve., Mar. 21, 1943; s. Theodore Eugene and Margaret Agnes (Vargo) Kramer; m. Jacqueline Marie Rini, May 30, 1969; children: Thomas, Kathleen, Anne. BA, John Carroll U., 1965; JD, Case Western Res. U., 1968. Bar: Ohio 1969. Law clk. Cuyahoga County Common Pleas Ct., Cleve., 1970—72, chief law clk., 1972—73; asst. counsel Jacobs, Visconsi & Jacobs Co., Cleve., 1973-78; corp. counsel Revco D.S. Inc., Twinsburg, Ohio, 1978-93, sr. corp. counsel, 1993-97; legal counsel CVS Pharmacy, Twinsburg, 1997-2000, sr. legal counsel, 2000—. Lectr. in field. Served with U.S. Army, 1968-70. Mem. Ohio State Bar Assn. Roman Catholic. Home: 31710 Birch Cir Solon OH 44139-1636 Office: CVS Pharmacy Inc 1920 Enterprise Pkwy Twinsburg OH 44087-2207

KRAMISH, ARNOLD, physicist, historian, author; b. Denver, June 6, 1923; m. Vivian Ruth Raker, Aug. 19, 1952; children: Pamela, Robert. BS, U. Denver, 1945; A.M., Harvard U., 1947. With Manhattan Project, 1944-46, AEC, 1946-51; sr. staff mem. Rand Corp., Santa Monica, Calif., 1951-68; v.p. Inst. for the Future, Washington, 1968-70; sci. attache U.S. Mission to UNESCO, Paris, 1970-73; counselor for sci. and tech. affairs U.S. Mission to OECD, Paris, 1974-76; sci. research R & D Assocs., Arlington, Va., 1976-81; ind. tech. cons., 1981—; tech. dir. White House Study preliminary to Strategic Def. Initiative, 1981—84; advisor Undersecretary of Def. for Policy, 1984—91; assoc. Global Bus. Access Ltd., 1991—. Prof. UCLA, 1965-66, London Sch. Econs., 1967-68; adj. prof. internat. studies U. Miami, Fla., 1969; fellow Woodrow Wilson Internat. Ctr. for Scholars, 1982-83; Rockefeller scholar, Bellagio, Italy, 1984; pres. Tech. Analysis Internat., 1983—. Author: Atomic Energy for Your Business, 1956, Atomic Energy in the Soviet Union, 1959, The Peaceful Atom in Foreign Policy, 1963, The Future of Non-Nuclear Nations, 1970, The Griffin, 1986; also numerous articles, book chpts.; patentee nuclear radiometer. Sci. advisor European Cmty., 1960-62. With AUS, 1943-46. Carnegie fellow Coun. on Fgn. Rels., 1958-59; John Simon Guggenheim fellow, 1966-67; Rsch. fellow Inst. for Strategic Studies, London, 1966-67; Sr. fellow Global Access Inst., 1994—. Mem. PEN, Authors Guild. Office: PO Box 2621 Reston VA 20195-0621 E-mail: Kramish@post.harvard.edu.

KRAMM, DEBORAH ANN, information technology executive; b. Pasadena, June 24, 1949; d. Donald F. and Mary (Roach) Coonan; m. Kenneth R. Kramm, Dec. 20, 1969; children: Deidre Lyn, Jonathan Russel. BA, U. Calif., Irvine, 1971; MS, Mich. Tech. U., 1981. Math. asst. NASA-Jet Propulstion Lab., Pasadena, 1967-70; libr. asst. U. Calif. Irving Libr., 1967-71; rsch. assoc. animal behavior lab. Mich. Tech. U., Houghton, 1971-80; programmer, analyst Shell Oil Co., Houston, 1981-85, corp. auditor EDP, 1985-87; team leader SLA, 1988-90, supr. resource planning adminstrn., 1990-91, adminstrv. coord. product devel. ctr.-design ctr., 1991-93, bus. analyst sr. systems analyst, 1993-96, engagement mgr., 1996-97, mgr. engagement svc., 1998-99, mgr. sales and contract support, 1999—2001; prin. cons. Shell IT Internat., 2001—03; sr. learning cons. Shell Learning, 2003—. Chmn. bd. MMARK, Houston, 1983-85. Contbr. articles to profl. jours.; designer (program application software) Shell Point-of-Sale Terminal, 1982-85. Treas. KFHS Orch., 1986-88; co-leader Boy Scouts Am., Houston, 1981-83. AAUW scholar, 1980, Calif. State scholar, 1967-71. Mem.: AAUW (pres. br. 1975—81), Inst. Mgmt. Cons., CMC, Shell Data Processors Club, Houston Bus. Forum (pres. bd. dirs.), Assn. for Women in Computing (membership bd. dirs.). Home: 5814 Pinewilde Dr Houston TX 77066-2324 Office: Shell Oil Co PO Box 2463 Houston TX 77252-2463

KRANE, JESSICA (AIDA JESSICA KOHNOP-KRANE), writer, educator; b. Chgo., July 5, 1920; d. Samuel Rubenstein and Esther Ginsburg; m. Louis Kohnop, Jan. 11, 1956. Student, Roosevelt U., 1952—55. Writer, concert pianist, lectr. Appearences on varous TV programs including The Tonight Show, To Tell the Truth, The Today Show. Author: Face-O-Metrics, How to Use Your Hands to Save Your Face, The Sensuous Approach to Looking Younger; contbr.: memoir Born Again Vision, deput as pianist: Orchestra Hall, 1956; musician (toured U.S. and Canada with): Louis Kohnop; musician: Bklyn. Mus., WNYC, NY Town Hall, cmty. concerts. Avocation: fashion design. Home: 4400 Hillcrest Dr Apt 720 Hollywood FL 33021

KRANE, STEPHEN MARTIN, physician, educator; b. N.Y.C., July 15, 1927; s. Daniel Golden and Bessie (Berman) K.; m. Cynthia Ramin, June 28, 1952; children: David Alan, Peter Jay, Ian Matthew, Adam. AB, Columbia U., 1946, MD, 1951; A.M. (hon.), Harvard U., 1968; MD (hon.), U. Geneva, 1989. Intern to chief resident in medicine Mass. Gen. Hosp., Boston, 1951-57, chief arthritis unit, 1961, physician, 1969—2001; research fellow Washington U., St. Louis, 1956; asst. in medicine Harvard U. Med. Sch., Boston, 1958, prof., 1972-87, Persis, Cyrus and Marlow B. Harrison prof. clin. medicine, 1987—. Contbr. articles to profl. jours. Served with USNR, 1945-46. Recipient Kappa Delta award Orthopedic Rsch. Soc., 1977, Herberden medal Herberden Soc., London, 1980; named Guggenheim fellow Oxford U., 1973-74. Fellow ACP, AAAS, Am. Acad. Arts and Scis., Am. Coll. Rheumatology (master, Disting. Investigator award 1995); mem. Am. Soc. Clin. Investigation, Assn. Am. Physicians, Am. Fedn. Clin. Rsch., Am. Soc. Biol. Chemistry, Molecular Biology, Soc. Bone Mineral Rsch., Endocrine Soc. Home: 101 Windsor Rd Newton MA 02468-1121 Office: Mass Genl Hosp Boston MA 02114 E-mail: krane.stephen@mgh.harvard.edu.

KRANE, STEVEN CHARLES, lawyer; b. Far Rockaway, N.Y., Jan. 20, 1957; s. Harry and Gloria (Christle) K.; m. Faith Marston, Oct. 1, 1983; children: Elizabeth Jordan, Cameron Marston. BA, SUNY, Stony Brook, 1978; JD, NYU, 1981. Bar: N.Y. 1982, U.S. Dist. Ct. (so. and ea. dists.) N.Y. 1982, U.S. Ct. Appeals (2d and 6th cirs.) 1987, U.S. Supreme Ct. 1987, U.S. Ct. Appeals (1st and 3d cir.) 2000. Ptnr. Proskauer Rose LLP, N.Y.C.; law clk. to Assoc. Judge Judith S. Kaye N.Y. Ct. Appeals, N.Y.C. and Albany, 1984-85. Lectr. in law Columbia U. Sch. Law, N.Y.C., 1989-92; vis. prof. Ga. Inst. of Tech., 1994-96; mem. departmental disciplinary com. Appellate divsn. 1st Jud. dept. Supreme Ct. N.Y., 1996-2000, spl. trial counsel, 1991-93. Editor articles, NYU Jour. Internat. Law and Politics, 1980-81. Securities Inst. NYU fellow, 1980-81; recipient Vol. Counsel award Legal Aid Soc., 1984. Fellow Am. Bar Found. (chmn. N.Y. state), N.Y. Bar Found.; mem. ABA, N.Y. Bar Assn. (com. on stds. of atty. conduct, chmn. 1999-, com. on profl. ethics 1990-94, spl. com. to rev. the code of profl. responsibility 1992-95, chmn. 1995-99, vice chair spl. com. on future of profession 1997-2000, ho. of dels. 1996—, com. on mass disaster response 1997—, com. on multidisciplinary practice and legal profession 1998-99, exec. com. 1998-2003, mem.-at-large, exec. com. 1998-2000, spl. com. on law gov. firm structure and ops., vice chair 1999—2002, chair 2002-, pres. 2001-02, pres. com. on access to justice, co-chair 2000-01, spl. assn. ho. com. chair 2000-2001), Assn. of Bar of City of N.Y. (com. on profl. and jud. ethics 1990-93, chmn. 1993-96, sec 1985-88, com. on profl. responsibility, chmn. subcom. provision legal svcs. 1985-88, com. on fed. cts. 1996-99, com. Marden Meml. lecture 2000—, chmn. del. to N.Y. State Bar Assn. ho. dels. 1997-98, internat. security affairs 2001-03), Am. Law Inst., Federalist Soc. (profl. responsibility practice group exec. com. 1999—), Hist. Soc. Cts. of State of NY (trustee 2001—), Phi Beta Kappa, Pi Sigma Alpha. Republican. Avocations: military history, meteorology, boston red sox baseball. Office: Proskauer Rose LLP 1585 Broadway 17th Fl New York NY 10036-8299 E-mail: skrane@proskauer.com.

KRANE, VIKKI, psychology educator; d. Mark and Penny Krane. PhD, Univ. of N.C., Greensboro, 1990. Prof. sport psychology Bowling Green State U., Bowling Green, Ohio, 1990—. Editor: The Sport Psychologist; contbr. Fellow Rsch. consortium fellow, AAHPERD, 1992. Fellow: Assn. for the Advancement of Applied Sport Psychology (secretary-treasurer 1994—97, cert. cons.); mem.: AAHPERD, N.Am. Soc. for the Psychology of Sport and Phys. Activity. Office: Bowling Green State U Sch HMSLS Eppler Ctr Bowling Green OH 43403

KRANEPOOL, HARRY ANTHONY, science educator; b. Bklyn., July 26, 1941; s. Harry M. and Marie R. (Sorrentino) K. BS, St. Francis Coll., Bklyn., 1962; MSED, Bklyn. Coll., 1972; MA in Edn., CCNY, 1977. Cert. sci., math., biology and chemistry tchr., N.Y., N.J., Pa. Sci. chmn. Bishop Loughlin Meml. H.S., Bklyn., 1968—. Author: Chemistry, A Modern Approach, 1977-87, rev. edits., 1992, 96. Recipient BQ Stanys Svc. award, 1999. NSTA Disting. Svc. award, 2002. Mem. Sci. Assn. Tchrs. N.Y. (fellows award), LIUNA-AFL-CIO (pres. LFA 1261), N.Y. State Coun. of Ednl. Assns. (pres. 1989-93), NSTA (dir. Region II 1990-92), Stanys (pres. 1987-89, Svc. award 1985), Sci. Coun. N.Y.C. (pres. 1998-2000), N.Y. State Sci. Olympiad (treas. 1995—). Democrat. Roman Catholic. Home: 31-31 138th St Apt 4D Flushing NY 11354-2625 Office: Lay Faculty Assn Local 1261 13825A 31st Dr Flushing NY 11354-2664 Fax: 718-539-6447. E-mail: lfahak@aol.com.

KRANIS, MICHAEL DAVID, lawyer, judge; b. N.Y.C., Aug. 17, 1955; s. Herbert and Mildred (Swartz) K.; m. Patricia Ann Pagano, Sept. 29, 1989. BA, SUNY, Albany, 1977; JD, Union U., 1980. Bar: N.Y. 1981, U.S. Dist. Ct. (so. and ea. dists.) N.Y. 1983. Law clk. to hon. judge Robert C. William N.Y. Supreme Ct., Monticello, 1980-82; prin. Michael D. Kranis, P.C., Poughkeepsie, N.Y., 1982-88; ptnr. Coombs, Kranis & Wing, Poughkeepsie, 1988-94; sole practitioner Poughkeepsie, 1995—. Asst. corp. counsel City of Poughkeepsie, 1983-85, hearing officer, 1985—; adj. prof. D.C. C.C., Poughkeepsie, 1984-87; judge Town of Pleasant Valley, N.Y., 1988-97; gen. counsel Grace Smith House, Inc., Poughkeepsie, 1983-95; adj. prof. Marist Coll., 1993. Mem. exec. com. Dutchess County Rep. Com., Pleasant Valley, 1997-2000, 2001-, Jud. Nominating Com., Dutchess County, 1987, 97-2000; mem. DC Republican Com., 1985-87, 97—; mem. Pleasant Valley Planning Bd., 1984-86; bd. dir., chmn., vice chmn. Task Force for Child Protection, Inc., 1992-2000; mem. bd. dir. Dutchess County Econ. Devel. Corp., 1994-2003, Child Abuse Prevention Ctr., Inc., 1994-2003, Pleasant Valley Little League, v.p., 2001—, chmn. Town of Pleasant Valley Rep. Com., 2001—. Mem. N.Y. State Bar Assn. (ho. of dels.), Dutchess County Bar Assn. (pres. 1998-99, treas., v.p. 1996, pres.-elect 1997, chmn. fee dispute com., chmn. bar endowment, v.p.), Dutchess County Magistrates Assn., N.Y. State Magistrates Assn., Rotary (pres., bd. dirs. Pleasant Valley chpt. 1985-97, Paul Harris fellow 1987). Office: 2 Jefferson Pl Poughkeepsie NY 12601

KRANITZ, THEODORE MITCHELL, lawyer; b. St. Joseph, Mo., May 27, 1922; s. Louis and Miriam (Saferstein) K.; m. Elaine Shirley Kaufman, June 11, 1944; children: Hugh David, Karen Gail and Kathy Jane (twins). Student, St. Joseph Jr. Coll., 1940-41; BS in Fgn. Svc., Georgetown U., 1948, JD, 1950. Bar: Mo. 1950, U.S. Supreme Ct. 1955. Pres., sr. ptnr. Kranitz & Kranitz, PC, St. Joseph, 1950—. Author articles in field Pres. St. Joseph Cmty. Theatre, Inc., 1958-60; bd. dirs. United Jewish Fund St. Joseph, 1957—, pres., 1958-63; sec. Boys' Baseball St. Joseph, 1964-68; trustee Temple Adath Joseph, 1970-74, 77-80; bd. dirs. B'nai Sholem Temple, 1976—, Lyric Opera Guild Kansas City, 1980-91; founder, pres. St. Joseph Light Opera Co., Inc., 1989-90; mem. St. Joseph Postal Customers Adv. Coun., 1993—, chmn., 1993-95; mem., sec. St. Joseph Downtown Assn., 1995-97. Mem. Mo. Bar, St. Joseph Bar Assn. (pres. 1977-78), Am. Legion, Air Force Assn., B'nai B'rith (dist. bd. govs. 1958-61). Home: 2609 Gene Field Rd Saint Joseph MO 64506-1615 Office: Kranitz & Kranitz PC Boder Bldg 107 S 4th St PO Box 968 Saint Joseph MO 64502-0968 Fax: (816) 232-8558. E-mail: kranitz@ponyexpress.net.

KRANSELER, LAWRENCE MICHAEL, lawyer; b. Newton, Mass., Oct. 28, 1958; s. Arthur Sheldon and Barbara Joan (Siegel) K.; m. Wendy Kranseler; children: Alex, Jenna, Lucas. BS in Econs., Boston Coll., 1980; MBA, JD, U. Pa., 1984. Bar: Mass. 1985, U.S. Dist. Ct. Mass. 1985. Assoc. Hale and Dorr, Boston, 1984-89; supervising sr. counsel Hasbro, Inc., Pawtucket, R.I., 1989-95, mng. atty., 1995-2000; v.p. Hasbro Inc., Pawtucket, R.I., 2001—; v.p., sec. Hasbro Interactive, Inc., Pawtucket, 1997—2000. Vol. mentor UCAP Mentoring Program. Bd. dirs., treas., chmn. fin. com., mem. exec. com., vol. Big Brother/Big Sister Assn.; fundraising capt. Am. Heart Assn., Combined Jewish Philanthropics; coach Town of Sharon Baseball, Town of Sharon Soccer, Town of Sharon Basketball. Recipient James E. Shaw Meml. award Pres. Boston Coll., 1980. Mem. ABA, Mass. Bar Assn., Boston Bar Assn., Phi Delta Phi. Home: 30 Sentry Hill Rd Sharon MA 02067-1522 Office: Hasbro Inc 1027 Newport Ave Pawtucket RI 02861-2500 E-mail: LKranseler@hasbro.com.

KRANTZ, DAVID S. medical psychology educator, researcher; b. N.Y.C., Feb. 9, 1949; s. Robert B. and Beatrice K.; m. Marsha L. Douma, June 27, 1982; children: Michael Douma, Della Krantz. BS, CCNY, 1971; PhD, U. Tex., 1975. Asst. prof. psychology U. So. Calif., L.A., 1975-78; asst. then assoc. prof. Uniformed Svcs. U. Health Scis., Bethesda, Md., 1978-87, prof. med. psychology, 1987—, prof., chmn. dept. med. and clin. psychology, 1999—; prof. psychiatry, medicine Georgetown U. Sch. Medicine, 1991—. Jour. editor, acad. leader med. sch. dept. Georgetown U. Sch. Medicine. Co-author: Behavior, Health and Environmental Stress, 1982, Introduction to Health Psychology, 1989, 97; assoc. editor: Health Psychology, 1988-93, editor-in-chief, 1994—2000; mem. editorial bd.: Psychosomatic Medicine, 1990—; contbr. more than 160 articles and chpts. to profl. publs. Named one of Outstanding Young Scientists in Am., Sci. Digest, 1984. Fellow APA (Outstanding Contbn. to Health Psychology award 1981, 2000, Disting. Sci. Early Career award 1982), Acad. Behavioral Medicine Rsch. (pres.1995), Am. Psychol. Soc. Achievements include research on the etiology of myocardial ischemia and arrhythmia, and research in behavioral cardiology. Office: Uniformed Svcs Univ of the Health Scis/Med Psychology 4301 Jones Bridge Rd Bethesda MD 20814-4712

KRANTZ, JUDITH TARCHER, novelist; b. N.Y.C., Jan. 9, 1928; d. Jack David and Mary (Brager) Tarcher; m. Stephen Falk Krantz, Feb. 19, 1954; children: Nicholas, Anthony. BA, Wellesley Coll., 1948. Fashion publicist, Paris, 1948-49; fashion editor Good Housekeeping mag., N.Y.C., 1949-56; contbg. writer McCalls, 1956-59, Ladies Home Jour., 1959-71; contbg. west coast editor Cosmopolitan mag., 1971-79. Author: Scruples, 1978, Princess Daisy, 1980, Mistral's Daughter, 1982, I'll Take Manhattan, 1986, Till We Meet Again, 1988, Dazzle, 1990, Scruples Two, 1992, Lovers, 1994, Spring Collection, 1996, The Jewels of Tessa Kent, 1998, Sex & Shopping: Confessions of a Nice Jewish Girl, 2000. Office: St Martin Press 175 5th Ave New York NY 10010*

KRANTZ, KERMIT EDWARD, physician, educator; b. Oak Park, Ill., June 4, 1923; s. Andrew Stanley and Beatrice H. (Cibrowski) K.; m. Doris Cole Krantz, Sept. 7, 1946; children: Pamela (Mrs. Richard Huffstutter), Sarah Elizabeth, Kermit Tripler. BS, Northwestern U., 1945, BM, MS in Anatomy, Northwestern U., 1947, MD, 1948; LittD (hon.), William Woods Coll., 1971. Diplomate Am. Bd. Ob-Gyn. Intern ob-gyn. N.Y. Lying-In Hosp., 1947-48; asst. resident, asst. ob-gyn. Cornell U. Med. Coll., N.Y. Lying-In Hosp., N.Y. Hosp., 1948-50; fellow, resident in ob-gyn Mary Fletcher Hosp., Burlington, Vt., 1950-51; dir. Durfee Clinic, 1952-55; instr., then asst. prof. U. Vt. Coll. Medicine, 1951-55; asst. prof. U. Ark. Med. Sch., 1955-59; prof., chmn. dept. ob-gyn. U. Kans. Med. Ctr., 1959-90, Univ. Disting. prof., 1990—92, prof. anatomy, 1963—, lectr. history medicine, 1959—, dean clin. affairs, 1972-74, chief staff, 1972-74, obstetrician and gynecologist in chief, 1959-90, assoc. to exec. vice chancellor for facilities devel., 1974-83; univ. disting. prof. emeritus ob/gyn. and anatomy U. Kans., 1994—. Cons. in field. Author numerous articles in field. Mem. Nat. Adv. Child Health and Human Devel. Council, NIH, 1974-76. Bowen-Brooks fellow N.Y. Acad. Medicine, 1948-50; recipient Found. award South Atlantic Assn. Obstetricians and Gynecologists, 1950, Found. award Am. Assn. Obstetricians and Gynecologists, 1950, Wyeth-Ayerst Pub. Recognition award 1st Am. Assn. Prof. of Gynecology and Obstetrics, 1988; named Outstanding Prof. in Coll. of Medicine Nu Sigma Nu, 1955; Robert A. Ross lectureship award Armed Forces Dist. meeting Am. Coll. Obstetricians and Gynecologists, 1972, Outstanding Civilian Service medal U.S. Army-Dept. Def., 1985; Charles A. Durham Meml. lectr. Ann. Session Tex. Med. Assn., 1978; Markle scholar med. sci., 1957-62; Kermit E. Krantz Soc. established at U. Kans. Med. Ctr., 1982. Founding fellow Am. Coll. Obstetricians and Gynecologists (Kermit E. Krantz Lectureship award established 1973, Outstanding Dist. Services award 1978, 82); fellow ACS, Am. Coll. Ob-Gyn (life); mem. Am. Assn. Anatomists, Am. Fedn. Clin. Research, AMA, Am. Med. Writers Assn., Am. Fertility Soc., AAUP, Soc. Exptl. Biology and Medicine, Aerospace Med. Assn., Endocrine Soc., Soc. Gynecologic Investigation, Central Assn. Obstetricians and Gynecologists, N.Y. Acad. Medicine, N.Y. Acad. Sci., Kans. Med. Soc., Assn. Mil. Surgeons U.S. (sustaining), Kans. Obstet. Soc., Sigma Xi, Alpha Omega Alpha. Home: 6711 Overhill Rd Shawnee Mission KS 66208-2263 Office: U Kans Med Ctr Kansas City KS 66160-0001

KRANTZ, LINDA LAW, librarian; b. Princeton, N.J., June 19, 1943; d. Harold Bell and Ruth Workman Law; m. David Walter Krantz, July 29, 1967. Student, Mt. Union Coll., 1961-63; BA in French Lit., U. Rochester, 1965; MLS, Rutgers State U., 1967. Libr. asst. Fine Hall Libr. Math. and Physics Princeton U., 1962—66; reference libr. Princeton Pub. Libr., 1966-67; cataloger NASA Lewis Rsch. Ctr., Cleve., 1967; reference libr. sci.-tech. Cleve. Pub. Libr., 1968-69; reference libr. Wright State U. Libr., Dayton, Ohio, 1969-73; libr. dir. Rockbridge Regional Libr., Lexington, Va., 1974—. Bd. dirs. Kendal. Musician (violinist): Rockbridge Orch., 1975—96, 1999—, Allegheny-Highlands Symphony Orch., 1997—. Mem.: ALA, Va. Pub. Libr. Dirs. Assn. (pres. 2002—03), Va. Libr. Assn. (go. co-chair 1997—99, George Mason award 1995), Lexington Rotary Club (bd. dirs. 1997, Paul Harris fellow 1996), Omicron Delta Kappa. Avocations: music, nature, reading, cats. Home: 151 Elliots Hill Ln Lexington VA 24450-7203 Office: Rockbridge Regional Libr 138 S Main St Lexington VA 24450-2316 E-mail: lkrantz@cfw.com., lkrantz@rrlib.net.

KRANTZ, STEVEN GEORGE, mathematics educator, writer; b. San Francisco, Feb. 3, 1951; s. Henry Alfred and Norma Oliva (Crisafulli) K.; m. Randi Diane Ruden, Sept. 7, 1974. BA, U. Calif., Santa Cruz, 1971; PhD, Princeton U, 1974. Asst. prof. UCLA, 1974-81; assoc. prof. Pa. State U., University Park, 1981-84, prof., 1984-86; prof. dept. math. Washington U., St. Louis, 1986—, chmn. dept. math., 1999—, divsn. head for sci. depts., 2002—. Adv. bd. Am. Inst. Math., Am. Math. Soc. book series; mng. editor Jour. Math. Analysis and Applications. Founder, mng. editor Jour. Geometric Analysis; editor-in-chief Jour. of Math. Analysis and Apps.; Author: Function Theory of Several Complex Variables (monograph), 1982, 2d edition, 1992, Complex Analysis: The Geometric Viewpoint, 1990, Real Analysis and Foundations, 1991, Partial Differential Equations and Complex Analysis, 1992, A Primer of Real Analytic Functions, 1992, Geometric Analysis and Function Spaces, 1993, How to Teach Mathematics, 1993, 2nd edit., 1999, A Tex Primer for Scientists, 1995, The Elements of Advanced Mathematics, 1995, 2d edit., 2002, Techniques of Problem Solving, 1996, Function Theory of One Complex Variable, 1997, A Primer of Mathematical Writing, 1996; (with H. R. Parks) The Geometry of Domains in Space, 1999, Contemporary Issues in Mathmatics Education, 1999, A Handbook of Complex Variables, 1999, A Panorama of Harmonic Analysis, 1999, Handbook of Typography for the Mathematical Sciences, 2000, The Implicit Function Theorem, 2002, Mathematical Apocrypha, 2002, Graduate School and Careers in Mathematics: A Survival Guide, 2003; cons. editor Birkhäuser Pub., 2002-, McGraw-Hill, 2002-; contbr. numerous rsch. articles to profl. publs. Recipient Disting. Tchg. award, UCLA Alumni Found., 1979:NSF

rsch. grantee, 1975—, Kemper grantee, 1994. Richardson fellow Australian Nat. U., 1995; mem. Am. Math. Soc. (prin. organizer summer rsch. inst. 1989), Math. Assn. Am. (Chauvenet prize, Beckenbach prize 1994), Textbook Authors Assn. E-mail: sk@math.wustl.edu.

KRANWINKLE, CONRAD DOUGLAS, broadcast executive; b. Elgin, Ill., Oct. 27, 1940; s. Conrad David and Helen Elvira (Walgren) K.; m. Susan Hall Warren, Aug. 24, 1962; children: Mark Conrad, Jane Shafer. BA, Northwestern U., 1962; JD, U. Mich., 1965. Bar: Calif. 1966, U.S. Dist. Ct. (ctrl. dist.) Calif. 1966, U.S. Ct. Appeals (9th cir.) 1966, N.Y. 1995. Law clk. to chief justice U.S. Supreme Ct., Washington, 1966-67; ptnr. Munger, Tolles & Olson, L.A., 1967-88, O'Melveny & Myers, L.A. and N.Y.C., 1989—, mng. ptnr., 1996—2000; exec. v.p. Univision Comms., INc., L.A., 2000—. Vis. prof. law U. Mich., winter 1993. Pres. Poly. Sch. Bd. Trustees, Pasadena, Calif., 1986-88; mgr. Rep. Gubernatorial campaign, Calif., 1973-74; chmn. U.S. Senate campaign, Calif., 1978. Mem. Am. Law Inst., Coun. on Fgn. Rels., Calif. C. of C. (bd. dirs. 1990-94), Calif. Club, Valley Hunt Club, River Club. Office: Univision Comms Inc 1999 Avenue of the Stars Los Angeles CA 90067 E-mail: dkranwinkle@univision.com.

KRANZ, JACK, university librarian, educator; b. L.A., Mar. 14, 1947; s. Leo and Blanche Kranz; m. Linda Kay Hoffman, Dec. 21, 1969; children: Jeremy Alan, Joshua Eli. BA, Calif. State U., 1970, MA, 1975; MLS, U. Calif., 1976. Libr. Calif. State U., Northridge, 1970—, instr. geography dept., 2001—; instr. L.A. Valley Coll., Valley Glen, 1998—, L.A. Pierce Coll., Woodland Hills, 1999—. Libr. rep. Calif. Faculty Assn., L.A., 1997—2000; bd. mem. Soc. Preservation Film Music, L.A., 1992—95. Democrat. Jewish. Achievements include research in web-based information access. Avocations: theater, travel. Office: California State U 18111 Nordhoff St Northridge CA 91330-8326 E-mail: jack.kranz@csun.edu.

KRANZ, KENNETH LOUIS, human resources company executive, entrepreneur; b. Evanston, Ill., July 7, 1946; s. Kenneth Louis Sr. and Florence A. (Knapton) K.; m. Susan Emilie Mueller, Apr. 3, 1976. BA, Tarkio Coll., 1969. Cert. compensation profl.; lic. IRS enrolled agt., adminstrv. svc. mgr., life and health agt. Cost acct. Fluid Power, Wheeling, Ill., 1969-71, Wells Lamont Corp., Chgo., 1971-74, sr. cost acct., 1974-76, acct. mgr. cost audit, 1977-80, acct. mgr. taxes, employee benefits, 1980-81, mgr. taxes, employee benefits, 1981-84; benefits mgr. Keeler Brass Co., Grand Rapids, Mich., 1984-86, employee benefits and compenstion mgr., 1986-90; human resources mgr. GRM Industries, Grand Rapids, 1990-92; co-owner Profl. Benefits Svcs., Inc., Grand Rapids, 1992-95; pres. MagnaCare Group Inc., Grand Rapids, 1995—. Mem. Home Health Svcs. (treas. 1986-90), Internat. Soc. Pre-Retirement Planners, West Mich. Compensation Assn., Am. Compensation Assn., Human Resource Mgmt. Assn., Life Underwriters Assn. Republican. Reformed Church America. Avocations: numismatics, all sports. Office: MagnaCare Group Inc 6140 28th St SE Ste 200 Grand Rapids MI 49546-6934

KRANZDORF, JEFFREY PAUL, lawyer, recording company executive, television producer; b. Phila., Jan. 28, 1955; s. Charles David and Hilda (Eisenberg-Nahama) K.; m. Perri Scott Lovell, Sept. 16, 1979; children: Charles David II, Caitlin Blair. AB, U. So. Calif., 1976; JD, Southwestern U., Los Angeles, 1979; student UCLA Graduate Sch. Mgmt. Bar: Calif. 1979, N.Y. 1989, U.S. Dist. Ct. (cen. dist.) Calif. 1979. Assoc., Davis & Cox, Los Angeles, 1980-81; dir. bus. affairs Am. Variety Internat. Inc., Los Angeles, 1981-82, gen. counsel, mng. dir., 1982-85; v.p., gen. mgr. LaBuick Media, Inc., 1985—, sr. v.p. LaBuick Media, Inc., Silver Eagle Records, Inc., 1988—; sec., dir. Ernie's Record Mart, Nashville, 1981-85; pres. Sun Classic Comm. Group, Inc., 1990-92; sr. v.p. bus. and legal affairs Goldstar Video Corp., 1993—; with U. So. Calif. Entertainment Law Inst., 1980—; internat. licensing cons. Ron V. Brown Internat., Pickwick License A/S Denmark; bus. affairs counsel Franklin Waterman Entertainment, 1993—. Prodr. Howard Keel Live at the Royal Albert Hall, Rockin' the Night Away, Ricky Nelson and Fats Domino Live at the Universal Amphitheatre, Blueberry Hill, A Tribute to Ricky Nelson; prodr., dir. Roy Orbison Live; supervising prodr. The Makeover Show with Jerome Alexander; exec. prodr. Rock U.K.; co-exec. prodr. Party In Progress, 1993—, The New Morton Downey Jr. Show, 1993—. Bd. dirs. Sports Archives, Inc., 1990-91. Office: Franklin-Waterman Entertainment Inc 2644 30th St Santa Monica CA 90405-3009 also: 777 N Palm Canyon Dr Ste 201 Palm Springs CA 92262-5548

KRANZDORF, NORMAN M(ELVIN), lawyer, real estate executive; b. Hanover, Pa., Sept. 28, 1930; s. Julius L. and Dora (Kaplan) K.; m. Hermina Goodman, Aug. 28, 1955; children: Betty, Michael. AB, Dickinson Coll., 1952; LLB, U. Pa., 1955. Bar: Pa. 1955. Pres. Amterre Devel. Inc.; v.p., gen. mgr. Food Fair Properties, Inc., counsel; ptnr. The Kranzco Group and Affiliates, Conshohocken, Pa.; CEO, pres. Kranzco Realty Trust, Conshohocken, Pa., 1980-2000; trustee Kramont Realty Trust, Plymouth Meeting, Pa., 2000—. Lectr. continuing edn. programs Mich. State U., U. Ariz.; lectr. Am. Mgmt. Assn., Practicing Law Inst., Aspen Law Inst., N.W. Ctr. for Profl. End., others. Author: Retailer Tenant Bankruptcy, 1997; contbr. articles to profl. jours. Former trustee Internat. Coun. Shopping Ctrs.; bd. govs. Nat. Assn. Real Estate Investment Trusts. Office: Urdang and Assoc 630 W Germantown Pike Plymouth Meeting PA 19462

KRANZLER, JAY D. pharmaceutical executive; b. Nyack, N.Y., Feb. 17, 1958; s. Moses Nathan Kranzler and Eveline Leah Shuchatowitz; m. Bryna Wincelberg, June 22, 1980; children: Michael Jared, Jesse Ryan. BA, Yeshiva U.; MD, D of Philosophy-Pharmacology, Yale U. Mgmt. cons. McKinsey & Co., 1985-89; pres., ceo Cytel Corp., San Diego, 1989—. Psychiatry prof. Yale U.; pres., ceo, chmn. bd. dirs. Sequel Therapeutics, San Diego, 1992—. Adj. mem. Rsch. Inst. of Scripps Clinic, 1989—. Office: Cypress Bioscience Inc Ste 325 4350 Executive Dr San Diego CA 92121

KRANZOW, RONALD ROY, lawyer; b. Chgo., Aug. 4, 1931; s. Roy Ludwig and Elsie Emma (Hennig) K.; m. Joan Carole Stromberg, June 7, 1952; children: Susan, Kenneth, Jill. Student, De Paul U., 1949-52, Syracuse U., 1952-53, Trinity U., 1953-54, Roosevelt U., 1956, John Marshall Law Sch., 1956-59; JD, Golden Gate U., 1961. Bar: Calif. 1961, Tex. 1977, U.S. Ct. Appeals (9th cir.) 1961, U.S. Ct. Appeals (2d cir.) 1969, U.S. Ct. Appeals (8th cir.) 1976, U.S. Ct. Appeals (fed. cir.) 1982. Sales corr. Internat. Cellucotton Products Co., Chgo., 1949-52; sales asst. Kaiser Aluminum & Chem. Corp., Oakland, Calif., 1956-61, trademark counsel, 1961-68, PepsiCo Inc., Purchase, N.Y., 1968-74, asst. gen. counsel, 1976-86, assoc. gen. counsel, 1986-96; v.p., legal counsel Frito-Lay Inc., Dallas, 1974-89, sr. v.p., legal counsel, 1989-95; assoc. gen. counsel Frito-Lay, Inc., Dallas, 1995-96. Contbr. articles to profl. jours. Trustee Grace Presbyn. Village, Dallas, 1995-96. Mem. ABA, Dallas Bar Assn. (chmn. antitrust and trade regulation sect. 1990-91), Am. Intellectual Property Law Assn., U.S. Trademark Assn. (chmn., com. mem. 1965—, pres., chmn. bd. dirs. 1977-78), Internat. Trademark Assn. Republican. Presbyterian. Avocations: church teaching, sports, reading.

KRARAS, GUST C. hotel executive; b. Terpsithea, Greece, Mar. 4, 1921; came to U.S., 1938; s. Christ I. and Ypapanti (Contos) K.; m. Stella Dialectos, Apr. 28, 1946; children: Christ, Angel, Ypapanti. *Gus and Stella Kraras started their family business in Wildwood, N.J., 1955. They developed their holdings from a small restaurant, now owning several motels and restaurants with their entire family. As an offshoot of this beginning, their son, Chris, founded a nationally known tour packaging company called White Star Tour and Travel that operates thousands of tours a year to destinations all over the U.S. and Canada from their different offices. In addition, the Kraras family owns several real estate developments, banquet facilities, and other small businesses throughout Pennsylvania and New Jersey.* Owner-operator Lorraine Hotel & Restaurant, Wildwood, N.J., 1955-73, White Star Motel, Wildwood, 1972—; owner-operator Nantucket Motel, Wildwood, 1973—, White Star Tours, Reading, Pa., 1975—; owner Two Mile Landing, Wildwood, 1982—; owner-operator Beach Terrace Motor Inn, Wildwood, 1985—, Rusty Rudder Restaurant, Wildwood, 1985—, Mansion Heights Assocs., Birdsboro, Pa., 1986—. Owner-operator G.C.M., Reading, 1980—, Hopewell Heights, Birdsboro, 1988—. *Gus and Stella's son, Chris, was instrumental in developing the family business. He founded a nationally known travel company called White Star Tour and Travel, and along with Gus and Stella's daughters Angel and Partricia and their husbands, Mauro Cammarano and Bernard Donahue, and Chris's wife, Ann, the entire family broadened their business interests to include real estate developments, banquet facilities, building companies, and additionall motels and restaurants. Their grandson, Dean, joined the business five years ago and is also intimately involved, rounding out three generations of family business endeavors.* Editor hist. jours., 1954, 70, 75, 89. Pres. St. Constantine Ch., St. Helen Ch., Reading, 1958-59, 77, chpt. 61 Am. Hellenic Ednl. Progressive Assn., Reading, 1957; dist. gov. 5th dist. AHEPA, N.J., Del., 1981-82. With OSS, 1943-45, ETO. Mem. Nat. Tour Assn., Archon Depoutatos of Ecumenical Patriarchate of Constantinople, Masons, Shriners. Democrat. Greek Orthodox. Office: White Star Tours Inc 26 E Lancaster Ave Reading PA 19607-2632

KRASA, ROBERT, manufacturing executive; b. Detroit; Various pos., to pres., CEO Dow Corning Toray Silicone, Tokyo; corp. v.p., gen. mgr. bus. unit Dow Corning Midland Hdqs.; pres., gen. mgr. N.Am. contract furniture sector Haworth, Inc., Holland, Mich., 2001—03, CEO, 2003—. Office: Haworth Inc 1 Haworth Ctr Holland MI 49423-9576*

KRASEAN, THOMAS KARL, historian; b. South Bend, Ind., Feb. 21, 1940; s. William Henry and Rose Ercelia (Mariottini) K.; m. Arleen Ruth Llewellyn, June 19, 1965 (div. Oct. 1970); children: Thomas Karl, David William, Elizabeth Rose; m. Liliane Siahou, Nov. 4, 1972. AA, Kellogg Community Coll., 1960; student, U. Ala., 1960-61; BA, East Mich. U., 1963; MA, Western Mich. U., 1965. Cert. in fund raising mgmt., 1996. Field rep. Ind. State Libr., Indpls., 1965-69, state archivist, 1969-70; dir. Byron Lewis Libr., Vincennes (Ind.) U., 1970-77; field rep. Ind. Hist. Soc., Indpls., 1977-82, dir. field svcs. divsn., 1982-92, dir. cmty. rels. divsn., 1992-97, dir. devel. and membership svcs., 1997—2001, spl. asst. to the pres., 2001—02, dir. planned giving, 2002—. Rep. Ind. Am. Revolution Bicentennial Commn., 1971-77; mem. Adv. Com. Historic Preservation, 1972-73, Adv. Com. Ind. Hist. Bur., 1980-2000; chmn. George Rogers Clark Trail Found., 1972-74; founder, pres. Old N.W. Corp., 1973-77; bd. dirs. Ind. Adv. Com. Nat. Hist. Publs. and Records Commn., 1979-97. Mem. White River Park Task Force, Indpls., 1981-83; bd. dirs. Friends of the State Archives, 2000--. Named Sagamore of the Wabash. Mem. Am. Assn. State and Local History (state chmn. awards com. 1981-92, regional chmn. awards com. 1988-92, nominating com. 1992-95), Soc. Am. Archivists, Midwest Archives Conf. (charter), Ind. Hist. Soc. (adv. coun. Ind. Jr. Hist. Soc. 1971-2001), Ind. Oral History Roundtable (charter), Soc. Ind. Archivists (founder, sec., treas. 1972-92), Civil War Roundtable (pres. 1970-71, 79-80, 93-94), Battle Creek (Mich.) Civil War Roundtable (life), Indpls. Lit. Club (pres. 1989, treas. 1991—), Contemporary Club Indpls. (bd. dirs. 1998-2000, pres. 2001-02), Devonshire Neighborhood Assn. (pres. 1998-2000). Republican. Roman Catholic. Avocations: travel, book collecting. Home: 6038 Castlebar Cir Indianapolis IN 46220-4107 Office: Ind Hist Soc 450 W Ohio St Indianapolis IN 46202-3269 E-mail: tkrasean@indianahistory.org.

KRASILOVSKY, GARY WAYNE, physical therapist, educator; b. N.Y.C., Nov. 21, 1949; s. Monroe and Gertrude K.; m. Linda Strauss; children: Michael, Steven. BS, U. Mo., 1971; MA, NYU, 1977, PhD, 1989. Lic. physical therapist, N.Y., Conn. Phys. therapist NYU Med. Ctr., N.Y.C., 1974-83; chief phys. therapist Norwalk (Conn.) Hosp., 1983-86; cons., Westport, Conn., 1986—; phys. therapist Nursing and Home Care, Wilton, Conn., 1994—; inst. phys. therapy Hunter Coll., CUNY, 1987-89, asst. prof., 1989-96, assoc. prof., 1997—, program dir., 1989—. Cons. Mediplex, Westport, 1986-94; adj. asst. prof. NYU, N.Y.C., 1993; adj. assoc. prof. L.I. U., Bklyn., 1996—. Contbr. articles to profl. jours. Recipient rsch. award Conn. Physical Therapy Assn., 1989. Am. Phys. Therapy Assn., N.Y. Phys. Therapy Assn. (program dir. 1994—, co-chmn. acad. adminstrs. spl. interest group). Office: CUNY Hunter Coll Phys Therapy Program 425 E 25th St New York NY 10010-2547 E-mail: gkrasilo@hunter.cuny.edu.

KRASLOW, DAVID, retired newspaper publishing executive, reporter, author, consultant; b. N.Y.C., Apr. 16, 1926; s. Frank and Goldie (Sirota) K.; m. Bernice Schonfeld, Sept. 18, 1949; children: Ellen Anne, Karen Leah, Susan Beth. BA in Journalism, U. Miami, Fla., 1948. Washington corr. L.A. Times, 1963-66, news editor Washington bur., 1966-70, chief Washington bur., 1970-72; asst. mng. editor Washington Star-News, 1972-74; chief Washington bur. Cox Newspapers, 1974-77; pub. Miami News, 1977-88, sports writer, 1947-48; successively sports writer, reporter, Washington corr. Miami Herald, 1948-63; panelist news program Sta. WPBT-TV, Miami, 1979-91; v.p. Cox Newspapers, Miami, 1989-91. Co-author: A Certain Evil, 1965, The Secret Search for Peace in Vietnam, 1968. Life trustee, mem. acad. affairs com., Sch. Medicine com., athletic adv. com. U. Miami; mem. Orange Bowl Com.; bd. dirs. Greater Miami Tennis Found., Inc., Internat. Oceanographic Found., U. Miami, Pub. Health Trust of Miami-Dade County; founding pres. Ctr. for Fine Arts (now Miami Art Mus.), Miami, 1979-84. With USAAF, 1944-46. Recipient George Polk award, 1969; Raymond Clapper award, 1969; Dumont award, 1969; Nieman fellow Harvard U., 1961-62 Mem. Gridiron Club (Washington). Jewish. E-mail: dkgables@aol.com.

KRASNA, ALVIN ISAAC, biochemist, educator; b. N.Y.C., June 23, 1929; s. Selig and Esther (Finer) K.; m. Elaine C. Cohen, Feb. 27, 1955; children—Susan Roni, Gary Marc, Allen Selig. BA, Yeshiva Coll., 1950; PhD, Columbia U., 1955. Mem. faculty Columbia U., 1956—; prof. biochemistry, 1970—, acting chmn., 1977-78, 88-90, vice chmn., 1978-88, 90—. Contbr. to profl. jours. Predoctoral fellow NSF, 1953; Guggenheim fellow, 1962; research grantee NSF; research grantee NIH; research grantee Am. Cancer Soc.; research grantee AEC, Dept. Energy Mem. Am. Chem. Soc., Am. Assn. Biol. Chemists, AAAS, Harvey Soc., Am. Soc. Microbiology, Sigma Xi. Home: 6 Arbor Dr New Rochelle NY 10804-1101 Office: 630 W 168th St New York NY 10032-3702

KRASNA, MARK JONATHAN, thoracic surgeon, researcher; b. Sault Ste Marie, Mich., Mar. 18, 1958; s. Irwin H and Anne M Krasna; m. Diane M Santagata; children: Vered E, Rachel D, Daniel E. Md, Tel Aviv U. Med. Sch., Tel Aviv, Israel, 1976—82. Surgery Am. Bd. Of Surgery, 1990, Thoracic Surgery Am. Bd. OF THORACIC SURGERY, 1992. Chief of thoracic surgery U. Of Md. Med. Sch., Baltimore, Md., 1999—; prof. of surgery U. Fo Mryland Med. Sch., Baltimore, Md., 1999—. Author: (medical text) The Atlas Of Thoracoscopic Surgery. Mem. Beth Tfiloh Cmty. Sch., Baltimore, Md., 1997—2000, Suburban Orthodox Congregation, Baltimore, Md., 1996—99. Recipient Humanitarian Of The Yr., Mildred Mindell Cancer Found., 1999, Intrenational Brotherhood Award, Bikur Cholim Hosp. Jerusalem, 2000. Fellow: ACS. R-Liberal. Jewish. Avocations: swimmin, sailing, camping, diving. Office: University Of Maryland Medical School N4e35 22 S Greene St Baltimore MD 21201 Home Fax: 410-328-0693; Office Fax: 410-328-0693. Personal E-mail: mkrasna@smail.umaryland.edu.

KRASNER, DANIEL WALTER, lawyer; b. N.Y.C., Mar. 18, 1941; s. Nathan and Rose Krasner; m. Ruth Pollack, Dec. 20, 1964; children: Jonathan, Lisa, Noah, Rebecca. BA, Yeshiva Coll., 1962; LLB, Yale U., 1965. Bar: N.Y. 1966, U.S. Dist. Ct. (so. dist.) N.Y. 1967, U.S. Dist. Ct. (ea. dist.) N.Y. 1968, U.S. Supreme Ct. 1978, U.S. Ct. Appeals (1st, 2d, 3d, 5th, 6th, 8th-11th dists.). Assoc. Pomerantz Levy Houdek & Block, N.Y.C., 1965-76; sr. ptnr. Wolf Haldenstein Adler Freeman & Herz, N.Y.C., 1977—. Vice chmn. Westchester Day Sch., Mamaroneck, N.Y., 1979-86; v.p., trustee Bd. Jewish Edn., N.Y.C., 1981—. Democrat. Avocations: tennis, golf, sailing. Office: Wolf Haldenstein Adler Freeman & Herz 270 Madison Ave New York NY 10016-0601 E-mail: krasner@whafh.com.

KRASNER, DAVID, education educator; b. Brooklyn, NY, Mar. 1, 1952; s. Milton and Anne Krasner; m. Lynda Intihar, Dec. 8, 2002. PhD in drama, Tufts U., 1996. Asst. prof. U. of Idaho, 1993—95, So. Ill. U., 1995—97; assoc. prof. Yale U., 1997—. Author: (book) A Beautiful Pageant, African American Theatre, Drama and Performance in the Harlem Renaissance, 2002, Method Acting Reconsidered, Theory, Practice, Future, 2000; editor: Resistance, Parody and Double Consciousness in African American Theatre, 1997, African American Performance and Theatre History: A Critical Reader, 2001; co-editor: Blackwell Companion to Twentieth Century American Drama. Mem.: Am. Soc. for Theatre Rsch. (Errol Hill award 1998, 2002). Home: 110 Blue Trail Hamden CT 06518 Office: Yale University Theater Studies 254 York St New Haven CT 06520-8296 Home Fax: 203-432-1308; Office Fax: 203-248-1374. E-mail: david.krasner@yale.edu.

KRASNER, MICHAEL ALAN, political science educator; b. Hot Springs, S.D., July 2, 1943; s. George David and Alice (Doress) K.; m. Deborah Jane Shapiro, June 16, 1974; children: Abigail Judith, Elizabeth Sara. AB, U. Chgo., 1964; PhD, Columbia U., 1977. Program analyst Office Econ. Oppty., Washington, 1967-68; adj. lectr. Lehman Coll. CUNY, Bronx, 1967-68, adj. lectr. Hunter Coll. N.Y.C., 1968-69; half-time lectr. Queens Coll., CUNY, Flushing, N.Y., 1970-72, instr., 1972-74, asst. prof., 1974-77, assoc. prof. polit. sci., 1977—. Vis. prof., rsch. fellow U. Aarhus, Denmark, 1985-86, Fulbright exch. prof., 1983-84; exch. prof. U. Paris, 1994; cons., trainer, evaluator U.S. Postal Svc., N.Y.C. and Boston, 1989—; cons. Townsend Harris H.S., Queens, 1996—; cons., project dir. Ctr. for Applied Rsch. in Social Scis., Bklyn., 1978-83. Author: Going For It: How to Organize a Grassroots Campaign, 1992; co-author: American Government: Structure and Process, 1982; contbr. articles to profl. publs. Vice-chmn. Queens Coll. chpt. Profl. Staff Congress, 1996—99; co-dir. Taft Inst. for Govt., 1996—, Michael Harrington Ctr., 2002—; guest tchr. Brattleboro Union H.S., 1995—; mem. county bd, Vt. Progressive Coalition, Brattleboro, 1990—; commentator WBAI-FM, N.Y.C., 1978—91. Tng./rsch. grantee U.S. Inst. of Peace, 1992-93; Cmty. Leadership Tng. Program grantee Rockefeller Bros. Fund, 2002-03; Hazen Found. grantee, 2003—. Mem. Internat. Peace Rsch. Inst. Jewish. Avocations: swimming, camping. Home: 192 Taylor Rd Putney VT 05346-9023 Office: CUNY Queens Coll Dept Polit Sci 65-30 Kissena Blvd Flushing NY 11367 E-mail: mkrasner@sover.net., michael_krasner@qc.edu.

KRASNER, WILLIAM, freelance/self-employed writer; b. St. Louis, June 8, 1917; s. Samuel and Bryna Persov Krasner; m. Juanita Frances Frazier, Oct. 13, 1956; children: David Ely, Daniel Asher, Lawrence Samuel, James Nathan. Student, Washington U., St. Louis, 1935—36, AAF Meterology Sch., 1942—46; BS in Psychology, Columbia U., 1948. Freelance writer, novelist, Berwyn, Pa., 1948—; prodr., writer CBS-TV, Radio, St. Louis, 1957—60; devel., speechwriter Washington U., St. Louis, 1961—63; article editor, co-founder Trans-Action Mag., St. Louis, 1964—69; writer, editor Smith-Kline Pharm., Phila., 1969; med. writer, editor U. Pa., Phila., 1969—74; brochure writer NIMH, Phila., 1974—75. Author: Burgos Gaol, 1939, Walk the Dark Streets, 1949, The Gambler, 1950, North of Welfare, 1954, Stag Party, 1957, Death of Minor Poet, 1984, Resort to Murder, 1986; contbr. articles to profl. jours. mags. and newspapers, poems and essays to publs., to Krasner archive spl. collections, Vets. Hist. Project. Warrant officer (j.g.) USAF, 1942—46, PTO. Fellow, Pa. Coun. on Arts, 1980; grantee, Nat. Inst. Arts and Letters, 1955. Jewish. Achievements include research in methods of forecasting development of tropical cyclones. Avocations: reading, helping people, time with children and grandchildren. Home: 538 Berwyn Ave Berwyn PA 19312

KRASNO, RICHARD MICHAEL, foundation executive, educator; b. Chgo., Jan. 20, 1942; s. Louis R. K. and Adeline G. (Glassman) Kaplan; children: Jeffrey Patrick, Eric Peter; m. Carin Blucher. BS, U. Ill., 1965; PhD, Stanford U., 1970; LittD (hon.), Coll. St. Rose, 1983; LLD (hon.), Sacred Heart U., 1984. Asst. prof. ednl. psychology U. Chgo., 1970-74; program advisor Brazil Ford Found., Rio de Janeiro, 1974-77, program advisor Latin Am. N.Y.C., 1977, program advisor Mid.-East & Africa, 1978-80; deputy asst. sec. of edn. U.S. Dept. Edn., Washington, 1980-81; exec. v.p. Inst. Internat. Edn., N.Y.C., 1981-83, pres., CEO, 1983-98; pres. Monterey (Calif.) Inst. Internat Stud, 1998-99, Kenan Charitable Trust, Chapel Hill, N.C., 1999—. Commr. U.S.-Brazil Fulbright Commn., 1975-77, U.S. Nat. Commn. UNESCO, 1983; chmn. Internat. Transition Team Dept. Edn., 1979, 80; mem. U.S.-Mex. Bilateral Commn., 1980, 84; sr. Fulbright lectr., 1973-74. Contbr. articles to profl. jours. Trustee Laspau, Cambridge, Mass., 1980—82, Eisenhower Exch. Program, 2002—. Nat. Defense Edn. fellow U.S. Govt., 1967-68. Mem. Coun. Fgn. Rels., Century Assn., Cosmos Club. Office: The Kenan Ctr PO Box 3858 Chapel Hill NC 27515-3858 E-mail: richard_krasno@unc.edu.

KRASNOSTCHEKOVA, ELENA ALEXANDER, language educator; b. Moscow, June 22, 1934; d. Alexander Michael Krasnostchekov and Donna Jacob Gruz; m. Sergey Michael Samoilov, Dec. 9, 1961; 1 child, Michael. M in Russian Lang. and Lit., Yaroslavl (Russia) Pedagogy Inst., 1955; PhD in Russian Lit., Moscow Lenin Pedagogy Inst., 1965. Sr. rsch. assoc. USSR Book Rsch. Inst., Moscow, 1966—81; prof. Moscow Lenin Pedagogy Inst., Moscow, 1966—81; vis. asst. prof. NYU, 1988—90; from asst. prof. to prof. U. Ga., Athens, 1991—98, prof., 1998—. Author: Oblomov by I.A. Gncharov, 1970, Vsevolod Ivanov's Creative World, 1980, I.A. Gorcharov: An Universe in Art, 1997. Fellow Fgn. Rsch. fellow, Slavic Rsch. Ctr. Hokkaido U., 1991—92. Mem.: Am. Assn. Tchrs. Slavic East European Langs., Am. Assn. Advancement Slavic Studies. Avocation: gardening. Home: 225 Hampton Park Dr Athens GA 30606 Office: U Ga Joseph E Brown Hall Athens GA 30602

KRASNOV, KIRILL, physicist, researcher; b. Kiev, Ukraine, Apr. 5, 1973; s. Vladimir Sergeyevich Krasnov and Nadezhda Charitonovna Krasnova; m. Tatiana Mechetnaya, July 28, 2000; 1 child, Nikita. PhD in Physics, Penn State U.; University Park, PA, 1996—99. Post grad. rschr. UC Santa Barbara, Santa Barbara, 1999—2002; long term rschr. Albert-Einstein-Institut, Golm/Potsdam, Germany, 2002—. Author: (scientific articles) Advances in Theoretical Mathematical Physics, Classical and Quantum Gravity, Physical Review D, Physical Review Letters, Journal of Mathematical Physics. Achievements include first to Quantum mechanical description of black holes. Office: Albert-Einstein-Institut Am Muehlenberg 1 Golm 14476 Germany Office Fax: +49 331 567-7297. E-mail: krasnov@aei.mpg.de.

KRASNOW, ERWIN GILBERT, lawyer; b. Bklyn., Jan. 8, 1936; s. Charles and Etta (Simowitz) K.; m. E. Judith Levine, Sept. 6, 1960 (dec. July 1994); children: Michael Andew, Catherine Beth; m. Jane Gasperini, Nov. 25, 1995. AB summa cum laude, Boston U., 1958; JD, Harvard U., 1961; LLM, Georgetown U., 1965. Bar: Mass. 1961, U.S. Dist. Ct. Mass. 1961, D.C. 1963, U.S. Ct. Appeals (D.C. cir.) 1963, U.S. Supreme Ct. 1965, U.S. Ct. Appeals (4th cir.) 1978, U.S. Ct. Appeals (5th and 11th cirs.) 1982. Rsch. asst. Harvard U. Law Sch., Cambridge, Mass., 1961; adminstr. asst. to Congressman Torbert H. Macdonald, U.S. Ho. of Reps., Washington, 1962-64; ptnr. Kirkland and Ellis, Washington, 1964-76; sr. v.p., gen. counsel Nat. Assn. Broadcasters, Washington, 1976-84; ptnr. Verner, Liipfert, Bernhard, McPherson & Hand, Washington, 1984—. Vis. prof. Ohio State U., 1974; disting. vis. lectr. Temple U., 1976; adj. prof. Am. U., 1975, Law Ctr., Georgetown U., 1984; professorial lectr. Grad. Sch. Arts and Scis., George Washington U., 1982, 83, adj. prof., 1998; professorial lectr. Sch. Law, Cath. U. Am., 1982; bd. dirs. Broadcast Capital Fund, Inc. (formerly Minority Broadcast Investment Fund), 1978—, treas., 1979-92, vice chmn., 1993—; mem. govt. industry adv. coun. Ctr. for Telecom. Studies, George Washington U., 1980-84; mem. adv. bd. Inst. for Comm. Law, Sch. Law, Cath. U. Am., 1982—; mem. bd. advisors Comm. Media Ctr., N.Y. Law Sch., 1982—; mem. adv. com. comm. law program UCLA, 1983-85. Co-author: A Candidate's Guide to the Law of Political Broadcasting, 1977, 3d edit., 1984, Buying and Building a Broadcast Station, 3d edit., 1987, 100 Ways To Cut Legal Fees and Manage your Lawyer, 1988, Radio Financing: A Guide for Lenders and Investors, 1990, Insider's Guide to Radio Acquisition Contracts, 1992; co-author: FCC Lobbying A Handbook of Insider Tips and Practical Advice, 2001; editor: National Association of Broadcasters Legal Guide to FCC Broadcast Rules, Regulations and Policies, 1977; bd. editors Fed. Comm. Bar Jour., 1973-75; mem. editl. adv. bd. Jour. Broadcasting, 1972-85, Telematics and Informatics, 1982—; mem. adv. com. COMM/ENT Law Jour., 1983—; contbr. articles to legal publs. Mem. ABA (vice chmn. agy. adjudication com. 1974-77, chmn. comm. law com. adminstrv. law sect. 1980-81), FBA (pres. Capitol Hill chpt. 1963-64, dep. co-chmn. comm. law com. 1967-69, co-chmn. 1970-71), Fed. Comm. Bar Assn. (exec. com. 1976-79, 84-85, treas. 1984-85), Capitol Hill Bar Assn. (past pres.), Boston U. Alumni Club Washington (pres. 1967-70), Boston U. Nat. Alumni Assn. (bd. dirs. 1966-68, regional v.p. 1971, 73), Phi Beta Kappa. Home: 3307 Q St NW Washington DC 20007-2717 Office: Shook Hardy & Bacon 600 14th St NW Ste 800 Washington DC 20005 Business E-mail: ekrasnow@shb.com.

KRASNOW, JORDAN PHILIP, lawyer; b. Malden, Mass., May 14, 1944; s. Louis and Roslyn (Packer) K.; children: Laura, Joshua, Abbey, Abigail. AB, Clark U., 1965; JD magna cum laude, Boston U., 1968. Bar: Mass. 1970. Law clk. to Presiding Justice Mass. Superior Ct., Boston, 1968-69; assoc. atty. Peabody & Arnold, Boston, 1969-71, Gaston Snow & Ely Bartlett, Boston, 1971-75, ptnr., 1975-86; officer, dir. Goulston & Storrs, Boston, 1986—; co-mng. dir., 1994-97. Lectr. Mass. Continuing Legal Edn., Boston, 1975-85;

adv. com. Boston U. Real Estate Program, 1988—; charter mem. Greater Boston Real Estate Bd.-Real Estate Fin., 1989. Mem. Mayor's Adv. Com. Housing Linkage, Boston, 1984; mem. exec. com. Anti Defamation League New Eng.; trustee Roxbury Prep. Charter Sch. Recipient Disting. Achievement award B'nai B'rith Realty Unit, 1995. Fellow Mass. Bar Found.; mem. Mass. Bar Assn., Boston Bar Assn., B'nai Brith (trustee realty unit New Eng. chpt.). Jewish. Avocations: travel, sports. Home: 94 Beacon St Apt 2 Boston MA 02108-3329 Office: Goulston & Storrs 400 Atlantic Ave Boston MA 02110-3333 E-mail: jkrasnow@goulstonstorrs.com.

KRASNOW, RICHARD P. lawyer; b. Bklyn., Feb. 12, 1947; s. Nathan A. and Doris (Pearson) K.; m. Nancy Meyrich, Oct. 3, 1982. AB, U. Chgo., 1968; JD, NYU, 1972. Assoc. Shereff, Friedman, Huffman & Goodman, N.Y.C., 1972-73; ptnr. Weil, Gotshal & Manges, N.Y.C., 1972—. Mem. ABA, N.Y. State Bar Assn., Assn. Bar City of N.Y. Office: Weil Gotshal & Manges 767 5th Ave Fl Concl New York NY 10153-0119

KRASNY, CHARLOTTE ALTHEA, volunteer; b. Detroit, Nov. 28, 1935; d. Harold Oliver and Charlotte Ruth (Lundberg) Jones; m. Mike S. Krasny, Dec. 21, 1958; children: Mitchell, Robin, Scott, Glenn, Keith. BEd cum laude, U. Miami, Coral Gables, Fla., 1958. Cert. secondary sch. tchr. (math.), lic. real estate agt. Tchr. Kinloch Park Jr. High, Miami, Fla., 1958-60; tchr. Rickards Jr. High, Tallahassee, Fla., 1960-62, Cen. Jr. High Sch., Melbourne, Fla., 1962-63; vol. Jr. League, Melbourne, Fla., 1964—; musician Melbourne Mcpl. Band, 1965—; tchr. Hoover Jr. High, Indialantic, Fla., 1983-84. Pres., chmn. bd. Melbourne Mcpl. Band, 1975-85; vice chmn. Melbourne Commn. on Bicentennial of U.S., 1986-89; mem. Com. on Centennial of Melbourne, 1987-88; membership chmn. Haven for Children Guild, 1996-2002; mem. women's adv. coun. Eau Gallie Yacht Club, 1997-2000. Mem. AAUW, South Brevard Panhellenic, Jr. League South Brevard. Republican. Avocations: scuba diving, snow skiing, music, travel. Home: 787 Malibu Ln Indialantic FL 32903-3617

KRASNY, HARVEY CHARLES, pharmaceutical executive, researcher; b. High Point, N.C., July 27, 1945; s. Morris Theodore and Elizabeth (Nurkin) K. BS, Lynchburg (Va.) Coll., 1967; MS, U. N.C., 1969, PhD, 1976. Rsch. biochemist Glaxo Wellcome Inc., Research Triangle Park, N.C., 1969-83, sr. rsch. scientist, 1983-95; v.p. licensing and new bus. devel. CaroTech, LLC, Research Triangle Park, 1995—. Contbr. articles to profl. jours. Mem. Am. Soc. Clin. Pharmacology and Therapeutics, Am. Soc. Pharmacology and Exptl. Therapeutics, Licensing Execs. Soc., Assn. of Univ. Tech. Mgrs., Soc. Toxicology, Sigma Xi (pres. chpt. 1993-95). Achievements include study of pharmacokinetics, bioavailability and drug metabolism of the antiviral agent acyclovir (Zovirax) in humans; pre-clinical development of AZT (Retrovir). Office: PO Box 13416 Research Triangle Park NC 27709-3416

KRASNY, MICHAEL P. computer company executive; BS in Fin., U. Ill., 1975. Founder, chmn., CEO, sec. CDW Computer Ctrs., Vernon Hills, Ill., 1984—2001, bd. mem. emeritus, 2001—. Bd. mem. Kellogg Sch. of Mgmt., Northwestern U. Recipient Entrepeneur of Yr., Ernest and Young, 1993, CEO of Yr., Fin. World, 1996, Torch award for marketplace ethics, Nat. BBB, 2000. Mem.: Young Pres. Orgn., Econ. Club of Chgo. Office: CDW 200 N Milwaukee Ave Vernon Hills IL 60061-1577*

KRASS, MARC STERN, lawyer; b. Detroit, June 23, 1949, s. Marvin David and Ruth B. (Stern) K.; m. Susan McAuley; children: Jonathan, Matthew. AB, Oberlin Coll., 1970; postgrad., U. Pitts., 1970-71; JD cum laude, Northwestern U., 1976. Bar: Ill. 1976, U.S. Dist. Ct. (no. dist.) Ill. 1976, U.S. Dist. Ct. (we. dist.) Tex. 1980, Ohio 1981, U.S. Dist. Ct. (so. dist.) Ohio 1982. Assoc. Seyfarth, Shaw, Fairweather & Geraldson, Chgo., 1976-80; assoc. gen. counsel Procter & Gamble Co., Cin., 1980—. Bd. dirs. United Home Care, Inc., Cin., 1983-88, Ctr. for Comprehensive Alcoholism Treatment, Cin., 1988-90. Mem. Cin. Bar Assn. Home: 9806 Indian Springs Dr Cincinnati OH 45241-3671 Office: Procter & Gamble Co One Procter & Gamble Pla Cincinnati OH 45202 E-mail: krass.ms@pg.com.

KRATE, NAT, artist; b. N.Y.C., Aug. 26, 1918; s. Samuel and Ida (Tuchschneider) K.; m. Helen Levy Krate, May 26, 1923; children: Iris Ann, David, Riva. Attended, WPA Art Sch., N.Y.C., 1934-35, Pratt Inst., 1935-36, Art Students League, 1936-38, 46-47, Syracuse U., 1943-44. Art dir. Erland Advtg. Agy., N.Y.C., 1946-48; creative dir. Krate/Basch Advtg. Agy., N.Y.C., 1948-61; owner & dir. Nat Krate Co. Inc., N.Y.C. and Pittsfield, Mass., 1961-80. Mem. adv. bd. Sarasota (Fla.) Art Assn., 1989-91, Longboat Key (Fla.) Art Ctr., 1986-88; art instr. Ringling Sch. of Art and Design, Sarasota, Fla., 1989-90. Solo exhbns. include Becket Art Gallery, Mass., 1978, Welles Gallery, Lenox, Mass., 1981, Ana Sklar Gallery, Bal Harbor, Fla., 1985, Foster Harmon Galleries Am. Art, Sarasota, Fla., 1986, 89, 92, 94, Arvida Gallery, Longboat Key, 1986, Longboat Key Art Ctr., Fla., 1989, Anna Howard Galleries, Washington, Conn., 1992, Lee County Alliance of the Arts, Ft. Myers, Fla., 1994, Donn Roll Galleries, Sarasota, 1994, 96, Hang-Up Gallery, Sarasota, 1998, Fla. West Coast Symphony Hall, 1999, Sarasota Visual Art Ctr., 2000, Venice Art Ctr., 2001, 02; group exhbns. include Soc. for the Four Arts, Palm Beach, Fla., 1989, 90, 91, 95, 99, 2002, Fla. Figure Show, Brevard Mus., Melbourne, Fla., 1993, 43d Ann All Fla. Boca Raton Mus., Fla., 1994-95, Fla. Artist Group, Mus. Arts and Sci., Daytona Beach, Fla., 1994, 4th Biennial Exhbn., Huntsville Mus., Ala., 1994, Mickelson Gallery, Washington, D.C.1994-95, Mobile Mus. of Art, Ala., 1996, Mus. Contemporary Art, Jacksonville, Fla., 1998, Hunter Mus. Am. ARt, Chattanooga, 1998, Venice (Fla.) Art Ctr., 1997, 99, Lee County Alliance of Arts, Ft. Myers, Fla., 1997, 99, Ridge Art Assn., Winter Haven, Fla., 1997-98, 99-2001, Hang-Up Gallery, Sarasota, 1998, Jacksonville (Fla.) Mus. Contemporary Art, 1998, Fla. Southern Coll., Lakeland, 1999, Charlotte County Visual Art Ctr., 2000-2002, Ringling Mus. Art, Sarasota, Fla., 2000, Edison C.C., Ft. Myers, Fla., 2000, Selby Gardens Mus., Sarasota, 2000-03, The Capitol in Tallahassee, 2001, Appalachian State U., 2001, The Art Ctr., St. Petersburg, Fla., 2002, Hilton Head Art League, S.C., 2002, BIG Arts, Fla., 2002, Zenith Gallery, Washington, 2002, 03, Bonita Springs Art Ctr., Fla., 2003. Mem. Longboat Key Art Ctr., Sarasota Visual Art Ctr., Mus. of Arts and Scis., Daytona Beach, Fla., Sarasota County Arts Coun.; co-founder, mem. bd. dirs. Pub. Interest Com., Longboat Key, 1985-95; adv. cons. various candidates for pub. office, 1986-95. Staff sgt. U.S. Army, 1941-45. Mem. Am. Artists Profl. League, Inc., Knickerbocker Artists U.S.A., Fla. Artists Group, The Salmagundi Club. Home: 4737 Sweetmeadow Cir Sarasota FL 34238-3398

KRATHWOHL, DAVID READING, education educator emeritus; b. Chgo., May 14, 1921; adopted by Marie (Reimold) K.; m. Helen Jean Abney, Dec. 20, 1943; children: James D. (dec. Nov. 1967), David A., Ruth Anne Krathwohl Cleghorn, Kristin Jeanne. BS, U. Chgo., 1943, MS, 1947, PhD, 1953. Asst. dir. unit on evaluation Bur. Ednl. Research, Coll. Edn., U. Ill., 1949-55, instr., 1949-53; asst. prof., 1953-55; asso. prof. Mich. State U., 1955-58, prof., 1958-65, research coordinator, 1955-63; chmn. Psychol. Found. Edn., 1960-63; dir. Bur. Ednl. Research, 1963-65; dean Sch. Edn. Syracuse (N.Y.) U., 1965-76; prof. Sch. Edn., Syracuse (N.Y.) U., 1965-91, Hannah Hammond prof. edn., 1982-91, Hannah Hammond prof. emeritus, 1991—. Chmn. bd. trustees Eastern Regional Inst. for Edn., 1966-71. Author: (with others) Taxonomy of Educational Objectives: Cognitive Domain, 1956, Affective Domain, 1964, Social and Behavioral Science Research: A New Framework for Conceptualizing, Implementing and Evaluating Research Studies, 1985, How to Prepare a Research Proposal, 3d edit., 1988, Methods of Educational and Social Science Research: An Integrated Approach, 2d edit., 1998; editor (with L.W. Anderson) A Taxonomy for Learning, Teaching, and Assessing: A Revision of Bloom's Taxonomy of Educational Objectives, 2001. Served with USAAF, 1943-46. Fellow Ctr. for Advanced Study in Behavioral Scis., 1980-81 Fellow AAAS, APA (v.p. ednl. psychology div.); mem. Am. Ednl. Rsch. Assn. (pres.), Am. Psychol. Soc. Home: 9 Thornwood Ln Fayetteville NY 13066-2529 Office: Syracuse U Sch Of Education Syracuse NY 13244-2340

KRATKA-SCHNEIDER, DOROTHY MARYJOHANNA, psychotherapist; b. New Britain, Conn., Apr. 29, 1934; d. Josef Matthew and Mari Catherine (Stifil) Kratka; m. Warren Andrew Schneider, Apr. 26, 1975. BS in Nursing, Columbia U., 1960, MSW, Fordham U., 1969; EdD in Counseling Psychology, U. San Francisco, 1983. RN, Conn.; bd. cert. diplomate in clin. social work. Instr. pub. health nursing U. Conn., Storrs, 1963-64; participant Voter Registration Drive, Greenwood, Miss., 1965; pub. health nurse Jesuit Med. Mission Bd., Tanzania, East Africa, 1965-67; chief psychiat. social worker Knickerbocker Hosp., N.Y.C., 1969-74; coordinator social services Rockefeller U. Hosp., N.Y.C., 1974-77; asst. prof. Calif. State U., Sacramento, 1985-88, assoc. prof., 1985-88; counseling psychologist VA, San Francisco, 1987-89; psychologist, social worker Dept. Transp., 1989-93; pvt. practice Corte Madera, Calif., 1993—. Bd. dirs. Nat. Assn. Soc. Work Referral Service, San Francisco, 1984-86. Bd. dirs. Health Systems Adv. Com., San Francisco, 1978, Cmty. Mental Health, Marin County, Calif., 1998—; mem. Cath. Charities Bd. for Aging, San Francisco, 1985, bd. dirs., 1983-85; apptd. to Marin County Cmty. Mental Health Bd., 1998—; apptd. to Marin County Grand Jury, Superior Ct., 1999—. NIMH grantee, 1967-69. Mem. APA, Internat. Assn. Profl. Counselors and Psychotherapists (diplomate psychotherapy), NASW (diplomate in clin. social work), Register for Clin. Social Workers of NASW, Amnesty Internat., Kappa Delta Pi. Democrat. Roman Catholic. Avocations: hiking, watercolors, flying, swimming. Office: Diablo Med Plz Ste 200 Novato CA 94947 E-mail: dorothyschneider@earthlink.net.

KRATOCHVIL, BYRON GEORGE, chemistry educator, researcher; b. Osmond, Nebr., Sept. 15, 1932; came to Can., 1967; s. Frank James and Mabel Louise (Schneider) K.; m. Marianne Spain; children: Susan, Daniel, Jean, John. BS, Iowa State U., 1957, MS, 1959, PhD, 1961. Asst. prof. chemistry U. Wis.-Madison, 1961-67; assoc. prof. chemistry U. Alta., Edmonton, Can., 1967-71, prof. chemistry, 1971-98, prof. emeritus, 1998—, dept. chmn., 1989-95, assoc. v.p. rsch., 1996-98, sr. advisor, v.p. rsch., 1998-2001; dir. planning and ops. Alta. Synchrotron Inst., 2002—. Co-author: (with W.E. Harris) Chemical Analysis, 1969, Chemical Separations and Measurements, 1974, Introduction to Chemical Analysis, 1981; analytical editor Can. Jour. Chemistry, Ottawa, Ont., 1985-88, sr. editor, 1988-93; contbr. numerous articles to sci. jours. Recipient merit award Iowa State U. Alumni, 1990. Fellow AAAS, Chem. Inst. Can. (bd. dirs. 1977-80, Fisher Lectr. award 1990); mem. Am. Chem. Soc. Office: U Alta Dept Chemistry Chemistry Centre Edmonton AB Canada T6G 2G2

KRATOCHVIL, L(OUIS) GLEN, lawyer; b. Highland, Wis., Oct. 11, 1922; s. John A. and Emma (Pusch) K.; m. Evelyn Gregory, Sept. 12, 1946; 1 son, Louis Glen Jr. LLB, U. Wis., 1951; JD. Bar: Wis. 1951, Tex. 1952, U.S. Dist. Ct. (so. dist.) Tex. 1956, U.S. Ct. Appeals (5th cir.) 1956, U.S. Supreme Ct. 1956, U.S. Dist. Ct. (ea. dist.) Tex. 1961. Landman Shell Oil Co., Houston, 1951-52; assoc. firm Murphy & Crystal, Houston, 1953-55; asst. U.S. atty. So. Dist. Tex., 1955-57; pvt. practice Houston, 1957—99. Pres. McGregor Terr. Civic Club, Houston, 1954, Young Rep. Club U. Wis., 1950. Lt. USNR, 1941-46, PTO. Mem.: FBA, ABA, U. Wis. Alumni Assn. (pres. Houston chpt. 1972—73), Maritime Law Assn., Houston Bar Assn., Wis. Bar Assn., Tex. Bar Assn., Brazos River Club (treas. 1970—99), Lions (pres. 1955), Phi Alpha Delta (chief justice 1950). Home: 302 Kickerillo Dr Houston TX 77079-7412 Office: Kratochvil and Powell 3303 Main St Ste 207 Houston TX 77002-9321

KRATOVIL, JANE LINDLEY, think tank associate, developer/fundraiser; b. Boston, Nov. 25, 1952; 1 child, Lindley. BA, Lynchburg Coll., 1974. Various positions U.S. Ho. of Reps., Washington, 1974-77, The Pittston Co., Greenwich, Conn., 1977-79; assoc. dir. City Sports Mgmt. Inc., Washington, 1979-82; adminstrv. asst. to spl. asst. to pres. for adminstrn. The White House, Washington, 1982-85; exec. asst. to gen. and dep. gen. counsel U.S. Dept. Treasury, Washington, 1985-88; exec. dir., sec. Eisenhower World Affairs Inst., Washington, 1988-2000; pres. Lindley & Assoc., Springfield, Va., 2000—. Office: 8340 Wickham Rd Springfield VA 22152-1739 E-mail: jkratovil@earthlink.net.

KRATT, PETER GEORGE, lawyer; b. Lorain, Ohio, Mar. 7, 1940; s. Arthur Leroy and Edith Ida (Dietz) K.; m. Sharon Amy Maruska, June 15, 1968; children: Kevin George, Jennifer Ivy. BA, Miami U., Oxford, Ohio, 1962; JD, Case Western Res. U., 1966. Bar: Ohio 1966. Atty. Cleve. Trust Co., 1966-74; assoc. counsel AmeriTrust Co., 1974-84, sec., assoc. counsel, 1985-87, sed., sr. assoc. counsel, 1987-92; ret. v.p., mgr. personal trust adminstrn. Huntington Trust Co., 1993-99. Mem. Am. Soc. Corp. Secs., Ohio Bar Assn., Rotary, Lions. Methodist. Avocations: hiking, gardening.

KRATZ, CHARLES E., JR., dean; b. Balt., Apr. 22, 1951; s. Charles Edward Sr. and Catherine Mary (Hudson) K. BA in History, U. Notre Dame, 1973, MA in History, 1974; M of Libr. Sci., U. Md., 1976. Asst. head of public svcs. U. Mo. Libr., Kansas City, 1979-80, head of public svcs., 1980-82; assoc. dir. Rider U., Lawrenceville, N.J., 1982-85; asst. dean of public svcs. Hofstra U., Hempstead, N.Y., 1985-91; libr. dean U. Scranton (Pa.) Libr., 1991—. V.p. to pres. bd. trustees PALINET, 1997-2002; v.p. to pres. OCIC Mems. Coun., 2003—. Author: (with others) Facts & Figures, 1987, Training Issues and Strategies, 1990, Staff Development: A Practical Guide, 1992, 3d edit., 2000; contbr., editor: The Personnel Manual: An Outline for Libraries, 1994; editor: Library Personnel Consultants List, 1990, Training Issues in Changing Technology, 1986; contbr. articles to profl. jours. Mem.: ACRL (coms.), LITA (coms.), LAMA (pres. 1997—98), ALA (coun. 1999—2002). Roman Catholic. Avocations: theatre, skating, sports. Home: 405 Kyle Dr Stroudsburg PA 18360-8788 E-mail: kratzc1@scranton.edu.

KRATZ, HOWARD RUSSEL, physicist, researcher; b. Mattoon, Wis., Nov. 2, 1916; s. Samuel H. and Clara A. (Jones) K.; m. Mary K. Bunsa, June 2, 1942; children: Marilyn Kratz Locker, William H. BA, Ripon Coll., 1938; PhD, U. Wis., 1942. Tchg. asst. U. Wis., Madison, 1938-41; rsch. asst. Princeton (N.J.) U., 1941-42; mem. staff Metall. Lab., U. Chgo., 1942-44; mem. staff Los Alamos (N.M.) Sci. Lab., 1944-46, GE Rsch. Lab., Schnectady, N.Y., 1946-59, Gen. Atomic, San Diego, 1959-72; sr. scientist Sys., Sci., and Software, San Diego, 1972-79; ret., 1979—. Contbr. articles to Phys. Revue, Rev. Sci. Instruments, Jour. Optical Soc. Am., Jour. Am. Instrument Soc. Recipient 1972 best paper award Am. Instrument Soc., 1973. Mem. Am. Phys. Soc., Sigma Xi. Democrat. Unitarian Universalist. Home: 600 Carolina Village Rd Hendersonville NC 28792

KRAUS, DAVID (DIRK) BRUCE, musician, educator; b. Marysville, Ohio, Dec. 28, 1968; s. Kenneth Martin and Alice Elizabeth Kraus; m. Jennifer Ann Simpson. BA, BS, Ohio No. U., 1992. Piano tchr. Conservatory Piano, Worthington, Ohio, 1996—2001; piano tchr., owner Piano Inst., Ft. Collins, Colo., 2001—. Mem.: Ft. Collins Music Tchrs. Assn. Office: Piano Inst 2839 S College # 3 Fort Collins CO 80525

KRAUS, DENNIS HARRY, surgeon; b. Indpls., Nov. 25, 1958; s. Ernest M. and Alice K.; m. Daryl Brook, Sept. 17, 1987; children: Cameron, Devon, Collin. BA, U. Rochester, 1984, MD, 1985. Intern, resident Cleve. Clinic Found., 1985-90; assoc. attending surgeon Meml. Sloan-Kettering Cancer Ctr., N.Y.C., 1991—, dir. speech and hearing ctr., 1992—; asst. assoc. prof. Cornell U., N.Y.C., 1998—. Chmn. ethics com. Meml. Sloan-Kettering Cancer Ctr., 1998. Author: Assessment of Patients with Suspected Sinonasal Neoplasms, 1997; co-author: (chpts.) Surgical Management of Unilateral Vocal Cord Paralysis in Thoracic Surgery, 1998, Neoplasms of the Neck in Pathology of the Head and Neck, 1998, Recurrent Nerve Paralysis Following Pneumonectomy, 1998. Recipient Travel award Nat. Cancer Inst., Park City, Utah, 1996, Am. Acad. Facial Plastics and Reconstructive Surgery Travel award, 1991. Fellow Am. Rhinologic Soc.; mem. Am. Acad. Otolaryngology-Head and Neck Surgery (Hon. award 1996), Med. Soc. State N.Y. Avocations: golf, skiing, travel, food and wine. Office: Meml Sloan-Kettering Cancer Ctr 1275 York Ave New York NY 10021-6094

KRAUS, JANICE, social worker, educator; b. Bridgeport, Conn., Nov. 1, 1950; d. John Francis and Helen Blanche (Ksiazak) Kraus; m. Alfred Harrington, Nov. 22, 1980 (div. 1982). BS, So. Conn. State U., New Haven, 1972; MS, So. Conn. State U., 1976, MSW, 1987. Tchr. Clinton (Conn.) Bd. Edn., 1972—; psychiat. clinician Lawrence and Meml. Hosp., New London, Conn., 1988-90; pvt. practice, 1980—. Mem. Nat. Assn. Social Workers, NEA, Land Conservancy, World Wildlife Fund, Cousteau Soc. Episcopalian. Avocations: antiques, gardening. Home: 324 Boston Post Rd Old Lyme CT 06371-1318

KRAUS, JOHN WALTER, former aerospace engineering company executive; b. N.Y.C., Feb. 5, 1918; s. Walter Max Kraus and Marian Florance (Nathan) Sandor; m. Janice Edna Utter, June 21, 1947 (dec. Feb. 1981); children: Melinda Jean Kraus Peters, Kim Kohl Kraus; m. Jean Curtis, Aug. 27, 1983. BS, MIT, 1941; MBA, U. So. Calif., 1972. From indsl. engr. to indsl. engring. mgr. TRW, Inc., Cleve., 1941-61; spl. asst. Atomics Internat., Chatsworth, Calif., 1961-65; br. chief McDonnell Douglas Astronautics Co., Huntington Beach, Calif., 1966-74; sr. mgr. McDonnell Douglas Space Systems Co., Huntington Beach, Calif., 1983-93; pres. Kraus and DuVall, Inc., Santa Ana, Calif., 1975-83, retired, 1993. Cons. Tech. Assocs. So. Calif., Santa Ana, 1974-75. Author: (handbook) Handbook of Reliability Engineering and Management, 1988. Mem. Nat. Def. Industries Assn. (formally Am. Def. Preparedness Assn., life, chmn. tech. div. 1954-57), Nat. Soc. Profl. Engrs. (life), Oasis Sailing Club (commodore 1996-2002, dir. 1996—), Friends of Oasis (dir. 1999—, treas. 2000-2002), MIT Club of So. Calif.. Republican. Avocations: sailing, reading, gardening. Home: 2001 Commodore Rd Newport Beach CA 92660-4307 E-mail: skprjohn6@netscape.net.

KRAUS, LESLIE JAY, lawyer; b. Bklyn., Sept. 6, 1943; s. George E. and Sylvia (Hornreich) K; adopted s. Bobbi (Needleman) K.; m. Susan J. Rosenthal, Dec. 21, 1968; 1 child, Erica. BS, Northeastern U., Boston, 1966; JD, Suffolk U., 1969. Bar: Mass. 1969. Assoc. Cohn, Riemer & Pollack, Boston, 1970, atty. estate tax IRS, Bridgeport, Conn., 1970-71; field atty. NLRB, Mpls., 1971-76; v.p. Indsl. Rels. Assocs., Mpls., 1976-82; pres. Leslie J. Kraus & Assocs., Inc., Edina, Minn., 1982—. Instr. U. Minn., Mpls., 1977-94. Co-chmn. YWCA Parent Coun., Mpls., 1985-86; vice chmn. Lake Fellowship of Unitarian Universalists, Excelsior, Minn., 1986-87, chmn. 1987-89, social action chair 1990—; mem. Southview Mid. Sch. Site Coun., 1993-97, chair, 1994. Mem. ABA (labor law sect.), Mass. Bar Assn., Northwest Athletic Club. Unitarian Universalist/Jewish. Office: Leslie J Kraus & Assocs Inc 4375 Thielen Ave Minneapolis MN 55436-1522 E-mail: leskraus@aol.com.

KRAUS, MARGERY, management consultant, communications company executive; b. Franklin, N.J., May 20, 1946; d. Soland Lily (Cvern) Rosen; m. Stephen Kraus, Sept. 4, 1966; children: Lisa, Evan, Mara. BA in Polit. Sci., Am. U., 1967, MA in Govt., 1970. With Close Up Found., Arlington, Va., 1971-84, v.p., 1976-84; exec. v.p. APCO Assocs., Inc., Washington, 1984-88, pres., CEO, 1988—. Bd. dirs. Internat. Mgmt. and Devel. Inst.; chair, Northwestern Mutual Financial Network, Govt'l Rels. Com., chair, Coun. of PR Firms, Pub. Affairs Coun., Catherine B. Reynolds Found., Interat. Mgmt. and Devel. Inst., Inst. for Public Rels., The Creative Coalition, Meridian Internat. Ctr.; previously served as bd. dirs., Rsch. Inst. of the Children's Nat. Medical Ctr., Washington, D.C.; cons., speaker in field; adv. bd. Kellogg Sch. Mgmt. Bd. dirs. Close Up Found., Pub. Affairs Coun. Washington Businesswoman of the Year, 1998, PR Professional of the Year, 1997, named Internat. Pub. Rels. Profl. of Yr., 2001. Mem., Adv. Bd., Terry Sanford Inst. of Public Policy, Duke Univ, Coun. on Am. Politics, George Washington Univ. Grad. Sch. of Political Mgmt. Home: 9609 Whitecedar Ct Vienna VA 22181-5423 Office: APCO Worldwide 1615 L St NW Ste 900 Washington DC 20036-5623

KRAUS, PANSY DAEGLING, gemology consultant, editor, writer; b. Santa Paula, Calif., Sept. 21, 1916; d. Arthur David and Elsie (Pardee) Daegling; m. Charles Frederick Kraus, Mar. 1, 1941 (div. Nov. 1961). AA, San Bernardino Valley Jr. Coll., 1938; student, Longmeyer's Bus. Coll., 1940; grad. gemologist diploma, Gemol. Inst. Gt. Britain, 1960, Gemol. Inst. Am., 1966. Clk. Convair, San Diego, 1943-48, San Diego County Schs. Publs., 1948-57; mgr. Rogers and Boblet Art-Craft, San Diego, 1958-64; part-time editl. asst. Lapidary Jour., San Diego, 1963-64, assoc. editor, 1964-69, editor, 1970-94, sr. editor, 1984-85; pvt. practice cons. San Diego, 1985—. Lectr. gems, gemology local gem, mineral groups; gem & mineral club bull. editor groups. Author: Introduction to Lapidary, 1987; editor, layout dir.: Gem. Cutting Shop Helps, 1964, The Fundamentals of Gemstone Carving, 1967, Appalachian Mineral and Gem Trails, 1968, Practical Gem Knowledge for the Amateur, 1969, Southwest Mineral and Gem Trails, 1972, Introduction to Lapidary, 1987; revision editor Gemcraft (Quick and Leiper), 1977; contbr. articles to Lapidary jour., Keystone Mktg. catalog. Mem. San Diego Mineral and Gem. Soc., Gemol. Soc. San Diego, Gemol. Assn. Gt. Britain, Mineral. Soc. Am., Gemol. Inst. Am., Epsilon Sigma Alpha. Home and Office: 6127 Mohler St San Diego CA 92120-3515

KRAUS, PETER LEO, librarian, educator; b. Mineola, N.Y., June 18, 1968; s. Leo Emil Kraus and Barbara Luise (Hausser) Kessler; m. Kristin Louise Borden, July 22, 1995. BA in History, Fla. State U., 1991, MS in Library Sci., 1993. Rsch. asst. Ctr. for Local Govt. U. North Fla., Jacksonville, 1991-92; libr. N.Y. Pub. Libr., N.Y.C., 1994-99; asst. libr. Marriott Libr., U. Utah, Salt Lake City, 1999—2003, asst. libr. Technology Assisted Curriculum Ctr., 2003—. Adj. instr. Salt Lake City C.C., 2002—. Mem. ALA, Am. Assn. Coll. and Rsch. Librs., Spl. Librs. Assn., Utah Libr. Assn., Mountain Plains Libr. Assn., We. Assn. Map Librs., Utah Mus. Assn., Utah Hist. Soc. Office: U Utah Marriott Libr Dept Documents & Microforms 295 S 1500 E Salt Lake City UT 84112 E-mail: peter.kraus@library.utah.edu.

KRAUS, ROBERT, physician; b. N.Y.C., July 10, 1936; s. Manny and Lillian Kraus; m. Myra H. Kraus; children: Richard Penn, Daniel. BS, Tufts U., 1957; MD, Albert Einstein Coll. Medicine, 1961. Diplomate in internal medicine and cardiovascular disease Am. Bd. Internal Medicine; cert. Am. Bd. Echocardiography. Intern Wadsworth V.A. Hosp., L.A., 1961-62, resident internal medicine, 1962-64, resident in cardiology, 1964-65; clin. dir. cardiology noninvasive lab. Cedars-Sinai Med. Ctr., L.A., 1970—; clin. prof. medicine UCLA Sch. Medicine, 1980—. Capt. U.S. Army, 1965-67. Avocations: bassoon playing, biking. Office: Cedars-Sinai Med Ctr 8700 Beverly Blvd Los Angeles CA 90048-1865

KRAUS, ROBERT H. lawyer; b. Teaneck, NJ, May 10, 1939; s. Henry and Alice R. K.; m. Carol A. Gerry, June 10, 1961; children: William R., Karen B., Kathryn L. AB, Rutgers Coll., 1961, JD, 1964. Bar: N.J. 1965, D.C. 1965. Assoc. Lowenstein & Sandler, Newark, 1966-69, Johnstone & O'Dwyer, Westfield, N.J., 1969-70, Shear & Kraus, Scotch Plains, N.J., 1971, Leib, Kraus, Grispin & Roth, Scotch Plains, N.J., 1972—. Gen. ptnr. Woodland Estates Partnership, RVS/RHK Co., LLC, Scotch Plains, 1987—2001, Flemington Trade Ctr., LLC, Fanwood Plaza Ptnrs., LLC. Bd. dirs., trustee Fanwood Scotch Plains YMCA, 1976—; trustee Scotch Plains-Fanwood Scholarship Found., 1982-88, Fanwood Cmty. Found., 1998—; chmn. Rotary-Garbe Found., Inc., 1994—. Capt. U.S. Army, 1965-66. Recipient William D. Mason Disting. Svc. award Fanwood-Scotch Plains Jaycees, 1977. Mem. ABA, NJ Bar Assn., Union County Bar Assn., Scotch Plains-Fanwood Soccer Assn. (gen. mgr., coach 1977-83). Home: 96 Forest Rd Fanwood NJ 07023-1305 Office: Leib Kraus Grispin & Roth 328 Park Ave Scotch Plains NJ 07076-0310 E-mail: rkraus@lkgrlaw.com.

KRAUS, SHERRY STOKES, lawyer; b. Richmond, Ky., Aug. 11, 1945; d. Thomas Alexander and Callie (Ratliff) Stokes; m. Eugene John Kraus, Aug. 27, 1966. Student, U. Ky., 1962-64; BS, Roosevelt U., 1966; JD cum laude, Albany Law Sch., 1975; LLM in Taxation, NYU, 1981. Bar: N.Y. 1976, U.S. Dist. Ct. (we. dist.) N.Y. 1976, U.S. Tax Ct. 1986. Law clk. U.S. Tax Ct., Washington, summer 1974; law clk. 4th dept. appellate divsn. N.Y. State Supreme Ct., Rochester, 1975-77; assoc. Nixon, Hargrave, Devans & Doyle, Rochester, 1977-81, 83-84, Harter, Secrest & Emery, Rochester, 1984-86; pvt. practice Rochester, 1986—. Faculty grad. tax program Sch. Law, NYU, N.Y.C., 1981-82; prin. tech. adv. to assoc. chief counsel - tech. IRS, Washington, 1983-84; mem. N.Y. State Tax Appeals Adv. Panel on Practice & Procedure, 1998—. Articles editor ABA Tax Articles Periodical, The Tax Lawyer, 1984-88; mng. editor NYU Tax Articles Periodical, NYU Tax Law Rev., 1981-82; lead articles editor Tax Articles Periodical, Albany Law Rev., 1973-75; contbr. articles to profl. jours. David J. Brewer scholar Albany Law Sch., 1973. Mem. ABA, N.Y. State Bar Assn. (tax sect. exec. com. 1984—), Monroe County Bar Assn. (treas. 1990-92), Monroe County Bar Found. (pres. 1994-95), Justinian Soc. Avocations: watercolors, guitar, dulcimer. Office: 513 Times Square Bldg Rochester NY 14614-2078 E-mail: sskraus@frontiernet.net.

KRAUS, STEVEN GARY, lawyer; b. Newark, Aug. 22, 1954; s. Leon Judah Kraus and Rose (Cohen) Turchin; m. Jane Susan Sukoneck, June 29, 1980; children: Adam. AB, Brandeis U., 1976; JD, Rutgers U., 1979. Bar: N.J. 1979, Pa. 1979, U.S. Dist. Ct. N.J. 1979, U.S. Supreme Ct. 2002. Jud. law sec. to assignment judge Charles A. Rizzi, Superior Ct. N.J., Camden, 1979-80; assoc. Kavesh & Basile, Vineland, N.J., 1980-81, Bennett & Bennett, West Orange,

N.J., 1981-82; pvt. practice, Warren, N.J., 1982—. Mem. ABA, N.J. State Bar Assn., Nat. Assn. Subrogation Profls. Home: 17 Regent Cir Basking Ridge NJ 07920-1900 Office: 122 Mount Bethel Rd Warren NJ 07059-5127 E-mail: steven.kraus@subrogationlawyer.com.

KRAUSE, CAROLYN H. state legislator, lawyer; m. David Krause. BA, U. Wis.; JD, IIT. Assoc. Foss, Schuman & Drake, Chgo., 1966-73; lawyer, solo practice Mt. Prospect, Ill., 1973-76; pvt. practice Krause & Krause, Mt. Prospect, Ill., 1976—; mayor Mt. Prospect, 1973-76; Dist. 56 rep. Ill. Ho. Reps., Springfield, 1993—. Spokesman appropriations, gen. svcs., cities and villages, fin. instns., healthcare, and human svcs. coms., Ill. Ho. Reps. Apptd. by Gov. James Thompson (Ill.) to local govt. fin. study commn., 1980, criminal justice info. authority, 1985-87; past dir. Clearbrook Ctr.; chair Mcpl. Conf.; dir. Pub. Action to Deliver Shelter of Northwest Cook County. Mem. Ill. and Chgo. Bar Assns. Home: 204 S George St Mount Prospect IL 60056-3430 Office: Ill Ho of Reps State Capitol Springfield IL 62706-0001 Also: 111 E Busse Ave Ste 605 Mount Prospect IL 60056-3249*

KRAUSE, CHARLES JOSEPH, otolaryngologist; b. Des Moines, Apr. 21, 1937; s. William H. and Ruby I. (Hitz) Krause; m. Barbara Ann Steelman, June 14, 1962; children: Sharon, John, Ann. BA, State U. Iowa, 1959, MD, 1962. Diplomate Am. Bd. Otolaryngology. Intern Phila. Gen. Hosp., 1962—63; resident in surgery U. Iowa, 1965—66, resident in otolaryngology, 1966—69; fellow dept. plastic surgery Marien Hosp., Stuttgart, Germany, 1970; asst. prof. otolaryngology U. Iowa, 1969—72, asso. prof., 1972—75, vice chmn. dept. otolaryngology, 1973—77, prof., 1975—77; prof., chmn. dept. otolaryngology U. Mich. Med. Sch., Ann Arbor, 1977—92; pres. Am. Bd. Otolaryngology, Houston. Chief clin. affairs U. Mich. Hosps., Ann Arbor, 1986—89; asst. dean for clin. affairs U. Mich., 1986—89, sr. assoc. dean med. sch., 1992—96, chief clin. affairs, 1992—95, sr. assoc. hosp. dir., 1995—96, prof. dept. otolaryngology, 1996—. Author: book in field; contbr. chapters to books, articles. Capt. USAF, 1963—65. Fellow: Am. Soc. Head and Neck Surgery (coun. 1980—83, chmn. rsch. com. 1980—83, pres. 1987—88); mem.: Am. Bd. Otolaryngology (bd. dirs. 1984—, exam. com. chair 1993—, pres.-elect 1996—98, pres. 1998—2000), Centurions of Deafness Rsch. Found., Am. Laryngol. Assn., Am. Laryngol., Rhinol. and Otol. Soc., Am. Cancer Soc. (med. adv. com. Washtenaw County unit), Walter P. Work Soc. (pres. 1987), Soc. United Otolaryngologists Am. Acad. Depts. Otolaryngology, Mich. Otolaryngol. Soc., Mich. State Med. Soc., Washtenaw County Med. Soc. (exec. com. 1979—82), Assn. Rsch. in Otolaryngology, Am. Asssn. Cosmetic Surgeons, Assn. Head and Neck Oncologists, ACS (adv. coun. otolaryngology 1979—83), Am. Acad. Facial Plastic and Reconstructive Surgery (regional v.p. 1977—80, chmn. rsch. com. 1977—80, pres. 1981—82), Am. Acad. Otolaryngology Head and Neck Surgery (bd. dirs. 1987—93, sec.-treas. 1987—93, pres.-elect 1995, pres. 1996), AMA. Republican. Presbyterian. Home and Office: 880 Sea Dune Ln Marco Island FL 34145-1840 E-mail: cjkrause1@aol.com.

KRAUSE, CHESTER LEE, publishing company founder; b. Iola, Wis., Dec. 16, 1923; s. Carl and Cora E. (Neil) K. Grad. high sch., Iola. Ind. contractor, 1946-52; chmn. bd. Krause Publs., Inc., Iola, 1952-95. Co-editor: Standard Catalog of World Coins. Chmn. bldg. fund drive Iola Hosp., 1975-80; active Village Bd., 1963-72, Assay Commn., 1961, Marshfield Clinic Nat. Adv. Coun., 1992-96. With AUS, 1943-46. Named Wis. Small Businessman of Yr. Wis. Small Bus. Adminstrn. Adv. Coun., 1990; Melvin Jones fellow, 1989; recipient Meguiar award, 1995, Friend of Automotive History award Soc. Automotive Historians, 1995, Marshfield Clinic Heritage Found. award, 2001. Mem. Soc. of Automobile Historians (Friends of Automobile Historians 1995), Am. Numis. Assn. (medal of merit, Farren Zerbe award, Hall of Fame, Lifetime Achievement award), Can. Numis. Assn. Home: 290 E Iola St Iola WI 54945-9620 Office: 160 N Washington St Iola WI 54945-9642 E-mail: ckrause@athenet.net.
To publish on time, all the time.

KRAUSE, DOROTHY SIMPSON, fine artist; b. Mobile, Ala., Sept. 22, 1940; d. Edwin Holland and Ethel Alberta (Simmons) Tuthill; m. Richard Alan Krause, July 7, 1978; 1 child, Lauren Simpson Miller. BA in Painting with honors, Montevallo U., 1960; MA in Art Edn., U. Ala., 1962; EdD in Art Edn., Pa. State U., 1968. Assoc. prof. Va. Commonwealth U., 1969-74; dir. grad. art programs Mass. Coll. Art, Boston, 1974-75, dean grad. and continuing edn., 1975-82, v.p. adminstrn. and fin., 1982-85, prof. computer graphics, 1985-2000. Artist-in-residence Kodak Ctr. Creative Imaging, 1991—95, Digital Atelier, Smithsonian Am. Art Mus., Washington, 1997. Represented in permanent collections Smithsonian Am. Art Mus., Washington, De Cordova Mus., Lincoln, Mass., Zimmerlie Mus., Rutgers U., Spencer Mus., Lawrence, Kans. Mem.: Women's Caucus for Art, Print Alliance, Photgraphic Resource Ctr., Boston Printmakers. Home: PO Box 421 Marshfield Hills MA 02051

KRAUSE, EDWARD CHARLES, priest, educator; b. Worcester, Mass., Sept. 11, 1940; s. Edward Krause and Elizabeth Linden. BA, Notre Dame U., 1963; STL, Gregorian U., Rome, 1967; PhD, Boston U., 1975. Priest Congregation of the Holy Cross. Prof., chaplain Stonehill Coll., North Easton, Mass., 1970—75, St. Mary's Coll., Notre Dame, Ind., 1975—80; prof., pastor Gannon U., Erie, Pa., 1980—. Mem. adv. bd. Scholars for Social Justice, St. Louis, Confraternity of Cath. Clergy. Author: (book) Democracy and J.C. Muray, 1975; contbr. essays to publs.; contbg. editor: Nat. Cath. Register Newspaper. Med. moral advisor St. Mary's Nursing Home, Erie, 1980—, St. Vincent's Hosp., Erie, 1982—96, Diocese of Erie, 1986—. Recipient Pro Ecclesia award, The Vatican, 1994; fellow, NEH, 1987. Mem.: Am. Soc. Christian Ethics, Am. Acad. Religion, Fellowship of Cath. Scholars, Soc. Cath. Social Scientists (bd. dirs.).

KRAUSE, GLORIA ROSE, music educator; b. Milw., Oct. 30, 1922; d. Carl Fred and Rose (Bremeier) Runge; m. George Tanner Krause Jr., June 24, 1960; 1 child, George Henry. MusB, U. Rochester, 1946; MusM, Northwestern U., 1954. Music tchr. Livingston Manor (N.Y.) Cen., 1946-59, Monticello (N.Y.) Cen. Sch., 1959-61, Liberty (N.Y.) Cen. Sch., 1966-67, Livingston Manor Sch., 1968-79, Narrowsburg (N.Y.) Ctrl. Sch., 1979-87. Dir. Ill. Winds Chamber Ensemble, Narrowsburg, N.Y., 1975—; gen. mgr. Delaware Valley Opera, Narrowsburg, 1986—. Music dir.: (operas) HMS Pinafore, Mikado, Pirates of Penzance, Princess Ida, Patience, Amahl and Night Visitors, The Medium, Gondoliers, Marriage of Figaro, Don Pasquale, Die Fledermaus, Gypsy Baron, The Beggars Opera, La Traviata, Madame Butterfly, La Boehme, The Medium, The Merry Widow, The Barber of Seville (Rossini), Student Prince, Orphans in the Underworld, Hansel and Gretel; bassoonist with Highland Symphony Orch., Middletown, NY, 1986-90, New Sussex Cmty. Orch., Sparta, NJ, 1984-90. Pres. Del. Valley Arts Alliance, 1980—; bd. dirs. Tusten-Cochecton Libr., Narrowsburg, 1988—. Recipient Svc. award Siddha Meditation Ashram Found., South Fallsburg, NY, 1990, Recognition award Alliance NY State Arts Couns., 1995; named Woman of Yr., Catskill Mountain Bus. and Profl. Women, 1995; Gloria R. Krause Recital Hall named in her honor Del. Valley Arts Alliance, 2002 Office: Del Valley Opera PO Box 188 Narrowsburg NY 12764-0188

KRAUSE, HARRY DIETER, law educator; b. 1932; came to US, 1951, naturalized, 1954; m. Eva Maria Disselnkötter, 1957; children: Philip Renatus, Thomas Walther, Peter Herbert. Student, Freie U., Berlin, 1950-51; BA, U. Mich., 1954, JD, 1958. Bar: Mich. 1959, D.C. 1959, Ill. 1963, U.S. Supreme Ct. 1963. With firm Covington & Burling, 1958-60; with Ford Motor Co., Dearborn, Mich., 1960-63; asst. prof. to prof. law U. Ill., Champaign, 1963-82, Alumni Disting. prof. law, 1982-89, Max L. Rowe prof. law, 1989-94, tchg. prof. emeritus, 1994—. Fulbright prof. U. Bonn, Germany 1976-77; vis. assoc. Ctr. Socio-Legal studies, 1977; vis. fellow Wolfson Coll. Oxford (Eng.) U., 1984; US Del. to Hague Conf. on Pvt. Internat. Law Treaty on Internat. Adoptions, 1990-93; commr. Uniform State Laws, Ill., 1991-97; reporter Uniform Parentage Act, 1969-73, Rev. Uniform Adoption Act, 1979-84, Uniform Putative Fathers Act, 1985, Nat. Conf. Commr. on Uniform State Laws; mem. Internat. Acad. Comparative Law Rapporteur US, Uppsala, 1966, Teheran, 1974, Budapest, 1978, Caracas, 1983, Sydney, 1986, Brisbane, 2002, gen. rep. Athens, 1994; cons. on family law and social legis. to fed. and state legis., jud. and exec. commns.; vis. prof. law U. Mich., 1981, U. Miami, 1987; Culverhouse prof. Stetson U., 1991. Author: Illegitimacy: Law and Social Policy, 1971, Family Law: Cases and Materials, 1976, 5th edit., (with others), 2003, Kinship Relations, 1976, Family Law in a Nutshell, 1977, 4th edit., Child Support in America: The Legal Perspective, 1981; law editor: (with R. Walker et. al.) Inclusion Probabilities in Parentage Testing, 1983, Family Law (West's Blackletter Series), 1988, 2d edit., 1996, International Library of Essays in Law and Legal Theory: Family Law I: Society and Family, 1992, Family Law II: Cohabitation, Marriage and Divorce, 1992, Child Law: Parent, Child and State, 1992; bd. editors Mich. Law Rev., 1957-58, Family Law Quar., 1971—, Jour. Legal Edn., 1988-91, Am. Jour. Comparative Law, 1991—, and others. With US Army, 1954-56. Recipient von Humboldt Found. rsch. prize, 1992; Guggenheim fellow, 1969-70; assoc. Ctr. Advanced Study U. Ill., 1970, 79; German Marshall Fund US fellow, 1977-78; Hewlett fellow, Australia, 1984; German Acad. Exch. Svc. fellow, 1985. Mem. ABA (past mem. coun. sect. family law, com. chmn.), Am. Law Inst. (adviser family law project 1990-2001), Ill. Bar Assn. (past mem. coun. sect. on family law, internat. law), Am. Assn. Comparative Study of Law (dir. 1980-2000), Internat. Soc. Family Law (v.p. 1973-77, exec. coun. 1977-97), Order of Coif. Office: U Ill Coll Law Champaign IL 61820

KRAUSE, HEATHER DAWN, data processing executive; b. Kansas City, Kans., May 6, 1956; d. Jack E. Firth and Bonnie Jo (Reeves) Cupps; m. Kerry Murray Krause, May 23, 1981. Cert., Kansas City Skill Ctr., 1980; BS in Computer Info. Sys., Friends U., Wichita, 2003. Cert. drafting tchr.; cert. in bus. supervision; cert. in Novell Netware system adminstrn. Assoc. drafter Black & Veatch, Kansas City, Mo., 1980; technician mech. design Wilcox Electric, Kansas City, 1980; network adminstr. Smith & Loveless, Inc., Lenexa, Kans., 1980—; owner Digital Design Technologies, Kansas City, Mo., 1989—; tech. editor Que Books Macmillan Computer Pub., 1994—. Instr. Longview C.C., Lee's Summit, Mo., 1987-93. Mem.: Phi Theta Kappa. Democrat. Avocations: camping, fishing, hiking, skiing, web site development. Home: PO Box 11319 Kansas City MO 64112-0319 E-mail: hkrause@krausehouse.com.

KRAUSE, HELEN FOX, physician, otolaryngologist; b. Boston, Mar. 20, 1932; d. Nathan and Frances Lena (Rich) Fox; children: Merrick Eli, Beth Riva Harper, Kim Debra Codd. BS, U. Maine, 1954; MD, Tuft U., 1958. Diplomate Am. Bd. Otolaryngology. Intern Health Ctr. Hosps. Pitts., 1958-59; resident Eye & Ear Hosp., Children's Hosp., VA Hosp., 1959-62; pvt. practice Pitts., 1962—. Mem. otolaryngology adv. bd. U.S. Pharmacopea, 1991-96, 2000—, chmn., 1995-2000; clin. assoc. prof. U. Pitts. Sch. Medicine; vis. prof. Pan Hellenic Otorhinolaryngology Soc., Crete, Greece, 1993, Panama, Argentina, 1998, China, Hong Kong, 1999, Thailand, China, Taiwan, 2000, Pan Am. Oto Soc., 2000; assoc. clin. prof. U. Pitts. Sch. Medicine; pres., dir. 1st World Congress of Otorhinolaryngologic Allergy, Endoscopy and Laser Surgery, Athens, 1998, 2001; bd. dirs. Bayer Pharm. Women's Health Initiative; vis. prof. Thailand, Sigapore; lectr. 2nd World Congress Otolaryngology, Allergy and Immunology, 2001. Author, editor: Otolaryngic Allergy and Immunology, 1989; lectr., vis. prof. Singapore, Bangkok, Hong Kong (multiple tng. programs 1990); contbr. chpts. to books and articles to profl. jours. Pres. North Hills Jewish Community Ctr., Pitts., 1973-74; cons. North Allegheny Sch. Bd., Pitts., 1977; lectr. North Allegheny Sr. High Sch., Wexford, 1979-84; chmn. Desert Storm Project, North Hills Bus. and Profl. Women, 1991. Recipient Disting. Svc. award, Pa. Acad. Otolaryngology, 1993, Hon. Achievement award, Am. Acad. Otolaryngology Head and Neck Surgery, 1993, Bd. govs. Chair award, 2000, award, Panhellenic Soc. ORL-HNS, 2001; scholar Jackson Meml. Labs., Bar Harbor, Maine, 1954. Fellow ACS, Am. Acad. Otolaryngology Head and Neck Surger (bd. govs. 1982-89, 90—), Am. Acad. Otolaryngologic Allergy (pres. 2984-85), Svc. award 1990, cert. appreciation 1991, Pres.'s award 1997, Spl. Achievement award 1997), Am. Acad. Facial Plastic and Rsch. Surgery; memb. Pa. Acad. Otolaryngology (pres. 1989-90), Internat. Soc. Otorhinolaryngic Allergy and Immunology (pres. 1995-98), Pitts. Otological Soc. (pres. 1983-85), Phi Beta Kappa, Phi Kappa Phi. Office: 9104 Babcock Blvd Ste 4110 Pittsburgh PA 15237-5866 E-mail: hfk@nauticom.net.

KRAUSE, JOHN L. optometrist; b. Portland, Oreg., Oct. 26, 1917; m. Nancy D., Sept. 30, 1942; children: Diana L., Karen L., Ronald L. OD, Ill. Coll. Optometry, 1947. Practice optometry, Niles, Ill., 1978—88. USAF Med. Service liaison officer, Northwestern U. Med. Sch., Chgo., 1964-91. Author: Sight Check Your Child, 1961, Holiday Fax, 1991, Win-Win, Inc., 1994; contbr. articles to nat. mags.; patentee card holder, 1967. Bd. overseers S.E. Univ. Coll. Optometry, North Miami Beach, Fla., 1993; liaison to optometry Nat. Alliance Mental Health, 1993; mem. ins. coun. City Tamarac, Fla., 1995—, chmn., 2002—; ombudsman State of Fla., Broward County, 1996-2000. Served with U.S. Army, 1941-45, to lt. col. USAF, ret., 1970. Decorated Bronze Star with cluster; inductee Broward County Fla. Sr. Hall of Fame, 2000. Mem. Am. Optometric Assn., Ill. Optometric Assn., Fla. Optometric Assn. Armed Forces Optometric Soc. (Honor award 2002), Air Force Assn., Fla. Pub. Health Assn. (chmn.-elect vision sect. 1992), Fla. Ret. Optometrists Assn. (pres. 1993-95, editor 1995-), Kappa Phi Delta, Phi Theta Upsilon, Phi Mu Delta. Achievements include patents for eyedrop transport apparatus. Avocations: golf, stamp collecting, autographs. Home: 7270 Fairfax Dr Tamarac FL 33321-4305

KRAUSE, KENNETH MICHAEL, music educator; b. Monmouth, N.J. s. Kenneth Alan and Jane Francis Krause. BS in Edn., Millersville U. Kodaly Cert. West Chester U., 1994, Choral Music Cert. CME Inst. Choral Tchr. Edn., 1995. Bus driver Eschbach Bus Co., Holtwood, 1987—96; elem. choral dir. Lebanon Sch. Dist., 1993—96; dir. of bands Lebanon H.S., 1996—99; dir. of secondary instrumental music Ea. Lebanon County Sch. Dist., Myerstown, 1999—; organist, choir dir. Christ Evang. Luth. Ch., Lancaster, 2001—. Dir. of youth soccer Lancaster Family YMCA, 1988—92; organist, choir dir. Bethel Evang. Congl. Ch., Conestoga, Pa., 1986—90; dir. of music, organist Zion Evang. Luth. Ch., East Petersburg, 1990—94; organist, choirmaster Covenant United Meth. Ch., Lebanon, 1995—2000. Mem.: Nat. Assn. for Music Educators, Assn. of Luth. Ch. Musicians, Am. Choral Directors Assn., Am. Guild of Organists, Organ Hist. Soc., Toastmasters Internat. (CTM, ATM 1990, 1996), Tri-M Music Honor Soc. (life). Avocations: public speaking, bowling, golf, soccer, travel. Home: 826 Olde Hickory Rd Lancaster PA 17601-4932 Office: Eastern Lebanon County School District 180 ELCO Dr Myerstown PA 17067 Personal E-mail: kmkrause@aol.com. E-mail: kkrause@elco.k12.pa.us.

KRAUSE, KURTH WERNER, aerospace executive; b. Milw., July 21, 1940; s. Eugene Ralph and Dorothy Mildred (Raffel) K.; m. Susan Ruth Firle, June 15, 1963; children: Scott Alan Krause, Sheryl Lynn Krause Gildea. BS in Math. and Physics, U. Wis., 1962; postgrad., MIT, 1966-67; cert. sr. mgmt. program, UCLA, 1985; cert., Stanford Exec. Inst., 1986. Project engr. AC Spark Plug div. GM, Milw., 1963-65; staff engr. MIT Instrumentation Lab., Cambridge, Mass., 1965-67; mem. tech. staff TRW, Houston, 1967-68, sect. head, 1969-73, dept. head, 1974-75, subproject mgr. and project mgr. Redondo Beach, Calif., 1975-79; asst. v.p. Ultrasystems, Inc., Irvine, Calif., 1979-83; dir. aerospace systems Intermetrics, Inc., Huntington Beach, Calif., 1983-84, gen. mgr. aerospace systems group, 1984-93; project mgr. Aerojet, Azusa, Calif., 1993-95; program mgr. TRW, El Segundo, Calif., 1995-99; ret., 1999. Mem. strategic adv. bd. So. Calif. Tech. Execs. Network, Tustin, Calif., 1986-93; mem. Air Force Assn./USAF Space and Missile Ctr. Exec. Forum, El Segundo, Calif., 1989-92. Contbr. articles to profl. jours. Mentor YMCA Bldg. Life Options Program, 1999—; mem. St. Andrews Presbyn. Ch., 2002—; hon. bd. dirs. Discovery Mus. of Orange County, Santa Ana, Calif., 1990—92. Recipient Apollo Achievement award NASA, Washington, 1969, cert. of commendation MIT, Cambridge, 1969, Skylab award NASA Manned Flight Awareness, Johnson Space Ctr., 1974, Apollo/Soyuz Test Project NASA Flight Crew, Johnson Space Ctr., 1975. Mem. AIAA, Am. Electronics Assn., So. Calif. Tech. Execs. Network, USAF Space and Missile Sys. Ctr. Exec. Forum, Mesa Verde Country Club (CFO 1980-81), Alpha Delta Phi (pres. Wis. chpt. 1961-62), Phi Eta Sigma. Republican. Avocations: golf, computers, writing, travel, bridge. E-mail: golfnspace@aol.com.

KRAUSE, LOIS RUTH BREUR, chemistry educator; b. Paterson, N.J., Mar. 26, 1946; d. George L. and Ruth Margaret (Farquhar) Breur; m. Bruce N. Pritchard, 1968 (div. May 1982); children: John Douglas, Tiffany Anne,; m. Robert H. Krause, June 16, 1990. Student, Keuka Coll., 1964-65; BS in Chemistry cum laude, Fairleigh Dickinson U., 1980, MAT summa cum laude, 1994; postgrad., Stevens Inst. Tech.; PhD, Clemson U., 1996. With dept. R & D UniRoyal, Wayne, N.J., 1966-68, Jersey State Chem. Co., North Haledon, 1968-69, Inmont, Clifton, N.J., 1969; from chemist to sr. analyst Lever Bros., Edgewater, N.J., 1976-80; process engr. Bell Telephone Labs., Murray Hill, N.J., 1980-84, RCA, Somerville, N.J., 1984-86; sr. engr. electron beam lithography ops. Gain Electronics Corp., Somerville, 1986-88; ind. tech. cons. Pritchard Assocs., Budd Lake, N.J., 1988-92; tchr. of math. and scis. Mt. Olive Bd. Edn. (temporary assignments), 1990-92; tchr. chemistry Morris Hills Regional Dist., 1992-93; vis. asst. prof. edn. Clemson U., 1994—95, instr. chem. labs., 1994-96, vis. asst. prof. edn., 1995-96, vis. asst. prof. chemistry, 1996-98, lectr. phys. scis. dept. geol. scis., 1998—. Faculty fellow Office of Tchg. Effectiveness and Innovation Clemson U., 1999-2000; presenter workshops and profl. papers for profl. confs. Author: How We Learn and Why We Don't: Student Survival Guide, 1999, 4th edit., 2003; contbr. articles to profl. jours. Troop leader, trainer, cons. Bergen County council Girl Scouts U.S., 1969-80, troop leader Morris Area council, 1980-83, head com. Mt. Olive twp., 1980-81; den leader, den leader coach, trainer Boy Scouts Am., 1973-76. Peter Sammartino scholar, 1994. Fellow: Soc. Antiquaries (Scotland), Am. Inst. Chemists; mem.: AAUW, APA, ASCD, NRA (endowment mem.), IEEE (sr.), AAAS, Nat. Sci. Tchrs. Assn., N.Y. Acad. Scis., Assn. Women in Sci., Law Enforcement Alliance Am. (life), Am. Chem. Soc., Soc. Women Engrs., Am. Soc. Quality Control, 2d. Amendment Sisters, Single Action Shooting Soc., Catawba Valley Scottish Soc. (life patron), Clan Farquharson U.S.A. (asst. commr. for S.C. 1997—98, commr. Carolinas region 1998—99, clan genealogist 1999), Arbor Day Found., Clan Morrison Soc. N.Am. (life), 2d Amendment Found. (life), Nat. Woodlot Owners Assn., Mensa (cert. proctor 1999—), Clan Stewart Soc. of Am., Scottish Am. Mil. Soc. (color guard), Marine Corps League Aux., Alpha Epsilon Lambda, Phi Delta Kappa (editor Clemson Kappan 1995—2000), Phi Omega Epsilon. Republican. Achievements include work in ultra fine line electron beam lithography, statis. process control, rsch. in learning and cognition; designed graduate course of student centered instruction. Home: 303 Cherokee Hills Dr Pickens SC 29671-8619 Office: Clemson U 442 Brackett Hl Clemson SC 29634-0001 E-mail: krause@clemson.edu., krause@cognitiveprofile.com., L_krause@bellsouth.net.

KRAUSE, MANFRED OTTO, physicist; b. Stuttgart, Germany, Mar. 11, 1931; came to U.S., 1960, naturalized, 1970; s. Friedrich Bernhard and Friedel Ernstine K.; m. Josephine Winifred Cammer, Dec. 26, 1963; m. C. Denise Caldwell, Sept. 15, 2001. BS, Technische Universitat Stuttgart, 1954, diploma in physics, 1957, PhD, 1960. Sr. physicist Wm. H. Johnston Labs., Inc., Balt., 1960-63; sr. scientist Oak Ridge Nat. Lab., 1963-95; exch. prof. U. Paris, 1975. Cons. Oak Ridge, 1995—, U. Ctrl. Fla. Contbr. articles on electron, charge and x-ray spectrometry to sci. publs., chpts. to books. Recipient Alexander von Humboldt award, 1975-76. Fellow Am. Phys. Soc.; mem. AAAS, Smithsonian Instn., Natural History Soc., Audubon Soc. Achievements include discoverer of x-ray spectrometry based on photoelectric effect, 1971. Home: 125 Baltimore Dr Oak Ridge TN 37830-7837

KRAUSE, PETER JAMES, pediatrician, researcher, educator; b. Denver, Mar. 17, 1945; s. Peter and Frances (Coles) K.; m. Carol Ann Blawie, May 24, 1975; children: Rebecca Ann, Peter John Paul, Kathleen Helen. BA with honors in Biology, Williams Coll., 1967; MD, Tufts U., 1971. Diplomate Am. Acad. Pediatrics. Intern in pediatrics Yale-New Haven Hosp., 1971-72, resident in pediatrics, 1972-73, Stanford U. Med. Ctr., Palo Alto, Calif., 1973-74; rsch. fellow pediatric infectious diseases UCLA Sch. Medicine, 1976-79; chief, pediatric infectious diseases Hartford (Conn.) Hosp., 1979-96; attending physician, dir. pediatric AIDS program Conn. Children's Med. Ctr., Hartford, 1996-98, chief, pediatric infectious diseases, 1998—. Asst. prof. pediatrics Sch. Medicine. U. Conn., Farmington, 1979-84, assoc. prof., 1985-91, prof., 1991—; speaker to profl. groups. Author: (with others) Textbook of Pediatric Infectious Diseases, 1987, 4th edit., 2001, Pediatrics: The National Medical Series for Independent Study, 1987, 4th edit., 1998, Conn's Current Therapy, 1991, Current Pediatric Therapy, 1992, Nelson Textbook of Pediatrics, 2000; co-editor: North American Parasitic Zoonoses, 2002; (with D.J. Richardson and P.J. Krause) North American Parasitic Zoonoses, 2002; mem. editl. bd. Jour. Clin. Microbiology, 1991-99; contbr. over 100 articles to profl. jours. Maj. U.S. Army, 1974-76. Recipient nat. rsch. svc. award NIH, 1977-79. Fellow Am. Acad. Pediatrics, Pediatric Infectious Diseases Soc., Infectious Diseases Soc. Am.; mem. AAAS, Am. Pediat. Soc., Am. Soc. Microbiology, Am. Fedn. Clin. Rsch. (sr.), Soc. Pediatric Rsch. (sr.), Assn. Clin. Scientists, Infectious Diseases Soc. Conn., N.Y. Acad. Scis., Am. Pediatric Soc., Sigma Xi. Office: Conn Children's Med Ctr 282 Washington St Hartford CT 06106-3322 E-mail: pkrause@ccmckids.org.

KRAUSE, RICHARD JOHN (RJ), elementary school educator, coach; b. East St. Louis, Ill., Dec. 26, 1950; s. Raymond John and Ruth Ivy (Fischer) K.; life ptnr. Victoria Stigar. AS, Southwestern Ill. Coll., 1970; BS, So. Ill. U., 1972. Cert. elem. tchr., secondary tchr., phys. edn. tchr. Produce clk. Kroger Food Co., East St. Louis, 1969; clk. Belleville (Ill.) Linen Co., 1969-70; tchr., coach St. Charles Sch., DuBois, Ill., 1973-76; county bd. mem. St. Clair County, Belleville, 1982—2002; tchr., coach East St. Louis Sch. Dist., 1976—. Co-founder RJ Krause All-Stars Sports Club, Ill., scout Chgo. Cubs, 1995. County bd. mem., St. Clair County, 1982-2002; Dem. precinct committeeman East St. Louis Dem. Orgn., 1982—; pres. Ill. Citizens for Better Govt., East St. Louis, 1972—; founder RJ Krause All-Stars Sports Club. Named Nat. Vol. Coach of the Yr. Gatorade, 1985, Hometown Hero Hardee's, 1992, Coach of Yr. St. Louis Sports Commn., 1999; recipient 40 Under 40 award St. Louis mag., KMOX Radio, 1990, Kimmel Cmty. Svc. award Belleville News-Dem. of So. Ill. U., 1993, award St. Louis Sports Commn., 1999, NFL Cmty. Quarterback award St. Louis Rams, 2001, St. Louis Focus award, 2003. Mem. RJ Krause All-Stars Sports Club (pres. 1977—), Ill. H.S. Assn. for Offcls., K.C., Knights of Peter Claver, Am. Fedn. of Tchrs., Ill. Fedn. of Tchrs. Democrat. Roman Catholic. Achievements include coached 5000th game in 1994. Avocations: Coaching, taking young people on field trips, collecting baseball cards, watching St. Louis sports and U. Mo. football. Home: 820 N 71st St East Saint Louis IL 62203 Office: Wilson Elem Sch 4817 Hallows Ave Washington Park IL 62204

KRAUSE, RICHARD MICHAEL, medical scientist, government official, educator, senior researcher; b. Marietta, Ohio, Jan. 4, 1925; s. Ellis L. and Jennie Mae (Waterman) Krause. BA, Marietta Coll., 1947, DSc (hon.), 1978; MD, Case Western Res. U., 1952; DSc (hon.), U. Rochester, 1979, Med. Coll. Ohio, Toledo, 1981, Hahnemann Med. Coll. and Hosp., 1982; LLD (hon.), Thomas Jefferson U., 1982. Rsch. fellow dept. preventive medicine Case Western Res. U., 1950—51; intern Ward Med. Svc., Barnes Hosp., St. Louis, 1952—53, asst. resident, 1953—54; asst. physician to hosp. Rockefeller Inst., 1954—57, asst. prof., assoc. physician to hosp., 1957—61; prof. epidemiology Sch. Medicine, Washington U., St. Louis, 1962—66, assoc. prof. medicine, 1962—65, prof. medicine, 1965—66; assoc. prof., physician to hosp. Rockefeller U., 1966—68, prof., sr. physician, 1968—75; dir. Rockefeller U. (Animal Rsch. Ctr.), 1974—75, Nat. Inst. Allergy and Infectious Diseases, NIH, HEW, Bethesda, Md., 1975—84; USPHS surgeon, 1975—77; asst. surgeon gen., 1977—84; dean Emory U. Sch. Medicine, Atlanta, 1984—89, Robert W. Woodruff prof. medicine, 1984—89; mem. program com. Inst. Medicine, 1986—87; sr. sci. adv. Fogarty Internat. Ctr. NIH, Bethesda, 1989—; sr. investigator NIAID NIH, Bethesda, 2000—. Bd. dirs. Mo.-St. Louis Heart Assn., 1962—66, mem. rsch. com., 1963—66; mem. exec. com. coun. on rheumatic fever and congenital heart disease Am. Heart Assn., 1963—66, chmn. coun. rsch. study com., 1963—66, mem. assn. rsch. com., 1963—66, mem. policy com., 1966—70; mem. commn. streptococcal and staphylococcal diseases U.S. Armed Forces Epidemiol. Bd., 1963—72, dep. dir., 1968—72; bd. dirs. N.Y. Heart Assn., 1967—73, chmn. adv. coun. on rsch., 1969—71, mem. dirs. coun., 1973—75; cons. WHO, 1967—, mem. coccal expert com., 1967—; mem. steering com. Biomed. Sci. Scientific Working Group, WHO, 1978; mem. infectious disease adv. com. Nat. Inst. Allergy and Infectious Disease, NIH, 1970—74; bd. dirs. Royal Soc. Medicine Found., Inc., 1971—77, treas., 1973—75; bd. dirs. Allergy and Asthma Found. Am., 1976—77, Lupus Found. Am., 1977—79. Assoc. editor: Jour. Immunology, 1963—71, sect. editor: Viral and Microbial Immunology, 1974—75; editor: Jour. Exptl. Medicine, 1973—75; adv. editor:, 1976—84, mem. editl. bd.: Bacteriological Revs., 1969—73, Infection and Immunity, 1970—78, Immunochemistry, 1973—80, Clin. Immunology and Immunopathology, 1976—78; contbr. articles to profl. jours. Served with U.S. Army, 1944—46. Decorated Gumhuria medal Egypt; recipient Disting. Svc. medal, HEW, 1979, C. William O'Neal Disting. Am. Svc. award, Robert Koch Medal in Gold, Berlin, 1985, Sr. U.S. Scientist award, Alexander Von Humboldt Found., Fed. Republic Germany, 1986. Mem.: AAAS, Am. Epidemiol. Soc., Practitioner's Soc. N.Y., Royal Soc. Medicine, Infectious Diseases Soc. Am., Am. Coll. Allergists, Harvey Soc., Am. Soc. Microbiology, Am. Assn. Immunologists, Am. Soc. Clin. Investigation, Am. Soc. Biol. Chemists, Am. Acad. Allergy, Assn. Am. Physicians, Inst. Medicine, U.S. Nat. Acad. Scis., Cosmos (Washington), Century Assn. (N.Y.C.). Achievements include research in pathogenesis and epidemiology of streptococcal

diseases; immunochem. studies on streptococcal antigens; immunogenetics; recognition of rabbit antibodies with molecular uniformity, genetics of immune response. Home: 4000 Cathedral Ave NW Apt 413B Washington DC 20016-5268 Office: NIAID NIH Rm 202 16 Center Dr Bldg 16 Bethesda MD 20892-0001 E-mail: richard_krause@nih.gov.

KRAUSE, SONJA, chemistry educator; b. St. Gall, Switzerland, Aug. 10, 1933; came to U.S., 1939; d. Friedrich and Rita (Maas) K.; m. Walter Walls Goodwin, Nov. 27, 1970 BS, Rensselaer Poly. Inst., 1954; PhD, U. Calif., Berkeley, 1957. Sr. phys. chemist Rohm & Haas Co., Phila., 1957-64; vol. U.S. Peace Corps, Nigeria, 1964-65; asst. lectr. Lagos U.; asst. prof. Gondar Health Coll. U.S. Peace Corps, Ethiopia, 1965-66; vis. asst. prof. U. So. Calif., L.A., 1966-67; chemistry faculty Rensselaer Poly. Inst., Troy, N.Y., 1967—, prof., 1978—. Mem. coun. Gordon Rsch. Conf., 1981-83; mem. com. on polymers and engrng. NRC, 1992-94; sabbatical Inst. Charles Sadron, Ctr. Rsch. on Macromolecules, Strasbourg, France, 1987. Author: (with others) Chemistry of Environment, 1978, 2d edit., 2002; editor: Molecular Electro-Optics, 1981; mem. editorial adv. bd. Macromolecules, 1982-84 Bd. dirs. Nat. Plastics Ctr. and Mus., Leominster, Mass., 1996-2000. Fellow Am. Phys. Soc. (coun. divsn. biol. physics 1980-93); mem. IUPAC (assoc.), Am. Chem. Soc. (chmn. ea. N.Y. sect. 1981-82, councillor 1991-95, adv. bd. petroleum rsch. fund 1979-81, assoc. mem. com. on edn. 1993-95, assoc. mem. internat. com. 1996), Biophys. Soc. (coun. 1977), N.Y. Acad. Scis., Sigma Xi (pres. Rensselaer Poly Inst. chpt. 1984-85). Office: Rensselaer Poly Inst Dept Chemistry Troy NY 12180 E-mail: krauss@rpi.edu.

KRAUSE, STEVEN ALBERT, writer; b. Wausau, Wis., Apr. 24, 1951; s. Albert and Jean (Otto) K. BS in Biology, U. Wis., Stevens Point, 1974. Freelance writer popular pubs. Author: Wines From the Wilds, 1982, 96, In Search of the Wild Dewberry, 1983, reprinted as Drinks From the Wilds, 1996. Mem.: Nat. Wildlife Fedn., Nature Conservancy. Home: 1313 Emter St Wausau WI 54401-6122

KRAUSE, THOMAS EVANS, record promotion and radio consultant; b. Mpls., Dec. 17, 1951; s. Donald Bernhard and Betty Ann (Nokleby) K.; m. Barbara Ann Kaufman, Aug. 17, 1974 (div. Apr. 1978); m. Nicole Michelle Purkerson, Aug. 13, 1988; children: Andrew Todd Evans, Allison Michelle. Student, Augsburg Coll., 1969-73; BA, Hastings Coll., 1975. Lic. 3d class with broadcast endorsement FCC. Air personality Sta. KHAS Radio, Hastings, Nebr., 1974-75; air personality, news dir. Sta. KWSL Radio, Sioux City, Iowa, 1975-76; asst. program dir. Sta. KISD Radio, Sioux Falls, S.D., 1976-78; music dir. Sta. KVOX Radio, Fargo, N.D., 1978; program dir. Sta. KPRQ Radio, Salt Lake City, 1978-79; air personality Sta. KIOA Radio, Des Moines, 1980; program dir., ops. mgr. Sta. KKSS Radio, Sioux Falls, 1981-83; program dir. Stas. KIYS/KBBK Radio, Boise, Idaho, 1983-87; program dir., ops. mgr. Sta. WSRZ AM/FM Radio, Sarasota, Fla., 1988-90; owner, cons. Tom Evans Mktg., Seattle, 1990—; editor., pub. Northwest Log, Seattle, 1991-96; mgr. never-MAN, 1994—. Co-founder Sta. KCMR Radio, Augsburg Coll., Mpls., 1973; TV show coord./host Z-106 Hottraxx, Sarasota, 1988-90; air personality/guest disc jockey various radio stas., Pacific N.W., 1990—; host Am. Music Report. Sta. KIX-106 Radio, Canberra, Australia, 1992; instr. Sta. KGRG-FM and KENU-AM, Green River Coll., Auburn, Wash., 1994—. Contbr. articles to various trade publs., mags. Bd. judges Loyola U. Marconi Awards, Chgo., 1992-93; bd. dirs. Habitat for Humanity, Snohomish County, Wash., 1992-96, Martin Luther King Day Celebration, Sarasota County, Fla., 1989-90, Shoreline/So. County YMCA, 1992-95, Puget Sound Sr. Baseball League, 2001—; dist. coord. Carter for Pres., Nebr. 1st Dist., 1975-76; hon. chair March of Dimes Walk Am., Sioux Falls, 1977; head coach Seattle Beavers Baseball Club, 1999—; bd. dirs. Puget Sound Sr. Baseball League, 2001—; media vol., MC or spokesperson M.S. Soc., MDA, Am. Diabetes Assn., Human Soc., others. Mem. Free Methodist Ch. Avocations: sports, films, science fiction, photography, travel. Office: Tom Evans Mktg 16426 65th Ave W Lynnwood WA 98037-2710

KRAUSE, TIMOTHY GILBERT, web site manager; b. Chippewa Falls, Wis., July 17, 1969; s. Gregory Mitchem and Donna Mae (Ripienski) K.; m. Kimberly Catherine Taft, June 18, 1994. BS in Acctg., St. Johns U., 1991; MA in English, St. Cloud State U., 1993; postgrad., Purdue U., 1997. Acct. St. Johns U., Collegeville, Minn., 1988-97; pvt. practice West Lafayette, Ind., 1995-97; dir. web comm. Cargill, Inc., Mpls., 1997—99, 2002—; dir. editl. ops. DirectAg.com., 1999—2001. Cons. Mpls. Pub. Libr.; instr. Princeton Rev., Chgo., 1994—96; educator St. Cloud (Minn.) State U., 1991—93, Purdue U., West Lafayette, Ind., 1993—97; lectr. Richard Hadley Profl. Devel., West Lafayette, 1996; mem. cmty. faculty Met. State U., 2003—; presenter in field. Author: Wired Resumes; reviewer IEEE Profl. Comm., 1996—, Tech. Comm. Quar., 1997—; contbr. articles to profl. jours. Mem. MLA, Nat. Coun. Tchrs. English, Assn. for Bus. Comm. (book rev. editor 1997-98), Rhetoric Soc. Am., Conf. on Coll. Composition and Comm., Alliance for Computers & Writing, Phi Kappa Phi. Avocations: web design, fishing. Home: 1110 Sunnyfield Rd N Minnetrista MN 55364 Office: PO Box 5625 Minneapolis MN 55440-5625 Personal E-mail: tkrause@concentric.net. Business E-Mail: tim_krause@cargill.com.

KRAUSEN, ANTHONY SHARNIK, plastic surgeon; b. Phila., Feb. 22, 1944; s. B. M. and Kay S. (Sharnik) Krausen; m. Susan Elizabeth Park, Sept. 6, 1970; children: Park, Allison. Student, Germantown Acad., 1949-61; BA, Princeton U., 1965; MD, U. Mich., 1969. Diplomate Am. Bd. Surgery. Intern Presbyn. Med. Ctr., Denver, 1969-70; resident St. Joseph Hosp., Denver, 1970-71, Barnes Hosp., St. Louis, 1972-76; with Milw. Med. Clinic, 1976—, head dept. facial plastic surgery, 1984—. Mem. staffs Columbia and St. Mary Hosp., Ozaukee. Pres. Contemporary Art Soc., Milw. Art Mus., 1983; bd. dirs. Friends of Art. With N.G. U.S. Army, 1970—76. Fellow: ACS, Am. Acad. Otalaryngology, Am. Acad. Facial Plastic and Reconstructive Surgery, Am. Acad. Cosmetic Surgery; mem.: Town Club (Milw.), Ivy Club (Princeton, N.J.). Office: 12203 N Corporate Pky Mequon WI 53092 E-mail: skrausen@execpc.com.

KRAUSER, JANICE, special education educator; b. Chgo., Apr. 30, 1951; d. John Francis and June (Fogle) K. BS, U. Tenn., 1973; MEd, Fla. Atlantic U., 1979. Tchr. John Sevier Elem. Sch., Knoxville, Tenn., 1973-76; substitute tchr. Broward County Schs., Ft. Lauderdale, Fla., 1976-78; tchr. Broward Estates Elem. Sch., Ft. Lauderdale, 1978-79, Attucks Mid. Sch., Hollywood, Fla., 1979-81; tchr., spl. edn. specialist South Broward High Sch., Hollywood, 1981-92; spl. edn. specialist New River Middle Sch., Ft. Lauderdale, 1992—. Selected mem. Fla. Spkrs. Bur., 1997—; state-wide design team mem. of inclusion materials for sch.-based adminstrs.; mem. Fla. Comprehensive Sys. Pers. Devel., 1997—. Co-author: (curriculum) Fundamental Math I and II, Consumer Math, Applied English I, II, and III, Fundamental English I, II, III; published photographer. Zone chmn. U.S.Water Polo, Colorado Springs, 1984-92, 98-2000, bd. dirs. 1998-2000; treas. Fla. Water Polo, 1982-97; dist. del. U.S. Masters Swimming, 1987-95; mem. internat. congress Internat. Swimming Hall of Fame, Ft. Lauderdale, 1994—, (bd. dirs. 1989-93); water polo referee VII World Master's Swimming Championships, Casablanca, Morocco, 1998. Named Swimming Coach of Yr. Hollywood Sun-Tattle, 1984-85, Head Water Polo Coach U.S. Olympic Festival, 1986, 90; selected to Pine Crest Sch. Athletic Hall of Fame, 1998, U.S. Water Polo Hall of Fame, 1998. Mem. Coun. Exceptional Children (v.p. Broward County 1998-2000), U. Tenn. Alumni Assn. (sec. Dade Broward chpt., 2003—), Pine Crest Alumni Assn. (bd. dirs. 1993-2000, sec. 1995-97, v.p. 1999-2000, pres. 2000), Brain Injury Assn. of Fla. (event com. 2001—), Phi Delta Kappa. Avocations: needlepoint, reading, sewing, volunteering. Home: 1610 NE 43rd St Oakland Park FL 33334-5509

KRAUSER, ROBERT STANLEY, health care executive; b. N.Y.C., Aug. 24, 1937; s. Benjamin and Eva (Ferester) K.; m. Mary Kay Edwards, June 12, 1977 (dec. May 1999); children: Robert Edwards, Kathryn Edwards. BA, U. Vt., 1958; MS, Columbia U., 1959. Rschr., portfolio analyst Merrill, Lynch, Pierce et al, N.Y.C., 1961-63; dir. spl. situations rschr. Orvis Bros., N.Y.C., 1964-66; dir. rsch. Amott, Baker, N.Y.C., 1966-69; v.p. rsch. counsel Bruns, Nordemann & Rea, N.Y.C., 1970-75; v.p. rsch. assoc. Rosenkrantz, Ehrenkrantz, N.Y.C., 1976-77; investment banker Herzfeld & Stern, Stamford, Conn., 1978-82; chmn., pres. Viral Response Sys., Inc., Greenwich, Conn., 1983—. Patentee in field. With U.S. Army, 1959, res. Recipient Certificate of Recognition Eli Whitney Mus., 1987. Mem. Nat. Assn. Chain Drug Stores, Am. Mensa (Philanthropic award 1987), Inventors Assn. Conn. (Inventor of Yr. 1988), U.S. Tennis Assn. (ranked 1995), The Wimbledon Soc., Landmark Club, East Hampton Tennis Club (mixed doubles champ 1972), Armonk Tennis Club, Grand Slam Tennis Club (singles champ 1977, 78), San Diego Tennis and Racquet Club. Republican. Avocations: tennis, skiing, swimming, travel, medical reading. Home: 444 Taconic Rd Greenwich CT 06831-2850 Office: Viral Response Sys Inc 444 Taconic Rd Greenwich CT 06831-2850

KRAUSER, SHERRIE L. judge; b. Washington, Sept. 11, 1950; 2 children. BA with honors, U. Md., 1972; JD, Duke U., 1973. Bar: Md. 1973, Pa. 1975, D.C. 1977, U.S. Dist. Ct. Md. 1978, U.S. Ct. Appeals (4th cir.) 1985. Trial atty. honors program, criminal divsn. U.S. Dept. Justice, 1973-74; asst. gen. counsel Pa. Crime Commn., 1975-77; pvt. practice Hyattsville, Md., 1977-79; assoc. county atty. Prince George's County, Md., 1979-89; assoc. judge dist. 5 Dist. Ct. Md., 1989-95; assoc. judge Cir. Ct. for Prince George's County, Md., 1995—, coordinating judge family divsn., 2001—. Mem. Youth Drug and Violence Prevention Program, 1996—; mem. Cen. Md. regional adv. bd. Md. Alt. Dispute Resolution Commn., 1999. Recipient award for promotion of equal access to the cts. Md. Hispanic Bar Assn., 1996, Md. Women Leading the Way award, 1997, Women of Achievement in Md. History award, 1998, Pres.'s award for extraordinary contbns. to bar and cmty., 1986, 99. Fellow Md. Bar Found. (life); mem. Nat. Assn. Women Judges (Md. task force on women in prison 1993—, mem. Md. chpt. 1991—), Women's Bar Assn. Md. (bd. dirs. 1985-86, 89-93, co-chair awards com. 1988-93, co-chair program com. 1988-89, co-chair membership com. 1985-86), Md. State Bar Assn. (sect. litigation 1983—, program com. 1985-89, chair program com. 1986-88, spl. com. on citizenship and law-related edn. 1983-90, planning com. 1988-90), Prince George's County Bar Assn. (bd. dirs. 1983-89, chair litigation sect. 1988-89, chair law-related edn. com. 1983-86, 96-00, chair Law Day com. 1982-83, co-chair Law Day com. 1996--), J. Franklyn Bourne Bar Assn., Md. Jud. Conf., Thurgood Marshall Am. Inns of Ct. (master 1998—), Charlotte E. Ray Am. Inns of Ct. (master 1994-96). Office: Prince George's County Cir Ct 14735 Main St Upper Marlboro MD 20772-3065

KRAUSHAR, JONATHAN POLLACK, communications and media consultant; b. Kew Gardens, N.Y., Apr. 26, 1948; s. Leo and Evelyn (Pollack) K.; m. Linda Marie Pekarski, Apr. 20, 1980; children: Matthew, Elizabeth. BA in English, U. Wis., 1969; MBA in Mktg. and Internat. Bus., NYU, 1981. Reporter The Hudson Dispatch, Union City, N.J., 1970, The Record, Hackensack, N.J., 1970-72; assoc. prodr. Sta. WPIX-TV News, N.Y.C., 1973, Sta. WCBS-TV News, N.Y.C., 1974-76; spl. projects supr. Philip Morris Internat., N.Y.C., 1976-82; v.p. Ailes Comms., Inc., N.Y.C., 1982, sr. v.p., 1984, pres. corp. comms. group, 1990, pres., 1991-95, Jon Kraushar and Assocs., Inc., N.Y.C., 1996—. Freelance writer N.Y. Times, N.Y.C., 1972-76, Washington Post, Washington, 1972-76. Author: (with Roger Ailes) You Are the Message, 1988; inventor (video) Electronic Resume, 1982. Media adviser Reagan/Bush Campaign, N.Y.C., 1984, Bush/Quayle Campaign, N.Y.C., 1988, Forbes for Pres., 1996, 2000; debate coach Dick Cheney, 2000. Recipient Feature Writing award N.J. Press Assn., 1972; pub. affairs reporting fellow Washington Journalism Ctr., 1974; fed. grantee U. Wis. Dept. Behavioral Disabilities, 1969. Mem. Internat. Assn. Bus. Communicators (bd. dirs. N.Y. chpt., chmn. main event spkrs. program 1983-85), Econ. Club. Republican. Jewish. Avocations: in-line skating, swimming, water sports. Office: Jon Kraushar and Assocs Inc 10 E 40th St Ste 1308 New York NY 10016-0201

KRAUSKOPF, JOHN, research scientist, educator; b. N.Y.C., Mar. 30, 1928; s. Daniel Melvin and Celia Krauskopf; m. Sharon L. Greene, June 14, 1997; children: Sara (Seeda), Jill Gellene, Lynn Bernstein, David Matthew Krauskopf-Greene. BA, Cornell U., 1949; PhD, U. of Tex., 1953. Mem. tech. staff Bell Labs., Murray Hill, NJ, 1966—86; adj. prof. Ctr. for Visual Sci., U. of Rochester, N.Y.C., 1983—; rsch. prof. Ctr. for Neural Sci., NYU, 1986—. President's adv. com. for dept. of psychology Lehigh U., Bethlehem, Pa. Author seminal sci. papers, book chpts.; editor: (book) Visual Psychophysics and Physiology; mem. editl. bd. Am. Jour. Psychology, Vision Rsch., Investigative Ophthalmology and Visual Sci., Clin. Vision Sci. 1st lt. Med. Svc. Corp. U.S. Army, 1953—55. Recipient Verriest medal, Internat. Color Soc., 1999; scholar N.Y. State and Cornell U., N.Y. State Regents, 1945—49, USPHS Post Doctoral Fellow, NIH, 1956—59, 1975—76, Rsch. Grant, Nat. Eye Inst., 1986—2002. Mem.: Soc. Exptl. Psychologists, Assn. for Rsch. in Vision and Ophthalmology, Ea. Psychol. Assn., APA, Optical Soc. of Am. Achievements include research in Exptl. study of color vision. Office: Ctr for Neural Sci 4 Washington Pl Rm 809 New York NY 10003 Fax: 212-995-4011. Personal E-mail: jkr@cns.nyu.edu.

KRAUSS, ALISON, country musician; b. July 23, 1971; Albums Too Late to Cry, 1987, Two Highways, 1989, I've Got That Old Feeling, 1990, Every Time You Say Goodbye, 1992, I Know Who Holds Tomorrow, 1994 (Grammy award Best Southern, Country or Bluegrass Gospel album), Now That I've Found You, 1995, (with Union Sta.) So Long So Wrong, 1997. Recipient Female Vocalist of Yr. award, Internat. Bluegrass Music Assn., 1990—91, 1993, 1995, Entertainer of Yr. award, 1991, 1995, Rising Video Star of Yr.-Europe award Country Music TV, 1995, Single of Yr. award, Country Music Assn, 1995, Vocal Event of Yr., 1995, Horizon award, 1995, Female Vocalist of Yr., 1995, Best New Country Artist Tour award Pollstar, 1995, Americana Artist of Yr. award Gavin, 1995, Country Artist of Yr. Rolling Stone, 1995, Grammy award Best Bluegrass Recording, 1992, Grammy award Best Country Collaboration with Vocals, 1995, Grammy award Best Female Country Vocal Performance, 1996, Bluegrass/Old-Time Music Album award, 1996, Best Female Vocalist, 1996, Grammy award Best Country Instrumental Performance, 1998, Grammy award Best Bluegrass Album, 1998, Grammy award Best Country Performance by a Duo or Group with Vocals, 1998. Office: DS Management c/o Denise Stiff 1017 16th Ave S Nashville TN 37212-2302

KRAUSS, CARL F. lawyer; b. St. Louis, Mar. 22, 1936; s. Frederick Emanuel and Jewell Edith (Bell) K.; m. Gladys Weber, July 27, 1972; children: Kenneth F., Stephen W. AB in Econs./Bus. Administrn., Knox Coll., 1958; JD, U. Mo., 1961. Bar: Mo. 1961, Kansas 1981, Tex. 1989. Assoc. Morrison & Hecker, Kansas City, Mo., 1961-67, ptnr., 1967-81, Morrison & Hecker, L.L.P, Overland Park, Kans., 1981—2003, Stinson Morrison Hecker, L.L.P, Overland Park, 2003. Bd. editors Mo. Law Review. Founding mem. Overland Park Econ. Devel. Coun., 1986. Mem. ABA, Mo. Bar Assn., Kansas Bar Assn., Tex. Bar Assn., Johnson County Bar Assn., Johnson County Farm Bur. (dir. 2002--), Kansas City Met. Bar Assn., Overland Park C. of C. (dir. 1991-97). Avocation: farming. Home: 1608 E Frontier Ln Olathe KS 66062-2243 Office: Stinson Morrison Hecker LLP 9 Corporate Woods 450 9200 Indian Creek Pkwy Overland Park KS 66210-2002

KRAUSS, GEORGE, metallurgist; b. Phila., May 14, 1933; s. George and Berta (Reichelt) K.; m. Ruth A. Oeste, Sept. 10, 1960; children: Matthew, Jonathan, Benjamin, Thomas. BS in Metall. Engring., Lehigh U., 1955; MS, MIT, 1958, Sc.D., 1961. Registered profl. engr., Colo., Pa. Devel. metallurgist Superior Tube Co., Collegeville, Pa., 1955-56; prof. Lehigh U., Bethlehem, Pa., 1963-75, Colo. Sch. Mines, Golden, 1975—; dir. Advanced Steel Processing and Products Research Ctr., 1984-93; Amax Found. prof., 1975-90; prof. dept. metall. engring. Colo. Sch. Mines, Golden, 1990-92, John Henry Moore prof., 1992-97, Univ. prof. emeritus, metallurg. cons., 1997—. Author: Principles of Heat Treatment of Steel, 1980, Steels: Heat Treatment and Processing Principles, 1990, Tool Steels, 5th edit., 1998; editor: Deformation Processing and Structure, 1984,, Carburizing: Processing and Performance, 1989; editor Jour. Heat Treating, 1978-82; co-editor Fundamentals of Microalloying Forging Steels, 1987; contbr. articles profl. jours. NSF fellow Max Planck Inst. fur Eisenforschung, 1962-63; recipient Adolf Martens medal, Wiesbaden, 1990, Disting. Alumni award Lehigh U., 1993, George R. Brown gold medal, 1998; named Outstanding Educator, Colo. Sch. Mines, 1990. Fellow ASM, The Metals Soc., Internat. Fedn. Heat Treatment and Surface Engring., Japan Soc. Promotion Sci.; mem. AIME, Iron and Steel Soc.-AIME (disting. mem. 1993, Howe lectr. 2003), Iron and Steel Inst. Japan (hon.), Am. Soc. Materials Internat. (hon.; trustee 1991-94, v.p. 1995-96, pres. 1996-97, C.S. Barrett silver medal 1998, Bodeen Heat Treating Achievement award 1999, A.E. White Disting. Tchr. award 1999, Campbell lectr. 2000), Internat. Fedn. Heat Treatment (pres. 1989-91). Home: 3807 S Ridge Rd Evergreen CO 80439-8517 Office: Colo Sch Mines Dept Metall Engring Golden CO 80401 E-mail: gkrauss@mines.edu.

KRAUSS, HENRY FREDERICK, JR., optometrist; b. Sewickley, Pa., Apr. 10, 1952; s. Henry Frederick and Mirella Anna (Guerrieri) K.; m. Sally Winston Miller, July5, 1975; children: Molly Anne, Henry Neil, Malinda Paige, Michael Winston. BS, Centre Coll., Ky., 1976; OD, U. Houston, 1980. Optometrist, owner Eye Care Assocs., Richardson, Tex., 1980—. V.p. ProComp Systems Inc., Albuquerque, 1983-86; ptnr. K-W Distbrs., Dallas, 1983-86, Summit Seminars, Richardson, 1985—; owner, operator Profl. Enhancement Strategies, 1997—. Bd. dirs. Found. for Edn. and Rsch. in Vision, 1988-89, S.W. Vision Svc. Plan, 1982-84. Fellow Am. Acad. Optometry; mem. Am. Optometric Assn., Tex. Optometric Assn. (Young Optometrist of Yr. award 1985), North Tex. Optometric Assn. (pres. 1983-84), Am. Pub. Health Assn. (vision care sect.). Republican. Mem. Lds Ch. Avocations: golf, tennis, photography, horsemanship, sailing, scuba diving. Office: Eye Care Assocs 660 W Campbell Rd Richardson TX 75080-3301

KRAUSS, HERBERT HARRIS, psychologist; b. Phila., June 13, 1940; s. Leon and Ethel Sarah (Cohen) K.; m. Beatrice Joy Osgood, Aug. 26, 1965, children: Michael Conal, Daniel Avram. BS, Pa. State U., 1961, MS, 1962; PhD, Northwestern U., 1966. Lic. psychologist, N.Y. Intern in med. psychology U. Oreg. Med. Sch., 1962-63; asst. prof. psychiatry, psychology U. Kans. Med. Sch., Kansas City, Kans., 1966-67; asst. prof. psychiatry, psychology, chief psychologist in child psychiatry Ohio State U. Coll. Medicine, Columbus, 1967-69; assoc. prof. psychology U. Ga., Athens, 1969-71; prof. psychology Hunter Coll., CUNY, N.Y.C., 1971-2001, chmn. dept. psychology, 1992-99; dir. rehab. rsch. and outcomes mgmt. Internat. Ctr. for the Disabled, N.Y.C., 1984—2002; prof., chmn. dept. psychology Pace U., 2001—. Cons. Managed Health Network, N.Y.C., 1979-90, PhD Program, NYU, rehab. counselling, 1991—; adj. assoc. prof. psychiatry Cornell Med. Sch., N.Y.C., 1978—; assoc. attending psychologist Payne Whitney Clinic, N.Y. Hosp., 1978—; ptnr. Health Resources Mgmt. Co-author: Living with Anxiety and Depression, 1974; co-editor: Between Survival and Suicide, 1976, A Provider's Guide to Psychiatric Services in the General Hospital, 1986, The Aging Workforce: A Guide for University Administrators, 1992; co-editor Internat. Jour. Group Tensions, 1995-2000, assoc. editor, 2000—; cons. editor Jour. Individual Psychology, 1996—. Cons. Irvington, N.Y. Drug Coun., 1983; coach football and wrestling Irvington Sunnysiders, 1978-83, soccer Am. Youth Soccer Orgn., Houston, 1976-78. Named Outstanding Teacher Psychology, N.Y. Psychol. Assn., 1972. Mem. APA, N.Y. Acad. Scis., Ea. Psychol. Assn., Internat. Organ for Study of Group Tensions (v.p., co-pres. 1999—), Am. Coun. on Germany, Am. Evaluation Assn., Cornell Club, Sigma Xi. Home: 520 Grand Ave Newburgh NY 12550-1929 Office: Pace Univ Dept Psychology 1 Pace Plz New York NY 10273-0048 E-mail: herbkrauss@wavelength.net.

KRAUSS, JOHN LANDERS, public policy, urban affairs consultant, mediator, arbitrator; b. Orange, N.J., Oct. 20, 1948; s. George Howard Krauss Jr. and Shirley Krauss; m. M. Elizabeth Wood, May 23, 1976 (div. Sept. 1988); m. Eleanor C. Werbe, June 29, 1991. BA with honors in Polit. Sci., Colo. Coll., 1971; JD, Ind. U., Indpls., 1976. Bar: Ind. 1976, U.S. Dist. Ct. (so. dist.) Ind. 1976, U.S. Ct. Appeals (7th cir.) 1979, U.S. Supreme Ct. 1986, D.C. 1999, cert.: (mediator). Spl. asst. to gov. Office of Gov. of Ind., Indpls., 1971-72; dep. dir. Greater Indpls. Progress Com. Inc., Indpls., 1972 73, exec. dir., 1973 81; dir. dept. met. devel. City of Indpls., 1981-82, dep. mayor, 1982-91; sr. fellow Ind. U. Ctr. for Urban Policy and Environment, Indpls., 1991—; exec. dir. Gov.'s Gambling Impact Study Commn., 1998-99. Mediator Ind. Dept. Edn., 1998—, U.S. Postal Svc., 1998—; mediator and fact finder Ind. Edn. Employment Rels. Bd., 1991—; exec. dir. Ind. Adv. Commn. on Intergovtl. Rels., 1995—; assoc. Kettering Found., Dayton, Ohio, 1997—; chmn. Charles L. Whistler Award Com.; chmn. bd. dirs. Nyhart Co., Inc.; cons. U.S. Govt. Projects, Ukraine, Morocco, Russia, Estonia, Turkey, South Africa; external mediator The World Bank, 2000—; adj. prof. law Ind. U. Sch. Law, Indpls., 2000—; mem. panel of arbitrators Nat. Arbitration Forum; commr. Ind. Supreme Ct. Commn. on Continuing Legal Edn., 2003—; pub. arbitrator NASD Dispute Resolution, 2003—; mem. Roster of Neutrals Internal Rev. Office of Appeals, 2003—. V.p. corp., mem. bd. govs., trustee Indpls. Art Mus.; trustee emeritus Ptnrs. for Livable Cmtys., Washington; bd. govs. Orchard Sch., Indpls.; vice chmn. Tourism for Tomorrow, Inc., 2000—; past mem. exec. com. Pan Am. games Organizing Com., 1987. Named Sagamore of the Wabash, State of Ind. Mem.: AIA (past bd. dirs. Indpls. chpt.), Am. Arbitration Assn. (comml. panel mediators and arbitrators 1998—), Am. Soc. Pub. Adminstrn. (pres. Ind. chpt. 1992—94, bd. dirs. Ind. chpt.), Assn. for Conflict Resolution, Dramatic Club, Pi Gamma Mu. Office: Ind U Ctr Urban Policy/Environment 342 N Senate Ave Indianapolis IN 46204-2630

KRAUSS, JONATHAN SETH, pathologist; b. Bklyn., May 25, 1945; s. Maurice Daniel and Rose (Halpern) K.; children: Timothy, Rachel; m. Janis Krauss, July 3, 2002. AB, Cornell U., 1966; MD, U. Fla., 1970. Intern Med. Coll. Va., Richmond, 1970-71; resident U. N.C., Chapel Hill, 1973-78; asst. prof. Med. Coll. Ga., Augusta, 1978-83, assoc. prof., 1983-93, prof., 1993—2001, prof. emeritus, 2001—. Contbr. articles to Am. Jour. Clin. Pathology, Thrombosis Rsch., Clin. Chemistry, Ann. Clin. Lab. Sci., Modern Pathology, Ob.-gyn. Pres. Augusta Authors Club, 1989-90; treas. Friends of Libr., Augusta, 1992-93. Lt. USNR, 1971-73. Fellow Coll. Am. Pathologists (insp. Ga. 1999—), ACP/ASIM; mem. Am. Soc. Hematology, Torch Club Augusta. Jewish. Achievements include research in crossed affinity electrophoresis of von Willebrand factor antigen, granulocytic fragments in sepsis suggestive of irreversible shock, Factor VII deficient individuals in Georgia, secondary neoplasia in ovarian cancer. Home: PO Box 12611 Augusta GA 30914-0611 Office: 3005 Vassar Dr Augusta GA 30909

KRAUSS, JUDITH BELLIVEAU, nursing educator; b. Malden, Mass., Apr. 11, 1947; d. Leo F. and Dorothy (Conners) Belliveau; m. Ronald L. Krauss, Sept. 5, 1970; children: Jennifer Leigh, Sarah Elizabeth. BS, Boston Coll., 1968; MSN, Yale U., 1970. RN, Conn. Clinical specialist Conn. Mental Health Ctr., New Haven, 1971-73; clin. instr. Yale Sch. Nursing, New Haven, 1971-73; asst. prof. rsch. Yale U. Sch. Nursing, New Haven, 1973-78, assoc. dean, 1978-85, prof., dean, 1985-98, prof., 1998—; master Yale U. Silliman Coll., 2000—. Cons. pharm. and pub. cons., sch., govt. agys. Author: The Chronically Ill Psychiatric Patient and the Community, 1982 (Am. Jour. Nursing Book of Yr. 1982); editor Archives of Psychiat. Nursing, 1986—; mem. editl. bd. Psychiat. Rehab., Psychiat. Svcs.; contbr. articles to profl. jours. Trustee Boston Coll., 1991-99, trustee assoc., 2000—. Am. Nurses Found. scholar, 1978; recipient Chamberlain award Soc. Edn. and Rsch. in Nursing, 1994; named Disting. Alumna Yale Sch. Nursing, 1984; Am. Acad. Nursing/Inst. of Medicine sr. scholar in residence, 1998-99. Mem. ANA (Disting. Contbn. to Psychiat. Nursing award 1992, Leadership citation 2002), Am. Acad. Nursing, Conn. Nurses Assn. (mem. cabinet on edn. 1987 89, bd. dirs. 1988 91, rep. to ANA house of dels. 1988-91, Josephine Dolan award 1989), Sigma Theta Tau (Disting. Lectr. award 1987), Delta Mu (Founders award 1987). Avocations: tennis, golf, hiking, skiing. Office: Yale U Sch Nursing Ste 200 100 Church St S New Haven CT 06536-0740 E-mail: judith.krauss@yale.edu.

KRAUSS, LEO, urologist, educator; b. N.Y.C., Nov. 5, 1928; s. Moe and Marie (Shapiro) K.; m. Harriet Powell, Dec. 4, 1955; children: Robert, Jennifer. BA summa cum laude, Syracuse U., 1948; MD, NYU, 1953. Diplomate Am. Bd. of Urology. Attending urologist N. Shore U. Hosp., Plainview, N.Y., 1963—, Manhasset, N.Y., 1987—; chief of urology Syosset (N.Y.) Comty. Hosp., 1963-78; urologist pvt. practice, Plainview, 1963—. Consulting urologist USAF, Plattsburgh, N.Y., 1961-63, VA Hosp., Tupper Lake, N.Y., 1961-63; asst. prof. urology SUNY, Stony Brook, 1976—. Contbr. articles and abstracts to profl. jours. Bd. dirs. Long Island Cancer Coun., Huntington, N.Y., 1977-79. Capt. USAF, 1954-56, Korea. Named Attending Urologist of Yr., Nassau County Med. Ctr., E. Meadow, N.Y., 1981. Fellow Am. Coll. Surgeons; mem. AMA, N.Y. State Urolog. Soc., Am. Assn. Clin. Urologists, Am. Fedn. for Clin. Rsch., Am. Urolog. Assn., Phi Beta Kappa, Alpha Omega Alpha. Avocations: tennis, travel, reading. Home: 33 Orchard Dr Woodbury NY 11797-2827 Office: Leo Krauss MD PC 875 Old Country Rd Plainview NY 11803-4942

KRAUSS, MICHAEL IAN, law educator; b. N.Y.C., Apr. 21, 1951; s. Alfred Emmanuel Krauss and Geraldine (Teitelbaum) Appleton, m. Cynthia Mary Conner, Sept. 18, 1971; children: Rebecca Liane, Joshua Charles. BA cum laude, Carleton U., 1973; LLL summa cum laude, U. de Sherbrooke, Que., Can., 1976; LLM, Yale U., 1978; postgrad., Columbia U., 1982-83. Bar: Que. 1978, Can. 1978, Va. 1990. With Le'Tourneau, Stein & Assocs., Quebec City,

1976-77; asst. prof. U. de Sherbrooke, 1978-82, assoc. prof.; vis. prof. law U. Toronto, Ont., Can., 1983-84; prof. law George Mason U., Arlington, Va., 1987—. Commr. Quebec Human Rights Comm., Montreal, 1982-87; dir. Inst. Economique de Montreal, 1985-89, Va. Inst. for Pub. Policy, 1999—; adj. faculty mem. Inst. for Justice. Editor: Affirmative Action: Theory and Consequences, 1989; mem. editorial bd. L'Analyste Mag., 1986-89, Foundations Mag., 1988—, (book) Fire and Smoke: Government Lawsuits and the Rule of Law, 2001, Legal Ethics in a Nutshell, 2003; contbr. articles to profl. jours. Named Commonwealth scholar Brit. Commonwealth Office, Ottawa, 1978; fellow Law and Econs. Inst. Law Sch. Columbia U., N.Y.C., 1982, Yale U., New Haven, 1977; Salvatori fellow Heritage Found., 1995; Mackenzie-Kign scholar Govt. of Can., 1977. Mem. ABA, Que. Bar Assn., Can. Bar Assn., Va. State Bar, Va. Assn. Scholars (pres. 19972002). Republican. Jewish. Office: George Mason U Sch Law 3301 Fairfax Dr Arlington VA 22201-4411

KRAUSZ, MICHAEL, philosopher, educator; b. Geneva, Sept. 13, 1942; s. Laszlo and Susan Beate (Strauss) K.; m. Constance Frances Costigan. BA, Rutgers U., 1965; spl. studies, London Sch. Econs., 1963-64; MA, Ind. U., 1966; PhD, U. Toronto, 1969; postgrad., Oxford U., 1969—70. Acting chmn. dept. Bryn Mawr Coll., Pa., 1983-84, chmn. dept., 1993—2003, Milton C. Nahm prof., chair dept. philosophy, 2003—. Vis. asst. prof. Am. U., Washington, 1973-74; vis. prof. lectr. Georgetown U., 1977-79, Hebrew U., Jerusalem, 1978, Swarthmore Coll., 1980-81, Haverford Coll., 1981-82, U. Nairobi, 1985; disting. vis. prof. Am. U. in Cairo, 1980; spl. lectr. U. Oxford, 1987, 88, 89; instr. Curtis Inst. of Music, 2002-03; chmn. external rev. com. Dept. Philosophy, Swarthmore Coll., 1987, Smith Coll., 1990; rsch. assoc. to vice prin. Linacre Coll., Oxford U., 1988, vis. sr. mem., 1986-90; vis. sr. mem. Linacre Coll., 1986-90, 98, 99; vis. prof. Indian Inst. Advanced Studies, Shimla, India, 1992, U. Ulm, 1997; co-dir. Confs. on Philosophy of Human Studies, 1981-88, chmn., 1988-94, Greater Phila. Philosophy Consortium; mem. emeritus fellowship selection panel, Anew W. Mellon Found. Princeton Inst. Advanced Study, 2003. Referee: NEH, 1978, 1982, Jour. Aesthetics and Art Criticism, 1986, Nous, 1996; author: Rightness and Reasons: Interpretation in Cultural Practices, 1993, Limits of Rightness, 2000; co-author (with Rom Harré): Varieties of Relativism, 1995; editor: Critical Essays on the Philosophy of R. G. Collingwood, 1972, Relativism: Interpretation and Confrontation, 1989, The Interpretation of Music, 1993, co-editor: The Concept of Creativity in Science and Art, 1981, Relativism: Cognitive and Moral, 1982, Rationality, Relativism, and the Human Sciences, 1986; editor: Is There a Single Right Interpretation?, 2002, Interpretation and Its Objects: Studies in the Philosophy of Michael Krausz, 2003; co-editor: Jewish Identity, 1993, Interpretation, Relativism & the Metaphysics of Culture, 1999; editor: (series) Philosophy of History and Culture, E.J. Brill, 1986—, Greater Phila. Philosophy Consortium Series, Philosophy in the Global Context, 1995; author: revs., papers; editor: Andreea Ritivoi. Bd. dirs. Solisti N.Y., 1987—88; founder, pres., assoc. artistic dir. Phila. Chamber Orch., 1984; guest condr. Pleven Philharm. Orch., Bulgaria, 1999, 2000, Vrasta Philharm., Bulgaria, 2001, Plovdiv Philharm., Bulgaria, 2002. Fellow Royal Soc. Arts, London, 1973—, Andrew Mellon, Aspen Inst. Humanistic Studies, 1977—78, Ossabaw Found., 1978, 1980, hon. fellow, Tata Energy Rsch. Inst., New Delhi; grantee Ford Found., 1971, Bryn Mawr Coll., 1973—74, 1976, 1985—86, 1989, Alfred Sloan Found., 1986. Fellow Ctr. Study Developing Soc.; mem. Am. Philos. Assn., Am. Soc. Aesthetics (program chmn. ea. div. 1987—, chmn. steering com. ea. div. 1989-90, program chmn. nat. div. 1991, mem. Am. steering com.), World Congress Philosophy, 1998, fellow, Ctr. for the study of Developing Soc., Delhi, 1998, 99. Jewish. Avocations: 20 solo national and international art shows, music (violin and conducting). Office: Bryn Mawr Coll Dept Philosophy Bryn Mawr PA 19010 E-mail: mkrausz@brynmawr.edu.

KRAUSZ, PETER THOMAS, artist, gallery director, educator; b. Brasov, Romania, Aug. 19, 1946; s. Tibor Thomas and Judith Noemi (Mozes) K.; m. Irina Kozak, Sept. 14, 1971; 1 child, Anne-Nathalie. Ed., Fine Arts Acad., Bucharest, Romania, 1964-69. Exhbn. dir. The Saidye Bronfman Ctr., 1980-91; prof. dept. history of art U. Montreal, 1991—. Lectr. Concordia U., Montreal, 1980-91. Exhbns. include Marlborough/Godard Gallery, Montreal, 1976, Forum/76, Montreal Mus. Fine Arts, 1976, Mira Godard Gallery, Toronto, 1979, 97, 99, 2001, Waddington Gallery, Montreal, 1979, Optica Gallery, Montreal, 1985, Galerie Articule Montreal, 1986, Galerie J. Yahouda Meir, Montreal, 1988, 89, Galerie Dresdnere, Toronto, 1988, 89, 90, 93, 94, 95, Robert McLaughlin Gallery, Oshawa, 1989, Mus. Que., 1990, Galerie Lallouz, Montreal, 1992, Concordia U. and Leo Kamen Gallery, Toronto, 1996, 97, Galerie de Bellefeuille, Montreal, 1997, 2000, Musee d'art de Joliette, 1999, Forum Gallery, N.Y., 2002; organizer, curator numerous exhbns.; author: Drawing--A Canadian Survey 1977-1982, 1983, Ten Aspects--Recent Concerns in Canadian Drawing, 1984. Can. Coun. grantee, 1975, 77, 79, 84, 86, 92, 98. Ministry of Cultural Affairs grantee, 1983, 88, 89, 92, 93, 98. Office: PO Box 6128 Sta A Montreal QC Canada H3C 3J7

KRAUSZ, SUSAN, musician, pianist, composer; b. Stuttgart, Fed. Republic of Germany; came to U.S., 1947; d. Moritz and Else (Stein) Strauss; m. Laszlo Krausz, Aug. 18, 1935 (dec. May 1979); children: Peter (dec.), Michael. Diploma in piano teaching, Stuttgart Musik Hoschschule, 1933, Columbia U., 1947-48; MA, Case Western Reserve U., 1956; postgrad., Columbia U. Accompanist N.Y. Coll. Music, 1947-48; piano tchr. Cleve. Music Sch. Settlement, 1949-55, Case Western Res. U., 26 yrs.; now pvt. piano tchr. Musician Orch. la Suisse Romande, Geneva (1st Viola solo), 1938-47, self-compositions TV, 1978-79, 92; composer Piano Picture Book, 1965, Piano Picture Book II, Piano Picture Book III, Variations for Piano Solo, Piano Sonata, Impressions for Piano, 9 Songs for Piano, 2002; 18 piano pieces, songs in four langs. for soprano and piano; accompanist mems. Met. Opera, Covent Garden Opera. Mem. Cleve. Composers Guild of Fortnightly Musical Club. Avocation: reading. Home and Studio: 3429 Blanche Ave Cleveland OH 44118-2129

KRAUT, HARRY JOHN, music producer, consultant; b. Bklyn., Apr. 11, 1933; s. Harry and Margaret Grace (Pflaum) K. AB, Harvard U., 1954, postgrad., 1954-56. Asst. to mgr. Boston Symphony Orch., 1958-68, assoc. mgr., 1968-71; adminstr. Tanglewood Music Ctr., Lenox, Mass., 1962-71; exec. v.p. Amberson, Inc., N.Y.C., 1971—; pres. Arts Planning and Design, Inc., Key West, Fla., 1988—, Pacific Music Festival Found., N.Y.C., 1991—; executor Estate of Leonard Bernstein, N.Y.C., 1990—; advisor Schleswig-Holstein Musik Festival, 1985-90, Pacific Music Festival (Sapporo), 1990—, Festival Bourgogne, 2000—; dir. Performing Arts Ctrs., Key West, Fla., 2002—. Mem. adv. bd. London Symphony Orch., 1995—, N.Y. Festival of Song, N.Y.C., 1992-, EOS Orch., N.Y.C., 1998—; trustee Peabody Conservatory, BAlt., 1983-87; pres. Harvard Glee Club Found., Cambridge, Mass., 1958-69. Exec. prodr. some 150 classic music films and videos, 1961—. Served with U.S. Army, 1956-58. Mem. Acad. TV Arts and Scis. (Emmy award 1978, 88), Harvard Musical Assn., Tennessee Williams Soc. (sec. 2003—). Democrat. Home: 1401 Tropical St Key West FL 33040-4905 Office: The Leonard Bernstein Office Inc 25 Central Park W New York NY 10023-7253 E-mail: harrykr@aol.com.

KRAUT, JOANNE LENORA, computer programmer, analyst; b. Watertown, Wis., Oct. 29, 1949; d. Gilbert Arthur and Dorothy Ann (Gebel) K. BA in Russian, U. Wis., 1971, MS in Computer Sci., 1973. Computer programmer U. Wis. Sch. Bus., Madison, 1969-72, Milw. Ins. Co., 1973-74; tech. coord. Wis. Dept. Justice, Madison, 1974-83; tech. svcs. supr. CRC Telecomm. (formerly Benchmark Criminal Justice Systems), New Berlin, Wis., 1983-89; sr. programmer/analyst Info. Comm. Corp., Pub. Safety Software, Inc., 1989-91; advanced systems engr. EDS, 1991-93; tech. specialist Time Ins., Milw., 1993-96; staff analyst Exacta Corp., Brookfield, Wis., 1996-98; prin. engr. Johnson Controls, Inc., 1998—. Mem. Lakewood Gardens Assn. (dir. 1981-83), Dundee Terrs. Condominium Assn. (officer 1983-99), Hartland Police & Fire Commn. (1998-99). Mem. AAUW, Phi Beta Kappa. Home: 37836 Division St Oconomowoc WI 53066-8910 Office: Johnson Controls Inc 507 E Michigan St Milwaukee WI 53202-5211

KRAUT, JOEL ARTHUR, ophthalmologist; b. Jersey City, July 21, 1937; s. Alan and Lillian Betty (Kravitz) K.; m. Cathy Jane Kleven, June 30, 1963 (div. 1998); children: David Terence, Amy Melissa. AB cum laude, Princeton U., 1958; MD, Columbia U., 1962. Diplomate Am. Bd. Ophthalmology. Intern Boston U. Med. Ctr., 1962-63; resident in ophthalmology NYU-Bellevue Med. Ctr., N.Y.C., 1963-66; chief ophthalmology USAF Hosp., Tachikawa, Japan, 1966-68; pvt. practice specializing in ophthalmology Brookline, Mass., 1968—; asst. prof. Ophthalmology Harvard Med. Sch., 1996—. Clin. assoc., clin. instr. ophthalmology Harvard U. Med. Sch.; clin. instr. ophthalmology Tufts U. Sch. Medicine, 1968-91, clin. assoc. prof. ophthalmology, 1991—, assoc. surgeon ophthalmology, 1981-91, surgeon in ophthalmology, 1991—; dir. Low Vision Ctr., Mass. Eye & Ear Infirmary, 1968—, med. dir. Rehab. Ctr., bd. surgeons, 1993—, pres. eye staff, 1994-96, pres. med. staff, 1995-96, bd. dirs.; mem. med. staff Beth Israel Deaconess Med. Ctr., 1991—; bd. dirs. physiol. optics dept. ophthalmology Tufts-New Eng. Med. Ctr., 1968-73; cons. U.S. 5th Air Force, Japan, 1966-68; ophthalmology adv. com. Tufts U. Health Plan; spl. gift com. Princeton U. Contbr. chpts. to textbooks, articles to med. and profl. jours. Chmn. United Way campaign, 1973; bd. dirs. Boston Aid to Blind, 1987-95 (Man of Vision award 1996); mem. adv. bd. Mass. Commn. for Blind, 1988-94 (Disting. Svc. award 1994). Recipient Disting. Svc. award Mass. Commn. for Blind, 1994, Disting. Svc. award Mass. Eye and Ear Infirmary, 1997; Cane scholar, 1954-58, St. John-Princeton scholar, 1958-62; U. Calif. Rsch. fellow, 1960. Fellow: ACS; mem.: Mass. Soc. Eye Physicians and Surgeons (exec. bd. 1988—, recorder 1991—94, treas. 1995—96, pres.-elect 1996, pres. 1996—98), Mass. Med. Soc. Greater Boston, New Eng. Implant Soc. (sec. 1979—81, pres. 1981—83), Intraocular Lens Soc., Soc. Geriatric Ophthalmology, Nat. Assn. Visually Handicapped (adv. bd. 1991—), Mass. Ophthal. Soc., New Eng. Ophthal. Soc. (mem. nominating com. 1997—, state councillor 1998—), Am. Acad. Ophthalmology (mem. low vision rehab. com. 1995—2001, Honor award 1991), Royal Soc. Medicine, du Bailliage de la Chaine des Rotissurs, Princeton U. Club (spl. gifts com. 1992—93, 1996—98, 2002—03), Hazel Hotchkiss Wightman Tennis Club, Sigma Xi, Phi Beta Kappa.

KRAUZE, TADEUSZ KAROL, sociologist, educator; b. Warsaw, Feb. 27, 1934; came to U.S., 1958; s. Alfons W. and Kazimiera (Plazewska) K.; m. Sharon Robin Reland, Mar. 17, 1967; 1 child, Andrzej. MA, U. Lodz, 1955; PhD, NYU, 1974. Lectr. sociology Rutgers U., Newark, 1966-69; lectr. polit. sci. Haverford (Pa.) Coll., 1970-72; rsch. assoc. sociology Cornell U., Ithaca, N.Y., 1975-78; asst. prof. sociology Hofstra U., Hempstead, N.Y., 1971-75, assoc. prof., 1978-85, prof., 1985—. Cons. Com. for Sci. Rsch., Warsaw, 1992; editor-in-chief, Internat. Jour. Sociology, 1995—. Editor: (with K. Slomczynski) Class Structure and Social Mobility in Poland, 1978, Social Stratification in Poland; Eight Empirical Studies, 1986, Internat. Jour. Sociology, 1996—; contbr. articles to Am. Sociol. Rev., European Sociol. Rev., Social Forces. Grantee Internat. Rsch. and Exch. Bd., 1976, 83, 84; Fulbright fellow USIA, 1981-82, Fulbright-Hays rsch. fellow, 1994. Achievements include rsch. in social stratification, sociology of sci. and quantitative methodology. Home: 4 Stuyvesant Oval Apt 9A New York NY 10009-2409 Office: Hofstra U Dept Sociology Hempstead NY 11550

KRAVATH, ALAN WOLFE, education evaluator; b. N.Y.C., Sept. 27, 1939; s. Reuben and Fanny (Tannenbaum) K.; m. Carla Friedman, June 11, 1967; children: Gabriel, Daniel (dec.). BA in English, CCNY, N.Y.C., 1965; MS in Spl. Edn., L.I. U., Bklyn., 1993. Cert. tchr. spl. edn., tchr. English, N.Y. Assoc. editor RSI Mag., N.Y.C., 1963-67; account exec. Creamer-Dickson-Basford Pub. Rels., N.Y.C., 1967-71; nat. dir. pub. info. United Svc. Orgns., Washington, 1971-77; evaluation educator, tchr. N.Y.C. Bd. Edn., 1987—. Founder, pub. (booklet) Westchester Media Directory, 1984. Pub. rels. advisor pub. rels. adv. com. New Rochelle (N.Y.) Bd. Edn., 1977. Mem. East Yonkers Kiwanis (sec. 1984-87). Home: 1245 California Rd Eastchester NY 10709 Office: PS 150 920 E 167th St Rm 114 Bronx NY 10459-2317

KRAVATH, RICHARD ELLIOT, retired pediatrician, educator; b. N.Y.C., May 25, 1935; s. Reuben and Fannie Kravath; m. Pauline Sara Hauser, Aug. 27, 1960; children: Robert, Peter, Caroline. AB, Columbia U., 1956; MD, SUNY, Bklyn., 1960. Diplomate Am. Bd. Pediatrics. Intern Montefiore Med. Ctr., 1960-61, pediatric resident, chief resident, 1964-66, pediatric pulmonary fellowship, 1966-68; dir. div. intensive care pediatrics Albert Einstein Coll. Medicine, Bronx, 1981-82, prof. pediatrics, 1982; dir. in-patient pediatrics King's County Hosp. Ctr., Bklyn., 1982-2000; prof. clin. pediatrics SUNY, Bklyn., 1982-2000; ret., 2000. Author, co-author: Pediatrics: Pretest, 1987, 89, 92, 95; co-author: Water and Electrolytes in Pediatrics, 1982, 2d edit., 1993; contbr. articles to profl. jours. Capt. USAF, 1961-64. Mem. Alumni Assn. SUNY-Bklyn. (pres. 1992). Achievements include patents for monitoring of stress and a partitioning device for pools. Home: 6 Scott St Dobbs Ferry NY 10522-2614

KRAVER, RICHARD MATTHEW, lawyer; b. Bklyn., Nov. 27, 1946; s. Barnett L. and Pearl (Aronson) K.; m. Harriet Shapiro, Sept. 7, 1970; children—Michael E., Barry S. B.S., NYU, 1968, J.D., Syracuse U., 1971. Bar: N.Y. 1972, Fla. 1975, U.S. Dist. Ct. (so. and ea. dist.) N.Y. 1973, U.S. Tax Ct. 1973, U.S. Ct. Appeals (2d cir.) 1973, U.S. Ct. Appeals (D.C. cir.) 1983, U.S. Supreme Ct. 1976, U.S. Dist. Ct. (no. dist.) N.Y. 1986, U.S. Ct. Appeals (3d cir.) 1986. Assoc. Feldshuh & Frank, N.Y.C., 1972-76; sole practice, N.Y.C., 1977-79; ptnr. Kraver & Martin, N.Y.C., 1979-85, Kraver & Parker, N.Y.C., 1985-88, Kraver & Levy, N.Y.C., 1989—. Mem. ABA, N.Y. State Bar Assn., Fla. Bar Assn. Home: 153 Albemarle Rd White Plains NY 10605-3303 Office: Kraver & Levy 767 3rd Ave Fl 35 New York NY 10017-2023

KRAVETZ, NATHAN, educator, author; b. NYC, Feb. 11, 1921; s. Louis and Anna (Thau) K. m. Evelyn Cottan, Dec. 10, 1944; children: Deborah Ruth, Daniel. BEd with hons., UCLA, 1941, MA, 1949, EdD, 1954. Cert. tchg., adminstrn., Calif. Tchr. Walnut Creek (Calif.) Elem Sch., 1941-42; tchr., prin. L.A. Unified Sch. Dist., 1946-64; dir. evaluation rsch. Ctr. for Urban Edn., N.Y.C. Schs., 1965-69; prof. Hunter/Lehman Coll., CUNY, N.Y.C., 1964-76, prof. emeritus, 1979; prof. internat. and gifted edn., dean Calif. State U., San Bernardino, 1976-91, prof. emeritus, 1991. Vis. prof. U. SC, 1985-87, UCLA, 1989, Calif. State U., Northridge, 1998—; fgn. svc. officer US Dept. State, Lima, Peru, 1958-60; staff officer UNESCO, Paris, 1969-72, cons. Venezuela, 1968; cons. Ford Found., Chile, 1964, UN Devel. Program, S.Am., 1973-74, US AID, Pakistan and Indonesia, 1974-75, Benin, 1977, Guatemala, 1992, Chulalongkorn U., Thailand, 1999; lectr. UCLA Humanities Ext., 2002 Author 10 children's books; editor Borgo Press, Calif., 1990-95. Sgt. Air Corps. U.S. Army, 1942—46. Univ. fellow Harvard U., 1951-52; grantee Fulbright Rsch. award, Argentina, 1980. Jewish. Avocation: reading history. E-mail: nathan.kravetz@csun.edu.

KRAVITCH, PHYLLIS A. federal judge; b. Savannah, Ga., Aug. 23, 1920; d. Aaron and Ella (Wiseman) K.. BA, Goucher Coll., 1941; LLB, U. Pa., 1943; LLD (hon.) (hon.), Goucher Coll., 1981, Emory U., 1998. Bar: Ga. 1943, U.S. Dist. Ct. 1944, U.S. Supreme Ct. 1948, U.S. Ct. Appeals (5th cir.) 1962. Practice law, Savannah, 1944—76; judge Superior Ct., Eastern Jud. Circuit of Ga., 1977—79, U.S. Ct. Appeals (5th cir.), Atlanta, 1979—81, U.S. Ct. Appeals (11th cir.), 1981—, sr. judge, 1996—. Mem. Jud. Conf. Standing Com. on Rules, 1994—2000. Trustee Inst. Continuing Legal Edn. in Ga., 1979—82; mem. Bd. Edn., Chatham County, Ga., 1949—55; mem. coun. Law Sch., Emory U., Atlanta, 1985—; mem. vis. com. Law Sch., U. Chgo., 1990—93; bd. visitors Ga. State U. Law Sch., 1994—; mem. regional rev. panel Truman Scholarship Found., 1993—2000; mem. vis. com. Goucher Coll., 2000—. Recipient Hannah G. Solomon award, Nat. Coun. Jewish Women, 1978, Trailblazer award, Greater Atlanta Hadassah, 2000, James Wilson award, U. Pa. Law Alumni Soc., 1992, Kathleen Kessler award, Ga. Assn. Women Lawyers, 2001, Shining Star award, Atlanta Women's Found., 2002. Fellow: Am. Bar Found.; mem.: ABA (Margaret Brent award 1991), Nat. Assn. Women Lawyers (Arabella Babb Mansfield award 1999), U. Pa. Law Soc., Am. Law Inst., Am. Judicature Soc. (Devitt award com. 1998—99), State Bar Ga., Savannah Bar Assn. (pres. 1976). Office: US Ct Appeals 11th Cir 56 Forsyth St NW # 202 Atlanta GA 30303-2205

KRAVITT, JASON HARRIS PAPERNO, lawyer; b. Chgo., Jan. 19, 1948; s. Jerome Julius and Shirley (Paperno) K.; m. Beverly Ray Niemeier, May 11, 1974; children: Nikola Wedding, Justin Taylor Paperno. AB, Johns Hopkins U., 1969; JD, Harvard U., 1972; diploma in comparative legal studies, Cambridge U., Eng., 1973. Bar: Ill. 1973, N.Y. 2002, U.S. Dist. Ct. (no. dist.) Ill. 1973, U.S. Dist. Ct. (so. dist.) N.Y. 2002. Assoc. Mayer, Brown Rowe & Maw (formerly Mayer, Brown & Platt), Chgo., 1973-78, ptnr., 1979—, co-chmn., 1998-2001. Adj. prof. law Northwestern U., Evanston, Ill., 1994—, adj. prof. fin. Kellogg Sch. Mgmt., 1998—. Editor: Securitization of Financial Assets, 2d edit., 1996. Bd. dirs. Chgo. Met. YMCA, 1998-2001, Mus. Contemporary Art, Chgo., 1974-75; dir., chmn. The Cameron Kravitt Found., 1984—; sec., chair legal, regulatory tax and acctg. com. Am. Securitization Forum. Fellow Am. Coll. Comml. Lawyers; mem. ABA, Chgo. Coun. Lawyers, Chgo. Bar Assn., N.Y. Bar Assn., Econ. Club of Chgo., Execs. Club Chgo. Home: 250 Sheridan Rd Glencoe IL 60022-1948 Office: Mayer Brown Rowe & Maw 190 S La Salle St Ste 3100 Chicago IL 60603-3441 E-mail: jkravitt@mayerbrownrowe.com.

KRAVITZ, EDWARD ARTHUR, neuroscientist; b. N.Y.C., Dec. 19, 1932; married, 1958; 2 children. BS, CCNY, 1954; PhD in Biochemistry, U. Mich., 1959. Fellow biochemistry Nat. Heart Inst., 1959—60; rsch. fellow neurophysiology and neuropharmacology Harvard Med. Sch., Boston, 1960—61, instr. neurophysiology and neuropharmacology, 1961—63, from asst. prof. to assoc. prof., 1963—69, prof. neurobiology, 1969—86, George Packer Berry Prof. neurobiology, 1986—. Dir. program neurosci. Harvard Med. Sch., 1982—90; bd. trustees, exec. com., dir. neurobiology course Marine Biol. Lab., 1975—79; governing coun. Inst. Medicine, 1991—93; lectr. in field. Recipient Von Humboldt award, 1991, Guggenheim award, 1992, Lifetime Achievement in Mentoring award, Harvard Med. Sch. Fellow: AAAS; mem.: Am. Acad. Arts and Sci., Soc. Neurosci. (co-founder neurobiology of disease workshops), Nat. Acad. Sci., Inst. Medicine. Achievements include research in neurohormones and behavior, neuroethology, serotonin and aggression. Office: Harvard Med Sch Dept of Neurobiology 220 Longwood Ave Boston MA 02115-5701 E-mail: edward_kravitz@hms.harvard.edu.

KRAVITZ, ELLEN KING, musicologist, educator; b. Fords, N.J., May 25, 1929; d. Walter J. and Frances M. (Prybylowski) Kokowicz; m. Hilard L. Kravitz, Jan. 9, 1972; children: Julie Frances, Heather Francesstepchildren: Kent, Kerry, Jay. BA, Georgian Ct. Coll., 1964; MM, U. So. Calif., 1966, PhD, 1970. Tchr. 7th and 8th grade music Mt. St. Mary Acad., North Plainfield, NJ, 1949-50; cloistered nun Carmelite Monastery, Lafayette, La., 1950-61; instr. Loyola U., L.A., 1967; asst. prof. music Calif. State U., L.A., 1967-71, assoc. prof., 1971-74, prof., 1974—99, emeritus prof., 1999—. Founder Friends of Music Calif. State U., L.A., 1976. Mem. editl. adv. bd.: Jour. Arnold Schenberg Inst., 1977—87; editor: Jour. Arnold Schoenberg Inst., Vol. I, No. 3, 1977, Jour. Arnold Schoenberg Inst., Vol. II, No. 3, 1978; author (with others): Catalog of Schoenberg's Paintings, Drawings and Sketches; author: (book) Music in Our Culture, 1996. Guest lectr. Schoenberg Centennial Com., 1969—, mem., 1974. Mem.: Hist. Assn. L.A. Music Ctr., Am. Musicol. Soc., L.A. County Mus. Art, Pi Kappa Lambda, Mu Phi Epsilon.

KRAVITZ, LEE, editor; Degree, Yale U.; MA in Journalism, Columbia U. Editor React, 1995—2000; v.p. Parade Pubs., 1995—2000; editor Parade Magazine, N.Y.C., 2000—; sr. v.p. Parade Pubs., 2000—. Office: Advance Publications Inc 711 3rd Ave New York NY 10017-4014*

KRAVITZ, LENNY, singer, guitarist; b. May 26, 1964; 1 child, Zoe. Albums Let Love Rule, 1989, Mama Said, 1991, Are You Gonna Go My Way, 1993 (2 Grammy nominations), Circus, 1995, Five, 1998 (Grammy), Greatest Hits, 2000, Lenny, 2001, Soundtrack Cutting Edge, Waterboy, 1998, Twice Upon a Yesteryear, Austin Powers, The Spy Who Shagged Me, 1999, appeared (films) Lennon: A Tribute, 1991, Lenny Kravitz: Video Retrospective, 1992, (voice films) Rugrats: The Movie, 1999. Recipient Grammy award, 1999. Office: care CAA 9830 Wilshire Blvd Beverly Hills CA 90212-1804 also: Virgin Records 550 Madison Ave New York NY 10022-3211 also: 2100 Columbia Ave Santa Monica CA 90404*

KRAVITZ, MARTIN JAY, lawyer; b. Phila., Oct. 3, 1950; s. Louis L. and Shirley (Best) K.; m. Donna Marie Fawcett, Nov. 26, 1978; children: Daniel Jay, Andrew Stephen. BA, U. Denver, 1972; JD, U. Pacific, 1977. Bar: Nev. 1977, U.S. Dist. Ct. Nev. 1977, U.S. Ct. Appeals (9th cir.) 1978, U.S. Supreme Ct. 1985. Law clk. to presiding justice Nev. Supreme Ct., Carson City, 1977-78; jr. ptnr., assoc. Goodman, Oshins, Brown & Singer, Las Vegas, 1978-82, Oshins, Brown, Singer & Wells, 1982-83; ptnr. Brown, Wells, Beller & Kravitz, Las Vegas, 1983-86, Brown, Wells & Kravitz, Las Vegas, 1986-88, Wells, Kravitz, Schnitzer, Sloane & Lindsey, Las Vegas, 1989—; assoc. prof. bus. law Clark County Community Coll., 1979-80. Chmn. lawyers div. United Jewish Appeal, Las Vegas, 1978— ; trustee Clark County Sch. Bd., 1988. Mem. ABA, Am. Trial Lawyers Assn., Clark County Bar Assn. Democrat. Jewish. Office: Wells Kravitz Schnitzer Sloane & Lindsey 520 S 4th St Las Vegas NV 89101-6524

KRAVITZ, RUBIN, chemist; b. Framingham, Mass., Mar. 22, 1928; s. Abe and Lillian (Cohen) K. m. Geraldine Pudaim, Aug. 20, 1950 (dec.); children: Richard Alan, Steven Jay, Stuart Paul; m. Annabelle S. Durieux, July 16, 1978; 1 child, Michelle Pearl. BS, Northeastern U., 1952, D in Pharm, 1982. Analytical chemist FDA, HEW, Boston, 1956-61; analytical chemist Alcohol and Tobacco div. U.S. Treasury Dept., Boston, 1961-65; supr. phys. testing lab. plastic div. Am. Hoechst Corp., Leominster, Mass., 1967-78, rsch. chemist plastic div., 1978-83; sr. devel. engr. EPS, 1983-85; pres. Nat. Plastics Mus. Inc., 1981-85; dir., pres. T.H.E. Hypnosis Ctr., Virginia Beach, Va., 1986-89; staff pharmacist MacDonald Army Hosp., Ft. Eustis, Va., 1987-89; chief pharmacist U.S. Army Health Clin., Fort Monroe, Va.; pres., chief exec. officer Cadet Labs., Virginia Beach, 1984—; chief pharmacist U.S. Army Health Clinic, Ft. Monroe, 1989—. Del. Va. Pharm. Assn., 1988; mem. Mid-Atlantic Cholesterol Coun. Cubmaster Boy Scouts Am., Worcester, Mass., 1967-68; trustee, founding pres. Nat. Plastics Ctr. and Mus., 1985—. With USAAF, 1946-48. Recipient Hygeia Bowl award, Wyeth Ayerst, 2002. Mem. Assn. Mil. Surgeons U.S., Soc. Plastic Engrs. (newsletter editor 1969-71, treas. Pioneer Valley sect. 1972-73, v.p. 1973-74, chmn. tech. com. 1973, pres. Pioneer Valley sect. 1975-76, chmn. sect. museum 1979-85, achievement award 1981), ASTM (chmn. compression molding 1969-70, vice chmn. publicity and papers com. D-20 on plastics 1972-76, chmn. subcom. specimen preparation, chmn. sect. plastic furniture, chmn. specimen preparation 1976, chmn. task group Kravitz impact test method 1976, chmn. D 20.12 Olefin Plastics com., mem. exec. com. 1982-85), Assn. Analytical Chemists, Assn. to Advance Ethical Hypnosis, Am. Soc. Rsch. and Clin. Hypnosis, K.P. (chancellor comdr. 1963-64).

KRAW, GEORGE MARTIN, lawyer, essayist; b. Oakland, Calif., June 17, 1949; s. George and Pauline Dorothy (Herceg) K.; m. Sarah Lee Kenyon, Sept. 3, 1983 (dec. Nov. 2001). BA, U. Calif., Santa Cruz, 1971; student, Lenin Inst., Moscow, 1971; MA, U. Calif., Berkeley, 1974, JD, 1976. Bar: Calif. 1976, U.S. Supreme Ct. 1980, D.C. 1992. Pvt. practice, 1976—; ptnr. Kraw & Kraw, San Jose, 1988—. Mem. adv. com. Pension Genefit Guaranty Corp., 2002—. Mem. ABA, Internat. Soc. Cert. Employee Benefit Specialists, Nat. Assn. Health Lawyers, Inter-Am. Bar Assn. Office: Kraw & Kraw 333 W San Carlos St Ste 200 San Jose CA 95110-2735

KRAWCZAK, KENNETH FRANCIS, lawyer; b. Saginaw, Mich., Mar. 5, 1951; s. Frank Vincent and Annabelle Kathleen Krawczak; m. Kimberlee Kaye Nelson, Oct. 25, 1986; children: Sarah Krawczak Steed, Joseph, Kerri. BA, We. Coll., Oxford, Ohio, 1974; JD, Ohio State U., 1976. Bar: Ohio 1977, U.S. Dist. Ct. (no. dist.) Ohio 2002. Hearing officer State Employee Compensation Bd., Columbus, Ohio, 1977-78, Ohio Ind. Commn., Toledo, 1978-81; claims atty. Gen. Tire Co., Akron, Ohio, 1981-82; atty. dept. law BP Am. Inc., Cleve., 1982—2002; atty. Swartz, Campbell LLC, Cleve., 2002—. Pres. Self-Insured Group Ohio, 1998—. Avocation: golf. Home: 19163 Seven Oaks Dr Strongsville OH 44136-7541 Office: Swartz Campbell & Detweiler 200 Public Sq # 1120 Cleveland OH 44113

KRAWCZENIUK, JOSEPH VOLODYMYR, humanities educator; b. Ternopil, Ukraine, Oct. 7, 1924; arrived in U.S., 1951; s. Volodymyr and Pelahiya (Murij) Krawczeniuk; m. Oksana Kolodij, Feb. 16, 1957; children: Borys V., Vsevolod J., Bohdan A., Andrij J. PhD, Ludwig-Maximilians-U., Munich, 1951; MLS, Columbia U., 1960. Asst. prof. fgn. lang., lit. and European history King's Coll., Wilkes-Barre, Pa., 1962—67, assoc. prof., 1968—72, prof., 1972—. Author: Metropolitan Andrew Sheptytsky in English Publications, 1963, Cult of Sts. Cyril and Methodius in Ukraine, 1969, Ukrainians on Hawaiian Islands, 1983. Fellow: Shevchenko Scientific Soc.; mem.: Ukrainian Acad. Arts and Scis. Avocations: reading, sports. Office: King's Coll 133 N River St Wilkes-Barre PA 18711 E-mail: jvkrawcz@kings.edu.

KRAWCZYK, EVA, information systems analyst, educator; b. Zgierz, Poland, Feb. 18, 1973; d. Tadeusz Ignacy and Stella Krawczyk. AS, Am. Acad. of Art, 1994; BA, Columbia Coll. of Chgo., 1996; MS in info. sci., Roosevelt U., 1998, MBA, 1999; PhD, Am. Coll. of Metaphysical Theology, 2002; DD, Trinity Coll. & U., 2002. Minister Minn., 2002. Mgr. Excel Mktg. and Comm., Inc., Chgo., 1999—; mergers & acquisitions bus. coord. Internat. Profit Assoc., Buffalo Grove, Ill., 1999—. Volunteering Mercy Home for Boys & Girls, Chgo., 2000—01. Author: (novel) The Investigation of Lived Experiences: From a Phenomenographic & Phenomenological Perspective in the Scope of a Metaphysical Aura and Knowledge Base, 2003, Addicted to a Degree, 2003, Eve's 365 Days of Christmas, 2003. Fund organizer Feed the Children, Chgo., 2000—02. Fellow Grad. Assistantship and fellowship, Walter E. Heller Coll. of Bus. Adminstrn., 1997—98. Mem.: IEEE (assoc.), Polish Am. Leadership Initiative PALI (assoc.), NAFE (assoc.), Nat. Hispanic Soc. (hon.). Independent Thinkers. Christian. Achievements include patents pending for doll and specific type of lamp. Avocations: art, reading, dancing, animation, travel. Home: 5115 N Nagle Ave Chicago IL 60630-1816 Home Fax: 773-594-0315. Personal E-mail: globeeve@aol.com.

KRAWCZYNSKI, TONY EDWARD, music educator; b. Springfield, Mass., Jan. 14, 1974; s. Richard Michael and Dorothy Ellen Krawczynski. MusB in Edn., U. Mass., 1999. Fla.Tchg. Cert. Fla. Dept. of Edn., 2001. Dir. bands Palm Harbor (Fla.) Mid. Sch., 1999—. Marching band asst. Dunedin (Fla.) H.S., 2000, 03. Mem. first no. region divsn. 9 USCG Aux., South Hadley, Mass., 1996. Grantee, Pinellas County Arts Coun., 2002. Mem.: Internat. Assn. Jazz Educators, Coll. Band Dir.'s Nat. Assn., Pinellas County Music Educator's Assn., Fla. Bandmaster's Assn., Music Educator's Nat. Conf. Independent. Roman Catholic. Avocation: baseball. Office: Palm Harbor Middle School 1800 Tampa Road Palm Harbor FL 34683 Office Fax: 727-669-1244. Personal E-mail: tony_krawczynski@places.pcsb.org. E-mail: tony_krawczynski@places.pcsb.org.

KRAWETZ, ARTHUR ALTSHULER, chemist, science administrator; b. Chgo., Oct. 30, 1932; s. John and Grace (Altshuler) K. BS in Chemistry, Northwestern U., 1952; MS in Phys. Chemistry, U. Chgo., 1953, PhD in Phys. Chemistry, 1955. V.p. Phoenix Chem. Lab., Inc., Chgo., 1950-73, tech. dir., 1958—, pres., 1974—. Contbr. articles to profl. jours. Mem. Nat. Safety Coun., 1980-2002. 1st Lt. USAF, 1956-58, capt. Res. Fellow Am. Inst. Chemists (life), Royal Soc. Chemistry (chartered chemist); mem. ASTM (chmn. sub-com. XI engring. scis., sub-com. N-VI fire resistance 1974-84, sub-com. IX-D oxidation 1974-81, task force on precautionary statements for hazardous material and lab. ops. 1976-84, com. mem.), Am. Chem. Soc., Instrument Soc. Am., Air & Waste Mgmt. Assn., Soc. for Applied Spectroscopy, Soc. Automotive Engrs., Soc. Tribologists and Lubrication Engrs., Nat. Lubricating Grease Inst., The Coblentz Soc., Nat. Fire Protection Assn. (com. on classification and properties of hazardous chemical data, phys. and chem. data consistency adv. com.), Chgo. Gas Chromatography Discussion Group, Internat. Assn. Stability and Handling Liquid Fuels (hon.), Phi Beta Kappa, Sigma Xi, Phi Lambda Upsilon, Pi Mu Epsilon. Achievements include patents for temperature control apparatus and method, method of determining acid content of oil sample, automatic oxygen measuring system, viscometers, measurement of bulk modulus and pressure viscosity, corrosion rate evaluation procedures; registered copyrights for various software. Office: Phoenix Chem Lab Inc 3953 W Shakespeare Ave Chicago IL 60647-3497 E-mail: pclinc@xnet.com.

KRAWETZ, STEPHEN ANDREW, molecular medicine and genetics scientist; b. Fort Frances, Ont., Can., Sept. 17, 1955; s. Stephen and Michaelene (Medynski) K.; m. Lorraine Ruth St. John, Aug. 19, 1977; children: Rhochelle Tairaesa, Alexandra Renée. BSc, U. Toronto, Ont., 1977, PhD, 1983. Tchr. Scarborough Bd. Edn., Ont., 1976-77; Alberta Heritage Found. Med. Rsch. postdoc. fellow U. Calgary, Alta., Can., 1983-89; asst. prof. rsch. ctr. for molecular biology Wayne State U., Detroit, 1989, asst. prof. molecular biology and genetics, 1989-92, asst. prof. obstetrics and gynecology and molecular biology and genetics, 1992-94, assoc. prof. ob/gyn. and molecular medicine and genetics, 1994-2000; prof. ob-gyn. and molecular medicine and genetics Inst. Scientific Computing, Detroit, 2000-01; Charlotte B. Failing prof. ob-gyn. and molecular medicine and genetics and Inst. Sci. Computing, Wayne State U., Detroit, 2001—. Biotech. cons., Calgary, 1985-89, Grosse Pointe Woods, Mich., 1989—; co-founder Genetic Imaging, Inc., 1988; mem. gene therapy group DMC, Detroit, 1997—. Mem. editl. bd. BioTechniques, Ag Biotech News and Info.; contbr. numerous articles to scholarly jours. Recipient B.C. Childrens Hosp. Rsch. award, Vancouver, 1984, Computer Applications in Molecular Biology award, IntelliGenetics Inc., Mountain View, Calif., 1988; Alta. Heritage Found. Med. Rsch. fellow, 1985-88. Mem. AAAS, Am. Soc. Human Genetics, Soc. for the Study of Reproduction, Internat. Soc. for Matrix Biology (founding mem.). Achievements include development of splinkers for sequencing DNA, of a computer-based imaging system for biological data, of VPCS cloning vectors, of the basis of biological sequence alignment algorithm; one of the first to describe overlapping reading frames in eucaryotes; first detailed analysis of a mammalian protamine gene; first definition of sequence interpretation errors in the GenBank database; first to define a genic domain in human sperm; research in gene therapy targeted to the amelioration of human disease; showed that selective potentiation of our genome mediates cell-phenotype. Home: 590 S Brys Dr Grosse Pointe Woods MI 48236-1285 Office: Dept Ob-Gyn Ctr Molecular Med Genetics Detroit MI 48201 E-mail: steve@compbio.med.wayne.edu.

KRAYZELBURG, LENNY, Olympic athlete; b. Odessa, Ukraine, Sept. 28, 1975; arrived in U.S., 1989, 1995; s. Oleg and Yelena Krayzelburg. Student, UCLA. Recipient Gold medal 100-meter backstroke, 200-meter backstroke, 4 x 100-meter medley (team) Sydney Olympics, 2000, Summer Nats. Phillips Performance award, 1997-99, Gold medal 100-meter backstroke, Silver medal 200-meter backstroke U.S. Open Championships, San Antonio, 1999, Gold medal 100-meter backstroke, Silver medal 200-meter backstroke Janet Evans Invitational, L.A., 2000; named USA Swimming Swimmer of Yr., 1999; broke 3 world records 50-meter backstroke, 100-meter backstroke, 200-meter backstroke Pan Pacific Championships, 1999, ranked 1st in the world for 50m backstroke, 100m backstroke, 200m backstroke, 1999. Avocations: reading history books, working with computers, basketball, L.A. Lakers. Office: USA Swimming 1 Olympic Plz Colorado Springs CO 80909-5746

KREAGER, EILEEN DAVIS, administrative consultant; b. Caldwell, Ohio, Mar. 2, 1924; d. Fred Raymond and Esther (Farson) Davis. BBA, Ohio State U., 1945. With accounts receivable dept. M & R Dietetic, Columbus, Ohio, 1945-50; complete charge bookkeeper Magic Seal Paper Products, Columbus, 1950-53, A. Walt Runglin Co., L.A., 1953-54; office mgr. Roy C. Haddox and Son, Columbus, 1954-60; bursar Meth. Theol. Sch. Ohio, Delaware, 1961-86; adminstrv. cons. Fin. Ltd., 1986—. Ptnr. Coll. Administrv. Sci., Ohio State U., 1975-80; seminar participant Paperwork Systems and Computer Sci., 1965, Computer Systems, 1964, Griffith Found. Seminar Working Women, 1975; pres. Altrusa Club of Delaware, Ohio, 1972-73. Del. Altrusa Internat., Montreal, 1972, Altrusa Regional, Greenbrier, 1973. Mem. AAUW, Assn. Am. Inst. Mgmt. (exec. coun. of Inst. 1979), Am. Soc. Profl. Cons., Internat. Platform Assn., Ohio State U. Alumna Assn., Columbus Computer Soc., Air Force Assn., Innovation Alliance, Toastmasters Internat., Ohio State U. Faculty Club, Univ. Club Columbus, Capital Club, Delaware Country Club, Columbus Met. Club, Friends Hist. Costume & Textile Collection Ohio State U., Internat. Order Police Ohio, Inc., Motha Michtag Mariner, Inc., Kappa Delta. Methodist. Home: PO Box 214 Columbus OH 43085-0214

KREAGER, WILLIAM, architect; BArch, U. Wash., 1967. Prin. Mithun, 1977—. Mem. Urban Land Inst. Residential Coun. Fellow: AIA (past chair housing profl. interest area 2000, chair nat. housing awards 2001, adv. group, juror honor awards). Office: Pier 56 Ste 200 1201 Alaskan Way Seattle WA 98101-2913*

KREAMER, CAROLYN LEE, nursing educator, community health nurse; b. Waynesboro, Pa., July 28, 1948; d. Martin Noah Kreamer and Manila Keturah Strauser Kreamer. Diploma in nursing, York (Pa.) Hosp. Sch. Nursing, 1969; BS, Pa. State U., U. Pk., Pa., 1975; MS, U. Md., Balt., 1980; PhD, U. Tex. at Austin. Staff nurse Milton S. Hershey Med. Ctr., Hershey, Pa., 1970—73, 1975; vis. nurse, pub. health status York Vis. Nurses Assn., Pa., 1975—76; assoc. instr. nursing York Hosp. Sch. Nursing, Pa., 1976—78; instr. nursing York Coll. of Pa., Pa., 1980—82, Pa. State U., Hershey, 1983—86; assoc. prof. nursing Messiah Coll., Grantham, Pa., 1986—, chairperson, 1986—. Treas. Pa. Higher Edn. Nursing Sch. Assn., Harrisburg, Pa., 2000—03; faculty adv. Lambda Kappa, Sigma Theta Tau Internat., Grantham, Pa., 2003—. Recipient Sci. award, York County Oilmen's Assn., 1969. Mem.: Am. Assn. Critical Care Nurses Assn., Am. Nurses Assn., Sigma Theta Tau. Democrat. Meth. Avocation: horseback riding. Home: 563 Fishing Creek Rd Lewisberry PA 17339 Office: Messiah College Dept Nursing PO Box 3031 One College Ave Grantham PA 17027

KREB, ROBERT JOSEPH, III, physiatrist; b. Phila., Apr. 30, 1945; s. Wellington D. and Elia (di Medici) K.; m. Patricia Napp Holstin, July 19, 1969 (div. July 1989); children: Ashley C., Whitney H., Amanda L., Hilary A.; m. Eileen Eagan, Oct. 6, 1990. BS, St. Joseph's U., Phila., 1967; MD, U. Pa., 1971; MPH, Harvard U., 1973. Pvt. practice, Phila., 1986—; chmn. phys. medicine and rehab. Chester County Hosp., Pa., 1986—, DCMH and Brandywine Hosp.; med. dir. inpatient rehab. Pa. Hosp., 2000—. Assoc. prof. U. Pa., Phila., 1980-90; cons. Johnson & Johnson, N.J., 1983-86, Merck, N.J., 1976-78, Becton-Dickinson, N.J., 1979-82. Inventor in field. With DCM Hosp. Found., Drexel Hill, Pa., 1990—, Brandywine Hosp. found., Calan, Pa., 1992—. Comdr. USPHS, 1972-73. NIH fellow, 1973-74. Fellow NIH, 1973-74; Robert W. Johnson Clinician fellow U. Pa., 1976-77. Fellow Am. Acad. Phys. Medicine and Rehab., Am. Soc. Clin. Evaluation, Am. Acad. Pain Mgmt., Am. Assn. Neurophysiology, Pa. Acad. Phys. Medicine and Rehab., Phila. Coll. Physicians; mem. Phila. Soc. Phys. Medicine and Rehab. Republican. Episcopalian. Avocations: golf, tennis, physical fitness.

KREBS, ARNO WILLIAM, JR., lawyer; b. Dallas, July 7, 1942; s. Arno W. and Lynette (Linnstaedter) K.; m. Peggy Sharon Stagg, Dec. 17, 1966; 1 child, Kirsten; m. Barbara Lyn Craig, Dec. 28, 1973 BA, Tex. A&M U., 1964; LL.B., U. Tex., 1967. Bar: Tex. 1967, U.S. Dist. Ct. (so. dist.) Tex. 1968, U.S. Ct. Appeals (5th cir.) 1971, U.S. Ct. Appeals (11th cir.) 1981, U.S. Dist. Ct. (we. and no. dists.) Tex. 1981, U.S. Supreme Ct. 1983, U.S. Dist. Ct. (ea. dist.) Tex. 1984. Assoc. Fulbright & Jaworski, Houston, 1967-75, ptnr., 1975—. Contbr. articles to profl. jours. Mem. Houston Bar Assn., ABA, Tex. Aggie Bar Assn. (pres. 1978-79), Tex. Bar Found., Houston Bar Found., Tex. A&M U. 12th Man Found. (pres. 1988), Houston Ctr. Club. Lutheran. Office: Fulbright & Jaworski 1301 Mckinney St Fl 51 Houston TX 77010-3031

KREBS, CARL F. architectural firm executive; b. Phila., Aug. 27, 1959; AB, Harvard U., 1981; MARch, Columbia U., 1985. Ptnr. Davis Brody Bond, 1984—. Ptnr.-in-charge Health Scis. Learning Ctr., U. of Wis.; ptnr.- in-charge Sch. of Vet. Medicine, Cornell U., Lang. Resource Ctr., Columbia U. Recipient Arch. Record award, Bus. Week, 2000. Office: Davis Brody Bond LLP 315 Hudson St 9th Fl New York NY 10013 Fax: 212-633-4762.

KREBS, CAROL MARIE, architect, psychiatric therapist; b. St. Louis, May 6, 1958; d. Festus John and Virginia (Klohr) K. B in Environ. Design, U. Kans., 1982; MA in Edn. Counseling, St. Louis U., 1995. Archtl. intern GSA, Kansas City, Mo., 1980-81, Old Post Office Renovation, St. Louis, 1980-81; free-lance archtl. designer St. Louis, 1981-84; archtl. designer Interior Space, St. Louis, 1984, Gina Ward and Assoc., St. Louis, 1984-85, Michael Fox and Assoc., St. Louis, 1985-86; mgr. facility design and constrn. Southwestern Bell Telephone, St. Louis, 1986-88; mgr. int. arch. and design exec. facilities Southwestern Bell Corp. Asset Mgmt., St. Louis, 1989-94; psychiat. therapist DePaul Health Ctr., St. Louis, 1994—, Comtrea, Inc. Therapist St. Mary's Health Ctr., Mo. Dept. Mental Health, Dept. of Developmental Disabilities, 1998-99, MCI WorldCom, 1999-2001, Generation D.; instr., counselor St. Louis C.C. Active Big sister Big Bros./Big Sisters of Greater St. Louis, 1986—; mem. Operation Food Search. Mem. AIA. Avocations: historic building rehabilitation, art and play therapy activities with children and adults. Home: 1030 N Harrison Ave Condo #502 Saint Louis MO 63122-2606 E-mail: cmakjack2@earthlink.net.

KREBS, EDWIN GERHARD, biochemistry educator; b. Lansing, Iowa, June 6, 1918; s. William Carl and Louise Helena (Stegeman) K.; m. Virginia Frech, Mar. 10, 1945; children: Sally, Robert, Martha. AB in Chemistry, U. Ill., 1940; MD, Washington U., St. Louis, 1943, DSc (hon.), 1995; DSc honoris causa, U. Geneva, 1979; hon. degree, Med. Coll. Ohio, 1993; DSc (hon.), U. Ind., 1993, U. Ill., 1995; D honoris causa, U. Nat. De Cuyo, 1993. Intern, asst. resident Barnes Hosp., St. Louis, 1944-45; rsch. fellow biol. chemistry Wash. U., St. Louis, 1946-48; prof., chmn. dept. biol. chemistry Sch. Medicine U. Calif., Davis, 1968-76; from asst. prof. to prof. biochemistry U. Wash., Seattle, 1948-66, prof., chmn. dept. pharmacology, 1977-83, prof. biochemistry and pharmacology, 1984-91; investigator, sr. investigator Howard Hughes Med. Inst., Seattle, 1983-90, sr. investigator emeritus, 1991—. Mem. Phys. Chemistry Study Sect. NIH, 1963-68, Biochemistry Test Com. Nat. Bd. Med. Examiners, 1968-71, rsch. com. Am. Heart Assn., 1970-74, bd. sci. counselors Nat. Inst. Arthritis, Metabolism and Digestive Diseases, NIH, 1979-84, Internat. Bd. Rev., Alberta Heritage Found. for Med. Rsch., 1986, external adv. com. Weis Ctr. for Rsch., 1987-91; mem. subgroup interconvertible enzymes IUB Spl. Interest Group Metabolic Regulation; internat. adv. bd. Advances in Second Messenger Phosphoprotein Rsch.; external adv. com. Cell Therapeutics Inc., Seattle; adv. bd. Kinetek, Vancouver, B.C. Mem. editorial bd. Jour. Biol. Chemistry, 1965-70; mem. editorial adv. bd. Biochemistry, 1971-76; mem. editorial and adv. bd. Molecular Pharmacology, 1972-77; assoc. editor Jour. Biol. Chemistry, 1971-93; mem. internat. adv. bd. Advances in Cyclic Nucleotide Rsch., 1972—; editorial advisor Molecular and Cellular Biochemistry, 1987—. Recipient Nobel Prize in Medicine or Physiology, 1992, Gairdner Found. award, Toronto, 1978, J.J. Berzelius lectureship, Karolinska Institutet, 1982, George W. Thorn award for sci. excellence, 1983, Sir Frederick Hopkins Meml. lectureship, London, 1984, Rsch. Achievement award Am. Heart Assn., Anaheim, Calif., 1987, 3M Life Scis. award FASEB, New Orleans, 1989, Albert Lasker Basic Med. Rsch. award, 1989, CIBA-GEIGY-Drew award Drew U., 1991, Steven C. Beering award, Ind. U., 1991, Welch award in chemistry Welch Found., 1991, Louisa Gross Horwitz award Columbia U., 1989, Alumni Achievement award Coll. Liberal Arts and Scis. U. Ill., 1992, Kaul Found. award for excellence, 1996; John Simon Guggenheim fellow, 1959, 66. Mem. NAS, Am. Soc. Biol. Chemists (pres. 1986, ednl. affairs com. 1965-68, councillor 1975-78), Am. Acad. Arts and Scis., Am. Soc. Pharmacology and Exptl. Therapeutics. Achievements include life-long study of the protein phosphorylation process. Office: U Wash HSB K540A PO Box 357750 Seattle WA 98195-7750

KREBS, LEO FRANCIS, lawyer; b. Botkins, Ohio, June 9, 1937; s. Eugene L. and Velma L. K.; m. Paula Anne Calvert, Nov. 4, 1961; children: Matthew, Mark, Thomas, Peter. BA, U. Dayton, 1959; JD, Georgetown U., 1965. Bar: Ohio 1966, U.S. Dist. Ct. (so. dist.) Ohio 1966, U.S. Ct. Appeals (6th cir.) 1974, U.S. Supreme Ct. 1975. Legal dep. Montgomery Probate Ct., 1966-68; assoc. Bieser, Greer & Landis, Dayton, Ohio, 1968-74, ptnr., 1974—. Assoc. editor Georgetown Law Rev., 1964-65. Chmn. fin. com. Holy Angels, 1986-98, former chmn., bd. dirs. parish coun.; former bd. dirs. Cath. Social Svcs. Dayton, 1987 90; former mem. Oakwood YMCA Baseball Commn.; coach YMCA baseball. 1st lt. U.S. Army, 1959-62. Fellow Am. Coll. Trial Lawyers, Ohio State Bar Found.; mem. ABA, Ohio State Bar Assn., Ohio Assn. Trial Attys., Dayton Bar Assn., Phi Delta Phi. Avocations: hiking, tennis. Office: Bieser Greer & Landis 6 N Main St Ste 400 Dayton OH 45402-1914 E-mail: lfr@bgl.com.

KREBS, MARGARET ELOISE, publishing executive; b. Clearfield, Pa., Apr. 20, 1927; d. Henry Louis and Della Louise (Beahan) Krebs. Grad. high sch. With Progressive Pub. Co., Inc., Clearfield, 1945—, bus. office mgr., 1959—60, bus. mgr., 1960—63, asst. to pub., 1963—69, dir., exec. v.p., 1969—77, pres., 1977—, assoc. pub., 1981—. V.p., sec. Clearfield Broadcasters, Inc., Stas. WCPA-AM and WQYX-FM, 1965—, dir., 1971—. Mem.: Pa. Newspaper Women's Assn., Lake Glendale Sailing Club (sec. 1966—70), Clearfield Bus. and Profl. Women's Club (pres. 1952—53, dist. membership chmn. 1952—53). Democrat. Roman Catholic. Home: 526 Ogden Ave Clearfield PA 16830-2146 Office: 206 E Locust St Clearfield PA 16830-2423

KREBS, MARTHA, physicist, federal science agency administrator; PhD in Theoretical Physics, Cath. U. America, Washington, D.C., 1975. Staff dir. House subcommittee on energy development and applications, Washington, 1977-83; assoc. dir. planning and devel. Lawrence Berkeley Lab., 1983-93; dir. office of sci. Dept. of Energy, 1993-99; sr. fellow Inst. Def. Analyses. Office: Inst Def Analyses 1801 N Beauregard St Alexandria VA 22311-1701

KREBS, MARY JANE SCHIRGER, psychiatric nurse specialist; b. Perth Amboy, N.J., June 2, 1948; d. John William and Eleanore Jean (Hydo) Schirger; m. Jeffrey Scott Krebs, Aug. 4, 1979; children: Derek Jon, Richard William. BS, Trenton (N.J.) State Coll., 1970; MA, NYU, 1977. Cert. clin. nurse specialist in psychiat./mental health nursing. Clin. nurse specialist in adult mental health N.Y. Hosp.-Cornell Med. Ctr., N.Y.C., 1977—83; rsch. assoc. dept. psychiatry Cornell U. Med. Coll., N.Y.C., 1984—87; psychiat. clin. nurse specialist Payne Whitney Clinic, N.Y.C., 1984—88; psychotherapist Assoc. Psychotherapists of Danbury, Conn., 1987—95; asst. dir. nursing Westchester divsn. N.Y. Hosp.-Cornell Med. Ctr., White Plains, 1988—94; dir. nursing Silver Hill Hosp., New Canaan, Conn., 1994—97; v.p. clin. svcs. Jackson Brook Inst., South Portland, Maine, 1997—99; chief clin. and nursing officer Spring Harbor Hosp., South Portland, 1999—. Nursing cons. Contbr. chpts. to books, articles to profl. jours; editor textbook in field. Mem. Orgn. Maine Nurse Execs., Am. Coll. Healthcare Execs., Sigma Theta Tau. E-mail: krebsm@springharbor.org.

KREBS, ROBERT ALAN, lawyer; b. Pitts., Dec. 12, 1958; s. James Arthur and Helen Marie (McGrogan) K.; m. Elizabeth Ann Bedford, Apr. 20, 1985; children: Stephen Vladimir, Diane Kathleen. BA, Pa. State U., 1981; student, U. Exeter, U.K., 1981; JD, Capital U., 1984. Bar: Pa. 1984, D.C. 1989, U.S. Dist. Ct. (ea. dist.) Pa. 1990, U.S. Dist. Ct. (we. dist.) Pa. 1984, U.S. Dist. Ct. (no. dist.) Ohio 1990, U.S. Dist. Ct. (D.C.) 1989, U.S. Ct. Appeals (D.C. cir.) 1989, U.S. Ct. Appeals (3d cir.) 1986, U.S. Supreme Ct. 1988. Assoc. Henderson & Goldberg, Pitts., 1985-87, Messer Shilobod & Crenney, Pitts., 1987-89, Klett Lieber Rooney & Schorling, Pitts., 1989-91, Conte, Melton & D'Antonio, Conway, Pa., 1992—2002, Morella & Assocs., Pitts., 2002—. Articles editor Capital Law Rev., 1983-84. Mem. Pa. Dem. State Com., 37th Dist., 1994-, Allegheny County Dem. Com., Pitts., 1991—; mem. com. on jud. issues Pa. Gov.-Elect Edward G. Rendell Transition Team, 2003; vol. Pitts.; mem. Pa. Workers Compensation Appeal Bd., 2003—. Recipient Am. Jurisprudence award Lawyers Coop. Pub. Co., 1982. Mem. ABA, FBA, D.C. Bar Assn., Pa. Trial Lawyers Assn. (amicus curiae com. 1996--), Allegheny County Bar Assn. (fed. ct. sect. coun. 1996-99), Capital U. Law Sch. Alumni Assn. (bd. dirs. 1995-2001, v.p. 1996-2001), Western Pa. Trial Lawyers Assn. (bd. govs. 1994—, chair edn. com. 1994-95, co-chair pres.'s scholarship com. 2001-03, co-chair comeback award com. 2001-03). Democrat. Roman Catholic. Home: 3235 Comanche Rd Pittsburgh PA 15241-1138 Office: 8150 Perry Hwy Ste 100 Pittsburgh PA 15237 E-mail: kakrebs@morellalaw.com.

KREBS, ROBERT DUNCAN, rail transportation company executive; b. Sacramento, May 2, 1942; s. Ward Carl and Eleanor Blauth (Duncan) K.; m. Anne Lindstrom, Sept. 11, 1971; children: Robert Ward, Elisabeth Lindstrom, Duncan Lindstrom. BA with distinction, Stanford U., 1964; MBA, Harvard U., 1966. Asst. gen. mgr. So. Pacific Transp. Co., Houston, 1974-75, asst. regional ops. mgr., 1975-76, asst. v.p., 1976-77, asst. to pres., 1977-79, gen. mgr., 1979, v.p. transp., 1979-80, v.p. ops., 1980-82, pres., 1982-83, also dir.; pres., chief operating officer Santa Fe So. Pacific Corp., 1983-88, pres., CEO, 1988-96; chmn., pres., CEO Burlington Northern Santa Fe Corp (merger Santa Fe So. Pacific Corp and Burlington Northern), 1997-99; chmn., CEO Burling No. Santa Fe Corp., 1999-2000, chmn., 2000—. Chmn. burlington Northern Santa Fe Corp., 2000—. Bd. dirs. Phelps Dodge Corp., Ft. Worth Symphony Orch. Assn., Tex. Christian U. Mem. Stanford U. Alumni Assn., Phi Beta Kappa, Kappa Sigma. Clubs: Onwentsia (Lake Forest, Ill.), Burlingame, Calif., Pacific Union, Bohemian, Chicago, City (Ft. Worth), Rivercrest Country (Ft. Worth). Office: Burlington Northern Santa Fe Corp PO Box 961052 Fort Worth TX 76161-0052

KREBS, ROCKNE, artist; b. Kansas City, Mo., Dec. 24, 1938; s. Arthur Sanford and Lorine (Fisher) Krebs; m. Nizette Brennan, Oct. 30, 1991; children: Heather, Rockne Brennan, Nizette Cameron. BFA, U. Kans., 1961. Exhbns. include Gallery of Modern Art, Washington, 1968, Corcoran Gallery Art, Washington, 1969, U.S. Pavilion Expo 70, Osaka, Japan, 1970, Art Inst. Chgo., 1970, L.A. County Mus., 1970, New Orleans Mus., 1971, Phila. Mus. Art, 1973, Omni-Internat. Complex, Atlanta, 1973-76, Walker Art Ctr., Mpls., 1974, Art Prk, Lewiston, N.Y., 1975, U.S. Bicentennial Expo Sci. and Tech. Kennedy Space Ctr., Cape Canaveral, Fla., 1976, Balt. Inner Harbor, 1977, Fort Worth Art Mus., 1978, Disneyland Hotel, Anaheim, Calif., 1979, The Mall, Washington, 1980, Cin. Contemporary Art Ctr., 1985, Meml. Art Gallery, Rochester, N.Y., 1987, U. Rochester (N.Y.), 1987, Okla. Art Ctr., 1988; executed laser and neon artwork Urban Scale-Pine Ave. and City of Long Beach, Calif., 1992, laser artwork Pegasus Cloud Projection at Downtown Plz., City of Sacramento, 1993, neon, laser, fiber optic and search lights artwork Red River Bridge, Shreveport, La., 1993-95, animated laser projection Olympics CNN Ctr., Atlanta, 1996, laser art, The Universe Exhbn. at Armory Art Ctr., Pasadena, Calif., 2001; pioneer use of lasers in art; rschr, author: The Laserman Letters to Myself, 1996-99; patentee in field. Lt. USN, 1961-64. Mem.: SAR. Office: PO Box 292 194 Old Mill Ln Burgess VA 22432

KREBS, WILLIAM HOYT, company executive, industrial hygienist; b. Detroit, Apr. 6, 1938; s. William Thomas and Mary Louise (Hoyt) K.; m. Susan Kathryn Bartholomew, Aug. 8, 1964 (div. July 1976); children: Elizabeth Louise, William Thomas II; m. Jane Germer Meikle, June 18, 1983; stepchildren: David Andrew, Sarah Elizabeth. BS, U. Mich., 1960, MPH (IH), 1963, MS, 1965, PhD, 1970. Rsch. asst. U. Mich., Ann Arbor, 1962-63; indsl. hygienist Lumbermens Mut. Casualty Co., Chgo., 1963-64, GM Corp., Detroit, 1970-77, mgr. toxic materials control activity, 1977-81, dir. toxic materials control activity, 1981-90, dir. indsl. hygiene activity, 1990-93; v.p. Indsl. Health Scis., Inc., Grosse Pointe Park, Mich., 1993—. Mem. asbestos adv. com. Mich. Occupational Health Standards Commn., Lansing, 1984—. Contbr. articles to profl. jours. Mem. Grosse Pointe Meml. Ch., Grosse Pointe Farms, 1954; mem. health and safety com. Detroit Area coun. Boy Scouts Am., 1980; mem. environment and energy com. Detroit Regional Chamber. Fellow Am. Indsl. Hygiene Assn. (hon. mem.; bd. dirs. 1976-79, v.p. 1986-87, pres. 1988-89); mem. AAAS, APHA, Mich. Indsl. Hygiene Soc. (pres. 1980-81), Brit. Occupational Hygiene Soc., Internat. Occupational Hygiene Assn. (v.p. 1990-91, pres. 1992-93), Internat. Commn. on Occpl. Health, Soc. Automotive Engrs. Presbyterian. Home: 1014 Bishop Rd Grosse Pointe Park MI 48230-1421 Office: Indsl Health Scis Inc 1014 Bishop Rd Grosse Pointe Park MI 48230-1421

KRECKLOW, DOUGLAS EARL, secondary education educator, coach; b. Omaha, July 6, 1952; s. Earl Harold and Evelyn Florence (Hammer) K.; m. Leslie Tamisiea, Aug. 25, 1973; children: Rebecca Anne, Kyle Douglas. BA in Edn., Wayne State Coll., 1974; MS, Pa State U., 1986. Interim instr. Wayne (Nebr.) State Coll., 1977-78; aquatics dir./coach Ames (Iowa) Parks and Recreation, 1978-79; aquatics dir., coach, chair Westside High Sch., Omaha, 1979—. Del. People to People Visit, Republic China, 1987, pres. Swim Omaha, Performance Enhancement Enterprises, Inc., Omaha, 1990—. Contbr. articles to profl. jours. Instr., trainer ARC; bd. dirs. U.S./USSR Fitness Testing Project for Nebr., 1988. Mem. AAHPERD, Nat. Interscholastic Coaches Assn. (Outstanding Svc. award 1995), Nat. Strength Coaches Assn., Am. Coll. Sports Medicine, Am. Swim Coaches Assn., Nat. High Sch. Athletic Coaches Assn., Nat. Fed. High Sch. Swimming Rules Commn., Nebr. Coaches Assn. (Coach of Yr. 1979-88, 90-95), Omaha Westside Swim Club (advisor 1979—). Republican. Presbyterian. Avocations: golfing, cycling, swimming. Home: 9711 Walnut St Omaha NE 68124-1159 Office: Westside High Sch 8701 Pacific St Omaha NE 68114-5298

KREDELL, CAROL RUTH, artist; b. Paterson, N.J., Oct. 20, 1924; d. Robert Blee and Stella Wilhelmina (Heffelfinger) K. BS, Pratt Inst., Bklyn., 1946; MS in Home Econs., U. Wis., 1957; MS in Art Edn., Syracuse U., 1968. Extension home economist York County/Pa. State U., State College, 1946-60; asst. prof. interior design Cornell U., Ithaca, N.Y., 1960 65; lectr. home econs. Syracuse (N.Y.) U., 1965-67; tchr. art and home econs. Ithaca City Sch. Dist., 1968-88; artist, vol. Trumansburg (N.Y.) Conservatory of Fine Arts, 1982—. Disaster vol. Tompkins County ARC, Ithaca, 1993—; vol. Trumansburg Conservatory fine arts and other shows, 1982—. Mem. Young Ladies Radio League, Second Area

Young Ladies Amateur Radio Club, Tompkins County Amateur Radio Club (operator for disasters), Epsilon Sigma Phi. Republican. Presbyterian. Home: 1 Sunrise Ter Trumansburg NY 14886-9102

KREEGER, MARGARET RYAN, lawyer; b. Torrance, Calif., Apr. 1, 1953; d. Robert Emmett and Margaret Caroline Ryan; m. Withold Udo Kreeger, Sept. 10, 1989; 1 child, Patrick Ryan. BA, U. Calif., Irvine, 1975; JD, U. San Francisco, 1978. Bar: Pa. 1979, Calif. 1981. Trial atty. EEO Commn., Balt., 1978-79, L.A., 1979-85; sr. atty. So. Calif. Edison, L.A., 1985-88; gen. counsel Utility Operation Cons., Pasadena, 1988; counsel Atlantic Richfield Co., L.A., 1989-2000; mng. atty. BP, 2000—. Mem. ABA, Calif. Bar Assn., Los Angeles County Bar Assn. Home: 1191 Shorecrest Ln Huntington Beach CA 92648-4162 Office: BP 6 Centerpointe Dr # 514 La Palma CA 90802

KREEK, LOUIS FRANCIS, JR., lawyer; b. Washington, Aug. 24, 1928; s. Louis F. and Esperance (Agee) K.; m. Gwendolyn Schoepfle, Sept. 12, 1970. BS, MIT, 1948; JD, George Washington U., 1952. Bar: D.C. 1952, U.S. Dist. Ct. D.C. 1952, U.S. Ct. Appeals (D.C. cir) 1952, Ohio 1955, N.Y. 1964, U.S. Dist. Ct. (so. and ea. dists.) N.Y. 1964, N.J. 1972. Patent examiner U.S. Patent Office, Washington, 1948-53; patent atty. Pitts. Plate Glass Co., 1953-54, Battelle Meml. Inst., Columbus, Ohio, 1954-56, Merck & Co., Inc., Rahway, N.J., 1956-60; divsn. patent counsel Air Reduction Co., Murray Hill, N.J., 1960-63; assoc. Kenyon & Kenyon, N.Y.C., 1963-66; patent atty. Johns-Manville Corp., Manville, N.J., 1967-68; sr. patent atty. Esso Rsch. and Engring. Co., Linden, N.J., 1968-73, ICI Ams. Inc, Wilmington, Del., 1973-85; assoc. Hahn Loeser & Parks LLP and predecessor firms, Akron, Ohio, 1985-94, of counsel, 1994—. Mem. ABA, Am. Intellectual Property Law Assn., N.Y. Intellectual Property Law Assn. (assoc.), Cleve. Intellectual Property Law Assn. (bd. dirs. 1991-92), Akron Bar Assn., MIT Alumni Assn. (bd. dirs. fund bd. 1977-80, officers conf. com. 1981-84, chmn. 1983), MIT Club Del. Valley (pres. 1978-80), MIT Club NE Ohio (pres. 1986-89), Am. Diabetes Assn. (bd. dirs. Akron chpt. 1989-90), Akron Roundtable (bd. dirs. 1989-90, 2001-02), Kiwanis (pres. 1989-90, 2001-02, lt. gov. 1992-93). Home: 2321 Stockbridge Rd Akron OH 44313-4512

KREEK, MARY JEANNE, physician; b. Washington; d. Louis Francis and Esperance (Agee) K; m. Robert A. Schaefer, Jan. 24, 1970; children: Robert A., Esperance Anne. BA, Wellesley Coll., 1950; MD, Columbia U. Coll. Physicians and Surgeons, 1962; D honoris causa (hon.), Uppsala U., Sweden, 2000. Med. rschr. NIH, Bethesda, Md., 1957-62; intern, resident Cornell N.Y. Hosp. Med. Ctr., N.Y.C., 1962-65, fellow, 1965-67; instr. medicine Cornell Med. Coll., 1966-67; acad. medicine specializing in internal medicine, endocrinology, gastroenterology, clin. pharmacology, neuroscience, molecular genetics N.Y.C., 1966—. Mem. staff N.Y.-Presbyn. Hosp.-Weill Sch. Medicine of Cornell U., 1968—77, clin. asst. prof., asst. attending physician, now assoc. attending physician, adj. assoc. prof.; asst. prof. Rockefeller U., 1967—72, sr. rsch. assoc., physician, 1972—83, assoc. prof., physician, 1983—94, prof., sr. physician, head of lab., 1994—; head Ind. Lab. on Biology of Addictive Disease, 1975—94, head of lab., 1994—; sr. physician Rockefeller U. Hosp., 1994—; adj. prof. Beijing Med. U., 1996—2000, Peking U., 2000—, Karolinska Inst., 2001; mem. gen. medicine study sect. NIH, 1973—77; co-chmn. John E. Fogarty (NIH) Internat. Conf. Hepatotoxicity Due to Drugs and Chems., 1977, charter mem. peer rev. oversight group, 1996—2000; vis. prof. Pahlavi U., Shiraz, Iran, 1977; spl. adv. Nat. Inst. Drug Abuse, 1976—86, mem. nat. adv. coun., 1991—95, mem. molecular genetics consortium, 1999—; prin. investigator Rsch. Ctr. Biol. Basis Addictive Diseases, 1987—; mem. gastroenterology adv. com. FDA, 1975—79, 1992—96, NIH Gen. Clin.; mem. gen. rsch. ctr. study sect. NIH, 1979—83, chmn., 1982—83; mem. exec. com. Coll. Problems Drug Dependence, 1982—87, 1989—94, chmn. exec. com., 1985—87, chair sci. program com., 1991—96; fellow CPDD, 1992—; dir. NIH-Nat. Inst. Drug Abuse Rsch. Ctr., 1987—. Recipient Borden Rsch. award, 1962, Career Scientist award Health Rsch. Coun. City N.Y., 1974-75, Dole/Nyswander award, Rsch. Scientist award NIH Gen. Clin. sect., 1978—, Mentor of Mentors award Am. Soc. Addiction Medicine, 1995, Assn. for Med. Edn. and Rsch. in Substance Abuse-Betty Ford award for outstanding rsch., 1996, R. Brinkley Smithers Disting. Scholar award Am. Soc. Addiction Medicine, 1999, Nathan B. Eddy award, Lifetime Rsch. award Coll. on Problems of Drug Dependence, 1999. Fellow: ACP, N.Y. Acad. Scis., Am. Fedn. for Clin. Rsch., Am. Coll. Neuropsychopharmacology; mem.: Assn. Am. Physicians, Coun. Fgn. Rels. (permanent mem. 2001—), Soc. on Neuroscis., Rsch. Soc. on Alcoholism, Internat. Narcotic Rsch. Conf. Group (exec. com. 1993—97, pres.-elect 2001—02, pres. 2002—), Internat. Assn. Study Liver, Am. Assn. Study Liver Diseases, Endocrine Soc., N.Y. Gastroent. Assn. (pres. 1987), Am. Gastroent. Assn., Shakespeare Soc. of Wellesley, Sigma Xi, Phi Beta Kappa. Office: Rockefeller U New York NY 10021

KREER, IRENE OVERMAN, association and meeting management executive; b. McGrawsville, Ind., Nov. 11, 1926; d. Ralph and Laura Edith (Sharp) Overman; m. Henry Blackstone Kreer, Dec. 22, 1946 (dec.); children: Laurene (dec.), Linda Kreer Witt. BS in Speech Pathology, Northwestern U., 1948. Speech pathologist Ill. pub. schs., 1947-49; staff asst., lectr. Art Inst. Chgo., 1962—; pres. Irene Overman Kreer & Assocs., Inc., Chgo., 1962—. Frequent lectr. on art, arch., Chgo. area; TV appearances representing Art Inst. edn. programs. Past bd. dirs. Glenview (Ill.) Pub. Libr.; mem. The Art Inst. Chgo., Glenview Cmty. Ch., Field Mus., Chgo. Architecture Found., Smithsonian Assocs. Mem. Nat. Trust Hist. Preservation, Assn. Alumnae Northwestern U. (bd. dirs. 1975—), Delta Delta Delta. Republican. Avocations: travel, archaeology, tennis (ranked in women's singles and doubles, Chgo.).

KREFETZ, GERALD SAUL, investment counselor, writer; b. N.Y.C., July 26, 1932; s. Samuel Frank and Dorothy (Karlikow) K.; widowed; children: Nadine Carol, Adriene Dara. BA, Bklyn. Coll., 1954; MA, Columbia U., 1957. Propr. Krefetz Mgmt. and Rsch., N.Y.C., 1985—. Author: Investing Abroad: A Guide to Financial Europe, 1965, Money Makes Money and the Money Money Makes Makes More Money: The Men Who Are Wall Street, 1970, the Dying Dollar, 1972, rev. edit., 1975, Book of Incomes, 1981, The Smart Investor's Guide: How To Make Money in the Coming Bull Market, 1982, Jews and Money: The Myths and the Reality, 1983, How to Read and Profit From Financial News, 1984, Leverage: The Key to Multiplying Money, 1985, All About Saving, 1986, Making the Most of Your Money Series, 1992, Paying for College, 1995, How to Read and Profit From Financial News, 1995, Parents Guide to Paying for College, 1998. With U.S. Army, 1954-56.

KREFTING, ROBERT J(OHN), publishing company executive; b. Peoria, Ill., Apr. 29, 1944; s. Walter and Rebecca Juliana K.; m. Sally Ann Kingsmill, Aug. 27, 1978; children: Matthew, Nicholas; children by previous marriage: Gordon, Melissa, Sarah. BA magna cum laude with honors in History, Williams Coll., 1966. Subscription sales mgr. Time, Inc., N.Y.C., 1966-71; assoc. pub. Psychology Today, Del Mar, Calif., 1971-74; with CBS Publs., N.Y.C., 1974-83, v.p., group pub. spl. interest mags., 1977-79, pres., 1979-83, City Home Pub., Houston, 1984-85; exec. v.p. McCall Pub. Co., 1985-87; pres. Park Ave. Pub., N.Y.C., 1987-90, Holly Hill Pub., Katanah, N.Y., 1991-98; sr. v.p. Reader's Digest Assn., Pleasantville, 1998—2001. Mem. Mag. Pubs. Assn., Young Presidents Orgn., Waccabuc Country Club, Sky Club, Phi Beta Kappa. Home: 4 Powder Hill Rd Waccabuc NY 10597-1004 E-mail: rkrefting@starband.net.

KREGEL, KEVIN R. astronaut; b. Amityville, N.Y., Sept. 16, 1956; s. Alfred H. and Frances T. Kregel. BS in Astronautical Engring., USAF Acad., Colo. Springs, Colo., 1978; MPA, Troy State U., 1988. Commd. 2d lt. USAF, 1978, student pilot, 1978—79; exchange officer RAF, Lakenheath, England, 1980—83, USN, Whidbey Island Seattle, 1984—86; student USN Test Pilot Sch., Patuxent River, Md., 1987—88; test pilot Eglin AFB, Fla., 1988—90; resigned USAF, 1990; aerospace engr., instr. pilot NASA Shuttle Flights, 1990—92; astronaut trainee Johnson Space Ctr., Houston, 1992—93; space flight crew mem., 1995—. Recipient 4 Space Flight medals, NASA, Exceptional Svc. award. Achievements include 4 Space flights; 5000 flight hours in 30 different aircraft; 66 carrier landings. Office: Astronauts Office CB Johnson Space Ctr Houston TX 77058

KREGER, MELVIN JOSEPH, lawyer; b. Buffalo, Feb. 21, 1937; s. Philip and Bernice (Gerstman) K.; m. Patricia Anderson, July 1, 1955 (div. 1963), children: Beth Barbour, Arlene Roux; m. Renate Hochleitner, Aug. 15, 1975. JD, Mid-valley Coll. Law, 1978; LLM in Taxation, U. San Diego, 1988. Bar: Calif. 1978, U.S. Dist. Ct. (cen. dist.) Calif. 1979, U.S. Tax Ct. 1979, U.S. Supreme Ct. 1995; cert. specialist in probate law, trust law and estate planning law, taxation law, Calif. Life underwriter Met. Life Ins. Co., Buffalo, 1958-63; bus. mgr. M. Kreger Bus. Mgmt., Sherman Oaks, Calif., 1963-78, enrolled agt., 1971—; pvt. practice North Hollywood, Calif., 1978—. Mem. Nat. Assn. Enrolled Agts., Calif. Soc. Enrolled Agts., State Bar Calif., L.A. Bar Assn., San Fernando Valley Bar Assn. (probate sect., tax sect.). Jewish. Avocations: computers, travel. Office: 11424 Burbank Blvd North Hollywood CA 91601-2301 E-mail: mel@meltaxlaw.com.

KREHBIEL, CARL, state representative; b. Sept. 13, 1948; BA in Internat. Rels. and German, U. Kans., 1970; MA in Internat. Rels., PhD in Internat. Rels., U. So. Calif. With U.S. Army, 1970—91; pres. tele. co.; mem. Kans. Ho. of Reps., 1999—. Bd. dirs. McPherson County Crimestoppers. Mem.: Moundridge C. of C., Kans. Telecom. Industry Assn. (bd. dirs.), Disabled Am. Vets., Am. Legion. Republican. Office: 112-S State Capitol 300 SW 10th Ave Topeka KS 66612 Address: PO Box 228 Moundridge KS 67107*

KREHBIEL, FREDERICK AUGUST, II, electronics company executive; b. Chgo., June 2, 1941; s. John Hammond and Margaret Ann (Veeck) K.; m. Kay Kirby, Dec. 21, 1973; children: William Veeck, Jay Frederick. BA, Lake Forest Coll., 1963. Export mgr., then v.p. internat. Molex Inc., Lisle, Ill., 1970-75, exec. v.p., dir., from 1976; vice chmn., CEO Molex Co., 1988-93; chmn., CEO Molex, Inc., Lisle, Ill., 1993—98, co-chmn., CEO, 1998—2001, co-chmn., 2001—. Bd. dirs. Tellabs Inc., Molex, Inc., No. Trust Bank, DeVry, Inc., Grainger Inc. Trustee Rush Med. Ctr., Chgo., Lyric Opera, Chgo., Chgo. Zool. Soc., Chgo. Hist. Soc., Mus. Sci. and Industry, Chgo., Chgo. Orch. Assn., Sch. of Art Inst., Chgo., Terra Mus. Mem. Hinsdale (Ill.) Golf Club, Chgo. Club, Casino Club (Chgo.), Chgo. Yacht Club, Racquet Club Chgo., Everglades Club, Bath and Tennis Club Palm Beach. Home: 505 S County Line Rd Hinsdale IL 60521-4725 Office: Molex Inc 2222 Wellington Ave Lisle IL 60532-3820

KREHTINKOFF-YARLOVSKY, NINA, nursing administrator, medical-legal consulting firm owner; b. Flin Flon, Man., Can., Oct. 5, 1955; d. Vasyl Nicolov and Milka Georgi (Krehtinkoff) Yarlovsky; m. Jay Richard Fisherman, June 26, 1983 (div. Dec. 1996). BS, Roanoke Coll., 1977; postgrad., Autonomous U. Guadalajara, 1977-79; MS, Pace U. Grad. Sch. Nursing, 1992. Cert. legal nurse cons. Staff nurse oncology Yonkers (N.Y.) Gen. Hosp., 1982-83, Montefiore Med. Ctr., Bronx, N.Y., 1984-85; br. mgr., nursing supr. Staff Builders, Health Care Svcs., Inc., Flushing, N.Y., 1985-88; inpatient nurse mgr. Ritter-Scheuer Hospice, Bronx, 1988-90; supr. home care Jacob Perlow Hospice, Beth Israel Med. Ctr., N.Y.C., 1990; patient care mgr. Westmoreland Hospice, Greensburg, Pa., 1992-93; dir. clin. svcs. Olsten Kimberly Quality Care, Inc., White Plains, N.Y., 1993-94; utilization review supr. Staff Builders, Health Care Svcs., Inc., Washington, 1994-95; sr. utilization rev. nurse ADP Integrated Med. Solutions, Rockville, Md., 1996—; pres., owner Med-Law Analysis, Inc., 2001—. Presenter AIDS conf. Mem.: Am. Bd. Quality Assurance and Utilization Rev. Physicians (diplomate 1997—), Nat. Alliance Cert. Legal Nurse Cons. (mem. 2001—). E-mail: medlaw@adelphia.net .

KREIDER, CLEMENT HORST, JR., neurosurgeon; b. Annville, Pa., Oct. 14, 1932; s. Clement Horst and Eleanor Lucille (Etter) K.; m. Yvonne Maria Vignone, Mar. 6, 1983; children: Clement H. III, John William H., George E. Etter (dec. Jan. 2001); stepchildren: Michael A. Ketcham (dec. July 1997), David C. Ketcham. Student, Yale U., 1949-51, 53-54; BS, Bethany (W.Va.) Coll., 1957; MD, Temple U., 1963. Lic. physician, Pa., N.J. Intern Pa. Hosp., Phila., 1963-64; resident in gen. surgery Temple U. Hosp, Phila., 1964-65, resident in neurosurgery, 1965-69; pvt. practice neurosurgery Harrisburg, Pa., 1969-72, Ocean, N.J., 1972-99; chief sect. neurosurgery Jersey Shore Med. Ctr., Neptune, N.J., 1972-96, attending neurosurgeon, 1996-99, emeritus, 2000—. Sr. attending Monmouth Med. Ctr., Long Branch, N.J., 1972-99, emeritus attending, 2000—; full attending Riverview Med. Ctr., Red Bank, N.J., 1972-99, emeritus, 2000; cons. emeritus CentraState Med. Ctr., Freehold, N.J.; courtesy staff emeritus Med. Ctr. of Ocean County, Point Pleasant, N.J., Kimball Med. Ctr., Lakewood, N.J., Bayshore Cmty. Hosp., Holmdel, N.J.; clin. instr. surgery Hershey (Pa.) Med. Ctr., 1970-72, Hahnemann Med. Ctr., Phila., 1970-72. Contbr. articles to profl. jours.; mem. com. on pub. N.J. Medicine, Lawrenceville, 1985-99. With U.S. Army, 1951-53. Fellow Stroke Coun., Am. Heart Assn.; mem. Congress of Neurol. Surgeons, Am. Assn. Neurol. Surgeons Joint Sect. on Cerebrovasc. Surgery, Med. Soc. N.J., N.J. Neurosurg. Soc., Monmouth County Med. Soc., Acad. Medicine of N.J. Avocation: boating.

KREIDER, JIM, farmer, former state legislator; b. Nurnburg, Germany, June 24, 1955; (parents Am. citizens); m. Debbie Kreider; children: Lacey, Neeley. Student, S.W. Mo. State U. Farmer, Nixa, Mo.; mem. Mo. Ho. of Reps., Jefferson City, 1992—2002, spkr. pro tem, 1997—2001, spkr., 2001—02. Mem. agr.-bus. com., agr. com., edn. com., energy environ. com. Mem. com. Am. Soil Conservation Svc. Named Farm Family of Yr., 1992. Mem. Christian County Farm Bur. (v.p., legis. chmn.). Democrat. Home and Office: PO Box 1980 Nixa MO 65714-1980*

KREIDER, LEONARD EMIL, economics educator; b. Newton, Kans., Feb. 25, 1938; s. Leonard C. and Rachel (Weaver) K.; m. Louise Ann Pankratz, June 10, 1963; children: Brent Emil, Todd Alan, Ryan Eric. Student, Bluffton Coll., 1956-58; BA, Bethel Coll., 1960; student, Princeton U., 1960-61; MA, Ohio State U., 1962, PhD, 1968. Economist So. Ill. U., Carbondale, 1965-70; asst. prof. Beloit (Wis.) Coll., 1970—, prof., 1978, chmn. dept. econs. and mgmt., 1984-89, acting v.p. acad. affairs, 1987-88, Allen Bradley prof. econs., 1991—. Chief of party Devel. Assocs., Asuncion, Paraguay, 1970; economist Deere and Co., 1973, Castle and Cooke, San Francisco, 1975-76, AmCore, Rockford, Ill., 1984, Rockford Meml. Hosp., 1990-91, Stone Container, San Jose, Costa Rica, 1996; cons. corps. and attys. Author: Development and Utilization of Managerial Talent, 1968; contbr. numerous articles, reports to profl. jours. Mem. Nat. Assn. Bus. Economists, Am. Econs. Assn., Am. Assn. Higher Edn., Soc. Internat. Devel. (pres. So. Ill. chpt. 1969), Indsl. Relations Research Assn. (elections com. 1974). Presbyterian. Home: 820 Milwaukee Rd Beloit WI 53511-5636 Office: Beloit Coll Dept Econ Mgmt Beloit WI 53511

KREIDLER, CHARLES W(ILLIAM), linguist, educator; b. Frankfort, Ky., Aug. 5, 1924; s. Christopher George and Elizabeth Allen (Best) K.; m. Carol Jane Kardos, Aug. 15, 1959; children: James Christopher, Julia Frances Hickey. AB in Spanish, U. Cin., 1948; MA in Linguistics, U. Mich., 1951, PhD, 1957. Teaching fellow U. Mich., Ann Arbor, 1953-54, asst. prof. English, 1959-63; instr., then asst. prof. modern langs. St. Peter's Coll., Jersey City, 1954-58; Fulbright lectr. in English Ctrl. Univ. Ecuador and U. Guayaquil, Ecuador, 1958-59; assoc. prof., then prof. linguistics Georgetown U., Washington, 1963-93, prof. emeritus, 1993—; Fulbright Prof. U. Sao Paulo, Brazil, 1990, Cath. U. of Asuncion, Paraguay, 1994. Lectr. U. P.R., 1965, U. So. Calif., 1968; guest prof. U. Regensburg, Germany, 1975; cons. in field. Author: (with Allen Glatthorn and Ernest Heiman) The Dynamics of Language, 1971, The Pronunciation of English: A Course Book in Phonology, 1989, Describing Spoken English, 1997, Introducing English Semantics, 1998; editor: Phonology: Critical Concepts, 2000; contbr. articles to profl. jours. With USNR, 1943-46. Home: 4512 Verplanck Pl NW Washington DC 20016-2432 E-mail: chak321@aol.com.

KREIDLER, FRANK ALLAN, lawyer; b. Cleve., Jan. 20, 1947; s. Emil J. and Dorothy M. K.; m. Mary Ann Kreidler, Oct. 4, 1980; children: Catherine Allison, James Fredrick, Kristine Anne, Kimberly Jaclyn. AA, Palm Beach Jr. Coll., Lake Worth, Fla., 1968; BS, Fla. State U., 1970, JD, 1973. Bar: Fla. 1973, U.S. Dist. Ct. (so. dist.) Fla. 1974, U.S. Tax Ct. 1974, U.S. Ct. Appeals (5th cir.) 1976, U.S. Supreme Ct. 1977, U.S. Ct. Mil. Appeals 1977, U.S. Dist. Ct. (mid. dist.) Fla. 1981, U.S. Ct. Appeals (11th cir.) 1982, U.S. Ct. Fed. Claims 1994; diplomate Congress of Cert. Cir. Mediators. Asst. state atty. 15th Circuit, West Palm Beach, Fla., 1973-75, asst. pub. defender Belle Glade, Fla., 1976-78; pvt. practice Belle Glade, 1975-78; city atty. City of Lake Worth, Fla., 1978-82; gen. couns. Lake Worth Utilities Authority, 1980-85; pvt. practice Lake Worth, 1982—. Adj. prof. Fla. Atlantic U., Boca Raton, 1984—; mediator Supreme Ct. Fla., Tallahassee, 1989—, U.S. Dist. Ct. Trial Bar (so. dist.) Fla., Miami, 1982—. Chmn. human rights adv. com. Dist. 9 State of Fla., West Palm Beach, 1992-96; chmn. adv. bd. Palm Beach Kidney Assn., West Palm Beach, 1985-87; mem. Criminal Justice Commn. Corrections Task Force, 1995-97, Nat. Com. for Employer Support of Guard and Res., 1998—, Palm Beach County Emergency Shelter Grants Program adv. bd., 1997-2001; mem. adv. coun. Lake Worth H.S., 1998—2002. Comdr. USNR, 1977—. Recipient Cmty. Svc. award Palm Beach Blood Bank, 1979, Donor of Month award, 1991, Harriette Glasner Freedom award Pal Beach chpt. ACLU, 2000. Mem. ABA, Am. Arbitration Assn., Palm Beach County Seminole Boosters (bd. dirs. 1990—, Pres.' award 1998), Leadership Palm Beach, Naval Res. Assn. (pres. Palm Beach chpt. 1991—2001), Legal Aid Soc., Palm Beach County Bar Assn. (Human Rights Advocacy award 1995), Fla. Bar Assn. (Pro Bono Svc. award 1997). Avocation: 1967 chrysler. Office: 1124 S Federal Hwy Lake Worth FL 33460-5244 E-mail: faklaw@yahoo.com.

KREIFELDT, JOHN GENE, mechanical engineering educator; b. Manistee, Mich., Oct. 7, 1934; s. Chester Edward and Bernadine (Janicki) K.; children: Max, Alexander. BS, UCLA, 1961; MS, EE, MIT, 1964; PhD, Case Western Res. U., 1969. Prof. Tufts U., Medford, Mass., 1969—2001, prof. emeritus, 2001—. Contbr. articles to profl. jours; inventor/patentee "Reach" toothbrush. Grantee NIH, NASA. Office: Dept Mech Engring Tufts Univ Medford MA 02155

KREIFELS, FRANK ANTHONY, lawyer, corporate executive; b. Omaha, Nov. 26, 1951; s. Robert Frank and Mary Ellen (Basan) K.; 1 child, Katherine Joy. BBA in Fin., Creighton U., 1974, MBA in Fin. and Acctg., 1975; JD, Hamline U., 1978. Bar: Minn. 1978, U.S. Dist. Ct. Minn. 1978, Nebr. 1983. Staff atty. NCR-Comten Inc., St. Paul, 1978-80; gen. counsel, sec. Agriventure Corp., Foxley & Co., Foxley Cattle Co., Herd Co., Flavorland Industries (and all affiliates), Omaha, 1980-85; mem. Ellsworth Law Firm, Omaha, 1985-87, exec. v.p., chief operating officer, Dale Beggs Devel. Co. (and all affiliates), 1987—; cons. Small Bus. Adminstrn., Omaha, 1974; corp. lobbyist Foxley Cattle Co./Herd Co., Omaha, 1981-85; appointed Neb. state reporter Am. Agrl. Law Update, 1985—. Campaign coord. Nebr. Rep. Com., 1982, 84. Recipient Cert. of Merit, Small Bus. Adminstrn., 1974. Mem. ABA, Am. Corp. Counsel Assn., Am. Agrl. Law Assn., Nebr. State Bar Assn., Phi Alpha Delta. Roman Catholic. Clubs: Omaha Barrister's, Omaha Westroads. Office: Montclair Profl Ctr 13057 W Center Rd Omaha NE 68144-3748

KREIG, ANDREW THOMAS, trade association executive; b. Chgo., Feb. 28, 1949; s. Albert Arthur and Margaret Theresa (Baltzell) K. AB, Cornell U., 1970; MSL, Yale U., 1983; JD, U. Chgo., 1990. Bar: D.C. 1991, Mass. 1991, Ill. 1991. Writer, editor Hartford (Conn.) Courant, 1970-84; media dir. Conn. House Spkr., Hartford, 1984; freelance author, journalist, lectr. Hartford and Chgo., 1985-89; law clk. U.S. Dist. Judge Mark L. Wolf, Boston, 1990-91; assoc. Latham & Watkins, Washington, 1991-93; v.p., comms. dir. Wireless Comms. Assn. Internat., Inc., Washington, 1993-96, v.p., gen. counsel, 1996, pres., CEO, 1997—. Ethics com. Soc. Profl. Journalists, 1987-90. Author: Spiked: How Chain Management, 1987, 2d edit., 1988; editor Spectrum, 1994—; bd. editors Pvt. & Wireless Cable, 1994—, Wireless Internat., 1996—; contbr. articles to profl. jours. V.p. Residences Market Square, Washington, 1993-98; co-chair Fixed Wireless Com. Coalition, 2000—. Ford Found. fellow Yale Law Sch., New Haven, 1982-83. Mem. Fed. Com. Bar Assn. (legis. com.). Home: PH8 701 Pennsylvania Ave NW Washington DC 20004-2608 Office: Wireless Comms Assn Ste 700 W 1333 H St NW Washington DC 20005 E-mail: president@wcai.com.

KREIMER, MICHAEL WALTER, financial planner, investment company official; b. N.Y.C., Aug. 29, 1963; s. Anthony Kreimer and Frieda (Göebel) Rath; m. Madeline Louise Lawler, Dec. 31, 1992; children: Jillian Marie, Maximilian Walter. BS cum laude, SUNY, Albany, 1985. Lic. ins. agt., N.Y.; CFP. Assoc. v.p. McLaughlin, Piven, Vogel Inc., Jericho, N.Y., 1985-88; fin. planner, br. mgr. A.G. Edwards & Sons, Smithtown, N.Y., 1988—. Agt. Ins. Dept. State of N.Y., 1989—. Cons (newsletter) Investing, 1992—. Fundraiser Big Bros./Big Sisters Suffolk, Commack, N.Y., 1989; mem. Nat. Parks Conservation Assn., Washington, 1992; coach Bellport Girls Soccer, 2002—. Mem. Nat. Assn. Securities Dealers (lic.), Internat. Bd. Standards and Practices for CFPs (CFP mark 1993), Inst. CFPs (direct pub. awareness program 1994-97, L.I. chpt.), Southampton C. of C., Rotary. Republican. Roman Catholic. Avocations: tennis, skiing, golf, running. Home: 2 Abets Creek Path East Patchogue NY 11772-5400 Office: AG Edwards & Sons 760 Montauk Hwy Water Mill NY 11976-2624

KREIMER, OSVALDO N. sociologist, consultant, lawyer; b. Buenos Aires, Dec. 15, 1936; arrived in U.S., 1970; 1 child, Julian. JD, U. Buenos Aires, 1965, postgrad. cert. in sociology, 1966; cert., U. Paris, 1968; PhD, Stanford U., 1976. Comm. mgr. Siam Di Tella, Buenos Aires, 1962—66; asst. prof. Boston U., Boston, 1976—77; unit chief-edn. OAS, Washington, 1977—86, dir. dept. edn., 1986—87, prin. specialist Inter-am. Com. Human Rights, 1989—2001, rapporteur-advisor Indian rights, 2001—; dir. project Indian rights WC.-Am. U., Washington, 2002—. Author: Education and Drug Abuse, 1985; dir. (jour.) La Educacion, 1986—89. Dir. Washington area U.S.-Argentine Coun., 2002—03. Achievements include drafting of American declaration on the rights of indigenous peoples. Avocation: sculpting. E-mail: osvaldokreimer@hotmail.com.

KREIN, CATHERINE CECILIA, broadcast and journalism educator; b. N.Y.C., July 2, 1938; d. Timothy T. and Catherine A. (Lavery) Mitchell; m. Robert Krein, Apr. 18, 1970; 1 child, Karyn Elise. BS, Fordham U., 1960; film cert., NYU, 1974; MA, Queens Coll., 1994. Various positions including prodr., editl. dir., writer CBS News, N.Y.C., 1963-86; chief spokesperson Bklyn. Dist. Atty., 1986-87; v.p. external affairs Molloy Coll., Rockville Centre, N.Y., 1987-99; adj. prof. Hofstra U., 1997—99, prof. journalism and media studies, 1999—. Mem.: IRTS, NATAS, L.I. Communicators Assn., L.I. Coalition Fair Broadcasting, Profl. Pub. Rels. of L.I., Soc. Profl. Journalists, Pub. Rels. Soc. Am., Radio TV News Dirs. Assn. Home: 151-20 88th St Howard Beach NY 11414-2008 E-mail: jrncck@hofstra.edu.

KREIN, DAVID FREDERICK, humanities educator; b. Mauston, Wis., Apr. 14, 1942; s. Gideon Isadore Krein, Dorothy Lillian (Bibb) Krein; m. Louise Ann Hall. BA magna cum laude, U. Dubuque, 1963; MA, Duke U., 1965; PhD, U. Iowa, 1974. Cert. tchg. Iowa, 1978. Instr. history Washburn U., Topeka, Iowa, 1965—67; asst. prof. history Clarke Coll., Dubuque., Iowa, 1967—69; assoc. prof. history Palmer Jr. Coll., Davenport, Iowa, 1976—79; coord. Dept. Social Sci. Scott C. C., Bettendorf, Iowa, 1979—. Author: The Last Palmerston Government: Foreign Policy, Domestic Politics, and the Genesis of "Splendid Isolation", 1978; contbr. articles. Mem. Quad Cities World Affairs Coun., Davenport, Iowa, 1979—85. Recipient Iowa Dist. Tchr. award, U. Iowa, 1986; fellow NDEA fellow, 1969—72; scholar, U. Dubuque, 1960—63. Mem.: The Hist. Soc., N.Am. Conf. British Studies, Am. Hist. Assn., Kappa Delta Pi, Pi Kappa Delta, Phi Alpha Theta. Avocations: fishing, boating, swimming. Home: 6304 Scott St Davenport IA 52806 Office: Scott Community Coll 500 Belmont Rd Bettendorf IA 52722 Personal E-mail: davidkrein@earthlink.net. Business E-Mail: dkrein@eicc.edu.

KREIN, SUZANNE RUTH, writer; b. Alexandria, Va., Feb. 24, 1954; d. June Boutchard and George Allen Rexroat; m. Robert Harold Krein (dec. June 19, 2001); children: Victoria R., Julianna R. BS in Math. and Physics, Mary Wash. Coll., Va., 1976; MS in Computer Sci., Va. Poly. Inst. and State U., 1984. Author: (curriculum) Youth in Action, (curriculum) Pursuits, Mission Mosaic, RA Lad and Crusader, Preteen Bible Study, Family Bible Series, Baptist Adults, T-Com 98 (Youth Vacation Bible School), Bible Discovers, Youth Discovery, (online files) Youth Extra! Adult Extra! Preteen Extra!, (reviews) www.sfsite-.com, (articles) Sunday School Leader. Dir. local chpt. Va. Soc. for Human Life, Fredericksburg, 1989—93; choir mem. Ramoth Bapt. Ch., Stafford, Va., 1976—2003, Sunday sch. tchr., 1977—2003, youth group dir., 1982—86, children's choir dir., 1993—2003. Mem.: Christian Writer's Cir. of Fredericksburg. Baptist. Avocations: writing christian science fiction, contemporary christian music, reading, bowling, homeschool teaching. Personal E-mail: kreinmousewriter@msn.com.

KREINDLER, PETER MICHAEL, lawyer; b. 1945; BA, Harvard U., 1967, JD, 1971. Bar: D.C. 1971, N.Y. 1989. Assoc. Hughes, Hubbard & Reed, 1975-77, ptnr., 1977-88, Arnold & Porter, 1990-91; sr. v.p., gen. counsel and sec. AlliedSignal, Morristown, NJ, 1992—95; sr. v.p., gen. counsel Honeywell Internat., 1999—. Office: Honeywell Inc 101 Columbia Rd Morristown NJ 07960-4640*

KREINES, JOSEPH MELVIN, conductor; b. Chgo., Feb. 3, 1936; s. Leon David and Beatrice (Schoenbaum) Kreines. BA, U. Chgo., 1955, BA in Music, 1956; MusM, U. South Fla., 1977. Conductor U. Chgo. Symphony, 1957—59; assoc. conductor Fla. Symphony Orch., Orlando, 1961—65; conductor Brevard Symphony Orch., Cocoa, Fla., 1965—76; assoc. conductor Fla. Orch., Tampa, 1968—74; conductor Treasure Coast Symphony, Ft. Pierce, Fla., 2000—03. Cons. in field. Author: Music for Concert Band, 1989; composer American Song-Set. Mem.: Music Educators Nat. Conf., Fla. Orch. Assn. (assoc.), Fla. Bandmasters Assn. (assoc.). Avocations: movies, theater. Home and Office: 635 Auburn Ave Melbourne FL 32901

KREINHEDER, HAZEL FULLER, genealogist, historian; b. Northampton, Mass., Aug. 27, 1935; d. John Herbert and Hazel Gertrude (Lamica) Fuller; m. Robert Frederick Kreinheder, Nov. 14, 1959; children: John Frederick, Paul Robert. BA, U. Mass., 1957. Lab. asst. dept. chemistry Amherst (Mass.) Coll., 1952-57; rsch. analyst Dept. Def., Fort George G. Meade, Md., 1957-63; libr. staff mem. Columbia Hist. Soc., Washington, 1976-77; hist. rschr. Washington, 1977-81; staff genealogist DAR, Washington, 1981-85, corrections genealogist, 1985-2001, ethnic and minority genealogist, 1997—, asst. dir. genealogy divsn., 2001—. Hist./geneal. cons. Washington Perspectives, Inc., 1977—90. Co-author/author: 5 booklets. Mem. exec. bd. Capitol Hill Babysitting Coop., 1966—68; mem. Com. 100 Fed. City, 1978—, mem. hist. preservation com., 1978—81; vol. pre-sch. vision screening program Prevention Blindness Soc., 1969—72; mem. Oldest Inhabitants DC, 0199—, Bryan Sch. Neighborhood Assn., 1995—, Nat. Bldg. Mus., 1999—; vol. Friends of Libr./U. Mass.; mem. Cir.-on-the-Hill, treas., 1964—65. Recipient Capitol Hill Citizen of the Yr., Capitol Hill Restoration Soc., 1970. Mem.: DAR (life; nat. vice chmn.'s assn., vice chair patriot index com. 1992—95, Marty Mattoon chpt. libr. 1996, vice chair minority rsch. lineage rsch. com. 1998—), Soc. Genealogique Canadienne-Francaise, Soc. Genealogy Que., Nat. Geneaology Soc., Am. Hist. Assn., Orgn. Am. Historians, Capitol Hill Restoration Soc. (sec. 1967—68, treas. 1968—70, co-chmn. hist. preservation com. 1979—81, chmn. ho. com. 1979—81), Friends of Evergreens, Friends of Libr., Nat. Assn. Rail Passengers, Nat. Mus. Am. Indian (charter mem.), Nat. Inst. Geneal. Rsch. Alumni Assn., Mass. Soc. DAR. Republican. Lutheran. Avocations: civic activities, reading, needlework. Home: 113 Kentucky Ave SE Washington DC 20003-1447 Office: Nat Soc DAR 1776 D St NW Washington DC 20006-5303

KREININ, MORDECHA ELIAHU, economics educator; b. Tel Aviv, Jan. 20, 1930; came to U.S., 1951, naturalized, 1960; m. Marlene Miller, Aug. 29, 1956; children: Tamara, Elana, Miriam. BA, U. Tel Aviv, 1951; MA, U. Mich., 1952, PhD, 1954. Asst. prof. econs. Mich. State U., East Lansing, 1957-59, assoc. prof., 1959-61, prof., 1961-90, univ. disting. prof. econs., 1990—. Vis. prof. econs. UCLA, 1969, UN, Geneva, 1971-73, NYU, 1975, 93, 96, U. Toronto, 1978, others; vis. scholar Inst. Internat. Econs. Studies, U. Stockholm, 1978-80, U. B.C., summer, 1983, Monash U., Melbourne, Australia, 1987-94, 2002, NYU, 1993, 96, Copenhagen Bus. Sch., Denmark, 1994-95, Kobe (Japan) U., 1997, Ctr. Southeast Asian Studies, U. Singapore, 1998, Johns Hopkins U., 2002; adj. rsch. assoc. East-West Ctr., Honolulu, 1990—, world lectr. tours on behalf of U.S. Info. Svc., 1974-96; cons. to Dept. Commerce, 1964-66, Dept. State, 1972-74, UN Coun. Fgn. Rels, N.Y.C., 1965-67, Brockings Instn., 1972-75, Ctrl. Am. Common Market, 1972-75, Internat. Monetary Fund, 1976, East-West Ctr., Honolulu, 1987—; mem. internat. econs. rev. bd. NSF, 1981, 85; bd. dirs. Internat. Trade and Fin. Assn., pres. 1993; sr. Fulbright specialist, 2001—. Author: Israel and Africa: A Study in Technical Cooperation, 1964, Alternative Commercial Policies*Their Effects on the American Economy, 1967, International Economics-A Policy Approach, 9th edit., 2002, Trade Relations of the EEC*An Empirical Investigation, 1974, International Commercial Policy: Issues for the 1990's, 1993, Contemporary Issues in Trade Policy, 1995, (with L. Officer) The Monetary Approach to the Balance of Payments: A Survey, 1978, Economics, 1983, 3d edit., 1999, 4th edit., 2003; co-author: Economic Integration on Asia, 2000, Economic Integration and Development, 2002; editor: Can Australia Adjust?, 1988, International Commercial Policy: Issues for the 90's, 1993, Contemporary Issues in Trade Policy, 1995, The U.S.-Canada Free Trade Agreement, 1999; co-editor: Asia-Pacific Economic Linkages, 1997; contbr. articles to profl. jours. NSF fellow, 1964-73, Ford Found. fellow, 1960-61; recipient Disting. Faculty award Mich. State U., 1968, State of Mich. Collegiate award, 1984, Whitefield Winslow Faculty award, 1994, Festschrift in his honor, Washington, 2003. Mem. AAUP, Am. Econ. Assn., Midwest Econ. Assn., Western Econ. Assn., Royal Econ. Assn., Internat. Trade and Fin. Assn. (bd. dirs. 1991-94). Jewish. Home: 1431 Sherwood Ave East Lansing MI 48823-1851 Office: Mich State U Dept Econs East Lansing MI 48824 E-mail: kreinin@msu.edu.

KREIPKE, MERRILL VINCENT, civil engineer, consultant; b. Evansville, Ind., Feb. 14, 1916; s. Charles Edwin and Ida Marguerite (Hufnagel) K.; m. Dorothy Louise Neu, July 17, 1937; children: Karen Jean Kreipke Walker, Jane Ann Kreipke Runyon. BSCE, Purdue U., 1936. Registered profl. engr., Ky., Ind., Va.; registered land surveyor, Ind. Various positions City Engr.'s Office, Evansville, 1936-39; from insp. to asst. engr. Louisville Dist. C.E., 1939-44, 46-51, chief soils and materials engring., 1951-56; civil engr. Chief of Engrs., Dept. Army, Washington, 1956-61; engr. geophys. scis. Chief of R&D, Dept. Army, Washington, 1961-69, chief geophys. scis., 1969-73, acting chief environ. scis., 1973-74; head mil. R&D C.E., Dept. Army, Washington, 1974-75; cons. Falls Church, Va., 1975—. Head U.S. del. NATO Sci. Studies, 1966, 68, 70. Mem. campsite devel. com. Girl Scouts of Am., No. Va., 1957-60; mem. retirement comty. task force Westminster at Lake Ridge, 1978-90, mem. integrated strategic plan com., 2003—; new site bldg. com., Covenant Presbyn. Ch., 2003—. Lt. (j.g.) USNR, 1944-46. Fellow ASCE; mem. NSPE, Internat. Soc. for Terrain-Vehicle Systems (founding), Va. Soc. Prof. Engrs. (Outstanding Svc. award 1979, No. Va. chpt. pres. 1978-79, Outstanding Svc. award 1988), Soc. Am. Mil. Engrs. Presbyterian. Home: Westminster at Lake Ridge 12191 Clipper Dr Apt 403 Woodbridge VA 22192-2240

KREISBERG, NEIL IVAN, advertising executive; b. N.Y.C., Feb. 1, 1945; s. Leo and Lucille (Levy) K.; children: Andrew Jay, Tracy Michelle (dec.); m. Linda Gering, Sept. 24, 1986; children: William Gering, James Gering. BS,BA, Rider Coll., Trenton, N.J., 1966. With Grey Worldwide, Inc., N.Y.C., 1966—, v.p., mgmt. supr., 1974-79, sr. v.p., account mgmt., 1979-85, exec. v.p., 1985-93, exec. v.p., group dir., 1993-99; group exec. v.p., exec. mng. dir. Grey Global Group, N.Y.C., 2000—. Bd. dirs. Advt. Edn. Found. Mem.: Brae Burn Country Club. Jewish. Office: Grey Advt Inc 777 3rd Ave New York NY 10017-1401

KREISBERG, ROBERT A. dean, medical educator; Student, U. Ala., U. South Ala.; MD, Northwestern U., 1958. Vice chair dept. medicine U. Ala., Birmingham, prof.; interim dean Univ. of South Alabama Coll. of Med., 2000, dean, 2001—. Med. dir. Univ. Consortium Clin. Rsch. Fellow Am. Coll. Physicians (gov. Ala., regent, chair scientific program subcom., edtl. policy com., gen. chair, Disting. Tchr. award 1994); mem. Am. Fedn. Clin. Rsch. (pres. 1974-75). Office: Coll of Med Univ of South Alabama 307 Univ Blvd, 170 CSAB Mobile AL 36688

KREISER, FRANK DAVID, real estate executive; b. Sept. 20, 1928; s. Harry D. and Olive W. (Quist) K.; m. Patricia Williams, Aug. 23, 1973; children: Sally, Frank David, Susan, Paul, Mark, Patti, Richard. Student, U. Minn., 1950-51. Cert. residential broker. Real estate developer, 1960—. Founder, owner Frank Kreiser Real Estate, Inc., Mpls., 1966-89, pres., 1979—; owner F. & P.K. Properties, 1973—; membership chmn. RELO, 1987-88; br. mgr. Merrill Lynch Realty, 1989-90, br. mgr., v.p. Burnet Realty, 1990-97; broker Coldwell Banker, 1998—; ptnr., founder B & K Properties Co., Mpls., 1976-96; chmn. bd., founder Transfer Location Corp., Atlanta, 1979-84. With U.S. Army, 1948-50, Korea. Mem. Nat. Assn. Realtors, Mpls. Bd. Realtors (dir. 1972), Minn. Assn. Realtors, Realtors Nat. Mktg. Inst., Minn. Multi Housing Assn., Edina C. of C., 50th France Bus. Assn. (pres. 2000-02), Edina Country Club. Lutheran. Address: 5036 France Ave S Minneapolis MN 55410-2033

KREISLE, WILLIAM ECKMAN, civil engineer, surveyor, research cartographer, writer; b. Tell City, Ind., Oct. 13, 1924; s. John David and Ruth Ann (Eckman) K.; m. Marilyn Jane Ramsey, Aug. 26, 1950; childrne: Jonathan, Peter, Kristine (dec.). BS in Civil Engring., Purdue U., 1948; postgrad., U. Md. Ext., Paris, 1955; MA in Humanities, U. Louisville, 1971. Registered profl. engr., Ind.; registered land surveyor, Ind., Ohio, Ill., Ky. Structural and project engr. Maxon Constrn. Co., Inc., Dayton, Ohio, 1948-51, Tell City, 1948-51; design engr. Tex. Gas Transmission Co., Owensboro, Ky., 1951-52; chief engring. and planning sect. Dept. Army, Civilian Dist. Engr., Wuerzburg, Germany, 1953; chief planning Port Dist. Engrs., Bordeaux, France, 1954-55; arch. engr. North Dist. Joint Constrn. Agy., Paris, 1955-56; arch., engr. K & I Engring., Tell City, 1956-63, U.S. Army Corps of Engrs., Louisville, 1963-66, chief survey br., 1967-81; chief terrain analysis br. Def. Mapping Agy., Louisville, 1981-83; prin., chief engr. W.E. Kreisle and Assocs., Profl. Engrs. and Land Surveyors, 1983—. Asst. instr. Topo Command Seminar, Washington, 1973; vis. lectr. U. Cin., 1978-83; lectr. and spkr. in field. Co-author: Engr. Svy. Manual, including Hist. Engr. Surveying; contbr. articles to profl. jours., monographs on history and devel. of Ohio River for navigation. Cpl. USMC, 1942-45, WWII. Recipient citations Nuc. Power Commn., 1978, U.S. Supreme Ct. 1985, Atty. Gen. of the State Ind., 1985, Atty. Gen. of the State of Ill., 1994, U.S. Dist. Ct. (we. dist.) Ky.; cited for devising method for permanently location 560 mile-boundary line between four states (Ohio, Ind., Ill., Ky.) and supervising all field work involved. Mem. ASCE (life, past editor Jour. Surveying Engring.), Libr. Congress (assoc.), Ind. Hist. Soc., Tell City Hist. Soc. (v.p.), Sigma Chi (life). Avocation: history. Home and Office: 14450 S Alton Rd Leavenworth IN 47137

KREISLER, ROCHELLE, psychologist; b. Bklyn., June 13, 1956; d. Abe Blass and Betty (Becker) Glass; children: Alanna, Adam. BA, Bklyn. Coll., 2000, postgrad., 2000—03. Legal sec. Eric H. Green, Esq., N.Y.C., 1985—91, Booker & Auerbach, N.Y.C., 1991—97, Gladstein & Isaac, N.Y.C., 1997—98; summer sch. tchr. Bklyn. pub. schs., 2001; elem. and jr. h.s. tchr. Yeshiva Rambam, 1998—2002; intern sch. psychologist Youth Dares O.E.S., Bklyn., 2002—. Author: (children's book) Johnny Compound, 2001. Mem.: Nat. Assn. Sch. Psychologists. Jewish. Avocations: reading, needlepoint, writing, swimming. Home: 2790 Bragg St 710 Brooklyn NY 11235 E-mail: RHKreisler@aol.com.

KREISMAN, ARTHUR, higher education consultant, humanities educator emeritus; b. Cambridge, Mass., June 7, 1918; s. Louis and Rose (Shechtell) K.; m. B. Evelyn Goulston, Apr. 20, 1940 (dec. July 1992); children: Peter Jon, Steven Alan, Richard Curt, James Bruce; m. Mamie Jewel Liles Tribble, July 17, 1994. AB, Brigham Young U., 1942; student, Harvard U., 1939; AM, Boston U., 1943, PhD, 1952; LittD (hon.), City U., 1988. Grad. asst. in English Boston U., 1942-43; with Signal Corps. U.S. Army, 1943-45, with Signal Corps. overseas, 1944-45; instr. U.S. Armed Forces Inst., 1945, So. Oreg. U., Ashland, 1946, asst. prof., 1947-51, assoc. prof., 1951-55, prof., 1955-81, chmn. dept. English, 1951-63, chmn. humanities div., 1955-69, dir. gen. studies, 1959-66, dean arts and scis., 1966-77, dir. curricular affairs, 1978-80, prof. emeritus, 1981—, appt. ofcl. univ. historian, 1985; co-founder with Evelyn Kreisman Edukon, Inc., 1982—. TV lectr. Network Ednl. TV, 1955-58, dir. Block Teaching Project, U.S. Office Edn., 1957-59, Nat. Def. Edn. Act Inst. for Advanced Study in English, 1966; cons. Fedn. Regional Accrediting Commns. in Higher Edn., 1974-75, Council on Postsecondary Accreditation, 1975-79, Chico (Calif.) State U., 1973-76, City U. Seattle, 1975-99, Lincoln Meml. U., 1976, Marylhurst Edn. Center, 1976, Oreg. Inst. Tech., 1977-79, Sheldon Jackson Coll., 1979-83, Council on Chiropractic Edn., 1982, 83, Griffin Coll., 1990-91; mem. Gov.'s Adv. Com. on Arts and Humanities, 1966-69, 71-76; mem. task force human services Oreg. Ednl. Coordinating Council, 1972; mem. steering com. Oreg. Joint Com. for Humanities, 1972-74; chmn. Seminar Coll. Evaluators NW Assn. Schs. and Colls., U. Wash., 1977-84; mem. nat. adv. bd. on quality assurance in experiential learning Council on Advancement Experiental Learning, 1978-80; team leader Danforth Found. Workshop on Liberal Arts Edn., Colo. Coll., 1972. Author: Correspondence Courses for State System, American Literature, 1955, World Literature, 1956, Contemporary Literature, 1961, Reader's Guide to the Classics, 1961, Remembering: The History of Southern Oregon University, 2002; editor: Oregon Centennial Anthology, 1959; Contbr. poetry and articles to periodicals. Mem. Ashland City Coun., 1950-54; co-founder Rogue Valley Unitarian Fellowship, 1953; bd. dirs. Comty. Chest, Inst. Renaissance Studies, 1956-64, Friends of Libr., 1991-96, pres., 1994-96; mem. steering com. Learning in Retirement Program, 1993-94; chmn. bd. trustees Ashland Comty. Hosp., 1960-64; bd. dirs. So. Calif. U. for Profl. Studies, 1997-99; chmn. bd. dirs. North Ctrl. U., 1998-99. Recipient Bicentennial anniversary prize in humanities Columbia U., 1954, disting. svc. award Ashland Cmty. Hosp. Found., 1998; prize for excellence in teaching, 1966, Outstanding Service award Indsl. Coll. Armed Forces, 1976, Disting. Service award Alumni Assn., 1977; Ford Found. fellow in Oriental philosophy and religion Harvard, 1954 Mem. AAUP (past pres. Oreg. coun.), Nat. Coun. Tchrs. English (past pres. Oreg. coun.), Commn. of Pacific Assn. of Schs. and Colls. (elected 1994-95), N.W. Assn. Schs. and Colls. (examiner 1958—, trustee 1976-80, mem. comm. colls. 1972-80), Am. Legion (past post comdr.), Lambda Iota Tau, Phi Kappa Phi, Tau Kappa Alpha. Office: 1880 Green Meadows Way Ashland OR 97520-3683

KREISSMAN, STARRETT, librarian; b. N.Y.C., Jan. 4, 1946; d. Bernard and Shirley (Relis) K.; m. David Dolan, Apr. 13, 1985; 1 child, Sonya. BA, Grinnell Coll., 1967; MLS, Columbia U., 1968. Asst. circulation libr. Columbia U., N.Y.C., 1968-70; sci. libr. N.Y. Pub. Libr., N.Y.C., 1970-71; outreach libr. Stanislaus County Free Libr., Modesto, Calif., 1971-73, Oakdale libr., 1974-79, acquisitions libr., 1979-85, br. supr., 1985-92, county libr., 1992—99; libr. dir. Ventura County Libr., 1999—. Writer book revs. Stanislaus County Commn. on Women. Mem. ALA, Pub. Libr. Assn., Calif. Libr. Assn. (legis. com. 1993-95, Libr. of Yr., 1998), Rotary. Office: Ventura County Library 646 County Square Dr Ste 150 Ventura CA 93003

KREITER-FORONDA, CAROLYN, poet, artist; b. Farmville, Va., Dec. 20, 1946; d. Victor William and Lucile Wildman Kreiter; m. Patricio J. Gomez-Foronda, Mar. 28, 1991. BA, Mary Washington Coll., 1969; MA, George Mason U., 1979, MEd, 1973, PhD, 1995. Cert. tchr. Va. Specialist, English specialist, dept. chair Fairfax County (Va.) Pub. Schs., 1969-2000. Adj. prof. George Mason U., Fairfax, 1985-89; writing cons. No. Va. Writing Project, Fairfax, 1978—; edtl. bd. SCOP Publs., Catonsville, Md., 1993-2001. Author: Contrary Visions, 1988, Gathering Light, 1993, Death Comes Riding, 1999, Greatest Hits, 2001; co-editor: In a Certain Place, 2000. Mem. alumni bd. dirs. George Mason U., 1983-88. Recipient meritorious educator of yr. award Rotary, 1997. Mem.: The Writers Ctr., Am. Pen Women, Rappahannock Art League, Poetry Soc. Va. (dir. Poetry in the Schs. program). Avocations: reading, walking, biking. E-mail: pforonda@oasisonline.com.

KREITLOW, BURTON WILLIAM, retired adult education educator; b. Howard Lake, Minn., Aug. 14, 1917; s. William Arthur and Esther Ingeborg (Nelson) K.; m. Doris J. Ounsworth, Sept. 13, 1944; children: Karen Neal, Candace Kreitlow. Tchg. cert., Cokato (Minn.) Normal, 1935; BS, U. Minn., 1941, MA, 1948, PhD, 1949. Rural tchr. Dist. 58, Montrose, Minn., 1935-37; county 4-H agt. Minn. Ext. Svc., Mankato, Minn., 1938-39, county agr. agt. Warren, Minn., 1941-42, dist. supr. 4H St. Paul, 1945-46; asst. prof. basic coll. Mich. State U., East Lansing, 1948-49; from asst. prof. to prof. U. Wis., Madison, 1949-81, prof. emeritus, 1981—. Vis. prof. Tex. A&M U., Fla. State U., Alaska-Pacific U., Wash. State U., Nat. Taiwan U., U. Hawaii (Hilo), U. Alaska, Anchorage; Disting. vis. prof. Ohio State U. Grad. Sch., 1975-76; workshop leader, lectr.; chmn. Commn. of Profs., 1961-63; bd. dirs. emeritus Coll. St. Scholastica, Duluth, Minn., 1992-93, Aging Trust Fund, Northland Found., Duluth, 1991-94. Author: Rural Education: Community Backgrounds, 1954, Leadership for Action in Rural Communities, 1960, (series) Steps to Learning, 1966-80; playwright (with others) Under the Stars and Stripes--Stories of World War II, 2002; editor: Examining Controversies in Continuing Education, 1981, Creative Planning for the Second Half of Life, 1997; contbr. column to (jour.) Adult Learning, 1989-91. Mem. Wisconsin Heights Sch. Bd., Mazomanie, Wis., 1959-62; pres. Homestead Coop. of Grand Marais (Minn.), 1992-94. Recipient Haight Travel fellowship U. Wis. Grad. Sch., 1967; named to Internat. Adult and Continuing Edn. Hall of Fame, Am. Assn. Adult and Continuing Edn., 1996. Mem. NEA (chair publs. com. rural dept. 1965-67), Minn. Gerontol. Soc., Lions (pres. 1959, 85), Phi Delta Kappa. Democrat. Mem. UCC Ch. Avocations: community volunteer, leading memoir writing groups, continued teaching and learning. Home: PO Box 865 Grand Marais MN 55604-0865 also: 78-7039 Kam 111 Rd Unit 145 Kailua Kona HI 96740-2530

KREITZ, HELEN MARIE, retired elementary education educator; b. Taylor, Tex., Aug. 22, 1929; d. Joseph Jr. and Mary Lena (Miller) K. BA, U. Mary Hardin-Baylor, 1950; MEd, U. Tex., 1959. Cert. tchr., Tex. Bookkeeper Singer Sewing Machine Co., Taylor, 1950-51; advt. salesperson Taylor Times, 1951-52; tchr. Temple (Tex.) Ind. Sch. Dist., 1952-88. Lector, eucharistic min. St. Mary's Cath. Ch., Temple, 1974—. Mem. Tex. Ret. Tchrs. (life, treas. Temple chpt. 1991-2002), Tex. State Tchrs. Assn. (life, treas. Temple chpt. 1954-55), Tex. Classroom Tchrs. Assn. (life, pres. Temple chpt. 1967-69), U. Tex. Execs. (life), Pi Lambda Theta. Roman Catholic. Avocations: sewing, handcrafts. Home: PO Box 3446 Temple TX 76505-3446

KREITZER, JACALYN BOWER, vocalist, voice educator; b. Silverton, Oreg., Feb. 16, 1956; d. Jack Allen and Coraliss Mae Bower; m. David M. Kreitzer, Nov. 26, 1987; children: Fredricka Jacalyn, Anatol. MusB, Univ. of Puget Sound, Tacoma, Wash.; MusM, Univ. of So. Calif., Los Angeles, Calif., 1982—85. Lead role Contessa/Andrea Chenier/San Francisco Opera, San Francisco, 1998, Erda/Das Rheingold/Deutsche Oper Berlin, Berlin, 1991, Brangane/Tristan und Isolde/Teatro Liceu, Barcelona, 1989, Ericlea/Ritorno di Ulisse/San Francisco Opera, San Francisco, 1986, Urlich & Mahler 2/Prague Radio Symphony, Prague, Czech Republic, 1999, Rossweisse/Die Walkure/Metropolitan Opera, New York, NY, 1984—87; participant Mother/The Consul, Spoleto, Italy, Sosostris/Midsummer Marriage/New York City Opera, NYC, Waltraute/Die Walkure/Theatre Chatelet, Utrica/Un Ballo in Maschera/Dublin Grand Opera, Waltraute, Fricka/Die Walkure/Chgo. Lyric Opera, Chgo., Brangane/Tristan Und Isolde/Los Angeles Opera, Los Angeles, Calif., Brangane/Tristan Und Isolde/Barcelona Opera, Barcelona, Erster Magd/Electra/Geneva Opera, Geneva, Norns/Gotterdammerung/Artpark New York, NY, Norns, Waltraute, Fricka, Erda/Der Ring Des Nibelungen/Seattle Opera, Seattle. Prodr., Marilyn Horne/frederica von Stadoe recitals; voice-diction tchr. Cal Poly Music Dept., San Luis Obispo, 1999, prodr., master, 2001—03. Received powerful reviews from the: "Kansas City Star"; "Spandauer Volksblatt", Berlin; "Kreitzer"; "Newark News Star"; R. Pontizious, "San Francisco Examiner"; "Los Angeles Times"; and Phillip Collins, "San Jose Metro". Mem.: NATS, AGMA. Republican. Luth. Achievements include Master classes with Elizabeth Schwarzkopt, Birgitt Nielson. Avocations: Koi fish, travel, camping. Home: 1442 12th St Los Osos CA 93402

KREITZER, LOIS HELEN, personal investor; b. Pitts., Feb. 2, 1933; d. Franklin and Helen Katherine (Leyda) Maroney; m. William Emil Kreitzer, Nov. 14, 1962. BS, Pa. State U., 1955. Stockbroker Parker Hunter (formerly McKelvy & Co.), Pitts., 1955-62; cons. Pitts., 1962-68; executrix of estates, 1968-82; personal investor, 1975—; shareholder activist, 1970—. Mem. AAUW (life, jrs. sec., v.p., pres. 1960-62), DAR (jrs. treas.-sec., v.p., pres. 1957-60), Nat. Assn. Investors Corp. (life), Pa. State U. Alumni Assn. (life), Colonial Dames 17th Century (charter treas.), Pa. State Club of Allegheny County (pres. 1963), Pitts. Athletic Assn., Coll. Club Pitts. (life, jr. v.p., pres. 1959-60), Soroptimists (life, v.p. Pitts. chpt. 1961). Republican. Presbyterian. Avocations: cooking, baking, theatre, traveling, walking.

KREITZMAN, RALPH J. lawyer; b. N.Y.C., Nov. 11, 1945; s. Emanuel M. and Hannah G. (Steinhardt) K.; m. Wendy A. Karpel, Nov. 24, 1968; children: Susan Beth, Emily Meg. BS in Acctg., Rider U., 1967; JD cum laude, Bklyn. Law Sch., 1970. Bar: N.Y. 1971, U.S. Dist Ct. (so. dist.) N.Y. 1971, U.S. Dist. Ct. (ea. dist.) N.Y. 1973, U.S. Ct. of Appeals (2nd cir.) 1975, U.S. Supreme Ct. 1976. Assoc. Hughes Hubbard & Reed LLP, N.Y.C., 1970-80; sr. ptnr. real estate group Hughes Hubbard & Reed LLC, N.Y.C., 1980—. Trustee Village of Great Neck, 2001-, former chair planning bd., former mem. archtl. rev. com.; dep. mayor Village Great Neck, N.Y., 2003—. Served with U.S. Army Res., 1968-74. Mem. ABA (real property law sect. and com. on fgn. investment in U.S. real estate), N.Y. State Bar Assn. (real property law sect., com. on comml. leases and com. on financings), Assn. of Bar of City of N.Y. (com. on real property law, former chair leasing subcom.). Office: Hughes Hubbard & Reed LLP 1 Battery Park Plz New York NY 10004-1482 E-mail: kreitzman@hugheshubbard.com.

KREIZINGER, LOREEN I. lawyer, nurse; b. Syracuse, N.Y., Apr. 16, 1959; d. David F. and Blanche L. (Heaney) Mosher; m. Kenneth R. Kreizinger, Aug. 30, 1985; 1 child, Katelyn Rose. Grad. in nursing, Crouse-Irving Meml. Hosp., Syracuse, 1981; BS in Bus. with honors, Nova U., 1987, JD, 1990. Bar: Fla. 1990; RN, N.Y., Fla. Nurse ICU and infants neonatal unit, Syracuse, Ft. Lauderdale, Fla., 1979-86; med. malpractice cons. Krupnick, Campbell et al, Ft.Lauderdale, 1986-90, assoc., 1990-92, of counsel, 1992—; pvt. practice, Ft.Lauderdale, 1992—. Instr. adult intensive care Crouse-Irving Meml. Hosp., 1981-82; adj. prof. Nova U., Ft. Lauderdale, 1994—; seminar instr. legal aspects of nursing Fla. Bd. Nursing, 1990-92; guest spkr. TV talk show Med. Malpractice, 1991. Sec., bd. dirs. Shepherd Care Ministries, Hollywood, Fla., 1993, 94; mem. choir 1st Bapt. Ch. Ft. Lauderdale, 1994—. Mem. ABA (law and medicine com. 1990—), FBA, ATLA (spl. L-Trytophen com. 1991-94), Fla. Bar Assn., Fla. Assn. Women Lawyers, Fla. Acad. Trial Lawyers, Broward County Women Lawyers Assn., Broward County Trial Lawyers Assn., Phi Alpha Delta. Republican. Avocations: sailing, snow skiing, rollerblading. Office: 515 E Las Olas Blvd Ste 1150 Fort Lauderdale FL 33301-2281

KREJCI, ROBERT HARRY, non-profit organizations development consultant; b. Chgo., June 4, 1913; s. John and Johanna (Tischer) K.; m. Marian Hallock, Mar. 28, 1941 (dec. Aug. 1986); 1 child, Susan Ann Krejci Stevens. BS in Forestry with honors, Mich. State U., 1940. Dist. exec. Boy Scouts Am., Chgo., 1940-48, asst. scout exec., 1948-50, scout exec. Herrin, Ill., Huntington, W.Va., 1950-65; devel. cons. The Cumerford Corp., Kansas City, 1965-73, dir. western divsn. Ft. Lauderdale, Fla., 1974-78; devel. cons. in pvt. practice, San Diego, 1978-90. Co-founder, pres. Philanthropy Coun., San Diego, 1987-93; dir. World War II Farm Labor Camp, State of Ill., 1942, 43. Author: How to Succeed in Fund Raising For Your Non-Profit Organization, 1989. Vol. organizer United Way, various cities, Ill., 1955, 56. Recipient George Washington medal Freedoms Found. at Valley Forge, 1953; named Vol. of Yr. Philanthropy Coun., 1996, Exemplar, Rancho Bernardo Rotary Found., 1995. Mem. Rotary Internat. (Paul Harris fellow). Avocations: travel, gardening, writing, collecting humor. Home: 16566 Casero Rd San Diego CA 92128-2743

KREJCI, ROBERT HENRY, aerospace engineer; b. Shenandoah, Iowa, Nov. 15, 1943; s. Henry and Marie Josephine (Kubicek) K.; m. Carolyn R. Meyer, Aug. 21, 1967; children: Christopher S., Ryan D. BS with honors in Aerospace Engring., Iowa State U., 1967, M Aerospace Engring., 1971. Commd. 2d lt. USAF, 1968, advanced thoru grades to capt., 1978; lt. col. USAFR; served with Sys. Command Space Launch Vehicles Sys. Program Office; advanced ICBM program officer Space Launch Vehicles Sys. Program Office; U.S. Dept. Energy rsch. assoc. Lawrence Livermore Lab.; dept. mgr. advanced Navy tech. programs ATK Thiokol Propulsion, Brigham City, Utah, 1978-84, mgr. space programs, 1984-85, mgr. Navy advanced programs, 1986—. Fellow AIAA (assoc.). Home: 885 North 300 East Brigham City UT 84302-1310 Office: ATK Thiokol Propulsion PO Box 707 Brigham City UT 84302-0707

KREKORIAN, JAMES EDMUND, stock options trader; b. Royston, Ga., June 15, 1952; s. Edmund Arthur and Patricia Ann (James) K.; m. Diane Leigh Appleton, Aug. 24, 1974 (div. Feb. 1984); m. Zoe Pomes Scherf, July 14, 2000. BSCE, Duke U., 1974. Lic. airline transport pilot, FAA. Tchr., cons. Am. Contract Bridge League, Atlanta and Charlotte, N.C., 1982-85, cons. N.Y.C., 1986—; options trader, market maker, floor ofcl. Am. Stock Exch., N.Y.C., 1986—; mgr., investing mem. Blue Hercules Trading LLC, N.Y.C., 1999—. Capt. USAF, 1974-81. Mem. Am. Contract Bridge League (grand life master 1993, Blue Ribbon Pairs Nat. Champion 1996), Am. Stock Exch. Avocations: tournament Bridge, running, phys. tng., music, theatre. Home: 424 W End Ave Apt 14E New York NY 10024-5784

KRELLE, WILHELM ERNST, emeritus economics educator; b. Magdeburg, Germany, Dec. 24, 1916; s. Willy and Elisabeth (Dienemann) K.; m. Rose-Alix Scholz, May 20, 1944 (dec.); children: Rainer (dec.), Axel, Heide, Gabriele. D, U. Freiburg, 1947, diploma in physics, 1948; DSc (hon.), U. St. Gall, 1970; PhD

(hon.), U. Vienna, 1971, U. Karlsruhe, 1976, U. Muenster, 1981, U. Mannheim, 1983, U. Berlin-Humboldt, 1994. Asst. U. Heidelberg, Germany, 1948—53, dozent, 1954—55; assoc. prof. U. St. Gall, Switzerland, 1956-58; prof. econs. U. Bonn, Germany, 1958-82, prof. emeritus, 1982—. Mem. bd. econ. advisers to Minister Commerce, Bonn, 1969—; mem. supervising bd. Krupp Stahl AG, Bochum, Fed. Republic Germany, 1972-90. Author: Produktionstheorie, 1969, Preistheorie II, 1976, Theorie des wirtschaflichen Wachstums, 1985, Economics and Ethics, 2003, others; contbr. articles to profl. jours. Fellow Econometric Soc.; mem. Gesellschaft fur Wirtschafts-und Sozialwissenschaften (pres. 1975-79), Rotary (pres. Bonn lodge 1982-83), Grosses Verdienst Kreuz des Verdienstordens of the Fed. Republic Germany. Rockefeller fellow, 1953-54; recipient Kondratieff gold medal Russian Acad. Scis., 1994. Mem. Synod Evang. Ch., 1973-85. Served with German Army, 1935-45. Avocations: music, hiking. Home: Am Domblick 15 D-53177 Bonn Germany Office: U Bonn Adenauerallee 24-42 D-53113 Bonn Germany

KRELSTEIN, RONALD DOUGLAS, lawyer; b. Memphis, May 7, 1942; LLB, Vanderbilt U., 1967. Bar: Tenn. 1967, U.S. Dist. Ct. (we. dist.) Tenn. 1969, U.S. Ct. Appeals (6th cir.) 1970, U.S. Supreme Ct. 1976. Pvt. practice, Memphis, 1967-70; asst. pub. defender Shelby County, Memphis, 1970-71; police legal adviser Memphis Police Dept., 1971-74; pvt. practice Memphis, 1974—. Pres. Tenn. Law Enforcement Legal Advisers Assn., 1973-74. Nat. Collegiate Pistol Champion 4 times; holder Disting. Pistol Shot and Disting. Rifleman awards; mem. Christian Bros. H.S. (Memphis) Hall of Fame, 1995—. Avocation: competitive rifle and pistol shooting.

KREMBS, GEORGE MICHAEL, computer and electrical engineer; b. Merrill, Wis., Sept. 2, 1934; BSEE, U. Notre Dame, 1956; PhDEE, Stanford U., 1959. Mgr. advanced display sys. IBM, Kingston, N.Y., 1964-87, total sys. strategist, 1987-98; ret., 1998; computer cons. Krembs Assocs., West Hurley, N.Y., 1998—. Contbr. articles to profl. jours. Home: 123 Pleasant Ridge Dr West Hurley NY 12491-5409 Fax: (845) 679-3326. E-mail: krembsg1@hotmail.com.

KREMENTZ, JILL, photographer, author; b. N.Y.C., Feb. 19, 1940; d. Walter and Virginia (Hyde) Krementz; m. Kurt, Jr. Vonnegut, Nov. 1979; 1 child, Lily Vonnegut. Student, Drew U., 1958—59; attended Art Students League. With Harper's Bazaar mag., 1959—60, Glamour mag., 1960—61; pub. rels. staff Indian Industries Fair, New Delhi, 1961; reporter Show mag., 1962—64; staff photographer N.Y. Herald Tribune, 1964—65, staff photographer Vietnam, 1965—66; assoc. editor Status-Diplomat mag., 1966—67; contbg. editor N.Y. mag., 1967—68; corr. Time-Life Inc., 1969—70; contbg. photographer People mag., 1974—. Contbr. ; one-woman shows include Madison (Wis.) Art Ctr., 1973, U. Mass., Boston, 1974, Nikon Gallery, N.Y.C., 1974, Del. Art Mus., Wilmington, 1975, Newark Mus., 1994, Staley-Wise Gallery, 1996, The Margaret Mitchell House, Atlanta, 1999, Represented in permanent collections Mus. Modern Art, Libr. of Congress, The Face of South Vietnam (text by Dean Brelis), 1968, Words and Their Masters (text by Israel Shenker), 1974; author (photographer): Sweet Pea: A Black Girl Growing Up in the Rural South (foreword by Margaret Mead), 1969, A Very Young Dancer, 1976, A Very Young Rider, 1977, A Very Young Gymnast, 1978, A Very Young Circus Flyer, 1979, A Very Young Skater, 1979, The Writer's Image, 1980, How It Feels When a Parent Dies, 1981, How It Feels to be Adopted, 1982, How It Feels When Parents Divorce, 1984, The Fun of Cooking, 1985, Lily Goes to the Playground, 1986, Jack Goes to the Beach, 1986, Katherine Goes to Nursery School, 1986, Jamie Goes on an Airplane, 1986, Tanya Goes to the Dentist, 1986, Benjy Goes to a Restaurant, 1986, Holly's Farm Animals, 1986, Zachary Goes to the Zoo, 1986, A Visit to Washington, D.C., 1987, How It Feels to Fight for Your Life, 1989, A Very Young Skier, 1990, A Very Young Musician, 1990, A Very Young Gardener, 1990, A Very Young Actress, 1991, How It Feels to Live With a Physical Disability, 1992, The Writer's Desk, 1996, The Jewish Writer, 1998. Recipient Nonfiction award, Washington Post/Children's Book Guild, 1984, ACCH Joan Fassler Meml. Book award, 1990, Equality, Dignity, Independence award, Nat. Easter Seals, 1992. Mem.: PEN. Address: care Alfred A Knopf Inc 201 E 50th St New York NY 10022-7703

KREMER, EUGENE R. architecture educator; b. N.Y.C., Jan. 4, 1938; s. John and Ida (Applegreen) K.; m. Sara Lillian Kimmel, June 26, 1960; children: Michael, Ian. BArch, Rensselaer Poly. Inst., 1960; postgrad., U. Pa., 1960-61; MArch, U. Calif., 1967; grad. coll. mgmt. program, Carnegie Mellon U., 1991. Registered architect, N.Y., Kans. Architect Ulrich Franzen Assoc., N.Y.C., 1963-66; asst. prof. Washington U., St. Louis, 1967-70; lectr. Portsmouth (Eng.) Poly. Inst., 1970-71, Poly. Ctrl. London, 1971-72; dir. Inst. Environ. Design, Washington, 1972-73; prof., head dept. architecture Kans. State U., Manhattan, 1973-85, 92-95, dir. program devel. Coll. Architecture and Design, 1985-92, asst. dean, 1988-90. Dir. Boston Architecture and Design, summer, 1983—90; vis. faculty mem. Czech Tech U., Prague, 1999; scholar in residence AIA, Washington, 2002; mem. State Bldg. Adv. Bd., Topeka, 1984—86, Topeka, 1992—95; mem. editl. bd. Jour. Arch. and Planning Rsch., College Station, Tex., 1983—. Author: Careers in Architecture, 1967, Leadership Meetings in Environmental Design, 1973; author/editor newsletter Architecture Update, 1984-86, 92—; editor Architecture and Design News, 1990-92; contbr. Architects Handbook of Professional Practice, 13th edit., also articles to profl publs. Chmn. Adv. Bd. Gifted, Talented, Creative, Manhattan, 1974-75; mem. Convocations Com., Manhattan, 1974-93, chn., 1984-88, 90-93; mem. Truman Scholarship Com., Manhattan, 1980—; pres. Friends Kans. State U. Librs., Manhattan, 1985-86. Fellow AIA (Spl. Svc. award Kans. 1984, 88, 91, 94, 98, 99, Presdl. citation Kansas City 1993); mem. Environ. Design Rsch. Assn., Assn. Collegiate Schs. Architecture (treas. 1976-80, pres. 1981-82, Svc. award 1983), AIA Kans. (sec. 1989, v.p./pres.-elect 1990, pres. 1991, past pres. 1992, univ. liaison 1993-2002, Henry Schirmer Disting. Svc. award 2002), AIA Flint Hills (pres. 1998), Golden Key (hon.), Tau Sigma Delta, Tau Beta Pi, SCARAB (hon.), Tau Epsilon Phi (pres. 1959-60). Avocations: reading, photography. Office: Kans State U Coll Architecture Planning and Design 211 Seaton Hall Manhattan KS 66506-2900

KREMER, HONOR FRANCES (NOREEN KREMER), real estate broker, small business owner; came to U.S., 1961; m. Manny Kremer; 1 child, Patrick David. BS, CUNY; MS, Baruch Coll. Group sec. Bentalls, Ltd.; office mgr. Aschner Assocs., N.Y.C., 1961-63; pub. rels. asst. McMaster U., Hamilton, 1963-64; office mgr. Packaging Components, N.Y.C., 1965-67; head acctg. Shaller Rubin Assocs., N.Y.C., 1967-72, v.p. fin. and adminstrn., 1979-82, sr. v.p., mem. exec. com., 1982—, sec.-treas. multi-media divsn., 1972-75. Pvt. practice bus. cons., 1986-89; sr. v.p., exec. v.p., fin. officer Lewis & Gace Med. Advt., N.Y.C., 1989-91; broker, owner Malone Kremer Realty, Leonia, N.J., 1991—; bus. cons., 1991—. Mem. Nat. Assn. Realtors, N.J. Assn. Realtors, Nat. Fedn. Bus. and Profl. Women (bd. dirs., v.p.), Advt. Fin. Mgmt. Group. Roman Catholic.

KREMER, MATTHEW MARKUS, lawyer, mediator, judge pro tem; b. San Antonio, Sept. 27, 1951; s. Donn Clarke Kremer and Shari Adler; m. Judy Lynn Ware, Dec. 30, 1978 (div. June 1985); children: Kailee, Maxwell; m. Mary Ann Wynne, Dec. 6, 1987; 1 child, Raoul. BS, Western State U., 1976; JD, Thomas Jefferson Sch. Law, 1978. Bar: Calif. 1978, U.S. Dist. Ct. (so. dist.) Calif. 1978; cert. specialist family law Calif. State Bd. Legal Specialization. Pvt. practice, San Diego, 1978—; judge pro tem San Diego Superior Ct, 1991—. Chmn. San Diego Regional Com. on Family Law, Exec. Com. of State Bar. Pres. Beth Sholom Synagogue, Chula Vista, Calif., 1982. Mem. Assn. Cert. Family Law Specialists, San Diego County Bar Assn., Foothills Bar Assn., Rep. Senate Club. Republican. Jewish. Avocations: writing, golf, skiing, Civil War re-enactments. Office: 9665 Chesapeake Dr Ste 310 San Diego CA 92123-1352 E-mail: Kremerlaw@aol.com., mmkremer@famlawcal.com.

KREMERS, CAROLYN SUE, writer, musician, educator; b. Denver, Nov. 2, 1951; d. Richard Treakle and Patricia Sue (Willson) K.; m. David L. Musgrave, July 3, 1999 (div. 2003). BA in English & Humanities with honors, Stanford U., 1973; BA in Flute Performance, Met. State Coll., 1981; MFA in Creative Writing, U. Alaska, 1991. Cert. secondary English lang. arts tchr., Alaska. Tchr. music and English, various schs., Ill., Colo., Alaska, 1974-88; vis. asst. prof. English, U. Alaska, Fairbanks, 1991-92, asst. prof. devel. studies Bethel, 1992-93, instr. English, Fairbanks, 1993-97; asst. prof. English and creative writing Ea. Wash. U., Spokane, 1997-2001; instr. English U. Alaska, Fairbanks, 2001—. Cons. Alaska State Writing Consortium, 1990—. Author: Place of the Pretend People: Gifts from a Yup'ik Eskimo Village, 1996; author numerous essays and poems. Individual Artist fellow Alaska State Coun. Arts, 1992. Avocations: flute and violin playing, skiing, backpacking, running, bicycling.

KREMIN, DANIEL PAUL, clinical forensic psychologist; b. Bklyn., Sept. 26, 1946; s. Harry and Ruth Kremin; m. Diane Joyce Siesel, Mar. 18, 1972; children: Sean, Todd. BA, Fairleigh Dickinson U., 1967, MA, 1974; MS, Yeshiva U., 1976, SpC., 1977, PhD, 1978. Diplomate Am. Bd. Forensic Medicine, Am. Bd. Forensic Examiners, Am. Bd. Adminstrv. Psychology, Am. Bd. Psychol. Specialties, Profl. Acad. Custody Evaluators; bd. cert. sch. and emergency crisis response; bd. cert. homeland security. Sr. psychologist Columbia Presbyn. Hosp., 1975-76; mem. com. on handicapped N.Y. Bd. Edn., 1977-81, psychologist, 1977-78, clin. coord., 1978-79, coord. learning disabilities identification program, 1979, asst. to regional coord., 1979-80, chmn., 1980-81; dir. spl. svcs. Teaneck (N.J.) Pub. Schs., 1981-89; dir. spl. edn. and pupil pers. svcs. Hicksville (N.Y.) Pub. Schs., 1989-92, asst. supt., 1992-2000; pvt. practice in psychology, 1992—. Fellow clin. psychology Rousso Ctr., Albert Einstein Coll. Medicine. Tchg. fellow Fairleigh Dickinson U., 1974. Fellow Am. Coll. Forensic Examiners, Am. Acad. Experts in Traumatic Stress (registered custody evaluator); mem. ASCD, APA, Soc. Pediat. Psychology, Nat. Honor Soc. Psychology, Nat. Assn. Sch. Psychologists, N.Y. State Psychol. Assn., Nassau County Psychol. Assn., Coun. Exceptional Children. Avocation: skiing. Office: Ste 102 990 Westbury Rd Westbury NY 11590-5309 E-mail: dockrem@aol.com.

KREMPASKY, FRANCES M. librarian; b. Detroit, Dec. 13, 1961; d. Stephen and Mary Margaret Krempasky. BA, Mich. State Univ., East Lansing, Mich., 1984; MA Libr. and Info. Sci., Wayne State Univ., Detroit, Mich., 1996. Libr. asst. Mich. State Univ. Libraries, Ea. Lansing, Mich., 1984—96; libr. I Southfield Pub. Libr., Southfield, Mich., 1996—98; libr. II, head of database mgmt. Wayne State Univ., Detroit, 1998—99, libr. II, head of cataloging, 1999—. Sec. Wayne State Univ. Pres. Comm. on the Status of Women, Detoit, Mich., 2002—03. Mem.: Am. Libr. Assoc. (co-chair, crative fIdeas in tech. svc. discussion group 2002—03), Mich. Libr. Assoc. (mem., access collections and tech. svc. roundtable 2001). Home: 20541 Charlton Sq #209 Southfield MI 48076 Office: Wayne State Univ Libr 5048 Gullen Mall Detroit MI 48202

KREMPEL, RALF HUGO BERNHARD, writer, artist, art gallery owner; b. Groitzsch, Saxony, Germany, June 5, 1935; came to U.S., 1964; s. Curt Bernhard and Liesbeth Anna Margarete (Franz) K.; m. Barbara von Eberhardt, Dec. 21, 1967 (div. 1985); 1 child, Karma. Student, Wood and Steel Constrn. Coll., Leipzig, German Democratic Republic, 1955. Steel constructor, worldwide, 1955-73; co-owner San Francisco Pvt. Mint, 1973-81; prin. artist San Francisco Painter Magnate, 1982—; dir. Stadtgalerie Wiprechtsburg Groitzsch, Germany, 1991—, Museumsgalerie am Markt, Groitzsch, 1994—. Exhbns. Centre Internat. d'Art Contemporain, 1985, Art Contemporain Cabinet des Dessins, 1986, Galerie Salammbo-Atlante, 1987 and others, Retrospective Mus.-gallery Borna, 1993; inventor, designer Visual Communication System, utilizing colors instead of letters to depict and transmit messages;Arrivaluation as the Origin of Species; 6 Order of the Universe registrations, Arrivalution as the Origin of Species, Libr. of Congress, Washington, 1991—. Avocations: art research, photography. Home: 2400 Pacific Ave San Francisco CA 94115-1280 Office: San Francisco Painter Magnate Rincon Ctr San Francisco CA 94119-3368 also: Brühl 2 04539 Groitzsch Germany

KREMPL, ERHARD, mechanics educator, consultant; b. Regensburg, Germany, Mar. 5, 1934; came to U.S., 1964, naturalized, 1983; m. Johanna A. Wunderlich, Dec. 19, 1961 (dec.); children: Christiane C., Ralph D. Dipl. Ing., Technische Hochschule Muenchen, W. Germany, 1956, Dr.Ing., 1962. Instr., research engr. Technische Hochschule Muenchen, 1956-59, wissenschaftl asst., 1959-64; mechanics of materials engr. Gen Electric Co., Schenectady, 1964-68; assoc. prof. Rensselaer Poly Inst., Troy, N.Y., 1968-75, prof. mechanics, 1975-93, dir. Mechanics of Materials Lab., 1975—, head dept. mech. engring., aero. engring. and mechanics, 1987-96, Rosalind and John J. Redfern Jr. prof. engring., 1993—. Vis. scientist Argonne Nat. Lab., Ill., 1974; Richard Merton guest prof. Institut für Statik und Dynamic der Luft und Raumfahrtkonstruktionen, Stuttgart, W.Ger., 1975-76 Author: (with Lai and Rubin) Introduction to Continuum Mechanics, 3d edit., 1993; contbr. numerous articles to profl. jours.; editor: Jour. Engring. Materials and Tech., 1981-84. Rsch. grantee NSF, Office Naval Rsch., NASA, Pressure Vessel Rsch. Com., Dept. Energy; Japanese Soc. Promotion Sci. fellow, 1984; Fulbright-Hayes grantee U. Innsbruck, Austria, 1985; recipient Sr. U.S. Scientist Humboldt award, 1993-94. Fellow ASME (chmn. materials div. 1977-78), Am. Acad. Mechanics; mem. ASTM, AAUP, Am. Soc. Engring. Edn., Soc. Engring. Sci.

KRENDEL, EZRA SIMON, systems and human factors engineering consultant; b. NYC, Mar. 5, 1925; s. Joseph and Tamara (Shapiro) K.; m. Elizabeth Spencer Malany, Aug. 20, 1950 (dec. Nov. 1983); children: David A., Tamara E. Krendel-Clark, Jennifer K. Hall; m. Janet Brownlee Allen, June 27, 1992. AB, Bklyn. Coll., 1945; Sc.M. in Physics, MIT, 1947; A.M. in Social Relations, Harvard, 1949; MA honoris causa, U. Pa., 1971. From research engr. to sr. staff engr. Franklin Inst. Research Labs., 1949-55, lab. mgr., 1955-63, tech. dir., 1963-66, sr. adviser, cons., 1961; dir. Mgmt. Sci. Ctr., Wharton Sch. U. Pa., Phila., 1967-69, prof. ops. research and stats., Wharton Sch., 1966-90, prof. emeritus, 1990—, prof. systems engring. Sch. Engring. and Applied Sci., 1983-93; prin. scientist Systems Tech., Inc., Hawthorne, Calif., 1987—89. Emeritus prof.; mem. rsch. adv. com. on control guidance and nav. NASA, 1964-65; various coms. Hwy. Rsch. Bd., NRC, 1964-74; vis. lectr. NATO, 1968, 71; mem. roster of arbitrators Fed. Mediation and Conciliation Svc.; cons. govt. agys., industry, legal profession. Author: Unionizing the Armed Forces, 1977; contbr. articles to profl. publs. Mem. Phila. Mayor's Sci. and Tech. Adv. Council. Recipient Louis E. Levy Gold medal Franklin Inst., 1960 Fellow IEEE, AAAS, APA, Am. Psychol. Soc., Human Factors Soc.; mem. Ergonomics Soc., Cosmos Club, Sigma Xi. Home: 211 Cornell Ave Swarthmore PA 19081-1933 E-mail: krendel@wharton.upenn.edu.

KRENDL, CATHY STRICKLIN, lawyer; b. Paris, Tex., Mar. 14, 1945; d. Louis and Margaret Helen (Young) S.; m. James R. Krendl, July 5, 1969; children: Peggy, Susan, Anne. BA summa cum laude, North Tex. State U., 1967; JD cum laude, Harvard U., 1970. Bar: Alaska 1970, Colo. 1972. Atty. Hughes, Thorsness, Lowe Gantz & Clark, Anchorage, 1970-71; adj. prof. U. Colo. Denver Ctr., 1972-73; from asst. prof. to prof. law, dir. bus planning program U. Denver, 1973-83; ptnr. Krendl, Krendl, Sachnoff & Way, Denver, 1983—. Author: Colorado Business Corporation Act Deskbook, 2002; editor: Colorado Methods of Practice, 8 vols. 1983-2003, Closely Held Corporations in Colorado, vols. 1-3, 1981; contbr. articles to profl jours. Named Disting. Alumna North Tex. State U., 1985. Mem. Colo. Bar Assn. (bd. govs. 1982-86, 88-91, chmn. securities subsect. 1986, bus. law sect. 1988-89, Professionalism award), Denver Bar Assn. (pres. 1989-90). Avocation: reading. Home: 1551 Larimer St Apt 1101 Denver CO 80202-1630 E-mail: csk@krendl.com.

KRENEK, DEBBY, newspaper editor; d. Ernest Reed and Elizabeth Pendleton (Brown) K.; m. James C. Roberts Jr., Feb. 28, 1987; children: Christine Elizabeth Roberts, Taylor James Roberts. BJ, Tex. A&M Univ., 1978. Copy editor Corpus Christi (Tex.) Caller-Times, 1978-81; news editor Dallas Times Herald, 1981-85, asst. bus. editor, 1985-86, exec. news editor, 1986-87; dep. news editor N.Y. Daily News, 1987-88, dep. mng. editor, 1988-91, mng. editor, 1991-93, exec. editor, 1993-97, editor-in-chief, 1997-2000; assoc. editor Newsday, 2001—. Chief creative officer Petplace.com, 2000—01. Named to Acad. of Women Achievers YWCA, N.Y., 1992. Avocations: photography, tennis, home renovation. Office: Newsday 235 Pinelawn Rd Melville NY 11747-4250*

KRENEK, MARY LOUISE, political scientist, researcher; b. Wharton, Tex., Dec. 8, 1951; d. George P., Jr. and Vlasta (Zahn) Krenek. AA, Wharton County Jr. Coll., 1972; BA, Tex. A&I U., Corpus Christi, 1974; MA, St. Mary's U., San Antonio, 1992; Czech lang. cert., Charles U., Prague, Czech Republic, 1994. Cert. secondary and elem. tchr. Tex. Polygraph examiner, San Antonio, 1979-81; ind. contractor market, polit. and social rschr. San Antonio, Houston, 1982—. Substitute tchr., tchr. San Antonio Ind. Sch. Dist., 1981—82, Houston Ind. Sch. Dist., 1991—98, 2002—; instr. govt. Wharton County Jr. Coll., 1997—99; assoc. J.C. Penney Co., Inc., 1994—2000; with Am. Acad. Excellence, Houston. Sec. Egypt Plantation Mus., 2003; del. Tex. Dem. Conv., 1971—72. 1st lt. U.S. Army, 1975—78, lt. col. USAR, 1978—2003, ret. USAR, 2003. Mem.: CESAT, Am. Polit. Sci. Assn., Nat. Assn. Self-Employed, Point/Counterpoint (Houston chpt.), Women in Mil. Svc. Am. Meml. Found. (charter), Houston Czech Cultural Ctr., Sharton County Hist. Mus. Assn. (assoc.), Ret. Officers Assn. (sec.-treas. Alamo chpt., jr. v.p. Dept. Tex., sec. Greater Houston chpt., ROTC coord.), St. Mary's U. Alumni Assn., Am. Legion, Pi Sigma Alpha. Roman Catholic. Avocations: reading, writing, travel. Home: 10502 Fountain Lake Dr Stafford TX 77477-3711 also: PO Box 310 Egypt TX 77436-0310 E-mail: marykrenek01@aol.com.

KRENK, CHRISTOPHER JOSEPH, human services professional; b. Eugene, Oreg., Jan. 20, 1949; s. Marvin A. and Mary S. K.; m. Nell Babcock, July 3, 1977; children: Hanna, Elliot, Miranda. BS, U. Oreg., 1971; MSW, U. Wash., 1977. Cert. social worker. Dir. program svcs. The Christie Sch., Marylhurst, Oreg., 1977-83; dir. social svcs. Cedar Hills Hosp., Portland, Oreg., 1983-85, CEO, 1985-90; pres., CEO Albertina Kerr Ctrs., Portland, 1990—. Pres. Oregon Alliance of Children's Programs, Salem, 2001. Chairperson Long Range Planning com. First Unitarian Ch., 1992-98; mem. social work adv. coun. Portland State U. Grad. Sch. Mem. NASW, Multnomah County Mental Health Adv. Coun. (chairperson 1999-2000), Portland City Club, Portland Indsl. Rotary Club. Home: 13401 SW Atwater Ln Lake Oswego OR 97034 Office: Albertina Kerr Ctrs 424 NE 22nd Ave Portland OR 97232 Fax: 503-239-8106. E-mail: ckrenk@comcast.net., chrisk@albertinakerr.org.

KRENKEL, PETER ASHTON, engineer, educator; b. San Francisco, Jan. 3, 1930; s. Harry Nichols and Daisy Genevieve (Ashton) K.; m. Jessica Ann Jones AA, Coll. City San Francisco, 1952; BS, U. Calif., Berkeley, 1956; MS, U. Calif.-Berkeley, 1958, PhD, 1960. Registered profl. engr., Ga., Tenn., Nev., N.C. Instr. U. Calif., Berkeley, 1958-60; founder Associated Water & Air Resources Engrs., Inc. (now Eckenfelder & Assoc., Inc.), Nashville, 1968-74; chmn., prof. dept. environ. and water resources engring. Vanderbilt U., Nashville, 1960-73; dir. div. environ. planning TVA, 1974-78; exec. dir. water resources ctr. U. Nev., Reno, 1978-82, dean coll. engring., 1982-87, prof. civil engring., 1987-96, prof. and dean emeritus coll. engring., 1996—. Disting. lectr. Am. Inst. Chem. Engrs.; cons. WHO, Internat. Joint Commn. on Great Lakes Water Quality, U.S. EPA, U.S. Dept. Energy, Roy F. Weston, Inc. Stauffer Chem. Co., G.M., Monsanto, Korean Advanced Inst. Sci. and Tech., Seoul, 1985, others; cons. Ministry of Water Resources and Power, Republic of China, 1980, chmn. thermal pollution panel Nat. Water Commn., Washington, 1970-72, Tenn. Air Conservation Commn., 1971-77; eminent overseas speaker Inst. Engrs., Australia, 1986; appointed to Air Pollution Hearing Bd., Washoe County, Nev., 1990-92; mem. Washoe County Water Commn., 1995—; mem. cmty. adv. bd. Nev. Test Site, U.S. Dept. Energy, 1997—. Author: (with V. Novotny) Water Quality Management, 1980, (handbook) (with V. Novotny, K.R. Imhoff, M. Olthof) Urban Drainage and Wastewater Disposal, 1989; editor: (with F.L. Parker) Thermal Pollution, Biological Aspects, 1970, Thermal Pollution, Engineering Aspects, 1970, Water Quality Monitoring in Europe, 1972, Heavy Metals in the Aquatic Environment, 1974; contbr. numerous articles on environ. control to profl. jours. Pres. Tenn. Lung Assn., 1974-75. With AUS, 1953-55. Fellow USPHS, 1963; recipient award outstanding research san. engring. ASCE, 1963, Skill, Integrity, Responsibility award Am. Gen. Contractors, 1984 Mem. ASCE (editor proc. nat. conf. on environ. engring. 1991), AIChE, APHA, Am. Water Works Assn., Water Pollution Control Fedn. (bd. control), Air Pollution Control Assn., Internat. Assn. Water Pollution Rsch. (governing bd.), Am. Acad. Environ. Engring. (diplomate), Sigma Xi, Tau Beta Pi, Chi Epsilon. Home: 3500 Cashill Blvd Reno NV 89509-5024

KRENS, THOMAS, museum director; b. N.Y.C., Dec. 26, 1946; BA in Polit. Economy with honors, Williams Coll., 1969; M in Art, SUNY, Albany, 1971, HHD (hon.), 1989; M in Pub. and Pvt. Mgmt., Yale U., 1984. Asst. prof. art Williams Coll., Williamstown, Mass., 1972-80, asst. prof. history art grad. program, 1977-80, adj. prof.; dir. Mus. Art Williams Coll. Mus. Art, Williamstown, Mass., 1981-88; cons. Solomon R. Guggenheim Mus., N.Y.C., 1986-88; dir. Guggenheim Mus. SoHo, N.Y.C., 1988—, The Peggy Guggenheim Collection, Venice, Italy, 1988—; dir., trustee Solomon R. Guggenheim Found. N.Y.C., 1988—. Adv. com. mus. project NEA and Am. Fedn. Arts, Washington; adj. prof. art history Williams Coll., 1988-91, dir. artist in residence program, 1976-80; lectr. in field. Author: Jim Dine Prints: 1970-77, 1977, The Prints of Helen Frankenthaler, 1980, The Drawing of Robert Morris, 1982, Robert Morris: The Mind/Body Problem, 1994; exhbns. include Jim Dine Prints, 1970-77, 1976, The Prints of Helen Frankenthaler, 1980, The Drawing of Robert Morris: 1956-82, 1982, Refigured Painting: The German Image, 1960-88, The Great Utopia: The Russian and Soviet Avant-Garde, 1915-1932, Marc Chagall and the Jewish Theatre, Robert Morris: The Mind/Body Problem. Honorary Award: Doctor of Humane Letters, SUNY. Mem. Aspen Inst. Italia (bd. dirs.), Soc. Kandinsky/Ctr. Georges Pompidou, Gesellschaft fur Moderne Kunst am Mus. Ludwig (adv. bd.), Coun. Fgn. Rels., Assn. Art Mus. Dirs. (assoc.), AFA (adv. com.), Yale Univ. Coun. (com. on the art gallery and Brit. Art Ctr). Office: Solomon R Guggenheim Mus 1071 5th Ave New York NY 10128-0112

KRENSKY, ALAN MICHAEL, pediatrician, educator; b. Chgo., Oct. 12, 1951; s. Arthur Melvin and Joanne Hope (Phillips) K.; m. Carol Ann Clayberger, Oct. 14, 1979; children: Andrew, Matthew, Lauren. BA, U. Pa., 1973, MD, 1977. Diplomate Am. Bd. Pediat. Resident in pediat. Boston Children's Hosp., 1977-80, clin. fellow in nephrology, 1980-81; rsch. fellow in immunology Dana-Farber Cancer Inst., Boston, 1981-83; instr. pediat. Boston Children's Hosp./Harvard Med. Sch., 1983-84; from asst. prof. pediat. to assoc. prof. pediat. Stanford (Calif.) U., 1984-94, prof. pediat., 1994—, Shelagh Galligan prof. pediatrics, chief divsn. immunology. Chmn. exptl. immunology study sect. NIH, 1993-95. Contbr. more than 200 articles to profl. jours. Recipient Young Investigator award Am. Soc. Histocompatibility and Immunogenetics, 1985, Award for Rsch. Excellence Am. Acad. Pediatrics, 1993; Burroughs Wellcome scholar in exptl. therapeutics, 1994-99. Mem. Am. Assn. Immunologists, Am. Soc. Nephrology (Young Investigator award 1990), Am. Soc. Clin. Investigation, Am. Soc. Pediat. Nephrologists, Soc. Pediat. Rsch. (pres. 2002, Young Investigator award 1985), Transplantation Soc. Office: Stanford U Sch Med Dept Pediatrics Med Ctr Stanford CA 94305-5164

KRENTZ, EUGENE LEO, university president, educator, minister; b. Edmonton, Alta., Can., June 16, 1932; came to U.S., 1958; s. Emil and Natalie (Martin) K.; m. Joyce Ann Triolet, Feb. 1, 1958; children— Paul, Cynthia, Tamara B.Th., Concordia Theol. Sem., Springfield, Ill., 1958, B.D., 1971, M.Div., 1973; MA, Eastern Mich. U., 1973; PhD, U. Mich., 1980; LHD (hon.), Dominican U., River Forest, Ill., 1995. Ordained to ministry Lutheran Ch. 1958. Pastor St. Paul Luth. Ch., Susanville, Calif., 1958-61; pastor Trinity Luth. Ch., St. Joseph, Mich., 1961-65; prof. Concordia Coll., Ann Arbor, Mich., 1965-83; pres. Concordia U., River Forest, Ill., 1983-95; exec. dir. Concordia Mission Soc., 2000. Contbg. author: Concordia Pulpit, 1974, 78, 80, 83, 85; contbg. editor: Luth. Edn., 1983-95. Chmn. coll. divsn. United Way, Ann Arbor; mem. troop com. Boy Scouts Am., Ann Arbor; peer reviewer U.S. Dept. Edn.; bd. dirs. Fedn. Ind. Ill. Colls. and Univs.; mem., past pres. Luth. Edn. Conf. N.Am. Recipient Servus Ecclaesiae Christi, Concordia Theol. Sem., Ft. Wayne, Ind., 1978, Servant of Christ award Condordia Coll., Bronxville, N.Y., 1995. Mem. Luth. Edn. Assn., Phi Delta Kappa Avocations: tennis; sailing; skiing; reading; travel. Home: 36395 N Tara Ct Ingleside IL 60041-8576

KREPS, JUANITA MORRIS, economics educator, former government official; b. Lynch, Ky., Jan. 11, 1921; d. Elmer M. and Cenia (Blair) Morris; m. Clifton H. Kreps, Jr., Aug. 11, 1944; children: Sarah, Laura, Clifton. AB, Berea Coll., 1942; MA, Duke U., 1944; PhD, 1948; LLD (hon.), Bryant Coll., 1972, U. N.C. at Chapel Hill, 1973, Tulane U., Colgate U., 1980, Trinity Coll., 1981, U. Rochester, Grove City Coll., 1984, Davidson Coll., 1990, Lenoir-Rhyne Coll., 1991, U. Notre Dame, 1992, Duke U., 1993; LittD (hon.), Cornell Coll., 1973, Western Md. Coll., 1982; LHD (hon.), Denison U., 1973, U. Ky., Queens Coll., St. Lawrence U., 1975, Wheaton Coll., 1976, Claremont Grad. Sch., Berea Coll., 1979. Instr. econs. Denison U., 1945-46, asst. prof., 1948-50; mem. faculty Duke U., 1955-77, asst. prof., 1962-68, prof. econs., 1968-77, James B. Duke prof., 1972-77, James B. Duke prof. emerita, 1979—, asst. provost, 1969-72, v.p., 1973-77, v.p. emerita, 1979—; sec. U.S. Dept. Commerce, 1977-79. Mem. adv. com. Congl. Commn. for the Future of Worker Mgmt. Rels., Secs. of Commerce and Labor, 1993-94. Author: (with C.E. Ferguson) Principles of Economics, 2d rev. edit, 1965, Lifetime Allocation of Work and Income, 1971, Sex in the Marketplace: American Women at Work, 1971,

Women and the American Economy, 1976; co-author: (with Richard Perlman and Gerald Somers) Contemporary Labor Economics, 1973; Editor: Employment, Income and Retirement Problems of the Aged, 1963, Technology, Manpower and Retirement Policy, 1966, Sex, Age and Work, 1975. Bd. dirs. Am. Coun. on Germany, Rsch. Triangle Found., Ednl. Testing Svc., 1972-77; mem. Nat. Manpower Policy Task Force; trustee Berea Coll., 1972-78, 80-98, Duke Endowment, 1979—, Nat. Humanities Ctr., 1983-86, U. N.C., Wilmington, 1993-2001, Humrro, 1980-83, Coun. Fgn. Rels., 1983-89, Kenan Inst. Pvt. Enterprise of U. N.C., Chapel Hill, 1995—; pres. bd. overseers Tchrs. Ins. and Annuity Assn., 1992-96; bd. dirs. TIAA, 1968-72, 85-96, Coll. Retirement Equities Fund, 1972-77. Named to Presl. Commn. on Nat. Agenda for the 80's, 1979; recipient N.C. Pub. Svc. award, 1976, Stephen Wise award, 1978, Woman of Yr. award Ladies Home Jour., 1978, Duke U. Alumni award, 1983, Haskins award Coll. Bus. and Pub. Adminstrn., NYU, 1984, First Corp. Governance award Nat. Assn. Corp. Dirs., 1987, Dir.'s Choice Leadership award Nat. Women's Econ. Alliance Found., 1987, Disting. Meritorious Svc. medal Duke U. Alumni, 1987. Fellow Gerontol. Soc. (v.p. 1971-72), Am. Acad. Arts and Scis.; mem. AAUP, AAUW (Achievement award 1981), Am. Econ. Assn. (v.p. 1983-84), So. Econ. Assn. (pres. 1975-76), Indsl. Rels. Rsch. Assn. (exec. com.).

KRESA, KENT, aerospace executive; b. N.Y.C., Mar. 24, 1938; s. Helmy and Marjorie (Boutelle) K.; m. Joyce Anne McBride, Nov. 4, 1961; 1 child, Kiren BSAA, MIT, 1959, MSAA, 1961, EAA, 1966. Sr. scientist rsch. and advanced devel. divsn. AVCO, Wilmington, Mass., 1959-61; staff mem. MIT Lincoln Lab., Lexington, Mass., 1961-68; dep. dir. strategic tech. office Def. Advanced Rsch. Projects Agy., Washington, 1968-73; dir. tactical tech. office Def. Advanced Rsch. Project Agy., Washington, 1973-75; v.p., mgr. Rsch. & Tech. Ctr. Northrop Corp., Hawthorne, Calif., 1975-76, v.p., gen. mgr. Ventura divsn. Newbury Park, Calif., 1976-82, group v.p. Aircraft Group L.A., 1982-86, sr. v.p. tech. devel. and planning, 1986-87, pres., COO, 1987-90; chmn. bd., pres., CEO Northrop Grumman Corp., L.A., 1990—2001, chmn. bd., CEO, 2001—03, now chmn. bd., 2003—. Bd. dirs. Avery Dennison Corp., Fluor Corp., Eclipse Aviation Corp., Trust Co. of the W., Advanced Bionics. Bd. dirs. John Tracy Clinic for the Hearing-Impaired, W.M. Keck Found., L.A. World Affairs Coun.; bd. govs. L.A. Music Ctr.; bd. visitors Anderson Sch. Bus., UCLA; bd. trustees Calif. Inst. Tech. Recipient Henry Webb Salsbury award MIT, 1959, Arthur D. Flemming award, 1975, Calif. Industrialist of Yr. Calif. Mus. of Sci. and Industry and the Calif. Mus. Found., 1996, Bob Hope Disting. Citizen award Nat. Security Indsl. Assn., 1996; Sec. of Def. Meritorious Civilian Svc. medal, 1975, USN Meritorious Pub. Svc. citation, 1975, Exceptional Civilian Svc. award USAF, 1987. Fellow AIAA; mem. Aerospace Industries Assn. (past bd. govs.), Naval Aviation Mus. Found., Navy League U.S., Soc. Flight Test Engrs., Assn. U.S. Army, Nat. Space Club, Am. Def. Preparedness Assn., L.A. Country Club, NAE. Office: Northrop Grumman Corp 1840 Century Park E Los Angeles CA 90067-2101

KRESGE, ALEXANDER JERRY, chemistry educator; b. Wilkes-Barre, Pa., July 17, 1926; married; 3 children. BA, Cornell U., 1949; PhD in Chemistry, U. Ill., 1953. Rsch. assoc. Purdue U., West Lafayette, Ind., 1954-55, MIT, 1955-57; assoc. chemist Brookhaven Nat. Lab., 1957-60; from asst. prof. to prof. chemistry Ill. Inst. Tech., Chgo., 1960-74, chmn. chem. group, 1974-78; prof. chemistry U. Toronto, Ont., Can., 1974-92, prof. emeritus, 1992—. Guest prof. MIT, 1965; vis. scientist Fritz Haber Inst., 1981, U. Goteborg, 1983; mem. Gordon Rsch. Conf. on Chemistry and Physics of Isotopes, vice chmn., 1967, chmn., 1968; lectr. in field. Mem. editorial adv. bd. Isotopes in Organic Chemistry, Jour. Phys. Organic Chemistry. Fulbright scholar U. London, 1953-54; NSF sr. fellow, 1964-65, Guggenheim fellow, 1964-65, Killam fellow, 1984-86, Yamada fellow, 1985; recipient Morley medal of Cleve. sect. Am. Chem. Soc., Syntex award Chem. Inst. Can. Fellow Royal Soc. Can., Chem. Inst. Can.; mem. AAAS, Am. Chem. Soc., Royal Soc. Chemistry (Ingold lectr. 1995), Argentinian Soc. Organic Chemistry (hon.). Achievements include rsch. in reaction mechanisms, isotope effects, flash photolysis, acid-base catalysis and kinetics. Office: Dept Chemistry Univ Toronto Toronto ON Canada M5S 3H6 E-mail: akresge@chem.utoronto.ca.

KRESGE, BRUCE ANDERSON, retired physician; b. Detroit, Dec. 20, 1931; s. Stanley Sebastian and Dorothy Eloise (McVittie) K.; m. Peggy Ann Sale, June 14, 1952; children— Deborah Kresge McDowell, Katherine Kresge Lutey, Susan Kresge Drewes, Cynthia Kresge Furlong, Stephen. BA, Albion Coll., 1953; MD, Wayne State U., 1956. Intern Detroit Receiving Hosp., 1956-57; resident U. Mich. Hosp., 1959-60; pvt. practice Rochester, Mich., 1960-90; mem. staff St. Joseph Mercy Hosp., Pontiac, Mich., also; Pontiac Gen. Hosp., 1960-67; Crittenton Hosp., Rochester, 1967—. Pres. Rochester br. YMCA, 1975-77; trustee Kresge Found.,, 1967—, Crittenton Hosp., 1993-99; hon. trustee Albion Coll., 1999—. With M.C., U.S. Army, 1957-59. Mem. AMA. Republican. Methodist. Home: 1071 N Lake Angelus Rd Lake Angelus MI 48326-1026

KRESGE, JENNIFER ALISON, physician assistant; b. Passaic, N.J., Aug. 28, 1970; d. Earl Harold and Diane (Pityinger) Greenleaf; m. Matthew Jason Kresge, Sept. 1, 2002. BS in Psychology cum laude, Hobart & William Smith, 1992; physician asst. cert., Bowman Gray Sch. Medicine, 1996. Cert. nursing asst. Nursing asst. Saratoga County Infirmary, Ballston Spa, NY, 1992—94; physician asst. Mansfield Family Practice, Storrs, Conn., 1997—98, Malta Family Medicine, 1998—2002; physician asst., Bariatric coord. Floch Surg. Assocs., 2002—. Mem. Am. Acad. Physician Assts. Episcopalian. Achievements include completing Ironman USA triathlon in Lake Placid, NY in 2002. Avocations: running, travel, triathlons, water and snow skiing. Home: 4 Maryland Ct Rexford NY 12148 E-mail: mjjakresge@aol.com.

KRESH, J. YASHA, cardiovascular researcher, educator; b. Russia, July 13, 1948; came to U.S., 1967; m. Myrna Blickman. BSEE, N.J. Inst. Tech., 1971; MSBME, Rutgers U., 1973, PhD, 1976. Rsch. assoc. Beth Israel Med. Ctr., Newark, 1976-79; dir. rsch. Jefferson Med. Coll., Phila., 1979-86; prof. medicine, dir. cardiovascular biophysics and computing Cardiovascular Rsch. Ctr., Phila., 1986—; prof., dir. rsch. cardiothoracic surgery MCP Hahnemann Sch. Medicine, Phila., 1986—. Prof. biomed. and mech. engring. Drexel U., 1984—. Author more than 175 publs. in physiol. cardiology and bioengring. jours.; patentee in field. Fellow Am. Coll. Cardiology, Am. Inst. Med. and Biol. Engring.; sr. mem. IEEE, Biomed. Engring. Soc., Am. Inst. Med. Biol. Engr.; mem. Am. Heart Assn., Am. Soc. Artificial Internal Organs, Sigma Xi, Tau Beta Pi, Eta Kappa Nu. Avocations: fractal art, porsche-phile, theoretical biology, computing. Office: Drexel U Coll Medicine MS # 111 245 N 15th St Philadelphia PA 19102-1192 E-mail: j.yasha.kresh@drexel.edu.

KRESKY, JEFFREY, music educator, writer, composer; b. Passaic, NJ, May 14, 1948; children: Emily, Ian. PhD, Princeton U., 1969—74. Prof. of music William Paterson U., Wayne, NJ, 1973—. Co-conductor NY Gilbert and Sullivan Players, NYC. Home: 325 Stillwell Pl Ridgewood NJ 07450 Office: William Paterson U 300 Pompton Rd Wayne NJ 07470 Office Fax: 973-720-2217. Personal E-mail: kreskyj@wpunj.edu. E-mail: kreskyj@wpunj.edu.

KRESS, NANCY, writer; b. Buffalo, Jan. 20; d. Henry Francis and Angelina (Canale) Koningisor; m. Michael Joseph Kress, July 14, 1973 (div. 1986); children: Kevin Michael, Brian Stephen. BS in Edn., SUNY, Plattsburgh, 1969; MEd, SUNY, Brockport, 1978, MA in English, 1979. Cert. tchr. N.Y. K-6 and English 7-12. Grade 4 tchr. Penn Yan (N.Y.) Schs., 1970-73; tchr. grade 9 English Holley (N.Y.) Ctrl. Schs., 1979-80; instr. SUNY, Brockport, 1980-83; copywriter Stanton & Hucko, Inc., Rochester, N.Y., 1984-89; freelance writer, 1990—. Author: (novels) An Alien Light, 1988, Beggars in Spain, 1993, Beggars and Choosers, 1995, Beggars Ride, 1996, Oaths & Miracles, 1996, Maximum Light, 1997, Stinger, 1998, Yanked, 1999, Probability Sun, 2001, Probability Spun, 2002, Crossfire, 2003; columnist Writer's Digest mag., 1992—, Dynamic Characters, 1998, The Aliens of Earth, 1998, Breaker's Dozen, 1998, Probability Moon, 2000. Winner 1997 Nebula awd for Flowers of Aulit Prison. Mem. Sci. Fiction Writers Am. (nebula awards for best short story 1985, best novella 1991, hugo award for best novella 1992). Office: c/o Tor Books 14th Fl 175 5th Ave Fl 14 New York NY 10010-7703*

KRESS, SIDNEY C. pathologist; b. Wadesboro, N.C., Mar. 29, 1940; s. Jacob Himi and Esta Joyce (Levy) Kress; m. June Anita Cohen; children: Jeffrey, Michael. BS in Chemistry, Duke U., 1962; MD, U. N.C., 1966. Diplomate Am. Bd. Pathology. Resident in pathology Kings County Hosp., Bklyn., 1966-71; pathologist Raritan Bay Med. Ctr., Perth Amboy, N.J., 1973—. Clin. asst. prof. pathology Robert Wood Johnson Sch. Medicine, Piscataway, N.J., 1978—. Maj. USAF, 1971-73. Fellow Coll Am. Pathology; mem. N.J. Med. Soc., Middlesex County Med. Soc. Avocations: computers, photography, gardening. Office: Raritan Bay Med Ctr 530 New Brunswick Ave Perth Amboy NJ 08861-3674 E-mail. skress@rbmc.org.

KRESS, THOMAS SYLVESTER, engineer, consultant; b. Kingsport, Tenn., Dec. 5, 1933; s. Samuel Arthur and Elsie Augusta Kress; m. Evelyn Dolores McConnell, June 2, 1956; children: Reid Leonard, Wendy Gail Collins, Tyler Andrew. BS, U. Tenn., Knoxville, 1953—56, MS, 1956—65, PhD, 1965—71. Lic. engr., Tenn., 1971. Engr. Pratt and Whitney Aircraft, East Hartford, Conn., 1956—59; engr., program mgr., sect. head, scientist Oak Ridge Nat. Lab., Tenn., 1959—94; cons. Oak Ridge, Tenn., 1994—; mem. Adv. Com. on Reactor Safeguards, Washington. Mem. Com. for Safety of Nuclear Installations group experts on source terms OECD, Paris, 1979-84; tech. expert in Chernobyl rev. IAEA, Vienna, 1986; mem. Savannah River Lab. severe accident adv. com. Dept. Energy, Oak Ridge, 1988-91, mem. waste tank adv. com., 1990—, mem. adv. com. for reactor safeguards. Contbr. articles to profl. jours. Fellow: Am. Nuc. Soc.; mem.: AAAS, NSPE, Am. Soc. Mech. Engrs. (sect. chmn. 1978—79), N.Y. Acad. Sci. Avocations: fly fishing, basketball, softball. Home: 102B Newridge Rd Oak Ridge TN 37830 Home Fax: 865-482-7548. Personal E-mail: tskress@aol.com.

KRESS, WILLIAM F. manufacturing company executive; Pres. Green Bay (Wis.) Packaging. Office: Green Bay Packaging 1700 Webster Ct Green Bay WI 54302-1166

KRESSEL, HENRY, venture capitalist; b. Vienna, Jan. 24, 1934; came to U.S., 1946, naturalized, 1955; s. Aaron and Hudi (Zauderer) K.; m. Bertha Horowitz, Sept. 16, 1956; children: Aron, Kim. BS magna cum laude, Yeshiva U., 1955; MS, Harvard U., 1956; MBA, U. Pa., 1959, PhD (David Sarnoff fellow), 1965. Engr. Solid State div. RCA, 1959-61, engring. leader, 1961-63, 65-66; mem. tech. staff RCA David Sarnoff Research Center, 1966-70, head semicondr. device research, 1970-78, dir. materials research lab., 1978-79, staff v.p. solid state research, 1979-83; sr. v.p. E.M. Warburg, Pincus & Co., N.Y.C., 1983-84, mng. dir., 1985—99, sr. mng. dir., 2000—. Regents lectr. U. Calif., San Diego, 1978-79; bd. dirs. Yeshiva U. Rsch. Inst.; cons. solar energy U.S. ERDA, 1975, USAF; adv. com. engring. NSF, 1996-99; engring. adv. coun. N.C. State U., 1985-88; mem. bd. dirs. several high tech. companies. Author: Semiconductor Lasers and Heterojunction LED's, 1977; editor: Characterization of Epitaxial Semiconductor Films, 1976, Semiconductor Devices for Optical Communication, 1980; assoc. editor: IEEE Jour. Quantum Electronics, 1978-81; chmn. coordinating com. Jour. Lightware Tech., 1981-82; contbr. numerous articles to sci. jours.; patentee in field. Served with Fin. Corps U.S. Army, 1959. Recipient David Sarnoff award RCA, 1974, Revel award Yeshiva U., 1980 Fellow IEEE (pres. Lasers and Electro-optics Soc. 1978-79, Centennial award 1984, Millennium award 2000, Sarnoff award 1985, Leos Svc. award 1992), Am. Phys. Soc.; mem. AIME, Nat. Acad. Engring. Home: 1056 Fifth Ave New York NY 10028 Office: E M Warburg Pincus & Co 466 Lexington Ave Fl 10 New York NY 10017-3147

KRESSEL, HERBERT YEHUDE, medical educator; b. Bklyn., Nov. 20, 1947; BA, Brandeis U., Waltham, Mass., 1968; MD, U. So. Calif., L.A., 1972. Diplomate Am. Bd. Radiology in diagnostic radiology, lic. physician, Calif., Pa., Wis., N.Y., N.J., Mass. Intern in medicine U. Wash. Hosp., Seattle, 1972-73; resident in radiology U. Calif., San Francisco, 1973-74, NIH fellow in diagnostic radiology, 1974-76, clin. instr. radiology, 1976-77, asst. prof., 1977-80, assoc. prof., 1980-85, prof., 1985-93; Miriam H. Stoneman prof. radiology Harvard Med. Sch., Boston, 1993—; attending physician GI radiology sect. dept. radiology Hosp. of U. Pa., 1977-82, dir. continung edn., 1979-93, attending physician, chief MRI sect., 1982-93; radiologist-in-chief Beth Israel Deaconess Med. Ctr., Boston, 1996—, pres., CEO, chief med. officer, 1998-2000, radiologist-in-chief, 2000—. Mem. plan devel. adv. task force on magnetic resonance for 1986 HealthSystems Plan-Health Systems Agy. Southeastern Pa., Inc., 1985-87; dir. R.I. Magnetic Resonance Imaging Network, Providence, 1988-93; mem. sci. adv. com. for rsch. grants Am. Cancer Soc., 1990-93; task force chmn. Com. on Studies Involving Human Beings, U. Pa., 1985-92; mem. coun. for continuing med. edn. U. Pa., 1990-93. Mem. editl. bds. Radiology, 1985-91, Magnetic Resonance in Medicine, 1987—; editor Magnetic Resonance Ann., 1985-88, Magnetic Resonance Quar., 1988-94; patentee in field. Mem. bd. dirs. Coregroup, 1996. Recipient Sylvia Sorkin Greenfield award Am. Assn. Physicists in Medicine, 1993. Fellow Am. Coll. Radiology (Commn. on Magnetic Resonance 1987-90, com. on pub. rels. 1987—, com. MR stds. and accreditation 1987—, chmn. com. on MR clin. applications 1987, Commn. on Govt. Rels. 1992—), Soc. Magnetic Resonance in Medicine (trustee 1987, sci. program com. chmn. 1989-90, pres.-elect 1990-91, pres. 1991-92, Crues Kressel award sect. magnetic resonance technologists 1991, Silver medal 1994), Radiol. Soc. N.Am. (refresher course com. 1992-93), Am. Roentgen Ray Soc., Soc. Gastrointestinal Radiologists, Soc. Computed Body Tomography (rsch. com. 1990-93), Mass. Radiol. Soc., New Eng. Roentgen Ray Soc. Office: Beth Israel Hosp Dept Radiology 330 Brookline Ave Rm Cc483B Boston MA 02215-5491 E-mail: hkressel@caregroup.harvard.edu.

KRESTON, MARTIN HOWARD, advertising, marketing, public relations, and publishing executive; b. N.Y.C., May 27, 1931; s. Henry and Frances (Stoll) Kreizvogel; m. Audrey Elizabeth Muir, Aug. 20, 1960 (dec. Jan., 1992); children: Mark Bradley, Rebecca Sarah; m. Judith Kate Stern, Dec. 15, 1996. BS in Econs, Wharton Sch., U. Pa., 1953; postgrad., N.Y. U., Northwestern U. Asst. dept. mgr. R.H. Macy & Co., N.Y.C., 1953-54; mktg. supr., account exec. Edward H. Weiss & Co., Chgo., 1956-60; with Doyle Dane Bernbach Inc., N.Y.C., 1960-86, v.p., mgmt. supr., 1970-72, sr. v.p., mgmt. supr., 1972, group sr. v.p., 1972-86, exec. v.p., 1984-86, cons., 1986-88; exec. v.p. England & Co. Pub. Rels., 1988-89; pres., chief exec. officer Caggiano, Kreston & Siebel, N.Y.C., 1989-90; dir. mktg. optical group Jobson Pub. Corp., N.Y.C., 1990; N.E. sales dir. USA Today, N.Y.C., 1991-98. With U.S. Army, 1954-56. Mem. Univ. Club, Met. Opera Club Republican. Jewish. Home: 930 Park Ave New York NY 10028-0209

KRETSCHMAR, WILLIAM EDWARD, state legislator, lawyer; b. St. Paul, Aug. 21, 1933; s. William Emanuel and Frances Jane (Peterson) K. BS, Coll. St. Thomas, 1954; LLB, U. Minn., 1961. Bar: N.D. 1961, U.S. Dist. Ct. N.D. 1961. Pvt. practice Kretschmar Law Office, Ashley, ND, 1962—; mem. N.D. Ho. of Reps., Bismarck, 1972-98, speaker, 1988-90, 2000—. Mem. N.D. Commn. Uniform State Laws, 1987—; bd. dirs. N.W. G.F. Mut. Ins. Co., Eureka, S.D.; del. N.D. Constl. Conv., Bismarck, 1971-72. Mem. ABA, State Bar Assn. N.D., Lions (pres. local club 1972-73, 93-94), Elks. Republican. Roman Catholic. Avocations: hunting, swimming, hiking, bicycling, skiing. Home: 201 E 3d St Venturia ND 58413-4015 Office: Kretschmar Law Office 117 1st Ave NW Ashley ND 58413-7037

KRETSCHMER, FRANK FREDERICK, JR., electrical engineer, researcher, consultant; b. Phila., July 31, 1930; m. Shirley J. Kretschmer; children: Frank F. III, John, Diane, Linda, Thomas. BSEE, Pa. State U., 1957; MSEE, Drexel Inst. Tech., 1961; PhD, Johns Hopkins U., 1970. Asst. devel. engr. Burroughs Corp., Paoli, Pa., 1957-58; project engr. Bendix Radio Corp., Towson, Md., 1958-64; rsch. assoc. Johns Hopkins U., Balt., 1964-70; supervisory electronics engr. Naval Rsch. Lab., Washington, 1970-90, 90—. Cons. in field. Author: Aspects of Radar Signal Processing, 1986; contbr. over 30 articles to profl. jours. and confs. With USN, 1948-52. Fellow IEEE (life). Achievements include over 20 patents in field.

KRETSCHMER, KEITH HUGHES, investor; b. Omaha, Oct. 20, 1934; s. John G. and Mary (Hughes) K.; m. Adine Williams, Oct. 1, 1960; children: Hugh, Dara, Kurt. AA, Wentworth Acad., 1954; BS, U. Nebr., 1956; student, UCLA, 1968. With J.G. Kretschmer & Co., Omaha, 1958-60; gen. agt. Lincoln (Nebr.) Life & Casualty, 1960-62; exec. v.p., sec. treas. Automated Mgmt. systems, Kansas City, Mo., 1962-68; investment exec. Shearson, Hammill & Co., Los Angeles, 1968-75; gen. ptnr. Bear Stearns & Co., Los Angeles, 1975-85; sr. mng. dir. Bear Stearns & Co. Inc., Boston, 1985-91, spl. assoc. dir., 1991-92; mng. dir. Oppenheimer & Co., Inc., Boston, 1993-94, Oppenheimer Capital, 1995-2001. Mem. stockholders com. Tosco Corp., Los Angeles, 1982 Author: Your Option, 1978. Advanceman Rep. Pres.'s Nixon and Ford, 1970-76; trustee Lighthouse Preservation Soc., 1986-88; active United Way Mass.; founding dir. Option Soc. So. Calif, 1974-85; bd. dirs. Pacific Palisades-Malibu YMCA, 1976-86, chmn. bd. dirs., 1980; bd. dirs. South Shore Art Ctr., Cohasset, Mass., 1988-97, pres., 1991-93; bd. dirs. World Affairs Coun. Boston, 1989-96; mem. pres.'s coun. Accion Internat., 1992—. Served to maj. U.S. Army, Airborne Ranger, 1956-58. Mem. The Explorers Club, Aircraft Owners and Pilots Assn., Experimental Aircraft Assn., Seaplane Pilots Assn., CEO Club, Angel Flight, AERO Club New England, Vintage Sports Car Club Am., Masons, Shriners. Congregationalist. Avocation: pilot since 1952. Office: 294 Sunshine Ave Sequim WA 98382 Home: 111 Lupine Dr Sequim WA 98382 E-mail: kkretsc@aol.com.

KRETZSCHMAR, WILLIAM ADDISON, JR., English language educator; b. Ann Arbor, Mich., Sept. 13, 1953; s. William Addison and Audrey June (Krauss) K.; m. Claudia Suzanne Miller. AB, U. Mich., 1975; MA in Medieval Studies, Yale U., 1976; PhD in English, U. Chgo., 1980. Instr. English Mundelein Coll., Chgo., 1977-82, dir. summer sch., 1979-81; asst. prof. English U. Wis., Whitewater, 1982-86, U. Ga., Athens, 1986-89, assoc. prof., 1989-95, prof., 1995—, dir. linguistics program, 1996-99. Author: Introduction to Quantitative Analysis of Linguistic Survey Data, 1996; editor: Dialects in Culture (R.I. McDavid, Jr.), 1979, Handbook of the Linguistic Atlas of the Middle and South Atlantic States, 1993, Oxford Dictionary of Pronunciation for Current English, 2001; editor: Linguistic Atlas Middle and South Atlantic States, Linguistic Atlas North-Central States, 1984—; editor Jour. English Linguistics, 1983-99, Empirical Linguistic Series, 1996-99; contbr. articles to profl. jours. Mem. MLA (regional del. 1983-86), Am. Dialect Soc. (exec. com. 1999-2003), Linguistic Soc. Am., Medieval Acad. Am., Assn. Computers Humanities (bd. dir. 1999-2003). Home: 125 Renfrew Dr Athens GA 30606-3936 Office: U Ga Dept English Athens GA 30602

KREUL, CAROL ANN, nurse; b. Dodgeville, Wis., Mar. 6, 1956; d. Norbert Francis and Rose Blanch (Winters) K. ADN, Madison (Wis.) Area Tech. Coll., 1981. RN, Wis.; cert. critical care, instr. ACLS. Staff nurse, dir. ICU Upland Hills Health, Inc., Dodgeville. Mem. AACN. Home: 506 Diagonal St Highland WI 53543-9709

KREUTER, GRETCHEN V. academic administrator; b. Mpls., May 7, 1934; d. Sigmund and Marvyl (Larson) von Loewe; m. Robert L. Sutton, 1993; children: David Karl, Betsy Ruth Rymes. BA, Rockford Coll., 1955; MA, U. Wis., 1958, PhD, 1961; LLD (hon.), Rockford Coll., 1992, Coll. St. Mary, 1994. Lectr. in Am. Studies Colgate U., Hamilton, N.Y., 1962-67; lectr. in history Coll. St. Catherine, St. Paul, 1969-71, Hamline U., St. Paul, 1971-72; prof. of history Macalester Coll., St. Paul, 1972-73, St. Olaf Coll., Northfield, Minn., 1975-80; asst. to pres. Coll. St. Catherine, St. Paul, 1980-84; asst. to v.p. acad. affairs U. Minn., Mpls., 1984-87; pres. Rockford Coll., Ill., 1987-92, Olivet (Mich.) Coll., 1992-93; sr. fellow Am. Coun. Edn., Washington, 1993-94; hon. fellow Inst. for Rsch. in Humanities U. Wis., Madison, 1994—; interim pres. Coll. of St. Mary, Omaha, 1995-96. Mem., chmn. Minn. Humanities Coun., St. Paul, 1974-83; mem. Mich. Humanities Coun., 1993; bd. dirs. Nat. Assn. State Humanities Commn., Washington, 1984-86. Author: An American Dissenter, 1969 (McKnight prize 1978), Running the Twin Cities: editor: Women of Minnesota, 1977, 2d edit., 1998, Two Career Family, 1978, Forgotton Promise: Race and Gender Conflict on a Small College Campus: A Memoir, 1996. Bd. dirs. Kobe Coll. Corp., Rockford Mus. Ctr., ACE Commn. on Minorities in Higher Edn., 1991-92, Mich. Humanities Coun., 1993-94. Address: 2402 Kendall Ave Madison WI 53705-3845 E-mail: gkreuter@facstaff.wisc.edu.

KREVANS, JULIUS RICHARD, university administrator, physician; b. N.Y.C., May 1, 1924; s. Sol and Anita Krevans; m. Patricia N. Abrams, May 28, 1950; children: Nita, Julius R., Rachel, Sarah, Nora Kate. BS Arts and Scis, N.Y. U., 1943, MD, 1946. Diplomate: Am. Bd. Internal Med. Intern, then resident Johns Hopkins Med. Sch. Hosp., mem. faculty, until 1970, dean acad. affairs, 1969—70; physician in chief Balt. City Hosp., 1963—69; prof. medicine U. Calif., San Francisco, 1970—, dean Sch. Medicine, 1971—82, chancellor, 1982—93, chancellor emeritus, 1993—. Contbr. articles on hematology, internal med. profl. jours. Served with M.C. AUS, 1948-50. Served with USMC, 1948—50, AUS. Mem. ACP, Assn. Am. Physicians. Address: 32 Birch Bay Dr Bar Harbor ME 04609

KREYCHE, GERALD FRANCIS, retired philosophy educator; b. Kenosha, Wis., June 19, 1927; s. Harold Joseph and Henrietta Fredericka (Oteman) K.; m. Eleanor Ann Okon, June 19, 1948. AB, DePaul U., 1949, AM, 1950; PhD cum laude, U. Ottawa, Can., 1958. Mem. faculty DePaul U., 1950-59, chmn. dept. philosophy, 1961-82, prof., 1965-89, prof. emeritus, 1989—; now also Danforth assoc. Aquinas lectr. Alverno Coll., Milw., 1963; vis. prof. St. Mary's Coll., Minn., 1977; bd. advisors Univ. Press Am. Condr.: radio programs What Do You Think? ; also What's the Big Idea?, 1960; frequent appearances ednl. and comml. TV, also radio, 1958— ; Author: Perspectives on God, 1972, Thirteen Thinkers; also articles religious publs.; Co-editor: Harbrace Philosophy series; Visions of the American West, 1988, Heroes of the American West, 2001; sr. editor: Am. Thought; sect. editor: U.S.A. Today; bd. advisors: Philos. Research and Analysis; former editor-in-chief Listening: A Journal of Religion and Culture; referee Archives of Philosophy With AUS, 1945-46. Recipient DePaul U. Distinguished Service award, 1969, Univ. award for excellence, 1984-85, Viam Sapientiae award, 1989 Mem. Am. Metaphys. Soc., Ill.-Ind. Am. Cath. Philos. Assn. (pres. 1960), Am. Cath. Philos. Assn. (pres. 1972-73), Chgo. Lit. Club (pres. 1986-87), Phi Kappa Theta, Phi Eta Sigma. Home: 15881 County Rd 28 Dolores CO 81323 E-mail: ellieok@fone.net.

KREYLING, EDWARD GEORGE, JR., railroad executive; b. St. Louis, June 1, 1923; s. Edward George and Mildred (Schroeder) K.; m. Mary Emily Gronemeyer, Sept. 4, 1943; children: Carol (Mrs. Robert D. Knight), Deborah Ann (Mrs. Hugh J. Risseeuw), Edward George III. BSBA, Washington U., St. Louis, 1947, MBA, 1954. Accountant Monsanto Chem. Co., 1947-50; chief statistician White Rodgers Elec. Co., St. Louis, 1950-54; dir. market research Laclede-Christy Co., St. Louis, 1954-55; with St. L.-S.F. Ry., 1955-69, dir. marketing, 1964-65, v.p. traffic and indsl. devel., 1965-69; v.p. traffic I.C. R.R., Chgo., 1969-70; exec. v.p. Penn Central Transp. Co., Phila., 1970-71; v.p. marketing So. Ry., 1971-79, sr. v.p. mktg. service, 1979-80, exec. v.p. mktg., 1981-82; v.p. mktg. services Norfolk So. Corp. (Va.), 1982-87, ret. Active Virginia Beach. Sch. Bd., 1992-94; dir. Seton House, 1995-98, Va. Christian Coalition, 1998-2001, v.p.; dir. Assist Crisis Pregnancy Ctr., 2001—. Served with AUS, 1943-45. Mem. Nat. Freight Traffic Assn. Home: 11307 Stones Throw Dr Reston VA 20194-1044

KRIBEL, ROBERT EDWARD, academic administrator, consultant physicist; b. Pitts., Sept. 17, 1937; s. Joseph P. and Helen M. K.; m. Ruth Ann Gropelli; children— Robert E., Karen A., Mark P., Gary P. BS, U. Notre Dame, 1959; MS, U. Calif., San Diego, 1966, PhD in Physics, 1968. Research scientist Gen. Atomic, Inc., 1965-69; assoc. prof. physics Drake U., 1970-73; vis. assoc. prof. applied physics Cornell U., 1973-74; prof., head dept. physics James Madison U., 1974-78, Auburn (Ala.) U., 1978-87, acting dean scis. and math., 1985-87, prof. physics, 1987-88; v.p. acad. affairs Jacksonville (Ala.) State U., 1988-92, prof. physics, 1992-93; dean natural scis. and math. Mesa State Coll., 1993-99; pres. REK Enterprises, Auburn, Ala., 1999—; chief acad. officer Air U., 2000—02. Contbr. articles to profl. jours. Served with U.S. Navy, 1959-62. Mem. Am. Phys. Soc., IEEE, Am. Assn. Physics Tchrs., Sigma Xi, Phi Kappa Phi. Personal E-mail: bkribel@aol.com.

KRICK, EDWIN HARRY, SR., medical educator, internal medicine physician; b. Takoma Park, Md., Aug. 13, 1935; s. Russell Kenneth and Flora Shaffer Parsons K.; m. Kay Saunders Kronquest, June 2, 1957 (dec. May 1982); children: Joylyn Marie Grant, Edwin Harry Krick Jr.; m. Beverly Kay Hardt, Oct. 9, 1983. BA in Chemistry, Atlantic Union Coll., 1957; MD, Loma Linda U., 1961, MPH, 1971. Diplomate in internal medicine and rheumatology Am. Bd. Internal Medicine; diplomate Am. Bd. Allergy and Immunology: Preventive Medicine, Nat. Bd. Medicine U.S. and Japan. Intern White Meml. Hosp., L.A., 1961-62; resident in internal medicine Loma Linda U. Med. Ctr., 1970-73; fellow in rheumatology and immunology Scripps Clinic and Rsch. Found., La Jolla, Calif., 1974-76; staff physician Tokyo Adventist Hosp., 1962-66; dir. Kobe Adventist Clinic Japan Mission Seventh-Day Adventists, 1966-70; instr.

preventive medicine Loma Linda (Calif.) U., 1971-76, asst. prof. medicine, 1976-80, assoc. prof. medicine, 1980—. Dir. preventive medicine Loma Linda U. Sch. Medicine, 1973-83, chief sect. rheumatology, 1977-84, dean Sch. Pub. Health, 1986-90, dir. rheumatology fellowship, 1993—. Treas. Loma Linda U. Sch. Medicine Alumni Assn., 1973-75, pres., 1979-80. Named Alumnus of Yr., Loma Linda U. Sch. Medicine Alumni Assn., 1988. Fellow ACP, Am. Coll. Rheumatology; mem. AMA, Calif. Med. Soc., San Bernardino County Med. Soc., Alpha Omega Alpha. Republican. Avocations: flying, amateur radio, hiking, white water rafting, fitness/exercise. Home: PO Box 2113 Redlands CA 92373-0681 Office: Faculty Med Offices Loma Linda U 11370 Anderson St Loma Linda CA 92354-3450 E-mail: ebhk@earthlink.net.

KRICKA, LARRY J. chemistry educator; b. Karlovy Vary, Czechoslovakia, Aug. 22, 1947; arrived in U.S., 1987; m. Barbara J. Kricka, July 25, 1970; children: Simon, Anna, Thomas. BA with honors, York (Eng.) U., 1968, DPhil, 1971. Rsch. asst. Liverpool (Eng.) U., 1971-73; from lectr. to sr. lectr. to reader Birmingham (Eng.) U., 1973-87; Med. Rsch. Coun. traveling fellow U. Calif., San Diego, 1981-82; prof. U. Pa., Phila., 1987—. Disting. vis. scholar Christ's Coll., Cambridge, England, 2002, Cambridge, 02. Author: (book) Ligand Binder Assays, 1985; editor: (book) Nonisotopic DNA Probe Techniques, 1992; co-author: (with J. Cheng) Biochip Technology, 2001; editor: Luminescence, 1983—; mem. editl. bd. Analytical Biochemistry, 1983—; contbr. articles to profl. jours. Recipient Rank prize for optoelectronics Rank Orgn., 1991. Fellow Royal Soc. Chemistry (SAC Silver medal 1981), Royal Coll. Pathologists, Nat. Acad. Clin. Biochemistry; mem. Assn. Clin. Biochemists, Am. Assn. Clin. Chemistry (pres. 2001, Kubasik Lectr. award Upstate N.Y. sect. 1997, Reimer award Capitol sect. 2000). Avocations: skiing, travel. Office: U Pa Med Ctr Dept Pathol/Lab Medicine 3400 Spruce St Philadelphia PA 19104 E-mail: kricka@mail.med.upenn.edu.

KRIEBEL, CHARLES HOSEY, management sciences educator; b. Tarrytown, N.Y., Nov. 6, 1933; s. Nelson Stearly and Elizabeth Grace (Hosey) K.; m. Jan Lilly McAuley, June 7, 1961; children: Paul Charles, Susan, James McAuley, Carl Nelson. BS in Econs., U. Pa., 1959, MA in Stats., 1961; PhD in Indsl. Mgmt., MIT, 1964. Instr. Wharton Sch. Fin., U. Pa., Phila., 1959-61; asst. prof. Sloan Sch., MIT, Cambridge, 1963-64, Grad. Sch. Indsl. Adminstrn., Carnegie-Mellon U., Pitts., 1964-67, assoc. prof., 1967-70, prof., 1970-2000, prof. emeritus, 2000—, head dept indsl. mgmt., 1981-86; dir. strategic tech. Met. Life, N.Y.C., 1987-88. Cons. McKinsey & Co., Inc., N.Y.C., Rand Corp., Santa Monica, Calif., Gulf Oil Corp., Pitts., Imperial Tobacco, Montreal, Que., Can., Mellon Bank (N.A.), Pitts., LTV STeel Co., Inc., Gen. Reins Corp., N.Y.C., Industrikonsulent I.K.O., Copenhagen, Westinghouse Electric Corp., Pitts., U.S. Steel Corp., Pitts., Rockwell Internat., Pitts., Am. Mgmt. Sys., Fairfax, Va., HAL Inst. Computer Tech., Osaka, Japan, other indsl. firms; rep. NAS; mem. adv. bd. NSF, 1985-88. Mem. editorial bd.: Internat. Fedn. Info. Processing, 1971—; editorial cons. Prentice-Hall, Inc., 1967-80; contbr. over 100 articles to profl. jours. With Signal Corps, U.S. Army, 1954-56. Fulbright-Hays advisor, 1965-79; Ford Found. fellow MIT, 1964. Fellow AAAS; mem. Assn. Computing Machinery (nat. lectr.), Inst. Mgmt. Scis. (dept. editor Mgmt. Sci.), Ops. Rsch. Soc. Am., Am. Econ. Assn., Am. Statis. Assn., Econometric Soc., N.Y. Acad. Scis., Info. Systems Rsch. (sr. editor bd.), Delta Kappa Epsilon (pres. 1959). Home: 108 Silent Run Rd Fox Chapel Pittsburgh PA 15238 Office: Carnegie-Mellon U Grad Sch Indsl Admin Pittsburgh PA 15213

KRIEG, ARTHUR M. pharmaceutical company executive, internist; b. Cleve., Aug. 17, 1957; m. Deborah Lanners Krieg, Oct. 11, 1985; children: Alexandra, Elizabeth, Peter. BS in Biology, Haverford Coll., 1979; MD, Washington U., St. Louis, 1983. Diplomate Am. Bd. Internal Medicine, Am. Bd. Rheumatology. Resident in internal medicine U. Minn., Mpls., 1983-86; med. staff fellow NIH, Bethesda, Md., 1986-91; prof. U. Iowa, Iowa City, 1991—; chief sci. officer Coley Pharm. Group, Wellesley, Mass., 1997—. Med. adv. bd. Kid Needs, 1998—. Mem. editl. bd. Lupus News, 1990—; adv. editor Arthritis and Rheumatism, 1996—; editor Antisense and Nucleic Acid Drug Development; contbr. articles to profl. jours.; patentee in field. Recipient Scholar award Pfizer, 1993; grantee Am. Soc. Clin. Investigation, Henry Kunkel Investigation award Am. Coll. Rheumatology, 1998. Mem. Alpha Omega Alpha. Avocations: hiking, camping, skiing. Office: 93 Worcester St Ste 101 Wellesley MA 02481-3609 E-mail: akrieg@coleypharma.com.

KRIEG, MARTHA FESSLER, software engineer; b. Canton, Ohio, May 31, 1948; d. Herbert Thoburn and Suzanne Marie (Smith) Fessler; m. Laurence John Krieg, June 1, 1968; children: Katherine Joy, Marjorie Elissa, Ian William Herbert. BA, Coll. of Wooster, 1970; MA in Romance Langs., MLS, U. Mich., 1971, 72, PhD in Romance Linguistics, 1976, MS in Computer Sci., 1989. Lectr. in Spanish Macomb County Community Coll., Warren, Mich., 1977; rsch. asst. Middle English Dictionary U. Mich., Ann Arbor, 1975-81; instr. Washtenaw Community Coll., Ann Arbor, 1985, 87; sr. user cons. Univ. Computing Ea. Mich. U., Ypsilanti, 1988-89, vis. lectr. dept. computer sci., 1985-90, lectr. dept. computer sci., 1990-93; lead analyst IntelliSys Automotive, 1995; sr. programmer, analyst Advantage Computing (formerly T and B Computing), Ann Arbor, Mich., 1995—. Co-author: Getting Started with dBase III+, 1991; author: Microsoft Works for IBM-PC, 1990, Microsoft Works for Macintosh, 1990, Paradox Database Management System, 1990, Manuals for Dress Shop 2.0, 1994; contbr. articles and revs. to profl. publs.; author help pages for various systems. Troop leader Huron Valley coun. Girl Scouts U.S., 1986-93, coun. del., 1987-88, 90-92; fin. sec. St. Luke Luth. Ch., Ann Arbor, 1989-92; host family Youth for Understanding, 1994—; area rep. Youth For Understanding internat. exchange program, 1996. Named Leader of Yr. Huron Valley coun. Girl Scouts U.S., 1991. Mem.: Gt. Lakes Lace Group, Sigma Delta Pi, Phi Beta Kappa, Mensa, Beta Phi Mu. Avocations: lacemaking, woodworking, music, embroidery, camping. Office: Advantage Computing 3850 Ranchero Dr Ann Arbor MI 48108-2772

KRIEGEL, LEONARD, English language educator; b. N.Y.C., May 25, 1933; s. Fred and Sylvia (Breittholz) K.; m. Harriet May Bernzweig, Aug. 27, 1957; children: Mark Benjamin, Eric Bruce. BA, Hunter Coll., 1955; MA, Columbia, 1956; PhD, N.Y. Univ., 1960. Prof. english City Coll. N.Y., 1976-92, assoc. prof. eng., 1972-76, asst. prof. eng., 1965-72, instr. eng., 1961-65; asst. prof. eng. L.I. Univ., 1960-61; prof. Leiden Univ., 1964-65, Groningen Univ., 1968-69, U. Paris, 1980. Author: The Long Walk Home, 1964, Edmund Wilson, 1972, Working Through, 1972, Notes for the Two-Dollar Window, 1976, On Men and Manhood, 1980, Quitting Time, 1982, Falling Into Life, 1991, Flying Solo, 1998. Recipient Rifkind fellow Rifkind Found., 1991, Guggenheim fellow Guggenheim Found., 1972, Rockfeller fellow Rockefeller Found., 1976. Home: 355 8th Ave New York NY 10001-4838 E-mail: len7373@aol.com.

KRIEGER, ABBOTT JOEL, neurosurgeon; b. N.Y.C., Apr. 29, 1939; m. Marsha Tomback; children: Lloyd, Lara, Dana. BA, Bklyn. Coll., 1959; MD, N.Y. Med. Coll., 1963; DMS in Pharmacology, Columbia U., 1970. Diplomate Am. Bd. Neurol. Surgery. Intern in surgery Montefiore Hosp., N.Y.C., 1963-64; resident in surgery, then in neuropathology Montefiore Hosp. and Med. Center, 1964-65; resident in neurol. surgery Albert Einstein Coll. Medicine, 1966-67, 70-71, resident in neurology, 1968; chief neurosurgery VA Hosp., Pitts., 1971-73; asst. prof. neurosurgery U. Pitts. Sch. Medicine, 1971-73; prof., chief program dir. neurosurgery N.J. Med. Sch., Univ. Medicine and Dentistry, Newark, 1974-94; pvt. practice Livingston, N.J., 1994—. Attendent St. Barnabas Med. Ctr., Beth Israel Hosp. Contbr. articles to med. jours. Served with USMCR, 1956-62. Fellow ACS; mem. Soc. Neurol. Surgeons, Congress Neurol. Surgeons, Am. Assn. Neurol. Surgeons, N.J. Neurosurg. Soc. Home: 1060 Park Ave New York NY 10128 Office: PO Box 385 22 Old Short Hills Rd Livingston NJ 07039-5605

KRIEGER, FREDERIC MICHAEL, lawyer; b. Wilmington, Del., Apr. 28, 1950; s. Arthur H. and Edythe (Ploener) K.; m. Alice T. Whittelsey, Oct. 28, 1979; children: Daniel Marsh, Anna Caroline. AB, U. Pa., 1972; J.D., Emory U., 1975; student U. Lancaster, Eng., 1970-71. Bar: Ga. 1975, D.C. 1976, Pa. 1978, Ill. 1984, U.S. Dist. Ct. (no. dist.) Ga. 1976, U.S. Dist. Ct. (ea. dist.) Pa. 1978, U.S. Dist. Ct. D.C. 1976, U.S. Ct. Appeals (3d cir.) 1979, U.S. Dist. Ct. (no. dist.) Ill. 1984. Trial atty. SEC, Washington, 1975-78; assoc. firm Morgan, Lewis & Bockius, Phila., 1978-82; ptnr. firm Miller Schreiber & Sloan, Phila., 1982-83; assoc. gen. counsel Chgo. Bd. Options Exchange, 1983— ; adj. faculty Am. U. Law Sch., 1977-78, Cath. U. Law Sch., 1977-78, IIT/Chgo. Kent. Coll., 1986—; lectr. Inst. for Paralegal Tng., Phila., 1982 . Contbr. articles to law jours. Bd. dirs. Friends of Glencoe (Ill.) Pub. Library, 1984; bd. dirs. Glencoe Human Relations Com., 1986—; mem. New Trier Democratic Assn., 1984. Mem. ABA (mem. subcom. on securities markets and market structure, fed. regulation of securities com.). Club: Univ. of Chgo.

KRIEGER, IRVIN MITCHELL, chemistry educator, consultant; b. Cleve., May 14, 1923; s. William I. and Rose (Brodsky) K.; m. Theresa Melamed, June 9, 1965; 1 dau., Laura. BS, Case Inst. Tech., 1944, MS, 1948; PhD, Cornell, 1951. Rsch. asst. Case Inst. Tech., Cleve., 1946-47; teaching fellow Cornell U., Ithaca, N.Y., 1947-49; instr. Case Western Res. U., 1949-51, asst. prof., 1951-55, assoc. prof., 1955-68, prof., 1968-88, prof. emeritus, 1988—; dir. Center for Adhesives, Sealants and Coatings, 1983-88. Vis. prof. U. Bristol, 1977-78; cons. for chem. firms; prof. invité Ecole Nat. Supérieure de Chimie de Mulhouse, 1987, Louis Pasteur U., Strasbourg, France, 1989. Contbr. articles to profl. jours. Served as ensign USNR, 1943-46. NSF fellow Université Libre De Bruxelles, 1959-60; sr. fellow Weizmann Inst., 1970 Mem. Am. Chem. Soc., Am. Inst. Chem. Engrs., AAUP, Soc. Rheology (pres. 1977-79, Bingham medalist 1989). Home: 3460 Green Rd Apt 101 Beachwood OH 44122-4076 Office: Case Western Reserve U Cleveland OH 44106 E-mail: imk@cwru.edu.

KRIEGER, JOSEPH BERNARD, physicist, physics educator; b. Bklyn., July 10, 1937; s. Samuel and Leah (Sussman) K.; m. Rose Meyerson, May 31, 1964; 1 child, Stephen. AB, Columbia Coll., 1959; PhD in Physics, Columbia U., 1965. Asst. prof. physics Poly. Inst. Bklyn., 1965-68, assoc. prof. physics, 1968-72; vis. assoc. prof. physics CUNY, Bklyn., 1971-72, assoc. prof. physics, 1972-73, prof. physics, 1973—, chmn., 1976-80, exec. officer PhD program, 1990—97. Cons. for govt. and industry, 1980—. Contbr. articles to profl. jours. Fellow Am. Phys. Soc.; mem. Sigma Xi. Home: 243 McDonald Ave Brooklyn NY 11218-1449 Office: Brooklyn Coll 2900 Bedford Ave Brooklyn NY 11210

KRIEGER, ROBERT ALAN, software engineer; b. West Allis, Wis., Feb. 7, 1968; s. George Phillip and Nancy Louise (Keller) K. BS in computer sci., U. Wis., 1990, MS in computer sci., 1994. Assoc. computer scientist Cooper Power Systems Thomas Edison Tech. Ctr., Franksville, Wis., 1990-94, software engr., 1995; product devel. software engr. Merge Tech., Inc., West Allis, Wis., 1995—2001; sr. software engr. Merge eFilm, 2002—. Lead software designer Cooper Power Sys., Franksville, 1990-95. Contbr. articles to profl. jours. Recipient Outstanding Scholar award U. Wis., 1986, Achievement award in Writing Nat. Coun. Tchrs. Eng., 1985. United Methodist. Achievements include work in unifying artificial intelligence theory of Bayesian networks; implementation of Bayesian network construction software and probabilistic inference mechanism; development of graphical front-end to electrical power systems database and analysis package; work in Ethernet communication and networking protocols to transfer medical imagery.

KRIEGER, ROBERT EDWARD, publisher; b. Chgo., Apr. 6, 1925; s. Nicholas Francis and Clara Maude (Larson) K.; m. Maxine Donalda Spooner, June 21, 1947; children: Robert Edward, Donald Eric, Thomas Eliot. Formerly exec. with multi-corp. book and pub. firms; chmn. bd. dirs. Krieger Pub. Co., Inc., Malabar, Fla., 1969—. Chmn. Tech. R&D Authority, 1988-92. Mem. ALA, Internat. Assn. Ind. Pubs., So. Pubs. Assn., Scholarly Pubs. Assn., Masons. Republican. Methodist. Office: Krieger Pub Co PO Box 9542 Melbourne FL 32902-9542

KRIEGER, SANFORD, lawyer; b. N.Y.C., Nov. 4, 1943; s. Harry and Ruth Krieger; m. Carol B. Bachenheimer, Aug. 19, 1967; 1 child, Paul Matthew. BA cum laude, Cornell U., 1965; JD cum laude, Harvard U., 1968. Bar: N.Y. 1971, U.S. Dist. Ct. (so. dist.) N.Y., U.S. Supreme Ct. 1974.3. Legal adviser to Ethiopian Govt., 1968-70; assoc. Simpson Thacher & Bartlett, N.Y.C., 1970-73, Fried Frank Harris Shriver & Jacobson, London, 1973-75, ptnr. N.Y.C., 1977—. Mem. ABA, Assn. Bar City N.Y. Office: Fried Frank Harris Shriver & Jacobson 1 New York Plz Fl 22 New York NY 10004-1980 E-mail: kriegsa@ffhsj.com.

KRIEGER, THEODORE KENT, poet; b. Charles City, Iowa, Sept. 26, 1950; s. Dale Theodore and Beverly (Clapp) K.; m. Elaine Marie Dorwin, Aug. 2, 1974 (div. July 1979). Diploma, Am. Sch. Photography, Lombard, Ill., 1973; BA in English summa cum laude, N.W. Mo. State U., 1977, postgrad.; MA in English, Am. Internat. U., 2001. Newspaper reporter, photographer Charles City Press, 1977-80, Atchison County Mail, Rock Port, Mo., 1983; freelance writer Charles City, 1983—; security guard Guard Sys., Ltd., Charles City, 1983—86. Ind. sales agt.; freelance photographer, 1998—. Author: (book of poems) Bearing It Alone, 1979 (Voices Internat. award 1981), Metal Monarch, 1999, Rainman, 2001, Gumbo Road (novel), 2003; contbr. poetry to literary mags. Grantee Author's League, 1982, Pen-Am. Ctr., N.Y., 2002. Mem. Acad. Am. Poets., Author's Guild. Roman Catholic. Avocations: photography, reading. Home: PO Box 452 Charles City IA 50616-0452

KRIEGER, WILLIAM CARL, English language educator; b. Seattle, Mar. 21, 1946; s. Robert Irving Krieger and Mary Durfee; m. Patricia Kathleen Callow, Aug. 20, 1966 (div. Jan. 2002); children: Richard William, Robert Irving III, Kathleen Elizabeth. BA in English, Pacific Luth. U., Tacoma, 1968, MA in humanities, 1973; PhD in Am. studies, Wash. State U., 1986. Instr. Pierce Coll., Tacoma, 1969-98, prof. English, 1969-98, chmn. English dept., 1973-79, 81-84, 95-98, chmn. humanities divsn., 1979-81, ombudsman, 1995-98; adj. prof., Hist. and English Ctrl. Wash. State U., Wash., 1980; vis. prof., Hist. and English So. Ill. U., Carbondale, Ill., 1981-84, Pacific Luth. U., Tacoma, 1981-84; head wrestling coach Gig Harbor HS, Wash., 1990-95; dean acad. edn., Walla Walla CC, Walla Walla, Wash., 1998—; instr., humanities and comm. Walla Walla CC, Walla Walla, Wash., 2002—. Bd. dir. Thoreau Cabin Project, Tacoma, 1979-98; project dir. Campus Wash. Centennial Project, Tacoma, 1984-89; spl. cons. Clover Park Sch. Dist., Tacoma, 1985; lang. arts cons., Inst. for Citizen Edn. in Law, U. Puget Sound Law Sch., 1990. Author: A Necessary Evil? Sports and Violence, 1998; contbr. Handbook of Pesticide Toxicology, 2nd edit., 2001. Apptd. Wash. State Centennial Commn., Constrn. Com., Pierce Couny Centennial Com.; mem. bd. dir. Tacoma Symphony; choir dir. Rosedale Ch.; mem. Peninsula Cmty. Chorus, 1993-97, pres., 1995; dir. Peninsula Madrigal Singers, 1995-97; active Tacoma Opera Chorus, 1997-98; co-prodr. summer musical Walla Walla Cmty. Coll. Found., 2001, 02, 03. Recipient: Disting. Achievement Award Wash. State Centennial Commn., 1989, Outstanding Achievement Award Pierce County Centennial Commn., 1989, Centennial Alumni recognition Pacific Luth. U., Tacoma, 1990; named Outstanding Tchr. Nat. Inst. Staff and Orgnl. Devel., 1992; NEH rsch. fellow Johns Hopkins U. and Peabody Conservatory of Music, 1994. Mem. (life) Thoreau Soc., Community Coll. Humanities Assn. (standing com. 1982-83), Am. Studies Assn., Wash. Community Coll. Humanities Assn. (bd. dir. 1982-84, grantee, 1984), Western Wash. Ofcl. Assn. Avocations: officiating high sch. and coll. football and wrestling, hiking, powerlifting, poetry, vocal music. Office: Walla Walla Comty Coll 500 Tausick Way Walla Walla WA 99362-9270 Home: 653 E Chestnut St Walla Walla WA 99362-3323 E-mail: blitz@bmi.net., william.krieger@wwcc.ctc.edu.

KRIEGHBAUM, DOUGLAS MATTHEW, music educator; b. Aurora, Ill, May 22, 1978; s. Kenneth Delmar and Mary Elizabeth Krieghbaum. MusB Edn, U. Ill., 2001. Cert. K-12 type 10 edn. Ill. Music dir. Plano H.S., Ill., 2001—; band dir. Centennial Elem. Sch., Plano, 2001—. Band dir. Plano H.S., Plano, 2001—, madrigal dir., 2001—02, marching band dir., 2001—02, jazz band dir., 2001—, choir dir., 2001—, head freshman/sophmore girls softball, coach, 2002; 5th grade band dir. Centennial Elem. Sch., Plano, 2001—02; pvt. instrumentalist instr., Plano, 2001—; mem. Aurora Summer Concert Band, Aurora, ILL., 1995—2002, Indian Valley Cmty. Band, Sandwich, 2002. Adult staff mem. Kendall County Operation Snowball, 2001—02. Mem.: NEA, Internat. Tub-Euphonium Assoc. (ITEA), Internat. Trombone Assoc. (ITA), Tchrs. Union, MENC. Office: Plano Cmty Sch Dist # 88 704 West Abe St Plano IL 60545 Personal E-mail: krieghb@aol.com.

KRIEGSMAN, ALAN M. retired critic; b. N.Y.C., Feb. 28, 1928; s. Harry Pickel and May (Cohn) K.; m. Sali Ann Ribakove, Nov. 28, 1957. Student, MIT, 1945-46; BS, Columbia U., 1951, MA, 1953. Lectr. in music Columbia U., N.Y.C., 1955-60; music and performing arts critic San Diego Union, 1960-65; asst. to the pres. Juilliard Sch., N.Y.C., 1965-66; music and performing arts critic Washington Post, 1966-74, dance critic, 1974-96, critic emeritus, 1996. Advisor-cons. vis. com. on arts and humanities, MIT, 1976-86; vis. lectr. Dance Critics Conf., Am. Dance Festival; adjudicator Pulitzer Prize juries in music, criticism, feature writing, 1980-94; bd. dirs. Choo-San Goh & H. Robert Magee Found., 1996—. Contbr. articles on performing arts to various publs. Mem. leadership group nat. dance/media project UCLA, 1999. With U.S. Army, 1946-47. Fulbright scholar U. Vienna, 1956-57; recipient Pulitzer prize in Criticism, 1976, Metro DC Dance awards, spl. citation for inestimable contbns., 2002. Mem. Dance Inst. Washington (bd. dirs. 1996—), Dance Critics Assn. (bd. dirs. 1996-98), Cunningham Dance Found. (bd. dirs. 1999—). Democrat. Jewish. Avocations: piano, mathematics, science. Home: 4701 Willard Ave Apt 1013 Chevy Chase MD 20815-4622 Fax: (301) 907-4682. E-mail: amkmike@attglobal.net.

KRIEGSMAN, EDWARD MICHAEL, lawyer; b. Bridgeport, Conn., Oct. 29, 1965; s. Irving Martin and Marlene Sonya (Kates) K.; m. Meryl Gail Dennis, June 11, 1989; children: Barry Alan, David Jacob, Rachel Lynn. BS in Biology, MIT, 1986; JD, U. Pa., 1989. Bar: Pa. 1989, U.S. Patent and Trademark Office 1989, Mass. 1990, U.S. Ct. Appeals (Fed. cir.) 1990, U.S. Dist. Ct. Mass. 1992. Assoc. Finnegan, Henderson, Farabow, et al, Washington, 1989-90; ptnr. Kriegsman & Kriegsman, Framingham, Mass., 1990—. Mem. ABA, Am. Intellectual Property Law Assn., Mass. Bar Assn., Fed. Cir. Bar Assn., Boston Patent Law Assn., South Middlesex Bar Assn. Jewish. Avocations: reading, sports. Home: 103 Richard Rd Holliston MA 01746-1213 Office: Kriegsman & Kriegsman 665 Franklin St Framingham MA 01702 E-mail: edward.kriegsman@kriegsmanlaw.com.

KRIEGSMAN, SALI ANN, arts executive, artistic director, writer, consultant; b. N.Y.C., Apr. 16, 1936; d. Aaron and Charlotte (Pomeranz) Ribakove; m. Alan M. Kriegsman, Nov. 28, 1957. MA, Goddard Coll., 1976. Rsch. assoc. Scripps Clinic and Rsch. Found., La Jolla, Calif., 1961-65; exec. editor Am. Film Inst., Washington, 1969-74; asst. prof. George Washington U., Washington, 1979-80; dance cons. Smithsonian Instn., Washington, 1979—84; dir. dance program NEA, Washington, 1986-95; exec. dir. Jacob's Pillow Dance Festival, Becket, Mass., 1995-98. Writer An Evening of Dance, In Performance at the White House, Sta. WETA-TV, 1998; mem. arts acad. adv. com. Coll. Bd., 1996-97; mem. nat. dance and media project leadership group UCLA, 1996-2000; mem. steering com. Am. Assembly Art, Tech. and Intellectual Property, 2000-02; sr. advisor Digital Dance Libr., 2002-03. Author: Modern Dance in America: The Bennington Years, 1981; contbr. Britannica Book Of The Year, 1984-86; contbg. author: International Encyclopedia of Dance, 1998. Bd. dirs. Mass. Mus. Contemporary Art, 1995-97, Meredith Monk/The House Found., 2001—; pres. Dance Heritage Coalition, 1999-2000. Recipient Flo-Bert award N.Y. Com. To Celebrate Nat. Tap Dance Day, 1997, Oklahoma City U. Preservation of Heritage Am. Dance award, 1999, Tap Preservation award, N.Y.C. Tap Festival, 2002. E-mail: saliann@attglobal.net.

KRIENKE, KENDRA CLIVER (KENDRA DANIEL), art dealer, artist; b. Plainfield, N.J. d. Edwin Kendall Cliver and Estelle (Blaine) Hufnagel; m. Douglas Elliot Krienke (div. 1991); m. Allan L. Daniel, June 1, 1993. BA, Drew U., 1969; student, Nat. Acad. Design. Owner, portrait painter, frame designer, art dealer Whistler's Daughter Art Gallery, Basking Ridge, N.J., 1974-84; owner, frame designer, art dealer Whistler Gallery, Basking Ridge, 1985-90; dealer in original vintage art by illustrators for children and fantasy N.Y.C., 1989—. Contbg. author: American Illustrator Art, 1991; prepared 10 exhbns. and catalogues, 1978-84; curator Childhood Enchantments--British and American Illustration for Children, Mus. Cartoon Art, 1989, Johnson & Johnson, 1990; designer walls of Pied Piper Room, Hotel Wales, N.Y.C.; contbr. to publs. including Decorating with Pictures, 1991, Myth, Magic and Mystery exhbn. and book, 1996, Famous American Illustrators (by Arpi Ermoyan - Soc. of Illustrators), 1998; contbr. articles to profl. mags.; 2 paintings from gallery were used in film You've Got Mail. Mem. Soc. of Illustrators, ATCA.. Avocations: collecting art and antiques, jazz, 19th and 20th century literature, interior decorating, animal rights.

KRIER, JAMES EDWARD, law educator, writer; b. Milw., Oct. 19, 1939; s. Ambrose Edward and Genevieve Ida (Behling) Krier; m. Gayle Marian Grimsrud, Mar. 22, 1962 (div.); children: Jennifer, Amy; m. Wendy Louise Wilkes, Apr. 20, 1974; children: Andrew Wilkes-Krier, Patrick Wilkes-Krier. BS, U. Wis., 1961, JD, 1966. Bar: Wis. 1966, U.S. Ct. Claims 1968. Law clk. to chief justice Calif. Supreme Ct., San Francisco, 1966-67; assoc. Arnold & Porter, Washington, 1967-69; acting prof., then prof. law UCLA, 1969-78, 80-83; prof. law Stanford U., Calif., 1978-80, U. Mich. Law Sch., Ann Arbor, 1983—, Earl Warren DeLano prof., 1988—. Cons. Calif. Inst. Tech., EPA; mem. pesticide panel NAS, 1972—75, mem. com. energy and the environment, 1975—77. Author: (book) Environmental Law and Policy, 1971; author: (with Stewart) Environmental Law and Policy, 2d edit., 1978; author: (with Ursin) Pollution and Policy, 1977; author: (with Dukeminier) Property, 1981, Property, 5th edit., 2002; contbr. articles to profl. jours. Served to lt. U.S. Army, 1961—63. Mem.: Order of Coif, Artus, Phi Kappa Phi. Office: U Mich Law Sch 625 S State St Ann Arbor MI 48109-1215 E-mail: jkrier@umich.edu.

KRIER, JOSEPH ROLAND, chamber of commerce executive, lawyer; b. Port Washington, Wis., Apr. 15, 1946; m. Cyndi Taylor. BA, U. Tex., 1968, JD, 1971. Bar: Tex. 1971. Assoc. real estate sect. Bracewell & Patterson, Houston, 1971-73; ptnr., mem. corp. and comml. litigation sect. Groce, Locke & Hebdon, 1973-83; ptnr. Grieshaber & Roberts, San Antonio, 1983-87; pres. The Greater San Antonio C. of C., 1987—. Head JK & Assocs., 1983-87. Mem. centennial commn. U. Tex.; mem. Tex. Higher Edn. Coordinating Bd.; coordinating chmn. task force Target '90: Goals for San Antonio project; past pres., bd. dirs. San Antonio Amateur Sports Found.; past chmn., bd. dirs. Arts Coun. San Antonio; founder, bd. dirs. San Antonio Winston Sch.; bd. dirs. Ctr. for Multiple Handicapped Children, Tex. Soc. for the Prevention of Blindness, San Antonio Cmty. Radio Corp., San Antonio chpt. Tex. Execs., Tex. Bus. Hall of Fame; bd. visitors M.D. Anderson Cancer Clinic, co-chmn. Annual Gift Campaign South Tex., 1987; mem. adv. bd. Tex. Lyceum. Fellow Tex. Bar Assn.; mem. San Antonio Bar Assn., Omicron Delta Kappa. Office: The Greater San Antonio C of C PO Box 1628 602 E Commerce St San Antonio TX 78205-2620

KRIESBERG, LOUIS, sociologist, educator; b. Chgo., July 30, 1926; s. Max and Bessie (Turner) K.; m. Lois Ablin, Aug. 23, 1959; children: Daniel A., Joseph A. PhB, U. Chgo., 1947, MA, 1950, PhD, 1953. Instr. sociology sch. gen. studies Columbia U., N.Y.C., 1953-56; Fulbright rsch. scholar U. Cologne, Germany, 1956-57; sr. fellow in law and behavior scis. U. Chgo., 1957-58; sr. study dir. Nat. Opinion Rsch. Ctr., 1958-62; assoc. prof. dept. sociology, 1962-67, Syracuse (N.Y.) U., 1962-67, prof., 1967-97, prof. emeritus, 1997—, dir. program on analysis and resolution conflicts, 1985-94, Maxwell prof. social conflict studies, 1994-97, Maxwell prof. emeritus social conflict studies, 1997—. Author: Mothers in Poverty, 1970, Social Inequality, 1979, Social Conflicts, 1973, rev. edit., 1982, International Conflict Resolution, 1992, Constructive Conflicts, 1998, 2d edit., 2003; editor: Social Processes in International Relations, 1968, Research in Social Movements, Conflicts, and Change, vols. 1-14, 1978-92; co-editor: Intractable Conflicts and Their Transformation, 1989, Timing the De-escalation of International Conflicts, 1991. Cons., lectr. Syracuse Area Middle East Dialogue Group. Grantee U.S. Inst. Peace, MacArthur Found., Hewlett Found. Fellow Am. Sociol. Assn. (chair peace and war sect. 1990-91, award for Disting. Career 1993), Internat. Peace Rsch. Assn. (co-chair internat. conflict resolution 1989-94), Internat. Studies Assn. (chair peace studies sect. 1998-99), Internat. Sociol. Assn. (rsch. com. 1, exec. com. 1982-86), Internat. Soc. Polit. Psychology (governing coun. 1992-94), Soc. for Study Social Problems (pres. 1983-84, Lee Founders award 1990), Ea. Sociol. Soc. (exec. com. 1977-81), Peace Studies Assn. (ann. award 1995), N.Y. State Sociol. Assn. (Disting. Svc. award 1999). Jewish. Avocations: swimming, travel. Home: 164 Summerhaven Dr East Syracuse NY 13057-3115 Office: Conflicts Analysis Resolution Syracuse U Syracuse NY 13244-1090

KRIESBERG, SIMEON M. lawyer; b. Washington, June 4, 1951; s. Martin and Harriet M. K.; m. Martha L. Kahn, Jan. 9, 1994. AB, Harvard U., 1973; M in Pub. Affairs, Princeton U., 1977; JD, Yale U., 1977. Bar: D.C. 1977, U.S. Dist. Ct. D.C. 1978, U.S. Ct. Appeals (D.C. cir.) 1978, U.S. Ct. Internat. Trade 1979, U.S. Ct. Appeals (Fed. cir.) 1981, U.S. Supreme Ct. 1982. Assoc. Leva, Hawes, Symington, Martin & Oppenheimer, Washington, 1977—83; sr. counsel internat. trade Sears World Trade Inc., Washington, 1983—85, v.p., gen. counsel, 1985—87; ptnr. Mayer Brown Rowe & Maw LLP, Washington, 1987—. Professional lectr. Nitze Sch. Advanced Internat. Studies, Johns

Hopkins U., 1991-93; mem. binat. dispute resolution panel under U.S.-Can. Free Trade Agreement, 1990-92; guest scholar Brookings Inst., 1992-93; mem. roster of dispute resolution panelists under NAFTA, 1996—. Mem. editorial adv. com. Internat. Legal Materials, 1991-97; article and book rev. editor Yale Law Jour., 1976-77. Officer or dir. Washington Hebrew Congregation, 1980-94, Jewish Cmty. Coun. Greater Washington, 1986-94, Interfaith Conf. of Met. Washington, 1989—, D.C. Jewish Cmty. Ctr., 1994—, Mid-Atlantic coun. Union Am. Hebrew Congregations, 1994—2002. Recipient Pro Bono Svc. award Internat. Human Rights Law Group, 1991, Lawrence L. O'Connor medal Sears, Roebuck and Co., 1984. Mem. ABA, Am. Law Inst., Am. Soc. Internat. Law, D.C. Bar. Office: Mayer Brown Rowe & Maw LLP 1909 K St NW Washington DC 20006-1101

KRIETOR, DAVID, airport authority executive; B in Fin., M in Pub. Adminstrn., Syracuse U. Former dir. Cmty. and Econ. Devel. Dept. City of Phoenix (Ariz.), dir. Aviation Dept., 2000—. Office: City of Phoenix Aviation Dept 3400 E Sky Harbor Blvd Phoenix AZ 85034-4403*

KRIGER, MARK PHILLIP, management education educator, consultant, writer; b. Boston, May 22, 1946; s. William and Sadee (Schlar) K.; m. Lucy Jane Miller, June 25, 1977; 1 child, Joshua Francis. BA, U. Mass., 1968; MA in Computer Sci., U. Calif., Berkeley, 1970; MS in Philosophy, MIT, 1975; DBA in Mgmt., Harvard U., 1983. Rsch. assoc. Harvard U., Cambridge, Mass., 1973-76; pvt. practice cons. Winchester, Mass., 1976-78; lectr. Northeastern U., Boston, 1980-82, asst. prof., 1982-88, assoc. prof., 1988, SUNY, Albany, 1988-95; prof. Norwegian Sch. Mgmt., 1995—. Co-author: The Hidden Side of Leadership, 1986; author chpts. in books; mem. editl. rev. bd. The Leadership Quar.; ad hoc reviewer Acad. Mgmt. Rev., Strategic Mgmt. Jour., and others; contbr. articles to profl. jours. Assoc. commr. Town Conservation Commn., Winchester, 1985-87. NDEA fellow MIT, 1968-69, U. Calif.-Berkeley fellow, 1969-70, Harvard U. Bus. Sch. fellow, 1981-82; recipient Beckhard award MIT, 1988. Mem. Nat. Acad. Mgmt. (internat. mgmt. div. 1986, Best Paper award), Strategic Mgmt. Soc., Eastern Acad. Mgmt. (membership chair N.Y. State chpt. 1989-90, track chair 1990-91), MIT Club Norway (dir. 1995—), Harvard Bus. Sch. Club Ea. N.Y. (dir. 1992-95). Office: Norwegian Sch Mgmt-BI PO Box 580 N-1301 Sandvika Norway E-mail: mark.kriger@bi.no.

KRIKEN, JOHN LUND, architect; b. Calif., July 5, 1938; s. John Erik Nord and Ragnhild (Lund) K.; m. Anne Girard (div.); m. Katherine Koelsch, Aug. 8, 1988. BArch, U. Calif., Berkeley, 1961; MArch, Harvard U., 1968. Ptnr. Skidmore, Owings and Merrill, San Francisco, 1970—. Tchr. Washington U., St. Louis, 1968, U. Calif., Berkeley, 1972, Rice U., Houston, 1979; design advisor, chief architect Ho Chi Minh City, Vietnam, 1994—; mem. design rev. bd. Port San Francisco, 1995—. Mem. Bay Conservation and Devel. Commn., Calif., 1984—; mem. Arts Commn. City and County of San Francisco, 1989-95; mem. design rev. bd. Berkeley campus U. Calif., 1986-92; bd. dirs. San Francisco Planning and Rsch., 1995—; vice chair, Eng. and Des. Advisory Panel (EDAP) for the rebuilding pf San Francisco Bay Bridge, 1997—; mem. GSD's alumni coun. Harvard U, 2000—; CED's dean's adv. coun. U. Calif., Berkeley, 2000—. Fellow AIA; mem. Am. Inst. Cert. Planners, Sunday Afternoon Watercolor Soc. (founding mem.), Lambda Alpha Internat. Office: Skimore Owings & Merrill 1 Front St San Francisco CA 94111-5303

KRIKOS, GEORGE ALEXANDER, pathologist, educator; b. Old Phaleron, Greece, Sept. 17, 1922; came to U.S., 1946; s. Alexios and Helen (Spyropoulou) K.; m. Aspasia Manoni, June 22, 1949; children: Helen, Alexandra, Alexios. DDS, U. Pa., 1949; PhD, U. Rochester, 1959; PhD (hon.), U. Athens, Greece, 1981. Asst. prof. pathology U. Pa. Sch. Dentistry, 1958-61, assoc. prof., 1961-67, prof., 1967-68, chmn. dept., 1964-68; assoc. prof. oral pathology U. Pa. Grad. Sch., 1962-68, prof. oral pathology, 1968; prof. pathobiology Sch. Dentistry, U. Colo., Denver, 1968-75, chmn. dept. pathobiology, 1968-73, prof. oral biology, 1975-86, chin. div. oral biology, 1986-91, prof. oral biology emeritus, 1991—, asst. dean basic sci. affairs, 1973-75, asso. dean oral biology affairs, 1975-76. Vis. prof. Sch. Dentistry, U. Athens, 1980-81; mem. dental study sect. NIH, 1966-70; mem. cancer com. Colo.-Wyo. Regional Med. Program, 1970-72; cons. oral pathology Denver VA Hosp., 1970-72 Served with AUS, 1949-54. Mem. Am. Soc. Investigative Pathology, Internat. Assn. Dental Rsch., Sigma Xi. Home: 350 Ivy St Denver CO 80220-5855

KRIKUN, BORIS LVOVICH, neurologist; b. Kiev, Ukraine, Feb. 17, 1923; arrived in U.S., 1975; s. Lev Osipovich Krikun and Roza Zacharovna Chernyavskaya; m. Ludmila Aleksandrovna Alekseeva, Jan. 25, 1991; m. Ludmila Alexandrovna Arsenieva, Nov. 14, 1953 (dec. Oct. 1988). MD with honors, 1st Moscow Med. Inst., 1952; PhD, Med. and Stomatol. Inst. Moscow, 1971. Virologist Gamaleya Inst. Microbiology and Epidemiology, Moscow, 1963—65; neurologist various med. ctrs., Russia, 1953—71; cons. neurologist Donolo Hosp., Tel Aviv, 1972—74; med. resident Hosp. Joint Disease and Med. Ctr., N.Y.C., 1978—80, Manhattan, 1980—81; solo practitioner Forest Hills, NY, 1981—99; pres. Herpes Virus Product Devel. Co., Queens, NY, 1999—; rsch. assoc. in antiviral chemotherapy Inst. Applied Biology, N.Y.C., 1975—77. Mem.: N.Y. Acad. Scis. Home: 66-36 Yellowstone Blvd Apt 8A Forest Hills NY 11375

KRIMENDAHL, HERBERT FREDERICK, II, investment banker; b. Cin., Oct. 28, 1928; s. Herbert F. and Mary Bess (Christian) K.; m. Constance Kathryn McCown, Sept. 21, 1957 (dec. Sept. 1989); children: Elizabeth Knowles, Nancy Christian; m. Emilia Alice Saint-Amand, Feb. 4, 1999. BA, Ohio State U., 1950; MBA, Harvard U., 1952. Assoc. Goldman, Sachs & Co., N.Y.C., 1953-62, ptnr., 1963-87, ltd. ptnr., 1987-99, sr. dir., 1999—; chmn. Petrus Ptnrs. Ltd., N.Y.C., 1992—. Trustee Philharm. Symphony Soc. N.Y., 1977—, pres., 1989-96, The James Madison Coun. of Libr. of Congress, 1995—, Bridgehampton Chamber Music Assocs., 1997—; Ohio State U. Found., 1998—. Mem. River Club, Maidstone Club, The Brook, The Links, Jupiter Island Club, Deepdale Golf Club. Office: Petrus Ptnrs Ltd 630 Fifth Ave Ste 3170 New York NY 10111-0100

KRIMM, SAMUEL, physicist, educator; b. Morristown, N.J., Oct. 19, 1925; s. Irving and Ethel (Stein) K.; m. Marilyn Marcy Neveloff, June 26, 1949; children: David Robert, Daniel Joseph. BS, Poly. Inst. Bklyn., 1947; MA, Princeton U., 1949, PhD, 1950. Postdoctoral fellow U. Mich., Ann Arbor, 1950-52, mem. faculty, 1952—, prof. physics, 1963-2001, prof. emeritus, 2001—, mem. Macromolecular Rsch. Ctr., 1968—, mem. biophysics rsch. divsn., 1962—, chmn. biophysics rsch. div., 1976-86, dir. program in protein structure and design, 1985-94, assoc. dean research Coll. Lit., Sci. and Arts, 1972-75. Chmn. infrared spectroscopy Gordon Rsch. Conf., 1968; mem. NAS/NRC NBS Polymers divsn. Evaluation Panel, 1973-76, chmn., 1975-76; mem. materials rsch. adv. com. NSF, 1981-86, chmn., 1984; mem. DOE Coun. on Material Scis., 1986-89; mem. program adv. com. Internat. Conf. on Raman Spectroscopy, 1984-86, mem. exec. com., 1988-90; Fraser Price Meml. lectr., 1988; disting. lectr. Inst. Materials Sci. U. Conn., 1995; mem. com. on promoting rsch. collaboration NAS/IOM, 1987-89; cons. B.F. Goodrich, 1956-86, Allied 1963-93, Monsanto, 1987-92; vis. prof. U. Mainz, 1983, U. Paris, 1991. Author papers on vibrational spectroscopy, x-ray diffraction studies of natural and synthetic polymers, potential energy function devel.; mem. editorial bd. Jour. Polymer Sci. Polymer Physics Edn., 1967-99; Biopolymers, 1973—; Macromolecules, 1968-71; Jour. Macromolecular Sci.-Rev. Macromolecular Chemistry, 1983-92. Served with USNR, 1944-46. Recipient Humboldt award, 1983; U. Mich. Disting. Faculty Achievement award, 1986; Textile Research Inst. fellow, 1947-50; NSF sr. postdoctoral fellow, 1962-63; sr. fellow U. Mich. Soc. Fellows, 1971-76 Fellow AAAS, Am. Phys. Soc. (High Polymer Physics prize 1977, chmn. div. biol. physics 1979, div. councilor 1981, exec. com. 1983, planning com. 1992); mem. Am. Chem. Soc., Biophys. Soc., Coblentz Soc. (hon., bd. mgr. 1967-70). Office: U Mich Biophysics Rsch Divsn 930 N University Ave Ann Arbor MI 48109 E-mail: skrimm@umich.edu.

KRINER, SALLY GLADYS PEARL, artist; b. Bradford, Ohio, Jan. 29, 1911; d. Henry Walter and Pearl Rebecca (Brubaker) Brant; m. Leo Louis Kriner, Feb. 28, 1933; children— Patricia Staab, Jane Palombo. Grad. Arsenal Tech. sch. Indpls.; student Ind. U.-Indpls., 1954, Herron Sch. Art, Indpls., 1958. Exhibited in one woman shows Hoosier Salon, Indpls., 1960, Village Art Gallery, Southport, Ind., 1967, 70, 73, Brown County Art Guild, Nashville, Ind., 1970, 74, 77, 80, 83, 87, 92; group shows include South Side Art League, Indpls., 1959-74, Indpls. Art League, 1959-64, Brown County Art Guild, 1969—, Hoosier Salon, 1961, 65, 67, 68, 73, 75, 76, 77, 82, 86, 87, 91, 95, Frames and Things Gallery, 1995; represented in permanent collections Riley Hosp., Indpls., others. Founder Southside Women's Symphony Com., Indpls., 1958; treas. Perry Twp. Republican Club, Ind., 1960-65; pres. State Assembly Women's Club, 1965-67; bd. dirs. ARC, Indpls., 1942-45, Southside Civic Orgn., Indpls., 1954, Clowes Hall Women's Com., Indpls., 1963. Recipient citation ARC, 1946; citation Marion County Meritorious Service Award, 1959; citation Greater Southside Civic Orgn., 1961; Art award Kappa Kappa Kappa, 1967, 68, 70, 71. Fellow Indpls. Art League Found. (numerous awards 1960-66); mem. Southside Art League, Inc. (pres. 1964-65, numerous awards 1964-75, founder), Ind. Artists Club, Inc. (Purchases award 1978), Ind. Heritage Arts, Inc., Rutland Art Assn., Brown County Art Guild (pres. 1980-83, v.p. 1983—), Ind. fedn. Arts Clubs (bd. dirs. 1963-73), Ind. Artist (chmn. prize fund 1974-75), Consignment and appraisal of fine arts, Hoosier Salon, Indpls. Mus. Arts, Nat. Soc. Arts and Letters, Nat. Mus. Women in Arts, Hoosier Group Women in Arts, Oil Painters of America (Master of Art award for contbg. to heritage Brown County Indiana Art Colony 1997). Presbyterian. Avocation: growing flowers. Home: 394 E Freeman Ridge Rd Nashville IN 47448-8871

KRING, CHARLES UDELL, retired civil engineer; b. Belle Rive, Ill., Aug. 31, 1910; s. Charles Harvey and Carolyn (Schoenmetzler) K.; m. Marguerite F. Kay, Aug. 25, 1945 (dec. Dec. 1999); children: Mary, Judith, Gary; m. Jeanne Millett, July 24, 2002. BSCE, U. Ill., 1932, MSCE, 1939, PhD in Civil Engring., 1948. Registered profl. engr., Calif. Field engr. San Francisco-Oakland Bay Bridge, 1934-35; engr. Golden Gate Bridge, 1936-37; supt. Ben Hur Constrn. Co., St. Louis and Indpls., 1937-38; bridge engr. Parsons, Brinkerhoff, Hall & Macdonald, N.Y., 1941-42; chief structural engr. Bermuda Architect-Engrs., 1942-43; cons. engr. Charles U. Kring Assocs., San Jose, Calif., 1946—; pres. Kring Constrn. Co., Inc., San Jose, 1948—; owner, mgr. Foxworthy Shopping Ctr., San Jose, Calif., 1956-84, Olympia Plaza Shopping Ctr., Seaside, Calif., 1966-77. Owner Kaydell Angus Farm, Los Gatos, Calif., 1959-96; lectr. Air U. Maxwell Field. Author: Selection of Weapons and Estimation of Force Requirements for Aerial Bombardment, 1947. Col. USAF, 1943-45, World War II. Decorated Medal of Freedom. Mem. ASCE, Commonwealth Club, San Jose Country Club, Tau Beta Pi. Republican. Avocations: photography, golf. Home: 7336 Via Laguna San Jose CA 95135-1332 Office: Kring Constrn Co Inc 1035 Minnesota Ave San Jose CA 95125-2431 E-mail: chaskring@aol.com.

KRINGEL, JEROME HOWARD, lawyer; b. Milw., Apr. 2, 1940; s. Lester E. and Irene A. (Kreutzer) K.; m. Mary Kathleen McAuliffe, Sept. 8, 1962; children: Anne, Mary Karen, Jennifer, Elisabeth, Katherine. AB, Marquette U., 1962; postgrad., U. Heidelberg, Germany, 1963; LLB, Yale U., 1966. Bar: Wis. 1966, U.S. Dist. Ct. (ea. dist.) Wis. 1966, U.S. Ct. Appeals (7th cir.) 1966. Ptnr., coord. bus. practice Michael, Best & Friedrich, Milw., 1966—. Trustee Shorewood (Wis.) Village Bd., 1974-80. Mem. ABA, Wis. Bar Assn. (chmn. bus. law sect. 1990-91), Milw. Bar Assn. Office: Michael Best & Friedrich LLP 100 E Wisconsin Ave Ste 3300 Milwaukee WI 53202-4108 E-mail: jhkringel@mbf-law.com.

KRINGELIS, KURT, portfolio manager; b. Tucson, Sept. 14, 1970; s. Imants Kringelis and Gesche Gengelbach. BS in Fin., U. Ill., 1991, MBA, JD, U. Ill., 1995. Bar: Ill. 1995; CFA; CPA, Ill. Fin. analyst Equitable Investment Svcs., DesMoines, 1995-96, assoc. portfolio mgr., 1996-97; investment mgr. ING Investment Mgmt., Atlanta, 1998, dir. high yield bonds, 1999—. Mem. AICPA, ABA, Assn. for Investment Mgmt. and Rsch., Ill. State Bar Assn., Ill. CPA Soc., Atlanta Soc. CFA. Office: ING Investment Mgmt Ste 300 5780 Powers Ferry Rd NW Atlanta GA 30327

KRINSKY, CAROL HERSELLE, art history educator; b. N.Y.C., June 2, 1937; d. David and Jane (Gartman) Herselle; m. Robert Daniel Krinsky, Jan. 25, 1959; 2 children. BA, Smith Coll., 1957; MA, NYU, 1960, PhD, 1965. Mem. faculty NYU, 1965—, assoc. prof. art history, 1973-78, prof., 1978—; Frederic Lindley Morgan prof. U. Louisville, 2001. Author: Vitruvius de Architectura, 1521. 1969, Rockefeller Center, 1978, Synagogues of Europe, 1985, rev. edit., 1996, Gordon Bunshaft of Skidmore, Owings & Merrill, 1988, Europas Synagogen, 1988, Contemporary Native American Architecture, 1996; contbr. articles to profl. jours. Bd. dirs. Internat. Survey Jewish Monuments, Syracuse, N.Y., 1981—, Soc. Archtl. Historians, 1978-80, 86-89, The Mac Dowell Colony, Inc., 1989—, Jewish Heritage Coun. World Monuments Fund; co-chair seminar on the city Columbia U., 1993-95. Am. Coun. Learned Socs. grantee, 1981, Nat. Endowment for the Arts grantee, 1993; recipient Arnold Brunner award N.Y.C. chpt. AIA, 1990. Fellow Soc. Archtl. Historians (pres. 1984-86, pres. N.Y.C. chpt. 1977-79); mem. Coll. Art Assn., Planning History Group, Am. Urban History Assn., Women's City Club, Century Assn., Phi Beta Kappa. Office: NYU Dept Fine Arts 100 Washington Sq E New York NY 10003-6688 E-mail: chk1@nyu.edu.

KRINSKY, FREDDA S. clinical chemist, consultant; b. Bklyn., May 17, 1952; d. Sam and Priscilla Krinsky. BS in Med. Biology, L.I. U., 1975, MS in Med. Biology, 1979; MBA in Corp. Fin., Adelphi U., 1987. Med. technologist Johns Hopkins Hosp., Balt., 1975-78; clin. chemist SmithKline Clin. Labs., Lake Success, N.Y., 1980-83; lab. adminstr. Cen. Gen. Hosp., Plainview, N.Y., 1983-86; cons. Strategies & Techs., Plainview, N.Y., 1987-96; corp. tech. staff Grumman Corp., Bethpage, N.Y., 1988-91, legal and patent staff liaison, 1990-91; adminstrv. ops. staff ROLM, Jericho, N.Y., 1991-92; cons. Chase Manhattan, N.Y.C., 1993-96; CEO Krinsky & Co. LLC, Highlands Ranch, Colo., 1998—. Clin. adj. instr. Sch. of Med. Biology, L.I. U., Greenvale, N.Y., 1983-86; coord. continuing lab. medicine-edn., Johns Hopkins Hosp., Balt., 1976-78. Grantee HEW, 1978-79. Mem. AAAS, Internet C. of C., Rockies Venture Club, Internat. Leadership Coun., Forum of Women Entrepreneurs, Women in Tech. Achievements include development of a database system for tracking intellectual properties, method for facilitating the technology transfer of the inventions within the appropriate strategic business unit for exploitation both internally and externally. Home and Office: 10073 Charissglen Ln Highlands Ranch CO 80126-5526 E-mail: krinskycompany@uswest.net.

KRINSKY, ROBERT DANIEL, consulting firm executive; b. Bklyn., Jan. 24, 1937; s. Milton and Josephine E. (Bachrach) K.; m. Carol M. Herselle, Jan. 25, 1959; children: Alice E., John D. BA, Antioch Coll., 1957. Various actuarial positions The Segal Co., N.Y.C., 1954-65, v.p. to exec. v.p., 1966-82, pres., 1982-93, chmn., 1994—; bd. dirs. Wiss, Janney, Elster Assocs., Inc., 2003—. Mem. working com. Nat. Coordinating Com. for Multi-employer Pension Plans, Washington, 1982—. Trustee Antioch U., Yellow Springs, Ohio, 1983-02, chmn., 1993-02; trustee Moses L. Parshelsky Found., 1982—; bd. dirs. Harbor Festival Found., N.Y.C., 1983-87; chmn. Conf. Bd. Chmn. Small Liberal Arts Colls. and Univs., 2000-02; bd. dirs. Elderhostel, Inc., 2001—, vice chmn., 2003—. Asst. health svc. officer USPHS, 1959-61. Fellow Conf. Actuaries in Pub. Practice; mem. Am. Acad. Actuaries, Soc. Actuaries (assoc.), Assn. Pvt. Pension and Welfare Plans (bd. dirs. 1982—, chmn. 1988-89), Nat. Dance Inst. (bd. dirs. 1987—, chmn. 1988-89, 93-2003), Century Assn. Office: The Segal Co 1 Park Ave New York NY 10016-5895 E-mail: rKrinsky@segalco.com., rdkactbird@aol.com.

KRIPKE, DANIEL FREDERICK, psychiatrist, educator; b. Washington, Dc, Oct. 12, 1941; m. Z Drescher, Apr. 23, 1965; children: Gawain M, Clarissa C. MD, Columbia Coll. of Physicians and Surgeons, New York City, 1961—65; BA, Harvard Coll., Cambridge, MA, 1958—61. License Calif., 1970. Prof. of psychiatry U. of Calif., San Diego, La Jolla, Calif., 1982—; adj. prof. of psychology San Diego State U., San Diego, Calif., 1997—. Author: (web site) http:/BrightenYourLife.info, http:/www.DarkSideOfSleepingPills.com. Capt. US Air Force, 1966—68, Holloman AFB, New Mexico. Recipient Fellow, Am. Psychiat. Assn. Achievements include research in In 1981, Dr. Kripke published the first controlled trial of bright light treatment of depression. Avocation: making glass jewelry. Home: 8437 Sugarman Dr La Jolla CA 92037 Office: UCSD 0667 9500 Gilman Dr La Jolla CA 92093-0667 E-mail: dkripke@ucsd.edu.

KRIPPNER, STANLEY CURTIS, psychologist; b. Edgerton, Wis., Oct. 4, 1932; s. Carroll Porter and Ruth Genevieve (Volenberg) Krippner; m. Lelie Anne Harris, June 25, 1966 (div. 2002). BS, U. Wis., 1954; MA, Northwestern U., 1957, PhD, 1961; PhD (hon.), U. Humanistic Studies, San Diego, 1982. Diplomate Am. Bd. Sexology. Speech therapist Warren Pub. Schs. (Ill.), 1954-55, Richmond Pub. Schs. (Va.), 1955-56; dir. Child Study Ctr. Kent (Ohio) State U., 1961-64; dir. dream lab. Maimonides Med. Ctr., Bklyn., 1964-73; prof. of psychology Saybrook Grad. Sch., San Francisco, 1973—. Adj. prof. psychology Calif. Inst. Human Sci., 1994—; vis. prof. U. P.R., 1972, Sonoma State U., 1972-73, U. Life Scis., Bogota, Colombia, 1974, Inst. for Psychodrama and Humanistic Psychology, Caracas, Venezuela, 1975, State U. West Ga.., 1976, John F. Kennedy U., 1980-82, Inst. for Rsch. in Biopsychophysics, Curitiba, Brazil, 1990; adj. prof. Calif. Inst. Integral Studies, 1991-97; lectr. Acad. Pedagogical Scis., Moscow, 1971, Acad. Scis., Beijing, 1981, Minas Gerais U., Belo Horizonte, Brazil, 1986-87. Author: (with Montague Ullman) Dream Telepathy, 1973, rev. edit., 1989, Song of the Siren: A Parapsychological Odyssey, 1975, (with Alberto Villoldo) The Realms of Healing, 1976, rev. edit., 1987, 2003, Human Possibilities, 1980, (with Jerry Solfvin) La Science et les Pouvoirs Psychiques de l'Homme, 1986, (with Alberto Villoldo) Healing States, 1987, (with Joseph Dillard) Dreamworking, 1988, (with David Feinstein) Personal Mythology, 1988, (with Patrick Welch) Spiritual Dimensions of Healing, 1992, (with Dennis Thong and Bruce Carpenter) A Psychiatrist in Paradise, 1993, (with David Feinstein) The Mythic Path, 1997, (with Andre de Carvalho) Sonhos Exoticos, 1998, (with Fariba Bogzaron and Andre de Carvalho) Extraordinary Dreams and How to Work with Them, 2002; editor: Advances in Parapsychological Research, Vol. 1, 1977, Vol. 2, 1978, Vol. 3, 1982, Vol. 4, 1984, Vol. 5, 1987, Vol. 6, 1990, Vol. 7, 1994, Vol. 8, 1997, Psychoenergetic Systems, 1979, Dreamtime and Dreamwork, 1990; co-editor: Galaxies of Life, 1973, The Kirlian Aura, 1974, The Energies of Consciousness, 1975, (with Susan Powers) Future Science, 1977, Broken Images, Broken Selves, 1997, (with Mark Waldman) Dreamscaping, 1999, (with Etzel Cardeña and Steven J. Lynn) Varieties of Anomalous Experience, 2000, (with Teresa McIntyre) The Psychological Effects of War: Trauma on Civilians, 2003; mem. editl. bd. Alternative Therapies in Health and Medicine, Jour. Humanistic Psychology, Jour. Transpersonal Psychology, Jour. Indian Psychology, Dream Network, Humanistic Psychologist; contbr. 800 articles to profl. jours. Mem. Joseph Plan Found.; Bd. dirs., adv. bd. Acad. Religion and Phys. Rsch., Survival Rsch. Found., Hartley Film Found. Recipient Svc. to Youth award YMCA, 1959, Citation of Merit Nat. Assn. Creative Children and Adults, 1975, Cert. Recognition Office Gifted and Talented, U.S. Office Edn., 1976, Volker medal South Africa Soc. Psychical Rsch., 1980, Bicentennial medal U. Ga., 1985, Charlotte and Karl Bühler award, 1992, Dan Overlade Meml. award, 1994, Humanist of Yr. award Ch. of Humanism, 1996, Career Achievement award Parapsychol. Assn., 1998, J.B. Rhine Award, 2002, Ashley Montague Peace prize, 2003; named to Wisdom Hall of Fame, 2001. Fellow APA (pres. divsn. 32, 1980, pres. divsn. 30, 1997, Disting. Contbns. to Profl. Hypnosis award 2002, Disting. Contbns. to Internat. Advancement of Psychology award 2002), Am. Soc. Clin. Hypnosis, Am. Psychol. Soc., Soc. Sci. Study Religion, Soc. Sci. Study Sexuality, Western Psychol. Assn.; mem. AAAS, ACA, Am. Soc. Psychical Rsch., Am. Ednl. Rsch. Assn., Internat. Coun. Psychologists, Assn. for Study of Dreams (pres. 1993-94), Soc. for the Anthropology Consciousness, Inter-Am. Psychol. Assn., Assn. Humanistic Psychology (pres. 1974-75), Assn. Transpersonal Psychology, Internat. Soc. Hypnosis, Internat. Soc. for Study of Dissociation, Nat. Assn. for Gifted Children, Sleep Rsch. Soc., Soc. Sci. Exploration, Biofeedback Soc. Am., Coun. Exceptional Children, Soc. Accelerative Learning and Tchg., Soc. Gen. Sys. Rsch., Swedish Soc. Clin. and Exptl. Hypnosis, Western Psychol. Assn., Internat. Soc. Gen. Semantics, Menninger Found., Nat. Soc. Study of Edn., Parapsychol. Assn. (pres. 1983), Soc. Clin. and Exptl. Hypnosis, World Future Soc. Office: Saybrook Grad Sch 450 Pacific Ave Rm 300 San Francisco CA 94133-4640 E-mail: skrippner@saybrook.edu.

KRISCH, ALAN DAVID, physics educator; b. Phila., Apr. 19, 1939; s. Kube and Jeanne (Freiberg) K.; m. Jean Peck, Aug. 27, 1961; 1 child, Kathleen Susan. AB, U. Pa., 1960; PhD, Cornell U., 1964. Instr. Cornell U., 1964; mem. faculty U. Mich., Ann Arbor, 1964—, assoc. prof. high energy physics, 1966-68, prof., 1968—. Vis. prof. Niels Bohr Inst., Copenhagen, 1975-76; trustee Argonne Nat. Lab., 1972-73, 80-82, chmn. zero gradient syncrotron users group, 1973-75, 78-79, chmn. internat. com. for high energy spin physics symposia, 1977-94, past chmn., 1995—, chmn. organizing com. conf. on particle and nuclear physics intersections, 1983-86, mem., 1987-91, hon. mem., 1994—; chmn.-elect, chmn. IUCF Users Group, 1997-2002; spokesperson NEPTUN-A Expt. at 400 GeV UNK accelerator in Russia, 1989-99, SPIN collaboration Fermilab, 1991-95, SPIN at HERA collaboration DESY in Germany, 1996-99, SPINatU-70 Exp. at 70 Gev IHEP accelerator in Protvino, Russia, 2000—, SPIN at COSY Expt. COSY accelerator, Jülich, Germany, 2002-. Trustee Ann Arbor Hands On Mus., 1999-. Fellow NSF, 1963, Guggenheim Found., 1971-72, Denmark Nat. Bank, 1975-76. Fellow Am. Phys. Soc.; mem. AAAS. Achievements include discovery of heavy elementary particles, of structure within the proton, of scaling in inclusive reactions, of spinning core within proton, of large spin forces in violent proton collisions, of precise confirmation of large spin forces; invention of inclusive reactions; development of first high energy spin-polarized proton beam, of first strong focusing spin-polarized proton beam; demonstration of "Siberian snake" technique for accelerating spin-polarized beams. Office: U Mich Randall Lab Ann Arbor MI 48109-1120

KRISE, PATRICIA LOVE, automotive industry executive; b. Indpls., July 28, 1959; d. John Bernard and Ann (Emmons) Love; m. Thomas Warren Krise, Sept. 5, 1987. BA magna cum laude, Hanover Coll., Ind., 1981; MBA with hons., Miami U., Oxford, Ohio, 1982. Substitute tchr. Henry County Sch. Dist., Knightstown, Ind., 1982-83; project mgr. Servaas Labs., Inc., Indpls., 1983-84; sales analyst Ford Motor Co., Mpls., 1984, outstate field mgr., 1984-86, met. field mgr., 1986-87, truck merchandising mgr., 1987-88, merchandising mgr., 1988-89, met. field dir. Denver dist., 1989, market representation specialist Denver dist., 1990-91; regional market rep. mgr. Infiniti divsn. Nissan Motor Corp., Naperville, Ill., 1991-92, regional merchandising mgr., 1992-93, dealer ops. cons., 1993—97, dealer ops. mgr., 1995-97; adminstrv./remktg. mgr. Fairlane Credit subsidiary Ford Motor Credit, Colorado Springs, 1997—99, mgr. nat. expansion, remktg. and adminstrn., 1999; acct. svcs. mgr. Ford Motor Credit, Colorado Springs, 2000—. Advisor/presenter Ford Dealer Advt. Fund, Mpls., 1987-88. Nat. sponsorship liaison Race for the Cure, Colorado Springs, 2002; vol. Marian House Soup Kitchen, 1997—2000; adult literacy tutor Jr. Achievement, 1998; mem. fund-raising com. Race for the Cure, Colorado Springs, 1999, co-chair ops. com., 2001; bd. dirs. Jr. Achievement, Colorado Springs, 2001—03. Recipient Outstanding Mktg. award Ctrl. Region Ford Motor Co., 1987, Wall St. Jour. award, 1982; named Internat. Woman of Yr., 1992. Mem. Twin Cities Sales Mgrs. Club, Hanover Coll. Alumni Assn., Women's Athletic Assn. (treas. 1979-80), Pre-Law Club (pres. 1980-81), Nat. Assn. Female Execs., Alpha Delta Pi., co-chair Race for the Cure for Fairlane Credit, 1998. Republican. Roman Catholic. Avocations: running, sailing, yoga. E-mail: PKrise@Ford.com.

KRISE, THOMAS WARREN, military officer, English language educator; b. Fort Sam Houston, Tex., Oct. 27, 1961; s. Edward Fisher and Elizabeth Ann (Bradt) K.; m. Patricia Lynn Love, Sept. 5, 1987. BS, USAF Acad., 1983; MSA, Cen. Mich. U., 1986; MA, U. Minn., 1989; PhD, U. Chgo., 1995. Commd. 2d lt. USAF, 1983, advanced through grades to lt. col.; dep. missile comdr. 742d Strategic Missile Squadron, Minot AFB, N.D., 1983-85, missile crew comdr., 1985-86, ICBM flight comdr., 1986-87; instr. English USAF Acad., Colorado Springs, 1989-91, asst. prof., 1991-92, 97-99, assoc. prof., 1999—2002, prof., 2002—. Sr. mil. fellow Inst. for Nat. Strategic Studies, 1995-97; vice-dir. Nat. Def. U. Press, 1995-97; dir. English major program USAF Acad., 1997-2000; dir. core lit. program, 1998-2000; dir. Air Force Humanities Inst., 1997—; vis. prof. U W.I., Mona, Jamaica, 1999. Asst. editor War, Literature and the Arts, 1991-92, assoc. editor, 1998-2003, mng. editor, 2003—; gen. editor: McNair Papers monograph series, 1995-97, Caribbeana: An Anthology of English Literature of the West Indies, 1657-1777, 1999; contbr. articles to profl. jours. Adult literacy tutor Coalition for Adult Literacy, Colorado Springs, 1989-91, literacy tutor trainer, Adult Literacy Network, Colorado Springs, 1991-92 Recipient Pres.' Student Leadership award U. Minn., 1989; Summer Inst. grantee Nat. Endowment for the Humanities, 1990, Seiler Rsch. grantee F.J. Seiler Rsch. Lab., A.F. Systems Command, 1991, Faculty Rsch Com. grantee, 1998-2003, Salzburg Seminar grantee, 2003, Rsch. grant USAF Inst. Nat. Security Studies, 1998, 99, CBS Bicentennial Narrators scholar, 1994; Fulbright fellow, 1999. Mem. SAR (Pikes Peak chpt. pres. 1991-92), Toastmasters Internat. (U. Minn. chpt. pres. 1988-89), MLA, Am. Soc. for 18th Century Studies (conf. dir. 2002), Soc. for 18th Century Am. Studies (sec.-treas. 1995-99), Soc. Early Americanists (exec. coord. 2003—), Colorado Springs Adult Literacy Network (pres. 1991-92), Assn. Grads. USAF Acad. (bd. dirs. 1991-95, Chgo. chpt. pres. 1993-95), Army and Navy Club (Washington), Royal Air Force Club (London), Phi Kappa Phi. Episcopalian. Avocations:

travel, sailing, skiing, hiking, scuba diving. Home: 2635 Edenderry Dr Colorado Springs CO 80919-3868 Office: Dept English and Fine Arts 2354 Fairchild Dr Ste 6d45 U S A F Academy CO 80840-6299

KRISHEN, ALOK, biostatistician; arrived in U.S., 1973; s. Viapak and Nirmal Krishen; m. Trieu Do, Sept. 10, 1977; 1 child, Calvin. BSc in Math. with honors, Panjab U., Chandigarh, Panjab, India, 1972, MSc in Math. with honors, 1973; MS in Stats., Fla. State U, 1976. Assoc. dir. biomed. data scis. Glaxo Smith Kline, Research Triangle Park, NC, 1997—2000, dir. biostatistics and programming, 2000—01, sr. dir. biostatistics and programming, 2001—02; sr. dir. biomed. data scis. Glaxo Smith Kline, Inc., Research Triangle Park, NC, 2003—. Mem.: Am. Statis. Assn. Achievements include research in Optimally Weighted, Fixed Sequence, and Gatekeeper Multiple Testing Procedures, Statistical Planning and Inference; statistical methodology, regulatory perspective on statistical issues in clinical research. Home: 12331 Wharton's Way Raleigh NC 27613-6029 Office: Glaxo Smith Kline 5 Moore Dr Research Triangle Park NC 27709

KRISHER, BERNARD, foreign correspondent; b. Frankfurt, Germany, Aug. 9, 1931; s. Joseph and Fella (Solnica) K.; m. Akiko Yaginuma, May 1, 1960; children: Deborah, Joseph. BA, Queens Coll., 1953; postgrad., Columbia U., 1961-62. From staffwriter to asst. editor mag. N.Y. World-Telegram & Sun, 1955-61; corr. Newsweek, 1963—, bur. chief, 1968-80; corr. Fortune, 1981-83; chief editorial advisor Focus Weekly Mag. Shincho-sha Pub. Co., Tokyo, 1981-97; editl. advisor Dohosha Pub. Co., Kyoto and Tokyo, 1984-98; editor at large Japan Avenue, 1991-94; editor at large Asia Wired mag., 1993-98; founder and pub. The Cambodia Daily, Phnom Penh, 1993—; editl. dir. Future Book series Tachibana Pub. Co., Tokyo, 1998—. Hon. research assoc., vis. scholar East Asian Research Ctr., Harvard U., 1978-79; Far East rep. The Media Lab. MIT, 1987—. Author: (with Alan Levy) Draftee's Confidential Guide, 1957, Interview, 1976, The Plus and Minuses of Being Japanese, 1978, Harvard Diary, 1979, How Harvard Sees Japan, 1979, We Who Lived in Japan, 1986; (with King Norodom Sihanouk) Charisma and Leadership, 1990, A Vision for a New Asia (with Cambodia Daily staff), 2003. Founder, vol. chmn. Japan Relief for Cambodia, 1992—; vol. chmn. Am. Assistance for Cambodia, 1993—, Internet Appeal for N. Korean Flood Victims, 1995—; chmn. Sihanouk (free charity) Hosp.- Ctr. of Hope, Phnom Penh, Cambodia, 1996—. Recipient Gleitsman Internat. Activist award, 2001, Ive Asia Pacific Culture prize, 2003. Mem Coun. Fgn. Rels., Signet Soc., Player's Club. Home: 4-1-7-605 Hiroo Shibuya-ku Tokyo 150-0012 Japan E-mail: bernie@krisher.com.

KRISHNA, HARI J. engineer; b. Madras, India, May 13, 1948; came to U.S., 1968; s. J. Raghotham Reddy and J. Sarojini Devi; m. Laxmi Krishna, Mar. 26, 1972. BS, Osmania U., Hyderabad, India, 1967; MS, Kans. State U., 1971; PhD, Utah State U., 1979. Registered profl. engr.; cert. profl. hydrologist Am. Inst. Hydrology. Internat. cons. FAO/UN, Bangkok, 1981-82; asst. prof. Utah Water Rsch. Lab., Logan, 1982-84; rsch. scientist Tex. A&M Blackland Rsch. Ctr., Temple, 1984-88; dir. assoc. prof. V.I. Water Resources Rsch. Inst., St. Thomas, 1988-93; team leader TCEQ, Austin, Tex., 1993—2000; sr. engr. Tex. Water Devel. Bd., Austin, 2000—. Recipient Disting. Alumnus award Utah State U., 1997. Mem. Am. Rainwater Catchment Sys. Assn. (pres.), Phi Kappa Phi, Tau Beta Pi. Office: TWDB PO Box 13231 Austin TX 78711-3231

KRISHNA, KISHORE BELLAMKONDA, biomedical researcher, educator; b. Visakhapatnam, India, Aug. 2, 1953; s. Dharma Rao and Kamala Devi Bellamkonda; m. Ratnavathi Rolla, Feb. 24, 1989; children: Satya, Dharma. MBBS, Sri Venkateswara U., Tirupathi, India, 1975; MD, Banaras Hindu U., Varanasi, India, 1980; PhD in Biomed Scis., Cath. U. Louvain, Belgium, 1990. Med. registration Andhra Med. Coun., India, 1977. Asst. prof. pharmacology Cath. U. Louvain, Brussels, 1991-92; vis. fellow Nat. Heart, Lung and Blood Inst. NIH, Bethesda, 1993-97; rsch. asst., prof. medicine divsn. nephrology & hypertension U. Cin. Med. Ctr., 1997-2001; rsch. assoc., prof. medicine nephrology & hypertension U. Utah Health Scis. Ctr., Salt Lake City, 2001—. R & D com. Salt Lake City Healthcare System; ad hoc mem. study sect. NIH. Mem. editl. bd. Am. Jour. Physiology; contbr. articles. Fellow Jap. Ministry of Edn., Sci. and Culture, 1981-83, Internat. Inst. Cellular and Molecular Pathology, Belgium, 1987-89, Sci. Devel. Found. Cath. U. Louvain, 1989-91. Mem.: AHA, Nat. Kidney Found., Am. Physiol. Soc., Internat. Soc. Nephrology, Am. Soc. Nephrology, Inst. Biology (chartered biologist 1988), Smithsonian Inst. Hindu. Avocations: classical music, photography, philosophical reading. Office: U Utah Health Scis Ctr Rm 4R312 50 N Medical Dr Salt Lake City UT 84132 Office Fax: (801) 581-4343. E-mail: Bellamkonda.Kishore@hsc.utah.edu.

KRISHNA, N(EPALLI) RAMA, biochemist; b. Masulipatam, Andhra, India; came to U.S., 1971; PhD, Indian Inst. Tech., Kanpur, 1972. Postdoctoral fellow Ga. Inst. Tech., Atlanta, 1972-73, U. Alta., Edmonton, Can., 1974-76; assoc. scientist Cancer Ctr. U. Ala., Birmingham, 1976-79, asst. prof. dept. biochemistry, 1979-85, assoc. prof., 1985-92, prof., 1992—, dir. nuclear magnetic resonance core facility, 1984—. Cons. Ortho Pharm. Corp., Raritan, N.J., 1979-83. Contbr. articles to profl. jours. Recipient Leukemia Soc. Am. Scholar award, 1982-87. Office: Univ Ala Dept Biochemistry and Molecular Genetics NMR Core Facility CH19-B31 1530 3d Ave S Birmingham AL 35294-2041 E-mail: nrkrishna@bmg.bhs.uab.edu.

KRISHNAMACHARI, SADAGOPA IYENGAR, mechanical engineer, consultant; b. Chidambaram, Tamil Nadu, India, Sept. 14, 1944; came to U.S., 1982; s. Renga Iyengar and Alamelu Sadagopan; m. Lalitha Ramanujam, June 2, 1969; children: Sriram, Parashar. BS in Math., U. Madras, India, 1963, BSME, 1966; MS in Mechanics, Ill. Inst. Tech., 1984. Engr. Bharat Heavy Elecs. Ltd., Tiruchi, Tamil Nadu, 1967-73, sr. engr., 1973-77, mgr. nuclear engring., 1977-82; mgr. product design and devel. L.J. Broutman & Assocs., Chgo., 1984-91, 1991-96; ind. cons. Pioneer Techs., Naperville, Ill., 1996—. Industry rep. Indian Boiler Regulatory Bd., 1976-77; mem. vis. faculty dept. mech. engring. Ill. Inst. Tech., Chgo., 1985—; bd. dirs. Soc. Plastics Engrs. PD3. Author: Applied Stress Analysis of Plastics--A Mechanical Engineering Approach, 1992. Founder classical music sch. for children, Tiruchi, 1978. Mem. ASME (sr.), Soc. Plastics Engrs. (bd. dirs. PD3 divsn., editor SPE/PD3, Outstanding Achievement award, Best Paper award 1999), Soc. Exptl. Mechanics. Hindu. Achievements include pioneered capabilities for stress analysis of pressure vessels, piping, thermal and mechanical design of nuclear heat exchangers, components made of non-metallic materials; development of stress analysis of non-metallic materials.

KRISHNAMURTHY, SANDEEP, writer, researcher; PhD, U. of Ariz., 1996. Author: (e-commerce textbook) E-Commerce Management: Text and Cases. Office: Univ Washington Bothell 18115 Campus Way NE Room UW1-233 Bothell WA 98033 E-mail: sandeep@u.washington.edu.

KRISHNAMURTY, SUNDAR, mechanical engineer; b. Tiruchy, Tamil Nadu, India, June 3, 1960; m. Shobana Venkataraman; children: Tara Murty, Surya Murty. BS, Ind. Inst. Tech., Kanpur, India, 1982; MS, U. Pa., 1984; PhD, U. Wis., 1989. Asst. prof. U. Mass., Amherst, 1989—95, assoc. prof., 1996—2000, assoc. head MIE dept., 2000—. Assoc. editor: Jour. Design and Mfg. Automation, 2000. Mem.: ASME, Mass. Soc. Profs. (v.p. 2000). Office: U Mass Mech and Indsl Engring Amherst MA 01003

KRISHNAN, HEMA A. finance educator; b. Coimbatore, India, June 28, 1961; arrived in U.S., 1989; d. Ananthakrishnan Sekaripuram and Anandam Krishnan; m. Babu Viswanathan, June 24, 1993; 1 child, Naveen. MS, Indian Inst. Tech., New Delhi, 1982; MBA, Indian Inst. Mgmt., Bangalore, 1988; PhD, U. Tenn., 1993. Sales officer Hindustan Petroleum Corp., Madras, India, 1983—86, regional coord., 1988—89; grad. asst. U. Tenn., Knoxville, 1989—93; asst. prof. Xavier U., Cin., 1993—98, assoc. prof., 1998—. Contbr. articles to profl. jours. Mem.: Strategic Mgmt. Soc., Acad. Mgmt., Beta Gamma Sigma. Avocations: reading, music. Office: Xavier U 3800 Victory Pky Cincinnati OH 45207 E-mail: krishnan@xavier.edu.

KRISHNAN, KRISHNASWAMY RANGA RAMA R. psychiatry educator; b. Madras, Tamilnadu, India, Apr. 22, 1956; came to U.S., 1981; s. N. Krishnaswamy and Sulochana Krishnaswamy Reddy; m. Sripriya Chitamoor, May 21, 1987; children: Vaishnavi, Prahlad. PUC, Loyola Coll., Madras, India, 1973; MBBS, U. Madras, India, 1978. Chief resident Duke Med. Ctr., Durham, 1981-83, asst. prof., 1984-89, assoc. prof., 1990-95, prof., 1995—, chmn. psychiatry, 1998—. Office: Duke U Med Ctr Box 3950 Durham NC 27710-0001 E-mail: krish001@acpub.duke.edu.

KRISHNAN, MAHESH, research scientist; PhD in pharm. sci., U. Iowa, 2001. Pharmacist Madras, 1991. Sr. rsch. scientist Therics, Inc., Princeton, NJ, 2001—. Author: Reactivity of Biodegradable Polymers (Jour. Publ., 2000). Mem.: Am. Assn. of Pharm. Scientist. Achievements include research in Controlled Release of Drugs for Bone Growth. Home: 4615 Ravens Crest Dr Plainsboro NJ 08536 Office: Therics Inc 115 Campus Dr Princeton NJ 08540 Personal E-mail: krish0923@yahoo.com. E-mail: mkrishnan@therics.com.

KRISHNAN, PALANIAPPA, agricultural engineering educator; b. Kanadukathan, Tamil Nadu, India, Apr. 25, 1953; came to U.S., 1974; s. Lakshmanan and Umayal (Thenappan) K.; m. Chitra Palaniappa Palaniappan, June 18, 1980; 1 child, Prashanth. BTech with honors, Indian Inst. Tech., Kharagpur, 1975; MS, U. Hawaii, 1976; PhD, U. Ill., 1979. Rsch. assoc. U. Ill., Urbana, 1979-80, Oreg. State U., Corvallis, 1980-83, asst. prof., 1983-85; asst. prof. agrl. engring. U. Del., Newark, 1985-91, assoc. prof., 1991—, dir. ops. rsch. program, 1996—. Cons. Am. Agrotech Lab., Sacaton, Ariz., 1983-86, Rodale Rsch. Ctr., Kutztown, Pa., 1986-91, Christiana Care, Newark, Del., 1998—; faculty advisor Indian Students Assn., Newark, 1988-92, Indian Graduate Students Assn., Newark, 2000—; chmn. career guidance com., 1990—, sect. found. liaison leader, 1992—. Assoc. editor: Food Process Engineering Institute, 1994-99; contbr. articles to profl. jours.; patentee in field. Hunter fellow U. Ill., Urbana, 1977-78; rsch. grantee Oreg. State U., Corvallis, 1981; teaching grantee U. Del., Newark, 1987; recipient Excellence in Advising award U. Del., 1997. Mem. INFORMS, ASQ (Del. chpt. v.chmn. 2000-01, chmn. 2001-02, del. conf. chmn. 2002-03), Am. Soc. Engring. Edn., Am. Soc. Agrl. Engrs. (sec., vice-chmn., chmn. agrl. pest control and fertilizer application com. 1988-92), Newark Lions (lion tamer 1989, bd. dirs. 1990-92, 94—, pres. 1991-92, 99-2000, 03—). Home: 45 Bristol Ln Newark DE 19711-2998 E-mail: baba@udel.edu.

KRISHNAN, RANGA RAMA, psychiatrist; b. Madras, India, Apr. 26, 1956; arrived in U.S., 1981; s. Krishnaswamy and Sulochana Krishnaswamy Reddy; m. Sripriya Chitamoor Krishnan, May 21, 1987; children: Vaishnavi, Prahlad. PUC, Loyola Coll., 1973; MBBS, U. Madras, 1978. Chief resident Duke Univ. Med. Ctr., Durham, NC, 1981—83, asst. prof., 1984—89, assoc. prof., 1990—95, chmn. psychiatry, 1998—. Office: Duke Univ Med Ctr Box 3950 Durham NC 27710 Fax: 919-681-5489. E-mail: krish001@mc.duke.edu.

KRISHNAN, RANJANI, finance educator; b. Calcutta, West Bengal, India, Aug. 2, 1965; d. S. S. Ananthakrishnan and Anandi Krishnan; m. Satish Joshi; children: Prithvi Joshi children: Tanvi Joshi. AA, Inst. Cost and Works Accts., India; MBA, U. Pitts., PhD, 1998. Assoc. prof. Mich. State U., East Lansing, 1998—. Contbr. articles. Mem.: Am. Acctg. Assn. (exec. com. 2001—02). Office: Mich State Univ Eli Broad Sch Mgmt East Lansing MI 48824 Business E-Mail: krishn15@msu.edu.

KRISHNAN, RAVI VENKATA, internist; b. Madras, India, Sept. 10, 1965; s. Venkata and Sakunthala Krishnan; m. Geetha Murthy Krishnan, June 21, 1993; children: Nisha, Anita, Rahul. MBBS, Stanley Med. Sch., Madras, 1988; MD, Case Western Res. U., 1995. Diplomate Am. Bd. Internal Medicine. Pvt. practice No. Ohio Med. Svcs., Inc., Cleve., 1995—. Mem. AMA, ACP. Avocations: internet surfing, travel. Office: 6803 Mayfield Rd Ste 412 Cleveland OH 44124-2214

KRISHNASAMY, BHARATH KUMAR, physician; b. June 30, 1945; MD, Andhra U., Visakhapatnam, India, 1969. Diplomate Am. Bd. Radiology, Am. Bd. Nuclear Medicine. Dir. nuclear medicine Howard U. Sch. Medicine, Washington, 1976-79; asst. prof. raidology Washington U. Sch. Medicine, St. Louis, 1979-85; asst. dir. nuclear medicine Mallinckrodt Inst. Radiology, St. Louis, 1979-85; med. dir., chief radiologist San Gabriel Valley Diagnostic Ctr., West Covina, Calif., 1985—. Contbr. chpt. to book, numerous articles to profl. jours. Office: 1509 W Cameron Ave Ste D West Covina CA 91790-2725

KRISLOV, MARVIN, lawyer, educator; b. Balt., Aug. 24, 1960; s. Joseph and Evelyn (Moreida) K.; m. Amy Ruth Sheon, Aug. 25, 1993; children: Zachary Jacob, Jesse Harris, Eve Rose. BA in Econs. summa cum laude, Yale U., 1982; BA/MA in Modern History, Oxford (Eng.) U., 1985; JD, Yale U., 1988. Bar: Calif. 1988, D.C. 1989, Mich. 1999. Law clk., Judge M.H. Patel U.S. Dist. Ct. (no. dist.) Calif., San Francisco, 1988-89; trial atty. U.S. Dept. Justice, Civil Rights Divsn., Washington, 1989-93; spl. asst. U.S. atty. U.S. Atty.'s Office, Washington, 1989-90; spl. counsel Office of Counsel to the Pres., Washington, 1993-94, asst. counsel, 1994, assoc. counsel, 1995-96; dep. solicitor U.S. Dept. Labor, Washington, 1996-98, acting solicitor, 1997-98; v.p., gen. counsel U. Mich., Ann Arbor, 1998—. Adj. prof. law, George Washington U. Law Sch., Washington, 1991-93; adj. prof. U. Mich. Law Sch., 2000—, U. Mich. polit. sci. dept., 2001—. Mem. New Haven Bd. Aldermen, 1982-83. Rhodes scholar, 1983. Mem. Phi Beta Kappa. Office: U Mich 4010 Fleming Adminstrn Bldg Ann Arbor MI 48109-1340

KRISS, GARY W(AYNE), Episcopal priest; b. Balt., Dec. 29, 1946; s. Warren B. and Margaret L. (Austin) K. AB cum laude, Dartmouth Coll., 1968; MDiv, Yale U. Divinity Sch., 1972; postgrad. studies, The Gen. Theol. Sem., N.Y.C., 1972, St. George Coll., Jerusalem, 1978; DD, Nashotah House, 2001. Ordained to ministry Episcopal Ch. as deacon, 1972, as priest 1972. Chaplain to the congregation Cathedral Ch. of St. Paul, Burlington, Vt., 1972-74; coord. Rock Point (Vt.) Summer Confs., 1973-77; vicar St. Mark's, St. Luke's Parishes, Castleton and Fair Haven, Vt., 1974-78; asst. to dean The Cathedral of All Saints, Albany, N.Y., 1978-79, canon precentor, 1979-84, dir. inst. Christian studies, 1979-84; dean Cathedral of All Saints, Albany, 1984-91; dean and pres. Nashotah (Wis.) House, 1992—2001; interim rector St. Paul's Epis. Ch., Troy, NY, 2001—02, assoc. priest, 2002—. Bd. dirs. Brookhaven Home for Boys, Chelsea, Vt., 1975-79, Albany Collegiate Interfaith Ctr., 1982-90, pres. 1984-90; Episcopal campus priest, SUNY, Albany, 1980-84; bd. dirs. Capital Area Coun. of Chs., Albany, N.Y., 1989-91, chmn. of Faith and Learning Commn.; The Living Ch. Found., 1994—. Bd. dirs. Samaritan Shelters, Glenmont, N.Y., 1979-91, The Child's Hosp., Albany, 1986-90, Child's Nursing Home, Albany, 1987-91, pres. 1990-91. Episcopalian. Home and Office: PO Box 26 Cambridge NY 12816

KRISS, GERARD ANTHONY, astronomer; b. Pitts., Mar. 2, 1956; children: Jonathan Robert, Katherine Elizabeth, Alexander Edward. SB in Physics, MIT, 1978, PhD in Physics, 1982. Asst. prof., post-doctoral scholar dept. astronomy U. Mich., Ann Arbor, 1982-85; from assoc. rsch. to rsch. scientist dept. physics and astronomy Johns Hopkins U., Balt., 1985-93, assoc. rsch. prof., 1993—98; assoc. astronomer Space Telescope Sci. Inst., Balt., 1998—. Mem. sci. rev. panels NASA, Washington, 1986—. Contbr. articles to Astrophys. Jour. and Astronomical Jour. and to The Physics of Active Galaxies (book)) also chpt. in Multiwavelength Astrophysics, 1988. Named jr. fellow Mich. Soc. of Fellows, Ann Arbor, 1982-85; recipient Nat. Sci. Found. fellowship, 1978-81 and long-term grant for astrophysics NASA, 1995. Mem. Internat. Astron. Union, Am. Astron. Soc., Sigma Xi. Achievements include: an x-ray survey of the emission from Seyfert galaxies (1980); far-ultraviolet spectra detecting strong neutral hydrogen absorption in the Seyfert type 1 NCG 4151 (1992); detection of ultraviolet line emission indicative of shock-heated gas in the Seyfert 2 Galaxy NGC 1068 (1992); resolved the structure of ionized helium in the intergalactic medium, 2001. Office: Space Telescope Sci Inst 3700 San Martin Dr Baltimore MD 21218

KRISS, ROBERT J. lawyer; b. Cleve., Dec. 15, 1953; BA summa cum laude, Cornell U., 1975; JD cum laude, Harvard U., 1978. Bar: Ill. 1978, U.S. Dist. Ct. (no. dist.) Ill. 1978, U.S. Ct. Appeals (7th cir.) 1983, U.S. Dist. Ct. (no. dist. trial bar) Ill. 1982, U.S. Ct. Appeals (5th cir.) 1984. Ptnr. Mayer, Brown, Rowe & Man, Chgo. Presenter in field; adj. prof. trial practice Northwestern U. Law Sch. Author short story. Chmn. consent degree task force Chgo. Park Dist., 1986-87; bd. dirs. Chgo. Legal Assistance Found., 1996-2000, Victory Gardens Theater. Mem. Nat. Inst. Trial Advocacy (faculty midwest regional program 1988-91, 94), Winnetka Caucus (chmn. schs. candidate selection com. 1997). Office: Mayer Brown Rowe & Man 190 S La Salle St Ste 3100 Chicago IL 60603-3441

KRISSEL, SUSAN HINKLE, transportation company executive; b. Miami, Nov. 21, 1947; d. Jack Boyd and Carolyn (Frates) Hinkle; m. Richard Krissel, Mar. 19, 1972; children: John Boyd, Carolyn Frates. BA, U. Miami, 1970, MEd, 1977. Grad. admissions counselor Fla. Internat. U., Miami, 1971-74, budget coord. external degree program, 1974-78, transcript officer, 1978-82; owner, dir. Southeastern Consolidated Industries, Inc., 1982—. Bd. dirs. Jr. League Miami, 1985-86, Beaux Arts, U. Miami, Coral Gables, 1980-84, Parents Assn. Trinity Episcopal Sch., Miami, 1988-91; pres. Woman's Cancer Assn., U. Miami, 1980-81, Palmer Trinity Parents Assn., 1992-93; trustee Palmer Trinity Sch., 1992-93; mem. Young Patronesses of the Opera, bd. govs., 1999—. Mem. The Flamingo Forum, Jr. League Miami, Beaux Arts. Episcopalian. Avocations: reading, boating, travel, needlepoint, golf. Home: 8750 SW 63rd Ct Miami FL 33143-8069

KRISTENSEN, DOUGLAS ALLAN, former state legislator; b. Kearney, Nebr., Jan. 4, 1955; s. Donald M. and Mary Lou (Martin) K.; m. Terri S. Harder; children: Morgan Claire, Paige Nicole. BA, U. Nebr., 1977; JD, Drake U., 1980. Ptnr. Lieske & Kristensen, 1981—; atty. Kearney County, 1982-88; mem. Nebr. Legislature from 37th dist., Lincoln, 1988—; chmn. transp. com. Nebr. Legislature, Lincoln, 1991-98, mem. intergovtl. coop. and revenue coms., mem. exec. bd., chair transp. com., 1991-97, speaker of the legislature, 1998—2002; chancellor U. Nebr. Bd. dirs. young lawyers ssect. Nebr. Bar, 1984-88, Nebr. CLE Inc., 1986-90. Henry Toll fellow, 1991; recipient Pres.' award Nebr. Assn. County Ofcls., 1987. Mem. Nebr. Bar Assn., Iowa Bar Assn., Nebr. County Atty.'s Assn. (bd. dirs. 1985—), Rotary Internat., Optimists Club. Office: University of Nebraska at Kearney 905 W 25th St Lincoln NE 68849 Home: 219 N Brown Ave Minden NE 68959-1524

KRISTENSEN, HANS M. think-tank executive, researcher; b. Esponderup, Denmark, Apr. 7, 1961; s. Hans M. and Johanne M. Kristensen; m. Sandra M. Marquardt, Mar. 5, 1959; 1 child, Adam Marquardt. Realeksamen, Ranum (Denmark) Statsskole, 1978; Studentereksamen, Vesthimmerlands Gymnasium, Aars, Denmark, 1981. Coord. Greenpeace Nat. Disarmament Campaign, Copenhagen, 1982—86; coord. Greenpeace Internat. Disarmament Campaign, Lewes, England, 1987—88, Greenpeace Scandanavian Disarmament Campaign, Copenhagen, 1988—91, rsch. assoc. Greenpeace International, Washington, 1991—96; cons. Western States Legal Found., Berkeley, Calif., 1996—97, Brit.-Am. Security Info. Coun., Washington, 1997—98; spl. advisor Danish Def. Commn., Copenhagen, 1997—98; sr. rschr. The Nautilus Inst., Berkeley, Calif., 1998—2002; cons. Natural Resources Def. Coun., 2003—. Co-author: (book) SIPRI Yearbook, (column) Bulletin of The Atomic Scientists, author several monographs on nuc. armament and disarmament. Grantee, Danish Inst. for Fgn. Policy (DUPI), Ploughshares Fund, John D. and Catherine T. MacArthur Found.

KRISTENSEN, JOHN, church organization administrator; b. Copenhagen, Jan. 2, 1948; arrived in Can., 1951; s. Magnus and Anna (Christensen) K.; m. Janet Mary Morris, Aug. 28, 1971; children: David, Joel, Evan. Honors BSc, U. Western Ont., London, Can., 1971. Ordained to ministry Apostolic Ch. in Can., 1981. Ops. rsch. analyst Govt. of Can., Ottawa, Ont., 1971-74; sys. cons. Quasar Sys., Ottawa, 1974-78; cons. Eco-Sys., Montreal, Que., Can., 1976-81, v.p., 1979-81; min. Apostolic Ch. in Can., Montreal, 1981-94, gen. sec., 1988-94, pres., 1994—. Home and Office: The Apostolic Church 685 Park St S Peterborough ON Canada K9J 3S9

KRISTENSEN, MARLENE, early childhood education educator; b. Baudette, Minn., Sept. 1, 1932; d. Glenn Edward and Frances Emma (Wilson) Munson; m. Robert A. Kristensen, June 5, 1955; children: Mary Kristensen-Quinlan, Debra Kristensen-Anderson. BA, Concordia Coll., Moorhead, Minn., 1954; student, Everett Community Coll., 1973, Edmonds Community Coll., 1974—; postgrad., Cen. Wash. U. From asst. dir. to dir. Lynnwood (Wash.) Day Care, 1974-84; kindergarten tchr. Edmonds (Wash.) Sch. Dist., 1957-58; tchr. trainer Children's World Learning Ctr., Edmonds, 1984-93; ret., 1993. Honor roll tchr., 1987-91. Mem. tchrs.' adv. bd. Weekly Reader Publs., 1991-93. Mem. ASCD, Nat. Assn. for Edn. Young Children.

KRISTEVSKI, ALEX C. clinical psychologist; b. May 12, 1956; BA, Ind. U., 1980, MS, 1983; PsyD, Chgo. Sch. Profl. Psychology, 1990. Bd. cert. med. psychologist Acad. Med. Psychology. Staff clin. psychologist ABJ-VA Outpatient Clinic, Crown Point, Ind., 1990—. VA faculty affiliate Northwestern U. Med. Sch., 1990—. Fellow Am. Bd. Med. Psychotherapists (diplomate), Internat. Coll. Prescribing Psychologists (diplomate), Prescribing Psychologists Register; mem. APA, Mich. Psychol. Assn., Soc. Clin. and Exptl. Hypnosis. Home: 2834 Painted Leaf Dr Crown Point IN 46307-8132 E-mail: drack@mail.icongrp.com.

KRISTIANSEN, MAGNE, electrical engineer, educator; b. Elverum, Norway, Apr. 14, 1932; came to U.S., 1958, naturalized, 1967; s. Martin and Ella (Sobye) K.; m. Aud Bohn, July 6, 1957; children: Sonja Bohn, Eric Bohn. BS in Elec. Engring., U. Tex., Austin, 1961, PhD (Ford Found. fellow), 1967. Registered profl. engr., Tex. Rsch. engr. U. Tex., Austin, 1964-66; faculty Tex. Tech U., Lubbock, 1966—, prof., 1971—, P.W. Horn prof., 1977—, C.B. Thornton prof., 1990—2002; dir. plasma lab. Ctr. for Pulsed Power and Power Electronics, Lubbock, 1966—, dir. pulsed power lab., 1980—; v.p. rsch. and engring. Enfitek, Inc., Lubbock, 1987-90; v.p. R & D Integrated Tech. Inc., Lubbock, 1990-98. Cons. def. products divsn. Varo, Inc., Garland, Tex., 1970-71; cons. Aerospace Corp., El Segundo, Calif., 1974-76, BDM Corp., Albuquerque, 1975-76, 85-87, Palisades Inst., N.Y. and NRC, 1977, Rockwell Internat., 1978, Maxwell Labs., 1979-83, LaJolla Inst., 1979, NASA, 1979, Norwegian Rsch. Coun., 1980, Sci. Applications, Inc., 1983-88, 91-92, Lawrence Livermore Nat. Lab., 1983-95, McDonnell Douglas, 1986, LTV Missiles and Electronics Group, 1987-89, NEA-Lindberg A/S, 1988, Physics Internat. Co., 1992-97, Rocket Rsch. Co., 1992, Swedish Def. Rsch. Inst., 1992-2000; Hazeltine Ocean Sys., 1995, Lockheed Martin, 1995-96, 2003, Integrated Technologies, Inc., 1998—; collaborator Los Alamos Nat. Lab., 1974-95, others; contractor DNA, 1986-97, NASA, 1990-2001, Wright Aeronautical Labs., 1994—. Co-author: An Introduction to Controlled Thermonuclear Fusion, 1977, Russian, Japanese, Chinese translations, 1980-81, Rotating Mirror Cameras, 1997; co-editor: Advances in Pulsed Power Technology, 1984—. Contbr. articles to profl. jours. Mem. USAF Sci. Adv. Bd., 1981-85. Served with Royal Norwegian Air Force, 1950-58. Recipient Meritorious Civilian Svc. award USAF, 1985, Excellence award Halliburton Found., 1994; grantee State of Tex., 1966-85, 88-94, NSF, 1967-87, AEC, 1968-71, Air Force Office Sci. Rsch., 1968—, Army Rsch. Lab., 1994—, Dept. Energy, 1978-79; sr. fellow in sci. NATO, 1975, fellow Japan Soc. for Promotion Sci., 1979. Fellow IEEE (life, Pulsed Power Conf. Peter Haas award 1987, Nuc. and Plasma Sci. Soc. Merit award 1991, Millennium medal), Am. Phys. Soc.; mem. AAAS, Russian Acad. Scis. (fgn. mem., Ural sect.), Am. Soc. Engring. Edn., Sigma Xi, Tau Beta Pi, Eta Kappa Nu, Phi Kappa Phi. Home: 3105 78th St Lubbock TX 79423-1815 Office: Tex Tech U Dept Elec/Computer Engring Lubbock TX 79409-3102 E-mail: m.kristiansen@coe.ttu.edu.

KRISTIN, KAREN, artist; b. L.A., Aug. 27, 1943; d. Earle Barnard and Ann Maxine (Taylor) Immel; m. Richard Edward Amend, Aug. 21, 1976 (div. Aug. 1981); m. Gary Marchal Lloyd, Oct. 1, 1985 (div. Sept.1989). Student, Art Ctr. Coll. Design, 1961, Valley Jr. Coll., 1962, Pierce Jr. Coll., 1967, 68, UCLA, 1969, 70. Lectr. UCLA Ext. Program, 1973-76; scenic artist Hollywood, Calif., 1978-83; ptnr., designer, lead painter Sky Art Scenic Art Svcs., Hollywood, Calif., 1983-88; owner, pres., lead painter, designer Sky Art Karen Kristin, Inc., Englewood, Colo., 1989—. Spkr., lectr. in field. Co-author (under Karen Kristin Amend): Handwriting Analysis: The Complete Basic Book, 1980, Achieving Compatbility with Handwriting-Analysis, vol. I, Understanding Your Emotional Relationships, 1992, vol. II, Exploring Your Sexual Relationships, 1992; prin. murals include The Cirque Du Soleil Theater, Las Vegas, 1993, N.Mex. Mus. Natural History, 1989, 90, Forum Shops at Caesars, Las Vegas, 1992, 97, Kansas City Station Hotel and Casino, Kansas City, Mo., 1996, Sunset Station Hotel and Casino, Las Vegas, 1997, Venetian Hotel Grand Canal Shoppes, Las Vegas, 1998, Chaitanya Joti Mus., Puttaparthy, India, 2000, Hyatt Casino, Blackhawk, Colo., 2001, Argosy Casino, Kans. City, Mo., 2003; sky art backdrops for numerous movies, commls., and TV. Mem. Am. Assn. Handwriting Analysts (spkr. 1991—), Am. Handwriting Analysis Found. (sprk. 1991—), Human Graphics Ctr., Graphex Internat. and Gold NIBS, Universal Soc. of

Integral Why (mentor 1994—). Democrat. Avocations: photography, reading, traveling, camping, fishing. Office: Sky Art Karen Kristin Inc 3051 S Broadway Englewood CO 80110-1528 E-mail: skyartkk@aol.com.

KRISTOF, KATHY M. journalist; b. Burbank, Calif., Feb. 4, 1960; d. Joseph E. and Frances S. Kristof; m. Richard R. Magnuson, Jr., Jan. 4, 1986 (div.); 2 children. BA, U. So. Calif., L.A., 1983. Reporter L.A. Bus. Jour., 1984-88, Daily News, Woodland Hills, Calif., 1988-89, L.A. Times, 1989—; syndicated columnist L.A. Times Syndicate, 1991—. Author: Kathy Kristof's Complete Book of Dollars and Sense, 1997, Investing 101, 2000, Taming the Tuition Tiger, 2003; contbr. articles to mags. and profl. jours. Recipient John Hancock Fin. Svcs. award, 1992, Personal Fin. Writing award ICI/Am. U., 1994, Consumer Adv. of Yr., Calif. Alliance for Consumer Edn., 1998. Mem. Soc. Bus. Editors and Writers (pres. 2003), Calif. Newspapers Pubs. Assn. (2nd pl. Bus. and Fin. Story award 1999). Office: Los Angeles Times 202 W 1st St Los Angeles CA 90012 E-mail: kathy.kristof@latimes.com.

KRISTOF, LADIS KRIS DONABED, political scientist, writer; b. Cernauti, Romania, Nov. 26, 1918; came to U.S., 1952, naturalized, 1957; s. Witold and Maria (Zawadzki) Krzysztofowicz; m. Jane McWilliams, Dec. 29, 1956; 1 son, Nicholas. Student, U. Poznan, Poland, 1937-39; BA, Reed Coll., Portland, Oreg., 1955; MA, U. Chgo., 1956, PhD, 1969. Regional exec. dir., Sovromlemn, Romania, 1948; sales mgr. Centre du Livre Suisse, Paris, France, 1951-52; lectr. U. Chgo., 1958-59; assoc. dir. Inter-Univ. Project History Menshevism, N.Y.C., 1959-62; mem. faculty dept. polit. sci. Temple U., 1962-64; research fellow Hoover Instn., Stanford U., 1964-67; faculty polit. sci. U. Santa Clara, 1967-68; asso. Studies Communist System, Stanford, 1968-69; mem. faculty polit. sci. U. Waterloo, Ont., Can., 1969-71; prof. polit. sci. Portland (Oreg.) State U., 1971-89, prof. emeritus, 1990—. Vis. prof. U. Wroclaw, Poland, 1990, U. Iasi, Romania, 1991, U. Punjab, India, 1992. Author: The Nature of Frontiers and Boundaries, 1959, The Origins and Evolution of Geopolitics, 1960, The Russian Image of Russia, 1967, The Geopolitical Contours of the Post-Cold War World, 1992; also articles in Romania; co-author, co-editor: Revolution and Politics in Russia, 1972. Active Internat. YMCA Center, Paris, 1950-52, NAACP, Chgo., 1957-59, Amnesty Internat., Portland, 1975— . Served with Corps Engrs. Romanian Army, 1940-45. Fulbright scholar Romania, 1971, 84 Mem. Am. Polit. Sci. Assn., Assn. Am. Geographers, Am. Assn. for Advancement of Slavic Studies, Internat. Polit. Sci. Assn., Western Slavic Assn. (pres. 1988-90), Am.-Romanian Acad. Arts and Scis. (v.p. 1995-00). Home: 23050 NW Roosevelt Dr Yamhill OR 97148-8336 Office: Portland State Univ Dept Polit Sci Portland OR 97207 E-mail: kristofj@pdx.edu. *War, want and concentration camps, exile from home and homeland, these have made me hate strife among men, but they have not made me lose faith in the future of mankind. Personal experience, including my own unsteady progress through life, has taught me to beware of man's capacity for plain stupid, irrational, as well as consciously evil behavior, but it also has taught me that man has an even greater capacity for recovery from lapses. In a short thrust of planned, wisely guided activity he is able to climb to higher levels of material and intellectual achievement than he ever reached before. In short, I remain a rationalist and an optimist at a time when the prophets of doom have the floor. My query is, if man has been able to create the arts, the sciences and the material civilization we know in America, why should he be judged powerless to create justice, fraternity and peace.*

KRISTOF, NICHOLAS DONABET, journalist; b. Chgo., Apr. 27, 1959; s. Ladis K.D. and Jane (McWilliams) K.; m. Sheryl WuDunn; children: Gregory, Geoffrey, Caroline. BA, Harvard U., 1981; BA and MA in Law, U. Oxford, Eng., 1983; diploma in Arabic, Am. U. in Cairo, 1983-84; student, Taipei Lang. Inst., 1987-88. Econs. reporter N.Y. Times, N.Y.C., 1984-85, fin. corr. L.A. bur., 1985-86, chief Hong Kong bur., 1986-87, chief Beijing bur., 1988-93, chief Tokyo bur., 1995-99, sr. writer, 1993-2000, assoc. mng. editor, 2000—01, columnist, 2001—. Vis. fellow East-West Ctr., 1993; vis. scholar Linfield Coll., 1994, 99. Author: (with S. WuDunn) China Wakes: The Struggle for the Soul of a Rising Power, 1994, Thunder from the East: Portrait of a Rising Asia, 2000. Recipient Pulitzer prize for fgn. reporting, 1990, George Polk award for fgn. reporting L.I. U., N.Y., 1990, Hal Boyle award Overseas Press Club, 1990, Citations for Excellence, 1994, 96, 2000; Rhodes scholar, 1981-83. Avocations: travel, reading, running. Office: New York Times 229 W 43rd St New York NY 10036-3959

KRISTOFF, KARL W. lawyer; b. Buffalo, Mar. 31, 1942; BA, SUNY, Buffalo, 1965; JD, John Marshall Law Sch., 1968. Bar: Ill. 1968, U.S. Supreme Ct. 1974, N.Y. 1976. Ptnr., v.p. dipute resolution divsn., chair edn. law practice group Hodgson, Russ, LLP, Buffalo. Mem. editorial bd. The John Marshall Jour. Practice and Procedure, 1968, active, 1967. Mem. N.Y. Vets. Affairs Commn., 2002—. Maj. gen. ret. N.Y. Air N.G. Mem. Am. Arbitration Assn. (comml. panel arbitrators), Nat. Pub. Employer Labor Rels. Assn., Nat. Coun. Sch. Attys., N.Y. State Assn. Sch. Attys., N.Y. State Pub. Employer Labor Rels. Assn., Edn. Law Assn. Office: Hodgson Russ LLPr One M&T Plz Ste 2000 Buffalo NY 14203-2391 E-mail: kkristof@hodgsonruss.com.

KRISTOFFERSON, KARL ERIC, writer; b. Jacksonville, Fla., Mar. 3, 1929; s. Gustave Edward and Oma Nancy (Reynolds) K.; m. Barbara Elaine Dalton, Jan. 22, 1954; children: Karol, Paul, Scott AA, Jacksonville U., 1961; BS with honors in Journalism, U. Fla., 1963. Engring. writer Pratt & Whitney Aircraft Co., West Palm Beach, Fla., 1963; publs. supr. Ling-Temco-Vought Ops. and Boeing Co., Kennedy Space Ctr., Fla., 1964-72; chief pub. affairs IRS Dist. Hdqrs., Greensboro, N.C., 1972-74; senior writer, editor NASA Pub. Affairs, Kennedy Space Ctr., 1974-88, news chief, 1988-93. Freelance writer for TV, motion pictures and maj. nat. mags. and publs., 1960—; regular assignment writer Reader's Digest; corr. Titusville Star Advocate, 1995—Fla. Today, 1995—. Served with USAF, 1950-53, Korea Decorated Air medal; recipient Apollo, Skylab, Apollo-Soyuz, Voyager, Space Shuttle Achievement awards NASA, 1969-93, Aviation Space Writers' Assn. award for articles writing, 1974 Mem. Canaveral Press Club.

KRISTOL, DANIEL MARVIN, lawyer; b. July 7, 1936; s. Abraham Louis and Pearl Cecile (Oltman) K.; m. Katherine Fairfax Chinn, Nov. 4, 1968; children: Sarah Douglas, Susan Fairfax. BA, U. Pa., 1958, LLB, 1961. Bar: Del. 1961, U.S. Dist. Ct. Del. 1962. Assoc., ptnr. Killoran & VanBrunt, Wilmington, Del., 1961-76; dir. Prickett, Jones, Elliott & Kristol, Wilmington, 1976-99; ptnr. predecessor Prickett, Ward Burt & Sanders, Wilmington, 1976-99; dir. Richards, Layton & Finger, Wilmington, 1999—. Pub. defender Ct. Common Pleas, Wilmington, 1966-69; asst. solicitor City of Wilmington, 1970-73; spl. counsel Div. Housing State of Del., 1972-87, gen. counsel Del. State Housing Authority, 1973-99. With USAR, 1964-67. Mem. ABA, Del. State Bar Assn. (chmn. real and personal property com. 1974-78, chmn. world peace through law com. 1980-81, chmn. sr. lawyers com. 1999—), Am. Coll. Real Estate Lawyers, Wilmington Country Club, Greenville Country Club, Mill Reef Club (Antigua, W.I.), Wilmington Club, Penn Club of N.Y.. Republican. Jewish. Office: PO Box 551 Wilmington DE 19899-0551 E-mail: kristol@rlf.com.

KRISTOL, WILLIAM, editor, political analyst; b. Dec. 23, 1952; s. Irving Kristol and Gertrude Himmelfarb; m. Susan Scheinberg, Dec. 28, 1975; children: Rebecca Louise, Anne Elizabeth, Joseph Max. AB, Harvard U., 1973, PhD, 1979. Instr., then asst. prof. polit. sci. U. Pa., Phila., 1978-83; asst. prof. pub. policy Harvard U., Cambridge, Mass., 1983-85; spl. asst., chief of staff Dept. Edn., Washington, 1985-89; campaign mgr. Alan Keyes for Senate, Md., 1988; domestic policy advisor Office of V.P., Washington, 1989, chief of staff to v.p., 1989-93; dir. Bradley Project of 90s, Washington, 1993; chmn. Project for the Rep. Future, Washington, 1993-95; editor The Weekly Standard, Washington, 1995—. Jewish. Office: 1150 17th St NW Ste 505 Washington DC 20036-4621

KRISTY, JAMES E. financial management consultant; b. Kenosha, Wis., Sept. 3, 1929; s. Eugene H. and Ann T. Kristy; m. Edith L. Reid, Feb. 19, 1955; children: James R., Ann E., Robert E. BS in Econs., U. Wis., 1951; MBA in Fin., U. So. Calif., 1964; postgrad., Claremont (Calif.) Grad. Sch.; PhD in Mgmt. and Edn., Columbia Pacific U., 1981. V.p. Lloyds Bank Calif., L.A., 1969-71; chief treasury officer Computer Machinery Corp., L.A., 1971-75; sr. v.p., CFO Century Bank, L.A., 1979; vis. prof. Chapman U., 1995—. Cons., writer and lectr. in field; seminar leader Frost & Sullivan, London, CEL Ltd., Hong Kong, U. Calif., U. Hawaii, U. Colo., Temple U., Rutgers U., Tulane U. Author: Analyzing Financial Statements: Quick and Clean, 6th edit., 2003, Handbook of Budgeting, 1992; (with others) Finance Without Fear, 1983, Commercial Credit Matrix Software, 2002. 1st. lt. U.S. Army, 1951-53, Korea. Recipient Pub. Svc. award SBA, 1971. Address: PO Box 113 Buena Park CA 90621-0113 E-mail: edskrs@msn.com.

KRITCHEVSKY, DAVID, biochemist, educator; b. Kharkov, Russia, Jan. 25, 1920; came to U.S., 1923, naturalized, 1929; s. Jacob and Leah (Kritchevsky) K.; m. Evelyn Sholtes, Dec. 21, 1947; children: Barbara Ann, Janice Eileen, Stephen Bennett. BS, U. Chgo., 1939, MS, 1942; PhD, Northwestern U., 1948; DSc (hon.), Purdue U., 2001. Chemist Ninol Labs., Chgo., 1939-46; postdoctoral fellow Fed. Inst. Tech., Zurich, Switzerland, 1948-49; biochemist Radiation Lab., U. Calif. at Berkeley, 1950-52, Lederle Lab., Pearl River, N.Y., 1952-57, Wistar Inst., Phila., 1957—; prof. biochemistry Sch. Vet. Medicine U. Pa., Phila., 1965—; prof. emeritus, 1992—; prof. biochemistry Sch. Medicine U. Pa., 1970—81, chmn. grad. group molecular biology, 1972-84. Mem. USPHS study sect. Nat. Heart Inst., 1964-68, 72-76; chmn. rsch. com. Spl. Dairy Industry Bd., 1963-70; food and nutrition bd. NAS, 1976-82. Author: Cholesterol, 1958; editor: (with G. Litwack) Actions of Hormones on Molecular Processes, 1964; co-editor: (with R. Paoletti) Advances in Lipid Research, 1963-89, (with P. Nair) 1973, Bile Acids, 1971; Western Hemisphere editor Atherosclerosis, 1978-90, cons. editor, 1990—; contbr. articles to profl. jours. Recipient Rsch. Career award Nat. Heart Inst., 1962, Herman award Am. Soc. Clin. Nutrition, 1992, Disting. Svc. award U. N.C. Inst. Nutrition, 1993, Auenbrugger medal U. Graz, Austria, 1994, SUPELCO/AOCS award, 1996, Lifetime Achievement award Am. Inst. for Cancer Rsch., 1996; Caspar Wistar scholar, 1992. Fellow: AAAS, Am. Soc. Oil Chemists (chmn. methods com. 1963—64), Am. Coll. Nutrition (award 1978), Am. Inst. Nutrition (pres. 1979, Borden award 1974), Am. Oil Chemists Soc.; mem.: Am. Oil Chemistry Soc., Internat. Soc. Fat Rsch., Am. Heart Assn. (spl. recognition coun. on atherosclerosis 1993), Arteriosclerosis Coun., Soc. Exptl. Biology and Medicine (pres. 1985—87), Am. Chem. Soc. (award Phila. sect. 1977), Am. Soc. Biol. Chemists. Achievements include research on role vehicle when cholesterol and fat produces atherosclerosis in rabbits, effects of saturated and unsaturated fat, deposition of orally administered cholesterol in aorta of man and rabbit, caloric restriction and cancer. Home: 136 Lee Cir Bryn Mawr PA 19010-3724 Office: Wistar Inst 36th And Spruce St Philadelphia PA 19104-4268 E-mail: kritchevsky@wistar.upenn.edu.

KRITCHEVSKY, STEPHEN BENNETT, epidemiologist, educator; b. Phila., July 15, 1960; s. David and Evelyn S. Kritchevsky; m. Nannette C. Gover, Feb. 2, 1982; children: Alexander, Samuel, Caleb. BA, U. Chgo., 1982; MSPH, U. N.C., 1986, PhD, 1989. Asst. prof. U. Tenn., Memphis, 1989—95, assoc. prof., 1995—2001, prof., 2001—03; prof. dept. internal medicine, sect. on gerontology and geriatric medicine Wake Forest U. Med. Sch., Winston-Salem, 2003—, dir. rsch. J. Paul Sticht Ctr. on Aging, 2003—. Mem. Soc. for Epidemiologic Rsch., Soc. Healthcare Epidemiology, Am. Coll. Epidemiology, Gerontol. Soc. Am., Am. Soc. for Nutritional Scis. Office: Wake Forest Univ J Paul Sticht Ctr on Aging Medical Center Blvd Winston Salem NC 27157

KRITIKOS, HARALAMBOS NICHOLAS, electrical engineering educator; b. Tripoli, Greece; PhD, U. Pa., 1961. Prof. elec. engring. U. Pa., until 1999, prof. emeritus, 1999—. Mem. IEEE (assoc. editor transactions 1986, 88, exec. editor 1981-85). Address: 200 S 33rd St Philadelphia PA 19104-6314

KRITZER, GLENN BRUCE, lawyer; b. Newark, June 13, 1947; s. Julius B. and Ethyl (Rosenthal) K.; children: Rebecca, Gary. Student, Lehigh U., 1965-67; BA with distinction, U. Wis., 1969; JD, NYU, 1972. Bar: N.Y. 1973, U.S. Dist. Ct. (so. dist.) N.Y. 1974, U.S. Dist. Ct. (ea. dist.) N.Y. 1975, U.S. Ct. Appeals (2d cir.) 1975, Calif. 1977, Fla. 1980, U.S. Ct. Appeals (5th cir.) 1980, U.S. Dist. Ct. (so. dist.) Fla. 1981, U.S. Ct. Appeals (11th cir.) 1981, U.S. Dist. Ct. (trial bar) Fla. 1982, U.S. Supreme Ct. 1985, U.S. Dist. Ct. (ea. dist.) Wis. 1985, U.S. Ct. Appeals (7th cir.) 1986, U.S. Dist. Ct. (mid. dist.) Fla. 1990. Examining atty. N.Y.C. Dept. Investigation, 1972-73, dep. dir. bur. city marshals, 1973-74, dir. bur. city marshals, 1974-76, spl. asst. dist. atty., 1975, spl. asst. corp. counsel, 1976; assoc. Herzfeld & Rubin P.C., N.Y.C., 1976-77; asst. U.S. atty. Office of U.S. Atty. (ea. dist.) N.Y., 1977-79, Office of U.S. Atty. (so. dist.) Fla., 1979-82; pvt. practice Miami, 1982—. Mem. Nat. Assn. Criminal Def. Lawyers, Fla. Assn. Criminal Def. Lawyers (bd. dirs. Miami chpt.), Fed. Bar Assn., Asst. U.S. Attys. Assn., Dade County Bar Assn. Office: 799 Brickell Plz Ste 700 Miami FL 33131-2805 E-mail: glennbkritzeresq@aol.com.

KRITZER, PAUL ERIC, media executive, communications lawyer; b. Buffalo, May 5, 1942; s. James Cyril and Bessie May (Biddlecombe) K.; m. Frances Jean McCallum, June 20, 1970; children: Caroline Frances, Erica Hopkins. BA, Williams Coll., 1964; MS in Journalism, Columbia U., 1965; JD, Georgetown U., 1972. Bar: U.S. Supreme Ct. 1978, Wis. 1980. Reporter, copy editor Buffalo Evening News, 1964, 69, 70; instr. English Augusta (Ga.) Coll., 1968-69; law clk. Office of FCC Commr., Washington, 1971, MCI, Washington, 1972; counsel U.S. Ho. of Reps., Washington, 1972-77; assoc. counsel Des Moines Register & Tribune, 1977-80; editor, pub. Waukesha (Wis.) Freeman, 1980-83; legal v.p., sec. Jour. Communications Inc., Milw., 1983—. Trustee Carroll Co., Waukesha, 1981-89; producer Waukesha Film Festival, 1982; bd. dirs. Des Moines Metro Opera, Inc., 1979-80; bd. dirs. Milw. Youth Symphony Orch., 1992-2001, pres. 1994-97; bd. dirs. Milw. Symphony Orch., 1997—; bd. dirs. United Performing Arts Fund, 1994-97. With U.S. Army, 1965-68. Presbyterian. Avocations: bridge, gardening. Home: 211 Oxford Rd Waukesha WI 53186-6263 Office: Jour Communications Inc 333 W State St PO Box 661 Milwaukee WI 53201-0661 Business E-Mail: pkritzer@jc.com.

KRITZMAN, LAWRENCE DAVID, humanities educator; b. N.Y.C. s. Melvin M. and Margy (Rosenstein) K.; m. Janie L. Kritzman; 1 child, Jeremy. BA, U. Wis., 1969; AM, Middlebury Coll., 1970; PhD, U. Mich., 1976. Lectr. Rutgers U., New Brunswick, N.J., 1976-77, asst. prof., 1977-82, assoc. prof., dir. grad. studies, 1982-87; prof. French civilization Ohio State U., Columbus, 1987-89; prof. French & comparative lit. Dartmouth Coll., Hanover, N.H., 1989—, Edward Tuck prof. French, 1994—, chair comparative lit. dept., 1992-95, Ted and Helen Geisel Third Century prof. in the humanities, 1995—2002, Pat and John Rosenwald rsch. prof. in Arts and Scis., 2002—. Chair Com. for Future of French Studies, French Embassy, N.Y., 1991—; vis. prof. U. Mich., Ann Arbor, 1991, 93, Duke NEH Inst., 1986, 90, Northwestern NEH Inst., assoc. dir., 1995; vis. prof. Stanford U., 1999, Harvard U., 2001, 2003. Author: Destruction/Découverte, 1980, Rhetoric of Sexuality and Literature fo French Renaissance, 1991; editor: Fragments, 1981, France Under Mitterand, 1984, Foucault: Politics, Philosophy, Culture, 1988, Le Signe et le Texte, 1989, Auschwitz & After: Race, Culture & The Jewish Question in France, 1995; mem. editl. bd.: Etudes Montaignistes, 1988, Montaigne Studies, Early Modern Culture, Studies in 20th Century Literature, Contemporary French Civilization Sites, French Forum, Sites, gen. editor: European Perspectives, 1989—, Columbia U. Press, —, mem. adv. bd.: French Politics and Society, —; contbr. . Chair Com. Future of French Studies in U.S.; dir. Edward Morot-Inst. French Cultural Studies, 1994, 1997, 1999, 2001, 2003. Recipient Chevalier de l'Ordre des Palmes Academics, French Govt., 1991, Ordre National de Merite by Pres. France, 2000; Officier des Palmes des Palmes Academics, 1994; sr. fellow Am. Coun. Learned Soc., 1989; Andrew W. Mellon Found. grant Duke U., 1980. Mem. MLA, Am. Coun. French Social and Cultural Affairs, Nat. Writer's Union, Am. Comparative Lit. Assn., Acad. Lit. Studies. Home: 24 Warwick Rd Brookline MA 02445 Office: Dept French Dartmouth Coll Hanover NH 03755

KRIVAI, GALINA, manufacturing executive; b. Odessa, Ukraine, Dec. 18, 1936; arrived in U.S., 1977; d. Alexander Sophia Batist; m. Michael Krivai, Apr. 27, 1962; children: Mark, Marat. Degree, Economy Coll. of Russia, 1962. Economist Russian Bank of Odessa, 1960—62; cosmetologist Rome, 1977—78; pres. Gleem Industries, Inc., Bklyn., 1992—. Avocation: gardening.

KRIVAN, HOWARD CALVIN, microbiologist; s. Edward D. and Irene Frazzini; m. Gail P. Popelka, Feb. 12, 2000; children: Mitchell Calvin, Madison Marie. BS, U. of N.Mex, 1980, MS, 1982; PhD, Va. Tech, 1986. Staff fellow NIH, Bethesda, Md., 1987—89; v.p. BioCarb, INc., Gaithersburg, Md., 1989—91; exec. v.p. MicroCarb Inc., Gaithersburg, Md., 1991—94; prof. Am. U. Caribbean, Plymouth, Montserrat, 1994—95; pres., chief sci. officer, bd. mem. Legere Pharmaceuticals, Ltd., Carson City, Nev., 1995—. Bd. dirs. MicroCarb, Inc., Gaithersburg, Md., 1991—94, Legere Pharmaceuticals, Ltd., Carson City, Nev., 1996—; vis. prof. Am. U. of Caribbean, Cupecoy, 2002. Author: (sci. article) Jour. Antimicrobial Chemotherapy, (sci. book) Bacterial Pathogenesis, (over 50 sci. articles) Infection & Immunity, J. Biol. Chem., Molecular Microbiology. Recipient Intramural Rsch. Tng. award, NIH, 1987; fellow, 1988. Mem.: AAAS, Am. Chem. Soc., Am. Soc. of Microbiology. Independent. Achievements include patents for 18 U.S. patents in Biotechnology/Microbiology; patents pending for 6 pending applications in Biotechnology. Avocations: scuba diving, fishing, camping, tennis, gardening. Office: Legere Pharmaceuticals Ltd 3123 Research Way Carson City NV 89706 Home Fax: 775-888-2063; Office Fax: 775-841-2263. Personal E-mail: biotahoe@earthlink.net.

KRIVKOVICH, PETER GEORGE, advertising executive; b. Bad Ischl, Austria, Oct. 25, 1946; came to U.S., 1953; s. George M. Krivkovich and Ada (Kalenkiewicz) Bajor; m. Linda J. Monken, Aug. 30, 1970; children: Peter A., Alexis C. BS, U. Ill., 1969; postgrad., Loyola U., Chgo., 1972-73. Advt. asst. Kemper Ins. Co., Chgo., 1969-71; account exec. Nader-Lief, Chgo., 1971-72; account mgr. Leo Burnett, Chgo., 1972-73; ptnr. Hackenberg, Normann, Krivkovich, Chgo., 1973-80; pres. Cramer-Krasselt, Chgo., 1981-86, pres., COO, 1987-98, pres., CEO, chmn. bd., 1999—; pres., CEO CKPR, 2002—. Mem. Nat. Advt. Rev. Bd. Bd. dirs. Off The Street Club, Prentice Hosp., Chgo. Humanities Festival, Mfrs. Bank, 1993—2002. Named One of 100 Best and Brightest Advt. Execs. of Yr. Advt. Age mag., 1986, Midwest Advt. Exec. of Yr. Adweek mag., 1987. Mem. Am. Assn. Advt. Agys. (chmn. Chgo. chpt. 1992, 93, regional bd. govs. 1996, 97, nat. bd. govs. 1998-2002), Direct Mktg. Assn., Chgo. Assn. Direct Mktg., Chgo. Advt. Club, Glenview (Ill.) C. of C., Tavern Club, Exec. Club. Office: Cramer-Krasselt 225 N Michigan Ave Ste 800 Chicago IL 60601-7690 E-mail: pkrivkov@c-k.com.

KRIVOSHEIN, ARCADIUS V. research scientist; b. Krasnodar, Russia, Aug. 28, 1973; MS in Biology, Kuban State U., Russia, 1995; PhD in Chemistry, Russian Acad. of Scis., Moscow, 1998. Cert. Tchr. Biology & Chemistry Ministry of Higher Edn., Russia, 1995. Rsch. assoc. Barrow Neurol. Inst., Phoenix, 1999—2000; postdoctoral assoc. Cornell U., Ithaca, NY, 2000—03, rsch. assoc., 2003—. Contbr. articles to profl. jours. Fellow Hon. Diploma Fellowship, Kuban State U., Russia, 1991—95. Mem.: N.Y. Acad. Scis., Soc. Neurosci., Biophys. Soc. Achievements include research in Biophysics and biochemistry of neurotransmitter receptors; discovery of Secondary structure of nicotinic receptor domains; Chemical compounds alleviating neuronal effects of cocaine; first to Mass Spectrometry of an Intact Neurotransmitter Receptor. Office: Cornell U 217 Biotechnology Bldg Ithaca NY 14853-2703

KRIZ, GEORGE JAMES, former agricultural research administrator; b. Brainard, Nebr., Sept. 20, 1936; s. George Jacob and Rose Agnes Kriz; m. Patricia Elizabeth Kelly (div. Feb. 1989); children: Rosalie Sue, Richard Patrick, Thomas George; m. Rhoda Mae Whitacre, June 23, 1989. BS in Agrl. Engring., Iowa State U., 1960, MS in Agrl. Engring., 1962; PhD, U. Calif., Davis, 1965. Lectr. U. Calif., Davis, 1965; asst. prof. agrl. engring. N.C. State U., Raleigh, 1965-68, assoc. prof., 1968-72, prof., 1972-99, assoc. dept. head, 1969-73, asst. rsch. dir., 1973-81, assoc. rsch. dir., 1981-99, prof. emeritus, 1999—. Operator bed and breakfast. Fellow Am. Soc. Agrl. Engring. (bd. dirs. 1983-85, found. trustee 1986-94, 96-97, pres. 1995-96, presdl. citation 1988, 91); mem. Coun. Agrl. Scis. and Tech. Avocations: gardening, walking. E-mail: gkriz@visuallink.com.

KRIZAN, KELLY JOE, physician, leather craftsman; b. Winner, SD, Jan. 16, 1951; s. Miles Woodrow and Sadie Mae (DeSmet) K.; m. Susan Barker, Aug. 21, 1971 (div. Aug. 1983); children: Jennifer Rebecca, Nicholas Miles; m. Cynthia Lydia Obras, Aug. 6, 1983. BS, SD State U., 1973; BS in Medicine, U. SD, 1976; MD, Tufts U., 1978. Diplomate Am. Bd. Family Practice. Commd., Am. Bd. Radiology. (first active duty capt. US Air Force, 1978, advanced through grades to lt. col., 1984. Intern USAF Med. Ctr., Scott AFB, Ill., 1978-79, resident, 1979-81; staff physicain USAF Hosp., Hill AFB, Utah, 1981-83; chief emergency svcs., chief family practice USAF Hosp., Hill AFB, Utah, Incirlik AB, Turkey, 1983-84, chmn. dept. family practice, 1985-86; resident radiology U. Wash., 1986-90, clin. asst. prof., 1990—; chmn. dept. radiology 13th AF Med. Ctr., Clark AB, Philippines, 1990-91, St. Mary's Health Care Ctr., Pierre, SD, 1993—, chmn. radiology, 1993—, chief of staff, 1997. Pres. bd. dir. Oahe Inc., 2001—; bd. dirs. Pierre Players, Short Grass Art Coun., St. Mary's Found.; Artist leather goods, winner various awards. U. SD Presdl. scholar, 1969. Am. Top Radiologists consumer's Rsch. Coun. of Am., Fellow Am. Acad. Family Physicians; mem. Am. Coll. Radiology (mem. rural econ. com. 2003—), mem. ACR Rural Econ. Comm. - 2003, Am. Roentgen Ray Soc., Radiol. Soc. N.Am., Phi Kappa Phi. Roman Catholic. E-mail: kellykrizan@catholichealth.net.

KRIZEK, RAYMOND JOHN, civil engineering educator, consultant; b. Balt., June 5, 1932; s. John James and Louise (Polak) K.; m. Claudia Stricker, Aug. 1964; children— Robert A., Kevin J. BE, Johns Hopkins U., 1954; MS, U. Md., 1961; PhD, Northwestern U., 1963. Instr. U. Md., College Park, 1957-61; rsch. asst. civil engring. Northwestern U., Evanston, Ill., 1961-63, asst. prof. civil engring., 1963-66, assoc. prof. civil engring., 1966-70, prof. civil engring., 1970—, chmn. dept. civil engring., 1980-92, dir. Master of Project Mgmt. program, 1994—, Stanley F. Pepper chair prof., 1987—. Cons. to industry Editor books; contbr. numerous articles to profl. jours. Served to lt. U.S. Army, 1955-57 Decorated Palmes Academiques (France), 1993; recipient Hogentogler award ASTM, 1970; named disting. vis. scholar NSF, 1972. Mem.: ASCE (pres. GEO Inst. 1997—98, Huber Rsch. prize 1971, Karl Terzaghi award 1997, Ill. sect. Civil Engr. of Yr. 1999, Hon. mem. 2002, Wallace Hayward Baker award Geo-Inst. 2003), Internat. Soc. Soil Mechanics and Geotech. Engring., Nat. Acad. Engring., Spanish Acad. Engring. (corr.). Roman Catholic. Home: 1366 Sanford Ln Glenview IL 60025-3165 Office: Dept Civil Engring Northwestern U 2145 Sheridan Rd Evanston IL 60208-3109

KRMPOTICH, FRANK ZVONKO, fiberglass company executive, consultant; b. Zagreb, Croatia, Feb. 17, 1948; came to U.S., 1983; s. Franjo and Anica (Pavlich) K.; m. Jana Snjezana Fabjanovich, May 25, 1973; children: Kris, Tomi. BSME, U. Zagreb, 1978; Degree in Arctic Engring. (hon.), U. Anchorage, 1985. Design engr. Fiberglass Fabricator, Zagreb, 1976-79; sr. design engr. Mech. Engring. Inst., Zagreb, 1979-84; prin. engr. Alaska Engring., Anchorage, 1984-87; sr. design engr. Test Co., Anchorage, 1987-89, Ershigs, Bellingham, Wash., 1989-90, Chemetics Internat., Vancouver, B.C., Can., 1991-93; sr. design cons. engr. Fiberglass Cons. Engring., Bellingham, 1990-91, CEO, 1994—. Cons. engr., Bellingham, 1990—. Author: FRP Equipment Design, 1994. Pres. Croatian Bus. Assn., Zagreb-Seattle, 1991. Mem. ASME, NSPE, Nat. Assn. Corrosion Engrs., Soc. Plastic Industry. Republican. Roman Catholic. Avocations: tennis, hockey, soccer. Home: 3111 Crestline Dr Bellingham WA 98226-4206 E-mail: zkrmpotich@home.com., fkrmpotich@asme.org.

KROB, MELANIE GORDON, writer; b. Houston, June 19, 1970; d. Robert Allen and Connie Marshall Gordon; m. Adam Nelson Krob, May 16, 1998. BA, U. of the South, 1992; PhD, Tulane U., 1998. Tchg. asst. Tulane U., New Orleans, 1992-98; freelance writer, 1998—. Contbr. articles to profl. jours. Exch. fellow Freie U., Berlin, 1995-96, Mellon fellow Mellon Found., Tulane U., 1997; rsch. grantee Deutscher Akademischer Austausch Dienst, Berlin, 1998, German Exile Rsch. grantee U. So. Calif., L.A., 1999. E-mail: mgkrob@hotmail.com.

KROBATH, KRISTA ANN, pharmacist; b. Pottsville, Pa., July 8, 1962; d. James Joseph and Gaye Diane (Anderson) E.; m. Gilbert Krobath. BS in Pharmacy, Temple U., 1985. Registered pharmacist. Pharmacist People's Drug, Harrisburg, Pa., 1985-86; pharmacist, mgr. Amcare Health Svcs., Harrisburg, 1986-96; pharmacist Pharmerica, Harrisburg, 1996-99, CFI Pharmacy, Harrisburg, 1999—. Mem. Pa. Pharm. Assn., Capital Area Pharm. Assn.

KROCHALIS, RICHARD F. municipal government official; BS in Environ. Sys. Engring., Cornell U.; M in City and Regional Planning, Harvard U. Dir. dept. constrn. and land use City of Seattle, Seattle, 1992-99, dir. dept. design, constrn. and land use, 1999—. Examiner Wash. State Quality Award Bd., 1995-96. Pres. bd. dirs. Sustainable Seattle; active Cornell U. Alumni Affairs;

mem. coun. Cornell U., 1991-98. Mem. Urban Land Inst., Am. Planning Assn., Am. Inst. Cert. Planners, Wash. State City Planning Dir.'s Assn. (pres.). Office: FederalTransit Adminstrn Ste 3142 915 Second Ave Seattle WA 98174 E-mail: rick.krochalis@ci.seattle.wa.us.

KROCK, CURTIS JOSSELYN, pulmonologist; b. Fort Smith, Ark., Oct. 11, 1935; s. Frederick Henry and Hazel Armiger (Josselyn) Krock; m. Ruth Leone Johnson, Apr. 27, 1968; children: Eric Gregory, Lynn Alyson. BA, Stanford U., 1957; MD, Johns Hopkins U. Sch. Medicine, 1961. Diplomate Am. Bd. Internal Medicine, Am. Bd. Pulmonary Medicine. Intern Barnes Hosp., St. Louis, 1961-62, resident in internal medicine, 1963-65; resident in pathology Johns Hopkins U. Sch. Medicine, Balt., 1962-63; pulmonary fellow Duke U., Durham, N.C., 1965-66; pvt. practice Holt-Krock Clinic, Ft. Smith, Ark., 1968-72, Carle Clinic, Urbana, Ill., 1972-2001, also bd. dirs., 1978-80, chief medicine dept., 1996-99; clin. asst. prof. U. Ill., Urbana, 1976-99, clin. assoc. prof., 2000—; assoc. program dir. med. residency program UICOM-UC; chief of medicine Carle Found. Hosp., 2003—. Capt. U.S. Army, 1966—68. Fellow: ACP; mem.: Sierra Club, Sigma Xi. Avocations: violin, reading. Home: 2125 Lynwood Dr Champaign IL 61821-6606 Office: Carle Clin Edn Ctr Forum Bldg 611 W Park Urbana IL 61801-2530 E-mail: curtis.krock@carle.com.

KROEBER, KARL, English language educator; b. Oakland, Calif., Nov. 24, 1926; s. Alfred Louis and Theodora Quinn (Kracaw) K.; m. Jean Taylor, Mar. 21, 1953; children— Paul Demarest, Arthur Romeyn, Katharine. AA, Coll. of Pacific, Stockton, Calif., 1945; AB, U. Calif., Berkeley, 1947; MA, Columbia U., 1951, PhD, 1956. Asst. prof. U. Wis.-Madison, 1956-61, asso. prof., 1961-63, prof., 1963-70; asso. dean U. Wis.-Madison (Grad. Sch.), 1963-65; prof. English and comparative lit. Columbia U., N.Y.C., 1970—, chmn. dept. English and comparative lit., 1973-76, Mellon prof. humanities, 1987. Author: Romantic Narrative Art, 1960, The Artifice of Reality, 1964, Studying Poetry, 1965, Backgrounds to British Romantic Literature, 1968, Styles in Fictional Structure, 1971, Romantic Landscape Vision, 1975, Images of Romanticism, 1978, Traditional Literatures of the American Indian, 1981, rev. edit. 1997, Wordsworthian Scholarship and Criticism, 1973-84, 1986, British Romantic Art, 1986, Romantic Fantasy and Science Fiction, 1988, Retelling/Rereading, 1992, Romantic Poetry: Recent Revisionary Criticism, 1993, Native American Persistence and Resurgence, 1994, Ecological Literary Criticism, 1994, Artistry in Native American Myths, 1998, Ishi in Three Centuries, 2003; emeritus editor Studies in American Indian Literatures; mem. editorial bd. The Wordsworth Circle, Native American Bibiliography Series, Studies in English Lit., Boundary 2, European Romantic Review. Served with USNR, 1944-46. Named Disting. Scholar, Keats-Shelley Assn., 1991; Fulbright Rsch. grantee Italy, 1960-61, U.S. Office Edn. Rsch. grantee, 1965-66; Guggenheim fellow, 1966-67; NEH fellow, 1991. Mem. MLA, Internat. Assn. Univ. Profs. English, N.Am. Soc. Study of Romanticism, Jane Austen Soc. N.Am., Acad. Lit. Studies, Byron Soc.., Assn. for Study of Native Am. Lit., Keats-Shelley Assn. Home: 226 Saint Johns Pl Brooklyn NY 11217-3406 Office: Columbia U Dept English & Comparative Lit New York NY 10027 Business E-Mail: kk17@columbia.edu.

KROEGER, ARTHUR, former university chancellor, former government official; b. Naco, Alta., Can., Sept. 7, 1932; s. Heinrich and Helena (Rempel) K.; m. Gabrielle Jane Sellers, May 7, 1966 (dec.); children: Alexandra, Kate. BA with honors, U. Alta., 1955; MA, Oxford U., Eng., 1958; LLD (hon.), U. Western Ontario, Can., 1991, U. Calgary, 1995, Carleton U., 2003. Fgn. service officer Can. Dept. External Affairs, 1958-71, treasury bd. secretariat, 1971-75, dep. minister Indian and No. affairs, 1975-79; dep. minister transport Can., Ottawa, Ont., 1979-83; sec. Ministry of State for Econ. Devel., Ottawa, Ont., 1983-84; spl. advisor to clk. Privy Council; dep. minister Regional Indsl. Expansion; dep. minister of Energy, Mines and Resources; dep. minister employment & immigration, 1988-92; chancellor Carleton U., Ottawa, Canada, 1993—2002. Vis. fellow Queen's U., Kingston, Ont., 1994-99; vis. prof. U. Toronto, 1993-94; chmn. Pub. Policy Forum, Ottawa, 1992-94. Program chmn. Gov. Gen.'s Study Conf., 1995; chmn. Can. Policy Rsch. Networks; bd. dirs. The Parliamentary Ctr., Social Rsch. and Demonstration Corp.; mem. Nat. Stats. Coun.; mem. Panel on Voluntary Sector Governance, 1997-99. Decorated companion Order of Can.; recipient Pub. Svc. Outstanding Achievement award, 1989, Disting. Alumnus award U. Alta.; Rhodes scholar, 1955; hon. fellow Pembroke Coll., Oxford. Mem. Can. Assn. Rhodes Scholars (exec. mem., pres. 1995-97). Clubs: Five Lakes Fishing. Home: 245 Springfield Rd Ottawa ON Canada K1M 0L1 E-mail: arthur.kroeger@sympatico.ca.

KROEGER, CATHERINE C. writer, editor, educator; b. St. Paul, Minn., Dec. 12, 1925; d. Homer Pierce Clark and Elizabeth Turner Dunsmoor; m. Richard Clark Kroeger, Dec. 22, 1950; children: Paul, Robert, Elizabeth, Marjorie, Mary. AB, Bryn Mawr Coll., 1947; MA, U. Minn., 1982, PhD, 1987. Founding pres. Christian for Bibl. Equality, Mpls., 1987-95; pres. emerita Christians for Bibl. Equality, Mpls., 1995—; Protestant chaplain Hamilton Coll., Clinton, N.Y., 1987-88; adj. assoc. prof. Gordon Conwell Theol. Sem., South Hamilton, Mass., 1992—. Founding organizer Women in the Bibl. World sect. Soc. Bibl. Lit., 1980-89. Author, editor: Women, Abuse and the Bible, 1996, Healing the Hurting, 1998; co-editor: Study Bible for Women, 1996; editor: InterVarsity Press Women's Bible Commentary, 2002; mem. editl. bd.: Jour. Religion and Abuse, 1999—; co-author (with Nancy Nason-Clark): No Place for Abuse: Biblical and Practical Resources to Counteract Domestic Violence, 2001; author: I Suffer Not A Woman, 1992. Bd. dirs. St. Paul Philharm Soc., 1964-66, Evangels. for Social Action, Phila., 1987-93; bd. dirs., pres. Minn. Sch. Missions, St. Paul, 1959-79; bd. dirs. emerita Whitworth Coll., Spokane, Wash. Fellow Inst. Bibl. Rsch. (exec. bd. 1995-97); mem. Am. Acad. Religion/Soc. Bibl. Lit., Women's Classical Caucus, Archaeol. Inst. Am., Am. Philological Assn. Presbyterian. Avocations: grandchildren, conducting study tours. Home: 1073 Stony Brook Rd Brewster MA 02631-2448 Office: Gordon Conwell Theol Sem 130 Essex St South Hamilton MA 01982-2317 E-mail: ckroeger@world.std.com.

KROEGER, SUSAN JEAN, accountant; b. Glenridge, N.J., July 3, 1961; d. John Alfred and Patricia Ann (Ferrante) Kroeger; m. George Clarence Merrill, June 18, 1983; children: C.J., B.J., G.J., P.J. BA, William Paterson Coll., 1986. CPA, N.J., ins. broker; lic. real estate sales person, N.J., lic. cosmetologist,N.J. Clk. Crum & Foster, Parsippany, N.J., 1980-86, internal auditor, 1986-87; sr. acct. Ernst & Young & Co., Iselin, N.J., 1987-89; pvt. practice Parsippany, 1989—; real estate sales assoc. ERA, Gallo & DeCroce, 1993—. Bd. dirs. PTA, Rockaway Meadow, exec. bd. dirs. Cen. Middle Sch.; exec. bd. dirs. Par Troy East Little League; coach Parsippany Soccer Club. Mem. AICPA, N.J. Soc. CPAs, North Ctrl. Jersey Real Estate Assn., Garden State Multiple Listing Svc. Republican. Roman Catholic. Avocations: camping, golfing.

KROEHLER, RALPH S. association executive; b. Chgo., Mar. 6, 1930; s. Henry G. and Laura S. K.; m. Marjorie A. Engel, Aug. 29, 1952; 1 child, Beth A. Student, Elmhurst Coll., 1947-50. Cert. fundraising exec. Dist. exec. Boy Scouts Am., Freeport, Ill., 1956-60, Allegan, Mich., 1960-63, fin. dir. Grand Rapids, Mich., 1963-67, asst. scout exec., 1967-69, scout exec., CEO Waukegan, Ill., 1969-71, Janesville, Wis., 1971-80, Peoria, Ill., 1980-95. Fundraising cons., Peoria, 1995—. Bd. dir. Peoria City Beautiful, 1982-88; chmn. devel. Peoria Symphony Orch., 2000—; chmn. nat. devel. campaign Palatines to Am., dir.-at-large, 2002—. With US Army, 1951. Mem. Nat. Soc. Fundraising Exec. (del. to nat. assembly 1992-95, pres. Ctrl. Ill. chpt. 1994-95, Outstanding Fundraising Exec. 1993), Rotary Club Peoria (pres. Beloit chpt. 1979-80). Mem. United Ch. of Christ. Avocations: civil war research, genealogy, photography. Home: 6910 N Rockvale Dr Peoria IL 61614-2341 E-mail: ralphkroehler@prodigy.net.

KROEMER, HERBERT, electrical engineering educator; b. Weimar, Germany, Aug. 25, 1928; Diplom-Physiker, Gottingen U., Germany, 1951, Dr. rer. nat., 1952; Doctorate (hon.), Tech. U. Aachen, Germany, 1985, U. Lund, Sweden, 1998, U. Colo., 2001. Prof. elec., computer engring. U. Calif., Santa Barbara; Faculty Rsch Lecturer U. Calif, 1985—96; Donald W. Whittier Chair in Electrical Engineering U. Calif., 1986—. J.J. Ebers Award of the Electron Devices Group of the IEEE, 1973, Heinrich Welker Medal of the Internat. Symposium on GaAs and related compounds, 1982, Nat. Lecturer, IEEE Electron Devices Soc., 1983, Jack Morton Award of the IEEE, 1986, Alexander von Humboldt Rsch. Award, 1994, Nat. Acad. of Engineering, 1997, Nobel Prize, 2000, Order of merit, Germany, 2001. Mem. Nat. Acad. Scis. (fgn. assoc.), IEEE (J.J. Ebers award 1973, Jack Morton award 1986, Medal of Honor, 2002), Am. Phys. Soc. Office: U Calif Elec-Computer Engring Dept Santa Barbara CA 93106

KROENER, WILLIAM FREDERICK, III, lawyer; b. N.Y.C., Aug. 27, 1945; s. William Frederick Kroener Jr. and Barbara (Mitchell) Kroener; m. Evelyn Somerville Bibb, Sept. 3, 1966; children: William F. Kroener IV(dec.), Mary Elizabeth, Evangeline Alberta, James Mitchell. AB, Yale Coll., 1967; JD, MBA, Stanford U., 1971. Bar: Calif. 1972, N.Y. 1979, D.C. 1983. Assoc. Davis, Polk & Wardwell, N.Y.C., London, 1971-79, ptnr. N.Y.C., 1979-82, Washington, N.Y.C., 1982-94; gen. counsel Fed. Deposit Ins. Corp., Washington, 1995—. Lectr. Stanford (Calif.) U. Law Sch., 1993—94, George Washington U. Law Sch., 1994—98, Washington Coll. Law, Am. U. Law Sch., Washington, 1996—; chmn. legal adv. group Fed. Fin. Instns. Exam. Coun., 2001—. Pres. Kroener Family Found.; gov. bd. mem. St. Albans Sch., 1991—95; fin. com. mem. Protestant/Episcopal Cathedral Found.-Wash. Nat. Cathedral, 1992—95; bd. visitors mem. Stanford U. Law Sch., 1983—92, deans adv. coun., 1992—93; nat. chair Stanford Law Fund, 1990—92; dir., gen. counsel Kenwood Citizens Assn., Inc., 1993—94; governing bd. FDIC Corp. Univ. Mem.: ABA, N.Y. Law Inst., Assn. of Bar of City of N.Y., Am. Law Inst., Kenwood Golf Club, Yale Club. Republican. Episcopalian. Home: 6412 Brookside Dr Chevy Chase MD 20815-6649 Office: Fed Deposit Ins Corp 550 17th St NW Washington DC 20429-0001

KROEPPEL, WARREN, airport terminal executive; Degree, Embry-Riddle Aeronautical U.; MBA, Adelphi U. Cert. comml. pilot, flight instr. FAA. Comml. pilot; mgr. airport ops., security and svcs. LaGuardia Airport Port Authority, Flushing, N.Y., mgr. ops. planning redevel. program JFK Airport, dep. gen. mgr. John F. Kennedy Internat. Airport, gen. mgr. LaGuardia Airport, 2000—. Office: LaGuardia Airport Hangar 7 Ctr 3rd Fl Flushing NY 11371*

KROESEN, FREDERICK JAMES, retired army officer, consultant; b. Phillipsburg, N.J., Feb. 11, 1923; s. Frederick James K. and Jean Ursula (Shillinger) Kroesen; m. Rowene Wilder McCray, Mar. 4, 1944; children: Karen McCray Kroesen Klare, Frederick J. III, Gretchen McCray Kroesen Tackaberry. BS in Agri., Rutgers U., 1944, LHD (hon.), 1983, BA in Internat. Affairs, George Washington U., 1962, MA in Internat. Affairs, 1966. Enlisted U.S. Army, 1942, commd. 2d lt., 1944, served with 63d Infantry div. WWII, advanced through grades to gen., 1976; served with 187th Airborne Regimental Combat Team, Korean War, 1953-55; instr. U.S. Army War Coll., 1962-65; mem. staff asst. chief of staff for force devel. U.S. Army, 1965-68, 70-71; served with Americal Div. Vietnam War, 1968 and 1971, comdr. Div., 1971; dep. comdr. XXIV Corps. U.S. Army, 1971-72, comdr. 1st Regn. Asst Command, VN, 1972, comdr. 82d Airborne Div., 1972-74, comdr. VII Corps in Europe., 1975-76, comdr. U.S. Army Forces Command, 1976-78, vice chief of staff U.S. Army, 1978-79; comdr.-in-chief U.S. Army, Europe, 1979-83; comdr. NATO Cen. Army Group Heidelberg, Germany, 1979-83; ret., 1983. Pvt. cons. in internat. security affairs; former mem. Army Sci. Bd. Decorated Def. D.S.M., Army D.S.M. with oak leaf cluster, Purple Heart with 2 oak leaf clusters, Silver Star with oak leaf cluster, Legion of Merit with 2 oak leaf clusters, D.F.C., Bronze Star with V and 2 oak leaf clusters, combat inf. badge with two stars; recipient Mil. Order of World War Disting. Svc. medal, 1985, Americanism award Am. Legion, 1993, State of N.J. Disting. Svc. medals, 1983, 95; named to Rutgers Hall Disting. Alumni, Rutgers Loyal Son, Cook Coll. Disting. Alumni award. Fellow Inst. Land Warfare (sr.), Assn. U.S. Army; mem. U.S. Army War Coll. Alumni Assn. (former pres.), U.S. Army War Coll. Found. (past bd. dirs.), 63d Div. Assn., 82d Airborne Div. Assn., Amcl Div. Vets. Assn., Rakkasan Assn., Soc. French Legion of Honor, Soc. Rhin et Danube, Rutgers Cap & Skull, Delta Upsilon. Home: 1250 S Washington St # 223 Alexandria VA 22314-4455

KROFT, STEVE, news correspondent, editor; b. Kokomo, Ind., Aug. 22, 1945; s. Fred and Margaret Kroft; m. Jennet Conant, June 29, 1991; 1 child, John Conant. BS, Syracuse U., 1967; MS in Journalism, Columbia U., 1975; DHL (hon.), Ind. U., SUNY. Reporter Sta. WSYR-TV, Syracuse, NY, 1972—74; investigative reporter Sta. WJXT-TV, Jacksonville, Fla., 1975—77; reporter Sta. WPLG-TV, Miami, Fla., CBS News, N.Y.C., 1980—81, corr. S.W. bur. Dallas, 1981—83, corr. Cen. Am. bur. Miami, 1983—84, corr. London, 1984—86, prin. corr. W. 57th program N.Y.C., 1986—89, corr., co-editor 60 Minutes, 1989—. Trustee Syracuse U. Sgt. U.S. Army, 1970—71, Vietnam. Recipient Ohio State award, Ohio State U., 1979, 1992, 1994, Emmy awards, 1982, 1984, 1990, 1993, 1999, 2001, Arents award, Syracuse U., 1992, George Foster Peabody award, 1992, 1998. Office: CBS News 60 Minutes 555 W 57th St New York NY 10019-2925*

KROGH-JESPERSEN, MARY-BETH, academic administrator; b. Schenectady, N.J., Aug. 10, 1949; d. George Henry and Barbara V. (Norton) Baillie; m. Karsten Krogh-Jespersen, Dec. 20, 1975; children: Erik, Sheila Ann, Michelle Grace. BA in Chemistry, Northeastern U., 1972; MBA, Pace U., 1990; PhD in Chemistry, NYU, 1976. Lectr. in chemistry Rutgers U., New Brunswick, N.J., 1979-81; prof. Pace U., N.Y.C., 1981-92, chair dept. chemistry, 1990-92; dean coll. of sci. Rochester (N.Y.) Inst. Tech., 1992-95; vice provost Rowan Coll., Glassboro, N.J., 1995-96; assoc. v.p. for acad. affairs Richard Stockton Coll., Pomona, N.J., 1996-2000; campus exec. officer Pa. State Worthington Scranton, 2000—. Contbr. articles to profl. jours. Mem. Am. Chem. Soc., Am. Phys. Soc. Roman Catholic. Office: Pa State Worthington Scranton 120 Ridgeview Dr Dunmore PA 18512-1602

KROGIUS, TRISTAN ERNST GUNNAR, international marketing consultant, lawyer; b. Tammerfors, Finland, Apr. 13, 1933; came to U.S., 1939; s. Helge Lorenz and Valborg Isolde (Antell) K.; m. Barbara Jane Brophy, Aug. 29, 1952; children— Ferril Anne, Lars Anthony, Karin Therese, Eric Lorenz, Marian Elaine, Rebecca Kristina BA, U. N.Mex., 1954; MA, Calif. State U.-Los Angeles, 1962; student Advanced Mgmt. Program, Harvard U., 1980; JD, Western State U., 1990. Bar: Calif. 1991. With Scott Paper Co., Phila., 1960-65, Hunt-Wesson Foods, Fullerton, Calif., 1965-75; pres. Hunt-Wesson Foods Can., Ltd., Toronto, Ont., 1969-71, pres. frozen and refrigerated foods div., 1971-75; pres., chief exec. officer Dalgety Foods, Salinas, Calif., 1975-78; v.p., gen. mgr. food div. Tenneco West, Inc., Bakersfield, Calif., 1978-80, pres., chief exec. officer, 1981-87; pres. Landmark Mgmt., Inc., 1987-88; ptnr. The Cons. Co., South Laguna, 1988-90, Internat. Mktg. Consultancy, 1990—; adj. prof. Western State U. Coll. of Law, 1992-97. Bd. dirs. South Coast Med. Ctr., Laguna Beach, Calif., 1969-74, pres., CEO, 1974; bd. dirs. South Sierra coun. Boy Scouts Am., 1981-87, Calif. State Coll. Found., Bakersfield, 1983-87, Found. for 21st Century, 1987-90; mgr. elder abuse program Pub. Law Ctr., 1992-93. Capt. USMC, 1954-60. Recipient World Food award Ariz. State U., Tempe, 1982 Republican. Episcopalian.

KROGSTAD, JACK LYNN, associate dean, accounting educator; b. Harlan, Iowa, Jan. 27, 1944; s. Chester Milo and Geraldine Elizabeth (Archibald) K.; m. Nancy Ellen Coffin, June 18, 1967; children: Kristine Ellen, Brian Lynn. BS, Union Coll., 1967; MBA, U. Nebr., 1971, PhD, 1975. Staff acct. Trachtenbarg & Grant CPAs, Lincoln, Nebr., 1967-68; asst. prof. U. Tex., Austin, 1975-78; assoc. prof. Kans. State U., Manhattan, 1978-80; John P. Begley prof. acctg. Crieghton U., Omaha, 1980-96, prof. acctg., 1997—, assoc. dean, 2000—. Vis. assoc. prof. U. Mich., Ann Arbor, 1980; vis. prof. U. Ill. 2000-; dir. rsch. Nat. Commn. Fraudulent Fin. Reporting, 1985-87. Editor: Auditing: A Journal of Practice and Theory; contbr. articles to profl. jours. With U.S. Army, 1968-70. Recipient Disting. Faculty Svc. award Crieghton U., 1988; Arthur Anderson & Co. doctoral fellow, 1974-75, Paton Acctg. Ctr. rsch. fellow, 1980, Barret Disting. Svc. award, 2002, Coll. Faculty of the Yr. award, 2001. Mem. AICPA, Nebr. Soc. CPAs (Acctg. Educator of Yr. award 1983), Am. Acctg. Assn. (regional v.p. 1984-85, auditing sect. chmn. 1984-85, Outstanding Auditing Educator award 1994), Beta Gamma Sigma, Beta Alpha Psi. Republican. Seventh-Day-Adventist. Home: 56717 Deacon Rd Pacific Junction IA 51561-4169 E-mail: jkrogstad@creighton..edu.

KROHN, CLAUS DANKERTSEN, insurance company executive; b. Oslo, Jan. 7, 1923; came to U.S., 1950; s. Dankert and Marie (Skjolden) K.; m. Madeline M. Moore, Oct. 10, 1954; 1 child, Christina Marie. Student, Oslo Katedralskole, Norway, 1947; student, Oslo U., 1947-49; MBA, Ind. U., 1951. Cons. Samvirke Ins. Co., Oslo, 1953-54; asst. sec. Manhattan Life Ins. Co., N.Y.C., 1954-59; sys. mgr. Raytheon Co., Andover, Mass., 1959-62; v.p. sys. Ohio Nat. Life Ins. Co., Cin., 1962-76, sr. v.p., 1977-88, also bd. dirs. Fellow Am. Scandinavian Found., 1950. Mem. LOMA/Life Ins. Assn. (adv. coun.), Den Gode Hensight Club (Bergen, Norway). Republican. Lutheran. Avocations: skiing, fishing. Home: 2324 Madison Rd Cincinnati OH 45208-2671

KROHN, FRANKLIN BERNARD, marketing specialist, educator; b. Erie, Pa., July 1, 1933; s. Lewis Harry and Marian (Post) K.; m. Alice Lester Krohn, July 4, 1954 (dec. Mar. 1969); children: Debra, Robert, Lynette; m. Inez Claire Judelsohn, Aug. 23, 1973. BA, SUNY, Buffalo, 1971, MA, 1974, PhD, 1977. Disting. Svc. prof. bus adminstrn. and mktg. SUNY, Fredonia, 1978—. Bd. dirs. Small Bus. Inst., SUNY, Fredonia, 1986—. Contbr. articles to profl. jours. Chmn. Brocton (N.Y.) Tourism Promotion Group, 1987-88. Served with U.S. Army, 1954-56. Recipient DeWitt Clinton Masonic award Lake Shore Lodge 851, 1988, Chancellor's award SUNY, 1987, Robert A. Beck Ethics Journalism award, 1992, 95, SUNY Disting. Svc. Prof. award, 1993, Pres. award for Excellence in Tchg. SUNY, Fredonia, 1999; Sam M. Walton Free Enterprise fellow Students in Free Enterprise, 1995—. Mem. Am. Mktg. Assn. (bd. dirs. Buffalo/Niagara chpt. 1984-90), Assn. for Bus. Communication, Assn. Mktg. Educators, Internat. Soc. for Gen. Semantics, Sml. Bus. Inst. Directors' Assn. (region II v.p. 1993-94). Home: 136 Old Mill Rd Brocton NY 14716-9630 Office: SUNY Dept Bus Adminstrn Fredonia NY 14063

KROHN, KENNETH ALBERT, radiology educator; b. Stevens Point, Wis., June 19, 1945; s. Albert William and Erma Belle (Cornwell) K.; 1 child, Galen. BA in Chemistry, Andrews U., 1966; PhD in Chemistry, U. Calif., 1971. Acting assoc. prof. U. Wash., Seattle, 1981-84, assoc. prof. radiology, 1984-86, prof. radiology and radiation oncology, 1986—, adj. prof. chemistry, 1986—. Guest scientist Donner Lab. Lawrence Berkeley (Calif.) Lab., 1980-81; radiochemist, VA Med. Ctr., Seattle, 1982—; affiliate investigator Fred Hutchinson Cancer Rsch. Ctr., 1997—. Contbr. articles to profl. jours.; patentee in field. Recipient Aebersold award, 1996; fellow, NDEA. Fellow AAAS; mem. Am. Assn. for Cancer Rsch., Am. Chem. Soc., Radiation Rsch. Soc., Soc. Nuclear Medicine, Acad. Coun., Sigma Xi. Home: 550 NE Lakeridge Dr Belfair WA 98528-8720 Office: U Washington Imaging Rsch Lab Box 356004 Seattle WA 98195-6004 E-mail: kkrohn@u.washington.edu.

KROHNKE, DUANE W. retired lawyer; b. Keokuk, Iowa, June 29, 1939; s. Ward Glenn and Marian Frances (Brown) K.; m. Mary Alyce Luschen, June 25, 1963; children: Alan Duane, Brian Douglas. BA, Grinnell (Iowa) Coll., 1961, Oxford U., 1963, MA, 1970; JD, U. Chgo., 1966; DHL, Grinnell Coll., 1999. Bar: N.Y. 1967, Minn. 1970, U.S. Supreme Ct. 1970, U.S. Ct. Appeals (2d cir.) 1967, U.S. Ct. Appeals (8th cir.) 1970, U.S. Ct. Appeals (D.C.) 1974, U.S. Dist. Ct. (so., ea. dists.) N.Y. 1967, U.S. Dist. Ct. Minn. 1970. Assoc. atty. Cravath, Swaine, Moore, N.Y.C., 1966-70, Faegre & Benson, Mpls., 1970-73, ptnr., 1974-2000, of counsel, 2001; ret., 2001. Adj. prof. U. Minn. Law Sch., 2002—. Editl. bd.: U. Chgo., 1964—66. Co-chair Bicentennial com. U.S. Dist. Ct. Minn. dist., Mpls., 1986-88; elder Westminster Presbyn. Ch., Mpls., 1985-91; trustee United Theol. Seminary, New Brighton, Minn., 1988-98. Recipient Alumni award Grinnell Coll., 1982; Rhodes scholar Rhodes Trustees, Oxford, Eng., 1961-63; Mecham scholar U. Chgo., 1963-66. Mem. Minn. State Bar Assn. (co-chair antitrust sect. 1982-84, co-chair ethics/standards of practice com. of ADR sect. 1995-96, chair elect ADR sect. 1996-97, chair ADR sect. 1997-98), Minn. Human Rights Advocates (vol. award 1991, 99, 2002), Order of Coif, Phi Beta Kappa. Avocations: reading, cultural events, exercise.

KROIS, AUDREY, artist; b. Boston, Mar. 14, 1934; d. Henry and Lillian Marie (Mueller) Haeberle; m. Richard Gamage, May 14, 1966 (div. Mar. 1975); m. Joseph E. Krois Jr., June 17, 1978. BA, Syracuse U., 1956; MSW, Columbia U., 1958; postgrad., Fashion Inst. Tech., 1964-66, Art Students League, 1973-76. Social worker Pleasantville (N.Y.) Cottage Sch., 1958-62; cons. to UNICEF UN, Bangkok, Thailand, 1963; supr. vol. program Henry St. Settlement, N.Y.C., 1964-66; dir. cmty. devel. program Anti Poverty Funding, N.Y.C., 1966-68; supervising dir., asst. v.p., cons. Divsn. Homemaker, Home Health Care, G.H.I., Inc., N.Y.C., 1969-78. One-woman shows include Clayton Liberatore Gallery, Bridgehampton, N.Y., 1995, 1996, 1999, 2002, South Palm Beach Town Hall Gallery, 1998, Southampton Town Hall, 1998, exhibited in group shows at Access to the Arts, Jamestown, N.Y., 1981, Embroiderers Guild Abigail Adams Smith Mus., N.Y.C., 1982, Arrowmont Sch., Gatlinburg, Tenn., 1982, Gayle Wilson Gallery, Southampton, N.Y., 1983, 1988, Discovery Art Gallery, Glen Cove, N.Y., 1989, Decatur House, Washington, 1990, Mus. Am. Quilter Soc., Paducah, Ky., 1992, Vanderbilt Mus., Centerport, N.Y., 1992, 1994, Wellspring Gallery, Santa Monica, Calif., 1993—94, Aullwood Audubon Ctr., Dayton, Ohio, 1996 (Best of Show), South Fla. Fair, 2002, Northern Trust Bank, 2002, Everglades Vis. Ctr., 2002, Water Mill Mus., Water Mill, N.Y., 2002, West Palm Beach Internat. Airport, 2002—03. Recipient 2d Pl. award Brookhaven Arts and Humanities Coun., 1997, 2d Pl. award East End Arts Coun., 1998. Mem. South Fork Craft Assn., Southampton Artists Assn. (bd. dirs. 1990-96, fin. dir. 1992-93, pres. 1994, Award of Excellence in Watercolor, 1994-96), Goodman Design Gallery (Award of Merit in Watercolor 1993), Palm Beach Watercolor Soc. Home: PO Box 2482 Palm Beach FL 33480-2482 also: PO Box 960 Southampton NY 11969-0960

KROL, JOHN CASIMIR, city manager, municipal planner; b. Chelmsford, Essex, Eng., June 1, 1949; came to U.S., 1951; s. Fortunat and Stanislawa (Kosowicz) K.; m. Linda Sue Wright, Jan. 2, 1971; children: Pamela, Suzanne, Michael. BS, Clarkson Coll. Technol., 1971; MS, SUNY, Buffalo, 1977. Credentialed city mgr. Planner St. Lawrence County, Canton, N.Y., 1971-74, county adminstrv. asst., 1984-85; sr. planner Town of Amherst, Williamsville, N.Y., 1974-77; planning dir. Clinton County, Plattsburg, N.Y., 1977-79, City of Ogdensburg(N.Y.), 1979-83; city mgr. City of Ogdensburg (N.Y.), 1987—; planning commr. Broome County, Binghamton, N.Y., 1986-87. Bd. dirs Soc. United Helpers, Ogdensburg, 1983-84, Ogdensburg Boys and Girls Club, 1990-93, Ogdensburg Minor Hockey Assn., 1993-97; co-chair annual city fund drive Am. Cancer Soc., Ogdensburg, 1982. Mem. Am. Inst. Cert. Planners, Mcpl. Mgmt. Assn. N.Y. State (dir. 1987-92, pres. 1992-93), Internat. City Mgrs. Assn., St. Lawrence County C. of C. (bd. dirs. 1988-94), Greater Ogdensburg C. of C. (bd. dirs. 1992-97). Presbyterian. Home: 515 John St Ogdensburg NY 13669-2007 Office: City of Ogdensburg 330 Ford St Ogdensburg NY 13669-1626 E-mail: jkrol@ogdensburg.org.

KROLEWSKI, BOZENA K. molecular biologist, researcher, cell biologist; b. Warsaw, Jan. 18, 1949; came to the U.S., 1981; d. Stefan and Zdzislawa M.S. (Zabielski) Checinski; m. Andrzej S. Krolewski, June 3, 1972; children: Martin A., Adam W. BA, Warsaw Med. Sch., 1971, MS, 1972, PhD, 1979. Rsch. asst. Warsaw Med. Sch., 1972—74; vis. fellow Harvard Sch. Pub. Health, Boston, 1981-84, rsch. fellow, 1984-87, scientist, 1987-92, sr. scientist, 1992—; rsch. assoc., cons. Joslin Diabetes Ctr., Boston, 1992—. Contbr. articles to profl. jours. Recipient Rsch. award NIH, Boston, 1984. Mem. Radiation Rsch. Soc., Cancer Rsch. Soc. Roman Catholic. Avocations: collecting antiques, walking, climbing, history, politics. Home: 639 Great Plain Ave Needham MA 02492 Office: Joslin Diabetes Ctr Genetics/Epidemiology 3d Flr One Joslin Pl Boston MA 02215

KROLIK, JULIAN HENRY, astrophysicist, educator; b. Detroit, Apr. 4, 1950; m. Elaine F. Weiss, Oct. 9, 1983; children: Theodore, Abigail. BS, MIT, 1971; PhD, U. Calif., Berkeley, 1977. Mem. Inst. for Advanced Study, Princeton, N.J., 1977-79; postdoctoral scientist MIT, Cambridge, Mass., 1979-81; rsch. assoc. Harvard U., Cambridge, Mass., 1981-84; asst. prof. Johns Hopkins U., Balt., 1984-86, assoc. prof., 1986-91, prof., 1991—. Office: Johns Hopkins Univ Dept Of Physics Astron Baltimore MD 21218

KROLIKOSKI, STANLEY JOSEPH, software company executive; b. Phila., Sept. 18, 1950; s. Stanley Joseph Krolikoski and Virginia Marie Sweeney; children: David, Mia. BA in Philosophy magna cum laude, U. Louvain, Belgium, 1972; MA in Philosophy, U. Kans., 1974; PhD in Philosophy, U. Ill., 1976, PhD in Computer Sci., 1980-85. Sr. sect. mgr. Honeywell, Inc., Mpls., 1985-89; adv. engr. IBM, Rochester, Minn., 1989-92; v.p. engring. CAD Lang. Sys., Inc., Columbia, Md., 1992-93; chief technologist, sr. fellow Compass Design Automation, San Jose, Calif., 1993-96; v.p. mktg. Cadence Design Sys., San Jose, 1996—, v.p. internat. stds. Mem. IEEE (chair internat. electrotech. com. of hardware lang. sect. 1993-94), VHDL (chair standardization group 1987-93, bd. dirs. 1996-2000), Open Verilog Internat. (bd. dirs. 1999-2001),

Open SystemC Intiative (chmn. bd., treas. 2001-03), Acellera (bd. dirs. 2001-03). Home: 584 Columbia Creek Dr San Ramon CA 94583 Office: Cadence Design Sys 2655 Seely Ave San Jose CA 95134 E-mail: stank@eda.org., stank@cadence.com.

KROLL, ARTHUR HERBERT, educator, consultant; b. N.Y.C., Dec. 2, 1939; s. Abraham and Sylvia Kroll; m. Lois Handmacher, June, 1964; children: Douglas, Pamela. BA, Cornell U., 1961; LLB cum laude, St. John's U., 1965; LLM in Taxation, NYU, 1969. Bar: D.C. Assoc. Patterson, Belknap, Webb & Tyler, N.Y.C., 1965-72, ptnr., 1972-90, Pryor, Cashman, Sherman & Flynn, N.Y.C., 1990-95; CEO KST Cons. Group, Inc. Adj. prof. U. Miami Sch. Law, NYU; lectr. numerous confs.; mem. adv. bd. Bur. Nat. Affairs Tax Mgmt., Inc., Practising Law Inst. Tax Adv. Bd., U. Miami Inst. Estate Planning, Bus. Laws, Inc.; mem. adv. com. NYU Ann. Inst. on Fed. Taxation. Author: Executive Compensation, 3 vols., Compensating Executives; monthly newsletter Family Bus. Profl.; mem. bd. contbg. editors and advisers Corporate Taxation; mem. editl. adv. bd. Jour. Compensation and Benefits. Mem. ABA (subcom. exec. compensation), Am. Pension Conf. (mem. steering com.). Office: KST Consulting Group Inc 250 E Hartsdale Ave Ste 30 Hartsdale NY 10530 E-mail: kstconsultinggroup@att.net.

KROLL, BARRY LEWIS, lawyer; b. Chgo., June 8, 1934; s. Harry M. and Hannah (Lewis) K.; m. Jayna Vivian Leibovitz, June 20, 1956; children: Steven Lee, Joan Lois Kroll Dolgin, Nancy Maxine Kroll Richardson. AB in Psychology with distinction, U. Mich., 1955, JD with distinction, 1958. Bar: Ill. 1958. Assoc. firm Jacobs & McKenna, Chgo., 1958-66, Epstein, Manilow & Sachnoff, Chgo., 1966-68, Schiff, Hardin, Waite Dorschel & Britton, Chgo., 1968-69; ptnr. Wolfberg & Kroll, Chgo., 1970-74, Kirshbaum & Kroll, Chgo., 1972-74; of counsel Jacobs, Williams & Montgomery, Ltd., Chgo., 1973-74; ptnr. Jacobs, Williams & Montgomery Ltd., Chgo., 1974-85, Williams & Montgomery Ltd., Chgo., 1985—2001; of counsel Williams Montgomery & John, Ltd., 2002—. Faculty John Marshall Law Sch., Chgo., 1969-73; atty. for petitioner in U.S. Supreme Ct. decision Escobedo vs Ill., 1964; mem. legal and legis. com. Internat. Franchise Assn., 1976-80 Asst. editor: Mich. Law Rev, 1957-58. Chmn. Park Forest Bd. Zoning Appeals, 1971-78. Served to capt. AUS, 1959 62. Named Outstanding Young Man Park Forest Jr. C. of C., 1966. Mem. Ill. Bar Assn., Chgo. Bar Assn. (chmn. legis. com. 1974-75), Ill. Appellate Lawyers Assn. (treas. 1978-79, sec. 1979-80, pres. 1981-82), Bar Assn. 7th Fed. Circuit, Order of Coif, Tau Epsilon Rho, Alpha Epsilon Pi. Jewish (trustee congregation 1966-70, 72-75, 90—, pres. men's club 1965-66). Home: 1440 N State Pkwy Chicago IL 60610-1564 E-mail: blk@willmont.com.

KROLL, BRIAN WALTER THOMAS, music educator; b. Mineola, NY, Mar. 29, 1974; s. Walter Albert Kroll and Lynda Alice Seelig; m. Mary Theresa Piekut, Dec. 23, 2000. BS in Edn., Hofstra U., 1997; Mus. M, Five Towns Coll., Dix Hills, NY, 2002. Cert. K-12 music tchr. NY. Vocal music tchr. Beach St. Mid. Sch., West Islip, NY, 1998—2000, Babylon Junior-Senior H.S., Babylon, NY, 2000—. Mem.: Music Educators Nat. Conf., Am. Choral Dirs. Assn., Suffolk County Music Educators Assn. (divsn. III east chorus chmn. 2001—), NY State Sch. Music Assn., Masons (sr. warden). Office: Babylon HS 50 Railroad Avenue Babylon NY 11702 Personal E-mail: bkroll@optonline.net.

KROLL, CONNIE RAE, librarian, information services consultant; b. Karlstad, Minn., June 12, 1955; d. Rudolph Julius and Irene Eleanor K. AAS, U. Minn., Crookston, Minn., 1975; BA, U. N.D., 1992; MLIS, U. Okla., 1993, postgrad. studies, Tex. Woman's U., 1993—. Circulation svcs. asst. N.W. Regional Libr., Thief River Falls, Minn., 1979-84, br. libr. substitute Warren, Hallock, Minn., 1985-88; libr. rsch. asst. U. N.D., Grand Forks, 1988-90; circulation asst. Grand Forks Pub. Libr., 1990-91; supr. interlibr. svcs. U. N.D. Med. Libr., Grand Forks, 1988-92; grad. asst. reference Bizzell Libr. U. Okla., Norman, 1993; grad. asst., vol. Tex. Woman's U., Denton, 1993-96; libr., dir. LRC Howard Coll., San Angelo, Tex., 1996—. Grant reviewer LSCA, State of Wash., Olympia, 1994; rsch. cons. Haynes & Boone Law Firm, Dallas, 1995-96; planning com., Tex. Tech. Visions of the Future, Lubbock, Tex., 1996—, instrl. coun. Howard Coll., San Angelo, Tex., 1996—; presenter: How to Avoid Vertical Stripes and an Empty Pocketbook, 1997. Vol. Christmas at Old Ft. Concho, San Angelo, Tex., 1996, 97, 99; catalog sale rep. Concho Kennel Club, San Angelo, 1997, hospitality chair, 1998, chair state employees contbn. campaign, 1998, chair Ann. Dog Show, 1999. Recipient Title IIB fellowship Dept Edn., Norman, Okla., 1993, Title IIB Dept. Edn., Denton, Tex., 1994-96, Mayo Drake scholarship State Employees Contbn. Campaign, Albuquerque, N. Mex., 1997. Mem. ALA, Tex. Libr. Assn. (com. mem.), Assn. Libr. and Info. Sci. Educators, N.D. Libr. Assn., Med. Libr. Assn. (s. ctrl. chpt. 1997). Office: Howard Coll 3197 Executive Dr San Angelo TX 76904-6801

KROLL, DAVID LEE, music educator; b. Grand Rapids, Mich., June 5, 1974; s. Micheal David and Jong Kim Kroll; m. Renee Lynn Groteleuschen, June 17, 2000. MusB in Edn., Concordia U., 1996. Min. of music Our Savior Luth. Ch. and Sch., Lansing, Mich., 1996—99, St. Petersburg, Fla., 1999—2002; organist Prince of Peace Luth. Ch., Coralville, Iowa, 2002—. Band dir. Gulf Coast Christian Sch., St. Petersburg, 2001—02. Grantee, U. Iowa, 2002—. Mem.: Music Educators Nat. Conf. Lutheran. Personal E-mail: krolldl@aol.com.

KROLL, DENNIS EDWARDS, industrial engineering educator; b. Chgo., June 7, 1947; s. Witold Charles and Lillian Mary (Zwic) K.; m. Susan Ann Michalski, May 26, 1973 (div. Dec. 1979); children: Steven Edward, Brian Christopher; m. Karen Elizabeth Wood, Jan. 13, 1990 (div. Sept. 1994); m. Carolyn S. Clark, Nov. 25, 2000. BS in Indsl. Engring., Bradley U., 1970; MS in Indsl. Engring., U. Wis., 1973; PhD, U. Ill., 1989. Devel. engr. Western Electric Co., Chgo., 1970-74; plant mgr. Junis Mfg. Co., Franklin Park, Ill., 1974-75; sr. indsl. engr. Sunbeam Appliance Co., Chgo., 1975-76; sr. mfg. engr. Victor Comptometer, Chgo., 1976; indsl. engr. Methode Mfg., Rolling Meadows, Ill., 1976-77; planning engr. Western Electric div. AT&T Tech., Lisle, Ill., 1977-81; prof. indsl. and mfg. engring. Bradley U., Peoria, Ill., 1981—. Founding editor Jour. Indsl. Engring. Design, 1995—; contbr. articles to profl. jours., chpts. to books. Precinct committeeman Peoria Rep. Com., 1981-82., Woodford County, 2002—; bd. dirs. West Peoria (Ill.) Street Light Dist., 1991-95; founding alderman City of West Peoria, 1993-2000; mem. Peoria Water Adv. Com., 1999-2000; mem. Eureka2000plus commn., 2001—; precinct committeeman Woodford Rep. Com., 2002—. Recipient lab. devel. award Soc. Mfg. Engrs., 1990, Simulation Lab. Devel. award St. Francis Med. Ctr., 1995, Bradley virtual course devel. award, 2001. Mem. Soc. Mfg. Engrs. (sr.), Inst. Indsl. Engrs. (sr.; cert. sys. integrator, chpt. pres. 1982-83, 94-95), Am. Legion, Planetary Soc., Am. Soc. for Engring. Edn. (IE Divsn. webmaster, sec., newsletter editor, chair). Roman Catholic. Avocations: fishing, gardening, cooking, history. Office: Bradley U IMET Morgan 110 1501 W Bradley Ave Peoria IL 61625-0003 E-mail: dek@bradley.edu.

KROLL, JOHN HENNIG, humanities educator; b. Washington, Feb. 12, 1938; s. John Henry and Ruth Waltner (Hennig) Kroll; m. Sandra Darin Puppel, Aug. 16, 1969 (div. Mar. 1999); children: Naomi, Jesse, Emily. BA, Oberlin Coll., 1959; MA, Harvard U., 1962, PhD, 1968. Jr. fellow Harvard U. Soc. Fellows, Cambridge, Mass., 1966—69; Agora rsch. fellow Agora Excavations, Athens, Greece, 1970—73; asst. prof., assoc. prof., prof. U. Tex.-Austin, 1974—. Lectr. Classics Harvard U., Cambridge, 1969; vis. prof. Am. Sch. Classical Studies, Athens, 2002—03. Author: Athenian Bronze Allotment Plates, 1973, Agora Excavation Greek Coins, 1992, Sylloge Nummorum-Munich-Athens, 2002; contbr. Fellow, NEH, 1979—80, Am. Coun. Learned Socs., 1985—86, Inst. for Advanced Study, 1985—86. Mem.: Am. Numismatic Soc. (2nd v.p. 2000—), Am. Assn. Ancient Historians, Am. Philol. Assn., Archaeol. Inst. Am. Avocations: music, travel. Office: Dept Classics Univ Texas Austin TX 78712*

KROLL, MARK, music educator; b. Bklyn., N.Y., Sept. 13, 1946; s. Eugene and Frances Kroll; m. Carol Lieberman, July 9, 1975; 1 child, Ethan. BA cum laude, CUNY Bklyn., 1968; MusM, Yale U., 1971. Lectr. U. Calif. Santa Cruz, 1971—74, Emerson Coll., Boston, 1976—78; prof. Boston U., 1978—2002, prof. emeritus, 2002—. Vis. prof. Zagreb Music Acad., Croatia, 1989, Belgrade Music Acad., Yugoslavia, 1989, Wurzburg Conservatory, Germany, 1993; founder, program chair Boston Early Music Festival, 1981—83; harpsichordist Boston Symphony Orch., 1979—; bd. dirs. Brookline Music Libr. Assn., Brookline, Mass., 1978—90. Author: La Belle Execution, 2003; editor: J.N. Hummel: Arrangements, 2000, 2003; performer: numerous rec., 1974—. Recipient Solo Recitalist award, Nat. Endowment Arts, 1981, Rsch. award, DAAD, 1996, 2002; fellow, NEH, 2003. Avocation: Black Belt 1984. Home: 59 Naples Rd Brookline MA 02446

KROLL, MARK WILLIAM, electrical engineer; b. Mpls, 1952; s. William H.O. and Irene Claudia Kroll; m. Lori Carolyn Kroll, Sept. 6, 1975; children: Braden, Mollie, Ryan, Chase. BS in Math., U. Minn., 1975, MSEE, 1983, PhDEE, 1987; MBA, U. St. Thomas, St. Paul, 1990. Circuit designer Medtronic, Fridley, Minn., 1970-72; teaching asst. U. Minn., Mpls., 1973-78; v.p. R & D Intercomp, Plymouth, Minn., 1978-84; v.p. of rsch. and devel. Cherne Med. Co., Edina, Minn., 1985-90; v.p. rsch. Angeion, Plymouth, 1991-95; v.p. Tachycardia Bus. Unit Pacesetter, 1995-97; v.p. and chief sci. officer St. Jude Med., Inc., St. Paul, 1997-98, sr. v.p., chief tech. officer cardiac rhythm mgmt. divsn., 1998—. Bd. dir. Harbinger, Inc., Mpls., Taser Internat., Scottsdale, Ariz., Arrowhead Offshore Capital. Co-editor: Implantable Cardioverter Defibrillator Therapy, 1996; contbr. over 75 papers to profl. publ. Bd. dirs. St. Peter's Luth. Sch., Edina, 1990—93. Alfred P. Sloan fellow, 1971. Fellow Am. Coll. Cardiology; mem. IEEE, Am. Heart Assn. (coun. on clin. cardiology), N.Am. Soc. Pacing and Electrophysiology. Achievements include 160 patents in field, issued US. Office: 15900 Valley View Ct Sylmar CA 91342-3577 E-mail: mkroll@sjm.com.

KROLL, PAUL BENEDICT, insurance consultant; b. Ft. Ord, Calif., Oct. 24, 1954; s. Harry Gardner and Jane Ellen (Cornwell) K.; 1 child, Dane Garcia. BA, Kans. Wesleyan U., 1977; MS, Emporia State U., 1979, MBA, 1983; cert. tchr., Washburn U., 1990. Cert. tchr., Tex. Pension adminstr. Kansas City (Mo.) Life Ins., 1980-82; actuary Victory Life Ins. Co., Topeka, 1983-85; actuarial analyst Security Trust Life Ins., Macon, Ga., 1985-87; policy examiner Kans. Ins. Dept., Topeka, 1987-88; adj. instr. math. Highland (Kans.) C.C., 1991-93; premium auditor Mountain States Mus. Cos., Albuquerque, 1995—2001; rep. Farmers Ins. Group. Kroll Ins. Cons., 2002—. Author: The Student's T Distribution, 1979. Mem. Ins. Inst. Am. (assoc. premium auditor), Am. Inst. Cert. Property and Casualty Underwriters (cert. property and casualty underwriter). Avocations: short wave listening, bird watching, bicycling. Office: 4255 Irving Ave N Minneapolis MN 55412 E-mail: krollic@juno.com.

KROLL, SANDRA L. retired healthcare facility administrator; b. Cleve., June 2, 1938; d. Gustave and Ruth (Davis) Donner; m. Charles Chung, Apr. 12, 1966 (dec. July 1994); m. Michael Kroll, Feb. 17, 1997. AAS in Nursing, Cuyahoga C.C.; MPH in Health Svcs. Adminstrn., Honolulu U., 1997. Staff nurse emergency dept. Kaiser Permanente Med. Care Program, Honolulu, 1968-76, supr., grant coord. family practice program, 1976-78, supr. med. subspecialty clinics, clin. supr., clinic supr. Hawaii Kai Clinic, 1978-97; clinic supr. Kaiser Permanente Med. Care Program, Hawaii Kai Clinic, 1984-97; clin. supr. Kailua Clinic, 1997-98; analyst/cons., informatics and clin. support svcs. Kaiser Permanente, Honolulu, 1998-99. Owner, operator Kroll Horse Ranch, Laupahoehoe, Hawaii. Past. pres. Am. Cancer Soc.; trustee Temple Emanu-El, Honolulu. Mem.: ANA (cert. nursing adminstr.), East Honolulu Pub. Health Nurses (chair adv. com.), Hawaii Kai Bus. and Profl. Women, Nat. Disting. Svc., Hawaii Nurses Assn. (past pres.), Oahu Quarter Horse Assn. (past pres.), Hawaii Quarter Horse Assn. (bd. dirs.), Hawaii Island Dressage and Combined Training Assn. (bd. dirs.), Hawaii Combined Tng. Assn. (bd. dirs.), Hawaii Horse Show Assn. (bd. dirs.). Home: PO Box 316 35-349 Kihalani Homestead Rd Laupahoehoe HI 96764

KROLL, SOL, lawyer; b. Russia, Aug. 10, 1918; m. Ruth Saslow; children: Gerald, Judy, Elise, Elliott. LLB, St. John's U., 1942. Bar: N.Y. 1942, U.S. Supreme Ct. 1956. Former U.S. counsel to Assn. Francaise des Socs. D'Assurances Transports; former mem. com. of interfraud task force N.Y. Ins. Dept.; sr. ins. counsel. County atty. Putnam County, N.Y. Contbr. articles on Am. ins. law to various ins. mags. Mem. ABA, Fed. Bar Assn., N.Y. State Bar Assn., N.Y.C. Bar Assn., Internat. Assn. Ins. Counsel, Industry Adv. Com. on Ins., Ins. Fedn. NY (bd. dirs.). Home: 600 Cantitoe St Bedford NY 10506-1107 Office: 1365 York Ave New York NY 10021 Fax: 212-755-9892.

KROLOPP, RUDOLPH WILLIAM, retired industrial designer, consultant; b. Chgo., June 7, 1930; s. Rudolph and Emma (Nice) K.; m. Dorcas S. Hall; children: Jacqueline, Mark, Joseph, Sharon, Lizabeth, John, Jennifer. BFA, U. Ill.-Champaign, 1956; postgrad., Lake Forest Coll., Ill., 1974-78. Staff designer Motorola Consumer Products, Chgo., 1956-59, chief designer, 1959-62, mgr. indsl. design communication div., 1962-82, dir. indsl. design, 1982-97, mem. patent com., 1981-97, chmn. corp. graphic standards council, 1983-97. Assoc. prof. indsl. design. U. Ill. Chgo. 1984; interviewed in CNN, MSNBC and Fox TV networks, and various publs., including Newsweek, Chgo. Sun Times, Reuters Am., others. Patentee in field. Instr. phys. fitness Oak Park YMCA, Ill., 1967; instr. cardiovascular health Buehler YMCA, Palatine, Ill., 1968—, bd. dirs., 1980—, chmn. program com., 1980—, sec. bd. dirs., 1983-84. Served with USMC, 1948-52. Recipient Master Design award Product Engring. Mag., 1961, Weson Design award Western Electronic Conv., 1970, Design Excellence award Indsl. Design Mag., 1972, Design Engring. award Nat. Marine Electronics Assn., 1972, Good Design award Hannover Fair, Germany, 1978, Nekkei Design award, 1990, Internat. Design award, 1991, Corp. award for good design, 1992, Design Excellence award, 1996, Idea Design award, 1997, Good Design award Hannover Fair, 1997. Fellow Indsl. Designers Soc. Am. (chmn. fellowship awards com. 1996, program chmn., sec., regional v.p., chmn. nat. nominating com., Spl. award 1993). Clubs: Parkers SAC (Chgo.) (pres. 1962-65). Roman Catholic. Home: 103 Golfview Rd Lake Zurich IL 60047-1290

KROMER, ANN MARIE, artist; b. Cin., Mar. 20, 1938; d. Albert David and Jane (Busch) Castellini; m. Frank Pierce Kromer, May 2, 1964; children: John, Edward, Elizabeth, James. BS, Marygrove Coll., 1960. Color seperator Gibson Greeting Cards, Cin., 1960-61; artist Mailway Advt., Cin., 1961-62; prodn. artist Long Advt., San Francisco, 1962-64; freelance graphic artist, painter, 1965-75; painter, 1975—. Art included in The Best of Acrylic Painting, 1996, The Best of Oil Painting, 1996, Postmarked Kentucky, 1989, Artist Mag., 1999, Water Color Expressions, 1999, Art of the Northeast, 1999; 13 solo exhbn. including Am. Artist, 2000. Recipient 1st in Mixed Media award Richter Art Ctr., 1st in Acrylic; finalist Arts for the Park, 1997. Mem. Catherine Lorillard Wolfe Art Club (Salmagundi award 1993, Lovell award 1994, DeCozen award 1997), Ridgefield Guild Artists (First in Acrylic 1996, Best in Show 2002), Rowayton Art Ctr. (First in Oil, Mixed Media 1996, First in Acrylic 1997, 99), Kent Art Assn. (Art of Merit award 1995). Avocations: gardening, travel, flower arranging, walking. Home and Office: 40 Beechwood Ln Ridgefield CT 06877-5803 E-mail: ackromer@yahoo.com.

KROMER, DEBRA GONZALES, researcher; b. Austin, Tex., Aug. 24, 1975; d. Alexander and Josie Gonzales; m. James Matthew Kromer, Mar. 5, 2000; 1 child, Miranda Gonzales. BA, Baylor Univ., Waco, Tex., 1997; graduate student, Univ. Tex., Austin, Tex., 2000—. Clin. rschr. Cedra Clin. Rsch., Austin, Tex., 1999—. Hispanic Scholarship fund, 2000—. Mem.: Am. Assn. of Pharm. Scientists, Pharmacy Graduate Students Assn. (tres. 2001—02), Capital City Dart Assn. (tres. 2000—). Cath. Avocation: darts.

KROMHOUT, ROBERT ANDREW, educator; b. Elgin, Ill., Oct. 23, 1923; s. Andrew and Sarah (Tiffany) K.; m. Ora Morlier, Dec. 21, 1950; children—Sharon, Brian, Ethan. BS, Kans. State U., 1947; MS, U. Ill., 1948, PhD, 1952. Asst. prof. U. Ill., 1952-56; asst. prof. Fla. State U., Tallahassee, 1956 58, assoc. prof., 1958-62, head dept. physics, 1959-62, prof. physics, 1962-92, prof. emeritus, 1992—; dir. Inst. for Cognitive Scis., 1985-92. Mem. Fla. Metric Coun., 1980-86 Served with AUS, 1943-46. Mem. Am. Phys. Soc., Am. Assn. Physics Tchrs., Sigma Xi, Phi Kappa Phi. Home: 206 Westminster Dr Tallahassee FL 32304-3519 E-mail: rkromhou@mailer.fsu.edu.

KROMINGA, LYNN, cosmetic and health care company executive, lawyer; b. L.A., May 16, 1950; d. Dale E. and Phyllis M. Krominga; m. Amnon Shiboleth, Apr. 9, 1992; 1 child, Karen Lee Shiboleth. BA in German, U. Minn., 1972, JD, 1974. Bar: Minn. 1974, N.Y. 1976. Assoc. firms in Mpls. and N.Y.C., 1974-77; assoc. counsel Am. Express Co., N.Y.C., 1977-80; sr. internat. counsel Revlon, Inc., N.Y.C., 1981-92, v.p. law, 1988-92, gen. counsel to exec. com., 1991-92, pres. licensing divsn., 1992-98, mem. exec. com., 1993-94, 97-99, exec. v.p. bus. devel., 1998-99; mem. bd. advisors MakeoverStudio.com, 1999—2001; bd. advisors Salonforce.com., 1999—2002; CEO Fashion Wire Daily, Inc., 2002; ptnr. KLS Mgmt. LLC, 2002—. Bd. dirs. StructuredWeb.com., 2000-02. Mem. ABA, Internat. Bar Assn. Cosmetic, Toiletry and Fragrance Assn. (vice chmn. govt. rels. com. 1991-92), Am. Arbitration Assn. (corp. counsel com. 1986-92, panel of arbitrators for large complex cases 1993-94, internat. panel of arbitrators 1997—), Phi Beta Kappa. Home: 418 E 59th St New York NY 10022-2341

KROMKA, JAMES THOMAS MICHAEL, designer, illustrator; b. Phoenix, Mar. 10, 1954; m. Linda Mae, Oct. 12, 1985. Student, Pasadena Coll. Design, 1972-74. Staff artist Riverside County Libr. System, 1969-72; circulation promotional artist Press Enterprise, Riverside, Calif., 1970-71; artist Lily div. Owens-Ill., Riverside, 1972-73; owner, mgr. Slinky Ink Graphics, Walnut Creek, Calif., 1974-76; co-designer, co-owner, constrn., mgr. Aesop's Restaurant, Riverside, 1976-78; owner, mgr. Bouhouze Custom Paint, Edgemont, Calif., 1978 79; graphic designer, dir. Robertshaw Controls, Corona, Calif., 1979-82; art dir., illustrator, prodn. artist Tobi's Graphics, Inc., El Monte, Calif., 1982 83; graphic designer, tech. illustrator Graphic Art Svcs., Chino, Calif., 1983-85, D. Sign Design Kustoms, 1985-98; tchr. animation MTI Coll., 1998-99; art dir., illustrator Interactive Illusion Inc., Costa Mesa, Calif., 1999-2000; designer, illustrator Wild West Media, Irvine, Calif., 2000-01, Shoreline Construction Co., Riverside, Calif., 2001—02; archtl. landscape and hardscape designer, illustrator Islander Pools, Temecula, Calif., 2002—. Home: 2556 Reservoir Dr Norco CA 92860-2327 E-mail: JKROMKA@Earthlink.net.

KROMMINGA, AN-MARIE, special education educator; b. Yakima, Washington, Mar. 23, 1936; d. Fred Henry and Edith Bessie Jackson; m. William Reynold Kromminga, Aug. 23, 1956. BA in Edn., Walla Walla College, 1958. Cert. profl. educator K-12 spl. edn., K-8 elem. edn., P-3 early childhood spl. edn., early childhood edn. Washington. Tchr. grades 1-7 Upper Columbia Conf. of Seventh-Day Adventist, Toppenish, Wash., 1955—56, tachr. grades 1-4 Wapato, Wash., 1959—60; tchr. grades 5-6 Ill. Conf. of Seventh-Day Adventist, Aurora, 1963—64, tchr. grades 1-8 Canton, 1972—74; substitute and homebound tchg. various schs., Ill., 1974—79; homemaking skills tchr. Ill. Dept. Children and Family Svcs., Sterling, 1979—81; home products ind. dealer, unit sales leader, to dist. leader Stanley Home Products Inc., Ill. and Wash., 1975—; presch./kindergarten tchr. Upper Columbia Conf. of Seventh-Day Adventists, Pasco, Wash., 1986—90; life skills spl. edn. tchr. Kiona-Benton Sch. Dist. 52, Benton City, Wash., 1990—. Chair Work Opportunities for Rural Kids, Benton City, 1990—96, Spl. Edn. Parent Group, Benton City, 1990—96; mem. Tri-Cities (Wash.) Transition Team, 1990—. Author: History of Benton City, Washington, 2000; contbr. articles to ch. newsletters and publs. Active disaster relief and cmty. svc. Seventh-Day Adventist Ch., 1963—79; leader for children's clubs and recreation programs for cmty. and ch., 1963—79. Recipient Tri City Crystal Apple award for excellence in edn., various cmty. svc. groups, bus., and orgns., 2002. Mem.: Coun. for Exceptional Children. Seventh Day Adventist. Avocations: dolls, music boxes, leathercraft, travel. Home: 1004 Frontier PR NE Benton City WA 99320

KRONDORFER, BJÖRN, religious studies educator; b. Frankfurt, Germany, Mar. 29, 1959; came to U.S., 1983; s. Paul and Ingrid (Podehl) K.; m. Katharina Von Kellenbach, May 18, 1991; children: Zadekia, Tabitha. BA, J.W. Goethe U., Frankfurt, Germany, 1981; MA, Temple U., 1984, PhD, 1990. Assoc. prof. St. Mary's Coll., St. Mary's City, Md., 1992—. Dir. biennial internat. study programs on Holocaust, 1989—; U.S. corr. Tribune-Jewish-German Jour., Frankfurt, 1992—96; cons. U.S. Holocaust Meml. Mus., Washington, 1991; mem. adv. bd. Inst. for Contemporary Midrash, 1996—2001; v.p. faculty senate St. Mary's Coll., 2002—; selected scholar Spkrs. Bur. Md. Humanities Coun., 1996—99, 2003—. Author: Remembrance and Reconciliation, 1995; editor: Body and Bible, 1992, Men's Bodies, Men's Gods, 1992, My Father's Testament (by E. Gastfriend), 2000; co-editor: Von Gott Reden im Land der Täter, 2001, Das Vermächtnis Annehmen, 2002; mem. editl. bd.: Living Text, 1997—2002, series editor: Cultural Criticism Series, 1998—2003, mem. publ. com.: Am. Acad. Religion, 1998—2002. Bd. dirs. Am. Friends Action Reconciliation, 1998—. Fellow Soc. Values in Higher Edn.; mem. Am. Acad. Religion (unit chair men's studies in religion 1997-2000), Am. Men's Studies Assn., Bibliodrama Gesellschaft. Office: St Mary's Coll Dept Philosophy-Religion Saint Marys City MD 20686 E-mail: bhkrondorfer@smcm.edu.

KRONE, CHERYL A. research scientist, consultant; b. Renton, Wa., May 25, 1948; d. Wilbur T. and Helen Faye K. BS, U. Washington, Seattle, 1978, MS, 1981, PhD, 1984. Vis. scientist U. Hawaii at Manoa, Honolulu, 1983; lectr. U. Washington, Seattle, 1983-84; rsch. chemist Nat. Oceanic and Atmospheric Adminstrn., Seattle, 1984-98; sr. rsch. scientist Applied Rsch. Inst., Seattle, 1998—. Deputy dir. Applied Rsch. Inst., Seattle, 1998—; cons. CK Consulting Svcs., Renton, Wa., 1998—. Author: (book chpt.) CRC Carcinogens and Mutagens in the Environment, 1982. Mem. Am. Chem. Soc., Inst. of Food Tech., New Zealand Assn. Scientists, Phi Beta Kappa, Sigma Xi. Avocation: triathlon. Office: Applied Rsch Inst PO Box 1969 Palmerston North 5301 New Zealand Fax: 64-6-353-1012. E-mail: cakrone@u.washington.edu.

KRONE, NORMAN BERNARD, commercial real estate developer, lawyer; b. Memphis, Sept. 13, 1938; s. Irving and Eva (Sauer) K.; m. Norma Lee Moon; children: John, Christine, David. LLB, Stetson U., 1964. Bar: Fla. 1964, Ohio 1987, US Dist. Ct. (mid. dist.) Fla. 1965, US Ct. Appeals (7th cir.) 1968; lic. real estate broker, Ohio, Mich., Ala. Atty. Lifsey & Johnston, Tampa, Fla., 1964—65; pvt. practice Tampa, Fla., 1965—66; property mgmt. atty. Ford Motor Co., Dearborn, Mich., 1966—67; audit mgr. Montgomery Ward & Co., Chgo., 1967—68, corp. real estate mgr., 1968—75; exec. v.p. Momtgomery Ward Properties Corp., Chgo., 1970—75; from v.p. to sr. v.p. Walgreen Co., Deerfield, Ill., 1975—85; pres., CEO The Hausman Co., Cleve., 1987—2001; sr. exec. v.p. Henry S. Miller, Grubb & Ellis Comml./Retail Svc., 1985—87; mng. prin. NK Devel. Ltd., 1996—2002; prin. NK Real Estate Adv. Ltd., 2002—; COO Olympia Devel. Group, 2004—. Trustee Internat. Coun. Shopping Ctr., NYC, 1976-79; dir. Myers Industries, Lincoln, Ill., 1976-83; instr. Intercoun. Shopping Ctr.-Inst. Profl. Devel.; dean U. Shopping Ctr. instructor - Law for Non-Lawyers, ednl. adv. com., small ctr. com., chmn. retail adv. com., 1975-76, cert. leasing specialist, 1995-; cons. Krone Group LLC, 2001-03; instr., spkr. in field, Law for Non-Lawyers. Author, editor: The Lease and Its Language, 1996, ICSC Study Lease, 2000, Anatomy of a Lease, 2001; contbr. articles to mags. Acting judge City of Tampa, 1964-66; bd. dir. Met. Housing and Planning Coun., Chgo., 1977-80, New City YMCA, 1976-78; mem. sch. bd. Palisades Cmty. Sch. Dist., 1968-69; mem. strategic planning com. Met. Chgo. YMCA, 1976-77; 1st pres. Cleve. Pops Orch.; bd. dir. Walgreen Hist. Found., 1984-87; co-founder, pres., mem. exec. com. Realty Resources (a network of comml. brokerage firms), 1987-2001. Named Entrepreneur of Yr. Operation Breadbasket, 1977. Mem. Cleve. Bar Assn., Real Estate Inst., Beachwood C. of C. (pres. 1996, exec. com. 1992-2001, life bd. dir.), Acacia Country Club (bd. dir. 1997-99, chmn. planning com. 1998-99, sec. 1998). Avocations: woodworking, golf. Office: NK Real Estate Advisors Ltd 9391 Mentor Ave PMB 281 Mentor OH 44060 Fax: 440-256-8360. E-mail: nbkrone@netscape.net.

KRONENBERG, S. ALLYX, poet, writer, lyricist; b. N.Y.C. d. William and Dorothy Kronenberg. BA in Psychology, CUNY; postgrad., NYU. Poetry and creative writing workshop facilitator C.E.T.A., N.Y.C., 1979—80, N.Y. State Coun. on the Arts, N.Y.C., 1980—83, Poets and Writers, N.Y.C., 1980—83; writing workshop facilitator Ptnrs. Ctr., L.A., 1996; creative writing resource tchr. Santa Monica -Malibu (Calif.) Unified Sch. Dist., 2003—. Panelist Nat. Writers' Club, Seattle, 1991. Author: (poetry book) Always, I Was Getting Ready to Go, 1989, Incantations of the Grinning Dream Woman, 1990, Confessions of a Travel Junkie, 2002; co-editor: Making Contact-Womens' Poetry Anthology, 1976; contbr. poetry to literary mags. Recipient Poetry Writing award, King County Arts Commn., Seattle, Bumber Shoot Arts Festival, Seattle. Mem.: ASCAP, Poets and Writers. Avocations: travel, hiking. Office: 502 Colorado Ave #405 Santa Monica CA 90401 E-mail: sakronenberg@hotmail.com., jardine@juno.com.

KRONENFELD, JENNIE JACOBS, medical sociologist; b. Hampton, Va., Aug. 11, 1949; d. Harry and Bessie (Pear) J.; m. Michael Reed Kronenfeld, Sept. 8, 1970; children: Shaun Jacobs, Jeffrey Brian, Aaron Benjamin. BA, U. NC, 1971; MA, Brown U., 1972, PhD, 1976. Asst. prof. U. Ala., 1975-80; assoc. prof. Sch. Pub. Health, U. S.C., Columbia, 1980-85, prof., 1985-90; prof.

sch. health adminstrn and policy Ariz. State U., 1990—; scientist Multi-purpose Arthritis Ctr. & Diabetes Research & Tng. Ctr., 1978-80; vis. faculty Princeton U., 1982. Author: Research in the Sociology Health Care, 1992-, Future: Schools of the Health of Children, 2000, Health Care Policy: Issues and Trends, 2002; -co-editor: Social and Economic Impact of Coronary Artery Disease, 1980; U.S. Health Policy, 1984; Sex Role Changes, 1986, Captive Populations, 1990, Controversial Issues In Health Care Policy, 1993, Research in the Sociology of Health Care, Vol. 10, 1993, Vol. 11, 1994; editor: Research in the Sociology of Health Care, Vol. 11, 1995; co-author: Getting Tenure, 1993, Dealing with Ethical Dilemmas on Campus, 1994. Assoc. editor Jour. Health and Social Behavior, 1983-85. Fellow Am. Acad. Health Behavior; mem. Am. Sociol. Assn. (sec., treas., chair med. sociol. sect. 1991-92), Assn. Social Scientists in Health (council mem. 1979-84, 89-91), Southern Sociol. Soc. (com. mem., v.p. 1989-90), Sociologists for Women in Soc. (pres.), NOW, Phi Beta Kappa, Delta Omega. Democrat. Jewish. Avocation: reading, gardening, swimming. Office: Ariz State U Coll Bus Sch Health Adminstrn and Policy PO Box 874506 Tempe AZ 85287-4506

KRONENFELD, JUDY ZAHLER, humanities educator, writer; b. N.Y.C., July 17, 1943; d. Samuel and Stella (Jupiter) Zahler; m. David Brian Kronenfeld, June 21, 1964; children: Daniel Aaron, Mara Gianna. BA in English summa cum laude, Smith Coll., 1964; MA in English Lit., Stanford U., 1966, PhD in English Lit., 1971. Asst. prof. English Purdue U., West Lafayette, Ind., 1976-77; lectr. U. Calif., Irvine, 1978-79, lectr. Creative Writing Dept. Riverside, 1984—. Vis. asst. prof. English U. Calif., Riverside, 1980-81, 88-89, Irvine, 1984, 85-87, vis. assoc. prof., 1987. Author: (poetry) Shadow of Wings, 1991, (critical study) King Lear and The Naked Truth: Rethinking the Language of Religion and Resistance, 1998; contbr. articles to profl. jours. Leverhulme Trust Fund fellow, 1968. Mem MLA, Renaissance Soc. Am., Assn. Lit. Scholars and Critics, Phi Beta Kappa. Home: 3314 Celeste Dr Riverside CA 92507-4051 Office: U Calif Creative Writing Dept Riverside CA 92521-0318 E-mail: jkronen@citrus.ucr.edu.

KRONER, FRED L. journalist; b. Champaign, Ill., Nov. 16, 1955; s. James Carlton and Naomi Ruth Kroner; m. Dee Siddens, Aug. 21, 1976 (div. Nov. 1996); 1 child, Devin Richard; m. Emily Sue Moon, June 6, 1999. BS, U. Ill., 1978. Sportswriter Champaign Courier, 1974-78, Bloomington (Ill.) Pantagraph, 1978-81, Champaign News-Gazette, 1981—. Contbg. author: Cascade of Memories, 1998, Nature's Echoes, 2000, Enlightened Shadows, 2001; author: Citizen Pain, Brian Cardinal, 2001, booklets and newspaper series. Coach Little League Baseball, Champaign, 1982—86, Summer League Baseball, Sullivan, Ill., 1990—93; guest commentator WDAN Radio, Danville, Ill., 1995—. Named Newsman of the Yr., Ill. Wrestling Coaches Assn., 1984, 1988, 2000, Sportswriter of the Yr. for Ill., Nat. Sportscasters & Sportswriters Assn., 2001; recipient awards, AP, 1985, 1989. Mem.: Nat. Sportswriters and Sportscasters Assn., Ill. Press Assn., Soc. Profl. Journalists. Methodist. Avocations: gardening, writing poetry. Home: 105 S Division St # 778 Mahomet IL 61853-9237 Office: Champaign-Urbana News-Gazette PO Box 677 Champaign IL 61824-0677 E-mail: ItsFred586@aol.com.

KRONEWITTER, FRANK DELL, software engineer, researcher; b. Flint, Mich., July 27, 1967; s. Barbara Zahn and Frank Dell Kronewitter. BS, U. Calif., Santa Barbara, 1991; MS, U. Calif., Irvine, 1993; PhD, U. Calif., San Diego, 2000. Software engr. Newport Sys. Solutions, Newport Beach, Calif., 1994—95; sr. software engr. Acterna, San Diego, 1999—. Author: (jour. article) Jour. of Linear Algebra and its Applications, Internat. Jour. of Robust and Nonlinear Control, (conf. article) IEEE Conf. in Decision and Control. Mem.: Am. Math. Soc., IEEE. Avocations: sailing, skiing. Office: Acterna 9855 Scranton Rd San Diego CA 92121 Personal E-mail: dell@ieee.org.

KRONFELD, EDWIN, natural gas company executive; m. Lydia Shepard Ballinger, Feb. 16, 1960; children: Nicholas, Alice, Alexander. Student, Harvard Coll., 1948—51; LLB, Georgetown U., 1961. Bar: N.Y., Washington, Okla. Staff atty. Securities & Exchange Commn., Washington, 1958-61; assoc. Lear & Scoutt, Washington, 1961-62; sole practice Washington, 1962-68; ptnr. Neal Siegler & Kronfeld, Washington, 1968-69, Morgan Lewis & Bockius, Washington, 1969-79, Thieman & Kronfeld, Tulsa, 1980-84, Kronfeld & Ribner, Tulsa, 1985-88; pres. Plymouth Resources Inc., Tulsa, 1982—. Lectr. Am. Law Inst.-ABA, Chgo., 1970-78; lectr. Practicing Law Inst., N.Y.C., 1970-78; adj. prof. law Georgetown U., Washington, 1971-78. Chmn. Tulsa Philharm., 1998 Mem. Okla. Ind. Petroleum Assn., Tulsa Assn. Petroleum Landmen, The Summit Club. Home: 2416 E 72d Pl Tulsa OK 74136 Office: Plymouth Resources Inc 15 W Sixth St Ste 2300 Tulsa OK 74119 E-mail: kronfeld@plymouthgas.com.

KRONGARD, HOWARD J. lawyer; b. Dec. 12, 1940; s. Raphael Harris and Rita (Keyser) K.; children: Kenneth, Mara Lynn. BA, Princeton U., 1961; JD, Harvard U., 1964; postgrad., Cambridge U., 1964-65. Bar: Md. 1965, N.Y. 1967, U.S. Dist. Ct. Md. 1965, U.S. Dist. Ct. (so. dist.) N.Y. 1967, U.S. Ct. Appeals (2d cir.) 1973, U.S. Ct. Appeals (8th cir.) 1980, U.S. Supreme Ct. 1991. Assoc. Piper & Marbury, Balt., 1964, Cravath, Swaine & Moore, N.Y.C., 1965, 66-73; law clk. to Hon. Kenneth B. Keating N.Y. Ct. Appeals, Albany, 1966; assoc., gen. counsel Peat, Marwick, Mitchell & Co., N.Y.C., 1973-86; gen. counsel Deloitte, Haskins & Sells, N.Y.C., 1986-89, Deloitte & Touche, LLP, N.Y.C., 1989-95; of counsel Freshfields Bruckhaus Deringer, London/N.Y.C., 1996—. Spkr. in field; bd. dirs. Lacrosse Found., Inc., Balt., 1981—, PCX Equities; U.S. rep. to Internat. Lacrosse Fedn.; legal adv. coun. Nat. Legal Ctr. Pub. Interest; pub. gov. Pacific Exch. Named Outstanding Player in U.S.A., U.S. Club Lacrosse Assn., 1968, 74; inducted into Lacrosse Hall of Fame, 1985, N.Y. Sports Hall of Fame, 1994; recipient Ames Briefwriting prize Harvard Law Sch., 1962; Frank Knox Meml. fellow, 1965. Mem. Assn. of Bar of City of N.Y., Harvard Club.

KRONHOLM, MARTHA MARY, elementary education educator; b. Wisconsin Rapids, Wis., July 28, 1952; d. Donald Edward and Ruth Marie (Albert) K. BS, U. Wis., LaCrosse, 1974; MEPD, U. Wis., Stevens Point, 1980; PhD, So. Ill. U., 1993. Cert. elem. sci. Nat. Sci. Tchrs. Assn. Elem. tchr. grades 4-6 Wisconsin Rapids Pub. Schs., 1974-88, sci. coord., 1986-88; ad hoc faculty U. Wis., Stevens Point, 1986-88; instr. sci. methods So. Ill. U., Carbondale, 1989-91; 6th grade tchr. Wisconsin Rapids (Wis.) Pub. Schs., 1992—, action rsch. team, 1993—. Mem. environ. edn. task force Wis. Dept. Pub. Instrn., Madison, 1983-85; rsch. asst. Earthwatch, Ethiopia, 1984, Borneo, 1985, Minn., Alaska, 1987; mem. bd. visitors U. Wis., Stevens Point, 1987—; mem. tchr. certification rev. com. Wis. Environ. Edn., State of Wis., 1981-83; ad hoc faculty U. Wis., Stevens Point, 1986-88, 96—. Co-author: (curriculum guides) Wisconsin Environmental Education Curriculum Planning Guide, 1985, Wisconsin Rapids Environmental Education Guide, 1989, Wisconsin Rapids Science Guide, 1988; contbr. articles to profl. jours. Mentor; mem. Habitat Restoration Com., 1992—; edn. chairperson Aldo Leopold chpt. Audubon Soc., Stevens Point, 1983-88; tchr. amb. Russian Expedition, 1995. Christa McAuliffe fellow U.S. Dept. Edn., 1987, 98; Delta Kappa Gamma Soc. Internat. scholar, 1989; Lifetouch Enrichment grantee, 1994, 96; recipient Kohl fellowship award, 1994; named Wisconsin Rapids Tchr. of Yr., 1994, 95, Wood County Conervation Tchr. of Yr., Regional Conservation Tchr. of Yr., 1995, Wis. Elem. Conservation Tchr. of Yr., 1995, Christa McAuliffe award 1998, Disting. Tchrs. award Wis. Elem. Sci. Teaching, 2002. Mem. Wis. Assn. for Environ. Edn. (sec., Aldo Leopold award 1990), AAUW (newsletter co-editor Wisconsin Rapids chpt. 1986-88, Project Renew scholar 1990), Ruffed Grouse Soc. (banquet com. 1983-87, Edn. and Conservation award 1986), Delta Kappa Gamma (sec. Sigma chpt. 2000-, Golden award 1988), Phi Kappa Phi, Kappa Delta Pi, Phi Delta Kappa (Howard M. Soule Ednl. Leadership fellow 1992). Democrat. Lutheran. Avocations: nature photography, travel, hiking, birdwatching. Home: 1430 23rd St N Ste G Wisconsin Rapids WI 54494-2192

KRONICK, NORMAN MARKS, real estate developer, investor, philanthropist; b. L.A., Sept. 19, 1928; s. Harry Bates and Rosina (Morris) K.; m. Josephine Taylor, Apr. 9, 1956 (dec. May 1997); 1 stepchild, Jane Brinley; m. Eva Dorothy Kronick, Oct. 19, 1997. BBA, U. Ga., 1949. Chmn. dir. Nat. Co. Inc., Honolulu and Ft. Worth, 1962—, Olinda Country Estates, Honolulu and Ft. Worth, 1979—, 710 Inc., Ft. Worth and El Paso, Tex., 1992—, Norman Kronick Tex. Inc., Ft. Worth-Houston, 1993—. Trustee Kronick Charitable Trust, Honolulu and Ft. Worth, 1988—; bd. dirs. Tarrant Area Food Bank, 1998-2001, Meals on Wheels, 2000-01. With U.S. Army, 1952-53, Korea. Jewish. Avocations: philanthropy, charities. Office: Riverbend Bus Park 2501 Gravel Dr Fort Worth TX 76118-6904

KRONIK, JOHN WILLIAM, Romance studies educator; b. Vienna, May 18, 1931; arrived in U.S., 1939, naturalized, 1944; s. Bernard and Melanie (Hollub) K.; m. Eva Kronik, Dec. 26, 1955; children: Theresa J., Geoffrey B. BA, Queens Coll., 1952; MA, U. Wis., 1953, PhD, 1960; DHL, Ill. Coll., 1979. Asst. prof. Romance lang. Hamilton Coll., Clinton, 1958-63; assoc. prof. Spanish, U. Ill., Urbana, 1963-66; prof. Romance studies Cornell U., Ithaca, N.Y., 1966-2000, prof. emeritus, 2001—. Vis. prof. Columbia U., 1968, Middlebury Coll., Vt., 1979, 80, 86, 91, Brigham Young U., 1982, U. Colo., 1989, U. Calif., Berkeley, 91, U. Calif., Irvine, 1994, U. Calif., L.A., 1999, 2000, U. Calif., Riverside, 2003; cons. NEH, 1973-92, Guggenheim Found., 1988—; corporator Internat. Inst. in Spain, Madrid, 1972—. Author: La farsa y el teatro espanol, 1971; co-editor: La familia de Pascual Duarte, 1961, Textos y Contextos de Galdos, 1994, Intertextual Pursuits: Literary Mediations in Modern Spanish Narrative, 1998; series editor Prentice-Hall, 1962-75; mem. editl. bd. MLA, N.Y.C., 1983-85; editor PMLA, 1985-92, Anales Galdosianos, 1986-90; contbr. articles to profl. jours. With U.S. Army, 1953—55. Fulbright fellow, 1960-61, 87-88; Rockefeller Found. rsch. resident, 1975; Guggenheim fellow, 1983-84; ACLS grantee, 1983-84. Mem. MLA, Internat. Assn. Hispanists, Internat. Galdos Assn. (pres.), Am. Assn. Tchrs. Spanish and Portuguese. Home: 1020 Highland Rd Ithaca NY 14850-1448 Office: Cornell U Dept Romance Studies Ithaca NY 14853-4701

KRONISH, JAN WARREN, ophthalmologist; b. Merrick, N.Y., Apr. 29, 1957; s. Robert and Selma Kronish. BS, MIT, 1979; MD, Harvard U., 1983. Diplomate Am. Bd. Ophthalmology (examiner 1994-97). Intern Cedars-Sinai Med. Ctr., L.A., 1983-84; resident Bascom Palmer Eye Inst./U. Miami, Fla., 1984-87; fellow U. Wis., Madison, 1987-88; vol. assoc. prof. Bascom Palmer Eye Inst., U. Miami, Fla., 1988-91; ptnr., ophthalmologist Delray Eye Assocs., Delray Beach, Fla., 1991—. Contbr. articles to profl. publs., chpts. to books. Fellow: ACS, Am. Acad. Ophthalmology (Honor award 1994); mem.: Am. Technion Soc. (bd. dirs. 1996—), Fla. Soc. Ophthalmology, Soc. Heed Fellows, Am. Soc. Ophthalmic Plastic and Reconstructive Surgery (sec. of edn. 2002—, Quickert Thesis award 1989). Office: Delray Eye Assocs 16201 Military Trl Delray Beach FL 33484-6503

KRONMAN, ANTHONY TOWNSEND, law educator, dean; b. 1945; m. Nancy I. Greenberg, 1982 BA, Williams Coll., 1968, PhD, 1972; JD, Yale U., 1975. Bar: Minn. 1975, N.Y. 1983. Assoc. prof. U. Minn., 1975-76; asst. prof. U. Chgo., 1976-79; vis. assoc. prof. Yale U. Law Sch., New Haven, 1978-79, prof., 1979—, Edward J. Phelps prof. law, 1985—, dean, 1994—. Editor: (with R. Posner) The Economics of Contract Law, 1979 (with F. Kessler and G. Gilmore) Cases and Materials on Contracts, 1986; past mem. editorial bd. Yale Law Jour.; author: Max Weber, 1983, The Lost Lawyer, 1993. Danforth Found. fellow, 1968-72 Fellow ABA, Am. Acad. Arts and Scis.; mem. Selden Soc., Conn. Bar Assn. (Cooper fellow), Coun. on Fgn. Rels. Office: Yale U Law Sch PO Box 208215 New Haven CT 06520-8215

KRONMAN, JOSEPH HENRY, orthodontist, educator; b. N.Y.C., Apr. 4, 1931; s. Jacob and Anna Rita (Dick) K.; m. Arlene Brenda Wice, Mar. 30, 1961; children: David Arthur, Bruce Edward, Lisa Sue. BS in Biology, NYU, 1952, D.D.S., 1955; cert. in orthodontics, Columbia U. Sch. Dentistry, 1959; PhD in Anatomy, Med. Coll. Va., 1962. Postdoctoral fellow Med. Coll. Va., 1959-61; mem. faculty Tufts U. Sch. Dental Medicine, Boston, 1962-94, prof. orthodontics, 1968-94, prof. anatomy, 1983-94, dir. postdoctoral studies, 1964-70, dir. continuing edn., 1982-88, asst. to dean Grad. Sch. Arts and Scis., 1964-69; pvt. practice orthodontics, 1963-78; prof. emeritus, 1994; prof. orthodontics and anatomy Nova S.E. U., 1997-2000. Cons. VA, 1966-68 Mem. editorial bd. Jour. Oral Surgery, Oral Medicine, Oral Pathology. Served to capt. Dental Corps U.S. Army, 1955-57, Korea. Recipient Oscar award Internat. Assn. Inventors and Compagnie 12 Pub., Paris, 1986. Fellow Internat., Am. colls. dentists; mem. ADA, Mass. Dental Soc., Internat. Assn. Dental Research, AAUP, Am. Assn. Orthodontists, Am. Assn. Anatomists, N.Y. Acad. Scis., Internat. Soc. Craniofacial Biology, AAAS, Mass. Assn. Orthodontists, Am. Assn. Dental Schs., Sigma Xi, Omicron Kappa Upsilon. Jewish. Achievements include co-inventing GK-101 caries removal agent, applicator (caridex), hydron root canal filling material and delivery system, root canal irrigation system, orthodontic headgear attachment. Home: 11755 Caracas Blvd Boynton Beach FL 33437-4081

KRONMILLER, JAN E. academic administrator; BS in Chemistry, DDS, Ohio State U.; PhD in Biomedical Scis., U. Conn. Cert. pediatric dentistry and orthodontics. NIH rsch. fellow U. Conn. Health Ctr.; asst. prof., pediatric dentistry U. Pitts.; pvt. practice; head, orthodontics section, Coll. Dentistry U. Ky.; prof. and chair., dept. orthodontics, Sch. Dentistry Oreg. Health Scis. U., prof., grad. program, Sch. Medicine; dean, Coll. Dentistry Ohio State U., 2001—. Recipient Nat. Rsch. Svc. award, NIH, Individual Physician Scientist award. Fellow: Internat. Coll. Dentists, Am. Coll. Dentists. Office: 305 W 12th Ave Columbus OH 43210

KRONSCHNABEL, ROBERT JAMES, retired manufacturing company executive; b. Green Bay, Wis., Jan. 13, 1935; s. Cyril E. and Margaret (Bierman) K. m. Catherine G. Murray, June 27, 1959; children: Frederick, Nina, Erich, Liesl, Mara. BSME, Marquette U., 1958; MBA, Harvard U., 1963. Field svc. engr. A.C. Electronics div. GM, Milw., 1958-61; mgr. materials Clark Contr. div. A.O. Smith, Cleve. and Lancaster, S.C., 1963-65; v.p., sr. cons. MSI, Appleton, Wis., 1965-67; plant mgr. Allis Chalmers, Port Washington, Wis., 1967-77, Simplicity Mfg. Co., Lexington, S.C., 1970-73; dir. mfg. bearings div. TRW, Jamestown, N.Y., 1977-79; v.p. mfg. bldgs. div. Butler Mfg. Co., Kansas City, Mo., 1979-83, v.p. corp. mfg., 1983-88, pres. Skylight div. Garland, Tex., 1988-91; pres. grain sys. divsn. CTB, Inc., Kansas City, 1991-99, retired, 1999. Mem. prison industries bd. Mo. Dept. Corrections, Jefferson City, 1986-88. Chmn. bd. dirs. Prime Health, Kansas City, 1980-88; bd. regents Rockhurst U., Kansas City, 1985—; bd. dirs. Whatsoever Cmty. Ctr., Kansas City, 1997—. Mem. Harvard Bus. Sch. Club. Republican. Roman Catholic. Avocations: gardening, golf, fishing. E-mail: robertk917@worldnet.att.net.

KRONSTEIN, WERNER J, lawyer; b. Heidelberg, Germany, Dec. 12, 1930; came to U.S., 1935; s. Heinrich D. and Kate (Brodnitz) K.; m Ilse Marie Engel, Feb. 10, 1962; 1 child, Phillip D. AB, Georgetown U., 1953, L.L.B., 1956. Bar: 1956. Law clk. U.S. Ct. Appeal for D.C. Circuit, Washington, 1956-57; ptnr. Arnold & Porter, Washington, 1957—. Trustee, Internat. Law Inst., Washington, 1983—, vice chmn., 1989—. Contbr. articles to profl. jours. Roman Catholic. Office: Arnold & Porter 555 12th St NW Washington DC 20004-1206

KRONZEK, CHARLES MICHAEL, lawyer; b. Pitts., Feb. 11, 1954; s. Morris and Shirley (Gorin) K.; m. Judith W.; children: Allison F., Jill L. BS, Geneva Coll., Pitts., 1991; JD, Mich. State U., 1994. Bar: Mich. 1995. Sr. ptnr. Kronzek & Cronkright PLLC, Lansing, Mich., 1994—. Office: Kronzek & Cronkright PLLC 4601 W Saginaw Ste 100 Lansing MI 48917-2741 E-mail: Kronzek@lawyer.com.

KRONZON, ITZHAK, physician, educator; b. Sept. 14, 1939; MD, Hebrew U., Jerusalem, 1964. Dir. noninvasive cardiology NYU, 1975—, prof. dept. medicine, 1993—. Author: (book) Mother, Sunshine, Homeland, 1985; editor, author: (book) Cardiogenic Embolism, 1996. Mem. N.Y. Echocardiography Soc. (pres. 1997-99). Office: 560 1st Ave New York NY 10016-6402

KROP, STEPHEN, retired pharmacologist; b. N.Y.C., Sept. 24, 1911; s. Dmetro Pantele Krop and Mary Badewko; m. Mary Lulick, July 28, 1934; children: Elaine, Marianne, Paul, Thomas. BS, George Washington U., 1939; MS, Georgetown U., 1940; PhD, Cornell U., 1942. Diplomate Fed. Exec. Inst., 1970. From asst. to instr. pharmacology Cornell U. Med. Coll., Ithaca, NY, 1939—44; chief pharmacology dept. reserach divsn. Ethicon Inc., 1957—63; chief drug pharmacology br. rsch. divsn. Bur. Sci. Rsch., 1963—79; cons. toxicologist EPA, others, Washington, 1979—85; from instr. to asst. prof. pharmacology Yale U. Sch. Medicine, 1944—46; chief pharmacology sect. med. divsn. CWS, U.S. Army, 1946—48; pres. Ethicon Rsch. Found., 1957—63; head pharmacodyamics dept. Squibb Inst. Med. Rsch., 1948—49; dir. pharmacology divsn. Warner Inst. Therapeutic Rsch., 1949—51; rsch. assoc. Chemical-Biological Coordination Ctr. NRC, 1951—52, asst. and acting dir., 1951—52; coord. physiology divsn. Med. Rsch. Labs., 1952—57; mil. chemicals rsch. and asst. chief divsn. physiology U.S. Army Chem. Warfare Med. Labs., 1952—57. Advisor grain infestation Nat. Grain Sanitation Conf., Kansas City, Kans., 1956—56; health edn. exch. scientist Polish Health Ministry, Poland, 1978—78; ret., 1979; Stephen and Mary Krop lectr. Georgetown U. Med. Ctr. First editor Military Chemicals Safety Manual. Fellow: Wash. Acad. Scis., NY Acad. Sciences; mem.: Am. Indsl. Hygiene Assn., Am. Physiol. Soc., Am. Soc. Pharmacology and Exptl. Therapeutics, The Harvey Soc., Soc. Exptl. Biology and Medicine, Am. Assn. Advancement Sci., Cosmos Club (Washington), Soc. Sigma Xi. Catholic. Achievements include research in Treatment Of Nerve Gas Poison; Treatment Of Hexachlorophene Poisoning. Avocations: music, genealogy, memoirs, history.

KROPF, RICHARD WILLIAM, priest, theologian; b. Milw., Jan. 9, 1932; s. Richard Bartlett Kropf and Aileen Katherine Foley. BA, Sacred Heart Sem., Detroit, 1954; ThM, St. John's Provincial Sem., Plymouth, Mich., 1958; PhD, U. Ottawa, Ont., Can., 1973; ThD, U. St. Paul, Ottawa, 1980. Assoc. prof. Roman Cath. Diocese, Lansing, Mich., 1958—67, adj. prof., 1972—80; canonically professed anchorite Roman Cath. Diocese Lansing, Montmorency, Mich., 1981—. Author: Teilhard, Scripture & Revelation, 1980, Evil & Evolution: A Theodicy, 1984, Faith: Security & Risk, 1990. Mem. Cath. Theol. Soc. Am., Am. Teilhard Assn., Internat. Thomas Merton Soc., Pigeon River Country Assn. (pres. 1994-97, mem. adv. coun. 1998—). Avocations: nature photography, environment, back-country sports, astronomy. Home and Office: Stella Maris Hermitage 19920 Black River Rd Johannesburg MI 49751 E-mail: rwkropf@fastmail.fm.

KROPF, SUSAN J. cosmetics company executive; married. BA in English, St. John's U.; MBA in Fin., NYU. Adminstrv. asst. Avon Products, Inc., N.Y.C., 1970, various mgmt. positions, 1970-85, v.p. purchasing and package devel., 1985-90, v.p., sr. officer product devel., 1990-92, v.p. R&D and mfg., 1992-97, sr. v.p. global ops. and bus. devel., 1992-97, exec. v.p., 1998-99, COO N.Am. & Global Bus. Ops., 1999—. Bd. dirs. Green Point Savs. Bank. Mem.: Fashion Group Internat., Cosmetic Exec. Women. Office: Avon Products Inc Ste C2-04 1251 Avenue Of The Americas New York NY 10020-1196

KROPINACK, JOHN FRANK, secondary education educator; b. Passaic, N.J., Apr. 28, 1947; s. Edward and Cecelia (Sepp) K.; m. Elaine Marie Bunsfield, Mar. 20, 1971 (div. May 1993); children: Michael, Brian, Laura, Allyson. BA in Secondary Edn., Fairleigh Dickinson U., 1969; postgrad., Jersey City State U., 1977-80, Glassboro State U., 1980. Cert. secondary math. tchr., N.J. Computer supr. N.J. Bell Telephone, Newark, 1969; instr. math Westwood (N.J.) Regional Mid. Sch., 1969-74, Cen. Regional High Sch., Bayville, N.J., 1974—. Trainer peer mediation for conflict resolution, 1991—, coord. conflict resolution program; ednl., computer cons.; adj. instr. in computer applications, mem. spkrs. bur. Ocean County Coll.; varsity bowling coach Cen. Regional High Sch., 1999-2001, varsity girls track coach, 2001. Author: (booklet) Peer Mediation/Conflict Resolution; author creative writings for personal improvement; chmn., editor computer curriculum. Pres. Stafford Twp. Bd. Edn., Manahawkin, N.J., 1980-88; scout master Troop 65 Boy Scouts Am., 1984-91; com. mem. Dist. 4-Ocean County Boy Scouts Am., 1987—; mem. King of Kings Ch., Manahawkin. Recipient Svc. award Dist. 4-Ocean County Boy Scouts Am., 1989, Merit award, 1991. Mem. Cen. Regional Edn. Assn. (v.p. 1981), Assn. Math. Tchrs. N.J., Parents without Partners (exec. bd., editor). mem. Ocean County Human Relations Commission, 1990-. Head Girl's Bowling Coach, 1999-. Head Girl's Track Coach, 2001-. Avocations: bible study, photography, sports, homemade kites, disc jockey. Home: 917 Bonita Ln Manahawkin NJ 08050-2102 Office: Ctrl Regional H S Forest Hills Pky Bayville NJ 08721 E-mail: jkropinack@yahoo.com.

KROPOTOFF, GEORGE ALEX, civil engineer; b. Sofia, Bulgaria, Dec. 6, 1921; came to Brazil, 1948, to U.S., 1952, naturalized, 1958; s. Alex S. and Anna A. (Kurat) K.; m. Helen P., July 23, 1972. BS in Engring., Inst. Tech., Sofia, 1941; postgrad., U. Calif., 1968. Registered profl. engr., Calif. With Std. Eletrica S.A., Rio de Janeiro, 1948-52, Pacific Car & Foundry Co., Seattle, 1952-64, T.G. Atkinson Assocs. Structural Engrs., San Diego, 1960-62, Tucker, Sadler & Bennett A-E, San Diego, 1964-74, Gen. Dynamics-Astronautics, San Diego, Incomtel, Rio de Janeiro, 1976, Bennett Engrs., 1976-82; project structural engr. Hope Cons. Group, San Diego, Saudi Arabia, 1982-84, ret., 1984. Warrant officer U.S. Army, 1945-46. Fellow ASCE; mem. Structural Engrs. Assn. San Diego (assoc.), Soc. Am. Mil. Engrs., Soc. Profl. Engrs. Brazil. Republican. Russian Orthodox. Pioneered engring. computer software. Home: 8712 N Magnolia Ave #133 Santee CA 92071

KROPP, EDWARD H. education educator, consultant; b. Reading, Pa., June 13, 1944; s. Karl Gustaf and Erna Mittag Kropp; m. Phyllis Ann Bauman, Nov. 5, 1966; children: Peter Alex, Julie Marie (Kropp) McKenzie. BA, Temple U., 1966; MA, George Mason U., 1994. PMP George Washington U. Staff mgr. Chesapeake and Potomac Tel., Roanoke, Va., 1969—81; dist. mgr. A T & T, Basking Ridge, NJ, 1981—96; comml. bids coord. Sci. Application Internat. Corp., San Diego, 1996—2000; sr. mgr. KPMG Cons. (Bearing Point), McLean, Va., 2000—02; prof. Keller Grad. Sch. of Mgmt., McLean, 2002—. Pres. E. H. Kropp & Assoc., Vienna, 2002—. Author: (book) A Guide to Repair Svc. Bur. Analysis, 1971, (manual) Land Mine Warfare (USMC), 1983. Exec. bd. Nat. Capital Area Coun., BSA, Wash., DC, 1998—. Col. USMC, 1966—94. Mem.: Nat. Contact Mgmt. Assn. Avocations: ednl. leadership rsch., in-prison literacy instrn.. Home: 8022 Kidwell Ct Vienna VA 22182 Office: Keller Grad Sch of Mgmt 1751 Pinnacle Dr Springfield VA 22152

KROPP, STACY ANNE, small business owner; b. Bklyn., Jan. 22, 1964; d. Alan Marc and Sheila Harriet (Friend) G.; 1 child, Ryan. Student, Suffolk C.C., 1981, Valencia C.C., 1982; grad., Fla. Coll. Natural Health, 2002. Lic. real estate agt., Fla., 1986. Owner, CEO Expert Restoration Techs., Inc., Sunrise, Fla., Bright Solutions, Inc.; ptnr., v.p. ops. Color All Techs. Inernat., Pompano Beach; owner Account Mgmt. Svcs., Inc., Ft. Lauderdale, Fla.; CEO Gold Power Supplements, Ft. Lauderdale; divsn. mgr. Alice Edwards Realty, Pembroke Pines, Fla.; gen. mgr. Gen. Accounts Svcs., Inc. Mem. NAFE, Nat. Assn. Self-Employed, Nat. Nutritional Foods Assn., Greater Miami Credit Assn., Am. Collectors Assn., Fla. Collectors Assn., Women in Network. Home: 14130 Langley Pl Fort Lauderdale FL 33325-6413

KROPP, WILLIAM RUDOLPH, physicist; b. Chgo., Nov. 10, 1936; s. William R. Sr. and Nora J. (King) K.; divorced; children: Marianne, Kathryn; m. Christa McDonnell, Feb. 2, 2001. BS, DePaul U., 1958; PhD, Case Inst. Tech., 1964. Postdoctoral fellow Case Inst. Tech., Cleve., 1964-66, U. Calif., Irvine, 1966-68, asst. prof. physics, 1968-74, research physicist, 1974—. Recipient Bruno Rossi prize, Am. Astron. Soc., 1989. Mem. AAAS, Am. Phys. Soc. Home: 11711 Via Rancho Santa Ana CA 92705-3153

KROPSCHOT, RICHARD HENRY, retired physicist, science laboratory administrator; b. Kalamazoo, May 25, 1927; s. Henry J. and Della (Burdorf) K.; m. Claire Mills, June 23, 1950; children: Susan, Anne. BS in Physics, Mich. State U., 1948, MS in Physics, 1950, PhD in Physics, 1958. Rsch. scientist N.Am. Aviation, Downey, Calif., 1950-51; physicist Nat. Bur. Standards, Boulder, Colo., 1951-79; dir. Office Basic Energy Scis., Dept. Energy, Washington, 1979-85; assoc. lab. dir. energy scis. Lawrence Berkeley (Calif.) Lab., 1985-90; liaison officer Office of Pres. U. Calif., Oakland, 1990-97, ret. Adj. prof. U. Colo., Boulder, 1969-79. Author: Technology of Liquid Helium, 1968; former editor Cryogenics, London, Rev. Sci. Instruments; contbr. articles to profl. jours. With USN, 1945-46, PTO, ETO. Recipient Gold medal U.S. Dept. Commerce, 1954, sci. fellow, 1976-77; recipient Disting. Svc. award U.S. Dept. Energy. Fellow Am. Phys. Soc. Presbyterian.

KROSSER, HOWARD S. aerospace company executive; b. Bklyn., Dec. 2, 1936; s. Samuel and Celia (Wexler) K.; m. Roslyn Elaine Rosenthal, Apr. 30, 1939; children: Scott A., Barry I. BS in Engring., Rutgers Coll., 1959; MS in Indsl. Mgmt., Ga. Inst. Tech., 1970; postgrad., Harvard U., 1985. Engr., engring. supr. Picatinny Arsenal, Dover, N.J., 1959-66; br. mgr., engr. Prodn. Modernization Agy., Dover, 1966-73; divsn. engring. mgr. Army Prodn. Agy., Dover, 1973-78; program mgr. Army Tank Command, Warren, Mich., 1978-85; dir. lab.

Army Armament R & D Ctr., Dover, 1985-86, tech. dir., 1986-88; v.p., gen. mgr. Hercules Aerospace, Wilmington, Del., 1988-89; pres. Hercules Def. Electronic Systems Inc., Wilmington, 1990-94; chmn. bd. dirs., pres. Alliant Def. Electronics Sys. Inc., Clearwater, Fla., 1994-96; v.p. smart weapons sys. Alliant Techsys., Inc., Mt. Arlington, N.J., 1996—. Mem. Army Sci. Bd., Washington, 1990-93. Recipient Meritorious Civilian Svc. award U.S. Army, 1986, Exceptional Civil Svc. award, 1988. Mem. Assn. of U.S. Army, Am. Def. Preparedness Assn. (Leslie Simon award 1988). Office: Alliant Techsys Inc PO Box 405 Wharton NJ 07885-0405

KROSTAG, DIANE THERESA MICHAELS, clinical informatics analyst; b. Wilkes-Barre, Pa., Apr. 13, 1959; d. William Adam Michaels and Theresa J. Zielinski Stauber; m. William Joseph Krostag, Oct. 20, 1979. AAS in Nursing, Luzerne County C.C., Nanticoke, Pa., 1979; student, U. N.Mex., Albuquerque, 1987-90; BS in Mgmt. Info. Systems, AAS in Computer Info. Syss. summa cum laude, Nat. Am. U., Rio Rancho, Albuquerque, 2000. Staff nurse pediat. U. Hosp., Albuquerque, 1979-80, staff nurse newborn nursery, 1980-81, asst. head nurse newborn nursery, 1981-85; charge nurse pediat. clinic U. Hosp.-Children's Hosp. N.Mex., Albuquerque, 1985-92; clin. info. specialist Shared Med. Sys. Action Sys. Univ. Hosp., Albuquerque, N. Mex., 1992-95; clin. informatics analyst Cerner Carenet Order Mgmt. Sys., Albuquerque, 1995—, Cerner Millennium Power Chart/Core, Albuquerque, 1999—, Cerner Millennium Orders, Albuquerque, 2001—. Recipient Disting. Nurse award Univ. Hosp., 1989. Mem. ANA, Am. Nursing Informatics Assn., N.Mex. Nurses Assn., Balloon Fedn. Am., Albuquerque Aerostat Ascension Assn. Avocation: pvt. pilot hot air balloon. Home: 77 Arizona Sunset Rd NE Albuquerque NM 87124-2538 E-mail: DKrostag@salud.unm.edu.

KROSZNER, RANDALL SCOTT, federal agency administrator, economist; b. Englewood, N.J., June 22, 1962; AB, ScB magna cum laude, Brown U., 1984; MA in Econs., Harvard U., 1987, PhD, 1990. Teaching asst. dept. econs. Brown U., Providence, 1983-84; tutor Winthrop House, Harvard U., Cambridge, Mass., 1985—, rsch. asst., 1985, teaching fellow, 1986; rsch. asst. Nat. Bur. Econ. Rsch., 1985; jr. staff economist Coun. Econ. Advisers, Exec. Office Pres., Washington, 1987—89; R.C. Hoiles postdoctoral fellow Harvard U., Cambridge, 1989-90; prof. bus. econs. U. Chgo. Grad. Sch. Bus., 1990—2001; mem. Coun. of Econ. Adv., Washington, 2001—. Referee Quar. Jour. Econs., Jour. Money, Credit and Banking, Jour. Polit. Economy, Jour. of Bus.; economist Econs. Rsch. Group, Cambridge, Mass., 1989-90. Contbr. articles to profl. jours. NSF fellow, 1984-87, Claude R. Lambe fellow, 1988-89; Richard M. Weaver scholar, 1988-89. Mem. Am. Econ. Assn., Phi Beta Kapa, Sigma Xi. Home: 2000 N Lincoln Park W Chicago IL 60614-4737 Office: Exec Off of the Pres Coun of Econ Adv EEOB, 17th & Pennsylvania Ave NW Washington DC 20502

KROTIUK, WILLIAM JOHN, mechanical engineer; b. Bklyn., July 7, 1948; s. William John and Regina Helen (Chrzanowski) K.; m. Claire Elise Guglielmelli, Oct. 20, 1973; 1 child, Elise Marie. BSME cum laude, Poly. U., Bklyn., 1970; MME, Poly. U., 1978; postgrad., Rensselaer Poly. Inst., 1970-71; MS in Nuclear Engring., Columbia U., 1972. Registered profl. engr., N.Y. R&D project engr. Combustion Engring., Windsor, Conn., 1970-71; supr. applied physics Ebasco Svcs., Inc., N.Y.C., 1972-85; prin. rsch. engr. Battelle Pacific Northwest Labs., Richland, Wash., 1985-87; staff engr. design Lockheed Martin, N.J., Pa., 1988-99; sr. tech. mgr. Dynatherm Corp. Inc., Hunt Valley, Md., 1999—2002; reactor engr. U.S. NRC, Washington, 2002—. Instr., organizer profl. symposia. Author, editor: Thermal-Hydraulics for Space Power, Propulsion and Thermal Management, 1990; contbr. articles, reports to profl. publs. Mem. ASME (reviewer fluids divsn. 1978—), AIAA (reviewer Jour. Thermophysics and Heat Transfer), Am. Nuclear Soc., Pi Tau Sigma, Tau Beta Pi. Avocations: model railroading, woodworking, gardening. Office: US NRC Washington DC

KROTKI, KAROL JOZEF, sociology educator, demographer; b. Cieszyn, Poland, May 15, 1922; emigrated to Can., 1964; s. Karol Stanislaw and Anna Elzbieta (Skrzywanek) K.; m. Joanna Patkowski, July 12, 1947; children—Karol Peter, Jan Jozef, Filip Karol. BA (hons.), Cambridge (Eng.) U., 1948, MA, 1952, Princeton U., 1959, PhD, 1960. Civil ser., Eng., 1948-49; dep. dir. stats. Sudan Govt., 1949 58; vis. fellow Princeton U., 1958-60; rsch. adviser Pakistan Inst. Devel. Econs., 1960-64; asst. dir. census rsch. Dominion Bur. Stats., Can., 1964-68; prof. sociology U. Alta., 1968-83, prof., 1983-91, prof. emeritus, 1991—. Vis. prof. U. Calif., Berkeley, 1967, U. N.C., 1970-73, U. Mich., 1975, U. Costa Rica, 1993; coord. program socio-econ. rsch. Province Alta., 1969-71; cons. in field. Author 14 books; contbr. articles to profl. jours. Served with Polish, French and Brit. Armed Forces, 1939-46. Decorated 10 wartime medals; recipient Achievement award Province of Alta, 1970, Commemorative medal for 125th Ann. of Can., 1992; hon. citizen Gizalki, Poland, 1994; grantee in field. Fellow Am. Statis Assn., Royal Soc. Can. (v.p. 1986-88), Acad. Humanities and Social Scis. (v.p. 1984-86, pres. 1986-88); mem. Fedn. Can. Demographers (v.p. 1977-82, pres. 1982-84), Can. Population Soc., Assn. des Demographes du Que., Soc. Edmonton Demographers (founder, pres. 1990-96, hon. advisor), Ctrl. and E. European Studies Soc. (pres. 1986-88), Population Assn. Am., Internat. Union Sci. Study Population, Assn. Internat. des Demographes de Langue Francaise, Internat. Statis. Inst., Royal Statis. Soc., Polish Culture Soc. (hon. mem.), Polish Soc. Arts & Scis. (London). Roman Catholic. Home: 10137 Clifton Pl Edmonton AB Canada T5N 3H9 Office: U Alta Dept Sociology Edmonton AB Canada T6G 2H4 E-mail: kkrotki@ualberta.ca.

KROTO, HAROLD WALTER, chemistry researcher, educator; b. Oct. 7, 1939; s. Heinz and Edith K.; m. Margaret Henrietta Hunter, 1963; 2 children. Student, U. Sheffield, 1958-64. Postdoctoral fellow NRCC, 1964-66; rsch. scientist Bell Tel. Labs., N.J., 1966-67; lectr. U. Sussex, Brighton Sussex, England, 1968-77, reader, 1977-85, prof. chemistry, 1985-91, Royal Soc. Rsch. prof., 1991—2001. Chmn. Vega Sci. Trust. Contbr. 280 articles to profl. jours. Created knight, 1996; recipient award Sunday Times Book Jacket Design Competition, 1964, Tilden lectr., 1981-82, Faraday lectr., 2002, Internat. New Materials prize Am. Phys. Soc., 1992, Italgas prize for innovation in chemistry, 1992, Longstaff medal Royal Soc. Chemistry, 1993, Hewlett Packard Europhysics prize, 1994, Science pour L'art prize Moet Hennessy Louis Vuitton, 1994; co-recipient Nobel prize in chemistry, 1996. Office: U Sussex Sch Chem Phys & Environ Sci Brighton Sussex BN1 9QJ England

KROTOSZYNSKI, RONALD JAMES, JR., law educator; b. Corpus Christi, Tex., Nov. 3, 1967; s. Ronald James and Barbara Carol (Jamison) K. BA, MA in Philosophy, Emory U., 1987; JD, LLM in Internat. and Comparative Law, Duke U., 1991. Bar: Ga. 1991, U.S. Ct. Appeals (11th cir.) 1991, D.C. 1992, U.S. Ct. Appeals (4th cir.) 1993. Law clk. to Judge Frank M. Johnson, Jr., Montgomery, Ala., 1991-92; assoc. Covington & Burling, Washington, 1992-95; asst. prof. law Ind. U., Indpls., 1995-99, Paul Bean Rsch. Fellow, assoc. prof., 1999-2000; from assoc. prof.to prof., Ethan Allen faculty fellow Washington & Lee U., Lexington, Va., 2000—. Contbr. articles to law jours. Page Miss. del. Dem. Nat. Conv., 1984. Grimes fellow Ind. U.,1996-97. Mem. ABA (vice chmn. publs. com. adminstrv. law sect. 1996 2001). Roman Catholic. Avocations: hiking, theater, wine. Office: Washington and Lee U Sch of Law 473 Sydney Lewis Hall Lexington VA 24450-0303 E-mail: krotoszynskir@wlu.edu.

KROTOWSKI, MARK H. physician; b. Germany, Dec. 12, 1947; came to U.S., 1949; s. Abraham and Eva K.; m. Sally Sendroff; 1 child, Laura. BA in Chemistry, Queens Coll., 1969; MD, Tel Aviv U., 1976. Diplomate Am. Bd. Family Practice. Pvt. practice, Bklyn., 1979—; clin. assoc. prof. Health Scis. Ctr./SUNY, Bklyn., 1980—. Dir., chmn. dept. family practice Brookdale U. Hosp. and Med. Ctr., Bklyn. Mem. World Orgn. Family Physicians, Am. Acad. Family Physicians, Soc. Tchrs. Family Medicine, Med. Soc. State N.Y., Kings County Med. Soc. (chmn. family practice divsn. 1980—). Avocation: computers. Office: 8923 Avenue A Brooklyn NY 11236-1206

KROTSENG, MARSHA VAN DYKE, higher education administrator; b. Indiana, Pa., May 10, 1955; d. Chester James and Helen Louise (Gibson) Van Dyke; m. Morgan Lee Krotseng, June 24, 1978. BA in Spanish, Coll. of William and Mary, 1977, MEd in Edn1. Adminstrn., 1981, EdD in Higher Edn., 1987. Spanish, journalism tchr. Lancaster County Pub. Schs., Irvington, Va., 1977-79; office mgr., computer programmer SEMCO, Inc., Newport News, Va., 1979-80; Spanish, German tchr. Newport News Pub. Schs., 1980-82; rsch. asst. Coll. of William and Mary, Williamsburg, Va., 1982-87; Gov.'s fellow Office of Sec. of Edn. Commonwealth of Va., Richmond, 1984; instnl. rsch. assoc., asst. prof. higher edn. U. Miss., Oxford, 1987-89; asst. dir., planning and inst. rsch. U. Hartford, West Hartford, Conn., 1989-91; dir. rsch. and info. systems State Coll. and Univ. Systems, Charleston, W.Va., 1991-98; assoc. provost Cleve. State U., 1998-99; vice provost, exec. asst. to pres. West Liberty State Coll., 1999—2002; chief planning officer Valdosta State Univ., 2002—. Proposal review panel mem. Assn. for Study of Higher Edn.-Ednl. Resource Info. Ctr. Higher Edn. Report Series, 1992—. Author: (chpt.) Politics and Policy in the Age of Education, 1990; co-editor: Developing Executive Information Systems in Higher Education, 1993; mem. editl. adv. bd. Ednl. Studies, 1990-93; assoc. editor Review of Higher Edn., 1991-94; editorial adv. bd. CASE Internat. Jour. Ednl. Advancement, 1999—. Unit coord. United Way Fund Drive, Hartford, 1989, 90; choir mem., soloist First Presbyn. Ch., South Charleston, 1998-99; mem. Charleston Women's Forum, 1994-98; mem. Leadership W.Va., 1995; mem. Valdosta Symphony Guild. Recipient Outstanding Doctoral Rsch. award Va. Poly. Inst., 1988; named one of Outstanding Young Women of Am., 1985, 86, Outstanding West Virginian, Gov. of W.Va., 1994, Leadership W.Va., 1995, Leadership Wheeling, 2001. Mem. Assn. for Study of Higher Edn. (bd. dirs. 1987-90, site selection com. chair 1990-93), Am. Assn. for Higher Edn., Am. Ednl. Rsch. Assn. (program co-chair divsn. J 1988-89), Am. Assn. Univ. Adminstrs., Assn. for Instnl. Rsch. (publs. bd. 1990-92, exec. com., forum chair 1992-94, v.p. 1998-99, pres. 1999-2000), Soc. for Coll. and Univ. Planning, Nat. Postsecondary Edn. Coop. Coun. on Postsecondary Edn. Stats., Valdosta Symphony Guild, Rotary Internat., Phi Beta Kappa, Kappa Delta Pi (Nat. Essay award 1987). Avocations: cantori montani choral ensemble, art, reading, travel. Office: Valdosta State U 1500 N Patterson St Valdosta GA 31698-0295 E-mail: krotseng@valdosta.edu.

KROUSE, CLYDE FRANCIS, writer; b. Minden, La., Dec. 3, 1946; s. Louis Prescott and Rita Florence Krouse; m. Sharon Ann Krouse, Nov. 4, 1988; children: Sheila, Paige, Justin, Rebecca, Daniel. Grad. h.s., Minden. Quality control inspector GE, Shreveport, La., 1971-78; supr. La. Army Ammunition Plant, Minden, 1979; sheet metal worker Ruskin Divsn.-Tomkins Industries, Minden, 1981-99. Author: (books) Thoughts of an Uneducated Man, 1975, Raccoons Don't Have Long, Floppy Ears, Do They?, 1995, Seen It, Done It, Been There—Ain't Back Yet, 1996, Warm Breezes, Soft Sunsets, Golden Moons, 1998. Mem. AAAS, La. Traditional Bowmen, Bayou State Bowhunters Assn., Masons (lodge 51, Honesty and Integrity award 1964), Mensa. Avocations: woodworking, archery, theorist-theoretical quantum astrophysics.

KROUSE, GEORGE RAYMOND, JR., lawyer; b. Atlantic City, N.J., Sept. 30, 1945; s. George R. and Viola (Rogers) K.; m. Susan Naylor, Aug. 5, 1967; children: Geoffrey, Alison. AB cum laude, Brown U., 1967; JD with distinction, Duke U., 1970. Bar: N.Y. 1971, U.S. Ct. Mil. Appeals 1971, U.S. Dist. Ct. (so. and ea. dists.) N.Y. 1975. Assoc. Simpson Thacher & Bartlett, N.Y.C., 1970-71, 75-78, ptnr., 1978—, chmn. corp. dept., 1991—2002, sr. adminstrv. ptnr., 2001—. Articles editor Duke Law Jour. Mem. bd. visitors Sch. Law, Duke U., Durham, N.C., 1986-92, chmn., 1997-2001; mem. nat. devel. coun. Duke U., 1994-2000, dir. Global Capital Markets Ctr. Capt. USAF, 1971-75. Decorated Air Force Commendation medal, Meritorious Svc. medal. Mem. ABA, N.Y. State Bar Assn., Assn. of Bar of City of N.Y. (com. on corps. 1985-88, com. art law 1990-93), Order of Coif, Montclair Golf Club, Cape Cod Nat. Golf Club, Bonita Bay Club. Avocation: golf. Home: 4 Erwin Park Montclair NJ 07042-3018 Office: Simpson Thacher & Bartlett 425 Lexington Ave 18th Fl New York NY 10017-3954 E-mail: g-krouse@stblaw.com.

KROUSE, HELENE JUNE, nursing educator; b. Bklyn., Mar. 24, 1955; d. Sidney and Gertrude Kempner; m. John H. Krouse, May 6, 1979; children: Beth Melissa, Daniel Jacob. BS cum laude, SUNY, Bklyn., 1976; MS, U. Rochester, 1979; PhD, Boston Coll., 1984. Cert. adult nurse practitioner, cert. otorhinolaryngology nurse. Staff nurse Downstate Med. Ctr., Bklyn., 1976-77; instr. in nursing Hunter Coll.-Bellevue Sch. Nursing, N.Y.C., 1979-80; asst. prof., coord. med.-surg. nursing Emmanuel Coll., Boston, 1980-84; asst. prof. nursing Boston Coll., Chestnut Hill, Mass., 1984-89; adult nurse practitioner Mass. Eye and Ear Infirmary, Boston; adminstr., nurse practitioner to Ear, Nose, Throat, Sinus and Allergy practice, Ormond Beach, 1989—2001; assoc. prof. U. North Fla., Jacksonville, 1995-97, acting chairperson dept. nursing, 1996-97; assoc. prof. U. Fla., 1997-2001; prof., asst. dean adult health Wayne State U., 2001—. Faculty fellow Boston Coll., 1988, rsch. fellow, 1987; bd. dirs. Nat. Certifying Bd. for Otorhinolaryngology and Head-Neck Nurses. Mem. rev. panel Nursing Rsch.; feature editor ORL-Head and Neck Nursing; contbr. articles on otolaryngology and allergy, compliance and decision making to profl. jours., also chpts. to books. Bd. dirs. Ear, Nose, Throat Nursing Found., 2002—, pres.-elect, 2003—. Recipient Ednl. award, ENT divsn. Smith and Nephew Inc., 1998, First Place in Ann. Videotape Contest, Soc. Otorhinolargyngology-Head and Neck Nurses, Sanders award for basic rsch., Am. Acad. Otolaryngic Allergy, 2001; grantee, U. Rochester Alumni Seed Found., 1978—79, Emmanuel Coll., 1981—83, Am. Acad. Otolaryngic Allergy Found., 2000—01; scholar, So. Nursing Rsch. Soc./Am. Nurses Found., 1998. Fellow Am. Acad. Nursing; mem. Oncology Nurse Soc., So. Nursing Rsch. Soc. (awards com. 2000), Soc. Otorhinolaryngology and Head-Neck Nurses, Inc. (chair nat. rsch. com., bd. dirs. 2000-2001, nat. cert. bd. 2001-2002, ENT-NF bd. 2002—, pres.-elect 2003), Sigma Theta Tau (Clin. Rsch. award 1986-87). Office: Wayne State U Coll Nursing 5557 Cass Ave Detroit MI 48202 E-mail: hjkrouse@wayne.edu .

KROWN, SEYMOUR RICHARD, film production executive; b. L.A., Feb. 17, 1931; s. Samuel P. and Frances Krown; m. Leatrice Krown, Nov. 19, 1955 (dec. 1990); children: Cheryl, Kenneth, Joel; m. Dena Mae Krown, 1998. Student, Calif. Poly. Inst., 1949-52. Engr. NBC, Hollywood, Calif., 1955-59; editor Paramount TV Prodns., Hollywood, 1959-63; prodn. mgr. United Prodns. Am., Burbank, Calif., 1963-75; v.p. prodn. L.A., 1977—; producer, dir. Walt Disney Prodns., Burbank, 1975-77, ret., 1965; cons., 1965. Dir. (TV show) The Mickey Mouse Club; producer: (films) An Evening with Stephen Leacock, The Gift, Inside the Mountain, Gold!, The First Metal, (TV documentary) Christopher Columbus: The Voyage of Discovery, 1987, I Made It Through The Rain, 1996, What's up Tiger Lily. Served as cpl. U.S. Army, 1953-55. Recipient Chris award Columbus Film Festival, 1970, Golden Babe award Chgo. Film Festival, 1986. Mem. Dirs. Guild Am., Pacific Pioneer Broadcasters.

KRPATA, STEVEN ALLEN, accountant, real estate company executive; b. Southington, Conn., Feb. 15, 1953; s. Edward Joseph Krpata Jr. and Nancy Jean (Davis) Niemi; m. Sheryl Jeanne Wilford, Sept. 1975 (div. Apr. 1990); m. Carole Lee Valente, Jan. 1, 1991 (div. Mar. 2002); stepchildren: Alexia M., Monica M.; m. Rebecca M. Alexander, July 19, 2003. BS, U. Conn., 1975, post-grad. studies Bus. Adminstrn., 1991-96; MBA, E. Carolina U., 1998. CPA, Conn. Controller U. Conn. Co-op, Storrs, 1975-78; v.p., controller Chase Enterprises, Hartford, Conn., 1978-85; pres. Diversified Enterprises, Inc., Hebron, Conn., 1985-90; prin. Steven A. Krpata CPA & Assocs., New Haven, 1991-96; CFO WEDCO Enterprises, Greenville, NC, 1997—2003; pres. SAK Devel., Greenville, 2003—. Treas. Assoc. Student Commissaries, Storrs., Conn., 1972-73, chmn. 1973-75 Treas. Bethany (Conn.) Congl. Ch., 1992; mem. Republican Orgn, Bethany, 1989-97, Greenville, N.C., 1997—; mem. exec. com. Pitt County GOP, 1999—. Mem. AICPA (fed. legis. com. 1993—), NRA (life), NRA-Inst. for Legis. Action. Avocations: flying (pvt. lic.), fly fishing, hunting. Office: WEDCo Enterprises PO Box 20443 Greenville NC 27858-0443

KRSUL, JOHN ALOYSIUS, JR., lawyer; b. Highland Park, Mich., Mar. 24, 1938; s. John A. and Ann M. (Sepich) K.; m. Justine Oliver, Sept. 12, 1958; children: Ann Lisa, Mary Justine. BA, Albion Coll., 1959; JD, U. Mich., 1963. Bar: Mich. 1963. Assoc. Dickinson Wright PLLP, 1963-71, ptnr., 1971-99, consulting ptnr., 2000—. Asst. editor: U. Mich. Law Rev, 1962-63. Recipient Disting. Alumnus award Albion Coll., 1984; Sloan scholar, 1958-59; Fulbright scholar, 1959-60; Ford. Found. grantee, 1964 Fellow: Am. Bar Found. (life; chmn. Mich. chpt. 1988—89); mem.: ABA (ho. of dels. 1979—2002, chmn. standing com. on membership 1983—89, exec. coun. 1984—91, chmn. sect. gen. practice 1989—90, tort and ins. practice sect., exec. coun. 1991—94, bd. govs. 1991—99, chmn. fin. com. 1993—94, exec. com. 1993—94, 1996—99, treas. 1996—99, editl. bd. ABA Jour. 1996—99, chmn. audit com. 2003—), Am. Bar Ins. Cons. Inc. (bd. dirs. sec. 1988—95), Am. Bar Endowment (bd. dirs. 1996—99), Nat. Conf. Bar Pres. (exec. coun. 1986—89), Am. Judicature Soc. (dir. 1971—79, exec. com. 1973—74), Fellows of Young Lawyers Am. Bar (bd. dirs. 1977—86, pres. 1983—84, chmn. bd. 1984—86), Mich. State Bar Found. (trustee 1982—83, 1985—99, chmn. fellows 1986—87), State Bar Mich. (commr. 1973—83, pres. 1982—83), Detroit Bar Assn. Found. (dir. 1971—84, pres. 1979—80), Detroit Bar Assn. (dir. 1971—80, pres. 1979—80), Am. Bar Retirement Assn. (bd. dirs. 1999—2003), Sixth Cir. Jud. Conf. (life), Detroit Club, Orchard Lake Country Club, Delta Tau Delta, Phi Eta Sigma, Omicron Delta Kappa, Phi Beta Kappa. Home: 7094 Huntington Dr Sawyer MI 49125-9319 Office: Dickinson Wright PLLC 500 Woodward Ave Ste 4000 Detroit MI 48226-3416

KRUCENSKI, LEONARD JOSEPH, secondary education educator; b. Buffalo, June 15, 1931; s. Stanislous and Anna Victoria (Pyzanowska) K.; m. Estelle Ann Gaik, Oct. 19, 1957; children: Leonard S., Brian M., William G. BS cum laude, SUNY, Buffalo, 1976, MS in Edn., 1980, EdD, 2001. Electronics technician Bell Aero Space Inc., Niagara Falls, N.Y., 1953-62, Moog Valve Inc, East Aurora, N.Y., 1962-69; engring. aid Cornell Aero. Labs. Inc., Buffalo, 1969-75; jr. engr. Kistler Instruments Inc., Clarence, N.Y., 1975-79; tchr. electronics Buffalo Pub. Sch. System, 1979—2000; ret., 2000. Recipient 85th Anniversary Alumni Disting. Svc. award Hutchinson Cen. Tech. High Sch., 1989. Mem. ASCD, NEA, Am. Vocat. Assn., Nat. Assn. Indsl. and Tech. Tchr. Educators, N.Y. State Occupational Edn. Assn., Vocat. Tech. Guild Buffalo, Buffalo Tchrs. Fedn. Avocations: woodworking, philately. Home: 176 Lorelee Dr Tonawanda NY 14150-4325

KRUCH, ALEKSANDR, retired gynecologist, educator; b. Volgograd, Russia, Apr. 4, 1933; s. Ilya A. and Nina B. Kruch; 1 child, Yelena A. MD, Volgograd U., 1957; PhD, Volgograd Med. U., 1965. Gynecologist, Dubovka, Russia, 1957—58, Hosp. No. 23, Volgograd, 1958—62; aspirant Med. U. Volgograd, 1962—65; prof. ob-gyn. Med. U. Kursk, 1965—98; ret., 1998. Author: Large Fetus (Macrosomia), 2001; contbr. Home: 100 Norway St Apt 308 Boston MA 02115

KRUCHKO, JOHN GREGORY, lawyer; b. Iowa City, Iowa, Sept. 3, 1948; s. Demitro M. and Caroline (Maloney) K.; m. Susan Lynn Clendaniel, Sept. 15, 1968; 1 child, Jennifer Lynn. B.A., Xavier U., 1970; M.A. in History, U. Cin., 1971, M.A. in Labor Relations, 1972; J.D., Coll. William and Mary, 1975. Bar: Pa. 1975, Md. 1977, D.C. 1983, U.S. Dist. Ct. (ea. and mid. dists.) Pa. 1976, Md. 1978, U.S. Ct. Appeals (4th cir.) 1978, (3d cir.) 1979, U.S. Supreme Ct. 1983. Assoc. Morgan, Lewis & Bockius, Phila., 1975-77, Venable, Baetjer & Howard, Balt., 1977-79; founder, sr. ptnr. Kruchko & Fries, Balt., 1979— . Author: Birth of a Union Local, 1973; The Maryland Employer's Guide to Labor and Employment Law, 1984. Contbr. articles to profl. jours. Chmn. fin. com. Balt. County Victory '84 Reagan/Bush, 1984. Mem. ABA (sect. labor and employment law, subcom. co-chmn. 1980—), Am. Acad. Hosp. Attys., Md. Bar Assn., Pa. Bar Assn. Roman Catholic. Clubs: Center (Balt.); University (Towson, Md.). Home: 7929 Westpark Dr Ste 202 Mc Lean VA 22102-4238

KRUCK, DONNA JEAN, special education educator, consultant; b. Peoria, Ill., Jan. 26, 1930; d. Walter George and Lois Irene (Newburn) Hagemeyer; m. Michael Roy Kruck Jr., June 27, 1948; children: Pamela Ann Kruck Hokanson, Michael Roy III, Quentin Robert; m. Somran Sirironrong, May 19, 1998. BS, Ill. State U., 1961; MEd, U. Ill., 1968. Cert. spl. edn. tchr. and adminstr., Ill. Tchr. New Lenox Dist. 122, Ill., 1956-61; tchr. spl. edn. Lincoln Way Area Joint Agreement, New Lenox, 1961-66; tchr. spl. edn., coord. Joliet Twp. High Sch. Dist. 204, Ill., 1966-86; pvt. practice cons. and diagnostician New Lenox, 1986-92. Child adv. New Lenox Dist. 122, 1986-88; instr. Chapel Christian U., 1994-96; LCMS missionary, ESL tchr., Bangkok, 1997—. Author: Let's Learn to Cook, 1971. Pres. Joliet Twp. Edn. Assn., 1971-76; donar Aurora Area Blood Bank, Joliet, 1974-90; v.p. Island Lakes Homeowners Assn., 1994-96; v.p. Luth. Women's Missionary League, 1993, pres., 1994-97; pres. Aid Assn. for Luths., 1995-97. Mem. AAUW, NEA (life), Nat. Ret. Tchr. Assn., Am. Assn. Retired Persons, Am. Assn. Mental Retardation, Am. Bus. Women's Assn., Coun. Exceptional Children (life), Coun. Adminstrs. Spl. Edn., Christian Edn. Assn., Ill. Edn. Assn. (life), Ill. Div. Learning Disabilities, Coun. for Ednl. Diagnostic Svcs. (div. learning disabilities), Lutherans for Life, Kappa Delta Pi, Delta Kappa Gamma. Lutheran. Avocations: traveling, presenting travelogues. Office: Concordia Gospel Ministry 205/20 Soi Chairyakiat 1 Ngam Wong Wan 10210 Bangkok Thailand Home: 1/121 Soi Chinnakhet 1/21 Ngam Wong Wan Rd Bangkok 10210 Thailand

KRUCKEBERG, ARTHUR RICE, botanist, educator; b. L.A., Mar. 21, 1920; s. Arthur Woodbury and Ella Muriel K.; m. Mareen Schultz, Mar. 21, 1953; children— Arthur Leo, Enid Johanna; children by previous marriage— Janet Muriel, Patricia Elayne, Caroline. BA, Occidental Coll., Los Angeles, 1941; postgrad., Stanford U., 1941-42; PhD, U. Calif.-Berkeley, 1950. Instr. biology Occidental Coll., 1946; teaching asst. U. Calif.-Berkeley, 1946-50; mem. faculty U. Wash., Seattle, 1950—, prof. botany, 1964-88, emeritus, 1988—, chmn. dept., 1971-77. Cons. in field. Co-founder Wash. Natural Area Preserves system, 1966. Served with USNR, 1942-46. Mem. Wash. Native Plant Soc. (founder 1976), Calif. Bot. Soc. Rsch. edaphics of serpentines, flowering plants. Home: 20312 15th Ave NW Shoreline WA 98177-2166 Office: U Wash PO Box 351330 Seattle WA 98195-1330 E-mail: ark@u.washington.edu.

KRUCKENBERG, TERESA MAY, research engineer, consultant; b. New Orleans, Aug. 23, 1963; d. Harold Dean and Joanna Marie (Clutter) K.; m. Matthew Reymond McDonald, Mar. 21, 1998; children: Emily Jane, Isabella Catherine. BSChemE, Okla. State U., 1985; MSME, San Diego State U., 1993. Composite structures rsch. and devel. engr. Hercules Aerospace, Salt Lake City, 1985-89; sr. rsch. engr. BF Goodrich Aerospace (Rohr), San Diego, 1989-94, CRC-ACS, Sydney, Australia, 1994—; cons. Wilson Composite Group, Folsom, Calif., 1998-99. Cons. BF Goodrich Aerospace, San Diego, 1999. Author chpt. Resin Transfer Moulding for Aerospace Structures, 1998; editor Resin Transfer Moulding for Aerospace Structures, 1998. Mem. Soc. Mfg. Eng., Soc. for Advancement of Materials and Process Engring. (chmn. Australia chpt. 1996-97). Avocations: scuba diving, hiking. Office: CRC-ACS 361 Milperra Rd NSW Bankstown 2200 Australia E-mail: tkruckenberg@crc-acs.com.au.

KRUCKS, WILLIAM NORMAN, lawyer; b. Chgo., Oct. 28, 1949; s. William and Lorraine (Rauland) K.; m. Linda C. Robertson; children: Kathryn Leigh, Greta Anne, Laura Elizabeth. BA, Tulane U., 1972; JD, U. Miss., 1976. Bar: Ill. 1976, Miss. 1976, U.S. Dist. Ct. (no. dist.) Ill. 1976, U.S. Dist. Ct. (no. dist.) Miss. 1976, U.S. Ct. Appeals (5th and 7th cirs.) 1976, U.S. Supreme Ct. 1980, U.S. Dist. Ct. (cen. dist.) Ill. 1984. Assoc. Rooks, Pitts and Poust, Chgo., 1976-83; founding ptnr. Freeborn & Peters, Chgo., 1983—. Chmn., gen. counsel, bd. dirs., corp. sec. Rauland Borg Corp. Editor Miss. Law Jour., 1974-76; contbr. articles to law jours. Atty. Chgo. Vol. Legal Svcs., 1982—. Named Outstanding Young Man Am., U.S. Jaycees, 1976; recipient Dean Robert T. Farley award U. Miss., 1977. Mem. Ill. Self-Insured Assn., Def. Rsch. Inst., Chgo. Assn. Commerce and Industry, Nat. Coun. Self-Insured, Beter Govt. Assn., Am. Jud. Soc., Tulane U. Alumni Assn., U. Miss. Alumni Assn., ABA, Ill. Bar Assn., Chgo. Bar Assn., Miss. Bar Assn., Workers Compensation Lawyers Assn., Legal Club Chgo., Union League Club (Chgo.), Chgo. Yacht Club, Internat. Assn. of Def. Counsel, Phi Delta Phi, Sigma Nu. Methodist. Home: 920 Sunset Rd Winnetka IL 60093-3623 E-mail: bkrucks@freebornpeters.com., wnk@krucks.com.

KRUDOP, DONALD W. music educator, choral director; b. Morristown, NJ, Apr. 18, 1953; s. Joan Ann Palmieri and Anthony Joseph Palmieri, Jr.(Stepfather); m. Susan Ann Steffe, June 14, 1986; children: James, Marc. MusB Edn., Shenandoah Coll. & Conservatory of Music, 1975; MusM in Conducting, Shenandoah U., 1992, postgrad., 1997—. Cert. k-12 music tchr. Vocal music specialist Holland Elem. Sch., Virginia Beach, Va., 1975—86; choral dir. Princess Anne Jr. H.S., Virginia Beach, 1986—89; dir. of choral music edn. Salem H.S., Virginia Beach, 1989—. Adj. faculty mem. Va. Wesleyan Coll., Virginia Beach, 1999—; dir. of music Heritage United Meth. Ch., Virginia Beach, 2000—; festival adjudicator Festivals of Excellence, Ashland, Va., 2002—, Fiesta-val, Richmond, Va., 1998—. Dir.: (invitational concert tour of great brita) Celebration of American Music, 1999. Recipient Disting. Alumni award, Shenandoah U., 2000. Mem.: Am. Choral Dirs. Assn. (va. repertoire & standards chmn. 1997—99), Va. Choral Dirs. Assn. (pres. 2002—), Va. Music Educators Assn. (Music Educator of Yr. dist. 2 2002), Music Educators Nat.

Conf. Home: 436 Cronin Rd Virginia Beach VA 23452 Office: Salem HS 1993 SunDevil Dr Virginia Beach VA 23464 Office Fax: 757-474-8483. Personal E-mail: dkrudop@aol.com. E-mail: dwkrudop@vbcps.k12.va.us.

KRUEGER, ANNE O. economist; b. Endicott, N.Y. BA, Oberlin (Ohio) Coll., 1953; MS, U. Wis., 1956, PhD, 1958, Georgetown U., 1992; PhD (hon.), Hacettepe U., Ankara, Turkey, 1990, Monash U., 1995. Asst. prof. econs. U. Minn., Mpls., 1959-63, assoc. prof. econs., 1963-66, prof. econs., 1966-82; v.p. econs. and rsch. The World Bank, Washington, 1982-86; art and scis. prof. econs. Duke U., Durham, N.C., 1987-93; Herald and Caroline L. Ritch prof arts and scis. in econs. Stanford (Calif.) U., 1993—, dir. Ctr. Rsch. Econ. Devel. and Policy Reform, 1996-2001; 1st dep. mng. dir. IMF, 2001—. Bd. dirs. Nordson Corp., Westlake, Ohio; mem. vis. com. Econs. Dept. Harvard U., 1990-98; sr. non-resident fellow Brookings Inst.; rsch. assoc. Nat. Bur. Econ. Rsch. Author: Trade Policies and Developing Nations, 1995, Economic Policies at Cross Purposes, 1993, Economic Policy Reform in Developing Countries, 1992, The Political Economy of Agricultural Pricing Policy, Vol. 5: A Synthesis of the Political Economy in Developing Countries, 1992, Economic Policy Reform: The Second Stage, 2000; co-author (with O. Aktan): Swimming Against the Tide: Turkish Trade Reform in the 1980s, 1992; editor: (with R.H. Bates) Political and Economic Interactions in Economic Policy Reform, 1993, The World Trade Orgnaization as an International Institution, 1998. Mem. N.Y. State Regents Commn. on Higher Edn., 1992-93. Recipient Robertson prize NAS, 1984, Bernhard Harms prize Inst. for World Economy, Kiel, 1990, Enterprise award Kenan Inst., 1990, Seidman prize, 1994. Fellow AAAS, Econometric Soc. (award 1984); mem. NAS, Am. Econ. Assn. (disting. fellow, chmn. com. rsch. 1988-92, chmn. commn. on grad. edn. in econs. 1989-90, v.p. 1977, pres.-elect 1995, pres. 1996, rep. to Internat. Econ. Assn. and mem. IEA exec. com. 1992-98, v.p. Internat. Econ. Assn. 1994-98). Office: Internat Monetary Fund Washington DC 20431

KRUEGER, ARLIN JAMES, physicist; b. Oct. 22, 1933; s. Rudolph August and Mathilda E. (Pooch) K.; m. Susan J. Peacock, Dec. 28, 1978; children: Sandra, Timothy, Terry. BA, U. Minn., 1955, postgrad., 1956-58, Colo. State U., 1976-78, PhD, 1984. Physicist Naval Weapons Ctr., China Lake, Calif., 1959-69; physicist-astrophysicist Goddard Space Flight Ctr., Greenbelt, Md., 1969-2000; W.H. Elkins prof. physics U. Md., Balt., 2000—01, rsch. prof., 2001—. Developer of rocket and satellite instruments: sensor sci. Nimbus-7 Total Ozone Mapping Spectrometer (TOMS), 1975—93, Rocoz Optical Rocket Ozonesonde, 1961—79, Volcanic Ash Mapper (VOLCAM), 1998—2000; mem. com. ext. U.S. Std. Atmosphere; instrument scientist U.S.-USSR Meteor 3/TOMS mission, U.S. Earth Probe/TOMS mission; prin. investigator Japanese ADEOS/TOMS mission, NASA Earth Sys. Scis. Pathfinder, Volcanic Ash Monitor (VOLCAM) Satellite Program, NASA Airborne Antarctic Ozone Experiment/TOMS Real-Time Support, NASA Airborne Arctic Experiment/TOMS Real Time Support; co-investigator Earth Observing Sys. Volcanic Eruption Investigation, Rsch. on Antarctic Ozone Hole; adv. volcanic hazards panel Office Fed. Coord. of Meteorology; invited lectr. Nat. Inst. Polar Rsch., Tokyo, AT&T Bell Labs., U.S. Naval Acad., Goddard Space Flight Ctr. Engring. Colloquium, Gordon Rsch. Conf. on Volcano-Climate, Fermi Sch. Physics, Italy, Russian Acad. Scis., Moscow; Quaternary Rsch. lectr. U. Wash.; invited participant and spkr. sci. workshops and confs. Contbr. articles to profl. publs. Recipient Exceptional Sci. Achievement medal, NASA, Exceptional Svc. medal, 2001, Goddard rsch. and study fellow 1976-78, Colo. State U., 1976—78. Mem. AAAS, Am. Meteorol. Soc., Internat. Assn. Meteorology and Atmospheric Physics (internat. ozone commn.), Am. Geophys. Union, Sigma Xi. Achievements include research on stratospheric ozone, remote sensing from satellites, volcanic eruptions, volcanic aviation hazards, atmosphere of Mars. Office: JCET U Md Baltimore County 1000 Hilltop Cir Baltimore MD 21250 E-mail: akrueger@umbc.edu.

KRUEGER, ARTUR W. G. international business consultant; b. Neuendorf, Ger., Jan. 16, 1940; came to U.S., 1975; s. Werner Georg and Charlotte (Klein) K. MS in Bus. Policy, Columbia U., 1978. Mktg. exec., gen. mgr. Rosenthal A.G. Subsidaries, Spain, Scandinavia, U.S., 1970-79; pres. Am. Euro Cons. Co., Inc., Houston, 1980—. Lectr. in field. Mem. Am. Mgmt. Assn., Space Found., Columbia Bus. Assocs., Internat. Bus. Coun., Marine Tech. Soc., Instrument Soc. Am., Houston World Trade Assn., Norwegian-Am. C. of C., U.S. C. of C., German Am. C. of C., Swiss Am. C. of C., French Am. C. of C. Office: Am European Cons Co Inc PO Box 19686 Houston TX 77224-9686

KRUEGER, BETTY JANE, telecommunications company executive; b. Indpls., Oct. 4, 1923; d. Forrest Glen and Hazel Luellen (Taylor) Burns; m. Alan Douglas Krueger, Apr. 4, 1975; 1 son by previous marriage--Michael J. Vornehm. Student, Butler U., 1948-49. Supr., instr. Ind. Bell Telephone Co., Indpls., 1941-54; supr. communications Jones & Laughlin Steel Co., Indpls., 1954-56, Ford Motor Co., Indpls., 1956-64, U.S. Govt., Camp Atterbury, Ind., 1964-66; dir. communications Meth. Hosp. of Ind., Indpls., 1966-79; pres., owner Rent-A-Radio, Inc. of Ind., Indpls., after 1979; sec.-treas. Communications Unltd., Inc. Former pres. Am. Legion Aux.; chmn. for Ind., Girls State U.S.A., 1972-77; probation officer vol., 1973-74; suicide prevention counselor, 1972-73; mem. Nat. Wildlife Fund. Recipient award for outstanding community service Ford Motor Co., 1961. Mem. Am. Soc. Hosp. Engring., Am. Hosp. Assn., Nat. Assn. Bus. and Ednl. Radio, Inc., Nat. Mus. Women in Arts, Internat. Teletypewriters for the Deaf, Assn. Public Safety Communications Officers, Inc., Am. Bus. Women. Methodist. Home: 6242 N 575 E Franklin IN 46131-8759 Office: 4545 Southeastern Ave Indianapolis IN 46203-2307

KRUEGER, BONNIE LEE, editor, writer; b. Chgo., Feb. 3, 1950; d. Harry Bernard and Lillian (Soyak) Krueger; m. James Lawrence Spurlock, Mar. 8, 1972. Student, Morraine Valley Coll., 1970. Adminstrv. asst. Carson Pirie Scott & Co., Chgo., 1969-72; traffic coord. Tatham Laird & Kudner, Chgo., 1973-74, J. Walter Thompson, Chgo., 1974-76, prodn. coord., 1976-78; editor-in-chief Assoc. Pubs., Chgo., 1978—, Sophisticate's Hairstyle Guide, 1978—, Sophisticate's Beauty Guide, 1978—, Complete Woman, 1981—; pub., editorial svcs. dir. Sophisticate's Black Hair Guide, 1983—, Sophisticate's Soap Star Styles, 1994-95. Mem. Statue of Liberty Restoration Com., N.Y.C., 1983; campaign worker Cook County State's Atty., Chgo., 1982; poll watcher Cook County Dem. Orgn., 1983; mem. Chgo. Architecture Found. Recipient Exceptional Woman in Pub. award, Women in Periodical Pub., 2000, Communicator of Yr. award, Am. Health and Beaty Aids Inst. Mem. Soc. Profl. Journalists, Am. Health and Beauty Aids Inst. (assoc. mem., Communicator of Yr. award), Lincoln Park Zool. Soc., Landmarks Preservation Coun. of Ill., Art Inst. Chgo., Chgo. Hist. Soc., Mus. Contemporary Art, Peta, Headline Club, Sigma Delta Chi. Lutheran. Office: Complete Woman 875 N Michigan Ave Chicago IL 60611-1803 *I approach my life like one would approach the climbing of a mountain— plenty of faith, determination, self criticism, hard work and the joy and knowledge that the top is there for everyone to reach, if you pursue it with a combination of fervor, patience and love.*

KRUEGER, DARRELL WILLIAM, academic administrator; b. Salt Lake City, Feb. 9, 1943; s. William T. and E. Marie (Nelson) K.; m. Verlene Terry, July 1, 1965 (dec. Jan., 1969); 1 child, William; m. Nancy Leane Jones, Sept. 2, 1969; children: Tonya, Amy, Susan. BA summa cum laude, So. Utah State Coll., 1967; MA in Govt., U. Ariz., 1969, PhD in Govt., 1971. Asst. prof. polit. sci. N.E. Mo. State U., Kirksville, 1971-73, v.p. acad. affairs, dean of instrn., 1973-89; pres. Winona State U., Minn., 1989—. Facilitator The 7 Habits of Highly Effective People, 1993, Crucial Conservations, 2003; mem. adv. bd. U.S. Bank, Rochester, Minn., 1989—. Mem. Gamehaven Coun. Boy Scouts Am., 1989—. Recipient Outstanding Alumnus award, So. Utah State, 1992. Mem.: Am. Assn. Higher Edn., Am. Assn. State Colls. and Univs., Rotary, Phi Beta Kappa. Mem. Lds Ch. Avocations: running, golf. Home: 1411 Heights Blvd Winona MN 55987-2519 Office: Winona State U Somsen 201 8th & Johnson Winona MN 55987

KRUEGER, DEBORAH A. BLAKE, school psychologist, consultant; b. Chgo., Aug. 22, 1954; d. Stanley Walter and Maryanne Lois Blake; m. Darrell George Krueger, May 31, 1986; children: Sarah, Joshua. BA, DePaul U., 1976, MEd, 1980; PhD, Loyola U., 1998. Lic. psychologist, Ill. Learning disabilities specialist Assocs. in Family Therapy, Lake Bluff, Ill., 1980-85; reading and learning disabilities specialist Proviso West H.S., Hillside, Ill., 1980-82; edn. therapist Hartgrove Hosp., Chgo., 1982-85; dir. spl. edn. Old Orchard Hosp., Skokie, Ill., 1985-87; program coord. One-to-One Learning Ctr., Northfield, Ill., 1995-98; sch. psychologist Winnetka (Ill.) Pub. Schs., 1997—. Cons. Naperville and Woodridge Schs., 1998—; lectr. Loyola U., Chgo., 1997—; pvt. practice, Northbrook, Ill., 2000—; third-party cons. Hartgrove Psychol. Hosp., Chgo., 1985-88, Old Orchard Psychol. Hosp., Skokie, 1987-89; co-founder Baby N'Me Mother-Infant Dyad Groups, 1991; spkr. Resolve Orgn., Good Samaritan Hosp., Downers Grove, Ill., 1991. Founder Living with Infertility and Experimentation (L.I.F.E.), Evanston, Ill., 1990-96; mem. steering com. Resolve for L.I.F.E. Group, Evanston, 1990-94. Grantee Loyola U., 1996. Mem. APA, Assn. for Advancement Therapeutic Edn., Nat. Assn. Sch. Psychologists, Soc. Personality Assessment, Ill. Sch. Psychol. Assn., Ill. Assn. for Infant Mental Health. Avocations: piano, fitness, personal reading, local school involvement. Home: 2434 Ridgeway Ave Evanston IL 60201-1858 Office: Winnetka Pub Schs 520 Glendale Ave Winnetka IL 60093-2135 also: 910 Skokie Blvd Northbrook IL 60062 E-mail: DbKrueger@aol.com.

KRUEGER, EUGENE REX, academic program consultant; b. Grand Island, Nebr., Mar. 30, 1935; s. Rudolph F. and Alma K.; m. Karin Schubert, June 9, 1957; children: Eugene Eric, Richard Kevin, Kristina. Student, Kans. State U., 1952-53; BS in Physics, Rensselaer Poly. Inst., 1957, MS in Math, 1960, PhD in Applied Math, 1962. Research physicist IBM, 1957-58; research fellow Army Math. Research Center, U. Wis., 1962-63; prof. U. Colo., Boulder, 1965-74; vice chancellor, prof. Oreg. State System of Higher Edn., Eugene, 1974-82; exec. cons. Control Data Corp., 1982-85, v.p., 1985-89; exec. dir. tech.-based engring. edn. consortium William C. Norris Inst., 1989-96, v.p., 1996-97. Adj. prof. computer sci. U. Minn., 1989-94; adj. prof. Western Sem., 1997-01; chmn. seminar for dirs. of acad. computing facilities, 1969-82; pres. Krueger & Assocs., 1989—; cons. on computer graphics computing facility mgmt.; dir. various research grants and contracts; U.S. acad. cons. African Virtual U./World Bank, 1995—; interim pres. Christian Heritage Coll., 1998. Contbr. research papers in field to publs. Mem. Sigma Xi, Phi Kappa Phi. E-mail: rex@bendcable.com.

KRUEGER, GERALD PETER, psychologist; b. Evanston, Ill., Apr. 3, 1944; s. Albert August and Pauline Mary (Didier) K.; m. Jessica Ann Prendergast, Aug. 26, 1967; children: Michael G., Deborah L., Kevin A. BA in Psychology, U. Dayton, 1966; MA in Exptl. and Engring. Psychology, Johns Hopkins U., 1975, PhD in Exptl. Psychology, 1977; grad., U.S. Army Command and Gen. Staff Coll., 1980, U.S. Army War Coll., 1988. Cert. profl. ergonomist Bd. Certification Profl. Ergonomics. Engring. psychology rschr. Bunker-Ramo Corp., Wright-Patterson AFB, Ohio, 1966-69; human factors rsch. psychologist U.S. Army Human Engring. Lab., Aberdeen, Md., 1969-71; R & D coord. Def. Advanced Rsch. Projects Agy., Saigon, Vietnam, 1971-72; mil. police ops. officer U.S. Army, Ft. Meade, Md., 1972, aviation psychologist Aeromed. Rsch. Lab. Ft. Rucker, Ala., 1976-80; R & D programs staff officer U.S. Army Med. R & D Command, Ft. Detrick, Md., 1980-84; dep. chief dept. behavioral biology Walter Reed Army Inst. Rsch., Washington, 1984-88; dir. biomed. applications rsch. divsn. U.S. Army Aeromed. Rsch. Lab., Ft. Rucker, 1988-90; comdr., scientific tech. dir. U.S. Army Rsch. Inst. Environ. Medicine, Natick, Mass., 1990-94; ret. col. U.S. Army, 1994; v.p. ergonomics R & D svcs. Biomechanics Corp. Am., Melville, N.Y., 1994-95; prin. rsch. scientist, ergonomist Star Mountain, Inc., Alexandria, Va., 1995-98; pres. Krueger Ergonomics Cons., Inc., 1998—; prin. scientist, ergonomist Wexford Group Internat., Vienna, Va., 2000—. Tchr. U.S. Armed Forces Inst., Saigon, 1971, Johns Hopkins U., 1974-75, U. So. Calif., 1977-80; adj. asst. prof. med.-clin. psychology Uniformed Svcs. U. Health Scis., Bethesda, Md., 1997—; mem. sci. coun. to UTEK Corp., Plant City, Fla., 1999—. Book review editor Ergonomics in Design Mag., 1995—; assoc. editor Mil. Psychology, 1991-2003, mem. editl. bd., 2003--; guest editor jours. in field; contbr. articles to profl. jours. Recipient Richard M. Griffith Meml. award So. Soc. Philosophy and Psychology, 1978, order of mil. med. merit for career contbns. army med. dept., 1992, numerous mil. awards, medals and skill proficiency badges, including Legion of Merit, 1994, Bronze Star U.S. Army, 1972, meritorious svc. medals with 2 oak leaf clusters. Fellow APA (pres. divsn. mil. psychology 1995-96, pres. divsn. engring. psychologists 2001-02); mem. Soc. for Indsl. Orgnl. Psychologists, Am. Indsl. Hygiene Assn., Assn. U.S. Army, Nat. Def. Indsl. Assn., Human Factors and Ergonomics Soc. (pres. Potomac chpt. 2003), Aerospace Med. Assn., Aerospace Human Factors Assn., Soc. for Human Performance in Extreme Environments, Army War Coll. Alumni Assn., VFW, Am. Legion. Roman Catholic. Avocations: participating in running events, organizing community activities. Office: Krueger Ergonomics Consultants 4105 Komes Ct Alexandria VA 22306-1252 E-mail: jerrykrueg@aol.com. *Pick good mentors. Mine taught me to: 1) Try new things, welcome challenges. 2) Develop a high level of competence. 3) Know your customers' needs. 4) Always give them more than they expect.*

KRUEGER, HERBERT WILLIAM, lawyer; b. Milw., Apr. 20, 1948; s. Herbert William Sr. and Lily (Kuphall) K.; m. Judith Ann Wanserske, July 20, 1970; children— Kara, Dana, Andrew, Christopher. B.A., U. Wis.-Milw., 1970; J.D., U. Chgo., 1974. Bar: Fla. 1974, Ill. 1975, U.S. Dist. Ct. (no. dist.) Ill. 1975. Instr. in law U. Miami Sch. Law, Coral Gables, Fla., 1974-75; assoc. Mayer, Brown & Platt, Chgo., 1975-80, ptnr., 1981—, head compensation dept., 1984—, mem. mgmt. com., 1989—. Contbg. author Continuing Legal Education Pension Practice and Securities Laws handbooks, Practising Law Inst. handbook Acquiring and Selling Privately Held Companies, Pension Investment Handbook; contbr. articles to profl. jours. State dir. Wis. Coll. Reps., 1969-70; exec. dir. Com. to Reelect Pres., Wis. Young Voters Campaign, 1972; chmn. fiduciary standards com. Ill. Study Commn. on Pub. Pension Investment Policies, 1981-82; mem. nat. adv. bd. NYU Real Estate Inst. Pension Fund Investment in Real Estate Conf. Mem. ABA, Pension Real Estate Assn. (mem. govt. affairs com.). Office: Mayer Brown & Platt 190 S La Salle St Ste 3100 Chicago IL 60603-3441

KRUEGER, JAMES A. lawyer; b. Sept. 21, 1943; s. A.A. and Margaret E. (Hurley) K.; m. Therese Eileen Connors, Aug. 2, 1968; 1 child, Colleen. BA cum laude, Gongaza U., 1965; JD, Georgetown U., 1968; LLM, NYU, 1972. Bar: Wash. 1969, U.S. Supreme Ct. 1972, U.S. Tax Ct. 1972, U.S. Dist. Ct. (we. dist.) Wash. 1980, U.S. Ct. Appeals (9th cir.) 1982. Mem. staff U.S. senator from Wash., 1967-68; mem. Vandebert, Johnson & Gandora (and predecessor firms), 1972—. Spl. dist. counsel Wash. State Bar Assn., 1984-94; adj. prof. law, U. of Puget Sound, 1974-76. Co-author: Representing the Close Corporation, 1979, Partnership Agreements, 1981, Planning for the Small Business Enterprise, 1982, The Partnership Handbook, 1984. Chmn. bd. Cath. Cmty. Svcs. of Pierce and Kitsap Counties, 1983-84; bd. dirs. United Way of Pierce County, 1973-82, 99—. Capt. U.S. Army, 1968-72. Decorated Bronze star. Mem. ABA, Wash. State Bar Assn. (spl. dist. counsel), Tacoma-Pierce County Bar Assn. Roman Catholic. Office: 1201 Pacific Ave Ste 1900 Tacoma WA 98402-4315

KRUEGER, JENNIFER ANN, librarian; b. New Orleans, Aug. 17, 1963; d. William Charles Jr. and Carol Ann Krueger; m. Mitchell Craig, Stein, Oct. 22, 1989. BS in Math., Tufts U., 1985; MLS, Simmons Coll., 1988; MBA in Mktg., Columbia U., 1993. Libr. Somerville (Mass.) Pub. Libr., 1985-87; info. asst. Lotus Devel. Corp., Cambridge, Mass., 1987; rsch. analyst PA Cons. Group, Hightstown, N.J., 1988-90; info. specialist AIG, N.Y.C., 1990-91; head info. svcs. N.Y. Pub. Libr., N.Y.C., 1993—96, asst. dir. electronic rsch., 1996—98, dep. to dir., 1998—2002, coord., 2003—. Named One of Top 40 New Yorkers under 40, Daily News, 1995. Mem. NAFE, Am. Soc. Info. Sci., Columbia U. Bus. Sch. Alumni Assn. Office: New York Pub Libr 475 Fifth Ave Rm 101M New York NY 10018

KRUEGER, KARLI ANN, music educator; b. Ventura, Calif., Apr. 23, 1976; d. James Raymond and Diane Marie Krueger. MusB, So. Oreg. U., 2002. Musician Ind., Ashland, Oreg., 2002—. Mem. So. Oreg. Repertoirie singers, Ashland, Oreg., 2002—, So. Oreg. U. Chamber Choir, Ashland, Oreg. Mem.: Oreg. Music Teachers Assn., Music Teachers Nat. Assn. (Student Achievement Recognition Award 2002). Independent. Christian Science. Avocation: sports. E-mail: krue5399@students.sou.edu.

KRUEGER, KEITH ROGER, non-profit management executive; b. St. Paul, Minn., Mar. 27, 1957; s. Richard Ernest and Shirley May (Popp) K. BA, George Washington U., 1979; MAPA, U. Minn., 1981. Fellow V.P. Walter Mondale, Washington, 1980; adminstrv. asst. Minn. Sen. Health Com., St. Paul, 1982; chief legis. asst. Cong. Gerry Sikorski, Washington, 1983-85; dir. gov. rels. Am. Optometric Assn., Washington, 1985-86; pres. Non-Profit Mgmt. Assoc., Washington, 1986—2002; CEO Consortium for Sch. Networking, Washington, 2002—. Episcopal. Office: Consortium for Sch Networking Ste 900 1710 Rhode Island Ave NW Washington DC 20036-3007 Office Fax: 202-861-0888. E-mail: Keith@cosn.org.

KRUEGER, KENNETH JOHN, nutritionist, educator; b. L.A., Jan. 29, 1946; s. Charles Herbert and Adelaide Marie K.; m. Ellen Santucci, June 16, 1979 (div. 1989); children: Kenneth, Michael, Scott, David. BA in Humanities, U. So. Calif., 1968; MS in Edn. (Psychology), Mt. St. Mary's Coll., 1972. English tchr. Corcoran (Calif.) High Sch., 1968, Charter Oak High Sch., Covina, Calif., 1969-90; nutrition and exercise instr. Mt. San Antonio Coll., Walnut, Calif., 1974-90; pres. Mega Group, Ltd., 1990, The Krueger Group, Malibu, Calif., 1991—2000; exec. Overnite Express, L.A., Calif., 1993, Calif. Parcel Express, Encino, 1994-95; nutritionist Swiss Nat. Team, 1995-99; phys. edn. tchr. Hiram Johnson H.S., Sacramento, 1995-96. Adj. prof. phys. edn. Sierra Coll., Rocklin, Calif., 1996; health instr. L.A. City Coll., 1996-97, West L.A. Coll., 1998; swim coach Mt. San Antonio Coll., Walnut, Calif., 1974-77; coach, v.p. Trojan Swim Club, Newport Beach, Calif., 1978-90; bd. dirs. Nutrition and Exercise Cons., Tustin, Calif.; nutrition and exercise dir. Health Am., 1987-90; chmn., nutrition and fitness com. Internat. Eating Disorders Com., 1988; U.S. nat. team nutritionist for (FINA) World Cup 1988 Champions; recruiter Club Med, Paris, 1976-78; program coord. Pacific Am. Inst., San Francisco, 1983; asst. coach Vevey Natation, Switzerland, 1972-73; asst. swim coach Swiss Nat. Team, 1968, 85; chief marshall U.S. Olympic Swim Trials, Irvine, 1980, linguistics chmn. protocol U. So. Calif. Venue, L.A. Olympic Com., 1983-84; mem.-at-large long distance com. U.S. Swimming, Colorado Springs, 1987-91, coach So. Calif. Long Distance Swimming, 1987-89; del. chief, coach and swimmer So. Calif. Swimming for Internat. Crossing of Lake Geneva, sponsored by Internat. Olympic Com., Switzerland, 1987; meet dir. U.S. 25K Long Distance Swimming Championships/FINA World Cup Trials, Long Beach, Calif., 1988, U.S. 25K Swim Championships, Long Beach, 1989. Author: Reflections and Refractions, 1973; contbr. articles to internat. profl. nutrition and sport jours. Bd. dirs. U.S.A. Athletes Hall of Fame, 1991-92. Recipient NCAA All Am. award U. So. Calif., 1966, NCAA Nat. Champ award, 1966, U.S. Masters Swimming Champion, 1972 and annually 1974-81, Internat. Sr. Olympics Champion, 1972 and annually 1974-85; recipient commendations U.S. Congress, Calif. Senate, L.A. County Bd. Suprs.; inducted into U.S.A. Athletes Hall of Fame. Mem. KC. Libertarian. Roman Catholic. Avocations: sports, reading. Mailing: 5435 Vesper Ave Sherman Oaks CA 91411

KRUEGER, KURT DONN, district court judge; b. Worthington, Minn., May 8, 1952; s. Donn Kurt and Lola (Lueck) K.; m. Kim Short, Jan. 2, 1983; children: Krista Marie, Kurt Derrick. BA in Gov., Mont. State U., 1974; JD, George Mason U., 1978. Bar: Va. 1978, U.S. Dist. Ct. (ea. dist.) Va. 1979, U.S. Ct. Appeals (4th and D.C. cirs.) 1979, Mont. 1980, U.S. Dist. Ct. Mont. 1980, U.S. Ct. Appeals (9th cir.) 1985, U.S. Supreme Ct. 1990. Law clk. to superior ct. judge, Washington, 1978-80; staff atty. Mont. Legal Svcs. Assn., Butte, 1980-83; pvt. practice Butte, 1984-2000; dist. ct. judge 2d Jud. Dist. State of Mont., 2001—. Bd. dirs Mont. Legal Svcs. Assn., Helena, 1984—, pres., 1988-89. State rep. Mont. State Legis., Helena, 1985-87; bd. dirs. Big Bros. and Big Sisters, Butte, 1985-88, Butte Silver Bow Zoning Bd. Adjustment, 1989-92; adv. bd. vigilante dist. Boy Scouts Am., 1989—; mem. Mont. Criminal Jury Instrns. Commn., 2001--, Mont. Interstate Compact State Coun., 2001--, Mont. Supreme Ct. Adv. Commn. on civil and appellate procedure, 2003--, Mont. Full Faith and Credit Coun., 2003--, Equal Justice Task Force, 2003--. Roscoe Pound fellow, ATLA, 2000—. Mem.: Mont. Wildlife Fedn. (bd. dirs. 1998—2000), Skyline Sportsmen (bd. dirs. 1997—2000). Methodist. Avocations: hiking, fishing, skiing, hunting, camping. Address: PO Box 485 Butte MT 59703

KRUEGER, RALPH ARTHUR, motel and food executive; b. Cleve., Apr. 14, 1952; s. Daniel and Florence (Myer) K. AA, Adirondack Community Coll., Glen Falls, N.Y., 1983; BS, Hudson Valley C.C. Dept. mgr./inventory Telescope Furniture Co., Granville, N.Y., 1970-82; owner, mgr. Pine Grove Motel, Diner and Bakery, Granville, 1979-89, Valley Food Ct., Granville, 1988-89; owner Eagles Nest Homes of Granville, N.Y., 1990-93; parts mgr. SAAB, SUBARU, 1990-97, Yamaha, 1997-98; mgr. Cumberland Farms, 1998—2002; real estate salesperson, 1991—; owner RAK Enterprises, 2000—. Editor, pub.: Border Rider News, 1987-92. Treas. Heritage Days Village of Granville, 1986; trustee Congl. Ch., 1985—. Recipient Scouters Key award Boy Scouts Am., 1984, dist. award of merit, 1985, Leaders Woodbadge-Honor Campers award, 1985. Mem. Internat. Media and Info. Coun. (co-chmn. 1988), Internat. Snowmobile Coun. (Va.), Border Riders Snowmobile Club (pres. 1974-76, 87-90), Washington County Assn. Snowmobile Clubs (pres. 1983-87, treas. 1990-95, Washington County coord. 1990-94), Granville C. of C., Wakpominee Order of Arrow. Republican. Avocations: camping, pipe organ restoration.

KRUEGER, RAYMOND ROBERT, lawyer; b. Portage, Wis., Aug. 29, 1947; s. Earl Andrew and Catherine Virginia (Klenert) K.; m. Barbara Bowen, June 21, 1969; children: Lindsey, Michael. BA in Econs., U. Wis., 1969, JD, 1972. Bar: Wis. 1972. Assoc. Charne, Glassner, Tehan, Clancy & Taitelman S.C., Milw., 1973-79, shareholder, 1979-91; ptnr. Charne Clancy Krueger Pollack & Corris S.C., Milw., 1991—92, Michael, Best & Friedrich, Milw., 1992—. Chmn. Georgia O'Keeffe Found., Abiquiu, N.Mex., 1989—; trustee Village of Whitefish Bay, Wis., 1989—2003; mem. Milwaukee River Revitalization Coun., 1988—, vice chair, 1989—96, chair, 1996—; dir. River Revitalization Found., Inc., 1998—, chair, 2001—; trustee Milw. Art Mus., 2003—, mem. bldg. com., 1996—; chair Whitefish Bay Cmty. Devel. Authority, 2002—. Capt. USAF, 1969—78. Mem. ABA (natural resources sect.), State Bar Wis. (environ. law sect.), Milw. Bar Assn. (environ. law sect.), Environ. Law Inst. Avocation: visual arts. Office: Michael Best & Friedrich 100 E Wisconsin Ave Ste 3300 Milwaukee WI 53202-4108 E-mail: rrkrueger@mbf-law.com.

KRUEGER, ROBERT CHARLES, former ambassador, former senator, congressman; b. New Braunfels, Tex., Sept. 19, 1935; s. Arlon E. and Faye (Leifeste) K.; m. Kathleen Tobin Krueger; children: Mariana, Sarah, Christian. BA, So. Meth. U., 1957; MA, Duke U., 1958; M.Litt., Oxford (Eng.) U., 1961, D.Phil., 1964; D.Litt. (hon.), U. St. Thomas; D.Pub.Service hon., Lycoming U., 2003. From instr. to assoc. prof. English Duke U., 1961-72; vice provost, dean Trinity Coll. Arts and Scis., Duke U., 1972-73; chmn. bd. Comal Hosiery Mills, 1973-75; ptnr. Krueger Brangus Ranch, 1974-86; mem. 94th-95th Congresses from 21st Tex. dist., 1975-79; U.S. ambassador-at-large, coord. for Mex. affairs, 1979-81; pres. Krueger Assocs., 1981-91; Bentsen prof. govt.-bus. rels. Lyndon B. Johnson Sch., U. Tex., 1985-86; commr. Tex. R.R. Commn., 1991—93; Tsanoff prof. pub. affairs Rice U., 1986-88; Disting. lectr. So. Meth. U., 1991; U.S. senator from Tex., 1993-94; amb. to Burundi, 1994-96; amb. to Botswana, 1996—2000; spl. rep. of sec. of state So. Africa Devel. Cmty., 1998—2000; rsch. fellow Merton Coll. Oxford (Eng.) U., 2000—01; cons. on nat. and internat. bus. and fgn. affairs, 2001—. Spkr. in field; bd. dirs. VIAD Corp.; mem. chancellor's bd. advisors U. Ill. Med. Ctr. Author: The Poems of Sir John Davies, 1975; contbr. over 300 articles to profl. jours. and newspapers. Mem. Tex. Philos. Soc. (pres. 1993), Blue Key, Phi Beta Kappa. Office: PO Box 311717 New Braunfels TX 78131-1717

KRUEGER, ROBERT EDWARD, manufacturing executive, mechanical engineer; b. L.A., Mar. 26, 1922; s. Edward Jr. and Ida Viola (Herren) K.; m. Elizabeth Westerfors, Sept. 10, 1949; children: Karen Elizabeth, Clarence Frederick (dec.), Roger Carl (dec.), Bruce Wayne, Glen Herren. Student, L.A. City Coll., 1939-40, Calif. Inst. Tech., 1940-43, 46-47, Yale U., Harvard U., MIT, Army Electronics Tng. Ctr., 1943-44; BSME, Stanford U., 1950, MBA, 1952. Lic. fed. firearms dealer and ammunition mfr. Bur. Alcohol, Tobacco and Firearms. Trainee Douglas Aircraft Co., Santa Monica, Calif., summers 1941-43; staff mem. Los Alamos (N.Mex.) Sci. Lab., 1947-49; chief engr. Rutishauser Corp., Pasadena, Calif., 1952-53; asst. to pres. Unitek Corp., El Monte, Calif., 1953-55; sales mgr. Donner Sci. Co., Concord, Calif., 1955-57, Shand & Jurs divsn. Gen. Precision Equipment Corp., Berkeley, 1957-58; v.p. sales Advanced Instruments, Richmond, Calif., 1958-60; sales mgr. Gilliland Instruments, Oakland, Calif., 1960-62; ptnr. Krueger & Smith, Berkeley, 1969-72; founder, pres. Tetra Valves, Inc., Berkeley, 1972-78; owner, propr. Krueger Mfg.-Engring., Lafayette, Calif., 1962—. Author or co-author books, manuals, other works; patentee in field. Donor portraits of U.S. Pres. George Bush and Barbara Bush, White Ho., Washington, 1995, portrait of U.S. Pres. George Bush, Nat. Portrait Gallery, Washington, 1995; v.p. Calif. Rep. Assembly, 1983-84. With USAAF, 1942-47; with USAFR, 1947-53. Recipient

John Singleton Copley medal Nat. Portrait Gallery, 1999. Mem. IEEE (life), AAAS, ASTM, NRA (life, endowment), Am. Soc. for Metals Internat. (life), Am. Def. Indsl. Assn. (life), James Smithson Soc./Smithsonian Instn. (Patron award Benefactors Cir. 1991), Nat. Mus. Am. Indian (charter), Colonial Williamsburg Found., Raleigh Tavern Soc., USN League (life), Spencer Baird Soc., Calif. Rifle and Pistol Assn. (life), Calif. State Sheriffs Assn., Contra Costa County Sheriffs Posse. Pantheist. Avocations: U.S. national heritage, art collections, politics, travel, photography. Home: 1084 Via Roble Lafayette CA 94549-2925 Office: Krueger Mfg-Engring 1084 Via Roble Lafayette CA 94549-2925

KRUEGER, ROBERT WILLIAM, management consultant; b. Phila., Nov. 16, 1916; s. Robert Henry and Frieda (Lehmann) K.; m. Marjorie Evelyn Jones, July 26, 1941; children: Arlene R. Krueger Pappan, Diane L. Krueger Lane. PhD in Physics, UCLA, 1942. Research engr. Douglas Aircraft Co., Santa Monica, Calif., 1942-46; asst. chief missiles div. RAND Corp., Santa Monica, 1946-53; missle systems cons. L.A., 1953-54; pres. Planning Research Corp., L.A., 1954-73, Profl. Services Internat., from 1973. Founder Profl. Svcs. Coun., 1970, bd. dirs. Chmn. 59th Dist. Republican Central Com., 1960-61; pres. 59th Dist. Rep. Assembly, 1960-61; mem. Calif. Rep. Central Com., 1962-66; Trustee U. Calif. Los Angeles Found. Mem. Am. Phys. Soc. Died Dec. 19, 2002.

KRUEGER, RONALD, aerospace engineer; b. Calw, Ger., Nov. 28, 1958; s. Roman Hupalo and Margit Evelin Nassi Krueger. Abitur, Kepler Gymnasium, Pforzheim, 1978; Diplom Ingenieur, U. Stuttgart, 1989, DSc, 1996. Asst. U. Stuttgart, 1989-96; NRC rsch. assoc. Langley Rsch. Ctr. NASA, Hampton, Va., 1997-2000; staff scientist ICASE, Hampton, Va., 2000—02; sr. staff scientist Nat. Inst. Aerospace, Hampton, Va., 2003—. With German Army, 1978-79. Mem. AIAA (sr.), ASTM, Am. Soc. Composites, Deutsche Gesellschaft für Luft- und Raumfahrt Lilienthal-Oberth e.V. DGLR. Home: 142 Pine Creek Dr Hampton VA 23669-1244 Office: NASA Langley Rsch Ctr Mail Stop 188E Hampton VA 23681-2199 E-mail: rKrueger@nianet.org.

KRUEGER, ROSS T. gastroenterologist; b. Springfield, Ohio, Aug. 13, 1941; s. Raymond Leslie and Adelaide Ruth Krueger; m. Jean C. Cox, Nov. 22, 1975; children: Celeste, Dean, Rose, Joy. BA, Coll. of Wooster, 1963; MD, Western Res. U., 1966. Diplomate in internal medicine and gastroenterology Am. Bd. Internal Medicine. Intern Balt. City Hosps., 1966-68, resident in internal medicine, 1970-71; fellow in gastroentorology Duke U. Hosp., Durham, N.C., 1971-73; pvt. practice gastroenterology Jacksonville, Fla., 1973—. Pres. Fla. Gastroenterol. Assn., 1986-87. Bd. dirs. Jacksonville Episcopal H.S., Riverside Presbyn. Day Sch., Jacksonville Symphony Assn.; mem. vestry Good Shepherd Episcopal Ch. Maj. U.S. Army, 1969-71. Fellow ACP, Am. Soc. Internal Medicine. Office: 1801 Barrs St Ste 605 Jacksonville FL 32204-4746 E-mail: rtkruegermd@hotmail.com.

KRUG, EDWARD CHARLES, environmental scientist; b. New Brunswick, N.J., Aug. 24, 1947; s. Edward and Regina (Bartkoviak) K.: m. Nancy Wegner, July 19, 1988. BS in Environ. Sci with highest honors, Rutgers U., 1975, PhD in Soil Sci., 1981. cert. profl. soil scientist. Asst. scientist Conn. Agrl. Expt. Sta., New Haven, 1980-85; assoc. scientist Ill. State Water Survey U. Ill., Champaign, 1985-90; advisor Com. for a Constructive Tomorrow, Washington, 1989-90, dir. environ. projects, 1991-93; ind. environ. cons. Winona, Minn., 1993—. Mem. sci. adv. com. Environ. Issues Coun., U.S.A., 1993—; mem. adv. bd. Media Rsch. Ctr., Alexandria, Va., 1991—; adj. profl. scientist Ill. State Water Survey, U. Ill., Champaign, 1999—; biogeochemist Office of the Chief, Ill. State Water Survey, Champaign, 2000—; mem. tech. adv. group Ill. Environ. Protection Agy., nutrient sci. com. Contbg. author: Ency. for Earth System Science, 1992; contbr. articles to profl. jours. Mem. N.J. Ad Hoc Water Quality Control Com., New Brunswick, 1972-73; reviewer, tech. advisor N.J. Pub. Interact Rsch. Group, New Brunswick, 1972-75; chmn. ch. and soc. coms. United Meth. Ch., Winona, Minn., 1990-91, 2000—; mem. regional tech. adv. group U.S. Environ. Agy., 2001—; mem. nutrient sci. com. Ill. Environ. Protection Agy. With USN, 1967-69. Recipient Frank G. Helyar award Rutgers U., 1973, Excellence in Rev. award Jour. Environ. Quality, 1991. Mem. Am. Geophys. Union, Soil Sci. Soc. Am., Internat. Union Soil Scientists, Ill. Soil Carbon Ptnrs. Working Group, Internat. Union Soil Scientists. Achievements include conception and development of organic acid buffering theory; generalization of Rosenquist land-use theory to include naturally increased acidity of watershed from accelerated loss of bases; unified theory of acid/base biogeochemistry. Address: 2404 Berniece Dr Champaign IL 61822-7254 E-mail: ekrug@uiuc.edu.

KRUG, FRED ROY, film and television director and producer; b. Bern, Switzerland, Aug. 30, 1929; came to U.S., 1951; s. Adalbert and Margot Panchaud de Bottens-Krug; m. Rosemary Wehner, Feb. 25, 1956; 1 child, Vivian Evelyn. BA, Columbia Coll., L.A., 1962, postgrad., 1963. Freelance cinematographer, writer, Europe and U.S., 1945-63; dir. Sta. KLYD-ABC TV, 1963; film and VTR dir. Sta. KCOP-TV, L.A., 1963-68; v.p. prodn. Bill Burrud Prodns., Los Angeles, 1968-72; producer, dir. Walt Disney Prodns., Burbank, Calif., 1972-74, Fred R. Krug Prodns., Hollywood, Calif., 1974—. Contr. articles to film mags. and profl. jours.; contbr. regular columns to European and U.S. newspapers; prodr., dir. (TV series) The Wonderful World of Disney, NBC; prodr. various news, pub. affairs and mus. shows for U.S. Army, radio and TV; producer, dir., cinematographer (TV series) Animal World, ABC, NBC, and CBS, The American West, The Challenging Sea, World of Women, Wild Kingdom; producer (spl.) Population Explosion, syndication; numerous TV commls. and promotional films in U.S. Europe, C.Am., French Polynesia; cinematographer "CHiPS", MGM; producer (feature film) Pacific Internat. Enterprises, 1977-79; assoc. producer Across the Great Divide; exec. producer Mountain Family Robinson. Mem. Hollywood adv. coun. Salvation Army, 1984—85; bd. dirs. Bob Hope USO Club, Hollywood, 1984—87; pilot USAF Aux. CAP, maj., 1988—. Mem. Dirs. Guild Am., Producers Guild Am., Rotary (Paul Harris fellow 1987, v.p. Hollywood club 1987-88, pres. Santa Ynez Valley club 1996-97). Avocation: flying. Home: Ranchito de los Ciervos 3398 Calzada Ave Santa Ynez CA 93460-8703 E-mail: fredroy@silcom.com.

KRUG, JEFFREY ALAN, b. Radford, Va., Jan. 21, 1959; s. Alan Sents and Elaine Myers Krug; m. Miriam Batista Siqueira; children: Viviane, Alan. BA, Pa. State U., 1982, MS, 1984; PhD, Ind. U., 1993. Fin. analyst Commerzbank, Duesseldorf, Germany, 1981; econ. analyst Austrian Postal Savings Bank, Vienna, 1982; instr., rsrch. asst. Pa. State U., 1983—84; fin. planning mgr. Tex. Instruments Inc., Dallas, 1984—88; mgr. of fin. PepsiCo, Inc., Louisville, 1988—89, instr. Ind. U., Bloomington, 1989—92; vis. prof. Coll. William & Mary, Williamsburg, Va., 1993—94; asst. prof. U. Memphis, Memphis, 1994—98, U. Ill., Champaign, 1998—2003; assoc. prof. Appalachian State U., Boone, NC, 2003—. Adj. prof. exec. MBA program U. Muenster, Germany, 2002—, U. Ill., 2003—. Lt. jg USNR, 1985—88. Mem.: So. Mgmt. Assn., Acad. of Mgmt., Strategic Mgmt. Soc., Delta Phi Alpha, Omicron Delta Epsilon, Beta Gamma Sigma. Methodist. Office: Appalachian State U Coll of Bus Adminstrn 4072 Raley Hall Boone NC 28608 Business E-Mail: Krugja@appstate.edu.

KRUG, JOHN CARLETON (TONY KRUG), college administrator, library consultant; b. Evansville, Ind., Nov. 27, 1951; s. John Elmer and Mary Ellen K.; m. Anna Marie Waters, July 3, 1983. BA, Ind. State U., 1972, MLS, 1973; PhD, So. Ill. U., Carbondale, 1985. Lic. to ministry Bapt. Ch. Exec. dir. Olney (Ill.) Carnegie Pub. Libr., 1973-74; assoc. dean Wabash Valley Coll., Mt. Carmel, Ill., 1974-84; mem. Com. for U.S. Depository State Plan, Springfield, Ill., 1982-84; dir. librs. Maryville Coll., St. Louis, 1984-88; dir. info. svcs. Bethany (W.Va.) Coll., 1988-97; dean libr. svcs. Carson Newman Coll., Jefferson City, Tenn., 1997—2002; dir. ctrl. libr. Appalachian Coll. Assn., Berea, Ky., 2002—. Coord. libr. activities, Appalachian Coll. Assn., 1997-2002; sec. pro-tem Ill. Basin Coal Mining Manpower Council, Mt. Carmel, 1974-79; governing bd. exec. com. Higher Edn. Ctr. Cable TV, 1986-88; conf. speaker Kans. State U., 1982. Author: Libraries Using/Planning for Microcomputers, 1986; also computer programs. V.p. bd. dirs. Wabash Area Vocat. Enterprises, Mt. Carmel, 1978 81; bd. edn. Wabash Cmty. Unit, Mt. Carmel, 1980-83; exec. com. Cmty. Edn. and Arts Assn., Carbondale, 1983-84; visual arts adv. com. Ill. Arts Coun., Chgo., 1982-84; pastor Hopewell United Meth. Ch., Bridgeport, Ill., 1976-77; minister Terre Haute (Ind.) 1st Bapt. Ch., 1972—; elder Gateway Christian Ch., 1986-88; bd. dirs. Fair Haven Christian Sch., 1986-88; pres. T3-Tchrs., Tech., Tomorrow; bd. dirs. Christian Coll. Librs., 1995-97. 1997-2002; dir., Appalachian coll. Assoc. cntrl. Libr., Berea Ky 2002- Mem. So. Bapt. Libr. Assn., Assn. Christian Librs. Office: Appalachian Coll Assn 210 Center St Berea KY 40403 E-mail: tonyk@acaweb.org.

KRUGER, BARBARA, audiologist, speech and language pathologist; b. Corpus Christi, Tex., Aug. 16, 1944; BA in Psychology cum laude, CUNY, 1967, MA in Speech Pathology, 1970, PhD in Audiology and Hearing Sci., 1975. Asst. prof. audiology, dir. hearing rsch. lab. Columbia U., N.Y.C., 1975-78; asst. prof. otolaryngology, dir. audiology and speech lang. pathology Albert Einstein Coll. Medicine, Montefiore Med. Ctr. Yeshiva U., Bronx, N.Y., 1978-87; cons. Kruger Assocs., Commack, N.Y., 1987—; dir. Audiology and Comm. Svcs., 1987—. Founder, bd. dirs. The Hearing Care Group; adj. prof. Columbia U., 1979-82; chmn. earphone calibration Internat. Electrotech. Commn., Am. Nat. Standards Inst., workgroup hearing aids real-ear probe microphone measurement; cons. Albert Einstein Coll. of Medicine, Kennedy Ctr., 1987-90; apptd. N.Y. State Hearing Aid Dispensing Adv. Bd. in Dept. of State, 1999 ; co chair Open Data structure Hearing Related Data. Spencer Found. grantee, 1976-78, Am. Otological Soc. grantee, 1978-79, Rose M. Badgeley Residuary Charitable Trust grantee, 1981-84; recipient Program Project award NIH, 1984-86. Fellow Am. Speech-Lang. Hearing Assn., Am. Acad. Audiology; mem. L.I. Speech-Lang. Hearing Assn.

KRUGER, CHARLES HERMAN, JR., mechanical engineering educator; b. Oklahoma City, Oct. 4, 1934; s. Charles H. and Flora K.; m. Nora Nininger, Sept. 10, 1977; children— Sarah, Charles III, Elizabeth, Ellen. S.B., M.I.T., 1956, PhD, 1960; D.I.C., Imperial Coll., London, 1957. Asst. prof. MIT, Cambridge, 1960; research scientist Lockheed Research Labs., 1960-62; prof. mech. engring. Stanford (Calif.) U., 1962—, chmn. dept. mech. engring., 1982-88, sr. assoc. dean engring., 1988-93, vice provost, dean rsch. and grad. policy, 1993—2003. Vis. prof. Harvard U., 1968-69, Princeton U., 1979-80; mem. Environ. Studies Bd. NAS, 1981-83; mem. hearing bd. Bay Area Air Quality Mgmt. Dist., 1969-83 Co-author: Physical Gas Dynamics, 1965, Partially Ionized Gases, 1973, On the Prevention of Significant Deteriorization of Air Quality, 1981; asso. editor: AIAA Jour, 1968-71; contbr. numerous articles to profl. jours. NSF sr. postodoctoral fellow, 1968-69; recipient Plasma Chemistr award Internat. Plasma Chemistry Soc., 2003, Cuthbertson Award, Stanford Univ., 2003. Fellow AAAS; mem. AIAA (medal, award 1979), ASME, Am. Phys. Soc., N.Y. Acad. Scis.

KRUGER, GUSTAV OTTO, JR., oral surgeon, educator; b. N.Y.C., Sept. 28, 1916; s. Gustav Otto and Anna Charlotte (Mellquist) K.; m. Helyn E. Hollingsworth, Apr. 12, 1947; children: Deborah Ann (Mrs. M. Henry King III), Tristram Coffin, Abigail Hollingsworth Imus. BS, George Washington U., 1938, AM, 1939; DDS, Georgetown U., 1939, ScD (hon.), 1977. Diplomate Am. Bd. Oral and Maxillofacial Surgery (pres. 1964). Intern Johns Hopkins Hosp., 1939-40; fellow Mayo Found., 1940-42, 45-48; mem. faculty Georgetown U. Sch. Dentistry and Grad. Sch., 1948-87, prof. oral surgery, chmn. dept., 1948-87, prof. emeritus, 1987—, assoc. dean, 1966-82. Chief dental dept. Georgetown U. Hosp., Washington, 1948 82; cons. VA hosps., Martinsburg, W.Va. and Washington, U.S. Naval Hosp., Bethesda, D.C. Gen. Hosp., Washington; cons. to Pres.'s physician, 1960-64; cons. Walter Reed Army Med. Ctr.; mem. cancer tng. com. Nat. Cancer Inst., USPHS, 1967-71, chmn., 1969-71. Author: Textbook of Oral and Maxillofacial Surgery, 1959, 6th edit., 1984; contbr. articles to profl. jours. Capt. Dental Corps AUS, 1942-45, CBI, PTO. Recipient Arnold K. Maislen award N.Y. U., 1970; Simon P. Hullihen award W.Va. Soc. Oral Surgeons and W.Va. Med. Ctr., 1980; named Man of Year Georgetown U. Alumni Assn., 1961, Disting. Svc. award, 1992. Fellow AAAS, Am. Coll. Dentists (chmn. D.C. sect. 1969-71, Disting. Svc. award 2002), Internat. Coll. Dentists (chmn. D.C. sect. 1967-70); mem. ADA (chmn. oral surgery sect. 1961, mem. rev. commn. on advanced edn. in oral surgery 1965-71, chmn. commn. 1969-71), D.C. Dental Soc. (pres. 1960, Sterling V. Mead award 1989), Am. Assn. Oral and Maxillofacial Surgeons (program chmn. 1961, 79th Ann. Meeting dedication 1997), Middle Atlantic Soc. Oral and Maxillofacial Surgeons (pres. 1952), Am. Assn. Dental Schs., Am. Acad. Oral Pathology, Am. Acad. Oral and Maxillofacial Radiology, Internat. Assn. Dental Research, Am. Coll. Oral and Maxillofacial Surgeons (Harry Archer award 1992), Wash. Dental Study Club (pres. 1993), Kiwanis (co-chmn. orthop. com. 1971-86), Xi Psi Phi, Sigma Gamma Epsilon, Omicron Kappa Upsilon. Home: 6806 Bradgrove Cir Bethesda MD 20817-3001

KRUGER, HARRY, retired conductor, retired music educator; b. Atlanta, July 20, 1929; s. Isaac and Sarah Kruger; m. Natalie Elizabeth Wyatt, Aug. 21, 1957; children: Rebecca, Anna, William. MusB, New Eng. Conservatory, Boston, 1953, MusM, 1955; Mus D, LaGrange Coll., Ga., 1991. Conductor Arlington Symphony, Mass., 1952—53; asst. conductor Atlanta Symphony, 1955—61; dir. orchestral activities Bowling Green State U., Ohio, 1961—65; conductor Columbus Symphony, Ga., 1965—87, Macon Symphony, Ga., 1977—83; conductor, dir. music LaGrange Symphony, 1989—2001, conductor emeritus, 2001—; ret. prof. music Columbus State U. Guest conductor Atlanta Symphony, 1983, 96, Birmingham Symphony, Ala., 1974, Tupelo Symphony, Miss., 1978, 79. Author: The Appreciation of Great Music, 2000. Conductor Atlanta Ballet Orch., 1956—61, Atlanta Cmty. Orch., 1957—61, So. Ballet Orch., Atlanta, 1958—61, Toledo Orch., 1961—65. Mem.: Am. Symphony Orch. League, Music Educators Nat. Conf., Ga. Music Educators Assn. (conductor ann. convs.). Democrat. Jewish. Avocations: swimming, travel, reading, camping, sports. Home: 4140 Oak Ferry Dr Kennesaw GA 30144

KRUGER, JEROME, materials science educator, consultant; b. Atlanta, Feb. 7, 1927; s. Isaac and Sarah (Stein) K.; m. Mollee Coppel, Feb. 20, 1955; children: Lennard, Joseph. BS, Ga. Inst. Tech., 1948, MS, 1949; PhD, U. Va., 1952. With Naval Rsch. Lab., Washington, 1952-55; with Nat. Bur. Standards, Commerce Dept., Washington, 1955-83, group leader Corrosion and Electrodeposition, 1966-83; prof. Johns Hopkins U., 1984-99, chmn. materials sci. and engring., 1986-88, prof. emeritus, 1999—. Cons. Argonne Nat. Lab., Lockheed, Balt. Gas & Electric, Teletech Thompson, Dalton & DeRose, Mueller Brass, S.W. Rsch. Inst., Dickenson, Wright, Moon, Van Dusen & Freeman, Haineness, Dickey & Pierce, W.O. Snead, H.M. Huber Co., DACCO Sci.; Jerome Kruger vis. scholar U. Va., 1998. Divisional editor Jour. Electrochem. Soc., 1966-83; subject area editor: Ency. of Materials Sci. and Engring.; also editor books; contbr. articles to tech. jours., chpts. to book. DuPont fellow U. Va., 1951-52; recipient Silver medal Commerce Dept., 1962, Gold medal, 1972; Blum award Nat. Capitol sect. Electrochem. Soc., 1966, Foley award, 1999; Samuel Wesley Stratton award Nat. Bur. Standards, 1982; Presdl. rank of Meritorious Exec. of Sr. Exec. Svc., 1982; U.R. Evans award Inst. Corrosion (U.K.), 1991, Hon. fellow, 1996; establishment of Jerome Kruger vis. scholar program at U. Va., 1998, 1st invited scholar, 1999. Fellow Electrochem. Soc. (treas. 1982-86, hon. mem. 1987, Outstanding Achievement award 1977, Olin Palladium medal 1995), fellow Nat. Assn. Corrosion Engrs. (bd. dirs. 1983-86, W.R. Whitney award 1976, Jerome Kruger award in corrosion sci., Balt.-Washington sect., 1997); mem. Am. Inst. Conservation, Internat. Corrosion Coun. (1st v.p. 1984-87, pres. 1987-90), Fedn. Materials Socs. (pres. 1977), Standards Alumni Assoc.(v.p.) Nat. Inst. Stds. and Tech., Sigma Xi, Tau Beta Pi. Jewish. Home and Office: 619 Warfield Dr Rockville MD 20850-1921 E-mail: jk2727@aol.com.

KRUGER, KENNETH, architect; b. Newark, Aug. 13, 1928; s. Rudolph Robert and Clarise Estelle (Goldman) K.; m. Elinor Margaret Kane, July 22, 1978; children: Jonathan, Karen, Kai. BArch, MIT, 1951, MS, 1953, postgrad., 1964; MArch, Harvard U., 1952; postgrad., U. Rome, 1955. Registered arch., Mass., N.J., N.Y., profl. engr., Mass.; cert. Nat. Coun. Archtl. Registration Bds.; lic. constrn. supr., home inspector, real estate broker, title 5 sys. inspector, Mass. Archtl. designer Carl Koch & Assoc., Cambridge, Mass., 1953-54; structural designer Frank Grad, Paris, 1955; arch. Marcel Breuer & Assocs., N.Y.C., 1956-57; structural engr. Simpson & Stratta, San Francisco, 1959-60, Chin & Hensolt, San Francisco, 1961-62, Internat. Engring. Co., Rio de Janeiro, 1963; arch., engr. Kenneth Kruger, Boston, 1964-68, Kruger Kruger Albenberg Archs. & Engrs., Cambridge, Mass., 1969—. Instr. arch. MIT, Cambridge, 1952-53. Mem. Fresh Pond Adv. Bd., Cambridge, 2002; Mass. Designer Selection Bd. Overseas fellow MIT, 1952, Rotch prize, 1951; Fulbright scholar, 1954-55. Fellow ASCE, AIA, Am. Soc. Home Inspectors (v.p. 1991, Pres.'s award 1991, exec. com. 1991-93, dir.-at-large 1988-90, 92-94, chmn. bylaws com. 1992-94; dir. New Eng. chpt. 1982), Boston Soc. Archs. (dir., commr. 1974-77), Boston Soc. Civil Engrs., Boston Assn. Structural Engrs., Constrn. Specification Inst., Sigma Xi, Alpha Epsilon Pi. Avocations: skiing, tennis, squash, backpacking, biking. Office: Kruger Kruger Albenberg 67 Grozier Rd Cambridge MA 02138-3314

KRUGER, KENNETH CHARLES, architect; b. Santa Barbara, Calif., Aug. 19, 1930; s. Thomas Albin and Chleople (Gaines) K.; m. Patricia Kathryn Rasey, Aug. 21, 1955; children: David, Eric. B.Arch., U. So. Calif., 1953. Registered architect, Calif. Pres. Kruger Bensen Ziemer, Santa Barbara, 1960-90; part-time instr. architecture dept. Calif. Poly., San Luis Obispo, 1993-95; part-time architect, 1993—. Regent Calif. Archtl. Found., 1997—. Bd. dirs. United Boys and Girls Club. Fellow AIA; mem. Archtl. Found. Santa Barbara (pres. 1987-89). Democrat. Home: 1255 Ferrelo Rd Santa Barbara CA 93103-2101

KRUGER, LON, coach; b. Topeka, Kans., Aug. 19, 1952; m. Barbara Miles; children: Angie, Kevin. BS in bus., Kansas State Univ., 1975; MS in physical edn., Pitts. State Univ., 1977. Asst. coach Pitts. State Univ., 1976-77; grad. asst. coach Kansas State Univ., 1977-78, asst. coach, 1978-82; head coach Pan American Univ., 1982-86; athletic dir. Pan American, 1982-85; head coach Kansas State Univ., 1987-90, Univ. Fla., 1991-96, Univ. Ill., 1996-99, Atlanta Hawks, 2000—. Head coach 1991 USA Jr. World Champion Team, USA World Univ. Games Team, 1995; appt. by NCAA to serve on USA Basketball Games Com.; head coach 1987 Big Eight Select Team, Beijing, China, asst. coach 1987 U.S. Pan American Team. Co-chairpersons Alachua County's Red Ribbon Campaign, 1991-93. Recipient Big Eight Player of Yr., 1973, 74, Gainesville Vol. of Yr., 1995. Office: Atlanta Hawks One CNN Ctr Ste 405 South Tower Atlanta GA 30303

KRUGER, MOLLEE COPPEL, writer; b. Bel Air, Md., Mar. 28, 1929; d. Benjamin and Mary Coppel; m. Jerome Kruger, Feb. 20, 1955; children: Lennard Gideon, Joseph Avrum. BA, U. Md., 1950. Columnist The Harford Gazette, Bel Air, Md., 1945-47; advt. copywriter Joseph Katz Co., Balt., 1951-55; TV scriptwriter Jewish Community Coun., Washington, 1960-72; columnist, feature writer various newspapers, Washington and N.Y.C., 1967-88; freelance writer various nat. publs., 1980—. Condr. writing workshop Montgomery County Cmty. Svcs., Rockville, Md., 1982; cons. Buddemeir Co., Balt., 1958-59; pres. Maryben Books, Rockville, 1970—; tchr. creative writing Jewish Cmty. Ctr., Rockville, 1974-78, cons. editor sr. adult publs., 1975, 76, 77; cons. editor Stds. Alumni Assn., 1992. Author: Unholy Writ, 1970, More Unholy Writ, 1973, Yankee Shoes, 1975 (Gold Ribbon Bicentennial award 1976), Daughters of Chutzpah, 1983, Admiral of the Mosquitoes, 1990, Ladies First, 1995 (mus. adaptation 1st prize Nat. Music Competition Nat. League Am. Pen Women); editor Std. newsletter Nat. Bur. Stds., 1978-80 (Excellence award 1979); performer one-woman show on Emma Lazarus, Jewish Cmty. Coun., Washington, 1976; playwright (one act plays) The Muted Note: A Pulpit Drama, 1965, Master of Dreams: S.Y. Agnon, 1968, President McKinley is Dead, 1977; playwright, prodr. hist. show for Md. 350 Com., Montgomery County, Rockville, 1982-84; contbr. articles to popular mags.; author numerous poems. Founding mem. Humanities Commn. Montgomery County, 1984-91; judge Md. Writing Contest for Sr. Citizens, Annapolis, 1987-91, Montgomery County Bd. Elections,l 1990-92. Recipient Cert. of Recognition US Dept. Commerce, Washington, 1979, Alice Sherry Meml. award Poetry Soc. Va., Charlottesville, 1988, Courage award Dystonia Med. Found., 1997, Gov. Arts award Md. Citizens for the Arts Found., 2002, Lifetime Achievement recognition U. Md. Librs., 2003; named Outstanding Md. Woman Writer Md. State Dept. Edn., Md. Commn. for Women, Balt., 1989; Millenium poetry displayed in Montgomery County, Md. Govt. Bldg., 2000-; named Notable Montgomery County Author, Friends of the Libr., 2001. Mem. Nat. League Am. Pen Women (Md. state letters chmn. 1990-92, 1999-2001, br. pres.-elect, nat. letters bd. 1992-94, founding mem. Chesapeake Mag., 1993, chmn. nat. letters com., nat. membership chmn. 1994-95, nat. exec. bd. 1994-96, nat. pub. rels. chmn. 1996-98, writing awards 1983, 85, 87, 89, 1st prize Nat. Adult Short Story contest 1994, 1st prize Nat. Catherine Leach Poetry competition 1994, 1st prize Nat. Miriam S. Rogers letters contest, 1995, 2d prize Chesapeake Short Story contest 1996, 2d prize Md. Form Poetry 1999, centennial com. 1997, 1st pl. 1998, millenium planning com. 1999), Mortar Bd. Alumni Club (pres. 1977-78, 50th ann. recognition cert. 2000, 50th Class Reunion com. 2000, Comcast Humanities Achievement award, 2001). Democrat. Jewish. Avocations: walking, travel.

KRUGER, PAUL, nuclear civil engineering educator; b. Jersey City, June 7, 1925; s. Louis and Sarah (Jacobs) K.; m. Claudia Mathis, May 19, 1972; children: Sharon, Kenneth, Louis. BS, MIT, 1950; PhD, U. Chgo., 1954. Registered profl. engr., Pa. Rsch. physicist GM, Detroit, 1954-55; mgr. dept. chemistry Nuclear Sci. and Engring. Corp., Pitts., 1955-60; v.p. Hazleton Nuclear Sci. Corp., Palo Alto, Calif., 1960-62; prof. civil engring. Stanford (Calif.) U., 1962-87, prof. emeritus, 1987—. Cons. Elec. Power Rsch. Inst., Palo Alto, 1975-95, Los Alamos (N.Mex.) Nat. Lab., 1985-98. Author: Principles of Activation Analysis, 1973, Geothermal Energy, 1972. 1st lt. USAF, 1943-46, PTO. Recipient achievement cert. U.S. Energy R & D Adminstrn., 1975. Fellow Am. Nuclear Soc.; mem. ASCE (divsn. chmn. 1978-79). Home: 819 Allardice Way Stanford CA 94305-1050 Office: Stanford U Civil Engring Dept Stanford CA 94305

KRUGMAN, GARY DAVID, lawyer; b. Bklyn., July 31, 1948; s. Irving and Thelma K.; m. Carla Christina Calcagno, Oct. 13, 1991. BSBA, SUNY, Albany, 1969; JD, Case Western Res. U., 1973. Bar: D.C. 1973. Trademark examining atty. U.S. Patent and Trademark Office, Arlington, Va., 1974-78, interlocutory atty. examiner, 1978-82, adminstrv. trademark judge, 1982-89, chair pub. adv. com., 1997-99; atty. Sughrue, Mion PLLC, Washington, 1989—. Adj. prof. Cath. U. Sch. Law, Washington, 1995-2000. Author: Trademark Trial and Appeal Board Practice and Procedure, 1997, 5th edit., 2003. Mem. ABA, Am. Intellectual Property Law Assn., D.C. Bar (mem. steering com. intellectual propery sect. 1993-98). Avocations: tennis, hiking, travel. Office: Sughrue Mion PLLC 2100 Pennsylvania Ave NW Washington DC 20037-3202

KRUGMAN, RICHARD DAVID, pediatrician, university administrator, educator; b. N.Y.C., Nov. 28, 1942; s. Saul and Sylvia (Stern) K.; m. Mary Elizabeth Kerber, July 9, 1966; children: Scott, Joshua, Todd, Jordan. AB, Princeton U., 1963; MD, NYU, 1968. Resident U. Colo. Sch. Medicine, Denver, 1968-71; staff assoc. Nat. Inst. Health, Bethesda, Md., 1971-73; asst. prof. U. Colo. Sch. Medicine, 1973-78, assoc. prof., 1978-87, prof. of pediatrics, 1988—, dean, 1992—. Author: The Battered Child, 5th edit., 1997; editor: (jour.) Child Abuse/Neglect, 1986-2001. Chmn. U.S. Adv. Bd. Child Abuse and Neglect, Washington, 1989-91; dir. Kempe Nat. Ctr. for Prevention and Treatment of Child Abuse and Neglect, Denver, 1981-92; trustee Princeton U., 2001—. Recipient C. Henry Kempe award Nat. Conf. on Child Abuse, 1989, St. Geme award U. Colo. Sch. Medicine, 1992, 98; Paul Harris fellow Rotary Internat., Sydney, Australia, 1992. Mem. Internat. Soc. Prevention of Child Abuse and Neglect (pres. 1992-94), Am. Acad. Pediatrics (Ray Helfer award 1995, Brandt Steele award 1996), Am. Pediatric Soc. Office: U Colo Sch Medicine 4200 E 9th Ave Denver CO 80262-0001

KRUGMAN, SCOTT DANIEL, pediatrician, educator; b. Denver, Colo., June 11, 1969; s. Richard David and Mary Elizabeth Krugman; m. Lynn Holley Holley, June 12, 1993; children: Daniel Watt, Ryan Scott. BA, Middlebury Coll., 1987—91; MD, Dartmouth Med. Sch., 1991—95. Pediatrics Am. Bd. of Pediat., 1998. Chmn., dept. of pediat. Franklin Sq. Hosp. Ctr., Balt., 2002—; clin. asst. prof. of pediat. U. of Md. Sch. of Medicine, Balt., 2000—. Mem. Md. State Child Fatality Rev. Team, 1999—2001, Balt. County Child Fatality Rev. Team, 2001, Balt. County Child Protection Rev. Panel, 2001, The Family Tree, Balt., 2000. Recipient Rolf Syvertson fellow, Dartmouth Med. Sch., 1995, Ciba-Geigy Cmty. Svc. award, 1993; grant; child abuse prevention program, Md. Children's Trust Fund, 2002. Fellow: Am. Acad. of Pediat. Avocations: tennis, travel, family. Office: Franklin Square Hosp Ctr 9000 Franklin Square Dr Baltimore MD 21237

KRUGMAN, STANLEY LEE, international management consultant; b. N.Y.C., Mar. 2, 1925; s. Harry and Leah (Greenberg) K.; m. Helen Schorr, June 14, 1947; children: Vicky Lee, Thomas Paul; m. Carolyn Schambra, Sept. 17, 1966; children: David Andrew, Wendy Carol; m. Gail Jennings, Mar. 17, 1974; children: Hillary Marie, Paul. B Chem. Engring., Rensselaer Poly. Inst., 1947; postgrad., Poly. Inst. Bklyn., Columbia U., 1947-51. Process devel. engr. Merck

& Co., Rahway, N.J., 1947-51; sr. process and project engr. C.F. Braun & Co., Alhambra, Calif., 1951-55; with Jacobs Engring. Co., Pasadena, Calif., 1955-76; from chief engr. to v.p. engring. and constrn. to v.p. gen. mgr. to exec. v.p. to pres., and dir.; exec. v.p., dir. Jacobs Engring. Group Inc., Pasadena, Calif., 1974-82; pres., dir. Jacobs Constructors of P.R., San Juan, 1970-82; pres. Jacobs Internat. Inc., 1971-82, Jacobs Internat. Ltd., Inc., Dublin, Ireland, 1974-82; dep. chmn. Jacobs LTA Engring., Ltd., Johannesburg, South Africa, 1981-82; pres. Krugman Assocs., 1982—; internat. mgmt. cons. Patentee in field. Served to lt. (j.g.) USNR, 1944-46, PTO. Mem.: Am. Chem. Soc., Am. Inst. Chem. Engrs., U.S. Naval Inst. Presbyterian. Home and Office: 24452 Portola Rd Carmel CA 93923-9327 E-mail: slkrugman@earthlink.net.

KRUGMAN, STANLEY LIEBERT, science administrator, geneticist; b. St. Louis, June 8, 1932; s. Bernard and Della (Goldberg) Krugman; m. Judith Raechel Alfend, June 28, 1958; children: Mark Bernard, Jeffrey Jon. BS in Forestry, U. Mo., 1955; MF, U. Calif., Berkeley, 1956, PhD in Plant Physiology, 1961. Rsch. aide U. Calif., 1956-61, rsch. assoc., 1961-62; rsch. physiologist U.S. Forest Svc., 1962-64, project leader, 1964-71, staff geneticist, 1971-80, staff dir., 1980-95; sr. for specialist, pvt. cons. World Bank Natural Resources, Washington, 1995—. Cons. in field. Editor: (book) Seeds of Woody Plants, 1974, Advances in Reproductive Biology, 1974, Management Biosphere Reserves, 1979, Advances in Forest Physiology, 1980. Recipient Sci. medal, USSR, 1995, Czech Republic, 1995, Poland, 1997. Fellow: AAAS, Soc. Am. Foresters (William Schlich medal 1990); mem.: Internat. Union Forestry Orgn. Jewish. Office: 6515 Dryden Dr Mc Lean VA 22101-4627 E-mail: SKRUGMAN@juno.com.

KRUH, LOUIS, advertising executive, lawyer; b. N.Y.C., Jan. 29, 1923; s. Jack and Ada (Levy) K.; m. Gladys Tina Kahn, July 3, 1952; children: David Scott, Nancy Lynn. BBA cum laude, CCNY, 1963; MBA with distinction, Pace U., 1973; JD, Touro Law Sch., 1984. Bar: N.Y. 1985. Adv. rep. Jewelry Mag., N.Y.C., 1949-54; sr. account exec. BBDO, N.Y.C., 1954-70; dir. adv. N.Y. Telephone, N.Y.C., 1970-90; lawyer pvt. practice Merrick, N.Y., 1990-92; sr. atty. N.Y. State Workers Compensation Bd., Hempstead, N.Y., 1992—. Mem. print adv. com. Assn. Nat. Advertisers, N.Y.C., 1987-90; mem. pub. rels. adv. bd. League for Hard of Hearing, N.Y.C., 1982-90. Author: The Family Guide to Long Island, 1970, The New Family Guide to Long Island, 1976; co-author: Machine Cryptography and Modern Cryptanalysis, 1985, Presidential Landmarks, 1992; co-founder, co-editor: Cryptologia Jour., 1977—; co-editor Cryptology: Yesterday, Today, and Tomorrow, 1987, Cryptology: Machines, History & Methods, 1989, Selections from Cryptologia: History, People and Technology, 1998; book rev. editor The Cryptogram Jour., 1975—; contbr. articles to profl. jours. Trustee Merrick Pub. Libr., N.Y., 1967-73, pres. 1969-71; trustee Nassau County Reference Libr., Garden City, N.Y., 1968-72; bd. dirs. Merrick Sch. Dist., 1973-80, 84—, pres. 1976-79, 90-92, 2000-02; speaker Nat. Sch. Bds. Assn., Alexandria, Va., 1978-79; chmn. pub. rels. com. N.Y. State Sch. Bds. Assn., Albany, 1979-80; co-founder, pres., bd. dirs. Hist. Soc. of the Merricks, 1975—; co-pres. Merrick Brotherhood Coun., 1995—; bd. dirs. Bellmore-Merrick Ctrl. H.S. Dist., 2000—, pres., 2001-02. With U.S. Army, 1943-46, ETO. With USAR, 1943—46, ETO. Decorated Purple Heart, Bronze Star. Recipient Merrick Man of Yr. Merrick C. of C., 1979. Mem. Am. Cryptogram Assn. (pres. 1984-86), Am. Radio Relay League (vol. counsel 1990-2002), N.Y. Cipher Soc. (pres.), Kiwanis (bd. dirs. Merrick 1979-80, 97—). Jewish. Avocations: cryptology, ham radio. Office: NY State Workers Comp Bd 175 Fulton Ave Hempstead NY 11550-3718

KRUIDENIER, DAVID, newspaper executive; b. Des Moines, July 18, 1921; s. David S. and Florence (Cowles) K.; m. Elizabeth Stuart, Dec. 29, 1948; 1 child, Lisa. BA, Yale U., 1946; MBA, Harvard U., 1948; LLD, Buena Vista Coll., 1960, Simpson Coll., 1963; LittD, Luther Coll., 1990; DHL, Drake U., 1990. With Mpls. Star and Tribune, 1948-52; with Des Moines Register and Tribune, 1952-85, pres., pub., 1971-78, chief exec. officer, 1971-85, chmn., chief exec. officer, 1982-85; with Cowles Media Co., 1983-93, pres., chief exec. officer, 1983-84, chmn., chief exec. officer, 1984-85, chmn., 1985-97. Trustee Gardner and Florence Call Cowles Found., Drake U., Des Moines Art Ctr., Grinnell Coll. Greater Des Moines Found. With USAAF, 1942-45. Decorated Air medal with three clusters, D.F.C. Mem. Coun. on Fgn. Rels., Des Moines Club, Mpls. Club, Sigma Delta Chi, Beta Theta Pi, Beta Gamma Sigma. Home: 3409 Southern Hills Dr Des Moines IA 50321-1318 Office: 715 Locust St Des Moines IA 50309-3703

KRUKOWSKI, JAN, communications executive; b. Lodz, Poland, Nov. 18, 1930; came to U.S., 1941; s. Edward and Alice (Landau) K.; m. Nancy Harrow; children: Damon, Anton. BA, NYU, 1952, MA, 1961. Writer Dem. Nat. Com., N.Y.C., 1952—56; account exec. Alfred Auerbach Assocs., N.Y.C., 1957; v.p. Press Release, Inc., N.Y.C., 1958; pres. Krukowski and Symington, Inc., N.Y.C., 1959-63; exec. v.p. Barton-Gillet Co., N.Y.C., 1964-80; pres. Jan Krukowski & Co., N.Y.C., 1980—. Trustee Am. Symphony Orch., 2001-, Tchrs. Coll., Columbia U., 2002-; dir. Norman and Rosita Winston Found., 1997-. Mem.: Century Assn. Office: Jan Krukowski & Co 74 E 79th St New York NY 10021

KRUKOWSKI, LUCIAN, philosophy educator, artist; b. N.Y.C., Nov. 22, 1929; s. Stefan and Anna (Belcarz) Krukowski; m. Marilyn Denmark, Jan. 14, 1955; 1 child, Samantha. BA, CUNY, 1952; BFA, Yale U., 1955; MS, Pratt Inst., 1958; PhD, Wash. U., St. Louis, 1977. Faculty mem. Pratt Inst., N.Y.C., 1955-69; dean Sch. Fine Arts Wash. U., St. Louis, 1969-77, prof. philosophy, 1977-96, chmn. dept. philosophy, 1986-89, prof. philosophy emeritus, 1996—. Author: Art and Concept, 1987, Aesthetic Legacies, 1992; contbr. articles to publs.; artist 10 one-person shows, 1960-92, outdoor murals for copr. bldgs., 1972, 83. Cpl. USMC, 1952—54. Mem.: Am. Philos. Assn., Am. Soc. Aesthetics. Avocations: climbing, hiking. Home: 6003 Kingsbury Blvd Saint Louis MO 63112 Office: Washington U Dept of Philosophy 1 Brookings Dr Dept Of Saint Louis MO 63130-4899 E-mail: LucianK@swbell.net.

KRUKS, SONIA R. social sciences educator, researcher; b. London, Feb. 15, 1947; arrived in U.S., 1980; d. Leo Kruks and Sima Horn; m. Benjamin G. Wisner, Jr., Feb. 9, 1978; 1 child, Gabrielle Kruks-Wisner. BA hons., Leeds U., England, 1968; MSc Econs., London Sch. Econs., 1970, PhD, 1977. Lectr. in politics City of London Polytechnic, 1971—77; asst., assoc. prof. politics Grad. Fac. New Sch. For Social Rsch., N.Y.C., 1981—90; Danforth prof. politics Oberlin (Ohio) Coll., 1990—. Author: Political Philosophy of Merlean-Ponty, 1981, Situation and Human Existence, 1990, Retrieving Experience, 2001; mem. editl. bd. Polity, 1989—95, Sartre Studies, 1997—, Hypatia, 2000—. Mem.: Am. Philosophical Assn., Am. Polit. Sci. Assn. (sect. treas. 1992—95, sect. sec. 1993—95, best paper award women and politics sect. 1992). Avocations: ceramics, walking, music. Office: Oberlin Coll Politics Dept Oberlin OH 44074 Office Fax: 440-775-8898.

KRULAK, CHARLES CHANDLER, marine officer; b. Quantico, Va., Mar. 4, 1942; s. Victor Harold and Amy (Chandler) K.; m. Zandra Lynn Meyers, June 27, 1964; children: David Chandler, Todd Cameron. BS, U.S. Naval Acad., 1964; MS, George Washington U., 1973; advanced mil. course, Amphib. War Sch., 1968, Army Command and Gen. Staff, Coll., 1976, Nat. War Coll., 1982. Commd. 2d lt. USMC, 1964, advanced through grades to gen., 1995, retired, 1999, rifle co. comdr., 1965-66, 69-70, bn. comdr., 1983-85; mil. asst. Asst. Sec. Def. for Command, Control, Comm. and Intelligence, Washington, 1986-87; dep. dir. White House Mil. Office, Washington, 1987-89; brigade comdr. and asst. divsn. comdr. USMC, N.C., 1989-91, force svc. support group comdr., 1989-90, force svc. support comdr., brigade comdr., 1990-91; dir. pers. mgmt., pers. procurement Hdqtrs. Marine Corps, 1991-92; comdg. gen. MCCDC, Quantico, Va., 1992-94; comdr. marine forces, Pacific and comdg. gen. Fleet Marine Forces, Pacific, Camp Smith, Hawaii, 1994-95; commandant USMC, 1995-99; sr. exec. MBNA Am. Corp., Wilmington, Del., 1999—. Contbr. articles to Marine Corps Gazette. Decorated D.S.M. (2), Def. D.S.M. (2), Silver Star, Bronze Star with combat V (3), Purple Heart (2). Avocations: running, reading. Office: MBNA Am 1100 N King St Wilmington DE 19884-0001

KRULAK, VICTOR HAROLD, newspaper executive; b. Denver, Jan. 7, 1913; s. Morris and Besse M. (Ball) K.; m. Amy Chandler, June 1, 1936; children: Victor Harold Jr., William Morris, Charles Chandler. BS, U.S. Naval Acad., 1934; LL.D., U. San Diego. Commd. 2d lt. USMC, 1934; advanced through grades to lt. gen.; service in China, at sea, with USMC (Fleet Marine Forces), 1935-39; staff officer, also bn. regimental and divsn. comdr. World War II, World War II; chief staff (1st Marine Div. Korea); formerly comdg. gen. (Marine Corps Recruit Depot), San Diego; formerly spl asst. to dir., joint staff counterinsurgency and spl. activities (Office Joint Chiefs Staff); comdg. gen. Fleet Marine Force Pacific, Pacific, 1964-68; ret., 1968; v.p. Copley Newspaper Corp., 1968-79; pres. Words Ltd. Corp., San Diego. Trustee Zool. Soc. San Diego. Decorated D.S.M., Navy Cross, Legion of Merit with 3 oak leaf clusters, Bronze Star, Air medal, Purple Heart (2) U.S.; Cross of Gallantry; Medal of Merit Vietnam; Distinguished Service medal (Korea), Order of Cloud and Banner, Republic of China. Mem. U.S. Naval Inst., U.S. Marine Corps Assn., Am. Soc. Newspaper Editors, InterAm. Press Assn., U.S. Strategic Inst. (chmn.). Home: # 307 2404 Loring St San Diego CA 92109 Office: Words Ltd 2404 Loring St San Diego CA 92110-4827

KRULEWICZ, RITA GLORIA, special education educator; d. Charles Lewis and Gloria Edna Perrine; m. Donald Joseph Krulewicz, Nov. 1981; 1 child, Clare. BS, Coll. Misericordia, 1976; MEd, Trenton State Coll., 1979. Multi-handicapped tchr. The Woods Sch., Langhorne, Pa., 1976-79, Mercer County Spl. Svcs. Sch. Dist., Hamilton, NJ, 1979-86; resource ctr. tchr. Princeton (N.J.) Regional Sch. Dist., 1992—, John Witherspoon Mid. Sch., Princeton, 1992—. Worker Dem. Orgn., Pa., 1976—; mem. Morrisville Hist. Soc., 1976—. Named Tchr. of Yr. Mercer County Spl. Svcs., 1986. Mem.: NEA, Coun. Exceptional Children (professionally recognized spl. edn. 1999—), N.J. Edn. Assn., Kappa Delta Pi. Roman Catholic. Avocations: reading, gardening, surfing the net, going to movies, traveling. Home: 136 Carlisle Ave Yardville NJ 08620-1244 Office: John Witherspoon Mid Sch 217 Walnut Ln Princeton NJ 08540-3484

KRULFELD, RUTH MARILYN, anthropologist, educator; m. Jacob Mendel Krulfeld, 1964; 1 child, Michael David. BA cum laude, Brandeis U., 1956; PhD, Yale U., 1974. Field rschr. micro-geog. rsch. farms, Singapore, Malaya, 1951-53; anthrop. rschr., Jamaica, 1957, 1958, 1960—62, 1993; anthrop. rschr. S.E. Asian refugees to U.S., 1981—; anthrop. rschr., Lombak, Indonesia and N.E. Thailand, 1993; asst. prof. anthropology, dir. grad. students George Washington U., Washington, 1964-72, 93-97, assoc. prof., 1973-76, prof., 1976-2000, chmn. dept. anthropology, 1984-87, founder spl. grad. program in internat. world devel.; prof. anthropology, internat. affairs; prof. emeritus anthropology, human scis., internat. affairs, 2000—. Bd. dirs. No. Va. Humanities Coun.; rschr. Laotian refugees in U.S., 1981—, also rsch. on culture change in villages in Indonesia; adv. bd. Successful New Ams. Project of S.E. Asian Resource Action Ctr.; adv. to bd. Newcomers Cmty. Svc. Ctr., Lao-Am. Women's Assn., Lao Cmty. Forum; cons. Human Rights Conf. of AAAS. Co-author: Reconstructuring Lives, Recapturing Meaning: Refugee Identity, Gender and Culture Change, 1994, Beyond Boundaries: Selected papers on Refugees and Immigrants, 1997, Power, Ethics, and Human Rights: Anthropological Studies of Refugee Research and Action, 1998; contbr. articles to profl. jours.; editl. bd. com. on refugees and immigrants. Bd. dirs. No. Va. Regional Humanities Coun. Currier scholar Yale U., 1958; Ford fellow, 1960-62; grantee Found. for Study of Man, 1957, Am. Coun., 1963, Cotlow faculty rsch. grantee, 1992-93, faculty rsch. grantee George Washington U., 1992-93, rsch. grantee Va. Found. for Humanities and Pub. Policy, 1995-96; recipient Banneker award Ctr. for Washington Area Studies, 1996, George Washington U. award, 2000. Mem. Anthrop. Soc. Washington, Am. Anthrop. Assn. (nominating com., com. on refugee issues gen. anthropology divsn., vice chair com. on refugees issues 1992-94, gen. anthropology divsn. 1993-94, exec. bd. com. on refugees and immigrants 1994-99, CORI editl. bd. 1998-99, CORI award for best paper on refugees issues 1992, Pedagogical Rsch. and Innovative Devel. in Edn. award 1994, award for leadership and contbn. to refugee studies com. on refugees and immigrants 2000). Office: George Washington U Dept Anthropology Washington DC 20052-0001 *Perhaps the major attitudes that have motivated my work have been a deep respect for my fellow human beings, and a need to learn from them, to experience their wondrous creativity, ability and diversity; as an anthropologist, to understand as much about human societies as I could, and as an educator, to ignite this enthusiasm and wonder in my students, to encourage them to go beyond our present understanding and abilities. As an advocate for human rights, I hope to instill in my students the wish to be involved in social action.*

KRULIK, BARBARA S. director, writer, curator; b. N.Y.C., June 13, 1955; d. Herbert Arnold and Irene Sylvia K. BA in Art History, Pa. State U., 1976; MA in Museology, Reinwardt Acad., Amsterdam, The Netherlands, 2000. Asst. to dir. Nat. Acad. of Design, N.Y.C., 1976—78; acting dir. NAD, N.Y.C., 1977-78, coord. exhbns., 1978-83, asst. dir., 1983-89, interim dir., 1989-90, dep. dir., 1990-92; assoc. dir. Forum Gallery, N.Y.C., 1992-94; dir. Grad. Sch. Figurative Art New York Acad. Art, N.Y.C., 1994-97; owner, dir. KECCS (Krulik Cultural Cons. Svcs.), 2001—. Ind. curator, 1997—; cons., 1997—. Author, editor exhbn. catalogues. Mem. Am. Assn. Mus. (curators and registrars coms.), Internat. Coun. on Mus. E-mail: bskrulik@xs4all.nl.

KRULITZ, LEO MORRION, financial executive; b. Wallace, Idaho, June 15, 1938; s. John Morrion and Myrtle (Parker) K.; m. Donna Eileen Ristau, June 18, 1960; children— Cynthia, Pamela. BA, Stanford U., 1960; JD cum laude, Harvard U., 1963; MBA, Stanford U., 1969. Bar: Idaho bar 1963, Ind. bar 1969, D.C. bar 1978, U.S. Supreme Ct. bar 1978. Ptnr. firm Moffatt, Thomas, Barrett & Blanton, Boise, Idaho, 1963-67; v.p., treas. Irwin Mgmt. Co., Columbus, Ind., 1969-77; solicitor Dept. of the Interior, Washington, 1977-79; gen. counsel Cummins Engine Co., Columbus, Ind., 1979-80, v.p., 1980-92; pres. Cummins Fin., Inc., 1984-92, Cummins Cash and Info. Svcs., Inc., 1988-92; pres., CEO Saunders, Inc., Birmingham, Ala., 1992-93; pres., CEO, dir. Parkland Mgmt. Co., Cleve., 1994—; endowment trustee Euclid Ave. Christian Ch., 1995-2001; dir. Horvitz Newspapers, Inc., Bellevue, Wash., 1994—. Trustee Lois U. Horvitz Found., 1998—; exec. dir. H.R.H. Family Found., 1994-98; treas. Irwin-Sweeney-Miller Found., Columbus, 1976-77; dir. L'Enfant Plaza Properties, Washington, 1974-77; mem. U.S. delegation Soviet Union Conf. on Environ. Law, 1978 Mem. Bartholomew Consol. Sch. Bd., 1982-88; trustee Wheelright Mus. of the Am. Indian, 2002—. Mem. Idaho Bar Assn., Ind. Bar Assn., D.C. Bar Assn., Harvard Club (N.Y.C.), Union Club (Cleve.). Democrat. Home: 20900 Colby Rd Shaker Heights OH 44122-1906 Office: 1001 Lakeside Ave E Ste 900 Cleveland OH 44114-1172

KRULL, EDWARD ALEXANDER, dermatologist; b. Oakville, Conn., Oct. 25, 1929; s. Alexander and Marian (Ruppert) K.; m. Joan Marie Adams, Sept. 7, 1955; children: Alisa M., Lael Adams, Edward Alexander. Student, Yale U., 1948-51, MD, 1955. Diplomate Am. Bd. Dermatology (bd. dirs. 1984-94, v.p. 1992-93, pres. 1994), Am. Bd. Med. Spltys. (chmn. dermatology sect. 1992-94). Intern San Francisco City-County Hosp., 1955-56; with Madigan Gen. Hosp., 1959-60; resident Henry Ford Hosp., Detroit, 1960-63, staff physician dept. dermatology, 1965-76, chmn. dept., 1976-97, chair emeritus dept. dermatology, 1997—, Edward Krull chair in dermatologic surgery, 2001—; dermatology practice Grand Rapids, Mich., 1963-65. Bd. dirs. Skin Cancer Found., 1977-80, Found. Internat. Dermatologic Edn., 1980-82; mem. residence rev. com. in dermatology, 1984-94, chmn., 1987-94. Mem. editl. bd. Jour. Dermatol. Surgery and Oncology, 1976-79, assoc. editor, 1993-96. Bd. govs. Henry Ford Hosp., trustee, 1986-94, mem. exec. com. bd. trustees, 1986-94, mem. fin. com. bd. trustees, 1986-94. Capt. M.C., U.S. Army, 1957-59, Iran. Recipient Disting. Svc. award Henry Ford Med. Alumni. Mem. AMA, Am. Dermatol. Assn. (pres. 1995-96), Am. Coll. Mohs Micrographic Surgery and Cutaneous Oncology, Am. Acad. Dermatology (hon.; editl. bd. jour. 1979-84, chmn. various task forces, bd. dirs. 1982-86, exec. com. bd. dirs. 1984-86, v.p. 1986-87, coun. sci. assembly 1991-95, chmn. 1995-96, Bronze award exhibit, 1969, Gold medal 1996, C.S. Livingood lecture 1998), Mich. Dermatol. Soc. (sec.-treas. 1973-75, pres. 1976-77), Mich. State Med. Soc. (sec. dermatology sect. 1972-73, pres. 1973-74), Wayne County Med. Soc. (Profl. Achievement award 1997), Am. Soc. Dermatologic Surgery (pres. 1982, bd. dirs. 1973-76, 78-82, chmn. edn. coordinating com. 1978-82, Leon Goldman Achievement award 1988, Pres.' award 2002), Assn. Profs. Dermatology (bd. dirs. 1988-89), Assn. Acad. Dermatologic Surgeons (pres. 1988-89). Episcopalian. Avocations: tennis, trout fishing, golf. Home: 422 University Pl Grosse Pointe MI 48230-1638 Office: Henry Ford Hosp Dept Dermatology 2799 W Grand Blvd Dept Detroit MI 48202-2689

KRULL, JEFFREY ROBERT, library director; b. North Tonawanda, N.Y., Aug. 29, 1948; s. Robert George and Ruth Otilie (Fels) K.; m. Alice Marie Hart, Apr. 12, 1969; children: Robert, Marla. BA, Williams Coll., Williamstown, Mass., 1970; MLS, SUNY, Buffalo, 1974. Cert. profl. libr., N.Y., Ohio, Ind. Traffic mgr. New England Tel. Co., Burlington, Vt., 1970-71; tchr. Harrisburg (Pa.) Acad., 1971-72; reference libr. Buffalo and Erie County Pub. Libr., 1973-76; head libr. Ohio U., Chillicothe, 1976-78; dir. Mansfield-Richland County Pub. Libr., Ohio, 1978-86, Allen County Pub. Libr., Ft. Wayne, Ind., 1986—. Mem. exec. com. Ft. Wayne Area Libr. Svc. Authority, 1986-90, v.p., 1989; mem. exec. com. Ind. Coop. Libr. Svcs. Authority, 1992—, pres., 1994-95; mem. Online Computer Libr. Ctr. Pub. Libr. Adv. Coun., 1994-97; pres. Ft. Wayne Area INFONET, 1995—. Pres. Three Rivers Literary Alliance, 1997—; trustee Ohionet, Columbus, 1984—86. Named Sagamore of the Wabash, Gov. Ind., 2001. Mem. ALA, Pub. Libr. Assn. (pres. met. librs. sect. 1990-91, statistical report adv. com.), Libr. Adminstrn. and Mgmt. Assn. (sec. libr. orgn. and mgmt. assn. 1996-97), Ohio Libr. Assn. (bd. dirs. 1985-86), Ind. Libr. Fedn. (vice chmn. legis. com. 1987—), Beta Phi Mu. Home: 3017 Oak Borough Run Fort Wayne IN 46804-7808 Office: Allen County Pub Libr PO Box 2270 900 Webster St Fort Wayne IN 46801-2270 E-mail: jkrull@acpl.lib.in.us.

KRUMBOLTZ, JOHN DWIGHT, psychologist, educator; b. Cedar Rapids, Iowa, Oct. 21, 1928; s. Dwight John and Margaret (Jones) K.; m. Helen Brandhorst, Aug. 22, 1954 (div. Aug. 1986); children: Ann, Jennifer; m. Betty Lee Foster, Nov. 8, 1987. BA, Coe Coll., Cedar Rapids, 1950; MA, Columbia Tchrs. Coll., 1951; PhD, U. Minn., 1955; PhD (hon.), Pacific Grad. Sch. Psychology, 1991. Counselor, tchr. W. Waterloo (Iowa) H.S., 1951-53; from teaching asst. to instr. U. Minn., 1953-55; from asst. prof. ednl. psychology to assoc. prof. Mich. State U., 1957-61; faculty Stanford U. Sch. Edn., 1961-66, prof. edn. and psychology, 1966—. Vis. sr. research psychologist Ednl. Testing Service, 1972-73; fellow Ctr. for Advanced Study in Behavioral Scis., 1975-76, Advanced Study Ctr., Nat. Ctr. for Research in Vocat. Edn., Ohio State U., 1980-81; vis. colleague dept. psychology Inst. Psychiatry, U. London, 1983-84 Author: (with others) Learning to Study, 1960; (with Helen B. Krumboltz) Changing Children's Behavior, 1972; editor: Learning and the Educational Process, 1965, Revolution in Counseling, 1966; (with Carl E. Thoresen) Behavioral Counseling: Cases and Techniques, 1969, Counseling Methods, 1976; (with Anita M. Mitchell and G. Brian Jones) Social Learning and Career Decision Making, 1979, (with Daniel A. Hamel) Assessing Career Development, 1982; contbr. articles to profl. jours. With USAF, 1955-57. Recipient Eminent Career award Nat. Career Devel. Assn., 1994; Guggenheim fellow, 1967-68. Mem. APA (pres. div. counseling psychology 1974-75, award for disting. profl. contbns. to knowledge 2002), Am. Ednl. Rsch. Assn. (v.p. div. E. 1966-68), Am. Pers. and Guidance Assn. (Outstanding Rsch. award 1959, 66, 68, Disting. Profl. Svcs. award 1974, Leona Tyler award 1990). Home: 933 Valdez Pl Stanford CA 94305-1008

KRUMHOLZ, ALLAN, medical educator; b. Lodz, Poland, Jan. 1, 1945; came to U.S., 1949; s. Jacob and Mera (Rosen) K.; m. Francine Iris Herzog, Aug. 20, 1967; children: Matthew, Andrea. BA, Queens Coll., 1966; MD, Chgo. Med. Sch., 1970. Intern, med. resident Balt. City Hosp., 1970-72; neurology resident Johns Hopkins Hosp., Balt., 1972-76, asst prof. neurology, 1978-85, EEG fellowship, 1979, assoc. prof. neurology, 1985-90; asst. prof. neurology SUNY (Stony Brook) Med. Sch., 1976-77; prof. neurology U. Md., Balt., 1989—. Chmn. profl. adv. bd. Epilepsy Found. Am., Landover, Md., 1995-97. Capt. Md. NG, 1970-76. Named Physician of Yr. Gov.'s Com. (Md.), 1987; recipient Outstanding Tchr. award U. Md. neurology residents, 1991. Fellow Am. Acad. Neurology, Am. Neurol. Assn., Am. Epilepsy Soc. Avocations: swimming, skiing. Home: 5404 Springlake Way Baltimore MD 21212-3444 Office: U MD Hosp Dept Neurology 22 S Greene St Baltimore MD 21201-1544 E-mail: akrumholz@som.umaryland.edu.

KRUMHOLZ, BURTON ALAN, obstetrician-gynecologist, educator; b. Bklyn., Dec. 12, 1928; s. Robert and Ruth (Kleinholz) K.; m. Ellen Claire Goldblatt, June 24, 1951 (div. Dec., 1970); children: Susan, Linda, Debra; m. Sheila Hope Odesky, Sept. 25, 1971; children: Andrew, Glenn. BA, Colby Coll., 1948; MD, N.Y. Med. Coll., 1953. Diplomate Am. Bd. Ob-Gyn. Intern Wm. McKinley Meml. Hosp., Trenton, N.J., 1954; resident Met. Med. Ctr. N.Y. Med. Coll., N.Y.C., 1954-55, U.S. Naval Hosp., Portsmouth, 1955-57. Dir. gynecology dept. Nassau County Med. Ctr., East Meadow, N.Y., 1973-75; dir. Ob-gyn, Queens Hosp. Ctr., Jamaica, N.Y., 1975-83; assoc. chmn. Ob-gyn. Long Island Jewish Med. Ctr., N. Hyde Park, 1976-94; prof. Ob-gyn. Albert Einstein Coll. Medicine, 1989. Fellow ACOG, ACS, Am. Soc. Colposcopy and Cervical Pathology, Am. Pub. Health Assn.; mem. AMA. Office: Women's Comprehensive Ctr 1554 Northern Blvd Manhasset NY 11030-3006 E-mail: krumholz@lij.edu.

KRUMHOLZ, RICHARD A. physician; b. Wilkes-Barre, Pa., Nov. 5, 1935; s. Manuel and Ella (Weber) K.; m. Sylvia Krumholz; children: Harlan, Susan, Lynne, Julie; m. Cheryl S. Kelley, Sept. 11, 1985; 1 child, Jill. Student, U. Pitts., 1953-55, U. Dayton, 1956; MD, St. Louis U., 1960. Practice medicine specializing in allergy and pulmonary diseases, Dayton, Ohio, 1965-91; Sarasota, Fla., 1994—. Served with USAF, 1963-65. Home: 2519 Riverview Blvd Bradenton FL 34205 Office: 2034 Bee Ridge Rd Ste 104 Sarasota FL 34239-6252 E-mail: Richard@krumholzgroup.com.

KRUMM, TAHLMAN, JR., communications educator; b. Columbus, Ohio, Sept. 9, 1941; s. Tahlman and Eleanor Ione (Beaton) Krumm; m. Elizabeth Chapman Egnor; children: Eric Tahlman, Jason Robert. BA in history, Ohio State U., Columbus, 1966; BA in English and linguistics, U. South Fla., Tampa, 1969; MA in journalism, Ohio State U., 1974, PhD in communication, 1978; participant pub. utility exec. program, grad. sch. bus. admin., U. Mich, 1979. Mktg. Columbus and So. Ohio Electric Co., 1964—65; reporter to reg. editor AP Ohio Bur., 1969—72, feature writer; broadcast editor AP Ohio Bur.; legis. corr. AP Ohio Bur.; grad. tchg. asst. sch. of journalism Ohio State U., 1972—76, admin. asst. to dir. sch. of journalism, 1972—73, asst. dir. comm. svcs. office of pub. affairs, 1976—78, adj. lectr. sch. of journalism, 1978—79; pres., chmn. Omnicomm Enterprises Inc., Columbus, 1979—87; ptnr. Kaderly Mini-Warehouse Co, Columbus, Ohio, 1980—84, First Worthington Co., Columbus, Ohio, 1980—85; dir. U.S. Healthstar, Columbus, 1985—91; pres., chmn. Avalanche Creek Projects Group, Columbus, 1992—2000; chmn. Inquesta LLC, 2000—. Dir. Kokomo (Ind.) Gas and Fuel Co., 1969—72; trustee Ralph Hastings Beaton Trust, 1970—2001; mem. grad. admissions com. sch. of journalism Ohio State U., 1972—76; prog. asst. mid-east sec. Dow Jones Newspaper Fund Editing Intern Program, 1979; dir., sec. Cage Media Inc., Celina, 1982—86; chmn. exec. com. Kokomo (Ind.) Gas and Fuel Co., 1984—92; dir., sec. Folly Beach Comm. Inc., Charleston, SC, 1984—87; dir., ptnr. Frontier Mktg. and Mgmt., Columbus, Ohio, 1998—2002; mem. Ohio Bd. of Regents, 1993—2002, chair various coms., vice chair, 1996—98, bd. chair, 1998—2000; mem. coun. of bd. chairs Assn. of Governing Bds., 2002—03; mem. bd. of trustees Columbus Coll. of Art and Design, 2003—. Mem. Ctr. Strategic and internat. studies working group Georgetown U., Washington, 1982—83; at large commr. U.S. comm. UNESCO, 1982—86, mem. Am. del. to 2nd session IPDC, 1982, pvt. sector rep. to 3rd session IPDC, 1982, mem. com. on comm. U.S. nat. commn., 1982—84, chmn. com. on reorganization, U.S. nat. commn., 1983—84; project coord. symposium on global comm. dev. and pvt. sector opportunities UNESCO-U.S. State Dept., 1984; spl. rep. of U.S. nat. commn. to exec. bd. UNESCO; mem. nat. steering com. George Bush Pres.; at large del. Rep. Nat. Conv., 1988; Ohio mem. com. on resolutions Rep. Nat Conv., 1988; mem. Nat. Adv. Coun. of the U.S. Peace Corps, 1990—91; regional selection panelist Pres. Commn. on White House Fellowships, St. Louis, 1990—92; at large del. Rep. Nat. Conv., 1992; alt. del. at large, Ohio Rep. primary, 1980; media cons. Betts for U.S. Senate, 1980; mem. Ohio Steering com. Bush Pres., 1987—88; sr. advisor and media coord. Ohio Bush Pres. Com., 1987—88; mem. transition team Gov. George V. Voinovich, Ohio, 1990—91; issues coord. ops. improvement task force Gov. of Ohio, 1992, exec. asst. to gov., 1991—92; mem. exec. steering com. Ohio Bush Reelection Campaign, 1992; spl. asst. higher edn. Gov. of Ohio, 1992—93; mem. charter rev. commn. City of Bexley, Ohio, 1998; spl. advisor U.S. nat. coun. world comm. yr. Internat. Telecom. Union, 1983—84; mem. exec. com. U.S. Nat. Commn. UNESCO, 1983—85, mem. membership com., 1983—85; mem. nat. steering com. Fund Am. Future, 1985—85; mem. Ohio Bd. of Regents, 1993—2002, Governor's Commn. on Student Success, 2000, co-chair standards com., 2000. With U.S. Army, 1962—68. Finalist Warren C. Price competition, History Divsn. Assn. Edn. in Journalism, 1974. Mem.: Columbus Mus. of Art, The Rev. Club, Rocky Fork Hunt and Country Club, The Athletic Club of

Columbus, Pres. Club, Ohio State U., Haverford Coll. Alumni Assn., Ohio U. Alumni Assn. (life), Columbus Acad. Alumni Assn., U. South Fla. Alumni Assn., The Golf Club, Kappa Tau Alpha. Avocations: reading, writing, golf, ecotourism, travel. Home: 2361 Clifton Avenue Bexley OH 43209 Office: 72 South 4th Street Columbus OH 43215

KRUMP, GARY JOSEPH, lawyer, judge; b. Breckenridge, Minn., June 27, 1946; m. Mary Kay Chermak; children: Adam, Jonathon. BA, N.D. State U., 1968; JD, U. Minn., 1971, postdoctoral, 1972; cert. in health care, So. Ill. U., Edwardsville, 1978, MBA, 1980; grad. cert., George Washington U., 1981; grad., Fed. Exec. Inst., 1988, U.S. Army Command & Gen. Staff Coll., 1989; grad. sr. mgrs. in govt. program, Harvard U., 1998. Bar: Minn. 1971, U.S. Ct. Mil. Appeals 1972, U.S. Supreme Ct. 1975, D.C. 1977. Commd. 2nd lt. U.S. Army, 1970, advanced through grades to capt., 1971, capt. with JAGC, 1972-76, chief internat. law-Japan, 1974-76; chief adminstrv. law Walter Reed Army Med. Ctr., 1976-77; sr. staff atty. office of gen. counsel VA, Washington, 1978-83, nat. coord. med. care recovery program, 1979, dep. asst. gen. counsel, 1983-87, assoc. dep., asst. sec. for acquisitions, 1988-89; v.p., gen. counsel JSA Healthcare Corp., 1989-91; dir., corp. sec. DKH Healthcare; dir. Office of Real Property Mgmt. Office Real Property Mgmt., U.S. Dept. VA, Washington, 1991-92, dep. asst. sec. acquisitions and material mgmt., 1992—2003, acting asst. sec. acquisitions and facilities, 1992-95; VA environ. exec., 1994—2003; chmn., chief adminstrv. judge VA Bd. Contract Appeals, 2003—; VA dispute resolution offcl., 2003. Mem. faculty Ctrl. Mich. U., U. Va.; apptd. to career Fed. Sr. Exec. Svc.; gen. counsel, dir. Soccerama Assn., Inc., 1987-93; bd. dirs. JSA Healthcare Inc., 1989-91, JSA Internat., Inc., 1989-91, VA; sec. DKH Healthcare, Inc., 1990-91; prin., dir., gen. counsel ISG, Inc., 1991-97; dir., gen. counsel Am. Health Group, Inc., 1993-97; mem. Interagy. Com. on Supply Mgmt. Steering Group, Nat. Performance Rev. Com. on Reinventing VA; chair Interagy. Procurement Reform Working Group, 1993-95; chair interagy. contracts group GSA; mem. Interagy. Contracts Adv. Group; chair nat. conf. reinventing small bus. partnerships VA, 1993; chair interagy contracts group GSA, mem. adv. group; apptd. Pres.' Com. for Purchase from Blind and Other Severely Disabled, 1992—, chair, 1996-2000; com. chmn. Subcom. on Procurement Reform, 1996-97, pres. com. disting. svc. award, 2000, chmn. subcom. on governance, 2002—; mem. nat. adv. bd. Fed. Prison Industries, 1995—, chair subcom. administrn.; VA environ. exec., 1994—; trustee Leadership VA, 1992-95; mem. Fed. Environ. Execs. Task Force, 1994—; mem. Interagy. Com. on Stds. Policy, 1995—, VA Stds. Exec., 1994—, VA Metrics Exec., 1994—; mem. Interagy. Electronic Commerce Task Force, 1994—; departmental co-chair Combined Fed. Campaign VA, 1994, departmental co-chair, campaign mgr., 1999; chair VA Departmental Environ. Adv. Group, 1994—; bd. dirs. VA Dept., 1992-95; chmn. bd. dirs. VA Supply Fund, 1993—; mem. Fed. Procurement Coun., 1991-97; mem. Procurement Execs. Coun., 1997—, vice chair, 2000-03, chair com. on electronic commerce, 1999—; mem. Interagy. e-Gov Task Force, Office Mgmt. & Budget, Exec. Office of Pres., 2000—; mem. VA e-Gov Steering com., 2000—; Creekmore lectr. on procurement law Judge Advs. Sch., Army, U. Va., 1997; mem. com. on ethics DC Bar, 2001—; judge VA Dispute Resolution Official, 2003—. Sec. Vets. Affairs Commendation, 1989, 95; mem. Ctr. for Pub. Resources Nat. Procurement Com., 1986-89, Adminstv. Conf. U.S. Alternative Disputes Resolution Symposium, 1988. Served to lt. col. JAGC, USAR, 1976—. Decorated U.S. Legion of Merit; recipient Presdl. Rank award, 1997, VA Meritorious Svc. award, 2000, Exceptional Svc. award, 2003. Fellow Nat. Contract Mgrs. Assn. (bd. advisors 1989-90, 93—, com. internat. contracting 1995—); mem. ABA (vice chair com. on healthcare contract law 1997—, com. on healthcare), VFW (life), Judge's Assn. (bd. contract appeals, 2003), BCA Bar Assn., Fed. Bar Assn. (nat. chmn. tort law com., health and human svcs. coun. chmn. 1980-81, chmn. Nat. Tort Conf. 1979, editor Tort Law Newsletter 1978-81, Superior Svc. awards 1979, 81), D.C. Bar Assn. (com. ethics), Nat. Forensic Ctr., Am. Coll.-Legal Medicine (assoc.), Internat. Soc. Mil. Law and Law of War, Internat. Legal Soc., Res. Officers Ass. (life), Mid-Atlantic Token Kai, Japanese Sword Soc. U.S., Fed. Acquisition Inst. Policy Bd., Fed. Procurement Coun., Contract Svcs. Assn. (procurement com. 1989-91), Interagency Med. Procurement Mgmt. Com., Govt. Procurement Tng. (adv. com.), Interagency Procurement Career Mgmt. Com., Fed. Real Property Execs. (interagy. adv. coun. 1991-93), Vets. of Am., Am. Legion (life), Bd. of Contract Appeals Judges Assn., Bd. of Contract Appeals Bar Assn., Beta Gamma Sigma, Tau Kappa Epsilon. Home: 13812 Town Line Rd Silver Spring MD 20906-2112 Office: US Dept Vets Affairs Acquisitions and Material Mgmt 810 Vermont Ave NW Washington DC 20420-0001 E-mail: gary.krump@mail.va.gov.

KRUPANSKY, BLANCHE, retired judge; b. Cleve., Dec. 10, 1925; d. Frank and Ann K.; m. Frank W. Vargo, Apr. 30, 1960. AB, Flora Stone Mather Coll., 1943-47; JD, Case Western Res. U., 1948, LLM, 1966. Bar: Ohio 1949. Gen. practice law, 1949-61, 83-84; asst. atty. gen. State of Ohio; asst. chief counsel Ohio Bur. Workmen's Compensation; judge Cleve. Mcpl. Ct., 1961-69; judge Common Pleas Ct. Cuyahoga County, 1969-77, Ct. Appeals Ohio 8th Appellate Dist., 1977-81; justice Supreme Ct. Ohio, 1981-83; judge 8th Dist. Ct. Appeals, 1983-95, chief justice, 1991; ret., 1995. Vis. com. Case Western U. Law Sch., 1974-78, bd. govs., 1975-76 Recipient Outstanding Jud. Service award Supreme Ct. Ohio, 1972-76, Law Book scholar award Cuyahoga Women's Polit. Caucus, 1981, outstanding contbn. to law award Ohio Assn. Civil Trial Attys., 1982, Disting. Alumna award, 1982, Disting. Service award Women's Space, 1982, award Democratic Women's Caucus, 1983, award Women's Equity Action League Ohio, 1983; Personal Achievement and Community Svc. award Case We. Res. U., 1988, Margaret Ireland award Women's City Club, 1984; named Woman of Achievement Inter-Club Council Cleve., 1969; inducted into Ohio Women's Hall of Fame, 1981 Mem. Nat. Assn. Women Lawyers, Nat. Assn. Women Judges, Ohio Bar Assn. (Cronise Lutes award 1997), Bar Assn. Greater Cleve., Cuyahoga County Bar Assn., Cleve. Women Lawyers, LWV, Ohio Ctrs. of Appeals Assn., Ohio Assn. Attys. Gen., Ohio Appellate Judges Assn., Soc. of Benchers (chair 1994-95), SAR (Silver Medal award 1995). Republic. Roman Catholic. Club: Woman's City (Woman of Achievement award 1981) (Cleve.).

KRUPANSKY, ROBERT BAZIL, federal judge; b. Cleve., Aug. 15, 1921; s. Frank A. and Anna (Lawrence) K.; m. Marjorie Blaser, Nov. 13, 1952. BA, Case Western Res. U., 1946, LLB, 1948, JD, 1968. Bar: Ohio 1948, Supreme Ct. Ohio 1948, Supreme Ct. U.S. 1948, U.S. Dist. Ct. (no. dist.) Ohio 1948, U.S. Ct. Appeals (6th cir.) 1948, U.S. Ct. Customs and Patent Appeals 1948, U.S. Customs Ct. 1948, ICC 1948. Pvt. practice law, Cleve., 1948—51; asst. atty. gen. State of Ohio, 1951—57; mem. Gov. of Ohio cabinet and dir. Ohio Dept. Liquor Control, 1957—58; judge Common Pleas Ct. of Cuyahoga County, 1958—60; sr. ptnr. Metzenbaum, Gaines, Krupansky, Finley & Stern, 1960—69; U.S. atty. U.S. Dist. Ct. (no. dist.) Ohio, Cleve., 1969—70, U.S. dist. judge, 1970—82; judge U.S. Ct. Appeals (6th cir.), Cleve., 1982—91, sr. judge, 1991—. Legal cons. City of Mayfield Heights, Ohio, 1960—64; spl. counsel Atty. Gen. Ohio, 1964—68; adj. prof. law Case Western Res. U. Sch. Law, 1969—70. 2d lt. U.S. Army, pilot USAAC, 1942—46, col. USAF Res. ret. Mem.: FBA, ABA, Assn. Asst. Attys. Gen. State Ohio, Am. Judicature Soc., Cuyahoga County Bar Assn., Cleve. Bar Assn. Office: Carl B Stokes US Courthouse 801 W Superior Ave Cleveland OH 44113-1832

KRUPAT, KITTY WEISS, writer, educator; b. N.Y.C., Feb. 9, 1938; d. Paul and Magda (Neumann) Weiss; m. Arnold Krupat, Aug. 1962 (div. 1968). BA, NYU, 1961, Master's, 1998, postgrad., 1999—. Rsch. editor Esquire mag., N.Y.C., 1966-70; mng. editor pocket books Simon & Schuster, N.Y.C., 1970-74; organizer, edn. dir. dist. 65 UAW, N.Y.C., 1974-89; organizer grad. student organizing com. NYU, N.Y.C., 1996—; edn. dir. Internat. Ladies' Garment Workers Union, N.Y.C., 1989-95; instr. Cornell U., N.Y.C., 1997—; tchg. asst. NYU, 1995—2003; assoc. dir. Queen's Coll. Labor Resource Ctr. CUNY, 2002—. Instr. Queens Coll., CUNY. Co-editor (anthology) Out at Work: Building A Gay Labor Alliance, 2001; contbr. articles to profl. jours. Organizer No Sweat Coalition NYU, 1996—. Mem. MLA, Am. Studies Assn., Labor at the Crossroads (bd. dirs. 1989—), Wagner Labor Archives (bd. dirs. 1987—), United Assn. Labor Educators (bd. dirs. 1981—), Nat. Writers Union. Avocations: music, art, theater, gardening, movies.

KRUPCHAK, TAMARA, artist; b. Lake Station, Ind., Apr. 15, 1956; d. John Charles Krupchak and Rose Marie Maretich-Krupchak. BS, Ball State U., 1978. Artist, spkr., creativity coach Tamara Krupchak Fine Art, San Diego, 1988—. Group shows include San Diego Tijuana Yokohama Art Exchange, 1992, San Diego Mus. Art, 1994, 97, 98, 99; artist (book) Getting Exposure, 1995. Bd. dirs. artist guild San Diego Mus. Art, 1994-97, trustee, 1996-97; mem. nat. devel. com. Coll. Fine Arts, Ball State U., 2001. Recipient art commn. St. Mary's Health and Learning Ctr., Grand Rapids, Mich., 1998, Sunland Christian Sci. Healing Ctr., San Diego, 1998. Mem. Toastmasters Internat. (winner Area 21 Internat. Speech Contest 1998). Office: 1090 University Ave Ste 201A San Diego CA 92103-3362

KRUPER, JOHN GERALD (JACK KRUPER), sales and marketing executive; b. Carbondale, Pa., Feb. 10, 1949; s. John Joseph and Evelyn (Bernosky) K.; m. Renee Jane Shugg, Aug. 4, 1973; children: Kevin John, Melissa Lynn, Abbey Renee. BSBA in Acctg., U. Scranton, 1970; postgrad., SUNY, 1974, U. Scranton, 1985. Store mgr. Endicott Johnson Corp., schenectady, 1970-71; retail mdse. distbr. Endicott, 1971-72; asst. mdse. buyer, 1972-74; full line mdse. buyer, 1974-76; dir. corp. advt. and sales promotion, 1976-79; gen. sales mgr. Ranger divsn., 1979-81; v.p. merchandising, 1981-84; v.p. granded footwear divsn., 1984-86; v.p. Continental Mktg. Group, Inc., 1986-90, v.p. sales and mktg. Lehigh divsn., 1990-92, Iron Age divsn. Childs Corp., 1992-94; nat. sales dir. hy-test divsn. Florsheim Shoe Co., 1994—; nat. sales and prodn. devel. mgr. to gen. mgr. Florsheim Work Group, 1996-97, 96-97; brand gen. mgr. John Deere Footwear divsn., 1997-99, John Deere Internat. divsn., 1999—2000; v.p. sales and mktg. Tatra Mfg. Co., Cary, Ill., 2001—. Served with Corps Engrs., U.S. Army, 1970. E-mail: Jack.Kruper@florsheim.com. Home: 201 Foxford Dr Cary IL 60013 Office: 700H Industrial Dr Cary IL 60013 E-mail: jgkruper@aol.com.

KRUPINSKI, CHRISTINE MARGARET, artist; b. Esslingen, Germany, Dec. 22, 1951; d. John Francis and Elfriede Gertrude (Klose) Newman; m. Dennis Krupinski, Mar. 19, 1977 (dec. Nov. 1995); children: Matthew, Kathleen, Andrew. Student, Edinboro St. Coll., Pa., No. Va. C.C., Annandale, Va. One woman exhibns. include Shirlington Artist's Guild, Va., 1994, Gallery Okuda Internat., Washington, 1996, Fishscale & Mousetooth Gallery, Manassas, Va., 1997, Market St. Bar and Grill Hyat Regency, Reston, Va., 1997, Glass Growers Gallery, Erie, Pa., 1997, The Art League, Alexandria, Va., 1998, The University Club, 1999; group shows include Va. Watercolor Soc., 1992, 93, 94, 95, 96, 97, 98, 99, 2000, Brea (Calif.) Civic and Cultural Ctr., 1992, 93, 97, 98, Kirkpatric Gallery, 1992, 94, 95, 96, Miss. Mus. Art, Jackson, 1993, 94, 95, 96, 98, 2000, Neville Pub. Mus., Green Bay, Wis., 1993, 94, 95, 98, 99, 2000, World Trade Ctr., New Orleans, 1993, 94, 95, 97, John Hopkins U. Gallery, Balt., 1993, 94, 95, Strathmore Hall, Bethesda, Md., 1998, 99, 2000, Pitts. Watercolor Soc., 1993, 94, Perry House Galleries, Alexandria, Va., 1993, 94, Torpedo Factory Art League Gallery, Alexandria, 1993, 94, 95, 96, 97, 98, 99, 2000, W.Va. Watercolor Soc., 1994, 96 (Best in Show), We. Colo. Ctr. for the Arts, Grand Junction, 1994, 95, 98, Wire Grass Mus. Art, Dothan, Ala., 1994, 95, 97, Tex. Watercolor Soc., San Antonio, 1994, 95, 96, 97, So. Watercolor Soc., 1994, 95, 96, 97, 98, Parkersburg (W.Va.) Art Ctr., 1994, 95, Red River Watercolor Soc., Fargo, N.D., 1994, 95, Phila. Watercolor Club, 1994, 95, Pa. Watercolor Soc., 1994, 95, N.W. Watercolor Soc., 1994, Keenan Ctr. Gallery, Lockport, N.Y., 1994, New Eng. Watercolor Soc., Boston, 1994, 95, Missoula (Mont.) Mus. Art, 1994, 95, Salmagundi Club, N.Y.C., 1994, 95, 96, 97, 98, 99, Nat. Arts Club, N.Y.C., 1994, 95, 97, 98, 99, 2000, Foothills Art Ctr., Golden, Colo., 1995, 97, 98, 99, 2000, others; permanent collections include Time Life Books, Eat'n Park Restaurants, Cellular Telecomms. Industry Am.; author: The Best of Watercolor, 1995, The Best of Watercolor 2, 1997, The Best of Watercolor 3, 1999; featured in Artist's mag., Am. Artist, others. Recipient Grumbacher award Miss. Watercolor Soc., 1993, Juror's award Nat. Watercolor Okla. Exhibn., 1993, 3rd place Pitts. Watercolor Soc. Aqueous Open, 1993, Merit award Niagara Frontier Watercolor Soc., 1994, Spl. award of 500 prints We. Colo. Watercolor Soc., 1994, Equal award The Art League (2) 1994, (2) 95, (3) 96, 97, 99, 2000, Hon. Mention The Art League, 1994, 95, Merit award Mid-Atlantic Regional Watercolor Soc., 1994, 95, Hon. Mention Arts coun. Fairfax County, 1995, Juror's Mention Nat. Watercolor Okla. Exhibn., 1995, Bd. Dirs. award We. Colo. Watercolor Soc., 1995, Strathmore Paper award Allied Artists of Am., Inc., 1997, Silver Medal of Honor, 2000, Gold Medal of Honor, 2001, Past Pres.'s award Watercolor Soc. Ala., 1997, Purchase award Watercolor USA, 1997, numerous others; named Best in Show Arts Coun. Fairfax County, 1994, 96, W. Va. Watercolor Soc., 1996, Adirondacks Exhib. Am. Watercolors Merit award 1999, Miss. Watercolor Soc. Merit award 1999, 2001, Rocky Mountain Watercolor Soc. (signature). Fellow Am. Artist's Profl. League (Maitland award 1994, Pres.'s award 1995, Medal of Honor 1997, Am. Artist's Profl. Fund award 1998); mem. Allied Artists Am. (Henry Gasser-Moses Worthman Meml. award 1998), Am. Watercolor Soc. (signature), Nat. Watercolor Soc. (signature), Ga. Watercolor Soc. (signature, Touring Exhibn. 1993, Ga. Peach award 2001), Ky. Watercolor Soc. (signature, Touring exhibn. 1993, 96, Purchase award 1995, 96, Merit award 1997, award 1999), Midwest Watercolor Soc. (signature, Merit award 1997), N.E. Watercolor Soc. (signature, Merit award 1993, 96, 98), Okla. Watercolor Soc. (signature), Pa. Watercolor Soc. (signature), Potomac Valley Watercolorists, So. Watercolor Soc. (signature, Hal P. Moore award 1994, Dr. Jim Congleton award 1995, George P. Shook Meml. award 1997. Merit award 1998), Watercolor Soc. Ala. (signature, Past Pres. award 1997), Okla. Watercolor Soc. (signature), Balt. Watercolor Soc. (signature, Dick Blick Co. award 1998, Merit award 1994, 95), Tex. Watercolor Soc. (signature, Juror's Choice award 1995, Touring Exhibn. 1995), Va. Watercolor Soc. (signature, Merit award 1993, 94, 95, 96, 97), Mo. Watercolor Soc. (signature), Watercolor West (signature, Founder's award 1993, Merit award 1999). Home: 10602 Barn Swallow Ct Fairfax VA 22032-3150 E-mail: artbychris@earthlink.net.

KRUPKA, ROBERT GEORGE, lawyer; b. Rochester, N.Y., Oct. 21, 1949; s. Joseph Anton and Marjorie Clara (Meteyer) Krupka; m. Pamela Banner Krupka; children: Kristin Nicole, Kerry Melissa. BS, Georgetown U., 1971; JD, U. Chgo., 1974. Bar: Ill. 1974, Colo. 1991, D.C., 1991, Calif. 1998, U.S. Dist. Ct. (no. dist.) Ill. 1974, U.S. Dist. Ct. (ea. dist.) Wis. 1974, U.S. Ct. Appeals (7th cir.) 1976, U.S. Supreme Ct. 1978, U.S. Dist. Ct. (cen. dist.) Ill. 1980, U.S. Dist. Ct. (no. dist.) Calif. 1980, U.S. Dist. Ct. (ctrl. and so. dists.) Calif. 1999, U.S. Ct. Appeals (4th and fed. cirs.) 1982, U.S. Ct. Appeals (6th cir.) 1985, U.S. Ct. Appeals (1st, 2d, 3d, 5th, 8th, 9th, 10th and 11th dists.) 1999. Assoc. Kirkland & Ellis, Chgo., 1974-79, ptnr., 1979—. Author: Infringement Litigation Computer Software and Database, 1984, Computer Software, Semiconductor Design, Video Game and Database Protection and Enforcement, 1984. Mem. bd. trustees Francis W. Parker Sch., 1987-98, pres., 1994-97. Mem. ABA (chmn. sec. com. 1982-88, chmn. div. 1988-90, 98—, coun. 1994-97), Computer Law Assn., U.S. Patent Quar. Adv. Bd., Am. Intellectual Property Law Assn. (chmn. subcom. 1988—), Mid-Am. Club. Office: Kirkland & Ellis 777 S Figueroa Ste 3700 Los Angeles CA 90017- E-mail: bob_krupka@kirkland.com.

KRUPMAN, WILLIAM ALLAN, lawyer; b. Cleve., Aug. 14, 1936; s. Joel and Betty (Button) K; m. Janice deLemos, June 19, 1960; children: Pamela, Theodore, Sally. BA, Amherst Coll., 1958; LLB, U. Mich., 1961; LLM in Labor Law, N.Y.U., 1962. Bar: Ohio 1961, N.Y. 1962. Ptnr. Jackson Lewis LLP, N.Y.C., 1962-75, mng. ptnr., 1975—. Author: Winning NLRB Elections, 1997. Bd. dirs. Children's Village, Dobbs Ferry, N.Y. Mem. N.Y. State Bar Assn. Home: 2 Ponds Ln Purchase NY 10577 Office: Jackson Lewis LLP 59 Maiden Ln New York NY 10038-4502

KRUPP, BARBARA D. artist; b. Elyria, Ohio, July 1, 1942; d. Edward G. and Wilma Mary Nuhn; m. James L. Krupp, July 27, 1942 (div. 2003); children: Rory, Rolf, Rachelle, Rodney. X-ray technician Elyria Meml. Hosp., 1969-74; ptnr. The Rockport (Mass.) Collection, 1983-92. Owner Barbara Krupp Gallery, Rockport, Mass., 1983-89. Exhibited in group show Ariel Gallery, N.Y.C., 1990, Raiford Gallery, Roswell, Ga., 1997-98, 99, Ft. Wayne Art Mus., 1999, Ambiance Gallery, Vero Beach, Fla., 2003; represented in permanent collections Musee des Duncan, Paris, Art Expo, N.Y., Art Expo Calif., L.A., Barbara Krupp Gallery, Miller Gallery, Cin., Ambiance Gallery, Vero Beach, Fla., Phoenix Gallery, Topeka, Kans., also numerous pub. and pvt. collections. Founder Krupp Bot. Gardens, 1997—. Recipient Bronze medal, Salon d'Aout. Mem. Rockport Art Assn. Roman Catholic. Avocation: gardening. Home and Office: 2125 Seagrape Dr Vero Beach FL 32963 E-mail: barbarakrupp@gte.net.

KRUPP, CLARENCE WILLIAM, lawyer, personnel and hospital administrator; b. Cleve., June 20, 1929; s. William Frederick and Mary Mae (Volchko) K.; m. Janice Margaret Heckman, June 28, 1952; children: Bruce, Carolyn. BBA cum laude, Cleve. State U., 1958, LL.B., 1959, LL.M., 1963; LL.D. (hon.), 1974. Bar: Wis. 1972. Dir. indsl. relations and indsl. engring. Buxbaum Co., Canton, Ohio, 1963-66; mgr. indsl. relations Trane Co., La Crosse, Wis., 1966-73; dir. personnel-labor relations environ. products div. ITT, Phila., 1973; v.p. indsl. relations, gen. counsel G. Heileman Brewing Co., La Crosse, 1973-76; atty., v.p. human resources-risk control, sec. Good Samaritan Hosp., Dayton, Ohio, 1976-80; mgr. compensation and benefits State of Ariz., Phoenix, 1980-83; personnel adminstr., land mgmt. agt. Salt River Project, 1983-94; Indian and sch. land specialist, 1992—; chmn., pres. C.W. Krupp P.C., 1986—. Cons. on labor rels., 1969, 81-83, 88—; elec. line land impact cons., western states, 2000—. Contbr. articles to profl. jours. Mcpl. arbitrator, La Crosse, 1976; pres., mem. La Crosse Bd. Edn., 1969-72; mem. Wis. Gov.'s Task Force on Edn., 1972-73, Ohio Little White House library del.; mem. Ariz. Spinal Injury Panel, 1984-2000. Served with U.S. Army, 1951-53. Named Outstanding Ariz. State Profl. Employee, 1982, Employee of Quarter, 1990, 91. Mem. Am. Bar Assn. (forum hosp. on law, labor law sect.), Am. Corp. Counsel Assn., Nat. Notary Assn., Wis Bar Assn. (Continuing Edn. award 1972), Am. Assn. Hosp. Attys., Ariz. Assn. Industries (healthcare com. 1983-97, chmn. legis. subcom. 1983-97), Am. Soc. Law and Medicine, Dayton C. of C., Electric League of Ariz. (ins. advisor 1985-97), Internat. Right of Way Assn. (regional cons. Native Am. land rights 1998—). Clubs: Rotary. Democrat. Roman Catholic. Home and Office: 8701 E Via De La Gente Scottsdale AZ 85258-4040 E-mail: clarewk@msn.com. *Understand and be tolerant of the views of others. With that insight your decisons will be respected and your judgment both honored and sought.*

KRUPP, FRED D. lawyer, environmental agency executive; b. Mineola, N.Y., Mar. 21, 1954; s. Arthur L. and Rosalind (Mehr) K.; m. Laurie Louise Devitt, Aug. 21, 1982; children: Alexander Mehr, Zachary Devitt, Jackson O'Connor. BS, Yale U., New Haven, 1975; JD, U. Mich., Ann Arbor, 1978. Ptnr. Albis & Krupp, New Haven, 1978-83; ptnr. Cooper, Whitney, Cochran & Krupp, New Haven, 1984; pres. Environ. Def., 1984—; gen. counsel Conn. Fund for the Environment, New Haven, 1978-84. Mem. Pres.'s Commn. on Environ. Quality, 1991-92; mem. Pres.'s Coun. on Sustainable Devel., 1993-99; mem. Pres.s' Adv. Com. Trade Policy and Negotiations, 1994-2002; bd. dirs. League of Conservation Voters, H. John Heinz III Ctr. for Sci., Econs. and Environment. Helen De Roy fellow U. Mich. Law Sch. 1986 Office: Environ Def 257 Park Ave S New York NY 10010-7304

KRUPP, JAMES ARTHUR GUSTAVE, consultant; b. Naples, Italy, Oct. 27, 1944; came to U.S., 1945; s. Ralph Gustave and Lydia (Guerroni) K.; m. Joyce Ann Draffan, Nov. 5, 1966; children: James Michael Douglas, Matthew Ralph Alexander. Student, U.S. Naval Acad., 1963-66; BSME magna cum laude, U. New Haven, 1971, EMBA, 1981. Cert. Fellow in Prodn. and Inventory Mgmt. Prodn. control mgr. Sargent & Co., New Haven, 1966-72; prodn. scheduling mgr. Stanley Tools, New Britain, Conn., 1972-75; materials mgr. Whitney Blake, Hamden, Conn., 1975-76; materials control mgr. Burndy Corp., Norwalk, Conn., 1976-79; prodn. and inventory mgr. Picker Corp., Northford, Conn., 1979-81; materials mgr. Carlyle Johnson Machine Co., Manchester, Conn., 1981-84; dir. advanced planning systems ITT Sealectro, New Britain, 1984-89; v.p. materials Echlin Inc., Branford, Conn., 1989-99; dir. materials planning Stanadyne Corp., Windsor, Conn., 1999—. Mem. editl. rev. bd. Prodn. and Inv. Mgmt. Jour., 1988—; contbr. over 50 articles to profl. jours. Chmn. Bd. Ethics, Wallingford, Conn., 1980-84; councilman Town Coun., Wallingford, 1984-85; mem. Charter Revision Commn., Wallingford, 1988-89. With USN, 1963-67. Mem. Am. Prodn. and Inventory Control Soc. (Romey Everdell award 1998), Assn. Internal Mgmt. Cons., Mensa. Democrat. Roman Catholic. Avocations: youth soccer and special olympics referee, fishing, chess. E-mail: jkrupp@stanadyne.com. *Whether in life or business, there are 3 guiding principles whose attainment surpass all measures of success: 1) An unfaltering tradition of the highest sense of personal honor. 2) An absolute respect for the dignity of all those with whom one comes in contact. 3) An unwavering commitment to excellence in all that one does.*

KRUPP, ROBIN RECTOR, illustrator, author; b. Bklyn., Mar. 29, 1946; d. Robert Wayman and Margaret (Hayden) R.; m. Edwin Charles Krupp, Dec. 31, 1968; 1 child, Ethan Hembree. BA in Art Practice cum laude, Pomona Coll., Claremont, 1968; MA in Painting, Calif. State U., 1970. Coll. art instr. Pierce Coll., Woodland Hills, Calif., 1971—85, 1988—93, 2001—01; design instr. Fashion Inst. of Design and Merchandising, Sherman Oaks/L.A., 1979-88; extension instr. Calif. State U., Northridge, Calif., 1987-89; author, illustrator Macmillan, William Morrow, Harper Collins, N.Y.C., 1985-2000; instr. Life Bible Coll., Woodbury U., 2000—. Presenter, performer various sch. and orgns., 1985—; painter. Author/illustrator: Get Set to Wreck!, 1987, Let's Go Traveling, 1992, (Crown Collection 1992), Let's Go Traveling in Mexico, 1996; illustrator: The Comet and You (Best Sci. Writing Am. Inst. Physics, 1986), The Big Dipper and You, 1989, The Moon and You, 1993, The Rainbow and You, 2000; solo shows include Sweeney Art Gallery, U. Calif., Riverside, 2001. Artist summer reading programs Met. Coop. Libr. System, So. Calif., 1988, 90. Recipient Living Legacy award Women's Internat. Ctr., 1998. Mem. Soc. of Children's Book Writers and Illustrators, Children's Authors Network, Year on the Young Reader (steering com.), Calif. Readers (adv. bd. 1988-89), So. Calif. Childrens Booksellers Assn. (author's rep. 1992-96), So. Calif. Coun. on Lit. for Children and Young People (Best Work of Nonfiction 1985, Dorothy C. McKenzie award 1998). Avocations: painting, travel, gardening, reading, sketching. Office: 5208 Mount Royal Dr Los Angeles CA 90041-1334 E-mail: rrkrupp@hotmail.com.

KRUSE, ANN GRAY, computer programmer; b. Oklahoma City, Jan. 4, 1941; d. Floyd and Bernice Florence (Follansbee) Gray; m. Roy Edwin Kruse, Mar. 20, 1971 (dec.). AB, Randolph Macon Woman's Coll., 1963; MBA, U. Chgo., 1973. Programming mgr. Ind. Info. Controls, Valparaiso, Ind., 1966-67; systems programmer Am. Steel Foundries, Hammond, Ind., 1970-73; engr. applications programming Bell Helicopter Textron, Fort Worth, 1974-76; lead systems programmer Harris Data Communications, Dallas, 1976-81; sr. systems programmer Lone Star Gas Co., Dallas, 1981-82; sr. software specialist Raytheon, Dallas, 1982—. Republican. Episcopalian. Home: 6128 Black Berry Ln Dallas TX 75248-4909 Office: PO Box 660023 Dallas TX 75266-0023 E-mail: akruse@gsb.uchicago.edu.

KRUSE, CHARLES THOMAS, lawyer; b. Tulsa, Sept. 26, 1963; s. Joseph Daniel and Judith Sue (Holleman) K.; m. Jennifer Jones, May 20, 1989; 1 child, Charles Thomas Jr. BA, Emory U., 1985; JD, Vanderbilt U., 1989. Bar: Tex. 1989, U.S. Dist. Ct. (so. dist.) Tex. 1990, U.S. Ct. Appeals (5th and 8th cirs.) 1991; bd. cert. civil trial law Tex. Bd. Legal Specialization. Law clk. to Hon. Ricardo H. Hinojosa U.S. Dist. Ct. (so. dist.) Tex., McAllen, Tex., 1989-90; assoc. Fulbright & Jaworski, Houston, 1990-91; ptnr. McDade & Fogler, Houston, 1992-95; counsel to ptnr. King & Spalding, Houston, 1995-2000; ptnr. Bracewell & Patterson, LLP, Houston, 2000—. Contbr. articles and papers to profl. publs. Bobby Jones scholar U. St. Andrews, 1985-86. Fellow Tex. Bar Found., Houston Bar Found.; mem. ABA, Houston Bar Assn., Houston Young Lawyer Assn. Republican. Episcopalian. Home: 10622 S Evers Park Dr Houston TX 77024-5528 Office: Bracewell & Patterson LLP Ste 2900 711 Louisiana St Houston TX 77002 E-mail: tkruse@bracepatt.com.

KRUSE, DOUGLAS CHARLES, financial industry consultant, educator; b. N.Y.C., Jan. 11, 1951; s. Harry Dayton and Mary Helen (Grayston) K.; m. Betty Anne Whelchel, June 20, 1987. AB magna cum laude, Princeton U., 1972; DPhil, U. Sussex, Falmer, Eng., 1977. Asst. treas. internat. dept. Bankers Trust, N.Y.C., 1977-80; internat. economist Office Internat. Banking U.S. Treasury, Washington, 1980-85; v.p. Merrill Lynch Internat., N.Y.C., 1985-86; mem. mgmt. com., dir. strategy, market planning and new products Merrill Lynch Japan, Tokyo, 1986-89; pres. DCK Internat. Strategic Mgmt., N.Y.C., 1989—. Lectr. U. Sussex, 1973; professorial lectr. Johns Hopkins U. Sch. Advanced Internat. Studies, Washington, 1982-84; mem., negotiator U.S.-Japan Yen-Dollar Working Group, Tokyo and Washington, 1984-85; staff of commr. for econ. and monetary affairs Commn. European Communities, Brussels, 1974; dir. Banking and Fin. Assistance Ctr., Budapest, Hungary, 1992-94; cons. IMF, IDB World Bank and pvt. fin. firms. Author: Monetary Integration in Western Europe, 1980; contbr. articles to profl. jours. Recipient Woodrow Wilson prize; Marshall scholar, 1972-76. Mem. Asia Soc., Japan Soc., Phi Beta Kappa. Office: DCK Internat Strategic Mgmt PO Box 501 New York NY 10163-0501

KRUSE, JOHN ALPHONSE, lawyer; b. Detroit, Sept. 11, 1926; s. Frank R. and Ann (Nestor) K.; m. Mary Louise Dalton, July 14, 1951; children: Gerard, Mary Louise, Terence, Kathleen, Joanne, Francis, John, Patrick. BS, U. Detroit, 1950, JD cum laude, 1952. Bar: Mich. bar 1952. Ptnr. Alexander, Buchanan & Conklin, Detroit, 1952-69, Harvey, Kruse, PC, Detroit, 1969—. Guest lectr. U. Mich., U. Detroit, Inst. Continuing Legal Edn.; city atty. Allen Park, Mich., 1954-59; twp. atty., Van Buren Twp., Mich., 1959-61. Co-founder Detroit and Mich. Cath. Radio. Past pres. Palmer Woods Assn.; mem. pres.'s cabinet U. Detroit; bd. dirs. Providence Hosp. Found.; trustee Ave Maria Coll. Named one of 5 Outstanding Young Men in Mich., 1959, Outstanding Alumnus, U. Detroit Sch. Law, 1989, Humanitarian award Neuromuscular Inst. 1988. Mem. Detroit Bar Assn., State Bar Mich. (past chmn. negligence sect.), Assn. Def. Trial Counsel (bd. dirs. 1966-67), Am. Judicature Soc., Internat. Assn. Def. Counsel, Equestrian Order of the Holy Sepulchre. Clubs: Detroit Golf (past pres.). Roman Catholic. Home: 5569 Hunters Gate Dr Troy MI 48098-2342 Office: 1050 Wilshire Dr Ste 320 Troy MI 48084-1526 E-mail: jkruse@harveykruse.com., johnakruse@comcast.net. *Start each day with a simple petition - Lord help me to do your will today. End each day in thanks for his divine guidance. Prayer is to the soul as exercise is to the body. Neglect neither!*

KRUSE, LAYNE E. lawyer; b. Emporia, Kans., Aug. 15, 1951; BA, Tex. A&M U., 1973; MSc, London Sch. Econs., 1974; JD, Yale U., 1977. Bar: Tex. 1978, cert.: Tex. Bd. Legal Specialization (civil trial law). Law clk. to Hon. John R. Brown U.S. Ct. Appeals (5th cir.); mem. Fulbright & Jaworski, L.L.P., Houston. Chair antitrust and bus. litigation sect. State Bar Tex. Mem.: ABA, Houston Bar Assn. Office: Fulbright & Jaworski LLP 1301 Mckinney St Ste 5100 Houston TX 77010-3031

KRUSE, MARYLIN LYNN, retired foreign language educator; b. Kansas City, Mo., June 26, 1940; d. Mildred Marie Goetsch; m. Richard Lee Weinberg, Dec. 26, 1962 (div. Oct. 1988); children: Eric H., Kerstin I; m. Leon Edward Kruse, Dec. 28, 1998. BA, Cornell Coll., 1962; MA, Marycrest Coll., 1982. English tchr. Galesburg (Ill.) Community Schs., 1962-63, Grant Community Schs., Fox Lake, Ill., 1963-64, Saydel Community Schs., Des Moines, 1965-66; English instr. Grandview Coll., Des Moines, 1966-70; behavior disorders cons. Western Ill. Assn., Galesburg, Ill., 1976-77; prevocational coord. Knox-Warren Spl. Edn. Dist., Galesburg, 1977-78; Spanish tchr. Winola Community Schs., Viola, Ill., 1979-80; spl. edn. tchr. Pleasant Valley (Iowa) Community Schs., 1980-86; English instr. Ea. Iowa Community Coll. Dist., Davenport, 1983-86; spl. edn. tchr. Davenport Community Schs., 1986-94; fgn. lang. tchr. Davenport Cmty. Schs., 1994—2002, ret., 2002. Co-author: Parent Prerogatives, 1979. Recipient Tchr. Incentive award State of Iowa Dept. Edn., 1982; chpt. II grant U.S. Office of Edn., Williams Jr. High, 1988. Mem.: Audubon Soc., Sierra Club. Republican. Lutheran. Avocations: home decorating, bird watching. Home: 4614 Hamilton Dr Davenport IA 52807-3427

KRUSE, PAMELA JEAN, lawyer; b. Miami, Fla., June 3, 1950; d. Robert Emil and Irma G. Kruse. BS, Mich. State U., 1973, MA, 1975, PhD, 1979; JD, U. Mich., 1985. Bar: Mich. 1986. Grad. asst. Mich. State U., East Lansing, 1976-77, asst. intramural dir., 1977-79, labor rels. rep., 1979-81, asst. dir. labor rels., 1981-82; resident mgr. 719 Oakland, Ann Arbor, Mich., 1982-83; rsch. asst. Law Sch. U. Mich., Ann Arbor, 1982-85; jud. clk. U.S. Dist. Ct. (we. dist.) Mich., 1985-86; assoc. Clary, Nantz, Wood, Hoffius, Rankin & Cooper, Grand Rapids, Mich., 1986-91; with Village Bike Shops, 1991—. Bd. dirs. Babe Zaharias Golf Tournament, Am. Cancer Soc., 1987-91. Recipient Gold and Silver medals U.S. Pan Am. Team, Winnipeg, Man., Can., 1967, Silver medal U.S. Olympic Team, Mexico City, 1968; holder world records swimming 400 meters freestyle, 1967, 200 meters freestyle, 1967, 440-yard freestyle, 1966; inducted to Greater Fort Lauderdale Sports Hall of Fame, 1979. Mem. ABA, State Bar Mich. (exec. coun. young lawyers sect. 1987-90), Grand Rapids Bar Assn. (chairperson, exec. bd. dirs. young lawyers sect. 1987-91), Mich. Pub. Employer Labor Rels. Assn. (bd. dirs. 1981-82, chmn. manual revision com. 1982), Mich. State U. Alumni Assn. (1st v.p., bd. dirs. 1988-89), U.S. Olympians, Phi Delta Kappa, Kappa Alpha Theta. Office: Village Bike Shop Ltd 450 A Baldwin St Jenison MI 49428

KRUSE, PAUL ROBERT, retired librarian, educator; b. What Cheer, Iowa, Feb. 26, 1912; s. Carl Fred and Phoebe (Mumby) K.; m. Esther Moe, June 3, 1939 (div.); 1 son, Robert Leroy; m. Carolyn Rector, June 12, 1980 (dec. Sept. 1995). AB, John Fletcher Coll., 1933; BS in L.S, U. Ill., 1940; PhD, U. Chgo., 1958. Librarian John Fletcher Coll., University Park, Iowa, 1932-33, Bolles Sch., Jacksonville, Fla., 1934-38; reference librarian Jacksonville Pub. Library, 1938-42; reference asst. in charge reference collections Library of Congress, Washington, 1942-45; established library for UN Conf., San Francisco, 1945; instr. Library Sch., Catholic U., Washington, 1943-48; bibliographer Ency. Brit., 1946-47; editor Who Knows and What, A.N. Marquis Co., 1949; vis. asst. prof. Library Sch., U. So. Calif., 1950, George Peabody Coll., 1950-51; reorganized library for Rollins Coll., Winter Park, Fla., 1951-52; vis. asso. prof. Library Sch., U. Ill., 1952-53; asso. prof. Library Sch., U. Denver, 1954-55; librarian Golden Gate U., San Francisco, 1955-63; assoc. prof. Sch. Library and Info. Scis., Univ. N. Tex., Denton, 1965-77. Fulbright lectr., library advisor U. Tehran, 1962-64, U. Ceylon, 1964-65; library cons. U.S. AID, Universidad Santa Maria la Antigua, Panama, 1968 Author: The Story of The Encyclopaedia Britannica, 1768-1943; Editor: Index for Lend Lease: Weapon for Victory, 1944; compiler bibliographies for: Ten Eventful Years, Ency. Brit, 1947, Profiles of Special Libraries, 2d edit, 1981; cons.: Pergamum Press, 1978; Contbr. articles to profl. jours. Active community and profl. theatre groups. Mem. ALA, Spl. Librs. Assn. (conf. chmn. 1961), Masons, Shrine. Republican. Methodist. Home: Foss Home 13023 Greenwood Ave N Seattle WA 98133-7397

KRUSE, PAUL WALTERS, JR., physicist, consultant; b. Hibbing, Minn., Nov. 24, 1927; s. Paul Walters and Marie Rae (Gibson) K.; m. Margaret Mary Fitzpatrick, Jan. 23, 1954; children— Paul II, Robert, John, Mary, Margaret, Charles, Thomas, Catherine, William. BS, U. Notre Dame, 1951, MS, 1952, PhD, 1954. Physicist Farnsworth Electronics Co., Ft. Wayne, Ind., 1954-56; sr. rsch. scientist Honeywell Corp. Tech. Center, Bloomington, Minn., 1956-59, prin. rsch. scientist, 1959-60, staff scientist, 1960-69, sr. staff scientist, 1969-77, prin. staff scientist, 1977-79, prin. rsch. fellow, 1979-83; chief rsch. fellow Honeywell Corp. Sci. and Tech., 1983-86, Honeywell Sensor and System Devel. Ctr., 1987-93; cons., 1993—; chief scientist Infrared Solutions, Inc., Mpls., 1994-98. Panel mem. Pres.'s Sci. Adv. Com., 1969-72; mem. Army Sci. Adv. Panel, 1965-77, Army Sci. Bd., 1978-82, 85-90; com. mem. Nat. Materials Adv. Bd., NRC-NAS, 1971-72, Adv. Bd. on Mil. Pers. Supplies, 1969-71; mem. planning com. 3d Internat. Photoconductivity Conf., 1968-69; chmn. Army ERADCOM Tech. Com., 1976; mem. com. on chem. and biol. sensor tech. NRC-Nat. Acad. Scis., 1982-84. Author: (with McGlauchlin and McQuistan) Elements of Infrared Technology, 1961, (with D.D. Skatrud) Uncooled Infrared Imaging Arrays and Systems, 1997, Uncooled Thermal Imaging Arrays, Systems and Applications, 2001; contbr. articles to profl. jours.; mem. editorial adv. bd.: Optics Letters, 1977-79, Infrared and Millimeter Waves, 1978-89, Infrared Physics, 1986-98; patentee in field. Bd. dirs. Benilde High Sch., 1970-74. Recipient H.W. Sweatt award for outstanding sci. accomplishment, 1966, Alan Gordon Meml. award Soc. Photo-Optical Instrumentation Engrs., 1981, Outstanding Civilian Service medal Dept. of Army, 1983, Levinstein award Infrared Info. Soc. Detector Splty. Group, 1999; selected by sec. def. for Joint Civilian Orientation Conf. 37, 1967 Fellow Am. Phys. Soc., Optical Soc. Am., AIAA (assoc.); mem. Am. Electronics Assn. (sci. and tech. com. 1990-93), Notre Dame Club Minn. (pres. 1974-75), Notre Dame Alumni Assn. (dir. 1979-82). Home: 6828 Oaklawn Ave Minneapolis MN 55435-1627

KRUSE, ROSALEE EVELYN, accountant, auditor, executive; b. Muscatine, Iowa, Aug. 23, 1953; d. Burr Arthur Beeding and Mary Ellen (Phillips) McGourty; m. Michael Raymond Kruse, May 20, 1972 (div. Oct. 1997); children: Lauretta Kathleen Kruse Tkaczyk, Matthew William Kruse. A in Gen. Studies, Muscatine C.C., 1986; BBA, U. Iowa, 1988; M of Acctg., St. Ambrose U., 1993. CPA, Iowa. Acct. Rock Island (Ill.) Arsenal, 1989-96, auditor, 1996-98, accountant, 1998, freelance consulting exec., 1999-2000, CEO, 2000—. Acctg. instr. Am. Inst. Commerce, 1989; adj. prof. St. Ambrose U., 1996. Mem.: Inst. Internal Auditors (bd. govs. 1996—99, pres. 1999—2000, bd. govs. 2000—01), Inst. Mgmt. Accts (program roster com. Iowa chpt. 1995—96, acad. rels. and ednl. project student affairs com. 1996—97, fin. and adminstrn. 1997—98, pres.-elect 1997—98, pres. 1998—99, pub. rels. com. 1999—2000, regional coun. exec. 1998—2001, members interest group 1999—2000, continuing profl. edn. com. 2000—01, bd. govs.), Iowa Soc. CPAs (membership com. 1995—96, auditing stds. and acctg. prin. com. 1996—98, pub. and profl. rels. com. 1996—97, info. tech. com. 1999—2000, continuing profl. edn. com. 2000—01), Am. Soc. Mil. Comptrs. (chairperson chpt. competition 1991—92, treas. 1993—94, 1st v.p. 1994—95, scholarship chair 1997—98). Methodist.

KRUSHKAL, VYACHESLAV S. mathematician, educator; b. Novosibirsk, Russia, 1971; arrived in U.S., 1991; s. Samuel and Tamara Krushkal. Student, Novosibirsk State U., 1988—91; PhD in Math., U. Calif., San Diego, 1996. Mem. IHES, Bures-sur-Yvette, France, 1995—95; vis. rsch. instr. Mich. State U., East Lansing, 1996—97; mem. Max Planck Inst., Bonn, Germany, 1997—98, Inst. for Advanced Study, Princeton, NJ, 1998—99; Gibbs instr. Yale U., New Haven, 1999—2001; asst. prof. U. Va., Charlottesville, 2001—. Hepps Grad. fellow, U. Calif. San Diego, J.M.Hepps Found., 1993—94, Sloan Doctoral Dissertation fellow, Alfred P. Sloan Found., 1994—95. Office: Univ Va Math Dept PO Box 400137 Charlottesville VA 22904-4137

KRUSKAL, JONATHAN BRUCE, radiologist, research scientist; s. Leonard and Jocelyn Kruskal; m. Pamela Kleviansk, Mar. 15, 1987; children: Joshua David, Jessica Rose. PhD, U of Cape Town, Cape Town, 1984—87; MB, U of Cape Town Med. Sch., Cape Town, 1977—82; BS chemistry, U of Cape Town, Cape Town. Cert. radiologist Am. Bd. of Radiology, 1992. Dir. body imaging, Beth Israel Deaconess Med. Ctr., Boston, 1999—, abdominal imaging fellowship program, Beth Israel deaconess Med. ctr., Boston, 1997—; co-dir. optical imaging lab., Beth Israel Deaconess Med. ctr., Boston, 2001—; dir. radiology quality improvement, Beth Israel Deaconess Med. Ctr., Boston, 2000—; exec. com. cancer ctr., Beth Israel deaconess Med. Ctr., Boston, 1998; rsch. com. Am. Roentgen Ray Soc., Reston, Va., 2002—; ednl. officer New Eng. Roentgen Ray Soc., Boston, 2002—; vis. prof. Soc. of Gastrointestinal Radiologists, 2003. Recipient Wylie Dodds Award, Soc. of GI Radiologists, 1999, 2000, Philip Meyers Award, 2000; grantee R21 rsch. Award, Nat. Cancer Inst., 1999-2002; scholar Rsch. Scholar Award, Radiol. Soc. of N.Am., 1999-2001. Mem.: New Eng. Roentgen Ray Soc. (ednl. coord. 2002), Am. Roentgen Ray Soc. (mem. of rsch. com. 2002), Radiol. Soc. of N.Am. Achievements include research in NCI funding: molecular imaging of formation of liver metastases. Office: Beth Israel Deaconess Hosp/Harvard M 1 Deaconess Rd Boston MA 02215

KRUSKAL, MARTIN DAVID, mathematical physicist, astrophysicist; b. N.Y.C., Sept. 28, 1925; married, 1950; 3 children. BS, U. Chgo., 1945; MS, NYU, 1948, PhD in Math., 1952. Rsch. scientist Plasma Phys. Lab., Princeton U., 1951—61, prof. astrophys. sci., 1961—, prof. math., 1981—89, emeritus, 1989—; David Hilbert prof. math. Rutgers U., New Brunswick, NJ, 1989—. Trustee Soc. for Indsl. & Applied Math., 1985—91, Math. Scis. Edn. Bd. of NRC, 1986—89; Ext. Adv. Com. Ctr. for Nonlinear Studies, Los Alamos Nat. Lab., 1980—. Recipient Dannie Heineman Math. Phys. prize, 1983, Potts Gold medal, Franklin Inst., 1986, Nat. medal Sci., NSF, 1993, John von Neumann Prize, Soc. Indsl. and Applied Math., 1994; fellow NSF (sr.), 1959—60, Weizmann Inst. Sci. (sr.), 1973—74, Japan Soc. Promotion Sci., 1979. Fellow: Am. Phys. Soc.; mem.: NAS (chmn. sect. of applied math. scis. 1990—93, award in Applied Math. and Numerical Analysis 1989), AAAS, Royal Soc. London (fgn.), Math. Assn. Am., Am. Math. Soc. (Gibbs lectr. 1979). Home: PO Box 49 Arroyo Seco NM 87514-0049 Office: Rutgers U Dept Math Hill Ctr Busch Campus New Brunswick NJ 08903

KRUSOR, MARK WILLIAM, lawyer; b. Topeka, Nov. 6, 1951; s. William Albert and Gladys Eleanor (Lyon) K.; m. Carolyn Kay Gish, May 19, 1973 (div. Aug. 1984); 1 child, Bethany Ellen; m. Teresa D. Garcia, Aug. 1, 1986. BA, Washburn U., 1973, JD, 1976. Assoc. Christenson, Mathews & Taylor, Winfield, Kans., 1976-79; ptnr. Mathews, Taylor & Krusor, Winfield, Kans., 1979—. Instr. Southwestern Coll., Winfield, 1978-86, Cowley County C.C. and Winfield State Hosp. and Tng. Ctr., 1981, 82, 84, 85, 86, St. John's Coll., Winfield, 1984; pres. adv. com. Kans. Dept. Corrections Winfield Pre-release Ctr., 1986. Chmn. bd. trustees Winfield Pub. Libr., 1981, 82; pres. bd. dirs. Winfield Child Care Ctr., 1979; chmn. drive Winfield United Way, 1978; pres. Holy Name Parish Coun., Winfield, 1981; county chmn. allegrucci for Congress com., Winfield, 1978; treas. Citizens Com. for Merit Sel. of Judges, Winfield, 1984; mem. resident rights com. Winfield State Hosp. and Tng. Ctr., 1980-82; mem. adv. com. Winfield State Hosp., 1982-90, Kans. Dept. Corrections-Winfield Ctr., 1984-90; pres. Winfield Pub. Sch. Found. Mem. ABA, Kans Bar Assn., Kans. Trial Lawyers Assn. (bd. govs. 1983-87), Cowley County Bar Assn. (sec.-treas. 1978, v.p. 1979, pres. 1980), Washburn Law Sch. assn., Kans. Hist. Soc., Cowley County Hist. Soc., Jaycees, Optimists (pres. 1980-81), Elks, KC. Democrat. Roman Catholic. Home: 7 Braid Hills Dr Winfield KS 67156-6303 Office: Taylor Krusor & Passiglia LLP First Nat Bank Bldg Winfield KS 67156 E-mail: markk@winfieldattorneys.com.

KRUSOS, DENIS ANGELO, communications company executive; b. N.Y.C., Oct. 27, 1927; s. Angelo and Mary (Razzi) K.; B.S., CCNY, 1949; M.S., Newark Coll. Engring., 1951; J.D., St. Johns U., 1968; m. Catherine Bezas, July 30, 1955; children— Peri Denise, Denis Zachary. Devel. engr. missile div. Republic Aviation & Fairchild Engring. Corp., 1952-56; sr. engr. Arma div. Am. Bosch Arma Corp., 1956-60; founder dir. Automation Labs., Inc., Mineola, N.Y., 1955-65; founder, chmn. bd., dir. Integrated Electronics Corp., Huntington Station, N.Y., 1966-83; chmn. bd. Color Q Inc., Dayton, Ohio, 1969-92; founder, pres., dir. Panafax Corp., Woodbury, N.Y., 1977-82; founder, chmn. bd., dir. Visual Scis., Inc., 1969-83; founder, chmn. bd., chief exec. officer, dir. CopyTele, Inc., Melville, N.Y., 1982—. Served with U.S. Army, 1946-47. Mem. Am., New York, Suffolk County bar assns., IEEE. Home: 1 Lloyd Harbor Rd Huntington NY 11743-9701 Office: CopyTele Inc 900 Walt Whitman Rd Melville NY 11747-2293

KRUSZYNSKI, TIMOTHY EDWARD, retired corrections officer, poet; b. Chgo., Sept. 21, 1949; s. Edward Michael and Dorothy Viola (Freske) K. BS in Psychology, DePaul U., 1971. Cert. Cook County Dep. Sheriff. Dishwasher Marshall Fields, Chgo., 1967-71; gen. duties clk. Continental Bank, Chgo., 1971-76; stockbroker, messenger Ernst & Co., Chgo., 1976-78; corrections officer Cook County, Chgo., 1978-99, sgt., 1992-99; ret., 1999. Author of poetry. Supporter Dem. Nat. Com., Washington, 1999-2000. Named Internat. Poet of Merit, Internat. Soc. Poets, Washington, 2000. Roman Catholic. Home: 14316 La Salle Riverdale IL 60827-2743

KRUTSICK, ROBERT STANLEY, retired science center executive; b. Lansford, Pa., Dec. 6, 1942; s. John Jacob and Mary Ann (Novak) K.; m. Charlotte Ann Harper, Feb. 18, 1977; children: Robert Steven, Laurie, Tracy, Andrew, Daniel. BS, Pa. State U., 1966; M in Local and State Govt., U. Pa., 1967. Sr. v.p., treas. Univ. City Sci. Ctr., Phila., 1978-88, acting pres., 1988-90, exec. v.p., 1988-97. Supr. Upper Merion Twp., King of Prussia, Pa., 1989; pres. Upper Merion Park and Hist. Found., 1997—; bd. dirs. Upper Merion Area Sch. Dist.; vice chair Upper Merion Twp. Planning Commn.; pres. Lafayette Ambulance Squad, 2002; mem. joint oper. com. Ctr. for Tech. Studies; bd. dirs. Cradle of Liberty coun., Boy Scouts Am., Girl Scouts of Freedom Valley. Mem.: Upper Merion Area Edn. Found. (pres.), Optimist Club (past pres.). Republican. Roman Catholic. Avocations: tennis, golf, basketball. Home: 210 Cedar Pl Wayne PA 19087-2170 E-mail: bkrutsick@aol.com.

KRUTTER, FORREST NATHAN, lawyer; b. Boston, Dec. 17, 1954; s. Irving and Shirley Krutter. BS in Econs., MS in Civil Engring., MIT, 1976; JD cum laude, Harvard U., 1978. Bar: Nebr. 1978, U.S. Supreme Ct. 1986, N.Y. 1991. Antitrust counsel Union Pacific R.R., Omaha, 1978-86; sr. v.p. law, sec. Berkshire Hathaway Group, Omaha, 1986—; pres. Republic Ins., Dallas, 2000—. Co-author: Impact of Railroad Abandonments, 1976, Railroad Development in the Third World, 1978; author: Judicial Enforcement of Competition in Regulated Industries, 1979; contbr. articles Creighton Law Rev. Mem. ABA, Phi Beta Kappa, Sigma Xi. Office: Berkshire Hathaway Group 4016 Farnam St Omaha NE 68131-3016 Business E-Mail: fkrutter@berkre.com.

KRUTZ, JONATHAN LAWRENCE, non-profit association administrator; b. Seward, Nebr., Mar. 28, 1962; s. Charles Herald and Mel Elaine Krutz; m. Kimiko Cunningham, Dec. 31, 1994; children: Amy Lynne, Carl Matthew. BA in Philosophy and Humanities, Valparaiso U., 1984; MBA, U. Iowa, 1993. Dir. publs. and mktg. Phi Mu Alpha Sinfonia Music Fraternity, Evansville, Ind., 1984-86; adj. prof. human resources Concordia Coll., Seward, 1996; computer mktg. specialist Tandy Corp., Chestnut Hill, Mass., 1986-87; gen. mgr. Oetting's Detasseling Inc., Seward, 1988-92; pres. North Caucasus Group Inc., Iowa City, 1994-96; adj. prof. econs. Doane Coll., Crete, Nebr., 1996-98; vis. scholar North Caucasus Ctr. for Edn. and Econ. Devel., Stavropol, Russia, 1993-96; exec. dir. S.E. Nebr. Mediation Ctr., Beatrice, 1996—2001, Nebr. Hospice and Palliative Care Assn., 2001—. Editor quar. music mag. The Sinfonian, 1984-86, monthly newspaper The Eaglet, 2000—; writer, prodr., editor travel video Stavropol, Russia: A Preview for Travelers, 1994. Rsch. dir. Gambling with the Good Life, Nebr., 1996—, chmn., 2002—; mem. Lincoln (Nebr.) Luth. Choir, 1988—, treas., 1990-91, pres., 1991-92, resource devel. chair, 1996-2001; mem. Omaha Symphonic Chorus, 2002; leader, lectr. Free Market Economy Program, Stavropol, 1993; bd. dirs. Eagle (Nebr.) Vision, Inc., 1998—, chmn., 2002—, sec., 2003; mem. Gage County Juvenile Diversion Adv. Bd., 1999-2001. Nat. Merit scholar, 1980; U.S. AID grantee, 1993. Mem. Nebr. Mediation Ctr. Assn. (bd. dirs. 2000-01), Nat. Assn. for Cmty. Mediation, Seward C. of C., Kappa Sigma Chpt. Corp. (bd. dirs. 1983-85). Avocations: singing, reading. Office: Nebr Hospice and Palliative Care Assn 21203 A St Eagle NE 68347

KRYDER, MARK HOWARD, computer and electrical engineering executive, educator, consultant; b. Oct. 7, 1943; Sr. v.p., dir. Seagate Rsch., Seagate Tech., Pitts. Univ. prof. Carnegie Mellon U., Pitts. Office: Seagate Tech 1251 Waterfront Pl Pittsburgh PA 15222-4215

KRYMSKAYA, VERA P. science educator; PhD, Moscow State U., 1991. Postdoctoral rschr./rsch. assoc. U. Pa., Phila., 1996—2001, rsch. asst. prof., 2001—. Contbr. articles to profl. jours. Recipient Lam Found. Rsch. Achievement award, 2002; grantee, Am. Heart Assn., 2000—01, Lam Found., 2000—05, NIH, 2002—. Mem.: AAAS, Am. Thoracic Soc., Am. Soc. For Biochemistry and Molecular Biology. Office: Univ Pa 421 Curie Blvd Philadelphia PA 19104 Office Fax: 215-573-4469. E-mail: krymskay@mail.med.upenn.edu.

KRYS, SHELDON JACK, retired foreign service officer, career minister; b. NYC, June 15, 1934; s. Martin and Anna K.; m. Doris M., May 24, 1964; children— Wendy M., Madeleine S., Susan Jennifer. N.D., U. Md., College Park, 1955; grad., Nat. War Coll., Washington, 1977; PhD (hon.), St. John Fisher Coll., 1996. Newscaster Radio Sta. KRSD, Rapid City, S.D., 1955-57; dir., producer Radio Sta. WWDC, Washington, 1957-59; prin. Chris Sheldon Pub. Relations, Washington, 1959-61; cons. to dir. FMCS, Washington, 1961-62; ednl. and cultural affairs officer, dir. reception ctrs. Dept. State, Washington, 1962-64, dir. personnel Latin Am., 1969-74, fgn. svc. insp., 1977-79, exec. dir. Bur. Near Eastern and South Asian Affairs, 1979-83, dep. dir. mgmt. ops., 1983-84, exec. asst. to under sec. for mgmt., 1984-85, mgmt. officer London, Eng., 1965-66, spl. asst. to ambassador, 1966-69, adminstrv. counselor Belgrade, Yugoslavia, 1974-76; amb. to Trinidad and Tobago, 1985-88; exec. sec. Laird Commn., 1987; asst. sec. state adminstrn. and info. mgmt., 1988-89; asst. sec. state diplomatic security, 1989-92; diplomat-in-residence George Washington U., Washington, 1992-93; cons. internat. and intergovtl. affairs Fletcher, Heald & Hildreth, P.L.C., Roslyn, Va., 1994—. Co-chmn. ambassadorial seminar Dept. of State, 1992—2003. Mem. bd. George Foster Peabody Awards, 1990-95, chmn. bd. 1993-95, chmn. emeritus 1996, chmn. editl. bd. Fgn. Svc. Jour., 1994-96; bd. dirs. Sr. Living Found., 1997—; bd. dirs., treas. Washington Inst. Fgn. Affairs, 1998—; trustee St. John Fisher Coll., 1997—. Recipient Meritorious Honor award, Dept. State, 1974, Disting. Honor award, 1981, Superior Honor award, 1983, Presdl. Meritorious Svc. award, 1983, Wilbur J. Carr award, 1994. Mem. Armed Forces Comm. and Electronics Assn. (bd. dirs. 1991-92), Nat. War Coll. Alumni Assn., Am. Fgn. Svc. Assn., Am. Broadcast Pioneers, Broadcast Found., City Tavern Club. Avocations: gardening, nature watching, tennis. Office: Fletcher Heald & Hildreth PLC 1300 North 17th St 11th Fl Arlington VA 22209-3801

KRYTER, KARL DAVID, retired research scientist; b. Indpls., Oct. 13, 1914; s. George David and Mary Matilda (Christoph) K.; m. Grace Irene Brown, June 21, 1946; children: Dianne, Victoria (Mrs. Myron I. Liebhaber), Kathryn (Mrs. Richard A. Rendon). AB, Butler U., 1939; PhD, U. Rochester, 1942. Rsch. tchr. fellow Harvard U., Cambridge, Mass., 1942-46; asst. prof. Washington U., St. Louis, 1946-48; dir. human resources research labs. Air Force Cambridge Rsch. Ctr., 1948-57; head dept. psychoacoustics Bolt Beranek & Newman, Inc., Cambridge, Mass., 1957-65; dir. Sensory Scis. Rsch. Ctr., Menlo Park, Calif., 1965-76; staff scientist Stanford Rsch. Inst., Menlo Park, 1976-85. Adj. prof. San Diego State U., 1990—; tchr. Colby Coll., 1960—63, MIT, 1958—59; advisor U.S. Pres.'s Office for Sci. and Tech., 1968—70; mem. SST environ. study com. Dept. Interior, 1969; past chmn. coun. com. hearing and bioacoustics NAS/NRC, 1960. Author: The Effects of Noise on Man, 1970-85, Handbook of Hearing and the Effects of Noise, 1994. Recipient Disting. Svc. award in sci. Am. Speech and Hearing Assn., medal U. Liege, Belgium. Fellow APA (coun. reps. 1966-69), Soc. Engring. Psychologists (pres. 1965, Franklin V. Taylor award), Acoustical Soc. Am. (coun., pres. 1972). Home: 1515 San Antonio Creek Rd Santa Barbara CA 93111-1319 E-mail: kdkryter@earthlink.net.

KRYZAK, LINDA ANN, educational administrator; b. Oak Park, Ill., Nov. 3, 1951; d. Eugene Joseph and Helen (Vlahos) K.; children: Melissa Lynn, Heather Rae. BS in Edn., No. Ill. U., 1973, MS in Edn., 1977; cert. advanced study in ednl. tech., Nat.-Louis U., 1998. Cert. gen. adminstr., elem. tchr., spl. edn., early childhood spl. edn. tchr., social/emotional disordered tchr., learning disabled, educable and trainable mentally handicapped, supervisory endorsements. Dir. career/life tng., rsch. project leader, ednl. cons. Grove Sch., Lake Forest, Ill., 1974-81; pvt. practice Addison, Ill., 1981-82; tchr. spl. edn. Sch. Dist. 83, Franklin Park, Ill., 1982-85; coord. spl. edn. Leyden Area Spl. Edn. Coop., Franklin Park, Ill., 1985-94; prin. South Elem. Sch., Franklin Park, Ill., 1994-99; dir. instrn. and tech. Franklin Park Sch. Dist. 84, 1999—2001, prin. East Early Childhood Ctr., dir. tech., 2001—. Founder Creative Learning Choices, 1992—; adj. prof. tech. in edn. Nat. Louis U., 2000—. Pub. speaker on computers, assistive technology, software and integration of spl. edn. students into regular classrooms, 1988—. Mem. Ill. Computing Educators.

KRZYSZTOFOWICZ, ROMAN, systems engineering and statistical science educator, consultant; b. Cieszyn, Poland, Sept. 27, 1947; came to U.S., 1974; naturalized, 1985; s. Janusz and Irena (Rogozinska) K.; m. Liana Balayan, May 27, 1995; son, Arman; daughter Nayiri. MS with highest distinction, Cracow (Poland) Tech. U., 1970; PhD, U. Ariz., 1978. Rsch. engr. Inst. for Meteorology and Water Resources, Cracow, 1970-72, head computer ctr., 1972-74; lectr. Chief Tech. Orgn., Cracow, 1973-74; asst. prof. systems engring. U. Ariz., Tucson, 1978-79; asst. prof. civil engring. MIT, Cambridge, Mass., 1979-82; assoc. prof. systems engring. U. Va., Charlottesville, Va., 1982-86, prof. systems engring., 1986—, dir. grad. program systems engring., 1984-89, assoc. dir. ctr. for risk mgmt. engring. systems, 1987-88, prof. statistics, 1995—. Vis. scientist Swiss Fed. Inst. Tech., Lausanne, 2002; lectr. George Washington U., 1982-83, NATO Advanced Study Inst., Tucson, 1985, Deauville, France, 1993, Coop. Program for Operational Meteorology, Edn. and Tng., Boulder, Colo., 1993-96; rep. NSF in coop. rsch. initiatives with Brazil and Poland, 1991; reviewer proposals NSF, 1980—, Natural Scis. and Engring. Rsch. Coun. Can., 1987—; rschr. Nat. Weather Svc., 1992, 1995; expert on flood forecasting, Commn. for Hydrology, World Meteorology Orgn., 1997-2000; mem. doctoral examination com. U. Que., 1997, 2000, U. Paris VI, 2002; reviewer articles for numerous jours. Editor Jour. of Hydrology, 1996—; mem. editl. bd. Stochastic Hydrology and Hydraulics, 1990-98, Control and Cybernetics, 1994—, Stochastic Environ. Rsch. and Risk Assessment, 1999—, Water Resources Monographs of the Polish Academy of Sciences, 2000—, Jour. Applied Meteorology, 2001—; contbr. articles to profl. jours., chpts. to books, entries to Systems and Control Ency., Concise Ency. Environ. Systems, Ency. Ops. Rsch. and Mgmt. Sci., Ency. of Sci. and Tech. Recipient Prof. W. Wierzbicki award Polish Soc. Civil Engrs. and Technicians, 1970, Rsch. award NSF, 1978-99, Presdl. Young Investigator award Pres. of U.S., 1984. Mem. IEEE, Am. Statis. Assn., Soc. for Judgment and Decision Making, Internat. Inst. Forecasters, Inst. for Ops. Rsch. and the Mgmt. Scis., Am. Geophys. Union, Am. Water Resources Assn., Am. Meteorological Soc., Tau Beta Pi (Eminent Engr. award 1985). Republican. Armenian Catholic. Avocations: opera, theater, skiing, sailing, hiking. Office: U Va PO Box 400747 151 Engineer's Way Charlottesville VA 22904-4747 E-mail:

rk@virginia.edu. *Education is a launchpad to a rewarding life. Research demands passion and endurance. The challenge for me as an academician is to turn learners into thinkers, to bring about in students a transition from acquiring knowledge to creating new knowledge, to graduate scientists and engineers who not merely perpetuate today's technology but invent a better one. For it is the creative element that uplifts the individual and benefits mankind.*

KRZYZAN, JUDY LYNN, automotive executive; b. Buffalo, Sept. 1, 1951; d. James Lambert and Janet Lucille (Grabau) McKellar; m. Ronald Edward Krzyzan, Dec. 21, 1974 (div. Jan. 1989); 1 child, Brian Edward. Student, Erie C.C., 1969-70. With counter and delivery M & H Auto Supply, Orchard Park, N.Y., 1973-75; parts counter person Crest Dodge Inc., Orchard Park, 1975-81; parts mgr. Case Chrysler Plymouth, Hamburg, N.Y., 1981-87, Mancuso Chrysler Plymouth, Hamburg, 1987-91, Transitowne Dodge, Williamsville, N.Y., 1991—. Supr. Profl. Inventory Assn., N.H., 1976-85. Named Mopar Parts Master, 1996. Mem. Chrysler Parts and Svc. Mgrs. Guild (v.p., sec. 1986-87, 89-92), The Greater Buffalo Auto Body Guild. Avocations: scuba diving, horseback riding, downhill skiing, cross-country skiing, trap shooting. Home: 2801 Creek Rd Hamburg NY 14075 Office: Transitowne Dodge 7408 Transit Rd Williamsville NY 14221-6091 E-mail: partzladi@aol.com.

KRZYZANOWSKI, RICHARD L. lawyer, corporate executive; b. Warsaw, Mar. 25, 1932; came to U.S., 1967, naturalized, 1972; s. Andrew and Mary K.; children: Suzanne, Peter, Christine. BA, U. Warsaw, 1956; ML, U. Pa., 1960; PhD, U. Paris, 1962. Bar: Pa. With Crown Cork & Seal Co., Inc., Phila., 1967—, dir., exec. v.p. gen. counsel, 1990-2001. Counselor John Paul II Found., Vatican, Rome, Italy; exec. trustee, founder Krzyzanowski Found., Phila. Mem. Int. Bar Assn. (London). Office: Crown Cork & Seal Co Inc 1 Crown Way Philadelphia PA 19154-4599

KRZYZANSKI, WOJCIECH, pharmacokineticist, consultant, mathematician; b. Leba, Poland, Aug. 30, 1965; s. Marian Krzyzanski and Jozefa Krzyzanska; m. Monika Gronska, June 29, 1991; children: Katarzyna, Anna. MSc with honors, Jagiellonian U., Cracow, Poland, 1989; PhD, SUNY at Buffalo, 1997. Asst. Inst. of Math., Jagiellonian U., Cracow, 1989—94; postdoctoral fellow dept. pharmaceutics SUNY at Buffalo, 1998; rsch. asst. prof. dept. pharm. scis. U. at Buffalo, 1998—. Cons. W. R. Johnson Pharm. Rsch. Inst., Raritan, NJ, 2001—. Contbr. articles to profl. jours. Recipient Giorgio Segre prize, European Fedn. for Pharm. Scis., 2000; fellow in pharmacokinetics and pharmacodynamics, InnaPhase Corp., 2001. Mem.: Am. Math. Soc., Am. Assn. Pharm. Scientists. Home: 123 Imperial Dr Amherst NY 14226 Office: Dept Pharm Scis 565B Hochstetter Hall Buffalo NY 14260

KRZYZEWSKI, MIKE, university athletic coach; b. Chgo., Feb. 13, 1947; m. Carol Mickie Marsh; children: Debbie Savarino, Linda Frasher, Jamie. BS, U.S. Mil. Acad., 1969. Capt. team, 1968—69; capt. second team All-NIT, 1969; capt. North-South game, 1969; head coach svc. teams, 1969—72; head coach U.S. Mil. Acad. Prep Sch., Ft. Belvoir, Va., 1972—74; grad. asst. Ind. U., 1974—75; head coach U.S. Mil. Acad., West Point, NY, 1975-80, Duke U. Blue Devils, Durham, NC, 1980—; head coach south team Nat. Sports Festival, 1983; instr. Olympic Trials, 1984. Chmn. Children's Miracle Network Telethon; bd. dirs. V Found.; with Comprehensive Cancer Ctr., NABC Coaches vs. Cancer; bd. dirs. K Lab Human Performance; fundraising leader Emily Krzyzewski Ctr. Immaculate Conception Cath. Ch., Durham, NC. Served U.S. Army, 1967—69, officer U.S. Army, 1969—74, ret. capt. U.S. Army, 1974. Named Nat. Coach of Yr., 8 times. Mem.: NCAA (basketball issues com.), Nat. Assn. Basketball Coaches (pres. 1998—99, Dist. Coach of Yr. 1977, 1984, 1992, 1994, 1999, 2000, Nat. Coach of Yr. 1991, 1999). Achievements include coaching team to NCAA Divsn. I Championship, 1991, 92, 2001, 2nd place, 1986, 90, 94, 99, final four, 1986, 88, 89, 90, 91, 92, 94, 99, 2001; ranked first in the Big Apple NIT Champion, ACC Champion, NCAA Tournament Finalist, equal NCAA record for most victories in a season, 1986; ranked first, ACC Champion, NCAA Champion, team ranked number 1 from start to finish, a first repeat NCAA Champion since 1972-73; ranked first, NCAA Tournament Finalist, ACC regular season champion, ACC Champion, equal for most victories in a season, 1999; ranked first, NCAA Champion, ACC regular season co-champion, ACC Champion, TiVo Preseason NIT champion, 2001; ranked first, ACC Champion, NCAA Tournament Sweet 16, Maui Invitational champion, 2002; only 4th coach in NCAA history to earn 3 or more national championships along with John Wooden, Adolph Rupp, and Bob Knight; led Duke to 3 NCAA titles and 9 Final Four appearances since 1986. Office: Duke Univ Cameron Indoor Stadium Durham NC 27708-0556

KSANSNAK, JAMES EDWARD, service management company executive; b. Hazleton, Pa., Mar. 13, 1940; s. Edward J. and Helen (Holodick) K.; m. Valerie M. Anderson, June 9, 1962 (div. 1986); children: Keith, Janet, Linda; m. Suzanne M. Teefy, Feb. 21, 1987. BS magna cum laude in Acctg., St. Joseph's U., Phila., 1962. C.P.A. With Arthur Andersen & Co., Phila., 1962-86, sr. mem. staff, 1964-67, mgr., 1967-71, ptnr., 1971-79, mng. ptnr., 1979-86; sr. v.p. ARAMARK Corp. (formerly ARA Svcs., Inc.), Phila., 1986-87, sr. v.p., CFO, 1987-91, exec. v.p., CFO, 1991-97, vice chmn., 1997—2001. Bd. dirs. CSS Industries, Inc., Aramark Corp.; chmn. Tasty BakingCo., 2003—. Contbr. articles to profl. jours. Mem. Cmty. Leadership Seminar, 1972, trustee, bd. dirs., 1984; treas., bd. dirs. Ambler (Pa.) Youth Svcs., 1974-79; bd. dris., mem. exec. com. Phila. YMCA, 1974-94, chmn. fin. com., chmn. ann. meeting, city fundraising chmn., 1974-83, maj. gifts chmn., 1984-87, chmn. 1987-91; mem. exec. com. Phila. Urban Affairs Coalition, 1978-95; bd. dirs. Greater Phila. Internat. Network, 1980-86, INROADS-Phila., Inc., 1981-90, Am. Cancer Soc., 1994-96, Thomas Jefferson U., 1994—, Main Line Health Sys., 1996-98; mem. Mayor's Com. on Literacy, Phila., 1984-85; mem. fin. com., exec. com. Presbyn.-U. Pa. Med. Ctr., 1981-90, chmn. found., 1986; vice chmn. United Way, 1982; trustee Coll. Bus., St. Joseph's U., 1982-85. Recipient alumni award St. Joseph's U., 1980; named Profl. of Yr., Phi Chi Theta, 1981 Mem. AICPA, Pa. Inst. CPAs (chmn. tech. meetings 1970, chmn. coop. with attys. 1972, exec. comm. Phila. chpt. 1980-82), Planning Execs. Inst. (chmn. bd. 1981, Neil Denen award 1984), Union League, Sunnybrook Golf Club, Loxahatchee Golf Club, Knights of Malta. Republican. Roman Catholic. Home: 205 Echo Dr Jupiter FL 33458 Office: ARAMARK Corp 1101 Market St Philadelphia PA 19107-2988

KSIENSKI, AHARON ARTHUR, electrical engineer; b. Warsaw, June 23, 1924; came to U.S., 1951, naturalized, 1959; s. Isreal and Rebecca K.; married; children: David, Ruth. B.E. in Mech. Engring, Inst. Mech. Engring., London, 1947; M.Sc. in Elec. Engring, U. So. Calif., 1952, PhD, 1958. Sr. staff engr., head antenna dept. research staff Hughes Aircraft Co., Culver City, Calif., 1958-67; prof. elec. engring., tech. dir. communication systems electrosci. lab. Ohio State U., 1967-76, prof. elec. engring., chmn. communication and propagation com. electrosci. lab., 1976-87, prof. emeritus, 1987—. Bd. dirs. Ohio State U. Research Found., 1975-79; cons. in field. Editor trans., revs. in field. Recipient Brabazon award Inst. Electronic and Radio Engrs., London, 1967, 76 Fellow IEEE; mem. Internat. Union Radio Sci. (chmn. commns. B and C 1972-75) Home: 1780 Lynnhaven Dr Columbus OH 43221-1410 Office: 1320 Kinnear Rd Columbus OH 43212-1156 E-mail: a-arthur@worldnet.att.net.

KU, ANCHI H. legal assistant; b. Ankara, Turkey, Apr. 12, 1957; came to U.S., 1977; d. Gregory S.L. and Shirley L. Hang; children: Andrew Ku, Amanda Ku. BS, U. Tex., Dallas, 1981; grad., Asian Am. Leadership Conf., Dallas, 1990. Real estate broker Realty World, Richardson, Tex., 1981-83; property mgr. Trammell Crow Co., Dallas, 1985-86; legal asst. Smith, Underwood & Perkins, Dallas, 1989-95; sr. legal asst. Friedman, Driegert & Hsueh, Dallas, 1995—. Bd. dirs. Tex. Dept. Human Svcs. Featured interview A World of Difference, Dallas Morning News, 1990. World Cup amb. Dallas Venue, 1994; mem. steering com. Walka Mile in My Shoe, 1993—; mem. adv. coun. Women's Bus. Issues Greater Dallas Chamber, 1994-96; co-chair City of Dallas 14-1 Redistricting Plan, 1990; alt. mem. bd. adjustment, 1990-92; mem. host com. Asian Ams. for Kay Bailey Hutchinson, 1990, 93-94; scheduling co-chair Bartlett mayoral campaign, 1991; asst. campaign dir. Driegert campaign for county Rep. chair, 1992; chair spl. events Rep. Party Dallas County, 1992-93; co-chair Dallas County George W. Bush gubernatorial campaign, 1994; co-chair VIP com. Rep. State Conv., Dallas, 1992; bd. dirs. Dallas Met. YWCA, 1989-92; bd. dirs. Asian Am. C. of C., 1989-94, vice chair, 1991-94. Recipient Pillar of Progress award Dallas Area Rapid Transit, Trinity River Bridge, 1992, Oustanding Cmty. Svc. award West End Pl., Dallas, 1991. Mem. NAFE, Exec. Women in Tex. Govt., Dallas Women Together. Avocations: traveling, photography, community service, politics, children and women's advocacy. Office: Friedman Driegert & Hsueh 8117 Preston Rd Ste 570 Dallas TX 75225-6337

KU, ANDREW, interventional neuroradiologist; b. Jan. 12, 1958; AB, Harvard Coll., 1980; MD, Columbia U., 1984. Diplomate Am. Bd. Radiology. Surg. intern U. Pa. Presbyn. Med. Ctr., 1985; resident in radiology Duke U., 1989; fellow in neuroradiology NYU Med. Ctr., 1990, fellow in interventional neuroradiology, 1991; asst. prof. U. Tex. Health Sci. Ctr., Houston, 1991-95; sr. attending physician Allegheny Gen. Hosp., Pitts., 1995—. Cons. neurologic devices panel FDA, Rockville, Md., 1995—. Mem. AMA, Am. Soc. Neuroradiology, Am. Soc. Interventional and Therapeutic Neuroradiology, Soc. Cardiovasc. and Interventional Radiology, World Fedn. Interventional and Therapeutic Neuroradiology, Sierra Club. Avocations: photography, hiking. Office: Allegheny Gen Hosp Dept Radiology 320 E North Ave Pittsburgh PA 15212-4756 E-mail: andrewku@pol.net.

KU, DAVID NELSON, medical educator; b. St. Louis, Mar. 15, 1956; DA, Harvard U., 1978; MS, Ga. Inst. Tech., 1982, PhD, 1983; MD, Emory U., 1984. Dir. vascular lab Hyde Park Cmty. Hosp., Chgo., 1985—86; from asst. prof. to assoc. prof. Ga. Inst. Tech., Atlanta, 1986—95, prof., 1995—98, Regents prof., 1998—; assoc. prof. Emory U., Atlanta, 1991—97, prof., 1997—. Mem. adv. bd. Ga. Inst. Tech., 1996—, mem. exec. bd., 1996—, mem. mech. engring. faculty recruiting com., 1996—; chair tenure com. Coll. Engring. Ga. Inst. Tech., 1996—. Assoc. editor: Jour. Vascular Investigation, 1994—, Jour. Biomech. Engring., 1995—. Mem. chorus Atlanta Symphony Orch., 1989—90. Mem.: AMA, ASME (Larson award 1996), Am. Coll. Angiology, Sigma Xi. Office: Ga Inst Tech Mech Engring Atlanta GA 30332-0001

KU, JENTUNG, mechanical and aerospace engineer; b. Hsinchu, Republic of China; came to U.S., 1974; m. Jung-Chen and Chun-Yin (Hsieh) K.; m. Shu-Mei Chen, Aug. 17, 1979; children: Lisa, Daniel, Brian. BS, Tsing Hua U., Hsinchu, 1972; MS, Purdue U., 1976, PhD, 1980. Rsch. asst. Purdue U., West Lafayette, Ind., 1976-80; mem. tech. staff Advanced Tech. Ctr., Bendix Corp., Columbia, Md., 1980-83; section head/program mgr. OAO Corp., Greenbelt, Md., 1983-91; group leader NASA Goddard Space Flight Ctr., Greenbelt, Md., 1991—. Contbr. articles on heat transfer and thermal control systems to profl. jours.; pioneer in developing capillary two-phase heat transport systems (1 honor medal, 2 Tech. Innovation awards NASA). Bd. dirs. Columbia Chinese Bapt. Ch., 1991—. Mem. ASME, AIAA, Am. Nuclear Soc., Tau Beta Pi, Phi Tau Phi. Baptist. Avocation: tennis. Home: 14208 Bradshaw Dr Silver Spring MD 20905-6503 Office: NASA Goddard Space Flight Ctr Greenbelt MD 20771-0001

KU, YI-YIN, organic chemist; b. Xian, PR China, May 15, 1959; arrived in USA, 1983; d. Wei-Qing and Jin-Hua Teng Ku; m. Yao-En Li, Dec. 25, 1985; children: Kory Li, Katie Li. BS, Northwestern U, Xian, China, 1982; MS, U of Ill., Chgo., Ill, 1985; PhD, U of Ill, Chgo., Ill, 1988. Sci. Abbott Labs., No. Chgo., Ill., 1989—92, sr. sci., team leader, 1992—96, rsch. invest., group leader, 1996—98, vol. assoc. rsch. fellow, 1998—2000, sr. group leader, 2000—. Contbr. articles to profl. jours. including Jour. Organic Chemistry, Organic Letters, Jour. Am. Chem. Soc., others. Recipient Sci. of the Year, Abbott Labs., 1992, Chmn., 1995, Rober Stein, 1996; Grad. fellow, U. Ill., Chgo., 1998. Mem.: Am. Chemical Soc. Achievements include 13 patents; 41 publications and national conference presentations. Home: 23 River Oaks Circle E Buffalo Grove IL 60089-4623 Office: Abbott Labs 1401 Sheridan Rd North Chicago IL 60064

KUAN, JACKSON HSUN, gastroenterologist; b. Taipei, Taiwan, Mar. 23, 1959; came to U.S., 1972; s. S.Y. and Ming C. (Liu) K.; m. Lana Choy, June 13, 1987; children: Kristen Candice, Eric Jackson. BA, NYU, 1980; MD, Albany Med. Coll. of Union U., 1986. Diplomate Am. Bd. Internal Medicine, Am. Bd. Gastroenterology. Resident Roosevelt Hosp., N.Y.C., 1986-89; fellow in gastroenterology Downstate Med. Ctr., Bklyn., 1989-91; pvt. practice, 1991-92; gastroenterologist Palmadessa & Kuan Gastroenterology Assocs., P.C., 1993—2002; asst. dir. gastroenterology N.Y. Flushing Hosp., 1997—2002; gastroenterologist pvt. practice, Flushing, NY, 2003—. Rsch. asst. Rockefeller U., 1980-82, summers 1983-84; admitting privilges Flushing Hosp. Med. Ctr., N.Y. Hosp. Queens, North Shore Univ. Hosp.; asst. dir. gastroenterology, adv. mem. nutrition com., internship admissions com. Flushing Hosp. Contbr. articles to profl. jours. Mem.: ACP, AMA, Med. Soc. of the State N.Y., Am. Gastroenterology Assn., Am. Coll. Gastroenterology. Avocations: computers, tennis, travel. Office: 132-59 41St Rd Ste 1A & 1B Flushing NY 11355-2281 also: 146-01 45th Ave Ste 205 Flushing NY 11355 E-mail: GIProf@aol.com.

KUBALE, BERNARD STEPHEN, lawyer; b. Reedsville, Wis., Sept. 5, 1928; s. Joseph and Josephine (Novak) Kubale; m. Mary Thomas, Apr. 21, 1956 (dec. Jan. 13, 2001); children: Caroline, Catherine, Anne. BBA, U. Wis., 1950, LLB, 1955; LLD (hon.), St. Norbert Coll., 1985. CPA Wis.; bar: Wis. 1955. Acct. John D. Morrison and Co., Marquette, Mich., 1950-51; atty., ptnr. Foley and Lardner, Milw., 1955—, chmn. mgmt. com., 1985-94. Bd. dirs. Green Bay Packers, Wis. E. R. Wagner Mfg. Co., Wausau Homes. Chmn. bd. dirs. St. Norbert Coll., DePere, Wis., 1980—84, Children's Hosp. Wis., Milw., 1982—91. 1st lt. USAF, 1951—53. Mem.: ABA, Milw. Bar Assn., Wis. Bar Assn., Wis. Inst. CPAs, Milw. Club, Milw. Country Club, Chenequa Country Club. Republican. Roman Catholic. Avocations: fishing, skiing, baseball. Home: 5935 Monclaire Rd Hartland WI 53029 Office: Foley & Lardner 1st Wisconsin Ctr 777 E Wisconsin Ave Ste 3800 Milwaukee WI 53202-5367

KUBAS, CHRISTINE, retired law enforcement officer; b. Passaic, N.J., Dec. 15, 1946; d. Patsy Carmelo and Carmela Angela (Colombo) Gatto; m. Emil R. Kubas, Apr. 28, 1974 (div. 1978); 1 child, Brian Patrick. Student, Ga. So. Coll., 1965-67, Bloomfield Coll., 1967-69, William Paterson Coll., 1972-73, Passaic County C.C., 1978, 81, 84, 87. Cert. EMT, tng. officer. Admitting technician St. Mary's Hosp., Passaic, 1967-68; apprentice Garden State Optical, Saddle Brook, N.J., 1969-70; children's supr. Passaic County Youth Ctr., Wayne, N.J., 1972-74; officer Passaic County Sheriff's Dept., Paterson, N.J., 1974-82, sgt., 1982-85, lt., 1985-86, capt., 1986-88, hostage negotiator on sheriff's emergency team, 1980-81; legal sec. Law Office W. Joseph Weiner, 1988-89; investigator Morris County Probation Svcs., Morristown, N.J., 1990-97, with parent locator svc., 1991-92, team leader, 1993-97; sr. judiciary investigator State of N.J., 1995-97, ret., 1997. Asst. tng. officer Passaic County Jail, 1980-81. Active Passaic County Dem. Women, 1974-88, pres., 1976-77; sec.-treas. Police Benevolent Assn. 286, Paterson, 1978-80, contract negotiator, 1978. Roman Catholic. Avocations: reading, music, esp, angels. Home: 45 Ramapo Ave Pompton Lakes NJ 07442-1731

KUBAS, GREGORY JOSEPH, research chemist; b. Cleve., Mar. 12, 1945; s. Joseph Arthur and Esther Kubas; m. Chrystal Henry, Dec. 22, 1973; children: Kelly Richmond (dec. 1997), Sherry Lopez. BS, Case Inst. Tech., 1966; PhD, Northwestern U., 1970. Postdoctoral fellow Princeton (N.J.) U., 1971-72, Los Alamos (N.Mex.) Nat. Lab., 1972-74, mem. staff, 1974—; lab. fellow, 1987—. Author: Metal Dihydrogen And Sigma Complexes, 2001; contbr. articles to profl. jours. Recipient E.O. Lawrence Meml. award US Dept. Energy, 1994. Mem. Am. Chem. Soc. (Inorganic Chemistry award 1993). Achievements include patents in field. Home: 29 Camino Cielo Santa Fe NM 87506-2114 Office: Los Alamos Nat Lab # Ms-j514 Los Alamos NM 87545-0001

KUBE, HAROLD DEMING, retired financial executive; b. Buffalo, Wyo., June 16, 1910; s. Carl Christen and Inez (Mather) K.; m. Shirley Smith; children: Robert Ford, Thomas Smith. BS, U. Nebr., 1932; MBA, Harvard U., 1934. Owner Beef Cattle Farm, Warrenton, Va., 1950—; co-owner Resources Devel. Assocs., 1965-80; dir. emeritus Jefferson Savs. and Loan Assn., Warrenton, 1980—, Greater Washington Investors, Inc., 1987—. Bd. dirs. A & K Land and Cattle Corp., Warrenton. Co-author: Manufacturing Distribution in U.S., 1938. With USN, 1944-46. Mem. Am. Econ. Assn. Episcopalian. Avocation: golf. Home and Office: 6470 Beverleys Mill Rd Broad Run VA 20137-2101

KUBEY, ROBERT WILLIAM, media educator, developmental psychologist, television analyst and researcher; b. Berkeley, Calif., July 20, 1952; m. Barbara Lewert Kubey, Nov. 14, 1981; children: Benjamin, Daniel. AB in Psychology with honors, U. Calif., Santa Cruz, 1974; MA in Behavioral Sci., U. Chgo., 1978, PhD in Behavioral Sci., 1984. NIMH postdoctoral fellow U. Calif., Irvine, 1984-85, vis. lectr., 1985; asst. prof. dept. comm. Rutgers U., New Brunswick, N.J., 1985-91, assoc. prof. dept. comm., 1991-99, assoc. prof. dept. journalism and media studies, 1999—, dir. Master's Comm. and Info. Studies, 1997—2000, dir. Ctr. for Media Studies, 1999—; dir. N.J. Media Literacy Project, 1999—. Mem. faculty Harvard U. Inst. on Media Edn., Cambridge, Mass., 1993, 94; vis. assoc. prof. dept. comm. Stanford (Calif.) U., 1995-96; rsch. dir. Media Edn. Lab. Rutgers U., Newark. Co-author: Television and the Quality of Life, 1990; editor: Media Literacy in the Information Age, Transaction, 1997; editor media edn. series Lawrence Erlbaum Assocs., 1994—; author: Creating Television, 2003; contbr. articles to profl. jours. Annenberg scholar in media edn. Annenberg Sch. Comm., U. Pa., 1993. Fellow Ctr. for Critical Analysis of Contemporary Culture, Gerontol. Soc. Office: Rutgers Univ Dept Jour/Media Studies 4 Huntington St New Brunswick NJ 08901-1071 E-mail: kubey@scils.rutgers.edu.

KUBIAK, ANDREA CELESTE, language educator; b. Orange, Calif., Aug. 14, 1975; d. Robert Joseph and Donna Jean Kubiak. AA, Coll. of the Desert, 1994; BA, U. of Calif., Riverside, Calif., 1996; MA, Ohio U., 2001. Tchg. asst. Ohio U., Athens, Ohio, 1999—2001; prof. of spanish Coll. of the Desert, Palm Desert, Calif., 2002—. Author: (plays) Tosca Bartola. Vol. English tchr. Peace Corps., Kleczew, Poland, 1997—99; translator children's ministry and jail ministry Glory to God Ministries Internat., Cathedral City, Calif., 1993—2003. Recipient Alumni Assn. award, Coll. of the Desert, 1994; scholar Golf scholarship, Idaho State U., 1994—95, Tchg. scholar, Ohio U., 1999—2001. Democrat. Avocations: sports, travel, languages, books, music. Home: 15382 Ave Mirola Desert Hot Springs CA 92240 Office: College of the Desert Monterey Ave Palm Desert CA 92260 Home Fax: 760-329-4532. Personal E-mail: toscaria@yahoo.com.

KUBIAK, JOHN MICHAEL, academic administrator; b. Pulaski, Wis., Jan. 15, 1935; s. Anton Joseph and Genevieve (McGuire) K.; m. Mary Dee Neville, Aug. 5, 1966; children: Michelle Jo, Leslie A. Welsh, Robert N. Welsh. BS in Mil. Engring., U.S. Mil. Acad., 1958; MBA, Washington U., St. Louis, 1976, M Data Processing, 1977; PhD, St. Louis U., 1981. Commd. 2d lt. USAF, 1958, advanced through grades to col., 1979; prof. aerospace studies Cornell U., Ithaca, N.Y., 1983-86; retired USAF, 1986; exec. dir. Emaudi Ctr. Internat. Studies, Cornell U., 1986-96; ret., 1997—. Trustee Boulder City Hosp., 2000—, v.p. bd. trustees, 2002—. Decorated Legion of Merit (2), Meritorious Svc. Medal (2), Air Force Commendation Medals (2), Air Medals (2). Mem. Air Force Assn., Rotary (pres. Boulder City 1998-99, asst. gov. dist. 5300 2001-02), Beta Gamma Sigma, Order Daedalians. Republican. Avocations: gardening, golf, aviation. E-mail: kubiak@west-point.org.

KUBIC, CHARLES RICHARD, naval officer; b. Greensburg, Pa., Dec. 7, 1950; s. William Louis and Josephine Roberta (Mologne) K.; m. Anne Renee Sheroda, July 29, 1972; children: Charles Brian, Kathryn Anne, Andrew William. BSCE, Lehigh U., 1972; MSCE, 1978. Registered profl. engr., Pa., Va. Commd. ensign CEC U.S. Navy, 1972, advanced through grades to rear admiral, 1998; asst. head constrn. dept. OICC, Thailand, Bangkok, 1973-75; co-comdr. NMCE Four, Port Hueneme, Calif., 1975-77; assignment officer Naval Mil. Pers. Command, Washington, 1978-80; asst. pub. works officer Nat. Naval Med. Ctr., Bethesda, Md., 1980-82; AOICC for design OICC Mediterranean, Madrid, 1982-85; White House fellow White House Office Policy Devel., 1985-86; dir. Strategic Programs Office Naval Facilities Engring. Command, Alexandria, Va., 1986-89; comdg. officer NMCB Three, Port Hueneme, Calif., 1989-91; prodn. officer Navy Pub. Works Ctr., Norfolk, Va., 1991-94; vice comdr. Atlantic Divsn. Navfacengcom, Norfolk, 1994-97; com 22NCR Norfolk, 1997-98; vice comdr. Navfacengcom, 1998-99; comdr. Third Naval Constrn. Brigade and PACNAVFACENGCOM, 1999—2002, Com First Naval Constrn. Divsn., 2002—. Contbr. articles to profl. jours. Scoutmaster Boy Scouts Am., Bangkok, 1973-75, cubmaster, Madrid, 1984, Va., 1985-87, 92-94. Decorated 3 Legion of Merit medals, 4 Meritorious Service medals; CNO scholar, 1977-78. Fellow Soc. Am. Mil. engrs.; mem. NSPE, U.S. Naval Inst., Phi Beta Kappa, Tau Beta Pi, Sigma Phi Epsilon. Republican. Roman Catholic. Avocations: golf, skiing, scuba diving, running. Office: First Naval Constrn Divsn 1310 8th St Norfolk VA 23521-2416 E-mail: kubicfam@worldnet.att.net.

KUBICEK, PAUL J. political scientist, educator; b. San Antonio, Tex., Aug. 11, 1968; s. Eben James and Sandra Lee Kubicek; m. Alyce Howarth, July 12, 1995; children: Jonah, Asher. BSFS, Georgetown U., 1989; MA, U. Mich., 1992, PhD, 1995. Asst. prof. Koc U., Istanbul, Turkey, 1995—98, U. Wyo., Laramie, 1999—2000; assoc. prof. Oakland U., Rochester, Mich., 2000—; rsch. assoc. Ctr. for Russian and Ea. European Studies U. Mich., Ann Arbor, 2001—. Author: The European Union and Democratization, 2003, Unbroken Ties: The State, Interest Associations and Corporation in Post-Soviet Ukraine, 2000. Grantee, IREX, 2002, Coun. Internat. Edn., 2000. Mem.: Am. Polit. Sci. Assn., Am. Assn. Advancement Slavic Studies. Avocations: fly fishing, travel. Office: Dept Political Sci Oakland Univ Rochester MI 48309

KUBICZKY, STEPHEN RALPH, lawyer; b. North Braddock, Pa., Oct. 8, 1947; s. Stephen Ralph and Helen (Kish) K. BS, U. Notre Dame, 1969, MS, 1977; JD, Northwestern U., 1972. Bar: Ill. 1972, U.S. Dist. Ct. (no. dist.) Ill. 1972, U.S. Ct. Claims 1978, U.S. Tax Ct. 1978, U.S. Ct. Appeals (7th cir.) 1979. Assoc. Altheimer & Gray, Chgo., 1973-75, 77-80, ptnr., 1980-91, counsel, 1991-92; pvt. practice Riverside, Ill. Chmn. planning com., materials author Ill. Inst. Continuing Legal Edn., 1983, 94, 87-88, 93, 97; pub. witness Pres.'s Commn. on Pension Policy, 1981; mem. instnl. rev. bd. Rush-Presbyn. St. Luke's Med. Ctr., 1999—. Vol. coord. Ill. state Bush/Quayle '92 Presdl. campaign; pres. Riverside Twp. Regular Rep. Orgn., 1994-98; trustee Triton Coll., 1995—. Recipient Hero of the Heart award, 2001, Caught in the Act of Caring award, 2003. Mem. ABA, Ill. State Bar Assn. (chmn. employee benefits sect. 1981-83, sect. coun. fed. taxation sect. 1980-84, contbr. newsletter 1980-85), Wigmore Club (exec. com. 1992-96), Henry Wade Rogers Soc., Ill. Cmty. Coll. trustees Assn. (sec. 1999-2000, chmn. north suburban region 1998-99, Spl. Achievement award 2000, Leadership award 2000, Edn. award 2000). Office: PO Box 86 Riverside IL 60546-0086

KUBIDA, JUDITH ANN, museum administrator; b. Chgo., Aug. 29, 1948; d. William and Julia Ann (Kun) K.; m. Benjamin Kocolowski, Nov. 22, 1980. Attended, Southeast Coll. Adminstrn. asst. in vis. svcs. and sci. and edn. depts. Mus. Sci. and Industry, Chgo. Columnist monthly community newspaper Pullman Flyer. Vice-pres. pub. rels. Hist. Pullman Found., Hist. Pullman Dist., Chgo., editor quarterly newsletter Update, create publicity brochures, liaison with Ill., Chgo. Film Offices, publ. chmn., mem. annual house tour com., prodr. commemorative plate. Democrat. Home: 11334 S Langley Ave Chicago IL 60628-5126 Office: Hist Pullman Found Hotel Florence 11111 S Forrestville Ave Chicago IL 60628-4649

KUBIDA, WILLIAM JOSEPH, lawyer; b. Newark, Apr. 3, 1949; s. William and Catherine (Gilchrist) K.; m. Mary Jane Hamilton, Feb. 4, 1984; children: Sara Gilchrist, Kathleen Hamilton. BSEE, USAF Acad., 1971; JD, Wake Forest U., 1979. Bar: N.C. 1979, U.S. Patent Office 1979, Ind. 1980, U.S. Dist. Ct. (no. dist.) Ind. 1980, U.S. Dist. Ct. (so. dist.) Ind. 1980, U.S. Ct. Appeals (7th cir.) 1981, U.S. Dist. Ct. Ariz. 1982, U.S. Ct. Appeals (9th and fed. cirs.) 1982, Ariz. 1982, Colo. 1990, U.S. Dist. Ct. Colo. 1990, U.S. Ct. Appeals (10th cir.) 1990. Patent and trademark atty. Lundy and Assocs., Ft. Wayne, Ind., 1979-81; patent atty. Motorola, Inc., Phoenix, 1981-85; intellectual property counsel Nippon Motorola, Ltd., Tokyo, 1985-87; ptnr. Lisa & Kubida, Phoenix, 1987-89; engring. law counsel Digital Equipment Corp., Colorado Springs, Colo., 1989-92; of counsel Holland & Hart, Denver, Colorado Springs, 1992-93, ptnr., chmn. intellectual property practice group, 1993-99; ptnr., dir. intellectual property practice group Hogan & Hartson LLP, Colorado Springs, 1999—. Bd. dirs. Colorado Springs Tech Incubator, Bd. dirs. Colorado Springs Tech. Incubator. 1st lt. USAF, 1971—76. Mem. Am. Intellectual Property Law Assn. (computer software sect.), Licensing Exec. Soc. (Pacific Rim subcom.), Country Club Colo., Mensa, Intertel, Aston Martin Owners Club, Phi Delta Phi. Republican. Presbyterian. Home: 4165 Regency Dr Colorado Springs CO 80906-4368

KUBIET, LEO LAWRENCE, newspaper advertising and marketing executive; b. Apr. 11, 1924; s. Joseph J. and Laura Agnes (Bucy) K.; m. Mary Jean Metz, Sept. 14, 1946; children: Lawrence Michael, Martin Alan. BA in Journalism and English, Fairmont State Coll., 1949; postgrad., U. Mich., 1950, Wayne State U., 1952, U. Detroit, 1953. With The News, Detroit, 1950-68; retail advt. mgr. St. Petersburg (Fla.) Times and Evening Ind., 1968-70, advt. mgr., 1970-75, advt. dir., 1975-76, corp. dir., 1976-89, v.p. advt., 1986-87, sr. v.p., 1987-89; dir. Modern Graphic Arts, Fla. Trend Mags., Inc. divsn. Semit Corp. Charter and hon. life mem. advt. adv. council U. Fla., 1978—, hon. life, 1995—; bd. dirs. U. Fla. Found., chmn. Embrace Excellence Campaign Fund, Coll. Journalism, 1989-93; bd. govs. St. Petersburg Area C. of C., 1979-83; bd. dirs. Fla. Orch., 1988-89, Hall of Fame Bowl, 1987-91; mem. fund raising com. St. Anthony's Hosp. Found., 1991-93; bd. dirs. Tampa Bay Coun., Nat. Assn. Investors Corp., 1995-2000. Bd. dirs. Pt. Brittany Condo Two Corp., 1995—2001, v.p., 2000—01, treas., 2001—03; mem. Fla. Lottery Commn. With Seabees USN, 1942—46. Mem.: Advt. Agy. Rev. Com., Newspaper Pubs. Assn. (plans com.), Newspaper Advt. Bur. Am., St. Petersburg Sales and Mktg. Execs., Inc., St. Petersburg Advt. Fedn. (past pres., bd. dirs. Silver medal 1977), Am. Press. Inst., So. Region Adv. Coun., Internat. Newspaper Advt. and Mktg. Execs. (hon.), Internat. Newspaper Advt. and Mktg. Execs. (life; past pres.), Commerce Club Pinellas County (past pres.), St. Petersburg Country Club, Pt. Brittany Yacht Club (bd. govs., treas. 2001—03, vice commdr. 2003—), St. Petersburg Yacht Club. Roman Catholic. Avocations: travel, computers. Home: 5108 Brittany Dr S Apt 308 Saint Petersburg FL 33715-1525 E-mail: le.jekub@verizon.net.

KUBILUS, NORBERT JOHN, information technology executive; b. Newark, Oct. 6, 1948; s. Vity Leo and Ursula Eva (Yarusavage) K.; m. Linda J. Ferri, July 23, 1988; 1 child from previous marriage, Jessica Leigh; 1 stepchild, James M. Feigert. ScB cum laude, Seton Hall U., 1970; MS, Rensselaer Poly. Inst., 1973. Rsch. asst. Rensselaer Poly. Inst., Troy, N.Y., 1971-72; systems programmer, analyst RAPIDATA, Fairfield, N.J., 1972-76, mgr. quality assurance, 1976-78, mgr. corp. support svcs., 1978-79, dir. software devel., 1979-81, asst. v.p., 1980-81; v.p., COO network svcs. divsn. NDC, Fairfield, 1981-83; v.p. info systems and tech. Ednl. Testing Svc., Princeton, N.J., 1983-86; mng. ptnr. Norda Group, Yardley, Pa., 1986-88; v.p., chief tech. officer Optimal Solutions Inc., Hoboken, N.J., 1987-91; v.p., chief info. officer BCM, Inc., Plymouth Meeting, Pa., 1991-94; v.p. ops., chief info. officer Leading Hotels of World, Ltd., N.Y.C., 1994-96; mng. ptnr. Kubilus Ferri & Assocs., Yardley, Pa., 1996-2000; dir. ops. and fin. Stellcom, Inc., San Diego, 2000—01; ptnr. Tatum CIO Ptnrs. LLP, San Diego, 2001—. Reviewer Reston (Va.) Pub. Co.; adj. prof. N.J. Inst. Tech., 1976—84; nat. lectr. Assn. Computing Machinery, 1976—80; prof. computer sci. Coll. of N.J., 1997—2001; mem. assoc. faculty U.S. Open U., 2000—01; advisor Ctr. for Commercialization of Advanced Tech., 2002—; chair CIO sig San Diego Telecom Coun., 2003—. Author: Developing Computer-Based Accounts Receivable, 1981, Manager's Guide to Distributed Data Processing, 1982, How to Implement Management Information Systems, 1983, How to Select Small Business Computer Software, 1984, Business Use of the Internet, 1997; contbr. articles to profl. jours. Treas. Cedar Grove (N.J.) Jaycees, 1977; bd. dirs. Gathering Internat. Families Together, 1983-86, Teraccenter, Inc., 2003—. Decorated Order of Cross and Crescent, 1970; NSF tng. grantee, 1972; recipient Physics medal Seton Hall U., 1970, Tech. Leadership award Hewlett Packard Corp., 1993; Faculty fellow Coll. of N.J., 1998-2001. Mem.: Am. Mgmt. Assn. (info. systems & tech. coun. 1985—, chmn.Year 2000 Forum 1998—2000, editor Mgmt. Handbook, 3d edition), Assn. Info. Tech. Profls. (legis. network 1985—93, bd. dirs. 1988—91, legis. network 1998—, bd. dirs. 2002—, vice president 2003, pres. 2004, Individual Performance award 1987, 1989—90, 1998, 2003), Digital Equipment Computer Users Soc. (U.S. exec. bd. 1977—81), Design Fin. Officers Group (vice chmn. 1992—93, chair 1993—94), Contingency Planning Exch., Assn. Computing Machinery (chair, Info. Mgmt. Working Group 2000—01), Inst. Cert. Computer Profls. (life; cert. data processor, cert. systems profl., cert. computing profl. 1980—82, cert. amb. 1980—82, N.J. state dir. 1989—90), Upsilon Pi Epsilon, Sigma Pi Sigma. Office: Tatum Ptnrs 3878 Ruffin Rd Ste B San Diego CA 92123 E-mail: norbert.kubilus@tatumpartners.com.

KUBINA, PAVEL, professional hockey player; b. Celadna, Czechoslovakia, Apr. 15, 1977; Defense Tampa Bay (Fla.) Lightning, 1997—. Office: Tampa Bay Lightning Ice Palace 401 Channelside Dr Tampa FL 33602

KUBISCH, ANNE CHRISTINE, political scientist; b. Niles, Mich., Nov. 25, 1955; d. Jack Bloom and Constance Rippe Kubisch; m. Mark Randolph Montgomery, June 18, 1988; children: Marina Kubisch Montgomery, Nicholas Kubisch Montgomery. BA cum laude, Tufts U., Medford, Mass., 1977; MS in Pub. and Internat. Affairs, Princeton U., 1984. Rsch. assoc. Battelle Meml. Inst., Washington, 1978—82; staff asst. to David Rockefeller N.Y.C., 1984—85; program officer for L.Am. The Ford Found., N.Y.C., 1985—87, rep. in Ngeria/asst. rep. for West Africa Lagos, Nigeria, 1987—90, program officer, urban poverty program N.Y.C., 1990—92, dep. dir., urban poverty program, 1992—94; dir. roundtable on comprehensive community initiatives The Aspen Inst., N.Y.C., NY, 1994—. Bd. dirs. United Neighborhood Houses of N,T, N.Y.C., 1994—, Nat. Cmty. Bldg. Network, Oakland, Calif., 2001—, Family Support Am., Chgo., 1999—; vice chair of bd. Inst. for Rsch. and Reform in Edn., Phila., 2001—, Youth Devel. Strategies, Inc., Phila., 2001—. Author (editor): (book) Voices from the Field II: Reflections on Comprehensive Community Change, Voices from the Field: Learning from the Early Work of Comprehensive Community Initiatives, New Approaches to Evaluating Community Initiatives, Volume II: Theory, Measurment and Analysis, New Approaches to Evaluating Community Initiatives; contbr. Co-chair of diversity forum The Brearley Sch., N.Y.C., NY, 2002. Achievements include research in Developed new theory about the relationship between racism and urban poverty, and developed approach to evaluating community change based on theory of change.

KUBISTAL, PATRICIA BERNICE, educational consultant; b. Chgo., Jan. 19, 1938; d. Edward John and Bernice Mildred (Lenz) Kubistal. AB cum laude, Loyola U., Chgo., 1959, AM, 1964, AM, 1965, PhD, 1968; postgrad., Chgo. State Coll., 1962, Ill. Inst. Tech., 1963, State U. Iowa, 1963, Nat. Coll. Edn., 1974-75. With Chgo. Bd. Edn., 1959-93, tchr., 1959-63, counselor, 1963-65, adminstrv. intern, 1965-66, asst. to dist. supt., 1966-69, prin. spl. edn. sch., 1969-75; prin. Simpson Sch., 1975-76, Brentano Sch., 1975-87, Roosevelt H.S., 1987, Haugan Sch., 1989; prin. Cook County Juvenile Temporary Detention Ctr. Sch. Jones Met. H.S. Bus. and Commerce, 1989-90, adminstr. dept. spl. edn., 1990-93; supr. Lake View Evening Sch., 1982-92, ednl. cons., 1993—. Lectr. Loyola U. Sch. Edn., Nat. Coll. Edn. Grad. Sch., Mundelein Coll., 1982-91, DePaul U., 1998-99; coord. Upper Bound Program of U. Ill. Circle Campus, 1966-68. Book rev. editor of Chgo. Prins. Jour., 1970-76, gen. editor, 1982-90. Active Crusade of Mercy; mem. com. Ill. Constnl. Conv., 1967-69; mem. Citizens Sch. Com., 1969-71; mem. edn. com. Field Mus., 1971; ednl. advisor North Side Chgo. PTA Region, 1975; gov. Loyola U., 1961-87; pres. St. Matthews Parish Coun., 1995-98. Recipient Outstanding Intern award Nat. Assn. Secondary Sch. Prins., 1966, Outstanding Prin. award Citizen's Sch. Com. of Chgo., 1986; named Outstanding History Tchr., Chgo. Pub. Schs., 1963, Outstanding Ill. Educator, 1970, one of Outstanding Women of Ill., 1970, St. Luke's Logan Sq. Cmty. Person of Yr., 1977; NDEA grantee, 1963, NSF grantee, 1965, HEW Region 5 grantee for drug edn., 1974, Chgo. Bd. Edn. Prins.' grantee for study robotics in elem. schs.; U. Chgo. adminstrv. fellow 1984. Mem. Ill. Personnel and Guidance Assn., NEA, Ill. Edn. Assn., Chgo. Edn. Assn., Am. Acad. Polit. and Social Sci., Chgo. Prins. and Adminstrs. Assn. (pres. aux.), Nat. Coun. Adminstrv. Women, Chgo. Coun. Exceptional Children, Loyal Christian Benevolent Assn., Kappa Gamma Pi, Pi Gamma Mu, Phi Delta Kappa, Delta Kappa Gamma (paliamentarian 1979-80, pres. Kappa chpt. 1988-90, Lambda state editor 1982-92, chmn. Lambda state comm. com. 1992, Internat. Golden Gift Fund award), Delta Sigma Rho, Phi Sigma Tau. Home and Office: 5111 N Oakley Ave Chicago IL 60625-1829

KUBLER, FRANK LAWRENCE, lawyer; b. Pensacola, Fla., July 4, 1957; s. Frank Martin and Esther Helen (Flora) K. AA, Miami-Dade Jr. Coll., 1978; BS in Mech. Enging., U. Miami, Coral Gables, Fla., 1981, BA in History, 1982, JD, 1986. Bar: Fla. 1986, U.S. Cir. Ct. (11th cir) 1988, U.S. Cir. Ct. (fed. cir.) 1989, U.S. Patent Office 1987. Assoc. Dominik, Stein, Saccocio, Reese, Colitz & Van der Wall, Miami Lakes, Fla., 1986-90; pres. Law Office of Frank L. Kubler, Miami Lakes, 1990—; cons. Oltman, Flynn & Kubler, Ft. Lauderdale, Fla., 1990-96, ptnr., 1996—. Mem. Inter-Am. Law Rev., 1985. Mem. Patent Law Assn. South Fla. (v.p. 1993-94, pres. 1994-95), Mensa, Rotary (dir. 1992-94, chmn. scholarship com. 1994-95), Tau Beta Pi. Office: 915 Middle River Dr Ste 415 Fort Lauderdale FL 33304-3561

KÜBLER-ROSS, ELISABETH, physician; b. Zurich, Switzerland, July 8, 1926; came to U.S., 1958, naturalized, 1961; d. Ernst and Emma (Villiger) K.; m. Emanuel Robert Ross, Feb. 7, 1958; children: Kenneth Lawrence, Barbara Lee. MD, U. Zurich, 1957; D.Sc. (hon.), Albany (N.Y.) Med. Coll., 1974, Smith Coll., 1975, Molloy Coll., Rockville Centre, N.Y., 1976, Regis Coll., Weston, Mass., 1977, Fairleigh Dickinson U., 1979; LL.D., U. Notre Dame, 1974, Hamline U., 1975; hon. degree, Med. Coll. Pa., 1975, Anna Maria Coll., Paxton, Mass., 1978; Litt.D. (hon.), St. Mary's Coll., Notre Dame, Ind., 1975, Hood Coll., 1976, Rosary Coll., River Forest, Ill., 1976; L.H.D. (hon.), Amherst Coll., 1975, Loyola U., Chgo., 1975, Bard Coll., Annandale-on-Hudson, N.Y., 1977, Union Coll., Schenectady, 1978, D'Youville Coll., Buffalo, 1979, U. Miami, Fla., 1976; D.Pedagogy, Keuka Coll., Keuka Park, N.Y., 1976. Rotating intern Community Hosp., Glen Cove, N.Y., 1958-59; rsch. fellow Manhattan State Hosp., 1959-62; resident Montefiore Hosp., N.Y.C., 1961-62; fellow psychiatry Psychopathic Hosp., U. Colo. Med. Sch., 1962-63; instr. psychiatry Colo. Gen. Hosp., U. Colo. Med. Sch., 1962-65; mem. staff LaRabida Children's Hosp. and Rsch. Ctr., Chgo., 1965-70; asst. prof. psychiatry, asst. dir. psychiatric consultation and liaison service Billings Hosp., U. Chgo., 1965-71; chief cons. and rsch. liaison sect. LaRabida Children's Hosp. and Rsch. Ctr., 1969-70; med. dir. Family Service and Mental Health Ctr. S. Cook County, Chicago Heights, Ill., 1970-73; pres. Ross Med. Assos. (S.C.), Flossmoor, Ill., 1973-77; pres., chmn. bd. Shanti Nilaya Growth and Health Ctr., Escondido, Calif., 1977—. Consulting psychiatrist Chicago Lighthouse for the Blind, 1965-71; consultant Peace Corps, 1965-71, Illinois State Psychiatric Inst., 1965-71; mem. numerous adv., cons. bds. in field. Author: On Death and Dying, 1969, Questions and Answers on Death and Dying, 1972, Death: The Final Stage, 1974, To Live Until We Say Goodbye, 1978, Working It Through, 1981, Living With Death and Dying, 1981, Remember The Secret, 1981, On Children and Death, 1985, AIDS: The Ultimate Challenge, 1988, On Life After Death, 1991, The Tunnel and The Light: On Life, Death and Life After Death, 1994, The Wheel of Life: Autobiography, 1997, Life Lessons, 2000, Real Taste of Life, 2002; contbr. articles, chapters to books. Named Woman of the Decade, Ladies Home Journ., 1979, One of the 100 Greatest Thinkers of the Century, Time Mag., 2000; recipient Teilhard prize, Teilhard Found., 1981, Golden Plate award, Am. Acad. Achievement, 1980, Modern Samaritan award, Elk Grove Village, Ill., 1976, numerous others. Mem. AAAS, Am. Holistic Med. Assn. (founder), Am. Med. Women's Assn., Am. Psychiat. Assn., Am. Psychosomatic Soc., Assn. Cancer Victims and Friends, Ill. Psychiat. Soc., Soc. Swiss Physicians, Soc. Psychophysiol. Research, Second Attempt at Living. Address: PO Box 6168 Scottsdale AZ 85261-6168

KUBO, KIMBERLY ANNETTE, entrepreneur; b. L.A., Calif., Apr. 30, 1969; d. Arnold Toshio Kubo and Sheryl J. Jai; children: Leah Marie Mortenson, Sarah Grace Mortenson. BA, U. Phoenix; Assoc. of Arts, Fashion Inst. Design and Merchandising. Sales exec. Tardus Fin. Group, Honolulu, 2002—; bus. owner jazziegirl.com, Honolulu, 2002—. Make-up artist He Did It Just For You, 1999. Mem. Kailua Christian Women's Club, 2001. Avocations: reading, pilates, walking. Home: Po Box 22662 Honolulu HI 96823 Home Fax: 808-595-5174. Personal E-mail: shinko25@hotmail.com.

KUBY, BARBARA ELEANOR, personnel director, management consultant; b. Medford, Mass., Sept. 1, 1944; d. Robert William and Eleanor (Frasca) Asdell; m. Thomas Kuby, July 12, 1969. BS in Edn./ Psychology, Kent State U., 1966, MEd, 1987. Tchr. Nordonia/Euclid (Ohio) Pub. Schs., 1966-78; chief tng. officer United Bldg. Factories, Manama, Bahrain, 1979-81; mgr. tng. and devel. Norton Co., Akron, Ohio, 1981-85; v.p. Kuby and Assocs. Inc., Chagrin Falls, Ohio, 1973-91, pres., 1992—2002; corp. dir. human resource devel. and systems TransOhio Savs. Bank, Cleve., 1985-88; asst. v.p. human resources and adminstrv. sys. Leasing Dynamics, Inc., Cleve., 1988-90; dir. human resources, orgnl. devel. GOJO Industries, Akron, 1990-93, v.p. human resources and orgnl. devel., 1993—. Adj. faculty cons. Buffalo State U., 1972—92, Lake Erie Coll., Cleve., 1985—95; lectr., cons. Cleve. State U., 1978—2000; program dir. Ctr. Profl. Advisors, East Brunswick, NJ, 1978—99. Cons., lectr. Girl Scouts U.S., Cleve., 1981—90; colleague Creative Edn. Found.; cons. project bus. Jr. Achievement, 1992—93; trustee Ohio Ballet, 1996—2002; bd. dirs. Apollo's Fire Baroque Orch. Friends, 2003—. Recipient Svc./Commitment award, Creative Edn. Found., 2001. Mem.: ACLU, Gestalt Inst. Cleve., Soc. Orgnl. Learning, Human Resource Planning Soc., Holocaust Meml. Mus., Greenpeace. Avocations: travel, gardening, photography. Home: 7236 Chagrin Rd Chagrin Falls OH 44023-1102

KUBY, RONALD LAWRENCE, lawyer; b. Cleve., July 31, 1956; s. Donald Joseph Kuby and Ruth Miller; m. Marilyn Vasta; 1 child, Emma Sojourner Vasta-Kuby. BA, U. Kans., 1979; JD magna cum laude, Cornell U., 1983. Bar: N.Y. 1984. Assoc. Kunstler & Kuby, N.Y.C., 1994—95, Law Office William M. Kunstler, N.Y.C., 1984—94; ptnr. Law Office Ronald L. Kuby, N.Y.C., 1996—. Contbr. articles to profl. jours. Mem. adv. bd. police misconduct task force N.Y. Civil Liberties Union, 1999—. Recipient Thurgood Marshall award, N.Y. City Bar Assn., 1998, N.Y. Metro Achievement in Radio award for best talk show host, 2000, N.Y. Metro Achievement in Radio award for best talk show, 2001, award for excellence in 9/11 broadcasting, UFA/UFOA (N.Y. Firefighters), 2003. Communist. Office: 740 Broadway Fl 5 New York NY 10003-9518 E-mail: ronkuby@aol.com.

KUC, JOSEPH A. education educator, consultant; b. N.Y.C., Nov. 24, 1929; s. Peter and Helen (Dubec) K.; m. Karola Ingrid Maywald, July 17, 1991; children: Paul D., Rebecca R., Miriam A. BS, Purdue U., 1951, MS, 1953, PhD, 1955. Asst. prof. Purdue U., West Lafayette, Ind., 1955-59, assoc. prof., 1959-63, prof., 1963-74, U. Ky., Lexington, 1974-95, prof. emeritus, 1995—. Contbr. numerous articles to profl. jours. Pres. Cen. Ky. ACLU, Lexington, 1977-79. Mem. Am. Chem. Soc., Am. Phytopathol. Soc., Am. Soc. Plant Physiologists, Am. Soc. for Biochemistry and Molecular Biology, N.Y. Acad. Sci., Phytochem. Soc., Ky. Acad. Sci., Sigma Xi. Avocations: hiking, gardening, conversation. Home and Office: 5502 Lorna St Torrance CA 90503

KUCERA, DANIEL WILLIAM, retired bishop; b. Chgo., May 7, 1923; s. Joseph F. and Lillian C. (Petrzelka) K.. BA, St. Procopius Coll., 1945; MA, Catholic U. Am., 1950, PhD, 1954. Joined Order of St. Benedict, 1944, ordained priest Roman Cath. Ch., 1949. Registrar St. Procopius Coll. and Acad., Lisle, Ill., 1945—49, St. Procopius Coll., Lisle, Ill., 1954—56, acad. dean, head dept. edn., 1956—59, pres., 1959—65; abbot St. Procopius Abbey, Lisle, 1964—71; pres. Ill. Benedictine Coll. (formerly St. Procopius Coll.), Lisle, 1971—76, chmn. bd. trustees, 1976—78; aux. bishop Joliet, Ill., 1977—80; bishop of Salina, 1980—83; archbishop of Dubuque, 1983—95; ret., 1995. Mem.: KC (4 degree). Roman Catholic.

KUCERA, GUSTAV, economics educator; b. Vienna, Nov. 25, 1937; m. Erika Sanitzer, Jul. 19, 1975. Dr jur, Univ. Vienna, 1960. Staff mem. Austrian Inst. Econ. Rsch., Vienna, 1961-62; asst. prof. dept. econs. Univ. Vienna, 1962-75; econ. prof. U. Goettingen, Germany, 1975—. Dir. Seminar fuer Handwerkswesen, Goettingen, 1986—; chmn. rsch. coun. Deutsches Handwerksinsitut, Bonn, 1995—. Author: Die Bedeutung des Nichpreiswettbewerbs fuer Wachstumsmodelle, 1977, Volkswirtschaftspolitik, 1987, Deregulierung des Handwerks, 1990; editor: Goettinger Handwerkswirtschaftliche Studien, 1986. Mem. Verein fur SocialPolitik, Nat. Econs. Gesellschaft, Goettinger Rechtswissenschaftliche Gesellschaft. Office: Univ Goettingen Platz der Goettinger Sieben 3 D 37073 Goettingen Germany

KUCERA, HENRY, linguistics educator; b. Trebarov, Czechoslovakia, Feb. 15, 1925; arrived in U.S., 1949, naturalized, 1953; s. Jindrich and Marie (Kral) K.; m. Jacqueline M. Fortin, Oct. 6, 1951; children: Thomas Henry, Edward James. MA, Charles U., Prague, Czechoslovakia, 1947, PhDr, 1991; PhD, Harvard U., 1952; MA ad eundem, Brown U., 1958; DSc (hon.), Bucknell U., 1984; PhilD (hon.), Masaryk U., Brno, Czechoslovakia, 1990. Asst. prof. fgn. langs. U. Fla., 1952-55; from mem. faculty to prof. emeritus Brown U., 1955—90, prof. emeriitus, 1990—; mem. Ctr. for Cognitive Sci., 1977-85, exec. com., 1980-86; mem. Ctr. for Neural Studies, 1973-90, exec. com., 1977-90; dir. Inst. for Cognitive and Neural Research, 1981-88. Fellow Russian Rsch. Ctr., Harvard U., 1952, 79-87, rsch. assoc. Slavic dept., 1977-79; rsch assoc. MIT, 1960-63; vis. prof. U. Mich., 1967, U. Calif. at Berkeley, 1969; vis. scholar U. Vienna, 1968-69; pres. Lang. Software Systems, Inc., 1982-2001. Author: The Phonology of Czech, 1961, (with W.N. Francis) Computational Analysis of Present-Day American English, 1967, (with G. Monroe) A Comparative Quantitative Phonology of Russian, Czech and German, 1968, Computers in Linguistics and in Literary Studies, 1975, (with K. Trnka) Time in Language, 1975, (with W.N. Francis) Frequency Analysis of English Usage, 1982; also linguistic and lit. articles.; Editor: American Contributions to the Sixth International Congress of Slavists, 1968. Bd. dirs. Internat. Inst. Providence, 1960-67; bd. adminstrn. Howard Found., 1977-95; mem. R.I. Com. for Humanities, 1986-90. Ford fellow, 1954-55; Howard Found. fellow, 1960-61; Guggenheim fellow, 1960-61; sr. fellow NEH, 1968-69; Am. Council Learned Socs. fellow, 1969-70 Hon. fellow Linguistic Soc. of Czech Acad. Scis.; mem. MLA, Linguistic Soc. Am., Czechoslovak Soc. Arts and Scis. in Am. (v.p. 1980-82), Prague Linguistic Circle (hon.), Phi Beta Kappa. Home: 107 Freedom Shores Rd Freedom NH 03836-5105 E-mail: Henry_Kucera@brown.edu.

KUCHARSKI, THOMAS EDWARD, secondary school educator; b. Chgo., Ill., Aug. 17, 1962; s. Chester and Anita Kucharski; m. Paula Walker, Oct. 11, 1986; children: Nicholas, Rachael. PhD, Loyola U., 2002. Cert. tchr. Ill. Tchr. Loyola U., Chgo., 1991—94, Loyola Acad., Wilmette, Ill., 1987—94, New Trier H.S., Winnetka, Ill., 1994—. Adviser New Trier H.S., Wilmette, 1995—2002, negotiator, Winnetka, 1996—2002; tour leader New Trier Ext., Winnetka, 1999—2002; pres. Loyola Acad. PA, Wilmette; presenter in field. Recipient grant to study Mozart in Vienna, NEH, 1998, Spl. Recognition for Tchg., MIT, Charlton Coll., others. Liberal. Avocations: travel, reading. Home: 1522 N Pine Arlington Heights IL 60004 Office: New Trier H S 385 Winnetka Ave Winnetka IL 60093 Personal E-mail: kucharst@nttc.org.

KUCHEMAN, CLARK ARTHUR, philosophy and religious studies educator; b. Akron, Ohio, Feb. 7, 1931; s. Merlin Carlyle and Lucile (Clark) K.; m. Melody Elaine Frazer, Nov. 15, 1986. BA, U. Akron, 1952; BD, Meadville Theol. Sch., 1955; MA in Econs., U. Chgo., 1959, PhD, 1965. Instr., then asst. prof. U. Chgo., 1961-67; prof. Claremont (Calif.) McKenna Coll., 1967—, Claremont Grad. Sch., 1967—. Co-author: Belief and Ethics, 1978, Creative Interchange, 1982, Economic Life, 1988; contbg. editor: The Life of Choice, 1978; contbr. articles to profl. jours. 1st lt. USAF, 1955-57. Mem. Am. Acad. Religion, Hegel Soc. Am., N.Am. Soc. for Social Philosophy. Democrat. Home: 10160 60th St Riverside CA 92509-4745 Office: Claremont McKenna Coll Dept Philosophy Religon Pitzer Hall 850 Columbia Ave Claremont CA 91711-6420 E-mail: clark.kucheman@claremontmckenna.edu. *Education and life itself have the same purpose, and, borrowing words from G. W. F. Hegel, "...the final purpose of education is liberation and the struggle for a higher liberation still."*

KUCHLER, JOSEPH ALBERT, surgeon; b. Feb. 20, 1948; BS, St. Joseph's U., 1970; MD, Jefferson Med. Sch., 1974. Resident gen. surgery Cooper Hosp. U. Med. Ctr., 1974-78; resident cardiothoracic surgery U. Louisville, 1978-80; attending surgeon Our Lady of Lourdes Med. Ctr., Camden, N.J., 1980—, Cooper Hosp., Camden, 1980—, West Jersey Health Sys., Marlton, N.J., 1980—. Home: 2 Tanbark Ct Kirkwood Voorhees NJ 08043-1544 Office: 455 Route 70 W Cherry Hill NJ 08002-3524 E-mail: jkuchler@erols.com.

KUCHNER, EUGENE FREDERICK, neurosurgeon, educator, neuroscientist; b. N.Y.C., 1945; s. Morton H. and Edna Estelle Kuchner; m. Joan Ruth Freedman, Sept. 2, 1968; children: Marc Jason, Eric Benjamin. AB, Johns Hopkins U., 1967; MD, U. Chgo., 1971. Diplomate Am. Bd. Neurol. Surgery, Am. Bd. Med. Examiners. Resident in surgery Yale U. Sch. Medicine, New Haven, 1971-72; resident in neurosurgery Montreal (Que., Can.) Neurol. Inst., McGill U., 1972-76, spine fellow, 1976; neurosurgeon SUNY Downstate Sch. Medicine, Bklyn., 1976-79, SUNY Sch. Medicine, Stony Brook, 1979—, assoc. prof., 1983—; cons. neurosurgeon North Shore U. Hosp./NYU Sch. Medicine, 1997—. Mem. staff North Shore U. Hosp.-Cornell Med. Ctr., 1977—97, cons. surgeon, 1977—97; mem. staff Univ. Hosp., Stony Brook, 1979—97, Nassau County Med. Ctr., 1977—2000, St. John's Hosp., 1976—99, Mt. Sinai-NYU Health Sys., 1997—, Nassau U. Med. Ctr., 2000—. Contbr. articles to profl. pubs.; specialist in microsurgery, magnetic resonance imaging, spinal trauma, pituitary surgery. Recipient K.G. McKenzie Meml. award Royal Coll. Physicians and Surgeons Can., 1976, Open Scholarship award Johns Hopkins U., yearly, 1963-66, Scholarship award U. Chgo., yearly, 1967-70; NSF fellow, MIT chemistry fellow, 1968, Blackman-Hoffman Found. fellow, 1969-70, USPHS fellow, 1969. Mem. ACS, AMA, Am. Assn. Neurol. Surgeons, Congress Neurol. Surgeons, N.Y. Acad. Scis., L.I. Neurosci. Acad., Suffolk Acad. Medicine, Montreal Neurol. Ins. Fellows Soc., N.Y. State Neurosurg. Soc., N.Y. State Med. Soc., N.Y. State Soc. Surgeons, Am. Coll. Med. Quality, Healthcare Info. and Mgmt. Sys. Soc., Am. Epilepsy Soc., Am. Soc. Law Medicine and Ethics, Yale Surg. Soc., Yale Club N.Y.C., Sigma Xi. Office: Stony Brook Med Ctr PO Box 721 Stony Brook NY 11790-0721

KUCHTA, BEATRICE L. ESKEN, English educator; b. Pitts., Sept. 29, 1944; d. Christopher and Betty Beatrice (Gerhold) Esken; m. Kenneth K. Worton, Apr. 3, 1965; children: Eric J. Worton, Jill A. Worton Peters, Joi L. Worton Schwartz; m. Edward A. Kuchta, July 18, 1981. BS in Secondary Edn. English, California U. of Pa., 1966, MS in Counseling Edn., 1983. Cert. tchr., Pa.; lic. life ins., real estate agt., Pa. Tchr. art, phys. edn., English Munhall (Pa.) H.S., 1966-68; real estate salesperson, realtor Mt. Lebanon, Pa., 1970-76; sales assoc. J.C. Penney Co., Inc., Bridgeville, Pa., 1976-78; tchr. English Baldwin-Whitehall Sch. Dist., Pitts., 1979; tchr. English, econs., Japanese lang. and culture South Park (Pa.) Sch. Dist., Pa., 1980—. Amb. to Japan, Pa. Dept. Edn., Harrisburg, 1994, del. to Australia, 1997. Author, illustrator: Which Age Is Best?, 1995. Sunday sch. tchr. Jefferson Hills (Pa.) Bible Ch., 1995-99. Recipient Tchrs. Excellence award, 1999, 2000; name inscribed on Wall of Tolerance. Mem. NEA, Nat. Coun. English Tchrs., South Park Edn. Assn. (bldg. rep. 1997-), Pa. State Edn. Assn., Western Pa. Real Estate Investors Assn., Steel Valley Mother of Twins Club (charter). Avocations: travel, flower arranging, real estate, gourmet cooking. Home: 255 Coleen Dr Pittsburgh PA 15236-4308 Office: South Park Sch Dist 2178 Ridge Rd Ste 2 South Park PA 15129-8806 E-mail: edward.kuchta@verizon.net.

KUCHTA, RONALD ANDREW, art museum director, magazine editor, curator; b. Lackawanna, N.Y., June 23, 1935; s. Andrew and Clara May (Barnes) K.; m. Sique Stoll, Oct. 1, 1970 (div. 1974). BA, Kenyon Coll., 1957; MA, Western Res. U., 1961; postgrad. in mgmt., Cornell U., 1979. Curator Chrysler Mus., Provincetown, Mass., 1961-68, Santa Barbara (Calif.) Mus. Art, (Calif.), 1968-74; dir. Everson Mus. Art, Syracuse, N.Y., 1974-95; editor Am. Ceramics mag., 1995; assoc. Loveed Fine Arts, N.Y.C., 1995. Adj. prof. Syracuse U., 1974—95; trustee Fondo del Sol, Washington, 1974—, Nat. Conf. Educators of Ceramic Arts, 1986, Quarry Rd. Sculpture Pk., Cazenovia, NY; founding dir. Syracuse China Ctr. for Study of Am. Ceramics; chmn. Urban Arts Commn., Syracuse, 1992—93; juror Mino '89 Internat. Competition for Ceramics, Gifu, Japan, 1989, Concorso Internat. della Ceramica d'Arte, Faenza, Italy, 1990, Biennale Nat. de Ceramique, Trois Rivieres, Que., Canada, 1992, 2d Cairo Internat. Biennale Ceramics, 1994, Millenium Art Ctr., Phila., 1997, San Angelo (Tex.) Ceramic Nat., 1998, Ariz. Commn. on the Arts, 1999, 1st World Biennale for Ceramics, Ichon, Republic of Korea, 2001, 2d World Biennale for Ichon, 2003, No. Clay Ctr. McKnight Awards, Mpls., 2003; bd. dirs. Watershed Ctr., North Edgecomb, Maine, Longhouse Res., Easthampton, NY, Mus. Ceramic Art, N.Y.C.; lectr. U. Regina, Sask., Canada, Mimar Sinan U., Istanbul, Turkey, Alta. Coll. Art, Calgary, Calif. Conf. Advancement of Ceramic Art, Davis, Nat. Mus. History, Taipei, Taiwan, 1993, Japan Soc., N.Y.C., 1994, Czech Ceramic Design Ctr., Cesky Krumlov, 1996, Internat. Acad. Ceramics, Nagoya, Japan, 1996, Nat. Arts Club, N.Y.C., Bard Coll., N.Y.C., 1997, Cleve. Mus. Art, Stetson U., DeLand, Fla., Washington U., St. Louis, 1997, Santa Barbara City Coll., 1998, Cotta Terra Symposium, Deruta, Italy, 1998, Konstfack U. Coll. Arts, Crafts and Design, Stockholm, 1998, Royal Coll. Art, London, 1998, Oslo (Norway) Internat. Ceramic Symposium, 2003; curator Enigmatic Visions/Sublime Forms Contemporary Japanese, 1998, Ceramic Longhouse Res., Easthampton; keynote spkr. Craft Futures Conf., Victoria and Albert Mus., London, 1998, consuming craft Buckinghamshire Chiltern U. Coll., 2000; keynote spkr., curator Oslo Internat. Ceramics Symposium, 2003. Author: Mayan Figurines, 1971, Interior Vision, 1971, Modern Mexican Art, 1972, Provincetown Painters, 1975, Batuz: Works in Paper, 1981, Robert Beauchamp: An American Expressionist, 1984, The Elegiac and the Primordial:

Ceramics at the End of the Twentieth Century, 1997, Consuming Ceramics: Its Classification and Place in the U.S. Art Market, 2001, Norwegian Clay and the Possible Superiority of Ceramics, 2003, Elimination and Affirmation: The Potent Process of the Jury; pub.: A Century of Ceramics in the U.S., 1979, American Ceramics: Collection of Everson Museum of Art, 1989; translator: Pre-Hispanic Art: Time and Culture, 1997. With U.S. Army, 1958-60. Mem.: Assn. Art Mus. Dirs. (emeritus), Nat. Arts Club, Internat. Acad. Ceramics, Phi Kappa Sigma. Democrat. Episcopalian. Home: 60 Sutton Pl S New York NY 10022-4168 Office: Am Ceramics Mag 9 E 45th St New York NY 10017-2425

KUCHYNSKI, MARIE, physician; b. Cleve., Sept. 23, 1964; d. Harry Gregory and Albina (Guarnera) K.; m. K. William Burdick; children: Nicole, Marie, Burdick. BA, Case Western Reserve U., 1986, MD, 1990. Diplomate in internal medicine and in rheumatology Am. Bd. Internal Medicine. Intern U. Hosps. Cleve., 1990-91, resident, 1991-93; physician pvt. practice, Elyria, Ohio, 1995-98; pvt. practice Brunswick, Ohio, 1998—. Mem. utilization mgmt. com Cleve Health Network, 1996 98; med. advisor Tri-City Lupus Project, 1997-98. Rheumatology fellow U. Hosps. Cleve., 1993-95. Mem. AMA, Am. Coll Physicians, Am. Coll. Rheumatology, Cleve. Soc. Rheumatology, Phi Beta Kappa. Democrat. Roman Catholic. Avocations: gardening, crafts, piano. Home: 21503 Brookfield Place Strongsville OH 44149 Office: Univ Primary Care Practice 3812 Center Rd Brunswick OH 44212-3024

KUCIC, JOSEPH, management consultant, industrial engineer, network engineer, information security specialist; b. Mali Losinj, Croatia, Yugoslavia, Dec. 21, 1964; came to U.S., 1967, naturalized, 1974; s. Roman Kucic and Esterina (Karcic) Milevoj; m. Gia Michelle Bonavisa, Sept. 11, 1992; children: Ann Marie, Jillian Michelle. AAS, Coll. of Aeronautics, 1984; BS, Thomas A. Edison State Coll., 1986; B in Tech., N.Y. Inst. Tech., 1986; MBA, St. John's U., Jamaica, N.Y., 1989. Workload planner Butler Aviation-Newark, Inc., Newark, 1984-85; tech. planner N.Y. Airlines, Flushing, N.Y., 1985-86; product support engr. United Techs.-Pratt & Whitney, East Hartford, Conn., 1986; indsl. engr. Montefiore Med. Ctr., Bronx, 1986-88; sr. work mgmt. analyst Bank Leumi Trust Co., N.Y.C., 1988-89; sr. methods analyst Salomon Bros., Inc., N.Y.C., 1989-92; mgmt. cons. United Mgmt. Techs., N.Y.C., 1992-93; sr. sys. analyst Met. Hosp. Ctr. N.Y.C. Health & Hosp. Corp. Metro. Hosp. Ctr., 1993; dir. info. svcs. N.Y.C. Health & Hosp. Corp. Bronx Mcpl. Hosp. Ctr., 1993-94; project mgr. Montefiore Med. Ctr., Bronx, N.Y., 1994-96, ANS Comms., Inc., Elmsford, N.Y., 1996; mgr. infrastructure planning, divsn. of Am. Online ANS Comms., Inc., 1996-97; mgr. KPMG Peat Marwick, Hawthorne, N.Y., 1997-98; sr. mgr. KPMG LLP, N.Y.C., 1998-2000; dir. profl. svcs. Network Assocs., Inc., 1999; mng. dir. Pricewaterhouse Coopers, LLP, N.Y.C., 2000—02; cons. GM Asset Mgmt., N.Y.C., 2002—. Spkr. in field. Contbr. articles to profl. jours. Mem.: Asn. Computing Machinery Computer Security Inst., Coll. Aeronautics Alumni Asn. (pres. 1990-92), SAE (affiliate), AIAA, IEEE (assoc.), Inst. Indsl. Engr. (chpt. pres. 1988-89, chmn. bd. N.Y.C. chpt. 1989-90, bd. govs. 1988-92, Cert. of Recognition 1988) (sr.), St. John's Univ. Col. Bus. Admin. Alumni Asn. (bd. dir. 1991-93), Wings Club N.Y., Tau Alpha Pi. Republican. Roman Catholic. Avocation: tennis. Home: 11B Relay Pl Cos Cob CT 06807-2714 also: 767 5th Ave New York NY 10153 E-mail: jkucic@mail.com.

KUCIJ, TIMOTHY MICHAEL, engineer, minister, musician; b. Whittier, Calif., Sept. 2, 1954; m. Paulina V Jimenez, 1979. Studied with Frank Sanucci, Edward D. Berryman, Thurla Wallis, Kathreen Prout, Eddy L. Manson, Henry Charles Smith, Joseph P. Free, Ronald Gearman, 1965—78; student, Sherwood Music Conservatory, Chgo., 1965-68; BA in Music, Calif. State Poly. U., Pomona, 1978; ThM cum laude, Christian Bible Coll., 1983; grad. studies, Maranatha Bapt. Bible Coll, Central Baptist Theological Seminary. Licensed minister Bapt. Ch., 1982. Tech. writer Honeywell Inc., West Covina (Calif.) and Mpls., 1977-84; hydromech. reliability engr. Advanced Systems divsn. Northrop Corp., Pico Rivera, Calif., 1984-86; sr. engr. quality and reliability Swedlow, Inc., Garden Grove, Calif., 1986-88, mgr., quality assurance, composites divsn., 1988-90, quality assurance staff specialist, 1990-92; div. quality assurance engr. Rexroth Corp. divsn. Piston Pump, Fountain Inn, SC, 1992-94; sr. quality engr. Hi-Shear Corp., Torrance, Calif., 1996-98; sr. quality sys. mgr. TRW Automotive, Carson, Calif., 1998—. Lectr. tech. and engring.; tchr. piano, organ and composition, 1971—81; active pulpit supply local Bapt. Chs., Calif., SC. Performer (pipe organ) Wiltern Theater, L.A., 1966—68, Busch-Reisinger Mus. Harvard U., Cambridge, Mass., 1972, 1973, 1974; composer: scores of original piano pieces including Persistence and The Storm, Purity, Remembrance, Your Song, Yearning, Compassion, A Little Jingle, A Familiar Song, Images, Paulina, Afterthought, Blue Fragrance, Sunset, Then, Piano Lesson # 1, Chase, Unrest, Nebulae, Distress, Retrograde, Frolic, The Happy Whistler, The Little Toy March, Hope, Teardrops, Reminisce, Wind Chimes, A Place Somewhere, Rainbows, The Bicentennial Rag, The Pulsar Rag, Dazzling Fingers, The Butterfly Rag, Serenity, first 25 original pieces written in honor of Am. bicentennial; compositions housed in numerous librs. including L.A. County Libr., St. Louis Pub. Libr., Atlanta-Fulton County Libr., The Master's Coll. Libr., Calif. State Poly. U. Libr., Archive of Contemporary Music, N.Y.C., Phila. Free Libr., Juilliard Sch. Music Libr., Calif. Bapt. Coll. Libr., Biola U. Libr., N.Y. Pub. Libr., Cleve. Pub. Libr., Boston Pub. Libr., Harvard U. Libr.; musician: debut, 1966, (recordings) KRC Records, 1993—, A Place Somewhere, 1993, 2003, LifeSongs, 1993, 2003; concertized nationally (piano, pipe organ), scored comprehensive piano arrangements Jesus Loves Me, Over the Rainbow, songwriter Jesus is the Answer, O Jesus; editor: The Golden State Baptist, 1995—96; contbr. articles. Asst. to local pastors Bapt. chs. in Tex., Ga., Wis., Minn., and Calif., 1978—82; pastor Victory Bapt. ch., Pine City, Minn., 1982—83; music dir., Bible tchr. Calvary Bapt. Ch., La Verne, Calif., 1988—92, mem. sch. bd., ch. coun., 1989—92; music dir., youth dir. Covina Bapt. Temple, 1985—87; pastor First Missionary Bapt. Ch., Gardena, Calif., 1994—96; bd. dirs. Garden Grove Symphony Orch., 1989—90. Named one of Outstanding Young Men in Am., U.S. Jaycees, 1980; recipient First prize, So. Calif. Organ Competition, 1966, Performer's cert., 1967, Disting. Alumnus award, Calif. State Poly. U., 1989. Mem.: Christian Fellowship Art Music Composers, Broadcast Music, Inc., Am. Symphony Orch. League, Am. Soc. Quality, Creation Rsch. Soc., Am. Composer's Forum. Republican. Home: 2239 W 236th Pl Torrance CA 90501-5950

KUCINICH, DENNIS J. congressman; b. Oct. 8, 1946; 1 child, Jackie. Student, Cleveland State U.; BA, MA, Case Western Reserve U. Pres. K Comm., Cleve.; v. pres. sales and mktg. Town and Country Printing, Cleve.; councilman City of Cleve., 1969-73, clk. of mcpl. ct., 1975-77, mayor, 1977-79; senator State of Ohio; mem. U.S. Congress from 10th Ohio dist., 1997—; mem. edn. and the workforce, govt. reform coms.; chair. Congress. Prog. Caucus. Named Outstanding Pub. Official, Internat. Eagles. Democrat. Office: US Ho of Reps 1730 Longworth Ho Office Bldg Washington DC 20515-3510*

KUCKELMAN, BRIAN THOMAS, architect; b. Kansas City, Kans., Aug. 11, 1954; s. Paul J. and Bernice J. (Neeley) K.; m. Pamela J. Uhlmeyer, July 6, 1979; children: Crystal, Tyler, Michelle. BA in Architecture, U. N.Mex., 1977. Draftsman McHugh/Grenfell Architects, Santa Fe, N.Mex., 1977-79; project architect Architectural Svcs., Hilo, Hawaii, 1979-84; project mgr. Pace Constrn., Tucson, 1984-89, Doubletree Hotels Corp., Phoenix, 1989-94; v.p. facility devel. Meta Assocs., Louisville, 1994-96; v.p. design and constrn. Omni Hotels, Irving, Tex., 1996—. Membership v.p. Lehua Jaycees, Hilo, 1984. Republican. Roman Catholic. Office: Omni Hotels 420 Decker Dr Irving TX 75062-3952

KUCZMARSKI, SUSAN SMITH, management consulting company executive; b. Portland, Oreg., Apr. 24, 1951; d. Fernando Martin and Bula Grace (Weddle) Smith; m. Thomas Dale Kuczmarski, Aug. 21, 1976; children: John Thomas, James Smith, Thomas Michael. BA, Colo. Coll., 1973; MIA, Columbia U., 1975, MEd, 1978, EdD, 1979. Instr. U. Ill., Chgo., 1976-77, Nat.-Louis U., Evanston, Ill., 1986-88; lectr. Dominican U., River Forest, Ill., 1977-78; asst. prof. Concordia U., River Forest, 1977-79; edn. dir. Constl. Rights Found., Chgo., 1979-81; assoc. dir. devel., instr. Northwestern U., Evanston, 1981-84; exec. v.p. Kuczmarski & Assocs., Chgo., 1984—. Instr. Colo. Coll., Colorado Springs, 1998; trustee Edward Lowe Found., Cassopolis, Mich., 1986-96. Author: The Family Bond: Inspiring Tips for Creating a Closer Family, 2000, The Sacred Flight of the Teenager: A Parent's Guide to Stepping Back and Letting Go, 2002; author, editor: Youth and Society: Rights and Responsibilities, 2d edit., 1980; co-author: Values-Based Leadership: Rebuilding Employee Commitment, Performance, and Productivity, 1995; book rev. editor Jour. Internat. Affairs, 1973-75. Vol. Harlem Tutorial Program, N.Y.C., 1973-74; trustee Chgo. City Day Sch., Chgo., 1996—. Internat. House fellow, 1974, Columbia U. Sch. Internat. Affairs fellow, 1974-75, Columbia U. internat. fellow, 1975-76. Mem. Com. on Fgn. Affairs, Kappa Alpha Theta. Democrat. Roman Catholic. Avocation: foreign travel. Office: 1165 N Clark St Chicago IL 60610-2702

KUCZWARA, THOMAS PAUL, postal inspector, lawyer; b. Dec. 21, 1951; s. Stanley Leo and Eleanore (Pawelko) K.; m. Diana Lynn Rychtarczyk, Sept. 8, 1979; 1 child, Paul Stanley. BA, Loyola U., Chgo., 1973; JD, U. S.C., 1976. Bar: Ill. 1976, U.S. Dist. Ct. (no. dist.) Ill. 1982. Assoc. Doria Law Offices, Chgo., 1977-78; asst. corp. counsel City of Chgo., 1978-80; asst. city atty. City of Aurora, Ill., 1980-82; postal insp. U.S. Postal Inspection Svc., Salt Lake City, 1982-85, regional insp. atty. cen. region Chgo., 1985—. Mem. St. Bartholomew's Parish Coun., Chgo., 1978; vol. atty. Lawyers for Creative Arts, 1978. Ill. state scholar, 1969. Mem. Sierra Club, Pi Sigma Alpha. Roman Catholic. Office: US Postal Inspection Svc Chgo Divsn 433 W Harrison 6th Fl Chicago IL 60669-2201 E-mail: tpkuczwara@uspis.gov.

KUCZYNSKI, JOHN-MICHAEL MAXIME, humanities educator, writer; b. Washington, Aug. 21, 1972; s. Pedro-Pablo Godard Kuczynski. BA, UCLA, 1997. Author: Elements of Virtualism: A Study in the Philosophy of Perception, 2003; contbr. articles to profl. jours. Home and Office: PO Box 14163 Santa Barbara CA 93107 Personal E-mail: jsbach@jps.net.

KUCZYNSKI, LES STANISLAUS, non-profit organization administrator; b. Lubeck, Germany, June 3, 1947; came to U.S., 1950; s. Lucjan Joseph and Maria (Szurminska) K.; m. Alice D. Borzym, June 14, 1986; 1 child, Andrew Lucas. BA, St. Thomas U., 1969; JD, U. Minn., 1972; MBA, Keller Grad. Sch. Mgmt., 1982. Gen. counsel Ill. Bur. Employment Security, Chgo., 1975-83, Polish Nat. Alliance, Chgo., 1985—; nat. exec. dir. Polish Am. Congress and Charitable Found., Chgo., 1990—. Mem. appeals panel forced labor compensation program Internat. Orgn. for Migration, Geneva; mem. nat. adv. com. Holocaust and War Victims Tracing and Info. Ctr., ARC; pres. coun. World Polonia, 2002—; mem. Senate Consultative Com. for Rels. with Polonia. Mem. scholar com. Gladstone-Norwood Bank, Chgo., 1991—; pres. Homeowners Assn. Condomunium Assn., Forest Park, Ill., 1980-82; dir. Homeowners Assn. Cmty. Group, Park Ridge, Ill., 1994; chmn. Polish-Am. Polit. League, Chgo., 1990—; mem. adv. bd. Litewska Children's Hosp., Chgo., 1994—; mem. sch. bd. Mary, Seat of Wisdom Sch., Park Ridge, 2002—. Mem. John Paul II Soc. (pres. 1986, sec. 1994). Avocations: reading, aerobics, movies, cross-country skiing, gardening.

KUCZYNSKI, PEDRO-PABLO, investor; b. Lima, Peru, Oct. 3, 1938; s. Maxime and Madeleine Louise (Godard) K.; married; 4 children. BA, Exeter Coll., Oxford (Eng.) U., 1959; M.P.A., Princeton U., 1961. Economist World Bank, 1961-67, sr. economist, 1971-73; dep. dir.-gen. Central Res. Bank Peru, 1967-69; sr. economist Internat. Monetary Fund, Washington, 1969-71; v.p., partner Kuhn, Loeb & Co. Internat., N.Y.C., 1973-75; dir. dept. econs. Internat. Finance Corp., Washington, 1975-77; pres., chief exec. officer Halco Mining Inc., Pitts., 1977-80; minister of energy and mines Peru, 1980-82; chmn., mng. dir. First Boston Internat. Co., N.Y.C., 1982-92; pres., CEO Westfield Capital Ltd., Miami, Fla., 1992—; minister of economy and finance Peru, 2001—02. Pres., CEO The Latin America Enterprise Fund L.P., 1995—; bd. dirs. ROC Taiwan Fund, Tenaris, Inc. Mem. Am. Econ. Assn., Univ. Club (Washington), Pitts. Golf Club, Racquet and Tennis Club. Home: 626 Coral Way Coral Gables FL 33134 Office: The Latin Am Enterprise Fund LLP 2665 S Bayshore Dr Miami FL 33133-5448 E-mail: pkuczynski@laef.com.

KUDDES, KATHRYN M. fine arts director; b. Midland, Tex., July 11, 1960; d. Fred M. and Dale M. Springer; m. Kenton C. Kuddes. MusB, Millikin U., 1983; Master in Music Edn., U. North Tex., 1995. Cert. provisional all-level music tchr. Tex., tchr. Kodály tng. Tex., profl. supr. Tex. . Choral dir. 6-12 Stafford Mcpl. Sch. Dist., Stafford, Tex., 1983—86; elem. music specialist Killeen Ind. Sch. Dist., Killeen, Tex., 1986—89, Coll. Sta. Ind. Sch. Dist., College Station, Tex., 1989—94; grad. tchg. fellow U. North Tex., Denton, Tex., 1994—95; elem. music specialist Plano Ind. Sch. Dist., Plano, Tex., 1995—98, K-12 coord. vocal music, 1998—2000, dir. fine arts. V.p. Kodály Educators Texas, 1992—97; pres. so. divsn. Orgn. Am. Kodály Educators, 1997—2001. Editor: (profl. newsletter) KET Encounter, 1997. Mem. P.E.O. Sisterhood, Allen, 1987—2002. Named nationally registered music educator, Music Educators Nat. Conf., 1993. Mem.: Assn. Supervision and Curriculum Devel., Am. Orff-Schulwerk Assn., Texas Music Adminstrs. Conf., Orgn. Am. Kodály Educators (pres. so. divsn. 1997—2001), Kodály Educators Tex. (v.p. 1992—97), Am. Choral Dirs. Assn., Tex. Choral Dirs. Assn., Music Educators Nat. Conf., Tex. Music Educators Assn. Avocations: music, folk instruments, travel. Office: Plano Ind Sch Dist 2700 W 15th St Plano TX 75075 Office Fax: 469-752-8039. Business E-Mail: kkuddes@pisd.edu.

KUDDUS, RUHUL HAQUE, medical educator; arrived in US, 1984; s. Mohammad Johurul Haque and Jalegan Nesa; m. Nahid Akhter Khanm, June 15, 1980; children: Nayema, Nasique, Raisa, Noah. MSc, U. Dhaka, Bangladesh, 1979; MS, George Mason U., 1987; PhD, U. Pitts., 1993. Rsch. assoc. U. Pitts., 1993—99, instr., 2000—01, asst. prof., surgery, 2001—02. Editor: Journ. of Bangladesh Studies, 1990, Development Issues of Bangladesh, 1995, Development issues of Bangladesh II, 2002. Pres. Bangladesh Devel. Initiative, Seattle, 1999—, Bangladesh Am. Assn., Pitts., 1999—2001. Recipient U. scholar, U. Dhaka, 1976, Deans scholar, U. Pitts., 1989. Mem.: Starzl Transplantation Inst., Am. Assn. for Advancement of Sci. Democrat. Home: 231 Greenfield Ave Pittsburgh PA 15217 Office: U of Pitts 200 Lothrop St Pittsburgh PA 15213 Office Fax: 412-624-6666. E-mail: kuddusrh@msx.upmc.edu.

KUDELKA, JAMES, choreographer, artistic director; b. Newmarket, Ont., Can. Student, Nat. Ballet Sch., Toronto. Dancer Nat. Ballet of Can., Toronto, 1972-81, artist in residence, 1992-96; prin. dancer Les Grands Ballets Canadiens, Montreal, 1981-84, resident choreographer, 1984-90; works created for San Francisco and Joffrey Ballets, Am. Ballet Theatre, Birmingham Royal Ballet; artistic dir. Nat. Ballet Can., 1996—. Choreographer (ballets) Sonata, Nat. Ballet of Can., 1973, A Party, 1976, Washington Square, 1977, The Rape of Lucrece, 1980, Playhouse, 1980, All Night Wonder, 1981, Pastorale, 1990, Musings, 1991, The Miraculous Mandarin, 1993, The Actress, 1994, Spring Awakening, 1994, The Nutcracker, 1995, The Four Seasons, 1997, Swan Lake, 1999, The Firebird, 2000, The Contract, Nat. Ballet Can., 2002, Genesis, Les Grands Ballets Canadiens, 1982, In Paradisum, 1983, Alliances, 1984, Le Sacre du Printemps, 1987, La Salle des Pas Perdus, 1988, Concerto Grosso, 1988, Cruel World, Am. Ballet Theatre, 1994, States of Grace, 1995, Dreams of Harmony, San Francisco Ballet, 1987, The End, 1992, Terra Firma, 1995, Some Women and Men, 1998, Le Baiser de la fée, Birmingham Royal Ballet, The Book of Alleged Dances, Australian Ballet, 1999, Fifteen Heterosexual Duets, Toronto Dance Theatre, Six Tableaus for the Sexually Challenged, Montreal Danse, Passage, 1981, Intimate Letter, 1981, Hedda, 1983, Court of Miracles, 1983. Office: The National Ballet of Canada 470 Queens Quay W Toronto ON Canada M5V 3K4 E-mail: info@ballet.ca.

KUDER, ARMIN ULRICH, lawyer; b. Phila., Nov. 14, 1935; s. David Dennis and Ethel Rose (Strasburger) Kuder; m. Patricia A. Hipple, June 28, 1959 (div. Mar. 1968); children: Carlyn Elizabeth, Eric David, Keith Ulrich; m. Margaret A. Trossen, July 26, 2002. AB, Lafayette Coll., 1956; LLB, Harvard U., 1959. Bar: D.C. 1959, Md. 1987, U.S. Ct. Mil. Appeals 1962, U.S. Dist. Ct. Md. 1968. Assoc. Coles & Goertner, Washington, 1963-65, Mehler, Smollar et al., Washington, 1965-67; ptnr. Smollar & Kuder, Washington, 1967-68, Kuder, Sherman et al., Washington, 1968-78, Kuder, Smollar & Friedman P.C., Washington, 1978—. Lectr. continuing legal edn., various locations. Chmn. Nat. Health Agys., NCAC, 1977—78, Ctr. Marine Conservation, Washington, 1981—83, NIMH human subjects rev. panel, 1978—83; vice chmn. Arthritis Found., Atlanta, 1979—80, 1990—92, chmn., 1992—94; pres. Arthritis and Rheumatism Internat., 1996—98, treas., 1998—; mem. internat. steering com. The Bone and Joint Decade, Lund, Sweden, 2000—; bd. dirs. Can. Arthritis Network, 2001—02; chmn. Hyde Sch., Bath, Maine, 1984—87, New Art Assn., Washington, 1986—87; sec. Combined Health Appeal, Washington, 1984; mem. Gov.'s Adv. Coun. on the Future of Nursing in Va., 2002—. Served to lt. comdr. JAGC USNR, 1959—63. Fellow Am. Acad. Matrimonial Lawyers, Internat. Acad. of Matrimonial Lawyers; mem. ABA, D.C. Bar Assn. (trustee client security fund 1984-92, chmn. 1991-92, hearing com. chmn. bd. on profl. responsibility 1985-91), Md. Bar Assn., Montgomery County Bar Assn., Bar Assn. D.C. Office: Kuder Smollar & Friedman PC 1925 K St NW Washington DC 20006-1105 E-mail: akuder@ksflaw.com.

KUDLACZ, MICHAEL S. career officer; b. Omaha; BS in Criminal Justice, U. Nebr., Omaha, 1971; student, Squadron Officer Sch., 1974; M in Sociology, Pepperdine U., 1977; student, Air Command and Staff Coll., 1983, Indsl. Coll. Armed Forces, 1989. Commd. 2d lt. USAF, 1971, advanced through grades to maj. gen., 1999; stationed at Beale AFB, Calif., 1972-76, Ellsworth AFB, S.D., 1976-79; RF-4C asst. flight comdr./flight comdr., asst. ops. officer 91st Tactical Reconnaissance Squadron, Bergstrom AFB, Tex., 1980-81; wing and base airspace mgr. then chief current ops. div. 67th Tactical Reconnaissance Squadron, Bergstrom AFB, Tex., 1981-82; chief programs and requirements div. Hdqs. Strategic Air Command, Offutt AFB, Nebr., 1983-84, chief officer assignments div., dep. chief staff personnel, 1984-85; comdr. 62d Bombardment Squadron, Barksdale AFB, La., 1985-86; chief aircrew tng. div. Hdqs. Strategic Air Command, Offutt AFB, Nebr., 1986-87, exec. officer dep. chief of staff ops., 1987-88; chief N. Am. br. joint staff J-5 Pentagon, Washington, 1989-91, dep. comdr. for ops. 42nd bomb wing, comdr. 42nd ops. group Loring AFB, Maine, 1993-95, comdr. 416th bomb wing Griffiss AFB, N.Y., 1995-97, comdr. 55th wing Offutt AFB, Nebr., 1997-98, dir. personnel programs edn. and tng., deputy chief of staff for personnel, 1998—, deputy dir. of ops. and tng. to dir. of ops. and tng., dir. Air and Space ops., 1998—. Decorated Legion of Merit with oak leaf cluster, Def. Meritorious Svc. medal, Meritorious Svc. medal with four oak leaf clusters, Air medal, Air Force Commendation medal with oak leaf cluster, Combat Readiness medal with 2 oak leaf clusters, Armed Forces Expeditionary medal. Address: HQ USAF/XOO 1480 Air Force Pentagon Washington DC 20330-1480

KUDO, EMIKO IWASHITA, former state official; b. Kona, Hawaii, June 5, 1923; d. Tetsuzo and Kuma (Koga) Iwashita; m. Thomas Mitsugi Kudo, Aug. 21, 1951; children: Guy J.T., Scott K., Candace F. BS, U. Hawaii, 1944; MS in Vocat. Edn., Pa. State U., 1950; postgrad., U. Hawaii, U. Oreg. Tchr. jr. & sr. h.s., Hawaii, 1945-51; instr. home econs. edn. U. Hawaii Tchrs. Coll., Honolulu, 1948-51, Pa. State U., State College, 1949-50; with Hawaii Dept. Edn., Honolulu, 1951-82, supr. sch. lunch svc., 1951-64, home econs. edn., 1964-68, adminstr. vocat.-tecy. edn., 1968-78; dep. supt. State Dept. Edn., Honolulu, 1978-82, cons. Am. Samoa vocat. edn. state plan devel., 1970-71; vocat. edn. U. Hawaii, 1986. Internat. secondary program devel. Ashiya Ednl. Sys., Japan, 1986-91; cons. to atty. gen. mental health svcs. for children and adolscents State of Hawaii, 1994; chief planner devel. State of Hawaii Children & Adolscents Mental Health Svcs. Implementation Plan, 1994-95; state coord. industry-labor-edn., 1972-76; mem. nat. task force edn. and tng. for minority bus. enterprise, 1972-73; mem. steering com. Career Info. Ctr. Project, 1973-78; co-dir. Hawaii Career Devel. Continuum project, 1971-74; mem. Nat. Accreditation and Instl. Eligibility Adv. Coun., 1974-77, cons., 1977-78; mem. panel Internat. Conf. Vocat. Guidance, 1978, 80, 82, 86, 88; state commr. edn. commn. of the states, 1982-90; mem. Hawaii edn. coun., 1982-90. Author handbooks and pamphlets in field. Dir. Dept. Parks and Recreation, City and County of Honolulu, 1982-84; bd. dirs. Honolulu Neighborhood Housing Svcs., 1991—; exec. bd. Aloha coun. Boy Scouts Am., 1978-88; bd. trustees St. Louis H.S., 1988-95; mem. Gov.'s Commn. on Sesquicentennial Observance of Pub. Edn. in Hawaii, 1990-91; mem. Commn. State Rental Housing Trust Fund, 1992-98; mem. steering com. Hawaii Long Term Care Coalition, 1992—. Japan Found. Cultural grantee, 1977; Pa. State U. Alumni fellow, 1982; named to Konawaea H.S. Hall of Fame, 1997. Mem. ASCD, NEA, Am. Assn. Retired Persons (mem. state legis. com. 1990-92), Pa. State U. Disting. Alumni, Western Assn. Schs. and Colls. (accreditation team mem. Ch. Coll. of Hawaii 1972-73), Am. Vocat. Assn., Hawaii Vocat. Assn., Hawaii Edn. Assn. (trustee 1992—), Hawaii State Ednl. Officers Assn., Am. Family Consumer Sci. Assn., Hawaii Assn. Curriculum & Devel., Am. Tech. Edn. Assn., Hawaii Recreation and Park Assn., Omicron Nu, Pi Lambda Theta, Phi Delta Kappa, Delta Kappa Gamma. Home and Office: 217 Nenue St Honolulu HI 96821-1811

KUDRAVETZ, DAVID WALLER, lawyer; b. Sumter, S.C., Feb. 2, 1948; s. George and Barbara (Waller) K.; m. Eleanor McCrea Snyder, June 21, 1969; 1 child, Julia McCrea. BS, U. Va., 1971, JD, 1974. Bar: Va. 1974, U.S. Tax Ct. 1974; CPA, Va. Assoc. Robert M. Musselman, Charlottesville, Va., 1974; ptnr. Carwile & Kudravetz, Charlottesville, Va., 1975-78, McClure, Callaghan & McCallum, Charlottesville, Va., 1979-81, McCallum & Kudravetz, P.C., Charlottesville, Va., 1982—. Instr. fed. income taxation U. of Va. Sch. Continuing Edn., 1975-79. Mem. AICPA, Va. State Bar Assn., Charlottesville-Albemarle Bar Assn., Am. Assn. Atty.-CPAs, Va. Soc. CPAs. Office: McCallum & Kudravetz PC 250 E High St Charlottesville VA 22902-5178 E-mail: DWK@MKPC.com.

KUDRLE, ROBERT THOMAS, economist, educator; b. Sioux City, Iowa, Aug. 23, 1942; s. Chester John and Helen Marguerite (Crakes) K.; m. Venetia Hilary Mary Thomas, July 20, 1970; children: Paul John Reginald, Thomas David Chester. AB, Harvard U., 1964, AM, 1969, PhD, 1974; MPhil., U. Oxford, Eng., 1967. Grad. rsch. assoc. Ctr. Internat. Affairs Harvard U., Cambridge, Mass., 1969-71; instr. Tex. A & M Univ., College Station, 1971-72; asst., assoc. prof. Humphrey Inst. U. Minn., Mpls., 1972-83, asst., assoc. dir. Ctr. Internat. Studies, 1972-82, prof. Humphrey Inst., 1983—, dir. MA program pub. affairs, 1984-86, dir. Freeman Ctr. Internat. Econ. Policy, 1990-97, assoc. dean rsch. Humphrey Inst., 1992-96. Cons. U.S. Dept. Justice, U.S. AID, Urban Inst., UN Ctr. Transnat. Corps., Consumer and Corp. Affairs Can., WHO, others. Author: Agricultural Tractors: A World Industry Study, 1975; co-author State Evaluation of Foreign Sales Efforts, 1988; co-editor Reducing the Cost of Dental Care, 1983, The Industrial Future of the Pacific Basin, 1984, Jour. Internat. Studies Quarterly, 1980-84, 85; mem. editorial bd. Internat. Political Economy Yearbook, 1983—, Jour. Health Politics, Policy & Law, 1981-92; contbr. articles to profl. jours., chpts. to texts. First v.p. UN Assn. Minn., Mpls., 1976-78, mem. adv. coun., 1978-88. Graduate prize fellow Harvard U., 1967-69, Pew Faculty fellow in Internat. Affairs Harvard U., 1990-91; Nuffield Coll. studentship, Oxford, Eng., 1966-67; Rhodes scholar, Oxford, Eng., 1964-67. Mem. Assn. Pub. Policy Analysis and Mgmt. (instl. rep. 1988-97), Internat. Studies Assn. (v.p. 1998-99), Am. Econ. Assn., Harvard Club Minn. Avocations: running, gardening. Home: 4650 Fremont Ave S Minneapolis MN 55409-2263 Office: Humphrey Inst Pub Affairs 301 19th Ave S Ste 300 Minneapolis MN 55455-0429

KUDROW, LISA, actress; b. Encino, Calif., July 30, 1963; m. Michael Stern, May 27, 1995; 1 child, Julian. BS in Biology, Vassar Coll., Poughkeepsie, N.Y., 1985. TV appearances include Bob, Cheers, Coach, Newhart, Flying Blind, Mad About You, 1991-99, Friends, 1994— (Emmy for outstanding supporting actress, 1997 & 1998, American Comedy Award, 2000, Emmy for outstanding performance by a female actor, 2000, Golden Satellite for best actress, 2000); appeared in (films) The Carazysitter, 1995, Romy and Michele's High School Reunion, 1997, Clockwatchers, 1997, The Opposite of Sex, 1998 (NY Film Critics Circle Award, 2000), Hercules (voice) 1998, Analyze This, 1998, Hanging Up, 2000, All Over the Guy, 2001, (voice) Dr. Dolittle 2, 2001, Analyze That, 2002.

KUDRYASHEVA, ALEXANDRA A. microbiologist, radiobiologist, biotechnologist, educator; b. Tula, Russia, Jan. 1, 1934; d. Andrew P. and Neonila K. (Volkonogova) Chernozhukov; m. Michael N. Kudryashev (div.); m. Dan B. Chopyk, Dec. 19, 1990. BS in Biology, All-Union Inst. Food Industry, Moscow, 1965, DSc, 1969; PhD in Tech. Biol. Scis., Russia, 1983; PhD (hon.), Volgograd Tech. Inst., 1996. Technologist Glavkonserv Food Ministry, Govt. of USSR, Eisk, 1954-61, head. of lab. irradiation microbiology Tula, 1962-71; from asst. prof. to prof. Russian Acad. Economy, Moscow, 1971-93, dean tech. and commodities, 1983-85, head dept. biotech., 1985-93; head food resources Inst. of Human Ecology, Moscow, 1993-97; pres. Internat. Ctr. Nutrition and Health Rehab., Toms River, N.J., 1997—; cons. UNO, 2001—02. V.p. radiology of food products, Russian Acad. Agr., Moscow, 1976-89; pres. Assn. of Commodities Specialists of USSR, 1985-91; chmn. cert. com. Coun. of Ministers of USSR, 1989-96; sec. commodities sect. Ministry of Edn., Govt. of USSR, 1978-85. Contbr. more than 400 articles to sci. and profl. jours., books; holder more than 50 patents. Mem. Russian Acad. Natural Scis. (silver medal), Union of Concerned Scientists, N.Y. Acad. Scis., Internat. Info. Acad. (internat. prize

1998). Achievements include new technologies of manufacture and application of natural bio-correctors for food, medicine, agriculture and ecology. Avocations: travel, photography, ethnic cooking, poetry. Home and Office: 106 Guadeloupe Dr Toms River NJ 08757

KUEBLER, CHRISTOPHER ALLEN, pharmaceutical executive; b. Hamilton, Ohio, Oct. 31, 1953; s. William E. and E. Dean (Morgan) K.; m. Susan Kuebler; children: Megan, Lauren, Samantha. BS, Fla. State U., 1975. Various sales and product mgmt. positions E.R. Squibb & Sons, Princeton, N.J., 1976-84; mgr. product devel. Monsanto Health Care, St. Louis, 1985-86; group product mgr. Abbott Pharms., Abbott Park, Ill., 1986-89, v.p. mktg. and sales, 1989-93; corp. v.p. European operation Abbott Internat., Abbott Park, 1993-95; chmn., CEO Covance Inc., Princeton, 1995—. Bd. mem. Nat. Pharm. Coun., Washington, Inhale Therapeutic Systems, San Carlos, Calif.; mem. mktg. steering com. Pharm. & Rsch. Mfrs. Assn., Washington, 2001--. Office: Covance Inc 210 Carnegie Ctr Princeton NJ 08540-6233

KUEBLER, DAVID WAYNE, insurance company executive, private investigator; b. New Orleans, Apr. 18, 1947; s. Royce Matthew and Rosemary (West) K.; children: Kira Louise. B. in Bus. Mgmt., Loyola U., New Orleans, 1969. Lic. ins. broker, investment mgr.; lic. investigator, La. Asst. mgr. Winn-Dixie, Inc., New Orleans, 1962-69; account exec. Travelers Ins. Co., St. Louis, 1969-74; sr. account exec. Gen. Am. Life., St. Louis, 1974-76; dist. mgr. Guardian Life Ins., New Orleans, 1976-81; pres. Profl. Planners, Inc., Kenner, La., 1981—, Louisiana-detectives.com, 2001, Pro-Care, Inc., 1983—. Asst. chief of staff civil mil. ops. 377 Taacom, New Orleans, 1987. Coach girls athletics, Metairie, La., 1987. Col. USAR. Mem.: Bus. Espionage Controls and Countermeasures Assn., Christian Investigators Am., Christian Legal Soc., Met Plus Group Millionaires, Million Dollar Round Table, Christian Motorcycle Assn. Democrat. Roman Catholic. Avocations: coaching girls softball and basketball. Home: 29 Chateau Haut Brion Kenner LA 70065 Office: Profl Planners Inc PO Box 640877 Kenner LA 70064-0877 E-mail: dwkuebler@cs.com.

KUECHLE, JOHN MERRILL, lawyer; b. Mpls., Dec. 18, 1951; s. Harry Bronson and Virginia (McClure) K.; m. Nancy Anderson, June 20, 1976; 1 child, David Michael. AB magna cum laude, Occidental Coll., 1974; JD cum laude, Harvard U., 1977. Bar: Calif. 1977. Assoc. Mitchell, Silberberg & Knupp, L.A., 1977-83, ptnr., 1983-2000, of counsel, 2001—. Mem. Phi Beta Kappa. Republican. Episcopalian. Avocations: masters track and field, orienteering, rock climbing. Home: 10733 Ranch Rd Culver City CA 90230-5458 Office: Mitchell Silberberg & Knupp 11377 W Olympic Blvd Los Angeles CA 90064-1625 E-mail: jmk@post.harvard.edu.

KUEHL, ALEXANDER EDWARD, physician, health facility administrator, medical educator, writer; b. St. John, Nfld., Can., Aug. 12, 1944; came to U.S., 1945; s. Frederick George and Olivia Kendall (Dwyer) K.; 1 child, Kendall Ann Warsaw. BA, Johns Hopkins U., 1966, MPH, 1976; MD, Syracuse U., 1970. Bd. cert. in orthopaedic surgery; bd. cert. in emergency medicine. Intern Univ. Hosp., Syracuse, 1970-71, resident, 1971-73, Johns Hopkins Hosp., 1974-78; fellow in emergency med. svc. and trauma Univ. Hosp., Balt., 1978-79; dir. med. affairs Md. Inst. Emergency Med. Svcs., Balt., 1979-81; v.p. med. dir. N.Y.C. Health & Hosps. Corp., 1981-89. Chairperson N.Y.C. Regional Coun., 1988—89, N.Y.C. Med. Adv. Com., 1981—97; med. dir. CVPH Emergency Care Ctr., 1997—2000, Noble Hosp., 2000—; commr. pub. health St. Lawrence County, 2001—; mem. adv. bd. WHO, 1985. Author: (textbooks) Medical Director's Handbook, 1989, Prehospital Systems and Medical Oversight, 2002. Chmn. Mayoral Transition (Health), N.Y.C., 1993. Lt. col. USAR. Fellow ACS, Am. Coll. Emergency Med. Dispatch (pres. 1994-99), fellow Am. Coll. Emergency Physicians; mem. Nat. Assn. Emergency Med. Svc. Physicians (founding mem., bd. dirs. 1986-97. Stewart award 1990), Clinton County Med. Soc. (pres. 1996-2002), Pub. Health Honor Soc. Johns Hopkins U. Home: 6 Rocky Edge Rd Morristown NY 13664 Office: EJ Noble Hosp 77 W Barney St Gouverneur NY 13642 E-mail: ejnoble-akuehl@northnet.org.

KUEHL, HANS HENRY, electrical engineering educator; b. Detroit, Mar. 16, 1933; s. Henry Martin and Hilde (Schrader) K.; m. Anna Meidinger, July 25, 1965; children: Susan, Michael. BS, Princeton U., 1955; MS, Calif. Inst. Tech., 1956, PhD, 1959. Asst. prof. elec. engring. U. So. Calif., 1960-63, assoc. prof., 1963-72, prof., 1972—, chmn. dept. elec. engring., electrophysics, 1987-98. Cons. Deutsch Co., L.A., 1973, Hughes Aircraft Co., Culver City, Calif., 1975. Contbr. articles to profl. jours. Recipient U. So. Calif. Teaching Excellence award, 1964, Haliburton award U. So. Calif., 1980. Fellow IEEE; mem. Am. Phys. Soc., Internat. Sci. Radio Union, Eta Kappa Nu (bd. dirs. 2000-02, Outstanding Faculty award 1977). Avocations: tennis, racquetball. Office: U So Calif Elec Engring Dept Phe 622 Mc 0271 Los Angeles CA 90089-0271 E-mail: kuehl@usc.edu.

KUEHL, KAREN SIMPSON, cardiologist, researcher; b. Memphis, Tenn., Mar. 15, 1940; d. William and Evelyn Berg S.; m. W. Michael Kuehl, Oct. 25, 1939; children: Peter, Sarah, Matthew. BA, Swarthmore Coll., Swarthmore, Pa., 1961; MD, Harvard U., Boston, 1965; MPH, Joohns Hopkins U., Balt., 1997. Diplomate Am. Bd. Pediats. Resident pediat. Cleve. Met. Gen. Hosp., 1965—67; fellow pediatric cardiology Children's Nat. Med. Ctr., Washington, 1967—69, cardiologist, 1981—85, prof. pediat., 1998—; staff physician Nat. Heart Lung and Blood Inst., Bethesda, Md., 1969—71; assoc. prof. Georgetown U. Sch. Medicine, Washington, 1987—98; asst. prof., cardiologist Einstein Coll. Medicine, Bronx, NY, 1971—75; asst prof., pediat. A. Einstein Sch. Medicine, New York, NY, 1971—72; fellow then asst. prof., adj. U. Va., Charlottesville, 1975—81, asst. prof., rsch. assoc.; assoc. prof. George Washington U. Sch. Medicine, Washington, 1982—89. Mem. and chmn. FDA Panel on Circulatory Devices, Washington, 1988—92. Contbr. articles. Devel. of Kids Cholesterol Club grant, Kellogg Co., 1985-1989. Fellow: Am. Coll. Cardiology (life), Am. Acad. Pediat. (life); mem.: Children's Nat. Health Network Bd. (assoc.), Internat. Soc. Adult Congenital Cardiac Disease (assoc.), Internat. Soc. Environ. Epidemiology (assoc.). Society Of Friends. Achievements include development of Education course for adults with congenital heart disease; Education Services for adults with congenital heart disease. Office: Children's Nat Med Ctr 111 Michigan Ave NW Washington DC 20010 Office Fax: 202-884-5700. E-mail: kkuehl@cnmc.org.

KUEHL, SHEILA JAMES, state legislator; b. Tulsa, Feb. 9, 1941; d. Arthur Joseph and Lillian Ruth (Krasner) K. BA, UCLA, 1962; JD, Harvard U., 1978. Actress, 1950-65; assoc. dean of students UCLA, 1969-75; pvt. practice L.A., 1978-85; law prof. Loyola U. of L.A., 1985-89; mng. atty. Calif. Women's Law Ctr., L.A., 1989-93; mem. Calif. State Assembly, Sacramento, 1995-2000, spkr. pro tem, 1997-99, chair jud. com., 1999-2000; mem. Calif. State Senate, 2001—, chmn. natural resource com., 2001—. Appeared in TV series Broadside, 1964-65, as Zelda Gilroy in Dobie Gillis, 1959-63, as Jackie Erwin in Trouble with Father, 1950-56. Mem. gender bias adv. com. Calif. Supreme Ct., 1985-91; bd. overseers Harvard U., 1997—. Named One of 20 Most Fascinating Women in Politics, George Mag., 1996, named One of 100 Most Influential Attys. in Calif., Calif. Law Bus., 1998; recipient Barry Goldwater Human Rights award, 1998, Legislator of Yr., Calif. Pks. and Recreation Soc., 1999, Pub. Svc. award UCLA Alumni Assn., 2000, Liberty award Lambda Legal Def. Edn. Fund, 2002, Women in Govt. award Good Housekeeping, 2003. Mem. Women Lawyers' Assn. of L.A. (pres. 1986-87). Office: State Capitol Sacramento CA 95814-4906

KUEHLING, ROBERT WARREN, lawyer, accountant; b. Madison, Wis., Aug. 31, 1952; s. Warren Ernest and Mary Alice (Jenkins) K.; m. Susan Mary O'Brien, July 8, 1978; children: Megan Ann, Jeffrey Robert. BBA, U. Wis., JD, 1976. Bar: Wis. 1977, U.S. Dist. Ct. (we. dist.) Wis. 1977; CPA. Ptnr. Kuehling & Kuehling, Madison, 1977—. Lawyer, accountant; b. Madison, Jr. Aug. 31, 1952; s. Warren Ernest and Mary Alice (Jenkins) K.; m. Susan Mary O'Brien, July 8, 1978; children— Megan Ann, Jeffrey Robert. B.B.A., U. Wis., J.D., 1976. Bar: Wis. 1977, U.S. Dist. Ct. (we. dist.) Wis. 1977; C.P.A. Ptnr. Kuehling & Kuehling, Madison, 1977— . Office: Kuehling & Kuehling 131 W Wilson St Ste 501 Madison WI 53703-3243 E-mail: kuehling@execpc.com.

KUEHN, FRANCES, painter; b. N.Y.C., Feb. 16, 1943; d. Irving and Sarah (Bauman) Tannenbaum; m. George C. Kuehn, Dec. 21, 1963 (div. Nov. 1979); 1 child, Beth Kuehn Monge; m. Raymond T. Hoobler, June 30, 1990. BA, Rutgers U., 1964, MFA, 1971. One-woman shows include Max Hutchinson Gallery, N.Y.C., 1974, N.J. State Mus., Trenton, 1976, A.M. Sachs Gallery, N.Y.C., 1978, Phoenix Gallery Project Rm., N.Y., 2001, Ben Shahn Gallery, William Paterson U., Wayne, N.J., 2002, exhibited in group shows at Whitney Mus. Am. Art, 1972, 1973, Lowe Art Mus., Coral Gables, Fla., 1974, Akron (Ohio) Art Inst., 1974, Voorhees Art Gallery, New Brunswick, N.J., 1977, Gallery Henoch, N.Y.C., 1994, Mitchell Algus Gallery, 2002, Tatischeff Gallery, 2003, Represented in permanent collections Allen Meml. Art Mus., Oberlin (Ohio) Coll., Newark Mus., Power Inst., U. Sydney (Australia), others. N.J. State Coun. Arts fellow, 1978—79, Nat. Endowment Arts fellow, 1982—83. Home and Office: 789 W End Ave Apt 4D New York NY 10025-5417 E-mail: rthcc@cunyvm.cuny.edu.

KUEHN, GEORGE E. lawyer, former beverage company executive; b. N.Y.C., June 19, 1946; m. Mary Kuehn; children: Kristin, Rob, Geoff. BBA, U. Mich., 1968, JD, 1973. Bar: Mich. 1974. Assoc. Hill, Lewis et al, Detroit, 1974-78; ptnr. Butzel, Long et al, Detroit, 1978-81; exec. v.p., gen. counsel, sec. The Stroh Brewery Co., Detroit, 1981-99—; shareholder Butzel Long, Detroit, 2000—. With U.S. Army, 1969-71. Office: Butzel Long Ste 900 150 W Jefferson Ave Detroit MI 48226 E-mail: Kuehn@butzel.com.

KUEHN, JAMES MARSHALL, newspaper editor; b. Mobridge, S.D., May 23, 1926; s. Christ A. and Selma (Brandon) K.; m. Phyllis Yvonne Larson, Apr. 3, 1950; children— Douglas James, Deborah Kay, Diana Lisa. BA, U.S.D., 1949. State editor Rapid City (S.D.) Jour., 1949-54, wire editor, 1954-58, mng. editor, 1958-66, exec. editor, 1966-73, v.p.-editor, 1973-86. Vice pres. Rapid City Library Bd., 1969-73; dir. Mt. Rushmore Nat. Meml. Soc., 1991—. Served with C.E. AUS, 1945-46. Mem. Rapid City C. of C. (v.p. 1970-73), S.D. C. of C. (dir. 1978-81), Lambda Chi Alpha. Lodges: Kiwanis (pres. 1973-74). Republican. Lutheran. E-mail: jmpykuehn@rushmore.com.

KUEHN, RICHARD ARTHUR, telecommunications consultant; b. Cleve., Jan. 31, 1939; s. Arthur John and Alice (Schilling) K.; m. Cynthia Louise Shideler, Dec. 31, 1984. BBA, Case Western Res. U., 1960. V.p. Warwick Communications, Cleve., 1957-62; pres. RAK Assocs., Cleve., 1962—. Author: Cost Effective Telecommunications; editor Telecom. Info. Mgmt. Jour., 1999; columnist Bus. Communications Rev., 1974—; contbr. 100 articles to profl. jours. Mem. Soc. Telecommunication Cons. (founder). Home and Office: RAK Assocs 17894 Clifton Park Ln Cleveland OH 44107-1027

KUEHN, RONALD L., JR., natural resources company executive; b. Bklyn., Apr. 6, 1935; m. Allison Spencer, June 7, 1986; children: Kathleen, Kelly, Erin, Coleen, Shannon, Caroline, Ronald L. III. BS, Fordham U., 1957, LL.B., 1964. Bar: N.Y. 1964. Assoc. Hughes, Hubbard & Reed, N.Y.C., 1964-68; exec. v.p., gen. counsel Allied Artists Pictures, N.Y.C., 1968-70; v.p., gen. counsel, sec. So. Natural Resources, Inc., Birmingham, Ala., 1970-79, exec. v.p., 1979-81; pres., COO Sonat Inc., 1982-83, pres., 1982-99, CEO, 1983-99, chmn., 1986-99; chmn. bd. El Paso Corp., 1999-2000, also bd. dirs., ret., 2001, chmn., CEO, 2003—. Bd. dirs. Transocean Offshore, Inc., AmSouth Bancorp., Praxair Inc., The Dun & Bradstreet Corp.; trustee Tuskegee U. 1st lt. U.S. Army, 1958-59. Mem. ABA, N.Y. State Bar Assn., Assn. of Bar of City of N.Y., Fed. Energy Bar Assn., Newcomen Soc. of U.S., Bretton Woods Com. Roman Catholic.*

KUEHNE, CARL W. food products executive; CEO, pres. Am. Foods Group, Dakota Pork Industries. Office: Am Foods Group PO Box 8547 544 Acme St Green Bay WI 54308-8547

KUEHNE, DALE STANWAY, minister, political science educator; b. Mpls., July 25, 1958; s. Norman William and Janet Mae (Stanway) K.; m. Rachel Brynne Gustafson, Aug. 30, 1980; children: Naomi, Leah, Ryan. BA, U. Minn., 1981; MA, Gordon-Conwell Theol. Sem., 1985, Georgetown U., 1989, PhD, 1993. Ordained min. Evangel. Covenant Ch. Byington fellow Gordon-Conwell Theol. Sem., South Hamilton, Mass., 1984-85; fellow Georgetown U., Washington, 1985-89; assoc. prof. polit. sci., dir. Pryor Program Leadership Studies William Jewell Coll., Liberty, Mo., 1989—94; assoc. prof. polit. sci. St. Anselm Coll., Manchester, NH, 1994—, founding dir. N.H. Inst. Politics, 1999—2002; pastor Emmanuel Covenant Ch., Nashua, NH, 2001—. Earhart Found. fellow, 1988-89. Mem. Am. Polit. Sci. Assn. Home: 136 Sagamore St Manchester NH 03104-3666 Office: St Anselm Coll 100 St Anselm Dr Manchester NH 03102

KUEHNLE, KENTON LEE, lawyer; b. Chgo., Nov. 10, 1945; s. Robert Louis and Mary Caroline (Recktenwald) K.; m. Sherry L. Esposito, June 6, 1970; children: Robert, Amanda, Matthew. BA, Augustana Coll., 1967; JD, Duke U., 1970. Bar: Ohio 1970, U.S. Dist. Ct. (so. dist.) Ohio 1971. Assoc. Dunbar, Kienzle & Murphey, Columbus, Ohio, 1970-77; ptnr. Loveland, Callard & Clapham, Columbus, 1977-80, Scott, Walker & Kuehnle, Columbus, 1980-86, Thompson, Hine & Flory, Columbus, 1986—2001, Roetzel & Andress, Columbus, 2001—, Allen, Kuehnle & Stovll, Columbus, 2003—. Mem., lectr. standard forms com. Columbus Bd. Realtors; instr. paralegal program Capital U. Law Sch., 1998-2001. Author: Ohio Real Estate Law; co-author: (seminar book) Foreclosure Law, 1989-98, Title Insurance Endorsements, 1991-97, Commercial Leasing, 1994-97, Condominium Law, 1981-97, Use of Internet for Real Estate Lawyer, 1997; contbr. articles to profl. jours. Mem. Augustana Coll. Alumni Bd., Rock Island, Ill., 1986-89; trustee Madison Plains Scholarship Found., Madison County, Ohio, 1986—; elder First Presbyn. Ch., Grove City, Ohio, 1990-93; pres. Computer Users Group, Columbus, 1985-86. Mem. ABA (sect. real property, probate and trust law 1973—, com. on condominium and coop. housing 1977—), Columbus Bar Assn. (chmn. real property com. 1976-78, chmn. micro computer subcom. 1986-87, 92-94, lectr. for bar assn. seminars), Ohio State Bar Assn. (bd. govs. real property sect. 1979-82, 90—, chmn. 1997-99, editor state real property sect. newsletter 1995-99, chmn. subcom. to rev. condominium statute 1980-81, lectr. continuing legal edn. programs), Am. Coll. Real Estate Lawyers (sec. title ins. subcom.), Coun. Ethics in Econs., Honesty in Bus., Legal Profession Task Force, Joseph Fletcher Lawyers Conf. (ann. ethics conf., spkr. selection chair). Avocations: computer programming, baseball, theology. Home: 11325 Big Plain Circleville Rd Orient OH 43146-9301 Office: Roetzel & Andress 155 E Broad St Ste 1200 Columbus OH 43215-3609 E-mail: kkuehnle@prodigy.net.

KUELBS, JOHN THOMAS, lawyer; b. Springfield, Minn., Sept. 8, 1942; s. Alois Nicholas and Lucille Marie (Neudecker) K.; m. J. Michele Norton; children: Susan, Thomas. BA, St. John's U., Collegeville, Minn., 1965; JD, Creighton U., 1973. Bar: Nebr. 1973, Calif. 1980, U.S. Ct. Claims, U.S. Ct. Appeals (9th circuit), U.S. Ct. Appeals (D.C. circuit), U.S. Supreme Ct. Sr. counsel Ford Aerospace, Newport Beach, Calif., 1976-78, divsn. counsel, 1978-81; group counsel Hughes Aircraft, El Segundo, Calif., 1981-86, staff v.p., asst. gen. counsel, 1986-88, v.p., assoc. gen. counsel L.A., 1988-94, sr. v.p., gen. counsel Arlington, Va., 1994-98; sr. v.p. legal Raytheon Sys. Co., Arlington, 1998-99, sr. v.p. acquisition policy, 1999. Col. (ret.) JAGC, U.S. Army, 1976. Mem. ABA (pub. contract law sect. coun. 1992-94, coun. officer 1994-96, sec. pub. contract law sect. chair 1996-97), FBA, Calif. Bar Assn., Nebr. Bar Assn.; fellow ABA Pub. Contract Law Assn., Nat. Contract Mgmt. Assn. Office: Raytheon Corp Ops 1100 Wilson Blvd Ste 1500 Arlington VA 22209-2297

KUELTHAU, PAUL STAUFFER, lawyer; b. West Bend, Wis., Mar. 31, 1912; s. George Herman and Marie Louise (Rix) K.; m. Laura Parish, Aug. 16, 1937; children: Karen Allan, Marline Holmes. AB, U. Wis., 1934, JD, 1936. Bar: Wis. 1936, U.S. Ct. Appeals (10th cir.) 1941, U.S. Ct. Appeals (7th cir.) 1947, Mo. 1953, U.S. Dist. Ct. (ea. dist.) Mo. 1954, U.S. Ct. Appeals (8th cir.) 1962, U.S. Dist. Ct. (so. dist.) Ill. 1964, U.S. Supreme Ct. 1973, U.S. Ct. Appeals (D.C. cir.) 1974. Regional atty. NLRB, various locations, 1939-46, chief counsel to chmn. Washington, 1946-53; assoc. Lewis, Rice, Tucker, Allen & Chubb, St. Louis, 1953-62; ptnr. Moller, Talent, Kuelthau, & Welch, St. Louis, 1962-88. Contbr. articles to profl. jours. Mem. ABA, Mo. Bar Assn., Bar Assn. St. Louis, Indsl. Relations Research Assn. Presbyterian. Home: 3 Rehabilitation Way Apt 417 Woburn MA 01801-6025

KUENNE, ROBERT EUGENE, economics educator; b. St. Louis, Jan. 29, 1924; s. Edward Sebastian and Margaret (Yochum) K.; m. Janet Lawrence Brown, Sept. 7, 1957; children: Christopher Brian, Carolyn Leigh Jeppsen. Student, Harris Jr. Coll., St. Louis, 1941-42; B.J., U. Mo., 1947; AB, Washington U., St. Louis, 1948, A.M., 1949, Harvard, 1951, PhD, 1953; PhD (hon.), Umea U., 1985. Asst. prof. econs. U. Va., 1955; mem. faculty Princeton (N.J.) U., 1956—, assoc. prof., 1960-69, prof. econs., 1969—. Cons. U.S. Naval War Coll., 1954, 55, Inst. Def. Analyses, Arlington, Va., 1968—2001, Inst. for Energy Analysis, Washington, 1978-82; vis. prof. mil. systems analysis U.S. Army War Coll., 1967-85; mem. sci. and mgmt. adv. com. U.S. Army Computer Systems Command. Author: The Theory of General Economic Equilibrium, 1963, The Attack Submarine: A Study in Strategy, 1965, The Polaris Missile Strike: A General Economic Systems Analysis, 1966, Monopolistic Competition Theory: Studies in Impact, 1967, Microeconomic Theory of the Market Mechanism, 1968, Eugen von Böhm-Bawerk, 1971, Rivalrous Consonance, 1986, Economics of Oligopolistic Competition, 1992, General Equilibrium Economics, 1991, Economic Justice in American Society, 1993, Price and Nonprice Rivalry in Oligopoly: The Integrated Battleground, 1999. Served with AUS, 1943-46. Named Oliver Ellsworth Bicentennial preceptor, 1975-60; fellow European Econs. and Fin. Ctr., 1992—. Mem. Princeton Club (N.Y.C.). Home: 63 Bainbridge St Princeton NJ 08540-3901 Office: Princeton U Dept Econs Princeton NJ 08544-0001 E-mail: kuenne@princeton.edu.

KUENNEN, THOMAS GERARD, journalist; b. St. Louis, June 30, 1953; s. George Glennon and Earline (Doherty) K.; m. Anne L. Gillette, Sept. 10, 1988; 1 child, Madeline Livingston. BJ, U. Mo., 1975. Copy editor Macon (Ga.) Telegraph & News, 1976-77; news editor Mascoutah (Ill.) Herald, and related newspapers, 1977-79; pub. rels. assoc. Booker Assocs., Inc., St. Louis, 1979-80, Fru Con Corp., St. Louis, 1980-81; assoc. editor Rock Products Mag., Chgo., 1981-84; editor Roads & Bridges Mag., Des Plaines, Ill., 1984-95; prin., editor Expresswaysonline.com, Wheeling, Ill., 1995—. Mem. editl. com. Am. Bus. Press, N.Y.C., 1984-85. Recipient Jesse H. Neal award Am. Bus. Press, 1983, Svc. award La. Associated Gen. Contractors, 1990, Editl. Excellence award Am. Soc. Bus. Press Editors, 1998. Mem. Constrn. Writers Assn. (bd. dirs. 1985-86, 95-99, Robert F. Boger award 1985, 93, 95, 98, Hon. Mention 2003), The Rd. Info. Program (bd. dirs. 1999—), Road Gang, Nat. Asphalt Pavement Assn. (Hot Mix Hall of Fame), Women in Comm. (treas. 1983-84, Cub's Cup 1985). Roman Catholic. Office: Expresswaysonline dot com 925 N Milwaukee Ave Ste 224B Wheeling IL 60090-1869

KUENSTER, JOHN JOSEPH, editor; b. Chgo., June 18, 1924; s. Roy Jacob and Katheryn (Holechek) Kuenster; m. Mary Virginia Maher, Feb. 5, 1947 (dec. Feb. 1983); m. Suely Brazâo, July 1, 1995. Editor The Columbian, Chgo., 1948-57; staff writer Chgo. Daily News, Chgo., 1957-65; dir. devel. and pub. rels. Mercy Hosp., Chgo., 1965-66; sr. writer The Claretians, Chgo., 1966—; editor Baseball Digest, Evanston, Ill., 1969—; exec. editor Century Pub. Co., Evanston. Author: (book) Cobb to Catfish, Heartbreakers, Home and Away, 2003, When St. Jude Came to Chicago, 2003, (booklet) The Police, Money, Mission in Guatemala, Honesty, Is it the Best Policy?; co-author: (book) To Sleep with the Angels. Mem.: Baseball Writers' Assn. Am. Roman Catholic. Office: Baseball Digest Century Publishing Co 990 Grove St Evanston IL 60201-6510 E-mail: jkuenster@centurysports.net.

KUES, IRVIN WILLIAM, health care financial executive; b. Balt., Apr. 23, 1936; s. Harry Irvin and Theresa Frances (Seliga) K.; m. Mary Carolyn Gaff, Oct. 24, 1959; Pamela, Janet, Lynne, Leslie. BS in Engring. Sci., Johns Hopkins U., 1957, M in Bus. Sci., 1959. Cert. data processer. Rsch. analyst Am. Newspaper Rsch. Inst., Chgo., 1957-59; mgmt. analyst Western Elec. Co., Balt., 1959-61; asst. supt. E.D.P. Bethlehem (Pa.) Steel Co., 1961-66; v.p. data processing Comml. Credit Corp., Balt., 1966-74; CFO Johns Hopkins Hosp., Balt., 1974-86, Johns Hopkins Health System, Balt., 1986-94; chmn. provider reimbursement rev. bd. U.S. Dept. HHS, Balt., 1994—. Bd. dirs. Francis Scott Key Hosp., Balt., Med. Svcs. Corp., Balt., Dome Corp., Balt., Med. Ctr. Ins. Co., Bermuda; mem. fin. coun. Md. Hosp. Assn., Towson, 1984. Co-author: Yearbook of Healthcare Mgmt., 1991—. Advisor Villa Julie Coll., Stevenson, Md., 1991. Fellow Healthcare Fin. Mgmt. Assn.; mem. Healthcare Rate Coun., Ctr. Club. Avocations: tennis, golf, reading. Home: 1214 Brook Meadow Dr Towson MD 21286-1751 Office: Provider Reimbursement Rev Bd Ste L 2520 Lord Baltimore Dr Baltimore MD 21244-2670 E-mail: ikues@cms.hhs.gov.

KUESEL, THOMAS ROBERT, civil engineer; b. Richmond Hill, N.Y., July 30, 1926; s. Henry N. and Marie D. (Butt) K.; m. Lucia Elodia Fisher, Jan. 31, 1959; children— Robert Livingston, William Baldwin B. Engring. with highest honors, Yale U., 1946, M. Engring., 1947. With Parsons, Brinckerhoff, Quade & Douglas, 1947-90, project mgr., 1967-68, ptnr., sr. v.p. N.Y.C., 1968-83, chmn. bd., dir., 1983-90; cons. engr., 1990—; vice chmn. OECD Tunneling Conf., Washington, 1970; mem U.S. Nat. Com. on Tunneling Tech., 1972-74. Chmn. Geotech. bd. NRC, 1988-89. Contbr. 60 articles to profl. jours.; designer more than 120 bridges, 135 tunnels and numerous other structures in 36 states and 20 fgn. countries, most recent L.A. Metro, 1982-98, Geo Coleman Bridge Replacement, Yorktown, Va., 1991-95, Boston Ctrl. Artery and Harbor Tunnel, 1994—, Boston Ocean Outfall Tunnel, 1988-90, Cumberland Gap Tunnel, Ky. and Tenn., 1986-90, Jamuna River Bridge, Bangladesh, 1985-95, Trans Koolau Tunnel, Hawaii, 1985-90, Ft. McHenry Tunnel, Balt., 1978-85, Rogers Pass Rwy. Tunnel, B.C., 1981-85, Glenwood Canyon Tunnel, Colo., 1981-88, subways Boston, N.Y., Balt., Wash., Atlanta, Pitts., San Francisco, Seattle, L.A., Caracas, Singapore and Taipei. Fellow: ASCE; mem.: Nat. Acad. Engring., Yale Club N.Y.C., Yale Sci. and Engring. Assn., Am. Underground Constrn. Assn. (hon.), Wee Burn Club, The Moles, Tau Beta Pi.

KUEST, KRISTINA M. manufacturing engineer; b. San Antonio, June 28, 1973; d. Albert Reinhold and Veronika Franziska Kuest. MSME, MIT, 1999. Mfg. engr. Kuest Corp., San Antonio, 1995—. Bd. dirs. San Antonio Dance Umbrella, 2001—. Mem. Soc. Mfg. Engrs.

KUETHE, ALLAN J. historian, educator; b. Waverly, Iowa, Feb. 1, 1941; s. Raymond F. and Margaret M. Kuethe; m. Lourdes de la Concepcion Ramox, Feb. 11, 1936; children: John, Jennifer, Allen, Christian. BA, U. Iowa, 1962; MA, U. Fla., 1963, PhD, 1967. Asst. to assoc. prof. Tex. Tech. U., Lubbock, 1967—79, prof., 1979—90, Paul Whitfield Horn prof., 1990—, chair history dept., 1992—2001. Author: Military Reform and Society in New Guanada, 1978, Cuba, 1753-1815: Crown, Military and Society, 1986; co-author: Relaciones de Puder y Comerico Colonial, 1999. Grantee, U.S.-Spanish Joint Com. Ednl. and Cultural Affairs, 1983—84; Woodrow Wilson fellow, 1962—63, Fulbright-Hays fellow, 1965—66, Fulbright-Hays Rsch. Abroad fellow, 1986—87. Home: 5519 83rd St Lubbock TX 79424 Office: Tex Tech Univ History Dept Lubbock TX 79409

KUETHER, ANNIE, state representative; b. St. Louis, Mar. 20, 1952; 2 children. Student, Bowling Green State U. Bd. dirs. Topeka City Homes. Mem.: Nat. Woman's Polit. Caucus, Topeka Conv. Visitor's Bur., Topeka Arts Coun. (bd. dirs.), Topeka Bar Aux., Mulvane Art Mus., Friends Topeka Zoo. Democrat. Episcopalian. Office: 279-W State Capitol 300 SW 10th Ave Topeka KS 66612 Home: 1346 SW Wayne Ave Topeka KS 66604*

KUFELDT, GEORGE, biblical educator; b. Chgo., Nov. 4, 1923; s. Henry and Lydia (Dorn) K.; m. Kathryn Rider, July 24, 1943 (dec. July 1956); children: Anita Kay Kufeldt Shelton, Kristina Sue Kufeldt Schmidt; m. Claudena Eller, June 21, 1957 (dec. Sept. 1978); m. Lydia Borgardt, Aug. 12, 1980. AB, Anderson Coll., Ind., 1945, ThB, 1946, MDiv, 1953; PhD, Dropsie U., 1974. Ordained to ministry Ch. of God, 1948. Pastor Ch. of God, Homestead, Fla., 1948-50, Cassopolis, Mich., 1954-57, Lansdale, Pa., 1957-61; prof. O.T. and Hebrew Anderson U., 1961-90, prof. emeritus O.T., 1990—. Contbr. to Wesleyan Bible Commentary, vol. II, 1968, Nelson's Expository Dictionary of the Old Testament, 1980, Educating for Service, 1984, The Genesis Debate, 1986, Listening to the Word of God, 1990. Author: The Book of Ezericl Asbury Bible Commentary, 1992. Dropsie U. fellow, 1961, 63; Land of the Bible Workshop grantee NYU, 1966. Mem.: Am. Hellenic Ednl. Progressive Assn. (pres., Achievement award 1990), Am. Hist. Soc. Germans from Russia (life; bd. dirs. 1991—98). Home: 907 N Nursery Rd Anderson IN 46012-2721 E-mail: gkufeldt@aol.com.

KUFFNER, GEORGE HENRY, dermatologist, educator; b. S.I., N.Y., Aug. 22, 1949; s. George Henry and Wilmouth Anne (Clendenin) K.; m. Lynne Diane Blakeslee, May 17, 1975; children: Kevin, Todd A. BA, Johns Hopkins U., 1971, MD, 1975. Intern U. Hosps. Cleve., 1975-78, resident, 1978-81; staff dermatologist Cleve. Clinic Wooster, Ohio, 1981—. Asst. clin. prof. dermatology U. Hosps. Cleve., 1981—. Contbr. articles to profl. jours. Fellow Am. Acad. Dermatology; mem. Ohio State Med. Assn., Ohio Dermatological Assn., Akron Dermatology Staff, Am. Med. Assn., Cleve. Dermatology Soc. Methodist. Avocations: swimming, piano, reading, video/stero electronics, travel. Office: Cleveland Clinic Wooster 1740 Cleveland Rd Wooster OH 44691-2204

KUFUS, MARTIN W. security specialist; b. Blackwell, Okla., Nov. 30, 1956; s. Wayne M. and Alberta L. (Ramsey) K.; m. Kim Gilbert, June, 2002; 1 stepchild, Josiah. BS in Journalism, Okla. State U., 1980; MS in Journalism, Ohio U., 1991. Staff reporter Morning Jour. and Evening News, Daytona Beach, Fla., 1980-81; Russian-speaking paratrooper 5th Spl. Forces Group, Ft. Bragg, N.C., 1983-85; Russian linguist in signal intelligence U.S. Army Field Sta., Augsburg, West Germany, 1985-88; free-lance mag. writer, 1989—; constrn. safety officer BDM Constrn. Co., Columbus, Ohio, 1993-94; news editor, sr. reporter Wilson County News, Floresville, Tex., 1994—95, 1997—2002; asst. editor Soldier of Fortune mag., Boulder, Colo., 1995-97; security mgr. Bexar Met. Water Dist., San Antonio, 2002—. Fgn. correspondence intern AP, Jerusalem, 1989; guest lectr. journalism Ohio U., Ohio, 2001. Firefighter Floresville Vol. Fire Dept., 1995, 1997; flood rescue technician Wilson County Vol. Emergency Response Team, 1998—; mem. Wilson County Local Emergency Planning Com., 2003—, Wilson County assistance adv. com. ARC, 2001—02. Sgt. U.S. Army, 1981—88. Recipient 1st pl. award best original news story Tex. Cmty. Newspaper Assn., 1996, Watermark Media award Am. Water Works Assn., Tex., 2001. Mem.: Alamo Silver Wings Airborne Assn., State Firemen's and Fire Marshals' Assn. Tex., Spl. Forces Assn. Methodist. Avocations: fishing, cross country skiing, snorkeling.

KUGLER, SHARON M.K. chaplain; b. Phoenix, Jan. 28, 1959; d. William R. and Grace D. Kugler; m. Duane A. Isabella, Sept. 4, 1982; 2 children. BS in Math., Santa Clara U., 1981; MA in Liberal Studies and Religious Studies, Georgetown U., 1998. Chaplain Johns Hopkins U., Balt., 1993—. Chaplain Balt. Mem.: Assn. Coll. and Univ. Religious Affairs (pres. 2000—02), Nat. Assn. Coll. and Univ. Chaplains (pres. 1999—2001), Theta Alpha Kappa. Roman Catholic. Office: Johns Hopkins Univ 3400 N Charles St Baltimore MD 21218 Office Fax: 410-261-1212. Personal E-mail: chaplain@jhu.edu. E-mail: chaplain@jhu.edu.

KUH, CHARLOTTE VIRGINIA, economist; b. Apr. 13, 1944; d. Peter Greenebaum and Frederica Angela (Coerr) K.; m. Roy Radner, Jan. 22, 1978; children: Siobhan Frederica, Michael Edwin. BA magna cum laude, Radcliffe Coll., 1967; MPhil (Univ. fellow), Yale U., 1969, PhD (Dept. Labor grantee), 1976. Rec. sec.-treas. Econometric Soc., New Haven, 1970-75; acting asst. prof. engrng. econ. systems Stanford U., 1974-76; asst. prof. Harvard U. Grad. Sch. Edn., 1976-79; staff mgr., dist. mgr. AT&T Corp., 1979-87; exec. dir. grad. records exams program Ednl. Testing Svc., 1987-95; exec. dir. Office of Sci. and Engrng. Personnel Nat. Rsch. Coun., 1995—2001; dep. exec. dir. policy & global affairs divsn. Nat. Rsch. coun., Washington, 2001—. Mem. rev. panel NSF, 1979, 81, mem. adv. panel policy rsch. and sci. resource studies, 1983-87; mem. rev. panel Nat. Inst. Edn., 1978-85; mem. com. study nat. needs for biomed. and behavioral research pers. NRC, 1980-85, mem. adv. panel Office Sci. and Engrng. Pers., 1983-90, mem. panel on stats. on supply and demand for precoll. sci. and math. tchrs., com. on nat. stats., 1986-89, mem. com. Women in Sci. and Engrng. NRC, 1991-95, vice chair, 1993-95, mem. com. to study strategies to strengthen excellence of the N.I.H. Intramural Research Program, Inst. of Medicine, 1988; mem. exec. com. of dels. Am. Coun. Learned Socs., 1999—2002, chmn. 2001-02, treas., bd. dirs., 2002—; mem. adv. com. Bunting Inst., Radcliffe Coll., 1998—2001; cons. in field. Author articles in field. Grantee Carnegie Coun. Higher Edn., Ford Found., Spencer Found. Fellow Assn. Women in Sci.; mem. Am. Econ. Assn., Econometric Soc. Office: Natl Research Council 500 5th St Washington DC 20001 E-mail: ckuh@nas.edu., cvkuh@concentric.net.

KUH, ERNEST SHIU-JEN, electrical engineering educator; b. Peking, China, Oct. 2, 1928; came to U.S., 1948, naturalized, 1960; s. Zone Shung and Tsia (Chu) K.; m. Bettine Chow, Aug. 4, 1957; children: Anthony, Theodore. BS, U. Mich., 1949; MS, MIT, 1950; PhD, Stanford U., 1952; DEng (hon.), Hong Kong U. Sci. and Tech., 1997; D Eng. (hon.), Nat. Chiao Tung U., Taiwan, 1999. Mem. tech. staff Bell Tel. Labs., Murray Hill, N.J., 1952-56; assoc. prof. elec. engrng. U. Calif., Berkeley, 1956-62, prof., 1962—, Miller rsch. prof., 1965-66, William S. Floyd Jr. prof. engrng., 1990—, William S. Floyd Jr. prof. engrng. emeritus, 1993—, chmn. dept. elec. engrng. and computer sci., 1968-72, dean Coll. Engrng., 1973-80. Cons. IBM Rsch. Lab., San Jose, Calif., 1957—62, NSF, 1975—84; mem. panel Nat. Bur. Stds., 1975—80; mem. vis. com. Gen. Motors Inst., 1975—79; mem. vis. com. dept. elec. engrng. and computer scis. MIT, 1986—91; mem. adv. coun. elec. engrng. dept. Princeton U., 1986—98; mem. bd. councilors Sch. Engrng. U. So. Calif., 1986—91; mem. sci. adv. bd. Mills Coll., 1976—80. Co-author: Principles of Circuit Synthesis, 1959, Basic Circuit Theory, 1967, Theory of Linear Active Network, 1967; Linear and Nonlinear Circuits, 1987 Recipient Alexander von Humboldt award, 1980, Lamme medal Am. Soc. Endrng. Edn., 1981, U. Mich. Disting. Alumnus award, 1970, Berkeley citation, 1993, C & C prize Japanese Found. for Computers and Comm. Promotion, 1996, 1998 EDAC, Phil Kaufman award; Brit. Soc. Engrng. and Rsch. fellow, 1982. Fellow IEEE (Edn. medal 1981, Centenial medal 1984, Circuits and Systems Soc. award. 1988), AAAS; mem. NAE, Acad. Sinica, Chinese Acad. Scis. (fgn. mem.), Sigma Xi, Phi Kappa Phi. Office: U Calif Elec Engrng & Computer Sci Berkeley CA 94720-0001

KUH, RICHARD HENRY, lawyer; b. N.Y.C., Apr. 27, 1921; s. Joseph Hellmann and Fannie Mina (Rees) K.; m. Joyce Dattel, July 31, 1966; children: Michael Joseph, Jody Ellen. BA, Columbia Coll., 1941; LLB magna cum laude, Harvard U., 1948. Bar: N.Y. 1948, U.S. Dist. Ct. (so. dist.) N.Y. 1948, U.S. Dist. Ct. (ea. dist.) N.Y. 1967, U.S. Supreme Ct. 1968. Assoc. firm Cahill, Gordon & Reindel, 1948-53; asst. dist. atty. N.Y. County Dist. Attys. Office, 1953-64, dist. atty., 1974; pvt. practice law N.Y.C., 1966-71; ptnr. firm Kuh, Goldman, Cooperman & Levitt, N.Y.C., 1971-73, Kuh, Shapiro, Goldman, Cooperman & Levitt, P.C., N.Y.C., 1975-78, Warshaw Burstein Cohen Schlesinger & Kuh, N.Y.C., 1978—. Adj. prof. NYU Law Sch. Author: Foolish Figleaves, 1967; mem. bd. editors: Harvard Law Rev, 1947-48; mem. adv. bd.: Contemporary Drug Problems, 1975—, Criminal Law Bull, 1976— ; contbr. articles to popular and profl. jours. Trustee Temple Israel, N.Y.C., 1975-84, Grace Ch. Sch., 1981-85. With U.S. Army, 1942-45, ETO. Walter E. Meyer Research and Writing grantee, 1964-65 Mem. ABA (chair criminal justice sect. 1983-84, chair spl. com. on evaluation jud. performance 1983-90, ho. dels. 1988-93, mem. jud. evaluation adv. com. Nat. Ctr. State Cts. 1990-91, chair 1st nat. conf. gun violence 1994), Assn. Bar City N.Y., Am. Bar Found., Harvard Law Sch. Assn. N.Y. (trustee 1989-92), Harvard Club (mem. admissions com. 1998-01), Phi Beta Kappa. Democrat. Jewish. Home: 14 Washington Pl New York NY 10003-6609 Office: 555 5th Ave New York NY 10017-2416

KUHENS, BRIAN SCOTT, investment company executive, publishing company exexcutive; b. Lowell, Mass., June 20, 1966; s. Culver LaVerne and Joan Avon (Madden) K.; m. Donna Gayle Hennequin, Dec. 27, 1986; 1 child, Sage Hennequin. BA in Philosophy, U. S.C., 1990. Series 7, 63, 65 lic. Nat. Assn. Securities Dealers; registered investment advisor Securities and Exch. Commn., Va. Commonwealth, S.C. Gen. mgr. Sound Advice, Inc., Columbia, SC, 1987—90; v.p., owner Wordsprint, Inc., Galax, Wytheville, Va., 1991—95; stockbroker, fin. cons., intermediate trainer Wheat First Butcher Singer, Galax, 1995—98; prodn. editor, pub. The History Project, Inc., Galax, 1996—; owner Magnolia Street, 2000—02; pub., owner POTC, L.L.C., 2000—; owner Whammy Corp., 2001—02; columnist, contbg. editor Gannett Newspapers, 2001—. Registered investment advisor, Wadena, Iowa, Galax, 1998—, Spartanburg, Va., 1998—. Editor COGITO, 1986, (plays) Character in Time: The US Presidents, 1997—; asst. editor Mobile Illustrated, 1989-90. Chmn. bd. trustees Twin County Regional Hosp., Galax, 1995-98, dir. ex officio, 1997-98; trustee Illyria Twp., Fayette County, Iowa, 1999-2000. Recipient Mgmt. Plus/Silver award Nat. Assn. Printers and Lithographers, 1994, 95, Highest Ranking-First Place/Mgmt. Excellence award Print Image Internat., 1995. Mem. Rotary Internat. (Paul Harris fellow 1997, William E. Skelton Charter fellow 1997), Rotary Club Galax (dir., pres. 1993-2002, Presdl. citation for integrity, love and peace 1995-96), Rotary Internat. (asst. gov. dist. 7570 1996-98, Dist. Gov.'s citation for outstanding svc. 1997). Avocations: music, hiking, numismatics, electronics, poker. Fax: 864-582-0059. E-mail: advisor@kunens.com.

KUHI, LEONARD VELLO, astronomer, university administrator; b. Hamilton, Ont., Can., Oct. 22, 1936; came to U.S., 1958; s. John and Sinaida (Rose) K.; m. Patricia Suzanne Brown, Sept. 3, 1960 (div.); children: Alison Diane, Christopher Paul; m. Mary Ellen Murphy, July 15, 1989. BS, U. Toronto, 1958; PhD, U. Calif., Berkeley, 1964. Carnegie postdoctoral fellow Hale Obs., Pasadena, Calif., 1963-65; asst. prof. U. Calif., Berkeley, 1965-69, assoc. prof., 1969-74, prof., 1974-89, chmn. dept. astronomy, 1975-76, dean phys. scis. Coll. Letters and Sci., 1976-81, provost, 1983-89; sr. v.p. for acad. affairs, provost U. Minn., Mpls., 1989-91, prof. astronomy, 1989—, chmn. dept. astronomy, 1997—. Vis. prof. U. Colo., 1969, Coll. de France, Paris, 1972-73, U. Heidelberg, 1978, 80-81; bd. dirs. Am. Inst. Physics. Contbr. articles to profl. jours. Recipient Alexander von Humboldt Sr. Scientist award, 1980-81; NSF research grantee, 1966—. Fellow AAAS; mem. Am. Astron. Soc. (treas. 1987, 96—), Astron. Soc. Pacific (pres. 1978-80), Internat. Astron. Union, Assn. Univ. for Rsch. Astronomy (chair bd. dirs. 1998-2001). Office: U Minn Dept Astronomy 116 Church St SE Minneapolis MN 55455-0149 E-mail: kuhi@astro.umn.edu.

KUHL, CHRISTOPHER FANELLI, music educator; b. Syracuse, N.Y., Feb. 8, 1956; s. Roger Anthony and Sirje Kuhl. MusB in Composition, SUNY, Potsdam, 1977; MusM in Composition, MusM in Musicology, Bowling Green State U., 1979; PhD in Comparative Arts, Ohio U., 1982. Music prof. Miss. U. for Women, Columbus, 1982—87; dept. chair, tchr. English and philosophy for gifted children Ill. Math. and Sci. Acad., Aurora, 1987—. Poet-in-residence Mary Anderson Ctr. for the Arts, Ind. Author: A Far Country, 1989; contbr. poetry to jours. Home: Apt 201 851 Staghorn Ln North Aurora IL 60542-1439

KUHL, DAVID EDMUND, physician, nuclear medicine educator; b. St. Louis, Oct. 27, 1929; s. Robert Joseph and Caroline Bertha (Waldemar) Kuhl; m. Eleanor Dell Kasales, Aug. 7, 1954; 1 child, David Stephen. AB, Temple U., Phila., 1951; MD, U. Pa., 1955; LHD (hon.), Loyola U. Chgo., 1992. Diplomate Am. Bd. Radiology, Am. Bd. Nuc. Medicine (a founder; life trustee 1977-). Intern, then resident in radiology Sch. Medicine and Hosp. U. Pa., 1955—56, 1958—63, mem. faculty, 1963—76, prof. radiology, 1970—76, vice chmn. dept., 1975—76, chief div. nuc. medicine, 1963—76; prof. radiol. scis. UCLA Sch. Medicine and Hosp., 1976—86, chief div. nuc. medicine, 1976—84, vice-chmn. dept., 1977—86; prof. internal medicine and radiology U. Mich. Sch. Medicine, Ann Arbor, 1986—2000, prof. radiology, 2000—, chief divsn. nuc. medicine, dir. PET Ctr., 1986—2002. Disting. faculty lectr. in biomed. rsch. U. Mich. Med. Sch., 1992, Henry Russel lectr., 98; mem. adv. com. Dept. Energy, NIH, Internat. Commn. on Radiation Units and Measures, Max Planck Soc.; prof. bioengring. Moore Sch. of Electrical Engrng., U. Pa., 1974—76. Mem. editl. bd.: various jours.; contbr. articles to med. jours. Served as officer M.C. USNR, 1956—58. Recipient Rsch. Career Devel. award, USPHS, 1961—71, Ernst Jung prize for medicine, Jung Found., Hamburg, 1981, Emil H. Grubbe gold medal, Chgo. Med. Soc., 1983, Berman Found. award peaceful uses atomic energy, 1985, Steven C. Beering award for advancement med. sci., Ind. U., 1987, Disting. Grad. award, U. Pa. Sch. Medicine, 1988, William C. Menninger Meml. award, ACP, 1989, Javits Neurosci. Investigator award, NIH, 1989, Charles F. Kettering prize, GM Cancer Rsch. Found., 2001, Hon. Lifetime Mem. award, Einstein Soc., Nat. Atomic Mus. Found., 2001. Fellow: Nat. Inst. for Med. and Biol. Engrng., Am. Coll. Nuc. Physicians, Am. Coll. Radiology; mem.: Inst. Medicine Nat. Aad. Scis., Soc. Neurosci., Am. Neurol. Assn. (Foster Elting Bennett Meml. lectr. 1981), Soc. Nuc. Medicine (ann. lectr. 1991, Nuc. Pioneer citation 1976, Herman L. Blumgart, M.D. Pioneer award 1995, Disting. Scientist award 1981, George Charles de Hevesy Nuc. Medicine Pioneer award 1995, Benedict Cassen prize for rsch. 1996), Radiol. Soc. N.Am. (ann. orator 1982, Outstanding Rschr. award 1996), Assn. Univ. Radiologists, Assn. Am. Physicians, Alpha Omega Alpha, Sigma Xi. Office: U Mich Hosp Divsn Nuc Medicine 1500 E Medical Center Dr Ann Arbor MI 48109-0005 E-mail: dkuhl@umich.edu.

KUHL, PAUL BEACH, lawyer; b. Elizabeth, N.J., July 15, 1935; s. Paul Edmund and Charlotte (Hetche) K.; m. Janey Mae Stadheim, June 24, 1967; children: Alison Lyn, Todd Beach. BA, Cornell U., 1957; LLB, Stanford U., 1960. Assoc. Law Offices of Walter C. Kohn, San Francisco, 1961-63, Sedgwick, Detert, Moran & Arnold, San Francisco, 1963-73, ptnr., 1973-99, of counsel, 2000—. Pro tem judge, arbitrator San Francisco Superior Ct., 1989—. Served to lt. USCG, 1961. Mem. ABA, Am. Coll. Trial Lawyers, Am. Bd. Trial Advocates, Def. Rsch. Inst., No. Calif. Assn. Def., Am. Platform Tennis Assn. (regional pres. and bd. dirs. 2003—), Mediation Soc., Tahoe Tavern Property Owners Assn. (sec. 1979-81, pres. 1981-83), Lagunitas Country Club (v.p. 1995-97). Avocations: tennis, reading. Home: PO Box 1434 Ross CA 94957-1434 Office: Sedgwick Detert Moran & Arnold 1 Embarcadero Ctr Ste 1600 San Francisco CA 94111-3716 E-mail: beach.kuhl@sdma.com.

KUHL, RONALD WEBSTER, retired marketing executive; b. Chgo., Dec. 12, 1938; s. Robert Emerson and Kathleen (Webster) K.; m. Mary Walls, Sept. 28, 1968; children: David Douglas, Kevin Lathrop. BS in Econs., U. Pa., 1960; MBA, Harvard U., 1964. Account exec. Young & Rubicam Advt., N.Y.C., 1964-71, v.p. mgmt. supr. San Francisco, 1988-90; mgr. promotion and design The First Ch. of Christ Scientist, Boston, 1971-75; account exec. BBDO Advt., San Francisco, 1975-77; acct. supr. Ketchum Communications, San Francisco, 1977-80; sr. v.p., mgmt. supr. Grey Adv., San Francisco, 1980-85; dir. mktg. ComputerLand Corp., Hayward, Calif., 1985-88; v.p. mktg. communications Ventura Software Inc., San Diego, 1990-92; v.p. mktg. Castelle, Santa Clara, Calif., 1992-94; v.p. advt. and mktg. svcs. Interactive Video Enterprises, San Ramon, Calif., 1994-96; v.p. mktg. and svcs. NetSoft, Irvine, Calif., 1996-98; v.p. mktg. E-Centrix, Walnut Creek, Calif., 1998-2000, ret., 2001. 1st lt. U.S. Army, 1960-62. Avocations: antique collecting, tennis, swimming, travel.

KUHLER, DEBORAH GAIL, grief therapist, former state legislator; b. Moorhead, Minn., Oct. 12, 1952; d. Robert Edgar and Beverly Maxine (Buechler) Ecker; m. George Henry Kuhler, Dec. 28, 1973; children: Karen Elizabeth, Ellen Christine. BA, Dakota Wesleyan U., 1974; MA, U. N.D., 1977. Outpatient therapist Ctr. for Human Devel., Grand Forks, N.D., 1975-77; mental health counselor Community Counseling Services, Huron, S.D., 1978-88, 91-93; owner, dir. bereavement svcs. Kuhler Funeral Home, Huron, 1978—; adj. prof. Huron U., 1979—83, 1990—2002; mem. from dist. 23 S.D. Ho. Reps., Pierre, 1987-90; mem. House Judiciary com., chair House Health and Welfare Com., Pierre, 1990. Active 1st United Meth. Ch. Named Young Alumnus of the Yr., Dakota Wesleyan U., 1989, Bus. and Profl. Women, 1989. Mem. ACA, AAUW (Achievement in Politics award 1987), PEO, Am. Mental Health Counselors Assn., Assn. for Death Edn. and Counseling, Phi Kappa Phi. Avocations: reading, breadmaking, sewing, piano.

KUHLER, RENALDO GILLET, museum official, scientific illustrator; b. Teaneck, N.J., Nov. 21, 1931; s. Otto August and Simonne L. (Gillet) K.; 1 child, Anne Marie Cooper. BA, U. Colo., 1961. Curator of history, illustrator exhibit, miniature diorama preparator Ea. Wash. State Hist. Soc. Mus., Spokane, 1962-67; mus. illustrator N.C. State Mus. Natural History, Raleigh, 1969—; semi-ret., 1999. Designer, executor of art work for sci. illustrations, awards, brochures, pamphlets and periodicals Dept. Agr. and Mus., N.C., 1972-74; designer 36 illustrations for Handbook of Reptiles and Amphibians of Florida, Part 1 (Ray E. Ashton), 1981; contbr. many illustrations Atlas of Freshwater Fishes of North America (David Lee), Endangered Threatened and Rare Fauna of N.C. (Ross, Rohde and Lindquist), Distribution Survey of N.C. Mammals (Lee, Funderburg and Clark); Endangered Threatened and Rare Fauna of N.C., part 1 (Mary K. Clark), Potential Effect of Oil Spills on Seabirds, etc. (Lee and Socci), Poisonous Snakes of N.C. (William M. Palmer), Reptiles of North Carolina (William M. Palmer and Alvin Braswell), Synopsis of North American Centipede (Rowland Shelley), 2002 ; gen. illustrator: American Firearms and the Changing Frontier (Waldo E. Rosebush); also contbr. to jours. and bulls. including Then.C.Naturalist; currently working on skull illustrations for Mammals of North Carolina (Mary Kay Clark); calligrapher; creator wood handicrafts; violin maker, 1949. Appearance as sci. illustrator (TV) Nat. Geog., June 2001. Mem. Dem. Nat. Com.; life mem. Raleigh Rhinoceros Club, 2000—. Mem. Nat. Trust Hist. Preservation, Nat. Smokers Alliance, Raleigh Rhinoceros Club (life). Democrat. Avocations: experimenting with laminated paper and models of ships and trains, carburator fittings for smoking pipes, designer hiking and summer office suits. Home: Apt 3 510 Tilden St Raleigh NC 27605-1524 Office: NC State Mus Natural Scis 210 N Salisbury St Raleigh NC 27603-1358

KUHLMAN, JAMES WELDON, retired county extension education director; b. Amarillo, Tex., Feb. 13, 1937; s. Herman and Alma Marie (Gerdsen) K.; m. Ann Bullock Davis, Dec. 23, 1967; children: Lisa Ann, Jennifer Shawn. BS, West Tex. State U., Canyon, 1959; MS, U. Nebr., 1961. Tchg. West Tex. State U., Canyon, 1958-59; grad. asst. U. Nebr., Lincoln, 1959—61; county ext. agt. Buffalo County, 1962—67; Buffalo County ext. agt., chair, 1967—72; Worth County ext. dir. Iowa State U., Northwood, 1972-81, Cerro Gordo County ext. edn. dir. Mason City, 1981-97; ret., 1997; farmer, 1955—, Buffalo County, Nebr., 1955-97. Spkr. various civic clubs, 1980—, flower garden Buchart Gardens in Victoria, Can., 1990-2001. Author: The History of the Nance Hereford Ranch, 1996, The Block Pasture, 1998, From Kirchhatten to Canyon, 2001. Past pres., past treas. No. Iowa Figure Skating Club, Mason City, 1984-98; active Mason City Iowa Conv. and Visitors Bur., chair grants com., 1998-2000; treas. River City Trees, 1998—; bd. dirs. Ctrl. Gardens Clear Lake, Iowa, 2003—. With U.S. Army Res., 1961-67. Recipient Disting. Pres. award Sertoma Club Internat., Kearney, Nebr., 1966, Top award Lions Club Internat., Northwood, Iowa, 1979. Mem. Nat. Assn. County Agrl. Agts. (nat. com., voting dir. 1984, 90, Disting. Svc. award 1984), Nat. Assn. Ret. Fed. Employees (pres. local chpt. 1998-1999), State Conv. of Nat. Assn. Ret. Fed. Employees (co-chair 2001), Iowa Fedn. of Nat. Assn. of Ret. Fed. Employees (chair nat. legislation com.), Am. Hereford Assn., Iowa Hereford Assn. (dir. 1991-99), Iowa Hereford Breeders Assn. (dir.), Nebr. Hereford Assn., Holstein Assn. Am., North Ctrl. Iowa Geneology Club (past vice chair, pres. 1999-2000), Rotary Club Mason City (com. chair 1988, 97—, bd. dirs. 2000-03), Mason City C. of C. (agr. com. 1981—, chmn. regional issues com. 1990-91), Iowa State U. Ext. Assn. (dir. 1980s), Iowa State U. Coun. Ex Profls. (chair retiree sect. 1999-2000), Epsilon Sigma Phi (dir.). Presbyterian. Avocations: cattle breeding and cattle history of Hereford breed, genealogy, writing, gardening, photography. Home: 722 N Hampshire Ave Mason City IA 50401-2440

KUHLMAN, RICHARD SHERWIN, lawyer, author; b. Chgo., Sept. 4, 1943; s. Milton and Florence (Rosenthal) K.; m. Wendy Sue Kremin, Aug. 13, 1971; children: Andrew Michael, Matthew Foster. BA, U. Ill., 1965; JD, Northwestern U., 1968. Bar: Ill. 1969, U.S. Dist. Ct. (no. dist.) Ill. 1969, U.S. Ct. Appeals (7th cir.) 1969. Former ptnr. Foss, Schuman, Drako & Barnard, Chgo., Gottlieb, Schwartz, Chgo.; with Kuhlman, Perlman, Chgo.; panel atty. fed. defender program U.S. Dist. Ct. (no. dist.) Ill., Chgo. 1969—. Contbr. Real Estate Litigation Handbook, Ill. Inst. for Continuing Legal Education, 1975, articles to profl. jours, bulls., and mags; author: Killer Roads from Crash to Verdict, 1985, Jury Trial, Progress and Democracy, 1981, Killer Roads, 1986, Safe Places, 1989; editor, prin. author: Transportation Negligence, 1981, 4th edition 1986. Chmn. Anti-Defamation League Appeal, Chgo., 1976-77; mem. Leadership Council for Met. Open Communities, 1979. Mem. Ill. State Bar Assn., ABA (TIPS sect., chmn., speaker Nat. Teaching Inst. on Transp. Nelligence 1985-86, chmn. automobile law com. 1986-87), ATLA, Ill. Inst. Continuing Legal Edn. Office: Kuhlman & Perlman 1 N La Salle St Chicago IL 60602-3902

KUHLMANN, FRED MARK, lawyer, business executive; b. St. Louis, Apr. 9, 1948; s. Frederick Louis and Mildred (Southworth) K.; m. Barbara Jane Nierman, Dec. 30, 1970; children: F. Matthew, Sarah Ann. AB summa cum laude, Washington U., St. Louis, 1970; JD cum laude, Harvard U., 1973. Bar: Mo. 1973. Assoc. atty. Stolar, Heitzmann & Eder, St. Louis, 1973-75; from tax counsel to staff v.p. McDonnell Douglas Corp., St. Louis, 1975—87, sr. v.p., gen. counsel, 1991—97; exec. v.p. McDonnell Douglas Health Systems Co., 1987—89; pres. McDonnell Douglas Systems Integration Co., 1989—91; of counsel Bryan Cave, St. Louis, 1997-98; pres. Sys. Svc. Enterprises, St. Louis, 1998—. Bd. dirs. Republic Health Corp., Dallas, 1988-90; mem. governing bd. Luth. Med. Ctr., 1989-95, chmn., 1990-92. Bd. dirs. Luth. Charities Assn., 1982-91, sec. 1984-86, chmn. 1986-89; elder Lutheran Ch. of Resurrection, 1977-80; mem. Regents Coun. Concordia Sem., 1981-84; chmn. cub scout pack 459 Boy Scouts Am., 1984-86; bd. dirs. Luth. High Sch. Assn., 1978-84, 91-97, pres. 1992-97, long range planning com. 1990-92, chmn. alumni assn. 1981; chmn. north star dist. Boy Scouts Am., 1990-93; bd. dirs. Mcpl. Theatre Assn., St. Louis, 1991—; chmn. long range planning com. St. Paul's Luth. Ch., 1988-91, 98-2001, pres., 1996-97, 2002-; bd. dirs., mem. exec. com. United Way of Greater St. Louis, 1994-97, chmn. Vanguard divsn., 1994-97; mem. amb. coun. Luth. Family and Children's Svcs. of St. Louis, 1998—; bd. dirs. Luth. Charities Found., 1998—; mem. adv. bd. Webster U. Bus. and Tech. Sch., 1999-2001; mem. bd mgrs. worker benefit plans Luth Ch.-Mo. Synod, 2001—. Recipient Disting. Leadership award Luth. Assn. for Higher Edn., 1981. Mem. ABA, Mo. Bar Assn., Bar Assn. Met. St. Louis, Bellerive Country Club, Phi Beta Kappa, Omicron Delta Kappa. Republican. Avocations: tennis, golf, racquetball. Home: 1711 Stone Ridge Trails Dr Saint Louis MO 63122-3546 Office: Sys Svc Enterprises 77 Westport Plz Ste 500 Saint Louis MO 63146-3126 E-mail: fmkuhlmann@sseinc.com.

KUHLMANN-WILSDORF, DORIS, materials scientist, educator; b. Bremen, Germany, Feb. 15, 1922; came to U.S., 1956. d. A. Friedrich and Elsa S. (Dreyer) K.; m. Heinz G.F. Wilsdorf, Jan. 4, 1950; children: Gabriele, Michael. BS in Physics, U. Göttingen, Germany, 1944, MS, 1946, PhD in Materials Sci., 1947; DS in Physics-Materials Sci., U. Witwatersrand, South Africa, 1954. Postdoctoral fellow U. Göttingen, 1947-48; postdoctoral fellow in physics U. Bristol, Eng., 1949-50; lectr. physics U. Witwatersrand, Johannesburg, 1950-56; from assoc. prof. metall. engring. to prof. U. Pa., Phila., 1957-63; prof. engrng. physics U. Va., Charlottesville, 1963-66, univ. prof. applied sci., 1966—. Co-founder, co-owner HiPerCon; inventor in field. Editor: 4 materials sci. books; contbr. articles to profl. jours. Recipient J. Shelton Horsley award Va. Acad. Sci., 1966, Americanism medal DAR, 1966, Heyn medal German Metall. Soc., 1988, Achievement award Soc. Women Engrs., 1989, Ragnar Holm Sci. Achievement award IEEE, 1991. Fellow Am. Soc. Materials Internat. (life, Edward DeMille Campbell Meml. lectr. 2002), Am. Phys. Soc.; mem. Am. Soc. Women Engrs. (life), Am. Soc. Engrng. Edn. (medal for excellence 1965, 66), AIME Metall. Soc., Nat. Acad. Engrng. Achievements include development of metal fiber brushes; patents in field. Office: U Va Dept Physics Charlottesville VA 22904-0001 Mailing: HiPerCon 717 Albermarle St Charlottesville VA 22903 E-mail: dw@virginia.edu.

KUHN, ALBERT JOSEPH, English educator; b. Dowell, Ill., Apr. 4, 1926; s. Albert and Elizabeth (Furjes) K.; m. Roberta Marshall, June 12, 1949 (dec. 1993); children— William, Frederick. BA, U. Ill., 1950; PhD, Johns Hopkins, 1954. Mem. faculty Ohio State U., 1954—, chmn. English dept., 1964-71, prof. English, 1965, provost, v.p. acad. affairs, 1971-79, dir. Univ. Honors, 1985-89, professor emeritus, 1989—. Contbr. to Romantic Bibliography, 1963, also articles.; editor: Three Sentimental Novels, 1970, Victorian Literature and Society, 1984 Mem. region VIII Woodrow Wilson Selection Com., 1961-68; mem. research bd. Children's Hosp., 1973-77; trustee Battelle Meml. Inst. Found., 1975-79. Served with USNR, 1944-46. Recipient Disting. Svc. award Ohio State U., 1991. Mem. MLA, North Cen. Assn. Colls. and Schs. (cons.-evaluator), Kit Kat Club (Columbus), Phi Beta Kappa, Phi Kappa Phi. Home: 35 Webster Park Ave Columbus OH 43214-3512

KUHN, BOWIE K. lawyer, former professional baseball commissioner, consultant; b. Takoma Park, Md., Oct. 28, 1926; m. Luisa Hegeler; four children. BA, Princeton, 1947; LL.B., U. Va., 1950. Bar: NY. 1951, U.S. Supreme Ct. 1972. With firm Willkie, Farr & Gallagher, N.Y.C.; legal counsel several baseball clients, 1950-69; rep. Maj. League club owners in negotiations with Maj. League Players Assn., 1968; commr. pro tempore of baseball, 1969; commr., 1969-84; of counsel Willkie, Farr & Gallagher, 1984-87; former ptnr. Myerson & Kuhn, N.Y.C., 1988-89; pres. The Kent Group Inc., Ponte Vedra Beach, Fla., 1990—, Sports Franchises, Inc., Milford, Conn., 1992—. Author: Hardball: The Education of a Baseball Commissioner, 1987. Office: The Kent Group Inc 136 Teal Pointe Ln Ponte Vedra Beach FL 32082-1935

KUHN, BRENT, advertising executive; BA in Comms., U. Ill. Account rep. Tatham, Laird & Rudner, Chgo.; with McCann Erickson; pres. Bennett Kuhn Varner Inc., Atlanta, 1989—. Office: Bennett Kuhn Varner Inc 2964 Peachtree Rd Ste 700 Atlanta GA 30305

KUHN, BRIAN LAWRENCE, lawyer; b. Memphis, Feb. 16, 1948; s. Edward William and Mattie (Mahaffey) K.; m. Nancy Brandenburg, June 17, 1970; children: Matthew Lawrence, Andrew Ryan, Anthony Mitchell. BSBA, U. Tenn., 1971, JD, 1974. Bar: Tenn. 1974, U.S. Dist. Ct. (we. dist.) Tenn. 1974. Asst. county atty. Shelby County, Memphis, 1974-81; ptnr. Kuhn, Kuhn & Kuhn, Memphis, 1980-82; county atty. Shelby County, Memphis, 1982-94; sr. counsel Ford & Harrison LLP, Memphis, 1998—. Chief adminstrv. officer, 1981. Bd. dirs. Boys' Clubs of Memphis, 1983—; chmn. bd. trustees, Raleigh United Meth. Ch., Memphis, 1982; parliamentarian, legal adviser, Shelby County Charter Commn., 1984. Mem. ABA, Memphis and Shelby County Bar Assn. (law libr. commn. 1982-92), Tenn. Bar Assn., Kiwanis of La.-Miss.-Tenn. (pres. Memphis, lt. gov., dist. chmn. 1976-80). Office: Ford & Harrison LLP 6750 Poplar Ave Ste 600 Memphis TN 38138 E-mail: bkuhn@fordharrison.com.

KUHN, DONALD MARSHALL, marketing professional; b. Miami, Fla., Nov. 2, 1922; s. Paul Carlton Kuhn and Helen (Merrick) Bond; m. Jane Emma Williams, Dec. 24, 1948 (dec. 1988); children: Marshall Merrick, Richard Williams, Diane Joan, Paul Willard; m. Kay Bardsley, Feb. 25, 1990. BA in Journalism and Drama, U. Miami, 1949. Cert. fundraising executive. Advt. copywriter Sears Roebuck and Co., Chgo., 1949-50; dir. pub. relations Tb Inst. Chgo. and Cook County, 1950-54; dir. fundraising Dade County Tb Assn., Miami, 1955-59, Minn. Tb and Health Assn., St. Paul, 1959-60, Mich. Lung Assn., Lansing, 1960-68, Am. Lung Assn., N.Y.C., 1968-78; nat. founder, dir. regional fin. program Rep. Nat. Com., Washington, 1978-79; exec. v.p., dir. fundraising div. Walter Karl, Inc., Armonk, N.Y., 1979-90, cons., 1990-93, May Devel. Svcs., Greenwich, Conn., 1993—. Mem. direct mktg. task force Am. Red Cross, Washington, 1983-84; mem. direct mail task force Am. Heart Assn., Dallas, 1982. Editor: Non-profit Council Info. Exchange, 1987-90; contbr. articles to Fundraising Mgmt. Mag. and other publs. Bd. dirs. Isadora Duncan Internat. Inst., N.Y.C., 1987—. Mem. Assn. Fundraising Profls. (bd. dirs. 1978-80), Direct Mktg. Assn. (mem. operating com., non-profit coun. 1987-90, recipient non-profit coun. fundraising achievement award 1991). Republican. Congregationalist. Avocations: personal computers, croquet. Home and Office: 6305 S Geneva Cir Englewood CO 80111-5437

KUHN, EDWIN P. travel company executive; BS, Ohio St. Univ. Pres., CEO TravelCenters of Am, 1992—. Mem. Nat. Assn. Truck Stop Operators (chmn. long-range planning com.). Office: TravelCenters of Am Inc 24601 Center Ridge Rd Ste 200 Westlake OH 44145-5677*

KUHN, HANS HEINRICH, retired chemist; b. Uzwil, St. Gallen, Switzerland; came to U.S., 1957; d. Werner and Gretchen (Haeberle) K.; m. Edith Lilly Peyer, Aug. 28, 1954; children: Johann Heinrich, Barbara Edith. Degree in Chem. Engring., Swiss Fed. Inst. Tech., Zürich, 1949, Doctor in Sci. Tech., 1954. Postdoctoral researcher Swiss Fed. Inst. Tech., Zürich, 1954-57; rsch. chemist Dewey & Almy, Div. W.R. Grace, Cambridge, Mass., 1957-60; group leader Deering Milliken Rsch. Co., Spartanburg, S.C., 1960-61, sect. leader, 1961-65, dep. mgr., 1965-80; sr. scientist Milliken Rsch. Co., Spartanburg, S.C., 1980-95, rsch. fellow, 1995-2000; ret., 2000. Contbr. articles to profl. jours. Consul of Switzerland for S.C. and N.C., Spartanburg, 1970-94. Recipient Olney medal Am. Assn. Textile Chemists and Colorists, 1997. Mem. Am. Chem. Soc., Swiss Chem. Soc., Rotary. Presbyterian. Home: 176 W Park Dr Spartanburg SC 29306-5045

KUHN, HOWARD ARTHUR, engineering executive, educator; b. Pitts., Dec. 6, 1940; s. Howard E. and Selma W. Kuhn; m. Beverly A. Burke, Dec. 23, 1961; children: Amy, Jeffrey, David, Stephen. BS, Carnegie-Mellon U., 1962, MS, 1963, PhD, 1966. Registered profl. engr., Pa., Fla., S.C. Prof. engring. Drexel U., Phila., 1966-74, U. Pitts., 1975-89, adj. prof., 1989-2000; v.p., CTO Scienda Bldg. Scis., 2000—02, cons. engr., 2002—. Dir. freshman engring. program, U. Pitts, 1981-88, indsl. adv. com.; cons. engr. Deformation Control Tech., Pitts., 1980-88; tech. dir. Concurrent Techs. Corp., 1988, tech. v.p., 1989-92, v.p., chief tech. officer, 1992-2000; bd. dirs. Pitts. Tech. Coun. Author: Powder Forging, 1990; editor: Powder Metallurgy Processing, 1978, ASM Handbook on Mechnical Testing, 2000; inventor powder metallurgy forging, aluminum plate rolling improvements. Pres. PTA, Gibsonia, Pa., 1976-77; mem. Civic Adv. Com., Gibsonia, 1978-82; chmn. Laurel Highlands Cancer Program, bd. dirs. Johnstown Chiefs Hockey Team, 1995-2000; dir. advanced tech. programs Cambria County Area C.C., 1994-96, bd. trustees C.C., 1996-2000; bd. dirs. Orangeburg-Calhoun Tech. Coll. Fellow Am. Soc. Materials Internat. (chmn. mfg. technology, nominating com., Zay Jeffries award, Edgar C. Bain award, Campbell lecture selection com.); mem. ASME, Am. Powder Metallurgy Inst., Soc. Mfg. Engrs., Light Gage Steel Engrs. Assn., Richland Athletic Assn. (pres.). Democrat. Methodist. Home: 128 McCaffrey Ln Johnstown PA 15905 Office: Industry Blvd Irwin PA 15642

KUHN, JAMES E. judge; b. Hammond, La., Oct. 31, 1946; s. Eton Percy and Mildred Louise (McDaniel) K.; m. Cheryl Aucoin, Dec. 27, 1969; children: James M., Jennifer L. BA, Southeastern La. U., 1968; JD, Loyola U. of South, 1973. Bar: La. 1973, Colo. 1995, U.S. Supreme Ct. 1978. Asst. dist. atty. 21st Jud. Dist., La., 1980-90, judge, 1990-95, Ct. Appeals (1st cir.), Baton Rouge, 1995—. Instr. history, and polit. sci. Southeastern La. U., Hammond, 1991—; past mem. appellate ct. performance and standards com. La. Supreme Ct.; lectr. in field. Founder For Our Youth; past bd. dirs. La. Coun. Child Abuse, past sec.-treas. Conf. of Ct. Appeal Judges for State of La. Recipient Am. Jurisprudence award Loyola Law Sch. Mem. ABA, La. State Bar Assn. (Professionalism and Quality of Life com.), Colo. State Bar Assn., 21st Jud. Bar Assn., Livingston Parish Bar Assn., Baton Rouge Bar Assn., Covington Bar Assn., Fla. Parishes Inns of Ct., Delta Theta Phi. Home: 253 W Oak St Ponchatoula LA 70454-3330

KUHN, JOHN HENRY, retired paper industry executive; b. N.Y.C., Aug. 1, 1930; s. Franz Alfred and Elfriede Engler K.; m. Theresa M. Kuhn, Nov. 29, 1958; children: Eric J., Elaine Kuhn Spear. BS, Rutgers U., 1952; MS, SUNY, Syracuse, 1957. Rsch. asst. Lowe Paper Co., Ridgefield, N.J., 1954-55; corp. mfg. mgr. domestic overseas Container corp. Am., Chgo., 1956-85; v.p. paper mills and mfg. Belkin Packaging Ltd., Toronto, Ont., Canada, 1985-87; v.p., gen. mgr. Cin. Paperboard Corp., 1987-90, ret., 1990. Cons. ops., 1990—; trustee Ctr. for Econ. Initiatives, Cin., 1994—. Bd. sch. dirs. Wissahickon Dist., Blue Bell, Pa., 1969-74; chmn. northwest br. Am. Cancer Soc., Phila., 1969-73; mem. Delnor Hosp. Men's Found., St. Charles, Ill., 1980-85. 1st lt. U.S. Army, 1952-54, Korea. Mem.: Tech. Assn. Pulp and Paper Industry (mem. Ohio sect., mem. exec. com. 1990—, Albert award 1957, Herman Schneider award for Disting. Engr. 2001), Ret. Engrs. and Scientists of Cin. (bd. dirs., pres.), Paper Industry Mgmt. Assn. (trustee emeritus, treas. 1975—82, Glen T. Renegar award 1991), Syracuse Pulp and Paper Found. (life), Optimist Club (dir. 1981—85). Republican. Roman Catholic. Avocations: golf, photography, travel, volunteer historical society archives. Home and Office: 5340 Aspenknoll Ct Cincinnati OH 45230-1376 E-mail: Kuhn5340@aol.com.

KUHN, KATHLEEN JO, accountant; b. Springfield, Ill., Aug. 9, 1947; d. Henry Elmer and Norma Florene (Niehaus) Burge; m. Gerald L. Kuhn, June 22, 1968; children: Gerald Lynn, Brett Anthony. BS in Bus., Bradley U., 1969. CPA Ill. Contr. Byerly Music Co., Peoria, Ill., 1969—70; staff acct. Clifton Gunderson & Cjo., Columbus, Ind., 1970—71; acct. Dept. of Transp., State of Ill., Springfield, 1972—76, Gerald L. Kuhn & Assocs., Springfield, 1976—78, ptnr., 1979—, quality control mgr., 1990—. Grad. asst. Dale Carnegie courses, 1979—80; writer, editor co. policy guideline, 1979—80; editor co. quality control manual, 1990. Pianist Trinity Luth. Ch. Recipient Attendance award, Continuing Profl. Edn. for Accts., 1979—. Mem.: AICPA, Nat. Bus. & Motivational Assn., Am. Woman's Soc. CPAs, Ill. Soc. CPAs, Met. Federated Jr. Women's Club, Springfield Art Assn., Olympic Swim Club. Lutheran. Home: 2511 Westchester Blvd Springfield IL 62704-5406 Office: 2659 Farragut Dr Springfield IL 62704-1462

KUHN, LESLIE ALVIN, cardiologist; b. S. Fallsburg, N.Y., May 10, 1924; Student, Harvard U., 1946; MD, SUNY, Downstate, 1948. Diplomate Am. Bd. Internal Medicine, Am. Bd. Cardiovascular Diseases. Intern Mt. Sinai Hosp., N.Y.C., 1948-49, resident medicine, 1951-52, fellow cardiology, 1952-53, attending cons., 1974—; resident medicine Boston City Hosp., 1949-51; clin. prof. medicine Mt. Sinai Sch. Medicine, N.Y.C., 1974—; pvt. practice. Cons. cardiologist Bronx (N.Y.) VA Hosp. Fellow Am. Coll. Cardiology, ACP; mem. Am. Fedn. Clin. Rsch., AHA, AMA. Address: 5410 Mosholu Ave Bronx NY 10471-2408

KUHN, MATTHEW, retired engineering company executive; b. Sacalaz, Banat, Romania, Mar. 19, 1936; came to U.S., 1967; s. Peter and Katherine (Gerres) K.; m. Betty Jane Ritchie, Aug. 20, 1966; children: Andrew Jason, Andrea Suzanne. BASc in Engring. Physics, Queen's U., Kingston, Ont., Can., 1962; MASc, U. Waterloo, Ont., 1963, PhDEE, 1967, D of Engring. (hon.), 1985; postgrad., Brown U., 1967-68. Supr. MTS Bell Tel. Labs., Murray Hill, NJ, 1968—73; from mgr. adv. tech. to asst. v.p. BNR Ltd., Ottawa, Canada, 1973—85; asst. v.p. BNR Inc., Research Triangle Park, NC, 1985—89; pres. Microelectronics Ctr. of N.C., Research Triangle Park, 1989—94, EconTech Cons. & Rsch. Mgmt. Svcs., 1994—99, ret., 1999. Adj. prof. engring. mgmt. Duke U., 1997-2000; presenter numerous profl. meetings. Contbr. articles to profl. jours. Mem. N.C. Bd. Sci. & Tech., 1991-94; chmn. adv. coun. Queen's U., 1983-84; chmn. engring. adv. coun. Duke U., Durham, N.C., 1989-94. Fellow IEEE (editor spl. issue Electron Devices Jour. Optoelectronics 1975). Roman Catholic. Achievements include discovery of quasi-static method measurement technique for integrated circuit development; co-development first generation fiber optics technology. Home: 2 Whisper Ln Chapel Hill NC 27514-1635 E-mail: mkuhnet@aol.com. *It is sometimes necessary to disagree but never to be disagreeable.*

KUHN, MERRILY A. nursing educator; b. Buffalo, June 16, 1945; d. Norbert and Audrey (Nihart) K. BSN, D'Youville Coll., 1967; MS, Canisius Coll., 1973; PhD in Rsch., Evaluation and Physiology, SUNY, Buffalo, 1981, MSN, 1983. RN, CCRN. Staff nurse Mercy Hosp., Buffalo, 1967; staff, asst. head nurse Dover (N.J.) Gen. Hosp., 1967-68; faculty adult health All Souls Hosp. Sch. Nursing, Morristown, N.J., 1968-69; instr. critical care cardiovascular/respiratory Millard Fillmore Sch. Nursing, Buffalo, 1969-77, asst. prof. D'Youville Coll., Buffalo, 1977-81; asst. prof. pathophysiology/pharmacology SUNY Grad. Nursing Sch., Buffalo, 1981-84; edn. dir. Ednl. Svcs., Hamburg, N.Y., 1980—; assoc. prof. Daemen Coll., Buffalo, 1992—. Cons. in intensive care nursing, pharmacology and complementary therapies throughout U.S. and Can.; nurse, coord., programdesigner for telephone lectr. network series Comm. in Learning, Buffalo, 1976-79; presenter in field. Author: Pharmcotherapeutics: A Nursing Process Approach, 1986, 4th edit., 1998, Manual of IV Drugs, 1996, 2d edit., 1998, Manual of Critical Care Nursing, 1996, Complementary Therapies for the Health Care Provider, 1999, Herbal Therapies & Supplements: A Traditional and Scientific Approach, 2001, (games) Critical Care Challenge, 1990, 1993, NCLEX Challenge Game, 1990, 2 Computer Packages IV Fast Facts and PO Fast Facts, 1992; mem. editl. bd. Critical Care Nurse, 1982—93, 1999—, Jour. N.Y. State Nurses Assn., 1993—; contbr. articles to profl. jours. Bd. dirs. N.Y. State Soc. Critical Care Medicine, 1982-83, Blue Cross Western N.Y., 1980-99; pres. cardiovascular Clin. Specialist Group, 1984, v.p., 1985; mem., coun. nurses Am. Heart Assn. Named Outstanding Young Woman of Am., 1978, 80-95. Mem. ANA, AACN (editor clin. issues 1992), ANA Coun. Computer Application, N.Y. State Nurses Assn. (chmn. edn. com. dist. 1 1995—), Am. Assn. Coun. Nurse Researchers, Hypertension Control Bd. Western N.Y. (bd. dirs. 1977-92), Sigma Theta Tau. Home: 6748 Boston State Rd Hamburg NY 14075-6607

KUHN, PAUL HUBERT, JR., investment counsel; b. Chattanooga, Sept. 7, 1943; s. P. Hubert and Pauline Anna (Byrnes) Kuhn; m. Jeanne Bartlett Elmore, June 7, 1966 (dec. 1996); children: Katherine, Christopher. BA, Vanderbilt U., 1965; MBA, Ind. U., 1971. Chartered investment counselor. V.p., prin. Stein Roe & Farnham, Chgo., 1971-89; v.p. Stein Roe Spl. Fund, Chgo., 1983-89; mng. ptnr. Davidson Ptnrs. Investment Counsel, Nashville, 1989-2000; ptnr. J.C. Bradford & Co., Nashville, 1989-2000. Prin. Woodmont Investment Counsel, 2000—. Bd. dirs. Augustana Hosp., Chgo., 1980-83, USO of Chgo.; pres. Lincoln Park Renewal Corp., Chgo. Lt. USN, 1965-69. Mem. Assn. Investment Mgmt. and Rsch., Nashville Soc. Fin. Analysis (bd. dirs. 1997-2001, pres. 2001-02), Nat. Orgn. Reform Marijuana Laws (bd. dirs. 1997—), Tavern Club (Chgo.) (bd. govs.), Woman's Athletic Club of Chgo. (hon.), Nashville City, Investment Analysts Soc. of Chgo., Phi Beta Kappa, Omicron Delta Kappa. Republican. Roman Catholic. Office: Woodmont Investment Counsel Ste 600 102 Woodmont Blvd Nashville TN 37205 E-mail: paul@woodmontcounsel.com.

KUHN, ROSE MARIE, language educator; b. UCCLE, Belgium; arrived in USA, 1974; m. Thomas H. Zynda. PhD, Catholic Univ., Wash., DC, 1988, MA, 1977, Universite Catholique, Louvain, Belgium, 1974; BA, Facultes Universitaires, St. Louis, 1971. Prof. of French Calif. State Univ., Fresno, Calif., 1988—; vis. asst. prof. of French Christian Bros. Univ., Memphis, 1987—88; asst. prof. of French Rhodes Coll., Memphis, 1983—87; vis. asst. prof. of German Hope Coll., Holland, Mich., 1982—83; lectr. in German Cath. Univ., Wash., DC, 1980—82; lectr. in French Oberlin Coll., Oberlin, Ohio, 1979—80; tchr. in French Nat. Cathedral HS, Wash., DC, 1977—79. Office: Calif State Univ Fresno EE96 Dept of Fgn Lang & Lit Fresno CA 93740-8030

KUHN, RYAN ANTHONY, information industry investment banker; b. Framingham, Mass., Sept. 15, 1947; s. Robert Anthony Kuhn and Julia (Scott) McMillan; m. Cynthia Lynn DeVore, June 4, 1988; 1 child, Ryan R. BA in Psychology, Trinity Coll., Hartford, Conn., 1970; MBA, Harvard U., 1979. Mgr. corp. acquisitions McGraw-Hill, N.Y.C., 1979-85; sr. assoc. venture capital Golder Thoma Cressey, Chgo., 1985-86; pres. Reid Psychol. Systems, Chgo., 1986-90, Lilly Pulitzer, Chgo., 1990-93; prin. Kuhn Capital, Chgo., 1990—. Contbr. articles to profl. publs. and mags.; guest spkr. TV and radio talk show. Bd. dirs. Infant Welfare Soc. Chgo., Harvard Bus. Sch. of Chgo. Republican. Episcopalian. Office: Kuhn Capital 440 N Wells Ste 650 Chicago IL 60610

KUHN, SARAH, educator, consultant; b. Boston, June 24, 1952; d. Thomas Samuel and Kathryn (Louise) Muhs K.; m. Ralph Edward LaChance, 1987. BA, Harvard U., 1974; PhD, MIT, 1987. Pvt. practice cons., researcher, 1984—; project mgr. Stone Ctr. Wellesley (Mass.) Coll., 1987-88; prof. policy and planning U. Mass., Lowell, Mass., 1990—. Instr., researcher MIT, 1980-83; economist, Econ. Lit. Project, Boston, 1979—; mem. High Tech Rsch. Group, Cambridge, 1981-87. Author: Computer Manufacturing in New England, 1982, (with others) The Retail Revolution, 1981, Massachusetts High Tech: The Promise and the Reality, 1984. Fellow Harvard-MIT Joint Ctr. Urban Studies, 1982-83, Eastern Women's Rowing Champion, Nat. Women's Rowing Assn., 1974. Mem. Assn. Computing Machinery, Am. Planning Assn. Jewish. Office: U Mass Lowell Dept Policy and Planning Coll Mgmt Lowell MA 01854

KUHN, THOMAS B, education educator; b. Zurich, Zurich, Switzerland, Dec. 23, 1960; s. Robert Bernard and Elisabeth Maria Kuhn; m. Amanda Jill Copus, June 3, 1995; children: Sally Liane, Ella Jane. PhD, U. of Zurich, 1981—91. Asst. prof. U. of Alaska, 1998—2002, U. of Mont., 2002—. Pres. Alaska Chpt. of the Soc. for Neuroscience. Mem. editl. bd. Jour. of Biol. Chemistry, 2000—. Spinal cord Regeneration Rsch., Christopher Reeve Paralysis Found., 2000—02, Alaska Basic Neuroscience Program, NIH, 2000—. Mem.: Am. Soc. for Biochemistry and Molecular Biology, Am. Soc. for Cell Biology, Soc. for Neuroscience. Office: University of Montana Dept of Pharmaceutical Sci Missoula MT 59812

KUHN, VIRGINIA R. lawyer; b. Neillsville, Wis., July 29, 1963; d. Bernard Herman and Ruby Violet K.; m. Michael Joseph Schlecht, Aug. 28, 1993. BA, U. Wis., 1985; JD, Hamline U., 1989. Bar: Minn. 1990. Reference atty. West Pub., St. Paul, 1990-91; atty. advisor Office of Hearings and Appeals, Mpls., 1991-95, sr. atty., 1995—. Lectr. Hennepin C.C., Mpls., 1993-98; coach mock trial team Hamline U., St. Paul, 1998; vol. atty. Legal Aid Svc., St. Paul, 1991-92. Vol. Salvation Army, Mpls., 1995—; bd. dirs. Minn. Stroke Assn., 1999; mentor Homework N'Hoops, Mpls., 1999. Mem. Minn. State Bar Assn., Hennepin County Bar Assn. Democrat. Avocations: reading, skiing, mountain biking, rollerblading. Office: Office of Hearings & Appeals 330 2nd Ave S Ste 650 Minneapolis MN 55401-2225

KUHN, WALTER F. emergency medicine physician; b. Harrisburg, Pa., Sept. 21, 1948; s. Walter F. and Estelle H. K.; m. Sharon C., June 1972; children: Joshua, Lydia. BS, U. N.C., 1970; MD, Pa. State U., 1974. Diplomate Am. Bd. Family Practice, Am. Bd. Emergency Medicine, Tropical Medicine and Travelers Health; cert. forensic examiners. Med. dir. CHAPA project, Bangladesh, 1977-81; asst. prof. Pa. State U., Hershey, 1983-85; staff physician Kent Gen. Hosp., Dover, Del., 1985-90; assoc. prof. Med. Coll. Ga., Augusta, 1990—2003, prof. emergency medicine, 2003—. Med. dir. Mission to the World Presbyn. Ch. of Am., 1999—. Office: Med Coll Ga 1120 15th St Augusta GA 30912-0006

KUHN, WHITEY, advertising executive; Pres. Kuhn & Wittenborn Advt., Kansas City, Mo., 1978—. Office: Kuhn & Wittenborn Advt Ste 600 2405 Grand Blvd Kansas City MO 64108

KUHN, WILLIAM FRANK, music educator; b. Piqua, Ohio, July 8, 1955; s. Frank C. and Emma Marie Kuhn; m. Kristine Lynn Tuchardt, Oct. 11, 1986; children: Michael William, Elizabeth Marie. BA, Concordia Tchrs. Coll., River Forest, Ill., 1977; MusM, Northwestern U., Evanston, Ill., 1985; EdD, U. Nebr., Lincoln, 2000. Dir. music Luther H.S. South, Chgo., 1977—80; dir. sec. music Hong Kong Internat. Sch., Repulse Bay, Hong Kong, 1980—93; chair, dept. of music, dir. instrumental music Concordia U. - Nebr., Seward, 1993—. Min. of music Ch. of All Nations - Luth., Repulse Bay, 1980—93; dir. Lincoln (Nebr.) Luth. Choir, 1998—2003. Composer: (choral composition) This Child, Lord, Lord of All Hopefulness. Recipient Leadermaker Award, Hong Kong Internat. Sch., 1993. Mem.: Assn. of Luth. Ch. Musicians, Nebr. Bandmasters Assn., Nebr. Music Educators Assn., Music Educators Nat. Conf., Pi Kappa Lambda. Lutheran. Avocations: travel, reading, cooking. Home: 947 North 12th St Seward NE 68434-1403 Office: Concordia Univ 800 North Columbia Ave Seward NE 68434 E-mail: wkuhn@cune.edu.

KUHN, WILLIS EVAN, II, lawyer, mediator; b. Indpls., July 20, 1948; s. Theodore Roosevelt and Theresa Anne (Lupinacci) K.; m. Virginia Katherine Williams, Apr. 12, 1983; children: William Franklin, Virginia Anne. BA, Vanderbilt U., 1970; JD with honors, U. Tex., 1973. Bar: Tex. 1973, cert. mediator. Assoc. Johnson & Gibbs, Dallas, 1973-75, Moore & Peterson, Dallas, 1975-80; ptnr. Baker, Smith & Mills, Dallas, 1980-85, Kuhn & Fishman, Dallas, 1985-90, Hopkins & Sutter, Dallas, 1990-93; pvt. practice Dallas, 1993—. Mem. Dallas So. Meml. Assn., 1992—. Mem. State Bar Tex., Dallas Bar Assn., Dallas Athletic Club, Order of Coif, Phi Kappa Psi. Republican. Avocations: golf, history. Home: 4118 Briargrove Ln Dallas TX 75287-6601 Office: 15851 N Dallas Pkwy #600 Dallas TX 75001-6030

KUHNS, CRAIG SHAFFER, business educator; b. Spokane, Wash., Apr. 14, 1928; s. Theodore Lewis and Audrey Grace (Shaffer) K. BS, U. Calif., Berkeley, 1950, BA, 1954, MBA, 1955. Analyst Standard Oil Co. of Calif., San Francisco, 1955-57; bus. educator U. Calif./San Jose State U., 1958-63, City Coll. of San Francisco, 1963—. Adj. faculty U. San Francisco, 1977-90. 1st lt. U.S. Army, 1951-52, col. Mil. Intelligence USAR, 1953-80, col. AUS, ret. Mem. Calif. Alumni Assn., U.S. Army War Coll. Alumni Assn., Res. Officers Assn,. Japan Soc. Republican. Avocation: travel. Home: 8 Locksley Ave Apt 8A San Francisco CA 94122-3850 Office: City Coll San Francisco 50 Phelan Ave San Francisco CA 94112-1821 E-mail: croco_dile123@msn.com.

KUHNS, NANCY EVELYN, minister; b. Coaldale, Pa., June 5, 1947; d. Calvin Joseph and Helen Mary (Gerber) K. BS in Bible, United Wesleyan Coll., 1969; MS in Early Childhood Edn., Marywood Coll., 1982; MDiv, Lancaster (Pa.) Theol. Sem., 1987. Ordained to ministry United Ch. of Christ, 1988. Organist, choir dir. Zion Stone Ch. of Snyder's, New Ringgold, Pa., 1976-86; pastor Rebersburg (Pa.) Charge United Ch. of Christ, 1987—. Gen. Synod Del., 1993, 95; dir. day care ctr. Jim Thorpe and Lehighton, Pa., 1976-86. Bd. dirs. Pa. Ctrl. Conf., United Ch. of Christ, 1991-93, 2000-2003, chair ch. and ministry com., 1996-99. Home: PO Box 156 Rebersburg PA 16872-0156

KUHRAU, EDWARD W. lawyer; b. Caney, Kans., Apr. 19, 1935; s. Edward and Dolores (Hardman) Kuhrau; m. Janiece Christal (div. 1983); children: Quentin, Clayton; m. Sandy Shreve. BA, U. Tex., 1960; JD, U. So. Calif., 1965. Bar: Calif. 1966, Wash. 1968, Alaska 1977. With Perkins Coie (and predecessor firms), Seattle, 1968—, ptnr., 1973—. Editor-in-chief Wash. Real Property Deskbook; contbr. articles to profl. jours. With USAF, 1955—58. Mem. ABA, Wash. Bar Assn., Am. Coll. Real Estate Lawyers, Pacific Real Estate Inst. (pres., founding trustee), Order of Coif, Seattle Yacht Club, Wing Point Golf and Country Club, Poulsbo Yacht Club. Office: Perkins Coie 1201 3rd Ave Fl 40 Seattle WA 98101-3029 E-mail: kuhre@perkinscoie.com.

KUHRT, SHARON LEE, nursing administrator; b. Denver, July 20, 1957; d. John Wilfred and Yoshiko (Ueda) Kuhrt. BSN, Loretto Heights Coll., 1982; MSN, Regis U., 1992. RN Colo., Mass., Maine. RN level III Porter Meml. Hosp., Denver, 1981-87; transport supr. Kapiolani Med. Ctr. Women & Children, Honolulu, 1987-89; dir. patient care unit Aspen Valley Hosp., Colo., 1989-91; dir. clin. practice Ctrl. Maine Med. Ctr., Lewiston, 1991-2000, dir. Sch. Nursing, 1998—. Home: 873 Oak Hill Rd North Yarmouth ME 04097-6242 E-mail: skhurts@cmhc.org.

KUJALA, WALFRID EUGENE, musician, educator; b. Warren, Ohio, Feb. 19, 1925; s. Arvo August and Elsie Fannie (Ojajarvi) K.; m. Sherry Henry, Dec. 29, 1989; children by previous marriage: Stephen, Gwen, Daniel. MusB, Eastman Sch. Music, 1948, MusM, 1950. Flutist Rochester Philharm. Orch., 1948—54; soloist, flutist, piccoloist Chgo. Symphony Orch., 1954—2001; prof. flute Northwestern U., Evanston, Ill., 1962—. Vis. prof. of flute Shepherd Sch. Music, Rice U., 1995-97. Author: The Flutist's Progress, 1970, The Flutist's Vade Mecum of Scales, Arpeggios, Trills and Fingering Technique, 1995; consulting editor Flute Talk Mag., 1991—; contbr. articles to profl. jours.; performed world premiere of Concerto for Flute by Gunther Schuller with Chgo. Symphony Orch., conducted by Sir Georg Solti, 1988. Served with AUS, 1943-45, ETO, PTO. Recipient Exemplar of Music Tchg. award, Northwestern U., 1992. Mem.: Nat. Flute Assn. (past pres., Lifetime Achievement award 1997). Office: Sch Music Northwestern U Evanston IL 60208-2400 E-mail: walfridkujala@aol.com.

KUJAWSKI, DANIEL, science educator; b. Bujenka, Poland, Feb. 23, 1948; came to U.S., 1996; s. Jan and Czeslawa Kujawska; m. Danuta Radziszewska, July 14, 1974; 1 child, Anna. MSc, Warsaw (Poland) Tech. U., 1973, DSc, 1992; PhD, Polish Acad. Scis., 1978. Lectr., sr. lectr. Warsaw Tech. U., 1975-89; lectr., sr. rsch. assoc. U. Alta., Edmonton, Can., 1989-96; from assoc. prof. to prof. Western Mich. U., Kalamazoo, 1996—. Co-chmn. low-cycle fatigue com. Polish Group Fracture, 1987-89. Author: (textbook) Fatigue Life of Metals, 1991, (book) Modeling of the Fatigue Life and Crack Propagation in Metals, 1991. Killam postdoctoral scholar U. Alta., Edmonton, 1983-85. Mem. ASME, SAE. Achievements include research in the mech. behavior of metals and composites, fatigue and fracture mechanics. Avocations: tennis, swimming, walking. Office: Western Mich U Mech and Aero Engring Kalamazoo MI 49008 Fax: (616) 387-3358. E-mail: daniel.kujawski@wmich.edu.

KUJAWSKI, ELIZABETH SZANCER, art curator, consultant; b. N.Y.C., Feb. 7, 1951; d. Henryk and Irene (Zilz) Szancer; children: Melissa, Stephanie. BA cum laude in Art History and Italian, Douglass Coll., 1972; MA in Art History, Queens Coll., 1975. Info. asst. Whitney Mus. Am. Art, N.Y.C., 1972-75; asst. curator Collection of Nelson A. Rockefeller, N.Y.C., 1975-79; asst. dir. SKT Galleries, Inc., N.Y.C., 1979-82; prin., art curator, cons. Elizabeth Szancer Kujawski Art Advisors, N.Y.C., 1982—. Mem. exhbn. com. Internat. Ctr. Photography, N.Y.C. Mem.: Art Table, Inc., Internat. Assn. Profl. Art Advisors (pres. 1998—2003, bd. dirs.). Avocations: tennis, piano, travel. Office: 767 5th Ave Ste 4200 New York NY 10153-0023

KUJAWSKI, MARIO JULIO, artist, educator; b. Buenos Aires, May 13, 1944; s. Richard and Irma Dorothea K. BA, Brown U., 1966; MA, Ohio State U., 1969. Instr. Dayton (OHio) Art Inst., 1969-71, U. Dayton, 1971-73, Wright State U., Dayton, 1973-75, Montgomery County, Dayton, 1975-81; asst. prof. Kent (Ohio) State U., 1984-91; lectr. Beck Ctr. Arts, Lakewood, Ohio, 1995—, Cons. Living Arts Ctr., Dayton, 1974—75; instr. adult program Cleve. Inst. Art, 1990—; artists adv. bd. New Orgn. Visual Arts, Cleve., 1993—99; workshop

leader State of Ohio, 1998—; bd. trustees Artist's Archives Western Res., 2001, archived artist, 2001—. Represented in collections of Dayton Mus. Art, State of Ohio, Chrysler Corp., Sherwin Williams, Mead Data Ctr., Chase Manhattan Bank. Judge Parma (Ohio) City Schs., 1999. Jewish. Avocations: swimming, painting, reading. Studio: 1900 Superior Ave # 116 Cleveland OH 44114 E mail: mariokujawski@aol.com.

KUK, MICHAEL LOUIS, protective services official; b. Clinton, Iowa, Jan. 11, 1949; s. Louis and Mary Ann (Popdan) K. MS, Columbia Pacific U., 1988; PhD in Religion, Univeral Life Ch. U., 1998. Cert. emergency med. tech., safety splst., fire officer IV, insp. II, Instr. III, HazMat tech., fire and arson investigator. Firefighter, emergency med. tech. Clinton (Iowa) Fire Dept., 1972-76; fire safety tech. Olin Chems., Lake Charles, La., 1976-81; fire chief PPG Industries, Westlake, La., 1979-81, Ward 1 Fire Dist., Moss Bluff, La., 1976-85; CEO, founder On Fire Cons., Clinton, 1985-89; fire chief Savanna (Ill.) Army Depot, 1989-2000; asst. fire chief Ft. Leavenworth, Kans., 2000—. Author: M.A.C.I. Modifications, 1993, 97; contbr. articles to profl. jours. Guest spkr. Fire Svc. Caucus, Washington, 1997. With U.S. Army, 1969 71; army civilian firefighter, 1998, fire chaplain. Recipient Purple Heart of Firefighting, Internat. Fire Inst., 1992; named Firefighter of Yr. VFW, 1982, 83, 84. Mem. Internat. Assn. Fire Chiefs, Musicians Union #67. Byzantine Catholic. Avocations: music, collecting firefighting memorabilia. Home: 918 Cottonwood Dr Lansing KS 66043-6264 E-mail: mlkuk@hotmail.com.

KUKER, ALAN MICHAEL, lawyer; b. Neptune, N.J., Oct. 7, 1942; s. Max Irving and Ruth (Lewis) K.; m. Belen Castillo. BA, Rutgers U., 1964; JD, Boston U., 1967. Bar: Fla. 1968, U.S. Dist. Ct. (so. dist.) Fla. 1968, U.S. Ct. Appeals (5th cir.) 1968, U.S. Supreme Ct., 1980. With Legal Svcs., South Fla., 1968-72; pvt. practice Miami, Fla., 1973; adminstrv. judge Miami-Dade & Monroe County Dist. Office, 1986—. V.p. Friends of 440 Scholarship Fund. Contbr. articles to profl. jours. Recipient Innovator award. Mem. Fla. Bar Assn., Dade County Bar Assn., Miami Beach Bar Assn. Office: Office of Judge of Compensation Cliams State of Fla 401 NW 2nd Ave 5-321 Miami FL 33128-1740 E-mail: amk022@hotmail.com.

KUKIELKA, GILBERT LEON, physician; b. San Jose, Costa Rica, Jan. 28, 1959; came to U.S., 1987; s. Zelman Kukielka and Regina Hedrych; m. Morissa J. Ladinsky, Sept. 1, 1991; children: Andrew, Nicole. MD with highest honors, U. Costa Rica, 1983. Diplomate in internal medicine, cardiovasc. disease and interventional cardiology Am. Bd. Internal Medicine. Intern U. Costa Rica, San Jose, 1982-83, resident internal medicine, 1984-87, chief med. resident, 1986-87; resident internal medicine Baylor Coll. Medicine, Houston, 1988-90, fellow cardiovascular scis., 1990-94, rsch. asst. prof., 1992-95, asst. prof., 1995-96, adj. asst. prof., 1996—; fellow in cardiology Johns Hopkins U. Sch. Medicine, Balt., 1995-98, interventional cardiology fellow, 1998-99; peripheral vascular interventional fellow Lindner Ctr. Cardiovascular Clin. Rsch./Christ Hosp., Cin., 1999-2000; asst. prof., dir. peripheral vascular intervention Ohio State U., Columbus. Sci. reviewer Jour. Leukocyte Biology, 1993—, Circulation, 1994—, Gene, 1994—; contbr. articles to profl. jours. Recipient Outstanding Achievement award for basic rsch. Curaflex, 1992, Young Investigator award So. Soc. Pediat. Rsch., 1992, Virginia and Ernest Cocknell Jr. award The Meth. Hosp. Found., Houston, 1995, Outstanding Young Ams., 1988, Am. Coll. Cardiology/Bristol-Myers Squibb award, 1999; named one of Am.'s Top Physicians, 2003; Baylor Coll. Medicine grantee, 1994. Fellow ACP, Am. Coll. Cardiology; mem. AMA, Johns Hopkins Med. and Surg. Assn., Soc. Leukocyte Biology (Young Investigator award 1994). Office: Ohio State U Heart Ctr 473 West 12th St 200 HL RI Columbus OH 43210 E-mail: gilk@osu.edu.

KUKLA, EDWARD RICHARD, rare books & special collections librarian; b. Detroit, Jan. 31, 1941; s. Stanley Frank and ClaraBelle (Morton) K. BA, Wayne State U., 1962; MA, U. Mich., 1963, MLS, 1973. Asst. instr. Mich. State U., East Lansing, 1970-72; media mobile libr. State Libr. of Mich., 1972; asst. libr. rare books and manuscripts libr. Greenfield Village and Henry Ford Mus., Dearborn, Mich., 1974-78; rare books and spl. collections libr. Wash. State U., Pullman, 1979-86; head spl. collections dept. Mpls. Pub. Libr., Mpls. Athenaeum Libr., 1987—. Educator, lectr. rare books, history of books and printing, book collecting; reviewer NEH. Author: Un estudio critico sobre Altazor de Vicente Huidobro, 1963, The Scholar and the Future of the Research Library Revisited, 1973, The Struggle and the Glory: A Special Bicentennial Exhibition, 1976. Recipient C. Allen Harlan scholarship, 1958, medal of distinction Fgn. Lang., 1958; tchg. fellow U. Mich, Ann Arbor, 1963-66. Mem. ALA, Assn. Coll. and Rsch. Librs. (rare books sect. 1990, local arrangements com.), U. Mich. Sch. Libr. Sci. Alumni Assn. (life), Am. Contract Bridge League, Am. Cut Glass Assn. (life), Am. Film Inst. (charter), Am. Swedish Inst., English First (life), Haviland Collectors Internationale Found., Minn. Film Arts Founders Club, Pickard Collectors Club (charter), Walker Art Ctr., Inst. Arts, Mpls. Friends of Libr. Assn., Mpls. Libr. Staff Assn., Mich. Jr. Acad. Sci., Art and Letters (jr. mem.), Ampersand Club, U. Mich. Union Club (life), Phi Beta Kappa, Sigma Delta Pi, Beta Phi Mu. Home: 2439 3rd Ave S Apt C-11 Minneapolis MN 55404-3518 Office: Mpls Pub Library 250 Marquette Ste 400 Minneapolis MN 55401-2188

KUKLA, MAIJA MEIJER, research scientist, educator; b. Riga, Latvia, May 10, 1965; d. Meijer Girsh and Iraida Ivanovna Kukla; children: Anna Belak, Mark Belak. BS, MSc, U. Latvia, Riga, 1988, DSc (hon.), 1996. Cert. lead rsch. scientist title. Vis. rschr. Zelinsky Inst. Organic Chemistry, Moscow, 1988—89; rsch. assoc. Inst. Chem. Physics, Riga, 1991—96, sr. rsch. assoc., 1996—98, lead rsch. scientist, 1998—2002; program dir. U.S. NSF, Arlington, Va., 2002—. Invited scientist UNESCO Internat. Ctr. Theoretical Physics, Trieste, Italy, 1994; Office Naval Rsch. postdoctoral fellow Mich. Technol. U., Houghton, 1997—2000, rsch. faculty, 2000—01; rsch. scientist U. Md., College Park, 2001—02, Naval Warfare Ctr., Indian Head, Md., 2001—; reviewer Jour. Am. Ceramic Soc., Jour. Applied Physics, NATO Rsch. Series, Thermochimica Acta, Physica Status Solidi, MRS Procs.; presenter in field. Contbr. articles to profl. jours. Mem.: Am. Phys. Soc., Materials Rsch. Soc., Am. Chem. Soc.

KUKLIN, ANTHONY BENNETT, lawyer; b. N.Y.C., Oct. 9, 1929; s. Norman B. and Deane (Cable) K.; m. Vivienne May Hall, Apr. 4, 1964; children: Melissa, Amanda. AB, Harvard U., 1950; JD, Columbia U., 1953. Bar: N.Y. 1953, D.C. 1970. Assoc. Dwight, Royall, Harris, Koegel & Caskey, N.Y.C., 1955-61, Paul, Weiss, Rifkind, Wharton & Garrison, N.Y.C., 1961-69, ptnr., 1969-95, counsel, 1995—. Lectr. in Law, Columbia Law Sch., 1997-2001; bd. dirs. Chgo. Title & Trust Co., Chgo. Title Ins. Co., 1986-96. Contbr. articles to legal jours. Mem. ABA (chmn., sec. real property, probate and trust law 1987-88), Internat. Bar Assn. (chmn. div. one 1985-88), N.Y. State Bar Assn. (chmn. sect. real property 1981-82), Assn. of Bar of city of N.Y., Am. Coll. Real Estate Lawyers (pres. 1981-82), Anglo-Am. Real Property Inst. (chmn. 1989), Am. Coll. Constrn. Lawyers. Home: 22 Pryer Ln Larchmont NY 10538-4022 Office: Paul Weiss Rifkind Wharton & Garrison Ste # 4200 1285 Ave of Ams Fl 22 New York NY 10019-6065

KUKOC, TONI, professional basketball player; b. Croatia, Sept. 18, 1968; Forward Chicago Bulls, 1993-99, Phila. 76ers, 1999—. Named European Player of the Yr.; recipient NBA Sixth Man of the Yr., 1995—96. Avocations: yachting, fishing, tennis, golf, movies. Office: Phila 76ers 1st Union Ctr Philadelphia PA 19148

KUKOVICH, ALLEN GALE, state legislator, lawyer; b. Greensburg, Pa., Sept. 5, 1947; s. Albert Francis and Catherine Thelma (Heasley) K.; m. Nancy Ruth Egeberg, Nov. 23, 1991; 1 child, Alexandra Gale. BA in Polit. Sci., Kent State U., 1969; JD, Duquesne U., 1973. Bar: Pa. 1973. Pvt. practice, 1973-77; mem. Pa. Ho. of Reps., Harrisburg, 1977-96, Pa. Senate, Dist. 39, 1996—; pvt. practice North Huntingdon, Pa., 1995—. Bd. dirs. Americans for Dem. Action, Childrens Trust Fund; pres. Pa. Inst. on Pub. Policy. Mem. Pa. Bar Assn. (legal svcs. to the pub. com.), Westmoreland County Bar Assn. Office: Senate Box 203039 185 Capitol Bldg Harrisburg PA 17120

KUKRAL, MICHAEL ANDREW, geographer, educator; b. Richfield, Ohio, Oct. 15, 1959; s. Clarence Ferdinand Kukral and Ada Mae Nemer. BS in Geography, Ohio U., 1982, MA in Polit. Sci., 1986, MSc in Environ. Sci., 1987; PhD in Geography, U. Ky., 1995. Prof. geography Ohio U., Athens, 1992—95, Ohio Wesleyan U., Delaware, Ohio, 1996—99; dir. Kukral Inst. Geography Exploration, Terre Haute, Ind., 1997—; prof. geography Rose-Hulman Inst. Tech., Terre Haute, Ind., 1999—. Author: Prague 1989: Theater of Revolution, 1997. Faculty advisor Lambda Chi Alpha Frat., Terre Haute, Ind., 2000—. Named to Hall of Fame, Revere H.S., Richfield, OH, 1998; fellow, U.S. Fulbright Commn., 1989—90; grantee Internat. Project, Lilly Found., 1992, Provost's Summer Pool grantee, Ohio U., 1994, 1995; scholar McCurty scholar, Bath Twp. Playhouse, 1978. Mem.: Ind. Acad. of Social Sciences (exec. dir. 2000), Assn. Am. Geographers (chair, Hoffman award com. 2001, Viola Hoffman Dissertation award 1989), Automatic Musical Instruments Collector's Assn. (life; historian), Phi Beta Delta (hon.), Kappa Kappa Psi (life; pres. 1981—82), Lambda Chi Alpha (life; faculty advisor). Green Party. Roman Catholic. Avocations: backpacking, travel, player piano restoration, music, naturalist. Home: 216 Madison Blvd Terre Haute IN 47803 Office: Rose-Hulman Institute of Technology 5500 Wabash Ave CM 92 Terre Haute IN 47803 Home Fax: 812-877-8909; Office Fax: 812-877-8909. Personal E-mail: kukral@rose-hulman.edu. E-mail: kukral@rose-hulman.edu.

KUKULINSKY, NANCY ELAINE, health care consultant; b. Pitts, Pa, Feb. 22, 1950; d. Henry Herman and Jennie Loretta (Guzeli) K.; children: Jeremy David Patches, Melissa Ann Patches BS, U. Pitts., 1971; MPA, Pa. State U., 1981; PhD, U. Pitts., 1987. Rsch. project asst. Pa. State U., University Park, 1971-80; exec. dir. Pathology Edn. and Rsch. Found., Pitts., 1980-90; dir. bus. ops. Sch. Medicine, U. Cin., 1991-98; exec. dir. Acad. Pathology Assoc. Inc., Cin., 1991-98; bus. mgr. Ctrl. Bapt. Hosp. Surgery Ctr., Lexington, Ky., 1999—2002; dir. admin. Gen. Clin. Rsch. Ctr., U. Ky. Coll. Medicine, 2002—. Cons. Physicians' Adv. Network, Pitts., 1990—; trustee No. Allegheny Found. for Excellence, Pitts., 1989-91, Path-Tek Diagnostics, Inc., Pitts., 1987-88. Contbr. articles to profl. jour. Trustee Montgomery County Sch. Dist. Ednl. Found., Mt. Sterling, Ky. Mem. Med. Group Mgmt. Assn., Acad. Practice Assn., Pathology Mgmt. Assn., Assn. Women Adminstr., Grad. Women in Sci. (pres. 1978-79). Democrat. Roman Catholic. Avocation: collecting turn of the century oak furniture and corvettes. Home: 409 W High St Mount Sterling KY 40353-1329 E-mail: kukuline@bellsouth.net.

KUKURA, RITA ANNE, pre-school educator; b. Tulsa, July 18, 1947; d. James Albert and Carmen Alberta (Parsons) Hayden; m. Joel Richard Graft, Oct. 28, 1967 (dec. Apr. 1969); m. Raymond Richard Kukura, Dec. 18, 1971 (div. 1981); children: Tiffany Carmen Noel, Austin Raymond. BS, Kent. State U., 1971; MS, Okla. State U., 1991. Cert. early childhood, nursery, elem. tchr., Okla., spl. edn. tchr. for emotionally disturbed. Tchr. kindergarten Southlyn Elem. Sch., Lyndhurst, Ohio, 1971-73; elem. tchr. Wakefield Acad., Tulsa, 1981-83, tchr. kindergarten, 1983-87; reg. early intervention coord. Okla. Dept. Edn., Tulsa, 1990-92; tchr. devel. delayed children, coord. integrated program Child Devel. Inst. Children's Med. Ctr., Tulsa, 1992-93; tchr. elem. sch. Prue (Okla.) Schs., 1993-95, Tulsa Pub. Schs., 1995—. Manuscript reviewer for profl. orgns., 1989-91; mem. human rights com. Ind. Opportunities of Okla., 1995—; Oklahoma Edn. Assn. Leadership Acad., 1998; del. Okla. Edn. Assembly, 1995; grant reviewer for spl. grants State Dept. Edn., 1996; presenter and lectr. in field. Den leader Cub Scouts Am., Tulsa, 1984-88; com. mem. Boy Scouts Am., Tulsa, 1984-88; vol. office worker Met. Tulsa Citizen Crime Commn., 1986; adv. com. Latchkey Project, Tulsa County, 1985; ad hoc task force on day care Interagy. Coord. Coun., 1989-91; nat. rep. Tourette Syndrome Assn. to Nat. Broadcasting Assn. AERho, 1990-93; mem. resource com. Ronald McDonald House, 1990-92, vol. Tulsa area, 1991-97, STARBASE, 1993—, Drug Edn. for Youth, 1994; mem. adv. bd. Tulsa Regional Coordinating Coun. for Svcs. to Children and Youth and Families, 1991-92; planning com. symposium Magic Coun. Girl Scouts Am., 1991-93; lt. sr. mem. Tulsa Composite Squadron CAP, 1992-94; presenter numerous confs.; workshop participant Alternatives to Violence Project, 1996. Recipient Den Leader Tng. award Boy Scouts Am., 1988, State Commendation medal Air N.G., 1993. Mem. AAUW (bd. dirs. Tulsa county chpt. 1991-93, mem., 1997-2000), Nat. Assn. Early Childhood Tchr. Educators, Nat. Tourette Syndrome Assn. (state pres. 1987-92, state dir. 1992-93, hon. mem. bd. dirs. 1993, area coord., fundraiser 1988-90), Gold Star Wives Am., Tulsa Classroom Tchrs. Assn. (bldg. del. 1997-98), Okla. Edn. Assn. (leadership acad. 1998), Okla. Edn. Assn. (mem. resolution com. 1998-2000), Kappa Delta Pi, Omicron Nu, Alpha Epsilon Rho (hon. mem. S.W. region 1990-93), Phi Delta Kappa. Roman Catholic. Avocations: piano, exercising, reading. Office: Burroughs Elem Sch 1927 N Cincinnati Tulsa OK 74106 E-mail: kukurri@tulsaschools.org.

KULA, KATHERINE SUE, dentist; b. Dayton, Ohio, Oct. 5, 1945; d. James Adam and Adelaide Charlotte (Thaler) Miller; m. Theodore John Kula Jr., Aug. 2, 1969; children: Stacy Charlotte, Theodore John III. BS, U. Dayton, 1966, MS, 1972; DMD, U. Ky., 1977; MS, cert. in pediat. dentistry, U. Iowa, 1979; cert. in orthodontics, U. Md., 1992. Sci. tchr. Lexington Cath. HS, Ky., 1969-71, chmn. sci. dept., 1971-73; resident U. Iowa Dental Sch., Iowa City, 1977-79; asst. prof. U. Md. Dental Sch., Balt., 1979-84, assoc. prof., 1984-92; assoc. prof. dept. orthodontics and pediatric dentistry U. NC Dental Sch., Chapel Hill, 1992-97, adj. prof., 1998—; chair dept. orthodontics & dentofacial orthopedics U. Mo., Kans. City, 1998—. Mem. staff U. N.C. Hosp., Chapel Hill, 1992-97, dental faculty practice, 1992—; outside grant reviewer NIH-NIDR, Washington, 1993—; manuscript reviewer Pediatric Dentistry Jour., Chgo., 1982—. Angle Orthodontist Contbr. articles to profl. jour. and chpts. to books. Bd. dir. Bridges-Leadership for Women, Chapel Hill, 1995-96, Virginia Brown Found., Kans. City, 2002—, Grantee NIH-Nat. Insts. Dental Rsch., 1994, Am. Assn. Dental Schs., 1997. Fellow Am. Coll. Dentists, Am. Acad. Pediatric Dentists, Am. Acad. Pediatric Dentists (1st pl. table clinic ednl. rsch. 1994, Rsch. award 1980); mem. Md. Soc. Dentistry for Children (pres., sec.-treas. 1979-92), Am. Assn. Dental Rsch. (sec.-treas. Balt. sect. 1979-92, Am. Assn. Dental Sch. (sec., chair, councilor orthodontics sect. 1993-2001, mem.-at-large coun. of sects. 2001-02, sec. 2002, chair-elect 2003, 1st pl. Rsch. award 2000, 1st pl. World Wide Web Instrnl. Materials 2002, chair-elect 2003), Am. Assn. Orthodontists, Internat. Assn. Dental Rsch. Avocation: gardening. E-mail: kulak@umkc.edu.

KULACKI, FRANCIS ALFRED, engineer, educator; b. Balt., May 21, 1942; s. Frank Alfred and Ida (Jarowski) K.; m. Jane H. Davidson, Nov. 29, 1985; children: Sarah, Nancy. BSME, Ill. Inst. Tech., 1963, MS in Gas Engring., 1966; PhD, U. Minn., 1971. From asst. prof. to assoc. prof. mech. engring. Ohio State U., Columbus, 1971-79; prof., chmn. dept. mech. and aerospace engring. U. Del., Newark, 1980-85; dean engring. Colo. State U., Ft. Collins, 1986-93; dean Inst. of Tech./U. Minn., 1993—95, prof., 1996—. Cons. in field; mem. Minn. High Tech. Coun., 1993-95; mem. ind. adv. bd. U. Md., Baltimore County; mem. engring. U. Ky. Contbr. numerous articles to profl. jours. Pres. Columbia Tech. Council, 1980; pres. Arbour Park Civic Assn., Newark, 1985; mem. engring. coun. Swarthmore Coll., 1985-93. Fellow ASME (chmn. heat transfer div. 1987-88, various bds. and coms.), AAAS, Am. Soc. Engring Edn., NSPE (ednl. adv. group, chair 1990-93); mem. Phi Kappa Sigma, Tau Beta Pi, Pi Tau Sigma. Home: 5020 Arden Ave Edina MN 55424-1314 Office: U Minn Dept Mech Engring 121 ME Minneapolis MN 55455

KULAK, DARYL WAYNE, holistic health business educator; b. Edmonton, Alta., Can., Mar. 20, 1963; s. Wayne and Eunice Kulak; m. Tamara Oakley, Jan. 29, 1999. Grad. in computer sys. tech., NO. Alta. Inst. Tech., Edmonton, 1983. Tech. arch. SHL Systemhouse, Inc., Edmonton, 1983-95; dir. corp. tng. Claremont Tech. Group, Columbus, Ohio, 1995-98; dir. e-bus. practice CBSI, Columbus, 1998-99; pres., CEO Water-Logic, Inc., Westerville, Ohio, 2000—02; pres. The Simplicity Inst., Westerville, Ohio, 2002—. Author: Use Cases: Requirements in Context, 2000, 2d edit., 2003. Mem. Natural Law Party, Green Energy Ohio. Avocations: reading, writing, travel, politics. E-mail: daryl@simplicity-institute.com.

KULAS, FREDERICK JOHN, computer company executive; b. Hanover, N.J., June 27, 1951; s. Walenty William and Liliane Maria (Cailliatte) K.; m. Mary Catherine Rodock, July 19, 1987. BSME, Worcester Poly. Inst., 1973; MBA, Harvard U., 1977; grad., GE Mfg. Mgmt. Program, 1975. EIT Mass. Mfg. mgr. GE, Schenectady, N.Y., 1973-74, Plainville, Conn., 1974-75; mktg. rep. IBM Corp., Waltham, Mass., 1977-80; product mktg. mgr. Digital Equipment Corp., Hudson, Mass., 1980 82, product mgr. Stow, Mass., 1982-84, mktg. mgr. Westborough, Mass., 1984-87, mktg. programs mgr., 1987-89, mktg. mgr. Marlborough, Mass., 1989-92, software bus. mgr. Stow, 1992-95, sys. bus. mgr., 1995-98; software bus. mgr. Compaq Computer Corp., Stow, 1998-2000, bus. devel. mgr., 2000—02; ops. mgr. Hewlett-Packard Co., Littleton, Mass., 2002—. Class agt. ann. alumni fund Worcester Poly. Inst.; mem. Sudbury Valley Trustees. Mem.: Appalachian Mountain Club, Harvard Bus. Sch. Club Boston, Pi Tau Sigma. Republican. Roman Catholic. Avocations: tennis, golf, photography, music. Home: 9 Travis Dr Framingham MA 01702-6131 Office: Hewlett-Packard Co 550 King St Littleton MA 01460-1289

KULAWIK, KRZYSZTOF ANDRZEJ, language educator; b. Knurów, Poland, Mar. 8, 1971; s. Andrzej and Maria (Szala) Kulawik; m. Luz Marcela Hurtado, Mar. 10, 1995. Magister in Iberian Philology, U. Jagiellonski, Cracow. Poland, 1994; MA, Instituto Caro y Cuervo, Bogota, Colombia, 1995; PhD, U. Fla., 2001. H.S. tchr. English Gimnasio de los Cerros, Bogota, 1995; tchg. asst. of linguistics-semantics Instituto Caro y Cuervo, Bogota, 1995; tchg. asst. and assoc. of Spanish and Portuguese U. Fla., Gainesville, 1996—2001; asst. prof. Spanish lang. and Spanish Am. lit. and culture Ctrl. Mich. U., Mount Pleasant, 2001—. Contbr. articles to profl. publs. Grantee, Ctrl. Mich. U., 2002; scholar, EEC, 1991—92, ICETEX, Govt. of the Republic of Colombia93 Dept. of Edn., 1993—95. Mem.: MLA (assoc.), Am. Assn. Tchrs. of Spanish and Portuguese (assoc.), L.Am. Studies Assn. (assoc.). Independent. Avocations: travel, reading, music, skiing, sailing. Home: 802 W Preston Ave Mount Pleasant MI 48858 Office: Ctrl Mich U Pearce Hall 312 Mount Pleasant MI 48859 Office Fax: 989-774-2323. Personal E-mail: k.kulawik@cmich.edu. E-mail: kulaw1ka@cmich.edu.

KULBICKI, MELVIN ANDREW, political science educator; b. Balt., Apr. 9, 1948; s. Michael and Florence M. (Koczrowski) K.; m. Lorraine C. Style; children: Elizabeth A., Kathryn M. BA, U. Md., Balt., 1970; MA, Pa. State U., 1972, PhD, 1979. Instr. York (Pa.) Coll., 1976-79, asst. prof., 1979-91, assoc. prof. polit. sci., 1991—2002, prof. polit. sci., chmn., 2002—. Host, producer TV program York Roundtable, 1983-84; asst. dir. Balt. Coun. on Fgn. Affairs, 1979-80. News columnist York Daily Record, 1992; contbr. articles, revs., papers to profl. publs. Mem. planning bd. York Suburban Schs., 1992-97; bd. dirs. Leadership York, 1979-83. Wye Inst. fellow, 1988; Pa. Coun. on Humanities grantee, 1985. Mem. AAUP, Nat. Assn. Scholars, Pa. Polit. Assn., N.E. Polit. Sci. Assn., Am. Polit. Sci. Assn. Roman Catholic. Avocations: chess, golf, jazz. Home: 761 Woodberry Rd York PA 17403-4115 Office: York Coll Polit Sci Dept York PA 17405 E-mail: mkulblck@ycp.edu.

KULCINSKI, GERALD LAVERNE, dean; b. La Crosse, Wis., Oct. 27, 1939; s. Harold Franklin and June Kramer K.; m. Janet Noreen Berg, Nov. 25, 1961; children: Kathryn, Brian, Karen. BS in Chem. Engring., U. Wis., 1961, MS in Nuclear Engring., 1962, PhD in Nuclear Engring., 1965. Rschr. Los Alamos (N.Mex.) Nuclear Lab., 1963; lectr. Ctr. Grad. Study, Richland, Wash., 1965-71; sr. rsch. sci. Battelle Northwest Lab., Richland, 1965-71; prof. U. Wis., Madison, 1972—, dir. Fusion Tech. Inst., 1973-75, 79—, Grainger Prof. Nuclear Engring., 1984—, assoc. dean coll. engring., 2001—. Vis. sci. Karlsruhe (Germany) Nuclear Rsch. Ctr., 1977, Bechtel Corp., San Francisco, 1989, 95; active Gov. Energy Policy Task Force, Wis., 1980; U.S. del. to Internat. Tokamak Reactor Project, Vienna, Austria, 1979-81; mem. adv. panel INTOR, 1987; mem. numerous review panels, including Los Alamos Nat. lab., Sandia Nat. Lab., Argonne Nat. Lab. Assoc. editor: Fusion Engring. and Design. Recipient Curtis W. McGraw Rsch. award Engring. Rsch. Com. Am. Assn. Engring. Edn., 1978, John Randle Grumman Achievement award Grumman Aircraft Corp., 1987, Leadership Fusion award Fusion Power Assocs., 1992, NASA Pub. Svc. medal, 1993, Disting. Faculty award Wis. Alumni Assn., 1994, Big 10 Centennial award, 1995. Fellow Am. Nuclear Soc. (sec. Richland sect. 1970, student advisor Wis. chpt. 1972-73, chmn. 2nd topical meeting on fusion tech. 1976, bd. dirs. 1987-90, Outstanding Achievement award 1980); mem. NAE. Home: 6013 Greentree Rd Madison WI 53711-3125 Office: U Wis 1500 Johnson Dr Madison WI 53706-1609 E-mail: kulcinski@engr.wisc.edu.

KULESHA, KEVIN JOHN, investment banker; b. Englewood, N.J., May 15, 1956; s. Kasmier J. and Florence L. (Anguissola) K. BSBA, Georgetown U., 1976; MSIA, Carnegie Mellon U., 1979. Field dir. Bradley for Senate Com., Bethesda, Md., 1975-76; commodity trader Chgo., 1977; assoc. Morgan Stanley & Co., N.Y.C., 1979-83; v.p. Lazard Fréres & Co., N.Y.C., 1983-86, Furman Selz Mager Dietz & Birney, N.Y.C., 1986-87, Merrill Lynch Capital Markets, N.Y.C., 1987-88, dir., 1989-91; mng. dir. The Sandstone Group, Denver, 1991—. With Andean Investment Advisors, LLC, Denver, 1998-99; bd. dirs. La Real Compania de Seguros Generales SA, Lima, Peru, 1998-99; chmn., CEO IncSurance Inc., Story, Wyo.

KULICK, RICHARD JOHN, computer scientist, researcher; b. New Kensington, Pa., Mar. 27, 1949; s. John Anthony and Anna Teresa (Tuzik) K. BS, Pa. State U., 1971; MBA, U. Md., 1973. Project acct. PPG Indusries, Inc., Ford City, Pa., 1973-75; programmer analyst Allegheny Ludlum Steel Corp., Brackenridge, Pa., 1975-77, systems analyst, 1977-82, sr. systems analyst, 1982, sr. MIS planner, 1982-86; system design specialist Allegheny Ludlum Corp., Brackenridge, Pa., 1986-91, mgmt. info. systems assoc. Vandergrift, Pa., 1991-2001, sr. info. sys. assoc., 2001—. Author: Heuristic Coil Slitting Optimization, 1986, (manual) Data Modeling Standards, 1988, Information Systems Integration Strategy, 1989. Mem. Computer Soc. of IEEE, Nat. Systems Programmers Assn., Assn. for Computing Machinery (voting), Tech. Coun. on Software Engring., Datamation High Tech. Panel, Compu Panel, IDC Corp. Computing Coun., Smithsonian Assocs., U.S. Tennis Assn., Racquet Club Pitts., Pa. State U. Club Alle-Kiski Valley. Avocations: music, reading, stamp collecting, running, fine art. Home: 483 Lillian Rd Leechburg PA 15656-8220 Office: Allegheny Ludlum Corp 132 Lincoln Ave Vandergrift PA 15690-1249 E-mail: RKulick@Alleghenyludlum.com.

KULIG, JOHN WALTER, pediatrician, educator; b. Providence, Sept. 23, 1949; s. John and Helena K.; m. Cynthia M., May 23, 1981; children: Jessica, Jillian. BA, Brown U., 1971; MD, U. Cin., 1975; MPH, Harvard U., 1990. Diplomate Am. Bd. Pediats. Fellow in adolescent medicine Children's Hosp. Med. Ctr., Cin., 1978-79; resident in pediat. New Eng. Med. Ctr., Boston, 1975-79, dir. adolescent medicine, 1979—; prof. pediat. Tufts U. Sch. Medicine, Boston, 2002—, prof. family medicine and cmty. health, 2002—. Adj. assoc. prof. maternal and child health Harvard Sch. Pub. Health, Boston, 1997—2003. Mem. Alpha Omega Alpha. Office: New England Medical Ctr 750 Washington St # 479 Boston MA 02111-1533 E-mail: JKulig@tufts-nemc.org.

KULIK, BETH A. physician assistant, educator; b. Allentown, Pa., Jan. 28, 1962; d. Ellwood C. and Martha J. Kulik. BS in Math., Moravian Coll., 1985; physician asst. cert., King's Coll., Pa., 1991. Cert. physician asst. Nat. Commn. on Certification of Physician Assts., 1992— and Commonwealth Pa., 1992—. Instr. math. and computer sci. Linden Hall Sch., Lititz, Pa., 1985-86; physician asst. Lehigh Valley Family Practice, Allentown, 1992-93, Affinity/Lehigh Valley Hosp., Allentown, 1993-94, Doylestown (Pa.) & Warrington Family Practice, 1994; math. tutor Northampton C.C., Bethlehem, Pa., 1997—2001, adj. prof., 1998—2001; instr. Quakertown (Pa.) Sch. Dist. Evening Sch., 1999—2001; instr. algebra Holy Child Sch., Bethlehem, 1999—2001. Emergency rm. vol. St. Luke's Quakertown Hosp., 1986-87, 2000—; ambulance attendant LifeStar, Quakertown, 1986—87; EMT, 1987—91; mem. St. Luke's Quakertown Hosp. Aux., 1993—97; sr. clk./circulation asst. James A. Michener Libr., Quakertown, Pa. Recipient Voluntary Svc. award VA Med. Ctr., Wilkes-Barre, Pa., 1991. Fellow Am. Acad. Physician Assts.; mem. Pa. Soc. Physician Assts. Avocations: reading, fishing. Home: 2560 Trumbauersville Rd Quakertown PA 18951-3723 Office: James A Michener Library 229 California Rd Quakertown PA 18951

KULIK, ROSALYN FRANTA, food company executive, consultant; b. Wilmington, Del., Aug. 29, 1951; d. William Alfred and Virginia Louise (Ellis) Franta. BS in Voc. Home Econs. Edn., Purdue U., 1972, MS in Foods and Nutrition, 1974; postgrad. in advanced mgmt. program, Harvard Bus. Sch., 1990. Registered dietitian. Home economist Kellogg Co., Battle Creek, Mich., 1974-75, nutrition and consumer specialist, 1975-77, mgr. advt. to children, 1977-79, corp. adminstrv. asst., 1979, dir. nutrition, 1979-82, dir. nutrition and analytical services, 1982, v.p. nutrition and chemistry, 1983, v.p. quality and nutrition, 1983-87, v.p., asst. to chmn., 1987-88; exec. v.p., gen. mgr. Fearn Internat., Franklin Park, Ill., 1988-90; cons., 1991—. Contbr. articles on food sci. and nutrition to profl. jours. Mem. ch. coun. Grace Luth. Ch., Tampa, Fla., 2000—03; bd. dirs. State Arthritis Found., County Vol. Ctr., Homeowners Property Assn. Avila, Neighborhood Property Owners Assn., 2002—. Recipient Ada Decker Malott Meml. scholarship, Purdue U., 1970, disting. alumna Purdue U. Sch. of Consumer and Family Sci. Fellow Am. Dietetic Assn.

(cofounder, exec. officer nutrition in complementary care dietetic practice group 1998—, chair 2002-03); mem. Inst. Food Technologists (profl. mem.), Am. Dietetic Assn., Phi Kappa Phi, Gamma Sigma Delta, Omicron Nu, Alpha Omicron Pi. Republican. Lutheran. Avocations: music, church work, travel, Jr. League volunteerism.

KULIKOWSKI, CASIMIR ALEXANDER, computer science and engineering educator; b. Hertford, Herts, Eng., May 4, 1944; arrived in U.S., 1961; s. Victor A. and Isabel S. (Tuckett) Kulikowski; m. Christine A. Wilk, May 31, 1969; children: Michael Edward, Victoria Anne. BE with honors, Yale U., 1965, MS, 1966; PhD, U. Hawaii, 1970. From asst. prof. to assoc. prof. Rutgers U., New Brunswick, NJ, 1970—77, prof., 1977—97, chmn. dept. computer sci., 1984—90, dir. Lab. Computer Sci. Rsch., 1985—96, bd. govs. prof., 1997—. Mem. bd. sci. counselors Nat. Libr. Medicine, Bethesda, Md., 1984—87; mem. biomed. libr. rev. com. NIH, 1994—99, chair, 1997—99. Author: A Practical Guide to Designing Expert Systems, 1984, Computer Systems that Learn, 1992; editor: Artificial Intelligence Expert Systems and Languages in Modeling & Simulation, 1988; co-editor: Yearbook of Medical Informatics, 2001—; assoc. editor: Artificial Intelligence in Medicine Jour., 2001—; mem. editl. bd. Computers in Biology and Medicine, 1980—, Jour. Am. Med. Informatics Assn., 1993—98, Methods Info. in Medicine, 1999—, Iterations: An Interdisciplinary Jour. of Software History, 2001—. Pres. Highland Park (N.J.) Residents Assn., 1983—88. Fellow: IEEE, AAAS, Am. Inst. Med. and Biol. Engring., Am. Coll. Med. Informatics, Am. Assn. Artificial Intelligence; mem.: NAS Inst. Medicine. Office: Rutgers U Dept Computer Sci Hill Ctr Busch Campus New Brunswick NJ 08903

KULIN, KEITH DAVID, cinematographer; b. Bogota, N.J., Jan. 24, 1948; s. Joseph Julius and Ava L. (Finestone) K.; m. Mary Mulroy, Nov. 24, 1993. BA, Ramapo Coll. N.J., 1973. News photographer Ridgewood Newspapers, Paramus, N.J., 1967; desk asst. TV news CBS Inc., N.Y.C., 1975-77, newsreel photographer, 1977-84, documentary photographer, 1984-98; prodr., editor A Few Minutes With Andy Rooney, 1998—. Staff documentary cinematographer for 60 Minutes, West 57th, CBS Reports, 48 Hours, Saturday Night with Connie Chung, other CBS news programs; judge Nat. Acad. TV Arts and Scis., 1995—. Contbr. photography to Ridgewood newspapers, N.Y. Times, Womens World, 1966-75. Served with U.S. Army, 1968-70, Vietnam. Recipient Outstanding Photog. Achievement award Eastman Kodak Co., 1985, Spot News and Feature News awards, 1967, Emmy award for CBS Sunday Morning Segment, 1997; nominee Emmy award, 1985. Mem. Internat. Brotherhood Elec. Workers, TV and Radio Working Press Assn. Avocations: computers, still photography. Home: 202 Maple Dr Wyckoff NJ 07481-2317 Office: CBS News 555 W 57th St New York NY 10019-2925 E-mail: kdk@cbsnews.com.

KULINSKY, LOIS, lawyer; b. Chgo., Mar. 17, 1946; d. Ben Albert and Florence Sylvia (Barth) Kay; m. Fred Martin Kulinsky, Sept. 4, 1967 (div. 1980); 1 child, Jeffrey. BS, U. Minn., 1967; MAT, U. Chgo., 1970; JD, Ill. Inst. Tech., 1980. Bar: Ill. 1980, U.S. Dist. Ct. (no. dist.) Ill. 1980, U.S. Supreme Ct. 1995. Tchr. Chgo. Pub. Schs., 1967-70, Maine Twp. Schs., Des Plaines, Ill., 1971-80; atty. John P. Biestek & Assocs., Arlington Heights, Ill., 1980-83; pvt. practice Wheeling, Ill., 1983—. Mem. Ill. Bar Assn., Chgo. Bar Assn., Lake County Bar Assn. Avocations: photography, art. Office: 395 E Dundee Rd Ste 200 Wheeling IL 60090-7003 Fax: (847) 459-4448. E-mail: lois@kulinskylaw.com.

KULIS, ELLEN MAE, elementary education educator; b. Punxsutawney, Pa., Jan. 19, 1943; d. John Williams and Julia (Knopick) Johnson; m. Raymond Edward Kulis, July 2, 1983. BS in Elem. Edn., Ind. U., Pa., 1966; MS in Elem. Edn., Clarion U., Pa., 1970; principalship, Penn State U., University Park, Pa., 1988. First grade tchr. Ridgway Sch. Dist., Ridgway, Pa., 1966-67; head start tchr. Jefferson County, Syskesville, Pa., summers 1967-70; first grade tchr. Punxsutawney Areas Schs., Punxsutawney, Pa., 1970-85, third grade tchr., 1985—. Co-op tchr. Ind. U., Pa., 1979-90. Asst. Encore Group, Punxsutawney, Pa., 1978-81; mem. Sodality, 1958-64, Newman Ctr., Indiana, Pa., 1983-90. Mem. PTO, PSEA, NEA, PAEA, RAEA, Delta Kappa Gamma. Democrat. Byzantine Catholic. Home: 921 Lilac St Indiana PA 15701-3332

KULKA, J(OHANNES) PETER, retired physician, pathologist; b. Vienna, Feb. 7, 1921; came to U.S., 1933; s. Ernest Walter and Anna Maria (Jolles) K. AB, Cornell U., 1941; MD, Johns Hopkins U., 1944. Diplomate Am. Bd. Pathology. Intern in pathology Strong Meml. Hosp., Rochester, N.Y., 1944-45; asst. resident in pathology Mass. Gen. Hosp., Boston, 1945-47; instr. anatomy Harvard U. Med. Sch., Boston, 1947-49, instr. pathology, 1949-52, clin. assoc., asst. clin. prof., assoc. clin. prof., 1952-70, clin. fellow in psychiatry, 1970-73; resident in psychiatry, then clin. fellow in psychiatry McLean Hosp., Belmont, Mass., 1970-74; child psychiatry trainee South Shore Mental Health Ctr., Quincy, Mass., 1973-74; pathologist Robert B. Brigham Hosp., Boston, 1955-58, 61-70, assoc. dir. grad. tng. grant, 1961-68, chmn. med. staff, 1965-67; assoc. in pathology Peter Bent Brigham Hosp., Boston, 1955-58, asst. in medicine, 1958-61; clin. instr. medicine, gen. physician Health Svc., Tufts U., Medford, Mass.; mem. courtesy staff Lawrence Meml. Hosp., Medford, 1975-79. Mem. editl. bd. Arthritis and Rheumatism, 1960-68; contbr. articles to med. jours. Capt. M.C., U.S. Army, 1953-55. Avocations: camping, canoeing, skiing. Home: PO Box 316 Lincoln MA 01773-0316

KULKARNI, ARUN DIGAMBAR, computer science educator; b. Poona, India, Dec. 14, 1947; came to U.S., 1984; s. Digambar D. and Sumati D. Kulkarni; m. Vasanti Arun Kulkarni, Oct. 15, 1978; children: Himani, Prathit, Shradha. BE, Poona U., 1969; MTech, India Inst. Tech., Bombay, 1971, PhD in Elec. Engring., 1978. Devel. engr. Sarabhai Electronics Rsch. Ctr., Ahmedabad, India, 1971-73; scientist Nat. Remote Sensing Agy., Hyderabad, India, 1976-84; postdoctoral researcher Va. Poly. Inst. and State U., Blacksburg, 1984-85; asst. prof. computer sci. U. Tex., Tyler, 1986-91, assoc. prof. computer sci., 1991-97, prof. computer sci., 1997—. Vis. faculty U. So. Miss., Hattiesburg, 1985-86 Author: (texts) Neural Networks for Image Understanding, 1995, Computer Vision and Fuzzy-Neural Systems, 2001; contbr. chpts. to books, articles to profl. jours. Recipient Chancellor's Coun. Outstanding Tchr. award, 2001—03, Alpha Chi Outstanding Faculty award, 1999—2000; Fulbright fellow, 1984, NASA/ASEE summer fellow, 1997. Mem. Assn. for Computing Machinery, Internat. Soc. Neural Networks. Home: 817 W Rieck Rd Tyler TX 75703-3528 Office: U Tex 3900 University Blvd Tyler TX 75701-6622 E-mail: akulkarn@mail.uttyl.edu.

KULKARNI, BIDY, reproductive endocrinologist, biomedical researcher, consultant; b. Janwa, Maharashtra, India, Apr. 18, 1930; arrived in U.S., 1961; s. Dhondu Y. Kulkarni and Sita Deshpande; m. Suman Sane, May 8, 1957; children: Neela, Bob. BS, Ferguson Coll., Poona, India, 1952; MS, U. Poona, 1956, PhD, 1962. Post doctoral fellow Clark U. and Worcester Found., Shrewsbury, Mass., 1961—64, Nat. Rsch. Coun., Ottawa, Canada, 1964—66; sect. chief dept. endocrinology S.W. Rsch. Found., San Antonio, 1967—70; asst. prof. ob-gyn. U. Chgo., 1970—73; dir. gynecol. endocrinology Michael Reese U., Chgo., 1970—72; dir. reproductive endocrinology Loyola U. Med. Ctr., Maywood, Ill., 1973—79, assoc. prof. ob-gyn., 1973—79; dir. reproductive endocrinology Cook County Hosp., Chgo., 1980—93; assoc. prof. ob-gyn. Chgo. Med. Sch., N. Chgo., 1981—93; pres. Rsch. and Edn. Svcs., Darien, Ill., 1991—. Cons. in field; dir. perinatal ctr. Loyola U. Med. Ctr., Maywood, 1975—77; hon. attending physician Cook County Hosp., Chgo., 1993—. Contbr. articles to profl. jours., chapters to books. Named Outstanding Citizen of Yr., Met. Chgo., 1973; grantee, Ctr. for Population Rsch., NIH, Agy. for Internat. Devel. Mem.: Internat. Fedn. Fertility Socs., Am. Fertility Soc., Nat. Acad. Biochemistry, Soc. for Study of Reprodn., Endocrine Soc., Chgo. Gynecol. Soc. (life), Chgo. Gynecol. Soc. (life Outstanding Scientist 2000), Soc. Reproductive Medicine (life). Democrat. Avocations: badminton, hiking, travel. Home: 9 S 155 Nantucket Darien IL 60561 Office: Rsch and Edn Svcs 9 S 155 Nantucket Darien IL 60561

KULKARNI, KISHORE GANESH, economics educator, consultant; b. Oct. 31, 1953; arrived in U.S., 1976; s. Ganesh Y. and Sindhu G. Dhekane; m. Jayu K., Aug. 17, 1980; children: Lina, Aditi. BA, U. Poona, India, 1974, MA, 1976, U. Pitts., 1978, PhD., 1982. Tchg. asst. U. Pitts., 1976—78, tchg. fellow, 1978—80, prof. semester at sea program, 1994, asst. prof. Johnstown, Pa., 1981—82, U. Ctrl. Ark., Conway, 1982—86; assoc. prof. N.E. La. U., Monroe, 1986—89, Met. State Coll., Denver, 1989—93, prof., 1993—, chmn. dept. econs., 1994—97. Author: Principles of Macro Monetary Theory, Modern Monetary Theory, Readings in International Economics; co-author: Role of LIC in Economic Development of India; editor: Indian Jour. of Econs. and Bus.; contbr. articles to profl. jours. Recipient 1st prize essay competition, Forum of Free Enterprise, Bombay, India, 1975, Rama Watumull Fund award, Honolulu, 1977; rsch. fellow, Winrock Internat., Morrilton, Ark., 1984—85, vis. rsch. fellow, Nat. Inst. Bank Mgmt., Pune, India, 1974. Mem.: Assn. Indian Econ. Studies, So. Econ. Assn., Southwestern Econ. Assn., Am. Econ. Assn., Golden Key Internat. Soc. Avocation: tennis. Home: 2249 S Miller Ct Lakewood CO 80227 E-mail: KulkarnK@mscd.edu.

KULKIN, HEIDI SHARON, education educator; b. Framingham, Mass., Apr. 23, 1968; d. Samuel G. and Arlene L. Kulkin. BA, R.I. Coll., 1995; MSW, Tulane U., New Orleans, 1996, PhD, 2001. LCSW La. Bd. of Social Work Examiners, 2001. Asst. prof. Southeastern La. U., Hammond, 2000—. Clinician Heidi S. Kulkin, PhD, LCSW, Metairie, La., 2001—. Author: (jour. article) Jour. of Homosexuality; author: (presenter) Distance edn.: Comparing apples and oranges. Mem. Nat. Assn. Social Workers, Washington, 1995, Coun. on Social Work Edn., Alexandria, Va., 2000. Office: Southeastern La U SLU 10686 Social Work Hammond LA 70402 Office Fax: 985-549-5046. Personal E-mail: hkulkin@selu.edu.

KULKOSKY, CHRIS JAMES, social worker; b. Newark, June 27, 1952; s. Peter Francis and Rose Kulkosky; m. Mary Anne Lynn, Jan. 31, 1990. BA, Columbia U., 1974. Cert. social worker, N.J.; cert. in supervisory mgmt., state core leadership. Paralegal MFY Legal Svcs., N.Y.C., 1977-78; vets. svc. officer N.J. Dept. Mil. and Vets. Affairs, Paterson, 1981-85, regional supr., 1985-97, chief Bur. Vets. Svcs. Trenton, 1997—. Author: Prison Ship, 1977, Poetry of Chris James Kulkosky Website, 1996 (Poem of the Month award A Little Poetry Website 1997). Mem. Columbia Alumni Secondary Schs. Com., N.Y.C., 1981—. Mem. Palisades Nature Assn. Democrat. Roman Catholic. Avocation: collecting baseball cards. Home: 72 Ocean Blvd Little Egg Harbor Twp NJ 08087 Office: NJ Dept Mil and Vets Affairs PO Box 340 Trenton NJ 08625-0340 Fax: (609) 530-6970. E-mail: chriskulkosky@webtv.net., Kulkosky@njdmava.state.nj.us

KULKOSKY, PAUL JOSEPH, psychology educator; b. Newark, Mar. 3, 1949; s. Peter Francis and Rose Mary (Leonetti) K.; m. Tanya Marie Weightman, Sept. 16, 1978. BA, Columbia U., N.Y.C., 1971, MA, 1972; PhD, U. Wash., 1975. Rsch. assoc. Cornell U., White Plains, N.Y., 1980-81, instr. psychiatry, 1981-82; asst. prof. psychology Colo. State U., Pueblo, 1982-86, assoc. prof., 1986-89, chmn. dept. psychology, 1988-91, prof., 1989—. Bd. advisors Pueblo Zool. Soc., 1984-85, 1988-91, bd. dirs., 1985-88; editorial cons. to pubs.; consulting editor Jour. Neurotherapy. Contbr. chpts. to books, articles to profl. jours.; referee psychol. jours. Liaison Rocky Mountain Region Coun. undergrad. psychology programs, 1990-91. Named Hon. Affiliate Prof. Am. U., Washington, 1977; rsch. grantee NIH, 1984-97; staff fellow Nat. Inst. Alcohol Abuse and Alcoholism, 1976-80. Mem.: AAAS (vice chmn. psychol. scis. sect. Southwestern and Rocky Mountain divsn. 1990—91, chmn. 1991—92, exec. com. Colo. rep. 1991—94, pres.-elect 1994—95, pres. 1995—96, past pres. 1996—), Colo.-Wyo. Acad. Sci. (exec. com. 1997—99, pres. 1999—2001, past pres. 2001—), Soc. for Study Ingestive Behavior (charter), Internat. Soc. Biomed. Rsch. on Alcoholism (charter), U. So. Colo. Club, Phi Kappa Phi (treas. USC chpt. 1998—2001), Sigma Xi (treas. USC chpt. 1986—96). Home: 417 Tyler St Pueblo CO 81004-1405 Office: U So Colo 2200 Bonforte Blvd Pueblo CO 81001-4901 Business E-Mail: paul.kulkosky@colostate-pueblo.edu.

KULL, BRYAN PAUL, business information/technology executive; b. Newark, Jan. 23, 1960; s. Paul and Joan Lorraine (Schell) K.; m. Lindsay Fairfield Patton, Nov. 26, 1983; children: Taylor Bryan, Kathryn. BS in Mgmt., Keene (N.H.) State Coll., 1982; MBA in Mktg., So. Ill. U., 1987. Sales rep. Warner-Lambert Co., Morris Plains, NJ, 1982—84; key account mgr. Clorox Co., Oakland, Calif., 1984—86; divsn. mgr. Alberto-Culver Co., Melrose Park, Ill., 1986—89; area mgr. Schering-Plough Corp., Memphis, 1989—90; nat. sales mgr. Shering-Plough Healthcare, Liberty Corner, NJ, 1991—94; v.p. spl. mkts. Sunshine Biscuits, Inc., Woodbridge, NJ, 1994—96; v.p. client svc. Info. Resources, Inc., Fairfield, NJ, 1997—2000; ptnr. Computer Sci. Corp., West Orange, NJ, 2000—01; client ptnr. Cambridge Technology Ptnrs., Mass., 2001—03; v.p. Intellinex LLC, N.Y.C., 2002—. Mem. Triathlon Fedn., Davis, Calif., 1988-89. Mem. Assn. MBA Execs., Nat. Assn. Chain Drug Stores (assoc.), Pres.'s Club at Schering-Plough. Republican. Presbyterian. Avocations: golf, tennis, skiing, cycling, wine collecting. E-mail: infores@yahoo.com.

KULL, JAMES ARTHUR, music educator; b. Chgo., Sept. 1, 1961; s. Victor James and Anita Kull; m. Jennifer Lynn Miller, June 20, 1992; children: Katherine, Morgan. MusB in Edn. summa cum laude, VanderCook Coll. Music, 1983; MS in Music Edn., U. Ill., 1988. Cert. spl. music K-12. Dir. bands Hufford Jr. H.S., Joliet, Ill., 1983—85, Champaign (Ill.) Ctrl. H.S., 1985—89, Wheeling (Ill.) H.S., Wheeling, 1989—91, St. Charles (Ill.) East H.S., 1994—; assoc. instr. dept. bands Ind. U., Bloomington, 1991—93; dir. jazz studies, asst. dir. bands Kans. State U., Manhattan, 1993—94. Band dir. Elgin (Ill.) C.C., 1997—. Musician (lead alto saxophone): Arts Ctr. Jazz Ensemble, 2002. Recipient Dr. Victor W. Zajec award, VanderCook Coll. Music, 2001, Excellence in Beginning Tchg. award, 1988, Stamey award for excellence in undergrad. tchg., 1993. Mem.: NEA, Music Educators Nat. Conf., Internat. Assn. Jazz Educators. Presbyterian. Home: 235 Pleasant Plains Dr Saint Charles IL 60175 Office: St Charles East HS 1020 Dunham Rd Saint Charles IL 60174 Personal E-mail: jamesakull@aol.com. E-mail: jkull@d303.org.

KULLAS, ALBERT JOHN, management and systems engineering consultant; b. Webster, Mass., May 5, 1917; s. Albert J. and Mary (Piechowiak) K.; m. Joyce M. Gladue, Jan. 31, 1942; children: Michael, Daniel, Mark, James. BS in Civil Engring., Worcester Poly. Inst., 1938; grad., Am. Mgmt. Assn., 1956; MS in Civil Engring., NYU, 1940; grad., Sloan Sch. Mgmt. Sr. Execs., MIT, 1973. Registered profl. engr. With Martin Marietta Corp., 1940-82, structures mgr., 1955-57, chief engr., 1957, design engring. mgr., 1957-59, tech. devel. mgr., 1959-60, Dyna Soar and Gemini Launch vehicle tech. dir., 1960-62, research and engring. dir., 1962-65, dir. tech. ops., 1965-66, dir. space sci., research, adv. tech., 1966-67, dir. Voyager program, 1967-68, dir. Planetary Systems, 1968, dir. Viking project, div. v.p., 1969-72, div. v.p. ops. rev., 1972-73, v.p. data systems, 1973-82; mgmt. and systems engring. cons. Littleton, Colo., 1982-98; pres. Albert J. Kullas, Inc. Rsch. and tech. panel space vehicles NASA, 1968-78; chmn. bd. Biax Corp., 1987-90; 1st v.p. The Highlands, Inc., 1999-. Contbr. articles to profl. jours. Mem. rsch. adv. coun. Colo. State U., 1971—; treas. Porter Hosp. Found., 1980-85, 1st v.p., 1986-88, pres., 1988-90, v.p., 1990-93, active, 1993—; bd. dirs. Colo. Jud. Inst., 1980-91, chmn., 1984-86; mem. exec. com. Rocky Mountain Sci. Council, 1964-65; bd. dirs. MIT Alumni Colo., 1990-2002. Recipient Robert H. Goddard award Worcester Poly. Inst., 1962 Fellow AIAA (award 1967); Asso. fellow (chmn. honors and awards com. 1973-81); mem. ASCE, Sigma Xi, Tau Beta Pi. Office: 5088 W Maplewood Ave Littleton CO 80123-6729 *I believe that being thorough, consistent, and persistent in pursuing one's convictions are necessary ingredients for personal and managerial success.*

KULLBERG, DUANE REUBEN, accounting firm executive; b. Red Wing, Minn., Oct. 6, 1932; s. Carl Reuben and Hazel Norma (Swanson) K.; m. Sina Nell Turner, Oct. 19, 1958 (dec. Sept. 1989); children: Malissa Kullberg, Caroline Godellas; m. Susan Turley, Dec. 30, 1992; stepchildren: Betsy Lucas, Jane Holtzermann. BBA, U. Minn., 1954. With Andersen Worldwide, 1954-89, ptnr., 1967-89, mng. ptnr., Mpls., 1970-74, dep. mng. ptnr., Chgo., 1975-78, vice chmn. acctg. and audit practice worldwide, 1978-80, mng. ptnr., CEO, 1980-89, ret., 1989. Bd. dirs. John Nuveen Co., Carlson Cos., Inc., Chgo. Bd. Options Exch. Life trustee Northwestern U., Art Inst. Chgo., U. Minn. Found., chmn. bd. trustees, 1993-95; chair Swedish Coun. Am. Found., 1999-2001. With U.S. Army, 1956-58. Decorated comdr. Royal Order of Polar Star (Sweden), 1989; recipient Legend in Leadership award Emory U., 1992, Regents award U. Minn., 1995, Outstanding Achievement award U. Minn., 1990. Mem. Chgo. Club, Comml. Club, Mpls. Club. Home: 179 E Lake Shore Dr Apt 1001 Chicago IL 60611-1306 also: 6444 N 79th St Scottsdale AZ 85250-7919

KULLBERG, GARY WALTER, advertising agency executive; b. White Plains, N.Y., Dec. 15, 1941; s. Walter George and Neva Virginia (Franz) K.; m. Audrey Ellen Greenwald, June 20, 1976; 1 child, Eric Alan. BS, U. R.I., 1963. Contr. WCD, Inc., N.Y.C., 1963-66; v.p., mgmt. supr. Ogilvy & Mather, N.Y.C., 1966-77; sr. v.p., account group head Wells, Rich, Greene, N.Y.C., 1977-83; CEO, CFO, co-founder Fredericks Kullberg Amato Pisacane, Inc., 1983-88; pres. Kullberg Amato Pisacane/ABP, Inc., 1987-89; pres., COO PanCom Internat. Corp., 1989-91; CEO PanCom Comm. Corp., 1991-93, Kullberg Cons. Group, N.Y.C., 1993—. Guest spkr. univs. Mem. bd. advisors, chmn. mktg., mktg. comm. com., exec. com. Manhattan Salvation Army; mem. bus. adv. coun. U. R.I. Coll. Bus., vice-chmn., co-chair publicity com. Mem. West Point Soc. N.Y. (career adv. com.), Am. Numismatic Assn., N.Y. Athletic Club, U. R.I. Alumni Assn. (exec. com., fin. com., govt. rels. com.), Phi Gamma Delta. Home and Office: Kullberg Cons Group LLC 171 Forge Rd North Kingstown RI 02852-1007

KULLEN, SHIRLEY ROBINOWITZ, psychiatric epidemiologist, consultant; b. Balt., Sept. 6, 1922; d. Joseph and Rose (Collins) Robinowitz; m. Joseph Stephen Reff, Sept. 14, 1941 (div. 1958); children: Richard Brian, Robert Alan; m. Sidney Irving Margolis, Oct. 28, 1973 (dec. Dec. 1988); m. Sol Kullen, Jan. 10, 1993. BS, Am. U., 1959, MBA, 1961, PhD, 1972. Statistician NIMH, Bethesda, Md., 1964-72, health scientist adminstrn., 1972-93; cons. psychiatric epidemiologist, Chevy Chase, Md., 1993—. Lectr. Am. U. Washington, 1961, 69, 70, 74, 87, seminar developer, 1987; lectr. Howard U., Washington, 1963-67. Bd. dirs. Jewish Cmty. Ctr. Greater Washington, Rockville, Md., 1979—90, Hebrew Home Washington, Rockville, 1980—85, Fed. Credit Union, Rockville, 1987—93; exec. v.p. S-K Family Partnership, 1996—. Mem. APHA (adv. bd. mental health sect. 1990-93), AAUW. Avocations: golf, music, writing. Home: 2100 S Ocean Blvd Apt 202N Palm Beach FL 33480-5201 Office: 5610 Wisconsin Ave Chevy Chase MD 20815

KULLER, JONATHAN MARK, lawyer; b. Paterson, N.J., Jan. 2, 1951; George and Muriel (Kaplan) K.; m. Mardi Risa Adelman, Oct. 8, 1977; children: Brett Louis, Devin Howard. BS, Livingston Coll., 1972; JD, Rutgers U., 1976. Bar: N.J. 1976, U.S. Dist. Ct. N.J. 1976, U.S. Supreme Ct. 1985. Law clk. to presiding judge N.J. Superior Ct., Hackensack, 1976-77; assoc. Miller & Platt, Paterson, 1977-78; ptnr. Markus, Kuller & Cohen, Parsippany, N.J., 1978-87, Blaustein & Wasserman, Woodbridge, N.J., 1987-98, L'Abbate, Balkan, Colavita & Contini, L.L.P., Livingston, NJ, 1998—2001, Podvey, Sachs, Meanor, Catenacci, Hildner & Cocziello, P.C., Newark, 2001—. Mem.: N.J. Bar Assn. Jewish. Office: Podvey Sachs Meanor Catenacci Hildner & Cocziello PC One Riverfront Plz Fl 8 Newark NJ 07102 E-mail: jkuller@podveysachs.com.

KULOK, WILLIAM ALLAN, entrepreneur, venture capitalist; b. Mt. Vernon, N.Y., July 24, 1940; s. Sidney Alexander and Bertha (Lembeck) K.; m. Susan B. Glick, June 26, 1965; children: Jonathan, Brian, Stephanie. BS in Econs., U. Pa., 1962. CPA, N.Y. Acct. David Kulok Co., N.Y.C., 1962-67; asst. to pres. Syndicate Mags., N.Y.C., 1967-70; founder Kulok Capital Inc., N.Y.C., 1970, pres., 1970—. Bd. dir. Listcomp Corp., Mail Mgmt. Corp., Mag. Devel. Fund, Lazard Spl. Equities Fund, ASA Internat. Ltd., N.Y. Import/Export Ctr., Inc., Ctr. for Exec. Edn., Arts & Events, Inc., World Trade Ctr., Palm Beach; lectr. Wharton Sch., U. Chgo., NYU. Pres. N.Y. Soc. Ethical Culture, 1978-80; vice chmn. bd. Ethical Culture Schs., 1979, chmn., 1982-86. Mem. AICPA, Sleepy Hollow Country Club, Loxahatchee Club, Tryall Golf and Beach Club (Jamaica, W.I.). Home: 116 Echo Dr Jupiter FL 33458-7716

KULONGOSKI, THEODORE RALPH, governor, former judge; b. Nov. 5, 1940; married; 3 children. BA, U. Mo., 1967, JD, 1970. Bar: Oreg., Mo., U.S. Dist. Ct. Oreg., U.S. Ct. Appeals (9th cir.). Legal counsel Oreg. State Ho. of Reps., 1973-74; founding and sr. ptnr. Kulongoski, Durham, Drummonds & Colombo, Oreg., 1974-87; deputy dist. atty. Multnomah County, Oreg., 1992; atty. gen. State of Oreg., 1993-97; justice Oreg. Supreme Ct., 1997—2001; gov., State of Oreg., 2003—. State rep. Lane County (Oreg.), 1974-77, state senator, 1977-83; chmn. Juvenile Justice Task Force, 1994, Gov.'s Commn. Organized Crime; mem. Criminal Justice Coun.; exec. dir. Met. Family Svc., 1992; dir. Oreg. Dept. Ins. and Fin., 1987-91. Mem. Oreg State Bar Assn., Mo. Bar Assn. Office: Gov's Office 254 Capitol Bldg 900 Court St NE Salem OR 97301*

KULP, EILEEN BODNAR, social worker; b. Glens Falls, N.Y., Sept. 25, 1941; d. Joseph and Bertha Bodnar; m. Randolph Heath Kulp, June 5, 1961; children: Kimberly, Randolph Heath II, Kevin Joseph. B in Sociology, Hampton U., 1978; MSW, Norfolk State U., 1981. LCSW Va., diplomate in clin. social work Nat. Bd. Examiners, cert. addictions specialist, lic. substance abuse treatment practitioner. Social worker II adult chem. dependency Peninsula Hosp., Hampton, 1981-82, leader treatment team adolescent chem. dependency unit, 1982-84, sr. clinician adult chem. dependency unit, 1984-86, program coord. adult chem. dependency unit, 1986-88, dir. adult treatment programs, 1988-92; pvt. practice Newport News, Va., 1986-93; dir. new founds drug and alcohol programs Riverside Regional Med. Ctr., Newport News, 1994—, dir. newfound drug and alcohol programs, dir. outpatient psychiat. svcs. Addictions profls. team People Exch. Program, Norway, Sweden, Germany, 1989—. Bd. dirs Hampton Count PTA's, pres., 1979-80; bd. dirs. Hampton City Schs. Bd. Edn., 1981-85, Safe Haven Home for Abused Children, 1993—, Commonwealth Va. Citizens Adv. Bd. Youth and Family Svcs., Dept. Corrections, 1989—; chmn. adv. bd. Hampton Juvenile and Domestic Rels. Ct., bd. dirs., 1984—. Mem. Va. Coun. Social Welfare (pres. Tidewater chpt. 1987-88), Nat. Assn. Social Workers, Va. Assn. Alcoholism and Drug Abuse Counselors, Am. Coun. Alcoholism, Hampton Mental Health Bd. (pres. 1988-89), Va. Soc. Clin. Social Workers, Va. Coun. PTA's (life), Acad. Cert. Social Workers (cert.), Alpha Kappa Mu. Roman Catholic. Avocations: jazz, classical music, theatre, traveling. Home: 26 Sarfan Dr Hampton VA 23664-1760 E-mail: eileen.kulp@rivhs.com.

KULP, JAMES, finance company executive; b. Seoul, Korea (South), June 22, 1961; m. Jacqueline Ann Kulp. MBA, Oklahoma City U., 1993. Regional dir. GE Aircraft Engines, Kuala Lumpur, Malaysia, 1989—2000; sr. v.p. quality GE Fin., GE Capital, Lynchburg, Va., 2001—. Office: General Electric Financial 700 Main St Lynchburg VA 24501

KULPA, ALDONA, pharmacist; b. Alytus, Lithuania, Apr. 2, 1958; arrived in U.S., 96; d. Antanas Janavicius and Anele Janaviciene; m. Algis R. Kulpa, July 1, 1996. Degree in pharmacy, Kaunas (Lithuania) Med. Acad., 1982. Registered pharmacist N.Y. Pharmacist Vilnius (Lithuania) Cathedral Pharmacy, 1982—85, pharmacy unit mgr., 1985—89; asst. dir. Vilnius U. Pharmacy, 1989—96; pharmacy tech. Hip Pharmacy, Hempstead, NY, 1997—98, pharmacy intern, 1998—99; pharmacist Pathmark Pharmacy, Seaford, NY, 2000—. Union pres. Vilnius Cathedral Pharmacy, 1985. Mem.: Am. Pharm. Assn. Avocations: computers, travel, reading. Home: 1291 Paul St Seaford NY 11783 Office: Pathmark Pharmacy 4055 Merrick Rd Seaford NY 11783

KULSKI, JULIAN EUGENIUSZ, architect, planner, educator; b. Warsaw, Mar. 3, 1929; came to U.S., 1948, naturalized, 1950; s. Julian Spitoslav and Eugenia Helena (Solecka) K; children: Helena E., Julian S., Stefan T.A. Student, Sch. Architecture Oxford (Eng.) U., 1947-48; BArch, Yale U., 1953, MArch, 1954; PhD, Warsaw Inst. Tech., 1966. Practice architecture, city planning, Conn., 1954-59, 1959—; prof. architecture U. Notre Dame, South Bend, Ind., 1960-65; prof., dir. urban and regional planning George Washington U., Washington, 1965-67; prof., dir. city and regional planning Howard U., 1967-90. Cons. World Bank, 1964-90; bd. dirs. Nat. Archtl. Accrediting Bd., 1971-76; chmn. accrediting com. Harvard U., 1972, 75, U. P.R., 1974, Pratt U., 1975, Carnegie-Mellon U., 1976, U. Va.1978. Author: Land of Urban Promise, 1967 (Book-of-Month award), Evolution of American Urban Systems, 1970, Architecture in a Revolutionary Era, 1971, Dying, We Live, 1979; contbr. numerous articles to profl. jours. Served with Polish Army, 1941-46. Decorated Home Army Cross, Army Cross (4), Combat medal (Poland); knight of Malta, Order St. John of Jerusalem; recipient cert. of achievement Nat. Archtl. Accrediting Bd., 1973, 76. Fellow AIA; mem. Am. Planning Assn., Am. Inst. Cert. Planners, AAUP. Office: PO Box 69 Orlean VA 20128-0069 *My life has been guided by the following philosophy: It is hard to work for freedom, harder yet to die for it, and hardest of all to suffer for it.*

KULSTAD, GUY CHARLES, public works official; b. Feb. 28, 1930; s. John Marlyn and Anne Mildred (Boyd) Kulstad Ibison; m. Bonnie Jane Sherman, Aug. 28, 1955 (div. Aug. 1996); children: Anne Marie Kulstad Hurst, Mark, Alice Kulstad Krause. BS in Civil Engring., U. Calif., Berkeley, 1958. Registered profl. engr., Calif., Oreg., Wash., traffic engr., Calif., land surveyor, Oreg.; cert. c.c. instr., Calif. Engring. aid County Rd. Dept., L.A., 1951, asst. civil engr., 1953-58; dir. pub. wks. Benicia, Calif., 1958-59; dep. dir. pub. wks. Solano County, Calif., 1959-65; dir. pub. wks. Humboldt County, Calif., 1965-92; mgmt. cons., 1992—. Gen. mgr. Humboldt Bay Wastewater Authority 1975, 82-89. Mem. Employer support of N.G. and Res. With AUS, 1951-53. Recipient Outstanding Svc. award North Bay chpt. Calif. Soc. Profl. Engrs., 1964, Boss of the Yr. award Arcata Jaycees, Recognition award Humboldt Toastmaster, Meritorious Leadership award, Surveyor award Calif. Land Surveyors Assn., Illmars Lagzdin award for engring. contbns., Guy C. Kulstad award Humboldt County Dept. Pub. Wks. Fellow ASCE; NSPE, mem. Nat. Soc. County Engrs., Calif. County Engrs., County Engrs. Assn. Calif., Commonwealth Club of Calif., Sons of Norway.

KULT, AMY ELAINE, marketing consultant; b. Lafayette, Ind., Nov. 7, 1972; d. Jerry Lynn and Gayle Ann (Neal) Biggs; m. Troy Mathew Kult, My 12, 1995. BFA, Purdue U., 1996. Asst. sales mgr. Claire's Boutique, Lafayette, 1995-96; intern Lafayette Mus. of Art, Lafayette, 1996; sales Lafayette Bank & Trust, Lafayette, 1996-97; account rep. Dontech-Yellow Pages, Hillside, Ill., 1997; program mgr. Sunflower Group, Des Plaines, Ill., 1997-99; mktg. cons. Bounty SCA Worldwide, Chgo., 1999—; account exec. EURO RSCGIMAPCT, 2002—. Artist numerous posters. Recipient scholarship Ball State U., Muncie, 1991-93. Mem. Nat. Mus. of Women in the Arts, Nat. Trust for Hist. Preservation, Delta Phi Delta (sec. 1993-96). Democrat. Avocation: artwork.

KULTERMANN, UDO, architectural and art historian, educator, author; b. Stettin, Germany, Oct. 14, 1927; came to U.S., 1967, naturalized, 1981; s. Georg and Charlotte (Schultz) K.; m. Judith Danoff, May 10, 1975. Student, U. Greifswald, Germany, 1946-50; PhD magna cum laude, U. Muenster, Germany, 1953. Curatorial asst. Kunsthalle, Bremen, Germany, 1954-55; art editor Bertelsmann Pubs., Guetersloh, Germany, 1955-56; program dir. Am. House, Bremen, Germany, 1956-59; dir. city art mus. Schloss Morsbroich, Leverkusen, Germany, 1959-64; dir. Morsbroicher Kunsttage, Leverkusen, Germany, 1961; lectr. Duesseldorfer Geschichtsverein, Duesseldorf, Germany, 1953, 62, Technische Hochschule, Braunschweig, Germany, 1962, Oslo U., 1963, Trondheim U., Harvard U., Yale U., U. Calif., Berkeley, UCLA, U. Pa., U. Minn., 1965—; prof. archtl. history Washington U., St. Louis, 1967-94, Ruth and Norman Moore Prof. of Architecture and Urbanism, 1986-94, prof. emeritus, 1994—. Ednl. leader study tours German architects to Japan, 1965, 67; arch. commn. Biennale Venice, 1979—82; ednl. leader Soviet-Am. Travelling Arch. Seminar, Russia, 1986—87; jury Nat. U., Al Ain, United Arab Emirates, Internat. Open Air Exhbn., Pistany, Czech Republic; ednl. leader Nat. Trust for Hist. Preservation, Cruise, Copenhagen, Amsterdam, Rouen, Mont St. Michel, Bordeaux, and Lisbon, 1989; participant in internat. confs.; participant 1st Internat. Congress African Culture, Salisbury, Southern Rhodesia; lectr. univs., Jerusalem, Calcutta, Cairo, Kyoto, Buenos Aires, Shanghai. Author: Architecture of Today, 1958, Hans und Wassili Luckhardt-Bauten und Projekte, 1958, Dynamische Architektur, 1959, New Japanese Architecture, 1960, New Architecture in Africa, 1963, Junge deutsche Bildhauer, 1963, Der Schluessel zur Architektur von heute, 1963, New Architecture in the World, 1965, History of Art History, 1966, 2d edit., 2002, paperback edit., 1981, rev. edit., 1993, Spanish edit., 1996, Italian edit., 1997, Korean edit., 1999, Croatian edit., 2001, The New Sculpture-Assemblage and Environments, 1967, Architektur der Gegenwart, 1967, Gabriel Grupello, 1968, The New Painting, 1969, rev. edit., 1978, New Directions in African Architecture, 1969, Art and Life: The Function of Intermedia, 1970, New Realism, 1972, Die Architektur im 20 Jahrhundert, 6th edit., 2003, Ernest Trova, 1978, I Contemporanei, Storia della Scultura nel Mondo, 1979, Architecture in the Seventies, 1980, Architects of the Third World, 1980, Zeitgenoessische Architektur in Osteuropa, 1985, Spanish edit., 1989, Kleine Geschichte der Kunsttheorie, 1987; : Japanese edit., 1996, Korean edit., 1997, rev. 2d edit., 1998, Visible Cities-Invisible Cities-Urban Symbolism and Historical Continuity, 1988, Kunst und Wirklichkeit-Von Fiedler bis Derrida-Zehn Annaeherungen, 1991, Die Maxentius-Basilika.Ein Schluesselwerk spaetantiker Architektur, 1996, Contemporary Architecture in the Arab States-Renaissance of a Region, 1999, Thirty Years After-The Future of the Past, 2002; co-author (with Werner Hofmann): Modern Architecture in Color, 1970; editor: Kenzo Tange: Architecture and Urban Design, 1970, paperback edits., 1978, 1989, Architektur der Welt, Verlag und Datenbank fuer Geisteswissenschaften, Weimar, 1996—, St. James Modern Masterpieces: The Best of Art, Architecture, Photography and Design Since 1945, 1998, vol. VI Architecture in South and Central Africa in: World Architecture: A Critical Mosaic 1900-2000, 2000. Faculty mem. Nat. Humanities Faculty, Atlanta, 1986—. Recipient Disting. Faculty award Washington U., 1985. Mem. Croatian Acad. Scis. and Arts (corr.).

KULWICKI, BERNARD MICHAEL, ceramics engineer, researcher; b. Detroit, July 3, 1935; s. Bernard Joseph and Rose Lorkowski Kulwicki. BChE, U. Detroit, 1958; MS in Engring., U. Mich., 1960, PhD, 1963. Exch. visitor Inst. Solid State Physics, Prague, Czech Republic, 1963—64; mem. tech. staff Tex. Instruments, Attleboro, Mass., 1964—98. Contbr. articles to profl. jours. Fellow: Am. Ceramic Soc.; mem.: AAAS, Sigma Xi, Materials Rsch. Soc. Achievements include patents in field. Avocations: golf, music, computer technology. Home: PO Box 1407 Attleboro Falls MA 02763-0407

KULWIN, DWIGHT ROBERT, surgeon, educator; b. Rochester, Minn., Oct. 4, 1948; m. Elizabeth H. Brown, Dec. 13, 1981; children: Charles, Robert. BS, U. Ill., 1969; MD, U. Chgo., 1973. Diplomate Am. Bd. Ophthalmology. Prof. U. Cin. Coll. Medicine, 1979—. Author books, papers, and articles in field. Fellow ACS, Am. Soc. Ophthalmic Plastic and Reconstructive Surgery (Wendell Hughes lectr. 1996), Royal Jordanian Soc. Ophthalmology, Hellenic Ophthalmology Soc.; mem. Cosmos Club. Home: 260 Sunny Acres Dr Cincinnati OH 45255-3903 Office: U Cin Med Ctr Barrett Ctr PO Box 670-670 Cincinnati OH 45267-0670

KULYK, KAREN GAY, visual artist; b. Toronto, July 19, 1950; d. Joseph and Natalie Melanie (Solowski) K. BFA with honors, York U., 1973. Founder, curator Seedlings Gallery, Toronto, 1973-75; established studios worldwide, 1975—. Tchr. various instns., Can., Thailand, Bermuda, and England. Solo exhbns. include Kitchener-Waterloo Art Gallery, 1994, Rodman Hall, St. Catharines, Ont., 1995, Harbinger Gallery, 1994—, Marianne Friedland Gallery, 1974-1996, Masterworks Found. Gallery, Hamilton, Bermuda, 1997, Henry Dyson Fine Art, London, 1996—, Carnegie Gallery, Dundas, Ont., Can., 1996, Nancy Poole's Studio, Toronto, 1996-99, Gallery on the Bay, Hamilton, Ont., 1997—, Wallack Gallery, Ottawa, Can., 1996—, Zwicker Gallery, Halifax, N.S., Can., 1999—, Nat. Gallery Thailand, Grey Coll. U. Durham, Eng., 2000; exhibited in group shows at Harbinger Gallery, Waterloo, Ont., Touchstone Gallery, Hong Kong, Marianne Friedland Gallery, Fla., Sotheby's, Toronto, Chgo. Internat. Art Exhbn., York U., U. Toronto, Offices of Gov. Gen. of Can., Carleton U. Art Gallery, numerous others; represented in collections at Kitchener-Waterloo Art Gallery, Wilfred Laurier U., Waterloo, Art Gallery of Hamilton, Carleton U., York U., Agnes Etherington Art Gallery, Nat. Gallery of Bermuda, Hartford Coll. Md., Can. Trust, Dominion Trust, Shell Can., Thai Airways Internat., Can. Airlines Internat., others, pvt. collections; illustration: Orff, 27 Dragons and a Snarkel; subject of several newpaper articles. Recipient Grollo d'Oro, award Treviso Intenrat. Art Competition, 1983; grantee Sheila Hugh Mackay Found., 1996. Home and Office: 5270 Morris St Halifax NS Canada B3J 1B4

KULZICK, KEN STAFFORD, retired lawyer, travel writer; b. Milw., July 20, 1927; s. Earl Joseph and Claire Agnes (Blask) K.; m. Patricia Louise Siekert, June 19, 1949; 1 child, Kate Kulzick Stafford. PhB, Marquette U., Milw., 1950; JD, UCLA, 1956. Bar: Calif. 1956, U.S. Dist. Ct. (no. and cen. dists.) Calif. 1956, U.S. Ct. Appeals (9th cir.) 1956. Tchg. asst., rschr. UCLA, 1953—56; asst. U.S. atty. (honor grad program) Dept. Justice, L.A., San Francisco, 1956-58; ptnr. Lillick, McHose & Charles, L.A., 1958-86, Liebig & Kulzick, L.A., 1987-91, Gipson, Hoffman & Pancione, L.A., 1991-94; copyright lawyer, past pres. L.A. Copyright Soc. Media cons. specializing in dramatic documentaries, 1958—; media advisor League of Women Voters, L.A., 1986, 90; lectr. UCLA, 1987—. Contbr. articles to L.A. Lawyer mag., EMMY mag., Entertainment Law Reporter, others; bd. editors UCLA Law Rev., 1954-56. Served to lt. USN, 1950-53; Korea Home: PO Box 1926 Eagle River WI 54521-1926 Home (Winter): 1520 Scenic Dr Felton CA 95018-9642

KUMA, HISAO, information systems educator; b. Shinjuku, Tokyo, Japan, Oct. 30, 1936; s. Haruo and Motoko (Ikuta) K.; m. Kyoko Murakami, Feb. 12, 1965; children: Kazue, Yuki. B of Engring., Chiba (Japan) U., 1960; D of Engring., Tokyo U., 1982. Chief rschr. System Devel. Lab., Hitachi, Japan, 1960-87; vis. prof. U. Alta., Edmonton, 1987-88; prof. Grad. Sch. Informatics Teikyo Heisei U., Chiba, 1987—. Vis. prof. Chiba U., 1991—2002. Author: Telemedicine, 1983, New Technology for the Medical Management Computer Systems in the Doctor's Office, The Computer in the Doctor's Office, 1980; contbr. articles to profl. jours. Recipient Faculty Enrichment award Can. Govt., 1993. Mem.: JAMI, IEICE, ACM, IEEE (sr.). Home: 17-10 Ohkubo 2 chome Shinjuku-ku Tokyo 169-0072 Japan Office: Teikyo Heisei Univ 2289 Uruido Ichihara 290 0193 Japan E-mail: hkuma@iccc.org.

KUMAKO, KUAMI MAWUNYO, agricultural scientist; b. Cotonou, Benin, Nov. 11, 1963; s. Martin Kouami Kumako and Felicia Kpogo. BS in Agrl. Sci. Engring., U. Bénin, Togo, 1995; MS in Agrl. Econs., U. Ky., 2000. Rsch. asst. devel. program UN, Lomé, Togo, 1994—95; rsch. asst. dept. agrl. econs. U. Ky., Lexington, 1998—2001. Rsch. cons. World Bank, Washington, 2000—01. Mem. Commité Action Renouveau, Togo, 1990—96. Achievements include discovery of principle of rainfall-based index contract application in insurance. Home: 6919 Woodstream Lane Lanham MD 20706-2145 Personal E-mail: kumako1@hotmail.com.

KUMAO, HEIDI ELIZABETH, artist, educator; b. Calif., Jan. 2, 1964; BS in Chemistry, BA in Art, U. Calif., Davis, 1989; MFA, Sch. Art Inst. Chgo., 1991; postgrad., Syracuse U., 1992-95, 97-98. Asst. prof. U. Md., Balt., 1991-92, Syracuse (N.Y.) U., 1992-95, 97-98; rsch. fellow U. Mich., Ann Arbor, 1995-96; adj. prof. CCNY, N.Y.C., 1997; vis. asst. prof. U. Mich., Ann Arbor, 2001—03, asst. prof., 2003—. Microsoft artist residency studio creative inquiry Carnegie Mellon U., 1999—. One person shows at Ariz. State U. Art Mus., 1996, Alternative Mus., N.Y.C., 1997, Yerba Buena Ctr. for Arts, San Francisco, 1998; artist, author brochure: Hidden Mechanisms, 1996, Joan Miro Found., Barcelona, Spain, 1998, Centro Cultural Light, Rio de Janeiro, 1998, Mus. Image and Sound, Sao Paulo, 1999, Mus. Modern Art, Buenos Aires, 1999, Lisa Sette Gallery, Ariz., 1999. Rsch. fellow in arts U. Mich., 1995-96, artist's fellow Art Matters, 1996, N.Y. Found. for Arts, 1997; grantee M.W. Sharpe Art Found., 1996-97, Creative Capital Found., 2002; Microsoft fellow Carnegie Mellon U., 1999-2000; McDowell Colony fellow, 2002. Mem. Coll. Art Assn., Art and Sci. Collaborators Inc. E-mail: hkumao@umich.edu.

KUMAR, ANIL, nuclear engineer; b. Agra, India, Aug. 3, 1952; came to U.S., 1988; s. Vedprakash and Satyawati (Sudhir) Parashar; m. Geeta Sharma, Nov. 29, 1979; children: Amitabh, Kishen. MSc in Physics, Agra U., 1973; PhD in Nuclear Engring., U. Bombay, India, 1981. Sci. officer Bhabha Atomic Rsch. Ctr., Bombay, 1974-81; sr. researcher Ecole Poly. Fed. Lausanne, Switzerland, 1982-88; devel. engr. UCLA, 1988-90, sr. devel. engr., 1990-99; dir. T.C. Rsch. Ctr., L.A., 1998—. Software developer Quest Software, Irvine, Calif., 1999—. Contbr. articles to Jour. Fusion Energy, Nuclear Sci. and Engring., Fusion Tech., Fusion Engring. and Design, Atom Kern Energie, proc. internat. confs. and symposia. Mem. Am. Nuclear Soc., Am. Phys. Soc., Soc. Indsl. and Applied Math. Achievements include research in modified wigner rational approximation in neutronics, Boltzmann Fokker Planck transport equation, measurements of induced radioactivity and nuclear heating in fusion neutron environment, inertial confinement fusion, low activation materials, fusion reactor design, muon catalyzed fusion. Office: 8001 Irvine Ctr Dr Irvine CA 92618

KUMAR, ASHIR, pediatrician, medical educator; b. Fatehpur, U.P., India, Mar. 11, 1945; m. Kusum Kumar. MBBS, All India Inst. Med. Scis., New Delhi, 1966, MD in Pediatrics, 1972. Diplomate Am. Bd. Pediat., Am. Bd. Pediat. Infectious Diseases. Asst. prof. Case Western U. Sch. Medicine, Cleve., 1977-83, Mich. State U., East Lansing, 1983-86, assoc. prof., 1986-92, prof. dept. pediat. and human devel., 1992—. Editor for Am., Indian Jour. Pediat., 1996. Fellow Infectious Diseases Soc. Am., Am. Acad. Pediat.; mem. Pediat. Infectious Diseases Soc., Am. Assn. Physicians of Indian Origin, Aiimsonians of Am. (chair acad. coun. 1995—). Office: Mich State U Dept Pediat & Human Devel C-203 East Fee Hall East Lansing MI 48824-1316 E-mail: kumara@msu.edu.

KUMAR, B. PREETHAM, engineering educator, researcher; b. Chennai, Tamilnadu, India, Mar. 29, 1960; came to U.S., 1992; s. R. and Jamuma Balasubramaniam; m. Priyadarsini Kumar, June 27, 1991; children: Veena, Vasanth. BEng, Coll. Engring. Guindy, Chennai, 1982, MEng, 1984; PhD in Engring., Indian Inst. Tech., Chennai, 1992. Cert. engr. Project assoc. Indian Inst. Tech., 1984-92; lectr., rschr. U. Calif., Davis, 1992—; asst. prof. Calif. State U., Sacramento, 1992—. Author: Encyclopedia of Electrical and Electronics Engineering, 1998; contbr. articles to IEEE Transactions on Antennas and Propagation, 1989—. Named Prof. of Yr., IEEE Sacramento br., 1999. Mem.: IEEE (sr.). Avocations: poetry, travel, cricket, table tennis. Home: 412 Russell Park #8 Davis CA 95616 Office: Calif State U 6000 J St Sacramento CA 95819-6019 E-mail: kumarp@ecs.csus.edu.

KUMAR, BINOD, materials engineer, educator; b. Jamalpur, Bihar, India, Jan. 13, 1946; came to U.S., 1971; s. Rambaran and Ramsunderi (Rai) Singh; m. Shyama Thakur, May 23, 1969; children: Vineet, Sunita. MS, Pa. State U., 1973, PhD, 1976. Glass technologist Seraikella Glass Works, Konnagar, India, 1968-71; rsch. engr. Anchor Hocking Corp., Lancaster, Ohio, 1976-79; sr. rsch. engr. U. Dayton, 1980—, prof., 1992. Cons. Zimmer, Inc., Warsaw, Ind., 1987-90, Mead, Inc., Dayton, 1988, JAFE, Inc., Greenville, Ohio, 1987-90, Rotor Seal Dynamics, Calif., 1995—, Tex. Tech. Industries, Maine, 1999—. Trustee India Found., Dayton, 1991-95. Mem. Am. Ceramic Soc., Electrochem. Soc., Indian Ceramic Soc. (life). Achievements include 100 publs. and patents contributing to the fields of glass tech., solid state ionics, lithium rechargeable batteries, fuel cells and high temperature superconductivity; also mentoring jr. profls., undergraduate and grad. students. Office: U Dayton 300 College Park Ave Dayton OH 45469-0001 E-mail: kumarb@udri.udayton.edu.

KUMAR, HARINATH V. urologist, surgeon; b. Hyderabad, Andhra Pradesh, India, Sept. 2, 1938; came to U.S., 1964; s. Ramchander and Seetha Rao; m. Leela Murthy, Mar. 13, 1967; children: Vivek, Naveen, Veena. MB BS, Gandhi Med. Coll., Hyderabad, 1963. Diplomate Am. Bd. Urology. Intern Lawrence and Meml. Hosp., New London, Conn., 1965; resident in surgery Norwalk (Conn.) Hosp., 1966-67; resident in urology Bellevue Hosp., VA Hosp., N.Y.C., 1967-68, Montefiore Hosp. and Med. Ctr., Bronx, N.Y., 1968-70, fellow in urology, 1970-72; attending urologist Morrisania City Hosp., Bronx, 1972-74, Northwestern Med Ctr., Oil City, Pa., 1975—, Franklin, Pa., 1980—, Titusville (Pa.) Area Hosp., 1976—. Fellow ACS, Internat. Coll. Surgeons; mem. AMA, Pa. Med. Assn., Urol. Assn. Pa. Inc. Home: 3 Crestview Dr Oil City PA 16301-2009 Office: 32 Seneca St Oil City PA 16301-1314 also: 422 N Monroe St Titusville PA 16354-1670 also: 621 Elm St Tionesta PA 16353-9717

KUMAR, KAPLESH, materials scientist; b. Lucknow, India, Nov. 9, 1947; came to U.S., 1970; s. Shiam and Vidya (Devi) Sunder; m. Savinder Kaur, May 27, 1974; children: Priyadarshini, Ruchira. B.Tech., Indian Inst. Tech., 1969; MS, Stevens Inst. Tech., 1971; ScD, MIT, 1975; JD magna cum laude, New Eng. Sch. Law, 1997. Bar: Mass. 1998; registered patent aty. Mem. tech. staff Charles Stark Draper Lab., Inc., Cambridge, Mass., 1975-80, chief materials devel. sect., 1980-88, chief materials sci. and tech. sect., 1988-91, prin. mem. tech. staff, 1992—. Vis. lectr. IIM-ASM Internat., 1989; chmn. workshop on superconductivity and its applications to nat. needs, 1991; session chmn. Structures, Dynamics & Materials Conf., AIAA, 1996, 97. Author: (with others) Plasma Spraying: Theory and Applications, 1993; patentee in materials processing; pub. Applied Physics Review monograph, 1988; contbr. articles to profl. jours. Recipient Patent award Charles Stark Draper Lab., Inc., 1982, Outstanding Performance award, 1994, Invention Disclosure award NASA, 1983. Mem. ASM Internat. (mem. internat. materials revs. com. 1991—), AIAA (mem. materials tech. com. 1991-98), MIT Sangam Club for India Affairs (pres. 1972-73), India Assn. Greater Boston, Inc. (pres. 1995-97), IIT Soc. New Eng. (v.p. 1993-95), Indian Am. Forum for Polit. Edn. (pres. New Eng. chpt. 1998-2000, bd. trustees 2000—). Achievements include research in intellectual property law; permanent and soft magnetic materials; structural materials; micromechanical devices, inertial instruments; subspecialties include materials; ceramics.

KUMAR, KRISHAN, management consultant company executive; b. Patiala, India, Aug. 17, 1944; came to U.S., 1970; naturalized, 1978; s. Sewa Ram and Savitri (Devi) Aggarwal; B.S.M.E. (Merit scholar), Birla Inst. Tech. and Sci., India, 1966; M.S.I.E., N.J. Inst. Tech., 1975; m. Saroj, July 23, 1969; children: Anuj, Amit. Engring. positions in U.S. and India, 1966-73; indsl. engr., then sr. indsl. engr. Berkey Photo, Inc., Clifton, N.J., 1973-76; assoc. Walter Frederick Friedman & Co., West Orange, N.J., 1977—, v.p., 1981-85; pres. Eskay Cons. Group, Edison, N.J., 1985—. Mem. Am. Inst. Indsl. Engrs. (sr.), Inst. Mgmt. Cons. (cert.), Coun. Logistics Mgmt., Am. Arbitration Assn. (panelist). Contbr. articles to profl. jours. Home and Office: 6 Vallata Pl Edison NJ 08820-1688

KUMAR, KRISHNA, retired physics educator; b. Meerut, India, July 14, 1936; came to U.S., 1956, naturalized, 1966; s. Rangi and Susheila (Devi) Lal; m. Katharine Johnson, May 1, 1960; children: Jai Robert, Raj David. BSc in Physics, Chemistry and Math., Agra U., 1953, MSc in Physics, 1955; MS in Physics, Carnegie Mellon U., 1959, PhD in Physics, 1964. Rsch. assoc. Mich. State U., 1963-66, MIT, 1966-67; rsch. fellow Niels Bohr Inst., Copenhagen, 1967-69; physicist Oak Ridge (Tenn.) Nat. Lab., 1969-71; assoc. prof. Vanderbilt U., Nashville, 1971-77; fgn. collaborator AEC of France, Paris, 1977-79; Nordita prof. U. Bergen, Norway, 1979-80; prof. physics Tenn. Tech. U., Cookeville, 1980-83, univ. prof. physics, 1983-99, prof. physics emeritus, 1999—. Tax assoc. H&R Block, 2003—; disting. hon. fellow Manibal Acad. Higher Edn., India, 2002—; lectr. in field; cons. various rsch. labs. Author: Nuclear Models and the Search for Unity in Nuclear Physics, 1984, Superheavy Elements, 1989, (with J.R. Kumar) The Redhead From Alpha Centauri, 2003; contbr. articles to profl. jours., books. Sec. India Assn., Pitts., 1958-59; faculty advisor, 1990-99, assoc. mem. Triangle Fraternity, 1990-99; deacon Presbyn. Ch., 1991-93, elder, 2000-02; faculty advisor Indian Assn. of Cookeville, 1994-95; mem. exec. com. Putnam County Dem. Party, 1999-2002. Recipient Gold medal Agra U., 1955; NSF rsch. grantee, 1972-75; Paul Harris fellow Rotary Internat., 1995. Mem. Indian Phys. Soc., Am. Phys. Soc., Tenn. Acad. Scis., Internat. Cmty. Hospitality Assn. (pres. 1992-94), Planetary Soc., Phi Kappa Phi, Sigma Pi Sigma, Sigma Xi (bd. dirs. 1992-93, charter mem. chpt. installation 1994). Unity Ch. Home: 718 W 12th St Cookeville TN 38501-7788 E-mail: kkaadmi_99@yahoo.com.

KUMAR, NANDA PRATIVADI, lawyer; s. Govinda Prativadi Rajamacharyar and Perindevi Prativadi Tayar; m. Christine Anne Cherris Kumar, Nov. 24, 1995. MS, Andhra U., Waltair, India, 1982; PhD, U. Delhi, 1999—99; JD, Temple U., 2000. Bar: U.S. Patent and Trademark Office 1999, Pa. 2000, N.J. 2000. Postdoctoral scientist AgBiotech Ctr., New Brunswick, NJ, 1992—95; rsch. scientist Phytotech, Inc., Monmouth Junction, NJ, 1995—96; sr. rsch. scientist NovaFlora, Inc., Phila., 1996—97; law clk. Dechert, Princeton, NJ, 1997—99, law clk., patent agt. Reed Smith, Phila., 1999—2000, patent atty., 2000—. Contbr. articles to sci. publs.; patentee in field. Recipient internat. travel award, Coun. of Sci. and Indsl. Rsch., India, 1991; Ctr. of Advanced Study's Rsch. fellow, Univ. Grants Commn., Govt. of India, 1983—88, postdoctoral rsch. fellow, Coun. of Sci. and Indsl. Rsch., India, 1990—94. Mem.: Pa. Bar Assn., Am. Intellectual Property Law Assn. Avocations: travel, swimming, aerobic excercise, music, basketball. Personal E-mail: nandapba@yahoo.com.

KUMAR, PANGANAMALA RAMANA, electrical and computer engineering educator; b. Nagpur, Maharashtra, India, Apr. 21, 1952; came to U.S., 1973; s. Panganamala Bhavanarayana and Panganamala Kamala (Avasarala) Murthy; m. Devarakonda Jayashree Sundaram, Jan. 22, 1982; children: P. Ashwin, Shilpa P. BTech., Indian Inst. Tech., Madras, India, 1973; MS, Washington U., 1975, DSc, 1977. Asst. prof. dept. math. and computer sci. U. Md., Baltimore County, 1977-82, assoc. prof. dept. math. and computer sci., 1982-84; assoc. prof. dept. elec. and computer engring. and coordinated sci. lab. U. Ill., Urbana, 1985-87, prof. dept. elec. and computer engring., 1987—, rsch. prof. coordinated sci. lab., 1987—, Franklin Woeltge prof. elec. and computer engring., 2000—. Co-author: Stochastic Systems, 1986; assoc. editor: Systems and Control Letters, 1984-93, Math. of Control, Signals and Systems, 1986—, SIAM Jour. on Control and Optimization, 1989-93, Jour. of Discrete Event Dynamic Systems: Theory and Application, 1993—; assoc. editor-at-large IEEE Trans. on Automatic Control, 1989-97; mem. editl. bd. Jour. on Adaptive Control and Signal Processing, 1986-99, Math. Problems in Engring., 1995—; contbr. articles to profl. jours. Recipient Donald P. Eckman award Am. Automatic Control Coun., 1985. Fellow IEEE. Avocation: table tennis. Office: U Ill Coordinated Sci Lab 1308 W Main St Urbana IL 61801-2307 E-mail: prkumar@uiuc.edu.

KUMAR, RAJ, psychologist, hypnotherapist; b. Dibai, India, Jan. 9, 1961; came to U.S., 1989; s. Dilbagh Rai and Laksmi Rani Kumar; m. Sunita M. Kumar, July 19, 1993; 1 child, Sapna. BA, Agra (India) Coll., 1981; MA, St. John's Coll., Agra, 1983; PhD, Agra U., 1987. Cert. hypnotist, Hawaii. Psychologist Dept. Health, Honolulu, 1989—. Author: From Darkness to Light, 2000, The Secrets of Health and Healing, The Spiritual Thoughts for the Day. Active Milan, Hawaii, 1999. Avocations: exercise, music, collecting books and antiques. Office: New Life Ctr 627 South St Honolulu HI 96813 E-mail: Raj@hgea.org.

KUMAR, RAJENDRA, electrical engineering educator; b. Amroha, India, Aug. 22, 1948; came to U.S., 1980; s. Satya Pal Agarwal and Kailash Vati Agarwal; m. Pushpa Agarwal, Feb. 16, 1971; children: Anshu, Shipra. BS in Math. and Sci., Meerut Coll., 1964; BEE, Indian Inst. Tech., Kanpur, 1969, MEE, 1977; PhD in Electrical Engring., U. New Castle, NSW, Australia, 1981. Mem. tech. staff Electronis and Radar Devel., Bangalore, India, 1969-72; rsch. engr. Indian Inst. Tech., Kanpur, 1972-77; asst. prof. Calif. State U., Fullerton, 1981-83, Brown U., Providence, 1980-81; prof. Calif. State U., Long Beach, 1983—. Cons. Jet Propulsion Lab., Pasadena, Calif., 1984-91, Aerospace Corp., El Segundo, Calif., 1995—. Contbr. articles. Recipient Best Paper award Internat. Telemetering Conf., Las Vegas, 1986, 10 New Technology awards NASA, Washington, 1987-91. Mem.: AAUP, AIAA, NEA, IEEE (sr.), Inst. of Navigation, Calif. Faculty Assn., Inst. Navigation, Auto Club So. Calif. (Cerritos), Tau Beta Pi (eminent mem.), Eta Kappa Nu, Sigma Xi. Achievements include patents for efficient detections and signal parameter estimation with applications to hihg dynamic GPS receivers; multiusage estimation of received carrier signal parameters under very high dynamic conditions of the receiver; fast frequency acquisition via adaptive least squares algorithms; Kalman filter ionospheric delay estimator, method and apparatus for reducing multipath signal error using deconvolution; others. Avocations: gardening, walking, hiking, reading. Home: 13910 Rose St Cerritos CA 90703-9043 Office: Calif State U 1250 N Bellflower Blvd Long Beach CA 90840-0001

KUMAR, ROMESH, chemical engineer; b. Rajpura, India, Oct. 18, 1944; came to U.S., 1966; s. Kundan Lal and Pushpa (Wati) Agarwal; m. Kumkum Khanna, Feb. 22, 1976. BS, Panjab U., India, 1965; MS, U. Calif., Berkeley, 1968, PhD, 1972. Postdoctoral appointee Argonne (Ill.) Nat. Lab., 1972-73, asst. chem. engr., 1973-76, chem. engr., 1976—; also head fuel cell dept. Chem. Engring. divsn. Argonne Nat. Lab. Tchr. fuel cell power sys. design and analysis for transp. applications. Contbr. to Weissberger's Techniques in Chemistry, 1975; patentee in field. Recipient Silver medal Panjab U., 1965 Hindu. Home: 1549 Ceals Ct Naperville IL 60565-6148 Office: 9700 Cass Ave Argonne IL 60439-4803 E-mail: kumar@cmt.anl.gov.

KUMAR, SANJAY, computer company executive; b. Colombo, Sri Lanka, 1962; came to the U.S., 1976; Dir. software devel. UCCEL Corp.; pres., COO Computer Assocs. Internat., Inc., Islandia, NY, pres., CEO, 2000—, chmn., 2002—. Office: Computer Assocs Internat Inc One Computer Assocs Plaza Islandia NY 11749*

KUMAR, SANJAYA, epidemiologist, statistician; m. Shalini Varma Kumar, Mar. 5, 1998. BvSc&AH, G.B. Pant U of Agrl. & Tech., India, 1988; MS in epidemiology, U of Guelph, Guelph,Can., 1998; PhD, Hamilton U., 2001. Rsch. scientist N.Y. State Dept. Health, Troy, NY, 1999—. Fellow: Royal Statis. Soc.; mem.: NSHS, ACE, Sigma Xi. Office Fax: 518-402-7959. E-mail: sxk10@health.state.ny.us.

KUMAR, SHAILENDRA, urologist, educator; b. Patna, Bihar, India, Oct. 7, 1941; came to U.S., 1969; m. Singh Meera; children: Yash, Pratish, Priya. MD, Patna Med. Coll., 1964. Resident in surgery Worcester (Mass.) City Hosp., 1969-70; resident in urology Howard U., Washington, 1970-73; fellow dept. urology Meml. Sloan-Kettering Cancer Ctr., N.Y.C., 1973-74; clin. assoc. prof. urology/surgery Howard U., 1978—. Mem. Am. Urol. Assn., Montgomery County Med. Assn. Office: 6510 Kenilworth Ave Ste 2200 Riverdale MD 20737-1342

KUMAR, SRIKANTA PONNATHPUR, electrical engineer, researcher; b. Ponnathpur, India, Aug. 13, 1954; arrived in U.S.A., 1976; s. Ramaswamy and Padmamma Ponnathpur; m. Tara Vishwanath, Aug. 2, 1982; children: Shruti, Kumar. BSc with hons., Bangalore (India) U., 1971; BEE, Indian Inst. Sci., 1974, MEE, 1976; PhD, Yale U., 1981. Asst. prof. of elec. engring. Rennselaer Polytechnic Inst., Troy, NY, 1982—85, Northwestern U., Evanston, Ill., 1985—89, assoc. prof. of elec. engring., 1989—96, dir. masters program in info. tech., 1996—98; sr. tech. advisor Nat. Inst. Standards and Tech., Gaithersberg, Md., 1998—99; program mgr. Def. Advanced Rsch. Projects Agy., Arlington, Va., 1999—. Co-editor: Proceedings of IEEE, 2003; editor: Jour. High Speed Networks, 1994—, Mag. of Signal Processing: IEEE, —. Mem.: IEEE, Assn. Computing Machinery. Avocations: music, meditation, walking. Office: Defense Advanced Rsch Projects Agency 3701 N Fairfax Drive Arlington VA 22203 Fax: 703-807-1793. E-mail: skumar@darpa.mil.

KUMAR, SUBODHA, information scientist, educator; b. Pathargama, Bihar, India, Feb. 8, 1975; arrived in U.S., 1999; s. Shiva Kumar Tekriwal and Mira Devi; m. Susmita Sarawgi, Feb. 15, 2002. BS in Engring., Bihar Inst. Tech., Sindri, India, 1994; M in Tech., Indian Inst. Tech., Kanpur, 1997; MBA, U. Tex., Dallas, 2000; PhD, U. Tex. Dallas, Richardson, 2001. Tchg. asst. Indian Inst. Tech., Kanpur, India, 1995—97; sr. engr. Tata Engring. and Locomotive Co., Janmshedpur, India, 1997—98; rsch. asst. U. Toronto, Canada, 1998—98; tchg. asst. U. Tex. at Dallas, Richardson, 1999—2000; rsch. asst. FSI Internat., Allen, Tex., 2000—01, rsch. scientist, 2001—01; asst. prof. U. Wash., Seattle, 2001—. Fellow, U. Toronto, 1998, U. Tex. at Dallas, 1999—2001; grantee, FSI Internat., 2000—01; Selden Leavell Merit Based scholar, U. Tex. at Dallas, 2000—01. Mem.: Assn. Info. Sys. Achievements include patents for robotic cell design. Office: Univ Wash Bus Sch 350 Mackienzie Box 353200 Seattle WA 98195 Office Fax: 205-543-3968. E-mail: subodha@u.washington.edu.

KUMAR, UDAYA, urologist; b. Gobi, Tamil Nadu, India, May 17, 1961; arrived in U.S., 1998; s. Marannan Gowder and Ponnammal Marannan; m. Anita Sundaresan; children: Anirudh, Aditi. MB, BChir, Stanley Med. Coll., Madras, India, 1983, MS in Gen. Surgery, 1989; Diploma in Urology, Inst. Urology and Nephrology, London, 1993. Fellow in renal transplant Cleve. Clinic Found., 1998—99; fellow in endourology and laparoscopy Loyola U., Chgo., 1999—2000; asst. prof. U. Ark. for Med. Scis., Little Rock, 2000—. Contbr. chapters to books, articles to profl. jours. Fellow: Royal Coll. Surgeons Edinburgh; mem.: Am. Urol. Assn. Office: Univ Ark for Med Scis Slot 540 4301 W Markham Rd Little Rock AR 72205 Office Fax: 501-686-5277. Business E-Mail: kumarudaya@uams.edu.

KUMAR, VERINDER, accountant, financial executive; b. Mirpur, Kashmir, India, Sept. 24, 1937; came to U.S., 1979; s. Basheshar Nath and Tara Wanti (Durga Devi) Mahajan; m. Manjula Mehandru, Oct.31, 1965; children: Monisha, Ayesha. BA, Punjab U., India, 1958. Cert. acct., U.K. Acct. Punjab Nat. Bank, New Delhi, 1958-62, Glenhurst Hayes, Ltd., London, 1963-65, George Cohen Group, London, 1965-68; fin. acct. Nuffield Nursing Homes Trust, London, 1968-79; comptr. Community Nutrition Inst., Washington, 1980-84, treas./cons., 1984—; CFO Wilcoxon Constrn., Inc., Rockville, Md., 1984—. Bd. dirs., sec., treas. Md. Pools, Balt., Topgun of Va., Lorton, Tyma-Kumar Joint Venture, Rockville; v.p. Avery Corp. Mem. Woodford Pk. Residents Assn. Republican. Hindu. Avocations: hiking, fishing, cricket, soccer, reading. Home: 8505 Bethany Ct Vienna VA 22182-5060

KUMAR, VIJAYA BHAGAVATULA, electrical engineering educator, consultant; b. Porumamilla, India, Aug. 15, 1953; came to U.S., 1977; s. Ramamurthy and Saradamba Bhagavatula; m. Latha Bhagavatula, July 1, 1982; children: Ramamurthy, Madhusudan, Chandrasekhar. B.Tech. in EE, IIT, Kanpur, India, 1975; M.Tech. in EE, IIT, 1977; PhD in EE, Carnegie Mellon U., 1980. Asst. prof. dept. elec. and computer engring. Carnegie Mellon U., Pitts., 1982-87, assoc. prof., 1987-91, prof., 1991—, assoc. dept. head, 1994-96, thrust leader, optical recording, 1998—. Cons. Raytheon Systems Ctr., Tucson, 1997—, U.S. Army MICOM, Huntsville, Ala., 1993-95, Mytec Tech. Inc., Toronto, Ont., Can., 1995-98, Baker & McKenzie, San Francisco, 1998-99. Co-author (sect.) Handbook of Brain, 1995, (chpt.) Biometric Encryption, 1999; contbr. over 300 articles to profl. engring. jours. Sec. S.V. Temple, Pitts., 1994, bd. dirs., pres. exec. com., 1992; mem. tri-svc. ATR tech. armament plan for conventional weapons com., 1995. Fellow: Optical Soc. Am., Internat. Soc. Optical Engrs.; mem.: IEEE (sr.), Sigma Xi. Avocations: traveling, bridge, table tennis. Office: Carnegie Mellon U Dept Electric & Computer E Pittsburgh PA 15213 E-mail: kumar@ece.cmu.edu.

KUMIN, MAXINE WINOKUR, poet, writer; b. Phila., June 6, 1925; d. Peter and Doll (Simon) Winokur; m. Victor Montwid Kumin, June 29, 1946; children: Jane Simon, Judith Montwid, Daniel David. AB, Radcliffe Coll., 1946, MA, 1948; LHD (hon.), Centre Coll., 1976, Davis and Elkins Coll., 1977, Regis Coll., 1979, New England Coll., 1982, Claremont Grad. Sch., 1983, U. N.H., 1984. Instr. Tufts U., Medford, Mass., 1958-61, lectr. English, 1965-68. Scholar Radcliffe Inst. for Ind. Study, 1961-63; vis. lectr. U. Mass., Amherst, 1973, Princeton U., 1979, 81-82; adj. prof. Columbia U., 1975; Fannie Hurst prof. of literature Brandeis U., 1975, Wash. U., St. Louis, 1977; vis. sr. fellow, lectr. Princeton U., 1977; Carolyn Wilkerson Bell vis. scholar Randolph-Macon Woman's Coll., 1978; writer in residence Fla. Internat. U., 1998; poet in residence Bucknell U., 1983; vis. prof. MIT, 1984, U. Miami, 1995, Pitzer Coll., 1996, Fla. Internat. U., 1998; McGee prof. of writing Davidson Coll., 1997; master artist Atlantic Ctr. for Arts, New Smyrna Beach, Fla., 1984; staff mem. Bread Loaf Writers' Conf., 1969-71, 73, 75, 77; poetry cons. Library of Congress, 1981-82; elector The Poet's Corner, The Cathedral of St. John the Divine, 1990—; mem. staff Sewanee Writer's Conf., 1993-94, Bucknell U. visiting poet, 2001. Author: (poetry) Halfway, 1961, The Privilege, 1965, The Nightmare Factory, 1970, Up Country: Poems of New England, 1972 (Pulitzer Prize for poetry 1973), House, Bridge, Fountain, Gate, 1975, The Retrieval System, 1978, Our Ground Time Here Will Be Brief, 1982, Closing the Ring, 1984, The Long Approach, 1985, Nurture, 1989, Looking for Luck, 1992, Connecting the Dots, 1996, Selected Poems 1960-1990, 1997; (novels) Through Dooms of Love, 1965, The Passions of Uxport, 1968, The Abduction, 1971, The Designated Heir, 1974; (essays) To Make A Prairie: Essays on Poets, Poetry, and Country Living, 1980, In Deep: Country Essays, 1987, Women, Animals and Vegetables: Essays and Stories, 1994; (short stories) Why Can't We Live Together Like Civilized Human Beings?, 1982; (juvenile) Sebastian and the Dragon, 1960, Spring Things, 1961, A Summer Story, 1961, Follow the Fall, 1961, A Winter Friend, 1961, Mittens in May, 1962, No One Writes a Letter to the Snail, 1962, (with Anne Sexton) Eggs of Things, 1963, Archibald the Traveling Poodle, 1963, (with Sexton) More Eggs of Things, 1964, Speedy Digs Downside Up, 1964, The Beach Before Breakfast, 1964, Paul Bunyan, 1966, Faraway Farm, 1967, The Wonderful Babies of 1809 and Other Years, 1968, When Grandmother Was Young, 1970, When Great-Grandmother Was Young, 1971, (with Sexton) Joey and the Birthday Present, 1971, (with Sexton) The Wizard's Tears, 1975, What Color Is Caesar?, 1978, The Microscope, 1984; contbr. poems to nat. mags. Recipient Lowell Mason Palmer award, 1960, William Marion Reedy award, 1968, Eunice Tietjens Meml. prize Poetry Mag., 1972, Borestone Mountain award, 1976, Radcliffe Coll. Alumnae Recognition award, 1978, Am. Acad. and Inst. Arts and Letters award for excellence in literature, 1980, Levinson award Poetry mag., 1987, The Poets' prize, 1994, Aiken Taylor Poetry prize, 1995, Centennial award Harvard Grad. Sch. Arts and Scis., 1996; grantee Nat. Endowment for the Arts, 1966; fellow Nat. Coun. on Arts and Humanities, 1967-68; fellow Acad. Am. Poets, 1986; fellow Woodrow Wilson, 1979-80, 91-93. Mem. Acad. Am. Poets (chancellor), Poetry Soc. Am., PEN Am., Authors Guild, The Writers Union. Address: Scott Waxman Agy Inc 1650 Broadway Ste 1011 New York NY 10019-6833

KUMJIAN, JOHN CHARLES, musician, educator; b. Detroit, Mar. 15, 1956; s. George Charles and Bessie Isabelle Kumjian; m. Cherilyn Ann Wright, Nov. 26, 1983. BME, No. Mich. Univ., 1985; MA in Ednl. Leadership, No. Mich. U., 2001. Cert. tchr. Mich. Dir. bands Sch. Dist. Florence (Wis.) County, 1988—99; dir. bands, music tchr. Glen Lake Cmty. Schools, Maple City, Mich., 1999—. Studio, live performer varied, 1979—. Musician: (albums) Slide Rules (Eric Erickson), 2000, I Can See (Jay Webber), 2000. Mem.: Wis. Sch. Music Assn., Mich. Sch. Band and Orch. Assn., Music Educators Nat. Conf. Avocations: travel, fishing. Home: 6746 Windwood Dr Lake Ann MI 49650-9551 E-mail: kumjiaj@glenlake.k12.mi.us.

KUMMER, GLENN F. retired manufacturing executive; b. Park City, Utah, 1933; BS, U. Utah, 1961. Sr. acct. Ernst & Ernst, 1961-65; trainee Fleetwood Enterprises Inc., Riverside, Calif., 1965-67, purchasing mgr., 1967-68, plant mgr., 1968-70, gen. mgr. recreational vehicle div., 1970-71, asst. v.p. ops., 1971-72, sr. v.p. ops., 1972-77, exec. v.p. ops., 1977-82, pres., 1982-98, chmn., CEO, 1998—2002, also bd. dirs. Office: Fleetwood Enterprises Inc PO Box 7638 3125 Myers St Riverside CA 92503-5544

KUMMEROW, ARNOLD A. superintendent of schools; b. Framingham, Mass., Mar. 25, 1945; s. Arnold A. Sr. and Elizabeth Patricia (Westfield) K.; m. Constance Booth, July 10, 1971. BME, Eastern Mich. U., 1968, MA, 1975; PhD, U. Mich., 1989. Cert. adminstrn., Mich. Instrumental music dir. Vandercook Lake Pub. Schs., Jackson, Mich., 1968-74; instrumental music dir., asst. prin., prin. L'Anse Creuse Pub. Schs., Mt. Clemens, Mich., 1975-89; asst. supt. curriculum and pers. Lincoln Consol. Schs., Ypsilanti, Mich., 1989-91; asst. supt. Ypsilanti Pub. Schs., 1991-93; mem. curriculum devel. staff Mich. Dept. Edn., 1993-94; supt. Carsonville-Port Sanilac (Mich.) Schs., 1994-97, Armada (Mich.) Area Schs., 1997—. Named Exemplary Sch. Prin., Mich. Dept. Edn. and U.S. Dept. Edn. Mem. AASA, MASA, ASCD. Home: 17201 Knollwood Dr Clinton Township MI 48038-2833 Office: Armada Area Schs 74500 Burk St Armada MI 48005-3314

KUMMETH, PATRICIA JOAN, nursing educator; b. Libertyville, Ill., Mar. 7, 1949; d. Francis Alphonse Kummeth, Elizabeth Claire Kummeth. BSN, Coll. St. Teresa, 1970; MSN, U. Wis., Eau Claire, 1988. Registered nurse. Staff RN med. Saint Marys Hosp., Rochester, Minn., 1970—72, clin. insvc. educator, 1972—76, head nurse med., 1976—78, staff RN hematology/nephrology, 1978—81; nursing edn. specialist Mayo Clinic Hosp., Rochester, 1982—. Nursing continuing edn. appraiser Am. Nurses' Credentialing Ctr., Washington, 1998—. Author: (booklet) Problem-Oriented Charting: A Study Guide, 1976; developer (nursing asst. model in jour.) Med.-Surg. Nursing, 2001. Sec. Rochester Women's Softball Assn., 1994—98. Recipient Breaking Barriers award, Minn. Coalition to Promote Women in Athletic Leadership, 2001. Mem.: ANA (congress on nursing practice and economics 1998—2002), Minn. Nurses Assn. (commn. nursing practice 1999—2003, sec. 1992—93, commn. on edn. 1991—92), Acad. Med.-Surg. Nurses (sec. Upper Miss. River Valley chpt. 1999—2001), Am. Soc.Healthcare Educators and Trainers (info. mgr. Minn. affiliate 1993—95), Minn. Nurses Assn. (pres. 6th dist. 1988—92, sec. 1995—99, dir. 2000—02), Sigma Theta Tau (Kappa Mu chpt.), American Nurses' Credentialing Center (Commn. Accreditation 1998—2002). Roman Catholic. Avocations: reading, golf, travel. Office: Mayo Clinic Hosp 1216 Second St SW - 7 Marian Hall Rochester MN 55902

KUMMINGS, DONALD DALE, English educator; b. Lafayette, Ind., July 28, 1940; s. Herman Wilhelm and Estelle Catherine (Easterwood) K.; m. Gail Nadine Savage, Mar. 23, 1963 (div. Aug. 1978); children: Kevin Scott (dec.), Jeremy William; m. Patricia Finnelly Larson, Mar. 21, 1987. BA, Purdue U., 1962, MA, 1964; PhD, Ind. U., 1971. Tchg. assoc. Purdue U., West Lafayette, Ind., 1963-64; instr. in English Adrian (Mich.) Coll., 1964-66; assoc. instr. Ind. U., Bloomington, 1966-70; asst. prof. English U. Wis.-Parkside, Kenosha, 1970-75, assoc. prof. English, 1975-85, prof. English, 1985—, chair dept. English, 1974-76, 91-94. Book rev. editor Rutgers U., Camden, N.J., 1983-90; panelist, reviewer NEH, Washington, 1992-98; lectr. in field; book manuscript cons. Harcourt Brace Jovanovich, U. Tenn. Press, Susquehanna U. Press, U. Iowa Press, Houghton Mifflin, W.W. Norton, Oxford (Eng.) U. Press. Author: Walt Whitman, 1940-1975: A Reference Guide, 1982, The Open Road Trip: Poems, 1989; editor: Approaches to Teaching Whitman's "Leaves of Grass," 1990; co-editor: Walt Whitman: An Encyclopedia, 1998; contbr. numerous articles to profl. jours. Mem. Honor Our Neighbors' Origins and Rights, 1991—. Named Wis. Prof. of Yr., Carnegie Found. for Advancement of Tchg., 1997. Mem. MLA (cons. reader 1993, 94), ACLU, Am. Lit. Assn., Acad. Am. Poets, Wis. Fellow of Poets, Walt Whitman Assn., Walt Whitman Birthplace Assn., Greenpeace. Avocations: travel, photography, jazz, racquetball. Office: U Wis-Parkside Dept English PO Box 2000 Kenosha WI 53141-2000 E-mail: kummings@uwp.edu.

KUMMLER, RALPH H. chemical engineer, educator, dean; b. Jersey City, Nov. 1, 1940; m. Jean Evelyn Helge, Aug. 25, 1962; children: Randolph Henry, Bradley Rolf, Jeffrey Ralf. BSChemE, Rensselaer Poly. Inst., 1962; PhD, Johns Hopkins U., 1966. Chem. engr. GE Space Scientist Lab., Valley Forge, Pa., 1965-69; assoc. prof. chem. engring. Wayne State U., Detroit, 1970-75, prof., 1975—, chmn. dept., 1974-93, dir. hazardous waste mgmt. programs, 1986—, assoc. dean rsch., 1997-2001, interim dean, 2001—. Contbr. articles to publs. Bd. dirs., past pres. Kirkwood Lake Assn. Fellow: Engr. Soc. Detroit (Young Engr. of Yr. award 1975, Gold award 1990, Disting. Svc. award 1994, Horace Rackham Humanitarian award 1999), Am. Inst. Chemists; mem.: AIChE (past pres. Detroit chpt.), Svc. award 1981, Chem. Engr. of Yr. award 1981), Mich. Air and Waste Mgmt. Assn. ((past pres.), Waste Mgmt. award 2002), Am. Chem. Soc., Tau Beta Pi, Sigma Xi. Achievements include co-patentee in chem. innovations. Office: Wayne State U Coll Engring Detroit MI 48202

KUM-NJI, PHILIP, pediatrician, educator; s. Nolbert and Esther NNsen Kum-Nji; m. Stella Yuh Yih, Sept. 9, 1958; children: Nicole Ndum, Germain Nji, George Temfung, Paul Che, Peter Feul. MD, U. of Yaounde Sch. of Medicine, Cameroon, 1971—77; MPH, Tulane Sch. of Pub. Health and Tropical Medicine, 1985—86. Pediatrics Am. Bd. of Pediat., 1994. Med. officer Ministry of Pub. Health, Mbouda, Mbengwi, and Buea, Cameroon, 1978—84; instr. in pub. health U. of Yaounde Med. Sch., Cameroon, 1984—85; asst. prof. of pediat. U. of Pitts. Sch. of Medicine. Med. dir. miss. children's health project Children's Health Fund, Clarksdale, Miss. Author (rsch.) numerous pubs. in med. jours. Fellow: Am. Acad. of Pediat.; mem.: So. Soc. of Pediatric Rsch., Ambulatory Pediatric Assn. Office: Children's Hosp of Pitts 3705 Fifth Ave Pittsburgh PA 15217 Office Fax: 412-692-5807.

KUMP, KARY RONALD, lawyer; b. Provo, Utah, Apr. 27, 1952; s. Ronald and Ann (Thomas) K.; m. Terri Renee Farley, Sept. 24, 1980; children: Kasey Ronald, Kyle Thomas, Kristopher Lewis, Kolby Lawrence, Karson Jack. AA, Rio Hondo Coll., 1972; BA, U. Calif., Fullerton, 1976; JD, Western State U., Fullerton, 1980; cert. trial advocacy, Hastings Law Sch., 1982. Bar: Calif. 1982, Utah 1995, U.S. Dist. Ct. (ctrl. dist.) Calif. 1982, (no. and so. dists.) Calif. 1985. Assoc. William G. Kellen & Assocs., Riverside, Calif., 1980-83, Kellen & Luchs, Riverside, 1983-84; ptnr. Luchs, Kump & Milelich, Riverside, 1984-85, Carter & Kump, Riverside, 1985-87; sole practice Riverside, 1987-90; ptnr. Kump & Kennedy, 1990-98, Kump & Earven, 1998-99, Law Offices of Farley & Kump, LLP, Carpinteria, Calif., 1999—2001, Ventura, Calif., 2001—. Panel atty. Lawyer Referral Svc., Riverside, 1982—, Coll. Legal Clinic, Riverside, 1984—, Montgomery Ward Legal Svcs. Plan, Riverside, 1986—; judge pro tem Riverside Mcpl. Ct.; arbitrator Riverside Superior Ct.; mediator 4th Dist. Ct. Appeals; hearing officer City of Riverside. Exec. post advisor Boy Scouts Am. Fellow Roscoe Pound Inst.; mem. ABA, State Bar Calif. (bd. govs., Svc. Contbn. award 1984), Riverside Bar Assn. (panel atty. 1982, co-chair pub. bar rels., fee arbitrator, mediator client rels.), Assn. Trial Lawyers Am., Santa Barbara Bar Assn., Inland Empire Bankruptcy Forum, Ventura/Santa Barbara Trial Lawyers Assn., Consumer Attys. Calif., Calif. Trustees Assn. Republican. Mem. L.D.S. Ch. Avocations: golf, tennis, fishing, scuba. Office: 592 Poli St Ventura CA 93001 E-mail: kary@j.farley.com.

KUMP, WARREN LEE, retired diagnostic radiologist; b. Jennings, Kans., June 30, 1926; s. Lee Robert and Hazel Jessie (Bobbitt) K.; m. Patricia Jeanne Burke, Oct. 16, 1950; children: Theresa, Lee, Mary, John. BA, U. Kans., 1947, MD, 1950. Diplomate Am. Bd. Radiology. Intern U. Ill., Chgo., 1950-51; med. officer USN/USMC, 1951-53; resident U. Minn., Mpls., 1953-56; staff radiologist North Meml. Med. Ctr., Mpls., 1957-96. Chief radiology North Meml. Med. Ctr., 1965-91, chief of staff, 1974-75, trustee, 1982-2001, chmn. bd. dirs., 1993-2000; pres. Mpls. Radiology Assocs., 1965-91. Bd. dirs. Newman Found., 1955-60, St. Therese Found., New Hope, Minn., 1962-94; pres. St. Therese Charitable Svcs., New Hope, 1991-94. Fellow Am. Coll. Radiology; mem. AMA, Radiol. Soc. N.Am., Am. Roentgen Ray Soc., Minn. Radiol. Soc. (pres. 1974-75), Minn. Med. Assn. Roman Catholic. Avocations: reading, traveling, historical research. Office: Mpls Rad Assocs 604 Oakdale Med Bldg Minneapolis MN 55422 E-mail: Wlkump@aol.com.

KUMPFER, KAROL LINDA, research psychologist; b. Neptune, N.J., July 30, 1943; d. Beverly Donald and Mary Belle (Campbell) K.; m. Henry Overton Whiteside, Mar. 6, 1978; 1 child, Jane H. BA, Colo. Women's Coll., 1966; MA, U. Utah, 1970, PhD, 1972; postdoctoral, U. Minn., 1975. Lic. psychologist, Utah. Asst. prof. psychology Oberlin (Ohio) Coll., 1971-73; research assoc. Inst. Child Devel. U. Minn., Mpls., 1975-76; asst. prof. Colo. Women's Coll., Denver, 1976-78; psychologist Salt Lake County Mental Health Dept., 1979-80; dep. dir. State Div. Alcoholism and Drugs, Salt Lake City, 1980-84; vis. assoc. prof. Grad. Sch. Social Work U. Utah, Salt Lake City, 1983—88, asst. prof. pyschiatry, 1986—88, assoc. prof. dept. health promotion and edn., 1988—; dir. Ctr. Substance Abuse & Prevention, Wash., DC, 1998—2000, Strengthening Families Program, Salt Lake City, 1982—. Editor/author: Childhood and Chemical Abuse: Prevention and Intervention, 1986, Social Facts: Utah in Perspective, 1986. Bd. dirs. Repetory Dance Theatre, Salt Lake City, 1983—, Western Assn. Concerned Adoptive Parents, Salt Lake City, 1985—, Utah Alliance for Mentally Ill, Salt Lake City, 1979-80, Indian Walk-in Ctr., 2000—; pres. U. Utah. Faculty Women's Club, 1974-75. Grantee Utah Dept. Social Services, Salt Lake City, 1984—; grantee Dept. Justice Office Juvenile Justice and Juvenile Delinquency Prevention, 1987—. Mem.: AAAS, Nat. Inst. Drug Abuse (spl. task force 1985—, grantee 1982—86, 1998—), Utah Mental Health Assn. (bd. dirs.), Evaln. Rsch. Soc., Coun. on Social Work Edn., Nat. Inst. Alcoholism and Alcohol Abuse (spl. task force 1985—, grantee 1980, 2000—), Am. Acad. Child Psychiatry (spl. task force 1986—88), Utah Psychol. Assn. (bd. dirs. 1985—88), Nat. Coun. Social Work Edn., Am. Pub. Health Assn., Am. Psychol. Assn., Utah Psychologists in Pvt. Practice Assn. (pres. 1985—90), Sigma Xi. Democrat. Unitarian Universalist. Avocations: skiing, sailing, travelling. Office: Health Promotion Edn U Utah 250 S 1850 East Salt Lake City UT 84112-0920

KUMRA, SANJIV, psychiatrist; b. Toronto, Ont., Can., Sept. 30, 1967; s. Surender and Asha Kumra; m. Neerja Suri-Kumra, Mar. 18, 1969; children: Amit, Rohit. MD, U. Toronto, 1990. Sr. staff fellow NIH, Bethesda, Md., 1995—98; asst. prof. psychiatry Albert Einstein Coll. Medicine, Bronx, NY, 2000—. Recipient Career Devel. award, NIH, 1990. Fellow: Royal Coll. Physicians and Surgeons. Achievements include research in Childhood-Onset Schizophrenia. Office: North Shore - Long Island Jewish Medical 75-59 263rd St Glen Oaks NY 11021

KUMTA, PRASHANT NAGESH, materials science educator, engineering educator, consultant; b. Madras, India, Aug. 17, 1960; arrived in U.S., 1984; s. Nagesh Shanker and Soomathee Nagesh (Marballi) Kumta; m. Ujwala Prashant Kamath; children: Tanay, Aniket. BTech, Indian Inst. Tech., Bombay, 1984; MS, U. Ariz., 1987, PhD, 1990. Undergrad. rsch. asst. Indian Inst. Tech., Bombay, 1983-84; grad. work asst. Oreg. Grad. Ctr., Beaverton, 1984-85; grad. tchg. asst. U. Ariz., Tucson, 1985-87, grad. rsch. asst., 1987-88, grad. rsch. assoc., 1988-90; asst. prof. Carnegie Mellon U., Pitts., 1990-95, assoc. prof., 1995-99, prof., 1999—; editor Materials Sci. and Engring. B, 2001—. Prin. investigator Eveready Battery Co., Cleve., 1993-2000, Mitsubishi Chem. Co., Japan, 2000—; cons. Changs Ascending, Taiwan, 2000—; prin. investigator Jet Propulsion Lab., Pasadena, Calif., 1997-2000, Pitts. Plate Glass (PPG) Industries, 1998-2000, Mitsubishi Chem. Co., Japan, 2000—; cons. Timo Industry, Pitts., 1992-93, EIC, Mass., 2001-02; mem. summer rsch. faculty Air Force Office, Washington, 1993. Author: Role of Ceramics in Advanced Electrochemical Systems, 1996, Covalent Ceramics: Science and Technology of Non-Oxides, 1996, Chemical Processing Aspects of Electronic Ceramics, 1998, Processing and Characterization of Electrochemical Materials and Devices, 2000, 2001, 2002; contbr. articles; editor: Materials Science of Engineering B, 2001—. Recipient Rsch. initiation award NSF, Washington, 1993; grantee NSF, Air Force Office, Army Rsch. Office Def., Advanced Rsch. Projects Agy., Washington, 1993—, Office of Naval Rsch., Washington, 2000—. Mem. Am. Ceramic Soc., Materials Rsch. Soc., Electrochem. Soc. Achievements include pioneering development of thio-sol-gel and hydrazide sol-gel processes to synthesize transition and rare-earth chalcogenides and nitrides, ceramics, novel complexed precursor approaches to new non-oxide ceramics, mechanochemical synthesis of oxide and non-oxide ceramics and composites, patents awarded related to development of novel cathode materials for primary batteries, novel processes to fabricate lithium-ion electrodes and new biomaterials for bone tissue engineering and gene delivery; patent for new class of polymer-ceramic composites for bone tissue engineering and new class of stable cathodes for lithium-ion batteries. Office: Carnegie Mellon U Dept Science 4309 Wean Hall 5000 Forbes Ave Pittsburgh PA 15213-3890 E-mail: kumta@cmu.edu.

KUN, JOYCE ANNE, secondary education educator, small business owner; b. Salem, Ohio, Oct. 20, 1946; d. Robert Malvern Slutz and Helen Roberta (Williams) Short; m. James Joseph Kun, June 10, 1978; 1 child, Jessica Erin. BS in Edn., Ohio U., 1969; MA in Tech., Kent State U., 1980. Cert. tchr., Ohio. Tchr. Ridgewood Local, West Lafayette, Ohio, 1970-71, Norton (Ohio) High Sch., 1971—; owner The Norton Pub, 1992—. Mem. NEA, Canton chpt. DAR, Ohio Edn. Assn., Ohio Tech. Edn. Assn., N.E. Ohio Tech. Edn. Assn. (officer 1972-78), Norton Classroom Tchrs. Assn. (exec. bd.), Norton Grange, Barberton Moose Lodge, Epsilon Pi Tau. Lutheran. Avocations: bowling, golf, flower gardening. Office: The Norton Pub 4020 Cleve Mass Rd Norton OH 44203-5601 Home: 3500 Greenwich Rd Norton OH 44203-5567 Office: Norton High Sch 4128 Cleve Mass Rd Norton OH 44203-5633 E-mail: joycekun@aol.com.

KUN, KENNETH A. business executive; b. Bklyn., July 14, 1930; s. Elemer and Elizabeth (Strom) K.; m. Carolyn C. Kun, July 3, 1955; children: Michael Eric, Deborah Kun LoBello. BS in Chemistry, Bklyn. Coll., 1952; MS in Chemistry, Bklyn. Poly. Inst., 1955, Yale U., 1959, PhD in Chemistry, 1961. Sr. rsch. chemist Rohm and Haas Co., Phila., 1961-66, from product mgr. to Far East regional indsl. product mgr. Tokyo, 1966-72, regional mgr. sales, mktg., and tech. for Latin Am. Miami, Fla., 1972-76, mgr. environ. and pollution control rsch. Phila., 1972-78; dir. mktg. splty. chems. divsn. Church and Dwight Co., 1978-79; dir. rsch. splty. chems. divsn. Calgon Corp., 1979-81; v.p. rsch., devel. and engring., chief tech. officer Polychrome Corp., 1981-83; pres., CEO, bd. trustees Syracuse (N.Y.) Rsch. Corp., 1983-91; pres. Kun Assocs., Collegeville, Pa., 1991—. Author: Oxidation-Reduction Polymers, 1965, Electron-Transfer Polymers, 1966; contbr. articles to Jour. Am. Chem. Soc., Jour. Organic Chemistry, Jour. Polymer Sci., others; patentee in field. Bd. dirs. Cen. N.Y. Tech. Devel. Orgn.; chmn. Econ. Devel. Commn. Town of Dewitt, N.Y.; active N.Y. Econ. Devel. Commn., United Way Syracuse. Fellow Am. Inst. Chemists; mem. AAAS, ASTM, Am. Assn. Lab. Accreditation (bd. dirs., treas., exec. com.), Am. Chamber Commerce in Japan (chmn. licenses, patent, trademark com.), Am. Chem. Soc. (chmn. Syracuse sect.), Am. Mgmt. Assn., N.Y. Acad. Scis., Bklyn. Coll. Chemist's Assn., Yale Chemists Assn., Yale Sci. & Engring. Assn., Syracuse Chamber Commerce, Assn. Old Crows, Sigma Xi. Home and Office: 1754 Morgan Ln Collegeville PA 19426-2876 E-mail: kenakun@aol.com.

KUNAKEMAKORN, NUMSIRI C, education educator; b. Toledo, Ohio; d. Pravit and Tiplada Kunakemakorn; m. John Goshert. BA in english, U. of Calif. at Santa Barbara, 1988—92; MA in internat. and mulitcultural edn., U. of San Francisco, 1992—93; MA in english, Sonoma State U., 1993—96; PhD in comparative lit., Purdue U., 1996—2003. Educator Purdue U., 1997—2001, Utah Valley State Coll., 2001—. Editor Multiplicities: Mediating Cultural Productions, West Lafayette, Ind., 2000; news anchor Channel 8, Thai Sky News, Bangkok, Thailand, 1996; editor-in-chief Sycamore Rev. 12.1, West Lafayette, Ind., 2000, Sycamore Rev. 12.2, West Lafayette, Ind., 2000,

Sycamore Rev. 13.1, West Lafayette, Ind., 2001, Sycamore Rev. 13.2, West Lafayette, Ind., 2001. Editor: (essay collection) Without Covers: Literary Magazines at the Digital Edge. Vol. Lafayette Crisis Ctr., Ind., 1999—2000; coordinating com. Cmty. Times, West Lafayette, Ind., 1998—99, co-prod. editor, 1998—99. Calif. State U. Pre-Doctoral scholarship, Calif. State U., 1994—95, Calif. State U. Forgivable Loan/Doctoral Incentive Program, 2000—03, Purdue Rsch. grant, Purdue U., 2001—02. Mem.: Am. Comparative Lit. Assn., Latin Am. Studies Assn., Modern Language Assn. (del., gt. lakes region 1999—2001), Multi-Ethnic Literatures of the US, Nat. Women's Studies Assn. (elections chair, women of color caucus 1999—2000). Avocation: public speaking.

KUNCHEVA, LUDMILA ILIEVA, engineering educator; b. Sofia, Bulgaria, Aug. 25, 1959; arrived in Wales, 1997; d. Ilia Ivanov and Svetla Radoslavova Tomov; m. Roumen Koumanov Kountchev, Apr. 11, 1981; children: Diana Kountchev, Kamelia Kountchev. MSc, Tech. U., Sofia, 1982, degree in engring. and math., 1983; PhD, Bulgarian Acad. Scis., 1987. Rsch. assoc. Bulgarian Acad. Scis., Sofia, 1987-96, sr. rsch. assoc., 1996-97; lectr. U. Wales, Bangor, 1997-2001, sr. lectr., 2001—. Author: (book) Fuzzy Classifier Design, 2000; contbr. articles to profl. jours. Fellow, European Cmtys. Commn., 1993, Royal Soc., 1995—96, U. West Fla., 1996—97; grantee, EUFIT '96, 1996. Home: Minafon Tyn Lon Treborth Bangor Gwynedd LL57 2NJ Wales Office: U Wales Sch Informatics Bangor Gwynedd LL57 1UT Wales E-mail: l.i.kuncheva@bangor.ac.uk.

KUNDEL, HAROLD LOUIS, radiologist, educator; b. N.Y.C., Aug. 15, 1933; s. John A. and Emma E. (Tolle) K.; m. Alice Marie Pape, Mar. 28, 1958; children: Jean, Catherine, Peter AB, Columbia U., 1955, MD, 1959; MS, Temple U., 1963; MA (hon.), U. Pa., 1980. Diplomate Am. Bd. Radiology. Asst. to assoc. prof. Temple U., Phila., 1967-73, prof. radiology, 1973-80; Matthew J. Wilson prof. research radiology U. Pa., Phila., 1980—2001, Matthew J. Wilson prof. emeritus radiology, 2001—. Dir. Pendergrass Diagnostic Imaging Labs. U. Pa., Phila., 1980—2001. Contbr. articles to profl. jours. Capt. USAF, 1963—65. Fellow: Am. Coll. Radiology; mem.: Soc. Thoracic Radiology, Am. Roentgen Ray Soc., Radiol. Soc. N.Am. (Honor award 1978), Assn. Univ. Radiologists (Meml. award 1963, Stauffer award 1982), Alpha Omega Alpha. Lutheran.

KUNDLA, JOHN ALBERT, retired coach; b. Star Junction, Pa., July 3, 1916; Student, U. Minn., 1939, ME, 1942. Head coach De La Salle (Minn.) H.S., 1946-68, Mpls. Lakers, 1947-59, U. Minn., 1960-69. Named to Basketball Hall of Fame, 1995. Achievements include coach of Championship Team, 1948, 50, 52-54, NBA, 1949, BBA.

KUNDTZ, JOHN ANDREW, lawyer; b. Cleve., June 23, 1933; s. Ewald E. and Elizabeth (O'Neill) K.; m. Helen Margaret Luckiesh, Aug. 31, 1957; children— John M., Helen E., Margaret L. BS in Social Studies, Georgetown U., 1955; JD, Case Western Reserve U., 1958. Bar: Ohio 1958, U.S. Dist. Ct. (no. dist.) Ohio 1961. Ptnr. Falsgraf, Kundtz, Reidy & Shoup, Cleve., 1961-69; ptnr. Thompson Hine and Flory, Cleve., 1970-90; pvt. practice Cleve., 1990—. Dir. Investment Advisors Internat., Inc., Cleve. Trustee Hathaway Brown Sch., Shaker Heights, Ohio, Chagrin River Land Conservancy, Chagrin Falls, Ohio, Cleve. Soc. for the Blind. 1st lt. USAF, 1958-60. Mem. Ohio State Bar Assn., Assn. Transp. Practitioners. Republican. Roman Catholic. Home: 32540 Creekside Dr Pepper Pike OH 44124-5224 Office: 3000 Aurura Rd Ste 250 Cleveland OH 44139

KUNDU, MUKUL RANJAN, physics and astronomy educator; b. Calcutta, India, Feb. 10, 1930; came to U.S., 1959; s. Makhan Lal and Monoroma K.; m. Sept. 9, 1958; children: Krishna, Rina, Sanjit. BS (with first class honors), U. Calcutta, India, 1949, MS, 1951; DSc, U. Paris, 1957. Assoc. prof. Cornell U., Ithaca, N.Y., 1962-65, Tata Inst. Fund Rsch., Bombay, India, 1965-68; prof. U. Md., College Park, 1968—, dir. astronomy, 1978-85. Editor: Radio Physics of the Sun, 1980, Unstable Current Systems and Plasma Instabilities in Astrophysics, 1984, Energetic Phenomena on the Sun, 1989; author: Solar Radio Astronomy, 1965; mem. editorial bd. Solar Physics, 1967—. Named Nat. Acad. Sci. fellow, 1967, 74-75, 86, U.S. Sr. Scientist awardee Humbolt Found., 1978, Am. Phys. Soc. fellow, 1989. Fellow Am. Phys. Soc.; mem. Am. Astron. Soc., Am. Geophys. Union, Internat. Astron. Union, Internat. Union Radio Sci. Office: U Md Dept Astronomy College Park MD 20742-0001 E-mail: kundu@astro.umd.edu.

KUNDU-RAYCHAUDHURI, SMRITI KANA, biomedical scientist; b. India, 1959; came to U.S., 1989; d. Mrityunjoy and Uma K.; m. Siba P. Raychaudhuri; 3 children. MD, All India Inst. Med. Scis., New Delhi, 1987. Postdoctoral fellow Stanford (Calif.) U. Med. Ctr., 1989—92, rsch. assoc., 1992—94, sr. rsch. scientist, 1994—. Mem. AIDS clin. trials unit NIH, Bethesda, Md., 1989—; mem. sci. rev. bd. FDA, 1995. Contbr. articles to profl. jours. Mem. Am. Assn. Immunologists, N.Y. Acad. Scis., Am. Soc. for Microbiologists. Avocations: reading, music.

KUNERT, PAUL CHARLES, lawyer; b. Hankinson, N.D., Jan. 14, 1935; s. Harry Firdinand Kunert and Mary Bernice Sisson; m. Sandra Kathryn Rood, Nov, 19, 1962 (dec. June 1994); children: Melissa, Kathryn, Miles Joseph; m. Paricia Joan McGraw, Oct. 11, 1997. Student, St. John's U., 1954-55; BA, U. Minn., 1957, JD cum laude, 1960. Bar: Minn. 1961, U.S. Dist. Ct. Minn. 1972. Assoc. Robins, Davis & Lyons, St. Paul, 1961-66; ptnr. Sahr, Kunert & Tambornino, Mpls., 1967-96, Kunert, Tambornino & Kuhar, Mpls., 1996-2000; sole practice Minnetonka, Minn., 2000—. Mem. Minn. Def. Lawyers Assn., Hennepin County Bar Assn. Office: 10285 Yellow Circle Dr Minnetonka MN 55343 Fax: (952) 933-8298.

KUNES, ELLEN, editor-in-chief; Cons. editor Mademoiselle Mag.; contbg. editor Omni Mag.; sr. editor Self Mag.; lifestyle dir. McCalls, 1991—94; exec. editor Redbook Mag., 1994—98; editor O Mag., 1999; editor-in-chief Redbook Mag., 2001—. Author: Living Well - Or Even Better, 1991. Office: Redbook 224 W 57th St New York NY 10019

KUNES, RICHARD W. cosmetics executive; MBA, Pace U. With Colgate-Palmolive Co.; internat. mfg. contr. internat. ops. group Estée Lauder Cos. Inc., N.Y.C., 1986, regional fin. officer Asia/Pacific markets, v.p., contr. global ops., v.p. ops. fin. worldwide, v.p. fin. adminstrn., corp. contr., 1998—2000, sr. v.p., CFO, 2001—. Office: Estée Lauder Co Inc 767 5th Ave New York NY 10153*

KUNG, DAVID, plastic surgeon; married; 2 children. BA with honors, Columbia Coll., 1984, DDS with distinction, 1989; MD, Harvard Med. Sch., 1992. Diplomate Am. Bd. Oral and Maxillofacial Surgery, Am. Bd. Plastic Surgery. Intern in surgery Mass. Gen. Hosp., Boston, 1989, resident in surgery, 1992-95; resident in plastic surgery U. N.C., 1996-98, fellow in craniofacial surgery, 1998; clin. instr. divsn. plastic surgery Georgetown U. Med. Ctr., Washington, 1998—. Clin. preceptor Harvard Med. Sch., 1995; reviewer, publ. rev. com. Harvard Med. Sch. Office of Med. Edn., 1990—92. Editor-in-chief: Columbia U. Office Profl. Edn., 1985—86. Pres. Honor and Rsch. Soc., Columbia U., 1985—88. Recipient Nat. Rsch. Svc. award NIH, 1986, award of achievement Am. Assn. Oral and Maxillofacial Surgery, 1989. Fellow: ACS (assoc.); mem.: Am. Soc. Plastic Surgeons, Chinese Am. Med. Soc. (bd. dirs. 2000—), Am. Soc. Maxillofacial Surgeons, Chinese Med. and Health Assn. (bd. dirs. 1998—), Nat. Capital Soc. Plastic Surgeons (mem. exec. bd. 1999—2000), Omicron Kappa Upsilon. Office: Ste 309 5100 Wisconsin Ave NW Washington DC 20016-4119 Fax: 202-966-4639. E-mail: dk@kungmd.com.

KUNG, FRANK F. biotechnology and life sciences investor, venture capitalist; b. 1948; BS, Nat. Tsing Hwa U., Taiwan, 1970; MBA, U. Calif., Berkeley, 1983, PhD in Molecular Biology, 1976. Post doctoral rsch. scientist Univ. Calif., Berkeley, 1976-77; rsch. dir. Clin. Bio-Rsch., Emeryville, Calif., 1977-79; scientist, asst. to pres. Cetus Corp., Berkeley, Calif., 1979-81; dir. Cetus Immune Corp. (subs. of Cetus Corp.), Palo Alto, Calif., 1980-84; pres., CEO Genelabs Techs., Inc., Redwood City, Calif., 1984-95, chmn., 1984-96, BioAsia Investments, Palo Alto, Calif., 1996—. Office: BioAsia Investments 575 High St Ste 201 Palo Alto CA 94301-1648 E-mail: fkung@bioasia.wm.

KUNG, PANG-JEN, materials scientist, electrical engineer; b. I-Lan, Taiwan, May 13, 1959; s. Ching-Yu and A-Se (Yu) K.; m. Tzyy-Yun Tzeng, May 18, 1986; children: Naihau, Naiwei. MSChemE, Nat. Tsing Hua U., 1983; MSEE, Auburn U., 1988; MMetE, Carnegie Mellon U., 1991, PhD in Materials Sci., 1993; MBA, U. Conn., 1998. Jr. engr. Tatung Co., Taipei, Taiwan, 1979—80; tchg. asst. Nat. Tsing Hua U., Hsin-Chu, Taiwan, 1981—82, rsch. asst., 1982—83; assoc. scientist Indsl. Tech. Res. Inst., Hsin-Chu, 1985—86; tchg. and rsch. asst. Auburn (Ala.) U., 1986—89; rsch. asst. Carnegie Mellon U., Pitts., 1989—91; staff rsch. asst. Los Alamos (N.Mex.) Nat. Lab., 1991—92, rsch. fellow, 1993—94; sr. scientist Advanced Fuel Rsch., Inc., East Hartford, Conn., 1995—98; chmn. Pioneer Techs., Inc., West Hartford, Conn., 1996—99; cons. InfiMed, Inc., Liverpool, NY, 1998—2000; product devel. engr. JDS Uniphase, Rsch. Triangle Park, NC, 2001—02; pres. Optotrack, Inc., Cary, NC, 2002—. Chmn. acad. affairs Tatung Inst. Tech., Taipei, 1979-80; tech. info. editor Indsl. Tech. Rsch. Inst., Hsin-Chu, 1985-86; translator tech. articles Super Tech. Books Co., Taipei, 1986. Author, editor: Unit Operations in Chemical Engineering, 1986; contbr. articles to profl. jours. 2nd lt. Chinese Air Force, 1983-85. Recipient Editor's Choice award Nat. Poetry Assn., 1989, 90; Am.-Chinese Engr. scholar Am.-Chinese Assn. Engrs., 1980; Liang Ji-Duan fellow Carnegie Mellon U., 1991. Mem. AAAS, IEEE, SPIE, Materials Rsch. Soc., Am. Vacuum Soc. (Tech. Paper award 1992), Acad. Am. Poets, Beta Gamma Sigma. Achievements include research in diamond thin films and high Tc superconductors; superconducting quantum interference devices and biomagnetic systems; surface characterization and microstructural analysis; ferroelectric devices, giant magnetoresistive sensors, high-speed microelectronics, epitaxial heterostructures, in-process monitors, pulsed laser deposition, thermal evaporation, sputtering; pyroelectric sensor arrays, gas sensors, plasma-enhanced chemical vapor deposition, x-ray imaging materials, digital radiography and fluoroscopy, microelectromechanical systems (MEMS); optical switches and waveguides; optical communication systems; nanotechnology, microfluidics, biol. and chem. assays. Office: Optotrack Inc PO Box 1242 Cary NC 27512 E-mail: ckung@optotrack.com.

KUNG, PATRICK CHUNG-SHU, biotechnology executive; b. Nanjing, China, July 10, 1947; came to U.S., 1969; s. Tao and Yuing (Li) K.; m. Yie Lu; children: Julia, Calvin, Charles Shen. BS, Fu Jen U., Taiwan, 1968; PhD, U. Calif., Berkeley, 1974. Rsch. fellow MIT, Cambridge, 1974-77; sr. rsch. fellow Ortho Pharm. Co., J & J, Raritan, NJ, 1978—81; v.p. rsch. Centocor Inc., Malvern, Pa., 1982-83; co-founder, exec. v.p. T Cell Scis., Inc./Avant Immunotherapies, Inc., Cambridge, 1984—98; bd. dirs. PhytoCeutica, Inc., New Haven, Ontogen Corp. Exec. bd. Coll. Letters and Scis. U. Calif., Berkeley, 1989-91; bd. dirs. Ontogen Corp.; bd. dirs. PhytoCeutica, Inc., pres., CEO, 1999-2003. Contbr. articles to profl. jours. Trustee Park Sch., Brookline, Mass., 1992-95. Recipient Philip Hoffman award Johnson & Johnson Co., 1979, Achievement award Chinese Inst. Engrs., 1988, Discoverers award U.S. Pharm. Mfrs. Assn., 1991, Thomas Alva Edison award N.J. Rsch. Coun., 1991. Mem. Soc. Chinese Bioscientists in Am. (pres. bio/pharm. scis. divsn. 1994, 95).

KUNG, SHAIN-DOW, molecular biologist, academic administrator; b. China, Mar. 14, 1935; came to U.S., 1971, naturalized, 1977; s. Chao-tzen and Chih (Zhu) K. Grad., Chung-Hsing U., Taiwan, China, 1958; PhD, U. Toronto, Can., 1968. m. Helen C.C. Kung, Sept. 5, 1964; children: Grace, David, Andrew. Rsch. fellow Hosp. for Sick Children, Toronto, 1968-70; biologist UCLA, 1971-74; asst. prof. biology U. Md., Baltimore County, 1974-77, assoc. prof., 1977-82, prof., 1982-86, acting chmn. dept., 1982-84, assoc. dean arts and sci., 1985-86, prof. botany College Park, 1986-93; acting dir. U. Md. Ctr. for Agrl. Biotech., 1986-88, dir., 1988-93; acting provost Md. Biotech. Inst., 1989-91; dean sch. sci. Hong Kong U. Sci. and Tech., 1991-92, v.p. for acad. affairs, 1992-98, acting v.p. for acad. affairs, 2000. Hon. prof. Fudan U., 1986, Beijing Agrl. U., 1987. Author 6 books; editor 14 books; contbr. chpts. to books, articles to profl. jours. Recipient PHilip Morris award for disting. achievement in tobacco sci., 1979, Outstanding Alumni award, 1990, Outstanding Svc. award, 1990; named Disting. Scholar, Nat. Acad. Sci., 1981; Fulbright grantee, 1982-83, grantee NSF, NIH. Mem. AAAS, Am. Soc. Plant Physiologists. Office: Hong Kong U Sci and Tech Clear Water Bay Kowloon Hong Kong

KUNIHOLM, BRUCE ROBELLET, university administrator; b. Washington, Oct. 4, 1942; s. Bertel Eric and Berthe Eugenie (Robellet) K.; m. Elizabeth Fairbank, June 29, 1968 (div. July 1987); children: Jonathan, Erin; m. Donna Slawson, Jan. 19, 2001. AB in English, Dartmouth Coll., 1964; MA in History, Duke U., 1972, MA in Pub. Policy Sci., PhD in History, Duke U., 1976. Instr. English Robert Acad./Robert Coll., Istanbul, Turkey, 1964-67; Coun. Fgn. Rels./NEH fellow Dept. State, Washington, 1979, internat. rels. officer policy planning staff, 1979-80; from instr. to lectr. policy studies and history Duke U., Durham, N.C., 1975-77, asst. prof. pub. policy studies and history, 1977-78, 80-84, assoc. prof. pub. policy studies and history, 1984-87, prof. pub. policy studies and history, 1987—, chmn. dept. public policy studies, 1989-94, dir. Terry Sanford Inst. Pub. Policy, 1989-94. Vis. prof. Internat. Rels. Koc U., Istanbul, Turkey, 1995-96, 2002; prof. pub. policy studies and history, 1996—; vice-provost for acad. and internat. affairs, Duke U., Durham, N.C., 1996—2001; chmn. acad. com.Can.-U.S. Fulbright Program, 2000—; dir. Ctr. for Internat. Studies, 1999—2001; guest scholar Woodrow Wilson Internat. Ctr. Scholars, 1982; cons. NEH, USMC, Dept. State, U.S. Army, United Tech. Corp.; invited lectr. numerous orgns., colls., univs., fgn. countries including U.S. Senate Fgn. Rels.Com., CIA, State Dept., Chase Manhattan Bank, Harvard U., Brown U., Dartmouth Coll., Yale U., Princeton U., France, Eng., Germany, Italy, Kuwait, Saudi Arabia, Sudan, Can., Turkey, also others. Author: Origins of the Cold War in the Near East, 1980 (Stuart L. Bernath prize 1981), The Persian Gulf and United States Policy, 1984, The Palestine Problem and United States Policy, 1986; contbr. articles to profl. jours.; contbr. chpts. books. Bd. dirs., chmn. acad. com. Found. for Ednl. Exch. between Can. and U.S., 2000—. Capt. USMC, 1967-71, Vietnam. Decorated Bronze Star with V device; recipient Disting. Teaching award Trinity Coll., Duke U., 1989; rsch. grantee Harry S. Truman Libr., 1984, Duke U. Rsch. Coun., 1985-86, Inst. Turkish Studies, 1986-87, travel grantee Ctr. Soviet and East European Studies, 1991; Fulbright sr. rsch. fellow, Turkey, 1986-87, Woodrow Wilson Internat. Ctr. Scholars fellow Smithsonian Instn., 1986-87, sr. fellow Nobel Inst., Oslo, 1994. Mem. Am. Hist. Assn., Fulbright Fellows, Coun. Fgn. Rels., Orgn. Am. Historians, Soc. Historians Am. Fgn. Rels., Middle East Inst., Middle East Studies Assn., Internat. Inst. Strategic Studies, Phi Beta Kappa. Democrat. Avocations: triathlons, bluegrass banjo, wine. Home: 613 Swift Ave Durham NC 27701 Office: Duke U Sanford Inst Public Policy Durham NC 27708

KUNIN, MADELEINE MAY, former ambassador to Switzerland, former governor; b. Zurich, Switzerland, Sept. 28, 1933; came to U.S., 1940, naturalized, 1947; d. Ferdinand and Renee (Bloch) May; children: Julia, Peter, Adam, Daniel BA, U. Mass., 1956; MS, Columbia U., 1957; MA, U. Vt., 1967; numerous hon. degrees. Newspaper reporter Burlington Free Press, Vt., 1957-58; guide Brussels World's Fair, Belgium, 1958; TV asst. producer Sta. WCAX-TV, Burlington, 1960-61; freelance writer, instr. English Trinity Coll., Burlington, 1969-70; mem. Vt. Ho. of Reps., 1973-78; lt. gov. State of Vt., Montpelier, 1979-82, gov., 1985-91; disting. vis. in Pub. Policy Bunting Inst., Cambridge, Mass., 1991-92, Dartmouth Coll., Hanover, N.H., 1992; dep. sec. edn. Dept. Education, Washington, D.C., 1993-96; U.S. amb. to Switzerland, 1996-99; scholar in residence Middlebury Coll., 1999; disting. vis. prof. St.Michael's Coll. and U. Vt., 2003—. Fellow Inst. Politics, Kennedy Sch. Govt., Harvard U., 1983; lectr. Middlebury Coll., St. Michael's Coll., 1984; disting. pub. policy visitor Rockefeller Ctr., Dartmouth Coll., 1992; pub. policy fellow Bunting Inst., Radcliffe Coll., Harvard U., 1991-92; Vt. Joint Fiscal Com., 1977-78; mem. exec. com. Nat. Conf. Lt. Govs., 1979-80; founder, pres. Inst. Sustainable Cmtys., Montpelier, Vt., 1991—; mem. 3 person com. to recommend v.p. to Bill Clinton; mem. transition team, co-chair nat. com. Women for Clinton, 1992; scholar-in-residence Middlebury (Vt.) Coll., 1999-2003; disting visitor U. of Vt. and St. Michael's Coll., 2003—; commentator Vt. Pub. Radio, 2001—. Author: Living a Political Life: A Memoir, 1994, The Big Green Book, 1976; contbr. articles to profl. jours., mags. and newspapers. Commentator Vt. Pub. Radio. Scholar in residence Middleburg Coll., 1999—; Named Outstanding State Legislator, Eagleton Inst. Politics, Rutgers U., 1975; Montgomery fellow Dartmouth Coll., 1991. Fellow Am. Acad. Arts & Scis.; mem. Nat. Gov.'s Assn. (mem. exec. com.), Nat. Govs.' Conf. (chair com. on energy and the environ.), New Eng. Gov.'s Conf. (chairperson). Democrat. Office: Middlebury College Robert A Jones House Middlebury VT 05753 E-mail: mkunin@middlebury.edu.

KUNIYASU, KEITH KAZUMI, secondary education educator; b. Honolulu, Apr. 16, 1955; s. Hajime and Betty Mieko (Yamamoto) K. AA in Liberal Arts, AS in Graphic Arts, U. Hawaii, Pearl City, 1978; BS in Tech. Edn., Western Wash. U., 1982; MEd in Tech. Edn., Oreg. State U., 1987. Cert. vocat. adminstr. Instrumental music instr. Aiea (Hawaii) Intermediate Sch., 1978-88; spl. edn. instr. Highlands Intermediate Sch., Pearl City, 1983-84; visual comm. instr. Oak Harbor (Wash.) High Sch., 1982-83; photography instr. Olympic Coll., Bremerton, Wash., 1984-85; comm. techs. instr. North Kitsap High Sch., Poulsbo, Wash., 1984-93; instr. comm. techs. River Ridge High Sch., Lacey, Wash., 1993—. Edn. rep. curriculum/competency validation com. Wash. State Supt. Pub. Instrn., Olympia, 1988-93; cons. Wash. SkillsUSA- Vocat. Indsl. Clubs Am., 1990—; mem. Nat. SkillsUSA- Vocat. Indsl. Clubs of Am. Leadership Handbook Revision Team, 1995; pvt. woodwind instr., 1974-94; counselor, woodwind specialist Maui (Hawaii) Intermediate Select Band Camps, 1975-80; advisor Leeward C.C. Graphic Arts Club, Pearl City, 1978-80; sch. accreditation teams for various high schs. throughout Wash., 1988—; writing com. leadership curriculum Wash. State Supt. Instrn. Edn., Olympia, 1993—. Author: (pamphlet series) Care of Single Reeds, 1983, (brochures) Addressing Technology Education, 1988-92, Communication Technologies, 1995, What Is Hawk Communications?, 1995, VisCom Student Study Guide, 1987, 2nd edit., 1990, 3rd edit., 1993, 4th edit., 1996, From Goods to Services, 1988, Technology Education Facility, 1988, Communication Technologies at North Kitsap High School, 1989, Visual Communications, 1990, Bob's Law's (Robert's Rules of Order), 1995, 2nd edit., 1997. Organizer, pres. Pacific Islanders Club at Western Wash. U., Bellingham, 1981-82; organizer, bd. dirs. Leeward Fine Arts Coun., Pearl City, 1981-94. Named Olympic Region Advisor of Yr., Wash. Skills USA-Vocat. Indsl. Clubs Am., 2003, Wash. State Advisor of Yr., 2003. Mem. NEA, Internat. Tech. Edn. Assn. (affiliate rep. 1990-94), Internat. Graphic Arts Educators Assn., Graphic Arts Tech. Found., Am. Vocat. Assn., Wash. Vocat. Assn., Wash. Tech. Edn. Assn., SkillsUSA-Vocat. Indsl. Clubs Am. (advisor, regional coord. 1990-96, 99-2000, 2002—). Avocations: travel, cooking, music, reading, working with young adults. Office: River Ridge H S 8929 Martin Way E Lacey WA 98516-5932 E-mail: kkuniyasu@nthurston.k12.wa.us.

KUNIYUKI, KEN TAKAHARU, lawyer; b. Honolulu, Nov. 30, 1947; s. Henry Seiya and Emi (Takami) K.; m. Noreen Kanai, Aug. 20, 1971; children: Patricia Satchie, Karen Cheimi. BA, U. Hawaii, 1969, MA, 1970; JD, U. Calif., Berkeley, 1973. Bar: Hawaii 1973, U.S. Dist. Ct. Hawaii 1973, U.S. Ct. Appeals (9th cir.) 1976. Assoc. David Schutter, Honolulu, 1973-74; ptnr. Turk & Kuniyuki, Honolulu, 1974-77, Kuniyuki & Pang, Honolulu, 1978-80; pvt. practice, Honolulu, 1980-81; ptnr. Kuniyuki & Chang, Honolulu, 1981—; arbitrator Hawaii Med. Claims Panel, Honolulu, 1979—, Ct. Annexed Arbitration, Circut Ct. 1st Cir., 1986—. Bd. dirs. ACLU, Hawaii, 1978-80, chmn. litigation com., 1978-81. Mem. Am. Arbitration Assn., Hawaii Chess Fedn. (pres. 1982-83). Office: Kuniyuki & Chang Pauahi Tower 1001 Bishop St #2660 Honolulu HI 96813

KUNKA, ROBERT L. pharmacist, researcher; s. Irvin L. and Mary M. Kunka; m. Alice K. Kirkman, July 21, 1952; children: Benjamin A., Emily Caroline. BS in Pharmacy, U. Ill., 1970; PhD, U. N.C., 1977. Asst. prof. U. Pitts., 1977—84; assoc. dir. drug devel. G.D. Searle, Rosemont, Ill., 1984—89; dir. clin. trials mgmt. Chugai-Upjohn, Rosemont, 1989—91; dir. full devel., clin. pharmacology and discovery medicine GlaxoSmithKline, Research Triangle Park, NC, 1991—. Contbr. articles. Men's ministry coord., bd. trustees Sunrise United Meth. Ch., Holly Springs, NC, 1997—2002; bd. dirs. Heart of Carolina Emmaus, Raleigh, NC, 1995—96. Syndor Barksdale Pennick and Charles J. Lynn Meml. fellow, Am. Found. Pharm. Edn., 1975—76. Mem.: Am. Soc. Clin. Pharmacology, Am. Assn. Pharm. Scientists. Avocations: kayaking, hiking. Home: 204 Birkhaven Dr Cary NC 27511 Office: GlaxoSmithKline Five Moore Dr 172241 Research Triangle Park NC 27709 Personal E-mail: bobkunka@aol.com. E-mail: robert.l.kunka@gsk.com.

KUNKEL, DAVID NELSON, lawyer; b. Rochester, N.Y., Apr. 5, 1943; s. Frederick W. and Dorothy Jean (Smith) K.; m. Gayle Kellogg Van Dussen, Aug. 21, 1965; children: Jennifer Dawn, Nelson Charles. BA with high honors, U. Va., 1965; LLB, U. Pa., 1968. Bar: Pa. 1969, N.Y. 1972. Assoc. Montgomery, McCracken, Walker & Rhoads, Phila., 1968, Nixon, Hargrave, Devans & Doyle, Rochester, N.Y., 1971-78, ptnr., 1978-95, sr. counsel, 1995; vice chair, exec. v.p. PSINet, Inc., Ashburn, Va., 1995—2000; cons. internat. and tech. cos., 2000—02; pres., CEO Hopeman Bros. Marine Interiors LLC; pres., COO AWH Corp., 2002—03; exec. v.p., gen. counsel Next Century Techs., Inc., 2003—. Mem. Bd. Edn. Bloomfield Ctrl. Sch., East Bloomfield, N.Y., 1982-85. Lt. USNR, 1969-71. Mem. ABA, Internat. Bar Assn. E-mail: davidkunkel@nxtcent.com.

KUNKEL, DOROTHY ANN, music educator; b. Weeping Water, Nebr., Nov. 24, 1934; d. Lloyd Nelson and Dorothy Grace (Holman) K. Student, Nebr. Wesleyan U., 1952-54; MusB, Am. Conservatory of Music, Chgo., 1958, B of Music Edn., 1960, M of Music Edn. cum laude, 1970. Cert. music instr. K-12, Mich. Music supr., orch. dir. Sch. Dist. 48, Villa Park, Ill., 1960-80; orch. condr. Nat. Music Camp, Interlochen, Mich., 1970-84; dir. of orchs. Traverse City (Mich.) Area Pub. Schs., 1983-96; pvt. violin studio, 1995—. Dir., founder Galena (Ill.) Music Acad., 1961-69; v.p. bd. dirs. Concord Acad., Petoskey, Mich., 1996-97; string methods instr. Sherwood Sch. of Music, Chgo., 1969-73, Am. Conservatory of Music, Chgo., 1978-79; guest condr. Ga. All-State Orch., 1976, 81, 93, Fla. All-State Orch., 1977, 82, Ill. All-State Orch., 1982, Mich. Youth Arts Honors Orch., 1995, Marquette Symphony Orch., 1998, Great Lakes Chamber Orch., 2002, 03; condr. Petito Promonades concerts Chgo. Symphony Orch., 1981, Old Town Playhouse, Traverse City, Mich., 1997—. Choir dir. Oakbrook (Ill.) Christian Ctr., 1977-80, Lake Ann (Mich.) Meth. Ch., 1981-90; condr. Benzie Area Symphony Orch., 1999—, Great Lakes Chamber Orch., 2002—; mem. chancel choir Ctrl. United Meth. Ch., Traverse City. Recipient They Are Making Am. Mus. award Sch. Musician, 1981, Best in Class award Adjudicators Nat. Invitational, Kennedy Ctr., Washington, 1992, 95. Mem. Am. String Tchrs. Assn. (pres. Ill. chpt. 1979-80), Nat. Sch. Orch. Assn., Mid-West Internat. Band and Orch. Clinic (bd. dirs. 1980—, Medal of Honor 1966, 70, 74, 2000), Mich. Sch. Band and Orch. Assn. (adjudicator 1990—, Orch. Tchr. of Yr. 1995), Music Educators Nat. Conf., Sigma Alpha Iota, Willard Sorority. Avocations: camping, cats, cross-country skiing, feeding birds and small animals. Home: 2426 E Kasson Rd Cedar MI 49621-8673 E-mail: dkmusic934@aol.com.

KUNKEL, GEORGE A., JR., civil engineer; b. Pitts., Oct. 25, 1958; s. George A. and Mary Ellen Kunkel; m. Elisabeth J. Shakin; children: George, Emily. BS in Civil Engring., Pa, State U., 1980; MS in Water Resources Engring., Drexel U., 1987. Registered profl. engr..; cert. water treatment plant operator Pa. Ops. engr. Phila. Water Dept., 1980—92, chief load control ctr., 1992—. Contbr. chapters to books, articles. Mem.: Am. Water Works Assn. (water loss control com. 1998—2002). Office: Phila Water Dept 2901 N 29th St Philadelphia PA 19132 Business E-Mail: george.kunkel@phila.gov.

KUNKEL, RICHARD LESTER, public radio executive; b. Syracuse, N.Y., Nov. 12, 1944; s. Lester DeLong Kunkel and Margaret Fanny Ralph; m. Mary Joan Goldsworthy, Aug. 10, 1968; children: Richard J., Charles J., Joseph B. BS, Syracuse U., 1967, MS, 1969. Lic. real estate broker, N.C. Program dir. Sta. WNBI, Northland Broadcasting, Park Falls, Wis., 1969-72; instr., prodn. dir. Sta. WMKY, Morehead (Ky.) State U., 1972-77; radio mgr. Maine Pub. Broadcasting Network, Orono, 1977-78; instr., sta. mgr. Sta. KNTU, U. North Tex., Denton, 1978-84; v.p., dean Southeastern Ctr. for Arts, Atlanta, 1985-88; pres., gen. mgr. Spokane (Wash.) Pub. Radio Inc., 1988—. Cons., 1978—. With Army N.g., 1968-74. Recipient Addy award 1975. Avocations: photography, computers. Home: 18212 N Atlantic Rd Colbert WA 99005-9608 Office: KPBX/KIBX and KSFC Spokane Pub Radio 2319 N Monroe St Spokane WA 99205-4586 E-mail: rkunkel@kpbx.org.

KUNKEL, SCOTT WILLIAM, strategic management and entrepreneurship educator; b. St. Louis, May 26, 1945; s. Robert Scott and Mary (Muldowney) K.; m. Cindy Jones; children: Mary C. Cronan, Deborah A. Hicks. BBA in Accountancy, Memphis State U., 1974, MS in Finance, 1979; PhD in Bus. Adminstrn., U. Ga., 1991. Asst. v.p., controller First Fed. Savs. & Loan, Memphis, 1976-79; v.p. Maury County Fed. Savs. & Loan, Columbia, Tenn., 1979-81, Great Southern Fed. Savs. & Loan, Gainesville, Ga., 1981-82; pres.

Career Apparel, Gainesville, 1981-85; assoc. prof. Brenau U., Gainesville, 1982-88; asst. prof. U. Nev., Reno, 1988-92; assoc. prof. U. San Diego, 1992—. Mem.: Internat. Coun. Small Bus., Acad. Entrepreneurship, Family Firm Inst., Acad. Mgmt., U.S. Assn. Small Bus. and Entrepreneurship. Republican. Avocations: sailing, singing, song writing, guitar, acting. Office: U San Diego Sch Bus San Diego CA 92110-2492

KUNKEN, KENNETH JAMES, lawyer; b. Mineola, N.Y., July 15, 1950; s. Leonard Yale and Judith Mae Kunken. BS, Cornell U., 1973, MA, 1977; MEd, Columbia U., 1976; JD, Hofstra U., 1982. Bar: U.S. Dist. Ct. (ea. and so. dist.) N.Y. 1983, U.S. Supreme Ct. 1997, U.S. Ct. Appeals (fed. cir.) 1997. Vocat. rehab. counselor Human Resources Ctr., Albertson, N.Y., 1977-79; asst. dist. atty. Nassau County Dist. Attys. Office, Mineola, N.Y., 1982—, dep. bur. chief, 1997—. Instr. Nat. Inst. Trial Advocacy, Hempstead, N.Y., 1993—. Recipient Judge Thomas E. Ryan award Nassau County Ct. Officers Benevolent Assn., 1996, George M. Estabrook Disting. Svc. award Hofstra Alumni Assn., Inc., 1999. Mem. N.C. Bar Assn., Hofstra U. Sch. of Law Alumni (adv. com. 1993-96). Office: Nassau County Dist Attys Office 262 Old Country Rd Mineola NY 11501-4251

KUNKLE, WILLIAM JOSEPH, lawyer; b. Lakewood, Ohio, Sept. 3, 1941; s. William Joseph and Georgia (Howe) K.; m. Sarah Florence Nesti, July 11, 1964; children: Kathleen Margaret, Susan Mary. BA, Northwestern U., Evanston, Ill., 1963; Jd, Northwestern U., 1969. Bar: Ohio 1969, U.S. Dist. Ct. (no. dist.) Ill. 1969, Ill. 1969, U.S. Ct. Appeals (7th cir.) 1991, U.S. Supreme Ct. 1991. Process control engr. Union Carbide Corp., Cleve., 1964-65, prodn. supr. Greenville, S.C., 1965-66; assoc. Hauxhurst, Sharp, Mollison & Gallagher, Cleve., 1969-70; asst. pub. defender Cook County Pub. Defender, Chgo., 1970-73; asst. states atty. Cook County States Atty., Chgo., 1973-85; ptnr. Phelan, Cahill & Quinlan, Ltd., Chgo., 1985-96, Cahill, Christian & Kunkle, Ltd., Chgo., 1996—2002, Wildman, Harrold, Allen & Dixon, Chgo., 2002—. Chmn. The Ill. Gaming Bd., 1990—93; dep. spl. outside counsel U.S. Ho. Reps., Washington, 1988—89; adj. prof. I.I.T. Chgo. Kent Sch. Law, 1980—84; instr. Nat. Inst. Trial Advocacy, 1978—82, 1986; lectr. Nat. Coll. Dist. Attys., 1979—85, Nat. Law Enforcement Inst., 1980—86; 1st asst. states atty. of Cook County, 1983—85; spl. state's atty. 18th Jud. Cir., DuPage County, 1995—99. Contbg. author: Punishment Prosecutor's Viewpoint, 1983, 1989, Trial Techniques Compendium, Nat. College of Dist. Attys. (2d, 3rd, 4th, 5th, 6th eds.). Recipient Disting. Faculty award Nat. Coll. Dist. Attys., 1980, Award for Prosecution Svc. Chgo. Assn. Commerce & Industry, 1981. Fellow Am. Coll. Trial Lawyers, ABA; mem. Internat. Soc. Barristers, Nat. Dist. Attys. Assn. (bd. dirs. 1984-85), Assn. Govt. Attys. in Capital Litigation (pres. 1983-84), Chgo. Bar Assn. (bd. mgrs. 1983-84), Ill. State Bar Assn. (LAWPAC trustee 1989-95), Internat. Assn. Gaming Attys., Chgo. Crime Commn. (bd. dirs.). Avocations: golf, softball, carpentry, motorcycling. Office: Wildman Harrold Allen & Dixon 225 W Wacker Dr Chicago IL 60606-1229

KUNKLER, ARNOLD WILLIAM, retired surgeon, educator; b. St. Anthony, Ind., Nov. 18, 1921; s. Edward J. and Selma (Hasenour) K.; m. Muriel Helen Burns, May 22, 1954; children: Lisa, Arnold William, Carolyn, Christine, Phillip, Kevin. AB, Ind. U., 1943, MD, 1949. Diplomate Am. Bd. Surgery. Intern Ind. U. Med. Ctr., Indpls., 1949-50, asst. resident in surgery, fellow vascular surg. research, 1950-54, resident in surgery, 1954-55, faculty, 1955—76, clin. prof. surgery, 1976-94; ret., 1994. Individual practice medicine specializing in gen. surgery, Terre Haute, Ind., 1955-94; dir. med. edn. Terre Haute Regional Hosp., 1970-79; staff Terre Haute Center Med. Edn.; chief of staff Terre Haute Regional Hosp., 1989-90. Contbr. articles to profl. jours. Pres. Terre Haute Med. Edn. Found., 1972-73, 78-81, bd. dirs., 1967-86; pres. cmty. adv. coun. Terre Haute Center Med. Edn., 1976-80; treas. Wabash Valley Cmty. Blood Program, 1974-78 ; trustee Terre Haute Regional Hosp., 1978-84, chmn. bd., 1981-84, Vigo County Bd. Health, 1990-97. With U.S. Army, 1943-46, ETO. Fellow ACS (pres. Ind. chpt. 1980-81); mem. Ind. State Med. Assn. (com. med. edn. 1986-92), Vigo County Med. Soc., Pam. Am. Med. Assn., Pan Pacific Surg. Assn., Midwest Surg. Assn., Aesculapian Soc. Wabash Valley, Ind. Soc. Chgo., Rotary Club of Terre Haute, Sagamore of the Wabash, Skyline Club, Country Club of Terre Haute. Democrat. Roman Catholic. Home: 3515 Ohio Blvd Terre Haute IN 47803-1938 *Success and service are interdependent.*

KUNOV, HANS, biomedical and electrical engineering educator; b. Copenhagen, Mar. 14, 1938; arrived in Can., 1967; s. Jens Christian and Ruth K.; m. Helle H.D. Jorgensen, Sept. 12, 1964 (div. 1972); children Mads Jacob, Niels Peter; m. D. Clare Lamb, Aug. 1, 1977. MASc, Tech. U. Denmark, Copenhagen, 1963, PhD, 1966. Registered profl. engr., Ont. Postdoctoral fellow Tech. U. Denmark, 1966-67; asst. prof. U. Toronto, Ont., Can., 1967-73, assoc. prof., 1973-82, prof., 1982—, dir. Inst. Biomed. Engring., 1989-99. Dir. Elec. Engring. Consociates, Toronto, 1972—; pres. Artel Engring., 1975—; dir. rsch., co-founder Poul Madsen Med. Devices Ltd., Toronto, 1992—93; co-founder Electrobiologics Corp., 1995—, Vivosonics, Inc., 1999—; mem. grant selection com. Natural Scis. and Engring. Rsch. Coun., Ottawa, Ont., 1990—93. Contbr. numerous sci. papers and publs. Chmn. United Way, U. Toronto, 1991-92; mem. Big Bros. Met. Toronto, 1980—, dir., 1988-92. Recipient Big Brother of Yr. award, Big Bros. Met. Toronto, 1985, 1986, Irving Pomerantz award, 1989, 2002, Queen's Golden Jubilee award, 2003. Mem. IEEE (assoc. editor BME Trans. 1991-93), Acoustical Soc. Am., Can. Med. Biol. Engring. Soc., Danish Engring. Soc. Achievements include development of novel audiometric techniques, of accurate mechano-acoustic models of human hearing and speech apparatus. Home: 4 Princeton Rd Etobicoke ON Canada M8X 2E2 Office: U Toronto 4 Taddle Creek Rd Toronto ON Canada M5S 3G9 E-mail: H.Kunov@utoronto.ca.

KUNSTADTER, GERALDINE SAPOLSKY, foundation executive; b. Boston, Jan. 6, 1928; d. Harry Herman and Nettie Sapolsky; m. John W. Kunstadter, Apr. 23, 1949; children: John W., Lisa, Christopher, Elizabeth Student, MIT, 1945-48. Draftsman U. Chgo. Cyclotron Project, 1948; engring. asst. Gen. Electric Corp., Lynn, Mass., 1948-49; pres. Capricorn Investments Corp., 1971—; chair, dir. A. Kunstadter Family Found., N.Y.C., 1966—. Host family program dir. N.Y.C. Commn. for UN, 1971-86; pres. Nat. Inst. Social Scis., 1979-81; adv. coun. hospitality com. UN Delegations. Mem. adv. coun. East Asia studies program MIT Sch. Arch.; mem. internat. hospitality com. Nat. Coun. Women; bd. dirs. Bridge to Asia Found., Nat. Com. on U.S.-China Rels., Atlantic Coun. of U.S., Ballets Tech. Found., N.Y.C., Ctr. US.-China Arts Exch., Inst. World Affairs; adv. coun. of thr hospitality com. UN Deleg. Recipient Windham award, 1970, Silver medal, Nat. Inst. Social Sci., 1981, Pres.'s medal, Archtl. Soc. China, 2001. Mem. Inst. Current World Affairs, Coun. on Fgn. Rels., Am. Women's Club, Hurlingham Club, Lansdowne Club (London), Cosmopolitan Club (N.Y.).com. of mgmt of network 20/20

KUNTZ, CHARLES, IV, neurological surgeon; b. Oct. 21, 1964; married; 2 children. BA in Chemistry magna cum laude, Holy Cross Coll., 1987; MD in Infectious Disease, Case Western Res. U., 1991. Intern, resident, fellow U. Washington Affiliated Hosps., Seattle, 1991-2000; asst. prof., dir. spine and peripheral nerve surgery Mayfield Clinic and Spine Inst., U. Cin., 2000—. Contbr. articles to profl. jours. Mem. AMA, Am. Assn. of Neurol. Surgeons, Congress of Neurol. Surgeons, North Am. Spine Soc., Phi Beta Kappa, Alpha Omega Alpha. Office: Ste 3100 222 Piedmont Ave Cincinnati OH 45219 Fax: (513) 475-8033. E-mail: charlesKuntz@yahoo.com.

KUNTZ, CHARLES POWERS, lawyer; b. L.A., May 7, 1944; s. Walter Nichols and Katherine (Powers) K.; m. June Emerson Moroney, Dec. 23, 1969; children: Michael Nicholas, Robinson Moroney, Katie Moroney. AB with honors, Stanford U., 1966, JD, 1969; LLM, NYU, 1971. Bar: Calif. 1970, N.Y. 1970, U.S. Dist. Ct. (no. dist.) Calif. 1970, U.S. Ct. Appeals (9th cir.) 1970, U.S. Supreme Ct. 1979. Staff atty. project for urban affairs Office Econ. Opportunity, N.Y.C., 1969-71; dep. pub. defender Contra Costa County Pub. Defender's Office, Martinez, Calif., 1971-75; assoc. Treuhaft, Walker & Brown, Oakland, Calif., 1976-78; ptnr. Hirsch & Kuntz, San Rafael, Calif., 1979-85; pvt. practice San Rafael, 1985-89; ptnr. Coombs & Dunlap, Napa, Calif., 1989—. Mem.: ABA, Napa County Bar Assn., Calif. Attys. Consumer Justice, Inns of Ct. Home: 48 Wild Rye Way Napa CA 94558-7014 Office: Coombs & Dunlap 1211 Division St Napa CA 94559-3372 E-mail: ckuntz@coombslaw.com.

KUNTZ, EDWARD LAWRENCE, health care executive; b. Phila., Feb. 22, 1945; s. Samuel J. and Mary S. (Shulman) K.; m. Caroline L. Lessner, Aug. 3, 1969; m. Stuart M., David M., Beth. BA, Temple U., 1966, JD, 1969, ML, 1978. Pvt. practice, Phila., 1970-78; asst. gen. counsel ARA Svcs., Phila., 1978-79, sector counsel, 1979-84, assoc. gen. counsel, 1984-85; exec. v.p. ARA Living Ctrs., Houston, 1985-92; chmn., CEO Living Ctrs. Am., Houston, 1992-97, Vencor Inc. (now Kindred Healthcare), Louisville, 1999—; pres. Kindred Healthcare, 1999—2002. Dir. Alzheimer's Assn., Houston, 1993—; advisor Woodway Fin. Group, Houston, 1994—; mem. com. Am. Health Care Assn., Washington, 1986—. Co-chmn. fundraising campaign United Way, Med. Ctr., Houston, 1993; bd. dirs. Alley Theater, 1994-97, mem. facilities com., 1994; bd. trustees, adminstrv. and pers. com. Enamu-El, 1996-97. Mem. Thyroid Soc. of Houston (bd. dirs., vice chmn. 1995—), Am. Health Care Assn. (chmn. multifacility steering com., bd. dirs., exec. com., long term financing task force 1997, former mem. numerous coms.), Alzheimer's Assn. (bd. dirs. 1992-97), Thyroid Soc. (vice chmn. bd. dirs., chmn. fund devel. 1996, chmn. bd. 1997), Anti-Defamation League (bd. dirs. 1996-97). Home: 8807 Stable Crest Blvd Houston TX 77024-7035 Office: Kindred Healthcare 680 S Fourth St Louisville KY 40202

KUNTZ, HAL GOGGAN, petroleum exploration company executive; b. San Antonio, Dec. 29, 1937; s. Peter A. and Jean (Goggan) K.; children: Hal Goggan, Peter, Michael B., Vesta. BS in Engring., Princeton U., 1960; MBA, Oklahoma City U., 1972. Line, staff positions Mobil Oil Corp., Dallas, Oklahoma City, and New Orleans, 1963-74; co-founder, pres. CLK Corp., New Orleans and Houston, 1974—, IPEX Co., New Orleans, 1974—, CLK Investments I, II, III, and IV, 1979—; pres. Gulf Coast Exploration Co., New Orleans, 1979—, CLK Producing, CLK Oil and Gas Co., CLK Exploration Co., 1980—. Bd. dirs. North Houston Bank. Mem. Mus. Fine Arts, Houston, 1978—; mem. condrs. cir. Houston Symphony, 1980; mem. governing bd. Houston Opera. With AUS, 1960-63. Mem. Am. Mgmt. Assn., Nat. Small Bus. Assn., Inter-Am. Soc., Soc. Exploration Geophysics, Am. Assn. Petroleum Geologists, Aircraft Owners and Pilots Assn., Houston C. of C., River Oaks C. of C., Petroleum Club, U. of Houston Club, Argyle Club, Order of Alamo, Coronado Club, Princeton Club, River Oaks Country Club, San Antonio Country Club. Republican. Roman Catholic. Avocations: golf, skiing, birdshooting. Office: CLK Co LLC 5 Post Oak Park Ste 2330 4400 Post Oak Pkwy Houston TX 77027 Office Fax: 713-871-0204. E-mail: hal_kuntz@sbcglobal.net.

KUNTZ, JOEL DUBOIS, lawyer; b. Dennis, Mass., Feb. 5, 1946; s. Paul Grimley Kuntz and Harriette (Hunter) Ainsworth; m. Karan Judd, June 29, 1968; children: Matthew Christopher, Kristin Lara. BA, Haverford Coll., 1968; JD, Yale U., 1971; LLM in Taxation, NYU, 1980. Bar: Conn. 1972, Oreg. 1974. Assoc. Stoel, Rives, Boley, Jones & Grey, Portland, Oreg., 1974-79, ptnr., 1979-94; v.p., gen. counsel Entek Internat. LLC, Lebanon, Oreg., 1994—. Author (with James S. Eustice): Federal Income Taxation of S Corporations, 1982, 4th edit., 2001; author: (with James S. Eustice, Charles S. Lewis, Thomas P. Deering) Tax Reform Act of 1986: Analysis and Commentary, 1987; author: (with Robert J. Peroni) U.S. International Taxation, 1992. Capt. USMC, 1971-74. Mem. Am. Coll. Tax Counsel, Internat. Fiscal Assn. Democrat. Home: 3910 Lakeview Blvd Lake Oswego OR 97035-5549 Address: PO Box 39 Lebanon OR 97355-0039 E-mail: jdkuntz@attglobal.net.

KUNTZ, LARRY E., JR., music educator; b. Harrisburg, Pa., Mar. 20, 1965; s. Larry E. and Patricia L. Kuntz; m. Debra Acor Kuntz, July 15, 1988; children: Scott J., Trevor J., Olivia J. BMus, Mansfield U., Pa., 1987; M. Music, VanderCook Coll. Music, Chgo., 1993. Tchr. music Town and Country Day Sch., Harrisburg, Pa., 1987—88; dir. bands Mt. Carmel Area Sch. Dist., Pa., 1988—89; tchr. music Corning-Painted Post Area Sch. Dist., Corning, NY, 1989—92; dir. orch. Hanover Pub. Sch. Dist., Pa., 1992—2002, South Western Sch. Dist., Pa., 2002—. Music dir. Hanover Symphony Orch., 1995—; choir dir. First Bapt. h., Painted Post, NY, 1991—92; prin. trumpet Hershey Symphony Orch., Pa., 1994—95. Condr. (CD) A Star Spangled Spectular, 2001, trumpeter From Telemann to Goemanne, 2000, condr. Pomp and Ceremony, 2000, At the Movies, 1999, A Global Experience, 1999, A Holiday Concert with Karen Bureau, 1998, Childhood Memories, 2002, Musical A-B-C's, 2002, From Russia, With Love, 2003. Coach Little League Baseball. Scholar Presser scholar, Presser Found., Mansfield U., 1985, Kreuscher Performance scholar, Mansfield U. Music Faculty, 1986. Mem.: Music Educators Nat. Conf., Internat. Trumpet Guild, Condrs. Inst. of S.C. (assoc.), Nat. Exchange Club. Republican. Lutheran. Avocations: ice skating, cooking, singing. Office: Hanover Symphony Orchestra PMB 151 1150 Carlisle St Hanover PA 17331

KUNTZ, LEE ALLAN, lawyer; b. Nashville, July 9, 1943; s. Irwin and Lucy (Kornman) K.; 1 child, Douglas. BA, Duke U., 1965; LLB, Columbia U., 1968. Bar: N.Y. 1968, U.S. Dist. Ct. (so. dist.) N.Y. 1973, U.S. Tax Ct. 1973. Assoc. Shearman & Sterling, N.Y.C., 1968-76, ptnr., 1976—, mng. ptnr., 1994-98, sr. ptnr. Real Estate Group, 1988-93. Mem. policy com. Shearman and Sterling, 1991-99. Contbr. articles to profl. jours. Bd. visitors Columbia Law Sch., 1998—; dir. Vols. Legal Svcs., 2000—, Am. Coll. Real Estate Lawyers, 2002-. Mem. ABA, Assn. Bar City N.Y., Am. Coll. Real Estate Lawyers. Office: Shearman & Sterling 599 Lexington Ave Fl C2 New York NY 10022-6069

KUNTZ, MARION LUCILE LEATHERS, classicist, historian, educator; b. Atlanta, Sept. 6, 1924; d. Otto Asa and Lucile (Parks) Leathers; m. Paul G. Kuntz, Nov. 26, 1970; children by previous marriage: Charles, Otto Alan (Daniels). BA, Agnes Scott Coll., 1945; MA, Emory U., 1964, PhD, 1969. Lectr. Latin Lovett Sch., Atlanta, 1963-66; mem. faculty Ga. State U., 1966—, assoc. prof., 1969-73, prof. Latin and Greek, 1973—, Regents' Prof., 1975—, chmn. dept. fgn. langs., 1975-84, research prof., 1984—, Fuller E. Callaway disting. prof., 1985—, alumni disting. prof., 1994. Author: Colloquium of the Seven About Secrets of the Sublime of Jean Bodin, 1975, Guillaume Postel, Prophet of the Restitution of All Things: His Life and Thought, 1981, Jacob's Ladder and the Tree of Life: Concepts of Hierarchy and the Great Chain of Being, 1987, Postello, Venezia e Il Suo Mondo, 1988, Venice, Myth and Utopian Thought, 1999, The Anointment of Dionisio: Prophecy and Politics in Renaissance Italy, 2002; also scholarly articles; mem. editl. bd. Library of Renaissance Humanism. V.p. acad. affairs Am.-Hellenic Found.; patron Michael C. Carlos Mus. Named Latin Tchr. of Yr. State Ga., 1965; Am. Classical League scholar, 1966, Gladys Krieble Delmas scholar, 1991; Am. Coun. Learned Socs. grantee, 1970, 73, 76, 81, 87, 90; recipient medal for excellence in Renaissance studies Pres. of Coun. Gen., Tours, France, 1995, Disting. Career Alumna award Agnes Scott Coll., 1995. Master: Soc. for Values in Higher Edn., Philosophy and Religion; mem.: Classical Assn. Midwest and South (Semple award 1965), Am. Philol. Assn., Archaeol. Inst. Am., Soc. di Philosophique Medievale, Soc. Medieval and Renaissance Philosophy (exec. bd. 1988—), Medieval Acad. Soc. de Culture Europèenne, Soc. des Seizièmistes, Soc. Christian Philosophers (exec. bd. 1987—), Internat. Soc. Neo-Latin Studies, Internat. Soc. Neo-Platonic Studies, Am. Hist. Assn., Am. Soc. Ch. History, Am. Cath. Philos. Assn., Am. Soc. Aesthetics, Renaissance Soc. Am. (coun. 1994—), Am. Philol. Assn., Am. Acad. Rome (sec.-treas. 1970—74), Friends of the Vatican Libr., Italia Nostra, Fondazione Ambiente Italiana, Amici di Querini-Stampalia Galleria e Biblioteca, Coun. Amici di Biblioteca Nazionale di San Marco, Italian Cultural Soc., Nat. Trust Hist. Preservation, Atlanta Hist. Soc., High Mus. of Art (patron), The Atlanta Symphony (patron), Friends of the Warburg Inst., World Monuments Fund, The Commerce Club, Omicron Delta Kappa, Phi Kappa Phi, Phi Beta Kappa. Roman Catholic. Home: Villa Veneziana 1655 Ponce De Leon Ave Atlanta GA 30307 also: Castello 6817 Venice Italy E-mail: marion@gsu.edu.

KUNTZ, WILLIAM FRANCIS, II, lawyer, educator; b. N.Y.C., June 24, 1950; s. William Francis I and Margaret Evelyn (Brown) K.; m. Alice Beal, May 20, 1978; children: William Thaddeus, Katharine Lowell, Elizabeth Anne. AB, Harvard U., 1972, AM, 1974, JD, 1977, PhD, 1979. Bar: N.Y. 1978. Assoc. Shearman & Sterling, N.Y.C., 1978-86; mem. Milgrim, Thomajan & Lee, N.Y.C., 1986-94; ptnr. Seward & Kissel, N.Y.C., 1994-2001, The Torys Law Firm, 2001—. Assoc. prof. Bklyn. Law Sch., 1987-2002. Author: Criminal Sentencing, 1988. Bd. dirs. MFY Legal Svcs., Inc., N.Y.C., 1984-90, Boys Brotherhood Republic, N.Y.C., 1986-90, Habitat for Humanity, N.Y.C., 1987-90; chmn. Resources for Children with Spl. Needs, N.Y.C., 1986-89; mem. N.Y. Civilian Complaint Rev. Bd., 1987—, chmn., 1994. Mem. ABA, N.Y. State Bar Assn., N.Y. County Lawyers Assn. (bd. dirs. 1991-96), Assn. of Bar of City of N.Y. (chmn. mcpl. affairs com. 1992-95, judiciary com., exec. com. 2002—), Bklyn. Bar Assn. (judiciary com. 1995—), Met. Black Bar Assn. Democrat. Roman Catholic. Office: The Torys Law Firm 237 Park Ave New York NY 10017-3142 Business E-Mail: wkuntz@torys.com.

KUNTZ, WILLIAM RICHARD, JR., lawyer; b. New Rochelle, NY, Oct. 6, 1949; s. William Richard and Mary Margaret (Kerkvliet) Kuntz. BSE, Princeton U., 1971; JD, U. So. Calif., 1974. Bar: Calif. 1974, US Dist. Ct. (cen. dist.) Calif. Assoc. McKenna & Fitting, LA, 1974—75, Stroock, Stroock & Lavan, LA, 1975—81, Hahn, Cazier & Leff, LA, 1981—82; ptnr. Hahn, Cazier & Smaltz, LA, 1982—87, Morgan, Lewis & Bockius, LA, 1987—88; from v.p., gen. coun. to exec. v.p., CFO Chart House Enterprises Inc., Solana Beach, Calif., 1988—97, exec. v.p., CFO, 1997; mng. dir. CB Richard Ellis, Inc., Newport Beach, Calif., 1997—99; of counsel Merrill, Schultz & Wolds, San Diego, 1999—. Mem.: ABA, State Bar Calif. Assn. Home: 13536 Kibbings Rd San Diego CA 92130-1242 Office: Merrill Schultz & Wolds Ltd 401 West A St Ste 2550 San Diego CA 92101 Business E-Mail: wrk@mswltd.com.

KUNTZMAN, RONALD, pharmacology research executive; b. Bklyn., Sept. 17, 1933; s. Herman and Fanny Kuntzman; m. Bernice Russman, May 29, 1955; children: Fred, Gary. BS, Bklyn. Coll., 1955; MS, George Washington U., 1957, PhD in Biochemistry, 1962. Biochemist lab. chem. pharmacology Nat. Heart Inst., NIH, Bethesda, Md., 1955-62; sr. biochemist Wellcome Research Labs.-Burroughs Wellcome & Co. U.S.A. Inc., Tuckahoe, N.Y., 1962-66, dep. head biochem. pharmacology dept., 1967-70; assoc. dir. dept. biochemistry and drug metabolism Hoffmann-La Roche Inc., Nutley, N.J., 1970-71, assoc. dir. biol. research, 1972-73, dir. therapeutics research, 1973-79, asst. v.p., 1974-81, dir. pharm. R & D, 1980-81, v.p. pharm. R&D, 1981-84, v.p. R&D, 1984-92; adj. prof. dept. chem. biology and pharmacognosy Rutgers U. Coll. Pharmacy, Piscataway, N.J., 1990—; adj. mem. Roche Inst. Molecular Biology, Nutley, N.J., 1992-96. Mem. adv. coun. Nat. Orgn. for Rare Disorders, 1987-91; adj. prof. Rutgers U., 1990—. Mem. editl. bd. Biochem. Pharmacology, 1966-68, Neuropharmacology, 1970-78, Xenobiotica, 1970-84, Archives of Biochemistry and Biophysics, 1971-78, Life Scis., 1973-78; contbr. numerous articles to profl. jours. Mem. AAAS, Am. Soc. Pharmacology and Exptl. Therapeutics (editorial bd. jour. 1968-75, nominating com. 1972, chmn. div. nominating com. 1977, chmn. div. drug metabolism 1978-81, sec.-treas. 1981-83, coun. 1981-83, chmn. long-range planning com. 1987-92, exec. com. div. drug metabolism 1975-76, John Jacob Abel award 1969), Am. Soc. Biol. Chemists, Am. Coll. Neuropsychopharmacology, Soc. Toxicology, George Washington U. Alumni Assn. (Dist. Alumni Achievement award 1988), Roche Inst. of Molecular Biology (adj. 1992-96), Sigma Xi. Achievements include research on steroids and other normal body constituents which are metabolized by drug metabolizing enzymes; discovered P448, the hemoprotein inducible by hydrocarbon; demonstrated that DOPA-5HTP decarboxylase are the same enzyme. Address: 16 Reunion Rd Rye Brook NY 10573-1085 E-mail: ronkfun@aol.com.

KUNZ, ALEXANDRA CAVITT, physician, anthropologist, researcher; b. Waukegan, Ill., Aug. 3, 1944; d. Howard Hamilton Cavitt and Evelyn Lucille (Becker) Goding; m. Louis William Kunz, Jan. 27, 1968 (div. July 1981); children: Jacob Alexander (dec.), Carmen Rachel. BS with Distinction, U. Nebr., 1966; MD, Ea. Va. Med. Sch., 1991; CPH, Harvard U., 1992, post-grad. Evolutionary Anthropology, 1995—2000. Registered dental hygienist. Mem U.S. Pub. Health Team, Hawaii, 1966; periodontal hygienist Nebr., 1966—91, 1966—91, 1966—91, 1966—91, 1966—91, 1966—91; med. rschr. Harvard U., Boston, 1992—. Mem. AAAS, Am. Assn. Neurol. Surgeons Rsch. Found., Internat. Neurotrauma Soc., Nat. Neurotrauma Soc., Physicians for Human Rights, Mass. Med. Soc., Physicians for Social Responsibility, Am. Fedn. Aging Rsch., Am. Found. AIDS Rsch. Avocations: ice skating, cross country skiing, piano.

KUNZ, APRIL BRIMMER, state legislator, lawyer; b. Denver, Apr. 1, 1954; divorced. AA, Stephens Coll., 1974; BS, U. So. Calif., 1976; JD, U. Wyo., 1979. Bar: Wyo. Pres. K and R Enterprises; mem. Wyo. Ho. Reps., Cheyenne, 1985-86, 90-92, Wyo. Senate, Cheyenne, 1992—, chair jud. com., pres., 2003—. Mem. Women's Civic League; mem. Laramie County Rep. Women's Club. Mem. ABA, Wyo. State Bar Assn, Laramie County Bar Assn. Republican. Office: PO Box 285 Cheyenne WY 82003-0285 also: Wyo Senate State Capitol Cheyenne WY 82002-0001*

KUNZ, PHILLIP RAY, sociologist, educator; b. Bern, Idaho, July 19, 1936; s. Parley P. and Hilda Irene (Stoor) K.; m. Joyce Sheffield, Mar. 18, 1960; children: Jay, Jenifer, Jody, Johnathan, Jana. BS, Brigham Young U., 1961, MS cum laude, 1962; PhD (fellow), U. Mich., 1967. Instr. Eastern Mich. U., Ypsilanti, 1964, U. Mich., Ann Arbor, 1965-67; asst. prof. sociology U. Wyo., Laramie, 1967-68; prof. emeritus sociology Brigham Young U., Provo, Utah, 1968—, acting dept. chmn., 1973; dir. Inst. Geneal. Studies, 1972-74; cons. various edn1. and rsch. instns., 1968—. Missionary Ch. Jesus Christ LDS, Ga. and S.C., 1956-58, mem. high coun., 1969-70, bishop; mission pres. La. Baton Rouge Mission, 1990-93. Author: 10 Critical Keys for Highly Effective Families, other books; contbr. articles on social orgn., family rels. and deviant behavior to profl. jours. Housing commr. City of Provo, 1984— . Served with AUS, 1954-56. Recipient Karl G. Maeser rsch. award, 1977 Mem. Am. Sociol. Assn., Rocky Mountain Social Sci. Assn., Am. Coun. Family Rels., Rural Sociol. Soc., Am. Soc. Criminology, Soc. Sci. Study of Religion, Religious Rsch. Assn., Sigma Xi, Phi Kappa Phi, Alpha Kappa Delta (Alcuin award 1997). Democrat. Home: 3040 Navajo Ln Provo UT 84604-4820 Office: Brigham Young Univ Dept Sociology Provo UT 84602

KUNZE, GEORGE WILLIAM, retired soil scientist; b. Warda, Tex., Sept. 16, 1922; s. John Paul and Hermine (Moerbe) K.; m. Flora Mae Rothmann, July 11, 1947; children: Brenda Kay, Wayne Lester. BS, Tex. A&M U., 1948, MS, 1950; PhD, Pa. State U., 1952. Mem. faculty Tex. A&M U., College Station, 1952—, asst. prof., 1952-56, assoc. prof., 1956-60, prof. soil mineralogy, 1960-84, assoc. dean Grad. Sch., 1967-68, dean, 1968-84, now ret. Cons. U. Alaska, 1963-66; cons. Bangladesh Agrl. U., 1970, Grad. Sch. Agrl. Scis., Castelar Argentina, 1972; mem. Fed. Adv. Com. on Affirmative Action in Employment Practices in Instns. of Higher Edn.; pres. Conf. So. Grad. Schs., 1980-81 Cons. editor Soil Science, 1958-84. With USAAF, 1943—45. Recipient Faculty Disting. Achievement award in research Tex. A&M U., 1966, in administration Tex. A.&M. U., 1984 Fellow: AAAS, Am. Soc. Agronomy, Mineral Soc. Am.; mem.: Clay Mineral Soc. Am. (councilor). Home: PO Box 107 Warda TX 78960-0107

KUNZE, LINDA JOYE, educator; b. Grand Rapids, Mich., Mar. 27, 1950; d. Elon George and Lillian (Wolbers) Benaway (dec.); children: Christopher Russel, Jason Scott. BS, Grand Valley State U., Allendale, Mich., 1971, MEd, 1990. Substitute tchr. Kent Intermediate Sch. Dists., Grand Rapids, 1972-76, 85; instr. YWCA, Grand Rapids, 1972-77, youth svcs. dir., 1977-79; CETA tng. specialist Grand Rapids Pub. Schs., 1977-79; student intern Cen. Elem. Sch., Sparta, Mich., 1986; tchr. Sparta High Sch., 1986, Hastings (Mich.) Mid. Sch., 1986-87; dir. Northview Extended Day Care, Grand Rapids, 1988-95; tchr. Mich. Reformatory, Ionia, Mich., 1995-97, Ionia Temp. Facility, 1997-2000; prin. Brooks Correctional Facility and Muskegon Temporary Facility, 2000—; tchr. Handlon Mich. Correctional Facility, 2001—. Cons. Forest Hills Pub. Schs., Grand Rapids, 1989, Rockford (Mich.) Pub. Schs., 1989—90, Godwin Pub. Schs., Grand Rapids, 1989—, Northview Child Care Network, Grand Rapids, 1989—; mem. Mich. Adult Edn. Profl. Devel. Instrnl. Leadership Team. Cons. Citizens League/Child Care Task Force, Grand Rapids, 1988-89, Campfire Inc., Grand Rapids, 1988-89. Recipient Funding awards Fed. Govt., 1977, State Mich., 1988. Mem. Mich. Reading Assn., Mich. Assn. for Adult and Cmty. Educators, Correctional Edn. Assn., Mich. Assn. Adult Basic Educators (founder), Mich. Dept. Corrections (mem. Adult Basics Edn. curriculum com., trainer Tchg. Adults with Learning Disabilities), Literacy 2000 Internat. Corrections Conf. (workshop presenter). Avocations: volleyball, softball, camping, tennis, swimming. Home: 2182 Daylor Dr NE Grand Rapids MI 49525-1520

KUNZE, OTTO ROBERT, retired agricultural engineering educator; b. Warda, Tex., May 27, 1925; s. John Paul and Hermine Amanda (Moerbe) K.; m. Alice Ruth Eifert, Aug. 5, 1951; children: Glenn, Allen, Charles, Karen. BS, Tex. A&M U., 1950; MS, Iowa State U., 1951; PhD, Mich. State U., 1964. Registered profl. engr., Tex. Agrl. and indsl. engr. Ctrl. Power and Light Co., San Benito, Tex., 1951-56; rsch. agrl. engring. dept. Mich. State U., East Lansing, 1961-64; assoc. prof. agrl. engring. dept. Tex. A&M U., College

Station, 1956-61, 64-69, prof. agrl. engring. dept., 1969-90, prof. emeritus agrl. engring. dept., 1990—. Vis. prof. Nanjing (China) Coll. Food, Grain and Oil Econs., 1993; lectr. Tsukuba U., Japan, 93; cons. and vis. prof. Nat. Chung Hsing U. in Taichung and Nat. Taiwan U. in Taipei, Taiwan, 1994; lectr., cons. Internat. Conf. on Grain Drying in Asia, Bangkok, Thailand, 1995; engring. cons. Advanced Dryer Sys., Inc., Alachua, 1997, Farmers Rice Coop., Sacramento, 1992, Post Harvest Process and Food Engring. Ctr., G.B. Pant U., Pantnagar, India, 1985, Rice Process Engring. Ctr., Indian Inst. Tech., Kharagpur, 1975, Rice Tec, Alvin, Tex., 1996; lectr. on rice harvesting Asian Productivity Orgn., Taichung, Taiwan, 1985, 87; lectr. U. P.R., Mayaguez, 1990; keynote spkr. P.R. sec. Am. Soc. Agrl. Engrs., Añasco, 1990; publ. coord. Rice Tech. Working Group, 1976-90. Co-author (with Finis T. Wratten and Yubin Lan): Physical and Mechanical Properties of Rice; co-author: (with David Calderwood) Rough Rice Drying-Moisture Absorption and Desorption; contbr. chpts. to 5 books, over 100 articles to profl. jours. Mem. A&M Consol. Bd. Equalization, College Station, 1969-71; mem. Tex. Air Control Bd., Austin, 1979-90; mem. pediatric scholarship com. M.D. Anderson Cancer Ctr., Houston, 1990—. With U.S. Army, 1944-46, ETO. Decorated 2 Bronze Stars; recipient Outstanding Svc. award Rice Tech. Working Group, 1990, Outstanding Agrl. Engring. achievement 20th Century, 2000; Faculty fellow NSF, 1961-62. Fellow Am. Soc. Agrl. Engrs. (tech. dir., numerous coms.), Am. Assn. Cereal Chemists (assoc. editor), Sigma Xi (sec. 1969-70, chmn. 1970-71), Phi Kappa Phi (pub. rels. officer 1984-85). Lutheran. Home: PO Box 3 Warda TX 78960-0003 Office: Tex A&M U Agrl Engring Dept College Station TX 77843-2117

KUNZE, RALPH CARL, retired savings and loan executive; b. Buffalo, Oct. 31, 1925; s. Bruno E. and Esther (Graubman) K.; m. Helen Hites Sutton, Apr. 1978; children by previous marriage: Bradley, Diane Kunze Cowgill, James. BBA, U. Cin., 1950, postgrad., 1962-63; grad., Ind. U. Grad. Sch. Savs. and Loan, 1956, U. Calif., 1973. With Mt. Lookout Savs. & Loan Co., Cin., 1951-63, sec., mng. officer, 1958-63; with Buckeye Fed. Savs. & Loan Assn., Columbus, Ohio, 1963-77, exec. v.p., sec., 1967-70, pres., sec., vice chmn. bd. dirs., 1970-77; pres., chief operating officer, dir. Gate City Savs. and Loan Assn., Fargo, N.D., 1977-81; chief exec. officer, dir. United Home Fed., Toledo, 1981-91, also chmn. bd. dirs., 1985-91, ret., 1991. Former trustee Ohio Savs. and Loan League, Toledo C. of C.; mem. investment adv. com. City of Toledo; mem. media contact group and legis. com. U.S. Savs. League. Mem. Toledo Com. 100, Toledo Zool. Soc., St. Vincent Hosp. Found.; past pres. Toledo Zoo; past pres. coun. Hope Luth. Ch.; pres. Toledo Neighborhood Housing Svcs., 1981-83; pres., chmn. pers. com. United Way Franklin County, Ohio; past pres. Ohio Soc. Prevention Blindness; bd. dirs. Revitalization Corp. Toledo, 1983-84, Bittersweet Farms, Autistic Cmty. of N.W. Ohio, Inc.; past mem., trustee Kidney Found. Northwestern Ohio and Luth. Social Svcs., Wesley Glen Retirement Meth. Ctr., Columbus, 1974-77. Served with USNR, 1944-45. Mem. Lambda Chi Alpha. Home: 2606 Emmick Dr Toledo OH 43606-2701

KUNZEL, ERICH, JR., conductor, arranger, educator; b. N.Y.C., Mar. 21, 1935; s. Erich and Elisabeth (Enz) Kunzel; m. Brunhilde Gertrud Strodl, Sept. 5, 1965. AB in Music with distinction, Dartmouth Coll., 1957; postgrad., Harvard U., 1957—58; AM, Brown U., 1960; LittD, No. Ky. State U., 1973; D of Arts, Coll. Mt. St. Joseph, 1996; D in Musical Arts, U. Cin., 2000. Condr. Sante Fe Opera, 1957, Santa Fe Opera, 1964, 1965; music faculty Brown U., 1958—65; asst. condr. R.I. Philharmonic, 1963—65; resident condr. Cin. Symphony Orch., 1965—77; condr. Cin. Summer Opera, 1966, 1973, Cin. Ballet Co., 1966—68; assoc. prof. U. Cin. Coll.-Conservatory Music, 1965—71, chmn. opera dept., 1968—70; music dir. Philharmonia Orch., 1967—71, New Haven (Conn.) Symphony Orch., 1974—77, San Francisco Art Commn. Pops, 1981—83; condr. Cin. Pops Orch., 1977—; prin. pops condr. Naples Philharm. Orch., 1993—. Guest condr. Boston Symphony, Cleve. Orch., Boston Pops, Phila. Orch., San Francisco Symphony, Buffalo Philharm., Rochester Philharm., Pitts. Symphony, Atlanta Symphony, Chgo. Symphony Orch., Interlochen Arts Festival, Dallas Symphony, Detroit Symphony, Toronto Symphony, Montreal Symphony, St. Louis Symphony, Nat. Symphony, London Symphony, China Nat. Symphony, Can. Opera Co., San Francisco Opera, others. Editor, arranger choral works, recs. for Decca Gold Label, Atlantic Records, Telarc Internat., Vox Records, Caedmon Records, Pro Arte Records, Fanfare, MMG, MCA Classics Gold. V.p. Pierre Monteux Meml. Found., Met. Opera Guild; chmn. Greater Cin. Arts and Edn. Ctr., 1998—. Named Billboard Crossover Artist of Yr., 1988, 1989, 1990, 1991; named to Hon. Order Ky. Cols.; recipient Grand Prix du Disque, 1989, Sony Tiffany award, 1989, Classical Record of Yr. award, Japan, 1989, Grammy nomination, 1989, 1991, 1993, 1995, Ohioana Pegasus award, 2000. Mem.: Am. Symphony Orch. League, Delta Omicron, Phi Mu Alpha Sinfonia, Phi Delta Theta (Disting. Alumnus award 1996). Office: Music Hall 1241 Elm St Cincinnati OH 45210-2231*

KUNZENDORF, ROBERT GODFREY, psychologist, educator, researcher; b. Lincoln, Nebr., Feb. 18, 1951; s. Godfrey and Mabel Roberta (Valentiner) Kunzendorf; m. Elizabeth Ann Ritvo, June 5, 1971; children: Jennifer Ritvo, Rebecca Ritvo. BA, Yale U., 1973; PhD, U. Va., 1979. Asst. prof. U. Lowell, Mass., 1979-85, assoc. prof., 1985-90; prof. U. Mass.-Lowell, 1990—. Editor: Mental Imagery, 1991; co-editor: The Psychophysiology of Mental Imagery, 1990, Hypnosis and Imagination, 1996, Individual Differences in Conscious Experience, 2000, Imagination Cognition and Personality, 2000—; contbr. chpts. to books and numerous articles to profl. jours. Grantee, NIMH, 1982—83; behavioral medicine rsch. fellow, Harvard Med. Sch., 1993—2002. Mem.: APA, Internat. Soc. Hypnosis, Am. Assn. for Study of Mental Imagery (pres. 1990—91), Am. Psychol. Soc. Avocation: alpine hiking. Office: U Mass-Lowell Dept Psychology Lowell MA 01854 Business E-Mail: robert_kunzendorf@uml.edu.

KUNZLER, JOHN EUGENE, physicist; b. Willard, Utah, Apr. 25, 1923; s. John Jacob and Freida (Meier) K.; m. Lois McDonald, Dec. 29, 1950; children: Carol Kunzler Blaine, Marilyn Kunzler Barker, Bonnie Kunzler Stein, Kim Kunzler Tomeo. BS in Chem. Engring, U. Utah; PhD, U. Calif., Berkeley. With AT & T Bell Labs., Murray Hill, N.J., 1952—, dir. electronic materials lab., 1969-73, dir. electronic materials and device lab., 1973-79, dir. electronic materials, processes and devices lab., 1979-83, dir. magnetic bubble subsystems and common tech. support lab., 1983-85, dir. future devices study ctr., 1985-86; retired, 1986. Contbr. articles to profl. jours.; patentee in field. Recipient John Price Wetherill medal Franklin Inst., 1964; Internat. prize for new materials Am. Phys. Soc., 1979; Kamerlingh Onnes medal, 1979 Fellow Am. Phys. Soc.; mem. Am. Chem. Soc., Nat. Acad. Engring., Sigma Xi, Tau Beta Pi, Alpha Chi Sigma. Home: 80 Stephensburg Rd Port Murray NJ 07865-3204

KUO, FRANKLIN F. computer scientist, electrical engineer; b. Apr. 22, 1934; came to U.S., 1950, naturalized, 1961; s. Steven C. and Grace C. (Huang) K.; m. Dora Lee, Aug. 30, 1958; children: Jennifer, Douglas. BS, U. Ill., 1955, MS, 1956, PhD, 1958. Asst. prof. dept. elec. engring. Poly. Inst. Bklyn., 1958-60; mem. tech. staff Bell Telephone Labs., Murray Hill, N.J., 1960-66; prof. elec. engring. U. Hawaii, Honolulu, 1966 82; exec. dir. SRI Internat., Menlo Park, Calif., 1982-94; founder, v.p. GWcom, 1994-98; sr. advisor Byair Corp., 1998—. Dir. info. systems Office Sec. of Def., 1976-77; liason scientist U.S. Office Naval Research, London, 1971-72; cons. prof. elec. engring. Stanford U., Calif., 1982—96; vis. prof. U. Mannheim, Germany, 1995-96, Nihon U. Global Bus. Sch., 1998-; mem. exec. panel Chief of Naval Ops., 1980-85; mentor, Stanford U. Grad. Sch. of Bus., 1999-; adv. China Vest, 2001-. Author: Network Analysis and Synthesis, 1962, (2d edit.), 1966, Linear Circuits and Computations, 1973; co-author: System Analysis by Digital Computer, 1966, Computer Oriented Circuit Design, 1969, Computer Communications Networks, 1973, Protocols and Techniques in Data Communication Networks, 1981, Multimedia Communications, 1997; cons. editor, Prentice-Hall Inc., 1967— ; mem. editorial bd. Future Generations Computer Systems; contbr. articles to profl. jours.; developer Alohanet packet broadcast radio network Mem. Pres. coun. U. Ill.; mem. adv. bd. Beckman Inst.; mem. dean's adv. bd. U. Calif. Santa Cruz, 2002—. Recipient Alexander von Humboldt Found. Rsch. award, 1994. Fellow IEEE; mem. The Internet Soc., Tau Beta Pi, Eta Kappa Nu Home: 824 La Mesa Dr Portola Valley CA 94028 E-mail: fkuo@ix.netcom.com.

KUO, JOHN TSUNGFEN, geophysicist, educator, researcher; b. Hangchow, Chejiang, China, Apr. 1, 1922; came to U.S., 1949; naturalized, 1967; s. Lee Kuo; m. Marilyn Dunlap, Apr. 14, 1957; children: Ping Andrea, Sonya Sue, J. David. BS in Geology with Physics and Math., U. Redlands, 1952, ScD (hon.), 1978; MS in Geophysics, Cal. Inst. Tech., 1954; PhD in Geophysics, Stanford U., 1958. Asst. prof. San Jose (Calif.) St. Coll., 1957-60; rsch. assoc. Stanford U., 1958-60; rsch. scientist Columbia U., N.Y.C., 1960-64, assoc. prof., 1964-67, prof., 1967-83, Vinton prof., 1983-85, Ewing and Worzel prof., 1985-92, Ewing and Worzel prof. emeritus, 1992—. Participant DEEPSCAN, 1963; dir. Aldridge Lab. Applied Geophysics, 1964-92, Lamont-Doherty's Underground Geophys. Obs., Ogdensburg, N.J., 1967-77, Columbia U., Project Migration, Inversion, Diffraction and Scattering, 1979-89; disting. sr. vis. scholar U. Cambridge, Eng., 1970-71; vis. prof. U. Tex., Austin, 1977-78, Cornell U., N.Y., 1978, 92-97, Tech. U. Clausthal, Fed. Rep. of Germany, 1987; adj. prof. Cornell U., 1992-98; Columbia U. del. People's Republic of China, 1979; tech. adv. 20th Dist. Congressman, 1983—; hon. prof. co-dir. integrated basin studies Chengdu Inst. Tech., People's Republic of China, 1986; hon. prof. Acad. Sinica, 1979—, China U. Geoscis., Beijing, 1992; hon. sr. rschr. Inst. Geophysics, China Seismological Bur., People's Republic of China, 1995—; expert World Bank, 1982. Mem. editl. bd. Bollettino di Geofisica, Italy, 1985-89; contbr. over 120 articles to profl. jours. Danforth Tchg. fellow, 1957—, Sr. Postdoctoral fellow NSF, 1970; Rsch. grantee NSF, NASA, U.S. Geol. Survey, Office Naval Rsch., Air Force Office Sci. Rsch., Air Force Geophysics, U.S. Bur. Mines; recipient Alexander von Humboldt award for disting. U.S. sr. scientist, Fed. Republic Germany, 1986, Hon. Knight for Life award Knights Round Table Internat., 1993, Alumni Career Achievement award U. Redlands, 2002. Fellow Geol. Soc. Am. (sr.), Royal Astron. Soc. U.K.; mem. Internat. Union Geodesy and Geophysics (fellow Assn. Geodesy, pres. permanent commn. for Earth tides 1979-87), Am. Geophys. Union (life, assoc. editor Geophysics Rev.), Soc. Exploration Geophysicists (rep.-at-large, com. mem., chmn. com.), Seismol. Soc. Am., Petroleum Exploration Soc. N.Y., Redlands Round Table (hon.), China Geophys. Soc. (fgn. corr.), Sigma Xi. Home: 11 Hoffman Ln Blauvelt NY 10913-1707 Office: Columbia U New York NY 10027

KUO, LIH, medical educator; b. Taipei, Taiwan, Aug. 28, 1957; came to U.S., 1983; BS in Biology, Tunghai Univ., Taichung, Taiwan, 1979; MS in Physiology, Nat. Taiwan U., 1983; DPhil, Med. Coll. Va., 1987. Rsch. asst. Dept. Physiology & Biophysics Nat. Def. Med. Ctr., 1979-81; tchg. asst. Dept. Physiology Nat. Taiwan U., 1981-83, Med. Coll. Va., Richmond, 1985-87; postdoctoral rsch. assoc. Dept. Med. Physiology Tex. A&M U., 1990-91; asst. prof. Tex. A&M U. Health Ctr., 1992-98, assoc. prof., 1998-2001, prof., 2001—, Kruse Centennial chair, 2003, dir. Ophthalmic Vascular Rsch. Program, 2003. Mem. exptl. cardiovascular scis. study sect. NIH, 1994-98; spkr. in field. Contbr. articles to profl. jours. Dr. Sun Yet Sen Sci. scholar Tunghai U., 1977-79, Ministry Edn. scholar Outstanding Student Coll. Medicine Nat. Taiwan U., 1981-83; A.D. Williams award Postdoctoral fellow Med. Coll. Va., 1983-85, Med. Coll. Va. Grad. fellow, 1985-87. Fellow Am. Heart Assn. (mem. basic cardiovasc. scis.), Am. Physiol. Soc. (cardiovasc. sect.); mem. Chinese Physiol. Soc., Microcirculatory Soc. (Grega-Zacharkow Young Investigator award 1990), Phi Kappa Phi. Office: Tex A&M U Dept Med Physiology Med Rsch Bldg 702 SW HK Dodgen Loop Temple TX 76504

KUO, MICHELLE CHEN (CHOU-HSIA CHEN), musician, educator; d. Shin-Yang and Yu-Shou Chen; m. Cheng Kuo, Aug. 12, 1983; children: Anthony Charles, Christopher Michael. B, U. Rochester, 1984; M, The Juilliard Sch., 1986. Lic. The Royal Schs. of Music, London. Pvt. tchr., Morris Plains, NJ, 1974—. Pianist numerous concert performances and competitions. Mem.: N.Y. State Music Tchrs. Assn. (assoc.), Nat. Guild Piano Tchrs. (assoc.), Music Educators Assn. (assoc.; v.p. 2002—).

KUO, PING-CHIA, historian, educator; b. Yangshe, Kiangsu, China, Nov. 27, 1908; s. Chu-sen and Hsiao-kuan (Hsu) K.; m. Anita H. Bradley, Aug. 8, 1946. A.M., Harvard U., 1930, PhD, 1933. Prof. modern history and Far Eastern internat. relations Nat. Wuhan U., Wuchang, China, 1933-38; editor China Forum, Hankow and Chungking, 1938-40; counsellor Nat. Mil. Council, Chungking, China, 1940-46, Ministry Fgn. Affairs, 1943-46; participated in Cairo Conf. as spl. polit. asst. to Generalissimo Chiang Kai-shek, 1943; during war yrs. in Chungking, also served Chinese Govt. concurrently in following capacities: mem. fgn. affairs com. Nat. Supreme Def. Council, 1939-46; chief, editorial and pubs. dept. Ministry Information, 1940-42, mem. central planning bd., 1941-45; tech. expert to Chinese delegation San Francisco Conf., 1945; chief trusteeship sect. secretariat UN, London; (exec. com. prep. commn. and gen. assembly), 1945-46; top-ranking dir. Dept. Security Council Affairs, UN, 1946-48; vis. prof. Chinese history San Francisco State Coll., summers 1954, 58; assoc. prof. history So. Ill. U., 1959-63, prof. history, 1963-72, chmn. dept. history, 1967-71, prof. emeritus, 1972—. Sr. fellow Nat. Endowment for Humanities, 1973-74; Pres. Midwest Conf. Asian Studies, 1964 Author: A Critical Study of the First Anglo-Chinese War, with Documents, 1935, Modern Far Eastern Diplomatic History (in Chinese), 1937, China: New Age and New Outlook, 1960, China, in the Modern World Series, 1970; Contbr. to Am. hist. pubs. and various mags. in China and Ency. Brit. Decorated Kwang Hua medal A-1 grade Nat. Mil. Council, Chungking, 1941; Auspicious Star medal Nat. Govt., Chungking, 1944; Victory medal, 1945 Mem. Am. Hist. Assn., Assn. Asian Studies. Clubs: Commonwealth (San Francisco). Home: 8661 Don Carol Dr El Cerrito CA 94530-2752

KUO, WAY, industrial engineer, researcher; b. Taipei, Taiwan, Jan. 5, 1951; m. Suzanne Lee, July 13, 1951; children: Tiffany, Wendy. BS in Nuclear Engring., Nat. Tsing-Hua U., Taiwan, 1972; MS in Indsl. Engring., Kans. State U., 1978, MS in Stats., PhD in Engring., 1980. Tech. staff mem. Bell Labs., Holmdel, N.J., 1981-84; from asst. prof. to prof. Iowa State U., Ames, 1984-88, prof., chair indsl. and mfg. sys. engring., 1988-93; prof., head indsl. engring. dept. Tex. A&M U., College Station, 1993—. Mem. adv. bd. NSF, Washington, 1990-92, Nat. Inst. Stds. and Tech., Washington, 1990-95. Co-author: Optimazation of Systems Reliability, 1985; editor: Quality through Engineering Design, 1993; contbr. numerous articles to profl. jours. Fellow IEEE, Am. Soc. Quality Control, Inst. Indsl. Engrs. Office: Texas A&M U Coll Engring 301 Wisenbaker Eng Rsch Ctr College Station TX 77843-3126 E-mail: way@tamu.edu.

KUPCHAK, KENNETH ROY, lawyer; b. Forrest Hills, Pa., May 15, 1942; s. Frank V. and Anne B. (Ruzanic) Kupchak; m. Patricia K. Geer, Jan. 27, 1967; children: Lincoln K., Robinson K. AB, Cornell U., 1964; BS, Pa. State U., 1965; JD in Internat. Affairs, Cornell U., 1971. Bar: Hawaii 1971, U.S. Dist. Ct. Hawaii 1971, U.S. Supreme Ct. 1988. Meteorology staff U. Hawaii, Honolulu, 1968; ptnr. Damon Key Leong Kupchak & Hastert, Honolulu, 1971—, v.p., 2002—, bd. dirs., 2002—. Chief minority counsel 8th legis. Hawaii Ho. Reps., Honolulu, 1974—75; legis. coord. Hawaii State Assn. Counties, Honolulu, 1988; bd. dirs. Fletcher Constrn. Co., N.Am. Ltd.; adj. prof. William S. Richardson Sch. Law, U. Hawaii, 1993; mem. Honolulu Common Fgn. Rels., 1995—; vice chair bd. counselors Mid-Pacific Inst., 1993—95, trustee, 1995—, chmn. pers. com., 1998—, chmn. edn. com., 2000—, chmn. rsch. evaluation com., 2002—; lectr. on constrn. law. Co-author: Fifty State Construction Lien and Bond Laws, 2000, The Design/Build Process, 1997, A State-By-State Guide to Architect, Engineer and Contractor Licensing, 1998, A State-By-State Guide to Construction and Design Law, 1998; contbr. articles to profl. jours. Chair agenda com. C.Z.M. Statewide Adv. Com., Hawaii, 1980—92; pres., bd. dirs. Hawaii Cmty. Svc. Coun., Honolulu, 1982—88; trustee Moanalua Gardens Found., 1985—88, Operation Raleigh (N.C.) U.S.A., 1986—90; bd. dirs. Hawaii Nature Ctr., 1989—, sec., 2001—02, pres., 2002—; chair Hawaii State Commn. on Korean and Vietnam War Meml., 1992—95. Capt. USAF, 1964—68, Vietnam. Fellow Centennial, Pa. State U., 1996. Fellow: Am. Coll. Constrn. Lawyers; mem.: ABA (constrn. industry forum, dispute resolution steering com. 1994—, chair 1998—2000, chair ann. meeting 2001, governing com. 2002—), USAF Assn. (v.p. Hawaii chpt. 1994—97), Am. Arbitration Assn. (panel arbitrators), Internat. Bar Assn., Hawaii Bar Assn., Cornell Law Alumni Assn. (exec. com. 1990—93), Hawaii Lacrosse Club (founder, dir., sec. 1990—2000), Volcano Golf and Country Club, Oahu Country Club, Cornell Club Hawaii (bd. dirs., chair scholarship com. 1994—2000). Avocations: lacrosse, hiking, photography. Office: 1600 Pauahi Tower 1001 Bishop St Honolulu HI 96813-3429 E-mail: krk@hawaiilawyer.com.

KUPCHELLA, CHARLES EDWARD, academic administrator, author, educator; b. Nanty Glo, Pa., July 7, 1942; s. Charles Francis and Margaret (Bouite) K.; m. R. Adele Kiel, July 20, 1963; children: Richard Charles, Michele Louise, Jason Charles. BS in Edn., Indiana U. of Pa., 1964; PhD, St. Bonaventure U., 1968. Asst. prof. Bellarmine Coll., Louisville, 1968-72, assoc. prof., 1972-73; assoc. dir. cancer rsch. ctr. Sch. of Medicine, assoc. prof. U. Louisville, 1973-79; prof., chmn. dept. biology Murray (Ky.) State U., 1979-85; dean Ogden Coll. Western Ky. U., Bowling Green, 1985-93; provost S. E. Mo. State U., Cape Girardeau, 1993—99; pres. U. N.D., 1999—. Author: Sights/Sounds: Special Senses, 1976, Environmental Science, 1986, 3rd rev. edit., 1993, Dimensions of Cancer, 1987; contbr. chpts. to books, over 50 articles to profl. jours. Bd. dirs. Ky. Ctr. for Pub. Issues, Lexington, 1990-93; mem. cancer edn. rev. com. NIH/Nat. Cancer Inst., 1993-97; mem. inst. rsch. grant rev. com. Am. Cancer Soc., 1993-96. NDEA fellow, 1964-68. Mem. AAAS (nominating com. sect. on sci. and engring. 1995-97), Ky. Acad. Sci. (pres. 1977), Ky. Sci. and Tech. Coun. (sec., treas. Lexington 1988-93), Am. Assn. Cancer Edn. (chair fin. com. 1990-93, treas. 1993-96, pres. 1999-2000, exec. coun.). Office: U of North Dakota Office of Pres Grand Forks ND 58202

KUPCINET, IRV, columnist; b. Chgo., July 31, 1912; s. Max and Anna (Paswell) K.; m. Essee Joan Solomon, Feb. 12, 1939; children: Karyn (dec.), Jerry Solomon. AB, Northwestern U., 1930-32, U. N.D., 1935. Columnist Chgo. Daily Times, 1935-43, Kup's Column, Chgo. Sun Times, 1943—; host TV program Kup's Show, Chgo., 1959—; commentator WBBM-TV, Chgo.; former commentator Chgo. Bears football broadcasts. Spl. cons. in charge of columnists for War Fin. Divsn., drives U.S. Treasury Dept. V.p. Dr. Jerome D. Solomon Meml. Found.; originator, host Purple Heart Cruise. Recipient 14 Emmy awards, numerous civic and profl. awards; Wabash Ave. Bridge, Chgo. renamed Irv Kupcinet Bridge, 1986. Mem. Newspaper Guild, Nat. Press Club (Washington), Chgo. Press Club, Tau Delta Phi. Office: Chgo Sun-Times 401 N Wabash Ave Chicago IL 60611-5642

KUPEL, FREDERICK JOHN, business executive; b. Burbank, Calif., Apr. 22, 1929; s. Martin Charles and Lorene (Murray) K.; m. Nancy Kathryn Eubank, 1952 (div. 1979); children: James Frederick, Douglas Edward; m. Karen J. Jensen, 1980 (div. 1992); 1 stepchild, John Robert Jensen, Jr. Student, Claremont McKenna Coll., 1948-50; BA, U. Calif., Berkeley, 1951; MA in Psychology, Sonoma State U., 1980. Lic. profl. counselor. Acctg., fin. and mgmt. positions, 1951-66; acctg. and ops. exec. Evans Products Co., Portland, Oreg., 1967-71; v.p. fin. Columbia Corp., Portland, 1971-77, Plantronics, Inc., Santa Cruz, Calif., 1977-78; counselor Yellow Brick Rd. Program, Portland, 1975-76; cons., 1978-84; dir. bus. devel. and acquisitions ITT Communication Services, Inc., 1985-87; v.p. fin., chief fin. officer Bohemia, Inc., Eugene, Oreg., 1987-89, pres. Bus. Devel. Corp., Lake Oswego, Oreg., 1989-93; bus. owner, 1994—2000; CEO, Kupel & Co., Portland, 2000—. With AUS, 1946-47. Mem.: Portland Indsl. Rotary (pres. 1999—2000). Office: 3735 SE Ogden St Portland OR 97202 E-mail: fred@kupel.com.

KUPER, ADAM JONATHAN, anthropologist, educator; b. Johannesburg, Transvaal, Republic of South Africa, Dec. 29, 1941; s. Simon Meyer and Gerty (Hesselson) K.; m. Jessica Sue Cohen, Dec. 16, 1966; children: Simon, Jeremy, Hannah. BA, U. Witwatersrand, Johannesburg, 1961; PhD, U. Cambridge, Eng., 1966; D (hons.), U. Gothenburg, Sweden, 1978. Lectr. in Social Anthropology Makerere U., Kampala, Uganda, 1967-70; lectr. in Anthropology U. Coll. U. London, 1970-76; prof. African Anthropology and Sociology U. Leiden, The Netherlands, 1976 85; prof. social anthropology, head human scis. dept. Brunel U., Middlesex, Eng., 1985—. Mem. Inst. for Advanced Study, Princeton, N.J., 1994-95. Author: Kalahari Village Politics: An African Democracy, 1970, Anthropologists and Anthropology: The British School, 1922-72, 1973, 2d rev. ed. 1983, 3rd rev. ed. 1996, Changing Jamaica, 1976, Regionaal Vergelijkend Onderzoek in Afrika, 1977, Wives for Cattle: Bridewealth and Marriage in Southern Africa, 1982, South Africa and the Anthropologist, 1987, The Invention of Primitive Society: Transformations of an Illusion, 1988; editor: The Social Anthropology of Radcliffe-Brown, 1982, The Social Science Encyclopedia, 1985, 2nd edit., 1996, Current Anthropology, 1985-93, Conceptualizing Society, 1992, The Chosen Primate, 1994, Culture: The Anthropologists' Account, 1999, Among the Anthropologists, 1999; contbr. more than 90 articles to profl. jours. Fellow British Acad.; mem. Acad. Europe. Avocation: golf. Home: 16 Muswell Rd London N10 2BG England E-mail: kuper@ajkuper.freeserve.co.uk.

KUPER, DANIELA F. writer, speaker; b. Chgo., June 18, 1950; d. Harry W. and Anne F. (Fisher) K.; children: Judah E., Sahra J. BA, So. Ill. U., 1971. Pres., creative dir. Kuper-Finlon Advt., Boulder, 1982-88. Writer, spkr., 1988—. Contbr. fiction to newspapers and mags.; author novel, 1998. Ucross Found. fellow, Djerassi Found. fellow. Mem. Colo. Author's League, Denver Ad Fedn., Boulder C. of C., Art Dirs. Club Denver (award 1985, 86).

KUPERMAN, FRANCES PERGERICHT, lawyer; b. Cleve., June 4, 1952; d. Joseph and Ann Pergericht; m. Roman G. Kuperman, Feb. 24, 1982; 1 child, Natalie Jill. BA magna cum laude, Case Western Res. U., 1974; JD, Washington U., St. Louis, 1978. Bar: N.H. 1979, Ill. 1981. Law clk. presiding justice U.S. Dist. Ct. No. Dist. Ill., Chgo., 1979-81; assoc. Jenner & Block, Chgo., 1981-83; asst. regional atty. Dept. Health and Human Svcs., Chgo., 1983-96, sr. counsel Office of Counsel to the Inspector Gen. Washington, 1996—. Topics editor Washington U. Law Quar., 1977-78. Mem. Phi Beta Kappa. Office: Office of Inspector Gen Dept Health and Human Svcs 330 Independence Ave SW Washington DC 20201-0003 E-mail: frankuperman@comcast.net.

KUPERMAN, MICHAEL ARON, language educator, writer; b. Chgo., June 22, 1971; s. Bonnie and Mike Walker(Stepfather); m. Mandy Chien Kuperman, July 21, 2002. BA, U. Fla., 1993. Lectr. Kao Yuan Inst. Tech., Lu Chu, Taiwan, 1987—. Contbr. articles to profl. jours.;, author poems.

KUPERMAN, ROBERT IAN, advertising agency executive; b. Bklyn., Dec. 31, 1941; s. Morris and Gertrude Kuperman; m. Ellen Rose, June 6, 1973; children: Jason, Molly. BFA, Pratt Inst., 1963. Vice pres., sr. art dir. Doyle Dane Bernbach, N.Y.C., 1963-71; v.p., creative dir. Della Femina Travisano & Ptnrs., N.Y.C., 1971-73; sr. v.p., creative dir. Wells, Rich & Greene, N.Y.C. and Los Angeles, 1973-80, BBDO/West, Los Angeles, 1980-82; exec. v.p., exec. creative dir. DDB, LA, 1982—87; exec. v.p., creative dir. chiat/Day, LA, 1987—98, pres., CEO, 1998—2001; chmn., CEO DDB Worldwide, NY, 2001—. Instr. Sch. Visual Arts, N.Y.C., 1968-74, Pratt Inst., Bklyn., 1966-68, Art Ctr., LA, 1975-79; adv. Jackson Lab. Art dir. TV comml. 1949 Auto Show, 1970 (Clio Hall of Fame award 1979), Volkswagen advertisements, (now in Smithsonian Mus. Art), other TV commls. Recipient Gold medals N.Y. Art Dirs. Show, 1969, 71, Andy award Advt. Club N.Y., 1970, Clio awards for excellence in worldwide advt., 1970, 72, 74, 78, 83. Mem. Los Angeles Creative Club (co-founder, chmn. bd. dirs.), Los Angeles Advt. Club (bd. dirs. 1979). Office: DDB Worldwide 437 Madison Ave New York NY 10022 Office Fax: 212-415-3414.

KUPERSMITH, JOEL, physician, medical school dean; b. Nov. 26, 1939; s. Charles Douglas and Sally K.; m. Judith Freidman, June 15, 1969; children: David, Rebecca, Adam. BS, Union Coll., Schenectady, 1960; MD, N.Y. Med. Coll., 1964. Prof., chief clin. pharmacology Mt. Sinai Sch. Medicine, NYC, 1974-86; chief cardiology divsn. Beth Israel Med. Ctr., NYC, 1985-86; prof., chief cardiology divsn. U. Louisville Sch. Medicine, East Lansing, 1986-91, V.V. Cooke prof. medicine Lubbock, 1987-91; prof., chair medicine Mich. State U., East Lansing, 1991-97; dean Sch. Medicine, dean Sch. Biomed. Sci. Tex. Tech U. Sch. Medicine, Lubbock, 1997—2001, v.p. clin. affairs, 1997—2001, prof. internal med., 1997—. Chief cardiac arrhythmia clinic Mt. Sinai Med. Ctr., 1977—85, assoc. prof. pharmacology, 1979—84; scholar-in-residence Inst. Medicine, 2003—. Author: Clinical Manual of Electrophysiology, 1997, The Pharmacologic Management of Heart Disease, 1993. Recipient Affirmative Action award U. Louisville, 1988, Alumni Assn. Disting. Achievement award N.Y. Med. Coll. Med. Sch., Coun. Deans, 1992. Mem.: AMA (med. sch. sect., governing coun.), Assn. Am. Med. Coll. (task force on fraud/abuse, Petersdorf scholar-in-residence 2003—), Am. Heart Assn. (exec. com. Coun. on Clin. Cardiology 1991—94), Assn. Profs. Medicine (program com. 1994), Am. Soc. Clin. Investigation (sr.). Office: Tex Tech U Sch Medicine 2450 N St NW Washington DC 20037

KUPFER, CARL, ophthalmologist, science administrator; b. N.Y.C., Feb. 9, 1928; s. James and Hannah Kupfer; m. Muriel I. Kaiser, Dec. 9, 1969; children: Charles, Sarah. AB, Yale U., 1948; MD, Johns Hopkins U., 1952; DSc (hon.),

U. Pa., 1982, SUNY, 1992. Diplomate Am. Bd. Ophthalmology. Intern, then resident Johns Hopkins U., 1952—55; asst. prof. Harvard U. Med. Sch., Boston, 1960—66; prof., chmn. dept. ophthalmology U. Wash. Sch. Med., Seattle, 1966—69; dir. Nat. Eye Inst. NIH, Bethesda, Md., 1970—2000, sr. clinician, 2000—; intern, then resident Johns Hopkins U., 1957—58. Bd. trustees Am. Found. for Blind, 2001. Recipient Migel award, Am. Found. for Blind, 1976, Pisart award, Lighthouse for the Blind, N.Y.C., 1984, Presdl. Rank award, 1991, Humanitarian award, Lions Club Internat., 1992. Mem.: Inst. Medicine of NAS, Johns Hopkins Soc. Scholars. Office: NIH Bldg 10 10 Center Dr Msc 1860 Bethesda MD 20892-0001

KUPFER, DAVID J. psychiatry educator; b. N.Y.C., Feb. 14, 1941; s. Alex and Muriel (Greenfield) Kupferstein; m. Barbara Stern Burstin, June 1963 (div. Mar. 1975); m. Ellen Frank, June 1975; children: Andrea, Jeffrey, Deborah, Nancy, Erica, Tonia. BA magna cum laude, Yale U., 1961, MD, 1965. Diplomate Am. Bd. Psychiatry and Neurology. Med. intern Montefiore Hosp. Ctr., N.Y.C., 1965—66; clin. fellow in psychiatry Yale U. Sch. Medicine, New Haven, 1966—67; postdoctoral fellow, chief resident in psychiatry Dana Psychiat. Clinic, Yale-New Haven Hosp., 1969—70; asst. prof. Yale U. Sch. Medicine, New Haven, 1970—73; assoc. prof. psychiatry U. Pitts., 1973—75, prof., 1975—, chmn. dept., 1983—; dir. rsch. Western Psychiat. Inst. and Clinic Western Psychiat. Inst. and Clinic, Pitts., 1973—, Thomas Detre prof., chmn. dept. psychiatry, 1994—. Office: U Pitts Western Psychiat Inst & Clinic 3811 Ohara St Pittsburgh PA 15213-2593

KUPFERMAN, DAVID COBB, painter; b. Boston, Mar. 10, 1946; s. Lawrence Kupferman and Ruth Cobb; m. Beth Ann Fried, Feb. 24, 1993. Student, U. Wis., 1964-66; BS in Creative Intelligence, Maharishi European Rsch. U., Seelisberg, Switzerland, 1976. Apprentice to Lawrence Kupferman Mass. Coll. Art; apprentice to sculptor Mirko Harvard U., Cambridge, Mass. Subject of TV documentary Impact: David Kupferman, 1994. One-man shows include Greenfield Gallery, N.Y.C., 1971, Harvard U., 1971, Harold Ernst Gallery, Boston, 1974-76, French Libr. of Boston, 1976, Gallery of World Art, Newton, Mass., 1978, Visual Images Gallery, Wellfleet, Mass., 1984, 85, Newton Free Libr. Gallery, 1988, 99, Galerie Mourlot, Boston, 1992, Cataumet Art Ctr., Cape Cod, Mass., 1994, 96, 2001, Kendall Ctr. for Arts, Belmont, Mass., 1991, 97, Swansborough Gallery, Wellfleet, 1995, 96, Thayer Acad., Braintree, Mass., 1997, Hodgell Gallery, Sarasota, Fla., 1997, 99, Gallery Szent-Gyorgyi, Falmouth, Mass., 1998, Hahn Gallery, Phila., 1999, Danforth Mus., Framingham, Mass., 2001, Judi Rotenberg Gallery, Boston, 2001, 02, 03, Harmon-Meek Gallery, Naples, Fla., 2002; group shows include Inst. Contemporary Art, Boston, 1974, 75, Midtown Gallery, N.Y.C., 1977, Wallace-Wentworth Gallery, Washington, 1985-87, Richard Green Gallery, N.Y.C., 1988-89, Galerie Keller, Paris, 1986, Allene LaPedes Gallery, Santa Fe, 1988-89, Jill George Gallery, London, 1991-2000, Boston Fine Arts, 1993-94, Lydon Fine Arts, Chgo., 1993-2002, DeCordova Mus., 1990-93, 98, 99, 2000, 2001, Armenian Mus., Watertown, Mass., 2000, Phila. Mus. Gallery, 1993, Cape Mus. Fine Art, Dennis, Mass., 1994-95, 99, 2002, Danforth Mus. Art, Framingham, Mass., 1995-97, 2002, Mus. Fine Arts, Boston, 1997, Cynthia Corbett Gallery, London, 2000, Art on Paper Fair, London, 2001; represented in permanent collections at Fuller Mus. Art, Brockton, Mass., McMullen Mus. Art/Boston Coll., Cape Mus. Fine Arts, Danforth Mus. Art, Boston Pub. Libr., Provincetown (Mass.) Art Assn. and Mus., DeCordova Mus., Lincoln, Mass., Stamford Mus., Conn., Mass. Coll. Art, Boston, Mus. Fine Arts, Springfield, Mass., Naples Mus., Fla., Davis Mus., Wellesley Coll., U. NH Art Gallery, Durham, Art Ctr. Sarasota, Fla., others; author, artist: Milkman Max, 1965. Mass. Arts Lottery grantee, 1988; Change Inc. Robert Rauschenberg's Artist Found. grantee, 1999; Adolph and Esther Gottlieb Found. grantee, 1999; Pollock-Krasner Found. grantee, 2000. Home: 115 Irving St Watertown MA 02472-2705 E-mail: dbkupferman@attbi.com.

KUPFERMAN, MEYER, composer; b. N.Y.C., July 3, 1926; s. Elias and Fanny (Hoffman) K.; m. Sylvia Kasten, June 16, 1946 (div.); 1 dau., Lisa; m. Pei-fen Chin, July 24, 1973. Student, Queens Coll., 1944-46. Co-dir. New Chamber Music Soc., 1946-48, Bolton Music Festival, Bolton Landing, N.Y., 1947-48; mem. forum group bd. N.Y. chpt. Internat. Soc. Contemporary Music, 1949-50; tchr. composition, chamber music, music for theatre Sarah Lawrence Coll., 1951-93, prof. emeritus, 1955—, chmn. music dept., 1979; dir., founder Sarah Lawrence Improvisational Ensemble, 1967—; composer-in-residence Calif. Music Ctr., 1977-80; pres. Soundspells Prodns., 1986—; composer-in-residence N.Y. Virtuosi, 1997; condr. Monte Carlo Orch., 1999. Concert lectr. Colgate U., 1996, SUNY-New Paltz, 1996. Composer: debut, Steinway Hall, N.Y.C., 1946, film scores Hallelujah the Hills, 1962, A X'mas Memory, 1966, Blast of Silence, 1960, Faces of America, 1965, Goldstein, 1964, Black Like Me, 1964, Cool Wind, 1961, Among the Paths to Eden, 1968; (operas) In a Garden, 1948, The Curious Fern, 1957, Voices for a Mirror, 1957, Draagenfut Girl, 1958, Doctor Faustus Lights the Lights, 1963, The Judgement, 1966-67, Prometheous, 1976, The Proscenium, 1991; symphony Symphony No. 10: FDR, 1982, Clarinet Concerto, 1984, Ode to Shreveport, 1985, Sound Phantoms, #8, 1983, Challenger (for large orch.), 1983, A Little Ivory Concerto, 1986, Jazz Symphony, 1988, Savage Landscape, 1989, Double Concerto for 2 clarinets and orch. commd. by Nassau Symphony for soloists Stanley and Naomi Druker, 4 Piano Retrospective on March 8, at Katheryn Bache Miller Theatre featuring premieres of Symphonic Odyssey, Vilnius, Lithuania, 1990, Red Sonata, Snow and In Quiet Measure, with pianists Morton Estrin, Kuzuko Hayami, Christopher Vassiliades and Svetlana Gorokhovich, 1992, Ice Cream Concerto, 1992, The Moor's Concerto, 1993, Fantasy Concerto for Violin and Orchestra, 1997, Strata for Solo Flute, N.Y.C., 1997, Percussion Symphony, Ithaea Percussion Ensemble, 1997, Quasar Symphony, Vilnius, 1997, Sound Phantoms # 8, Sinfonia Brevis II, Vilnius, 1997; chamber music Cycle of Infinities, 1962-67, Images of Chagall, 1988, (recs.) Images of Chagall, Jazz Symphony and Challenger with Lithuanian Nat. Philharm., Clarinet Concerto with Pro Arte Chamber Orch. of Boston; (choreographed by Martha Graham) ballet score O Thou Desire, 1977, Concerto for Guitar and Orch. premiered by Orquesta de Baja Calif., Chaccone Sonata premiered by Laurel Ann Mauer, Hexagon Skies for guitar and orch., Infinites Projection for small orch., winter symphony for orch., 1999; author: Atonal Jazz; Third Piano Concerto, commd. by Christopher Vassiliades, 1999, Speculum Symphony '99 and Music for Guitar and Orchestra commd. by Robert Limon and the Orquestra de Baja Calif., 1998; commd. Concerto Brevis for Flute and Orch., Nat. Flute Assn., 1999: Concerto Brevis, A Faust Concerto, Lunar Symphony, 1999, Speculum Symphony, 1999, Tinker Hill, 1999, Fly by Night (for two solo clarients and orch.), 2000, Icon Symphony, 2000, Quantum Symphony, 2000, Structures for Orchestra, 2001, Elegy for the Vanished, 2001, Violin Concerto: The Voyager, 2001, Concerto for Guitar and Strings, Tuba and Orchestra, 2002. First recipient La Guardia Meml. award outstanding achievement field music, 1958, Music award Am. Acad. and Inst. Arts and Letters, 1981, Dutchess County Individual Artist's award, 1991; Nat. Endowment Arts grantee, 1974; Guggenheim fellow, 1974-75; Ford Found. grantee, 1975-76 Mem. ASCAP (mem. Deems Taylor Award com. of judges). E-mail: mkupferman@msn.com.

KUPIETZKY, MOSHE J. lawyer; b. N.Y.C., May 17, 1944; s. Jacob Harry and Fanny (Dresner) K.; m. Arlene Debra Usdan, June 22, 1966; children: Jay, Jeff, Jacob. BBA cum laude, CCNY, 1965; LLB, JD magna cum laude, Harvard U., 1968. Bar: N.Y. 1969, Calif. 1970. Law clerk to Hon. William B. Herlands U.S. Dist. Ct., N.Y.C., 1968-69; assoc. Mitchell Silberberg & Knupp, L.A., Calif., 1969-74, ptnr., 1974-80; ptnr., prin. Hayutin Rubinroit Praw & Kupietzky, L.A., 1980-87; ptnr. Sidley, Austin, Brown & Wood, L.A., 1987—. Bd. dirs. Nat. Inst. Jewish Hospice, Beverly Hills, Calif., 1986-98, L.A. Econ. Devel. Corp.; bd. advisors Graziadio Sch. Bus. and Mgmt. Pepperdine U., L.A., 1996-98. Mem. ABA, Beverly Hills Bar Assn., L.A. County Bar Assn. Office: Sidley Austin Brown & Wood 555 W 5th St Ste 4000 Los Angeles CA 90013-3000 E-mail: mkupietzky@sidley.com.

KUPP, JOHN C. music educator; b. Pottstown, Pa., June 25, 1950; s. John C. and Marguerite (Endy) Kupp. M, Montclair State U., N.J.; B, Susquehanna U., Pa., 1972. Dir. orchestra Bergenfield H.S., NJ, 1972—, tchr. instrumental music; dir. Bergenfield Summer Music Program. Mgr. North Jersey Region I H.S. Orch., North Jersey Region I H.S. Symphonic Band, Bergen County H.S. Band; coord. Bergen County H.S. Band and Choir Festival. Mem.: Music Educators of Bergen County, Am. String Tchrs. Assn. with Nat. Sch. Orch. Assn. Avocations: saxophone, travel. Office: Bergenfield HS 80 S Prospect Ave Bergenfield NJ 07621

KUPPER, KETTI, artist; b. L.A., Oct. 14, 1951; d. Charles Parnell Kupper and Donna Corrine Callen; m. Steven Robert Ford Feb. 9, 1978 (div. Mar. 1994); children: Ashley Elizabeth, Kimberly Brianna. BS, Brigham Young, 1974; student, Acad. Art, San Francisco, 1974-76; MFA in Visual Art, Norwich U., 1994. Freelance painter, illustrator, 1980—; prin., co-owner Fordesign Mktg., Wilton, Conn., 1990-93; chmn. of art U. Bridgeport, 1991-96; ind. cons. Milford, Conn., 1994-98; mentor, tchr. Conn. Commn. Arts, Hartford, Conn., 1996-98; non resident studio tchr. Vt. Coll., Monpelier, 1998—; pres. Exquisite Gardens Landscape Design. Commd. paintings include portrait Clint Murchison for Dallas Times Herald Mag., 1984, Am. Express Olympiadas Barcelona for commercial, 1992, portrait U. Bridgeport Pres. Edwin Eigel, 1995; collections include: Nestle Corp., Ptnrs. Nat. Health Plans, Tex. Instruments; art pub. in Times, Newsweek, Conn. Mag., Dallas Life Mag., Readers Digest. Curator Focus on Environ. U. Bridgeport Coll.; cmty. environ. activist Bridgeport Area Arts Coun.; dir. contest Smithsonian Nat. Mus. Am. Indian, N.Y.C., 1994; grantwriter, mural dir. Conn. commn. Arts, 1995; bd. dirs. Women's Caucus for Art, L.A. Recipient Addy 14th Dist. Region award Am. Adv. Fedn., 1984, Painting award The Discovery Mus., 1995, Painting award Silvermine Artists Guild, 1996, Painting award Artworks Gallery, 1997. Mem. AIA, Coll. Art Assn., Women's Caucus for Arts (chpt. pres. 1996-98), N.Y. Soc. Illustrators, Calif. Lawyers for Arts, Nat. Art Educators Assn., Assn. Profl. Landscape Designers. Democrat. Avocations: writing, gardening, remodeling, construction design. Office: 4208 1/2 Camero Ave Los Angeles CA 90027-4519 E-mail: kettik@sbcglobal.net.

KUPPER, PHILIP LLOYD, chemist; b. Louisville, Ky., Sept. 7, 1940; s. Louis James and Mary Sylvia (Noonan) K.; m. Lynn Anne Abbinanti, Dec. 28, 1968; children: Nicole Marie, Rachel Ann Mary. BS in Chemistry, U. Md., 1963; MBA, Ga. State U., 1970. Tech. counselor Nat. Soft Drink Assn., Washington, 1964-68; dir., rsch. & devel. Moxie Monarch NuGrape, Atlanta, 1968-69; chief chemist GRAF/S Beverages, Milw., 1970-75; rsch. mgr. Crush Internat., Evanston, Ill., 1975-81; flavor chemist Procter & Gamble, Cin., 1981—. Patentee in field. With USAR, 1963-69. Mem. Soc. Flavor Chemists (cert.), Soc. Soft Drink Techs., Inst. Food Tech. Roman Catholic. Avocations: golf, sports, reading. Home: 254 Mystic Ave Cincinnati OH 45216-1404 Office: Procter & Gamble Winton Hill Tech Ctr 6210 Center Hill Ave Cincinnati OH 45224-1797 E-mail: philker7@webtv.net.

KUPPER, THOMAS S. dermatologist, educator; BS, U. of Calif., LA, 1977; MD, Yale U. Sch. of Medicine, LA, 1981. Diplomate Am. Bd. of Dermatology, 1989. Asst. resident in surgery Yale- New Haven Hosp., 1981—83; postdoctoral fellow Yale U. Sch. of Medicine, New Haven, 1983—85, assoc. rsch. scientist, 1985—86, asst. prof. dermatology and surgery, 1987—89; assoc. prof. medicine Wash. U. Sch. of Medicine, St. Louis, 1989—92; TB Fitzpatrick prof. dermatology Harvard Med. Sch., Boston, 1992—; chief divsn. of dermatology Brigham and Women's Hosp., Boston, 1995—2000, chmn. dept. of dermatology, 2000—; resident in dermatology Yale New-Haven Hosp. Dir. Harvard Skin Disease Rsch. Ctr., Boston, 1994—; prin. investigator SPORE in Skin Cancer, Boston, 2001—. Grantee Immunophysiology of Keratinocyte Cytokines, NIH/NIAID, 1989—, Skin Disease Rsch. Ctr., NIH/NIAMS, 1994—, Skin Homing T Cells: Molecular Characterization of CLA, NIH/NIAID, 1997—, SPORE in Skin Cancer, NIH/NCI, 2001—. Office: Brigham and Women's Hosp 75 Francis St Boston MA 02115

KUPPER, WILLIAM P., JR., publishing executive; Mgr. advtsg. sales Sports Illustrated Time, Inc., advtsg. dir. Life mag., internat. advtsg. dir. Time mag.; pub. Health mag., 1992—95; sr. v.p. U.S. advtsg. sales Bus. Week Mc-Graw Hill Cos., New York, 1995-99, pub. Bus. Week, 1999-2000, pres. Bus. Week Group, 2000—, pub. Bus. Week Group, 2000—. Office: The McGraw Hill Cos Inc McGraw Hill Bldg 43rd Fl 1221 Ave of the Americas New York NY 10020-1093

KUPPERMAN, STEPHEN HENRY, lawyer; b. New Orleans, Sept. 17, 1953; s. Abraham Bernard and Jo-Ellyn (Levy) K.; m. Mara Rothstein, Oct. 18, 1980; children: Zachary Hart, Shane Levi, Jake Benjamin. BA, Duke U., 1974; JD, Tulane U., 1977. Bar: La. 1977, U.S. Dist. Ct. (ea. dist.) La. 1977, U.S. Dist. Ct. (mid. dist.) La. 1978, U.S. Dist. Ct. (we. dist.) La. 1981, U.S. Ct. Appeals (5th cir.) 1977, U.S. Ct. Appeals (11th cir.) 1982, U.S. Supreme Ct. 1980. Assoc. Stone Pigman Walther Wittmann & Hutchinson, New Orleans, 1977—81, ptnr., 1981—2003; founding mem. Barrasso Usdin Kupperman Freeman & Sarver, L.L.C., New Orleans, 2003—. Adj. prof. Tulane Law Sch., 1988—; mem. Tulane Law Rev., 1975-77, adv. bd., 1992—. Articles editor Tulane Law Rev., 1976-77, mem. 1975-76; contbr. articles to law revs., profl. jours. Bd. dirs. Goodwill Industries, 1980-87, mem. adv. bd. 1987-91; bd. dirs. Jewish Family Svcs., New Orleans, 1978-93, treas. 1986, v.p. 1987-88, pres., 1988-90; bd. dirs. Jewish Fedn., New Orleans, 1989-93, 95-2001, treas. 1991-93; mem. adv. bd. Jewish Endowment Found., New Orleans, 1979—, Tulane Continuing Legal Edn. Program, 1983—; mem. adv. bd. B'nai B'rith Anti-Defamation League S. Ctrl. Region, 1987—, vice-chmn., 1991-95, chmn. 1995-99; mem. Young Leadership Cabinet United Jewish Appeal, 1990-92; bd. dirs. Touro Infirmary Found., 1998—, Touro Synagogue, New Orleans, 1991-2000, sec. 1995-97, v.p. 1997-99, Touro Infirmary, 2000—, vice-chmn., 2002—. Fellow Am. Bar Found.; mem. ABA, La. Bar Assn. (continuing legal edn. com. 1986-88, disciplinary conduct com. 1995—), New Orleans Bar Assn. (mem. Inn of Ct. 1994—), Fed. Bar Assn. (bd. dirs. New Orleans chpt. 1989-94), Securities Industry Assn., Metro Vision C. of C. (exec. com. 2002-2003), Order of Coif. Democrat. Jewish. Office: Barrasso Usdin Kupperman Freeman and Sarver LLC Ste 1800 909 Poydras St New Orleans LA 70112 E-mail: skupperman@barrassousdin.com.

KUPPERMANN, ARON, physical chemist, educator; b. Sao Paulo, Sao Paulo, Brazil, May 6, 1926; arrived in U.S., 1953, naturalized, 1965; s. Jacob and Mary Kuppermann; m. Roza Davidson, Jan. 21, 1951; children: Baruch, Miriam Kuppermann M, Nathan, Sharon. BSc in Chem. Engring., U. of Sao Paulo, Sao Paulo, SP, Brazil, 1944—48; BSc in Civil Engring., U. of Sao Paulo, Brazil, 1951; PhD, U. of Notre Dame, Notre Dame, Indiana, 1955. Asst. prof. of chemistry Inst. Tech. of Aeronautics, Sao Jose dos Campos, Brazil, 1949—51; instr. of phys. chemistry U. of Ill., Urbana, Ill., 1955—57, asst. prof. of phys. chemistry, 1958—60; rsch. assoc. Inst. Atomic Energy, Sao Paulo, Brazil, 1960—61; assoc. prof. of phys. chemistry U. of Ill., Urbana, Ill., 1961—63; prof. of chem. physics Calif. Inst. of Tech., Pasadena, Calif., 1963—. Cons. Jet Propulsion Lab., Pasadena; cons. World Bank, Washington, 1983—2002; Reilly lectr. U. of Notre Dame, Notre Dame, 1965; Venable lectr. U. of NC, Raleigh, NC, 1967—67; Werner lectrer U. of Kans., Kansas City, 1968; Boys-Rahman lectr. Royal Soc. of Chemistry, London, 1999; Guggenheim fellow Weizmann Inst. of Sci., Rehovot, Israel, 1976—77; fgn. expert Shandong U., Jinan, Shandong, China, 1984—84; Forcheimer vis. prof. Hebrew U., Jerusalem, 1998; mem. adv. bd. Internat. Jour. of Radiation Physics and Chemistry, Washington, 1968—76; mem. editl. bd. Jour. of Phys. Chemistry, Wahington, DC, 1965—70; mem. US-Brazil Sci. Cooperation Panel in Chemistry, Nat. Acad. of Sci., Washington, 1969—73; chmn. US-Brazil Sci. Cooperation Program in Chemistry, NAS, Washington, 1973—76. Bd. dirs. Villa Esperanza, Pasadena, Calif. Recipient Centennial of Sci. award, U. of Notre Dame, 1965. Fellow: Am. Inst. Chemists, Am. Phys. Soc.; mem.: Am. Chem. Soc. Home: 2487 Morslay Rd Altadena CA 91001 Office: California Inst Tech 1201 E California Blvd Pasadena CA 91125

KUPPUSAMY, PERIANNAN, medical educator, medical researcher; b. Apr. 4, 1954; m. Lakshmi Kuppusamy; 2 children. BSc in Math., Physics and Chemistry, U. Madras, India, 1975, MSc in Chemistry, 1977; PhD in Electron Paramagnetic Resonance Spectroscopy, Indian Inst. of Tech., 1985. Lectr. dept. chemistry Pachaiyappa's Coll., Madras, India, 1978—80, asst. prof. dept. chemistry, 1985—86; tchr. fellow dept. chemistry Indian Inst. of Tech., Madras, 1980—85; rsch. fellow divsn. cardiology Johns Hopkins U. Sch. of Medicine, Balt., 1987—90, instr. medicine, 1990—92, asst. prof., asst. dir. dept. medicine, 1992—. Mem. editl. rev. bd.: Shock, Stroke, Magnetic Resonance in Medicine; contbr. articles to profl. jours., chpts. to books. Recipient tchr. fellowship, Univs. Grants Commn., Govt. of India, 1984, Fogarty fellowship, NIH, 1987, rsch. award, Chesapeake Ednl. & Rsch. Trust, 1991. Mem.: Oxygen Soc., Biophys. Soc., NY Acad. Scis., Am. Heart Assn. (Established Investigator award 1996), Am. Chem. Soc. Home: 2910 Brightwater Ln Abingdon MD 21009-1829 Office: Johns Hopkins U Sch Medicine EPR Labs Divsn Cardiology 5501 Hopkins Bayview Cir # 14 Baltimore MD 21224-6821

KUPPUSWAMI, NARMADHA, physician, educator; b. June 7, 1946; MD, U. Madras India, 1971. Bd. cert. ObGyn. Pvt. practice ob-gyn., 1976—; clin. asst. prof. ob-gyn. Chgo. Med. Sch., 1984—88; attending med. staff, vice chmn. dept. ob-gyn. Good Samaritan Hosp., Downers Grove, Ill., chmn. dept. ob-gyn., 2003—. Office: 3825 Highland Ave Downers Grove IL 60515-1552

KUPPUSWAMY, CARTHY, network engineer; b. Madras, TamilNadu, India, Oct. 16, 1977; s. Kuppuswamy Sundaraman and Lalitha Kuppuswamy. B in Mech. Engring., U. Madras, 1999; MS in Indsl. Engring., Okla. State U., 2001. Auto CAD cert. CADD Ctr., Madras, India, 1998. Rsch. asst. Okla. State U., Stillwater, 2000—01, tchg. asst., 2001—01; assoc. network engr. Sprint, Overland Park, Kans., 2002—02, network engr., 2002—. Mem. Indian Student Assn., Stillwater, 2000—01. Scholar, Okla. State U., 2000—01. Mem.: INFORMS (hon.; pres. 2001—01), SAE (assoc.), Soc. Mech. Engrs. (assoc.). Achievements include research in VPN and Data Security; Industrial Enginnering Research for FAA; first to Designed and Implemented a Performance Plan for Sprint; development of Found ways to measure work loads when none existed. Avocations: travel, racquetball, working out, learning, computers. Home: 11602 Stearns St #226 Overland Park KS 66210 Office: Sprint 5454 West 110th St Overland Park KS 66211 Personal E-mail: carthy.kuppuswamy@mail.sprint.com. E-mail: carthy.kuppuswamy@mail.sprint.com.

KUPST, MARY JO, psychologist, researcher; b. Chgo., Oct. 4, 1945; d. George Eugene and Winifred Mary (Hughes) K.; m. Alfred Procter Stresen-Reuter Jr., Aug. 21, 1977. BS, Loyola U., 1967, MA, 1969, PhD, 1972. Lic. psychologist, Ill., Wis. Postdoctoral fellow U. Ill. Med. Ctr., Chgo., 1971—72; rsch. psychologist Children's Meml. Hosp., Chgo., 1972—89; assoc. prof. psychiatry and pediatrics Northwestern U. Med. Sch., Chgo., 1981—89; prof. pediatrics Med. Coll. Wis., Milw., 1989—, dir. pediatric psychology, 1995—. Practice clin. psychology, Chgo., 1975-89, McHenry, Ill., 1987-89; co-chair pediat. oncology group psychology com., 1995-2001, vice chair psychology discipline Children's Oncology Group, 2002—. Editor: (with others) The Child with Cancer, 1980; contbr. articles to profl. jours. V.p. McHenry County Mental Health Bd., 1997—2001. Fellow APA (charter fellow; pres.-elect Divsn. 54); mem. Wis. Psychol. Assn. Office: Med Coll Wis Dept Pediats 8701 W Watertown Plank Rd Milwaukee WI 53226-3548 E-mail: mkupst@mail.mcw.edu.

KUPSTAS, CORRINE LYNN, environmental director, chemical engineer; b. Springfield, Mass., Jan. 25, 1964; d. Richard Paul and Nancy Horridge, Ann Funicello (Stepmother) and Robert Horridge(Stepfather); m. Gregory Kupstas, Jan. 24, 1987; children: Anastasia, Joel. BS in Chem. Engring., U. of RI, 1985. Environ. engr. U.S. EPA, Boston, 1985—89, Monsanto Co., Springfield, Mass., 1989—92, environ. regulatory specialist St. Louis, 1992—94, mfg. supr. Luling, La., 1994—96, roundup bus. unit leader Fayetteville, NC, 1996—98; bus. unit leader Searle/Monsanto Co., Augusta, Ga., 1998—2000; environ. dir. Pharmacia Corp., Kalamazoo, 2000—. Mem., tchr. Richland Bible Ch., Mich., 2000—02. Mem.: Soc. of Women Engrs., AIChE. Avocation: hiking. Home: 3938 Fieldstone Cir Galesburg MI 49053 Office: Pharmacia Corp 7000 Portage Rd Kalamazoo MI 49001 Office Fax: 269-833-8611. Personal E-mail: gjkups@aol.com. E-mail: corrine.l.kupstas@pharmacia.com.

KURAHASHI, YUKO, theater educator; d. Ken and Sumiko Kurahashi. BA in English, Keio U., Tokyo, 1984; MA in English, Waseda U., Tokyo, 1986; MA in Theatre, Ind. U., 1990, PhD in Theater, 1996. Vis. asst. prof. Miami U., Oxford, Ohio, 1999—2001; asst. prof. Kent State U., Kent, Ohio, 2001—. Author: Asian American Culture on Stage: The History of the East West Players; contbr. articles to profl. jours. Fellow, AAUW, 1993—94; Allen Lee Hughes fellow, Arena Stage, 1996—97, Summer Rsch. and Creativity Activity grantee, Kent State U., 2003. Mem.: Assn. Theatre for Higher Edn. (assoc.), Am. Soc. Theatre Rsch. (assoc.).

KURATA, PHILLIP CEDOMIR, journalist; b. Coaldale, Pa., Oct. 28, 1946; s. Fred and Virginia May (Mefford) Kurata; m. Chialing Chang, July 5, 1980 (div. Apr. 1995); 1 child, Shana Rebecca. BA, Kans. U., 1968, MA, 1982. Tchr. English Peace Corps, Tunis, Tunisia, 1968—70; pub. health tchr. Project Hope, Tunis, 1970—71; corr. Far Eastern Econ. Rev., 1979—81, 1979—81, UPI, Hong Kong, 1981—82; editor/translator Agence France-Presse, Paris, 1982—85; journalist Voice of Am., Tokyo, Beijing and Washington, 1985—98; writer U.S. State Dept., Washington, 1998—. Profl. boxer All-Japan Kickboxing Assn., Tokyo, 1972—74. Author: (novels) The Reluctant Agent, 2000 (Fiction prize, Washington Writers' Pub. House, 2000). Bahai. Home: 3409 Pendleton Dr Silver Spring MD 20902

KURATKO, DONALD F. entrepreneur, educator, consultant; b. Chgo., Aug. 27, 1952; s. Donald W. and Margaret M. (Browne) K.; m. Deborah Ann Doyle, Dec. 28, 1979; children: Christina Diane, Kellie Margaret. BA in Econs., John Carroll U., 1974; MS in Mortuary Sci. and Adminstrn., Worsham Coll., 1975; MBA in Mktg.-Mgmt., Benedictine U., 1979; DBA in Small Bus. Mgmt., Nova Southea. U., 1984. Lic. funeral dir., Ill. Prof. bus. Benedictine U., Lisle, 1979-83; prof., exec. dir. entrepreneurship program Ball State U., Muncie, Ind., 1983—, disting. prof., 1990—; funeral dir. Kuratko Funeral Home, North Riverside, Ill., 1975-83. Cons. Kendon Assocs., Riverside, 1983-88, Intrapreneurial Group, 1989—, Acordia, AT&T, GTE, United Techs., Ameritech, Union Carbide Corp.; dir. Pathologists Assocs., Acordia Ctrl. Ind., Ind. monument advisors, Beacon Venture Capital. Author: Management, 1988, 3rd edit., 1991, Effective Small Business Management, 1986, 7th edit., 2001, Entrepreneurship, 1989, 5th edit., 2001, Entrepreneurship and Innovation in the Corporation, 1987; Entrepreneurial Strategy, 1994, The Entrepreneurial Decision, 1997, The Breakthrough Experience, 1998, Strategic Entrepreneurial Growth, 2001, Human Resource Function in Emerging Enterprises, 2002, Corporate Entrepreneurship, 2002; mem. editl. bd. Mid-Am. Bus. Jour., 1985-95, Jour. Bus. Venturing; cons. editor Entrepreneurship Theory & Practice Jour., Small Bus. Forum; contbr. 150 articles in field to profl. jours. Named Outstanding Young Hoosier, Ind. Jaycees, 1985, one of Outstanding Young Men of Am., 1983, 84, #1 Entrepreneurship Program Dir. in USA, Entrepreneur Mag., Disting. Tchg. Professorship, 1990, Stoops Disting Prof. Bus., 1990, Outstanding Univ. Prof., 1996, Entrepreneur of Yr. in Ind., Ernst & Young, Inc. Mag. and Merrill Lynch, 1990; 21st Century Entrepreneurship Rsch. fellow; Disting. scholar U.S. Assn. for Small Bus. and Entrepreneurship, 2003; recipient George Washington medal of honor, 1987, Leavey Found., 1988, Excellence award N.F.I.B. Found., 1993, Nat. Outstanding Entrepreneurship Educator of Yr. award, 1993, Kauffman Found. Entrepreneurship Educator award, 1994, Entrepreneural World of Differences award, 1998, Thomas W. Binford meml award, 2000, Outstanding Rschr. award, 1999; developed nationally-ranked entrepreneurship program, Top 20 Business Week, Top 25 Success Mag., Top 20 Entrepreneur Mag., Top 5 U.S. News and World Report, Nat. Model Prog. award, 1990, Nat. Model Prog. award, grad. level, 1998, Nat. Innovative Pedagogy award, 2001. Mem. U.S. Assn. Small Bus. and Entrepreneurship (pres. 1993-94), Nat. Acad. Mgmt., Internat. Coun. Small Bus., Midwest Bus. Adminstrn. Assn. (pres. entrepreneurship divsn. 1992-93), Nat. Consortium Entrepreneurship Ctrs. Roman Catholic. Avocations: weightlifting, jogging. Home: 2309 N Kensington Way Muncie IN 47304-2484 Office: Ball State U Coll Bus Muncie IN 47306-0001 E-mail: dkuratko@bsu.edu.

KURDI, RAMSEY, music educator; MusM in Edn., New Eng. Conservatory, 1997. Tchr. choral music Worcester (Mass.) Pub. Schs., Worcester, Mass., 1998—. Mem.: Nat. Assn. Music Educators.

KURE, KATSUHIRO, plastic surgeon; b. Nov. 11, 1957; MD, Showa U., Tokyo, 1984. Diplomate Am. Bd. Plastic Surgery, Am. Bd. Pathology. Chief resident in neuropathology Albert Einstein Coll. Medicine, Bronx, N.Y., 1989-90; clin. instr. Showa U., Tokyo, 1990-92; surg. resident U. Hawaii, 1992-93, resident in neurosurgery, 1994-97; chief resident in neurosurgery U. Miami, Fla., 1997-98; resident, chief resident in plastic surgery UCLA, 1998—2000; pvt. practice plastic surgery Beverly Hills, Calif., 2000—. Office: 436 N Roxbury Dr # 207 Beverly Hills CA 90210

KUREPA, ALEXANDRA, mathematician, educator; b. Zagreb, Croatia, Dec. 31, 1956; came to U.S., 1985; d. Svetozar and Zora (Lopac) K.; m. Rodney Anthony Waschka II, June 24, 1988; children: Andre Kurepa Waschka, Lana

Kurepa Waschka. BS, U. Zagreb, 1978, MS, 1982; PhD, U. North Tex., 1987. Asst. prof. math. U. Zagreb, 1987-88, Tex. Christian U., Ft. Worth, 1989-93, N.C. A&T State U., Greensboro, 1993-96, assoc. prof., 1996-2001, prof., 2001—. Author: Matematika 2, 1989, 2000, Matematika 4, 2001; contbr. articles to profl. jours. Rsch. grantee UNESCO, 1988, 89, U.S. Dept. Edn., 1995-2000, Assn. Women in Math.-Nat. Security Agy., 1997-2000, NSF, 1997-2000,2003-, Math. Assn. Am./Tensor Found., 2002, Office Naval Rsch., 2003--. Mem. Am. Math. Soc., Math. Assn. Am., Assn. for Women in Math., Nat. Coun. Tchrs. Math. Office: NC A&T State U Dept Math Greensboro NC 27411-0001 E-mail: kurepa@ncat.edu.

KURFEHS, HAROLD CHARLES, real estate executive; b. Jersey City, Dec. 10, 1939; s. Harold Charles and Matilda Gertrude (Ruschman) Kurfehs; m. Linda Roberta Lepis, Aug. 1, 1964; children: Harold Charles III, Diane E., Robert C. BS (Oaklawn Found. scholar), St. Peter's Coll., 1962; MBA, Wharton Sch. U. Pa., 1964. Product mgr. Am. Brands, Inc., N.Y.C., 1958-62, 64-66, account exec. Benton & Bowles, N.Y.C., 1966-68; account mgr. Wells, Rich, Greene, Inc., N.Y.C., 1968-69; v.p., dir. mktg. Meta-Language Products, Inc., N.Y.C., 1969-70; sr. acct. exec. McCaffrey & McCall, Inc., N.Y.C., 1970-71; dir. advt. Ethan Allen, Inc., N.Y.C., Danbury, Conn., 1971-75; v.p., gen. mgr. retail/franchise divsn. N.Am. Ops. Reed Ltd., Toronto, 1975-76; v.p., gen. mgr. fabric divsn. Reed Nat. Drapery Co. and Sanderson Fabrics, Toronto, 1975-76; pres. Fairfield Book Co., Inc., Harlin House, Ltd., Brookfield, Conn., 1977-83; dir. advt. and pub. rels., bd. dirs., mem. mktg. planning bd. Ethan Allen, Inc., Danbury, Conn., 1983-85; sr. comml. investment broker William Raveis Comml. Investment Real Estate, Danbury, CT, 1985-96; sr. comml. broker Century 21, Scalzo Realty, Inc., Bethel, Conn., 1996—2002; v.p. Coldwell Banker Comml. CCS, 2002—. Lectr. We. Conn. State U., 1985—86; chmn. Real Estate United Way No. Fairfield County, Conn., 1990, 91, account exec., bus. and industry divsn., 2001; mem. policies and procedures com. lead mgmt. Conn. Econ. Resource Ctr., 1995—96; alt. mem. Brookfield Planning Commn., 1997, 98, elected mem., 1999—, vice chmn., 2002—03; ex-officio mem. Brookfield Econ. Devel. Commn., 2002—. Contbr. Named Top Prodr., State of Conn., 1988, 1989, Broker of Month, Conn. Real Estate Jour., 1990, Broker of Yr., Scalzo Comml., 1998, Listing Agt. of Yr., 2001, Broker of Yr., Coldwell Banker Comml., 2002. Mem.: NRA (life), Conn. Assn. Realtors (comml.-investment divsn., regl. treas. 1992, v.p. 1993, 1994, pres. 1995—96, state dir. 1993, 1994, 1998, state sec. 1994, state v.p. 1995, state pres.-elect 1996, state pres. 1997), Wharton Grad. Club N.Y., Pi Sigma Phi. Home: 42 Obtuse Rd N Brookfield CT 06804-3140 Office: 2 Stony Hill Rd Bethel CT 06801-1028

KURFEHS, JOSEPH MORRIS, information security executive; b. Jersey City, N.J., Sept. 21, 1965; s. Frederick Joseph and Maria (Linfante) K.; m. Debra Lynn Kubinak, Oct. 26, 1992; children: Casey Jo, Sydney Lynn, Kaitlyn Taylor. AS in Mgmt., Middlesex County Coll., Edison, N.J., 1989; BS in Mgmt. Sci., Kean U., 1995. Cert. LAN Mgr., Microsoft U. Tax specialist First Investors, Woodbridge, NJ, 1985—86; systems project mgr. Prudential Investments, Edison, 1987—2002; pres., CEO, Info. Security Mgmt., LLC, 2002—. Percussionist, Old Bridge (N.J.) Theater Guild, 1981-88; v.p. Italian Club, Old Bridge, 1982. Recipient Outstanding Sr. Indsl. Edn. award Madison Ctrl. H.S., Old Bridge; recipient Nebisco Art Gallery Expo award for fine art/woodworking, 1994. Mem.: St. Lupo Soc. ((Jersey City), Internat. Sys. Security Assn, Alpha Sigma Lambda Nat. Honor Soc. Republican. Roman Catholic. Avocations: computer games, drums, golf, woodworking. E-mail: SurfKurf@aol.com.

KURIAN, GEORGE THOMAS, publisher; b. Changanacherry, Kerala, India, Aug. 4, 1931; came to U.S., 1968; s. Thomas Kurian and Mary (Abraham) George; m. Annie Cyriack, Aug. 22, 1966; 1 child, Sarah Claudine. MA, Madras (India) Christian Coll., 1951. Dir. Indian Univs. Press, Madras, 1960-68; editor Clarence L. Barnhart, Bronxville, N.Y., 1968-71, Macmillan Inc., N.Y.C., 1971-72; pres. George Kurian Reference Books, Baldwin Place, N.Y., 1972—. Bd. dirs. Fgn. Affairs Info. Svc., Baldwin Place, 1982—. Editor: Ency. of Third World, 1978 (ALA award 1978), World Press Ency., 1982, World Edn. ency., 1988 (ALA award 1988), Ency. of First World, 1990, Ency. of the Future, 1995, World Christian Encyclopedia, 2000, also 10 other encys. and 18 books. Mem. The Encyclopedists: Internat. Ency. Soc. (pres. 1990—), World Future Soc. Republican. Avocation: carpentry. Home: 3689 Campbell Ct Yorktown Heights NY 10598-1808 Office: George Kurian Reference Books PO Box 519 Baldwin Place NY 10505-0519

KURIAN, PIUS, nephrologist, educator; b. Arpookara, Kerala, India, May 9, 1959; s. Pylo and Mariamma Kurian; m. Sally Kurian, May 11, 1986; children: Michelle Maria, Matthew Paul, Catherine Tresa. BSc, Kuriakose (India) Elias Coll., 1979; MB, BChir, Kottayam (India) Med. Coll., India, 1986. Diplomate Am. Bd. Internal Medicine, Am. Bd. Nephrology, Am. Bd. Forensic Examiners; specialist clin. hypertension, Am. Soc. Hypertension. Resident in internal medicine Nassau County Med. Ctr., East Meadow, N.Y., 1988-91, fellow in nephrology, 1991-94; attending physician in nephrology Mercy Med. Ctr. and Cmty. Hosp., Springfield, Ohio, 1994—. Asst. prof. dept. medicine Wright State U., Dayton, Ohio, 1998; chief divsn. internal medicine Mercy Med. Ctr., Springfield, Ohio, 1999, chmn., dir. dept. medicine Mercy Med. Ctr., Springfield, Ohio, 2000; mem. governing bd. Covenant Health Sys.; med. dir. Cmty. Physicians Dialysis, Springfield, 2000—. Fellow ACP; mem. AAAS, AMA, Am. Soc. Hypertension (specialist in clin. hypertension), Am. Soc. Nephrology, Am. Coll. Physicians Execs., Internat. Soc. Nephrology, Renal Physicians Assn., N.Y. Acad. Scis, Am. Diabetes Assn., Nat. Kidney Found. Roman Catholic. Office: 247 S Burnett Rd Springfield OH 45505-2639

KURIEN, SANTHA T. psychiatrist; b. Perumpavoor, Kerala, India, June 15, 1945; came to U.S., 1973; d. Varghese and Mary (Thomas) Koshy; m. Thomas K. Kurien; children: Susan, Miriam. MD, Calicut Med. Coll., Kerala, India, 1970. Diplomate Am. Bd. Psychiatry and Neurology; cert. geriatric psychiatry; cert. addiction psychiatry, clin. psychopharmacology. Sr. house surgeoncy Vellore (Madras) Med. Coll., 1970-71; gen. med. practice St. Thomas Memorial Hosp., Vadasserikara, Kerala, India, 1971-72; psychiat. residency Fairfield Hills Hosp., Newtown, Conn., 1973-76, staff psychiatrist, 1976-77, Danbury (Conn.) Hosp., 1977-82; psychiatrist pvt. practice, Danbury, 1982—. Consulting psychiatrist Pope John Paul Ctr., Danbury, Conn., 1991-2000. Mem. Am. Psychiat. Assn., Am. Assn. Geriatric Psychiatry, New Haven County Med. Assn., Danbury Med. Soc., Assn. Kerala Med. Grads., Am. Soc. Clin. Psychopharmacology (cert.). Office: 27 Hospital Ave Ste 304 Danbury CT 06810-5954

KURILOFF, EFFIE HANNAH, education educator; b. Bklyn., Mar. 31, 1931; d. Morris and Nora Kuriloff; m. Bert Schwarzschild, Aug. 5, 1956 (div. 1986); children: David Mark, Nomi, Daria Ida. BS, N.J. Coll. for Women, 1952; MS, Bank St. Coll., 1954. Cert. tchr., N.Y., Calif. Tchr. Walden Sch., N.Y.C., 1954, Bedford Elem. Sch., Westport, Conn., 1955-56, San Francisco Unified Sch. Dist., 1956-65; instr. child devel. and family studies City Coll., San Francisco, 1965—. Dir., parent educator Mission Cooperative Nursery Sch./Rocky Mountain Participation Nursery Sch., San Francisco, 1965—; cons. in field, 1977—. Author: Maya: A Pre-schooler Meets the Death of Her Father, 1993; featured in documentary film The Tricycle Solution: Teachable Moments for Parents and Preschoolers, 2002. Chair Seward St. Mini-Park, San Francisco, 1975, Mural Project Eureka Valley Promotion Assn., San Francisco, 1977, Children's Fair Castro St. Fair, San Francisco, 1982; homeless educator Episc. Sanctuary Shelter, San Francisco, 1992-99. Recipient Ventures Beneficial to the Cmty. award Mayor of San Francisco, 1976. Mem. Nat. Assn. for Edn. Young Children. Democrat. Jewish. Avocations: pottery, singing, gardening, painting, hiking. Home: 363 Douglass St San Francisco CA 94114-2432 Office: Rocky Mountain Participation Nursery Sch 2475 15th St San Francisco CA 94114-1225

KURILOFF, EMILY ANNE, psychologist, educator; b. N.Y.C., Apr. 10, 1959; d. Myron Abraham and Ruth (Benn) Wassell; m. Daniel Benjamin Kuriloff, Aug. 28, 1983; children: Allison, Melissa. AB, Vassar Coll., 1980; D in Psychology, Yeshiva U., 1985; cert. psychoanalysis, William A. White Inst., 1997. Lic. psychologist N.Y. Intern Postgrad. Ctr., 1984—85; therapist, supr. N.Y. Foundling Hosp., 1986—89; supr., faculty William A. White Inst., N.Y.C., 1997—. Faculty, supr. Inst. Contemporary Psychotherapy, N.Y.C., 1999—; supr., adj. assoc. clin. prof. Tchrs. Coll. Columbia U., N.Y.C., 1997—; adj. asst. prof. Psychology New Sch. Social Rsch., N.Y.C., 1987—90. Contbr. Mem.: APA, Inst. Contemporary Psychotherapy, Phi Beta Kappa. Democrat. Jewish. Home: 43 Hawkes Close Irvington NY 10533 Office: 5 W 86th St 1BB New York NY 10024

KURIN, RICHARD, museum program director; b. Bronx, N.Y., Nov. 27, 1950; m. Allyn Bland; children: Danielle, Jaclyn. BA, SUNY, 1972; MA in Anthropology, U. Chgo., 1974; cert. in Urdu lang., U. Calif., Berkeley, 1974; PhD in Anthropology, U. Chgo., 1981. Vis. asst. prof. dept. anthropology So. Ill. U., Carbondale, 1981-84, asst. prof., 1984-85; program coord., curator, cons. Festival of India, Aditi & Mela Exhbns., Smithsonian Instn., Washington, 1984-85; chair 150th Anniversary Program Com. Smithsonian Instn., Washington, 1993—, chair deciduous group, 1997-98, dep. dir. Ctr. for Folklife Programs & Cultural Studies, 1985-87, acting dir., 1987-90, dir., 1990—; professorial lectr. Johns Hopkins U., Paul Nitze Sch. Adv. Internat. Studies, 1985-95. Collector Am. Mus. Natural History, Punjabi Indian village artifacts, 1970; vis. instr. cmty. devel. program So. Ill. U., Carbondale, 1979-81; program coord. Indian Puppetry Program, Smithsonian Instn., 1980, cons. anthropologist Harza Engring. Co., UNDP and World Bank, Indus Basin Master Planning Project, 1977; ethnic tours mgr. divsn. performing arts On-Tour India Program, Pakistan Program, Smithsonian Instn., 1976; cons. anthropologist U. Karachi, U.S. HEW Family Planning Project, 1977; mem. adv. bd. Coun. Overseas Rsch. Ctrs., 1989; adj. prof. George Washington U., 1999. Author: Aditi: The Living Arts of India, 1986, Reflections of a Culture Broker: A View From the Smithsonian, 1997, Smithsonian Folklife Festival: Culture Of, By, and For the People, 1998; (film) Aditi: The Living Arts of India, 1986; lead writer, organizer: Iowa Folklife: Our People, Traditions and Communities, 1996-97; advisor film: Jerusalem: Gateways to the City, 1995, Hosay: Muslim Transnationalism in Trinidad, 1994—, White House Workers, 1994; edtl. advisor film Kathputli: An Indian Puppetry Tradition, 1986—; recs. Smithsonian Folkways Records, 1986—. Bd. trustees, Smithsonian Sec.'s Rep., Libr. of Congress, Am. Folklore Ctr., 1989—; trustee Am. Pakistan Rsch. Orgn., 1989—; mem. Fairfax County Citizen Assn. Edn. Com., 1991—; pres. Bailey's Elem. Sch. P.T.A., 1989-91. Recipient fellowships NDEA, Title VI, 1973, Fulbright-Hayes, HEW, 1976, Social Sci. Rsch. Coun., 1976, 83, Am. Inst. Pakistan Studies, 1983, Sec.'s Gold medal for exceptional svc. Smithsonian Instn., 1996; grantee, Smithsonian Instn., 1979, 86, 89, 90, 92, 95, 96, NEH, 1982, 1991—, Nat. Endowment Arts, 1987. Fellow Soc. Applied Anthropology; mem. Am. Folklore Soc. (Benjamin Botkin lifetime achievement award 1999), Am. Ethnological Soc., Assn. Asian Studies, Am. Anthropol. Assn. Office: Ctr Folklife & Cultural Heritage Smithsonian Instn Washington DC 20560-0953 E-mail: kurin@folklife.si.edu.

KURIT, NEIL, lawyer; b. Cleve., Aug. 31, 1940; s. Jay and Rose (Rainin) K.; m. Doris Tannenbaum, Aug. 9, 1964 (div.); m. Donna Chernin, Aug. 24, 1986. BS, Miami U., Oxford, Ohio, 1961; JD, Case Western Res. U., 1964. Bar: Ohio 1964. Prin. Kahn, Kleinman, Yanowitz & Arnson Co., L.P.A., Cleve., 1964—. Co-author Handbook for Attys. and Accts., Jewish Cmty. Fedn. Endowment Fund. Trustee, v.p. Montefiore Home, 1983-87; trustee Jewish Cmty. Fedn. Cleve., 1983-86, 90-95. Mem. ABA, Ohio State Bar Assn. Home: 2870 Courtland Blvd Cleveland OH 44122-2802 Office: Kahn Kleinman Yanowitz & Arnson Co LPA 2600 Tower at Erieview Cleveland OH 44114 E-mail: nkurit@kahnkleinman.com

KURITA, KYOKO, education educator; m. Jamies Ezra Lipson, June 24, 1980. PhD, Yale U., 1982—90. Assoc. prof. Pomona Coll., Claremont, Calif., 1990—. Fellow Rsch. Fellowships, Japan Found., SSRC, 1997-8; 2001-2. Mem.: MLA (assoc.), AAS (assoc.). Office: Pomona Coll 550 N Harvard Ave Claremont CA 91711

KURK, KATHERINE CHENAULT, education educator; d. Victor John Kurk and Elizabeth Dean Guy. BA, U. of Ky., 1968—72, MA, 1972—74, PhD, 1974—79. Asst. prof. Drury Coll., Springfield, Mo., 1979—84; dir. Le Village Francais, Springfield, Mo., 1980—84; assoc. prof. Drury Coll., Springfield, Mo., 1983—84; asst. prof. No. Ky. U., Highland Heights, 1986—90, assoc. prof., 1990—97; vis. assoc. prof. Davidson Coll., NC, 1994, U. of Ky., Lexington; french ap and ib prof. Holmes H.S., Covington, Ky., 2002; prof. of modern languages No. Ky. U., Highland Heights, 1997—. Editor: French Forum Inc., 1984—2000; asst. editor Ky. Philol Rev., 1990—. Mem.: Ky. Philol Assn. (exec. com., editor 1990—2003), Am. Assn. of Teachers of French Nat. Fgn. Languages in the Elem. Sch. Commn. (assoc.). Independent. Avocation: gardening. Office: Northern Kentucky University Dept of Lit & Language Highland Heights KY 41099

KURK, MITCHELL, physician; b. N.Y.C., Aug. 25, 1931; s. Benjamin and Frieda (Steinbaum) K.; m. Marcia Carol Leon (dec. 1981); children: Hope, Nancy, Cindy. BS, MS, Columbia U., 1954; OD, Mass. Coll. Optometry, 1955; DO, Phila. Coll. Osteopathic, 1960; MD, U. Calif., 1962. Diplomate Am. Bd. Family Practice. Pvt. practice, N.Y.C., 1962—. Attending physician Peninsula Hosp. Ctr. Author: Prescription for a Long Life, 1997. Fellow Internat. Coll. Applied Nutrition, Am. Acad. Family Physicians; mem. Internat. Acad. Preventive Medicine, Am. Holistic Med. Assn., AMA, N.Y. State Med. Soc., Nassau County Med. Soc., Nassau Acad. Medicine. Republican.

KURKUL, WENYI WANG, musician, educator, administrator; b. Taipei, Taiwan, Oct. 30, 1964; arrived in U.S., 1986; d. Shih-Ming and Hsieh-Chu Wang. MusM, Ohio U., 1988; MusD, U. Mo., 1995; D in Music Edn., Ind. U., 2000. Prof., adminstr. Sch. Music Tainan (Taiwan) Coll., 1989-92; prof. Nat. Taiwan Acad. Arts, 1989-92, Nat Sun Yat-Sen U., Kaohsiung, Taiwan, 1990-92; mem. vis. faculty Sch. Music Ind. U., Bloomington, 1999—2000; prof. dept. music George Mason U., 2000—03, dir. music edn. dept. music Coll. Visual and Performing Arts, 2001—03, exec. dir. Orff Schulwerk Tchr. Tng. and Cert. Program, 2001—03. Soloist-in-residence Nat. Chiang Kai Shek Cultural Ctr., Taipei, 1991-94; flutist Asian Composers League, Taipei, 1990-92; asst. prin. flutist Taiwan Symphony Orch., Taichung, 1984-86; contbr. articles to profl. publs. Nat. Art and Sci. Coun. scholar, Taiwan, 1989-92; Nat. rsch. grantee Ministry of Edn., Taiwan, 1989-92; named New Performing Star of Yr. Nat. Theatre and Concert Hall Planning and Mgmt. Coun., Taiwan, 1991. Mem.: APA, AAUP, Internat. Soc. Philosophy Music Edn. (founding), Pub. Rels. Soc. Am., Am. Edml. Rsch. Assn., Am. Orff-Schulwerk Assn., Internat. Soc. for Music Edn. (Eng.), European Recorder Tchrs. Assn., Soc. for Rsch. in Music Edn., Music Edn. Nat. Conf., Coll. Music Soc., Nat. Flute Assn. (life), Phi Kappa Lambda. Home: 10716 Kings Riding Way Ste 102 Rockville MD 20852 E-mail: wkurkul@gmu.edu.

KURLAN, MARVIN ZEFT, surgeon, educator; b. Wilkes-Barre, Pa., Feb. 20, 1934; s. Ephraigm Joseph and Fannye Lillian Kurlancheek; m. Eleanor Frank, June 21, 1964; 1 child, Todd. BA, Wilkes Coll., 1957; MS, U. Ill., 1958; MD, SUNY, Buffalo, 1964. Diplomate Nat. Bd. Med. Examiners, Am. Bd. Surgery. Intern then resident in surgery Millard Fillmore Hosp., Buffalo, 1964-69, dir. trauma svcs., 1974-82, sr. attending surgeon, 1984-95; surgeon emeritus, 1995—; plant surgeon Bethlehem (Pa.) Steel Corp., 1969-74; med. dir. Bros. of Mercy Health Facilities, Clarence, N.Y., 1974-82. Assoc. examiner Am. Bd. Surgery, Phila., 1987-95; chmn. James Platt White Soc., Sch. Medicine and Biomed. Scis., SUNY, Buffalo, 1992-94 (Dean's adv. coun., 1995-97); cons. in surgery Walter Reed Army Med. Ctr., Washington. Contbr. articles to profl. jours. Vol. Empire State Games, Buffalo, 1986; mem. Jack Kemp Forum, Buffalo, 1985-91; bd. dirs. Jewish Fedn. Allentown, Pa., 1972-74. Served AUS (res.) to lt. col. Med. Corps, 1965-91, active duty operation Desert Shield and Desert Storm. Decorated Army Svc. medal with Oak Leaf Cluster, Army Achievement medal. Fellow Am. Coll. Gastroenterology, Am. Trauma Soc. (founder), N.Y. Acad. Scis.; mem. ACS (life fellow leadership soc.), Assn. Mil. Surgeons U.S., Hastings on Hudson Bioethics Ctr., Buffalo Surg. Soc. (sec. 1986-88, v.p. 1988-89, pres. 1989-90), SUNY at Buffalo Found. (pres.'s assoc.), Grand Coun. World Parliament, Confedn. Chivalry, Knight of Humanity, Order White Cross Internat. (dist. comdr. N.Y., U.S.), Chevalier Grand Cross, Ordre Soverain et Militaire de Milice du St. Sepulcre, Phi Lambda Kappa (nat. pres. 1993), Nu Sigma Nu. Clubs: Sci. Progress Research (Buffalo) (v.p. 1983-84). Lodges: Masons, Shriners. Republican. Avocation: world travel. Home and Office: 413 Dan Troy Dr Buffalo NY 14221-3558

KURLAND, HAROLD ARTHUR, lawyer; b. N.Y.C., Jan. 20, 1952; s. Jordan Emil and Anita (Siegel) K.; m. Christine Rogers, June 28, 1975; children: Thomas Philip, Andrew Rogers. AB, Dartmouth Coll., 1973; JD, Cornell U., 1976. Bar: N.Y. 1977, D.C. 1977, U.S. Dist. Ct. (we. dist.) N.Y. 1977, U.S. Dist. Ct. (no. dist.) N.Y. 1983, U.S. Dist. Ct. (no. dist.) Tex. 1981, U.S. Ct. Appeals (2d cir.) 1980, U.S. Dist. Ct. (D.C. dist.) 1986, U.S. Ct. Appeals (D.C. cir.) 1986, U.S Ct. Appeals (3d cir.) 1988, U.S. Dist. Ct. (mid. dist.) Pa. 1988, U.S. Dist. Ct. (ea. and so. dists.) N.Y. 1991, U.S. Supreme Ct. 1980. Assoc. Nixon, Hargrave, Devans & Doyle LLP (now Nixon Peabody LLP), Rochester, N.Y., 1976-84, ptnr., 1985-2000; founding ptnr. Ward Norris Heller & Reidy LLP, Rochester, 2000—. Mediator, arbitrator Am. Arbitration Assn.; mem. adv. com. on civil practice N.Y. Office Ct. Adminstrn. Past chmn. bd. dirs. Rochester Philharm. Orch.; bd. dirs. Vol. Legal Svcs. Project. Mem. ABA, N.Y. State Bar Assn., D.C. Bar Assn., Monroe County Bar Assn. (chair judicary com., past. chmn. cts. com., fed. ct. com., exec. com., trustee), Rochester Inn of Ct. (past. pres., master), Am. Bd. Trial Advocates (assoc.). Democrat. Home: 154 Council Rock Ave Rochester NY 14610-3335 Office: Ward Norris Heller & Reidy LLP 300 State St Rochester NY 14614 E-mail: hak@wnhr.com.

KURLAND, PAUL CARL, lawyer, educator; b. Bklyn., May 28, 1946; s. Marvin and Beatrice (Marmer) K.; m. Phyllis Pfeffer, Sept. 1, 1968; children: Joshua Ethan, Abigail Sara. BA, Bklyn. Coll., 1967; JD, NYU, 1970. Bar: N.Y. 1971, U.S. Ct. Appeals (2d cir.) 1971, U.S. Dist. Ct. (so. and ea. dists.) N.Y. 1972, U.S. Supreme Ct. 1974. Assoc. Cahill, Gordon & Reindel, N.Y.C., 1970-73, Emil, Korbin, Klein & Garbus, N.Y.C., 1973-77; ptnr. Kurland and Scheiman, N.Y.C., 1977-79, Baer, Marks & Upham, N.Y.C., 1979-85, Snow, Becker & Krauss, P.C., N.Y.C., 1986—. Mem. faculty Nat. Inst. Trial Advocacy, 1980—, faculty trial techniques program Hofstra U., 1980—, Emory U., 1982-91, Cardozo Law Sch., 1987—; arbitrator U.S. Dist. Ct. (ea. dist.) N.Y., Am. Arbitration Assn. Pres. Manhasset (N.Y.) Dem. Club; mem. Nassau County Dem. Com.; bd. dirs. World Hunger Yr.; bd. dirs. Sing Out mag., 1998-2000. Mem. ACLU, ABA, Assn. Bar City of N.Y., N.Y. U. Law Sch. Alumni Assn. (v.p. bd. dirs.). Home: 142 Hemlock Rd Manhasset NY 11030-1216 Office: Snow Becker Krauss PC 605 3rd Ave Fl 25 New York NY 10158-0125 E-mail: pkurland@sbklaw.com.

KURLANDER, HONEY WACHTEL, artist, educator; b. Bklyn. d. Charles Bernard and Sara F. (Alexander) Wachtel; m. Neale Kurlander, June 25, 1949; children: Harold Michael, Susan Laurie. Student, Parsons Sch. Design; cert. in illustration, Pratt Inst., 1948. Freelance textile designer, N.Y.C., 1948-58; freelance children's book illustrator, 1950-60; art instr. East Meadow (N.Y.) High Sch., 1958-60, Kurlander Studio, East Meadow, 1958-79, Kurlander Art Studio, Old Westbury, N.Y., 1979-2000. Exhibited in one-man shows at Garden City (N.Y.) Galleries Ltd., 1960-90, Robley Gallery, Roslyn, N.Y., 1971, Madison Ave. Gallery, N.Y.C., 1975, Salmagundi Club, N.Y.C., 1978, Gallerie Marcel Bernheim, Paris, Kaigado Gallery, Tokyo; executed mural Astoria Queens, 1985, mural Oyster Bay-East Norwich Libr., 1998, poster Centennial Celebration of Statue of Liberty; represented in permanent collections at Dietz Mus., Wasserberg, Germany, C.W. Post Coll. Art Ctr., Brookville, N.Y., DeSeversky Conf. Ctr., Greenvale, N.Y. Recipient 1st prize Heckscher Mus., 1966; 1st prize Eastern Regional Exhibit, 1968. Mem. Nat. League Am. Penwomen (Best in Show award 1978, 81, 84, 90, 95, awards 1962—, Nat. Biennial 2000), Art League Nassau County, Salmagundi Club (Williams award 1979). Avocations: photography, gardening, sewing, travel. Home: Kurlander Studio 6185 Wooded Run Dr Columbia MD 21044

KURLANDER, NEALE, accounting and law educator, lawyer; b. Bklyn., Jan. 1, 1924; s. Sol and Eleanor Kurlander; m. Honey Wachtel, June 25, 1949; children: Harold M., Susan L. BS, Long Island U., 1948; JD, N.Y. Law Sch., N.Y.C., 1951; MBA, Adelphi U., 1967. Bar: N.Y. 1952; CPA, N.Y. V.p., chief fin. officer Profit Motivation Svcs., Inc., Garden City, N.Y., 1967-71; cons.-reviewer Ernst & Ernst, Garden City, 1967-72; lectr. Practicing Law Inst., N.Y.C., 1974; chmn. dept. accting and law Adelphi U., Garden City, 1964-82; cons. Regent's External Degree, Albany, N.Y., 1974-87; pvt. practice law Old Westbury, N.Y., 1952—; pvt. practice acct., CPA, 1960—; prof. acctg. and law Adelphi U., Garden City, 1962—. Profl. developer Harris, Kerr, Forster & Co., N.Y.C., 1969-71, treas. Fin. Execs. Inst., Long Island, N.Y., 1974-76, chmn. acad. rels., 1975—, bd. dirs. 1975—; faculty Found. for Acctg. Edn., 1975—, bd. trustees, 1976-79. Author: Basic Accounting, 1962, Auditing, Vol. I and II, 1978; contbr. articles to profl. jours. Cmdr. post 6081 VFW, Bklyn., 1953-54; mem. Bd. Elections, Nassau County, N.Y., 1964-70, Citizens' Adv. Com. N.Y. State Dept. Taxation, Albany, 1975-87, Bd. Appeals, Old Westbury, 1988-93; legis. adv. coun. N.Y. State Assembly 15th Dist., 1991-93. Recipient cert. Delta Mu Delta, 1982, Dr. Emanuel Saxe Outstanding CPA in Edn. award N.Y. State Soc. Cert. Pub. Accts., 2000; named Outstanding Acctg. Educator, Found. for Acctg. Edn., N.Y., 1982, Acct. of Yr. Acctg. Soc., 1992. Mem. AICPA, N.Y. State Soc. CPA's (Dr. Emanuel Saxe Outstanding CPA in Edn. award 2000), Am. Acctg. Assn., Nassau County Bar Assn., N.Y. State Assembly 15th Dist. (legis. adv. coun.). Avocations: reading, woodworking, traveling, walking, swimming. Home: 6185 Wooded Run Dr Columbia MD 21044 E-mail: nkurlander@aol.com.

KURLINSKI, JOHN PARKER, physician; b. Buchanon, W.Va., Jan. 17, 1948; s. John Peter and Jean (Holloway) K.; m. Claire Sawyer, June 12, 1971; children: Joshua John, Ryan Edward, Seth Parker. AB cum laude, Williams Coll., 1970; MD, Johns Hopkins Sch. Medicine, 1974. Intern, then resident Johns Hopkins Hosp., Balt., 1974-77; fellowship neonatal/perinatal medicine U. Calif., San Diego, 1977-79; chief resident pediatrician Johns Hopkins Hosp., 1979-80; pediatrician, co-dir. neonatology S.W. Regional Neonatal Ctr. at Sunrise Hosp. and Med. Ctr., Las Vegas, 1980-93; vice chief pediat. Sunrise Children's Hosp., Las Vegas, 1983-90, vice chief of staff, 1989-90, chief of staff, 1990-95, dir. NICU, 1994—2002; clin. assoc. prof. pediatrics U. Nev. Sch. Medicine, Reno, 1994—. Bd. dirs. S.W. Regional Neonatal Ctr. Edn. Found.; chmn. bd. dirs. Sunrise Children's Hosp. Found.; mem. Med.-Legal Screening Panel, Nev., 1986—; many hosp. coms., 1980—. Bd. dirs. So Nev. chpt. March of Dimes, Las. Vegas, 1984—. Mem. AMA, Am. Acad. Pediatrics (v.p. Nev. chpt. 1987-90, pres. 1990-93, coun. mem. dist. VIII sect. on perinatal pediatrics), Clark County Med. Soc., Las Vegas Pediatric Soc. (founding), Phi Beta Kappa. Avocations: rugby, skiing, hiking, camping. Home: 3322 Beam Dr Las Vegas NV 89139-5902 Office: Sunrise Childrens Hosp 3186 S Maryland Pky Las Vegas NV 89109-2317 E-mail: kurli@lvcm.com.

KURMAN, JUTA, educator; b. Wändra, Parnu, Estonia, Nov. 7, 1912; d. August and Maria (Reier) Tomberg; m. Alexander Pooman, Sept. 17, 1938 (dec. 1938); m. Hugo Kurman, Jan. 18, 1940; children: Jaan, Juri-George. Tchrs. Lic., Tchrs. Sem., Estonia, 1934; Artist Dipl., State Conservatory of Music, Estonia, 1940, N.Y. Coll. of Music, 1952. Tchr. Tallinn (Estonia) Pub. Schs., 1934-38; performing artist concerts, state radio, and theater Estonia, 1932-40; TV voice soloist Maj. Bowes Original Amateur Hour, Radio City, N.Y., 1949-50; with Claire Mann Show, Channel 5, N.Y.C., 1952; pres. Estonian Music Ctr., N.Y.C., 1973—. Club and ch. soloist; lectr in field; music critic Free Estonian Word, 1948—, Baltic Papers. Co-editor: Haapsalu Shawl, 1972, Kompiling Mart Saar VocalAlbum, 1965, Kompiling Kaljo Raid Estonian Volksongs Album, 1991; contbr. articles to profl. jurs. Sustaining mem. Rep. Nat. Com., 1990—; sustaining sponsor Ronald Reagan Presdl. Found., 1987—. Named Laureate of Estonian Letters and Scis. Found.; N.Y. Coll. Music grantee, 1948. Mem. Estonian Music Sorority (pres. 1951-63), Estonian Women's Club of N.Y. (pres.), Estonian Ednl. Soc. (hon. mem. elders coun.), World Fedn. Estonian Women's Clubs in Exile (West) (founding pres. 1966—). Republican. Lutheran. Avocations: music, poetry, writing, gardening. Home: 68-50 Juno St Forest Hills NY 11375-5728 Office: Estonian Music Ctr 243 E 34th St New York NY 10016-4852

KURN, NEAL, lawyer; b. Springfield, Mass., July 19, 1934; s. Samuel and Jane Etta (Freeman) K.; m. Barbara Agron, June 9, 1957; children: Jeffrey Howard, Sharon Ilene Marcus-Kurn, Jennifer Rose Endsley. BSBA with high honors, U. Ariz., 1956, JD with honors, 1963. Bar: Ariz. 1963; cert. specialist tax and estate and trust law, Ariz.; CPA, Ariz. Staff mem. Price Waterhouse & Co., San Francisco, L.A. and Phoenix, 1956, 58-60; assoc., ptnr. Moore, Romley, Kaplan, Robbins & Green, Phoenix, 1963-71; ptnr. Powers, Ehrenreich, Boutell & Kurn, Phoenix, 1971-82; ptnr., also bd. dirs. Fennemore Craig, Phoenix, 1982—. Adj. prof. law Ariz. State U., 1980-82. Editor-in-chief Ariz. Law Rev., 1962-63. Past chmn. tax adv. commn. Ariz. State Bd. Legal

Specialization; bd. dirs. Ariz. Cmty. Found., 1986—, chmn. 1994-96; bd. dirs. Ariz. Bar Found., 1983-89, chmn., 1988; bd. dirs. Jewish Fedn. Greater Phoenix, pres., 1977-79; bd. dirs. U. Ariz. Found., 1998—; bd. visitors U. Ariz. Law Sch.; v.p. coun. Jewish Fedn., 1988-90; chmn. Jewish Cmty. Found. Greater Phoenix, 1998-2001; bd. dirs. Trust for Jewish Philanthropy, 2000-2003; chmn. adv. bd. Leave a Legacy, State of Ariz., 2001—. With U.S. Army, 1956-58. Fellow Am. Coll. Tax Counsel, Am. Bar Found., Am. Coll. Trust and Estate Counsel; mem. ABA, State Bar Ariz. (past chmn. taxation sect., bd. govs. 1991-93), Maricopa County Bar Assn., Phi Kappa Phi, Beta Gamma Sigma. Democrat. Jewish. Office: Fennemore Craig 3003 N Central Ave Ste 2600 Phoenix AZ 85012-2913 E-mail: nkurn@fclaw.com.

KURNICK, NATHANIEL BERTRAND, retired oncologist-hematologist; b. N.Y.C., Nov. 8, 1917; s. Jacob and Celia (Levine) K.; m. Dorothy Manheimber, Oct. 4, 1940 (dec. Dec. 1985); children: John E., Katherine(dec.), James T.; m. Sally Ann Kreeger, June 23, 1989. BA, Harvard U., 1936, MD, 1940. Diplomate Am. Bd. Internal Medicine, Am. Bd. Med. Oncology, Am. Bd. Hematology, Am. Bd. Med. Examiners. Intern Mt. Sinai Hosp., N.Y.C., 1941-42, chief resident internal medicine, 1946; asst. prof. medicine Tulane U. Med. Sch., New Orleans, 1949-54; chief hematology svc. VA Hosp., Long Beach, Calif., 1954-59, cons., 1959—; assoc. clin. prof. medicine U. Calif., L.A., 1954-64, clin. prof. medicine Irvine, 1964-99; pvt. practice Long Beach, 1959-83; dir. Bixby Hematology-Oncology Lab. Long Beach Cmty. Med. Ctr., 1982—99. Chmn. cancer activities, 1968—90; chmn. dept. medicine, 1966—68; chmn. dept. med. oncology and hematology, 1982—87; pres. Long Beach Soc. Internal Medicine, 1971; chmn. Franklin Bank of Calif., Orange, Calif., 1988—. Contbr. articles to jours. in field. Trustee Garden Grove, Calif. Union High Sch.Dist., 1960-64. Capt. M.C., U.S. Army, 1942-46. Am. Cancer Soc./NRC fellow, 1946-47, Rockefeller Inst., 1946-47, Nobel Inst., 1947-49; NIH/Am. Cancer Soc. grantee, 1949-1972; Henry Hunter Workman rsch. fellow Harvard Med. Sch./Mass. Gen. Hosp., 1940-41. Fellow ACP; mem. Intern. Soc. Exptl. Hematology, Am. Soc. Hematology, Western Soc. Clin. Rsch., Cen. Soc. Clin. Rsch., Sigma Xi (fellow 1951). Democrat. Jewish. Avocations: sailing, skiing, travel. E-mail: nbkurnick@post.harvard.com.

KURNIT, RICHARD ALAN, lawyer, educator; b. N.Y.C., Mar. 22, 1951; s. Shepard and Jean (Zinsher) Kurnit; m. Diane Ruth Katzin, Sept. 9, 1979; 1 child, Katrina. AB magna cum laude, Columbia U., 1972; JD cum laude, Harvard U., 1975. Bar: N.Y. 1976, U.S. Dist. Ct. (so. dist.) N.Y. 1976, U.S. Ct. Appeals (D.C. cir.) 1977, U.S. Ct. Appeals (2d cir.) 1978, U.S. Supreme Ct. 1980, U.S. Dist. Ct. (ea. dist.) N.Y. 1981. Law clk. to Thomas P. Griesa U.S. Dist. Ct. (so. dist.) N.Y., N.Y.C., 1975-76; assoc. Paul, Weiss, Rifkind, Wharton & Garrison, N.Y.C., 1976-81; ptnr. Frankfurt Kurnit Klein & Selz, N.Y.C., 1981—. Instr. advt. law New Sch., N.Y.C., 1981—; lectr. Am. Assn./Advt. Agys., ABA, Am. Promotional Mktg. Assn., ALI, 1985—, Am. Advt. Fedn., 1988—. Author: Libel Claims Based on Fiction, 1985. Recipient Citizens Communications Ctr. award, 1975. Mem. ABA., N.Y.C. Bar Assn. (advt. industry subcom.), Phi Beta Kappa. Home: 110 Riverside Dr Apt 16F New York NY 10024-3734 Office: Frankfurt Kurnit Klein & Selz 488 Madison Ave Fl 9 New York NY 10022-5754

KURNOW, ERNEST, statistician, educator; b. Bklyn., Oct. 21, 1912; s. Harry and Sarah Malka (Shagaloff) K.; m. Joyce Litzky, Oct. 6, 1938; children: Ruth (Mrs. Jeffrey Jarrett), Susan Carol (Mrs. Leonard Weistrop), Alice Rose (Mrs. Claude Morin). BS cum laude, CCNY, 1932, MS in Edn, 1933; PhD, NYU, 1951. Tchr. N.Y.C. Bd. Edn., 1935-40, statistician, 1941-48; mathematician ordnance div. War Dept., 1940-41; mem. faculty NYU, 1948—, prof. econs., 1960-63, prof. bus. stats., chmn. dept., 1963-86, prof. emeritus bus. stats., adj. prof. bus. stats., 1986—, chmn. dept., 1963-76; chmn. doctoral program N.Y. U., 1976-85, dir. Careers in Bus. program, 1979-88. Cons. N.Y. State Tax Structure Study Commn., 1959—64, Mayor N.Y.C. Com. Mgmt. Survey, 1950-51, Turkish Ministry Finance, 1955-56; cons. temporary commn. Revision N.Y. State Constn., 1958; temporary commn. fiscal affairs N.Y. State Govt., 1953-54; cons. Tri-State Transp. Commn., 1964-66, 73-75; participant Brazilian capital markets program, 1968; study dir. Govs.' Spl. Commn. on Financing Mass Transp., 1970-71; cons. Commn. on Charter Revision, City of N.Y., 1973-74, Temporary Commn. on City Finances, 1975-76 Author: The Turkish Budgetary Process, 1956; also articles. Statistics for Business Decisions, 1959, Theory and Measurement of Land Rent, 1961. Recipient Gt. Tchr. award NYU Alumni Assn., 1974; named Tchr. of Yr., 1999-2000; Fulbright grantee to Greece, 1966-67; Kurnow Classroom established in his honor, NYU, 1993. Fellow Am. Statis. Assn.; mem. Internat. Statis. Inst. (elected), Am. Econ. Assn., Econometric Soc., Inst. Mgmt. Scis., Nat. Tax Assn., Am. Soc. Quality Control, Sphinx, Beta Gamma Sigma, Sigma Eta Phi, Delta Pi Sigma, Alpha Phi Sigma, Delta Sigma Pi. Jewish. Home: 3 Washington Square Vlg Apt 17I New York NY 10012-1810 Office: New York Univ Dept Stats Washington Sq N New York NY 10003-6635 E-mail: ekurnow@stern.nyu.edu.

KURODA, YASUMASA, political science educator, researcher; b. Tokyo, Apr. 28, 1931; arrived in U.S., 1951; s. Shohei and Take (Ishii) Kuroda; m. Alice Kassis, Mar. 21, 1961 (div. Mar. 1995); children: Kamilla, Kamil; m. Miyoko Otaguro, Aug. 14, 1998. Student, Waseda U., 1951; BA, U. Oreg., 1956, MA, 1958, PhD, 1962. From instr. to asst. prof. polit. sci. Mont. State U., Bozeman, 1960-64; asst. prof. polit. sci. U. So. Calif., L.A., 1964-66; assoc. program officer advanced projects East-West Ctr., Honolulu, 1967-69; assoc. prof. U. Hawaii-Manoa, Honolulu, 1969—71, prof. polit. sci., 1971—2002, prof. emeritus, 2002—; lectr. Japan-Am. Inst. Mgmt. Sci., Honolulu, 1973-90; pres. Election Svcs. Hawaii, Inc., 1996—2001; exch. rschr. Waseda U., Tokyo, 2002—. V.p. Minerva Rsch., Inc., Honolulu, 1981-96; vis. scholar Waseda Grad. Sch. Asia-Pacific Studies, 2002—03. Author: Reed Town, Japan, 1974, Chiho Toshi no Kenryokukozo, 1976, (with others) Palestinians Without Palestine, 1978; co-editor: Studies in Political Socialization in the Arab States, 1987, Japan in a New World Order: Contributing to the Arab-Israeli Peace Process, 1994, Japanese Culture in Comparative Perspective, 1997. Bd. of govs. Japanese Cultural Ctr. Hawaii, Honolulu, 1988—, program com., 1988—. Recipient Disting. Vis. Lectr. award SUNY, 1994; Rockefeller Found. grantee, 1963-64, Social Sci. Rsch. Coun. grantee, 1966-67, Toyota Found. grantee, 1984-87, 87-90; vis. rsch. fellow Harry S. Truman Rsch. Inst. of the Advancement of Peace, Hebrew U., 1992, Inst. Legal Studies, Kansai U., 1994. Mem. Am. Polit. Sci. Assn., Internat. Polit. Sci. Assn., Internat. Assn. Middle Ea. States (coll. of fellows 1986—). Democrat. Avocation: stamp collecting. Home: 1-19-31 A604 Nakatehara Kohoku ku Yokohama 222 0023 Japan

KUROKAWA, SUSUMU, management educator, researcher; b. Himeji, Japan, Aug. 3, 1956; s. Masako Kurokawa; m. Kazuko Saito, July 28, 1985; children: Umpei, Shohei, Shimpei. PhD, Mass. Inst. Tech., 1992. Asst. prof. Dept. Mgmt. Drexel U., Phila., 2001; rsch. assoc. prof. Vanderbilt U., Nashville, 1996—2001. Advisor Min. Internat. Trade & Industry, Tokyo, 1993—94. Contbr. scientific papers. Adviser Waseda U., Tokyo, 1995—99. Recipient Best Japanese Book in Entrepreneurship award, Shoukou Chukin, 1996; fellow Abe fellowship, Social Sci. Rsch. Coun., 1994; scholar Fulbright scholarship, Fulbright Found., 1985. Mem.: Acad. Mgmt. Avocations: martial arts, guitar, ham radio. Home: 547 Howe Rd Merion Station PA 19066 Office: Drexel U Dept Mgmt 101 N 33rd St Philadelphia PA 19104 Home Fax: 215-895-2891. Personal E-mail: sk92@drexel.edu.

KUROSKY, ALEXANDER, biochemist, educator; b. Windsor, Ont., Can., Sept. 12, 1938; came to U.S., 1972; s. Peter and Stella (Gemper) K.; m. Anna Kinik, May 18, 1963; children: Lisa Kathryn, Tanya Kristine, Stephanie Ann. BSc, U. B.C., 1965; MSc, U. Toronto, 1969, PhD, 1972. Research technician Can. Dept. Agr., Harrow, Ont., Vancouver, B.C., 1959-64; chemist research and devel. Can. Breweries Ltd., Toronto, Ont., 1965-67; faculty Med. Br., U. Tex., Galveston, 1973—, assoc. prof., 1978-82, prof., 1982—, dir. Biomolecular Resource Facility; dir. Nat. Heart., Lung, and Blood Inst. NIH Ctr., Galveston. Contbr. articles to sci. publs. Province of Ont. grad fellow, 1968-71; grantee Burkitt Found., NIH, Nat. Cancer Inst.; recipient Disting. Teaching award U. Tex. Med. Br. Grad. Sch., 1981 Mem. Am. Soc. Biochemistry and Molecular Biology, Am. Chem. Soc., AAAS, Can. Biochem. Soc., Am. Soc. Human Genetics, Sigma Xi (John G. Sinclair award 1988) Achievements include research on prohormone processing and structure, function and genetics of proteins. Home: 6605 Golfcrest Dr Galveston TX 77551-1821 Office: U Tex Med Br Dept Human Biol Chem And Genetics Galveston TX 77555-0001

KUROTSUCHI, ROY YUTAKA, obstetrician, gynecologist; b. San Jose, Calif., July 30, 1927; s. Zenich and Fumi (Kuchii) K.; m. Nancy Akiko Ishikawa; children: Susan Rachael, James Alan, Karen Ann. BS, Elmhurst Coll., 1951; MD, U. Ill., 1955. Diplomate Am. Bd. Ob-Gyn. Intern to resident in ob-gyn. West Suburban Hosp., Oak Pk., Ill., 1955-56, 56-60; physician VA. Attending physician (hon.) La Grange Meml. Hosp., Ill. Fellow AMA; mem. ACOG.

KURRUS, THOMAS WILLIAM, lawyer; b. Carmel, N.Y., May 13, 1947; s. Theo Hornsby and Jean Ellen (Cumming) K. BS magna cum laude, U. Fla., 1975, JD, 1979. Bar: Fla. 1980, U.S. Dist. Ct. (no. dist.) Fla. 1980, U.S. Ct. Appeals (5th cir.) 1980, U.S. Dist. Ct. (mid. dist.) Fla. 1981, U.S. Ct. Appeals (11th cir.) 1981, U.S. Ct. Appeals (4th cir.) 1984, U.S. Supreme Ct. 1984. Assoc. Law Firm Larry G. Turner, Gainesville, Fla., 1981-83; ptnr. Turner, Kurrus & Griscti, Gainesville, 1983-88; prin. Law Offices of Thomas W. Kurrus, Gainesville, 1988—. Mem. Fla. Supreme Ct. commn. on jury instructions, 1995. Contbr. articles to profl. jours. Mem. ACLU (Gainesville chpt. legal panel chmn. 1999), Nat. Assn. Criminal Defense Lawyers (Fla. chpt. bd. dirs., chmn. continuing legal edn. com., local legis. liaison, pres. award 1993, appreciation award 1998). Avocations: fishing, art, horses. Office: PO Box 838 Gainesville FL 32602-0838

KURSEWICZ, LEE Z. marketing consultant; b. Chgo., Oct. 26, 1916; s. Antoni and Henryka (Sulkowska) K.; ed. Chgo. and Bata ind. schs.; m. Ruth Elizabeth Venzke, Jan. 31, 1940; 1 son, Dennis. With Bata Shoe Co., Inc., 1936-78, plant mgr., Salem, Ind., 1963-65, v.p., mng. dir., Batawa, Ont., Can., 1965-71; v.p., dir. Bata Industries, Batawa, 1965-71, plant mgr., Salem, 1971-76; pres. Bata Shoe Co., Inc., Belcamp, Md., 1976-77, sr. v.p., dir., 1977-79; gen. mgr. Harford Insulated Panel Systems div. Hazleton Industries, 1981-82. City mgr. City of Batawa, 1965-71; vice chmn. Trenton (Ont.) Meml. Hosp., 1970-71; pres. Priestford Hills Community Assn., 1979-80; chmn. adv. bd. Phoenix Festival Theatre, Hartford County Community Coll., 81; vice chmn. Harford County chpt. ARC, 1980-81, chmn., 1982-83; chmn. Harford County Econ. Devel. Adv. Bd., 1983-85; mem. Susquehanna Region Pvt. Industry Council, 1983-85. Mem. Am. Mgmt. Assn. Clubs: Rotary, Bush River Yacht (commodore 1966), Bush River Power Squadron (comdr. 1967), Western Hills Country of Salem (pres. 1975), Trenton Country (pres. 1968-69), Md. Country. Home and Office: 31445 East Nine Drive Laguna Niguel CA 92677

KURT, JOHNNY THOMAS, music educator; s. Thomas James Kurt and Sandra Sue Abel-Kurt. MusB, U. Nebr., Omaha, 1991; Med in Ednl. Adminstrn., U. Nebr., Lincoln, 1995; Endorsement in Gifted/Talented Edn., U. Iowa, 2002. Cert. tchr., adminstr. Iowa, cert. tchr., adminstr. Nebr. Grad. tchg. asst. Baylor U., Waco, Tex., 1991; substitute tchr. Omaha Pub. Sch. Dist., 1992—95; instrumental music instr. Lewis Ctrl. Pub. Sch. Dist., Council Bluffs, Iowa, 1995—. Instr. in gifted/talented summer programs Creighton U., Omaha, 2001—. Contbr. articles to profl. publs., procs. in field. (Publ., 1991). Vol. Nebr. Humane Soc., Omaha, 1998. Fellow Belin-Blank Gifted/Talented Educator fellowship, U. of Iowa, 2001. Mem.: NEA, Iowa Bandmasters Assn. (mem. R&D state bd. 1997—99), Iowa H.S. Music Assn. (adjudicator 1998—), Omicron Delta Kappa, Phi Delta Kappa. Office: Lewis Ctrl Sch Dist 1600 East South Omaha Bridge Rd Council Bluffs IA 51503 E-mail: jkurt@lewiscentral.k12.ia.us.

KURTH, LIESELOTTE, foreign language educator; b. Wuppertal, Germany; came to U.S., 1951; s. Otto and Emmi (Klammer) Voigt. MA, Johns Hopkins U., 1960, PhD, 1963. Asst. prof. German Johns Hopkins U., Balt., 1964-68, assoc. prof., 1968-73, prof., 1973-89, chmn. dept., 1980-87; prof. emeritus, 1989—. Author: Die Zweite Wirklichkeit, 1969, Perspectives and Points of View, 1974, Continued Existence, Reincarnation, and the Power of Sympathy in Classical Weimar, 1999; contbr. articles top profl. jours. and yearbooks; editor collections and edits. Gilman fellow, 1958-62; Gail fellow, 1962-63 Mem. MLA (mem. exec. com. South Atlantic br. 1982-84, pres. br. 1985-86), Lessing Soc., Goethe Soc. of N.Am., Phi Beta Kappa. Home: 800 Southerly Rd Apt 914 Towson MD 21286-8409 Office: Johns Hopkins U Dept German 34th and Charles Sts Baltimore MD 21218

KURTH, REBECCA JANE, physician; b. Lawrence, Mass., Sept. 2, 1961; d. Wilfred and Margaret Mary Kurth; m. Randolph Stewart Marshall, Apr. 10, 1960; children: Trevor Kurth Marshall, Virginia Rose Marshall, Zoe Samantha Marshall. BA, Harvard U., 1983; MD, Coll. of Physicians & Surgeons, Columbia U., 1987. Diplomate Am. Bd. of Internal Medicine, 1990. Instr. in clin. medicine Columbia U., NY, 1990—94, asst. clin. prof. of medicine, 1994—2002, assoc. prof. of clin. medicine, 2002—. Dir. Columbia Eastside PrimeCare, NY, 2000—. Mem.: Assn. of Am. Med. Colleges, ACP. Achievements include research in Researcher in the structure and content of medical education. Office: Columbia Presbyn Eastside 16 East 60th New York NY 10022 Office Fax: 212-326-8746.

KURTH, RONALD JAMES, university president, retired naval officer; b. Madison, Wis., July 1, 1931; s. Peter James and Celia (Kuehn) K.; m. Esther Charlene Schaefer, Dec. 21, 1954; children: Steven, Audrey, John, Douglas. BS, U.S. Naval Acad., 1954; MPA, Harvard U., 1961, PhD, 1970. Commd. ensign U.S. Navy, 1954, advanced through grades to rear adm., 1981; U.S. naval attache Moscow, 1975-77; comdg. officer NAS, Memphis at Millington, Tenn., 1977-79; mil. fellow Council Fgn. Relations, N.Y.C., 1979-80; exec. asst. to dep. chief naval ops. Dept. Navy, Washington, 1980-81, dir. Pol-Mil Policy and Current Plans, 1981-83, dir. Long Range Planning Group, 1983-84; U.S. def. attache Moscow, 1985-87; pres. U.S. Naval War Coll., Newport, R.I., 1987-90, Murray (Ky.) State U., 1990-94; dean acad. affairs Air War Coll., Maxwell AFB, Ala., 1994-98; pres. St. John's Northwestern Mil. Acad., Delafield, Wis., 1998—. Teaching fellow Harvard U., Cambridge, Mass., 1969-70. Author: The Politics of Technological Innovation in the Navy, 1970. Mem. nat. adv. bd. Boy Scouts Am. Decorated Def. D.S.M., Navy D.S.M., Legion of Merit with 2 gold stars, Meritorious Svc. medal with gold star. Mem. Am. Acad. Polit. Sci., U.S. Naval Inst. (life), Naval War Coll. Found. (life), U.S. Naval Acad. Alumni, Harvard U. Alumni, Rotary. Episcopalian. Home: 505 Saint Johns Rd Delafield WI 53018-1440 Office: St John's Northwestern Mil Acad Delafield WI 53018 E-mail: rkurth@sjnma.org. *Among those who know you, ponder whose respect you have and whose you do not. It will provide you with a measure of your worth.*

KURTICH, JOHN WILLIAM, architect, film-maker, educator; b. Salinas, Calif., Oct. 18, 1935; s. John Joseph and Elizabeth (Lyons) K. BA in Theatre and Cinematography, UCLA, 1957; BArch, U. Calif., Berkeley, 1966; MS in Architecture and Urban Design, Columbia U., 1968. Film-maker SMP Architects, San Francisco, 1960-61; film-maker, archtl. draftsman McCue & Assocs., San Francisco, 1962-66; freelance film-maker, designer Friedberg, N.Y., 1968; instr. Sch. of Art Inst., Chgo., 1968-70, asst. prof., 1970-74, assoc. prof., 1974-82, prof., 1982—, chmn. dept. design and communication, 1981-85, area head interior arch., 1987-94, chmn. undergrad. divsn. Staff arch. Am. Excavations, Samothrace, Greece, 1970—; archtl. cons. Fed. Res. Bank Chgo., 1978; William Bronson Mitchell and Grayce Slovet Mitchell endowed chair in Interior Architecture, 1995—. Multi-media prodns. include: Hellas, Columbia U., N.Y.C., 1968, Art Inst. Chgo., 1971, 79, Muncie: Microsm of America (NEA grante), Muncie, Ind., 1972, Legend of the Minotaur, Art Inst. Chgo., 1973, The Seasons, Shapes, Contrasts, Art Inst. Chgo., 1977, 83, 84, Canal du Midi, Art Inst. Chgo., 1987, Light: A History of Architecture from Stonehenge to the Fall Of Western Civilization, Graham Found., 1988, The Desert of Rets, Graham Found., 1989, The Mysteries of Samothrace, Art Inst. Chgo., 1989, Echoes of Eternity, Art Inst. Chgo., 1989, Porno Versailles, Graham Found., 1990, Monuments and Memorials, State Ill. Art Gallery, 1990, The Art Institute of Chicago: The Corporation, Art Inst. Chgo., 1990, The Seven Wonders of the World, Mus. Contemporary Art, 1991, Design in the Fourth Dimension Space-Time, Neo Con/Chgo. Architecture Found., 1993, The Ancient World, Art Inst. Chgo., 1994, Ilumine: The Architecture of Light, Graham Found., 1995, Recent Excavations at Samothrace, Graham Found., 1996. Served with USNR, 1957-60. Recipient Architecture medal Alpha Rho Chi, 1966; William Kinne fellow Columbia U., Fgn. Travelling fellow; grantee NEA, 1972, Woman's Bd. Art Inst. Chgo., 1973, Union Ind. Colls. Art, 1974, Fulbright-Hays (Eng.), 1976, Fulbright-Hays (Jordan), 1981, Ford Foun./Art Inst Chgo. Faculty Enrichment, 1982, 87, 91, 93, 2000, Graham Found. for Advanced Studies in Fine Arts, 1988. Fellow Royal Soc. Arts (London); mem. AIA (corp. mem.), Soc. Archtl. Historians, Nat. Com. for Interiors, Chgo. Archtl. Club. Home: 4737 S Ellis Ave Chicago IL 60615-1807 Office: Sch of Art Inst Chgo Office of Interior Arch 37 S Wabash Ave Chicago IL 60603-3103 E-mail: jkurtich@artic.edu.

KURTZ, ALFRED BERNARD, radiologist; b. Albany, N.Y., May 1, 1944; s. Leonard David and Esther (Lederman) K.; m. Barbara Ellen, July 3, 1973; children: Dana, Liza, Amy. BA, NYU, 1966; MD, Stanford U., 1972. Diplomate Am. Bd. Radiology. Internal medicine intern Montefiore Hosp. and Med. Ctr., Bronx, N.Y., 1972-73, resident in internal medicine, 1973-74, resident in diagnostic radiology, 1974-77; from fellow in ultrasound and body CT to prof. Jefferson Med. Coll. Thomas Jefferson Univ. Hosp., Phila., 1977—85; prof. ob-gyn. Jefferson Med. Coll. Thomas Jefferson U. Hosp., Phila., 1985—, vice chmn. Dept. Radiology Jefferson Med. Coll., 1989—2002. Examiner oral bds. in ultrasound category Am. Bd. Radiology, 1985—; med. advisor Blue Shield of Pa., Phila., 1983—; mem. adv. com. Ctr. of Excellence in Biomed. Imaging, Phila., 1987—. Author: Ultrasound: The Requisites, 1995, Obstetrical Measurements in Ultrasound: A Reference Manual, 1988; editor: Atlas of Ultrasound Measurements, 1990; assoc. editor Radiology; contbr. articles to profl. jours. Grantee Nat. Cancer Inst., NIH, 1993-96. Fellow Am. Inst. Ultrasound in Medicine (bd. govs. 1990-92, sec. 1993-97, pres.-elect 1999-2001, pres. 2001-03, immediate past pres., 2003—), Am. Coll. Radiology (chmn. com. on edn. and tng. of commn. 1987-93, commn. on ultrasound 1987-93), Soc. Radiologists in Ultrasound (pres. 1991-93), Coll. Physicians Phila. Achievements include advancement of the ability of ultrasound to establish an accurate fetal age; establishment of ultrasound patterns for analysis of diffuse liver disease; advancement of ultrasound in evaluation of obstetrical and gynecologic problems including by intravaginal scanning and cross sectional imaging evaluation for ovarian cancer. Home: 1050 Indian Creek Rd Wynnewood PA 19096-3407 Office: Thomas Jefferson U Hosp 111 S 11th St Philadelphia PA 19107-5084

KURTZ, ANTHONY DAVID, physicist; b. N.Y.C., May 3, 1929; s. Jacob Kurtz and Claire Juscow; m. Nora Morcos, May 27, 1985; 1 child, Sandria; m. Margery Geilich, Apr. 3, 1955 (div. May 1985); children: Jennifer Kurtz Unger, John. BS in Physics, MIT, 1951, MS in Physics, 1952, ScD in Phys. Metallurgy, 1955. Staff mem. semiconductor physics Lincoln Lab., 1952—55; project mgr. diffused device rsch. Clevite Transistor Products, 1955—56; dir. semiconductor applied rsch. Mpls.-Honeywell Regulatory Co., 1956—59; dir. R&D, sr. scientist, CEO Kulite Semiconductor Products, Inc., Leonia, NJ, 1959—. Adj. prof. dept. mech. engring. Columbia U., N.Y.C., 2002—. Contbr. articles to profl. jours. Named to N.J. Inventors Congress and Hall of Fame, State N.J., 1991; recipient I R 100 for miniature semiconductor pressure transducer, Indsl. Rsch. Inc., 1968, Si Fluor Tech. award, Instrument Soc. Am., 1978. Achievements include patents in field; invention of MEMS technology. Home: 256 Hempstead Rd Ridgewood NJ 07450 Office: Kulite Semiconductor Products Inc 1 Willow Tree Rd Leonia NJ 07605

KURTZ, CHARLES JEWETT, III, lawyer; b. Columbus, Ohio, May 13, 1940; s. Charles Jewett, Jr. and Elizabeth Virginia (Gill) K.; m. Linda Rhoads, Mar. 18, 1983. BA, Williams Coll., 1962; JD, Ohio State U., 1965. Bar: Ohio 1965, D.C. 1967, U.S. Dist. Ct. (so. dist.) Ohio 1967, U.S. Dist. Ct. (no. dist.) Ohio 1976, U.S. Ct. Appeals (6th cir.) 1992. Law clk. to justice Ohio State Supreme Ct., Columbus, 1965-67; assoc. Porter, Wright, Morris & Arthur, Columbus, 1967-71, ptnr., 1972—, mng. ptnr. litigation dept., 1988-91, mem. directing ptnrs. com., 1988-89. Mem. faculty Ohio Legal Ctr. Inst. Trustee Ballet Met., Columbus, 1990-94; mem. vestry St. Albans Episcopal Ch., 1986-89. Mem. ABA, Am. Arbitration Assn. (mem. panel comml. arbitrators), Ohio Bar Assn. (mem. workers compensation com.), Columbus Bar Assn. (sustaining mem., common pleas ct. com.), Columbus Bar Found., Columbus Def. Assn. (pres. 1976), Athletic Club, Columbus Country Club, Capital Club. Office: Porter Wright Morris & Arthur 41 S High St Ste 2900 Columbus OH 43215-6194 E-mail: Ckurtz@porterwright.com.

KURTZ, DOLORES MAY, civic worker; b. Reading, Pa., Oct. 27, 1933; d. Harry Claude and Ethel Gertrude (Fields) Filbert; m. William McKillips Kurtz, Oct. 26, 1957. Sec. cert., Pa. State U., 1980. Legal sec. Snyder, Balmer & Kershner, Reading, 1951-53; head teletype operator E.. duPont de Nemours, Reading, 1953-56; exec. sec. Ford New Holland (Pa.) Inc. (formerly Sperry New Holland), 1956-91; ret., 1991. Active Lancaster County Rep. Com., 1983-85; pres. New Holland Area Womans Club, 1982-84; bd. dirs. Cmty. Meml. Park Assn., New Holland, 1957-82, Lancaster County Fedn. Womens Clubs, 1982—, 2d v.p., 1984-86, 1st v.p., 1986-88, pres. 1988-90; founding mem. Summer Arts Festival, New Holland, 1980—, bd. dirs., 1985-91; membership chair S.E. dist. Pa. Fedn. Womens Clubs, 1984-86; area rep., bd. dirs. Womens Rep. Club Lancaster County, 1982-84; com. mem. New Holland Boro, 1983-85; v.p. Lancaster-Lebanon Arthritis Found. Guild, 1992, pres., 1993. Recipient Outstanding Vol. for Pa. award Pa. Fedn. Womens Clubs, 1984, Woman in the Arts award, 1998. Mem. Gen. Fedn. Womens Clubs Pa. (conservation divsn. chair 1996-98, credentials com. 1998-2000, chmn. Caps for Kids project Lancaster County chpt. 1999-2003). Methodist. Avocations: arts and crafts, travel, photography.

KURTZ, ELLEN R. journalist; b. Bklyn., May 22, 1934; d. George and Gertrude (Troiansky) Rabinowitz; m. Raymond J. Kurtz, June 26, 1954 (dec. May 1988); children: Jill A., Michael S., Jack L.; m. Sol T. Horowitz. BA, Bklyn. Coll., 1955. Tchr. N.Y.C. Pub. Schs., 1955-56; lectr. Weight Watchers of N.J., Livingston, 1969-83; owner, dir. Livingston Coll. Bd. Rev., 1975-83; mng. editor On the Scene, Livingston, 1984-86; editor Regional Weekly News, East Hanover, N.J., 1986; writer spl. sects. Star-Ledger, Newark, 1987—2000. Cons. editor Hosp. News of N.J., Colonia, 1989—90; feature writer Drew U., Madison, NJ, 1996—2000; publicist Drew U. Ctr. for Holocaust Study, 1997—98; instr. The Adult Sch. of the Chathams, Madison and Florham Park, 1999; Holocaust coun. MetroWest, 2001—; lectr. Jewish Edn. Assn. MetroWest NJ, 2000—. Contbr. articles to newspapers, mags. Judge essay contest B'nai Brith/Albert Adler Meml. Scholarship Fund, Livingston, 1987—2002; active Vols. for Israel, 1989. Mem.: Livingston Writers' Group, N.J. Press Women (office holder, com. chairperson, Communicator of Achievement award 1997, Communicator of Achievement Award 1984). Jewish. Avocations: travel, aerobics, reading, bowling. Home and Office: 1305 Bush Circle Rockaway NJ 07866

KURTZ, EUGENE ALLEN, composer, educator, consultant; b. Atlanta, Dec. 27, 1923; s. Wilbur George and Annie Laurie (Fuller) K. BA in Mus., U. Rochester, 1947; MA in Mus., Eastman Sch. Mus., 1949; studied with Arthur Honegger and Darius Milhaud, Ecole Normale de Musique, Paris, 1949-51; studied with Max Deutsch, Paris, 1953-57. Guest prof. composition U. Mich., Ann Arbor, 1967-68, 70-71, 73-74, 80-81, 88, Eastman Sch. Mus., Rochester, N.Y., 1975, U. Ill., Urbana, 1976, U. Tex., Austin, 1977-78, 85-86, Hartt Sch. Mus., Hartford, Conn., 1989; cons. Editions Jobert, Paris, 1972—; lectr. in field. Compositions include The Solitary Walker, 1964, Conversations for 12 Players, 1966, Ca...Diagramme Pour Orchestre, 1972, The Last Contrabass in Las Vegas, 1974, Mècanique, 1975, Logo, 1979, Five-Sixteen for piano, 1982, World Enough and Time, 1982, String Trio, Time and Again, 1984-85, From Time to Time for violin and piano, 1986-87, The Broken World for string quartet, 1993-94, Shadows on the Wind for 17 players, 1995-96, Icare for solo flute, 1997, also film scores and incidental music for radio, theatre and TV; commd. by U. Mich., 1958, Am. Cultural Ctr., Paris, 1966, Ministère de la Culture Français, 1972, 82, U. Nev., 1974, Radio France, 1975, 79, 85, Musical Arts Assn., Cleve., 1976. Sgt. inf. U.S. Army, 1942-46, ETO. NEA grantee, 1982-83; recipient Am. Acad. Inst. Arts and Letters award, 1992, French Acad. des Beaux-Arts award, 1997. Mem. Société des Auteurs, Compositeurs et Editeurs de Musique. Office: 6 Rue Boulitte 75014 Paris France

KURTZ, HAROLD PAUL, foundation executive; b. Milw., May 21, 1936; s. Henry John and Minnie Christina (Olson) K.; m. Grace Jahn, June 16, 1963; children: Steven, David. BA, Wartburg Coll., 1958; MS, U. Wis., 1961. Journalist Post-Crescent, Appleton, Wis., 1961-63; dir. pub. rels. Luth. Gen. Hosp., Park Ridge, Ill., 1963-73, Med. Coll. Wis., Milw., 1973-77; v.p. Children's Hosp., St. Paul, 1977-90; dir. devel. U. Minn., 1990-95; exec. dir. Lyngblomsten Found., 1995—2002; pres. Wright-Berglund Found., 2002—. Author: Public Relations for Hospitals, 1969; Public Relations and Fund Raising for Hospitals, 1981; (with M. Burrows) Effective Use of Volunteers,

1971; editor: Toward a Creative Chaplaincy, 1973, Fly the Banner High, 1991. Bd. dirs. Bd. Edn., Dist. 621, Mounds View, 1985-95; bd. dirs. Spl. Intermediate Sch. Dist. 916, 1986-95; bd. dirs. Wright-Berglund Found., 1980—. Recipient Community Svc. citation Wartburg Coll., 1970; named Boss of Yr., Internat. Assn. Bus. Comms. Mem. Chgo. Hosp. Pub. Rels. Soc. (pres. 1971-72), Wartburg Coll. Alumni Assn. (bd. dirs. 1962-66). Lutheran. Home: 1465 17th Ave NW Saint Paul MN 55112-5524

KURTZ, HARVEY A. lawyer; b. Baraboo, Wis., July 9, 1950; s. Walter R. and Henrietta M. (Hinze) K.; m. Yvonne Larme, Jan. 28, 1978; children: Benjamin L., Leah L. BA, U. Wis., 1972; JD, U. Chgo., 1975. Bar: Wis. 1975, U.S. Dist. Ct. (ea. dist.) Wis. 1980. Atty. Whyte & Hirschboeck S.C., Milw., 1975-89, shareholder, 1981-89; ptnr. Foley & Lardner, Milw., 1989—. Mem. ABA, State Bar of Wis. Assn., Milw. Bar Assn. (chmn. employee benefits sect. 1993-94), Greater Milw. Employee Benefit Coun., Wis. Retirement Plan Profls. (pres. 1987-88), Internat. Pension and Employee Benefits Lawyers Assn., Kiwanis, Phi Beta Kappa. Home: 3927 N Stowell Ave Milwaukee WI 53211-2461 Office: Foley & Lardner Ste 3800 777 E Wisc Ave Milwaukee WI 53202 E-mail: hkurtz@foleylaw.com.

KURTZ, JAMES EUGENE, freelance writer, minister; b. Altoona, Pa., June 28, 1928; s. Harry F. and Mildred (Sipes) K. LittD, Berean Coll., 1976; ThD, Ridgedale Theol. Sem., Chatanooga, 1974. Editorial writer Altoona Tribune, 1952-55; minister Jackson Park Ch., Chgo., 1957-58, First Congregational Ch., East Machias, Maine, 1991-93; advt. mgr. Pacific Flush Tank Co., Chgo., 1964-77; freelance news corr. Chgo., 1978-82; freelance corr. Joliet, Ill., 1987-88; pub.'s rep. Antioch Pub., Joliet, 1985-88. Editor Opinion mag., 1993—; editorial page editor Patriot Newspapers; contbr. articles to popular mags. Mem. Nat. Assn. Scholars, Soc. Profl. Journalists, Acad. Am. Poets. Home: PO Box 239 Peru IL 61354-0239

KURTZ, JAMES P. administrative law judge; b. Highland Park, Mich., Dec. 5, 1932; s. A.T. and Virginia C. (Riley) K.; m. Barbara A. Gonczy, Feb. 2, 1957; children: Mary T., Christina M., Ann V., J. Peter, Karen M., Eileen M. AB, U. Detroit, 1955, JD, 1958. Bar: Mich. 1958, U.S. Dist. Ct. (ea. dist.) Mich. 1958, U.S. Ct. Appeals (6th cir.) 1964. Supervisory atty. 7th region NLRB, Detroit, 1958-67; ptnr. firm Brennan & Kurtz, Detroit, 1967-69; adminstrv. law judge Employment rels. commn. State of Mich. Dept. CIS, Detroit, 1969-2001; retired, 2001. Instr. labor and real estate Detroit Coll. Bus., Dearborn, 1968-73; adj. prof. adminstrv. law U. Detroit, 1969-72. Editor-in-chief U. Detroit Law jour., 1957-58; editor procs. Nat. Acad. Arbitrators, 1971-75. Mem. Mich. Bar Assn. (Labor Law sect.). Roman Catholic. Home: RR 1 Craig Beach 401 Erieview Harrow ON Canada N0R 1G0 E-mail: jpkurtz@sympatico.ca.

KURTZ, JEROME, lawyer, educator; b. Phila., May 19, 1931; s. Morris and Renee (Cooper) K.; m. Elaine Kahn, July 28, 1956; children: Madeleine, Nettie Kurtz Greenstein. BS with honors, Temple U., 1952; LLB magna cum laude, Harvard U., 1955. Bar: Pa. 1956, N.Y. 1981, D.C. 1982; CPA, Pa. Assoc. Wolf, Block, Schorr & Solis-Cohen, Phila., 1955-56, 57-63, ptnr., 1963-66, 68-77; tax legis. counsel Dept. Treasury, Washington, 1966-68; commr. IRS, 1977-80; ptnr. Paul, Weiss, Rifkind, Wharton & Garrison, 1980-90; prof. law NYU, 1991-2001, dir. grad. tax program, 1995-98. Instr. Villanova Law Sch., 1964-65, U. Pa., 1969-74; vis. prof. law Harvard U., 1975-76; mem. adv. group to commr. IRS, 1976. Editor: Harvard Law Rev, 1953-55; contbr. numerous articles to profl. jours. Pres. Ctr. Inter-Am. Tax Adminstrn., 1980; bd. dirs. Common Cause, 1984-90, chmn. fin. com., 1985-88; bd. dirs. Nat. Capitol Area ACLU, 1990-91; mem. adv. bd. NYU Tax Inst., 1988-97, Little, Brown Tax Practice Series, 1994-96. Recipient Exceptional Service award Dept. Treasury, 1968, Alexander Hamilton award, 1980 Mem. ABA (chmn. tax shelter com. 1982-84), N.Y. Bar Assn. (exec. com. tax sect. 1981-82), Pa. Bar Assn., Phila. Bar Assn. (chmn. tax sect. 1975-76), Assn. of the Bar of the City of N.Y. (chmn. tax coun. 1993-95), Am. Law Inst. (cons. fed. inc. tax project taxation of pass through entities), Am. Coll. Tax Counsel, Beta Gamma Sigma. Home: 17 E 16th St New York NY 10003-3116 E-mail: jeromekurtz2@aol.com.

KURTZ, JOEL, construction company executive; b. Paterson, N.J., June 13, 1940; Student, Paul Smith Coll., 1961-63. Lumbering contractor JK Forest Products, N.Y, Pa., 1965-67; v.p., owner Martin Hermann Lumber Co., Callicoon, N.Y., 1968-75; pres., owner Transea Rsch. & Devel., Callicoon, 1976—. Inventor, patentee split keel system for sailboats. Served in U.S. Army, 1963-65. Mem. Soc. Naval Architects & Marine Engrs., Cocheton Men's Club. Republican. Avocations: art, science, travel, sailing. Home: 252 Hortonville-main St Callicoon NY 12723-5616

KURTZ, JOEL BARRY, finance executive; b. Bklyn., Aug. 2, 1944; BBA, Pace U., 1970; MBA, C.W. Post Coll., 1981. Staff acct. Arthur Andersen & Co., Melville, N.Y., 1970-73; divsn. contr. Elec. Comp. divsn. Gould Inc., Farmingdale, N.Y., 1973-78; contr. CBS-Holt, Rinehart & Winston, N.Y.C., 1979-80, Siemans Data Switching Systems, formerly Databit Inc., Hauppage, N.Y., 1981-87; v.p. fin. Linotype-Hell Co., Hauppage, 1987-93; CFO INS Devel. Inc., Hauppage, 1993-96; sr. dir. Nortel Networks Inc. (formerly Periphonics Corp.), Bohemia, N.Y., 1996—. Home: 84 Vera Ln Commack NY 11725-1922 Office: 425 Oser Ave Hauppauge NY 11788-3640

KURTZ, JUDITH MARSHA, elementary education educator; b. Bklyn., Apr. 15, 1947; d. Henry Leonard and Florence (Goldsamt) Austin; m. Joel Barry Kurtz, Aug. 2, 1944; children: Brian David, Steven Joshua, Stacey Lynne. BS, SUNY, Cortland, 1968; MS, Hofstra U., 1971. Tchr. elem. sch. Lynbrook (N.Y.) Pub. Schs., 1968-74, Massapequa (N.Y.) Pub. Schs., 1988—. Home: 84 Vera Ln Commack NY 11725-1922 Office: RJ Lockhart Pittsburg Ave Massapequa NY 11758

KURTZ, LARRY, corporate communications executive; m. Melissa Kurtz. AB in Econs., Princeton U.; postgrad., U. Mo. V.p., tech. group mgr. Burson-Marsteller, N.Y.C., Chgo., San Francisco and Houston, 1974-84; asst. dir. corp. comm. Crown Zellerbach Corp., San Francisco, 1984-86; dir. corp. comm. Chiron Corp., 1988-92, past v.p. corp. comm.; v.p. corp. comm. and investor rels. McKesson HBOC, Inc., San Francisco, 1997—. Office: McKesson HBOC Inc 1 Post St Ste 3275 San Francisco CA 94104-5236

KURTZ, MAXINE, personnel consultant, lawyer; b. Mpls., Oct. 17, 1921; d. Jack Isadore and Beatrice (Cohen) K. BA, U. Minn., 1942; MS in Govt. Mgmt., U. Denver, 1945, JD, 1962; postdoctoral student, U. Calif., San Diego, 1978. Bar: Colo. 1962, U.S. Dist. Ct. Colo., 1992. Analyst Tri-County Regional Planning, Denver, 1945-47; chief rsch. and spl. projects Planning Office, City and County of Denver, 1947-66; dir. tech. and evaluation Model Cities Program, 1966-71; pers. rsch. officer Denver Career Svc. Auth., 1972-86, dir. pers. svcs., 1986-88, sr. pers. specialist, 1988-90, pub. sector pers. con., 1990-95, atty., 1990—, pers. and human resources cons., 1996-98. Expert witness nat. com. on urban problems U.S. Ho. of Reps., U.S. Senate. Author: Law of Planning and Land Use Regulations in Colorado, 1966; co-author: Care and Feeding of Witnesses, Expert and Otherwise, 1974; bd. editors: Pub. Adminstrn. Rev., Washington, 1980-83, 88-92; editl. adv. bd. Internat. Pers. Mgmt. Assn.; prin. investigator: Employment: An American Enigma, 1979. Active Women's Forum of Colo., Denver Dem. Com.; chair Colo. adv. com. to U.S. Civil Rights Commn., 1985-89, mem. 1989-2002. Sloan fellow U. Denver, 1944-45; recipient Outstanding Achievement award U. Minn., 1971, Alumni of Notable Achievement award, 1994. Mem. ABA, Am. Inst. Planners (sec. treas. 1968 70, bd. govs. 1972-75), Am. Planning Assn., Am. Soc. Pub. Adminstrn. (nat. coun. 1978-81, Donald Stone award), Colo. Bar Assn., Denver Bar Assn., Order St. Ives, Pi Alpha Alpha. Jewish. Home and Office: 2361 Monaco Pky Denver CO 80207-3453

KURTZ, MYERS RICHARD, hospital administrator; b. Schaefferstown, Pa., June 18, 1924; m. Linda Bewan, Dec. 26, 1988; 1 child, Ronald Hayden; 1 stepchild, Erin B. Brown. BS, U. Md., 1958; MBA, Ind. U., 1963. Served as enlisted man U.S. Army, 1942-51, commd. 2d lt., 1951; advanced through grades to lt. col. Med. Svc. Corps, 1965; mem. staff Army Surgeon Gen., Washington, 1963-67; ret., 1967; affiliation adminstr. NYU Med. Ctr., N.Y.C., 1967-69; exec. dir. Ephrata Community Hosp., Pa., 1969-76; supt. Longview State Hosp., Cin., 1976-79; asst. dir. Ohio Dept. Mental Health and Mental Retardation, Columbus, 1979-81, dir., 1981-82; sr. v.p. Cleve. Met. Gen. Hosp., 1982-83; supt., CEO Ctrl. State Hosp., Milledgeville, Ga., 1983-93; adminstr., CEO G. Pierce Wood Meml. Hosp., Arcadia, Fla., 1995-98. Adj. asst. prof. dept. psychiatry U. Cin., 1977-83. V.p., bd. dirs. Coordinated Home Care Agy., Inc., Lancaster County; pres. Lancaster County Hosp. Coun.; bd. dirs. Pa. Hosp. Assn., Baldwin County United Way, 1986-91, Baldwin County Salvation Army; mem. adv. bd. Youth Devel. Ctr., 1984 91. Decorated Legion of Merit, Army Commendation medal with oak leaf cluster, Soldiers medal. Fellow Royal Soc. Health; mem. Am. Coll. Hosp. Adminstrs. (life diplomate), Am. Acad. Med. Adminstrs., Am. Hosp. Assn., Milledgeville-Baldwin County C. of C. (bd. dirs. 1984-87, exec. com. 1986—, treas. 1987—), Nassau County Vol. Ctr. (bd. dirs., 1998-, pres. 2002-2003), Sigma Iota Epsilon, Rotary Internat. Home: 95485 Captains Way Fernandina Beach FL 32034-4346 E-mail: LmKurtz@earthlink.net.

KURTZ, MYRA BERMAN, microbiologist; b. N.Y.C., July 20, 1945; d. Milton Robert and Shirley Berman; m. Stuart Jacob Kurtz, Aug. 16, 1970; 1 child, Rachel Linda. AB, Goucher Coll., 1966; PhD, Harvard U., 1971. Rsch. assoc. SUNY, Albany, 1971-72; assoc. prof. microbiology Universidade Fed. de Sao Carlos, Brazil, 1972-74; rsch. assoc. Waksman Inst. Microbiology, Piscataway, N.J., 1975-76, asst. rsch. prof., 1976-82; sr. rsch. scientist E.R. Squibb & Sons, Princeton, N.J., 1982-87; sr. rsch. fellow Merck Rsch. Labs., Rahway, N.J., 1987-89, dir., 1989-95, sr. dir., 1995—. Reviewer various jours. and granting orgns.; chmn. Gordon Rsch. Conf., 1992. Editor: Genetics of Candida; assoc. editor: Expl. Mycology Jour. (name changed to Fungal Genetics & Biology 1996), 1988-2001; contbr. articles to profl. jours. Del. Dem. Nat. Conv., Miami, Fla., 1970. Mem. AAAS, Am. Soc. for Microbiology. Avocations: cross-country skiing, hiking.

KURTZ, PAUL, philosopher, author, educator, publisher; b. Newark, Dec. 21, 1925; s. Martin and Sara (Lasser) K.; m. Claudine C. Vial, Oct. 6, 1960; children: Valerie L., Patricia A., Jonathan, Anne. BA, NYU, 1948; MA, Columbia U., 1949, PhD, 1952. Instr. Queens Coll., 1950-52; instr. philosophy Trinity Coll., Hartford, Conn., 1952-55, asst. prof., 1955-58, assoc. prof., 1958-59, Vassar Coll., Poughkeepsie, N.Y., 1960-61; vis. prof. New Sch. Social Rsch., N.Y.C., 1960-65; assoc. prof. Union Coll., Schenectady, 1961-64, prof., 1964-65; vis. prof. U. Besancon, France, 1965; prof. philosophy SUNY, Buffalo, 1965-91, prof. emeritus, 1992—. Moderator TV series. Author (with Rollo Handy): A Current Appraisal of the Behavioral Sciences, 1964; author: Decision and the Condition of Man, 1965, The Fullness of Life, 1974, Exuberance, 1977, In Defense of Secular Humanism, 1983, A Skeptics Handbook of Parapsychology, 1985, The Transcendental Temptation, 1986, Forbidden Fruit, 1988, Eupraxophy, 1989, Philosphical Essays in Pragmatic Naturalism, 1990, The New Skepticism, 1992, Toward a New Enlightenment, 1994, The Courage to Become, 1997, Humanist Manifesto 2000, 1999, Embracing the Power of Humanism, 2000, Skepticism and Humanism: The New Paradigm, 2001; editor: American Thought Before 1900, 1966, American Philosophy in the Twentieth Century, 1966, Sidney Hook and the Contemporary World, 1968, Moral Problems in Contemporary Society, 1969; co-editor: International Directory of Philosophy and Philosophers, 4th edit., 1978—81, Tolerance and Revolution, 1970, Language and Human Nature, 1971, A Catholic/Humanist Dialogue, 1972, The Humanist Alternative, 1973, Idea of a Modern University, 1974, The Philosophy of the Curriculum, 1975, The Ethics of Teaching and Scientific Research, 1977, University and State, 1978, Sidney Hook: Philosopher of Democracy and Humanism, 1983, Building a World Community, 1989, Challenges to the Enlightenment, 1994, Skeptical Odysseys, 2001; editor: The Humanist, 1967—78; co-editor: Science and Religion, 2003; ; mem. editl. bd.: The Humanist, 1964—78, Philosophers Index, 1969—85, Question, 1969—81, pres.: Prometheus Books, 1970—, mem. editl. bd.: The Skeptical Inquirer, 1976—, editor-in-chief: Free Inquiry Mag., 1980—, pub.: The Sci. Rev. of Alternative Medicine, 2002—. Chmn. Coun. for Secular Humanism, 1980—, Coun. on Internat. Studies and World Affairs, 1966-69, Ctr. for Inquiry, 1995—; trustee Behavioral Rsch. Coun., Great Barrington, Mass.; bd. dirs. U.S. Bibliography of Philosophy, 1958-70, Univ. Ctrs. for Rational Alternatives, 1969-96; bd. dirs. Internat. Humanist and Ethical Union, 1968—, co-chmn., 1986-94; chmn. Com. for Sci. Investigation Claims of Paranormal, 1976—2002. With AUS, 1944-46. Behavioral Rsch. Coun. fellow, 1962-63, French Govt. fellow, 1965, John Dewey fellow, 1986-87; recipient Bertrand Russell Soc. award, 1988, Internat. Humanist award, 1999, Chancellor Charles Norton award, 2001. Fellow: AAAS; mem.: U.K. Rationalists Press Assn. (v.p. 1990—), Acad. Humanism (Laureate, pres. 1983—). Office: Prometheus Books Inc 59 John Glenn Dr Amherst NY 14228-2197 E-mail: paulkurtz@aol.com. *Two passions have dominated my intellectual and professional life: (1) a commitment to critical intelligence-I am skeptical of the false beliefs and mythologies that have motivated other men and women; and (2) a belief in the importance of human courage, particularly in defending reason in society and in attempting to reconstruct ethical values so that they are more democratic and humane.*

KURTZ, PAUL MICHAEL, law educator; b. Bronx, NY, Sept. 22, 1946; s. Louis and Helen (Mechanic) K. m. Carol Porter, June 6, 1971; 1 child, Benjamin. BA, Vanderbilt U., 1968, JD, 1972; LLM, Harvard U., 1974. Bar: Tenn. 1972, U.S. Ct. Appeals (6th cir.) 1973, U.S. Ct. Appeals (5th cir.) 1977, U.S. Supreme Ct. 1978. Law clk. to chief judge U.S. Ct. Appeals (6th cir.), 1972-73; instr. Boston U. Law Sch., 1973-74, Boston Coll. Law Sch., 1974-75; asst. prof. law U. Ga., Athens, 1975-78, assoc. prof., 1978-83, prof., 1983-94, assoc. dean, 1991—, J. Alton Hosch prof., 1994—. Vis. prof. U. Mo. Law Sch., 1982, Mercer Law Sch., 1984, U. Tex., 1986, Vanderbilt U., 1987; commr. on Uniform State Laws, 2001—; reporter Nat. Conf. Commrs. on Uniform State Laws, Com. on Interstate Child Support Enforcement, Com. on Status of Children of Aided Conception; reporter Ga. Supreme Ct. Com. on Indigent Def. Reform, 2000-03. Author: Criminal Offenses in Georgia, 1980, Family Law: Cases, Text, Problems, 1986, 3d edit., 1998; contbr. articles to profl. jours.; mem. editl. bd. Family Law Quar., 1983—. Mem. Am. Assn. Law Schs. (chmn. sect. family and juvenile law), ACLU, Am. Humane Assn. (bd. dirs. 1998—), Common Cause, Soc. Am. Law Tchrs., Am. Law Inst. (reporter 1995-96), Supreme Ct. Hist. Soc., Order of Coif, B'nai B'rith (Ga. state sec., pres. Athens lodge). Democrat. Avocations: reading, travel, bowling, politics. Home: 362 W Cloverhurst Ave Athens GA 30606-4212 Office: U Ga Law Sch Athens GA 30602 E-mail: pmkurtz@uga.edu.

KURTZ, ROBERT ARTHUR, finance company executive; b. Holyoke, Mass., June 16, 1943; BS in Fin., Am. Internat. Coll., Springfield, Mass., 1967; MBA in Fin., U. Okla., 1969. Sr. fin. analyst corp. treas. office Gulf Oil Internat., Pitts., 1969-71; with corp. fin. staff Humble Oil div. Exxon, Houston, 1971-73; account mgr. Merrill Lynch, Atlanta, 1973-75; personal and corp. fin. advisor Atlanta, 1975-77; pres., founder Internat. Trade and Mktg. Corp., Atlanta, 1977-84; chmn. Kray Fin. Corp., Atlanta, 1984—. Author: Diagnosing the Customer's Decision Strategy, 1994, Pick 'em Right the First Time, 1997. Mem. Soc. Neuro-Linguistic Programming (cert. trainer), Am. Assn. for Counseling and Devel. Lutheran. Home: 1630 Broadwell Oaks Dr Alpharetta GA 30004-1580

KURTZ, ROSEMARY, state representative; b. Richmond, Ind., Aug. 11, 1930; m. James Kurtz (dec.); children: Jennifer, Donna, Tamara. BA, U. Okla., 1952; MA, U. Kans., 1955; postgrad., U. Iowa, 1968—70. Tchr., Phoenix, St. Louis, 1953—65; instr. McHenry County Coll., 1970—77; tchr. High Sch. Dist. 155, 1978—90; mem. Ill. Ho. of Reps., 2001—. Asst. instr. U. Kans., 1953—55. Appointee Zoning Bd. Appeals, Crystal Lake, 1978—98; treas. City of Crystal Lake, 1997—2001; appointee Firefighters Pension Bd., 1997—2001; Rep. election judge, 1994—97. Recipient, Women in Mgmt., 1997—2000. Mem.: Delta Gamma Found. for Blind. Republican. Roman Catholic. Office: 200-3N Stratton Office Bldg Springfield IL 62706 Address: 1301 Pyott Rd Ste 201c Lake In The Hills IL 60156*

KURTZ, SHELDON FRANCIS, lawyer, educator; b. Syracuse, N.Y., May 18, 1943; s. Abraham Kurtz and Rosalyn (Bronstein) Stern; m. Alice Kaufman, June 22, 1968; children: Andrea, Emily. AB, Syracuse U., 1964, JD, 1967. Bar: N.Y. 1967, Iowa 1973. Assoc. Nixon, Mudge, Guthrie, Alexander & Mitchell, N.Y.C., 1967-69, Cleary, Gottlieb, Steen & Hamilton, N.Y.C., 1970-73; prof. U. Iowa Coll. Law, Iowa City, 1973-89, U. Va. Sch. Law, Charlottesville, 1979-80; dean Coll. Law, Fla. State U., Tallahassee, 1989-91; prof. Coll. Law U. Iowa, Iowa City, 1991—, prof. Coll. Med. Author: Kurtz on Iowa Estates, 3 vols., 1981, 2d edit., 2 vols., 1989, Problems, Cases and Materials on Family Estate Planning, 1983, (with Hood and Shors) Estate Planning for Shareholders of a Closely Held Corporation, 2 vols. and supplement, 1986, (with Hovenkamp) American Property Law, 1987, 3d edit., 1999, (with McGovern) Wills, Trusts and Estates, 2d edit., 2001, (with Hovenkamp) The Law of Property, 2001 (with Moynihan) Introduction to the Law of Real Property, 3d edit., 2002; also articles. Recipient Burlington No. tchg. award U. Iowa, 1987, Michael J. Brody Disting. Svc. award, 2001. Mem. Iowa Bar Assn. (commr. Uniform State Laws), Am. Law Inst. Avocations: cooking, hiking. Office: U Iowa Coll Law Rm 446 Iowa City IA 52242 E-mail: sheldon-kurtz@uiowa.edu.

KURTZ, THOMAS EUGENE, mathematics educator; b. Oak Park, Ill., Feb. 22, 1928; s. Oscar Christ and Helen (Bell) K.; m. Patricia Anne Barr, June 13, 1953 (div. Aug. 1973); children— Daniel Barr, Timothy David, Beth Louise; m. Agnes Seelye Bixler, June 10, 1974. BA, Knox Coll., Galesburg, Ill., 1950; PhD, Princeton, 1956; DSc, Knox Coll., 1985. Mem. faculty Dartmouth, 1956-93, prof. math. and computer sci., 1966-93, chmn. Program in Computer and Info. Sci., 1966-93, dir. Kiewit Computation Ctr., 1959-75; dir. Office Acad. Computing, 1975-78. Author: Basic Statistics, 1963, (with J.G. Kemeny) Basic Programming, 1967, 2d edit., 1971, 3d edit., 1980, (with J.G. Kemeny) Structured Basic Programming, 1987. Trustee, chmn. coun. EDUCOM, 1974-78; chmn., bd. dirs. NERComp, Inc., 1970-78; trustee, vice chmn. Dartmouth Time Sharing Sys., Inc., 1972-78; chmn. X3J2 sub. com. Am. Nat. Standards Inst., 1974-84, convenor WG8 Internat. Standards Orgn. Basic Com., 1987-94; bd. dirs., vice chmn. True Basic, Inc., 1983—; mem. panel uses of computers in edn. Pres.'s Sci. Adv. Com., 1965-66. Democrat. Mem. United Ch. Christ. Achievements include co-designing BASIC computer lang. and Dartmouth time sharing system. Home: 3 Lakeview Dr Hanover NH 03755-3407

KURTZBERG, HOWARD, lawyer; b. N.Y.C., Apr. 14, 1958; s. Theodore R. and Charlotte (Taubman) K.; m. Carmelinda Ann Amedo, Nov. 21, 1982; children: Timothy Joseph, Alyssa Lauren. BA, Queens Coll., 1979; JD, Benjamin N. Cardozo Sch. Law, 1982. Bar: N.Y. 1983. Labor rels. asst. L.I. Jewish Med. Ctr., New Hyde Park, N.Y., 1982-83; in-house counsel Rose Assocs., N.Y.C., 1983-84; assoc. gen. counsel Intercontinental Monetary, N.Y.C., 1984-89; sr. assoc. Albanese, Albanese & Fiore, Garden City, N.Y., 1989-91; v.p., gen. counsel Inter-Market Fin. Corp., Westbury, N.Y., 1991-92; pvt. practice Jericho, N.Y., 1992—. Office: 380 N Broadway Ste 300 Jericho NY 11753-2109 Fax: 516-932-8353. E-mail: kurtzlaw@aol.com.

KURTZER, BENJAMIN LOUIS, networking engineer; b. Elizabeth, NJ, Dec. 19, 1958; s. Nathan and Sylvia Kurtzer; m. Melissa Ancell, Dec. 8, 1991; children: Ellianna Michal, Chaim Ezra, Bracha Tikva, Leora Batya, Avraham Aryeh. BA, Yeshiva U., 1979. Cert. Cisco Systems, Inc. Oper. systems mgr. Toys R Us, Paramus, NJ, 1987—95; ops. mgr. Neodata, Longmont, Colo., 1995—97; network engr. AT&T, Denver, 1997—98, Qwest Comm., Denver, 1998—2000; optical engr. Cisco Systems, Inc., Centennial, Colo., 2000—. Networking and computing cons. Texsure, Denver, 1998—. Pres. Knesset Israel Torah Ctr., Sacramento, Calif., 1991—93. Mem.: Assn. of Support Profls.

KURTZER, DANIEL, ambassador; b. Elizabeth, N.J. BA, Yeshiva U., 1971; MA, MA, Columbia, PhD, 1976. Dean Yeshiva Coll., Yeshiva U., N.Y.C., until 1979; joined Fgn. Svc., Dept. State, Washington, 1976, from 1979, with Bur. Internat. Orgn. Affairs, from 1976; 2d sec. for polit. affairs Am. Embassy, Cairo, 1979-82, 1st sec. for polit. affairs Tel Aviv, 1982-86; dep. dir. for Egyptian affairs Dept. State, from 1986, speechwriter, mem. sec.'s policy planning staff, until 1989, dep. asst. sec. for Nr. Ea. Affairs, 1989-94, prin. dep. asst. sec. for intelligence and rsch., 1994-97, acting asst. sec., 1997; amb. to Egypt, Am. Embassy, Cairo, 1997—. Office: Am Embassy Cairo Unit 64900 Apo AE 09839-4900

KURTZKE, JOHN FRANCIS, SR., neurologist, epidemiologist; b. Bklyn., Sept. 14, 1926; s. John Ambrose and Teresa Rose (Knipper) K.; m. Margaret Mary Nevin, June 30, 1950; children: John Francis Jr., Catherine Kurtzke Brown, Elizabeth Kurtzke Siebert, Joan Kurtzke Brennan, Robert, James, Christine Kurtzke Hughes. BS summa cum laude, St. John's U., 1948; MD, Cornell U., 1952; MD (hon.), U. Ferrara, Italy, 2000. Diplomate in neurology Am. Bd. Psychiatry and Neurology (asst. examiner, then examiner and sr. examiner in neurology 1964-96, cert. appreciation 1969, 90). Intern Kings County Hosp., Bklyn., 1952-53; resident in neurology VA Hosp., Bronx, N.Y., 1953-56, chief neurology svc. Coatesville, Pa., 1956—63, Washington, 1963—95; chief neuroepidemiology sect. VA Med. Ctr., Washington, 1995—2002, cons. in neurology, 1995—, cons. in neuroepidemiology, 2002—. Mem. faculty Jefferson Med. Coll., Phila., 1958-63, asst. prof. clin. neurology, 1963; mem. faculty Georgetown Med. Sch., Washington, 1963—, prof. neurology, 1968-2000, prof. emeritus, 2000—, vice chmn. dept. neurology, 1976-95, prof. cmty. and family medicine, 1968-95; Disting. prof. neurology uniformed svcs. U. Health Scis., Bethesda, 1992—. USN med. student liaison officer, 1979-85; vis. prof. neurology and neuroepidemiology Temple U. Sch. Medicine, 1984-89; cons. neurology Nat. Naval Med. Ctr., Bethesda, 1966-2000, Surgeon Gen. Navy, 1970-97; mem. med. adv. bd. Nat. Multiple Sclerosis Soc., 1966-94, hon. mem., 1995—, mem. working group on design of clin. studies in multiple sclerosis, 1976-84, mem. exec. com., 1981-83; med. adv. bd. Internat. Fedn. Multiple Sclerosis Socs., 1972—, hon. mem., 1998—; mem. com. multiple sclerosis World Fedn. Neurology, 1967—, com. neuroepidemiology, 1977—; chmn. epidemiology sect. NIH Epilepsy Adv. Com., 1973-76; med. rsch. program specialist for neurology and neurobiology VA Rsch. Svc., 1977-80; chmn. work group epidemiology HEW Commn. Control of Huntington's Disease, 1976-78; mem. naval exam. bd. Naval Med. Command, 1980-83; mem. Residency Rev. Com. Neurology, 1983-88, vice chmn., 1985-86, chmn., 1987-88; chmn. U.S. Naval Res. Med. Flag Coun., 1985-86; mem. instnl. rev. bd. Nat. Inst. Neurol. Diseases and Stroke, 1989-98; established investigator Nat. Multiple Sclerosis Soc., 1987—; mem. spl. panel Inst. Medicine, 1990; mem. Am. Com. Treatment and Rsch. in Multiple Sclerosis, L.Am. Com. on Treatment and Rsch. in Multiple Sclerosis, Consortium of Multiple Sclerosis Ctrs. Author, co-author: Epidemiology of Multiple Sclerosis, 1968, Epidemiology of Cerebrovascular Disease, 1969, Epidemiology of Neurologic and Sense Organ Disorders, 1973, Neuroepidemiology, 1998, Psychiatry/Neurology, 1998, Practice Questions. Book One, 1998, Psychiatry Neurology, 1998, Book Two, 1998; mem. editl. bd. Neuroepidemiology, 1980—, Neurology, 1984-92, Stroke, 1986-2000, Jour. Clin. Epidemiology, 1988—, Jour. Neurol. Sci., 1990-96, Acta Neurologica Scandinavica, 1990-97; contbr. over 450 articles to profl. jours., chpts. to books. Served with USN, 1944-46; rear adm. M.C., USNR, 1946-86, ret. 1986. Decorated Legion of Merit (2), Navy Commendation medal, Armed Forces Res. medal with gold hourglass, others; recipient cert. of merit, Surgeon Gen. Navy, 1969, Gold Bicennial medal, Georgetown U., 1982, Sec.'s Disting. Career award, Dept. Vets. Affairs, 1998, Charcot award, Internat. Fedn. MS Socs., 1999, others. Fellow: AHA (stroke coun. 1991—2000), ACP, AAAS, Am. Heart Assn., Pan Am. Med. Assn. (coun. neurology sect.), N.Y. Acad. Sci., Am. Coll. Epidemiology, Am. Coll. Preventive Medicine, Am. Acad. Neurology (chmn. sect. on neuro-epidemiology 1971—75, chmn. com. nat. needs in neurology 1981—85, subcom. nat. needs in neurology 1985—86, mem. work force task force 1997, John Jay Dystel prize for mulitple sclerosis rsch. 1997); mem.: AMA, AAUP, Consortium Multiple Sclerosis Ctrs. (Lifetime Achievement award 2003), Lat. Am. Com. Treatment and Rsch. in Multiple Sclerosis, Am. Com. Treatment and Rsch. in Multiple Sclerosis, Soc. Med. Cons. to Armed Forces (com. on res. affairs 1980—83, com. on manpower 1984—98), Sr. Stroke Soc., Res. Officers Assn. (life), Naval Inst. (life), Fleet Res. Assn. (life), Naval Officers Assn. Am. (life), Am. Neurol. Assn. (hon.; chmn. bylaws ad hoc com. 1990—91), Danish Neurol. Soc. (hon.), French Soc. Neurology (hon.; fgn.), Assn. Nicoló Copernico (hon.), German Soc. Neurology (hon.), Assn. Mil. Surgeons (life), Naval Res. Assn. (life), Naval Order U.S. (life), Internat. Stroke Soc., Am. Soc. Microbiology, Am. Epilepsy Soc., Assn. Rsch. in Nervous and Metal Disease, Internat. Epidemiol. Assn., Am. Epidemiol. Soc., So. Med. Assn., Navy League (life). Home: 7509 Salem Rd Falls Church VA 22043-3240 Office: 7509 Salem Rd Falls Church VA 22043-3240 Office Fax: 703-560-6490. Business E-Mail: kurtzke2@aol.com. *To be a physician demands recognition of the intrinsic value and dignity of human life while pursuing the goal of relieving pain and impairment due to disease or injury.*

KURTZMAN, NEIL A. medical educator; b. Bklyn., June 18, 1936; s. Louis S. and Roselie (Yegla) K.; m. Sandra Sabatini, Feb. 14, 1976; children from previous marriage: Jonathan, Laura. BA with honors, Williams Coll., 1957;

MD, N.Y. Med. Coll., 1961. Intern Robert Packer Hosp., Sayre, Pa., 1961-62; resident Ohio State U. Hosp., Columbus, 1962-63; asst. chief med. services Nobel Army Hosp., Ft. McClellan, Ala., 1963-64; med. resident William Beaumont Gen. Hosp., El Paso, Tex., 1964-65, chief med. resident, 1965-66; fellow in nephrology U. Tex. Southwestern Med. Sch., Dallas, 1966-68; chief renal div. Brooke Army Med. Ctr., Ft. Sam Houston, Tex., 1969-72; prof., chief nephrology sect. U. Ill. Coll. Medicine, Chgo., 1972-84; prof. Tex. Tech U. Health Scis. Ctr., Lubbock, 1985—99, chief nephrology divsn., 1985-94, chief of staff univ. med. ctr., 1990-92, chmn. dept. internal medicine, 1985-98, prof., 1999—. Mem. gen. medicine B study sect. Nat. Inst. Arthritis, Metabolic and Digestive Diseases, Bethesda, Md., 1978-83; mem. merit rev. bd. VA, Washington, 1979-82, chmn., 1981-82; mem. sci. adv. bd. Nat. Kidney Found., N.Y.C., 1981-92, chmn., 1988-90, v.p., 1990-92, pres., 1992-94; prin. investigator regulation urinary acidification NIH, Bethesda, 1978—. Author: Handbook of Urinalysis and Urinary Sediment, 1974, Pathophysiology of the Kidney, 1977, Doing Nothing, 2000; also more than 300 sci. papers, more than 600 sci. presentations; editor-in-chief Seminars in Nephrology, 1981—, Am. Jour. Kidney Diseases, 1997-2002; assoc. editor Am. Jour. Nephrology; mem. editorial bd. 7 sci. jours.; referee 16 sci. jours. Faculty advisor Alpha Omega Alpha, U. Ill., 1977-84, Tex. Tech U. Health Sci. Ctr., 1985-2002. lt. col. U.S. Army, 1963-72. Decorated U.S. Army Meritorious Svc. award; recipient Pres.'s award Nat. Kidney Found., 1990, Outstanding Acad. Achievement award N.Y. Med. Coll., 1993, So. Soc. for Clin. Investigation's Founder's award, 1996, Tex. chpt. Am. Coll. Physicians Laureate award, 1996, David M. Hume award Nat. Kidney Found., 1999, Headliner award, 2003. Fellow AAAS; mem. Am. Physiol. Soc., Am. Soc. Clin. Investigation, Assn. Am. Physicians, Ctrl. Soc. Clin. Research, So. Soc. Clin. Investigation, Alpha Omega Alpha. Office: Dept of Int Med TTUHSC 3601 4th St Lubbock TX 79430-0001 E-mail: neil.kurtzman@ttuhsc.edu.

KURUVILLA, KOLLANPARAMPIL, electrical engineer; b. Kodukulanji, Kerala, India, July 20, 1943; came to U.S., 1988; s. Thomas and Susanna (Idicula) K.; m. Elizabeth Kuruvilla, Oct. 23, 1967 (dec. Jan. 1971); 1 child, Susan, m. Santha Mathew, Feb. 12, 1972; children: Babita, Nandita, Oscar. BSc in Engring., Kerala U., 1965; PhD, Kennedy Western U., 1997; postgrad., Trinity Coll./Theol. Sem., Newburgh, Ind., 1998—. Lectr. in elec. engring. Mar. Athanasius Coll. Engring., Kerala, 1965-66; elec. engr., exec. engr. Kerala State Electricity Bd., Trivandrum, 1966-87; elec. engr. Zambia Electricity Supply Corp., Lusaka, 1972-75; chief power sta. Soiedade Hidroelectrico do Révue, Mininstry of Power, Chimoio, Mozambique, 1979-81; project engr., design engr. Southeastern Pa. Transp. Authority, Phila., 1989—. Author: In Nature's Lap, 1995, A Smell of Africa (Safe in his Arms), 1998, It's Spring in America, 1999; inventor in field of safety and security measures; patentee in field. Nat. assoc. Libr. of Congress. Named Citizen of Yr., Hutt River Province, Australia, 1994, 96. Mem. Instn. Engrs. India, World Affairs Coun. of Phila., Handi Ham Club. Achievements include invention of in field of safety and security measures; patents for in field. Avocations: reading, music, painting, writing, amateur radio, reading, music, reading about nature, painting, amateur radio, writing. Home: 133A Dawn Dr Lansdale PA 19446-5251 Office: Southeastern Pa Transp Authority 1234 Market St Ste 13 Philadelphia PA 19107-3721 E-mail: VU2KKLN3ilq@prodigy.net.

KURVONEN, TIMO LAURI, research scientist; b. Orimattila, Finland, Oct. 14, 1964; s. Lasse Allan and Saara Kaija (Keskinen) K.; m. Marjo Tuulia Seppanen, July 1, 1994; children: Sampo, Jenni. MS, Helsinki U. Tech., 1991; PhD, Helsinki U. Tech., Espoo, Finland, 1994. Rsch. asst. Helsinki U. Tech., Lab. Space Tech., Espoo, Finland, 1989-91, rsch. scientist, 1991-95, 97—; prof. space & aviation Rovaniemi Inst. Tech., Finland, 1997-2000; chief technologist Nat. Bd. Edn., Helsinki, Finland, 2000—. Contbr. articles to profl. jours. Rsch. grantee Commn. European Union, Italy, 1995-97; rsch. fellow Joint Rsch. Ctr. European Commn., Ispra, Italy, 1995-97; rsch. scholar Antti and Jenny Wihuri Fund, Finland, 1993, Emil Aaltonen Found., Finland, 1996, 97, Tech. Devel. Found., Finland, 1997, 98. Avocations: old automobiles, sailing, skiing, cross-country skiing. Office: Nat Bd Edn Hakaniemenkatu 2 PO Box 380 FIN-00531 Helsinki Finland Fax: 358-9-7747 7715. E-mail: lauri.kurvonen@oph.fi.

KURY, FRANKLIN LEO, lawyer; b. Sunbury, Pa., Oct. 15, 1936; s. Barney and Helen (Witkowski) K.; m. Elizabeth Heazlett, Sept. 14, 1963; children: Steven, David, James. Bar: Pa. 1962. Atty. Pa. Dept. Justice, Harrisburg, 1961-62; ptnr. Kury & Kury, Sunbury, 1963-80, Tive, Hetrick & Pierce, Harrisburg, 1981-82, Reed, Smith, Shaw & McClay, Harrisburg, 1983—. Adj. prof. immigration law, Harrisburg, Widener Law Sch., 1999-2000. Mem. Pa. Ho. of Reps., Harrisburg, 1967-72, Pa. Senate, Harrisburg, 1973-80; del. at large Dem. Nat. Conv., San Francisco, 1984; bd. dirs. Hawk Mountain Sanctuary Assn. 1st lt. USAR, 1962-66. Mem.: Pa. Bar Assn. (chmn. environ. sect. 1984, 1st award for Outstanding Contbn. to Profession of Environ. Law Practice 1993), Am. Immigration Lawyers Assn. Democrat. Avocation: golf. Office: Reed Smith LLP 213 Market St Ste 900 Harrisburg PA 17101-2108 E-mail: fkury@reedsmith.com.

KURYK, DAVID NEAL, lawyer; b. Balt., Aug. 24, 1947; s. Leon and Bernice G. (Fox) K.; m. Alice T. Lehman, July 8, 1971; children: Richard M., Robert M., Benjamin A. BA, U. Md., 1969; JD, U. Balt., 1972. Bar: Md. 1972, U.S. Dist. Ct. Md. 1973, U.S. Ct. Mil. Appeals 1973, D.C. 1974, U.S. Ct. Appeals (4th cir.) 1974, U.S. Supreme Ct. 1976, U.S. Ct. Appeals (Fed. cir.) 1982. Assoc. Harold Buchman, Esq., Balt., 1970-76; pvt. practice Balt., 1976—. Mem. editl. bd. Md. Bar Jour., 1973-76. Sgt. USAF, 1967-73. Mem. ABA (products gen. liability and consumer law com. 1976—, com. auto law 1977), Md. State Bar Assn., Bar Assn. Balt. City, ATLA, U. Balt. Alumni Assn., Zeta Beta Tau. Democrat. Jewish. Home: 11200 5 Springs Rd Lutherville MD 21093-3520 Office: Am Bldg 231 E Baltimore St Ste 702 Baltimore MD 21202-3446 E-mail: david@kuryk.com.

KURZ, ALAN SCOTT, retired small business owner; b. N.Y.C., N.Y., May 8, 1951; s. Marvin Roy Kurz and Barbara Yarmus; m. Kathleen Turmer, Sept. 8, 1976 (div. Sept. 2, 1981). BA, Boston U., 1974. Owner Travel in Style (5 agys.), Great Neck and Little Neck, NY, 1974—79, Galaxy Travel (28 agys.), L.A., 1980—88; gen. mgr. Oasis Reservations, Miami, 1989—96; owner Askme Computers, Miami, 1996—2001; ret., 2001. Cons. to travel agys., tour opers., computer bus., Fla., 1997—; keynote spkr. Am. Soc. Travel Agts. Avocations: reading, scuba diving, snow skiing. E-mail: askme2005@aol.com.

KURZ, JAMES ECKHARDT, retired chemist; b. Louisville, Ky., Oct. 8, 1934; s. Margaret Freda and Eckhardt Kurz; m. Ann Brookes, Nov. 29, 1964; children: James, Jeffrey. BA, Centre Coll. Ky., 1956; MA, Duke U., 1958, PhD, 1961. Mgr. rsch. & develop. Monsanto Co., St. Louis, 1961—85; tech. fellow Boeing Co., St. Louis, 1986—2000; ret., 2000. Cons., St. Louis, 2000—. Contbr. chapters to books. Mem.: Am. Chem. Soc. Presbyterian. Home: 14317 Aitken Hill Ct Chesterfield MO 63017

KURZ, MARY ELIZABETH, lawyer; b. Scranton, Pa., May 13, 1944; m. William H. Bright III. Student, U. Paris, Sorbonne, summer 1965; BA in French magna cum laude, Marywood Coll., 1966; postgrad., U. Md., 1966-67, U. N.C., 1967, U. Wis., 1969; JD with honors, U. Md., 1971. Bar: Md. 1972, D.C. 1978, Mont. 1982, Mich. 1988, Tex. 1994, N.C. 1996, U.S. Dist. Ct. (we. dist.) Mich., U.S. Supreme Ct., U.S. Ct. Appeals (4th, 6th, D.C. cirs.), U.S. Dist. Ct. Mont. Law clk. to presiding justice Ct. Spl. Appeals Md., 1971-72; asst. atty. gen. criminal div. State of Md., 1972-74, asst. legis. officer to gov., 1974-75, asst. atty. gen. representing U. Md., 1975-82; legal counsel U. Mont., Missoula, 1982-87; gen. counsel, v.p. legal affairs Mich. State U., East Lansing, 1987-94; vice chancellor and gen. counsel Tex. A&M U. System, 1994-96; vice chancellor, gen. coun. N.C. State U., Raleigh, 1996—. Speaker numerous confs. and profl. meetings; mem. Commn. to Study Sovereign Immunity, 1975. Mem. staff Md. Law Rev. Reginald Heber Smith fellow, 1969. Mem. ABA, Nat. Assn. Coll. and Univ. Attys. (mem. numerous coms., chmn. com. site selection 1985-86, chmn. com. continuing legal edn. 1986-89, bd. dirs. 1985-88, 2d v.p. 1989-90, 1st v.p. 1990-91, pres.-elect 1991-92, pres. 1992-93) Home: 102 King George Loop Cary NC 27511-6334 Office: NC State U 3rd Fl Holladay Hall Raleigh NC 27695

KURZ, MORDECAI, economics educator; b. Natanya, Israel, Nov. 29, 1934; came to U.S., 1957, naturalized, 1973; s. Moshe and Sarah (Kraus) K.; m. Lillian Rivlin, Aug. 4, 1963 (div. Mar. 1967); m 2d Linda Alice Cahn, Dec. 2, 1979. BA in Econs. and Polit. Sci., Hebrew U., Jerusalem, 1957; MA in Econs., Yale U., 1958, PhD in Econs., 1962; MS in Stats., Stanford U., 1960. Asst. prof. econs. Stanford U., 1962-63, assoc. prof., 1966-68, prof., 1969—, Joan Kenney prof. econs., 1997—, dir. econs. sect. Inst. for Math. Studies, 1971-89; sr. lectr. in econs. Hebrew U., 1963-66. Cons. econs. SRI Internat., Menlo Park, Calif., 1963-78; spl. econ. advisor Can. health and Welfare Ministry, Ottawa, Ont., 1976-78; spl. econ. advisor Pres.'s Commn. on Pension, Washington, 1979-81; rsch. assoc. Nat. Bur. Econ. Rsch., 1979-82; Lady Davis vis. prof. Hebrew U., Jerusalem, 1993; prin. investigator Smith Richardson Found., 2001—. Author: (with Kenneth J. Arrow) Public Investment, The Rate of Return and Optimal Fiscal Policy,1970, Endogenous Economic Fluctuations: Studies in the Theory of Rational Beliefs, 1997; co-editor Econ. Theory, 1997—. Bd. dirs. Ben-Gurion U. of the Negev, Israel, 1998—. Ford Found. faculty fellow Stanford U., 1973; Guggenheim Found. fellow Stanford U., Harvard U., Jerusalem, 1977-78; Inst. Advanced Studies fellow Hebrew U., Mt. Scopus, Jerusalem, 1979-80; prin. investigator NSF, 1969-93, Smith-Richardson Found., 2001—. Fellow Econometric Soc. (assoc. editor Jour. Econ. Theory 1976-90); mem. Am. Econ. Assn. Democrat. Jewish. Office: Stanford U Econs Dept Serra St at Galvez Stanford CA 94305-6702 E-mail: mordecai@stanford.edu.

KURZ, THOMAS PATRICK, lawyer; b. Stevens Point, Wis., Dec. 26, 1951; s. Edward Albert and Bertha Marie (Schmidt) K.; m. Debra Kay Gentz, Jan. 6, 1979; children: Natalie Jean, Thomas Patrick Jr. BA, U. Wis.-Madison, 1974; JD, Georgetown U., 1977. Bar: Wis. 1977, U.S. Dist. Ct. (ea. dist.) Wis. 1977, Ill. 1982, Tex. 1989. Assoc. Foley & Lardner, Milw. and Madison, 1977-82; atty. A.E. Staley Mfg. Co., Decatur, Ill., 1982-85; corp. counsel Staley Continental, Inc., Rolling Meadows, Ill, 1985-88; gen. counsel, asst. sec. Sysco Corp., Houston, 1988-99; of counsel Andrews & Kurth, Houston, 2000-2002; dep. gen. counsel, asst. sec. Sysco Corp., Houston, 2002—. Mem. Georgetown Law Jour., 1975-76, editor, 1976-77. Recipient Eagle Scout award Samoset coun. Boy Scouts Am., 1967; Wis. honors scholar, 1970. Fellow Tex. Bar Found.; mem. ABA, Ill. Bar Assn., State Bar Tex., Phi Beta Kappa. Roman Catholic. Home: 20010 Sky Hollow Ln Katy TX 77450-5218 Office: Sysco Corp 1390 Enclave Pkwy Houston TX 77077-2099 E-mail: kurz.tom@corp.sysco.com.

KURZBAN, IRA JAY, lawyer; b. Bklyn., May 9, 1949; s. Benjamin and Irene (Weiss) K.; m. Magda Montiel Davis, Apr. 15, 1989; children: Kathryn Montiel Davis, Paula Lindsay Davis, Magda Marie Davis, Sadie Bethany Kurzban, Benjamin Kurzban. BA magna cum laude, Syracuse U., 1971; MA, U. Calif., Berkeley, 1973, JD, 1976; hon. fellow, U. Pa. Law Sch., 1987. Bar: Calif. 1976, Fla. 1976, U.S. Dist. Ct. (no. dist.) Calif., 1976, U.S. Dist. Ct. (so. dist.) Fla., 1976, U.S. Dist. Ct. (ctrl. dist.) Calif. 1999, U.S. Ct. Appeals (5th cir.) 1978, U.S. Ct. Appeals (11th cir.) 1981, U.S. Ct. Appeals (4th cir.) 1994, U.S. Ct. Appeals (6th cir.) 2002, U.S. Ct. Appeals (2d cir.) 2003, U.S. Supreme Ct. 1980. Ptnr. Kurzban, Kurzban, Weinger & Tetzeli P.A., Miami, Fla., 1977—99; Fla. counsel Nat. Energy Civil Liberties Com., 1979-98; gen. counsel Am. Immigration Lawyers Assn., 1992-93. Adj. prof. immigration and nationality law U. Miami Sch. of Law, 1979—, Nova Southeastern Law Sch., 1982—; instr. polit. sci. U. Calif. Berkeley, 1973; mem. civil justice adv. com. U.S. Dist. Ct. (so. dist.) Fla., 1993-94; mem. certification com. in immigration and nationality law Fla. Bar, 1994-96; lectr. in field. Author: Kurzban's Immigration Law Sourcebook: A Comprehensive Outline and Reference Tool, 8th edit., 2002; contbr. articles to profl. jours. Founder Berkeley Law Found. Recipient Tobias Simon pro bono svc. award Fla. Supreme Ct., 1982, Trial Lawyer of Yr. award Trial Lawyers for Public Justice, Carol King award Nat. Lawyers Guild, 1996, Lawyer of the Ams. award U. Miami Sch. Law, 1992, Edith Lowenstein Meml. award for excellence in immigration scholarship, 2002; Polit. Sci. Dept. fellow U. Calif., Berkeley, 1971, Kent fellow Danforth Found., 1974-77, Law and Society fellow U. Calif., Berkeley, 1975-76, Wasserstein fellow Harvard Law Sch., 2003. Fellow Am. Immigration Law Found. (hon.); mem. ABA (chair refugee legal assistance com. 1983-84, mem. immigration coord. com. 1991-93), Am. Immigration Lawyers Assn. (pres. so. Fla. chpt. 1980-81, nat. pres. 1987, Jack Wasserman award for excellence in federal litigation 1983, Edith Lawenstein award for excellence in writing in immigrant law 2002), Am. Inns of Ct., Phi Beta Kappa, Phi Kappa Phi. Office: Kurzban Kurzban Weinger & Tetzeli PA 2650 SW 27th Ave Miami FL 33133-3003 E-mail: ira@kkwtlaw.com.

KURZBAN, ROBERT OWEN, psychologist, researcher; b. Poughkeepsie, N.Y., Sept. 29, 1969; s. Stanley Abbot Kurzban and Nina Irene Liben. BA, Cornell U., 1991; PhD, U. Calif., Santa Barbara, 1998. Post-doctoral fellow Internat. Found. Rsch. in Exptl. Econs. U. Ariz., Tucson, 1998—2000; post-doctoral fellow U. Calif./Calif. Inst. Tech., L.A., 2000—02. Asst. prof. U. Pa., Phila., 2002—. Fellow post-doctoral fellowship, Intern. Found. Rsch. in Exptl. Econs., 1998-2000, post-docotoral fellowship, McArthur Found., 2000-2002; grantee Russell Sage Found. Behavioral Econs. Roundtable Small grants program, Russell Sage Found., 1999. Office: U Pa 3815 Walnut St Philadelphia PA 19104 Office Fax: 215-898-7301. Business E-Mail: kuraban@psych.upenn.edu.

KURZDORFER, PETER JOHN, chess educator, writer, editor; b. Buffalo, Dec. 30, 1949; s. Joseph and Elizabeth (Fernandez) K.; m. Kathleen R. Wing, May 21, 1994. Grad. h.s., Kenmore East, N.Y. Ch. organist various, Buffalo, 1964-69, 72-79, stock boy, 1968-69, ch. organist, 1982-84, laborer Buffalo and Lockport, N.Y., 1969-72; cellist, singer Kurzdorfer & Cady, Buffalo, 1978-79, 82-87; home health care aide Boston, San Diego, Buffalo, 1979-89; Bradford (Pa.) resident chess master Am. Chess Sch., 1989-97; owner, operator Kurzdorfer's Chess Svc., Bradford, 1997. Author: The Everything Chess Basics Book, 2003; (software) Chessmaster 5000, 1995; co-author: (CD-ROM) How to Play Chess, Zane, 1996; contbr. articles to profl. jours.; columnist Bradford Jour., 1989-96; asst. editor Chess Life mag., 1997-2000, editor, 2000—; editor School Mates mag., 2000-03. Mem. Am. Chess Sch. (pres. 1992-96), U.S. Chess Fedn. (cert. nat. master, life master, coach, tournament dir.), Chess Journalists of Am. (judge 1992-95). Avocations: singing, piano. Home and Office: 6666 Bennett Rd Franklinville NY 14737-9712 E-mail: magazines@uschess.org.

KURZMAN, HAROLD PHILIP, transportation economist, consultant; b. N.Y.C., Dec. 14, 1936; s. Harold P and Eleanor Hess Kurzman; m. Udine Y Bowen, Sept. 3, 1966 (dec. July 2002); children: Cecelia, Philip. BA, Haverford Coll., 1958; MA, Johns Hopkins U., 1960; Program for Mgmt. Devel., Harvard Bus. Sch., 1975. Dir. and project mgr. Louis Berger Internat., Washington, 1967-85; advisor Govt. of Malawi, Lilongwe, 1986-88; assoc. Lukehart Thornill Assocs., Falls Church, Va., 1990—. Consult Inter-Am Develop Bank, Washington, 1990—91, World Bank, Washington, 1991—92; dir. planning and econs. PBI, 1994—99. Contbr. articles to profl jours. Mem.: Transport Research Forum, Nat Economists Club. Avocations: tennis, photography. Home: 11801 Rockville Pike Apt 503 Rockville MD 20852-2720 Personal E-mail: hardu@msn.com.

KURZMAN, ROBERT GRAHAM, lawyer, educator; b. N.Y.C., July 3, 1932; s. Benjamin E. and Betty Kurzman; m. Carol Ellis, Aug. 26, 1956; children: Marc, Nancy, Amy. BA, Hofstra U., 1954; JD, Cornell U., 1957. Bar: N.Y. 1959, U.S. Dist. Ct. (no., so., ea. and we. dists.) N.Y. 1964, U.S. Supreme Ct. 1964. Assoc. Wynn, Blattmachr & Campbell, N.Y.C., 1959-63; ptnr. Leaf, Kurzman, Deull & Drogin, N.Y.C., 1963-79, Goldschmidt, Fredericks, Kurzman & Oshatz, 1979-83, Kurzman & Eisenberg and precedessor firms, White Plains, N.Y., 1982—. Adj. prof. law NYU; dir. Stratton Industries, Inc.; acting city ct. judge City of New Rochelle (N.Y.), 1981. Author: (with Rita Gilbert) Paralegals and Successful Law Practice, 1981; contbr. articles to profl. jours. Mem. adv. bd. So. Meth. U. Sch. Law, Estate Planning Inst.; coord. estates and trusts paralegal program Manhattanville Coll., 1974-75; pres. West Putnam coun. Boy Scouts Am., 1981; trustee, pres. Temple Israel; former chmn. New Rochelle Rep. Com. Capt. USAR, 1957-59. Recipient Silver Beaver award Boy Scouts Am., Silver Antelope aawrd; named Man of Yr., New Rochelle B'nai B'rith, 1977. Fellow Am. Coll. Probate Counsel; mem. ABA, N.Y. State Bar Assn., Assn. Bar City N.Y., Masons, Ridgeway Country Club (White Plains), Cornell Club of N.Y.C. (pres.). Home: 166 Tewksbury Rd Scarsdale NY 10583-6036 Office: 1 N Broadway White Plains NY 10601-2310 E-mail: rkurzman@kelaw.com.

KURZMAN, STEPHEN ALAN, accountant, educator; b. Boston, Feb. 24, 1945; s. H. Edward and Gertrude (Blake) K.; m. Marilyn Verna Baker, June 30, 1968; children; David Eric, Jessica Susan. BS, Northeastern U., 1968; MS, Bentley Coll., 1977. Asst. to treas. Home Owners Fed. Savs. & Loan Assn., Boston, 1968-70; sr. acct. Martin D. Braver & Co., Chestnut Hill, Mass., 1970-73; tax supr. Laventhol & Horwath, Boston, 1973-76; ptnr. Kurzman, Scibetta & Dempsey, Canton, Mass., 1976—. Adj. asst. prof. taxation Bentley Coll., 1978—, chmn. tax adv. bd., grad. tax program adv. com.; bd. dirs., treas. Congregation Mishkan Tefila; chmn. IRS Dist. Dirs. Liaison Commn. for New Eng.; program chmn. Bentley Coll. Nat. Tax Conf. Contbr. articles to profl. jours. Memm. AICPA (instr. 1982—), Mass. Soc. CPAs (past chmn. fed. tax com., bd. dirs., chmn. tax forum com., cochmn. tax conf.), Bentley Coll. Alumni Assn., B'nai B'rith, Beta Alpha Psi. Home: 8 David Rd Newton MA 02459-2712 Office: Kurzman Scibetta & Dempsey 1017 Turnpike St Canton MA 02021-2828 Personal E-mail: sakaye224@aol.com. E-mail: skurzman@ksdcpa.com.

KURZROCK, RAZELLE, internist, educator; b. Toronto, Sept. 29, 1954; d. David and Matilda Kurzrock; m. Philip Cohen, Sept. 28, 1985; children: Benjamin A., Jonathan A., Rena A., Tali A. BS with honors, U. Toronto, 1974, MD, 1978. Asst. prof. U. Tex. M.D. Anderson Cancer Ctr., Houston, 1984-89, prof. medicine sect. biologic medicine, 1994—, chief, 1990—. Vis. prof. The Wistar Inst., Phila., 1987-88. Contbr. articles on molecular biology and cancer treatment to profl. jours. Fellow: ACP. Office: U Tex MD Anderson Cancer Ctr 1515 Holcombe Blvd Box 422 Houston TX 77030-4009

KURZWEG, ULRICH HERMANN, engineering science educator; b. Jena, Germany, Sept. 16, 1936; came to U.S., 1947, naturalized, 1952; s. Hermann Herbert and Erna Herta (Michaelis) K.; m. Sophia Speth, Dec. 21, 1963; 1 dau., Tina. BS, U. Md., 1958, MA (Woodrow Wilson fellow 1958-59), Princeton U., 1959, PhD in Physics, 1961. Sr. theoretical physicist United Tech. Research Labs., East Hartford, Conn., 1962-68; adj. assoc. prof. math. Rensselaer Poly. Inst., Hartford (Conn.) Grad. Center, 1964-68; mem. faculty U. Fla., Gainesville, 1968, prof. engring. scis., 1968—. Contbr. numerous articles to sci. and tech. publs. Fulbright grantee, 1961-62; recipient Cert. of Recognition, NASA, 1984, award for excellence in undergrad. teaching U. Fla., 1991. Mem. AAAS, Am. Phys. Soc., N.Y. Acad. Scis., Sigma Xi. Home: 8407 NW 4th Pl Gainesville FL 32607-1414 Office: U Fla Dept Mech and Aerospace Engring Gainesville FL 32607

KURZWEIL, ALAN DENNIS, social worker, marriage and family therapist, consultant; b. N.Y.C., May 27, 1950; s. Raffael and Hilda Molly (Meisel) K.; m. Paula Lee Backstrom, Oct. 24, 1971; children: Jeffrey Michael, Justin Henry. BA in Psychology, Allegheny Coll., 1971; MSSA, Case Western Reserve, 1976. Lic. ind. social worker, Ohio. Theraeputic activities worker Polk (Pa.) State Sch., 1972-74; planning intern Geauga County Mental Health Bd., Chardon, Ohio, 1974-75; clin. social worker intern Akron Child Guidance Ctr., Barberton, Ohio, 1975-76; clin. social worker Western Res. Human Svcs., Akron, Ohio, 1976-88; psychiat. social worker Kaiser-Permanente, Akron, 1988-91, regional coord. psychiat. social work, Ohio region, 1991-97; pvt. practice marriage and family therapist Fairlawn, Ohio, 1983-99; co-dir. Stages, Fairlawn, 1984—; individual and family therapist Summit Mental Health Group, Fairlawn, 1999—. Coach N.W. Akron Indoor Soccer, 1986-87; asst. coach Revere Soccer Club, 1991-94; team capt. Summit County Slow Pitch Club, 1984-94, 97; mgr. Akron Silver League, 2002. Mem. NASW (dist. sec. 1980-82, dist. treas. 1982-86, mental health chairperson 1980-91, dist. v.p. 1986-89, Social Worker of Yr. 1988), Registry Clin. Social Workers. Democrat. Avocations: softball, racquetball, volleyball, jogging, basketball. Home: 4035 Meadowvale Ct Akron OH 44333 Office: Summit Mental Health Group 3094 W Market St Ste 105 Fairlawn OH 44333-3617 E-mail: adkurzweil@adelphia.net.

KURZWEIL, EDITH, sociology educator, editor; b. Vienna; d. Ernest W. and Wilhelmine M. (Fischer) Weiss; m. Charles H. Schmidt, June 24, 1945 (div. 1958); children: Ronald J., Vivien A.; m. Aug. 2, 1958 (widowed 1966); 1 child, Allen J. BA, Queens Coll., CUNY, 1967; MA, New Sch. Social Rsch., 1969, PhD, 1973. Asst. prof. sociology Hunter Coll., N.Y.C., 1972-75, Montclair State Coll., Upper Monclair, N.J., 1973-78; assoc. prof. sociology Rutgers U., Newark, 1979-85, prof. sociology, chmn., 1985-92; Disting. Olin. Prof. Adelphi U., 1993, univ. prof., 1994—2001, univ. prof. emeritus, 2001—. Vis. prof. Goethe U., 1984. Author: The Age of Structuralism, 1980, Italian Entrepreneurs, 1983, The Freudians: A Comparative Perspective, 1989, Freudians and Feminists, 1995, Briefe aus Wien: Nazi Laws & Jewish Lives, 1999, (German translation only); editor: The Partisan Century: 60 Years of Partisan Review, 1996, (with others) Literature and Psychoanalysis, 1983, Writers and Politics, 1983, Cultural Analysis, 1984; exec. editor Partisan Rev., Boston, 1978-94, editor, 1994—; editl. bd. Psyche, 1990—, Psychoanalytic Books, 1990-2000; series editor Psychiatry and Psychology Transaction, 1995—. Bd. govs. New Sch. Univ., 1999—; adv. bd. N.Y. Civil Rights Coalition, 2001—. Rockefeller Humanities fellow, 1982-83, NEH fellow, 1987-88; NEH grantee, 1989-90, 91-92; NYCH grantee, 1995. Mem. Am. Sociol. Assn., Tocqueville Soc., Internat. Assn. History of Psychoanalysis, Internat. Sociol. Assn., Women's Freedom Network (bd. dirs. 1994—), P.E.N. Home: 1 Lincoln Plz New York NY 10023-7129 E-mail: partisanek@aol.com.

KURZWEIL, HARVEY, lawyer; b. Bklyn., Mar. 23, 1945; s. Martin E. Kurzweil and Muriel (Krause) Kanow; m. Barbara Kramer, Aug. 17, 1969; children: David, Paul (dec.), Emily, Elizabeth. AB, Columbia Coll., 1966, JD, 1969. Bar: N.Y. 1970. Assoc. Dewey, Ballantine, Bushby, Palmer & Wood, N.Y.C., 1969-77, ptnr., 1977-90, Dewey Ballantine, N.Y.C., 1990—, chmn. litigation dept., mem. mgmt. and exec. coms. Bd. dirs. Menninger Clinic; trustee Menninger Found.; bd. visitors Columbia Law Sch. Fellow Am. Bar Found., Internat. Acad. Trial Lawyers; mem. ABA, N.Y. State Bar Assn., D.C. Bar Assn., Assn. of Bar of City of N.Y. (trade regulation com. 1982-85), Univ. Club. Jewish. Avocations: sports cars, reading, gardening, sports. Home: 1025 5th Ave New York NY 10028 Office: Dewey Ballantine 1301 Avenue Of The Americas New York NY 10019-6022 also: PO Box 370 Saddle River NJ 07458-0389 E-mail: hkurzweil@deweyballantine.com.

KURZWEIL, RAYMOND C. computer scientist, entrepreneur; b. N.Y.C., Feb. 12, 1948; s. Fredric and Hannah Kurzweil; m. Sonya Rosenwald, Aug. 3, 1975. BS, MIT, 1970; DHL (hon.), Hofstra U., 1982, Misericordia Coll., 1989; D of Music (hon.), Berklee Coll. Music, 1987; DSc (hon.), Renssalaer Polytech. Inst., 1988, Northeastern U., 1988, N.J. Inst. Tech., 1990, Queens Coll., CUNY, 1991, Dominican Coll., 1993; D of Engring. (hon.), Merrimack Coll., 1989. Founder, CEO Kurzweil Computer Products, Inc. (now Xeroc Imaging Systems), Cambridge, Mass., 1974—80; chmn., CEO Kurzweil Music Systems, Inc., Waltham, Mass., 1982—90; founder, CEO Kurzweil Applied Intelligence, Inc. (acquired by Lernout & Hauspie), Waltham, Mass., 1982—97; founder, chmn., CEO Kurzweil Technologies Inc., 1995—; founder, CEO Kurzweil Ednl. Systems Inc. (acquired by Lernout & Hauspie), 1996—98; founder, pres., CEO Med. Learning Co. Inc. and FamilyMed.com, 1997—; founder, chmn., CEO FAT KAT Inc., 1999—. Chmn. exhbn. bd. Age of Intelligent Machines Exhbn. Mus. of Sci., Boston, 1985—; bd. dirs. Wang Labs., Med. Mgr. Corp. Author: The Age of Intelligent Machines, 1990, The 10% Solution for a Healthy Life, 1993, The Age of Spiritual Machines, When Computers Exceed Human Intelligence, 1999; contbr. articles to profl. jours., chapters to books. Former mem. tech. adv. com. Nat. Ctr. Adult Literacy U. Pa.; chmn. The Kurzweil Found.; trustee Beth Israel Hosp.; overseer New Eng. Conservatory of Music; incorporator Boston Mus. Sci.; mem. vis. com. MIT Sch. Music and MIT. Sch. Humanities. Named New Eng. Inventor of Yr., 1988; named to Computer Design Hall of Fame, Computer Design Mag., 1982; recipient Grace Murray Hopper Outstanding Young Computer Scientist of Yr. award, Assn. for Computing Machinery, 1978, Personal Computing to Aid the Handicapped Nat. award, Johns Hopkins U., 1981, Francis Joseph Campbell award, Am. Libr. Assn., 1983, Entrepreneurial Excellence award, White Ho. Conf. on Small Bus., 1986, Founders award, MIT, 1989, Engr. of Yr. award, Design News mag., 1990, Louis Braille award, Associated Svcs. for the Blind, Mass. Quincentennial award for innovation and discovery, 1992, Gordon Winston award, Can.

Nat. Inst. Blind, 1994, Dickson prize, Carnegie Mellon U., 1994, Access prize, Am. Found. Blind, 1995, Software Industry Achievement award, Mass. Software Coun., 1996, Pres.'s award, Assn. Higher Edn. and Disability, 1997, Vision award, Stevie Wonder/SAP, 1998, Nat. Medal of Tech., 1999. Fellow: Boston Computer Soc. (former bd. dirs.), Assn.. Computing Machinery (Grace Murray Hopper Outstanding Young Computer Scientist of Yr. 1978). Avocation: music. Office: Kurzweil Technologies Inc 15 Walnut St Wellesley Hills MA 02481-2101

KUSAMICHI, MASATAKE, investment company executive; CEO Nishho Iwai Corp., Tokyo, until 1999, exec. advisor, 1999—. Office: Nissho Iwai Corp 4-5 Akasaka 2 chome Minato-ku Tokyo 107-0052 Japan Fax: 81-3-3588-4136.

KUSCHELL, DANIEL J, radio personality; Mem.: Nat. Speakers Assn. (assoc.). Office: A Champion Vision Inc 3370 N Hayden #123-146 Scottsdale AZ 85251 Office Fax: 623-907-4720. Personal E-mail: danchampion03@msn.com. E-mail: dan@achampionvision.com.

KUSH, CHARLES ANDREW, III, telecommunications executive, internet entrepreneur; b. Somerville, N.J., Dec. 30, 1964; s. Charles A. Jr. and Barbara A. (Zuris) K. BS in Mech. and Aerospace Engring., Rutgers U., 1987. Registered profl. engr. in tng., N.J. Prodn. engr. ITT Avionics, Clifton, N.J., 1987-88, project engr., 1988, program transition engr., 1988-89; pres. Creative Products, Middlesex, N.J., 1989—; info. mgr. AT&T, Piscataway, N.J., 1990-93, bus. mgr., 1994-97; portfolio mgr. Beechwood, Clark, N.J., 1997-99; dir. Network OSS, Woodbridge, N.J., 2000-01. Recipient George R. Bolmer Meml. scholarship Bound Brook Rotary, 1983, Fisk Assocs. Engring. scholarship Fisk Assocs., 1983, Carl Rabke award for Citizenship and Scholarship, 1983, ITT Avionics Presdl. citations, 1988. Mem. CEO Club, ASME, AIAA, Nat. Soc. Profl. Engrs., Soc. Mfg. Engrs. (sr.), Internat. Platform Assn., Soc. Automotive Engrs., Assn. Old Crows, Nat. Mail Order Assn., Middlesex Borough Computer Com. Avocations: exercise, photography, travel, automobiles, boating. E-mail: info@cproducts.com.

KUSHALKUMAR, M. BAID, chemical engineer; BSChemE, Bombay U, Bombay U, 1965; MSChemE, Ill. Inst. Tech., 1967; DSChemE, U Del., 1973. Sr. ChemE Union Carbide Corp., Chgo., 1967—69; tech. spl.,proj. mgmt. Xerox Corp., Webster, NY, 1973—79; staff engr.,mgr.,grplor Champion Internat. Corp/St. Regis Corp., W. Nyack, NY, 1979—86; sr. rsch. mgr. Avery Dennison Corp., Painesville, Ohio, 1987—91, tech. dir., 1991—99, dir. tech. ops., 1998—2000; v.p., mf., prod. devel. Jenmar Visual Sys., Fremont, Calif., 2000—01; cons. Pvt. Practice, Concord, Ohio, 2002—. Contbr. articles. Pres. Jain Soc. of Greater Cleve.(Ohio), 2003—04. Grantee rsch. assistantships,fellowships, various U. Del., ITT Chgo., 1969—73. Mem.: Soc. of Plastics Engr., Am. Inst. of ChemE. Achievements include patents in field of on in-mold labelling; on digital printing. Avocations: reading, swimming, walking. Home: 11340 Pelican Grove Concord OH 44077

KUSHEL, GLENN ELLIOT, lawyer; b. Bklyn., May 5, 1945; BME, CUNY, 1968; MSME, Columbia U., 1970; JD, Seton Hall U., 1974; LLM, NYU, 1978; cert., Coll. Fin. Planning, 1987. Bar: N.J. 1974, N.Y. 1977, U.S. Supreme Ct. 1978. Mem. tech. staff Bell Telephone Labs., Whippany, N.J., 1968-71, cost engr. Exxon Resource and Engr. Co., Florham Park, N.J., 1971-72; dep. atty. gen. State of N.J., Trenton, 1974-76; assoc. Rosenman and Colin, N.Y.C., 1976-81; pvt. practice Bklyn., 1981—2001; assoc. Bivona & Cohen, N.Y.C., 2001—. Mem. N.Y. State Sum/Um Arbitrators, 1995-2001. Assoc. mem. malpractice panel N.Y. State Supreme Ct., Kings County, 1986-90. Atomic Energy Commn. fellowship, 1968. Mem. Pi Tau Sigma, Tau Beta Pi. Avocations: skiing, running, financial planning. Office: Wall Street Plz New York NY 10005

KUSHEN, ALLAN STANFORD, retired lawyer; b. Chgo., Oct. 5, 1929; s. Barney and Ethel (Friedman) K.; m. Betty Cohen, Sept. 2, 1951 (dec. Jan. 2000); children: Annette Joyce, Robert Allan; m. Natalie Best, June 1, 2001. BBA cum laude, LLB cum laude, U. Miami, Fla., 1952; LLM, NYU, 1955. Bar: Fla. 1952, N.Y. 1956. Atty. Schering Corp., Bloomfield, N.J., 1955-67, atty. counsel labs. divsn., 1967-69, atty. domestic ops. divsn., 1969-73; v.p., gen. counsel Schering-Plough Corp., Kenilworth, N.J., 1973-80, sr. v.p. pub. affairs Madison, N.J., 1980-94; ret., 1994. Adv. com. Allendale Ins. Co., N.Y., 1986-94; lectr. in field. Trustee Food and Drug Law Inst., 1972-94, trustee emeritus, 1994—; trustee Montclair Art Mus., 2000. 1st lt. JAG, U.S. Army, 1952-54. Food and Drug Law Inst. fellow NYU, 1955. Mem. Phi Delta Phi, Omicron Delta Kappa, Iron Arrow. Home: Millbrook Rd New Vernon NJ 07976

KUSHINSKY, JEANNE ALICE, SAT tutor; b. Reading, Pa, Jan. 12, 1937; d. Otis Jacob and Alice Elizabeth (Kurtz) Rothenberger; m. Sheldon Melvin Wallerstein, May 9, 1959 (div. July 1978); children: Seth, Gail Wallerstein Melichar; m. David Lazar Kushinsky, Apr. 11, 1987. BS, Cedar Crest Coll., 1958; postgrad., Kean U N.J., 1978—92, Rutgers U., 1993. Tchr. East Orange Bd. Edn., NJ, 1958—60; editor Dept. Testing and Assessment State Dept. Edn., Trenton, NJ, 1974—76; tchr. Edison Township Bd. Edn., NJ, 1974—2000; pvt. tutor SAT verbal sect. Edison, NJ, 1980—. Mem. Citizen's Adv. Coun. Edn., Edison, NJ, 1991—93. Fashion show com. Rahway Hosp. Found., 2002—; chairperson gala Edison Arts Soc., 2003—, bd. trustees, 2000—; active Dist. VIII Middlesex County Bd. Atty. Ethics, Trenton, NJ, 2000—. Grantee grant, N.J. Coun. for Humanities, 1996. Mem.: Brandeis Univ. Nat. Women's Comm., NJ Edn. Assn., NEA, Metuchen-Edison Hist. Soc., Proprietary House, Nat. Trust for Hist. Preservation, Borough Improvement League. Democrat. Jewish. Avocations: historic preservation architecture, feminist issues, mentoring young people, film studies, reading. Home: 119 Turner Ave Edison NJ 08820 Home Fax: 732-225-2353.

KUSHLAN, JAMES A. biologist, research administrator, author, educator; b. Cleve., Oct. 11, 1947; BS in Biology and Chemistry cum laude, U. Miami, 1969, MS in Biology, 1972, PhD in Biology, 1974; DSc (hon.), Thiel Coll., Greenville, Pa., John Cabot U., Rome, Italy. Rsch. biologist U.S. Dept. of Interior, 1975-84; dir. ctr. water resources studies Tex. A&M U., Commerce, 1986-88, assoc. prof. biology, 1984—87, prof. biology, 1987-88, U. Miss., 1988-98, chmn. dept. biology, 1988—95; dir. Patuxent Wildlife Rsch. Ctr., 1995-2001; sr. sci. advisor U.S. Geol. Survey, 2001—02; sr. rsch. assoc. Smithsonian Environ. Rsch. Ctr., 2001—. Author: The Herons Handbook, 1984, Freshwater Fishes of Southern Florida, 1987, Storks, Ibises and Spoonbills of the World, 1992, Heron Conservation, 2000; contbr. to Dictionary of Birds, 1985, Encyclopedia of Birds, 1985, Ecosystems of Florida, 1990, The Rivers of Florida, 1991; editor Fla. Field Naturalist, 1981-86, Colonial Waterbirds, 1985-88; mem. editl. bd. Wetlands, 1982, assoc. editor, 1993-95; author 200 papers, revs., commentaries; contbr. articles to profl. jours. Mem. United Way Planning Coun., Oxford, Miss., 1991-92; past bd. dirs. Miss. Nature Conservancy, 1991-95; bd. dirs. John Cabot U., Am. Bird Conservancy, Wetland Internat., N.Am. Bird Conservation Initiative, U.S., Hawk Mountain Sanctuary, Md. League Conservation Voters; com. chair Waterbird Conservation for Ams. Recipient Citizen award WIOD Radio, Miami, 1980; Paul Harris fellow Rotary Internat., 1989. Fellow Am. Ornithologists' Union (life, mem. coun., v.p. 1998-99, pres.-elect 2002—), mem. Soc. Wetland Scientist (life, assoc. editor), Waterbird Soc. (bd. dirs., pres. 1996-98), Herons Specialist Group (chair 1985-97), Orithol. Coun. (bd. dirs. 1996-99), Rotary (chpt. pres. 1987-88), Sigma Xi (chpt. pres. 1983-84). Achievements include research in ornithology, wetland sciences, international wetland and biodiversity conservation, and waterbirds. Office: Smithson Environ Rsch Ctr PO Box 1930 Edgewater MD 21037-

KUSHLAN, SAMUEL DANIEL, physician, educator, hospital administrator; b. New Britain, Conn., Feb. 17, 1912; s. H. David and Bessie M. K.; m. Ethel Ross, June 24, 1934; children: Nancy Kushlan Wanger, David Ross. BS, Yale U., 1932, MD, 1935. Diplomate: Am. Bd. Internal Medicine with subsplty in gastroenterology. Intern New Haven Hosp., 1935-36, asst. resident, 1937; vol. research fellow Mass. Gen. Hosp., 1938; assoc. physician-in-chief Yale-New Haven Hosp., 1967-82, cons. to chief staff, 1982—; clin. prof. medicine Yale U., 1967—. Contbr. numerous articles to profl. jours. Chmn. bequest and endowment program Yale Med. Sch. Alumni Fund, 1977-90; cons. to office of alumni affairs Yale Med. Sch., 1990—. Named Physician of Yr. Conn. Digestive Disease Soc., 1975 Mem. Am. Gastroenterol. Assn., Am. Soc. Gastrointestinal Endoscopy, AMA, Conn. State Med. Soc., New Haven Med. Assn., Conn. Regional Soc. for Gastrointestinal Endoscopy, World Med. Assn., Assn. Yale Alumni in Medicine (pres. 1957-59), Yale Alumni Fund (bd. dirs. 1986-91), Sigma Xi, Alpha Omega Alpha. Office: Suite 1063 CB Yale-New Haven Hosp New Haven CT 06504 *Life must have Meaning.*

KUSHMA, DAVID WILLIAM, journalist; b. Phila., Oct. 27, 1954; s. John Joseph and Helen Elizabeth (Pusti) K.; m. Sandra Joe Cummins, June 2, 1989. BA in English, U. Pa., 1975; MA in Journalism and Mass Comm., U. Minn., 1977. Staff writer Phila. Bull., 1977-80, Detroit Free Press, 1980-87, editorial writer, 1987-92, assoc. editor, 1992-97; editl. page editor The Comml. Appeal, Memphis, 1997—. Mem. Am. Soc. Newspaper Editors, Nat. Conf. Editorial Writers. Office: The Comml Appeal 495 Union Ave Memphis TN 38103-3221 E-mail: kushma@gomemphis.com., dkushma@msn.com.

KUSHMAR, NEAL, accountant; b. Detroit, Oct. 16, 1924; s. Harry and Dora K. BBA, U. Detroit, 1955; MDiv, St. Olaf's Coll., 1962. Acct. Neil's Acctg. Svc., Royal Oak, Mich., 1946—. Scoutmaster Boys Scouts Am., Detroit, 1962-73. With U.S. Army, 1943-44. Mem. Am. Legion, Disabled Am. Vets., Nat. Tax Accts., Nat. Assn. Tax. Preparers. Avocations: reading, camping, hiking, sr. citizen activities, swimming.

KUSHNER, AILEEN, medical/surgical nurse; b. Bklyn., Jan. 26, 1947; d. Harold and Gloria (Ostrofsky) Jarashow; divorced; Michelle, Adam, Brad. AS, SUNY, Farmingdale, 1983; student, SUNY, Stony Brook, 1988-89, Adelphi U., 1990-91, SUNY Regents Coll., 1993-96; BSN, Molloy Coll., 2000. RN, N.Y. Staff nurse medicine, surgery Nassau U. Med. Ctr., East Meadow, NY, 1983-89, med. head nurse, 1989-97, nurse liaison dept. phys. medicine and rehab., 1997—2002, nurse liaison dept. quality assurance, 2002—. Home: 3042 Lowell Ave Wantagh NY 11793-3221

KUSHNER, EVA, academic administrator, educator, author; b. Prague, Czechoslovakia, June 18, 1929; d. Josef and Anna (Kafkova) Dubsky; m. Donn Jean Kushner, Sept. 15, 1949 (dec. 2001); children: Daniel Peter, Roland Joseph, Paul Joel. PhB, Coll. Marie de France, Montreal, 1946; BA, McGill U., 1948, MA, 1950, PhD in French Lit., 1956; D (hon.), Acadia U., 1988, United Theol. Coll., 1992, St Michael's U., 1993, U. Western Ont., 1996, U. Szeged, 1997. Lectr. French McGill U., Montreal, 1952-55, instr. French, 1956, 58, 61-62, 67-69, prof. French lang. and lit., 1976-87, chair dept. French, 1976-80; pres., vice chancellor Victoria U. U. Toronto, 1987-94, dir. ctr. comparative lit., 1994-95; vis. prof. Princeton U., 2000; Mary Rowell Jackman and Mary Coyne Rowell prof. Victoria Coll., 2001—. Sessional lectr. philosophy Sir George Williams U., 1952-53; lectr. U. Coll., London, 1958-59; lectr. Carleton U., 1961; asst. prof. French & comparative lit., 1963, assoc. prof., 1965, prof., 1969-76, chmn. comparative lit., 1965-69, 70-72, 75-76, adj. prof. lit., 1976-79; mem. exec. com. Can. Coun., 1975-81; v.p. Social Scis. & Humanities Rsch. Coun. Can., 1983-86; mem. adv. bd. Nat. Libr. Can.; pres. Humanities Rsch. Coun. Can. 1970-72; vice-chmn. George R. Gardiner Mus. Ceramic Arts, 1990-94. Author: Patrice de La Tour de Pin, 1961; Le Mythe d'Orphée dans la Littérature Française Contemporaine, 1961; Chants de Bohême, 1963; Rina Lasnier, Collection Ecrivains Canadiens d'Aujourd'Hui, 1964; Poètes d'Aujourd'Hui, 1969; Saint-Denys Garneau, 1967; François Mauriac, 1972, Japanese transl., 1976; co-author anthology Que. poetry, transl. into Hungarian, 1978, Polish, 1985, The Living Prism. Itineraries in Comparative Literature, 2001, Pontus de Tyard et son oeuvre poétique, 2001; editor Renewals in the Theory of Literary History; co-editor/co-author: L'Avènement de l'Esprit Nouveau (1400-80), 1988, Crises et essors nouveaux (1560-1610), 2000, Théorie Littéraire: Problèmes et Perspectives, 1989, Histoire des Poétiques, 1997; editor, co-author La Problématique du Sujet chez Montaigne, 1995; co-dir. rsch. Renaissance vols. Histoire Comparée des Littératures de Langues Européennes; mem. editorial com. Can. Comparative Lit. Rev., Dalhousie French Studies, Etudes Montaignistes; mem. internat. adv. bd. Synthesis, Lit. Rsch., 1990-95; contbr. articles to profl. publs. Named Officer Order of Can., 1997. Fellow Royal Soc. Can. (v.p. 1980-82); mem. Académie Européenne des Lettres, des Sciences et des Arts, Am. Comparative Lit. Assn. (adv. bd.), Internat. Comparative Lit. Assn. (pres. 1979-82, co-editor proc. 7th and 9th ICLA Congress, 11th Congress, vols. IV-V, 1991, VI, 1992, VII VIII, 1993, IX, 1994, X, 1995), Internat. Fedn. for Modern Langs. and Lits. (v.p. 1987-93, pres. 1996-99), MLA (del. assembly, chmn. 16th century French lit. divsn., mem. exec. coun. 1983-86, nominating com. 1986-88), Assn. Internat. des Études Françaises, Assn. Canadienne de Littérature Comparée (v.p. 1969-71), Internat. Assn. Neo-Latin Studies, Soc. Canadienne d'Études de la Renaissance, Assn. des Littératures Canadienne et Québecoise, Can. Soc. Semiotic Rsch., Assn. des Professeurs de Français des Universités Canadiennes, Renaissance Soc. Am. (discipline rep. for French studies 1996-99). Office: Victoria Coll 73 Queen's Park Toronto ON Canada M5S 1K7

KUSHNER, FREDERICK GARY, cardiologist, medical educator; b. N.Y.C., May 20, 1948; s. Jack and Gloria Kushner; m. Ivy Erica Sommerstein, May 8, 1977; children: Adam Benjamin, Jared Scott. BA, Columbia U., 1970, MD, 1974. Med. intern, resident Harvard Beth Israel, Boston, 1974—76; cardiology fellow U. Pa., Phila., 1976—78, Mass. Gen. Hosp., Boston, 1978—79; clin. assoc. prof. medicine Tulane U. Sch. Medicine, New Orleans, 1993—; med. dir. Heart Clinic La., Marrero, 1995—. Chmn. credentials com. Leadership Com. of the Coun. on Clin. Cardiology of the Am. Heart Assn., Dallas, 1999—2001; com. mem. Guidelines Com. for mgmt. of ST Elevation MI of the Am. Heart Assn. and Am. Coll. of Cardiology, Washington, 2001—. Exhibitions include World Trade Ctr., New Orleans Acad. Fine Arts, others. Pres. The New Orleans Friends Music, 2000—03; bd. mem. Touro Synagogue, New Orleans, 2002—, Columbia Coll. Alumni Assn., N.Y.C., 1996; alumni coun. bd. mem. Columbia Coll. Physicians and Surgeons, N.Y.C., 1996—. Fellow: ACP (licentiate), Am. Heart Assn., Soc. Cardiac Angiography and Interventions (licentiate), Soc. Nuc. Cardiology (licentiate), Am. Coll. Cardiology (licentiate; v.p. La. chpt. 1990). Achievements include research in nuclear cardiology and perfusion scanning. Avocations: painting, sailing, travel, reading, golf. Home: 6026 St Charles Ave New Orleans LA 70118 Office: Heart Clinic La Suite 613 Physicians Center North Marrero LA 70072 Home Fax: 504-897-6767; Office Fax: 504-349-6621. Personal E-mail: fjakush@aol.com.

KUSHNER, HAROLD JOSEPH, mathematics educator; b. N.Y.C., July 29, 1933; s. Hyman and Harriet Kushner; m. Linda Rosen, Sept. 20, 1960; children: Diana, Nina. BA, CCNY, 1955; MS, U. Wis., 1956, PhD, 1958. Mem. staff Lincoln Lab., Lexington, Mass., 1955-63, Rias, Balt., 1963-64; prof. applied math. Brown U., Providence, 1964—, dir. Lefschtez Ctr. Dynamical Systems, 1980-87, 95-99, chmn. divsn. applied math., 1988-91. Cons. numerous govt. agys. and cos., 1964—. Author: Stochastic Stability and Control, 1967, Introduction to Stochastic Control Theory, 1972, Probability Methods for Approximations in Stochastic Control, 1977, Stochastic Approximation, 1978, Weak Convergence Methods and Applications to Stochastic Systems, 1984, Weak Convergence Methods and Singularly Perturbed Stochastic Control and Filtering Problems, 1991, Numerical Methods for Stochastic Control Problems in Continuous Time, 1992, Stochastic Approximation Algorithms and Applications, 1997, Heavy Traffic Analysis of Controlled Queuing and Communication Networks, 2001. Recipient numerous grants U.S. govt. agys., 1964—, Louis E. Levy award Franklin Inst., 1994. Fellow IEEE (Control Systems award 1992), mem. Inst. Math. Stats., Soc. Indsl. and Applied Math. (W.T. and Idalia Reid prize 2003), Ops. Rsch. Soc. Am., Inst. Mgmt. Sci. Home: 560 Lloyd Ave Providence RI 02906-5427 Office: Brown U Divsn Applied Math Providence RI 02912-0001

KUSHNER, HARVEY DAVID, management consultant; b. N.Y.C., Dec. 28, 1930; s. Morris K. and Hilda Kushner; m. Rose Rehert, Jan. 14, 1951 (dec. 1990); children: Gantt A., Todd R., Lesley K.; m. Patricia E. Sacks, Jan. 1992. BS in Engring., Johns Hopkins U., 1951. Assoc. engr. U.S. Navy Bur. Ships, 1951-53; mem. tech. staff Melpar Inc., 1953-54; with ORI Inc., 1955-88, pres., 1969-83; chmn. bd., CEO ORI, Inc., 1977-88; chmn. bd., pres. The ORI Group, Inc., 1985-88; v.p. Reliance Group Inc. (parent co. of ORI, Inc.), 1970-77; pres. Disclosure Inc., 1972-77; group pres., sr. v.p. Atlantic Rsch. Corp. parent co. of ORI Group, Inc., 1987-88; pres. Kushner Mgmt. Planning Corp., Bethesda, Md., 1988—; chmn. bd. trustees Maryland Venture Capital Trust, 1990-2001. Cons. in bus. and tech. devel., mgmt. and orgn.; bd. dirs. Computer Tech. Assocs., 1988-01, MRJ Tech., Inc., 1988-00, Naviant Tech., Inc., 1998-00, Stamet, Inc., 1994—, Hyperspace Comms., Inc., 2002—. Pub. Rose Kushner's If You've Thought About Breast Cancer. Chmn. Commn. Higher Edn. in Sci. and Tech., Montgomery County, Md., 1984-85, Md. Govs. High Tech. Roundtable, Annapolis, Md., 1983-86, United Way Campaign, Montgomery County, 1980, mem. exec. bd., 1981-85; bd. dirs. Suburban Md. High Tech. Coun., 1986-96, chmn. 1986-1991; chmn. bd. dirs. Rose Kushner Breast Cancer Adv. Ctr., 1990—; mem. nat. subcom. on breast cancer detection and control Am. Cancer Soc., 1991-95; mem. bd. vis. Sch. Pub. Affairs, U. Md., 1988-93, chmn., 1991-92; mem. nat. adv. coun. Sch. Engring. Johns Hopkins U., 1987—; mem. bd. vis. U. Md. Biotech. Inst., 1993—. Recipient Superior Pub. Svc. medal Dept. of Navy, 1988. Fellow AAAS, N.Y. Acad. Scis.; mem. ASME, IEEE (sr.), Nat. Security Indsl. Assn. (chmn. exec. com. 1987-88, chmn. anti-submarine warfare com. 1986-88, mem. bd. trustees 1982-97, vice-chmn. bd. trustees 1987-88, chmn. bd. 1988-89, Vice-Adm. Charles E. Weakley award 1991), Profl. Svcs. Coun. (bd. dirs. 1974-2002, v.p. 1983-88, chmn. bd. dirs. 1991-92), Inst. for Ops. Rsch. and the Mgmt. Scis., Am. Inst. Aerospace Sci., Nat. Def. Industry Assn. (trustee 1997-2001), (assoc.) Sigma Xi. Cosmos Club. E-mail: harveydk@aol.com.

KUSHNER, JACK, retired physician executive; b. Montgomery, Ala., Dec. 5, 1939; s. Louis Harry and Rose (Feldman) K.; m. Annetta Esther Horwitz, June 21, 1964; children: Reyna, Eve. BA, Tulane, 1960; MD, U. Ala., 1964; MGA, U. Md., 1990. Diplomate Am. Bd. Neurosurgery. Intern George Washington U. Hosp., Washington, 1964-65; resident in surgery U. Mich., Ann Arbor, 1965-66; resident in neurosurgery Bowman Gray Sch. Medicine Wake Forest U., Winston-Salem, N.C., 1968-72; pvt. practice neurosurgery, Annapolis, Md., 1972-95; pres., CEO, Futuristic Instruments, Annapolis, 1995-98; chmn., bd. dirs. Telehealth, 1999; ret., 2000; cons. in field. Bd. dirs. E-Global Telehealth, 1999—; chmn. bd. Second Opinion USA; chmn., CEO Am. Opportunity Portal. Author: Preparing To Tack: When Physicians Change Careers, 1995; contbr. articles to profl. jours. With U.S Army, 1966-68, Vietnam. Decorated Bronze Star; recipient Most Disting. Alumnus award U. Md., 2001. Fellow Am. Coll. of Surgeons (emerging tech. and edn. com.), Internat. Coll. of Surgeons; mem. Am. Assoc. Neurol. Surgeons, Congress of Neurol. Surgeons, So. Neurosurgical Soc., Pan Pacific Neurosurgical. Avocations: golf, yacht racing. Home: Ferry Farms 2030 Homewood Rd Annapolis MD 21402-1005 E-mail: jackkushner@msn.com.

KUSHNER, JEFFREY L. manufacturing company executive; b. Wilmington, Del., Apr. 7, 1948; s. William and Selma (Kreger) K.; m. Carolyn Patricia Hypes, May 2, 1975; children: Tawnya Lynne. BBA summa cum laude, U. Hawaii, 1970; MBA, Columbia U., 1972. Sr. fin. analyst Black & Decker, Towson, Md., 1972-73, div. controller Solon, Ohio, 1973-74; asst. div. controller Rockwell Internat., Pitts., 1974-75; div. contr. Carborundum Corp., Niagara Falls, N.Y., 1975-77; mgr. fin. planning United Techs. Corp., Hartford, Conn., 1977-80, corp. v.p. fin. planning, 1986-88, corp. v.p. asset mgmt., 1989-92; asst. contr. Sikorsky Aircraft, Stratford, Conn., 1980-82, div. controller, 1982-83, v.p. fin., chief fin. officer, 1983-85; v.p. fin. and adminstrn. MasterBrand Industries Inc., Deerfield, Ill., 1993-98; sr. v.p. fin. and CFO Lorillard Tobacco Co., 1998; exec. v.p., CFO Cookson Electronics, 1999—. Bd. dirs. ACR, Hartford, 1987-88, Recipient Bronfman Found. fellowship, 1970-71. Mem. Conf. Bd. (coun. 1987-88), Fin. Execs. Inst. Home: 195 Woodland Rd Westwood MA 02090-2631 E-mail: jeffkushner@hotmail.com.

KUSHNER, LAWRENCE MAURICE, physical chemist, consultant; b. N.Y.C., Sept. 20, 1924; s. Hyman Tobias and Mary (Malkin) K.; children: Robb Adam, Leslie Meryl; m. Shirley Gayle Brown, June 24, 1972. BS, Queens Coll., 1945; A.M., Princeton U., 1947, PhD, 1949. Teaching asst. Princeton U., 1947-48; with Nat. Bur. Standards, 1948-73, chief, metal physics sect., 1956-61, chief, metallurgy div., 1961-66; dep. dir. Inst. Applied Tech., 1966-68, dir., 1968, dep. dir. bur., 1969-73, acting dir. bur., 1972-73; commr. Consumer Product Safety Commn., Washington, 1973-77; policy devel. Nat. Bur. Standards, 1977-80; mem. div. staff Mitre Corp., McLean, Va., 1980-85, cons. scientist, 1985-89; adj. prof. engring. and public policy Carnegie-Mellon U., 1981-91. Lectr. chemistry Am. U., 1952-60; spl. asst. for legis. to asst. sec. of commerce for sci. and tech., 1964-65; mem. ad hoc internat. group metal physics OECD, 1961 Recipient Superior Accomplishment award Dept. Commerce, 1954, gold medal, 1968; Meritorious Svc. award Am. Nat. Standards Inst., 1973. Mem. Am. Phys. Soc., AAAS, Fed. Profl. Assn., Am. Chem. Soc., Washington Acad. Scis., ASTM (hon.), Sigma Xi (nat. pres. 1976, bd. dirs.) Achievements include spl. rsch. crystal properties, surface phenomena in chemistry and metallurgy, materials sci., product safety and environ. regulation, sci. and tech. policy, technol. innovation. Home: 20506 Beaver Ridge Rd Montgomery Village MD 20886

KUSHNER, MARK JAY, physics and engineering educator; b. L.A., Dec. 21, 1952; s. Leonard Harry and Muriel (Chelin) K. BA, BS, UCLA, 1976; MS, Calif. Inst. Tech., 1977, PhD, 1979. Postdoctoral Calif. Inst. Tech., Pasadena, 1979-80; physicist Sandia Nat. Labs, Albuquerque, 1980-81, Lawrence Livermore (Calif.) Nat. Labs, 1981-83; dir. electron, atomic and molecular physics Spectra Tech., Bellevue, Wash., 1983-86; prof., Founder prof. engring. U. Ill., Urbana, 1986—. Chairperson Gaseous Electronics Conf., 1996-98; mem. plasma sci. com. NRC, 1998-2003. Assoc. editor Transactions Plasma Sci., 1989—; editl. bd. Plasma Sources Sci. and Tech., 1991—, Jour. Vacuum Sci. & Tech. A, 1998-2000; contbr. over 185 articles to tech. jours. Fellow IEEE (Plasma Sci. and Applications award 2000), Am. Phys. Soc., Optical Soc. Am., Inst. Physics, Am. Vacuum Soc. (Plasma Sci. and Tech. award 1999); mem. Materials Rsch. Soc. Office: U Ill 1406 W Green St Urbana IL 61801-2918 E-mail: mjk@uiuc.edu.

KUSHNER, MICHAEL JAMES, neurologist, consultant, educator; b. Hackensack, N.J., July 18, 1951; s. Samuel and Ruth Ellen (Paul) K.; m. Sarah Joan Warden, Aug. 14, 1976; children: Hunter Paul, Paul Macrae (dec.). BA in Physics, Yale U., 1973; MD, NYU, 1977. Diplomate Am. Bd. Psychiatry, Am. Bd. Neurology, Am. Bd. Med. Examiners; cert. Am. Bd. Electrodiagnostic Medicine, Am. Bd. Pain Medicine. Intern Parkland Meml. Hosp., U. Tex., Dallas, 1977-78; resident in neurology Neurol. Inst., Columbia-Presbyn. Med. Ctr., N.Y.C., 1978-81; rsch. assoc. U. Pa., Phila., 1981-83, asst. prof. neurology, 1983-90; attending physician Hosp. of U. Pa., Phila., 1983-90; with Wilson (N.C.) Neurology Ctr., 1992—; clin. asst. prof. East. Carolina U. Sch. Medicine, 1997—. Dir. SPECT facility Hosp. of U. Pa., 1986-90, asst. dir. neurovascular lab., 1987-90; mem. sensory disorders and lang. study sect. NIH, Bethesda, Md., 1988-90; cons. Dupont Med. Products Div., Billerica, Mass., 1987—; staff neurologist Wilson (N.C.) Neurology Ctr.; legal medicine cons.; neurology physician advisor N.C. Blue Cross/Blue Shield; asst. prof. East Carolina U. Sch. Medicine; dir. Wilson Regional MRI Ctr. Contbr. numerous articles to profl. jours. Interviewer alumni schs. com. Yale U., Phila., 1984—. Fellow Am. Acad. Neurology, Am. Heart Assn. (stroke coun.); mem. AMA, Internat. Soc. for Blood Flow and Metabolism, N.C. Neurol. Soc. (pres. 1995-97), Yale of N.Y.C., Yale of Cen. N.C., Yale of N.C. Republican. Episcopalian. Avocations: oenology, travel, swimming, golf. Home: 1110 Salem St NW Wilson NC 27893-2137 Office: Wilson Neurology Ctr PO Box 3148 Wilson NC 27895-3148

KUSHNER, ROBERT ELLIS, artist; b. Pasadena, Calif., Aug. 19, 1949; s. Joseph and Dorothy (Browdy) K.; m. Ellen Saltonstall, Oct. 27, 1978; children: Max Saltonstall, Lila Saltonstall, Josef Nathaniel. BA, U. Calif., San Diego, 1971. One-man shows include DC Moore Gallery, N.Y.C., 1995, 96, 97, 98, 2000, Holly Solomon Gallery, N.Y.C., 1976, 79, 80, 82, 85, 87, 89-91, 94, Michael Lord Gallery, Milw., 1988-90, 93, 2000, Gallery Rudolf Zwirner, Cologne, Germany, 1982, 86, U. Colo. Art Gallery, Boulder, 1982, Am. Graffiti Gallery, Amsterdam, Netherlands, 1982, Studio Marconi, Milan, Italy, 1982, U. So. Calif. Helen Lindhurst Gallery, Los Angeles, 1982, James Mayor Gallery, London, 1978, 82, 86, 93, Castelli-Goodman-Solomon, East Hampton, N.Y., 1982, Whitney Mus., 1985, Inst. Contemporary Art, Phila., 1987-88, J.B. Speed Art Mus., Louisville, 1988, Aspen Art Mus., Colo., 1988, Wichita Art Mus., 1989, Staller Art Ctr., SUNY, Stony Brook, 1990, Am. Ctr. Tokyo, Osaka, Fukuoka and Sapporo, Japan, 1990-91, First Gallery, Moscow, 1991, Yoshiaki Inoue Gallery, Osaka, 1992, 94, 96, 97, 2000, Gallery APA, Nagoya, Japan, 1994, 99, Midtown Payson Galleries, N.Y.C., 1992, 93, 95, Timothy Brown Fine Art, Aspen, Colo., 1992, 93, David Floria Gallery, Aspen, 1995, Hiroshima (Japan) Prefectural Mus., 1997, Lizan-Tops Gallery, East Hampton, N.Y., 1997, 99, 2000, N.J. Ctr. Visual Arts, Summit, N.J., 1998, Parchman Stremmel Gallery, San Antonio, Tex., 1998, D.C. Moore Gallery N.Y.C., 1995, 96, 98,

2001, 2003, Bellas Artes Gallery, Santa Fe, N.Mex., 1997, 99, Takada Gallery, San Francisco, 1999, 2001, Hiromi Art Internat., 1998, The Contemporary Mus., Honolulu, 2001, Oxy Gallery, Osake, Japan, 2001, Takada Gallery, 2002, Holland Am. Line, 2002, Tribeca Contemporary, N.Y.C., 2002, ; exhibited numerous group shows including Whitney Mus. Am. Art, N.Y.C., 1975, 81, 82, 83, 85, 99, 2000, Mus. Modern Art, N.Y.C., 1978, 80, 81, 83, 84, Karen McCready Fine Art, N.Y.C., 1998, The Monmouth Mus., Lincroft, N.J., 1998, Brandts Klaedefabrik Odense, Denmark, 2001, Albright-Knox Gallery, Buffalo, 1979, Bklyn. Mus., 1984, 86, Mpls. Inst. Arts, 1983, Phila. Inst. Contemporary Art, 1987, Tweed Mus. Art, 1999, 2000, Sydney Art Mus., 1982, Venice Biennale, 1980, 84, Guggenheim Mus., Soho, N.Y., 1997, White Columns, N.Y., 1998, Katonah (N.Y.) Mus. Art, 1999, D.C. Moore Gallery, 1999, 2000, William Havu Gallery, Denver, 2000, Frontstore, Basel, Switzerland, 1999, 2000, 2001, Sarajevo Mus. Quartier, 1998, Mus. Moderner Kunst Stiftung Ludwig, Vienna, 1998, 99, D.C. Moore Gallery, 2001, Bellas Artes Gallery, Santa Fe, 2001, 02, others; represented in permanent collections, Mus. Modern Art, Albright-Knox Mus., Buffalo, Tate Gallery, London, Whitney Mus. Am. Art, Met. Mus. Art, N.Y.C., Bklyn. Mus., Phila. Mus. Art, L.A. County Mus. Art, Balt. Mus. Art, Milw. Art Mus., Uffizzi Gallery, Florence; pub. commns. include Entex Bldg., Houston, 1985, 1270 Avenue of the Americas, Rockefeller Center, N.Y.C., 1991, Tower Place, Cin., 1991, Capital Group, L.A., 1996, Equitable Life Assurance Corp., N.Y., 1996, Royal Pines Golf Course, Kobe, Japan, 1996, Tabla Restaurant, N.Y.C., 1998, Yoshiaki Inoue Gallerry, Osaka, 2000, Michael Lord Gallery, Milw., 2000, Lizan Tops Gallery, East Hampton, n.Y., 2000, Public Market Bldg., Sacramento, Calif., 2001, Blue Smoke, N.Y.C., 2001, Oxy Gallery, Osaka, Japan, 2001, Moore Gallery, Washingon, 2001, 2003, Contemporary Mus., Honolulu, 2001, Bellas Artes, Santa Fe, 2002, Tkada Gallery, San Francisco, 2002; artist numerous art performances, 1971-82; designer costumes, sets; author: (with Ed Friedman and Katherine Landman) The New York Hat Line, 1979; subj. of numerous publs. including Robert Kushner: Gardens of Earthly Delight, 1997. Office: DC Moore Gallery 724 5th Ave New York NY 10019-4106 E-mail: r2knyc@mindspring.com.

KUSHNER, ROBERT F, physician; b. Chicago, Ill., Oct. 6, 1953; s. Irving and Pearl Kushner; m. Nancy Kushner, May 29, 1977; children: Sarah Ann, Steven Harris. MD, U. Ill., Chicago, 1979; MS, U. Chgo., 1984. Assoc. prof. medicine U. of Chgo. Sch. of Medicine, 1992—98; prof. medicine Northwestern U., Feinberg Sch. of Medicine, Chicago, 1998—. Med. dir. wellness inst. Northwestern Meml. Hosp., Chicago, 1998—2003. Recipient Dannon Inst. Award for Excellence in med./dental nutrition edn., Am. Soc. for Clin. Nutrition, 2002. Mem.: Am. Soc. for Parenteral and Enteral Nutrition (pres. 2000—01), Am. Soc. for Clin. Nutrition, North Am. Assn. for Study of Obesity. Achievements include board certified physician nutrition specialist, having taken a leading role in education, clinical research, patient care and advocacy regarding the importance of diet, nutrition and obesity. Office: Wellness Inst 150 East Huron Ste 1100 Chicago IL 60611 Home Fax: 847-256-0352; Office Fax: 312-926-5444. E-mail: rkushner@nmh.org.

KUSHNER, TODD ROGER, computer scientist, software engineer; b. Bethesda, Md., June 18, 1956; s. Harvey David and Rose Molly (Rehert) K.; m. Lea Louise Friedman, Nov. 11, 1990; children: Joshua Philip, Daniel Stuart. BS in Life Scis., MIT, 1976; MS in Computer Sci., U. Md., 1980, PhD in Computer Sci., 1982. Rsch. technician NIH, Bethesda, 1976-77; programmer Tech. Mgmt. Inc., Washington, 1977-78, GTE-Telenet, McLean, Va., 1978-79; grad. rsch. asst. U. Md., College Park, 1980-82, mem. rsch. staff, 1985-88; computer scientist SRI Internat., Menlo Park, Calif., 1982-83; sr. software engr. Vicom Sys. Inc., San Jose, Calif., 1983-85; sr. engr. Stanford Telecoms., Reston, Va., 1988-89; adv. programmer IBM Corp., Gaithersburg, Md., 1989-93; sr. scientist CTA Inc., Rockville, Md., 1993-96; mem. sr. software staff Lockheed Martin Fed. Systems, Denver, 1996-99; mem. tech. staff Lucent Techs., Denver, 1999—2002; sr. programmer CSG Systems, Inc., 2002—. Adj. lectr. U. Santa Clara, Calif., 1983, U. Md., Gaithersburg, 1989-90, Johns Hopkins U., Gaithersburg, 1989-93; participant Software Process Interchange Network, McLean, Va., 1993—. Contbr. articles to profl. publs. Grad. fellow Air Force Office Sci. Rsch., 1980. Mem. IEEE Computer Soc., Assn. Computer Machinery. Democrat. Jewish. Avocations: swimming, racquetball, skiing, golf.

KUSHNER, TONY, playwright; Student, Columbia U., NYU. Assoc. artistic dir. N.Y. Theatre Workshop, 1987; adj. faculty dramatic writing program NYU. Author: (plays) A Bright Room Called Day, 1990, Angels in America: A Gay Fantasia on National Themes Part I "Millenium Approaches", 1992 (Pulitzer Prize for drama, 1993, Tony award Best Play, 1993), Part II "Perestroika", 1993 (Tony award Best Play, 1994), Slavs!, 1994; adaptor The Illusion (Pierre Corneille), 1988; dir.(writer): Yes Yes No No: The Solice of Solstice, Apogee/Perigee, Bestial/Celestial Holiday Show, 1985, In Great Eliza's Golden Time, 1986. Recipient Writers award Whiting Found., 1990, AAAL award, 1994; grantee NEA, 1985, 1987, 1993.

KUSHNER-COHEN, CAROL ANN, school nurse; b. Phila., May 28, 1943; d. Sidney and Frances (Ferdman) Kushner; m. Robert N. Cohen, Aug. 30, 1981; children: Stephanie, Michael. Diploma, Albert Einstein Med. Ctr., 1964; BSN, U. Pa., 1973, MSN, 1975; cert. sch. nurse, Trenton State Coll., 1994. Staff nurse ICU Albert Einstein Med. Ctr., Phila., 1964-65; asst. head nurse Daroff Div., Phila., 1965-66; head nurse ICU Hahnemann Hosp., Phila., 1966-70, instr. staff devel., 1970-71; clin. supr. Hosp. Med. Coll. Pa., Phila., 1975-78, head nurse, 1978-80, nurse recruiter, 1980-82; nursing instr. Mercer Med. Ctr. Sch. Nursing, Trenton, N.J., 1982-93; sch. nurse Trenton Bd. Edn., 1994-96, Three Bridges Sch., Readington Twp. Bd. of Edn., 1996—. Clin. panel mem. RN Mag., 1980, 81. Mem. Nat. Sch. Nurse Assn., N.J. Sch. Nurse Assn., Hunterdon County Sch. Nurse Assn., Sigma Theta Tau (Xi chpt.). E-mail: ckushner-cohen@readington.k12.nj.us.

KUSHNIR, ANDREI, artist, consultant; b. Regensberg, Germany, Aug. 30, 1947; s. Wasyl and Maria Kushnir; m. Raissa Shyshko Kushnir; children: Basil, Larissa. BA, U. Ill., Chgo., 1969; MA, Georgetown U., 1971; JD, Howard U., Washington, 1975. Bar: D.C., Ill. Atty. FAA, Washington, 1975—81; assoc. counsel Dept. Navy, Office Gen. Counsel, Washington, 1981—97; cons. in litigation U.S. Dept. Justice, Washington, 1997—; artist Taylor & Sons Fine Art, Washington, 1999—2001; owner Andrei Kushnir/Michele Taylor, LLC, Ellicott City, Md., 2002—. Guest instr. outdoor painting workshop South Fla. C., Sebring, 2002; ofcl. artist USCG. Book, My River, 1999, American Light, 2001, Represented in permanent collections USCG, D.C. Commn. of Arts and Humanities, Univ. Club, Washington, one-man shows include Mus. Fla. Art & Culture, Sebring, Fla., 1998, Capital Hill Art League, Wash., 1998, Univ. Club, 1999, Taylor & Sons Fine Art, 1999, 2001, one-man shows include Rehoboth Art League, Rehoboth Beach, Del., 2003, paintings included in, Along the Potomac, Philip Ogilvie, Arcadia Pub., Rock Creek Park, Gail Silsbury, Johns Hopkins Press, exhibited in group shows, Holter Mus. Art, Helena, MT, 1998, Art Inst. & Gallery, Salisbury, Md., 1998, Mus. Contemporary Art, Wash., 1999, Nat. Parks Acad. Arts, 2001, 2002, exhibited in group shows, 2003, paintings included in group shows at, Alexandria Art League, Va., 1991—98, Arts Coun., Md., 1995, Blue Ridge Arts Coun., Front Royal, Va., 1995—2002, Foundry Gallery, Wash., 1995, Touchstone Gallery, 1996, Artists Atelier, Atlanta, Ga., 1996, Capitol Hill Art League, Howard County, Md., 1998, Serendipity Gallery, Boca Grande, Fla., 1997—2003, Coun. for the Arts, Chambersburg, PA, 1998, Nagano Olympics Ofcl. Art Exhbn., Japan, 1998, Spectrum Gallery, Wash., 1999, Hudson Valley Art Assn., NY, 1999, Nat. Oil & Acrylic Painters Soc. Annual Exhibits, 2000, 2001, Schoharie County Arts Coun., Cobleskill, NY, 2001, 2002, Crane Collection, Wellesley, Mass., 2002, 2003, Alexander Gallery, NY, 2002, Mill Atelier, Santa Fe, N.Mex, 2003, Period Gallery, Omaha, 2000. Recipient First place oils, Casper Artist Guild, Wyo., 2002, Award of Excellence, Period Gallery, Omaha, 2000, Best in Show, Blueridge Arts Coun., Front Royal, Va., 2000. Mem.: Nat. Oil and Acrylic Painters Soc., Miniature Painters, Gravers and Sculptors Soc. (v.p. 1999—2001), Washington Soc. Landscape Painters, Salmagundi Club N.Y. Avocations: banjo, guitar. Office: Andrei Kushnir/Michele Taylor LLC 8289 Main St Ellicott City MD 21041

KUSHWAHA, SUDHIR SINGH, internist, cardiologist, educator; b. Gwalior, India, June 29, 1958; came to U.S., 1992; MB, BChir, U. London, 1981, MD, 1992. Diplomate Am. Bd. Internal Medicine, Am. Bd. Cardiology. Intern London Hosp., 1991-92; resident in internal medicine Ctrl. Middlesex Hosp., London, 1983-84, resident in cardiology, 1985-87, Harefield Hosp., England, 1987-92, Mass. Gen. Hosp., Boston, 1992-95; asst. prof. Mt. Sinai Hosp., NYC, 1995-99; assoc. prof. U. NC, Chapel Hill, NC, 1999-2000, dir. heart failure and transplant program, 1999-2000; assoc. prof., cons. Mayo Clin./Mayo Med. Sch., Rochester, Minn., 2000—. Fellow Am. Coll. Cardiology. E-mail: kushwaha.sudhir@mayo.edu.

KUSIK, CHARLES LEMBIT, chemical engineer; b. Apr. 24, 1934; s. Charles and Mary (Jackson) K. BS, MIT, 1956, MS, 1958; ScD, N.Y. U., 1961. Registered profl. engr., Mass. Scientist ops. rsch. group MIT, Cambridge, 1961-62; project officer U.S. Army, Aberdeen, Md., 1962—63; engr. Avco Corp., Wilmington, Mass., 1963-64; mem. profl. staff Arthur D. Little, Inc., Cambridge, Mass., 1964—2002, mgr. metals and energy mgmt., 1980-89, dir., 1989—2002; with ICF Consulting, Cambridge, 2002—03; pvt. practice cons. Lincoln, Mass., 2003—. Author: (with Kenahan) Energy Use Patterns for Metal Recycling, 1978, (with Makar and Mounier) Availability of Critical Scrap Metals Containing Chromium in the United States, 1980; contbr. articles to profl. jours. Mem. AIME, Am. Inst. Chem. Engrs., Assn. Iron and Steel Engrs. Office: 209 Lincoln Road Lincoln MA 01773-5100 E-mail: kusik773@alum.mit.edu.

KUSIN, GARY M. consumer products company executive; b. Texarkana, Tex. married; 4 children. BA, U. Tex., Austin; MBA, Harvard U. V.p., gen. mgr. Sanger-Harris divsn. Federated Dept. Stores; pres., co-founder Babbage's Inc., Dallas, 1983—95; co-founder Laura Mercier Cosmetics, Dallas, 1995—98; pres., CEO OmniOffices, Inc. (later HQ Global Workplaces), 1998—99; CEO HQ Global Workplaces, 1999—2001; pres., CEO Kinko's Inc., Dallas, 2001—. Bd. dirs. Electronic Arts, Inc. Bd. trustees St. Mark's Sch. Tex.; chmn. Dallas Young Pres.' Orgn.; mem. Dallas Citizen's Coun. Named Entrepreneur of Yr., Inc. Mag. Mem.: Dallas C. of C. (bd. dirs.). Office: Kinko s Inc Three Galleria Tower 13155 Noel Rd Ste 1600 Dallas TX 75240*

KUSKA, JOHN JOSEPH, JR., accountant, management consultant; b. Balt., Feb. 27, 1953; s. John Joseph and T. Virginia (Branham) K.; 1 child, Jennifer L. BA magna cum laude, Lycoming Coll., 1975. CPA, Md., W.Va.; registered rep. Staff acct. Deloitte & Touche (H & S), Balt., 1975-76; sr. acct. Henry E. Pear & Co., Laurel, Md., 1977-78; corp. sec. Nu-Homes, Inc., Columbia, Md., 1979-80; mgr. Barry S. Fishman & Assocs., Bethesda, Md., 1981-87; prin. John J. Kuska, Jr. & Co., 1987—. Winner Durant Furey Meml. award (first in acctg. class) Lycoming Coll., 1975. Mem. AICPA, Md. Assn. CPAs. Republican. Avocations: bicycling, hunting. E-mail: kuskacpa@frontiernet.net.

KUSMA, KYLLIKKI, lawyer; b. Tartu, Estonia, Dec. 8, 1943; came to U.S., 1951; d. August and Helju Kusma. BA, Ohio U., 1966; MA (VA Rehab. fellow), Ohio State U., 1967; JD, Ohio No. U., 1976; MLT, Georgetown U., 1980. Bar: Ohio 1977, D.C. 1978. Speech and hearing therapist Lima (Ohio) Meml. Hosp., 1967-70, Tipp City (Ohio) Schs., 1970-74; atty.-adv. Office Chief Counsel, IRS, Washington, 1977-81; v.p., assoc. tax counsel Security Pacific Nat. Bank., L.A., 1981-83; ptnr. Brownstein Zeidman & Lore, Washington, 1983-95, Ernst & Young LLP, Columbus, Ohio, 1995—2002. Instr. Wright State U., 1972-76. Author: (with others) Mortgage-Backed Securities Special Update: REMICs, 1988; contbr. articles to profl. jours. Vol. local civic and polit. activities. Mem. ABA, Ohio Bar Assn., Columbus Bar Assn., Columbus Women Execs. (v.p., sec.), Phi Kappa Phi. E-mail: llikki@msn.com.

KUSMER, KENNETH LESLIE, historian, educator; b. Cleve., June 19, 1945; s. Andrew Luke and Dorothy Dean K.; m. Holly Beth Jay (div.). AB, Oberlin Coll., 1968; MA, PhD, U. Chgo., 1980. Ins. Cleve. State U., 1969-71; asst. prof. Temple U., 1976-81, assoc. prof., 1981-87, prof., 1987—. Vis. prof. U. Pa., 1984-85, U. Goettingen, Germany, 1987-88, U. Genoa, Italy, 2001. Author: A Ghetto Takes Shape, 1976, Down and Out, On the Road: The Homeless in American History, 2001; editor: Black Communities and Urban Development, 1991; mem. editl. bd. Jour. Urban History, 1998—; contbr. articles to profl. jours. Adv. Bd. Balch Inst. of Ethnic Studies, Phila., 1985—. Mem. Orgn. of Am. History (nominating bd.), Am. Historical Assn., Am. Immigration Hist. Soc., Urban Hist. Assn., Penn. Acad. of Fine Arts. Home: 167 Sycamore Rd Havertown PA 19083-3507 Office: Dept Hist Temple U Philadelphia PA 19122

KUSMIERSKI, JANET LOUISE, painter, illustrator, graphic designer; b. Queens, N.Y., Oct. 22, 1953; d. Henry Kusmierski and Irene Mastro; m. Greg G. Singer, Jan. 24, 1985; children: Avery K. Singer, Calder K. Singer. BFA, Parsons Sch. Design/New Sch. for Social Rsch., 1974; MA, Hunter Coll. of CUNY, 1978. One-woman shows include Elizabeth Harris Gallery, 1999, exhibited in group shows at Snug Harbor Cultural Ctr./Newhouse Gallery, 1997, Aisling Gallery, 1996, Artwalk-Studio Tours, 1995, Heckscher Mus., 1995, Women's Caucus for Art, N.Y.C. chpt., 1992, Everson Mus., 1986 (Honorable Mention), The Drawing Ctr., 1982. Artist grantee Artists Space, 1985; recipient Mary Duke Biddle Found. honorarium Mary Duke Biddle Found., 1981. Democrat. Roman Catholic. Office: 9 Murray St 6 SE New York NY 10007-2243

KUSPIT, DONALD BURTON, art historian, art critic, educator; b. N.Y.C., Mar. 26, 1935; s. Morris and Celia (Schmukler) Kuspit Sigmund; m. Judith Clements Price, Mar. 22, 1962. BA in Philosophy with distinction, Columbia U., 1955; MA in Philosophy, Yale U., 1957; DPhil magna cum laude, U. Frankfort, 1960; PhD in Art History, U. Mich., 1971; DFA (hon.), Davidson Coll., 1993; DFA, San Francisco Art Inst., 1996; LHD (hon.), U. Ill., 1998. Asst. prof. Pa. State U., State College, 1960-66; assoc. prof. U. Windsor, Ont., Can., 1966-70; prof. U. N.C., Chapel Hill, 1970-78; Univ. Disting. prof. Rutgers U., New Brunswick, N.J., 1982-83; prof. art, chmn. dept. art SUNY-Stony Brook, 1978-83; editorial cons. UMI Rsch. Press, Ann Arbor, Mich., 1980-90; Andrew Dixon White prof. at large Cornell U., Ithaca, N.Y., 1991-97. Editl. cons. Cambridge U. Press, 1991—, Ency. Brit. European Art 1900-1950, Art Criticism and Theory; mem. overview com. visual arts sect. NEA, Washington, 1983-85. Author: Clement Greenberg, ARt Critic, 1979, the Critiic as Artist: The Intentionality of Art, 1984, Leon Golub: Existentialist/Activist Painter, 1985, The New Subjectivism: Art of the 1980's, 1988, Eric Fischl, 1988, Louise Bourgeois, 1989, Alex Katz: Night Paintings, The Dialectic of Decandence, 1993, Alex Katz: Night Paintings, The Dialectic of Decandence, reprinted, 2000, The Cult of the Avant-Garde Artist, 1993, Signs of Psyche in Modern and Post-Modern Art, 1993, Albert Renger-Patzch, 1993, Primordial Prosences: The Sculpture of Karel Appel, 1994, Idiosyncratic Indentities: Artists at the End of Avant-Garde, 1986, Health and Happiness in Twentieth Century Avant-Garde Art, 1996, Dale Chihuly, 1997, Jamali, 1997, Joseph Raffael, 1998, The Rebirth of Painting in the Late 20th Century, 2000, Psychostrategies of Avant-Garde Art, 2000, Redeeming Art: Critical Reveries, 2000, Don Eddy, 2001; contbg. editor: Art in Am., 1978—92, Contemporanea, 1988—90, ArtForum, 1982—, Sculpture Mag., 1992—, New Art Examiner, 1993—; editor: Art Criticism, 1984—. Recipient award for disting. contbn. to the visual arts Nat. Assn. Schs. Art and Design, 1997; Younger humanist fellow NEH, 1973, critic fellow Nat. Endowment for Arts, 1977, Guggenheim fellow, 1977. Fellow Asian Cultural Coun.; mem. PEN, Coll. Art Assn. (Frank Jewett Mather award 1983), Am. Soc. Aesthetics, Internat. Assn. Art Critics (v.p. Am. sect. 1982-84), Am. Psychoanalytic Assn. Home: 38 W 26th St New York NY 10010-2012 Office: SUNY Dept Art Stony Brook NY 11794-5400

KUSSEROW, RICHARD PHILLIP, government official, business executive; b. San Jose, Calif., Dec. 9, 1940; s. Roger Berthold and Eve W. (Larson) K.; m. Rebecca Hatchell, Sept. 14, 1985; 1 child, Carrie Elizabeth. BA in Polit. Sci, UCLA, 1963; MA in Govt., Calif. State U., L.A., 1964; postgrad., So. Meth. U., 1965, John Marshall Sch. Law, 1972, Harvard U., 1984. Cert. internal auditor, cert. govt. auditor; cert. govt. fin. mgr., cert. fraud examiner. Lectr. Calif. State U., L.A., 1963, 64; case officer CIA, 1968-69; spl. agt. supr. in white collar and organized crime FBI, 1969-81; Insp. Gen., U.S. Dept. HHS, 1981-92; mem. Pres.'s Coun. on Integrity and Efficiency, 1981-92, vice chmn., 1986-89, chmn. legislation com., 1982-85, 89-92; mem. Pres.' Council on Mgmt. Improvement, 1986-89, 91-92; chair Nat. Task Force of Implementation of Chief Fin. Officers Act, 1990-91; chmn. Chief Fin. Officers Task Force, 1991; pres., CEO Strategic Mgmt. Sys., Inc., 1992—; ptnr. O.K. Real Estate, 1993—; pres. Govt. Mgmt. Sys., Inc., 1995—2002; pres., CEO, chmn. bd. Nat. Hotline Svcs., Inc., 1995—; CEO Corp. Compliance Svcs., Inc., 1995—. Presdl. appointee to Nat. Adv. Commn. on Law Enforcement, 1989; mem. CFOs Coun., 1990-92, Def. Procurement Round Table, 1993—; lectr. white collar crime, asset protection, health care, fraud and abuse, internal controls, corporate compliance programs, others; mem. Atty. Gen.'s Econ. Crime Coun., 1988-90; nat. chmn. Am Compliance Inst., 1995. Author: Principles of Investigative Targeting, 1974 Management Principles for Asset Protection, 1986, Corporate Compliance Policies & Procedures, 2000, Compliance Training Manual, 2001; contbr articles on corp. compliance investigations, auditing and mgmt. to profl. jours. Pres. Nat. Honor Svc., 1996—. Capt. USMCR, 1964-68. Recipient Sec.'s Bronze medal for good govt., 1983, Outstanding Leadership award Pres. Coun. on Mgmt. Improvement, 1988, Cert. of Svc. Appreciation, Pres. of U.S., 1989, Donald L. Scantlebury award for fin. mgmt. excellence Assn. Govt. Accts., 1992; H. Horton Rontree Disting. lectr. in health law, 1990. Mem. Assn. Fed. Investigators (nat. pres. 1984-85, chmn. awards com. 1986-87), Soc. Former FBI Agts., Assn. Govt. Accts. (nat. task force on fed. fin. mgmt. 1983-88, pres. Balt. chpt. 1987, chmn. nat. profl. devel. conf. 1989, nat. pres. 1990, nat. leadership awards Boston chpt. 1985, No. Va. chpt., Washington chpt., D.C. chpt. 1985, Nat. Assn. 1987), Am. Health Lawyers Assn., Nat. Health Care Anti-Fraud Assn. (pub. svc. award 1989), Inst. Internal Auditors (cert.), Am. Compliance Inst. (governing bd. 1996-2001), Army-Navy Club. Presbyterian. Avocations: reading, travel, tennis. E-mail: strategicm.com. also: 620 Kenmore Ave ste B Fredericksburg VA 22401-5759 E-mail: rkusserow@strategicm.com.

KUSSMAN, ELEANOR (ELLIE KUSSMAN), retired educational superintendent; b. Bklyn., Mar. 17, 1934; d. Mortimer Joseph and Eleanor Mary (O'Brien) Gleeson; m. Karl Kussman, June 30, 1956 (dec. Oct. 1988); children: Katherine Ann, Kristine Sue. BA, Wheaton Coll., Norton, Mass., 1955; MS, LaVerne Coll., Claremont, Calif., 1974. Cert. tchr. K-C.C., cert. in pupil pers. and adminstrn., Calif. Tchr. sci. and math. Norwood (Mass.) Jr. H.S., 1955-56; tchr. phys. edn. Brawley (Calif.) Union H.S., 1956-58, Ctrl. Union H.S., El Centro, Calif., 1958-74, tchr. health careers, 1974-80, state and fed. project dir., 1980-85; instr. horse husbandry and equitation Imperial Valley Coll., Imperial, Calif., 1974-76; supr. Imperial Valley (Calif.) Regional Occupational Program, 1985-95. Cons. E.E. Kussman Cons., El Centro, 1992—, Calif. Joint Gender Equity Com., Sacramento, 1991-96, State of Calif. Gender Equity, Sacramento, 1986-96; grad. instr. program in counseling and guidance U.Calif., Redlands, 1989. Mem. fin. com. United Way, El Centro, 1987-93; sec.-treas. Pvt. Industry Coun., El Centro, 1985-95; past sec.-treas. Calif. Regional Occupational Ctrs./Programs, 1986-88; bd. dirs. Imperial Valley Coll. Desert Mus., 1998-2000. Named Educator of Yr. Imperial Valley Chpt. Phi Delta Kappa, 1995. Mem. AAUW, ASCD, Assn. Calif. Sch. Adminstrs. (past local and regional officer), Rotary Internat. (bd. dirs. 1994-97). Avocations: camping, travel, gardening, reading, horses. Home and Office: PO Box 83 El Centro CA 92244-0083

KUSSMAUL, WILLIAM GUY, III, cardiologist; b. N.Y.C., Mar. 9, 1949; s. William Guy Kussmaul Jr. and Dorothy (Sturm) Kussmaul; m. Linda Marie Herman, Aug. 23, 1980; children: Mary, Susannah, Jonathan, Matthew. BS, Yale U., 1971; MD, U. Pa., 1976. Diplomate Am. Bd. Internal Medicine, cert. medicine, cardiovasc. diseases, interventional cardiology. Asst. prof. medicine U. Pa., Phila., 1985—94; assoc. prof. medicine MCP, Hahnemann U., Phila., 1994—. Assoc. editor Annals of Internal Medicine. Contbr. articles to prof. jours. Lt. comdr. USN. Fellow: ACP, Soc. Cardiac Angiography and Intervention, Am. Coll. Cardiology. Office: Cardiology Cons Phila 227 N Broad St Ste 200 Philadelphia PA 19107

KUSSROW, NANCY ESTHER, educational association administrator; BA, Valparaiso U., 1952; MA, U. N.C., 1954. Exec. dir. Nat. Assn. prins. of Schs. for Girls; ret., 1996.

KUSTER, LARRY DONALD, lawyer; b. Kewanee, Ill., July 27, 1947; s. Donald Carl and Rosemary Ann (Riggins) Kuster; m. Mary Catherine Whitmore, July 11, 1970; children: David, Ryan. BA, Augustana Coll., 1969; JD with honors, U. Iowa, 1973. Bar: Ill. 1973, U.S. Dist. Ct. (cen. dist.) : Ill. 1980, U.S. Dist. Ct. (so. dist.): Ill. 1996, U.S. Ct. Appeals (7th cir.) : 1982, U.S. Tax Ct. : 1979. Assoc. Rammelkamp, Bradney, Kuster, Keaton, Fritsche & Lindsay PC, Jacksonville, Ill., 1973—75, ptnr., 1976—. Moderator continuing legal edn. program Ill. Inst. Continuing Legal Edn., 1985—86; lectr. in field; master barrister Lincoln-Douglas Inn of Ct., 1993—. Contbr. articles to profl. jours. Active Am. Coun. on Germany, 1982—2002, City of Jacksonville Heritage Cultural Ctr. Bd., 1986—91, Fedn. Def. and Corp. Coun., 1989—; pres. West Central Ill. Council on World Affairs, 1982—83; bd. dirs. Sherwood Eddy Meml. YMCA, 1975—80, Jacksonville Area C. of C., 1981—84, pres., 1990; bd. dirs. Jacksonville Area Visitors and Tourism Bur., 1986—91; trustee MacMurray Coll., Jacksonville, 1991—2001; pres. Ill. Assn. Hist. Preservation Commns., 1982; vice-chmn. Jacksonville Hist. Preservation Commn., 1981—83, chmn., 1983—84. Mem.: Ill. Bar Assn. (civil practice and procedure coun. 1976—77, 1986—90, sec. workers' compensation sect. 1982—83, vice-chmn. 1983—84, chmn. 1984—85), Morgan County Bar Assn. (pres. 1977—78), Am. Arbitration Assn. Home: RR 1 Box 19 Chapin IL 62628-9801 Office: Rammelkamp Bradney 232 W State St Jacksonville IL 62650-2002

KUSTER, ROBERT KENNETH, former scientist; b. Los Angeles, July 11, 1932; s. Arthur Rollo Kuster and Ermine Rosebud (Prittchett) Woodward. AS, Gavilan Coll., 1974, AA in Humanities, 1981; student, San Jose State U., 1955, 1974-76, UCLA, 1977. Installer Western Electric Co., Inc., Corpus Christi, Tex., 1951-52, 1955, San Jose, Calif., 1957-58, 1960-83; ptnr., scientist, cons. WE-Woodward's Enterprises, Morgan Hill, Calif., 1975—; technician Lucent Tech., Inc., San Jose, 1983-85, ret., 1985. Scientist pvt. practice, Gilroy, 1978—. Served to sgt. U.S. Army Corps Engrs., 1952-54. Mem. AAAS, Astron. Soc. Pacific, Calif. Acad. Scis., N.Y. Acad. Scis., Am. Legion, VFW. Lodges: Elks. Baptist. Avocations: photography, golf, camping, hiking, music. Home: 17506 Hoot Owl Way Morgan Hill CA 95037-6524

KUSTERER, THOMAS, project administrator; b. Balt., July 9, 1946; s. Edward Thomas and Anne Thelma (Ekas) K.; m. Janet Elizabeth Polunas, Sept. 16, 1972; children: David, Robert. BS, Loyola Coll., 1968, MBA, 1982; MS, Rutgers U., 1972. Instr. Balt. C.C., 1968-69; tchg. asst. Rutgers U., 1969—71; cons. Benedict (Md.) Estuarine Lab., 1971-72; planner Harford County (Md.) Govt., Bel Air, Md., 1972-84; natural resources mgr. Md. Dept. of the Environ., Balt., 1984-89; program mgr. Montgomery County Govt., Rockville, Md., 1989—. Mem. Md. Coastal Resources Adv. Com., 1984-88, Govs. Solid Waste Mgmt. Task Force, 1987, Md. Acid Deposition Adv. Com., 1984-88, nat. round table on unit pricing for solid waste collection and disposal U.S. EPA, 1992, nat. round table on full cost acctg. for solid waste mgmt. systems, 1994. Contbg. author/advisor: Pay As You Throw: Lessons Learned about Unit Pricing, 1994; contbg. author Developing Agreements on the Siting of Waste Management Facilties, 1994, Innovative Approaches to Siting Solid Waste Management Facilities, 1992; editor (newsletter) Md. Environ., 1986, 87; contbr. articles to profl. jours. Mgr. youth sports teams Parks and Recreation Depts., Howard and Balt. Counties, 1983-97; officer Md. Save Our Streams, Annapolis, 1973-76; officer Hist. Ellicott City, Inc. Recipient Environtl. Svcs. award Pub. Technology Inst., 1991, Environtl. Merit award Take Pride in Am., 1990. Mem. Air and Waste Mgmt. Assn., Water Environment Fedn., Howard County Hist. Soc., Balt. Mus. Art, Sierra Club. Democrat. Roman Catholic. Avocations: tennis, swimming, birding. Home: 3796 Dorsey Search Cir Ellicott City MD 21042-3753 Office: Montgomery County Recycling Ctr 16105 Frederick Rd Derwood MD 20855

KUSTIN, KENNETH, chemist; b. Bronx, N.Y., Jan. 6, 1934; s. Alex and Mae (Marvisch) K.; m. Myrna May Jacobson, June 24, 1956; children: Brenda Jayne, Franklin Daniel, Michael Thorpe. B.Sc., Queens Coll., Flushing, N.Y., 1955; PhD, U. Minn., 1959. Postdoctoral fellow Max Planck Inst. for Phys. Chemistry, Göttingen, Germany, 1959-61; asst. prof. chemistry Brandeis U., Waltham, Mass., 1961-66, assoc. prof., 1966-72, prof., 1972-97, prof. emeritus, 1997—, chmn. dept. chemistry, 1974-77. Vis. prof. pharmacology Harvard U. Med. Sch., 1977-78; Fulbright-Hays lectr., 1978; program dir. NSF, 1985-86; adj. rsch. scientist U.S. Army, Natick RD&E Ctr., 1991—. Editor: Fast Reactions, vol. 16 of Methods in Enzymology, 1969; bd. editors Internat. Jour. Chem. Kinetics, 1983-90, Inorganic Chemistry, 1993-95; rsch. and publs. in field. Mem. AAAS, Am. Chem. Soc. (councilor 1983-85), Phi Beta Kappa. E-mail: kmkuskin@ix.netcom.com.

KUSUKAWA, AKIRA, demographer, educator; b. Fukuoka, Kyushu, Japan, May 13, 1925; s. Tokuzo Tanaka and Ko Kusukawa; m. Emiko Fujita, June 3, 1952. BS, Yamaguchi Coll., 1944; MPH, Johns Hopkins U., 1953; MD, Kyushu

U., 1948, D of Med. Sci., 1956. Tech. advisor to Coun. of Mins. Govt. of Sudan, 1959—60; sec. UN Population Commn., N.Y.C., 1964—74; spl. asst. UN Population Fund, N.Y.C., 1974—77, dir., 1977—86; ret., 1986. Prof. Moscow State U., Russia, 1988, N.Y. Med. Coll., 1986—, L.I. U., N.Y.C., 1986—, UN Demographic Centre, India, 1963—64. Author: Cardiovascular Epidemiology, 1956; co-author: Ageing Research, 1999; contbr. Recipient Medal of Peace, State Coun. Bulgaria, 1986, Golden Order Labor, Presdl. Coun. Hungary, 1986. Mem.: Japanese Med. Soc. Am. (dir.), Population Assn. Am., Internat. Union Sci. Study Population. Avocations: swimming, music, oil painting. Home: 214 Harriman Dr #2023 Goshen NY 10924-2425 Office: Long Island Univ Hoxie Hall 720 Northern Blvd Brookville NY 11548-1300

KUSY, ROBERT PETER, biomedical engineering and orthodontics educator; b. Worcester, Mass., Oct. 19, 1947; s. Stanley J. and Mary B. (Rutkiewicz) K.; m. Gisela Bauer, June 27, 1969; children: Kimberly, Kevin. BSME, Worcester (Mass.) Poly. Inst., 1969; MSMetE, Drexel U., 1971, PhD in Materials Sci., 1973. Rubber rsch. technician Vellumoid Gasket Corp. divsn. Fed.-Mogul Corp., Worcester, 1966-69; rsch. asst. dept. metall. engring. Drexel U., Phila., 1969-72, rsch. assoc. U. N.C. Dental Rsch. Ctr., Chapel Hill, 1972-74; asst. prof. oral biology dept. orthodontics U. N.C. Dental Rsch., Chapel Hill, 1974-79, assoc. prof. orthodontics dept. orthodontics, 1979-89; assoc. prof. biomed. engring. U. N.C. Sch. Medicine, Chapel Hill, 1985-89; prof. orthodontics, prof. biomed. engring. U. N.C. Sch. Dentistry and Medicine, Chapel Hill, 1989—, adj. prof. curriculum applied scis., 1990-96; adminstrv. bd. U. N.C. Grad. Sch., Chapel Hill, 1989-95; prof. curriculum applied and materials scis. U. N.C., Chapel Hill, 1996—. Engring. design, testing and mgmt. cons. Internat. Nickel, Structure-Probe, DuPont, Kodak, CTL Tech., Rising Star, Smiling Faces, Epolin, Dental Rsch. Corp., Tracor Aerospace, Enron Chem., Unitek, 3M, Ormco Corp., Flexmedics Corp., Lancer Orthodontics, Aristech, Orthodontic Ptnrs., Hutchinson Tech., Wyeth-Ayerst Rsch., Composite Products, A-Company, Ortho Organizers, U. N.C., Tom's of Maine, Implant Scis.; reviewer small projects grants NIH, 1985—, project site visitor, 1986—; mem. bd. sci. adv. com. Epolin Corp., 1986-89. Mem. rev. staff Am. Jour. Orthodontics, 1982—, Polymer, 1985—, Jour. Applied Polymer Sci., 1985—, Dental Materials, 1986—, Jour. Polymer Sci., 1987—, Jour. Biomed. Materials Rsch.-Applied Biomaterials, 1989—, The Angle Orthodontist, 1989—, scanning Microscopy Internat., 1995—, Jour. Dental Rsch., 1994—, Jour. Biomechanics, 1996—; mem. adv. bd. Jour. Materials Sci., Materials in Medicine; contbr. over 200 articles to profl. jours. Pres. Hills of the Haw Home Owners' Assn., 1986-88; mem. pastoral coun. Newman Ctr., 1986-87; organizer Sr. Basketball Club, Chapel Hill Cmty. Ctr., 1985-88; coach Children's Basketball League, Chapel Hill, Carrboro, 1981-82, 83-86; mem. ch. choir, 1987-89, 92—. Capt. U.S. Army, 1969-77. Recipient Spl. Dental Rsch. award, 1977-81, Rsch. Career Devel. award, 1977-82, both from NIH, Nat. Inst. Dental Rsch.; recipient Focused Giving award Johnson & Johnson Co., 1993-96, B.F. Dewel Hon. Rsch. award Am. Assn. Orthodontists Found., 1995, Orthodontics Tchg. award U. N.C., Chapel Hill, 1996. Mem. N.Am. Thermal Analysis Soc., Am. Soc. Materials, Am. Chem. Soc. (divsn. polymer chemistry divsn. phys. chemistry), Internat. Assn. Dental Rsch., Am. Assn. Dental Rsch., Internat. Metallographic Soc., Soc. Biomaterials, Soc. Plastics Engrs. Roman Catholic. Office: U NC Bldg 210H CB 7455 Rm 313 Chapel Hill NC 27599-0001

KUTCHIN, EDWARD DAVID, lawyer; b. Bklyn., Sept. 1, 1953; s. Melvin and Maxine (Lampert) K.; m. Jill C. Pollack, Aug. 18, 1979. BA, Muhlenberg Coll., 1975; JD, New Eng. Sch. Law, 1978; LLM in Taxation, Boston U., 1981. Bar: Mass. 1978, U.S. Dist. Ct. Mass 1978, U.S. Tax Ct. 1978, U.S. Ct. Appeals (1st cir.) 1978. Law clk. Atty. Gen.'s Advocacy Inst. U.S. Dept. Justice, Washington, 1977; assoc. Law Offices Robert Smith, Boston, 1978-81, Kline & Gordon, Boston, 1981-85; ptnr. Lapping & Kutchin, Boston, 1985-88, Kutchin & Rufo, P.C., Boston, 1988—. Bd. trustees Merrimack Valley Jewish Fedn., 1996—; chmn. Muhlenberg Coll. New Eng. Regional Alumni Assn., 1995—. Mem. ABA, Mass. Bar Assn., Boston Bar Assn. Democrat. Jewish. Avocations: tennis, soccer, exercise, weightlifting, travel. Home: 68 Sunset Rock Rd Andover MA 01810-5001 Office: Kutchin & Rufo PC 175 Federal St Boston MA 02110-2210 E-mail: ekutchin@kutchinrufo.com.

KUTEMEYER, PETER MARTIN, industrial engineering executive; b. Freiburg, West Germany, Nov. 19, 1938; came to U.S., 1954, naturalized, 1956; s. Martin Henry and Gertrude Barbara (Buechel) K.; m. Fresquez, June 25, 1961 (div. Aug. 1986); children: Michael, Kristina. BME with distinction, Ariz. State U., 1968, MS in Engring. Mechanics, 1969; MBA, U. Utah, 1977. Enlisted USAF, 1958, commd. 2d lt., 1967, advanced through grades to capt., 1970, aero. engr., 1969-71, sys. devel. engr., 1971-74, tech. liaison officer to W. German Fed. Govt., 1974-78; ret., 1978; indsl. mgr. Mining Progress, Inc., Highland Mills, N.Y., 1978-79, prodn. mgr., 1979-81; gen. mgr. Bischoff Environ. Sys. divsn. Intertech Inc., Highland Mills, N.Y., 1981-89; pres. PMK Enterprises, Inc., Wilmington, Del., 1989—. Mem. ASME, AIAA. Home: 5225 Pooks Hill Rd Apt 1020S Bethesda MD 20814-6718 E-mail: p.kutemeyer@verizon.net.

KUTER, KAY E. writer, actor; b. L.A., Apr. 25, 1925; s. Leo E. and Evelyn Belle (Edler) K. Student, Pomona Coll., 1943, UCLA, 1944; BFA in Drama, Carnegie Inst. Tech., 1949. Radio actor NBC, 1944; actor, 1944—. Actor in 198 musicals, off-Broadway, stock, repertory, touring, and Shakespearean stage prodns.; 51 feature films; more than 435 TV shows including 7 yrs. as a series regular (Newt Kiley) in Green Acres and Petticoat Junction; voiceover actor for cartoon series Aladdin, The Little Mermaid, Prince Valiant, Biker Mice From Mars, Fantastic Four, Julius and Friends; in cartoon spls. Olympic Mascot Izzy, Annabelle's Wish, The Jungle Book: Mowgli's Story, The Little Mermaid II; in CD-ROMS The Beast Within, Ultima 9, Grim Fandango, The Curse of Monkey Island, Heretic II, Emperor Dune, Arcanum; in radio prodns. Getting Married, Treasure Island, Macbeth, Satanic Verses, Heartbreak House; author: Carmen Incarnate, 1946, Ships That Never Sailed, 1994, Hollywood Houdini, Picture Perfect World, 1995; voiceover spokesman Hershey's Kisses, 1989—; editor: The Jester, 1956-60, The Jester 35th Anniversary, 1960, 50th Anniversary, 1976; contbr. to Nat. Libr. Poetry anthologies, 1995, 96, 97, 99, 2000 (Editor's Choice award); dir. more than 50 stage prodns. including Steve Allen's The Wake. Bd. dirs. Family Svc. of L.A., 1950-70. Mem. SAG (bd dirs. 1970-73), AEA, AFTRA, ADA, ACLU, NOW, NARAL, UNICEF, UN Assn. U.S., Nat. Trust Hist. Preservation, Smithsonian, Carnegie Mellon U. Westcoast Drama Alumni Clan (founding mem., officer, bd. dirs. 1968-80), Ephebian Soc., Internat. Soc. Poets (disting. mem.), Albert C. May Soc., Acad. Am. Poets, Andrew Carnegie Soc., Pacific Pioneer Broadcasters, Carnegie Mellon U. Alumni Assn. (regional v.p. 1976-79, Svc. award 1979), Van Nuys H.S. Alumni Assn., Interfaith Alliance, Libr. Found. L.A., Nat. Audubon Soc., Hist Soc. So. Calif., L.A. Conservancy, Nat. Trust Pub. Edn., Theatre 40, Calif. Artists Radio Theatre, Am. Film Inst., Libr. Congress Assocs., Ams. United, Masquers Club (bd. dirs. 1953-75, rec. sec. 1956-70, corr. sec. 1957-69. v.p. 1971-75), Actors' Fund of Am. (life mem.), others. Democrat. Avocations: composing, piano. Home: 6207 Satsuma Ave North Hollywood CA 91606-3819

KUTHER, TARA L. psychology educator; d. Philip John Kuther and Irene Lopez. BA, Western Conn. State U., 1993; MA, Fordham U., 1995, PhD, 1998. Assoc. prof. Western Conn. State U., Danbury, Conn., 1998—, assoc. program, 2003. Bd. dir. Danbury Regional Commn. on Childcare Rights and Abuse, Danbury, 1998—. Author: The Psychology Majors Handbook, 2003, Careers in Psychology: Opportunities in a Changing World, 2004; contbr. articles to profl. jour. Putting Children First fellow Tchrs. Coll. Columbia U., 1995. Mem. APA, Assn. for Practical and Profl. Ethics, Soc. for Rsch. in Adolescence, Soc. for Rsch. into Child Devel., Sigma Xi. Office: Western Conn State U Dept Psychology 181 White St Danbury CT 06810 6826 E-mail: kuthert@wcsu.edu.

KUTKA, NICHOLAS, nuclear medicine physician; b. Czechoslovakia, Dec. 17, 1926; s. Vladimir and Agatha (Flenko) Kutka; m. Anna Cizmar, Apr. 14, 1965 (dec. Oct. 1996); children: Andrew, Gregory; m. Veronika Filova, Apr. 28, 2001. MD, Comenius U., Bratislava, Czechoslovakia, 1951; PhD, Slovak Acad. Scis., Bratislava, 1962. Diplomate in internal medicine Postgrad. Edn. of Physicians; diplomate Am. Bd. Nuclear Medicine, Am. Bd. Disability Analysts. Asst. prof. Inst. Physiology Comenius U., Bratislava, 1951; intern, resident in internal medicine Mil. Hosp., Bratislava, 1952-55, chief dept. Inst. Endocrinology Slovak Acad. Scis., Bratislava, 1956-69; tech. asst. Internat. Atomic Engery Agy., Bogota, Colombia, 1969-70; resident in nuclear medicine Duke U., 1971-73; asst. prof. radiology Baylor Coll. Medicine, Houston, 1973-95, assoc. prof. radiology, 1995—; dir. nuclear medicine Ben Taub Gen. Hosp., Houston, 1978-81; chief nuclear medicine service VA Med. Ctr., Houston, 1982-96, staff physician, 1996—2001, chief nuclear medicine sect., 2001—. Mem. med. staff univ. affiliated hosps. Houston, faculty Sch. Nuclear Medicine Tech.; fellow Internat. Atomic Energy Agy., Rome, 1962-63. Contbr. numerous articles to profl. jours; mem. editl. bd. Endocrinologia Experimentalis. Served with Health Service Czechoslovak Army, 1952-54. Recipient prize in nuclear medicine J.E. Purkyne, 1965. Mem. Harris County Med. Soc., Tex. Med. Assn., Soc. Nuc. Medicine, Am. Coll. Nuc. Physicians, Am. Soc. Nuc. Cardiology. Address: VA Med Ctr #115 2002 Holcombe Blvd PO Box 20183 Houston TX 77225-0183 E-mail: nkutka@aol.com.

KUTLAR, FERDANE, genetics educator, researcher; b. Turkey, Apr. 15, 1945; came to U.S., 1984; d. Mehmet and Sidika Tanrikulu; m. Abdullah Kutlar, Feb. 7, 1975. MD, Istanbul (Turkey) Med. Sch., 1971. Bd. cert in internal medicine, Turkey, 1976. Resident in internal medicine Istanbul U. Sch. Medicine, 1972-76; chief resident dept. medicine Istanbul Hosp., 1977-81; rsch. fellow Med. Coll. Ga., Augusta, 1982, hematology fellow Istanbul U. Sch. Medicine, 1983; rsch. fellow Med. Coll. Ga., Augusta, 1984, asst. prof., 1985-99, assoc. prof. medicine, 1999—. Dir. DNA lab. Med. Coll. Ga., Augusta, 1994—; presenter in field. Contbr. articles to profl. jours. Mem. Am. Soc. Hematology, Am. Soc. Human Genetics, Med. Coll. Ga. Pres.'s Club. Avocations: oil painting, gardening, decorating, chess. Home: 623 Sawgrass Dr Martinez GA 30907-9137 Office: Med Coll Ga Dept Medicine 15th St AC-1000 Augusta GA 30912-2100 E-mail: fkutlar@mail.mcp.edu.

KUTLER, STANLEY IRA, history and law educator, author; b. Cleve., Aug. 10, 1934; s. Robert P. and Zelda R. (Coffman) K.; m. Sandra J. Sachs, June 24, 1956; children: Jeffrey, David, Susan, Andrew. BA, Bowling Green State U., 1956; PhD, Ohio State U., 1960. Instr. history Pa. State U., State College, 1960-62; asst. prof. San Diego State U., 1962-64; from asst. prof. to prof. U. Wis., Madison, 1964-80, E. Gordon Fox prof. Am. instns., law and history, 1980—. Disting. exchange scholar to China Nat. Acad. Scis., 1982; Kenneth Keating lectr. Tel Aviv U., 1984; sr. Fulbright lectr. to Japan, 1977, to Israel, 1985, China, 1986; disting. vis. Fulbright scholar, Peru, 1987; Bicentennial prof. Tel Aviv U., 1985; cons. NEH, 1975—, The Constitution Project, 1985—; disting. chair Polit. Sci., U. Bologna, 1991; hist. cons. BBC/Discovery series Watergate, 1994. Author: Judicial Power and Reconstruction, 1968, Privilege and Creative Destruction, 1971, 2d edit., 1990, The American Inquisition, 1983, The Wars of Watergate: The Last Crisis of Richard Nixon, 1990, 92, Abuse of Power: The New Nixon Tapes, 1997; editor: Supreme Court and the Constitution, 1969, 3d edit., 1984, Looking for America, 1975, 80, The Encyclopedia of the Vietnam War, 1995, Encyclopedia of 20th Century America, 1995, American Perspectives: Historians on Historians, 1996, Watergate: The Fall of Richards Nixon, 1996, Dictionary of American History, 10 vols., 1996—; founding editor Rev. in Am. History, 1972-97; mem. adv. editor Greenwood Pub., 1968-73, Johns Hopkins U. Press, 1982—. Recipient Silver Gavel award ABA; fellow Sage Found., 1967-68, Emmy award, 1994, Peabody award, 1994, Best Reference Work award, Am. Assn. Pubs., 1996; fellow Guggenheim Found., 1971-72, Rockefeller Found., 1979-80. Jewish. Office: U Wis Dept History Madison WI 53706

KUTLICH, ANNA, writer; b. Detroit, Nov. 12, 1948; d. Nikola and Sophie (Bulat) Kutlich. BA in English, Oakland U., 1983. Reporter Oakland Press, Pontiac, Mich., 1980—83; copywriter, copyeditor Leo Burnett Advt., Southfield, Mich., 1984—85; tech. writer Time Engring., Troy, Mich., 1986; documentation analyst Henry Ford Hosp. Data Ctr., Rochester Hills, Mich., 1986—88; reporter Reminder Newspaper, Clarkston, Mich., 1989; project leader, copywriter, editor Electronic Data Systems, Troy, Mich., 1989—93; tech. writer VSE Corp., Sterling Heights, Mich., 1993—94; substitute tchr. Madison Dist. Pub. Schs., Madison Heights, Mich., 1994—95; process mgr., writer, editor U.S. Coun. Automotive Rsch., Southfield, 1995—99; engring. tng. coord. DaimlerChrylser Corp., Auburn Hills, Mich., 1999—2000; documentation specialist, trainer Ford Motor Co., Dearborn, Mich., 2000—01. Author (as Candy Stevans): (book) Eight O'Clock Blues, 2001. Precinct del., Rochester, Mich., 1996—98. Avocations: swimming, bicycling, walking. Office: Book One Pub Inc PO Box 80781 Rochester MI 48308-0781 Business E-Mail: Candystevans@aol.com.

KUTLINA, MARY LOUISE, elementary education educator; b. Niagara Falls, N.Y., Dec. 1, 1963; d. Joseph William and Frida Marlene (Reumel) K. BA in Communications, Niagara U., 1985, MS in Edn., 1988. Cert. elem. tchr., English tchr. Elem. tchr., jr. high English tchr. St. Joseph Elem. Sch., Niagara Falls, 1988-90; sub. tchr. Niagara Falls Bd. of Edn., 1990—97, 1999—; Eng. tchr. St. Peter's Luth. Sch., 1997-99; sub. tchr. Grand Island Ctrl. Sch. Dist., 2001—. Lectr. St. Stanislaus Kostka, 1977—; newsroom intern Sta. WIVB-TV, Buffalo, 1984—; prodn. asst. Niagara Frontier Cable TV, 1986. Author: (teleplay) Friends of Blondin, 1985, (children's play) Silly Sarah Becomes Smart, 1990, (book of poetry) Friends of Mary, 1991, also numerous radio and TV commls., news stories, charcoal and ink drawings. Vol. Blind Info. Svc., 1978-87; fundraiser, clerical aide March of Dimes Birth Defects Found., 1981-85, YMCA, 1990-94, Music Sch. Niagara, 1992-96, Friends of Niagra Falls Pub. Libr., 1990—, Friends of Niagara U. Theater; mem. Niagara U. Alumni Admissions Program, 1994. Mem. Internat. Platform Assn., 1994-01, Substitute Tchrs. United (newsletter staff, bd. dirs.-sec. 1991-92, editor SUB NEWS 1994), Pi Lambda Theta. Avocations: aerobics, reading biographies, writing poetry, volunteer work. Home: 2634 Welch Ave Niagara Falls NY 14303-1956 Office: Grand Island Central Sch 1100 Ransom Rd Grand Island NY 14072

KUTNER, JANET, art critic, book reviewer; b. Dallas, Sept. 20, 1937; m. Jonathan D. Kutner, Jan. 15, 1961. Student, Stanford U., 1955-57; BA in English, So. Meth. U., 1959. Asst. dir. Dallas Mus. Contemporary Arts, 1959-61; art critic, book reviewer Dallas Morning News, 1970—; Dallas/Ft. Worth corr. ARTnews Mag., 1975—. Mem. arts adv. panel Dallas Mcpl. Libr., 1981-91; mem. adv. bd. Arts Magnet H.S. of Dallas, 1980-92; mem. adv. com. Sch. Architecture and Environ. Design, U. Tex., Arlington, 1985-87; mem. long range planning com. Dallas Mus. Art, 1985-86; mem. visual arts and architecture adv. panel Tex. Com. on Arts, 1980-82. Contbr. articles to profl. jours.; juror various art exhbns. Bd. trustees Greenhill Sch., Dallas, 1980-81. Art critic's grantee Nat. Endowment for Arts, 1976-77, art critic's fellow Nat. Gallery Art, 1991—. Mem. Am. Assn. Museums, Dallas Mus. Art, Internat. Coun. Museums, ArtTable, Dallas Press Club (Critics award 1997). Office: Dallas Morning News PO Box 655237 Dallas TX 75265-5237

KUTOSH, SUE, artist; b. Elizabeth, N.J., Dec. 25, 1947; d. Stephen and Irene (Ribecky) K. BFA, Carnegie-Mellon U., 1971; MA, Kent State U., 1973. One-woman shows include Keane Mason Gallery, N.Y.C., 1978, West Broadway Gallery, N.Y.C., 1981, Kristen Richards Gallery, N.Y.C., 1983, Mussavi Arts Gallery, N.Y.C., 1987, N.Y. Bot. Garden, Bronx, 1992, Montserrat Gallery, N.Y.C., 1996, Pleiades Gallery, N.Y.C., 1997; art included in books: The Films of Jane Fonda, 1981, Hispanic Hollywood, 1990, The Lavender Screen, 1993, Hollywood Babble On, 1994, New Art Interna., 1998-2000; scenic art contbns. Sesame Street. Recipient Daytime Emmy for Seseame Street, 1993-94. Mem. United Scenic Artists, Local 829, Catharine Lorillard Wolfe Art Club, N.Y. Artists Equity, Nat. Assn. Women Artists. Avocation: photography. Home: 200 E 16th St Apt 2-d New York NY 10003-3708

KUTRZEBA, JOSEPH S. theatrical and film producer, director; b. Lodz, Poland, Oct. 11, 1927; came to U.S., 1950; s. Israel and Malka (Hakman) Fajwiszys; m. Valerie M. Hageman, Sept. 1955 (div. 1959); 1 child, Karen Janina; m. Michaela Lacher, Jan. 14, 1979; children: Marcus, Claudia Nina. BA, U. Munich, 1950; MFA, Yale U., 1956; PhD, NYU, 1974. Rschr., prodn. coord., dir., stage mgr. CBS-TV, N.Y.C., 1956-73; prodr., dir., writer, narrator UN Radio, N.Y.C., 1959-69; dir.-mem. Actors Studio, N.Y.C., 1960-62; founder, prodr., artistic dir. Queens Playhouse, Flushing Meadows, N.Y., 1972-74, also mem. bd. dirs., pres.; mem. faculty New Sch. for Social Rsch., N.Y.C., 1975-77. Prodr., dir. documentary film Children in the Holocaust, 1980; dir. 4 stage prodns., N.Y.C., 1995-97, (English and Polish versions) Helena: the Emigrant Queen, 1996 at La Mama and Kosciuszko Found.; presented Shakespeare's Sonnets at St. Peter's Ch. with Sam Waterston and Jan Englert. Mem. citizens com. Study N.Y. Theater, 1971-72; aux. mounted officer N.Y.C. Police Dept., 1974-77; a founder Warsaw Ghetto Resistance Orgn.; exec. sec., dep. presiding officer Hidden Child Found. Lt. U.S. Army, 1950-52, Korea. Recipient Tony award, Drama Desk award nominations for prodr. Best Broadway mus. The Lieutenant, 1975; recipient bronze award Internat. Film and TV Festival N.Y. for Children in the Holocaust with Liv Ullman, 1980; MacDowell Colony fellow, 1973. Mem. Dirs. Guild Am., Yale U. Alumni Assn. Avocations: tennis, skiing, horseback riding.

KUTSCHER, RONALD EARL, retired federal government executive; b. Hebron, Nebr., Apr. 18, 1932; s. Earl Harvey and Doris Lillian (Zong) K.; m. Elizabeth Elin Granholm, Dec. 28, 1963; children: Laura Ingrid, Steven Ronald. BA, Doane Coll., 1955; postgrad., U. Ill., 1955-56. Economist Bur. Labor Stats., Washington, 1957-68, asst. chief for rsch. divsn. of econ. growth, 1968-76, asst. commr., 1976-82, assoc. commr., 1982-96. Contbr. articles to profl. jours. With U.S. Army, 1952-54. Mem. Am. Statis. Assn. (chair com. on coms. 1989-91, chair program com. 1985, Prize Best Econ. Forecast 1973). Lutheran. Avocations: photography, golf. E-mail: brekutsch@aol.com.

KUTSCHER, THOMAS ALAN, electrical engineer; b. Mpls., Nov. 7, 1950; s. Richard Helmuth and Dorothy (Faulkner) K. BSEE, U. Minn., 1972; MBA, U. Kans., 1982. Registered profl. engr. Elec. engr. Black & Veatch, Kansas City, Mo., 1972-73, Overland Park, Kans., 1973-99, sr. elec. engr., 1980-83, project engr., 1984-90, project engring. mgr., 1990-93, project mgr., 1993-99; pres. Kutscher Rsch., Overland Park, Kans., 1999—. Author: Multi-Layered Reality, 2000; contbr. articles to profl. jours. Active Big Bros./Big Sisters of Greater Kansas City, 1974-80, Am. Red Cross Greater Kans. City, 2000—; mktg. mgr. Heart of Am. region U.S. Volleyball Assn., Kansas City, 1985-87, newsletter editor, 1985-87. Mem. IEEE (sr.).

KUTSENOK, VICTOR Y. mathematician, educator, mathematician, researcher; b. Kiev, Ukraine, Nov. 24, 1956; s. Yefim V. and Fira B. Kutsenok; m. Irina L. Kyner, Jan. 15, 1982; children: Alex V., Anya V. PhD in Tchg. Math., Moscow Sci. Rsch. Inst. Gen. Edn., 1992. Lic. tchr. Ind., 1997. Math. tchr. Secondary Sch. #79, Kiev, 1978—91; math. instr. Physics-Mathematics Lycium, Kiev, 1989—92; math. prof. U. St. Francis, Fort Wayne, Ind., 1993—, chair math. dept., 2000—. Mem.: Math. Assn. Am. Achievements include research in finding optimized methods of teaching mathematics. Home: 7922 Sedgewick Pl Fort Wayne IN 46835 Office: Univ St Francis 2701 Spring St Fort Wayne IN 46808 Personal E-mail: victork@mixi.net. E-mail: vkutsenok@sf.edu.

KUTSIN, LEONID, engineering educator, researcher; b. Belaya Tserkov, Ukraine, Jan. 12, 1935; arrived in U.S., 1993; s. Kutsin and Mitnitsky; m. Genya Vishnevetsky, Nov. 11, 1961; children: Igor Vishnevetsky, Renata Dielman. MS in Mechanics, Petrozavodsk (Russia) State U., 1957; Candidate in Tech. Scis., Kuban State Agrointstitut, Krasnodar, Russia, 1967; D in Tech. Scis., Rostov (Russia) State Inst. Machinery, 1982. Sr. rschr., dept. head State Rsch., Tech. and Design Inst. for Mechanization Livestock Farms, Kiev, Ukraine, 1960—87; prof., head mech. engring. dept. Saratov (Russia) State Agroengineering U., 1987—93; cons. Bion Techs., Inc., Amherst, NY, 1998; prof. Erie Coll., Amherst, 1998—99; cons. N.Am. Acad. Info. Scis., Toronto, Canada, 2000—03. Cons. Pan-Am. Environmental, Inc., Buffalo, 1999—2000. Author: (textbook) Distribution of Furage, 1971; contbr. articles to profl. jours. Mem.: N.Y. Acad. Scis., Am. Assn. Agrl. Engring., Internat. Info. Acad. Jewish. Achievements include patents in field. Home: 420 Old Falls Blvd North Tonawanda NY 14120 Office: SEAM, Inc. Director of Technologies 1576 Sweet Home Rd Amherst NY 14228

KUTTLER, CARL MARTIN, JR., academic administrator; b. Daytona Beach, Fla., Jan. 31, 1940; s. Carl M. and Winona (Ellis) K.; m. Evelyn Flathmann, June 29, 1963; children— Cindy, Carl Martin III, Erika. AA, St. Petersburg Jr. Coll., 1960; BS in Mgmt., Fla. State U., Tallahassee, 1962; JD, Stetson U., 1965. Bar: Fla. bar 1965. Research aide 2d Dist. Ct. Appeals, Lakeland, Fla., 1965-66; instr. St. Petersburg (Fla.) Jr. Coll. (now St. Petersburg Coll.), 1965-76; asst. to v.p. for adminstrn. St. Petersburg (Fla.) Jr. Coll., 1966-67, dean. adminstrv. affairs, 1967-78, pres., 1978—. Adj. instr., cons. grad. edn. program U. Tex., Austin; judge Templeton Prize in Religion. Co-author: 1,001 Exemplary Practices in America's Two-Year Colleges, 1994. Mem. pres.'s Coun. Div. Cmty. Colls., 1978—; candidate for Fla. Commr. Edn., 1974; mem. judging panel selecting outstanding high schs. in Am. for U.S. Sec. Edn.; apptd. by Pres. U.S. Nat. Adv. Coun. Ednl. Rsch. and Improvement; apptd. by U.S. Sec. VA to Adminstr.'s Ednl. Assistance Adv. Com. Named Most Disting. Alumnus, Stetson U. Alumni Assn., 1978, 1988, Hon. Father of C.C. Sys. in Russia, Assn. Edn. for Everybody, 1994, Outstanding C.C. Pres. in Am., Assn. of C.C. Trustees, 1998; recipient Disting. Floridian award, Phi Theta Kappa, 1986, Nat. Disting. Coll. Pres. award, 1991, Internat. Leadership award, 1990, vis. scholar award, 1987, master tchr. award, 1988, 1992, 1993, U. Tex. Disting. Pres.'s award, PTK Fla., 1991, Alumnus award, Fla. State U., 1981, 1988, Liberty Bell award, St. Petersburg Bar Assn., 1992, Werner Kubsch award for outstanding achievement in internat. edn., C.C. for Internat. Devel., Inc., 1997, top Phi Theta Kappa chpt. award of 1200 cmty. colls., 2001, Chmn.'s award, St. Petersburg C. of C., 2001, C.W. Bill Young Pinellas Pinnacle award, Dept. Econ. Devel., 2002, Pres. award Profl. Excellence, Fla. Assn. C.C., 2002. Mem.: Fla. Bar Assn., Fla. Assn. C.C.s (Pres.'s award for profl. excellence 2002), Am. Assn. C.C.s, Nat. Assn. Coll. and Univ. Attys. Republican. Presbyterian. Home: 8336 40th Ave N Saint Petersburg FL 33709-3935 Office: St Petersburg Coll PO Box 13489 Saint Petersburg FL 33733-3489 E-mail: kuttlerc@spcollege.edu.

KUTTNER, BERNARD A. retired judge; b. Berlin, Jan. 13, 1934; arrived in U.S., 1939; s. Frank B. and Vera (Knopfmacher) Kuttner; children: Karen M., Robert D., Stacey M. Gilby. AB cum laude, Dartmouth Coll., 1955; postgrad., U. Va. Law Sch., 1956; JD, Seton Hall U., 1959; postgrad., NYU, 1960. Bar: N.J. 1960, U.S. Supreme Ct. 1964, U.S. Ct. Mil. Appeals 1967, N.Y. 1982, DC 1982, cert.: N.J. (civil trial lawyer). Assoc. Toner, Crowley, Woelper & Vanderbilt, 1959-62; pvt. practice Newark, 1962-75; corp. counsel Irvington, NJ, 1963-66; judge N.J. State Divsn. Tax Appeals, 1977-79; instr. civil litigation Montclair State Coll., 1979-82. Del. Jud. Conf. N.J. Supreme Ct., 1974—81; vice chmn. dist. ethics com. Supreme Ct. N.J., 1984—85, chmn., 1985—86. Contbr. articles to profl. jours. Commr. Essex County (N.J.) Pk. Commn., 1973—79; apptd. bd. trial atty. cert. N.J. Supreme Ct., 1986—90; founding mem. Cesar E. Chavez Found. Served to lt. comdr. USNR, 1964—74. Mem.: ATLA, ABA (co-editor trial techniques newsletter sect. tort and ins. practice, chmn. trial techniques com. 1988—89, mem. sect. litig.), Am. Counsel Assn., Essex County Bar Assn. (chmn. 1973—75, trial and appellate litig., jud. com. 1972—75, treas. 1975—79, pres. 1980—81, products liability com. 1981—), Irvington Bar Assn. (pres. 1968—70), DC Bar Assn., Inst. Ethical Behavior (pres. 1985—). Jewish. Office: Kuttner Law Offices 24 Lackawanna Pl Millburn NJ 07041-1618 E-mail: Kuttnerbuck@aol.com.

KUTTNER, ROBERT LOUIS, editor, columnist; b. N.Y.C., Apr. 17, 1943; s. Arthur Paul Kuttner and Pauline M. Levy; m. Sharland Grace Trotter, Dec. 19, 1971 (dec. Nov. 1997); children: Gabriel A., Jessica A.; m. Joan Fitzgerald, May 7, 2000. AB, Oberlin Coll., 1965; MA, U. Calif., Berkeley, 1966; cert., London Sch. Econs., 1963-64; LLD (hon.), Swarthmore Coll., 1999. Asst. to I.F. Stone, Washington, 1966; legis. asst. to Congressman W.F. Ryan, 1967-68; corr. program dir. Pacifica Radio, N.Y.C., 1968-71; editor The Village Voice, Washington, 1971-73; staff writer Washington Post, 1974-75; chief investigator Senate Banking Com., Washington, 1975-78; editor Working Papers, Mass., 1980-83; econs. writer, editor The New Republic, 1983-91; columnist Bus. Week, 1984—, Boston Globe and Washington Post Syndicate, 1985—; co-editor The Am. Prospect, 1989—. Contbr. editor More Mag., Washington, 1973-78; lectr. Boston U., 1980-82, W. Colston Leigh Bur., N.J., 1987—; vis. prof. U. Mass., 1987-88, Brandeis U., Mass., 1991-92, 2003—. Author: Revolt of the Haves, 1980, The Economic Illusion, 1984, The Life of the Party, 1987, The End of Laissez-Faire, 1991, Everything for Sale, 1997, Family Reunion, 2002; nat. policy corr.: New Eng. Jour. Medicine, 1996—2000. Exec. dir. Nat. Commn. on Neighborhoods, Washington, 1978; bd. dirs. Econ. Policy Inst. Washington, 1986—, Families USA, Boston, 1989-96, Florence Fund, 1999—. Recipient Jack London award, United Steelworkers Am., 1982, John Hancock award, John Hancock Co., 1988, Paul Hoffman award UN Devel. Program, 1996, Sidney Hillman award Sidney Hillman Found., 1998; Woodrow Wilson fellow U. Calif., 1965-66, Kennedy fellow, Harvard U., 1979, fellow John

Guggenheim Meml. Found., 1988, McCormack Inst, 1987-88, Radcliffe Pub. Pollicy Ctr., 1998-2000. Mem. Nat. Acad. Social Ins. Avocations: tennis, photography, writing poetry. Office: Am Prospect 5 Broad St Boston MA 02109-2901

KUTYNA, DONALD JOSEPH, air force officer; b. Chgo., Dec. 6, 1933; s. Frank A. and Isabel E. (Kmiec) K.; m. Lucille Mae Moellering, June 5, 1957; children: Dale J., Douglas J. Student, U. Iowa, 1951-53; BS, U.S. Mil. Acad., 1957; MS in Aero./Astronautics, MIT, 1965. Commd. 2d lt. USAF, 1957, advanced through grades to 4 star gen., 1990; pilot trainee Vance AFB, Enid, Okla., 1958; comdr. B-47 crew March AFB, Riverside, Calif., 1958; test pilot Edwards AFB, Calif., 1965-69; pilot 44th Tactical Fighter Squadron, Royal Takhli AFB, Thailand, 1969-70; planner R&D Pentagon, Washington, 1971-72; exec. officer Undersec. of Air Force, Washington, 1973-76; program mgr. Air Force Electronics Systems Div., Bedford, Mass., 1976-82; mgr. Dept. Def. Space Launch Program, L.A., 1982-84; dir. space systems Pentagon, Washington, 1984-86; vice comdr. Space Div., L.A., 1986-87; comdr. USAF Space Command, Peterson AFB, Colo., 1987-90; comdr.-in-chief N.Am. Aerospace Def. Command, U.S. Space Command, Peterson AFB, 1990-92; v.p. advanced space systems Lockheed Martin Corp. (formerly Loral Corp.), N.Y.C., 1993-99; v.p. space tech. Loral Space & Comm. Corp., N.Y.C., 1999—. Recipient Space award Nat. Geog. Soc., 1987, James V. Hartinger award Nat. Security Indsl. Assn., 1990. Mem. Air Force Assn. (Schriever award 1991). Avocations: skiing, surfing, fishing, hunting, antique cars.

KUTZ, JOSEPH EDWARD, hand surgeon, educator; b. Standish, Mich., June 11, 1928; s. Joseph M. and Hazel (Stock) K.; m. Mary Jane Templeton, June 15, 1957; children: Anthony, Karen, Bradley. BS, U. Detroit, 1953, MS, 1955; MD, U. Mich., 1958. Diplomate Am. Bd. Surgery. Rotating intern Springfield (Ohio) City Hosp., 1958-59; resident in gen. surgery U. Louisville Med. Sch., 1959-63; fellow in surgery of hand U. Louisville, 1963-64, asst. clin. prof. surgery, 1968-74, assoc. clin. prof., 1974-88, clin. prof. surgery, 1988—. Contbr. numerous articles to profl. jours. With AUS, 1946-48. Mem. ACS, Am. Soc. Surgery of Hand, Caribbean Soc. Surgery of Hand, Am. Med. Assn., Ky. Med. Assn., Jefferson County (Ky.) Med. Soc. (pres. 1988-89), Louisville Surg. Soc., Pan-Pacific Surg. Soc., Southeastern Surg. Congress., Am. Soc. Plastic Surgeons, Internat. Soc. Reconstructive Microsurgery (founder, treas. 1983-91), World Soc. for Reconstructive Microsurgery (founding mem.), Am. Soc. for Reconstructive Microsurgery (pres. 1986-87), Sunderland Soc. (charter), SC Orthop. Assn. (hon.), Group for Advancement Microsurgery. Office: 225 Abraham Flexner Way Louisville KY 40202-1846

KUTZ, KENNETH JOHN, retired mining executive; b. Elrose, Sask., Can., Nov. 16, 1926; came to U.S., 1957, naturalized, 1962; s. John and Leah (Lefevre) K.; B.S. summa cum laude in Geol. Engring., U. Sask., 1948; m. Nora M. Marchand, Nov. 10, 1948; children— Shirley Mae Kase, Gerald John. Surveyor Howe Sound Co., Britannia Beach, B.C., 1947-48, research engr., 1950-51, asst. chief engr., 1951-54, chief engr., maintenance supt., Snow Lake, Man., 1954-55, mine supt., Cobalt, Idaho, 1956-57; mine supt. Lakeview Mining Co. (Oreg.), 1958-59, Sunshine Mining Co., Kellogg, Idaho, 1960-61; mining engr. Texasgulf Inc., Moab, Utah, 1961-62, mine supt., 1963-65, tech. asst. to gen. mgr., 1965-66, tech. asst. to v.p. Potash div., Salt Lake City, 1966-68, adminstrv. asst., 1968-69, asst. to pres., mgr. Australian iron ore projects, 1969-73, v.p. Internat. div., 1973-82; pres. Texasgulf Minerals & Metals, 1983-90; pres. Texasgulf Panama, Pandora Mining (Pty.), 1983-90; ret., 1990. Registered Profl. engr., B.C., Oreg. Mem. AIME, Mining and Metall. Soc. Am. (past pres.), Can. Inst. Mining and Metallurgy (life), Australian Inst. Mining and Metallurgy, Mining Club N.Y. (bd. govs., past pres.), Innis Arden Golf Club, Collectors Club of N.Y. Republican. Roman Catholic. Author: Gold Fever, 1988, Nome Gold, 1991, Victoria Gold, 1993, California Gold, 1994, Black Gold, 1995, Klondike Gold, 1996, Untold Wealth, 1998; patentee in field. Home: 7 Whaling Rd Darien CT 06820-5930

KUURE, BOJAN MARLENA, operating room nurse; b. Jakobstad, Finland, Nov. 14, 1942; d. Anders Arne and Aina Viktoria (Back) Sundqvist; m. Arvo Antero Kuure, Nov. 3, 1965; 1 child, Saara Bojan. Diploma, Helsingfors Svenska Sjukvardsinstitut, Helsinki, Finland, 1964; specialty nursing in anesthia & surgery, Helsingfors Svenska Sjukvards, Helsinki, Finland, 1967-68; Aprubatur in Edn., U. Helsinki, 1972. Staff nurse U. Finland Hosp., 1964-67, specialty nurse, 1968-70; tchr. dir. Nursing Inst., Helsinki, 1970-72; oper. rm. nurse Island Hosp., Anacortes, Wash., 1972-83, surg. dir., 1983. Vol. Interplast, Inc., Healing the Children. Paul Harris fellow Rotary Internat.; recipient Women Helping Women award Soroptimists Internat., 2002. Mem. Am. Assn. Oper. Rm. Nurses, Oper. Rm. Mgrs. Wash., Wash. State Coun. Peri-op Nursing, Wash. Orgn. Nurse Execs. Home: 1201 5th St Anacortes WA 98221-1709 Fax: 360-299-1382. E-mail: bojank@island-health.org.

KUWABARA, JAMES SHIGERU, research hydrologist; b. Honolulu, Apr. 26, 1953; s. Donald Shigeyuki and Setsue (Ogawa) K.; m. Rie Rita Kimura, June 6, 1982; children: Sara Mie, Annie Mako. BSCE, U. Hawaii, 1975; MS in Environ. Engring., Calif. Inst. Tech., 1976, PhD in Environ. Engring., 1980. Computer operator Computer Info. Svcs., Honolulu, 1971; engring. rschr. U. Hawaii, Honolulu, 1971-73; aquacultural rschr. Sea Grants Program, Honolulu, 1973-75; grad. rsch. fellow NSF, Pasadena, Calif., 1975-78; grad. rsch. asst. Calif. Inst. Tech., Pasadena, Calif., 1978-80; postdoctoral rsch. fellow Nat. Rsch. Coun., Menlo Park, Calif., 1980-82; rsch. hydrologist U.S. Geol. Survey, Menlo Park, Calif., 1982—. Conf. chmn. West Coast Water Chem. Workshop, Stanford, 1986; final rev. panel Water Res. Rsch. Grants, Reston, Va., 1988-89; session organizer Estuarine Rsch. Conf., San Francisco, 1991; session moderator Am. Chem. Soc., Washington, 1992; coord. San Francisco Bay Toxic Substances Hydrology Program, 1994—. Editor Estuaries, 1993; assoc. editor Water Resources Rsch., 2001, dep. editor, 2003; contbr. chpts. to books, numerous articles to Geochimica et Cosmochimica Acta, Limnology and Oceanography, Sci., other profl. jours. Mem. Eagle Scout rev. bd. Boy Scouts Am., Honolulu, 1974-75. Hawaii State Acad. scholar U. Hawaii, 1972; NSF Grad. fellow Calif. Inst. Tech., 1975; Nat. Rsch. Coun. postdoctoral rsch. assoc. U.S. Geol. Survey, 1980. Mem. ASCE, Am. Inst. Chemists, Estuarine Rsch. Fedn., Phycological Soc. Am. Achievements include development of a larval culturing system of State of Hawaii's prawn industry; optimization of gametophytic culturing of giant kelp for biomass conversion program; design of toxicant introduction device, process-interdependent solute transport modeling; modeling benthic flux of contaminants. Office: US Geol Survey 345 Middlefield Rd # MS439 Menlo Park CA 94025-3591 E-mail: kuwabara@usgs.gov.

KUWAYAMA, S. PAUL, physician, allergist, immunologist; b. Sapporo, Hokkaido, Japan, Nov. 8, 1932; s. Satoru and Chiyoko (Nishikawa) K.; m. Barbara Ann Dresback, June 29, 1974; children: David, Steven, Jason. BS, Hokkaido U., Sapporo, 1955, MD, 1959. Diplomate Am. Bd. Pediatrics, 1965, Am. Bd. Allergy & Immunology, 1972, Am. Bd. Pediatric Allergy, 1970; lic. Nat. Bd. Med. Examiners of Japan, 1960, Wis. State Bd. Med. Examiners, 1968, Ariz. State Bd. Med. Examiners, 1987, N.Mex. State Bd. Med. Examiners, 1987, Tenn. State Bd. Med. Examiners, 1992. Intern U.S. Naval Hosp., Seattle, 1959-60, St. Mary's Hosp., Milw., 1960-61; jr. resident in pediatrics Temple U. Sch. of Medicine, Phila., 1961-62; chief pediat. resident W.Va. U. Sch. of Medicine, Morgantown, 1962-63; postdoctoral fellow in immunology, jr. fellow in pediatric allergy The Children's Mercy Hosp.-U. Kans. Sch. of Medicine, Kansas City, 1964-65; staff pediatrician Atomic Bomb Casualty Commn. in Hiroshima, U.S. Nat. Acad. of Scis.-U.S. Atomic Energy Commn., 1966-67; sr. pediatric allergist, dept. immunobiology U. Kans. Sch. of Medicine, 1967-68. Asst. clin. prof. pediatric allergy and immunology Med. Coll. Wis., Milw., 1970—. Contbg. author texts and forward to books. Fulbright scholar, 1960-63. Fellow Am. Acad. Pediatrics (sect. on allergy and immunology), Am. Coll. Allergy, Asthma and Immunology, Am. Assn. Cert. Allergists, Am. Acad. Allergy, Asthma and Immunology, Am. Assn. Clin. Immunology and Allergy; mem. AMA, Fulbright Scholarship Grantee Alumni Assn., State Med. Soc. of Wis., Milw. Pediatric Soc. Office: 11035 W Forest Home Ave Hales Corners WI 53130-2541

KUYATH, RICHARD NORMAN, lawyer; b. Sacramento, Calif., Jan. 25, 1948; s. Norman John and Marie Elizabeth (Engelhardt) Kuyath; m. Laura Ann Brumfield, Aug. 12, 1972; children: Brian James, Bradford David;1 child, Matthew Lawrence. BA, U. Minn., 1971; JD, William Mitchell Coll. Law, St. Paul, 1975. Bar: Minn. 1975. Contract specialist FMC Corp., Naval Systems Divsn., Mpls., 1975-80, sr. contract specialist, 1980-87, sr. contract counsel, 1988-89, mgr. contract counsel, 1989—; govt. contract counsel 3M Co., St. Paul, 1989-91, sr. counsel, 1991—. Contbr. articles to profl. jours. Fellow: Am. Bar Found. (vice chair pub. contract law sect. R&D and intellectual property com.); mem.: Nat. Contracts Mgmt. Assn. (cert. assoc. contracts mgr. 1980). Republican. Congregationalist. Home: 6103 Jeffrey Ln Minneapolis MN 55436-1206 E-mail: rnkuyath1@mmm.com.

KUYKENDALL, CRYSTAL ARLENE, educational consultant, lawyer; b. Chgo., Dec. 11, 1949; d. Cleophus Campbell and Ellen (Campbell) Logan; m. Roosevelt Kuykendall, Apr. 10, 1969 (dec. Aug. 1972); children: Kahlil, Rasheki, Kashif. BA, Southern Ill. U., 1970; MA, Montclair State U., 1972; EdD, Atlanta U., 1975; JD, Georgetown U., 1982; LHD (hon.), Lewis and Clark Coll., Portland, 2002. Bar: D.C. 1988. Instr. Seton Hall U., South Orange, N.J., 1971-73; adminstrn. intern D.C. Pub. Schs., 1974-75; dir. citizens tng. inst. Nat. Com. for Citizens in Edn., Washington, 1975-77; dir. urban and minorities rels. dept. Nat. Sch. Bd. Assn., Washington, 1977-79; edn. dir. PSI Assocs., Inc., Washington, 1979-80; exec. dir. Nat. Alliance of Black Sch. Educators, Washington, 1980-81; dir. mktg. Roy Littlejohn Assoc., Inc., Washington, 1983—; pres., gen. counsel K.I.R.K., Inc. (Kreative and Innovative Resources for Kids), Washington, 1981—. Cons. to Ministry of Sport and Recreation, Western Australia Govt., 1990; chmn. U.S. Pres. Nat. Adv. Coun. on Continuing Edn., Washington, 1978-81; cons. U. Pitts. Race Desegregation Assistance Ctr., 1982-87, J.H. Lowry Assn., Chgo., 1982, U.S. Dept. of Edn. Transition Team, Washington, 1980. Author: Developing Leadership for Parent/Citizen Groups, 1975, You & Yours: Making the Most of this School Year, 1987, Improving Black Student Achievement by Enhancing Self Image, 1989, From Rage to Hope: Strategies for Reclaiming Black and Hispanic Students, 1992, rev. edit., 2003, Dreaming of a PHAT Century, 2000, 2nd edit., 2003. Mem. adv. bd. Inst. of the Black World, Atlanta, 1975-81; mem. steering com. Nat Conf. on Parental Involvement, Denver, 1977-78; mem. edn. task force Martin Luther King Jr. Ctr. for Social Change, Atlanta, 1978-80; mem. bd. dirs. Health Power, Inc., 1995-2001, Shiloh Bapt. Ch. of Washington Family Life Ctr. Fedn., 1996—. Named Honorary Citizen of New Orleans, Mayor's Office, 1976; Ford found. fellow, 1973-74; Honorary Ky Colonel award, 1993, 99, 2002; Cert. Congl. Recognition, 2001. Mem. Nat. Bar Assn., Nat. Alliance of Black Sch. Edn., Alpha Kappa Alpha. Democrat. Baptist. Avocations: poetry writing, card playing, swimming, jogging, skiing. Office: KIRK Inc PO Box 60115 Potomac MD 20859-0115

KUYKENDALL, JOHN WELLS, academic administrator, educator; b. Charlotte, N.C., May 8, 1938; s. James Bell and Emily Jones (Frazer) K.; m. Nancy Adams Moore, July 15, 1961; children— Timothy Moore, James Frazer BA cum laude, Davidson Coll., 1959; BD cum laude, Union Sem., Richmond, Va., 1964; STM, Yale U., 1965; MA, Princeton U., 1972, PhD, 1975; DD (hon.), Hanover Coll., 1999; LHD (hon.), Wofford Coll., 1999. Ordained to ministry Presbyterian Ch., 1965. Campus minister Presbyn. Ch., Auburn, Ala., 1965-70; faculty Auburn U., 1973-84; pres. Davidson (N.C.) Coll., 1984—97, pres. emeritus, prof. religion, 1997—2003. Author: (with others) Presbyterians: Their History and Beliefs, 1978, Southern Enterprize: The Work of Evangelical Societies in the Antebellum South, 1982; contbr. articles to profl. jours. Recipient Algernon Sydney Sullivan award Auburn U., 1982 Mem. Am. Soc. Ch. History, Phi Beta Kappa, Omicron Delta Kappa, Phi Kappa Phi. Democrat.

KUYKENDALL, RICHARD G. music educator; s. F. G. and Mary Frances Kuykendall, Ruby Kuykendall (Stepmother); m. Susan M. Kuykendall, Aug. 22, 1993. BA, McNeese State U., Lake Charles, LA, 1974—78, MusM, 1982—84. Band dir. Calcasieu Parish Sch. Board,J.I. Watson Mid. Sch., Iowa, La., 1995—; band dir., lagrange h.s. Calcasieu Parish Sch. Bd., Lake Charles, La., 1993—95. Band director,leesville h.s. Vernon Parish Sch. Bd., Leesville, La., 1985—93; band dir., carencro h.s. Lafayette Parish Sch. Bd., Lafayette, La., 1983—85; band dir., leesville h.s. Vernon Parish Sch. Bd., Leesville, La., 1979—82; band dir., hackberry h.s. Cameron Parish Sch. Bd., Hackberry, La., 1978—79; adj. instr. of low brass U. of La. at Lafayette, Lafayette, La., 1984—85; mem. of mcneese faculty brass quintet McNeese State U., Lake Charles, La., 1982—83; mem. u. of la. at lafayette faculty brass quintet U. of La. at Lafayette, Lafayette, La., 1984—85; mem. of so. assn. of colleges and schools com. (twice) S.A.C.S., La., 1981—82; teacher-computer music composition(summer) Calcasieu Parish Sch. Bd., Lake Charles, La., 2000—01. Performer for armed forces, civic groups and nursing homes, 1976—; bd. chmn., vice chmn., deacon First Christian Ch., Lake Charles, La., 2000—. Recipient Commendation for Ednl. Achievements at Leesville H.S., La. State Legislature, 1982, J.I. Watson Mid. Sch. Tchr. of the Yr., J.I. Watson Sch., 1998-99, KPLC TV Class Act Award, KPLC TV (Local NBC affiliate), 1998, Mayoral Proclomation designating May 23, 2002 as Rick Kuykendall Day in the town of Iowa, La., Town of Iowa, 2002, Commendation for Achievements at Leesville H.S., Vernon Parish Sch. Bd., 1982, Commendation for Outstanding Civilian Support, US Army, Ft. Polk, La., 1982. Mem.: Dist. V Band Directors Assn. (pres. (twice) 1998—2000), Music Educators Nat. Conf., Am. Fedn. of Teachers. Office: JI Watson Middle School 201 E First St Iowa LA 70647

KUYKENDALL, STEVEN THOMAS, former congressman; b. McAlester, Okla., Jan. 27, 1947; s. Henry and Frances (Campbell) K.; m. Janice E. Francis, Oct. 3, 1970; children: Kerry D., Brent T., Craig S. BS in Bus., Oklahoma City U., 1968; MBA, San Diego State U., 1974. Pres. Lockheed Mortgage Corp., 1981-84; prin. David Buxton Fin. Group, 1984-94; mem. 54th Assembly Dist., 1994-98, minority whip, vice chmn. utilities and commerce com., mem. banking and fin., local govt. and budget coms.; mem. 106th Congress from 36th Calif. dist. U.S. Ho. Reps., Washington, 1999-2001, mem. armed svcs. com., mem. sci. com., mem. transp. and infrastructure com.; lobbyist Evente, 2002—. Past pres., trustee Peninsula Edn. Found., 1988-93. Mayor, coun. mem. City of Rancho Palos Verdes, Calif., 1991-94. Capt. USMC, 1968-73, Vietnam. Republican. Presbyterian. Mailing: 21311 Hawthorne Blvd, Ste 107 Torrance CA 90503-5693

KUYPER, JOAN CAROLYN, foundation administrator; b. Balt., Oct. 22, 1941; d. Irving Charles and Ethel Mae (Pritchett) O'Connor; m. L. William Kuyper, Dec. 20, 1964; children: Susan Carol, Edward Philip. BA in Edn., Salisbury State U., 1963; postgrad. Columbia U., 1978; MA in Arts Mgmt. and Bus., NYU, 1988. Elem. sch. tchr. Prince Georges County Schs., Md., 1963-68; free lance singer, opera, oratorio, chamber music Amato Opera, N.Y.C., 1967-80; owner, mgr. Privette Artists' Registry, Placement Service for Singers, Teaneck, N.J., 1969-78; exec. dir. Teaneck Artists Perform-Chamber Music Series, 1975-80; program dir. Vols. in Arts & Humanities, Vol. Bur. Bergen County, N.J., 1978-81; dir. Bergen Mus. Art and Sci., 1981-83; cons. Am. Soc. Prevention Cruelty to Animals, 1984, Am. Coun. for Arts, 1987; dir. ops. Isabel O'Neil Found. and Studio, 1984-85. Dir. vol. svcs. March of Dimes Birth Defects Found. of Greater N.Y., 1985-88; dir. chpt. devel. Huntington's Disease Soc. Am., 1988-91; bd. dirs Pro Arte Chorale and adv. bd. on arts, Teaneck, 1976-81; mgmt. cons. Girl Scouts U.S., 1992-2000; dep. dir. for orgnl. advancement Soc. Women Engrs., 2000—; sr. counsel The Forbes Group. Mem. N.Y. Soc. Assn. Execs. (membership com. 1991-94, Cert. Assn. Execs. chair 1995-96, program planning com. 1996-98, chmn. profl. devel. com. 1998—), Am. Soc. Assn. Execs. (cert.), Assn. Mus., Mus. Coun. N.J., Am. Mktg. Assn. (bd. dirs. 1990-96), Assn. for Vol. Adminstrn. (author handbook), Nat. Soc. Fund Raising Execs., Orgnl. Devel. Network, SearchNet, Exec. Women in Golf Assn, Altrusa Club (bd. dirs. 1984-86, 90-93, 96—, pres. 1986-88), PEO, Phi Alpha Theta. Democrat. Presbyterian. Home: 345 W 58th St Apt 14X New York NY 10019-1142 also: 1275 Pebble Beach Rd Tobyhanna PA 18466-9119 E-mail: joankuyper@aol.com.

KUZEL, TIMOTHY MICHAEL, hematologist, oncologist, consultant; s. William M. and Grace Kuzel; m. Sylvia A. Kuzel; children: Timothy G., Annmarie H. MD, U. of Mich., 1978—84. Lic. medical doctor ABIM-PA, 1987, hematology ABIM-Pennsylvania, 1990, oncology ABIM-Pennsylvania, 1989. Assoc. prof. of medicine Feinberg Sch. of Medicine, Chicago, 1990—. Achievements include research in American Cancer Society clinical oncology career development award. Office: Feinberg School of Medicine 676 N St Clair Suite 850 Chicago IL 60611 Office Fax: 312-695-6189.

KUZIEMSKI, NAOMI ELIZABETH, counselor, education consultant; b. Phila., Dec. 22, 1925; d. Andrew Raymond and Elizabeth M. (Graham) Hartman; m. Walter William Kuziemski, Dec. 28, 1943 (dec. Feb. 2000); children: Nancy Kuziemski Simpson, Sandra Ruth McElroy. BS in Bus. Edn., Temple U., 1945, MS in Counseling, 1949. Tchr. Sch. Dist. Phila., 1945-58; coll. counselor Phila. H.S. for Girls, 1958-96; ednl. cons., 1996—. V.p. Nat. Assn. Coll. Admissions Counselors, Alexandria, Va., 1985-87, dir. Tools of the Trade workshop, 1992-95; pres. Pa. Assn. Coll. Admissions Counselors, 1991-93; focus group mem. U.S. News and World Report, Washington, 1995-96; panelist and presenter in field. Del., instnl. rep. Coll. Bd., N.Y., 1978-96. Recipient Bernard P. Ireland award Coll. Bd., Phila., 1996, Gayle C. Wilson award Nat. Assn. Coll. Admission Counselors, Alexandria, 1996, Recognition award PASSCAC, 1998; named Counselor of the Yr., Inroads, Phila., 1982. Mem. AAUW (Phila. br., v.p. 1997-99), Coll. Bd.-Middle States (planning com. 1995-97). Home: 7 Lawnside Rd Cheltenham PA 19012-1812 E-mail: naomikuz@aol.com.

KUZMA, GEORGE MARTIN, retired bishop; b. Windber, Pa., July 24, 1925; s. Ambrose and Anne (Marton) K.. Student, Benedictine Coll., Lisle, Ill.; BA, postgrad., Duquesne U., U. Mich.; grad., SS Cyril and Methodius Byzantine Cath. Sem. Ordained priest Byzantine Cath. Ch., 1955. Asst. pastor SS Peter and Paul Ch., Braddock, Pa., 1955—57; pastor Holy Ghost Ch., Charleroi, Pa., 1957—65, St. Michael Ch., Flint, Mich., 1965—70, St. Eugene Ch., Bedford, Ohio, 1970—72, Annunciation Ch., Anaheim, Calif., 1970—86; rev. monsignor Byzantine Cath. Ch., 1984, titular bishop, 1986, consecrated bishop, 1987; aux. bishop Byzantine Cath. Diocese of Passaic, NJ, 1987—90; bishop Van Nuys, Calif., 1991—2000; ret., 2000. Judge matrimonial tribunal, mem. religious edn. commn., mem. commn. orthodox rels. Diocese of Pitts., 1955—69; judge matrimonial tribunal, vicar for religious Diocese of Parma, 1969—82; treas., bd. dirs., chmn. liturgical commn., mem. clergy & seminarian rev. bd., liaison to ea. Cath. dirs. religious edn., bd. dirs. Diocese of Van Nuys, 1982—86, diocesan credit un, chmn. diocesan heritage bd., chmn. diocesan ecumenical commn., 1982—86; vicar gen. Diocese of Passaic; Episcopal vicar for Ea. Pa.; chmn. Diocesan Retirement Plan Bd.; pres. Father Walter Cizsek Prayer League; chaplain Byzantine Carmelite Monastery, Sugarloaf, Pa. Assoc. editor: Byzantine Cath. World; editor: The Apostle. With USN, 1943—46, PTO. Office: Byzantine Cath Eparchy of Van Nuys 8131 N 16th St Phoenix AZ 85020-3901

KUZMANOVIC, JANE VIOLET, director; b. Akron, Ohio, Apr. 9, 1962; d. Ljubomir Emanuel and Viorika Violet Boujanac, m. Dragan Kuzmanovic, May 1, 1983; children: Miriam Violeta, Lorraine Ljubica, Michael Miroslav, Daniel Branislav, Thomas Dragoslav, Stefanie Adela, Julianne Jovana, Melanie Dragana. BS in Bus. Mgmt., U. of Phoenix, 2003. Publications prodn. coord. Hughes Aircraft Co., El Segundo, Calif., 1984—93; dept. sec. Norstan Cabling Svcs., Van Nuys, Calif., 1995; exec. asst. AVEX, Inc., Camarillo, Calif., 1995—97; faculty and curriculum coord. Kennedy-Western U., Thousand Oaks, Calif., 1997—2000, sr. faculty and curriculum coord., 2000—02, faculty and curriculum mgr., 2002—. Translator, office asst. Star Upholstering, Beverlywood, Calif., 1976—98; tchr., Sunday sch. Apostolic Christian Ch., Nazarean, Carson and Van Nuys, Calif., 1989—. Singer (alto): Apostolic Christian Ch. Choir; dir.: (children's Sunday sch. choir) Apostolic Christian Ch., Nazarean. Supporter Habitat for Humanities, LA, 2002; fund-raiser participant of 10k walk The Nat. Multiple-Sclerosis Soc., Santa Barbara, 2003; mem. Apostolic Christian Ch., Nazarean, Van Nuys, Calif., 1976. Grantee Pell, NAFSA, 2003. Avocations: gardening, winemaking, travel, cooking, canning. Office: Kennedy-Western U 501 MarinSt #200 Thousand Oaks CA 91360 Office Fax: 805-379-1092. E-mail: jkuzmanovic@kw.edu.

KUZNESOF, ELIZABETH ANNE, history educator; BA, U. Wash., 1961, MA, 1968; PhD, U. Calif., Berkeley, 1976. Vis. prof. history U. Kans., Lawrence, 1976-77, asst. prof. history, 1977-80, assoc. prof., 1980-85, prof., 1985—, asst. prof. history, 1977-80, assoc. prof., 1981-87, prof., 1987—, dir. L.Am. Studies, 1992—. Author: Household Economy and Urban Development in Sao Paulo 1765 to 1836, 1986; guest editor, author Jour. Family History, 1985; contbr. articles to profl. jours. Numerous fellowships and grants NEH, 1980, 91, Social Sci. Rsch. Coun., 1991-92, Fulbright/S.Am. Today Grant, 1986, Fulbright Tchg. Rsch. Grant to Brazil, 1988; Tinker fellow, 1981-82; John Carter Brown Libr., Hall Found. for Humanities, 1985-86, Utah Eccles Fellowship, 1991-92. Office: Univ of Kansas Ctr Latin Am Studies Lawrence KS 66045-0001

KUZNETSOV, ANDREY VALER'EVICH, science educator; b. Magadan, Russia, Mar. 20, 1966; arrived in U.S., 1994; s. Valerii G. Kuznetsov and Ljudmila A. Safonova; m. Marina F. Bykova, Oct. 22, 1960; 1 child, Ivan. MS in Mech. Engring., Moscow State Tech. U., 1988; PhD in Mech. Engring., Russian Acad. Scis., Moscow, 1992. Sr. rsch. scientist Vienna (Austria) U. Tech., 1995-97; asst. prof. N.C. State U., Raleigh, 1998—2002, assoc. prof., 2002—. Rsch. fellow Alexander von Humboldt Found., 1993. Mem. ASME. Office: NC State U Box 7910 3182 Broughton Hall Raleigh NC 27695-7910 Fax: (919) 515-7968. E-mail: avkuznet@eos.ncsu.edu.

KUZNETSOV, VLADIMIR A. biomedical researcher, computational biologist; s. Andrey D. and Mariya M. (Zazulina) K.; m. Anna V. Ivshina, May 12, 1981; 1 child, Andrey. Ms. Sci., Kyrghyz State U., Russia, 1966—71; Ph. D., Moscow State U., Moscow, Russia, 1984—84. Dr. of Physical and Matematical Sciences Scietific&Technical Union, Russian Acad. of Sciences, St.-Peterburg, 1992. Sr. rsch. fellow Nat. Inst. of Child Health and Human Devel., NIH, Bethesda, Md., 1999—; chief scientist Civilized Software, Inc., Bethesda, Md., 1998—99; head of lab. The Inst. of Chem. Physics, Russian Acad. of Sciences, Moscow, Russia, 1992—98, sr. rschr., 1982—91, Moscow Acad. of Vet. Medicine, Moscow, Russia, 1981—82; rschr. Rsch. Inst. of Oncology & Radiology, Frunze, 1972—81. Rsch. scholar Ctr. for Biol. Evaluation&Research, FDA USA, Bethesda, Md., 1995—97. Author: Dynamics of Immune Processes During Tumor Growth, 1992; editl. bd. book series: Advances in Math for Applied Science, 1994. Recipient Medal, Russian acad. Natural Sci., 1994; am. Cancer Soc. grantee, 1995-97; Nat. Cancer Inst./NIH grantee, 1997-98. Fellow Russian Acad. Natural Scis.; mem. Am. Math. Soc., Am. Assn. Cancer Rsch. (corr.), London Math. Soc. Achievements include research in Computational & Systems Biology, Statistical Genomics And Evolution, Mathematical Immunology, Cancer Biology, Infectious Diseases; discovery of Mathematical theory of cancer immunobiology; development of Probability models of gene expression and molecular evolution; Voting prediction methods in clinical trials based on limited data; contributions to substantiation & development of basic mathematical models of tumor & immune system internations; leadership in mathematical immunology of cancer and computational clinical immunology; inventor of the statistically weighted syndromes methods for prognosis of fuzzy systems; inventor of a family of skewed statistical distributions associated with evolution of conserved sequences encoded in the genomes. Avocations: archaeology, tourism, swimming. Office: Limb/Nichd/Nih 9 South Dr Rm 1N-124E Bethesda MD 20892 Personal E-mail: vk28u@nih.gov. E-mail: vk28u@nih.gov.

KUZON, WILLIAM M., JR., plastic surgeon, muscle physiologist; b. Kenmore, N.Y., Aug. 7, 1955; s. William M. Sr. and Arleen C. (Belcher) K.; m. Linda Anne Blaszcyzkiewicz, July 17, 1977; children: Aniela Jacqueline, Robert Edward, Cecelia Arleen. BA magna cum laude, U. Rochester, 1977, MD, 1981; MSc, U. Toronto, 1984, PhD, 1990. Diplomate Am. Bd. Plastic Surgery. Surgery intern Toronto Gen. Hosp., 1981-82; plastic and reconstruction surgery residency U. Toronto, 1984-91, asst. prof., 1989-91, U. Mich., Ann Arbor, 1992—, assoc. prof., 1997—, sr. assoc. rsch. scientist, 1998—, assoc. chmn. dept. surgery, 1998—, sect. head plastic surgery, dir. residency program, 2002—. Attending surgeon VA, Ann Arbor, 1992—; jour. editl. bd. Annals Plastic Surgery, Microsurgery, Plastic Reconstructive Surgery; jour. referee; book reviewer; session chmn. or panel participant at numerous sci. meetings; lectr. various colls. and univs. Contbr. over 70 articles to profl. jours.; presenter in field to over 80 sci. socs. Bd. dirs. Loch Alpine Improvement Assn., 1996-98. Fellow Med. Rsch. Coun. Can., 1983-87, Easter Seal Rsch. Inst., 1989-90; scholarAm. Assn. Plastic Surgeons, 1992-95; grantee U. Mich. Dept. Surgery, 1993-94, U. Mich. Rsch. Adv. Com., 1994-95, R.W. Johnson Pharm. Rsch. Inst., 1994-95, U.S. Army Med. Rsch. and Devel. Command, 1994-98, Parexel Internat. Corp., 1995-96, NIH, 1995-2000, 1996-2001, 98-2003, Dept. Vet. Affairs, 1996, U.S. Fulbright Program, 1996; recipient Davis and Geck Plastic Surgery Clin. Rsch. award, 1989,90. Fellow ACS, Royal Coll. Physicians and Surgeons (plastic surgery); mem. AAAS, Internat. Microsurgical Soc., Ont. Coll. Physicians and Surgeons, Can. Soc. Exercise Physiology, Am. Assn. Plastic Surgeons, Am. Soc. Plastic and Reconstructive Surgeons, Can. Soc.

Plastic Surgeons, Plastic Surgery Rsch. Coun., Am. Soc. Peripheral Nerve, Group for Advancement of Microsurgery, Am. Soc. Reconstructive Microsurgery, Reed O. Dingman Soc. Tissue Engring. Soc., Harry Benjamin Internat. Gender Dysphoria Assn. Inc., Midwestern Assn. Plastic Surgeons, Mich. Acad. Plastic Surgeons, Soc. Univ. Surgeons. Avocations: guitar, steelhead fishing, hockey, soccer, skiing. Office: U Mich 2130 Taubman Ctr 1500 E Medical Center Dr Ann Arbor MI 48109-0005

KUZUHARA, LOREN WYATT, management consultant, educator; b. Evanston, Ill., Nov. 15, 1962; s. Daniel Kei Kuzuhara, Toyoko Teresa Kuzuhara; m. Lavina Mohanlal Harjani, Dec. 28, 1990; children: Daniel, Carolyn. PhD, U. Wis.-Madison, 1994, MBA, 1993; BS, U. Ill.-Champaign-Urbana, 1985. Prof. Sch. Bus. U. Wis.-Madison, 1998—2002; strategic rschr. Am. Family Ins., Madison, 1995—98; mgmt. cons. Orgnl. R&D, MADISON, 2001—. Trustee Madison Country Day Sch., 1996—. Author: Organizational Behavior and Management: An Integrated Skills Approach, 2002, Applied Organizational Behavior, 2003. Recipient Dr. Brenda Pfaehler award of excellence, Trio Student Support Svcs. Program, U. Wis.-Madison, 2001, Dean's Acad. Staff Excellence in Tchg. award, Sch. of Bus., U. Wis.-Madison, 2001, Reggie Tate Excellence in Tchg. award, Sch. Bus., U. Wis.-Madison, 1989, Svc. award, Madison Country Day Sch., 2002. Mem.: ASTD, Soc. Human Resource Mgmt., Acad. Mgmt. Avocation: travel, movies, auto racing, reading. Home: 9 Apostle Island Madison WI 53719 Office: Sch Bus Univ Wis-Madison 975 University Ave Madison WI 53706-1323 Home Fax: 608-262-8773; Office Fax: 608-262-8773. Personal E-mail: lkuzuhara@bus.wis.edu. Business E-Mail: LKUZUHARA@BUS.WISC.EDU.

KVALSETH, TARALD ODDVAR, mechanical engineer, educator; b. Brunkeberg, Telemark, Norway, Nov. 7, 1938; married; 3 children. BS, U. Durham, King's Coll., Eng., 1963; MS, U. Calif.-Berkeley, 1966, PhD, 1971. Research asst. engring. expt. sta. U. Colo., Boulder, 1963-64, teaching asst. dept. mech. engring.; mech. engr. Williams & Lane Inc., Berkeley, 1964-65; research asst. dept. indsl. engring. and ops. research U. Calif.-Berkeley, 1965-71, research fellow, 1973; asst. prof. Sch. Indsl. and Systems Engring. Ga. Inst. Tech., Atlanta, 1971-74; sr. lectr. indsl. mgmt. div. Norwegian Inst. Tech. U. Trondheim, 1974-79, head indsl. mgmt. div., 1975-79; assoc. prof. dept. mech. engring. U. Minn., Mpls., 1979-82, prof., 1982—. Guest worker NASA Ames Research Ctr., Calif., 1973; mem. organizing com. 1st Berkeley-Monterey Conf. Timespan, Pay and Discretionary Capacity, 1973; mem. steering com. Internat. Conf. Human Factors in Design and Op. Ships, Gothenburg, Sweden, 1977; mem. bd. Norwegian Ergonomics Com., 1977-80; gen. session chmn. Conf. Work Place Design and Work Environ. Problems, Trondheim, 1978 Author book chpts., articles, presentations, reports in field; editor text books; mem. editl. bd., reviewer for numerous profl. jours., patentee in field. Fellow AAAS; mem. IEEE, Inst. Indsl. Engrs. (sr.), Human Factors and Ergonomics Soc. (pres. upper Midwest chpt.), Nordic Ergonomics Soc. (coun. 1977-80), Internat. Ergonomics Assn. (gen. coun. 1977-80, v.p. 1982-85), Ergonomics Soc., Psychonomic Soc., Am. Psychol. Soc., Am. Statis. Assn., Sigma Xi. Lutheran. Home: 4980 Shady Island Cir Mound MN 55364 Office: U Minn Dept Mech Engring Minneapolis MN 55455 E-mail: kvals001@umn.edu.

KVAMME, MARK D. marketing professional; BA in French, Econs. and Lit., U. Calif., Berkeley. Programmer Apple Computer; founding mem., then internat. product mgr. in U.S. Apple France; founder, pres., CEO Internat. Solutions, 1984-86; dir. internat. mktg. Wyse Tech., 1986-89; ptnr. CKS Group, Cupertino, Calif., 1989-91, chair, CEO, 1991-98; chair USWEB/CKS, Cupertino, Calif., 1998—; ptnr. Sequoia Capital, Menlo Park, Calif., 1999—. Office: Sequoia Capital 3000 Sand Hill Rd Bldg 4 Menlo Park CA 94025-7113

KVANVIG, JONATHAN L. philosophy educator; b. Dickinson, Md., Dec. 7, 1954; s. Kenneth George and Alice Mae K., Edith Mae Kvanvig (Stepmother); m. Carol Dobbs Dobbs, June 9, 1958; children: Jared Daniel, Brittany Mae. BA, Evangel Coll., Springfield, Mo., 1977; MA, U. of Mo., Columbia, 1979; PhD, U. of Notre Dame, South Bend, Ind., 1982. Philosophy prof. Tex. A&M U., College Station, Mo., 1983—2001, U. Mo., Columbia, Mo., 2001—, dept. chair, 2001. Bd. govs. Clarendon Found., Washington, 1991—2003. Fellow, NEH, 1986, summer fellow, 1991. Mem.: Southwestern Philos. Soc. (sec.-treas. 1995—98), Soc. Christian Philosophers (exec. com. 1999—2001), Am. Philos. Assn. Avocations: cycling, coaching, umpiring. Home: 4705 Newcastle Dr Columbia MO 65203 Office: U Mo 436 Gcb Columbia MO 65211 Home Fax: 573-884-8949; Office Fax: 573-884-8949. Personal E-mail: kvanvigj@missouri.edu. E-mail: kvanvigj@missouri.edu.

KVILEKVAL, KARA HELLE VICTORIA, vascular surgeon; b. Rome, May 14, 1954; d. Axel and Pamela (Dane) K. BA, B.A. Simmons Coll., 1975; MD, SUNY, Stony Brook, 1983. Intern and resident Dept. Surgery, SUNY, Stony Brook, 1983-88, vascular fellowship, 1988-89; clin. instr. dept. surgery SUNY, Stony Brook, 1989-92; attending vascular surgeon VA Med. Ctr., Northport, N.Y., 1989-99, Univ. Hosp., Stony Brook, 1989-99, asst. prof. clin. surgery, 1992-99; vascular surgeon Vascular Assocs. of L.I., Stony Brook, 1999—. Contbr. articles to profl. publs. Fellow ACS (assoc.); mem. AMA, Am. Med. Women's Assn., N.Y. Soc. Cardiovascular Surgery. Office: Vascular Assocs LI 2500-21 Rte 347 Ste 78 Stony Brook NY 11790

KVINT, VLADIMIR LEV, economist, educator, mining engineer; b. Krasnoyarsk, Siberia, Russia, Feb. 21, 1949; s. Lev V. Kvint and Lidia E. Adamskaya; children: Liza, Valeria. MS in Mining Engring., Inst. Non-Ferrous Metals, Krasnoyarsk, 1972; PhD in Managerial Econs., Inst. Nat. Economy, Moscow, 1975; D of Econs., Inst. Econs., Acad. Scis., Moscow, 1988; life-title: Prof. Pol. Economy, Inst. Economy, Acad. of Scis., Moscow, 1989; HHD, U. Bridgeport, 1997. Asst. prof. Inst. of Non-Ferrous Metals, 1972; chief of dept. non-ferrous metals co., Norilsk, Russia, 1975—76; dep. chair, chief economist Automation of non-ferrous metals com., 1976—78; chief dept. sci.-tech. progress Siberian br. Acad. of Scis., Novosibirsk, 1978—82; part-time prof. various Russian univs., 1976—89; leading rschr., fellow Inst. Econs., Acad. Scis., Moscow, 1982—89; econ. adviser Govt. of Albania, 2002—; chmn. expert econ. coun. Ministry of Sport, Russia, 2002—. Cons. GE, N.Y.C., 1989—94, Cable & Wireless, London, 1989—97; econ. adviser Pres. of the UN, 1997—98, King of Bulgaria, 1996—2001; vis. prof. Vienna (Austria) Econ. U., 1989—90; prof. Fordham U. Grad. Sch., N.Y.C., 1990—; disting. prof. Babson Coll. Bus., Mass., 1991; mng. dir. emerging markets Arthur Andersen, 1992—97; dir. for govtl. affairs Metromedia Internat. Telecom. Inc., 1997—2000; adj. prof. Stern Grad. Sch. Bus. NYU, 1995—2000. Author: The Acceleration of Technological Development of Production, 1976, The Introduction and Use of Automation Systems, 1981, The Krasnoyarsk Experiment, 1982, Management of Scientific-Technical Progress, 1986, The Economic and Scientific-Technical Information, 1987, Development of Economy of Daghestan, 1988, The Barefoot Shoemaker: Capitalizing on the New Russia, 1993, A Different Perspective on Emerging Markets, 1995, Incorporating the Global Risk Management in the Strategic Decision Making Process, 1997, The Global Emerging Market in Transition, 1999; co-author: Creating and Managing International Joint Ventures, 1996, International M&A, Joint Ventures and Beyond, 1998, Investing Under Fire: Winning Strategies, 2003; editor-in-chief: Emerging Market of Russia: Sourcebook for Investment and Trade, 1997; contbr. articles to CNN, Forbes, Harvard Bus. Rev., others. Bd. dirs. USSR Exporters Assn., Moscow, 1988-90; mem. internat. com. Muhlenberg Coll., Allentown, Pa., 1992-99; chmn. Summits Instl. Investors & Global Risk Management, World Econ. Devel. Congress, Washington, 1995-97. Recipient Silver medal for achievements in nat. economy, USSR Main Nat. Com., Moscow, 1986, Gold medal Hon. Lawyer of Russia, 2003, US Fulbright Scholar award, 2001. Fellow: Wexner Heritage Found. (N.Y.C.), New Eng. Ctr. for Internat. and Regional Studies (hon.); mem.: Internat. Acad. Emerging Markets (pres.), Bretton Woods Com. (Washington), Am. Econ. Assn., Russian Acad. Natural Scis. (life), Internat. Acad. Regional Devel. (life), Internat. Informatization Acad. of UN (hon.), Philos. Soc., N.Y. Acad. Scis., World Jewish Acad. Scis. (pres.). Achievements include devel. of theory of regionalization of scientific tech. progress; evaluation of role of scientific-technical policy in devel. of regional economy; devel. of regional programs, developed a theory of emerging markets, developed a system of optimization models of strategies of companies in new emerging markets, economic solutions to poverty. Office: Fordham U 113 W 60th St Fl 6 New York NY 10023-7484 E-mail: drvkvint@hotmail.com. *In our life, we have to be prepared to face not only problems; we must also be prepared to face happiness. Those not prepared can lose the opportunity.*

KVINTA, CHARLES J. lawyer; b. Hallettsville, Tex., Feb. 16, 1932; s. John F. and Emily (Strauss) K.; m. Margie N. Brenek, Oct. 9, 1954; children: Charles, Sherri, Kenneth, Christopher. BA in Govt., U. Tex., 1954, LLB, 1959. Bar: Tex. 1959. Atty. Tex. Hwy. Dept., Yoakum, 1959-61; ptnr. Gaus & Kvinta, Yoakum, 1962-67, Kvinta, Young & Frietsch, Yoakum, 1975—, Kvinta & Kvinta Attys., Yoakum, 1986—, Exec. v.p. First State Bank, Yoakum, 1968-74, atty., 1975—; city atty. City of Yoakum, 1980—. Co-founder Bluebonnet Youth Ranch, Yoakum, 1968, bd. trustees, bd. dirs., pres. Yoakum Ind. Sch. Dist.; judge Lavaca County. 1st lt. U.S. Army, 1954-56. Recipient Outstanding Cmty. Svc. award Sons of Hrman, 1984, Outstanding Svc. award Bluebonnet Youth Ranch, 1975, Yoakum Little League, 1982, Yoakum Lions, 1982, Paul Gustwick Outstanding Cmty. Svc. award, 1986, Tex. Rd. Hand award for outstanding support Tex. Hwy. Tex. Dept. Transp. Mem. Tex. Bar Assn., Am. Legion. Democrat. Roman Catholic. Home: 713 Coke St Yoakum TX 77995-4415 Office: Kvinta & Kvinta Attys 403 W Grand Ave Yoakum TX 77995-2617

KVITKO, ARKADY, mathematician, researcher; b. Slavyanka, Hasansky, Russia, June 6, 1949; came to U.S., 1989; s. Nikolay Zilberg and Leonora K.; m. Rachel Kravchenko, Apr. 30, 1974; children: Marina, Max. BS in Math. and Physics, City Coll., Odessa, Ukraine, 1970; MS in Ops. Rsch., Odessa State U., Odessa, Ukraine, 1974; PhD in Ops. Rsch., State U., Minsk, Russia, 1982. From asst. prof. to adj. prof. Odessa State U. City Coll., 1975-89; from SAS programmer, analyst to sr. statistician Merrill Lynch, N.Y.C., 1990-97, sr. ops. rsch. analyst, 1997—. Cons., presenter in field. Co-author: (with M. Zholdak) Probabitlity Theory and Information Systems, 1989; contbr. articles to profl. jours. Polytech. U. grant, 1982-89. Avocations: chess, reading. E-mail: Alex_Kvitko@yahoo.com.

KWAAN, JACK HAU MING, retired physician; b. Hong Kong, Apr. 9, 1928; came to U.S., 1953; s. Y.K. and Rose W. Kwaan; m. Min K. Ho, Feb. 11, 1973; children: Mary, Peter, Rebecca, Nicholas. MD, U. Hong Kong, 1952. Diplomate Am. Bd. Radiology, Am. Bd. Surgery, Am. Bd. Thoracic Surgery. Resident in radiology Roswell Park Meml. Inst., 1955-56; chief resident Peter Bent Brigham Hosp., 1956-57; rsch. fellow in radiology Harvard Med. Sch., Boston, 1956-57; sr. cancer rsch. radiol. therapist Roswell Park Meml. Inst., Buffalo, 1958-59; asst. prof. radiology U. Ky., Lexington, 1963-65; resident in surgery U. Calif., Irvine, 1965-68; rsch. fellow oncologic surgery M.D. Anderson Hosp., Houston, 1968-69; resident in thoracic U. Calif., Irvine, 1969-71, chief resident thoracic surgery, 1970, asst. prof. surgery, 1972-73; chief vascular surgery sect., co-dir. vascular surgery tng. program U. Calif. Irvine/Long Beach VA Med. Ctr., 1974-87; prof. surgery U. Calif., Irvine, 1983 87; sr. resident in thoracic surgery U. So. Calif./L.A. County Med. Ctr., 1971; staff thoracic cardiovasc. surgeon Long Beach VA Hosp., 1972-73; asst. chief dept. surgery Valley Med. Ctr., Fresno, Calif., 1973-74; prof. surgery U. Okla., Tulsa, 1987-93; ret., 1993. Chief dept. surgery Valley Med. Ctr., Fresno, Calif., 1973-74; chief vascular surgery sect. Long Beach VA Med. Ctr., 1974-87; surgical cons. Kaiser Permanente Hosp. Contbr. articles to profl. jours. Fellow Am. Coll. Surgeons; mem. Brit. Med. Assn., Gen. Med. Coun. London (registrant), Assn. Mil. Surgeons of U.S. (life), Assn. VA Surgeons, Internat. Cardiovascular Soc. Home: PO Box 50183 Long Beach CA 90815-6183

KWAK, SEUNG-KEON, research scientist; b. Seoul, Republic of Korea, Feb. 2, 1967; arrived in U.S., 1992; s. Sebom Kwak, Kyungja Lim; m. Jeong Eun Rhee; 1 child, Bethia. BS, Hankook Aviation U., Kyunggi, Korea, 1989; MS, W.Va. U., 1994; PhD, Ohio State U., 1999. Postdoctoral rschr. Ohio State U., Columbus, 1999—2001; dir. rsch. and devel. Quality Rsch., Devel. and Cons., Inc., Chaska, Minn., 2001—. Tech. reviewer IEEE Trans. on Automatic Control, IEEE Conf. on Decision and Control, Am. Control Conf. Contbr. articles to profl. jours. Lt. Republic of Korea Air Force, 1989—92. Mem.: ASME (mem. organizing com. 2000 Conf. 1999—2000, tech. reviewer ASME Internat. Mech. Engring. Congress and Exposition). Home: 12142 86th Ave N Maple Grove MN 55369 Office: Quality Rsch Devel and Cons Inc Ste 6 125 Columbia Ct Chaska MN 55318 Office Fax: 952-556-5206. Business E-Mail: skwak@qrdc.com.

KWALWASSER, HELEN, musician, music educator; b. Syracuse, N.Y., Oct. 11, 1927; d. Jacob and Pearl Little Kwalwasser; m. Harvey Wedeen; children: Lisa, Laura. Student, Juilliard Sch. Music, 1945—47. Prof. violin and chamber music Bowling Green (Ohio) State U., 1961—64, Temple U., Phila., 1970—; violinist N.Y. Chamber Soloists, N.Y.C., 1970—; mem. Galimir String Quartet. Soloist, chamber musician Mozart Festival, 1975—2001; musical advisor, prin. soloist Davidsbund Chamber Players, Phila., 1985—; judge young artists competitions Nat. Can. Music Competition, others. Mem.: Phi Mu Alpha (advisor 1990), Sigma Alpha Iota (hon.; Delta Mu chpt., advisor 1986). Avocations: photography, reading, travel. Office: Temple Univ Rock Hall Broad St Philadelphia PA 19122 Home: Academy House 1420 Locust St Philadelphia PA 19102

KWAN, BENJAMIN CHING KEE, ophthalmologist; b. Hong Kong, July 12, 1940; came to U.S., 1959; s. Shun Ming and Lurk Ming (Lai) K.; m. Catherine Ning, Aug. 29, 1964; children: Susan San, David Daiwai. MD, Wash. U., St. Louis, 1967. Diplomate Am. Bd. Ophthalmology. Ptnr. So. Calif. Permanente Med. Ctr., Harbor City, 1976—, chief of svc. ophthalmology, 1976-88; clin. prof. dept. ophthalmology UCLA, 1995—. Chmn. winter blossom ball Chinese Am. Debutante's Guild, 1993. Capt. U.S. Army, 1969-71. Recipient Svc. award Asian Am. Sr. Citizens Svc. Ctr., 1993, Proclamation award Calif. Sec. of State, 1993, Svc. award East L.A. Chinese Everspring Sr. Assn., 1994. Fellow Am. Acad. Ophthalmology; mem. Chinese Am. Ophthal. Soc. (pres. elect 1997-99, pres. 1999-00, Svc. award 1994), Chinese Physician's Soc. So. Calif. (bd. dirs., pres. 1983, Svc. award 1983, 89), Orgn. Chinese Ams. (pres. L.A. chpt. 1986-87). Roman Catholic. Avocations: ballroom dancing, singing, snow skiing. Home: 6327 Tarragon Rd Rancho Palos Verdes CA 90275-5834 Office: 1050 Pacific Coast Hwy Harbor City CA 90710-3509

KWAN, MICHELLE, professional figure skater; b. Torrance, Calif., July 07; Grad. H.S. Nat. spokesperson Children's Miracle Network, co-chair ProKids program. Recipient Skating Mag. Readers' Choice award for figure skater of the year, 1993-94, 95-96, Dial award, 1997, Skating Mag. Reader's Choice award, 2003; named 1996 Female Athlete of Yr., U.S. Olympic Com, finalist, Women's Sports Found. Sportswoman of the Yr., 2003 Achievements include being the youngest World Champion in U.S. history; third youngest World Champion; victories include: World Junior Championships, 1994, 96, Hershey's Kisses Internat. Challenge, 1995, 96, 97, Skate Am., 1995, Skate Can., 1995, Nations cup, 1995, U.S. Postal Svc. Challenge, 1995, State Farm U.S. Championships, 1996, 1999, 2001, 2003, Champions Series Final, 1996, Japan Open, 1997, 99, Thrifty Car Rental Skate Am., 1997, 1999, 2000, Skate Can., 1997, 1999, U.S. Championships, 1998, 99, World Championships, 1998, 99, 2000, 2001, 2003, Goodwill Games, 1998, 1998 Ultimate Four, 1998, Grand Slam Figure Skating, 1998, U.S. Pro Classic, 1998, Masters of Figure Skating, 1999, 1998 Keri Lotion Figure Skating Classic, 1998, 1998 Masters Figure Skating, World Prof. Championships, 1998, Smart Ones Skate Am., 2001. Office: USFSA 20 1st St Colorado Springs CO 80906-3624

KWAN, PAUL W. science educator; b. Hong Kong; BS, U. Md., 1966; MS, Clark U., 1971, PhD, 1975. Asst. rsch. prof. Tufts U. Sch. Medicine, Boston, 1985—. Avocation: martial arts. Office: Tufts U Sch Medicine 136 Harrison Ave Boston MA 02111 E-mail: paul.kwan@tufts.edu.

KWART, ARNOLD MARTIN, urologic surgeon; b. N.Y.C., May 29, 1942; s. Sam and Esther Molly (Goldberg) K.; m. Cathryn Kahn, May 13, 1984. BS cum laude, U. Fla, 1964; MD, Duke U., 1968. Diplomate Am. Bd. Urology. Intern/resident physician NYU, N.Y.C., 1968-70; resident physician urology Johns Hopkins Hosp., Balt., 1970-74; urologic surgeon U.S. Army, Seoul, Korea, 1974-77; asst. prof. urology George Washington U., Washington, 1977-80, assoc. clin. prof. urology, 1980-87, clin. prof. urology, 1988—97; ptnr. Urologic Surgeons Washington, D.C., 1980-97; assoc. clin. prof. urology and urologic oncology Georgetown U. Hosp., 1996—; chmn. dept. urology Washington Hosp. Ctr., Washington, 1997—. Pres. Attending Physicians Assn., George Washington U. Hosp., 1985-86; mem. various coms. George Washington U. including cost containment com., 1980, joint conf. com., 1983-86, 86-89, working group GWU/AMI study, 1984, exec. com. faculty senate, 1985-86, chmn. com. on pub. rels., 1986-88, search com., v.p. med. affairs, 1988, physicians adv. coun., 1989—, med. ctr. devel. com., 1989, chmn. ad hoc med. staff com., 1989-90, chmn. oper. rm. com., 1990-96, chmn. urologic com., 1996—; mem. tumor bd. Sibley Meml. Hosp., 1980—, tumor bd. com., 1981, continuing med. edn., 1981-83, tranfusion com., 1988—, organized prostate cancer awareness week, 1990—; presenter in field. Contbr. articles to profl. jours. Lectr. Fed. Res. Sys., 1985, Multiple Sclerosis Soc., 1985; vol. Am. Cancer Soc., 1977—, adv. bd. Md. Ostomy Assn., 1989—, vol. physician Jewish Social Svcs. Agy., 1991—. Maj. U.S. Army, 1974-77. Recipient Johns Hopkins Med. and Surg. Assn. Best Presentation award The Brady Urologic Inst., 1981, First Pl. Sci. Exhibit, Percutaneous Removal of Kidney Stones, D.C. Med. Soc., 1983; recognized as one of the best urologists in Washington, D.C. area by Washingtonian Mag., 1986, 91, 93, 97, 2002. Fellow ACS; mem. AMA, Am. Urol. Assn. (alt. to socioeconomics com. 1989, mem. mid-Atlantic sect. 1977—, membership com. 1987-90, chmn. membership com. 1990, credentials com. 1987-88), D.C. Med. Soc. (cancer com. 1980-85, grievance com. 1988-90, long-range planning com. 1989, nominating com. 1989, vice chmn. utilization and peer rev. com. 1990, chmn. utilization and peer rev. com. 1993, chmn. sci. program com. 1996—), Washington Urologic Soc. (membership chmn. 1989, treas. 1990, sec. 1991, v.p. 1992, pres. 1993), Soc. Univ. Urologists, Jacobi Med. Soc., Am. Cancer Soc., Endourological Soc., Phi Beta Kappa, Phi Kappa Phi, Phi Eta Sigma, Alpha Epsilon Delta. Jewish. Achievements include inventor of Kwart Retroinject Stent-Cook Urol. Mfr., Endosnare-Cook Urol. Mfr. Office: Washington Hospital Center Department of Urol 110 Irving St NW Ste 3b19 Washington DC 20010-2976

KWASNICK, PAUL JACK, retail executive; b. N.Y.C., Apr. 8, 1925; s. Joseph and Dorothy (Ginsberg) K.; m. Selma Marcus, Sept. 7, 1947; children: Raymond, Diane, Robert. BBA, CCNY, 1947, MBA, 1957. Fin. exec. M.H. Fishman Co., Inc., N.Y.C., 1947-61; asst. sec.-treas. Zayre Corp., Natick, Mass., 1961-66, v.p., asst. sec.-treas., 1966-68, v.p., treas., 1968-72, sr. v.p., treas., 1972-73; exec. v.p., gen. mgr. Kings Dept. Stores, Inc., Newton, Mass., 1973-75, pres., chief operating officer, 1975-78, pres. retail div., chief operating officer, dir., mem. exec. com., 1981; chmn., pres., chief exec. officer, dir., mem. exec. com. Mars Stores, Inc., North Dighton, Mass., 1982-89; pres., chief exec. officer Landmark Advisors, Inc., Boston, 1989—. Pres., chief exec. officer, chmn. Data Printer Corp., Malden, Mass., 1978-80, bd. dirs., 1967-83; regional dir., bd. dirs. Shawmut Community Bank, Framingham, Mass. Bd. dirs., asst. treas. Mass. Easter Seal Soc., 1986-88, treas., 1988-89, vice chmn., 1989-91, chmn. 1991-93; trustee Combined Jewish Philanthropies of Greater Boston, 1977—, The West Suburban YMCA, Newton, 1984-2000, chmn., 1991-2000; dir. Mass. Conn. Compulsive Gambling, 1990-91. With AUS, 1943-46. Mem. Internat. Mass Retail Assn. (bd. dris. 1981-89, treas. 1986-89). Jewish.

KWEMBE, TOR ANTHONY, mathematical educator, researcher; b. Gboko, Nigeria, Nov. 23, 1955; came to U.S., 1981; s. Peter Wundu and Adzuai Margerite K.; m. Azungwe Isabel Kwembe, July 15, 1980; children: Terfa, Fanen, Wundu. BS, U. Calabar, Nigeria, 1980; MS, U. Ill., 1983, PhD, 1989. Acad. coord. U. Ill. Engring., Chgo., 1985-88, postdoctoral rsch. assoc., 1988-90; asst. lectr. U. Sokoto, Nigeria, 1980-81; asst. prof. Chgo. State U., 1990 93, assoc. prof., 1993-98, prof., 1998—. Chairperson dept. math. Chgo. State U., 1994, chair faculty senate, 1997-98; coord. minority engring. program U. Ill., Chgo., 1987-90. Contbr. articles to profl. jours. Dwight E. Eisenhower grant Ill. Bd. of Higher Edn., 1993. Mem. Math. Assn. of Am., Soc. for Math. Biology, Internat. Fedn. of Non Linear Analyst, U. Profls. of Ill. (chpt. treas. 1996-98). Avocations: traveling, table tennis, lawn tennis, music. Home: 4100 Poplar Ave Richton Park IL 60471 Office: Dept Math Chgo State U 9501 S King Dr Chicago IL 60628 E-mail: tkwembe@csu.edu.

KWESKIN, EDWARD MICHAEL, lawyer; b. Stamford, Conn., June 26, 1946; s. Sydney C. and Ethel (Jaffe) K.; m. Helen S. Truss, Aug. 17, 1969; children: Abigail, Adam. BA, U. Pa., 1968; JD with honors, George Washington U., 1971. Bar: Conn. 1971, U.S. Dist. Ct. Conn. 1971, U.S. Ct. Appeals (2d cir.) 1971, Pa. 1971, U.S. Dist. Ct. (ea. dist.) Pa. 1971, U.S. Supreme Ct. 1979. Staff atty. Cmty. Legal Svcs., Phila., 1971-73; assoc. Wofsey Rosen Kweskin & Kuriansky, Stamford, 1973-79, ptnr., 1979—. Spl. master family law Superior Ct., State of Conn., 1995—. Commn. Sixth Taxing Dist., Norwalk, Conn., 1993—, chmn., 1999—; pres. Temple Sinai, Stamford, 1994-96, counsel, 2001—. Mem. ABA (mem. family law sect.), Conn. Bar Assn. (mem. exec. com. family law sect. 1997—), Stamford-Norwalk Regional Bar Assn. (past pres., past family law chmn.), U. Pa. Alumni Club of Fairfield County (pres. 1973-77, chmn. secondary sch. com. 1992—). Home: 3 Plant Ct Norwalk CT 06853-1824 Office: Wofsey Rosen Kweskin & Kuriansky LLP 600 Summer St Stamford CT 06901-1490 E-mail: ekweskin@wrkk.com.

KWETKAUSKIE, JOHN A. medical technologist; b. Elizabeth, N.J., June 25, 1947; s. Albert and Genevieve Kwetkauskie; m. Patricia Manning, May 13, 1972; children: Brian R., Lara A. BS in Life Scis., N.Y. Inst. Tech., 1970. Registered med. technologist. Med. technologist Geisinger Wyoming Valley Med. Ctr., Wilkes-Barre, Pa., 1974-96, Med. Transport, Inc., Hazleton, Pa., 1988—, Columbia Diagnostics, Inc., Canton, Mass., 1997-99, Greiner Vacuette N.Am., Monroe, N.C., 1999—. Part-time EMT, ed. coord. & designated officer Med. Transport, Inc., Hazleton, Pa., 1988—; EMT, instr. Pa. Dept. Health, Harrisburg, 1990—; adj. faculty Luzerne County C. C., 1994—, Lehigh Carbon County C.C., 1992—; cons. Ea. Safety Health, Inc., Nanticoke, Pa. Author: (instrn. manual) Prevention of Infectious Diseases - for EMS Providers, 1996. With U.S. Army, 1970-74, 90-91. Mem. Am. Med. Technologists, Nat. Assn. EMS Educators, Am. Socl Clin. Lab. Scis., Clin. Lab. Mgmt. Assn. Avocations: camping, boating, outdoor activities. Office: Greiner Vacuette NAm PO Box 1026 Monroe NC 28111

KWIAT, DAVID MARK, educator, actor; b. Mpls., May 9, 1951; s. Joseph J. and Charlotte (Adler) K. BA summa cum laude, U. Minn., 1974; MFA, Fla. State U., 1976. Actor, dir. Actors Theatre of St. Paul, Minn., 1978-80, 81-89; actor Ariz. Theatre Co., Tucson, 1980-81; prof. New World Sch. of the Arts, Miami, Fla., 1989—. Author: (play) John Barrymore: Confessions of an Actor, 1976, (collection of poetry) Travelers in Residence, 1999. Endowed tchg. chair, Miami-Dade Comty. Coll., 1996; named Best Supporting Actor, Miami New Times, 2003. Mem. Actors' Equity Assn., S. Fla. Theatre League, Fla. Assn. for Theater Edn. (bd. dirs. 1991-96), voting mem. Carbonell awards S. Fla. Entertainments Writers Assn., Miami, 1992-95, Phi Beta Kappa. Home: 11207 SW 114th Lane Cir Miami FL 33176-3863 Office: New World Sch of the Arts 300 NE 2d Ave Miami FL 33132 E-mail: david.Kwiat@mdc.edu.

KWIK-KOSTEK, CHRISTINE IRENE, physician, retired air force officer; b. Lvov, Poland, Sept. 12, 1939; d. Karol Stanislaus and Leonarda Fryderica (Seniuk) Kostek; widowed; children: Christine, Catherine. Grad. summa cum laude, Med. Acad. Cracow, Poland, 1956-62; grad. primary flight medicine, Brooks AFB, Tex., 1985; completed chief of profl. staff course, Sheppard AFB, Tex., 1988. Diplomate Am. Bd. Emergency Medicine, Am. Bd. Internal Medicine, Poland; cert. Edni. Coun. Fgn. Med. Grads.; recert. Extended Allergy Care Provider. Intern. Med. Acad. Cracow, Poland, 1962-63; residency in internal medicine II-Clinic of Internal Diseases, Cracow, Poland, 1963-66, staff, 1966-69; gen. med. officer Gen. Hosp., Sokoto, Nigeria, 1969-72; intern. Frankford Hosp., Phila., 1972-73; house physician Holy Redeemer Hosp., Meadowbrook, Pa., 1973-74; emergency room physician John F. Kennedy Hosp., Phila., 1974-76, emergency room dir., 1976-78; commd. capt. USAF Med. Corps, 1978, advanced through grades to col., 1993; emergency rm., primary care physician USAF Clinic, Ramstein, West Germany, 1978-81; officer in charge Emergency Room and Gen. Practice Clinic, Peterson Field, Colo., 1981-84; primary care physician Malcolm Grow Med. Ctr., Andrews AFB, Md., 1984-88; chief clinic svcs. 63d Med. Group/SGH, Norton AFB, Calif., 1988-93; staff physician 60th Med. Group, Travis AFB, Calif., 1993-96, Occupl. and Environ. Health and Safety Svcs., Ft. George Meade, Md., 1996-99; ret., 1999—; reg. med. ofcr. Dept. of State. Asst. tchr., sr. asst. tchr. Inst. Descriptive Anatomy, Cracow, 1963-69; emergency physician on call First Aid Sta., Cracow, 1966-69. Fellow Am. Coll. Emergency Physicians; mem. AMA, Am. Coll. Emergency Physicians, World Med. Assn., Am. Coll. Physician Execs. Avocations: photography, travel, gourmet cooking. Home: 6201 Berlee Dr Alexandria VA 22312 Office: Dept State Office of Med Svcs 2401 E St NW Washington DC 20522 Home and Office: US Embassy Cairo Unit 64900 Box 19 Apo AE 09839-4900 E-mail: kwikci@state.gov.

KWIRAM, ALVIN L. physical chemistry educator, university official; b. Riverhills, Man., Can., Apr. 28, 1937; came to U.S., 1954; s. Rudolf and Wilhelmina A. (Bilske) K.; m. Verla Rae Michel, Aug. 9, 1964; children: Andrew Brandt, Sidney Marguerite. BS in Chemistry, BA in Physics, Walla Walla (Wash.) Coll., 1958; PhD in Chemistry, Calif. Inst. Tech., 1963; DS (hon.), Andrews U., 1995. Alfred A. Noyes instr. Calif. Inst. Tech., Pasadena, 1962-63; research asso. physics dept. Stanford (Calif.) U., 1963-64; instr. chemistry Harvard U., Cambridge, Mass., 1964-67, lectr., 1967-70; assoc. prof. chemistry U. Wash., Seattle, 1970-75, prof., 1975—, chmn. dept. chemistry, 1977-87, vice provost, 1987-88, sr. vice provost, 1988-90, vice provost for rsch., 1990—2002. Bd. dirs. Seattle Biomed. Rsch. Inst., 1992—2002; mem. divsn. rev. com. Pacific N.W. Nat. Lab., Environ. and Health Scis. Divsn., 1998—2001; mem. adv. com. Pacific N.W. Nat. Lab., 2000—; mem. adv. bd. for univ. connections U. Hawaii, 1999—2001; exec. dir. NSF Ctr. for Materials and Devices for Info. Tech. Rsch., 2002—. Contbr. numerous articles to sci. jours. Bd. dirs. Seattle Econ. Devel. Commn., 1988-92, Wash. Rsch. Found., 1989-94, Seattle-King County Econ. Devel. Coun., 1989-98, Helen R. Whiteley Found., 1997—; mem. vis. com. divsn. chemistry and chem. engring. Calif. Inst. Tech., 1991-96; chmn. adv. bd. Sch. Engring., Walla Walla Coll., 1992—. Recipient Eastman-Kodak Sci. award, U.-Industry Relations award Council for Chem. Research, 1986; Woodrow Wilson fellow, 1958; Alfred P. Sloan fellow, 1968-70; Guggenheim Meml. Found. fellow, 1977-78 Fellow: AAAS (chmn.-elect, chmn., past chmn. sect. on chemistry 1991—94, program com. 1994—98), Am. Phys. Soc.; mem.: Worldwide Univ. Network (acad. adv. bd. 2002—), Coun. Chem. Rsch. (bd. dirs. 1980—84, chmn. 1982—83), Am. Chem. Soc. (sec.-treas. divsn. phys. chemistry 1976—86, divsn. councilor 1986—, com. on sci., chmn. subcom. on fed. funding for rsch. 1990—94, adv. bd. for grad. edn. 2000—), Nat. Assn. State Univs. and Land Grant Colls. (exec. com., coun. rsch. policy and grad. edn., chmn.-elect, chmn., past chmn. 2000—03), Sigma Xi. Office: Univ Wash Dept Chem Seattle WA 98195-1700 E-mail: kwiram@u.washington.edu.

KWOK, REGINALD YIN-WANG, urban planning and development educator, architect; b. Hong Kong, Jan. 24, 1937; came to U.S., 1967; s. On and Yee Fong (Pun) K.; m. Annette Holmes, Aug. 29, 1964; 1 child, Zoe Song-Yi Diploma in architecture, Poly., London, 1963; Diploma in tropical studies, Archtl. Assn., London, 1967, MS in Architecture, MS in Urban Planning, Colombia U., N.Y.C., 1969, PhD in Urban Planning, 1973. Asst. architect Chamberlin Powell and Bon, London, 1960-61; architect Denys Lasdun and Ptnrs., London, 1963-64, 65-66, Palmer and Turner, Hong Kong, 1965; ind. architect London, 1971; rschr. Inst. Urban Environment, 1968-69; asst. prof. divsn. urban planning Columbia U., 1972-76, assoc. prof., 1976-80, assoc. East Asian Inst., 1975-80; prof. Ctr. Urban Studies and Planning, U. Hong Kong, 1980-89; prof. Sch. Hawaiian/Asian/Pacific Studies, Coll. Social Sci. U. Hawaii at Manoa, Honolulu, 1989—. Vis. prof., Zhongshan (China) U., 1983—, Tsinghua (China) U., 1985—, Wuhan (China) Acad. Urban Constrn., 1985—; vis. fellow Princeton U., 1986, Inst. Urban and Regional Devel. U. Calif., Berkeley, 1987; adv. prof. Tongji U., Shanghai, 1987—; dir. planning program for developing nations Columbia U., 1976-80; dir. Ctr. Urban Studies and Urban Planning U. Hong Kong, 1980-89; chairperson internat. affairs planning coun. U. Hawaii at Manoa, 1990—, advisor MA in Chinese Studies program; vis. scholar Harvard U., 1996-97. Author: (with M. Castells and L. Goh) The Shek Kip Mei Syndrome: Economic Development and Public Housing in Hong Kong and Singapore, 1990, General Theories of Urban Planning (transl. and edited by H. Chen), 1992, (with Alvin Y. So) The Hong Kong-Guangdong Link, 1996; editor: (with W.L. Parish and A.G.O. Yeh) Chinese Urban Reforms: What Model Now?, 1990, . Mem. bldg. com. Hong Kong Housing Authority, 1982-83, mem. mgmt. com., 1983-88; mem. planning bd. Lands and Works Br., 1985-89; mem. met. study steering group Hong Kong, 1987-89; mem. spl. econ. zone Shenzhen (China) City Planning Com., 1986; bd. dirs. Chinatown Planning Coun., N.Y.C., 1976-80; mem. adv. com. to borough pres. Manhattan Overall Econ. Devel. Program, N.Y.C., 1978-80; mem., sec. econ. devel. com., Chinatown Improvement Com., N.Y., 1975-76. Rsch. and study grantee, most recently Min. des Affaires Etranges, France, and Consulat Gen. de France, Hong Kong, 1988, Hawaii Com. of Humanities, 1990, Eu Tong Sen Endowment, 1992-93, 98. Mem. Assn. Asian Studies, Internat. Fedn. Housing and Planning, Archtl. Soc. China (hon. mem. coun. 1983—), Royal Inst. Brit. Architects (assoc.), Ea. Regional Orgn. Planning and Housing (mem. coun., mem. exec. com. Kuala Lumpur 1984—, dep. pres. 1984-86, hon. pres. 1986—), Hong Kong Inst. Architects, Internat. Sociol. Assn., Regional Sci. Assn., Geog. Soc. China. Office: U Hawaii at Manoa Moore Hall 409 Honolulu HI 96822

KWOLEK, STEPHANIE LOUISE, chemist, researcher; b. New Kensington, Pa., July 31, 1923; d. John and Nellie (Zajdel) Kwolek. BS, Carnegie-Mellon U., 1946; DSc (hon.), Worcester Poly. Inst., 1981, Clarkson U., 1997, Carnegie Mellon U., 2001. Chemist E.I. duPont de Nemours & Co., Inc., Wilmington, Del., 1946—59, rsch. chemist, 1959—67, sr. rsch. chemist, 1967—74, rsch. assoc., 1974—86, cons. in polymer chemistry, 1986—. Contbr. articles to profl. jours.; prodr.:. Named a Women in Tech. Internat., 1996; named to U. Akron Polymer Processing Hall of Fame, 1985, Dayton, Ohio Engring. and Sci. Hall of Fame, 1992, Nat. Inventors Hall of Fame, 1995; recipient award for contbns. to Kevlar, Am. Soc. Metals, 1978, Engring./Tech. award, Soc. Plastics Engrs., 1985, Harold deWitt Smith award, ASTM, 1988, George Lubin Meml. award, SAMPE, 1991, Medal of Excellence in composite materials, U. Del., 1992, Jack Kilby award, Kilby Awards Found., 1994, Am. Innovation award, Patent and Trademark Office, 1995, Achievement award, Indsl. Rsch. Inst., Inc., 1996, Nat. Medal of Tech. award, U.S. Dept. of Commerce Tech. Adminstrn., 1996, Perkin medal, Soc. Chem. Industry, 1997, Commonwealth award, Commonwealth Trust and PNC Bank, 1998, Lemelson-MIT Lifetime Achievement award, 1999, Henry E. Millson award, AATCC, 2001. Mem.: Phi Kappa Phi, Franklin Inst. Phila. (Howard N. Potts medal 1976), Nat. Acad. Engring., Am. Inst. Chemists (Chem. Pioneer award 1980), Am. Chem. Soc. (award for creative invention 1980), Carnegie Mellon U. Alumni Assn. (Merit award 1983, Disting. Achievement award 1998), DuPont Country Club, Phi Beta Kappa, Sigma Xi. Achievements include patents in field. Home and Office: 312 Spalding Rd Wilmington DE 19803-2422

KWON, CHUL SOO, psychiatrist; b. Seoul, Korea, Sept. 10, 1948; m. Sung Hee Chung, Apr. 6, 1974; 1 child, Soon Jeong (Susan). MD, Seoul Nat. U., Korea, 1974. Diplomate Am. Bd. Psychiatry and Neurology. Intern Washington Hosp. Ctr., 1975-76, resident in gen. surgery, 1976-77; resident in psychiatry Johns Hopkins Hosp., Balt., 1977-80; fellow in behavioral sci. Johns Hopkins U., Balt., 1977-80, asst. in psychiatry, 1980-86; dir. partial hospitalization program North Charles Genl. Hosp., Balt., 1981-88; med. dir. partial hospitalization program Homewood Hosp. Ctr., Balt., 1988-91; med. dir. psychiat. partial hospitalization program Union Meml. Hosp., Balt., 1991—; physician St. Joseph Med. Ctr., Towson, Md., 1991—, Church Hosp., Balt., 1991-99, Md. Gen. Hosp. (U. Md. Med. System), Balt., 1991-98, 2000—, Taylor Manor, Ellicott City, Md., 1987-98; mgmt. mem. EHP Group Practice, 1993—; physician JL Kernan Hosp., Balt., 1995—, Sheppard-Enoch Pratt Hosp., 1998—; physician, subinvestigator Ctr. for Behavioral Health, 1999—. Instr. psychiatry Johns Hopkins U., 1986—96; physician, sub-investigator Ctr. Behavioral Health, 1999—; psychiat. cons. U. Splty. Hosp. (U. Md. Med. System), 2001—; psychiatrist-in-charge, cons. Harbor Hosp. (Medstar Health Sys.), Balt., 2001—. Mem.: AMA, Internat. Neuropsychiat. Assn., Korean Am. Med. Assn., Internat. Psychogeriatric Assn., Am. Soc. Clin. Psychopharmacology (cert.), Am. Acad. Clin. Psychiatrists, Md. Psychiat. Soc., Johns Hopkins Med. and Surg. Assn., Am. Neuropsychiat. Assn. Home: 2908 Chainita Ct Ellicott City MD 21042-7625 Office: Union Meml Hosp Dept Psychiat 201 E University Pkwy Baltimore MD 21218-2829 Fax: 410-313-9641; 410-554-6603. E-mail: cskwon@jhu.edu.

KWON, JOON TAEK, retired chemistry researcher; b. Kimpo, Kyunggi Do, Republic of Korea, Mar. 10, 1935; came to U.S., 1955; s. Young Tae and Byoung Soon (Kim) K.; m. Moon Ja You, Aug. 15, 1964; children: Howard Albert, Daphne Elsa. BS in Chemistry, U. Ill., 1957; MS in Chemistry, Cornell U., 1959, PhD in Chemistry, 1962; postdoctoral fellow, U. B.C., Vancouver, Can., 1962-64. Instr. II dept. chemistry U. B.C., 1964-65; assoc. rsch. chemist Chemcell Ltd., Edmonton, Alta., Can., 1965-66; rsch. chemist Celanese Corp., Summit, N.J., 1967-70; sr. rsch. chemist Lummus Co., Bloomfield, N.J., 1970-78; prin. rsch. chemist ABB Lummus Global Inc., Bloomfield, N.J., 1978-99. Co-author: Handbook of Chemical Production Process, 1986; contbr. articles to profl. jours. Disting. commr. and mem. Silver Beaver lodge Monmouth council 347 Boy Scouts Am., vigil mem. Order of the Arrow. Indsl. matching grantee Nat. Rsch. Coun., Ottawa, Can., 1966-67. Fellow Am. Inst. Chemists (ret.); mem. Korean Chem. Soc. (life, rec. sec. N.Am. 1975-93), Korean Scientists and Engrs. in Am. (pres. N.J. chpt. 1976-77), U. Ill. Alumni Assn. (life), Cornell U. Alumni Assn. Methodist. Achievements include patent for prodn. process for propylene oxide and 13 other patents in field of organometallic chemistry and process rsch. Home: 142 Derby Dr Freehold NJ 07728-2767 E-mail: jtkwon1@aol.com.

KWON, OH CHAE, researcher; b. Seoul, Korea, July 11, 1967; s. Young Gul Kwon and Sang Soon Shim; m. Hye Yeon Lee, Apr. 6, 1994; children: Hyukjae, Huynjae. BS in Engring., Seoul Nat U., Korea, 1990, MS in Engring., 1994; PhD, U. Mich., 2000. Rsch. engr. Korea Inst. Aero. Tech., Seoul, 1993-96; teaching asst., rsch. asst. U. Mich., Ann Arbor, 1996-2000, rsch. fellow, 2000-01; mem. rsch. staff Princeton U., 2001—02; rsch. assoc. U. So. Calif., L.A., 2002—. With Korean Res., 1991-92. Rackham fellow U. Mich., 1998-99. Mem. Combustion Inst., Sigma Xi. Avocation: travel. Home: 1717 N Verdugo Rd # 216 Glendale CA 91208 Office: U So Calif AME Dept OHE 430 Los Angeles CA 90089 Business E-Mail: okwon@usc.edu.

KWONG, DONALD, contracts administrator, consultant; b. Sacramento, Calif., Feb. 10, 1968; s. Dewey and Wai Ying (Chin) K. BA, U. Calif., Santa Cruz, 1991; DD, Universal Life Ch., 1996. Purchasing agt. U.S. Dept. Energy, Sacramento, 1991-93; procurement specialist PRC Environ. Mgmt., San Francisco, 1993-95; cons. San Jose MBDC, 1995-96; contracts adminstr. Aerotherm Corp., Mountain View, Calif., 1996-98; staff aide II City of Santa Clara, 1999—2001, staff analyst, 2001—. Mem. Industry Coun. for Small Bus. Devel., 1996-98, Dept. of Def. Small Bus. Coun., 1996-98. Editor: (literary jour.) Seaweed Soup, 1990-91; columnist Stir Mag., 1999-02. No. sec. Asian Pacific Caucus, Calif. Dem. Party, 1995-96; treas. Asian Pacific Dem. Club, San Francisco, 1995. Mem.: Club Asean (dir. fundraising 1999-2000, pres. 2001, dir. profl. devel. 2001-) (advisor Wilcox H.S. key club), Orgn. Chinese Ams. bd. dirs. 1996-2002, sec. 1997-98, v.p. 1999-2000, parliamentarian 2000, pres. 2001), Alumni Assn. U. Calif. Santa Cruz (life), Nat. Contract mgmt. (chpt. v.p. 1994-95), Nat. Assn. Asian am. Profls. (nat. bd. dirs. 1999-2000). Democrat. Office: City of Santa Clara Housing & Comty Svcs 1500 Warburton Ave Santa Clara CA 95050-3792

KWONG, EVA, artist, educator; b. Hong Kong, 1954; came to the U.S., 1967; d. Tony and Ivory Kwong; m. Kirk Mangus, 1976; children: Una, Jasper. BFA, RISD, 1975; MFA, Tyler Sch. Art/Temple U., Phila., 1977. Vis. artist, 1977—; vis. faculty Cleve. (Ohio) Inst. Art, 1982-83; part-time faculty U. Akron, Ohio, 1987, 89, 95, Kent (Ohio) State U., 1990—. Lectr. in field. Works in over 300 exhbns. Visual Arts Regional fellow Arts Midwest, Mpls., 1987, Visual Arts fellow Nat. Endowment for the Arts, Washington, 1988, Ohio Arts Coun., Columbus, 1988, 94, 99. Mem. Nat. Coun. on Edn. for the Ceramic Arts (dir.-at-large 1995-97). Office: Kent State Univ Art Dept Main St Kent OH 44242-0001

KWORTNICK, LINDA MARIE, emergency nurse; b. Phila., Sept. 3, 1954; d. Robert Leroy and Mary Dolores (Murray) Schnee; m. William J. Kwortnick, Sept. 23, 1978; children: Angela Nicole, William Robert. Diploma, St. Josephs Hosp. Sch. Nursing, Phila., 1976. Cert. emergency nurse. Head nurse emergency dept. St. Mary Hosp., Phila., 1980-82; staff nurse Jeans Hosp., Phila., 1983—; nursing supr. Cheltenham York Rd. Nursing Home, Phila., 1985-86; relief nursing supr. Lawndale Hosp., Phila., 1989-92; ind. contractor Med. Tex. Industries, Inc., Phila., 1993—; office nurse Dr. Anthony Palazzolo, M.D., Phila., 1995—2001; disease mgr. Corsolutions, Inc., 2001—. First aid and CPR instr., Nat. Safety Coun., 1994—. Mem. Emergency Dept. Nurses Assn. Home: 528 Quarry Rd Harleysville PA 19438-2411

KYBAL, ELBA GOMEZ DEL REY, economist, non-profit organization executive; b. Santa Fe, Argentina, Apr. 1, 1915; came to U.S., 1942; d. J. Ignacio and Concepción (del Rey) Gómez; m. Milic Kybal, July 16, 1950 (dec. July 1977); children: Cynthia, Alexander. BA in Internat. Rels., U. Litoral, Rosario, Argentina, 1940; MA in Econs., Harvard U., 1945, PhD in Econs., 1946. Economist Fed. Res. Bank, N.Y.C., 1946-47; economist, polit. affairs officer UN, N.Y.C., 1947-56, sr. economist; head specialized conf., chief L.Am. econ. integration Orgn. Am. States, Washington, dir. under secretariat for econ. and social affairs, 1956—80. Cons. Argentine Govt., Buenos Aires. Contbr. articles to profl. jours. Advisor InterAm. com. of women OAS, Washington, 1960—80; vol. cons. Pan Am. Devel. Found., Washington, 1980—82; vol. Argentine, Ecuadorian and Peruvian Found., Washington, 1988—90; pres. Pan Am. Roundtable, Washington, 1999—2001, Pan Am. Liaison Com. of Women's Orgns., 1995—99, Retirees Assn. Orgn. Am. States, Washington, 2001—03; bd. dirs. Gala Hispanic Theatre, Washington, 1997—2001. Named Vol. of the Yr., Pan Am. Devel. Found., 1981, Bus. and Profl. Women's Club, 1984. Mem.: Phi Beta Kappa. Roman Catholic. Avocation: travel. Home: Watergate South # 801 700 New Hampshire Ave NW Washington DC 20037-2406

KYDD, WILLIAM, former medical association administrator; Pres. Alzheimer's Soc. Can., Toronto, Canada, 1999—2001.

KYE, HOON TAIK, retired anesthesiologist, educator; b. Korea, 1936; came to U.S., 1964; MD, Seoul Nat. U., 1961. Med. officer Korean Air Force, 1961-64; intern Newark City Hosp., 1964-65; resident anesthesiology U. Chgo., 1965-68, instr., 1968-70, asst. prof., 1970; attending physician St. Joseph Hosp., Chgo., 1971; asst. clin. prof. Loyola U., 1972-81. Mem. AMA, Am. Coll. Anesthesiologists, Am. Soc. Anesthesiologists.

KYES, HELEN G. (MRS. ROGERS M. KYES), civic leader; b. Marion, Ohio; d. Benjamin and Bess (Gilmore) Jacoby; B.A., Oberlin Coll., 1926; Ph.D. (hon.), Oakland U., 1980; m. Roger M. Kyes, June 5, 1931; children— Carolyn Kyes Eggert (dec.), Frances (dec.), Katharine Kyes Leab, Anne Kyes Spence. Sec., pres. Federated Women's Club, Marion, Ohio, 1927-31; bd. dirs. Cleve. Coll. Club, 1936-41, Cleve. YWCA, 1938-41; mem. bd. Woman's Nat. Farm and Garden, 1943-56, 60—, sec., 1943-45, 54-55; dir. Children's Aid and Home Friendless, 1949—, v.p., 1961— ; bd. dirs. Brookside Sch., Cranbrook, 1952-58, sec., 1957-58; bd. dirs. Kingswood Sch., Cranbrook, 1968— ; charter mem. bd. trustees Oakland U. Found., 1958, v.p. exec. bd., 1960— ; trustee Oakland U., 1970— ; mem. Woman's Assn. Detroit Symphony; com. 100 Detroit Met. Opera; capt. spl. gifts Detroit United Fund, 1959-61; mem. Detroit Mus. Art Founders Soc.; mem. com. Detroit Foster Home Edn. and Recruitment Program, 1960— . Mem. DAR, AAUW (past treas., v.p. Marion). Presbyterian (vice moderator deacons). Clubs: Bloomfield Hills Country, Detroit, Village Woman's. Home: 945 Cranbrook Rd Bloomfield Hills MI 48304-2724 also: 6861 N Ocean Blvd Boynton Beach FL 33435-3339

KYHOS, THOMAS FLYNN, lawyer; b. Cheverly, Md., May 13, 1947. B.A. in Econs., DePauw U., 1969; J.D., Cath. U., 1973. Bar: Md. 1974, D.C. 1974, U.S. Tax Ct. 1974, U.S. Supreme Ct. 1978. sole practice, Washington, 1974— ; pres. First Oxford Corp., Washington, 1976— . Mem. ABA, Md. Bar Assn., D.C. Bar Assn. Home: 5714 Massachusetts Ave Bethesda MD 20816-1929 Office: 3528 K St NW Washington DC 20007-3503

KYIN, SAW WILLIAM, chemist, consultant; b. Rangoon, Burma, Aug. 6, 1954; came to U.S., 1981; s. U Shin Nga and Daw (Swa) Khin; m. Cynthia H. Hsuan-Hung, Jan. 30, 1975; children: Tim, Maureen., Michelle. BS, Rangoon Arts and Sci. U., 1977; MS, Western Ill. U., 1984. Dir. biotech. ctr. Genetic Engring. Facility, U. Ill., Urbana-Champaign, 1984-92; dir. molecular biology dept. Synthesis/Sequencing Facility, Princeton, N.J., 1992—. Mem. AAAS, Am. Chem. Soc., Am. Peptide Soc., Am. Soc. Mass Spectrometry, N.Y. Acad. Scis., Assn. Biomolecular Resource Facilities, Protein Soc. Office: Princeton Univ Dept Molecular Biology Washington Rd Princeton NJ 08544-0001 E-mail: skyin@molbio.princeton.edu.

KYL, JON L. senator; b. Oakland, Nebr., Apr. 25, 1942; s. John and Arlene (Griffith) K.; m. Caryll Louise Collins, June 5, 1964; children: Kristine Kyl Gavin, John Jeffry. BA, U. Ariz., 1964, LLB, 1966. Atty. Jennings, Strouss & Salmon, Phoenix, 1966-86; mem. U.S. Ho. Reps. 100th-103rd Congresses from 4th Ariz. dist., 1987-94; U.S. senator from Ariz., 1994—. Mem. Fin. Com., Jud. Com., Energy and Natural Resources Com. Chmn. Rep. Policy Com.; founding dir. Crime Victim Found. Mem. Ariz. State Bar Assn. Republican. Office: US Senate 730 Hart Senate Bldg Washington DC 20510-0001*

KYLE, CORINNE SILVERMAN, management consultant; b. N.Y.C., Jan. 4, 1930; d. Nathan and Janno (Harra) Silverman; m. Alec Kyle, Aug. 29, 1959 (div. Feb. 1969); children: Joshua, Perry (dec.), Julia. BA, Bennington Coll., 1950; MA, Harvard U., 1953. Assoc. editor Inter-Univ. Case Program, N.Y.C., 1956-60; co-founder, chief editor Financial Index, N.Y.C., 1960-63; rsch. analyst McKinsey & Co., N.Y.C., 1963-64; sr. rsch. assoc. Mktg. Sci. Inst., Phila., 1964-67; founding ptnr. Phila. Group, 1967-70; sr. assoc. Govt. Studies and Systems, Phila., 1970-72, cons. program planning and control, 1972-78; sr. assoc. Periodical Studies Svc., 1978-81; v.p., dir. rsch. Total Rsch. Corp., Princeton, N.J., 1981-82; mgr. social rsch. The Gallup Orgn., Princeton, 1982-86; v.p. Response Analysis Corp., 1986-91; dir. rsch. Gallup Internat. Inst., 1991-97; assoc. Krog & Ptnrs., Inc., 1997-99; survey rsch. cons., 1999—. Lectr. rsch. methods Temple U., 1981-82; vis. prof. Fairleigh Dickinson U., 1990-91, 93; dir. Verbena Corp., N.Y.C. Contbr. numerous articles to profl. publs. Mem. adv. coun. to 8th Dist. city councilman, Phila., 1971-79; mem. 22nd Ward Dem. Exec. Com., 1971-78, State Dem. Com., 1974-76; mem. Pa. Gov.'s Council on Nutrition, 1974-76; v.p. Miquon Upper Sch. Bd., Phila., 1977-78; trustee Princeton Regional Scholarship Found., 1982-85, pres., 1984-85; mem. bd. edn. Princeton Regional Sch. Dist., 1984-93, pres. 1987, 89; mem. exec. bd. Mercer County (N.J.) Sch. Bds. Assn., 1987-92, v.p., 1991-92; mem. exec. com. Princeton Community Dem. Orgn., 1992-97; mem. Princeton Regional Planning Bd., 1994-99, chair, 1997-99, Princeton Environ. Commn., 1994-97; chair Princeton Borough task force on consolidation, 1995; chair One Princeton, 1996-97; mem. West Orange Bd. Edn., 2002--. Mem.: West Orange Advocates, N.J. Assn. for Pub. Opinion Rsch. Home: 32 Randolph Pl West Orange NJ 07052-4808

KYLE, DAVID L. gas industry executive; b. Wichita, Kans. BS in Indsl. Engring. and Mgmt., Okla. State U., 1974; MBA, U. Tulsa, 1987; grad. advanced mgmt. program, Harvard U., 1992. Joined ONEOK, Inc., Tulsa, 1974, pres. ONG, 1995, pres., COO, 1997, chmn., CEO, 2000—, also bd. dirs. Office: ONEOK Inc 100 W Fifth St Tulsa OK 74103

KYLE, JOHN EMERY, mission executive; b. San Diego, July 7, 1926; s. John E. and Agnes (McDaniel) K.; m. Lois Ellen Rowland, June 8, 1947; children: Arlette Marie, Jayson Duane, Marcus Justin, Darlene Patricia. BS in Agriculture, Oreg. State U., 1950; BDiv, Columbia Theol. Sem., 1961, MDiv, 1971; D in Ministry (hon.), Belhaven Coll., 1999. Ordained to ministry Presbyn. Ch. in U.S., 1961. Sr. buyer Easwest Produce Co.-Safeway Stores Inc., San Francisco, 1951-57; pastor Presbyn. Ch. in U.S., Hazard, Ky., 1961-63; adminstr. Wycliffe Bible Translators, Manila, Philippines, 1964-73; coord. Mission to the World, Presbyn. Ch. in Am., Decatur, Ga., 1974-77, Wycliffe Bible Translators, Washington, 1977-79; missions dir., v.p. Intervarsity Christian Fellowship, Madison, Wis., 1979-88; exec. dir. Mission to World Presbyn. Ch. in Am., Atlanta, 1988-94; sr. v.p. Evang. Fellowship of Mission Agys., Norcross, Ga., 1994—. Trustee Columbia Bible Coll. and Sem., 1982—86, Concerts of Prayer Internat., Mpls., 1988—99, Berkeley Hts., NJ, Overseas Missionary Fellowship, Robesonia, Pa., 1982—86, A.D. 2000 Movement, Colorado Springs, Colo., 1989—2000, Co mission, 1992—98, World Relief Bd., 1997—, Christ's Coll., Taipei, Taiwan, 1992—98; dir. World Student Mission Convention, 1979, 81, 84, 87, Urbana, Ill. Author: Now This Generation, 1990; editor: The Unfinished Task, 1982, Finishing the Task, 1987, Urban Missions, 1988. Midshipman USNR, 1944-45. Recipient Presdl. Merit medal Pres. of Philippines. Mem. Evang. Fgn. Missions Assn. (trustee 1989-94), Nat. Assn. Evang., Assn. Ch. Missions Com., World Evang. Fellowship, Concerts of Prayer Internat. Presbyterian. Office: 2343-A Granville Place Monroe NC 28110-E-mail: 76453.2026@compuserve.com.

KYLE, NICHOLAS SCOTT, art educator, artist; b. Ft. Worth, Tex., Aug. 17, 1942; s. Chester Scott and Desolee Mcmanus Kyle; m. Rose Gayle Allison, Dec. 1, 1979; m. Jerolyn Joan Fowler, Feb. 1, 1963 (div. May 24, 1979); 1 child, Christian Scott. MA, Purdue U., West Lafayette, Ind., 1970—71; BA, U. of Ctrl. Okla., Edmond, Okla., 1964—65. Cert. K-12 Teaching - Visual Art Okla., 1965. Art instr. South Jr. H.S., Joplin, Mo., 1965—67; art instr. and chair, practical arts dept. Western Oaks Jr. H.S., Okla. City, Okla., 1972—77; art instr. Putnam City West H.S., Okla. City, Okla., 1977—80; art instr. and chair, fine arts dept. Putnam City H.S., Okla. City, Okla., 1980—97; adj. art instr. Okla. City C.C., Okla. City, Okla., 1972—82; assoc. prof. art, head art dept. Mo. So. State U., Joplin, 1997—. One-man shows include Three Rivers C.C., Pine Bluff, Mo., Bartlesville (Okla.) Ctr., Kirkpatrick Mus. Complex, Oklahoma City, Firehouse Art Ctr., Norman, Okla. Art Ctr. Annex, Oklahoma City, Mus. Art, U. Ctrl. Okla., John Porter Gallery, Oklahoma City, Governor's Gallery Okla. State Capitol, Labette C.C., Parsons, Kans., Spiva Gallery Mo. So. State Coll., Coty Coll., Nevada, Mo., Locus Gallery, St. Louis, exhibited in group shows at Individual Artists of Okla., Phoenix, City Arts Ctr., Oklahoma City, Donna Nigh Gallery, U. Ctrl. Okla., Edmond, Md. Mansion, Ponca City, Okla., Individual Artists of Okla. Gallery, Oklahoma City, Arts Pl. II Gallery, Keyes Gallery, Springfield, Mo., Ponca City (Okla.) Art Gallery, Back Door Gallery, Dallas, Fred Jones Mus. Art, U. Okla., Norman, Lafayette Art Ctr., West Lafayette, Ind., Tar Box Gallery, San Diego, Calif., Stephen F. forte Gallery, Shreveport, La., Norick Art Ctr., Okla. City U., Spiva Art Mus., Joplin, Mo., Untitled Gallery, Oklahoma City, Mullsjo Folkhogskola, Sweden, East Gallery, Okla. State Capitol, Oklahoma City, U. Ctrl. Okla., Edmond, Represented in permanent collections Nestle Purina Corp., St. Louis, Tinnin Mus. Three Rivers C.C., Plne Bluff, Mo., Okla. State Art Collection, Oklahoma City, Kirkpatrick Ctr. Mus., Maybee-Gerrer Mus. Art, Shawnee, Okla.; appeared on PBS Can Johnny Think, 1992, subject (video prodn.) Creative Expression. Okla. city arts festival edn. com. and opening night new years eve celebration com. Arts Coun. of Okla., Okla. City, Okla., 1990—97; project assistance and artist in residence selection committees State Arts Coun. of Okla., Okla. City, Okla., 1986—97; pres. 2000-2002, dir. of exhibits 1998-2003 George Spiva Ctr. for the Arts Regional Mus., Joplin, Mo., 1998—2003; representing the visual art edn. members Okla. Alliance for Arts Edn., Okla. City, Okla., 1986—97; alumni dir. Okla. Arts Inst., Okla. City, Okla., 1990—2003; founding bd. mem., treas., v.p. Okla. Visual Arts Coalition, Okla. City, Okla., 1988—97. Recipient Tchr. of the Yr., Western Oaks Jr. H.S., Okla. City, Okla., Putnam City Sch. Dist. and the Okla. Edn. Assn., Okla. City, Okla., 1976, Tchr. of the Yr., Putnam City H.S., Okla. City, Okla., 1983, Tchr. of the Yr., 1983, Okla. County Tchr. of the Yr., Okla. State Dept. of Edn., 1983, Nat. Visual Art Tchr. of the Yr., Disney Am. Tchr. Awards, LA, Calif., 1991, Okla. Art Educator of the Yr., Okla. Art Edn. Assn. and the Nat. Art Edn. Assn., 1991, Award of Excellence, Okla. Edn. Assn., 1992, Mayor Ron Norick and Okla. City Coun., 1992, Medal of Excellence in Tchg., Okla. Found. for Excellence, 1992, The Governor's Art Award, Okla. State Arts Coun., 1992, Judge - Arts Festival Okla., Okla. City C.C., 1992, Judge - Ctrl. Art Assn. Arts Festival, Okla. City, Okla., Ctrl. Art Assn., 1995 and 1996, Judge - El Reno Arts Festival, El Reno, Okla., El Reno Arts and Humanities Coun., 1996, Judge - Okla. Sculpture Soc. Ann. Exhbn., Okla. City, Okla., Okla. Sculpture Soc., 1997, Judge - Ponca City Arts Festival, Ponca City, Okla., Ponca City Arts Coun., 1997; grantee Nat. Arts Edn. Rsch. Ctr. Visual Arts Rsch. Grant, NY U., NY, NY, Nat. Arts Edn. Rsch. Ctr. funded by Nat. Endowment for the Arts and U.S. Dept. of Edn., 1988. Mem.: AAUP, Coll. Art Assn., NEA, Okla. Edn. Assn., Putnam City Assn. of Classroom Teachers (exec. bd. mem. 1996—97), Mo. Art Edn. Assn., Nat. Art Edn. Assn. (western region secondary dir. 1996—97), Okla. Art Edn. Assn. (pres. 1986—88, Okla. Art Educator of the Yr. 1991), Kappa Delta Pi, Internat. Honor Soc. in Edn. Home: 9805 County Lane 185 Carthage MO 64836 Office: Mo So State College 3950 East Newman Rd Joplin MO 64801-1595 Office Fax: 417-625-3046. E-mail: kyle-n@mssu.edu.

KYLE, RICHARD HOUSE, federal judge; b. St. Paul, Apr. 30, 1937; s. Richard E. and Geraldine (House) K.; m. Jane Foley, Dec. 22, 1959; children: Richard H. Jr., Michael F., D'Arcy, Patrick G., Kathleen. BA, U. Minn., 1959, LLB, 1962. Bar: Minn. 1962, U.S. Dist. Ct. Minn. 1992. Atty. Briggs & Morgan, St. Paul, 1963-68, 1970-92; solicitor gen. Minn. Atty. Gen. Office, St. Paul, 1968-70; judge U.S. Dist. Ct., St. Paul, 1992—. Pres. Minn. Law Rev., Mpls., 1962. Mem. Minn. State Bar Assn., Ramsey County Bar Assn. Republican. Episcopal. Office: US Dist Ct Federal Courts Bldg 316 Robert St N Saint Paul MN 55101-1495

KYLE, ROBERT ARTHUR, medical educator, oncologist; b. Bottineau, N.D., Mar. 17, 1928; s. Arthur Nichol and Mabel Caroline (Crandall) K.; m. Charlene Mae Showalter, Sept. 11, 1954; children: John, Mary, Barbara, Jean. AA, N.D Sch. Forestry, 1946; BS, U. N.D., 1948; MD, Northwestern U., 1952; MS, U. Minn., 1958. Diplomate Am. Bd. Internal Medicine; subsplty. Hematology. Fellow Mayo Grad. Sch., Rochester, Minn., 1953-59; clin. asst. Tufts U. Sch. Medicine, Boston, 1960-61; cons. internal medicine Mayo Clinic, Rochester, 1961—; prof. medicine and lab. medicine Mayo Med. Sch., Rochester, 1975—. Pres. med. subjects unit Am. Topical Assn., Johnstown, Pa., 1976-81; chmn. standards, ethics and peer rev. orgn. Cancer & Acute Leukemia Group B, Scarsdale, N.Y., 1978-82; Robert A. Hettig lectr. in hematology Baylor U. Coll. of Medicine, Houston, 1984; Waldenström lectr., Stockholm, 1988; Redlich Meml. lectr Cedars-Sinai Med. Ctr., U. Calif., L.A.; vis. prof. St. Elizabeth's Med. Ctr., Tufts U. Sch. Medicine, Boston, 1998. Author: The Monoclonal Gammopathies, 1976, Medicine and Stamps, vols. 1 and 2, 1980; author/editor: Neoplastic Disease of the Blood, 4th edit., Myeloma: Biology and Management, 1995, 2nd edit. 1998. Chmn. bd. trustees First Presbyn. Ch., Rochester, Minn., 1967; chmn. Rochester Med. Ctr. Ministry, 1979-86; chmn. adv. bd. Internat. Waldenstrom's Macroglobulinemia Found. Capt. USAF, 1955-57. Named Disting. Topicl Philatelest, Am. Topical Soc., 1982; Recipient Waldenström award Internat. Workshop for Myeloma, Italy, 1991, Henry S. Plummer Distinguished Internist award Mayo Clin., 1995, Mayo Distinguished Clinician award 1996, Sioux award U. N.D., 1998; Bruce Wiseman lectr. Ohio State U., 1991, Kauffman Meml. lectr. Meml. Sloan Kettering Med. Ctr., N.Y.C., 1997; Clement Finch prof. U. Wash., 1993. Master ACP; mem. Royal Coll. Pathologists (hon.), N.Y. Acad. Scis., Am. Soc. Hematology, Internat. Soc. Hematology (sec.-gen. Inter-Am. divsn. 1990), Am. Assn. Cancer Rsch., Internat. Myeloma Found. (chmn. sci. adv. bd. 1995), Internat. Soc. Amyloidosis (pres. 2001-), Phi Beta Kappa. Republican. Avocation: philately. Home: 1207 6th St SW Rochester MN 55902-1918 Office: Mayo Clinic 200 1st St SW Rochester MN 55905-0002 also: 920 Hilton Rochester MN 55905-0001

KYLE, ROBERT CAMPBELL, II, publishing executive; b. Cleve., Jan. 6, 1935; s. Charles Donald and Mary Alice (King) K.; children: Peter F., Kit C., Scott G. BS, U. Colo., 1956; MA, Case Western Res. U., 1958; MBA, Harvard U., 1963, DBA, 1966. Ptnr. McLagan & Co., Chgo., 1966-67; founder, pres. Devel. Sys. Corp. (subs. Longman Group USA), Chgo., 1967-82; pres. Longman Group USA, Chgo., 1982-89; chmn., CEO Dearborn Pub. Group, Inc. (formerly Longman Group USA), 1989-98. Chmn. CTS Fin. Pub., 1997-2000. Author: Property Management, 1979; co-author: Modern Real Estate Practice, 1967, How to Profit From Real Estate, 1988 (Chgo. Book Clinic Lifetime Achievement award 1998). Mem. dean's adv. coun. Coll. Bus. U. Colo., 1992-98, Ctr. for Entrepreneurship Adv. Bd., U. Colo., 1996-2002; trustee Mystic Seaport Mus., 1989—, exec. com., 1999—, vice chair, 2001—; dir. Chgo. Maritime Soc., pres. 1999-2000; trustee The Burnham Inst., 2002—, San Diego Maritime Mus., 2002—, exec. com., 2003—. Mem. Real Estate Educators Assn. (pres. 1981), Internat. Assn. Fin. Planning, Chgo. Book Clinic (dir.), Harvard Club N.Y., Econs. Club, San Diego Yacht Club, N.Y. Yacht Club. Avocations: yacht racing, tennis. Home: 2910 Owens St San Diego CA 92106

KYLER, ARLENE, advertising executive; b. N.Y.C., Apr. 21, 1944; d. Abraham S. and Evelyn Estrin Hoberman; m. Jerry Kyler, June 20, 1964; children: Elizabeth Amy, Alison Eve. *Father Abraham S. Hoberman was chairmen of the math department and head of the photography club at Seth Low Junior High School in Brooklyn, New York. In addition, he was assistant director at Camp Swago in Callicoon, New York. Mother Evelyn Estrin Hoberman was executive secretary for Linens of the Week in New York City. She also served as president of the Brooklyn Young Ladies Aid Society. Sister Barbara Hoberman Levine is the author of "Your Body Believes Every Word You Say." Sons-in-law are Gregory Allen Wank and Jakob Karlsmark. Grandson is Jaden Michael Kyler-Wank.* BA, Bklyn. Coll., 1964. Cert. tchr. common branches subjects SUNY-State Edn. Dept. Elem. sch. tchr. Pub. Sch. 216K, Bklyn., 1964—67; pres. Parties Unlimited Entertainment, Inc., East Rockaway, NY, 1974—86, Take My Card, Inc., East Rockaway, 1985—. Founder PTA's 1st Pub. Pre-Sch. Program, Oceanside, NY, 1973—79; pre-sch. chairperson Nassau Dist. PTA, L.I., NY, 1976—79; initiator PTA's Pre-Sch. Hearing Screening, L.I., NY, 1976; legis. co-chairperson PTA Coun., Oceanside, 1978—79; trustee Temple Avodah Sisterhood, Oceanside, NY, 1976—80; co-founder Free Sons and Daughters Investment Club, L.I., NY, 2000. Recipient United Jewish Appeal award Honoring Free Sons of Israel, Chai Lodge Long Is., N.Y., 1994. Mem.: Workmen's Benefit Fund of the U.S.A. (charter sec.-treas. br. #849), N.Y. Soc. for Profl. Inventors (trustee 1995—99), Free Sons of Israel (dist. dep. 1984, founder Chai Singles' Lodge #230 1992, 2nd dep. grand master 1993—96, 1st dep. grand master 1996—99, U.S. Grand Master 1999—2002, United Jewish Appeal award). Achievements include patents for card display stands; card display apparatus; display and dispensing apparatus. Avocations: theater, travel, watersports, cats. Office: Take My Card Inc 3445 Park Ave Oceanside NY 11572

KYLES-OMARI, CYNTHIA LEE, editor, career consultant; b. San Francisco, Feb. 1, 1965; d. Troy and Nancy Lee Kyles; m. Omar Ali Omari, Feb. 21, 1997; 1 child, James Jamil. BA in Polit. Sci., Cambridge State U., 2001. Dir. John Robert Powers, L.A., 1988-89; career cons. U. Sound Arts, Hollywood, Calif., 1989-90, Banking Inst., L.A., 1991-92, Barbizon Models, L.A., 1992-93; lobbyist Ga. Trial Lawyers, Atlanta, 1995; campaign asst. Re-Elect Willie Brown Campaign, San Francisco, 1999; legis. editor State Net, Sacramento, 2000—01; bd. dirs. Oreg. Coun. for Multiracial Affairs, 2001—02. Co-founder Orgn. for Bi-Racial Studies, Portland, Oreg., 1981; campaign worker Tom Torlakson for Senate, Martinez, Calif., 2000. Mem. Multi-Racial Ams. So. Calif. (bd. dirs. 1988-89). Democrat.

KYLLONEN ROSE, JULIE FRANCES, college program administrator; b. Columbia, Mo., Mar. 18, 1943; d. Toimi Enoch Kyllonen and Frances Aileen Thompson; m. Charles Lincoln Rose, Mar. 17, 1972 (div. 1974). AA in Liberal Arts, Stephens Coll., 1963; AB in Polit. Sci., U. Mo., Columbia, 1965; MS in Fgn. Svc., Georgetown U., 1968. Clk.-typist US Peace Corps, Washington, 1965-67; jr. profl. Fgn. Census Rsch. Br. of U.S. Census Bur., Washington, 1967-68; office mgr. Teknekron Inc., Washington, 1968; archivist Eisenhower Presdl. Libr. Nat. Archives, Washington and Abilene, Kans., 1968-72; dir. admissions ELS Lang. Ctr., Oakland, Calif., 1974-78; program coord. for Sponsored Students Iowa State U., Ames, 1978-88; dir. internat. student/scholar/faculty svcs. Western Ill. U., Macomb, 1988—. Cons. Macomb Area Indsl. Devel. Corp., 1989-98; presenter and spk. in field, in U.S. and internationally. Fulbright-Hays fellow U.S. Dept. of Edn., Egypt, 1988, Malone fellow Nat. Coun. U.S.-Arab Rels., Saudi Arabia, 1996; scholar Rotary Internat. Group Study Exch. program, Korea, 1994, scholar NAFSA, China, 1989. Mem.: SIETAR-U.S.A., Soc. for Intercultural Edn., Tng. and Rsch. Internat., NAFSA: Assn. Internat. Educators (coord. Nigerian Student Concerns 1980—85, chmn. Mid-East spl. interest group 2000—03, Region IV newsletter editor), Macomb Area C. of C., Univ. Women's Club (2d v.p. 1994—96), Altrusa Internat. (bd. dirs. 1993—95), Delta Kappa Gamma. Avocations: artwear designer, fiber artist, weaver, mysteries. Office: Western Ill U Office Internat Edn One Univ Cir Macomb IL 61455 E-mail: J-Rose@wiu.edu.

KYLSTRA, JOHANNES ARNOLD, physician; b. Manado, Indonesia, Nov. 30, 1925; s. Jan Arnold and Johanna Leonore (Van Praag) K.; m. Carol S. Rous (dec.); children: Jan Andrew, Kimberly; m. Yvonne C. Alden. MD, U. Leiden, 1952, PhD, 1958. Asst. prof. physiology U. Leiden, Netherlands, 1961-63; vis. asst. prof. physiology SUNY, Buffalo, 1963-65; asst. prof. medicine and physiology Duke U., Durham, N.C., 1965-66, assoc. prof. medicine, 1966-72, prof. medicine, 1972-89, prof. emeritus medicine, 1989—, assoc. prof. physiology, 1972-89; TB control physician N.C. Dept. Environ., Health & Natural Resources, 1989-98. Contbr. numerous articles on respiratory physiology, liquid breathing and lung lavage to profl. jours. Served with Royal Netherlands Navy, 1955-58. Recipient Lockheed award Marine Technology Soc., 1970, Disting. Research award Sigma Xi, 1974, Stover-Link award Undersea Med. Soc., 1979 Home: 3615 Ocean Dr Corpus Christi TX 78411-1342

KYNCL, JOHN JAROSLAV, pharmacologist; b. Prague, Czechoslovakia, Aug. 16, 1936; came to U.S. 1971; s. Jan Petr and Marie (Mikesova) K.; m. Mila Marie Tomaides, Mar. 4, 1961; children: Marketa Kyncl Leisure, John Anthony. PhD, Komensky U., Bratislava, 1963; ScC, Czech. Acad. Sci., 1967. Pharmacologist Rsch. Inst. for Biochemistry & Pharmacy, Prague, 1963-68; A. von. Humboldt fellow U. Heidelberg, Ger., 1968-71; rsch. fellow Cleveland Clinic Found., 1971-72; E. Volwiler rsch. fellow Abbott Labs., North Chicago, Ill., 1972—. Contbr. over 100 articles to profl. jours. Fellow Coun. for High Blood Pressure Rsch. Am. Heart Assn.; mem. Am. Hypertension Soc., Am. Endocrine Soc., Internat. Hypertension Soc. (Paris), FASEB. Achievements include over 20 patents including invention of terazosin (Hytrin) and terlipressin (Glypressin). Home: 800 Green Bay Rd Lake Bluff IL 60044-1829

KYOMEN, HELEN H. psychiatrist; b. Long Beach, Calif., July 11, 1959; d. Keiso and Yoshie Kyomen. MD, U. So. Calif., 1986; MS, Harvard Sch. Pub. Health, 1993. Diplomate Am. Bd. Psychiatry. Rsch. fellow divsn. on aging Harvard Med. Sch., Boston, 1990-92; asst. psychiatrist McLean Hosp., Belmont, Mass., 1992-95, asst. attending psychiatrist, 1995—. Mentored clin. scientist Harvard Med. Sch./Nat. Inst. Aging, 2000—. Contbr. articles to profl. jours. John A. Hartford scholar Harvard Med. Sch., 1990-91, fellow in geriatric medicine/psychiatry, 1990-92, fellow in clin. effectiveness, 1991-93; grantee Claude D. Pepper Older ams. Independence Ctr. rsch. devel. pilot project Harvard Med. Sch. Divsn. Aging, 1999; recipient mentored clinical scientist devel. program award Sch. Nat. Inst. Aging/Divsn. Aging Harvard Med. Sch., 2000. Mem. AMA, Am. Psychiat. Assn., Am. Assn. Geriatric Psychiatry, Am. Geriatrics Soc. (postdoctoral fellow 1992-94; New Investigator award 1997, Pres. Poster award 1997), Assn. Rsch. in Nervous and Mental Disease, N.Y. Acad. Scis. Avocations: guitar, singing, painting, sketching, ballroom dancing, tennis. Office: McLean Hosp 115 Mill St Belmont MA 02478-1048

KYRIAZIS, ARTHUR JOHN (ATHANASIOS IOANNIS KYRIAZIS), lawyer, biotechnologist; b. Thessaloniki, Greece, Nov. 2, 1958; came to U.S., 1960; s. George A. and Elpis (Halkedis) K.; m. Maria M. Zissimos, Aug. 31, 1986; children: Cassandra Hope, Michael John, George Athanasios II. AB, Harvard U., 1981; postgrad, Pepperdine U., 1982-83; JD cum laude, Temple U., 1985; postgrad., U. Pa., 1993—98. Bar: Pa. 1985, U.S. Dist. Ct. (ea. dist.) Pa. 1985, U.S. Bankruptcy Ct. (ea. dist.) Pa. 1985, U.S. Bankruptcy Ct. N.J., 1986, Calif. 1987, U.S. Dist. Ct. (ea. dist.) Calif. 1988, U.S. Ct. Appeals (3d cir.) 1991, U.S. Supreme Ct. 1994. Assoc. Cardillo & Corbett, N.Y.C., 1983; law clk. to Hon. Norma J. Shapiro U.S. Dist. Ct. (ea. dist.) Pa., 1984; assoc. Needleman Needleman Caney Stein & Kratzer, 1984—85; law clk. to Hon. James Gardner Colins Commonwealth Ct. Pa., Phila., Harrisburg, 1985—86; assoc. Rawle & Henderson, Phila. and Marlton, NJ, 1987—88, Lesser & Kaplin and predecessor firm, Phila., Blue Bell, Pa. and Marlton, NJ, 1988—89; prin. Kyriazis & Assocs., Phila., Cherry Hill, N.J. and Delaware County, Pa., 1989—. Arbitrator Phila. Ct. Common Pleas, 1988—, Delaware County Ct. Common Pleas, 1993—; pro bono counsel Am. Assn. Univ. Students, 1989—; solicitor to Register of Wills, Montgomery County, 2000. Author: (with H. Caldwell) Unchecked Discretion: The Buck Stops Here: Is There a Fourth Amendment at the International Borders of the United States, 1993, Whittier Law Rev. Pa. co-coord. Dukakis for Pres., 1987-88; del. Nat. Fin. Com., Dem. Conv., Atlanta, 1988; mem. Hellenic Am. for Dukakis, Pa., 1987-88; founder Am. Assn. Univ. Students, Cambridge, Mass. and Phila., 1978-79; v.p. Hercules-Spartan Phila. chpt. 26 Am. Hellenic Progressive Edn. Assn., 1989-90, pres., 1990-91, bd. govs., 1987 93; mem. alumni assn. bd. trustees The Haverford Sch., 1999—. Mem. ATLA, ABA (young lawyers div., litigation and bus. law sect., bus., real estate sects.), Am. Hellenic Lawyers Assn. (founder, treas. 1992-94), Phila. Bar Assn. (exec. com. young lawyers sect. 1988-90, fin. sec. exec. com. 1990, sec. exec. com. 1989, co-chmn. law related edn. com. 1988—, mem. bar edn. found. com. 1988—, mem. Bill Rights 200 coms., mem. fed. cts. 200 com., chmn. debate com. and mock trial 1987—, debate dir. fed. cts. 200 nat. high sch. debate tournament 1990—), Camden County Bar Assn. (young lawyers, pub. benefits, debtor-creditor relations), Pa. Bar Assn. (litigation, young lawyers jud. administrn.), N.J. Trial Lawyers Assn., Pa. Trial Lawyers Assn., Am. Arbitration Assn. (comml. arbitrator 1988—), Pa. Bar Assn., State Bar Calif. (litigation, intellectual property, entertainment), Am. Assn. Univ. Students (legal counsel 1989—), Coll. Admissions Inst. Am. (adv. bd. 1992—), Hellenic Univ. Club (bd. trustees 1996-98), Harvard Club (N.Y., Washington), Penn Club (N.Y.), Maxwell Football Club, Nat. Press Club, Harvard-Radcliffe Club Phila. (schs. com.), Penn Faculty Club. Republican. Greek Orthodox. Office: 1806 Garrett Rd Lansdowne PA 19050-1005 also: 336 Bay Ave Unit 503 Ocean City NJ E-mail: akyriazis@msn.com.

KYRILLOS, JOSEPH M. state legislator, political organization worker; b. Middletown, N.J., Apr. 12, 1960; BA, Hobart Coll., 1982; MS, Boston U., 1983. Spl. asst. U.S. Sec. Interior, 1985-87; mem. N.J. Gen. Assembly, 1987-91, N.J. Senate, Dist. 13, Trenton, 1992—; senate majority conf. leader; mem. senate budget and appropriations com.; mem. senate econ. growth com. Chmn. conservation, natural resources and energy com. N.J. State Assembly, appropriations com., edn. com., select com. on ocean and beach protection; mem. com. Mid-Atlantic Health Group; dir. bus. stds. and ethics com. N.J. State Senate. Host cable tv program Tour of N.J. Mem. Garden State Arts Ctr. Found., Count Basie Theater, Rainbow Found., Monmouth County Hist. Assn., Women's Ctr. of Monmouth County, Bayshore Sr. Day Ctr., Christian Ministry in the Nat. Parks, N.J. State Tourism Adv. Coun. Mem. No. Monmouth C. of C., Lions (Middletown club), Elks (Middletown club). Address: 1715 Highway 35 Middletown NJ 07748-1867 Office: State House Box 099 Trenton NJ 08625-0099*

KYSOR, DANIEL FRANCIS, psychologist; b. Corry, Pa., Aug. 3, 1956; s. Darrell Francis and Louise Mary (Col) K.; m. Kate Galbraith Morrison, Sept. 7, 1991; children: Kenneth Jon Kron, Samuel Morrison, Charles Col. BS, Edinboro U., 1980; MS in Ednl. Psychology, Edinboro U., Pa., 1988; MEd in Secondary Sch. Adminstrn., Edinboro U., 1994; postgrad., Miss. State U., 1991—. Cert. elem. edn., guidance, elem. and secondary adminstr., sch. psychologist; lic. psychologist, Pa. Tchr. Calhoun County Schs., Grantsville, W.Va., 1982; counselor, tchr. Bradford (Pa.) Children's Home, Pa., 1983; residential program counselor Assn. for Retarded Citizens, Meadville, Pa., 1984-86; resident hall dir. Edinboro (Pa.) U., 1984-86, counselor Edinboro Summer Acad. for the Gifted, 1985-96; guidance counselor Cranberry Sch. Dist., Seneca, Pa., 1986; dropout prevention counselor Erie (Pa.) Sch. Dist., 1988; sch. psychologist Seneca Highlands IU #9, Coudersport, Pa., 1989—. Pvt. practice Addis & Assocs., Bradford, Pa., 1994-97; CEO, dir. psychol. svc. Por t Psychol. Svcs., Inc., 1996—. Pa. Rural Leadership Program scholar Pa. State U., 1989; Rsch. grantee St. Bonaventure (N.Y.) U.; recipient citations Pa. House of Reps., 1991, 93, 95. Mem. ACA (life), NASP, Am. Sch. Counselor Assn., Nat. Fedn. Interscholastic Ofcls. Assns., Pa. Interscholastic Athletic Assn., Ea. Wrestling League, Ea. Ind. Officials Wrestling Assn., Nat. Wrestling Officials Assn., Clowns of Am. Internat., Inc./POCO Clowns. Democrat. Presbyterian. Avocations: wrestling officiating, reading, biking, backpacking. Home: 109 Chestnut St Port Allegany PA 16743-1248 Office: Seneca Highlands IU #9 306 N Main St Coudersport PA 16915-1626 E-mail: kysor@penn.com.

KYTE, SHANNAN DYAN, multimedia designer; BS in Info. Sci., Christopher Newport U., 1997. Tech. comm. coord. Thomas Jefferson Nat. Accelerator Facility, Newport News, Va., 1998—2000, electronic media mgr., 2000—. Mem.: Phi Mu Frat. (philanthropic chair 1997—99, alumnae pres. 1999—2003). Office: Jefferson Lab 12000 Jefferson Ave Newport News VA 23606